MLRC 50-State Survey

Employment Libel & Privacy Law

2013

Prepared by Leading Media Attorneys and Law Firms
in All Fifty States, the District of Columbia
and Puerto Rico

Edited by
The Media Law Resource Center
www.medialaw.org

Oxford University Press, Inc., publishes works that further Oxford University's objective of excellence in research, scholarship, and education.

Published by Media Law Resource Center, Inc.
520 Eighth Avenue, North Tower, 20th Floor, New York, New York 10018
and
Oxford University Press, Inc.
198 Madison Avenue, New York, New York 10016

ISBN: 978-0-19-993110-1

Printed in the United States of America on acid-free paper

Note to Readers

This publication is designed to provide accurate and authoritative information in regard to the subject matter covered. It is based upon sources believed to be accurate and reliable and is intended to be current as of the time it was written. It is sold with the understanding that the publisher is not engaged in rendering legal, accounting, or other professional services. If legal advice or other expert assistance is required, the services of a competent professional person should be sought. Also, to confirm that the information has not been affected or changed by recent developments, traditional legal research techniques should be used, including checking primary sources where appropriate.

(Based on the Declaration of Principles jointly adopted by a Committee of the American Bar Association and a Committee of Publishers and Associations.)

CONTENTS

EDITORS' NOTE

The 2013 edition of the Media Law Resource Center 50-STATE SURVEY OF EMPLOYMENT LIBEL & PRIVACY LAW reflects the current law of libel and privacy in the employment context throughout the United States and its territories. New legal developments since publication of last year's edition are printed in bold in each chapter, and while we endeavor to make the MLRC 50-STATE SURVEY as current as possible, no such annual work can ever be fully up to date.

Readers should also understand that each of the reports is an outline and not a treatise on the law. Each tends to focus on black letter law and may to some extent not give full treatment to gray areas or exceptions to rules.

All of the chapters are based on a standard outline. Since the law on any given topic may be more developed in some jurisdictions than it is in others, it is possible that some topics included in the general survey outline will have no entries in a particular chapter, or that a new topic will be added in an appropriate section. The index of issues in the back of the SURVEY allows for quick comparisons among jurisdictions on particular issues.

The SURVEY is the result of the diligent work of our nationwide network of preparers, whose names and firms appear at the beginning of each chapter. They take time from their busy practices to share with us the latest developments in employment libel and privacy law in the jurisdictions that they cover, and we sincerely thank all of them for their efforts.

We also thank the members of MLRC's Employment Law Committee, who help oversee this publication and contribute to its continuing success.

The Media Law Resource Center is a non-profit information clearinghouse organized by the media to monitor developments and promote First Amendment rights in the libel, privacy, access, reporter's privilege, and related media law fields. Besides the 50-STATE SURVEY OF EMPLOYMENT LIBEL & PRIVACY LAW, we also publish similar annual surveys of libel and privacy and related law in the media context – the MLRC 50-STATE SURVEY: MEDIA LIBEL LAW and the MLRC 50-STATE SURVEY: MEDIA PRIVACY & RELATED LAW.

We would like to extend our heartfelt thanks to all of MLRC's media and defense counsel members, see infra, who support this work. Many of attorneys at these companies and firms are also contributors to this and our other SURVEYS. Without their continuing financial and moral support, an effort of such magnitude as this publication would not be possible.

Media Law Resource Center
New York, New York
December 2012

MEDIA LAW RESOURCE CENTER, INC.
520 Eighth Avenue, North Tower, 20th Floor
New York, NY 10018
212-337-0200 | www.medialaw.org

MLRC MEDIA MEMBERSHIP
(as of December 2012)

A & E Television Networks
A. H. Belo Corp.
ABC, Inc.
Advance Publications, Inc.
Allbritton Communications Company
ALM Media, LLC
American Media, Inc.
AOL Inc.
ARTstor
Associated Newspapers Ltd
The Associated Press
Association of American Publishers
The Authors Guild, Inc.
AXIS PRO
Bauer Publishing Group
Belo Corp.
Bloomberg L.P.
Broadway Video Entertainment
California Newspaper Publishers Association
Capitol Broadcasting Company, Inc.
CBS Broadcasting Inc.
CBS Corporation
CBS Interactive
CBS Outdoor
CBS Radio, Inc.
Chubb Specialty Insurance
CNA Insurance
Connecticut Broadcasters Association
Consumers Union of U.S., Inc.
Courthouse News Service
Cox Enterprises, Inc.
Crain Communications Inc.
Daily News, L.P.
Discovery Communications, LLC
Dow Jones & Company
E! Entertainment
The E. W. Scripps Company
ESPN, Inc.
Fairfax Media Limited
The First Amendment Center
First Amendment Coalition
Forbes, Inc.
Fox News Network, LLC
Fox Television Stations, Inc.
Future US, Inc.
Gannett Company, Inc.
Gawker Media, LLC
Getty Images
The Globe and Mail, Inc.
Globosat Comercialização De Conteúdos S.A.
Google Inc.
Greenpeace International
Guardian News & Media Ltd
Hachette Book Group
The Hearst Corporation
Hiscox Media
Home Box Office, Inc.
Hubbard Broadcasting, Inc.
International Media Lawyers Project - Media Entities
Investigative News Network
Jacqueline Anne Sutton
John Wiley & Sons, Inc.
Journal Communications, Inc.
LIN Media
Macmillan
Marsh, Inc.
The McClatchy Company
The McGraw-Hill Companies, Inc.
Media Insurance Brokers Limited
Meredith Corporation
Microsoft Corporation
Motion Picture Association of America, Inc.
MPA - The Association of Magazine Media
MTV Networks
Mutual Insurance Company, Limited
National Association of Broadcasters
National Geographic Society
National Press Photographers Association
NBCUniversal
New York Public Radio
The New York Times Company
The New Yorker Magazine
News Corporation
News International
Newsday LLC/News 12 Networks LLC
Newspaper Association of America
The Newsweek/Daily Beast Company
North Jersey Media Group, Inc.
NPR
OneBeacon Professional Insurance
Oxford University Press Inc.
Penguin Group (USA) Inc.
Pennsylvania Newspaper Association
PR Newswire Association, LLC
Promotion Marketing Association, Inc.
ProPublica
Radio Free Europe/Radio Liberty
Radio Television Digital News Association
Random House, Inc.
Reuters America LLC
SBS
Scottsdale Insurance Co.
Showtime Networks Inc.
Simon & Schuster
Stephens Media LLC
Telegraph Media Group
Thai Public Broadcasting Service
Time Inc.
Time Warner Cable, Inc.
Tribune Company
Turner Broadcasting System, Inc.
Village Voice Media
The Washington Post Company
Wenner Media LLC
WGBH Educational Foundation
WNET.ORG

MLRC Defense Counsel Section Membership
(as of December 2012)

Adams and Reese LLP
Alice Neff Lucan, Attorney At Law
Allied Law Group LLC
Alston Hunt Floyd & Ing
Archer & Greiner, P.C.
Arnall Golden & Gregory LLP
Baker & Hostetler LLP
Banki Haddock Fiora
Banner & Bower, P.C.
Barnes & Thornburg
Benn Law Firm
Bernardi, Ronayne & Glusac, P.C.
Bernstein, Shur, Sawyer & Nelson
Bersenas Jacobsen Chouest Thomson Blackburn LLP
Bingham Greenebaum Doll LLP
Bingham McCutchen LLP
Blake, Cassels & Graydon LLP
Blish & Cavanagh, LLP
Bond, Schoeneck & King, PLLC
Bose McKinney & Evans LLP
Bostwick & Jassy LLP
Bradley Arant Boult Cummings LLP
Brian MacLeod Rogers, Barrister & Solicitor
Brooks, Pierce, McLendon, Humphrey & Leonard, LLP
Brown Rudnick LLP
Bryan Cave LLP
Buchanan Ingersoll & Rooney PC
Burch Porter & Johnson, PLLC
Butler, Snow, O'Mara, Stevens & Cannada, PLLC
Butzel Long
Byelas & Neigher
C. Thomas Dienes, Attorney At Law
Cades Schutte LLP
Cahill Gordon & Reindel LLP
Cameron A. Stracher, Esq.
Campbell & Williams
Charles A. Brown, Attorney At Law
Cooper, White & Cooper LLP
Counts Law Group
Covington & Burling LLP
Cowan, DeBaets, Abrahams & Sheppard LLP
Cravath, Swaine & Moore LLP
David M. Snyder, P.A.
Davis Wright Tremaine LLP
Debevoise & Plimpton LLP
Devereux Chatillon, Esq.
Dinsmore & Shohl LLP
DLA Piper US LLP
Doerner, Saunders, Daniel & Anderson
Donald M. Craven, P.C.
Donaldson & Callif, LLP
Dorsey & Whitney LLP
Dow Lohnes PLLC
Doyle & McKean, LLP
Edwards Wildman Palmer LLP
Epstein Becker & Green, P.C.
Faegre Baker Daniels LLP
Faruki Ireland & Cox P.L.L.
Fenno Law Firm, LLC
Fenwick & West LLP
Finers Stephens Innocent LLP
Fishman Haygood Phelps Walmsley Willis & Swanson LLP
Foley & Lardner LLP
Fox Rothschild LLP
Frankfurt Kurnit Klein & Selz, P.C.
Frost Brown Todd LLC
Funkhouser Vegosen Liebman & Dunn Ltd.
George & Brothers
Giordano, Halleran & Ciesla, PC
Godfrey & Kahn, S.C.
Golenbock Eiseman Assor Bell & Peskoe LLP
Goodwin Procter LLP
Gordon Silver
Gowling Lafleur Henderson LLP
Graham & Dunn
Gravel & Shea
Graves, Dougherty, Hearon & Moody, P.C.
Graydon, Head & Ritchey
Greenberg Traurig
Hall, Estill, Hardwick, Gable, Golden & Nelson
Hangley Aronchick Segal Pudlin & Schiller
Haynes and Boone LLP
Henry R. Kaufman, P.C.
Hinckley, Allen & Snyder LLP
Hiscock & Barclay LLP
Hogan Lovells US LLP
Holland & Knight LLP
Holmes Weinberg, PC
Honigman Miller Schwartz and Cohn LLP
Hunton & Williams
International Media Lawyers Project - Law Firms
Jackson Walker LLP
Jenner & Block LLP
Johnson Winter & Slattery
Johnston Barton Proctor & Rose LLP
Jorden Burt LLP
Joshua Koltun, Attorney
K & L Gates LLP
Katten Muchin Rosenman LLP
Kelley Drye / White O'Connor
King & Ballow
King & Spalding LLP
Koley Jessen P.C., L.L.D.
Lathrop & Gage LLP
Law Office of John J. Lynch
Law Office of Michael A. Pezza Jr.
Law Office of Paul Steinberg
Law Offices of D. John McKay

Law Offices of Jennifer A. Klear
Law Offices of Judith B. Bass
Law Offices of Kathleen Conkey
LeClairRyan
Leopold, Petrich & Smith PC
Levine Sullivan Koch & Schulz, L.L.P.
Lewis, Rice & Fingersh, L.C.
Lightfoot Franklin & White, LLC
Loeb & Loeb LLP
Lowe, Stein, Hoffman, Allweiss & Hauver L.L.P.
Lowenstein Sandler PC
Lucas and Cavalier, LLC
Mandell Menkes LLC
Mayer Brown LLP
McCusker Anselmi Rosen & Carvelli, PC
McGuireWoods LLP
McKenna Long & Aldridge LLP
Media Risk Consultants LLC
Miller Korzenik Sommers LLP
Minter Ellison
Mintz, Levin, Cohn, Ferris, Glovsky and Popeo, P.C.
Montgomery McCracken Walker & Rhoads LLP
Munger, Tolles & Olson
Nesbitt, Vassar & McCown, L.L.P.
Nixon Peabody LLP
Norwick, Schad & Goering
Ogden, Gibson, Broocks, Longoria & Hall, LLP
Orr & Reno, P.A.
Owen Bird Law Corporation
Parr Brown Gee & Loveless
Parsons Behle & Latimer
Patterson Belknap Webb & Tyler LLP
Paul, Hastings, Janofsky & Walker LLP
Peifer, Hanson & Mullins, P.A.
Pepper Hamilton LLP
Perkins Coie LLP
Phelps Dunbar LLP
Pillsbury Winthrop Shaw Pittman LLP
Preti Flaherty Beliveau & Pachios, LLP
Prince Lobel Tye LLP
Proskauer Rose LLP
Quattlebaum, Grooms, Tull & Burrow PLLC
Quinn Emanuel Urquhart & Sullivan, LLP
Rahdert, Steele, Reynolds and Driscoll, P.A.
Ram & Olson
Reed Smith LLP
Rodey, Dickason, Sloan, Akin & Robb, P.A.
Rothwell, Figg, Ernst & Manbeck, P.C.
RPC
Rushton, Stakely, Johnston & Garrett, P.A.
Satterlee Stephens Burke & Burke LLP
Saul Ewing LLP
Schiff Hardin LLP
Schnader, Harrison, Segal & Lewis
Sedgwick LLP
Sheppard Mullin Richter & Hampton LLP
Sidley Austin LLP
Skadden, Arps, Slate, Meagher & Flom LLP
Smallman Law PLLC
Smith Moore Leatherwood LLP
SmithAmundsen LLC
SmithDehn LLP
SNR Denton US LLP
Stephen Fuzesi, Jr.
Steptoe & Johnson LLP
Steven P. Suskin, Attorney At Law
Stevens Martin Vaughn & Tadych, PLLC
Stites & Harbison
Stokes Lawrence, P.S.
Strassburger, McKenna, Gutnick & Gefsky
Tantalo & Adler LLP
The Bussian Law Firm PLLC
The Maneke Law Group, L.C.
Thomas & LoCicero PL
Thompson & Knight LLP
Thompson Coburn LLP
Troutman Sanders LLP
Venable LLP
Vinson & Elkins
Waller Lansden Dortch & Davis, LLP
Walter & Haverfield
Weil, Gotshal & Manges LLP
Willcox & Savage, P.C.
Williams & Anderson PLC
Williams & Connolly
Willkie Farr & Gallagher LLP
Wilmer Cutler Pickering Hale and Dorr LLP
Wilson Sonsini Goodrich & Rosati
Womble Carlyle Sandridge & Rice LLP
Wyatt, Tarrant & Combs LLP
Wyche, Burgess, Freeman & Parham, P.A.

Associate Members

Broadcasting Board of Governors/Voice of America
Clifford Chance Europe LLP
David Price Solicitors & Advocates
Doughty Street Chambers
Gabriella Rubagotti, Barrister, Fifth Floor Selborne Chambers
GRAEF Rechtsanwälte
Kennedy Van der Laan
Melkonian & Co.
Simpson Grierson
Taylor Wessing LLP

Below is the generic outline which preparers of the specific state chapters were asked to follow. The individual chpaters may slightly vary from this structure, depending on the law of the jurisdiction involved. Any bracketed material in this Topic Outline is considered as instruction to the SURVEY preparers and is not reproduced in the final SURVEY reports.

SURVEY OF [STATE] EMPLOYMENT LIBEL LAW

Survey Preparers
Name of Firm
Firm Address
Telephone; Facsimile

(With Developments Reported Through **November 1, 2012**)

GENERAL COMMENTS

[comments or caveats regarding structure of local court system, the manner in which local cases are reported or cited, etc.]

SIGNIFICANT DEVELOPMENTS SINCE THE 2012 *SURVEY*

I. GENERAL LAW

A. General Employment Law

1. ***At Will Employment.*** [including whether jurisdiction permits claims of wrongful discharge]

B. Elements of Libel Claim

1. ***Basic Elements.***

2. ***Fault.*** [including whether jurisdiction distinguishes between issues of public and private concern; identification of matters found or not found to be "of public concern"; fault standard applicable in cases involving issues of private concern, including whether different standard is applied in cases involving public figure/official plaintiff as opposed to private figure plaintiff]

a. **Private Figure Plaintiff/Matter of Public Concern.**

b. **Private Figure Plaintiff/Matter of Private Concern.**

c. **Public Figure Plaintiff/Matter of Public Concern.**

3. ***Falsity.***

4. ***Defamatory Statement of Fact.***

5. ***Of and Concerning Plaintiff.***

6. ***Publication.***

a. **Intracorporate Communication.** [including circumstances in which publication within a company does or does not constitute publication for defamation purposes]

b. **Compelled Self-Publication.** [including whether jurisdiction has recognized claims of defamation by compelled self-publication and, if recognized, burdens of proof]

c. **Republication.** [distinguishing among original speaker's liability for *its own* republications, "foreseeable" republications *by others*, and the republisher's independent liability for its own republication]

7. ***Statements versus Conduct.*** [including extent to which jurisdiction permits defamation claims based on conduct, such as hand gestures or using an armed security guard to escort a discharged employee from the premises]

8. ***Damages.*** [including discussion of various damages available, e.g., general, compensatory, special, nominal, or any others recognized in your jurisdiction, detailing requirements for each]

a. **Presumed Damages and Libel Per Se.** [including whether jurisdiction permits presumed damages and the effect, if any, of Gertz v. Robert Welch, Inc., 418 U.S. 323 (1974) and Dun & Bradstreet, Inc. v. Greenmoss Builders, Inc., 472 U.S. 749 (1985)]

(1) **Employment-Related Criticism.**

(2) **Single Instance Rule.**

b. **Punitive Damages.** [including applications, if any, of Dun & Bradstreet, supra]

II. PRIVILEGES AND DEFENSES

A. Scope of Privileges

1. ***Absolute Privilege.***

2. ***Qualified Privileges.***

a. **Common Interest.**

b. **Duty.**

c. **Criticism of Public Employee.**

d. **Limitation on Qualified Privileges.**

(1) **Constitutional or Actual Malice.**

(2) **Common Law Malice.**

e. **Question of Fact or Law.**

f. **Burden of Proof.**

B. Standard Libel Defenses [including definitions, examples, scope of defenses, and burdens of proof]

1. ***Truth.*** [including concepts of "substantial truth"/"substantial falsity"]

2. ***Opinion.*** [including extent to which courts apply privilege derived from Gertz, supra; effect of Milkovich v. Lorain Journal Co., 497 U.S. 1 (1990) on opinion privilege; and test used to distinguish opinion from fact]

3. ***Consent.***

4. ***Mitigation.***

III. RECURRING FACT PATTERNS

[including whether governed by statutory or common law and any applicable privileges]

A. Statements in Personnel File

B. Performance Evaluations

C. References

D. Intracorporate Communication

E. Statements to Government Regulators

F. Reports to Auditors and Insurers

G. Vicarious Liability of Employers for Statements Made by Employees

1. ***Scope of Employment.***

a. **Blogging** [employers' liability for comments on employees' (authorized and unauthorized) blogs.]

2. ***Damages.***

H. Internal Investigations [cases and statutes regarding the application of libel law to an employer's internal investigations, including those regarding improper behavior, theft, etc.]

IV. OTHER ACTIONS BASED ON STATEMENTS

[including whether plaintiffs may use these causes of action to circumvent requirements of defamation law]

A. Negligent Hiring, Retention, and Supervision

B. Intentional Infliction of Emotional Distress

C. Interference with Economic Advantage

D. Prima Facie Tort

V. OTHER ISSUES

A. Statute of Limitations

[indicating if different limitation periods apply to defamation and slander; recognition of single publication rule]

B. Jurisdiction [statutes, court rules or decisions regarding jurisdiction over employment privacy claims]

C. Workers' Compensation Exclusivity.

[the extent to which employment privacy claims fall within exclusive jurisdiction of the workers' compensation system]

D. Pleading Requirements

[including degree of specificity required]

Below is the generic outline which preparers of the specific state chapters were asked to follow. The individual chapters may slightly vary from this structure, depending on the law of the jurisdiction involved. Any bracketed material in this Topic Outline is considered as instruction to the SURVEY preparers and is not reproduced in the final SURVEY reports.

SURVEY OF [STATE] EMPLOYMENT PRIVACY LAW

Survey Preparers
Name of Firm
Firm Address
Telephone; Facsimile

(With Developments Reported Through **November 1, 2012**)

GENERAL COMMENTS

[including comments or caveats regarding structure of local court system, the manner in which local cases are reported or cited, etc.]

SIGNIFICANT DEVELOPMENTS SINCE THE 2012 *SURVEY*

[Please discuss any significant developments which have occurred since the last update of the chapter. Text should appear in bold, and should also be placed in appropriate outline section below.]

I. GENERAL LAW OF PRIVACY

A. Legal Basis of Privacy Claims

[note whether constitutional, statutory, or common law]

B. Causes of Action

[describe whether jurisdiction has explicitly accepted/rejected the tort and, if accepted, the substantive elements of the tort and the applicable procedural requirements, including statute of limitations]

1. ***Misappropriation/Right of Publicity.***

2. ***False Light.***

3. ***Publication of Private Facts.***

4. ***Intrusion.***

C. Other Privacy-related Actions

[including whether accepted in the jurisdiction, substantive and procedural requirements, and available remedies; any applicable privileges or defenses, especially those established by cases rejecting "end runs" around the protection of privacy or other law]

1. ***Intentional Infliction of Emotional Distress***

2. ***Interference With Prospective Economic Advantage***

3. ***Prima Facie Tort***

II. EMPLOYER TESTING OF EMPLOYEES

[including which tests have been specifically rejected or approved and any procedures employers must follow]

A. Psychological or Personality Testing

1. ***Common Law and Statutes.***

2. ***Private Employers.***

3. ***Public Employers.***

B. Drug Testing

1. ***Common Law and Statutes.***

2. ***Private Employers.***

3. ***Public Employers.***

C. Medical Testing

1. ***Common law and statutes***

2. ***Private Employers.***

3. ***Public Employers.***

D. Polygraph Tests

E. Fingerprinting

III. SEARCHES

[including applicable constitutional or statutory provisions]

A. Employee's Person

1. ***Private Employers.***

2. ***Public Employers.***

B. Employee's Work Area

C. Employee's Property

1. ***Private Employers.***

2. ***Public Employers.***

IV. MONITORING OF EMPLOYEES

A. Telephones and Electronic Communications [including whether law requires consent of all parties or only one party]

1. ***Wiretapping (Telephone).***

2. ***Electronic Communications (E-mail).***

3. ***Other Electronic Monitoring.*** [including monitoring of employees key strokes, signing on and off, etc.]

B. Mail

C. Surveillance/Photographing

V. ACTIVITIES OUTSIDE THE WORKPLACE

A. Statute or Common Law

B. Employees' Personal Relationships

1. ***Romantic Relationships Between Employees.***

2. ***Sexual Orientation.***

3. ***Marital Status.***

C. Smoking

D. Blogging

VI. RECORDS

[including record-keeping requirements and public accessibility of the records]

A. Personnel Records

B. Medical Records

C. Criminal Records

D. Subpoenas / Search Warrants

[This section, which formerly focused solely on subpoenaes to employers seeking information about employees, should now also address search warrants served on employers seeking to search employee files or an employee's workspace.]

VII. ACTIONS SUBSEQUENT TO EMPLOYMENT.

[viability of claims made after conclusion of the employment relationship]

A. References

B. Non-compete agreements.

VIII. OTHER ISSUES

A. Statutes of Limitations

[including whether same period applies to privacy, negligent hiring/retention/supervision, intentional infliction of emotional distress, and prima facie tort; if different, whether other claims may be used to circumvent shorter privacy limitation period]

B. Jurisdiction

[statutes, court rules or decisions regarding jurisdiction over employment privacy claims]

C. Workers' Compensation Exclusivity.

[the extent to which employment privacy claims fall within exclusive jurisdiction of the workers' compensation system]

D. Pleading Requirements

[including degree of specificity required]

SURVEY OF FEDERAL EMPLOYMENT LIBEL LAW

Gerron L. McKnight
Frost Brown Todd LLC
3300 Great American Tower, 301 East Fourth Street
Cincinnati, Ohio 45202
Telephone (513) 651-6802; Facsimile (513) 651-6981
E-mail: gmcknight@fbtlaw.com

(With Developments Reported Through **November 1, 2012**)

GENERAL COMMENTS

While most of the principles of libel and privacy law applicable to employment situations are matters of state law, there are a number of federal provisions with impact on the workplace and libel and privacy issues which arise in that environment. This chapter outlines the federal statutes applicable to libel cases in the employment context.

SIGNIFICANT DEVELOPMENTS SINCE THE 2012 *SURVEY*

None.

I. GENERAL LAW

A. General Employment Law

1. ***At Will Employment.*** The applicability and parameters of the employment at will doctrine are matters of state law. However, even when employment is at will under state law, an employer's right to discharge an at will employee for any reason or no reason is subject to numerous limitations imposed by federal statutes which make it unlawful to terminate or take other adverse action against an employee on certain specified grounds. See, e.g., Title VII of the Civil Rights Act of 1964, 42 U.S.C. § 2000e et seq. (prohibiting discharge on the basis of race, color, religion, sex, pregnancy, and national origin or for complaining of such discrimination); the Age Discrimination in Employment Act, 29 U.S.C. § 621 et seq. (prohibiting discharge on the basis that employee is aged 40 years or older or for complaining of such discrimination); the Americans with Disabilities Act, 42 U.S.C. § 12101 et seq. (prohibiting discharge on the basis of disability or for complaining of such discrimination); the Civil Rights Act of 1866, 42 U.S.C. § 1981 (prohibiting discharge on the basis of race); the Family and Medical Leave Act, 29 U.S.C. § 2601 et seq. (prohibiting discharge for exercising right to take leave under the statute); the Genetic Information Nondiscrimination Act of 2008, 42 U.S.C. § 2000ff et seq. (prohibiting discharge on the basis of genetic information); the National Labor Relations Act, 29 U.S.C. § 151 et seq. (prohibiting discharge because of membership or non-membership in a labor organization or union); the Uniform Services Employment and Reemployment Rights Act of 1994, 38 U.S.C. § 4301 et seq. (prohibiting discharge on the basis of past, present, or future membership in a uniformed service); the Occupational Safety and Health Act, 29 U.S.C. § 654 et seq. (prohibiting discharge or adverse action against an employee who files a complaint related to workplace safety or institutes or testifies at a proceeding related to workplace safety); the Employee Retirement Income Security Act of 1974, 29 U.S.C. § 1001 et seq. (prohibiting discharge for the purpose of prohibiting attainment of vested pension rights); the Jury Systems Improvements Act of 1978, 28 U.S.C. § 1875 (prohibiting discharge based on employees jury service in any court of the U.S.); the Consumer Credit Protection Act, 15 U.S.C. § 1671 et seq. (prohibiting discharge based on garnishment of wages); the Bankruptcy Act, 11 U.S.C. § 525 et seq. (prohibiting discharge because employee has filed for bankruptcy protection); the Sarbanes-Oxley Act, 18 U.S.C. 1514(A) (granting protection to employees of companies with publicly traded securities who provide evidence of certain types of fraud) and 1513(e) (establishing criminal penalties for retaliation against a witness, victim or informant); federal whistleblower statutes containing anti-retaliation protections for employees who report safety concerns, including the Whistleblower Protection Act of 1989, 5 U.S.C. § 2302 et seq.; Federal Mine Safety and Health Act § 105(c)(1), 30 U.S.C. § 815(c)(1); Federal Water Pollution Control Act, 33 U.S.C. § 1367; Federal Deposit Insurance Act § 2[33], 12 U.S.C. § 1831j; and the Clean Air Act, 42 U.S.C. § 7622.

B. Elements of Libel Claim

1. ***Basic Elements.*** Defamation claims based on statements made during procedures required under collective bargaining agreements may be preempted by the National Labor Relations Act. Compare Aubuschon v. Intl Mill Serv., 522 N.E.2d 898 (Ill. 1988), rev'd, 530 N.E.2d 976 (Ill. 1988), cert. denied., 490 U.S. 1106 (1989) (defamation claim preempted where employer was required to inform union of plaintiffs discipline by grievance proceeding set out in collective bargaining agreement) with Tellez v. Pac. Gas & Elec. Co., 817 F.2d 536 (9th Cir.), cert. denied, 484 U.S. 908 (1987) (defamatory letter that employees manager sent to 11 other company managers regarding employees suspension for

suspected involvement in on-the-job cocaine sale not preempted; defamation claim did not implicate collective bargaining agreement because collective bargaining agreement did not require or suggest sending of such letters).

Similarly, Section 301 of the Labor Management Relations Act will preempt a defamation claim if the claim is founded directly on rights created by a collective bargaining agreement or if a resolution of the claim is substantially dependent on analysis of the collective bargaining agreement. Rogers v. Nstar Elec., 389 F. Supp. 2d 100, 111 (D. Mass. 2005) (defamation claim preempted when claim necessarily requires a determination of the limits of employers power to discipline employees under collective bargaining agreement); DeCoe v. General Motors Corp., 32 F.3d 212 (6th Cir. 1994) (defamation claim by employee accused of sexual harassment required consideration of CBAs detailed sexual harassment policy and required proof of an unprivileged publication, which necessarily implicated examining the CBA, and so was preempted).

Defamation claims may be preempted by the Employee Retirement Income Security Act (ERISA) when "the existence of an ERISA plan is a critical factor in establishing liability. Mayeaux v. Louisiana Health Service and Indem. Co. 376 F.3d 420, 433 (5th Cir. 2004) (so holding where defamation claim arose from the manner in which the ERISA plan administrator determined not to cover Hymans high dosage antibiotic treatments and the subsequent notification to patients that the treatments would not be covered under the Plan).

The Second Circuit Court of Appeals held that the Railway Labor Act did not preempt state defamation claims when those claims were minor disputes reviewable only by arbitral panels under 45 U.S.C.S. § 184 of the Railway Labor Act (RLA). See Sullivan v. Am. Airlines, Inc., 424 F.3d 267, 278 (2005). The RLA commits to arbitral panels, not to federal courts, disputes between airlines and their employees that grow out of grievances, or out of the interpretation or application of agreements concerning rates of pay, rules, or working conditions . . . . 45 U.S.C. § 184. Because such disputes cannot be brought in federal court in the first instance, federal courts may not take jurisdiction over them simply to dismiss them on the basis that they are defensively preempted and belong before arbitral panels. Am. Airlines, Inc., 424 F.3d at 278.

2. ***Fault.*** The Supreme Court's decisions in New York Times Co. v. Sullivan, 376 U.S. 254, 1 Media L. Rep. 1527 (1964), and its progeny – Gertz v. Robert Welch, Inc., 418 U.S. 323, 1 Media L. Rep. 1633 (1974); Dun & Bradstreet, Inc. v. Greenmoss Builders, Inc., 472 U.S. 749, 11 Media L. Rep. 2417 (1985); Philadelphia Newspapers, Inc. v. Hepps, 475 U.S. 767, 12 Media L. Rep. 1977 (1986); and Milkovich v. Lorain Journal Co., 497 U.S. 1, 17 Media L. Rep. 2009 (1990) – held that the First Amendment prohibits defamation plaintiffs who are public officials and "public figures" – which includes both "pervasive," general public figures and "vortex," limited-purpose public figures – from recovering for an admittedly defamatory statement unless that statement is both false and made with "actual malice;" that is, with knowledge that it was false or with reckless disregard of whether it was false or not.

The New York Times Co. v. Sullivan "actual malice" requirement applies only to cases in which the plaintiff is a public official or public figure, which are unlikely to arise in most defamation cases in an employment context. But individual states may apply the Sullivan "actual malice" requirement on other cases, and some have done so.

Of more relevance to the employment context, in Gertz the Court imposed a lower requirement to private-plaintiff cases, holding that the First Amendment prohibits recovery without some showing of "fault" by the defendant. Gertz at 347. The exact level of fault required is a question of state law; courts in some states have imposed different standards based on whether the matter discussed in the statement at issue is a "matter of public concern" or a "matter of private concern." Also, because the Supreme Court left the issue unclear, courts in some states have held that the Gertz fault requirement applies only in cases with media defendants.

The National Labor Relations Act ("Act"), 29 U.S.C. §§ 151-169, provides protection against statements made in the context of a "labor dispute" (as defined in 29 U.S.C. § 152(9)). Thus, litigants bringing defamation lawsuits in that context are required to prove New York Times actual malice as a condition of recovery. Linn v. United Plant Guard Workers of America, Local 114, 383 U.S. 53, 65 (1966). The Act is administered by the National Labor Relations Board ("Board"). And "although the Board tolerates intemperate, abusive and inaccurate statements made by the union during attempts to organize employees," the Act does not give "either party license to injure the other intentionally by circulating defamatory or insulting material known to be false." *Id.* (emphasis added). Also, states are not federally preempted on such lawsuits. Id.

a. **Private Figure Plaintiff/Matter of Public Concern.** See discussion supra.

b. **Private Figure Plaintiff/Matter of Private Concern.** See discussion supra.

c. **Public Figure Plaintiff/Matter of Public Concern.** See discussion supra.

3. ***Falsity.*** No applicable federal provisions.

4. ***Defamatory Statement of Fact.*** No applicable federal provisions.

5. ***Of and Concerning Plaintiff.*** No applicable federal provisions.

6. ***Publication.***

a. **Intracorporate Communication.** No applicable federal provisions.

b. **Compelled Self-Publication**. No applicable federal provisions.

c. **Republication.** No applicable federal provisions.

7. ***Statements versus Conduct.*** No applicable federal provisions.

8. ***Damages.***

a. **Presumed Damages and Libel Per Se.**

(1) **Employment-Related Criticism.** No applicable federal provisions.

(2) **Single Instance Rule.** No applicable federal provisions.

b. **Punitive Damages.** To recover punitive damages for a false and defamatory statement, a public figure plaintiff or a private-figure plaintiff in a case involving a matter of public concern – both unlikely in an employment case – must prove actual malice as defined by the federal constitutional standard of New York Times v. Sullivan, 376 U.S. 254, 1 Media L. Rep. 1527 (1964), by showing that the defendant published the defamatory material with "actual malice;" that is, with knowledge that it was false or with reckless disregard of whether it was false or not. Gertz v. Robert Welch, Inc., 418 U.S. 323, 350 1 Media L. Rep. 1633 (1974)

II. PRIVILEGES AND DEFENSES

A. Scope of Privileges

1. ***Absolute Privilege.*** The Federal Tort Claims Act, 28 U.S.C. § 2671 et seq., (FTCA) provides individuals injured by the tortious acts of federal government employees with an avenue to seek compensation from the federal government where they otherwise would be barred by sovereign immunity. The federal government is liable ... in the same manner and to the same extent as a private individual under like circumstances, but shall not be liable for interest prior to judgment or for punitive damages. 28 U.S.C. § 2674. However, the FTCA excludes from the waiver of sovereign immunity defamation claims, and any claims arising out of defamatory acts. 28 U.S.C. § 2680(h); Popovic v. United States, 175 F.3d 1015 (4th Cir. 1999) (unpublished table decision); Edmonds v. United States (2006), 436 F. Supp. 2d 28 (dismissing claims of negligent disclosure, negligent endangerment, negligent infliction of emotional distress, and negligent interference with prospective economic opportunity under the libel and slander exception because all of these claims arise out of libel or slander). Thus, the government retains its sovereign immunity against claims of defamation, libel, and slander. However, where an action is not excluded, courts determine the nature and extent of tort liability by applying the law of the state in which the cause of action arose. See 28 U.S.C. § 1346.

A federal employee making false statements in the course of performing discretionary acts within the scope of his duties is absolutely immune under the federal common law from a defamation action under state tort law. Burgoyne v. Brooks, 76 Md. App. 222, 544 A.2d 343 (Md. Ct. Spec. App. 1988).

Statements allegedly made by union, employee, and union steward during meetings and investigations of grievance are protected by absolute privilege under § 1 of the National Labor Relations Act. Stiles v. Chrysler Motor Corp., 89 Ohio App. 3d 256, 624 N.E.2d 238 (Ohio App. 6 Dist. 1993), dismissed, jurisdictional motion overruled, 67 Ohio St. 3d 1502, 622 N.E.2d 651, interpreting 29 U.S.C. § 151.

2. ***Qualified Privileges.***

a. **Common Interest.** No applicable federal provisions.

b. **Duty.** No applicable federal provisions.

c. **Criticism of Public Employee.** No applicable federal provisions.

d. **Limitation on Qualified Privileges.**

(1) **Constitutional or Actual Malice.** When the plaintiff is a public official or public figure, even if the plaintiff can prove that the defendant published false and defamatory statements concerning the plaintiff with common law malice, in order to prevail, constitutional considerations require the plaintiff to prove by clear and convincing evidence that the defendant published the complained-of statement with "actual malice:" knowledge that the statements were false or with actual serious doubts as to whether the statements were true or false. St. Amant v. Thompson, 390 U.S. 727, 731 (1968). Courts in many states have held that qualified privileges may be defeated with a showing of actual malice.

(2) **Common Law Malice.** No applicable federal provisions.

e. **Question of Fact or Law**. No applicable federal provisions.

f. **Burden of Proof.** No applicable federal provisions.

B. Standard Libel Defenses

1. ***Truth.*** No applicable federal provisions.
2. ***Opinion.*** No applicable federal provisions.
3. ***Consent.*** No applicable federal provisions.
4. ***Mitigation***. No applicable federal provisions.

III. RECURRING FACT PATTERNS

A. Statements in Personnel File

No applicable federal provisions.

B. Performance Evaluations

No applicable federal provisions.

C. References

No applicable federal provisions.

D. Intracorporate Communication

No applicable federal provisions.

E. Statements to Government Regulators

No applicable federal provisions.

F. Reports to Auditors and Insurers

No applicable federal provisions.

G. Vicarious Liability of Employers for Statements Made by Employees

1. ***Scope of Employment***. No applicable federal provisions.

   a. **Blogging.** No applicable federal provisions.

2. ***Damages.*** No applicable federal provisions.

H. Internal Investigations

No applicable federal provisions

IV. OTHER ACTIONS BASED ON STATEMENTS

As with defamation claims, Section 301 of the Labor Management Relations Act will also act to preempt any state law claim arising from the breach of a collective bargaining agreement and any state law tort claim that is substantially dependent on, rather than only tangentially related to, the terms of a collective bargaining agreement. Alongi v. Ford Motor Co., 386 F.3d 716, 724 (6th Cir. 2004).

A. Negligent Hiring, Retention, and Supervision

Although the existence of a collective bargaining agreement does not necessarily cause federal preemption of this common law claim, if the existence of such an agreement were to become relevant, federal preemption questions might be raised under the Labor Management Relations Act, 29 U.S.C. § 185(a). For example, in making a determination of proximate cause, "a court might have to resort to the collective bargaining agreement to discover whether contractual limitations on the power of the employer to deal with the employee precluded it from taking steps to prevent the harm." Retherford v. AT&T Comms., 844 P.2d 949, 974 (Utah 1992).

B. Intentional Infliction of Emotional Distress

No applicable federal provisions.

C. Interference with Economic Advantage

No applicable federal provisions.

D. Prima Facie Tort

No applicable federal provisions.

V. OTHER ISSUES

A. Statute of Limitations

No applicable federal provisions.

B. Jurisdiction

No applicable federal provisions.

C. Worker's Compensation Exclusivity

The Federal Employee Compensation Act (FECA), 5 U.S.C. § 8101 et seq., establishes a workers' compensation program for federal employees injured while working. The Secretary of Labor has exclusive authority to administer FECA and to decide all questions, including questions of coverage, under FECA. 5. U.S.C. § 8145. FECA provides the exclusive means by which federal employees may recover from the federal government for employment-related injuries. 5 U.S.C. § 8116(c). As such, a determination that FECA applies to a libel claim precludes the assertion of state law libel claims against the federal government. See Hightower v. U.S., 205 F.Supp.2d 146, 151-153 (S.D.N.Y. 2002) (holding that the district court lacked subject matter jurisdiction to hear a state law claim for malicious prosecution, libel, slander, and intentional infliction of emotional distress because the plaintiff had already recovered for the injuries in a FECA claim).

D. Pleading Requirements

No applicable federal provisions.

SURVEY OF FEDERAL EMPLOYMENT PRIVACY LAW

Gerron L. McKnight
Frost Brown Todd LLC
3300 Great American Tower, 301 East Fourth Street
Cincinnati, Ohio, 45202
Telephone (513) 651-6802; Facsimile (513) 651-6981
E-mail: gmcknight@fbtlaw.com

(With Developments Reported Through **November 1, 2012**)

GENERAL COMMENTS

The law protecting an employee's right to privacy varies greatly depending on whether the employee works in the public or private sector. Constitutional protection of individual privacy rights, such as the prohibition against unreasonable searches and seizures, applies only to actions by the government and not to those of private employers. In contrast, employee privacy rights in the private sector are largely dependent upon diverse legal protections that vary from subject matter to subject matter and from state to state. In addition, various federal statutes, which apply in both the public and private employment context, affect employees' privacy interests. This chapter outlines the federal law on workplace privacy.

SIGNIFICANT DEVELOPMENTS SINCE THE 2012 *SURVEY*

None.

I. GENERAL LAW OF PRIVACY

A. Legal Basis of Privacy Claims

1. ***Constitutional Law.*** Courts have recognized privacy protections for employees under the First, Third, Fourth, Fifth, Ninth, and Fourteenth Amendments to the U.S. Constitution, which are applicable only in the public employment context. See, e.g., City of Ontario v. Quon, 130 S. Ct. 2619 (2010) (the City's review of a police officer's personal text messages sent on City-issued pagers where there was a question of improper personal use did not constitute an unreasonable search under the Fourth Amendment where the City limited the search to a reasonable time frame and to messages sent during work hours); Richards v. County of Los Angeles, 775 F.Supp.2d 1176 (C.D. Cal. 2011) (the County's covert videotaping of multiple employees in a meal and break room who had not been implicated by an anonymous complaint against an individual employee violated non-implicated employees' Fourth Amendment rights where individual who monitored surveillance admitted to watching all employees on tapes, and employees performed acts they would not have performed in public; Thorne v. El Segundo, 726 F.2d 459 (9th Cir. 1983), cert. denied, 469 U.S. 979 (1984) (police clerk's First Amendment privacy rights were abridged when she was forced, through polygraph exam, to disclose information regarding personal sexual matters which was later considered in decision to deny her admission to police academy); Engblom v. Carey, 677 F.2d 957 (2d Cir. 1982) (correction officers employed by state prison brought action against state officials claiming that their constitutional rights were violated when, during a strike, members of the National Guard were quartered in staff housing buildings; court held that correction officers had a legitimate expectation of privacy protected by the Third Amendment, in their living quarters, which were located on grounds of correction facility and made available to correction employees); Am. Fed'n of Gov't Employees, R.R. Ret. Bd. Council, AFL-CIO v. United States R.R. Ret. Bd., 742 F. Supp. 450 (N.D. Ill. 1990) (requiring applicants to answer certain questions as a condition of employment impermissibly infringed upon their Fifth Amendment right against self-incrimination); Nelson v. National Aeronautics and Space Admin., 131 S.Ct. 746 (2011) (reversing the 9th Circuit, and holding that reasonable background checks in an employment background investigation did not violate federal contractor employees' constitutional right to informational privacy where employees challenged questions contained in employment background investigation forms for non-sensitive contract positions regarding "details, including information about 'treatment or counseling received'" for recent illegal drug use and "open-ended questions" regarding the "employee's 'honesty and trustworthiness.'"); Mindel v. United States Civil Serv. Comm'n, 312 F. Supp. 485 (N.D. Cal. 1970) (postal clerk's termination because of his private sex life violated right to privacy guaranteed by Ninth Amendment); **Garlitz v. Alpena Reg'l Med. Ctr., 834 F. Supp. 2d 668 (E.D. Mich. 2011) (questions regarding private sex life of applicant for per diem position, including whether she experienced pain during sex, whether she was or ever had been pregnant, whether she ever had an abortion, miscarriage, or live birth, and whether she was on birth control implicated plaintiff's Fourteenth Amendment right to privacy and were not relevant to the performance or functions of the position she applied for).**

2. ***Statutory Law***

a. **Privacy Act of 1974.** This Act governs the maintenance and disclosure of records, including personnel records, by a federal agency. The Privacy Act was enacted to promote respect for privacy of citizens by requiring all departments and agencies of the executive branch and their employees to observe privacy protections afforded by the Constitution in the computerization, collection, management, use, and disclosure of individuals' personal information. The Privacy Act is limited in scope because it applies only to federal government employees. 5 U.S.C. § 552(a) et seq. See V.A.1, infra. The Act provides that "[n]o agency shall disclose any record which is contained in a 'system of records' by any means of communication to any person . . , except pursuant to . . . prior written consent of, the individual to whom the record pertains." *Krieger v. United States DOJ*, 529 F. Supp. 2d 29, 37 (D.D.C. 2008). The fact that electronic records are searchable does not make the records a "system of records" under the Act. For purposes of determining whether electronic records are stored as a system of records, the court will consider whether the files and folders are labeled in an organized fashion ("computer files are like paper documents . . . and hard drives are like file cabinets."). *Id.*

b. **Fair Credit Reporting Act.** This Act establishes requirements that employers must meet to obtain a consumer report (a report dealing with an applicant's or employee's credit history) or an investigative consumer report (a report concerning an applicant's or employee's character, general reputation, personal characteristics, or mode of living based on interviews with neighbors, friends, or associates).

Employers may obtain either type of report only for legitimate employment purposes, including evaluating a consumer for employment, promotion, reassignment or retention as an employee. However, employers must comply with notice and disclosure requirements and must receive the consumer's written authorization, on a document separate from the employment application, before a report may be obtained. In addition, before obtaining an investigative consumer report, employers must give written notice to the employee or applicant that a report including information as to his character, general reputation, personal characteristics, and mode of living may be made; provide notice that, upon request, a complete disclosure of the nature and scope of the investigation will be supplied; and give the employee or applicant a summary of a consumer's rights under the Act. 15 U.S.C. § 1681 et seq.

The Act also entitles the consumer to a copy of the report and a summary of a consumer's rights under the Act before any adverse employment action is taken based, in whole or in part, on information contained in either a consumer report or an investigative consumer report. **See, e.g., Goode v. LexisNexis Risk & Info. Analytics Group, 848 F. Supp. 2d. 532 (E.D. Pa. 2012) (adjudication of plaintiffs as "noncompetitive" in application process based on background check was an adverse employment action requiring defendant to comply with FCRA notice and disclosure requirements prior to making such a determination).**

The Federal Trade Commission, which enforces the Act, has issued an opinion letter stating that employers engaging outside counsel or investigators to investigate alleged harassment, discrimination, or other workplace issues must comply with the notice and disclosure requirements of the Act if such outside counsel and investigators regularly conduct investigations of workplace misconduct because in such circumstances they may be considered "consumer reporting agencies." FTC Letter Opinion on Sexual Harassment Investigators and the Fair Credit Reporting Act, 96 Daily Lab. Rep (BNA) at E-1 (May 19, 1999).

c. **Fair and Accurate Credit Transactions Act of 2003.** This Act, which became law in December 2003, required the Federal Trade Commission (FTC) and other federal agencies to issue regulations governing the disposal of consumer credit information. The FTC final rule became effective June 1, 2005, and, as the commentary makes clear, creates broad responsibilities for employers. This rule requires that any person who maintains or otherwise possesses consumer information for a business purpose must properly dispose of such information by taking reasonable measures to protect against unauthorized access to or use of the information in connection with its disposal. 16 C.F.R. § 682.3(a) (2005).

This Act amended numerous Fair Credit Reporting Act provisions. Very few courts that have analyzed Section 311(a) of this Act have found that 15 USC § 1681m(h)(8) bars private enforcement of the Act in its entirety. See, e.g., Murray v. GMAC Mortgage Corp., 434 F.3d 948 (7th Cir. 2006); Putkowski v. Irwin Home Equity Corp., 423 F. Supp. 2d 1053 (N.D. Cal. Mar. 23, 2006); Murray v. Cross Country Bank, 399 F. Supp. 2d 843 (N.D. Ill. Aug. 15, 2005). Instead, such violations are administratively enforced. 15 U.S.C. § 1681m(h)(8)(B) (2004). Two federal district courts, however, have held that § 1681m(h)(8) only bars private rights of action to enforce § 1681m(h) (holding that because §312(f) of FACTA provides that "nothing in this section, the amendments made by this section, or any other provision of this Act shall be construed to effect any liability under section 616 or 617 or the Fair Credit Reporting Act. . . that existed on the day before the enforcement of this Act," private individuals may still enforce the requirements of the Act. Barnette v Brook Road, Inc., 429 F.Supp.2d 741, 2006 WL 1195913 (E.D. Va. 2006); Kubbany v. Trans Union LLC, 2009 WL 1844344 (N.D. Cal. June 10, 2009); but see Bourdelais v. J.P. Morgan Chase, 2011 WL 1306311 (E.D. Va. April 1, 2011) (disagreeing with

Barnette and Kubbany and holding that no private right of action exists for the Act). **See also Haley v. Citibank N.A., 2012 WL 2403501 (S.D. Tex. June 25, 2012) (discussing current circuit split regarding private rights of action).**

d. **Omnibus Crime Control and Safe Streets Act.** This Act proscribes deliberate interceptions of wire or oral communications. An interception of an employee's communications under conditions which justify the employee's subjective expectation of confidentiality is prohibited. 18 U.S.C. § 2510 et seq. See IV.A.1, infra.

e. **Electronic Privacy Communications Act of 1986.** This Act amends the Omnibus Crime Control and Safe Streets Act, which focuses on older technologies such as the telephone, and provides protections against unauthorized interception of, and access to, transmitted and stored electronic communications. 18 U.S.C. § 2510 et seq., 18 U.S.C. § 2701 et seq. See IV.A.2, infra.

f. **Employee Polygraph Protection Act of 1988.** This Act prohibits most private employers from using lie detector tests to screen job applicants or to penalize employees or applicants who refuse to submit to a lie detector test. The Act has been found not to apply to situations where a union, not the employer, requested the polygraph exam. Watson v. Drummond Co., 436 F.3d 1310, 1313-14 (11th Cir. 2006). Also, there are substantial exceptions to the Act, including all government employers, private security firms, and employers conducting investigations involving economic loss, such as theft or embezzlement. 29 U.S.C. § 2001 et seq. See II.D.1, infra; See Veazey v. Comms. & Cable, Inc., 194 F.3d 850, 861 (7th Cir. 1999) (reinstating the claim under EPPA of an employee who was discharged after he refused to provide his superiors with a tape-recorded voice exemplar of him reading a transcript of a threatening voicemail message that had been sent to another employee, because the results of the tape recording were to be used to render a diagnostic opinion regarding the honesty or dishonesty of the plaintiff when evaluated by a voice stress analyzer); Polkey v. Transtecs Corp., 404 F.3d 1264 (11th Cir. 2005) (affirming grant of summary judgment to plaintiff where employer could not satisfy its burden of establishing reasonable suspicion of subject employee's involvement in mail tampering incident under investigation and therefore could not rely on ongoing investigation exemption); Drummond Co., 436 F.3d at 1315 (affirming summary judgment for the Defendant where the ongoing investigation exemption applied).

g. **Health Insurance Portability and Accountability Act of 1996 (HIPAA).** The privacy rules under HIPAA apply generally to all "health plans." HIPAA's privacy standards address the use and disclosure of individuals' health information, or "protected health information" (PHI), by organizations subject to the statute, called "covered entities." PHI is information that relates to i) an individual's past, present, or future physical or mental health or condition, ii) health care provided to the individual, or iii) past, present, or future payment of health care provided to the individual. 45 C.F.R. §§ 160.103. Individual and group plans that provide or pay the cost of medical care are "covered entities." 45 C.F.R. §§ 160.102, 160.103.

While employers or plan sponsors are not themselves covered entities, the group health plans established for their employees are covered entities under the privacy rules. Often these plans do not have a separate corporate existence, thereby requiring the plan sponsor to ensure compliance with HIPAA's privacy rules regarding PHI. However, employment records, i.e. those maintained by a covered entity in its capacity as an employer, are specifically excluded from the definition of PHI. Id.

Generally, a covered entity may not use or disclose Protected Health Information unless the use or disclosure is allowed by the privacy rules (usually a health-care purpose) or the individual subject of the information provides written authorization. 45 C.F.R. §§ 164.502(a). Particularly, the privacy rules prohibit the use of PHI for employment or personnel decisions. 45 C.F.R. §§ 164.504(f)(1).

B. Causes of Action

Federal causes of action involving privacy exist only by virtue of the constitutional and statutory provisions discussed supra.

C. Other Privacy-related Actions

Federal causes of action involving privacy exist only by virtue of the constitutional and statutory provisions discussed supra.

II. EMPLOYER TESTING OF EMPLOYEES

A. Psychological or Personality Testing

1. ***ADA.*** The Americans with Disabilities Act, 42 U.S.C. § 12101 et seq., prohibits employers from conducting pre-employment medical tests as a condition of employment. See Karraker v. Rent-A-Center, Inc., 411 F.3d 831,

834 (7th Cir. 2005). Psychological tests that are designed to identify a mental disorder or impairment qualify as medical examinations, but psychological tests that measure personality traits such as honesty, preferences, and habits do not. Id. at 835 (citation omitted). If a psychological test is used only to identify personality traits, but also has the capacity to test for mental disorders, the test is impermissible if it has the effect of screening out candidates with mental disorders. Id. at 835-37 (holding that Minnesota Multiphasic Personality Inventory qualified as a medical examination and that pre-employment use violated Americans With Disabilities Act). See also II.A.1, supra.

2. ***Fair Credit Reporting Act.*** An employer's use of a consumer reporting agency to inquire into an employee's or job applicant's character, general reputation, personal characteristics, or mode of living is governed by the Fair Credit Reporting Act. See I.B.2, supra.

B. Drug and Alcohol Testing

1. ***Constitutional Law.*** Workplace drug and alcohol testing of government employees and job applicants is subject to the protections afforded by the U.S. Constitution.

a. **Fourth Amendment.** Under the Fourth Amendment of the U.S. Constitution, individuals are guaranteed the right to be free from unreasonable governmental searches and seizures. Thus, when drug or alcohol testing is done directly by a state entity, or at the direction of the government, the Fourth Amendment is implicated. The courts have generally held that the taking of blood, urine, or breath samples for drug or alcohol testing constitutes a search and/or seizure sufficient to trigger the protections of the Fourth Amendment of the U.S. Constitution. See Skinner v. Ry. Labor Exec. Assn., 489 U.S. 602 (1989).

To determine if a drug or alcohol testing program is constitutionally valid, courts engage in a two-step test: first determining if a special need for the testing exists and then, if it does, determining if the employee's privacy rights are outweighed by the employer's or the public's interest in testing. The courts' balancing test includes factors such as the reasonableness of the privacy expectations of the employees; the intrusiveness of the testing involved; the dangerousness of the employee's job; the threat to the public from these dangers; the effectiveness of the testing program as a deterrent to drug use; and the drawbacks of requiring testing only upon reasonable individualized suspicion. See Skinner v. Ry. Labor Exec. Assn., 489 U.S. 602, 624-31 (1989); Carroll v. City of Westminster, 52 F. Supp. 2d 546 (D. Md. 1999), aff'd, 233 F.3d 208 (4th Cir. 2000) (rejecting challenge to constitutionality of defendant police departments drug testing policy because city's substantial interests in insuring that its police officers are drug free justifies departure from the warrant or individualized suspicion requirement necessary to conduct a Fourth Amendment search).

b. **First Amendment**. The First Amendment to the U.S. Constitution guarantees that the government will not interfere with the free exercise of religion. It is unlikely that drug testing would be found to interfere with a government employee's free exercise of religion, but the use of sacramental peyote has been claimed to implicate the First Amendment. In Employment Div., Dep't of Human Resources of Oregon v. Smith, 494 U.S. 872, reh'g denied, 496 U.S. 913 (1990), a member of the Native American Church was fired because of his sacramental use of peyote. He was subsequently denied unemployment compensation because he was fired for conduct that was illegal under Oregon law. The U.S. Supreme Court held that Oregon's prohibition of the sacramental use of peyote did not violate the First Amendment's guarantee of freedom of religion. In response to Employment Div., Dep't of Human Resources of Oregon v. Smith, Congress enacted the Religious Freedom Restoration Act of 1993 (RFRA). Among other things, RFRA prohibits the Federal Government from substantially burdening a person's exercise of religion even if the burden is a result of a generally applicable rule. 42 U.S.C. § 2000bb-1(a) unless the rule meets the standards of strict scrutiny. Id.

2. ***Statutes.***

a. **ADA.** Although the ADA prohibits discrimination against a qualified individual with a disability because of the disability, the ADA specifically provides that the term individual with a disability does not include an individual who is currently engaging in the illegal use of drugs. 42 U.S.C. § 12114 (a). The ADA does, however, protect drug addicts who either are participating in, or who have completed, a supervised drug rehabilitation program and are no longer current illegal drug users. These provisions did not change under the ADA Amendments Act of 2008 (ADAAA).

The EEOC's Interpretive Guidance to the regulations covering the ADA provides that [t]he term currently engaging is not intended to be limited to the use of drugs on the day of, or within a matter of days or weeks before, the employment action in question. Rather, the provision is intended to apply to the illegal use of drugs that has occurred recently enough to indicate that the individual is actively engaged in such behavior. The courts have generally endorsed this approach. See, e.g., Shafer v. Preston Mem'l Hosp. Corp., 107 F.3d 274 (4th Cir. 1997) (Congress intended to exclude from ADA protection an employee who uses drugs in the weeks and months prior to discovery, even if the employee is participating in rehabilitation at the time the employer terminates the employment) abrogated on other grounds, Baird ex rel.

Baird v. Rose, 192 F.3d 462 (4th Cir. 1999); but see, Hernandez v. Hughes Missile Systems Company, 292 F.3d 1038 (9th Cir. 2002) (question of fact precluding summary judgment existed with respect to whether decision not to rehire was based on the plaintiffs record of disability, where former employee who had tested positive for cocaine use reapplied for a position with the employer and was rejected, even though plaintiff had not premised his claim on any current addiction) *vacated on other grounds*, Raytheon Co. v. Hernandez, 540 U.S. 44, *51 (2003). The ADA does not preclude employers from instituting testing practices to monitor illegal drug use. The ADA provides specifically that none of its provisions regarding the illegal use of drugs in the workplace or its identification of certain substances users as disabled should be construed to "encourage, prohibit, or authorize a covered entity to conduct drug tests of job applicants or employees to determine the illegal use of drugs or to make employment decisions based on such test results." 42 U.S.C.A. § 12114 (d), 29 C.F.R. § 1630.16(c).

b. **Drug-Free Workplace Act of 1988.** This Act requires federal contractors with contracts exceeding $100,000 and grantees receiving any amount of federal funds to certify to the appropriate federal agency that they provide a drug-free workplace and implement workplace drug abuse prevention programs. The Act applies only to the specific workplace where work on the federal contract or grant is taking place and only to those employees doing work directly related to the contract or grant. A copy of an anti-drug abuse policy must be given to every employee doing work under the contract or grant. The policy must include: a written statement (the policy) prohibiting the manufacture, possession, distribution, or use of controlled substances in the workplace; a list of the disciplinary actions that will be taken against employees who violate the policy; a drug-free awareness program to educate employees about the dangers of illegal drugs, including information on the availability of drug counseling, rehabilitation, and employee assistance programs; and a notice to each employee that he or she must inform the employer of drug-related convictions within five days of the conviction. If an employee's drug-related conviction involves drug abuse in the workplace, the employer must report the conviction to the contracting federal agency within 10 days of being notified of the conviction. Within 30 days of the workplace drug-conviction notice, the employer must discharge or otherwise discipline the employee or enroll the employee in a government-approved rehabilitation program. Failure to adopt an anti-drug policy can result in a loss of the contract or grant and debarment from further federal work for up to five years. 41 U.S.C. § 701 et seq.

c. **Omnibus Transportation Employee Testing Act of 1991.** Pursuant to this Act, five operating administrations of the Department of Transportation have promulgated rules requiring private employers in the transportation industry to implement alcohol and drug testing. 49 U.S.C. § 5331. Employers whose employees operate aircraft, public transportation, or commercial motor vehicles are subject to the provisions of this Act. The regulations require that airlines, railroads, commercial motor carriers, and operators of mass transportation conduct pre-employment, reasonable suspicion, random, and post-accident drug and alcohol testing of employees performing safety-sensitive functions. Employers and drivers found to be in violation of the regulations may be subject to civil forfeiture penalties of up to $10,000. 49 U.S.C. § 521. There is no private right of action.

d. **Rehabilitation Act.** Public employers and government contractors or subcontractors are prohibited from discriminating against individuals on the basis of a physical handicap. 29 U.S.C. § 701 et seq. This Act, like the ADA, seeks to prevent an employer from discriminating against qualified handicapped individuals. Unlike the ADA, it applies only to those employers receiving federal contracts in excess of a certain dollar amount and to participants in federally funded programs. For purposes of the Rehabilitation Act, a handicapped individual includes alcoholics and drug addicts. To attain handicapped status, employees must demonstrate that they are alcoholics or addicted to drugs; casual alcohol or drug use is insufficient. However, despite the Rehabilitation Acts inclusion of alcoholism and drug addiction as covered impairments, it specifically provides that a handicapped employee does not include an alcoholic or drug abuser whose current use prevents the individual from performing the duties mandated by the position, or poses a direct threat to property or another individuals' safety. The Act also has been held to prohibit discrimination of individuals with past drug-use problems. See D'Amico v. City of New York, 132 F.3d 145 (2d Cir.), cert. denied, 524 U.S. 911 (1998).

An employer will be required to reasonably accommodate a handicapped individual under the Rehabilitation Act and determine if performance problems are caused by the handicap. Courts differ as to whether an employer may distinguish an individual's disability from its consequences. For example, in Teahan v. Metro-North Commuter R.R. Co., 80 F.3d 50 (2d Cir. 1996), the court ruled that the employer could not separate the employee's alcoholism from his absenteeism. A second federal appeals court, however, upheld the discharge of a college football coach who alleged that his arrest for drunk driving, for which he was terminated, was attributable to his alcoholism. This court concluded that the Rehabilitation Act permitted the discharge for misconduct even if the misconduct could be traced to the employee's disability. The court reasoned that if this were not so, employers would be required to tolerate behavior from alcoholics that would not be tolerated from sober or nonalcoholic intoxicated employees. See Maddox v. Univ. of Tenn., 62 F.3d 843 (6th Cir. 1995). Overall, in the majority of cases, the courts have found no violation of the Rehabilitation Act when the employee is fired due to egregious or criminal conduct which would result in termination if the employee were not disabled. See Newland v. Dalton, 81 F.3d 904, 906 (9th Cir. 1996), and cases cited therein.

Under the Rehabilitation Acts regulations, pre-employment drug tests are prohibited unless they are "job related," compelled by "business necessity," and administered after a conditional employment offer has been extended. The Rehabilitation Act prohibits the administering of drug tests to current employees without reasonable suspicion of substance abuse.

e. **Public Health and Welfare Act.** This Act prohibits discrimination against a federal civilian employee solely on the basis of prior substance abuse. 42 U.S.C. § 290dd. Certain federal agencies, such as the Central Intelligence Agency, are not subject to the provisions of this Act. Nothing in the Act, however, is intended to exempt such agencies from the provisions of the Rehabilitation Act. The Act does not prohibit dismissal from employment of a federal civilian employee who cannot function in his/her employment. Under the Act, there is no private right of action.

f. **Federal Credit Reporting Act.** Some employees have successfully challenged drug and alcohol testing under the Federal Credit Reporting Act, by analogizing drug and alcohol tests to consumer reports. See Hodge v. Texaco, Inc., 975 F.2d 1093 (5th Cir. 1992), reh'g denied (1992) (there was no basis in the statutory language or the legislative history to conclude that medical-type reports were meant to be excluded from [FCRAs] coverage.).

3. ***Executive Order.*** In September 1986, President Reagan issued Executive Order 12564, commonly referred to as the drug-free federal workplace policy. This Executive Order mandated that all federal executive agencies develop plans for achieving a drug-free workplace, including the implementation of drug-testing programs. In response, a vast majority of federal agencies have approved plans for workplace drug testing of their employees. The U.S. Department of Health and Human Services has issued mandatory guidelines governing the implementation of federal employee drug and alcohol programs.

A common characteristic of the testing policies adopted is the requirement that employees in sensitive positions (where drug use would pose a danger to the public or national security) be tested along with (1) applicants for government employment; (2) government employees reasonably suspected of using drugs or alcohol; (3) employees involved in workplace accidents; and (4) employees in drug rehabilitation programs. Agencies are to conduct their drug programs pursuant to scientific and technical guidelines established by the Secretary of Health and Human Services. Any employee testing positive must be discharged unless the individual receives counseling or rehabilitation, and remains drug-free.

4. ***Union Employees.*** The unilateral implementation of drug testing has been found by the National Labor Relations Board to be a mandatory subject of bargaining because it was plainly germane to the working environment. See Memorandum of the General Counsel of the National Labor Relations Board, issued September 24, 1987, Daily Lab. Rep. (BNA) No. 184, at D-1 (Sept. 24, 1987) (citing Dubo Mfg. Corp., 142 N.L.R.B. 431 (1963); Collyer Insulated Wire, 192 N.L.R.B. 837 (1971)).

C. Medical Testing

1. ***The Americans with Disabilities Act.*** The Americans with Disabilities Act (ADA), although not enacted as a statute to protect employees' privacy rights, has that effect as a result of certain of its provisions. The statute applies to both public and private employers. 42 U.S.C. § 12112 et seq.

a. **Pre-offer stage.** The ADA prohibits an employer from conducting or requiring any medical examination of an applicant prior to making an offer of employment. The ADA also restricts employers from making inquiries of a job applicant as to whether such applicant is an individual with a disability or as to the nature or severity of such a disability.

b. **Conditional offer stage.** Once a conditional offer of employment has been made, an employer may require a medical examination of an applicant, provided that all entering employees in the same job category are subjected to such an examination regardless of disability and any information obtained regarding the medical condition or history of the applicant is collected and maintained on separate forms and in separate medical files and is treated as a confidential medical record. See V.B.1.a, infra.

c. **Employees.** An employer may conduct voluntary medical examinations, including voluntary medical histories, which are part of an employee health program available to employees at a work site. An employer also may make inquiries into the ability of an employee to perform essential functions of a position. However, an employer may neither require a medical examination nor make inquiries of an employee as to whether such employee is an individual with a disability or as to the nature or severity of the disability, unless such examination or inquiry is shown to be job-related and consistent with business necessity. However, non-disabled applicants may not be entitled to challenge such inquiries under the ADA. Compare Armstrong v. Turner Indus., 141 F.3d 554 (5th Cir. 1998) (questioning, but not deciding, whether a non-disabled applicant has a right of action under the ADA) with Fredenburg v. Contra Costa County Dep't Health Servs., 172 F.3d 1176 (9th Cir. 1999) (allowing claims by non-disabled employees).

2. ***HIV/AIDS.*** AIDS is a protected disability under the ADA. 28 C.F.R. § 36-104. Therefore, pre-offer HIV tests are unlawful under the ADA. An HIV carrier who has not developed AIDS but is perceived as having the disease is also protected. However, employees would not be protected where the absence of exposure to the virus may be a legitimate job requirement, as in certain health-care positions. See, e.g., Scoles v. Mercy Health Corp., 887 F. Supp. 765 (E.D. Pa. 1994) (doctor infected with HIV not qualified to perform as orthopedic surgeon). But see Doe v. District of Columbia, 796 F. Supp. 559, 569 (D.D.C. 1992) (based on state of medical knowledge, there is no measurable risk of [HIV positive firefighter] transmitting HIV to other firefighters or the public during the performance of official firefighting duties.).

3. ***Genetic Testing.*** The Genetic Information Nondiscrimination Act of 2008 (GINA), 42 U.S.C. § 2000ff et seq., was signed into law by President George W. Bush on May 21, 2008. The law includes two titles. Title I amends portions of the Employee Retirement Income Security Act (ERISA), the Public Health Service Act, and the Internal Revenue Code. These amendments address the use of genetic information in health insurance. Title I went into effect May 22, 2009 for individual health insurers, and at the start of the "plan year" beginning one year after GINA's enactment for group health plans.

Title II applies to private and state and local government employers with 15 or more employees, employment agencies, labor unions, and joint labor-management training programs. It also covers Congress and federal executive branch agencies. Title II prohibits the use of genetic information in making decisions related to the compensation, terms, conditions, or privileges of employment; prohibits harassment based on genetic information; prohibits the intentional acquisition of genetic information about applicants and employees; imposes strict confidentiality requirements; and prohibits retaliation. Also, though formerly allowed under the ADA, GINA prohibits covered entities from obtaining family medical history or conducting genetic tests of job applicants after an offer of employment has been made. Title II of GINA went into effect on November 21, 2009.

In addition to Title II of GINA, several other statutes addressing the workplace may provide employees some protection. For example, the ADA does deal with genetic testing privacy issues peripherally in that a genetic test may be considered a medical examination. 42 U.S.C. § 12112(d). Title VII of the Civil Rights Act of 1964, as amended, 42 U.S.C. § 2002e et seq. (Title VII). Title VII may prohibit genetic discrimination, at least in cases in which there is a disparate impact along the lines of race, color, religion, sex, or national origin. Employers cannot fail or refuse to hire or discharge any individual or otherwise to discriminate against any individual because of any of these factors. Inasmuch as some genetic traits seem to be associated with race, ethnicity, or sex, genetic testing may have a disproportionate effect on members of a protected class. See, e.g., Norman-Bloodsaw v. Lawrence Berkley Lab., 135 F.3d 1260, 1272 (9th Cir. 1998).

The Health Insurance Portability and Accountability Act of 1996 (HIPAA), which amends the Employee Retirement Income Security Act (ERISA), 29 U.S.C. §§ 1001-461, provides some federal protection against genetic discrimination in health insurance. Before HIPAA took effect, employers and health insurers had the ability to limit or deny health insurance coverage to individuals with preexisting medical conditions. Under HIPAA, group health plans and health insurance issuers offering group health insurance coverage may impose a preexisting condition exclusion only under certain limited circumstances. The key aspect to HIPAA, with regard to genetic information, is that it prohibits employers and health insurers from denying coverage to those who undergo genetic testing, unless the testing results in the "diagnosis of the condition." 29 U.S.C. §§ 1181(b)(i)(B).

Federal sector applicants and employees may seek protection under Executive Order 13145, which prohibits discrimination in federal employment based on genetic discrimination.

4. ***Vocational Rehabilitation Act of 1973.*** The same rules as under the ADA apply to medical examinations of employees under the Vocational Rehabilitation Act of 1973 (Rehabilitation Act). 29 U.S.C. § 701 et seq.; HR Rep No. 101-485, 101st Cong., 2nd Sess. (1990), at 43. This Act applies only to public employers and government contractors or subcontractors. See II.B.2.d, infra.

D. Polygraph Tests

1. ***Employee Polygraph Protection Act of 1988.*** This law prohibits most private employers from using lie detector tests to screen job applicants or to penalize employees or applicants who refuse to submit to such tests. 29 U.S.C. § 2001 et seq.

a. **Definition of lie detector.** The law defines a lie detector as any mechanical or electrical device used to render a diagnostic opinion about the honesty or dishonesty of an individual. This includes polygraph, voice stress analyzers, psychological stress evaluators, and similar devices. Only mechanical and electrical devices are prohibited under the Act, not paper-and-pencil tests, chemical testing, or other non-mechanical or non-electrical means that purport to measure an individual's honesty.

b. **Exceptions.** The Act exempts from its coverage all government employers. It also contains an exemption that allows certain departments of the federal government engaged in national defense and security to administer lie detector tests to any experts or consultants under contract and their employees. Also exempted are FBI contractors, security services, and drug manufacturers, and employers conducting an ongoing investigation of economic loss or injury to the employer's business, such as theft, embezzlement, misappropriation, or an act of unlawful industrial espionage.

2. ***Constitutional Law.*** A polygraph does not constitute a search within the meaning of the Fourth Amendment. See Stehney v. Perry, 907 F. Supp. 806 (D.N.J. 1995), aff'd, 101 F.3d 925 (3d Cir. 1996); Chesna v. Dep't of Defense, 850 F. Supp. 110, 116-17 (D. Conn. 1994).

E. Fingerprinting

1. ***Public vs. Private Employers***. No applicable federal provisions.

III. SEARCHES

A. Employee's Person

1. ***Private Employers.*** Unlike public section employers, see infra, private sector employers are not constrained by the Fourth Amendment unless they are acting under the auspices of the government.

2. ***Public Employers.*** The Fourth Amendment of the U.S. Constitution protects individuals from unreasonable searches and seizures at the hands of any state actor. This protection extends into the workplace of all federal and, through the Fourteenth Amendment, state employers. See O'Connor v. Ortega, 480 U.S. 709 (1987). However, the protections provided by the Fourth Amendment are limited. Only unreasonable searches performed where the employee has a reasonable expectation of privacy are unconstitutional. Also, to be lawful, a search by a public employer of an employee's person must either be necessary for a non-investigatory work-related purpose or be based on reasonable grounds to suspect that the search will produce evidence of work-related misconduct.

Employees whose Fourth Amendment rights have been violated may recover for the emotional shock or physical harm of the unlawful search, but may not recover for any resulting injury to their employment status or position. See Bivens v. Six Unknown Agents of the Fed. Bureau of Narcotics, 456 F. 2d 1339 (2d Cir. 1972).

B. Employee's Work Area

The same standards apply to searches of a public employee's person and work area. See United States v. Horowitz, 806 F.2d 1222, 1224 (4th Cir. 1986) (whether employee's privacy interest will be recognized depends upon whether the individual had a reasonable expectation of privacy in the area searched, not merely in the items found); see, e.g., United States v. Simons, 206 F.3d 392 (4th Cir. 2000) (employee had legitimate expectation of privacy in his office because he did not share it, and there was no evidence of any workplace practices, procedures, or regulations that had the effect of lowering such expectation); cf. Schowengerdt v. United States, 944 F.2d 483, 485, 488-89 (9th Cir. 1991) (holding that civilian employee of Navy weapons plant lacked legitimate expectation of privacy in private office when office was regularly searched in employee's absence, employee was aware that such searches occurred, and employee had participated in searches of coworkers' offices); United States v. Taketa, 923 F.2d 665, 672-73 (9th Cir. 1991) (rejecting argument that government employee lacked a legitimate expectation of privacy in his office because regulation requiring clean desks implied that office was subject to inspection, in part on ground that the regulation had not been enforced by a practice of inspections).

C. Employee's Property

1. ***Private Employers.*** Unlike public section employers, see infra, private sector employers are not constrained by the Fourth Amendment unless they are acting under the auspices of the government.

2. ***Public Employers.*** Whether or not a governmental employer's search of an employee's property is improper will be tested by a standard of reasonableness under all the circumstances, which requires a balancing of the employee's privacy expectations against the governmental employer's need for supervision, control and an efficient workplace. O'Connor v. Ortega, 480 U.S. 709 (1987) (employee doctor had an expectation of privacy in his desk and file cabinets because they were used only by the doctor and he had kept personal items there for a long time); Faulkner v. State of Maryland, 317 Md. 441, 564 A.2d 785 (Md. 1989) (search of locker for drugs or alcohol not unreasonable where the employer reserved the right to conduct such a search); McDonell v. Hunter, 809 F.2d 1302 (8th Cir. 1987) (search of correctional officers' vehicles within prison confines found reasonable); Shields v. Burge, 874 F.2d 1201 (7th Cir. 1989) (police officers' search of another officer's closed, personal briefcase found inside automobile being lawfully searched as part of internal misconduct investigation was reasonable); but see, Leventhal v. State of New York, 266 F.3d 64 (2d Cir.

2001) (state agency employee had reasonable expectation of privacy in contents of his office computer where employee occupied private office with door and had exclusive use of computer, and agency did not routinely conduct searches of office computers nor had it adopted policy against mere storage of personal files, as opposed to use of agency time for personal business; however, agency possessed individualized suspicion justifying search).

IV. MONITORING OF EMPLOYEES

A. Telephones and Electronic Communications

1. ***Wiretapping (Telephone).*** All employers are subject to the provisions of the Omnibus Crime Control and Safe Streets Act, which prohibits the interception of oral communications, including telephone communications. 18 U.S.C. § 2511 et seq. The term oral communications is broadly defined to include those communications "uttered by a person exhibiting an expectation that such communication is not subject to interception."

Section 2511 (1)(c) makes intentional disclosure of any illegally-intercepted conversation a criminal offense if the person disclosing the communication knew or had "reason to know" that it was so acquired. Under the First Amendment, § 2511(1)(c) is invalid as applied to individuals who lawfully obtained a tape of such a conversation and then disclosed it. See Bartnicki v. Vopper, 532 U.S. 514, 535 (2001). The U.S. Court of Appeals for the District of Columbia, however, imposed liability upon a Congressman who published an illegally intercepted conversation that was provided to him by a third party. See Boehner v. McDermott, 441 F.3d 1010, 1015-17 (D.C. Cir. 2006). The Court found that the Congressman illegally obtained the tape because he had knowledge the conversation was illegally intercepted when it was provided to him. See id. The decision is important because it found that a private party has a cause of action against a person (including an employer) who knowingly obtains and publishes an illegally recorded conversation, even if that person was not involved in illegally intercepting the conversation. See id.

a. **Exceptions.** This Act provides for a telephone extension exception which is important in the employment context. Under this exception, employers may monitor employee calls in the ordinary course of business. A court ruled that an employer which informed employees that telephone calls were being monitored to help improve service was protected under the telephone extension exception. See James v. Newspaper Agency Corp., 591 F.2d 579 (10th Cir. 1979). Similarly, an employer was entitled to record an employee's business calls to determine if the employee was violating previous warnings not to disclose confidential information to competitors. See Briggs v. Am. Air Filter Co., 630 F.2d 414 (5th Cir. 1980). In another case, a hospital monitored calls between two employees of the hospital in which they made disparaging remarks about the hospital supervisory personnel. The court held that the hospital had not violated the Act because the intercepted call was a business call and monitoring of it was in the ordinary course of business. Epps v. St. Mary's Hosp. of Athens, 802 F.2d 412, reh'g denied, 807 F.2d 999 (11th Cir. 1986). However, while monitoring business calls, employers may not purposefully listen in on personal phone calls once it is clear that the nature of the call is not business-related. See Watkins v. L.M. Berry & Co., 704 F.2d 577 (11th Cir. 1983). For example, a court found no legitimate business purpose was served by an employer's recording of personal calls, many involving conversations of a sexual nature, in an effort to discover whether an employee had participated in the theft of $16,000. See Deal v. Spears, 980 F.2d 1153 (8th Cir. 1992).

A second exception, the provider exception, permits providers of wire communication services, such as telephone companies, to monitor calls for mechanical or service checks.

b. **Defenses.** The consent defense provides that if one party consents to interception prior to the communication, no violation occurs. An employee may either expressly or impliedly consent to an otherwise impermissible monitoring of a communication. See Simmons v. Southwestern Bell Tel. Co., 452 F. Supp. 392 (W.D. Ok. 1978), aff'd, 611 F.2d 342 (10th Cir. 1979) (finding that implied consent existed after acknowledging that the defendant company had a well-known monitoring policy and prohibition against using monitored phones for personal calls and that employee had received numerous warnings regarding excessive use of these lines for personal reasons); but see, Watkins v. L.M. Berry & Co., 704 F.2d 577 (11th Cir. 1983) (rejecting claim that the employee had impliedly consented to the interception of a personal call after determining that the employee had consented to the company's policy of monitoring business calls but not personal calls); Deal v. Spears, 980 F.2d 1153 (8th Cir. 1992) (consent to tape record an employee's telephone calls could not be implied merely because the employer had warned the employee that an employee's phone calls might be monitored to cut down on personal use of the phone).

c. **Penalties.** Violations of this statute may give rise to criminal and civil liability. Violators may be imprisoned or fined, and an individual whose communications are unlawfully intercepted may recover damages, including punitive damages and attorneys fees. The penalty for a violation is the sum of the actual damages suffered by the plaintiff and any profits made by the violator as a result of the violation; or statutory damages of whichever is the greater of $100 a day for each day of violation, or $10,000. 18 U.S.C. § 2520.

2. ***Electronic Communications (E-mail).*** The Electronic Privacy Communications Act of 1986 (ECPA) updates the Omnibus Crime Control and Safe Streets Act and provides protections against unauthorized interception of, and access to, transmitted and stored electronic communication. Title I of the Act, 18 U.S.C. § 2510 et seq., prohibits the interception of electronic communication, while Title II, 18 U.S.C. § 2701 et seq., prohibits unauthorized access to stored communication. The ECPA applies to both citizens of the United States and foreign citizens. See Suzlon Energy Ltd. V. Microsoft Corp., 2011 WL 4537843 (9th Cir. Oct. 3, 2011) (holding that Microsoft did not have to produce emails from the account of a citizen of India for a civil fraud proceeding against the citizen in Australia where Microsoft had the emails stored on a server in the United States because the plain text of the ECPA states that the ECPA applies to "any person"). Because of several exceptions applicable in the employment context, this law does not create substantial privacy rights for employees utilizing electronic communication instruments at work.

Title I makes it illegal for anyone to intercept electronic communication and prohibits the disclosure or use of the contents of an electronic communication if the disclosing individual knows or has reason to know that the communication was intercepted.

a. **Limitations.** Although nothing in Title I of the ECPA explicitly excludes the workplace from the scope of the Act, the limitations apparent on the face of the statute, as well as judicial interpretation of the Act, have substantially limited its applicability to the office environment. For example, most courts that have considered the issue have limited its scope by defining intercept narrowly. See Fraser v. Nationwide Mut. Ins. Co., 352 F.3d 107, 113 (3rd Cir. 2003) (holding that intercept within the meaning of Title I can only occur contemporaneously with transmission and employer's retrieval of stored e-mails does not violate the EPCA); Steve Jackson Games, Inc. v. United States Secret Serv., 36 F.3d 457 (5th Cir. 1994) (seizing unread e-mail messages stored in a bulletin board is not an interception since electronic communication is intercepted for purposes of Title I only when it is acquired by an outsider during the actual transmission of the message from one party to another); Wesley College v. Pitts, 974 F. Supp. 375 (D. Del. 1997), aff'd, 172 F.3d 861 (3d Cir. 1998) (there can be no interception under Title I if the acquisition of the contents of electronic communication is not contemporaneous with their transmission); Fraser v. Nationwide Mut. Ins. Co., 135 F. Supp. 2d 623, 635 (E.D. Penn. 2001) (an employer that retrieves stored e-mails that have already been received by the recipient does not violate the EPCA, because such conduct does not constitute interception under the Act); See also, United States v. Simons, 29 F. Supp. 2d 324 (E.D. Va. 1998). Since e-mail is often in transit for only a few seconds, under this interpretation Title I offers little protection in the e-mail context.

But a 2005 decision by the 1st Circuit holding otherwise casts doubt on this conclusion. In U.S. v. Councilman, 418 F.3d 67 (1st Cir. 2005) (en banc) (vacating 373 F.3d 197 (1st Cir. June 29, 2004)), an en banc panel reversed the trial court's dismissal of charges under the ECPA, and vacated the appellate panels affirmance of the dismissal, concluding that the term electronic communication includes transient electronic storage that is intrinsic to the communication process, and hence that interception of an e-mail message in such storage is an offense under the Wiretap Act. See also, Theofel v. Farey-Jones, 359 F.3d 1066, 1076-77 (9th Cir. 2004) (holding that copies of opened emails on ISP servers are in electronic storage); U.S. v. Szymuskiewicz, 2009 WL 1873657 (E.D. Wis. June 30, 2009) (applying Councilman). Additionally, the District Court for the Southern District of New York has held that the ECPA not only applies to e-mails being stored temporarily during transmission, but also to those being stored in post transmission storage. Rozell v. Ross-Holst, 2007 U.S. Dist. LEXIS 46450 (S.D.N.Y. June 21, 2007).

b. **Exceptions.** Title I also contains several exceptions which limit its applicability in the work context. For example, it is not unlawful to intercept the contents of an electronic communication when the intercepting party has obtained the consent of one of the parties to the communication. In addition, employers intercepting employees' electronic communications may also avail themselves of the business use exception which applies where (a) the employer is the provider of the e-mail service and (b) the interception occurs in the normal course of the individual's employment.

An employer which is the provider of the e-mail service is free to access stored e-mail messages and other electronic communication irrespective of the nature (personal or professional) of the message and without regard to whether the employer has first received the employee's consent. See Fraser, 352 F.3d 107 (3rd Cir. 2003) (holding that email stored on employer's system was excepted from Title II protection); Bohach v. City of Reno, 932 F. Supp. 1232 (D. Nev. 1996) (§ 2701(c)(1) allows service providers to do as they wish when it comes to accessing communications in electronic storage); McLaren v. Microsoft Corp., 1999 Tex. App. Lexis 4103 (Texas Ct. App. May 1999) (dismissing employee's claim that his employer's review and dissemination of e-mail stored in the employee's workplace personal computer constituted an invasion of privacy, despite the fact that the plaintiff's personal e-mail folder was protected by a password, because the e-mail was transmitted over Microsoft's network).

c. **Penalties.** Title I provides substantial civil penalties for violators, including a $10,000 per day, per incident fine, along with the potential for attorneys fees and punitive damages. Compensatory damages may be awarded in the amount of plaintiff's actual damages and profits made by the violator; or a statutory amount of the greater of $100 a day for each day of violation or $10,000.

Title II applies once an electronic communication has been transmitted and stored, whether temporary or otherwise. Title II makes it unlawful to access, without authorization, a facility through which an electronic communication service is provided. 18 U.S.C. § 2701(a). As a practical matter, Title II provides little protection for employees because of the Act's broad exemptions.

An individual may bring a civil action for relief under Title II and potentially receive attorney's fees and punitive damages. However, unlike under Title I, compensatory damages are limited to plaintiff's actual damages and profits made by the violator, or $1,000 per incident, whichever is higher. 18 U.S.C. § 2707(c).

3. ***Other Electronic Monitoring.*** One court has found that the monitoring of key strokes that records the internal transmission from the computer to the CPU is beyond the regulation of the Electronic Privacy Communications Act because it does not affect interstate commerce. See U.S. v. Ropp, 347 F. Supp. 2d 831 (C.D. Cal. 2004); see also Rene v. G.F. Fishers, Inc., 2011 WL 4349473 (S.D. Ind. Sept. 16, 2011). But another court disagreed, finding that the keystroke data affects interstate commerce even though it is intercepted before it travels in interstate commerce. Potter v. Havlicek, 2007 U.S. Dist. LEXIS 10677, *21 (S.D. Ohio February 14, 2007). Also, phone numbers dialed and dates of calls are encompassed by the definition of "electric communication" under § 2510(12) of the ECPA. McEwen v. SourceResources.com, 2007 U.S. Dist. LEXIS 10156 (S.D. Tex. Feb. 13, 2007).

B. Mail

1. ***Tampering***. It is a federal offense to knowingly and willfully obstruct or retard the passage of the mail. 18 U.S.C. § 1701. A package is in the mail from the time it is placed in the mailbox until it reaches the addressee. Garmon v. Foust, 741 F.2d 1069 (8th Cir. 1984).

A person's reasonable expectation of privacy in his mail is viewed as the same whether the mail is in his possession or in the hands of private parties en route to the addressee. In United States v. Van Leeuwen, 397 U.S. 249 (1970), the Supreme Court clearly stated that the Fourth Amendment right against unreasonable searches and seizures applied with equal force whether those papers were in transit in the mail or locked at home. While in the mail, papers and packages can only be opened and examined under [a] warrant ... as is required when papers are subjected to search in one's own household. Id. at 251.

C. Surveillance/Monitoring

1. ***Constitutional Law.*** The key factor in determining the legality of a public employer's surveillance of employees is whether the employees had a reasonable expectation of privacy under the particular circumstances. Employees have attempted to invoke the U.S. Constitution to challenge their employers' workplace surveillance and monitoring, albeit largely unsuccessfully. For example, a court held that a quasi-public telephone company did not violate the Fourth Amendment when it installed surveillance cameras in the company's common workspace areas, reasoning that employees do not have an objectively reasonable expectation of privacy in the open areas of their workplace. Vega-Rodriguez v. Puerto Rico Tel. Co., 110 F.3d 174 (1st Cir. 1997).

2. ***The USA Patriot Act.*** The USA Patriot Act, which is formally titled Uniting and Strengthening America by Providing Appropriate Tools Required to Intercept and Obstruct Terrorism Act of 2001, Pub. L. No. 107-56, 115 Stat. 272 (2001) (Patriot Act) changed significantly the government's ability to conduct surveillance under the Federal Wiretap Act, 18 U.S.C. § 1343 et seq. (which requires a court order issued by a judge who must conclude that there is probable cause to believe that one of the crimes contained in the Act has been or is about to be committed) and the Foreign Intelligence Surveillance Act of 1978, 50 U.S.C. §§ 1801 et seq. (FISA) (which allows wiretapping of aliens and citizens in the United States based on a finding that there is probable cause to believe that the target is a member of a foreign terrorist group or an agent of a foreign power, and for U.S. citizens and permanent resident aliens, there must be probable cause to believe that the person is engaged in activities that may involve a criminal violation).

Under the Patriot Act, terrorism is a predicate act for which a wiretap can be authorized. § 201 (amending 18 U.S.C. § 2516(q)). It also authorized wiretapping for crimes related to computer fraud and abuse. § 202. The Patriot Act lowered the threshold for which surveillance pursuant to FISA is permitted. §§214, 216 (amending 19 U.S.C. §§ 3121, 3123, 3127; 50 U.S.C. §§ 1842, 1843). It also lowered the barriers that had been erected between the law-enforcement and national security agencies, thus allowing for greater sharing of information gained through surveillance, by whatever means. § 203 (amending 18 U.S.C. §§ 2510, 2517). It also makes it easier for law-enforcement officers to obtain surreptitious warrants, which allow them to delay notifying a target that a search of seizure has been conducted. § 213 (amending 18 U.S.C. §3103a).

The Patriot Act permits roving taps, which allow the government to obtain a court order that does not name a specific telephone line or e-mail account to be tapped, but instead allows the government to tap any phone line, cell phone or Internet account that a suspect uses. This may have a significant impact upon the workplace because employees have access to many different phones and computers, including those of their co-workers. Since the government would be interested in tapping all of the electronic equipment that is reasonably accessible to a suspected terrorist, a broad web of means of communication in the workplace potentially are affected. In addition, the Patriot Act provides explicit legal authorization for government surveillance of e-mail and Internet communications, and may allow a government agency such as the FBI to access their target's communications, as well as the communications of non-targets who use the same Internet Service Provider. Thus, it is likely that these added powers could affect the privacy interests of co-workers and those with whom they communicate.

The Patriot Act also lowered the standard for the government to be allowed to listen to stored communications such as voicemail and clarified the standard for obtaining stored e-mails by deleting the electronic storage of such communication from the definition of wire communication in 18 U.S.C. § 2510(1) and adding the word wire to 18 U.S.C. § 2703. § 209. The government can now obtain voicemail and other stored communications without an intercept order; only a search warrant is needed. In May 2011, President Obama signed a four year extension of the Patriot Act's provisions regarding roving wiretaps, court-ordered searches of business records, and surveillance of non-American "lone wolf" suspects who do not have confirmed ties to terrorist groups.

3. ***Union Employees***. Under the National Labor Relations Act, employer surveillance may be viewed as interfering with employees' right to organize. 29 U.S.C. § 151 et seq. The National Labor Relations Board has held that the installation and use of video surveillance equipment is a mandatory subject of bargaining and that the union has a statutory right to bargain over the installation of video surveillance equipment. Colgate-Palmolive Co., 323 NLRB 515 (1997). But see, Cramer v. Consol. Freightways, Inc., 255 F.3d 683 (9th Cir. 2001), cert. denied, 534 U.S. 1078 (2002) (holding that even though the collective bargaining agreement allowed for employer surveillance, the agreement did not supercede state law and constitutional privacy claims and finding that the surveillance violated California's state law prohibiting the use of two-way mirrors).

4. ***Anti-retaliation.*** The Hatch Act protects the political association rights of federal employees and provides protection for whistleblowing. A federal government agency or employer may not retaliate against an employee or applicant for disclosing what he or she believes to be a violation of law, rule, or regulation or waste, fraud and mismanagement. 5 U.S.C. §§ 1501(4), 2302(b)(8), 7324, 7325. Several other federal whistleblower statutes contain specific anti-retaliation provisions for employees who report safety concerns. These statutes often expressly preempt other common law remedies. See, e.g., Whistleblower Protection Act of 1989, 5 U.S.C. § 2302; Federal Mine Safety and Health Act § 105 (c)(1), 30 U.S.C.§ 815(c)(1); Federal Water Pollution Control Act, 33 U.S.C. § 1367; Federal Deposit Insurance Act § 2[33], as amended, 12 U.S.C. § 1831j; Clean Air Act, 42 U.S.C. § 7622.

V. ACTIVITIES OUTSIDE THE WORKPLACE

A. Statute or Common Law

No applicable federal provisions.

B. Employees' Personal Relationships

1. ***Romantic Relationships Between Employees.*** No applicable federal provisions.

2. ***Sexual Orientation.*** No applicable federal provisions.

3. ***Marital Status.*** No applicable federal provisions.

C. Smoking

No applicable federal provisions.

D. Blogging

As the use of blogs and social networking websites become more common, the federal courts are beginning to encounter lawsuits challenging an employer's right to terminate an employee based upon information written on their blogs or social networking websites. See, e.g., Shaver v. Davie County Pub. Sch., 2008 U.S. Dist. LEXIS 29084 (M.D.N.C. April 7, 2008) (dismissing wrongful termination claims brought by a bus driver who claimed he was terminated for information contained on his MySpace blog regarding his practice of Wicca religion).

Also, some employers have tried to bring information contained in their former employee's blog as evidence of their conduct at trial. For example, in Mackelprang v. Fidelity National Title Agency, 2007 U.S. Dist. LEXIS 2379; 99 Fair Empl. Prac. Cas. (BNA) 997 (D.C. Nev. January 9, 2007), an employer faced with sexual harassment claims attempted to introduce evidence found on an employee's MySpace page that suggested the employee was promiscuous. The court refused to admit the evidence, making a distinction between relevance of non-work sexual conduct and sexual conduct in the workplace. Id. But see Equal Employment Opportunity Commission v. Simply Storage Mgmt., LLC, 270 F.R.D. 430 (S.D. Ind. 2010) (allowing limited discovery of claimants' Facebook and MySpace posts revealing the claimants' emotional state where "severe emotional distress" was alleged in a sexual harassment case); **Mailhoit v. Home Depot U.S.A., Inc., 2012 WL 393063 (C.D. Cal. Sept. 7, 2012) (holding that multiple discovery requests regarding social networking sites similar to the requests made in Simply Storage Mgmt. were overbroad and vague, but allowing discovery of plaintiff's social networking communications "between Plaintiff and any current or former Home Depot employees, or which in any way refer…to her employment with Home Depot or this lawsuit").**

Additionally, under the National Labor Relations Act, the termination of employees for posting comments regarding work-related issues on social networking websites may be viewed as interfering with the employees' right to engage in protected, concerted activities under the Act. In the September 2011 decision in Hispanics United of Buffalo, Inc., Case No. 3-CA-27872, a National Labor Relations Board Administrative Law Judge held that five employees who were discharged after posting comments on Facebook concerning their working conditions (including job performance, work load, and staffing issues) had to be reinstated with backpay because they were unlawfully discharged under the Act. **See also Karl Knauz BMW, Knauz Auto Group, 358 NLRB 164 (2012) (finding that employee who complained on Facebook that low quality food being served by the employer during a sales event would impact his sales commissions was engaged in protected, concerted activity, but holding that employer did not terminate employee based on that activity).** But see JT's Porch Saloon & Eatery Ltd., No. 13-CA-46689, 2011 WL 2960964 (NLRB 2011) (holding that a bartender's Facebook posting complaining about the employer's tipping policy was not concerted because it did not attempt to mobilize employees and was simply an individual gripe); Lee Enterprises, Inc. d/b/a Arizona Daily Star, No. 28-CA-23267, 2011 WL 1825089 (NLRB 2011) (holding that a non-union newspaper reporter who insulted rival news reporting agencies on a twitter account promoted by his employer did not engage in concerted activity, as his speech did not involve terms and conditions of employment).

VI. RECORDS

A. Personnel Records

1. ***Statutes.*** The Privacy Act of 1974 requires federal agencies to inform individuals of personal data record-keeping systems and to permit individuals to inspect and correct personal information concerning them. It also limits the type of information agencies may collect, prohibits disclosure of personal information without the written consent of the individual, and authorizes civil suits for damages resulting from willful or intentional violation of the Act. The records protected under this Act include anything containing the name or the identifying number, symbol, or other identifying particular assigned to the individual. Subject to several exceptions, records may not be released unless pursuant to the individuals written request or prior consent. 5 U.S.C. § 552(a) et seq.

2. ***Unions.*** Under the Labor Management Relations Act, employers may refuse to release employee personnel records to a union for a grievance hearing, absent employee consent. See, e.g., New Jersey Bell Tel. Co. v. N.L.R.B., 720 F.2d 789 (3d Cir. 1983) (attendance records); Intl Union of Elec., Radio & Mach. Workers v. N.L.R.B., 648 F.2d 18 (D.C. Cir. 1980) (discrimination complaints); but see Safeway Stores v. N.L.R.B., 691 F.2d 953 (10th Cir. 1982) (requiring disclosure of employment records).

B. Medical Records

1. ***Statutes.***

a. **Americans with Disabilities Act**. The Americans with Disabilities Act requires that any information relating to the medical condition or medical history of an applicant or employee be collected on separate forms, kept in separate medical files from the general personnel information, and treated as confidential. 42 U.S.C. § 12112(c)(3)(B). Disclosure of medical records or information is allowed only in three situations under the ADA: (1) when supervisors and managers need to be informed regarding necessary restrictions on work or duties of the employee and necessary accommodations; (2) when first-aid and safety personnel need to be informed about a disability that might require emergency treatment; and (3) when government officials investigating compliance with the ADA request access to such records or information.

b. **Occupational Health and Safety Act**. The Occupational Health and Safety Act requires general industry, maritime and construction employers which have access to employee exposure or medical records pertaining to employees exposed to toxic substances or harmful physical agents, to conduct employee medical surveillance and maintain records concerning employee occupational health. An employee is entitled to access to those records. 29 C.F.R. § 1910.1020 et seq.

c. **Public Health and Welfare Act.** The Public Health and Welfare Act requires that the records of the identity and treatment of any patient which are maintained in connection with the performance of any activity relating to substance abuse education conducted with a federal agency should be kept confidential, unless the patient consents to their release. 42 U.S.C. § 290dd-2.

d. **Genetic Information Nondiscrimination Act.** The Genetic Information Nondiscrimination Act requires that employers keep genetic information confidential and in a separate medical file. To meet this requirement, an employer may keep the genetic information in the same file as it keeps medical information in compliance with the Americans with Disabilities Act. An employee is entitled to access those records, and five additional, albeit narrow, exceptions to the limitations on disclosure are prescribed by GINA. 42 U.S.C. § 2000ff et seq.

2. ***Constitutional Law.*** The Supreme Court has recognized that medical records fall within the ambit of information protected by the constitutional right to privacy. See Whalen v. Roe, 429 U.S. 589 (1977). However, the individual's interest must be weighed against the government's interest. See, e.g., Doe v. Southeastern Pa. Transp. Auth., 72 F.3d 1133 (3d Cir. 1995), cert. denied, 519 U.S. 808 (1996) (employers need for access to its employees' HIV prescription information outweighed the employees' interest in keeping the information confidential, where employer had minimized the possibility of future disclosure and the plaintiff suffered no adverse job-related actions); United States v. Westinghouse Elec. Corp., 638 F.2d 570, 577 (3rd Cir. 1980) (due to the very personal and confidential nature of an employee's medical information, employee's interest outweighed governments interest in seeking medical records of company's employees in conjunction with a governmental investigation of a potentially hazardous work area); A.F.G.E. v. HUD, Am. Fed'n of Gov't Employees v. Dep't of Hous. & Urban Dev., Gov't Employees v. Perry, 118 F.3d 786 (D.C. Cir. 1997) (employees have a protected constitutional privacy right in information relating to any mental health counseling and treatment which they have received; governments interest in such information to determine employees' continued suitability for secret security clearance does not outweigh the privacy rights of employees who do not perform job duties affecting national security and have not demonstrated any emotional problems affecting their work); Plowman v. Dep't of the Army, 698 F. Supp. 627 (E.D. Va. 1988) (employee's constitutional right to privacy in information concerning his AIDS status was neither absolute nor unqualified); Redmond v. City of Overland Park, 672 F. Supp. 473 (D. Kan. 1987) (police department had a substantial and valid interest in obtaining psychiatrists statements concerning probationary police officer in order to determine the officers fitness for duty).

3. ***Drug Records.*** In Ellison v. Cocke County, Tennessee, 63 F.3d 467 (6th Cir. 1995), a county employee brought suit against a county hospital alleging a violation of his privacy rights based on the hospitals disclosure of the employee's medical records relating to the diagnosis, prognosis, and treatment of the employee's drug use. The employee had been discharged after hospitalization for alleged drug use. The employee's hospital records were disclosed during a grievance hearing, and later published in two local newspapers, despite the employee's request that his grievance and related medical information be kept strictly confidential. The Sixth Circuit refused to recognize an implied private right of action under the confidentiality provision of the criminal prohibition of disclosure of substance abuse records under the Public Health and Welfare Act.

C. Criminal Records

Employer use of arrest or conviction records as a basis for making employment decisions may be challenged as discriminatory on the ground that the use of such information has a disproportionate impact on minorities. See Gregory v. Litton Sys., Inc., 472 F.2d 631 (9th Cir. 1972). Policies that automatically disqualify applicants based on a conviction record have, in some instances, been rejected as discriminatory. See, e.g., Green v. Missouri Pac. R.R. Co., 549 F.2d 1158 (8th Cir. 1977). On the other hand, policies that consider such information as merely one component in its hiring process have been upheld. See, e.g., Hill v. U.S. Postal Serv., 522 F. Supp. 1283 (S.D.N.Y. 1981). When there is a legitimate business need to consider conviction history, such action may survive a disparate impact challenge. For example, where a hotel rejected applicants who had been convicted of serious crimes for safety-sensitive positions, such as bellstaff, that involved access to guests' luggage and rooms, the court found that the policy was narrowly tailored to fit its legitimate needs and was not unlawful. See Richardson v. Hotel Corp. of Am., 332 F. Supp. 519 (E.D. La. 1971), aff'd, 468 F.2d 951 (5th Cir. 1972). **Additionally, on April 24, 2012, the Equal Employment Opportunity Commission issued its Enforcement Guidance on the Consideration of Arrest and Conviction Records in Employment Decisions listing best practices for employers. Available at http://www.eeoc.gov/laws/guidance/arrest_conviction.cfm.**

D. Subpoenas / Search Warrants

All search warrants are subject to the restraints of the Fourth Amendment, discussed supra.

All subpoenas issued by a federal court are governed by Rule 45 of the Federal Rules of Civil Procedure.

E. Bankruptcy

The federal Bankruptcy Act provides that an employee or job applicant may not be discriminated against in employment solely because the individual has filed for bankruptcy protection. 11 U.S.C. § 525.

VII. Actions Subsequent to Employment.

A. References

No applicable federal provisions.

B. Non-compete agreements

No applicable federal provisions.

VIII. OTHER ISSUES

A. Statutes of Limitations

No applicable federal provisions.

B. Jurisdiction

Federal courts lack jurisdiction on claims that have already been determined by the Secretary of Labor to be covered by the Federal Employee Compensation Act (FECA), 5 U.S.C. § 8101 et seq. See VIII.C., infra.

C. Workers' Compensation Exclusivity

The Federal Employee Compensation Act, 5 U.S.C. § 8101 et seq., (FECA) establishes a workers' compensation program for federal employees injured while working. The Secretary of Labor has exclusive authority to administer FECA and to decide all questions, including questions of coverage, under FECA. 5 U.S.C. § 8145. FECA provides the exclusive means by which federal employees may recover from the federal government for employment-related injuries. 5 U.S.C. § 8116(c). Where the Secretary determines that FECA applies, courts have no jurisdiction over claims brought under the Privacy Act regardless of whether the Secretary ultimately allows benefits under FECA. 5 U.S.C. § 8128(b). See, e.g., Smith v. Nicholson, 287 Fed. Appx. 402 (5th Cir. 2008) (holding that the district court lacked jurisdiction to try an employee's Privacy Act claim against employer federal government because the employee had already sought benefits under FECA), Scott v. United States Postal Service, 2006 U.S. Dist. LEXIS 68963 (D.D.C. September 26, 2006) (holding that the court lacked jurisdiction for Privacy Act claim even though the Secretary denied employee benefits under FECA for claim arising out of the same facts).

D. Pleading Requirements

No applicable federal provisions.

SURVEY OF ALABAMA EMPLOYMENT LIBEL LAW

James P. Pewitt and Don B. Long III
Johnston Barton Proctor & Rose LLP
Colonial Brookwood Center
569 Brookwood Village, Suite 901
Birmingham, Alabama 35209
Telephone: (205) 458-9400; Facsimile: (205) 458-9500

(With Developments Reported Through **November 1, 2012**)

GENERAL COMMENTS

Alabama has a three-tier court system: (1) trial courts (circuit courts, generally for civil cases in which more than $10,000.00 is at issue and for criminal cases, Ala. Code ' 12-11-30 (1975), and district courts, generally for civil cases in which no more than $10,000.00 is at issue and for receiving guilty pleas in felony cases not punishable by death, Ala. Code § 12-11-31 (1975)); trial court opinions are not reported in an official reporter or the West reporter but are sometimes published in specialty reporters such as the Media Law Reporter; (2) intermediate courts of appeal (the Alabama Court of Criminal Appeals; the Alabama Court of Civil Appeals, whose jurisdiction is limited by a dollar amount of $50,000.00, among other criteria, Ala. Code § 12-3-10 (1975), unless the Supreme Court of Alabama transfers one of its cases to the Court of Civil Appeals pursuant to Ala. Code § 12-2-7(6) (1975)); and (3) the Supreme Court of Alabama (which has jurisdiction coextensive with the state, including jurisdiction of appeals from the two intermediate courts of appeal, Ala. Code § 12-2-7 (1975)). Until 1969, the Court of Criminal Appeals and the Court of Civil Appeals were one court, the Court of Appeals, which was referred to in citations as "Ala. Ct. App." Beginning in 1969, those decisions are designated "Ala. Crim. App." or "Ala. Civ. App.," respectively. Decisions of the Supreme Court of Alabama are published with the designation "Ala." From 1910 through 1976, Alabama appellate opinions appeared in both an official state reporter and West's Southern reporter. From 1977 to the present, all of Alabama's appellate decisions appear in West's Southern reporter (and one or more specialty reporters in some cases), but not in a separate official reporter. Alabama appellate decisions are also published electronically by ALALINC (www.alalinc.net), Westlaw (www.westlaw.com), and LEXIS (www.lexis.com).

Much of Alabama's defamation law, whether growing out of employment matters or not, has been federalized by New York Times Co. v. Sullivan, 376 U.S. 254, 1 Media L. Rep. 1527 (1964), and its progeny – most notably, Gertz v. Robert Welch, Inc., 418 U.S. 323, 1 Media L. Rep. 1633 (1974); Dun & Bradstreet, Inc. v. Greenmoss Builders, Inc., 472 U.S. 749, 11 Media L. Rep. 2417 (1985); Philadelphia Newspapers, Inc. v. Hepps, 475 U.S. 767, 12 Media L. Rep. 1977 (1986); and Milkovich v. Lorain Journal Co., 497 U.S. 1, 17 Media L. Rep. 2009 (1990). Ex parte Rudder, 507 So. 2d 411, 416, 13 Media L. Rep. 2289, 2292 (Ala. 1987) ("We recognize that the courts of this State are bound by the constitutional principles enunciated in these Supreme Court cases."). Alabama's defamation law is also interpreted and applied in federal district courts and in federal circuit courts of appeal when a federal district court retains an Alabama state-law defamation claim pursuant to supplemental jurisdiction, 28 U.S.C. § 1367, or diversity jurisdiction, 28 U.S.C. § 1332.

SIGNIFICANT DEVELOPMENTS SINCE THE 2012 *SURVEY*

In 2012, the Supreme Court of Alabama addressed whether a claim for defamation arising out of an investigation by a local church should be dismissed because it implicated ecclesiastical affairs over which the court lacked jurisdiction. Ex parte Bole, 2012 Ala. LEXIS 110 (Ala. Aug. 31, 2012). In 2011, a parishioner sent a letter to the church supervisor accusing a retired church minister of financial mismanagement and malfeasance. Id. at *3-6. The supervisor conducted an investigation that did not result in official charges but did lead to the retired minister being cut off from ongoing contact with the church. Id. at *7-*8. Following the investigation, the retired minister brought suit against the parishioner for defamation. Id. at *1. The parishioner moved to dismiss the claim on the grounds that the court did not have jurisdiction over the claim because it implicated internal church decisions. Id. The Supreme Court of Alabama began its opinion by noting that under the First and Fourteenth Amendment to the United States Constitution it did not have jurisdiction "to resolve disputes regarding [churches'] spiritual or ecclesiastical affairs." Id. at *31. The court then held that the claim at issue should be dismissed because it was "intertwined with the underlying investigation by the [supervisor], with the resolution, and with the [supervisor's] ultimate decision to remove" the retired minister. Id. at *83.

In 2011, the Alabama Court of Civil Appeals addressed what punitive damages were appropriate in the case of per se defamation. Tanner v. Ebbole, 88 So. 3d 856 (Ala. Civ. App. 2011). In this action, tattoo parlor employees had told customers that a competitor was using needles infected with communicable diseases, knowing the accusation to be false. This was found to be per se defamatory. The competitor was awarded nominal damages of $1 and punitive damages of $100,000. Id. at 870. The court began by stating that under the BMW v. Gore guideposts per se

defamatory conduct is particularly reprehensible. Id. at 872-74. The court then upheld the punitive damages award, finding that the reprehensibility of the conduct justified deviation from the standard ratio allowed between compensatory and punitive damages. Id. at 876-77.

I. GENERAL LAW

A. General Employment Law

1. ***At Will Employment.*** "Alabama has a well-established 'employment-at-will' doctrine, under which an employer may terminate an employee at its discretion, if no provision in the employment contract provides for a specific term of employment or sets forth terms and conditions for dismissal." Ex parte Gardner, 822 So. 2d 1211, 1217 (Ala. 2001) (quoting Gardner v. State Farm Mut. Ins. Co., 822 So. 2d 1201, 1207 (Ala. Civ. App. 2001)).

Generally, Alabama does not permit a "wrongful discharge" exception to its at-will employment doctrine. Willis v. Ideal Basics Industries, Inc., 484 So. 2d 444, 446 (Ala. 1986). There are two exceptions to this general rule, however. Alabama recognizes claims of wrongful discharge or retaliatory discharge in cases where one's employment was terminated because the employee filed a workers' compensation claim or filed notice of the employer's violation of a safety rule. Ala. Code § 25-5-11 (1975); Ala. Power Co. v. Aldridge, 854 So. 2d 554, 562 (Ala. 2002). It also recognizes claims of wrongful discharge in cases where one's employment is terminated because the employee reported the violation of a state ethics law. Ala. Code § 36-25-24 (1975); see Thompson v. Colbert County Tourism and Convention Bureau, 782 So. 2d 313 (Ala. Civ. App. 2000), cert. denied, 782 So. 2d 323 (Ala. 2000). Otherwise, "employment may be terminated for 'a good reason, a wrong reason, or no reason.'" Cunningham v. Dabbs, 703 So. 2d 979, 981 (Ala. Civ. App. 1997) (quoting Hinrichs v. Tranquilaire Hospital, 352 So. 2d 1130, 1131 (Ala. 1977)). An at-will employee in Alabama may have a claim for wrongful termination under federal law, however. See, e.g., Sunshine Investments, Inc. v. Brooks, 642 So. 2d 408, 410-11 (Ala. 1994) (Brooks' award of damages from the jury for wrongful discharge under 29 U.S.C. § 215(a)(3) and for libel, affirmed).

B. Elements of Libel Claim

1. ***Basic Elements.*** "The elements of a cause of action for defamation are: 1) a false and defamatory statement concerning the plaintiff; 2) an unprivileged communication of that statement to a third party; 3) fault amounting at least to negligence on the part of the defendant; and 4) either the actionablity of the statement irrespective of special harm or the existence of special harm caused by the publication of the statement." Wal-Mart Stores, Inc. v. Smitherman, 872 So. 2d 833, 840 (Ala. 2003) (quoting McCaig v. Talladega Publ'g Co., 544 So. 2d 875, 877 (Ala. 1989)). A written statement grounds a libel claim; while an oral statement grounds a claim for slander. See Butler v. Town of Argo, 871 So. 2d 1 (Ala. 2003). Radio and television broadcasts, however, whether read from a script or not, "must be declared upon as libel rather than slander." Gray v. WALA-TV, 384 So. 2d 1062, 1065 (Ala. 1980), overruled on other grounds by Nelson v. Lapeyrouse Grain Corp., 534 So. 2d 1085, 1091 n.3 (Ala. 1988); First Indep. Baptist Church of Arab v. Sutherland, 373 So. 2d 647, 649-50 (Ala. 1979). A defamation claim "cannot be brought after the death of the alleged victim," Larrimore v. Dubose, 827 So. 2d 60, 62 (Ala. 2001), and if the defamed plaintiff dies after filing suit and before resolution of the case, the plaintiff's defamation claim does not survive, Ala. Code § 6-5-462 (1975), Daugherty v. Mut. Life Ins. Co. of New York, 649 So. 2d 857, 857 (Ala. 1994).

2. ***Fault.*** "If a plaintiff is determined to be a public official, public figure, or limited-purpose public figure, then the plaintiff has the burden of establishing by clear and convincing evidence that the defamatory statement was made with 'actual [constitutional] malice -- that is, with knowledge that it was false or with reckless disregard of whether it was false or not.'" Cottrell v. NCAA, 975 So. 2d 306, 333 (Ala. 2007) (quoting New York Times Co. v. Sullivan, 376 U.S. 254, 280, 1 Media L. Rep. 1527, 1551 (1964)). Alabama courts sometimes confuse constitutional malice with common law malice, which is synonymous with bad faith or malicious intent and is proven by evidence of ill will, spite, hostility, and the like. Barnett v. Mobile County Pers. Bd., 536 So. 2d 46, 53-54 (Ala. 1988); see also Butler v. Town of Argo, 871 So. 2d 1, 26-27 (Ala. 2003). As the Supreme Court of Alabama observed in a 1979 opinion, "The trial court was apparently confused about the multisense term 'malice.' Although the United States Supreme Court has used the term 'actual malice,' it is clear from Sullivan and its progeny that the term as used by that Court is synonymous with, and only with, 'knowledge of falsity or reckless disregard of truth or falsity.' This is because a false and defamatory publication may be made purposefully to do harm, yet if it is made without knowledge of its falsity and without reckless disregard of its truth or falsity, the defamed public figure may not recover." Mobile Press Register, Inc. v. Faulkner, 372 So. 2d 1282, 1287, 5 Media L. Rep. 1108, 1112 (Ala. 1979) (emphasis added) (citations omitted), overruled on other grounds by Nelson v. Lapeyrouse Grain Corp., 534 So. 2d 1085, 1091 n.3 (Ala. 1988). The public figure or public official must prove constitutional malice by clear and convincing evidence. Wiggins v. Mallard, 905 So. 2d 776, 786, 33 Media L. Rep. 1025, 1035 (Ala. 2004).

The Supreme Court of Alabama declared Alabama's criminal defamation statute, Ala. Code § 13A-11-163, unconstitutional in Ivey v. State, 821 So. 2d 937, 29 Media L. Rep. 2089 (Ala. 2001), because the statute did not require a showing of "actual malice" in a prosecution for criminal defamation as required by Garrison v. Louisiana, 379 U.S. 64, 1 Media L. Rep. 1548 (1964). In reaching that determination, the Supreme Court of Alabama considered whether it could interpret the term "maliciously" to have the same meaning as "actual malice" (i.e., knowledge of falsity or reckless disregard for truth or falsity). The court concluded that the terms were not interchangeable and that it could not interpret "maliciously" to have the same meaning as "actual malice" without exceeding the court's constitutional limitations. Ivey, 821 So. 2d 937, 29 Media L. Rep. 2089 (Ala. 2001).

A private figure has the burden of establishing by a preponderance of the evidence that the defendant was at least negligent in publishing defamatory statements. Cottrell v. NCAA, 975 So. 2d 306, 333 (Ala. 2007). In determining whether a defendant acted negligently in publishing defamatory statements, a court may consider: "(a) the thoroughness of the check that a reasonable person would make before publishing the statement, (b) the nature of the interests that [the defendant] was seeking to promote in publishing the statement, and (3) [sic] the extent of damage to which the statement exposed the plaintiff's reputation." Marous Brothers Construction, LLC v. Alabama State Univ. No. 2:07-cv-384-ID, 2008 U.S. Dist. LEXIS 95848, at *23 (M.D. Ala. Nov. 24, 2008).

"[W]here it is determined that a private individual is alleging defamation, there must be a determination of whether the defamatory speech involves a matter of public concern." Cottrell v. NCAA, 975 So. 2d 306, 344 (Ala. 2007) (quoting Ex parte Rudder, 507 So. 2d 411, 416, 13 Media L. Rep. 2289, 2292 (Ala. 1987)). As discussed infra at I.B.2.a, I.B.2.b, and I.B.5, the status of the plaintiff and of the allegedly defamatory speech determines whether presumed or punitive damages may be recovered, whether proof of special damages is required, and whether the plaintiff bears the burden of proving that the allegedly defamatory statements are false. See, e.g., Forrester v. WVTM TV, Inc., 709 So. 2d 23, 25, 26 Media L. Rep. 1111, 1113 (Ala. Civ. App. 1997).

Alabama courts have held the following subjects, among others, to be matters of public concern within the circumstances of the particular case: the welfare of a community's children, the welfare of children at a community-sponsored event, and whether adults are putting too much pressure on children in sports, Forrester, 709 So. 2d at 26, 26 Media L. Rep. at 1113; alleged abusive prescriptive drug practices, Ex parte Rudder, 507 So. 2d at 417, 13 Media L. Rep. at 2293; alleged mismanagement by administrators of an electric co-operative, McCaig v. Talladega Publishing Co., 544 So. 2d 875, 880, 16 Media L. Rep. 1946, 1950 (Ala. 1989); and dissemination of explicit photographs on a high school campus, S. B. v. St. James Sch., 959 So. 2d 72, 99 (Ala. 2006). Alabama courts have held the following subjects, among others, to be matters not of public concern within the circumstances of the particular case: the alleged theft of grain by a grain elevator employee, Nelson v. Lapeyrouse Grain Corp., 534 So. 2d 1085, 1091, 1096 (Ala. 1988); allegedly defamatory statements about a relatively prominent local businessman that were not made in connection with the businessman's involvement in local affairs or in connection with any matter of public controversy, Mead, 448 So. 2d at 310-11, 10 Media L. Rep. at 1032; and theft by an individual from a private foundation, Cottrell, 975 So. 2d at 344.

The court determines, as a matter of law, whether the defamation plaintiff is a public official or figure or a private figure and whether the allegedly defamatory speech involves a matter of public concern. Ex parte Rudder, 507 So. 2d at 416, 13 Media L. Rep. at 2292. For Alabama state-law defamation claims, the principles of defamation law do not differ for media and for non-media defendants. Beneficial Management Corp. of America v. Evans, 421 So. 2d 92, 96 (Ala. 1982), overruled on other grounds by Nelson v. Lapeyrouse Grain Corp., 534 So. 2d 1085, 1091 n.3 (Ala. 1988). The reported defamation decisions thus include numerous cases for each type of defendant without making any distinction as to the legal principles that apply for media defendants as opposed to non-media defendants.

a. **Private Figure Plaintiff/Matter of Public Concern.** In a defamation action brought by a private figure plaintiff for statements involving a matter of public concern, the plaintiff must prove that the defendant was at least negligent in making the complained-of statements. Forrester v. WVTM TV, Inc., 709 So. 2d 23, 25, 26 Media L. Rep. 1111, 1113 (Ala. Civ. App. 1997). If, in such a case, there is no clear and convincing evidence of constitutional malice (Sullivan "actual malice," which requires that the defamation defendant either knew that the complained-of statements were false or in fact had serious doubts as to the truth or falsity of such statements), damages cannot be presumed, and the plaintiff must offer competent evidence of actual injury caused by the complained-of statements. Ex parte Rudder, 507 So. 2d 411, 415, 13 Media L. Rep. 2289, 2292 (Ala. 1987).

b. **Private Figure Plaintiff/Matter of Private Concern.** In a defamation action brought by a private figure plaintiff involving a matter of purely private concern, the plaintiff must prove that the defendant was at least negligent in making the complained-of statements. Wal-Mart Stores, Inc. v. Smitherman, 872 So. 2d 833, 840 (Ala. 2003). If the court determines in such a case that the statement complained of is libelous or slanderous per se, the plaintiff may recover nominal or presumed damages and need not prove actual damages. Drill Parts & Serv. Co. v. Joy Mfg. Co., 619 So. 2d 1280, 1289 (Ala. 1993). Libel per se is a statement that on its face, without resort to external matters, "charges an offense punishable by indictment, or . . . tends to bring an individual into public hatred, contempt, or ridicule, or charges an act odious and disgraceful in society." McGraw v. Thomason, 265 Ala. 635, 639, 93 So. 2d 741, 744 (1957). A statement is slanderous per se if it imputes to the plaintiff an indictable offense involving infamy or moral turpitude. Delta Health Group, Inc. v. Stafford, 887 So. 2d 887, 896 (Ala. 2004), or, if referable to a woman, want of chastity, Ala. Code § 6-5-181 (1975). In addition, a statement that imputes to another an existing venereal disease or other communicable disease is considered slanderous per se. See Tanner v. Ebbole, 88 So. 3d 856, 863-64 (Ala. 2011) (holding that statements that plaintiff had hepatitis and HIV/AIDS were slanderous per se).

c. **Public Figure Plaintiff/Matter of Public Concern.** In a defamation action brought by a public figure or official, the plaintiff must prove by clear and convincing evidence that the complained-of statements were published with constitutional malice. Deutcsh v. Birmingham Post Co., 603 So. 2d 910, 20 Media L. Rep. 1483 (Ala. 1992) (where City Police Chief was criticized in newspaper editorials for matters concerning his performance of public duties, Chief must prove by clear and convincing evidence that the newspaper made false and defamatory statements of fact with knowledge of falsity or with actual serious doubts as to truth); Barnett v. Mobile County Pers. Bd., 536 So. 2d 46, 54 (Ala. 1988) (in a suit against the County Personnel Board and other public officers for libel, Town Clerk, who was accused of granting unauthorized pay raises to Town employees, must establish by clear and convincing proof that Defendants made the complained-of false and defamatory statements about her with constitutional malice); Gary v. Crouch, 923 So. 2d 1130 (Ala. Civ. App. 2005) (police officer, as a public official, must present clear and convincing evidence that Police Chief acted with constitutional malice when he caused his letter containing criticism of the police officer to be published in local newspaper). Whether evidence is sufficient to support a finding of actual malice is a question of law. Sanders v. Smitherman, 776 So. 2d 68 (Ala. 2000).

The threshold question of whether the actual-malice standard applies in a defamation action involves a two-pronged inquiry: (1) whether the defendant is a public official, and if so, (2) whether the allegedly defamatory comments related to his conduct as a public official. Smith v. Huntsville Times Co., 888 So. 2d 492, 496 (Ala. 2004). This is because "the Constitution protects statements made about public officials when those statements concern 'anything which might touch on an official's fitness for office . . . .' " Id. (quoting Soke v. Plain Dealer, 632 N.E.2d 1282, 1284 (Ohio 1994)). In Smith v. Huntsville Times Co., 888 So. 2d at 496, the plaintiff police investigator conceded that he was a public official, but argued that the actual malice standard did not apply to his claim because he was "not on duty" at the time of the incident recounted in the allegedly defamatory newspaper article and that, therefore, the article defamed him in his private business. The Supreme Court of Alabama declined to attach considerable significance to the fact that the plaintiff was off duty at the time of the alleged incident, finding it clear that the plaintiff's alleged official conduct (racial animus in law enforcement) lay at the heart of the criticisms contained in the allegedly defamatory article. Id. at 498.

The Supreme Court of Alabama recognizes the three-pronged test for determining whether a plaintiff is a limited-purpose public figure that was previously established by the D.C. Circuit Court of Appeals, in Waldbaum v. Fairchild Publications, Inc., 201 U.S. App. D.C. 301 (D.C. Cir. 1980), and then adopted by the Eleventh Circuit Court of Appeals, in Silvester v. American Broadcasting Co., 839 F.2d 1491 (11th Cir. 1988). See Cottrell v. NCAA et al, 975 So. 2d 306 (Ala. 2007). Under this test, for the Court to determine whether a plaintiff is a limited-purpose public figure with regard to a public controversy it must (1) isolate the public controversy; (2) examine the plaintiff's involvement in the controversy; and (3) determine whether the alleged defamation [was] germane to the plaintiff's participation in the controversy. Cottrell, 975 So. 2d at 334. Applying the test in that case, the Court held that a public controversy existed with regard to the NCAA's investigation and treatment of the University of Alabama athletic program. See id. at 334-36. The Court concluded, however, that statements suggesting Cottrell had stolen funds from a charitable foundation and that he had "abandoned his family" were not germane to the public controversy and that for purposes of those particular statements Cottrell was in fact a private person. Id. at 342-43. Whether a plaintiff should be characterized as a limited-purpose public figure is a threshold question of law for the court to decide. See Marous Bros. Constr., LLC v. Ala. State Univ., No. 2:07-cv-384-ID, 2008 U.S. Dist. LEXIS 10867, at *6 (M.D. Ala. Feb. 11, 2008) (citing Cottrell, 975 So. 2d 307). That question, however, is generally more appropriate for resolution at the summary judgment stage than on a motion to dismiss. Marous Bros. Constr., 2008 U.S. Dist. LEXIS 10867, at *11.

3. ***Falsity.*** Unless the plaintiff is a private figure and the publication complained of is a matter of only private concern, the defamation plaintiff has the burden of proving that the allegedly libelous statements are false. Forrester v. WVTM TV, Inc., 709 So. 2d 23, 26, 26 Media L. Rep. 1111, 1113-14 (Ala. Civ. App. 1997).

If a statement is true in its most literal sense, then it cannot support a claim for defamation, which requires a false and defamatory statement of fact. McCaig v. Talladega Publishing Co., 544 So. 2d 875, 878-79, 16 Media L. Rep. 1946, 1949 (Ala. 1989) ("The undisputed testimony of the parties indicates that facts set out in the article are in their most literal sense true. Given the truthfulness of the published statements, the trial court correctly determined that the statements, as a matter of law, were not capable of having a defamatory meaning."). See also Forrester, 709 So. 2d at 26, 26 Media L. Rep. at 1113-14 ("The video aired by WVTM truthfully depicts what occurred at the ball field. The video and the reporters' corresponding explanations as to what occurred are true in their most literal sense."). In Wal-Mart Stores, Inc. v. Smitherman, 872 So. 2d 833, 840 (Ala. 2003), the Supreme Court of Alabama held that allegedly defamatory statements that were true in a literal sense, even if they could be construed as accusing the plaintiff of committing a crime of theft, did not support a claim for defamation. See also S. B. v. Saint James School, 959 So. 2d 72 (Ala. 2006) (rejecting arguments that a "false statement" was to be inferred from a photograph that was undisputedly posed for by plaintiffs); **Jackson v. Waff, LLC, 2012 Ala. Civ. App. LEXIS 295 (Ala. Civ. App. Oct. 23, 2012) (holding that plaintiff had no claim for defamation against broadcaster that accurately reported a story based on information that later proved inaccurate).**

If a statement is substantially true, then it cannot support a claim for defamation. Williams v. Fox Television Stations, Inc., No. CV 04-4000 (Jeff. Co. Cir. Ala. Oct. 3, 2005). In Williams, summary judgment was entered in favor of a television station that reported on the arrival of an unknown substance included in a letter mailed to a downtown law office—just one month after the terrorist attacks of September 11, 2001—the resulting scare that the arrival of the letter caused, and the subsequent arrest of Williams, who mailed the letter. Williams sued the television station claiming that the unknown substance was not hazardous, and, therefore, any statement broadcast by the television station that he had been arrested for sending "a threatening letter" was defamatory. In entering the summary judgment, the Court found that the undisputed evidence showed that the recipients of the letter and others who were in the vicinity when the letter was opened felt threatened by the letter and that the "gist" or "sting" of a broadcast that Williams had been arrested for sending a "threatening letter" was justified and "would have been at the very least substantially true." Accordingly, summary judgment was entered in favor of the television station on the ground of substantial truth. See also Drill Parts & Serv. Co. v. Joy Mfg. Co., 619 So. 2d 1280, 1290 (Ala. 1993) ("When the trial court entered the summary judgment for the defendants as to the defamation claim, it specifically referred only to the October 20, 1982, article in the Birmingham News, stating that that article was 'substantially correct' and that the plaintiffs had not presented any evidence to the contrary. We infer from the trial court's order that it also concluded that the other articles were substantially correct. Because we conclude that a jury, when reading these articles in their entirety, could not find that they conveyed a false meaning, we affirm the summary judgment as to the plaintiffs' defamation claim."); Pemberton v. Birmingham News Co., 482 So. 2d 257, 264, 12 Media L. Rep. 1465, 1470 (Ala. 1985) (in a libel action by a state public official, who must prove constitutional malice, "[t]he jury verdict exonerating [the reporter] is necessarily based on the conclusion that either the statements [complained of] are essentially accurate or there was insufficient evidence that they were written by [the reporter] with [constitutional] malice").

A categorical denial of an alleged defamatory statement, such as, "I know I didn't do it," is not substantial evidence creating a fact question regarding the truth or falsity of the statement. Dudley v. Bass Anglers Sportsman Soc'y, 777 So. 2d 135 (Ala. Civ. App. 2000); see also Little v. Consol. Publ'g Co., 83 So. 3d 517, 524 (Ala. Civ. App. 2011) ("Surely liability under the clear and convincing proof standard of Sullivan cannot be predicated on mere denials, however vehement; such denials are so commonplace in the world of polemical charge and countercharge that, in themselves, they hardly alert the conscientious reporter to the likelihood of error.") (quotations omitted). Similarly, the fact that a newspaper publishes an article criticizing a police officer's conduct despite the "naked aspersions" of a spokesperson for the police department, which questioned the veracity of the citizen's allegations of police misconduct before the police department's investigation had been concluded, does not support an inference of actual malice. Smith v. Huntsville Times Co., 888 So. 2d 492, 501 (Ala. 2004) ("To require that a reporter withhold such a story or face potential liability for defamation because a police officer denies a citizen's allegation of misconduct is exactly the type of self-censorship the New York Times rule was intended to avoid.") (quoting Roberts v. Dover, 525 F. Supp. 987, 993 (M.D. Tenn. 1981)).

4. ***Defamatory Statement of Fact.*** Defamation may take the form of libel or slander. The general rule is that "[l]ibel is expressed by print, writing, pictures, or signs; slander is expressed orally." JENELLE MIMS MARSH & CHARLES W. GAMBLE, ALABAMA LAW OF DAMAGES § 36-26 (5th ed.2004). "Because of the greater deliberation and permanency of a libel, the courts have come to hold certain things to be libelous per se that would have been sufficient to be a bases of an action for slander without a showing of special damages." MARSH & GAMBLE, ALABAMA LAW OF DAMAGES § 36-26.

"A decision whether a statement is reasonably capable of a defamatory meaning is a question of law." Cottrell v. NCAA, 975 So. 2d 306, 346 (Ala. 2007). Generally, "any false and malicious publication, when expressed in printing or writing, or by signs or pictures, is a libel [if it] charges an offense punishable by indictment or . . . tends to bring an individual into public hatred, contempt, or ridicule, or charges an act odious and disgraceful in society. This general definition may be said to include whatever tends to injure the character of an individual, blacken his reputation, or imputes fraud, dishonesty, or other moral turpitude, or reflects shame, or tends to put him without the pale of social intercourse." McGraw v. Thomason, 265 Ala. 635, 639, 93 So. 2d 741, 744 (1957). "The test to be applied in determining whether a newspaper article makes a defamatory imputation is whether an ordinary reader or a reader of average intelligence, reading the article as a whole, would ascribe a defamatory meaning to the language." Drill Parts & Serv. Co. v. Joy Mfg. Co., 619 So. 2d 1280, 1289 (Ala. 1993).

Alabama law recognizes that the First Amendment "protects mere rhetorical hyperbole or statements that cannot reasonably be interpreted as representing actual facts." Finebaum v. Coulter, 854 So. 2d 1120, 1125, 31 Media L. Rep. 1560 (Ala. 2003) (citing Milkovich v. Lorain Journal Co., 497 U.S. 1, 20 (1990)). Words and terms must be read in context to determine whether they are reasonably capable of a defamatory meaning. In Blevins v. W.F. Barnes Corp., 768 So. 2d 386 (Ala. Civ. App. 1999), the court held that since the meaning of the word "extort" is not confined to the crime of extortion and because the use of the word in the context in which it was spoken indicates that it was rhetorical hyperbole, the defendant's statement that Blevins "tried to extort money out of me because I refused to pay his demands" was not slanderous per se. In Finebaum v. Coulter, 854 So. 2d 1120, 31 Media L. Rep. 1560 (Ala. 2003), plaintiff radio sportscaster sued defendant radio sportscaster for defamation based on a comment made on defendant's radio show while discussing the deferential treatment that football recruiters receive from sportscasters and coaches. As an example of such treatment, defendant referenced a conversation he had heard on another radio program between plaintiff and a recruiter, stating: "[T] hese two guys really slobbered over each other, I mean, I really thought they were going to start performing oral sex on one another, it was so sickening." Finebaum, 854 So. 2d at 1123. Plaintiff alleged that, by making that comment on his radio program, defendant had implied that plaintiff was a homosexual. The Supreme Court of Alabama held that defendant's statement was "only rhetorical hyperbole" and was therefore protected by the First Amendment. Id. at 1129.

One Alabama opinion from 1947 colorfully makes the point that what is defamatory in one era may not be defamatory in another: "In the time of Elizabeth it was actionable to call a person a witch"; "[i]n the time of Charles II it was actionable libel to say of a person in publication that he was a Papist and that he went to Mass"; other terms defamatory because of the particular reference of the times are: "an odious, foul, or despised animal [such as] a skunk"; a frozen snake, with reference to the fable of the frozen snake; a hoary-headed filcher; Judas-like; anarchist; dead-beat; slacker; profiteer. Tidmore v. Mills, 33 Ala. App. 243, 251-53, 32 So. 2d 769, 775-76 (1947). A 1912 decision opines, "The term 'damn rascal' is an opprobrious expression and is one of the strongest expressions to convey the idea of moral turpitude." Smith Bros. & Co. v. W.C. Agee & Co., 178 Ala. 627, 635, 59 So. 647, 649 (1912). Alabama courts are not fooled by appearances: "One of the known forms of libel is a publication cloaked in irony – censure in the guise of praise. Another subtle type is open abuse under color of a jest . . . . The courts look through all such disguises, and take note of the real imputations of such utterances." Berry v. City of New York Ins. Co., 210 Ala. 369, 370-71, 98 So. 290, 292 (1923).

5. ***Of and Concerning Plaintiff***. "In an action for libel or slander, the plaintiff must prove, unless it shall be admitted by the defendant, the facts showing that the alleged defamatory matter was published or spoken of the plaintiff." Ala. Code § 6-5-182 (1975); see also Foley v. State Farm Fire & Cas. Ins. Co., 491 So. 2d 934, 937 (Ala. 1986) ("Ala. Code 1975, § 6-5-182, requires that in an action for slander, the plaintiff must prove the facts showing that the allegedly defamatory matter was published or spoken of the plaintiff."); Forrester v. WVTM TV, Inc., 709 So. 2d 23, 25, 26 Media L. Rep. 1111, 1113 (Ala. Civ. App. 1997) (where boy and father are "clouded over" in television broadcast and never identified by name in broadcast, court fails "to see how the television station could defame a 'blue dot' "; summary judgment for Defendant affirmed on other grounds). We know of no support under Alabama law for the proposition that a corporate officer, as opposed to his or her corporate employer, may recover for the publication of a defamatory communication about the corporation.

6. ***Publication.*** "A libel or slander action will lie only if the defendant publishes defamatory material about the plaintiff to a third party." Rowe v. Isbell, 599 So. 2d 35, 36 (Ala. 1992). "In an action for libel or slander, the plaintiff must prove, unless it shall be admitted by the defendant, the facts showing that the alleged defamatory matter was published or spoken of the plaintiff." Ala. Code § 6-5-182 (1975). "Publication is not 'established by rumor or report.'" K-Mart Corp., Inc. v. Pendergrass, 494 So. 2d 600, 604 (Ala. 1986). Likewise, publication is not established by the mere physical receipt of documents. Butler v. Town of Argo, 871 So. 2d 1, 20 (Ala. 2003) (noting that, in order to show publication, plaintiff must demonstrate more than defendant's mere physical receipt and handing over of documents to the clerk at a city council meeting to be stamped and signed as received).

There is a "long-established rule of Alabama law that a rebuttable presumption exists that a letter, postage prepaid, mailed to a person at his place of residence, was received by that person." Pittman v. Gattis, 534 So. 2d 293, 295 (Ala. 1988). A newspaper is published in the county where the newspaper is printed. Ex parte Windom, 763 So. 2d 946, 949 (Ala. 2000).

In at least one case, the defamation claim was based on the publication of a retraction of prior allegedly defamatory statements. A. G. Edwards & Sons, Inc. v. Clark, 558 So. 2d 358, 359 (Ala. 1990) (Defendant had "offered to issue a public retraction, and [Plaintiff] agreed that a public retraction would be appropriate but warned [Defendant] not to do further damage to his reputation when making the retraction. [Defendant] then published a 'retraction' . . . which repeated the allegedly defamatory remarks, and which publication, [Plaintiff] claimed, further damaged his reputation.").

a. **Intracorporate Communication.** Publication to at least one third party is an element of a defamation claim, but "a communication between corporation employees, within the line and scope of the employees' duties with the corporation, is not publication to a 'third party.'" Burks v. Pickwick Hotel, 607 So. 2d 187, 189 (Ala. 1992); see also Wilson v. Southern Med. Ass'n, 547 So. 2d 510, 514 (Ala. 1989). The "intracorporate communications" rule applies also to companies and businesses that are not corporations. Burks v. Pickwick Hotel, 607 So. 2d 187, 189-90 (Ala. 1992); see also Willow Lake Residential Ass'n v. Juliano, 80 So. 3d 226, 247 (Ala. Civ. App. 2010) (holding that communications between a homeowners association and homeowners were intracorporate communications). Alabama courts have held that communication within a company in the following circumstances, among others, does not constitute publication for purposes of a libel claim: "[W]here [an allegedly defamatory] letter is dictated by a corporate employee to a fellow corporate employee in the course of transacting the corporation's business and in the line of their duty as employees of the corporation and the letter is sent to another fellow corporate employee and it is in respect to that employee's relations to the corporation, there is not sufficient publication to sustain an action for libel," Burney v. Southern Ry. Co., 276 Ala. 637, 642, 165 So. 2d 726, 730-31 (1964); where Brothers (the corporation's president) made allegedly defamatory statements about Nelson (a corporate employee suspected of thievery of grain from the company's grain elevator) to other corporate employees, and "Brothers's communications were necessary in determining the culpability of Nelson and other employees, they concerned corporate business and fell within the McDaniel/Burney 'no publication' rule," Nelson v. Lapeyrouse Grain Corp., 534 So. 2d 1085, 1093 (Ala. 1988); and where employees of a credit union made allegedly defamatory statements concerning their supervisor in response to questions posed by an auditor, who was acting as an agent of the credit union, during an investigation of apparent improprieties in the files of a former credit union employee, the employees' statements fell within the parameters of the "no publication" rule, Brackin v. Trimmier Law Firm, 897 So. 2d 207, 221-22 (Ala. 2004). Alabama courts have held that communication within a company in the following circumstances, among others, does constitute publication for purposes of a defamation claim: "Brothers's [a corporate officer] communications in the presence of a polygraph test operator [who was not an employee of the corporation] and Jacob's [a corporate employee] communications to Bolar [a customer of the corporation] do not fall within the McDaniel/Burney ['no publication'] Rule," Nelson, 534 So. 2d at 1094.

b. **Compelled Self-Publication.** The Supreme Court of Alabama does not accept a plaintiff's compelled self-publication as satisfaction of the publication element of the plaintiff's libel claim. Gore v. Health-Tex, Inc., 567 So. 2d 1307, 1308-09 (Ala. 1990) ("Ms. Gore also contends that the fact that she was required to self-publicize the reason for her termination [alleged falsifying of company records] was sufficient to find Health-Tex guilty of slander. We disagree. We are not prepared to hold that a plaintiff's own repetition of allegedly defamatory statements can supply the element of publication essential in a slander action").

c. **Republication.** Alabama courts adhere to the "general rule" that "one who publishes a defamatory statement will not be held liable for the repetition of it by others." Barnette v. Wilson, 706 So. 2d 1164, 1166 (Ala. 1997) (quotations omitted); see also Age-Herald Publ'g Co. v. Waterman, 188 Ala. 272, 288-89, 66 So. 16, 21 (1913) ("It is too well settled to be now questioned that one who utters a slander is not responsible, either as on a distinct cause of action, or by way of aggravation of damages of the original slander, for its voluntary and unjustifiable repetition, without his authority or request, by others over whom he has no control, and who thereby make themselves liable to the person slandered, and that such repetition cannot be considered in law a necessary, natural, or probable consequence of the original slander.") (quotations omitted). "When, however, the second publication is a natural and probable consequence of the first, the initial publisher is responsible for it. Where there were circumstances, known to the original defamer at the time of his publication that might reasonably lead him to expect a repetition, he is responsible for it." Barnette, 706 So. 2d at 1166 (quotations omitted). A republisher is, however, "protected by [the initial speaker's] conditional privilege [if any] to the extent that it reported fairly and accurately the information released at the press conference." Fulton v. Advertiser Co., 388 So. 2d 533, 540, 7 Media L. Rep. 1351, 1356 (Ala. 1980), overruled on other grounds by Nelson v. Lapeyrouse Grain Corp., 534 So. 2d 1085, 1091 n.3 (Ala. 1988).

7. ***Statements versus Conduct.*** Although we are not aware of case law directly on point, we surmise that Alabama would recognize a defamation claim based on conduct as well as on statements. The pertinent language in Alabama cases is, arguably, broad enough to include false and defamatory conduct as grounds for a defamation claim. See, e.g., McGraw v. Thomason, 265 Ala. 635, 639, 93 So. 2d 741, 744 (1957) ("Generally, any false and malicious publication, when expressed in printing or writing, or by signs or pictures, is a libel, [if it] charges an offense punishable by indictment, or . . . tends to bring an individual into public hatred, contempt, or ridicule, or charges an act odious and disgraceful in society."). On the other hand, silence by one who knows the facts of a case but who does nothing to quell rumors does not rise to the level of slander "per se." "[T]here must be some certain link connecting the expressive behavior disputed to a charge of infamy and turpitude." Shook v. St. Bede Sch., 74 F. Supp. 2d 1172, 1180 (M.D. Ala. 1999) (a school official's refusal to offer reasons for the nonrenewal of the plaintiff's contract did not impute moral turpitude to the plaintiff).

8. ***Damages.*** For a defamation claim in Alabama, the following types of damages are permitted, in the appropriate circumstances: compensatory damages (including actual damages – both general and special – nominal damages, and presumed damages) and punitive damages. Actual compensatory damages may be awarded only if the plaintiff has proved each element of the defamation claim and has proved, by competent evidence, actual injury or damage as a proximate result of the defamation, the purpose being to "fairly and reasonably compensate the injured party [in a monetary award] for the loss or injury sustained." Alabama Pattern Jury Instructions, Civil (Lawyers Coop. Publ'g, 2d ed. 1993) §§ 11.01, 11.02. Mere conjecture regarding the cause of certain damages is insufficient. See Casey v. McConnell, 975 So. 2d 384, 390 (Ala. Civ. App. 2007). Special damages are the monetary loss that must be proved by the plaintiff if the statements complained of are libel per quod (i.e., if the statements do not, without resort to extrinsic facts, expose the plaintiff to public ridicule or contempt) or if the statements complained of are slander per quod (i.e., if the statements do not impute to the plaintiff an indictable offense involving infamy or moral turpitude). See Clark v. America's First Credit Union, 585 So. 2d 1367, 1371 (Ala. 1991); Anderton v. Gentry, 577 So. 2d 1261, 1264 (Ala. 1991). Emotional distress and anguish arising from the plaintiff's knowledge that he has been defamed constitute general damages and will not sustain a claim of slander per quod. Shook v. St. Bede Sch., 74 F. Supp. 2d 1172, 1181 (M.D. Ala. 1999). The amount of special damages does not have to be proved to a precise certainty. Smith v. Atkinson, 771 So. 2d 429, 436 (Ala. 2000). The following statutory exception to the requirement of proving special damages is still "on the books" in the Alabama Code: "Any words written, spoken, or printed of any woman falsely imputing to her a want of chastity are actionable without proof of special damages." Ala. Code § 6-5-181 (1975). Nominal damages, often in the amount of $1.00, may be awarded if the defamation plaintiff proves every element of the libel or slander complained of, the defamation complained of is either libel per se or slander per se, and the plaintiff has not proved any substantial injury. The main purpose of such an award is, of course, to vindicate the plaintiff's reputation by showing that the plaintiff prevailed. In Alabama, however, the primary importance of nominal damages may be to support a claim for punitive damages; any award of compensatory damages, no matter how small, can support a punitive damages award. **See Tanner v. Ebbole, 88 So. 3d 856, 882 (Ala. Civ. App. 2011) (upholding a punitive damages award in a defamation action where the jury awarded only nominal compensatory damages).** Punitive damages, which are usually the tail that wags the dog in tort cases in Alabama including defamation cases, are described in part I.B.8.b, infra. The defendant in a defamation action is entitled to mitigate damages if he can show "that the charge was made in good faith by mistake or through inadvertence or misapprehension, and that he has retracted the charge in the same medium of publication as the charge was originally promulgated and in a prominent position therein." Ala. Code § 6-5-184 (1975).

a. **Presumed Damages and Libel Per Se.** If the plaintiff is a private figure for purposes of the statement that is complained of, and the publication that is complained of involved a matter of purely private concern, and the statement complained of is libelous per se (i.e., the language of the statement, without resort to extrinsic facts, exposes the plaintiff to public ridicule or contempt, even if the statement contains no accusation of crime) or slanderous per se (i.e., the statements impute to the plaintiff an indictable offense involving infamy or moral turpitude), the law in Alabama presumes damage to the plaintiff's reputation without special proof, and the plaintiff may be awarded such sum of compensatory damages as would reasonably compensate the plaintiff for damage to reputation. Myers v. Mobile Press-Register, Inc., 266 Ala. 508, 511, 97 So. 2d 819, 822 (1957); see also Delta Health Group, Inc. v. Stafford, 887 So. 2d 887 (Ala. 2004) (where defendant accused plaintiff of stealing its building materials, that accusation constituted slander per se, and plaintiff was relieved of the requirement that he prove actual harm to his reputation or any other actual damage); but see Edwards v. Hyundai Motor Mfg. Alabama, LLC, 603 F.Supp.2d 1336, 1355 (M.D. Ala. Mar. 27, 2009) (a "vague statement" by the defendant that he and the plaintiff had a "'thing going'" does not constitute slander per se). In 1988, the Supreme Court of Alabama affirmed the constitutionality of § 6-5-180 of the Alabama Code regarding presumed damages in light of Dun & Bradstreet, Inc. v. Greenmoss Builders, Inc., 472 U.S. 749, 11 Media L. Rep. 1633 (1985). See Nelson v. Lapeyrouse Grain Corp., 534 So. 2d 1085, 1092 n.3 (Ala. 1988).

The Supreme Court of Alabama has determined that the presumption of injury to the plaintiff's reputation that arises in an action for defamation per se is not rebutted by a plaintiff's testimony at trial that his reputation is excellent. In Liberty National Life Insurance Co. v. Daugherty, the Supreme Court of Alabama expressed its reluctance to "permit evidence that would have the effect of 'destroying, or at least seriously jeopardizing, the prevailing presumption of injury to reputation,' " and refused to "elevate [the plaintiff's] testimonial evidence of good character to the status of a judicial admission." Liberty Nat'l Life Ins. Co. v. Daugherty, 840 So. 2d 152, 161 (Ala. 2002). The court noted that even if the plaintiff's testimony regarding his excellent reputation had negated any injury to his reputation, the plaintiff would still be entitled to recover for mental anguish because the action involved defamation per se. Daugherty, 840 So. 2d at 162. In Horton Homes, Inc. v. Brooks, the Supreme Court of Alabama established the quantum of proof necessary to support damages for mental anguish as "some evidence of mental anguish." Horton Homes, Inc. v. Brooks, 832 So. 2d 44, 53 (Ala. 2001). "Mental anguish includes anxiety, embarrassment, anger, fear, frustration, disappointment, worry, annoyance, and inconvenience." Id.

One Alabama court has found that a plaintiff in a defamation action was "libel-proof" because the plaintiff already had such an "extensive criminal background" that, as a matter of law, he could show "no significant damage to his reputation as a result of [television] broadcasts regarding his [most recent] arrest." Williams v. Fox Television Stations, Inc., No. CV 04-4000 (Jeff. Co. Cir. Ala. Oct. 3, 2005).

(1) **Employment-Related Criticism.** "Words are defamatory per se if they directly tend to prejudice anyone in his office, profession, trade, or business, or in any lawful employment by which he may gain his livelihood." Kelly v. Arrington, 624 So. 2d 546, 549, 21 Media L. Rep. 2217, 2219 (Ala. 1993) ; but see Edwards v. Hyundai Motor Mfg. Alabama, LLC, 603 F.Supp.2d 1336, 1355 (M.D. Ala. 2009) (holding that a "vague statement" by the defendant, in the work environment, that he and the plaintiff had a "'thing going'" does not constitute slander per se). In discussing whether an allegedly libelous statement directly prejudiced the plaintiff in his profession, the court in Blevins v. W.F. Barnes Corp., 768 So. 2d 386 (Ala. Civ. App. 1999), adopted the following analysis by the Missouri Supreme Court: "'[The defamatory] words . . . must be such, if true . . . as would disqualify a person or render him less fit properly to fulfill the duties incident to the special character he has assumed. Words to be actionable as disparaging a person in his calling must touch his office, profession, or trade. They must impeach either his skill or his knowledge, or his official or professional conduct. . . . [T]he disparaging words . . . must affect the plaintiff in some way which is peculiarly harmful to one engaged in his trade.'" Blevins v. W.F. Barnes Corp., 768 So. 2d 386 (Ala. Civ. App. 1999) (quoting Jacobs v. Transcon. & Western Air, 358 Mo. 674, 678, 216 S.W.2d 523, 525 (1948)).

Criticism of one who holds a political office or is a candidate for political office is subject to a different set of rules. "Debate concerning [a state senator's] conduct while pursuing his duties as a member of the Senate . . . deserves the highest protections provided by the First Amendment." Sanders v. Smitherman, 776 So. 2d 68, 74 (Ala. 2000). Remarks regarding the conduct of a legislator are political speech concerning matters of public concern and are, therefore, subject to the full measure of protection under the First Amendment. Id.

(2) **Single Instance Rule.** The single instance rule, which holds that publication of a single instance of false and defamatory information is not actionable because to err (at least once) is human, and publication regarding a single instance is unlikely to lower a person in the estimation of others, has not, to our knowledge, been considered in Alabama. See ROBERT D. SACK, SACK ON DEFAMATION § 2.4.15 (Practicing Law Institute 3d ed. 1999).

b. **Punitive Damages.** Except for particular provisions to the contrary noted within this paragraph, punitive damages may be awarded in a libel case if there is any award of compensatory damages and: (1) the plaintiff has proved by clear and convincing evidence that the defendant consciously or deliberately engaged in oppression, fraud, wantonness, or common law malice (ill will, spite, etc.) with regard to the plaintiff, Ala. Code § 6-11-20 (1975); **Tanner v. Ebbole, 88 So. 3d 856, 882 (Ala. Civ. App. 2011) (upholding a punitive damages award in a defamation action where the jury awarded only nominal compensatory damages)**; (2) the plaintiff has proved by clear and convincing evidence that the statement that is complained of was published by the defendant with knowledge that the statement was false or with actual serious doubts as to the truth of the statement, Ala. Code § 6-5-186 (1975); and (3) the plaintiff has proved that at least five days before commencement of the libel action the plaintiff made written demand upon the defendant for a public retraction of the charge or matter published, which the defendant failed or refused to publish within five days in as prominent and public a place or manner as the charge or matter published occupied, Ala. Code § 6-5-186 (1975). Punitive damages may not be awarded in a libel case if the defendant proves that he retracted the statement within ten days of the date of publication in the same medium of publication as the complained-of statement was originally published and in a prominent position therein. Ala. Code § 6-5-185 (1975).

Except for particular provisions to the contrary noted in this paragraph, punitive damages may be awarded in a slander case if there is any award of compensatory damages and: (1) the plaintiff has proved by clear and convincing evidence that the statement that is complained of was published with knowledge that the statement was false or with actual serious doubts as to whether the statement was true, Nelson v. Lapeyrouse Grain Corp., 534 So. 2d 1085, 1091 n.3 (Ala. 1988); **Tanner v. Ebbole, 88 So. 3d 856, 882 (Ala. Civ. App. 2011) (upholding a punitive damages award in a defamation action where the jury awarded only nominal compensatory damages)** (2) the plaintiff has proved by clear and convincing evidence that the defendant consciously or deliberately engaged in oppression, fraud, wantonness, or common law malice (ill will, spite, etc.) with regard to the plaintiff, Ala. Code § 6-11-20 (1975); and (3) the slander case is not a private-plaintiff/matter-of-purely-private-concern case. In a slander case with a private plaintiff and a matter of purely private concern, punitive damages may be awarded to the plaintiff if any compensatory damages are awarded and: (1) the plaintiff has proved to the jury's reasonable satisfaction that the defendant published the complained-of statement with common law malice, Nelson, 534 So. 2d at 1096; and (2) the plaintiff has proved by clear and convincing evidence that the defendant consciously or deliberately engaged in oppression, fraud, wantonness, or common law malice with regard to the plaintiff, Ala. Code § 6-11-20 (1975). Punitive damages may not be awarded to the plaintiff in a slander case if the defendant proves that he retracted the statement within ten days of the date of publication in the same medium as the original publication and in a prominent position therein. Ala. Code § 6-5-185 (1975).

Alabama Code § 6-11-27 (1975) governs the award of punitive damages against an employer for the acts of the employer's agent (including employees). Because of one of the several provisions of that statute, a plaintiff who proves a claim for wanton hiring and supervision will also, in most cases, be able to obtain an award of punitive damages from the employer. For the statutory requirements to recover punitive damages from an employer for the actions of the employer's agent, see III.G.2, infra.

"Punitive damages may not be awarded against the State of Alabama or any county or municipality [of the State], or any agency [of the State], except any entity covered under the Medical Liability Act now codified as Section 6-5-480 et seq., or any acts [amending that section]." Ala. Code § 6-11-26 (1975).

Alabama's punitive damages law, Alabama Code § 6-11-21, establishes the following monetary limitations and procedural requirements, in pertinent part: "(a) Except as provided in subsections (b), (d), and (j) . . . no award of punitive damages shall exceed three times the compensatory damages of the party claiming punitive damages or . . . $500,000 . . . , whichever is greater; (b) Except as provided in subsections (d) and (j) . . . no award of punitive damages [against a defendant who is a small business] shall exceed . . . $50,000 . . . or 10 percent of the business' worth, whichever is greater; (c) 'Small business' for purposes of this section means a business having a net worth of two million dollars . . . or less at the time of the occurrence made the basis of the suit; . . . (e) Except as provided in Section 6-11-27 [liability of principal, etc., for act of agent], no defendant shall be liable for any punitive damages unless that defendant has been expressly found by the trier of fact to have engaged in conduct, as defined in Section 6-11-20 [summarized in I.B.8.b, supra], warranting punitive damages, and such defendant shall be liable only for punitive damages commensurate with that defendant's own conduct; (f) As to all the fixed sums for punitive damage limitations set out . . . in sections (a) (b) and (d), those sums shall be adjusted as of January 1, 2003, and as of January 1 at three-year intervals thereafter, at an annual rate in accordance with the Consumer Price Index rate; (g) The jury may neither be instructed nor informed as to the provisions of this section; (h) this section shall not apply to class actions . . . ."

II. PRIVILEGES AND DEFENSES

A. Scope of Privileges

1. ***Absolute Privilege.*** "In defamation actions [in Alabama], the only absolutely privileged communications recognized under the law are those made during legislative or judicial proceedings (or, in such circumstances as those dealt with in Webster v. Byrd, [494 So. 2d 31 (Ala. 1986),] quasi-judicial proceedings), or contained in legislative acts of this state which are made under authority of law." Butler v. Town of Argo, 871 So. 2d 1, 24 (Ala. 2003) (quoting Walker v. Majors, 496 So. 2d 726, 730 (Ala. 1986)).

"[A] defamatory publication made before the commencement of an action in court is absolutely privileged when made with some relation to a contemplated proceeding . . . ." Walker, 496 So. 2d at 729-30 (adopting the standard presented in Restatement (Second) of Torts § 587 (1977) for absolute privilege). See also Hollander v. Nichols, 19 So. 2d 184, 90 (Ala. 2009) (holding that allegedly defamatory material contained in medical records disclosed in a small claims collections proceeding was covered by absolute privilege); Wright v. State, 757 So. 2d 457 (Ala. Civ. App. 2000) ("[S] tatements made by correctional officers during, or in the course of instituting, a prison disciplinary proceeding are absolutely privileged."). In Cutts v. Am. United Life Ins. Co., 505 So. 2d 1211 (Ala. 1987), the Supreme Court of Alabama determined that statements in a letter from the defendant to the Assistant District Attorney concerning an investigation regarding the termination of insurance benefits for the plaintiff's company were covered by the absolute privilege for "those involved in judicial proceedings." Cutts, 505 So. 2d at 1215 ("[A]n absolute privilege exists in favor of those involved in judicial proceedings, including judges, lawyers, jurors, and witnesses, shielding them from an action for defamation."). "[C] ommunications made in the course of quasi-judicial proceedings" in Alabama are also protected by an absolute privilege. See Webster v. Byrd, 494 So. 2d 31, 34 (Ala. 1986) (letter of termination from president of a state junior college to a full-time technical instructor at the college absolutely privileged because it begins a possible contest of the termination by the instructor); Surrency v. Harbison, 489 So. 2d 1097, 1103-04 (Ala. 1986) (overruling prior Alabama law and holding that grievance proceedings are quasi-judicial and communications made during the course of grievance proceedings are absolutely privileged); and Sullivan v. Smith, No. 2040335 (Ala. Civ. App. Oct. 7, 2005); see also Sweeney v. Alabama Alcoholic Beverage Control Bd., 94 F. Supp. 2d 1241 (M.D. Ala. 2000), vacated in part and superseded by 117 F. Supp. 2d 1266 (M.D. Ala. 2000) (testimony at a termination hearing for a Board employee is absolutely privileged since such a hearing is "quasi-judicial"). "The determination of whether a statement is privileged is a question of law for the trial judge." Atkins Ford Sales, Inc. v. Royster, 560 So. 2d 197, 200 (Ala. 1990).

The rationale behind the absolute privilege, and the limits of the privilege, have been explained by the Supreme Court of Alabama as follows: "In questions falling within [the] absolute privilege the question of malice has no place. However malicious the intent, or however false the charge may have been, the law, from considerations of public policy, and to secure the unembarrassed and efficient administration of justice, denies to the defamed party any remedy through an action for libel or slander. This privilege, however, is not a license which protects every slanderous publication or statement made in the course of [the privileged] proceedings. It extends only to such matters as are relevant or material . . . , or, at least, it does not protect slanderous imputations plainly irrelevant and impertinent, voluntarily made, and which the party making them could not reasonably have supposed to be relevant." O'Barr v. Feist, 292 Ala. 440, 446, 296 So. 2d 152, 157 (1974) (quoted and applied in Barnett v. Mobile County Pers. Bd., 536 So. 2d 46, 51 (Ala. 1988)). Publications that are only incidentally related to legislative activities do not fall within the ambit of the absolute legislative privilege. See Butler v. Town of Argo, 871 So. 2d 1, 25 (Ala. 2003) (finding that circulating a petition, talking with numerous people, playing a tape-recorded conversation containing allegedly defamatory statements for a reporter, distributing the transcript to reporters, and granting interviews to reporters were, at most, only incidentally related to a city council member's legislative activities, and therefore not absolutely privileged).

In Hillman v. Yarbrough, 936 So. 2d 1056 (Ala. 2006), the Supreme Court of Alabama stated that some actions by local legislators, "such as explaining reasons for voting on legislation or engaging in activities only incidentally related to legislative affairs," fall outside of a legislative function and thus are not protected by the absolute privilege. Hillman v. Yarbrough, 936 So. 2d at 1064 (quoting Butler v. Town of Argo, 871 So. 2d 1, 24 (Ala. 2003). The court stated that "[t]he fact that an action is undertaken in the course of a legislator's fulfilling his or her responsibilities does not necessarily indicate that the action was taken in the performance of a legislative duty or act." Id. at 1062. Instead, it is the occasion in which the statements are made that is privileged. Id. The court again reversed the trial court's grant of the commissioner's motion to dismiss based on its finding that the plaintiff might have been able to prove that the county commissioner's "presence at the meeting of the [county parks and recreation] Board was not a legislative function but rather a 'public discussion outside of a legislative function.'" Id. at 1065 (quoting Butler, 871 So. 2d at 24).

In Rowe v. Isbell, 599 So. 2d 35 (Ala. 1992), the Supreme Court of Alabama noted that, under Ala. Code § 25-4-116 (1975), communications of allegedly false and defamatory information to the Department of Industrial Relations' Unemployment Compensation Agency were absolutely privileged only if made "in connection with the requirements and administration of Chapter 4, Title 25, Code of Alabama. . . ." Rowe, 599 So. 2d at 36 (emphasis added). The United States District Court for the Middle District of Alabama, however, has clarified the scope of the absolute privilege provided by the statute. See Johnson v. Fed. Express Corp., 147 F. Supp. 2d 1268 (M.D. Ala. 2001). The federal district court in Johnson noted that although "Alabama law provides that 'all' communications from an employer to [the Alabama Department of Industrial Relations] 'shall be absolutely privileged and shall not be made the subject matter or basis for any civil action for slander or libel in any court,' . . . the Supreme Court of Alabama has deliberately avoided ruling whether the privilege is qualified or absolute." Johnson, 147 F. Supp. 2d at 1277 (citations omitted) (quoting Ala. Code § 25-4-116 (1975)). Noting that such indecision "chills free speech," the court "[had] no trouble finding that the statute means what it says: the privilege is absolute." Id.

2. ***Qualified Privileges.*** The defense of qualified privilege gives protection to defendants in those cases in which the defendant "acted in the discharge of any public or private duty, whether legal or moral, which the ordinary exigencies of society, or his own private interest, or even that of another, called upon him to perform." Ex parte Blue Cross & Blue Shield, 773 So. 2d 475, 479 (Ala. 2000). A qualified privilege shields a defamation defendant from liability for false and defamatory statements made of and concerning a defamation plaintiff in the circumstances described in parts II.A.2.a through II.A.2.f, infra, unless the plaintiff proves that the defendant published the false and defamatory statements with common law malice (ill will, hostility, threats, rivalry, other legal actions, former libels or slanders, and the like). Gore v. Health-Tex, Inc., 567 So. 2d 1307, 1308 (Ala. 1990). In 1912, the Supreme Court of Alabama announced a corollary to the qualified privilege, as follows: "While there are authorities to the contrary, we think the sounder, better rule is that merely exceeding the privilege, in consequence of excitement or of intemperance of speech, does not per se destroy the [qualified] privilege; but that such unnecessarily defamatory expression, upon the privileged occasion, may be considered by the jury in determining actual [common law] malice vel non in the utterance; and which, if present, negatives an essential element of qualified privileged communication and defeats the defense based upon that character of privilege." Smith Bros. & Co. v. W. C. Agee & Co., 178 Ala. 627, 635-36, 59 So. 647, 649 (1912). Whether the statement is protected by a qualified privilege is a question of law for the court. Butler v. Town of Argo, 871 So. 2d 1, 26 (Ala. 2003).

In addition to the qualified privileges described below, the Supreme Court of Alabama has also acknowledged both a statutory and common law fair report privilege. See Wilson v. Birmingham Post Co., 482 So. 2d 1209, 1211, 12 Media L. Rep. 1668, 1670 (Ala. 1986). In Wilson, the court construed and applied § 13A-11-161 of the Alabama Code, which it described as an "explicit statutory privilege protecting fair and accurate reports of criminal charges and official investigations." Wilson v. Birmingham Post Co., 482 So. 2d at 1212. The Court, after observing that the Alabama statute "is a codification of the common law as reflected in the Restatement (Second) of Torts § 611 (1977)," held that the publication at issue was "conditionally privileged under § 13A-11-161 *and* the common law." Wilson v. Birmingham Post Co., 482 So. 2d at 1211, 1213 (emphasis added). This statutory application of the fair report privilege can be defeated if the defendant publishes with common law malice or the defendant refuses or neglects "to publish in the same manner in which the publication complained of appeared, a reasonable explanation or contradiction . . . by the plaintiff," or the publisher refuses, upon written request from the plaintiff, "to publish the subsequent determination of [the] suit, action or investigation" that the defendant initially reported. Ala. Code § 13A-11-161 (1975). The extent to which Alabama would apply a common law fair report privilege to situations not otherwise covered by § 13A-11-161 is not yet clear. For example, in WKRG-TV, Inc. v. Wiley, 495 So. 2d 617, 618-19, 13 Media L. Rep. 1680, 1681 (Ala. 1986), the court declined to apply the formulation of the fair report privilege set out in § 611 of the Restatement (Second) of Torts to a report of a meeting of private citizens at a local church. **In Jackson v. Waff, LLC, 2012 Ala. Civ. App. LEXIS 295 (Ala. Civ. App. Oct. 23, 2012), the Alabama Court of Civil Appeals held that, because the police had in fact stated that it considered the plaintiff a suspect in a shooting, the plaintiff could not state a claim for defamation against a broadcaster who reported the statement, despite the plaintiff's innocence, despite the police having concluded he was innocent, and despite the broadcaster's refusal "to publish the subsequent determination of [the] suit, action or investigation" as required by Ala. Code § 13A-11-161 (1975). The case is noteworthy because the court found it unnecessary even to reach the fair report privilege.**

A number of Alabama statutes provide immunity for communications that are made within the purview of the particular statute. The statute that provides for mandatory reporting of suspected child abuse, for example, extends absolute immunity from civil or criminal liability for such reporting. Ala. Code § 26-14-9 (1975); Brown v. Pound, 585 So. 2d 885, 886 (Ala. 1991) (absolute immunity for physician and medical center that complied with the mandates of the statute in reporting suspicions of child abuse). This absolute privilege does not extend to defamatory communications, however. See, e.g., Harris v. City of Montgomery, 435 So. 2d 1207, 1212 (Ala. 1983) ("allegations of tortious conduct on the part of the [police] officer beyond those actions protected by the immunity statute . . . , if proved, would remove the officer from the purview of § 26-14-9"; "allegations of false imprisonment, false arrest, and, apparently, defamation in the complaint").

Despite the Supreme Court of Alabama's recognition of absolute immunity in Harris, 435 So. 2d at 1212, and in Brown, 585 So. 2d at 886, pursuant to the immunity statute for reporting of suspected child abuse, the court has refused to recognize absolute immunity pursuant to the statute that protects communications relating to an unemployment benefits claim under state law, notwithstanding the fact that the statute specifically provides that such communications "shall be absolutely privileged and shall not be made the subject matter or basis for any civil action for slander or libel in any court." Ala. Code § 25-4-116 (1992) (emphasis added); Cantrell v. North River Homes, Inc., 628 So. 2d 551, 554 (Ala. 1993) (acknowledging that in a 1983 decision the court had "raised, but did not decide, the question of '[w]hether [this statutory privilege] is an absolute privilege or merely a qualified one,' " the court again ducked the question in 1993, finding that " '[even] if the statutory privilege is only a qualified one, [Defendants have] carried [their] burden, and summary judgment was proper' " because Plaintiff "presented no substantial evidence that [Defendant's] statements were attended by [common law] malice").

The Constitution of the State of Alabama provides that the State of Alabama, its agencies, and its officers and agents are immune from tort liability in their official capacity except that "a suit may be made against State officials in their official capacity for acts allegedly committed fraudulently, in bad faith, beyond their authority, or under a mistaken interpretation of the law." Rutledge v. Baldwin County Comm'n, 495 So. 2d 49, 52 (Ala. 1986). As with the child-abuse reporting statutes, the immunity does not extend to defamatory communications. Gibson v. Abbott, 529 So. 2d 939, 941 (Ala. 1988). Public officers acting in their official capacity as state employees are protected in defamation actions by a qualified privilege, however. That privilege can be defeated only by a showing of common law malice, which must be pleaded and proved by the defamation plaintiff. Gibson, 529 So. 2d at 941-42.

All public officers in Alabama are protected from tort liability by the qualified privilege that is set forth in Restatement (Second) of Torts § 895D (1974), as follows: "A public officer acting within the general scope of his authority is not subject to tort liability for an administrative act or omission if (a) he is immune because engaged in the exercise of a discretionary function, (b) he is privileged and does not exceed or abuse the privilege, or (c) his conduct was not tortious because he was not negligent in the performance of his responsibility." Gibson v. Abbott, 529 So. 2d 939, 941-42 (Ala. 1988). Discretionary function immunity does not protect a public official or employee in the negligent performance of ministerial acts. Tuscaloosa County v. Henderson, 699 So. 2d 1274, 1277 (Ala. Civ. App. 1997) (citing Phillips v. Thomas, 555 So. 2d 81, 83 (Ala. 1989)). "Furthermore, [a public officer or] employee is not protected by discretionary function immunity if his actions were committed fraudulently, willfully, maliciously, or in bad faith." Henderson, 699 So. 2d at 1277-78. Federal officers and employees are protected by applicable federal privileges, which are not discussed in this survey of Alabama law.

In Key v. City of Cullman, 826 So. 2d 151 (Ala. Civ. App. 2001), cert. denied, 826 So. 2d 159 (Ala. 2002), a bank customer and her two sons sued a police officer and the city that employed him after a photograph of the plaintiffs with a caption identifying them as suspects in a check forgery case was published in the "Crimestoppers" section of the local paper. The Alabama Court of Civil Appeals affirmed the trial court's summary judgment in favor of the officer and the city, noting that although it was "debatable" whether the officer conducted the investigation in a negligent or even reckless manner, that matter was "within the discretion afforded the investigator of a crime," and therefore, within the scope of State-agent immunity for discretionary acts. Key, 826 So. 2d at 158 (citing Ex parte Butts, 775 So. 2d 173 (Ala. 2000)).

In addition to the categories of qualified privilege that are discussed below, Alabama law also recognizes a fair response privilege. See, Morrison v. Mobile County Bd. of Educ., 495 So. 2d 1086, 1090, 1092 (Ala. 1986) (Where defendants alleged that their "comments were not 'accusations' but merely constituted fair response to charges leveled by the plaintiffs," the court side-stepped the question whether board members' statements at a board meeting "enjoy an absolute privilege" and held simply that "defendants' comments were fair response to charges leveled by the plaintiff.").

a. **Common Interest.** "Where a party makes a communication and that . . . communication is one in which the party has an interest and it is made to another having a corresponding interest, the communication is privileged, if it is made in good faith and without [common law] malice[,] . . . [which can be] shown by [substantial] evidence of previous ill will, hostility, threats, rivalry, other actions, former libels or slanders, and the like, emanating from the defendant, or by the violence of the defendant's language, the mode and extent of the publication, and the like." Cantrell v. North River Homes, Inc., 628 So. 2d 551, 553-54 (Ala. 1993); **see also Ex parte Bole, 2012 Ala. LEXIS 110, *46-47 (Ala. Aug. 31, 2012) (recognizing the qualified privilege of members of religious associations in communications between them in furtherance of their common purpose or interest);** Ex parte Blue Cross & Blue Shield, 773 So. 2d 475 (Ala. 2000) (where an insurance company wrote letters explaining that claims were being denied because the services performed by the plaintiff were outside of the scope of his license to practice dentistry, those statements were protected by the defense of qualified privilege because both the insurance company and its insureds had an interest in the reason for the denial of the claims); Brown v. Chem. Haulers, Inc., 402 So. 2d 887, 891 (Ala. 1981) (where a former employer tells a prospective employer that a former employee's negligence was the cause of an accident, those communications are protected by common-interest qualified privilege); Camp v. Corr. Med. Serv., 668 F. Supp 2d 1338, 1364 (M.D. Ala. 2009) (holding communications between the Alabama Department of Corrections and its dental supplier were made under a common interest).

b. **Duty.** "'Where a party makes a communication, and such communication is prompted by duty owed either to the public or to a third party, or the communication is one in which the party has an interest, and it is made to another having a corresponding interest, the communication is privileged, if made in good faith and without actual malice. The duty under which the party is privileged to make the communication need not be one having the force of legal obligation, but it is sufficient if it is social or moral in its nature and defendant in good faith believes he is acting in pursuance thereof, although in fact he is mistaken.'" Clack v. America's First Credit Union, 585 So. 2d 1367, 1370 (Ala. 1991) (quoting Berry v. City of New York Ins. Co., 210 Ala. 369, 371, 98 So. 290, 292 (1923)); see also Reynolds Metals Co. v. Mays, 547 So. 2d 518, 524-25 (Ala. 1989) (communications by employer to telegraph operators protected by a qualified privilege where employer had a duty to give employee written notice of suspension and of polygraph test); Webster v. Byrd, 494 So. 2d 31, 36 (Ala. 1986) (duty of community college president to the public and students to eliminate instructors who were incompetent or insubordinate rendered his communications regarding termination of tenured professor protected by a qualified privilege); Smith v. Equifax Services, Inc., 537 So. 2d 463, 469 (Ala. 1988) (holding "the furnishing of information in a business context by an information reporting company" is protected by qualified privilege as a duty owed to the party requesting the information in a business context); Tidwell v. Winn-Dixie, Inc., 502 So. 2d 747, 748 (Ala. 1987) (a store manager's statement to a police officer regarding the plaintiff, who was subsequently convicted for disturbing the peace at the store, was protected by qualified privilege as a statement prompted by duty). "The privilege may be lost if the publication goes beyond what the occasion requires." Gary v. Crouch, 867 So. 2d 310, 317 (Ala. 2003) (noting that, even if a police chief had a duty to respond to a letter from a city councilman, such duty did not immunize him from his decision to send the letter containing allegedly defamatory statements to local media outlets).

c. **Criticism of Public Employee.** There is no qualified privilege in Alabama for criticism of public employees as such. Statements of criticism regarding public employees may be protected by the constitutional malice standard for public officials. See Deutcsh v. Birmingham Post Co., 603 So. 2d 910, 20 Media L. Rep. 1483 (Ala. 1992). Criticism of lower level public employees may be protected by the common interest, duty, or fair report privilege. See, e.g., Fulton v. Advertiser Co., 388 So. 2d 533, 537-40, 7 Media L. Rep. 1351, 1354-56 (Ala. 1980) (press conference by State Finance Director regarding alleged abuses and misconduct within the Alabama Building Commission held to be protected by qualified privilege based upon duty; summary judgment for State Finance Director reversed and remanded nonetheless), overruled on other grounds by Nelson v. Lapeyrouse Grain Corp., 534 So. 2d 1085, 1091 n.3 (Ala. 1988).

d. **Limitation on Qualified Privileges.**

(1) **Constitutional or Actual Malice.** When the plaintiff is a public official or figure, even if the plaintiff can prove that the defendant published false and defamatory statements concerning the plaintiff with common law malice, in order to prevail, constitutional considerations require the plaintiff to prove by clear and convincing evidence that the defendant published the complained-of statement with knowledge that the statements were false or with actual serious doubts as to whether the statements were true or false. Finebaum v. Coulter, 854 So. 2d 1120, 31 Media L. Rep. 1560 (Ala. 2003) ("Mere negligence does not suffice. Rather, the plaintiff must demonstrate that the author [or speaker] 'in fact entertained serious doubts as to the truth of his publication,' or [that he] acted with a 'high degree of awareness of . . . probable falsity.") (citations omitted); Little v. Consol. Publ'g Co., 83 So. 3d 517, 522 (Ala. Civ. App. 2011) ("When a plaintiff in a libel action is a public official and the alleged defamatory statement relates to his conduct as a public official, the plaintiff must establish constitutional malice by clear and convincing evidence.") (quotations omitted); Gary v. Crouch, 923 So. 2d 1130, 1136-38 (Ala Civ. App. 2005) (noting that while a showing of common law malice is sufficient to defeat a qualified privilege, a public official defamation plaintiff must prove the defendant acted with constitutional malice).

(2) **Common Law Malice.** "'Common law malice' in its traditional sense may be shown by evidence of previous ill will, hostility, threats, rivalry, other actions, former libels or slanders, and the like . . . or by violence of the defendant's language, the mode and extent of publication and the like." Banks, Finley, White & Co. v. Wright, 864 So. 2d 324, 329 (Ala. Civ. App. 2001), cert. denied, 864 So. 2d 333 (Ala. 2003) (quoting Fulton v. Advertiser Co., 388 So. 2d 533 (Ala. 1980)). If a defamation plaintiff proves that the defendant published with common law malice, that proof defeats the defendant's claim of a qualified privilege, including the statutory fair report privilege. Wilson v. Birmingham Post Co., 482 So. 2d 1209, 1213, 12 Media L. Rep. 1668, 1671-72 (Ala. 1986). Alabama courts sometimes confuse constitutional malice with common law malice, perhaps because each is occasionally referred to simply as "actual malice" in the case law. See, e.g., Brackin v. Trimmier Law Firm, 897 So. 2d 207, 224 (Ala. 2004) ("In order to overcome that conditional privilege, [plaintiff] was required to establish by substantial evidence that [auditor] made those defamatory communications with common law or actual malice. . . . Actual malice may be shown by 'evidence of previous ill will, hostility, threats, rivalry, other actions, former libels or slanders, and the like.' "); Barnett v. Mobile County Pers. Bd., 536 So. 2d 46, 54 (Ala. 1988) ("The 'actual malice' that a private party plaintiff must prove in order to defeat this qualified or conditional privilege is the traditional common law malice, and it must be distinguished from the 'actual malice' required in defamation cases brought by public figures and public officials under New York Times Co. v. Sullivan and its progeny.") (citation omitted).

The amount of compensation a defendant in a defamation suit receives for the publication or broadcast that contains an allegedly libelous statement is not probative of actual malice. In Ex parte Crawford Broadcasting Company, 904 So. 2d 221 (Ala. 2004), the Supreme Court of Alabama held that the compensation paid to two radio talk-show hosts who, during their morning radio show broadcast, aired an allegedly libelous statement was not relevant to show actual malice. "The fact that the [employees] were paid any particular amount for their work does not indicate whether they were concerned with the truth of their statements." Id. at 225. In reaching its decision, the Court in Crawford reaffirmed an 1854 opinion, Ware v. Cartledge, 24 Ala. 622 (1854), which held that the wealth of a defendant in a defamation action is wholly irrelevant to determining whether that defendant is sufficiently influential to affect the plaintiff's reputation. The Crawford Court equated "wealth" as the term was used in Ware with the term "compensation" in the current case. Id. at 226. As the Court explained, "[a] person can be a highly compensated social pariah or a low-paid social exemplar. The public's perception of that person is connected less to the amount of that person's paycheck than to what he does with his life." Id.

In Wiggins v. Mallard, 905 So. 2d 776, 33 Media L. Rep. 1025 (Ala. 2004), the Supreme Court of Alabama held that a private party defamation plaintiff may overcome a qualified immunity defense with testimony indicating that the defendant intentionally lied about the plaintiff. "Thus, common-law malice may be shown, not only by 'evidence of hostility, rivalry, the violence of the language, [or] the mode and extent of publication,' but, also, by proof of 'the recklessness of the publication and prior information regarding its falsity.'" Id. at 788. In its analysis, the Supreme Court of Alabama noted that, "[i]n reality, evidence needed to establish constitutional malice and common-law malice overlap[s] significantly . . . insofar as the same evidence bears both on the defendant's motive, for purposes of common-law malice, and on the defendant's attitude toward the truth or falsity of his published material, for purposes of constitutional malice." Id. at 787 (internal citations quotations). In Camp v. Corr. Med. Serv., 668 F. Supp 2d 1338, 1364 (M.D. Ala. 2009), the defendant's lack of firsthand knowledge regarding the truth of the defamatory statements he made was not sufficient to show actual malice.

e. **Question of Fact or Law.** The issue as to whether an absolute privilege or a qualified privilege (or no privilege at all) applies in a particular defamation case is a question of law for the court. Butler v. Town of

Argo, 871 So. 2d 1, 24 (Ala. 2003). The credibility of witnesses, however, is "a matter within the exclusive province of the jury." Wiggins, 905 So. 2d 776, 783. In Wiggins, where "[t]he unequivocal testimony of each defendant [was] substantial evidence of the untruthfulness of the other's testimony," the Supreme Court of Alabama held that the application of the privilege was a question for the jury. Id. at 788.

f. **Burden of Proof.** In Ex parte Blue Cross & Blue Shield, 773 So. 2d 475 (Ala. 2000), the Supreme Court of Alabama resolved the conflicting case law concerning which party has the burden of proving the presence or absence of "actual malice" (i.e., common law malice) when a qualified privilege is interposed as a defense in a defamation action. The Court made clear that the defendant does not have the burden of proving absence of actual malice to avail himself of the qualified privilege defense. Id. The plaintiff bears the burden of proving defamation with actual malice to prevail against a defense of qualified privilege. Id.

B. Standard Libel Defenses

1. ***Truth.*** Truth is a "complete and absolute defense to defamation." **Fed. Credit, Inc. v. Fuller, 72 So. 3d 5, 10 (Ala. 2011).** Truth includes literal truth and substantial truth. McCaig v. Talladega Publ'g Co., 544 So. 2d 875, 878-79, 16 Media L. Rep. 1946, 1949 (Ala. 1989) (the "facts set out in the article are in their most literal sense true"); Drill Parts & Serv. Co. v. Joy Mfg. Co., 619 So. 2d 1280, 1290 (Ala. 1993) ("When the trial court entered the summary judgment for the defendants as to the defamation claim, it specifically referred only to the October 20, 1982, article in The Birmingham News, stating that that article was 'substantially correct' and that the plaintiffs had not presented any evidence to the contrary. We infer from the trial court's order that it also concluded that the other articles were substantially correct."). In every type of defamation case but one, it is the plaintiff who bears the burden of proving that the complained-of statements are false. Only in private-figure-plaintiff cases in which the allegedly defamatory statements involve a matter of purely private concern must the defendant prove truth in order to succeed on the truth defense. Forrester v. WVTM TV, 709 So. 2d 23, 26, 28, 26 Media L. Rep. 1111, 1113 (Ala. Civ. App. 1997) ("Because this case involves a matter of public concern, the burden is on [Plaintiff] to show that the broadcast was false," [from the majority opinion]. "Because I believe [Plaintiff's] reprimand of his child was essentially a private matter, and not a matter of public concern, I do not think [Plaintiff] had the burden of proving that the broadcast was false," [from the dissenting opinion].); but cf. Sanders v. Smitherman, 776 So. 2d 68 (Ala. 2000) (in the context of a motion for summary judgment, once the defendants submitted substantial evidence in support of their motion indicating that their statements were true, the burden shifted to the plaintiffs to present substantial evidence indicating that the statements made about them were false).

2. ***Opinion.*** One cannot recover in a defamation action because of another's expression of an opinion based upon disclosed, non-defamatory facts, no matter how derogatory the expression may be, because the recipient of the information is free to accept or reject the opinion based upon his or her independent evaluation of the disclosed, non-defamatory facts. Sanders v. Smitherman, 776 So. 2d 68 (Ala. 2000). Where a statement of opinion on a matter of public concern reasonably implies false and defamatory facts regarding a public figure or official, the burden of proof is on the plaintiff to show that such statements were made with knowledge of their false implications or with reckless disregard of their truth. Deutcsh v. Birmingham Post Co., 603 So. 2d 910, 911-12, 20 Media L. Rep. 1483, 1484-85 (Ala. 1992). In Sanders, a city mayor expressed concern over possible violations of state ethics laws by a state senator based on information that had been presented to him by a member of the county school board. Under Alabama law, the underlying facts that form the basis of a defendant's opinion are the relevant area of inquiry. Sanders, 776 So. 2d at 74. Noting that the underlying facts in Sanders had not been refuted, the court found that this case presented a classic example of statements of opinion relating to matters of public concern. Id. Where a former police officer filed a libel claim against the police chief and the town based upon an allegedly false and defamatory letter from the police chief to a bullet-proof vest manufacturer, the letter was found to be the police chief's opinion and thus not actionable in libel. Williams v. Marcum, 519 So. 2d 473, 477 (Ala. 1987) (pre-Milkovich decision) ("As indicated by the wording of the letter itself, the statement made the basis of this claim was [the chief's] opinion. The law is clear that an opinion can never be false. Because a statement must be false to be actionable defamation, an opinion is simply not actionable defamation."). In a post-Milkovich decision, the Supreme Court of Alabama held a Birmingham newspaper not liable for libel for its criticisms (in editorials and articles) of the city's police chief and based its holding at least in part on a finding that the complained-of statements were expressions of opinion. Deutcsh v. Birmingham Post Co., 603 So. 2d 910, 912 (Ala. 1992) ("'[A] statement of opinion relating to matters of public concern which does not contain a provably false factual connotation will receive full constitutional protection.'") (quoting Milkovich v. Lorain Journal Co., 497 US. 1, 20, 17 Media L. Rep. 2009, 2017 (1990)).

3. ***Consent.*** Where a physician, who was required to obtain one million dollars in medical malpractice insurance in order to maintain privileges at the local hospitals, signed a general release and hold-harmless agreement in order to absolve the three other physicians who gave the malpractice carrier information regarding the physician who was applying for the insurance, the appellate court found there was no defamation because there was no publication, since the statements given by the three other physicians were both authorized and invited by the physician who

needed insurance. Reece v. Finch, 562 So. 2d 195, 198 (Ala. 1990). Although the Reece decision was based on a "no publication" holding that was itself based upon agency law, the gist of the decision is consent or authorization.

4. ***Mitigation.*** "In all actions of slander or libel, the truth of the words spoken or written or the circumstances under which they were spoken or written may be given in evidence under a general denial in mitigation of damages." Ala. Code § 6-5-183 (1975). "The defendant in an action of slander or libel may prove under a general denial in mitigation of damages that the charge was made in good faith by mistake or through inadvertence or misapprehension, and that he has retracted the charge in the same medium of publication as the charge was originally promulgated and in a prominent position therein." Ala. Code § 6-5-184 (1975). "In an action of slander or libel, if a retraction as provided in Section 6-5-184 shall be published in such medium within 10 days of the date of the publication, then the plaintiff in such case shall recover only actual damages." Ala. Code § 6-5-185 (1975). "Vindictive or punitive damages shall not be recovered in any action for libel on account of any publication unless (1) it shall be proved that the publication was made by the defendant with knowledge that the matter published was false, or with reckless disregard of whether it was false or not, and (2) it shall be proved that five days before the commencement of the action the plaintiff shall have made written demand upon the defendant for a public retraction of the charge or matter published; and the defendant shall have failed or refused to publish within five days, in as prominent and public a place or manner as the charge or matter published occupied, a full and fair retraction of such charge or matter." Ala. Code § 6-5-186 (1975). "If the [defamation] defendant, after or before an action is commenced, makes the retraction recited in Sections 6-5-184 through 6-5-186 and also tenders to the plaintiff a compensation in money, bringing the same into court, the plaintiff can recover no costs if the jury believes and finds the tender was sufficient." Ala. Code § 6-5-188 (1975). "The receipt of money tendered before [a defamation] action is commenced is a bar to the action and, if after an action is commenced, such releases the defendant from all damages and costs, except the costs which accrued before the tender and receipt of the money." Ala. Code § 6-5-189 (1975).

Although "the partial truth of a matter asserted may mitigate the need to punish the wrongdoer or to deter similar wrongs as it relates to punitive damages, it does not mitigate the mental anguish suffered by the offending statement." Slack v. Stream, 988 So. 2d 516, 533 (Ala. 2008) (declining to remit compensatory damages award for mental anguish where defendants argued partial truthfulness of his statements against plaintiff).

III. RECURRING FACT PATTERNS

A. Statements in Personnel File

The reported defamation decisions in Alabama regarding statements in personnel files are governed by general libel law. See, e.g., K-Mart Corp. v. Pendergrass, 494 So. 2d 600 (Ala. 1986) (former employee's libel action against former employer fails for lack of publication where the "separation report" [which included the following statement: "Violated company policy by failing to report and turn in money found at register #1 the same day it was found. It was discovered in her possession two days later."] was communicated only to K-Mart management and thus was an intracorporate communication, which is not legally a publication); but see Hughes v. Alabama Dep't of Pub. Safety, 994 F. Supp. 1395, 1407 (M.D. Ala.1998), aff'd, 166 F.3d 353 (11th Cir. 1998). ("In the Eleventh Circuit, when a personnel file becomes a public record by law, the personnel file has been made public. Under the Alabama Code, records of the Personnel Department are public records open to public inspection. See Ala. Code § 36-26-44.") (citations omitted).

B. Performance Evaluations

We know of no reported "performance evaluation" defamation decision from an Alabama state court. But see Hughes v. Alabama Dep't of Pub. Safety, 994 F. Supp. 1395, 1407 (M.D. Ala. 1998), aff'd, 166 F.3d 353 (11th Cir. 1998) (where Plaintiff alleged that defamatory and stigmatizing statements on his Probationary Performance Appraisal and Performance Planning Form were contained in his state personnel file, "which is a matter of public record," the trial court stated, "In the Eleventh Circuit, when a personnel file becomes a public record by law, the personnel file has been made public. Under the Alabama Code, records of the Personnel Department are public records open to public inspection. See Ala. Code § 36-26-44.") (citations omitted).

The Supreme Court of Alabama has, however, considered whether a plaintiff in an action for libel and slander can subpoena documents that were generated during a hospital committee's peer review of a physician. In Kingsley v. Sachitano, 783 So. 2d 824 (Ala. 2000), the court held that the trial court correctly determined that documents generated during a peer review of a physician are subject to Ala. Code § 22-21-8, which preserves the confidentiality of quality assurance, credentialing, and similar materials of a hospital, clinic, or medical staff. This statute also prevents a party from obtaining these materials through discovery or introducing them into evidence.

The United States District Court for the Middle District of Alabama recently addressed the boundaries of peer review in Marshall v. Planz, 145 F. Supp. 2d 1258 (M.D. Ala. 2001). In particular, the court examined how far the notion of "peer review committee" extends under two Alabama statutes. Section 6-5-333 of the Alabama Code applies to "information . . . furnished to" a committee; section 22-21-8 of the Alabama Code applies to information obtained through "involvement . . . in the preparation" of committee materials. Marshall, 145 F. Supp. 2d at 1265. In determining whether certain statements had been "furnished to" a peer review committee, the court examined whether the communication at issue encouraged the policy behind the peer review privilege as articulated by the Supreme Court of Alabama, namely to encourage full candor in the peer review proceedings. Marshall, 145 F. Supp. 2d at 1266. In finding that certain statements made outside of a formal peer review process were covered by the peer review privilege, the court emphasized that context was dispositive; the statements had been made for the purpose of peer review, and the court would not "exalt form over function." Marshall, 145 F. Supp. 2d at 1267. On the other hand, the court was unwilling to abandon the distinction between a mere conversation between doctors and a peer review process, finding that because other statements "[did] little to encourage full candor in the peer review proceedings," the defendant could not assert the peer review privilege. Marshall, 145 F. Supp. 2d at 1268. The court also concluded that under Alabama law, the peer review privilege from testifying in a civil case is not subject to a good-faith requirement, and that the Supreme Court of Alabama's broad interpretation of the peer review privilege calls for a policy of limited waiver. Marshall, 145 F. Supp. 2d at 1274.

C. References

In Brown v. Chem. Haulers, Inc., 402 So. 2d 887, 891 (Ala. 1981), the Supreme Court of Alabama considered whether a plaintiff had been defamed if his former employer was telling the plaintiff's prospective employers that the plaintiff's negligence had caused a tractor trailer accident. The plaintiff also contended that his former employer's "failure to verify [the plaintiff's] version of the cause of the accident" constituted slander regarding the plaintiff. Brown, 402 So. 2d at 891. The court found that "even if [the former employer] actually told [plaintiff's] prospective employers that [plaintiff's] negligence was the underlying cause of the accident, such communication would appear to be at least conditionally privileged because it was a communication by a party with an interest 'made to another party with a corresponding interest.'" Id. Finding no evidence of common law malice, which would defeat defendant's conditional privilege, the court affirmed summary judgment for the defendant. Id. In Gore v. Health-Tex, Inc., 567 So. 2d 1307, 1308 (Ala. 1990), the Supreme Court of Alabama noted that "both parties [in the case] agree that any publication made between a previous employer and a prospective employer is protected by a conditional privilege" if made with common interest or because of a duty owed and if made without common law malice.

D. Intracorporate Communication

The Supreme Court of Alabama "has held that communications among employees in the course of transacting the company's business and in the proper scope of the employees' duties do not constitution a publication" for purposes of a defamation claim. Atkins Ford Sales, Inc. v. Royster, 560 So. 2d 197, 201 (Ala. 1990) (employer's "communications to employees that were necessary in determining the reason for [a] $1,500 shortage did not constitute publication"). "However, communications made to individuals outside this limited group of employees do not fall within this 'no publication' rule." Id. ("It cannot reasonably be argued that [the employer's] statements to [plaintiff's] parents and to [the] employee hired to replace [plaintiff] were necessary in determining the location of the missing funds or were within the line of [the employer's] duties."). Even if employers or employees of a company publish defamatory statements to a third party, the statements may be protected by a qualified privilege based upon a common interest or duty, and, if so, the plaintiff can prevail on the defamation claim only with proof that the publication was made with common law malice. Nelson v. Lapeyrouse Grain Corp., 534 So. 2d 1085, 1094 (Ala. 1988); see also Brackin v. Trimmier Law Firm, 897 So. 2d 207 (Ala. 2004) (where auditor had been retained as an agent of a credit union to conduct an investigation, auditor's communications with the state agency that had directed the credit union to perform the investigation were protected by a qualified privilege).

E. Statements to Government Regulators

The Supreme Court of Alabama held in Rowe v. Isbell, 599 So. 2d 35 (Ala. 1992), that "communications of allegedly false and defamatory information to the Department of Industrial Relations' Unemployment Compensation Agency are absolutely privileged only if the communications were made "in connection with the requirements and administration of Chapter 4, Title 25, Code of Alabama, so as to be privileged under [Ala. Code] § 25-4-116 (1975)." Rowe, 599 So. 2d at 36. The United States District Court for the Middle District of Alabama, however, has taken a stronger stand on the meaning of the very same statute. See Johnson v. Fed. Express Corp., 147 F. Supp. 2d 1268 (M.D. Ala. 2001). The federal district court in Johnson noted that although "Alabama law provides that 'all' communications from an employer to [the Alabama Department of Industrial Relations] 'shall be absolutely privileged and shall not be made the subject matter or basis for any civil action for slander or libel in any court,' . . . the Supreme Court of Alabama has deliberately avoided ruling whether the privilege is qualified or absolute." Johnson, 147 F. Supp. 2d at 1277 (citations omitted) (quoting Ala. Code § 25-4-116 (1975)). Noting that such indecision "chills free speech," the court "[had] no trouble finding that the statute means what it says: the privilege is absolute." Id.

For a discussion of the scope of absolute privilege for "those involved in judicial proceedings," see Cutts v. Am. United Life Ins. Co., 505 So. 2d 1211, 1215 (Ala. 1987), determining that statements in a letter from the defendant to the Assistant District Attorney concerning an investigation regarding the termination of insurance benefits for the plaintiff's company were covered by the privilege. For a discussion of qualified privilege, see Tidwell v. Winn-Dixie, Inc., 502 So. 2d 747, 748 (Ala. 1987), where a store manager's statement to a police officer regarding the plaintiff, who was subsequently convicted for disturbing the peace at the store, was protected by a qualified privilege as a statement prompted by duty.

F. Reports to Auditors and Insurers

Allegedly false and defamatory statements to auditors and insurers may be protected by a qualified privilege, usually pursuant to a finding that the auditor or insurer was acting as an agent for the plaintiff and the plaintiff's insurer, with authorization by the plaintiff. Reece v. Finch, 562 So. 2d 195, 198 (Ala. 1990); see also Interstate Electric Co. v. Daniel, 227 Ala. 609, 613-14, 151 So. 463, 464-66 (1933) (where allegedly false and libelous material in the proof of loss statement was filed by defendant company with the bond company, based on an investigation and full audit by the company's auditor, "the persons who made [the alleged libelous statements in the proof of loss] were acting as officers or agents of [defendant company] and within the line and scope of their authority, and they were made to the person or persons to whom the provisions of the bond required them to be made, and if made in good faith, believing that they were true, without [common law] malice, the communication was privileged, and the defendants are not liable").

In Brackin v. Trimmier Law Firm, 897 So. 2d 207 (Ala. 2004), the plaintiff argued that the auditor's failure to investigate the accuracy of the employees' statements constituted evidence of actual malice. The Supreme Court of Alabama, however, found that the auditor could not have determined the validity of the employees' statements concerning the plaintiff because of the nature of those statements. Id. at 225. The court noted that the auditor was not a trier of fact over allegations of wrongdoing; she was merely investigating loan transactions. Id. Her role as an investigator required her to report her findings from the investigation to the appropriate entities or persons. Id. The court found no evidence that the auditor knew that any of the statements made in her report were false or that she acted with reckless disregard for their falsity. Id.

Where, in the context of investigating the reason why certain materials purchased could not be accounted for at a nursing home, the employer summarily concluded that a former employee had stolen the materials, reported the loss to the insurance company, classified the loss as a crime, and informed the insurance agent that the police probably would not take action because the former employee was related to the police chief, the court found that the plaintiff had presented sufficient evidence to create a jury question as to whether the company's communications to the insurer were made with common law malice. Delta Health Group v. Stafford, 887 So. 2d 887 (Ala. 2004).

G. Vicarious Liability of Employers for Statements Made by Employees

1. ***Scope of Employment.*** "'Communications among the managerial personnel of a corporation about the company's business do not constitute a publication, under the rule of McDaniel v. Crescent Motors, Inc., 249 Ala. 330, 31 So. 2d 343 (1947).'" Hanson v. New Technology, Inc., 594 So. 2d 96, 100 (Ala. 1992) (quoting K-Mart Corp. v. Pendergrass, 494 So. 2d 600, 603 (Ala. 1986)). "[A]s long as a communication to a non-managerial employee falls within the proper scope of that employee's knowledge or duties, the McDaniel/Burney rule applies to non-managerial employees as well as to managerial employees." Id. at 101 (quotations omitted).

"[E]ven if plaintiff ha[s] established with legally sufficient evidence that there was a communication from [an] employee to an outsider, plaintiff still [must prove] that [the employer] itself . . . had published the alleged defamation. Basic principles of agency law operate within the area of defamation law, of course, and . . . if 'publication is sought to be shown by an agent, it does not bind the principal as a publication . . . , unless the act of such agent was within the line and scope of the agent so acting or employed.' Furthermore, 'where the evidence is undisputed, agency vel non, its character and extent, are questions of law for the court.'" K-Mart Corp. v. Pendergrass, 494 So. 2d 600, 604 (Ala. 1986) (citations omitted). When an employee makes the allegedly false and defamatory publication, the employer will be liable for the employee's defamatory statements only if the employee acted within the scope of the employee's authority from the employer or the employer ratified the employee's statements. Walton v. Bromberg & Co., 514 So. 2d 1010, 1011-13 (Ala. 1987) ("Bromberg's management . . . told the employees not to talk about the incident [concerning an investigation as to whether employee Walton had stolen a diamond ring] with customers or among themselves; however, after Rose Washington took the polygraph test, she called a friend, who was a former employee of Bromberg's, and told her what had been happening. After Walton was terminated, she and her husband brought this suit, claiming that Washington's actions constituted defamation by Bromberg's." . . . "The Waltons failed to produce a scintilla of evidence to support a finding that Rose Washington, a gift wrapper at Bromberg's, had authority to speak on behalf of Bromberg's in making allegedly defamatory statements about Walton.").

a. **Blogging**. No Alabama authority on point.

2. ***Damages.*** "A principal, employer, or other master shall not be liable for punitive damages for intentional wrongful conduct or conduct involving malice based upon acts or omissions of an agent, employee, or servant of said principal, employer, or master unless the principal, employer, or master either: (i) knew or should have known of the unfitness of the agent, employee, or servant, and employed him or continued to employ him, or used his services without proper instruction with a disregard of the rights or safety of others; or (ii) authorized the wrongful conduct; or (iii) ratified the wrongful conduct; or unless the acts of the agent, servant or employee were calculated to or did benefit the principal, employer or other master, except where the plaintiff knowingly participated with the agent, servant, or employee to commit fraud or wrongful conduct with full knowledge of the import of his act." Ala. Code § 6-11-27(a) (1975). The corporation's employee who makes the false and defamatory statements is individually liable even if the statements were made within the line and scope of the employee's employment with the corporation when the statements were made. Sunshine Invs., Inc. v. Brooks, 642 So. 2d 408, 410 (Ala. 1994) ("Ahn first argues that he cannot be held individually liable for any defamatory statements, because, he argues, he was acting within the line and scope of his employment when he made the statements. For example, he argues that there was no evidence to justify 'piercing the corporate veil.' Ahn cites no authority to support the proposition that if he engaged in tortious conduct, only the corporation and not he can be held liable. Ahn misconstrues the law if he assumes that, merely because he is employed by a corporation, that employment protects him from all civil liability for tortious conduct. A person is liable for the torts that he commits, regardless of the capacity in which he acts.").

H. Internal Investigations

The Supreme Court of Alabama has held that certain communications made in conjunction with an internal investigation do not constitute a "publication." See Atkins Ford Sales, Inc. v. Royster, 560 So. 2d 197, 201 (Ala. 1990) (employer's "communications to employees that were necessary in determining the reason for [a] $1,500 shortage did not constitute publication"). Communications made to individuals outside this limited group of employees, however, do not fall within this "no publication rule." Id. ("It cannot reasonably be argued that [the employer's] statements to [plaintiff's] parents and to [the] employee hired to replace [plaintiff] were necessary in determining the location of the missing funds or were within the line of [the employer's] duties."); see also Nelson v. Lapeyrouse Grain Corp., 534 So. 2d 1085, 1094 (Ala. 1988) (distinguishing statements made between and among employees or officers of the corporation and statements made in the presence of a polygraph operator and a customer of the corporation; the court held the latter two constituted third parties and the publication requirement was satisfied).

IV. OTHER ACTIONS BASED ON STATEMENTS

We know of no Alabama state court decision that has considered the question whether a defamation plaintiff may use causes of action other than defamation, such as intentional infliction of emotional distress ("outrage," in Alabama) or interference with contract or business, to circumvent the requirements of defamation law. Defamation plaintiffs in Alabama often include other tort claims and sometimes a breach of contract claim, as shown infra at IV.B. and C., but we know of no Alabama decision in which a non-defamation tort or contract claim has succeeded based upon the allegedly defamatory statements in the case. In multiple-tort defamation cases, Alabama courts typically rule upon each claim separately (except for claims that are merely duplicative), with no reference to the possibility that the non-defamation claims that are based upon allegedly defamatory statements might enable the plaintiff to avoid the requirements of defamation law. See, e.g., Williams v. A. L. Williams & Assocs., Inc., 555 So. 2d 121, 125 (Ala. 1989) ("Williams's allegations and the evidence he presented do not support a cause of action for outrage. The actions of which he complains are little more than a restatement of his claims for libel and tortious interference with business relations.") (tort claims considered separately).

A. Negligent Hiring, Retention, and Supervision

Alabama recognizes causes of action for negligent or wanton supervision, see Jones Express v. Jackson, 86 So. 3d 298, 304 (Ala. 2010), and for negligent or wanton retention as a form of negligent entrustment, see Ex parte McCullough, 747 So. 2d 887, 891 (Ala. 1999), but we know of no published Alabama state court decision that has addressed the question of liability for defamation in the context of negligent hiring, retention, or supervision. But see Mills v. Wex-Tex Industries, Inc., 991 F. Supp. 1370, 1381-91 (M.D. Ala. 1997) (trial court considered plaintiff's state-law claims for assault and battery, invasion of privacy, outrage, defamation, and negligent hiring, training, and supervision separately; the actions complained of included allegedly defamatory speech and other conduct) (applying Alabama law to the state-law claims). A plaintiff who proves a claim for wanton hiring and supervision will also, in most cases, be able to obtain an award of punitive damages from the employer under Alabama Code § 6-11-27 (1993). See III.G.2, supra.

B. Intentional Infliction of Emotional Distress

Claims for defamation and outrage (intentional infliction of emotional distress) are often paired. See, e.g., S. B. v. St. James Sch., 959 So. 2d 72, 99 (Ala. 2006) (invasion of privacy, defamation, and outrage claims pleaded; all failed, independently); Anderton v. Gentry, 577 So. 2d 1261 (Ala. 1991) (defamation and outrage claims pleaded; both failed, independently); Bailey v. Avera, 560 So. 2d 1038, 1039-40 (Ala. 1990) (defamation and outrage claims pleaded; both failed, independently); Fitch v. Voit, 624 So. 2d 542, 543-44, 21 Media L. Rep. 1863, 1864 (Ala. 1993) (claims for violation of privacy, for libel, and for outrage; all failed, independently).

C. Interference with Economic Advantage

Claims for defamation and for interference with contract or business also appear together rather frequently. See, e.g., Espinoza v. Rudolph, 46 So. 3d 403 (Ala. 2010) (claims for tortious interference with business relations, slander, defamation, and libel); Peterson v. City of Abbeville, 1 So. 3d 38 (Ala. 2008) (counterclaim alleging inference with contractual relationships and defamation); Hanson v. New Technology, Inc., 594 So. 2d 96 (Ala. 1992) (claims for breach of contract, breach of implied covenant of good faith and fair dealing, defamation, fraud, intentional interference with contractual or business relations, and outrage; summary judgment for defendant on all claims affirmed).

D. Prima Facie Tort

Alabama courts have not yet recognized a claim of prima facie tort. See Liberty Nat'l Life Insurance Co. v. Univ. of Ala. Health Servs. Found., 881 So. 2d 1013, 1025 (Ala. 2003) ("In light of our holding in Polytec, the presence in the case of the alternative claim alleging business interference, and the early stage of this case, we do not determine whether a claim for prima facie tort should be a recognized cause of action in this State under the claims and factual underpinnings involved here."); see also Ex parte Lumbermen's Underwriting Alliance, 662 So. 2d 1133, 1135 (Ala. 1995) (Plaintiff alleged "intentional infliction of emotional distress and outrageous behavior, breach of a third-party beneficiary contract, bad faith, fraud, misrepresentation, and 'prima facie tort'"; where all counts were dismissed except for outrage, appellate court denied defendant's petition for writ of mandamus to compel dismissal of the outrage claim) (quotation marks around prima facie tort added by Supreme Court of Alabama).

V. OTHER ISSUES

A defamation claim is subject to arbitration if an agreement to that effect exists between the parties. Ex parte Hagan, 721 So. 2d 167 (Ala. 1998), writ of cert. dismissed sub nom., Minnesota Mut. Life Ins. Co. v. Hagan, 525 U.S. 1119 (1999). "The rule, applied in the federal courts, that ambiguities in arbitration clauses will be construed in favor of arbitration, applies only if there is an ambiguity." Ex parte Hagan, 721 So. 2d at 173-74. Defamation claims are subject to the Alabama Rules of Civil Procedure, Alabama Rules of Evidence, pertinent portions of the Alabama Code and Constitution, local rules, and applicable federal law. See I.B.8.b, supra.

The Supreme Court of Alabama has demonstrated a willingness to consider via interlocutory appeal whether a trial court properly denied the defendants' motion for summary judgment in a defamation action. In Coulter v. Finebaum, No. CV-99-1395 (Jefferson Cir. Ct. May 30, 2001), the defendants to an action for defamation moved for summary judgment on several grounds. The trial court denied the defendants' motion in its entirety, but the trial court certified the pertinent questions to the Supreme Court of Alabama for interlocutory review. Initially, the Supreme Court of Alabama rejected the petition for interlocutory review, but upon the defendants' request for reconsideration, the court agreed to hear the interlocutory appeal. The Supreme Court of Alabama held that the trial court in Coulter v. Finebaum erred in denying the motion for summary judgment filed by the defendants, finding that the statement at issue was "only rhetorical hyperbole," and as such, was protected by the First Amendment. Finebaum v. Coulter, 854 So. 2d 1120, 1129, 31 Media L. Rep. 1560 (Ala. 2003).

A. Statute of Limitations

The statute of limitations for a libel or slander claim in Alabama is two years. Ala. Code § 6-2-38(k) (1975). "The single publication rule provides that "repetition or republication of [an] identical libel [and slander] is not a new cause of action for which a separate suit may be maintained, but is merely an aggravation of the pre-existing cause, and in proper cases may tend to show actual malice." Poff v. Hayes, 763 So. 2d 234, n.5 (Ala. 2000) (quoting Age-Herald Publ'g Co. v. Huddleston, 92 So. 193 (1921)). However, "a different publication of the [complained of] matter — that is, a subsequent publication of the same matter in other newspapers than that of the defendant"—is a republication, which may be the basis for a different cause of action than that contained in the original complaint, or may be added to the original complaint, but in either case, the republication claim is barred if filed more than two years after the republication. Age-Herald Publ'g Co. v. Waterman, 188 Ala. 272, 278-79, 66 So. 16, 18 (1913)

"The statute of limitations for actions alleging libel or slander prescribes a period that runs from the date of publication -- that is the date on which the injury to the plaintiff's reputation occurs and the cause of action is completed." Poff v. Hayes, 763 So. 2d 234, 242 (Ala. 2000). "Under Alabama defamation law . . . the statute [of limitations] does not toll during the length of time that the plaintiff allegedly suffers the effect of the injury." Doyle v. Univ. of Alabama in

Birmingham, 680 F.2d 1323, 1326 (11th Cir. 1982) (Plaintiff's defamation claim accrued upon her receipt of a letter advising her of the imposition of a probationary period, not at the end of the probationary period, where Plaintiff's defamation claim is based upon the inclusion of a memo about Plaintiff's alcoholism in her personnel file) (applying Alabama law). The Supreme Court of Alabama has stated that "language in Poff suggests that a nonspecific allegation of the publication of allegedly defamatory material is sufficient to defeat a defendant's motion for summary judgment" (on a statute of limitations defense), and that such a nonspecific allegation, along with "other allegations" in additional pleadings was sufficient to determine that publication had occurred within the statutory period. Hollander v. Nichols, 19 So. 2d 184, 90 (Ala. 2009), discussing Poff v. Hayes, 763 So. 2d 234, 241 (Ala. 2000). The Court held in Hollander, however, that one specific allegation of republication within the statutory period (that was covered by absolute privilege), coupled with other generalized allegations of republication, was not sufficient to survive summary judgment. Hollander v. Nichols, 19 So. 2d 184, 90 (Ala. 2009).

Where a federal court has initially retained an Alabama defamation claim pursuant to the court's pendant jurisdiction under 28 U.S.C. § 1367, and thereafter dismisses the Alabama claim without prejudice, the statute of limitations on the Alabama claim is tolled while the claim is in the federal court and for 30 days after that court's dismissal of the claim. See, e.g., DeVaughn v. City of Clanton, 992 F. Supp. 1318, 1327 (M.D. Ala. 1997) ("Plaintiff's claim of defamation and/or slander per se is based upon a state law cause of action. Because the court finds that Defendant's motion for summary judgment on Plaintiff's federal causes of action are due to be granted, the court no longer has jurisdiction over the defamation claim. See 28 U.S.C. § 1367(c)(3). The court emphasizes that dismissal of the defamation claim is without prejudice. The statute of limitations on that claim has been tolled while this action was pending in federal court. 28 U.S.C. § 1367(d).").

Alabama's "discovery" provision for tolling of the statute of limitations states as follows: "In actions seeking relief on the ground of fraud where the statute [of limitations] has created a bar, the claim must not be considered as having accrued until the discovery by the aggrieved party of the fact constituting the fraud, after which he must have two years within which to prosecute his action." Ala. Code § 6-2-3 (1975). For more than 25 years, Alabama decisions have recognized that this statutory tolling provision "may be 'applied to other torts not arising in fraud in appropriate cases, and applies to a fraudulent concealment of the existence of [the] cause of action.' " Holdbrooks v. Central Bank of Alabama, N.A., 435 So. 2d 1250, 1251 (Ala. 1983). For the tolling statute to apply, however, the person who (arguably) concealed the existence of the cause of action must have had an obligation to disclose the facts necessary for the aggrieved party to discover the cause of action; such obligation arises only in a confidential relationship or because of the presence of special circumstances. Holdbrooks, 435 So. 2d at 1252. We know of no reported decision in which a court has found, under Alabama law, a duty to disclose an alleged libel. See, e.g., Tonsmeire v. Tonsmeire, 285 Ala. 454, 458, 233 So. 2d 465, 467 (Ala. 1970) (separated but not yet divorced husband and wife cannot have a confidential relationship, because they are antagonistic toward one another; estranged husband had no duty to inform wife of his allegedly defamatory statements about her to others); Holdbrooks, 435 So. 2d at 1252 (Plaintiff and bank were not in confidential relationship with each other at the time the bank issued the allegedly defamatory credit report regarding plaintiff, because plaintiff's loan had already "been declared in default and [plaintiff] had been informed of the bank's intention to file for foreclosure."); Hovater v. Equifax, Inc., 823 F.2d 413, 414-16 (11th Cir. 1987) (where Equifax prepared an investigatory report for Penn National insurance company that "accused [plaintiff] . . . of associating with known arsonists and of having accumulated large gambling debts," plaintiff's claim for libel is barred by statute, because no confidential relationship or "particular circumstances" triggered the tolling provisions of Alabama Code § 6-2-3) (applying Alabama law to plaintiff's state-law claim for libel), later proceeding at Hovater v. Equifax Servs., Inc., 669 F. Supp. 392 (N.D. Ala. 1987).

For all claims for damages against an Alabama municipality that grow out of torts, the Alabama municipal non-claim statute requires the potential plaintiff to present the claims to the municipal clerk within six months from the accrual date of the claims. Alabama Code § 11-47-23 (1994). The potential plaintiff who fails to comply with the non-claim statute is barred from suit even if the plaintiff's claims are not barred by the applicable statute of limitations (two years for defamation claims, Alabama Code § 6-2-38(k) (1993)). Harris v. City of Montgomery, 435 So. 2d 1207, 1213 (Ala. 1983). A companion statute, Alabama Code § 11-47-192 (1994), requires that on a claim for personal injury (which would include a defamation claim), the person who was injured, or a representative of the injured person, must file a sworn statement with the municipal clerk that states "substantially the manner in which the injury was received, the day and time and the place where the accident occurred and the damages claimed." Harris, 435 So. 2d at 1213-14.

The Supreme Court of Alabama has held that the municipal non-claim statute does not require that tort claims against city employees be presented within six months, even where the allegedly tortious acts of the city employee were "nothing more than ministerial acts done in carrying out the policies of the City." Harris, 435 So. 2d at 1214.

B. Jurisdiction

Alabama is a "minimum contacts" state for purposes of personal jurisdiction, coextensive with the limits permissible under the principles of Int'l Shoe Co. v. State, 326 U.S. 310 (1945), and its progeny, and thus requires that an out

-of-state resident have "some minimum contacts with [Alabama] so that, under the circumstances, it is fair and reasonable to require the person to come to this state to defend an action." Ex parte MONY Fed. Credit Union, 668 So. 2d 552, 556-59 (Ala. 1995), on remand sub nom., SouthTrust Bank v. Empire Corporate Fed. Credit Union, 668 So. 2d 560 (Ala. Civ. App. 1995); Ala. R. Civ. P. 4.2(a). In the context of a defamation claim, the court will consider such factors as the extent to which the defamatory statements were published in Alabama, whether the defamatory statements were of and concerning an Alabama resident, and, if a mass publication is the vehicle for the alleged defamation, the extent to which subscriptions and advertisements are solicited in Alabama. See, e.g., Army Times Publ'g Co. v. Watts, 730 F.2d 1398, 10 Media L. Rep. 1974 (11th Cir. 1984) (applying federal minimum contacts analysis to state-law defamation claim brought in federal court in Alabama against a newspaper based in Washington, D.C.). Alabama's long-arm procedure for service of process on nonresidents implements Alabama's minimum-contacts basis for personal jurisdiction. Ala. R. Civ. P. 4(b).

The Alabama Court of Civil Appeals addressed the issue of whether the posting of an allegedly defamatory statement in an Internet forum by an out-of-state defendant constitutes sufficient contacts with the State of Alabama so as to give rise to personal jurisdiction over the defendant. Novak v. Benn, 896 So. 2d 513 (Ala. Civ. App. 2004). After noting that the record contained no evidence to support a finding of general personal jurisdiction over the defendant, the court found that the defendant's conduct related to the cause of action did not evidence "an action of the defendant purposefully directed toward" Alabama. Id. at 517. Rather, the statement at issue "was made in a forum accessible by practically every person whose computer has access to the Internet, not just Alabama residents." Id. Therefore, the court held that the trial court lacked personal jurisdiction over the defendant, concluding: "Although it can be inferred that [defendant] knew of [plaintiff's] status as an Alabama resident, it cannot reasonably be said that [defendant] expressly aimed his allegedly tortious conduct at Alabama . . . ." Id. at 520.

Alabama's defamation law is interpreted and applied to Alabama state-law defamation claims in federal courts when those claims are retained by the federal court pursuant to pendant jurisdiction, 28 U.S.C. § 1367, or diversity jurisdiction, 28 U.S.C. § 1332. If a state-law defamation claim, whether brought in state or federal court, "is substantially dependent upon analysis of the terms of an agreement made between the parties in a labor contract, that claim must either be treated as a § 301 claim or dismissed as pre-empted by federal labor-contract law . . . ." Surrency v. Harbison, 489 So. 2d 1097, 1102 (Ala. 1986) (citations deleted).

The question of federal preemption is raised again in the context of the Fair Credit Reporting Act. If a plaintiff brings an action in state court alleging that the defendant published defamatory or libelous statements, but does not invoke any specific state or federal law, a defendant cannot remove the action to federal court by asserting that the plaintiff's allegations could have supported a claim under the Fair Credit Reporting Act. Watkins v. Trans Union, L.L.C., 118 F. Supp. 2d 1217, 28 Media L. Rep. 2557 (M.D. Ala. 2001). When state law defamation claims are brought in federal court, they may be preempted by the Fair Credit Reporting Act. See Sigler v. RBC Bank, 712 F. Supp 2d 1265, 1270 M.D. Ala. 2010).

If the alleged defamation occurs on a federal military enclave, federal law applies, not state law. See, e.g., Parker v. Main, 804 F. Supp. 284, 285-86 (M.D. Ala. 1992) (Where the allegedly defamatory statements occurred at Fort Rucker, Alabama, federal law applies, but "the federal law applied to conduct occurring in the [federal military] enclave incorporates much of the state law of the surrounding state.").

The Supreme Court of Alabama has made clear that in libel actions involving newspaper publication, venue lies in the county in which the newspaper is primarily published and not in other places where it is merely circulated. Ex parte Windom, 763 So. 2d 946 (Ala. 2000). Venue lies in the county in which the newspaper was printed whether the libel action is against a newspaper publisher or an individual reporter. Ex parte Arrington, 599 So. 2d 24, 26, 20 Media L. Rep. 1292, 1293-94 (Ala. 1992), later proceeding sub nom., Kelly v. Arrington, 624 So. 2d 546 (Ala. 1993).

The Supreme Court of Alabama further clarified the meaning of "injury" for the purpose of determining venue in libel actions involving newspaper publications in Ex parte Windom, 840 So. 2d 885 (Ala. 2002), where the defendant's defamatory statements were made at a press conference in one county and were subsequently reprinted in other counties as reports by the Associated Press. The court noted that for venue purposes, "the word injury commonly refers not to the damage allegedly suffered by the plaintiff, but to the wrongful act or omission allegedly committed by the defendant." Windom, 840 So. 2d at 893 n.2 (Ala. 2002) ("[A]lthough the libelous damage may accrue in separate counties, the injury happens in only one county, the county of original publication.") (citing Ex parte Wilson, 408 So. 2d 94, 96 (Ala. 1981)).

If a case involves allegedly defamatory matter that was contained in a letter, venue is proper "at the place of posting or at the place of receipt by the addressee." Ex parte First Alabama Bank of Montgomery, N.A., 461 So. 2d 1315, 1318 (Ala. 1984).

Under the forum non conveniens statute, Ala. Code §6-3-21.1(a), the court may order a transfer of venue based on the interest of justice and the convenience of the parties and witnesses. See Ex parte Verbena United Methodist Church, 953

So.2d 395 (Ala. 2006) (transferring defamation case from a county with a "weak connection" to the case to a county where a majority of the contact between the parties occurred and where most of the parties and witnesses resided).

Alabama's general venue laws are stated at Alabama Code § 6-3-2 (proceedings against individuals generally), § 6-3-4 (insurance actions), § 6-3-6 (unincorporated organizations or associations), § 6-3-7 (actions against corporations, including domestic and foreign corporations and class actions against corporations), § 6-3-9 (actions involving the prison system), § 6-3-10 (counties having two courthouses), and § 6-3-11 (actions against county or municipality for damages).

The Supreme Court of Alabama has concluded that courts are prohibited by the First Amendment of the United States Constitution from determining the truth or falsity of alleged defamatory remarks whose adjudication requires the court to opine on disputes regarding a church's spiritual or ecclesiastical affairs. Ex parte Bole, 2012 Ala. LEXIS 110, *31 (Ala. Aug. 31, 2012). Further, the Alabama Court of Civil Appeals has concluded that courts are prohibited from determining the truth or falsity of alleged defamatory remarks made by a religious organization or that organization's pastor as to the "conformity of its members to standards of faith and morality," and, therefore, "may not entertain claims pertaining to those issues." Reynolds v. Wood, 998 So. 2d 1058, 1059 (Ala. Civ. App. 2007).

C. Worker's Compensation Exclusivity

Alabama's Worker's Compensation statute provides an exclusive remedy for an employee seeking compensation or damages from his employer for an "injury or death occasioned by an accident or occupational disease proximately resulting from and while engaged in the actual performance of the duties of [his] employment." Ala. Code § 25-5-52. The Worker's Compensation statute provides redress only for an employee's physical injuries. Jones v. Bancgroup, 735 So. 2d 1163, 1165 (Ala. Civ. App. 1998). "Purely psychological" injuries are not covered by the Worker's Compensation statute exclusivity provision. Jones v. Bancgroup, 735 So. 2d 1163, 1165 (Ala. Civ. App. 1998) (both holding that the plaintiff employee's invasion of privacy claims were not barred by the worker's compensation exclusivity provision).

D. Pleading Requirements

"Alabama is a 'notice pleading' state. Therefore, even though [plaintiff's] complaint was inartfully drawn, . . . [plaintiff] put the defendants on notice . . . ." Surrency v. Harbison, 489 So. 2d 1097, 1099, 1104 (Ala. 1986). "A pleading which sets forth a claim for relief . . . , shall contain (1) a short and plain statement of the claim showing that the pleader is entitled to relief, and (2) a demand for judgment for the relief the pleader seeks." Rule 8(a), Alabama Rules of Civil Procedure. "Under this rule the prime purpose of pleadings is to give notice." Rule 8, Alabama Rules of Civil Procedure, Committee Comments on 1973 Adoption.

"Although Rule 8(a) eliminates many technical requirements of pleading, it is clear that it envisages the statement of circumstances, occurrences, and events in support of the claim presented." Id. See Davis v. Marshall, 404 So. 2d 642, 644-45 (Ala. 1981), overruled on other grounds by Elmore County Comm'n v. Ragona, 540 So. 2d 720, 725 (Ala. 1989). In a defamation case, the plaintiff must identify the specific communications upon which the claim is based. See Peinhardt v. West, 22 Ala. App. 231, 236, 115 So. 80, 84 (1927) ("The law requires, with a few exceptions not necessary to be here noted, that the complaint set out the particular defamatory words as published, and the authorities hold that it is not sufficient to set out the publication in substance and effect."), rev'd on other grounds, 217 Ala. 12, 115 So. 88 (1927); see also Cleveland v. Cleveland, 263 Ala. 530, 532, 83 So. 2d 281, 282 (1955) ("So far as we can ascertain the weight of authority, where a complaint for libel is involved, holds that the complaint should set out the particular defamatory words as published."); Lightfoot v. Floyd, 667 So. 2d 56, 69 (Ala. 1995) (where "there [was] no reference to particular written communications or to the substance of any oral communications in which [plaintiff] may have been characterized as a 'drug dealer,'" plaintiff's defamation claims were properly dismissed on defendants' motion for summary judgment).

In response to a defamation plaintiff's complaint, the defendant must plead all applicable affirmative defense—whether in the answer to the complaint or in a motion under Rule 12 that is filed prior to the answer. Ala. R. Civ. P. 8, 12; Sims v. Lewis, 374 So. 2d 298 (Ala. 1979). Although privilege is an affirmative defense for a defamation defendant that the defendant must raise and prove, Tonsmeire v. Tonsmeire, 281 Ala. 102, 107, 199 So. 2d 645, 648 (1967), the defamation defendant is not required to plead absence of actual malice to invoke the defense of qualified privilege, Ex parte Blue Cross & Blue Shield, 773 So. 2d 475 (Ala. 2000). The defamation plaintiff must plead, and prove, common law malice "in order to recover in an action for defamation against an individual under a qualified privilege." Gibson v. Abbott, 529 So. 2d 939, 942 (Ala. 1988), see also Butler v. Town of Argo, 871 So. 2d 1, 27 (Ala. 2003). On defamation claims where special damages are required or will be demanded, special damages must be specifically pleaded. Delta Health Group, Inc. v. Stafford, 887 So. 2d 887, 897 (Ala. 2004).

SURVEY OF ALABAMA EMPLOYMENT PRIVACY LAW

Bethany L. Bolger
Rushton, Stakely, Johnston & Garrett, P.A.
Post Office Box 270
Montgomery, Alabama 36101-0270
Telephone: (334) 206-3100; Facsimile: (334) 262-6277

(With Developments Reported Through **November 1, 2012**)

GENERAL COMMENTS

None.

SIGNIFICANT DEVELOPMENTS SINCE THE 2012 *SURVEY*

None.

I. GENERAL LAW OF PRIVACY

A. Legal Basis of Privacy Claims

The common law right of privacy gives rise to a tort action for violation of that right. Smith v. Doss, 251 Ala. 250, 37 So. 2d 118 (Ala. 1948). It is generally accepted that the right of privacy, or, alternatively, the tort of invasion of privacy consists of four limited and distinct wrongs: (1) intruding into the plaintiff's physical solitude or seclusion; (2) giving publicity to private information about the plaintiff that violates ordinary decency; (3) putting the plaintiff in a false, but not necessarily defamatory, position in the public eye; or (4) appropriating some element of the plaintiff's personality for a commercial use. See Minnifield v. Ashcraft, 903 So. 2d 818, 821 (Ala. Civ. App. 2004); Butler v. Town of Argo, 871 So. 2d 1 (Ala. 2003). Each of these categories of invasion of privacy (intrusion into seclusion, public disclosure of private information, putting a person in a false light, and appropriation of an element of a person's personality for commercial use) has distinct elements, and each category establishes a separate privacy interest that may be invaded. See Regions Bank v. Plott, 897 So. 2d 239 (Ala. 2004).

Under Alabama law, the right of privacy is a personal right, and the courts have not recognized a "relational right" to privacy. Woods v. SunTrust Bank, 81 So. 3d 357 (Ala. Civ. App. 2011) (holding trial court properly excluded evidence of calls made by creditor to debtors' home because it was not relevant to the debtors' caregiver's individual claim for invasion of privacy).

Compensatory and punitive damages may be available to the prevailing plaintiff. See Slack v. Stream, 988 So. 2d 516 (Ala. 2008) (upholding $662,000 award in favor of college professor based on claims of defamation, invasion of privacy, and intentional interference with a business contract against department chairman).

B. Causes of Action

1. ***Misappropriation/Right of Publicity.*** Alabama has not denominated the interest protected by its commercial appropriation invasion of privacy tort as the right of publicity. See Minnifield v. Ashcraft, 903 So. 2d 818, 824 (Ala. Civ. App. 2004). However, Alabama's commercial appropriation privacy right represents the same interests and addresses the same harms as does the right of publicity as customarily defined. Id. at 824. The elements of Alabama's commercial appropriation invasion of privacy tort, which bases liability on commercial, rather than psychological interests, do not differ significantly from those of the tort of violation of the right of publicity. Liability for this wrong arises when one's name or likeness is appropriated by another to the other's use or benefit. See Schifano v. Greene County Greyhound Park, 624 So. 2d 178 (Ala. 1993).

In order to establish a cause of action for misappropriation right of publicity, the plaintiff must show (1) the defendants use of the plaintiff's identity; (2) the appropriation of plaintiff's name or likeness to defendant's advantage, commercially or otherwise; (3) lack of consent; and (4) resulting injury. See Minnifield v. Ashcraft, 903 So. 2d 818, 824 (Ala. Civ. App. 2004). Thus, the use of an employee's name or likeness, such as for use in advertising, without obtaining the employee's prior consent, may form the basis for a claim of invasion of privacy. However, there is no claim simply because someone's name or likeness is brought before the public. It is only when publicity is given for the purpose of appropriating to the defendant's benefit the commercial or other values associated with the name or likeness that the right of privacy is invaded. See Schifano v. Greene County Greyhound Park, 624 So. 2d 178, 181 (Ala. 1993) relying on Restatement (Second) of Torts. No one has the right to object merely because his name or his appearance is brought before the public, since neither is in any way a private matter and both are open to public observation. It is only when the publicity is given for the purpose of appropriating to the defendant's benefit the commercial or other values associated with a name or the likeness that the right of privacy is invaded. See Minnifield v. Ashcraft, 903 So. 2d 818, 822 (Ala. Civ. App. 2004). Alabama courts have distinguished this tort from the tort of conversion, stating that the tort of invasion of privacy does not require proof of a wrongful taking of property or of an illegal assertion of ownership; it is sufficient to show an appropriation of some element of the plaintiff's personality for a commercial use. Tanner v. Ebbole, 88 So. 3d 856 (Ala. Civ. App. 2011).

While waiver may be a defense, it does not arise from the mere fact that one is a public figure. See Bell v. Birmingham Broadcasting Company, 96 So. 2d 263, 265 (Ala. 1957) (waiver is limited to those circumstances where the information is legitimately necessary and proper). One who is a public figure or is presently newsworthy may be the proper subject of news or informative presentations; however, the privilege does not extend to commercialization of his personality through a form of treatment distinct from the dissemination of news or information. Id. With regard to the defense of consent, the court held, "even the most famous have a right to be protected against the unauthorized commercial appropriation of their names and photographs." Id.

2. ***False Light***. Alabama has adopted the Restatement (Second) of Torts § 652E with regard to this cause of action. See Norris v. Moskin Stores, Inc., 132 So. 2d 321, 323 (Ala. 1961). One who gives publicity to a matter concerning another that places the other before the public in a false light is subject to liability to the other for invasion of his privacy if (a) the false light in which the other was placed would be highly offensive to a reasonable person, and (b) the actor had knowledge of or acted in reckless disregard as to the falsity of the publicized matter and the false light in which the other would be placed. Regions Bank v. Plott, 897 So. 2d 239, 244 (Ala. 2004); see also Cottrell v. National Collegiate Athletic Association, 975 So. 2d 306 (Ala. 2007) (holding summary judgment in favor of NCAA proper where false statements had been posted on NCAA's website due to clerical error).

A false-light claim does not require that the information made public be private; instead, the information made public must be false. Butler v. Town of Argo, 871 So. 2d 1, 17 (Ala. 2003) (emphasis in original). "Unlike defamation, truth is not an affirmative defense to a false light claim; rather, falsity is an element of the plaintiff's claim, on which the plaintiff bears the burden of proof." Martin v. Patterson, 975 So. 2d 984 (Ala. Civ. App. 2007). Further, it is integral to a false light claim that the untrue information be publicly communicated. Id.; see also S.B. v. St. James School, 959 So. 2d 72 (Ala. 2006) (school investigation of student conduct sufficiently narrow in scope to preclude liability on false light claim).

In a case where a police lieutenant alleged false light invasion of privacy against his police chief, claiming that the chief violated ordinary decency by publicizing the lieutenant's substandard job performance, the court affirmed a summary judgment motion for the chief, based on the idea that the lieutenant's job performance was already a matter of public record. Gary v. Crouch, 867 So. 2d 310 (Ala. 2003). The Alabama Supreme Court has also held that a city could not be liable for false light invasion of privacy because the claim requires proof that the city's agent acted knowingly or recklessly, and liability against a city is statutorily limited to acts of neglect, carelessness, or unskillfulness. Walker v. City of Huntsville, 62 So. 3d 474, 501-02 (Ala. 2010).

3. ***Publication of Private Facts.*** There are three basic elements of the cause of action for invasion of privacy based on public disclosure of private information: (1) there must be a public disclosure; (2) the facts disclosed must be private facts, rather than public ones; and (3) the matter made public must be one which would be offensive and objectionable to a reasonable person of ordinary sensibilities. See McCaig v. Talladega Publishing Company, 544 So. 2d 875 (Ala. 1989). A disclosure of private facts claim can be defended by showing waiver, consent, or that the matter published was of public concern. Grimsley v. Guccione, 703 F.Supp. 903 (M.D. Ala. 1988) (plaintiff claimed that a Penthouse magazine article titled "Birth of a Hemorrhoid" constituted an invasion of privacy but the court found that the plaintiff had consented to and assisted in publication of facts by a competing publisher); McCaig v. Talladega Publishing Company, 544 So. 2d 875 (Ala. 1989) (the defendant published an article describing improper and irregular business practices but the court held that the broadcast of matters of legitimate public concern or general interest is not prohibited and that if the community has a legitimate interest in the publication of the information in question, there is no invasion of privacy). But see Daily Times Democrat v. Graham, 162 So. 2d 474 (Ala. 1964) (verdict affirmed against newspaper who published a photograph of a woman whose dress was blown up at a carnival funhouse); Horne v. Patton, 287 So. 2d 824 (Ala. 1973) (employer does not have a right to obtain from physician each and every detail of employee's health).

A distinction exists, however, between publicity and publication as utilized under this cause of action. "Publicity, as it is used in this section [Restatement (Second) of Torts § 652D] differs from publication, as that term is used...in connection with liability for defamation. Publication, in that sense, is a word of art, which includes any communication by the defendant to a third person. Publicity on the other hand, means that the matter is made public, by communicating it to the public at large, or to so many persons that the matter must be regarded as substantially certain to become one of public knowledge. The difference is not one of the means of communication, which may be oral, written or by any other means. It is one of a communication that reaches or is sure to reach, the public." See Johnston v. Fuller, 706 So. 2d

700, 703 (Ala. 1997). It is not an invasion of the right of privacy to communicate a fact concerning the plaintiff's life to a single person or even a small group of persons. See Jones v. Hamilton, 53 So. 3d 134 (Ala. Civ. App. 2010).

In S.B. v. St. James School, the state supreme court held that lewd photographs taken by four teenage students of each other, which they emailed to two other students, had not been publicized in such a way as to establish a prima facie case of invasion. 959 So. 2d 72 (Ala. 2006). The plaintiff-students argued that the school had publicized the photographs to a large number of people through teachers, students, and parents. The court disagreed, stating that there was no evidence that anyone associated with the faculty had disseminated or communicated to the public at large the existence of the photographs. Further, the evidence indicated that knowledge of the photographs was pervasive throughout the school community, and "the students could no longer have had an expectation of privacy regarding the photographs because there is no privacy in that which is already public." The court also held that the students could no longer claim a right to privacy because the matter had become one of legitimate public concern.

4. ***Intrusion.*** In Phillips v. Smalley Maintenance Services, Inc., 435 So. 2d 705 (Ala. 1983), the Supreme Court of Alabama adopted the Restatement (Second) of Torts § 652B definition of the wrongful-intrusion branch of the invasion of privacy tort under which it is actionable to make an unauthorized intrusion on a person's physical or mental solicitude or seclusion. To succeed on a claim alleging invasion of privacy, a plaintiff must show: (1) that the matters intruded into are of a private nature; and (2) that the intrusion would be so offensive or objectionable that a reasonable person subjected to it would experience outrage, mental suffering, shame or humiliation. See Busby v. Truswal Systems Corp., 551 So. 2d 322, 323 (Ala. 1989). There must be something in the nature of prying or intrusion and the intrusion must be something which would be offensive or objectionable to a reasonable person. Two primary factors are considered in determining whether or not an intrusion concerning private information is actionable. The first is the means used. The second is the defendant's purpose for obtaining the information. Johnson v. Corporate Special Services, 602 So. 2d 385 (Ala. 1992) (citing W. Prosser and W. Keeton, The Law of Torts, p. 851, 856 (5th ed. 1984)). Of course, the intrusion must also be an intentional act. See Jones v. Hamilton, 53 So. 3d 134 (Ala. Civ. App. 2010).

The Alabama Supreme Court has held that a plaintiff who made a significant worker's compensation claim should have expected a reasonable investigation regarding his physical capacity. I.C.U. Investigations, Inc. v. Jones, 780 So. 2d 685 (Ala. 2000). Videotaping by defendant investigation firm hired by the claimant's employer observing claimant's daily activities, including urinating in his own front yard, was legitimate and did not constitute unwarranted publicity. Additionally, the court held that means employed by the firm to investigate were not wrongful "[b]ecause the activities Jones carried on in his front yard could have been observed by any passerby." In Nipper v. Variety Wholesalers, Inc., 638 So. 2d 778 (Ala. 1994), the plaintiff-employee's intrusion claims were not actionable where a loss prevention manager, responding to negative hotline tips, interviewed the plaintiff as well as other employees in the store's back room regarding allegations that the plaintiff committed theft, drug use and brandishing a firearm on the job. The court found that communications made in furtherance of the investigation were only published to the plaintiff's fellow employees and to that extent reasonably necessary to investigate the hotline complaints. Since communications were published only to fellow employees (a small group of people) the plaintiff's claims could not stand. See also S.B. v. St. James School, 959 So. 2d 72 (Ala. 2006) (school investigation of student conduct sufficiently narrow in scope to preclude liability on wrongful intrusion claim); Martin v. Patterson, 975 So. 2d 984 (Ala. Civ. App. 2007) (holding defendants' driving by plaintiff's work site, honking their horn and indicating that they were filming him not sufficiently personal in nature to rise to level of wrongful intrusion).

5. ***Sexual Harassment.*** Alabama recognizes that a cause of action exists for invasion of privacy relating to sexual harassment. See Phillips v. Smalley Maintenance Services, 435 So. 2d 705, 709 (Ala. 1983) (extensive inquiries into one's sex life or looking up one's skirt may constitute an invasion of privacy). The elements for this claim are the same as for the cause of action for invasion of privacy based on public disclosure of private facts, discussed supra. Ex parte Birmingham News, Inc., 778 So. 2d 814 (Ala. 2000). For examples of such cases, see Ex parte Atmore Community Hospital, 719 So. 2d 1190 (Ala. 1998) (the fact that supervisor made several lewd comments and asked a female employee to meet him outside of work hours for other than business purposes and looked up the female's skirt on more than one occasion presents substantial evidence that supervisor committed an invasion of privacy) and Busby v. Truswal Systems Corp., 551 So. 2d 322 (Ala. 1989) (trial court erred in granting summary judgment for employer on invasion of privacy claim where evidence showed that supervisor invited plaintiffs to swim in supervisor's pool in the nude, asked to put his hands in employee's pockets, told plaintiff he would "put a stick on their machines" so they could masturbate while working, said that he could perform intercourse as fast as one of the machines at the plant could operate and made numerous other comments of this nature). But see McIsaac v. WZEW-FM Corp., 495 So. 2d 649 (Ala. 1986) (the claim fell short of invasion of privacy where allegations were that supervisor told female employee that he had an affair with another female employee and asked her to dinner. Furthermore, supervisor was alleged to have "given her a look that you don't normally get from just your everyday association with your boss" and other suggestive lurks and innuendos. The court found, "even the dire affront of inviting an unwilling woman to illicit intercourse has been held by most courts to be no such outrage as to lead to liability").

An employer may be liable for invasion of privacy in the employment context if there is ratification of the conduct. Busby v. Truswal Systems Corp., 551 So. 2d 322, 327 (Ala. 1989). A finding by the Alabama Unemployment Compensation Agency that an employee terminated employment due to sexual harassment is not deemed imputed knowledge to an employer of improper sexual harassment in the workplace to support ratification. See Moman v. Gregerson's Foods, Inc., 570 So. 2d 1215 (Ala. 1990); see also Armstrong v. Standard Furniture, 197 Fed. Appx. 830 (11th Cir. 2006) (holding employer did not ratify alleged conduct of employees where it had no knowledge of harassment as to one defendant-employee and where it investigated allegations of harassment and harassment then ceased as to other defendant-employee). Where a co-employee defendant's behavior is aimed at "satisfying (the co-employee's) own lustful desires," no corporate purpose could conceivably be served and there would be no liability to the employer. Busby v. Truswal Systems Corp., 551 So. 2d 322, 327 (Ala. 1989); Ex parte Atmore Community Hospital, 719 So. 2d 1190 (Ala. 1998).

While an employer is generally not liable for the intentional torts of its employees or agents, there is an exception to this general rule for common carriers. See Connell v. Call-A-Cab, Inc., 937 So. 2d 71 (Ala. 2006).

C. Other Privacy-related Actions

1. **Intentional Infliction of Emotional Distress.** Alabama first recognized the tort of intentional infliction of emotional distress, more commonly known as the tort of outrage, in American Road Service v. Inmon, 394 So. 2d 361 (Ala. 1980). The elements of the action consist of the following: (1) that the employer intended to inflict emotional distress or should have known that it would result; (2) that the conduct was extreme and outrageous; (3) that the actions of the employer were the cause of the plaintiff's distress; and (4) that the emotional distress of the plaintiff was severe. Ex parte Crawford & Co., 693 So. 2d 458 (Ala. 1997). The tort of outrage is a very limited cause of action, and cases are generally decided on a fact-specific basis. See American Road Service, supra, (no outrage even though the evidence showed that the plaintiff had been harassed, investigated without cause, humiliated, accused of improper dealings, treated uncustomarily, terminated without justification and that this caused emotional distress resulting in a loss of weight and insomnia).

Although Alabama courts have recognized the viability of outrage claims in the employment context under certain circumstances, the courts have also taken pains to emphasize that an outrage claim will not lie in a mere run-of-the-mill employment dispute arising from dismissal of an employee at will. Less v. Sea Breeze Health Care Ctr., Inc., 391 F. Supp. 2d 1103 (S.D. Ala. 2005). "[R]eview of pertinent Alabama authorities reveals that the line of demarcation between non-actionable outrage claims and actionable outrage claims in the employment arena is found in the determination of whether the termination is for reasons that contravene public policy. Where a plaintiff complains that his discharge contravenes public policy, particularly if the discharge was the culmination of a protracted pattern of discrimination in violation of public policy, he may properly pursue a claim of outrage because the violation of public policy furnishes the requisite "sound of fury" to accompany the termination. Id. (noting that this line of authority may be limited by another strand of case law suggesting that being subjected to unlawful discrimination over an abbreviated time period, or facing unlawful conduct falling short of discharge, may be inadequate to sustain a claim of outrage, even if the employer's acts otherwise are irreconcilable with sound public policy). Where an employee was discharged in the middle of a personal financial crisis, the Court held the discharge not so shocking as to go beyond the bounds of decency as required for an outrage claim. Carraway Methodist Health Systems v. Wise, 986 So.2d 387 (Ala. 2007).

Claims for outrage are often joined with a claim for invasion of privacy. Busby v. Truswal Systems Corp., 551 So. 2d 322 (Ala. 1989) (claim stated for outrage where there is extensive sexual harassment). See also I.B.4, supra. Employees may recover compensatory and punitive damages under this tort. American Road Service v. Inmon, 394 So. 2d 361 (Ala. 1980).

2. **Interference With Prospective Economic Advantage.** Alabama first recognized the tort of intentional interference with business or contractual relations in Gross v. Lowder Realty Better Homes and Gardens, 494 So. 2d 590 (Ala. 1986). The current elements of the claim are: (1) the existence of a protectable business relationship; (2) of which the defendant knew; (3) to which the defendant was a stranger; (4) with which the defendant intentionally interfered; and (5) damage. White Sands Group, L.L.C. v. PRS II, LLC, 32 So. 3d 5, 14 (Ala. 2009); Thomas v. Williams, 21 So. 3d 1234 (Ala. Civ. App. 2008) (reversing order granting motion to dismiss and holding allegations that defendant's phone call to plaintiff's employer resulted in job loss were sufficient to assert a valid claim of intentional interference with a business or contractual relations). In the context of a corporate employee interfering with a contract of the corporation, the plaintiff must also show that the employee acted outside the scope of his employment and that the employee acted with actual malice, shown by a pattern of interference. See Rhodes v. Unisys Corp., 170 Fed. Appx. 681 (11th Cir. 2006).

The damages recoverable for intentional interference with a contractual relationship include: (1) the pecuniary loss of the benefits of the relation; (2) consequential losses for which the interference is a legal cause; (3) emotional distress or actual harm to reputation if either is reasonably to be expected to result from the interference; and (4) punitive damages. James Roberson & Penhall Co. v. C.P. Allen Constr. Co., 50 So. 3d 471, 477 (Ala. Civ. App. 2010); see also Slack v. Stream, 988 So. 2d 516 (Ala. 2008) (upholding $662,000 jury award in favor of college professor based on claims of defamation, invasion of privacy, and intentional interference with a business contract against department chairman). Punitive damages may be awarded if the wrongful acts are carried out wantonly, spitefully or maliciously. Gross, 494 So. 2d at 594.

It is essential to a claim of tortious interference with contractual relations that the plaintiff establish that the defendant is a third party, i.e., a "stranger" to the contract with which the defendant allegedly interfered. See Waddell & Reed, Inc., v. United Investors Life Ins. Co., 875 So. 2d 1143, 1153 (Ala. 2003) ("[a] party to a contract or a business relationship cannot be liable for tortious interference with [that] contract or business relationship"). A defendant is not a "stranger" to a contract or business relationship when: (1) the defendant is an essential entity to the reported injured relations; (2) the allegedly injured relations are inextricably a part of or dependent upon the defendant's contractual or business relations; (3) the defendant would benefit economically from the alleged injured relations; or (4) both the defendant and plaintiff are parties to a comprehensive interwoven set of contracts or relations. Id. at 1156. **A co-employee of a plaintiff will be deemed a third party or a stranger to a business or contractual relationship between the plaintiff and the employer only if the co-employee was acting outside the scope of his or her authority or employment and was acting with actual malice. McGlathery v. Ala. Agric. & Mech. Univ., No. 2101017, 2012 Ala. Civ. App. LEXIS 201, *26-28 (Aug. 3, 2012).**

A separate, but related, tort is interference with prospective employment opportunities, which can be viable despite the lack of an existing contract or business relation. See White Sands Group, L.L.C. v. PRS II, LLC, 998 So. 2d 1042 (Ala. 2008) ("The two torts [tortious interference with a contractual relationship and interference with a business relationship or expectancy] are initially distinguished by their primary elements -- one tort deals with the interference with a fixed-term contract that is already in existence; the other tort deals with 'mere expectancies.' The latter element determines which interests along the continuum of business dealings are protected") (emphasis in original). The extension of this cause of action in the employment-opportunity context is based on the reasoning that the interference would prevent the plaintiff from securing employment or deprive him of earning a livelihood. Smith v. Boyd Bros. Transp., Inc., 406 F. Supp. 2d 1238 (M.D. Ala. 2005). Thus, a plaintiff's interference-with-employment-opportunity claim does not lie when the plaintiff obtains in full, and without hindrance, the employment opportunity sought. Id.

Justification for the interference is an affirmative defense that may be pled and proved by the defendant. See Pegram v. Hebding, 667 So. 2d 696 (Ala. 1995). Alabama has also adopted the "competitor's privilege" expressed in Restatement (Second) of Torts §76. Tom's Foods, Inc. v. Carn, 896 So. 2d 443, 457 (Ala. 2004).

3. **Prima Facie Tort.** There is no prima facie tort in the state of Alabama.

II. EMPLOYER TESTING OF EMPLOYEES

A. Psychological or Personality Testing

1. ***Common Law and Statutes***. There is no common law or statutory basis to prevent employers in the private or public sector to conduct tests that are intended to reveal information about an employee's predisposition to act in a certain way.

2. ***Private Employers***. See II.A.1, supra.

3. ***Public Employers***. See II.A.1, supra.

B. Drug Testing

1. ***Common Law and Statutes***. There is no drug testing statute in the state of Alabama that specifically addresses an employer's right to conduct drug tests. However, employers may qualify for a five percent workers compensation insurance premium discount by voluntarily implementing a drug free workplace that complies with specific criteria and that is approved by the Workers Compensation Division of the Alabama Department of Industrial Relations. Ala. Code §25-5-332 (1975).

2. ***Private Employers***. Private sector employers are free to test applicants and employees for drug and alcohol use. An employer is free to conduct for cause testing, random testing and testing following an accident. See Nipper v. Variety Wholesalers, Inc., 638 So. 2d 778 (Ala. 1994) ("Variety [the employer] had the right to reasonably investigate complaints made about the store and against Nipper [the plaintiff] in relation to [the plaintiff's] status as manager of the store. It was not unreasonable for [the employer] to be concerned about complaints such as it received, particularly in light of the $30,000 worth of inventory that had been lost from the store. This alleged intrusion into [the plaintiff's] private concerns fall short of that required to constitute the invasion of privacy tort.") An employee in Alabama can be terminated

for refusing to take a required drug test as employment in the State of Alabama is "at will." See Stevenson v. Precision Standard, Inc., 762 So. 2d 820 (Ala. 1999) (upholding summary judgment in favor of a corporation who randomly administered seven drug tests in four-month period as was required by the Federal Aviation Administration). Employers are advised to obtain consent to test forms from its employees and to advise in personnel manuals that testing is required. This eliminates the employee's claim that he did not anticipate testing. Under the general principals discussed above, employer liability may be created by the publication of results to individuals who have no need to know the results (publication of private facts), publication of false results (false light) or requiring the employee to give blood or urine samples in an intrusive fashion (wrongful intrusion). See I.B.2.-4, supra.

On a related matter, Ala. Code §25-4-78(3)(a) provides for total disqualification for unemployment benefits for individuals who are separated from employment and who are disqualified solely for testing positive to illegal drugs.

3. ***Public Employers***. The collection of breath, blood or urine samples for drug tests is a "search" governed by the Fourth Amendment. See Skinner v. Railway Labor Executive Association, 489 U.S. 602, 617 (1989). Therefore, the constitutionality of a drug-testing program must be determined by balancing the privacy interests of the employees with the interests of the governmental entity served by the drug testing. Skinner, 489 U.S. at 619. Numerous state and local governments maintain random and for-cause drug testing programs. In English v. Talladega County Board of Education, 938 F. Supp. 775 (N.D. Ala. 1996), the court upheld the employer's drug testing program for individuals operating commercial motor vehicles. Id. at 779. See also Jefferson County Board of Education v. Moore, 706 So. 2d 1147 (Ala. 1997) (court upheld reinstatement of employees on the basis that employees who tested positive for drugs and alcohol maintained excellent employment records and held that employees should be reinstated after successfully completing rehabilitation programs). See also Ex parte Athens State College, 795 So. 2d 709 (Ala. 2000); Bessemer State Tech. College v. Hosea-Studdard , 851 So. 2d 46 (Ala. Civ. App. 2002).

C. Medical Testing

1. ***Common Law and Statutes***. There are no Alabama cases or statutes on point with regard to this topic. But see II.C.3, infra

2. ***Private Employers***. Some Alabama employers may have obligations in this area under the Americans with Disabilities Act (ADA). The ADA covers private employers with fifteen or more employees and all state and local government agencies.

3. ***Public Employers***. Alabama law prohibits state employers from discrimination based upon handicap (including blindness, visual impairments, and any other physical disability), unless the handicap prevents the performance of the job in question. Ala. Code §21-7-8 (1975). Therefore, medical or physical testing to determine if a public employee can perform a job should be in accordance with the Americans with Disabilities Act and should not occur prior to the time that a job has been offered to the potential employee.

D. Polygraph Tests

There is no Alabama statute or case law addressing the issue of polygraph tests in the private employment setting. However, under the Federal Employee Polygraph Protection Act (EPPA), most private employers are prohibited from requiring employees or prospective employees to submit to lie detector tests. 29 U.S.C. §2001, et seq. However, certain employers, i.e., governmental employers, certain governmental contractors, drug companies, and employers whose primary business is to provide security services are exempt from the Act and may require polygraph testing of their employees.

The law defines a lie detector as any mechanical or electrical device used to render a diagnostic opinion about the honesty of dishonesty of an individual. This includes polygraph, voice stress analyzers, psychological stress evaluators, and similar devices. An employer may not discipline an employee for refusing to take a test, nor may discipline be imposed in retaliation for a complaint if the employer has violated the law. Moreover, even though employees of federal, state and local governments are specifically excluded from the protections of the Employee Polygraph Protection Act, 29 U.S.C. §2006, state employers are prohibited from requiring a polygraph as a condition of employment. Ala. Code §36-1-8 (1975). However, in Montgomery v. Big B, Inc., 460 So. 2d 1286 (Ala. 1984), the court found that an allegedly defamatory communication made by corporate employees to a polygraph test operator concerning the plaintiff's alleged complicity in a misappropriation of corporate funds was admissible because the corporate employees had a privilege to disclose a co-employee's criminal conduct in the presence of a polygraph test operator. Id. The polygraph test operator had a corresponding interest in receiving pertinent information concerning alleged theft in order to administer the polygraph test in a competent manner. Id. The co-employees lost their privilege to disclose potentially damaging information only if the disclosures were made with bad faith or with actual malice. Id. In Ex parte N.J.J., 9 So.3d 455 (Ala. 2008), a workers' compensation case, results from a polygraph test administered as part of the investigation of a criminal attack were admitted as evidence.

E. Fingerprinting

There is no Alabama case or statute addressing the issue of fingerprinting of employees.

III. SEARCHES

A. Employee's Person

1. ***Private Employers***. There is no case in this jurisdiction addressing an employer's right to search an employee's person, however, employees have the right to be protected from unreasonable intrusions into their private affairs. See I.B.1,4, supra. Thus, the employee's right to privacy would depend on his or her expectations and whether they are reasonable under the circumstances. If the employer notifies employees at the time of their hiring that their desk, lockers, vehicles and person are subject to examination whenever they are on company property, the employee should have no expectation of privacy with regard to a search.

2. ***Public Employers***. A search of a public employee's person, property or work area is governed by O'Connor v. Ortega, 480 U.S. 709, 715, 724-725 (1987). There, the court considered the applicability of the Fourth Amendment privacy rights to non-court ordered searches of public employees' offices. Where a state-run hospital in California, having been made aware of allegations of wrongdoing by an employee, searched the employee's office and confiscated personal items the court concluded that the employee had a reasonable expectation of privacy within the confines of his office. Therefore, government employers must first have a reasonable ground for making warrantless searches. A search of an employee's person and belongings is proper if there is a reasonable suspicion that the employee has engaged in misconduct such as bringing contraband into a prison. See Smith v. Alabama State Personnel Board, 521 So. 2d 35 (Ala. Civ. App. 1987) (even though the Department of Corrections had personnel regulations which established that the Board of Corrections had the right to search personal property and vehicles, the court held that a search could be properly conducted only on "reasonable suspicion").

B. Employee's Work Area

An employee may establish the legitimacy of the expectation of privacy by showing a subjective expectation of privacy and societal acceptance of this expectation as objectively reasonable. See United States v. Scrushy, No. CR-03-BE-0530-S, 2005 U.S. Dist. LEXIS 42842 (N.D. Ala. Jan. 21, 2005). The question of whether an employee has a reasonable expectation of privacy must be addressed on a case-by-case basis. Id. In Scrushy, the court found the defendant, who had consistently and successfully tightly limited and controlled access by others to his work spaces and computers, "clearly had a subjective expectation of privacy in his office suite." Id. However, the court found that this expectation was not reasonable or legitimate in light of company policies, which clearly authorized the employer to search the work spaces and electronic devices of any and all employees on its property. Id. Thus, "the defendant's assertion that he held an objectively reasonable expectation of privacy in his office suite located on corporate property [was] totally unfounded and unsupported." Id.; see also III.A.1-2, supra.

C. Employee's Property

1. ***Private Employers***. No specific case or statute in this jurisdiction. See III.A.1-2, supra.

2. ***Public Employers***. See III.A.1-2, supra.

IV. MONITORING OF EMPLOYEES

A. Telephones and Electronic Communications

The Electronic Communications Privacy Act (ECPA) of 1986, part of Title III of the Omnibus Crime Control and Safe Streets Act, 18 U.S.C §2510, prohibits the interception of, and introduction into evidence of, telephone communications unless one party to the communications gives consent. Under the ECPA, a plaintiff may be able to recover damages for violation of workplace privacy by showing that personal telephone calls were monitored by an employer without consent (even if the calls were made on a business telephone during working hours). An employer may have the right to monitor an employee's phone calls for a legitimate business purpose, such as quality control, investigation of a theft, or even determining whether an employee is making personal calls, so long as the interception is narrowly tailored to meet the particular need prompting the interception. See, Stephanie L. Schaeffer, Esq., Cause of Action Against a Public Employer for Violation of Privacy in the Workplace, 15 COA2D 139, 2003; Watkins v. L.M. Berry & Co., 704 F. 2d 577 (11th Cir. 1983); Walker v. Darby, 911 F. 2d 1573 (11th Cir. 1990).

Under Alabama statute, a person is guilty of criminal eavesdropping, a Class A misdemeanor, if he intentionally uses any device to eavesdrop, whether or not he is present at the time. Ala. Code §13A-11-31 (2001). The term eavesdrop is defined in §13A-11-30 as "To overhear, record, amplify or transmit any part of the private communication of others without the consent of at least one of the persons engaged in the communication of others,..." Id. Note also that such eavesdropping may involve a taking of the individual's property, e.g., ideas, thoughts and other products of the human mind. Because the aforementioned products are properties of value, when an individual's conversation is unlawfully and electronically recorded, there might also be a theft under Chapter 8, Article 1 of the Alabama Criminal Code. Additionally, under Article 1, Section 5 of the Alabama State Constitution, Alabama guarantees against "unreasonable seizure or searches," but the Alabama State Constitution only protects against intrusions of state actors.

Another potential claim can be derived from the "invasion of privacy" common law action. Alabama has specifically recognized the tort of invasion of privacy, which is implicated by a "wrongful intrusion onto one's private activities in such a manner so as to outrage or to cause mental suffering, shame or humiliation to a person of ordinary sensibilities." Hogin v. Cottingham, 533 So. 2d 525, 530-31 (Ala. 1988). In a case where the plaintiff-employee left her job after learning that her personal calls were being intercepted, recorded and examined by the defendant-employer, the court refused to grant a summary judgment motion to dismiss in favor of the employee because a trial question existed as to whether the employer intruded upon the affairs of the employee. Smith v. Devers, No. CIV.A.01-T-551-N, 2002 WL 75803 (M.D. Ala. Jan. 17, 2002).

1. ***Wiretapping***. Restatement (Second) of Torts, §652B (1977) Comment c states in part: "The defendant is subject to liability under the rule stated in this Section only when he has intruded into a private place, or has otherwise invaded a private seclusion that the plaintiff has thrown about his person or affairs." The wrongful intrusion may be by physical intrusion into a place where the plaintiff has secluded himself, by discovering the plaintiff's private affairs through wiretapping or eavesdropping, or by some investigation into the plaintiff's private concerns, such as opening private mail or examining a private bank account. Id. See also Vernars v. Young, 539 F.2d 966 (3rd Cir. 1976) (holding that invasion of privacy occurred when mail addressed to plaintiff was opened by defendant without plaintiff's consent); see generally, W. Page Keeton, et al., Prosser and Keeton on the Law of Torts, §117, at 854-55 (5th ed. 1984); 62 Am. Jur. 2d Privacy §§ 51-57 (1990). Further, if the means of gathering the information are excessively objectionable and improper, a wrongful intrusion may occur. See Hogin v. Cottingham, 533 So. 2d 525 (Ala. 1988) (wrongful intrusion occurs when there has been abrupt, offensive, and objectionable prying into information that is entitled to be private).

18 U.S.C.S. §2515 of Title III of the Omnibus Crime Control and Safe Streets Act of 1968, 18 U.S.C.S. §§ 2510-2520, states: "Whenever any wire or oral communication has been intercepted, no part of the contents of such communication and no evidence derived therefrom may be received in evidence in any trial, hearing, or other proceeding in or before any court, grand jury, department, officer, agency, regulatory body, legislative committee, or other authority of the United States, a State, or a political subdivision thereof if the disclosure of that information would be in violation of this chapter."

2. ***Electronic Communications***. Although no Alabama case has addressed the issue, communications via e-mail and voice mail receive the same degree of protection as telephonic communications referenced above under the ECPA. See E-Mail and Voice Mail, Employee Privacy and the Federal Wire Tap Statute, 44 Am. Univ. Law Rev. 219, 245 (1994), Stephanie L. Schaeffer, Esq., Cause of Action Against a Public Employer for Violation of Privacy in the Workplace, 15 COA2D 139, 2003. In Myrick v. Barron, 820 So. 2d 81 (Ala. 2001), the court held, "[t]he wrongful intrusion may be by. . . discovering the plaintiff's private affairs through wiretapping or eavesdropping or by some investigation into the plaintiff's private concerns, such as opening private mail or examining a private bank account." Id.; referencing Restatement (Second) of Torts §652B.

3. ***Other Electronic Monitoring***. There is no specific Alabama case or statute addressing this issue.

B. Mail

According to Johnson v. Stewart, 854 So. 2d 544 (Ala. 2002), "One who intentionally intrudes, physically or otherwise, upon the solitude or seclusion of another or his private affairs or concerns, is subject to liability to the other for invasion of his privacy, if the intrusion would be highly offensive to a reasonable person." Comment c to Restatement (Second) of Torts, §652B (1977) states in part: "The defendant is subject to liability under the rule stated in this Section only when he has intruded into a private place, or has otherwise invaded a private seclusion that the plaintiff has thrown about his person or affairs." The wrongful intrusion may be by physical intrusion into a place where the plaintiff has secluded himself, by discovering the plaintiff's private affairs through wiretapping or eavesdropping, or by some investigation into the plaintiff's private concerns, such as opening private mail or examining a private bank account." Id. (emphasis added); see also Hogin v. Cottingham, 533 So. 2d 525 (Ala. 1988) (wrongful intrusion occurs when there has been abrupt, offensive, and objectionable prying into information that is entitled to be private). The general principals discussed in I.B.1-4, supra, would apply as well.

C. Surveillance/Photographing

Violation of the right of privacy may be actionable against an employer where the investigation of a person being watched, trailed, shadowed or being kept under surveillance is pursued in an offensive or improper manner. Martin v. Patterson, 975 So. 2d 984 (Ala. Civ. App. 2007) ("generally, surveillance is not an actionable intrusion as long as it is conducted in a reasonable and nonobtrusive manner"). Thus, in those areas where an employee has an expectation of privacy such as in restrooms and dressing rooms (areas set aside for private activities), surveillance may constitute an invasion of privacy under the Fourth Amendment. However, according to Ex parte Doster Constr. Co., 772 So. 2d 447 (Ala. 2000), if an employer has acquired videotape surveillance of an employee committing an act there is no duty under the law that the employee be allowed to see the surveillance video prior to deposition. Id. at 449. "We see no apparent advantage to requiring disclosure of videotape before an employee is deposed, except for the advantage that would ensure to the employee if he intended to lie or pursue a fraudulent claim." Id. at 451.

V. ACTIVITIES OUTSIDE THE WORKPLACE

A. Statute or Common Law

There is no Alabama statute that speaks to the issue of employer involvement in employee activity outside the workplace; however, the Supreme Court of Alabama upheld summary judgment for a workmen's compensation carrier who hired an investigator to investigate an employee/workman's compensation claimant at his place of residence from a vehicle parked outside of the claimant's home. Johnson v. Corporate Special Services, Inc., 602 So. 2d 385 (Ala. 1992). The Court held that the purpose of the investigation was legitimate and invasion of privacy did not occur in that the employee could have expected reasonable investigation of his alleged condition. Id. For discussion of common law prohibitions, see V.B.1-3, infra.

B. Employees' Personal Relationships

1. ***Romantic Relationships Between Employees***. Employers in Alabama are entitled to discourage or prohibit romantic relationships between employees. Employment actions concerning employees engaged in romantic relationships should be consistent with Title VII of the Civil Rights Act. 42 U.S.C. §2000(e), et seq. Inquiries regarding romantic relationships or relationships with a spouse may subject the employer to liability for invasion of privacy. Phillips v. Smalley Maintenance Services, 435 So. 2d. 705 (Ala. 1983) (supervisor inquired of employee as to how often she and her husband had sex and what positions they used).

2. ***Sexual Orientation***. No case in Alabama finds that inquiries about sexual orientation create liability to the employer. See Logan v. Sears, 466 So. 2d 121 (Ala. 1985) (cause of action against employer did not exist where employee stated that customer, an admitted homosexual, was "as queer as a three dollar bill").

3. ***Marital Status***. The analysis here is the same as V.B.1.-2, supra.

C. Smoking

No cases or statutes in this jurisdiction.

D. Blogging

No cases or statutes in this jurisdiction.

VI. RECORDS

A. Personnel Records

Alabama does not have a law allowing employees access to their own personnel records. Several Alabama statutes require that employers keep specific records about employees: (1) employer must keep certain records with regard to child labor (Ala. Code §25-8-38 (1975)); (2) employer must record all employee injuries for which compensation is paid or claimed and a report must be made to the Department of Industrial Relations within fifteen days of an accident (Ala. Code §25-5-4 (1975)); and (3) employers must keep true and accurate work records for each employee for unemployment compensation purposes. (Ala. Code §25-4-116 (1975)). Personnel records of public employees are generally governed by the Alabama Open Records Act. Ala. Code § 36-12-40, *et seq.*; Graham v. Alabama State Employees Ass'n, 991 So. 2d 710 (Ala. Civ. App. 2007) (holding personnel files of administrative law judge and others in the possession of the State Personnel Department were subject to disclosure). In addition, federal record keeping requirements are extensive.

B. Medical Records

An employee or designated representative may examine, upon written request, any x-rays, laboratory reports, and medical records associated with the person's workers compensation claim. Ala. Code §25-5-77 (1975).

C. Criminal Records

Alabama law prohibits employers without a "right to know" or a "need to know" from obtaining non-conviction arrest records. Ala. Code §§41-9-601, -636, -642 (1975). There is no prohibition against obtaining criminal convictions or copies of criminal convictions in Alabama.

D. Subpoenas / Search Warrants

There are no cases or statutes in this jurisdiction regarding subpoenas to employers seeking information about employees or search warrants served on employers seeking to search employee files or an employee's workspace. But see III.B., supra.

An employer cannot retaliate against an employee for responding to a subpoena for jury duty. Ala. Code § 12-16-8.1 titled "Discharge from employment prohibited" reads in pertinent part: "(a) No employer in this state may discharge any employee solely because he serves on any jury empanelled under any state or federal statute; provided, however, that the employee reports for work on his next regularly scheduled hour after being dismissed from any jury." Id. Employee is entitled to be compensated for actual and punitive damages for being laid off from work because of jury duty. Birmingham Drywall, Inc. v. Moore, 598 So. 2d 970 (Ala. Civ. App. 1992); Given v. Heilig-Meyers Co., 738 So. 2d 1282 (Ala. Civ. App. 1999) (while this section prohibits an employer from terminating an employee because of his or her service on a jury, it does not prohibit an employer from terminating an employee because he is called to appear as a witness before a grand jury).

VII. Actions Subsequent to Employment

A. References

No cases or statutes on point in this jurisdiction.

B. Non-Compete Agreements

Ala. Code §8-1-1 provides, in pertinent part: "(a) Every contract by which anyone is restrained from exercising a lawful profession, trade, or business of any kind otherwise than is provided by this section is to that extent void. (b) ... One who is employed as an agent, servant or employee may agree with his employer to refrain from carrying on or engaging in similar business and from soliciting old customers of such employer within a specified county, city, or part thereof so long as the ... employer carries on a like business therein." Id.

Section 8-1-1 expresses the public policy in Alabama disfavoring contracts in restraint of trade; such contracts are disfavored "because they tend not only to deprive the public of efficient service but also... to impoverish the individual." Robinson v. Computer Servicenters, Inc., 346 So. 2d 940, 943 (Ala. 1977)). A covenant not to compete that does not fall within the limited exceptions set out by §8-1-1(b) is void. Construction Materials, Ltd. v. Kirkpatrick Concrete, Inc., 631 So. 2d 1006, 1009 (Ala. 1994). In adopting §8-1-1, the Legislature has declared the public policy of this state against noncompete agreements. Cherry Bekaert & Holland v. Brown, 582 So. 2d 502 (Ala. 1991). Contractual provisions linking the right of an individual to leave a company's employ in order to compete with the concomitant payment of money are prohibited. See Hendrich v. Pan Am. Fin. Servs., No. 06-0034-BH, 2006 U.S. Dist. LEXIS 39157 (S.D. Ala. June 13, 2006). However, a non-compete agreement has been upheld as valid and enforceable where the court found that it did not prevent the plaintiff from "practicing the only trade that he knows," even though the court acknowledged the trial court's suggestion that the plaintiff had made a "good argument concerning the issue of undue hardship." Eastis v. Veterans Oil, Inc., 65 So. 3d 443 (Ala. Civ. App. 2010) (rejecting plaintiff's additional arguments that the agreement was not sufficiently limited in geographic scope and that the defendant did not have a protectable interest).

VIII. OTHER ISSUES

A. Statutes of Limitations

The statute of limitations for bringing an action for invasion of privacy or outrage is two years. Ala. Code §6-2-38 (1) (1975); see Archie v. Enterprise Hospital, 508 So. 2d 693 (Ala. 1987). In cases where an employee alleges that she was improperly touched in the workplace as part of a claim for invasion of privacy or outrage, the statute of limitations may be circumvented by bringing a claim for assault. Actions for assault and battery must be brought within six years. Ala. Code §6 -2-34(1)(1975).

B. Jurisdiction

The circuit courts have original jurisdiction over civil actions where the matter in controversy exceeds $10,000, exclusive of interest and costs, and concurrent jurisdiction with the district courts if the matter in controversy exceeds $3,000. Ala. Code §12-11-30. Thus, the circuit court would generally be the trial court where the initial complaint would be filed in an employment case. Few Alabama court decisions have focused on jurisdictional issues in the context of privacy or related claims against employers. However, in International Brotherhood of Electrical Workers v. Morton, 428 So. 2d 15 (Ala. 1983), the supreme court held that federal law preempted the trial court from exercising jurisdiction over a cause of action by plaintiff-employees, who alleged invasion of their right to privacy due to a union's dissemination of their salary information, when such dissemination arose out of the organizing activities of the union.

C. Worker's Compensation Exclusivity

The exclusivity provisions of Alabama's workers' compensation laws are found at Ala. Code §25-5-52 and -53. In Busby v. Truswal Systems Corp., 551 So. 2d 322 (Ala. 1989), the Alabama Supreme Court held that tort actions for "purely psychological injuries inflicted during the course of employment" are not barred by the exclusivity provisions of the Workers' Compensation Act. In Busby, the plaintiffs alleged that they had been sexually harassed, both verbally and physically, and asserted claims of invasion of privacy and the tort of outrage. In another case, the Alabama Court of Civil Appeals followed Busby and similarly held that the plaintiff's allegations of verbal and physical harassment by a supervisor were not barred by the exclusivity provisions of the Workers' Compensation Act. Jones v. Bancgroup, 735 So. 2d 1163 (Ala. Civ. App. 1998). Like Busby, the plaintiff in Jones asserted claims of invasion of privacy and tort of outrage and sought damages for psychological injuries. Id.; see also Bullin v. Corr. Med. Servs., 908 So. 2d 269 (Ala. Civ. App. 2004) (holding employees' claims that employer failed to protect them from the wrongful conduct of the prison population were not barred as a matter of law because each employee testified that injuries were purely psychological in nature).

D. Pleading Requirements

Rule 8(a) of the Alabama Rules of Civil Procedure requires that a pleading which sets forth a claim shall contain (1) a short and plain statement of the claim showing that the pleader is entitled to relief; and (2) a demand for judgment for the relief the pleader seeks. Rule 9(g) provides that when special damages are sought, they shall be specifically stated. With regard to defenses, Rule 8(c) provides that "waiver, and any other matter constituting an avoidance or affirmative defense" shall be set forth affirmatively. Thus, if waiver or consent is a defense to a false light or misappropriation claim, these matters should be specifically pled. Furthermore, if an employer defends an interference with contractual relations case on the basis of justification, this defense should be pled as an affirmative defense. White Sands Group, L.L.C. v. PRS II, LLC, 32 So. 3d 5, 12 (Ala. 2009).

SURVEY OF ALASKA EMPLOYMENT LIBEL LAW

James H. Juliussen
Elizabeth P. Hodes
Davis Wright Tremaine, LLP
701 W. 8th Avenue, Suite 800
Anchorage, Alaska 99501

Telephone: (907) 257-5300; Facsimile: (907) 257-5399

(With Developments Reported Through **November 1, 2012**)

GENERAL COMMENTS

The state of Alaska is divided into four judicial districts. Alaska's judicial system consists of four courts: the Supreme Court, the Court of Appeals, the Superior Court and the District Court. Jurisdiction of the Court of Appeals is limited to criminal matters. The Superior Court is Alaska's trial court of general jurisdiction and sits as an intermediate court of appeals for decisions from District Court and administrative agencies. In civil matters, the jurisdiction of the District Court is, in general, limited to matters involving less than $100,000.00. Alaska courts are likely to follow the restatements of the law in the absence of pertinent Alaska statutory or case law.

Alaska does not follow the "American Rule" concerning the award of attorneys' fees. Rather, under Alaska Civil Rule 82(a)(1), a portion of actual attorneys' fees are awarded to the prevailing party, unless the court, in its discretion, directs otherwise.

SIGNIFICANT DEVELOPMENTS SINCE THE 2012 *SURVEY*

None.

I. GENERAL LAW

A. General Employment Law

1. ***At Will Employment.*** In Alaska, an employment contract is deemed to create an at will employment relationship when such contract is not for a determinable length of time, Luedtke v. Nabors Alaska Drilling, Inc., 768 P.2d 1123 (Alaska 1989); see also Mitford v. de Lasala, 666 P.2d 1000 (Alaska 1983), whereas employees hired for a specific term may not be discharged before the expiration of such term except for good cause. Id. In describing the nature of at will employment, the Luedtke court held that "[e]mployees hired on an at-will basis can be fired for any reason that does not violate the implied covenant of good faith and fair dealing." Luedtke, 768 P.2d at 1131. The Alaska Supreme Court has acknowledged that a violation of public policy could constitute a breach of this implied covenant. Knight v. American Guard & Alert, Inc., 714 P.2d 788 (Alaska 1986).

Note, however, that the Alaska Supreme Court has determined that an employer's promise of employment until retirement is enforceable and transforms at will employment to employment terminable only with cause, even if no additional consideration is tendered by the employee. Eales v. Tanana Valley Medical-Surgical Group, Inc., 663 P.2d 958 (Alaska 1983) (employer's promise of "permanent employment" is for a specific term and terminable only with cause).

Alaska clearly permits claims of wrongful discharge in a variety of settings. See, e.g., Zoerb v. Chugach Electric Association, Inc., 798 P.2d 1258 (Alaska 1990); Reed v. Municipality of Anchorage, 782 P.2d 1155 (Alaska 1989); Thorstenson v. ARCO Alaska, Inc., 780 P.2d 371 (Alaska 1989).

B. Elements of Libel Claim

1. ***Basic Elements.*** In actions for defamation, Alaska courts overtly follow the lead of the Restatement (Second) of Torts (1977). In French v. Jadon, Inc., 911 P.2d 20 (Alaska 1996), for example, the court quoted directly from § 558 of the Restatement in holding that "to prevail on a defamation claim, a plaintiff has to establish (1) a false and defamatory statement; (2) an unprivileged publication to a third party; (3) fault amounting at least to negligence on the part of the publisher; and (4) the existence of either 'per se' actionability or special harm." Id. at 32. See also McAdoo v. Diaz, 884 P.2d 1385, 1390 (Alaska 1994). In defining what constitutes a defamatory statement, Alaska courts similarly use the Restatement for guidance. The Alaska Supreme Court has held that "[a] communication is defamatory if it tends to harm the reputation of another so as to lower him [or her] in the estimation of the community or to deter third persons from associating or dealing with him." Green v. Northern Publishing Co., Inc., 655 P.2d 736, 739, 8 Media L. Rep. 2515 (Alaska 1982), cert. denied, 463 U.S. 1208, 103 S. Ct. 3539, 77 L. Ed. 2d 1389 (1983) (citing Restatement (Second) of Torts § 559 (1977)).

2. ***Fault.*** Alaska courts have followed the standard definition of "actual malice." See, e.g., Rybacheck v. Sutton, 761 P.2d 1013, 15 Media L. Rep. 2291 (Alaska 1988); Urethane Specialties, Inc. v. City of Valdez, 620 P.2d 683 (Alaska 1980); Lull v. Wick Construction Co., 614 P.2d 321 (Alaska 1980). Reckless disregard consists of "conduct that is heedless and shows a wanton indifference to consequences; it is conduct which is far more than negligent . . . . There must be sufficient evidence to permit the inference that the defendant must have, in fact, subjectively entertained serious doubts as to the truth of his statement." Green v. Northern Publishing Co., 655 P.2d 736, 742, 8 Media L. Rep. 2515 (Alaska 1982) (emphasis in original; citations omitted), cert. denied, 463 U.S. 1208 (1983); accord Mount Juneau Enterprises, Inc. v. Juneau Empire, 891 P.2d 829, 23 Media L. Rep. 1684 (Alaska 1995); Beard v. Baum, 796 P.2d 1344 (Alaska 1990).

a. **Private Figure Plaintiff/Matter of Public Concern.** The standard of care applicable in cases of public concern is actual malice, regardless of whether the defendant is a private or public figure. See Taranto v. North Slope Borough, 992 P.2d 1111 (Alaska 1999), cert. denied, 529 U.S. 1130, 120 S.Ct. 2006, 146 L.Ed.2d 956 (2000) (cabdriver's illegal sales of alcohol and drugs deemed matter of public concern); Mount Juneau Enterprises, 891 P.2d 829 (presence of hazardous materials on site of proposed tramway project is an issue of public concern). Previously, a federal district court had erroneously predicted that Alaska courts would follow Gertz rather than continue to apply the Rosenbloom standard under the State Constitution. Sisemore v. U.S. News & World Report, 662 F. Supp. 1529, 14 Media L. Rep. 1590 (D. Alaska 1987).

b. **Private Figure Plaintiff/Matter of Private Concern.** The negligence standard applies to statements concerning a private figure plaintiff that are not of public concern. See, e.g., French v. Jadon, Inc., 911 P.2d 20 (Alaska 1996).

c. **Public Figure Plaintiff/Matter of Public Concern.** The applicable standard of care is actual malice. See Mt. Juneau, I.B.2.a, supra; Beard v. Baum, 796 P.2d at 1353-54 (state employee was public figure with respect to issue of job performance, as well as allegations of corruption at public agency, and for purposes of defamation, actual malice standard applied to allegedly defamatory statements on both issues).

3. ***Falsity.*** Private figure plaintiffs have the burden of proving falsity. Sisemore v. U.S. News & World Report, 662 F. Supp. 1529, 14 Media L. Rep. 1590 (D. Alaska 1987).

4. ***Defamatory Statement of Fact.*** Whether a statement is capable of defamatory meaning is for the judge to determine. Fairbanks Publishing Co. v. Pitka, 376 P.2d 190, 194 (Alaska 1962). If the publication is libelous per se on its face, the judge may tell the jury that the words are defamatory, but if a statement is capable of two meanings, only one of which is defamatory, the issue of defamation is for the trier of fact. Id. See also, Suulutaaq, Inc. v. Williams, 782 F.Supp.2d 795, 807-808, 39 Media L. Rep. 1103 (D.Alaska 2010) (under state law, defamatory meaning may be express or implied and may be implied by omission or juxtaposition of facts even if individual statements are "true" when viewed in isolation). To determine whether a statement is one of fact or opinion, Alaska courts consider the language used, the contextual meaning of the statement, whether the statement can be verified, and the circumstances under which the statement was made. Sands v. Living Word Fellowship, 34 P.3d 955 (Alaska 2001), rehearing denied. A statement may be defamatory even though expressed as opinion if it implies underlying factual knowledge. Kinzel v. Discovery Drilling, Inc., 93 P.3d 427, 441 (Alaska 2004).

5. ***Of and Concerning Plaintiff.*** Libelous words must have been published concerning plaintiff, and understood by at least one third person to have concerned plaintiff. Golden North Airways v. Tanana Publishing Co., 15 Alaska 303, 315, 218 F.2d 612, 618 (9th Cir. 1954). A libel directed at a group may constitute the basis of an action by an individual if the group is small enough so that a person reading or hearing the words would readily identify a specific person in the group. Id. at 316.

6. ***Publication.*** Publication of defamatory material occurs when it is communicated to someone other than the person defamed. McCutcheon v. State, 746 P.2d 461 (Alaska 1987). Gay v. Williams, 486 F. Supp. 12, 5 Media L. Rep. 1785 (D. Alaska 1979), suggests that Alaska will apply the same liability standard in defamation cases regardless of whether the alleged defamation occurred through broadcast or print media. Communication to an attorney can be publication in the absence of evidence that the attorney was authorized to receive such communication by the person defamed. City of Fairbanks v. Rice, 20 P.3d 1097, 1107 (Alaska 2000) (upon rehearing).

a. **Intracorporate Communication.** Communications among employees of a corporation apparently are deemed to have been published, see Jones v. Central Peninsula General Hospital, 779 P.2d 783 (Alaska 1989) and Schneider v. Pay 'N Save Corp., 723 P.2d 619 (Alaska 1986), but are protected by a conditional privilege. See III.A-B, infra.

b. **Compelled Self-Publication.** No reported Alaska cases deciding this issue. But see, Odom v. Fairbanks Memorial Hosp., 999 P.2d 123, 133-34 (Alaska 2000) (Fabe, J., concurring and dissenting in part) (noting appellant's failure to contest the superior court's conclusion that self-publication is not grounds for defamation action).

c. **Republication.** Defendants are generally liable for republication of defamatory statements. Suulutaaq, Inc. v. Williams, 782 F.Supp.2d 795, 809, 39 Media L. Rep. 1103 (D.Alaska 2010). Nonetheless, reliance on a statement of a third party will not create liability unless the speaker is negligent or unreasonable in such reliance. Id. See also, Gay v. Williams, 486 F. Supp. 12, 5 Media L. Rep. 1785 (D. Alaska 1979) (defendants found not liable for republication of defamatory wire service statements). Reliance upon a statement about a public figure will not create liability unless the speaker knows that the statement is probably false or has some obvious reason to doubt its accuracy. Suulutaaq, 782 F.Supp.2d at 809.

7. ***Statements versus Conduct.*** Conduct, unaccompanied by words, can be defamatory per se. Alaska State Bank v. Fairco, 674 P.2d 288 (Alaska 1983) (bank's repossession of collateral and dishonoring of checks damaged plaintiffs' business reputations and was defamatory per se).

8. ***Damages.***

a. **Presumed Damages and Libel Per Se.** Presumed damages are recoverable in cases not involving matters of public interest or concern. Odom v. Fairbanks Memorial Hosp., 999 P.2d 123 (Alaska 2000); Alaska State Bank v. Fairco, 674 P.2d 288 (Alaska 1983).

The Alaska legislature, however, made substantial changes to the laws governing the civil justice system in tort reform legislation that went into effect on August 7, 1997. The changes apply only to causes of action that accrue on or after that date. This law places limits on the amount of non-economic damages that can be awarded in civil litigation. Alaska Stat. § 09.17.010(a). It caps damages that may be awarded by a court or jury for such non-economic losses arising out of a single injury or death at $400,000 or the injured person's life expectancy in years multiplied by $8,000, whichever is greater. Alaska Stat. § 09.17.010(b). The statute provides for different caps when damages are awarded for severe permanent physical impairment or severe disfigurement. Alaska Stat. § 09.17.010(c). No cases have yet been reported applying this legislation to defamation actions.

(1) **Employment-Related Criticism.** No reported Alaska cases. See statutory discussion of qualified privileges, II.A.2, infra.

(2) **Single Instance Rule.** No reported Alaska cases.

b. **Punitive Damages.** Actual malice must be shown before punitive damages are awarded. Fairbanks Publishing Co. v. Pitka, 376 P.2d 190 (Alaska 1962). The Fairbanks court applied the common law "ill will" or "hatred" standard for malice sufficient to allow an award of punitive damages. Alaska courts have not decided whether the current "actual malice" liability test is also the proper test for determining whether punitive damages should be awarded. Punitive damages must be supported by clear and convincing evidence. Alaska Stat. § 09.17.020. Where an employer is vicariously liable for the act of its employee, punitive damages may not be awarded against the employer unless the employer or employer's managerial agent (A) authorized the act or omission and the manner in which it was performed or occurred; or (B) ratified or approved the act or omission after it occurred; or (2) the employee was (A) unfit to perform the act or avoid the omission and the employer or the employer's managerial agent acted recklessly in employing or retaining the employee; or (B) was employed in a managerial capacity and was acting within the scope of employment. Alaska Stat. § 09.17.020(k).

Tort reform measures enacted in 1997 impose significant limitations upon the availability of punitive damages, and also specify certain procedures to be followed before punitive damages may be awarded. These provisions require a bifurcated proceeding in actions in which a claim of punitive damages is presented to the fact-finder. In the first portion, the fact-finder must determine, concurrently with all other issues presented, whether punitive damages shall be allowed. The fact-finder may make an award of punitive damages only if the plaintiff has proven by clear and convincing evidence that the defendant's conduct (1) was outrageous, including acts done with malice or bad motives, or (2) evidenced reckless indifference to the interest of another person. Alaska Stat. § 09.17.020(a), (b). Unless the evidence is relevant to another issue in the case, discovery of evidence that is relevant to the financial condition of the defendant or the amount of financial gain the defendant gained or expected to gain as a result of its conduct may not be conducted until after the fact-finder has determined that an award of punitive damages is allowed. The court may issue orders as necessary, including directing the parties to have the information relevant to these issues available for production immediately at the close of the initial trial in order to minimize the delay between the initial trial and the separate proceeding to determine the amount of punitive damages. Alaska Stat. § 09.17.020(e).

If the fact-finder, applying the standards set out above, determines that punitive damages are to be allowed, a separate proceeding is conducted to determine the amount of punitive damages to be awarded. The statute sets forth seven factors that the fact-finder "may consider" at this separate proceeding, including: (1) the likelihood at the time of the conduct that serious harm would arise from the defendant's conduct; (2) the degree of the defendant's awareness of the likelihood described in (1) of this subsection; (3) the amount of financial gain the defendant gained or expected to gain as a result of the defendant's conduct; (4) the duration of the conduct and any intentional concealment of the conduct; (5) the attitude and conduct of the defendant upon discovery of the conduct; (6) the financial condition of the defendant; and (7) the total deterrence of other damages and punishment imposed on the defendant as a result of the conduct, including compensatory and punitive damages awards to persons in situations similar to those of the plaintiff and the severity of the criminal penalties to which the defendant has been or may be subjected. Alaska Stat. § 09.17.020(c).

An award of punitive damages is generally limited under the statute to the greater of (1) three times the amount of compensatory damages awarded to the plaintiff in the action; or (2) the sum of $500,000. There are two exceptions to this general cap on punitive damages. One limits the imposition of punitive damages, in actions against defendant employers to recover damages for certain unlawful employment practices, to amounts ranging from $200,000 to $500,000, depending on the number of employees that the employer has. The other exception, which is subject to the cap on damages for employment practice claims noted above, allows for recovery of substantially higher punitive damages in cases where conduct for which punitive damages may be recovered was motivated by financial gain. Specifically, the law now provides that where conduct giving rise to punitive damage awards "was motivated by financial gain and the adverse consequences of the conduct were actually known by the defendant or the person responsible for making policy decisions on behalf of the defendant," the fact-finder may award punitive damages not to exceed the greatest of (1) four times the amount of compensatory damages awarded to the plaintiff; (2) four times the aggregate amount of financial gain that the defendant received as a result of the defendant's misconduct; or (3) the sum of $7 million. Alaska Stat. § 09.17.020(g). The law also requires that 50 percent of any punitive damage award be deposited into the general fund of the state. Alaska Stat. § 09.17.020(j). This provision was challenged and upheld by the Supreme Court of Alaska in State v. Carpenter, 171 P.3d 41, 67 (2007).

II. PRIVILEGES AND DEFENSES

A. Scope of Privileges

1. ***Absolute Privilege.*** Absolute privilege exists for testimony in judicial proceedings. Nizinski v. Currington, 517 P.2d 754 (Alaska 1974).

2. ***Qualified Privileges.*** Alaska provides two statutory privileges. Alaska Stat. § 09.65.160 provides immunity for good faith disclosures of job performance information. An employer who discloses information about the job performance of an employee or former employee to a prospective employer of the employee or former employee at the request of the prospective employer or the employee is presumed to be acting in good faith and, unless the lack thereof is shown by a preponderance of the evidence, may not be held liable for the disclosure or its consequences. The presumption of good faith is rebutted upon a showing that the employer or former employer (1) recklessly, knowingly, or with a malicious purpose disclosed false or deliberately misleading information; or (2) disclosed information in violation of a civil right of the employee or former employee that is protected under Alaska Stat. § 18.80 or under comparable federal law. Alaska Stat. § 09.65.160.

Alaska Stat. § 23.10.610 places limits on causes of action for certain disclosures. A person may not bring an action for defamation of character, libel, slander, or damage to reputation against an employer who has established a program of drug testing or alcohol impairment testing under Alaska Stat. §§ 23.10.600 - 23.10.699 if the action is based on drug or alcohol testing unless (1) the results of the test were disclosed to a person other than the employer, an authorized employee, agent or representative of the employer, the tested employee, the tested prospective employee, or another person authorized or privileged by law to receive the information; (2) the information disclosed was a false positive test result; (3) the false positive test result was disclosed negligently; and (4) all elements of an action for defamation of character, libel, slander, or damage to reputation as established by law are satisfied. Alaska Stat. § 23.10.610.

The Alaska Supreme Court has also recognized a common-law conditional privilege on speech that addresses matters of public health and safety. Taranto v. North Slope Borough, 992 P.2d 1111, 1114 (Alaska 1999), cert. denied, 529 U.S. 1130, 120 S.Ct. 2006, 146 L.Ed.2d 956 (2000); Urethane Specialties, Inc., v. City of Valdez, 620 P.2d 683 (Alaska 1980); see also, Maddox v. Hardy, 187 P.3d 486, 497 (Alaska 2008) (communications with state and federal officials alleging illegal activities likely subject to qualified privilege); Smith v. Stafford, 189 P.3d 1065, 1072–73 (Alaska 2008) (social workers entitled to qualified immunity conducting investigations for child custody matters).

a. **Common Interest.** Alaska recognizes a conditional privilege based on circumstances where any one of several persons having a "common interest" in a particular subject matter believes that there is information that another sharing the common interest is entitled to know. See, e.g., Briggs v. Newton, 984 P.2d 1113 (Alaska 1999) (subcontractor has common interest privilege to disclose contractor's statements to building owner); Lull v. Wick Construction Co., 614 P.2d 321 (Alaska 1980) (privilege based on joint business interest); Schneider v. Pay 'N Save Corp., 723 P.2d 619 (Alaska 1986) (privilege based on common interests arising from employer/employee relationship).

b. **Duty.** Furthermore, in Schneider, the court held alternatively that the defendant's statements are conditionally privileged arising under his duty, as an employee, to make the allegedly defamatory statements. Schneider v. Pay 'N Save Corp., 723 P.2d 619 (Alaska 1986).

c. **Criticism of Public Employee.** Alaska has yet to recognize a conditional privilege based for criticism of a public employee beyond that imposed by New York Times Co. v. Sullivan, 376 U.S. 254, 84 S. Ct. 710, 11 L. Ed. 2d 686 (1964), and its progeny. See, e.g., Green v. Northern Publishing Co., Inc., 655 P.2d 736 (Alaska 1982) (holding that a physician contracted to provide medical services for state correctional facilities is a public official under New York Times); Beard v. Baum, 796 P.2d 1344 (Alaska 1990) (state employee alleging corruption in state agency is a limited use public figure for purposes of newspaper article criticizing his job performance). However, if the employee's duties pertain to public safety, the conditional privilege of Taranto, 992 P.2d at 1114, would apply.

d. **Limitations on Qualified Privilege.** The Alaska court follows the comments to the Restatement (Second) of Torts § 599 in determining whether a conditional privilege has been abused. Specifically, a conditional privilege is abused where (i) the publisher has knowledge of, or a reckless disregard for, the falsity of the defamatory matter; (ii) the defamatory matter is published for some purpose other than that for which the particular privilege is given; (iii) the publication is made to some person not reasonably believed to be necessary for the accomplishment of the purpose of the particular privilege; or (iv) the publication includes defamatory matter not reasonably believed to be necessary to accomplish the purpose for which the occasion is privileged. Schneider v. Pay 'N Save Corp., 723 P.2d 619 (Alaska 1986).

(1) **Constitutional or Actual Malice.** A showing of actual malice (i.e., knowledge of falsity or reckless disregard for the truth) negates the invocation of a conditional privilege. Olivit v. City and Borough of Juneau, 171 P.3d 1137, 1143 (2007); Taranto v. North Slope Borough, 992 P.2d 1111 (Alaska 1999), cert denied, 529 U.S. 1130, 120 S.Ct. 2006, 146 L.Ed.2d 956 (2000).

(2) **Common Law Malice.** No reported Alaska cases.

e. **Question of Fact or Law.** Whether an occasion gives rise to a privilege is a question of law for the court, however, where facts are in dispute, whether a conditional privilege has been abused is a question for the jury. Schneider v. Pay 'N Save Corp., 723 P.2d 619 (Alaska 1986).

f. **Burden of Proof.** Defendant has burden of establishing privilege; plaintiff then has burden of proving abuse. Schneider v. Pay 'N Save Corp., 723 P.2d 619 (Alaska 1986).

B. Standard Libel Defenses

1. ***Truth.*** Truth is a complete defense. Fairbanks Publishing Co. v. Pitka, 376 P.2d 190 (Alaska 1962). Alaska courts follow the standard rule of requiring only "substantial accuracy." See, e.g., Fairbanks Publishing Co. v. Francisco, 390 P.2d 784 (Alaska 1964).

2. ***Opinion.*** In a pre-Milkovich case, the Alaska Supreme Court held that when a defamatory comment concerns a matter of public interest, the defense of opinion extends to nonmalicious misstatements of fact. Pearson v. Fairbanks Publishing Co., 413 P.2d 711 (Alaska 1966). However, the Alaska Supreme Court held that an editorial was capable of defamatory meaning since it could be interpreted as meaning that the newspaper believed a physician was at least partially responsible for the death of an inmate. Green v. Northern Publishing Co., 655 P.2d 736, 8 Media L. Rep. 2515 (Alaska 1982), cert. denied, 463 U.S. 1208 (1983).

To ascertain whether a statement is one of fact or opinion, courts consider "the type of language used, the meaning of the statement in context, whether the statement is verifiable, and the broader social circumstances in which the statement was made." Sands v. Living Word Fellowship, 34 P.3d 955, 960 (Alaska 2001), rehearing denied, quoting Milkovich v. Lorain Journal Co., 497 U.S. 1, 20 (1990). A statement couched in terms of an opinion may still be actionable if the statement implies underlying factual knowledge. Kinzel v. Discovery Drilling, Inc., 93 P.3d 427, 441 (Alaska 2004).

3. ***Consent.*** No reported Alaska cases, however, see Cox v. Nasche, 70 F.3d 1030 (9th Cir. 1996) (concluding that Alaska courts would confer absolute privilege for statements covered by previously signed release).

4. ***Mitigation.*** There are no cases addressing the effect of publishing a retraction, correction, or clarification, but the court in Mount Juneau Enterprises, Inc. v. Juneau Empire, 891 P.2d 829, 23 Media L. Rep. 1684 (Alaska 1995), held that a refusal to retract, without more, does not raise an inference of actual malice sufficient to preclude summary judgment.

III. RECURRING FACT PATTERNS

A. Statements in Personnel File

The court in Jones v. Central Peninsula General Hospital, 779 P.2d 783 (Alaska 1989) relied specifically on a construction of the Restatement (Second) of Torts § 595 (1977) in finding that employers have a conditional privilege to make statements in a personnel file, as such publication affects a "sufficiently important interest of the recipient" where a supervisor makes the statement "under a legal duty to publish the defamatory matter." Id. at 790; citing Restatement (Second) of Torts § 595 (1977). In Jones, a supervisor's statement that employee was "paranoid," on the verge of a "breakdown," and in need of "help and fast" was found to be conditionally privileged under this analysis.

B. Performance Evaluations

Although the case did not concern a written performance evaluation, in Schneider v. Pay 'N Save Corp., 723 P.2d 619 (Alaska 1986), the Alaska Supreme Court held that statements between a store manager and an employee of an independent performance evaluation corporation that plaintiff "stole" from the store was protected by a conditional privilege rooted in the employee/employer relationship. Specifically, the Schneider court found that the publication reflected a "'sufficiently important interest' of [the defendant] to warrant such communication." Schneider, 723 P.2d at 624 (quoting Restatement (Second) of Torts § 595 (1977)).

C. References

Alaska Stat. § 09.65.160 provides immunity for good faith disclosures of job performance information. An employer who discloses information about the job performance of an employee or former employee to a prospective employer of the employee or former employee at the request of the prospective employer or the employee or former employee is presumed to be acting in good faith and, unless lack of good faith is shown by a preponderance of the evidence, may not be held liable for the disclosure or its consequences. For purposes of this section, the presumption of good faith is rebutted upon a showing that the employer or former employer (1) recklessly, knowingly, or with a malicious purpose disclosed false or deliberately misleading information; or (2) disclosed information in violation of a civil right of the employee or former employee that is protected under Alaska Stat. § 18.80 or under comparable federal law.

D. Intracorporate Communication

The Alaska Supreme Court has adopted the Restatement position that the common interest of members of religious, fraternal, charitable or other non-profit associations, whether incorporated or unincorporated, supports a privilege for certain communications among those members. Marshall v. Munro, 845 P.2d 424, 429 (1993) (citing Restatement (Second) of Torts § 596 cmt. e. (1977)). This rule applies to communications regarding the qualifications of the officers and members, alleged misconduct of those members and officers, and their participation in the activities of the organization. Id. Likewise, the rule applies to communications between members and officers of an organization regarding the conduct of activities for which it was organized. Id. See also III.A-B, supra.

E. Statements to Government Regulators

In Odom v. Fairbanks Memorial Hospital, 999 P.2d 123 (Alaska 2000), the Alaska Supreme Court recognized that a limited immunity applies to statements made in compliance with federal reporting requirements. The immunity applies unless the reporter has knowledge that the report is false. Id.

F. Reports to Auditors and Insurers

No cases, but conditional privilege of Jones, Schneider, and Odom likely applies. See III.A-B, E, supra.

G. Vicarious Liability of Employers for Statements Made by Employees

1. ***Scope of Employment.*** In accordance with the Restatement (Second) of Torts § 228A and § 229, Alaska does not alter the traditional doctrine of respondeat superior for defamation torts. See Taranto v. North Slope Borough, 909 P.2d 354, 358 (Alaska 1997) (employers may be vicariously liable for the defamatory statements of employees where (i) the activities leading to publication occurred within authorized time and space limits, (ii) it is "inferable" that the

employee acted in an effort to serve the employer's interests, and (iii) the employee acted with the knowledge of his or her supervisors).

a. **Blogging.** There are no reported Alaska cases dealing with employee blogs, whether authorized by the employer or not.

2. ***Damages.*** No Alaska cases.

H. Internal Investigations

There are no reported Alaska cases or statutes addressing the application of libel law to an employer's internal investigations, including investigations of employee misconduct. But see, Cameron v. Chang-Craft, 251 P.3d 1008, 1014-15, n. 7 (Alaska 2011) (noting jury verdict against defendant employer and co-worker for defamatory statements allegedly made in connection with co-worker complaint and investigation of same, which verdict was not at issue on appeal).

IV. OTHER ACTIONS BASED ON STATEMENTS

A. Negligent Hiring, Retention, and Supervision

In Broderick v. King's Way Assembly of God, 808 P.2d 1211, 1221 (Alaska 1991), the Alaska Supreme Court held that an employer, in selecting an employee, must exercise a degree of care commensurate with the nature and danger of the business in which he is engaged and the nature and grade of service for which the employee is intended. Compare Sievers v. McClure, 746 P.2d 885 (Alaska 1987) (general contractor entitled to rely on independent contractor's general reputation and past history of competence and general contractor is not liable to independent contractor's employees for allegedly negligent selection and hiring). The Alaska Supreme Court has not squarely addressed issues of negligent supervision and retention. However, Alaska's Supreme Court recently noted that claims for negligent hiring, training, supervision and retention require proof that the employer knew or should have known the employee posed a risk. Ayuluk v. Red Oaks Assisted Living, Inc., 201 P.3d 1183 (Alaska 2009) (assisted living facility could be held vicariously liable under an "aided in agency" theory for employee caregiver's sexual battery of facility resident, though such theory is not applicable to all employers).

B. Intentional Infliction of Emotional Distress

Alaska recognizes the tort of intentional infliction of emotional distress, generally adopting the definitions and approach of the Restatement (Second) of Torts. See also Tommy's Elbow Room v. Kavorkian, 727 P.2d 1038 (Alaska 1986). Liability will be imposed for the infliction of emotional distress where (i) the emotional distress is "severe," (ii) the conduct of the tortfeasor is intentional or reckless, and (iii) such conduct is capable of being characterized as extreme or outrageous. King v. Brooks, 788 P.2d 707 (Alaska 1990); Teamsters Local 959 v. Wells, 749 P.2d 349 (Alaska 1988); Croft by Croft v. Wicker, 737 P.2d 789 (Alaska 1987). In Lincoln v. Interior Reg. Housing Authority, 30 P.3d 582, 589 (Alaska 2001), the Alaska Supreme Court recognized that a cause of action for intentional infliction of emotional distress may lie where an employee was discharged in retaliation for cooperating with a governmental investigation of the employer.

C. Interference with Economic Advantage

In Alaska, the elements of the tort of intentional interference with prospective economic advantage are (1) the existence of a prospective business relationship between the plaintiff and a third party; (2) knowledge by the defendant of the prospective relationship, and intent to prevent its fruition; (3) conduct by the defendant interfering with the relationship; (4) failure of the prospective relationship to culminate in pecuniary benefit to the plaintiff; (5) causation of the plaintiff's damages by the defendant's conduct; and (6) absence of privilege or justification for the defendant's actions. Hayes v. A.J. Associates, Inc., 960 P.2d 556, 571 (Alaska 1998).

D. Prima Facie Tort

No reported Alaska cases.

V. OTHER ISSUES

A. Statute of Limitations

Alaska applies a two-year limitations period to defamation actions. Alaska Stat. § 09.10.070. Normally, the period begins to run when the libelous statement is communicated to a third party. Chiei v. Stern, 561 P.2d 1216 (1977). Application of the discovery rule to the statute of limitations in defamation cases was rejected in McCutcheon v. State, 746 P.2d 461 (Alaska 1987). The court found a defamed person's knowledge of the defamation is not a necessary element for a libel action but hinted that the discovery rule might be applied where the manner of publication is "inherently secretive."

B. Jurisdiction

The superior courts have jurisdiction over all civil matters within the state, Alaska Stat. § 22.10.020; see id. § 09.05.010. Apparently there are no geographic restrictions on where an action may be brought within the state apart from those in Alaska R. Civ. P. 3, but venue may be changed to serve the convenience of witness and the ends of justice. Alaska Stat. § 22.10.040. Jurisdiction over nonresidents is authorized under Alaska's long-arm statute, Alaska Stat. § 09.05.015.

C. Worker's Compensation Exclusivity

The exclusive remedy provision of Alaska's Workers' Compensation Act bars any claim against an employer or fellow employee for injuries arising out of and during the course of employment. Alaska Stat. § 23.30.055; Gordon v. Burgess Construction Co., 425 P.2d 602, 605 (Alaska 1967) ("The remedies provided by a workmen's compensation act are intended to be in lieu of all rights and remedies as to a particular injury whether at common law or otherwise."). However, the exclusivity provision does not bar claims for intentional torts. Elliot v. Brown, 569 P.2d 1323, 1327 (Alaska 1977); Van Biene v. ERA Helicopters, 779 P.2d 315, 318-19 (Alaska 1989). The intentional tort exception will only apply if a plaintiff can establish specific intent to injure, and not merely willful or knowing conduct that leads to an injury. Fenner v. Municipality of Anchorage, 53 P.3d 573, 576-77 (Alaska 2002).

D. Pleading Requirements

In Alaska, a pleading which sets forth a claim for relief "shall contain (1) a short and plain statement of the claim showing that the pleader is entitled to relief, and (2) a demand for judgment for the relief the pleader seeks. Relief in the alternative or of several different types may be demanded." Alaska R. Civ. P. 8(a). In general, pleadings are intended merely to serve as a means of arriving at fair and just settlements of controversies between litigants and should not raise barriers that prevent the achievement of that end. Mitchell v. Land, 355 P.2d 682 (Alaska 1960). Special damages must be specifically stated. Alaska R. Civ. P. 9(h).

SURVEY OF ALASKA EMPLOYMENT PRIVACY LAW

James H. Juliussen
Elizabeth P. Hodes
Davis Wright Tremaine, LLP
701 W. 8th Avenue, Suite 800
Anchorage, Alaska 99501
Telephone: (907) 257-5300; Facsimile: (907) 257-5399

(With Developments Reported Through **November 1, 2012**)

GENERAL COMMENTS

The state of Alaska is divided into four judicial districts. Alaska's judicial system consists of four courts: the Supreme Court, the Court of Appeals, the Superior Court and the District Court. Jurisdiction of the Court of Appeals is limited to criminal matters. The Superior Court is Alaska's trial court of general jurisdiction and sits as an intermediate court of appeals for decisions from District Court and administrative agencies. In civil matters, the jurisdiction of the District Court is, in general, limited to matters involving less than $100,000.00. Alaska courts are likely to follow the restatements of the law in the absence of pertinent Alaska statutory or case law.

Alaska does not follow the "American Rule" concerning the award of attorneys' fees. Rather, under Alaska Civil Rule 82(a)(1), a portion of actual attorneys' fees are awarded to the prevailing party, unless the court, in its discretion, directs otherwise.

SIGNIFICANT DEVELOPMENTS SINCE THE 2012 *SURVEY*

None.

I. GENERAL LAW OF PRIVACY

A. Legal Basis of Privacy Claims

The right to privacy is specifically enumerated in the Alaska Constitution. Alaska Const. art. I, § 22. The Alaska Supreme Court has held, however, that the constitutional right to privacy is a right against government action, not against the actions of private parties. Chizmar v. Mackie, 896 P.2d 196, 206 (Alaska 1995) (citing Luedtke v. Nabors Alaska Drilling, Inc., 768 P.2d 1123, 1130 (Alaska 1989)). The Court has also recognized the existence of a public policy supporting the privacy rights of employees, as well as the common law right to be free from harassment and constant intrusion into one's daily affairs. Luedtke, 768 P.2d at 1131-32, 1137. In general, the common law right of privacy in Alaska mirrors Dean Prosser's approach to the tort or invasion of privacy as adopted by the Restatement (Second) of Torts. Id. at 1127, 1137. Following the Restatement's approach, the Court has commented favorably on four categories of invasion of privacy: (1) intrusion upon the plaintiff's seclusion or solitude, or into his private affairs; (2) public disclosure of embarrassing facts about the plaintiff; (3) publicity which places the plaintiff in a false light in the public eye; and (4) appropriation, for the defendant's advantage, of the plaintiff's name or likeness. Id. at 1127. There are no statutes in Alaska that give rise to a civil cause of action for invasion of privacy.

B. Causes of Action

1. ***Misappropriation/Right of Publicity.*** Although the tort of misappropriation was acknowledged by the Alaska Supreme Court in 1989, no reported cases in Alaska have specifically applied this tort. Luedtke v. Nabors Alaska Drilling, Inc., 768 P.2d 1123, 1127 (Alaska 1989).

2. ***False Light.*** Alaska's Supreme Court has affirmed the Restatement position that a false light claim arises where one publicizes a matter that places another before the public in a false light, and that liability requires at least knowing or reckless disregard of the falsity of the publicized assertion of fact. State v. Carpenter, 171 P.3d 41, 53 (2007) (citing Restatement (Second) of Torts § 652E (1977)). "Because opinions cannot be proved false, they cannot give rise to false light liability." Id. False light invasion of privacy, in contrast to defamation, redresses mental distress from exposure to public view rather than damage to reputation. Id.

3. ***Publication of Private Facts.*** Although the tort of publication of private facts was recognized by the Alaska Supreme Court in 1989, no reported cases in Alaska have specifically applied this tort. Luedtke, 768 P.2d at 1127.

4. ***Intrusion.*** The Alaska Supreme Court has held that "[o]ne who intentionally intrudes . . . upon the solitude or seclusion of another or his private affairs or concerns, is subject to liability . . . if the intrusion would be highly

offensive to a reasonable person." Luedtke, 768 P.2d at 1137. Publication of the facts obtained is not necessary. Id. An "offensive intrusion" in this context requires "either an unreasonable manner of intrusion, or intrusion for an unwarranted purpose." Id. The Supreme Court has also recognized that a person may have a claim for intrusion even if a search was legally undertaken. Wal-Mart, Inc., v. Stewart, 990 P.2d 626, 632 (Alaska 1999).

C. Other Privacy-Related Actions

1. ***Intentional Infliction of Emotional Distress.*** Under Alaska law, there are three elements to a claim for intentional infliction of emotional distress: (1) the defendant's conduct is extreme and outrageous; (2) the conduct is intentional or reckless; and (3) the conduct causes severe emotional distress. Bishop v. Municipality of Anchorage, 899 P.2d 149, 155 (Alaska 1995). Liability will be found "only where the conduct has been so outrageous in character, and so extreme in degree, as to go beyond all possible bounds of decency, and to be regarded as atrocious, and utterly intolerable in a civilized community." Oaksmith v. Brusich, 774 P.2d 191, 199-200 (Alaska 1989) (quoting the Restatement (Second) of Torts § 46 comment d). Although the concept of continuing tort may prevent the running of the statute of limitations on these claims, damages cannot be recovered for harm suffered outside the limitations period. Id. at 199-200. The question of whether a claim for intentional infliction of emotional distress by an employee against an employer is barred by the exclusive remedy provisions of Alaska's workers' compensation statute has not been addressed by the Alaska Supreme Court. However, the Court has recognized the general viability of the claim against an employer if the elements of the tort are met. Finch v. Greatland Foods, 21 P.3d 1282 (Alaska 2001) (wrongful termination and retaliation claim).

2. ***Interference With Prospective Economic Advantage.*** In Alaska, the elements of the tort of intentional interference with prospective economic advantage are (1) the existence of a prospective business relationship between the plaintiff and a third party; (2) knowledge by the defendant of the prospective relationship, and intent to prevent its fruition; (3) conduct by the defendant interfering with the relationship; (4) failure of the prospective relationship to culminate in pecuniary benefit to the plaintiff; (5) causation of the plaintiff's damages by the defendant's conduct; and (6) absence of privilege or justification for the defendant's actions. Hayes v. A.J. Associates, Inc., 960 P.2d 556, 571 (Alaska 1998).

3. ***Prima Facie Tort.*** No reported Alaska cases.

II. EMPLOYER TESTING OF EMPLOYEES

A. Psychological or Personality Testing

1. ***Common Law and Statutes***. No Alaska statutes or reported cases.

2. ***Private Employers.*** No reported Alaska cases.

3. ***Public Employers.*** No reported Alaska cases.

B. Drug Testing

1. ***Common Law and Statutes.*** Alaska statutes permit employers to test employees and prospective employees for the presence of drugs as a condition of hiring or continued employment. Alaska Stat. §§ 23.10.600 – 23.10.699. An employer's ability to conduct drug and alcohol testing is not predicated on compliance with the statute. Alaska Stat. § 23.10.615. However, employers who establish testing policies that comply with the requirements of the statute are provided significant protection from actions by employees. Alaska Stat. § 23.10.600. The statute requires an employer to establish a written policy regarding drug testing and specifies requirements for collecting samples and testing employees. Alaska Stat. §§ 23.10.620, .630, .640. Employees who fail drug tests may be disciplined, up to and including termination. Alaska Stat. § 23.10.655.

2. ***Private Employers.*** In a case that predates Alaska's drug and alcohol testing statute, the Alaska Supreme Court affirmed a private employer's right to require employees to submit to drug testing. Luedtke v. Nabors Alaska Drilling, Inc., 768 P.2d 1123, 1136-1137 (Alaska 1989). Under the Court's analysis in Luedtke, drug testing must be reasonably contemporaneous with the employee's work time (to protect an employee's privacy interest in off-duty conduct) and an employee must receive adequate notice of the employer's adoption of a drug testing program. Id.

3. ***Public Employers***. Public employers are not excluded from the definition of an employer under Alaska statutes that permit testing of employees and prospective employees for the presence of drugs as a condition of hiring or continued employment. See Alaska Stat. § 23.10.699(5). However, random drug testing unsupported by a showing of "special needs" violates state constitutional privacy rights. Police Dept. Employees Assn. v. Municipality of Anchorage, 24 P.3d 547, 559 (Alaska 2001).

C. Medical Testing

1. ***Common Law and Statutes.*** No applicable Alaska statutes or case law exist. However, Alaska employers are subject to the provisions of the Americans With Disabilities Act of 1990, 42 U.S.C. § 12101 et seq. The ADA allows employers to make an offer of employment conditioned on the results of a medical examination. However, such an offer must meet the following requirements: (1) the examination must be given to all entering employees, not just those whom the employer may believe are disabled; (2) the results must be kept confidential; and (3) such an examination may not be used to discriminate against individuals with disabilities, unless the results make the individuals unqualified for the particular job. 42 U.S.C. § 12112 (d)(3). A physical examination includes any kind of medical or psychological test that is done for the purpose of measuring biological condition or response. After a worker is employed, a physical examination can be required only if it is job related and consistent with business necessity. 42 U.S.C. § 12112 (d)(4)(A). Arguably, the Alaska Human Rights Act's prohibitions against employment discrimination on the basis of mental or physical disabilities are broad enough to prohibit discriminatory medical testing. See Alaska Stat. § 18.80.220(a)(1).

2. ***Private Employers.*** No reported Alaska cases.

3. ***Public Employers.*** No reported Alaska cases.

D. Polygraph Tests

Alaska employers are prohibited from requesting, suggesting or requiring that an employee submit to a polygraph as a condition of employment. Alaska Stat. § 23.10.037(a). The prohibition is not applicable to employment of police officers by public employers. Alaska Stat. § 23.10.037(b).

E. Fingerprinting

No Alaska statute prohibits employers from fingerprinting employees. Certain employees, including health care workers who provide services to vulnerable individuals, are required to submit fingerprints for purposes of criminal background checks. See Alaska Stat. § 47.05.310(e).

III. SEARCHES

The only Alaska cases dealing with searches stem from criminal matters. In general, those cases interpret the scope of the constitutional prohibition against unreasonable searches and seizures. See, e.g., Cowles v. State, 961 P. 2d 438, 442 (Alaska Ct. App. 1998), aff'd 23 P.3d 1168 (Alaska 2001). Pursuant to constitutional provisions, a person is protected from unreasonable government intrusion whenever (1) the person manifests a subjective expectation of privacy in the property or activity being subjected to government scrutiny, and (2) that expectation of privacy is one that society recognizes as reasonable. Id.

A. Employee's Person

1. ***Private Employers.*** No reported Alaska cases.

2. ***Public Employers.*** No reported Alaska cases.

B. Employee's Work Area

In Cowles, the Alaska Court of Appeals ruled that a public employee did not have a reasonable expectation of privacy in her work area that precluded use of a concealed video camera. 961 P.2d at 444. The court's conclusion stemmed from the fact that the work area was readily observable by any member of the public who visited the area, and that the employee, who was suspected of theft, worked in a fiduciary capacity in an office where members of the public exchanged cash for theater tickets: "[B]ased upon the open and public nature of the place where Cowles worked, and the fiduciary nature of the work she was doing, we conclude that Cowles did not have a reasonable expectation of privacy from video surveillance in the box office." Id. There are no reported Alaska cases involving a private employer's search of an employee's work area.

C. Employee's Property

1. ***Private Employers.*** No reported Alaska cases.

2. ***Public Employers.*** No reported Alaska cases. But see, Smith v. State Dept. of Transportation, 253 P.3d 1233 (Alaska 2011) (employer did not breach covenant of good faith and fair dealing implied in Alaska employment contracts when it discharged employee for theft and dishonesty relating to disappearance of fuel and fuel tank after employee refused to allow employer to test fuel to determine whether it was the fuel stolen from employer).

IV. MONITORING OF EMPLOYEES

A. Telephones and Electronic Communications

1. ***Wiretapping.*** Alaska statutes prohibit persons from using "an eavesdropping device to hear or record all or any part of an oral conversation without the consent of a party to the conversation." Alaska Stat. § 42.20.310(a). Eavesdropping devices include "any device capable of being used to hear or record oral conversation whether the conversation is conducted in person, by telephone, or by any other means." Alaska Stat. § 42.20.310(b). The statute exempts reception of conversations broadcast by radio, overheard by publicly made "radio communications of any sort" and conversations of employees of a "common carrier by wire incidental to the normal course of their employment." Alaska Stat. § 42.20.320(a).

2. ***Electronic Communications.*** As discussed above, a person may not intercept an oral communication without the consent of one of the parties to the communication. Alaska Stat. § 42.20.310(a). No Alaska statutes specifically prohibit interception of other electronic communications.

3. ***Other Electronic Monitoring.*** No reported Alaska cases.

B. Mail

Alaska statutes prohibit persons from opening sealed mail not addressed to the person unless the person was authorized to do so either by the writer or by the person to whom it was addressed. Alaska Stat. § 11.76.120.

C. Surveillance/Photographing

As discussed above, in Cowles v. State, 961 P.2d 438, 444 (Alaska Ct. App. 1998), the Alaska Court of Appeals ruled that a public employee did not have a reasonable expectation of privacy in her work area that precluded use of a concealed video camera. The court's conclusion stemmed from the fact that the work area was readily observable by any member of the public who visited the area, and that the employee, who was suspected of theft, worked in a fiduciary capacity in an office where members of the public exchanged cash for theater tickets: "[B]ased upon the open and public nature of the place where Cowles worked, and the fiduciary nature of the work she was doing, we conclude that Cowles did not have a reasonable expectation of privacy from video surveillance in the box office." Id. There are no reported Alaska cases involving the use of video or still cameras by private employers.

V. ACTIVITIES OUTSIDE THE WORKPLACE

A. Statute or Common Law

Employer constraints on the off-duty conduct of employees has been addressed by the Alaska Supreme Court on at least two occasions. In Conway, Inc. v. Ross, 627 P.2d 1029, 1030-32 (Alaska 1981), the Court held that a topless dancer who engaged in an off-premises act of prostitution was wrongfully terminated by her employer. In the view of the Court, the employee's off-duty activities did not warrant discipline by the employer because:

> Ross's prostitution was unrelated to Conway's business. She did not solicit any of [Conway's] customers. Her single act of prostitution involved a gentleman she met apart from [Conway's business]. Ross's encounter with this gentleman occurred at her own premises and during the hours she was not working for Conway. In short, there was nothing to connect Ross's act of prostitution with her employment [as a topless dancer] at [Conway's business].

Id. at 1030-31.

Later, in Luedtke v. Nabors Alaska Drilling, Inc., the Court restated the proposition that an employer's right to control the off-duty conduct of its employees is predicated on the existence of a sufficient nexus between the off-duty conduct and the workplace:

> Where the public policy supporting the Luedtkes privacy in off-duty activities conflicts with the public policy supporting the health and safety of other workers, and even the Luedtkes themselves, the health and safety concerns are paramount. As a result, [the employer] is justified in determining whether the Luedtkes are impaired on the job by drug usage off the job.

Luedtke v. Nabors Alaska Drilling, Inc., 768 P.2d 1123, 1136 (Alaska 1989).

In Police Dept. Employees Assn. v. Municipality of Anchorage, 24 P.3d 547, 569-70 (Alaska 2001), the Court recognized that the nature of the duties of some public employees, such as police officers and firefighters, may give rise to a diminished expectation of privacy with regard to their off-duty activities.

B. Employees' Personal Relationships

1. ***Romantic Relationships Between Employees.*** No reported Alaska cases.

2. ***Sexual Orientation.*** No reported Alaska cases address private employers. In Alaska Civil Liberties Union v. State, 122 P.3d 781 (Alaska 2005), Alaska's Supreme Court held that spousal limitations in public employers' benefit plans were unconstitutional as applied to public employees with same-sex domestic partners. By restricting the availability of benefits to "spouses," the benefits programs were deemed to discriminate against same-sex couples (who are barred by law from marrying in Alaska or having any marriage performed elsewhere recognized in Alaska) in violation of the equal protection clause of Alaska's Constitution. Id. at 788–94.

3. ***Marital Status.*** The Alaska Human Rights Act prohibits employers from discriminating against employees or potential employees on the basis of marital status. Alaska Stat. § 18.80.220(a)(1). The statutory prohibition against marital status discrimination does not prevent employers from establishing anti-nepotism policies because the statutory definition of marital status was not intended to include the identity of one's spouse. Muller v. BP Exploration Inc., 923 P.2d 783, 791 (Alaska 1996). A denial of benefits to the dependents of unmarried employees that are available to the dependents of married employees does constitute discrimination on the basis of marital status, however. University of Alaska v. Tumeo, 933 P.2d 1147, 1156 (Alaska 1997). The Alaska legislature amended the Alaska Human Rights Act to permit employers to provide greater health and retirement benefits to employees who have a spouse or dependent children than are provided to other employees. Alaska Stat. § 18.80.220(c)(1).

C. Smoking

No Alaska statutes or reported cases specifically address the right of employers to prohibit employees from smoking outside the workplace. By statute, however, smoking is prohibited in many vehicles and indoor facilities, including vehicles of public transportation, buildings or other facilities owned, leased or operated by a public entity, schools and day care centers, courthouses, health facilities, food service establishments with seating capacities of 50 persons or more, grocery stores, and any "place of employment in which the owner, manager, proprietor, or other person who has control of the premises posts a sign stating that smoking is prohibited by law." Alaska Stat. § 18.35.300. Limited exceptions exist for designated smoking sections. Alaska Stat. §§ 18.35.310, .320.

D. Blogging

No reported Alaska cases address employee blogging, either at the request of the employer or at the employee's own initiative.

VI. RECORDS

A. Personnel Records

Alaska law requires employers to grant employees access to employment files. Alaska Stat. § 23.10.430. The statute requires access to the employee's "personnel file and other personnel information maintained by the employer concerning the employee." Id. Other Alaska statutes mandate that employers keep accurate records of employees' names, addresses, occupations, daily and weekly hours worked, and of the wages paid to each employee. Alaska Stat. § 23.05.080. Such records must be maintained for a period of at least three years. Id.

Under the Alaska Public Records Act, certain public employee information is available for public review. Alaska Stat. § 39.25.080(a). However, only basic information about the employee is considered public record, such as "position titles," "dates of appointment and separation," and "compensation authorized," while "employment applications" and "examination materials" of employees are exempted. Alaska Stat. § 39.25.080(a-b); see also Alaska Wildlife Alliance v. Rue, 948 P.2d 976 (Alaska 1997) (finding that timesheets of public employees were not subject to confidentiality provisions of Public Records Act).

Personnel records of police officers have been subject to *in camera* review and disclosure in litigation against officers and the State and in criminal proceedings, despite the officer's legitimate expectation of privacy, where the records are relevant the disclosure will occur in a manner which is least intrusive with respect to the officer's right to confidentiality. Jones v. Jennings, 788 P.2d 732 (Alaska 1990); Booth v. State, 251 P.3d 369 (Alaska App. 2011).

B. Medical Records

No Alaska statutes or reported cases address an employer's obligation to maintain confidentiality with respect to employees' medical records. Alaska employers are required to maintain the confidentiality of their employee's medical records under federal law. See, e.g., 42 U.S.C. § 12112(d)(3)(B) (ADA requires that employers maintain the confidentiality of an applicant's or employee's occupational injury or workers' compensation claim). Employers with drug and alcohol testing programs that comply with Alaska's drug testing statutes must maintain confidentiality with respect to records pertaining to the results of drug and alcohol tests. Alaska Stat. § 23.10.660.

C. Criminal Records

No Alaska statutes or reported cases address an employer's obligation to maintain confidentiality with respect to employees' criminal records.

D. Subpoenas / Search Warrants

No Alaska statutes or reported cases address an employer's obligation to maintain confidentiality in responding to subpoenas or search warrants. **But see Peterson v. State, 280 P.3d 559 (Alaska 2012) (recognizing union-relations privilege under Public Employee Relations Act, preventing employer from discovering in litigation with former employee information about communications between an employee (or the employee's attorney) and union representatives made in confidence, in connection with representative services relating to anticipated or ongoing disciplinary or grievance proceedings, and by union representatives acting in official representative capacity).**

VII. ACTIONS SUBSEQUENT TO EMPLOYMENT

A. References

Employers are protected by statute from liability for good faith disclosure of information about an employee's or former employee's job performance to a prospective employer where such information is provided at the request of the prospective employer or the employee. Alaska Stat. § 09.65.160. Under the statute, an employer is presumed to have been acting in good faith, and the presumption can be rebutted only by showing by a preponderance of the evidence that the employer (1) recklessly, knowingly, or maliciously disclosed false or deliberately misleading information; or (2) disclosed information in violation of a civil right to the employee that is protected under Alaska Stat. § 18.80 (which prohibits discrimination in employment) or under comparable federal law. **However, an employer may waive immunity under the statute by promising that it will not disclose information about an employee to prospective employers. Boyko v. Anchorage School Dist., 268 P.3d 1097 (Alaska 2012) (genuine issue of material fact whether employer statements and resignation agreement waived School District's protection under AS 09.65.160).**

B. Non-Compete Agreements

Non-compete agreements are strictly construed in Alaska because they are generally disfavored as restraints on trade, and because they impose hardships upon individuals seeking to make a living. DeCristofaro v. Security National Bank, 664 P.2d 167 (Alaska 1983). Non-compete agreements that are ancillary to employment contracts are typically viewed with more scrutiny than those ancillary to the sale of a business because employment contracts are often the product of unequal bargaining power. Wenzell v. Ingrim, 228 P.3d 103, 110 (Alaska 2010). Alaska courts consider the following factors in evaluating a non-compete agreement: (1) the absence or presence of limitations as to time and space; (2) whether the employee represents the sole contact with the customer; (3) whether the employee possesses confidential information or trade secrets; (4) whether the covenant seeks to eliminate competition which would be unfair to the employer or merely seeks to eliminate ordinary competition; (5) whether the covenant seeks to stifle the inherent skill and experience of the employee; (6) whether the benefit to the employer is disproportional to the detriment to the employee; (7) whether the covenant operates as a bar to the employee's sole means of support; (8) whether the employee's talent which the employer seeks to suppress was actually developed during the period of employment; and (9) whether the forbidden employment is merely incidental to the main employment. Data Management, Inc. v. Greene, 757 P.2d 62 (Alaska 1988).

A clause restricting a person from performing services for two years for clients of a former employer was neither unreasonably restrictive nor a violation of public policy in Wirum & Cash, Architects v. Cash, 837 P.2d 692 (Alaska 1992). Even overreaching covenants not to compete may be enforceable in part if the covenant can reasonably be reformed to comply with the intent of the parties. Data Management, 757 P.2d at 65. An employer bears the burden of proving the covenant was drafted in good faith before a court will reform an overbroad covenant. Id.

A non-compete agreement may be void for public policy reasons "if it unreasonably restrains trade, either because: (a) the restraint is greater than is needed to protect the promisee's legitimate interest, or (b) the promisee's need is outweighed by the hardship to the promisor and the likely injury to the public." Wenzell, 228 P.3d at 110 (citing Restatement (Second) on Contracts §§ 186, 188). An agreement restraining the activities of a dentist should be more closely scrutinized and may be void for public policy reasons because of the importance to the community of the particular services provided. Id. at 111 (dentist subject to non-compete was working for an organization "providing an important, low-cost service to a population in need of such care.") (citing Richard A. Lord, 6 Williston on Contracts § 13:6 (4th ed. 2009)).

The standard measure of damages for breach of a non-compete agreement is the lost profits of the party asserting the breach. National Bank of Alaska v. J.B.L. & K. of Alaska, Inc., 546 P.2d 579 (Alaska 1976).

VIII. OTHER ISSUES

A. Statutes of Limitations

In Alaska, the statute of limitations for torts and personal injury actions is two years. Alaska Stat. § 09.10.070.

B. Jurisdiction

The superior courts have jurisdiction over all civil matters within the state, Alaska Stat. § 22.10.020; see id. § 09.05.010. Apparently there are no geographic restrictions on where an action may be brought within the state apart from those in Alaska R. Civ. P. 3, but venue may be changed to serve the convenience of witness and the ends of justice. Alaska Stat. § 22.10.040. Jurisdiction over nonresidents is authorized under Alaska's long-arm statute, Alaska Stat. § 09.05.015.

C. Workers' Compensation Exclusivity

The exclusive remedy provision of Alaska's Workers' Compensation Act bars any claim against an employer or fellow employee for injuries arising out of and during the course of employment. Alaska Stat. § 23.30.055; Gordon v. Burgess Construction Co., 425 P.2d 602, 605 (Alaska 1967) ("The remedies provided by a workmen's compensation act are intended to be in lieu of all rights and remedies as to a particular injury whether at common law or otherwise."). However, the exclusivity provision does not bar claims for intentional torts. Elliot v. Brown, 569 P.2d 1323, 1327 (Alaska 1977); Van Biene v. ERA Helicopters, 779 P.2d 315, 318-19 (Alaska 1989). The intentional tort exception will only apply if a plaintiff can establish specific intent to injure, and not merely willful or knowing conduct that leads to an injury. Fenner v. Municipality of Anchorage, 53 P.3d 573, 576-77 (Alaska 2002).

D. Pleading Requirements

In Alaska, a pleading which sets forth a claim for relief "shall contain (1) a short and plain statement of the claim showing that the pleader is entitled to relief, and (2) a demand for judgment for the relief the pleader seeks. Relief in the alternative or of several different types may be demanded." Alaska R. Civ. P. 8(a). In general, pleadings are intended merely to serve as a means of arriving at fair and just settlements of controversies between litigants and should not raise barriers which prevent the achievement of that end. Mitchell v. Land, 355 P.2d 682, 687 (Alaska 1960). Special damages must be specifically stated. Alaska R. Civ. P. 9(h).

In cases where punitive damages are allowed, a separate proceeding must be conducted to determine the amount of such damages. Alaska Stat. § 09.17.020(a). In order for punitive damages to be awarded, the plaintiff must prove by clear and convincing evidence the defendant's conduct was (1) outrageous, including acts done with malice or bad motives; or (2) evidenced reckless indifference to the interests of another person. Alaska Stat. § 09.17.020(b). In general, punitive damages are capped at the greater of three times the amount of compensatory damages or $500,000, unless the trier of fact finds that the defendant's conduct was motivated by financial gain and the consequences of the conduct were actually known by the defendant, in which case, punitive damages are capped at the greater of four times the amount of compensatory damages, four times the aggregate amount of the financial gain that the defendant received as a result of the conduct, or the sum of $7,000,000. Alaska Stat. § 09.17.020(f), (g). In actions against employers for violations of the Alaska Human Rights Act, punitive damages are limited to an amount between $200,000 and $500,000, depending on the number of employees the employer has in Alaska. Alaska Stat. § 09.17.020(h). Fifty percent of all punitive damage awards must be deposited into the general fund of the state. Alaska Stat. § 09.17.020(j). Where damages are based on an employer's vicarious liability for the act of its employee, punitive damages may not be awarded against the employer unless the employer or employer's managerial agent (A) authorized the act or omission and the manner in which it was performed or occurred; or (B) ratified or approved the act or omission after it occurred; or (2) the employee was (A) unfit to perform the act or avoid the omission and the employer or the employer's managerial agent acted recklessly in employing or retaining the employee; or (B) was employed in a managerial capacity and was acting within the scope of employment. Alaska Stat. § 09.17.020(k).

SURVEY OF ARIZONA EMPLOYMENT LIBEL LAW

Daniel C. Barr and Jill L. Ripke
Perkins Coie LLP
2901 North Central Avenue
Phoenix, Arizona 85012
Telephone: (602) 351-8000; Fax (602) 648-7085
Email: dbarr@perkinscoie.com; jripke@perkinscoie.com

(With Developments Reported Through **November 1, 2012**)

GENERAL COMMENTS

None.

SIGNIFICANT DEVELOPMENTS SINCE THE 2012 *SURVEY*

None

I. GENERAL LAW

A. General Employment Law

1. ***At Will Employment.*** Employment is at will and therefore severable at the pleasure of either party absent a written contract to the contrary. Employment handbooks or manuals are contractual only if expressly so stated. A writing signed by the employer alone qualifies as a contract. A.R.S. § 23-1501(2). An employee's partial performance is not sufficient to avoid the requirement of a written contract. See id. Employees may sue for wrongful discharge in violation of public policy, but only for those policies that arise out of the Arizona Constitution or state statutes. Thirteen statutes presently provide a basis for a wrongful termination claim. A.R.S. § 23-1501(3)(b), (c); see generally Jenny Clevenger, Comment, Arizona's Employment Protection Act: Drawing a Line in the Sand Between the Court and the Legislature, 29 ARIZ. ST. L.J. 605 (1997).

2. ***Legislative Exceptions to the "At Will" Doctrine.*** Prior to the Arizona Legislature's 1996 enactment of the Employment Protection Act (the "Act"), A.R.S. § 23-1501, policies in an employee handbook or manual that impliedly promised job security, such as disciplinary procedures, presumptively altered the at-will relationship between an employee and employer, although an employer could overcome that presumption with an appropriate disclaimer in the handbook or manual. The Act, however, provides that an employment handbook or manual is not an implied contract, and does not alter the at will relationship, unless the "document expresses the intent that it is a contract of employment."

The Act also imposes two important restrictions on the tort action for wrongful discharge in violation of public policy, which is an exception to the "at will" doctrine. First, the public policy on which a terminated employee relies must be found in an Arizona statute or the Arizona Constitution. See Galati v. America West Airlines, Inc., 205 Ariz. 290, 69 P.3d 1011 (Ct. App. 2003) (Federal regulations cannot form basis of wrongful termination claim). Second, where the statute itself provides remedies for its violation, those remedies (including damages provisions) are exclusive. This second portion of the Act survived a constitutional challenge in Cronin v. Sheldon, 195 Ariz. 531, 542, 991 P.2d 231, 242 (1999).

3. ***Judicially-Made Exceptions to the "At Will" Doctrine.*** In Demasse v. ITT Corp., 194 Ariz. 500, 506-07, 984 P.2d 1138, 1144-45 (1999), the Arizona Supreme Court considered whether an employer may unilaterally change a policy in an employee handbook given that the policy has become an implied-in-fact contract as a result of the employee's legitimate expectations and reliance on the policy. The Demasse court concluded that an employer cannot unilaterally modify and thus negate the effect of implied-in-fact contractual terms. Modification of the terms of implied-in-fact contracts are governed by traditional contract law principles, which require assent and consideration to the offer of modification. Continued employment alone will not suffice as consideration.

In North Valley Emergency Specialists v. Superior Court, 208 Ariz. 301, 93 P.3d 501 (2004), the Arizona Supreme Court held that mandatory arbitration agreements between employers and employees are unenforceable under the Arizona Uniform Arbitration Act, A.R.S. § 2-1517.

In Leikvold v. Valley View Community Hospital, 141 Ariz. 544, 548, 688 P.2d 170, 174 (1984), the Arizona Supreme Court recognized that an employer's promises, policies, and practices that create a reasonable expectation of job security among employees constitute implied-in-fact employment contracts. The court in Leikvold held that whether an implied-in-fact contract exists is a jury question.

In Vermillion v. AAA Pro Moving & Storage, 146 Ariz. 215, 216, 704 P.2d 1360, 1361 (Ct. App. 1985), an Arizona court first recognized the public policy exception to the at will doctrine. In Wagenseller v. Scottsdale Memorial Hospital, 147 Ariz. 370, 378-79, 710 P.2d 1025, 1033-34 (1985), the Arizona Supreme Court reaffirmed Vermillion and held that judicial decisions, in addition to Arizona's statutes and constitution, were sources of public policy. In 1996, however, the Arizona Legislature enacted the Employment Protection Act, which expressly abrogated Wagenseller's holding that judicial decisions were sources of public policy.

In Mullenaux v. Graham County, 207 Ariz. 1, 82 P.3d 362 (Ct. App. 2004), the Arizona Court of Appeals held that the Arizona Employment Protection Act, A.R.S. § 23-1501, applies to public, as well as private, employers. The Court further held that a classified public employee must exhaust his or her administrative remedies under A.R.S. § 11-351 through 11-356 before filing an action for breach of contract and wrongful discharge.

B. Elements of Defamation Claim

1. ***Basic Elements.*** Defamation consists of (1) a false and (2) defamatory statement, (3) published to a third party, (4) that impeached the plaintiff's honesty, integrity, virtue, or reputation. See Turner v. Devlin, 174 Ariz. 201, 203-04, 848 P.2d 286, 288-89 (1993); Phoenix Newspapers, Inc. v. Church, 103 Ariz. 582, 596-97, 447 P.2d 840, 854-55 (1968).

2. ***Fault.*** The plaintiff's burden regarding the level of fault depends on whether the plaintiff is a public or a private figure, and on whether the allegedly defamatory statement refers to a public or a private matter.

a. **Private Figure Plaintiff/Matter of Public Concern.** Plaintiff must show that the defendant acted with (1) knowledge that the statement was false and defamatory, (2) reckless disregard regarding whether the statement was false and defamatory, or (3) negligent failure to determine whether the statement was false and defamatory. See Dombey v. Phoenix Newspapers, Inc., 150 Ariz. 476, 481, 724 P.2d 562, 567 (1986).

b. **Private Figure Plaintiff/Matter of Private Concern.** Same as for private figure plaintiff/matter of public concern. See Peagler v. Phoenix Newspapers, Inc., 114 Ariz. 309, 315, 560 P.2d 1216, 1222 (1977).

c. **Public Figure Plaintiff/Matter of Public Concern.** Plaintiff must show that the defendant acted with actual malice. See Scottsdale Publ., Inc. v. Superior Ct., 159 Ariz. 72, 75, 764 P.2d 1131, 1134 (Ct. App. 1988). Actual malice consists of reckless disregard for the truth or actual knowledge of falsity. See id. Arizona courts have held the following categories of persons to be public figures: (1) student senators, see Klahr v. Winterble, 4 Ariz. App. 158, 166, 418 P.2d 404, 412 (1966); (2) police officers, see Rosales v. City of Eloy, 122 Ariz. 134, 135, 593 P.2d 688, 689 (Ct. App. 1979); (3) teachers, see Sewell v. Brookbank, 119 Ariz. 422, 425, 581 P.2d 267, 270 (Ct. App. 1978); (4) narcotics agents, see Hansen v. Stoll, 130 Ariz. 454, 457, 636 P.2d 1236, 1239 (Ct. App. 1981); (5) county sheriffs, see Godbehere v. Phoenix Newspapers, Inc., 162 Ariz. 335, 344, 783 P.2d 781, 790 (1989); and (6) inspectors of the Federal Aviation Administration, see Lewis v. Oliver, 178 Ariz. 330, 336-37, 873 P.2d 668, 674-75 (Ct. App. 1993).

3. ***Falsity.*** Where the plaintiff is a public figure, he bears the burden of proving with convincing clarity that the defendant acted with knowledge of falsity or in reckless disregard of the truth. Phoenix Newspapers, Inc. v. Church, 103 Ariz. 582, 591-92, 447 P.2d 840, 849-50 (1968).

4. ***Defamatory Statement of Fact.*** Only statements that reasonably appear to be factual are actionable. Courts must determine from a statement's general tenor whether it states or implies an assertion of objective fact, or was merely figurative or hyperbolic. "The key inquiry is whether the challenged expression, however labeled by defendant, would reasonably appear to state or imply assertions of objective fact." Yetman v. English, 168 Ariz. 71, 76, 811 P.2d 323, 328 (1991) (quoting Immuno A.G. v. Moor-Jankowski, 77 N.Y.2d 235, 243, 566 N.Y.S.2d 906, 909, 567 N.E.2d 1270, 1273 (1991)).

5. ***Of and Concerning Plaintiff.*** Plaintiff must show that the statement was about him or her. While the individual need not be named, the plaintiff must show that the publication was "of and concerning" him. Hansen v. Stoll, 130 Ariz. 454, 458, 636 P.2d 1236, 1240 (Ct. App. 1981).

6. ***Publication.*** Plaintiff must show that some other person heard or read the allegedly defamatory statement. See Lally v. Cash, 18 Ariz. 574, 582, 164 P. 443, 446 (1917).

a. **Intracorporate Communication.** In Dube v. Likins, 216 Ariz. 406, 167 P.3d 93 (Ct. App. 2007), the Arizona Court of Appeals adopted Restatement (Second) of Torts § 577 cmt. i, which states, "A communication within the scope of his employment by one agent to another agent of the same principal is a publication ... and this is true whether the principal is an individual, a partnership or a corporation." This means that when there is a communication between two agents of the same principal, a publication has occurred for defamation purposes. The defamation claim, however, may be subject to a qualified privilege. Id. at *11.

b. **Compelled Self-Publication.** No Arizona court has recognized a defamation tort based on compelled self-publication, and a federal district court in Arizona predicted that Arizona courts would not do so. See Spratt v. N. Auto. Corp., 958 F. Supp. 456, 465 (D. Ariz. 1996). But see Ashway v. Ferrellgas Inc., 59 Fair Empl. Prac. Cas. (BNA) 375, 379 n.12 (D. Ariz. 1989) (suggesting in dictum that a discharged employee's "foreseeable compelled self-publications" can constitute sufficient publication to give rise to employment defamation claims), aff'd in part, rev'd in part, 945 F.2d 408 (9th Cir. 1991). The court in Spratt reasoned that Arizona will follow the Restatement (Second) of Torts § 577 cmt.m, which provides that "there is no defamation where the defamed person is the recipient of the communication and then publishes it to a third person." 958 F. Supp. at 465.

c. **Republication.** The court in Peagler v. Phoenix Newspapers, Inc., 131 Ariz. 308, 312, 640 P.2d 1110, 1114 (Ct. App. 1981), held that liability for republication must be predicated on some fault or neglect of the republisher. The court also held that "story balance" is not a substitute for the exercise of due care. The court upheld the following jury instruction: "Repetition of another's words does not release one of responsibility if the repeater knows that the words are false or inherently improbable, or there are obvious reasons to doubt the veracity of the person quoted or the accuracy of his reports." 131 Ariz. at 310, 640 P.2d at 1112. In Chilton v. Center for Biological Diversity, Inc., 214 Ariz. 47, 148 P.3d 91, 97 (Ct. App. 2006), the Court of Appeals found that the defendants had not supported their position that republishing material on a website that had previously been submitted to the U.S. Forest Service was subject to an absolute or qualified privilege.

7. ***Statements versus Conduct.*** No pertinent Arizona cases.

8. ***Damages.*** General damages refer to "damages for loss of reputation." A.R.S. § 12-653.01(3). Special damages relate to the plaintiff's "property, business, trade, profession, or occupation." Id. § 12-653.01(5). Plaintiffs must plead special damages unless they allege that the defendant's communication was defamatory per se. See Berg v. Hohenstein, 13 Ariz. App. 583, 586, 479 P.2d 730, 733 (1971). The court or jury in its discretion may award punitive damages if the plaintiff proves actual malice. See Dombey v. Phoenix Newspapers, Inc., 150 Ariz. 476, 481, 724 P.2d 562, 567 (1986).

a. **Presumed Damages and Defamation Per Se.** Statements that are defamatory per se are "actionable without proof of special damages because damages are presumed." See Peagler v. Phoenix Newspapers, Inc., 114 Ariz. 309, 316, 560 P.2d 1216, 1223 (1977) (holding that publication charging auto dealership with "highly questionable sales methods" was defamatory per se); Broking v. Phoenix Newspapers, Inc., 76 Ariz. 334, 337-38, 264 P.2d 413, 415 (1953) (holding that publication charging that individual committed crime was defamatory per se); Modla v. Parker, 17 Ariz. App. 54, 56 n.1, 495 P.2d 494, 496 n.1 (1972) (stating in dictum that words charging that individual has contagious or venereal disease were defamatory per se). But cf. Berg v. Hohenstein, 13 Ariz. App. 583, 586, 479 P.2d 730, 733 (1971) (holding that former salesman's publication that he was no longer responsible for making good on real estate broker's representations regarding lots was not defamatory per se); MacConnell v. Mitten, 131 Ariz. 22, 25, 638 P.2d 689, 692 (1981) (holding that employer's statement that it terminated employee who managed collection facility because the facility had been losing money was not defamatory per se). Courts look to the language alone to determine whether a statement is defamatory per se because such statements do not require innuendo. See Phoenix Newspapers, Inc. v. Church, 103 Ariz. 582, 587, 447 P.2d 840, 845 (1968).

(1) **Employment-Related Criticism.** "An utterance is slander per se when . . . [it] tends to injure a person in his profession, trade or business ... ." Modla v. Parker, 17 Ariz. App. 54, 56 n.1, 495 P.2d 494, 496 n.1 (1972).

(2) **Single Instance Rule.** No pertinent Arizona cases.

b. **Punitive Damages.** Arizona courts have put forth two overlapping standards regarding punitive damages in defamation cases. In Dombey v. Phoenix Newspapers, Inc., 150 Ariz. 476, 481, 724 P.2d 562, 567 (1986), the court held that a plaintiff must show that the defamer acted with actual malice. A plaintiff satisfies the actual malice standard by proving that the defendant "entertained serious doubts as to the truth of his publication." Scottsdale Publ., Inc. v. Superior Ct., 159 Ariz. 72, 82 n.7, 764 P.2d 1131, 1141 n.7 (Ct. App. 1988) (quoting St. Amant v. Thompson, 390 U.S. 727, 731 (1968)). The court in Linthicum v. Nationwide Life Insurance Co., 150 Ariz. 326, 330-31, 723 P.2d 675, 679-80 (1986), held that punitive damages were warranted if the plaintiff showed that the defamer acted with an "evil mind." A plaintiff may establish an "evil mind" by proving that the defendant "consciously pursued a course of conduct knowing that it created a substantial risk of significant harm to others." Gurule v. Illinois Mut. Life & Cas. Co., 152 Ariz. 600, 602, 734 P.2d 85, 87 (1987) (quoting Rawlings v. Apodaca, 151 Ariz. 149, 162, 726 P.2d 565, 578 (1986)). The court later explained in dictum that these two standards may be indistinct, and that at the least they considerably overlap. See Scottsdale Publ., 159 Ariz. at 82 n.7, 764 P.2d at 1141 n.7.

No actual malice is required in order to sustain an award of punitive or presumed damages in cases brought by a private plaintiff where no matter of public concern is involved. Hirsch v. Cooper 153 Ariz. 454, 457, 737 P.2d 1092, 1095 (Ct. App. 1986).

II. PRIVILEGES AND DEFENSES

A. Scope of Privileges

1. ***Absolute Privilege.*** Whether an absolute privilege exists is a question for the court. See Darragh v. Superior Ct., 183 Ariz. 79, 81, 900 P.2d 1215, 1217 (Ct. App. 1995). In general, an absolute privilege arises in the context of judicial proceedings, legislative proceedings, and administrative or executive functions of the government. See Ross v. Duke, 116 Ariz. 298, 301, 569 P.2d 240, 243 (Ct. App. 1976). Absolute privileges recognized in Arizona include: (1) statements made by legislators in the context of legislative proceedings, see Sanchez v. Coxon, 175 Ariz. 93, 95-97, 854 P.2d 126, 128-30 (1993); (2) statements by a public official while performing an act in the course of his official duty that he is specifically directed by law to perform, see Wyatt v. Ruck Constr., Inc., 117 Ariz. 186, 190, 571 P.2d 683, 687 (Ct. App. 1977); (3) statements made in judicial pleadings if connected with or related to subject of the inquiry, Drummond v. Stahl, 127 Ariz. 122, 125-26, 618 P.2d 616, 619-20 (Ct. App. 1980); (4) testimony of witnesses at judicial proceedings, Todd v. Cox, 20 Ariz. App. 347, 359-60, 512 P.2d 1234, 1236-37 (1973), including witness statements made in a private contractual arbitration proceeding. Yeung v. Maric, 224 Ariz. 499, 232 P.3d 1281 (Ct. App. 2010); (5) statements relating to a pending judicial proceeding made to persons with a direct interest in the litigation or who possess evidentiary information directly relevant to it, see Johnson v. McDonald, 197 Ariz. 155, 159-60, 3 P.3d 1075, 1079-80 (Ct. App. 1999); Hall v. Smith, 214 Ariz. 309, 152 P.3d 1192 (Ct. App. 2007) (absolute immunity applies to communications with non-parties who have a sufficiently close or direct relationship to the judicial proceeding); (6) complaints filed with the State Bar of Arizona, see Ashton-Blair v. Merrill, 187 Ariz. 315, 317, 928 P.2d 1244, 1246 (Ct. App. 1996); (7) information contained in a personnel file that is shared with the E.E.O.C. during an investigation of a charge of discrimination, see Paros v. Hoemako Hosp., 140 Ariz. 335, 337, 681 P.2d 918, 921 (Ct. App. 1984); (8) complaints filed with the Board of Legal Document Preparers, see Sobol v. Marsh, 212 Ariz. 301, 130 P.3d 1000, 1003 (Ct. App. 2006); Sobol v. Alarcon, 212 Ariz. 315, 131 P.3d 487, 490 (Ct. App. 2006); and (9) putative crime victims are entitled to absolute immunity when they file complaints with the police, see Ledvina v. Cerasani, 213 Ariz. 569, 575, 146 P.3d 70, 76 (Ct. App. 2006).

2. ***Qualified Privilege.*** In general, a defendant's communication is qualifiedly privileged if he was under some obligation to speak. See Green Acres Trust v. London, 141 Ariz. 609, 616, 688 P.2d 617, 624 (1984). A statement subject to a qualified privilege is immune from liability unless plaintiff proves that the defendant abused the privilege through actual malice or excessive publication. See id.

a. **Common Interest.** Statements made to others on a matter of common interest are qualifiedly privileged. See Hirsch v. Cooper, 153 Ariz. 454, 458, 737 P.2d 1092, 1096 (Ct. App. 1986). Statements made in editorials published in the "public interest," including "caustic criticism and biting ridicule," are qualifiedly privileged. See Klahr v. Winterble, 4 Ariz. App. 158, 168-70, 418 P.2d 404, 414-16 (1966). In the employment context, an employee's statements to her employer reporting sexual harassment are qualifiedly privileged. Miller v. Servicemaster by Rees, 174 Ariz. 518, 520, 851 P.2d 143, 145 (Ct. App. 1992).

b. **Duty.** Statements made pursuant to a duty are qualifiedly privileged. See Chamberlain v. Mathis, 151 Ariz. 551, 558, 729 P.2d 905, 912 (1986) (statements made by high-level executive government officials within the scope of their duties); Carlson v. Pima County, 141 Ariz. 487, 491-92, 687 P.2d 1242, 1246-47 (1984) (statements required by law to be contained in public records); Lewis v. Oliver, 178 Ariz. 330, 334-35, 873 P.2d 668, 672-73 (Ct. App. 1993) (communications made to public officials concerning matters that affect the discharge of their duties); Aspell v. American Contract Bridge League, 122 Ariz. 399, 400-01, 595 P.2d 191, 192-93 (Ct. App. 1979) (statements made pursuant to a legal, moral, or social duty); Ross v. Duke, 116 Ariz. 298, 301-02, 569 P.2d 240, 243-44 (Ct. App. 1976) (publication of documents by union official acting pursuant to official duties); Goddard v. Fields, 214 Ariz. 175, 150 P.3d 262, 267 (Ct. App. 2007) (statements made to the press by the Attorney General).

c. **Criticism of Public Employee.** Persons who criticize public officials regarding matters of public concern are not liable for defamation unless they act with actual malice. See Lewis v. Oliver, 178 Ariz. 330, 335, 337, 873 P.2d 668, 673, 675 (Ct. App. 1993) (inspectors of the Federal Aviation Administration are public officials); Rosales v. City of Eloy, 122 Ariz. 134, 135-36, 593 P.2d 688, 689-90 (Ct. App. 1979) (police officers are public officials); Sewell v. Brookbank, 119 Ariz. 422, 425, 581 P.2d 267, 270 (Ct. App. 1978) (teachers are public officials).

d. **Limitations on Qualified Privileges.** A defendant will lose the protection of a qualified privilege if the plaintiff proves either that the defendant acted with actual malice or excessively published the defamatory statement. See Burns v. Davis, 196 Ariz. 155, 164, 993 P.2d 1119, 1128 (Ct. App. 1999); Green Acres Trust v. London, 141 Ariz. 609, 616, 688 P.2d 617, 624 (1984); Melton v. Slonsky, 19 Ariz. App. 65, 68, 504 P.2d 1288, 1291 (1973).

e. **Question of Law or Fact.** Whether a communication is privileged is a question of law for the court. See Aspell v. American Contract Bridge League, 122 Ariz. 399, 401, 595 P.2d 191, 193 (Ct. App. 1979). Whether the defendant abused the privilege is a jury question, except that the court may decide the issue if the plaintiff presents no evidence of malice. See id.

f. **Burden of Proof.** A qualified privilege is an affirmative defense that must be pleaded by the defendant. See Chamberlain v. Mathis, 151 Ariz. 551, 554, 729 P.2d 905, 908 (1986). The plaintiff then must show that the defendant acted with actual malice to defeat a qualified privilege. See 151 Ariz. at 559, 729 P.2d at 913.

B. Standard Defamation Defenses

1. ***Truth.*** Truth is an absolute defense. See Central Ariz. Light & Power Co. v. Akers, 45 Ariz. 526, 543, 46 P.2d 126, 134 (1935). Substantial truth also is a complete defense and is determined by the court as a question of law. See Fendler v. Phoenix Newspapers Inc., 130 Ariz. 475, 478-80, 636 P.2d 1257, 1260-62 (Ct. App. 1981) (adopting Restatement (Second) of Torts § 581(A)). In matters of public concern, the statement is presumed to be true, and plaintiff has the burden of proving falsity. See Turner v. Devlin, 174 Ariz. 201, 205, 848 P.2d 286, 290 (1993).

2. ***Opinion.*** Arizona law once held that pure opinion was not actionable. See Glaze v. Marcus, 151 Ariz. 538, 540, 729 P.2d 342, 344 (Ct. App. 1986). The Arizona Supreme Court abandoned that position, however, following the U.S. Supreme Court's decision in Milkovich v. Lorain Journal Co., 497 U.S. 1 (1990). See Yetman v. English, 168 Ariz. 71, 76, 811 P.2d 323, 328 (1991); Burns v. Davis, 196 Ariz. 155, 164-65, 993 P.2d 1119, 1128-29 (Ct. App. 1999). Thus, Arizona currently does not recognize a dichotomy between opinion and fact. Nevertheless, statements that cannot "reasonably be interpreted as stating actual facts" about an individual are not actionable. Yetman, 168 Ariz. at 76, 811 P.2d at 328. Courts must determine from a statement's general tenor whether it stated or implied an assertion of objective fact, or was merely figurative or hyperbolic. "The key inquiry is whether the challenged expression, however labeled by defendant, would reasonably appear to state or imply assertions of objective fact." Id. (quoting Immuno v. Moor-Jankowsky, 77 N.Y.2d 235, 243, 566 N.Y.S.2d 906, 909, 567 N.E.2d 1270, 1273 (1991)) (emphasis omitted). See Hunley v. Orbital Sciences Corp., 2006 WL 2460631, *3 (D. Ariz. 2006) (An employer's statement that employee had poor interpersonal skills and was unable to work with management was as a matter of law not defamatory and merely an opinion).

3. ***Consent.*** The court in Glaze v. Marcus, 151 Ariz. 538, 540, 729 P.2d 342, 344 (Ct. App. 1986), held that consent is a defense to defamation.

4. ***Mitigation.*** In Boswell v. Phoenix Newspapers, Inc., 152 Ariz. 9, 19, 730 P.2d 186, 196 (1986), the Arizona Supreme Court invalidated a statutory provision that a plaintiff may recover general damages from a media defendant only if the defendant refused the plaintiff's timely request for a retraction. The Boswell court suggested in dictum, however, that "nothing prevents the legislature from requiring that retraction be considered in mitigation of damages." Id.

III. RECURRING FACT PATTERNS

A. Statements in Personnel File

No Arizona case specifically addresses whether statements in personnel files are conditionally privileged. However, the combination of defamatory remarks in a public employee's personnel file plus the employer's failure to rehire or the discharge of that public employee constitutes a deprivation of a liberty interest. See Montoya v. Law Enforcement Merit Sys. Council, 148 Ariz. 108, 109-10, 713 P.2d 309, 310-11 (Ct. App. 1985) (citing Paul v. Davis, 424 U.S. 693, 709 (1976); Doe v. United States Dep't of Justice, 753 F.2d 1092, 1106-07 (D.C. Cir. 1985)).

B. Performance Evaluations

Employers are absolutely privileged to forward employee evaluations to the E.E.O.C. in the course of the commission's investigation of a charge of discrimination. See Paros v. Hoemako Hosp., 140 Ariz. 335, 338, 681 P.2d 918, 921 (Ct. App. 1984). Evaluations of businesses by mercantile agencies, such as the Better Business Bureau, are conditionally privileged. See Antwerp Diamond Exch. of Am., Inc. v. Better Bus. Bureau, 130 Ariz. 523, 528, 637 P.2d 733, 738 (1981).

C. References

An employer who in good faith provides information requested by a prospective employer, or to a government body or agency, about the reason for termination of a former employee or about the job performance or professional conduct of a current or former employee is immune from civil liability. This qualified privilege applies only if the information concerns the current or former employee's education, training, experience, qualifications, and job performance, and the employer has no reason to doubt the accuracy of the information. A plaintiff may defeat the privilege by showing that the employer disclosed the information with actual malice or with an intent to mislead. A.R.S. § 23-1361. No reported cases from Arizona's state or federal courts involve an employee suing an employer because of a job reference.

D. Intracorporate Communication

In Dube v. Likins, 216 Ariz. 406, 167 P.3d 93 (Ct. App. 2007), the Arizona Court of Appeals adopted Restatement (Second) of Torts § 577 cmt. i, which states, "A communication within the scope of his employment by one agent to another agent of the same principal is a publication ... and this is true whether the principal is an individual, a partnership or a corporation." This means that when there is a communication between two agents of the same principal, a publication has occurred for defamation purposes. The defamation claim, however, may be subject to a qualified privilege. *Id.* at *11.

E. Statements to Government Regulators

Employers are absolutely privileged to forward employee performance evaluations to the E.E.O.C. in the course of the agency's investigation of a charge of discrimination. See Paros v. Hoemako Hosp., 140 Ariz. 335, 338, 681 P.2d 918, 921 (Ct. App. 1984). A defendant's statements during a meeting of the State Liquor Board are qualifiedly privileged. See Melton v. Slonsky, 19 Ariz. App. 65, 68, 504 P.2d 1288, 1291 (1973). Employers have a qualified privilege to submit records to the National Association of Securities Dealers regarding employment and disciplinary history. Wietecha v. Ameritas Life Insurance Corp., 2006 WL 2772838, *11 (D. Ariz. 2006).

F. Reports to Auditors and Insurers.

No pertinent Arizona cases.

G. Vicarious Liability of Employers for Statements Made by Employees

1. ***Scope of Employment.*** Employers are liable for defamatory statements made by an employee acting within the scope of his employment. See Phoenix Newspapers, Inc. v. Church, 24 Ariz. App. 287, 301, 537 P.2d 1345, 1359 (1975) (citing Restatement (Second) of Agency § 247). Where an employer's liability is premised on principles of respondeat superior, the employer cannot be held liable if the jury finds in favor of the employee who actually committed the tort. Wiper v. Downtown Dev. Corp., 152 Ariz. 309, 311, 732 P.2d 200, 202 (1987).

a. **Blogging.** No pertinent Arizona cases.

2. ***Damages.*** Arizona allows punitive damages against an employer for acts of its employees "so long as committed in the furtherance of the employer's business and acting within the scope of employment." Wiper v. Downtown Dev. Corp., 152 Ariz. 309, 310, 732 P.2d 200, 201 (1987) (quoting Western Coach Co. v. Vaughn, 9 Ariz. App. 336, 338-39, 452 P.2d 117, 119-20 (1969)). An award of punitive damages against an employer is improper where no punitive damages have been awarded against the employee and the employer's liability is based solely on the doctrine of respondeat superior. See Wiper, 152 Ariz. at 312, 732 P.2d at 203.

H. Internal Investigations.

No pertinent Arizona cases.

IV. OTHER ACTIONS BASED ON STATEMENTS

A. Negligent Hiring, Retention, and Supervision

1. ***Elements.*** An employer may be liable for negligent hiring, retention, or supervision if it knew or should have known that its employee presented an unreasonable risk of harm to others. See Quinonez v. Andersen, 144 Ariz. 193, 197, 696 P.2d 1342, 1346 (Ct. App. 1984). For an employer to be held liable for the negligent hiring, retention, or supervision of an employee, a court must first find that the employee committed a tort. See Kuehn v. Stanley, 208 Ariz. 124, 130, 91 P.3d 346, 352 (2004). Workers' compensation benefits are an employee's "exclusive remedy" for injuries suffered on the job "against the employer or any co-employee acting in the scope of his employment." A.R.S. § 23-1022(A). "[T]he trial court must first determine whether a co-worker was acting within the scope of employment when the harm occurred before ruling that workers' compensation benefits preclude an injured employee from suing [a] co-worker for damages." Smithey v. Hansberger, 189 Ariz. 103, 105, 938 P.2d 498, 500 (Ct. App. 1996).

2. ***Claims Based on Statements.*** No pertinent Arizona cases.

B. Intentional Infliction of Emotional Distress

1. ***Elements.*** To prevail on a claim of intentional infliction of emotional distress, a plaintiff must show that: (1) the defendant's conduct was "extreme and outrageous," (2) the defendant intended to cause emotional distress or recklessly disregarded the near certainty that distress would result from the conduct, and (3) the defendant's conduct caused severe emotional distress manifested as a physical injury. See Lucchesi v. Frederic N. Stimmel, M.D., Ltd., 149 Ariz. 76, 78-79, 716 P.2d 1013, 1015-16 (1986); Citizen Publishing Co. v. Miller, 210 Ariz. 513, 115 P.3d 107, 110 (2005). While this tort parallels defamation, it is intended to compensate for injured feelings, rather than reputation. See Godbehere v. Phoenix Newspapers, Inc., 162 Ariz. 335, 340-41, 783 P.2d 781, 786-87 (1989).

In Bodett v. Coxcom, Inc., 366 F.3d 736, 747 (9th Cir. 2004), the Ninth Circuit noted that Arizona courts have typically found false accusations alone not enough to constitute an intentional infliction of emotional distress. In light of the extremely high burden of proof for demonstrating intentional infliction of emotional distress in Arizona, the action causing the emotional distress must be so outrageous in character, and so extreme in degree, as to go beyond all possible bounds of decency, and to be regarded as atrocious and utterly intolerable in a civilized community. Id. (quoting Cluff v. Farmers Ins. Exch., 10 Ariz. App. 560, 460 P.2d 666, 668 (1969), overruled on other grounds, Godbehere v. Phoenix Newspapers, Inc., 162 Ariz. 335, 783 P.2d 781, 784 (1989)).

2. ***Claims Based on Statements.*** The factual basis for a claim of defamation may overlap the factual basis for a claim of intentional infliction of emotional distress. See Wallace v. Casa Grande Union High Sch. Dist. No. 82, 184 Ariz. 419, 427-28, 909 P.2d 486, 494-95 (Ct. App. 1995) (plaintiff sued for defamation and intentional infliction of emotional distress partially on the ground that her supervisor had slandered and ridiculed her); Lewis v. Oliver, 178 Ariz. 330, 332-33, 338, 873 P.2d 668, 670-71, 676 (Ct. App. 1993) (plaintiff sued for defamation and intentional infliction of emotional distress because of defendant's repeated complaints to plaintiff's superiors regarding plaintiff's work performance); Hunley v. Orbital Sciences Corp., 2006 WL 2460631, *4 (D. Ariz. 2006) (employer's verbal criticism and hostile manner towards an employee did not state a claim for intentional infliction of emotional distress); St. George v. Home Depot U.S.A., Inc., 2007 WL 604925, *12 (D. Ariz. 2007) (employees' allegations of sexual harassment, including allegations of lewd gestures, name calling, and physical threats, did not meet the high threshold for intentional infliction of emotional distress); Craig v. M & O Agencies, Inc., 2007 WL 2264635, *9 (9th Cir. 2007) (employee's allegations of sexual harassment, including allegations that her supervisor repeatedly propositioned her, followed her to the bathroom, and grabbing her and sticking his tongue in her mouth, stated a claim for intentional infliction of emotional distress with regard to the supervisor but not the employer).

C. Interference with Contract or Economic Advantage

1. ***Elements.*** To establish a prima facie case of intentional interference with contractual relations, a plaintiff must prove: (1) the existence of a valid contractual relationship or business expectancy, (2) the interferer's knowledge of the relationship or expectancy, (3) intentional interference inducing or causing a breach or termination of the relationship or expectancy, and (4) resultant damage to the party whose relationship or expectancy has been disrupted. See Antwerp Diamond Exch. of Am., Inc. v. Better Bus. Bureau, 130 Ariz. 523, 529-30, 637 P.2d 733, 739-40 (1981); Miller v. Hehlen, 209 Ariz. 462, 471, 104 P.3d 193, 202 (App. 2005). Additionally, the interference must be improper to be actionable. See Wagenseller v. Scottsdale Memorial Hosp., 147 Ariz. 370, 387-88, 710 P.2d 1025, 1042-43 (1985). In determining whether interference was improper, the fact finder should consider: "a) the nature of the actor's conduct, (b) the actor's motive, (c) the interests of the other with which the actor's conduct interferes, (d) the interests sought to be advanced by the actor, (e) the social interests in protecting the freedom of action of the actor and the contractual interests of the other, (f) the proximity or remoteness of the actor's conduct to the interference and (g) the relations between the parties." Id. (quoting Restatement (Second) of Torts § 767).

2. ***Claims Based on Statements.*** Statements that are harmful to reputation may also improperly interfere with contractual relationships or business expectations. See Antwerp Diamond Exch. of Am., Inc. v. Better Bus. Bureau, 130 Ariz. 523, 530, 637 P.2d 733, 740 (1981).

D. Prima Facie Tort

The prima facie tort is designed to provide a remedy for intentional and malicious actions that cause harm and for which no traditional tort provides a remedy. No reported Arizona cases have adopted or applied the prima facie tort, although the Arizona Supreme Court has acknowledged that other states recognize the tort. See State v. Bolt, 142 Ariz. 260, 268, 689 P.2d 519, 527 (1984).

V. PROCEDURAL ISSUES

A. Statute of Limitations

Arizona law provides a one year statute of limitations "for injuries to character or reputation by libel and slander." A.R.S. § 12-541(1). The limitations period generally "begins to run upon publication" of the defamatory statement. Lim v. Superior Ct., 126 Ariz. 481, 482, 616 P.2d 941, 942 (Ct. App. 1980). Courts toll the limitations period, however, when the defamatory statement is "peculiarly likely to be concealed from plaintiff, such as in a confidential memorandum or credit report." Clark v. Airesearch Mfg. Co., 138 Ariz. 240, 242, 673 P.2d 984, 986 (Ct. App. 1983). The statute of limitations will not be tolled when the alleged defamation occurred in public documents that were available to the plaintiff at any time. Wietecha v. Ameritas Life Insurance Corp., 2006 WL 2772838, *5 (D. Ariz. 2006).

B. Jurisdiction

Arizona courts exercise personal jurisdiction to the maximum extent permitted by the United States Constitution and the Arizona Constitution. See Ariz. R. Civ. P. 4.2(a). The Arizona Constitution and the United States Constitution are coextensive for the purposes of personal jurisdiction. See Houghton v. Piper Aircraft Corp., 112 Ariz. 365, 367, 542 P.2d 24, 26 (1975). Arizona does not place particular limits on its long-arm jurisdiction in defamation cases.

In Arizona, an internet business can be subject to jurisdiction for purposefully causing an injury within the state. In one case, a New Mexico software company sent defamatory email and made defamatory web postings about an Arizona company. A federal court in Arizona held there was personal jurisdiction because the defamatory statements were intentionally aimed at an Arizona business and caused an injury (defamation) within the state. See EDIAS Software Intern. v. BASIS Intern., Ltd., 947 F. Supp. 413 (D. Ariz. 1996). However, a merely passive website that does not conduct any commercial activity is insufficient for personal jurisdiction. See Cybersell, Inc. v. Cybersell, Inc., 130 F.3d 414, 418 (9th Cir. 1997); Mesa Airlines, Inc. v. Uslan, 2007 WL 1821298 (D. Ariz. 2007).

C. Complaint

Arizona law provides that: "In an action for libel or slander, the complaint need not state the extrinsic facts applying to the plaintiff the defamatory matter out of which the claim arose, but may allege generally that the libel or slander was published or spoken concerning the plaintiff, and if the allegation is controverted the plaintiff shall establish on the trial that it was so published or spoken." Ariz. R. Civ. P. 9(h).

D. Exhaustion of Administrative Remedies

In Bodett v. Coxcom, Inc., 366 F.3d 736, 740 n. 2 (9th Cir. 2004), the Ninth Circuit held that an employee waived her state law claims of retaliation under the Arizona Civil Rights Act by failing to file a prior administrative complaint with the Arizona Civil Rights Division pursuant to A.R.S. § 41-1481.

SURVEY OF ARIZONA EMPLOYMENT PRIVACY LAW

David J. Bodney, Peter S. Kozinets and Aaron J. Lockwood
Steptoe & Johnson LLP
201 East Washington Street, Suite 1600
Phoenix, Arizona 85004
Telephone: (602) 257-5200; Facsimile: (602) 257-5299

(With Developments Reported Through **November 1, 2012**)

GENERAL COMMENTS

The Arizona Supreme Court, Arizona's highest tribunal, set forth the essential discussion of invasion of privacy and the application of constitutional privilege to publication-related torts in Godbehere v. Phoenix Newspapers, Inc., 162 Ariz. 335, 338, 783 P.2d 781, 784 (1989). In the absence of contrary authority, Arizona courts follow the Restatement (Second) of Torts. Jesik v. Maricopa County Cmty. Coll. Dist., 125 Ariz. 543, 546, 611 P.2d 547, 550 (1980). The court has cautioned, however, that it will not follow the Restatement blindly. Reed v. Real Detective Pub. Co., 63 Ariz. 294, 303, 162 P.2d 133, 138 (1945) (establishing action for invasion of privacy). Additionally, the court has indicated that, although it is not bound by the decisions of federal circuit courts of appeals, if the Ninth Circuit has announced a clear rule on an issue of substantive federal law, it will look to the Ninth Circuit rule for guidance. Weatherford v. State, 206 Ariz. 529, 533, 81 P.3d 320, 324 (2003).

SIGNIFICANT DEVELOPMENTS SINCE THE 2012 *SURVEY*

In Judicial Watch, Inc. v. City of Phoenix, 228 Ariz. 393, 267 P.3d 1185 (Ct. App. 2011), a case involving Arizona's public records law, the Court of Appeals held that the mayor's privacy interests in the logs of his security detail, which reflected the mayor's personal and unscheduled events, failed to overcome the presumption in favor of public access once those logs were redacted for confidentiality and security concerns. The Court rejected the City's characterization of the public's interest as "insubstantial" because the redacted logs provided information already available in other records, such as the mayor's public calendar and his Twitter posts. Id. ¶ 25, 267 P.3d at 1190. The Court emphasized that the City raised only global generalities of possible harm to the mayor's privacy interests. Id. ¶ 29, 267 P.3d at 1192. Without a showing that the disclosure of specific information on the logs would adversely impact the mayor's interests, Judicial Watch was not required to justify its request, and the trial court was not required to balance the parties' interests. Id.

I. GENERAL LAW OF PRIVACY

A. Legal Basis of Privacy Claims

Arizona recognizes the tort of invasion of privacy as a matter of common law. See Godbehere v. Phoenix Newspapers, Inc., 162 Ariz. 335, 338, 783 P.2d 781, 784 (1989). Though the Arizona Constitution contains a privacy right, that provision has been held insufficient to give rise to a privacy-based action in the employment context. See Ariz. Const. Art. II, § 8 (No person shall be disturbed in his private affairs, or his home invaded, without authority of law.); Hart v. Seven Resorts, Inc., 190 Ariz. 272, 276, 947 P.2d 846, 850 (Ct. App. 1997) (holding that Arizona's constitutional right to privacy did not provide requisite public policy to support employees' wrongful termination suit against private employer based on employees' failure to submit to drug testing).

B. Causes of Action

The Arizona Court of Appeals has recognized the four-part classification of the invasion of privacy tort set forth in Restatement § 652. Rutledge v. Phoenix Newspapers, Inc., 148 Ariz. 555, 556, 715 P.2d 1243, 1244 (Ct. App. 1986). Because Rutledge imposed stringent proof requirements beyond those prescribed by the Restatement, however, the Arizona Supreme Court in Godbehere overruled Rutledge to the extent it conflicted with the Restatement's formulation of false light invasion of privacy. Godbehere, 162 Ariz. at 338, 783 P.2d at 784. Although the Godbehere court expressly adopted the Restatement's formulation of false light, it did not reach the other forms of invasion of privacy. Nonetheless, in view of the limited extent to which Godbehere overruled Rutledge and Arizona's general reliance on the Restatement in the absence of contrary authority, Arizona courts have continued to recognize each of the four forms of invasion of privacy as set forth in the Restatement. See, e.g., Hart, 190 Ariz. at 279, 947 P.2d at 853.

Arizona courts recognize numerous privileges against liability for invasion of privacy pursuant to statute and common law, specifically: (1) Arizona recognizes a privilege for publication of a fair and accurate abridgement of the public record. Sallomi v. Phoenix Newspapers, Inc., 160 Ariz. 144, 147, 771 P.2d 469, 472 (Ct. App. 1989); A.R.S. § 39-121 et seq. (2) Legally protectable privacy interests may not exist (a) where there has been consent to publication, (b) where the plaintiff has become a public character and thereby waived his right to privacy, (c) in the ordinary dissemination of news and events, (d) in connection with the life of a person in whom the public has a rightful interest, and (e) where the information would be of public benefit. Reed v. Real Detective Pub. Co., 63 Ariz. 294, 304, 162 P.2d 133, 138 (1945). Though Reed was an early misappropriation case, its broad focus makes it a useful guide in all invasion of privacy actions. (3) While no reported Arizona decisions have held expressly that common law defamation privileges serve as defenses to actions for false light invasion of privacy, the Court of Appeals has noted that traditional common law privileges against defamation liability whose underlying policies apply equally to privacy actions can act to bar liability for invasion of privacy. Star Publishing Co. v. Parks, 178 Ariz. 604, 605 n.1, 875 P.2d 837, 838 n.1 (Ct. App. 1993) (citing Time, Inc. v. Hill, 385 U.S. 374 (1966)). (4) Publishers of newspapers or periodicals are not liable for damages on account of publication of statements at the instance of a public officer acting in compliance with law. A.R.S. § 12-653. (5) In In re Med. Lab. Management Consultants, 931 F. Supp. 1487, 1492 (D. Ariz. 1996), the court held that the wire service privilege (which had not formally been recognized in Arizona) applies equally to invasion of privacy and defamation actions, and stated as a matter of law that there can be no content-based liability where a local broadcaster acts as a mere conduit for a nationally produced program.

Actions for invasion of privacy are governed by Arizona's two-year statute of limitations applicable to personal injury actions. A.R.S. § 12-542; Hansen v. Stoll, 130 Ariz. 454, 460, 636 P.2d 1236, 1242 (Ct. App. 1981). Defamation actions, however, are governed by a one-year statute. A.R.S. § 12-541(1). Actions for invasion of privacy do not survive the death of the person injured. A.R.S. § 14-3110.

1. ***Misappropriation/Right of Publicity.*** Arizona recognizes a cause of action for misappropriation. See Reed, 63 Ariz. at 304, 162 P.2d at 138. Reed held that publication of plaintiff's photograph falls within the scope of the misappropriation tort. Relying on Godbehere, trial courts have followed the formulation of the misappropriation tort as set forth in the Restatement. See, e.g., Lemon v. Harlem Globetrotters Int'l, Inc., 437 F. Supp. 2d 1089, 1100 (D. Ariz. 2006) (addressing claims by professional basketball players against licensor and promoter of Globetrotters-related apparel). Proper damages in misappropriation cases may include the fair market value of the unauthorized use or disgorgement of net profits attributable to the unauthorized use. Id. at 1103.

2. ***False Light.*** Arizona recognizes the tort of false light invasion of privacy as articulated by Restatement § 652E. Godbehere, 162 Ariz. at 342, 783 P.2d at 788. The Arizona Supreme Court has recognized Dean Prosser's view that disclosure must be public to support a claim for false light invasion of privacy. Godbehere, 162 Ariz. at 338, 783 P.2d at 784. No reported Arizona decision, however, has addressed the standards by which the sufficiency of a public disclosure should be measured. Unlike defamation, a false light cause of action may arise when something untrue has been published about an individual *or when the publication of true information creates a false implication about the individual.* In the latter type of case, the false innuendo created by the highly-offensive presentation of a true fact constitutes the injury. Godbehere, 162 Ariz. at 341, 783 P.2d at 787. Thus, a plaintiff may bring a false light invasion of privacy action even though the publication is not defamatory, and *even though the actual facts stated are true.* Id. In dictum, the Godbehere court suggested that false light by false association is sufficient to give rise to a claim under Arizona law. 162 Ariz. at 341 n.2, 783 P.2d at 787 n.2 (citing Douglass v. Hustler Magazine, Inc., 769 F.2d 1128 (7th Cir. 1985), cert. denied, 475 U.S. 1094 (1986) (publication of photograph in Hustler Magazine of model who consented to appearance in Playboy, though not false in itself, placed model in false light)).

Following the Restatement, Arizona requires that a publication involve a major misrepresentation of the plaintiff's character, history, activities or beliefs, not merely minor or unimportant inaccuracies. Godbehere, 162 Ariz. at 341, 783 P.2d at 787 (quoting Restatement § 652E cmt. c). Arizona has adopted the rule that a defendant is not liable in a false light case unless the publication places the plaintiff in a false light highly offensive to a reasonable person. Thus, the plaintiff's subjective threshold of sensibility is not the measure, and trivial indignities are not actionable. Godbehere, 162 Ariz. at 340, 783 P.2d at 786; see also Reed, 63 Ariz. at 305, 162 P.2d at 139 ("[A]ct must be of such a nature as a reasonable man can see might and probably would cause mental distress and injury to anyone possessed of ordinary feelings and intelligence.").

Noting that many jurisdictions have held that a false light action must relate only to the private affairs of the plaintiff and cannot involve matters of public interest, the Godbehere court held that a plaintiff cannot sue for false light if he or she is a public official and the publication relates to the performance of his or her public duties. 162 Ariz. at 343, 783 P.2d at 789. The court stopped short of saying, however, that a public official has no privacy rights at all and may never bring an action for invasion of privacy. Id. No reported decisions have addressed the burdens of proof set forth in Dun & Bradstreet, Inc. v. Greenmoss Builders, Inc., 472 U.S. 749 (1985), as they related to invasion of privacy claims.

3. ***Publication of Private Facts.*** In the past, Arizona courts have recognized a variant of the private facts tort. See, e.g., Rutledge v. Phoenix Newspapers, Inc., 148 Ariz. 555, 715 P.2d 1243 (Ct. App. 1986), overruled in part by Godbehere v. Phoenix Newspapers, Inc., 162 Ariz. 335, 783 P.2d 781 (1989). Godbehere expressly overruled Rutledge's requirement that the plaintiff establish intentional infliction of emotional distress to state a claim for the private facts tort.

See I.B, supra. Because Godbehere did not purport to reject Arizona's earlier recognition of the four-part classification of invasion of privacy, it is likely that the private facts tort remains viable as defined by the Restatement. Importantly, Arizona has recognized that "privacy rights are absent or limited . . . where the information would be of public benefit." Godbehere, 162 Ariz. at 343, 783 P.2d at 789 (quoting Reed, 63 Ariz. at 604, 162 P.2d at 138).

4. ***Intrusion.*** Arizona courts have never directly recognized the intrusion tort by name as a distinct cause of action. See Craig v. M&O Agencies, Inc., 496 F.3d 1047, 1060-61 (9th Cir. 2007) (concluding that under Arizona law a supervisor's conduct did not amount to an invasion of privacy when he followed an employee into the common area of a women's public restroom). Arizona has recognized, however, that a generic invasion of privacy can occur where a creditor takes unreasonable measures to collect a debt. Fernandez v. United Acceptance Corp., 125 Ariz. 459, 610 P.2d 461 (Ct. App. 1980). In Fernandez, the court held that an unfounded threat to repossess the plaintiff's car if an unrelated debt were not immediately repaid could constitute an actionable invasion of privacy where the defendant knew that it had no right to repossess the car. 125 Ariz. at 463, 610 P.2d at 464. The Fernandez court reasoned that conduct that will "probably result in extreme mental anguish, embarrassment, humiliation or mental suffering and injury to a person possessed of ordinary sensibilities under the same or similar circumstances" is actionable. 125 Ariz. at 461, 610 P.2d at 464 (quoting Rugg v. McCarty, 476 P.2d 753 (Colo. 1970)).

Arizona statutes criminalize the surreptitious viewing or recording of people in certain private settings, such as restrooms, regardless of whether a camera or other device is employed. A.R.S. § 13-3019. Viewing without a device is class 6 felony, the lowest classification under Arizona law, but use of a device is a class 5 felony. Id. If the person recorded is recognizable, the offense becomes a class 4 felony. Id. Arizona statutes also make invasion of privacy "for the purpose of sexual stimulation" a class 5 felony if the person depicted is unrecognizable, and a class 4 felony if the person is recognizable. Id. § 13-1424.

C. Other Privacy-Related Actions

1. ***Intentional Infliction of Emotional Distress.*** Arizona recognizes the tort of intentional infliction of emotional distress ("IIED") as defined in Restatement (Second) of Torts § 46. See Ford v. Revlon, Inc., 153 Ariz. 38, 43, 734 P.2d 580, 585 (1987). Arizona requires proof of intentional conduct to recover for IIED. Where reckless conduct makes the occurrence of emotional distress nearly certain, the element is satisfied. Ford, 153 Ariz. at 43, 734 P.2d at 585. Satisfaction of this element requires proof of conduct that falls at the very extreme edge of the spectrum of possible conduct. See Watts v. Golden Age Nursing Home, 127 Ariz. 255, 258, 619 P.2d 1032, 1035 (1980) (delay in reporting terminal illness held insufficient); see also Nelson v. Phoenix Resort Corp., 181 Ariz. 188, 888 P.2d 1375 (Ct. App. 1994) (humiliating termination of employment photographed by media held insufficient); Duhammel v. Star, 133 Ariz. 558, 653 P.2d 15 (Ct. App. 1982) (false allegations of police misconduct to city council held insufficient to support claim). Only when reasonable minds would differ in determining whether conduct is sufficiently extreme or outrageous does the issue go to a jury. Mintz v. Bell Atl. Sys. Leasing, 183 Ariz. 550, 554, 905 P.2d 559, 563 (Ct. App. 1995); see also Nelson v. Pima Community College, 83 F.3d 1075 (9th Cir. 1996) (holding that Arizona law supported dismissal as a matter law of an IIED claim based on termination of employment because defendants' conduct was not sufficiently extreme and outrageous). In rare cases, the courts have found the facts sufficient to present a jury question. See Ford, 153 Ariz. at 43, 734 P.2d at 585 (employer's failure to investigate complaints of sexual harassment for a period of months held sufficient to state a claim); Lucchesi v. Stimmel, 149 Ariz. 76, 78-79, 716 P.2d 1013, 1015-16 (1986) (physician's failure to attend properly to complications in delivery of child, resulting in decapitation of fetus, held sufficient to present jury question); Citizen Publishing Co. v. Miller, 210 Ariz. 513, 115 P.3d 107 (2005) (letter urging that "we should proceed to the closest mosque and execute five of the first Muslims we encounter" cannot be subject to an IIED claim because it was not likely to incite imminent violence and did not specifically target the plaintiffs or anyone else).

Arizona requires proof of severe emotional distress to recover for IIED. "A line of demarcation should be drawn between conduct likely to cause mere 'emotional distress' and that causing 'severe emotional distress.'" Midas Muffler Shop v. Ellison, 133 Ariz. 194, 199, 650 P.2d 496, 501 (Ct. App. 1982). Crying, being stressed and upset, and having headaches are not enough to establish severe harm. Spratt v. Northern Auto. Corp., 958 F. Supp. 456, 461 (D. Ariz. 1996). Nor is difficulty sleeping sufficient. Midas Muffler Shop, 133 Ariz. at 199, 650 P.2d at 501. Shock, moodiness, and estrangement from friends and coworkers are likewise not severe enough to warrant a claim. Bodett v. Coxcom, 366 F.3d 736, 747 (9th Cir. 2004). The Arizona Supreme Court has held, however, that medical and other evidence, combined with the plaintiff's testimony about her distress and evidence of physical complications, supports an award of damages. Ford, 153 Ariz. at 44, 734 P.2d at 586.

Notwithstanding the high standards required for a viable IIED claim under Arizona law, a federal district court allowed a claim against a supervisor arising from the supervisor's sexually harassing conduct to survive a motion to dismiss. Coffin v. Safeway, Inc., 323 F. Supp. 2d 997 (D. Ariz. 2004). The court reasoned that the cases cited by the supervisor were all distinguishable on the facts and that, with a single exception, were not decided at the pleading stage but on motions for summary judgment or a procedural equivalent. Id. at 1005-06. Finding no controlling Arizona or federal precedent, the court in Coffin concluded that plaintiff's allegations met basic pleading requirements under the Federal Rules of Civil Procedure. Id. at 1006-07.

Similarly, in Craig v. M&O Agencies, Inc., the Ninth Circuit sent an IIED claim against a supervisor to the jury. 496 F.3d 1047, 1059 (9th Cir. 2007). Over the course of several months, plaintiff's supervisor made inappropriate comments to her regarding her appearance and his sexual desire for her. At one point, he followed her into a women's bathroom at an off-site restaurant, "grabbed her arms [and] gave her an open-mouthed kiss." Id. at 1052. Unsatisfied with her employer's subsequent investigation and remedial actions, Craig filed claims under Arizona and federal law, naming her employer and supervisor as defendants. Id. at 1053. On appeal, the Ninth Circuit reversed summary judgment in the supervisor's favor on Craig's IIED claim. Id. at 1051. The court did not, however, allow the IIED claim to proceed against the employer. Id. at 1059-60.

2. ***Interference With Prospective Economic Advantage.*** Arizona recognizes a cause of action for interference with contract. Safeway Ins. Co. v. Guerrero, 210 Ariz. 5, 10, 106 P.3d 1020, 1025 (2005); Snow v. Western Sav. & Loan Ass'n, 152 Ariz. 27, 33, 730 P.2d 204, 211 (1986). Arizona also recognizes a distinct cause of action for interference with business expectancies. Pre-Fit Door, Inc. v. Dor-Ways, Inc., 13 Ariz. App. 438, 440, 477 P.2d 557, 559 (1970); see also Restatement § 766 (discussing interference with prospective advantage).

To prove the tort of intentional interference with contractual relations, a plaintiff must show: (1) the existence of a valid contractual relationship or business expectancy; (2) the interferer's knowledge of the relationship or expectancy; (3) intentional interference inducing or causing a breach or termination of the relationship or expectancy; and (4) resultant damage to the party whose relationship or expectancy has been disrupted. Neonatology Assocs., Ltd. v. Phoenix Perinatal Assocs., Inc., 216 Ariz. 185, 187, 164 P.3d 691, 693 (Ct. App. 2007). The interference must also be improper as to motive or means before liability will attach. Id. The Arizona Supreme Court has adopted the factors expressed in Restatement 2d of Torts, § 767 for determining whether conduct is improper for purposes of a tortious interference claim. Id. at 188, 164 P.3d at 694 (citing Wagenseller v. Scottsdale Mem'l Hosp., 147 Ariz. 370, 387, 710 P.2d 1025, 1042 (1985)). An attorney does not have a qualified privilege against such claims when acting on behalf of a client. Safeway Ins. Co. v. Guerrero, 210 Ariz. 5, 11-12, 106 P.3d 1020, 1026-27 (2005) (assertions of privilege are considered on a case-by-case basis, and Arizona courts follow the analysis in the Restatement for determining whether a plaintiff has shown improper conduct).

In Dube v. Desai, 218 Ariz. 362, ¶ 21, 186 P.3d 587, 593 (Ct. App. 2008), the Court of Appeals held that because a public-university employee was acting within the scope of his employment, the 180-day limitations period under the notice-of-claim statute applied to plaintiff's claim for tortious interference with prospective economic advantage against the employee.

3. ***Prima Facie Tort.*** No reported Arizona decisions. See Nicholas Homes, Inc. v. M&I Marshall & Ilsley Bank, N.A., 2010 WL 1759453, *5 (D. Ariz. April 30, 2010) ("[N]o Arizona court has ever adopted the prima facie tort doctrine as a viable cause of action in Arizona.").

II. EMPLOYER TESTING OF EMPLOYEES

A. Psychological or Personality Testing

1. ***Common Law and Statutes.*** No Arizona statutes; no reported Arizona decisions.

2. ***Private Employers.*** At-will employees may be discharged for refusing to sign employer's consent form for required psychological test. See Larsen v. Motor Supply Co., 117 Ariz. 507, 509, 573 P.2d 907, 909 (Ct. App. 1977).

3. ***Public Employers.*** No Arizona statutes; no reported Arizona decisions.

B. Drug Testing

1. ***Common Law and Statutes.*** By statute, Arizona law provides specific guidelines governing drug testing of employees. A.R.S. § 23-493 et seq. The statute sets forth numerous detailed procedural requirements governing the physical handling of samples, the testing methods, confirmation of positive results and employer policies. A.R.S. § 23-493.01-11.

Failure to pass, or the refusal to take, a drug test or alcohol impairment test administered by (or at the request of) the employer constitutes willful or negligent misconduct connected with employment pursuant to A.R.S. § 23-619.01. An employer may take adverse employment action based on a positive drug or alcohol impairment test, or based on a refusal of an employee or prospective employee to provide a drug testing sample. A.R.S. § 23-493.05. The disciplinary or rehabilitative action may include: (1) enrolling the employee in rehabilitation, treatment or counseling program as a condition of employment, (2) suspension of the employee, with or without pay, (3) termination of employment, (4) in case of drug testing, refusal to hire a prospective employee, or (5) other adverse employment action. A.R.S. § 23-493.05.

Drug test or alcohol impairment test results are confidential and may not be used or received in evidence, obtained in discovery or disclosed in any public or private proceeding, except in a proceeding related to action taken by an employer, or except disclosure to: (1) the tested employee or any person designated in writing by that employee, (2) individuals designated by the employer to evaluate test results or hear employee's explanation, or (3) an arbitrator, mediator, court or governmental agency as authorized by state or federal law. A.R.S. § 23-493.09.

However, Article 18, Section 8 of the Arizona Constitution bars the state from disallowing workers' compensation claims of employees whose work-related injuries are partially caused by their alcohol use, or who fail employer drug tests. Grammatico v. Indus. Comm'n, 211 Ariz. 67, 68, 72, 117 P.3d 786, 787, 791 (2005).

The Arizona Medical Marijuana Act allows qualifying patients with a debilitating medical condition to obtain marijuana from nonprofit dispensaries. Qualifying patients must register with the Arizona Department of Health Services ("DHS") and obtain a registry identification card before participating in the program. Employers may then use an online verification system – to be established by DHS – to verify identification cards provided by current employees or job applicants who have received a conditional offer of employment. A.R.S. § 36-2807(A). Unless doing so would cause an employer to lose a monetary or licensing benefit under federal law, an employer may not discriminate against a person in hiring, termination or any other term or condition of employment based on the person's status as a cardholder or positive drug test for marijuana. Id. § 36-2813(B). In addition, the Act treats confidentially and exempts from disclosure under the Arizona Public Record Law, A.R.S. § 39-121 et seq., all information relating to applicants for identification cards and dispensaries. Id. § 36-2810(A), (D). Anyone who violates the confidentiality of cardholder and dispensary information may be found guilty of a class 1 misdemeanor. Id. § 36-2816(D).

2. ***Private Employers.*** Employees may be terminated for refusing to submit to drug testing. See Hart v. Seven Resorts, Inc., 190 Ariz. 272, 276, 947 P.2d 846, 850 (Ct. App. 1997) (holding that Arizona's constitutional right to privacy did not provide requisite public policy to support employees' wrongful termination suit against private employer based on employees' failure to submit to drug testing).

A positive drug test may disqualify an employee from receiving unemployment compensation if the employer establishes that drug use adversely affected the workplace or termination of the employee was work-related. See Weller v. Arizona Dep't of Econ. Sec., 176 Ariz. 220, 224-25, 860 P.2d 487, 491-92 (Ct. App. 1993) (reversing Department of Economic Security Appeals Board denial of unemployment benefits to an employee who tested positive for marijuana because employer's rule that positive test for any level of cannabinoid metabolites in urine alone warranted termination of employment was not work-related or reasonable, as required to disqualify an employee from receiving unemployment compensation). See also Golden Eagle Distrib., Inc. v. Arizona Dep't of Econ. Sec., 180 Ariz. 565, 568, 885 P.2d 1130, 1133 (Ct. App. 1994) (holding that an employee who is discharged for failing a federally mandated drug test may be disqualified from receiving unemployment insurance benefits if positive drug test disqualified employee from continuing to work in his normal capacity).

3. ***Public Employers.*** An Arizona statute requires drug and alcohol testing for school transportation employees if a supervisor or his designee has probable cause that the employee's job performance has been impaired by use of alcohol or drugs. A.R.S. § 15-513. Probable cause is based on observance of employee by district personnel or other personnel furnishing transportation services to the school district. The person who observes the employee under the influence of alcohol or drugs must document the incident on a signed affidavit and obtain the signature of the employee's supervisor. A.R.S. § 15-513 does not exhaust the circumstances under which school districts may test transportation and non -transportation employees and does not require that transporting the pupils be a transportation employee's primary job. Op. Att'y Gen. No. I91-021.

Employers are required to provide an annual written certification to the Department of Economic Security if they maintain a drug or alcohol impairment testing policy in compliance with A.R.S. § 23-493.

A city's interests are not sufficiently compelling to permit random, suspicionless drug and alcohol testing on its firefighters. See generally Petersen v. City of Mesa, 207 Ariz. 35, 83 P.3d 35 (2004), cert. denied, 543 U.S. 814 (2004). While firefighters have reduced expectations of privacy because they work in a highly regulated occupation, "[b] alancing [firefighter's] privacy interests against the interests the City advances in favor of the [testing] Program's random component, . . . the City's generalized and unsubstantiated interest in deterring and detecting alcohol and drug use among the

City's firefighters by conducting random drug tests is insufficient to overcome even the lessened privacy interests of the firefighters in this case." Id. at 43.

C. Medical Testing

1. ***Common Law and Statutes.*** No Arizona statutes; no reported Arizona decisions.

2. ***Private Employers.*** No Arizona statutes; no reported Arizona decisions. Private employers may test for AIDS, but must be careful to avoid extreme and outrageous conduct that could create liability for intentional infliction of emotional distress. Op. Att'y Gen. No. I87-159.

3. ***Public Employers.*** No Arizona statutes; no reported Arizona decisions. Of course, any public employer is limited by Fourth Amendment considerations. Op. Att'y Gen. No. I87-159.

D. Polygraph Tests

1. ***Private Employers.*** In State v. Hess, 9 Ariz. App. 29, 31-32, 449 P.2d 46, 48-49 (1969), abrogated on other grounds by State v. Rodriguez, 192 Ariz. 58, 63, 961 P.2d 1006, 1011 (1998), the Court of Appeals held that private persons are not required to provide Miranda warnings when conducting a polygraph interrogation of store employees during an internal investigation.

In a case involving unemployment benefits, the Arizona Court of Appeals has held that an employee's termination for refusing to take a polygraph test constituted a discharge rather than a voluntary quit. See Valley Vendors, Inc. v. Jamieson, 129 Ariz. 238, 244, 630 P.2d 61, 67 (Ct. App. 1981) ("[R]efusal of the employee-claimant to submit to the polygraph examination in this case did not constitute willful or negligent misconduct connected with his employment and did not bar his right to receive unemployment insurance benefits.").

2. ***Public Employers.*** A police officer may be ordered to submit to a polygraph test and may be dismissed for refusal to take such a test during an internal investigation. Eshelman v. Blubaum, 114 Ariz. 376, 378, 560 P.2d 1283, 1285 (Ct. App. 1977); A.R.S. § 38-1101.

City officials may be ordered to take a polygraph test for purposes of an internal investigation. In Rivera v. City of Douglas, 132 Ariz. 117, 121, 644 P.2d 271, 275 (Ct. App. 1982), the Court of Appeals held that there was no Fifth Amendment violation in the requirement that city employees submit to polygraph examination because the employees were notified that the questions raised would specifically relate to performance of their official duties, that answers would not be used against them in a criminal prosecution and that the penalty for refusing would be dismissal. The court noted that ordering the employee to submit to a polygraph was not unreasonable, arbitrary or capricious because other investigative tools had been exhausted and the polygraph was only an alternative method of acquiring information. 132 Ariz. at 122, 644 P.2d at 276.

Under the Arizona Public Records Law, all data and reports from a polygraph examination of a law-enforcement or probation officer are confidential. A.R.S. § 38-1101(N). This data and reports may be used only for purposes of employment, peace officer certification or recertification, or the administrative matter for which the polygraph was taken. Id. The polygraph data and reports must be destroyed as soon as practicable three years after the date of appointment or employment, but not more than 90 days after that date, except for a pre-employment polygraph in which an applicant was not hired or in the case of an active investigation or appeal. Id. § 38-1101(O).

E. Fingerprinting

Arizona statutes mandate fingerprinting for certain specified groups of employees, including: (1) applicants for certification as school teachers, id. § 15-534; (2) non-certified school personnel and volunteers who provide services directly to pupils or who have independent access to or unsupervised contact with pupils, A.R.S. § 15-512; (3) all persons engaged in instructional work directly as a classroom, laboratory or other teacher or indirectly as a supervisory teacher, speech therapist or principal in charter schools, id. § 15-183; (4) employees of the Arizona State School for the Deaf and Blind, id. § 15-1330; (5) private investigators, id. § 32-2442; (6) personnel providing services directly to juveniles in children's behavioral health programs, id. § 36-425.03; (7) child care personnel and volunteers, id. §§ 36-883.02, 36-897.03; (8) domestic violence shelter employees and volunteers, id. § 36-3008; (9) licensees and contractors with the Department of Economic Security, id. § 46-141; (10) contractors and personnel providing services directly to juveniles, id. §§ 46-141, 41-2814; (11) child protective services workers, id. § 8-802; (12) probationary employees in a sworn, reserve or volunteer firefighter position, id. § 48-805; (13) registered nurse practitioners and nursing assistants, id. § 32-1606; (14) private process servers, id. § 11-445; and (15) every principal officer, agent or employee of a medical marijuana dispensary, id. § 36-2819.

III. SEARCHES

A. Employee's Person

No Arizona statutes; no reported Arizona decisions.

B. Employee's Work Area

No Arizona statutes; no reported Arizona decisions.

C. Employee's Property

No Arizona statutes; no reported Arizona decisions. The Arizona Attorney General has indicated that a state hospital's security personnel may search employees' packages and automobiles brought onto hospital grounds as well as employees' locked areas within the hospital as long as proper procedures are followed. Op. Att'y Gen. No. I87-159. The Department of Health Services would have to adopt appropriate regulations and would have to post signs at the entrances warning that searches will be conducted. Id. Those entering would then be on notice of the rights of security personnel and would therefore have no expectation of privacy. Id.

D. Employee's Electronic Communications and Files

A public employee's email messages maintained on a government system are not automatically public records under Arizona's public records law, A.R.S. § 39-121 et seq. Griffis v. Pinal County, 215 Ariz. 1, 5, 156 P.3d 418, 422 (2007). If a "substantial question" exists about the email's status as a public record, the requesting party may seek *in camera* review, and the party opposing disclosure has the burden of demonstrating that the email is purely personal and has no nexus with government duties. Id. at 6, 156 P.3d at 423.

See also VI, infra (discussing Lake v. City of Phoenix, 222 Ariz. 547, 218 P.3d 1004 (2009)).

IV. MONITORING OF EMPLOYEES

A. Telephones and Electronic Communications

1. ***Wiretapping (Telephone).*** A.R.S. § 13-3005 prohibits the intentional interception of an electronic communication by a non-party to the communication, as well as the intentional interception of a conversation or discussion at which the interceptor is not present. The statute also prohibits aiding, authorizing, employing, or permitting of another to commit an interception. One-party consent is sufficient to authorize an interception. The statute provides numerous exceptions immunizing the conduct of law enforcement and telephone service-providers in certain circumstances. See A.R.S. § 13-3012. Intentional unauthorized interception is a Class 5 felony (the second least serious felony under Arizona law). A.R.S. § 13-3005(A). A.R.S. § 12-731 authorizes an aggrieved party to bring a civil action based on unlawful electronic wiretapping, and provides for equitable relief, statutory damages and actual damages.

2. ***Electronic Communications (E-mail).*** A.R.S. § 13-3001 defines electronic communication to include transmission of any data of any nature by any electronic means, except for tone-only paging devices and tracking systems. Presumably, this definition is broad enough to include e-mail. The criminal prohibitions of A.R.S. § 13-3005 apply to interceptions of all electronic communications not only traditional wire communications.

3. ***Other Electronic Monitoring.*** No Arizona statutes; no reported Arizona decisions.

B. Mail

A.R.S. § 13-3003 provides: "A person who knowingly opens or reads or causes to be read a sealed letter not addressed to himself, without being authorized to do so either by the writer of such letter, or by the person to whom it is addressed, or a person who, without like authority, publishes the contents of such letter, knowing it to have been unlawfully opened, is guilty of a class 2 misdemeanor."

C. Surveillance/Photographing

A.R.S. § 13-3019 prohibits the photographing, videotaping or secret viewing of another person (1) in a restroom, bathroom, locker room, bedroom or other location where the person has a reasonable expectation of privacy; or (2) while the person is urinating, defecating, dressing, undressing, nude or involved in sexual intercourse or sexual contact. The statute does not prohibit photographing, videotaping or filming for security purposes where notice of the use of photographic equipment is clearly posted in the location, or by law enforcement officers pursuant to an investigation that is otherwise lawful. Undertaking such viewing or record-making for the purpose of "sexual stimulation" is a class 4 felony if the person depicted is recognizable, or a class 5 felony otherwise. A.R.S § 13-1424.

V. ACTIVITIES OUTSIDE THE WORKPLACE

A. Statute or Common Law

In the unemployment compensation context, an Arizona regulation recognizes a public policy against employers holding employees accountable for off-duty conduct, unless it is shown that such behavior affects the workplace. See A.A.C. R6-3-5185; see also Ariz. Const. Art. 2, § 8; Weller v. Arizona Dep't of Econ. Sec., 176 Ariz. 220, 226, 860 P.2d 487, 493 (Ct. App. 1993) (citing A.A.C. R6-3-5185(B) for the proposition that rules infringing without substantial justification on a worker's bodily privacy and personal life are unreasonable).

B. Employees' Personal Relationships

1. ***Romantic Relationships Between Employees.*** No reported Arizona decisions.

2. ***Sexual Orientation.*** Arizona's Code of Judicial Conduct prohibits judges, in the performance of their official duties, by words or conduct, from manifesting bias or prejudice, or engaging in harassment, including bias, prejudice or harassment based upon race, sex, gender, religion, national origin, ethnicity, disability, age, sexual orientation, marital status, socioeconomic status or political affiliation. See Ariz. R. Sup. Ct. 81, Code of Judicial Conduct, Rule 2.3 (2009). Judges may not permit court staff, court officials or others subject to their direction and control, including lawyers, to do so. Id.

Executive Order 2003-22, signed by the governor in January 2003, directs that no state agency "shall discriminate in employment solely on the basis of an individual's sexual orientation." The Order also directs the heads of state agencies to take measures to ensure that their procedures for complaints on employment discrimination reflect the Executive Order's policy, and to provide "appropriate requirements for confidentiality in cases arising from complaints of discrimination based on sexual orientation."

An employer's policy does not discriminate on the basis of sexual orientation because it prevents an employee under disciplinary investigation from discussing the case with anyone other than an attorney, minister, union representative or spouse. Patches v. City of Phoenix, 68 Fed. Appx. 772, 775 (9th Cir. 2003) (unpublished opinion). Such a policy tracks established communications privileges by prohibiting *all* unmarried employees from discussing the investigation with their partners. Id. Nor does a disciplinary investigation violate any right of privacy if the employee feels compelled to disclose her homosexuality when it was already apparent from the nature of her relationship with a subordinate. Id.

Pursuant to the Ninth Circuit's Employment Dispute Resolution (EDR) Plan and the U.S. Constitution, Ninth Circuit Judge Stephen Reinhardt, writing for the Judicial Council of the Ninth Circuit, ordered that benefits be provided to spouses of federal public defenders without regard to the spouse's gender. In re Levenson, 560 F.3d 1145 (9th Cir. 2009). Rejecting the argument that the federal Defense of Marriage Act (DOMA) precluded the provision of benefits to same-sex spouses, Judge Reinhardt reasoned that the denial of benefits violated the EDR Plan's prohibition of discrimination on the basis of gender or sexual orientation. Id. at 1147. He also found DOMA to be unconstitutional as applied to the Federal Employee Health Benefits program, concluding that there is no rational basis to deny benefits to same-sex spouses while providing them to opposite-sex spouses. Id. at 1149.

In 2011, the Ninth Circuit upheld a preliminary injunction against the implementation of an amendment to an Arizona statute that would have terminated coverage on January 1, 2011 for same-sex partners of public employees enrolled in the State's family benefits plan. Diaz v. Brewer, 656 F.3d 1008 (9th Cir. 2011). The amendment limits "dependents," which previously included "domestic partners," to qualifying children and "spouses." A.R.S. § 38-651(O). The Ninth Circuit found that this change discriminated against homosexual employees because heterosexual employees could continue receiving benefits by marrying their partners, while the Arizona Constitution's prohibition on same-sex marriage precludes homosexual employees from doing the same. Id. at 1014. The Ninth Circuit rejected the State's argument that this limitation on benefits – which affected only homosexual employees – was rationally related to the State's interest in saving money. Id.

3. ***Marital Status.*** No reported Arizona decisions.

C. Smoking

A.R.S. § 36-601.01 declares that smoking tobacco in any form is a public nuisance and dangerous to public health if done in any of the following places: Any elevator, indoor theater, library, art museum, lecture or concert hall, or bus which is used by or open to the public; waiting room, rest room, lobby or hallway of any health care institution; public waiting room of health associated laboratories or facilities; public waiting room of any physician, dentist, psychologist, physiotherapist, podiatrist, chiropractor, naturopath, optometrist or optician; or school building. State law does not prohibit smoking in such places if confined to areas designated and posted as smoking areas. Many local governments have enacted even stricter bans on smoking in public places. See, e.g., City of Tucson v. Grezaffi, 200 Ariz. 130, 134-35, 23 P.3d 675, 679-80 (Ct. App. 2001) (upholding City of Tucson's restaurant smoking ordinance).

D. Blogging

No Arizona statutes; no reported Arizona decisions.

VI. RECORDS

Under the Arizona Public Records Law, A.R.S. § 39-121 et seq., public records are presumed open to public inspection. Public records maintained pursuant to the Public Records Law are available for inspection subject to official's discretion to restrict access when privacy interests, confidentiality or best interests of the state in carrying out its legitimate activities outweigh the general policy of open access. See Carlson v. Pima County, 141 Ariz. 487, 491, 687 P.2d 1242, 1246 (1984). Where Arizona law does not directly address an issue concerning disclosure of public records, Arizona courts look to the federal Freedom of Information Act for guidance. See, e.g., Salt River Pima-Maricopa Indian Cmty. v. Rogers, Inc., 168 Ariz. 531, 540-41, 815 P.2d 900, 909-10 (1991). Arizona law permits a court to award attorneys' fees and costs to a party who substantially prevails in a lawsuit seeking the release of public records. A.R.S. § 39-121.02.

When a government entity withholds documents generated or maintained on a government-owned computer system on the grounds that the documents are "personal," the requesting party may ask the trial court to perform an *in camera* inspection to determine whether the documents fall within the public records law. Griffis v. Pinal County, 215 Ariz. 1, 2-3, 156 P.3d 418, 419-20 (2007). During this process, "[t]he party claiming that the disputed documents are not public records bears the burden of establishing its claim." Id. at 6, 156 P.3d at 423.

The Arizona Court of Appeals has refused to read into the Public Records Law a deliberative process privilege that would shield from inspection pre-decisional materials, such as opinions, recommendations and advice about agency policies. Rigel Corp. v. State, 225 Ariz. 65, ¶ 41, 234 P.3d 633, 641 (Ct. App. 2010). While the federal Freedom of Information Act contains a deliberative process privilege, 5 U.S.C. § 552(b)(5), the Arizona Public Records Law does not, and the court declined to create one via case law in light of Arizona's strong presumption in favor of public access and legal precedent limiting non-disclosure to specific statutory exemptions. Id. ¶¶ 40-41, 234 P.3d at 640-41.

Nothing in the Arizona Public Records Law "requires disclosure from a personal file by a law enforcement agency or employing state or local government entity of the home address or telephone number of eligible persons." A.R.S. § 39-123(A). The statute identifies the following persons as "eligible" for such protection: (1) peace officers, (2) justices, (3) judges, (4) commissioners, (5) public defenders, (6) prosecutors, (7) code enforcement officers, (8) adult or juvenile corrections officers, (9) corrections support staff members, (10) probation officers, (11) members of the board of executive clemency, (12) law enforcement support staff members, (13) national guard members who are acting in support of a law enforcement agency, (14) persons who are protected under an order of protection or injunction against harassment, (15) firefighters assigned to the Arizona counterterrorism center in the department of public safety, and (16) border patrol agents. Id. § 39-123(F)(4). The statute provides that the home address and telephone numbers for these individuals may be released only if (1) the person consents in writing, or (2) the records custodian determines that release of the information "does not create a reasonable risk of physical injury to the person or the person's immediate family or damage to the property of the person or the person's immediate family." Id. § 39-123(B). Any public employer who knowingly violates § 39-123 by releasing home addresses or phone numbers is guilty of a class 6 felony. Id. § 39-124.

"Eligible persons" may also request that various state agencies withhold similar information from disclosure. See, e.g., A.R.S. § 11-483 (requests that public be prohibited from accessing residential address, telephone number, unique identifier and recording date information in recorded instruments maintained by county recorder), § 11-484 (county assessor and treasurer), and § 28-454 (department of transportation). Additionally, "eligible persons" and anyone who cohabitates with "eligible persons" that are also registered to vote may request that their voter registration information, including residential address, telephone number and voting precinct number, be kept confidential. See id. § 16-153.

County recorders in counties with populations that exceed 800,000 persons must redact social security numbers from records available on the recorders' websites. A.R.S. § 11-461(G). In smaller counties, county recorders must redact this information from records upon request.

The Arizona Supreme Court has held that electronic records – including any embedded metadata – created by public employees and maintained by a public entity are "public records" subject to disclosure under the Arizona Public Records Law, A.R.S. § 39-121 et seq. Lake v. City of Phoenix, 222 Ariz. 547, 218 P.3d 1004 (2009). The court reasoned that "metadata in an electronic document is part of the underlying document; it does not stand on its own. When a public officer uses a computer to make a public record, the metadata forms part of the document as much as the words on the page." Id. at

550, 218 P.3d at 1007. The court rejected the City's argument that disclosure of metadata could create an "administrative nightmare," noting that the City could satisfy disclosure obligations by producing electronic documents in native format when responsive and appropriate, and that unduly burdensome or harassing requests can be addressed under existing law. Id. at 551, 218 P.3d at 1008.

In a part of the Court of Appeals' decision in Lake not addressed by the Supreme Court, the court held that police reports involving a police officer as a suspect or victim are public records. Lake v. City of Phoenix, 220 Ariz. 472, 481-82, 207 P.3d 725, 734-35 (Ct. App. 2009). The court rejected the City's argument that disclosure of such reports was prohibited because it would require the City to search the Arizona Department of Public Safety's Criminal Justice Information System and the National Crime Information Center, which are restricted to authorized users. The report was a public record, and the method of searching for that record was irrelevant. Id. at 481, 207 P.3d at 734.

In Judicial Watch, Inc. v. City of Phoenix, 228 Ariz. 393, 267 P.3d 1185 (Ct. App. 2011), the Court of Appeals held that the mayor's privacy interests in the logs of his security detail, which reflected the mayor's personal and unscheduled events, failed to overcome the presumption in favor of public access once the logs were redacted for confidentiality and security concerns. The Court rejected the City's characterization of the public's interest as "insubstantial" because the redacted logs provided information already available in other records, such as the mayor's public calendar and his Twitter posts. Id. ¶ 25, 267 P.3d at 1190. The Court emphasized that the City raised only global generalities of possible harm to the mayor's privacy interests. Id. ¶ 29, 267 P.3d at 1192. Without a showing that the disclosure of specific information on the logs would adversely impact the mayor's interests, Judicial Watch was not required to justify its request, and the trial court was not required to balance the parties' interests. Id.

A. Personnel Records

In Scottsdale Unified School District No. 48 v. KPNX Broadcasting Co., 191 Ariz. 297, 301, 955 P.2d 534, 538 (1998), the Arizona Supreme Court held that teachers had confidentiality or privacy interests in their birth dates, and that the Public Records Law did not compel disclosure of such records. Arizona Administrative Code § R2-5-105(F) enumerates the employee information that the State of Arizona will release upon a Public Records Law request, including: (1) name of employee; (2) date of employment; (3) current and previous class titles and dates received, (4) name and location of current and previous agencies to which the employee has been assigned, (5) current and previous salaries and dates of each change, and (6) name of employee's current or last known supervisor.

Arizona Supreme Court Rule 123 governs access to the state's judicial records. Under that Rule, records of court employees or volunteers are closed, except for information falling into six categories similar to those identified in § R2-5-105 (F). Ariz. R. Sup. Ct. 123(e)(1). In addition, Rule 123 allows inspection of information authorized to be released to the public by the individual employee or volunteer, unless otherwise prohibited by law. Id.

In Bolm v. Tucson Police Dep't, 193 Ariz. 35, 40, 969 P.2d 200, 205 (Ct. App. 1998), the Court of Appeals recognized that there is no blanket exemption for personnel and internal affairs documents from disclosure under the Public Records law. The court held that the balancing test adopted in KPNX Broadcasting Co. supported the Department's decision to withhold personnel evaluations and internal affairs records from public view. The court affirmed, however, the trial court's order compelling the production of the officers' hiring records, commendations and reprimands.

In City of Phoenix v. Peterson, 11 Ariz. App. 136, 140, 462 P.2d 829, 833 (Ct. App. 1969), plaintiff served a subpoena *duces tecum* to discover certain disciplinary records contained in a police department personnel file. The Court of Appeals held that, although the requested records were confidential as to the public at large, Arizona law did not prohibit the production of their "essence," such as the fact, nature and outcome of disciplinary proceedings, in response to a subpoena. The names of informants, confidential communications and irrelevant parts could be deleted.

Since Peterson, the Arizona Public Records Law has been amended to state explicitly that the disciplinary records of public employees are public records. A.R.S. § 39-128(A). However, this statute does not require the disclosure of the home address, telephone number or photograph of any person protected by A.R.S. §§ 39-123 and 39-124. Id. § 39-128(B).

Records relating to ongoing investigations of law enforcement and probation officers are not subject to public inspection. Arizona law prohibits an employer from including information about an investigation of a law enforcement or probation officer in those portions of the officer's personnel file that are open to public inspection until the investigation is complete or has been terminated. A.R.S. § 38-1101(L).

B. Medical Records

After a faculty member at Maricopa County Community College underwent gender reassignment surgery, several minor students complained about a man using the women's restrooms. Kastl v. Maricopa County Cmty. Coll. Dist., 2006

WL 2460636, *22 (D. Ariz. August 22, 2006), aff'd, 325 Fed. Appx. 492 (2009). In response, the school sought information regarding Kastl's medical condition. The district court stated that individuals have a protected interest in avoiding disclosure of personal matters, including medical information, but that interest is conditional. Id. at *21. The school had a compelling interest in protecting the privacy rights of other individuals who use the restrooms and had chosen a minimally intrusive means of obtaining information regarding Kastl's biological gender. Id. at *22-*23.

Arizona law allows emergency medical personnel who are under investigation by the Department of Health Services to obtain certain records in support of their defense. A.R.S. § 36-2227. The statute provides for access to records relevant to the investigation, including the name of the charging party, witness statements and even patient records. The employee who receives records pursuant to this statute cannot disclose the records to others, and may use them only for purposes of the investigation.

C. Criminal Records

A.R.S. § 41-1750(G)(2) addresses the dissemination of Arizona criminal history records to non-criminal justice agencies authorized by statute, ordinance or executive order for the purpose of evaluating the fitness of current or prospective licensees, employees, contractors or volunteers. The following organizations are authorized to receive criminal history record information: (1) Department of Liquor Licenses and Control, Executive Order No. 79-5; (2) State Board of Pharmacy, Executive Order No. 80-2; (3) State Lottery, Executive Order No. 81-2; (4) Office of Manufactured Housing, Executive Order No. 82-1; (5) State Board of Nursing, Executive Order No. 82-2; (6) Registrar of Contractors, Executive Order No. 82-4; (7) State Board of Dispensing Opticians, Executive Order No. 82-6; (8) Naturopathic Physicians Board of Examiners, Executive Order No. 82-7; (9) Department of Revenue, Executive Order No. 82-8; (10) State Board of Funeral Directors and Embalmers, Executive Order No. 82-9; (11) Structural Pest Control Board, Executive Order No. 83-1; (12) Veterans' Service Commission, Executive Order No. 83-3; (13) Department of Transportation Motor Vehicles Division, Executive Order No. 84-2; (14) Maricopa Juvenile Court, Executive Order No. 84-3; (15) State Labor Department, Executive Order No. 84-4; (16) State Athletic Commission, Executive Order No. 84-6; (17) Department of Revenue, Executive Order No. 84-9; (18) State Board of Technical Registration, Executive Order No. 85-3; (19) Compliance Section, Taxation Division, Department of Revenue, Executive Order No. 85-4; (20) Department of Health Services, Executive Order No. 85-14; (21) Arizona Department of Racing, Executive Order No. 86-1; (22) Mesa Public School District, Executive Order No. 86-3; (23) Department of Public Safety Licensing Section, Executive Order No. 86-6; (24) Game and Fish Department, Executive Order No. 86-7; (25) Department of Building and Fire Safety, Executive No. 86-8; (26) Supreme Court Foster Care Review Board, Executive Order No. 86-11; (27) Department of Transportation, Motor Vehicle Division, Executive Order No. 86-12; (28) Pima County Juvenile Court, Executive Order No. 86-13; (29) Mohave County Juvenile Court, Executive No. 86-14; (30) Governor of Arizona, Executive Order No. 87-4; (31) Health Care Cost Containment System, Executive Order No. 87-5; (32) Department of Environmental Quality, Executive Order No. 87-10; (33) Daisy Mountain Fire Department, Executive Order No. 91-22; (34) Medical Radiologic Technology Board of Examiners, Executive Order No. 91-22; (35) Board of Respiratory Care Examiners, Executive Order No. 91-23; Tribal Gaming office of any Indian Tribe having executed a Tribal-State Compact with the State of Arizona, Executive Order Nos. 94-8 and 2000-1; (36) Arizona Board of Examiners of Nursing Care Institution Administrators and Adult Care Home Managers, Executive Order No. 94-17; (37) Pinal County Department of Long Term Care, Executive Order No. 94-15; (38) Sun City Fire District, Executive Order No. 97-11; (39) Mayer Fire District, Executive Order No. 99-3; (40) Linden Fire District, Executive Order No. 2001-10; (41) Fountain Hills Fire Department, Executive Order No. 2001-11; (42) Bullhead City Fire Department, Executive Order No. 2004-02.

This statute also authorizes the Department of Public Safety to provide criminal history record information to the fingerprinting division for the purpose of screening applicants for fingerprint clearance cards. Id. § 41-1750(A)(12).

D. Subpoenas / Search Warrants

Under A.R.S. § 25-520 et seq., in a child support action the Department of Economic Security (DES) may issue a subpoena to a person or entity believed to have information needed for the establishment of paternity or the establishment, modification or enforcement of a child support order, requiring appearance before DES and the production of all records or documents related to an investigation or child support proceeding. Furthermore, A.R.S. § 41-1954(L) states that DES has access to certain records held by private entities with respect to child support obligors or obligees, or individuals against whom such an obligation is sought. Through a child support subpoena issued by DES pursuant to § 25-520, DES may discover the names and addresses of those persons, and the names and addresses of their employers, as they appear in customer records of public utilities, cable television companies or financial institutions.

The Equal Employment Opportunity Commission (EEOC) may subpoena general employment records as part of an investigation into a charge of systemic discrimination. In EEOC v. Federal Express Corp., 558 F.3d 842 (9th Cir. 2009), the court held as a matter of first impression that the EEOC retains authority to issue a subpoena even after it provides a right-to-sue letter and the charging party has initiated litigation. Id. at 848. The court reasoned that, once a charge is filed, the EEOC is required to investigate, and the issuance of a right-to-sue letter does not necessarily end that investigation. Id. at 849-50. The court also upheld the scope of the subpoena even though the EEOC did not seek specific information about any specific employee. Id. at 846. Rather, the EEOC requested information about FedEx's computer files reflecting, among other things, hiring, promotions, testing, discipline, evaluations, pay, transfers and terminations. Id. Although the requested information was not directly relevant, it was within the bounds of permissible discovery because it could assist the EEOC draft future requests that could produce evidence of discriminatory treatment. Id. at 854-55.

See also VI.A, supra (discussing City of Phoenix v. Peterson, 11 Ariz. App. 136, 462 P.2d 829 (1969)).

VII. ACTIONS SUBSEQUENT TO EMPLOYMENT

A. References

Arizona's anti-blacklisting statute establishes that "blacklisting" employees is illegal but also makes clear that it is not intended to prohibit employment references by providing: "It is not unlawful for a former employer to provide to a requesting employer, or agents acting in his behalf, information concerning a person's education, training, experience, qualifications, and job performance to be used for the purpose of evaluating the person for employment." A.R.S. § 23-1361(B).

A.R.S. § 23-1361(C) provides: "An employer who in good faith provides information requested by a prospective employer about the reason for termination of a former employee or about the job performance, professional conduct or evaluation of a current or former employee is immune from civil liability for the disclosure or the consequences of providing the information. There is a presumption of good faith if either: (1) the employer employs less than one hundred employees and provides only the information authorized by this subsection[, or] (2) the employer employs at least one hundred employees and has a regular practice in this state of providing information requested by a prospective employer about the reason for termination of a former employee or about the job performance, professional conduct or evaluation of a current or former employee." That presumption of good faith is rebuttable by showing that the employer disclosed the information with actual malice or with an intent to mislead. Id. § 23-1361(D).

B. Non-Compete Agreements

A covenant not to compete in an employment agreement is "valid and enforceable by injunction when the restraint does not exceed that reasonably necessary to protect the employer's business, is not unreasonably restrictive of the rights of the employee, does not contravene public policy, and is reasonable as to time and space." Phoenix Orthopaedic Surgeons, Ltd. v. Peairs, 164 Ariz. 54, 57, 790 P.2d 752, 755 (Ct. App. 1989), disapproved on other grounds, Valley Med. Specialists v. Farber, 194 Ariz. 363, 982 P.2d 1277 (1999). Arizona considers both non-compete agreements and other post-employment agreements under the same reasonableness analysis. Fearnow v. Ridenour, Swenson, Cleere & Evans, 213 Ariz. 24, 26, 138 P.3d 723, 725 (2006). A restrictive covenant is reasonable and enforceable when it protects some legitimate interest of the employer beyond the mere interest in protecting itself from competition, such as preventing "competitive use, for a time, of information or relationships which pertain peculiarly to the employer and which the employee acquired in the course of the employment." Farber, 194 Ariz. at 367, 982 P.2d at 1281 (quoting Harlan M. Blake, Employee Agreements not to Compete, 73 Harv. L. Rev. 625, 647 (1960)). An employer may also have a legitimate interest in having a "reasonable amount of time to overcome the former employee's loss, usually by hiring a replacement and giving that replacement time to establish a working relationship." 194 Ariz. at 370, 982 P.2d at 1284 (quoting Blake, 73 Harv. L. Rev. at 659). While Arizona courts may "blue pencil" a restrictive covenant by eliminating grammatically severable unreasonable terms, the court cannot add provisions or rewrite them. 194 Ariz. at 372, 982 P.2d at 1286.

Arizona law prohibits a "broadcast employer" from "requir[ing] a current or prospective employee to agree to a noncompete clause" as a condition of employment. A.R.S. § 23-494(A). A "broadcast employer" is defined as "a television station, television network, radio station or radio network." Id. § 23-494(B).

In Sogeti USA LLC v. Scariano, 606 F. Supp. 2d 1080 (D. Ariz. 2009), the District Court addressed the question – unanswered by Arizona courts – whether an employer must obtain the consent of a former employee to assign a non-compete agreement to a successor entity. Some jurisdictions require the employee's express consent on the grounds that a restrictive covenant in an employment agreement is "personal" to the employee. Id. at 1083. The Scariano court reasoned, however, that in Arizona contracts are presumptively assignable, and that Arizona law is "less concerned with the personal relationship between the employer and employee and more concerned with protecting employees from overreaching or other unconscionable arrangements." Id. at 1086. The court also determined that, in the absence of controlling precedent, a new public-policy restriction on contractual rights should not be created. Id.

The Arizona Court of Appeals has held that a former corporate officer had no duty to disclose his plans to resign and form a competing business, even though he had access to confidential business information and trade secrets, including new product ideas, strategies and failure rates, operational issues and marketing programs. Taser Int'l, Inc. v. Ward, 224 Ariz. 389, ¶ 4, 231 P.3d 921, 924 (Ct. App. 2010). The court reasoned that such an obligation "would create an undesirable impediment to free competition," particularly when defendant was an at-will employee unbound by any employment, non-compete or non-disclosure agreement. Id. ¶¶ 3, 39, 231 P.3d at 923, 932. The court clarified, however, that if defendant's "pretermination development efforts constituted competition, rather than merely preparation to compete, or involved the use of proprietary information, he had a duty to disclose his activities to Taser." Id. ¶ 40, 231 P.3d at 932.

VIII. OTHER ISSUES

A. Statutes of Limitations

Actions for invasion of privacy are governed by Arizona's two-year statute of limitations applicable to personal injury actions. A.R.S. § 12-542; Hansen v. Stoll, 130 Ariz. 454, 460, 636 P.2d 1236, 1242 (Ct. App. 1981). The same limitations period applies to actions for intentional infliction of emotional distress.

B. Jurisdiction

No Arizona statutes; no reported Arizona decisions.

C. Workers' Compensation Exclusivity

Work related injury claims in Arizona are redressed almost exclusively by the workers' compensation system. A.R.S. § 23-901 et seq.; Gamez v. Brush Wellman, Inc., 201 Ariz. 266, 269, 34 P.3d 375, 378 (Ct. App. 2001). When employers are properly insured, or self-insured, the workers' compensation laws provide immunity from suit, and an injured employee is limited to the recovery provided by the system. A.R.S. §§ 23-906, 23-1022. However, if an injury is caused by an employer's, or a co-employee's, willful misconduct, the injured employee may either file a claim for compensation or initiate a civil action for damages against the person or entity alleged to have engaged in the willful misconduct. Id. § 23-1022(A); Irvin Investors, Inc. v. Superior Court, 166 Ariz. 113, 800 P.2d 979 (Ct. App. 1990) (holding that workers' compensation laws barred employee's tort action against employer absent allegations of intentional misconduct or reckless disregard of the alleged sexual harassment). Additionally, employees are not confined to the workers' compensation system when their damages arise from an independent tort, even one closely related to the underlying injury. See, e.g., Mendoza v. McDonald's Corp., 222 Ariz. 139, 213 P.3d 288 (Ct. App. 2009) (holding that employee's recovery of damages for pain and suffering, lost earnings and medical expenses were not barred by workers' compensation laws to the extent her damages arose from distinct bad faith claim against McDonald's for its handling of her workers' compensation claim).

D. Pleading Requirements

No reported Arizona decisions or rules of court require special pleading formalities in privacy-related claims. See Coffin v. Safeway Inc., 323 F. Supp. 2d 997, 1004 (D. Ariz. 2004) (rejecting higher pleading standard for claim of intentional infliction of emotional distress).

SURVEY OF ARKANSAS EMPLOYMENT LIBEL LAW

Allen C. Dobson
Cross, Gunter, Witherspoon & Galchus, P.C.
500 President Clinton Avenue, Suite 200
Little Rock, Arkansas 72201
Telephone: (501) 371-9999; Facsimile: (501) 371-0035

Philip S. Anderson, Jess Askew III,
and Andrew King
Williams & Anderson, PLC
2200 Stephens Building, 111 Center Street
Little Rock, Arkansas 72201
Telephone : (501) 372-0800; Facsimile: (501) 372-6453

(With Developments Reported Through **November 1, 2012**)

GENERAL COMMENTS

None.

SIGNIFICANT DEVELOPMENTS SINCE THE 2012 *SURVEY*

None.

I. GENERAL LAW

A. General Employment Law

1. ***At Will Employment.*** It is the general rule in Arkansas that when the term of employment in a contract is left to the discretion of either party, or left indefinite, or terminable by either party, either party may put an end to the relationship at will or without cause. Crawford County v. Jones, 365 Ark. 585, 590, 232 S.W.3d 433, 438 (Ark. 2006). Under the employment at will doctrine, an employer may terminate an employee for good cause, bad cause or no cause at all. Lynn v. Wal-Mart Stores Inc, 102 Ark. App. 65, 280 S.W.3d 574 (Ark. App. 2008). An oral contract may be as binding on the employment relationship as a written employment contract. Moline Lumber Co. v. Harrison, 128 Ark. 260, 194 S.W. 25 (1917). Arkansas courts also have held that a handbook may modify the at-will relationship if the handbook expressly states that an employee may only be discharged for cause. Riddles v. Mid-Town Apartments Ltd. P'ship, No. CA 03-1189, 2004 WL 1399846 (Ark. App. 2004) (unreported opinion) (holding that a set of circumstances describing grounds for dismissal is at most an implied agreement, which is not sufficient to trump the at-will status); Palmer v. Ark. Council on Econ. Educ., 344 Ark. 461, 468, 40 S.W.3d 784, 788 (2001); Gladden v. Ark. Children's Hosp., 292 Ark. 130, 728 S.W.2d 501 (1987). In addition, Arkansas courts have held that where a handbook mentions "tenure" for good performance an implied employment contract will be recognized. Cisco v. King, 90 Ark. App. 307, 205 S.W.3d 808 (2005). Arkansas has recognized that an at-will employee has a cause of action for wrongful discharge if the employee is fired in violation of a well-established public policy of the state. Cross v. Coffman, 304 Ark. 666, 805 S.W.2d 44 (1991). The exception is limited and not meant to protect merely private or proprietary interests. Id. **A violation of procedural policy is not a violation of public policy. Tripcony v. Arkansas School for the Deaf, 2012 Ark. 188, at 9–11. Rather, a state's public policy is found in its constitution and statutes, such as whistleblower statutes, criminal statutes, and statutes designed to protect the public from harm. Id. at 9–11.** There are two other exceptions to the at-will doctrine: (1) where an employee relies upon a personnel manual that contains an express agreement against termination except for cause, and (2) where the employment agreement contains a provision that the employee will not be discharged except for cause, even if the agreement has an unspecified term. Magic Touch Corp. v. Hicks, 99 Ark. App. 334, 260 S.W.3d 322 (2007). The fact that employment is public rather than private does not change the at-will status of employment in Arkansas. Hogue v. Clinton, 791 F.2d 1318 (8th Cir. 1986), cert. denied, 479 U.S. 1008 (1986). One who maliciously makes false statements, threats, or induces an employer to discharge an employee is liable in tort to the employee for damages sustained regardless of whether employment was fixed or terminable at-will. Mason v. Funderburk, 247 Ark. 521, 446 S.W.2d 543 (1969). An exception is created to the general rule that an at-will public employee is not entitled to a discharge hearing when a state employer creates and disseminates a false and defamatory impression about the at-will employee in connection with the discharge. Speer v. City of Wynne, Ark., 276 F.3d 980 (8th Cir. 2002). Ark. Code Ann. § 11-9-107 eliminated the cause of action for retaliatory discharge in the worker's compensation context. Tackett v. Crain Automotive, 321 Ark. 36, 899 S.W.2d 839 (1995).

B. Elements of Libel Claim

1. ***Basic Elements.*** To support a claim of defamation, whether it is for slander due to spoken word or libel due to written work, the following elements must be proven: (1) the defamatory nature of the statement of fact; (2) the statement's identification of or reference to the plaintiff; (3) the publication of the statement by the defendant; (4) the defendant's fault in the publication; (5) the statement's falsity; and (6) damages. Dodson v. Allstate Insurance Co., 365 Ark. 458, 464, 231 S.W.3d 711, 716 (Ark. 2006). An essential element of slander or libel is that the statement must be published or communicated to a third person, someone other than the person slandered or libeled, to be actionable. Navarro-Monzo v.

Hughes, 297 Ark. 444, 763 S.W.2d 635 (1989). The publication to a third party must be unprivileged. Wal-Mart Stores, Inc. v. Dolph, 308 Ark. 439, 825 S.W.2d 810 (1992). A defamation action turns on whether the communication or publication tends or is reasonably calculated to cause harm to another's reputation. Thomson Newspaper Publ'g, Inc. v. Coody, 320 Ark. 455, 896 S.W.2d 897, 23 Media L. Rep. 2270 (1995); Little Rock Newspapers, Inc. v. Fitzhugh, 330 Ark. 561, 954 S.W.2d 914, 26 Media L. Rep. 1801 (1997), cert. denied, 523 U.S. 1095 (1998); **Lancaster v. Red Robin International, Inc., 2011 Ark. App. 706, at 8.** An alleged defamatory statement must imply an assertion of an objective verifiable fact. Faulkner v. Ark. Children's Hosp., 347 Ark. 941, 69 S.W.3d 393 (2002). In determining whether a statement implies an assertion of an objectively verifiable fact, the courts will weigh these factors: 1) whether the author used figurative or hyperbolic language that would negate the impression that the author was seriously asserting or implying such a fact; 2) whether the general tenor of the publication negates such an impression; and 3) whether the published assertion is susceptible of being proven true or false. Id. "Also, a defamatory statement must imply an assertion of an objective, verifiable fact; it should, for example, be capable of being proved true or false." Addington v. Wal-Mart Stores, Inc., 81 Ark. App. 441, 105 S.W.3d 369 (2003). "A basic rule of defamation law is that courts must construe a statement in light of its context and surrounding circumstances." Mercer v. City of Cedar Rapids, 308 F.3d 840 (8th Cir. 2002). Generally. continuing defamation is "unknown to Arkansas," and the District Court for the Eastern District of Arkansas has recently held that Arkansas Courts would probably not apply the doctrine in that specific case. Hillhouse v. U.S. Dep't of Treasury, No. 3:12-cv-97-DPM, 2012 U.S. Dist. LEXIS 128466 at *10 (E.D. Sept. 7, 2012).

2. ***Fault.*** The level of fault that must be shown depends on the plaintiff's private or public status and the private or public nature of the defendant's statement. Arkansas has adopted the minimum constitutional requirement of negligence as the appropriate level of fault for recovery by private figure plaintiffs under Gertz v. Robert Welch, Inc., 418 U.S. 323, 94 S. Ct. 2997, 41 L. Ed. 2d 789, 1 Media L. Rep. 1633 (1974). The publisher of a libelous article shall be liable to the defamed private individual for failure to exercise ordinary care prior to publication to determine the defamatory potential of its statements. Dodrill v. Ark. Democrat Co., 265 Ark. 628, 590 S.W.2d 840, 5 Media L. Rep. 1385 (1979). See also Little Rock Newspapers, Inc. v. Dodrill, 281 Ark. 25, 660 S.W.2d 933, 10 Media L. Rep. 1063 (1983). A public figure or public official must prove actual malice for statements relating to his public status. Little Rock Newspapers, Inc. v. Fitzhugh, 330 Ark. 561, 954 S.W.2d 914, 26 Media L. Rep. 1801 (1997), cert. denied, 523 U.S. 10953 (1998).

a. **Private Figure Plaintiff/Matter of Public Concern.** All plaintiffs in defamation cases must prove reputational injury in order to recover damages. In defamation per se actions, damages will no longer be presumed. United Ins. Co. of Am. v. Murphy, 331 Ark. 364, 961 S.W.2d 752 (1998); Faulkner v. Ark. Children's Hosp., 347 Ark. 941, 69 S.W.3d 393 (2002). A private or limited public figure plaintiff attempting recovery on matters of public concern must prove actual malice by clear and convincing evidence. See Fuller v. Russell, 311 Ark. 108, 842 S.W.2d 12, 21 Media L. Rep. 1254 (1992); Dodson v. Dicker, 306 Ark. 108, 812 S.W.2d 97, 19 Media L. Rep. 1124 (1991).

b. **Private Figure Plaintiff/Matter of Private Concern.** Arkansas has adopted the minimum constitutional requirement of negligence as the appropriate level of fault for recovery by private figure plaintiffs under Gertz v. Robert Welch, Inc., 418 U.S. 323, 94 S. Ct. 2997, 41 L. Ed. 2d 789, 1 Media L. Rep. 1633 (1974). The publisher of a libelous article shall be liable to the defamed private individual for failure to exercise ordinary care prior to publication to determine the defamatory potential of its statements. Dodrill v. Ark. Democrat Co., 265 Ark. 628, 590 S.W.2d 840, 5 Media L. Rep. 1385 (1979). See also Little Rock Newspapers, Inc. v. Dodrill, 281 Ark. 25, 660 S.W.2d 933, 10 Media L. Rep. 1063 (1983). Traditionally, making a false statement that the plaintiff was guilty of a crime or was afflicted with a loathsome disease, or making statements that prejudiced the plaintiff's ability to engage in his or her profession was considered defamatory per se, injurious, and sufficient to support an award of presumed damages. Now, in defamation per se actions, damages will no longer be presumed. All plaintiffs in defamation cases must prove reputational injury to recover damages. Stanley v. Gen. Media Communications, Inc., 149 F. Supp. 2d 701, 707, 29 Media L. Rep. 1631 (W.D. Ark. 2001); United Ins. Co. of Am. v. Murphy, 331 Ark. 364, 961 S.W.2d 752 (1998); Faulkner v. Ark. Children's Hosp., 347 Ark. 941, 69 S.W.3d 393 (2002). The evidence was sufficient to support a charge of slander when the plaintiff, a former employee, alleged that a current employee told customers that the plaintiff had been fired for stealing. Tandy Corp. v. Bone, 283 Ark. 399, 678 S.W.2d 312 (1984). Evidence that an employer and supervisor reported allegations of misconduct by nurses to the State Office of Long Term Care and police department was sufficient to support a jury's verdict of damage to nurses' reputations and a $265,000 damage award. Northport Health Servs., Inc. v. Owens, 82 Ark. App. 355, 107 S.W.3d 889 (2003), aff'd as modified, 356 Ark. 630, 158 S.W.3d 164 (2004). Former insurance agency employees successfully sued agency owners and insurance company with which agency was under contract and recovered damages for defamation based upon the owners' statements following the employees' resignations from the agency. Yeldell v. Tutt, 913 F.2d 533 (8th Cir. 1990). Corporate employees made statements imputing a pro-union disposition to the industrial relations manager of a plant. The statements were per se defamatory because they were of such a nature as to be injurious to the business relationship between the plaintiff and his employer. Andrews v. Mohawk Rubber Co., 474 F. Supp. 1276 (E.D. Ark. 1979). A university student who had been employed as a clerk at a motel prevailed in a slander action against the president of the motel who had accused the student of theft. McCorkle v. Jefferson, 252 Ark. 204, 478 S.W.2d 47 (1972). A retail store was held liable for defamation when information regarding a suspected theft by an employee was relayed to a police detective over a police radio and in the presence of third parties and was overhead by others, including the local press. Wal-Mart Stores, Inc. v. Lee, 348 Ark. 707, 74 S.W.3d 634 (2002).

c. **Public Figure Plaintiff/Matter of Public Concern.** Whether an individual is a "public official" or a "public figure" is a mixed question of law and fact to be determined by the trial court before the case is submitted to the jury. Southall v. Little Rock Newspapers, Inc., 332 Ark. 123, 964 S.W.2d 187, 26 Media L. Rep. 1815 (1998). "Public figures" are individuals who have assumed roles of special prominence in the affairs of society. Dodrill v. Ark. Democrat Co., 265 Ark. 628, 590 S.W.2d 840, 5 Media L. Rep. 1385 (1979) (citing Gertz v. Robert Welch, Inc., 418 U.S. 323, 94 S. Ct. 2997, 41 L. Ed. 2d 789, 1 Media L. Rep. 1633 (1974)). A "public official" is an individual holding a position of considerable public responsibility. Drew v. KATV Television, 293 Ark. 555, 739 S.W.2d 680, 14 Media L. Rep. 2078 (1987). The responsibilities must be of sufficient importance that the public has an interest in the position and the manner in which it is performed. Id. Public and limited public figures must prove by clear and convincing evidence that an allegedly defamatory statement was published with "actual malice." Pritchard v. Times Sw. Broad., 277 Ark. 458, 642 S.W.2d 877, 9 Media L. Rep. 1048 (1982). "Actual malice" means that the utterance was knowingly false or was made in reckless disregard of whether it was true or false. Lancaster v. Daily Banner-News Publ'g Co., 274 Ark. 145, 622 S.W.2d 671, 8 Media L. Rep. 1093 (1981). In order to find actual malice, there must be sufficient evidence that the defendant in fact entertained serious doubts as to the truth of the publication. Thomson Newspaper Publ'g, Inc. v. Coody, 320 Ark. 455, 896 S.W.2d 897, 23 Media L. Rep. 2270 (1995). Whether the evidence in the record is sufficient to support a finding of actual malice is a question of law. Fuller v. Russell, 311 Ark. 108, 842 S.W.2d 12, 21 Media L. Rep. 1254 (1992). An assistant dean and professor in a state university law school is a "public official," and communications relating to his qualifications as a scholar and professor of law involve "matters of public or general concern." Id. Determining whether the speech involves matters of public concern is the threshold issue. If the speech addresses a matter of public concern, then the Court must balance the interests of the employee, as a citizen, in commenting upon matters of public concern, and the interests of the state, as an employer, in promoting the efficiency of the public services it performs through its employees. Harper v. Crockett, 868 F. Supp. 1557 (E.D. Ark. 1994) (citing Shands v. City of Kennett, 993 F.2d 1337, 1342 (8th Cir.1993); Connick v. Myers, 461 U.S. 138 (1983)). For media defendants, publishing emotionally tinged documents or failing to investigate will not of itself establish bad faith or actual malice. Gallman v. Carnes, 254 Ark. 987, 487 S.W.2d 47 (1973) (citing St. Amant v. Thompson, 390 U.S. 727 (1968)). The plaintiff, a former federal prosecutor for eight years, was not a limited public figure or an all-purpose public figure in a defamation action arising from the newspaper's mistaken use of his picture in an article about the indictment of a lawyer with the same last name in a scandal unconnected with the plaintiff's former duties as a federal prosecutor and when the plaintiff had not achieved such general notoriety throughout the state where the newspaper was circulated so as to render him a public personality for all aspects of his life. Little Rock Newspapers, Inc. v. Fitzhugh, 330 Ark. 561, 954 S.W.2d 914, 26 Media L. Rep. 1801 (1997), cert. denied, 523 U.S. 1095 (1998). A political consultant was a limited public figure, and a local political race was found to be a matter of public concern. A limited public figure suing a non-media defendant over alleged defamatory statements which are a matter of public concern has the burden of proving such statements false and, by clear and convincing evidence, that such statements were made with actual malice. Fuller v. Russell, 311 Ark. 108, 842 S.W.2d 12, 21 Media L. Rep. 1254 (1992). A deputy sheriff considered to be a public official was fired primarily because of "immoral conduct" but failed to prove that the newspaper published with actual malice the story describing his termination. Hollowell v. Ark. Democrat Newspaper, 293 Ark. 329, 737 S.W.2d 646, 14 Media L. Rep. 2280 (1987). A deputy sheriff "having substantial responsibility for or control over the conduct of government affairs at least where law enforcement and police functions are concerned" was a public official but failed to prevail on his libel claim against the sheriff because he did not prove that the sheriff acted recklessly or with actual malice when discussing the deputy's termination with the news media. Karr v. Townsend, 606 F. Supp. 1121 (W.D. Ark. 1985). A police officer determined to be a public employee challenged the police department's suspension of him alleging that the suspension violated his right to free speech. The court found that the police officer's statement regarding the adequacy of future police protection made in frustration over a bank's check cashing policy was not a matter of public concern and therefore not protected by the First Amendment. Harper v. Crockett, 868 F. Supp. 1557 (E.D. Ark. 1994). In a recent case arising in the U.S. District Court for the Eastern District of Arkansas, the Eighth Circuit Court of Appeals held there was no evidence of actual malice where defendants produced and released a video indicating that two law enforcement officers had been implicated in the deaths of two teenage boys and a subsequent cover-up. Campbell v. Citizens for an Honest Gov't, Inc., 255 F.3d 560, 29 Media L. Rep. 2155 (8th Cir. 2001). Plaintiffs failed to prove by even a preponderance of the evidence that statements in the video were false. Plaintiffs also failed to prove with clear and convincing evidence that the statements in the video were published with reckless awareness of their probable falsity or actual belief in their falsity. Id.

3. ***Falsity.*** Publication with knowledge that a statement was false or made with reckless disregard of whether it was true or false must be proved. Pritchard v. Times Sw. Broad., 277 Ark. 458, 642 S.W.2d 877, 9 Media L.

Rep. 1048 (1982). Plaintiffs bear the burden of pleading and proof that the defendant negligently or knowingly published a false and defamatory fact. Dodson v. Allstate Ins. Co., 345 Ark. 430, 47 S.W.3d 866 (2001). Truth is a complete defense to a charge of defamation. Wirges v. Brewer, 239 Ark. 317, 389 S.W.2d 226 (1965).

4. ***Defamatory Statement of Fact.*** Plaintiffs bear the burden of pleading and proof that the defendant negligently or knowingly published a false and defamatory fact. Dodson v. Allstate Ins. Co., 345 Ark. 430, 47 S.W.3d 866 (2001). The common-law privilege of fair comment is recognized in Arkansas, so long as the facts charged are true and the comment is made without malice. State Press Co. v. Willett, 219 Ark. 850, 245 S.W.2d 403 (1952). In Dodson v. Dicker, 306 Ark. 108, 812 S.W.2d 97, 19 Media L. Rep. 1124 (1991), the Arkansas Supreme Court applied Milkovich v. Lorain Journal Co., 497 U.S. 1, 17 Media L. Rep. 2009 (1990), and weighed three factors in determining whether a statement could reasonably be viewed as implying an assertion of fact: "(1) whether the author used figurative or hyperbolic language that would negate the impression that she was seriously maintaining implied fact; (2) whether the general tenor of the publication negates this impression; and (3) whether the published assertion is susceptible of being proved true or false." Id. See also Faulkner v. Ark. Children's Hosp., 347 Ark. 941, 69 S.W.3d 393 (2002). The court cautioned that every set of circumstances weighed under this analysis must be considered on a case-by-case basis. Opinions, as opposed to verifiable statements of fact, are not actionable. Brown v. Tucker, 330 Ark. 435, 954 S.W.2d 262 (1997). The words "incompetent and unable to function in his position" claimed to have been used by defendant about plaintiff possessed the general tenor of an opinion as opposed to a verifiable statement of fact. Id. See also II.B.2, infra.

5. ***Of and Concerning Plaintiff.*** The plaintiff in a defamation case must prove that the statement was "of and concerning" him or her. Whether the words, taken together with the attendant circumstances, refer to the plaintiff is a question of fact for the jury to resolve. Little Rock Newspapers, Inc. v. Fitzhugh, 330 Ark. 561, 954 S.W.2d 914, 26 Media L. Rep. 1801 (1997), cert. denied, 523 U.S. 1095 (1998). There was sufficient evidence for the jury to conclude that an article was "of and concerning" the plaintiff, J. Michael Fitzhugh, when the plaintiff's photograph accompanied the story; the caption under the photograph and the article repeatedly referred to merely "Fitzhugh"; and several witnesses, all friends and acquaintances of the plaintiff, testified that they initially believed the article was about the plaintiff due to the inclusion of the plaintiff's photograph. Id. An individual cannot complain of a statement about an indefinite class. Wirges v. Brewer, 239 Ark. 317, 389 S.W.2d 226 (1965). Before a plaintiff can recover for libel to a group, the libelous statement must be understood by its hearers or readers of having reference to plaintiff. Id. The publication of an unsigned letter to the editor which recited several charges against city policemen as a class, including indecent exposure, was not libelous as a matter of law since the writer did not specifically refer to plaintiff. Pigg v. Ashley County Newspaper, Inc., 253 Ark. 756, 489 S.W.2d 17 (1973).

6. ***Publication.*** An unprivileged publication of slanderous statements to a third party is the central element in a defamation suit. Wal-Mart Stores, Inc. v. Dolph, 308 Ark. 439, 825 S.W.2d 810 (1992). In Dolph, testimony of shoplifting accusations made by an officer within a few feet of the check-out counter and exit where there were a number of customers justified a reasonable inference that the statements were published. Id. Publication can be either intentional or negligent communication of defamatory statements to a third party. Navorro-Monzo v. Hughes, 297 Ark. 444, 763 S.W.2d 635 (1989). Publication occurs when the defamatory matter is communicated to someone other than the person defamed. Northport Health Servs., Inc. v. Owens, 82 Ark. App. 355, 107 S.W.3d 889 (2003), aff'd as modified, 356 Ark. 630, 158 S.W.3d 164 (2004). A defamation action turns on whether the communication or publication tends or is reasonably calculated to cause harm to another's reputation. Southall v. Little Rock Newspapers, Inc., 332 Ark. 123, 964 S.W.2d 187, 26 Media L. Rep. 1815 (1998); **Lancaster v. Red Robin International, Inc., 2011 Ark. App. 706**. It is not necessary that the defamed person is present at the time of the publication. Braman v. Walthall, 215 Ark. 582, 225 S.W.2d 342, (1949) (overruled on other grounds by United Ins. Co. of Am. v. Murphy, 331 Ark. 364, 961 S.W.2d 752 (1998)). The defamatory statements do not need to be made to the public generally, or even to a considerable number of persons. Id. Publication is sufficient even though the third party does not believe what is said of the defamed person. Id. Circumstantial evidence that a defamatory statement was overheard can be enough evidence of publication to support a defamation claim. Wal-Mart Stores, Inc. v. Lee, 348 Ark. 707, 74 S.W.3d 634 (2002). **The plaintiff must allege facts that would allow a court to make a reasonable inference that the defendant published the material on its own accord. Neely v. NameMedia, Inc., 2012 U.S. Dist. LEXIS 107296, *6-7, 40 Media L. Rep. 2270 (W.D. Ark. 2012). When a plaintiff uploads his own images to online websites, search engine defendants are not liable for defamation when some of those images are accessible through internet searches. Id.**

a. **Intracorporate Communication.** Communications between members of the board of directors of a corporation are protected by a qualified privilege because all the parties present have a common interest in the subject matter of the statements. Navorro-Monzo v. Hughes, 297 Ark. 444, 763 S.W.2d 635 (1989). Communications between different branches of a corporation in the course of corporate business do not constitute publication to third persons for purposes of a defamation claim. Halsell v. Kimberly Clark Corp., 683 F.2d 285 (8th Cir. 1982), aff'g 518 F.Supp. 694 (E.D.Ark. 1981), cert. denied, 459 U.S. 1205 (1983).

b. **Compelled Self-Publication.** An Arkansas district court allowed plaintiff's defamation claim when one of the employee's allegations was that he had been injured through self-publication because he was forced to repeat the charges to the unemployment agency, prospective employers, fellow employees, and friends. Coatney v. Enterprise Rent-A-Car Co., 897 F. Supp. 1205 (W.D. Ark. 1995).

c. **Republication.** When a defamatory statement is repeated by someone other than the initial publisher, the second publisher may be liable for simply repeating what he has heard. Nance v. Flaugh, 221 Ark. 352, 253 S.W.2d 207 (1952). In Jones v. Commercial Printing Co., 249 Ark. 952, 463 S.W.2d 92 (1971), the defendant newspaper published a second article providing an answer to the plaintiff's suit after a first allegedly defamatory article. There, the plaintiff sought to introduce the subsequent article as a republication of the original to demonstrate aggravating circumstances for the purpose of awarding damages. Id. The court determined that the second article should be considered by the jury if they indeed found that the first article was defamatory. Id. The initial publisher of a libelous statement is liable for republication by others if the republication was foreseeable as a natural and probable consequence of the original publication. Luster v. Retail Credit Co., 575 F.2d 609 (8th Cir. 1978). Arkansas courts have not discussed a republisher's independent liability. See Ewing v. Cargill, Inc., 324 Ark. 217, 919 S.W.2d 507 (1996) (noting that the Supreme Court of Arkansas has "never decided whether one is liable for republication of a defamatory statement.") (overruled on other grounds by United Ins. Co. of Am. v. Murphy, 331 Ark. 364, 961 S.W.2d 752 (1998)) see also Wal-Mart Stores, Inc. v. Lee, 348 Ark. 707, 74 S.W.3d 634 (2002) (the court again declined to address the issue of liability for republication of defamation, stating that the issue, as a defense in a defamation lawsuit, was raised for the first time on appeal and was not properly preserved for appellate review).

7. ***Statements versus Conduct.*** No Arkansas cases on point.

8. ***Damages.*** All plaintiffs in defamation cases must prove reputational injury in order to recover damages. United Ins. Co. of Am. v. Murphy, 331 Ark. 364, 961 S.W.2d 752 (1998); Faulkner v. Ark. Children's Hosp., 347 Ark. 941, 69 S.W.3d 393 (2002). Damage to reputation cannot be presumed in any case. Little Rock Newspapers, Inc. v. Dodrill, 281 Ark. 25, 660 S.W.2d 933, 10 Media L. Rep. 1063 (1983). To prove reputational injury, plaintiffs must prove both that the defamatory statement was communicated to others, and that the statement detrimentally affected those relations. Northport Health Servs., Inc. v. Owens, 82 Ark. App. 355, 107 S.W.3d 889 (2003), aff'd as modified, 356 Ark. 630, 158 S.W.3d 164 (2004); Suggs v. Stanley, 324 F.3d 672 (8th Cir. 2003); Wal-Mart Stores, Inc. v. Lee, 348 Ark. 707, 74 S.W.3d 634 (2002). The required showing of harm to reputation is slight. **Lancaster v. Red Robin International, Inc., 2011 Ark. App. 706, at 8.** Proof that the defamatory statement detrimentally affected plaintiff's relations with others is enough, and proof of out-of-pocket losses is not required. **Id.**; Ellis v. Price, 337 Ark. 542, 990 S.W.2d 543 (1999). "It is not necessary to prove the literal truth of the accusation in every detail but that the imputation is substantially true, or as it is often put, to justify the gist, the sting, or the substantial truth of the defamation". Boellner v. Clinical Study Ctrs., LLC, 2011 Ark. 83, at 18, ___ S.W.3d ___, ___ (citing Pritchard v. Times Sw. Broad., Inc., 277 Ark. 458, 642 S.W.2d 877 (1982)). In order for liability to attach, there must be evidence that demonstrates a causal connection between defamatory statements made by the defendant and the injury to the plaintiff's reputation. Northport Health Servs., Inc. v. Owens, 82 Ark. App. 355, 107 S.W.3d 889 (2003), aff'd as modified, 356 Ark. 630, 158 S.W.3d 164 (2004) (citing Ellis, supra). In an unpublished opinion, the Arkansas Court of Appeals held that, although allegedly defamatory statements about plaintiff corporation were published twice in a local newspaper, testimony by the corporation's owner that the statements hampered his ability to market his corporation's services to other customers and that "no other company would do business with him" did not amount to proof that the allegedly defamatory statements were communicated to potential customers and that the corporation sustained damage to its reputation as required under Ellis. Cannon Computer Co. v. Douglas, No. CA00-890, 2001 WL 295233 (Ark. App. 2001) (unpublished). Nevertheless, a plaintiff's testimony that his or her reputation was injured is generally sufficient to take the issue to the jury. Northport Health Servs., Inc. v. Owens, 82 Ark. App. 355, 107 S.W.3d 889 (2003), aff'd as modified, 356 Ark. 630, 158 S.W.3d 164 (2004); see also Suggs v. Stanley, 324 F.3d 672 (8th Cir. 2003) (holding that "[u]nder Arkansas law, a plaintiff's testimony that her reputation has been injured by defamatory statements can be sufficient evidence of harm."). **But see Lancaster, 2011 Ark. App. 706, at 9 (affirming summary judgment against plaintiff where plaintiff's co-worker told another employee that plaintiff was dealing drugs but where plaintiff offered no evidence that the co-worker's statements caused damage to plaintiff).**

a. **Presumed Damages and Libel Per Se.** Traditionally, making a false statement that the plaintiff was guilty of a crime or was afflicted with a loathsome disease, or making statements that prejudiced the plaintiff's ability to engage in his or her profession was considered defamatory per se, injurious, and sufficient to support an award of presumed damages. Now, in defamation per se actions, damages will no longer be presumed. All plaintiffs in defamation cases must prove reputational injury in order to recover damages. Faulkner v. Ark. Children's Hosp., 347 Ark. 941, 69 S.W.3d 393 (2002); United Ins. Co. of Am. v. Murphy, 331 Ark. 364, 961 S.W.2d 752 (1998).

(1) **Employment-Related Criticism.** The words "incompetent and unable to function in his position" claimed by the plaintiff, a state police officer, to have been said by the defendant, the Governor,

about the plaintiff possessed the general tenor of an opinion as opposed to a verifiable statement of fact and therefore were not actionable. Brown v. Tucker, 330 Ark. 435, 954 S.W.2d 262 (1997). Statements made by faculty members and resident physicians named as defendants in a defamation action by former resident, including opinions regarding resident's personal competence or personal characteristics related to her job performance, including her "germ phobia," were either true or were opinions and therefore not actionable. Asaad-Faltas v. Griffin, 708 F. Supp. 1035 (E.D. Ark. 1989), aff'd, 902 F.2d 1572 (8th Cir.), cert. denied, 498 U.S. 905 (1990). Former insurance agency employees successfully sued agency owners and insurance company with which agency was under contract and recovered damages for defamation based upon the owners' statements following the employees' resignations from the agency. The owners claimed that the former employees had been terminated for "fraud doings [they] got involved in when the owner of the company was away." Yeldell v. Tutt, 913 F.2d 533 (8th Cir. 1990). The evidence was sufficient to support a charge of slander when the plaintiff, a former employee, alleged that a current employee told customers that the plaintiff had been fired for stealing. Tandy Corp. v. Bone, 283 Ark. 399, 678 S.W.2d 312 (1984). A statement by the plaintiff's immediate supervisor to one of the plaintiff's fellow employees and others that the plaintiff was "fired because he was caught stealing" was actionable and did not come within the qualified privilege afforded an employer, where the statement was factually incorrect and obviously injurious to the plaintiff. Dillard Dept. Stores, Inc. v. Felton, 276 Ark. 304, 634 S.W.2d 135 (1982). Corporate employees made statements imputing a pro-union disposition to the industrial relations manager of a plant. The statements were per se defamatory because they were of such a nature as to be injurious to the business relationship between the plaintiff and his employer. Andrews v. Mohawk Rubber Co., 474 F. Supp. 1276 (E.D. Ark. 1979).

(2) **Single Instance Rule.** No Arkansas cases on point.

b. **Punitive Damages.** To support an award of punitive damages in a defamation case, the jury must find that the defamatory statements were made with ill will, malice, or bad intent. Yeldell v. Tutt, 913 F.2d 533 (8th Cir. 1990); Suggs v. Stanley, 324 F.3d 672 (8th Cir. 2003). Whether there was a showing of express malice sufficient to support an award of punitive damages is a question of fact for the jury. Express malice may be shown by the defamatory words themselves and the manner of their publication. Express malice need not be proven by extrinsic evidence, but may not be inferred from the facts alone that the words were false and injurious to the plaintiff. The amount of punitive damages to award is within the province of the jury, subject to proper instruction from the court. Braman v. Walthall, 215 Ark. 582, 225 S.W.2d 342 (1949) (overruled on other grounds by United Ins. Co. of Am. v. Murphy, 331 Ark. 364, 961 S.W.2d 752 (1998), which concluded presumed damages would no longer be awarded in defamation per se cases). An award of punitive damages is proper where the jury could have concluded from the evidence that defendants acted with malice, displayed a conscious indifference for plaintiff, acted with deliberate intent to injure plaintiff, and acted with reckless indifference to the effect their allegations would have on plaintiff. Allstate Ins. Co. v. Dodson, 2011 Ark. 19, at 24; Ellis v. Price, 337 Ark. 542, 990 S.W.2d 543 (1999). Although a finding of express malice requires no extrinsic proof and can be inferred by the jury from all the circumstances of the case, an award of punitive damages cannot be upheld where the totality of the evidence is such that fairminded people could not infer malice. Dillard Dept. Stores, Inc. v. Felton, 276 Ark. 304, 634 S.W.2d 135 (1982). When reviewing an award of punitive damages, the extent and enormity of the wrong, all the circumstances, and the financial and social condition and standing of the erring party should be considered. Punitive damages are to be a penalty for conduct that is malicious or done with deliberate intent to injure another. United Ins. Co. of Am. v. Murphy, 331 Ark. 364, 961 S.W.2d 752 (1998). Two million dollar punitive damage award did not "shock the conscience" when the evidence showed that the plaintiff's former supervisor intentionally made defamatory statements because he did not like to work with women and did not want the plaintiff under his supervision; that the supervisor tried to enlist plaintiff's customers as his own; and that the company's officers knew that the supervisor had made the defamatory statements, were aware that the supervisor was not following company procedures to substantiate his claim that the plaintiff was stealing, and did nothing to stop the supervisor, even allowing the supervisor to fire the plaintiff. Such evidence could lead the jury to conclude that the company displayed conscious indifference and that such acts were done with deliberate intent to injure the plaintiff. Id. A six million dollar award did not "shock the conscience" of the court when the evidence showed the defendant insurance company's conduct occurred over a period of several years, was a part of its national claims practices and procedures, and was taken by a nationally-recognized insurance agency. Allstate. 2011 Ark. 19, at 27. When the evidence did not support an award of punitive damages but the jury was instructed to believe that it could award punitive damages and the amount of the verdict indicated that such an award had been made, the court ordered remittitur or, in the alternative, announced that the decision would be reversed and the cause remanded for a new trial. Joslyn Mfg. & Supply Co. v. White, 211 Ark. 362, 200 S.W.2d 789 (1947).

II. PRIVILEGES AND DEFENSES

A. Scope of Privileges

Determination of the existence of a privilege is a matter of law. See, e.g., Pogue v. Cooper, 284 Ark. 202, 680 S.W.2d 698 (1984). Arkansas recognizes the following privileges: (1) Statements and pleadings in judicial and quasi-judicial proceedings; (2) Justices of state court of last resort in publication of court opinion; (3) Physician testifying in a lunacy hearing; (4) Attorney's relevant and pertinent statements preliminary to a proposed judicial proceeding; (5) Communications between members of board of directors of a corporation; (6) Intra-company work-performance evaluation; (7) Communications between supervisors of employee; (8) Communication between former and prospective employers; (9) Communication pursuant to public duty; (10) Statements made to employer's personnel with duty of investigating employee theft; (11) Letter from party having an interest in a matter to another interested party; (12) Statements made by mercantile agency to customer having an interest in a matter; (13) Complete, impartial and accurate report of a judicial proceeding; (14) Publication requested or provoked by injured party; (15) Accurate report of issuance of Governor's investigation report; (16) Statement before police committee and at public hearing; (17) Publication of statement in good faith to protect one's own interest; (18) "Fair Report" privilege for substantially true account of an official action or proceeding, or of a meeting open to the public that deals with a matter of public concern.

1. ***Absolute Privilege.*** Statements made prior to the commencement of judicial proceedings are absolutely privileged if made in connection with possible litigation. This privilege covers statements made by both attorneys and parties to the possible litigation. The privilege is narrowed closely by "relevancy" and "pertinency" requirements and does not cover the publication of defamatory matter that has "no connection whatever" with the possible litigation. Jones v. Clinton, 974 F. Supp. 712 (E.D. Ark. 1997), appeal dismissed, 161 F.3d 528 (8th Cir. 1998); Pinkston v. Lovell, 296 Ark. 543, 759 S.W.2d 20 (1988); Selby v. Burgess, 289 Ark. 491, 712 S.W.2d 898 (1986). Statements made in the institution of or during the course and as a part of a judicial proceeding by an attorney participating as counsel which relate to the proceeding and are relevant and pertinent to the issues in the case are absolutely privileged also. Selby v. Burgess, 289 Ark. 491, 712 S.W.2d 898 (1986). Letters recounting events precipitating action against union employees by employers are absolutely privileged and cannot form the basis of an employee's defamation claim when those letters are sent pursuant to a collective bargaining agreement. Duke v. Domtar, No. 05-CV-4044, 2006 WL 2228830 (W.D. Ark. 2006).

2. ***Qualified Privileges.*** The fact that a third party learns of libelous matter is not necessarily publication; some communications are protected by a qualified privilege. Farris v. Tvedten, 274 Ark. 185, 623 S.W.2d 205 (1981). A publication may be conditionally privileged if the circumstances induce a correct or reasonable belief that the information affects a sufficiently important interest of the recipient or a third person and if the recipient is one to whom the publisher is under a legal duty to publish the defamatory matter or is a person to whom its publication is otherwise within generally accepted standards of decent conduct. Dillard Dept. Stores, Inc. v. Felton, 276 Ark. 304, 634 S.W.2d 135 (1982) (citing RESTATEMENT (SECOND) OF TORTS ' 595 (1981)); Duke v. Domtar, No. 05-CV-4044, 2006 WL 2228830 (W.D. Ark. 2006). The Arkansas Supreme Court clarified that a qualified privilege may be invoked if it is made in good faith upon any subject matter in which the person making the communication has an interest or in reference to which he has a duty, and to a person having a corresponding interest or duty, although it contains matters which, without such a privilege, would be actionable. Suggs v. Stanley, 324 F.3d 672 (8th Cir. 2003); Wal-Mart Stores, Inc. v. Lee, 348 Ark.707, 74 S.W.3d 634 (2002); Addington v. Wal-Mart Stores, Inc., 81 Ark. App. 441, 105 S.W.3d 369 (Ark. App. 2003); Navorro-Monzo v. Hughes, 297 Ark. 444, 763 S.W.2d 635 (1989). Immunity does not extend to irrelevant defamatory statements that have no relation to the interest entitled to protection, and the privilege is also lost if it is abused by excessive publication, if the statement is made with malice, or if the statement is made with a lack of grounds for belief in the truth of the statement. Id. If defendant publishes a defamatory statement under a qualified privilege, plaintiff bears the burden of proving that the publication exceeded the scope of the privilege. Ikani v. Bennett, 284 Ark. 409, 682 S.W.2d 747 (1985). The question of whether a particular statement falls outside of the scope of the qualified privilege is a question of fact. Wal-Mart Stores, Inc. v. Lee, 348 Ark. 707, 74 S.W.3d 634 (2002). In Lee, the court found that the scope of the employer's qualified privilege had been exceeded. The jury found that certain statements in the employer's loss-prevention case synopsis were not privileged because the employer did not have sufficient grounds to believe the statements were true. Wal-Mart Stores, Inc. v. Lee, 348 Ark. 707, 737, 74 S.W.3d 634 (2002) ("the trier of fact is free to believe all or part of any witness's testimony and may resolve questions of conflicting testimony and inconsistent evidence"). Qualified privilege must be exercised in a reasonable manner and is lost if abused. Suggs v. Stanley, 324 F.3d 672 (8th Cir. 2003).

a. **Common Interest.** The common interest privilege protects communications between persons having a corresponding interest. Navorro-Monzo v. Hughes, 297 Ark. 444, 763 S.W.2d 635 (1989). **However, the communication must be "of a kind reasonably calculated to protect or further [that common interest]." Lancaster, 2011 Ark. App. 706, at 8.** Employers and supervisory employees have a qualified privilege against liability for defamation regarding matters that affect their business. Freeman v. Bechtel Constr. Co., 87 F.3d 1029 (8th Cir. 1996). Therefore, a claim will fail unless there is an abuse of the privilege or the communication was to a non-privileged third party. Pighee v. L'Oreal USA Products, Inc., 351 F. Supp. 2d 885 (E.D. Ark. 2005). Communications between members of the board of directors of a corporation are protected by a qualified privilege because all of the parties present have a legitimate common interest in the subject matter of the statements. Id. Allegedly defamatory work-performance evaluation or other supervisory communication regarding employee is privileged so long as not published or communicated to anyone outside of company management. Puckett v. Cook, 864 F.2d 619 (8th Cir. 1989). In Ikani v. Bennett, 284 Ark. 409, 682 S.W.2d 747 (1985), the

Arkansas Supreme Court held that communication between supervisors of a counselor at the Department of Corrections, concerning his alleged gun smuggling to a foreign country, was privileged since it was an exchange of information between two supervisory employees concerning an employee under their charge, for whose performance they were responsible. See also Dillard Dept. Stores, Inc. v. Felton, 276 Ark. 304, 634 S.W.2d 135 (1982). **When two managers of a restaurant conducted an investigation of an employee, and those managers made statements to each other, and other employees made statements to those managers, such communications were privileged because they were made in connection with the investigation. Lancaster, 2011 Ark. App. 706, at 9.** Communications between former and prospective employers are qualifiedly privileged. Scholtes v. Sign Delivery Serv., Inc., 548 F. Supp. 487 (W.D. Ark. 1982). A letter from a doctor to a nurse criticizing the nurse and insinuating that she had substituted medication, thereby committing a crime, was deemed a privileged publication since it was made by one with an interest or duty in a matter to another who had a like interest. Farris v. Tvedten, 274 Ark. 185, 623 S.W.2d 205 (1981). Statements by a mercantile agency to a customer having an interest in the matter are privileged. Luster v. Retail Credit Co., 575 F.2d 609 (8th Cir. 1978) (credit report). Arkansas also recognizes a qualified privilege to publish a defamatory statement in good faith to protect one's own interest provided publication is reasonably necessary and the privilege is not abused by excessively broad publication, and this qualified privilege extends to a small-town employer's explanation to local media of the results of a newsworthy investigation into employee dishonesty or misconduct. Richmond v. Southwire Co., 980 F.2d 518, 21 Media L. Rep. 1284 (8th Cir. 1992).

b. **Duty.** A qualified privilege is extended to a communication made in good faith in which the communicating party has a duty, either legal, moral, or social. Ikani v. Bennett, 284 Ark. 409, 682 S.W.2d 747 (1985). Communications pursuant to public duty are privileged. Baker v. Mann, 276 Ark. 278, 634 S.W.2d 125 (1982) (letter from city council to prosecuting attorney requesting state police investigation of conduct in city police department not defamatory). Statements were not defamatory when made to an employer's personnel representative who had a duty to investigate an employee's possession of merchandise without a receipt. Dillard Dept. Stores, Inc. v. Felton, 276 Ark. 304, 634 S.W.2d 135 (1982). An employer's duty to report to the Employment Security Division carries a qualified privilege. Id; see also Addington v. Wal-Mart Stores, Inc., 81 Ark. App. 441, 105 S.W.3d 369 (2003). Statements made by employees of a defendant to the Employment Security Division also carry the qualified privilege afforded an employer, if the statements are made in good faith with reasonable grounds for believing them to be true on a subject matter in which the author had a public or private duty to a person having a corresponding duty. Duke v. Domtar, 2006 WL 2228830 (W.D. Ark. 2006) (citing Dillard Dept. Stores, Inc. v. Felton, 276 Ark. 304, 634 S.W.2d 135 (1982)). In Domtar, a human resources manager had a public duty to testify truthfully to an unemployment officer about the circumstances of an employee's termination. Id. Because the manager's testimony was made in good faith and with reasonable grounds for believing it to be true, his statements fell within the qualified privilege. Id. There is no explanation in the case why the defendant did not assert the governmental privilege under Ark. Code Ann. § 11-10-314, which states that information obtained by the Director of the Department of Workforce Services from an employer or individual, and any determination "as to the rights or status of any employer or individual made by the director" pursuant to administering the statute is confidential and privileged, and "shall not be used in any action or proceeding before any court…unless the Department is a party, a real party in interest, or a complainant therein…." Ark. Code Ann. § 11-10-314.

c. **Criticism of Public Employee.** Public interest usually calls this privilege into being. In Thiel v. Dove, 229 Ark. 601, 317 S.W.2d 121 (1958), statements concerning a policeman made by a witness at a police committee investigatory hearing and later before a public city council meeting were conditionally privileged. Communications by a city mayor and members of city council to a prosecuting attorney about a police chief's misconduct also were conditionally privileged. Baker v. Mann, 276 Ark. 278, 634 S.W.2d 125 (1982). Communications concerning a schoolteacher's discharge at a school board meeting were considered to be conditionally privileged when made by the school board members. McClain v. Anderson, 246 Ark. 638, 439 S.W.2d 296 (1969). "To state a procedural due process claim against a state employer for depravation of a protected liberty interest in a public employee's reputation, it is necessary to show defamation by a state actor during the course of termination." Eddings v. City of Hot Springs, 323 F.3d 596 (8th Cir. 2003).

d. **Limitation on Qualified Privileges.** This privilege is not absolute but rather must be exercised in a reasonable manner and for a proper purpose. **Lancaster v. Red Robin International, Inc., 2011 Ark. App. 706, at 8,;** Navorro-Monzo v. Hughes, 297 Ark. 444, 763 S.W.2d 635 (1989). If the publication is not within the confines of the privilege, abuses the privilege, or is not made pursuing a common interest, the privilege is lost. Id. Privileges do not protect defendant from publications to individuals other than those whose hearing is reasonably believed to be necessary and useful. **Lancaster, 2011 Ark. App. 706, at 9;** Ikani v. Bennett, 284 Ark. 409, 682 S.W.2d 747 (1985). A privilege does not extend to insubstantial libelous statements that have no bearing on the interests entitled to protection. Navorro-Monzo v. Hughes, 297 Ark. 444, 763 S.W.2d 635 (1989). The qualified privilege is gone if one publishes defamatory communications with malice. Id. Privileges may also be lost through excessive publication. Ark. Associated Tel. Co. v. Blankenship, 211 Ark. 645, 201 S.W.2d 1019 (1947). The question of whether malice has been established and the communication shown not to be privileged is a question of fact for the jury. Suggs v. Stanley, 324 F.3d 672 (8th Cir. 2003). Qualified immunity is an entitlement not to stand trial under certain circumstances. On the plaintiffs' defamation claim, the employer's qualified immunity granted by Ark. Code Ann. § 5-28-215 (Repl. 1997) for reporting alleged nursing home abuse was waived by the employer's bad faith in making the report. Northport Health Services, Inc. v. Owens, 356 Ark. 630, 158 S.W.3d 164 (2004).

(1) **Constitutional or Actual Malice.** The Arkansas Supreme Court used this standard in the privilege context in Dun & Bradstreet, Inc. v. Robinson, 233 Ark. 168, 345 S.W.2d 34 (1961) (overruled on other grounds by United Ins. Co. of Am. v. Murphy, 331 Ark. 364, 961 S.W.2d 752 (1998)). In that case, negligent investigation was enough to eliminate the qualified privilege. Id. Defendant's failure to confirm the truthfulness of its comments amounted to a "conscious indifference and reckless disregard" of plaintiff's rights. Id.

(2) **Common Law Malice.** Arkansas courts have defined malice as something other than "legal malice" imposing strict liability in unprivileged defamation cases and something less than "express malice" or "ill will." Navorro-Monzo v. Hughes, 297 Ark. 444, 763 S.W.2d 635 (1989). In Navorro-Monzo, the court did not find that the members of the board of directors of the corporation acted maliciously when the statements were not "exceptionally harsh" or "motivated by spite or revenge." Id. Rather, the statements were those made by an investor who was concerned about his investment. Id. In Duke v. Domtar, the burden of showing malice that would justify a loss of the qualified privilege was on the terminated employees making the claim of malice. Duke v. Domtar, No. 05-CV-4044, 2006 WL 2228830 (W.D. Ark. 2006). Because investigations into potential employee wrongdoing are already tinged with antagonism, and because there was no indication that statements made during investigatory interviews had crossed the line into malice, the court in Domtar determined that the qualified privilege applied to all communications in the investigatory interviews of the terminated employees. Id.

e. **Question of Fact or Law.** The existence of a privilege is determined as a matter of law. Minor v. Failla, 329 Ark. 274, 946 S.W.2d 954 (1997) (overruled on other grounds by United Ins. Co. of Am. v. Murphy, 331 Ark. 364, 961 S.W.2d 752 (1998)). The issue of whether the defamatory statement falls outside the scope of being a qualified privilege is a question of fact for the jury. Minor v. Failla, 946 S.W.2d 954 (1997) (overruled on other grounds by United Ins. Co. of Am. v. Murphy, 331 Ark. 364, 961 S.W.2d 752 (1998)); Addington v. Wal-Mart Stores, Inc., 105 S.W.3d 369 (2003).

f. **Burden of Proof.** Plaintiffs bear the burden of pleading and proof on each of the six elements of a defamation claim. See I.B.1, supra; Dodson v. Allstate Ins. Co., 345 Ark. 430, 47 S.W.3d 866 (2001). Plaintiffs bear the burden of pleading and proof that the defendant knowingly or negligently published a false and defamatory fact. Id. Plaintiffs must prove the falsity of the statements at issue by a preponderance of the evidence. Campbell v. Citizens for an Honest Gov't, Inc., 255 F.3d 560, 29 Media L. Rep. 2155 (8th Cir. 2001) (applying that burden of proof to public-figure plaintiffs). The defendant has the burden of proving that the defamatory statements were privileged. Ikani v. Bennett, 284 Ark. 409, 682 S.W.2d 747 (1985). When the defense of privilege is pleaded and established, the burden shifts to the plaintiff to prove that the privilege has been "abused by excessive publication, by use of the occasion for an improper purpose, or by lack of belief or grounds for belief in the truth of what is said." Id. A private libel plaintiff must prove fault, i.e., the defendant's negligence in the publication, only by a preponderance of the evidence. Little Rock Newspapers, Inc. v. Dodrill, 281 Ark. 25, 660 S.W.2d 933, 10 Media L. Rep. 1063 (1983). A private or limited public figure plaintiff attempting recovery on matters of public concern, and all public figures, must prove actual malice by clear and convincing evidence. See Thomson Newspaper Publ'g, Inc. v. Coody, 320 Ark. 455, 896 S.W.2d 897, 23 Media L. Rep. 2270 (1995); Fuller v. Russell, 311 Ark. 108, 842 S.W.2d 12, 21 Media L. Rep. 1254 (1992); Dodson v. Dicker, 306 Ark. 108, 812 S.W.2d 97, 19 Media L. Rep. 1124 (1991).

B. Standard Libel Defenses

1. ***Truth.*** Proof that a statement is substantially true will serve as a defense to a charge of defamation. Pritchard v. Times Sw. Broad., 277 Ark. 458, 642 S.W.2d 877, 9 Media L. Rep. 1048 (1982); Wirges v. Brewer, 239 Ark. 317, 389 S.W.2d 226 (1965) (holding that truth is a complete defense to a defamation charge). Truth is a defense to criminal libel even when the offending material is published without good motives or for justifiable ends. Weston v. State, 258 Ark. 707, 528 S.W.2d 412 (1975). In United Ins. Co. of Am. v. Murphy, 331 Ark. 364, 961 S.W.2d 752 (1998), the defendants challenged a jury instruction placing the burden of proof on them, but the Supreme Court of Arkansas held that the issue had not been preserved for appeal.

2. ***Opinion.*** Only statements alleging facts are properly the basis for an action sounding in defamation. Dodson v. Dicker, 306 Ark. 108, 812 S.W.2d 97, 19 Media L. Rep. 1124 (1991). As discussed supra I.B.4, the following three factors are relevant when distinguishing fact from opinion, but no one factor is dispositive: (1) whether the author used figurative or hyperbolic language that would negate the impression that he or she was seriously maintaining the implied fact; (2) whether the general tenor of the publication negates this impression; and (3) whether the published assertion is susceptible of being proved true or false. Id. (relying upon Milkovich v. Lorain Journal Co., 497 U.S. 1, 17 Media L. Rep. 2009 (1990)). Faulkner v. Ark. Children's Hosp., 347 Ark. 941, 69 S.W.3d 393 (2002). See also Bland v. Verser, 299 Ark.

490, 774 S.W.2d 124 (1989) (stating a slightly altered version of this test). The words "incompetent and unable to function in his position" claimed by the plaintiff, a state police officer, to have been said by the defendant, the Governor, about the plaintiff possessed the general tenor of an opinion as opposed to a verifiable statement of fact. Brown v. Tucker, 330 Ark. 435, 954 S.W.2d 262 (1997). Assertions regarding the role of the husband of the President of the State Board of Therapy Technology in the Board's business, even though stated in intemperate language, when expressed in terms of "opinion" and "protest" are not the type of assertions of objective facts that give rise to a defamation claim. Dodson v. Dicker, 306 Ark. 108, 812 S.W.2d 97, 19 Media L. Rep. 1124 (1991). Statements made by faculty members and resident physicians named as defendants in defamation action by former resident, including opinions regarding resident's personal competence or personal characteristics related to her job performance, including her "germ phobia," were either true or were opinions and therefore not actionable. Asaad-Faltas v. Griffin, 708 F. Supp. 1035 (E.D. Ark. 1989), aff'd, 902 F.2d 1572 (8th Cir. 1990), cert. denied, 498 U.S. 905 (1990).

3. ***Consent.*** Ark. Code Ann. § 11-3-204 allows an employer who obtains written consent from a current or former employee to disclose the following information about an employee: date and duration of employment; current pay rate and wage history; job description and duties; the last written performance evaluation prepared prior to the date of the request; attendance information; results of drug or alcohol tests administered within one year prior to the request; threats of violence, harassing acts, or threatening behavior related to the workplace or directed at another employee; whether the employee was voluntarily or involuntarily separated from employment and the reason for the separation; and whether the employee is eligible for rehire. An employer disclosing this information upon consent of the employee shall be presumed to be acting in good faith and shall be immune from civil liability for the disclosure or any consequence of the disclosure unless the presumption is rebutted with evidence that the information disclosed was false, and the employer had knowledge of its falsity or acted with malice or reckless disregard for the truth.

4. ***Mitigation.*** No Arkansas cases on point.

III. RECURRING FACT PATTERNS

A. Statements in Personnel File

Applying Arkansas law, the Eighth Circuit held that a report placed in an employee's permanent file stating that the employee was investigated on a charge of sexual harassment or disciplined would not constitute false statements for purposes of defamation. Freeman v. Bechtel Constr. Co., 87 F.3d 1029 (8th Cir. 1996). The employee in Freeman demonstrated no specific defamatory statements nor showed that the reports were communicated to an unprivileged third party. This fell within the scope of the qualified privilege allowing employers and supervisory employees to speak on matters that affect their business. Id. **In a recent case, the Arkansas Court of Appeals held that a qualified privilege applied to statements made between two managers and two employees regarding allegations that a third employee was dealing drugs at work. Lancaster v. Red Robin International, Inc., 2011 Ark. App. 706, at 9. While this case did not involve a personnel file, it did involve an employer's internal investigation of an employee's alleged misconduct. Id.**

B. Performance Evaluations

Arkansas law recognizes a qualified privilege for employers and supervisory employees, and this privilege also applies to intra-company performance evaluations. Puckett v. Cook, 864 F.2d 619 (8th Cir. 1989). The privilege remains unless the allegedly libelous statements were published or communicated to anyone outside company management. Id.

C. References

Ark. Code Ann. § 11-3-204 allows an employer who obtains written consent from a current or former employee to disclose the following information about an employee. See II.B.3, supra.

When a consent has not been signed, an individual may sue his or her current or former employer for defamation where such employer provides a prospective employer with information which the employee claims is defamatory. Scholtes v. Signal Delivery Serv., Inc., 548 F. Supp. 487 (W.D. Ark. 1982). There are no Arkansas cases discussing the application of the common interest privilege as a defense in the context of references provided by a current or former employer. See supra II.A.2.a. This must be raised as a defense by the employer. There is some support for the proposition that the common interest privilege would apply to this situation. For example, in Richmond v. Southwire Co., 980 F.2d 518, 21 Media L. Rep. 1234 (8th Cir. 1992), the qualified privilege to publish defamatory matter extended to a small town employer's explanation to local media of the results of an investigation into employee dishonesty or misconduct.

D. Intracorporate Communication

Communications between different branches of a corporation in the course of corporate business do not constitute publication to third persons for purposes of defamation. Halsell v. Kimberly-Clark Corp., 683 F.2d 285 (8th Cir. 1982), aff'g

518 F.Supp. 694 (E.D.Ark. 1981), cert. denied, 459 U.S. 1205 (1983). See supra II.A.2.a for more on the common interest privilege and its application in the intracorporate communications context.

E. Statements to Government Regulators

A letter sent by mayor and city council members to a prosecuting attorney pertaining to the former police chief's possible misconduct was conditionally privileged where the mayor and city council members were carrying out a public duty, the statements were not found to be untrue, and the plaintiff did not show that the sending of the letter was malicious. Baker v. Mann, 276 Ark. 278, 634 S.W.2d 125 (1982). A statement made by defendant before the police committee and at a public hearing of the city council that the defendant saw a particular policeman through an apartment window, only in an undershirt and with a nude woman, was conditionally privileged. Thiel v. Dove, 229 Ark. 601, 317 S.W.2d 121 (1958). A nursing home's report of alleged abuse to patients by nurses was not privileged under Ark. Code Ann. § 5-28-215 (Repl. 1997) because the employer made the report in bad faith. Northport Health Servs., Inc. v. Owens, 356 Ark. 630, 158 S.W.3d 164 (2004).

F. Reports to Auditors and Insurers

No Arkansas cases on point.

G. Vicarious Liability of Employers for Statements Made by Employees

Where the alleged slanderous statement is made by an employee of a corporation and the plaintiff is attempting to hold the corporation liable, the plaintiff must show that the statements were made in furtherance of the company's business. Smedley v. Life & Cas. Co. of Tenn., 221 F. Supp. 119 (W.D. Ark. 1963) (citing Sinclair Refining Co. v. Fuller, 190 Ark. 426, 79 S.W.2d 736 (1935); Safeway Stores, Inc. v. Rogers, 186 Ark. 826, 56 S.W.2d 429 (1933)).

1. ***Scope of Employment.*** For a corporation to be liable for a libelous statement made by an employee, the employee must have been acting within the scope of his employment. Smedley v. Life & Cas. Ins. Co. of Tenn., 221 F. Supp. 119 (W.D. Ark. 1963); Waters-Pierce Oil Co. v. Bridwell, 103 Ark. 345, 147 S.W. 64 (1912).

a. **Blogging.** No Arkansas cases.

2. ***Damages.*** A corporation is liable in damages for slander as it is for other torts. Waters-Pierce Oil Co. v. Bridwell, 103 Ark. 345, 147 S.W. 64 (1912). In addition to compensatory damages, under the doctrine of respondeat superior, an employer may also be liable for punitive damages for his employee's acts if the employee was acting within the scope of his employment at the time of the incident. Regions Bank v. Stone County Skilled Nursing Facility, Inc., 73 Ark. App. 17, 21, 38 S.W.3d 916, 919 (2001), aff'd, 345 Ark. 555, 49 S.W.3d 107 (2001); Gordon v. Planters & Merchs. Bancshares, Inc., 326 Ark. 1046, 935 S.W.2d 544 (1996). Whether an employee is acting within the scope of his employment depends on whether the employee is carrying out the purpose of the business, rather than acting solely on his own. Id.

H. Internal Investigations

No Arkansas cases.

IV. OTHER ACTIONS BASED ON STATEMENTS

A. Negligent Hiring, Retention, and Supervision

The Arkansas Supreme Court has stated that under the theories of negligent hiring, negligent retention, and negligent supervision, "the employer's liability rests upon proof that the employer knew or, through the exercise of ordinary care, should have known that the employee's conduct would subject third parties to an unreasonable risk of harm." Paulino v. QHG of Springdale, Inc., 2012 Ark. 55, at 13. For the most part, Arkansas case law on this subject is confined to employees' conduct other than statements. For example, a radiologist was not liable for negligently hiring a radiology technician where the technician had the highest ultrasound degree available, the radiologist had known the technician for eight years and the patient showed no evidence that a background check would have led the radiologist to believe that the technician was predisposed to commit a sexual assault. Porter v. Harshfield, 329 Ark. 130, 948 S.W.2d 83 (1997). The radiologist was not liable for negligent retention when the radiologist was unaware of a prior sexual assault complaint against the technician. Id. Furthermore, the radiologist was not liable for negligent supervision after the technician had described himself as being homosexual and the radiologist did not require another employee present in the room when the technician examined a male patient. Id. In a recent case, an attorney was found liable for negligently hiring and supervising another attorney who defrauded the plaintiffs in an adoption case. The court held that the employer was not immune under Ark. Code Ann. § 16-22-310 because the claim was for negligent hiring and supervision rather than malpractice. Madden v. Aldrich, 346 Ark. 405, 58 S.W.3d 342 (2001). Where an employee sexually assaulted a patient, the court held that a genuine issue of material fact existed as to the employer's negligent supervision where an affidavit of a home health consultant alleged that the employer's policies were not in keeping with accepted nursing practices. Regions Bank v. Stone County Skilled Nursing Facility, Inc., 73 Ark. App. 17, 38 S.W.3d 916 (2001) (reversed in part on other grounds by Regions Bank v. Stone County Skilled Nursing Facility, Inc., 345 Ark. 555, 49 S.W.3d 107 (2001), aff'd, 345 Ark. 555, 49 S.W.3d 107 (2001)). The court found negligent supervision in a case where the employer provided no formal training, no training manuals, materials or workbooks, and no written rules or regulation governing the conduct of its security guard in ejecting patrons from its nightclub. Kristie's Katering, Inc. v. Ameri, 72 Ark. App. 102, 35 S.W.3d 807 (2000). In another case, the court found negligent supervision when an employer failed to use reasonable care to avoid harm to patrons when he entrusted two ex-convicts, one of whom normally drank on the job, to forcibly remove patrons from an automobile auction. Am. Auto. Auction, Inc. v. Titsworth, 292 Ark. 452, 730 S.W.2d 499 (1987). Additionally, when a medical center employee sexually abused a patient, the court found that the medical center negligently supervised the employee following previous reports of his abuse of other patients. Sparks Reg'l Med. Ctr. v. Smith, 63 Ark. App. 131, 976 S.W.2d 396 (1998).

B. Intentional Infliction of Emotional Distress

To establish a claim of intentional infliction of emotional distress, known as the "tort of outrage" in Arkansas, the plaintiff must demonstrate that: (1) the defendant intended to inflict emotional distress or knew or should have known that emotional distress was the likely result of such conduct; (2) the conduct was "extreme and outrageous," was "beyond all possible bounds of decency," and was "utterly intolerable in a civilized community"; (3) the actions of the defendant were the cause of the plaintiff's distress; and (4) the emotional distress sustained by the plaintiff was so severe that no reasonable person could be expected to endure it. E.g., Miller v. Kroger Co., 82 Ark. App. 281, 105 S.W.3d 789 (2003); Palmer v. Council on Econ. Educ., 344 Ark. 461, 40 S.W.3d 784 (2001); Brown v. Tucker, 330 Ark. 435, 954 S.W.2d 262 (1997). The trial court must initially determine whether the conduct may reasonably be regarded as so outrageous as to permit recovery. Freeman v. Bechtel Constr. Co., 87 F.3d 1029 (8th Cir. 1996). Liability for the tort of outrage does not extend to mere insults, indignities, threats, annoyances, petty oppressions, or other trivialities. Ingram v. Pirelli Cable Corp., 295 Ark. 154, 747 S.W.2d 103 (1988). **Indeed, "discomfort, upset, embarrassment, anxiety, loss of sleep, and depression do not meet the 'mental distress' element of the tort of outrage." Coombs v. J.B. Hunt Transport, Inc., 2012 Ark. App. 24, at 10. Although an outrage claim does not survive a party, survivors can sue on their own behalf for emotional distress suffered by the survivors upon learning of the invasion into a decedent's privacy. Cannady v. St. Vincent Infirmary Med. Ctr., 2012 Ark. 369, at *9-10.** Arkansas courts have taken a somewhat strict approach to this cause of action. Tandy Corp. v. Bone, 283 Ark. 399, 678 S.W.2d 312 (1984). However, Arkansas does recognize the tort of outrage in an employment setting. Island v. Buena Vista Resort, 352 Ark. 548, 103 S.W.3d 671 (2003). Review of outrage claims in employment situations is particularly strict because "an employer must be given a certain amount of latitude in dealing with employees." Sterling v. Upjohn Healthcare Servs., Inc., 299 Ark. 278, 772 S.W.2d 329 (1989). Conduct not otherwise outrageous and extreme can be elevated to satisfy the test if the employer knows of an employee's inability to deal with emotional stress. Tandy Corp. v. Bone, 283 Ark. 399, 678 S.W.2d 312 (1984) (determining that the allegations were sufficient when an employee who was on Valium was being interrogated for suspected theft, requested the right to take his medication, was denied that right, and continued to be subjected to the interrogation). Mechanics Lumber Co. v. Smith, 296 Ark. 285, 752 S.W.2d 763 (1988) (determining that the actions of an employer in administering a polygraph to an employee who the employer knew suffered from multiple sclerosis and in rescheduling a second test did not rise to the level of conduct required for the tort of outrage). Cf. Givens v. Hixson, 275 Ark. 370, 631 S.W.2d 263 (1982) (involving an employer who was totally unaware of the physical or emotional condition of the employee). Because of the employer's right to discharge an at-will employee, a claim of outrage by an at-will employee cannot be predicated upon the fact of the discharge alone. However, the manner in which the discharge is accomplished or the circumstances under which it occurs may render the employer liable. City of Green Forest v. Morse, 316 Ark. 540, 873 S.W.2d 155 (1994) (citing Harris v. Ark. Book Co., 287 Ark. 353, 700 S.W.2d 41 (1985)). See also Employment Privacy Outline, VII.A.

C. Interference with Economic Advantage

Under Arkansas law, malicious and willful interference with the contractual rights and relationships of another has been recognized as an actionable tort. This action applies to situations in which a party, without a privilege to do so, purposely causes another not to employ a third person as well as to situations in which a party induces or purposely causes an employer to terminate a relationship with an employee, even if the employment was at-will. Palmer v. Ark. Council on Econ. Educ., 344 Ark. 461, 473, 40 S.W.3d 784, 791 (2001); Mason v. Funderburk, 247 Ark. 521, 446 S.W.2d 543 (1969). To state a prima facie case for this tort, the following elements must be alleged: (1) the existence of a valid contractual relationship or business expectancy; (2) knowledge of the relationship or expectancy on the part of the interferor; (3) intentional and improper interference inducing or causing a breach or termination of the relationship or expectancy; and (4) resultant damage to the party whose relationship or expectancy has been disrupted. Schueller v. Goddard, 631 F.3d 460, 463 (8th Cir. 2011); Palmer v. Ark. Council on Econ. Educ., 344 Ark. 461, 473, 40 S.W.3d 784, 791 (2001); Mason v. Wal-Mart

Stores, Inc., 333 Ark. 3, 969 S.W.2d 160 (1998) (citing Restatement (Second) of Torts § 766). See also Scholtes v. Signal Delivery Serv., Inc., 548 F. Supp. 487 (W.D. Ark. 1982) (recognizing such a claim when the plaintiff alleged that the defendants gave false information to prospective employers); Brown v. Tucker, 330 Ark. 435, 954 S.W.2d 262 (1997); Mason v. Funderburk, 247 Ark. 521, 446 S.W.2d 543 (1969); Ark. Life Ins. Co. v. Am. Nat'l Life Ins. Co., 110 Ark. 130, 161 S.W. 136 (1913) (recognizing this tort and determining that it does not survive and is not assignable).

The existence of a valid contract is not a prerequisite to maintaining an action for interference with prospective economic advantage. Cross v. Ark. Livestock & Poultry Comm'n, 328 Ark. 255, 943 S.W.2d 230 (1997). "[A]n action for tortious interference with a contractual relationship is based upon a defendant's conduct toward a third party." Baptist Health v. Murphy, 2010 Ark. 358, at 18. The tort requires a showing of "improper" conduct on the part of the alleged interferor. To determine whether the alleged conduct is improper or not, the following factors may be considered: (1) the nature of the actor's conduct; (2) the actor's motive; (3) the interests of the other with which the actor's conduct interferes; (4) the interests sought to be advanced by the actor; (5) the social interests in protecting the freedom of action of the actor and the contractual interests of the other; (6) the proximity or remoteness of the actor's conduct to the interference; and (7) the relations between the parties. Mason v. Wal-Mart Stores, Inc., 333 Ark. 3, 969 S.W.2d 160 (1998) (citing Restatement (Second) of Torts § 767). Filing a civil lawsuit is improper for purposes of intentional interference if it is done with no belief of its merits or is done in bad faith. Carmical v. McAfee, 68 Ark. App. 313, 7 S.W.3d 350 (1999). A party to a contract and its agents acting in the scope of their authority cannot be held liable for interfering with the party's own contract. Faulkner v. Ark. Children's Hosp., 347 Ark. 941, 69 S.W.3d 393 (2002) (hospital employees were acting within the scope of their employment and thus could not be liable for tortious interference with contractual relations when they allegedly jeopardized another employee's position with the hospital.) Johnson v. Sentinel-Record, No. 2002 WL 22036 (unreported opinion) (Ark. App. 2002); Palmer v. Ark. Council on Econ. Educ., 344 Ark. 461, 473, 40 S.W.3d 784, 791 (2001); Cross v. Ark. Livestock & Poultry Comm'n, 328 Ark. 255, 943 S.W.2d 230 (1997); St. Joseph's Reg'l Health Ctr. v. Munos, 326 Ark. 605, 934 S.W.2d 192 (1996). To prevail on a claim for interference, the plaintiff must prove that a third party failed to continue a contractual relationship with the plaintiff as a result of the defendant's improper conduct. First Commercial Bank, N.A. v. Walker, 333 Ark. 100, 969 S.W.2d 146 (1998), cert. denied, 525 U.S. 965 (1998). This cause of action is subject to the same law regarding qualified privilege to which other causes of action based upon defamatory statements are subject. Scholtes v. Signal Delivery Serv., Inc., 548 F. Supp. 487 (W.D. Ark. 1982). Compensatory and punitive damages are recoverable. Benny M. Estes & Assocs. v. Time Ins. Co., 980 F.2d 1228 (8th Cir. 1992). See also Employment Privacy Outline, VII.B, infra.

D. Prima Facie Tort

Although the Arkansas Supreme Court noted that this action had been asserted by a plaintiff in an employment claim, the court did not describe the action. England v. Dean Witter Reynolds, Inc., 306 Ark. 225, 811 S.W.2d 313 (1991).

V. OTHER ISSUES

A. Statute of Limitations

The limitations period applicable to libel actions is three (3) years. Ark. Code Ann. § 16-56-105. Slander actions must be brought within one (1) year. Ark. Code Ann. § 16-56-104. If an action is time-barred, the burden shifts to the plaintiff to prove by a preponderance of the evidence that the defendant's fraudulent concealment tolled the statute of limitations. Milam v. Bank of Cabot, 327 Ark. 256, 937 S.W.2d 653 (1997). The act of concealment must have been committed by those invoking the benefit of the statute of limitations. Id.

B. Jurisdiction

Effective July 1, 2001, circuit courts have original jurisdiction in all matters previously cognizable by the circuit and chancery courts. Prior to Amendment 80 to the Arkansas Constitution, when Arkansas had separate courts of law and equity, circuit court alone had jurisdiction to try a slander action. Axley v. Hammock, 185 Ark. 939, 50 S.W.2d 608 (1932). Although 16-60-116 previously controlled with respect to venue, the Civil Justice Reform Act of 2003, Ark. Code Ann. § 16-55-213, has repealed that statute by implication. Dotson v. City of Lowell, 375 Ark. 89, 289 S.W.3d 55 (2008). Generally, the venue for tort claims is now governed by the Civil Justice Reform Act. Venue is proper in the county where a substantial part of the events or omissions occurred that gave rise a claim; in the county where the individual defendant resides, or, if the defendant is not an individual, then in the county where the entity had its principal office at the time of the accrual of the action; or in the county where the plaintiff resided. Ark. Code Ann. § 16-55-213.

C. Worker's Compensation Exclusivity

Under Arkansas law, the rights and remedies granted to an employee for injury or death pursuant to the Workers Compensation statutes are exclusive. Ark. Code Ann. § 11-9-106. However, Arkansas has an intentional tort exception to the exclusive jurisdiction of Workers Compensation Commission. To remove a claim from the Commission's jurisdiction, there must be proof that an employer deliberately or intentionally acted with the purpose of bringing about certain consequences that harmed the employee. Hill v. Patterson, 313 Ark. 322, 855 S.W.2d 297 (1993). The Workers Compensation Commission has exclusive, original jurisdiction to determine the facts that establish jurisdiction unless the facts are so one-sided that the issue is a matter of law, not fact, such as with an intentional tort. International Paper Co. v. Clark County Circuit Court, 375 Ark. 127, 2008 WL 4949339 (Ark. Nov. 20, 2008) (citing VanWagoner v. Beverly Enters., 334 Ark. 12, 970 S.W. 2d 810 (1998)). Intentional torts, like slander or libel, are not heard before the Worker's Compensation Commission. Braman v. Wathall, 215 Ark. 582, 225 S.W.2d 342 (1950) (overruled on other grounds by United Ins. Co. of Am. v. Murphy, 331 Ark. 364, 961 S.W.2d 752 (1998)). The courts have held that even if such a claim arose out of or in the course of employment, it does not fall within the grounds for compensation under the Workers Compensation statutes. Id.

D. Pleading Requirements

Arkansas requires "fact pleading." Ark. R. Civ. P. 8.; Faulkner v. Ark. Children's Hosp., 347 Ark. 941, 69 S.W.3d 393 (2002). Simply because the complaint purports to state a specific cause of action does not make it so; the court will look to the alleged facts. "Notice pleading" allowed under the Federal Rules of Civil Procedure may be insufficient in Arkansas state court. Harvey v. Eastman Kodak Co., 271 Ark. 783, 610 S.W.2d 582 (1981). Unless a complaint alleging defamation sets forth the alleged defamatory statements and identifies the persons to whom such statements were published, the defendant will be unable to form a responsive pleading, and the complaint should be dismissed. Freeman v. Bechtel Constr. Co., 87 F.3d 1029 (8th Cir. 1996). When a defamation complaint fails to state a claim, it may be error to dismiss the complaint or strike the deficient allegations without giving the plaintiff a chance to amend, when the plaintiff requests to do so. Id. Qualified privilege may not be raised by demurrer. It must be pleaded by answer. Ottinger v. Ferrell, 171 Ark. 1085, 287 S.W. 391 (1926). No person shall be permitted to prosecute an action of slander or libel in forma pauperis. Ark. R. Civ. P. 72(d). Federal employees were acting within the scope of their employment when they wrote and sent a letter complaining of improper job performance by an administrative law judge, and the United States was properly substituted as the named defendant in lieu of the individual employees in the libel action instituted by the administrative law judge. Lawson v. United States, 103 F.3d 59 (8th Cir. 1996).

SURVEY OF ARKANSAS EMPLOYMENT PRIVACY LAW

Allen C. Dobson
Cross, Gunter, Witherspoon & Galchus, P.C.
500 President Clinton Avenue, Suite 200
Little Rock, Arkansas 72201
Telephone: (501) 371-9999; Facsimile: (501) 371-0035

Philip S. Anderson, Jess Askew III,
and Andrew King
Williams & Anderson, PLC
2200 Stephens Building, 111 Center Street
Little Rock, Arkansas 72201
Telephone : (501) 372-0800; Facsimile: (501) 372-6453

(With Developments Reported Through **November 1, 2012**)

GENERAL COMMENTS

None.

SIGNIFICANT DEVELOPMENTS SINCE THE 2012 *SURVEY*

None.

I. GENERAL LAW OF PRIVACY

A. Legal Basis of Privacy Claims

Arkansas courts have recognized certain privacy claims based upon tort common law. Dunlap v. McCarty, 284 Ark. 5, 678 S.W.2d 361 (1984); Dodrill v. Ark. Democrat Co., 265 Ark. 628, 590 S.W.2d 840, 5 Media L. Rep. 1385 (1979), cert. denied, 444 U.S. 1076 (1980).

B. Causes of Action

Arkansas courts have recognized the four following privacy claims: (1) appropriation: the use of the plaintiff's name or likeness for the defendant's benefit; (2) false light in the public eye: publicity that places the plaintiff in a false light before the public; (3) public disclosure of private facts: publicity of a highly objectionable kind even though it is true and no action would lie for defamation; and (4) intrusion: the invasion by a defendant upon the plaintiff's solitude or seclusion. Ark. Dep't Human Servs. v. Cole, 2011 Ark. 145; Jegley v. Picado, 349 Ark. 600, 80 S.W.3d 332 (2002). In Wal-Mart Stores, Inc. v. Lee, 348 Ark. 707, 74 S.W.3d 634 (2002), the court applied a privacy claim in an employment case. The privacy tort covers behavior harmful to the plaintiff even though there is no injury to reputation. Id.

1. ***Misappropriation/Right of Publicity.*** Mere publication of a person's likeness in a commercial newspaper or magazine does not create a cause of action for misappropriation. Murphy v. LCA-Vision, Inc., 776 F. Supp. 2d 886, 889 (E.D. Ark. 2011); Stanley v. Gen. Media Communications, Inc., 149 F. Supp. 2d 701, 706, 29 Media L. Rep. 1631 (W.D. Ark. 2001). The public must be able to identify the person from the photograph or drawing and the defendant must have capitalized upon the likeness of that person to sell more magazines or newspapers. The tort of appropriation requires commercial use of a person's name or likeness. Murphy, 776 F. Supp. 2d at 889; Stanley, 149 F. Supp. at 706.

2. ***False Light.*** Causes of action for invasion of privacy and libel may be joined in the same suit, but there can only be one recovery for any particular publication. Murphy v. LCA-Vision, Inc., 776 F. Supp. 2d 886, 889 (E.D. Ark. 2011); Wal-Mart Stores, Inc. v. Lee, 348 Ark. 707, 74 S.W.3d 634 (2002); Dodson v. Dicker, 306 Ark. 108, 812 S.W.2d 97, 19 Media L. Rep. 1124 (1991). The plaintiff must demonstrate: (1) the false light in which he was placed by the publicity would be highly offensive to a reasonable person, and (2) the defendant had knowledge of or acted in reckless disregard as to the falsity of the publicized matter and the false light in which the plaintiff would be placed and (3) the plaintiff sustained damages proximately caused by the defendant's giving of such publicity. Murphy v. LCA-Vision, Inc., 776 F. Supp. 2d 886, 889 (E.D. Ark. 2011). Where the plaintiff is a private figure and the publication is of public concern, the plaintiff must prove actual malice by clear and convincing evidence as a part of his prima facie case of invasion of privacy. Stanley, 149 F. Supp. 2d at 707; Addington v. Wal-Mart, 81 Ark. App. 441, 105 S.W.3d 369 (2003). Actual malice in this context involves publication of false information with the intention that the public construe the information as factual. Id. Statements made with actual malice are those made with knowledge that the statements were false or with reckless disregard of their falsity. The constitutional definition of malice is concerned with the author's subjective disregard for the accuracy of statements made. Wal-Mart Stores, Inc. v. Lee, 348 Ark. 707, 74 S.W.3d 634 (2002). In Lee, the court, citing Restatement (Second) of Torts, left open the question of whether liability could be based upon a showing of negligence as to truth or falsity. Id.

3. ***Publication of Private Facts.*** To state a claim for public disclosure of private facts, "...the complaint must make specific allegations of facts demonstrating either actual knowledge [by the defendant] of the tortious

nature of the book or facts giving rise to a duty to investigate." Steinbuch v. Hachette Book Group, No. 4:08-CV-00456 JLH, 2009 U.S. Dist. LEXIS 34756, at *8 (E.D. Ark. Apr. 8, 2009) (quoting Lewis v. Time Inc., 83 F.R.D. 455, 456 (E.D. Cal 1979) (the district court, in dismissing the plaintiff's claim, premised upon a publication of private facts, applied the knowledge requirements for a libel claim against distributor)). In Dunbar v. Cox Health Alliance, LLC, the court, following numerous other bankruptcy courts and the Restatement (Second) of Torts, held that filing an unredacted proof of claim was not a public disclosure of private facts because being "deemed 'public records' does not satisfy the 'publicity' element necessary to state a claim for invasion of privacy under [the Restatement]." In re Dunbar, 446 B.R. 306, 315 (Bankr. E.D. Ark. 2011) (quoting In re French, 401 B.R. 295, 318 (Bankr. E.D. Tenn. 2009)).

4. ***Intrusion.*** In order to state a cause of action for intrusion upon seclusion the plaintiff must prove: (1) an intrusion (2) that is highly offensive (3) into some matter in which a person has a legitimate expectation of privacy. Addington v. Wal-Mart, 81 Ark. App. 441, 105 S.W.3d 369 (2003); Fletcher v. Price Chopper Foods of Trumann, Inc., 220 F.3d 871 (8th Cir. 2000). "A legitimate expectation of privacy is the touchtone of the tort of intrusion." Id. Intrusion occurs when an actor believes or is substantially certain that he lacks the legal or personal permission to commit the intrusive act. Id. Unauthorized release of medical records does not constitute highly offensive conduct when that information could otherwise have been obtained by proper means. Id. The plaintiff in an invasion of privacy case must have conducted himself in a manner consistent with an actual expectation of privacy. Id. "[I]ntrusion requires a specific intrusive act as opposed to disclosing private information." Dunbar, 446 B.R. at 313-14. **However, in Coombs v. J.B. Hunt Transp., Inc., 2012 Ark. App. 24, the court found that inviting others into the employee's hotel room for the purpose of looking at him while intoxicated may be intrusive despite the fact that the employee was not in his own bed, was sharing a hotel room with another person, and had voluntarily become intoxicated.** In Wal-Mart Stores, Inc. v. Lee, the court held that evidence supported a finding that the employer committed the tort of intrusion in searching the employee's home and shop for allegedly stolen merchandise and that the employer published false and defamatory statements. Wal-Mart Stores, Inc. v. Lee, 348 Ark. 707, 74 S.W.3d 634 (2002). The action taken by the alleged tortfeasor must be offensive or objectionable to a reasonable person. Steinbuch v. Hachette Book Group, No. 4:08-CV-00456 JLH, 2009 U.S. Dist. LEXIS 34756 (E.D. Ark. Apr. 8, 2009). Although consent is a defense to an improper search, the consent to search must have been given freely and voluntarily where viewed in the light of the totality of the circumstances. Wal-Mart Stores, 348 Ark. at 724, 74 S.W.3d at 647. In a civil case, the issue of whether consent was valid is a question of fact to be decided by the trier of fact. Id. **Further, only living individuals may maintain an action for invasion of privacy. Cannady v. St. Vincent Infirmary Med. Ctr., 2012 Ark. 369, at 8. Arkansas case law and Ark. Code Ann. § 16-62-101(a)(1) do not provide for a claim of invasion of privacy that survives the death of the decedent. Id.**

C. Other Privacy-Related Actions

1. ***Intentional Infliction of Emotional Distress.*** The cause of action for intentional infliction of emotional distress is commonly referred to in Arkansas as the tort of outrage. M.B.M. Co., Inc. v. Counce, 268 Ark. 269, 596 S.W.2d 681 (1980). To establish a claim of outrage, the plaintiff must demonstrate that: (1) the defendant intended to inflict emotional distress or knew or should have known that emotional distress was the likely result of such conduct; (2) the conduct was "extreme and outrageous," was "beyond all possible bounds of decency," and was "utterly intolerable in a civilized community"; (3) the actions of the defendant were the cause of the plaintiff's distress; and (4) the emotional distress sustained by the plaintiff was so severe that no reasonable person could be expected to endure it. Crawford County v. Jones, 365 Ark. 585, 232 S.W.3d 433 (2006); Templeton v. United Parcel Serv. Inc., 364 Ark. 90, 216 S.W.3d 563 (2005); Stockton v. Sentry Ins., 337 Ark. 507, 989 S.W.2d 914 (1999); Brown v. Tucker, 330 Ark. 435, 954 S.W.2d 262 (1997). The trial court must initially determine whether the conduct may reasonably be regarded as so outrageous as to permit recovery. Freeman v. Bechtel Constr. Co., 87 F.3d 1029 (8th Cir. 1996). Liability for outrage does not extend to mere insults, indignities, threats, annoyances, petty oppressions, or other trivialities. Ingram v. Pirelli Cable Corp., 295 Ark. 154, 747 S.W.2d 103 (1988).

Arkansas courts have taken a somewhat strict approach to this cause of action. Tandy Corp. v. Bone, 283 Ark. 399, 678 S.W.2d 312 (1984). Review of outrage claims in employment situations is particularly strict because, "...an employer must be given a certain amount of latitude in dealing with employees." Sterling v. Upjohn Healthcare Servs., Inc., 299 Ark. 278, 280, 772 S.W.2d 329 (1989). Recovery for outrage was permitted when an employee who was suspected of theft was told that she was being laid off because of too many employees but was later told that she had to submit to a polygraph test before she could receive her last paycheck. M.B.M. Co., Inc. v. Counce, 268 Ark. 269, 596 S.W.2d 681 (1980). Although she passed the test, the employer deducted money from her final paycheck to cover her share of the missing money and she was denied unemployment benefits due to the employer's stated reasons for her dismissal. Id. However, an employer's conduct allegedly designed to force a suspected "whistle blower" to resign was insufficient to support a jury verdict for outrage. Sterling Drug, Inc. v. Oxford, 294 Ark. 239, 743 S.W.2d 380 (1988), reh'g denied, 294 Ark. 239, 747 S.W.2d 579 (1988). An employer's interpretation of an employment handbook or manual in regard to terminating an employee was insufficient to state a claim for outrage. Coatney v. Enterprise Rent-A-Car Co., 897 F. Supp.

1205 (W.D. Ark. 1995). Allegations that an employer informed the employee's dentist mid-procedure that the employee's insurance would not cover the procedure, thereby causing the dentist to cease working until he received assurances that he would be paid, and who informed the employee's pregnant wife that the employee was a "lazy s.o.b." who was not good enough for her and would be terminated while she was pregnant were insufficient to state a claim for the tort of outrage. Stockton v. Sentry Ins., 337 Ark. 507, 989 S.W.2d 914 (1999). The inaction of a national company and the area general manager to prevent or remedy sexual advances directed at an employee from the store manager was insufficient to state an action for outrage. Bare v. NPC Int'l., No. 09-2092, 2009 U.S. Dist. LEXIS 116138, at *10-11 (W.D. Ark. 2009). Allegations that an employee's co-workers used "crude and used profane language" around her, made "inappropriate sexual remarks about themselves and her," and one co-worker dropping his pants and exposing himself to her were inappropriate, but not "so extreme to support a claim of outrage." Sharbine v. Boone Exploration, Inc., No. 09-CV-1025, 2010 U.S. Dist. LEXIS 21628, at *6-8 (W.D. Ark. 2010).

Conduct not otherwise outrageous and extreme can be elevated to satisfy the test if the employer knows of an employee's inability to deal with emotional stress. Tandy Corp. v. Bone, 283 Ark. 399, 678 S.W.2d 312 (1984) (determining that the allegations were sufficient when an employee who was on Valium was being interrogated for suspected theft, requested the right to take his medication, was denied that right, and continued to be subjected to the interrogation); Mechanics Lumber Co. v. Smith, 296 Ark. 285, 752 S.W.2d 763 (1988) (determining that the actions of an employer in administering a polygraph to an employee who the employer knew suffered from multiple sclerosis and in rescheduling a second test did not rise to the level of conduct required for the tort of outrage). Cf. Givens v. Hixson, 275 Ark. 370, 631 S.W.2d 263 (1982) (involving an employer who was totally unaware of the physical or emotional condition of the employee). Because of the employer's right to discharge an at-will employee, a claim of outrage by an at-will employee cannot be predicated upon the fact of the discharge alone. However, the manner in which the discharge is accomplished or the circumstances under which it occurs may render the employer liable. Crawford County v. Jones, 365 Ark. 585, 232 S.W.3d 433 (2006); City of Green Forest v. Morse, 316 Ark. 540, 873 S.W.2d 155 (1994) (citing Harris v. Ark. Book Co., 287 Ark. 353, 700 S.W.2d 41 (1985)). A claim for negligent infliction of emotional distress is not recognized in Arkansas. Mechanics Lumber Co. v. Smith, 296 Ark. 285, 752 S.W.2d 763 (1988).

2. ***Interference With Prospective Economic Advantage.*** Under Arkansas law, malicious and willful interference with the contractual rights and relationships of another has been recognized as an actionable tort. Yupei Wang v. Wal-Mart Stores, Inc., 2010 U.S. Dist. LEXIS 79323, *at 13 (2010); Faulkner v. Ark. Children's Hosp., 347 Ark. 941, 69 S.W.3d 393 (2002); Palmer v. Ark. Council on Econ. Educ., 344 Ark. 461, 40 S.W.3d 784 (2001). This action applies to situations in which a party, without a privilege to do so, purposely causes another not to employ a third person as well as to situations in which a party induces or purposely causes an employer to terminate a relationship with an employee, even if the employment was at will. Mason v. Funderburk, 247 Ark. 521, 446 S.W.2d 543 (1969). "[A]n action for tortious interference with a contractual relationship is based upon a defendant's conduct toward a third party." Baptist Health v. Murphy, 2010 Ark. 358, at 18. The fact that the language alleged to have induced the discharge of an employee might be set forth in the complaint in such a manner as to form the basis of an action for libel or slander does not prevent the employee from maintaining an action for wrongful interference with his contract of employment. Mason v. Wal-Mart Stores, Inc., 333 Ark. 3, 969 S.W.2d 160 (1998) (citing Restatement (Second) of Torts § 766); Scholtes v. Signal Delivery Serv., Inc., 548 F. Supp. 487 (W.D. Ark. 1982) (recognizing such a claim when the plaintiff alleged that the defendants gave false information to prospective employers). To state a prima facie case for this tort, the following elements must be alleged: (1) the existence of a valid contractual relationship or business expectancy; (2) knowledge of the relationship or expectancy on the part of the interferor; (3) intentional interference inducing or causing a breach or termination of the relationship or expectancy; and (4) resultant damage to the party whose relationship or expectancy has been disrupted. Yupei Wang v. Wal-Mart Stores, Inc., 2010 U.S. Dist. LEXIS 79323, *at 13 (2010); Palmer v. Ark. Council on Econ. Educ., 344 Ark. 461, 473, 40 S.W.3d 784, 791 (2001); Mason v. Wal-Mart Stores, Inc., 333 Ark. 3, 969 S.W.2d 160 (1998) (citing Restatement (Second) of Torts § 766). See also Scholtes v. Signal Delivery Serv., Inc., 548 F. Supp. 487 (W.D. Ark. 1982); Brown v. Tucker, 330 Ark. 435, 954 S.W.2d 262 (1997); Mason v. Funderburk, 247 Ark. 521, 446 S.W.2d 543 (1969); Ark. Life Ins. Co. v. Am. Nat'l Life Ins. Co., 110 Ark. 130, 161 S.W. 136 (1913) (recognizing this tort and determining that it does not survive and is not assignable). "Some precise business expectancy or contractual relationship must be obstructed in order to commit the tort . . . ." Forever Green Athletic Fields, Inc. v. Lasiter Constr., Inc., 2011 Ark. App. 347 at 19 (citing Stewart Title Guar. Co. v. Am. Abstract & Title Co., 363 Ark. 530, 215 S.W.3d 596 (2005)). Interference with another's business expectancy is not actionable when the expectancy is subject to a contingency. Deck House, Inc. v. Link, 98 Ark. App. 17, 249 S.W.3d 817 (2007). The court in Deck held that a home builder's alleged interference, which was using the plaintiff designer's drawings without authorization, was not actionable because the agreement between the designer and the property owner was contingent in nature; it expressly contemplated the possibility that the property owner might not purchase the package that included the drawings, and the contract did not bind the property owner to purchase the package. Id. at 827.

One who intentionally causes a third person not to enter into a prospective contract with another who is his competitor or not to continue an existing contract terminable at-will is not liable for tortious interference if: (a) the relation concerns a matter involved in the competition between the actor and the other; (b) the actor does not employ wrongful means; (c) his action does not create or continue an unlawful restraint of trade; and (d) his purpose is at least in part to advance his interest in competing with the other. Office Machines, Inc. v. Mitchell, 95 Ark. App. 128, 234 S.W.3d 906 (2006) (citing Kinco, Inc. v. Schueck Steel, Inc., 283 Ark. 72, 671 S.W.2d 178, 181-2 (1984)).

The existence of a valid contract is not a prerequisite to maintaining an action for interference with prospective economic advantage. Cross v. Ark. Livestock & Poultry Comm'n, 328 Ark. 255, 943 S.W.2d 230 (1997). The tort requires a showing of "improper" conduct on the part of the alleged interferor. To determine whether the alleged conduct is improper or not, the following factors may be considered: (1) the nature of the actor's conduct; (2) the actor's motive; (3) the interests of the other with which the actor's conduct interferes; (4) the interests sought to be advanced by the actor; (5) the social interests in protecting the freedom of action of the actor and the contractual interests of the other; (6) the proximity or remoteness of the actor's conduct to the interference; and (7) the relations between the parties. Mason v. Wal-Mart Stores, Inc., 333 Ark. 3, 969 S.W.2d 160 (1998) (citing Restatement (Second) of Torts § 767). A party to a contract and its agents acting in the scope of their authority cannot be held liable for interfering with the party's own contract. Palmer v. Ark. Council on Econ. Educ., 344 Ark. 461, 473, 40 S.W.3d 784, 791 (2001); Cross v. Ark. Livestock & Poultry Comm'n, 328 Ark. 255, 943 S.W.2d 230 (1997); St. Joseph's Reg'l Health Center v. Munos, 326 Ark. 605, 934 S.W.2d 192 (1996). To prevail on a claim for interference, the plaintiff must prove that a third party failed to continue a contractual relationship with the plaintiff as a result of the defendant's improper conduct. First Commercial Bank, N.A. v. Walker, 333 Ark. 100, 969 S.W.2d 146 (1998), cert. denied, 525 U.S. 965 (1998).

This cause of action is subject to the same law regarding qualified privilege to which other causes of action based upon defamatory statements are subject. Scholtes v. Signal Delivery Serv., Inc., 548 F. Supp. 487 (W.D. Ark. 1982). Compensatory and punitive damages are recoverable. Benny M. Estes & Assocs. v. Time Ins. Co., 980 F.2d 1228 (8th Cir. 1992). Wal-Mart did not act "improperly," thereby intentionally interfering with the plaintiff's contractual relationship with the manufacturers he represented, by eliminating manufacturers' representatives from Wal-Mart's purchasing process to increase its profits. Mason v. Wal-Mart Stores, Inc., 333 Ark. 3, 969 S.W.2d 160 (1998). State police officer's claim that the Governor forced the officer's supervisor to demote the officer in the hope that the officer would resign failed to state a claim for tortious interference because there were no facts demonstrating that the officer had a valid contractual relationship or business expectancy in his job or that he was damaged. Brown v. Tucker, 330 Ark. 435, 954 S.W.2d 262 (1997).

3. ***Prima Facie Tort.*** Although the Arkansas Supreme Court noted that a "*prima facie* tort" claim had been asserted by a plaintiff in an employment lawsuit, the court did not reach the issue of whether such a cause of action exists under Arkansas law. England v. Dean Witter Reynolds, Inc., 306 Ark. 225, 811 S.W.2d 313 (1991).

II. EMPLOYER TESTING OF EMPLOYEES

A. Psychological or Personality Testing

1. ***Common Law and Statutes.*** While there are no Arkansas cases that address personality or psychological testing of private employees, the Law Enforcement Standards Act sets forth certain standards and qualifications for the hiring of law enforcement officers. Ark. Code Ann. § 12-9-108(a) (Supp. 1999). The statute provides that mere failure to meet the standards set forth by the statute or the Arkansas Commission on Law Enforcement Standards does not necessarily make an action by an unqualified officer invalid. Id. The Arkansas Supreme Court, however, has required "strict compliance" with these standards. Johnson v. City of Kensett, 301 Ark. 592, 787 S.W.2d 651 (1990). One standard requires that an individual seeking employment by a law enforcement unit be examined by a licensed psychiatrist or psychologist, who then must submit a report of his or her recommendations to the potential employer to be maintained in the employee's personnel file. Id.

2. ***Private Employers.*** No Arkansas cases on point.

3. ***Public Employers.*** Because the personnel file of a law enforcement officer contained no recommendation by a psychological examiner and no fingerprint check as required by the Law Enforcement Standards Act, the criminal charge the officer brought against the defendant was invalid. Johnson v. City of Kensett, 301 Ark. 592, 787 S.W.2d 651 (1990). **It is not unreasonable for a city to require officers to submit to drug testing without a warrant and probable cause because the city has an interest in maintaining efficient police departments and providing for the public safety. Green v. City of N. Little Rock, 2012 Ark. App. 21.**

B. Drug Testing

1. ***Common Law and Statutes.*** If an employer implements a drug-free workplace program, it may require its employees to submit to a test to detect the presence of drugs or alcohol. Ark. Code Ann. § 11-14-101 (Supp. 2009). Any employee who tests at a level higher than a prescribed level may be terminated and will lose eligibility for

workers' compensation medical and indemnity benefits. Id. The employer must notify all employees that it is a condition of employment to report to work free of the presence of drugs or alcohol. Id. The dangerous nature of an employer's industry, an employee's job duties, and the existence of risk factors are all elements that may justify a drug-free policy as reasonable when the policy is implemented to promote safety. George's Inc. v. Dir., Employment Sec. Dep't, 50 Ark. App. 77, 900 S.W.2d 590 (1995). In fact, an employee's refusal to comply with an employer's drug testing policy may constitute "misconduct" for purposes of unemployment compensation. This occurs when the employee disregards the employer's interests, violates the employer's rules, neglects the employer's standards of behavior expected from employees, and disregards the duties and obligations owed to the employer. Niece v. Dir., Employment Sec. Dep't, 67 Ark. App. 109, 922 S.W.2d 169 (1999). Arkansas law prohibits a person from attempting to defeat a drug or alcohol-screening test by urine substitution or spiking. Ark. Code Ann. § 5-60-201 (Repl. 2005). It is also illegal for a person to sell, give away, or market urine with the intent to defraud a drug-screening test in Arkansas. Id. A violation of this law is punishable as a Class B Misdemeanor. Id.

2. ***Private Employers.*** An employee who tested positive for drugs and who failed to be retested within 30 days or accept treatment pursuant to the employer's policy was discharged for misconduct connected with work, so that she was disqualified from receiving unemployment benefits. White v. Dir., Ark. Employment Sec. Dep't, 54 Ark. App. 197, 924 S.W.2d 823 (1996). A positive test result constituted a deliberate violation of the employer's rules and a willful disregard of the standard of behavior when the employer's safety policy authorized immediate termination if the employee had any detectable level of drug in the body. Grace Drilling Co. v. Dir. of Labor, 31 Ark. App. 81, 790 S.W.2d 907 (1990). But, an employer's failure to follow its urine specimen collection procedures resulted in insufficient evidence of misconduct, so the claimant was entitled to benefits. Ark. Midland R.R. v. Dir., ESD, 87 Ark. App. 311, 191 S.W.3d 544 (2004). An employee who was terminated after refusing a drug test was not allowed unemployment benefits when evidence did not support the notion that the employee was under duress in consenting to the condition of employment. Riceland Foods, Inc. v. Dir. of Labor, 38 Ark. App. 269, 832 S.W.2d 295 (1992). Although an employee was off-duty when he smoked marijuana, his discharge for testing positive for drugs in excess of a certain minimum level amounted to discharge for misconduct in connection with work, thereby denying him unemployment benefits. Rucker v. Price, 52 Ark. App. 126, 915 S.W.2d 315 (1996).

3. ***Public Employers.*** The State Police Department's failure to follow procedures set forth in the department's Drug Free Workplace Policy, which mandated that certain steps be taken in the chain of custody to ensure the reliability of drug testing and to prevent tampering and that any positive results be reviewed by a licensed physician who would then consult the employee and the employee's physician, required the reversal of a police officer's removal from his position for testing positive for marijuana during a random drug screening. Stueart v. Ark. State Police Comm'n, 329 Ark. 46, 945 S.W.2d 377 (1997).

C. Medical Testing

1. ***Common Law and Statutes.*** An employer may not require any employee or applicant for employment, as a condition of employment or continued employment, to submit to or take a physical or medical examination unless the examination is free of charge to the employee or applicant and he is provided a true and correct copy, either the original or duplicate original, of the examiner's report of the examination free of charge. Ark. Code Ann. § 11-3-203(a)(1) (Supp. 2009). However, if the employee tests positive for an illegal drug, then the employee and employer may make a written agreement concerning who will bear the cost of future tests or screens required as a condition of continued employment. Ark. Code. Ann. § 11-3-203(a)(3) (Supp. 2009). "An employer shall not seek to obtain or use a genetic test or genetic information of the employee or the prospective employee for the purposes of distinguishing between or discriminating against or restricting any right of benefit otherwise due or available to an employee or prospective employee." Ark. Code Ann. § 11-5-403(a) (Repl. 2002). "An employer shall not require a genetic test of or require genetic information from the employee or prospective employee for the purposes of distinguishing between or discriminating against or restricting any right or benefit otherwise due or available to an employee or prospective employee." Ark. Code Ann. § 11-5-403(b). The penalty for violating the above statute is a misdemeanor and may be punished by a fine of not more than twenty five thousand dollars or by imprisonment up to 1 (one) year, or both. Ark. Code Ann. § 11-5-404 (Repl. 2002). As for workers' compensation claims, an injured employee who claims to be entitled to compensation shall submit to a physical examination and treatment by another qualified physician, as the Workers' Compensation Commission may require from time to time if reasonable and necessary. Ark. Code Ann. § 11-9-511(a) (Repl. 2002). The places of examination and treatment must be reasonably convenient for the employee. Ark. Code Ann. § 11-9-511(b). A physician that the employee, employer, or insurance carrier chooses and pays for, may participate in the examination if requested. Ark. Code Ann. § 11-9-511(c).

2. ***Private Employers.*** No specific distinction between private and public employees in this context.

3. ***Public Employers.*** No specific distinction between private and public employees in this context.

D. Polygraph Tests

Arkansas does not have a specific statute addressing polygraph testing. However, an action against an employer and a polygraph examination administrator who administered one polygraph to and scheduled a second polygraph for an employee when the employer knew the employee suffered from multiple sclerosis did not rise to the level required for the tort of outrage. Mechanics Lumber Co. v. Smith, 296 Ark. 285, 752 S.W.2d 763 (1988). The consent form for acceptance of a polygraph must be executed freely with full knowledge and free of duress. Id.

E. Fingerprinting

Because the personnel file of a law enforcement officer contained no recommendation by a psychological examiner and no fingerprint check as required by the Law Enforcement Standards Act, the criminal charge the officer brought against the defendant was invalid. Johnson v. City of Kensett, 301 Ark. 592, 787 S.W.2d 651 (1990).

III. SEARCHES

A. Employee's Person

No Arkansas cases on point.

B. Employee's Work Area

No Arkansas cases on point.

C. Employee's Property

In Wal-Mart Stores, Inc. v. Lee, 348 Ark. 707, 74 S.W.3d 634 (2002), the court held that evidence supported a finding that the employer committed the tort of intrusion in searching the employee's home and shop for allegedly stolen merchandise and that the employer published false and defamatory statements. Although consent is a defense to an improper search, the consent to search must have been given freely and voluntarily viewed in the light of the totality of the circumstances. Id. In a civil case, the issue of whether consent was valid is a question of fact to be decided by the trier of fact. Id.

IV. MONITORING OF EMPLOYEES

A. Telephones and Electronic Communications

An intentional interception of wire or electronic communication, or disclosure of contents of interception, gives rise to criminal and civil liability under the Omnibus Crime Control and Safe Streets Act, 18 U.S.C. §§ 2510-2520. Deal v. Spears, 980 F.2d 1153 (8th Cir. 1992), aff'g 780 F.Supp. 618 (W.D. Ark 1991). Actual consent to interception of calls, which will exempt a party from civil liability, may be implied from the circumstances, although constructive consent is ineffective at creating an exemption. Id.

1. ***Wiretapping.*** An employee's consent to tape recording of intercepted telephone calls could not be implied merely when the employer warned the employee that he may monitor phone calls to cut down on personal use of the phone or because an extension telephone was located in the owners' residence. Deal v. Spears, 980 F.2d 1153 (8th Cir. 1992), aff'g 780 F.Supp. 618 (W.D. Ark 1991). Two elements of the "business use of telephone extension defense" are that the intercepting equipment is provided by the telephone company to the user and that the equipment is used in the ordinary course of business. Id. In Deal, the exemption of civil liability did not apply to business owners who recorded 22 hours of an employee's personal calls since the recorder was purchased at a store rather than furnished by the phone company, was connected to the extension phone rather than the phone line, and the scope of the interception was beyond the ordinary course of business. Id.

2. ***Electronic Communications.*** Electronic communications are treated the same as wiretapping and electronic surveillance under the Omnibus Crime Control and Safe Streets Act, 18 U.S.C.A. §§ 2510-2520 (1993). Deal v. Spears, 980 F.2d 1153 (8th Cir. 1992), aff'g 780 F.Supp. 618 (W.D. Ark 1991). Personal and business electronic communications "indistinguishably intertwined" on a publicly owned computer system are subject to Freedom of Information Act ("FOIA") requests. Pulaski County v. Arkansas Democrat-Gazette, 371 Ark. 217, 264 S.W. 3d 465, 35 Media L. Rep. 2313 (2007) (upholding release of emails pertaining to an extra-marital relationship between a government contractor and government employee). Communications may be reviewed *in camera* to determine if the content has a "substantial nexus" to governmental activities. Pulaski County v. Arkansas Democrat-Gazette, 370 Ark. 435, 260 S.W.3d 718 (2007) (per curiam). The communicating party who is not a public official has standing to intervene in the FOIA request

even if not an a citizen of Arkansas. Pulaski County v. Arkansas Democrat-Gazette, 371 Ark. 217, 264 S.W. 3d 465, 35 Media L. Rep. 2313 (2007).

3. ***Other Electronic Monitoring.*** No Arkansas cases on point.

B. Mail

No Arkansas cases on point.

C. Surveillance/Photographing

It is unlawful to use any image-recording device to photograph or film a person present in a place of business where that person has a reasonable expectation of privacy. Ark. Code Ann. § 5-16-101 (Supp. 2009). However, security monitoring operated by the employer is exempt from this statute. Id. Other than Deal v. Spears, 980 F.2d 1153 (8th Cir. 1992), aff'g 780 F. Supp. 618 (W.D. Ark 1991), the electronic surveillance case that has already been discussed, no other Arkansas cases are on point. As for photographing employees, no Arkansas cases are on point.

V. ACTIVITIES OUTSIDE THE WORKPLACE

A. Statute or Common Law

No Arkansas cases or statutes on point.

B. Employees' Personal Relationships

An employee unsuccessfully sought recovery for the tort of outrage when he was terminated for fraternizing with a subordinate in violation of the company policy. Coatney v. Enterprise Rent-A-Car Co., 897 F. Supp. 1205 (W.D. Ark. 1995). In Coatney, the employment manual contained a disclaimer indicating that the employment was at-will and contained a policy prohibiting fraternization between supervisors and their subordinates. Id.

1. ***Romantic Relationships Between Employees.*** No Arkansas cases on point.

2. ***Sexual Orientation.*** No Arkansas cases on point.

3. ***Marital Status.*** No Arkansas cases on point.

C. Smoking

No Arkansas cases on point.

D. Blogging

No Arkansas cases on point.

VI. RECORDS

A. Personnel Records

Arkansas does not have a statute addressing access to personnel records of private-sector employees, but the Personal Information Protection Act of 2005 governs the use of personal information such as social security numbers, driver's license numbers, account numbers, and medical information by businesses and state agencies. Ark. Code Ann. §§ 4-110-101 et seq. The Act requires businesses and state agencies to: (a) take all reasonable steps to destroy personal information that is no longer to be retained, and (b) maintain security procedures as appropriate to protect the information from unauthorized access, destruction, use, modification, or disclosure. Ark. Code Ann. § 4-110-104. The business or state agency must disclose certain security breaches to the owner of the personal information. Ark. Code Ann. § 4-110-105(a). The Act may be enforced by the Arkansas Attorney General. Ark. Code Ann. § 4-110-108.

Employees of private-sector employers do not have a right to inspect or copy their personnel records. Personnel records of public-sector employers are not available to the public if their disclosure would constitute a "clearly unwarranted invasion of personal privacy." Ark. Code Ann. § 25-19-105(b)(12). Disclosure under the Freedom of Information Act of police department records pertaining to an assessment center evaluation portion of a lieutenant examination as it related to candidates other than the applicant would constitute a clearly unwarranted invasion of privacy. Young v. Rice, 308 Ark. 593, 826 S.W.2d 252, 20 Media L. Rep. 1029 (1992). The public's right to know the contents of the records is normally weighed against an individual's right to privacy, so that when the public's interest is substantial, it will usually outweigh any individual privacy interests, and disclosure will be favored. Id. Balancing these considerations, the Arkansas Supreme Court found that police officers' home addresses were also exempt from disclosure. Stilley v. McBride, 332 Ark. 306, 965 S.W.2d 125 (1998). In privacy violation claims under 42 U.S.C. § 1983, a city's disclosure of police officers' personnel files, without notice or any attempt to redact sensitive personal information, may constitute negligence or gross negligence depending on the circumstances, but in order to sustain substantive due process claims such disclosure must be made with deliberate indifference. Hart v. City of Little Rock, 432 F.3d 801 (8th Cir. 2005), cert. denied, 547 U.S. 1207 (2006).

B. Medical Records

In contemplation of, preparation for, or use in any legal proceeding, a patient of a doctor, hospital, ambulance provider, medical health care provider, or other medical institution is entitled to access to the information in medical records, upon written request and payment of copying costs. Ark. Code Ann. § 16-46-106 (Supp. 2009). Medical records also are excluded from disclosure under the Freedom of Information Act. Id. However, the proceedings, minutes, records, or reports of organized committees of hospital medical staffs or medical review committees of local medical societies having the responsibility for reviewing and evaluating the quality of medical or hospital care shall not be subject to discovery pursuant to the Arkansas Rules of Civil Procedure, the Freedom of Information Act, or admissible in any legal proceeding and shall be absolutely privileged communications. Ark. Code Ann § 16-46-105(a) (2004). The Personal Information Protection Act of 2005 requires businesses and state agencies to take all reasonable steps to destroy medical information that is no longer to be retained. Ark. Code Ann. § 4-110-104(a). The Act also requires businesses and state agencies to maintain security procedures as appropriate to protect medical information from unauthorized access, destruction, use, modification, or disclosure. Ark. Code Ann. § 4-110-104(b).

C. Criminal Records

The Arkansas Crime Information Center shall make criminal records on persons available only to criminal justice agencies with specific statutory authority of access, and to any person or his attorney who has reason to believe that a criminal history record is being kept on him, or wherein the criminal defendant is charged with either a misdemeanor or felony. Ark. Code Ann. § 12-12-211(a) (Repl. 2009). However, the recently enacted "Arkansas State Criminal Records Act" allows employers and professional licensing boards to obtain felony arrest information and all conviction information held by the Arkansas Crime Information Center on an applicant or employee. Ark. Code Ann. §§ 12-12-1501 to -1513. (Repl. 2009).

D. Subpoenas/Search Warrants

An individual has a personal right in the information in his personnel file and therefore has standing to challenge a subpoena issued to an employer for that file. Smith v. Frac Tech Servs. No. 4:09CV00679 JLH, 2010 U.S. Dist. LEXIS 98751 at *5-6 (E.D. Ark. Sept. 1, 2010) (citing Richard v. Convergys Corp., 2007 U.S. Dist. LEXIS 9131 (D. Utah Feb 7, 2007) and Johnson v. Guards Mark Security, 2007 U.S. Dist. LEXIS 97915 (N.D. Ohio Mar, 31, 2007)). In Smith v. Frac Tech Services, Ltd., the plaintiff successfully quashed subpoenas improperly issued to out-of-state employers. Id. at *6.

VII. ACTIONS SUBSEQUENT TO EMPLOYMENT

A. References

Ark. Code Ann. § 11-3-204 allows an employer who obtains written consent from a current or former employee to disclose the following information about an employee: date and duration of employment; current pay rate and wage history; job description and duties; the last written performance evaluation prepared prior to the date of the request; attendance information; results of drug or alcohol tests administered within one year prior to the request; threats of violence, harassing acts, or threatening behavior related to the workplace or directed at another employee; whether the employee was voluntarily or involuntarily separated from employment and the reason for the separation; and whether the employee is eligible for rehire (Repl. 2002). An employer disclosing this information upon consent of the employee shall be presumed to be acting in good faith and shall be immune from civil liability for the disclosure or any consequence of the disclosure unless the presumption is rebutted with evidence that the information disclosed was false, and the employer had knowledge of its falsity or acted with malice or reckless disregard for the truth.

B. Non-Compete Agreements

Arkansas courts, like the courts in most states, do not favor non-compete agreements because they constitute restraints on trade. "Covenants not to compete are not looked upon with favor by the law." Moore v. Midwest Distrib., 76 Ark. App. 397, 65 S.W.3d 490 (2002) (citing Federated Mut. Ins. Co. v. Bennett, 36 Ark. App. 99, 818 S.W.2d 596 (1991)). The test for determining whether a non-compete will be upheld is stated below:

> "A contract in restraint of trade is valid when founded on a valuable consideration, if the restraint imposed is reasonable as between the parties and not injurious to the public by reason of its effect upon trade. Whether or not the restraint is reasonable is to be determined by considering whether it is such only as to afford a fair protection to the interest of the party in whose favor it is given, and not so large as to interfere with the interests of the public."

Girard v. Rebsamen Ins. Co., 14 Ark. App. 154, 685 S.W.2d 526 (1985) (citing Orkin Exterminating Co. v. Murrell, 212 Ark. 449, 206 S.W.2d 185 (1947)). In Girard, the Arkansas Court of Appeals found that Rebsamen's customer list and related information were protected interests. Id. at 159, 685 S.W.2d at 528.

Arkansas courts generally consider three factors to determine if a covenant not to compete is reasonable: there must be a valid interest to protect, the geographical restriction must not be overly broad and a reasonable time period must be imposed. Moore v. Midwest Distrib., 76 Ark. App. 397, 65 S.W.3d 490 (2002).

VIII. OTHER ISSUES

A. Statutes of Limitations

The limitation period for a tort of outrage claim is three (3) years. Ark. Code Ann. § 16-56-105 (Repl. 2005). Orlando v. Alamo, 646 F.2d 1288 (8th Cir. 1981). The limitation period for a claim of intentional interference with a contract is also three (3) years. Ark. Code Ann. § 16-56-105; Bishop v. Tice, 622 F.2d 349 (8th Cir. 1980) (citing Bankston v. Davis, 262 Ark. 635, 559 S.W.2d 714 (1978)).

B. Jurisdiction

A claim may be brought for violations of the Federal Privacy Act in a federal district court. 5 U.S.C. § 552(g)(1). Pursuant to Amendment 80 of the Arkansas Constitution, circuit courts have original jurisdiction in all matters previously cognizable by the circuit and chancery courts. Generally, the venue for tort claims is now governed by the Civil Justice Reform Act. Venue is proper in the county where a substantial part of the events or omissions occurred that gave rise a claim; in the county where the individual defendant resides, or, if the defendant is not an individual, then in the county where the entity had its principal office at the time of the accrual of the action; or in the county where the plaintiff resided. Ark. Code Ann. § 16-55-213 (Repl. 2005).

C. Worker's Compensation Exclusivity

Under Arkansas law, the rights and remedies granted to an employee for injury or death pursuant to the Workers Compensation statutes are exclusive. Ark. Code Ann. § 11-9-105 (Repl. 2002). However, Arkansas has an intentional tort exception to the exclusive jurisdiction of Workers Compensation Commission. To remove a claim from the Commission's jurisdiction, there must be proof that an employer deliberately or intentionally acted with the purpose of bringing about certain consequences that harmed the employee. Hill v. Patterson, 313 Ark. 322, 855 S.W.2d 297 (1993). The Workers Compensation Commission has exclusive, original jurisdiction to determine the facts that establish jurisdiction unless the facts are so one-sided that the issue is a matter of law, not fact, such as with an intentional tort. International Paper Co. v. Clark County Circuit Court, 375 Ark. 127, 289 S.W.3d 103 (2008) (citing VanWagoner v. Beverly Enters., 334 Ark. 12, 970 S.W. 2d 810 (1998)). Intentional torts, like slander or libel are not heard before the Worker's Compensation Commission. Braman v. Wathall, 215 Ark. 582, 225 S.W. 2d 342 (1950) (overruled on other grounds by United Ins. Co. of Am. v. Murphy, 331 Ark. 364, 961 S.W.2d 752 (1998)). The courts have held that even if such a claim arose out of or in the course of employment, it does not fall within the grounds for compensation under the Workers Compensation statutes. Id.

D. Pleading Requirements

Arkansas requires "fact pleading." Ark. R. Civ. P. 8; Faulkner v. Ark. Children's Hosp., 347 Ark. 941, 69 S.W.3d 393 (2002). Simply because the complaint purports to state a specific cause of action does not make it so; the court will look to the alleged facts. "Notice pleading" allowed under the Federal Rules of Civil Procedure may be insufficient in Arkansas state court. Harvey v. Eastman Kodak Co., 271 Ark. 783, 610 S.W.2d 582 (1981).

SURVEY OF CALIFORNIA EMPLOYMENT LIBEL LAW

Jennifer S. Baldocchi, Esq.
Gina Guarienti Cook, Esq.
Paul Hastings LLP
515 South Flower Street, 25th Floor
Los Angeles, California 90071
Telephone (213) 683-6000; Facsimile (213) 627-0705

(With Developments Reported Through **November 1, 2012**)

GENERAL COMMENTS

There are three levels of courts in California, the Superior Courts, the Appellate Courts and the Supreme Court. The Courts of Appeal provide intermediate review for decisions reached in the trial courts. Cases are decided by three-judge panels. Not all decisions of the Courts of Appeal are published. Rather, an opinion is only published if it meets certain criteria, such as establishing a new rule of law, criticizing existing law, or contributing to legal literature in a significant manner. Cal. Const. art. VI, § 14. Both courts and parties are prohibited from citing or relying upon unpublished decisions, except in limited circumstances relating to res judicata, collateral estoppel, or criminal proceedings. Cal. R. Ct. 8.1115(a-b). California's highest court is the Supreme Court. Its decisions are binding on all other California courts.

SIGNIFICANT DEVELOPMENTS SINCE THE 2012 *SURVEY*

None.

I. GENERAL LAW

A. General Employment Law

1. ***At Will Employment.*** California law presumes that employees are terminable at will. Cal. Lab. Code § 2922; Foley v. Interactive Data Corp., 47 Cal. 3d 654, 677, 254 Cal. Rptr. 211, 223, 765 P.2d 373, 385 (1988). This means that absent an agreement to the contrary, an employer may discharge an employee at any time, for any reason, or for no reason. Guz v. Bechtel Nat'l, Inc., 24 Cal. 4th 317, 327, 100 Cal. Rptr. 2d 352, 358, 8 P.3d 1089, 1095 (2000). Although California courts generally recognize an employer's right to administer its own workplace, an employee may nevertheless bring an action for wrongful discharge against an employer where the employer's conduct violates public policy. Foley, 47 Cal. 3d at 665, 254 Cal. Rptr. at 214, 765 P.2d at 376; Gould v. Md. Sound Indus., Inc., 31 Cal. App. 4th 1137, 1147, 37 Cal. Rptr. 2d 718, 723 (1995). Among other things, employers may be held liable for taking an adverse employment action against an employee for complaining in good faith about working conditions or practices he or she reasonably believes to be unsafe or unlawful. See Franklin v. Monadnock Co., 151 Cal. App. 4th 252, 260, 59 Cal. Rptr. 3d 692, 697 (2007). Employers may also be held liable under the California Fair Employment and Housing Act for a host of other wrongful conduct, including discrimination based on age, race, national origin, gender or religious preference. Cal. Gov't Code § 12900 et seq.

B. Elements of Defamation Claim

1. ***Basic Elements.*** Defamation is the invasion of the interest of reputation. Shively v. Bozanich, 31 Cal. 4th 1230, 1242, 7 Cal. Rptr. 3d 576, 583, 80 P.3d 676, 683, 32 Media L. Rep. 1097 (2003). The basic elements of this tort include the intentional publication of a statement of fact that is false, unprivileged, and has a natural tendency to injure or which causes special damage. **Summit Bank v. Rogers, 206 Cal. App. 4th 669, 696, 142 Cal. Rptr. 3d 40, 59 (2012);** Gilbert v. Sykes, 147 Cal. App. 4th 13, 27, 53 Cal. Rptr. 3d 752, 764 (2007); Nygard, Inc. v. Uusi-Kerttula, 159 Cal. App. 4th 1027, 1047-48, 72 Cal. Rptr. 3d 210, 225 (2008). Defamation traditionally has two forms, libel and slander, which are defined by statute in California. See Cal. Civ. Code §§ 44, 45, 45a, and 46.

In general, libel is a written communication that is false, that is not protected by any privilege, and that exposes a person to contempt or ridicule or certain other injuries to reputation. Shively, 31 Cal. 4th at 1242, 7 Cal. Rptr. 3d at 583, 80 P.3d at 683 (citing Cal. Civ. Code § 45). Slander is a false and unprivileged oral publication attributing to a person specific misdeeds or certain unfavorable characteristics or qualities, or uttering certain other derogatory statements regarding a person. Id. (citing Cal. Civ. Code § 46).

2. ***Fault.*** The level of fault that needs to be shown to give rise to an actionable claim for defamation depends upon: (i) whether or not the defamatory statement at issue concerns a public or private figure; and (ii) whether or not the statement concerns matters of public or private interest. See Brown v. Kelly Broad. Co., 48 Cal. 3d 711, 257 Cal. Rptr. 708, 771 P.2d 406, 16 Media L. Rep. 1625 (1989).

a. **Private Figure Plaintiff/Matter of Public Concern**. A private figure is someone who has neither engaged in purposeful activity inviting criticism nor acquired substantial media access in relation to the controversy at issue. Khawar v. Globe Int'l, Inc., 19 Cal. 4th 254, 265, 79 Cal. Rptr. 2d 178, 184, 965 P.2d 696, 702, 26 Media L. Rep. 2505 (1998). Where the speech at issue involves matters of public concern, the plaintiff bears the burden of proving falsity, regardless of whether or not plaintiff is a public or private figure. Carver v. Bonds, 135 Cal. App. 4th 328, 344, 37 Cal. Rptr. 3d 480, 493, 34 Media L. Rep. 1257 (2005) (because statements regarding consumer protection were matters of public concern under First Amendment, plaintiff required to prove falsity, even if not public figure).

Whether or not a given statement addresses matters of public concern is generally determined by the content, form, and context of the statement. Kirchmann v. Lake Elsinore Unified Sch. Dist., 57 Cal. App. 4th 595, 601, 67 Cal. Rptr. 2d 268, 273 (1997); see also **Price v. Operating Eng'rs Local Union No. 3, 195 Cal. App. 4th 962, 973, 125 Cal. Rptr. 3d 220, 227-28 (2011) (statements in union flyer did not address a matter of public concern because they did not relate to "a topic of widespread community interest or prior media coverage, or even a topic of interest to a substantial number of people . . . The fact that the flyers' distribution took place during a labor dispute and was undertaken by members of organized labor did not cause the action to rise to the level of a matter of public interest.").** Matters which "do not genuinely implicate any broad public interest nor materially enhance the self-governing ability of the public" are likely not matters of public concern. Hofmann Co. v. E.I. Du Pont de Nemours & Co., 202 Cal. App. 3d 390, 407, 248 Cal. Rptr. 384, 394 (1988), criticized on other grounds, Kahn v. Bower, 232 Cal. App. 3d 1599, 284 Cal. Rptr. 244, 19 Media L. Rep. 1236 (1991).

Certain specific rules govern a public employer's relations with its employees. For example, the First Amendment may prohibit the dismissal of a public employee for criticizing his or her employer, unless the employee's free speech interest is outweighed by the employer's interest in avoiding disruption. Pickering v. Bd. of Educ., 391 U.S. 563, 572-73, 88 S. Ct. 1731, 1737, 20 L. Ed. 2d 811, 820-21 (1968). In these situations, the critical element to determining whether First Amendment protection applies is whether the speech at issue addresses a matter of public concern. Kirchmann, 57 Cal. App. 4th at 601, 67 Cal. Rptr. 2d at 273 If the employee's speech involves a matter of public concern, an employer seeking to take action against the employee is faced with the burden of persuasion in showing that the employee's free speech rights were outweighed by the employer's interests in protecting the efficiency of the public services it performs through its employees. Id.

b. **Private Figure Plaintiff/Matter of Private Concern**. A private figure plaintiff need not prove actual or constitutional malice to prevail when the defamatory statements at issue do not involve matters of public concern. Nizam-Aldine v. City of Oakland, 47 Cal. App. 4th 364, 378 n.11, 54 Cal. Rptr. 2d 781, 790 n.11 (1996). Rather, the private figure plaintiff need only prove negligence. Comedy III Prods., Inc. v. Gary Saderup, Inc., 25 Cal. 4th 387, 398, 106 Cal. Rptr. 2d 126, 134, 21 P.3d 797, 803 (2001); Kelly Broad. Co., 48 Cal. 3d at 742, 257 Cal. Rptr. at 727, 771 P.2d at 425.

c. **Public Figure Plaintiff/Matter of Public Concern**. Defamation law applies heightened First Amendment protection to speech about public figures. Public figures must prove that the "defendant's defamatory statements were made with actual malice, i.e., actual knowledge of falsehood or reckless disregard for the truth, whereas private figures need prove only negligence." Comedy III Prods., Inc., 25 Cal. 4th at 398, 106 Cal. Rptr. 2d at 134, 21 P.3d at 803. The rationale for this is (1) that public figures have greater access to the media to rebut defamatory statements, and (2) such individuals invite attention and comment by voluntarily becoming public figures. Id.

There are two types of public figures – all-purpose public figures and limited-purpose public figures. See Gertz v. Robert Welch, Inc., 418 U.S. 323, 351, 94 S. Ct. 2997, 41 L. Ed. 2d 789 (1974). All-purpose public figures or public officials include those who occupy positions of persuasive power and influence. Id. Limited-purpose public figures include those who thrust themselves to the forefront of particular public controversies in order to influence the resolution of the issues involved. Id. Individuals in the latter category will be deemed public figures for a limited range of issues only. Ampex Corp. v. Cargle, 128 Cal. App. 4th 1569, 1577, 27 Cal. Rptr. 3d 863, 869-70 (2005); Khawar v. Globe Int'l, Inc., 19 Cal. 4th 254, 263, 79 Cal. Rptr. 2d 178, 183, 965 P.2d 696, 701, 26 Media L. Rep. 2505 (1998).

The determination of "whether a plaintiff in a defamation action is a public figure is a question of law for the trial court." Khawar, 19 Cal. 4th at 264, 79 Cal. Rptr. 2d at 183, 965 P.2d at 701. To constitute an all-purpose public figure, the plaintiff's name typically must be a "household word," meaning that the person is a celebrity or is recognizable by the population at large for his or her opinions or activities. See Waldbaum v. Fairchild Publ'ns, Inc., 627 F.2d 1287, 1292, 1294, 5 Media L. Rep. 2629 (D.C. Cir. 1980); Harris v. Tomczak, 94 F.R.D. 687, 703, 8 Media L. Rep. 2145 (E.D. Cal. 1982). To be a public official, among other things, the person involved must appear to have substantial control over governmental affairs and have greater access to mass media than an ordinary official. See Ghafur v. Bernstein, 131 Cal. App. 4th 1230, 1240, 32 Cal. Rptr. 3d 626, 633 (2005) (superintendent of charter school system is a public official); Kahn v. Bower, 232 Cal. App. 3d 1599, 1610-13, 284 Cal. Rptr. 244, 251-53, 19 Media L. Rep. 1236 (1991) (child welfare worker is a public official). Not all federal, state or local government officials are "public officials." See James v. San Jose Mercury News, Inc., 17 Cal. App. 4th 1, 10, 20 Cal. Rptr. 2d 890, 895, 21 Media L. Rep. 1624 (1993) (deputy public defender is not a public official); Franklin v. Benevolent & Protective Order of Elks, 97 Cal. App. 3d 915, 922-25, 159 Cal. Rptr. 131, 135-37, 5 Media L. Rep. 1977 (1979) (public high school teacher is not a public official). A defendant charged with defamation cannot, through his or her own conduct, create a defense by making the claimant a public figure. Hailstone v. Martinez, 169 Cal. App. 4th 728, 736, 87 Cal. Rptr. 3d 347, 352 (2008) (otherwise private information is not turned into a matter of public interest simply by its communication to a large number of people).

To be a limited-purpose public figure, three elements must be present. First, there must be a public controversy, meaning the issue was debated publicly and had foreseeable and substantial ramifications for non-participants. Second, the plaintiff must have voluntarily and actively sought to influence the resolution of the issue. Khawar, 19 Cal. 4th at 265, 79 Cal. Rptr. 2d 178 (1998) ("assuming a person may ever be accurately characterized as an *involuntary* public figure," this characterization is reserved for "an individual who, despite never having *voluntarily* engaged the public's attention in an attempt to influence the outcome of a public controversy, nonetheless has acquired such public prominence in relation to the controversy as to permit media access sufficient to effectively counter media-published defamatory statements."); **see Cole v. Patricia A. Meyer & Assocs., APC, 206 Cal. App. 4th 1095, 1122, 142 Cal. Rptr. 3d 646, 668 (2012) (noting that legal actions by themselves do not turn individuals into limited purpose public figures).** Third, the alleged defamation must be germane to the plaintiff's participation in the controversy. Gilbert v. Sykes, 147 Cal. App. 4th 13, 24, 53 Cal. Rptr. 3d 752, 762 (2007) (citations omitted).

To prove constitutional or actual malice, a plaintiff must show by clear and convincing evidence that the defamatory statement was made with knowledge of its falsity or with reckless disregard for whether or not it was false. Nguyen-Lam v. Cao, 171 Cal. App. 4th 858, 868, 90 Cal. Rptr. 3d 205, 212-13 (2009); Khawar, 19 Cal. 4th at 275, 79 Cal. Rptr. 2d at 191, 965 P.2d at 709. In applying this test, the standard for recklessness is whether the speaker entertained serious doubts as to the truth of his publication. Christian Research Inst. v. Alnor, 148 Cal. App. 4th 71, 84, 55 Cal. Rptr. 3d 600, 611 (2007). Although evidence of ill will by the defendant against the plaintiff may constitute circumstantial evidence of malice, such evidence does not of itself establish constitutional malice, absent knowledge of falsity or reckless disregard. Live Oak Publ'g Co. v. Cohagan, 234 Cal. App. 3d 1277, 1291-92, 286 Cal. Rptr. 198, 206 (1991).

3. ***Falsity***. For any statement to be defamatory, it must be "provably false." Carver v. Bonds, 135 Cal. App. 4th 328, 344, 37 Cal. Rptr. 3d 480, 493, 34 Media L. Rep. 1257 (2005) (statement is not defamatory unless it can reasonably be viewed as declaring or implying provably false factual assertion). A statement's falsity must be established by a preponderance of the evidence. See Christian Research Inst. v. Alnor, 148 Cal. App. 4th 71, 82, 55 Cal. Rptr. 3d 600, 610 (2007) (even where plaintiff is a public figure, no need to establish falsity by "clear and convincing" standard).

The general standard for determining whether a given statement is provably false is whether the statement is capable of being shown to be false by reference to concrete, objectively verifiable data. Vogel v. Felice, 127 Cal. App. 4th 1006, 1021, 26 Cal. Rptr. 3d 350, 361 (2005) (minor inaccuracies do not amount to falsity if the substance of a statement is true). The context of the statement is examined to determine whether it is correct, not whether every single detail contained within it is accurate. Henry v. Chapa, No. 1:07-CV-00336-DGC, 2009 WL 1748697, at *4 (E.D. Cal. June 19, 2009) (defendant need not justify every word of alleged defamatory matter; sufficient if "gist or sting" of matter was true); Balzaga v. Fox News Network, LLC, 173 Cal. App. 4th 1325, 1338, 93 Cal. Rptr. 3d 782, 792, 37 Media L. Rep. 1737 (2009) ("Defamation actions cannot be based on snippets taken out of context.") (citation and internal quotation marks omitted).

4. ***Defamatory Statement of Fact***. To be actionable, a purportedly defamatory publication must contain a statement of fact. Gregory v. McDonnell Douglas Corp., 17 Cal. 3d 596, 600, 131 Cal. Rptr. 641, 643, 552 P.2d 425, 427 (1976). As with the test for falsity, the general standard for determining whether a statement of fact exists is whether or not the statement can be objectively verified. See Campanelli v. Regents of Univ. of Cal., 44 Cal. App. 4th 572, 581, 51 Cal. Rptr. 2d 891, 897 (1996) (statements incapable of being objectively verified are opinions, not statements of fact). In determining whether a given utterance constitutes an actionable statement of fact, courts must evaluate the statement not as lawyers and judges but in the way a general hearer or reader would. **Summit Bank v. Rogers, 206 Cal. App. 4th 669, 699, 142 Cal. Rptr. 3d 40, 62 (2012) (statements on online message board "must be viewed from the perspective of the average reader of an Internet site such as [the one at issue], not the Bank or a banking expert who might view them as conveying some special meaning.").** Balzaga, 173 Cal. App. 4th at 1342, 93 Cal. Rptr. 3d at 796 (recognizing that "the use of hyperbole or language in a loose figurative sense is constitutionally protected and not actionable" as defamation (citation and internal quotation marks omitted)); Hufstedler, Kaus & Ettinger v. Superior Court, 42 Cal. App. 4th 55, 67, 49 Cal. Rptr. 2d 551, 559 (1996). "'[R]hetorical hyperbole,' 'vigorous epithet[s],' 'lusty and imaginative expression[s] of . . . contempt,' and language used 'in a loose, figurative sense' have all been accorded constitutional protection." Ferlauto v. Hamsher, 74 Cal. App. 4th 1394, 1401, 88 Cal. Rptr. 2d 843, 849, 27 Media L. Rep.

2364 (1999) (citations omitted; first alteration added); **Summit Bank v. Rogers, 206 Cal. App. 4th 669, 697, 699, 142 Cal. Rptr. 3d 40, 60, 62 (2012) ("online blogs and message boards are places where readers expect to see strongly worded opinions rather than objective facts"; "context . . . belies the claim that anyone . . . could reasonably interpret his use of the words 'problem Bank,' 'CEO's personel [sic] bank,' and Bank customers left 'high and dry' as implying provable assertions of fact");** Seelig v. Infinity Broad. Corp., 97 Cal. App. 4th 798, 810, 119 Cal. Rptr. 2d 108, 117 (2002) (comments on a morning radio program that contestant on television program was a "big skank," "local loser" and "chicken butt" did not constitute actionable statements of fact); Overhill Farms, Inc. v. Lopez, 190 Cal. App. 4th 1248, 1252, 119 Cal. Rptr. 3d 127, 132 (2010) (accusation that an employer engaged in a mass employment termination based upon racist and ageist motivations is clearly a "provable fact"). See II.B.2, infra.

5. ***Of and Concerning Plaintiff***. To be actionable, a defamatory statement must be "of and concerning" the plaintiff. The "of and concerning" requirement has been held to mean that the statement at issue must either expressly mention plaintiff or refer to him or her by reasonable implication. Blatty v. New York Times Co., 42 Cal. 3d 1033, 1044, 232 Cal. Rptr. 542, 548, 728 P.2d 1177, 1183, 13 Media L. Rep. 1928 (1986). The "of and concerning" requirement is specifically intended to grant a right of recovery to those who are the direct objects of injurious falsehoods, while denying such rights to those who merely complain of nonspecific statements that they subjectively believe caused them some harm. Id. The "of and concerning" requirement has been applied to deny recovery to individual members of large groups who sue based on defamatory statements about an organization or group to which they belong. See Noral v. Hearst Publ'ns, Inc., 40 Cal. App. 2d 348, 350, 104 P.2d 860, 862 (1940); Barger v. Playboy Enters., Inc., 564 F. Supp. 1151, 1153, 9 Media L. Rep. 1656 (N.D. Cal. 1983), aff'd, 732 F.2d 163 (9th Cir. 1984).

6. ***Publication***. For any defamatory statement to be actionable, it must be published to a third party. "Publication means communication to some third person who understands the defamatory meaning of the statement and its application to the person to whom reference is made." Smith v. Maldonado, 72 Cal. App. 4th 637, 645, 85 Cal. Rptr. 2d 397, 402, 27 Media L. Rep. 1814 (1999); Ruiz v. Harbor View Cmty. Ass'n, 134 Cal. App. 4th 1456, 1476, 37 Cal. Rptr. 3d 133, 146-47 (2005) (to be actionable, libel must be published, i.e., communicated to third party who understands its defamatory meaning). Publication need not be to a large group; communication to a single person is sufficient. Ringler Assocs. Inc. v. Md. Cas. Co., 80 Cal. App. 4th 1165, 1179, 96 Cal. Rptr. 2d 136, 148, 29 Media L. Rep. 1033 (2000). If publication occurs, the general rule is that everyone who takes a responsible part in the publication is liable for the defamation. Jones v. Calder, 138 Cal. App. 3d 128, 134, 187 Cal. Rptr. 825, 829, 9 Media L. Rep. 1314 (1982), aff'd, 465 U.S. 783, 10 Media L. Rep. 1401 (1984). Nevertheless, innocence can be a defense for secondary actors who merely disseminate information published by another, unless they knew or should have known it was defamatory. Osmond v. EWAP, Inc., 153 Cal. App. 3d 842, 852, 200 Cal. Rptr. 674, 679-80 (1984). Finally, the plaintiff must offer admissible evidence showing the defendant made the alleged defamatory statement; this cannot be based on inadmissible hearsay. See Gallagher v. Connell, 123 Cal. App. 4th 1260, 1268, 20 Cal. Rptr. 3d 673, 679 (2004) (plaintiff cannot use inadmissible hearsay to prove defamation; but defendant's failure to object could result in waiver).

a. **Intracorporate Communications**. In California, an intracorporate communication constitutes a publication for purposes of a defamation claim. Kelly v. Gen. Tel. Co., 136 Cal. App. 3d 278, 284, 186 Cal. Rptr. 184, 186 (1982). Indeed, sufficient publication of defamatory material occurs whenever a statement is communicated to parties other than the person defamed. Id.; Duste v. Chevron Prods. Co., 738 F. Supp. 2d 1027, 1042 (N.D. Cal. 2010) (statement made to internal investigator met the publication requirement). However, the publication is likely to be covered by the common interest privilege, which protects communications made without malice on subjects of mutual interest. See II.A.2.a, infra.

b. **Compelled Self-Publication**. California recognizes the doctrine of compelled self-publication in narrow circumstances where an individual is compelled to publish defamatory statements concerning himself or herself. Under California law, self-publication of a defamatory statement is actionable if the plaintiff can show he or she was "operating under a strong compulsion to republish the defamatory statement and the circumstances . . . are known to the originator of the defamatory statement at the time he communicates it to the person defamed." McKinney v. County of Santa Clara, 110 Cal. App. 3d 787, 797-98, 168 Cal. Rptr. 89, 94 (1980). In the employment context, this rule is often applied to job interviews and other attempts by a former employee to obtain a new job in the face of an adverse reference by the former employer. Id. at 798; Live Oak Publ'g Co. v. Cohagan, 234 Cal. App. 3d 1277, 1287, 286 Cal. Rptr. 198, 203 (1991). To that end, it has been held that self-publication or republication of a defamatory statement is often foreseeable to employers and therefore actionable if a job-seeker must tell a prospective employer what is in his personnel file in order to explain away a negative job reference. Id.; see also Reese v. Barton Healthcare Sys., 693 F. Supp. 2d 1170, 1189, 22 Am. Disabilities Cas. (BNA) 1719, 1731 (2010) (triable issue of fact as to whether employer's disciplinary notice would need to be explained away to future employers by plaintiff precluded summary judgment). But see, Davis v. Consol. Freightways, 29 Cal. App. 4th 354, 373, 34 Cal. Rptr. 2d 438, 448 (1994) (granting summary judgment against plaintiff who failed to show "strong compulsion" to republish defamatory matter; former employer not liable if employee voluntarily disclosed defamatory statement).

c. **Republication**. Generally, reprinting or recirculating a libelous writing is treated as having the same effect as the original publication. Ringler Assocs. Inc., 80 Cal. App. 4th at 1180, 96 Cal. Rptr. 2d at 148, 29 Media L. Rep. 1033 (2000); see Carver v. Bonds, 135 Cal. App. 4th 328, 348, 37 Cal. Rptr. 3d 480, 496, 34 Media L. Rep. 1257 (2005) (republisher not liable where no probability of prevailing against originator of alleged defamation). The originator of a defamatory statement may be liable for every republication of that statement, if it was reasonably foreseeable to the originating party that the defamatory material would be republished. Mitchell v. Superior Court, 37 Cal. 3d 268, 281, 208 Cal. Rptr. 152, 160, 690 P.2d 625, 633, 11 Media L. Rep. 1076 (1984) (originator is liable for authorized or intended republications). In some circumstances, the mere fact that a defendant knowingly allowed defamatory material to remain available for viewing by others after having been given a reasonable opportunity to remove such material may give rise to liability for republication. Hellar v. Bianco, 111 Cal. App. 2d 424, 426, 244 P.2d 757, 759 (1952) (involving defamatory material in tavern). In the employment context, an employer may limit its liability for any republication of defamatory material by adhering to strict policies of not providing reasons for an employee's termination and refraining from publishing any potentially defamatory statements outside of the company. Consol. Freightways, 29 Cal. App. 4th at 373, 34 Cal. Rptr. 2d at 448.

The Uniform Single Publication Act is codified in California Civil Code section 3425.1 et seq. Under that section, "[n]o person shall have more than one cause of action for damages for libel or slander . . . or any other tort founded upon any single publication or exhibition or utterance." Cal. Civ. Code § 3425.3; see also Jackson v. Balanced Health Prods., Inc., No. C 08-05584 CW, 2009 WL 1625944, at *5 (N. D. Cal. June 10, 2009) (holding that false advertising, unjust enrichment, and breach of warranty are not traditional torts as contemplated by Cal. Civ. Code § 3425.3). The application of the Single Publication Act in California is limited, however. As a general matter, the Act was instituted to protect mass media publication of a single issue of book or newspaper. Miller v. Collectors Universe, Inc., 159 Cal. App. 4th 988, 998, 72 Cal. Rptr. 3d 194, 201 (2008). The California Supreme Court recently remanded a case involving product labels, directing the trial court to consider whether the production of a product label over a period of years is a single integrated publication that triggers the running of the statute of limitations when the first such label is distributed to the public. Christoff v. Nestle USA, Inc., 47 Cal. 4th 468, 481-82, 97 Cal. Rptr. 3d 798, 807-09, 213 P.3d 132, 140-41 (2009). In addition, the Act does not apply to situations where the defendant republishes defamatory material with knowledge that it is defamatory. Schneider v. United Airlines, Inc., 208 Cal. App. 3d 71, 76-77, 256 Cal. Rptr. 71, 74-75 (1989).

7. ***Statements versus Conduct***. In California, a cause of action for defamation must challenge communications and not conduct. Joel v. Valley Surgical Ctr., 68 Cal. App. 4th 360, 371-72, 80 Cal. Rptr. 2d 247, 254 (1998). This is because the two forms of defamation are slander and libel. Cal. Civ. Code § 44. Libel requires publication and slander requires an oral utterance. Cal. Civ. Code §§ 45, 46. Additionally, at least one court has noted that there is a difference between protected free speech and mere offensive conduct. See generally In re Steven S., 25 Cal. App. 4th 598, 612, 31 Cal. Rptr. 2d 644 (1994).

8. ***Damages***. To recover general or actual damages, a plaintiff must establish the specific damage he or she suffered as a result of the publication. Burnett v. Nat'l Enquirer, Inc., 144 Cal. App. 3d 991, 1013, 193 Cal. Rptr. 206, 214, 9 Media L. Rep. 1921 (1983). "Defamatory language not libelous on its face is not actionable unless the plaintiff alleges and proves that he has suffered special damage as a proximate result thereof." Cal. Civ. Code § 45a. The requisite showing typically involves proof of lost time at work, medical expenses attributable to the defamation, and any other economic losses in one's employment. See O'Hara v. Storer Commc'ns, Inc., 231 Cal. App. 3d 1101, 1114, 282 Cal. Rptr. 712, 720, 19 Media L. Rep. 1225 (1991). In any action for defamation, special damages must be pled with specificity. Gomes v. Fried, 136 Cal. App. 3d 924, 939, 186 Cal. Rptr. 605, 614 (1982); Anschutz Entm't Group, Inc. v. Snepp, 171 Cal. App. 4th 598, 643, 90 Cal. Rptr. 3d 133, 165, 37 Media L. Rep. 1605 (2009) (plaintiff's allegations that the "conduct of [d] efendants was intentional, and done willfully, maliciously, with ill will ..., and with conscious disregard for Plaintiff's rights" and that "[p]laintiff's injuries were exacerbated" by such conduct lacked the required degree of specificity).

a. **Presumed Damages and Defamation Per Se**. As a general matter, statements that are defamatory per se are those publications which on their face are reasonably susceptible of defamatory meaning without the introduction of additional explanatory material. Selleck v. Globe Int'l, Inc., 166 Cal. App. 3d 1123, 1130, 212 Cal. Rptr. 838, 843 (1985); Douglas v. Janis, 43 Cal. App. 3d 931, 939 n.8, 942 n.10, 118 Cal. Rptr. 280, 285 n.8, 287 n.10 (1974); Duste v. Chevron Prods. Co., 738 F. Supp. 2d 1027, 1044 (N.D. Cal. 2010) (statement that plaintiff had "frequented" gentlemen's clubs and "brothels" was sufficient to create a triable issue of fact as to whether it was such that it injured him in respect to his profession and trade, which is sufficient to establish slander per se); Cal. Civ. Code § 45a (defining libel per se as any libel "which is defamatory of the plaintiff without the necessity of explanatory matter, such as an inducement, innuendo or other extrinsic fact"). Upon a showing of constitutional malice, presumed damages may be recovered for a defamatory statement even if plaintiff cannot show actual damages. Weller v. Am. Broad. Cos., 232 Cal. App. 3d 991, 1011-12, 283 Cal. Rptr. 644, 654, 19 Media L. Rep. 1161 (1991); but see Sommer v. Gabor, 40 Cal. App. 4th 1455, 1472, 48 Cal. Rptr. 2d 235, 246, 24 Media L. Rep. 1225 (1995) (limiting damages to "those damages that necessarily result from the publication of defamatory matter" and refusing to allow jurors to speculate regarding future damage was proper (citation and internal quotation marks omitted)).

(1) **Employment-Related Criticism**. See II.A.2.a, III.B, infra.

(2) **Single Instance Rule**. California has not addressed the single instance rule.

b. **Punitive Damages**. A plaintiff must demonstrate constitutional malice before punitive damages may be awarded with regard to a matter of public concern. Khawar v. Globe Int'l, Inc., 19 Cal. 4th 254, 274-75, 79 Cal. Rptr. 2d 178, 190-91, 965 P.2d 696, 708-09, 26 Media L. Rep. 2505 (1998); Carney v. Santa Cruz Women Against Rape, 221 Cal. App. 3d 1009, 1022, 271 Cal. Rptr. 30, 37, 18 Media L. Rep. 1123 (1990); Crane v. Ariz. Republic, 972 F.2d 1511, 1524-26, 20 Media L. Rep. 1649 (9th Cir. 1992) (applying California law). Also, state law sets forth general requirements that a plaintiff prove "oppression, fraud, or malice" to recover punitive damages. See Cal. Civ. Code §§ 3294, 3295 (setting forth traditional burdens of proof for punitive damages under California law).

II. PRIVILEGES AND DEFENSES

A. Scope of Privileges

California Civil Code section 47 codifies a number of absolute and qualified privileges available in California. As a general matter, if a statutory or common law privilege covering certain forms of communication does not already exist, California courts are predisposed to hold that no such privilege applies. Cruey v. Gannett Co., 64 Cal. App. 4th 356, 369, 76 Cal. Rptr. 2d 670, 678 (1998); Slaughter v. Friedman, 32 Cal. 3d 149, 158, 185 Cal. Rptr. 244, 249, 649 P.2d 886, 891 (1982). At least two nonstatutory privileges are available. These include the privilege of "fair-comment," and the privilege of "consent." See II.A.2.c and II.B.3, infra. Finally, a claim of privilege is an affirmative defense to defamation, and should be pled as such in the answer. Beroiz v. Wahl, 84 Cal. App. 4th 485, 492, 100 Cal. Rptr. 2d 905, 909 (2000).

1. ***Absolute Privileges***. Absolutely privileged publications are not actionable even if they are entirely false and malicious. Action Apartment Ass'n, Inc. v. City of Santa Monica, 41 Cal. 4th 1232, 1241, 63 Cal. Rptr. 3d 398, 406, 163 P.3d 89, 95 (2007). "Put another way, application of the privilege does not depend on the publisher's 'motives, morals, ethics or intent.'" Kashian v. Harriman, 98 Cal. App. 4th 892, 913, 120 Cal. Rptr. 2d 576, 592 (2002) (citation omitted); Wise v. Thrifty Payless, Inc., 83 Cal. App. 4th 1296, 1302, 100 Cal. Rptr. 2d 437, 441 (2000). The absolute privilege for such publications is based on the notion that certain publications require absolute immunity from the threat of civil action. Civil Code section 47 expressly codifies absolute privileges for publications by executive officers, publications in judicial proceedings, publications in legislative proceedings or other proceedings authorized by law, and publications in procedures authorized by law and reviewable by mandate. See Cal. Civ. Code § 47.

Significant case law exists interpreting each of the absolute privileges codified in Section 47. See, e.g., **Kerner v. Superior Court, 206 Cal. App. 4th 84, 121, 141 Cal. Rptr. 3d 504, 532 (2012) ("The privilege is interpreted broadly in order to further its principal purpose of affording litigants and witnesses the utmost freedom of access to the courts and to other official proceedings without fear of harassment in derivative tort actions.");** Rohde v. Wolf, 154 Cal. App. 4th 28, 37-38, 64 Cal. Rptr. 3d 348, 356 (2007) (litigation privilege bars all tort causes of action except malicious prosecution); Komarova v. Nat'l Credit Acceptance, Inc., 175 Cal. App. 4th 324, 336, 95 Cal. Rptr. 3d 880, 888-89 (2009) (communications with some relation to an anticipated lawsuit fall within the litigation privilege); Navarro v. IHOP Props., Inc., 134 Cal. App. 4th 834, 843-44, 36 Cal. Rptr. 3d 385, 392-93 (2005) (statements relating to settlements fall within absolute litigation privilege); Hagberg v. Cal. Fed. Bank FSB, 32 Cal. 4th 350, 373-75, 7 Cal. Rptr. 3d 803, 819-22, 81 P.3d 244, 257-59 (2004) (discussion of the "broad reach" of Section 47(b) privilege, which applies not only to defamation, but to all tort actions seeking to impose liability based upon a covered communication, except malicious prosecution); Moore v. Conliffe, 7 Cal. 4th 634, 652-53, 29 Cal. Rptr. 2d 152, 163, 871 P.2d 204, 215 (1994) (absolute privilege covering communications in proceedings reviewable by mandate applies to private parties).

In the employment context, the absolute privileges of Civil Code section 47 tend to apply most often to matters such as reports of sexual harassment or discrimination made to government officials, like the Equal Employment Opportunity Commission or the Department of Fair Employment and Housing. See Cruey, 64 Cal. App. 4th at 368, 76 Cal. Rptr. 2d at 677; Knoell v. Petrovich, 76 Cal. App. 4th 164, 169-70, 90 Cal. Rptr. 2d 162, 165 (1999) (litigation privilege applies to demand letters and prelitigation communications, even if fraudulently published to coerce settlement); Slaughter, 32 Cal. 3d at 156, 185 Cal. Rptr. at 247, 649 P.2d at 889. An employer will not be liable for defamation arising out of the employer's communication with the police regarding the employee. Section 47 gives all persons the right to report crimes to the police, the local prosecutor or an appropriate regulatory agency, even if the report is made in bad faith. Cabesuela v. Browning-Ferris Indus. of Cal., Inc., 68 Cal. App. 4th 101, 112, 80 Cal. Rptr. 2d 60, 66 (1998), superseded in irrelevant part by 2000 Cal. Stat. 98 § 1 (AB 2719); see Brown v. Dep't of Corr., 132 Cal. App. 4th 520, 529-30, 33 Cal. Rptr. 3d 754, 761 (2005) (dismissing employment retaliation claims based on statements, reports and actions privileged under section 47(b)). **The absolute privileges of Civil Code section 47 may also apply to reporting suspected criminal activity. Kerner, 206 Cal. App. 4th at 121, 141 Cal. Rptr. 3d at 532 (unqualified privilege applies when a citizen contacts law enforcement to report suspected criminal activity).**

The litigation privilege may also be implicated if an employer makes statements to customers or clients regarding a former employee. Neville v. Chudacoff, 160 Cal. App. 4th 1255, 73 Cal. Rptr. 3d 383 (2008) (letter sent by employer, several months prior to filing lawsuit against former employee, to customers accusing the former employee of breach of contract and misappropriation of trade secrets and suggesting that customers should not do business with former employee if they wished to avoid involvement in litigation protected by litigation privilege).

2. ***Qualified Privileges***. California Civil Code section 47 codifies a number of qualified privileges in addition to the absolute privileges it sets forth. A qualified privilege protects all communications made by parties to it, except those made with malice. Cruey, 64 Cal. App. 4th at 367, 76 Cal. Rptr. 2d at 676-77. The type of malice needed to defeat a qualified privilege is "actual malice." This is shown by evidence that the publication was motivated by hatred or ill will, or by evidence that the defendant lacked reasonable grounds for belief in the truth of the publication and therefore acted in reckless disregard of the truth. Noel v. River Hills Wilsons, Inc., 113 Cal. App. 4th 1363, 1370, 7 Cal. Rptr. 3d 216, 221-22 (2003). Mere negligence, oversight, or unintentional error does not constitute malice. Id.

Additional qualified privileges are codified in California Civil Code sections 43.7 and 43.8. California Civil Code section 43.7 grants qualified immunity to the peer review activities of members of mental health professional quality assurance committees, medical special societies, hospital staff peer review committees, and professional societies. California Civil Code section 43.8 grants qualified immunity for communications to hospitals and other specified medical establishments that are intended to aid in the evaluation of the qualifications, fitness, or character of a medical practitioner. See Hassan v. Mercy Am. River Hosp., 31 Cal. 4th 709, 724, 3 Cal. Rptr. 3d 623, 633, 74 P.3d 726, 734 (2003) (section 43.8 privilege may be defeated by proof that the person or entity asserting the privilege, when it made the communication, knew the information was false or otherwise lacked a good faith intent to assist in the medical practitioner's evaluation).

a. **Common Interest**. California Civil Code section 47(c) codifies the common law privilege of common interest, which protects communications made without malice on subjects of mutual interest. See Noel, 113 Cal. App. 4th at 1369, 7 Cal. Rptr. 3d at 220.

By its express terms, Section 47(c) renders a qualified privilege to any "communication[s made] without malice, to a person interested therein[] (1) by one who is also interested, or (2) by one who stands in such a relation to the person interested as to afford a reasonable ground for supposing the motive for the communication to be innocent, or (3) who is requested by the person interested to give the information." Section 47(c) expressly applies a qualified privilege to a "communication concerning the job performance or qualifications of an applicant for employment, based upon credible evidence, made without malice, by a current or former employer of the applicant to, and upon request of, one whom the employer reasonably believes is a prospective employer of the applicant."

In the employment context, Section 47(c) has been interpreted by case law to protect conditionally nonmalicious employment-related communications. See, e.g., Yanke v. City of Oakland, No. C-08-04379 EDL, 2009 WL 2581294, at *9 (N.D. Cal. Aug. 20, 2009) (common interest privilege applied to communications between a doctor who conducted fitness-for-duty psychiatric examination and employer where plaintiff could not show that doctor was motivated by negative feelings or ill will toward plaintiff and could, at best, theorize that the doctor provided his report to employer in order to further his relationship with the employer); Lee v. Eden Med. Ctr., 690 F. Supp. 2d 1011, 1022-23 (N.D. Cal. 2010) (human resource manager's communications with hospital management and counsel for Board of Registered Nurses regarding former employee's mental fitness evaluation subject to common interest privilege); London v. Sears, Roebuck & Co., 619 F. Supp. 2d 854, 864-65 (N.D. Cal. 2009) ("'[B]ecause an employer and its employees have a common interest in protecting the work place from abuse, an employer's statements to employees regarding the reasons for termination of another employee generally are privileged.'"; statements concerning former employee taking money from someone and subsequently being fired are privileged communications so long as they are not made with malice) (citation omitted; alteration in original); Deaile v. Gen. Tel. Co. of Cal., 40 Cal. App. 3d 841, 849, 115 Cal. Rptr. 582, 587 (1974) (holding that employer's publication to other employees of reasons for another employee's termination is conditionally privileged); Cruey, 64 Cal. App. 4th at 368-69, 76 Cal. Rptr. 2d at 677 (holding that employee's complaints of discrimination and harassment to private employer's human resources department are conditionally privileged). In the employment reference context, the common-interest privilege applies even when a defendant's reference is defamatory due to negligence, oversight, or unintentional error. Noel, 113 Cal. App. 4th at 1371, 7 Cal. Rptr. 3d at 222; but see III.C, infra.

Typically, the common interest protected is private or pecuniary, the relationship between the parties close (a family, business, or organizational interest, for example), and the information is shared in the course of the relationship. Kashian v. Harriman, 98 Cal. App. 4th 892, 914-15, 120 Cal. Rptr. 2d 576, 593-94 (2002). However, the cases have taken an "eclectic approach" toward interpreting the statute, and the common-interest privilege is not capable of precise or categorical definition. Its application to a case "depends upon an evaluation of the competing interests which defamation law and the privilege are designed to serve." Id. (citations omitted); see also Deaile, 40 Cal. App. 3d at 847, 115 Cal. Rptr. at 585 (defendant and recipients shared a "common interest" because all recipients of allegedly libelous communications were employed by defendant and worked at same facility which plaintiff had managed, or were plaintiff's superiors). The common-interest privilege may be lost not only if uttered with malice, but also if the communicator abuses the privilege by excessive publication or the discussion of immaterial matters with no bearing on the protected interest. Id.; see also Brown v. Kelly Broad. Co., 48 Cal. 3d 711, 742-43, 257 Cal. Rptr. 708, 727, 771 P.2d 406, 425 (1989) (no common interest between member of news media and general public); Kelly v. Gen. Tel. Co., 136 Cal. App. 3d 278, 285, 186 Cal. Rptr. 184, 187 (1982) (common interest exists in communications among employees designed to ensure honest and accurate records); Swift & Co. v. Gray, 101 F.2d 976, 980 (9th Cir. 1939) ("Mere idle curiosity on the part of the hearer is not enough" to establish that the hearer has an "interest" in the disclosure.").

b. **Duty**. California Civil Code section 47 recognizes an absolute privilege for communications made in "the proper discharge of an official duty." Cal. Civ. Code § 47(a). This privilege does not apply to private parties in California. Slaughter v. Friedman, 32 Cal. 3d 149, 156, 185 Cal. Rptr. 244, 247, 649 P.2d 886, 889 (1982). California has failed to adopt the absolute privilege contained in the Restatement (Second) of Torts Section 592A (1977), which provides that "[o]ne who is required by law to publish defamatory matter is absolutely privileged to publish it." Slaughter, 32 Cal. 3d at 157, 185 Cal. Rptr. at 249, 649 P.2d at 891.

c. **Criticism of Public Employee**. The common law "fair comment" privilege protects statements or expressions of fact or opinion about public officials, scientists, artists, composers, performers, authors, and other persons who place themselves or their work in the public eye. Kelly Broad. Co., 48 Cal. 3d at 732 n.18, 257 Cal. Rptr. at 720 & 732 n.18, 771 P.2d at 418 n.18; Inst. of Athletic Motivation v. Univ. of Ill., 114 Cal. App. 3d 1, 8 n.4, 170 Cal. Rptr. 411, 415 n.4 (1980). Also, the absolute executive privilege protects statements by an executive officer regarding public employees. This privilege has been extended to lower public officials, such as a school superintendent. Cal. Civ. Code § 47 (a); Morrow v. L.A. Unified Sch. Dist., 149 Cal. App. 4th 1424, 1443, 57 Cal. Rptr. 3d 885, 900 (2007).

Criticism of public employees for official conduct occurring within the scope of their employment arguably falls within the terms of California's anti-SLAPP (i.e., Strategic Lawsuit Against Public Participation) statute, California Code of Civil Procedure section 425.16. Under the terms of the statute, a defendant in any lawsuit "arising from any act of [a] person in furtherance of the person's right of petition or free speech . . . in connection with a public issue" may bring a special motion to strike a complaint or any cause of action therein within 60 days of service, and the statute requires that the motion must be granted, unless the plaintiff establishes "a probability that the plaintiff will prevail" on the merits. Cal. Code Civ. Proc. § 425.16(b)(1); see V.E, infra.

e. **Limitations on Qualified Privileges**.

(1) **Malice**. The qualified privileges established by California Civil Code section 47(c) may be overcome by showing the defamatory statement was made with actual malice. See Gallant v. City of Carson, 128 Cal. App. 4th 705, 714, 27 Cal. Rptr. 3d 318, 324 (2005) (manager's false statement that plaintiff was terminated for incompetence could support malice if made in retaliation for whistle-blowing activity) overruled in irrelevant part on other grounds by Reid v. Google, Inc., 50 Cal. 4th 512, 532, 113 Cal. Rptr. 3d 327, 344, 235 P.3d 988, 1002 (2010). The showing of actual malice necessary is the common law definition of malice, meaning "a state of mind arising from hatred or ill will, evidencing a willingness to vex, annoy or injure another person" or a showing that the defendant lacked reasonable grounds for belief in the truth of the publication and therefore acted in reckless disregard of the plaintiff's rights. Brown v. Kelly Broad Co., 48 Cal. 3d at 723, 257 Cal. Rptr. at 713, 771 P.2d at 411 (citation omitted); Bierbower v. FHP, Inc., 70 Cal. App. 4th 1, 3, 82 Cal. Rptr. 2d 393, 394 (1999) (holding that a discrepancy in an office memo concerning the date on which an alleged incident of sexual harassment took place is insufficient evidence of malice; malice cannot be derived from negligence); Roemer v. Retail Credit Co., 44 Cal. App. 3d 926, 936, 119 Cal. Rptr. 82, 88 (1975); Mamou v. Trendwest Resorts, Inc., 165 Cal. App. 4th 686, 81 Cal. Rptr. 3d 406 (2008) (evidence that alleged defamers had been hostile to plaintiff during his employment suggested that publication might have been motivated by hostility or ill will and precluded application of common interest privilege); Duste v. Chevron Prods. Co., 738 F. Supp. 2d 1027, 1044 (N.D. Cal. 2010) (fact

that statement was made with knowledge of its inaccuracy and with knowledge that it exposed plaintiff to possible disciplinary measures was sufficient to create issue of fact on common interest privilege).

(2) **Constitutional Malice**. A showing of constitutional malice may be insufficient to defeat the assertion of a qualified privilege. As noted above, the rule in California is that common law malice constitutes the necessary showing to be made to defeat a qualified privilege. See Lundquist v. Reusser, 7 Cal. 4th 1193, 1206 n.12, 31 Cal. Rptr. 2d 776, 783 n.12, 875 P.2d 1279, 1286 n.12 (1994); Aronson v. Kinsella, 58 Cal. App. 4th 254, 264, 68 Cal. Rptr. 2d 305, 311 (1997).

(3) **Excessive Publication**. The common interest privilege may be lost if the communicator abuses the privilege by excessive publication or the discussion of immaterial matters with no bearing on the protected interest. Deaile, 40 Cal. App. 3d at 847, 115 Cal. Rptr. at 585.

(4) **Question of Fact or Law**. The question of whether or not a qualified privilege applies is generally a question of fact for the jury, if the facts are in dispute. Otherwise, the issue may be resolved by the court. Lundquist, 7 Cal. 4th at 1203 n.9, 31 Cal. Rptr. 2d at 781 n.9, 875 P.2d at 1284 n.9.

(5) **Burden of Proof**. In any defamation action, where the defamatory statement in question was made within the parameters of a qualified privilege, the plaintiff has the burden of proving that the statement was made with malice such that the privilege does not apply. Lundquist, 7 Cal. 4th at 1209-10, 31 Cal. Rptr. 2d at 786, 875 P.2d at 1288-89; Williams v. Taylor, 129 Cal. App. 3d 745, 752, 181 Cal. Rptr. 423, 427 (1982); see also Smith v. Pac. Bell Tel. Co., 649 F. Supp. 2d 1073, 1101 (E.D. Cal. 2009) (granting summary judgment for employer where plaintiff failed to show that employer discussed internal investigation or answered co-workers' questions regarding plaintiff's termination with "actual malice"). The defendant bears the initial burden of establishing that the allegedly defamatory statement was made upon an occasion giving rise to a qualified privilege. Lundquist, 7 Cal. 4th at 1202-03, 31 Cal. Rptr. 2d at 781, 875 P.2d at 1284.

B. Standard Libel Defenses

1. ***Truth***. In California, truth is an absolute defense to any defamation action, regardless of the defendant's bad faith or malicious purpose in publishing the statements in question. Smith v. Maldonado, 72 Cal. App. 4th 637, 648, 85 Cal. Rptr. 2d 397, 404, 27 Media L. Rep. 1814 (1999). Generally, the defendant bears the burden of pleading and proving truth. Smith, 72 Cal. App. 4th at 647 n.5, 85 Cal. Rptr. 2d at 403 n.5. However, the First Amendment requires the plaintiff to bear the burden of proving falsity in actions involving public figures or matters of public concern. Id.; see also Comedy III Prods., Inc. v. Gary Saderup, Inc., 25 Cal. 4th 387, 398, 106 Cal. Rptr. 2d 126, 134, 21 P.3d 797, 803 (2001); Phila. Newspapers, Inc. v. Hepps, 475 U.S. 767, 106 S. Ct. 1558, 89 L. Ed. 2d 783 (1986).

To establish truth, a defendant need not prove the literal truth of the allegedly defamatory statement so long as the "gist" or "sting" of the statement is substantially true. Hughes v. Hughes, 122 Cal. App. 4th 931, 936, 19 Cal. Rptr. 3d 247, 251 (2004); Campanelli v. Regents of Univ. of Cal., 44 Cal. App. 4th 572, 582, 51 Cal. Rptr. 2d 891, 897 (1996); Weller v. Am. Broad. Cos., 232 Cal. App. 3d 991, 1010 n.17, 283 Cal. Rptr. 644, 656 n.17, 19 Media L. Rep. 1161 (1991).

2. ***Opinion***. California courts have consistently distinguished between actionable statements of fact and nonactionable statements of opinion. Eisenberg v. Alameda Newspapers, Inc., 74 Cal. App. 4th 1359, 1385, 88 Cal. Rptr. 2d 802, 822-23, 27 Media L. Rep. 2441 (1999). In contrast to false assertions of fact, publications of opinion generally cannot form the basis for a defamation action, even if they are objectively unjustified and are made in bad faith. Jensen v. Hewlett-Packard Co., 14 Cal. App. 4th 958, 970-71, 18 Cal. Rptr. 2d 83, 89-90 (1993). "Nevertheless, a statement of opinion may be actionable '. . . if it implies the allegation of undisclosed defamatory facts as the basis for the opinion.'" Ringler Assocs. Inc. v. Md. Cas. Co., 80 Cal. App. 4th 1165, 1181, 96 Cal. Rptr. 2d 136, 149, 29 Media L. Rep. 1033 (2000) (quoting Okun v. Superior Court, 29 Cal. 3d 442, 451-52, 175 Cal. Rptr. 157, 629 P.2d 1369 (1981); alteration in original).

Test For Opinion. In determining whether a statement is actionable fact or nonactionable opinion, courts use a "totality of the circumstances test," which involves an examination of both the statement and the context in which the statement was made. Franklin v. Dynamic Details, Inc., 116 Cal. App. 4th 375, 386, 10 Cal. Rptr. 3d 429, 437 (2004). First, the language of the statement is examined to determine whether the words would be understood in a defamatory sense. Next, the context in which the statement was made must be considered, looking to the nature and full content of the communication and the knowledge and understanding of the audience to whom the publication was directed. Seelig v. Infinity Broad. Corp., 97 Cal. App. 4th 798, 809-10, 119 Cal. Rptr. 2d 108, 117 (2002) (comments on a morning radio program that contestant on television program was a "big skank," "local loser" and "chicken butt" not actionable statements of fact); Vogel v. Felice, 127 Cal. App. 4th 1006, 1021, 26 Cal. Rptr. 3d 350, 361 (2005) (statements that plaintiffs were a "deadbeat dad" and bankrupt capable of conveying provably false factual imputation); San Francisco Bay Guardian, Inc. v. Superior Court, 17 Cal. App. 4th 655, 658, 21 Cal. Rptr. 2d 464, 465, 21 Media L. Rep. 1791 (1993); Yuin Univ. v. Korean Broad. Sys., 131 Cal. Rptr. 3d 919, 924, 199 Cal. App. 4th 1098, 1105 (2011) ("slanted reporting" is not actionable, and characterization of university as a "suspected degree factory" is an expression of opinion). Under the totality of the circumstances test, the court must place itself in the situation of an average reader and decide the natural and probable effect of the statements in question. Jackson v. Paramount Pictures Corp., 68 Cal. App. 4th 10, 29, 80 Cal. Rptr. 2d 1, 11 (1998); MacLeod v. Tribune Publ'g Co., 52 Cal. 2d 536, 551, 343 P.2d 36, 44 (1959).

Opinions Protected After *Milkovich*. California's general application of the rule providing that statements of opinion are not actionable has survived the Supreme Court's holding in Milkovich v. Lorain Journal Co., 497 U.S. 1, 17, 110 S. Ct. 2695, 2705, 111 L. Ed. 2d 1, 17, 17 Media L. Rep. 2009 (1990). Opinions, however, are not categorically protected from defamation claims. Rather, the dispositive question is whether the statement declares or implies a provably false assertion of fact. Overstock.com, Inc., v. Gradient Analytics, Inc., 151 Cal. App. 4th 688, 701, 61 Cal. Rptr. 3d 29, 39, 35 Media L. Rep. 2135 (2007). Thus, an opinion is not actionable, unless it could be reasonably understood as declaring or implying actual facts capable of being proved true or false. Integrated Healthcare Holdings, Inc., v. Fitzgibbons, 140 Cal. App. 4th 515, 527-28, 44 Cal. Rptr. 3d 517, 526-27 (2006) (discussion of when statement of opinion is actionable); Nygard, Inc. v. Uusi-Kerttula, 159 Cal. App. 4th 1027, 1052, 72 Cal. Rptr. 3d 210, 228 (2008) (a description of working environment as "horrible" and a "horror" would not be understood by any reasonable reader to be a statement of fact); Mamou v. Trendwest Resorts, Inc., 165 Cal. App. 4th 686, 728, 81 Cal. Rptr. 3d 406, 440 (2008) (assertions that individuals had "documentary proof" of alleged acts "all but precludes a finding that their accusations constituted non-actionable statements of opinion"); Overhill Farms, Inc. v. Lopez, 190 Cal. App. 4th 1248, 1252, 119 Cal. Rptr. 3d 127, 132 (2010) (accusation that an employer engaged in a mass employment termination based upon racist and ageist motivations is clearly a "provable fact").

Question of Fact or Law. The issue of whether a given communication constitutes a statement of fact or a constitutionally protected opinion is a question of law for the court. Melaleuca, Inc. v. Clark, 66 Cal. App. 4th 1344, 1353-54, 78 Cal. Rptr. 2d 627, 632 (1998); Kahn v. Bower, 232 Cal. App. 3d 1599, 1608, 284 Cal. Rptr. 244, 249, 19 Media L. Rep. 1236 (1991). However, some statements are ambiguous and cannot be characterized as factual or nonfactual as a matter of law. In such cases, the jury must determine whether an ordinary reader would have understood the statements as a factual assertion. Kahn, 232 Cal. App. 3d at 1608, 284 Cal. Rptr. at 249; Ruiz v. Harbor View Cmty. Ass'n, 134 Cal. App. 4th 1456, 1471, 37 Cal. Rptr. 3d 133, 144 (2005) (whether statement declares or implies provably false assertion is question of law for court unless statement is susceptible of both an innocent and libelous meaning, in which case jury must decide).

3. ***Consent***. A plaintiff who consents to the publication of defamatory matter cannot recover for defamation because consent establishes an absolute defense or privilege to the claim. Royer v. Steinberg, 90 Cal. App. 3d 490, 498, 153 Cal. Rptr. 499, 503 (1979) (holding that by publishing in a newspaper a confidential letter describing the reasons for his demotion along with his answers to these reasons the plaintiff consented to the publication); Kelly v. William Morrow & Co., 186 Cal. App. 3d 1625, 1635, 231 Cal. Rptr. 497, 503 (1986) (trier of fact must determine dispute about scope of consent given prior to publication of defamatory material).

4. ***Mitigation***. California Civil Procedure Code section 461 allows a defendant in a defamation case who is unable to prove the truth of the matter asserted to establish "mitigating circumstances" in an effort to limit the damages awarded to plaintiff. See Cal. Code Civ. Proc. § 461. Mitigating circumstances may include evidence which tends to show that, in publishing the defamatory statement, the defendant acted in good faith with honesty of purpose, and not maliciously. Roemer v. Retail Credit Co., 44 Cal. App. 3d 926, 940, 119 Cal. Rptr. 82, 91 (1975); Clay v. Lagiss, 143 Cal. App. 2d 441, 448, 299 P.2d 1025, 1030 (1956).

5. ***Contractual Limitations***. In general, contracts that purport to exempt persons or entities for intentional wrongs, gross negligence, and violations of the law are invalid in California as being against public policy. Cal. Civ. Code § 1668. In a limited context, however, at least one court has held that contractual provisions which limited the liability of certain actors for defamation were enforceable. Farnham v. Superior Court, 60 Cal. App. 4th 69, 77-78, 70 Cal. Rptr. 2d 85, 90 (1997) (holding that contractual provision absolving officers and directors of corporation for defamatory remarks by limiting recovery for defamation to those rights plaintiff held against the corporation was enforceable). The rationale for upholding a limited defamation waiver is that "no public policy opposes private, voluntary transactions in which one party, for a consideration, agrees to shoulder a risk which the law would otherwise have placed upon the other party." Farnham, 60 Cal. App. 4th at 77-78, 70 Cal. Rptr. 2d at 88 (quoting Tunkl v. Regents of Univ. of Cal., 60 Cal. 2d 92, 101, 32 Cal. Rptr. 33, 38, 383 P.2d 441, 446 (1963)).

6. ***Workers' compensation***. See VI., B., infra.

III. RECURRING FACT PATTERNS

A. Statements in Personnel File

California courts have found that intracorporate communications fall within an employer's qualified privilege. See Deaile v. Gen. Tel. Co. of Cal., 40 Cal. App. 3d 841, 846, 115 Cal. Rptr. 582, 585 (1974); Biggins v. Hanson, 252 Cal. App. 2d 16, 20, 59 Cal. Rptr. 897, 899-900 (1967). This rule covers statements contained in the personnel file of an employee that are made for the purpose of keeping honest and accurate records. Kelly v. Gen. Tel. Co., 136 Cal. App. 3d 278, 285, 186 Cal. Rptr. 184, 187 (1982). Accordingly, any such statements are not actionable, unless they were made with malice. Biggins, 252 Cal. App. 2d at 21, 59 Cal. Rptr. at 900 (court held that an interoffice memorandum discharging plaintiff for disloyalty, insubordination, and threat of sabotage to equipment was not privileged where the employer had no knowledge of the threat of sabotage to equipment at the time of the publication).

B. Performance Evaluations

In California, there is a strong policy disfavoring defamation suits based on communications that are part of, or related to, employee performance reviews, which are generally considered statements of opinion. McKinney v. Apollo Group, Inc., No. 07cv2373 WQH (CAB), 2009 WL 937142, at *11 (S.D. Cal. April 3, 2009); Jensen v. Hewlett-Packard Co., 14 Cal. App. 4th 958, 964, 970, 18 Cal. Rptr. 2d 83, 84-85, 89 (1993); Campanelli v. Regents of Univ. of Cal., 44 Cal. App. 4th 572, 581, 51 Cal. Rptr. 2d 891, 896 (1996). Indeed, the courts have expressly acknowledged the important business purpose of evaluations by noting:

> Clearly, there is a legitimate *raison d'etre* for such records, and management has an unquestioned obligation to keep them. We would therefore be loathe to subject an employer to the threat of a libel suit in which a jury might decide, for instance, that the employee should have been given a rating of 'average,' rather than 'needs improvement,' or that the employee had an ability, unrecognized and unappreciated by a foolish supervisor, to get along with and lead others.
>
> Jensen, 14 Cal. App. 4th at 965, 18 Cal. Rptr. 2d at 85.

Pursuant to their recognition of the importance of certain employer records, California courts have held that statements contained in an employee's performance evaluation are not actionable unless they falsely accuse an employee of criminal conduct, lack of integrity, incompetence, or reprehensible personal characteristics or behavior. Id. "This is true even when the employer's perceptions about an employee's efforts, attitude, performance, potential or worth to the enterprise are objectively wrong and cannot be supported by reference to concrete, provable facts." Id.; but see Rotella v. Emeritus Corp., No. C 10-03202 SI, 2010 WL 5141857, at *5 (N.D. Cal. Dec. 13, 2010) (statements by subordinate that plaintiff regularly failed to communicate with staff members, failed to perform other aspects of her job, and/or made degrading or disparaging statements about her regional team, and that the members of her team disliked her and expressed that she was a poor manager were capable of being proven false and therefore not protected statements of opinion). To the extent that any defamatory statements in personnel evaluations are actionable, at least one court has suggested that the plaintiff's remedy may be limited solely to contract damages for breach of the implied covenant of good faith and fair dealing. Id.; see also Sheppard v. Freeman, 67 Cal. App. 4th 339, 349, 79 Cal. Rptr. 2d 13, 18 (1998) (claim for libel may be brought against coworkers with respect to plaintiff's evaluation if coworkers acted with malice); but see Graw v. L.A. Cnty. Metro. Transp. Auth., 52 F. Supp. 2d 1152 (C.D. Cal. 1999) (rejecting analysis of Sheppard v. Freeman).

C. References

Under California law, the subject of references occasionally presents a problem for employers because they are required to walk a fine line between avoiding any defamatory comments and still disclosing a sufficient amount of information. See, e.g., Marshall v. Brown, 141 Cal. App. 3d 408, 412, 416, 190 Cal. Rptr. 392, 397 (1983) (wrongful interference liability based on negative comments in former employer's evaluation letter). To make matters difficult for both employers and employees, at least two California statutes purport to address an employer's reference obligations with somewhat conflicting conclusions.

The Blackballing Statute. California Labor Code sections 1050 and 1052 prohibit any party from making a misrepresentation that prevents or attempts to prevent a former employee from obtaining employment. The provisions of this "blackballing" statute have widespread application because any person who knowingly causes or permits a violation of this section or who fails to "take all reasonable steps within his power" to prevent a violation is guilty of a misdemeanor. See Cal. Lab. Code §§ 1050, 1052. Although under California Labor Code section 1053, employers may provide the reason for a discharge or resignation when a request is made, if any statement in a reference by an employer ". . . furnishes any mark, sign, or other means conveying information different from that expressed by words therein, such fact, or the fact that such statement or other means of furnishing information was given without a special request therefor is prima facie evidence of a violation of sections 1050 to 1053." In addition to criminal penalties, violations are subject to civil actions in which the claimant can seek treble damages. Cal. Lab. Code § 1054.

California Civil Code Section 47(c). Despite the provisions of Labor Code section 1050, California Civil Code section 47(c) provides employers with a qualified immunity for giving employment-related references. As more fully set forth in II.A.2, supra, section 47(c) states that employers cannot be held liable for providing a reference (even if the information given is inaccurate), as long as the statements made are not malicious and are based on credible evidence. See Cal. Civ. Code § 47(c); see also Smith v. Pac. Bell Tel. Co., 649 F. Supp. 2d 1073, 1101 (E.D. Cal. 2009) (granting summary judgment to employer, based on Civil Code section 47(c), on a blacklisting claim brought under Labor Code section 1050).

Common Law. In Conkle v. Jeong, 853 F. Supp. 1160, 1170 (N.D. Cal. 1994) (applying California law), aff'd, 73 F.3d 909 (9th Cir. 1995), the court found an employer's statement about a former employee to a prospective employer to be privileged because the employer merely provided candid responses about the former employee. Id. at 1169. Furthermore, the court held that malice could not be inferred from the former employer's statement that he did not want the employee to return. Id. In Dorn v. Mendelzon, 196 Cal. App. 3d 933, 943, 242 Cal. Rptr. 259, 264 (1987), the court similarly held that a response by a hospital administrator to an inquiry from another hospital about a doctor formerly employed by the administrator was privileged. According to the court, the statements made concerned restrictions placed on the doctor while at the first hospital, were not malicious, and served an important interest to the second hospital in assessing the qualifications of the doctor. Id. at 942, 242 Cal. Rptr. at 263.

In certain circumstances, an employer may be liable for misrepresentation if he or she fails to disclose material facts to a potential employer in an employment reference. See Randi W. v. Muroc Joint Unified Sch. Dist., 14 Cal. 4th 1066, 1083 -84, 60 Cal. Rptr. 2d 263, 273-74, 929 P.2d 582, 592-93 (1997) (dealing with a former employer's failure to disclose in a reference an employee's propensity for violent attacks). In Randi W., however, the California Supreme Court distinguished the case from traditional reference situations because Randi W. involved a voluntary letter submitted by a former employer, and not a reference furnished on the request of a prospective employer. Accordingly, the Court did not fully address whether the qualified privilege of Civil Code section 47(c) would bar an action for misrepresentation on different facts.

D. Intracorporate Communications

Communications among a company's employees that are designed to ensure honest and accurate records involve a common interest and therefore are protected by a qualified privilege against liability, where it is shown that the communicator and the recipient have a common interest and the communication is reasonably calculated to further that interest. Cal. Civ. Code § 47(c); London v. Sears, Roebuck & Co., 619 F. Supp. 2d 854, 864-65 (N.D. Cal. 2009) ("'[B]ecause an employer and its employees have a common interest in protecting the work place from abuse, an employer's statements to employees regarding the reasons for termination of another employee generally are privileged.'"; statements concerning a former employee taking money and subsequently being fired are privileged communications if not made with malice) (citations omitted; alteration in original); Kelly v. Gen. Tel. Co., 136 Cal. App. 3d 278, 285, 186 Cal. Rptr. 184, 187 (1982). See II.A.2, supra.

E. Reports to Auditors, Insurers, and Others

Reports made by an employer to its insurance adjusters and others are generally held to be subject to a qualified privilege. Williams v. Taylor, 129 Cal. App. 3d 745, 752, 181 Cal. Rptr. 423, 427 (1982); Cuenca v. Safeway S.F. Employees Fed. Credit Union, 180 Cal. App. 3d 985, 996, 225 Cal. Rptr. 852, 858 (1986).

F. Statement to Governmental Regulators

Statements made to government regulators are privileged under California Civil Code section 47. Fontani v. Wells Fargo Invs., LLC, 129 Cal. App. 4th 719, 734, 28 Cal. Rptr. 3d 833, 842 (2005) (statements regarding why employee was terminated made in a Form U-5 filing with the National Association of Securities Dealers absolutely privileged under California Civil Code § 47(b)), overruled in part on other grounds, Kibler v. N. Inyo County Local Hosp. Dist., 39 Cal. 4th 192 (2006); Garamendi v. Golden Eagle Ins. Co., 128 Cal. App. 4th 452, 478, 27 Cal. Rptr. 3d 239, 259 (2005) (letter to Insurance Commissioner absolutely privileged); see II.A, supra.

G. Vicarious Liability of Employers for Statements Made by Employees

Under principles of respondeat superior, an employer or principal is liable for compensatory damages for defamatory matter published by an employee or agent acting within the scope of his or her employment. See, e.g., Correia v. Santos, 191 Cal. App. 2d 844, 855-56, 13 Cal. Rptr. 132, 138 (1961); Swift & Co. v. Gray, 101 F.2d 976, 980-81 (9th Cir.

1939); but see Murray v. Bailey, 613 F. Supp. 1276, 1281, 11 Media L. Rep. 1369 (N.D. Cal. 1985) (stating that agency theory should be inapplicable for defamation liability where the First Amendment is implicated). Further, the California Labor Code requires an employer to indemnify its employees for all necessary expenditures or losses incurred by the employees as a direct result of the discharge of their duties. Cal. Labor Code § 2802(a). Because a corporation acts through individuals, it can only be liable for defamation derivatively, that is, through the defamatory conduct of specific employees. Thus, a judgment in favor of the employee accused of defamation bars recovery against the employer. Shaw v. Hughes Aircraft Co., 83 Cal. App. 4th 1336, 1347, 100 Cal. Rptr. 2d 446, 453-54 (2000).

1. ***Scope of Employment***. See III.G, supra.

a. **Blogging**. An employer's liability for comments on its employees' blogs will be analyzed under the Communications Decency Act of 1996 ("CDA"), which provides that "[n]o provider or user of an interactive computer service shall be treated as the publisher or speaker of any information provided by another information content provider." 47 U.S.C. § 230(c)(1). Furthermore, "[n]o cause of action may be brought and no liability may be imposed under any State or local law that is inconsistent with" the CDA. 47 U.S.C. § 230(e)(3). The California Supreme Court has recognized that "[t]hese provisions have been widely and consistently interpreted to confer broad immunity against defamation liability for those who use the Internet to publish information that originated from another source." Barrett v. Rosenthal, 40 Cal. 4th 33, 39, 51 Cal. Rptr. 3d 55, 58, 146 P.3d 510, 513, 34 Media L. Rep. 2537 (2006). The active involvement in the creation of defamatory Internet postings will expose a defendant to liability as an original source. Users or providers, however, who merely republish defamatory material, even if they actively select it for publication, are immune from liability. Barrett, 40 Cal. 4th at 62-63, 51 Cal. Rptr. 3d at 77, 146 P.3d at 529. In the employment context, an employer who plays no role in the creation or development of actionable statements posted by its employee on the Internet will be immune from liability, even if the statements originated from the employer's computer system. Delfino v. Agilent Techs., Inc., 145 Cal. App. 4th 790, 806-07, 52 Cal. Rptr. 3d 376, 390-91 (2006), cert. denied, 552 U.S. 817 (2007).

2. ***Damages***. See I.B.8, supra.

H. Internal Investigations

The common-interest privilege may protect statements made in connection with an employer's internal investigations, including those regarding employee complaints of sexual harassment. Bierbower v. FHP, Inc., 70 Cal. App. 4th 1, 3, 82 Cal. Rptr. 2d 393, 394 (1999); see also Cruey v. Gannett Co., 64 Cal. App. 4th 356, 369, 76 Cal. Rptr. 2d 670, 677 (1998) ("The conditional privilege set out in subdivision (c) of section 47 potentially applies in the present case because Lacy's letter of complaint to Gannett pertains to a subject of mutual interest to Gannett and its employees, an accusation of workplace harassment and discrimination."). See II.A.2.a, supra.

IV. OTHER ACTIONS BASED ON STATEMENTS

A. Negligent Hiring, Retention, and Supervision

It is well settled in California that a plaintiff may not evade any constitutional, statutory, or common law rights or privileges which protect certain forms of speech by asserting claims based on statements made by a party by labeling its claims as infliction of emotional distress, interference with prospective advantage, or as any other claims, except malicious prosecution. Long v. The Walt Disney Co., 116 Cal. App. 4th 868, 872-73, 10 Cal. Rptr. 3d 836, 840, 32 Media L. Rep. 1944 (2004) (holding that plaintiff cannot avoid defamation statute of limitations by proceeding on another theory); Reader's Digest Ass'n, Inc. v. Superior Court, 37 Cal. 3d 244, 265-66, 208 Cal. Rptr. 137, 151, 690 P.2d 610, 624, 11 Media L. Rep. 1065 (1984); Polygram Records, Inc. v. Superior Court, 170 Cal. App. 3d 543, 557, 216 Cal. Rptr. 252, 261, 11 Media L. Rep. 2363 (1985).

B. Intentional Infliction of Emotional Distress

Where the complaint is based on an offensive statement that is defamatory, a plaintiff cannot avoid the requirements of a defamation action by labeling a claim as emotional distress. See Long, 116 Cal. App. 4th at 872-73, 10 Cal. Rptr. 3d at 840. Thus, a public figure cannot recover for intentional infliction of emotional distress involving publications without showing that the publication contained a false statement of fact, i.e., that it was not an opinion. Lam v. Ngo, 91 Cal. App. 4th 832, 848-49, 111 Cal. Rptr. 2d 582, 595 (2001) (citing Hustler Magazine v. Falwell, 485 U.S. 46, 108 S. Ct. 876, 99 L. Ed. 2d 41 (1988)).

An employer could potentially be found liable for intentional infliction of emotional distress where the employer knew, or should have known, about a manager's constant verbal use of derogatory racial epithets directed at certain employees, but the employer took no action to prevent such conduct. See, e.g., Aguilar v. Avis Rent A Car Sys., Inc., 21 Cal. 4th 121, 126-27, 87 Cal. Rptr. 2d 132, 136-37, 980 P.2d 846, 849 (1999). But see IV.A, supra.

C. Interference with Economic Advantage

"[L]iability cannot be imposed on any theory for what has been determined to be a constitutionally protected publication." Reader's Digest Ass'n, Inc., 37 Cal. 3d at 265, 208 Cal. Rptr. at 151, 690 P.2d 610, 624, 11 Media L. Rep. 1065; Fellows v. Nat'l Enquirer, Inc., 42 Cal. 3d 234, 240, 228 Cal. Rptr. 215, 219, 721 P.2d 97, 100, 13 Media L. Rep. 1305 (1986). Accordingly, no claim for interference with prospective advantage based on statements can exist where no claim for defamation could be made.

D. Prima Facie Tort

California has generally rejected the legal doctrine of prima facie tort. Francis v. Dun & Bradstreet, Inc., 3 Cal. App. 4th 535, 541, 4 Cal. Rptr. 2d 361, 365 (1992); Della Penna v. Toyota Motor Sales, U.S.A., Inc., 11 Cal. 4th 376, 45 Cal. Rptr. 2d 436, 902 P.2d 740 (1995).

E. Trade Libel

Trade libel is "an intentional disparagement of the quality of property, which results in pecuniary damage to plaintiff." Polygram Records, Inc. v. Superior Court, 170 Cal. App. 3d 543, 548, 216 Cal. Rptr. 252, 254, 11 Media L. Rep. 2363 (1985) (quoting Erlich v. Etner, 224 Cal. App. 2d 69, 73, 36 Cal. Rptr. 256, 258 (1964)). To be actionable, trade libel requires a false statement. ComputerXpress, Inc. v. Jackson, 93 Cal. App. 4th 993, 1010, 113 Cal. Rptr. 2d 625, 641 (2001). In addition, because the gravamen of any action for trade libel is that false statements of fact were made that damaged plaintiff's business, "the limitations that define the First Amendment's zone of protection" are applicable. Blatty v. New York Times Co., 42 Cal. 3d 1033, 1042, 232 Cal. Rptr. 542, 547, 728 P.2d 1177, 1182, 13 Media L. Rep. 1928 (1986).

F. FEHA Violations

An action based on pure speech may be brought under the Fair Employment and Housing Act. Cal. Gov't Code § 12900 et seq. ("FEHA"). More specifically, the First Amendment permits the imposition of civil liability under FEHA for speech that creates a racially hostile or abusive work environment. Aguilar v. Avis Rent A Car Sys., Inc., 21 Cal. 4th 121, 135, 87 Cal. Rptr. 2d 132, 142-43, 980 P.2d 846, 855 (1999). However, this issue has been the subject of some debate among First Amendment scholars. Aguilar, 21 Cal. 4th at 137 n.5, 87 Cal. Rptr. 2d at 136 n.5, 980 P.2d at 855 n.5.

V. PROCEDURAL ISSUES

A. Statute of Limitations

The statute of limitations for any action for libel or slander is one year. Cal. Code Civ. Proc. § 340(c); Knoell v. Petrovich, 76 Cal. App. 4th 164, 168, 90 Cal. Rtpr. 2d 162, 164 (1999). In defamation actions, the one-year statute typically runs from the date of utterance or publication of the defamatory matter. Id. (citing Bernson v. Browning-Ferris Indus. of Cal., Inc., 7 Cal. 4th 926, 931, 30 Cal. Rtpr. 2d 440, 873 P.2d 613, 22 Media L. Rep. 2065 (1994)); Robert J. v. Catherine D., 171 Cal. App. 4th 1500, 1526, 91 Cal. Rptr. 3d 6, 25-26 (2009). Even under the discovery rule, accrual of the cause of action does not begin when the plaintiff finds out about the statements made about him or her. Instead, the statute of limitations begins to run as of the date that the plaintiff discovered or should have discovered a factual basis for the defamation claim. Burdette v. Carrier Corp., 158 Cal. App. 4th 1668, 1692, 71 Cal. Rptr. 3d 185, 203 (2008) (citing Shively v. Bozanich, 31 Cal. 4th 1230, 1248, 7 Cal. Rptr. 3d 576, 588, 80 P.3d 676, 686 (2003)). The fact that a plaintiff does not know the identity of each and every defendant who has caused the harm does not toll the running of the statute of limitations. Burdette, 158 Cal. App. 4th at 1692, 71 Cal. Rptr. 3d at 203 (citing Browning-Ferris Indus., 7 Cal. 4th at 932, 30 Cal. Rtpr. 2d at 443, 873 P.2d at 616).

Exceptions to the above rule exist, however. First, where the plaintiff does not know, and in the exercise of reasonable diligence should not know, of the accrual of her cause of action on the date of publication, the discovery rule tolls the accrual date on her claim until the date it should have been discovered. Manguso v. Oceanside Unified Sch. Dist., 88 Cal. App. 3d 725, 731, 152 Cal. Rptr. 27, 31 (1979). Second, the doctrine of fraudulent concealment can be asserted to estop a defamer who has intentionally concealed his or her identity from relying on the statute of limitations as a defense to what would otherwise be a stale claim. Browning-Ferris Indus. of Cal., Inc., 7 Cal. 4th at 937-38, 30 Cal. Rptr. 2d at 446, 873 P.2d at 619-20, 22 Media L. Rep. 2065 (1994). Finally, where the defamatory act in question is but one step in a continuing conspiracy which results in the plaintiff's discharge or damage, the statute of limitations does not commence to run until the commission of the last overt act in furtherance of the conspiracy. Rodriguez v. N. Am. Aviation, Inc., 252 Cal. App. 2d 889, 892-93, 61 Cal. Rptr. 579, 580-81 (1967); Schessler v. Keck, 125 Cal. App. 2d 827, 832-33, 271 P.2d 588, 592 (1954).

The statute of limitations is not tolled, however, if the single publication rule applies. The single publication rule generally provides that for any single edition of a newspaper, book, or other publication, there is but a single potential action for a defamatory statement contained therein, and the statute of limitations commences on its first general distribution to the public. Shively, 31 Cal. 4th at 1245-46, 7 Cal. Rptr. 3d at 585-87, 80 P.3d at 684-85, 32 Media L. Rep. 1097 (discovery may not delay accrual of cause of action for defamation beyond point at which defamation is no longer secret). **The single publication rule also applies to Internet publications regardless of how many people actually see it. Cole v. Patricia A. Meyer & Assocs., APC, 206 Cal. App. 4th 1095, 1121, 142 Cal. Rptr. 3d 646, 667 (2012).** The discovery rule does not apply to defamation claims based on the publication of defamatory material in a book, because applying the rule would undermine the single publication rule and reinstate the indefinite tolling of the statute of limitations. Shively, 31 Cal. 4th at 1251, 7 Cal. Rptr. 3d at 591, 80 P.3d at 688-89. In Traditional Cat Ass'n, Inc., v. Gilbreath, 118 Cal. App. 4th 392, 400-01, 13 Cal. Rptr. 3d 353, 359-60, 32 Media L. Rep. 1998 (2004), the court held that statements made on internet web sites are equally protected by the single publication rule. The California Supreme Court recently remanded a case involving product labels, directing the trial court to consider whether the production of a product label over a period of years is a single integrated publication that triggers the running of the statute of limitations when the first such label is distributed to the public. Christoff v. Nestle USA, Inc., 47 Cal. 4th 468, 481-82, 97 Cal. Rptr. 3d 798, 807-09, 213 P.3d 132, 140-41 (2009). Moreover, the single publication rule applies to all claims based on defamatory statements, regardless of label. This includes claims for emotional distress, violation of the right of publicity, and the appropriation of likenesses. Long v. The Walt Disney Co., 116 Cal. App. 4th 868, 872-73, 10 Cal. Rptr. 3d 836, 840, 32 Media L. Rep. 1944 (2004) ("In essence, plaintiffs claim that the complained-of acts are not like defamation at all, but constitute a new 'morph-tort' that has caused them emotional distress rather than loss of reputation. This distinction has already been considered and rejected.").

B. Jurisdiction

An individual defendant has the right to have any defamation case tried in the county of his or her residence. Buck v. James McClatchy Publ'g Co., 105 Cal. App. 248, 251-52, 287 P. 364, 365 (1930). In contrast, a plaintiff may generally sue a media defendant in the county where plaintiff resides if the media defendant has circulated copies of the defamatory publication there even though it was originally published in another county. Shores v. Chip Steak Co., 130 Cal. App. 2d 627, 630, 279 P.2d 595, 597 (1955).

The choice of law which applies to a defamation claim brought in California depends upon the so-called "governmental interest" test. The analysis of the choice of law question proceeds in three steps: "'(1) determination of whether the potentially concerned states have different laws, (2) consideration of whether each of the states has an interest in having its law applied to the case, and (3) if the laws are different and each has an interest in having its law applied (a "true" conflict), selection of which state's law to apply by determining which state's interests would be more impaired if its policy were subordinated to the policy of the other state.'" Sommer v. Gabor, 40 Cal. App. 4th 1455, 1467, 48 Cal. Rptr. 2d 235, 243, 24 Media L. Rep. 1225 (1995) (citation omitted); see also In re Yagman, 796 F.2d 1165, 1170-71, 13 Media L. Rep. 1545 (9th Cir. 1986) (the determining factor is California's "governmental interest" in application of privileges to alleged defamatory statements); Fleury v. Harper & Row, Publishers, Inc., 698 F.2d 1022, 1025, 9 Media L. Rep. 1200 (9th Cir. 1983), overruled on other grounds In re McLinn, 739 F.2d 1395 (9th Cir. 1984).

C. Worker's Compensation Exclusivity

The exclusive remedy provisions of the workers' compensation statute sometimes will constitute a defense used by employers in California to cut off an employee's claims for civil liability. Workers' compensation laws do not provide an employer with a defense to claims of defamation, however. Davaris v. Cubaleski, 12 Cal. App. 4th 1583, 1591, 16 Cal. Rptr. 2d 330, 335 (1993); Howland v. Balma, 143 Cal. App. 3d 899, 906, 192 Cal. Rptr. 286, 290 (1983).

D. Pleading Requirements

The specific words giving rise to a claim for defamation must be specifically identified in the complaint, if not pleaded verbatim. Gilbert v. Sykes, 147 Cal. App. 4th 13, 31, 53 Cal. Rptr. 3d 752, 767 (2007) (citations omitted). In view of this rule, a court would be justified in disregarding any evidence or argument concerning statements not explicitly set forth in the complaint. Vogel v. Felice, 127 Cal. App. 4th 1006, 1017 n.3, 26 Cal. Rptr. 3d 350, 359 n.3 (2005). If a statement is not defamatory on its face, the plaintiff also must plead and prove a defamatory meaning and special damages. Savage v. Pac. Gas & Elec. Co., 21 Cal. App. 4th 434, 447, 26 Cal. Rptr. 2d 305, 313, 22 Media L. Rep. 1737 (1993). Finally, if the plaintiff is a public figure, he or she must plead the defamatory statements were made with actual malice, that is, "with knowledge that it was false or with reckless disregard of whether it was false or not." Vogel, 127 Cal. App. 4th at 1017, 26 Cal. Rptr. 3d at 359 (citation omitted).

With respect to the answer, a defendant in California should plead any applicable defamation privilege as an affirmative defense, unless the application of the privilege is apparent on the face of the complaint. Peoples v. Tautfest, 274 Cal. App. 2d 630, 636, 79 Cal. Rptr. 478, 482 (1969). A privilege previously unpled also may be raised for the first time in a summary judgment proceeding, absent a showing of prejudice to the opposing party. Cruey v. Gannett Co., 64 Cal. App. 4th 356, 367, 76 Cal. Rptr. 2d 670, 676 (1998); Camarillo v. McCarthy, 998 F.2d 638, 639 (9th Cir. 1993).

E. Prior Restraints

Prior restraints entail the strictest scrutiny known to First Amendment jurisprudence. Se. Promotions, Ltd. v. Conrad, 420 U.S. 546, 558-59, 95 S. Ct. 1239, 1246-47, 43 L. Ed. 2d 448, (1975). A prior restraint is a judicial order forbidding certain communications when issued in advance of the time that such communications occur. Examples of prior restraints include temporary restraining orders and permanent injunctions that forbid speech. DVD Copy Control Ass'n, Inc. v. Bunner, 31 Cal. 4th 864, 885-86, 4 Cal. Rptr. 3d 69, 88, 75 P.3d 1, 17 (2003) (allowing content neutral injunction against posting decryption program that defeated copy protections for DVDs). Only content-based injunctions, however, are subject to prior restraint analysis. Id. Also, "a remedial injunction prohibiting the continued use of racial epithets in the workplace does not violate the right to freedom of speech if there has been a judicial determination that the use of such epithets will contribute to the continuation of a hostile or abusive work environment and therefore will constitute employment discrimination." Aguilar v. Avis Rent A Car Sys., Inc., 21 Cal. 4th 121, 126, 87 Cal. Rptr. 2d 132, 135, 980 P.2d 846, 848 (1999). Where a specific pattern of speech violates the Fair Employment and Housing Act, Cal. Gov't Code § 12900 et seq., an injunction prohibiting the repetition, perpetuation, or continuation of that practice is not a prohibited prior restraint of speech. Aguilar, 21 Cal. 4th at 140, 87 Cal. Rptr. 2d at 146, 980 P.2d at 858. Finally, following a trial at which it is determined that a defendant defamed the plaintiff, a court may issue an injunction prohibiting the defendant from repeating the defamatory statements. Such an injunction does not constitute a prior restraint. Balboa Island Vill. Inn, Inc. v. Lemen, 40 Cal. 4th 1141, 1155-56, 57 Cal. Rptr. 3d 320, 331, 156 P.3d 339, 349 (2007); see also Peralta Cmty. Coll. Dist. v. Fair Emp't & Hous. Comm'n, 52 Cal. 3d 40, 53, 276 Cal. Rptr. 114, 122, 801 P.2d 357, 365 (1990) (California Fair Employment and Housing Commission empowered to order employer to cease and desist verbal harassment).

F. Summary Judgment

In General. The court must grant a motion for summary judgment if there is no triable issue as to any material fact and the moving party is entitled to judgment as a matter of law. Raghavan v. Boeing Co., 133 Cal. App. 4th 1120, 1131-32, 35 Cal. Rptr. 3d 397, 405 (2005) (citing Cal. Code Civ. Proc. § 437c; granting summary adjudication of defamation claim). Summary judgment is a favored remedy in defamation cases in California because it affords a speedy resolution of actions involving First Amendment rights. Due to the chilling effect of protracted litigation on First Amendment rights, the courts impose more stringent burdens on one who opposes the motion and require a showing of high probability that the plaintiff will ultimately prevail in the case. Alszeh v. Home Box Office, 67 Cal. App. 4th 1456, 1460, 80 Cal. Rptr. 2d 16, 17 (1998). On summary judgment, "'whether published material is reasonably susceptible of an interpretation which implies a provably false assertion of fact – the dispositive question in a defamation action – is a question of law for the court. This question must be resolved by considering whether the reasonable or "average" reader would so interpret the material.'" Id. at 1461, 80 Cal. Rptr. 2d. at 18 (citations omitted; alteration omitted); see also Reader's Digest Ass'n, Inc. v. Superior Court, 37 Cal. 3d 244, 251, 208 Cal. Rptr. 137, 140, 690 P.2d 610, 613, 11 Media L. Rep. 1065 (1984); Wasser v. San Diego Union, 191 Cal. App. 3d 1455, 1461, 236 Cal. Rptr. 772, 775-76, 14 Media L. Rep. 1083 (1987).

The Anti-SLAPP Statute. Rather than filing a motion for summary judgment, the defendant should consider a special motion to strike when the complaint challenges the exercise of free speech rights in connection with a public issue. This motion is governed by the Strategic Litigation Against Public Participation ("SLAPP") provisions of California Code of Civil Procedure. Cal. Civ. Proc. Code § 425.16 et seq.; **Steed v. Dep't of Consumer Affairs, 204 Cal. App. 4th 112, 119, 138 Cal. Rptr. 3d 519, 524 (2012) (noting that the statute authorized the filing of a special motion to strike to expedite the early dismissal of these unmeritorious claims in order to encourage continued participation in matters of public significance and to ensure that this participation should not be chilled through abuse of the judicial process; noting that the Legislature expressly provided that the anti-SLAPP statute "shall be construed broadly."); Price v. Operating Eng'rs Local Union No. 3, 195 Cal. App. 4th 962, 969, 125 Cal. Rptr. 3d 220, 224 (2011) (applying anti-SLAPP statute to defamation);** Wilbanks v. Wolk, 121 Cal. App. 4th 883, 901, 17 Cal. Rptr. 3d 497, 508 (2004) (same); Kashian v. Harriman, 98 Cal. App. 4th 892, 905, 120 Cal. Rptr. 2d 576, 585-86 (2002) (same); Dowling v. Zimmerman, 85 Cal. App. 4th 1400, 1418, 103 Cal. Rptr. 2d 174, 189 (2001) (same). The defendant may file the special motion to strike, also known as an Anti-SLAPP motion, "within 60 days of the service of the complaint or, in the court's discretion, at any later time upon terms it deems proper." Cal. Code Civ. Proc. § 425.16(f); see Cal. Code Civ. Proc. § 425.17 (anti-SLAPP provision does not apply to certain lawsuits, including some actions brought solely in public interest or on behalf of general public).

A two-step process is applied to determine whether the anti-SLAPP motion should be granted. First, the defendant has the burden of making a threshold prima facie showing that the defendant's acts, of which the plaintiff complains, were taken in furtherance of the defendant's constitutional rights of petition or free speech in connection with a public issue. **Steed v. Dep't of Consumer Affairs, 204 Cal. App. 4th 112, 119, 138 Cal. Rptr. 3d 519, 525 (2012); Price v. Operating**

Eng'rs Local Union No. 3, 195 Cal. App. 4th 962, 970, 125 Cal. Rptr. 3d 220, 225 (2011); Balzaga v. Fox News Network, LLC, 173 Cal. App. 4th 1325, 1336, 93 Cal. Rptr. 3d 782, 791-92, 37 Media L. Rep. 1737 (2009); see also Raining Data Corp. v. Barrenechea, 175 Cal. App. 4th 1363, 1368, 97 Cal. Rptr. 3d 196, 199-200 (2009) (citing Equilon Enters. v. Consumer Cause, Inc., 29 Cal. 4th 53, 67, 124 Cal. Rptr. 2d 507, 518, 52 P.3d 685, 694 (2002)). If such a showing is made, the burden shifts to the plaintiff, who must provide sufficient evidence to demonstrate a probability of prevailing on the claim. Balzaga, 173 Cal. App. 4th at 1336, 93 Cal. Rptr. 3d at 791-92; Rivero v. Am. Fed'n of State, Cnty., and Mun. Employees, AFL-CIO, 105 Cal. App. 4th 913, 918-19, 130 Cal. Rptr. 2d 81, 85-86 (2003) (to qualify as a public issue, statements must concern a person or entity in the public eye, or a topic of widespread, public interest; unlawful workplace activity below some threshold level of significance is not an issue of public interest); Kashian, 98 Cal. App. 4th at 915, 120 Cal. Rptr. 2d at 594. A defendant who makes a successful anti-SLAPP motion to strike is entitled to mandatory attorney fees. Ketchum v. Moses, 24 Cal. 4th 1122, 1131, 104 Cal. Rptr. 2d 377, 383, 17 P.3d 735, 741 (2001). **Anti-SLAPP motion rulings are reviewed on appeal de novo. Cole v. Patricia A. Meyer & Assocs., APC, 206 Cal. App. 4th 1095, 1105, 142 Cal. Rptr. 3d 646, 655 (2012); Price v. Operating 'Eng'rs Local Union No. 3, 195 Cal. App. 4th 962, 970, 125 Cal. Rptr. 3d 220, 225 (2011);** Carver v. Bonds, 135 Cal. App. 4th 328, 342, 37 Cal. Rptr. 3d 480, 491, 34 Media L. Rep. 1257 (2005) (de novo review of alleged defamatory statements, which were provided along with other information to assist patients in choosing doctors and thus involved matter of public concern protected under anti-SLAPP law).

SURVEY OF CALIFORNIA EMPLOYMENT PRIVACY LAW

Rachel A. Miller, Esq.
Sheppard, Mullin, Richter & Hampton LLP
501 W. Broadway, 19th Floor
San Diego, CA 92101
Telephone: (619) 338-6536
Facsimile: (619) 515-4137

(With Developments Reported Through **November 1, 2012**)

GENERAL COMMENTS

The cornerstone of California employment privacy law is the guarantee of privacy provided by article 1, section 1, of the California Constitution. This right of privacy applies to all employees, both public and private sector; no state action is required to establish a violation of privacy under the California Constitution. Thus, there are few, if any, differences between the privacy rights of California public sector and private sector employees. While the California Supreme Court has suggested, in dicta, that private sector employees may possess lesser privacy rights, it does not appear that there is any distinction between the privacy rights of public sector and private sector employees. See Hill v. Nat'l Collegiate Ass'n, 7 Cal. 4th 1, 26 Cal. Rptr. 2d 834, 865 P.2d 633 (Cal. 1994). In addition, the California Supreme Court has also stated that public and private employees generally possess similar, if not equal, rights of privacy. Long Beach Employees Ass'n v. City of Long Beach, 41 Cal. 3d 937, 227 Cal. Rptr. 90, 719 P.2d 660 (Cal. 1986).

Although invasion of privacy claims based on the California Constitution are the most frequently seen invasion of privacy claims in California employment law, California courts have also recognized common-law invasion of privacy claims such as intrusion into private affairs, wrongful termination in violation of the public policy prohibiting invasion of privacy, and breach of employment contract (where an employer terminates an employee without good cause for exercising his or her rights to privacy).

SIGNIFICANT DEVELOPMENTS SINCE THE 2012 *SURVEY*

On September 24, 2012, Governor Jerry Brown signed AB 1844 into law, which goes into effect on January 1, 2013. AB 1844 prohibits employers from asking employees or applicants for access to their social media accounts (i.e., user names, passwords, or any other information related to social media accounts) or requiring employees to access such accounts for the employer. See IV.A.3, infra.

I. GENERAL LAW OF PRIVACY

A. Legal Basis of Privacy Claims

1. ***Constitutional Law***. The California Constitution, article 1, section 1, guarantees a right to privacy: "All people are by nature free and independent and have inalienable rights. Among these are enjoying and defending life and liberty, acquiring, possessing, and protecting property, and pursuing and obtaining safety, happiness, and privacy."

The privacy guarantee of the California Constitution is broader than the implied federal constitutional right to privacy. Am. Acad. of Pediatrics v. Lungren, 16 Cal. 4th 307, 326, 66 Cal. Rptr. 2d 210, 221-22, 940 P.2d 797 (Cal. 1997). Indeed, the California constitutional right to privacy applies to both private and public sector employees. Hill v. Nat'l Collegiate Ass'n, 7 Cal. 4th 1, 15-20, 26 Cal. Rptr. 2d 834, 842-45, 865 P.2d 633, 641-44 (Cal. 1994). Thus, unlike federal law, there is no "state action" requirement under California law. See White v. Davis, 13 Cal. 3d 757, 775, 120 Cal. Rptr. 94, 106, 533 P.2d 222, 234 (Cal. 1975); Porten v. Univ. of San Francisco, 64 Cal. App. 3d 825, 829,134 Cal. Rptr. 839, 842 (Cal. Ct. App. 1976); Wilkinson v. Times Mirror Corp., 215 Cal. App. 3d 1034,1040-45, 264 Cal. Rptr. 194, 198-200 (Cal. Ct. App. 1989).

However, it is unclear whether California's privacy guarantee applies identically to public and private employees. The California Supreme Court has issued conflicting guidance on this issue. In Long Beach Employees Ass'n v. City of Long Beach, 41 Cal. 3d 937, 227 Cal. Rptr. 90, 719 P.2d 660 (Cal. 1986), the California Supreme Court stated that public employees have been generally held to possess similar, if not equal, rights of privacy: The mere status of being employed by the government should not compel a citizen to forfeit his or her fundamental right of privacy. However, the California Supreme Court has also suggested that a different and more lenient standard may apply to California's private employers. Hill v. Nat'l Collegiate Ass'n, 7 Cal. 4th 1, 26 Cal. Rptr. 2d 834; 865 P.2d 633 (Cal. 1994).

2. ***Statutory Law***. There are numerous statutory protections of the privacy rights of employees found throughout California law, including but not limited to: California Code of Civil Procedure section 1985.6 (personnel files may only be produced pursuant to subpoena with notice to employee or authorization from employee); California Labor Code section 432.7 (limiting discovery of arrest information upon application); California Civil Code sections 1785.1-1786.56 (prescribing rules for use of credit and background checks); California Labor Code section 1051 (governing fingerprint testing); California Labor Code section 432.2 (prohibiting submission to polygraphs or similar examinations as a condition of employment); California Penal Code section 637.3 (limiting use of voice stress analysis testing); California Labor Code section 2930 (setting conditions for use of a shopping investigator's report); California Penal Code sections 630-637.5 (prohibiting wiretapping and eavesdropping); and California Labor Code section 435 (prohibiting employer from videotaping or audio taping employees in restrooms, locker rooms, or changing rooms).

Many of these statutory sections will be discussed in more detail, infra.

3. ***Common Law***. The California courts have recognized several types of common law invasion of privacy claims in the employment context. These claims include wrongful termination in violation of the public policy prohibiting privacy intrusions, breach of employment contract/implied covenant, and intrusion into private affairs. These causes of action will be discussed in more detail in 1.B, infra.

B. Causes of Action

1. ***Misappropriation/Right of Publicity***. There do not appear to be any reported California cases in which an employee has successfully brought a claim against his or her employer for common law misappropriation of name, picture or identity. See, e.g., Slivinsky v. Watkins-Johnson Co., 221 Cal. App. 3d 799, 270 Cal. Rptr. 585 (Cal. Ct. App. 1990) (dismissing former employee's claim for misappropriation of name on summary judgment because employee failed to show how employer's truthful and laudatory statement regarding plaintiff resulted in any injury to her). Despite employees' lack of success in bringing claims for misappropriation, this common law invasion of privacy claim is generally recognized by California courts.

Elements. The elements of appropriation of name or likeness are: (i) the defendant used plaintiff's name, likeness, or identity without plaintiff's permission; (ii) the defendant gained a commercial benefit or some other advantage by using plaintiff's name, likeness, or identity; (iii) the plaintiff was harmed; (iv) the defendant's conduct was a substantial factor in causing the plaintiff's harm and (v) that the privacy interests of plaintiff outweigh the public interest served by defendant's use of plaintiff's name, likeness, or identity. See Cal. Civil Jury Instructions No. 1803 (2007). In addition to the common law cause of action for misappropriation of name, picture or identity, there is a statutory claim for "commercial appropriation of a right of publicity" provided by California Civil Code section 3344. See, e.g., Miller v. Collectors Universe, Inc., 159 Cal. App. 4th 988, 72 Cal. Rptr. 3d 194 (Cal. Ct. App. 2008) (former employee may recover statutory damages where business used his name without consent on certificates of authenticity).

Defenses and Privileges. No cause of action for common law misappropriation will lie for the publication of matters in the public interest. A matter in the public interest is not restricted to current events but may extend to the reproduction of past events. Montana v. San Jose Mercury News, Inc., 34 Cal. App. 4th 790, 40 Cal. Rptr. 2d 639, 640 (Cal. Ct. App. 1995). Plaintiff's consent to the appropriation is a complete bar to the misappropriation claim. However, consent is not an affirmative defense to the common law misappropriation/invasion of privacy claim. Instead, lack of consent is an element of the claim that the plaintiff must plead and prove. The absolute and qualified privileges that apply to libel/defamation claims in California also apply to claims for misappropriation of name, picture, or identity. See II.A, California Employment Libel Outline.

2. ***False Light***. There do not appear to be any reported California cases in which an employee has successfully brought a claim against his or her employer for common law false light invasion of privacy. Couch v. San Juan Unified Sch. Dist., 33 Cal. App. 4th 1491, 39 Cal. Rptr. 2d 848 (Cal. Ct. App. 1995) (upholding summary judgment for employer on employee's claim for a "false light" invasion of privacy because the false light claim was identical to plaintiff's defamation claim and, therefore, was "superfluous"). However, this common law invasion of privacy claim is generally recognized by California courts.

Elements. The elements of false light invasion of privacy are: (i) the defendant publicized information or material that showed the plaintiff in a false light; (ii) the false light created by the publication would be highly offensive to a reasonable person in the plaintiff's position; (iii) there is clear and convincing evidence that the defendant knew the publication would create a false impression about the plaintiff or acted with reckless disregard for the truth OR the defendant was negligent in determining the truth of the information or whether a false impression would be created by its publication; (iv) the plaintiff was harmed OR the plaintiff sustained harm to his/her property, business, profession, or occupation including money spent as a result of the statement; and (v) the defendant's conduct was a substantial factor in causing the plaintiff's harm. See Cal. Civil Jury Instructions No. 1802 (2007).

Defenses and Privileges. Consent is a complete defense to false light invasion of privacy. The absolute and qualified privileges that apply to libel/defamation claims in California also apply to claims for false light invasion of privacy. See II.A, California Employment Libel Outline.

3. ***Publication of Private Facts***. There do not appear to be any reported California cases in which an employee has successfully brought a claim against his or her employer for common law publication of private facts. See e.g. Morrow v. Los Angeles Unified School Dist., 149 Cal.App.4th 1424 (Cal.App. 2 Dist. 2007) (principal could not prevail in invasion of privacy claim based on publication of private facts against school district because statements were of legitimate public concern). However, this common law invasion of privacy claim is recognized by California courts.

Elements. The elements of public disclosure of private facts are: (i) the defendant publicized private information concerning the plaintiff; (ii) a reasonable person in the plaintiff's position would consider the publicity highly offensive; (iii) the defendant knew, or acted with reckless disregard of the fact, that a reasonable person in the plaintiff's position would consider the publicity highly offensive; (iv) the private information was not of legitimate public concern or did not have a substantial connection to a matter of legitimate public concern; (v) the plaintiff was harmed; and (vi) the defendant's conduct was a substantial factor in causing the plaintiff's harm. See Cal. Civil Jury Instructions No. 1801 (2007); Moreno v. Hanford Sentinel, Inc., 172 Cal.App.4th 1125, 91 Cal.Rptr.3d 858 (Cal.App. 5 Dist. 2009).

Defenses and Privileges. Consent is a complete defense to a claim for public disclosure of private facts. The absolute and qualified privileges that apply to libel/defamation claims in California also apply to claims for publication of private facts. See II.A, California Employment Libel Outline.

4. ***Intrusion***. After invasion of privacy claims based on the California Constitution, the common law claim of intrusion is the next most commonly raised privacy invasion claim by California employees. However, very few of these cases are reported. The tort of intrusion frequently arises in the context of employee searches, drug testing, workplace surveillance, and monitoring of e-mail, voice mail, and Internet use.

Elements. The elements of intrusion into private affairs are: (i) the plaintiff had a reasonable expectation of privacy in the place, conversation, or other circumstances at issue; (ii) the defendant intentionally intruded in the place, conversation, or other circumstances at issue; (iii) the defendant's intrusion would be highly offensive to a reasonable person; (iv) the plaintiff was harmed; and (v) the defendant's conduct was a substantial factor in causing the plaintiff's harm. See Cal. Civil Jury Instructions No. 1800 (2007); see also Miller v. Nat'l Broad. Corp., 187 Cal. App. 3d 1463, 1482-83, 232 Cal. Rptr. 668, 678-79 (Cal. Ct. App. 1986); Restatement (Second) of Torts § 652B (1977); see Hernandez v. Hillsides, Inc. and Hillsides Children Center, Inc., 47 Cal.4th 272, 211 P.3d 1063, 97 Cal.Rptr.3d 274 (August 3, 2009).

Defenses and Privileges. Consent is a complete defense to a claim for intrusion into private affairs. The absolute and qualified privileges that apply to libel/defamation claims in California also apply to claims for intrusion. See II.A, California Employment Libel Outline.

5. ***Invasion of Privacy Based on the California Constitution***. Invasion of privacy based on article 1, section 1, of the California Constitution is probably the most frequently raised privacy invasion claim by California employees. In the employment context, most invasion of privacy claims based on the California Constitution turn on whether the employer's interest in conducting the allegedly intrusive activity outweighs the employee's privacy interest at stake.

Elements. In Hill v. Nat'l Collegiate Ass'n, 7 Cal. 4th 1, 26 Cal. Rptr. 2d 834, 865 P.2d 633 (Cal. 1994), the California Supreme Court set forth the elements of a California constitutional invasion of privacy claim: (i) a legally protected privacy interest; (ii) a reasonable expectation of privacy; and (iii) a serious invasion of privacy interest. Id. at 39-40, 26 Cal. Rptr. 2d at 859, 865 P.2d at 657. A legally recognized privacy interest generally falls into one of two classes: (1) informational privacy, which is the interest in precluding the dissemination or misuse of sensitive and confidential information; or (2) autonomy privacy, which is the interest in making intimate personal decisions or conducting personal activities without observation, intrusion, or interference. Pettus v. Cole, 49 Cal. App. 4th 402, 440, 57 Cal. Rptr. 2d 46, 70-71 (Cal. Ct. App. 1996). A reasonable expectation of privacy is an objective standard founded on widely accepted community norms. The customs, practices, and settings surrounding particular activities may create or inhibit a reasonable expectation of privacy. See Dietemann v. Time, Inc., 449 F.2d 245 (9th Cir. 1971) (applying California law). A serious invasion of privacy is one that constitutes an egregious breach of the social norms underlying the privacy right. Hill v. Nat'l Collegiate Ass'n, 7 Cal. 4th 1, 37, 26 Cal. Rptr. 2d 834, 857, 865 P.2d 633, 655 (Cal. 1994). When the intrusion is unintended or not highly offensive to a reasonable person, it is not actionable. Miller v. Nat'l Broad. Corp., 187 Cal. App. 3d 1463, 1482-83, 232 Cal. Rptr. 668, 678-79 (Cal. Ct. App. 1986).

Defenses and Privileges. There is no violation of the California constitutional right of privacy if the defendant can show the invasion was justified because it substantively furthered one or more legitimate and important countervailing interests. Hill v. Nat'l Collegiate Ass'n, 7 Cal. 4th 1, 40, 26 Cal. Rptr. 2d 834, 859, 865 P.2d 633, 657 (Cal. 1994). A countervailing interest is one of equal value, importance, or significance to the right of privacy. This defense requires a balancing of the competing interests to determine whether the non-privacy interest is as important as the privacy interest of the plaintiff. Even if the defendant is successful in establishing that the privacy invasion was justified by an important countervailing interest, the plaintiff may still prevail by showing there were feasible and effective alternatives to defendant's conduct that would have had a lesser impact on plaintiff's privacy interest. Hill v. Nat'l Collegiate Ass'n, 7 Cal. 4th 1, 40, 26 Cal. Rptr. 2d 834, 859, 865 P.2d 633, 657 (Cal. 1994).

Some courts view consent as a complete defense to a constitutional claim for invasion of privacy in California. Feminist Women's Health Ctr. v. Superior Court, 52 Cal. App. 4th 1234, 1249, 61 Cal. Rptr. 2d 187, 196 (Cal. Ct. App. 1997). Other courts view consent as a factor in a balancing analysis rather than a complete defense. Kraslawsky v. Upper Deck Co., 56 Cal. App. 4th 179, 193, 65 Cal. Rptr. 2d 297, 306 (Cal. Ct. App. 1997); see also TBG Ins. Servs. Corp. v. Superior Court, 96 Cal. App. 4th 443, 117 Cal. Rptr. 2d 155 (Cal. Ct. App. 2002) (discussing cases that view consent as a complete defense and those that view consent as one of several factors). Consent may be actual or apparent. Cal. Civil Jury Instructions No. 1302 (2007).

6. ***Breach of Contract/Covenant***. An employee who is terminated for refusing to submit to any type of search or drug test may contend that such action was both an invasion of privacy and a termination without good cause. Luck v. S. Pac. Transp. Co., 218 Cal. App. 3d 1, 267 Cal. Rptr. 618 (Cal. Ct. App. 1990), cert. denied, 498 U.S. 931 (1990).

Elements. The elements for breach of employment contract are: (i) the plaintiff and the defendant entered into an employment relationship; (ii) the defendant promised, by words or conduct, to discharge/demote the plaintiff only for good cause; (iii) the plaintiff substantially performed his/her job duties unless the plaintiff's performance was excused or prevents; (iv) the defendant discharged/demoted the plaintiff without good cause; and (v) the plaintiff was harmed by the discharge/demotion. See Cal. Civil Jury Instructions No. 2401 (2007).

Defenses and Privileges. The common law defenses of failure of consideration, waiver of breach, impossibility, illegality, impracticability and frustration have not been successfully asserted by an employer in any recently reported breach of employment contract case in California. However, an employer can successfully defend against a breach of contract/breach of implied covenant claim by showing that the plaintiff was an at-will employee and/or that there was good cause for the termination. Neither of these are affirmative defenses; therefore, the employer does not bear the burden of proof.

7. ***Termination in Violation of Public Policy***. California appellate courts appear to be split on whether an employee can use a privacy violation as the basis for bringing a claim for wrongful termination in violation of public policy, although the trend is to recognize such claims. In Luck v. S. Pac. Transp. Co., 218 Cal. App. 3d 1, 267 Cal. Rptr. 618 (Cal. Ct. App. 1990), the court held that an employee terminated for refusal to submit to a random drug test was denied the right to bring a claim for wrongful termination in violation of public policy based on an alleged privacy violation. The court reasoned that the right to privacy is a private right, not a public one; therefore, the violation of this right could not constitute a termination in violation of a public policy.

In contrast, in Semore v. Pool, 217 Cal. App. 3d 1087, 266 Cal. Rptr. 280 (Cal. Ct. App. 1990), the court held that an employee who was terminated for refusing to submit to a drug test could state a claim for termination in violation of public policy. The court found that a public policy was implicated because "a [p]laintiff's right not to participate in a drug test is a right he share[s] with all other employees. Semore, Id. at 1097, 266 Cal. Rptr. at 285. Similarly, in Pettus v. Cole, 49 Cal. App. 4th 402, 57 Cal. Rptr. 2d 46 (Cal. Ct. App. 1996), the court held that an employee could state a claim for wrongful termination in violation of public policy based on a finding that the employer had invaded the plaintiff's "informational and autonomy privacy rights when it procured personal medical and psychiatric information without the employee's knowledge or consent.

However, Ross v. RagingWire Telecomms., Inc., 42 Cal. 4th 920, 70 Cal. Rptr. 3d 382, 174 P.3d 200 (Cal. 2008), may have resolved the split among California appellate courts on whether an employee can use a privacy violation as the basis for bringing a claim for wrongful termination in violation of public policy. In Ross, an employee fired for medical marijuana use brought a claim for termination in violation of public policy based on the common law and the privacy clause of the California constitution, which encompasses the right "to determine whether or not to submit to lawful medical treatment." The Supreme Court of California held that an employer's refusal to accommodate an employee's marijuana use does not implicate the employee's right to refuse medical treatment. While the court found that Ross failed to state a cause of action for wrongful termination in violation of public policy, it suggests that an employee can use a privacy violation as a basis for a termination in violation of public policy claim.

Elements. The elements for proving wrongful discharge/demotion in violation of public policy are: (i) the plaintiff was employed by the defendant; (ii) the defendant discharged/demoted the plaintiff; (iii) the alleged violation of public policy (e.g., the plaintiff's refusal to engage in price fixing) was a motivating reason for the plaintiff's discharge/ demotion; and (iv) the discharge/demotion caused the plaintiff's harm. See Cal. Civil Jury Instructions No. 2430 (2007).

Defenses. The employer may prevail against a wrongful termination in violation of public policy claim if it can show that the termination was for a reason that was not violative of public policy. However, this is not an affirmative defense; therefore, plaintiff bears the burden of proof to establish that the termination was violative of public policy.

C. Other Privacy-Related Actions

1. ***Intentional Infliction of Emotional Distress.*** California recognizes the right to recover for injury resulting from the intentional infliction of emotional distress. This is an independent tort for which damages may be recovered without proof of a conventional tort, or physical impact or injury (mental suffering is sufficient). State Rubbish Collectors Ass'n v. Siliznoff, 38 Cal. 2d 330, 337-38, 240 P.2d 282, 285-86 (Cal. 1952). Thus, any common law claim for invasion of privacy or constitutional claim for invasion of privacy could also support a claim for intentional infliction of emotional distress if the plaintiff can show the invasion: (1) was extreme and outrageous; (2) made with the intent to cause, or a reckless disregard of the probability of causing, emotional distress; and (3) caused the plaintiff to suffer severe emotional distress. Cervantes v. J.C. Penney Co., 24 Cal. 3d 579, 593, 156 Cal. Rptr. 198, 206, 595 P.2d 975, 983 (Cal. 1979).

2. ***Interference With Prospective Economic Advantage.*** California recognizes a claim for intentional interference with prospective economic advantage. Shamblin v. Berge, 166 Cal. App. 3d 118, 122-123, 212 Cal. Rptr. 313, 315-16 (Cal. Court. App. 1985). California also recognizes the tort of negligent interference with prospective economic advantage. J'Aire Corp. v. Gregory, 24 Cal. 3d 799, 803, 157 Cal. Rptr. 407, 410, 598 P.2d 60, 62 (Cal. 1979).

To assert a claim for interference with prospective economic advantage, plaintiff must plead and prove: (1) an economic relationship evincing the probability of future economic benefits accruing to the plaintiff; (2) defendant's knowledge of the existences of that relationship; (3) defendant's intentional and wrongful commission of acts designed to disrupt the relationship; (4) actual disruption of the relationship; and (5) damages proximately caused by defendant's wrongful conduct. Delta Penna v. Toyota Motor Sales, U.S.A., Inc., 11 Cal. 4th 376, 45 Cal. Rptr. 2d 436, 447, 902 P.2d 740, 751 (Cal. 1995); see also Cal. Civil Jury Instructions No. 2202-03 (2007).

In Korea Supply Company v. Lockheed Martin Corp., 29 Cal. 4th 1134, 131 Cal. Rptr. 2d 29, 63 P.3d 937 (Cal. 2003), the court held that: (1) this tort does not require a specific intent to interfere or disrupt, but does require either the intent to interfere or disrupt or acting with the knowledge that interference or disruption was certain or substantially certain to result; and (2) the wrongful conduct requirement relates to conduct that is independently actionable, that is, it is proscribed by some constitutional, statutory, regulatory, common law, or some other determinable legal standard.

There do not appear to be any reported California cases in which interference with prospective economic advantage was alleged that involved invasion of privacy claims in the employment context.

3. ***Prima Facie Tort.*** The prima facie tort theory has not been recognized by the California Supreme Court, and it was rejected in the context of an illegal public employee strike. City and County of San Francisco v. United Ass'n of Journeymen & Apprentices of the Plumbing & Pipefitting Indus. of United States & Canada, Local 38, 42 Cal. 3d 810, 818-19, 230 Cal. Rptr. 856, 861-62, 726 P.2d 538, 543-44 (Cal. 1986).

4. ***Negligent Hiring.*** California recognizes the tort of negligent hiring if an employer has or should have had notice of an antecedent problem. However, employers are not required to investigate private facts prior to hiring an employee. See Roman Catholic Bishop of San Diego v. Superior Court, 42 Cal. App. 4th 1556, 50 Cal. Rptr. 2d 399 (Cal. Ct. App. 1996) (church leaders could not be held accountable for hiring abusive priests if they had no reason to believe there was any risk of trouble in the first place; there was no compelling state interest to require the employer to investigate the sexual practices of its employees and the employer who queries employees on sexual behavior is subject to claims for invasion of privacy and sexual harassment by that employee); Flores v. Autozone West, Inc., 161 Cal. App. 4th 373, 74 Cal. Rptr. 3d 178 (Cal . Ct. App. 2008) (an employer does not have a legal duty to investigate the juvenile record of a prospective employee, or to conduct extensive background checks or screening tests on each employee who is expected to have contact with the public prior to hiring).

II. EMPLOYER TESTING OF EMPLOYEES

A. Psychological or Personality Testing

1. ***Common Law and Statutes***. California has no express statutory provision prohibiting psychological or personality testing. However, California's anti-discrimination statute limits the use of such tests in certain situations, and the courts have held that such tests may be invasive of the state constitutional right of privacy.

The California Fair Employment and Housing Act (Cal. Gov't Code 12940 et seq.) ("FEHA") restricts the use of pre-employment tests or examinations that are intended to ascertain whether a job applicant has a medical disability and/or the nature of the disability. Many psychological tests may fall within the FEHA's restrictions because they are intended to assess whether an applicant has a mental disability. Indeed, any psychological or personality test is governed by the FEHA's pre-employment test restrictions if it is: (1) designed to provide evidence of a mental disorder or impairment, (2) used to assess whether an applicant has a mental impairment or (3) used to assess general psychological health. 29 C.F.R. 1607. 29 C.F.R. 1607 sets forth regulations to the federal Americans With Disabilities Act. These regulations are frequently followed by California courts in interpreting the disability discrimination portions of the FEHA. See e.g. Muller v. Auto. Club of S. Cal., 61 Cal. App. 4th 431, 71 Cal. Rptr. 2d 573 (Cal. Ct. App. 1998) (overruled, in part, on other grounds in Colmenares v. Braemar Country Club, Inc., 29 Cal. 4th 1019, 130 Cal. Rptr. 2d 662 (2003)).

On the other hand, if the test is solely designed to elicit information about personality traits (i.e., leadership abilities, sense of responsibility, industriousness, etc.), it will not constitute a medical exam and, therefore, will not be subject to the limitations of the FEHA. Such tests, however, may still give rise to invasion of privacy lawsuits. See II.C.1, infra.

Employers can be held liable if, as part of the job application process, they make employment decisions based on improperly validated tests that are irrelevant to the skills needed for successful job performance. Accordingly, employers should approach psychological testing with caution.

Case Law. Psychological and personality testing may give rise to invasion of privacy lawsuits. The questions on these tests generally focus on personal attitudes, relationships, and life experiences. See Soroka v. Dayton Hudson Corp., 18 Cal. App. 4th 1200, 1 Cal. Rptr. 2d 77 (Cal. Ct. App. 1991), depublished for unrelated reasons. Furthermore, a California Supreme Court case suggested that any type of employment exam that did not "specifically, directly and narrowly relate to the performance of [an employee's] official duties could be inappropriate. Long Beach Employees Ass'n v. City of Long Beach, 41 Cal. 3d 937, 227 Cal. Rptr. 90, 719 P.2d 660 (Cal. 1986).

2. ***Private Employers***. See I.A.1, supra.

3. ***Public Employers.*** There do not appear to be any reported California case addressing the difference between the rights of private employers and public employers to test their employees. However, the California Supreme Court has issued conflicting guidance on whether the state constitutional right to privacy applies identically to public and private employers. See I.A.I., supra. In addition, under federal law, it is arguable that public employers are more restricted in performing any type of employee test due to the United States Constitution's fourth amendment prohibition against unreasonable searches and seizures. Skinner v. Ry. Labor Executives' Ass'n, 489 U.S. 602 (U.S. 1989).

B. Drug Testing

1. ***Common Law and Statutes***. Although California has no statutory provisions expressly governing drug testing, the FEHA considers drug tests to be a type of medical test and, therefore, pre-employment drug tests are subject to the same limitations as any pre-employment medical examination. See II.C.1, infra. Thus, the process of deciding whether such policies and procedures pass legal muster has been left to the courts to determine on a case-by-case basis.

Generally, drug testing of applicants has been upheld; however drug testing of current employees, unless it involves a reasonable suspicion of drug use or a safety sensitive position, has been struck down.

Drug Testing of Applicants. The California Supreme Court has upheld across-the-board drug and alcohol screening for job applicants under both the United States and California Constitutions. Loder v. City of Glendale, 14 Cal. 4th 846, 59 Cal. Rptr. 2d 696, 927 P.2d 1200 (Cal. 1997), cert. denied, 118 S. Ct. 44 (1997). The court held that when a drug screening program is administered in a reasonable fashion as part of the lawful pre-employment medical examination that is required of each job applicant, drug testing of all job applicants is constitutionally permissible under the U.S. Constitution's Fourth Amendment and the California Constitution's privacy clause. In reaching its conclusion, the court weighed the applicant's privacy interests against the legitimacy and strength of the employer's interest in conducting the tests. The court concluded that job applicants have a diminished expectation of privacy, because the application process often requires the applicant to undergo a pre-employment medical examination, which may even require urinalysis. The court also concluded that an employer has a legitimate interest in screening job applicants, because drug use creates many workplace problems and the employer has no ongoing opportunity to observe the applicant for signs of drug use. Finally, the court noted that the intrusion into privacy was mitigated by the fact that the specific testing procedure was not overly intrusive as it did not involve visual observation of urination but only aural monitoring.

An employer lawfully may refuse to employ a person who fails a drug test that is a precondition of employment, even if the person has begun to work for the employer prior to taking the drug test. Ross v. Ragingwire Telecommunications, Inc., 33 Cal. Rptr. 3d 803 (Cal. App. 3d Dist. 2005).

However, a court has held that direct observation of an employee's urination violates that employee's privacy rights under the California Constitution. Hansen v. Cal. Dept of Corr., 920 F. Supp. 1480 (N.D. Cal. 1996) (applying California law). Similarly, in Wilkinson v. Times Mirror Corp., 215 Cal. App. 3d 1034, 264 Cal. Rptr. 194 (Cal. Ct. App. 1989), a California appellate court held that drug testing of applicants was reasonable under the circumstances because the employer had minimized the intrusiveness of the urinalysis test by: (1) advance notice, (2) use of a medical facility and personnel to administer the test, (3) no direct observation of applicant giving the sample, (4) guarantee of confidentiality, and (5) follow-up report to applicant, with opportunity to question and challenge the test results if believed to be erroneous.

Drug Testing of Current Employees. In general, California courts have struck down drug testing of current employees unless the employee fills a safety sensitive position or the employer has a reasonable, particularized suspicion of drug use.

In Loder v. City of Glendale, 14 Cal. 4th 846, 59 Cal. Rptr. 2d 696, 927 P.2d 1200 (Cal. 1997), cert. denied, 118 S. Ct. 44 (1997), the California Supreme Court held that drug testing of current employees was a violation of the U.S. Constitution's Fourth Amendment. The court found that the city's interest in maintaining a drug-free work force was insufficient to justify a policy requiring drug testing for current employees. The court reasoned that the need to test a current employee is not as great as the need to test an applicant because the employer has the opportunity to observe the employee, is knowledgeable about his/her work history and can thus determine whether there is any reason to suspect abuse of drugs or alcohol. See also Semore v. Pool, 217 Cal. App. 3d 1087, 266 Cal. Rptr. 280 (Cal. Ct. App. 1990) (current employee's right of privacy invaded by submission to a pupilary reaction drug test). See also Luck v. S. Pac. Transp. Co., 218 Cal. App. 3d 1, 267 Cal. Rptr. 618 (Cal. Ct. App. 1990) (California Court of Appeal held that random drug testing of current employee violated the state constitutional right to privacy); Farley v. Estelle Doheny Eve Hosp., L.A.S.C. Case No. C 629354 (1987) (random involuntary drug testing of current employees violates their reasonable expectation of privacy, and the desirability of preventing drug abuse does not justify this invasion of the right to privacy in the absence of reasonable suspicion that a particular employee is under the influence of drugs while on duty).

The clear distinction California courts draw between drug testing of current employees and applicants was highlighted in Pilkington Barnes Hind v. Superior Court, 66 Cal. App. 4th 28 (Cal. Ct. App. 1998). The question in Pilkington was whether an individual who had been on the job for four days was still considered an applicant for purposes of drug testing. The plaintiff had accepted an offer of employment specifically conditioned on passage of a drug test. Due to a series of events that were out of the control of the employer, the drug testing was not completed until four days after the plaintiff began work. The drug test was positive, and the employer withdrew its offer. The court in Pilkington held that because the drug test was delayed through no fault of the employer, the employee was essentially an applicant for the purposes of determining the propriety of drug testing.

However, some California courts have held that testing of current employees is permissible in certain situations. For example, testing employees in positions that have a direct impact on public safety is more likely to be upheld than testing the entire work force. Am. Fed'n of Lab. v. Unemployment Ins. App. Bd., 23 Cal. App. 4th 51, 28 Cal. Rptr. 2d 210 (Cal. Ct. App. 1994). Employees who do not have positions that have a direct impact on public safety may still be subject to random drug testing if aspects of their position pose a safety risk to their coworkers. Smith v. Fresno Irrigation Dist., 72 Cal. App. 4th 147 (Cal. Ct. App. 1999).

In addition, if the employer has a reasonable individualized suspicion of substance abuse, testing in such circumstances is more likely to be upheld. For example, in Loder v. City of Glendale, 14 Cal. 4th 846, 59 Cal. Rptr. 2d 696, 927 P.2d 1200 (Cal. 1997); cert. denied, 118 S. Ct. 44 (1997), the California Supreme Court stated in dicta that reasonable suspicion drug testing does not violate the right to privacy provided for in article I, section 1, of the California Constitution. See also Luck v. S. Pac. Transp. Co., 218 Cal. App. 3d 1, 267 Cal. Rptr. 618 (Cal. Ct. App. 1990) (the court suggests in dicta that testing of current employees may be permissible if the employee holds a safety-sensitive position). However, even if reasonable suspicion testing is permissible under the California Constitution, employers may still be exposed to liability if reasonable suspicion for believing an individual employee to be under the influence did not in fact exist at the time the employee was asked to submit to a drug test. Kraslawsky v. Upper Deck Co., 56 Cal. App. 4th 179, 65 Cal. Rptr. 2d 297 (Cal. Ct. App. 1997).

Recovery Agreements. In 2000, a California Court of Appeal held that: (1) a recovery agreement between an employer and an employee is valid when the employee cannot substantiate claims of undue influence and unconscionability, and (2) it is not arbitrary and capricious for an employer to fire an employee based on his failure to comply with a drug treatment program. The court reasoned that it could not require an employer to await a drug-related accident before allowing the employer to fire an employee who is not complying with a drug treatment program. Robison v. City of Manteca, 78 Cal. App. 4th 452, 92 Cal. Rptr. 2d 748 (Cal. Ct. App. 2000).

Drug Testing. Due to the fact that drug testing frequently involves a medical screening, drug testing is considered a medical test under California law. See II.B, supra. Moreover, any type of medical testing could run afoul of California's constitutional right to privacy, unless there is an important business interest in conducting the test that outweighs the privacy interest of the employee. See I.B, supra. In addition, the California Supreme Court has stated in dicta that any type of employment test that does not specifically, directly and narrowly relate to the performance of [an employee's] official duties could be violative of the employee's right to privacy. Long Beach Employees Ass'n v. City of Long Beach, 41 Cal. 3d 937, 227 Cal. Rptr. 90, 719 P.2d 660 (Cal. 1986). Employers should be sure to articulate clearly their rules against drug use or possession to all employees. Wilkinson v. Times Mirror Corp., 215 Cal. App. 3d 1034, 264 Cal. Rptr. 194 (Cal. Ct. App. 1989).

2. ***Private Employers.*** The California Supreme Court has suggested in dicta that private employers may be entitled to more leeway than public employers in instituting a drug testing program. Hill v. Nat'l Collegiate Ass'n, 7 Cal. 4th 1, 26 Cal. Rptr. 2d 834, 865 P.2d 633 (Cal. 1994). Despite the Supreme Court's dicta in Hill, it appears that the trend of the California courts is to treat public and private sector employers the same when analyzing the legality of their drug testing programs. For a general discussion of the legality of drug testing in California, see II.B.1, supra.

3. ***Public Employers.*** There do not appear to be any reported California cases specifically addressing whether drug testing of public employees should be subject to different standards than testing of private employees. Indeed, California case law seems to treat drug testing of public and private sector employees consistently.

The California Supreme Court's decision in Loder v. City of Glendale, 14 Cal. 4th 846, 59 Cal. Rptr. 2d 696, 927 P.2d 1200 (Cal. 1997) sets forth the general rules regarding permissibility of drug and alcohol testing of public employees. Loder is discussed in detail in II.B.1, supra.

C. Medical Testing

1. ***Common Law and Statutes.*** Medical testing that is conducted as part of a pre-employment examination or inquiry is restricted by the portions of the FEHA prohibiting disability discrimination. California law provides that an employer may make a pre-employment, pre-offer inquiry as to a medical condition only if the information is directly related either to the position for which the individual is applying or to a determination of whether the applicant would endanger his or her health or safety or the health or safety of others. Cal. Gov. Code 12940(d); 2 Cal. Code Regs. 7287.3(b)(1).

Post-offer pre-employment medical testing is somewhat less restrictive than pre-offer testing. An employer may condition an offer of employment on successful completion of a physical to determine fitness for the job in question, provided that: (1) all entering employees in similar positions are also given the exam, (2) the applicant may submit an independent medical opinion before a final determination on disqualification is made, and (3) the results are maintained in a separate, confidential file. 2 Cal. Code Regs. 7294.0(d). However, the medical examination should not be conducted unless the employer has extended a "real" offer of employment, which means the employer has evaluated all relevant non-medical information that it reasonably could have obtained and analyzed prior to giving the offer. Leonel v. American Airlines, Inc., 400 F.3d 702, 708-709 (9th Cir. 2005) (applying California law). Extreme caution should be taken before retracting an offer of employment due to the results of a post-offer, pre-employment medical test. Basing any employment decision on a disclosed disability is likely to run afoul of the FEHA, unless the employer can establish that the absence of such a disability is a bona fide occupational qualification for the position.

California Health and Safety Code Restrictions on AIDS Testing (Health and Safety Code sections 120975 through 121015) expressly prohibit discrimination based on AIDS or testing for AIDS. Section 120980 specifically prohibits any person from disclosing the results of such a test to any third party, in a manner that identifies or provides identifying characteristics of the person to whom the test results apply, unless authorized by that person. Health and Safety Code section 120980(f) also prohibits employers from using the results of an HIV test to determine an individual's suitability for employment.

2. ***Private Employers.*** See II.C.1, supra.

3. ***Public Employers.*** There do not appear to be any reported California cases addressing any difference between the rights of private employers and public employers to perform medical tests of their employees. However, the California Supreme Court has issued conflicting guidance on whether the state constitutional right to privacy applies identically to public and private employers. See I.A.I., supra. In addition, under federal law, it is arguable that public employers are more restricted in performing any type of employee test due to the United States Constitution's fourth amendment prohibition against unreasonable searches and seizures. U.S. Const., 4th Amend; Skinner v. By. Labor Executives' Ass'n, 489 U.S. 602 (U.S. 1989).

D. Polygraph Testing

California Labor Code section 432.2 prohibits all private employers from demanding that prospective or current employees submit to polygraph tests under any circumstances. Although the federal Employee Polygraph Act of 1988 allows companies to give polygraph tests to current employees in certain circumstances involving ongoing investigations of in-house thefts, California law does not have a similar exception. The prohibition of polygraph testing for private employers contained in California Labor Code section 432.2 does not apply to public employers.

E. Fingerprinting

California Labor Code section 1051 prohibits an employer from requiring a job applicant to provide photographs or fingerprinting samples for the purpose of forwarding them to law enforcement officials. There are exceptions to this rule in certain occupations (such as day care where employers may be required to submit fingerprint samples of job applicants to local law enforcement agencies). Violation of this statute is a misdemeanor and an employer may be liable for treble damages in a civil action. Cal. Lab. Code 1054.

III. SEARCHES

The California Constitution's search and seizure clause closely mirrors the Fourth Amendment. Cal.Const. art. I, § 13 ("The right of the people to be secure in their persons, houses, papers, and effects against unreasonable seizures and searches may not be violated; and a warrant may not issue except on probable cause, supported by oath or affirmation, particularly describing the place to be searched and the persons and things to be seized."). In 1982, California passed Proposition 8, which adopted the federal constitutional standard for criminal search and seizure jurisprudence. In re Lance W., 694 P.2d 744, 752 (Cal. 1985). With respect to criminal searches and seizures, California courts essentially adopt the most recent pronouncement by the Supreme Court. Hill v. National Collegiate Athletic Ass'n, 865 P.2d 633 (Cal. 1994) ("Under the Fourth Amendment and the *parallel* search and seizure clause of the California Constitution (art. I, § 13), the reasonableness of particular searches and seizures is determined by a general balancing test 'weighing the gravity of the governmental interest or public concern served and the degree to which the [challenged government conduct] advances that concern against the intrusiveness of the interference with individual liberty.'") (citations omitted) (emphasis added).

Protections against unreasonable searches and seizures only apply to governmental action, and do not apply to private employers, except when they are acting under the direction and control of law enforcement officers. Therefore, the majority of reported cases involving search and seizures in the workplace deal with public employees and governmental action.

A. Employee's Person

There do not appear to be any reported California cases in the employment context aside from cases related to drug and alcohol testing. See II.B, supra.

The Ninth Circuit Court of Appeals, applying California law, found an applicant for employment whose pre-employment medical examination included an undisclosed blood test for HIV/AIDS could state a claim for violation of the constitutional right to privacy. Leonel v. American Airlines, Inc., 400 F.3d 702, 714 (9th Cir. 2005).

B. Employee's Work Area

There do not appear to be any reported California cases in the employment context. In United States v. Ziegler, 474 F.3d 1184 (9th Cir. 2007), the Ninth Circuit held that an employer who exercised common authority over defendant's office and workplace computer, and could consent to search of contents of hard drive of defendant's workplace computer under the Fourth Amendment.

In Schowengerdt v. United States, 944 F.2d 483 (9th Cir. 1991), the court found that a Navy employee who possessed a security clearance and worked in a secure area could not have an objectively reasonable expectation of privacy in his office or desk. Even if the search in question was outside the scope of regular security procedures, the nature of the secured environment, where supervisors had keys to all areas rendered any expectation of privacy unreasonable.

C. Employee's Property

In Delia v. City of Rialto, 621 F. 3d 1069 (9th Cir. 2010), a public employee (firefighter) began to feel ill while working to control a toxic spill and was thereafter placed off-duty for several shifts by his treating physician. The employee became the subject of an internal investigation after surveillance of the employee showed him purchasing insulation from a home improvement store while being on off-duty status due to illness. During an internal affairs interview, the employee was asked to consent to the search of his house for the rolls of insulation he allegedly purchased. The employee refused.

The city then ordered the employee to enter his home, bring the rolls of insulation out, and lay them on his front lawn or face direct sanctions, including the possible loss of his position. The employee complied and subsequently sued the city for violation of his Fourth and Fourteenth Amendment rights. The court held that the warrantless compelled search of the employee's own home, requiring him to retrieve and display the rolls of insulation in public view on his front yard, violated the employee's right under the Fourth Amendment to be free from an unreasonable search of his home by his employer.

In United States v. Gonzalez, 300 F.3d 1048 (9th Cir. 2002), a case arising from the Western District of Washington, a store detective searched an employee's backpack as the defendant was exiting a military exchange store. Because the employee had clear notice of the store's policy of searching employee's belongings, and prevention of theft was a legitimate justification of the search, there was no evidence that the search went beyond its justification, and the search was therefore reasonable.

IV. MONITORING OF EMPLOYEES

A. Telephone and Electronic Communications

The California Invasion of Privacy Act prohibits a variety of intrusions on an individual's privacy. Cal. Penal Code 630-638. Section 631 prohibits intentional wiretapping, including: (1) making any unauthorized connection with a telephone or telegraph; (2) attempting, without the consent of all parties to the communication, to run the "contents or meaning of any ... communication that is in transit or passing over any wire ... or is being sent from, or received at any place within this state over such wire; (3) making use of, attempting to make use of, or communicating information obtained by such improper means; or (4) aiding, agreeing, employing, or conspiring to commit, permit or cause any such conduct. In sum, the Invasion of Privacy Act prohibits almost all incidents of eavesdropping or audio recording of a communication unless consent is obtained from all of the parties to the confidential communication.

California Penal Code section 632 prohibits intentional eavesdropping on or recording, by means of any electronic amplifying or recording device, a confidential communication without the consent of all parties to that communication. Id. Confidential communication is defined in section 632(c) as any communication carried on in circumstances as may reasonably indicate that any party to the communication desires it to be confined to the parties thereto, but excludes a communication made in a public gathering or in any legislative, judicial, executive, or administrative proceeding open to the public, or in any other circumstance in which the parties to the communication may reasonably expect that the communication may be overheard or recorded. The California Supreme Court resolved a disagreement among California's Courts of Appeal regarding the meaning of confidential communication under the California Invasion of Privacy Act. The Court held that a communication is deemed confidential if one party to the conversation reasonably expects that the conversation is not being overheard or recorded. Flanagan v. Flanagan, 27 Cal. 4th 766, 768, 41 P.3d 575, 576-77, 117 Cal. Rptr. 2d 574, 575 (Cal. 2002). Flanagan expressly disapproved of the line of authority providing that a conversation is confidential only if the party asserting confidentiality has an objectively reasonable expectation that the content of the conversation will not be divulged to third parties. Id.

California Penal Code section 632.7 prohibits intentionally recording, without the consent of all parties to the communication, a private cellular or cordless telephone conversation. Section 634 prohibits trespasses on any property for the purpose of committing a violation of any of the aforementioned Penal Code sections.

Notably, the California Supreme Court determined that California Penal Code sections 630, 637.2, and 632, prohibiting the secret recording of telephone communications, applied to an out of state company when it recorded telephone conversations between its employees and its customers in California. Kearney v. Salomon Smith Barney, Inc., 39 Cal. 4th 95, 128, 137 P.3d 914, 937, 45 Cal. Rptr. 3d 730, 757 (Cal. 2006).

Additionally, employees may also base their invasion of privacy tort claims on California's state constitution, which recognizes certain inalienable rights, including the right of privacy. Cal. Const. art. I, Section 1. This constitutional right has been held explicitly to create a right of action against both governmental entities and private parties. See Hill v. Nat'l Collegiate Athletic Ass'n, 7 Cal. 4th 1, 15-16, 26 Cal. Rptr. 2d 834, 842-843, 865 P.2d 633, 641 (Cal. 1994).

1. ***Wiretapping***. See Cal. Penal Code 631, discussed in IV.A, supra. Although Penal Code section 631 is aimed primarily at eavesdropping by wiretapping, it has been held to prohibit far more than illicit wiretapping. Ribas v. Clark, 38 Cal. 3d 355, 360, 212 Cal. Rptr. 143, 696 P.2d 637 (Cal. 1985). For example, eavesdropping on a confidential communication by means of an extension telephone is a violation of section 631. Ribas v. Clark, 38 Cal. 3d 355, 361-62, 212 Cal. Rptr. 143, 696 P.2d 637 (Cal. 1985).

See also Cal. Penal Code 632, discussed in IV.A, supra; Coulter v. Bank of America, 28 Cal. App. 4th 923, 33 Cal. Rptr. 2d 766 (Cal. Ct. App. 1994) (employee suing his employer for wrongful termination was ordered to pay former employer $132,000 because he secretly recorded his conversations with coworkers while preparing for litigation).

2. ***Electronic Communications***. The Invasion of Privacy Act discussed in IV.A, supra, preceded the advent of voice mail, electronic mail and the Internet and, thus, was not intended to apply to such forms of communication. However, unless employers implement policies advising employees that e-mail and voice mail are the property of the employer and may be accessed by the employer, employees may argue that they had a reasonable expectation of privacy in such forms of communication. This could give rise to claims for intrusion or violation of the California constitutional right to privacy if the employer accesses or monitors such communications.

Where, however, an employee signs an employer's electronic and telephone equipment policy statement consenting to monitoring of company-owned computers, the employee has no reasonable expectation of privacy for data stored on a company-owned computer even though the computer is located in the employee's home. TBG Ins. Servs. Corp. v. Superior Court, 96 Cal. App. 4th 443, 117 Cal. Rptr. 2d 155 (Cal. Ct. App. 2002).

Moreover, in Holmes v. Petrovich Development Company, LLC, 191 Cal. App. 4th 1047, 119 Cal. Rptr. 3d 878 (Cal. Ct. App. 2011) the court concluded that e-mails sent by an employee to her attorney regarding possible legal action against her employer did not fall within the attorney-client privilege as a "confidential communication" because the employee used an employer-owned computer to send the emails and (1) she had been told of the employer's policy that its computers were to be used only for company business and that employees were prohibited from using them to send or receive personal e-mail, (2) she had been warned that the employer would monitor its computers for compliance with this policy and might inspect files and messages "at any time," and (3) she had been explicitly advised that employees using company computers to maintain personal information or messages have "no right of privacy with respect to that information or message." Sending emails to her attorney in such a manner was, according to the court, "akin to consulting her attorney in one of the employer's conference rooms, in a loud voice, with the door open, yet expecting the conversation overheard by the employer would be privileged." Id. This case reiterates the importance of having an electronic communications policy that is shared with and, preferably, acknowledged in writing by, employees.

3. ***Other Electronic Monitoring.*** In certain circumstances, public employees may have a reasonable expectation of privacy in the content of text messages, and an employer's review of those messages may violate California's constitutional right to privacy where the employer does not have a clear policy stating otherwise. See, e.g., City of Ontario v. Quon, 130 S. Ct. 2619, 177 L. Ed. 2d 216 (2010) (reversing the Ninth Circuit's holding that an informal policy of not auditing text messages created an expectation of privacy in those text messages; the Court held that the employer's review of employee text messages was reasonable under the circumstances).

On September 24, 2012, Governor Jerry Brown signed AB 1844 into law, which goes into effect on January 1, 2013. AB 1844 prohibits emplpyers from asking employees or applicants for access to their social media accounts (i.e., user names, passwords, or any other information related to social media accounts) or requiring employees to access such accounts for the employer. The law applies widely to any employee online information, including e-mail, photos, social media accounts, blogs, texts, and instant messages, and videos. While the law generally prohibits employers from requesting access to such online information, a few exceptions exist: (1) where the employer "reasonably believes" access is relevant to an investigation of misconduct in violation of the law, or (2) where the log-in and password information is needed to access an "employer-issued electronic device." The law also prohibits employers from retaliating against or taking adverse employment action against employees or applicants who refuse to divulge social media information.

B. Mail

California Penal Code section 618 provides: Every person who willfully opens or reads, or causes to be read, any sealed letter not addressed to himself, without being authorized so to do, either by the writer of such letter or by the person to whom it is addressed, and every person who, without the like authority, publishes any of the contents of such letter, knowing the same to have been unlawfully opened, is guilty of a misdemeanor.

C. Surveillance/Photographing

Videotaping has been treated as eavesdropping by California courts and a video recorder has been treated as a recording device within the meaning of the California Invasion of Privacy Act. Cal. Penal Code 630-637.9; see also People v. Gibbons, 215 Cal. App. 3d 1204, 1208, 263 Cal. Rptr. 905 (Cal. Ct. App. 1989). California's Invasion of Privacy statute contained in California Penal Code 632 does not extend to taking of timed, still photographs without accompanying sound. People v. Drennan, 84 Cal. App. 4th 1349, 1358, 101 Cal. Rptr. 3d 584, 590 (Cal. Ct. App. 2000).

Even when conversations can be overheard by coworkers, employees have a reasonable expectation of privacy that their workplace conversations will not be secretly videotaped or recorded. Sanders v. Am. Broad. Cos., 20 Cal. 4th 907, 85 Cal. Rptr. 2d 909, 978 P.2d 67, 85 (Cal. 1999). However, in Hernandez v. Hillsides, 47 Cal.4th 272, 211 P.3d 1063, 97

Cal.Rptr.3d 274 (2009), the California Supreme Court recently held that an employer's videotape surveillance of its employees was permissible because it was "narrowly tailored in place, time and scope [and] prompted by legitimate business concerns." Likewise, another California court found that videotaping employees, at least where there were no audio capabilities, in a non-private office in a county jail, was not offensive enough to provide the basis for overturning a summary judgment order against the plaintiff's intrusion claim. Sacramento County Deputy Sheriffs' Ass'n v. Sacramento County, 51 Cal. App. 4th 1468, 1487, 59 Cal. Rptr. 2d 834 (Cal. Ct. App. 1996).

California explicitly prohibits the use of two-way mirrors or other surveillance methods in publicly accessible washrooms or dressing rooms. Cal. Penal Code 653n. California also prohibits employers from video or audio recording its employees in restrooms, locker rooms or other changing rooms. Cal. Labor Code 435.

Any employer who disciplines or discharges an employee on the basis of a shopping investigator's report prepared by a licensed private investigator must provide the employee with a copy of the report prior to discharging or disciplining the employee based on information in the report. If an employee is interviewed and the results of the interview could result in the employee's termination for dishonesty, the employee must be given a copy of the report during the interview. Cal. Lab. Code 2930. (A similar requirement is imposed on public service corporations who use spotters to investigate, obtain and report information regarding the employer's employees. Cal. Pub. Util. Code 8251.) The disclosure requirements imposed by the California Labor Code do not apply if the shopper is not a licensed private investigator or if the licensed private investigator is employed exclusively by the employer provided an employer-employee relationship exists and the investigation is conducted solely for the employer. Cal. Lab. Code 2930.

V. ACTIVITIES OUTSIDE THE WORKPLACE

A. Statutory or Common Law

The constitutional right of privacy under California law protects the freedom of intimate association with others (e.g., marriage, family and sex life) and the freedom of expressive association (e.g., political, social, economic, religious and cultural groups). See Warfield v. Peninsula Golf & Country Club, 10 Cal. 4th 594, 624-626, 42 Cal. Rptr. 2d 50, 68-69 (1995); Ortiz v. Los Angeles Police Relief Ass'n., 98 Cal. App. 4th 1288, 1306, 120 Cal. Rptr. 2d 670, 681 (2002).

California also has various statutes that prohibit employers from discriminating against employees for certain types of activities conducted outside the workplace. For example, California law prohibits employers from discriminating against individuals on the basis of their political affiliations. Cal. Lab. Code 1101, 1102. California employers are also prohibited from discriminating on the basis of marital status; however, employers have the right to prohibit spouses from working in the same department or facility if the prohibition is imposed for reasons of supervision, security, or morale. Cal. Gov't. Code 12940(a)(3); 2 Cal. Code Reg. 7292.5(a). California's Fair Employment and Housing Act prohibits on the basis of an employee's sexual orientation. Cal. Gov't. Code 12940(a).

In addition, California employers may not ask applicants about arrests that did not result in a conviction, any misdemeanor conviction for which probation has been successfully completed or otherwise discharged, and any marijuana convictions more than two years old. Cal. Lab. Code 432.7, 432.8.

Most significantly, the California Labor Code authorizes the Labor Commissioner to pursue an employee's claim of wage loss resulting from the employer demoting, suspending, or discharging the employee for lawful conduct occurring during nonworking hours away from the employer's premises. Cal. Lab. Code 96(k). For example, the Labor Commissioner can now pursue a claim for lost wages on behalf of an employee who was terminated for attending a protest rally on nonworking time. Some commentators have expressed concern that this provision, taken to its extreme, could be read to prohibit employers from disciplining or terminating employees for engaging in conduct that, although lawful, is detrimental to the employer (e.g. violation of a "no moonlighting" policy). The only two published decisions involving this provision have found that the statute does not state a public policy that can be used as a predicate for wrongful termination actions. See Barbee v. Household Automotive Finance Corp., 113 Cal. App. 4th 525, 6 Cal. Rptr. 3d 406 (2003); Grinzi v. San Diego Hospice Corp., 120 Cal. App. 4th 72, 14 Cal. Rptr. 3d 893 (2004). However, employers should continue to exercise caution in taking any adverse action against an employee for lawful conduct that occurs outside work.

B. Employees' Personal Relationships

1. ***Romantic Relationships Between Employees***. In Crosier v. United Parcel Serv., 150 Cal. App. 3d 1132, 198 Cal. Rptr. 361 (Cal. Ct. App. 1983), disapproved on other grounds by Foley v. Interactive Data Corp., 47 Cal. 3d 654, 254 Cal. Rptr. 211, 765 P.2d 373 (1988), the court upheld a company policy which prohibited management personnel from dating non-management employees. The purposes of the policy were to avoid misunderstandings, complaints of favoritism, and possible claims of sexual harassment.

In contrast, in Rulon-Miller v. IBM, 162 Cal. App. 3d 241, 208 Cal. Rptr. 524 (Cal. Ct. App. 1984), disapproved on other grounds by Foley v. Interactive Data Corp., 47 Cal. 3d 654, 254 Cal. Rptr. 211, 765 P.2d 373 (Cal. 1988), the court found that the employer's termination of an employee who was engaged in a romantic relationship with a competitor was a violation of the employee's right to privacy. In holding for the plaintiff, the California Court of Appeal found that IBM had no legitimate interest in its employees' off the job activities unless those activities interfered with its employees' work. The court also sustained the jury's award of punitive damages to the plaintiff because IBM had invaded the plaintiff's right to privacy in a manner that was outrageous.

Although at first glance the rulings in Crosier and Rulon-Miller appear to be inconsistent, they are not. In Crosier, there was a well-articulated employer policy prohibiting fraternization. In contrast, in Rulon-Miller, there was no such policy at issue; the employer decided after the fact that the employee's romantic relationship was somehow detrimental to the company. Thus, non-fraternization policies may be acceptable in California if the employer: (1) provides clear and unambiguous notice to the employees of the policy, and (2) has legitimate reasons for instituting the policy.

2. ***Sexual Orientation***. See V.A., supra.

3. ***Marital Status***. See V.A., supra. In Ortiz v. Los Angeles Police Relief Ass'n, 98 Cal. App. 4th 1288, 120 Cal. Rptr. 3d 670 (Cal. Ct. App. 2002), where an employee of the Los Angeles Police Relief Association Inc. ("LAPRA") who had access to confidential information regarding current and former police officers was terminated after LAPRA learned of the employee's impending marriage to an incarcerated felon, the court held that the employee's right to marry, as guaranteed by the privacy provision of the California Constitution, was not violated because LAPRA had a legitimate interest in protecting the safety of its police officers and ensuring that Ortiz would not divulge the confidential information regarding police officers to inmates. Id. at 1314, 682. More recently, in Bautista v. County of Los Angeles, 190 Cal. App. 4th 869, 118 Cal. Rptr. 3d 714 (Cal. Ct. App. 2010), the court upheld the termination of a police officer for violation of the Department's policy prohibiting association with persons of known criminal activity, where such association was detrimental to the image of the Department. The police officer at first befriended a woman with a long history of drug addiction and prostitution, developed a personal relationship with her, and eventually married her. The police officer sued after being terminated for violating the Department's policy. The court held that the policy did not violate the police officer's First Amendment right to freedom of association because the Department had a legitimate interest in regulating the behavior of its sworn officers to minimize conflicts of interest and protect its credibility and integrity.

C. Smoking

Smoking is banned in most areas of all California workplaces. Cal. Lab. Code 6404.5. There is no reported California case in which an employee has challenged a ban on smoking during off-duty hours; however, it is likely that such a policy would be viewed as an invasion of the employee's autonomy privacy rights unless the employer could show some countervailing business reason that outweighed the privacy interest at stake.

D. Blogging

There do not appear to be any reported California cases on point. However, Cal. Lab. Code 96(k) prohibits an employer from discriminating against an employee for lawful conduct occurring during nonworking hours away from the employer's premises which arguably includes blogging on an employee's own time.

Though it does not arise in the employment context, Moreno v. Hanford Sentinel, Inc., 172 Cal.App.4th 1125, 91 Cal.Rptr.3d 858 (Cal.App. 5 Dist. 2009), certainly provides employers with guidance related to invasion of privacy claims that might stem from accessing a current or prospective employee's online postings (on MySpace.com, facebook.com, etc.) that are accessible to the public even if the author only intended that such postings be accessible by a particular audience.

VI. RECORDS

A. Personnel Records

California courts have found that employee personnel records are protected by the right of privacy. Harding Lawson Assocs. v. Superior Court, 10 Cal. App. 4th 7,12 Cal. Rptr. 2d 538 (Cal. Ct. App. 1992); Board of Trustees v. Superior Court, 119 Cal. App. 3d 516, 174 Cal. Rptr. 160 (Cal. Ct. App. 1981); El Dorado Sav. & Loan Ass'n v. Superior Court, 190 Cal. App. 3d 342, 235 Cal. Rptr. 303 (Cal. Ct. App. 1987). In addition, peace officer personnel records are confidential, including records relating to citizen complaints, even if they are not associated with disciplinary proceedings against the subject officers. Cal. Penal Code. 832.5, 832.7, Cal. Evid. Code 1040. See Berkeley Police Ass'n v. City of Berkeley, 84 Cal. Rptr. 3d 130, 167 Cal. App.4th 385 (2008).

California Code of Civil Procedure section 1985.6 sets forth procedures to be followed when personnel files are sought in litigation. Pursuant to section 1985.6, a party seeking production of employment records via a subpoena must include either: (1) proof of service that the employee whose records are being sought has been notified of the subpoena; or (2) an express, written authorization from the employee for the production of the records.

California employers are required to permit employees to inspect their personnel files at reasonable times and intervals. Cal. Lab. Code 1198.5. "Personnel file" is defined very broadly to include virtually any document regarding the employee, whether found in the employee's "official" personnel file or not.

Contact Information. Employees have a reasonable expectation that their contact information provided to their employer as a condition of employment will not be divulged externally except to required government agencies such as the IRS. Belaire-West Landscape, Inc. v. Superior Court, 149 Cal. App. 4th 554, 561 (Cal. App. 2 Dist. 2007). In a putative class action against an employer alleging wage and hour violations, a California Court of Appeal considered whether the employer's disclosure to the class action plaintiffs of the names, last known addresses and last known telephone numbers of all of its current and former employees violated the employees' privacy rights. The court noted that the contact information of current and former employees deserves some privacy protection. However, the court determined that a pre-certification opt-out notice to the current and former employees, requiring them to object in writing in order to prevent contact information about them from being disclosed, adequately protected their privacy rights. The court found that it was likely employees would want information revealed to class action plaintiffs, the invasion of privacy was not serious, the identity of class members was discoverable, and fundamental public policy of payment of wages was at stake. Belaire-West Landscape, Inc. v. Superior Court, 149 Cal. App. 4th 554 (Cal. App. 2 Dist. 2007), applying Pioneer Electonics (USA) Inc. v. Superior Court, 40 Cal. 4th 360 (Cal. 2007) (concluding that an opt-out notice to customers of disclosure of their personal information in discovery unless they affirmatively asserted their right to privacy was sufficient to protect their privacy rights in consumer class action lawsuit). The same procedural requirements of notice and an opportunity to object may be extended to non-union employees whose contact information is requested by the union as part of its representation duties. See County of Los Angeles v. Los Angeles County Employee Relations Commission, 192 Cal. App. 1409, 122 Cal. Rptr. 3d 464 (Cal. Ct. App. 2011), review granted July 11, 2011.

Salary Information. Public employees do not have a reasonable expectation of privacy in the amount of their salaries. In August 2007, the California Supreme Court determined that disclosure of the gross salaries of all city employees who earned at least $100,000 to a newspaper that sought the information did not violate the state constitutional right to privacy, despite potential commercial exploitation of list of high earning city employees. Disclosure of the information contributed to the public's understanding and oversight of governmental operations by allowing interested parties to monitor expenditure of public funds. International Federation of Professional and Technical Engineers, Local 21, AFL-CIO v. Superior Court, 42 Cal 4th 319 (Cal. 2007). Several recent cases have expanded the disclosure of salary information to the disclosure of pension benefits received by public employees. See Sacramento County Employees' Retirement System v. Superior Court, 195 Cal. App. 4th 440, 125 Cal. Rptr. 655 (Cal. Ct. App. May 11, 2011) (ordering the disclosure of the names and pension benefit amounts of retirees); San Diego County Employees Retirement Association v. Superior Court, 196 Cal. App. 4th 1228, 127 Cal. Rptr. 3d 479 (Cal. Ct. App. June 28, 2011) (holding that the disclosure of public employees' pension payments, the amounts, and the calculation methods was not a violation of the public employees' privacy rights); Sonoma County Employees' Retirement Association v. Superior Court, 198 Cal. App. 4th 986 (Cal. Ct. App. Aug. 26, 2011) (permitting the disclosure of the names of all persons receiving county pension benefits and the gross amount of each recipient's benefit because the public had a substantial interest in knowing the names and pension amounts to prevent unfair practices relating to pensions).

Disclosure Of Information In The Public's Interest. In Marken v. Santa Monica-Malibu Unified School District, 136 Cal. Rptr. 3d 395 (Cal. Ct. App. 2012), the court upheld the release of information contained in an public school teacher's personnel file pertaining to a sexual harassment complaint against the teacher and the School District's subsequent investigation and reprimand of the teacher. A request for the information had been lodged under the California Public Records Act, Government Code § 6250 et seq., by a parent at the school where the teacher taught. When the School District notified the teacher it intended to comply with the request for information, the teacher sought an injunction and argued that the documents were protected by his federal and state constitutional privacy rights. The court disagreed. Although the court recognized that the teacher had a legally protected privacy interest in his personnel file, the court found these privacy interests were outweighed by the public's interest in disclosure, noting, the "public has a significant interest in the competence and misconduct of public school teachers teaching their children, especially allegations of misconduct that have a negative impact on their children. The public also has a significant interest in knowing how a school district responds to allegations of misconduct or improper behavior towards students by teachers." Id.

B. Medical Records

Pursuant to the Confidentiality of Medical Information Act ("CMIA") (Cal. Civ. Code 56 et seq.), all employers who receive medical information from a provider of health care are required to establish appropriate procedures to ensure the confidentiality and protection from unauthorized use and disclosure of that information. An employer may not use, disclose or knowingly permit its employees or agents to use or disclose medical information about an employee without the employee first having signed an authorization under California Civil Code section 56.11 or 56.21 permitting such use or disclosure. Cal. Civ. Code section 56.20. See also Pettus v. Cole, 49 Cal. App. 4th 402, 57 Cal. Rptr. 2d 46 (Cal. Ct. App. 1996) (provider who examined plaintiff pursuant to requirements of the employer's disability leave policy violated CMIA, as did the employer, where the provider released information to the employer without a valid CMIA authorization; information which may be disclosed without authorization is limited to that necessary to achieve a legitimate purpose, i.e., the "functional limitations of the patient" and more detailed descriptions regarding hostility toward the company and drinking habits went beyond that purpose); Kina v. United Airlines, 2008 WL 5071045 (N.D. Cal. 2008) (plaintiff properly stated a claim under CMIA when health care provider disclosed, without first obtaining his information, detailed sensitive confidential, personal and medical information to employer following fitness for duty evaluation). Disclosure of employment-related health assessments are authorized when they described functional limitations that may limit the patient's (employee's) fitness to perform his or her present employment, provided no statement of medical cause is included in the information disclosed. See Cal. Civ. Code. 56.10(c)(8)(B); Espinoza v. City of Imperial, 2008 WL 2397430 (S.D.Cal. 2009).

C. Criminal Records

California law prohibits an employer from asking job applicants about any arrest that did not result in a conviction. Cal. Lab. Code 432.7. Intentional violation of this section may result in actual damages, treble damages, and attorneys' fees. But see Faria v. San Jacinto Unified Sch. Dist., 50 Cal. App. 4th 1939, 59 Cal. Rptr. 2d 72 (Cal. Ct. App. 1996) (court held that in the case of an assistant principal demoted due to an alcohol-related misdemeanor offense, that only applicants, and not existing employees, may obtain treble damages; existing employees are limited to actual damages). California Labor Code 432.8 expands Section 432.7's prohibition by precluding an employer from asking questions regarding convictions for certain drug offenses that are more than two years old. See Starbucks v. Superior Court, 168 Cal. App. 4th 1436, 86 Cal. Rptr.3d 482 (2008) (holding nationwide, one-size-fits all employment application failed to unambiguously direct California applicants not to disclose prohibited marijuana convictions)

Moreover, the FEHA guidelines state that an employer should not ask an applicant about his or her arrest record because studies have shown that minorities tend to be arrested more frequently than non-minorities. The only acceptable inquiry is one that asks whether the applicant has ever been convicted of a crime, other than: (1) a conviction for which the record has been judicially expunged, sealed or eradicated, or (2) any misdemeanor conviction for which probation has been completed and the case has been judicially dismissed. The FEHA guidelines require the employer to indicate, however, that such a conviction does not automatically disqualify the applicant from employment. Accordingly, an employer may inquire as to whether the applicant has been convicted of a felony, but this question must be accompanied by a statement that a conviction will not necessarily disqualify the applicant from employment. In addition, employers (or their agents) cannot ask job applicants to reveal any convictions for possession or use of marijuana that occurred more than two years prior to their application. Cal. Lab. Code 432.7, 432.8. See also Flores v. Autozone West, Inc., 161 Cal. App. 4th 373, 74 Cal. Rptr. 3d 178 (Cal . Ct. App. 2008) (attempt to uncover juvenile records would be inconsistent with the confidentiality of juvenile delinquency records protected by law).

However, it is important to note that certain industries may be preempted by federal law with respect to this issue. Pursuant to the federal Combat Methamphetamine Epidemic Act of 2005 (CMA), retail pharmacies may ask applicants whether they have ever been convicted of any crime involving controlled substances "notwithstanding state law." 21 U.S.C. § 830(e)(1)(G). Thus, a California Court of Appeal recently held that the CMA permits retail pharmacies in California to inquire about convictions involving controlled substances regardless of the requirements in California Labor Code 432.8. See Rankin v. Longs Drugs Stores, 169 Cal. App. 4th 1246, 87 Cal. Rptr. 3d 543 (2009).

Notwithstanding the above, a licensed securities broker-dealer or affiliate, or any officer or employee thereof, may submit to the Department of Justice fingerprints of an applicant for employment for the purpose of obtaining information as to whether the applicant has a conviction or an arrest for which the applicant was released on bail or on his/her own recognizance pending trial, as established by the Department of Justice. Cal. Corp. Code 25221.

D. Background Checks and Investigations

An employer's ability to conduct background checks on applicants or employees and, to some extent, to investigate employee conduct using an outside service is governed by the California Investigative Consumer Reporting Agencies Act. This law requires the employer to make certain disclosures anytime it uses an "investigative consumer reporting agency to obtain an investigative report," defined as a report in which information about the character, general reputation, personal characteristics or mode of living of the consumer (i.e. the employee or applicant) is obtained through any means. An investigative consumer agency generally includes any person who engages in the practice of collecting, assembling, compiling, reporting, transmitting or communicating consumer information for a fee. In general, employers who use third parties to conduct background checks or investigations are subject to this law. Cal. Civil Code section 1786 et seq.

Assembly Bill 22, effective January 12, 2012, bans the use of pre-employment credit checks for many employers. The new law prohibits employers and prospective employers in California – with the exception of certain financial institutions – from obtaining consumer credit reports to use in the hiring and promotion process unless the position of the person for whom the report is sought is one of the following: (1) a managerial position; (2) a position in the state Department of Justice; (3) a sworn peace officer or other law enforcement position; (4) a position for which the information contained in the report is required by law to be disclosed or obtained; (5) a position that involves regular access to specified personal information for any purpose other than the routine solicitation and processing of credit card applications in a retail establishment; (6) a position in which the person is or would be named as a signatory on the employer's bank or credit card account, or authorized to transfer money or enter into financial contracts on the employer's behalf; (7) a position that involves access to confidential or proprietary information; or (8) a position that involves regular access to $10,000 or more in cash. Cal. Labor Code section 1024.5. AB 22 also requires that employers or prospective employers obtain the written consent of the person for whom the credit report is sought and to also inform the person of the specific reason for obtaining the report. Cal. Civil Code section 1785.20.5; Cal. Civil Code section 1786.16. There is also certain information which may not be included in the report. This includes bankruptcies, judgments, tax liens and criminal records of a certain age as well as criminal records of a certain disposition. Cal. Civil Code section 1786.18. With the passage of this bill, generally speaking, employers should use caution and not use credit checks unless there is a clear business justification related to the job in question.

Where an employer gathers information on an applicant's or employee's character, general reputation, personal characteristics or mode of living through criminal, civil or certain other public records, and does so itself instead of through an outside agency, it must provide that record to the applicant or employee within seven days. Where the public record is used as part of an investigation into suspected wrongdoing or misconduct by the subject, the employer can wait to provide a copy of the record until the investigation is complete. There are provisions allowing the employee or applicant to waive the right to receive the records. Cal. Civil Code section 1786.53.

Employers who fail to comply with the law can be sued civilly and held liable for actual damages or $10,000, whichever is greater, plus costs and reasonable attorneys' fees. Punitive damages may be available where the violation was grossly negligent or willful. Cal. Civil Code section 1786.50.

E. Social Security Numbers

California Civil Code 1798.85 prohibits persons and entities from: 1) posting or displaying someone's SSN; 2) printing a SSN on a card required to access products or services; 3) requiring someone to input his SSN over the Internet unless the connection is secure; 4) requiring someone to input his SSN to access a website unless a password or PIN is also required; and 5) printing someone's SSN on materials mailed to him unless federal or state law otherwise requires. This law does not prohibit including SSNs on applications and forms sent by mail, for example as part of an application or enrollment process. The law also includes an exception for using and releasing SSNs for internal verification or administrative purposes or where otherwise required by law. Cal. Civil Code section 1798.85.

In addition, effective January 1, 2008, employers are prohibited from listing an employee's SSN on wage statements. Employers must use only the last four digits of an employee's SSN or an existing employee identification number other than a SSN on the check. Cal. Labor Code section 226(a)(7).

F. Subpoenas / Search Warrants

A current or former employee's personnel records are considered private and may not be obtained absent compliance with the procedures set forth in California Code of Civil Procedure section 1985.6. See VI.A.

VII. ACTIONS SUBSEQUENT TO EMPLOYMENT

A. References

California Civil Code section 47(c) provides a qualified privilege for employers to communicate, without malice, with persons who have a common interest in the subject matter of the communication. The statutory privilege specifically applies to communications about an individual's job performance or qualifications for employment made by a current or former employee to a prospective employer of the individual. See also Neal v. Gatlin, 35 Cal. App. 3d 871, 111 Cal. Rptr. 117 (1973). A showing of malice will overcome the privilege. Malice in this context is a state of mind arising from hatred or ill will, evidencing a willingness to vex, annoy or injury another person. Agarwal v. Johnson, 25 Cal.3d 932, 160 Cal. Rptr. 141 (1979).

California Labor Code section 1050 also makes misrepresentations by a former employer about a discharged employee a misdemeanor. California Labor Code section 1053 sets forth an employer's right to respond to requests by providing a truthful statement concerning the reason for the discharge of an employee or why an employee voluntarily left the service of the employer.

B. Non-Compete Agreements

Covenants not to compete are generally void under California law. See Cal. Bus. & Prof. Code section 16600 (Except as provided in this chapter, every contract by which anyone is restrained from engaging in a lawful profession, trade, or business of any kind is to that extent void.)

The California Supreme Court has held that non-competition agreements are invalid in California, even if they are narrowly drafted and leave a substantial portion of the market available to the affected individual, unless they fall within few statutory or trade secret exceptions. Edwards v. Arthur Andersen, LLP, 44 Cal.4th 937, 189 P.3d 285, 81 Cal.Rptr.3d 282 (Cal. 2008). In Edwards, the Supreme Court addressed whether the "narrow restraint" exception adopted by the Ninth Circuit was a proper interpretation of California law. Under the "narrow restraint" exception, employers could enforce non-competition agreements that did not "entirely preclude" an employee from practicing his or her trade. The Supreme Court summarily rejected this "narrow restraint" exception created by the federal courts in Edwards. It expressed a stark disapproval for judicially created exceptions to California Business and Professions Code 16600 and stated that any time an agreement restricts an employee's "ability to practice his [] profession" in any way, it is void. However, the court expressly did not address the "trade secrets exception" long recognized by California courts, nor did it address covenants not to solicit employees. After Edwards, non-competition agreements must fall squarely within one of the few explicit statutory exceptions in order to be enforceable. See also Comedy Club Inc. v. Improv West Associates, 553 F. 2d 1277 (2009) (extending the reach of Section 16600's prohibition on non-compete agreements to licensing provisions in franchise agreements between two companies and directly stating that covenants not to compete may only be permitted under California law either when the statutory sale-of-business or dissolution of partnership situations provided in §16600 and 16602 apply, or when "they are necessary to protect trade secrets.").

VIII. OTHER ISSUES

A. Statute of Limitations

Most tort claims in California, including all four branches of the common law claim of invasion of privacy, are subject to a two-year statute of limitations. Cal. Civ. Code Proc. 335.1.

B. Jurisdiction

Privacy claims arising under the California constitution or California common law are subject to the jurisdiction of the California state courts.

C. Worker's Compensation Exclusivity

The California Department of Industrial Relations, Workers Compensation Appeals Board is not an exclusive venue for employer-employee disputes in the context of privacy claims against employers.

D. Pleading Requirements

California's modern pleading rules are quite liberal and have the following characteristics:

1. **Single Form of Action**: In California, the complaint may join causes of action of any kind (tort, contract, property etc.) in a single lawsuit. The complaint also may pursue both legal and equitable remedies at the same time. Cal. Civ. Proc. Code section 307.

2. **Fact Pleading**: Fact pleading requires somewhat more precision and detail than the notice pleading that is required in federal courts. However, as a practical matter, cases in California are pled almost identically as they are pled in federal court. Cal. Civ. Proc. Code section 425.10.

3. **California's Policy is to Construe Pleadings Liberally:** California courts construe complaints liberally in favor of the plaintiff. See, e.g., Fredericks v. Filbert Co., 189 Cal. App. 3d 272, 234 Cal. Rptr. 395 (Cal. Ct. App. 1987).

4. **Format Requirements**: Complaints filed in Superior Court must be drafted in accordance with California Rule of Court 2.1 et seq.. In addition, there may be format requirements under local rules and policies. Accordingly, it is essential to check with the specific branch of the court in which you intend to file your case.

SURVEY OF COLORADO EMPLOYMENT LIBEL LAW

Sarah E. Benjes
Thomas W. Carroll
Faegre Baker Daniels LLP
3200 Wells Fargo Center, 1700 Lincoln St.
Denver, Colorado 80203
Telephone: (303) 607-3500; Facsimile: (303) 607-3600
www.FaegreBD.com

(With Developments Reported Through **November 1, 2012**)

GENERAL COMMENTS

The District Courts of Colorado are the courts of general jurisdiction in Colorado. District courts also hear appeals from the County Courts. The Colorado Court of Appeals hears appeals from the District Courts. The Colorado Supreme Court is the court of last resort in Colorado.

The Colorado Supreme Court has adopted a set of jury instructions for use in libel cases in Colorado courts. These are the work of a committee appointed by the Colorado Supreme Court to study the law and prepare pattern instructions, annotations of legal authority, and "Notes on Use." Chapter 22 of Colorado Jury Instructions Civil (CJI-Civ.) (2012) represents the committee's attempt to reconcile and harmonize the various decisions applying the common law and constitutional law of libel. While not binding in the same sense that appellate decisions are, the instructions and annotations thereto have been approved by the Colorado Supreme Court and are considered persuasive authority in the trial courts.

SIGNIFICANT DEVELOPMENTS SINCE THE 2012 *SURVEY*

In Air Wisconsin Airline Corporation v. Hoeper, --- P.3d ---, 2012 WL 907764 (Colo. Mar. 19, 2012), the Colorado Supreme Court, *en banc*, in a divided opinion, affirmed a $1.2 million jury verdict for a former pilot on his defamation claim based on the airline's report to the Transportation Security Administration (TSA) that the pilot's employment had been terminated and he was mentally unstable and could be armed. The court considered: (1) whether Air Wisconsin was entitled to immunity, under federal law; and (2) whether the evidence demonstrated Air Wisconsin's statements were false, made with actual malice, and not protected opinions, under Virginia law. The court held that the lower court had erred in submitting to the jury the question of whether Air Wisconsin was entitled to immunity under the American Transportation Safety Act (ATSA). Under the ATSA, the immunity applies both to the suit and damages. Accordingly, the trial court must determine before trial whether an air carrier is immune from suit and instructing the jury on this topic was erroneous. However, the court held it was harmless error because Air Wisconsin was not entitled to immunity. The ATSA provides generally that an air carrier that makes a voluntary disclosure of any suspicious transaction related to air piracy, threats to aircrafts or passenger safety, or terrorism is immune from civil liability. However, the immunity does not apply to any disclosure made with: (1) "actual knowledge that the disclosure was false, inaccurate, or misleading;" or (2) "reckless disregard as to the truth or falsity of that disclosure." See 49 U.S.C. § 44941. The court drew upon the New York Times Co. v. Sullivan standard to interpret "reckless disregard" under the ATSA and find that the statements made to the TSA that Hoeper was mentally unstable, had been terminated earlier that day, and may have been armed were made with reckless disregard of their truth or falsity. Specifically, an Air Wisconsin manager knew when he made the statements only that Hoeper was angry when he failed a job-related test and would likely be terminated for failing the test. Further, the manager knew only that Hoeper had been issued a firearm because of his status as a federal flight deck officer. In addition, for the same reasons, the court concluded that the trial court record showed clear and convincing evidence of actual malice to support the defamation claim. Finally, the court rejected Air Wisconsin's arguments that its statements were protected opinions and substantially true. On September 11, 2012, Air Wisconsin filed a petition for a writ of certiorari to the U.S. Supreme Court to review the Colorado Supreme Court's decision.

I. GENERAL LAW

A. General Employment Law

1. ***At Will Employment.*** Under Colorado law, an employee who is hired for indefinite period of time is an "at-will employee" whose employment may be terminated by either party without cause and without notice. Cont'l Air Lines, Inc. v. Keenan, 731 P.2d 708 (Colo. 1987). Colorado courts have noted several exceptions to this doctrine.

In Continental Air Lines, Inc. v. Keenan, the Colorado Supreme Court recognized an exception where an employee could show that the employer and employee entered into a contract (in that case contained in an employee manual) that modified the at-will nature of the employee's employment. 731 P.2d at 711-12. See also Friedel v. Mountain View Fire Prot. Dist., 2008 WL 435280 (D. Colo. Feb. 14, 2008) (recognizing that "an employee handbook containing statements 'limiting an employer's right to discharge employees' may give rise to a cause of action under a theory of implied contract or promissory estoppel"). But see Watson v. Pub. Serv. Co. of Colo., 207 P.3d 860 (Colo. App. 2008) (holding that where an internet job posting only solicits responses from prospective applicants and explicitly disclaims any modification of at-will employment, the posting does not constitute a sufficiently definite offer, and thus did not create an implied contract upon the employee's acceptance). One method by which a plaintiff may defeat the at-will presumption is by demonstrating an express stipulation as to the duration of employment in exchange for consideration over and above plaintiff's existing performance. Kerstien v. McGraw-Hill Cos., Inc., 2001 WL 327167 (10th Cir. Apr. 4, 2001) (unpublished). Statements to employees about termination procedures or other types of policies or procedures may also be enforceable under an implied contract theory. See Young v. Dillon Co., Inc., 468 F.3d 1243, 1253-54 (10th Cir. 2006). But see Romero v. Denver Pub. Schs., Dist. No. 1, 2010 WL 2943528 (D. Colo. July 22, 2010) (holding that policies failed to establish implied employment contract when former school employee was unaware of one policy and other policies included disclaimers of any intent to change the at-will status of classified employees).

However, the statute of frauds may provide a defense to breach of contract claims based on oral statements. In Whatley v. Crawford & Co., 2001 WL 744979 (10th Cir. 2001) (unpublished), the Tenth Circuit Court of Appeals affirmed the dismissal of Whatley's breach of contract claim. Applying Colorado law, the court held that because the statute of frauds permits enforcement only of contracts that may be performed within one year, both plaintiff's open-ended contract for at-will employment with defendant and any alleged oral contract regarding conditions of employment were unenforceable. The court further held that the mere allegation that an employment contract was breached within one year does not place it beyond the reach of the statute of frauds. Additionally, Colorado Revised Statutes § 38-10-112(1)(a) precludes enforcement of an oral contract that cannot be performed within one year.

Even in the absence of an express or implied contract, an at-will employee may have a claim under the doctrine of promissory estoppel. See, e.g., Young v. Dillon, 468 F.3d 1243 (10th Cir. 2006). The employee must demonstrate that: (1) "the employer should reasonably have expected the employee to consider its offer to the employee to be a commitment to follow [certain] termination procedures," (2) "the employee reasonably relied on [those] procedures to his detriment," and (3) "injustice can be avoided only by enforcement of those termination procedures." However, the employer's promise must be "sufficiently specific" such that a mere description of an employer's present policies would not be considered a promise. See id. See also, e.g., Watson v. Pub. Serv. Co. of Colo., 207 P.3d 860 (Colo. App. 2008) (applying the elements of promissory estoppel); Laird v. Gunnison County, 2007 WL 108391 (D. Colo. Jan. 10, 2007) (unpublished) (granting summary judgment for employer on promissory estoppel claim based on employer's failure to provide a hearing and appeal prior to termination).

However, if an employer "clearly and conspicuously" disclaims intent to enter into a contract or disclaims intent to modify the at-will employment relationship, an employee will not be successful under contract or a promissory estoppel theories. See Ferrera v. Nielson, 799 P.2d 458, 461 (Colo. App. 1990) (noting that claims based on discharge procedures in a handbooks should not survive summary judgment when an employer "has clearly and conspicuously disclaimed intent to enter a contract limiting the right to discharge employees"); Friedel v. Mountain View Fire Prot. Dist., 2008 WL 43520 (D. Colo. Feb. 14, 2008) (granting defendant's summary judgment motion on promissory estoppel claim because disclaimers contained in employee manual stated nothing in the manual is intended to alter employees' at-will status). **But see Trujillo v. Atmos Energy Corp., 2012 WL 2390353 (D. Colo. Jun. 25, 2012) (concluding that a disclaimer in the employee handbook which was buried in the middle of a paragraph with no preceding language to highlight its importance and no reference to an employee's at-will status was not clear and conspicuous and thus failed to disclaim potential liability based upon the progressive discipline policy).**

In Martin Marietta v. Lorenz, 823 P.2d 100 (Colo. 1992), the Colorado Supreme Court recognized an at-will employee's tort claim for wrongful discharge predicated on the employee's refusal to comply with an employer's order or directive to perform an unlawful act. This is commonly referred to as the "public policy exception" to the at-will employment doctrine. The elements of a wrongful discharge claim based upon public policy are:

> (1) The employer directed the employee to perform an illegal act as part of the employee's work-related duties or prohibited the employee from performing a public duty or exercising an important job-related privilege;
>
> (2) That action directed by the employer would violate a specific statute relating to the public health, safety or welfare, or would undermine a clearly expressed public policy relating to the employee's basic responsibility as a citizen or the employee's right or privilege as a worker;

(3) The employee was terminated for refusing to perform the act;

(4) The employer was aware or reasonably should have been aware that the employee's refusal to comply with the employer's orders was based on the employee's reasonable belief that the action ordered by the employer was illegal, contrary to clearly expressed statutory policy, or a violation of the employee's legal right or privilege as a worker.

But see Dodson v. Bd. Of County Comm'rs, 2012 WL 2878009 (D. Colo. July 13, 2012) (noting that plaintiff's pure speculation and conclusory allegations that his termination was due to complaints of alleged misuse of building permit fees and poor air quality in the workplace were not sufficient to survive summary judgment where plaintiff failed to present any evidence of an act that his employer directed him to take or prohibited him from taking, identify a specific statute or express public policy that was violated, or show that he was terminated for refusing to perform an order given by his employer).

In Bonidy v. Vail Valley Center for Aesthetic Dentistry, P.C., 186 P.3d 80 (Colo. App. 2008), cert. denied, 2008 Colo. LEXIS 678 (Colo. June 23, 2008) (Bonidy I), the Colorado Court of Appeals held that regulations pertaining to rest and lunch breaks may give rise to a private cause of action for wrongful discharge in violation of public policy where a plaintiff presents evidence that public safety could be jeopardized if he or she is not permitted to receive rest and lunch breaks. In Rocky Mountain Hospital & Medical Services v. Mariani, 916 P.2d 519 (Colo. 1996), the Colorado Supreme Court indicated that the public policy exception applies not only to statutory violations but also to violations of professional rules of conduct, such as accountancy rules. In Lathrop v. Entenmann's, Inc., 770 P.2d 1367 (Colo. App. 1989), the Colorado Court of Appeals recognized a similar claim for wrongful discharge in retaliation for an employee filing a worker's compensation claim.

In Jaynes v. Centura Health Corp., 148 P.3d 241 (Colo. App. 2006), the Colorado Court of Appeals affirmed the dismissal of Jaynes' claim for wrongful discharge in violation of public policy. Jaynes argued that both the American Nurses Association ("ANA") code of ethics and the Colorado quality management functions statute, Colo. Rev. Stat. § 25-3-109 ("QM Statute"), created a public policy mandate that her employer had violated. In rejecting Jaynes' argument, the Court determined that the ANA Code, unlike the accountancy code of ethics in Mariani, did not support a public policy claim because it was a purely private pronouncement that did not emanate from governmental action. Moreover, because Jaynes was not an ANA member and the ANA's rules were not mandatory, she would not be subject to adverse consequences for violations of its rules even if the court concluded that it constituted public policy. The Court further concluded that the QM Statute failed to qualify as public policy under the Lorenz criteria because it did not clearly articulate a "public duty," and did not create "an important job-related right or privilege." In addition, the Court held that the action purportedly directed by the employer in this case, even if assumed true, did not "violate a specific statute."

In Coors Brewing Co. v. Floyd, 978 P.2d 663 (Colo. 1999), the Colorado Supreme Court held that an employee, who was allegedly fired to cover-up his employer's involvement in an illegal undercover narcotics investigation that he was instructed to conduct, could not bring a wrongful discharge action under the public policy exception to the employment at-will doctrine, where the employee never expressed an unwillingness to follow his superiors' instructions, never refused to participate in the illegal activity, and did not blow the whistle on the alleged criminal enterprise before he was terminated. The Court held that the public policy exception to the employment at-will doctrine only protects an employee from being forced to choose between committing a crime and losing his or her job. The public policy rationale behind the exception does not apply when the employee commits the crime and only points the finger at his or her employer after being fired.

In Boone v. MVM, Inc., 2007 WL 549833 (D. Colo. Feb. 15, 2007), the court denied MVM's motion for judgment on the pleadings as to Boone's claims for breach of contract and wrongful discharge in violation of public policy. Boone, hired to perform private security services in Iraq, alleged that MVM breached its contract to deploy him as stated in a written agreement and verbally. In addition, Boone argued that he was terminated for refusing to sign an "After Action Report" which contained statements he believed were false. Boone identified a specific federal statute, 18 U.S.C. § 1001(a), which prohibits false statements on a government contract, in his complaint and successfully alleged that his termination resulted from his attempt to comply with the statute.

In Mowry v. United Parcel Service, Inc., 280 Fed. App'x 702 (10th Cir. 2008), the Tenth Circuit affirmed summary judgment in favor of the employer ("UPS") on the employee's wrongful discharge in violation of public policy claim in which the employee was unable to prove the fourth element of the Lorenz test. In Mowry, the plaintiff's supervisor sent two other supervisors to follow Mowry, a package trailer driver, to determine if he was falsifying trip records. During the trip, Mowry stopped his truck at a rest area allegedly due to adverse road conditions. State and federal laws require drivers of commercial vehicles to pull off the road during adverse road and/or weather conditions. The two supervisors believed the road conditions were not sufficiently severe to warrant pulling off the road and concluded Mowry was making an unauthorized stop. Mowry recorded the time spent at the rest stop in his time card as "breakdown on road" and his supervisor discharged him for dishonesty. Mowry argued he had been terminated in violation of public policy because continuing his journey would have been in violation of federal and state safety regulations. The court rejected Mowry's argument that the two supervisors' knowledge of the adverse road conditions should be imputed to UPS as a whole to satisfy the knowledge element of the Lorenz test. The court noted that Mowry failed to cite any authority indicating that knowledge of the corporation as a whole, rather than that of an individual decisionmaker, is sufficient to prove the knowledge element of a Lorenz tort.

In Kearl v. Portage Environmental, Inc., 205 P.3d 496 (Colo. App. 2009), the Colorado Court of Appeals concluded that Colorado has a clearly expressed public policy against terminating an employee in retaliation for the employee's good faith attempt to prevent the employer's participation in defrauding the government. There, the defendant employer secured a contract with the U.S. Department of Energy to provide remediation services at a uranium enrichment plant. The plaintiff employee was terminated after objecting to the use of a flawed cleanup technology that allowed the spread of toxic substances. The Court held that the employee's allegations were sufficient to put the employer on notice of the "clearly expressed public policy" element of his claim for wrongful discharge under the public policy exception to the at-will employment doctrine, and it was error for the district court to grant the employer's motion to dismiss on this ground.

In Bonidy v. Vail Valley Center For Aesthetic Dentistry, P.C., 232 P.3d 277 (Colo. App. 2010) (Bonidy II), the Colorado Court of Appeals concluded "that when an employee objects to performing an act that satisfies the second element of a claim for wrongful termination of public policy and is immediately fired before having an opportunity to refuse to perform the directed act, the refusal element of the Lorenz test is satisfied." In that case, the plaintiff dental assistant objected to her work conditions relating to rest and lunch breaks and the court found that any formal complaint by her would be futile. Because of the futility of a formal complaint and because the plaintiff was fired before she had the opportunity to refuse to follow the objectionable directives, the court found the plaintiff met the refusal requirement. The court further concluded that, even if it were to require refusal under Lorenz, such a requirement would necessarily be excused when the employee is terminated so quickly as to have no opportunity to refuse.

B. Elements of Libel Claim

1. ***Basic Elements.*** The tort of defamation consists of two types of communication, "libel" and "slander"; "libel" is usually written communication while "slander" is generally an oral communication. Keohane v. Stewart, 882 P.2d 1293 (Colo. 1994). Under Colorado law, the elements of a defamation claim are: (1) a defamatory statement concerning plaintiff; (2) published to a third party; (3) with the publisher's fault amounting to at least negligence; and (4) either actionability of the statement irrespective of special damages (in the case of libel or slander per se) or the existence of special damages caused by the publication. See Graziani v. Epic Data Corp., 305 F. Supp. 2d 1192, 1197 (D. Colo. 2004); Brown v. O'Bannon, 84 F. Supp. 2d 1176, 1181 (D. Colo. 2000); Stump v. Gates, 777 F. Supp. 808 (D. Colo. 1991); Keohane v. Stewart, 882 P.2d 1293 (Colo. 1994). One court has held that deliberateness or recklessness is also a necessary element of a claim for defamation under Colorado law. See Zerr v. Johnson, 894 F. Supp. 372 (D. Colo. 1995).

2. ***Fault.*** The Civil Jury Instruction Committee takes the position that the standard of fault depends only upon the status of the plaintiff and the subject matter of the defamation (public concern versus private), but the status of the defendant (media versus nonmedia) is not relevant. See CJI-Civ. 22:1, 22:2, 22:4, 22:5 (2012). Colorado distinguishes between matters of private and public concern. In a defamation action under Colorado law, the New York Times v. Sullivan, 376 U.S. 254 (1964) actual malice standard of proof is to be applied in all cases involving a media defendant and where the plaintiff is a public figure, or the plaintiff is a public official, or the plaintiff is a private individual and the case involves matters of public interest or general concern. See Spacecon Specialty Contractors, LLC v. Bensinger, 782 F. Supp. 2d 1194 (D. Colo. 2011); Ramsey v. Fox News Network, L.L.C., 351 F. Supp. 2d 1145, 1148 (D. Colo. 2005); Zimmerman v. Board of Publ'ns of Christian Reformed Church, Inc., 598 F. Supp. 1002 (D. Colo. 1984); In re Green, 11 P.3d 1078, 1083 (Colo. 2000); see, e.g., Wilson v. Meyer, 126 P.3d 276 (Colo. App. 2005).

In addition, damages may be affected. In Rowe v. Metz, 579 P.2d 83, 4 Media L. Rep. 1431 (Colo. 1978), the Colorado Supreme Court held that the Gertz v. Robert Welch, Inc., 418 U.S. 323 (1974) damage rules do not apply to publications by nonmedia defendants, when the subject matter is not of public or general concern. See CJI-Civ. 22:1, 22:4, 22:5 (2012).

a. **Private Figure Plaintiff/Matter of Public Concern.** When a defamatory statement has been published concerning one who is not a public official or public figure but the matter involved is of public or general concern, the publisher will be liable to the person defamed if, and only if, he knows the statement to be false or made the statement with reckless disregard of whether it was true. Ramsey v. Fox News Network, L.L.C., 351 F. Supp. 2d 1145, 1148 (D. Colo. 2005); Walker v. Colorado Springs Sun, Inc., 538 P.2d 450 (Colo. 1975); Brudwick v. Minor, 2006 WL 1991755 (D. Colo. July 13, 2006). Examples of private figure plaintiffs have included bankers and land developers, Diversified Mgt. Inc. v. The Denver Post, 653 P.2d 1103 (Colo. 1982); proprietors of antique shops, Walker, 538 P.2d at 451; a commercial airplane pilot, Williams v. Cont'l Airlines, Inc., 943 P.2d 10 (Colo. App. 1996); a man accused of murdering a neighbor's child, Miles v. Ramsey, 31 F. Supp. 2d 869 (D. Colo. 1998); parents suspected of murdering their child, Ramsey v. Fox News Network, L.L.C., 351 F. Supp. 2d 1145 (D. Colo. 2005); and a couple whose residence was searched pursuant to a search warrant, Brudwick v. Minor, 2006 WL 1991755 (D. Colo. July 13, 2006).

Generally, a matter is of public concern whenever it embraces an issue about which information is needed or is appropriate, or when the public reasonably may be expected to have a legitimate interest in what is being published, but the boundaries of public concern cannot be readily defined and must be determined on a case-by-case basis. See Williams, 943 P.2d at 10. See also Spacecon, 782 F. Supp. 2d 1194 (D. Colo. 2011) (holding that film about misclassification of employees, failure to pay taxes, discrimination and abuse of workers, and human trafficking was a matter of public concern); TMJ Implants, Inc. v. Aetna, Inc., 498 F.3d 1175, 1185-86 (10th Cir. 2007) (holding that information in insurance bulletins about medical devices was a matter of public concern because thousands of people had a legitimate interest in the utility of the devices, including patients, physicians, and dentists); Brudwick v. Minor, 2006 WL 1991755 (D. Colo. July 13, 2006) (holding that the plaintiffs' defamation claims, based on newspaper and radio reports in which law enforcement personnel asserted that they remained suspicious of the plaintiffs, constituted a public controversy); Miles v. Ramsey, 31 F. Supp. 2d 869 (D. Colo. 1998) (holding that statements in a tabloid newspaper suggesting that the neighbor of a child murder victim was responsible for the murder involved a matter of public concern and, therefore, the heightened "reckless disregard" standard). The question of whether a subject is of public concern is a matter of law. See Williams v. Cont'l Airlines, Inc., 943 P.2d 10 (Colo. App. 1996).

In Arndt v. Koby, 309 F.3d 1247 (10th Cir. 2002), the Court held that the plaintiff's speech was not a matter of public concern. The plaintiff was a Boulder police officer who was criticized in the media for her alleged mishandling of the JonBenet Ramsey murder investigation. Stating that "neither the form nor the context of her proposed speech compel the conclusion that her proposed speech was a matter of public concern for First Amendment purposes," the Court concluded that plaintiff's speech was not a matter of public concern because the content of her speech was purely personal in that it "sought to restore her personal reputation." Id. at 1254.

In 2003, the Tenth Circuit held in Quigley v. Rosenthal, 327 F.3d 1044 (10th Cir. 2003), that the defendant's statements made at a press conference and during a radio show summarizing a federal civil rights lawsuit were not on a matter of public concern. Although the plaintiffs' neighbors alleged religious and/or ethnic discrimination in a lawsuit against the plaintiffs, these allegations did not constitute a matter of public concern. First, the neighbors were not claiming that a public employer discriminated against them. Second, the defendants should have known that the neighbors' allegations against the plaintiffs were false.

In Ramsey v. Fox News Network, L.L.C., 351 F. Supp. 2d 1145 (D. Colo. 2005), the district Court found that a story aired by a news network regarding the murder of plaintiffs' daughter, JonBonet Ramsey, was a matter of public concern. Accordingly, plaintiffs were required to prove actual malice in their defamation *per se* claim against the network. In granting the defendant's motion to dismiss, the Court noted that the constitutional protections afforded defendants in defamation cases based on matters of public concern not only protect broadcast media, but also protect "webloggers" who can "in a matter of hours point out key errors in reporting by mainstream media outlets." Id. at 1153.

To establish that a defamation plaintiff is a public figure by virtue of his or her involvement in a matter of public concern, i.e., a limited-purpose public figure, the defendant bears the burden of showing that: (1) public controversy existed on a specific question having ramifications for nonparticipants; (2) plaintiff had a significant role in the controversy, either by voluntarily attempting to affect the outcome or by being drawn into the controversy and assuming a central role; and (3) the alleged defamation was germane to the plaintiffs participation in the controversy. See Quigley v. Rosenthal, 43 F. Supp. 2d 1163(D. Colo. 1999), aff'd in part, rev'd in part, 327 F.3d 1044 (10th Cir. 2003).

b. **Private Figure Plaintiff/Matter of Private Concern.** The protections afforded the press when it reports on public officials and public figures do not shield it from liability when it publishes defamatory statements concerning private individuals. See Dixson v. Newsweek, Inc., 562 F.2d 626 (10th Cir. 1977). In nonconstitutional defamation cases (i.e., those not involving public figures, public officials or matters of public interest and concern), the burden of proving the material elements to sustain a claim based on libel or slander are on the plaintiff and the standard applied is a preponderance of the evidence. See CJI-Civ. 22:4, 22:5 (2012). See also Rowe v. Metz, 579 P.2d 83 (Colo. 1978).

Where the reputation of a private plaintiff has been injured by a nonmedia defendant in a purely private context, and remarks are defamatory per se, the common-law rule permitting a presumption of damages remains applicable. Rowe v. Metz, 579 P.2d 83 (Colo. 1978). In Sky Fun 1, Inc. v. Schuttloffel, 8 P.3d 570 (Colo. App. 2000), aff'd in relevant part, rev'd in part on other grounds, 27 P.3d 361 (Colo. 2001), statements by a former employer (a private, non-media individual) that defendant, a private person, was "not a good pilot" and was "a threat to passengers" were made not to protect public safety but to thwart defendant's employment opportunities. Accordingly, the statements, made with malice (in the common sense of the word, as distinguished from actual malice as defined by New York Times v. Sullivan, 376 U.S. 254 (1964), were not matters of public concern, but nonetheless were sufficient to support an award of compensatory and punitive damages.

Defamatory statements by a flight attendant and supervisor that a pilot attempted to rape a flight attendant were made by private non-media defendants about a private plaintiff did not become matters of public concern simply because the pilot flew for a commercial airline; there was no claim or evidence that the pilot was unsafe or less skilled because he allegedly raped or attempted to rape women during off-duty hours, nor did the evidence support a conclusion that members of the flying public were in danger of being sexually assaulted by the pilot. See Williams v. Cont'l Airlines, Inc., 943 P.2d 10 (Colo. App. 1996).

c. **Public Figure Plaintiff/Matter of Public Concern.** Publications that concern either a public figure such as a state judge, Keohane v. Stewart, 882 P.2d 1293 (Colo. 1994), or a county commissioner, Manuel v. Ft. Collins Newspapers, Inc., 599 P.2d 931 (Colo. App. 1979), or a municipal hospital board member, Wilson v. Meyer, 2005 Colo. App. LEXIS 1346, 19-21 (Colo. App. Aug. 25, 2005), or a matter of public concern are constitutionally protected, and a showing of actual malice is necessary to defeat the protection and make a defamatory publication actionable. See Seible v. Denver Post Corp., 782 P.2d 805 (Colo. App. 1989). Therefore, plaintiffs in defamation cases involving matters of public concern or public figures may not recover without showing that the publication was made with actual malice. See In re Green, 11 P.3d 1078, 1083 (Colo. 2000); Lewis v. McGraw-Hill Broad. Co., Inc., 832 P.2d 1118 (Colo. App. 1992); Cache La Poudre Feeds v. Land O'Lakes, Inc., 438 F. Supp. 2d 1288 (D. Colo. 2006).

In Wilson v. Meyer, 126 P.3d 276, 284 (Colo. App. 2005), the Colorado Court of Appeals affirmed the district court's award of summary judgment to an attorney for a municipal hospital board against a defamation claim by a candidate for the board. The claim was based on statements made by the attorney at a hospital board meeting. The plaintiff, as a candidate for public office, was a public figure, and therefore needed to prove by clear and convincing evidence not only that the attorney's statements were false, but that he acted with malice. Id. at 283. As the plaintiff did not allege that the attorney knew the allegedly defamatory statements were false, her claim could not survive. Id. at 283-84.

In order to balance the competing needs of an individual's right to be free from false and defamatory assertions and society's interest in encouraging and fostering vigorous public debate, the privilege of "fair comment" was incorporated into the law of defamation; "fair comment" protects statements that concern a matter of public concern, based upon true or privileged facts, that represented the actual opinion of the speaker and was not made solely for the purpose of causing harm. See Keohane v. Stewart, 882 P.2d 1293 (Colo. 1994). See also Wedbush Morgan Sec., Inc. v. Kirkpatrick Pettis Capital Mgmt., Inc., 2007 WL 1097872 (D. Colo. Apr. 9, 2007).

Unlike a private figure plaintiff, a public figure asserting a claim for slander per se must establish actual damages, which may be established by evidence of harm to reputation, personal humiliation, mental anguish and suffering or physical suffering. See Keohane v. Stewart, 882 P.2d 1293 (Colo. 1994).

3. ***Falsity.*** In civil or criminal libel actions brought by public officials, only false statements made with "actual malice" are subject to sanctions. People v. Ryan, 806 P.2d 935 (Colo. 1991). Opinion will support a defamation action if the language is defamatory and the underlying defamatory facts that provide the basis for the opinion are false and not disclosed in context. See Teilhaber Mfg. Co. v. Unarco Materials Storage, a Div. of Unarco Indus., Inc., 791 P.2d 1164 (Colo. App. 1989); cf. In re Green, 11 P.3d 1078, 1084 (Colo. 2000) (holding that "if a statement of opinion implies an undisclosed false statement of fact then the statement loses the protection of the First Amendment"); TMJ Implants, Inc. v. Aetna, Inc., 498 F.3d 1175, 1196-97 (10th Cir. 2007) (indicating that a statement might be considered defamatory if it omits a relevant material fact); Keenan v. Colo. Dep't of Human Servs., 2007 WL 2028118 (D. Colo. July 10, 2007) (holding defendant's statement that it was premature to determine whether plaintiff would be criminally investigated was not false or defamatory because it did not falsely insinuate that plaintiff had engaged in criminal conduct).

A defamation plaintiff must allege enough facts as to the alleged defamatory statement for a court to assess whether it is a fact or opinion or whether it is provably false. **See Rader v. Elec. Payment Sys., LLC, 2012 WL 4336175 (D. Colo. Sept. 21, 2012) (dismissing the libel claim and noting that without a "clear description" or quotation of the alleged defamatory statement, merely alleging that the statement is "defamatory" is not sufficient to state a claim for relief). But see Garland v. Bd. of Educ., 2012 WL 1018740 (D. Colo. Mar. 26, 2012) (factual allegations by school employee that an assistant principal who reported to the police that the employee threatened to burn the school down and was disgruntled were sufficient to show falsity and malice and survive a motion to dismiss where the employee alleged that the assistant principal had failed to investigate the report before relaying it to the police and had shown overt hostility to the employee in the days prior to the report).**

Colo. Rev. Stat. § 13-25-125 provides that the defendant may allege both truth of the matter charged as defamatory, and any mitigating circumstances to reduce the amount of damages; and that whether he proves the justification or not, he may give in evidence the mitigating circumstances. One who is alleged to have defamed another has a constitutional and statutory right to assert the truth of the defamatory statement as a defense and have a jury decide such a defense. Churchey v. Adolph Coors Co., 759 P.2d 1336 (Colo. 1988). This issue turns not upon the literal truth of every word published, but on the truth of "the gist, or the sting" of the published matter. Stated differently, the question is whether the publication as a whole "produces a different effect upon the reader than that which would be produced by the literal truth of the matter." Gomba v. McLaughlin, 504 P.2d 337, 339 (Colo. 1972); Broker's Choice of Am., Inc. v. NBC Universal, Inc., 2011 WL 97236 (D. Colo. Jan. 11, 2011) (holding that several allegedly defamatory statements were substantially true); Smiley's Too, Inc. v. Denver Post Corp., 935 P.2d 39 (Colo. App. 1996) (holding that a jury instruction was not grounds for reversal when it stated: "In order for the plaintiff to recover you must find that the substance or gist of the statement was false at the time the article was published, and the falsity was such that the article as a whole would produce a materially more damaging effect upon the reader than the truth of the matter."); see also Pierce v. St. Vrain Valley Sch. Dist. RE-1J, 944 P.2d 646 (Colo. App. 1997) (holding that statements that there were "allegations of sexual harassment" against a school superintendent were substantially true, regardless of whether the actual underlying allegations were themselves true), rev'd on other grounds, 981 P.2d 600 (Colo. 1997); Miles v. Ramsey, 31 F. Supp. 2d 869 (D. Colo. 1998) (finding, on summary judgment, that plaintiff's assertions that he had never been convicted of a sex offense and had never had sex with males under the age of consent were sufficient to overcome the National Enquirer's defense of substantial truth to its assertions that plaintiff was a "pedophile" and a "sex offender."). In Walker v. Colorado Springs Sun, Inc., 538 P.2d 450 (Colo. 1975), the Court suggested that the "state of mind" burden cannot be met where the gist of the defamation is substantially true.

4. ***Defamatory Statement of Fact.*** A statement is not opinion if it is susceptible to proof of truth or falsity. See Milkovich v. Lorain Journal Co., 497 U.S. 1 (1990). Before and after Milkovich, Colorado used and still uses a contextual approach to distinguish statements of opinion from statements of fact. See Keohane v. Stewart, 882 P.2d 1293 (Colo. 1994); NBC Subsidiary (KCNC-TV), Inc. v. Living Will Ctr., 879 P.2d 6 (Colo. 1994); Burns v. McGraw-Hill Broad. Co., 659 P.2d 1351 (Colo. 1983); Bucher v. Roberts, 595 P.2d 239 (Colo. 1979); see also Mink v. Knox, 613 F.3d 995 (10th Cir. 2010) (holding that no reasonable reader would believe that statements in satirical editorial column were said by university professor and that no reasonable person would believe they were statements of fact, rather than hyperbole or parody); TMJ Implants, Inc. v. Aetna, Inc., 498 F.3d 1175, 1183 (10th Cir. 2007) (holding that statements in an insurance bulletin that a medical device is "experimental and investigational" are not provably false, and therefore not defamatory); Jefferson County. Sch. Dist. No. R-1 v. Moody's Investor's Servs., Inc., 175 F.3d 848 (10th Cir. 1999) (applying Milkovich standard and factors outlined in Living Will Ctr., supra, and affirming that Moody's "outlook" on school district's financing bonds was not provably false and thus constituted protected opinion); **Shrader v. Biddinger, 2012 WL 976032 (D. Colo. Feb. 17, 2012) (finding that alleged defamatory statements in an internet bulletin board posting and email were opinions and not actionable where the defendant merely discussed reasoning for dissolution of his partnership with plaintiff, which included the defendant's opinion that the price of plaintiff's published materials was not justified because the defendant believed that most of the plaintiff's ideas were already addressed in other less expensive published materials)**; Kelley v. N.Y. Life Ins. & Annuity Corp., 2008 WL 5423343 (D. Colo. Dec. 30, 2008) (finding that defamatory statements that plaintiff, a political candidate, "beats women" were expressions of the defendant's personal animosity toward the plaintiff and could not reasonably be understood as factual assertions to form the basis of a slander claim when those who heard the statements did not believe them to be factual); Keenan v. Colo. Dep't of Human Servs., 2007 WL 2028118 (D. Colo. July 10, 2007) (holding statement to the press that defendant lost confidence in plaintiff's ability to perform his job responsibilities, even if based on audit results without independent investigation, did not support a claim of defamation because plaintiff could not show that information contained in the audit was both false and defendants knew or recklessly disregarded the possibility it was based on false facts); Seidl v. Greentree Mortg. Co., 30 F. Supp. 2d 1292 (D. Colo. 1998) (finding reasonable persons would not view statements made by plaintiff and his attorney in their demand letter and press release as assertions of fact); Lockett v. Garrett, 1 P.3d 206 (Colo. App. 1999) (ruling that, because allegedly defamatory statements had been made in recall petitions, no reasonable person could conclude that statements were assertions of fact rather than political opinions of dissatisfied citizens); Arrington v. Palmer, 971 P.2d 669 (Colo. App. 1998) (ruling that although statements made about plaintiff were defamatory per se, statements were protected because they were made in midst of political campaign and could not reasonably be interpreted as stating actual facts about plaintiff). In Sky Fun 1, Inc. v. Schuttloffel, 27 P.3d 361, 369-69 (Colo. 2001), the Court held that the limited liability provisions of 49 U.S.C. § 44936(g) do not preempt a state common law defamation claim, when the oral statements contain knowingly false information or are made with reckless disregard of the truth and are not based on the previous employer's records that it is required to transmit to the prospective employer. The Court thereby implicitly affirmed the Court of Appeals' previous decision, 8 P.3d 570 (Colo. App. 2000), that the former employer's statements that defendant was "not a good pilot" and constituted a "threat to passengers" were not protected opinion because a reasonable person would see the assertions as statements of fact, and the statements were deemed sufficiently factual to be susceptible of being proven true or false.

When a statement of opinion is based upon disclosed facts, with no suggestion that it is based upon undisclosed information, the statement is "pure opinion" and not a statement of fact. See NBC Subsidiary (KCNC-TV), Inc. v. Living Will Ctr., 879 P.2d 6 (Colo. 1994); Wilson v. Meyer, 126 P.3d 276 (Colo. App. 2005); cf. In re Green, 11 P.3d 1078, 1084 (Colo. 2000) (statement of opinion loses protection of First Amendment if it implies an undisclosed false statement of fact); **Nagim v. Douglas, 2012 WL 113433 (D. Colo. Jan. 13, 2012) (where the only third parties to receive the alleged defamatory comment were able to evaluate the alleged defamatory language because they had also received the email which was the basis for the alleged defamatory comment, there were no undisclosed facts to support a finding of a defamatory statement of fact).**

In NBC Subsidiary (KCNC-TV), Inc. v. Living Will Center, the Colorado Supreme Court recognized the Milkovich test of (1) whether a statement is verifiable and (2) whether it is susceptible of being understood as an assertion of actual fact, but held that the Milkovich formulation did not represent a departure from prior Colorado law. The court declared that Colorado courts would continue to utilize the following contextual factors adopted and applied in pre-Milkovich decisions to determine whether a statement reasonably could be understood to convey a factual proposition: first, the phrasing of the statement and the use of terms of apparency; second, the entirety of the statement, not just the objectionable word or phrase, and the context in which it appears; and third, all the circumstances surrounding the statement, including the medium through which it is disseminated and the audience to whom it is directed. In applying these factors, the courts should also consider whether the statement implies the existence of undisclosed facts that support it. See, e.g., Wedbush Morgan Sec., Inc. v. Kirkpatrick Pettis Capital Mgmt., Inc., 2007 WL 1097872 (D. Colo. Apr. 9, 2007) (applying the above analysis to a series of allegedly defamatory statements).

Whether allegedly defamatory language is constitutionally privileged as nonfactual in nature "is a question of law and a reviewing court must review the record de novo . . . ." NBC Subsidiary (KCNC-TV), Inc. v. Living Will Ctr., 879 P.2d 6, 11 (Colo. 1994). See also Keohane v. Stewart, 882 P.2d 1293, 1299 n.8 (Colo. 1994); Bucher v. Roberts, 595 P.2d 239 (Colo. 1979).

5. ***Of and Concerning Plaintiff.*** Colo. Rev. Stat. § 13-25-124 provides that it "shall not be necessary to plead extrinsic facts for the purposes of showing the application to the plaintiff of the defamatory matter" but that it "shall be sufficient to state generally that the same was published . . . concerning plaintiff," subject to proof at trial if controverted. Nonetheless, in Lininger v. Knight, 226 P.2d 809 (Colo. 1951), the Court held that when extrinsic facts are required to show application to plaintiff, the publication is not libelous per se and is subject to dismissal in the absence of pleading and proof of special damages. This is a departure from the majority rule, in which the per se/per quod distinction is relevant only with respect to the issue of defamatory meaning, and not the "of and concerning" requirement. See also Inter-State Detective Bur., Inc. v. Denver Post, Inc., 484 P.2d 131 (Colo. App. 1971) (plaintiff must allege, by way of innuendo, that words were published "of and concerning" plaintiff, where words standing alone do not refer to plaintiff); Dorr v. C.B. Johnson, Inc., 660 P.2d 517 (Colo. App. 1983) (publication not actionable when it does not refer to plaintiff). More recently, however, the Colorado Court of Appeals held that "whether the statement is directed at the plaintiff can be established by extrinsic proof without rendering the publication defamatory per quod." Gordon v. Boyles, 99 P.3d 75, 80 (Colo. App. 2004). See also Lee v. Colo. Times, Inc., 222 P.3d 957, 962 (Colo. App. 2009) ("We choose to follow the reasoning and holding in Gordon that extrinsic evidence may be used to prove a publication refers to the plaintiff without rendering the statement defamatory per quod."). In Stump v. Gates, 777 F. Supp. 808 (D. Colo. 1991), aff'd, 986 F.2d 1429 (10th Cir. 1993) (unpublished), the United States District Court for the District of Colorado held that publication of a police report that the plaintiffs' father committed suicide was not libelous per se of the plaintiffs because it was specifically directed at the deceased, not at the plaintiffs. In Keohane v. Stewart, 882 P.2d 1293 (Colo. 1994), the Colorado Supreme Court held that references to an unnamed judge in a letter to the editor was shown by sufficient extrinsic proof to apply to the plaintiff for purposes of fulfilling the "statement of fact" requirement.

6. ***Publication.*** Defamatory matter is "published" if it is communicated intentionally or by negligent act to one other than person defamed. Card v. Blakeslee, 937 P.2d 846 (Colo. App. 1996). In Colorado, publication is considered defamatory if it impeaches the honesty, integrity, or reputation of the plaintiff and thereby exposes him to public hatred, contempt, or ridicule. See Zimmerman v. Bd. of Publ'ns of Christian Reformed Church, Inc., 598 F. Supp. 1002 (D. Colo. 1984). The element of publication is not met by silent acquiescence while another makes a defamatory statement. Wilson v. Meyer, 126 P.3d 276 (Colo. App. 2005). Moreover, a plaintiff who is unable to produce evidence of a specific defamatory statement made by the defendant to a third party has failed to establish a prima facie showing of publication. Vinton v. Adam Aircraft Indus., Inc., 232 F.R.D. 650 (D. Colo. 2005).

a. **Intracorporate Communication.** In order to prove a claim of defamation against an employer, the employee must show that the employer published a false statement of defamatory fact and, if the communication is protected by a qualified privilege, that the employer published the material with malice. See Thompson v.

Pub. Serv. Co. of Colo., 800 P.2d 1299 (Colo. 1990); see also Sky Fun 1, Inc. v. Schuttloffel, 8 P.3d 570 (Colo. App. 2000) (former employer lost qualified privilege for statements defaming employee's safety record because they were made with malice, not to protect the public but to preclude employee's employment with another company), aff'd in relevant part and rev'd in part on other grounds, 27 P.3d 361 (Colo. 2001). With regard to a communication of allegedly libelous interoffice memoranda, the privilege with regard to the communication is qualified and not absolute, and will be lost where the publishers are motivated by express malice. See Abrahamsen v. Mountain States Tel. & Tel. Co., 494 P.2d 1287 (Colo. 1972). In an unpublished case, the Tenth Circuit Court of Appeals stated it was in "general accord" with the proposition that "circulation of a statement within an institution or agency does not, by itself, constitute publication." See Mercer v. Bd. of Trs., 2001 WL 980760 (10th Cir. Aug. 28, 2001).

A letter from the plaintiff's supervisor, a copy of which was delivered to each supervisor's superior, which contained the statement "you must realize your job was created for you because of your handicap," standing alone, did not charge the plaintiff, a paraplegic, with lack of capacity or fitness to perform his assigned duties as an underwriter for the State Compensation Insurance Fund and was not libelous per se. Paris v. Div. of State Comp. Ins. Fund, 517 P.2d 1353 (Colo. App. 1973).

b. **Compelled Self-Publication.** "Self-publication, either orally or in writing, of the defamatory statement to a third person by the person making such allegation shall not give rise to a claim for libel or slander against the person who originally communicated the defamatory statement." Colo. Rev. Stat. § 13-25-125.5. This statute superceded the holding of Churchey v. Adolph Coors Co., 759 P.2d 1336 (Colo. 1988), that even though the originator of a defamatory statement makes the statement to the defamed person, rather than to others, if the originator has reason to believe that the person defamed will be under strong compulsion to republish the contents of the defamatory statement to a third person, the originator is liable for defamation.

c. **Republication.** Each publication of a libel is a separate and independent claim, and each must be pleaded as a separate cause of action. Lininger v. Knight, 226 P.2d 809 (Colo. 1951). See also TMJ Implants, Inc. v. Aetna, Inc., 498 F.3d 1175, 1196 (10th Cir. 2007) ("[O]ne who republishes a defamatory statement may be liable to the same extent as the original speaker because each publication causes a new harm to the plaintiff's reputation.") (quoting Restatement (Second) of Torts § 578 cmt. b (1977)). Colorado has not formally adopted but would probably apply the single publication rule. See Source & Authority to CJI-Civ. 22:24 (2012); see also Spears Free Clinic & Hosp. for Poor Children v. Maier, 261 P.2d 489 (Colo. 1953). Otherwise, because each republication constitutes a distinct claim for relief, Pittman v. Larson Distrib. Co., 724 P.2d 1379, 1387 (Colo. App. 1986), each republication, being a separate publication, also must be pleaded as such, see Spears, 261 P.2d 489 (Colo. 1953); Lininger, 226 P.2d 809 (Colo. 1951), and is subject to a discrete statute of limitations bar. See Walker v. Associated Press, 417 P.2d 486 (Colo. 1966); Corporon v. Safeway Stores, Inc., 708 P.2d 1385, 1390 (Colo. App. 1985). Only redelivery, rereading, or other repetition of a libelous statement to others than the person libeled by further voluntary act of the person making the statement constitutes republication of libel by him. See Spears, 261 P.2d 489 (Colo. 1953); **Sandmeier v. Sadler, 2012 WL 3155841 (D. Colo. July 20, 2012)**.

In addition to the republisher, the original publisher is also responsible for foreseeable republications as an element of damages. See CJI-Civ. 22:25 (2012). "The rationale for making the originator of a defamatory statement liable for its foreseeable republication is the strong causal link between the actions of the originator and the damage caused by the republication." See Churchey v. Adolph Coors Co., 759 P.2d 1336 (Colo. 1988) (superseded by statute with regard to republication by the subject of the libel, or self-publication, as noted at I.B.6(b) supra).

7. ***Statements versus Conduct.*** No reported cases found.

8. ***Damages.*** Actual damages available for defamation include economic and reputation damages, damages for personal humiliation, emotional distress, and mental anguish and suffering. See Hayes v. Smith, 832 P.2d 1022 (Colo. App. 1991). Because damages for personal humiliation, emotional distress, and mental anguish do not require initial proof of reputation or economic loss, a person will be compensated even if there is a failure of proof as to reputational or economic damages. New methods for proving economic and reputational damages in defamation cases, including expert testimony, lessen the need for per se classifications before plaintiffs can recover damages. See id.

In an action brought by a public official or public figure, actual damages are an essential element of the claim, whether per se or per quod, even if constitutional actual malice is proven. Keohane v. Stewart, 882 P.2d 1293 (Colo. 1994); Rowe v. Metz, 579 P.2d 83, 84 (Colo. 1978); Notes on Use to CJI-Civ. 22:1 (2012). In Keohane, the Court held that the plaintiff had adequately shown actual damage in the form of emotional distress that the plaintiff claimed to have suffered because these words had been uttered, even though the sole hearer of the remarks disclaimed receiving any defamatory meaning from them.

"'Special damages' are limited to specific monetary losses. Special damages 'must result from the conduct of a person other than the defamer or the one defamed and must be legally caused by the defamation.'" Lind v. O'Reilly, 636 P.2d 1319, 1321 (Colo. App. 1981) (citing Restatement (Second) of Torts § 575 cmt. b (1965)). The evidence of causation must be more than speculative. Sunward Corp. v. Dun & Bradstreet, Inc., 811 F.2d 511 (10th Cir. 1987). A plaintiff proceeding under a theory of libel per se need not plead or prove special damages. See Keohane v. Wilkerson, 859 P.2d 291 (Colo. App. 1993). However, a plaintiff asserting a claim of slander per quod must plead and prove special damages. See id.; Carani v. Meisner, 2010 WL 3023805, *2-4 (D. Colo. July 30, 2010). Damages for loss of reputation, absent evidence of pecuniary harm, are considered non-economic damages. See James v. Coors Brewing Co., 73 F. Supp. 2d 1250 (D. Colo. 1999).

a. **Presumed Damages and Libel Per Se.** The law presumes that damages result from the publication of words actionable per se. See Melcher v. Beeler, 110 P. 181 (Colo. 1910). Statements need not be defamatory per se, or on their face, in order to sustain a cause of action; where statements are defamatory on their face, the law merely presumes that the plaintiff incurred some damages and it therefore exempts such a plaintiff from the requirement of proving damages. See Williams v. Burns, 540 F. Supp. 1243 (D. Colo. 1982). The law presumes damages for a private plaintiff when the defendant commits a libel per se regardless of whether the defendant is a media outlet. Denver Publ. Co. v. Bueno, 54 P.3d 893 (Colo. 2002); Rowe v. Metz, 579 P.2d 83 (Colo. 1978).

Presumed damages are not recoverable by a public figure, or by a private individual when the publication involves a matter of public or general concern. See Keohane v. Stewart, 882 P.2d 1293 (Colo. 1994); Notes on Use to CJI-Civ. 22:1 (2012).

Accusations of homosexuality are not libel per se. Hayes v. Smith, 832 P.2d 1022 (Colo. App. 1991).

(1) **Employment-Related Criticism.** Publication of words that injuriously affect the profession, business, or employment of a person by imputing to him want of capacity or fitness to perform duties thereof is actionable per se. See Sky Fun 1, Inc. v. Schuttloffel, 8 P.3d 570, 574 (Colo. App. 2000), aff'd in relevant part, rev'd in part on other grounds, 27 P.3d 361 (Colo. 2001); Paris v. Div. of State Comp. Ins. Fund, 517 P.2d 1353 (Colo. App. 1973).

A corporate officer's statement referring to a former employee was slanderous per se where the officer stated to the employee personally, "Oh, by the way, I told [other officers] that you have done a bad job or terrible job" in the area of credit and collections, and the other officers had testified they had discussions with the corporate officer concerning "inadequacies" in the former employee's job performance. Meehan v. Amax Oil & Gas, Inc., 796 F. Supp. 461 (D. Colo. 1992).

(2) **Single Instance Rule.** Words claimed to be actionable per se must be taken in the context and in the light of all the circumstances attendant upon the utterances. See Cinquanta v. Burdett, 388 P.2d 779 (Colo. 1963). Words spoken in reference to one particular bill about which the parties were in dispute did not impute a general charge of mercantile dishonesty and, therefore, were not actionable. See id.

b. **Punitive Damages.** To recover punitive damages, the plaintiff must plead and prove that the injury complained of was attended by circumstances of fraud, malice, insult or a wanton and reckless disregard of the plaintiff's rights and feelings. See Colo. Rev. Stat. § 13-21-102. By statute, the amount of exemplary damages generally may not exceed an amount equal to the amount of actual damages awarded to the injured party, although the court has the discretion to increase an award of exemplary damages to a sum not to exceed three times the amount of actual damages under certain aggravated circumstances. See id.; Sky Fun 1, Inc. v. Schuttloffel, 27 P.3d 361, 370-71 (Colo. 2001) (reversing court of appeals' decision that upheld trial court's awarding of exemplary damages in the amount of $5,000.00). The Supreme Court held that this restriction on exemplary damages applies equally to bench and jury trials. Sky Fun 1, 27 P.3d at 370; see also Ramos v. City of Pueblo, 28 P.3d 979 (Colo. App. 2001). In James v. Coors Brewing Co., 73 F. Supp. 2d 1250 (D. Colo. 1999), the Court held that prejudgment interest on damages should be considered as a part of the "actual damages" in assessing an award of punitive damages under Colo. Rev. Stat. § 13-21-102. But see Vickery v. Vickery, --- P.3d ----, 2010 WL 963204 (Colo. App. Mar. 18, 2010), cert. granted, 2010 WL 4159683 (Oct. 18, 2010) (declining to follow James and affirming reduction of punitive damages based on amount of compensatory damages assessed by the jury without the addition of prejudgment interest).

Evidence of the income or net worth of a party may not be considered in determining the appropriateness or amount of such damages. Colo. Rev. Stat. § 13-21-102. The standard of proof for this element is beyond a reasonable doubt. Colo. Rev. Stat. § 13-25-127. This is an addition to the constitutional requirement that the plaintiff prove his case by clear and convincing evidence under the standard of New York Times v. Sullivan, 376 U.S. 254 (1964). Walker v. Colo. Springs Sun, Inc., 538 P.2d 450 (Colo. 1975).

II. PRIVILEGES AND DEFENSES

A. Scope of Privileges

1. ***Absolute Privilege.*** Colorado courts have taken a broad view of the traditional absolute privilege attaching to publications made in the course of and reasonably related to judicial, quasi-judicial or legislative proceedings. See, e.g., Renner v. Chilton, 351 P.2d 277 (Colo. 1960); Glasson v. Bowen, 267 P. 1066 (Colo. 1928); Buckhannon v. US W. Commc'ns., Inc., 928 P.2d 1331 (Colo. App. 1996). The defense of absolute privilege permits a defendant to escape liability for conduct that would otherwise be actionable on the ground that the defendant acted in furtherance of some interest of social importance entitled to protection even at the expense of uncompensated harm to the plaintiff's reputation, and the interest may be one of the defendant himself, of a third person, or of the general public. See Walters v. Linhof, 559 F. Supp. 1231 (D. Colo. 1983).

Communications relating to legislative and judicial proceedings and other acts of the state are absolutely privileged. See Lininger v. Knight, 226 P.2d 809 (Colo. 1951); Cache La Poudre Feeds v. Land O'Lakes, Inc., 438 F. Supp. 2d 1288 (D. Colo. 2006); see also Keenan v. Colo. Dep't of Human Servs., 2007 WL 2028118 (D. Colo. July 10, 2007) (holding that statements reporting that the defendants' board motions for plaintiff's termination for "failure to meet established job performance (as specified by the State of Colorado) and shoddy work" were likely covered by absolute privilege for communications relating to legislative and judicial proceedings and other acts of the state). Attorneys are absolutely privileged to make defamatory remarks during preparation for judicial proceeding so long as the remarks have some relation to the proceeding. See Buckhannon v. US W. Commc'ns., Inc., 928 P.2d 1331 (Colo. App. 1996). Statements of a public employee made in disciplinary proceedings against supervisor for sexual harassment were privileged as quasi-judicial statements, and were entitled to immunity from civil damages liability. However, this immunity does not extend to subsequent personnel disciplinary proceedings brought against her by the employer for making false statements in an official investigation. See Hoffler v. State Pers. Bd., 27 P.3d 371 (Colo. 2001); **cf. Churchill v. Univ. of Colo. at Boulder, 2012 WL 3900750 (Colo. Sept. 10, 2012) (discussing and applying standards for quasi-judicial immunity of public officials)**. In contrast, the court in Seidl v. Greentree Mortgage Co., 30 F. Supp. 2d 1292 (D. Colo. 1998), held that, under Colorado law, an attorney did not have an absolute privilege to make statements to the press or to post statements on the Internet for the purpose of publicizing the case. Likewise, in Moore v. Gunnison Valley Hospital, 170 F. Supp. 2d 1080 (D. Colo. 2001), the defendants, hospital administrators, were not entitled to absolute, quasi-judicial immunity from 42 U.S.C. § 1983 action for issuing letters of admonition and summarily suspending a doctor, where the committee was appointed on an *ad hoc* basis suggesting a threat of influence, and there were limited procedural and appeal rights. See also Partminer Worldwide Inc. v. Siliconexpert Techs. Inc., 2010 WL 502718, at *5 n.5 (D. Colo. Feb. 10, 2010) (expressing "doubt as to whether the privilege protects communications to third parties . . . that are unconnected to the pending lawsuit").

If a person requests, or consents to, publication of a matter that is defamatory, the resulting defamation is subject to an absolute privilege. See Dominquez v. Babcock, 696 P.2d 338 (Colo. App. 1984).

Statements concerning an employee contained in a report that had to be filed pursuant to the Workmen's Compensation Act following an accident in which the employee received injuries while driving a truck in the course of his employment were absolutely privileged. See Dorr v. C.B. Johnson, Inc., 660 P.2d 517 (Colo. App. 1983). However, the absolute privilege that attached to statements concerning the employee in the report filed pursuant to the Workmen's Compensation Act did not extend to allegedly defamatory statements concerning the employee published by the employer and a manager to third persons not involved in the workmen's compensation proceedings. See Dorr v. C.B. Johnson, Inc., 660 P.2d 517 (Colo. App. 1983).

In Smith v. Board of Education of School District Fremont RE-1, 2003 WL 21664790 (Colo. App. July 17, 2003), a former employee of a school district brought, among other claims, a claim for outrageous conduct and intentional infliction of emotional distress against her supervisor, alleging that he repeatedly pinched her under her arms, hovered over her, and made derogatory gestures and remarks. The jury returned a verdict in favor of defendant. Plaintiff appealed, claiming that the court gave an erroneous instruction to the jury because the court included an additional element to the outrageous conduct claim – that defendant's conduct was willful and wanton. The Court noted that under the Colorado Governmental Immunity Act, defendant was entitled to qualified immunity as a public employee, unless his conduct was willful and wanton. Thus, the Court held that because the burden of overcoming defendant's affirmative defense is on plaintiff, the additional element in the jury instruction properly shifted the burden of proof on the qualified immunity issue to plaintiff.

The common law doctrine of fair report protects a news provider from a defamation claim when it reports allegedly defamatory statements made during judicial proceedings, even if the reporter believes or knows the statements to be false. In Wilson v. Meyer, 126 P 3d 276 (Colo. App. 2005), the Court found that a newspaper's reporting of allegedly defamatory statements made during a public proceeding was also protected by the fair report doctrine.

A defamation or other related claim by a pastor against his or her former church, which cannot be evaluated independently from the church's decision to terminate the pastor's employment, is prohibited by both the Free Exercise Clause and the Establishment Clause of the First Amendment. In Seefried v. Hummel, 148 P.3d 184 (Colo. App. 2005), the Colorado Court of Appeals rejected defamation claims brought by pastors against their former church for statements made by church members during a public meeting called to make a determination as to their continued employment. Because an evaluation of the defamation allegations could not occur without a subjective evaluation of the members' choice of spiritual leaders, the Court had no authority to consider the plaintiffs' claims.

2. ***Qualified Privileges.*** Qualified privileged communications are those that are fairly made by a person in the discharge of some public or private duty, whether moral or legal, or in the conduct of his own affairs and in matters where his interest is concerned; the immunity that is conferred is not absolute but is conditioned upon publication in a reasonable manner and for a proper purpose. See Graziani v. Epic Data Corp., 305 F. Supp. 2d 1192, 1198 (D. Colo. 2004) (citing Sunward Corp. v. Dun & Bradstreet, Inc., 568 F. Supp. 602 (D. Colo. 1983)).

Qualified privilege can apply to inter-office memoranda, Abrahamsen v. Mountain States Tel. & Tel. Co., 494 P.2d 1287 (Colo. 1972), and it protects the right of corporate officers to communicate with one another about their employees' conduct. Denver Pub. Warehouse Co. v. Holloway, 83 P. 131 (Colo. 1905).

a. **Common Interest.** If persons involved share common interests in the subject matter of an allegedly defamatory statement, a qualified privilege exists. See Price v. Conoco, Inc., 748 P.2d 349 (Colo. App. 1987). A qualified privilege is extended to a communication upon any subject in which the communicating party has a legitimate interest to persons having a corresponding interest. See Coopersmith v. Williams, 468 P.2d 739 (Colo. 1970); cf. Signer v. Pimkova 2007 WL 4442327, at *5 (D. Colo. Dec. 14, 2007) (concluding that defendant was not entitled to the common interest privilege, in part, because there was no evidence to establish those receiving the defamatory statement had anything in common other than that they had invested money through the plaintiff stock broker).

Communications between members of fraternal, social, professional, religious or labor organizations concerning the conduct of other members or officers in their capacity as such are qualifiedly privileged. See Willenbucher v. McCormick, 229 F. Supp. 659 (D. Colo. 1964). The Colorado Supreme Court has stated that an employer's communication to an employee is subject to a qualified privilege because the interests of employers and employees in assuring that employees know the reasons for their discharges and are not fired based on mistaken beliefs outweigh any harm that the knowledge of a negative reason may cause an employee. Churchey v. Adolph Coors Co., 759 P.2d 1336 (Colo. 1988). In Price v. Conoco, Inc., 748 P.2d 349 (Colo. App. 1987), the Court held that the defendant's written evaluation of the plaintiff's work performance was subject to a qualified privilege, but the privilege may be lost if the plaintiff could show the privilege had been abused. Likewise, in Williams v. Continental Airlines, Inc., 943 P.2d 10 (Colo. App. 1996), the Court recognized a qualified privilege for statements made in the course of an employer's investigation of alleged sexual harassment. See also Sky Fun 1, Inc. v. Schuttloffel, 8 P.3d 570 (Colo. App. 2000) (comments of former employer, relating to employee's safety record and made to a prospective employer, were privileged but privilege was lost because comments were made with malicious intent of preventing employee from obtaining employment), aff'd in relevant part, rev'd in part on other grounds, 27 P.3d 361 (Colo. 2001).

Employees of a company share a common interest in information relating to turnover or status of personnel and thus, upon an employee being discharged, a qualified privilege exists for the employer to inform other employees of the reason for the change in personnel. See Patane v. Broadmoor Hotel, Inc., 708 P.2d 473 (Colo. App. 1985). See also Forgacs v. Eye Care Ctr. of N. Colo., 2006 WL 2331084, at *2 (D. Colo. Aug. 10, 2006) (holding that the qualified privilege employers have to communicate about personnel matters applies to statements made during staff meeting about plaintiff's alleged theft). Under Colorado law, alleged statements made by former employees to a former supervisor in the presence of another managerial employee at the former employees' termination interviews, accusing the former employees of falsifying records, were subject to a qualified privilege between the employer and the employee and, therefore, could not form the basis for a defamation claim. See Silchia v. MCI Telecomms. Corp., 942 F. Supp. 1369 (D. Colo. 1996).

In Graziani v. Epic Data Corp., 305 F. Supp. 2d 1192, 1198-99 (D. Colo. 2004), the Court granted summary judgment to co-defendant UPS, finding that a qualified privilege applied to UPS's statement to plaintiff's former employer, Epic Data, that plaintiff had attempted to embezzle funds owed by UPS to Epic Data. The Court found that the information related to a legitimate interest in plaintiff's business integrity, and that Epic Data and UPS shared a common interest as the payor and payee of the funds that plaintiff allegedly sought to embezzle. Id. at 1198-99. Further, the Court observed that no evidence showed that UPS had acted with malice. Id. at 1199. Based on the existence of a qualified privilege, and the absence of malice, summary judgment was entered in favor of UPS. Id.

In Thompson v. Public Service Co. of Colorado, 800 P.2d 1299 (Colo. 1990), the Colorado Supreme Court held that national labor policy does not preempt state law and does not require the recognition of an absolute privilege for statements germane to the subject made to persons involved in contractual grievance proceedings under a collective bargaining agreement. The Court held that a defamation action relating to such statements may go forward when state law recognizes a qualified privilege.

b. **Duty.** Communication to an employer concerning an employee is privileged only if made in good faith by one having an interest or duty, though the duty need not be a legal one. See Radovich v. Douglas, 268 P. 575 (Colo. 1928). In Williams v. Boyle, 72 P.3d 392 (Colo. App. 2003), the Colorado Court of Appeals held that "[a] qualified privilege exists for communications by a party with a legitimate interest or duty to persons having a corresponding interest or duty in communications promoting legitimate individual, group, or public interests."

c. **Criticism of Public Employee.** The actual malice standard set forth in New York Times v. Sullivan, 376 U.S. 254 (1964), holding that a public official suing a newspaper for libel must bear the burden of showing by clear and convincing evidence that the defamatory publication was made with actual malice, was meant to remove the inhibitory effect of defamation laws, in essence creating a constitutional privilege for good-faith critics of public officials. See Kuhn v. Tribune-Republican Publ'g Co., 637 P.2d 315 (Colo. 1981). Unless the alleged defamatory statements are published with actual malice, that is, with knowledge that the statements are false or with reckless disregard for whether they are false or not, the reporting of a matter involving a public official is protected. See Russell v. McMillen, 685 P.2d 255 (Colo. App. 1984).

d. **Limitation on Qualified Privileges.** A qualified privilege will be lost if the plaintiff shows that the privilege has been abused; thus, if a person making a defamatory statement is motivated primarily by purposes other than the protection of the interest for which the privilege was given, the privilege is negated. See Sky Fun 1, Inc. v. Schuttloffel, 8 P.3d 570 (Colo. App. 2000), aff'd in relevant part, rev'd in part on other grounds, 27 P.3d 361 (Colo. 2001); Price v. Conoco, Inc., 748 P.2d 349 (Colo. App. 1987).

(1) **Constitutional or Actual Malice.** One who publishes defamatory or false material loses the qualified privilege for that publication if he publishes the material with malice, that is, knowing the matter to be false, or acting in reckless disregard as to its veracity. See Dominquez v. Babcock, 727 P.2d 362 (Colo. 1986); Cache La Poudre Feeds v. Land O'Lakes, Inc., 438 F. Supp. 2d 1288 (D. Colo. 2006).

To establish malice, a plaintiff must produce clear and convincing evidence that the defamation was published with actual knowledge of its falsity or in reckless disregard for its truth or falsity; reckless disregard exists when the defendant, in fact, entertained serious doubts about truth of his publication. See In re Green, 11 P.3d 1078, 1085 (Colo. 2000). The mere falsity of a statement alone cannot establish malice. Ling v. Whittemore, 343 P.2d 1048, 1051 (Colo. 1959). If a qualified privilege exists, mere negligence cannot supply the malice requirement for a defamation claim. See Williams v. Cont'l Airlines, Inc., 943 P.2d 10, 16 (Colo. App. 1996); Dominguez v. Babcock, 696 P.2d 338 (Colo. App. 1984), aff'd, 727 P.2d 362 (Colo. 1986).

(2) **Common Law Malice.** The Court in People v. Ryan, 806 P.2d 935, 938 (Colo. 1991) defined common law malice as spite or ill will. In Sky Fun 1, Inc. v. Schuttloffel, 8 P.3d 570 (Colo. App. 2000), aff'd in relevant part, rev'd in part on other grounds, 27 P.3d 361 (Colo. 2001), the Court of Appeals held that a privilege "will be lost if the publisher is actuated by express malice." There, a former employer lost its qualified privilege to make defamatory statements about the safety record of the former employee (a pilot) to a prospective employer because the former employer made the statements "with some malice," intending "to stop or alter the career of defendant" and the statements "were not made to protect the safety of the flying public, but instead to preclude defendant's employment." Id. at 575-75. The Colorado Supreme Court, affirming in relevant part on appeal, noted that it was the case that the speaker knew the statements to be false, or made in reckless disregard of their truth or falsity. See Sky Fun 1, Inc. v. Schuttloffel, 27 P.3d 361, 368 (Colo. 2001).

(3) **Other Limitations on Qualified Privileges.** The Colorado cases discussing the circumstances under which the qualified privilege may be lost focus primarily upon malice. However, the privilege may also be lost where the defendant abuses the privilege in one of the following ways: (a) defendant "knew the statement to be false, or acted with reckless disregard for whether the statement was false;" (b) defendant "acted primarily for purposes other than the protection of the interest for which the privilege was given;" (c) defendant "knowingly published the statement to a person to whom its publication was not otherwise privileged, unless [s/he] reasonably believed that the publication was a proper means of communicating such matter to the person to whom its publication was privileged;" or (d) defendant "did not reasonably believe the publication of the statement to be necessary to accomplish the purpose for which the privilege was given." CJI-Civ. 22:18 (2012).

e. **Question of Fact or Law.** Whether a qualified privilege protects a communication is a question of law requiring the court to balance the interest protected by the privilege and the interest served by allowing the defamation action. See Churchey v. Adolph Coors Co., 759 P.2d 1336 (Colo. 1988); Graziani v. Epic Data Corp., 305 F. Supp. 2d 1192, 1198 (D. Colo. 2004).

f. **Burden of Proof.** In Dominguez v. Babcock, 727 P.2d 362 (Colo. 1986), the Colorado Supreme Court held that where the alleged defamatory matter is qualifiedly privileged, the plaintiff, to defeat a motion for summary judgment, must show a genuine factual issue as to the existence of actual malice. See also Churchey v. Adolph Coors Co., 759 P.2d 1336 (Colo. 1988).

To prove a claim for defamation against an employer, a plaintiff must show that the employer published a false statement of defamatory fact. See Thompson v. Pub. Serv. Co. of Colo., 800 P.2d 1299, 1306 (Colo. 1990). If the communication is protected by a "qualified privilege," then the plaintiff may recover only if he proves that the defendant "published the material with malice, that is, knowing the matter to be false, or acted with reckless disregard as to its veracity." Id.

B. Standard Libel Defenses

1. ***Truth.*** In civil or criminal libel actions brought by public officials, truth is an absolute defense. See People v. Ryan, 806 P.2d 935 (Colo. 1991); Gordon v. Boyles, 99 P.3d 75, 81 (Colo. App. 2004). The common-law tort of defamation only requires the plaintiff to prove the defendant's publication of the defamatory statement by a preponderance of the evidence, and the defendant then may assert truth as an affirmative defense. See Smiley's Too, Inc. v. Denver Post Corp., 935 P.2d 39 (Colo. App. 1996).

To assert truth as a defense to a libel claim, the defendant need not prove the literal truth of the statement. Rather, Colorado courts have adopted the notion of "substantial truth" as a defense. That is, the "defendant asserting truth as a defense in a libel action is not required to justify every word of the alleged defamatory matter; it is sufficient if the substance, the gist, the sting, of the matter is true." Gomba v. McLaughlin, 504 P.2d 337, 338 (Colo. 1972); see also Gordon v. Boyles, 99 P.3d 75, 81 (Colo. App. 2004); **Rose Bud Catering v. Street Eats Ltd., 2012 WL 468522 (D. Colo. Feb. 13, 2012) (granting summary judgment for defendants on defamation claim based on defendants' undisputed affidavit and exhibits showing the alleged defamatory statements were true)**; Broker's Choice of Am., Inc. v. NBC Universal, Inc., 2011 WL 97236, 39 Media L. Rep. 1557 (D. Colo. Jan. 11, 2011) (holding that several allegedly defamatory statements were substantially true). Courts in other jurisdictions recognize that the substantial truth defense may not be available where the facts published are substantially true but the defendant "omitted material facts which caused the publication to create a defamation impression." See Allen v. Nelnet, Inc., 2007 WL 2786432 (D. Colo. Sept. 24, 2007) (citing cases from other jurisdictions). However, Colorado appellate courts have not yet addressed this issue. See id. The determination of whether an allegedly defamatory statement is true is an issue of fact, and the relevant inquiry is whether a substantial difference exists between the truth and the allegedly libelous statement. Gomba, 504 P.2d at 339; Gordon, 99 P.3d at 81; see also Bustos v. A & E Television Network, 646 F.3d 762, 39 Media L. Rep. 2049 (10th Cir. 2011) (noting that defamation requires significant impact on the plaintiff's public reputation when compared to the truth and holding that it was not defamation to say a prisoner was a member of the Aryan Brotherhood when he in fact merely conspired with the Brotherhood).

2. ***Opinion.*** In NBC Subsidiary (KCNC-TV), Inc. v. Living Will Center., 879 P.2d 6 (Colo. 1994), the Colorado Supreme Court recognized the Milkovich v. Lorain Journal Co., 497 U.S. 1 (1990) test of (1) whether a statement is verifiable and (2) whether it is susceptible of being understood as an assertion of actual fact, but held that the Milkovich formulation did not represent a departure from prior Colorado law. The Court declared that Colorado courts would continue to utilize the contextual factors adopted and applied in pre-Milkovich decisions in determining whether a statement reasonably could be understood to convey a factual proposition: first, the phrasing of the statement and the use of terms of apparency; second, the entirety of the statement, not just the objectionable word or phrase, and the context in which it appears; and third, all the circumstances surrounding the statement, including the medium through which it is disseminated and the audience to whom it is directed. In applying these factors, the courts also should consider whether the statement implies the existence of undisclosed facts that support it.

In general, statements of pure opinion cannot be the basis of a libel claim because they are constitutionally privileged. See NBC Subsidiary (KCNC-TV) v. Living Will Ctr., 879 P.2d 6, 9 (Colo. 1994); In re Green, 11 P.3d 1078, 1084 (Colo. 2000); Wilson v. Meyer, 2005 Colo. App. LEXIS 1346, 8-10 (Colo. App. Aug. 25, 2005); Brudwick v. Minor, 2006 WL 1991755 (D. Colo. July 13, 2006). However, a statement in the form of an opinion is actionable under Colorado law if it implies the allegation of undisclosed defamatory facts as the basis of the opinion. See TMJ Implants, Inc. v. Aetna, Inc., 498 F.3d 1175, 1183 (10th Cir. 2007); Simmons v. Prudential Ins. Co. of America, 641 F. Supp. 675 (D. Colo. 1986); cf. In re Green, 11 P.3d 1078, 1084 (Colo. 2000) (holding attorney could be disciplined for statements of opinion, that labeled a judge a "racist and bigot," if the comments implied an undisclosed false statement of fact).

Although an opinion that implies the existence of undisclosed false facts is not permitted, an opinion is absolutely protected when the author sets forth the facts upon which it is based. See Reddick v. Craig, 719 P.2d 340 (Colo.

App. 1985). An erroneous opinion is constitutionally protected under Colorado law and cannot be the subject of a defamation action. Id. In addition, a statement of opinion relating to matters of public concern is actionable only if it contains *provably* false facts. See TMJ Implants, Inc. v. Aetna, Inc., 405 F. Supp. 2d 1242 (D. Colo. 2005) (emphasis added), aff'd, 498 F.3d 1175 (10th Cir. 2007) (holding that the defendant's statement of opinion was not actionable because it related to a matter of public concern and depended, at least in part, on factors not provably true or false); cf. Wedbush Morgan Sec., Inc. v. Kirkpatrick Pettis Capital Mgmt., Inc., 2007 WL 1097872 (D. Colo. Apr. 9, 2007) (holding that statements about a matter of public concern that were evaluations based on subjective factors were protected under the fair comment privilege).

3. ***Consent.*** Consent is a complete defense to a defamation claim under some circumstances, see Churchey v. Adolph Coors Co., 759 P.2d 1336 (Colo. 1988), but only to the extent of that consent. See Dominquez v. Babcock, 727 P.2d 362 (Colo. 1986). Furthermore, if a party requests the reasons motivating another person's actions, the party consents to publication of those reasons. Id.

In Costa v. Smith, 601 P.2d 661 (Colo. App. 1979) two co-workers were discussing their jobs as data-processors while at a party. The plaintiff suggested that they work together, but the defendant said he would not consider working with the plaintiff. The plaintiff asked why the defendant would not work with him, and the defendant responded that the plaintiff was an incompetent word processor. The Court found that the plaintiff consented to the defendant's defamatory remarks by demanding to know the defendant's reasons for not wanting to work with him. Id.

4. ***Mitigation.*** A defendant in a defamation action may present any evidence that tends to mitigate damages. See Williams v. Dist. Court, Second Judicial Dist., City & Cnty. of Denver, 866 P.2d 908 (Colo. 1993). Such evidence may include any publications by third persons that deal with same subject and were made before or at about the same time as the date of publishing by the defendant. See id.

5. ***Sovereign Immunity.*** A state employee who makes potentially defamatory statements while performing within the scope of his or her employment will be immune from tort liability for defamation. Gallagher v. Board of Trustees for the Univ. of N. Colo., 54 P.3d 386 (Colo. 2002). See also Romero v. Denver Pub. Schs., Dist. No. 1, 2010 WL 1235635, at *5 (D. Colo. Mar. 18, 2010) (applying Colorado Governmental Immunity Act and dismissing libel per se claim against public school employee's supervisor).

III. RECURRING FACT PATTERNS

A. Statements in Personnel File

Although a qualified privilege protected an employer's statements in a letter of reprimand, a copy of which was placed in the employee's personnel file, the employee could recover on a libel claim by showing that the employer published the material knowing it to be false or acted with reckless disregard as to its veracity. Thompson v. Pub. Serv. Co. of Colo., 800 P.2d 1299 (Colo. 1990); **see also Garland v. Bd. of Educ., 2012 WL 1018740 (D. Colo. Mar. 26, 2012) (noting that malice "is required under the qualified privilege applicable to many employer statements about employee conduct").**

The Pilot Records Improvement Act, 49 U.S.C. § 44936(g), prevents lawsuits "based on the pilot records provided to a potential employer, including the personnel records, and oral statements made in connection with explaining the circumstances and contents of such records." Sky Fun 1 v. Schuttloffel, 27 P.3d 361, 368 (Colo. 2001). However, this provision did not prevent a pilot's defamation action where his former employer's "defamatory statements were either knowingly false or made in reckless disregard of the truth and were not based on records the [former] employer was required to transmit to the prospective pilot employer." Id. at 371.

B. Performance Evaluations

A written evaluation of an employee's performance prepared by his immediate supervisor, former supervisor and manager, was subject to a qualified privilege, but the privilege could be lost if the plaintiff could show that the privilege had been abused. See Price v. Conoco, Inc., 748 P.2d 349 (Colo. App. 1987). In Moore v. Gunnison Valley Hospital, 170 F. Supp. 2d 1080 (D. Colo. 2001) the defendant hospital administrators were not entitled to absolute, quasi-judicial immunity for issuing letters of admonition and summarily suspending a doctor, where committee was appointed on an *ad hoc* basis leading to a threat of influence, and there were limited procedural and appeal rights. The complaint was also held sufficient to survive a motion to dismiss on the basis of qualified immunity, where the plaintiff alleged he had no patients at the hospital and thus there was no factual basis for an emergency suspension to protect hospital patients. See id.

C. References

Colorado's Employee Reference Statute provides qualified immunity from civil liability to an employer who provides information about a current or former employee's job history or job performance to a prospective employer upon request of the employee or prospective employer. This immunity is lost if the employee can show by a preponderance of evidences both: (1) the information the employer disclosed was false and (2) the employer knew or reasonably should have known that the information was false. See Colo. Rev. Stat. § 8-2-114(3). Under this same statute, it is unlawful for an employer to "blacklist" an employee. That is, an employer may not maintain a blacklist or notify another employer that a current or former employee has been blacklisted. See Colo. Rev. Stat. § 8-2-114(2). Any person, firm, or corporation who violates this statute is guilty of a misdemeanor.

An elementary school teacher's defamation claim failed as a matter of law because the teacher did not establish the falsity of the principal's alleged statements to a prospective employer, knowledge or reckless disregard of such falsity, or willfulness or wantonness generally. See Zerr v. Johnson, 894 F. Supp. 372 (D. Colo. 1995). In Sky Fun 1 v. Schuttloffel, 8 P.3d 570 (Colo. App. 2000), the court held that while a written "Termination Report" concerning a pilot was privileged under the Pilot Records Improvement Act ("PRIA"), 49 U.S.C. § 44936(g), oral statements to the employee's prospective employer were not. The Colorado Supreme Court granted certiorari as to the oral statements and affirmed on this issue, holding that the PRIA does not pre-empt a common law defamation claim for "verbal assertions that the speaker knew to be false or the speaker made in reckless disregard of the truth, when the verbal statements are not based upon the previous employer's records." See Sky Fun 1 v. Schuttloffel, 27 P.3d 361, 368 (Colo. 2001). The Court of Appeals had previously held, in an issue not explicitly considered on certiorari, that the oral comments lost their common law qualified privilege because the former employer made them with (common law) malice in an attempt to "stop or alter" the pilot's career. See Sky Fun 1 v. Schuttloffel, 8 P.3d 570 (Colo. App. 2000).

D. Intracorporate Communication

With regard to communication of allegedly libelous interoffice memoranda, the privilege with regard to the communication is qualified and not absolute, and will be lost where the publishers are actuated by express malice. See Abrahamsen v. Mountain States Tel. & Tel. Co., 494 P.2d 1287 (Colo. 1972).

Although an employer's statements in a letter stating reasons for disciplinary action were subject to a qualified privilege, the employee could still recover on a libel claim by showing that the employer published the material knowing it to be false or acted with reckless disregard as to its veracity. See Thompson v. Pub. Serv. Co. of Colo., 800 P.2d 1299 (Colo. 1990). In an unpublished case, the Tenth Circuit Court of Appeals stated it was in "general accord" with the proposition that "circulation of a statement within an institution or agency does not, by itself, constitute publication." See Mercer v. Bd. of Trs., 2001 WL 980760 (10th Cir. Aug. 28, 2001).

E. Statements to Government Regulators

No reported cases found.

F. Reports to Auditors and Insurers

An action for libel by an employee against his employer based on claims filed by the employer with a surety company by which the employee was bonded to secure reimbursement for alleged irregularities was not barred by the fact that such claims were privileged, since the privilege was only qualified, but the employee had the burden of overcoming the privilege by proof of actual malice. See Interstate Transit Lines v. Crane, 100 F.2d 857 (10th Cir. 1939).

G. Vicarious Liability of Employers for Statements Made by Employees

1. ***Scope of Employment.*** A principal may be sued for slander committed by an agent without the agent being named as a defendant, if the agent acted within the course and scope of his agency, or if the agent was outside the scope of his agency and the defamation was ratified by the principal. See Kendall v. Lively, 31 P.2d 343 (Colo. 1934); Gordon v. Boyles, 99 P.3d 75, 82 (Colo. App. 2004) (finding that plaintiff had produced evidence sufficient to create issue of fact on whether talk show host's statements were made within the scope of employment). However, those who only deliver or transmit the defamatory statement, e.g., a newsboy, are not liable for republication because they do not "publish" the statement. Notes on Use to CJI-Civ. 22:7 (2012).

a. **Blogging** No reported cases found.

2. ***Damages.*** Where statements are actionable per se and vicariously attributed to an employer, requiring the employer to pay damages is reasonable since damages are presumed. See Kendall v. Lively, 31 P.2d 343 (Colo. 1934).

H. Internal Investigations

Statements made during the course of an employer's internal investigation into employee wrongdoing may be the subject of a defamation claim. See Williams v. Cont'l Airlines, Inc., 943 P.2d 10, 20 (Colo. App. 1996) (affirming trial court's slander verdict for plaintiff based on manager's statements made during course of employer's internal investigation for sexual harassment). Colorado has refused to recognize a separate tort claim for "negligent investigation." See id. In addition, where a court determines a communication during an investigation is subject to a qualified privilege and plaintiff is attempting to show abuse, a failure to investigate or a negligent investigation alone are not sufficient to show actual malice. See, e.g., Dominguez v. Babcock, 696 P.2d 338 (Colo. App. 1984), aff'd, 727 P.2d 362 (Colo. 1986).

IV. OTHER ACTIONS BASED ON STATEMENTS

A. Negligent Hiring, Retention, and Supervision

Colorado has recognized the tort of negligent hiring in cases where an employer hires a person under circumstances that give the employer reason to believe that the person, by reason of some attribute of character or prior conduct, would create an undue risk of harm to others in carrying out his or her employment responsibilities. See Connes v. Molalla Transp. Sys., Inc., 831 P.2d 1316 (Colo. 1992); Van Osdol v. Vogt, 908 P.2d 1122 (Colo. 1996).

The negligent hiring doctrine subjects an employer to liability for acts of an employee even if the employee's improper acts are not within the scope of his employment. Moses v. Diocese of Colorado, 863 P.2d 310 (Colo. 1993). But see State Farm Fire & Cas. Co. Inc., v. United States, 2008 WL 5083502 (D. Colo. Nov. 25, 2008) (where U.S. Forest Service employee accidentally started a fire in violation of a fire ban which resulted in destruction of property, the employee acted in violation of a policy established by the employer and thus the requirements for vicarious liability were not met).

The elements of a negligent hiring claim are: (1) an employment or agency relationship existed between the defendant and the employee; (2) the defendant owed the plaintiff a duty to exercise reasonable care in hiring the employee; (3) the defendant breached that duty; (4) the plaintiff suffered injury; and (5) there is a sufficient causal relationship between the defendant's breach of duty and the plaintiff's injury. Connes v. Molalla Transp. Sys., Inc., 831 P.2d 1316, 1320 (Colo. 1992). See also Johnson v. USA Truck, Inc., 2007 WL 2461645 (D. Colo. Aug. 27, 2007) (denying defendant employer's summary judgment motion on negligent hiring claim because plaintiff presented evidence that defendant employer knew, prior to hiring employee, about employee's unsatisfactory safety record from previous position); Prymak v. Contemporary Fin. Solutions, Inc., 2007 WL 4250020 (D. Colo. Nov. 29, 2007) (holding the primary inquiry in negligent hiring actions is "whether *at the time of hiring* the employer had reason to foresee the complained of harm") (citation omitted).

Whether an employment or agency relationship existed between the defendant and the employee is a question of fact. Moses v. Diocese of Colo., 863 P.2d 310, 324 (Colo. 1993). By contrast, whether the defendant owed a duty to exercise reasonable care in hiring the employee is a question of law for the court to decide. See Casebolt v. Cowan, 829 P.2d 352, 356 (Colo. 1992). Such a duty arises when there is a foreseeable risk of injury to others from defendant's conduct or failure to act. Connes, 831 P.2d at 1320. The scope of that duty will turn on the "anticipated degree of contact which the employee will have with other persons in performing his or her duties." Id. at 1321. Where an employee will have little or no contact with members of the public in performing his duties, the employer may have no duty to investigate the job applicant's background. Where an employee will have frequent contact with the public, however, the employer should conduct a background check on the applicant by verifying the applicant's employment history, calling references and past employers, asking the applicant about any gaps in his employment record, and even seeking to obtain any criminal records pertaining to the job applicant with the applicant's consent.

In Dolin v. Contemporary Financial Solutions, Inc., 622 F. Supp. 2d 1077 (D. Colo. 2009), the court found that the defendant employer owed the plaintiff investors a duty of care even though the plaintiffs did not have an account with the defendants. Referencing a case involving the same Ponzi scheme, the court reasoned that regardless of whether the plaintiffs had a formal account with defendant, once a fiduciary relationship is established between a broker and a client, it necessarily extends to the broker-dealer. Id. at 1083. The court held that by allowing the employee to act as a registered representative of the employer, the defendant employer essentially sanctioned his relationship with the client-plaintiffs as a securities dealer and thus created a special relationship and corresponding duty of care to the plaintiffs. Id. at 1084.

The tort of negligent supervision also has been recognized in Colorado. In Moses v. Diocese of Colorado, 863 P.2d 310, 329 (Colo. 1993), the Colorado Supreme Court held that an employer may be liable for negligent supervision if it knows or should have known that an employee's conduct would subject third parties to an unreasonable risk of harm. The tort arises from allegations that the employee was improperly supervised and that the plaintiff was injured as a result. See Restatement (Second) of Agency § 213 (1958). In Destefano v. Grabrian, 763 P.2d 275, 287-88 (Colo. 1988), the Colorado Supreme Court reversed the Colorado Court of Appeals' dismissal of the plaintiff's negligent supervision claim, holding that the plaintiff's allegations that she was injured as a result of having been seduced by a clergyman/marriage counselor whose employer knew or should have known of his propensity to engage in such misconduct but failed to supervise him properly were sufficient to state a claim for relief. In a case involving claims that a radio station was negligent in supervising a talk show host who had broadcast allegedly defamatory statements, the Colorado Court of Appeals reversed an award of summary judgment in favor of the radio station, finding that the station "had no internal practices or procedures to determine whether its employees were evaluating the credibility of confidential sources." Gordon v. Boyles, 99 P.3d 75, 81 (Colo. App. 2004).

Negligent retention is a distinct concept involving allegations that an employer improperly retained an employee after the employer knew or should have known that the employee's conduct could cause harm to a third person. Restatement (Second) of Torts § 317 (1965). Nevertheless, it has in common with the torts of negligent hiring and negligent supervision the concept that an employer may be liable if it knew or should have known that an employee's attributes or prior conduct presented an unreasonable risk of harm. See Van Osdol v. Vogt, 892 P.2d 402, 408 (Colo. App. 1994), aff'd, 908 P.2d 1122 (Colo. 1996).

Colorado has refused to recognize a separate tort claim for "negligent investigation" based upon statements made during course of a sexual harassment investigation. See Williams v. Cont'l Airlines, Inc., 943 P.2d 10 (Colo. App. 1996).

The statute of limitations for claims for negligent hiring, supervision, and retention is two years from the date of accrual. Colo. Rev. Stat. § 13-80-102(1)(a). Sandoval v. Archdiocese of Denver, 8 P.3d 598 (Colo. App. 2000) concerned claims of negligence, respondeat superior and ratification, and outrageous conduct against the principal and the owner and entity in control of a school where a teacher had a four-year sexual relationship with a student. The Court held that the two year statute of limitations in Section 13-80-102(1)(a) governed the claims against the principal and the archdiocese, not Section 13-80-103.7, which provides a six-year period of limitations in cases "based on a sexual offense against a child." See id. Claims against public or governmental entities, however, may be governed by the one-year limitations period established by Section § 13-80-103.

B. Intentional Infliction of Emotional Distress

The tort of intentional infliction of emotional distress has four elements: (1) the defendant engaged in extreme and outrageous conduct; (2) recklessly or with the intent of causing the plaintiff severe emotional distress; (3) the plaintiff suffered severe emotional distress; and (4) the distress was caused by the defendant's conduct. CJI-Civ. 23:1 (2012); see Restatement (Second) of Torts § 46 (1965). The Colorado Supreme Court adopted this tort in Rugg v. McCarty, 476 P.2d 753, 756 (Colo. 1970). The Rugg Court emphasized that the conduct alleged to have distressed the plaintiff must truly be offensive, stating that the defendant's behavior must have "been so outrageous in character, and so extreme in degree, as to go beyond all possible bounds of decency, and to be regarded as atrocious, and utterly intolerable in a civilized community." 476 P.2d at 756. The Rugg Court continued that, for facts to be actionable under the intentional infliction of emotional distress tort, they must be such that their "recitation . . . would arouse . . . resentment" against the defendant of "an average member of the community" and "lead him to exclaim, 'Outrageous.'" Id.; see also Churchey v. Adolph Coors Co., 759 P.2d 1336, 1349-51 (Colo. 1988); Brudwick v. Minor, 2006 WL 1991755 (D. Colo. July 13, 2006) (noting that claims for intentional infliction of emotional distress and outrageous conduct are essentially the same). In a similar vein, the Tenth Circuit has explained that the defendant's conduct must be more than just "unreasonable, unkind, or unfair; it must truly offend community notions of acceptable conduct." Grandchamp v. United Air Lines, 854 F.2d 381, 383 (10th Cir. 1988). While the conduct must be outrageous, atrocious, or utterly intolerable, it does not need to be physical or coercive in nature; verbal conduct alone may be sufficient. Archer v. Farmer Bros. Co., 70 P.3d 495 (Colo. App. 2002).

In general, Colorado courts will recognize an intentional infliction of emotional distress claim only when the defendant "has engaged in a pattern of conduct that either was intended to cause or recklessly did cause severe emotional distress." Rawson v. Sears Roebuck & Co., 530 F. Supp. 776, 780 (D. Colo. 1982) (emphasis added). Nevertheless, "it is possible for a single, isolated activity to be a sufficient basis for a cause of action," as "where a public or quasi-public official has severely abused his discretion or a private individual has blatantly and severely harassed another." Id.; see also Llewellyn v. Shearson Fin. Network, Inc., 622 F. Supp. 2d 1062 (D. Colo. 2009) (recognizing a valid claim for outrageous conduct where defendant creditor knowingly reported false information about plaintiff borrower's loan being in default to credit reporting agencies despite the plaintiff advising defendant of the inaccuracy of that information). The totality of the circumstances must be considered in determining whether "outrageous conduct" is alleged. Zalnis v. Thoroughbred Datsun Car Co., 645 P.2d 292, 294 (Colo. App. 1982). Importantly, Colorado courts will characterize a defendant's actions as outrageous only in the most extremely egregious circumstances, where the alleged conduct was "so extreme in degree as to go beyond all possible bounds of decency so as to be regarded as atrocious and utterly intolerable in a civilized community." Green v. Qwest Services Corp., 155 P.3d 383, 385 (Colo. App. 2006) (quoting Destefano v. Grabrian, 763 P.2d 275, 286 (Colo. 1988); Bob Blake Builders, Inc. v. Gramling, 18 P.3d 859, 865 (Colo. App. 2001)). In addition, it is the nature of the defendant's conduct, and not the consequences of that conduct, which must be sufficiently egregious so as to establish a cause of action for outrageous conduct. Green, 155 P.3d at 385-87 (holding that while the result of defendants' grossly negligent conduct, which included the loss of an entire home, was severe, the defendants' conduct itself was accidental and not sufficiently egregious to establish a cause of action for outrageous conduct).

Proof of physical injury resulting from the outrageous conduct is not required, but proof of severe emotional distress is required. Espinosa v. Sheridan United Tire, 655 P.2d 424 (Colo. App. 1982). The Colorado Jury Instructions on intentional infliction of emotional distress define "severe emotional distress" as "highly unpleasant mental reactions . . . so extreme that no person of ordinary sensibilities could be expected to tolerate and endure it." CJI-Civ. 23:4 (2012). The duration and intensity of the distress are factors to be considered in determining whether it is "severe." Id.

The items of damages recoverable for intentional infliction of emotional distress may include: (1) emotional distress, such as nervous shock, fright, horror, grief, shame, humiliation, embarrassment, anger, chagrin, disappointment, or worry; (2) any physical discomfort or inconvenience; (3) any physical illness or injury; (4) any reasonable medical expenses; (5) any loss of reputation; (6) any loss of earnings; and (7) any other elements of compensable damage for which there is sufficient evidence. CJI-Civ. 23:6 (2012). However, there is no Colorado authority for "loss of reputation" as a compensable item of damages for intentional infliction of emotional distress. Pecuniary losses are recoverable if they are a natural consequence of the defendant's conduct. Meiter v. Cavanaugh, 580 P.2d 399 (Colo. 1978). Punitive damages are recoverable if the plaintiff pleads and proves that the injury was attended by circumstances of fraud, malice, insult, or a wanton and disregard for the plaintiff's rights and feelings. Colo. Rev. Stat. § 13-21-102. The standard of proof for an award of punitive damages is beyond a reasonable doubt. Colo. Rev. Stat. § 13-25-127.

It is clear that an intentional infliction of emotional distress claim can arise in the employment context. For example, in Gwin v. Chesrown Chevrolet, Inc., 931 P.2d 466 (Colo. App. 1996), a black employee who alleged that his termination was motivated by race discrimination and accompanied by public humiliation and abusive treatment stated a claim for intentional infliction of emotional distress. Similarly, in Barham v. Scalia, 928 P.2d 1381, 1386 (Colo. App. 1996), a tenured professor who alleged that the dean had tried to have him removed from his job for personal reasons and instructed other faculty not to communicate with him stated an intentional infliction of emotional distress claim. In Pearson v. Kancilia, 70 P.3d 594 (Colo. App. 2003), the court held that there was sufficient evidence to support the jury's finding that a chiropractor engaged in outrageous conduct against his employee, who alleged that he forced her to have sex with him, by exploiting his position of authority over the employee to obtain what he wanted. However, in Pascouau v. Martin Marietta Corp., 185 F.3d 874 (10th Cir. 1999) (unpublished), the court held that comments made to a woman who alleged sexual harassment in the workplace and the conduct of her co-workers, although sexually explicit, immature, and rude, were not "egregious" enough for any reasonable juror to find they constitute outrageous conduct. In addition, in Coors Brewing Co. v. Floyd, 978 P.2d 663 (Colo. 1999), the court held that the employer's conduct, in instructing the employee to conduct an illegal undercover narcotics investigation, laundering money to fund the investigation and firing the employee as a scapegoat to cover up the employer's involvement in the criminal activity, was not sufficiently outrageous to support the employee's claim for intentional infliction of emotional distress. The court held that the outrageousness of the employer's conduct towards society, rather than the individual employee, is irrelevant. Furthermore, in Gruppo v. Fedex Freight Systems, Inc., 2007 WL 1964080 (D. Colo. June 29, 2007), the court held that a supervisor's "brusque," "demanding," and "insensitive" conduct toward an employee was not sufficiently "indecent and atrocious" to support a claim for outrageous conduct. In LaBrecque v. L3 Communications Titan Corp., 2007 WL 1455850 (D. Colo. May 16, 2007), aff'd sub nom. Sydnes v. United States, 523 F.3d 1179 (10th Cir. 2008) the court granted summary judgment for the employer because derogatory statements made by a supervisor about the employees, requiring employees to move their workspace to a different building far from their worksite, and the employees' termination, which was accompanied by insults and indignities, were not sufficiently outrageous to support a claim for intentional infliction of emotional distress. Also, in Silver v. Primero Reorganized School District, 2008 WL 700171 (D. Colo. Mar. 13, 2008), the court held that a principal's conduct of sending emails, leaving thirty phone messages, and following the plaintiff (teacher's aide) on at least two occasions was not outrageous conduct because the plaintiff never specifically asked the defendant to cease his activities, and the plaintiff and the defendant had been involved in a lengthy, consensual, romantic relationship.

On the other hand, Colorado courts have made clear that a termination from employment by itself is insufficient to support an intentional infliction of emotional distress claim, even when the termination allegedly violates a contractual promise or handbook provision on which the plaintiff purportedly relied. See Therrien v. United Air Lines, Inc., 670 F. Supp. 1517, 1524 (D. Colo. 1987) (citing Colorado cases); see also, e.g., Steinbach v. Dillion Cos., Inc., 253 F.3d 538, 541 (10th. Cir. 2001); Barham v. Scalia, 928 P.2d 1381, 1385 (Colo. App. 1996).

Claims for intentional infliction of emotional distress based on employment actions accompanied by allegedly defamatory remarks have not fared well either. In Pierce v. St. Vrain Valley School District RE-1J, 944 P.2d 646 (Colo. App. 1997), rev'd on other grounds, 981 P.2d 600 (Colo. 1999), the plaintiff, a school superintendent, commenced an intentional infliction of emotional distress against a school board for revealing to the press the fact that he had been asked to resign following an investigation into his sexually harassing conduct, despite their agreement to keep such information confidential. The Court of Appeals affirmed summary judgment in the school board's favor, holding that "[a] public figure may not maintain a claim for outrageous conduct when the conduct complained of is expressive behavior directed at his public persona." Id. at 652.

In Lindemuth v. Jefferson County School District, 765 P.2d 1057, 1058 (Colo. App. 1988), the plaintiff, a high school basketball coach, alleged that he was constructively discharged in part because his supervisor referred to him as a convicted child molester and distributed court records showing that he had pleaded "no contest" to assaulting a minor fourteen years earlier. The court concluded that the plaintiff's allegations failed to state an intentional infliction of emotional distress claim. Id. at 1059.

In Dorr v. C.B. Johnson, Inc., 660 P.2d 517, 520 (Colo. App. 1983), the plaintiff employee was driving a truck in the course of his employment when he was injured in an accident. The employee brought an outrageous conduct claim against his employer alleging, among other things, that his employer filed an accident report containing false and libelous statements that he had been intoxicated at the time of the accident. The court dismissed the plaintiff's claim, finding that he, too, failed to state an intentional infliction of emotional distress claim. Id. at 521.

In Schioppi v. Costco Wholesale Corp., 2007 WL 735702 (D. Colo. Mar. 7, 2007), the court granted the employer's motion to dismiss the employee's claim for intentional infliction of emotional distress because the employer's conduct was not sufficiently extreme and outrageous. The employee alleged she was terminated, in part, because one supervisor falsely accused her of theft, represented she had admitted to theft and ignored proof that she had not admitted the theft. While the court agreed the employer's conduct was "hardly becoming," it was not egregious enough to support a claim for intentional infliction of emotional distress. See id.

Plaintiffs in defamation cases involving matters of public concern or public figures may not recover from media defendants for the tort of intentional infliction of emotional distress by reason of defamatory publications without showing that the publication was made with actual malice. See Lewis v. McGraw-Hill Broad. Co., Inc., 832 P.2d 1118 (Colo. App. 1992). The "actual malice" requirement also was stated by the Colorado Court of Appeals in Pierce v. St. Vrain Valley School District RE-1J, 944 P.2d 646, 646-47 (Colo. App. 1997), rev'd on other grounds, 981 P.2d 600 (Colo. 1999).

Two relatively recent cases have found allegedly defamatory statements to constitute outrageous conduct. In GLN Compliance Group, Inc. v. Ross, 2011 WL 1085696 (D. Colo. Mar. 24, 2011), the court found both defamation and outrageous conduct where the plaintiffs-counterclaim defendants "undertook a campaign of willful and malicious defamation per se" resulting in substantial damages to the victim's reputation and emotional well-being. In Lee v. Colorado Times, Inc., 222 P.3d 957 (Colo. App. 2009), the Colorado Court of Appeals reversed summary judgment in favor of the defendant newspaper on the plaintiff's outrageous conduct claim. The court held that reasonable jurors could find outrageous conduct where the newspaper printed a column suggesting that the killer of the plaintiff's husband went free because the plaintiff did not testify, when in fact the plaintiff did testify. Because the trial court did not address whether the column involved a matter of public concern, the appellate court did not address the question either.

Currently it is unclear whether a federal employee's claim for intentional infliction of emotional distress against the government must be compensated by the Federal Employee's Compensations Act (FECA). If FECA applies, the employee's claim under the Federal Tort Claims Act (FTCA) would be precluded. In Tippetts v. United States, 308 F.3d 1091 (10th Cir. 2002), the Tenth Circuit transferred such a claim to the Secretary of Labor for a determination of whether FECA applies to claims of intentional infliction of emotional distress.

C. Interference with Economic Advantage

The Colorado Jury Instructions set forth the elements of a claim for interference with economic advantage, also known as interference with contractual relations or contractual obligations. The elements a plaintiff must prove are: (1) the plaintiff had a contract with a third party; (2) the defendant knew or reasonably should have known of the contract; (3) the defendant, by words, conduct, or both, intentionally induced the third party not to perform or to terminate the contract, or interfered with his performance under the contract; (4) the defendant's interference was improper; (5) thereby causing the plaintiff to incur damages. CJI-Civ. 24:1 (2012). The Court of Appeals in Lutfi v. Brighton Community Hospital Association, 40 P.3d 51 (Colo. App. 2001), adopted a modified version of the Colorado Jury Instructions elements for the interference with a contract. The elements needed to establish tortious interference with a contract requires that: (1) the plaintiff had a contract with another party; (2) the defendant knew or should have known of such contract's existence; (3) the defendant intentionally induced the other party to the contract not to perform the contract with the plaintiff; and (4) the defendant's actions caused the plaintiff to incur damages. Furthermore, the Court stated "regarding the third element, the interference with a prospective business relationship must be both intentional and improper." A defendant will avoid liability for actions that tortiously interfere with another party's contract, however, if the defendant's actions were undertaken in the "exercise of an absolute right." Omedelena v. Denver Options, Inc., 60 P.3d 717, 721 (Colo. App. 2002). Furthermore, an individual cannot intentionally interfere with a contract to which it is a party. Thus, a corporate agent for a particular entity cannot be liable for allegedly interfering with that entity's contract unless the agent is solely motivated by the desire to harm one of the contracting parties or interfere with the contractual relations. Chambers v. Prowers Cnty. Hosp. Dist., 2009 WL 902416 at *15 (D. Colo. Mar. 31, 2009) (citing W.O. Brisben Cos, Inc. v. Krystkowiak, 66 P.3d 113, 136 (Colo. App. 2002)).

In order to sustain a claim for interference with business relationships under Colorado law, the plaintiff must establish that the defendant was not a party to the contractual relationship at issue; the tort exists to punish individuals who are not parties to a contract for inducing a breach or preventing the performance of a contract between the plaintiff and a third party. In Vinton v. Adam Aircraft Industries, Inc., 232 F.R.D. 650 (D. Colo. 2005), the district court dismissed an employee's claims of tortious interference with business relationships against his former employer and its CEO. The Court concluded that his claim against his former employer, with whom he had a contract, was legally untenable. The Court also rejected his claim against the CEO after concluding that an employment relationship existed between the plaintiff and the CEO.

Colorado courts also have recognized a claim of interference with prospective economic advantage, alternatively referred to as a claim of intentional interference with prospective financial advantage or prospective contractual relations, as a cognizable cause of action. See Occusafe, Inc. v. EG&G Rocky Flats, Inc., 54 F.3d 618 (10th Cir. 1995); Vinton v. Adam Aircraft Industries, Inc., 232 F.R.D. 650 (D. Colo. 2005). The crucial question in determining liability for tortious interference with prospective financial advantage is whether the defendant's interference was intentional and improper. See id. Generally, under Colorado law, the plaintiff cannot sue one of its competitors for intentional interference with prospective economic advantage. See id.

To establish liability for interference with prospective economic advantage, the plaintiff is not required to show that a formal, binding contract was contemplated, Amoco Oil Co. v. Erwin, 908 P.2d 493, 500 (Colo. 1995), nor is the plaintiff required to prove that the defendant had knowledge of a specific prospective purchaser. See Pers. Dept., Inc. v. Prof'l Staff Leasing Corp., 297 Fed. App'x 773 (10th Cir. 2008). Rather, the plaintiff need only show that the defendant intentionally and improperly interfered with "the voluntary conferring of commercial benefits in recognition of a moral obligation." See Amoco Oil Co. v. Erwin, 908 P.2d 493, 500 (Colo. 1995). To establish that a person acted "improperly" requires a balancing of the parties' conflicting interests to determine whether the interference was warranted under the particular circumstances. The factors set out in Restatement (Second) of Torts § 767 are: (a) the nature of the actor's conduct, (b) the actor's motive, (c) the interests of the other with which the actor's conduct interferes, (d) the interests sought to be advanced by the actor, (e) the social interests in protecting the freedom of action of the actor and the contractual interests of the other, (f) the proximity or remoteness of the actor's conduct to the interference, and (g) the relations between the parties. Steinbach v. Dillion Cos., Inc., 253 F.3d 538 (10th. Cir. 2001). But see MDM Group Assocs., Inc. v. CX Reinsurance Co. Ltd., 2007 WL 528800 (Colo. App. Feb. 22, 2007) (stating that interference with prospective contractual relationship is tortious "only if there is a reasonable likelihood or reasonable probability that a contract would have resulted").

In addition, a party asserting an interference claim must be a party to the prospective quasi-contract. See id. In MDM Group, the court held that an insurance broker did not have prospective contractual relations where the insurance company, but not the broker, would be a party to any insurance policy that the broker sold. See id.

Furthermore, in Steinbach, the Tenth Circuit also held that when a corporate agent interferes with a contract between the corporation and the plaintiff, such interference is generally privileged if the agent acted for a bona fide organizational purpose. See Steinbach, 253 F.3d 538; see also Zelinger v. Uvlade Rock Asphalt Co., 316 F.2d 47, 52 (10th Cir. 1963) (holding that any interference with a corporation's contract by an officer, director or employee of the corporation who is in good faith serving the corporate interests is privileged). Additionally, the Steinbach Court held that § 301 of the Labor Management Relations Act preempted plaintiff's tortious interference and outrageous conduct claims.

Even an at-will contract is entitled to some protection from improper interference by a stranger to the contract. See Bithell v. W. Care Corp., 762 P.2d 708, 712 (Colo. App. 1988); Zappa v. Seiver, 706 P.2d 440, 442 (Colo. App. 1985). Further, improper interference may include conduct such as fraud, violence, and the threat of civil litigation or criminal prosecution, Electrolux Corp. v. Lawson, 654 P.2d 340 (Colo. App. 1982), but it is not limited to these "predatory means." See, e.g., Trimble v. City & County of Denver, 697 P.2d 716, 726 (Colo. 1985) (applying Restatement (Second) of Torts § 767 factors cited above to determine whether defendant improperly interfered with the performance of a settlement agreement).

Colorado courts have found that a defendant's untruthful defamatory statements about the plaintiff to others satisfy the "improper conduct" requirement of an interference with economic advantage claim. See Trimble v. City & Cnty. of Denver, 697 P.2d 716 (Colo. 1985); Bithell v. W. Care Corp., 762 P.2d 708 (Colo. App. 1988); cf. Wedbush Morgan Sec., Inc. v. Kirkpatrick Pettis Capital Mgmt., Inc., 2007 WL 1097872 (D. Colo. Apr. 9, 2007) (noting that defamation with actual malice would qualify as improper conduct to state a claim for tortious interference with prospective business relations in a case involving a matter of public concern); TMJ Implants, Inc. v. Aetna, Inc., 498 F.3d 1175, 1201 (10th Cir. 2007) (noting that only "actionable" defamatory statements can support an interference claim). In Bithell, for example, the plaintiff executed a management agreement with Western Care Corporation to manage one of its nursing home facilities. See 762 P.2d at 709. One of the defendants, an Associate Director with the Colorado Department of Health, informed a shareholder of Western Care Corporation that the plaintiff was "out of control and causing problems" at the nursing home, and that Western Care would lose its operating license if the plaintiff was not removed from his position. Id. at 710. The plaintiff was removed and thereafter filed an interference with contractual relations claim, alleging, among other things, that the defendant's statements about him were untruthful and defamatory and, thus, they improperly interfered with his contract with Western Care. Id. The plaintiff's claim survived the defendant's summary judgment motion. Id. at 712.

The measure of damages in an action for interference with economic advantage is the loss caused by the interference. Restatement (Second) of Torts § 774 (1977). A prevailing plaintiff may be awarded lost profits and chance for gain, reasonably foreseeable mental suffering, other compensatory and consequential damages, as well as punitive damages under Colo. Rev. Stat. § 13-21-102.

D. Prima Facie Tort

No reported cases found.

V. OTHER ISSUES

A. Statute of Limitations

The statute of limitations for an action for defamation in Colorado is one year after the cause of action accrues. Colo. Rev. Stat. § 13-80-103(1)(a).

Colorado has not legislatively adopted the Uniform Single Publication Act. Colorado appellate courts have not considered the question of whether the single publication rule will be applied in determining when the statute of limitations begins to run with respect to newspapers, books, or magazines, but the rule probably would be applied. See Source & Authority, CJI-Civ. 22:24 (2012).

A defamation action is deemed to accrue on the date both the injury and its cause are known or should have been known by the exercise of reasonable diligence. Colo. Rev. Stat. § 13-80-108(1); see Taylor v. Goldsmith, 870 P.2d 1264, 1265 (Colo. App. 1994); **cf. Sandmeier v. Sadler, 2012 WL 3155841 (D. Colo. July 20, 2012) (dismissing plaintiff's libel and slander claims because they were not brought within one year of the making or publication of the alleged libelous or slanderous statement and plaintiff failed to allege any republication of the statements)**.

The statute of limitations for all privacy related torts, including intrusion upon seclusion, false light, publication of private facts, negligent hiring, negligent supervision, negligent retention, and intentional infliction of emotional distress, is two years. Colo. Rev. Stat. § 13-80-102(1)(a). However, if the privacy related tort is brought against a sheriff, coroner, police officer, firefighter, or other law enforcement authority, a one-year statute of limitations applies. Colo. Rev. Stat. § 13-80-103(1)(c). Privacy related tort claims are deemed to accrue on the date when both the injury and its cause are known or should have been known in the exercise of reasonable diligence. Colo. Rev. Stat. § 13-80-108(1); Winkler v. Rocky Mountain Conference of United Methodist Church, 923 P.2d 152, 158 (Colo. App. 1995). Normally, the question of when the plaintiff's claim accrued is a question of fact, but if the undisputed facts show that the plaintiff discovered or reasonably should have discovered the tortious conduct as of a particular date, the question may be decided as a matter of law. Winkler, 923 P.2d at 158.

B. Jurisdiction

In University of Colorado v. Booth, 78 P.3d 1098 (Colo. 2003) the Supreme Court of Colorado held that the University of Colorado is a "public entity other than the state" for purposes of the Colorado Governmental Immunity Act's notice provision. Colo. Rev. Stat. § 24-10-109(3). Under this provision, a plaintiff is required to give notice of a claim within 180 days after the discovery of the injury to either the governing body of the public entity, here the Board of Regents, or the attorney representing the public entity, here the Attorney General. Failure to give timely notice is jurisdictional, whereas failure to give notice to the proper person or entity gives rise to an affirmative defense. See Booth, 78 P.3d at 1100 (citation omitted); see also Pfenninger v. Exempla, Inc., 17 P.3d 841 (Colo. App. 2000) (holding that that the Committee on Anti-Competitive Conduct did not have jurisdiction to consider plaintiff's common law defamation claim that arose out of professional review committee activity, and thus plaintiffs were not required to exhaust their administrative remedies before filing their defamation claim in the district court).

With regard to choice of law, the United States District Court for the District of Colorado has ruled that, under Colorado conflict of law rules, the law to be applied in a defamation action is that of the state having the most significant relation with the parties in communication. See Zimmerman v. Bd. of Publ'ns, 598 F. Supp. 1002 (D. Colo. 1984). In single-state defamation cases this is usually the law of the state where publication occurred, Restatement (Second) of Conflict of Laws § 149 (1971), while in multistate cases the law of the state of the plaintiff's domicile usually applies. Id., § 150. In Zimmerman v. Board of Publications, 598 F. Supp. 1002 (D. Colo. 1984), the allegedly defamatory article, though printed in Michigan, was "published" in Colorado through distribution of the same in the state; the plaintiff and its affiliated organizations, the subjects of the article, were Colorado residents; and the harm allegedly suffered by the plaintiff was suffered in Colorado. In light of these factors, Colorado had the most significant relationship to the plaintiff's defamation claim and its law applied. See id. **In Shrader v. Biddinger, 2012 WL 976032 (D. Colo. Feb. 17, 2012), the court applied Colorado law even though the plaintiff was an Oklahoma resident at the time the alleged injury occurred and a Missouri resident thereafter. The court applied the Restatement (Second) of the Conflict of Laws factors and concluded that Colorado had the most significant relationship to the occurrence and to the parties. The defendants were a Colorado corporation and a Colorado resident/individual. Further, the place where the injury occurred, the place where the conduct causing the injury occurred, and the place where the relationship between the parties was centered was considered to be in Colorado. The emails and on-line bulletin board postings containing the alleged defamatory statements were considered to occur in Colorado because they were sent/posted by the Colorado defendants.** The party asserting jurisdiction has the burden of supporting jurisdictional allegations with competent proof. See Zerr v. Johnson, 894 F. Supp. 372 (D. Colo. 1995). Where the issue of the district court's subject matter jurisdiction is intertwined with the merits of the case, district court may treat the motion to dismiss for lack of subject matter jurisdiction as one for summary judgment. See id.

C. Worker's Compensation Exclusivity

An employer who complies with Title 8, Articles 40 to 47 of the Colorado Revised Statutes ("Workers' Compensation Statute") is not subject to liability "for the death of or personal injury to any employee, except as provided" in the Workers' Compensation Statute. Colo. Rev. Stat. § 8-41-102. An employer's purchase and retention of a workers' compensation insurance policy constitutes a surrender by the employer and employee of all civil claims "for or on account of such personal injuries or death of such employee," except as provided in the Workers' Compensation Statute. Colo. Rev. Stat. § 8-41-104.

Workers' compensation was not the exclusive remedy of an employee who alleged defamation based on his employer's statements made after an accident and injury covered by workers' compensation, where the employee did not claim damages "for personal injury or aggravation of personal injury." Dorr v. C.B. Johnson, Inc., 660 P.2d 517, 520 (Colo. App. 1983). For this reason, and because the employee's injuries from the employer's statements did not occur "while he was performing any service arising out of and in the course of his employment," the Colorado Court of Appeals reversed the dismissal of the employee's defamation claims. Id. Although an absolute privilege protected the employer's statements in a report required by the Workers' Compensation Statute, the privilege did not extend to the employer's similar statements "to third persons not involved in the [workers'] compensation proceedings." Id. at 519.

D. Pleading Requirements

A plaintiff in a libel suit must state a claim upon which relief may be granted, and a trial court may grant a motion to dismiss in libel actions as well as in other suits. See Knowlton v. Cervi, 350 P.2d 1066 (Colo. 1960).

Each publication of libel is a separate cause of action and should be separately pleaded. See Lininger v. Knight, 226 P.2d 809 (Colo. 1951)

Claims for libel and slander are not subject to the heightened pleading requirements of Rule 9 of the Colorado Rules of Civil Procedure. Colorado Revised Statutes § 13-25-124 provides that, "[i]n an action for libel or slander":

> it shall not be necessary to state in the complaint any extrinsic facts for the purpose of showing the application to the plaintiff of the defamatory matter out of which the cause of action arose. It shall be sufficient to state generally that the same was published or spoken concerning the plaintiff; and, if such allegation is controverted, the plaintiff shall establish on the trial that it was so published or spoken.

The test to be applied is whether the plaintiff's complaint gives sufficient notice of the claim to the defendant to enable him to answer the complaint and prepare for trial. J & K Constr. Co. v. Molton, 390 P.2d 68, 70 (Colo. 1964); see also Colo. R. Civ. P. 8(a) (requiring a plaintiff to set forth in the complaint a "short and plain statement of the claim showing that the pleader is entitled to relief" and a demand for the "relief to which he deems himself entitled"). Nevertheless, a plaintiff seeking specific monetary losses allegedly resulting from a defamatory publication (i.e., special damages) must plead them in the complaint specifically. In Castillo v. United Parcel Service, 2008 WL 486082 (D. Colo. Feb. 19, 2008), the court granted summary judgment in favor of the defendant on plaintiff's defamation claim because he did not identify the actual statements alleged to be defamatory with adequate specificity. Moreover, plaintiffs proceeding on a libel per quod theory must plead special damages to avoid dismissal of their claim. See Stump v. Gates, 777 F. Supp. 808, 825 (D. Colo. 1991), aff'd, 986 F.2d 1429 (10th Cir. 1993); Keohane v. Wilkerson, 859 P.2d 291, 301 (Colo. App. 1993), aff'd sub nom. Keohane v. Stewart, 882 P.2d 1293 (Colo. 1994).

The Colorado Court of Appeals has ruled that, when a default has been entered, but damages have not been proven, there is no final judgment. Singh v. Mortensun, 30 P.3d 853 (Colo. App. 2001). In Singh the plaintiff's motion to set aside the entry of default was granted. In order to vacate a default judgment the court must use a three prong test: (1) whether the neglect was excusable; (2) whether the moving party has alleged a meritorious defense; and (3) whether relief from the challenged judgment would be consistent with equitable considerations such as protection of action taken in reliance on the judgment and prevention of prejudice by reason of evidence lost or impaired by the passage of time. Colo. R. Civ. P. 60(b).

SURVEY OF COLORADO EMPLOYMENT PRIVACY LAW

Natalie Hanlon-Leh
Morgan A. Word
Faegre & Benson LLP
2500 Republic Plaza
370 17th St.
Denver, Colorado 80202
Telephone: (303) 592-9000
Facsimile: (303) 820-0600

Jessica Brown
Gibson, Dunn & Crutcher LLP
1801 California Street
Suite 4200
Denver, Colorado 80202-2694
Telephone: (303) 298-5700
Facsimile: (303) 296-5310

(With Developments Reported Through **November 1, 2012**)

GENERAL COMMENTS

None.

SIGNIFICANT DEVELOPMENTS SINCE THE 2012 *SURVEY*

There were significant new developments this year in Colorado privacy law. First, in Judd v. Cedar St. Venture (In Re: District Court, City and County of Denver), 256 P.3d 687, 691 (Colo. 2011), the Colorado Supreme Court articulated a new test for assessing all discovery requests that implicate the right to privacy. The Court's prior decisions had applied different tests depending on the type of information requested. Id. Under the new test, the requesting party must first prove that the requested information is relevant to the action. Id. Next, the party opposing the request must show that he or she has a legitimate expectation of privacy in the requested information. Id. If so, the requesting party must demonstrate a compelling need for the information. Id. Finally, the requesting party must show that the information is not available from other, less intrusive sources. Id. at 692.

Second, in Denver Post Corp. v. Ritter, 255 P.3d 1083, 1088 (Colo. 2011), the Colorado Supreme Court considered whether Governor Bill Ritter's mobile telephone bills for his private phone account were public records and, therefore, whether the Colorado Open Records Act (CORA), COLO. REV. STAT. § 24-72-201 et seq. (2009), required their disclosure to the public. Under CORA, any person may request access to inspect and obtain a copy of any public record. Id. at 1086 (citing § 24-72-203(1)(a)). CORA defines a public record as any writing "made, maintained or kept by . . . any . . . political subdivision of the state . . . for use in the exercise of functions required or authorized by law or administrative rule." Id. (citing § 24-72-202(6)(a)(I)). Because both parties agreed that the Governor kept and used the billing statements only for their payment, did not obtain reimbursement from the state, and had not otherwise turned the bills over to any state agency or official, the court found that the plaintiffs had failed to allege that the governor kept the bills in his official capacity. Id. at 1088. The court further stated that merely alleging a potential future official use was insufficient to state a claim under CORA. Id. The court made its ruling despite the parties' stipulation that the vast majority of the calls placed on the cell phone involved discussions of public business in an official capacity. Id. at 1087. The dissent expressed concern that the majority's decision could allow public officials to shield their official conduct from scrutiny. Id. at 1098 (Rice, J., dissenting).

I. GENERAL LAW OF PRIVACY

A. Legal Basis of Privacy

Colorado first expressly recognized the tort of invasion of privacy in 1970, in Rugg v. McCarty, 476 P.2d 753 (Colo. 1970). The court in Rugg found that the Legislature recognized a right to privacy in Colorado's wiretapping and eavesdropping statute (former COLO. REV. STAT. § 40-4-33) and held that oppressive conduct by a creditor in connection with his efforts to collect from a debtor could infringe on this right. Id. at 756. The Rugg court did not attempt to define comprehensively the scope or elements of the right to privacy. Subsequent cases, including Robert C. Ozer, P.C. v. Borquez, 940 P.2d 371, 377 (Colo. 1997) and Doe v. High-Tech Institute, Inc., 972 P.2d 1060, 1067 (Colo. App. 1998), suggest that Colorado follows the traditional division of the right to privacy into four separate subdivisions: (a) unreasonable intrusion upon one's seclusion; (b) false light in the public eye; (c) appropriation of likeness; and (d) publication of private facts. See generally Gilbert v. Med. Econ. Co., 665 F.2d 305, 7 Media L. Rep. 2372 (10th Cir. 1981); Restatement (Second) of Torts § 652 (1977). Although the four privacy claims concern the concept of being left alone, each tort is made up of distinct elements and establishes a separate interest that may be invaded. See Doe, 972 P.2d at 1065. The Colorado Supreme Court recognized the privacy tort of intrusion when it denied certiorari in High-Tech Institute, Inc. v. Doe, No. 98SC574, 1999 Colo. LEXIS 198, at *1 (Colo. Mar. 1, 1999). The Colorado Supreme Court recognized the privacy tort of appropriation in Joe Dickerson & Associates, LLC v. Dittmar, 34 P.3d 995, 1001 (Colo. 2001), and the privacy tort of disclosure in Robert C.

Ozer, P.C. v. Borquez, 940 P.2d 371, 377 (Colo. 1997). But in Denver Publishing Co. v. Bueno, 54 P.3d 893, 897 (Colo. 2002), the Colorado Supreme Court declined to recognize the tort of false light invasion of privacy, finding that it was duplicative of the tort of defamation.

B. Causes of Action

Colorado state courts have adopted three of the four separate torts that fall under the generic term "invasion of privacy": (1) appropriation of another's name and likeness; (2) public disclosure of private facts; and (3) unreasonable intrusion upon the seclusion of another. See Slaughter v. John Elway Dodge Southwest/AutoNation, 107 P.3d 1165, 1171 (Colo. App. 2005). But see Bueno, 54 P.3d at 894 (refusing to recognize the fourth tort of "publicity that unreasonably places another in a false light before the public").

1. ***Misappropriation/Right of Publicity***. Other than the Colorado analogue of the Fourth Amendment found in Article II, Section 7 of Colorado's Constitution, there are no constitutional provisions or Colorado statutes specifically relating to misappropriation of publicity. But in December 1999, the Colorado Court of Appeals recognized a claim for invasion of privacy based on misappropriation/right of publicity under Colorado law. See Dittmar v. Joe Dickerson & Assocs., LLC, 9 P.3d 1145, 1146 (Colo. App. 1999). In Dittmar, the defendants, Joe Dickerson and his private investigation firm, were hired to investigate the plaintiff, Rosanne Marie Dittmar, in a child custody dispute. Id. During the course of their investigation, the defendants inquired into the circumstances under which Ms. Dittmar came to possess bearer bonds and reported the results of their investigation to the police. Id. Ms. Dittmar was subsequently charged and found guilty of theft of $15,000 or more. Id. The defendants published an article in their newsletter about Ms. Dittmar's conviction and their role in the events leading to her arrest. Id. The article included Ms. Dittmar's name and photograph. Id. Ms. Dittmar filed an action alleging that the defendants had maliciously appropriated her photograph and name for their own commercial advantage without her consent, resulting in an invasion of her right to privacy. Id. The trial court granted summary judgment for the defendants on Ms. Dittmar's invasion of privacy claim and Ms. Dittmar appealed. Id.

On appeal to the Colorado Court of Appeals, Ms. Dittmar argued that the essence of an invasion of privacy claim based on misappropriation of likeness/right of publicity is whether the defendant appropriates the plaintiff's name and likeness for his or her own commercial gain, and not whether the plaintiff is portrayed in a positive or negative light. Id. Ms. Dittmar characterized the defendant's newsletter as an "infomercial" designed to promote and attract business to their private investigation firm. Id. The Court of Appeals noted that the Restatement (Second) of Torts § 652C provides "one who appropriates to his own use or benefit the name or likeness of another is subject to liability to the other for invasion of his privacy." Id. The court further noted that "Colorado appellate courts have not addressed 652C" and that a claim for appropriation of another's name or likeness has never been recognized in Colorado. Id. However, the court reasoned, Colorado courts have recognized other types of claims for invasion of privacy, including invasion of privacy by publication of private facts and invasion of privacy by intrusion upon seclusion. Id. (citing Robert C. Ozer, 940 P.2d at 371, and Doe v. High-Tech Inst., 972 P.2d 1060 (Colo. App. 1998)). Thus, the court concluded, "We see no reason why a claim for appropriation of another's name or likeness should not be recognized in Colorado." Id.

The Colorado Court of Appeals found it was undisputed that Ms. Dittmar could be identified from the defendants' use of her name and likeness in their newsletter and that such use was without Ms. Dittmar's consent. Id. at 1148. The court also observed that other articles in the same publication simply referred to "our clients" with no identifying information given. Id. What was unclear to the court of appeals, however, was the purpose of the publication, whether the defendants derived any benefit from the appropriation, and whether Ms. Dittmar was harmed. Id. Thus, the court reversed the grant of summary judgment and remanded for further proceedings. Id.

The Colorado Supreme Court granted the defendants' petition for writ of certiorari. See Joe Dickerson & Assocs., LLC v. Dittmar, 34 P.3d 995, 29 Media L. Rep. 2618 (Colo. 2001). The Colorado Supreme Court agreed to review "whether the tort of invasion of privacy through appropriation of another's name or likeness is cognizable under Colorado law," "whether a claim for appropriation of name or likeness can be sustained where there is no evidence of an exploitable value to respondent's name or likeness," and "whether, under the circumstances, petitioners' communications were protected under the First Amendment of the United States Constitution." Id. at 999 n.2.

The Colorado Supreme Court, sitting en banc, reversed the judgment of the appellate court. Id. at 997. Joe Dickerson & Associates set forth the elements of an invasion of privacy by appropriation tort in Colorado: "(1) the defendant used the plaintiff's name or likeness; (2) the use of the plaintiff's name or likeness was for the defendant's own purposes or benefit, commercially or otherwise; (3) the plaintiff suffered damages; and (4) the defendant caused the damages incurred." Id. An invasion of privacy by appropriation tort will fail if the defendant's use of the plaintiff's name or likeness is considered privileged under the First Amendment. Id. In this case, although agreeing that the tort of invasion of privacy by appropriation of another's name or likeness is cognizable in Colorado, the Supreme Court found that the defendant's use of the plaintiff's name and likeness in this instance was privileged. Id. at 997. "[T]he defendant's use of the plaintiff's name and likeness in the context of an article about the plaintiff's crime and felony conviction is a matter of legitimate public concern" and is therefore protected by the First Amendment, despite some commercial aspects of the defendant's publication. Id. at 997, 1004.

The Colorado Supreme Court also made it clear that a plaintiff need not prove the value of her name or likeness when seeking only personal damages. Id. at 999. Disagreeing with the trial and appellate courts, as well as the Colorado Civil Jury Instructions, the court stated that "[t]he market value of the plaintiff's identity is unrelated to the question of whether she suffered mental anguish as a result of the alleged wrongful appropriation." Id. at 1002. As a consequence, it would be "illogical" to require a plaintiff, seeking only personal damages, to prove the value of her name or likeness. Id. The Colorado Supreme Court was careful to note, however, that it did not reach the question of whether the value of the plaintiff's name or likeness is a required element of the tort if the plaintiff is attempting to seek commercial damages. Id. at 1002.

Before Dittmar and Joe Dickerson & Associates were decided, the federal district court for the District of Colorado had considered but rejected a claim based on misappropriation of likeness/right of publicity. In PAM Media, Inc. v. American Research Corp., 889 F. Supp. 1403, 1409 (D. Colo. 1995), the United States District Court granted summary judgment dismissing an invasion of privacy/misappropriation claim brought by the producer and syndicate of Rush Limbaugh's radio talk show against the producer of a competing radio talk show entitled "After the Rush," in which the plaintiffs alleged misappropriation of Limbaugh's identity for commercial purposes. After noting that "[t]here is no Colorado case adopting this principle," the federal court assumed that the Colorado courts would follow the Restatement (Third) of Unfair Competition (1995), and granted the defendants' summary judgment motion because the plaintiffs did not make a sufficient showing that the defendants attempted to exploit the persona of Rush Limbaugh for their commercial benefit. Id. The court explained:

> None of the defendants' promotional material suggests that Rush Limbaugh, himself, is involved with "After the Rush." His name is used because it symbolizes a particular perspective on the public issues which are the grist for the mills of both programs. The ideology of Rush Limbaugh is not protectable by a right of publicity. The publication of a celebrity's opinions and commentaries invites the use of his name by other commentators expressing their contrasting opinions. Id.

The federal court held that "public disagreement with Rush Limbaugh on a competing radio talk show is not the exploitation of his identity." Id.

The court further distinguished the right of publicity, and a claim for misappropriation of publicity, from a claim for unfair competition:

> Likelihood of confusion about production and syndication of the two programs because of their titles is different from suggesting personal endorsement or sponsorship by the person whose name is well known. The rationale for a right of publicity is distinct from that supporting the law of unfair competition. The latter is based on the need for protecting the integrity of the process by which goods and services are marketed. The former is for protection of a person. The right of publicity is not involved here. Id.

Although there are no Colorado statutes specifically relating to the misappropriation of publicity, the Colorado Consumer Protection Act, COLO. REV. STAT. § 6-1-113, gives consumers a private right of action against any person who has engaged in or caused another to engage in any deceptive trade practice. A person engages in a deceptive trade practice when, in the course of such person's business, vocation, or occupation, such person: (a) knowingly passes off goods, services, or property as those of another; (b) knowingly makes a false representation as to the source, sponsorship, approval, or certification of goods, services, or property; (c) knowingly makes a false representation as to the characteristics, ingredients, uses, benefits, alterations or quantities of goods, food, services, or property or a false representation as to the sponsorship, approval, status, affiliation, or connection of a person therewith. COLO. REV. STAT. § 6-1-105(1). But see PAM Media, Inc., 889 F. Supp. at 1409 (D. Colo. 1995) (distinguishing between rights protected by unfair competition claims under the Colorado Consumer Protection Act and claims for misappropriation or publicity). Remedies under § 6-1-113 include treble damages and attorney fees.

In King v. PA Consulting Group, Inc., 485 F.3d 577, 593 (10th Cir. 2007), the Tenth Circuit held that the plaintiff was entitled to prevail on his invasion of privacy claim based on the misappropriation of his name. Though the plaintiff had resigned his employment with the defendant consulting company, the company continued to distribute promotional materials listing the plaintiff as the contact person for a particular practice area, changed the plaintiff's voice mail to indicate that he was unavailable but that the caller should leave a message, and had all messages sent to the plaintiff's email account forwarded to his replacement. Id. at 583. The defendant argued that the plaintiff, King, had failed to present evidence showing that his name had commercial value. Id. at 592. The court observed that the defendant's marketing manager had testified that King's name was included in the company's promotional materials because "he was a 'famous consultant[]' with a 'high profile' who was 'well known' in the industry." Id. In addition, King had introduced several advertisements, including one in the Wall Street Journal, in which King was described as a "'noted' management consultant and economist." Id. The court reasoned, "Although this evidence might not place King's name in the same league as a Hollywood celebrity or a professional athlete, that was not King's burden. Our sole inquiry . . . is whether this evidence would allow a jury to reasonably conclude that King's name held commercial value . . . [and we] are satisfied that it would." Id.

For invasion of privacy claims based upon misappropriation, the applicable statute of limitations is two years from the date when the plaintiff knew or should have known by the exercise of reasonable diligence of the misappropriation. COLO. REV. STAT. § 13-80-102(1)(a).

2. ***Publication of Private Facts***. In Robert C. Ozer, P.C. v. Borquez, 940 P.2d 371, 377 (Colo. 1997), the Colorado Supreme Court recognized that a cause of action exists in Colorado for giving unreasonable publicity to facts about an employee's private life. The elements of such a claim are: (1) the fact or facts disclosed must be private in nature; (2) the disclosure must be made to the public; (3) the disclosure must be one that would be highly offensive to a reasonable person; (4) the fact or facts disclosed cannot be of legitimate concern to the public; and (5) the defendant acted with reckless disregard of the private nature of the fact or facts disclosed. Id.; see also Fire Ins. Exch. v. Sullivan, 224 P.3d 348, 352-53 (Colo. App. 2009) (summarizing the invasion of privacy elements for the tort of unreasonable publicity).

In Ozer, the plaintiff, Borquez, was an associate attorney employed by the defendant law firm. 940 P.2d at 373. The law firm's named shareholder, Ozer, learned that the plaintiff was not only gay, but needed immediate AIDS testing because he had a companion who had been diagnosed with AIDS. Id. at 374. Ozer fired Borquez within a week after this disclosure. Id. Although the plaintiff had asked Ozer to keep this information confidential, Ozer told other members of the firm, and within two days, all employees and shareholders in the firm had learned about the plaintiff's personal life and his need for AIDS testing. Id.

Borquez initiated action against Ozer and the law firm for wrongful discharge under a Denver anti-discrimination statute and under the "lawful activities" provision of the Colorado Anti-Discrimination Act ("CADA"). Id.; see COLO. REV. STAT. § 24-34-402.5 (forbidding employers from requiring "as a condition of employment, that any employee or prospective employee refrain from engaging in any lawful activity during non-working hours"). Borquez also sued for invasion of privacy by public disclosure of private facts. 940 P.2d at 374. The jury awarded him approximately $30,000 in economic damages, $20,000 for "embarrassment and humiliation," and $40,000 in punitive damages. Id.

Both the Colorado Court of Appeals and the Colorado Supreme Court affirmed recognition of the tort. Id. at 375, 379. The Colorado Supreme Court, however, found that the jury instructions on the "publicity element" were erroneous, in that they did not state that the disclosure must be made to "a large number of persons or the general public." Id. at 379. The case was remanded for a new trial. Id. at 380.

Relying on Borquez, the plaintiff in A.T. v. State Farm Mutual Automobile Insurance Co. sought to amend her complaint to add a claim for invasion of privacy based on publication of private facts by State Farm. 989 P.2d 219, 220 (Colo. App. 1999). The plaintiff was a chiropractor who sustained injuries in a car accident and sued State Farm. Id. In the context of an arbitration to resolve her claims, she provided State Farm her medical records, which revealed treatment for a psychological disorder. Id. Subsequently, the plaintiff testified as a medical expert witness in litigation between one of her patients and State Farm. Id. In that litigation, State Farm cross-examined her about her psychological history and treatment, using the records it had obtained in the arbitration. Id. The plaintiff contended that State Farm's use of her medical records in the subsequent action was unauthorized and an invasion of her privacy. Id.

The Colorado Court of Appeals disagreed, stating that one element of the tort of invasion of privacy based on publication of private facts "is that the published information is private." Id. at 221. Because the plaintiff had disclosed the information in an arbitration that was not made private or confidential, the plaintiff waived, at least as to State Farm, the confidentiality that might otherwise attach to that information. Id. Thus, "the claim of invasion of privacy would necessarily fail." Id. Judge Rothenberg dissented, arguing that the court erred by treating "confidentiality" and "privacy" as synonymous. Id. at 222. "Importantly," Judge Rothenberg noted, "Borquez did not require that the fact or facts disclosed by defendant be confidential, only that they be private in nature." Id. at 221-22.

Judge Rothenberg later authored the opinion in Tonnessen v. Denver Publishing Co., 5 P.3d 959, 963 (Colo. App. 2000), which rejected an invasion of privacy claim based on publication of private facts because the facts had been made public before the defendant published them. In Tonnessen, the defendant newspaper printed two articles about the plaintiff's divorce proceeding, focusing on the unusual circumstances of his ex-wife's pregnancy. Id. at 962. Specifically, Tonnessen's ex-wife had given birth to twin girls fathered by two different men. Id.

The Tonnessen court, citing Robert C. Ozer, P.C. v. Borquez, 940 P.2d 371 (Colo. 1997), noted that the right of privacy may be invaded in several different ways, including unreasonable publicity given to one's private life. Id. at

966. "It is undisputed," the court observed, "that the basic facts of Tonnessen's dissolution of marriage case had already been revealed to the public through intense media scrutiny before publication of the articles at issue here." Id. "Hence," the court continued, "a requisite element"—that the facts disclosed be private in nature—"is missing." Id. Accordingly, the court affirmed the dismissal of Tonnessen's invasion of privacy claim. Id.

The tort of invasion of privacy by publication of private facts is difficult to establish under Colorado law. See Silver v. Primero Reorganized Sch. Dist. No. 2, 619 F. Supp. 2d 1074, 1080-81 (D. Colo. 2007). In Silver, a district court dismissed a claim by a school employee who alleged that she had confided in a school counselor regarding personal matters and the school counselor conveyed some or all of that information to the school's principal. Id. 1076. The principal later entered into a wager with another employee as to whether he could have sex with Ms. Silver before the end of the school year. Id. Using the information from the counselor, the principal allegedly preyed on Ms. Silver's emotions "and the two began a sexual relationship." Id. When Ms. Silver learned of the principal's wager, however, she tried to end the relationship and ultimately was forced to obtain a restraining order against the principal. Id. Thereafter, Ms. Silver was told that she would no longer enjoy unfettered access to the school as she had during her relationship with the principal. Id. Instead, she was limited to her immediate work area, the gym, the cafeteria, and if necessary, the office. Id. At the end of the school year, her employment was terminated. Id.

Among other claims, Ms. Silver brought a claim for invasion of privacy against the school counselor based upon his disclosure of her confidential communications to the principal. Id. at 1076-77. After setting forth the elements of the claim, the court found that Ms. Silver failed to allege that the information she revealed to the counselor was "private in nature." Id. at 1080. Although the complaint alleged that Ms. Silver discussed with the counselor "issues going on in [her] life," it did not allege that those issues were not publicly known. Id. For instance, the court hypothesized, Ms. Silver might have talked to the school counselor about a divorce or allegations of criminal conduct, both of which likely would constitute public information. Id. at 1080 n.8. In addition, the court reasoned, although the complaint alleged that Ms. Silver communicated to the counselor "privately and in confidence," that allegation "merely describe[d] the manner of the communication," and said nothing about its contents. Id. at 1080. The court went on to question whether the complaint adequately alleged "dissemination of the information to the public" (which can be met by showing the defendant "merely initiate[d] the process whereby the information is eventually disclosed to a large number of persons"), but refrained from deciding that issue, having concluded that Ms. Silver failed to allege that the information in issue was private in nature. Id. at 1081 n.9. The court then dismissed the claim, but gave Ms. Silver an opportunity to amend her complaint to allege adequately an invasion of privacy claim. Id. at 1081.

The statute of limitations for the tort of invasion of privacy by publication of private facts is two years from the date when the plaintiff knew, or should have known by the exercise of reasonable diligence, of the publication. COLO. REV. STAT. § 13-80-102(1)(a).

3. ***Intrusion.*** Although the Colorado Supreme Court did not label it as such, the general recognition of the tort of invasion of privacy in Rugg v. McCarty, 476 P.2d 753, 754 (Colo. 1970), was a right to privacy based on intrusion upon seclusion. In Rugg, the plaintiff complained about repeated and harassing calls from the defendant.

Subsequent Colorado decisions on intrusion mainly have concerned unwarranted intrusion by the defendant into the plaintiff's financial matters. See, e.g., Tollefson v. Safeway Stores, Inc., 351 P.2d 274, 276 (Colo. 1960) (rejecting invasion of privacy claim when defendant simply reminded plaintiff of an obligation to reimburse for a bounced check); Wells v. Premier Indus. Co., 691 P.2d 765, 767 (Colo. App. 1984) (rejecting invasion of privacy claim when employer complied with summons from IRS); Otten v. Birdseye, 527 P.2d 925, 927 (Colo. App. 1974) (not selected for official publication) (rejecting invasion of privacy claim when a mother-in-law obtained a writ of attachment to be issued for the son-in-law's property, despite no indication of a fraudulent transfer).

In Doe v. High-Tech Institute, Inc., 972 P.2d 1060 (Colo. App. 1998), the Colorado Court of Appeals recognized the tort of intrusion upon one's seclusion. The court noted that "intrusion upon seclusion clearly encompasses an intrusion upon a physical space" as well as "intrusions into a person's private concerns based upon a reasonable expectation of privacy in that area." Id. at 1068. Specifically, the court held that individuals have privacy interests in their bodies and information regarding their health. Id.

The plaintiff in Doe was a student in a medical assistant training program. Id. at 1064. Shortly after beginning the course, the student informed the instructor that he had tested positive for human immunodeficiency virus (HIV) and requested that the instructor keep the information confidential. Id. Later that month, the instructor informed students that they were required to be tested for rubella and obtained consent forms for blood tests for rubella. Id. Without telling the plaintiff, the instructor requested that the laboratory doing the testing also test plaintiff's blood sample for HIV. Id. The test results were positive and the laboratory reported plaintiff's name, address, and positive HIV status to the school and to the Colorado Department of Health, as required under COLO. REV. STAT. § 25-4-1402(1). Recognizing the tort of intrusion upon seclusion, the Court of Appeals held that the unauthorized HIV test under these circumstances "would be considered by a reasonable person as highly invasive, and therefore, sufficient to constitute an unreasonable or offensive intrusion." 972 P.2d at 1071.

According to Doe, the elements of a claim for intrusion upon seclusion are: (1) another person has intentionally intruded, physically or otherwise; (2) upon the plaintiff's seclusion or solitude; and (3) such intrusion would be offensive or objectionable to a reasonable person. Id. at 1067. The Tenth Circuit clarified the first element of this tort in Pascouau v. Martin Marietta Corp., No. 98-1099, 1999 U.S. App. LEXIS 15712, at *37 (10th Cir. 1999). The court stated that "in the usual case, intrusion upon seclusion involves physical intrusion into a place where a plaintiff has secluded herself--such as a defendant forcing his way into the plaintiff's home." Id. at *37–38. In addition, the court explained, intrusion upon seclusion "may occur by the use of physical senses to eavesdrop on or observe the plaintiff's private affairs." Id. at *38. The Pascouau plaintiff, however, did not allege a physical invasion, inappropriate spying, or improper eavesdropping. Instead, she asserted an "intrusion upon seclusion" privacy claim based on the same factual allegations as her Title VII hostile work environment and quid pro quo sexual harassment claims. The court determined that the plaintiff's claim failed because, even assuming the plaintiff's co-workers "bothered her with questions about her sex life and sexual preferences," such "sexually suggestive questions were only requests for information." Id. The court explained that the tort of intrusion upon seclusion "requires more than a mere inquiry that reveals nothing; liability attaches only to an uncontested invasion through physical or other means that actually gleans private information." Id. at *38–39. Therefore, the court affirmed summary judgment on the privacy claim for the plaintiff's employer.

Referencing Doe, the court in Quigley v. Rosenthal, 327 F.3d 1044 (10th Cir. 2003), cert. denied sub nom., mot. granted, Anti-Defamation League v. Quigley, 124 S. Ct. 1507 (2004), further addressed the scope of liability in an intrusion action. In Quigley, a feud broke out between two neighboring families, the Aronsons and the Quigleys. The Aronsons began recording the Quigley family's cordless telephone conversations. Id. at 1050. Mr. Aronson met with the Anti-Defamation League ("ADL") to report that the Quigleys were engaging in threatening, anti-Semitic behavior. Id. at 1052. The ADL and the Aronsons met with two lawyers to discuss whether it was legal to record the conversations. Id. at 1051–52. What both lawyers said in that meeting is disputed, but, in any event, the Aronsons continued to record the Quigleys' conversations. Id. at 1052. Eventually the Aronsons filed a lawsuit and held a press conference concerning the Quigleys' behavior, both activities revealing topics the Quigleys had discussed during their intercepted phone conversations. Id. at 1052–56.

The court in Quigley was called upon to decide whether the "use" of the phone conversations by the ADL and the lawyers involved with the case constituted intrusion (the court noted that the actual act of interception clearly qualified as intrusion). Id. at 1073. The court held that an intrusion claim could not be based on "use" alone, though "use" alone might result in another type of privacy action such as "unreasonable publicity given to another's private life." Id. at 1073.

In Pearson v. Kancilia, 70 P.3d 594, 599 (Colo. App. 2003), the Colorado Court of Appeals held that an employee could bring a claim for unreasonable intrusion upon the seclusion of another against a supervisor who allegedly forced the employee to engage in sexual intercourse. Pearson, the plaintiff, based her claim on evidence that her employer came to her apartment early in the morning three times a week for sex. Id. The court found that "the absence of a definitive refusal to engage in sex does not defeat, as a matter of law, a claim for privacy." Id.

The statute of limitations for intrusion upon seclusion is two years from the date when the plaintiff knew, or should have known by the exercise of reasonable diligence, of the intrusion. COLO. REV. STAT. § 13-80-102(1)(a) (§ 13-80-102(1)(a) also provides a two-year period of limitations for trespass).

4. ***False Light.*** In 2002, the Colorado Supreme Court held that the tort of false light invasion of privacy is not recognized in Colorado. Denver Publ'g Co. v. Bueno, 54 P.3d 893, 894 (Colo. 2002); Fire Ins. Exch. v. Sullivan, 224 P.3d 348, 353 (Colo. App. 2009). Bueno held that while the tort of false light had been recognized by lower courts, it had only been expressly adopted or applied in one case, McCammon & Assoc. v. McGraw-Hill Broad. Co., 716 P.2d 490, 492 (Colo. App. 1986) (adopting the "actual malice" test of Time, Inc. v. Hill, 385 U.S. 374 (1967), with regard to an action for false light invasion of privacy). Bueno, 54 P.3d at 897. The Supreme Court cited three of the four district court cases in the Tenth Circuit that had applied Colorado law to false light claims, apparently assuming Colorado had adopted the tort, noting that they all failed on the merits. Id. The cases cited by the Supreme Court were: Brown v. O'Bannon, 84 F. Supp. 2d 1176, 1180–81 (D. Colo. 2000), Seidl v. Greentree Mortg. Co., 30 F. Supp. 2d 1292, 1302 (D. Colo. 1998), and Smith v. Colo. Interstate Gas Co., 777 F. Supp. 854, 857 (D. Colo. 1991).

In overturning the appellate court, the Colorado Supreme Court compared the elements of the torts of libel per se, defamation by libel per quod, and false light invasion of privacy. Bueno, 54 P.3d at 899-900. It found the elements of all three torts to be similar, the main difference being that "publicity" under a false light claim requires publication to the public at large, whereas under the other two torts only one other person is needed to have understood the statement. Id. at

899. The court also considered the different interests protected by the different torts, concluding that false light deals more with a personal sense of offense. Id. at 901. While the court found this to be a valid distinction, it held that "recognition of the different interests protected rests primarily on parsing a too subtle distinction between an individual's personal sensibilities and his or her reputation in the community." Id. at 902.

The court concluded its decision by cautioning against utilizing privacy to undermine First Amendment principles. Id. at 903-04. According to the court, "because tort law is intended to recompense wrongful conduct and to prevent it, it is important that it be clear in its identification of that wrongful conduct. The tort of false light fails that test. The sole area in which it differs from defamation is an area fraught with ambiguity and subjectivity . . . ." Id. at 903.

Chief Justice Mullarkey dissented, observing that precluding duplicative damage awards could cure the overlap problem between defamation and false light torts. Id. at 905. Chief Justice Mullarkey also found it problematic that the majority decision places Colorado outside the majority of states on this issue. Id.

In Gordon v. Boyles, 99 P.3d 75 (Colo. App. 2004), a police officer and his wife sued a radio talk show host for asserting on the air that the officer had a history of domestic violence and had engaged in an extramarital affair. Plaintiffs brought claims for false light and defamation. The claims were dismissed and plaintiffs appealed the dismissal of the defamation claim, but not the false light claim. Id. at 78. On appeal, the court concluded that the radio host's comments about the affair could support a defamation claim, but that the comments about domestic violence could not, because they were true. Id. at 81. The Colorado Supreme Court granted certiorari, Boyles v. Gordon, No. 04SC211, 2004 Colo. LEXIS 809, at *2 (Colo. Oct. 18, 2004), but the parties stipulated for voluntary dismissal before the action was decided. Boyles v. Gordon, No. 04SC211, 2004 Colo. LEXIS 1059, at *1 (Colo. Nov. 24, 2004).

In Howard v. Las Animas County Sheriff's Office, No. 09-cv-00640, 2010 U.S. Dist. LEXIS 27684 (D. Colo. Feb. 23, 2010), aff'd, Civil Action No. 09-cv-00640-PAB-KLM, 2010 WL 1235673 (D. Colo. Mar. 22, 2010), a former employee of the Las Animas County Sheriff's Office brought various claims against the Sheriff's Office, including defamation, libel, and false light. To support his claims, the employee cited two newspaper articles that discussed his arrest and commitment to a state mental hospital. Id. at *23. The district court dismissed the claims, noting that "[t]he elements of a defamation, libel or false light claim are essentially identical" and that the employee's allegations were insufficient to support any of the claims. Id. The court held that since the employee acknowledged that he had been arrested and committed to a state hospital, he had failed to show that the published statements were false. Id. at *24.

C. Other Privacy-Related Actions

1. **Intentional Infliction of Emotional Distress.** The Colorado Supreme Court has recognized that the tort of intentional infliction of emotional distress through extreme and outrageous conduct is applicable in Colorado. See, e.g., DeCicco v. Trinidad Area Health Ass'n, 573 P.2d 559 (Colo. 1977). This tort cannot apply to conduct not directed towards the plaintiff or conduct occurring when the plaintiff was not present. Bradshaw v. Nicolay, 765 P.2d 630 (Colo. App. 1988); Green v. Qwest Servs. Corp., 155 P.3d 383, (Colo. App. 2006). To establish liability for this tort, the plaintiff must prove that the defendant engaged in extreme and outrageous conduct recklessly or with the intent of causing the plaintiff severe emotional distress and that plaintiff incurred severe emotional distress as a result of defendant's conduct. C.J.I. Civ. 3d 23:1 (1990); Dolin v. Contemporary Fin. Solutions, Inc., 622 F. Supp. 2d 1077, 1089 (D. Colo. 2009).

A state tort claim of extreme and outrageous conduct is preempted by federal law where determining the authority of the employer in question requires reference to a collective bargaining agreement. See, e.g., Steinbach v. Dillon Cos., Inc., 253 F.3d 538 (10th Cir. 2001) (holding that a claim for extreme and outrageous conduct was preempted by § 301 of the Labor Management Relation Act because the "plaintiff's outrageous conduct claim cannot be determined without reference to the collective bargaining agreement").

Intentional or Reckless Conduct. The conduct not only must be extreme and outrageous, but also must be engaged in recklessly or with the intent of causing the plaintiff severe emotional distress. C.J.I. Civ. 3d 23:3 (1990).

Extreme and Outrageous Conduct. To state a claim for outrageous conduct, it must appear from the face of the complaint that the defendant's alleged conduct "was so outrageous in character, and so extreme and to such a degree, as to go beyond all possible bounds of decency, and to be regarded as atrocious, and utterly intolerable in a civilized community." Rugg v. McCarty, 476 P.2d 753, 756 (Colo. 1970). The tort was "designed to create liability for a very narrow type of conduct." Green v. Qwest Servs. Corp., 155 P.3d 383, 385 (Colo. App. 2006). Colorado courts are more likely to find conduct outrageous if it involves a course or pattern of conduct rather than an isolated incident. City of Lafayette v. Barrack, 847 P.2d 136, 139 (Colo. 1993); Dukeminier v. K-Mart Corp., 651 F. Supp. 1322, 1323 (D. Colo. 1987); Rawson v. Sears Roebuck & Co., 530 F. Supp. 776, 780 (D. Colo. 1982). See also Card v. Blakeslee, 937 P.2d 846 (Colo. App. 1996) (dismissing plaintiff's claim for outrageous conduct based on defendant psychotherapist's alleged publication of letter to plaintiff's daughter and other third parties accusing plaintiff of sexually abusing her daughter because defendant's conduct was "not sufficiently heinous to create a submissible claim"); Mass v. Martin Marietta Corp., 805 F. Supp. 1530 (D. Colo. 1992) (outrageous conduct claim allowed to go to jury where plaintiff presented evidence of significant racial harassment).

Courts repeatedly have held that termination from employment, without more, is not conduct rising to the level required for intentional infliction of emotional distress. See, e.g., Kerstien v. McGraw-Hill Cos., Inc., 7 F. App'x 868 (10th Cir. 2001); Yarbrough v. ADT Security Servs., No. 07-cv-01546, 2008 U.S. Dist. LEXIS 59477, at *7 (D. Colo. Aug. 6, 2008). An employer's failure to follow its own policies also does not rise to that level. See, e.g., Oberhamer v. Deep Rock Water Co., No. 06-cv-02284, 2009 U.S. Dist. LEXIS 36289, at *46–48 (D. Colo. Apr. 29, 2009) (finding an employer's disregard of contractual obligations not to be conduct rising to the requisite level of outrageous). Even a discharge coupled with alleged defamatory remarks or allegations of unlawful discrimination does not support an intentional infliction of emotional distress claim. Katz v. City of Aurora, 85 F. Supp. 2d 1012, 1021 (D. Colo. 2000), aff'd, 2001 13 F. App'x 837 (10th Cir. 2001) (citing cases); see also Preston v. Atmel Corp., 560 F. Supp. 2d 1035, 1040 (D. Colo. 2008).

Indeed, the Colorado Supreme Court has signaled that it is very difficult for a plaintiff to allege conduct that will be regarded as "outrageous" in the employment context. In Coors Brewing Co. v. Floyd, 978 P.2d 663 (Colo. 1999), the Colorado Supreme Court held that the court of appeals erred in reversing the trial court's dismissal of the plaintiff's claim for intentional infliction of emotional distress. There, the plaintiff was an investigator in the Security Department at Coors Brewing Company. Id. at 664. He alleged that his supervisors ordered him to participate in illegal undercover drug investigations of other employees and a related money-laundering scheme. Id. He further alleged that he was fired by Coors executives seeking to conceal their involvement in the unlawful investigations and place all of the blame on him. Id. at 665. The Colorado Supreme Court began its analysis of the trial court's decision to dismiss the plaintiff's intentional infliction of emotional distress claim by noting that, to state such a claim, "a plaintiff must allege behavior by a defendant that is extremely egregious." Id. The court further noted that "[l]iability has been found only where the conduct has been so outrageous in character, and so extreme in degree, as to go beyond all possible bounds of decency, and to be regarded as atrocious, and utterly intolerable in a civilized community." Id. at 666. It then discussed a court of appeals case in which one plaintiff alleged that he was fired because he asked for a transfer away from a supervisor who was directing him to engage in unlawful activities and another plaintiff claimed he was fired for giving truthful testimony to the Public Utilities Commission during their investigation of these activities. See id. (discussing Cronk v. Intermountain Rural Elec. Ass'n, 765 P.2d 619, 621 (Colo. App. 1988)). The Cronk plaintiffs' claims were dismissed as a matter of law because they did not meet the high standard for intentional infliction of emotional distress claims that was established in Rugg v. McCarty, 476 P.2d 753, 756 (Colo. 1970). Id.

The Floyd court continued, "Applying this high standard here, we hold that the conduct Floyd alleges is insufficient to state a claim for intentional infliction of emotional distress by outrageous conduct." Id. The court accepted Floyd's allegations as true, including his allegations that "Coors engaged in an extensive criminal conspiracy involving illegal drugs and money laundering and that Coors fired Floyd to scapegoat him for these crimes." Id. But the court found that the outrageousness of Coors' alleged criminal conduct towards society was "irrelevant"; what mattered, for purposes of assessing Floyd's claim, was "Coors' behavior toward Floyd." Id. No reasonable person could find that Coors' "alleged scapegoating of Floyd arose to the high level of outrageousness required by our case law," the court concluded. Id. Thus, the court of appeals should not have reversed the trial court's dismissal of the plaintiff's claim. Id.

After Floyd, as the federal district court for the District of Colorado has correctly observed, "the tort of intentional infliction of emotional distress is extremely limited." Katz v. City of Aurora, 85 F. Supp. 2d 1012, 1021 (D. Colo. 2000), aff'd, 13 F. App'x 837 (10th Cir. 2001); see also Silver v. Primero Reorganized Sch. Dist. No. 2, 619 F. Supp. 2d 1074, 1079 (D. Colo. 2007) (dismissing plaintiff's outrageous conduct claim despite allegations that she was fired for ending a sexual relationship with the school principal after she learned that he had made a wager that he would have sex with her and used confidential information from a school counselor to initiate the relationship because a "breach of trust by a supposed confidant . . . or the loss of that attention when the relationship ends . . . are events so common in everyday society that no reasonable person could find such behavior to be 'utterly intolerable'"); Abrahamson v. Sandoz, Inc., No. 06-cv-00636, 2008 U.S. Dist. LEXIS 26163, at *29 (D. Colo. Mar. 31, 2008) (granting summary judgment to the defendant because the plaintiff's allegations that he was compelled to help the company break the law and that his working conditions were so intolerable that he was constructively discharged did not constitute outrageous conduct); Holdbrook v. Saia Motor Freight Line, LLC, No. 09-cv-02870, 2011 U.S. Dist. LEXIS 43078, at *16-18 (D. Colo. Apr. 20, 2011) (holding that an employer requiring an employee to drive trucks that the employee believed were unsafe did not constitute outrageous conduct). But see GLN Compliance Group, Inc. v. Ross, No. 01-cv-2313, 2011 U.S. Dist. LEXIS 34913 (D. Colo. Mar. 24, 2011) (finding outrageous conduct where the defendant engaged in a coordinated campaign to ruin the plaintiff both professionally and financially, published and disseminated defamatory statements about the plaintiff, and left a threatening voice message on the plaintiff's home answering machine) aff'd, No. 11-1246, 2012 U.S. App. LEXIS 8913 (10th Cir. Colo. May 2, 2012).

The Tenth Circuit has allowed a claim of intentional infliction of emotional distress to go to a jury. In Riske v. King Soopers, 366 F.3d 1085 (10th Cir. 2004), a bakery manager for King Soopers brought an intentional infliction of emotional distress claim against the company and her manager based on evidence that, over a two-year period, her manager sent her anonymous notes, flowers, and other "gifts," followed her around, and whistled in a "taunting manner." Id. at 1087–88. The court observed that the case "presents a close question," but determined that the "conduct here comes so close to the bounds of decency that reasonable people could disagree about whether it constitutes actionable conduct." Id. at 1089. The court repeatedly emphasized the fact that the alleged stalker was the plaintiff's manager, and thus had authority over the plaintiff, as well as the fact that her manager was aware of how upsetting to the plaintiff the anonymous notes and deliveries had been. Id. at 1089–90. The court commented, "[t]his may or may not be enough to convince a reasonable jury that the conduct went beyond a hurtful prank and is actionable as outrageous conduct. But in close cases like this, the issue should be resolved by the jury." Id. at 1090.

District Courts in Colorado have since used Riske as a bar for measuring the outrageousness of conduct. In Silver v. Primero Reorganized School District No. 2, the court drew a direct comparison between the facts at hand, which allegedly involved stalking and harassment by an employer, to the facts in Riske. No. 06-cv-02088, 2008 U.S. Dist. LEXIS 20791, at *33–38 (D. Colo. March 13, 2008). The court concluded that summary judgment for the defendant was warranted because the length of the harassment period was much shorter and the employee had been involved in a consensual relationship with the employer. Id. at *33–38 ("When compared to the facts of a 'close case' like Riske, the Court finds that the facts of this case are insufficient to constitute actionable outrageous conduct."); see also Preston v. Atmel Corp., 560 F. Supp. 2d 1035, 1040 (D. Colo. 2008) (dismissing plaintiff's outrageous conduct claim because, compared to Riske, "the instant case presents no such 'close question'").

Severe Emotional Distress. To state a claim for intentional infliction of emotional distress, proof of accompanying physical injury is not needed, but proof of severe emotional distress is required. Espinosa v. Sheridan United Tire, 655 P.2d 424 (Colo. App. 1982). The applicable jury instruction, Colo. Jury Instr. Civ. 23:4 (1990), defines "severe emotional distress" as "highly unpleasant mental reactions . . . (nervous shock, fright, horror, grief, shame, humiliation, embarrassment, anger, chagrin, disappointment, or worry) . . . so extreme that no person of ordinary sensibilities could be expected to tolerate and endure it. The duration and intensity of emotional distress are factors to be considered in determining its severity."

In Baker v. Echostar Comm. Corp., No. 06-cv-01103, 2007 U.S. Dist. LEXIS 89111, *35-39 (D. Colo. Dec. 4, 2007), the Colorado District Court held that a plaintiff waived her claim to severe emotional distress, and hence her intentional infliction of emotional distress claim, by arguing that her emotional distress was only of "garden variety."

Causation. Causation of emotional distress is required. C.J.I. Civ. 23:1 (1990).

Privileges and Defenses. In the defamation context, the actual malice requirement applies to intentional infliction of emotional distress claims against media defendants based upon Lewis v. McGraw-Hill Broadcasting Co., 832 P.2d 1118, 20 Media L. Rep. 1240 (Colo. App. 1992). In Lewis, the Colorado Court of Appeals held that the plaintiff could not recover for the independent tort of intentional infliction of emotional distress based on a false publication by a media defendant without showing that it was made with actual malice. Id. at 1125. Actual malice in this context requires a plaintiff to prove that the defendant knew the statement was false or acted with reckless disregard of its truth or falsity. See Barnett v. Denver Publ'g Co., Inc., 36 P.3d 145 (Colo. App. 2001), cert. denied, 535 U.S. 1056 (2002). In Books v. Paige, 773 P.2d 1098, 15 Media L. Rep. 2353 (Colo. App. 1988), the Colorado Court of Appeals cited Hustler Magazine v. Falwell, 485 U.S. 46 (1988), for the proposition that the First Amendment prohibited a public figure from maintaining a claim for outrageous conduct when the conduct complained of is expressive behavior directed at his "public persona." Then, in Seefried v. Hummel, 148 P.3d 184, 191 (Colo. App. 2005), the appeals court affirmed the dismissal of a claim for outrageous conduct that arose during a church meeting where church members decided to fire their pastor, finding that such a claim was barred by the First Amendment.

In addition, when an employee is eligible for benefits under the Worker's Compensation Act, the employee is barred from initiating personal injury actions against his or her employer. See, e.g., Tolbert v. Martin Marietta Corp., 759 P.2d 17, 21 (Colo. 1988). In Smith v. Colorado Interstate Gas Co., an employee's claim for intentional infliction of emotional distress was barred because the Worker's Compensation Act provided an exclusive remedy for the employee's injuries. 794 F. Supp. 1035, 1042 (D. Colo. 1992).

Damages. The applicable jury instruction, C.J.I. Civ. 23:6 (1990), lists the following items for which damages can be recovered for claims involving outrageous conduct: (1) emotional distress, including those forms of emotional distress enumerated in Colo. Jury Instr. Civ. 23:4 (1990), which are appropriate in light of the evidence in the case; (2) any physical discomfort or inconvenience; (3) any physical illness or injury; (4) any reasonable medical expenses; (5) any loss of reputation; (6) any loss of earnings; and (7) any other elements of compensable damage for which there is sufficient evidence. There is no Colorado case authority for "loss of reputation" as a compensable item of damages for this tort. COLO. REV. STAT. § 13-21-102.5(3)(a) limits damages for "non-economic loss or injury" to $468,010, unless the court finds justification by clear and convincing evidence for greater damages. In no case shall the amount of such damages exceed $936,030. These limitations were adjusted for inflation on January 1, 2008. COLO. REV. STAT. § 13-21-102.5(3)(c). COLO. REV. STAT. § 13-21-102.5(2)(b) defines "non-economic loss or injury" as "non-pecuniary harm for which damages are recoverable by the person suffering the direct or primary loss or injury, including pain and suffering, inconvenience, emotional distress, and impairment of the quality of life."

Pecuniary losses are recoverable if they are a natural consequence of the defendant's conduct. Meiter v. Cavanaugh, 580 P.2d 399, 402 (Colo. App. 1978).

Regarding non-pecuniary losses, the Colorado Court of Appeals has held that the "sentimental and emotional value" of a loss may be considered in awarding damages for extreme outrageous conduct. Chryar v. Wolf, 21 P.3d 428, 430 (Colo. App. 2000). But "only a reasonable, and not unusual, sentimental and emotional value may be considered in such actions." Id.

Punitive damages are recoverable for outrageous conduct. See Meiter v. Cavanaugh, 580 P.2d 399 (Colo. App. 1978). Punitive damages are governed by COLO. REV. STAT. § 13-21-102, which allows punitive damages where the plaintiff pleads and proves that the injury complained of was attended by circumstances of fraud, malice, insult, or a wanton and reckless disregard for the plaintiff's rights and feelings. The amount of exemplary damages generally may not exceed an amount equal to the actual damages awarded to the injured party, although the court has the discretion to increase an award of exemplary damages to a sum not to exceed three times the amount of actual damages under certain aggravated circumstances. COLO. REV. STAT. § 13-21-102(3)(b). Evidence of the income or net worth of a party may not be considered in determining the appropriateness or amount of such damages. COLO. REV. STAT. § 13-21-102. The standard of proof for this element is beyond a reasonable doubt. COLO. REV. STAT. § 13-25-127.

2. **Interference With Prospective Economic Advantage.** Colorado courts have recognized a claim for interference with prospective economic advantage, also referred to as a claim for interference with prospective financial advantage or prospective contractual relations, as a cognizable cause of action distinct from tortious interference with a contract. Amoco Oil Co. v. Ervin, 908 P.2d 493, 500 (Colo. 1995); see also Castillo v. Hobbs Mun. Sch. Bd., 315 F. App'x 693, 698 (10th Cir. 2009) (employer's failure to renew employee's contract after hearing sexually explicit messages the employee sent to his secretary did not infringe upon employee's prospective economic advantage because he received other employment positions).

Colorado follows the Restatement definition of this tort, which provides that "One who intentionally and improperly interferes with another's prospective contractual relation . . . is subject to liability to the other for the pecuniary harm resulting from loss of the benefits of the relation, whether the interference consists of (a) inducing or otherwise causing a third person not to enter into or continue the prospective relation or (b) preventing the other from acquiring or continuing the prospective relation."

RESTATEMENT (SECOND) OF TORTS, § 766B; see also Amoco, 908 P.2d at 500 (holding that Colorado recognizes the tort and giving the Restatement definition). This tort does not require the existence of an underlying agreement, but it does require the plaintiff to show "a reasonable likelihood or reasonable probability that a contract would have resulted" absent the defendant's interference. MDM Group Assocs., Inc. v. CX Reinsurance Co. Ltd., UK, 165 P.3d 882, 886 (Colo. App. 2007). But the prospective agreement need not be a formal contract:

It is not necessary that the prospective relation be expected to be reduced to a formal, binding contract. It may include prospective quasi-contractual or other restitutionary rights or even the voluntary conferring of commercial benefits in recognition of a moral obligation.

Amoco, 908 P.2d at 500 (quoting RESTATEMENT (SECOND) OF TORTS § 766B cmt. c (1979)). See also Tara Woods Ltd. P'ship v. Fannie Mae, 731 F. Supp. 2d 1103, 1119-20 (D. Colo. 2010) (interference with purchase offers from prospective buyers is sufficient to establish a claim for interference with prospective economic advantage).

The crucial question in determining liability for tortious interference is generally whether the defendant's interference was intentional and improper. See Harris Group, Inc. v. Robinson, 209 P.3d 1188, 1196 (Colo. App. 2009) ("Thus, to achieve the balance between protecting contracts and preserving privileges, a plaintiff must show more than that a defendant intentionally interfered with . . . prospective contractual relations. There must also be proof that such interference was 'improper.'"); Chambers v. Prowers County Hosp. Dist., No. 07-cv-01736, 2009 U.S. Dist. Lexis 28297, at *47 (D. Colo. Mar. 31, 2009).

Intentional interference includes interference that the actor knows is substantially certain to occur as a result of his action, even if interference was not the *purpose* of the action. Natural Wealth Real Estate, Inc. v. Cohen, No. 05-cv-01233, 2006 U.S. Dist. LEXIS 87439, at *16 (D. Colo. Dec. 4, 2006) (citing the Restatement (Second) of Torts § 766B cmt. d). A defendant's purpose is used instead to determine whether any interference was improper. Id. at *17. Improper interference includes conduct such as fraud, violence, and the threat of civil litigation or criminal prosecution, Electrolux Corp. v. Lawson, 654 P.2d 340 (Colo. App. 1982), but it is not limited to these "predatory means." The Restatement (Second) of Torts § 768 enumerates the factors courts should consider to determine whether the interfering conduct was improper: (1) the nature of the conduct; (2) the defendant's motive; (3) the interests of the party with whom the defendant's conduct interferes; (4) the interests sought to be advanced by the defendant; (5) the social interests in protecting the freedom of the defendant's action and the other party's contractual interests; (6) the proximity or remoteness of the defendant's conduct to the interference; and (7) the relations between the parties. See also Wedbush Morgan Sec., Inc. v. Hartman, No. 06-cv-00510, 2007 U.S. Dist. LEXIS 14390, at *23 (D. Colo. Mar. 1, 2007) (noting that "defamation with actual malice," if proven, "would certainly qualify as 'wrongful'" and thus improper).

Interfering with a prospective contract by exercising a lawful right does not constitute improper interference. For example, in Lufti v. Brighton Community Hospital Ass'n, 40 P.3d 51 (Colo. App. 2001), the Colorado Court of Appeals held that an emergency room doctor whose work as an independent contractor was terminated failed to establish the requirements of tortious interference with contractual relations. The court noted that the contract between the plaintiff and the hospital stated that the hospital "may at any time, require [the contractor] to remove any of the individual Physicians from the Department coverage schedule." Id. at *58. Because the actions of the hospital fell within the scope of the lawful contract, the plaintiff failed to show tortious interference. Similarly, in TMJ Implants, Inc. v. Aetna, Inc., the Tenth Circuit held that a statement that was not an actionable defamation "could not form the basis (for) interference claims because such activity was not improper." 498 F.3d 1175, 1198 (10th Cir. 2007). In Sweeney v. Marvin Windows, Inc., 2010 U.S. Dist. LEXIS 112159 (D. Colo. Oct. 20, 2010), a window dealer alleged interference with prospective economic advantage when the manufacturer refused to promote the dealer's business. The District Court held that this conduct did not interfere with prospective economic advantage because the manufacturer's actions were lawful. In Martin v. Montezuma-Cortez School District RE-1, the Colorado Supreme Court held that a school district could not state a claim against striking school teachers for tortious interference with economic advantage based upon the teachers' exercise of their lawful right to strike. 841 P.2d 237, 251 (Colo. 1992).

Likewise, the Colorado Supreme Court has indicated that, because "competition and an economic interest of seeking to acquire business are not usually improper interference," a competitor may exert some "economic pressure" without subjecting himself to liability for tortious interference with prospective economic advantage. See Amoco, 908 P.2d at 500, 501–02; Seefried v. Hummel, 148 P.3d 184 (Colo. App. 2005) (finding that an action for intentional interference with business relationships arising out of statements made by church members during the termination proceedings for a pastor was barred by the First Amendment). **Furthermore, under the "competitor's privilege," a "plaintiff cannot sue one of its competitors for intentional interference in prospective economic advantage." Zimmer Spine, Inc. v. EBI, LLC, Civil Case No. 10-cv-03112-LTB-CBS, 2011 WL 4089535, at *5 (D. Colo. Sept. 14, 2011). The privilege states that the defendant is not liable for intentional interference if (1) "it concerns a matter of competition between the defendant and plaintiff; (2) the defendant does not employ wrongful means; (3) the action does not amount to an unlawful restraint of trade; and (4) the defendant's purpose is, at least in part, to advance its own interest." Id. at 5. Although the privilege is an affirmative defense, it may nevertheless provide grounds for dismissal if its existence is clear on the face of the complaint. Id. at 7 (finding that the wooing away of sales personnel to a competitor fell under the privilege).**

Additionally, a defendant cannot be liable for interference with a contract to which it is a party. Rader v. Electronic Payment Sys., LLC, Civil Action No. 11-cv-01482, 2012 WL 4336175, at *4 (D. Colo. Sept. 21, 2012) (citing MDM Group Assocs. v. CX Reinsurance Co., 165 P.3d 882, 886 (Colo. App. 2007)). In Rader, the plaintiff, an independent sales representative for EPS, brought an action against EPS for tortious interference with prospective economic advantage after EPS independently entered into a sales contract with a client the plaintiff had recruited. Id. at *1-2. The plaintiff claimed that EPS "did not have any relationship" with the client and that EPS was "an outsider without any participation in [the] formed plan" for sale to the client. Id. at *4. The court held that the plaintiff failed to state a claim for tortious interference, noting that EPS made the final decision as to whether an order for its product was accepted or rejected. Id. The sales contracts that the plaintiff arranged were ultimately concluded between EPS and the client, not between the plaintiff and the client. Id. Because a tortious interference claim cannot lie against a defendant when the defendant itself is a party to the contract, the court dismissed the plaintiff's claim. Id. at *4-5.

The measure of damages in an action for interference with prospective economic advantage is the loss caused by the interference. RESTATEMENT (SECOND) OF TORTS § 774A (1979). A prevailing plaintiff may be awarded damages for lost profits and chance for gain, reasonably foreseeable mental suffering, other compensatory and consequential damages, and punitive damages. COLO. REV. STAT. § 13-21-102.

3. **Prima Facie Tort.** Colorado does not recognize this concept.

II. EMPLOYER TESTING OF EMPLOYEES

A. Psychological or Personality Testing

1. ***Common Law and Statutes.*** The Americans with Disabilities Act ("ADA"), 42 U.S.C. §§ 12101 et seq., prohibits the use of psychological testing in the pre-employment process to the extent the tests are designed to reveal mental impairments that may constitute a disability within the meaning of the ADA. Psychological tests that seek only to reveal traits or attributes of the applicant are not barred by the ADA. They may constitute an invasion of privacy, however, particularly if the questions ask employees to reveal highly personal information about religious and political beliefs or sexual preferences. Cf. McKenna v. Fargo, 451 F. Supp. 1355 (D.N.J. 1978), aff'd, 601 F.2d 575 (3d Cir. 1979) (holding that such a psychological test administered to firefighters did not violate their rights of privacy where the employer did not see their individual answers but only the results of the examination). Although there is no specific Colorado statute, regulation, or case addressing this issue, Colorado's anti-discrimination statute, COLO. REV. STAT. § 24-34-402, parallels the ADA and applies to all employers with one or more employees in Colorado.

2. ***Private Employers.*** There are no reported Colorado decisions on this subject.

3. ***Public Employers.*** There are no reported Colorado decisions on this subject.

B. Drug Testing

1. ***Common Law and Statutes.*** Colorado's anti-discrimination statute prohibits employers from discriminating against individuals on the basis of disability. See COLO. REV. STAT. § 24-34-402. However, a person currently involved in the illegal use of, or having an addiction to, a controlled substance is not "disabled" within the meaning of the statute. See COLO. REV. STAT. § 24-34-301(2.5)(b)(I). Accordingly, Colorado's statutory prohibition on disability discrimination cannot be used as a basis for challenging an employer's drug testing policy.

Moreover, COLO. REV. STAT. § 8-73-108(5)(e)(IX.5) provides that an employer shall not be charged for unemployment benefits when it has a previously established written drug policy and terminates an employee as the result of a drug test showing the presence of marijuana in the employee's system during working hours. **Although an employee's use of marijuana may be exempt from state criminal prosecution under the "medical use" provisions of the Colorado Constitution, an employee who uses marijuana under those provisions may still be denied unemployment benefits. Beinor v. Indus. Claim Appeals Office of Colo. & Serv. Group, Inc., 262 P.3d 970, 977 (Colo. App. 2011) (construing Colo. Const. art. XVIII, § 14(2)(b). But see id. at 978 (Gabriel, J., dissenting, and asserting that the Medical Marijuana amendment created not only a constitutional exemption to state prosecution, but also a constitutional right to possess marijuana).**

In 2001, the Colorado Supreme Court determined that an employer's personnel records of employee drug tests or other physical ability tests are not considered medical records under the medical records theft statute, COLO. REV. STAT. § 18-4-412(1). People v. Palomo, 31 P.3d 879 (Colo. 2001). Noting that even the ADA does not consider employment drug-screening tests to be medical examinations, the court reasoned that the medical information contained in personnel files was closer to employment examinations than medical examinations. Id. at 883. As a result, neither the district attorney's office nor the personnel manager were guilty of medical records theft when the personnel manager turned over employment records containing medical information to the district attorney's office. Id. at 883-85.

A case involving a challenge to a Colorado Department of Revenue Division of Racing regulation requiring "random, suspicionless drug testing of licensed dog trainers" was remanded by the Colorado Court of Appeals after the trial court had granted summary judgment in favor of the Department concerning the regulation. Timm v. Reitz, 39 P.3d 1252, 1254 (Colo. App. 2001). The appellate court found there was insufficient evidence in the record to demonstrate a special need to test dog trainers. Id. at 1256.

2. ***Private Employers.***

In Slaughter v. John Elway Dodge Southwest/AutoNation, 107 P.3d 1165 (Colo. App. 2005), an at-will employee was terminated for refusing to submit to a drug test by her employer. The employee filed suit, claiming that her termination violated public policy. Id. at 1167. She argued that the court should prevent private employers from requiring employee drug tests absent reasonable suspicion of drug use or health and safety issues. Id. at 1169. The court of appeals disagreed. Id. First, the court noted that the Fourth Amendment, which prohibits a public employer from drug testing without individualized suspicion of wrongdoing, only "limits government conduct, not private conduct." Id. Second, the court observed that Colorado "does not have a clearly expressed employee right to refuse drug testing"—to the contrary, COLO. REV. STAT. § 8-73-108(5)(e)(IX.5) establishes that it is acceptable for an employer to terminate an employee if a drug test shows the presence of marijuana in the employee's system during working hours. Id. at 1170. Finally, the tort of invasion of privacy by intrusion "does not clearly mandate a public policy that an employer may not direct an employee to take a drug test in compliance with a previously established drug policy." Id. at 1171. Thus, the court held, no public policy entitles an at-will employee to refuse to comply with an employer's previously existing policy requiring drug testing. Id.

In Roe v. Cheyenne Mountain Conference Resort, 124 F.3d 1221 (10th Cir. 1997), an employee alleged that her employer's drug policy, which included random drug testing, a requirement that employees disclose prescription drugs that they were taking, and a ban on the use of non-prescription drugs, violated her right to privacy under Colorado law. Specifically, the employee argued that the policy constituted an "intrusion upon seclusion," a tort that does not depend upon publication of private facts. Id. at 1236. The Tenth Circuit held that the employee had shown a substantial basis for the possibility that the Colorado courts would uphold a claim for invasion of privacy by intrusion upon seclusion and remanded the case to the Colorado courts. Id. at 1237. The plaintiff successfully used this theory to win the case on remand. (See Roe v. Cheyenne Mountain Conference Resort, No. 98-1138, 1999 U.S. App. LEXIS 2611 (10th Cir. 1999)). The Tenth Circuit's published decision in Roe constituted a departure from its earlier decision in Mares v. Conagra Poultry Co., 971 F.2d 492 (10th Cir. 1992), in which the court held, as a matter of law, that the "suggested intrusion" on the employee's privacy by the employer's policy requiring disclosure of prescription drugs was "insignificant."

The Colorado Supreme Court found that the results of an employer's mandatory drug screening test could become the basis of a defendant's criminal prosecution. People v. Alvarado, 31 P.3d 145, 146 (Colo. 2001) (sitting en banc). Defendant Luis Alvarado was out on bail pending his trial. Id. at 145. The bonding company requested his bail be revoked because the defendant had been using drugs. Id. The bonding company informed the district attorney's office that Alvarado had failed a drug test given by his employer, Westaff. Id. The district attorney's office was told by at least two of Westaff's employees that Alvarado had been terminated "because of drugs." Id. As a result, the district attorney's office obtained the results of the drug test from the laboratory Westaff used for Alvarado's drug testing, Clinical References Laboratories. Id. The court stated that "[a]ssuming without deciding that the seizure of the test results from Westaff was the result of an illegal search and relying on the trial court's redacted affidavit, we conclude that there remained sufficient probable cause to support the warrant for the evidence procured from Clinical References Laboratories." Id. at 146. Thus, the urine sample tested for the employer, which was retained by the laboratory because it tested positive, was held to be admissible evidence. Id.

3. ***Public Employers.*** Random Drug Testing. Where a public employer adopts a policy that requires its employees to submit to random drug testing, the testing constitutes a search under the Fourth Amendment and therefore must be reasonable. See 19 Solid Waste Dep't Mechanics v. City of Albuquerque, 156 F.3d 1068, 1072 (10th Cir. 1998). In determining whether the search is reasonable, a court must balance the nature of the privacy interest upon which the search intrudes and the character of the intrusion against the nature and immediacy of the governmental concern and the efficacy of the challenged test for meeting that concern. Id. Prior to conducting this balancing test, however, the court must determine whether the public employer has demonstrated that the drug testing program at issue is warranted by a "special need." Id. If the government cannot make such a showing, the drug testing program must be struck down as unconstitutional. Id.

In order to demonstrate a "special need" for its random drug testing program, a public employer must meet two requirements. First, the employer must show that the drug testing program was adopted in response to a documented drug abuse problem or that drug abuse among the target group would pose a serious danger to the public. Id. at 1073. Second, the employer must show that its drug testing program meets the related goals of detection and deterrence. Id. Where the drug tests occur infrequently and in predictable intervals, enabling the employees being tested to evade detection by avoiding drug use prior to the tests, the drug testing program lacks any deterrent effect and, accordingly, does not satisfy the "special need" showing. See id.

In 2000, the Tenth Circuit decided two cases involving the termination of public employees based on the positive results of random drug tests. Unlike Solid Waste, the issues on appeal in these two cases did not involve the "special needs" aspect of the Fourth Amendment. Nevertheless, the Tenth Circuit's treatment of these cases is significant because it helps to define the scope of public employees' rights in situations of random drug testing.

In Garcia v. City of Albuquerque, 232 F.3d 760, 771 (10th Cir. 2000), Silas Garcia, the plaintiff, was a bus driver for the Transit Department of the City of Albuquerque. Under federal regulations, vehicle operators such as Garcia are classified as "safety sensitive employees," and thus subject to random, suspicionless urinalysis drug tests. Id. at 763. In 1996, Garcia's urinalysis revealed the presence of metabolites for marijuana, upon which the City terminated Garcia's employment. Id. The Personnel Board, however, reinstated Garcia's employment, subject to his enrollment in a drug rehabilitation program and regular drug tests. Id. The City appealed the Personnel Board's decision to state court and, because Garcia failed to respond to the City's motion, the court entered a default judgment against him. Id. at 765. Pending the state court's review of the Personnel Board's decision, the City agreed to reassign Garcia as a security guard at the same pay and benefits of a bus driver. Id. at 764. Garcia failed to report to his security guard reassignment and, therefore, the City withdrew its offer of employment altogether. Id.

Garcia filed a complaint alleging that the City had violated his right of due process by infringing upon his property and liberty interests. Id. at 763. With respect to procedural due process, Garcia claimed that his rights had been violated by the City's refusal to return him to work "without any hearing and without justification." Id. at 769. The Tenth Circuit held that Garcia's procedural due process rights had not been violated. Id. at 770. The court accepted the City's argument that it had complied with the Personnel Board's order to reinstate Garcia by offering him employment as a security guard, but that Garcia had resigned that post by refusing to report for work. Id. at 770. The court further noted that Garcia had numerous opportunities to challenge the City's actions before neutral bodies, but that he had failed to do so. Id.

Garcia also alleged that his substantive due process rights had been violated by the City's arbitrary actions in terminating his employment and in refusing to return him to his bus route. Id. The Tenth Circuit held that Garcia was a tenured public employee entitled to substantive due process protection, but that the City's actions had not infringed upon his rights. Id. at 771. The court noted that substantive due process protects employees from actions that are "arbitrary." Id. Regarding Garcia's claim that his termination was arbitrary, the court noted that the Personnel Board terminated him based on the default judgment entered against him in state court, and that "compliance with a valid state court judgment is not an 'arbitrary action.'" Id. With respect to Garcia's claim that the City's refusal to return him to work as a bus driver constituted an arbitrary action, the court noted that Garcia's therapist concluded that he was "unable to drive motorcoach," and therefore the City's decision was not arbitrary. Id.

In Sigmon v. CommunityCare HMO, Inc., 234 F.3d 1121, 1122 (10th Cir. 2000), Don Sigmon, an employee of the City of Tulsa, tested positive for marijuana in a random drug test. The test was conducted pursuant a Tulsa policy designed to prevent drug use by City employees. Id. The City conditioned Sigmon's continued employment upon his completion of a substance abuse program run by the private corporation CommunityCare HMO, Inc. Id. While attending the substance abuse program, Sigmon claimed he was confronted with religious content that ran contrary to his predilections. Id. Sigmon sued the City of Tulsa and CommunityCare "for conspiring to force him to undergo an offensive religious experience on threat of termination of his employment, in violation of 42 U.S.C. § 1983." Id.

Because a § 1983 action will only lie where the defendants have acted "under color of law," id. at 1125, the issue for the Tenth Circuit was "whether Tulsa's act of threatening discipline against Sigmon in reliance on [CommunityCare's] report and recommendation converts [CommunityCare's] conduct into state action." Id. at 1126. In support of his claim, Sigmon alleged that CommunityCare representatives had "engaged in a conspiracy to violate his civil rights because they referred Sigmon to a religiously-based treatment program and then reported his non-compliance to the City, aware that this would likely prompt Tulsa to begin termination proceedings." Id. at 1126–27. The court, however, disagreed with Sigmon. According to the Tenth Circuit, Sigmon had "miss[ed] the fundamental point that Tulsa retained complete authority to enforce its drug policy, while [CommunityCare] merely acted as an independent contractor in identifying and referring employees to treatment services." Id. Therefore, Sigmon failed to satisfy the test for state action and the dismissal of his § 1983 claim was affirmed. Id. at 1127-28.

Drug Testing Based on Reasonable Suspicion. Where a public employer adopts a policy providing that employees will be required to take a drug test upon reasonable suspicion of drug abuse, the drug testing policy is constitutional if it provides for mandatory testing of employees who hold safety or security-sensitive positions based on reasonable suspicion of either on-duty or off-duty drug use. Individuals who do not hold safety or security-sensitive positions cannot be subjected to drug testing absent reasonable suspicion of on-duty drug use. See City & County of Denver v. Casados, 862 P.2d 908 (Colo. 1993), cert. denied, 511 U.S. 1005 (U.S. 1994).

The Exclusionary Rule and Employment Termination Proceedings. Because drug testing is subject to the Fourth Amendment's protections, public employees terminated for drug use have asserted that the exclusionary rule requires the suppression of drug test results obtained by means in violation of the Fourth Amendment. In Ahart v. Colorado Department of Corrections, a prison warden heard that two Department of Corrections employees used drugs and ordered them to submit to drug tests. 964 P.2d 517, 519 (Colo. 1998). Both employees tested positive and were fired. Id. The Administrative Law Judge ("ALJ") held that the warden lacked reasonable suspicion to order the employees to take the drug tests, but determined that there was no basis for applying the exclusionary rule to preclude the test results from the termination proceedings. Id. The State Personnel Board reversed the ALJ, holding that the exclusionary rule applied. Id. The Colorado Supreme Court agreed with the ALJ, however. It noted that the exclusionary rule does not apply in all civil cases, but only in civil cases where the benefits of applying the rule outweigh the costs. Id. at 520. Here, the court reasoned, the societal costs of applying the rule were "substantial" in view of the "security and safety-sensitive nature" of the prison workers' jobs. Id. at 523. Thus, the court held that the exclusionary rule was inapplicable.

C. Medical Testing

1. ***Common Law and Statutes.*** Both the Americans with Disabilities Act ("ADA") and the regulations promulgated under the Colorado Anti-Discrimination Act ("CADA") prohibit pre-offer medical examinations. See Americans with Disabilities Act of 1990, 42 U.S.C. § 12112(D)(2)(A) (1990) (the ADA applies to employers in Colorado with 15 or more full-time employees); 3 COLO. CODE REGS. § 708-1, Rules 60.1–60.2 (2007) (prohibiting pre-employment medical examinations and inquiries but permitting inquiries about an individual's ability to perform job related functions). CADA prohibits discrimination in employment against otherwise qualified handicapped persons and applies to all employers with ats least one employee in Colorado. COLO. REV. STAT. § 24-34-402(1). Furthermore, the regulations under CADA explicitly state that, where possible, CADA should be interpreted in a manner similar to the interpretation of rules and regulations under the ADA. COLO. CODE REGS. § 708-1, Rule 60.1(C).

An employer may require medical testing after making an offer of employment, provided the medical examination is required of all new hires within the same professional category. Regulations under the ADA require post-offer medical examinations to be related to the specific functions of employment and consistent with a business necessity. 29 C.F.R. § 1630.14(b)(3). Colorado law is more restrictive in regulating post-offer medical examinations. Regulations under CADA permit post-offer employment examinations *only* if they test for capabilities essential to employment. 3 COLO. CODE REGS. § 708-1, Rule 60.2(D). Although there is no Colorado law addressing the testing of employees or job applicants for HIV or AIDS, state law does regulate the procedures used for such testing. COLO. REV. STAT. § 10-3-1104.5. Colorado state law regulates what type of consent must be given to test for HIV and prohibits the release of test information to anyone who is not the patient's physician or involved in an underwriting decision. Id. One exception to this rule against disclosure is a Colorado law that requires any physician, hospital, or clinic to disclose to the State Department of Public Health the identity and address of every individual who tests positive for HIV or AIDS. COLO. REV. STAT. § 25-4-1402.

2. ***Private Employers.*** There are no reported Colorado decisions on this subject.

3. ***Public Employers.*** There are no reported Colorado decisions on this subject.

D. Polygraph Tests

The Federal Employee Polygraph Protection Act of 1988 generally prohibits the use of polygraph testing by private employers. 29 U.S.C. §§ 2001 et seq. There are no Colorado statutes governing the use of polygraph tests by employers. However, a few Colorado cases have touched upon their use.

In Everitt Lumber Co. v. Industrial Commission, two employees of Everitt Lumber were terminated for refusing to take a polygraph test that the company asked its employees to take during an investigation of inventory losses. 565 P.2d 967, 968 (Colo. App. 1977). Both employees previously had signed forms consenting to take such a test at any time during the course of their employment. Id. Following their terminations, the two employees filed claims for unemployment benefits and were awarded full benefits after a hearing. Id. The employer appealed, arguing that it could not be held responsible for the employees' terminations. Id. The Colorado Court of Appeals held that the employer must be deemed responsible, given that the employees were requested not only to submit to a polygraph but also to waive their Fifth Amendment rights against self-incrimination. Id. at 969; see also Johnson v. City Council for City of Glendale, 595 P.2d 701, 704 (Colo. App. 1979) (declining to decide whether a public employee's refusal to submit to a polygraph test may constitute sufficient cause to terminate his employment).

Subsequently, in Ellis v. Buckley, the plaintiff's employer hired an outside firm to investigate cash shortages that had been discovered at the store where the plaintiff was employed. 790 P.2d 875, 876 (Colo. App. 1989). The plaintiff took a polygraph test at her employer's request. Id. According to the outside firm that administered the test, the plaintiff "failed," and the employer terminated her employment. Id. The plaintiff commenced an action against the outside firm that administered the polygraph, alleging that the manner in which it had treated her during and following the test was outrageous. Id. She prevailed on her claims for negligence and intentional infliction of emotional distress. Id. at 877. Evidently, she did not sue her employer.

Finally, in Jones v. Geneva Pharmaceuticals, Inc., an employee was terminated for assaulting a co-worker. 132 F. App'x 772 (10th Cir. 2005). The employee denied the assault and offered to take a polygraph test to prove it. Id. at 773. Thereafter, she sued her employer for alleged age discrimination and sought to introduce into evidence her offer to take the polygraph. Id. The district court excluded the evidence, and the Tenth Circuit upheld the district court's exercise of discretion. Id. at 776. The appeals court stated, "Polygraph tests are generally inadmissible in this circuit. If a party seeks to admit a polygraph test, that party must satisfy the criteria for admission under Daubert." Id. (citation omitted). Because the plaintiff did not "demonstrate the polygraph's reliability or effectiveness," the probative value of the evidence she sought to admit—her offer to take the polygraph—was substantially outweighed by the danger of unfair prejudice to the employer." Id.

E. Fingerprinting

In Pacific Frontier v. Pleasant Grove City, 414 F.3d 1221 (10th Cir. 2005), door-to-door solicitors sued Pleasant Grove City under 42 U.S.C. § 1983, claiming that a city ordinance licensing procedure for solicitors violated their commercial speech rights under the First Amendment. The plaintiffs obtained a preliminary injunction enjoining two aspects of the licensing procedure, one of which was the fingerprinting provision. Id. at 1226. In upholding the injunction as to this provision, the Tenth Circuit noted, "Pleasant Grove failed to establish below that its fingerprinting requirement has had any impact on crime committed by solicitors. . . . Any speculation that fingerprints would assist with crime prevention is further undercut by evidence that residential burglaries committed in Pleasant Grove by those posing as solicitors involved individuals who did not apply for a license. The city has no evidence other than conjecture to support its argument that having solicitors' fingerprints on file would either deter crime or aid the investigation of a burglary." Id. at 1234-35. Because the city could not show that fingerprinting advanced its legitimate interest in protecting its citizens from crime and in preserving the privacy of its residents, the district court did not abuse its discretion in enjoining the fingerprinting element of the licensing procedure. Id. at 1235.

III. SEARCHES

The Fourth Amendment to the United States Constitution and Article II, Section 7 of the Colorado Constitution protect individuals from unreasonable searches and seizures by state actors. Hoffman v. People, 780 P.2d 471, 473 (Colo. 1989). Article II, Section 7 of the Colorado Constitution mimics the privacy protections in the United States Constitution. Derdeyn v. Univ. of Colo., 832 P.2d 1031, 1035 (Colo. App. 1991), aff'd, 863 P.2d 929 (Colo. 1993). Therefore, federal cases interpreting the United States Constitution are relevant to interpreting and understanding the scope of the privacy protections in Colorado Constitution. In the employment context, legal issues can arise if an employer conducts a search that infringes on its employees' expectation of privacy. The legality of an employer-sanctioned search depends on the manner in which the search was conducted and whether the employer is a government entity or a private company.

It is well established that drug testing is considered a "search" under the Fourth Amendment and Article II, Section 7 of the Colorado Constitution. See, e.g., Derdeyn v. University of Colorado, 832 P.2d 1031, 1033 (Colo. App. 1991). Several of the cases applying Colorado law on searches in the workplace arise in the context of employee challenges to drug testing programs.

A. Employee's Person

1. ***Private Employers.*** Unless acting as an agent of the government, private employers are not considered state actors. Thus, private employers are not constrained by the privacy protections in either the Federal Constitution or the Colorado Constitution. However, Colorado courts have developed common law invasion of privacy principles prohibiting private employers from conducting unreasonable searches. Thompson v. Johnson County Cmty. Coll., 108 F.3d 1388 (10th Cir. 1997). But see John R. Paddock, Searches of Employee's Property by Private Colorado Employers, 16 COLO. PRAC. § 1.34 (2nd ed. 2008) ("With regard to workplace searches, people employed by private companies do not have reasonable expectations of privacy within their employers' premises if they have prior notice that their work areas and property may be searched.").

In Roe v. Cheyenne Mountain Conference Resort, 124 F.3d 1221 (10th Cir. 1997), an employee alleged that her employer's drug policy, which included random drug testing, a requirement that employees disclose prescription drugs that they were taking, and a ban on the use of non-prescription drugs, violated her right to privacy under Colorado law. Specifically, the employee argued that the policy constituted an "intrusion upon seclusion." Id. at 1236. The Tenth Circuit held that the employee had shown a substantial basis for the possibility that the Colorado courts would uphold a claim for invasion of privacy by intrusion upon seclusion, and remanded the case to the Colorado courts. Id. at 1237. The Tenth Circuit's decision in Roe constituted a departure from its earlier decision in Mares v. Conagra Poultry Co., 971 F.2d 492 (10th Cir. 1992), in which the court held, as a matter of law, that the "suggested intrusion" on the employee's privacy by the employer's policy requiring disclosure of prescription drugs was "insignificant."

"Assuming without deciding" that the seizure of an employee's drug test results from an employer was "the result of an illegal search," the Colorado Supreme Court found sufficient evidence to sustain a finding of probable cause supporting a warrant issued to obtain the drug test results from the laboratory used by the employer. People v. Alvarado, 31 P.3d 145 (Colo. 2001). The trial court had previously ruled that the drug test results could not be used as evidence, as the search warrant to obtain the results of the test from the testing laboratory had been acquired based on information in the defendant's employment record. Id. at 145. Determining that the employment record had been obtained in violation of the defendant's Fourth Amendment rights, the trial court concluded there was an insufficient independent basis for the search warrant and, as a result, the drug test results must be suppressed. Id. at 145–46. The Supreme Court reversed, finding sufficient evidence supported the search warrant without reliance on the defendant's employment record. Id. at 146. The decision culminated in the drug test results required by the defendant's employer as a condition of employment being used in his criminal prosecution.

2. ***Public Employers.*** As government actors, public employers are constrained by the Federal Constitution and the Colorado Constitution when conducting workplace searches. When a public employee challenges his employer's policy requiring employees to submit to random drug testing, the court must balance the nature of the privacy interest upon which the search intrudes and the character of the intrusion, against the nature and immediacy of the public employer's concern and the efficacy of the challenged test for meeting that concern. Prior to conducting this balancing test, however, the court must determine whether the employer has demonstrated that the drug testing program at issue is warranted by a "special need." If the government cannot make such a showing, the drug testing program must be struck down as unconstitutional. See 19 Solid Waste Dep't Mechanics v. City of Albuquerque, 156 F.3d 1068 (10th Cir. 1998).

B. Employee's Work Area

The Tenth Circuit Court of Appeals has noted that the "expectation of privacy in commercial premises . . . is different from, and indeed less than, a similar expectation in an individual's home." United States v. Leary, 846 F.2d 592, 597 n.6 (10th Cir. 1988). See also Mainstream Mktg. Servs., Inc. v. Fed. Commc'n Comm'n, 358 F.3d 1228, 1233 (10th Cir. 2004) (upholding do-not-call registry despite First Amendment challenge by telemarketers because "the do-not-call registry targets speech that invades the privacy of the home, a personal sanctuary that enjoys a unique status in our constitutional jurisprudence"); McCarty v. City of Bartlesville, 8 F. App'x 867, 877 (10th Cir. 2001) ("It is unquestioned that there is a 'diminished expectation of privacy in the workplace.'"). Nevertheless, it is "well established that an employee has a reasonable expectation of privacy in his office." See, e.g., United States v. Anderson, 154 F.3d 1225, 1230 (10th Cir. 1998), cert. denied, 526 U.S. 1159 (1999); Leary, 846 F.2d at 595. With respect to work areas outside of an employee's office, the law is less certain. According to the United States Supreme Court, "Given the great variety in work environments . . . the question whether an employee has a reasonable expectation of privacy" in his work area "must be addressed on a case-by-case basis." O'Connor v. Ortega, 480 U.S. 709, 718 (1987).

1. ***Private Employers.*** In United States v. Anderson, 154 F.3d 1225, 1230 (10th Cir. 1998), cert. denied, 526 U.S. 1159 (1999), the Tenth Circuit considered whether the Vice President of Research and Development for ATD Corporation had a reasonable expectation of privacy in a particular room in the company's office building where the FBI made a search without a warrant. The court noted that "[the room] was not Anderson's office." Id. at 1230. Rather, it was an empty room with no desk, files, or telephone, that could be used by all personnel of ATD Corporation. Id. at 1230 n.1. The court further noted that a corporate employee cannot challenge searches of corporate offices solely because he has access to or control over them. Id. For instance, possession of a key to the premises searched is insufficient to confer standing on an employee. See id. at 1230.

To determine whether Anderson had a reasonable expectation of privacy in the searched room and thus standing to challenge the FBI's warrantless search, the court began by applying the "business nexus" test, which examines the relationship or "nexus" of the employee to the area searched. Id. "Certainly," the court stated, "an employee should be able to establish standing by demonstrating that he works in the searched area on a regular basis." Id. However, the court stated, the fact that an employee does not work in a particular area "should not categorically control his ability to challenge a warrantless search of that area." Id. Rather, the "better approach is to examine all of the circumstances of the working environment and the relevant search." Id. The court faulted the "business nexus" test for failing to take into account actions the employee may have taken to maintain his privacy in the searched area. Id. at 1232. Therefore, the court stated, "in determining whether an employee has standing to challenge seizure of an item from the workplace, we do not limit our analysis to the 'business nexus' test," but consider:

(1) the employee's relationship to the item seized;

(2) whether the item was in the immediate control of the employee when it was seized; and

(3) whether the employee took actions to maintain his privacy in the item.

Id. In light of those factors, the court concluded that Anderson had a reasonable expectation of privacy in Room 222 and, accordingly, standing to challenge the FBI's seizure of items from that room. Id. at 1233.

A member of a cleaning crew does not have an expectation of privacy in "the whole of the premises" the employee was retained to clean. United States v. Higgins, 282 F.3d 1261, 1270 (10th Cir. 2002). The defendant, Scott Higgins, testified he had a verbal agreement to clean and fix up a house that prosecutors asserted was used for methamphetamine manufacture. Id. at 1267. Following a complaint from a neighbor, the police arrived at the house that was supposed to be unoccupied and undergoing condemnation proceedings. Id. at 1266. Upon arrival, the police officers were confronted by two women, both claiming to be at the residence in order to clean it. Id. The police entered the house and found drug-making paraphernalia in plain view. Id. Defendant Higgins drove up to the house about an hour after the police had arrived and readily admitted to having chemicals in the car, chemicals that were later identified by a government witness to be used in the manufacture of methamphetamine. Id. at 1267. Higgins maintained that he found the chemicals at the house while cleaning and had taken the chemicals to the owner of the residence to determine what was to be done with them. Id.

The district court, while not specifically deciding that Higgins was or was not an employee, did observe that as a member of a cleaning crew, an individual may have a privacy interest in his supplies or work vehicle. Id. at 1269. However, this privacy interest did not extend to the entire property the member of the cleaning crew was employed to clean. Id. As a result, the defendant could not claim a privacy interest in the house. Agreeing with the district court, the Tenth Circuit held that the defendant's work could not "serve as a basis for an objectively reasonable expectation of privacy in the whole of the premises." Id. at 1270. The court also rejected the defendant's argument that he had moved into the house and therefore had a legitimate expectation of privacy in his residence. Id. at 1270–72.

In Narotzky v. Natrona County Memorial Hospital Board of Trustees, 610 F.3d 558 (10th Cir. 2010), the Tenth Circuit explained that, even if there is a reasonable expectation of privacy in the area searched, there will be no Fourth Amendment violation if the search is "not unreasonable in light of the circumstances and context." For a search to be reasonable, it must be (1) justified at its inception; and (2) reasonably related in scope to the circumstances that justified it. Id. at 564. In Narotzky, the plaintiffs were surgeons who filed suit against the hospital where they had medical staff privileges, alleging violation of their Fourth Amendment rights. Id. at 567. Following various disputes with the hospital, the plaintiffs resigned their privileges and removed their equipment from the hospital. Id. at 562. Shortly after the plaintiffs had left with their equipment, several medical instruments were discovered to be missing from the hospital. Id. After unsuccessfully attempting to contact the plaintiffs, hospital personnel opened and searched locker space belonging to the plaintiffs, but did not find the missing instruments. Id. Plaintiffs claimed that the search of their lockers violated the Fourth Amendment, but the Tenth Circuit disagreed, holding that, though the plaintiffs had a reasonable expectation of privacy in their lockers, the search did not violate the Fourth Amendment because it was both justified at its inception and reasonable in its scope. Id. at 567-68.

Finally, in People v. Galvadon, 103 P.3d 923 (Colo. 2005), the Colorado Supreme Court considered whether Carlos Galvadon, the night manager of a liquor store, had a reasonable expectation of privacy in the back room of the liquor store, where police officers without a search warrant discovered marijuana belonging to Galvadon. The court noted that a government search of a business in a "highly regulated industry" might be subject to less Fourth Amendment protection, but that the expectation of privacy in the liquor industry "is only diminished to the extent that searches are specifically authorized pursuant to constitutional administrative inspection regulations and conducted pursuant to the purpose of the regulatory scheme," suggesting that the degree of limitation on Fourth Amendment protections must be determined on an industry-by-industry basis. Id. at 929.

The court then held that the presence of video surveillance equipment in the liquor store meant that Galvadon had no reasonable expectation of privacy in the back room vis-à-vis his employer, the owner of the liquor store. Id. at 932. But the court went on to say that employees "may have little or no expectation of privacy from their employer, but still maintain a reasonable expectation of privacy from government intrusion." Id. Because the video surveillance system was "viewable only to Galvadon and the owner of the liquor store," this equipment was "insufficient to terminate Galvadon's reasonable expectation of privacy from government intrusion." Id. at 933. Thus, the court upheld the trial court's decision to grant Galvadon's motion to suppress the evidence discovered as a result of the warrantless search of the back room. Id. at 933–34.

2. ***Public Employers.*** Colorado courts also have recognized that government employees have a reasonable expectation of privacy in their offices and workplaces. City & County of Denver v. Casados, 862 P.2d 908 (Colo. 1993); People v. Rosa, 928 P.2d 1365 (Colo. App. 1996). "However," the Rosa court explained, "that expectation of privacy may be limited." Id. at 1369. Quoting O'Connor v. Ortega, 480 U.S. 709, 718 (1987), the court stated:

> Public employees' expectations of privacy in their offices, desks, and file cabinets, like similar expectations of employees in the private sector, may be reduced by virtue of actual office practices and procedures, or by legitimate regulation . . . . [I]t is the nature of government offices that others, such as fellow employees, supervisors, consensual visitors, and the general public, may have frequent access to an individual's office . . . . [S]ome government offices may be so open to fellow employees or the public that no expectation of privacy is reasonable. Id. at 1369.

In Rosa, an employee sought to challenge incriminating evidence that one of his supervisors had found at his work station. The court found that the employee "worked in an open area where desks were next to each other," that personnel "had access to other people's work areas," that, although each employee "was given a separate lock and key for his or her desk," employees "would commonly give the key to another person in case he or she was to be absent for an extended period of time," and that, according to a supervisor, everyone in the building was "subject to search at all times." Id. Thus, the court concluded, the employee had no reasonable expectation of privacy in his work area and his challenge to the evidence his supervisor had discovered failed. Id. at 1369–70.

In United States v. Soderstrand, 412 F.3d 1146 (10th Cir. 2005), the defendant Michael Soderstrand was an Engineering Department head at Oklahoma State University. A clerical employee in Dr. Soderstrand's department, Doris Al-Harake, noticed a safe in a department supply room and opened it. Inside, she discovered child pornography images and letters addressed to Dr. Soderstrand. Id. at 1149–50. Ms. Al-Harake notified the Dean of the College of Engineering, who notified campus police. Id. at 1150. Based on Ms. Al-Harake's report, law enforcement officers obtained a search warrant to access the contents of the safe. These contents then formed the basis of a thirteen-count indictment against Dr. Soderstrand. Id.

Dr. Soderstrand moved to suppress the evidence yielded by the search of the safe. Id. The court rejected his motion. It stated, "Even if we assume that Dr. Soderstrand had a reasonable expectation of privacy in the safe, which he never identified as belonging to him and which he left unattended in a common storage room accessible to a number of employees, we find that Al-Harake was not a state actor in her initial search of the safe, and the later search of the safe by law enforcement officers was supported by a valid search warrant . . . ." Id. at 1152. The court continued, "While Al-Harake may be an employee of the Government due to her state employment at OSU, she was in this case acting solely on her own account." Id. at 1153. Thus, Dr. Soderstrand's Fourth Amendment rights were not violated and he was not entitled to the exclusionary remedy he sought. Id. at 1153–54.

In 2002, the Tenth Circuit addressed an Oklahoma State University professor's expectations of privacy in child pornography Internet files. United States v. Angevine, 281 F.3d 1130 (10th Cir. 2002), cert. denied, 537 U.S. 845 (2002). There, Eric Neil Angevine pled guilty to the knowing possession of child pornography. Id. at 1131. Because he was a professor, the University provided Angevine with a computer, which was networked to other university computers and provided access to the Internet. Id. at 1132. Using this computer, Angevine downloaded over 3,000 pornographic images. Id. He deleted the files after viewing, and in some cases printing, the images. Id. Despite Angevine's deletion of the files, a police computer expert using "special technology" retrieved the data. Id. Denying the defendant's motion to suppress the images, the district court found that Oklahoma State University's computer-use policies prevented Angevine from having a "legitimate expectation of privacy in the data on the seized University computer." Id.

On appeal, the Tenth Circuit first cited Anderson's two core inquiries—subjective expectation of privacy and reasonable expectation of privacy—and then proceeded to the workplace factors also outlined in Anderson—the employee's relationship to the item, the immediate control of the item, and whether the employee took actions to maintain privacy in the item. Id. at 1134. The court emphasized that the University's computer-use policies and procedures provided notice to Angevine that random audits of Internet use and monitoring of users suspected of abusing those policies would occur, preventing Angevine from reasonably expecting privacy in the information downloaded onto the computer. Id. In addition, the computer was issued to Angevine solely for work use and the information seized from the computer was not in his immediate control. Id. at 1134–35. Finally, he had not taken actions to maintain his privacy interest in those files, as he downloaded the images on a computer he knew was monitored. Id. at 1135. Given that he had been warned through the University's computer-use policy and procedures that administrators would log deleted files, his deletion of the images was insufficient to establish a reasonable expectation of privacy. Id. The court stated, "Although we have found a reasonable expectation of privacy in information stored within offices, United States v. Leary, 846 F.2d 592, 598 (10th Cir. 1988), we have never held the Fourth Amendment protects employees who slip obscene computer data past network administrators in violation of a public employer's reasonable office policy." Id.

Similarly, in United States v. Sims, an engineer for the Department of Energy, Stanley Sims, began using an Internet chat room to converse with two young girls who used a single screen name. 428 F.3d 945 (10th Cir. 2005). The true identity of these girls was in fact another man, who reportedly took on the identity of young girls as a gag. Id. at 950. After conversing with Sims frequently for several months, this man reported Sims's sexually explicit communications to law enforcement. Id. Sims was arrested when he appeared at the location where he had arranged to meet the girls. Id.

Police conducted two separate searches of Sims' office computer. Id. at 954. The first search was conducted without a warrant by an information systems security manager at the behest of law enforcement. Id. The district court found that this search violated Sims's Fourth Amendment rights. Id. The second search was conducted pursuant to a warrant, but that warrant relied in part on the fruits of the first search. Id. The court of appeals' primary issue was to determine whether the second search warrant was valid. Id. The court declined to determine whether Sims had a reasonable expectation of privacy in his home computer, and therefore whether the first search violated his Fourth Amendment rights, because it determined that the warrant for the second search was supported by probable cause regardless of whether it relied on the disputed fruits of the first search. Id. at 954 n.3. It therefore affirmed the district court's decision that the warrant for the second search was valid. Id.

C. Employee's Property

1. ***Private Employers***. A Tenth Circuit Court opinion sheds light on how the privacy principles developed in the workplace context can be applied to employee property. United States v. Easterling, 41 F. App'x 201 (10th Cir. 2002), cert. denied, 537 U.S. 916 (2002). John Easterling, a garage employee, challenged police officers' seizure of his gun, which was found by the officers in the office of the garage. Id. at 202. Easterling attempted to convince the court that he resided in the garage office and, as a result, his Fourth Amendment rights were violated when the officers entered the garage during posted business hours, observed and seized the gun, and arrested Easterling for a violation of 18 U.S.C. § 922 (g)(1) (possession of a firearm by a convicted felon). Id. at 203. Both the trial court and the Tenth Circuit found that Easterling, while "camping out in the garage," did not have the same reasonable expectation of privacy in the garage office as he would have had in his personal residence. Id. at 203–04.

The Tenth Circuit also dismissed the notion that Easterling's Fourth Amendment claim could be grounded in the privacy expectations that employees have in their property. Id. at 204-05. While conceding that "[i]f Easterling [could] be afforded any Fourth Amendment protection regarding the search in this case, it would be the protection afforded him as an employee of a business," the court went on to explain that there is a lesser expectation of privacy in commercial buildings than residential buildings and "[t]here is [an even] lesser expectation of privacy in commercial premises open to the public during business hours." Id. at 204. Additionally, "an employee's expectation of privacy in the workplace [is addressed] on a case-by-case basis." Id.

Restating the factors outlined in Anderson and Angevine, the court found that, although the gun was a personal item, Easterling had taken "no action to keep the gun private." Id. In fact, Easterling left the gun on the floor of the office and was leaving the unlocked garage when he was arrested. Id. Quoting Angevine, the court stated, "We are reluctant to find a reasonable expectation of privacy where the circumstances reveal a careless effort to maintain a privacy interest." Id.

In Bastible v. Weyerhaeuser, the Tenth Circuit affirmed a district court ruling that a private employer's search of employees' cars for firearms did not violate the Fourth Amendment. 437 F.3d 999 (10th Cir. 2006). In Bastible, the employer's policy prohibited bringing firearms onto the work premises, including into the employee parking lot. Id. at 1001. After suspecting problems with substance abuse, the employer conducted a search of the parking lot with dogs to search for both drugs and firearms. Id. at 1002. Before conducting the search, the employer contacted the sheriff's department to enlist their help in identifying the owners of any cars that might be tagged by the dogs. Id. The security personnel contacted the sheriff's department any time a dog alerted them to a car, and the sheriff's department then disclosed the name of the registered owner of the car. Id. The owners of the cars asserted that their Fourth Amendment rights had been violated, invoking 42 U.S.C. § 1983. Id. at 1008. The appeals court affirmed the district court's findings that the employer's security personnel were not acting under color of law as required by § 1983, despite the assistance of the state sheriff's office. Id.

In People v. Gutierrez, 222 P.3d 925 (Colo. 2009), the Supreme Court of Colorado considered a Weld County Sheriff's Department investigation in which investigators confiscated and searched over five thousand tax return files in a tax preparer's office, looking for evidence of identity theft by undocumented immigrants. Id. at 929–32. The search warrant for the investigation was based on the confession of a single undocumented immigrant, who told investigators that "everyone [who is an undocumented immigrant] knows to go to [Amalia's Tax Service] for their taxes." Id. at 930 (internal quotation marks omitted) (second alteration in original). The warrant did not list any particular suspect by name, leading the trial court to describe it as "'an exploratory search' designed to permit the sheriff to rummage through 'the confidential records of thousands of persons based on nothing more than a suspicion that one or more of them may have committed a crime.'" Id. at 931.

The Colorado Supreme Court held that the defendant had an objectively reasonable expectation of privacy in his tax returns and additional tax-return-related information even though that information was stored in a client file on the premises of a tax preparer. Id. at 936. Further, the court noted that "probable cause [was] required to intrude upon (through search and seizure) each constitutionally protected privacy interest an individual may have, irrespective of whether that interest is in his person or his tax returns." Id. at 937. The warrant used did not satisfy the probable-cause requirement with respect to the defendant's return information because it did not point to him with any specificity. Id. at 940. Finally, the court held that the "good faith" exception to the exclusionary rule did not apply in this case because the warrant was "so lacking in indicia of probable cause that official belief in its existence [was] unreasonable." Id. at 941.

2. ***Public Employers.*** Public employers have a genuine interest in the proper and efficient functioning of their operations, without interference from misbehaving employees. Therefore, when evaluating the legality of a search conducted by a public employer, the public entities' interest should be balanced against the employee's legitimate expectation of privacy. See United States v. Collamore, 330 F. App'x 708, 712 (10th Cir. 2009) (reiterating the district court's holding that an employer's search of an employee's illegally parked vehicle was permissible because it was related to the employer's investigation into employee malfeasance, but affirming decision on other grounds).

In McCarty v. City of Bartlesville, 8 F. App'x 867 (10th Cir. 2001), the Tenth Circuit considered whether police officers who were terminated for double-billing had a reasonable expectation of privacy in their timesheets or payroll records. In McCarty, the Police Chief instructed a sergeant, Sergeant Shively, to investigate the suspicious conduct of the plaintiffs. Id. at 871. As part of his investigation, Shively reviewed the plaintiffs' timesheets and other payroll records being held by a local property management corporation. Id. The plaintiffs alleged that Shively's possession and examination of the timesheets and Department records violated their right to be free from unreasonable searches or seizures. Id. at 876. The Tenth Circuit held that the plaintiffs lacked standing to assert such a claim because they did not have a reasonable expectation of privacy in the items searched. Id. The court noted that the "operational realities and practices of the Department," where payroll records were routinely "made available for inspection by all members of the Department," compelled the conclusion that the plaintiffs did not have an objectively reasonable expectation of privacy in these items. Id. at 877.

In United States v. Barrows, 481 F.3d 1246 (10th Cir. 2007), the court considered whether a city employee had a reasonable expectation of privacy in a personal computer that he brought to work with him when another employee discovered pornographic images on his computer. The court observed that "private ownership is an important factor telling in favor of Fourth Amendment protection," but it is "not dispositive." Id. at 1248. The "significance of personal ownership is particularly weakened when the item in question is being used for business purposes." Id. In addition, the city employee had brought his personal computer to work and failed to password-protect it, turn it off, or otherwise secure it from third parties. Id. Moreover, he "knowingly networked his machine to the city computer for the express purpose of sharing files." Id. at 1249. Thus, even if he had a subjective expectation of privacy in his computer, it was objectively unreasonable and there was, accordingly, no Fourth Amendment violation. Id.

In Denver Post Corp. v. Ritter, 255 P.3d 1083, 1088 (Colo. 2011), the Colorado Supreme Court considered whether Governor Bill Ritter's mobile telephone bills for his private phone account were public records and, therefore, whether the Colorado Open Records Act (CORA), COLO. REV. STAT. § 24-72-201 et seq. (2009), required their disclosure to the public. Under CORA, any person may request access to inspect and obtain a copy of any public record. Id. at 1086 (citing § 24-72-203(1)(a)). CORA defines a public record as any writing "made, maintained or kept by . . . any . . . political subdivision of the state . . . for use in the exercise of functions required or authorized by law or administrative rule." Id. (citing § 24-72-202(6)(a)(I)). Because both parties agreed that the Governor kept and used the billing statements only for their payment, did not obtain reimbursement from the state, and had not otherwise turned the bills over to any state agency or official, the court found that the plaintiffs had failed to allege that the governor kept the bills in his official capacity. Id. at 1088. The court further stated that merely alleging a potential future official use was insufficient to state a claim under CORA. Id. The court made its ruling despite the parties' stipulation that the vast majority of the calls placed with the cell phone involved discussions of public business in an official capacity. Id. at 1087. The dissent expressed concerns that the majority's decision could allow public officials to shield their official conduct from scrutiny. Id. at 1098 (Rice, J., dissenting).

IV. MONITORING OF EMPLOYEES

A. Telephones and Electronic Communications

1. ***Wiretapping.*** COLO. REV. STAT. § 18-9-303 prohibits wiretapping of telephone, telegraph, and electronic communications. Wiretapping occurs when a person who is neither the sender nor the intended receiver of a telephone, telegraph, or electronic communication "[k]nowingly overhears, reads, takes, copies or records a telephone, telegraph, or electronic communication" without the consent of one party. Id. § 18-9-303(1)(a). The consent provision of § 18-9-303(1)(a) has been interpreted to mean that "the consent of the owner of the telephone line is irrelevant to the issue of consent to tap the phone line. Consent can only be given by a party to the conversation." United States v. Borrayo-Gutierrez, 119 F. Supp. 2d 1168, 1180 (D. Colo. 2000). Wiretapping also occurs when such a person "intentionally overhears, reads, takes, copies, or records a telephone, telegraph, or electronic communication for the purpose of committing or aiding or abetting the commission of an unlawful act." Id. § 18-9-303(1)(b). It occurs when such a person knowingly uses or discloses the contents of any such communication, or attempts to do so, while knowing or having reason to know the information was obtained in violation of the statute. COLO. REV. STAT. § 18-9-303(1)(c). Wiretapping occurs when such a person knowingly taps or makes any connection with a telephone or telegraph line, wire, or cable, or electronic, mechanical, or other device that permits the interception of messages. Id. § 18-9-303(1)(d). It occurs when such a person knowingly prevents, obstructs, or

delays the sending, transmission, or delivery of any message through a telegraph or telephone line, wire, or cable, or electronic, mechanical, or other device. Id. § 18-9-303(1)(e). And wiretapping occurs when such a person "[k]nowingly uses any apparatus to unlawfully do, or cause to be done, any act prohibited by this section or aids, authorizes, agrees with, employs, permits, or intentionally conspires with any person to violate the provisions of this section." Id. § 18-9-303(1)(f).

Wiretapping, as defined by § 18-9-303(1), is a class 6 felony, unless it involves a cordless telephone, in which case it is a class 1 misdemeanor. Id. § 18-9-303(2).

In 1999, the Colorado Supreme Court twice rejected challenges to the constitutionality of COLO. REV. STAT. § 18-9-303. In People v. Shepard, the defendant was charged with wiretapping in violation of § 18-9-303(1)(e), in connection with an alleged incident of domestic violence in which the defendant had prevented a call for help by cutting the phone cord. 983 P.2d 1, 2 (Colo. 1999). The trial court held that COLO. REV. STAT. § 18-9-303 was facially overbroad because it proscribed some conduct that is constitutionally protected, like when a parent disciplines a child by removing a phone from his room or hangs up a phone to prevent the child from making an unauthorized long-distance call. Id. at 3.

The Colorado Supreme Court disagreed, stating that "even if such conduct is constitutionally protected, the wiretapping statute's potential proscription on such conduct is not real and substantial as compared to the statute's prohibition of a whole range of easily identifiable and constitutionally proscribable conduct." Id. at 4. The court further noted that parents' right to privacy in matters related to childrearing is not absolute. Id. Thus, the "potential infringement on familial privacy" was not real or substantial in relation to the "plainly legitimate" proscriptions on wiretapping. Id. Furthermore, the court found, "[p]reventing the obstruction of private telephone calls, especially during an episode of domestic violence, is reasonably related to the public health, welfare, or safety." Id. at 5. Accordingly, the court upheld the statute as constitutional. Id.

The Colorado Supreme Court decided People v. Richardson, 983 P.2d 5 (Colo. 1999), on the same day. On similar facts (the defendant was charged with wiretapping in violation of § 18-9-303(1)(e) after interfering with his girlfriend's attempt to call the police), the trial court held that the statute violated the equal protection clauses of the United States and Colorado Constitutions by distinguishing between corded and cordless telephones. Id. at 6; see also COLO. REV. STAT. § 18-9-303(2). The Supreme Court disagreed, finding that users of corded telephones have a greater expectation of privacy than cordless phone users. See Richardson, 983 P.2d at 8. Thus, the court concluded, there was a rational basis for the classification and the statute did not violate equal protection. Id.

In Quigley v. Rosenthal, 327 F.3d 1044, 1062–63 (10th Cir. 2003), cert. denied sub nom., mot. granted, Anti-Defamation League v. Quigley, 540 U.S. 1229 (2004), the Tenth Circuit found the Anti-Defamation League ("ADL") violated the federal wiretap actby "using" the contents of a recorded telephone conversation. The ADL claimed it did not actually "use" the information; rather the information was "used" by its attorneys who had already settled with the plaintiffs. The court rejected the ADL's argument. Id. at 1063.

a. **Eavesdropping**. COLO. REV. STAT. § 18-9-304 prohibits eavesdropping on the conversation or discussion of another. Id. § 18-9-304(1). Eavesdropping occurs when any person not visibly present "knowingly overhears or records such conversation or discussion without the consent of at least one of the principle parties thereto." Id. § 18-9-304(1)(a). Eavesdropping also occurs when any person "intentionally overhears or records such conversation or discussion for the purpose of committing or aiding and abetting the commission of an unlawful act." Id. § 18 -9-304(1)(b). Eavesdropping further encompasses the knowing disclosure, or attempt at disclosure, of the contents of any conversation or discussion obtained in violation of this section. Id. § 18-9-304(1)(c). Lastly, eavesdropping occurs when any person knowingly "aids, authorizes, agrees with, employs, permits, or intentionally conspires with any person to violate the provisions of this section." Id. § 18-9-304(1)(d).

In Guara v. City of Trinidad, Civil Action No. 10-cv-02529-WJM-KMT, 2012 U.S. Dist. LEXIS 78994 (D. Colo. June 7, 2012), the plaintiff, David Guara, was a suspended firefighter employed by the City of Trinidad, Colorado. After his suspension, Guara brought claims against the city under Title VII of the Civil Rights Act, 42 U.S.C. § 2000e et seq. ("Title VII"), alleging retaliation and discrimination based on race and national origin. Id. at 10. In its defense, the city claimed that Guara was fired for surreptitiously tape recording his co-workers, in violation of Colorado's anti-eavesdropping statute. Id. at 16 (citing COLO. REV. STAT. § 18-9-304(1)(a)). The city referenced a letter sent to the plaintiff at the time of the suspension, stating that eavesdropping was both criminal and an impediment to the effective functioning of the department. Id. The court found that if the recording had been made in the presence of the co-workers (as Guara claimed), it would not violate the eavesdropping statute. Id. at 19. Nevertheless, it held that the relevant inquiry was whether the suspension decision was based on a sincere belief by the city that the recording violated the statute. Id. at 19. Relying on this logic, the court found that the city had articulated a non-pretextual, non-discriminatory basis for the plaintiff's suspension. Id. at 20.

The Colorado Court of Appeals has rejected a challenge to the constitutionality of COLO. REV. STAT. § 18-9-304. See People v. Lesslie, 24 P.3d 22 (Colo. App. 2000), cert. denied, 2001 Colo. LEXIS 401 (Colo. May 21, 2001). The defendants in this case, the sheriff and deputy sheriff of Hinsdale County, were charged with illegal eavesdropping and conspiracy to commit eavesdropping after they installed an electronic listening device in the men's bathroom of a bar for the purpose of intercepting narcotics transactions. Id. at 24. The defendants challenged the constitutionality of the eavesdropping statute, alleging that the statute should be deemed void for vagueness. Id. The defendants contended that the statute was ambiguous because it is not clear from the language of the statute that electronic listening devices are prohibited. Id. at 28.

Rejecting the defendants' allegations, the court noted that in determining whether a set of circumstances justifies a belief that interception is permissible, the relevant test is the same as that for determining when an investigative activity amounts to a search, i.e., whether there is a reasonable expectation of privacy at the time and place of the communication. Id. Under the circumstances of this case, the court held that patrons in the men's restroom did have a reasonable expectation of privacy in their communications and a reasonable person would not need to guess at the applicability of the eavesdropping statute. Id. Therefore, COLO. REV. STAT. § 18-9-304 was not constitutionally vague as applied to these circumstances. Id. Nevertheless, the court recognized that "this criminal statute requires a case-by-case analysis as to whether the participants in the intercepted conversations have a justifiable expectation of privacy and, in turn, whether they believe that their conversation is subject to interception." Id.

2. ***Electronic Communications.*** As stated above, Colorado's wiretapping law applies not only to telephones and telegraphs, but also to "electronic communications." COLO. REV. STAT. § 18-9-303. "Electronic communications" are defined as "any transfer of signs, signals, writing, images, sounds, data, or intelligence of any nature transmitted in whole or in part by a wire, radio, electromagnetic, photoelectronic, or photooptical system that affects interstate commerce but does not include: (a) any wire or oral communication; (b) any communication made through a tone-only paging device; or (c) any communication from a tracking device." COLO. REV. STAT. § 18-9-301(3.3). In 1997, this definition was amended to take out the exclusion of "the radio portion of a cordless cellular phone communication that is transmitted between the cordless telephone handset and the base unit." H.B. 97-1268, 61st Gen. Assembly (1997) (enacted). Therefore, such communications between the cordless phone's handset and base unit are covered by the wiretapping prohibition. Id.

3. ***Other Electronic Monitoring.*** There are no reported Colorado decisions on this subject.

B. Mail

There are no reported cases or statutes regarding monitoring of employee postal mail. Because Colorado's prohibition on wiretapping prohibits only the interception of information in transit, it would not apply to employer's monitoring of stored electronic mail messages of employees.

C. Surveillance/Photographing

In People v. Galvadon, 103 P.3d 923 (Colo. 2005), the Colorado Supreme Court implicitly seemed to approve the use of video surveillance equipment in the employment context. There, a liquor store night manager was found to have no reasonable expectation of privacy in the back room of the liquor store vis-à-vis his employer, the owner of the store, because of the presence of a video surveillance system. Id. at 932. The court went on to conclude, however, that the night manager did have a reasonable expectation of privacy in the back room of the liquor store vis-à-vis the government, because only he and the liquor store owner could view the video surveillance monitor or video recording. Id. at 933.

Outside the employment context and with regard to photography, the parents and husband of a murder victim brought suit against the officers investigating the murder for displaying nude photographs of the victim and her husband on their honeymoon and revealing other personal information about them to newspaper reporters. See Donohue v. Hoey, 109 F. App'x 340 (10th Cir. 2004). The Tenth Circuit concluded that the victim's husband had a legitimate expectation of privacy in the nude photographs; the officers' disclosure of the photographs did not advance any compelling state interest and the disclosure was not made through the least intrusive means. Id. at 359–61. Nevertheless, the Court found the claim as to the photographs barred by the statute of limitations applicable to claims for violations of 42 U.S.C. § 1983. Id. at 361–62.

Colorado's wiretapping law does not address video or photographic surveillance. To the extent a sound recording was also made, it would be subject to the prohibition found in COLO. REV. STAT. § 18-9-303. Likewise, an argument could be made that a video surveillance would constitute an unlawful interception if it results in the acquisition of the "contents" of communications such as the substance of a conversation between two parties. COLO. REV. STAT. §§ 18-9-303, 18-9-304.

D. Internet Files

The Tenth Circuit has addressed the privacy rights of government employees in Internet files downloaded onto government-issued computers. See United States v. Angevine, 281 F.3d 1130 (10th Cir. 2002), cert. denied, 537 U.S. 845 (2002). Neil Angevine, a professor at Oklahoma State University, was arrested and conditionally pled guilty to the knowing possession of child pornography. Id. at 1131. As part of his employment, the University provided Angevine with a computer, which was networked to other university computers and provided access to the Internet. Id. at 1132. Using this computer, Angevine downloaded over 3,000 pornographic images of young boys. Id. He attempted to completely erase the files after viewing, and in some cases printing, the images. Id. Despite Angevine's deletion of the files, a police computer expert was able to retrieve the data. Id. Denying the defendant's motion to suppress the images, the district court found that Angevine did not have a "legitimate expectation of privacy in the data on the seized University computer." Id.

On appeal, the Tenth Circuit, relying heavily on the employee privacy analysis in United States v. Anderson, 154 F.3d 1225 (10th Cir. 1998), cert. denied, 526 U.S. 1159 (1999), emphasized that the University's computer-use policies and procedures provided notice to Angevine that Internet use might be audited and monitored and, as a result, Angevine could not reasonably expect privacy in the information downloaded onto the computer. Angevine, 281 F.3d at 1132. In addition, the computer was issued to Angevine solely for work use and he did not have immediate control of the information seized. Id. at 1134–35. Lastly, the court determined that Angevine had not taken actions to maintain his privacy interest in those files, despite his attempt to erase the images. Id. at 1135. Given that he had been warned through the University's computer-use policy and procedures that administrators would log deleted files, the court concluded his deletion of the images was insufficient to establish a reasonable expectation of privacy. Id. Thus, "[c]onsidering 'all of the relevant circumstances,'" the court found that Angevine did not have an objectively reasonable expectation of privacy in the information downloaded onto his work computer. Id. (quoting Anderson). Further, the court stated, "Although we have found a reasonable expectation of privacy in information stored within offices, United States v. Leary, 846 F.2d 592, 598 (10th Cir. 1988), we have never held the Fourth Amendment protects employees who slip obscene computer data past network administrators in violation of a public employer's reasonable office policy." Id.

The Colorado Supreme Court has also addressed the privacy rights of state employees in their personal email files. In Denver Publishing Co. v. Board of County Commissioners of Arapahoe County, 121 P.3d 190 (Colo. 2005), Tracy Baker, a county clerk and recorder, was accused of sexual harassment by a former employee. While investigating the matter, the county found 570 sexually explicit emails sent by Baker to a current employee, Sale. Id. at 192. A dispute arose over whether the emails were "public records" within the Colorado Open Records Act ("CORA"). Id. at 191. The court noted that CORA defines "public records" as "all writings made, maintained, or kept by the state, any agency, institution, . . . or political subdivision of the state . . . for use in the exercise of functions required or authorized by law or administrative rule or involving the receipt or expenditure of public funds." Id. at 195 (quoting COLO. REV. STAT. § 24-72-202). In addition, "public records" include "the correspondence of elected officials" to the extent it is "demonstrably connected to the exercise of functions required or authorized by law or administrative rule" or involves the "receipt or expenditure of public funds." Id. (quoting COLO. REV. STAT. § 24-72-202(6)(a)(II)(B)). The court further noted that CORA was never meant to cover information held by a government official in his private capacity. Id. Finally, the court determined that the Colorado General Assembly intended that "email must meet the same requirements as any other record to be deemed a 'public record.'" Id. at 199.

The court noted that Baker and Sale had conceded that a number of emails were "public records" because they had a "demonstrable connection to Baker's function as an elected official." Id. at 204. As to the remaining emails, the court divided them into three categories: (1) messages that address the performance of public functions and do not contain sexually explicit content; (2) messages that do not address the performance of public functions and contain sexually explicit content; and (3) mixed messages containing both types of communications. Id. The court held that the first group of emails would be disclosed as "public records," the second group would not, and the third group would be disclosed only after those portions that did not address the performance of public functions were redacted. Id. at 204–05. In conclusion, the court stated, "[W]e believe this resolution best balances the competing interests involved and is consistent with the General Assembly's intent to do the same." Id. at 205.

V. ACTIVITIES OUTSIDE THE WORKPLACE

A. Statute or Common Law

The Colorado Anti-Discrimination Act ("CADA"), COLO. REV. STAT. § 24-34-402.5 (2008), prohibits employers from terminating employees for their participation in lawful activities during nonworking hours. Under CADA, wrongfully terminated employees can recover damages, including lost wages and benefits, from their former employers. The statute of limitations for actions filed with the Colorado Civil Rights Commission under this section is only six months; however, an exhaustion of administrative remedies is not required prior to initiating action. See Galieti v. State Farm Mut. Auto. Ins. Co., 840 F. Supp. 104, 106 (D. Colo. 1993) (the six-month statute of limitations applies only to claims filed with the Colorado

Civil Rights Commission, not to claims filed in district court). If the employee prevails in an action initiated under CADA, the employer must pay costs and attorney's fees. COLO. REV. STAT. § 24-34-402.5 (2)(b).

The statutory evaluation under CADA's lawful-activities provision requires the court to determine (1) whether the employee was terminated for participation in a lawful activity; and (2) whether the underlying reason for termination qualifies under a statutory exception. Marsh v. Delta Air Lines, Inc., 952 F. Supp. 1458 (D. Colo. 1997). CADA provides the following exceptions:

(1) Restrictions related to a bona fide occupational requirement;

(2) Restrictions reasonably related to the employment activities and responsibilities of a particular employee or a particular group of employees rather than to all employees of the employer; or

(3) When the restriction is necessary to avoid a conflict of interest.

COLO. REV. STAT. § 24-34-402.5.

The "lawful activities" provision of CADA was designed to prevent employers from firing smokers. See Evans v. Romer, 882 P.2d 1335, 1346 (Colo. 1994) (noting this purpose in dictum). But employees have used CADA to challenge discharges due to a wide variety of other lawful practices. Marsh held that CADA was created to "provide a shield to employees who engage in activities that are personally distasteful to their employer, but which activities are legal and unrelated to an employee's job-related duties." 952 F. Supp. at 1462. The court stated that the statute "should protect the job security of homosexuals who otherwise would be fired by an employer who discriminates against gay people, members of Ross Perot's new political party who are employed by a fervent Democrat, or even smokers who are employed by an employer with strong anti-tobacco feelings." Id. However, the court recognized that the duty of loyalty was a bona fide occupational requirement encompassed within the scope of COLO. REV. STAT. § 24-34-402.5(1)(a). Cf. Osborn v. Qwest Corp., 398 F. Supp. 2d 1161, 1169 n.5 (D. Colo. 2005) (observing that Qwest's requirement that off-duty misconduct must result in "injury to Qwest" may be an "acknowledgement of the applicability of [§ 24-34-402.5] to the termination policy of Qwest management employees in Colorado"). **Despite the provision's early purpose of protecting smokers, as well as a Colorado state constitutional amendment allowing the use of medical marijuana, recent decisions demonstrate that employers can nevertheless deny unemployment benefits to employees who use medical marijuana during non-working hours. Beinor v. Indus. Claim Appeals Office of Colo. & Serv. Group, Inc., 262 P.3d 970, 980-981 (Colo. App. 2011) (Gabriel, J., dissenting).**

As recognized in Yarbrough v. ADT Security Services, No. 07-cv-01546, 2008 U.S. Dist. LEXIS 59477, at *7 (D. Colo. Aug. 6, 2008), there have been relatively few cases addressing the applicability of CADA. In Yarbrough, the plaintiff challenged her termination for "creating a distraction in the workplace that negatively impacted co-workers." Id. The plaintiff argued that the given reason was simply a pretext and that she was really fired in retaliation for seeking a temporary restraining order against her co-worker. Id. The court disagreed, finding insufficient evidence indicating the termination violated CADA, and granted summary judgment in favor of the plaintiff's employer. Id. at *18.

In Gwin v. Chesrown Chevrolet, 931 P.2d 466, 468 (Colo. App. 1996), the Colorado Court of Appeals upheld a jury verdict finding that CADA applied to an employee who was fired because he demanded a refund from a motivational speaker at a sales seminar, which the employee was attending on his own time. The court rejected the employer's argument that the statute requires an employer to first restrict its employee's off-the-job activities. Id.

In 2008, the Colorado Court of Appeals expanded the scope of CADA's "lawful activities" provision by holding that it protects employees from discharge due to certain off-duty, job-related activities like whistle-blowing. Watson v. Pub. Serv. Co. d/b/a/ Xcel Energy, 207 P.3d 860, 865 (Colo. App. 2008); see also Thomas v. City of Blanchard, 548 F.3d 1317, 1323 (10th Cir. 2008) (holding that employees cannot be terminated for speaking out on a subject as a concerned citizen, even if the subject is related to their official duties). But see Gelfand v. Cherry Creek Sch. Dist., No. 07-cv-01923, 2009 U.S. Dist. Lexis 48931, at *19 (D. Colo. June 10, 2009) (holding that an employee who called the police to report child abuse did so out of a sense of professional duty, not as a concerned citizen). In Watson, Xcel Energy fired the plaintiff after he reported unsafe working conditions to the Occupational Safety and Health Administration. 207 P.3d at 864. Xcel, relying on precedent from Marsh, argued that the employee could not initiate a claim under CADA because the statute only shields employees engaging in off-the-job activities *unrelated* to their professional duties. Id. The Colorado Court of Appeals held that CADA's lawful activities provision applies to *all* lawful, off-duty conduct. Id. at 865. Watson also held that because CADA provides equitable relief, claims initiated under the statute are not entitled to jury trials. Id.

In Kennedy v. Colo. RS, LLC, Civil Action No. 10-cv-02240-WYD-MJW, 2012 U.S. Dist. LEXIS 12363, at *7-14 (D. Colo. Feb. 1, 2012), the plaintiff premised his common law claim for wrongful discharge on the defendant's

alleged violations of the CADA and the Americans with Disabilities Act. The court held that, despite the general rule that wrongful discharge claims are unavailable when premised on a statute that already provides a remedy (thus barring claims premised on ADA violations), wrongful claims premised on the CADA may nevertheless go forward. Id. at 13-14.

B. Employee's Personal Relationships

1. ***Romantic Relationships Between Employees.*** There are no reported cases under COLO. REV. STAT. § 24-34-402.5 that address non-marital romantic relationships between employees. However, at least one plaintiff has successfully argued that Colorado's "lawful activities" statute should apply to homosexual relationships outside of work. See Borquez v. Robert C. Ozer, P.C., 923 P.2d 166 (Colo. App. 1995), rev'd on other grounds, 940 P.2d 371 (Colo. 1997). Therefore, arguably the statute also could apply to romantic relationships between co-workers, provided the relationship is conducted entirely off the premises during non-working hours. Notably, the Tenth Circuit has held that there is no "fundamental right" to privacy in sexual activities that occur in the public employment context. In Seegmiller v. Laverkin City, a married police officer, Sharon Johnson, had an affair with another police officer during an out-of-town training seminar. 528 F.3d 762, 764 (10th Cir. 2008). The City reprimanded Ms. Johnson, concluding that her personal life had interfered with her duties as an officer. Id. Ms. Johnson alleged that the reprimand violated her federal constitutional right of privacy. Id. The court disagreed, noting that, although "no one disputes a right to be free from government interference in matters of consensual sexual privacy," the right Ms. Johnson sought to vindicate was narrower—it was the right to engage in sexual conduct with a fellow officer at a training conference paid for in part by the City. Id. at 769, 770. Ms. Johnson could not show that "the right thus asserted [was] 'objectively, deeply rooted in this Nation's history and tradition, and implicit in the concept of ordered liberty.'" Id. at 770. Thus, the court applied the rational basis test (rather than a heightened scrutiny analysis) to conclude that the City was entitled to restrict Ms. Johnson's sexual conduct, consistent with its code of ethics requiring officers to avoid the appearance of impropriety. Id. at 772.

2. ***Sexual Orientation.*** Colorado employers cannot discriminate on the basis of sexual orientation. COLO. REV. STAT. § 24-34-401(7.5). The prohibition of discrimination based on sexual orientation was enacted in Colorado in 2007. Prior to this enactment, the "lawful activities" provision of CADA had been construed to apply to a wrongful discharge based upon a plaintiff's homosexual relationship. See Borquez v. Robert C. Ozer, P.C., 923 P.2d 166, 178 (Colo. App. 1995), rev'd on other grounds, 940 P.2d 371 (Colo. 1997). **However, claims brought under the "lawful activities" provision of the CADA must be based on specific non-working conduct, not simply the plaintiff's sexual orientation. See Larson v. United Air Lines, No. 11-1313, 2012 U.S. App. LEXIS 11066, at *21-22 (10th Cir. June 1, 2012) (finding that, despite numerous anti-gay remarks made by an employee's supervisor, there was a plausible alternative explanation for the employee's suspension).**

In the context of religious employment, however, the First Amendment places significant restraints on the ability of courts to remedy situations involving sexual orientation. See, e.g., Bryce v. Episcopal Church in Diocese of Colo., 121 F. Supp. 2d 1327, 1337 (D. Colo. 2000) (holding that a lesbian youth minister whose employment was terminated because of her sexual orientation was barred by the Ministerial Exception from asserting Title VII sexual harassment claims against the church or its officers), aff'd, 289 F.3d 648, 655–59 (10th Cir. 2002) (determining the defendant's actions were ecclesiastical, not secular, and confirming the vitality of the Ministerial Exception and Church Autonomy doctrines despite the U.S. Supreme Court's decision in Employment Div. v. Smith, 494 U.S. 872 (1990)).

3. ***Marital Status.*** For employers with more than twenty-five employees, it is unlawful for an employer to discharge or refuse to hire a person solely because that person is married to or plans to marry another employee. COLO. REV. STAT. § 24-34-402(1)(h). The statute, however, provides three exceptions under which an employer may terminate or refuse to hire a person married to an employee:

(1) When one spouse directly or indirectly would supervise or exercise disciplinary authority over the other spouse;

(2) When one spouse would audit, verify, receive, or be entrusted with moneys received or handled by the other spouse; or

(3) When one spouse has access to the employer's confidential information, including payroll and personnel records. Id.

C. Smoking

When it was enacted in 1990, Colorado's "lawful activities" statute was commonly referred to as the "Smokers' Rights Bill" because it was allegedly designed to prohibit employers from terminating employees who smoke off the premises during non-work hours. See Evans v. Romer, 882 P.2d 1335, 1346 (Colo. 1994) (stating this purpose in dictum).

D. Blogging

There are no reported Colorado decisions on this subject.

VI. RECORDS

A. Personnel Records

Record-Keeping Requirements. Personnel records are "business records" that are subject to the requirements of the Uniform Records Retention Act. COLO. REV. STAT. §§ 6-17-101 et seq. Pursuant to this Act, any record required by any state or local law or regulation may be destroyed after three years from the date of creation, unless a specific law or regulation establishes a definite records retention period or a specific procedure to be followed prior to destruction. COLO. REV. STAT. § 6-17-104. Pursuant to the Colorado Wage Claim Act, COLO. REV. STAT. § 8-4-102, field labor contractors are required to keep certain payroll records for migratory laborers for three years.

Public Accessibility. The Colorado Open Records Act ("CORA"), COLO. REV. STAT. §§ 24-72-201 et seq., provides that "[a]ll public records shall be open for inspection by any person at reasonable times, except as provided in this part 2 or as otherwise provided by law." Id. § 24-72-203(1)(a). Although the plain language of the statute applies only to public entities, the Colorado Court of Appeals has applied the statute to a private, nonprofit Colorado corporation because a public entity exerted significant control over the private corporation. See Denver Post Corp. v. Stapleton Dev. Corp., 19 P.3d 36 (Colo. App. 2000) (holding that the Colorado Open Records Act required Stapleton Development to disclose to the Denver Post its proposals concerning the development of municipal property because of the municipality's significant control over the defendant corporation).

In Land Owners United, LLC v. Waters, No. 10CA1006, 2011 WL 3616176, at *15 (Colo. App. Aug. 18, 2011), the Colorado Court of Appeals held that the trial court may direct redaction of specific confidential information contained in public records. Although redaction is not expressly recognized under CORA, it is an appropriate method for balancing the interest in disclosure against the interest in protecting personal privacy. Id. (granting landowners' request for documents relating to the Colorado Division of Real Estate's suspension of an appraiser).

Generally, personnel files, except applications and performance ratings, are exempted from the public disclosure requirements of the Colorado Open Records Act, COLO. REV. STAT. § 24-72-204(3)(a)(II)(A). In defining what constitutes a personnel file, the Colorado Court of Appeals has held that this statutory exception to CORA applies only to documents that are actually present in an employee's personnel file, not to any document relating to an employee's employment. Denver Post Corp. v. Univ. of Colo., 739 P.2d 874, 878 (Colo. App. 1987). Thus, the Colorado Court of Appeals has held that information about severance payments made to public employees is not "personnel file" information exempt from disclosure. Freedom Newspapers, Inc. v. Tollefson, 961 P.2d 1150, 1154 (Colo. App. 1998).

The question of what constitutes a "personnel" file was addressed again in City of Boulder v. Avery, No. 01CV1741, 2002 WL 31954865, at *2 (D. Colo. Mar. 18, 2002). In Avery, a report was issued evaluating the workings of the Boulder municipal court. Part of the report concerned confidential questionnaires and interviews of employees. Carrigan, the plaintiff, was a Boulder Municipal Court judge who claimed that public disclosure of the report would invade her privacy rights and good name. Id. The court held that the report was not a personnel file under COLO. REV. STAT. § 24-72-202(4.5) because it did not include "home addresses, phone numbers, financial information [or] other demographic-type data kept by one's employer." Id. The court then considered whether Carrigan had a legitimate privacy interest in the material in the report but found that the public's interest in the reason for a judge's abrupt resignation outweighed Carrigan's privacy interest in her job performance. Id. at *3. However, the court ordered that some "highly personal recommendations proposed in the Report for Ms. Carrigan to follow had she remained judge" be redacted. Id. at *4.

Where documents are sought from a public employee's personnel file, the applicant must prove that the custodian's denial of inspection was arbitrary or capricious. Tollefson, 961 P.2d at 1154. As to documents which are not present in an employee's personnel file but which involve privacy rights, the custodian bears the burden under COLO. REV. STAT. § 24-72-204(6) of showing that disclosure would do substantial injury to the public interest by invading the confidential right to privacy of the individuals involved. Id. In addition, records of sexual harassment complaints and investigations that are maintained pursuant to any rule of the general assembly on a sexual harassment policy are exempt. COLO. REV. STAT. § 24-72-204(3)(a)(x)(A). However, in Daniels v. City of Commerce City, 988 P.2d 648, 650 (Colo. App. 1999), the trial court ruled that, despite § 24-72-204(3)(a)(x)(A), records relating to complaints of sexual harassment, gender discrimination, and retaliation against Commerce City were subject to disclosure, except where "the internal investigation of the City resulted in a non-confirmation of accusations and/or exoneration, the records may be redacted with reference to the names of [the] accused." Id. The Colorado Court of Appeals affirmed, holding that the "personnel file" exemption to CORA was inapplicable because the information sought was "not the type of personal, demographic information," such as "home addresses, telephone numbers, [and] financial information" that the personnel-file exemption protects from disclosure. Id. at 651. The court also rejected the city's argument that the "public interest" exception to CORA applied, holding that the trial court appropriately found that "members of the general public have a compelling interest to see that public entities, when conducting internal reviews of these kinds of maters, do so efficiently, clearly, and effectively." Id. at 652.

In Denver Publishing Co. v. Board of County Commissioners of Arapahoe County, 121 P.3d 190 (Colo. 2005), the Colorado Supreme Court considered whether CORA applied to sexually explicit personal email between state employees. The court held that emails of a purely personal nature did not meet the definition of "public records," and thus were not required to be disclosed. Id. at *50. See section V, part D for a detailed discussion of the court's reasoning.

The results of an employer's mandatory drug screening test, part of the defendant's employment record, can become the basis of the defendant's criminal prosecution. People v. Alvarado, 31 P.3d 145, 146 (Colo. 2001) (sitting en banc) (employee's personnel file, which contained documentation of a failed drug test was inappropriately given to the district attorney's office, but a subpoena forcing disclosure of results from the company administering the drug test was lawful and the evidence could be used against the defendant in a criminal trial).

In Romero v. City of Fountain, No. 11CA0690, 2011 Colo. App. LEXIS 732 (Colo. App. May 12, 2011), Romero sought a temporary restraining order to prevent his employer, the City of Fountain, from releasing an internal investigation report concerning Romero's actions while employed as a police officer. Romero attempted to preclude disclosure under CORA and the Colorado Criminal Justice Records Act (CCJRA). Id. at *2. The district court denied the preliminary injunction request, but stayed its order for fourteen days to allow Romero to file an appeal. Id. at *3. The district court analyzed the case under the CCJRA, rather than CORA, because internal affairs investigation files are treated as criminal justice records. Id. at *13. The court of appeals held that the district court properly analyzed the case under CCJRA because Romero's privacy interest in the nondisclosure of the records must be weighed against the public interest in disclosure, and CCJRA is more restrictive than CORA regarding access to public records. Id. at *13-14. The court stated that the "CCJRA preference for disclosure is tempered by the privacy interests and dangers of adverse consequences involved in the inspection request." Id. at *14. Nevertheless, the court of appeals affirmed the district court's denial of the temporary restraining order, holding that, in his decision to disclose the report, the police chief properly balanced Romero's privacy interest with the public interest in disclosure of the report. Id. at *15.

In Denver Post Corp. v. Ritter, 255 P.3d 1083, 1088 (Colo. 2011), the Colorado Supreme Court considered whether Governor Bill Ritter's mobile telephone bills for his private phone account were public records and, therefore, whether the Colorado Open Records Act (CORA), COLO. REV. STAT. § 24-72-201 et seq. (2009), required their disclosure to the public. Under CORA, any person may request access to inspect and obtain a copy of any public record. Id. at 1086 (citing § 24-72-203(1)(a)). CORA defines a public record as any writing "made, maintained or kept by . . . any . . . political subdivision of the state . . . for use in the exercise of functions required or authorized by law or administrative rule." Id. (citing § 24-72-202(6)(a)(I)). Because both parties agreed that the Governor kept and used the billing statements only for their payment, did not obtain reimbursement from the state and had not otherwise turned the bills over to any state agency or official, the court found that the plaintiffs had failed to allege that the governor kept the bills in his official capacity. Id. at 1088. The court further stated that merely alleging a potential future official use was insufficient to state a claim under CORA. Id. The court made its ruling despite the parties' stipulation that the vast majority of the calls placed with the cell phone involved discussions of public business in an official capacity. Id. at 1087. The dissent expressed concerns that the majority's decision could allow public officials to shield their official conduct from scrutiny. Id. at 1098 (Rice, J., dissenting).

Three-Part Balancing Inquiry Required. When employees raise privacy objections to the disclosure of personnel files, the Colorado Supreme Court has established that courts must conduct a three-part balancing inquiry: (1) whether the employee has a legitimate expectation of nondisclosure; (2) whether disclosure is nonetheless required to serve a compelling state interest; and (3) where a compelling state interest necessitates disclosure of otherwise protected information, how disclosure may occur in a manner that is least intrusive with respect to the right to privacy. Corbetta v. Albertson's, Inc., 975 P.2d 718, 721 (Colo. 1999) (citing Martinelli v. District Court, 199 Colo. 163, 173–76 (1980)). In addition, "it must be apparent from the order compelling discovery that the trial court conducted the foregoing test." Id. See also Am. Civil Liberties Union of Colo. v. Whitman, 159 P.3d 707, 710–11 (Colo. App. 2006) (noting that the Martinelli/Corbetta balancing test controls the question of whether internal police files could give rise to a reasonable expectation of privacy, which "must be analyzed on a case-by-case basis"); Estate of Rice v. City & County of Denver, No. 42381, 2008 U.S. Dist. LEXIS 42381, at *18 (D. Colo. May 27, 2008) (denying a motion for a protective order preventing discovery of the personnel records of the defendant deputy sheriffs through application of the Martinelli test as construed by the Tenth Circuit in Denver Policeman's Protective Ass'n v. Lichtenstein, 660 F.2d 432, 435 (10th Cir. 1981)). But see Grady v. Jefferson County Bd. of County Comm'rs, No. 07-cv-01191, 2008 U.S. Dist. LEXIS 19824, at *6 (D. Colo. Mar. 3, 2008) (noting the special privacy interests of police officers in the information in their personnel files).

In Judd v. Cedar St. Venture (In Re: District Court, City and County of Denver), 256 P.3d 687, 690 (Colo. 2011), the Colorado Supreme Court articulated a new test for assessing discovery requests that implicate privacy rights. Judd involved a discovery request for information regarding an attorney's compensation, as well as the methodology used to calculate that compensation, as a part of a malpractice claim. Although the court noted that it had previously utilized different tests for assessing discovery requests for personnel files and tax returns, it declined to apply either test for the request. Id. at 691. Instead, the court outlined a new test for all discovery requests implicating the right to privacy. Id. First, the requesting party must prove that the information is relevant to the action. Id. Next, the party opposing the request must show that it has a legitimate expectation that the requested information is confidential and will not be disclosed. Id. If the court determines that a legitimate expectation of privacy exists, the requesting party must either prove that disclosure is required to serve a compelling state interest, or that there is a compelling need for the information. Id. The requesting party must then also show that the information is not available from other sources. Id. at 692. Lastly, if the information is available from other sources, the requesting party must prove that it is using the least intrusive means to obtain the information. Id. Accord Scholl v. Pateder, Civil Action No. 09-cv-02959-PAB-KLM, 2011 U.S. Dist. LEXIS 94556, at *6 (D. Colo. Aug. 23, 2011) (involving a request for employment files so as to impeach an expert witness). Judd suggests that the principles outlined in Martinelli, while informative, will no longer be the governing test for discovery requests involving personnel files. Judd, 256 P.3d at 691.

In re Marriage of Wiggins, 279 P.3d 1, 3 (Colo. 2012), dealt with a subpoena of personnel records in relation to a child custody dispute. The father's attorney made arrangements with the mother's former employer for the production of the mother's employment file without her consent and before she had noticed the existence of the subpoena. Id. The court held that, under Colorado Rule of Civil Procedure 45, subpoenaed documents are to be produced only at the deposition, hearing, or trial specified in the subpoena. Id. The court stated that Rule 45 "balances the right to obtain information and evidence with the right to shield information from disclosure by ensuring sufficient opportunity for the subpoenaed witness, other parties to the case, or any other person claiming an interest in the subpoenaed documents to object to the subpoena." Id. at *8.

B. Medical Records

Record-Keeping Requirements. Outside of confidentiality restrictions and the requirement that medical information must be kept separate from other personnel information, there are no specific state record-keeping requirements for employers with custody of employee medical records or medical information. **However, under the Americans with Disabilities Act, any medical information collected by an employer must be kept in "separate medical files and . . . treated as a confidential medical record." EEOC v. Western Trading Co., Civil Action No. 10-cv-02387-WJM-MEH, 2012 WL 1460025, at *8 (D. Colo. Apr. 27, 2012) (citing 42 U.S.C. § 12112(c)(3)(B) (2006)). Intermingling such records with non-medical personnel records – even for the same employee – may violate the ADA. Id.**

Confidentiality. To the extent an employer has custody of medical records or medical information, Colorado law regarding confidentiality and theft restricts the employer's right to copy, misappropriate, or disclose such information. Colorado's theft of medical records statute, COLO. REV. STAT. § 18-4-412, prohibits obtaining a medical record or information for one's own use or the use of another without proper authorization, stealing or disclosing to an unauthorized person a medical record or medical information, or copying a medical record or medical information without authorization. Violation of the theft of medical records statute is a class 6 felony, punishable by up to 12–18 months imprisonment. COLO. REV. STAT. § 18-1.3-401.

"Medical record" includes any type of record documenting medical services performed on behalf of a patient by, and at the direction of, a physician, dentist, nurse, technician, or other health care provider. COLO. REV. STAT. § 18-4-412(2)(a). "Medical information" includes any information contained in the medical record or any information pertaining to the medical services performed at the direction of a physician or other licensed health care provider who is protected by the physician-patient privilege. See COLO. REV. STAT. §§ 13-90-107(1)(d), 18-4-412(2)(b).

Other statutes that address confidentiality of medical information include: COLO. REV. STAT. § 13-90-107(1)(d) (defining the physician-patient, nurse-patient privilege); COLO. REV. STAT. §§ 12-43-218, 13-90-108(1)(g) (privilege for licensed mental health practitioners); COLO. REV. STAT. § 12-33-126(1) (privilege for chiropractors); COLO. REV. STAT. § 25-4-1404 (prohibiting release of certain health care reports except in specified circumstances); and COLO. REV. STAT. § 10-3-1104.7(3) (information derived from genetic testing is confidential and privileged requiring written consent of person tested for disclosure of such information).

The Colorado Court of Appeals has recognized a privacy interest in a "person's body" and "information concerning one's health." Doe v. High Tech Inst., Inc., 972 P.2d 1060 (Colo. App. 1998). As part of its holding recognizing the tort of intrusion upon seclusion (see section I.B.4, supra), the court held that the extraction of a blood sample, the unauthorized disclosure of health records generally, or the release of medical information obtained from a blood sample could constitute an intrusion upon seclusion.

Likewise, the Tenth Circuit Court of Appeals has ruled that "there is a constitutional right of privacy that protects an individual from the disclosure of information concerning a person's health." Herring v. Keenan, 218 F.3d 1171, 1172 (10th Cir. 2000), cert. denied, 534 U.S. 840 (2001). This right includes a probationer's right to privacy regarding information concerning his or her medical condition. Id. at 1175. In Herring, the plaintiff's probation officer (the defendant) disclosed to the probationer's employer (a restaurant manager) and his sister that he had tested positive for HIV. Id. at 1176. Because this right was not clearly established in late 1993, the court held the defendant, who "believed that it was unlawful for a restaurant to employ a waiter who tested positive for HIV," was entitled to qualified immunity. Id. at 1177.

The Tenth Circuit has also addressed a claim brought under the Federal Tort Claims Act ("FTCA") alleging invasion of privacy and intentional infliction of emotional distress. Tippetts v. United States, 308 F.3d 1091, 1093 (10th Cir. 2002). In Tippetts, the Postal Service investigated the plaintiff's medical records in order to address his Worker's Compensation claim. Id. The postal service then issued an erroneous report of the plaintiff's past military record. Id. The report stated Mr. Tippetts had been diagnosed as having psychotic features. Id. Mr. Tippetts alleged that the report caused him to be placed on administrative leave. Id. The court found lack of jurisdiction by virtue of the Federal Employees Compensation Act ("FECA"). Id. at 1094. The court refused to address whether the FECA covers invasion of privacy claims and remanded to the Secretary of Labor. Id. at 1096.

Public Accessibility. The Colorado Open Records Act, which generally requires disclosure of public records, provides an exemption for state and local government records containing medical, psychological, sociological, and scholastic-achievement data on individual persons. COLO. REV. STAT. § 24-72-204(3)(a)(1); see also Sargent Sch. Dist. No. RE 33J v. Western Servs., Inc., 751 P.2d 56 (Colo. 1988).

Certain statutes also provide that specific kinds of medical information are confidential and may not be disclosed to the public. Reports concerning positive tests for AIDS are required to be submitted to the State Department of Health under COLO. REV. STAT. §§ 25-4-1402, 25-4-1403, but are declared to be strictly confidential by COLO. REV. STAT. § 25-4-1404(1). See also COLO. REV. STAT. § 25-4-1405. Any physician, state employee, or other person who makes confidential AIDS information public is guilty of a misdemeanor and subject to a $5,000 fine and two years in jail. COLO. REV. STAT. § 25-4-1409(2).

In Hunt v. Ortiz, 84 F. App'x 34 (10th Cir. 2003), cert. denied, 541 U.S. 1014 (2004), a prisoner contended that his constitutional privacy rights were violated when he was subjected to mandatory testing for HIV/AIDS and when the defendants disclosed to non-medical personnel that he refused to provide a blood sample for AIDS testing. Id. at 35. The prisoner pointed to the "strict regulations regarding the unauthorized disclosure of the 'strictly confidential' reports and records concerning persons who are diagnosed with AIDS." Id. at 37 (citing § 25-4-1404). Nevertheless, in light of the prison's substantial interest in pursuing a program to treat those infected with the disease and prevent its further transmission, the district court dismissed the prisoner's claims as legally frivolous under 28 U.S.C. § 1915A. Id. at 36. The Tenth Circuit held that. though the prisoner failed to state a claim, his contention that the disclosure of his refusal to take the HIV test was not frivolous. Id. at 37. The court noted that, although the refusal to take a medical test does not qualify as confidential information, the "unnecessary dissemination of such information may result [in] uncalled for ridicule of an inmate." Id.

Records from alcohol treatment facilities concerning alcoholics and intoxicated persons are confidential under COLO. REV. STAT. § 25-1-312(1). Records from drug abuse treatment facilities concerning drug abuse patients are confidential under COLO. REV. STAT. § 25-1-1108(1). Mental health records are declared confidential by COLO. REV. STAT. § 27-10-120(1).

In Weinman v. Adam (In re Adam Aircraft Industries, Inc.), 422 B.R. 263 (Bankr. D. Colo. 2009), a bankruptcy trustee sought to discover the medical records of a corporate debtor's former officer in order to determine the value of three "key man" insurance policies on the officer's life. Id. at 265, 266. The trustee contended that the officer had placed the policies' value at issue and waived his right to privacy by asserting an affirmative defense that he was a transferee for value in response to the trustee's fraudulent-transfer claim. Id. at 267. The court disagreed, holding that the trustee's duty "to collect and preserve potential assets of the estate does not trump a non-debtor's right to privacy in his medical records and health information," and issued a protective order preventing the records' discovery. Id. at 270.

In Roe v. Catholic Health Initiatives Colo., Civil Action No. 11-cv-02179-WYD-KMT, 2012 WL 12840, at *1 (D. Colo. Jan. 4, 2012), an employee brought claims against her employer under the Americans with Disabilities Act, alleging that her employer had forced her to disclose confidential medical information related to her disability and had disseminated that information to other employees. She sought to proceed under a pseudonym to avoid further disclosure of the confidential information. Id. In granting the motion, the court found that the employee's

"substantial privacy right" outweighs the public's interest in the "openness of judicial proceedings," particularly when the defendant is a private, rather than public, employer. Id. at *5.

C. Criminal Records

In Connes v. Mollala Transport System, Inc., 831 P.2d 1316 (Colo. 1992), the Colorado Supreme Court recognized the tort of negligent hiring. The court stated that employers have a responsibility to look beyond personal data disclosed by the applicant in a job application or interview in cases where the duties of the job will bring the employee into frequent contact with members of the public or will involve close contact with particular individuals as a result of a special relationship between such persons and the employer. Id. at 1321. However, the court held that employers do not have a duty to search for and review official records of a job applicant's criminal history in the absence of circumstances giving the employer reason to believe that an applicant, by reason of some attribute of character or prior conduct, would constitute an undue risk of harm. Id. at 1322.

In Raleigh v. Performance Plumbing & Heating, 130 P.3d 1011 (Colo. 2006), the Colorado Supreme Court considered a case in which the plaintiffs were struck and injured by the defendant's employee's vehicle while the employee was commuting home from work. The employer had failed to check the employee's driving record upon hiring him, despite the fact that the job involved driving. Id. at 1013–14. The court held that conduct of the employee outside of his or her employment *can* be actionable as a breach of the employer's duty of care in a negligent hiring case if the employer owed a duty of care to plaintiff when making the hiring decision. Id. at 1016. Under the specific circumstances of this case, however, the court held that the employer did not have a duty of care to the plaintiffs. Id. at 1013. The court reiterated that the scope of the employer's legal duty depends on the employer's actual knowledge or reason to believe at the time of hiring that the person being hired would create an undue risk of harm in carrying out his or her employment responsibilities. Id. at 1016; Connes v. Molalla Transp. Sys., Inc., 831 P.2d 1316 (Colo. 1992). Since the employee was commuting from work when the accident occurred, he did not come into contact with the plaintiffs through his employment and therefore the plaintiffs were not among those members of the public to whom the employer owed a legal duty. Id. at 1019. The Colorado Supreme Court agreed with the cautionary precedent that argued against extending the tort of negligent hiring to off-duty accidents, observing that any employer who fails to check the license status of his employees and who knows that it is necessary that employees commute to and from work could face liability. Id. at 1018.

In Keller v. Koca, 111 P.3d 445 (Colo. 2005), the Colorado Supreme Court considered negligent supervision, a tort akin to negligent hiring. There, an employee at a dry-cleaning business sexually assaulted a twelve-year-old girl on the premises of the business during non-working hours. Id. at 447. After the employee was sentenced, the child's parents sued the owner and operator of the business, alleging that he had known that "his employee was a sexual predator," because three former women employees at the business had been victims of the employee's harassment, and had quit their positions and informed the owner. Id. The court stated that the plaintiff must prove that the employer had a duty to prevent an unreasonable risk of harm to third persons. Id. at 448. The question of duty, the court continued, "boils down to issues of knowledge and causation—whether the employee's acts are 'so connected with the employment in time and place' such that the employer knows that harm may result from the employee's conduct and that the employer is given the opportunity to control such conduct." Id. at 448–49. The court noted that the plaintiff did not present any evidence that the employer knew or should have known that the manager would bring a child to the dry cleaners when it was closed and sexually assault her there. Id. at 450. "Nor was there any evidence that it was reasonably foreseeable that an employee who created a sexually hostile work environment would then abuse his access to the premises and take a young girl with no connection to the business to that place of employment for the purposes of committing a sexual assault." Id. The court acknowledged that "[t]his case arguably presents a close question of whether the employer's knowledge created a duty to take reasonable steps to prevent a particular harm from occurring." Id. But the court refused to "embrace a theory of negligent supervision that would be an open invitation to sue an employer for the intentional torts of an employee founded upon a generalized knowledge of that employee's prior conduct." Id. at 450–51.

Under Colorado law, the fact that a person has been convicted of a felony or another offense of moral turpitude does not, in itself, prevent the person from obtaining public employment or from receiving a license, certification, permit, or registration. COLO. REV. STAT. § 24-5-101. This rule does not apply when the employment involves contact with vulnerable persons under COLO. REV. STAT. § 27-1-110, when certification or authorization for an educator is sought under COLO. REV. STAT. § 22-60.5-107(2), or when the employment involves hiring for correctional or juvenile facilities under COLO. REV. STAT. §§ 17-1-109.5, 19-2-403.3. However, such prior offenses may be considered by any state or local agency if it is required to make a finding that an applicant for a license, certification, permit, or registration is a person of good moral character. COLO. REV. STAT. § 24-5-101; see also, e.g., id. § 12-25.5-109 (e) (escort services); id. § 12-47-111(1)(a)(III) (liquor licenses); id. §§ 12-47.1-302, 12-47.1-801(2)(a) (limited gaming key employees); id. § 12-48.5-105 (massage parlors); Squire Restaurant & Lounge, Inc. v. City & County of Denver, 890 P.2d 164 (Colo. 1994); R & F Enterprises, Inc. v. Board of County Comm'rs of Adams County, 606 P.2d 64 (Colo. 1980); Moya v. Colo. Ltd. Gaming Control Comm'n, 870 P.2d 620 (Colo. App. 1994).

Additionally, COLO. REV. STAT § 24-5-101(2) requires consideration of rehabilitation evidence before a convicted felon's license may be revoked. Colo. Real Estate Comm'n v. Bartlett, 272 P.3d 1099, 1103 (Colo. App. 2011) (requiring the Colorado Real Estate Commission to consider evidence of a convicted sex offender's rehabilitation before revoking his real estate license). **After a convicted felon's license has been revoked, however, the burden of producing evidence demonstrating rehabilitation falls on the license applicant. Colorado State Bd. of Pharmacy v. Priem, 272 P.3d 1136, 1140 (Colo. App. 2012). The agency does not have to disprove rehabilitation in order to deny reinstatement of a license. Id. Even if a convicted felon can prove rehabilitation, an agency is under no obligation to reinstate the felon's license automatically. Id. at 1141. "The fact of rehabilitation would not, of itself, prove entitlement to licensure." Id. Agencies may consider the pertinent details of a license applicant's crimes in determining whether to reinstate his license. Id.**

Applicants for teaching certificates are required to disclose and certify under penalty of perjury to the Colorado Department of Education any felony or misdemeanor conviction, except for misdemeanor traffic offenses or traffic infractions. COLO. REV. STAT. § 22-60-105.2. Likewise, the State Department of Human Services may establish fees and check on the criminal backgrounds of applicants for child care licenses and any persons living with or employed by an applicant for a child care license. COLO. REV. STAT. § 26-6-105. Disclosure of criminal records that are in the public domain, even if a great deal of time has passed, cannot form the basis of a privacy claim. Lindemuth v. Jefferson County Sch. Dist., 765 P.2d 1057, 1059 (Colo. App. 1988).

The Colorado Supreme Court has recognized a right of privacy for citizens in arrest records compiled by government officials. See Davidson v. Dill, 180 Colo. 123, 503 P.2d 157 (1972). Thus, the court held that justice requires "the existence of a right of privacy in the fingerprints and photographs of an accused who has been acquitted, to be at least placed in the balance, against the claim of the state for a need for their retention." Id. at 131.

In Petition of R.J.Z. v. State, the Colorado Court of Appeals held that the trial court erred in denying the petitioner's request to seal his arrest and criminal records. 104 P.3d 278, 283 (Colo. App. 2004), cert. denied, 2004 Colo. LEXIS 1029 (Colo. Dec. 20, 2004). The petitioner had been acquitted of multiple counts of sexual assault on a child, based on a woman's allegations that the petitioner, a youth pastor, had made unlawful sexual contact with her when she was younger. Id. at 279. The trial court had concluded that the public interest in keeping the petitioner's records open to the public and to potential employers outweighed any harm to the petitioner's privacy interests and potential damage to his reputation and future employability. Id. The court of appeals disagreed, citing § 24-72-408 and reasoning that "more than half the charges against petitioner were dismissed, and the jury acquitted him of the rest after a trial on the merits" and there was "no evidence that petitioner had been arrested or charged with any crimes subsequent to his acquittal on the charges at trial." Id. at 281. The appeals court was undaunted by the fact that the petitioner admittedly sought to obtain a position in school administration. Id. at 282. "We acknowledge the concerns of the [trial] court and of employers who must consider applicants for positions involving supervision of children and teenagers. Nevertheless, in the circumstances presented here, given the absence of other factors supporting the denial of the petition and the significant harm to the petitioner if the records remain unsealed, this consideration alone could not warrant keeping the records unsealed." Id.

By contrast, in Doe v. Federal Bureau of Investigation, 218 F.R.D. 256, 260 (D. Colo. 2003), the federal district court denied the request of a sitting judge in Colorado's state judicial system to seal court records in a case in which he served as a confidential informant to expose drug use by Colorado public officials. The court held that the informant's concerns regarding "damage to his personal and professional reputation," though valid, did "not outweigh the public's interest in having the case open." Id. at 259. Notably, the Doe case did not involve application of COLO. REV. STAT. § 24-72-308.

D. Subpoenas / Search Warrants

There are no recent Colorado cases dealing with subpoenas or search warrants in the context of employment law.

VII. ACTIONS SUBSEQUENT TO EMPLOYMENT

A. References

Negative employment references can support a retaliation claim under Title VII, Robinson v. Shell Oil, 519 U.S. 337, 341 (1997), or a defamation claim under state law, Churchey v. Adolph Coors Co., 759 P.2d 1336 (Colo. 1988). Section 704(a) of Title VII, codified at 42 U.S.C. § 2000e-3(a), makes it unlawful for employers to discriminate against "employees or applicants for employment." According to the Supreme Court, although the term "employees" in § 704(a) is ambiguous, it should be interpreted to include former employees. Robinson, 519 U.S. at 341. Thus, a former employee may sue a former employer for negative employment references given to a prospective employer in retaliation for the former employee's participation in a protected activity. See id. (former employee initiated action for negative references given in retaliation for filing a discrimination charge with the EEOC). The elements of a retaliation claim are (1) a protected activity, (2) an adverse employment action, and (3) a causal connection between the protected activity and the adverse action. Montes v. Vail Clinic, Inc., 497 F.3d 1160, 1176 (10th Cir. 2007). The circuits have split regarding what constitutes an "adverse employment action" in the context of post-employment references. In Hillig v. Rumsfeld, 381 F.3d 1028 (10th Cir. 2004), the Tenth Circuit held that a negative job reference is itself an "adverse employment action" for purposes of a retaliation claim and the plaintiff is not required to show that he or she missed out on a particular job opportunity as a result. See id. at 1033–35 (rejecting the position of the Second and Eleventh Circuits and joining that of the Ninth and D.C. Circuits).

In Getachew v. Google, Inc., Civil Action No. 12-cv-00896-BNB, 2012 U.S. Dist. LEXIS 68819, at *5-6 (D. Colo. May 17, 2012), the court held that to state a retaliation claim under Title VII, the plaintiff must have been in an employer-employee relationship with the individual or entity that provided the negative reference. Thus, although the defendant's search engine provided negative information about the plaintiff that may have adversely affected his employment opportunities, the provision of such information was insufficient to state a Title VII retaliation claim. Id.

The elements of a defamation claim are: (1) an oral or written communication concerning the plaintiff, (2) published to a third party, (3) which is false, and (4) which results in injury to the plaintiff's reputation. See Churchey, 759 P.2d 1336 (Colo. 1988) ("A cause of action for defamation requires, at a minimum, publication of a false statement of defamatory fact."). Statements that concern especially sensitive issues, like professional integrity or medical conditions, can be considered per se defamatory. Pittman v. Larson Distrib. Co., 724 P.2d 1379, 1387 (Colo. App. 1986).

As liability due to negative references began to increase, the Colorado General Assembly took action to protect employers. COLO. REV. STAT. § 13-25-125.5 made clear that self-publication by the plaintiff to a third person cannot give rise to a defamation action. Likewise, to assist employers with respect to potential liability for defamation claims in the context of post-employment references, a law went into effect that gives qualified immunity to employers for providing information about job history and job performance to a prospective employer. COLO. REV. STAT. § 8-2-114(3) provides that an employer cannot be liable for giving a negative employment reference about a current or former employee unless the plaintiff proves that the information disclosed was false and that the employer knew or reasonably should have known the information was false. See Alexander v. Walmart Stores, Inc., No. 08-cv-00070, 2009 U.S. Dist. LEXIS 37698, at *11 (D. Colo. May 4, 2009) (requiring proof that the former employer provided negative references and that prospective employers based decisions on those references in order to sustain a claim). The statute further gives the current or former employee about whom the information is disclosed the right to request and obtain copies of any written information sent to a prospective employer. § 8-2-114(5).

B. Noncompete Agreements

Under Colorado law, noncompete agreements are void unless they fall within one of several enumerated exceptions. COLO. REV. STAT. § 8-2-113. These exceptions permit noncompete agreements for executive and management personnel, for professional staff to management personnel, and for the protection of trade secrets. See id. The exceptions to the general rule of § 8-2-113 are to be "narrowly construed." Gold Messenger v. McGuay, 937 P.2d 907, 910 (Colo. App. 1997).

Management personnel are those employees who are "in charge" of the business and who act in an unsupervised manner. Atmel Corp. v. Vitesse Semiconductor Corp., 30 P.3d 789, 794 (Colo. App. 2001); see also Mgmt. Recruiters of Boulder, Inc. v. Miller, 762 P.2d 763, 765 (Colo. App. 1988) (an "account executive" who was primarily an "information gatherer" was not a manager or executive). Professional employees and professional staff to management have been defined narrowly to include "such persons as legal, engineering, scientific and medical personnel together with junior professional assistants." Boulder Med. Ctr. v. Moore, 651 P.2d 464 (Colo. App. 1982).

"To meet the trade secret exception, the primary purpose of the covenant not to compete must be the protection of trade secrets and the covenant must be reasonably limited in scope." Haggard v. Synthes Spine, No. 09-cv-00721, 2009 U.S. Dist. LEXIS 54818, at *14 (Dist. Colo. June 12, 2009); see also Colo. Accounting Machs. v. Mergenthaler, 609 P.2d 1125, 1226 (Colo. App. 1980) (prohibiting general competition will generally not be upheld if an employer can be adequately protected by a clause prohibiting disclosure of trade secrets). But see Saturn Sys. v. Militare, 252 P.3d 516 (Colo. App. 2011) (where a nonsolicitation clause and a nondisclosure clause are both part of an explicit confidentiality provision designed to protect trade secrets, the nonsolicitation clause is a permissible restriction, rather than an impermissible bar on all competition like in Mergenthaler). Moreover, courts will modify the restrictions so that they only apply to information that meets the definition of trade secrets under Colorado law. See Mgmt. Recruiters of Boulder, 762 P.2d at 765. Focused nonsolicitation agreements may provide an attractive middle ground between a noncompete agreement and a nondisclosure agreement for the protection of trade secret information. See id. (refusing to enforce a noncompete agreement but upholding a narrow nonsolicitation provision based on a finding that the identity, needs, and qualifications of the employer's clients were trade secrets and thus entitled to protection).

Even noncompete agreements that meet the exceptions set forth in § 8-2-113 must be reasonable in scope and no broader than necessary to protect the employer's legitimate interests. Whittenberg v. Williams, 135 P.2d 228, 229 (Colo. 1943). Compare In re Marriage of Fischer, 834 P.2d 270, 273–74 (Colo. App. 1992) (finding a three-year covenant was reasonable when it restricted the former husband of a small business owner from competing within 20 miles of the town where the business was located), with Knoebel Mercantile Co. v. Siders, 439 P.2d 355, 399 (Colo. 1968) (finding a two-year covenant prohibiting competition by a food and paper supply salesman in any state in which his former employer transacted business to be overbroad and unreasonable). Although Colorado courts may reform noncompete agreements to render them reasonable in scope, courts are not required to do so and may strike them altogether instead. See Gulick v. Robert Strawn & Assocs., 477 P.2d 489, 493 (Colo. App. 1970) (upholding trial court's reformation of an agreement that prevented an employee from competing with his former employer for eighteen months within thirty-five miles of any city where the employer transacted business). In addition, proper consideration for entering into the noncompete agreement must be demonstrated before the agreement can be enforced; but for at-will employees, continued employment (i.e., forebearance from the right to terminate the employee) is now sufficient consideration. Lucht's Concrete Pumping, Inc. v. Horner, 255 P.3d 1058, 1061 (Colo. 2011).

In BIAX Corp. v. Brother Int'l Corp, Civil Action No. 10-cv-03013-PAB-KLM, 2011 WL 5240403, at *2, *7-8 (D. Colo. Nov. 1, 2011), the defendant requested, as a condition for allowing the plaintiff's expert witness to view its computer source code, that the court add provisions to the protective order that would require the expert to agree not to work in his chosen field for the next four years. The court denied the request, noting that such a restriction would unduly infringe on the expert's ability to find employment and could also deprive the plaintiff of its expert witness. Id. at *3.

Under Colorado law, confidentiality, nondisclosure, and nonsolicitation agreements may not be characterized as covenants not to compete if they serve different purposes. Harvey Barnett, Inc. v. Shidler, 338 F.3d 1125, 1134 (10th Cir. 2003). If the agreements permit the employee to work wherever he wishes, for whomever he wishes, subject only to the prohibition against misusing his former employer's proprietary information, then they will not be analyzed under the provisions of § 8-2-113. See id.

VIII. OTHER ISSUES

A. Statutes of Limitations

The statute of limitations for most privacy related torts is two years. COLO. REV. STAT. § 13-80-102(1)(a) (creating a two-year statute of limitations for tort actions not involving a motor vehicle); see also, e.g., Galvan v. Spanish Peaks Regional Health Ctr., 98 P.3d 949, 951 (Colo. App. 2004) (reversing the trial court, which had determined that the employee's claim for wrongful termination for engaging in lawful off-duty conduct was barred by a six-month statute of limitations and holding that the claim was governed by the two-year statute of limitations in § 13-80-102); Sandoval v. Archdiocese of Denver, 8 P.3d 598 (Colo. App. 2000) (dismissing the plaintiff's claim for intentional infliction of emotional distress based on the two-year statute of limitations set forth in § 13-80-102(1)(a)). Privacy related tort claims are deemed to accrue on the date when both the injury and its cause are known or should have been known in the exercise of reasonable diligence. COLO. REV. STAT. § 13-80-108(1); Winkler v. Rocky Mountain Conference of United Methodist Church, 923 P.2d 152, 158 (Colo. App. 1995), cert. denied, 519 U.S. 1093 (1997). Normally, the question of when the plaintiff's claim accrued is a question of fact, but if the undisputed facts show that the plaintiff discovered or reasonably should have discovered the tortious conduct on a particular date, the question may be decided as a matter of law. Winkler, 923 P.2d at 158.

If the privacy related tort is brought against a sheriff, coroner, police officer, firefighter, or other law enforcement authority, a one-year statute of limitations applies. COLO. REV. STAT. § 13-80-103(1)(c). The statute of limitations for defamation claims is also one year. Lininger v. Knight, 226 P.2d 809, 812 (Colo. 1951) (claims must be filed within one year from the date both the injury to reputation and its cause are known or reasonably should be known). Each publication of a defamatory statement constitutes a separate cause of action; thus each publication attains its own one-year limitation period. Id.

B. Jurisdiction

Article VI, § 9(1) of the Colorado Constitution grants broad jurisdiction to district courts in Colorado. COLO. CONST. art. VI, § 9(1) (providing that "district courts shall be trial courts of record with general jurisdiction, and shall have original jurisdiction in all civil, probate, and criminal cases."). The Colorado Court of Appeals has appellate jurisdiction over final judgments from district courts and from the final decisions of several administrative commissions. COLO. REV. STAT. § 13-4-102. The Colorado Supreme Court is the highest appellate court in the state and has the final say on issues of civil and criminal litigation. COLO. REV. STAT. § 13-4-108.

In order to attain jurisdiction over employment privacy claims, courts must have proper personal and subject matter jurisdiction. Subject matter jurisdiction tends to be a non-issue regarding employment privacy claims initiated in state courts because of the broad jurisdictional grant to district courts. However, employers based outside of Colorado may contest personal jurisdiction. The analysis for personal jurisdiction over a nonresident involves a two-part test: (1) whether the nonresident defendant has "minimum contacts" with the forum state that justify an appearance in court there; and (2) whether the exercise of personal jurisdiction would offend traditional notions of fair play and justice. AST Sport Sci., Inc. v. CLF Dist., Ltd., 514 F.3d 1054, 1057 (10th Cir. 2008). In evaluating personal jurisdiction, it is important to consider that the Colorado long-arm statute was intended to confer "the maximum jurisdiction permitted by the due process clause of the United States and Colorado constitutions." Id.; see also Vogan v. City of San Diego, 193 P.3d 336, 339 (Colo. App. 2008) (internal quotation marks omitted).

C. Worker's Compensation Exclusivity

The Worker's Compensation Act of Colorado is designed to compensate workers for employment-related injuries and occupational diseases. The Act provides exclusive remedies for injuries sustained in the course of employment and injuries arising out of employment. 46 COLO. REV. STAT. §§ 8-40-102(1), 8-41-301(1)(b). Injuries sustained in the "course of employment" are injuries that actually occur while performing a job-related activity. See Popovich v. Irlando, 811 P.2d 379, 383 (Colo. 1989) ("'In the course of employment' generally refers to the time, place and circumstances under which the injury occurred. The 'course of employment' requirement is satisfied when it is shown that the injury occurred within the time and place limits of the employment relation and during an activity that had some connection with the employee's job-related functions."). Perhaps more relevant to employment privacy litigation are claims that "arise out of" employment. "An injury or occupational disease 'arises out of' employment when it has its origin in an employee's work-related functions and is sufficiently related thereto as to be considered part of the employee's service to the employer in connection with the contract of employment." Id.

The Worker's Compensation Act provides immunity for employers facing personal injury claims initiated by employees, provided that the employer remains compliant with the Act's requirements and the employee is eligible for compensation under the Act. See Ventura v. Albertson's, Inc., 856 P.2d 38, 39 (Colo. App. 1992) (describing how employers who intentionally cause injuries may lose immunity). Employers can lose immunity under the Act if they face wrongful discharge claims because the claims are not sustained during the course of employment. Ferris v. Bakery, Confectionery & Tobacco Union, 867 P.2d 38, 42 (Colo. App. 1993). But see Weissman v. Crawford Rehab. Servs., Inc., 938 P.2d 540, 542 (Colo. 1997) (Act's exclusivity provisions provided immunity for outrageous conduct claim based on wrongful termination), rev'd on other grounds, Crawford Rehab. Servs., Inc. v. Weissman, 938 P.2d 540 (Colo. 1997). Although there is not a case under Colorado law where the Act provided immunity for employment privacy claims, in Smith v. Colorado Interstate Gas Co. an employee's claim for intentional infliction of emotional distress was barred by the exclusivity remedy. 794 F. Supp. 1035, 1042 (D. Colo. 1992); see also Abrahamson v. Sandoz, Inc., No. 06-cv-00636, 2008 U.S. Dist. LEXIS 26163, at *28 (D. Colo. Mar. 31, 2008) (holding that the Act provided an exclusive remedy for plaintiff's intentional infliction of emotional distress claims, which were based on work-related retaliation, work-related performance reviews, and work-related hostile environment).

D. Pleading Requirements

Claims for intrusion upon seclusion, false light, publication of private facts, negligent hiring, negligent supervision, negligent retention, and intentional infliction of emotional distress are not subject to the heightened pleading requirements of Colo. R. Civ. P. 9. However, an employee who alleges that an act or omission of a public employee was willful or wanton must plead the "specific factual basis of such allegations." COLO. REV. STAT. § 24-10-110(5)(a). "Failure to plead the factual basis of an allegation that an act or omission of a public employee was willful and wanton shall result in dismissal of the claim for failure to state a claim on which relief can be granted." § 24-10-110(5)(b). The Colorado Court of Appeals has held that a claim for intentional infliction of emotional distress "intrinsically contains issues concerning willful and wanton conduct." Barham v. Scalia, 928 P.2d 1381, 1385 (Colo. App. 1996); see also Martin v. North Metro Fire Rescue Dist., No. 07-cv-00977, 2007 U.S. Dist. LEXIS 95113, at *13–16 (D. Colo. Dec. 13, 2007) (holding that the plaintiff's negligent supervision claim was not barred by the Colorado Governmental Immunity Act because the plaintiff had adequately pleaded willful and wanton misconduct). Arguably, claims for invasion of privacy do as well. Thus, an employee who seeks to assert an intentional-infliction-of-emotional-distress or an invasion-of-privacy claim against a public employer should seek to satisfy the heightened pleading requirements of § 24-10-110(5).

SURVEY OF CONNECTICUT EMPLOYMENT LIBEL LAW

Carla R. Walworth
Raymond W. Bertrand
Paul, Hastings, Janofsky & Walker LLP
75 East 55th Street
New York, NY10022
Tel: (212) 318-6000
Fax: (212) 319-4090

(With Developments Reported Through **November 1, 2012**)

GENERAL COMMENTS

There are three levels of courts in Connecticut: the Superior Court of Connecticut, the Appellate Court of Connecticut and the Supreme Court of Connecticut. A plaintiff has one appeal as of right in Connecticut. The Supreme Court exercises discretion in determining whether to accept a case on appeal.

SIGNIFICANT DEVELOPMENTS SINCE THE 2012 *SURVEY*

None.

I. GENERAL LAW

A. General Employment Law

1. ***At Will Employment.*** Under Connecticut law, absent a contract to the contrary or illegal discriminatory motive, an employer has the right to terminate an employee at any time without liability. Cweklinsky v. Mobil Chem. Co., 267 Conn. 210, 225-26, 837 A.2d 759, 768 (2004) (citing Thibodeau v. Design Group One Architects, LLC, 260 Conn. 691, 697, 802 A.2d 731, 735 (2002)). Thus, employment at will "remains the general rule." Cweklinsky, 267 Conn. at 226 n.13, 837 A.2d at 769 n.13; see also D'Ulisse-Cupo v. Bd. of Dirs. of Notre Dame High Sch., 202 Conn. 206, 212 n.l, 520 A.2d 217, 218 n.1 (1987) ("[a]s a general rule, contracts of permanent employment, or for an indefinite term, are terminable at will.") (citations omitted); **Lopes v. Hubbel Inc., No. DBDCV116007127, 2012 WL 1292601, at *2 (Conn. Super. Ct. Mar. 23, 2012) (same).**

Connecticut recognizes a narrow exception to the at-will rule, permitting a common law cause of action for wrongful discharge when an employee is terminated for reasons that contravene a clear mandate of public policy. Cweklinsky, 267 Conn. at 226 n.13, 837 A.2d at 769 n.13; see also Iosa v. Gentiva Health Servs., Inc., 299 F. Supp. 2d 29, 35 (D. Conn. 2004) (noting that the Connecticut Supreme Court "has repeatedly emphasized the narrowness of the exception"). Acknowledging the difficulty in defining the precise contours of the public policy exception, the Connecticut Supreme Court stated that the court looks to whether the discharge violated any explicit statutory or constitutional provision or contravened any judicially conceived notion of public policy. Thibodeau, 260 Conn. at 699, 802 A.2d at 736; Daley v. Aetna Life and Cas. Co., 249 Conn. 766, 798, 734 A.2d 112, 130 (1999). Additionally, if an employer genuinely fires an at-will employee for more than one reason and any of those bona fide reasons fails to offend an important public policy, there is no cause of action. Knofla v. Eastern Conn. Health Network, Inc., 2009 WL 4916366, at *3 (Conn. Super. Ct. Dec. 1, 2009). An employer's defamation of an employee is not recognized as a violation of public policy sufficient to state a cause of action for wrongful discharge. See Epworth v. Journal Register Co., No. CV940065371, 1995 Conn. Super. LEXIS 475, at *4-6 (Conn. Super. Ct. Feb. 15, 1995). In Epworth, the superior court stated that "[t]o the extent Connecticut has a public policy against defamation, the law of defamation, not [sic] the law of wrongful discharge, provides the appropriate judicial remedy." Id. at *5 n.2; see also Burnham v. Karl and Gelb, P.C., 252 Conn. 153, 161-62, 745 A.2d 178, 183 (2000) (affirming summary judgment for the defendant employer because even if the plaintiff's termination violated public policy, her wrongful discharge claim was precluded because of the existence of a statutory remedy); **Varley v. Regional School Dist. No. 4, No. MMXCV126007682S, 2012 WL 5936267, at *4 (Conn. Super. Ct. Nov. 8, 2012) (noting "when a statutory remedy exists to address a particular public policy concern, the plaintiff is precluded from bringing a common-law wrongful discharge action based upon a violation of that public policy").** However, an employer's termination of an employee allegedly in retaliation for the employee's family member considering litigation against the employer may give rise to a wrongful discharge claim in violation of public policy. Fortunato v. Silston, 48 Conn. Supp. 636, 856 A.2d 530 (2004). In Fortunato, the plaintiff claimed that she was terminated from her employment in a dental office after the business learned that her adult daughter was contemplating bringing a dental malpractice action against the office. Id. at 638 n.1, 856 A.2d at 532 n.1. The court accepted the plaintiff's argument that her daughter's actions invoked her daughter's right to access the judicial system as guaranteed by the Connecticut Constitution, and allowed the claim to proceed despite that it was the plaintiff who allegedly suffered the unlawful retaliation. See id. at 641, 856 A.2d at 534. The Fortunato court thus expanded the cause of action for wrongful discharge in violation of public policy despite the repeated characterizations by courts of it as a "narrow" exception to Connecticut's at-will employment rule. The court reasoned that "courts have not insisted that the right exercised lie in the very hand of the person fired." Id. at 640, 856 A.2d at 533. Whether this new development will spawn similar decisions or be overturned or rejected by other Connecticut courts remains to be seen.

B. Elements of Libel Claim

1. ***Basic Elements.*** Under Connecticut law, a defamatory statement is "a communication that tends to harm the reputation of another as to lower him in the estimation of the community or to deter third persons from associating or dealing with him." Iosa v. Gentiva Health Servs., Inc., 299 F. Supp. 2d at 37 (D. Conn. 2004) (internal quotations omitted) (quoting QSP, Inc. v. Aetna Casualty & Surety Co., 256 Conn. 343, 356, 773 A.2d 906, 916 (2001)); Gagnon v. Housatonic Valley Tourism Dist. Comm'n, 92 Conn. App. 835, 847, 888 A.2d 104, 114 (2006) (citation omitted). "Defamation is comprised of the torts of libel and slander. . . . Slander is oral defamation." DeVito v. Schwartz, 66 Conn. App. 228, 234, 784 A.2d 376, 381 (2001). "Libel is defamation which is made in a more permanent and proliferative form such as by the written word or electronic broadcast." Reaves v. Hartford Courant Co., No. X07CV020079871S, 2003 Conn. Super. LEXIS 525, at *3 (Conn. Super. Ct. Feb. 28, 2003). To establish a defamation claim, a plaintiff must establish four essential elements: (1) the defendant published a defamatory statement; (2) the defamatory statement identified the plaintiff to a third party; (3) the defamatory statement was published to a third party; and (4) the plaintiff's reputation suffered injury as a result of the statement. Gambardella v. Apple Health Care, Inc., 291 Conn. 620, 627-28, 969 A.2d 736, 742 (2009) (quoting Cweklinsky, 267 Conn. at 217, 837 A.2d at 763-64); Hopkins v. O'Connor, 282 Conn. 821, 838, 925 A.2d 1030, 1042 (2007); Torosyan v. Boehringer Ingelheim Pharms., Inc., 234 Conn. 1, 27, 662 A.2d 89, 103 (1995).

2. ***Fault.*** To establish a claim for defamation, Connecticut requires the plaintiff to prove fault amounting to at least negligence on the part of the publisher. Whether a level of fault greater than negligence must be established depends on the plaintiff's status as a public versus a private figure. See Miles v. Perry, 11 Conn. App. 584, 588, 529 A.2d 199, 203 (1987) ("The determination of whether a plaintiff is a public figure is dispositive of the . . . degree of fault of the defendants which the plaintiff ha[s] to prove.").

a. **Private Figure Plaintiff**. The Supreme Court of Connecticut has not ruled on the level of fault required to be proven by a private figure plaintiff alleging defamation. The Connecticut Appellate Court, however, has held that private persons may recover in defamation if they prove a negligent publication of a false, defamatory statement by a preponderance of the evidence. See Cowras v. Hard Copy, No. 3:95CV99, 1997 U.S. Dist. LEXIS 23514, at *45 (D. Conn. Sept. 29, 1997) (citing Miles v. Perry, 11 Conn. App. at 589, 529 A.2d at 203); see also Fuller v. Day Publ'g Co., No. 030565104, 2004 WL 424505, at *5 (Conn. Super. Ct. Feb. 23, 2004), aff'd, 89 Conn. App. 237, 872 A.2d 925 (2005).

No Connecticut court has ruled as to whether a level of fault greater than negligence is required to be proven by a private figure plaintiff where the publication at issue concerns a matter of public interest as opposed to one of purely private concern. But cf. Cowras, 1997 U.S. Dist. LEXIS 23514, at *46 (applying Connecticut law, the federal district court cited Milkovich v. Lorain Journal Co., 497 U.S. 1, 15 (1990), for the proposition that a level of fault greater than negligence is inappropriate for a private person attempting to prove he was defamed on matters of public interest), with Gomez v. Larson, No. CV980084646, 1999 Conn. Super. LEXIS 1535, at *19 (Conn. Super. Ct. June 8, 1999) (stating that "[c]onsiderable latitude is given to defendants commenting on matters of public concern regardless of whether or not the individual is a private or public figure").

b. **Public Figure Plaintiff**. Where the plaintiff is a public figure, Connecticut courts require clear and convincing proof of fault based on the higher "actual malice" standard set forth in New York Times Co. v. Sullivan, 376 U.S. 254, 84 S. Ct. 710 (1964); see also Woodcock v. Journal Publ'g Co., Inc., 230 Conn. 525, 535, 646 A.2d 92, 97 (1984); Holbrook v. Casazza, 204 Conn. 336, 342, 528 A.2d 774, 777 (1987), cert. denied, 484 U.S. 1006 (1988); Cox v. Galazin, 460 F. Supp. 2d 380, 389 (D. Conn. 2006). To prove actual malice, the plaintiff must show that "the statement, when made, [was] made with actual knowledge that it was false or with reckless disregard of whether it was false." Gambardella, 291 Conn. at 628, 969 A.2d at 742 (2009)(quoting Woodcock, 230 Conn. at 535, 646 A.2d 92). A determination of reckless disregard requires "sufficient evidence to permit the conclusion that the defendant in fact entertained serious doubts as to the truth of his publication." Woodcock, 230 Conn. at 546 (citation omitted). **A plaintiff must also "prove a person's 'responsibility' for publication by clear and convincing evidence." Dongguk Univ. v. Yale Univ., No. 08-cv-0441, 2012 WL 2087420, at *4 (D. Conn. June 8, 2012).**

"[T]hose classified as 'public figures' have thrust themselves 'to the forefront of particular controversies in order to influence the resolutions of the issues involved,' and they invited attention and comment." Lyons v. Heid, Nos. CV940311175S and CV940312019S, 1998 Conn. Super. LEXIS 1516, at *17 (Conn. Super. Ct. May 29, 1998) (quoting Gertz v. Robert Welch, Inc., 418 U.S. 323, 345, 94 S. Ct. 2997, 3009 (1974)). There is a distinction, though, between a "general purpose" public figure, where a person has achieved such notoriety that he or she is a public figure for all purposes, and a "limited purpose" public figure who "voluntarily injects himself or is drawn into a particular public controversy and thereby becomes a public figure for a limited range of issues." Fuller, 2004 WL 424505, at *5 (citing Jones v. New Haven Register, Inc., 46 Conn. Supp. 634, 643, 763 A.2d 1097, 1102 (2000), which in turn cited to Gertz. See also Fuller, 2004 WL 424505, at *5 (plaintiff found to be a limited purpose public figure since she "voluntarily injected herself into the lime light by committing a crime"). Whether a plaintiff qualifies as a public figure is a question of law for the court to decide. See Zupnik v. Assoc. Press, Inc., 31 F. Supp. 2d 70, 72 (D. Conn. 1998).

Not all public employees are considered public figures under Connecticut law. Certain "lower ranks of government employees" are not extended the public figure designation. Kelley v. Bonney, 221 Conn. 549, 580, 606 A.2d 693, 702 (1992). In Kelley, the Court concluded that a public school teacher is a public figure because "[r]obust and wide open debate concerning the conduct of the teachers in the schools of this state is a matter of great public importance." Id. at 581, 606 A.2d at 710. See also Belier v. Milford Board of Educ., No. 054002886S, 2005 Conn. Super. LEXIS 1932, at * 3 (Conn. Super. Ct. June 23, 2005) (reaffirming a public school teacher's status as a public official). Additionally, a police patrolman has been held to be a public official because a patrolman "has, or appears to the public to have, substantial responsibility for or control over the conduct of government affairs, at least where law enforcement and police functions are concerned . . ." Moriarty v. Lippe, 162 Conn. 371, 378, 294 A.2d 326, 329 (1972). However, in McIntire v. Piscottano, No. CV010076151, 2005 Conn. Super. LEXIS 1526, at *15 (Conn. Super. Ct. May 23, 2005), the court ruled that a town recreation director was not a "public figure" because he lacked "substantial authority over or control of the conduct of an important governmental function and [which] authority, if abused, has the potential to cause great social harm." Id. The defendant had argued that although plaintiff's position did not typically fall within the public figure rubric, the controversial issue relating to the allegedly defamatory statement was of public concern so as to deem plaintiff a public figure. In ruling for the plaintiff, the court stated that "[t]he employee's position must be one which would invite public scrutiny and discussion of the person holding it, entirely apart from the scrutiny and discussion occasioned by the particular charges in controversy." Id.

3. ***Falsity.*** To sustain an action for defamation in Connecticut, there must be an unprivileged publication of a false defamatory statement. Abdul-Salaam v. Lobo-Wadley, 665 F. Supp. 2d 96, 101 (D. Conn. 2009); see also Battistoni v. Lakeridge Tax Dist., No. LLICV075002223S, 2008 Conn. Super LEXIS 1618, at *4 (Conn. Super. Ct. June 17, 2008) (granting motion to strike slander claim where the plaintiff failed to allege that the statements at issue were false); Raye v. Wesleyan Univ., CV020098865S, 2003 Conn. Super. LEXIS 983, at *9 (Conn. Super. Ct. Apr. 10, 2003) (striking defamation claim where plaintiff failed to allege that the defamatory statements were false). However, it is unclear whether the plaintiff bears the burden of proving the falsity of the statement in light of the fact that truth is an affirmative defense, which the defendant must prove. See discussion infra II.B.1 regarding truth as an affirmative defense. The Supreme Court of Connecticut has stated that "[w]hile at common law, truth was an affirmative defense to be pleaded by the defendant, as a practical matter the burden of proving the falsity of the publication has been shifted to the plaintiff, in light of New York Times Co. and its progeny." Goodrich v. Waterbury Republican-American, Inc., 188 Conn. 107, 113 n.6, 448 A.2d 1317 n.6, 1322 (1982). See also Giannecchini v. Hosp. of St. Raphael, 47 Conn. Supp. 148, 164, 780 A.2d 1006, 1015 (2000) ("a defamation plaintiff bears the burden of proving that the statements made concerning him were false.") (citing Daley, 249 Conn. at 795, 734 A.2d at 129). However, some Connecticut courts have refused to place the burden of proving the falsity of the statements on the plaintiff where the plaintiff was a private figure alleging defamation on a matter of private concern. See Snyder v. Cedar, No. CV010454296, 2006 Conn. Super LEXIS 520, at *36 (Conn. Super. Ct. Feb. 16, 2006) ("[a]lthough cases that involve public comment on public figures . . . make clear that the burden of establishing falsity rests on the plaintiff when the 'actual malice' standard applies, there is no indication in these cases that the common-law rule has been altered for defamation by a private party of a non-public figure. Accordingly the falsity of the defamatory statement is presumed."); Kuselias v. S. New Eng. Tel. Co., No. CV910322295S, 1996 Conn. Super. LEXIS 2829, at *27-33 (Conn. Super. Ct. Oct. 28, 1996) ("where the plaintiff is a private figure and the matter involved is not one of public concern, it is difficult to see how any constitutional issues under the First Amendment are raised that would require a change in the common law allocations of the burden of proof.").

4. ***Defamatory Statement of Fact.*** "To be actionable, the [allegedly defamatory] statement in question must convey an objective fact, as generally, a defendant cannot be held liable for expressing a mere opinion." Indiaweekly.com, LLC v. Nehaflix.com, Inc., 596 F. Supp. 2d 497, 503 (D. Conn. 2009) (citing Daley, 249 Conn. at 795, 734 A.2d at 129)); accord Iosa, 299 F. Supp. 2d at 38 (under Connecticut law, "[t]here can be no claim of defamation in the absence of a false statement of fact"). (See II.B.2, infra, regarding opinion as a defense to defamation). A statement is factual "if it relates to an event or state of affairs that existed in the past or present and is capable of being known." Goodrich, 188 Conn. at 111, 448 A.2d at 1321 (citation omitted). In actions for defamation, such statements of fact are usually concerning a person's character or conduct. See id. "An opinion, on the other hand, is a personal comment about another's conduct, qualifications or character that has some basis in fact. . . . [W]hile this distinction may be somewhat nebulous, . . . [t]he important point is whether ordinary persons hearing or reading the matter complained of would be likely to understand it as an expression of the speaker's or writer's opinion, or as a statement of existing fact." Id. at 111-12. (citations and internal quotation marks omitted). Statements perceived as a joke by an ordinary person are treated as an opinion and are, therefore,

not defamatory. See McClain v. Pfizer, Inc., No. 3:06-CV-1795 (VLB), 2008 U.S. Dist. LEXIS 17757, at *22-23 (D. Conn. Mar. 27, 2008) (holding that statements by supervisor that the plaintiff was overly sensitive, that supervisor disagreed with employee's opinion during a meeting, and that employee's work did not meet expectations were expressions of opinion); Victoria Square, LLC v. Glastonbury Citizen, 49 Conn. Supp. 452, 454-56 (2006) (dismissing plaintiff's defamation claim because the newspaper's April Fool's Edition was clearly a parody). Merely stating a fact in the form of an opinion, however, does not render the statement unactionable. See Sweeney v. Faracalas, 2010 WL 150830, at *5 (Conn. Super. Ct. Mar. 10, 2010) ("[s]imply couching [factual] statements in terms of opinion" does not render them "opinions" for purposes of a defamation action); Shea v. City of Waterbury, No. CV085007926, 2009 Conn. Super. LEXIS 794, at *13-14 (Conn. Super. Ct. Feb. 20, 2009) ("A defamatory communication may consist of a statement in the form of an opinion [and] a statement of this nature is actionable… if it implies the allegation of undisclosed defamatory facts as the basis for the opinion.") (quoting RESTATEMENT (SECOND) OF TORTS § 566 (1976)). The court determines, as a matter of law, whether a statement is a fact or an opinion but where the court cannot "reasonably characterize" the statement as either fact or opinion, because, for example, innuendo is present, the determination becomes an issue for the jury. Goodrich, 188 Conn. at 112 n.5, 448 A.2d at 1322 n.5 (citation omitted).

5. ***Of and Concerning Plaintiff.*** To prevail on a defamation claim, the plaintiff must show that the defamatory statement identified the plaintiff to a reasonable third person. See QSP, 256 Conn. at 356-57, 773 A.2d at 916 (citation omitted). In Hamzi v. Goldstein, No. CV960324501S, 1999 Conn. Super. LEXIS 279, at *9-12 (Conn. Super. Ct. Feb. 4, 1999), the superior court held that the plaintiff, a nurse anesthetist, was unable to establish libel where he failed to show that the allegedly defamatory memorandum identified him by name, or that the radiology technologists to whom the memorandum was addressed understood the memorandum to be referring to the plaintiff. In Siena v. Meredith Corp., No. CV075002360, 2009 Conn. Super. LEXIS 884, at *13 (Conn. Super. Ct. Mar. 30, 2009), the court held that, given the "unique facts" of the case, there was a genuine issue of material fact preventing summary judgment for the defendant, a television news station, which aired reports about the plaintiff's brother who was alleged to have viewed pornography on police department computers. The court in Siena found that the reports, although not about the plaintiff, could be actionable because viewers might believe that the reports were "of and concerning" the plaintiff given that the two brothers were identical twins who looked very similar, both were police officers with the same department, and the report included references to the plaintiff's brother as simply "Siena" and "Officer Siena."

Where the defamatory statement refers to a general class of persons, such as doctors or lawyers, no cause of action exists for an individual member of the class without specific reference, either directly or by innuendo, to the individual member. See Bowen v. Poli-New Enc. Theatres, Inc., 12 Conn. Supp. 28 (1943) (citation omitted); Dontigney v. Paramount Pictures Corp., 411 F. Supp. 2d 89, 92-93 (D. Conn. 2006) (relying on Bowen and dismissing defamation claim based on depiction of Native Americans in a film where the plaintiff was not named in the film and it could not be said "that the group or class of Native Americans is so small that a reasonable viewer necessarily would believe the film was directed toward [the plaintiff]").

6. ***Publication.*** In order to establish a prima facie case of defamation, the plaintiff must prove that the defamatory statement was published to a third person. See QSP, 256 Conn. at 356, 773 A.2d at 916 (2001) (citation omitted). No action for defamation exists if the defendant publishes the defamatory statements only to the plaintiff, a rule generally true even if the plaintiff thereafter disseminates those same statements to a third party. Cweklinsky, 267 Conn. at 217, 837 A.2d at 764 (2004). See II.B.6.b, infra.

a. **Intracorporate Communication.** Connecticut recognizes that the dissemination of a defamatory communication among employees of a corporation or the inclusion of a libelous statement in an employee's personnel file may satisfy the publication element of a prima facie claim of defamation. See Cassidy v. Hartford Fin. Servs. Group, No. CV05009159S, 2008 Conn. Super. LEXIS 107, at *16 (Conn. Super. Ct. Jan. 8, 2008) (citing Torosyan v. Boehringer Ingelheim Pharm., Inc., 234 Conn. 1, 662 A.2d 89 (1995)); Wilk v. Abbott Terrace Health Ctr., Inc., No. CV065001328S, 2007 Conn. Super. LEXIS 2220, at *24-28 (Conn. Super. Ct. Aug. 15, 2007) (same); Cweklinsky v. Mobil Chem. Co., 364 F.3d 68, 73 (2d Cir. 2004) (same). However, while communications among employees of a corporation—or in certain situations among employees of multiple, connected corporations—may constitute publication, they are also protected by a qualified privilege that can be defeated by proof of malice on the part of the employer in making the communication. See II.A.2.a, infra, regarding qualified privilege for intracorporate communications.

b. **Compelled Self-Publication.** The Supreme Court of Connecticut expressly considered and rejected this theory of defamation in Cweklinsky, 267 Conn. at 217, 837 A.2d at 764 (2004). In this case, originally filed in the United States District Court for the District of Connecticut, the plaintiff was terminated from his job for disciplinary reasons and claimed that he was defamed by being forced to repeat the allegedly false reasons for his discharge to potential future employers. The District Court recognized compelled self-publication as satisfying the "publication" element of a defamation claim under Connecticut law. The plaintiff went on to prevail on the claim with a jury verdict and award of

$500,000 in lost earnings. The defendant-employer appealed the judgment to the United States Court of Appeals for the Second Circuit. Confronted with unsettled law in Connecticut, the Second Circuit requested certification from the Connecticut Supreme Court as to whether, under Connecticut law, a plaintiff can satisfy the publication element of defamation solely by proof that he himself repeated to a third party the defamatory statements made by his employer. Cweklinsky, 297 F.3d 154, 156 (2d Cir. 2002). The Court determined that for reasons of public policy— primarily society's interest in the free flow of information in the workplace — the doctrine of compelled self-publication defamation should be rejected. Cweklinsky, 267 Conn. at 217, 837 A.2d at 764. The Court also reasoned that recognition of the doctrine would undermine a plaintiff's duty to mitigate damages, since in a self-publication defamation action, "the party repeating the publication . . . essentially controls the cause of action, having the ability to increase damages by continually repeating the defamatory statement to different prospective employers." Id. at 223, 837 A.2d at 768. After the Supreme Court resolved the issue, the Second Circuit in Cweklinsky, which was now "[e]quipped with a newly delineated map of Connecticut's defamation law," vacated the jury verdict and $500,000 damages award. It also remanded the case for a new trial solely on the alternative theory of defamation by intracorporate publication. Cweklinsky, 364 F.3d at 74-75.

c. **Republication.** Repetition of a defamatory statement is itself defamation, see Wilkinson v. Schoenhorn, No. CV960565559S, 1999 Conn. Super. LEXIS 868, at *5 (Conn. Super. Ct. Mar. 24, 1999) (citing Charles Parker Co. v. Silver City Crystal Co., 142 Conn. 605, 611-12, 116 A.2d 440, 443 (1955)), subject to the rule discussed in I.B.6.b, supra, that an action will generally not lie when a plaintiff himself publishes the statements to third parties. One who repeats or otherwise republishes defamatory statements is subject to liability as if he had originally published the statements. See id. (citing Cianci v. N.Y. Times Publ'g Co., 639 F.2d 54, 61 (2d Cir. 1980)). The defendant does not escape liability by phrasing the statement as "something he had heard." Harris v. Deafenbaugh, No. CV91-0320379, 1993 Conn. Super LEXIS 2578, at *4 (Conn. Super. Ct. Oct. 4, 1993). For the re-publisher to claim the defense of truth (see II.B.1, infra, regarding truth as a defense), he must prove that the substance of the statements are, in fact, true, not that the original publisher did indeed utter the statements. See Wilkinson, 1999 Conn. Super. LEXIS 868, at *4-5 (citations omitted); Harris, 1993 Conn. Super. LEXIS 2578, at *3-4.

7. ***Statements versus Conduct.*** In Connecticut, to establish a claim of defamation, the defendant must have made a false defamatory statement. See Raye, 2003 Conn. Super. LEXIS 983, at *6. There are no Connecticut cases in which the court has recognized a cause of action for defamation based on the conduct of the defendant. However, in Britton Mfg. Co. v. Conn. Bank and Trust Co., 20 Conn. Supp. 113, 115, 125 A.2d 315, 315 (1956), the superior court suggested that had the plaintiff alleged that the defendant bank returned the plaintiff's check and charged the plaintiff's account for insufficient funds, as opposed to failing to honor the check, the requisite publication element of a defamation claim would have been alleged so as to constitute a cause of action for defamation. The court noted that the action of a drawer issuing a check without insufficient funds reflected on the personal integrity of the drawer and subjected the drawer to criminal prosecution. Therefore, returning a check and charging the drawer's account for insufficient funds, if false, is libelous per se. See discussion infra I.B.8.a regarding libel per se.

8. ***Damages.*** Libel claims are based on one of two theories: libel per quod and libel per se.

A claim of libel per quod is based on words that are not obviously defamatory on their face and thus require proof of extrinsic facts known to the plaintiff to establish their alleged defamatory meaning. A plaintiff asserting a libel per quod claim must plead and prove actual (or special) damages in order to recover. See Demorais v. Wisniowski, 81 Conn. App. 595, 603-04, 841 A.2d 226, 232, cert denied, 268 Conn. 923, 848 A.2d 472 (2004), (citing Battista v. United Illuminating Co., 10 Conn. App. 486, 491, 523 A.2d 1356, 1359, cert. denied, 204 Conn. 802, 803, 525 A.2d 1352 (1987)) see, e.g., Lowe v. City of Shelton, 83 Conn. App. 750, 767-68, 851 A.2d 1183, 1196 (2004) (affirming dismissal of claim of libel per quod because no evidence of any actual damages suffered by plaintiff). Special damages are "actual pecuniary" losses suffered as a result of the defamatory statements. Reaves, 2003 Conn. Super. LEXIS 525, at *4 (citation omitted).

A claim of libel per se (discussed in I.B.8.a, infra) is based on words alleged defamatory meaning of which is apparent on their face. See Pianin v. Thru Way Shopping Ctr., No. CV010186828, 2005 Conn. Super. LEXIS 2244, at *8 (Conn. Super. Ct. Aug. 24, 2005) (calling plaintiff a "thief" constituted libel per se). For such claims, a successful plaintiff is presumed to be injured and is entitled to general damages without proof of special damages. Demorais, 81 Conn. App. at 603 -04, 841 A.2d at 232 (citing Battista, 10 Conn. App. at 491-92, 523 A.2d at 1359). General damages are damages awarded for injury to reputation, and for the humiliation and mental suffering that the defamation caused the plaintiff. See DeVito v. Schwartz, 66 Conn. App. 228, 234-35, 784 A.2d 376, 381 (2001) ("[E]conomic damages are akin to special damages, and non economic damages are akin to general damages.") (citation omitted); but see Pianin, 2005 Conn. Super. LEXIS 2244, at *8 (finding nominal damages of one dollar adequate where plaintiff was unable to prove "a causal connection between the libelous statement and any damages suffered").

At the same time, in any action alleging libel, as opposed to slander, Connecticut statutory law provides for the mitigation of damages where a defendant offers prima facie proof of benign intent in making the defamatory statement.

See discussion infra II.B.4, regarding defendant's mitigation of damages. Where the defendant offers such proof, Conn. Gen. Stat. § 52-237 (2008) provides that for a plaintiff alleging libel to recover any damages other than actual damages alleged and proved, the plaintiff must prove either (1) malice in fact or (2) the defendant's failure to retract the libelous charge after the plaintiff's written request for a retraction. In Gambardella v. Apple Health Care, Inc., 291 Conn. 620, 969 A.2d 736 (2009), the Supreme Court of Connecticut clarified the difference between "malice in fact" as used in the statute and "actual malice" (discussed supra, I.B.2.b) defining actual malice as "the publication of a false statement with knowledge of its falsity or reckless disregard for its truth" and malice in fact as "the publication of a false statement with bad faith or improper motive." 291 Conn. at 634, 969 A.2d at 746; see also Haxhi v. Moss, 25 Conn. App. 16, 591 A.2d 1275 (1991) (stating that Connecticut courts have defined "malice in fact" as any improper or unjustifiable motive); Wolinsky v. Standard Oil of Conn., Inc., 712 F. Supp. 2d 46, 63 (D. Conn. 2010) (noting that, because defendant retracted the allegedly libelous statement upon plaintiff's request, and because plaintiff did not allege special damages, plaintiff could only recover on his libel claim if he could prove malice in fact).

a. **Presumed Damages and Libel *Per Se*.** As discussed supra, when the defamatory words are actionable per se, the law conclusively presumes the injury to a plaintiff's reputation. The plaintiff is required neither to plead nor to prove it. See Gaudio v. Griffin Health Servs. Corp., 249 Conn. 523, 551, 733 A.2d 197, 215 (1994) (citing Urban v. Hartford Gas Co., 139 Conn. 301, 308, 93 A.2d 292, 295 (1952)). Two categories of defamatory statements which Connecticut courts generally recognize as actionable per se are: (1) statements alleging a crime involving moral turpitude or to which an infamous penalty is attached; and (2) statements alleging improper conduct or lack of skill or integrity in one's profession or business, and which are of such a nature that they are calculated to cause injury to one in his profession or business. See Proto v. Bridgeport Herald Corp., 136 Conn. 557, 566, 72 A.2d 820, 825-26 (1950); Shea, 2009 Conn. Super. LEXIS 794, at *19-21 (concluding that defendant's statements that "plaintiffs were "gaming" the city's disability pension system" were "legally sufficient" to support a defamation per se claim because the comment diminishes the ""esteem, goodwill or confidence in which the plaintiff is held, or excite adverse, derogatory, or unpleasant feelings or opinions against him."") (quoting Lega Siciliana Social Club, Inc. v. St. Germaine, 77 Conn.App. 846, 851-52, 825 A.2d 827, cert. denied, 267 Conn. 901, 838 A.2d 210 (2003)); Integrated Sec. Solutions, LLC v. Sec. Tech. Sys., LLC, No. 4001811, 2007 Conn. Super. LEXIS 2397, at *6 (Conn. Super. Ct. Sept. 11, 2007) (allegations of "theft and dealing drugs" are libelous per se if proven false). Cf. Troche v. Smith, No. CV950370542S, 1998 Conn. Super. LEXIS 2251, at *6-8 (Conn. Super. Ct. Aug. 6, 1998) (employer's statements that plaintiff "had been a major problem" and that "even the blacks do not like him" were not libel per se since no reference was made to plaintiff's professional skills or competence).

Whether a publication is libelous per se is a question of law. See Battista,10 Conn. App. at 492, 523 A.2d at 1360. The determination of whether a published article is libelous per se must be based upon the face of the article itself. See Lyons v. Heid, Nos. CV940311175S and CV9403120195, 1998 Conn. Super LEXIS 1516, at *13 (Conn. Super. Ct. May 29, 1998) (citation omitted). The statements contained within the article must be taken "in the sense in which common and reasonable minds would understand them," and may not, for this purpose, be varied or enlarged by innuendo. Id.

(1) **Employment-Related Criticism.** Statements regarding an employee's general incompetence and allegations of theft have both been found to be actionable per se in Connecticut. See Miles, 11 Conn. App. at 602, 529 A.2d at 209 (1987). But see III.B. infra, regarding an employer's statements about an employee's work performance as mere expressions of opinion, which are not actionable as defamation.

(2) **Single Instance Rule.** No Connecticut cases discuss the "single instance rule."

b. **Punitive Damages.** Punitive damages may be recovered on account of malicious defamation and are limited to expenses of litigation less taxable costs. See Craney v. Donovan, 92 Conn. 236, 238, 102 A. 640, 641 (1917). The plaintiff's proof of mere negligence by the publisher is not enough to recover punitive damages. Id. See also King v. Cablevision Servs., No. CV940 135727S, 1998 Conn. Super. LEXIS 2380, at *27-29 (Conn. Super. Ct. Aug. 24, 1998) (setting aside a punitive damages award arising out of the employment context in the absence of proof of "outrageous conduct which is malicious, wanton, reckless or in willful disregard for another's rights") (citation omitted). But see Brown v. K.N.D. Corp., 7 Conn. App. 418, 423, 509 A.2d 533, 537 (1986), rev'd on other grounds, 205 Conn. 8, 529 A.2d 1292 (1987) ("[I]f a statement is of exclusively private concern and refers to a private figure, the common law controls and actual malice need not be proven in order to recover punitive or compensatory damages.").

II. PRIVILEGES AND DEFENSES

A. Scope of Privileges

1. ***Absolute Privilege.*** Under Connecticut law, damages cannot be recovered from a party who enjoys an absolute privilege, even if the statement is published falsely and maliciously. See Petyan v. Ellis, 200 Conn. 243, 245-46, 510 A.2d 1337, 1338 (1986). "[T]he class of absolutely privileged communications is narrow, and practically limited

to legislative and judicial proceedings, and acts of State." Leua Siciliana Soc. Club, Inc. v. St. Germaine, 77 Conn. App. 846, 855, 825 A. 2d 827, 834 (2003), cert. denied, 267 Conn. 901, 838 A. 2d 210 (2003).

Connecticut follows the long-standing common law rule that statements published in the course of judicial proceedings are absolutely privileged so long as the statements are pertinent to the subject of the proceeding. Petyan, 200 Conn. at 245-46, 510 A.2d at 1338. While to be considered an absolutely privileged statement, the statement must be related to a court pleading or court hearing, it is not essential that the statement be made in a pleading or during a hearing. See Hopkins, 282 Conn. at 832, 925 A.2d at 1038 ("The scope of privileged communication extends not merely to those made directly to a tribunal, but also to those preparatory communications that may be directed to the goal of the proceeding."). For example, the Superior Court in Snyder v. Cedar, held that the allegedly defamatory statements made by a pro se defendant to the plaintiff's lawyer as part of child support negotiations prior to the child support matter being presented to the court that same day were made during a judicial proceeding, and thus, privileged, even though the statements were only tangentially related to the subject matter of the negotiations. No. CV010454296, 2006 Conn. Super. LEXIS 520, at *53 (Conn. Super. Ct. 2006); but see Gallo v. Barile, 284 Conn. 459, 471, 935 A.2d 103, 111 (2007) (holding that statements made to police in connection with a criminal investigation are qualifiedly privileged but not absolutely privileged). The privilege afforded to statements made during the course of judicial proceedings can extend to persons who are not parties to the litigation. See McKinney v. Chapman, 103 Conn. App. 446, 452, 929 A.2d 355, 359-60 (2007).

An absolute privilege also shields relevant statements made during administrative proceedings that are "quasi-judicial" in nature. Petyan, 200 Conn. at 246 (citations omitted). Factors helpful in determining if a proceeding qualifies as quasi-judicial in nature include "'whether the [administrative] body has the power to: (1) exercise judgment and discretion; (2) hear and determine or to ascertain facts and decide; (3) make binding orders and judgments; (4) affect the personal property rights of private persons; (5) examine witnesses and hear the litigation of the issues on a hearing; and (6) enforce decisions or impose penalties."' Craig v. Stafford Constr., Inc., 271 Conn. 78, 85, 856 A.2d 372, 377 (2004) (quoting Kelley, 221 Conn. at 565-67, 606 A.2d at 703). Further, "it is important to consider whether there is a sound public policy reason for permitting the complete freedom of expression that a grant of absolute immunity provides." See id. **The Connecticut Superior Court also applied a test consisting of three elements in determining whether a person is entitled to qualified immunity: "[1] whether the official in question perform[s] functions sufficiently comparable to those of officials who have traditionally been afforded absolute immunity at common law ... [2] whether the likelihood of harassment or intimidation by personal liability [is] sufficiently great to interfere with the official's performance of his or her duties ... [and 3] whether procedural safeguards [exist] in the system that would adequately protect against [improper] conduct by the official." Osuch v. Hull, No. FSTCV084014443S, 2012 WL 3264058, at *7 (Conn. Super. Ct. July 17, 2012) (holding that probation officers preparing presentence investigation reports are entitled to absolute quasi-judicial immunity).** An internal affairs investigation conducted by a municipal police department is a quasi-judicial proceeding, Craig, 271 Conn. . at 89, 856 A.2d at 379, as is an affirmative action investigation opened by the department of correction to look into alleged wrongdoing in the workplace, see Morgan v. Bubar, 115 Conn. App. 603 (2009) (relying on the above-listed six factors from Kelley), and as are proceedings before the Equal Employment Opportunity Commission and the Connecticut Commission on Human Rights and Opportunities. Blake McIntosh v. Cadbury Beverages, Inc., No. 3:96-CV -2554, 1999 U.S. Dist. LEXIS 12801, at *25 (D. Conn. 1999) (holding that Equal Employment Opportunities Commission and the Connecticut Commission on Human Rights and Opportunities proceedings are quasi-judicial in nature); see also Shea, 2009 Conn. Super. LEXIS 794, at *6 ("The judicial proceeding to which [absolute] immunity attaches... includes any hearing before a tribunal which performs a judicial function, ex parte or otherwise, ... whether the hearing is public or not, ...lunacy, bankruptcy, or naturalization proceedings, .. an election contest, . . . [and some] proceedings of administrative officers, such as boards and commissions...") (citing Craig, 271 Conn. at 84-85, 856 A.2d at 376); Ventres v. Goodspeed Airport , LLC, Nos. X07CV01402085S, X07CV014025127S, X07CV075012545S, 2008 Conn. Super. LEXIS 1363, at *76-77 (Conn. Super. Ct. May 27, 2008) (statements made to the inland wetlands and watercourses commission in the course of fact finding and cease and desist proceedings are privileged); McClain,2008 U.S. Dist. LEXIS 17757, at *17-20 (holding that an OSHA investigation and hearing were quasi-judicial in nature); Milne v. Filene's, Inc., No. CV054018766S, 2007 Conn. Super. LEXIS 543, at *18 (Conn. Super. Ct. Feb. 21, 2007) (statements made to the state Department of Labor during the Department's investigation of the plaintiff's termination are privileged); Calderon v. Dinan & Dinan PC, No. 3:05-CV-1341 (JBA), 2006 U.S. Dist. LEXIS 39024, at *27 (D. Conn. June 13, 2006) (holding that workers' compensation hearings are quasi-judicial); **Carbone v. Diez, No. FSTCV085005902S, 2011 WL 6976574, at *9 (Conn. Super. Ct. Dec. 15, 2011) (holding that a Board of Ethics proceeding involving witnesses, admission, of evidence, etc. were quasi-judicial)**; but see Chadha v. Charlotte Hungerford Hosp., 272 Conn. 776, 788, 865 A.2d 1163, 1171 (2005) (holding that participants in quasi-judicial proceedings before medical review panels are not entitled to an absolute privilege but only qualified immunity).

An absolute privilege also shields complaints seeking to initiate quasi-judicial proceedings, even in cases where the complaint does not result in a full hearing. Rhea v. Uhry, 354 Fed. Appx. 469, 471 (2d Cir. 2009). But see Wolinksy v. Standard Oil of Conn., Inc., 712 F. Supp. 2d at 61 (holding that absolute privilege did not apply to a letter sent to all employees because it was not aimed at "marshalling evidence" for a potential investigation but rather was "primarily aimed at discrediting [plaintiff's] allegations; reassuring the . . . employees that their employer was not engaging in illegal behavior; and encouraging them to not let the matter distract from their work").

Even though "'judicial proceeding' has been defined liberally," employers should be cautioned that communications may not come within that definition and, therefore, are not privileged, if they were made to individuals (including co-workers of the plaintiff) "unconnected" with the proceedings and "in no way directed toward the achievement of the objects of litigation or any other proceedings." Hopkins, 282 Conn. at 848-849, 925 A.2d at 1048 (2007). See also Orsini v. Zimmer, 2009 WL 5698148, at *6 (Conn. Super. Ct. Dec. 24, 2009) (explaining that courts must consider the relevance of the communication to "the furtherance of the litigation"); **Fiondella Ins. v. Reiner, Reiner, & Bendett, No. HHDCV085025357, 2011 WL 6945229, at *9-10 (Conn. Super. Ct. Nov. 17, 2012) (holding that the circulation of a complaint to a limited number of lawyers was privileged).**

Once a proceeding is found to be quasi-judicial in nature, then the absolute privilege granted to statements made in furtherance of the proceeding extends to every step of the proceedings until their final disposition. Craig, 271 Conn. at 93, 856 A.2d at 381; see also Dlugokecki v. Vieira, No. 040184600S, 2005 Conn. Super. LEXIS 2020, at *11-13 (Conn. Super. Ct. July 7, 2005) (granting defendant's motion to dismiss slander per se and slander per quod claims when statements were made in relation to a pending application before a local inland wetlands commission). To the contrary, the privilege falls away when the challenged statements are not made during the course of any quasi-judicial proceeding. Compare Craig, 271 Conn. at 80, 856 A.2d at 374 (citizen's complaint commenced the police department's internal affairs process), with Lega Siciliana Soc. Club, Inc. v. St. Germaine, 77 Conn. App. 846, 856, 825 A. 2d 827, 834 cert. denied, 267 Conn. 901, 838 A.2d 210 (2003) (statements in letters sent to city officials and city zoning board not absolutely privileged because the complaints were not made during the course of any quasi-judicial proceeding, no governmental proceeding was ever initiated by the defendant claiming absolute immunity, and there was no evidence that the defendant's letters were an effort to initiate such a proceeding); Albert v. Shaikh, No. CV030825352S, 2003 WL 22904562 (Conn. Super. Ct. Nov. 25, 2003) (rejecting defendant's argument that his allegedly slanderous comments were entitled to absolute immunity since there was no allegation that defendant's statements were made as part of police investigation of misconduct; "[t]he mere fact that those statements led ultimately, by some unspecified procedural process, to the imposition of professional discipline against the plaintiff does not mean that the interview in which he made them was either part of an ongoing internal affairs investigation, or even a preliminary step in preparing to initiate such an investigation."); and Dickinson v. Merrill Lynch, Pierce, Fenner & Smith Inc, 431 F. Supp. 2d 247 (D. Conn. 2006) (rejecting the argument that statements on the NASD's Form U-5 are protected by absolute immunity; although the NASD has quasi-judicial responsibilities, the submission of a Form U-5 is not a stage in the NASD's quasi-judicial regulatory process.); Petyan, 200 Conn. at 246-52, 510 A.2d 1337 (statements made by employer on a form used in a fact-finding prior to an unemployment compensation hearing are absolutely privileged); Magnan v. Anaconda Indus., Inc., 37 Conn. Supp. 38, 44-46, 429 A.2d 492, 495 (1980) (applying an absolute privilege to information supplied on an "unemployment notice" as required by regulations). In Barrett v. La Petite Academy, Inc., No. CV030827112S, 2005 Conn. Super. Lexis 748, at *15 (Conn. Super. Ct. March 18, 2005), the Defendant reported plaintiff employee to the Department of Children and Families ("DCF") on suspicion of child abuse. In response to plaintiff's claim of defamation, defendant claimed that pursuant to Conn. Gen. Stat. § 17a-101a, it was required to report its suspicions of child abuse, and as such, was entitled to absolute immunity to plaintiff's claims. The court ruled that La Petite Academy was, in fact a mandatory reporting entity and as such was immune to plaintiff's claims, pursuant to Conn. 17a-101e(b). Id. The court disagreed with plaintiff's assertion that defendants were required to independently investigate their suspicions before contacting DCF. Id. In sustaining the absolute privilege, the court stated "[t]he plaintiff in the present case claims that [the defendant] should have realized that there was no basis to the allegations, but this implies a duty on [the defendant's] part to further investigate Welker and Monroe's claims, but Romero had no such duty." Id. at *7.

2. ***Qualified Privileges.*** In order for a qualified (or "conditional") privilege to protect an otherwise defamatory communication, five essential elements must be established: (1) an interest to be upheld, (2) a statement limited in its scope to this purpose, (3) good faith, (4) a proper occasion, and (5) a publication in a proper manner only to proper parties. Lowe v. City of Shelton, 83 Conn. App. at 771 n.5, 851 A.2d at 1198 (citing Miles, 11 Conn. App. at 595, 529 A.2d at 199). See also Bleich v. Ortiz, 196 Conn. 498, 501, 493 A.2d 236 (1985) (for qualified privilege to attach, defendant must assert an objective interest sufficiently compelling to warrant protection of an otherwise defamatory communication). But see Wolinksy v. Standard Oil of Conn., Inc., 712 F. Supp. 2d at 62, n. 5 (qualified privilege did not apply because the allegedly libelous statement was made "in furtherance of Defendants' business interests. However, "the immunity of privilege is lost if the defendant can be shown to have made the claimed defamatory [communication] for a purpose other than that for which the immunity was designed to afford protection." Hogan v. N.Y. Times Co., 211 F. Supp. 99, 108 (D. Conn. 1962).

a. **Common Interest**. "A [qualified] privilege is recognized in many cases where the publisher and the recipient have a common interest, and the communication is of a kind reasonably calculated to protect or further it." Miles, 11 Conn. App. at 597 n.9, 529 A.2d at 206. Thus, for example, Connecticut recognizes a qualified privilege for intracorporate communications, which permits an employer internally to communicate information that would otherwise be defamatory. See Torosyan, 234 Conn. at 29, 662 A.2d at 99; Gaudio, 249 Conn. at 545, 733 A.2d at 211. This privilege is overcome, however, by a showing that the statements were made with actual malice or malice in fact. Gambardella, 291 Conn. at 634. Communications between managers regarding the review of an employee's job performance and the preparation of documents regarding an employee's termination are protected by the qualified privilege, as "such communications and documents are necessary to effectuate the interests of the employer in efficiently managing its business." Strode v. Town of Hamden, No. CV990432459, 2002 Conn. Super. LEXIS 3604, at *10 (Conn. Super. Ct. Nov. 08, 2002) (quoting Torosyan, 234 Conn. at 29, 662 A.2d 89); see also McClain, No. 3:06-CV-1795 (VLB), 2008 U.S. Dist. LEXIS 17757, at *21-22 (holding that a qualified privileged applies to the contents of a performance review). A qualified privilege may also protect certain intercorporate communications that are necessary in order to make "efficient, intelligent employment decisions." Julian v. Securitas Security Servs. U.S.A., Inc., 2010 WL 1553778, at *5 (D. Conn. Apr. 19, 2010) (noting that examples of such relationships include an employer providing an employee reference, or between an employer and its IT or security provider). Similarly, a "physician/patient qualified privilege" may attach to insulate a physician from liability for defamatory statements made in a medical chart for the purpose of alerting other medical staff, who shared common interest in patient's care and safety, of potential medical problems. Kalams v. Giacchetto, 268 Conn. 244, 255-56, 842 A.2d 1100, 1108 (2004).

b. **Duty**. A qualified or conditional privilege attaches when one acts in the bona fide discharge of a public or private duty. See Flanagan v. McLane, 87 Conn. 220, 221-22, 87 A.2d 727, 728 (1913) ("The law implies malice from a libelous publication, except in certain cases of privilege, one of which is when the author and publisher of the alleged slander acted in the bona fide discharge of a public or private duty, or in the prosecution of his own rights or interests.") (citation and internal quotation marks omitted). See also Kalams, 268 Conn. at 256, 842 A.2d at 1108 ("To be entitled to claim the physician/patient qualified privilege, the physician must demonstrate he was acting in a professional capacity and in good faith with respect to the defamatory words."); Olumide v. Travelers Ins. Co., Inc., No. CV910505575, 1994 Conn. Super. LEXIS 265, at *16 (Conn. Super. Ct. Feb. 4, 1994) (stating that "as a general rule, a communication derogatory of the character or attributes of an employee [are] qualifiedly privileged if made between persons having a common business duty. . . "); Malik v. Carrier Corp., 202 F.3d 97, 108-09 (2d Cir. 2000) (discussing privileged intracorporate communications where employer had an affirmative duty to investigate the report of an allegation of sexual harassment).

c. **Criticism of Public Employee**. In Lieberman v. Gant, 474 F. Supp. 848 (D. Conn. 1979), aff'd, 630 F.2d 60 (2d Cir. 1980), the District of Connecticut upheld a qualified privilege where the defendant's statements attacked the credentials of a public university teacher whose tenure was being reviewed. The district court did not extend nor limit the scope of the qualified privilege by virtue of the fact that the criticism was directed at an employee of a public institution as opposed to a private entity.

d. **Other Limitations on Qualified Privileges**. An employer's qualified privilege may be lost if the employer "acts with an improper motive or if the scope or manner of a publication exceeds what is reasonably necessary to further the interest." Bleich, 196 Conn. at 501-04, 493 A.2d at (stating that "malice is not restricted to hatred, spite or ill will against a plaintiff, but includes any improper or unjustifiable motive") (citations omitted). But cf. Kelly vs. City of Meriden, 120 F. Supp. 2d 191, 199 (D. Conn. 2000) ("The actual malice sufficient to destroy th[e] immunity [of a qualified privilege] is shown where the defendant utters the statement with knowledge that it was false or with reckless disregard of the truth or falsity of the facts stated.") (citation omitted). See also Graham, No. CV040488908S, 2007 Conn. Super. LEXIS 2816, at *11-13 (denying summary judgment for the defendant and finding that the intracorporate communication privilege did not apply where there was a material issue of fact as to whether an employee of the defendant who reported that the plaintiff threatened to engage in workplace violence made the allegation knowing that it was untrue); see also Cassidy, 2008 Conn. Super. LEXIS 107, at *20-22 (malice was not found such as to overcome the qualified privilege where the only purported proof of malice was that the defendant failed to follow proper procedure in conducting its investigation of plaintiff's alleged workplace misconduct).

In Miles, 11 Conn. App. at 594 n.8, 529 A.2d 199, the Appellate Court of Connecticut held that the trial court did not err in concluding that a church pastor and trustees could not invoke a qualified privilege for defamatory statements made about the church's financial secretary where the defendants failed to confine the statements to the church board or an appropriate investigatory agency. Cf. Lieberman v. Gant, 474 F. Supp. 848 (D. Conn. 1979), aff'd 630 F.2d 60 (2d Cir. 1980) (upholding a qualified privilege where the publication of allegedly defamatory statements about a teacher's credentials were confined to the Dean's advisory counsel).

The privilege may also be lost if the employer fails to raise it as a special defense. See Harris v. Deafenbaugh, No. CV91-0320379, 1993 Conn. Super. LEXIS 2578, at **4-5 (Conn. Super. Ct. Sept. 30, 1993).

e. **Question of Fact or Law**. Under Connecticut law, whether a defamatory communication is protected by a privilege is a question of law. See Bleich, 196 Conn. at 501, 493 A.2d at 238 (citation omitted); Dlugokecki,

98 Conn. App. at 256-57, 907 A.2d at 1272; Alexandru v. Dowd, 79 Conn. App. 434, 439, 830 A.2d 352 (2003). The "pivotal factor" in determining if an absolute privilege is available "is frequently to whom the matter is published," since the privilege may be lost by unnecessary or unreasonable publication. McManus v. Sweeney, 78 Conn. App. 327, 335-36, 827 A.2d 708, 712 (2003). Whether a privilege is lost through its abuse is a question of fact decided by the jury. Bleich, 196 Conn. at 501, 493 A.2d 237.

f. **Burden of Proof**. Connecticut law places the burden of proving that a qualified privilege exists on the defendant. See Griffin v. Clemow, 28 Conn. Supp. 109, 251 A.2d 415 (1968). But as to whether a qualified privilege was abused, the burden of proof is on the plaintiff. See Cassidy, 2008 Conn. Super. LEXIS 107, at *18 Hogan, 211 F. Supp. at 109.

B. Standard Libel Defenses

In addition to privilege, other common defenses raised by employers who are accused of making defamatory communications, include the following:

1. ***Truth.*** Truth is an absolute defense to an action for libel in Connecticut. See Strada v. Conn. Newspaper, Inc., 193 Conn. 313, 316, 477 A.2d 1005 (1984) (citation omitted); Cweklinsky, 364 F.3d at 75. Contrary to the common law, the modern rule is that only substantial truth need be shown. See Estate of Gomez v. Larson, No. CV980084646, 1999 Conn. Super. LEXIS 1535, at *14 (Conn. Super. Ct. June 8, 1999) ("It is not necessary for the defendant to prove the truth of every word of the libel. If he succeeds in proving that 'the main charge, or gist, of the libel' is true, he need not justify statements or comments which do not add to the sting of the charge or introduce any matter by itself actionable.") (citation omitted). The issue is whether the libel, as published, would have a different effect on the reader than the pleaded truth would have produced. See Goodrich, 188 Conn. at, 113, 448 A.2d 1317.

Further, where all of the stated facts have been proven to be true or substantially true, a statement is not defamatory regardless of its tone or innuendo unless there exists additional material facts which, if disclosed, would alter the tone of the statement. See Strada, 193 Conn. at 323; see also Dickinson v. Lovely, No. CV05403643S, 2006 Conn. Super. LEXIS 1080, at *11 (Conn. Super. Ct. Apr. 6, 2006) (concluding that defendant's statements were reasonably perceived as truthful by defendant and as such were true statements and not defamatory.)

2. ***Opinion.*** The Connecticut Supreme Court has stated that "[t]o be actionable [as defamation], the statement in question must convey an objective fact, as generally, a defendant cannot be held liable for expressing a mere opinion." Daley, 249 Conn. at 795, 734 A.2d 112. See I.B.4, supra, regarding the distinction between facts and opinions. Employer statements about an employee's work performance is often found to be the employer's opinion instead of a factual statement. See, e.g., McClain, 2008 U.S. Dist. LEXIS 17757, at *22-23 (holding that statements by supervisor that the plaintiff was overly sensitive, that supervisor disagreed with employee's opinion during a meeting, and that employee's work did not meet expectations were expressions of opinion); Iosa, 299 F. Supp. 2d at 38 (applying Connecticut law, district court found that employer's statement in performance memorandum that it had "serious concerns" about plaintiff's performance was "an opinion . . . about the adequacy of Plaintiff's work"); Grossman v. Computer Curriculum Corp., 131 F. Supp. 2d 299, 312-13 (D. Conn. 2000) (finding, under Connecticut law, that an employer's statements about work performance are merely expressions of opinion and, thus not actionable); Torok v. Proof, No. CV900113204, 1993 Conn. Super. LEXIS 266, at *6 (Conn. Super. Ct. Feb 1, 1993) (holding that an employer's statement that a former employee was "not a good accountant" was not defamation because it was an opinion not capable of being proven true or false).

Connecticut also recognizes that where an opinion or comment is expressed in regards to a matter of public interest, such statements are guaranteed constitutional protection under the First Amendment. See Goodrich, 188 Conn. at 114-15, 448 A.2d at 1323 (stating that while the common law privilege of "fair comment" was traditionally a qualified privilege to express an opinion or otherwise comment on matters of public interest, the privilege has been "elevated to constitutional status," by a number of United States Supreme Court cases starting with New York Times Co., 376 U.S. 254).

To determine whether a statement of opinion is constitutionally protected, Connecticut courts distinguish between expressions of "pure" opinion and those of "mixed" opinion. Where a statement is an expression of "pure" opinion-based on facts which are stated, common knowledge, or readily accessible—the statement is guaranteed virtually complete constitutional protection. See Lizotte v. Welker, 45 Conn. Supp. 217, 709 A.2d 50, 57-8 (1996), aff'd 244 Conn. 156, 709 A.2d 1(1998) (citing Goodrich, 188 Conn. at 118-19, 448 A.2d at 1329). Where a statement is an expression of "mixed" opinion—based on facts which are neither known nor stated—such statements are protected only when made: (1) by members of the press or news media; (2) about matters of public interest or concern; and (3) without knowingly or recklessly distorting the facts upon which they are based. See Goodrich, 188 Conn. at 118-19, 448 A.2d 1317.

3. ***Consent.*** A plaintiff's consent to the publication of defamatory statements concerning the plaintiff is a complete defense to his action for defamation. See Olivas v. DeVivo Indus. Inc., No. CV990335908, 2002 Conn. Super. LEXIS 2504, at *12 (Conn. Super. Ct. July 26, 2002). However, where the person defamed did not consent but instead made an honest inquiry to ascertain the existence, source or meaning of the defamatory publication, the inquiry is not a defense to an action for its republication by the defamer. See id. at *1243. See discussion supra I.B.6.c regarding republication of defamatory statements.

4. ***Mitigation.*** Connecticut statutory law provides for the mitigation of damages in all actions alleging libel. In any action for libel, a defendant may offer prima facie proof of a benign intent in making the allegedly defamatory statements. See Conn. Gen. Stat. § 52-237 (2004). See also Lowe v. City of Shelton, 2003 Conn. Super. LEXIS 2206, at *6-7 (finding proof of defendant's benign intent by evidence disclosing no intent to defame the character of the plaintiff nor any indication of malice). When such proof is given, the plaintiff's recovery of damages is limited to actual damages alleged and proven, unless the plaintiff proves either (1) malice in fact or (2) the defendant's failure to retract the libelous charge following the plaintiff's written request for a retraction. See Conn. Gen. Stat. § 52-237; see also discussion supra I.B.8 regarding recovery of damages in actions alleging libel.

III. RECURRING FACT PATTERNS

A. Statements in Personnel File

As discussed in I.B.6.a, supra, the inclusion of a libelous statement in an employee's personnel file is a dissemination satisfying the publication element of a prima facie case of defamation. See Blake-McIntosh v. Cadbury Beverages, Inc., No. 3:96- CV-2554, 1999 U.S. Dist. LEXIS 12801, at *25 (D. Conn. June 25, 1999) (citing Torosyan, 234 Conn. at, 27-28, 662 A.2d 89; Gaudio, 1997 Conn. Super. LEXIS 1179, at *3. However, where a document in a personnel file simply describes an employee's work mistakes, and the employee concedes having made the errors, there is no false statement on which to base a defamation claim. Iosa, 299 F. Supp. 2d at 38. Also, while communications among employees of a corporation may constitute publication, they may also be protected by a qualified privilege. See Blake-McIntosh, 1999 U.S. Dist LEXIS 12801, at *25 (citing Torosyan, 234 Conn. at 29). See II.A.2.a, supra, regarding Connecticut's recognition of a qualified privilege for intracorporate communications.

Under Connecticut statutory law, an employer is required to permit an employee to inspect his or her personnel file following the employee's written request to do so. See Conn. Gen. Stat. § 31-128b (2003). If, upon inspection, the employee disagrees with any of the information contained within the file, the employee can request to have corrected or removed any information with which the employee disagrees. See id. § 31-128e. If the employer and employee cannot agree upon the removal or correction, the employee may then submit a written statement explaining his or her position regarding the information. See id. The employer must then maintain the statement as part of the employee's personnel file and include the statement when making any transmittal or disclosure from the personnel file to a third party. See id. Other than in the case of a number of statutorily enumerated exceptions, statements in an employee's personnel file may not be disclosed to any person not employed by or affiliated with the employer without the written consent of the employee. See id. § 31-128f.

B. Performance Evaluations

The District of Connecticut, applying Connecticut law, has held that an employer's statements concerning an employee's work performance are merely expressions of opinion and, therefore, not actionable as defamation. See Grossman, 131 F. Supp. 2d at 312-13; Coleman v. S. Cent. Conn. Reg'l Water Auth., 2009 U.S. Dist. LEXIS 10586, at *15 (D. Conn. Feb. 12, 2009). See II.B.2, supra, regarding opinion as a defense. See also Torok, 1993 Conn. Super. LEXIS 266, at *6 (Conn. Super. Ct. Feb. 1, 1993) (concluding that an employer's statement that a former employee was "not a good accountant" was not defamation because it was an opinion); Rafalko v. Univ. of New Haven, 2009 Conn. Super. LEXIS 2557, at *11-14 (Conn. Super. Ct. Sept. 25, 2009) (concluding that defendant was "entitled to his opinion about whether the plaintiff's work was impressive"). But cf. Miles, 11 Conn. App. at, 603, 529 A.2d at 206 (holding that an allegation of general incompetence is actionable per se); McPhee Elec. Ltd., LLC v. Konover Constr. Corp., 2009 Conn. Super. LEXIS 3110, at *118, *127-28 (Conn. Super. Ct. Oct. 22, 2009) (defendant's opinions regarding plaintiff's business integrity were defamatory per se and not privileged as fair comment); **Cohen v. Meyers, No. 2010CV115008047S, 2012 WL 4377824, at *9 (Conn. Super. Ct. Aug. 27, 2012) (holding that plaintiff's statements, which "charge[d] the defendants with improper conduct, lack of integrity in their business practices and profession and general incompetence in the performance of their work," were actionable per se).**

However, even if a statement regarding an employee's performance is held to be a defamatory statement of fact, Connecticut courts recognize a qualified privilege for communications among managers regarding the review of an employee's job performance. See Blake-McIntosh, 1999 U.S. Dist. LEXIS 12801, at *25 (citing Torosyan, 234 Conn. at 27-28, 662 A.2d 89). See II.A.2.a, supra, regarding Connecticut's recognition of a qualified privilege for intracorporate communications.

C. References

Statements made by a plaintiff's former employer to a prospective employer may form the basis for a defamation claim. E.g., Abbott v. ABCO Welding & Indus. Supply, 2009 Conn. Super. LEXIS 3049, at *1-3 (Conn. Super. Ct. Nov. 10, 2009) (denying motion to strike when plaintiff adequately alleged that former employer made defamatory to prospective employer who then rescinded its offer of employment). However, the Connecticut Supreme Court has held that a qualified privilege applies to employment references where the employee consents to such references. See Miron v. Univ. of New Haven Police Dep't, 284 Conn. 35 (2007). Recently, a District of Connecticut court held that there should be no distinction between individualized job references and publication of information on an electronic clearinghouse. Belanger v. Swift Transp., Inc., 552 F. Supp. 2d 297, 302-303 (D. Conn. 2008) (privilege applied where the defendant recorded the fact that it terminated the plaintiff, a truck driver, on an electronic driving record clearinghouse used by trucking companies to vet job applicants' safety records and work histories).

In Giannecchini v. Hosp. of St. Raphael, 47 Conn. Supp. 148, 164-65, 780 A.2d 1006 (2000), the superior court granted summary judgment in favor of the defendant on the plaintiff's defamation claim where the plaintiff failed to prove the falsity of the statement made by the former employer to the prospective employer that the plaintiff was "discharged." Id. at 164-65. The court held that while it was true that Giannecchini had been allowed to resign, the former employer presented "incontrovertible documentary proof that the employer had terminated Giannecchini's employment. Id. A former employer's refusal to provide an employee with a reference, however, cannot constitute defamation. See Calderon v. Dinan & Dinan PC, No. 3:05cv1341 (JBA), 2006 U.S. Dist LEXIS 39024 (D. Conn. 2006) (holding that a refusal to provide a reference fails to meet the publication requirement of a defamation claim).

As stated supra, Connecticut statutory law provides that an employer may not disclose statements in an employee's personnel file to any person not employed by or affiliated with the employer without the employee's written consent. See Conn. Gen. Stat. § 31-128f. This provision also applies in the context of references to prospective employers since an "employee," as defined in the statute, includes a former employee as well as a current employee. Id. § 31-128a. The statute also provides, however, that where the information disclosed is limited to "the verification of dates of employment and the employee's title or position and wage or salary or where the disclosure is made," no written authorization by the employee is required. Id. § 31-128f.

D. Intracorporate Communications

As discussed supra I.B.6.a, Connecticut recognizes that the dissemination of a defamatory communication among employees of a corporation may satisfy the publication element of a prima facie case of defamation. See Blake-McIntosh, No. 1999 U.S. Dist. LEXIS 12801, at *25 (citing Torosyan, 234 Conn. at 27-28, 662 A.2d at 99).

But while communications among employees of a corporation may constitute publication, they are also protected by a qualified privilege. See Gambardella v. Apple Health Care, Inc., 291 Conn. 620, 969 A.2d 736 (2009); see also Cassidy, 2008 Conn. Super. LEXIS 107, at *19-22 (intracorporation privilege applied where the findings of the employer's investigation into fraud by the plaintiff were communicated to the "appropriate individuals" within the company and the "communications concerned the investigation into the plaintiff's involvement"); Wilk v. Abbott Terrace Health Ctr., Inc., No. CV065001328S, 2007 Conn. Super. LEXIS 2220, at *24-28 (Conn. Super. Ct. Aug. 15, 2007). The employer's qualified privilege may be lost, however, if the employer acts with "actual malice" (i.e., publication of a statement with knowledge of the statement's falsity or reckless disregard for its truth) or "malice in fact" (i.e., publication of a false statement with bad faith or improper motive). Gambardella, 291 Conn. 620, 969 A.2d 736; see also Graham, 2007 Conn. Super. LEXIS 2816, at *11-13 (denying summary judgment and holding that the qualified privilege for intracorporate communications did not apply where there was a genuine issue of material fact as to the whether the statements at issue were made with knowledge they were false); Julian v. Securitas Sec. Servs. United States, Inc., 2010 U.S. Dist. LEXIS 38129, at *30 (D. Conn. Apr. 19, 2010) (although employer would ordinarily be entitled to a qualified privilege, court denied summary judgment because it was unclear whether its employees communicated false information "motivated by bad faith or an improper motive"); **Weber v. Fujifilms Med. Systs. USA, Inc., 854 F. Supp 2d, 219, 235 (D. Conn. 2012) (denying summary judgment to employer because evidence showed plaintiff's termination may have been based on discriminatory animus, which may constitute malice).** See II.A.2, supra, regarding the scope of the qualified privilege for intracorporate communications.

Pursuant to Connecticut statutory law, where information contained in an employee's personnel file or medical records is being disseminated to an employee or affiliate of the employer, the employee's consent is not required for disclosure. See Conn. Gen. Stat. § 31-128f.

E. Statements to Government Regulators

In addition to shielding statements made in judicial proceedings, an absolute privilege protects communications made during administrative proceedings that are quasi-judicial in nature. See II.A.1, supra, regarding the scope of the absolute privilege.

Under Connecticut statutory law, where an employer is providing information contained in an employee's personnel file or medical records pursuant to an administrative summons or judicial order, or in response to a government audit, or to comply with federal, state or local laws or regulations, the employee's consent is not required for disclosure. See Conn. Gen. Stat. § 31-128f.

F. Reports to Auditors and Insurers

There are no reported cases in which a Connecticut court has addressed a cause of action for defamation in the context of an employer's reporting information to auditors and insurers. However, where a defendant transmitted incorrect information in the course of its business of reporting claim information to insurance carriers, the court held that a qualified privilege applied to the allegedly defamatory statements. See VanEck v. Choicepoint., Inc., No. CV000443842S, 2000 Conn. Super. LEXIS 3628, at *2 (Conn. Super. Ct. Dec. 21, 2000).

Pursuant to Connecticut statutory law, an employer is not required to obtain an employee's consent to disclose information contained in the employee's personnel or medical records if the information is being disseminated to a third party that maintains or prepares employment records or performs other employment-related services for the employer. See Conn. Gen. Stat. § 31-128f.

G. Vicarious Liability of Employers for Statements Made by Employees

1. ***Scope of Employment.*** Under Connecticut law, an employer may be held liable for the defamatory statements of its employee based upon the doctrine of respondeat superior. See Smith v. Bridgeport Futures Initiative, Inc., No. 326697, 1996 Conn. Super. LEXIS 2158, at *10 (Conn. Super. Ct. Aug. 13, 1996) (citations omitted). For the employer to be held liable, the employee must be acting within the scope of his employment and in furtherance of the employer's business. See id. at *11. But it must be the affairs of the employer and not solely the affairs of the employee, which are being furthered in order for the doctrine to apply. See id. An employer will not be held liable for the defamatory statements of independent contractors. Ceslik v. Miller Ford, Inc., 584 F. Supp. 2d 433, 444-45 (D.Conn. 2008).

a. **Blogging.** There are no Connecticut decisions of note regarding employers' liability for comments on employees' (authorized and unauthorized) blogs.

2. ***Damages.*** A plaintiff may recover compensatory damages from an employer who is held vicariously liable for the defamatory statements of an employee. See 4 at *1748. However, in order to recover punitive damages from the employer for the statements of an employee, it must be shown that there was "some misconduct of the [employer] beyond that which the law implies from the mere relation of principal and agent. See Smith v. Bridgeport Futures Initiative, 1996 Conn. Super. LEXIS 2158, at *18 (quoting Maisenbacker v. Soc'y Concordia, 71 Conn. 369, 379, 42 A. 67, 70 (1899)). In Smith, the court held that the plaintiff's allegation that certain "upper management" authorized the libelous statements was insufficient to sustain a punitive damages award because it was "too unclear that the authorization extended to the alleged libelous statements in particular." Id. at *18-19.

H. Internal Investigations

Connecticut takes a broad view of the qualified privilege amongst managers so they can effectively communicate regarding employee performance and workplace issues. See Torosyan, 234 Conn. at 29, 662 A.2d at 103 ("communications between managers regarding the review of an employee's job performance and the preparation of documents regarding an employee's termination are protected by a qualified privilege. Such communications and documents are necessary to effectuate the interests of the employer in efficiently managing its business."). See also Julian, 2010 U.S. Dist. LEXIS 38129, at *15 (evidence of negligence in an investigation insufficient to support a finding of actual malice). Courts also have recognized that the qualified privilege will prevent chilling speech during internal investigations. See Raye, 2003 Conn. Super. LEXIS 983, at *14-15.

IV. OTHER ACTIONS BASED ON STATEMENTS

The Connecticut Supreme Court has concluded that a supervisor's false statements to an at-will vice president of sales about her job security were sufficient to support a jury verdict in her favor and award of $850,000 on her claim of promissory estoppel. In Stewart v. Cendant Mobility Servs. Corporation, 267 Conn. 96, 837 A.2d 736 (2003), both the vice president of sales and her husband worked for Cendant Mobility Services Corporation, a company that provides relocation services to domestic and international corporations and their employees. The husband was terminated as part of Cendant's reorganization. The vice president of sales went to her supervisor to express her concern that her employment might be negatively affected if her husband accepted a new job at a competitor. The supervisor told her that she should not be concerned, and that her husband's employment with an industry competitor would have no bearing on her job at Cendant. He further relayed to her that Cendant's CEO and president also valued her as a Cendant employee and wished to assure her that she need not be concerned about her job if her husband worked for a competitor. Id. at 99-100, 837 A.2d at 739. The employee continued on with Cendant. Later Cendant limited the employee's interaction with clients after her husband began working with a competing firm and also reduced her job duties. Eventually she was terminated, which she claimed was due to her refusal to sign a document delineating her job duties relative to her husband's work with any competitors. Id. at 100, 837 A.2d at 740. She brought several claims against the employer, including a negligent misrepresentation claim and promissory estoppel claim, both of which were based on the supervisor's false statements. The jury awarded the employee damages of $850,000 on each of the two claims, but it was undisputed that $850,000 was the total award for both claims since they were based on the same facts. Id. at 99, 837 A.2d at 739 n.1. The Connecticut Supreme Court found the evidence sufficient to support the jury's verdict on the promissory estoppel claim alone, and therefore declined to "reach Cendant's claim that the evidence was insufficient to support the plaintiff's negligent misrepresentation claim." Id. at 99, 837 A.2d at 739. At the same time, the fact that the negligent misrepresentation claim went all the way to the jury confirms that it is yet another viable cause of action, as well as promissory estoppel, available under Connecticut law based on employer statements. See also Harris v. Kupersmith, 2009 Conn. Super. LEXIS 2427, at *32-33 (Conn. Super. Ct. Aug. 31, 2009) (allegation that defendant misrepresented that plaintiff would be compensated for his work was sufficient to survive motion to strike negligent misrepresentation claim); Simoes v. Olin Corp., 2010 Conn. Super. LEXIS 1478, at *13-16 (Conn. Super. Ct. June 4, 2010) (plaintiff's promissory estoppel claim based on statements in employee handbook and defendant's representations of a progressive discipline policy were sufficient to survive summary judgment); Jasmin v. New Eng. Plasma Dev. Corp., No. CV044000706, 2005 Conn. Super. LEXIS 2001 (Conn. Super. Ct. July 7, 2005) (allegation of former employer's specific promise of "permanent" employment sufficient to survive motion to strike promissory estoppel claim). In Suntoke v. PSEG Power Connecticut, LLC, No. 3:06-CV-1520 (EBB), 2009 U.S. Dist. LEXIS 11434, at *30-33 (D. Conn. Feb. 13, 2009), the plaintiff's promissory estoppel claim failed to survive summary judgment as the court rejected his efforts to rely on Stewart v. Cendant. The court distinguished the case from Stewart because in Suntoke, the plaintiff did not claim he was told that his employment would continue past the end date of his temporary assignment; rather, he was simply told he would be "involved" in "training" and "we need someone with your experience and background and training." See also Nygren v. Greater N.Y. Mut. Ins. Co., 2009 U.S. Dist. LEXIS 26078, at *21-22 (D. Conn. Mar. 27, 2009) (granting defendant summary judgment on promissory estoppel claim because defendant never promised to use plaintiff "in perpetuity" or that plaintiff could not be terminated); **Desrosiers v. Diageo North Am., Inc., 137 Conn. App. 446, 461-62, 49 A.3d 233, 242-43 (2012) (rejecting promissory estoppel claim based on a supervisor's alleged statements to an employee that the employee's performance was satisfactory and that she no longer had to worry about past performance issues).** Other actions based on statements are discussed below.

A. Negligent Hiring, Retention, and Supervision

Connecticut recognizes the common law torts of negligent hiring, retention, and supervision. See Shippee v. Caswell, No. 559094, 2002 Conn. Super. LEXIS 2523, at * 16 (Conn. Super. Ct. July 26, 2002); Shore v. Town of Stonington, 187 Conn. 147, 155, 444 A.2d 1378, 1383 (1982). An employer may be held liable where a third party is injured as a result of the employer's negligence in hiring, retaining or supervising an employee, but the plaintiff must show that the employer knew or reasonably should have known of the employee's propensity to engage in the type of conduct about which the plaintiff complains. See Perry v. SBC/SNET, No. CV04085367, 2005 Conn. Super. LEXIS 2533, at *10 (Conn. Super. Ct. Sept. 12, 2005) (granting motion to strike plaintiff's negligent supervision claim because plaintiff failed to assert that the defendant knew or should have known that its employees had a propensity for tortious conduct); DeMaria v. Country Club of Fairfield, No. CV02392621S, 2003 Conn. Super. LEXIS 232, at *1142 (Conn. Super. Ct. Jan. 17, 2003); Mazurek v. Great Am. Ins. Co., 2009 Conn. Super. LEXIS 20, at *3-9 (Conn. Super Ct. Jan. 8, 2009) (granting summary judgment to general contractor for negligent hiring and retention claims brought by subcontractor's employee because there was no evidence that general contractor knew or should have known that subcontractor was negligent); Pursuit Ptnrs, LLC v. UBS AG, 2009 Conn. Super. LEXIS 1852, at *44-45 (Conn. Super. Ct. July 8, 2009) (granting motion to strike negligent supervision claim because plaintiffs failed to allege "that the defendants' employees had a propensity to engage in the alleged harmful conduct"); but see Maisano v. Congregation Or Shalom, 2009 Conn. Super. LEXIS 3108, at *7-10 (Conn. Super. Ct. Nov. 19, 2009) (denying summary judgment to employer on negligent supervision claim because employer failed to present evidence that "his actions constituted ordinary negligence, rather than flagrant indifference to the rights or safety of plaintiff"); Andreoni v. Forest Enters., 2010 Conn. Super. LEXIS 1047, at *20-23 (Conn. Super. Ct. Apr. 21, 2010) (denying summary judgment to defendant on plaintiff's negligent supervision and retention claims when plaintiff had reported discriminatory conduct to defendant).

However, where the injured third party is also an employee of the employer, Connecticut's Workers' Compensation Act, Conn. Gen. Stat. § 31-284(a) bars any negligent hiring, retention or supervision suits by the employee where the employee's claims are premised on physical injury. See DeMaria, 2003 Conn. Super. LEXIS 232, at *1142 (stating that "worker's compensation is an employee's only remedy for injuries that arise during the course of his employment, and. . . the exclusivity provision of 31- 284(a) applies whether the employee's claim is predicated on common-law tort, statute or contract") (citation omitted); Perodeau v. City of Hartford, 259 Conn. 729, 744-45, 792 A.2d 752, 761 (2002) (holding that the Workers' Compensation Act does not bar claims for emotional injuries that are not premised on a physical injury).

B. Invasion of Personal Privacy and Invasion of Privacy by False Light

The existence of a cause of action for invasion of privacy was recognized by the Connecticut Supreme Court in Goodrich. In recognizing this cause of action, the Supreme Court adopted the definition and categories of invasion of privacy as set forth in 3 Restatement (Second) of Torts § 652A: (a) unreasonable intrusion upon the seclusion of another; (b) appropriation of the other's name or likeness; (c) unreasonable publicity given to the other's private life; or (d) publicity that places the other in a false light before the public. Goodrich, 188 Conn. at 128 (emphasis added).

Section 652D of the Restatement (Second) of Torts defines a tort action for the invasion of personal privacy as being triggered by public disclosure of any matter that (a) would be highly offensive to a reasonable person and (b) is not of legitimate concern to the public. 3 Restatement (Second) of Torts § 652D. The Restatement describes the types of personal and private information that are given protection under the law of torts: "Sexual relations, for example, are normally entirely private matters, as are family quarrels, many unpleasant or disgraceful or humiliating illnesses, most intimate personal letters, most details of a man's life in his home, and some of his past history that he would rather forget. When these intimate details of his life are spread before the public gaze in a manner highly offensive to the ordinary reasonable man, there is an actionable invasion of his privacy, unless the matter is one of legitimate public interest." 3 Restatement (Second) of Torts § 652D cmt. c. See, e.g., Miron v. McNeil, 2010 Conn. Super. LEXIS 593, at *10-11 (Conn. Super. Ct. Mar. 12, 2010) (granting defendant's motion to strike when plaintiff failed to plead that disclosure of report was not a matter of legitimate public concern). Additionally, "[t]he circumstances under which there is an absolute privilege to publish matter that is an invasion of privacy are in all respects the same as those under which there is an absolute privilege to publish matter that is personally defamatory." 3 Restatement (Second) of Torts § 652F cmt. a. See also Fiondella, Inc. v. Reiner, Reiner & Bendett, 2009 Conn. Super. LEXIS 3366, at *23-24 (Conn. Super. Ct. Dec. 4, 2009) (explaining that "the absolute privilege will bar recovery for an invasion of privacy claim") (citing Alexandru v. Dowd, 79 Conn.App. 434, 441, cert. denied, 266 Conn. 925 (2003)). See discussion II.A.1, supra, regarding the scope of absolute privilege.

For example, in Burns v. Chapman, No. FBTcv0440033095, 2008 Conn. Super. LEXIS 3228 at *43 (Conn. Super. Ct. Dec. 12, 2008), the Superior Court found in favor of the plaintiff on her invasion of privacy claim. The claim was brought after the police chief of Bridgeport gave a newspaper interview following a police standoff with the plaintiff's boyfriend, during which the boyfriend shot and killed himself. The court found statements by the police chief concerning the couple's troubled relationship were not actionable because they were true and there was a legitimate public interest in disclosing the information in the context of the deadly domestic dispute. However, the court found in plaintiff's favor on her claim regarding statements by the police chief about the fact that the plaintiff began her relationship with the boyfriend while he was still married and that she had "tak[en] a husband from a family." The court found these statements were "gratuitous," they "gave high publicity to a private aspect of the plaintiff's life that would be highly offensive to a reasonable person" and the comments were "not of legitimate public concern." Id. at *43, 45.

In order to establish invasion of privacy by false light, the plaintiff must show "(a) the false light in which the other was placed would be highly offensive to a reasonable person, and (b) the actor had knowledge of or acted in reckless disregard as to the falsity of the publicized matter and the false light in which the other would be placed." 3 Restatement (Second) of Torts § 652E; See Goodrich, 188 Conn. at 131. This form of invasion of privacy protects one's interest in not being placed before the public in an objectionable false light or false position, "or in other words, otherwise than as he is." 3 Restatement (Second) of Torts, § 652E cmt. b. The essence of a false light privacy claim is that the matter published concerning the plaintiff (1) is not true and (2) is such a "major misrepresentation of his character, history, activities or beliefs that serious offense may reasonably be expected to be taken by a reasonable man in his position." Id., comment c. Goodrich supra, 131.

In Jonap v. Silver, 1 Conn. App. 550, 559-560, 474 A.2d 800,806 (1984), the plaintiff was marketing director for the defendant company. The President of that company requested, without the plaintiff's consent, that the editor of "Animal Nutrition and Health" magazine publish a letter, which was attributed to the plaintiff. The letter criticized at length certain FDA policies which had seriously interfered with the company's marketing efforts. The plaintiff testified that he agreed "in part" with the judgments and beliefs attributed to him in the letter, but steadfastly maintained that portions of the letter did not accurately reflect his beliefs or judgments, and that the facts and allegations in the letter were not true. The court found that a jury "could reasonably have found this to be highly offensive to a reasonable person because there is sufficient evidence to establish that there was a 'major misrepresentation of his character, history, activities or beliefs.'" See also Abdul-Salaam v. Lobo-Wadley, 665 F. Supp. 2d 96, 102 (D. Conn. 2009) (denying summary judgment because "any reasonable person would be offended if falsely accused of having been terminated for obscenity" and because reasonable people could disagree whether statement was false). In Kindschi v. City of Meriden, No. CV064022391, 2006 Conn. Super. LEXIS 3666 at *6-7 (Conn. Super. Ct. Nov. 27, 2006), a firefighter sued two fellow firefighters and the city that employed them for, inter alia, invasion of privacy by false light, alleging the defendants made false comments about the plaintiff to individuals or in closed meetings with fire department employees or agents. The court found that these facts only showed that the statements were made in private and were insufficient to establish that they were made in or to the public: "According to the Restatement comment in section 652D, whereas 'publication' includes any communication by the defendant to a third person[,] '[p] ublicity' . . . means that the matter is made public, by communicating it to the public at large, or to so many persons that the matter must be regarded as substantially certain to become one of public knowledge." Id. (citations omitted). See also Decker v. Martin, 2010 Conn. Super. LEXIS 168, at *21-26 (Conn. Super. Ct. Jan. 19, 2010) ("false light invasion of privacy requires publicity to the public at large or to enough persons so that the false and defamatory statements must be substantially certain to become public knowledge").

C. Intentional Infliction of Emotional Distress and Negligent Infliction of Emotional Distress

To support a claim of intentional infliction of emotional distress, a plaintiff must show: "(1) that the actor intended to inflict emotional distress; or that he knew or should have known that emotional distress was a likely result of his conduct; (2) that the conduct was extreme and outrageous; (3) that the defendant's conduct was the cause of the plaintiff's distress; and (4) that the emotional distress sustained by the plaintiff was severe." Petyan, 200 Conn. at 253, 510 A.2d at 1341. (citations omitted). Liability under this tort is reserved "for conduct exceeding all bounds usually tolerated by decent society, of a nature which is especially calculated to cause, and does cause, mental distress of a very serious kind." Id. at 254 n.5 (quoting W. Page Keeton et al., Prosser & Keeton on the Law of Torts § 12, at 60 (5th ed. 1984)). Although there is no bright line test for determining what constitutes "mental distress of a very serious kind," most trial courts look to the standard set forth in the Restatement, which "provides that '[emotional distress] includes all highly unpleasant mental reactions.... The law intervenes only where the distress inflicted is so severe that no reasonable [person] could be expected to endure it.'" Le v. Saporoso, 2009 Conn. Super. LEXIS 2878, at *9 (Conn. Super. Ct. Oct. 19, 2009) (quoting Restatement (Second) of Torts § 46 cmt. j (1965)). See also Julian, 2010 U.S. Dist. LEXIS 38129, at *33 (requiring plaintiff to tell his wife and children that he was fired for having accessed pornographic websites was sufficient evidence of severe emotional distress to survive summary judgment on intentional infliction of emotional distress claim).

Examples of employment-related conduct deemed extreme and outrageous include public ridicule, a hostile work environment involving repeated racially motivated statements, repeated taunts about a mental disability, false comments made to law enforcement and termination for exercising a right protected by statute. See, e.g., Crocco v. Advance Stores Co., Inc., 421 F.Supp.2d 485 (D. Conn. 2006) (plaintiff's supervisors indicated to police that plaintiff may have been responsible for a shooting on the employer's premises); Russack-Baker v. Billings P. Learned Mission, Inc., No. 566008, 2004 WL 423984, at *10 (Conn. Super. Ct. Feb. 9, 2004) (citing Knight v. Southeastern Council on Alcoholism & Drug Dependency, No. CV000557182, 2001 Conn. Super. LEXIS 2732 (Conn. Super. Ct. Sept. 21, 2001)); Maltz v. Stango, 2009 Conn. Super. LEXIS 2879, at *8 (Conn. Super. Ct. Oct. 29, 2009) (denying defendant's motion to strike when defendant reneged on promise to provide plaintiff with good recommendations because "this Court believes that in effect he was lying to the plaintiff, and that is serious enough to be extreme and outrageous under these circumstances"); Burke v. State, 2010 Conn. Super. LEXIS 282, at *24-25 (Conn. Super. Ct. Feb. 2, 2010) (plaintiff's allegations of co-worker's verbal and/or physical abuse sufficient to survive motion to strike); **Craig v. Yale Univ. School of Med., 838 F. Supp. 2d 4, 12-13 (D. Conn. 2011) (Plaintiff's "allegations of sleeplessness, loss of appetite, and emotional and psychological distress, in addition to his other symptoms" were sufficient to defeat motion to dismiss).** Conduct falling short of the extreme and outrageous standard includes, for example, an employer telling an employee he could resign and accept five weeks of severance or be terminated immediately and affording him no time to consider his options and making condescending comments about plaintiff's ability to read in presence of his colleagues. Appleton v. Board of Educ., 254 Conn. 205, 211, 757 A.2d 1059, 1063 (2000). See also Coleman, 2009 U.S. Dist. LEXIS 10586, at *13-14 (granting summary judgment to employer when "the most egregious comments concerning the plaintiff were uttered outside his presence and there is no evidence he was aware of them"); Julian, 2010 U.S. Dist. LEXIS 38129, at *18-19 (negligence in conducting an investigation of plaintiff did not approach the type of extreme behavior required for intentional infliction of emotional distress); Shea v. City of Waterbury, 2009 Conn. Super. LEXIS 794, *24-27 (Conn. Super. Ct. Feb. 20, 2009) (granting defendant's motion to strike because "[a]t best, the defendants were directing insults toward the plaintiffs and arguably may have been insinuating immoral or criminal behavior on the part of the plaintiffs," which the Supreme Court of Connecticut has determined is not "extreme and outrageous"); Skaats v. State, 2009 Conn. Super. LEXIS 2514, at *20 (Conn. Super. Ct. Sept. 4. 2009) (removal from an assignment, written reprimand, and threats of termination insufficient to constitute intentional infliction of emotional distress as a matter of law); Boulanger v. Eyelematic Mfg., Inc., 2010 Conn. Super. LEXIS 457, at *1-2 (Conn. Super. Ct. Mar. 2, 2010) (finding that "requiring impossible tasks, ordering work performed without proper backup or support and by way of yelling, insulting and berating the plaintiff on a regular basis" do not rise to the level of extreme or outrageous conduct); Winner v. Charlotte Russe, Inc., 2010 Conn. Super. LEXIS 1212, at *2-9 (Conn. Super. Ct. May 13, 2010) (plaintiff did not meet extreme or outrageous standard despite her allegations that defendants insulted and mocked her, suggested she quit, told her she was under investigation and would fired, assigned her unreasonable amounts of work, sent her "unwarranted and unreasonable" warning letters, and eventually terminated her for creating a hostile work environment, did not "satisf[y] the requirement of conduct so atrocious that it exceeds all bounds of decency and is utterly intolerable in a civilized society"); **Neron v. Cossette, No. CV116003350S, 2012 WL 1592174, at *9-10 (Conn. Super. Ct. Apr. 13, 2012) (holding that publishing allegedly false information in plaintiff's personnel file and telling others that plaintiff had lied on his employment application did not rise to the level of extreme and outrageous conduct); Rice v. Ryders Health Mgmt., No. CV 116008602, 2012 WL 2899096, at *6 (Conn. Super. Ct. June 18, 2012) (conduct that is merely "hurtful or distressing" is not extreme and outrageous).**

Yet even extreme and outrageous conduct may be privileged. Connecticut follows the Restatement of Torts, which provides that "conduct, although it would otherwise be extreme and outrageous, maybe privileged under the circumstances." Id. at 253 (quoting Restatement (Second) of Torts § 46 cmt. g (1965)). In Petyan, 200 Conn. 243, 510 A.2d 1337, the Connecticut Supreme Court held that regardless of how the defendant's conduct was categorized, her comment in the fact-finding supplement solicited by the employment security division was absolutely privileged and she could not be held liable for intentional infliction of emotional distress. See also Elbert v. Connecticut Yankee Council, Inc., No. CV010456879S, 2004 WL 1832935, at *10 (Conn. Super. Ct. July 16, 2004) (striking intentional infliction of emotional distress claim because defendant had absolute privilege in reporting child abuse to government agency, and "[t]hat absolute privilege applies regardless of whether the representations at issue could be characterized as false, extreme or outrageous"). See discussion II.A.1, regarding the scope of absolute privilege.

Connecticut also recognizes a separate cause of action for negligent infliction of emotional distress. The plaintiff must establish that the defendant knew or should have known that his conduct involved an unreasonable risk of causing emotional distress and that the distress, if it were caused, might result in illness or bodily harm. See Perodeau v. City of Hartford, 259 Conn. at 749, 792 A.2d at 761 (citation omitted). In the employment context, conduct giving rise to such a claim is actionable only if it occurs in the termination process. See id. at 762-63 (holding that there can be no claim for "negligent infliction of emotional distress arising out of conduct occurring within a continuing employment context, as distinguished from conduct occurring in the termination of employment"); **Grasso v. Conn. Hospice, Inc., 138 Conn. App. 759, 772, 54 A.3d 221, 230 (2012) (noting that the "termination" language in Perodeau is "restrictive" and that constructive termination, as opposed to actual termination, cannot support a claim for negligent infliction of emotional distress).** Yet the mere act of firing an employee, even wrongfully motivated, does not transgress the bounds of socially tolerable behavior, and thus is not enough, by itself, to sustain a claim for negligent termination of employment. Hanna v. Infotech Contract Servs., Inc., No. 3:01 CV680, 2003 U.S. Dist. LEXIS 7056, at *29-30 (D. Conn. Apr. 21, 2003). See also Perodeau, 259 Conn. at 751, 792 A.2d 752 ("[i]n cases where the employee has been terminated, a finding of a wrongful termination is neither a necessary nor a sufficient predicate for a claim of negligent infliction of emotional distress. The dispositive issue in each case [is] whether the defendant's conduct during the termination process was sufficiently wrongful that the defendant should have realized that its conduct involved an unreasonable risk of causing emotional distress and that [that] distress, if it were caused, might result in illness or bodily harm.") (citation and internal quotation marks omitted). The timing of the employer's alleged acts and the termination may be significant in determining whether an employee has a valid negligent infliction of emotional distress claim). See, e.g., Dichello v. Marlin Firearms Co., 2009 Conn. Super. LEXIS 1984, at *11 (Conn. Super. Ct. July 9, 2009) (declining to consider events six months prior to employee's actual termination to be part of her termination process); Boulanger, 2010 Conn. Super. LEXIS 457, at *1 (concluding that defendants' conduct did take place during the termination process because the "plaintiff was out sick as a result of the defendants' conduct and was [therefore] terminated"); Tomick v. United Parcel Servs., 2010 Conn. Super. LEXIS 1067, at *6-8 (Conn. Super. Ct. Apr. 23, 2010) (denying summary judgment when a factual question existed as to when the termination process began); **Lopes v. Hubbel Inc., No. DBDCV116007127, 2012 WL 1292601, at *7 (Conn. Super. Ct. Mar. 23, 2012) (granting defendant's motion to strike plaintiff's claim for negligent infliction of emotional distress; plaintiff's allegations that she was discharged after 31 years of employment while employees with less seniority assumed her job duties "were not so unreasonable as to support a cause of action for negligent infliction of emotional distress").**

D. Tortious Interference with a Contract

The essential elements of a cause of action for tortious interference with a contract (also termed interference with an advantageous business relationship) are: (1) the existence of a contractual or beneficial relationship; (2) the alleged wrongdoer's knowledge of the contract or relationship; (3) his intentional and tortious interference; and (4) actual loss suffered by the plaintiff as a result of the wrongdoer's interference. See Solomon v. Aberman, 196 Conn. 359, 364, 493 A.2d

193 (1985); Warner v. Dembinski, No. CV020079206, 2003 Conn. Super. LEXIS 1103, at *6-7 (Conn. Super. Ct. April 4, 2003). See also Vecchitto v. Vecchitto, 2009 Conn. Super. LEXIS 2813, at *5-8 (Conn. Super. Ct. Oct. 20, 2009) (granting defendant's motion to strike because plaintiff's tortuous interference claim was premised "on an unenforceable partnership agreement"). To satisfy the element of tortious interference, the plaintiff must prove that the defendant is guilty of fraud, misrepresentation, intimidation or molestation, or that the defendant acted maliciously. See Par Painting, Inc. v. Greenhorne & O'Mara, Inc., 61 Conn. App. 317, 324, 763 A.2d 1078, 1083 (2001) (citing Blake v. Levy, 191 Conn. 257, 260, 464 A.2d 52, 54 (1983)); Daley, 249 Conn. at 805-806, 734 A.2d 112; Harris v. Bradley Mem. Hosp. & Health Ctr., Inc., 296 Conn. 315, 345-48 (2010), rev'd on other grounds, 306 Conn. 304 (2012); Wilcox v. Schmidt, 2010 Conn. Super. LEXIS 1407, at *41-43 (Conn. Super. Ct. June 3, 2010) (holding that defendant's tortious interference counterclaim failed because although "credible evidence" showed that plaintiff intentionally and maliciously informed vendors that defendant was stealing from company and they should be careful about extending credit and payments to the company, the defendants failed to prove that economic loss resulted from plaintiff's actions).

Where the wrongdoer is also an agent of a party to the contract, Connecticut courts have held that there can be no intentional interference with contractual relations by someone who is directly or indirectly a party to the contract. See e.g., Lenart v. City Clerk of Derby, No. CV89028714S, 1990 Conn. Super. LEXIS 1508, at *2-3 (Conn. Super. Ct. Oct. 24, 1990) (stating that "[a]n agent acting legitimately within the scope of his authority cannot be held liable for interfering with or inducing his principal to breach a contract between his principal and a third party, because to hold him liable would be, in effect, to hold the corporation liable in a tort for breaching its own contract.") (citation and internal quotation marks omitted); Malik, 202 F.3d at 109 (same). Thus, in the employment context, whether an employee sues his employer or a coworker who is acting within the scope of his authority, the suit is barred. An agent can, however, be held liable for tortious interference if the agent "did not act legitimately within his scope of duty but used the corporate power improperly for personal gain." Winner, 2010 Conn. Super. LEXIS 1212, at *13-15 (finding that allegation that plaintiff's manager "tortiously interfered with plaintiff's employment contract by making false, malicious and defamatory statements about her and/or requiring her subordinates and co-workers to write similar statements" sufficient to state a tortious interference claim) (internal citations and quotations omitted).

Where an intentional interference with contractual relations claim is based on statements made in the course of a judicial or quasi-judicial proceeding, the defendant enjoys the defense of absolute immunity just as it would with a defamation claim. See Rioux v. Barry, 283 Conn. 338, 351, 927 A.2d 304, 311-312 (2007) (absolute privilege applies to statements made during police department's internal affairs investigation); Golden v. Hamer, 2009 Conn. Super. LEXIS 2309, *36-40 (Conn. Super. Ct. Aug. 25, 2009) (confirming that only those "statements made within the confines" of a judicial or quasi-judicial proceeding enjoy absolute immunity); Cox, 2010 Conn. Super. LEXIS 774, at *2-4 (absolute privilege applies to allegedly defamatory complaints that generated internal affairs investigations by the Department of Public Safety); **Perugini v. Guiliano, No. CV105016077, 2012 WL 3518047, at *2-3 (Conn. Super. Ct. July 26, 2012) (explaining that "participants in judicial and quasi-judicial proceedings . . . are afforded absolute immunity for statements and conduct arising out of those proceedings.").**

E. *Prima Facie Tort*

"The last time the Connecticut Supreme Court - or any appellate court in Connecticut - addressed the viability of . . a cause of action [for prima facie tort] was nearly a century ago." Grigorenko v. Pauls, 297 F. Supp. 2d 446, 450 (D. Conn. 2003) (referencing Connors v. Connolly, 86 Conn. 641, 647, 86 A. 600 (1913)). See e.g., McAnerney v. McAnerney, 165 Conn. 277, 283-84, 334 A.2d 437, 442 (1973) (stating that while the plaintiff relied on Connors and Morrison v. National Broad. Co., 24 App. Div. 2d 284, 266 N.Y.S.2d 406 (1965) as authority for the doctrine of "prima facie" tort, these cases had no application to the defendant because the complaint alleged no duty owed by the defendant to the plaintiff); S.A. Candelora Enter. v. Wild, No. CV010447877S, 2002 Conn. Super. LEXIS 283, at*13-17 (Conn. Super. Ct. Feb. 4, 2002) (holding that the plaintiff's claim of prima facie tort survived the defendant's motion to strike on the ground that it was barred by the economic loss doctrine because, as an intentional tort, it could conceivably be independent of the contractual breach). As the Grigorenko court went on to note, to the extent such a tort exists, its genesis shows that it consists of "intentional infliction of harm, resulting in damage, without legal excuse or justification." Id. Notably, in Brandt v. Walker Digital, LLC, X08CV0194566, 2004 Conn. Super. LEXIS 3221, at *1348 (Conn. Super. Ct. November 1, 2004) the superior court, relying primarily upon the Connors and Grigorenko decisions, stated that a cause of action for prima facie tort was viable in Connecticut and allowed plaintiff's claim to survive defendant's motion to strike. The court stated that this cause of action was only appropriate when the "intentional, culpable and unjustified conduct causing injury does not fall into any other theory of tort liability." Id. **See also Deutsch v. Backus Corp., No. X07CV106022074S, 2012 WL 1871398, at *12 (Conn. Super. Ct. May 2, 2012) (noting all traditional torts must be unavailable in order to assert the prima facie tort).**

V. OTHER ISSUES

A. Statute of Limitations

The statute of limitations for libel and slander is "two years from the date of the act complained of." Conn. Gen. Stat. § 52-597 (2004). Further, the statute of limitations on such a defamation claim begins on the date of publication. Cweklinsky, 267 Conn. at 224, 837 A.2d at 768. Federal courts sitting in Connecticut have consistently applied the "single publication rule" in multi-state defamation cases, holding that a plaintiff has only one cause of action for a single aggregate publication to a large number of persons at one time. See Valtec Int'l v. Allied Signal Aero. Co., No. 3:93CV01 171(WWE), 1997 U.S. Dist. LEXIS 7670, at *17 (D. Conn. Mar. 7, 1997) (citing Buckley v. N.Y. Post Corp., 373 F.2d 175, 179 (2d Cir. 1967); Fouts v. Fawcett Publ'ns, Inc., 116 F. Supp. 535, 536 (D. Conn. 1953); Dale Sys., Inc. v. Time, Inc., 116 F. Supp. 527, 530 (D. Conn. 1953)). Recently, in Hechtman v. Conn. Dep't of Pub. Health, 2009 Conn. Super. LEXIS 3277, at *26-27 (Conn. Super. Ct. Dec. 3, 2009), a Connecticut trial court adopted the single publication rule to internet postings. Therefore, "defamatory statements posted on the Internet are considered published on the date they are initially posted and not every time a third party views the statements."

B. Jurisdiction

Under Connecticut's long-arm statute, jurisdiction over nonresidents is specifically excluded in actions for defamation. See Conn. Gen. Stat. § 52-59b(a) (2004). However, where the alleged defamation arises from the nonresident's transaction of business within Connecticut, long-arm jurisdiction may be available. See id. ("a court may exercise personal jurisdiction over any nonresident individual, foreign partnership or over the executor or administrator of such nonresident individual or foreign partnership, who in person or through an agent . . . [t]ransacts any business within the state.) See also Jones v. Trump, 919 F. Supp. 583 (D. Conn. 1996) (holding that the defamatory statements made by New York residents to out-of-state news media that is disseminated in Connecticut does not constitute "business transactions" within the meaning of Connecticut's long-arm statute, and thus, are not actionable in Connecticut).

Further, before bringing common law defamation actions, federal and state law require an employee to "at least attempt to exhaust exclusive grievance and arbitration procedures, such as those contained in the collective bargaining agreement." Hedges v. Town of Madison, 2010 U.S. Dist. LEXIS 30415, at *17-19 (D. Conn. Mar. 30, 2010) (quoting City of Hartford v. Hartford Municipal Employees Ass'n., 259 Conn. 251, 788 A.2d 60, 79-80 (Conn. 2002) (citations omitted)), **aff'd in part and rev'd in part, 456 Fed. Appx. 22 (2d Cir. 2012).**

Additionally, absent certain egregious circumstances, the First Amendment bars courts from exercising jurisdiction over defamation claims against churches and in the context of the employment relationship between a minister and a church. Thibodeau v. Am. Baptist Churches of Conn., 120 Conn. App. 666, 679-84 (2010) (concluding that the lower court appropriately dismissed defamation and promissory estoppel claims when "the gravamen of the dispute is the decision of the defendant, a religious organization, not to recommend the plaintiff for a position in the ministry"); Guerrier v. S. New Eng. Conf. Ass'n of Seventh-Day Adventists, Inc., 2009 Conn. Super. LEXIS 2962, at *19 (Conn. Super. Ct. Nov. 12, 2009) (dismissing, inter alia, wrongful termination, negligent infliction of emotional distress, intentional infliction of emotional distress, and false light claims because of the ministerial exception to judicial jurisdiction over employment disputes).

C. Worker's Compensation Exclusivity

Connecticut's Worker's Compensation Act, Conn. Gen. Stat. §31-284, provides, in part, that worker's compensation is the exclusive remedy for any action by an employee "for damages on account of personal injury sustained by an employee arising out of and in the course of his employment." Notably, the Worker's Compensation Act excludes from the definition of "personal injury" any "mental or emotional impairment which results from a personnel action, including, but not limited to, a transfer, promotion, demotion or termination." Id. at 31-275. There are no published opinions addressing whether worker's compensation is the exclusive remedy for a workplace defamation claim. But see Cherry v. McDonald, No. CV 91 0502657S, 1995 Conn. Super. LEXIS 1653, at *7-9 (Conn. Super. Ct. June 2, 1995) (denying summary judgment to the defendant -- which argued that the plaintiff's slander claim fell within the exclusivity provision of the Worker's Compensation Act -- because there was a genuine issue of fact as to whether the plaintiff was injured during the course of employment).

D. Pleading Requirements

Connecticut is a fact pleading, not a notice pleading jurisdiction. See Conn. R. Super. Ct. Civ. § 10-1 ("Each pleading shall contain a plain and concise statement of the material facts on which the pleader relies, but not of the evidence by which they are to be proved). Thus, Connecticut courts have required the plaintiff in a defamation action to specifically allege when, where and to whom each statement was allegedly made. See e.g., 2500 SS Ltd. P'ship v. White, No. 328934, 1996 Conn. Super. LEXIS 2174, at *8-9 (Conn. Super. Ct. Aug. 19, 1996) (holding that although the plaintiff's complaint alleged the substance of the allegedly defamatory remarks, the complaint failed to adequately apprise the defendant of the claims against him because it did not allege when, where and to whom each remark was allegedly made); Chertkova v. Conn. Gen. Life Ins., No. CV980486346S, 2002 Conn. Super. LEXIS 2348, at *14 (Conn. Super. Ct. July 12, 2002) ("a complaint for defamation must, on its face, specifically identify what allegedly defamatory statements were made, by whom, and to whom. . . .") (citations and internal quotation marks omitted), aff'd, 76 Conn. App. 907, 822 A.2d 372 (2003); Raye, 2003 Conn. Super. LEXIS 983, at *10-11 (striking the plaintiff's defamation claim where the complaint did not state the actual language nor identify any source from which the actual language might be determined, and failed to specify when the allegedly defamatory statement was made); Pro Performance Corporate Servs., Inc. v. Goldman, No. CV010186618, 2003 Conn. Super. LEXIS 2414, at *5 (Conn. Super. Ct. Aug. 25, 2003) ("[i]n order to sufficiently state a claim for defamation, the specific statements, the exact words, must be alleged.").

When actions for defamation are brought in federal court in Connecticut, where notice pleading rules apply, the statements do not need to be stated "in haec verba." See Kloth v. Citibank, 33 F. Supp. 2d 115, 121 (D. Conn. 1998) ("[a]lthough the Second Circuit does not require in haec verba pleading, i.e., of the exact alleged defamatory words, Fed. R. Civ. P. 8 requires that the complaint 'afford defendant sufficient notice of the communications complained of to enable him to defend himself.'") (citations omitted); Julian, 2010 U.S. Dist. LEXIS 38129, at *13-14 (same); see also Barbusin v. E. Conn. State Univ., Case No. 3:05-CV-1171 (RNC), 2006 U.S. Dist. LEXIS 28083, at *4 (D. Conn. May 10, 2006) (holding that "[i]n defamation cases, the liberal pleading standard of Rule 8 of the Federal Rules of Civil Procedure is satisfied if the complaint provides sufficient notice of the communications complained of to enable the defendant to prepare a defense. The plaintiff need not allege the exact words of the statements at issue.") (citations omitted).

SURVEY OF CONNECTICUT EMPLOYMENT PRIVACY LAW

Lawrence Peikes
Wiggin and Dana LLP
Two Stamford Plaza
281 Tresser Boulevard
Stamford, CT 06901
Telephone: (203) 363-7600; Facsimile: (203) 363-7676

(With Developments Reported Through **November 1, 2012**)

GENERAL COMMENTS

There are three levels of courts in Connecticut; the Superior Court, the Appellate Court, and the Supreme Court. A plaintiff has one appeal as of right in Connecticut. The Supreme Court exercises discretion in determining whether to accept a case on appeal.

SIGNIFICANT DEVELOPMENTS SINCE THE 2012 *SURVEY*

Effective October 1, 2012, an important amendment was made to Connecticut's data breach law, Conn. Gen. Stat. § 36a-701b. The statute currently requires a person or business which "owns, licenses or maintains computerized data that includes personal information" to provide, "without unreasonable delay," "notice of any breach of security following the discovery of the breach to any resident of this state whose personal information was, or is reasonably believed to have been, accessed by an unauthorized person through such breach of security." Conn. Gen. Stat. § 36a-701b(b)(1). The amendment now requires the person or business to also "provide notice of the breach of security to the Attorney General" of Connecticut no later than "the time when notice is provided to the resident." Conn. Gen. Stat. § 36a-701b(b)(2). The "without unreasonable delay" standard contained in subsection (b)(1) therefore applies to subsection (b)(2) as well, though it may be subject to delays resulting from requests of law enforcement officials, Conn. Gen. Stat. § 36a-701b(d), and "the completion of an investigation" by the person or business "to determine the nature and scope of the incident, to identify the individuals affected, or to restore the reasonable integrity of the data system." Conn. Gen. Stat. § 36a-701b(b)(1). The notification "shall not be required if, after an appropriate investigation, and consultation with…law enforcement, the person reasonably determines that the breach will not likely result in harm to the individuals whose personal information has been acquired and accessed." Id. Absent these specific circumstances, however, notification must be promptly provided to affected residents and the Attorney General alike. Failure to comply with these requirements will constitute an unfair trade practice under Connecticut's Unfair Trade Practices Act, Conn. Gen. Stat. § 42-110b, which permits the recovery of punitive damages, attorneys' fees, and costs. Conn. Gen. Stat. §§ 36a-701b(g); 42-110g.

I. GENERAL LAW OF PRIVACY

A. Legal Basis of Privacy Claims

Common law provides the legal basis for a tort action for an invasion of privacy in Connecticut. See Goodrich v. Waterbury Republican-Am., Inc., 188 Conn. 107, 127-28, 448 A.2d 1317, 1329, 8 Media L. Rep. 2329 (1982); Venturi v. Savitt, Inc., 191 Conn. 588, 591, 468 A.2d 933, 10 Media L. Rep. 1155 (1983); Jonap v. Silver, 1 Conn. App. 550, 557, 474 A.2d 800 (1984).

B. Causes of Action

In recognizing a cause of action for invasion of privacy, the Connecticut Supreme Court has adopted the definition and categories of invasion of privacy as set forth in Restatement (Second) of Torts § 652A (1977). See, e.g., Goodrich, 188 Conn. at 128; Venturi, 191 Conn. at 591; **Bremmer-McLain v. City of New London, No. CV115014142S, 2012 Conn. Super. LEXIS 1428, at *42-43 (June 1, 2012)**. "[T]he law of privacy has not developed as a single tort, but as a complex of four distinct kinds of invasion of four different interests of the plaintiff, which are tied together by the common name, but otherwise have almost nothing in common except that each represents an interference with the right of the plaintiff to be let alone ...." Foncello v. Amorossi, 284 Conn. 225, 234, 931 A.2d 924 (2007). The four categories of invasion of privacy are: (a) misappropriation of another's name or likeness; (b) publicity that unreasonably places another in a false light before the public; (c) unreasonable publicity given to another's private life; and (d) unreasonable intrusion upon the seclusion of another.

1. ***Misappropriation/Right of Publicity.*** The court in Venturi, 191 Conn. 588 (1983), failed specifically to address plaintiff's claim that his case fell squarely within the ambit of Restatement (Second) of Torts § 652C, which states, "[o]ne who appropriates for his own use or benefit the name or likeness of another is subject to liability to the

other for invasion of his privacy." Nonetheless, the Court did acknowledge that Connecticut recognized the tort of misappropriation as set forth in the Restatement. In Korn v. Rennison, 21 Conn. Sup. 400, 403, 156 A.2d 476, 478 (1959), the court predicated the finding of misappropriation of one's name or likeness upon the defendant's knowledge, noting that the defendant "should have realized that [the conduct] would be offensive to persons of ordinary sensibilities." The Court therefore appeared to merge the elements of a private facts claim with those of misappropriation. In a later case, however, the Appellate Division of the Circuit Court in Steding v. Battistoni, 3 Conn. Cir. Ct. 76, 80-81, 208 A.2d 559 (1964), adopted the language of the Restatement and held that plaintiff had adequately proved a claim for misappropriation by demonstrating that defendant had used plaintiff's name for commercial advantage without plaintiff's permission. See also Jonap v. Silver, 1 Conn. App. 550 (1984); **Gleason v. Smolinski, 2012 Conn. Super. LEXIS 2086, at *37-38 (Aug. 10, 2012)("Gleason II") (noting that comment (b) to Restatement § 652C provides that "[e]ven if the appropriation of the name or likeness is not for a commercial purpose...there can be liability if it is done to obtain some benefit").**

Although the Connecticut Supreme Court "has never provided the courts with the elements required to state a claim sounding in appropriation of name or likeness," Connecticut courts recognize such a cause of action, and rely on the Restatement (Second) of Torts for guidance. See Gleason v. Smolinski, 2009 WL 2506607 (Conn. Super. July 20, 2009) ("Gleason I"). In Gleason I, a private citizen sued a newspaper owner for publishing a story that described her multiple marriages and divorces, the death of one of her sons, and other details of her life, in connection with a report on the disappearance of a man with whom she was romantically involved. The plaintiff alleged that "the defendant ... tortiously appropriated [her] name and likeness." Id. at *3. In his motion to strike the misappropriation claim, the defendant argued that the plaintiff did not "allege facts necessary to complete the tort of appropriation of likeness, and thus fail[ed] to state a claim upon which relief can be granted." Id. The plaintiff counter argued that, by publishing the story of the disappearance of a man, the defendant "ha[d] indeed attempted to market his newspaper through the use of the plaintiff's private information, her name, and her secretly photographed likeness." Id.

In granting the motion to strike, the court noted that the plaintiff did "little more than allege that [defendant] wrote an article about the circumstances surrounding the disappearance of [a man], which included a discussion of [plaintiff's] past activities." Id. at *4. The court relied on the Restatement Second of Tort, § 652C, and explained:

One who appropriates to his own use or benefit the name or likeness of another is subject to liability to the other for invasion of his privacy. The restatement also provides, however, that the value of the plaintiff's name is not appropriated by mere mention of it, or by reference to it in connection with legitimate mention of his public activities; nor is the value of his likeness appropriated when it is published for purposes other than taking advantage of his reputation, prestige, or other value associated with him, for purposes of publicity. No one has the right to object merely because his name or his appearance is brought before the public, since neither is in any way a private matter and both are open to public observation. It is only when the publicity is given for the purpose of appropriating to the defendant's benefit the commercial or other values associated with the name or the likeness that the right of privacy is invaded. The fact that the defendant is engaged in the business of publication, for example of a newspaper, out of which he makes or seeks to make a profit, is not enough to make the incidental publication a commercial use of the name or likeness. Thus a newspaper, although it is not a philanthropic institution, does not become liable under the rule stated in this Section to every person whose name or likeness it publishes. Id. at *4 (internal quotations and citations omitted).

Thus, the court concluded that, unless the plaintiff alleged "facts evidencing an actual appropriation," her claim was legally insufficient because it relied "on the mere fact that [the defendant] published [plaintiff's] name and photograph in his newspaper article." Id. at *4.

2. ***False Light.*** In order to establish invasion of privacy by false light, the plaintiff must show "(a) the false light in which the other was placed would be highly offensive to a reasonable person, and (b) the actor had knowledge of or acted in reckless disregard as to the falsity of the publicized matter and the false light in which the other would be placed." Restatement (Second) of Torts § 652E (1977); see Goodrich, 188 Conn. at 128; Crist v. O'Keefe & Associates, 2002 WL 1042152 *4 ("The essence of a false light privacy claim is that the matter published concerning the plaintiff (1) is not true ... and (2) is such a major misrepresentation of his character, history, activities or beliefs that serious offense may reasonably be expected to be taken by a reasonable man in his position."). To satisfy the second element of a false light claim, a plaintiff does not need to plead that "a statement on its face attempted to represent his character, history, activities or beliefs." Jenkins v. American Chiropractic Bd. of Nutrition, 2008 WL 4073424, at *6 (Conn. Super. Aug. 19, 2008). In other words, certain alleged statements "automatically carr[y] the implication of representing [a plaintiff's] credentials." Id. (denying defendant's motion to strike false light claim where plaintiff alleged that an organization that establishes educational and professional standards posted in a website that it decertified plaintiff). However, the plaintiff must identify with some degree of specificity the misrepresentations that are alleged to have cast her in a false light. Weissman v. Koskoff, Koskoff & Bieder, P.C., 2011 Conn. Super. LEXIS 181 (Jan. 19, 2011) (allegation that third parties

directed smirks and glances at plaintiff following her departure from law firm was insufficient to establish that employer published falsehoods about the circumstances of her separation from employment).

The information must be disseminated to the public at large. 3 Restatement (Second), Torts § 652D, Comment (a), pp. 384-85 (1976); **Gleason v. Smolinski, 2012 Conn. Super. LEXIS 2086, at *44-45 (Aug. 10, 2012) ("Gleason II").** "The form of invasion of privacy covered by the cause of action for publicity placing a person in a false light before the public 'does not depend upon making public any facts concerning the private life of the individual. On the contrary, it is essential to [that cause of action] that the matter published concerning the plaintiff is not true.'" Handler v. Arends, 1995 WL 107328, 1995 Conn. Super. LEXIS 660 (Conn. Super. 1995), citing 3 Restatement (Second), Torts § 652E, comment (a) (1971). As would be expected, publishing a statement on a website "satisfies the publicity requirement because the internet publications communicate to the public at large." American Chiropractic Bd. of Nutrition, 2008 WL 4073424, at *6.

"The standard governing the tort of false light invasion of privacy is similar to the standard governing the tort of defamation concerning a public official or public figure; that the publisher of the false statement knew that the statement was false or acted in reckless disregard of the falsity of the statement. A finding of reckless disregard requires sufficient evidence to permit the conclusion that the defendant in fact entertained serious doubts as to the truth of the publication." Rice v. Meriden Housing Auth., 2004 WL 870816, at *8 (Conn. Super. Mar. 31, 2004). Thus, an agency charged with administering drug tests on behalf of an employer will not be liable on a false light invasion of privacy theory for reporting a false positive result where the agency did not act with reckless disregard for the truth and made the report to a single representative of the employer. Stapleton v. Concentra Health Services, 2007 WL 2366946, at *1-2 (Conn. Super. Aug. 1, 2007). **Two key distinctions between false light and defamation claims should be noted, however: (1) "a false light claim is not limited to actually defamatory matters but would apply to any 'highly offensive false portrayal;'" and (2) "any publication of the defamation to another person permits a defamation action whereas a false light privacy invasion 'usually is required to come to the notice of at least a substantial portion of the general public or at least to be of such character and subject to such dissemination as to be reasonably certain of such exposure.'" Gleason II, 2012 Conn. Super. LEXIS 2086, at *44-45 (quoting 62A Am. Jur. 2d at § 128 p. 763-64).**

"Liability for false light invasion of privacy is limited to situations in which the false information regarding the plaintiff is given publicity." Crist v. O'Keefe & Assoc., 2005 WL 2364880, at *4 (Conn. Super. Aug. 31, 2005). "'Publicity'... means that the matter is made public, by communicating it to the public at large, or to so many persons that the matter must be regarded as substantially certain to become one of public knowledge." Id., quoting 3 Restatement (Second), Torts 652D, comment (a) (finding false bills sent to five individuals or business entities insufficient to establish information was communicated to the public at large); see also Deutsch v. Backus Corp., 2011 Conn. Super. LEXIS 70, at *38-39 (Jan. 14, 2011) (publicity element was not established where allegedly defamatory statements about physician were not disseminated outside the context of internal hospital review proceedings); Orsini v. Zimmer, 2009 Conn. Super. LEXIS 3442 (Dec. 24, 2009) (holding that letter sent to nine people in connection with contentious custody battle did not satisfy "publicity" requirement for tort of false light); Negron v. Rexam Cosmetic Packaging, Inc., 2006 WL 240528 (Conn. Super. Jan. 11, 2006) (posting of offensive photos of employee for less than one hour on company bulletin board and in restrooms of factory with two hundred employees was neither directed at the public at large nor substantially certain to become the subject of public knowledge).

Employers may defend against a false light invasion of privacy claim on the grounds that publicized information regarding an employee is true. See Burns v. Chapman, 2008 WL 5511264, at *17 (Conn. Super. Dec. 12, 2008) (police chief's comments to a newspaper regarding the private life of a police officer whose husband had committed suicide after a standoff, which included statements that the couple's dispute began over child support and that they had a "very stormy" relationship, were "essentially true," and therefore did not support a false light invasion of privacy claim); see also Miles v. City of Hartford, 2010 U.S. Dist. LEXIS 2185 (D. Conn. Jan. 12, 2010) (press release that accurately described plaintiff's arrest and the charges brought against her could not serve as basis for false light claim).

Where a plaintiff files a claim of false light invasion of privacy against a media defendant, such as a newspaper, Connecticut courts require that the plaintiff allege in the complaint that statements in the article were false. See Gleason v. Smolinski, 2009 WL 2506607, at *7 (Conn. Super. July 20, 2009)("Gleason I"). Thus, where a media defendant is involved, the courts balance the plaintiff's right to privacy against the media defendant's First Amendment's freedom of speech right and the constitutional right to a free press. Accordingly, Connecticut courts show some level of deference to the media's "editorial control and judgment," and generally acknowledge that, "[a]s long as the matter published is substantially true, the [media] defendant [is] constitutionally protected from liability for a false light invasion of privacy, regardless of its decision to omit facts that may place the plaintiff under less harsh public scrutiny." Id. (citation omitted).

Interestingly, at least one Connecticut Superior Court has recognized that a company may bring a false light invasion of privacy claim in connection with a defamation claim against a former employee for initiating a "campaign of harassment" by contacting existing and former employees to encourage them to file false and disparaging complaints about the company's staffing and safety inadequacies and filing over seventy unsubstantiated safety complaints with regulatory agencies. Southern Air, Inc. v. Raymond, 2009 WL 659296, at *6 (Conn. Super. Feb. 17, 2009).

3. ***Publication of Private Facts.*** In Connecticut, "in order to successfully litigate a cause of action for giving unreasonable publicity to the plaintiff's private life, the plaintiff must plead and prove: (1) that the defendant gave publicity; (2) to a matter concerning the private life of the plaintiff; and (3) that the matter publicized was of a kind that (a) would be highly offensive to a reasonable person, and (b) would not be of legitimate concern to the public." Handler v. Arends, 1995 WL 107328, 1995 Conn. Super. LEXIS 660 (Conn. Super. 1995), citing Restatement (Second) of Torts § 652D. **The Connecticut Superior Court has observed that in order to sustain a viable claim for this tort, "the action must be based on 'the disclosure of facts that are truly private, secluded, secret....'" Gleason II, 2012 Conn. Super. LEXIS 2086, at *42 (citations omitted). As the requirement of "publicity" differs from that of "publication," which can be satisfied by publication to only one person,** "[t]here is [no] magic number of persons, applicable to each situation, which constitutes a minimum for purposes of publicity in an invasion of privacy claim." Id., Beveridge v. Briston Spring Mfg. Co., 2000 WL 254654, 2000 Conn. Super. LEXIS 430 (Conn. Super. 2000). See also Pace v. Bristol Hospital, 964 F. Supp. 628 (D. Conn. 1997) (former employer's dissemination of information regarding former employee's discharge to management personnel, interested co-workers and an independent contractor with whom plaintiff worked did not constitute "publicity" necessary for a false light claim); Daconto v. Trumbull Housing Authority, 2004 WL 304325, at *4, 2004 Conn. Super. LEXIS 212 (Conn. Super. Jan. 30, 2004) (holding that comments made about employee at a meeting attended by plaintiff, defendant, and four other employees, do not meet the requisite standard of communication to constitute "publicity"); Evans v. Blanchard, 2005 WL 407846, at *2-3 (Conn. Super. Jan. 11, 2005) (not only does "publicity" require more widespread dissemination than mere "publication," but that publicity must also be direct).

In Connecticut, claims of unreasonable publicity given to another's private life are "governed by first amendment principles." Gleason v. Smolinski, 2009 WL 2506607, at *5 (Conn. Super. July 20, 2009)("Gleason I")(citation omitted). Consequently, if a defendant publishes information about a plaintiff's personal or romantic life in connection with a news story covering the disappearance of plaintiff's former love interest, as long as the published information is considered to be "a legitimate concern of the public" or "newsworthy," the defendant will not be liable. See Id. (striking plaintiff's claim of unreasonable publicity given to her private life where the court found that the disappearance of plaintiff's former love interest, and "reports of suicide, overdose and incarceration" were "typically considered newsworthy" and the published story did "not delve into the depths of these happenings, unearthing the most intimate private matters, but rather merely inform[ed] the reader of their existence"); see also Burns v. Chapman, 2008 WL 5511264, at *15 (Conn. Super. Dec. 12, 2008)(majority of police chief's comments to a newspaper regarding the private life of a police officer whose husband had committed suicide after a standoff were privileged as matters of legitimate public concern because the public had an interest in learning that the gunfire and ensuing standoff were unrelated to the duties of the police officer; however police chief's comment that the couple had begun their romantic relationship while the deceased husband was still married to another woman and involved "taking a husband from a family" was an invasion of plaintiff's privacy because it "gave high publicity to a private aspect of the plaintiff's life that would be highly offensive to a reasonable person" and "was not of legitimate public concern.")

4. ***Intrusion.*** In order to establish a claim for unreasonable intrusion upon the seclusion of another, a plaintiff must prove "an intentional physical intrusion [by the defendant] upon the private affairs or concerns of the plaintiff[] which would be highly offensive to a reasonable person." **Bremmer-McLain v. City of New London, No. CV115014142S, 2012 Conn. Super. LEXIS 1428, at *43 (June 1, 2012)**; Fields v. Kichar, 14 Conn. L. Rptr. No. 7, at 230, 231 (Jul. 3, 1995), quoting Mashantucket Pequot Tribe v. State, 1994 Conn. Sup. Ct. 8327, 1994 Conn. Super. LEXIS 2108 (Aug. 19, 1994). Whether the intrusion is "highly offensive to a reasonable person" is for a jury to decide. Rafferty v. Hartford Courant, 36 Conn. Sup. 239, 240-241, 416 A.2d 1215 (1980); Mashantucket Pequot Tribe v. State, supra; see also Tapia v. Sikorsky Aircraft Div. of United Tech. Corp., 1998 WL 310872, 1998 Conn. Super. LEXIS 1576 (Conn. Super. June 3, 1998) (defendant entered into plaintiff's personal locker while plaintiff was under suspension and inventoried contents; allegation that discovery of plaintiff's personal and private items contributed to decision to terminate plaintiff's employment failed to support allegation that the intrusion was highly offensive to a reasonable person). Although Connecticut appellate courts have not addressed the issue, at least two Superior Court decisions have held that "an allegation of physical contact is not necessary to successfully state a claim for invasion of privacy via an unreasonable intrusion upon the seclusion of another." Guccione v. Paley, 2006 WL 1828363, at *3 (Conn. Super. June 14, 2006), quoting Bonanno v. Dan Perkins Chevrolet, 26 Conn. L. Rptr. No. 368 (Conn. Super. Feb. 4, 2000); see also Slowick v. Morgan Stanley & Co., 2006 WL 573926 (Conn. Super. Feb. 21, 2006) (trier of fact could find comments regarding plaintiff's sex life, appearance, and values were highly offensive to reasonable person and sufficient to support invasion of privacy claim). **In addition, another recent Superior Court decision held that the intrusion must be "substantial." Gleason II, 2012 Conn. Super. LEXIS 2086, at *40 (finding that plaintiff's receipt of several threatening phone calls at home, only one of which could be attributed to defendant, "is not the type of 'substantial' intrusion on another's seclusion envisaged by this tort") (citing Comment (d) to the Restatement § 652).**

A plaintiff filing a claim of intrusion upon the seclusion of another does not need to allege that the defendant disseminated personal information about the plaintiff to the public at large. See Daconto v. Trumbull Housing Authority, 2008 WL 442147, at *9 (Conn. Super. Jan. 31, 2008) (denying defendant's motion for summary judgment premised on the fact that the defendant did not publish to the public at large a statement that an employee had sex with a director of operations in exchange for more favorable work assignments). A Superior Court decision holds that "[a] secret video recording of a private conversation [between co-workers] can certainly be considered an intrusion upon one's seclusion or their private affairs or concerns." Vasyliv v. Adesta, LLC, 2010 Conn. Super. LEXIS 3329, at *9 (Dec. 20, 2010).

Worth noting, "[p]ublication of private information alone is not legally sufficient to sustain [an intrusion] cause of action, which is concerned with the methods used when obtaining private information, rather than its subsequent dissemination." Gleason v. Smolinski, 2009 WL 2506607, at *3 (Conn. Super. July 20, 2009)(citation omitted)("Gleason I"). Therefore, the mere fact that a newspaper published a story describing details of a plaintiff's family and romantic life will not support a cause of action of unreasonable intrusion, unless the plaintiff alleges that the defendant obtained the private information in an offensive way. See Id. (granting defendant's motion to strike intrusion cause of action because plaintiff did not allege that the defendant obtained her personal information in an improper way). The Gleason I decision gives some examples of the allegations that a plaintiff would have to raise in support of a claim that the defendant improperly obtained plaintiff's private information. Id. (citing Restatement (Second), at § 652B, comment (b)).

An intrusion claim does not always require a defendant actively seeking to obtain a plaintiff's private information. One Connecticut Superior Court found that an employer may be liable to an employee for an unreasonable intrusion upon the employee's seclusion, even where the employer did not directly solicit the employee's personal information. Garces v. R & K Spero Co., LLC, 2009 WL 1814510, at *9 (Conn. Super. May 29, 2009) (denying defendant's motion to strike invasion of privacy intrusion claim where a reasonable jury could find that the supervisors constructively demanded information about plaintiff's menstrual cycle because they repeatedly refused to give the plaintiff the keys to use the bathroom at the fast food restaurant where she worked). However, it has been held that the intrusion must actually be committed by the defendant and not vicariously through a third party. Rizzitelli v. Thompson, 2010 Conn. Super. LEXIS 1992 (Aug. 2, 2010)(striking claim of intrusion where defendant did not enter plaintiff's property, but rather allegedly provided false information that resulted in police executing a search warrant at plaintiff's home).

In instances in which a plaintiff alleges that there was physical intrusion upon the plaintiff's privacy, a defendant may not invoke as a defense the fact that the plaintiff consented to such an intrusion, unless the consent was informed. See Birge v. Medical Electronic Distributors, Inc., 2009 WL 1959393, at *6 (Conn. Super. June 5, 2009) (denying defendant's motion to strike patient's invasion of privacy claim, where patient alleged that a medical distributor's salesman was improperly present during her therapy procedure involving the patient wearing a medical gown and the salesman applying heat therapy, in part, because the patient was never informed that the salesman was not a medical professional, and therefore her consent to the salesman being present was not informed).

Invasion of privacy claim sounding in intrusion is an intentional tort, and thus may not be brought against a governmental entity based on the doctrine of governmental immunity embodied in Connecticut General Statutes § 52-557n(a)(2). O'Connor v. Board of Education, 90 Conn. App. 59, 65, 877 A.2d 860 (2005).

C. Other Privacy-Related Actions

1. ***Intentional Infliction of Emotional Distress.*** The tort of intentional infliction of emotional distress was recognized by the Connecticut Supreme Court in Petyan v. Ellis, 200 Conn. 243, 253, 510 A.2d 1337 (1986), superseded by statute on other grounds as stated in Chadha v. Charlotte Hungerford Hosp., 272 Conn. 776 , 865 A.2d 1163 (2005). "'In order for a plaintiff to prevail on an intentional infliction of emotional distress claim, four elements must be established: (1) that the actor intended to inflict emotional distress; or that he knew or should have known that emotional distress was a likely result of his conduct; (2) that the conduct was extreme and outrageous; (3) that the defendant's conduct was the cause of the plaintiff's distress; and (4) that the emotional distress sustained by the plaintiff was severe.'" See Petyan, 200 Conn. at 243 (citation omitted). See also Hiers v. Cohen, 31 Conn. Sup. 305, 329 A.2d 609 (1973); Restatement (Second) of Torts § 46 (1965); Murray v. Bridgeport Hosp., 40 Conn. Sup. 56, 480 A.2d 610 (1984). "'Liability has been found only where the conduct has been so outrageous in character, and so extreme in degree, as to go beyond all possible bounds of decency, and to be regarded as atrocious, and utterly intolerable in a civilized community.'" Mellaly v. Eastman Kodak Co., 42. Conn. Supp. 17, 18, 597 A.2d 846 (1991), quoting 1 Restatement (Second) of Torts § 46, comment (d). Whether a defendant's conduct is sufficient to satisfy the requirement that it be extreme and outrageous is initially a question for the court to determine. Id.; see also Bell v. Board of Ed., 55 Conn. App. 400, 410, 739 A.2d 321 (1999); Garces v. R & K Spero Co., LLC, 2009 WL 1814510, at *4 (Conn. Super. May 29, 2009)(denying defendant's motion to strike intentional infliction of emotional distress claim where the court observed that requiring the employee-plaintiff to beg for a bathroom key to the point where she bleeds through her clothing given that she was on her menstrual cycle could lead an average member of

the community to exclaim, "outrageous!"); Burke v. State of Connecticut, Dep't. of Children & Families, 2010 Conn. Super. LEXIS 282 (Feb. 2, 2010) (allegations that co-worker engaged in verbal and physical abuse of plaintiff for nineteen months sufficient to survive motion to strike claim against co-worker for intentional infliction of emotional distress).

Only where reasonable minds disagree does it become an issue for the jury. Mellaly, at 18. "[I]n assessing a claim for intentional infliction of emotional distress, the court performs a gatekeeping function. In this capacity, the role of the court is to determine whether the allegations of a complaint, counterclaim or cross complaint set forth behaviors that a reasonable fact finder could find to be extreme or outrageous. In exercising this responsibility, the court is not fact finding, but rather it is making an assessment whether, as a matter of law, the alleged behavior fits the criteria required to establish a claim premised on intentional infliction of emotional distress." Hartmann v. Gulf View Estates Homeowners Ass'n, Inc., 88 Conn. App. 290, 295, 869 A.2d 275 (2005).

"In the workplace context, the threshold for extreme and outrageous behavior is even higher: It is clear that individuals in the workplace reasonably should expect to experience some level of emotional distress, even significant emotional distress, as a result of conduct in the workplace." Perodeau v. City of Hartford, 259 Conn. 729, 757 (Conn. 2002) (further holding that individuals in the workplace "should expect to be subject to…performance evaluations, both formal and informal; decisions related to such evaluations, such as those involving transfer, demotion, promotion and compensation; similar decisions based on the employer's business needs and desires, independent of the employee's performance; and disciplinary or investigatory action arising from actual or alleged employee misconduct. In addition, such individuals reasonably should expect to be subject to other vicissitudes of employment, such as workplace gossip, rivalry, personality conflicts and the like"); Michel v. Bridgeport Hospital, 2011 Conn. Super. LEXIS 538, at *27 (Mar. 7, 2011)(rejecting intentional infliction of emotional distress claim predicated on allegations that plaintiff was escorted to a private conference room where she was questioned in a menacing manner and not free to leave, accused of improperly accessing patient files and escorted from the premises). Thus, an employee's allegations that her supervisor and others undertook an investigation into her job performance in connection with a vindictive conspiracy to terminate her employment were deemed insufficient to satisfy the extreme and outrageous conduct element of proof. Gillians v. Vivanco-Small, 128 Conn. App. 207, 15 A.3d 1200 (2011). See also **Neron v. Cossette, 2012 Conn. Super. LEXIS 1019, at *28-30 (Apr. 13, 2012) (granting defendant's motion to strike because plaintiff's allegations that manager maliciously published cruel statements in plaintiff's personnel file, told others that plaintiff lied on his employment application, and spoke about plaintiff being "strange and creepy" were not sufficiently extreme and outrageous to sustain a cause of action for intentional infliction of emotional distress);** Fogarty v. The Forman School, 2011 Conn. Super. LEXIS 580 (Mar. 10, 2011)(observing that, in the employment context, extreme and outrageous conduct sufficient to sustain a cause of action sounding in intentional infliction of emotional distress usually involves "physical intimidation, vulgar remarks and public ridicule"); Albino v. Orca, Inc., 2011 Conn. Super. LEXIS 390 (Feb. 16, 2011)(striking intentional infliction of emotional distress claim premised on allegations that employer, inter alia, required plaintiff to work off the clock without compensation, circulated false information regarding the validity of plaintiff's workers' compensation claim, imposed unreasonable demands on, and made sarcastic and disparaging remarks to, plaintiff while he was on light duty assignment, and terminated plaintiff's employment based on pretext that there was a lack of work). But see Davis v. Benchmark Assisted Living, LLC, 2010 Conn. Super. LEXIS 3116 (Nov. 23, 2010)(advising patients' families that plaintiff had been suspended and then terminated "could be construed as a gratuitous rubbing of salt in the wound" so as to be outrageous); Mendez v. Utopia Home Care, Inc., 2010 Conn. Super. LEXIS 2870 (Nov. 5, 2010)(allegations that employer, inter alia, removed records from patient charts and then asked plaintiff for the missing records, reduced plaintiff's case load, back-dated an evaluation, conditioned issuance of plaintiff's final paycheck on her recreating previously submitted paperwork, and made false and defamatory statements to the department of public health were sufficient to establish extreme and outrageous conduct).

In Saporoso v. Aetna Life & Casualty Co., 221 Conn. 356, 603 A.2d 1160 (1992), the Connecticut Supreme Court held that a former employee who had recovered in workers' compensation for emotional distress allegedly caused intentionally by her employer could not subsequently pursue a common law tort action for the same injury. The Saporoso case was later overruled on different grounds. See Santopietro v. City of New Haven, 239 Conn. 207, 682 A.2d 106 (1996).

An employee's claim for intentional infliction of emotional distress against a public employer is barred by the doctrine of governmental immunity. Pane v. City of Danbury, 267 Conn. 669, 685, 841 A.2d 684, 695 (2004). Similarly, the absolute privilege that attaches to employers' statements made during a judicial or quasi-judicial proceeding bars recovery for intentional infliction of emotional distress allegedly stemming from those statements. McKinney v. Chapman, 103 Conn. App. 446, 929 A.2d 355 (2007).

2. ***Negligent Infliction of Emotional Distress.*** The Connecticut Supreme Court resolved a split in authority by holding that an employer may be found liable for negligent infliction of emotional distress only in the context of conduct during the course of an employment termination. Perodeau v. City of Hartford, 259 Conn. 729, 748, 792 A.2d 752, 764 (2002). Thus, there is no liability for negligent infliction of emotional distress for conduct occurring within the context of a continuing employment relationship. Id.; see also Leone v. New England Communications, 2002 WL 1008470 (Conn. Super. 2002) (applying Perodeau to dismiss negligent infliction of emotional distress claim based on conduct during continuing employment relationship); Martinez-Ruiz v. Centimark Corporation, 2002 WL 853606 (Conn. Super. 2002) (same); O'Connor v. Board of Education, 90 Conn. App. 59, 69, 877 A.2d 860 (2005)("Perodeau applies regardless of whether the defendant is an individual or a government entity").

The Perodeau Court also noted that wrongful termination claims and claims of negligent infliction of emotional distress via employment termination are independent of each other. Perodeau, 259 Conn. at 749-50. The issue in wrongful termination cases is whether the termination itself is wrongful because it violates an important public policy, while negligent infliction of emotional distress cases concern the manner of termination (i.e., unreasonable conduct in the termination process). Id. A jury verdict in favor of a certified nursing assistant on her claim for negligent infliction of emotional distress was sustained by the Connecticut Appellate Court where the jury could reasonable have found that the employer directed the plaintiff to assume the heaviest workload in the facility, in effect forcing her "to choose between her own health and well-being and that of her unborn child, and her continued employment ..." Davis v. Manchester Health Center, Inc., 88 Conn. App. 60, 73, 867 A.2d 876 (2005).

The Connecticut Appellate Court also sustained a claim for negligent infliction of emotional distress alleged by an employee suffering from multiple sclerosis where a co-worker, "aware of the nature of the plaintiff's condition and of the plaintiff's acknowledgement that her condition made her incapable of performing her nursing function, nevertheless falsely accused the plaintiff of willful misconduct" resulting in her termination. Olson v. Bristol-Burlington Health Dist., 87 Conn. App. 1, 6, 863 A.2d 748 (2005). See also Laros v. International Insights, Inc., 2011 Conn. Super. LEXIS 644 (Mar. 17, 2011)(allegations that employer terminated plaintiff's employment knowing she was worried about her financial situation in Chicago after falsely leading her to believe her employment there was secure sufficed to state cognizable claim for negligent infliction of emotional distress).

Connecticut courts are divided as to whether a constructive discharge can form the basis of a claim sounding in negligent infliction of emotional distress. Thus, while a Superior Court case holds that "an allegation of constructive discharge is insufficient to satisfy the requirement that the unreasonable conduct occurred in the termination process," Grasso v. Connecticut Hospice, Inc., 2011 Conn. Super. LEXIS 1091, at *24 (Apr. 28, 2011), a federal district court applying Connecticut law concluded "that allegations of constructive discharge may qualify as 'termination'" and will support a claim for negligent infliction of emotional distress where the employer behaved unreasonably in the resignation process. Tomby v. Community Renewal Team, Inc., 2010 U.S. Dist. LEXIS 132571 (D. Conn. Dec. 15, 2010).

The Connecticut Appellate Court resolved a split among the Superior Courts in determining that a plaintiff employee need not demonstrate that the defendant employer's conduct was extreme and outrageous in order to establish a claim for negligent infliction of emotional distress. Benton v. Simpson, 78 Conn. App. 746, 756-57 (2003). The Court stated that "where the defendant did not have such a malevolent state of mind [as to make out a claim of intentional infliction of emotional distress], but merely was negligent, the plaintiff may recover without having to prove that the conduct engaged in by the defendant was extreme and outrageous."

Claims of negligent infliction of emotional distress which implicate decisions involving religious doctrine and practice cannot be brought against religious organizations. See Thibodeau v. American Baptist Churches of Connecticut, 120 Conn. App. 666, 994 A.2d 212 (2010); Guerrier v. Southern New England Conference Association of Seventh-Day Adventists, Inc., 2009 Conn. Super LEXIS 2962 (Nov. 12, 2009). In Thibodeau, the plaintiff, an ordained Baptist Minister, brought a four count complaint against a regional organization of the American Baptist congregations. "The gravamen of each of the plaintiff's claims [which included a claim for negligent infliction of emotional distress] was that the defendant did not assist him in obtaining employment as an ordained minister, but rather harmed him by withdrawing its recognition of his ordination." The Appellate Court determined that "the conduct complained of occurred in the context of, or was germane to, a dispute over the plaintiff's fitness or suitability for his ordination to continue to be recognized and whether his resume should be circulated to churches associated with the defendant." As this would require the Court to inquire into "defendant's decisions regarding its internal management and decisions as to whether a person is suited for the clergy," the claim was barred under the First Amendment. Id. at 689.

3. ***Interference With Prospective Economic Advantage.*** This tort has not been recognized by the Supreme Court of Connecticut. One Connecticut court has stated that a cause of action for interference with economic advantage must include some independent "'conduct tortious in itself, such as fraud, duress, or defamation.'" Hiers, 31 Conn. Supp. at 310 (citation omitted). A separate but similar tort exists in Connecticut entitled tortious interference with a contract.

The tort of tortious interference with a contract (often termed interference with an advantageous business relationship) typically occurs when the relationship between two parties is threatened by the actions of a third party. See Selby v. Pelletier, 1 Conn. App. 320, 327 n.4, 472 A.2d 1285 (1984). However, "[a]n agent acting legitimately within the scope of his authority cannot be held liable for interfering with or inducing his principal to breach a contract between his principal and a third party, because to hold him liable would be, in effect, to hold the corporation liable in tort for breaching its own contract." Murray, 40 Conn. Supp. at 60-61; see also Metcoff v. Lebovics, 123 Conn. App. 512, 2 A.3d 942 (2010).

The elements of a cause of action for intentional interference with contractual relations are: 1) the existence of a contract; 2) the alleged wrongdoer's knowledge of the contract; 3) his intentional and tortious interference; 4) proof that the interference caused the harm sustained; and 5) damages resulting therefrom. See Solomon v. Aberman, 196 Conn. 359, 364, 493 A.2d 193, 196 (1985); Hart, Nininger & Campbell Assocs., Inc. v. Rogers, 16 Conn. App. 619, 627, 548 A.2d 758, 764 (1988); Selby v. Pelletier, 1 Conn. App. 320, 472 A.2d 1285 (1984). The intentional interference must be tortious conduct, which requires that the defendant be guilty of fraud, misrepresentation, intimidation, molestation, or have acted maliciously. See Blake v. Levy, 191 Conn. 257, 260, 464 A.2d 52, 54 (1983).

Remedies for intentional interference with existing or prospective contractual relations may be in the form of legal damages or injunctive relief, and the awarding of damages does not preclude the recovery of injunctive relief. See Hart, 16 Conn. App. at 632-33.

4. ***Prima Facie Tort.*** A cause of action for prima facie tort has not been recognized by any appellate court in Connecticut. However, in a case not arising in the employment context, a Superior Court held that a prima facie tort claim may be asserted against one who intentionally causes injury where redress under another traditional tort is not available. Deutsch v. Backus Corp., 2012 Conn. Super. LEXIS 1165, at *36 (May 2, 2012) ("[T]he prima facie tort doctrine is not intended to supplant traditional tort elements or traditional tort defenses."); Ballard v. Hartford Life Ins. Co., 2011 Conn. Super. LEXIS 81, at *13 (Jan. 18, 2011).

II. EMPLOYER TESTING OF EMPLOYEES

A. Psychological or Personality Testing

1. ***Common Law and Statutes.*** Employers in Connecticut are prohibited from requiring that employees or prospective employees take lie detector tests (see II.D, infra), and thus any psychological or personality test must be drafted carefully to avoid being challenged as an "honesty test."

2. ***Private Employers.*** No Connecticut case law on point.

3. ***Public Employer.*** No Connecticut case law on point.

B. Drug Testing

1. ***Common Law and Statutes.*** Employers in Connecticut may not "determine an employee's eligibility for promotion, additional compensation, transfer, termination, disciplinary or other adverse personnel action solely on the basis of a positive urinalysis drug test result unless (1) the employer has given the employee a urinalysis drug test, utilizing a reliable methodology, which produced a positive result and (2) such positive test result was confirmed by a second urinalysis drug test, which was separate and independent from the initial test, utilizing a gas chromatography and mass spectrometry methodology or a methodology which has been determined by the Commissioner of Public Health to be as reliable or more reliable than the gas chromatography and mass spectrometry methodology." An employer may not report, transmit or disclose any positive result unless a second result has been confirmed according to the statute. Conn. Gen. Stat. § 31-51u(a), (b).

Employers in Connecticut may not "require a prospective employee to submit to a urinalysis drug test as part of the application procedure for employment with such employer unless (1) the prospective employee is informed in writing at the time of application of the employer's intent to conduct such a drug test, (2) such test is conducted in accordance with the requirements of [Conn. Gen. Stat. § 31-51u], and (3) the prospective employee is given a copy of any positive urinalysis drug test result." The results of any test are to be kept strictly confidential. Conn. Gen. Stat. § 31-51v.

"No employer or employer representative, agent or designee engaged in a urinalysis drug testing program shall directly observe an employee or prospective employee in the process of producing the urine specimen." Conn. Gen. Stat. § 31-51w(a).

Results of urinalysis drug tests must be maintained along with other employee medical records and are subject to the privacy protections provided for in sections 31-128a to 31-128h, inclusive of the Connecticut General Statutes. Conn. Gen. Stat. § 31-51w(b). Results from urinalysis drug testing "conducted by or on behalf of an employer [are] inadmissible in any criminal proceeding." Conn. Gen. Stat. § 31-51w(b).

Employers in Connecticut may not require a current employee "to submit to a urinalysis drug test unless the employer has reasonable suspicion that the employee is under the influence of drugs or alcohol which adversely affects or could adversely affect such employee's job performance." Conn. Gen. Stat. § 31-51x(a). Reasonable suspicion is determined by the totality of the circumstances. Imme v. Federal Express Corp., 193 F. Supp. 2d 519 (D. Conn. 2002) (finding employer's suspicion reasonable where "(1) [plaintiff] engaged in a verbal altercation with another employee; (2) he made unusual and apparently incoherent comments over the radio; (3) he appeared to be walking back and forth quickly without any particular purpose; (4) he was chewing vigorously on a large plastic tie used for securing document bags, which was unusual behavior; and (5) he was unusually loud, energetic, and aggressive, even for him. In addition, [the supervisor] observed [plaintiff] being louder and more rambunctious than usual, yelling at people, and generally behaving out of the ordinary.").

An employer may require an employee to submit to random urinalysis drug testing if "(1) such test is authorized under federal law, (2) the employee serves in an occupation which has been designated as a high-risk or safety-sensitive occupation pursuant to regulations adopted by the Labor Commissioner, or (3) the urinalysis is conducted as part of an employee assistance program sponsored or authorized by the employer in which the employee voluntarily participates." Conn. Gen. Stat. § 31-51x(b). Either an employee or an employer may make a written request to the Commissioner of the Department of Labor to designate an occupation as "high-risk or safety-sensitive." An employer seeking such designation must prove that the occupation: 1) presents a clearly significant life threatening danger; 2) is separate from any ability to discern affected performance by either direct or indirect supervision; and 3) is not reasonably subject to other means of observation and evaluation. Conn. Agencies Regs. § 31-51x-1.

"Any aggrieved person may enforce the [foregoing provisions of the Connecticut General Statutes] by means of a civil action. Any employer, laboratory or medical facility that violates any [of the foregoing provisions], or who aids in the violation of any [of the foregoing provisions] shall be liable to the person aggrieved for special and general damages, together with attorney's fees and costs." Conn. Gen. Stat. § 31-51z(a). An action for injunctive relief may be brought by any aggrieved person, "by the Attorney General or by any person or entity which will fairly and adequately represent the interests of the protected class" and such injunctive relief may be granted by any court of competent jurisdiction. Conn. Gen. Stat. § 31-51z(b). "No provision of any collective bargaining agreement may contravene or supersede any of the provision of [the statute] so as to infringe on the privacy rights of any employee." Conn. Gen. Stat. § 31-51aa. A supervisor is not an "employer" subject to liability for violating Connecticut's drug testing statute. Ortega v. All-Star Transportation, LLC, 2009 Conn. Super. LEXIS 3521 (Dec. 17, 2009).

The Appellate Court has rejected the assertion that actual submission to a drug test is required to bring a claim under § 31-51x. Tomick v. United Parcel Service, Inc., 135 Conn. App. 589, 606-09, 43 A.3d 772 (2012). In Tomick, the plaintiff-employee was ordered by his supervisor to submit to a urinalysis drug test under threat of termination. Plaintiff acquiesced and was taken to a medical clinic where, upon completing various field sobriety tests, a physician determined that urinalysis was unnecessary. The next day, the supervisor again asked plaintiff to submit to urinalysis, and again plaintiff agreed. The Supervisor then told plaintiff that the second test would be unnecessary. The Appellate Court wrote that "[o]n these facts, where the plaintiff went to the medical clinic, under threat of termination, to submit to a drug test...and the next day was again ordered to submit to the test and acquiesced, a cause of action lies under § 31-51x." Id. at 609. The fact that plaintiff never took the urinalysis test was, according to the Court, "of no consequence." Id.

None of the foregoing provisions may be construed to "prevent an employer from conducting medical screenings, with the express written consent of the employees, to monitor exposure to toxic or other unhealthy substances in the workplace or in the performance of their job responsibilities. Any such screenings or tests shall be limited to the specific substances expressly identified in the employee consent form." Conn. Gen. Stat. § 31-51y(a). Nothing in the provisions of the statute may be construed to "restrict an employer's ability to prohibit the use of intoxicating substances during work hours or restrict an employer's ability to discipline an employee for being under the influence of intoxicating substances during work hours." Conn. Gen. Stat. § 31-51y (b) (1997). Likewise, nothing in the statute restricts or prevents "a urinalysis drug testing program conducted under the supervision of the Division of Special Revenue within the Department of Revenue Services relative to [persons] participating in activities upon which paramutual wagering is authorized . . . ." Conn. Gen. Stat. § 31-51y(c).

Employers must also be cognizant of Public Act No. 12-55, effective October 1, 2012, regarding the palliative use of marijuana. Section 17(b)(3) prohibits an employer from refusing to hire a prospective employee, or taking an adverse employment action against an existing employee, because of their status as a "qualifying patient" or "primary caregiver" under the Act. The Act defines a "qualifying patient" as "a person who is 18 years of age or older, is a resident of Connecticut and has been diagnosed by a physician as having a debilitating medical condition" permitting the palliative use of marijuana. A "primary caregiver" is defined anyone over 18 who "has agreed to

undertake responsibility for managing the well-being of the qualifying patient with respect to the palliative use of marijuana." Nothing in Section 17(b)(3) restricts an employer from prohibiting the use of intoxicating substances during work hours or disciplining employees for being under the influence at work.

2. ***Private Employers.*** For the purposes of the Drug Testing sections of the Connecticut General Statutes the term "Employer" "means any individual, corporation, partnership or unincorporated association, excluding the state or any political subdivision thereof." Conn. Gen. Stat. § 31-51t(2). The Connecticut Supreme Court has held that Conn. Gen. Stat. § 31-51x "was intended to provide the same protections to private employees in Connecticut as those protections that are afforded to employees of the federal government by the fourth amendment." Poulos v. Pfizer, Inc., 244 Conn. 598, 606-07, 711 A.2d 688 (1998); see also Schmidt v. Southern New England Telephone Co., 2006 WL 3317694 (Conn. Super. Nov. 1, 2006) (employee's cause of action for wrongful termination resulting from an improper drug test accrues at the time of the improper test, not on the date of termination) (citing Poulos, supra, at 606-07).

3. ***Public Employers.*** See II.B.2, supra.

C. Medical Testing

1. ***Common law and statutes.*** Employers in Connecticut may conduct medical screenings, "with the express written consent of their employees, to monitor exposure to toxic or other unhealthy substances in the workplace or in the performance of their job responsibilities. Any such screenings or tests shall be limited to the specific substances expressly identified in the employee consent form." Conn. Gen. Stat. § 31-51y(a).

The provisions of Conn. Gen. Stat. §46a-60 "concerning age [discrimination] shall not prohibit an employer from requiring medical examinations for employees for the purpose of determining such employees' physical qualification for continued employment." Conn. Gen. Stat. § 46a-60(b)(3).

2. ***Private Employers.*** For the purposes of the Medical Testing sections of the Connecticut General Statutes the term "Employer" "means any individual, corporation, partnership or unincorporated association, excluding the state or any political subdivision thereof." Conn. Gen. Stat. § 31-51t(2).

3. ***Public Employers.*** See II.B.3, supra.

D. Polygraph Tests

Employers in Connecticut are prohibited from requesting or requiring "any prospective employee or any employee to submit to, or take, a polygraph examination as a condition of obtaining employment or of continuing employment . . . ." Conn. Gen. Stat. § 31-51g(b)(1). An exception is made in the case of polygraph tests given "to persons to be employed by the state or any local government or any political subdivision thereof in any police department except for civilian employees within the department . . . ." Conn. Gen. Stat. § 31-51g(d).

E. Fingerprinting

Employers in Connecticut who hire "an agent, operator, assistant, guard, watchman or patrolman, shall make application to register such employee with the Commissioner of Public Safety. Such application shall be made on forms furnished by the commissioner, and, under oath of the employee, . . . and be accompanied by two sets of fingerprints of the employee . . . ." Conn. Gen. Stat. § 29-156a(c).

Clerks, stenographers, inspectors, agents and other employees, under the supervision of the Division of Special Revenues within the Department of Revenue Services shall be fingerprinted before being employed. Conn. Gen. Stat. § 12-559.

III. SEARCHES

Article I §7 of the Connecticut Constitution provides that "The people shall be secure in their persons, houses, papers and possessions from unreasonable searches and seizures; and no warrant to search any place, or to seize any person or things, shall issue without describing them as nearly as may be, nor without probable cause supported by oath or affirmation." Conn. Const. art. I § 7. This provision is virtually identical to the Fourth Amendment to the U.S. Constitution, which applies to public employees. Connecticut courts have not decided whether Article 7 provides additional protection. For "searches" via electronic monitoring, etc. See IV, infra.

A. Employee's Person

1. ***Private Employers.*** Private employees are not protected by the Fourth Amendment from searches by their employers. Privacy claims could be brought under an unreasonable intrusion theory despite the lack of case law on point.

2. ***Public Employers.*** In O'Connor v. Ortega, 480 U.S. 709, 719-20 (1987), the justices of the Supreme Court concluded that the Fourth Amendment applied to offices of public employees. The court further determined that a finding of "reasonableness" (a standard much less than probable cause) must be applied when searching a public employee's office.

B. Employee's Work Area

According to other jurisdictions, an employee's work area may generally be searched if the employer is looking for an item that is needed in the employee's absence, or in carrying out an investigation of alleged misconduct. In Tapia v. Sikorsky Aircraft Division of United Technologies Corp., 1998 WL 310872, 1998 Conn. Super. LEXIS 1576 (Conn. Super. 1998), the defendant entered into plaintiff's personal locker while plaintiff was under suspension and inventoried contents. The court held that the allegation that the discovery of plaintiff's personal and private items contributed to decision to terminate plaintiff's employment failed to support claim for intrusion.

C. Employee's Property

1. ***Private Employers.*** No Connecticut case law on point.

2. ***Public Employers.*** No Connecticut case law on point.

IV. MONITORING OF EMPLOYEES

A. Telephones and Electronic Communications

An employer in Connecticut must notify its employees when it electronically monitors their work or other activities. Conn. Gen. Stat. § 31-48d. The Act requires that employers conspicuously post a written notice which states the types of electronic monitoring that the employer is using. The Act defines "Electronic Monitoring" as those types of activities in which an employer collects data on its premises about an employee's activities or communications which can include using a computer, telephone, wire, radio, camera, electromagnetic, photo electronic or photo-optical systems. The act provides a limited exception that allows employers to electronically monitor the workplace to investigate illegal activities. Violations of the foregoing provisions may result in monetary penalties.

"No employer or agent or representative of an employer [in Connecticut] shall operate any electronic surveillance device or system, including but not limited to the recording of sound or voice or a closed circuit television system, or any combination thereof, for the purpose of recording or monitoring the activities of his employees in areas designed for the health or personal comfort of the employees or for safeguarding of their possessions, such as rest rooms, locker rooms or lounges." Conn. Gen. Stat. § 31-48b(b). Likewise, "[no] employer or his agent or representative and no employee or his agent or representative shall intentionally overhear or record a conversation or discussion pertaining to employment contract negotiations between the two parties, by means of any instrument, device or equipment, unless such party has the consent of all parties to such conversation or discussion." Conn. Gen. Stat. § 31-48b(d). Violations of the foregoing provisions may result in monetary fines or imprisonment. The Connecticut Supreme Court has held that this section does not provide a private right of action in favor of an aggrieved employee. Gerardi v. City of Bridgeport, 294 Conn. 461 985 A.2d 328 (2010).

1. ***Wiretapping.*** "No person shall use any instrument, device or equipment to record an oral private telephonic communication unless the use of such instrument, device or equipment (1) is preceded by consent of all parties to the communication and such prior consent either is obtained in writing or is part of, and obtained at the start of, the recording, or (2) is preceded by verbal notification which is recorded at the beginning and is part of the communication by the recording party, or (3) is accompanied by an automatic tone warning device which automatically produces a distinct signal that is repeated at intervals of approximately fifteen seconds during the communication while such instrument, device or equipment is in use." Conn. Gen. Stat. § 52-570d(a). The foregoing provision generally does not apply to federal, state or local criminal enforcement officials and related individuals, and any person claiming an illegal recording of a private telephonic communication may bring a civil action to recover damages, together with costs and reasonable attorney's fees. Conn. Gen. Stat. § 52-570d(c). A plaintiff seeking redress under Conn. Gen. Stat. § 52-570d need not plead or prove actual damages; nominal damages alone are sufficient to maintain a claim. Tarbox v. Tarbox, 2005 WL 1097228, *2 (Conn. Super. April 6, 2005).

2. ***Electronic Communications.*** In Brown-Criscuolo v. Wolfe, 601 F. Supp. 2d 441 (D. Conn. 2009), the United States District Court for the District of Connecticut considered whether a school principal's claims of improper search and seizure of her work computer in violation of the Fourth Amendment and common-law claims for invasion of privacy could survive the school's motion for summary judgment. In analyzing the plaintiff's Constitutional claim, the court set forth a four-part test to determine whether an employee has an expectation of privacy in e-mails sent or received on an employer's computer or e-mail system: "(1) does the corporation maintain a policy banning personal or other objectionable use, (2) does the company monitor the use of the employee's computer or e-mail, (3) do third parties have a

right of access to the computer or e-mails, and (4) did the corporation notify the employee, or was the employee aware, of the use and monitoring policies?" Id. at 449 (citations omitted).

Applying the four-part test, the court concluded that the plaintiff had a reasonable expectation of privacy as to her work e-mail account, then turned to the second part of the Fourth Amendment analysis, whether the defendant's search of plaintiff's e-mail account was conducted pursuant to a reasonable and justified investigatory search. Id. at 451. The court explained that, "[e]ven if a plaintiff has a reasonable expectation of privacy in the workplace, an investigatory search for evidence of suspected work-related employee misfeasance will be constitutionally reasonable if it is justified at its inception and of appropriate scope." Id. (internal quotation marks and citation omitted). But the court denied the defendant's motion for summary judgment on the plaintiff's Fourth Amendment claim because if concluded that a reasonable jury could find the school's conduct in the search of the plaintiff's e-mails "to be excessively intrusive." Id.

Similarly, the court refused to grant the defendant's motion for summary judgment as to the plaintiff's common-law invasion of privacy claims because a jury question existed by virtue of the fact that "[t]he Defendant accessed the Plaintiffs e-mail account without permission and looked at a correspondence that was not addressed to him." Id. at 455.

3. ***Other Electronic Monitoring.*** One Connecticut Superior Court has concluded that an employer installing a GPS tracking device in a vehicle owned by the employer and operated by an employee in the course of his employment does not violate Conn. Gen. Stat. §§ 31-48b or 31-48d. See Gerardi v. City of Bridgeport, 2007 WL 4755007, at * 6-8, 44 Conn. L. Rptr. 752 (Conn. Super. Dec. 31, 2007). The Superior Court reasoned that § 31-48b does not apply to a GPS tracking devise installed in a company vehicle because, "even when viewing the facts most favorably to [a] plaintiff. That statute applies 'in areas designed for the health or personal comfort of the employees or for safeguarding of their possessions, such as rest rooms, locker rooms or lounges.'" Id. at *5. Likewise, the Superior Court concluded that a GPS devise in a company vehicle does not constitute electronic monitoring under § 31-48d because "the clear and unambiguous language of the statute is that the monitoring take place 'on the premises' of the employer," and "[s]ince 31-48d was enacted in 1998, the legislature has not amended the statute to include GPS systems," even if such systems have been available to the public for many years. Id. at *7. This decision was affirmed by the Connecticut Superior Court on alternative grounds. See Gerardi, 294 Conn. 461.

B. Mail

No Connecticut case law on point.

C. Surveillance/Photographing

No Connecticut case law on point.

V. ACTIVITIES OUTSIDE THE WORKPLACE

A. Statute or Common Law

Connecticut fair employment laws prohibit discrimination on the basis of race, color, religion, age, gender, marital status, national origin, sexual orientation, and mental or physical handicap. Conn. Gen. Stat. §§ 46a-60(a)(1), 46a-81b. The Connecticut Commission on Human Rights and Opportunities ("CHRO") has the primary responsibility for administering and enforcing these laws. The Connecticut fair employment laws cover all public and private employers that employ three or more people. Employers may not refuse to hire, or discharge from employment, or discriminate against in compensation or other terms and conditions of employment, any person because of membership in any protected group. Employers should not ask job applicants for information about membership in a protected group.

B. Employees' Personal Relationships

1. ***Romantic Relationships between Employees.*** Employers who adopt anti-nepotism rules do not violate either Title VII or the Constitution. There is also no Connecticut case law that suggests anti-nepotism rules would violate the Connecticut Fair Employment Practices Act.

2. ***Sexual Orientation.*** No employer, "by himself or his agent, except in the case of a bona fide occupational qualification or need, [can] refuse to hire or employ or to bar or to discharge from employment any individual or to discriminate against him in compensation or in terms, conditions or privileges of employment because of the individual's sexual orientation. [Likewise, no] person, employer, employment agency or labor organization, except in the case of a bona fide occupational qualification or need, to advertise employment opportunities in such a manner as to restrict such employment so as to discriminate against individuals because of their sexual orientation." Conn. Gen. Stat. § 46a-81c.

3. ***Marital Status.*** The Connecticut Fair Employment Practices Act ("CFEPA") expressly protects individuals from discrimination based on marital status. Conn. Gen. Stat. § 46a-60(a)(1).

C. Smoking

For the purposes of sections of the Connecticut General Statutes regarding smoking in the workplace, "'Employer' means a person engaged in business who has employees, including the state and any political subdivision thereof ...'Business Facility' means a structurally enclosed location or portion thereof at which employees perform services for their employer. The term 'business facility' shall not include: (A) Facilities listed in subparagraph (A), (C) or (G) of subdivision (2) of subsection (b) of section 19a-342; (B) any establishment with a permit for the sale of alcoholic liquor pursuant to section 30-23 issued on or before May 1, 2003; (C) for any business that is engaged in the testing or development of tobacco or tobacco products, the areas of such business designated for such testing or development; or (D) during the period from October 1, 2003, to April 1, 2004, establishments with a permit issued for the sale of alcoholic liquor pursuant to section 30-22a, 30-26 or the bar area of a bowling establishment holding a permit pursuant to subsection (a) of section 30-37c." Conn. Gen. Stat. § 31-40q(a)(3)-(4).

Employers in Connecticut with fewer than five employees in a business facility are required to "establish one or more work areas, sufficient to accommodate nonsmokers who request to utilize such an area, within each business facility under his control, where smoking is prohibited. The employer shall clearly designate the existence and boundaries of each nonsmoking area by posting signs which can be readily seen by employees and visitors. In the areas ... where smoking is permitted, existing physical barriers and ventilation systems shall be used to the extent practicable to minimize the effect of smoking in adjacent nonsmoking areas." Conn. Gen. Stat. § 31-40q(b).

Every employer with five or more, "shall prohibit smoking in any business facility under said employer's control, except that an employer may designate one or more smoking rooms" and "[e]ach employer that provides a smoking room pursuant to this subsection shall provide sufficient nonsmoking break rooms for nonsmoking employees." Conn. Gen. Stat. § 31-40q(c). If a smoking room is provided, it must meet the following requirements: "(A) Air from the smoking room shall be exhausted directly to the outside by an exhaust fan, and no air from such room shall be recirculated to other parts of the building; (B) the employer shall comply with any ventilation standard adopted by (i) the Commissioner of Labor pursuant to chapter 571 (ii) the United States Secretary of Labor under the authority of the Occupational Safety and Health Act of 1970, as from time to time amended, or (iii) the federal Environmental Protection Agency; (C) such room shall be located in a nonwork area, where no employee, as part of his or her work responsibilities, is required to enter, except such work responsibilities shall not include any custodial or maintenance work carried out in the smoking room when it is unoccupied; and (D) such room shall be for the use of employees only." Conn. Gen. Stat. § 31-40q(c). Employers are permitted to designate an entire business facility as a nonsmoking area. Conn. Gen. Stat. § 31-40q(d).

No employer in Connecticut may require, "as a condition of employment, that any employee or prospective employee refrain from smoking or using tobacco products outside the course of his employment, or otherwise discriminate against any individual with respect to compensation, terms, conditions or privileges of employment for smoking or using tobacco products outside the course of his employment." Conn. Gen. Stat. § 31-40s(a). Non-profit organizations or corporations whose primary purpose is to discourage the use of tobacco products by the general public are exempt from the foregoing provision. Conn. Gen. Stat. § 31-40s(a).

D. Blogging

No Connecticut case law on point.

VI. RECORDS

A. Personnel Records

Under the Connecticut Personnel Files Act, a personnel file is broadly defined to include any document that is used or has been used by an employer to make employment-related decisions affecting an employee. Personnel files in Connecticut expressly do not include: "stock option or management bonus plan records, medical records, letters of reference or recommendations from third parties including former employers, materials which are used by the employer to plan for future operations, information contained in separately maintained security files, test information, the disclosure of which would invalidate the test, or documents which are being developed or prepared for use in civil, criminal or grievance procedures." Conn. Gen. Stat. § 31-128a(3). Simply because a report or file contains information about an employee does not necessarily mean it falls within the statutory definition of a personnel file. See Banknorth, N.A. v. Blackrock Realty, 2010 Conn. Super LEXIS 919 (Apr. 13, 2010) (investigative report prepared by bank in connection with a foreclosure action is not subject to protection as a personnel file under Conn. Gen. State. §31-128a(3) simply because it contained "individually identifiable information" regarding an employee).

Employers must, within a reasonable time after receipt of a written request from an employee, permit that employee to inspect his personnel file, during regular business hours at a location at or reasonably near the employee's place of employment. Conn. Gen. Stat. § 31-128b. In Connecticut, employees are allowed to obtain copies of their personnel files, or review those files, up to twice per calendar year. Conn. Gen. Stat. §§ 31-128g, 31-128h. Employers have the right to protect their files and records from loss, damage, or alteration by prohibiting employees from physically removing files from the premises or requiring that inspection of any personnel file take place in the presence of a designated official. Conn. Gen. Stat. § 31-128d.

The Connecticut Personnel Files Act affords strict confidentiality to personnel files of employees. Employers may not disclose the contents of a personnel file without the employee's written consent, except where the information is limited to the verification of dates of employment and the employee's title or position and wage or salary or where the disclosure is made: to a third party that maintains or prepares employment records or performs other employment-related services for the employer; pursuant to a lawfully issued warrant or subpoena; pursuant to certain requests by law enforcement agencies; where necessary in response to an apparent medical emergency; or where the disclosure is permitted under an applicable collective bargaining agreement. Conn. Gen. Stat. § 31-128f. Connecticut courts have held "that the contents of personnel files, though not immune from discovery, must only be disclosed in response to requests that directly relate to legitimate issues in the case [] that is clearly material and relevant" and that "[t]he proper procedure for the court to follow in making a determination on the discovery of documents contained in [an employee's] personnel file is to conduct an in camera inspection of the documents involved." Dotson v. Hartford Roman Catholic Diocesan Corp., 2011 Conn. Super. LEXIS 386, at *17-18 (Feb. 17, 2011). **Pursuant to Public Act No. 11-12, effective October 1, 2011, penalties for violating the Personnel Files Act have increased. Conn. Gen. Stat. § 31-69a(b) now provides a $500 penalty for the first violation of the statute related to an individual employee, and $1,000 for each subsequent violation related to the individual employee.**

If an employee disagrees with any of the information contained in his or her personnel file, removal or correction of such information may be agreed upon by such employee and his or her employer. If an agreement cannot be reached then such employee may submit a written statement explaining his or her position and such statement shall be maintained as part of such employee's personnel file and shall accompany any transmittal or disclosure from such file made to a third party. Conn. Gen. Stat. § 31-128e.

In Dir., Ret. & Benefits Servs. Div. v. Freedom of Info. Comm'n., 256 Conn. 764 (2001), the Connecticut Supreme Court held that if public employees had taken significant steps to protect their privacy (such as obtaining unlisted phone numbers, using a post office box, or removing their names from mailing lists) and did not want their personal information disclosed, then home addresses of those employees are exempt from the Freedom of Information Act ("FOIA"), pursuant to Conn. Gen. Stat. §1-210(b)(2). However, in Pane v. City of Danbury, 267 Conn. 669, 841 A.2d 684 (2004), the Court held that the FOIA does not provide a private right of action, so that the proper cause of action for a public employee whose personnel records were allegedly disclosed in violation of the FOIA, is a tort claim for invasion of privacy. "[T]he general rule developed in Connecticut case law is that a municipality is immune from liability for [its tortuous acts] unless the legislature has enacted a statute abrogating that immunity." Id., at 677, citing Spears v. Garcia, 263 Conn. 22, 818 A.2d 37 (2003).

On June 10, 2008, Connecticut approved Public Act No. 08-167, An Act Concerning the Confidentiality of Social Security Numbers. Effective October 1, 2008, Public Act No. 08-167 requires employers who collect Social Security numbers in the course of business to create a privacy protection policy which shall be published or publicly displayed (e.g., posting on an Internet web page).

To comply with Public Act No. 08-167, the privacy protection policy shall: (1) Protect the confidentiality of Social Security numbers, (2) prohibit unlawful disclosure of Social Security numbers, and (3) limit access to Social Security numbers. Public Act No. 08-167 also requires that employers in possession of employees' personal information (e.g., Social Security numbers, drivers' license numbers, state identification card numbers, account numbers, credit or debit card numbers, passport numbers, alien registration numbers or health insurance identification numbers) shall safeguard the data, computer files and documents containing the personal information from misuse by third parties, and shall destroy, erase or make unreadable such data, computer files and documents prior to disposal. Any person or entity that violates the provisions of Public Act No. 08-167 shall be subject to a civil penalty of five hundred dollars for each violation, provided such civil penalty shall not exceed five hundred thousand dollars for any single event. Public Act No. 08-167, however, provides a safe harbor for unintentional violations.

B. Medical Records

The Connecticut Personnel Files Act also applies to medical records. "Medical records" are defined as "all papers, documents, and reports prepared by a physician, psychiatrist or psychologist that are in the possession of an employer and are work-related or upon which such employer relies to make any employment-related decision." Conn. Gen. Stat. § 31-128a(4). The confidentiality provisions of the Connecticut Personnel Files Act apply to medical records as well.

Each employer in Connecticut who has personnel files is "required to keep any personnel file pertaining to a particular employee for at least one year after the termination of such employee's employment." Conn. Gen. Stat. § 31-128b. Likewise, each employer in Connecticut who has medical records is required to keep any medical records pertaining to a particular employee for at least one year after the termination of such employee's employment. "Medical records, if kept by an employer, shall be kept separately and not as part of any personnel file." Conn. Gen. Stat. § 31-128c.

C. Criminal Records

Conn. Gen. Stat. § 31-51i states, *inter alia,*:

(a) For the purposes of this section, "employer" means any person engaged in business who has one or more employees, including the state or any political subdivision of the state.

(b) No employer or any employer's agent, representative or designee may require an employee or prospective employee to disclose the existence of any arrest, criminal charge or conviction, the records of which have been erased pursuant to section 46b-146, 54-76o or 54-142a.

(c) An employment application form that contains any question concerning the criminal history of the applicant shall contain a notice, in clear and conspicuous language: (1) That the applicant is not required to disclose the existence of any arrest, criminal charge or conviction, the records of which have been erased pursuant to section 46b-146, 54-76o or 54-142a, (2) that criminal records subject to erasure pursuant to section 46b-146, 54-76o or 54-142a are records pertaining to a finding of delinquency or that a child was a member of a family with service needs, an adjudication as a youthful offender, a criminal charge that has been dismissed or nolled, a criminal charge for which the person has been found not guilty or a conviction for which the person received an absolute pardon, and (3) that any person whose criminal records have been erased pursuant to section 46b-146, 54-76o or 54-142a shall be deemed to have never been arrested within the meaning of the general statutes with respect to the proceedings so erased and may so swear under oath.

(d) No employer or any employer's agent, representative or designee shall deny employment to a prospective employee solely on the basis that the prospective employee had a prior arrest, criminal charge or conviction, the records of which have been erased pursuant to section 46b-146, 54-76o or 54-142a or that the prospective employee had a prior conviction for which the prospective employee has received a provisional pardon pursuant to section 54-130a.

(e) No employer or any employer's agent, representative or designee shall discharge, or cause to be discharged, or in any manner discriminate against, any employee solely on the basis that the employee had, prior to being employed by such employer, an arrest, criminal charge or conviction, the records of which have been erased pursuant to section 46b-146, 54-76o or 54-142a or that the employee had, prior to being employed by such employer, a prior conviction for which the employee has received a provisional pardon pursuant to section 54-130a.

(f) The portion of an employment application form which contains information concerning the criminal history record of an applicant or employee shall only be available to the members of the personnel department of the company, firm or corporation or, if the company, firm or corporation does not have a personnel department, the person in charge of employment, and to any employee or member of the company, firm or corporation, or an agent of such employee or member, involved in the interviewing of the applicant.

(g) Notwithstanding the provisions of subsection (f) of this section, the portion of an employment application form which contains information concerning the criminal history record of an applicant or employee may be made available as necessary to persons other than those specified in said subsection (f) by: (1) A broker-dealer or investment adviser registered under chapter 672a in connection with (A) the possible or actual filing of, or the collection or retention of information contained in, a form U-4 Uniform Application for Securities Industry Registration or Transfer, (B) the compliance responsibilities of such broker-dealer or investment adviser under state or federal law, or (C) the applicable rules of self-regulatory organizations promulgated in accordance with federal law; (2) An insured depository institution in connection with (A) the management of risks related to safety and soundness, security or privacy of such institution, (B) any waiver that may possibly or actually be sought by such institution pursuant to section 19 of the Federal Deposit Insurance Act, 12 USC 1829 (a), (C) the possible or actual obtaining by such institution of any security or fidelity bond, or (D) the compliance responsibilities of such institution under state or federal law; and (3) An insurance producer licensed under chapter 701a in connection with (A) the management of risks related to security or privacy of such insurance producer, or (B) the compliance responsibilities of such insurance producer under state or federal law.

In addition, it is the policy of the state of Connecticut "to encourage all employers to give favorable consideration to providing jobs to qualified individuals, including those who may have criminal conviction records." Conn. Gen. Stat. § 46a-79. Unless the state, or any of its agencies determines that an applicant is not suitable for the position of employment sought or the specific occupation, trade, vocation, profession or business for which a license, permit, certificate or registration is sought, an applicant "shall not be disqualified from employment by the state of Connecticut or any of its agencies, nor shall a person be disqualified to practice, pursue or engage in any occupation, trade, vocation, profession or business for which a license, permit, certificate or registration is required to be issued by the state of Connecticut or any of its agencies solely because of a prior conviction of a crime." Conn. Gen. Stat. §§ 46a-80(a), (b). Additionally, "[i]n no case may records of arrest, which are not followed by a conviction, or records of convictions, which have been erased, be used, distributed or disseminated by the state or any of its agencies in connection with an application for employment or for a permit, license, certificate or registration." Conn. Gen. Stat. § 46a-80(d).

D. Credit Records

Public Act No. 11-223, effective October 1, 2011, prohibits Connecticut employers from requiring as a condition of employment that an employee or applicant consent to the employer obtaining a credit report containing the individual's credit score, credit account balances, payment history, savings or checking account balances or account numbers. The law exempts financial institutions, and allows employers to obtain such reports where required to do so by law, the employer reasonably believes the employee has engaged in specific activity that constitutes a violation of the law related to the employee's employment, or the report is substantially related to the job in question or the employer has a bona fide purpose for requesting a credit report that is substantially job-related provided the request is disclosed in writing. The "substantially related" standard applies to managerial positions as well as positions that involve access to financial information, a fiduciary responsibility with respect to issuing payments, collecting debts, transferring money or entering into contracts, an expense account or corporate credit or debit card, or access to confidential and proprietary information or trade secrets. There is no private right of action under the statute. However, aggrieved employees and applicants may file a complaint with the Connecticut Department of Labor, which is empowered to impose a civil penalty of $300 per violation.

E. Subpoenas/Search Warrants

The Connecticut Personnel Files Act provides specific exceptions allowing production of information contained in an employee's personnel file pursuant to a lawfully issued subpoena or a search warrant. Conn. Gen. Stat. 31-128f. However, in an employment case where the plaintiff seeks discovery of other employees' personnel files, "[a]lthough the material in the personnel files may be disclosed, the decision to allow disclosure requires the court to balance the plaintiff's need for the material in the files against the privacy rights of the non-parties." Weston v. Wellcare Health Plans, Inc., 2006 WL 337216, at *2 (Conn. Super. Jan. 20, 2006). See also Section III, *supra*.

VII. ACTIONS SUBSEQUENT TO EMPLOYMENT

A. References.

Pursuant to the Connecticut Personnel Files Act, absent the consent of the employee, an employer may only verify the employee's dates of employment and the employee's title or position and wage or salary. Conn. Gen. Stat. § 31-128f. The Superior Court, however, has repeatedly held that the Connecticut Personnel Files Act does not confer a private right of action. Kelly v. Seacorp, Inc., 2002 WL 31050779, *9 (Conn. Super. Aug. 13, 2002.). But see Majewski v. Bridgeport, 2005 WL 469135, *17 (Conn. Super. Jan. 20, 2005)(recognizing that "courts have held that a failure to provide post-employment reference letters is an adverse employment action.")(citing Hawkins v. Astor Home for Children, 1998 WL 142134 (S.D.N.Y. 1998)). In addition, the Connecticut Supreme Court has recognized that statements made by employers in the context of an employment reference, authorized by the employee, are subject to a qualified privilege when made in good faith and without an improper motive or malice. Miron v. University of New Haven Police Department, 284 Conn. 35, 931 A.2d 847 (2007).

B. Non-Compete Agreements

The Connecticut Supreme Court has recognized that employees may be subject to covenants not to compete so long as the covenant is "partial and restricted in its operation 'in respect to either time or place ... and ... reasonable." Scott v. General Iron & Welding Co., 171 Conn. 132, 137, 368 A.2d 111 (1976). "The five factors to be considered in evaluating the reasonableness of a restrictive covenant ancillary to an employment agreement are: (1) the length of time the restriction operates; (2) the geographical area covered; (3) the fairness of the protection accorded to the employer; (4) the extent of the restraint on the employee's opportunity to pursue his occupation; and (5) the extent of interference with the public's interests. Robert S. Weiss and Associates, Inc. v. Wiederlight, 208 Conn. 525, 529 n. 2, 546 A.2d 216 (1988). This test is meant to be viewed in the disjunctive so a finding of unreasonableness in any factor will render the non-compete agreement unenforceable. New Haven Tobacco Co. v. Perrelli, 18 Conn. App. 531, 534, 559 A.2d 715 (1989) (New Haven Tobacco II).

A non-compete agreement which protects the employer in areas in which it does not do business or is unlikely to do business is unreasonable with respect to area. Id.; see also Webster Ins. Inc. v. Levine, 2007 WL 4733105 (Conn. Super. Dec. 21, 2007) (refusing to enforce non-solicitation agreement where former employer was attempting to prohibit former employee and his new employer from providing insurance clients with a product that former employer itself could not provide; "It is unreasonable to bar these clients from doing business with someone who actually has the particular expertise they need.") Moreover, Connecticut courts consider three additional factors when testing the reasonableness of a non-compete agreement's interference with the public's interests: (1) the extent of the effect on the public; (2) the likelihood that the agreement will create or maintain a monopoly; and (3) the extent of the interest protected by the agreement. New Haven Tobacco Co. v. Perrelli, 11 Conn. App. 636, 641, 528 A.2d 865 (1987) (New Haven Tobacco I); see also Fairfield County Bariatric and Surgical Associates, P.C. v. Ehrlich, 2010 Conn. Super. LEXIS 568, at *115-16 (Mar. 8, 2010) (restriction preventing physician from performing bariatric surgery at certain hospitals did not cause significant detriment to the public interest where surgeries could be performed at other area hospitals and there was no geographic restriction on surgeon's provision of follow up care).

The "time and geographical restrictions are to be reviewed as intertwined considerations when a determination is made on the reasonableness of the limitations on an employee's post-termination activities." Van Dyck Printing Co. v. DiNicola, 43 Conn. Supp. 191, 197, 648 A.2d 898 (1993), aff'd., 231 Conn. 272, 648 A.2d 877 (1994). See Stay Alert Safety Services, Inc. v. Fletcher, 2005 WL 2009036 (Conn. Super. Jul. 13, 2005) (2-year non-compete agreement covering area of 200 miles found reasonable); Aetna Retirement Servs. v. Hug, 1997 WL 396212 (Conn. Super. June 18, 1997) (global covenant barring insurer's former senior customer relations executive from working in a similar job for another insurer or a financial services company reasonable where term was for one year, and employer sought enforcement for only six months). Where courts find the restrictions to be unreasonable, they may modify or "blue pencil" the restrictions to the extent that the terms are severable. Beit v. Beit, 135 Conn. 195, 205, 63 A.2d 161 (1998). See Grayling Associates, Inc. v. Villota, 2004 WL 1784388 (Conn. Super. Jul. 12, 2004) (modifying non-compete agreement covering 100 mile radius to limit agreement to county in which employer was located, where 2-year duration and limitation of non-competition to employer's specific industry were otherwise reasonable). In early 2009, a Connecticut Superior Court opined that a non-compete covenant may be enforceable where the covenant had a time limit of the greater of two years or for so long as the former employee received benefits under a deferred compensation plan. Webster Financial Corp. v McDonald, 2009 WL 416059, at *5 (Conn. Super. Jan. 28, 2009). Remarkably, the McDonald court concluded that the mere fact that a covenant could be "unlimited in duration" did not make the covenant "per se unreasonable," where the covenant contained other limitations, such as prohibiting the former employee from participating in the insurance business within a twenty-five mile radius from the former employer's offices, the anti-solicitation of customers provision was applicable only to "former and present clients," and the covenant was not completely unlimited in duration because it was tied to the cessation of the former employee's participation in a deferred compensation plan. Id.

The signing of a non-compete agreement at the inception of employment has been implicitly held to have been supported by consideration. Hart, Nininger, Campbell Assocs. v. Rogers, 16 Conn. App. 619, 636-37, 548 A.2d 758 (1988). There is a split, however, as to whether continued employment may constitute valid consideration for a non-compete agreement. Compare Addison v. Torres, 2008 WL 1971028 (Conn. Super. Apr. 18, 2008) ("Continued employment, as opposed to new employment, is not adequate consideration.") (citing Dick v. Dick, 167 Conn. 210, 224, 355 A.2d 110 (1974)) and North American Outdoor Products, Inc. v. Dawson, 2004 WL 2284289, *4 (Conn. Super. Ct. 2004) ("It is well settled law in Connecticut that continued employment is not consideration for a covenant not to compete entered into after the beginning of the employment.") (citing, *inter alia*, Torosyan v. Boehringer Ingelheim Pharmaceuticals, Inc., 234 Conn. 1, 18, 662 A.2d 89 (1995)) with Piscitelli v. Pepe, 2004 WL 2898630, *4, 38 Conn. L. Rptr. 219 (Conn. Super. Nov. 5, 2004) (holding continued employment to be valid consideration for a non-compete agreement) (citing Roessler v. Burwell, 119 Conn. 289, 293, 176 A. 126 (1934)). Non-compete agreements signed after the start of employment are valid so long as they are supported by additional consideration. See Innovative Financial Services, LLC. V. Urban, 2005 WL 941342, *3 (Conn. Super. Feb. 23, 2005) (employer's payment of tuition for employee's on-line class sufficient consideration to support non-compete agreement entered into after start of employment).

Moreover, at least one Connecticut Superior Court has held that non-compete agreements signed by independent contractors after the start of a contractual engagement are not enforceable for want of consideration. Express Courier Systems, Inc. v. Brown, 2006 WL 3878086, *4 (Conn. Super. Dec. 18, 2006). In Deming v. Nationwide Mutual Ins. Co., 279 Conn. 745 (2006), the Supreme Court of Connecticut concluded that a contract provision under which an employee's deferred compensation is forfeited if s/he engages in a competing business "does not differ meaningfully from a covenant not to compete. The total prohibition against competition, enforced by a forfeiture of accrued benefits, subjecting the employee to an economic loss undoubtedly is designed to deter competition." Id. at 767. Therefore, a "forfeiture for competition clause ... must be analyzed under the reasonableness test for covenants not to compete." Id. at 769.

It should also be noted that "[e]ven after the employment has ceased ... the employee remains subject to a duty not to use trade secrets, or other confidential information, which he has acquired in the course of his employment, for his own benefit or that of a competitor to the detriment of his former employer." Elm City Cheese Co. v. Federico, 251 Conn. 59, 68-69, 752 A.2d 1037 (1999).

What is more, multiple violations of a non-compete agreement may be sufficient to establish "substantial injury to a competing business," potentially triggering liability under Connecticut's Unfair Trade Practices Act ("CUTPA"). See Greene v. Orsini, 50 Conn. Sup. 312, 316, 926 A.2d 708 (2007); see also Webster Financial Corp. v McDonald, 2009 WL 416059, at *15 (Conn. Super. Jan. 28, 2009)(allegation that an individual repeatedly breached a non-compete covenant and spread "false rumors to the [the former employer's] customers concerning [its] employees" raised a viable CUTPA claim).

VIII. OTHER ISSUES

A. Statutes of Limitations

The statute of limitations for invasion of privacy claims is governed by Conn. Gen. Stat. § 52-577. Section 52-577, provides that "[n]o action founded upon a tort shall be brought but within three years from the date of the act or omission complained of." Conn. Gen. Stat. § 52-577. It is well-settled that it is not the date of injury, but rather the date of the conduct that starts this statute running. If the action is to recover damages for injury to the person, or real or personal property and is caused by negligence, the action shall be brought "within two years from the date when the injury is first sustained or discovered or in the exercise of reasonable care, should have been discovered, except that no action may be brought more than three years from the date of the act or omission complained of." Conn. Gen. Stat. § 52-584.

B. Jurisdiction

The Appellate Court of Connecticut has noted that Connecticut Superior Courts have subject matter jurisdiction over claims for invasion of privacy and intentional infliction of emotional distress initiated by non-resident plaintiffs. Talenti v. Morgan and Brother Manhattan Storage Co., Inc., 113 Conn. App. 845, 853, 968 A.2d 933 (2009).

C. Worker's Compensation Exclusivity

The Connecticut Supreme Court has "consistently interpreted the exclusivity provision of the [Workers' Compensation Act], General Statutes § 31-284(a), as a total bar to common law actions brought by employees against employers for job related injuries with one narrow exception that exists when the employer has committed an intentional tort or where the employer has engaged in wilful or serious misconduct." Suarez v. Dickmont Plastics Corp., 229 Conn. 99, 106, 639 A.2d 507 (1994) (quoting Jett v. Dunlap, 179 Conn. 215, 217, 425 A.2d 1263 (1979)). To invoke this narrow exception, an employee must show that the employer either actually intended to injure the employee or intentionally created a dangerous condition that made the employee's injuries substantially certain to occur. Motzer v. Haberli, 300 Conn. 733, 744, 15 A.3d 1084 (2011). Connecticut's Supreme Court has held "that the failure to comply with safety regulations and the failure to train employees properly are insufficient to satisfy the substantial certainty standard without further evidence that the employee knew or believed that injury to the employee was substantially certain to occur." Id. at 745; **see also Maruszewski v. Ducci Elec. Contrs., Inc., No. CV106001601S, 2012 Conn. Super. LEXIS 1002, at *9 (Apr. 10, 2012) (granting employer's motion to strike negligence claim on workers' compensation exclusivity grounds where plaintiff failed to allege facts sufficient to show employer had reason to believe plaintiff's injury, sustained while removing cement from a cement mixer drum, was substantially certain to occur despite the fact that employer's initial attempt to remove cement failed and supervisor urged that the drum be cleaned quickly).**

Under this standard, if a work supervisor who assaults an employee can be identified as the alter ego of the employer, or if the employer has directed or authorized the assault, then the employer may be liable in common-law tort. See Jett, 179 Conn. at 219, 425 A.2d 1263. However, if the assailant is only another employee who could not be identified as a corporate alter ego, "then the strict liability remedies provided by Workmen's Compensation Act are exclusive and cannot be supplemented with common-law damages." Id. Consequently, employers in Connecticut may successfully move to strike an invasion of privacy claim relying on the worker's compensation exclusivity provision, so long as the employee alleged to have violated another employee's privacy is not the alter ego of the corporation, and the employer did not order the invasion of privacy. Note, however, that "the statute allows an employee to bring a tort action against his employer if the employer has failed to provide workers' compensation insurance." Graham v. Stonehouse Construction, LLC, 2011 Conn. Super. LEXIS 1590, at *4 (June 28, 2011).

For example, in Cintron v. Ademco Distribution, Inc., 2003 WL 943857 (Conn. Super. Feb. 24, 2003), the defendant hired the plaintiff in 1998. In February 1999, the plaintiff walked into the women's bathroom where she observed a co-employee, John Alberino, with a female co-employee. Upon seeing the plaintiff, Alberino made a lewd remark to the plaintiff. After this incident Alberino began making other lewd comments to the plaintiff. For instance, Alberino told the plaintiff that the way he deals with disgruntled employees is by getting his gun and blowing them away. Additionally, the plaintiff's supervisor began making lewd comments in front of the plaintiff. The plaintiff complained to Alberino's supervisor and to human resources about the conduct of Alberino and her supervisor. Because of the aforementioned conduct, the plaintiff was passed over for promotions and subsequently terminated. In response, the plaintiff filed a six-count complaint against the defendant alleging, inter alia, invasion of privacy. In support of this claim, the plaintiff specifically alleged that "[t]he statements, words and conduct made by the defendant's employees, and ratified by the [defendant], invaded plaintiff's right to privacy by intruding upon a privacy interest that is highly offensive to a reasonable person." Id. at *3. The plaintiff further contended that the defendant endorsed the harassment she suffered because it did not take adequate preventative steps.

In striking the plaintiff's invasion of privacy claim, the court noted that the plaintiff failed to allege that the defendant's actions fell under the Jett exception to the Workers Compensation exclusivity provision. "More specifically, the plaintiff [did] not allege that the defendant directed or authorized the conduct of its employees and supervisors. Although the plaintiff plead[] that the defendant ratified and condoned the acts of its employees, 'condoning is not an intentional tort on the part of the employer.'" Id. at *3. The court further reasoned that "[t]he plaintiff also fail[ed] to plead that the employees were of 'such a status in the defendant's organization as to be characterized as the alter ego of the corporation.'" Id. (citations omitted). The court added, "[i]f the [co-worker who invades an employee's privacy] is of such rank in the corporation that he may be deemed the alter ego of the corporation under the standards governing disregard of the corporate entity, then attribution of corporate responsibility for the [the invasion of privacy] is appropriate. It is inappropriate where the actor is merely a foreman or supervisor." Id. (citation omitted).

D. Pleading Requirements

Connecticut Practice Book § 10-1 provides that "[e]ach pleading shall contain a plain and concise statement of the material facts on which the pleader relies, but not of the evidence by which they are to be proved." In Rice v. Meriden Housing Authority, 2004 WL 870816, at *9 (Conn. Super. Mar. 31, 2004), the court granted the defendant's motion to strike an invasion of privacy claim where the plaintiff failed to specifically allege that defendant "entertained serious doubt as to the truth of [their] publication." Id., citing Woodstock v. Journal Publishing Co., 230 Conn. 525, 546, 646 A.2d 92 (1994). See also, Sidiropoulos v. Bridgeport Hosp., 2004 WL 202256, at *2 (Conn. Super. Jan. 9, 2004) (granting motion to strike invasion of privacy claim where plaintiff failed to allege the matter was publicized); Pickering v. St. Mary's Hospital, 2005 WL 1971003, at *3 (Conn. Super. June 29, 2005) (granting motion to strike invasion of privacy claim where plaintiff failed to allege the extent of publication, the size of the audience, or the likelihood of dissemination); but see Slowick v. Morgan Stanley & Co., 2006 WL 573926 (Conn. Super. Feb. 21, 2006) (failure to precede word "offensive" with word "highly" in pleading was "linguistic ambiguity" and not fatal to the cause of action).

Emphasizing that a plaintiff's right to recover is limited to the allegations of his complaint, in Foncello v. Amorossi, 284 Conn. 225, 931 A.2d 924 (2007), the Supreme Court of Connecticut held that it had no authority to consider an invasion-of-privacy claim that was not alleged in a town selectman's amended complaint. In Foncello, the town selectman sued two political opponents for alleged invasion of his privacy. Following the conclusion of selectman's case-in-chief, the Superior Court dismissed the action as to one of the defendants and, after trial, rendered judgment in favor of other defendant. The town selectman appealed. In affirming the Superior Court, the Supreme Court of Connecticut held that the Superior Court could not consider evidence that a political opponent had allegedly disseminated the town selectman's social security number to the press after the town selectman's original complaint had been filed, where the town selectman's amended complaint did not include allegations that the political opponent disseminated private information about the town selectman to any other person or member of the press after the original complaint had been filed.

SURVEY OF DELAWARE EMPLOYMENT LIBEL LAW

Peter L. Frattarelli
Archer & Greiner, P.C.
300 Delaware Avenue
Suite 1370
Wilmington, Del. 19801
Phone: (302) 777-4350; Facsimile: (302) 777-4352

(With Developments Reported Through **November 1, 2012**)

GENERAL COMMENTS

The law of defamation balances two competing societal interests in Delaware: protecting the individual's reputation, and encouraging free and open communication. Spence v. Funk, 396 A.2d 967, 969, 4 Media L. Rep. 1981 (Del. 1978). Delaware courts rely on the Restatement (Second) of Torts as an authoritative source on Delaware's law of defamation.

Citations to "Del." reference the Delaware Supreme Court, Delaware's highest court. Citations to "Del. Ch." references Delaware's trial court of equity. Citations to "Del. Super." reference Delaware's trial court of law.

SIGNIFICANT DEVELOPMENTS SINCE THE 2012 *SURVEY*

In Mimm v. Vanguard Dealer Services, L.L.C. et al, C.A. No. 11-736 GMS, 2012 U.S. Dist. LEXIS. 143936 (D. Del. Oct. 4, 2012), the federal court adopted the doctrine previously espoused by state courts that an employee's at will status does not, *per se*, preclude a claim of promissory estoppel. In that case, the employee advised a prospective employer that he was subject to a non-compete restriction from his then-current employer which that employer had indicated it would enforce, but the prospective employer verbally advised him it wished to hire him despite the non-compete. Despite his at will status, the promises combined with the reliance was sufficient to withstand a motion to dismiss the promissory estoppel claim.

I. GENERAL LAW

A. General Employment Law

1. ***At-Will Employment.*** "In determining the nature of an employment contract, Delaware law 'provides a heavy presumption that a contract for employment, unless otherwise expressly stated, is at-will in nature, with duration indefinite.'" Bloss v. Kershner, C.A. No. 93C-04-282-CHT, 2000 WL 303342, at *5 (Del. Super. Mar. 9, 2000) (citations omitted). An individual employed for an indefinite period of time is considered an at-will employee. Lankford v. Scala, C.A. No. 94C-04-023, 1995 WL 156220, at *2 (Del. Super. Feb. 28, 1995). At-will employees may be terminated at any time with or without cause in Delaware. E.I. DuPont de Nemours & Co. v. Pressman, 679 A.2d 436, 437 (Del. 1996).

The Supreme Court, however, has recognized one main exception to this general rule of termination without cause, specifically that every employment contract includes an implied covenant of good faith and fair dealing. Merrill v. Crothall-Am., Inc., 606 A.2d 96, 101 (Del. 1992). Under this implied covenant, if an employer acts in bad faith in the hiring or firing of an employee, he or she may be liable under a contract theory. Id. Nevertheless, the Delaware courts have narrowly interpreted the Merrill decision. The Delaware Supreme Court concluded that although it "recognize[s] an implied covenant of good faith and fair dealing as being part of employment contracts ... [s]uch a claim requires some aspect of fraud, deceit, or misrepresentation." Peterson v. Beebe Med. Ctr., Inc., C.A. No. 565, 1992, 1993 WL 102560, at *2 (Del. Mar. 24, 1993). In Merrill, the court held that a corporation that hired an employee knowing the employment to be temporary, but not disclosing that fact, violated an implied covenant of good faith when it terminated the employment without justification. Merrill v. Crothall-Am., Inc., 606 A.2d 96 (Del. 1992). The [employment-at-will] doctrine generally permits the dismissal of employees without cause and regardless of motive. Williams v. Cato Oil, Co., C.A. No. CPU5-09-001555, 2010 Del. C.P. LEXIS 42, at *10 (Del. Com. Pl. Sept. 7, 2010). The covenant [of good faith and fair dealing] permits a cause of action against an employer for the deceitful acts of its agent in manufacturing materially false grounds to cause an employee's dismissal. Id. Delaware case law demonstrates that the breach of the covenant of good faith and fair dealing can be claimed only when an employee has been fired or constructively discharged. Meltzer v. City of Wilmington, C.A. No. 07C-12-197, 2008 WL 4899230, at *2 (Del. Super. Aug. 6, 2008). Withholding or denying future promotions "is insufficient as a matter of law to support a claim for constructive discharge." Id.

2. ***Exceptions.*** The exceptions falling under the implied covenant of good faith provide an avenue for claims of wrongful discharge, but are limited to the following: (1) the termination violated public policy; (2) the employer misrepresented an important fact and the employee relied "thereon either to accept a new position or remain in a present one";

(3) the employer used its superior bargaining power to deprive an employee of clearly identifiable compensation related to the employee's past service; or (4) the employer falsified or manipulated a record to create fictitious grounds to terminate the employee. Lord v. Souder, 748 A.2d 393, 400 (Del. 2000) (citing E.I. DuPont de Nemours & Co. v. Pressman, 679 A.2d 436, 442-44 (Del. 1996)). See also Wharton v. Worldwide Dedicated Servs, C.A. No. 04C-02-035, 2007 WL 404770, at *6 (Del. Super. Feb. 2, 2007), reargument denied, 2007 WL 1653131 (Del. May 31, 2007). Courts have long recognized that an employer has wide latitude in terminating an at-will employee, and aside from these narrowly construed exceptions, the court will not disturb an employer's decision. Id. Additionally, plaintiffs cannot assert a common law claim for the breach of the implied covenant of good faith and fair dealing where the Delaware state statute, 19 Del. C. § 712(b), provides the exclusive remedy. Wilcoxon v. Red Clay Consol. Sch. Dist. Bd. of Educ., 437 F. Supp. 2d 235, 247 (D. Del. 2006).

Bad faith on the part of the employer can constitute an exception to the at-will doctrine. Bad faith has been defined as "not simply bad judgment or negligence, but rather it implies the conscious doing of a wrong because of dishonest purpose or moral obliquity; it is different from the negative idea of negligence in that it contemplates a state of mind affirmatively operating with furtive design or ill will." Cornely v. Hartco, Inc., C.A. No. 12817, 1994 WL 30520, at *3 (Del. Ch. Jan. 27, 1994). In Cornely, Vice Chancellor Chandler cited the New Hampshire case Monge v. Beebe Rubber Co., 316 A.2d 549, 551 (N.H. 1974), as an example of bad faith on the part of the employer where the employer terminated the plaintiff after she refused to date her foreman. See also Schuster v. Derocili, 775 A.2d 1029 (Del. 2001) (recognizing for first time that a person may assert a cause of action for breach of an implied covenant of good faith based upon a termination alleged to have resulted from a refusal to condone sexual advances). The Schuster decision is also important because it holds that an implied covenant of good faith claim exists when the employer deceitfully manufactures false grounds for termination. Id. at 1040. See also Miller v. Aramark Healthcare Support Servs., Inc., 555 F. Supp. 2d 463, 464, (D. Del. 2008) (holding that an action for a breach of good faith lies when the employer falsified records that led to the employee's dismissal).

Moreover, an employer cannot rely on the at-will doctrine as justification to discharge an employee for refusing to commit an illegal act. See Henze v. Alloy Surfaces Co., C.A. 91C-06-20, 1992 WL 51861 (Del. Super. Mar. 16, 1992) (holding that terminating employee for refusing to commit an illegal act is a violation of public policy). Further, despite the at will doctrine, an employer may bring a claim for promissory estoppel of the employee can show: (i) the making of a promise; (ii) with the intent to induce action or forbearance based on the promise; (iii) reasonable reliance; and (iv) injury. Lord v. Sauder, 748 A.2d 393 (Del. 2000). See also Scott-Douglas Corp. v. Greyhound Corp., 304 A.2d 309 (Del. Super. 1973); **Mimm v. Vanguard Dealer Services, L.L.C. et al, C.A. No. 11-736 GMS, 2012 U.S. Dist. LEXIS. 143936, *6 (D. Del. Oct. 4, 2012) at *6.**

Delaware has specific acts in various statutes that prohibit the employer from engaging in specific actions. First, by statute, an employer cannot force an employee to take a lie detector test as a condition of employment. 19 Del. C. § 704. Second, an employer cannot take any disciplinary action against employees who refuse to participate in abortions. 24 Del. C. § 1791. Third, employers cannot discharge an employee who is called for jury service. 10 Del. C. § 4515.

An employer's statements and conduct can alter the at-will status if such change is stated with a reasonable degree of specificity. Lord, 748 A.2d at 398. An employee's at-will status can be modified by either the promissory estoppel doctrine or contract. Bunting v. Citizens Fin. Group, Inc., No. 05C-03-013-ESB, 2006 WL 1067321, at *5 (Del. Super. Apr. 13, 2006).

B. Elements of Libel Claim

1. ***Basic Elements.*** The elements required to maintain an action for libel are: (1) a false statement, (2) which is defamatory, (3) which is of and concerning the plaintiff, (4) which was made in an unprivileged publication to a third party, and (5) the making of which was a consequence of fault amounting at least to negligence on the publisher's part. Durig v. Woodbridge Bd. of Educ., C.A. No. 90C-NO-22, 1992 WL 301983 (Del. Super. Oct. 9, 1992), aff'd, 622 A.2d 1095 (Del. 1993) (TABLE) (citing Gonzalez v. Avon Prods., Inc., 609 F. Supp. 1555, 1559 (D. Del. 1985)); Layfield v. Beebe Med. Ctr., Inc., C.A. No. 95C-12-007, 1997 WL 716900 (Del. Super. July 18, 1997). It is essential for the plaintiff to identify the defamatory communication, because otherwise "it is impossible to know whether the communication gives rise to a cause of action." Layfield, 1997 WL 716900, at *6 (citations omitted). In Bloss v. Kershner, the court laid out the elements of a claim for defamation, which include the following: (1) a defamatory communication; (2) publication; (3) that the communication refers to the plaintiff; (4) a third party's understanding of the communication's defamatory character; and (5) injury. Bloss v. Kershner, C.A. No. 93C-04-282, 2000 WL 303342, at *6 (Del. Super. Mar. 9, 2000). However, the scope of liability in Delaware for libel is broader than it is for slander. Spence v. Funk, 396 A.2d 967, 970, 4 Media L. Rep. 1981 (Del. 1978). Specifically, "while all slanderous statements would be libelous if written, not all libelous statements would be slanderous if spoken." Id.

2. ***Fault.*** The level of fault, if any, that must be shown depends on whether the plaintiff is a public or private figure and whether the nature of defendant's statement was public or private. Q-Tone Broad. Co. v. MusicRadio of Md. Inc., C.A. No. 93C-09-021, 24 Media L. Rep. 1929, 1995 WL 875438, at *4 (Del. Super. Dec. 22, 1995) (advancing the notion that a "public figure, as opposed to a private figure, must overcome heightened scrutiny by not only establishing the publication of a defamatory falsehood but also by establishing that the publisher acted with 'actual malice' – knowledge that the publication was false or with reckless disregard of whether the publication was false").

a. **Private Figure Plaintiff/Matter of Public Concern.** In Gannett Co. v. Re, 496 A.2d 553, 11 Media L. Rep. 2327 (Del. 1985), the Delaware Supreme Court addressed the constitutional limitations set forth by the United States Supreme Court. See, e.g., Hutchinson v. Proxmire, 443 U.S. 111, 5 Media L. Rep. 1279 (1979) (disallowing public expenditures from falling within the public controversy realm of understanding); Gertz v. Robert Welch, Inc., 418 U.S. 323, 1 Media L. Rep. 1633 (1974) (setting forth a distinction between a public and private figure); N.Y. Times Co. v. Sullivan, 376 U.S. 254, 1 Media L. Rep. 1527 (1964) (applying an actual malice standard to defamation claims). In Gannett, the plaintiff had developed an air-powered car which, after several unsuccessful trials, had ultimately succeeded in running for a short time. The defendant's publication stated, however, that the "car failed to start." Gannett, 496 A.2d at 556. The court held that the trial court had correctly applied a negligence standard in judging liability for defamation because the plaintiff was a private figure in regards to a matter of public concern. The court explained that the plaintiff had not thrust himself into a controversy that would have made him a public figure, but was involved in a matter of public interest, specifically energy conservation.

In Wilcoxon v. Red Clay Consol. Sch. Dist. Bd. of Education, 437 F. Supp. 2d 235, 244 (D. Del. 2006), the district court found that a record of a public school teacher's "dereliction of duty to her students and co-workers" constituted a matter of public concern and was protected speech under the First Amendment.

Speech directed to internal personnel and operational matters is not protected by the First Amendment. Johnson v. George, Jr., 2007 WL 1697276, at *6 (D. Del. June 12, 2007). In Johnson, the court determined that the employee's speech did not target matters of public concern because she was acting in her role as director and she spoke on certain issues as director of the campus. Id.

In Houllihan v. Sussex Technical School District, the court concluded that the employee failed to allege that her statements concerning noncompliance were made in her role as a citizen. 461 F. Supp. 2d 252, 260 (D. Del. 2006). Instead, the court was persuaded that the allegations in the employee's complaint and attached exhibits established the opposite, that the employee was speaking in connection with her official duties as school psychologist and/or special education coordinator. Id. at 261. "Indeed, some of [the employee's] concerns went to the very heart of the manner in which [the employee] carried out her job, and therefore, the Court concluded that [the employee] has not established that her speech was protected by the First Amendment." Id. at 260-61. Accordingly, the court dismissed the employee's First Amendment retaliation claim. Id.

In Yatzus v. Appoquinimink School District, the employee testified at her deposition that it was part of her job "to report what she perceived as illegal behavior" and to assist parents with complaints. Yatzus v. Appoquinimink School District, 458 F. Supp. 2d 235, 245 (D. Del. 2006). The employer argued that the employee was not acting as a citizen. Id. Rather, the employee's statements were not protected by the First Amendment because the employee's communications regarding the problems with the special education program and her assistance to parent's groups were part of her job responsibilities. Id. at 246. The court agreed and granted the employer's motion for summary judgment. Id. at 249.

For a private individual, the state may impose liability, though not a strict liability on a negligence, basis when the defamatory statement is on a subject of public interest. Q-Tone Broad. Co. v. MusicRadio of Md., Inc., C.A. No. 93C-09-021-WTQ, 24 Media L. Rep. 1929, 1995 WL 875438 (Del. Super. Dec. 22, 1995).

b. **Private Figure Plaintiff/Matter of Private Concern.** The Delaware Superior Court has held that a private figure plaintiff need only show fault on the part of the publisher and that the alleged libelous statements are defamatory when they do not involve a subject of public interest. Connolly v. Labowitz, 519 A.2d 138, 140 (Del. Super. 1986). In effect, the Superior Court has chosen a strict liability standard. Compare Connolly, 519 A.2d 138 with Q-Tone Broad. Co., 1995 WL 875438, supra, I.B.2.a. In Kanaga, the Delaware Supreme Court held that an opinion could also be actionable and would not be protected if it was directed toward a nonpublic figure. Kanaga v. Gannett Co., 687 A.2d 173, 181, 25 Media L. Rep. 1684 (Del. 1996). "The analysis in Kanaga does not apply to the disclosure resulting from criminal prosecutions which, by their nature, are public proceedings." Helman v. State, 784 A.2d 1058, 1071 (Del. 2001).

c. **Public Figure Plaintiff/Matter of Public Concern.** Delaware is bound by the Supreme Court's holding in N.Y. Times Co. v. Sullivan, 376 U.S. 254, 279-80, 1 Media L. Rep. 1527 (1964), and Gertz v. Robert

Welsh, Inc., 418 U.S. 323, 1 Media L. Rep. 1633 (1974). These cases held that the U.S. Constitution prohibits public officials and "public figures" from recovering from an admittedly defamatory statement unless that statement is both false and made with actual malice; that is, with knowledge that it was false or with reckless disregard of whether it was false or not. Ramada Inns, Inc. v. Dow Jones & Co., 543 A.2d 313, 319 (Del. Super. 1987) (citing Phila. Newspapers, Inc. v. Hepps, 475 U.S. 767, 12 Media L. Rep. 1977 (1986), and Gertz v. Robert Welch, Inc., 418 U.S. 323, 1 Media L. Rep. 1633 (1974)). The actual malice standard will apply when the plaintiffs are public figures. Id. Further, the Delaware Supreme Court has stated that actual malice means that the statement was published with the knowledge that it was false or with reckless disregard of whether it was false or not. Ross v. News-Journal Co., 228 A.2d 531, 532 (Del. 1967). The publisher must act with a high degree of awareness of the probable falsity of the statement. Q-Tone Broad. Co., 1995 WL 875438, at *4.

3. ***Falsity.*** Normally, Delaware courts adhere to the common law presumption that defamatory speech is false. Connolly, 519 A.2d at 140-41. However, a public figure plaintiff in a defamation action is constitutionally required to bear the burden of proving falsity. Ramada Inns, Inc., 543 A.2d at 318 (applying the decision of Phila. Newspapers, Inc. v. Hepps, 475 U.S. 767, 12 Media L. Rep. 1977 (1986)); Q-Tone Broad., 1995 WL 875438, at *4. Private figure plaintiffs do not have to prove this additional requirement. Connolly, 519 A.2d at 140-41. In Blake v. Minner, C.A. No. 07-230-JJF, 2007 WL 1307564, at *3 (D. Del. May 1, 2007), because there was no falsity of statement, the plaintiff's claims for defamation and slander failed. Therefore, the court dismissed the claims for failure to state a claim upon which relief may be granted. Id.

4. ***Defamatory Statement of Fact.*** Libel itself consists of a false and defamatory statement of fact concerning the plaintiff made in an unprivileged publication to a third party. Gonzalez v. Avon Prods., Inc., 609 F. Supp. 1555, 1558 (D. Del. 1985). Nevertheless, a statement is not defamatory unless it "tends so to harm the reputation of another as to lower him in the estimation of the community or to deter third persons from associating or dealing with him." Spence v. Funk, 396 A.2d 967, 969, 4 Media L. Rep. 1981 (Del. 1978) (citing Restatement (Second) of Torts § 559 (1977)). Additionally, a statement of fact is not libel if it is "substantially true." Gannett Co., 496 A.2d at 557. The courts will not find libel where the statement is no more damaging to the plaintiff's reputation in the mind of the average reader than a truthful statement would have been. Ramunno v. Cawley, 705 A.2d 1029, 26 Media L. Rep. 1651 (Del. 1998).

"It is generally true that courts are reluctant to impose liability for the expression of opinions." Ramunno, 705 A.2d at 1036 (citing Gertz v. Robert Welsh, Inc., 418 U.S. 323, 339, 1 Media L. Rep. 1633 (1974)). The Delaware Supreme Court has held that a speaker may not insulate himself or herself from liability simply by phrasing the defamatory statements as opinions or by imbedding statements so that a defamatory fact may be inferred. Ramunno, 705 A.2d at 1036. In determining whether a statement is one of fact or opinion, the four factors to consider are: (1) common usage, (2) objective verifiability, (3) context, and (4) social setting. Id.

5. ***Of and Concerning Plaintiff.*** It is not necessary that the individual defamed in writing be positively identified in the defamatory language itself. It may be shown by extrinsic evidence that the plaintiff was intended to be referred to by the writer and was understood to be referred to by the reader. Spence v. Funk, 396 A.2d 967, 972, 4 Media L. Rep. 1981 (Del. 1978); Klein v. Sunbeam Corp., 94 A.2d 385, 391 (Del. 1952), aff'd on reh'g, 95 A.2d 460 (Del. 1953). **The use of "John Doe," i.e., fictitious name, pleading when the alleged user of the defamatory language is unknown, is not permitted under Delaware law. Lorenzetti v. Hodges, C.A. No. S10C-07-007 RFS (Del. Super. Jan. 27, 2012) at *14-15.**

6. ***Publication.***

a. **Intracorporate Communication.** A supervisor's communication to other employees by spoken word and by written copy would be deemed publication. Cf. Bloss v. Kershner, C.A. No. 93C-04-282, 2000 WL 303342, at *6 (Del. Super. Mar. 9, 2000) (standing for the fact that the court may have let the libel case stand if the evidence demonstrated a communication to a third party); Gonzalez v. Avon Prods., Inc., 609 F. Supp. 1555 (D. Del. 1985). Statements that are made in evaluation reports are also considered publication. Durig v. Woodbridge Bd. of Educ., C.A. No. 90C-No-22, 1992 WL 301983 (Del. Super. Oct. 9, 1992), aff'd, 622 A.2d 1095 (Del. 1993) (TABLE).

However, statements made solely in the presence of the employee's supervisors are not considered publication. Schuster v. Derocili, 775 A.2d 1029 (Del. 2001). And because allegedly defamatory information (incorrect criminal history) contained in the plaintiff's personnel file was never published to a third party, summary judgment for the employer was proper. Bray v. L.D. Caulk Dentsply Int'l, 748 A.2d 406 (Del. 2000) (TABLE). Similarly, "the relaying of customer complaints to the individual about whom they are made is not publication." Laymon v. Lobby House, Inc., C.A. No. 07-129, 2008 WL 1733354, at *6 (D. Del. Apr. 14, 2008). As such, the employee's slander claim was properly dismissed on summary judgment. Id. See also Eaton v. Raven Transport, Inc., C.A. No. S08C-07-033-RFS, 2010 Del. Super. LEXIS 29 (Del. Super. Jan. 26, 2010) (employer's motion to dismiss employee's claims of character assassination, defamation of character and libel granted where employee failed to allege that employer made or published any defamatory statement about employee), employer's summary judgment granted in part, C.A. No. S08C-07-033 (RFS), 2010 Del. Super. LEXIS 487 (Del. Super. Nov. 15, 2010) (ruling that employer's oral statements were inadmissible hearsay and therefore could not support employee's *prima facie* case of slander).

Summary judgment was improper where a factual issue existed regarding whether a former director made statements for his own personal reasons or for the protection of the company, thereby entitling him to indemnity for costs of a defamation suit. See Westphal v. U. S. Eagle Corp., C.A. No. 18540-NC, 2002 WL 31820973 (Del. Ch. Nov. 27, 2002).

b. **Compelled Self-Publication.** Self-publication occurs when a plaintiff publishes an allegedly defamatory communication to a third party instead of the defendant publishing it to a third party. Harrison v. Hodgson Vocational Technical High School, C.A. No. 07C-06-301, 2007 WL 3112479, at *2 (Del. Super. Oct. 3, 2007). In 1992, the Delaware Superior Court rejected compelled self-publication as a method to satisfy the *prima facie* publication requirement under Delaware law. Lynch v. Mellon Bank, C.A. No. 90C-JA-125, 1992 WL 51880, at *3 (Del. Super. Mar. 12, 1992). Specifically, the Lynch court held that "[a]lthough the concept of self-publication has been accepted in a minority of other jurisdictions, it is not the law in Delaware." Id.; see also Bickling v. Kent Gen. Hosp., Inc., 872 F. Supp. 1299, 1310 (D. Del. 1994) (deciding that it need not predict whether the Supreme Court of Delaware would recognize compelled self-publication as the law of Delaware because defendant's qualified privilege would apply regardless).

c. **Republication.** The Delaware Supreme Court has stated, in dictum, that absent a privilege "the publisher and republisher of defamatory matter are strictly accountable and liable in damages to the person defamed, and neither good faith nor honest mistake constitutes a defense, serving only to mitigate damages." Short v. News-Journal Co., 212 A.2d 718, 719 (Del. 1965). But see Ramada Inns, Inc., 543 A.2d at 318 (asserting that republication is not libel if references to prior libelous material are minimal and do nothing more than provide a context for the new material). In Short, the defendant was absolved of liability because of an applicable privilege. Id. No other Delaware case addresses republication.

7. ***Statements versus Conduct.*** No Delaware court has decided whether conduct can be defamatory. But the Delaware Superior Court discussed, without deciding, whether publications can consist solely of acts or gestures. See O'Neill v. White, C.A. No. 82C-AP-31, 1987 WL 17680 (Del. Super. Sept. 28, 1987). The O'Neill court did not reach a decision on whether it is the law of Delaware because the court was satisfied that any communications inherent in the defendant's actions were well within the employer's privilege. Id. at *3. The plaintiff had alleged a claim of slander against the employer for unreasonably searching her bags by arguing that the defendant's actions communicated to all store employees that the store believed she was a thief. Id.

8. ***Damages.*** It is the law of Delaware that damages proximately caused by a publication deemed to be libelous need not be proved in order to recover nominal or compensatory damages, at least as to private figure plaintiffs. Kanaga v. Gannett Co., 687 A.2d 173, 182-83, 25 Media L. Rep. 1684 (Del. 1996). See also Davis v. W. Ctr. City Neighborhood Planning Advisory Comm., Inc., C.A. No. 02C-03-249-JEB, 2003 WL 908885, at *4 (Del. Super. Mar. 7, 2003) (holding that libel is actionable without special damages, whether the defamatory nature is apparent on the face of the statement or only by reference to extrinsic facts).

a. **Presumed Damages and Libel Per Se.** The alleged defamatory statements must "1) malign one in a trade, business, or profession; 2) impute a crime; 3) imply that one has a loathsome disease; or 4) impute unchastity to a woman" to be actionable without proof of special damages. Battista v. Chrysler Corp., 454 A.2d 286, 290 (Del. Super. 1982). See also Durig v. Woodbridge Bd. of Educ., C.A. No. 90C-NO-22, 1992 WL 301983, at *6 (Del. Super. Oct. 9, 1992), aff'd, 622 A.2d 1095 (Del. 1993) (TABLE). In Delaware, libel per se and libel per quod (established through extrinsic evidence) are actionable without alleging special damages. Edwards v. Lutheran Soc. Serv. of Dover, Inc., C.A. No. 83C-JN-22, 1987 WL 10271, at *4 (Del. Super. Apr. 8, 1987) (citing Spence v. Funk, 396 A. 2d 967, 971, 4 Media L. Rep. 1981 (Del. 1978)). But Delaware still follows the general rule that oral defamation – slander – is not actionable without allegation of special damages. Spence, 396 A.2d at 970. Slander per se, however, does not require proof of special damages. Id.

The plaintiff needs to show actual injuries absent a showing of knowledge of falsity or reckless disregard for the truth, but injury is not limited to out-of-pocket loss. Gannett Co., Inc. v. Kanaga, 750 A.2d 1174, 1183, 29 Media L. Rep. 1697 (Del. 2000) (citing Gertz and Dun & Bradstreet in support).

(1) **Employment-Related Criticism.** Delaware recognizes that there are four categories of defamation that are actionable per se without proof of special damages, specifically including statements that malign one in a trade, business or profession. Spence, 396 A.2d at 970. A memorandum by a supervisor that described the

plaintiff as uncooperative and stated that his work needed to be repeated and that he engaged in unsafe work practices would normally be actionable per se since it maligns the plaintiff in his trade. Stafford v. Air Prods. & Chems., Inc., C.A. No. 84C-JL-85, 1985 WL 189259, at *2 (Del. Super. Sept. 5, 1985). However, in the employment setting, Delaware courts recognize certain qualified or conditional privileges that insulate an employer from liability for those communications made between persons who share a common interest. Id. See infra II.

In Kelly v. Blum, the defendant made allegedly slanderous statements about the plaintiff's work and performance, which the plaintiff alleged maligned him in his business and profession. C.A. No. 456-VCP, 2010 Del. Ch. LEXIS 31, at *69 (Del. Ch. Feb. 24, 2010). In his motion to dismiss, the defendant argued that the plaintiff failed to state a claim for defamation because making "statements which are critical of an employee's job performance and are uncomplimentary in nature are not defamatory." Id. Assuming the accuracy of the allegations and drawing all inferences in the plaintiff's favor, the court denied the defendant's motion to dismiss, holding that the defendant made factual statements, or statements of opinion, relying on a strong factual predicate, defaming the plaintiff. Id. at *71.

An employer is only liable for defamatory statements of its employees if such statements were made within the scope of employment. Subh v. Wal-Mart Stores Inc., C.A. No. 08-410-SLR-LPS, 2009 U.S. Dist. LEXIS 108565, at *34 (D. Del. Nov. 19, 2009), aff'd, 2010 U.S. App. LEXIS 13903 (3d Cir. July 8, 2010).

In Tani v. FPL/NextEraEnergy, an employee filed a defamation/libel claim against his former employer alleging that the employer placed him on a "critical group list" or, in other words, a "watch list" as a means of blacklisting him. C.A. No. 10-860-LPS, 2011 U.S. Dist. LEXIS 105206, at *44 (D. Del. Sept. 16, 2011). The court granted the employer's motion to dismiss the defamation/libel claim because it was "far from clear" that the statement was defamatory. Id. at *46. In addition, the complaint did not identify the person or entity who allegedly defamed the employee, that the email communication referred to the employee, that the publisher understood that the communication was defamatory, or that the employee sustained an injury. Id. Even if the statement could be considered defamatory, the court held that the complaint did not identify the third parties to whom the email was published. Id.

(2) **Single Instance Rule.** Under Delaware law, a single instance of irresponsible failure to heed an employer's instructions will not constitute just cause for termination where the employer has tolerated previous misconduct of a similar severity without warning. Morris v. Southern Metals Processing Co., 1987 WL 37999, at *1 (Del. July 2, 1987).

b. **Punitive Damages.** The Delaware Supreme Court has held that in order to recover punitive damages in an action for libel, a private figure must show that the defendant acted with reckless disregard for the truth of the published statements or with knowledge that the published statements were false. Kanaga v. Gannett Co., 687 A.2d 173, 183, 25 Media L. Rep. 1684 (Del. 1996). Of course, public figures must still show actual malice. Ramada Inns, Inc. v. Dow Jones & Co., 543 A.2d 313, 319 (Del. Super. 1987) (citing Gertz v. Robert Welch, Inc., 418 U.S. 323, 342, 1 Media L. Rep. 1633 (1974)). The element of malice must be proven with convincing clarity. Id. (citing N.Y. Times v. Sullivan, 376 U.S. 254, 185, 1 Media L. Rep. 1527 (1964)).

II. PRIVILEGES AND DEFENSES

A. Scope of Privileges

1. ***Absolute Privilege.*** Delaware limits the absolute privilege to legislative and judicial proceedings. Barker v. Huang, 610 A.2d 1341 (Del. 1992). In Delaware, the absolute privilege is not confined to events occurring inside a courtroom, but extends to all communications relating to the litigation, including communications with witnesses and the drafting and filing of pleadings. Bove v. Goldenberg, C.A. No. 05C-10-134 (CHT), 2007 WL 446014, at *2 (Del. Super. Feb. 7, 2007). The well-recognized policy supporting the absolute privilege of facilitating the flow of communication between persons involved in judicial proceedings must be balanced against another important interest, namely, a person's right to be free from defamatory statements. Paige Capital Management, LLC v. Lerner Master Fund, LLC, C.A. No. 5502-VCS, 22 A.3d 710, 716 (Del. Ch. 2011). In Nelson v. Kamara, C.A. No. 08C-07-058-MMJ, 2009 WL 1964788, at *3 (Del. Super. June 30, 2009), the court declined to determine whether or not the witness's statements to the attorney general's office and police were substantially true because they were protected by the absolute privilege. The privilege typically operates to bar any cause of action against a witness for defamation or disparagement for statements made in a judicial proceeding, upon a showing that: (1) the statements issued were part of a judicial proceeding; and (2) the statements were relevant to a matter at issue in the case. Hughes v. Kelly, C.A. No. 4814-VCN, 2010 Del. Ch. LEXIS 152, at *25 (Del. Ch. June 30, 2010). The absolute privilege did not apply to statements made by the defendant during judicial proceedings in Rader v. ShareBuilder Corp. because the plaintiff's claims involved conspiracy to defraud, blackmail, extortion and constitutional violations rather than a claim for defamation. C.A. No. 10-398-LPS, 772 F. Supp. 2d 599, 605 (D. Del. 2011). According to the court, the

absolute privilege provides a basis for dismissal in actions involving defamation and any other action involving a false statement. Id. Article II, § 13 of the Delaware Constitution provides that for any speech or debate in either House, members of the General Assembly shall not be questioned in any other place. This is the only absolute privilege given by Delaware law to legislative proceedings, and it does not apply to other legislative bodies of the state, such as members of the Wilmington City Council. McClendon v. Coverdale, 203 A.2d 815 (Del. Super. 1964).

2. ***Qualified Privileges.***

a. **Common Interest.** There is a qualified privilege for communications made between persons who have a common interest for the protection of which such statements were made. Pierce v. Burns, 185 A.2d 477, 479 (Del. 1962). The Delaware courts have specifically adopted Section 596 of the Restatement (Second) of Torts, which states that "[a]n occasion makes a publication conditionally privileged if the circumstances lead any one of several persons having a common interest in a particular subject matter correctly or reasonably to believe that there is information that another sharing the common interests is entitled to know." O'Neill v. White, C.A. No. 82C-AP-31, 1987 WL 17680, at *3 (Del. Super. Sept. 28, 1987) (citing Gonzalez v. Avon Prods., Inc., 609 F. Supp. 1555, 1559 (D. Del. 1985)). "This [common interest] qualified privilege is particularly germane to the employer-employee relationship...." Battista v. Chrysler Corp., 454 A.2d 286, 291, (Del. Super. 1982). For example, in Simpler v. El Paso Polyolefins Co., C.A. No. 83C-JL-18, 1986 WL 4575 (Del. Super. Apr. 3, 1986), the privilege was applied to a communication to an employer regarding the conduct of an employee in relation to a customer. Another example of when the privilege applies is a statement made by a plant manager to plant employees that the plaintiffs were terminated for theft of plant property. Gonzalez v. Avon Prods., Inc., 609 F. Supp. 1555 (D. Del. 1985). The privilege was also applied to statements made by a plant supervisor that the plaintiff was demoted because he could not adequately perform his job. Battista, 454 A.2d 286. Similarly, this qualified privilege reaches co-employees when the allegedly defamatory statements relate to the plaintiff's ability to perform his or her job. Miller v. Aramark Healthcare Support Servs., 555 F. Supp. 2d 463, 474 (D. Del. 2008). In Miller, the employee remarked to the plaintiff that he performed like a technician with five years of experience, rather than twenty-five years. Miller, 555 F. Supp. 2d 474. Because the allegedly defamatory statements related to plaintiff's ability to perform his job, the statements fell within the privilege. Id. Conditional/qualified privilege can be raised as an affirmative defense to a defamation action. Gilliland v. St. Joseph's at Providence Creek, C.A. No. 04C-09-042, 2006 WL 258259, at *9 (Del. Super. Jan. 27, 2006). Conditional privilege has been held as a matter of law to include the publication of letters to the board of directors of a not-for-profit Delaware corporation when it pertained to the conduct of a board member. Id. There exists a qualified privilege for co-employees when statements relate to an employee's ability to perform his job. Hansen v. E.I. du Pont de Nemours & Co., C.A. No. 09-266 (LPS-MPT), 2011 U.S. Dist. LEXIS 12531, at *18 (D. Del. Feb. 9, 2011). Purported defamatory statements by coworkers that relate to an employee's conduct and attitude in the workplace are statements of opinion, not fact, that fall within the privilege. Id.

If the defamatory statement is made in the course of the defamed party's employment and on behalf of the employer, it is a privileged statement and the defendant is presumed not liable. Meades v. Wilmington Housing Authority, C.A. No. 03C-05-013 WCC, 2006 WL 1174005, at *2 (Del. Super. Apr. 28, 2006), aff'd, 918 A.2d 339 (Del. 2006) (TABLE). Thus, a conditional privilege exists that protects the employer if the statements were made in the context of the employee's ability to perform his job. Id.; see also Miller v. Aramark Healthcare Support Servs., 555 F. Supp. 2d 463, (D. Del. 2008). "This qualified privilege is particularly germane to the employer-employee relationship and had been recognized as such by the Delaware Supreme Court." Battista v. Chrysler Corp., 454 A.2d 286, 291 (Del. Super. 1982).

In sum, under the law of defamation, liability does not attach to a defamatory statement if the statement is privileged. Henry v. Del. Law Sch. of Widener Univ., Inc., C.A. No. 8837, 1998 WL 15897, at *9 (Del. Ch. Jan. 12, 1998), aff'd, 718 A.2d 527 (Del. 1998) (TABLE). A qualified privilege will extend to communications made between persons who have a common interest for the protection of which the alleged defamatory statements were made. Pierce, 185 A.2d at 479 (citing Restatement (Second) of Torts, § 593). Further, the qualified privilege protects statements disclosed to any person who has a legitimate expectation in the subject matter. Burr v. Atl. Aviation Corp., 332 A.2d 154, 155 (Del. Super. 1974), rev'd on other grounds, 348 A.2d 179 (Del. 1975). See also Stiner v. University of Delaware, 243 F. Supp. 2d 106 (D. Del. 2003) (finding qualified privilege where statement made to university accreditation board for purposes of accreditation).

b. **Duty.** Delaware's peer review statute, 24 Del. C. § 1768, titled "Immunity of Boards of Review, Confidentiality of Review Board Records," provides qualified immunity for peer review committee members whose function is to review records and medical care for quality assurances. Lipson v. Anesthesia Services, P.A., 790 A.2d 1261 (Del. Super. 2001) (statute can be utilized by private practitioners to extent complying with spirit of law).

The release to the full board of a community agency of a board member's allegedly harassing note to an employee was protected by a qualified privilege, and the letter in which it was enclosed was protected by the absolute defense of truth. See Davis v. W. Ctr. City Neighborhood Planning Advisory Comm., Inc., CA. No. 02C-03-249-JEB, 2003 WL 908885, at *4 (Del. Super. Mar. 7, 2003). Documents that had been used by or published to any person outside the peer review credentialing committee were not subject to the protections of 24 Del. C. § 1768(b) and were discoverable. Cain v. Villare, No. 04C-01-179-JRJ, 2005 WL 2710854, at *2 (Del. Super. Oct. 19, 2005).

c. **Criticism of Public Employee.** Citizens enjoy a qualified privilege to make complaints about government employees. In Jackson v. Filliben, 281 A.2d 604 (Del. 1971), a citizen complained of police brutality to the police officer's supervisor in writing. The court held that police officers must be considered public officials. Id. "Under settled law, a public officer may not recover for defamatory statements relating to his official conduct unless he proves that the statement was made with actual malice, that is, with knowledge that the statement was false or with reckless disregard of whether it was false or not." Id. at 605 (citing Ross v. News-Journal Co., 228 A.2d 531 (Del. 1967)). In Jackson, the court held that the statement was based in truth and therefore its publication was insufficient to establish malice. Id.

Government officials acting in capacity maintain immunity generally from defamation claims. Davis v. Town of Georgetown, C.A. No. 99C-04-006, 2001 WL985098, at *1 (Del. Super. Aug. 22, 2001) (police officer's defamation claim against his employer was barred by governmental immunity). **While such individuals may still be sued in an individual capacity, such an immunity exception will not apply to most defamation claims because only emotional distress and not bodily injury is present, and bodily injury is a requirement for this personal liability-immunity exception. Dickerson et al v. Phillips et al., C.A. No. N10C-08-221 PLA (Del. Super. June 13, 2012) at *5-6.**

d. **Limitation on Qualified Privileges.** Qualified privileges must be exercised with good faith, without malice, and absent any knowledge of falsity or desire to cause harm. Battista, 454 A.2d at 291; Burr, 348 A.2d at 181. The qualified privilege can be lost by (1) excessive or improper publication; (2) the use of the occasion not embraced within the privilege; (3) the making of the statement which the speaker knows as false; (4) expressed malice; (5) any desire to cause harm; or (6) bad faith in the exercise of the privilege. Gonzalez, 609 F. Supp. 1559 (citations omitted); Battista, 454 A.2d at 291; Layfield v. Beebe Med. Ctr., Inc., C.A. No. 95C-12-007, 1997 WL 716900 (Del. Super. July 18, 1997) (plaintiff must show that defendant knew the matter to be false or that defendant acted in reckless disregard as to the truth or falsity of the statement). The different ways to abuse the privilege are closely related and involve some inquiry into the mind of the publisher. Id. The question of whether a conditional privilege has been abused by malice or intent to harm is ordinarily a factual question for the jury. Battista, 454 A.2d at 291. The court in Wooleyhan v. Cape Henlopen School District held that the school administrator's attempt to invoke conditional privileges for her allegedly defamatory remarks failed because the conditional privilege could be lost if the jury determined that the privilege was abused by making a statement that the administrator knew was false. C.A. No. 10-153, 2011 U.S. Dist. LEXIS 102904, at * 26 (D. Del. Sept. 12, 2011). This privilege carries a rebuttable presumption of good faith. Eaton v. Miller Brewing Co., C.A. No. 507C-08 033 RFS, 2009 WL 1277991, at *3 (Del. Super. April 30, 2009). In addition, "the affirmative defense of conditional privilege may not be considered in the context of a motion to dismiss pursuant to Rule 12(b)(6)." Meades v. Wilmington Hous. Auth., No. 3762004, 2005 WL 1131112, at *2 (Del. May 12, 2005).

(1) **Constitutional or Actual Malice.** In Sheeran v. Colpo, the Delaware Supreme Court explained that actual malice is to make a statement with a deliberate intention to falsify or with reckless disregard for its truth or falsity. Sheeran v. Colpo, 460 A.2d 522, 524 (Del. 1983) (citing Old Dominion Branch No. 496, Nat'l Ass'n of Letter Carriers v. Austin, 418 U.S. 264 (1974)); see also Q-Tone Broad. Co. v. MusicRadio of Md., Inc., C.A. No. 93C-09-021-WTQ, 24 Media L. Rep. 1929, 1995 WL 875438, at *4 (Del. Dec. 22, 1995) (holding that actual malice is a high degree of awareness of the probable falsity). The actual malice standard will apply when the plaintiffs are public figures even if the speech at issue is commercial. Q-Tone Broad. Co., 1995 WL 875438. Evidence of malice can be presented through incident of excessive or improper publication or making statements known to be false. See Lipson v. Anesthesia Servs., P.A., 790 A.2d 1261, 1283 (Del. Super. Oct. 3, 2001). However, a public figure plaintiff does not have to produce evidence of actual malice to "satisfy a 'summary judgment' standard before obtaining the identity of an anonymous defendant" through discovery. Doe v. Cahill, 884 A.2d 451, 457, 464 (Del. 2005).

(2) **Common Law Malice.** In distinguishing the term "actual malice" from the legal concept of malice, the Delaware Superior Court has only offered a brief, indirect explanation based on a New Jersey ruling. Battista v. Chrysler Corp., 454 A.2d 286, 291 (Del. Super. 1982) (citing Coleman v. Newark Morning Ledger Co., 149 A.2d 193 (N.J. 1959)). The Coleman court noted that while something less than spite, ill will or desire to do harm may satisfy actual malice, a qualified privilege, once established by the occasion and proper purpose, is not forfeited by the mere addition of the fact that a defendant feels indignation and resentment towards the plaintiff and enjoys making such statements. Battista, 454 A.2d at 291 (citing Coleman v. Newark Morning Ledger Co., 149 A.2d 193, 202 (N.J. 1959)). When the occasion gives rise to a qualified privilege in a defamation context, there is a *prima facie* presumption to rebut the inference of malice, and the burden is on a plaintiff to show actual malice or that the scope of the privilege has been exceeded. Hampshire Group, Ltd. v. Kuttner, C.A. No. 3607-VCS, 2010 Del. Ch. LEXIS 144, at *185 (Del. Ch. July 12, 2010). In

Hampshire Group, Ltd., the Delaware Chancery Court clarified that malice is proven by showing that the defendant was motivated by ill will seeking to injure the plaintiff, or that the defendant acted in reckless disregard of the plaintiff's rights. Id.

f. **Question of Fact or Law.** Under Delaware law, the existence of a qualified privilege in a given set of circumstances is a matter to be determined by the court. Pierce v. Burns, 185 A.2d 477, 480 (Del. 1962). Nevertheless, Delaware has traditionally reserved the question of abuse of a qualified privilege for jury consideration. Battista, 454 A.2d at 291; Pierce, 185 A.2d at 480. "In the context of a motion to dismiss a libel suit, it is for the court to determine as a matter of law whether the allegedly defamatory statements are protected expressions of opinion, and whether statements of fact are susceptible of a defamatory meaning." Ramunno v. Crawley, 705 A.2d 1029, 1035 n.14, 26 Media L. Rep. 1651 (Del. 1998). Whether a statement is defamatory is a question for the court. Lucent Info. Mgmt., Inc. v. Lucent Tech., Inc., 5 F. Supp. 2d 238, 243 (D. Del. 1998).

Before a Delaware court reaches the question of actual malice in a libel action, it must determine two questions of law: (1) whether alleged defamatory statements are expressions of fact or protected expressions of opinion, and (2) whether challenged statements are capable of a defamatory meaning. Riley v. Moyed, 529 A.2d 248, 251, 14 Media L. Rep. 1379 (Del. 1987). Because the court determines these questions of law, the summary judgment procedure is often applied in this area of the law to avoid unnecessary legal fees and discourage frivolous suits. Id. at n.2.

g. **Burden of Proof.** A finding of a conditional privilege conditionally negates the presumption of malice and shifts the burden to the plaintiff to show actual malice. Battista, 454 A.2d at 290-91 & n.6. Conditional privileges are raised as affirmative defenses. Id. Absent a finding of express malice, the privilege, if not abused, defeats the action. Id. The question of whether a conditional privilege has been abused by malice or intent to harm is ordinarily a factual question for the jury. Id. (citing Pierce v. Burns, 185 A.2d 477 (Del. 1962)).

B. Standard Libel Defenses

1. ***Truth***. The Delaware Supreme Court has stated: "It is hornbook law that truth is an absolute defense to a defamation action." DeBonaventura v. Nationwide Mut. Ins. Co., 428 A.2d 1151, 1155 (Del. 1981). Sometimes a challenged writing may not be true in all respects. In that case, the writing is not libelous if either: (1) the plaintiff is "libel-proof," i.e., the portion of the article containing the alleged libel cannot be said to have damaged the plaintiff's reputation beyond the harm inflicted by the truthful portions of the remainder of the article; or (2) the writing is "substantially true," i.e., the alleged libel was no more damaging to the plaintiff's reputation in the mind of the average reader than a truthful statement would have been. Riley, 529 A.2d at 253. In making this evaluation of whether a statement is substantially true, the court will consider the "gist" or "sting" to determine "if it produces the same effect on the mind of the recipient which the precise truth would have produced." Id. at 253-54 (citations omitted). See also Nelson v. Kamara, C.A. No. 08C-07-058-MMJ, 2009 WL 1964788, at *3 (Del. Super. June 30, 2009) (holding that the "gist" of the letter dealt with the plaintiff's refusal to pay back money owed, which was substantially true and therefore not defamatory); Helman v. State, 784 A.2d 1058, 1071 (Del. 2001) (convicted sex offender's constitutionally grounded ability to seek redress from libel or defamation does not extend to truthful, public information disseminated by the state pursuant to sex offender registration and notification statute).

In Subh v. Wal-Mart Stores, Inc., the employee accused his former supervisor and his former employer of falsely and maliciously accusing him of a crime. C.A. No. 08-410-SLR-LPS, 2009 U.S. Dist. LEXIS 108565, at *34 (D. Del. Nov. 19, 2009), aff'd, 2010 U.S. App. LEXIS 13903 (3d Cir. July 8, 2010). The court granted the employer's motion for summary judgment because the employee pled "no contest" to a crime and the statements made by the employee's supervisor were substantially true. Id. at *35.

2. ***Opinion.*** Pure expressions of opinion are protected under the First Amendment. Riley, 529 A.2d at 251 (citing Gertz v. Robert Welch, Inc., 418 U.S. 323, 1 Media L. Rep. 1633 (1974)). A pure opinion is one based on stated facts or facts that the parties know or assume. Id.

Whether a statement constitutes a statement of fact or an expression of opinion is a question of law for the court to determine, not a question for the jury. Riley v. Moyed, 529 A.2d 248, 251, 14 Media L. Rep. 1379 (Del. 1987). In determining whether a statement is one of fact or opinion, four factors to consider are: (1) common usage, (2) objective verifiability, (3) context, and (4) social setting. Ramunno v. Cawley, 705 A.2d 1029, 1036, 26 Media L. Rep. 1651 (Del. 1998) But see Gannett Co., Inc. v. Kanaga, 750 A.2d 1174, 29 Media L. Rep. 1697 (Del. 2000) (appears to overrule Riley, but never discusses other prior cases that held it to be a question for court to decide).

In Kanaga v. Gannett Co, 687 A.2d 173, 177, 25 Media L. Rep. 1684 (Del. 1996), the Delaware Supreme Court recognized the Milkovich standard and adopted it as a standard for Delaware law. See also Milkovich v. Lorain Journal Co., 497 U.S. 1, 17 Media L. Rep. 2009 (1990). Thus, where an article contained the implied fact that a surgeon recommended an unnecessary hysterectomy for her own pecuniary gain, a jury could reasonably find that the article contained a false assertion of fact, even though the article was couched as an opinion. Kanaga, 687 A.2d at 179. To receive protection as opinion, it must be clear to the average reader that he or she is being offered conjecture, not solid information. Id. at 180. If the average reader could infer the existence of undisclosed facts, then the issue must be presented to a jury to decide whether or not they are being offered pure conjecture. Id. at 181; see also Ramunno v. Cawley, 705 A.2d 1029.

In Jacques-Scott v. Sears Holdings Corp., a former employee filed suit against her employer alleging that her character was defamed by her coworkers, in addition to claims of discrimination and hostile work environment. C.A. No. 10-422-LPS-MPT, 2011 U.S. Dist. LEXIS 29149, at *25 (D. Del. Mar. 22, 2011). In support of her defamation claim, the employee asserted that she was called a "noisey nip picking bitch and typical New York bitch" and was subject to comments like "I just don't like the bitch." Id. at *26. The court held that the employee's allegations did not constitute defamation because they merely showed opinions and dislike of the employee. Therefore, her allegations were insufficient to support a defamation claim. Id.

3. ***Consent.*** Consent can be an absolute defense to defamation. Edwards v. Lutheran Soc. Servs. of Dover, Inc., C.A. No. 83C-JN-22, 1987 WL 10271 (Del. Super. Apr. 8, 1987) (citing W. Keeton, Prosser and Keeton on Torts, § 114 (5th ed. 1984). However, "at the same time, of course, it is not every request to speak which manifests consent to slander.... As in other cases of consent, the privilege is limited by the scope of the assent apparently given and consent to one form of publication does not confer a license to publish to other persons, or in a different manner." Id. at *4.

4. ***Mitigation.*** Good faith or honest mistakes are not defenses, but serve to mitigate damages. Short v. News-Journal Co., 212 A.2d 718, 719 (Del. 1965).

III. RECURRING FACT PATTERNS

A. Statements in Personnel File

The only case dealing with particular information within a personnel file in connection with defamation in Delaware appears to be Bray v. L.D. Caulk Dentsply Int'l., 748 A.2d 406 (Del. 2000) (TABLE). In Bray, the plaintiff filed a defamation claim based on her personnel file containing false information regarding her criminal history. The defendant's motion to dismiss was granted due to the fact that the only individuals to whom this information was published were officers and managers of the defendant company, all of whom had a qualified privilege to the information. Id.

B. Performance Evaluations

Most statements made in the context of a performance evaluation do not rise to the level of being defamatory. For example, in Andres v. Williams, 405 A.2d 121, 122 (Del. 1979), statements were made that a sportscaster and statistician employed by a college did not work well within the supervisory structure, made excessive telephone calls, did not attend sporting events, had a conflict of interest because of his work for a newspaper, and did not deal well with students and coaches. The court held that these statements were not defamatory because they did not tend to lower the person in the estimation of the relevant community. Id.

The court reached a similar conclusion in Durig v. Woodbridge Bd. of Educ., C.A. No. 90C-NO-22, 1992 WL 301983, at *1 (Del. Super. Oct. 9, 1992). In Durig, the court found that disparaging statements made on the plaintiff's evaluation report, criticizing his performance as a school administrator, did not rise to a level that would lower the plaintiff in the opinion of the community or discourage third persons from associating with him. Id. at *6.

In the context of employee evaluations, the employer must be careful to make sure that the information transmitted is accurate, that the evaluator has no knowledge that the information is in fact false, and, most importantly, that the evaluation information is not transmitted outside the employment context to others who have no need for it. Id. at *7. If the evaluator acts with bad faith or with malice, the employer will lose the benefit of the privilege, subjecting the employer to the possibility of liability if the statements are subsequently found to be defamatory. Id.

If the evaluator includes statements of opinion, such as the individual manager's view as to the employee's style, work habits and interpersonal skills, those opinions are not defamatory. Id. at *6. However, if the evaluator's opinion is based on false facts that are defamatory, then the opinion may not be protected. See, e.g., Schuster v. Derocili, 775 A.2d 1029, 1040 (Del. 2001) (claim of breach of implied duty of good faith can exist where employer intentionally creates fictitious grounds for discipline or termination). A supervisor at the state department of corrections (DOC) was not entitled to qualified immunity for his alleged conduct of giving an employee a mediocre performance evaluation that included false criticism because of the employee's support for his labor union, a protected activity. Balas v. Taylor, 567 F. Supp. 2d 654, 665 (D. Del. 2008).

In Stafford v. Air Prods. & Chems., Inc., C.A. No. 84C-JL-85, 1985 WL 189259 (Del. Super. Sept. 5, 1985), the plaintiff made several unsuccessful demands to have alleged defamatory memoranda removed from his personnel file. These memoranda were job evaluations of the plaintiff. The comments in the job evaluations referred to the plaintiff's work habits and ability to interact harmoniously with other employees. Accordingly, the court held that they were proper subjects to come within the ambit of an employer's qualified privilege. Id. at *4. Moreover, the plaintiff believed that because his employer disliked him and the job evaluations reflected negatively upon him, that they therefore must have been defamatory. Id. Even assuming that an employer does not like a particular employee, malice is still required to lose the qualified privilege since publication is made for a proper purpose. Id. The presence of critical, disparaging statements and the fact that they may have been inspired in part by resentment or dislike does not constitute abuse of a qualified privilege. Battista v. Chrysler Corp., 454 A.2d 286, 291 (Del. Super. 1982).

C. References

"An employer or any person employed by the employer who discloses information about a current or former employee's job performance to a prospective employer is presumed to be acting in good faith; and unless lack of good faith is shown, is immune from civil liability for such disclosure or its consequences. For purposes of this section, the presumption of good faith may be rebutted upon a showing that the information disclosed by such employer was knowingly false, was deliberately misleading or was rendered with malicious purpose; or that the information was disclosed in violation of a nondisclosure agreement, or was otherwise confidential according to applicable federal, State or local statute, rule or regulation." 19 Del. C. § 709(a).

In Bickling v. Kent Gen. Hosp., Inc., 872 F. Supp. 1299 (D. Del. 1994), the district court held that statements of one hospital president to another hospital president concerning the plaintiff, who was the former vice president of the first hospital, were not defamatory because the statements would not lower the plaintiff in the estimation of the community or deter third persons from associating or dealing with him. The defendant had stated that the plaintiff had tried to usurp the defendant's position. Id. at 1308; see also Henry v. Del. Law Sch. of Widener Univ., Inc., C.A. No. 8837, 1998 WL 15897 (Del. Ch. Jan. 12, 1998), aff'd, 718 A.2d 527 (Del. 1998) (TABLE) (nonpositive statements by tenure committee not found to be defamatory).

D. Intracorporate Communication

A former sports writer at a state college sued the president of the college and its director of athletics for slander and libel. The Delaware Supreme Court held that the plaintiff was not defamed by remarks of the athletic director before the athletic council when he stated that the plaintiff did not "work within the supervisor's structure," because the statements did not lower the plaintiff in the estimation of the community or deter third persons from associating with him. Andres v. Williams, 405 A.2d 121, 122 (Del. 1979); See also Petrocelli v. Daimler Chrysler Corp., No. 04-943-KAJ, 2006 WL 733567, at *8 (D. Del. Mar. 22, 2006) (finding qualified privilege because statements accusing employee of theft were made in furtherance of the common interest); Meades v. Wilmington Hous. Auth., No. 03C-05-013 WCC, 2006 WL 1174005, at *2 (Del. Super. Apr. 28, 2006) (finding qualified privilege when employer discussed with staff, union members and lawyer incidents necessary to effectuate termination of employee).

E. Statements to Government Regulators

In Layfield v. Beebe Med. Ctr., Inc., C.A. No. 95C-12-007, 1997 WL 716900 (Del. Super. July 18, 1997), the plaintiff alleged that the medical center had defamed her when it filed a complaint with the Delaware Board of Nursing. The court held that the plaintiff's claim failed as a matter of law because in Delaware, a qualified privilege shields "communications made between persons who have a common interest for the protection of which the allegedly defamatory statements are made." Id. at *7 (quoting Pierce v. Burns, 185 A.2d 477, 479 (Del. 1962)). The medical center's complaint to the Board of Nursing was protected by a qualified privilege due to the fact that both the medical center and the board shared a common interest in the competence and professionalism of nurses who practice in the state. Id.

Delaware courts recognize the conditional privilege for quasi-judicial proceedings. Segars v. Alexander, C.A. No. 85C-MY-138, 1986 WL 4276 (Del. Super. Apr. 2, 1986), aff'd, 516 A.2d 483 (Del. 1986) (TABLE). The Delaware courts follow the Restatement (Second) of Torts Section 598, which states:

> An occasion makes a publication privileged if the circumstances induce a correct or reasonable belief that: (a) there is information that affects a sufficiently important public interest, and (b) the public interest requires the communication of the defamatory matter to a public officer or a private citizen who is authorized or privileged to take action if the defamatory matter is true.

Id. at *2. If there is a conditional privilege, that privilege affords protection to the publisher only in the absence of malice. Short v. News-Journal Co., 212 A.2d 718, 720 (Del. 1965).

In Stiner v. Univ. of Del., 243 F. Supp. 2d 106, 116 (D. Del. 2003), the court held that stating that a professor was "academically unqualified" to a university accreditation board for purposes of accreditation review may have a defamatory meaning in that it would tend to harm the reputation of the plaintiff in the community or deter third persons from associating or dealing with him. However, given the context of the communication, the court also concluded that the statement is subject to qualified privilege.

F. Reports to Auditors and Insurers

There are no reported cases in Delaware on this issue.

G. Vicarious Liability of Employers for Statements Made by Employees

1. ***Scope of Employment.*** The employer will be liable for the tortious acts of an employee under the doctrine of respondeat superior if those acts are performed within the scope of employment. Drainer v. O'Donnell, C.A. No. 94C-08-062, 1995 WL 338700 (Del. Super. May 30, 1995). The conduct is within the scope of employment if it: (1) is of the type the employee was hired to perform; (2) takes place within the authorized time and space limits; and (3) is at least partially motivated by a purpose to serve the employer. Wilson v. Joma, Inc., 537 A.2d 187, 189 (Del. 1988). The question of whether conduct was within the scope of employment is generally a question for the jury, unless the facts are so clear that they must be decided as a matter of law. Draper v. Olivere Paving & Constr. Co., 181 A.2d 565, 569 (Del. 1962).

In Mongelli v. Red Clay Consolidated School Dist. Board of Education, 491 F. Supp. 2d 467, 475 (D. Del. June 4, 2007), the issue before the court was whether a teacher, such as the plaintiff, may sue the school district for which she works for causes of action stemming from sexual harassment allegedly committed by one of the teacher's students. The employer argued that they are "not liable for alleged sexual harassment of a teacher by a special education student" because "[t]he classroom setting and the relationship between a public school teacher and her students is simply not analogous to so-called hostile environment scenarios involving workplace incidents between coworkers." Id. at 475-76. The court held that employers may, under certain circumstances, be held vicariously liable for sexual harassment suffered by their employees at the hands of nonemployees. Id. at 476.

a. **Blogging.** No reported cases in Delaware in connection with libel.

2. ***Damages.*** No reported cases in Delaware in connection with libel.

H. Internal Investigations

No reported cases in Delaware in connection with internal investigations.

IV. OTHER ACTIONS BASED ON STATEMENTS

A. Negligent Hiring, Retention and Supervision

The plaintiff, who failed to prove a defamation claim because statements made by the supervisor were privileged, also claimed unsuccessfully that the employer should be held liable for negligent hiring and retention of that supervisor. Park v. Georgia Gulf Corp., C.A. No. 91-569, 1992 WL 714968, at *10 (D. Del. Sept. 14, 1992). The district court held that the plaintiff failed to show requisite serious harm as a result. Id. An employer is liable for negligent hiring or supervision where the employer is negligent in the employment of improper persons involving the risk of harm to others or in the supervision of the employee's activities. Fanean v. Rite Aid Corp. of Del., Inc., 984 A.2d 812, 826 (Del. Super. 2009). The court established that this is direct liability of the employer rather than the employee's negligence imputed through vicarious liability. Id. An action for negligent supervision is based upon the employer's negligence in failing to exercise due care to protect third parties from the foreseeable tortious acts of an employee. Id.

In Smith v. Williams, a trucking company argued that it could not be held liable for alleged negligent hiring, retention or supervision of one of its employees because (1) the employee's accident with the plaintiff was minor; (2) the employee's previous accidents involved insignificant property damage and minor personal injury; (3) the employee's physician certified that he was capable of driving; and (4) the employer attended his employer's training and safety meetings. Smith v. Williams, C.A. No. 05C-10-207 PLA, 2007 WL 2677131, at *1 (Del. Super. Sept. 11, 2007). The court disagreed and allowed the plaintiff to proceed against the trucking company with a direct negligence claim in addition to his respondeat superior claim. Id. at *7.

B. Intentional Infliction of Emotional Distress

Delaware has recognized claims of intentional infliction of emotional distress in wrongful discharge cases. Mattern v. Hudson, 532 A.2d 85 (Del. Super. 1987); Correa v. Pa. Mfg. Ass'n Ins. Co., 618 F. Supp. 915, 928 (D. Del. 1985). Because emotional injuries are personal injuries for statute of limitation purposes, a two-year limitation will apply to claims of intentional infliction of emotional distress. Wright v. ICI Americas Inc., 813 F. Supp. 1083 (D. Del. 1993). Nevertheless, Delaware courts reject most intentional infliction claims in employment cases either because the conduct was not sufficiently outrageous, as in Avallone v. Wilmington Med. Ctr., Inc., 553 F. Supp. 931 (D. Del. 1982), or because it was preempted by Delaware's workers' compensation statute, as in Battista v. Chrysler Corp., 454 A.2d 286 (Del. 1982). See also Riley v. DRBA, 457 F. Supp. 2d 505 (D. Del. 2006) (granting defendant's motion to dismiss because common law actions against an employer for intentional infliction of emotional distress are barred by the Delaware Workers' Compensation Act). See also Lankford v. Scala, C.A. No. 94C-04-023, 1995 WL 156220 (Del. Super. Feb. 28, 1995) (infliction of emotional distress in sexual harassment claim dismissed under statute of limitations).

However, the Delaware Supreme Court has held that "an independent action for intentional infliction of emotional distress does not lie where, as here, the gravamen of the complaint sounds in defamation." Barker v. Huang, 610 A.2d 1341, 1351 (Del. 1992). The Supreme Court reasoned that permitting a cause of action for intentional infliction of emotional distress on the basis of the same acts that supported the defamation claim would swallow up the law of defamation because the defamation defenses would not apply. Id. See also Bickling v. Kent Gen. Hosp., Inc., 872 F. Supp. 1299, 1312 (D. Del. 1994) (discussing Barker v. Huang in dismissing an intentional infliction of emotional distress claim because it sounds in defamation). The rationale for this rule is to preclude one from reviving a defective defamation claim by pleading it as a claim for intentional infliction of emotional distress. Drainer v. O'Donnell, C.A. No. 94C-08-062, 1995 WL 338700 (Del. Super. May 30, 1995) (citing Barker v. Huang). In Drainer, the court held that the plaintiff employee could not simultaneously allege slander and intentional infliction of emotional distress. Id. Regardless, in Drainer, the alleged injuries would be compensated only by the Workers' Compensation Act. Id. at *3. See also Ramey v. Del. Materials Inc., 399 A.2d 205 (Del. 1979) (mental trauma has been held to be compensated under the Workers' Compensation Act).

To establish a cause of action for intentional infliction of emotional distress, a plaintiff must allege that as a result of the defendant's extreme and outrageous conduct, he or she suffered severe emotional distress. Cummings v. Pinder, 574 A.2d 843, 845 (Del. 1990). Such conduct must be considered extreme and offensive to the degree that it goes beyond all bounds of decency. Id. The plaintiff need not allege accompanying bodily harm. Id. The conduct must be so severe that "no reasonable man could be expected to endure it." Schlifke v. Trans World Entm't Corp., 479 F. Supp. 2d 445, 453 (D. Del. 2007). Courts are to consider both intensity and duration in deciding whether the conduct has reached this level. Id. However, allegations of headaches, irritability and loss of sleep fail to rise to the level necessary to establish severe emotional distress. Goldsborough v. 397 Properties, LLC, C.A. No. 98C-09-001, 2000 WL 33110878, at *3 (Del. Super. Sept. 29, 2000) (citing Hostetter v. Hartford Ins. Co., C.A. No. 85C-06-28, 1992 WL 179423 (Del. Super. July 13, 1992)). In O'Leary v. Telecom Resources Service, LLC, C.A. No. 10C-03-108-JOH, 2011 Del. Super. LEXIS 36, at *20 (Del. Super. Jan. 14, 2011), the court held that employees' claims that their reputations have been compromised, they cannot work in a chosen field, their wages have been reduced, and they have suffered embarrassment, anger, chagrin, disappointment, worry, frustration, and a deep sense of injustice as a result of a discharge were insufficient to support an intentional infliction of emotional distress claim.

In Subh v. Wal-Mart Stores East, LP, C.A. No. 07-479-SLR-LPS, 2009 WL 866798, at *20 (D. Del. Mar. 31, 2009), the court granted summary judgment for the employer on the plaintiff's intentional infliction of emotional distress claim. The plaintiff alleged that his claim for intentional infliction of emotional distress was closely tied to his other discrimination and retaliation claims against his employer because they arose from the same operative fact. Id. The court found that the record was devoid of evidence from which a reasonable fact finder could reach such a finding, particularly given that the employee continued to work for the employer after what he claims to have been months of severe discrimination. Id. The record indicated that the employer's conduct toward the employee could not be characterized as outrageous, nor was there evidence of the employee's severe mental distress. Id.

C. Interference with Economic Advantage

A plaintiff may maintain separate causes of action for tortious interference of employment or occupation and for libel or slander. DeBonaventura v. Nationwide Mut. Ins. Co., 428 A.2d 1151 (Del. 1981). To maintain a cause of action for tortious interference with prospective business opportunities, a plaintiff must prove the following elements: (1) the reasonable probability of a business opportunity; (2) the intentional interference by the defendant with that opportunity; (3) proximate causation; and (4) damages. Id. at 1153. The factors must be considered in light of the defendant's privilege to compete or to protect his business interest in a fair and lawful manner. Id. (citing Bowl-Mor Co. v. Brunswick Corp., 297 A.2d 61 (Del. Ch. 1972); Regal Home Distrib., Inc. v. Gordon, 66 A.2d 754 (Del. Super. 1949)). In DeBonaventura, an auto body repair shop brought an action against an insurance company for interfering with prospective business opportunities by diverting potential customers to a competitor's shops by stating that the plaintiff's pricing was higher than those at other shops and higher than the competitive prices generally prevailing in the appropriate market. DeBonaventura, 428 A.2d 1151. The court denied all claims because the statements were true. Id. at 11, 55.

The Delaware Supreme Court allowed a plaintiff to state a cause of action for interference with prospective economic benefits simultaneously with a cause of action for slander and libel. Andres v. Williams, 405 A.2d 121 (Del. 1979). However, the plaintiff, who had been employed under a one-year contract, was not entitled to recover under this claim because he did not have an expectancy to secure a new contract, and the defendants had the privilege of selecting persons for its business relations. Id. at 122.

Although the Delaware Supreme Court has not yet opined on the tort of intentional interference with prospective contractual relations, "Delaware courts have long recognized the persuasiveness of the Restatement of Torts in the area of contractual interference." Am. Original Corp. v. Legend, Inc., 652 F. Supp. 962, 969 (D. Del. 1986) (citing Bowl-Mor Co., Inc. v. Brunswick Corp., 297 A.2d 61, 64 (Del. Ch. 1972)). The United States District Court for the District of Delaware allowed a plaintiff to state a claim for intentional interference with prospective contractual relations, alleging that the decision to eliminate his position was made in retaliation for various statements he had made. McHugh v. Bd. of Educ. of the Milford Sch. Dist., 100 F. Supp. 2d 231, 247 (D. Del. 2000). "One who intentionally and improperly interferes with another's prospective contractual relation (except a contract to marry) is subject to liability to the other for the pecuniary harm resulting from loss of the benefits of the relation, whether the interference consists of (a) inducing or otherwise causing a third person not to enter into or continue the prospective relation or (b) preventing the other from acquiring or continuing the prospective relation." Id. at 246 (quoting Restatement (Second) of Torts § 766B (1979)). See also Acierno v. Preit-Rubin Inc., 199 F.R.D. 157 (D. Del. 2001) (discussing elements necessary to prove tortious interference in landowner/property action).

Delaware courts other than the Supreme Court have set forth the following elements that must be proved in a claim for tortious interference with prospective contractual relations: (1) the existence of a valid business relationship or expectancy; (2) knowledge of the relationship or expectancy on the part of the interferer; (3) intentional interference that induces or causes a breach or termination of the relationship or expectancy; and (4) resulting damages to the party whose relationship or expectancy has been disrupted. Lucent Info. Mgmt., Inc. v. Lucent Techs., Inc., 5 F. Supp. 2d 238, 243 (D. Del. 1998) (quoting Dionisi v. DeCampli, No. 9425, 1995 WL 398536 (Del. Ch. June 28, 1995), opinion amended by, C.A. No. 9425, 1996 WL 39680 (Del. Ch. Jan. 23, 1996)). But the requirements set forth in Lucent were in the context of a summary judgment motion, and courts may not be willing to apply them to a motion to dismiss. Enzo Life Science, Inc. v. Digene Corp., 295 F. Supp. 2d 424 (D. Del. 2003) (denying defendant's motion to dismiss even though plaintiff failed to identify the specific prospective business relationship with which the defendant interfered). Liability attaches if one induces a third person not to enter or continue a business relation with another or prevents a third person from continuing a business relation with another. Bove v. Goldenberg, C.A. No. 05C-10-134 (CHT), 2007 WL 446014, at *9 (Del. Super. Feb. 7, 2007). The essential element separating unfair competition from legitimate market participation is an unfair action on the part of the defendant by which he prevents the plaintiff from legitimately earning revenue. EDIX Media Group, Inc. v. Mahani, C.A. No. 2186-N, 2006 WL 3742595 (Del. Ch. Dec. 12, 2006).

A successful plaintiff's damages on a claim for interference with prospective contractual relations is not limited to the value of the stolen records or destroyed assets. Empire Financial Services Inc. v. Bank of New York (Delaware), 900 A.2d 92 (Del. 2006). The plaintiff can also recover for the lost profits that it would have earned but for the defendant's wrongful interference. Id. at 97.

In Rimmax Wheels LLC v. RC Components, Inc., the Delaware District Court granted the defendant's motion for summary judgment because the plaintiff failed to cite any evidence of record that would substantiate its claims that the defendant's actions caused the plaintiff's business relationships with any of its actual or prospective customers to fail. Rimmax Wheels LLC v. RC Components, Inc., 477 F. Supp. 2d 670, 676 (D. Del. 2007). The plaintiff did not identify any customers, did not describe any specific contracts or lost business opportunities, and did not provide any record evidence relating to the defendant's intent and or knowledge of any interference. Id. In Triton Construction Co. v. Eastern Shore Electrical Services, Inc., C.A. No. 3290-VCP, 2009 WL 1387115, at *1 (Del. Ch. May 18, 2009), the employer filed an action against its former employee for tortious interference with prospective economic advantage, along with several other claims. The employer argued that the former employee tortiously interfered with the employer's business by assisting a competitor with entering bids for various construction jobs in competition with the employer. Id. at *18. The court held that the employer failed to prove that it had a reasonable probability of a business opportunity because the employer failed to demonstrate that it had a reasonable business expectancy as to the vast majority of the jobs at issue. Id. at *19. In Triton, the court found that the plaintiff could not maintain a claim for tortious interference because the employee lacked a valid employment contract. Triton Constr. Co. v. E. Shore Elec. Servs., Inc., C.A. No. 3290-VCP, 2009 Del. Ch. LEXIS 88, at *17 -18 (Del. Ch. May 18, 2009). However, the at-will nature of an employment relationship will not automatically vitiate contractual obligations arising from a validly executed employment contract See Great American Opportunities, Inc. v. Cherrydale Fundraising, LLC, C.A. No. 3718-VCP, 2010 Del. Ch. LEXIS 15, at *37 (Del. Ch. Jan. 29, 2010) (holding that claims for tortious interference with a contract apply just as readily to an at-will employee who has executed a valid employment contract as they do to an employee contractually obligated to remain with a company for a specified period of time).

The tortious interference with prospective business relations standard is arguably more favorable to a defendant than the tortious interference with contractual relations standard because, under the former standard, a court must consider the defendant's privilege to compete or protect his business interests in a fair and lawful manner. Beard Research, Inc. v. Kates, C.A. No. 1316-VCP, 2010 Del. Ch. LEXIS 75, at *81 (Del. Ch. Apr. 23, 2010). However, in Beard Research, Inc., because the plaintiffs were able to show only that the contract was terminated by its terms rather than a contractual breach, they failed to show an essential element of their tortious interference with contractual relations claim. Id. at *79. Conversely, the plaintiffs were able to prove that the defendants tortiously interfered with prospective business relations because certain defendants misappropriated the plaintiff's proprietary information and trade secrets and used this information to steal the plaintiff's business. Id. at *87, **aff'd, 11 A.3d 749 (Del. 2010).**

D. *Prima Facie* Tort

Prima facie tort was first recognized as a cause of action in Kaye v. Pantone, Inc., 395 A.2d 369 (Del. Ch. 1978). However, in Kaye the facts were related to corporate matters and did not involve any claims of defamation or employee-related actions. Importantly, Delaware law does not recognize a *prima facie* tort claim in an employment context. Le T. Le v. City of Wilmington, C.A. No. 08-615-LPS, 2010 U.S. LEXIS 93175, at *44 (D. Del. Sept. 7, 2010).

In Delaware, the cause of action of *prima facie* tort has been defined as the intentional infliction of harm, absent excuse or justification, resulting in damage by an act or series of acts that would otherwise be lawful and that do not fall within the categories of traditional tort. Nix v. Sawyer, 466 A.2d 407, 412 (Del. Super. 1983). In Nix, the court noted that the plaintiff's assertion that certain acts by the defendant constituted a *prima facie* tort was inconsistent because the plaintiff had also alleged and labeled these actions as defamation, abuse of process and malicious prosecution. Id. at 413. Therefore, the court dismissed the claim. Id.; see also DeBonaventura v. Nationwide Mut. Ins. Co., 419 A.2d 942 (Del. Ch. 1980), aff'd, 428 A.2d 1151 (Del. 1981) (denying relief on the claim of *prima facie* tort and denying defamation claim). In Lord v. Souder, 748 A.2d 395 (Del. 2000), the terminated plaintiff claimed *prima facie* tort against the employer for recklessly disseminating information the plaintiff had provided during investigation of another employee. The court dismissed the claim because it was inconsistent with the employment-at-will doctrine. Id. at 403. The court determined that the *prima facie* tort claim was an indirect effort to expand the exceptions to the at-will employment presumption. Id. ("Such a precedent would, in effect, topple the precarious legal balance that ensures that at-will employment remains the general rule rather than the exception.").

V. OTHER ISSUES

A. Statute of Limitations

In DeMoss v. News-Journal Co., 408 A.2d 944, (Del. 1979), the Delaware Supreme Court held that an action for libel was governed by the two-year period of 10 Del. C. § 8119. In Shearin v. E.F. Hutton Group, Inc., 652 A.2d 578 (Del. Ch. 1994), the Chancery Court applied the DeMoss holding to slander, specifically stating that "most of the communications alleged in this instance to be defamatory were spoken, not written, but that difference presents no principled basis to distinguish the DeMoss holding, which...is applicable and binding." Id. at 584. In Golod v. Bank of America Corp., C. A. No. 08-746, 2009 WL 1605309, at *4 (D. Del. June 4, 2009), the Delaware District Court granted the defendant's motion to dismiss because the plaintiff's defamation claim was barred by the two-year statute of limitations. Similarly, in Clark v. Delaware Psychiatric Center, C.A. No. 11C-01-012 MMJ, 2011 Del. Super LEXIS 371 (Del. Super. Aug. 9, 2011), the Delaware Superior Court granted the defendant's motion to dismiss because the plaintiff's defamation and invasion of privacy actions were barred by the 10 Del. C. § 8119 two-year statute of limitations.

Delaware's borrowing statute, 10 Del. C. § 8121, implemented to prevent forum shopping, shortens the limitations period for actions arising in a foreign jurisdiction if the foreign statute specifies a shorter period. See Cerullo v. Harper Collins Publishers, Inc., C.A. No. 01C-03-21-CHT, 2002 WL 243387 (Del. Super. Feb. 19, 2002) (defamation action brought by two plaintiffs, one residing in Delaware and one in New York, and only Delaware plaintiff's claim survives). Where a resident of the state brings an action against a defendant who is subject to the state's jurisdiction, however, the borrowing statute will not shorten the statute of limitations even if the cause of action arose outside the state. Id. at *3.

B. Jurisdiction

To obtain jurisdiction over a nonresident defendant, a plaintiff should look to 10 Del. C. § 3104 for the numerous ways a court may exercise personal jurisdiction over a nonresident. On a motion to dismiss for lack of personal jurisdiction, the plaintiff bears the burden of making a *prima facie* case to establish the basis for jurisdiction. This burden is satisfied if the plaintiff shows that Delaware's long-arm statute, 10 Del. C. § 3104(c), confers jurisdiction. Universal Capital Mgmt. v. Micco World, Inc., C.A. No. 10C-07-039 RRC, 2011 Del. Super. LEXIS 255, at *9 (Del. Super. June 2, 2011). In a recent case, the Delaware Superior Court dismissed a defamation action for lack of personal jurisdiction. Clayton v. Farb, C.A. No. 97C-10-306, 1998 WL 283468 (Del. Super. Apr. 23, 1998). The plaintiff had alleged that the defendant was using an internet open discussion forum to post libelous and slanderous false statements about the plaintiff. Id. at *1. The defendant was a nonresident of Delaware. The plaintiff had asserted that Delaware had personal jurisdiction over this matter because the posted internet statements could be, and were, accessed in Delaware. Id. However, the court found that it could not properly exercise personal jurisdiction over the defendant on that basis. Id. at *2.

With respect to the choice of law governing a negative employment reference given by a Delaware employer to a New York employer, the defamation was determined to be a matter of New York law (and barred by its shorter statute of limitations) because the reference was received, and therefore given, within New York State, even though it was written and authored in Delaware. Smith v. Delaware State University, 47 A.3d 472, 480 (Del. 2012).

C. Workers' Compensation Exclusivity

The "exclusivity rule" of the workers' compensation statute provides that every employer and employee, adult and minor, shall be bound by the workers' compensation statute respectively to pay and to accept compensation arising out of and in the course of employment, regardless of the question of negligence and to the exclusion of all other rights and remedies. 19 Del. C. § 2304. In order to be exempted, the wrongful acts must be "completely unrelated to the conditions existing in, or created by, the workplace." Konstantopoulos v. Westvaco Corp., 690 A.2d 936, 939 (Del. 1996). For example, it is well settled that an employee's common law claim against an employer for intentional infliction of emotional distress is barred by the exclusivity provision of the Workers' Compensation Act. Meltzer v. City of Wilmington, C.A. No. 07C-12-197, 2008 WL 4899230, at *4 (Del. Super. Aug. 6, 2008). In order to be afforded the protections and limitations under the exclusivity provision of the Workers' Compensation Act, however, an employer must be in compliance with the act by either carrying workers' compensation liability insurance through an organization approved by the Delaware Department of Labor (the "DDOL"), or providing the DDOL with satisfactory proof of the employer's financial ability to directly pay the compensation, as provided under the act. Wisniewski v. Ocean Petroleum, LLC, C.A. No. 08-26-GMS, 2010 U.S. Dist. LEXIS 55695 (D. Del. June 7, 2010); 19 Del. C. § 2372. If an employer fails to maintain the required workers' compensation liability insurance, an employee may bring an action at law for damages. 19 Del. C. § 2374(e)(3). Furthermore, in defending that action, the employer cannot raise as a defense that the employee was negligent, assumed the risk of the injury, or was injured as the result of the negligence of a fellow employee. Id.; 19 Del. C. § 2364(e)(3)(a)-(c). In Deuley v. DynCorp International, Inc., 8 A.3d 1156, 1164 (Del. 2010), cert. denied, 131 S. Ct. 2119 (2011), an injured employee and surviving spouse's derivative claims of wrongful death and survival, personal injuries, and loss of consortium based on the employees' employment agreements were barred under the workers' compensation statute because the exclusivity provision extinguished the predicate claim.

D. Pleading Requirements

In Delaware, defamation requires (1) a defamatory communication, (2) publication, (3) communication that refers to the plaintiff, such that (4) a third party understands the communication's defamatory character, and (5) there is an injury. EDIX Media Group, Inc. v. Mahani, C.A. No. 2186-N, 2006 WL 3742595 (Del. Ch. Dec. 12, 2006). Four types of defamatory statements do not require the plaintiff to show any special damages: maligning a person in his trade or business, imputing a crime of moral turpitude, implying a person suffers from a loathsome disease, or imputing the unchastity of a woman. Id. at *12. Additionally, for the letter to be defamatory to the plaintiff, as opposed to the plaintiff's employees, it must contain statements that "reflect discredit upon the method by which the corporation conducts its business." Id. at *12. If the defamation claim is not for libel or slander per se, then special damages must be pled specifically. See Spence v. Funk, 396 A.2d 967, 969-70, 4 Media L. Rep. 1981 (Del. 1978). A public-figure defamation plaintiff must only plead and prove facts with regard to elements of the claim that are within his control when the defendant's identity remains unknown. Doe v. Cahill, 884 A.2d 451, 464 (Del. 2005). Only when it appears with reasonable certainty that a plaintiff could not prove any set of facts that would entitle him to relief may the court dismiss the complaint under Rule 12(b)(6). Ramunno v. Cawley, 705 A.2d 1029, 1034, 26 Media L. Rep. 1651 (Del. 1998). To survive a motion to dismiss, the complaint need only give general notice of the claim asserted. Id. (citing Solomon v. Pathe Communications Corp., 672 A.2d 35, 38 (Del. 1996)).

SURVEY OF DELAWARE EMPLOYMENT PRIVACY LAW

Peter L. Frattarelli
Archer & Greiner, P.C.
300 Delaware Avenue
Suite 1370
Wilmington, Del. 19801
Phone: (302) 777-4350; Facsimile: (302) 777-4352

(With Developments Reported Through **November 1, 2012**)

GENERAL COMMENTS

Citations to "Del." reference the Delaware Supreme Court, Delaware's highest court. Citations to "Del. Ch." reference Delaware's trial court of equity. Citations to "Del. Super." reference Delaware's trial court of law. Citations to "D. Del." reference the United States District Court for the District of Delaware.

SIGNIFICANT DEVELOPMENTS SINCE THE 2012 *SURVEY*

In Lee et al v. The Picture People, Inc., C.A. No. K10C-07-002 RBY, 2012 Del. Super. LEXIS 159 (Del. Super. March 19, 2012), the Court adopted Comment c to Restatement (Second) Torts § 652B, regarding the tort of intrusion, which requires a showing that the defendant intruded into a private place, or has otherwise invaded a private seclusion that the plaintiff has thrown about his person or affairs.

I. GENERAL LAW OF PRIVACY

A. Legal Basis of Privacy Claims

Delaware follows the Restatement (Second) of Torts for privacy claims. See, e.g., Shearin v. E.F. Hutton Group, Inc., 652 A.2d 578 (Del. Ch. 1994) (in determining whether plaintiff had stated a privacy claim, the court looked to the elements listed in the Restatement (Second) of Torts). The right of privacy is not an absolute right, but rather is qualified by the circumstances and also by the rights of others. Guthridge v. Pen-Mod, Inc., 239 A.2d 709, 714 (Del. Super. 1967); Slibeck v. Union Oil Co. of California, C.A. No. 85C-FE-7, 1986 WL 11542, at *3 (Del. Super. Sept. 18, 1986); Martin v. Widener Univ. Sch. of Law, C.A. No. 91C-03-255, 1992 WL 153540, at *18 (Del. Super. June 4, 1992); Wilcher v. City of Wilmington, 60 F. Supp. 2d 298, 302 (D. Del. 1999). The right of privacy has been defined generally as the unwarranted appropriation or exploitation of one's personality, the publicizing of one's affairs with which the public has no legitimate concern, or the wrongful intrusion into one's private activities in such a manner as to outrage or cause mental suffering, shame or humiliation to a person of ordinary sensibility. Reardon v. News-Journal Co., 164 A.2d 263 (Del. 1960). See also Colonial Ins. Co. of California v. Sudler, C.A. No. 97A-02-016-CHT, 1997 WL 1048174, at *1 (Del. Super. Sept. 25, 1997).

B. Causes of Action

The right of privacy is not an absolute right, but is a right qualified by the rights of others. Guthridge v. Pen-Mod, Inc., 239 A.2d 709, 714 (Del. Super. 1967); Slibeck, 1986 WL 11542, at *3; Martin, 1992 WL 153540, at *18; Wilcher, 60 F. Supp. 2d at 302. The Delaware Supreme Court has delineated the four varieties of the tort of invasion of privacy as the following: (1) intrusion on plaintiff's physical solitude; (2) publication of private matters violating the ordinary senses; (3) putting plaintiff in a false position in the public eye; and (4) appropriation of some element of plaintiff's personality for commercial use. Barker v. Huang, 610 A.2d 1341, 1350 (Del. 1992). These four varieties of the tort of invasion of privacy are discussed below.

1. *Misappropriation/Right of Publicity.*

a. **In General.** The Delaware Superior Court has recognized the tort of misappropriation. See Slibeck v. Union Oil Co., C.A. No. 85C-FE-7, 1986 WL 11542, at *1 (Del. Super. Sept. 18, 1986).

b. **Elements.** A *prima facie* case of misappropriation requires a showing of (1) the appropriation of an individual's identity or persona, (2) that is done by another for their use or benefit.

(1) **Appropriation of Plaintiff's Identity or Persona.** Misappropriation applies to a person's name or likeness; however, it does not include a person's telephone number or address. Slibeck, 1986 WL 11542, at *1.

(2) **For Use or Benefit of Defendant.** The defendant must gain some value through the use of the misappropriation beyond what one is entitled to as a result of the relationship of the parties. Slibeck, 1986 WL 11542, at *3. In Slibeck, the court found that because defendant Union Oil was Slibeck's employer, it was entitled, in its business, to use Slibeck's name, and thus such use was not misappropriation. Id.

c. **As Applied to Employment.** No reported cases.

d. **Procedural Matters.** There are no Delaware cases that discuss any special rules or issues involving burden of proof with regard to claims for misappropriation. The applicable statute of limitations is two years pursuant to 10 Del. C. § 8119.

2. ***False Light.***

a. **In General.** The Delaware courts recognize the tort of false light. See Shearin v. E.F. Hutton Group, Inc., 652 A.2d at 578 (Del. Ch. 1994); Price v. Chaffinch, C.A. Nos. 04-956 (GMS), 04-1207 (GMS), 2006 WL 1313178, at *6 (D. Del. May 12, 2006).

b. **Elements.** Delaware looks to the Restatement (Second) of Tort § 652(e) for the definition of such a claim, specifically that "[o]ne who gives publicity to a matter concerning another that places the other before the public in a false light is subject to liability to the other for invasion of his privacy, if: (a) the false light in which the other was placed would be highly offensive to a reasonable person, and (b) the actor had knowledge of or acted in reckless disregard as to the falsity of the publicized matter and the false light in which the matter would be placed. "Shearin v. E.F. Hutton Group, Inc., 652 A.2d 578, 596 n.23 (Del. Ch. 1994). See also Q-Tone Broad., Co. v. MusicRadio of Md., Inc., C.A. No. 93C-09-021, 1994 WL 555391 (Del. Super. Aug. 22, 1994); Wyshock v. Malekzadeh, C.A. No. 91C-09-22, 1992 WL 148002 (Del. Super. June 10, 1992). **See Lee et al v. The Picture People, Inc., 2012 Del. Super. LEXIS 159, at *8-9 (no false light claim for using studio photographs of customers without permission).**

In Shearin v. E.F. Hutton Group, Inc., the court held that the plaintiff had not stated a valid claim for the tort of false light because there was no public dissemination of information relating to the plaintiff. 652 A.2d at 595. The court stated, "The essence of a claim for the tort of being shown in a false light is an invasion of one's privacy, which cannot be accomplished unless there is some public dissemination of information relating to the plaintiff." Id. Likewise, in Price the court held that the plaintiff had no cause of action for false light invasion of privacy. 2006 WL 1313178, at *6.

c. **As Applied to Employment.** The Shearin case discussed above was in the employment context. See also Price, 2006 WL 1313178, at *7 ("Although the act of publicly shedding false light on a person's job performance can be deeply offensive and hurtful, there is simply no invasion of *privacy* when the person being criticized is a public figure and the performance being criticized is the very activity that gave rise to the person's public-figure status in the first place.") (emphasis in original).

d. **Procedural Matters.**

(1) **Burden of Proof.** Public-figure plaintiffs must prove falsity by clear and convincing evidence. Ramada Inns, Inc. v. Dow Jones & Co., 543 A.2d 313 (Del. Super. 1987). "One who seeks the public eye cannot complain of publicity if the publication does not violate ordinary notions of decency." Barbieri v. News-Journal Co., 189 A.2d 773, 774 (Del. 1963). Special damages must be pled if the statements are not slanderous per se or libel. Wyshock v. Malekzadeh, C.A. No. 91C-09-22, 1992 WL 148002 (Del. Super. June 10, 1992). Private individuals must prove actual malice when information that is disseminated is of public interest. Martin v. Widener Univ. Sch. of Law, C.A. No. 91C-03-255, 1992 WL 153540, at *17 (Del. Super. June 4, 1992).

(2) **Statute of Limitations.** The statute of limitations in a libel action is two years, pursuant to 10 Del. C. § 8119, because the damages are considered personal injuries. See DeMoss v. News-Journal Co., 408 A.2d 944 (Del. 1979). Accordingly, the claim of false light also would most likely be subject to 10 Del. C. § 8119. See generally Shearin, 652 A.2d 578.

3. ***Publication of Private Facts.***

a. **In General.** The Delaware courts recognize the tort of publication of private facts. See Martin, 1992 WL 153540, at *17. In Barbieri, the plaintiff's claim involved statements by the defendant that the plaintiff had been the last person subjected to the whipping post. 189 A.2d 773 (Del. 1963). The story was printed in connection with proposed legislation to reintroduce the whipping post. Id. The court, however, disallowed the plaintiff's claim. Id. The plaintiff unsuccessfully argued that his once-public whipping had become a private matter with the passage of time. Id. Because the matter was once again a matter of public interest, the publication of the story was nonactionable. Id.; see generally Helman v. State, 784 A.2d 1058 (Del. 2001) (stating that no privacy interest is implicated by community provisions of state sex offender registration and community notification statute); Atamian v. Gorkin, C.A. No. 97C-08-001, 1999 WL 743663 (Del. Super. Aug. 13, 1999), aff'd, 746 A.2d 275 (Del. 2000) (TABLE) (stating that a doctor's consult note was not public disclosure for purposes of supporting invasion of privacy cause of action). See also Barker v. Huang, 610 A.2d 1341, 1350 (Del. 1992); Slibeck v. Union Oil Co., C.A. No. 85C-FE-7, 1986 WL 11542, at *1 (Del. Super. Sept. 18, 1986).

b. **Elements.** The tort only applies to true statements of facts, not to false allegations, because the tort of defamation is designed to deal with falsehoods. Barker, 610 A.2d at 1350. The facts must be private to the plaintiff. Martin v. Baehler, C.A. No. 91C-11-008, 1993 WL 258843 (Del. Super. May 20, 1993). Also, the facts must be publicized. Id. (the publication element will not be satisfied if the disclosure is by a doctor to a patient's family). Although this claim is often referred to as the "publication of private facts" claim, the implicit requirement is not that the private facts be *published*, but that they be *publicized.* See Martin, 1993 WL 258843, at *2 ("Although the word 'publication' is used in the cases of Barbieri and Barker, the word used in the Restatement is publicity, and the Court adopts the definition of publicity as set forth in comment a as defining this tort's perimeters."). For this claim to be raised, there must be a public communication of the information. Id. (stating that a doctor's disclosure to a patient's family did not fulfill the publicity requirement because it did not reach the public). Private communications that only reach "a single person or even to a small group of persons" are insufficient to support an invasion of privacy claim. Id.

c. **As Applied to Employment.** No reported cases.

d. **Procedural Matters.** The burden of proof for a claim of publication of private facts is that which is likely to be offensive to a reasonable person. Atamian v. Gorkin, 1999 WL 743663 (Del. Super. Aug. 13, 1999), aff'd, 746 A.2d 275 (Del. 2000) (TABLE). The applicable statute of limitations is two years, pursuant to 10 Del. C. § 8119.

4. ***Intrusion.***

a. **In General.** The Delaware courts recognize the tort of intrusion. Slibeck, 1986 WL 11542, at *1. See also Barker v. Huang, 610 A.2d 1341 (Del. 1992); Beckett v. Trice, C.A. No. 92C-08-029, 1994 WL 710874 (Del. Super. Nov. 4, 1994), aff'd, 660 A.2d 393 (Del. 1995) (TABLE); Guthridge v. Pen-Mod, Inc., 239 A.2d 709, 714 (Del. Super. 1967) (the court instructed the jury that the defendant creditor could be liable for invasion of privacy if it had used unreasonably harassing methods of debt collection).

The claim for invasion of privacy was unsuccessful in Wallace v. Capital Cities/ABC, Inc., C.A. No. 88C-AP-4-1-CV, 1989 WL 100423 (Del. Super. Aug. 29, 1989). In Wallace, the defendant was granted summary judgment after his employees had photographed and broadcast on television the plaintiff's residence and portions of the interior. Id. The court, in its decision, explained that there were two decisive facts: (1) there was a legitimate public interest in the plaintiff's activities because the plaintiff had been arrested earlier that day on criminal charges of endangering the lives and welfare of children; and (2) anyone could have seen what the defendant had photographed. Id. See also Postell v. Eggers, C.A. No. 06C-11-021 (JTV), 2008 WL 134830, at *1 (Del. Super. Jan. 15, 2008).

b. **Elements.** A *prima facie* case for the tort of intrusion requires the plaintiff to show that the defendant had published private information concerning the plaintiff and that such intrusion would be highly offensive to a reasonable person. Slibeck, v. Union Oil Co., C.A. No. 85C-FE-7, 1986 WL 11542, at *1 (Del. Super. Sept. 18, 1986). In Beckett v. Trice, the court held that the plaintiff had not made out a *prima facie* case because she had invited the defendant into her life. Beckett v. Trice, C.A. No. 92-C-08-029, 1994 WL 710874 (Del. Super. Nov. 4, 1994), aff'd, 660 A.2d 393 (Del. 1995) (TABLE). In Barker, the court recognized the Restatement (Second) Torts § 652B as the standard to apply. Barker v. Huang, 610 A.2d 1341, 1350 (Del. 1992).

In Barker v. Huang, the Delaware Supreme Court held that the plaintiff had not made out a *prima facie* case of intrusion upon seclusion. 610 A.2d at 1350. It was not enough for the plaintiff to claim that the defendant participated in newspaper interviews in which he intentionally made false allegations of conspiracy against the plaintiff. Id. The defendant's actions "may have drawn unwanted public attention to [the plaintiff], but such acts do not trigger liability" under this tort. Id.

In Lee et al v. The Picture People, Inc., 2012 Del. Super. LEXIS 159, at *7-8, the Court also adopted Comment c to Restatement (Second) Torts § 652B, which requires a showing that the defendant intruded into a private place, or has otherwise invaded a private seclusion that the plaintiff has thrown about his person or affairs.

Also, in Fanean v. Rite Aid Corp. of Del., Inc., a customer of the defendant was receiving treatment for a chronic, communicable disease in the form of prescription medication supplied by the defendant, a pharmacy.

984 A.2d 812, 815 (Del. Super. Dec. 3, 2009). An employee of the defendant provided sensitive information detailing the plaintiff's prescription and medical history to third parties without justification, including the plaintiff's daughter and her fiancé's son. Id. The plaintiff alleged an intrusion upon seclusion claim, but the court dismissed the claim, holding that a pharmacy and its employees' access to confidential information is reasonable and cannot constitute intrusion for the sake of a breach of privacy claim. Id.

c. **As Applied to Employment.** No reported cases.

d. **Procedural Matters.** There are no Delaware cases that discuss any special rules or issues involving burden of proof. The applicable statute of limitations is two years, pursuant to 10 Del. C. § 8119.

C. Other Privacy-Related Actions

1. ***Intentional Infliction of Emotional Distress.*** Along with all invasion of privacy claims, an employer might see a "tag-along" claim for emotional distress or mental anguish. See McKnight v. Voshell, 513 A.2d 1319 (Del. 1986) (an appeal from rulings of the Superior Court in a tort action asserting claims of invasion of privacy and intentional infliction of emotional distress). Delaware has recognized claims of intentional infliction of emotional distress in wrongful discharge cases. Correa v. Pa. Mfg. Ass'n Ins. Co., 618 F. Supp. 915, 927-28 (D. Del. 1985); see also Mattern v. Hudson, 532 A.2d 85 (Del. Super. 1987) (adopting the Restatement (Second) of Torts § 46 standard for the requirements of the tort of intentional infliction of emotional distress). Because emotional injuries are personal injuries for statute of limitation purposes, a two-year limitation will apply to claims of intentional infliction of emotional distress. Wright v. ICI Americas Inc., 813 F. Supp. 1083 (D. Del. 1993). Nevertheless, Delaware courts reject most intentional infliction claims in employment cases either because the conduct was not sufficiently outrageous, as in Avallone v. Wilmington Med. Ctr., Inc., 553 F. Supp. 931 (D. Del. 1982), or because it was preempted by Delaware's workers' compensation statute, as in Battista v. Chrysler Corp., 454 A.2d 286 (Del. Super. 1982). See also Limehouse v. Steak & Ale Rest. Corp., No. 86, 2004, 2004 WL 1280400 (Del. June 7, 2004) (upholding the trial court's conclusion that plaintiff's claim for intentional infliction of emotional distress was barred by the exclusivity provision of the Workers' Compensation Act); Konstantopoulos v. Westvaco Corp., 690 A.2d 936 (Del. 1996) (same). See also Nieves v. Acme Markets, Inc., 541 F. Supp. 2d 600, 611 (D. Del. 2008) (plaintiff's claim did not fall within "intent to injure" exception); Riley v. DRBA, 457 F. Supp. 2d 505 (D. Del. 2006) (granting defendant's motion to dismiss because common law actions against an employer for intentional infliction of emotional distress are barred by the Delaware Workers' Compensation Act); Lankford v. Scala, C.A. No. 94C-04-023, 1995 WL 156220 (Del. Super. Feb. 28, 1995) (infliction of emotional distress in sexual harassment claim dismissed under statute of limitations).

However, the Delaware Supreme Court has held that "an independent action for intentional infliction of emotional distress does not lie where, as here, the gravamen of the complaint sounds in defamation." Barker v. Huang, 610 A.2d 1341, 1351 (Del. 1992). The Supreme Court reasoned that permitting a cause of action of an intentional infliction of emotional distress on the basis of the same acts that supported the defamation claim would swallow up the law of defamation because the defamation defenses would not apply. Id.; see also Bickling v. Kent Gen. Hosp., Inc., 872 F. Supp. 1299, 1312 (D. Del. 1994) (discussing Barker v. Huang in dismissing the intentional infliction of emotional distress claim because it sounds in defamation). The rationale for this rule is to preclude one from reviving a defective defamation claim by pleading it as a claim for intentional infliction of emotional distress. Drainer v. O'Donnell, C.A. No. 94C-08-062, 1995 WL 338700 (Del. Super. May 30, 1995) (citing Barker v. Huang). In Drainer v. O'Donnell, the court held that the plaintiff employee could not simultaneously allege slander and intentional infliction of emotional distress. Id. Regardless, in Drainer, the alleged injuries would be compensated only by Delaware's Workers' Compensation Act. Id. at *3; see also Ramey v. Del. Materials Inc., 399 A.2d 205 (Del. 1979) (mental trauma has been held to be compensated under the Workers' Compensation Act).

To establish a cause of action for intentional infliction of emotional distress, a plaintiff must allege that, as a result of the defendant's extreme and outrageous conduct, he or she suffered severe emotional distress. Cummings v. Pinder, 574 A.2d 843, 845 (Del. 1990). See also Tekstrom, Inc. v. Savla, C.A. No. 03-06-0033, 2005 WL 994524, at *1 (Del. Com. Pl. Apr. 27, 2005), aff'd in part, 2006 WL 2338050, at *12 (Del. Super. July 31, 2006); Brett v. Berkowitz, 706 A.2d 509, 513 n.10 (Del. 1998); Atamian v. Nemours Health Clinic, C.A. No. 01C-07-038 HDR, 2001 WL 1474819, at *2 (Del. Super. Nov. 14, 2001). Such conduct must be considered extreme and offensive to the degree that it goes beyond all bounds of decency. Cummings, 574 A.2d at 845. In such an instance, the plaintiff need not allege accompanying bodily harm. Id. The conduct must be so severe that "no reasonable man could be expected to endure it." Schlifke v. Trans World Entm't Corp., 479 F. Supp. 2d 445, 453 (D. Del. 2007). Courts are to consider both intensity and duration in deciding whether the conduct reached this level. Id. However, allegations of headaches, irritability and loss of sleep fail to rise to the level necessary to establish severe emotional distress. Goldsborough v. 397 Properties, L.L.C., C.A. No. 98C-09-001, 2000 WL 33110878, at *3 (Del. Super. Sept. 29, 2000) (citing Hostetter v. Hartford Ins. Co., C.A. No. 85C-06-28, 1992 WL 179423 (Del. Super. July 13, 1992)). In Jones v. Milford School District, a student alleged that school district personnel employed "harsh and unconscionable remarks" when they suggested that the student should attend an adult high school because he would be almost 20 years old when he graduated. C.A. No. 3194-VCN, 2010 Del. Ch. LEXIS 84, at *14 (Del. Ch. Apr. 29, 2010). The court held that this allegation was not supported by any fact-specific allegations and therefore dismissed the student's intentional infliction of emotional distress claim. Id.

In Subh v. Wal-Mart Stores East, LP, C.A. No. 07-479-SLR-LPS, 2009 WL 866798, at *20 (D. Del. Mar. 31, 2009), the court granted summary judgment for the employer on the plaintiff's intentional infliction of emotional distress claim. The plaintiff alleged that his claim for intentional infliction of emotional distress was closely tied to his other discrimination and retaliation claims against his employer because they arose from the same operative facts. Id. The court found that the record was devoid of evidence from which a reasonable fact finder could reach such a finding, particularly given that the employee continued to work for the employer after what he claims to have been months of severe discrimination. Id. The record indicated that the employer's conduct toward the employee could not be characterized as outrageous, nor was there evidence of the employee's severe mental distress. Id. The court in Wooleyhan v. Cape Henlopen School District dismissed an intentional infliction of emotional distress claim filed by a student against public school administrators because their alleged failure to conduct a proper investigation before and after suspending the student was not utterly outrageous conduct and was therefore insufficient to establish an intentional infliction of emotional distress claim. C.A. No 10-153, 2011 U.S. Dist. LEXIS 53541, at *48-49 (D. Del. May 17, 2011).

2. ***Interference With Prospective Economic Advantage.*** A plaintiff may maintain separate causes of action for both tortious interference of employment or occupation and libel or slander. DeBonaventura v. Nationwide Mut. Ins. Co., 428 A.2d 1151 (Del. 1981). To maintain a cause of action for tortious interference with prospective business opportunities, a plaintiff must prove the following elements: (1) the reasonable probability of a business opportunity; (2) the intentional interference by the defendant with that opportunity; (3) proximate causation; and (4) damages. Id. at 1153; Empire Fin. Servs., Inc. v. Bank of New York (Delaware), 900 A.2d 92, 98 n.19 (Del. 2006); TruePosition, Inc. v. Allen Telecom, Inc., C.A. No. 01-823 GMS, 2003 WL 151227, at *2 (D. Del. Jan. 21, 2003). The factors must be considered in light of the defendant's privilege to compete or to protect his business interest in a fair and lawful manner. DeBonaventura, 428 A.2d at 1153 (citing Bowl-Mor Co. v. Brunswick Corp., 297 A.2d 61 (Del. Ch. 1972); Regal Home Distrib., Inc. v. Gordon, 66 A.2d 754 (Del. Super. 1949)). Liability attaches if one induces a third person not to enter into or continue a business relation with another or prevents a third person from continuing a business relation with another. Bove v. Goldenberg, C.A. No. 05C-10-134, 2007 WL 446014, at *4 (Del. Super. Feb. 7, 2007). The essential element separating unfair competition from legitimate market participation is an unfair action on the part of the defendant by which he prevents the plaintiff from legitimately earning revenue. Edix Media Group, Inc. v. Mahani, C.A. No. 2186-N, 2006 WL 3742595, at *11 (Del. Ch. Dec. 12, 2006). In DeBonaventura v. Nationwide Mut. Ins. Co., an auto body repair shop brought action against an insurance company for interfering with prospective business opportunities by diverting potential customers to competitors' shops by stating that the plaintiff's pricing was higher than those at other shops and higher than the competitive prices generally prevailing in the appropriate market. DeBonaventura, 428 A.2d 1151. The court denied all claims because the statements were true. Id. at 1155. See also Cooper v. Anderson-Stokes, Inc., C.A. No. 85C-JA-13, 1987 WL 16749 (Del. Super. Aug. 21, 1987) (where plaintiff's claim for interference with a prospective business relationship failed because plaintiff did not have a legally protected expectancy of future relations with defendant).

The Delaware Supreme Court, in Andres v. Williams, allowed a plaintiff to state a cause of action for interference with prospective economic benefits simultaneously with stating a cause of action for slander and libel. Andres v. Williams, 405 A.2d 121, 122 (Del. 1979). However, the plaintiff, who had been employed under a one-year contract, was not entitled to recover under this claim because he did not have an expectancy to secure a new contract, and the defendants had the privilege of selecting persons for its business relations. Id. at 122.

Furthermore, the "Delaware courts have long recognized the persuasiveness of the Restatement of Torts in the area of contractual interference." Am. Original Corp. v. Legend, Inc., 652 F. Supp. 962, 969 (D. Del. 1986) (citing Bowl-Mor Co. v. Brunswick Corp., 297 A.2d 61, 64 (Del. Ch. 1972)). See also Empire, 900 A.2d at 98. In McHugh v. Bd. of Educ. of the Milford Sch. Dist., the United States District Court for the District of Delaware allowed a plaintiff to state a claim for intentional interference with prospective contractual relations, alleging that the decision to eliminate his position was made in retaliation for various statements he had made. 100 F. Supp. 2d 231, 247 (D. Del. 2000). "One who intentionally and improperly interferes with another's prospective contractual relation (except a contract to marry) is subject to liability to the other for the pecuniary harm resulting from loss of the benefits of the relation, whether the interference consists of (a) inducing or otherwise causing a third person not to enter into or continue the prospective relation or (b) preventing the other from acquiring or continuing the prospective relation." Id. at 246 (quoting Restatement (Second) of Torts § 766B (1979)).

Recently, the Delaware Supreme Court noted that the intentional interference with prospective contractual relations requires proof of the same elements required to prove a claim for tortious interference with prospective business opportunities. Empire, 900 A.2d at 98 n.19. But see Lucent Info. Mgmt., Inc. v. Lucent Techs., Inc., 5 F. Supp. 2d 238, 243 (D. Del. 1998) (quoting Dionisi v. DeCampli, C.A. No. 9425, 1995 WL 398536 (Del. Ch. June 28, 1995), opinion amended by, 1996 WL 39680 (Del. Ch. Jan. 23, 1996) (stating that the following elements must be proved in a claim for tortious interference with prospective contractual relations: (1) the existence of a valid business relationship or expectancy; (2) knowledge of the relationship or expectancy on the part of the interferer; (3) intentional interference that induces or causes a breach or termination of the relationship or expectancy; and (4) resulting damages to the party whose relationship or expectancy has been disrupted)). See also Cryovac Inc. v. Pechiney Plastic Packaging, Inc., 430 F. Supp. 2d 346, 357 (D. Del. 2006) (same); Del. Express Shuttle, Inc. v. Older, C.A. No. 19596, 2002 WL 31458243, at *22 (Del. Ch. Oct. 23, 2002) (same). The tortious interference with prospective business relations standard is arguably more favorable to a defendant than the tortious interference with contractual relations standard because, under the former standard, a court must consider the defendant's privilege to compete or protect his business interests in a fair and lawful manner. Beard Research, Inc. v. Kates, 8 A.3d 573, 608 (Del. Ch. 2010), aff'd. sub nom., ASDI, Inc. v. Beard Research, Inc., 11 A.3d 749 (Del. 2010). However, in Beard Research, Inc., because the plaintiffs were able to show only that the contract was terminated by its terms rather than a contractual breach, they failed to show an essential element of their tortious interference with contractual relations claim. Id. at *79. Conversely, the plaintiffs were able to prove that the defendants tortiously interfered with prospective business relations because certain defendants misappropriated the plaintiff's proprietary information and trade secrets and used this information to steal the plaintiff's business. Id. at *87.

A successful plaintiff's damages on a claim for interference with prospective contractual relations is not limited to the value of the stolen records or destroyed assets. Empire Fin. Servs., Inc. v. Bank of New York (Delaware), 2007 WL 1991179 (Del. Super. June 19, 2007), aff'd, 945 A.2d 1167 (Del. 2008) (TABLE). The plaintiff can also recover for the lost profits that it would have earned but for defendant's wrongful interference. Id. at *2.

In Rimmax Wheels LLC v. RC Components, Inc., the Delaware District Court granted the defendant's motion for summary judgment because the plaintiff failed to cite any evidence of record that would substantiate its claims that the defendant's actions caused the plaintiff's business relationships with any actual or prospective customers to fail. Rimmax Wheels LLC v. RC Components, Inc., 477 F. Supp. 2d 670, 676 (D. Del. 2007). The plaintiff did not identify any customers, did not describe any specific contracts or lost business opportunities, and did not provide any record evidence relating to the defendant's intent and or knowledge of any interference. Id.

In Triton Construction Co. v. Eastern Shore Electrical Services, Inc., C.A. No. 3290-VCP, 2009 WL 1387115, at *1 (Del. Ch. May 18, 2009), the employer filed an action against its former employee for tortious interference with prospective economic advantage, along with several other claims. The employer argued that the former employee tortiously interfered with the employer's business by assisting a competitor with entering bids for various construction jobs in competition with the employer. Id. at *18. The court held that the employer failed to prove that it had a reasonable probability of a business opportunity because the employer failed to demonstrate that it had a reasonable business expectancy as to the vast majority of the jobs at issue. Id. at *19. In Triton, the court found that the plaintiff could not maintain a claim for tortious interference because the employee lacked a valid employment contract. Triton, 2009 LEXIS 88, at *17-18. However, the "at-will" nature of an employment relationship will not automatically vitiate contractual obligations arising from a validly executed employment contract. (See Great American Opportunities, Inc., holding that claims for tortious interference with a contract apply just as readily to an "at-will" employee who has executed a valid employment contract as they do to an employee contractually obligated to remain with a company for a specified period of time. 2010 Del. Ch. LEXIS 15, at *37 (Del. Ch. Jan. 29, 2010)).

A claim for interference with prospective economic advantage must be forward-looking; thus an employee's claim of interference with respect to not paying back-pay and commissions does not fall within this tort. Nikolouzakis et al v. Exinda Corp. et al., C.A. No. 11-1261-LPS-MPT, 2012 U.S. Dist. LEXIS 109976 (Del. Super. Aug. 7, 2012) at *35-36.

3. ***Prima Facie Tort.*** *Prima facie* tort was first recognized as a cause of action in Kaye v. Pantone, Inc., 395 A.2d 369 (Del. Ch. 1978). However, in Kaye, the facts were related to corporate matters and did not involve any claims of defamation or employee-related actions.

In Delaware, the cause of action of *prima facie* tort has been defined as the intentional infliction of harm, absent excuse or justification, resulting in damage by an act or series of acts that would otherwise be lawful and that do not fall within the categories of traditional tort. Nix v. Sawyer, 466 A.2d 407, 412 (Del. Super. 1983). In Nix v. Sawyer, the court noted that the plaintiff's assertion that certain acts by the defendant were a *prima facie* tort was inconsistent because the plaintiff had also alleged, and labeled these actions, as defamation, abuse of process and malicious prosecution. Id. at 412-13. Therefore, the court dismissed the claim. Id.; see also DeBonaventura v. Nationwide Mut. Ins. Co., 419 A.2d 942 (Del. Ch. 1980), aff'd, 428 A.2d 1151 (Del. 1981) (denying relief on the claims of *prima facie* tort and defamation); Lynch v. Mellon

Bank of Del., C.A. No. 90C-JA-125, 1992 WL 51880 (Del. Super. Mar. 12, 1992) (holding that the claims for *prima facie* tort, negligence and breach of the implied covenant of good faith and fair dealing were barred by the exclusivity provision of the law). Ota v. Health-Chem Corp., C.A. No. 83C-FE-99, 1986 WL 15559 (Del. Super. Dec. 22, 1986) (finding for the employer on the claims of defamation and *prima facie* tort).

In Lord v. Souder, the terminated plaintiff claimed *prima facie* tort against the employer for recklessly disseminating information the plaintiff had provided during investigation of another employee. 748 A.2d 393, 403 (Del. 2000). The court dismissed the claim because it was inconsistent with the employment-at-will doctrine. Id. The court determined that the *prima facie* tort claim was an indirect effort to expand the exceptions to the at-will employment presumption. Id. ("Such a precedent would, in effect, topple the precarious legal balance that ensures that at-will employment remains the general rule rather than the exception."). In sum, Delaware law does not recognize a *prima facie* tort claim in the employment context. Le T. Le v. City of Wilmington, 2010 Dist. U.S. LEXIS 93175, at *44 (D. Del. Sept. 7, 2010), **aff'd, 2012 U.S. Appl. LEXIS 8206 (3d. Cir. April 14, 2012).**.

II. EMPLOYER TESTING OF EMPLOYEES

A. Psychological or Personality Testing

1. ***Common Law and Statutes.*** There are no reported cases or relevant statutes in Delaware that discuss psychological or personality testing.

2. ***Private Employers.*** No Delaware cases.

3. ***Public Employers.*** No Delaware cases.

B. Drug Testing

1. ***Common Law and Statutes.*** Department of Corrections may administer drug tests to inmates. 11 Del. C. § 6531.

2. ***Private Employers.*** Delaware generally allows pre-employment drug testing if implemented in a nondiscriminatory manner. Drug testing is mandated for applicants for certain positions. Testing is mandated for applicants for a position with a nursing home and current employees of a nursing home where the Department of Health and Social Services has a reasonable suspicion that an employee has been convicted of a disqualifying crime since becoming employed. 16 Del. C. § 1141, et seq. Aircraft personnel are subject to discretionary drug testing after reasonable suspicion. 2 Del. C. § 502.

In Seaford Nylon Employees Council, Inc. v. E.I. duPont de Nemours & Co., No. 1222, 1986 WL 11533 (Del. Ch. Oct. 10, 1986), a union contended, among other things, that the employer's expanded drug screening plan violated its members' privacy rights. The court ultimately determined that the union lacked standing to assert its members' individual privacy claims because the claims were not germane to the union's purpose.

In Wharton v. Worldwide Dedicated Services, the Delaware Superior Court determined that the employee's claim for wrongful termination failed where the employee's drug test was positive after an accident and the employee was later terminated after release of the verified positive drug test. C.A. No. 04C-02-035, 2007 WL 404770, at *7 (Del. Super. Feb. 2, 2007); see also Mann v. Cargill Poultry, Inc., C.A. No. 88C-AU37, 1990 WL 91102, at *6 (Del. Super. June 13, 1990) (DOT is not required to hold a job open for those who test positive).

In Wright v. Claymont Steel, C.A. No. 07A-12-005, 2008 WL 3021098, at *1 (Del. Super. Aug. 4, 2008), pursuant to the employer's policy, any employee who tested positive for any level of an illegal drug was subject to immediate termination. However, if the employee voluntarily disclosed a substance abuse problem, the employer would select and pay for an appropriate treatment program which the employee was required to successfully complete. Id. The policy also set forth a procedure for testing for illegal drugs. Id. If an employee's urine tested positive for an illegal substance, the test was not considered positive until a laboratory test confirmed the initial result. Id. The plaintiff voluntarily disclosed a substance abuse problem with alcohol and cocaine. Id. After the employer sent the plaintiff for treatment, it obtained a urine sample from the plaintiff which came back positive for cocaine. Id. at *2. Pursuant to the policy, the employer sent the sample to an outside lab, which reconfirmed the presence of cocaine. Id. Thereafter, the plaintiff was terminated, and he later filed for unemployment benefits. The claims referee determined that the plaintiff was terminated for just cause because the employer's in-house drug tests were sufficiently reliable. Id. On appeal, the Unemployment Insurance Appeal Board again determined that the employer terminated the plaintiff for just cause because the employee failed to successfully complete the drug program, as required by the employer's drug policy. Id. at *3. After reviewing all the evidence, the court affirmed the board's decision that the employee was terminated for just cause. Id. at *4.

In Gude v. Rockford Center Inc., the plaintiff alleged, in part, that she was discriminated against by her employer based upon her age because she was forced to submit to a drug test. 699 F. Supp. 2d 671, 675 (D. Del. Mar. 26, 2010). According to the court, the record did not support a finding that she was discriminated against on the basis of age. Id. at 681. The record reflected that employees, over and under the age of forty, were required to undergo the testing and that the employer provided a nondiscriminatory reason for the drug testing, specifically, missing narcotics, which the plaintiff could not rebut. Id.

Before the results of an employee's drug testing will be admitted before Delaware's Unemployment Insurance Appeal Board (UIAB), the employer must call a witness to establish the manner in which the specimen was obtained and preserved, as well as the person who tested the specimen. In Hertrich Nissan v. Unemployment Insurance Appeal Board, the employer appealed a decision of the UIAB which granted unemployment benefits to a former employee. C.A. No. K10A-07-005 JTV, 2011 Del. Super. LEXIS 334, at *1 (Del. Super. July 27, 2011). The former employee was involved in an accident at work and returned to work a few days after the accident. Id. Upon his return, he was administered a drug test. Id. The result was positive for marijuana. Id. The employee admitted to consuming marijuana a few days after the accident, but otherwise denied the use of marijuana at any time relevant to his claim for unemployment benefits. Id. As a result of the positive drug test, the employee was terminated from employment on the grounds that his drug use was in violation of the employer's drug policy. Id. at *2. In awarding unemployment benefits to the employee, the UIAB refused to consider the drug test results under the hearsay rule because the employer did not produce a witness qualified to testify as to the sample-taking procedures and the chain of custody. Id. The Delaware Superior Court affirmed the decision-holding that the UIAB acted within its legitimate discretion when it excluded the drug test results as hearsay evidence. Id. at *9.

3. ***Public Employers.*** The court will consider three factors when judging the constitutionality of public employee drug tests: (1) the nature of the privacy interest upon which the search intrudes; (2) the extent to which the search intrudes on the employee's privacy; and (3) the nature and immediacy of the governmental concern at issue, and the efficacy of the means employed by the government for meeting that concern. Wilcher v. City of Wilmington , 139 F.3d 366, 374 (3d Cir. 1998) (citing Vernonia Sch. Dist. 47J v. Acton, 515 U.S. 646 (1995)). In Wilcher v. City of Wilmington, the court opined that the Fourth Amendment's reasonableness test, as respects searches and seizures, was not violated by requiring the city's firefighters to subject themselves to urine tests. 60 F. Supp. 2d 298, 376 (D. Del. 1999) (on remand from 3d Cir.). The court found that Delaware state law provided greater protection to individuals with regard to searches and seizures. Id. at 380. The court found that Delaware's "reasonable person" standard was the proper standard to apply to those individuals affected by such a requirement. Id. On appeal, the Third Circuit held that under Delaware law, as predicted by federal court, the requirement that firefighters urinate while under observation was not sufficiently offensive to constitute invasion of privacy. Wilcher, 60 F. Supp. 2d at 304-05.

Testing is mandated for certain public employees. Department of Correction employees in sensitive security positions are subject to random drug testing and incident-triggered testing. 29 Del. C. § 8922. All applicants for these positions initially must submit to testing for illegal use of drugs. 29 Del. C. § 8922. School bus drivers are subject to drug testing. 21 Del. C. § 2708.

In Chapman v. Delaware Department of Health and Social Services, C.A. No. 08A-04-009, 2009 WL 2386090, at *6 (Del. Super. July 31, 2009), the court reversed the Merit Employee Relations Board's decision upholding the state's rescission of the employee's termination for her failure to provide a sufficient urine sample. The court determined that the state failed to follow its own three-step grievance process before the decision was made to rescind the promotion. Id.

C. Medical Testing

1. ***Common Law and Statutes***. There are few cases in Delaware addressing medical testing.

2. ***Private Employers***. In Frazier, following a work-related injury, the claimant refused to take a video urodynamics test to see if there was damage to her bladder, due to fear of radiation. Frazier v. Barrett Bus. Servs., Inc., C. A. No. 01A-07-010HDR, 2001 WL 1469150 (Del. Super. Oct. 5, 2001). After the Industrial Accident Board ordered her to submit to the test, the claimant appealed to the Superior Court. Id. The Superior Court held that the appeal was interlocutory and, as such, the court did not have jurisdiction. Id.

3. ***Public Employers***. In Bowers v. City of Wilmington, the plaintiff, a City of Wilmington police officer, sustained an injury while on the job which required medical treatment and made it impossible for her to return to work for a period of time. 2010 U.S. Dist. LEXIS 71514, at *2 (D. Del. July 15, 2010). More than one year later, the city terminated her employment. Id. The plaintiff filed suit against the city alleging that it violated the city's Code and her due process rights by terminating her without giving her an opportunity to voice opposition and undergo required medical examinations to determine her fitness to return to work. Id. The court concluded that the plaintiff could not overcome the

heavy presumption under Delaware law that her employment was at-will. Id. at *22. Therefore, she could not establish that she had a property right in her continued employment. Id.

D. Polygraph Tests

Delaware has enacted an anti-polygraph statute at 19 Del. C. § 704. Polygraph, lie detector, or similar tests or examinations are prohibited as a condition of employment or a continuation of employment. Id. Employers can be subject to a fine or imprisonment, and the Superior Court of Delaware shall have exclusive jurisdiction of offenses under this section. Id. at § 704(c).

In Heller v. Dover Warehouse Mkt., Inc., 515 A.2d 178 (Del. Super. 1986), an employer forced an employee to take a polygraph test, and as a result of the test, the employee was dismissed. The question for the court in Heller was whether a private cause of action may be maintained by an employer for violation of the provisions of 19 Del. C. § 704. The court found that a private cause of action was actionable. The court noted that "[a] polygraph test impinges on an employee's right to privacy and against involuntary self-incrimination." Id. at 181. The Delaware General Assembly has declared that the public policy of Delaware is that polygraph examinations in the employment context are offensive to the public welfare. Id. In response, the employer argued that the at-will doctrine should bar the plaintiff's claim. However, the court held that the plaintiff's complaint stated a claim upon which relief may be granted for any damages proximately caused by the violation of 19 Del. C. § 704, and therefore this cause of action constituted a statutory exception to the at-will employee doctrine. In the same case, at a later hearing for cross motions for partial summary judgment, the Superior Court examined whether Heller's consent waived any right to legal recourse resulting from the examination. Heller v. Dover Warehouse Mkt., Inc., C.A. No. 85C-FE-10, 1988 WL 97858, at *1 (Del. Super. Sept. 1, 1988). The court noted that "[t]he legal effect of an employee's consent to a polygraph examination is a question of first impression in Delaware." Id. at *2. The court held that the validity of an employee's consent depends upon a jury determination of whether the waiver was compelled as a condition of continued employment. Id. Under this test, if the jury finds the plaintiff was required to sign the waiver as a condition of employment, then the waiver and/or the consent is invalid. Because the test was applicable, the court denied the motions for partial summary judgment.

E. Fingerprinting

There are no reported cases in Delaware on this issue in the employment context.

III. SEARCHES

Del. Const. of 1897, art. I, § 6 (stating that there shall be no unreasonable searches and seizures).

A. Employee's Person

No Delaware cases, except to the extent of drug testing or other similar forms of testing discussed above in Section II.

1. ***Private Employers.*** No Delaware cases on searches of an employee's person.

2. ***Public Employers.*** No Delaware cases on searches of an employee's person.

B. Employee's Work Area

No Delaware cases on searches of an employee's person.

C. Employee's Property

1. ***Private Employers.*** No Delaware cases on searches of an employee's property.

2. ***Public Employers.*** A vice principal, as a state employee, must have probable cause before conducting a search. State v. Baccino, 282 A.2d 869, 870 (Del. Super. 1971).

IV. MONITORING OF EMPLOYEES

A. Telephones and Electronic Communications

1. ***Wiretapping.*** Employers must provide notice to employees prior to monitoring telephone use. Acknowledgment of this notice must be signed by the employee. If the monitoring policy is included in the employee handbook, the employee's signature acknowledging receipt of the handbook is sufficient. 19 Del. C. § 705.

Delaware's statutory wiretap laws are found at 11 Del. C. § 2401, et seq. In general, it is illegal to intercept a wire, oral or electronic communication when privacy is expected without the consent of at least one party to the communication. 11 Del. C. § 2402. Violation of this statute is a Class E felony and will result in a fine of not more than $10,000. Id. Likewise, a person is guilty of violation of privacy when he or she intercepts without the consent of all parties a message by telephone. 11 Del. C. § 1335(a)(4). Such a violation is a Class A misdemeanor. 11 Del. C. § 1335(c).

2. ***Electronic Communications.*** By statute, a person may not obtain, alter, prevent authorized access to, or divulge the contents of a wire or electronic communication while it is in electronic storage in an electronic communications system without the consent of at least one party to the communication. 11 Del. C. § 2421, et seq. Properly authorized law enforcement officers and certain other persons are exempted from the restrictions. Id. Sanctions include: (1) criminal: a class B misdemeanor for first-time offenders and a class A misdemeanor for subsequent offenders when the offense is committed for commercial advantage, malicious destruction or private commercial gain; fines range from $5,000 to $250,000, 11 Del. C. § 2421(b); (2) civil: plaintiffs may recover appropriate equitable or declaratory relief. The court may assess damages in a civil action not less than $1000, and attorneys' fees and costs. 11 Del. C. § 2427.

In State v. Appleby, 2002 WL 1613716 (Del. Super. July 18, 2002), the police were entitled to use information obtained from the hard drive in possession of the employee's estranged wife as part of their application for a warrant to search and seize the hard drive's other contents as evidence in an investigation of the employee's illegal interception of the employer's electronic communications.

3. ***Other Electronic Monitoring.*** In Brandewie v. State, the Delaware District Court denied an employer's motion for summary judgment on a sexual harassment claim based in part on the employer's failure to timely block internet access to a sexually charged website that the employer knew its employees accessed. C.A. No. 05-625-MPT, 2006 WL 3623817, at *5 (D. Del. Dec. 11, 2006). Further, the fact that the employees even had access to the site was "alarming" to the court. Id. In Mattern & Assoc. v. Seidel, a former employee was found to have breached his fiduciary duty of good faith, loyalty, and fair dealing that he owed to his employer when he misappropriated confidential and proprietary trade secrets by taking an image of a hard drive from the employer's laptop of his sales efforts, which included the employer's customer lists and client proposals. 678 F. Supp. 2d 256, 263 (D. Del. Jan. 14, 2010).

B. Mail/E-Mail

Employers must provide notice to employees prior to monitoring electronic mail or internet access. Acknowledgment of this notice must be signed by the employee. If the monitoring policy is included in the employee handbook, the employee's signature acknowledging receipt of the handbook is sufficient. 19 Del. C. § 705.

The use of e-mail by employees for personal business has been held to be a sufficient transgression in support of termination. McCormick v. Bd. of Educ. of Del., C.A. No. 97A-10-003, 1998 WL 960732 (Del. Super. July 22, 1998).

E-mails have also been used to demonstrate the presence of antagonism in the tenure application process, Hudson v. Wesley Coll., Inc., C.A. No. 1211, 1998 WL 939712 (Del. Ch. Dec. 23, 1998), and in attempts to prove the employee received notice of a particular policy that she allegedly violated. Palmer v. Lenfest Group, C.A. No. 99A-08-008 CG, 2000 WL 303315 (Del. Super. Feb. 4, 2000), aff'd, 755 A.2d 390 (Del. June 5, 2000) (TABLE).

In Rockwell Automation, Inc. v. Kall, the Delaware Chancery Court held that the employer could access proprietary documents stored in the computers it supplied to the employee. C.A. No. 526-N, 2005 WL 2266592, at *1 (Del. Ch. Sept. 9, 2005).

The employer in Beard Research, Inc. v. Kates, C.A. No. 1316-VCP, 2009 WL 1515625, at *1 (Del. Ch. May 29, 2009), brought an action for sanctions for alleged spoliation of evidence by a former employee in an action for tortious interference with business relations and misappropriation of trade secrets. The employer argued that the former employee's laptop computer, which included various incriminating e-mails, was irretrievably altered after a duty to preserve that evidence had arisen, and that the former employee and his subsequent employer were responsible for that alteration. Id. Although the court declined to grant a judgment in favor of the employer because of the spoliation of evidence, the court deemed it appropriate to draw an inference against the former employee for his actions in deleting key documents and having his hard drive replaced. Id. at *11. The court also awarded the employer attorneys' fees and expenses, including expert fees associated with the motion for sanctions, because of the former employee's "egregious" and "callous disregard for proper discovery in this Court." Id. at *13.

After a complaint by a coworker about an explicit e-mail sent by the plaintiff, an investigation revealed that numerous offensive and explicit e-mails were sent to several coworkers from a computer used by the plaintiff. Parkstone v. Coons, C.A. No. 07-465-SLR, 2009 WL 1064951, at *1 (D. Del. Apr. 20, 2009). The plaintiff's computer had been used to view pornographic pictures and videos, access a personal America Online account, prepare personal taxes, and send numerous offensive e-mails. Id. at *2. The investigation also revealed that the plaintiff failed to secure his password because some of the improper activity occurred on dates when the plaintiff was not in the office. Id. Thereafter, the plaintiff's employment was terminated and he brought a claim for invasion of privacy, among other claims, alleging that the computer he accessed was the property of the union, not his employer. Id. at *7. The court held that the plaintiff failed to show that the employer's actions of inspecting the computer breached an expectation of privacy and constituted an intrusion in his private affairs. Id. at *7. The court noted that the facts in the record showed that the employer had control over the computer and that the plaintiff routinely consented to its control by way of an acknowledgement that the plaintiff clicked on each time he keyed in his password. Id. Further, the court held that the individual defendants were entitled to immunity because they were employed by the county, a governmental agency. Id.

The Delaware Supreme Court in Butler v. Safe Check East, Inc. held that there was substantial evidence before the Unemployment Insurance Appeal Board to support its decision that the employee was terminated for just cause and therefore not entitled to unemployment benefits. No. 44, 2011, 2011 Del. LEXIS 368, at *5 (Del. 2011). The vulgar emails sent from the employee's computer clearly were prohibited by the employee handbook and against the employer's interest. Id. at *6.

C. Surveillance/Photographing

Installation of a camera in a private place without the consent of a person entitled to privacy for the purpose of photographing that person is a Class A misdemeanor. 11 Del. C. § 1335(a)(2), § 1335(c). Installation of listening devices in private places or using devices that amplify sound is a Class A misdemeanor. 11 Del. C. § 1335(a)(3), § 1335(c). 11 Del. C. § 1335 is modeled after 47 U.S.C. § 605. United States v. Vespe, 389 F. Supp. 1359 (D. Del. 1975), aff'd, 520 F.2d 1369 (3d Cir. 1975).

In State v. Dietz, an employer teamed up with police to conduct surveillance in a plant to investigate possible illegal drug transactions by employees. 1998 WL 109835 (Del. Super. Mar. 4, 1998). The Unemployment Insurance Appeals Board's decision to deny benefits was affirmed by the court because there was substantial evidence in the record, including surveillance video that showed the employee assaulting a coworker. Ramey v. Wal-Mart Stores East, LP, C.A. No. 08A-09-001, 2009 WL 2507173, at *2 (Del. Super. Aug. 13, 2009).

Employers can hire private investigators for employees' workers' compensation claims. See, e.g., Jarman v. Willow Grove Meats, C.A. No. 93A-07-001, 1994 WL 146031 (Del. Super. Mar. 30, 1994), aff'd, 650 A.2d 1306 (Del. Sept. 16, 1994) (TABLE). In McCoy v. BJ's Wholesale Club, C.A. No. 08A-11-005, 2009 WL 1299112, at *1 (Del. Super. May 11, 2009), the court upheld a decision by the Industrial Accident Board that granted the employer's petition to terminate workers' compensation benefits based, in part, on surveillance video of the employee bending, carrying fishing supplies, standing several hours while fishing, and walking with a normal gait. Similarly, in Miller v. Layton Home, C.A. No. 08A-08-004, 2009 WL 1231064, at *4 (Del. Super. April 29, 2009), the Industrial Accident Board relied upon a surveillance DVD presented at the hearing in reaching its decision as to the employee's disability status.

A motion to suppress evidence obtained as result of video surveillance of a self-storage locker in a commercial facility was denied where the defendant worked in the locker, with the door open, and there was no reasonable expectation of privacy. See State v. Bailey, 2001 Del. Super. LEXIS 471 (Del. Super. Nov. 30, 2001).

Videotape evidence and other evidence of an employee justified the jury's finding that the defendant employees were guilty of conspiracy to steal copper wire from the employer's locked shed. State of Delaware v. Nichols, 2010 Del. Super. LEXIS 259, at *4 (Del. Super. June 17, 2010).

V. ACTIVITIES OUTSIDE THE WORKPLACE

A. Statute or Common Law

See below.

B. Employees' Personal Relationships

1. ***Romantic Relationships Between Employees.*** In Baynard v. Kent County Motor & Sales Co., C.A. No. 87A-SE-1, 1988 WL 31972 (Del. Super. Mar. 10, 1988), aff'd, 548 A.2d 778 (Del. 1988) (TABLE), in an appeal from a decision of the Unemployment Insurance Appeal Board, the Superior Court affirmed the findings that a supervisor had been fired for just cause after engaging in an affair with a coworker's wife. The court found that this relationship was extremely disruptive to the working relationship between the supervisor and the coworker, especially because the supervisor had supervisory powers over that coemployee. Disqualification of unemployment benefits is not limited to misconduct that takes place only on the job site and only during working hours if there is sufficient nexus between the off-site misconduct and the individual's job performance. Id. at *1 (citing Taylor v. UIAB and Delaware Olds, C.A. No. 78A-NO-10, Stiftel, P.J. (Del. Super. Sept. 22, 1980)).

In Toomey v. Dep't. of Corr. for State of Del., C.A. No. 96A-02-003, 1997 WL 127009 (Del. Super. Jan. 29, 1997), aff'd, 700 A.2d 735 (Del. 1997) (TABLE), a case before the Unemployment Insurance Appeal Board, the Superior Court reversed the appeal board's finding that the prison had just cause for terminating its employee who had cohabited with a former inmate against prison policy. The Superior Court found that the prison did not establish the reasonableness of the rule, which, until this case, had not been enforced. Id. at *3. Violation of a reasonable company rule may constitute just cause for discharge, but the employee must be aware that the policy exists and that it may be cause for discharge. Ringer v. State Personnel Office, C.A. No. 91A-04-002, 1995 WL 562127 (Del. Super. Aug. 9, 1995).

In Kemp v. Peninsula Oil/Uncle Willie's, C.A. No. 98A-05-001, 1998 WL 1029273 (Del. Super. Dec. 8, 1998), on appeal, the court upheld the Unemployment Insurance Appeal Board's findings of just cause for termination of an employee who, on more than one occasion, was seen kissing her boyfriend (a nonemployee) and engaging in sexual conduct on the employer's premises.

2. ***Sexual Orientation.*** By a newly amended statute, in Delaware it is an unlawful employment practice for an employer to discriminate against an applicant or employee based on his or her sexual orientation, among other protected classes. (See below). 19 Del. C. § 711(a) (as amended by 77 Del. Laws ch. 90, § 24 (2009)). Before adoption of the revised statute, the Superior Court affirmed the decision of the Unemployment Insurance Appeal Board to deny benefits to a homosexual employee who alleged he was terminated as a result of the employer inadvertently opening a pornographic magazine sent to the employee at the employer's address. Weikel v. Village Printing, Inc., C.A. No. 95A-03-015, 1995 WL 862124 (Del. Super. Aug. 17, 1995).

3. ***Marital Status.*** By statute, in Delaware it is an unlawful employment practice for an employer to fail or refuse to hire or to discharge any individual or otherwise to discriminate against any individual with respect to his compensation, terms, conditions or privileges of employment because of such individual's race, *marital status*, color, age, religion, sex or national origin. 19 Del. C. § 711(a). "For purposes of evaluating a state law claim of discrimination under 19 Del. C. § 711(a), Delaware courts have adopted the framework established by federal courts for dealing with actions under Title VII of the Civil Rights Act of 1964 which requires a fact-finder to make 'explicit findings.'" Gallucio's v. Kane, C.A. No. 94A-12-010, 1995 WL 656818, at *3 (Del. Super. Oct. 19, 1995) (citations omitted).

C. Smoking

Delaware's amended Clean Indoor Air Act, which went into effect on November 27, 2002, prohibits smoking in any indoor enclosed area to which the general public is invited or in which the general public is permitted, including all workplaces. 16 Del. C. § 2902, et seq.

D. Blogging

In a nonemployment matter, the Delaware Supreme Court held that in order to recover, a plaintiff having a defamation claim based on a statement made in an internet chat room or on a blog must prove that a statement is factually based and thus capable of a defamatory meaning. Doe v. Cahill, C.A. 884 A.2d 451 (Del. Oct. 5, 2005) (holding also that a defamation plaintiff must satisfy a summary judgment standard to require disclosure of an anonymous defendant's identity).

VI. RECORDS

A. Personnel Records

Pursuant to 19 Del. C. § 732, "[a]n employer shall, at a reasonable time, upon request of an employee, permit that employee to inspect that employee's own personnel files used to determine that employee's own qualifications for employment, promotion, additional compensation, termination or disciplinary action." The employer must make these records available for an employee during regular business hours, but may require the employee to inspect such records on the employee's free time. Id. The employer may require the employee to file a written form requesting such access. Id.

If, upon inspection of the employee's personnel file, an employee disagrees with any of the information contained in such file or records, the employer and employee may agree to a removal or correction of such information. 19 Del. C. § 734. If agreement is not possible, then the employee may submit a written statement explaining the employee's position. Id. The statement shall be made part of the employee's personnel file or medical records and shall accompany any disclosure made to a third party. Id.

There are no Delaware cases that interpret these statutes.

B. Medical Records

If an employee chooses to make a claim under Delaware's Workers' Compensation Act, the employee shall have the right upon application to the employee's employer to inspect, copy, and reproduce any medical records pertaining to that employee that are in the possession of his or her employer or the employer's insurance carrier. 19 Del. C. § 2322(d). Medical records shall include physician reports, hospital reports, diagnostic reports, treatment reports, X-rays, and X-ray reports. Id.

Other types of employee medical records, however, have been held to some extent private. In In re Petition of Greenwood Trust Co., the Industrial Accident Board limited discovery and redacted certain information of other employees' medical history in a claim by some employees that the place of employment is a "sick building" and they have suffered an occupational disease as a result of the air quality. C.A. No. 98M-03-007-WTQ, 1999 WL 167792 (Del. Super. Mar. 3, 1999), aff'd sub nom., Greenwood Trust Co. v. Delaware Inds. Accid. Bd., 737 A.2d 530 (Del. 1999). "There can be no question that an employee's medical records, which may contain facts of a personal nature, are well within the ambit of privacy protection." Id. at *3 (citations omitted). See also Monstanto Co. v. Aetna Cas. and Sur. Co., C.A. No. 88C-JA-118, 1992 WL 182320 (Del. Super. May 26, 1992) (discussing discovery issues of employees' medical records). Likewise, in a libel case where a doctor claimed loss of patients and income as damages, the court allowed inspection of redacted versions of the doctor's patient medical records. Kanaga v. Gannett Co., C.A. No. 92C-12-182-JOH, 2002 WL 143819, 2002 Del. Super. LEXIS 29 (Del. Super. Jan. 10, 2002).

C. Criminal Records

Delaware law does not statutorily limit the use of criminal background checks for making hiring decisions.

Pursuant to 11 Del. C. § 8561, any person seeking employment with a child-care provider must provide an entire criminal history record or shall submit to fingerprinting, and provide other information necessary to obtain a report of the person's entire criminal history record from the State Bureau of Identification and a report of the person's entire federal criminal history record pursuant to the Federal Bureau of Investigation.

Pursuant to 11 Del. C. § 8571, any person seeking employment with a public school shall be required to submit fingerprints and other necessary information in order to obtain the individual's entire criminal history record.

Moreover, pursuant to 11 Del. C. § 8608, no person shall be appointed, promoted, or transferred to any position within a state agency that had or has access to criminal history record information facilities, systems, operating environments, or data file contents, without a criminal history record check being performed prior to employment.

Any person seeking employment for a position that has direct access to lottery ticket sales, agents, video lottery agents, or vendors must submit fingerprints and other relevant information in order to obtain the individual's entire federal and state criminal history record. 29 Del. C. § 4805(a)(25).

In Cannon v. News Journal, 962 A.2d 916 (Del. 2008), a job applicant brought an action against a potential employer, alleging that the defendant improperly discriminated against him because it refused to hire him based upon his criminal record. The Superior Court, New Castle County, dismissed the complaint for failure to state a claim upon which relief may be granted. Id. On appeal to the Supreme Court, the court affirmed the lower court's decision because the applicant failed to demonstrate that having a criminal record placed him within a protected class under the Delaware Discrimination in Employment Act. Id. See also Cannon v. News Journal, 2009 WL 1834776, * (D. Del. June 25, 2009) (dismissing the complaint under the doctrine of *res judicata* because the plaintiff filed suit against the same defendants on the same theories as those in his state filing, which was litigated and determined by a valid and final judgment.)

D. Subpoenas / Search Warrants

No Delaware cases.

VII. ACTIONS SUBSEQUENT TO EMPLOYMENT

A. References

Delaware recognizes a privilege for employers who provide references to a prospective employer concerning the applicant's job performance or work-related characteristics, violations of the law and ability to do the job. Delaware law, 19 Del. C. § 709(a), provides as follows:

An employer or any person employed by the employer who discloses information about a current or former employee's job performance to a prospective employer is presumed to be acting in good faith; and unless lack of good faith is shown, is immune from civil liability for such disclosure or its consequences. For purposes of this section, the presumption of good faith may be rebutted upon a showing that the information disclosed by such employer was knowingly false, was deliberately misleading or was rendered with malicious purpose; or that the information was disclosed in violation of a nondisclosure agreement, or was otherwise confidential according to applicable federal, State or local statute, rule or regulation.

"Information" includes: (1) information about an employee's or former employee's job performance or work-related characteristics; (2) any act committed by such employee that would constitute a violation of federal, state, or local law; or (3) an evaluation of the ability or lack of ability of such employee or former employee to accomplish or comply with the duties or standards of the position held by such employee or former employee. 19 Del. C. § 709(b)(1)-(3).

To prove a violation of 19 Del. C. § 709, a plaintiff must identify a specific false or defamatory communication by his or her employer to a third party. Collier v. Target Stores Corp., C.A. No. 03-1144-SLR, 2005 WL 850855 (D. Del. Apr. 13, 2005) (dismissing nonspecific claims by plaintiff that former employer gave false and misleading information to prospective employers). Such communications must not be knowingly false, deliberately misleading, made with malicious purpose, made in violation of a nondisclosure agreement, or otherwise confidential.

Absent evidence that the employer provided negative information about the plaintiff to her potential employers after the termination of employment, the plaintiff could not prove that she was retaliated against for filing a charge of discrimination. Gude v. Rockford Center Inc., 699 F. Supp. 2d 671 (D. Del. Mar. 26, 2010).

The employee in Eaton v. Raven Transport, Inc. argued that his former employer defamed him in oral statements to prospective employers and in oral statements to USIS, the entity which maintains a federally mandated database for motor carriers. C.A. No. S08C-07-033 RFS, 2010 Del. Super. LEXIS 487 (Del. Super. Nov. 15, 2010). As to the oral statement, the court ruled that the employee could not make out a case of slander because he offered only inadmissible hearsay to support his allegation. Id. at *10. Regarding the written statements, the court denied summary judgment because the truthfulness of the statement was still a question for the jury. Id. at *19.

B. Noncompete Agreements

All actions in Delaware regarding covenants not to compete are brought in the Court of Chancery. In order for a covenant not to compete to be enforceable, it must (1) meet general contract law requirements; (2) be reasonable in scope and duration, both geographically and temporally; (3) advance a legitimate economic interest of the party enforcing the covenant; and (4) survive a balance of the equities. Del. Express Shuttle, Inc. v. Older, C.A. No. 19596, 2002 WL 31458243 (Del. Ch. Oct. 23, 2002); Elite Cleaning Co. v. Capel, C.A. No. 690-N, 2006 WL 1565161 (Del. Ch. June 2, 2006); Am. Homepatient, Inc. v. Collier, C.A. No. 274-N, 2006 WL 1134170, at *2 (Del. Ch. Apr. 19, 2006); All Pro Maids, Inc. v. Layton, C.A. No. 058-N, 2004 WL 1878784, at *5 (Del. Ch. Aug. 10, 2004); TriState Courier and Carriage, Inc. v. Berryman, C.A. No. 20574-NC, 2004 WL 835886, at *10 (Del. Ch. Apr. 15, 2004). When seeking specific performance of a covenant not to compete, the plaintiff has the burden of establishing its case by clear and convincing evidence. Elite, 2006 WL 1565161, at *3. Delaware courts are strongly in favor of enforcement of contracts freely entered into by parties, and the court will only set aside the agreement "upon a strong showing that dishonoring the contract is required to vindicate a public policy interest even stronger than the freedom of contract." O'Leary v. Telecom Resources Service, LLC, C.A. No. 10C-03-108-JOH, 2011 Del. Super. LEXIS 36, at *16 (Del. Super. Jan. 14, 2011). In O'Leary, the plaintiffs, employees, moved for a judgment on the pleadings challenging the validity of the covenant not to compete provisions in both the senior management and asset purchase agreements. Id. at *8. The court held that the employees failed to meet the heavy burden of entitling them to a judgment on the pleadings because they failed to show that as a matter of Delaware law the non-compete clause was overbroad and thus facially invalid. Id. at *16.

A covenant not to compete is considered to be reasonably limited in scope if the geographic area extends only as far as the actual area of the plaintiff's business. Id. If the court finds that the territorial limits imposed on a former employee are unreasonable, it may enforce another limit that it does find reasonable, essentially rewriting the contract. Singh v. Batta Env. Assoc., Inc., C.A. No. 19627, 2003 WL 21309115 (Del. Ch. May 21, 2003). In Delaware Elevator, Inc. v. Williams, a former employee argued that the restrictive covenant was facially invalid and therefore the court should decline to exercise its blue pencil. C.A. No. 5596-VCL, 2011 Del. Ch. LEXIS 47, at *19 (Del. Ch. Mar. 16, 2011). Applying Maryland law, the Delaware court exercised its blue pencil and carved back the overly broad three-year, 100-mile radius restrictive covenant to a two-year, 30-mile radius restriction. Id. at *34. However, the court noted that when a restrictive covenant is unreasonable, the court should consider striking the provision in its entirety because "[t]he threat of losing all protection gives employers an incentive to restrict themselves to reasonable clauses." Id. at *31. A covenant not containing a geographic restriction may be unenforceable, Caras v. Am. Original Corp., C.A. No. 1258, 1987 WL 15553 (Del. Ch. July 31, 1987), but is not *per se* unreasonable. Gas-Oil Prods., Inc. of Del. v. Kabino, C.A. No. 9150, 1987 WL 18432 (Del. Ch. Oct. 13, 1987).

The reasonableness of the time period covered in a covenant not to compete depends on many factors, such as the nature of the employee's position, the nature of the interest to be protected, and the geographic scope of the agreement. The court will refuse to enforce an agreement that is more restrictive than necessary or "oppressive" to the employee. Norton Petroleum Corp. v. Cameron, C.A. No. 15212-NC, 1998 WL 118198 (Del. Ch. Mar. 5, 1998). For example, in All Pro Maids, Inc. v. Layton, the defendants conceded that the restrictive covenant at issue that was limited to one year and an area defined by specific zip codes where the majority of the plaintiff's clients were located was reasonable as to time and geography. 2004 WL 1878784, at *5.

A noncompetition agreement will only be enforced to protect the legitimate interests of the employer. "Interests which the law has recognized as legitimate include protection of employer goodwill and protection of employer confidential information from misuse." Research & Trading Corp. v. Pfuhl, C.A. No. 12527, 1992 WL 345465, at *12 (Del. Ch. Nov. 18, 1992). In many cases, the court will also enjoin the former employee from soliciting customers, using information concerning customers, or using customer lists. Id. The former employee must also be causing specific economic harm to the former employer, Norton Petroleum Corp., 1998 WL 118198; potential or future harm will not be considered. Take-A Break Coffee Servs., Inc. v. Grose, C.A. No. 11217, 1990 WL 67392 (Del. Ch. May 14, 1990 *revised* May 30, 1990).

VIII. OTHER ISSUES

A. Statutes of Limitations

The statute of limitations for personal injuries, which is governed by 10 Del. C. § 8119, is two years. This statute should be applicable for privacy-related torts. In Clark v. Delaware Psychiatric Center, C.A. No. 11C-01-012 MMJ, 2011 Del. Super LEXIS 371 (Del. Super. Aug. 9, 2011), the Delaware Superior Court granted the defendant's motion to dismiss because the plaintiff's defamation and invasion of privacy actions were barred by the 10 Del. C. § 8119 two-year statute of limitations.

B. Jurisdiction

A plaintiff should look to 10 Del. C. § 3104 for the numerous ways a court may exercise personal jurisdiction over a nonresident defendant. On a motion to dismiss for lack of personal jurisdiction, the plaintiff bears the burden of making a *prima facie* case to establish the basis for jurisdiction. This burden is satisfied if the plaintiff shows that Delaware's long-arm statute, 10 Del. C. § 3104(c), confers jurisdiction. Universal Capital Mgmt. v. Micco World, Inc., C.A. No. 10C-07-039 RRC, 2011 Del. Super. LEXIS 255, at *9 (Del. Super. June 2, 2011).

The Delaware Superior Court dismissed a defamation action for lack of personal jurisdiction. Clayton v. Farb, C.A. No. 97C-10-306, 1998 WL 283468 (Del. Super. Apr. 23, 1998). The plaintiff had alleged that the defendant was using an internet open-discussion forum to post libelous and slanderous false statements about the plaintiff. Id. at *1. The defendant was a nonresident of Delaware. The plaintiff had asserted that Delaware had personal jurisdiction over this matter because the posted internet statements could be, and were, accessed in Delaware. Id. However, the court found that it could not properly exercise personal jurisdiction over the defendant on that basis. Id. at *2.

C. Workers' Compensation Exclusivity

The "exclusivity rule" of the workers' compensation statute provides that every employer and employee, adult and minor, shall be bound by the workers' compensation statute respectively to pay and to accept compensation arising out of and in the course of employment, regardless of the question of negligence and to the exclusion of all other rights and remedies. 19 Del. C. § 2304. In order to be exempted, the wrongful acts must be "completely unrelated to the conditions existing in, or created by, the workplace." Konstantopoulos v. Westvaco Corp., 690 A.2d 936, 939 (Del. 1996). For example, it is well settled that an employee's common law claim against an employer for intentional infliction of emotional distress is barred by the exclusivity provision of the Workers' Compensation Act. Meltzer v. City of Wilmington, C.A. No. 07C-12-197, 2008 WL 4899230, at *4 (Del. Super. Aug. 6, 2008); Shockley v. General Foods Corp., 568 A.2d 491 (Del. 1989).

In order to be afforded the protections and limitations under the exclusivity provision of the Workers' Compensation Act, however, an employer must be in compliance with the act by either carrying workers' compensation liability insurance through an organization approved by the Delaware Department of Labor (the "DDOL"), or providing the DDOL with satisfactory proof of the employer's financial ability to pay directly the compensation, as provided under the act. Wisniewski v. Ocean Petroleum, LLC, 2010 U.S. Dist. LEXIS 55695 (D. Del. June 7, 2010), 19 Del. C. § 2372. If an employer fails to maintain the required workers' compensation liability insurance, an employee may bring an action at law for damages. 19 Del. C. § 2374(e)(3). **However, if an employee has already recovered from the workers compensation fund, he cannot try and receive a double recovery for the same injury from his employer, even if the employer did not have workers compensation insurance or coverage. Lyon and Lyon v. In Bocca Al Luppo Trattoria, C.A. No. 12C-03-023 RBY, 2012 Del. Super. LEXIS 433 (Del. Super. Sept. 18, 2012).** Furthermore, in defending that action, the employer cannot raise as a defense that the employee was negligent, assumed the risk of the injury, or was injured as the result of the negligence of a fellow employee. Id. § 2374(e)(3)(a)-(c). In Deuley v. DynCorp International, Inc., 8 A.3d 1156, 1164 (Del. 2010), cert. denied, 131 S. Ct. 2119 (2011), an injured employee and surviving spouse's derivative claims of wrongful death and survival, personal injuries, and loss of consortium based on the employees' employment agreements were barred under the workers' compensation statute because the exclusivity provision extinguished the predicate claim.

D. Pleading Requirements

The court may dismiss a complaint under Rule 12(b)(6) only when it appears with reasonable certainty that a plaintiff cannot prove any set of facts that would entitle him to relief. Ramunno v. Cawley, 705 A.2d 1029, 1034 (Del. 1998). To survive a motion to dismiss, the complaint need only give general notice of a claim asserted. Id. at 1034 (citing Solomon v. Path Communications, Corp., 672 A.2d 35, 38 (Del. 1996)). Absent claims for fraud, negligence, or mistake, the standard is notice pleading. Del. Super. Ct. Civ. R. (8)(c), R. 9(b).

SURVEY OF DISTRICT OF COLUMBIA EMPLOYMENT LIBEL LAW

Kevin T. Baine, Thomas G. Hentoff, and Julia H. Pudlin
Williams & Connolly LLP
725 12th Street, N.W.
Washington, DC 20005
Telephone: (202) 434-5000; Facsimile: (202) 434-5029

(With Developments Reported Through **November 1, 2012**)

GENERAL COMMENTS

Since August 1, 1970, the District of Columbia Court of Appeals has been the highest court of the District of Columbia, and the Superior Court has been the local trial court of general jurisdiction. Prior to that time, the U.S. Court of Appeals for the District of Columbia Circuit was the highest court and the U.S. District Court for the District of Columbia was the trial court of general jurisdiction, at least for claims in excess of $50,000.

SIGNIFICANT DEVELOPMENTS SINCE THE 2012 *SURVEY*

None.

I. GENERAL LAW

A. General Employment Law

1. ***At Will Employment.*** At will employees do not have written contracts and are employed for an unspecified term. Under D.C. law, either party can terminate the employment relationship for any or no reason. Elliot v. Healthcare Corp., 629 A.2d 6, 8 (D.C. 1993); International City Mgt. Ass'n Retirement Corp. v. Watkins, 726 F. Supp. 1, 8 (D.D.C. 1989). D.C. courts reject claims of wrongful discharge by at will employees. See Fleming v. AT&T Information Servs., Inc., 279 U.S. App. D.C. 15, 878 F.2d 1472, 1474 (1989) (finding no breach of contract); Kerrigan v. Britches of Georgetowne, Inc., 705 A.2d 624, 627 (D.C. 1997) (finding no breach of the implied covenant of good faith and fair dealing). D.C. law has carved out two exceptions to this rule, permitting at will employees to sue for wrongful discharge: (1) based on the employee's refusal to break the law at the employer's direction, Adams v. George W. Cochran & Co., 597 A.2d 28, 30 (D.C. 1991), and (2) where the employer's conduct violates "public policy." Carl v. Children's Hospital, 702 A.2d 159, 160 (D.C. 1997). See also Liberatore v. Melville Corp., 335 U.S. App. D.C. 26, 168 F.3d 1326, 1329-30 (1999). The D.C. Court of Appeals has not defined the scope of the public policy exception, advising that "'[f]uture requests to recognize [public policy] exceptions" to the at will doctrine "should be addressed only on a case-by-case basis. This court should consider seriously only those arguments that reflect a clear mandate of public policy – i.e., those that make a clear showing, based on some identifiable policy that has been "officially declared" in a statute or municipal regulation, or in the Constitution, that a new exception is needed.'" Fingerhut v. Children's Nat'l Med. Ctr., 738 A.2d 799, 803 (D.C. 1999) (quoting Carl, 702 A.2d at 164). In addition, "'there must be a close fit between the policy thus declared and the conduct at issue in the allegedly wrongful termination,'" and "exceptions must be 'firmly anchored either in the Constitution or in a statute or regulation which clearly reflects the particular "public policy" being relied upon.'" Id. at 803 n.7 (quoting Carl, 702 A.2d at 162, 164).

The D.C. Court of Appeals has not addressed the question of whether individual supervisors can be held liable for employees' wrongful discharge, but the U.S. District Court has held that the "D.C. Court of Appeals would allow claims against individual supervisors for wrongful discharge if it was shown that their conduct was sufficiently wrongful and violative of an important public policy." Myers v. Alutiiq Int'l Solutions, LLC, 811 F. Supp. 2d 261, 269 (2011).

B. Elements of Defamation Claim

1. ***Basic Elements.*** "To prevail in a defamation suit, Plaintiff must prove that the statements complained of were i) defamatory; ii) capable of being proven true or false; iii) 'of and concerning' the Plaintiff; iv) false and v) made with the requisite degree of intent or fault." Coles v. Washington Free Weekly, Inc., 881 F. Supp. 26, 30, 23 Media L. Rep. 1695 (D.D.C. 1995) (citing Liberty Lobby, Inc. v. Dow Jones & Co., 267 U.S. App. D.C. 337, 838 F.2d 1287, 1292-93, 14 Media L. Rep. 2249 (1988)). See also Moss v. Stockard, 580 A.2d 1011, 1022 (D.C. 1990); Benic v. Reuters America, Inc., 357 F. Supp. 2d 216, 220-21 (D.D.C. 2004). A plaintiff must also prove that the statements were vi) published to a third party, vii) published "without privilege," and viii) either "actionable as a matter of law irrespective or special harm or that [their] publication caused the plaintiff special harm." Crowley v. North Am. Telecommuns. Ass'n, 691 A.2d 1169, 1173 n.2 (D.C. 1997) (quotation omitted).

2. ***Fault.***

a. **Private Figure Plaintiff/Matter of Public Concern.** The D.C. Court of Appeals has held that matters of public concern are those that "relate[] to the ordering of government and society at large," Ayala v. Washington, 679 A.2d 1057, 1065 (D.C. 1996), and not merely those matters that attract "public interest," id. When a private figure plaintiff sues over a statement involving a matter of public concern, the standard of liability is negligence, see Moss, 580 A.2d at 1022 n.23, which must be proved by a preponderance of the evidence, see Ollman v. Evans, 242 U.S. App. D.C. 301, 750 F.2d 970, 976 n. 10, 11 Media L. Rep. 1433 (1984).

Examples of statements involving matters of public concern: A letter from an airline pilot's ex-girlfriend to the FAA accusing the agency of gender discrimination for failing to address her claims. Ayala, 679 A.2d at 1068. Allegations regarding the ethics of a government employee who controls government contracts. Lewis v. Elliot, 628 F. Supp. 512, 521 (D.D.C. 1986).

b. **Private Figure Plaintiff/Matter of Private Concern.** When a private figure sues over a matter of private concern, the standard of liability also is negligence. See Phillips v. Evening Star Newspaper Co., 424 A.2d 78, 87, 6 Media L. Rep. 2191 (D.C. 1980).

Examples of matters of private concern: A letter from an airline pilot's ex-girlfriend to the pilot's employer accusing him of off-duty marijuana use involved a matter of private concern. Although the alleged misconduct "could have a significant effect on public safety[, t]he allegations did not . . . address any issue concerning the conduct of government or the structure of society or any social issue." Ayala, 679 A.2d at 1068. See also Moss, 580 A.2d at 1033 (firing of a college basketball coach).

c. **Public Figure Plaintiff/Matter of Public Concern.** When a plaintiff is a public official or a public figure, the actual malice standard of New York Times Co. v. Sullivan, 376 U.S. 254, 280 (1964), applies, whether or not the challenged statement relates to a matter of public concern.

Examples of public figure plaintiffs. A woman who elected to be one of the first two women combat pilots while knowing of the preexisting public controversy over the appropriateness of women in combat positions "could reasonably have been expected to know that she was assuming a position of special prominence in the controversy about women in combat roles" and was, therefore, a voluntary limited-purpose public figure. Lohrenz v. Donnelly, 350 F.3d 1272, 1282, 32 Media L. Rep. 1065 (D.C. Cir. 2003) (internal quotation omitted); see also Bannum, Inc. v. Citizens for a Safe Ward 5, Inc. 383 F.Supp.2d 32 (D.D.C. 2005) (holding that an operator of community corrections centers is a limited-purpose public figure); Lapointe v. Van Note, 2006 WL 3734166, 35 Media L. Rep. 1065 (D.D.C. 2006) (holding that the Secretary General of a UN environmental program is a limited purpose public figure).

3. ***Falsity.*** "[I]n a defamation case the plaintiff has the burden of proving that the challenged statements are both false and defamatory." Kendrick v. Fox Television, 659 A.2d 814, 819, 24 Media L. Rep. 1065 (D.C. 1995). See also Ayala, 679 A.2d at 1069; Vereen v. Clayborne, 623 A.2d 1190, 1194-95 (D.C. 1993). A private-figure libel plaintiff may establish falsity by a preponderance of the evidence. See Ayala, 679 A.2d at 106. One court has held that a public-figure plaintiff must establish falsity by clear and convincing evidence. See Robertson v. McCloskey, 666 F. Supp. 241, 248, 14 Media L. Rep. 1437 (D.D.C. 1987). "A defendant can defend against a plaintiff's defamation claim by demonstrating that the gist of the statement is true or that the statement is substantially true, as it would be understood by its intended audience." Benic v. Reuters America, Inc., 357 F. Supp. 2d 216, 224 (D.D.C. 2004) (internal quotation omitted).

4. ***Defamatory Statement of Fact.*** A statement is defamatory if it tends to injure the plaintiff in his trade, profession, or community standing, or lower him in the estimation of the community. Clawson v. St. Louis Post-Dispatch, LLC, 906 A.2d 308 (D.C. 2006) (holding that the words "informer" and "FBI informer" are not defamatory); Howard Univ. v. Best, 484 A.2d 958, 989 (D.C. 1984); Afro-American Publ'g Co. v. Jaffe, 125 U.S. App. D.C. 70, 366 F.2d 649, 654 (1966). "[A]n allegedly defamatory remark must be more than unpleasant or offensive; the language must make the plaintiff appear "'odious, infamous, or ridiculous.'" Howard Univ., 484 A.2d at 989 (quoting Johnson v. Johnson Publ'g Co., 271 A.2d 696, 607 (D.C. 1970)); see also Ihebereme v. Capitol One, N.A., No. 10-1106 (ESH), 2010 WL 3118815, *11-12 (D.D.C. Aug. 9, 2010) (statements sent to credit bureaus were reasonably susceptible of defamatory meaning); Benic v. Reuters America, Inc., 357 F. Supp. 2d 216, 222-23 (D.D.C. 2004) (statement was not defamatory because "the average reasonable reader would not have interpreted [it] to mean that [plaintiff] had acted in a manner that was 'odious, infamous, or ridiculous'"). Press release by the District of Columbia CFO stating that fired city employees lacked the skills to perform their jobs was a charge of incompetence that was capable of being defamatory. Leonard v. District of Columbia, 794 A.2d 618, 628 (D.C. 2002) (denying motion to dismiss defamation claims). See also Klayman v. Segal, 783 A.2d 607, 611, 617-618 (D.C. 2001) (allegedly false quotation in newspaper article about chairman of nonprofit organization's efforts to appear on television talk shows was not capable of defamatory meaning when read in context of entire article). In Clampitt v.

American University, 957 A.2d 23 (D.C. 2008), the D.C. Court of Appeals found that the plaintiff's allegations raised a jury question about whether the university had defamed her "by publicly appearing to adopt the allegations of financial mismanagement" that appeared in pre-termination press reports. Id. at 41.

The court determines, as a threshold matter, if the statement is capable of bearing a defamatory meaning. "'It is only when the court can say that the publication is not reasonably capable of any defamatory meaning and cannot be reasonably understood in any defamatory sense that it can rule as a matter of law, that it was not libelous.'" White v. Fraternal Order of Police, 285 U.S. App. D.C. 273, 909 F.2d 512, 518, 17 Media L. Rep. 2137 (1990) (quoting Levy v. American Mut. Ins. Co., 196 A.2d 475, 476 (D.C. 1964)). **Failure to submit evidence regarding the contents of allegedly defamatory statements prevents a court from determining whether the statements at issue are capable of bearing a defamatory meaning and may lead to dismissal of defamation claims. See Queen v. Schultz, --- F. Supp. 2d ----, 2012 WL 3743856, at *24 (D.D.C. Aug. 30, 2012) (granting summary judgment on defamation claim where the claimant failed "to submit any evidence whatsoever" regarding contents of statements at issue).** If the court has determined that the statement is capable of a defamatory meaning, the jury decides whether the statement was understood in the defamatory sense. Moss, 580 A.2d at 1023. The plaintiff bears the burden of proof on this issue. Kendrick v. Fox Television, 659 A.2d 814, 819, 24 Media L. Rep. 1065 (D.C. 1995).

5. ***Of and Concerning Plaintiff.*** A plaintiff must show that the statement complained of was "of and concerning" the plaintiff, Coles v. Washington Free Weekly, Inc., 881 F. Supp. 26, 33, 23 Media L. Rep. 1695 (D.D.C. 1995), which means that a listener or reader would have to reasonably believe that the statements referred to the plaintiff. Caudle v. Thomason, 942 F. Supp. 635, 638 (D.D.C. 1996). District of Columbia courts have held that to be actionable, a defamatory statement "'must leave no doubt . . . in the minds of those familiar with the situation'" as to the identity of the person discussed. Id. (quoting Cunningham v. United Nat'l Bank of Wash., 710 F. Supp. 861, 863 (D.D.C. 1989)). Nevertheless, the "of and concerning" element may be satisfied if "the statements at issue lead the listener to conclude that the speaker is referring to the plaintiff by description, even if the plaintiff is never named or is misnamed." Croixland Properties Ltd. P'ship v. Corcoran, 335 U.S. App. D.C. 377, 174 F.3d 213, 216 (D.C. Cir. 1999); see also Jankovic v. Int'l Crisis Group, 494 F.3d 1080, 1088-1091 (D.C. Cir. 2007) (addressing whether namesake of corporation can be defamed when false misdeeds are attributed to his company). Although the legal standard in this regard is "not entirely settled," more recent courts have used the "leave no doubt" standard. Standardized Civil Jury Instructions for the District of Columbia, No. 17-5 (1998).

6. ***Publication.***

a. **Intracorporate Communication.** The D.C. Court of Appeals has held that because "[i]t is clear that any communication to someone other than the person defamed is a publication," circulating a defamatory statement within an organization is actionable. District of Columbia v. Thompson, 570 A.2d 277, 292 (D.C. 1990), vacated in part on other grounds, 593 A.2d 621 (D.C. 1991). **See also Owens v. District of Columbia, --- F. Supp. 2d ----, 2012 WL 2873945, at *4 (D.D.C. July 13, 2012) (fact issue as to whether plaintiff's performance evaluations were disseminated online precludes summary judgment on defamation claim).** "[T]he basis, if any, for excusing dissemination of a defamatory report . . . within an employment group . . . is not the lack of a publication." Id. Cf. Pinkney v. District of Columbia, 439 F. Supp. 519, 527 (D.D.C. 1977) (allegedly defamatory statement placed in plaintiff's personnel record was not yet a publication because "the statement complained of here is not alleged to have been sent to anyone other than the plaintiff himself"); **LeFande v. District of Columbia, --- F. Supp. 2d ----, 2012 WL 1865393, at *6 (D.D.C. May 21, 2012) (threat that allegedly defamatory material might be read by third parties fails to satisfy publication element).** In light of the Free Exercise Clause of the First Amendment, however, the D. C. Court of Appeals has held that the trustees of a church are protected against a pastor's defamation claims "when (1) such a claim flows entirely from an employment between a church and its pastor so that the consideration of the claims in isolation from the church's decision as to the pastor is not practical, (2) the alleged "publication" is confined within the church, and (3) there are no unusual or egregious circumstances." Heard v. Johnson, 810 A.2d 871, 885 (D.C. 2002).

b. **Compelled Self-Publication.** The District of Columbia does not recognize defamation claims based on compelled self-publication. Austin v. Howard Univ., 267 F. Supp. 2d 22, 30 (D.D.C. 2003); see also El-Hadad v. Embassy of the United Arab Emirates, 2006 WL 826098, at *17 (D.D.C. Mar. 29, 2006). In Atkins v. Industrial Telecommunications Association, Inc., 660 A.2d 885, 886, 892 (D.C. 1995), the D.C. Court of Appeals affirmed the dismissal of a libel count by the trial court, which had held that neither the District of Columbia nor Virginia recognized a cause of action based on compelled self-publication. *Id.* at 886. Although the Court of Appeals held that only Virginia law applied to the claim, the court repeated its previously stated view that "'there are few discernible differences between Virginia and District of Columbia defamation law,'" *id.* at 888 (quoting Sigal Constr. Corp. v. Stanbury, 586 A.2d 1204, 1208 (D.C. 1991)), and observed that "[o]nly a minority of jurisdictions have recognized a defamation claim based on compelled self-publication," Atkins, 660 A.2d at 894 (rejecting claim by former employee that he was compelled to publish a defamatory termination letter in response to questions from prospective employers).

c. **Republication.** Each publication of a defamatory statement, including each republication, is a separate tort; each republisher is responsible for the effects of his republication. Ingber v. Ross, 479 A.2d 1256, 1269 (D.C. 1984); Caudle v. Thomason, 942 F. Supp. 635, 639 (D.D.C. 1996). The originator of a defamatory statement may be liable for republication by a third party only if "'the repetition was reasonably to be expected.'" Ingber, 479 A.2d at 1269 (quoting Restatement (Second) of Torts § 576(c)).

7. ***Statements versus Conduct.*** "Actionable defamation is not necessarily restricted to verbal conduct. Indeed, it has been 'extended to . . . conduct carrying a defamatory imputation, such as hanging the plaintiff in effigy [or] erecting a gallows before his [or her] door.'" Wallace v. Skadden, Arps, Slate, Meagher & Flom, 715 A.2d 873, 878 n.5 (D.C. 1998) (quoting W. Page Keeton, Prosser and Keeton on the Law of Torts § 112, at 786 (5th ed. 1984)). Locking a terminated attorney out of her office by deactivating her access key can convey a defamatory meaning, if the evidence shows that the law firm has reserved such treatment for attorneys who had engaged in criminal or unethical activity. Wallace, 715 A.2d at 878.

8. ***Damages.*** Compensatory damages can be awarded for injury to reputation; for mental anguish, distress, and humiliation; and for any monetary and economic loss suffered as a result. Moss v. Stockard, 580 A.2d 1011, 1033 n.40 (D.C. 1990); Standardized Civil Jury Instructions for the District of Columbia, No. 17-13, Comment (1998). "It is an open question under D.C. law whether a plaintiff may recover damages for mental anguish without proof of injury to reputation." Id.

a. **Presumed Damages and Libel Per Se.** District of Columbia law permits the recovery of presumed damages for statements that are libelous per se. These are damages without proof of actual harm, "'presumed from the fact of publication.'" Moss, 580 A.2d at 1033 n.40 (quoting Gertz v. Robert Welch, Inc., 418 U.S. 323, 349, 1 Media L. Rep. 1633 (1974)); Robertson v. McCloskey, 680 F. Supp. 414, 415-16 (D.D.C. 1988). The District of Columbia applies a negligence standard for the recovery of presumed damages in cases involving private figures and matters of private concern. See Moss, 580 A.2d at 1033 n.40. Pursuant to Gertz, a plaintiff suing over matters of public concern must prove actual malice in order to recover presumed damages. See Ingber v. Ross, 479 A.2d 1256, 1265 (D.C. 1984). It is an open question in the District of Columbia whether a preponderance of the evidence or a clear and convincing evidence standard applies. See Moss v. Stockard, 580 A.2d 1011, 1033 n.40 (D.C. 1990).

The false imputation of criminal conduct is libelous per se. Washington Annapolis Hotel Co. v. Riddle, 83 U.S. App. D.C. 288, 171 F.2d 732, 736 (1948); Raboya v. Shrybman & Assocs., 777 F. Supp. 58, 60, 19 Media L. Rep. 1669 (D.D.C. 1991); Farnum v. Colbert, 293 A.2d 279, 281 (D.C. 1972); Harmon v. Liss, 116 A.2d 693, 695 (D.C. 1955).

(1) **Employment-Related Criticism.** "'One who publishes a slander that ascribes to another conduct, characteristics or a condition that would adversely affect [her] fitness for the proper conduct of [her] lawful business, trade or profession . . . is subject to liability without proof of special harm.'" Wallace v. Skadden, Arps, Slate, Meagher & Flom, 715 A.2d 873, 877-78 (D.C. 1998) (quoting Restatement (Second) of Torts § 573 (1977)). An allegation that an attorney is often out of the office during normal work hours could reasonably be construed, in context, as a reflection on her professional performance, Wallace, 715 A.2d at 878, as can an allegation that a dentist works only as a hygienist and does not handle complex cases. Ingber, 479 A.2d at 1264.

(2) **Single Instance Rule.** There are no reported cases in the District of Columbia concerning the application of the "single instance rule."

b. **Punitive damages.** To recover punitive damages in a defamation action, a plaintiff must establish by clear and convincing evidence that the defendant (1) published with knowledge of falsity or reckless disregard for truth, and (2) acted with spite, ill will, vengeance or deliberate intent to harm the plaintiff. See Columbia First Bank v. Ferguson, 665 A.2d 650, 657-58 (D.C. 1995); Standardized Civil Jury Instructions for the District of Columbia, No. 17-14 (1998). A plaintiff must prove at least nominal compensatory damages in order to collect punitive damages. See Ayala v. Washington, 679 A.2d 1057, 1070 (D.C. 1996). Proof of common law malice that is sufficient to overcome a qualified privilege is not, by itself, sufficient to satisfy the standard required for recovery of punitive damages. See Ferguson, 665 A.2d at 657-58.

II. PRIVILEGES AND DEFENSES

A. Scope of Privileges

1. ***Absolute Privilege.*** "[T]he District of Columbia has long recognized an absolute privilege for statements made preliminary to, or in the course of, a judicial proceeding, so long as the statements bear some relation to the proceeding." Finkelstein, Thompson & Loughran v. Hemispherx Biopharma, Inc., 774 A.2d 332, 338 (D.C. 2001); Messina v. Krakower, 439 F.3d 755, 760 (D.C. Cir. 2006) (citing cases). See In re Spikes, 881 A.2d 1118, 1123 (D.C. 2005) ("The

privilege for statements made in the course of judicial proceedings . . . is intended to afford an attorney absolute immunity from actions in defamation . . .") (emphasis omitted); Am. Petroleum Institute v. Technomedia Int'l, Inc., 699 F. Supp. 2d 258, 268-69 (D.D.C. 2010) (applying privilege to letter raising the specter of future litigation); Messina v. Fontana, 260 F. Supp. 2d 173, 177-78 (D.D.C. 2003) (letter sent by an attorney proposing a settlement prior to the filing of a lawsuit was absolutely privileged because it was "preliminary to a judicial proceeding") (quoting Finkelstein); Hinton v. Shaw Pittman Potts & Trowbridge, 257 F. Supp. 2d 96, 99 (D.D.C. 2003) (in-court testimony by employer and supervisor was absolutely privileged and would not support defamation claim); Browning v. Clinton, 292 F.3d 235, 246-47 (D.C. Cir. 2002) (memorandum produced by former President in direct response to document request in sexual harassment suit against him was absolutely privileged and would not support defamation claim) (quoting Finkelstein). The same privilege applies to statements made in legislative, administrative, or arbitral proceedings. See Mazanderan v. McGranery, 490 A.2d 180, 181 (D.C. 1984); Webster v. Sun Co., 252 U.S. App. D.C. 335, 790 F.2d 157, 162 (1986); Sturdivant v. Seaboard Serv. Sys., 459 A.2d 1058, 1059-60 (D.C. 1983). The D.C. Court of Appeals has held privileged statements made in an attorney's correspondence that was preliminary to a judicial proceeding that had been threatened against his client. McBride v. Pizza Hut, Inc., 658 A.2d 205, 208 (D.C. 1995); Marsh v. Hollander, 2004 WL 2106414, at *4 (D.D.C. 2004) ("statements made for the purpose of preparing for litigation, or . . . attempting to settle issues prior to commencing litigation are covered by this absolute privilege"). The Court of Appeals recently held that the privilege extends even to statements related to potential litigation made by attorneys "during preliminary consultations with prospective clients, including contacts that may be characterized as client solicitation," Finkelstein, 774 A.2d at 345, and that the privilege provides an absolute immunity from suit, not merely a defense to liability, see id. at 340 (permitting interlocutory appeal of denial of privilege's applicability). The privilege "applies to the range of potential participants in a legal proceeding—including attorneys, parties, judicial officers, witnesses, and jurors." Marsh, 2004 WL 2106414, at *5 (citing Brown v. Collins, 402 F.2d 209, 212 nn. 3-4 (D.C. Cir. 1968)). The privilege applies as well to a report to an unemployment compensation bureau. See Elliot v. Healthcare Corp., 629 A.2d 6, 9 (D.C. 1993); Goggins v. Hoddes, 265 A.2d 302, 303 (D.C. 1970). The absolute privilege also applies to statements made by an employer to the EEOC in the course of an EEOC investigation of an employee's discrimination claim, see Stith v. Chadbourne & Parke, LLP, 160 F. Supp. 2d 1, 8 (D.D.C. 2001), and to "statements made to the police for the purpose of initiating a criminal proceeding," id. at 7. A government official has absolute immunity from defamation claims when he is "performing an act required by law" or when the official's conduct was "(1) . . . within the outer perimeter of his official duties, and (2) the particular government function at issue was discretionary as opposed to ministerial." District of Columbia v. Simpkins, 720 A.2d 894, 897 (D.C. 1998). See also Liser v. Smith, 254 F. Supp. 2d 89, 101 (D.D.C. 2003) (holding that police detective's public release of information about ongoing criminal investigation was absolutely privileged); Trifax Corp. v. District of Columbia, 53 F. Supp. 2d 20, 25 (1999) (holding that statements set forth in report by the Office of Inspector General are absolutely privileged); Moss v. Stockard, 580 A.2d 1011, 1020 (D.C. 1990); Ribas v. Macher, 687 F. Supp. 684, 686 (D.D.C. 1988); Newbury v. Love, 100 U.S. App. D.C. 79, 242 F.2d 372, 373 (1957). "Accordingly, whenever a government official's conduct meets the test for absolute privilege based on the performance of an official mandatory or discretionary duty, no claim for defamation may be premised on statements published in the exercise of that duty." Simpkins, 720 A.2d at 897. Members of the Committee on Unauthorized Practice of Law (CUPL) have "absolute immunity for damages conferred on the Committee and its members." See In re Banks, 2002 WL 1988478, at *7 (D.C. Aug. 29, 2002).

2. ***Qualified Privileges.*** The existence of a qualified privilege is a complete defense to libel, but will be lost if the privilege is abused, such as if the defendant publishes a statement with malice, or if he publishes a statement in circumstances beyond those covered by privilege. "A qualified privilege is lost through publication that is outside normal channels, or otherwise excessive, or that is made with malicious intent." Tacka v. Georgetown Univ., 193 F. Supp. 2d 43, 52-53, 30 Media L. Rep. 1065 (D.D.C. 2001). See also Mosrie v. Trussell, 467 A.2d 475, 477 (D.C. 1983) (malice); Moss v. Stockard, 580 A.2d 1011, 1024 (D.C. 1990) (excessive publication). "District of Columbia law makes it very difficult for a plaintiff to overcome a qualified privilege." Novecon, Ltd. v. Bulgarian-Am. Enter. Fund, 338 U.S. App. D.C. 67, 190 F.3d 556, 567 (1999). There must be a "reasonable ground" for making the statement, "either in the legitimate interest of the person uttering it, or of the person to whom it is communicated." Collins v. Brown, 268 F. Supp. 198, 200 (D.D.C. 1967). Absent a family or other special relationship, a qualified privilege is less likely to be accorded when the statement is volunteered. Brown v. Collins, 131 U.S. App. D.C. 68, 402 F.2d 209, 211-12 (1968). The qualified privileges most pertinent in the employment context are set out below.

a. **Common Interest.** "To come within the protection of the common interest privilege, the statement must have been (1) made in good faith, (2) on a subject in which the party communicating has an interest or in reference to which he has, or honestly believes he has, a duty to a person having a corresponding interest or duty, (3) to a person who has such a corresponding interest." Millstein v. Henske, 772 A.2d 850, 856 (D.C. 1999) (citing Moss, 580 A.2d at 1024); see also Blodgett v. Univ. Club, 930 A.2d 210, 223-24 (D.C. 2007); Mastro v. Potomac Elec. Power Co., 447 F.3d 843, 858 (D.C. Cir. 2006); Armenian Assembly of America, Inc. v. Cafesjian, 692 F. Supp. 2d 20, 48-52 (D.D.C. 2010); Stark v. Zeta Phi Beta Sorority, Inc., 587 F. Supp. 2d 170, 176 (D.D.C. 2008); Slovinec v. American Univ., 565 F.Supp.2d 114, 119 (D.D.C. 2008); Catalyst & Chemical Services, Inc. v. Global Ground Support, 350 F. Supp. 2d 1, 21 (D.D.C. 2004). "Two circumstances foreclose asserting the privilege: first, excessive publication, defined as 'publication to those with no common interest in the information communicated, or publication not reasonably calculated to protect or further the interest,' and, second, publication with malice, which, within the context of the common interest privilege, is 'the equivalent of bad faith' . . ." Mastro, 447 F.3d at 858 (internal citations omitted) (quoting Moss, 580 A.2d at 1024, 1025). Applying the common interest privilege to protect statements that were made in an appraisal of the work of a university employee and that were passed on to university officials, the D.C. Court of Appeals observed that "[t]he privilege is an important one, because 'if [its] protection were not given, true information that should be given or received would not be communicated because of fear of the persons capable of giving it that they would be held liable in an action of defamation if their statements were untrue.'" Millstein, 722 A.2d at 856 (quoting Restatement (Second) of Torts, Ch. 25, Topic 3, Title A Scope Note (1977)). Statements made to the police to ensure plaintiff's peaceful removal from a place of business, but not made for the purpose of instituting judicial proceedings, are covered by the qualified common interest privilege (as opposed to the absolute judicial proceedings privilege). See Stith v. Chadbourne & Parke, LLP, 160 F. Supp. 2d 1, 8-9 (D.D.C. 2001). **The qualified common interest privilege also protects statements made by anyone who communicates in good faith with District of Columbia agencies during an investigation into alleged misconduct by District employees. See Payne v. Clark, 25 A.3d 918, 927 (D.C. 2011).** "It is a question of law for the court to determine whether a communication is privileged when the facts surrounding its publication are undisputed. . . . The issue of whether a party abused the privilege by acting with malice, recklessness, or dishonesty is a question of fact for the jury." Catalyst & Chemical Services, 350 F. Supp. 2d at 21.

The District of Columbia also recognizes the related qualified privilege of "self defense." See Washburn v. Lavoie, 437 F.3d 84, 90 (D.C. Cir. 2006); Mosrie, 467 A.2d at 477. "The privilege applies 'if the circumstances induce a correct or reasonable belief that (a) there is information that affects a sufficiently important interest of the publisher, and (b) the recipient's knowledge of the defamatory matter will be of service in the lawful protection of the interest." Washburn, 437 F.3d at 90 (quoting Restatement (Second) of Torts § 594 (1977)). See Mosrie, 467 A.2d at 479 ("self defense" privilege applied to protect statements by deputy chief against one of his accusers, where deputy chief made statements in context of internal investigation into his own misconduct, in order to shed light on motives of accusers); Dickins v. International Bhd. of Teamsters, 84 U.S. App. D.C. 51, 171 F.2d 21, 23-24 (1948) (privilege applied to statements about plaintiff that defendant's magazine circulated to more than 400,000 people, where defendant was responding to the plaintiff's accusations against its members, which were published in thousands of newspapers nationally); Novecon, Ltd., 190 F.3d at 566-69 (privilege applied to defendants' letter to more than 500 individuals and organizations making accusations against the plaintiffs, where the defendants were responding to an op-ed piece in the Wall Street Journal that, although favorable to the plaintiffs, was written by a third party). "[T]he privilege is not limited to replies to known attackers." Novecon, Ltd., 190 F.3d at 569. "[A] showing of 'excessive publication or express malice' can destroy [the] qualified privilege." Washburn, 437 F.3d at 91 (quoting Curry v. Giant Food Co., 522 A.2d 1283, 1294 (D.C. 1987)).

b. **Duty**. A qualified privilege protects statements made pursuant to official duty, Columbia First Bank v. Ferguson, 665 A.2d 650, 655 (D.C. 1995), such as statements by law enforcement authorities about suspected wrongdoing, see id.

Examples of statements held to be privileged or unprivileged: A bank security officer's report to regulators of alleged bank fraud is covered by the privilege. Columbia First Bank, 665 A.2d at 655. Officers and faculty members of educational organizations have a qualified privilege to discuss the qualifications of other officers and faculty members, as long as their statements are pertinent to the functioning of the educational institution. Greenya v. George Washington Univ., 167 U.S. App. D.C. 379, 512 F.2d 556, 563 (1975); McConnell v. Howard Univ., 260 U.S. App. D.C. 192, 818 F.2d 58, 70-71 (1987). An officer of a union can inform the union of any wrongdoing by its officers, attorneys, or members. Manbeck v. Ostrowski, 128 U.S. App. D.C. 1, 384 F.2d 970, 974 (1967). A hospital security guard's statements accusing an orderly of theft were covered by the privilege; a nurse administrator's allegations against the orderly regarding the same incident were not. Smith v. District of Columbia, 399 A.2d 213, 221 (D.C. 1979). Privilege applies to reports on employees that had been requested by prospective employers. Siegert v. Gilley, 282 U.S. App. D.C. 392, 895 F.2d 797, 803, aff'd, 500 U.S. 226 (1990); Collins v. Brown, 268 F. Supp. 198, 200 (D.D.C. 1967). A statement of wrongdoing made in good faith to law enforcement authorities is covered by the privilege. Columbia First Bank v. Ferguson, 665 A.2d 650, 655 (D.C. 1995); see also In re Spikes, 881 A.2d 1118, 1124 (D.C. 2005) ("a qualified privilege attaches to reports made to law enforcement authorities for investigation"). Store operator's claim that plaintiff committed theft by cashing an invalid check may or may not be privileged, depending on jury determination whether claim to investigators was made in bad faith. Carter v. Hahn, 821 A.2d 890, 894 (D.C. 2003) (reversing dismissal of defamation claim). Statements necessary for the smooth and efficient operation of a congressmen's office are covered by the privilege. Roland v. D'Arazien, 222 U.S. App. D.C. 203, 685 F.2d 653, 655 (1982).

c. **Criticism of Public Employee.** Criticism of public officials or public figures is protected by the actual malice standard of New York Times v. Sullivan. See Thompson v. Evening Star Newspaper Co., 129 U.S. App. D.C. 299, 394 F.2d 774, 775-76 (1968). "If a private citizen may be held liable in tort for a particular defamatory statement, then a public employee is equally liable in tort for the same statement." American Postal Workers Union v. United States Postal Serv., 265 U.S. App. D.C. 146, 830 F.2d 294, 308 (1987).

d. **Limitation on Qualified Privileges.** The D.C. Court of Appeals has held that to overcome a qualified privilege, a plaintiff must prove that the defendant acted with common law malice. See Moss v. Stockard, 580 A.2d 1011, 1026 n.29 (D.C. 1990). But see White v. Fraternal Order of Police, 285 U.S. App. D.C. 273, 909 F.2d 512, 524-25, 17 Media L. Rep. 2137 (1990) (stating that proof of actual malice can defeat qualified privilege). In Moss, the D.C. Court of Appeals applied a preponderance of the evidence, rather than a clear and convincing evidence, standard in finding that the existence of malice defeated a qualified privilege. 580 A.2d at 1033.

(1) **Constitutional or Actual Malice.** "The New York Times rule of actual malice redirects the focus of inquiry from the common law's emphasis on the defendant's attitude toward the plaintiff as the animus for defamatory publication to the defendant's attitude toward the truth or falsity of the content of such a publication." Nader v. de Toledano, 408 A.2d 31, 40, 5 Media L. Rep. 1550 (D.C. 1979). A plaintiff can establish actual malice only by proving by clear and convincing evidence that the defendant published a false statement with knowledge of falsity or reckless disregard for truth. "'[R]eckless conduct is not measured by whether a reasonably prudent man would have published, or would have investigated before publishing. There must be sufficient evidence to permit the conclusion that the defendant in fact entertained serious doubts as to the truth of his publication. Publishing with such doubts shows reckless disregard for truth or falsity and demonstrates actual malice.'" Id. at 41 (quoting St. Amant v. Thompson 390 U.S. 727, 731 (1968)).

(2) **Common Law Malice.** Common law malice is equivalent to bad faith or evil motive. Moss, 580 A.2d at 1026 n.29; Mosrie v. Trussell, 467 A.2d 475, 477 (D.C. 1983). It is "'the doing of an act without just cause or excuse, with such a conscious indifference or reckless disregard as to its results or effects upon the rights of feeling of others as to constitute ill will.'" Mosrie, 467 A.2d at 477. Ill will, by itself, is not enough to overcome the privilege. Id. at 477-78. See also Alade v. Borg-Warner Protective Servs. Corp., 28 F. Supp. 2d 655, 656 (D.D.C. 1998). Nor is ordinary negligence, such as the failure to inquire about the truth of an assertion prior to publication. Moss, 580 A.2d at 1025.

(3) **Other Limitations on Qualified Privileges.** The District of Columbia's qualified privileges may also be lost through excessive publication. "'Excessive publication,' defined as publication to those with no common interest in the information communicated, or publication not reasonably calculated to protect or further the interest, will render the statement non-privileged." Moss, 580 A.2d at 1024. In the context of the "self defense" privilege, the D.C. Circuit stated that "the common law privilege . . . does not demand that defendants demonstrate failsafe precision in identifying third parties with a sufficient interest in [defendants'] public controversy." Novecon, Ltd. v. Bulgarian-Am. Enter. Fund, 338 U.S. App. D.C. 67, 190 F.3d 556, 569 (1999) (quotation omitted). To retain the protection of the privilege, it is sufficient that the defendants "attempted to reach persons whose opinions of [defendants] were, or reasonably could have been, affected by plaintiffs' comments and the ensuing wave of negative publicity." Id. at 570 (quotation omitted). More generally, "'If on an occasion giving rise to a conditional privilege the publisher mistakenly communicates the defamatory matter to some person to whom he is not otherwise privileged to publish it, he is protected if . . . he reasonably believes that the person to whom he communicates it is a person whose knowledge of the matter would be useful in the protection of the interests in question.'" Id. at 569 n.8 (quoting Restatement (Second) of Torts § 604 cmt. e).

e. **Question of Fact or Law.** The existence of a qualified privilege is a question of law for the court to decide. Whether the privilege was abused by the defendant is a question of fact for the jury. Mosrie v. Trussell, 467 A.2d 475, 477 (D.C. 1983).

f. **Burden of Proof.** The plaintiff bears the burden of proving that the privilege does not apply, and a defendant is presumed to have acted in good faith. Moss v. Stockard, 580 A.2d 1011, 1024 (D.C. 1990); Mosrie, 467 A.2d at 477.

B. Standard Libel Defenses

1. ***Truth.*** Although truth has traditionally been considered a defense to a defamation claim, after Philadelphia Newspapers, Inc. v. Hepps, 475 U.S. 767, 776-77, 12 Media L. Rep. 1977 (1986) (holding that the First Amendment requires that plaintiff bear the burden of proving falsity of statements involving issues of public concern), courts applying D.C. law have held that falsity is as an essential element of the cause of action. See, e.g., Farrington v. BNA, Inc., 596 A.2d 58, 59-60 (D.C. 1991); Moss, 580 A.2d at 1022 n.23. In order to prove falsity, a plaintiff must prove that the challenged statement is not "substantially true." **If a statement is substantially true, then it is considered to be true as a legal matter for defamation purposes. See Farouki v. Petra Int'l Banking Corp., 811 F. Supp. 2d 388, 403 (D.D.C. 2011).** A statement is "substantially true" if the alleged falsity does not alter the statement's "gist" or "sting" in the mind of the reader or listener. See Prins v. IT& T, 757 F. Supp. 87, 91 (D.D.C. 1991).

2. ***Opinion.*** Following Milkovich v. Lorain Journal Co., 497 U.S. 1 (1990), D.C. courts hold that the First Amendment protects from liability statements that are not objectively verifiable as false. See White v. Fraternal Order of Police, 285 U.S. App. D.C. 273, 909 F.2d 512, 522, 17 Media L. Rep. 2137 (1990) (citing Milkovich); Coles v. Washington Free Weekly, Inc., 881 F. Supp. 26, 31, 23 Media L. Rep. 1695 (D.D.C. 1995). In Sigal Construction Corp. v. Stanbury, 586 A.2d 1204, 1210 (D.C. 1991), the D.C. Court of Appeals used a four-part test to distinguish actionable facts from constitutionally protected opinions in which the court considered: (1) "the allegedly defamatory words in the context of the document in which they appear"; (2) whether the statements "could be said to imply undisclosed defamatory facts"; (3) "whether the allegedly defamatory words are susceptible to proof of their truth or falsity"; and (4) "the context in which the document containing the allegedly defamatory reference is published." Id. (quoting Myers v. Plan Takoma, Inc., 472 A.2d 44, 47 (D.C. 1983)). **In Rosen v. American Israel Public Affairs Committee, Inc., 41 A.3d 1250 (D.C. 2012), the D.C. Court of Appeals held that an employer's allegedly defamatory statement to a newspaper, asserting that its former employee's behavior did not comport with its expected standards, was not provably false and thus was not defamatory. The court found that the challenged statement was not defamatory because it did not refer to particular, identifiable standards but merely to a general, subjective term capable of multiple meanings. Id. at 1258.**

3. ***Consent.*** Although "[c]onsent is an absolute defense to a claim of defamation," Farrington v. BNA, Inc., 596 A.2d 58, 59 (D.C. 1991); Kraft v. William Alanson White Psychiatric Found., 498 A.2d 1145, 1150 (D.C. 1985); Watwood v. Credit Bureau, Inc., 97 A.2d 460, 461-62 (D.C. 1953); Marsh v. Hollander, 2004 WL 2106414, at *8 (D.D.C. 2004), District of Columbia courts continue to address circumstances in which a priori consent to publication of negative evaluations affords a defendant a qualified privilege only. See Woodfield v. Providence Hospital, 779 A.2d 933, 938 (D.C. 2001) (accepting *arguendo* plaintiff's argument that a showing of malice can defeat consent defense). Traditionally, D.C. courts have held that "[t]he publication of a defamatory statement is privileged if: (1) there was either express or implied consent to the publication; (2) the statements were relevant to the purpose for which consent was given; and (3) the publication of those statements was limited to the those with a legitimate interest in their content." Farrington, 596 A.2d at 59. See also Joftes v. Kaufman, 324 F. Supp. 660, 662 (D.D.C. 1971) (consent found because of employee's agreeing to union membership that requires written notice of dismissal). Kraft, 498 A.2d at 1149 (by enrolling as a student in training program, plaintiff impliedly consented to intra-school publication of allegedly defamatory statements); Marsh, 2004 WL 2106414, at *8 (plaintiff consented to accounting-related communications from defendant by entering into an agreement with defendant that contained provisions for resolving accounting disputes). More recently, courts have suggested that, even given a priori consent to the publication of performance evaluations, where such consent is "merely implicit" the privilege is qualified and may be defeated by a showing of malice or excessive publication. Tacka v. Georgetown Univ., 193 F. Supp. 2d 43, 52, 30 Media L. Rep. 1065 (D.D.C. 2001); see also Wallace v. Skadden, Arps, Slate, Meagher & Flom, 715 A.2d 873, 881 (D.C. 1998) ("in the absence of a contract or of some affirmative act of consent, the defendants' allegedly defamatory communications were protected by a qualified privilege only").

4. ***Mitigation.*** "Facts indicating that the degree of injury ordinarily assumed to flow from particular defamation was not sustained are admissible in mitigation of compensatory damages." Manbeck v. Ostrowski, 128 U.S. App. D.C. 1, 384 F.2d 970, 977 n.38 (1967) (citations omitted). "The trier of fact may consider such relevant factors as 'the character of the defamatory publication and the probable effect of the language used as well as the effect which it is proved to have had. So too, it may consider the area of dissemination and the extent and duration of the circulation of the publication.'" Id. (quoting Restatement of Torts § 621 cmt. c (1938)) (holding that evidence of assertedly privileged nature of statement, even if insufficient to establish privilege, was admissible with regard to damages because it "might have given additional color to the effort to minimize [plaintiff's] actual injury").

III. RECURRING FACT PATTERNS

A. Statements in Personnel File

The qualified privilege to discuss the qualifications of colleagues, if the matter communicated is pertinent to the functioning of the organization, "extends to internal records in which such matters are discussed or recorded." Greenya v. George Washington Univ., 167 U.S. App. D.C. 379, 512 F.2d 556, 563 (1975); see also Miller v. Health Serv. for Children Foundation, 630 F.Supp.2d 44, 49 (D.D.C. 2009). Placing a statement in an employee's personnel record that has not yet been viewed by a third party is not an actionable publication. Pinkney v. District of Columbia, 439 F. Supp. 519, 527 (D.D.C. 1977).

B. Performance Evaluations

D.C. courts have found statements made in performance evaluations to be protected on the ground of either qualified privilege or implied consent. See Millstein v. Henske, 722 A.2d 850, 856 (D.C. 1999) (statements that are part of an employee's work performance appraisal are subject to the qualified "common interest" privilege); Greenya v. George Washington Univ., 167 U.S. App. D.C. 379, 512 F.2d 556, 563 (1975) (qualified privilege); Farrington v. BNA, Inc., 596

A.2d 58, 59-60 (D.C. 1991) (consent found when employer was mandated by collective bargaining agreement to provide written performance evaluation of employees); Kraft v. William Alanson White Psychiatric Found., 498 A.2d 1145, 1150 (D.C. 1985) (implied consent found because plaintiff student, before enrollment, had been given literature about the program he was entering and thus "was on notice that his supervisors would evaluate his work and would of necessity communicate their evaluations to the chairman of the training program"). Cf. Wallace v. Skadden, Arps, Slate, Meagher & Flom, 715 A.2d 873, 881-82 (D.C. 1998) (consent to receiving performance evaluations does not necessarily immunize other allegedly defamatory statements about plaintiff's performance).

C. References

A qualified privilege applies to references provided to prospective employers. See Sigal Constr. Corp. v. Stanbury, 586 A.2d 1204,1215 (1991) (finding abuse of qualified privilege because employer failed to disclose that he had not actually worked with employee and reference was based on "rumor," "gossip," or "scuttlebutt"); Hargrow v. Long, 760 F. Supp. 1, 2 (D.D.C. 1989).

D. Intracorporate Communications

Atkins v. Industrial Telecommuns. Ass'n, Inc., 660 A.2d 885,892-93 (D.C. 1995) (staff memo about employee's firing may give rise to libel action); Roland v. D'Arazien, 222 U.S. App. D.C. 203, 685 F.2d 653, 655 (1982) (interoffice allegation of sexual misconduct by plaintiff, an intern, was protected by the common interest privilege).

E. Statements to Government Regulators

Ayala v. Washington, 679 A.2d 1057 (D.C. 1996) (pilot suing ex-girlfriend for libel after she sends letters to FAA about pilot's off-duty marijuana use); Columbia First Bank v. Ferguson, 665 A.2d 650, 655 (report of possible wrongdoing of bank employee qualifiedly privileged); McBride v. Pizza Hut, Inc, 658 A.2d 205, 207(1995) (report to unemployment board is absolutely privileged); Miller v. Health Serv. For Children Foundation, 630 F.Supp.2d 44, 49 (D.D.C. 2009) (same); Lewis v. Elliott, 628 F. Supp. 512 (D.D.C. 1986) (libel claim based on bid protest letter about government contract).

F. Reports to Auditors and Insurers

There are no reported D.C. cases discussing libel defenses in the context of reports to auditors or insurers.

G. Vicarious Liability of Employers for Statements Made by Employees

1. ***Scope of Employment***. For an employer to be liable for statements made by one of its employees, the statement must be "'foreseeable as being within the range of responsibilities entrusted to the employee.'" Sigal Constr. Corp. v. Stanbury, 586 A.2d 1204, 1217 (D.C. 1991) (quoting Johnson v. Weinberg, 434 A.2d 404, 408 (D.C. 1981)). See also Hawthorne v. WMATA, 702 F. Supp. 285, 288 (D.D.C. 1988) ("A prerequisite for imposing liability for defamation against [an employer], as with any other tort, is that the actions complained of occur during the scope of the employee's official duties"). The employer has the burden of proof that the employee was not acting within the scope of employment. Sigal, 586 A.2d at 1217. Scope of employment is a question of law for the court only if there is insufficient evidence from which a reasonable juror could find the action came within the scope of employment. Boykin v. District of Columbia, 484 A.2d 560, 562 (D.C. 1984). Liability may be imposed when the employee acts under express or implied authority. Providing a reference is an example of implied authority. Sigal, 586 A.2d at 1218. Liability also may be imposed when the employee acts under apparent authority. See id. at 1218-19.

a. **Blogging.** There are no reported D.C. cases on point.

2. ***Damages.*** Punitive damages may not be recovered against an employer unless it has authorized or ratified the conduct at issue. See Woodard v. City Stores Co., 334 A.2d 189, 191 (D.C. 1975); May Dep't Stores Co., Inc. v. Devercelli, 314 A.2d 767, 778 (D.C. 1973).

H. Internal Investigations

In Blodgett v. University Club, 930 A.2d 210, 223-24 (D.C. 2007), the D.C. Court of Appeals held that the qualified common interest privilege protected the creation and use of an internal investigative report by a private club's board of directors during an investigation into a member's conduct.

IV. OTHER ACTIONS BASED ON STATEMENTS

A. Negligent Hiring, Retention, and Supervision

A common law claim of negligent hiring, training, or supervision must be predicated on causes of action or duties otherwise imposed by the common law. See Griffin v. Acacia Life Ins. Co., 925 A.2d 564, 576 (D.C. 2007); **Coleman v.**

District of Columbia, 828 F. Supp. 2d 87, 95-97 (D.D.C. 2011) (holding that plaintiff failed to properly allege a claim for negligent hiring, training, and supervision based on court's conclusion that the plaintiff had failed to properly allege an underlying claim of wrongful discharge in violation of public policy). To withstand dismissal of a negligent supervision claim against an employer, a plaintiff must establish that the employer knew or should have known that its employee behaved in a dangerous or otherwise incompetent manner and that, armed with that actual or constructive knowledge, the employer failed to adequately supervise its employee. See Bond v. U.S. Dep't of Justice, 828 F. Supp. 2d 60, 82 (D.D.C. 2011). In Bond, the district court dismissed plaintiff's negligent supervision claim against a newspaper because the plaintiff failed to allege that the newspaper knew about any allegedly dangerous or incompetent behavior on the part of its reporter and failed to allege any action on the part of the reporter that occurred after the newspaper's ombudsman was on notice of the plaintiff's concerns. Id.

B. Intentional Infliction of Emotional Distress

The tort of intentional infliction of emotional distress requires proof of (1) "'extreme or outrageous conduct'" that (2) "'intentionally or recklessly'" causes (3) "'severe emotional distress to another.'" Kerrigan v. Britches of Georgetowne, Inc., 705 A.2d 624, 628 (D.C. 1997) (quoting Bernstein v. Fernandez, 649 A.2d 1064, 1075 (D.C. 1991)). Conduct must be "so outrageous in character, so extreme in degree, as to go beyond all possible bounds of decency, and to be regarded as atrocious, and utterly intolerable in a civilized community." Id. (quoting Restatement (Second) of Torts § 46 comment d (1965)). See Crowley v. North Am. Telecommuns. Ass'n., 691 A.2d 1169, 1171-73 (D.C. 1997) (dismissing intentional infliction of emotional distress claim because statement was not outrageous, but reinstating defamation claim because of lack of qualified privilege); Elliott v. Healthcare Corp., 629 A.2d 6, 9 (D.C. 1993) (as a matter of law, employee discharge was not sufficiently extreme or outrageous to support claim of intentional infliction of emotional distress).

The D.C. Court of Appeals has reiterated that "[t]he requirement of outrageousness is not an easy one to meet," and that "this court has been particularly demanding as to the proof required to support a claim of intentional infliction of emotional distress in an employment context." Paul v. Howard Univ., 754 A.2d 297, 307 (D.C. 2000) (citations omitted). The U.S. District Court has added that "[e]specially in the employment context, the standard is exacting." Evans v. District of Columbia, 391 F. Supp. 2d 160, 170 (D.D.C. 2005) (citing Futrell v. Dep't of Labor Fed. Credit Untion, 816 A.2d 793, 808 (D.C. 2003)). See also Duncan v. Children's Nat'l Med. Ctr., 702 A.2d 207, 211-12 (D.C. 1997) ("[G]enerally, employer-employee conflicts do not rise to the level of outrageous conduct.")).

C. Interference with Economic Advantage

A claim of tortious interference with contractual relations requires: (1) existence of a legal contract; (2) defendant's knowledge of the contract; (3) intentional interference without justification; and (4) resulting damages. International City Management Assoc. Retirement Corp. v. Watkins, 726 F. Supp. 1, 5 (D.D.C. 1989). Connors, Fiscina, Swartz & Zimmerly v. Rees, 599 A.2d 47, 51, 15 Media L. Rep. 1721 (D.C. 1991); Kassman v. American Univ., 178 U.S. App. D.C. 263, 546 F.2d 1029 (1976).

D. Prima Facie Tort

"District of Columbia courts have not embraced a form of generic tort like the prima facie tort recognized by New York courts." Art-Metal-U.S.A., Inc. v. United States, 577 F. Supp. 182, 184 (D.D.C. 1983).

V. OTHER ISSUES

A. Statute of Limitations

The statute of limitations for defamation is one year. D.C. Code § 12-301(4). "Defamation occurs on publication, and the statute of limitations runs from the date of publication." Wallace v. Skadden, Arps, Slate, Meagher & Flom, 715 A.2d 873, 882 (D.C. 1998) (quotation omitted); see also Jankovic v. Int'l Crisis Group, 494 F.3d 1080, 1086-87 (D.C. Cir. 2007) (discussing statute of limitations and possible tolling under theories of equitable estoppel, the "lulling doctrine," and equitable tolling). **Hu v. George Washington Univ., 766 F. Supp. 2d 236, 243 (D.D.C. 2011) ("[I]n the District of Columbia a claim of common law defamation must be brought within one year of when a plaintiff knows or through the exercised of due diligence should have known the defamation occurred").** D.C. adheres to the single publication rule, and the republication of an allegedly libelous document on the Internet was not sufficient to restart the statute of limitations for a defamation claim. Jankovic, 494 F.3d at 1087. Where other torts with longer limitations periods arise out of the alleged defamation, the one-year period applies to those torts as well. See Mittleman v. United States, 322 U.S. App. D.C. 367, 104 F.3d 410, 415-16 (1997); Jovanovic v. US-Algeria Business Council, 561 F.Supp.2d 103, 113-14 (D.D.C. 2008). In the case of mass media publication, a defamation claim accrues at the time of publication, not at the time of discovery. See Mullin v. Washington Free Weekly, 785 A.2d 296, 299, 30 Media L. Rep. 1092 (D.C. 2001). If the allegedly defamatory statement was not made in a mass media context, and was otherwise not discoverable by the plaintiff, the statute of limitations may run from the date on which the plaintiff discovered the allegedly defamatory statement. Maupin v. Haylock, 931 A.2d 1039 (D.C. 2007).

B. Jurisdiction

Personal Jurisdiction: The District of Columbia's long-arm statute is found at D.C. Code § 13-423, and its application to defendants "transacting any business" in the District has been called coextensive with the Due Process Clause of the U.S. Constitution. See Mouzavires v. Baxter, 434 A.2d 988, 991 (D.C. 1981). However, to protect news organizations from being subject to unrelated lawsuits in the District solely by virtue of their newsgathering presence in the nation's capital, D.C. courts have created an exception to the statute providing that "the mere collection of news material here for use in subsequent publication elsewhere . . . is not a doing of business here, within the meaning of the statute." Moncrief v. Lexington Herald-Leader Co., 257 U.S. App. D.C. 72, 807 F.2d 217, 222, 13 Media L. Rep. 1762 (1986) (quotation omitted). For a recent discussion of personal jurisdiction in a defamation case, see Charlton v. Mond, 987 A.2d 436, 438-40 (D.C. 2010).

Subject-Matter Jurisdiction: The exclusive remedy for defamation suits brought by employees of the District of Columbia government as a result of statements made in connection with personnel issues is provided by the Comprehensive Merit Personnel Act, D.C. Code §§ 1-603.1, 1-606.1, 1-606.2, 1-606.3, 1-617.52, 1-617.53. See Stockard v. Moss, 706 A.2d 561, 566 (D.C. 1997). Thus, "a supervisor's explanation of his handling of adverse employment actions, even if made outside the formal process, falls within the scope of the CMPA because the explanation relates to a personnel issue." Sanders v. District of Columbia, 16 F. Supp. 2d 10, 15 (D.D.C. 1998) (quotations omitted). Any such claims brought in court will be dismissed for lack of subject-matter jurisdiction, with the plaintiff directed to file the suit in an administrative forum pursuant to the CMPA's procedures. See District of Columbia v. Thompson, 593 A.2d 621, 636 (D.C. 1991). A defamation claim based on an allegedly false sexual harassment allegation does not fall under the exception to the CMPA for sexual harassment claims. See Baker v. District of Columbia, 785 A.2d 696, 698 (D.C. 2001) (affirming dismissal for lack of jurisdiction for failing to comply with CMPA).

C. Worker's Compensation Exclusivity

There are no reported decisions directly addressing the interplay between a common law defamation claim and the D.C. Workers' Compensation Act ("WCA"), D.C. Code 32-1501 *et seq.* However, as the D.C. Circuit recently recognized, the Act "covers only '*accidental* injury or death arising out of and in the course of employment . . . and . . . injury caused by the *willful act* of third persons directed against an employee because of his employment.' *Id.* 32-1501(12) (emphases added). Thus, the statute excludes intentional torts of the employer, but the D.C. Court of Appeals has explained that the WCA does cover injuries intentionally caused by a co-worker: 'From the perspective of the employer' such 'injury is still "accidental" and the employer is liable' under the WCA, but not in tort, 'so long as the injury arose out of and occurred in the course of employment.'" Johnson v. District of Columbia, 528 F.3d 969, 978 (D.C. Cir. 2008) (quoting Grillo v. Nat'l Bank of Washington, 540 A.2d 743, 748 (D.C. 1988)). Based on this precedent, it is possible that the WCA may provide the exclusive remedy for certain employment-related defamation claims.

D. Pleading Requirements

Federal courts in the District of Columbia have held that "[d]efamation claims are subject to a 'heightened pleading standard.'" Black v. NFLPA, 87 F. Supp. 2d 1, 6 (D.D.C. 2000) (quoting Wiggins v. Phillip Morris, Inc., 853 F. Supp. 458, 466 (D.D.C. 1994)); see also Vreven v. Am. Ass'n of Retired Persons, 604 F. Supp. 2d 9, 15 (D.D.C. 2009). In such cases, a plaintiff must plead the alleged defamatory statements with particularity, including "'the time, place, content, speaker and listener of the alleged defamatory matter.'" Caudle v. Thomason, 942 F. Supp. 635, 638 (D.D.C. 1996) (quoting Wiggins, 853 F. Supp. at 465). Accord Stovell v. James, 810 F. Supp. 2d 237, 248 (D.D.C. 2011). "Furthermore, the allegedly defamatory statements must, wherever possible, be set forth in precise terms." Ruf v. ABC, Inc., 1999 U.S. Dist. LEXIS 1092, *20 (D.D.C. Feb. 1, 1999). A plaintiff's claim will be dismissed if he fails to state time and place of alleged defamatory communication, set forth the content of the alleged statement, or identify the speaker or listener. Hoffman v. Hill and Knowlton, Inc., 777 F. Supp. 1003 (D.D.C. 1991); Rauh v. Coyne, 744 F. Supp. 1186, 1193 (D.D.C. 1990).

The D.C. Court of Appeals has advised that "[u]nlike some jurisdictions, which apply a 'heightened pleading rule' to claims of defamation, we instead focus our inquiry on whether 'the factual allegations in the appellant's complaint are sufficient to permit the opposing party to form responsive pleadings, [since that is] the principal reason that some courts demand a heightened standard of pleading in defamation [] cases.'" Solers, Inc. v. Doe, 977 A.2d 941, 948 (quoting Oparaugo v. Watts, 884 A.2d 63, 76-77 (D.C. 2005) (emendations in original)). Under this standard, the Court of Appeals has dismissed complaints where the plaintiffs "failed to allege either the language or the substance of the libelous statements." (citing Watwood v. Credit Bureau, Inc., 68 A.2d 905, 906 (D.C. 1949)). But see Williams v. District of Columbia, 9. A.3d 484, 493 (D.C. 2010) (reversing dismissal, holding that the complaint had sufficiently identified the speaker of an allegedly defamatory statement as one of a "subset of 'senior' District officials" who would have been displeased with public testimony given by the plaintiff).

SURVEY OF DISTRICT OF COLUMBIA EMPLOYMENT PRIVACY LAW

Barbara B. Brown and Cody D. Knight
Paul Hastings LLP
875 15th Street, N.W.
Washington, D.C.
Telephone: (202) 551-1700; Facsimile: (202) 551-1705

(With Developments Reported Through **November 1, 2012**)

GENERAL COMMENTS

The Superior Court of the District of Columbia is the court of general jurisdiction for civil and criminal matters in the District of Columbia. D.C. Code §§ 11-921(a), 11-923(b) (2001). Superior Court decisions may be appealed to the District of Columbia Court of Appeals, id. at § 11-721(a), which is the District's highest court. Id. at § 11-102. Final judgments of the Court of Appeals are reviewable by the Supreme Court of the United States. Id.

The District of Columbia's local courts are analogous to state courts, United States Jaycees v. Superior Court, 491 F. Supp. 579, 582 (D.D.C. 1980), and the Court of Appeals has the status of a state supreme court. Hickey v. Dist. of Columbia Court of Appeals, 457 F. Supp. 584, 586 (D.D.C. 1978). In accordance with the federal statute providing for removal of state court actions to federal courts, defendants who are sued in Superior Court may remove cases to the United States District Court for the District of Columbia. D.C. Code § 11-503 (2001); see also Dist. of Columbia ex rel. John Driggs Co. v. Ranger Constr. Co., 394 F. Supp. 801, 802 (D.D.C. 1974) (defendants in the District of Columbia have right of removal concomitant to that of state court defendants).

SIGNIFICANT DEVELOPMENTS SINCE THE 2012 *SURVEY*

None.

I. GENERAL LAW OF PRIVACY

A. Legal Basis of Privacy Claims.

1. ***Constitutional Law.*** District of Columbia courts have recognized a right to "bodily integrity" that, in addition to being "ingrained in our common law," is "of constitutional magnitude." In re A.C., 573 A.2d 1235, 1243-1247 (D.C. 1990) (citing cases where courts have found a basis in the Constitution for the right to bodily integrity and a limited right to refuse medical treatment).

2. ***Statutory Law.*** Employees of the District of Columbia or its agencies (including current or former employees and applicants for employment) have a "right to individual privacy" under the "Whistleblower Protection Act." D.C. Code § 1-615.58(6) (2001). Thus, D.C. government employees have the "right to freely express their opinions on all public issues, including those related to the duties they are assigned to perform." D.C. Code § 1-615.58(1). However, District of Columbia agencies may promulgate rules "requiring that any such opinions be clearly disassociated from that agency's policy." Id. The Act prohibits a District of Columbia supervisor from taking adverse personnel action or otherwise retaliating against an employee or applicant because of the person's protected disclosure of information that evidences gross mismanagement, abuse of authority, violation of the law, or threats to public health or safety, or because of the person's refusal to comply with an illegal order. Id. at § 1-615.53; Williams v. Johnson, 701 F. Supp. 2d 1, 14–16 (D.D.C. 2010); Williams v. Johnson, 537 F. Supp. 2d 141, 155-56 (D.D.C. 2008); Wilburn v. Dist. of Columbia, 957 A.2d 921 (D.C. 2008). "For a disclosure to be protected by the whistleblower statute, it must contain information that is not publicly known." Mentzer v. Lanier, 677 F. Supp. 2d 242, 250–51 (D.D.C. 2010). However, a 2009 amendment to the Whistleblower Protection Act revised the definition of "protected disclosure" so that protection is extended even if a prior disclosure has been made by another employee or applicant. D.C. Law 12-160 ("Whistleblower Protection Amendment Act of 2009"), codified at D.C. Code § 1-615.52(a)(6); see also Saint-Jean v. District of Columbia, 846 F. Supp. 2d 247, 260 (D.D.C. 2012).

However, the right of District of Columbia employees to make protected disclosures shall not be construed to permit "the disclosure of the contents of personnel files, personal medical reports, or any other information in a manner to invade the individual privacy" of an employee or United States citizen, D.C. Code § 1-615.58(2), and nothing in the Act shall limit a District of Columbia employee's "access to his or her own personnel file, medical report file, or any other file or document concerning his or her status or performance within his or her agency," except as discussed in Section VI, infra. Id. at § 1-615.58(6).

Statute Applicable to D.C. Employees Only. By definition, the provisions of the Whistleblower Protection Act, including the restrictions against disclosing private information, apply only to persons who are current or former employees of the government of the District of Columbia and to applicants for employment by the District government. Id. at § 1-615.52(a)(3).

3. ***Common Law.*** The right of privacy in the District of Columbia has its basis in common law. Vassiliades v. Garfinckel's, 492 A.2d 580, 587 11 Med. L. Rptr. 2057 (D.C. 1985) ("The District of Columbia has long recognized the common law tort of invasion of privacy.") (citing Afro-American Publ'g Co. v. Jaffe, 366 F.2d 649, 653 (D.C. Cir. 1966) (en banc) (other citations omitted)). District of Columbia court decisions follow the Restatement (Second) of Torts formulation of the right of privacy and the causes of action for invasion of that right. Kitt v. Capital Concerts, Inc., 742 A.2d 856, 859, 28 Med. L. Rptr. 1538 (D.C. 1999) (citing Vassiliades, 492 A.2d at 587). Although "[t]he right of privacy stands on high ground, cognate to the values and concerns protected by constitutional guarantees," Afro-American Publ'g Co., 366 F.2d at 654, the "right of privacy is not absolute." Vassiliades, 492 A.2d at 586; Wolf v. Regardie, 553 A.2d 1213, 1220 (D.C. 1989).

B. Causes of Action

Invasion of privacy consists of "not one tort, but a complex of four, each with distinct elements and each describing a separate interest capable of being invaded." Wolf at 1216-17 (D.C. 1989); Garay v. Liriano, 839 F. Supp. 2d 138, 144 (D.D.C. 2012). The "four constituent torts" are (1) appropriating one's name or likeness for another's benefit; (2) publicity that places one in a false light in the public eye; (3) public disclosure of private facts; and (4) intrusion upon one's solitude or seclusion. Wolf, 553 A.2d at 1217 (citing Vassiliades v. Garfinckel's, 492 A.2d 580, 587 (D.C. 1985)). A cause of action for invasion of privacy "'represents a vindication of the right of private personality and emotional security.'" Vassiliades, 492 A.2d at 587 (quoting Afro-American Publ'g Co., 366 F.2d at 653). Invasion of privacy is an intentional tort. Randolph v. ING Life Ins. & Annuity Co., 973 A.2d 702, 711 (D.C. 2009).

1. ***Misappropriation/Right of Publicity***. Appropriation of likeness or personal identity, infringement of right of publicity, and misappropriation of celebrity "are indistinguishable as a legal matter." Lane v. Random House, Inc., 985 F. Supp. 141, 145-46, 23 Med. L. Rptr 1385 (D.D.C. 1995). In most instances, a plaintiff must allege "that the defendant's commercial benefit was derived from the identity of the plaintiff and the value or reputation which the public associates with that identity." Barnako v. Foto Kirsch, Ltd., Civ. A. No. 86-1700, 1987 WL 10230, at *2, 13 Med. L. Rptr. 2373 (D.D.C. Apr. 16, 1987). The plaintiff in Barnako failed to state a cause of action because "[h]e cannot demonstrate that Foto Kirsch derived any commercial benefit from a misperceived association between himself and Foto Kirsch." Id. "[I]t is not enough to demonstrate that a defendant profited directly from the unauthorized use of the plaintiff's photograph." Id.

However, "the rule stated is not limited to commercial appropriation. It applies also when the defendant makes use of the plaintiff's name or likeness for his own purposes and benefit, even though use is not a commercial one, and even though the benefit sought to be obtained is not a pecuniary one." Tripp v. United States, 257 F. Supp. 2d 37, 41 (D.D.C. 2003). The benefits that a defendant might seek to appropriate for his own use include "the reputation, prestige, social or commercial standing, public interest or other values of the plaintiff's name or likeness." Teltschik v. Williams & Jensen, PLLC, 683 F. Supp. 2d 33, 55 (D.D.C. 2010). Plaintiff in Tripp, a "high profile" witness to an investigation into wrongdoing by the President, stated a cause of action for misappropriation where she alleged that the defendants misused her name for their political benefit. 257 F. Supp. 2d at 42. Her notoriety was "significant enough to give plaintiff's name 'value' to defendant necessary to serve as a predicate for a misappropriation claim and remove th[e] case from the ambit of those in which persons' names were used for 'incidental' or 'informational' purposes only." Id. at 43.

Incidental use of a photograph, name or likeness "for a purpose other than taking advantage of a person's reputation or the value associated with his name will not result in actionable appropriation." Vassiliades v. Garfinckel's, 492 A.2d 580, 592 (D.C. 1985). See also Tripp, 257 F. Supp. 2d at 41 ("[T]he value of [a plaintiff's] likeness [is not] appropriated when it is published for purposes other than taking advantage of his reputation, prestige or other value associated with him for purposes of publicity."); Lane, 985 F. Supp. at 147 ("A person's name or likeness 'is not appropriated by mere mention of it, or by reference to it in connection with legitimate mention of his public activities . . . .'" (quoting Restatement (Second) of Torts § 652C (1977))); Pearce v. The E.F. Hutton Group, Inc., 664 F. Supp. 1490, 1500 (D.D.C. 1987) ("The essence of a misappropriation of name action is that the defendant has used another's name to take advantage of some value associated with it—not merely for informational purposes.").

A newsworthiness privilege applies to publications concerning matters of public interest. Lane, 985 F. Supp. at 146. "[I]t has always been considered a defense to a claim of invasion of privacy by publication . . . that the published matter complained of is of general public interest." Id. (quoting Pearson v. Dodd, 410 F.2d 701, 703 (D.C. Cir. 1969)). See also Peay v. Curtis Publ'g Co., 78 F. Supp. 305, 309 (D.D.C. 1948) ("An exception necessarily exists in respect to individuals who by reason of their position or achievements have become public characters."). Plaintiff cannot recover for misappropriation "based upon the use of his identity or likeness in a newsworthy publication unless the use has 'no real relationship' to the subject matter of the publication." Lane, 985 F. Supp. at 146 (holding that conspiracy theorist could not recover for use of his image in advertisement for book which sought to discredit conspiracy theories).

2. ***False Light.*** A cause of action for false light invasion of privacy lies where "[o]ne . . . gives publicity to a matter concerning another that places the other before the public in a false light . . . if (a) the false light in which the other was placed would be highly offensive to a reasonable person, and (b) the actor had knowledge of or acted in reckless disregard as to the falsity of the publicized matter and the false light in which the other would be placed." Lane v. Random House, Inc., 985 F. Supp. 141, 148 (D.D.C. 1995) (quoting Restatement (Second) of Torts § 652E (1977)). "[A]n invasion of privacy-false light claim . . . requires a showing of: (1) publicity, (2) about a false statement, representation or imputation, (3) understood to be of and concerning the plaintiff, and (4) which places the plaintiff in a false light that would be offensive to a reasonable person." Bean v. Gutierrez, 980 A.2d 1090, 1093 (D.C. 2009) (quoting Blodgett v. Univ. Club, 930 A.2d 210, 222 (D.C. 2007)).

The "publicity" element requires that the matter involve "a communication that reaches, or is sure to reach, the public"; communication of "a fact concerning the plaintiff's private life to a single person or even to a small group of persons" is insufficient. Bean, 980 A.2d at 1095 (affirming judgment in the defendant's favor where the defendant's communications about the plaintiff were made to a single individual who subsequently, without the defendant's knowledge, published the communications in a newsletter). See also White v. Fraternal Order of Police, 909 F.2d 512, 522, 17 Med. L. Rptr. (D.C. Cir. 1990); Saha v. Lehman, 537 F. Supp. 2d 122, 127 (D.D.C. 2008) (granting summary judgment on plaintiff's false light claim where there was no publicity of events at issue and plaintiff failed to demonstrate how defendants' conduct constituted a false statement, representation, or imputation); Lohrenz v. Donnelly, 223 F. Supp. 2d 25, 32-33 (D.D.C. 2002); Kitt v. Pathmakers, Inc., 672 A.2d 76, 78, 80 n.6 (D.C. 1996), appeal after remand, Kitt v. Capital Concerts, Inc., 742 A.2d 856, 859 (D.C. 1999).

False light invasion of privacy differs conceptually from defamation in the sense that "a defamation tort redresses damage to reputation while a false light privacy tort redresses mental distress from having been exposed to public view." White, 909 F.2d at 518. However, because the elements of a false light claim "are 'similar to those of a [defamation] claim,' . . . where a plaintiff brings defamation and false light claims based on the same underlying allegations, 'the claims will be analyzed in the same manner.'" Shipkovitz v. Washington Post Co., 571 F. Supp. 2d 178, 183 (D.D.C. 2008) (quoting Blodgett v. University Club, 930 A.2d 210, 222-23 (D.C. 2007)). "[A] plaintiff may only recover on one of the two theories based on a single publication, but is free to plead them in the alternative." Weyrich v. New Republic, Inc., 235 F.3d 617, 628, 29 Med. L. Rptr. (D.C. Cir. 2001).

The same constitutional limitations apply to a claim of false light invasion of privacy as to a claim for defamation. Farah v. Esquire Magazine, Inc., 40 Med. L. Rptr. 1926 (D.D.C. June 4, 2012). As with defamation, truth or assertion of opinion is a defense to an allegation of false light invasion of privacy. Zandford v. Nat'l Ass'n of Sec. Dealers, Inc., 19 F. Supp. 2d 1, 3 (D.D.C. 1998); White, 909 F.2d at 518; see also Shipkovitz, 571 F. Supp. 2d at 183-84. The "fair report" defense is also available where a defendant publishes a "fair and accurate report" of a qualified government source and properly attributes the statement to the official source in the publication. Jankovic v. Int'l Crisis Group, 593 F.3d 22, 26 (D.C. Cir. 2010) (citing Phillips v. Evening Star Newspaper Co., 424 A.2d 78, 89, 6 Med. L. Rptr. 2191 (D.C. 1980)).

The offensiveness of the alleged conduct is measured by an "ordinary, reasonable person" standard, and not that of a reasonable person in the particular profession of the complainant. Kitt, 742 A.2d at 860 (rejecting clarinetist's contention that offensiveness of concert promoter's alleged misconduct should be judged by a "reasonable performing artist" standard). Moreover, while the determination of offensiveness "is usually the province of the jury," the trial court must make "a threshold determination" of offensiveness in discerning the existence of a cause of action. Id. (citing Wolf v. Regardie, 553 A.2d 1213, 1219 (D.C. 1989)); see, e.g., Parnigoni v. St. Columba's Nursery Sch., 681 F. Supp. 2d 1, 18–20 (D.D.C. 2010).

False light invasion of privacy may be shown where a materially true communication conveys facts from which a false light representation may reasonably be inferred and where the communication, either by "the particular manner or language in which the true facts are conveyed," provides "additional, affirmative evidence" that the defendant intends or endorses the false light inference. White, 909 F.2d at 520-22; see Parnigoni, 661 F. Supp. 2d at 19–20.

For example, in White, the court could not conclude as a matter of law that a high-ranking police officer was not placed in a false light where letters from the Fraternal Order of Police went "beyond merely reporting materially true facts" relating to the officer's promotion after his urine sample tested positively at an inconclusive first stage of a drug test and after his urine samples were not handled according to police department procedures. Id. at 521-22. While the reporting of these facts alone is insufficient to support a cause of action, the letters' assertions that the initial test result "should easily have been confirmed" supplies "additional evidence" to support an inference that the officer in fact used drugs. Id. at 521.

3. ***Publication of Private Facts.*** A cause of action for the tort of public disclosure of private facts requires (1) publicity (2) absent any waiver or privilege (3) given to private facts (4) in which the public has no legitimate concern and (5) which would be highly offensive or cause suffering, shame, or humiliation to a reasonable person of ordinary

sensibilities. White v. Fraternal Order of Police, 909 F.2d 512, 517-18 (D.C. Cir. 1990) (citing Dresbach v. Doubleday & Co., 518 F. Supp. 1285, 1287 (D.D.C. 1981)).

To be actionable, the facts must be disseminated to the public. Publication to a single person does not constitute invasion of privacy. Mesumbe v. Howard Univ., 706 F. Supp. 2d 86, 97 (D.D.C. 2010) (citing Restatement (Second) of Torts § 652D cmt. a). In addition, the facts publicized must be private, rather than facts about events which take place in public view. Parnigoni v. St. Columba's Nursery Sch., 681 F. Supp. 2d 1, 22 (D.D.C. 2010) (citing Harrison v. Washington Post Co., 391 A.2d 781, 784 (D.C. 1978)).

Publicity of the private facts must be highly offensive to a reasonable person. Vassiliades v. Garfinckel's, 492 A.2d 580, 588 (D.C. 1985) ("The protection afforded to the plaintiff's interest in his privacy must be relative to the customs of the time and place, to the occupation of the plaintiff and to the habits of his neighbors and fellow citizens." (quoting Restatement (Second) of Torts § 652D (1977))). This is a factual question that is usually for the jury's consideration, Vassiliades, 492 A.2d at 588 (citation omitted), but the trial court makes "a threshold determination" of offensiveness in discerning the existence of a cause of action. Kitt v. Capital Concerts, Inc., 742 A.2d 856, 860, 28 Med. L. Rptr 1538 (D.C. 1999).

A person who publicizes private facts about another will not be subject to liability if the publicized matter is of general public interest. Vassiliades, 492 A.2d at 589 (citing Pearson v. Dodd, 410 F.2d 701, 703 (D.C. Cir. 1969)); Harrison v. Washington Post Co., 391 A.2d 781, 784 (D.C. 1978) (mistakenly arrested plaintiff cannot sue for telecast of event that happened on public sidewalk because "it is well settled law that an invasion of privacy action does not lie as to events which take place in public view") (citation omitted); White, 909 F.2d at 514, 517 (granting summary judgment to defendants where results of police officer's drug tests "involved a legitimate matter of public concern"); Restatement (Second) of Torts § 652D (1977). The defense is not limited to publicizing news related to current events or public affairs; it "also protects 'information concerning interesting phases of human activity and embraces all issues about which information is needed or appropriate so that that individual may cope with the exigencies of their period.'" Vassiliades, 492 A.2d at 589 (quoting Campbell v. Seabury Press, 614 F.2d 395, 397 (5th Cir. 1980)).

A police officer's claim of publication of private facts concerning the results of his drug tests failed "as a matter of law" because he is a public official and whether he used drugs "was squarely a matter of public concern." White, 909 F.2d at 517-18. "The public's interest 'extends to anything which might touch on an official's fitness for public office.'" Id. at 517 (quoting Gertz v. Robert Welch, Inc., 418 U.S. 323, 344-45 (1974)). "We think it axiomatic," the court stated, "that personal drug use is relevant to fitness for public office, especially for officials charged with enforcing the law." White, 909 F.2d at 517. Quoting the Restatement (Second) of Torts § 652D (1977), the court observed that "with public officials, 'the legitimate interest of the public . . . may include information as to matters that would otherwise be private.'" White, 909 F.2d at 517.

The privilege to publicize matters of general public interest, however, is not absolute, as "[c]ertain private facts about a person should never be publicized, even if the facts concern matters which are, or relate to persons who are, of legitimate public interest." Vassiliades, 492 A.2d at 589 (internal citations omitted). Resolving the conflict between the public's right to information and a person's right to privacy requires "a balancing of the competing interests." Id.

Damages are recoverable for the publicity's harm to reputation or interest in privacy and also for emotional distress or humiliation "if it is of the kind that normally results from such an invasion and it is normal and reasonable in its extent." Vassiliades, 492 A.2d at 594 (quoting Restatement (Second) of Torts § 652H, comment b (1977)). Harm need not be based on pecuniary loss. Id.

4. ***Intrusion.*** Intrusion upon seclusion consists of (1) an invasion or interference by physical intrusion, by use of a defendant's sense of sight or hearing, or by use of some other form of investigation or examination (2) into a place where a plaintiff has secluded himself or into his private or secret concerns (3) that would be highly offensive to an ordinary, reasonable person. Pearson v. Dodd, 410 F.2d 701, 704, 1 Med. L. Rptr. 1809 (D.C. Cir. 1969); Danai v. Canal Square Assocs., 862 A.2d 395, 399-400 (D.C. 2004); Wolf v. Regardie, 553 A.2d 1213, 1217 (D.C. 1989) (citing Restatement (Second) of Torts § 652B (1977)); Alexander v. FBI, 971 F. Supp. 603, 608 (D.D.C. 1997); Helton v. United States, 191 F. Supp. 2d 179, 181 (D.D.C. 2002). See also Jackson v. Dist. of Columbia, 412 A.2d 948, 954 (D.C. 1980) (mistakenly arrested plaintiff precluded from asserting privacy claim by court's finding that the arrest was reasonable and that the mistake was unintentional; plaintiff did not suffer an "unreasonable and serious interference with protected interests").

The acquisition of information "is not a requisite element" of the tort of intrusion. In addition, "[u]nlike some other types of invasion of privacy," a cause of action for intrusion does not require publication of information that is obtained. The "nature of the intrusion" initially determines liability. Wolf, 553 A.2d at 1217; Rogers v. Loews L'Enfant

Plaza Hotel, 526 F. Supp. 523, 528-29 (D.D.C. 1981). However, publication affects the amount of damages. Rogers, 526 F. Supp. at 528 n.8.

Invasions that are "intrinsic in the tort of intrusion upon seclusion" include those such as harassment, "peeping through windows or into other locations in which a plaintiff has chosen to seclude himself," opening another's personal mail, "eavesdropping on private conversations," entering another's home without permission or searching his or her belongings, and examining another's private bank account. Wolf, 553 A.2d at 1217-18; see also Randolph v. ING Life Ins. & Annuity Co., 973 A.2d 702 (D.C. 2009) ("[U]nauthorized viewing of personal information such as a plaintiff's Social Security number and other identifying information can constitute an intrusion that is highly offensive to any reasonable person, and may support an action for invasion of privacy (irrespective of whether the plaintiff alleges that economic or other resultant injuries have already come to pass); Helton, 191 F. Supp. 2d at 181-82 (holding that alleged unlawful strip search by U.S. Marshals stated a claim for intrusion upon seclusion). In contrast, the District of Columbia Court of Appeals has held that an individual has no legitimate expectation of privacy with respect to a discarded letter in a community trash room even where she had thrown out that letter in her office wastepaper basket. Danai, 862 A.2d at 399-403. Whether intrusion upon seclusion also encompasses the wrongful disclosure of personal information is unclear in the District of Columbia; that question was certified to the District's highest court in 2004, but left undecided upon the parties' joint motion for dismissal. Schuchart v. La Taberna del Alabardero, 365 F.3d 33, 36-38 (D.C. Cir. 2004).

A cause of action for intrusion is stated where plaintiff alleged that her supervisor made "improperly intrusive" phone calls to her at home and at work in which he made sarcastic and leering comments about her personal and sexual life. Rogers v. L'Enfant Plaza Hotel, 526 F.Supp. 523 (D.D.C. 1981). The situation is analogous to "persistent and unwanted" telephone calls by debt collectors, an area where invasion of privacy has been found. Rogers, 526 F. Supp. at 528. See also Klugel v. Small, 519 F. Supp. 2d 66, 76 (D.D.C. 2007) (denying motion to dismiss claim of invasion of privacy where plaintiff's employer asked her questions regarding her physical relationship with her husband and her sexuality); Rochon v. FBI, 691 F. Supp. 1548, 1551-52, 1564 (D.D.C. 1988) (black FBI agent adequately pled invasion of privacy claim where he alleged that co-workers and supervisors harassed him through hate mail and obscene phone calls, and defaced pictures of his children).

In a case popularly known as "Filegate," Alexander v. FBI, 971 F. Supp. 603 (D.D.C. 1997), former Reagan and Bush political appointees and government employees sufficiently alleged intrusion against the FBI, First Lady Hilary Rodham Clinton and others for use of the employees' FBI files to obtain potentially embarrassing information on Reagan and Bush personnel. Id. (overruled on other grounds in Alexander v. FBI, 691 F. Supp. 2d 182, 188 (D.D.C. 2010)). The court reasoned that, although a third party (the FBI) maintained the files, plaintiffs had a privacy interest in the files because, "when plaintiffs cooperated with the FBI during their field examinations, they did so with the belief that their FBI files would not be available for any purpose other than the required government clearance. Thus the files, although not in plaintiffs' direct control, were still a part of their private and secret concerns." Alexander v. FBI, 971 F.Supp. at 609 (ordering further discovery to determine the extent of plaintiffs' cooperation in creating the files and the resulting privacy interest).

C. Other Privacy-related Actions

1. *Intentional Infliction of Emotional Distress*

a. **Elements.** The District of Columbia recognizes the tort of intentional infliction of emotional distress, the elements of which are (1) extreme and outrageous conduct by defendant which (2) intentionally or recklessly (3) causes plaintiff severe emotional distress. Duncan v. Children's Nat'l Med. Ctr., 702 A.2d 207, 211 (D.C. 1997); Kerrigan v. Britches of Georgetowne, Inc., 705 A.2d 624, 628 (D.C. 1997); Than v. Radio Free Asia, 496 F. Supp. 2d 38, 51 (D.D.C. 2007); Rogers v. Loews L'Enfant Plaza Hotel, 526 F. Supp. 523, 529-30 (D.D.C. 1981).

There is no general duty of care to avoid causing mental distress, and liability is not imposed for all conduct causing mental distress. Liability attaches only for acts "so outrageous in character, and so extreme in degree, as to go beyond all possible bounds of decency." Duncan, 702 A.2d at 211 (quoting Dist. of Columbia v. Thompson, 570 A.2d 277, 290 (D.C. 1990) modified, 593 A.2d 621 (D.C. 1991)); Kerrigan, 705 A.2d at 628; Harris v. Dist. of Columbia, 696 F. Supp. 2d 123, 137–38 (D.D.C. 2010) (dismissing a claim for intentional infliction of emotional distress because the alleged conduct was not outrageous where plaintiff alleged only that he was arrested without a warrant during a search of his workplace, that excessive force was used by twelve officers who approached him with guns drawn, that he was detained overnight, and that another officer lied in his affidavit); Ihebereme v. Capital One, N.A., 730 F.Supp.2d 40, 50 (D.D.C. 2010). "This very demanding standard is only infrequently met." Brown v. Children's Nat'l Med. Ctr., 773 F. Supp. 2d 125, 137-38 (D.D.C. 2011) (internal quotations omitted). To recover, a plaintiff must demonstrate "an intent on the part of the alleged tortfeasor to cause a disturbance in [the plaintiff's] emotional tranquility so acute that harmful physical consequences might result." Sterling Mirror of Md., Inc. v. Gordon, 619 A.2d 64, 67 (D.C. 1993).

Considerations for determining whether conduct is extreme and outrageous as a matter of law include (1) applicable community standards, (2) the nature of the activity at issue, (3) the relationship between the parties, and (4) the particular environment in which the conduct took place. Duncan, 702 A.2d at 211 (citing King v. Kidd, 640 A.2d 656, 668 (D.C. 1993)).

b. **Relationship to Employment Law.** "Perhaps recognizing the often bitter quality of employee-employer disputes, courts in this jurisdiction are especially skeptical of intentional infliction of emotional distress claims in employment cases." Anderson v. Ramsey, 2006 WL 1030155, at *8 (D.D.C. Apr. 19, 2006). District of Columbia courts are "particularly demanding as to the proof required to support a claim of intentional infliction of emotional distress in an employment context." Paul v. Howard Univ., 754 A.2d 297, 307 (D.C. 2000); see also Williams v. District of Columbia, 9 A.3d 484, 292 (D.C. 2010); Ben-Kotel v. Howard Univ., 156 F. Supp. 2d 8, 14-15 (D.D.C. 2001), aff'd, 319 F.3d 532 (D.C. Cir. 2003).

While conduct in the context of an employer-employee relationship can support a claim for intentional infliction of emotional distress, employer-employee conflicts involving intra-workplace mistreatment generally do not rise to the level of outrageous conduct. Duncan, 702 A.2d at 211-12, 212 n.4 (citing Thompson, 570 A.2d at 290; Howard Univ. v. Best, 484 A.2d 958, 986 (D.C. 1984)) (internal citation omitted). "[I]t has been specifically held . . . that harassment in a professional context, including exclusion from business meetings and the spreading of unfavorable rumors, is not the type of conduct that gives rise to" a cause of action for intentional infliction of emotional distress. Shewmaker v. Minchew, 504 F. Supp. 156, 163 (D.D.C. 1980), aff'd, 666 F.2d 616 (D.C. Cir. 1981). Likewise, "'discharge of an employee is not conduct that goes beyond all possible bounds of decency and [is] regarded as atrocious and utterly intolerable in a civilized society.'" Anderson, 2006 WL 1030155, at *8 (quoting Crowley v. North Am. Telcoms. Ass'n, 691 A.2d 1169, 1172 (D.C. 1997)). See also Kerrigan, 705 A.2d at 628 ("In the employment context, we traditionally have been demanding in the proof required to support an intentional infliction of emotional distress claim.") (citing King v. Kidd, 640 A.2d 656, 670-74 (D.C. 1993); Adams v. George W. Cochran & Co., 597 A.2d 28, 35 (D.C. 1991); Waldon v. Covington, 415 A.2d 1070, 1077-78 (D.C. 1980); Hoffman v. Hill and Knowlton, Inc., 777 F. Supp. 1003, 1005 (D.D.C. 1991)); Thompson v. Jasas Corp., 212 F. Supp. 2d 21, 28 (D.D.C. 2002) ("In an employment context, the proof required to support a claim for intentional infliction of emotional distress is particularly demanding.") (citing Lockamy v. Truesdale, 182 F. Supp. 2d 26, 38 (D.D.C. 2001)).

An employee alleges sufficiently extreme and outrageous workplace conduct to survive a motion to dismiss where she claims that her supervisor "informed her that the ideal female employee was small-breasted, publicly criticized plaintiff for the 'hump' on her back and her large breasts, and joked about AIDS in plaintiff's presence knowing that plaintiff's brother was suffering from the syndrome." Garvin v. Am. Ass'n of Retired Persons, No. Civ. A. 89-3348, 1992 WL 693382, at *4 (D.D.C. Feb. 27, 1992). Similarly, a "reasonable jury could conclude that [a supervisor's] repeated disparaging comments regarding plaintiff's pregnancy and pattern of making crude gestures and sexual advances towards her constituted extreme and outrageous conduct exceeding the bounds of decency." Wade v. WMATA, 2005 WL 1513137, at *6 (D.D.C. June 27, 2005); see also Parnigoni v. St. Columba's Nursery Sch., 681 F. Supp. 2d 1, 22–23 (D.D.C. 2010) (collecting cases).

An employee fails to state a claim for intentional infliction of emotional distress where he alleges that his employer targeted him for a sexual harassment investigation, manufactured evidence against him to support a false claim of harassment, leaked information about the investigation to other employees, and unjustifiably promoted someone over him. "This conduct, even construed as true, was of the type attributable to 'employer-employee conflicts that do not, as a matter of law, rise to the level of outrageous conduct.'" Kerrigan, 705 A.2d at 628 (citing Howard Univ. v. Best, 484 A.2d 958, 986 (D.C. 1984)).

Public employees of the Washington Area Metro Transit Authority ("WMATA") cannot sustain actions against the District for defamation, wrongful termination, or intentional infliction of emotional distress based on WMATA's hiring, training, or supervision because these are governmental functions for which the District law provides WMATA shall not be liable. D.C. Code § 9-1107.01(80); Headen v. Wash. Metro. Area Transit Auth., No. 10-0784, 2010 WL 3905066, *5 (D.D.C. Oct. 5, 2010).

Although claims for negligent infliction of emotional distress ("NIED") previously required a showing that the defendant's negligent conduct put the plaintiff in danger of bodily harm, the District of Columbia Court of Appeals in Hedgepeth v. Whitman Walker Clinic, 22 A.3d 789, 810-11 (D.C. 2011), held that this "zone of danger" rule will not preclude recovery for an NIED claim if the plaintiff can show that "the defendant has a relationship with the plaintiff, or has undertaken an obligation to the plaintiff, of a nature that necessarily implicates the plaintiff's emotional well-being." Hedgepeth, however, envisioned such NIED claims as continuing to arise in the context of a doctor-patient relationship, and at least one court has dismissed an NIED claim on the basis that the employer-employee relationship at issue did not implicate the employee's emotional wellbeing. Id. at 813; Etoh v. Fannie Mae, 2011 WL 4431140. at *21 (D.D.C. Sept. 23, 2011) (dismissing an NIED claim in the employment context).

2. ***Interference With Prospective Economic Advantage***

a. **Elements.** To establish a claim for tortious interference with prospective economic advantage, a plaintiff must allege (1) the existence of a valid business relationship or expectancy, (2) knowledge of the relationship or expectancy on the part of the interferer, (3) intentional interference inducing or causing a breach, termination of the relationship or expectancy, or failure of performance and (4) resultant damage. NCRIC, Inc. v. Columbia Hosp. for Women Med. Ctr., Inc., 957 A.2d 890 (D.C. 2008); Bennett Enters. Inc. v. Domino's Pizza, Inc., 45 F.3d 493, 499 (D.C. Cir. 1995); see AMTRAK v. Veolia Transp. Servs., 2011 WL 1872199 (D.D.C. May 9, 2011); Genetic Sys. Corp. v. Abbott Labs., 691 F. Supp. 407, 422-23 (D.D.C. 1988). The actor's "interference must be improper." Furash & Co., Inc. v. McClave, 130 F. Supp. 2d 48, 56 (D.D.C. 2001).

Plaintiff must demonstrate more than general intent to interfere or knowledge of probable consequences. Sheppard v. Dickstein, Shapiro, Morin & Oshinsky, 59 F. Supp. 2d 27, 34 (D.D.C. 1999); Genetic Sys., 691 F. Supp. at 423. "A competitor's conduct must be more egregious, for example, it must involve libel, slander, physical coercion, fraud, misrepresentation, or disparagement." Id. But see Canady v. Providence Hosp., 942 F. Supp. 11, 18 (D.D.C. 1996) (stating that "arbitrary or capricious failure to afford . . . process" to physicians facing disciplinary proceedings satisfies the intent element for intentional interference with prospective economic advantage, but finding that plaintiff had not proven arbitrary or capricious action). To be actionable, the interference need not cause an actual breach of the business relationship, but instead may cause "merely a failure of performance" by one of the parties. Casco Marina Dev., L.L.C. v. District of Columbia Redevelopment Land Agency, 834 A.2d 77, 84 (D.C.2003). "For the most part the 'expectancies' thus protected have been those of future contractual relations, such as the prospect of obtaining employment or employees, or the opportunity of obtaining customers." Carr v. Brown, 395 A.2d 79, 84 (D.C. 1978). The expectancy must revolve around an existing relationship or a specifically anticipated transaction. Jankovic v. International Crisis Group, 593 F.3d 22, 29 (D.C. Cir. 2010). It is not enough to allege interference with "generic opportunities of any successful enterprise," a situation which is better addressed by a claim for defamation. Id.

A defendant may avoid liability if he "can establish that his conduct was legally justified or privileged." Onyeoziri v. Spivok , 44 A.3d 279, 287 (D.C. 2012) (internal quotations omitted); see also Murray v. Wells Fargo Home Mortg., 953 A.2d 308, 326 (D.C. 2008). This would include, for example, "protecting a present, existing economic interest." Id. (internal quotations omitted). After the plaintiff establishes a prima facie case, the burden then shifts to the defendant to prove that the interference was legally justified or privileged. Alfred A. Altimont, Inc. v. Chatelain, Samperton & Nolan, 374 A.2d 284, 288 (D.C.1977)); NCRIC, Inc. v. Columbia Hosp. for Women Med. Ctr., Inc., 957 A.2d 890, 901 (D.C. 2008).

The District of Columbia has not recognized the tort of negligent interference with contract or prospective contractual relations. Furash & Co. v. McClave, 130 F. Supp. 2d 48, 56 (D.D.C. 2001).

b. **Relationship to Employment Law.** To survive a motion to dismiss his or her claim of intentional interference with prospective economic advantage, an employee must allege "business expectancies, not grounded on present contractual relationships but which are commercially reasonable to anticipate and are considered to be property." McManus v. MCI Commc'ns Corp., 748 A.2d 949, 957 (D.C. 2000) (holding that employee cannot maintain suit for interference with prospective advantage where her expectancy is based on at-will relationship). See also Houlahan v. World Wide Ass'n of Specialty Programs & Sch., 2006 WL 785326, at *4 (D.D.C. Mar. 28, 2006) (employment relationship "of freelance news journalist and news service organization" insufficient "to show the existence of a valid business relationship" required for claim of intentional interference with prospective economic advantage); Sheppard, 59 F. Supp. 2d at 34 (holding that plaintiff who alleged that supervisors' conduct interfered with his expectation of continued employment with employer failed to demonstrate damage to any future business relationship or expectancy).

Tortious interference with employment arises only upon "interference with a contract between the plaintiff and a third party." Hopkins v. Blue Cross & Blue Shield Ass'n, No. 10-900, 2010 WL 5300536, at *8 (D.D.C. Dec. 21, 2010). An employer that chooses not to promote an existing employee due to statements made by the employee's supervisor thus cannot be held liable for tortious interference of a prospective economic advantage. Id. However, a supervisory employee is not shielded from personal liability merely because of his supervisory status when the employee "'maliciously' procures the discharge of another by their common employer." Garvin v. Am. Ass'n of Retired Persons, No. Civ. A. 89-3348, 1992 WL 693382, at *1, 3 (D.D.C. Feb. 27, 1992) (refusing to dismiss tortious interference claim alleging that supervisor gave employee assignments that aggravated an age-related back condition, unfairly disciplined and evaluated her, and publicly criticized her personal appearance, leading to employee's discharge); Sorrells v. Garfinckel's, 565 A.2d 285, 290-91 (D.C. 1989).

A discharged university employee survived a motion to dismiss her claim of tortious interference with prospective business advantage based on her allegations that the university tortiously interfered with her "valid business expectancy that she would be able to teach, and possibly also serve as an administrator, in higher education until her retirement," that the university "intentionally interfered with this business expectancy by spreading false and defamatory lies about her to the *Washington Post* and the NCAA," and that at least three potential sources of prospective employment disappeared as a result of these actions." Kimmel v. Gallaudet Univ., 639 F. Supp. 2d 34, 45 (D.D.C. 2009) (internal quotation and citation omitted). The court noted, however, that alleged interference with an alleged expectancy of continued employment is not enough to state a claim for tortious interference. Id. at 45 n.7.

Former general counsel of the International Trade Commission failed to state a prima facie case for "interference with his professional career" because he did not sufficiently allege damage. Plaintiff alleged that he was reassigned to a position as senior advisor, which precluded him from "utiliz[ing] his legal background and experience" and hampered his professional development. Shewmaker v. Minchew, 504 F. Supp. 156, 163 (D.D.C. 1980), aff'd, 666 F.2d 616 (D.C. Cir. 1981). "Such an allegation," the court concluded, "does not state a claim of damages to plaintiff's economic interests and commercial dealings." Id.

3. **Prima Facie Tort.** District of Columbia courts have not recognized a cause of action for prima facie tort. Nix v. Hoke, 139 F. Supp. 2d 125, 132 n.5 (D.D.C. 2001) (citing Schwartz v. Franklin Nat'l Bank, 718 A.2d 553, 556-57 (D.C. 1998)).

II. EMPLOYER TESTING OF EMPLOYEES

The Employment Guidelines of the District of Columbia Office of Human Rights and the District's Commission on Human Rights adopt and incorporate by reference the United States Equal Employment Opportunity Commission's Guidelines for Employment Selection Procedures, which appear at 29 C.F.R § 1607 (2012). D.C. Mun. Regs. tit. 4, § 504 (2009).

A. Psychological or Personality Testing

1. ***Common Law and Statutes.*** See II.A.3, infra.

2. ***Private Employers.*** See II.A.3, infra.

3. ***Public Employers.*** Rejection of "psychiatrically disqualified" applicants by the District of Columbia Fire Department on the basis of the Minnesota Multiphasic Personality Inventory-2 ("MMPI-2") test, a sentence completion test, a figure drawing test and a clinical interview, raises a factual issue as to whether the employer violated the Rehabilitation Act of 1973. Does I-IV v. Dist. of Columbia, 962 F. Supp. 202 (D.D.C. 1997) (denying defendant's motion for summary judgment).

B. Drug Testing

1. ***Common Law and Statutes.*** Mayor's Order 90-27, January 31, 1990, requires employees under the Mayor's personnel authority to "abide by" the District's policy of providing a drug-free workplace for all employees. The Order prohibits District employees from "engaging in the unlawful manufacture, distribution, dispensing, possession or use of a controlled substance in the workplace." Employees who perform work under federal contracts or grants and who violate a criminal drug statute are required to "notify [their] immediate supervisor, in writing, no later than five days after [a] conviction . . . or a plea of guilty" for a violation occurring in the workplace. Id.; see also Federal Drug Free Workplace Act of 1988, 41 U.S.C.A. § 701(a). Additionally, Mayor's Order 96-139, September 17, 1996, requires D.C. government employees who are drivers of commercial motor vehicles to abide by the testing provisions set forth in the implementing regulations of 49 U.S.C. § 31306. The Order also provides that candidates for employment as drivers of commercial motor vehicles shall be subject to alcohol and controlled substances testing as a pre-employment condition and that D.C. employees who operate commercial motor vehicles in the performance of their duties shall be subject to random, post-accident, reasonable suspicion, return-to-duty, and follow-up testing for the use of alcohol and controlled substances. Id.

2. ***Private Employers.*** No statutes or case law.

3. ***Public Employers.*** Employees of several District of Columbia departments are subject to drug and alcohol testing pursuant to provisions of the District of Columbia Code.

The Department of Corrections shall perform drug and alcohol tests on (1) applicants, (2) employees who have had a referral based on "reasonable suspicion" (defined as "a belief by a supervisor that an employee is under the influence of an illegal substance or alcohol to the extent that the employee's ability to perform his or her job is impaired"), (3) post-accident employees, and (4) randomly on "high potential risk employees" (defined as any employee who has inmate care and custody responsibilities or who works within a correctional institution). D.C. Code §§ 24-211.21, 24-211.22 (2001). Confirmed positive test results or refusal to submit to the test shall be grounds for termination. Id. at § 24-211.24. The results of a random test cannot be turned over to law enforcement without the employee's written consent. Id.

Department of Corrections employees who operate motor vehicles in the District of Columbia are deemed to have provided their consent to urine or breath testing whenever a supervisor has a reasonable suspicion or a police officer arrests them and has reasonable grounds to believe they were operating or in control of a vehicle within the District while their alcohol concentration was 0.08 grams or more per 210 liters of breath, while under the influence, or while their ability to operate a motor vehicle was impaired by the consumption of an intoxicating beverage. D.C. Code § 24-211.23(e).

The Department of Human Services and the Commission on Mental Health Services are authorized to conduct drug and alcohol tests on (1) applicants for positions that would qualify them as "high potential risk employees" (defined as employees with resident care or custody responsibilities in a secured facility or who work in a residential facility), (2) employees who have had a probable cause referral from a supervisor, (3) post-accident employees, and (4) randomly on "high potential risk employees." D.C. Code § 1-620.22. An employee is given one opportunity to seek treatment following his or her first positive test result. Thereafter, any confirmed positive test result or a refusal to submit to a test shall be grounds for termination of employment. D.C. Code § 1-620.25. The results of a random test cannot be turned over to law enforcement without the employee's written consent. Id.

Certain District of Columbia employees who serve children are also subject to a drug and alcohol testing policy. D.C. Code § 1-620.35. Additionally, the District of Columbia Housing Authority is authorized to establish a program of pre-employment, random, reasonable suspicion, post-accident, return to duty, and follow-up testing. However, "[o]nly employees whose duties include responsibility for safety-sensitive or high-risk potential functions may be subject to random testing." D.C. Code § 6-217.

District of Columbia procedures for mandatory and individualized drug testing of employees have been analyzed under the Fourth Amendment's protection against "unreasonable searches and seizures" by government officials. See Piroglu v. Coleman, 25 F.3d 1098, 1101 (D.C. Cir. 1994); Turner v. Fraternal Order of Police, 500 A.2d 1005 (D.C. 1985). The District of Columbia's collection and analysis of a urine sample from a District of Columbia employee constitutes a "search" subject to the Fourth Amendment's reasonableness requirement. Piroglu, 25 F.3d at 1101 (holding that District of Columbia's collection of urine sample from emergency medical technician under mandatory testing program constitutes search).

Reasonableness of the search is determined by balancing the search's intrusion upon the individual's legitimate expectation of privacy against the government interest in conducting the search. Turner, 500 A.2d at 1007; Piroglu, 25 F.3d at 1101. Where the government's interest outweighs the intrusion upon the individual's privacy, the search is constitutionally permissible. See e.g., Piroglu, 25 F.3d at 1101-03 (District's "strong interest" in protecting the public from emergency medical technicians who are under the influence of drugs outweighs "relatively slight" invasion of employee's privacy).

When a drug test is conducted without any individualized suspicion (i.e., on a blanket basis), the government must show a "special need" for testing without individualized suspicion. Nat'l Fed'n of Fed. Employees-IAM v. Vilsack, 681 F.3d. 483, 492 (D.C. Cir. 2012). A governmental agency must further provide an evidentiary foundation to support a conclusion that the alternative of only suspicion-based testing is impractical in the specific context. Id. Applying this test, the United States Court of Appeal for the D.C. Circuit found a policy of the United States Forest Service requiring drug testing of all employees at twenty-eight Job Corps Civilian Conservation Centers to be facially unconstitutional. The court found insufficient the Forest Service's stated special circumstances that the employees were residential employees of the centers in isolated areas and had safety and oversight responsibility for youth participating in Job Corps programs at the centers, given the absence of evidence that suspicion-based testing was impractical as an alternative solution. Id.

C. Medical Testing

1. ***Common law and statutes.*** Under District of Columbia law, employers are not permitted to request or require genetic tests or to obtain or use genetic information of an employee or applicant. D.C. Mun. Regs. tit. 4 § 509.2. The use of family medical history, or request for such information in connection with employment, is also prohibited. Id.

2. ***Public Employers.*** The Mayor of the District of Columbia is authorized by statute to establish an employee health services program that provides for, among other things, "pre-employment and other physical examinations, including fitness-for-duty examinations." D.C. Code § 1-620.07 (2001); *see also* D.C. Mun. Regs. Subt. 6-B § 2049.

3. ***Private Employers.*** No reported cases.

D. Polygraph Tests.

Employers or prospective employers cannot (1) "administer, accept or use the results of any lie detector test" in connection with an individual's employment or application or consideration for employment, or (2) "have administered" within the District of Columbia a lie detector test to any employee or, during or in any hiring procedure, any prospective employee whose employment "as contemplated at the time of administration of the test" would occur in whole or in part in the District of Columbia. D.C. Code § 32-902(a) (2001).

The prohibition does not apply to any criminal or internal disciplinary investigation or to a pre-employment investigation done by the Metropolitan Police, the Fire Department, or the Department of Corrections. However, applicants may not be denied employment even by these public safety agencies based solely on the results of a pre-employment lie detector test. D.C. Code § 32-902(b). The use by the United States Secret Service of a pre-employment polygraph examination that included questions about prospective employees' medical, psychological, sexual, criminal, and drug use history was deemed to be permitted under the Fourth Amendment to the Constitution because those individuals "were applying for positions of public trust concerning the security of the nation and of our elected officials." Croddy v. FBI, 2006 WL 2844261, at *4 (D.D.C. Sept. 29, 2006).

A "lie detector test" is "any polygraph, lie detector, or other test which by any mechanical, electrical, chemical, or physiological means attempts to determine whether a person is telling the truth, or the truth to the best of the person's knowledge." D.C. Code § 32-901(4) (2001). An "employer" is broadly defined for purposes of the Act to include anyone (with the exception of the federal government) who employs any natural person and who does business in the District of Columbia. D.C. Code § 32-901(2).

Administration of a lie detector test to any employee or applicant in violation of the statute is "an unwarranted invasion of privacy" and is "compensable by damages for tortious injury." D.C. Code § 32-903(a) (2001). Employers who violate the statute "shall be guilty of a misdemeanor" and subject to a $500 fine and/or 30 days in jail. D.C. Code § 32-903 (c). Where an employer is civilly liable for violation of the statute, the court shall establish the amount of damages plus reasonable attorney's fees. D.C. Code § 32-903(d).

E. Fingerprinting

See infra VI.C.

Employees of the District of Columbia Lottery and Charitable Games Control Board are required to be fingerprinted as a condition of employment. D.C. Code § 3-1304.

III. SEARCHES

A. Employee's Person

1. ***Private Employers.*** No reported cases.

2. ***Public Employers.*** Similar to the courts' analysis of drug testing of public employees, bodily searches of public employees by the District of Columbia have been analyzed under the Fourth Amendment's protection against unreasonable searches and seizures by government officials. Profitt v. Dist. of Columbia, 790 F. Supp. 304 (D.D.C. 1991).

Determining the reasonableness of a search "'requires a balancing of the need for the particular search against the invasion of personal rights that the search entails.'" Id. at 305. Factors to consider include 'the scope of the particular intrusion, the manner in which it is conducted, the justification for initiating it, and the place in which it was so conducted.'" Id. (quoting Bell v. Wolfish, 441 U.S. 520, 559 (1979)). The court in Profitt determined that a visual body cavity search of a Department of Corrections employee was reasonable where there was a reasonable basis for suspicion (an anonymous tip) and a "compelling government interest at stake" (protecting public safety). 790 F. Supp. at 307-08.

B. Employee's Work Area

"It has been long settled that one has standing to object to a search of [one's] office, as well as of [one's] home." Gatlin v. United States, 833 A.2d 995, 1005 (D.C. 2003) (quoting O'Connor v. Ortega, 480 U.S. 709, 722 (1987)). Whether an employee has a "reasonable" expectation of privacy is "addressed on a case-by-case basis." Gatlin, 833 A.2d at 1005 (employees had no legitimate expectation of privacy in the halls and gathering places of a D.C. charter school); Harris v. Dist. of Columbia, 696 F. Supp. 2d 123, 131–32 (D.D.C. 2010) (a police officer did not have a reasonable expectation of privacy while on duty at a daycare center that was part of the public school system).

In the context of ruling that a warrantless search by police violated an employee's Fourth Amendment right to privacy, the United States Court of Appeals for the District of Columbia Circuit has indicated that, where an area is assigned to an employee's exclusive use, an employer may not search the area for property that is not work-related. United States v. Blok, 188 F.2d 1019 (D.C. Cir. 1951). Blok was a government office employee arrested on suspicion of petty larceny. With the consent of Blok's supervisor, the police conducted a warrantless search of "a desk assigned to [Blok's] exclusive use" and seized alleged evidence. Id. at 1019. Noting that Blok "was entitled to, and did, keep private property of a personal sort in her desk," the court held that Blok had enough of a possessory interest in the desk to make the search unreasonable. Id. at 1021. "We think appellee's exclusive right to use the desk assigned to her made the search of it unreasonable." Id. Cf. Freeman v. United States, 201 A.2d 22, 24 (D.C. 1964) (Veterans Administration employee's Fourth Amendment privacy rights not violated by search of table, where employee "did not have the exclusive right to use the table" and where "the table was open for common use by other employees of the agency").

The Blok court further observed that an unconsented-to search of the desk "would have been reasonable if made by some people in some circumstances." 188 F.2d at 1021. Blok's "official superiors might reasonably have searched the desk for official property needed for official use." Id. However, her supervisors "could not reasonably search the desk for her purse, her personal letters, or anything else that did not belong to the government and had no connection with the work of the office." Id. Nor did the supervisor's consent make the search by the police reasonable. Id.

The ruling in Blok occurred prior to the United States Supreme Court's decision in O'Connor v. Ortega, 480 U.S. 709, 107 S.Ct. 1492, 94 L.Ed.2d 714 (1987), in which the Court held that a public employer may conduct a work-related search, which is not criminal in nature, of a public employee's office, desk and file cabinets, as long as the search is "for noninvestigatory, work-related purposes, as well as for investigations of work-related misconduct," and the search satisfies "the standard of reasonableness under all the circumstances." Id. at 725–26. The extent to which Blok remains good law in the District in light of the later ruling in O'Connor is unclear, although the case has never been expressly overruled.

C. Employee's Property

1. ***Private Employers.*** No reported cases.

2. ***Public Employers.*** Public employees can state a claim under the Fourth and Fifth Amendments for personal property that is unlawfully seized by their employer and not returned. Harris v. Dist. of Columbia, 696 F. Supp. 2d 123, 132–33 (D.D.C. 2010) (noting the plaintiff has stated a claim for the personal property seized at his arrest, but dismissing his claim for failure to identify the property that was seized).

IV. MONITORING OF EMPLOYEES

A. Telephones and Electronic Communications

1. ***Wiretapping (Telephone).*** The District of Columbia permits wiretapping with "one-party consent." As a general matter, it is unlawful for a person in the District of Columbia to willfully intercept, endeavor to intercept, or procure any other person to intercept or endeavor to intercept the contents of any wire or oral communication or to willfully use or disclose the contents of such communication. D.C. Code § 23-542(a)(1) (2001). Willfully disclosing or endeavoring to disclose to any other person or willfully using or endeavoring to use the contents of any wire or oral communication, or evidence derived therefrom, knowing or having reason to know that the information was obtained through the interception of a wire or oral communication is likewise unlawful. Id. at § 23-542(a)(2-3).

A person "acting under color of law," however, may lawfully intercept a wire or oral communication where such person is a party to the communication or where one of the parties to the communication gives prior consent to such interception. D.C. Code § 23-542(b)(2); United States v. Sell, 487 A.2d 225, 228–29 (D.C. 1985). In addition, a person "not acting under color of law" may lawfully intercept a wire or oral communication where such person is a party to the communication or where one of the parties to the communication gives prior consent to such interception. Id. at § 23-542(b)(3).

"Wire communication" means any communication made in whole or in part through the use of facilities for the transmission of communications by the aid of wire, cable, or other like connection between the point of origin and the point of reception furnished or operated by any person engaged as a common carrier in providing or operating such facilities. Id. at § 23-541(1). "Oral communication" means any oral communication uttered by a person exhibiting an expectation that the communication is not subject to interception under circumstances justifying the expectation. Id. at § 23-541(2). "Intercept" means the aural acquisition of the contents of any wire or oral communication through the use of any electronic, mechanical, or other device or apparatus. Id. at § 23-541(3) and (4).

"The District of Columbia wiretapping statute is 'virtually identical' to the federal wiretapping statute." Napper v. United States, 22 A.3d 758, 767 (D.C. 2011). Consequently, the analysis applied by the Supreme Court in the Fourth Amendment right-to-privacy context is used to determine "whether an act of electronic surveillance runs afoul of [the District of Columbia wiretapping statute]." Id. (affirming finding by lower court that criminal suspect did not have a reasonable expectation of privacy and thus no violation of the Fourth Amendment or D.C. statutory law occurred when suspect made cell phone calls that were recorded by clearly visible cameras in interrogation room despite suspect's attempts to shield his calls from the cameras by covering his mouth when speaking). But see Council on American-Islamic Relations

Action Network, Inc. v. Gaubatz, 793 F.Supp.2d 311, 329 (D.D.C. 2011) (stating in dicta that there are "textual differences" between District of Columbia and federal wiretapping statutes).

D.C. Code § 23-554(a) (2001) establishes a civil cause of action against any person who improperly intercepts, discloses or uses, or procures another to intercept, disclose, or use wire or oral communications. A defendant may be liable under this section for: a) actual damages not less than liquidated damages computed at the rate of $100 a day for each day of violation, or $1,000, whichever is higher; b) punitive damages; and c) reasonably incurred attorneys' fees and other litigation costs. Id.

2. ***Electronic Communications (E-mail).*** No reported cases.

3. ***Other Electronic Monitoring.*** The Court of Appeals for the District of Columbia Circuit held that the use of a global positioning device attached to a vehicle for an extended period constituted a Fourth Amendment search, thus suggesting that public employees could not be so monitored. United States v. Maynard, 615 F.3d 544, 563-65 (D.C. Cir. 2010). **This ruling was affirmed by the United States Supreme Court in United States v. Jones, 132 S.Ct. 945, 954 (2012). The Supreme Court declined to consider the question of whether the search was carried out with reasonable suspicion or probable cause due to waiver of the argument by the United States. Id.**

B. Mail

No relevant statutes or case law.

C. Surveillance/Photographing

No relevant statutes or case law.

V. ACTIVITIES OUTSIDE THE WORKPLACE

A. Statute or Common Law

The District of Columbia Human Rights Act ("DCHRA") prohibits employment discrimination by employers, employment agencies, and unions on the basis of sexual orientation, political affiliation, marital status, personal appearance, family responsibilities, gender identity or expression, genetic information, race, color, religion, national origin, sex, age, disability, or matriculation. D.C. Code § 2-1402.11 (2001). See Underwood v. Archer Mgmt. Servs. Inc., 857 F. Supp. 96, 97 -98 (D.D.C. 1994); Jackson v. Dist. of Columbia Bd. of Elections and Ethics, 999 A.2d 89 (D.C. 2010) (detailing history of D.C. Human Rights Act). "Given the substantial similarity between Title VII and the DCHRA, the District of Columbia relies on interpretations of Title VII when interpreting DCHRA claims." Kimmel v. Gallaudet Univ., 639 F. Supp. 2d 34, 41 (D.D.C. 2009) (internal quotation omitted).

B. Employees' Personal Relationships

1. ***Romantic Relationships.*** No District of Columbia statutes, regulations, or cases are directly on point. However, The court in Atlantic Richfield Co. v. D.C. Comm'n on Human Rights, 515 A.2d 1095, 1097 (D.C. 1986), affirmed a ruling that defendant constructively discharged plaintiff and discriminated against her based on her appearance where plaintiff's supervisor "frequently questioned [her] about her after-work activities and asked her if she got phone numbers from men visiting the office." Id. Taken together with the plaintiff's other claims, including allegations that her supervisor criticized the fit and quality of her clothing, and that a company official had described her behavior at a party as "resembl[ing] that of a prostitute," the court found there was "ample evidence" to support the plaintiff's contention of constructive discharge. Id. at 1101.

2. ***Sexual Orientation.*** The District of Columbia Human Rights Act prohibits an employer from discharging, suspending, or refusing to hire or promote an individual and from subjecting a person to different terms, conditions and privileges of employment because of the person's sexual orientation. D.C. Code § 2-1402.11. See also D.C. Mun. Regs. tit. 4 § 519. The Human Rights Act defines "sexual orientation" to mean "male or female homosexuality, heterosexuality and bisexuality, by preference or practice." D.C. Code § 2-1401.02(28).

See Howard Univ. v. Green, 652 A.2d 41, 49 n.11 (D.C. 1994) (noting in dicta that rumors concerning the sexual orientation of three university hospital employees "intruded in an offensive manner on the women's privacy and held them up to ridicule").

3. ***Marital Status.*** The D.C. Human Rights Act prohibits employment discrimination on the basis of marital status. D.C. Code § 2-1402.11. Specifically, the Marital Status Guidelines of the District's Office of Human Rights and the District's Commission on Human Rights prohibit an employer's "[d]ecisions on hiring, promotion, compensation, lay

-off, and other terms and conditions of employment" from being "related to marital status." D.C. Mun. Regs. tit. 4 § 510.3. The guidelines also forbid recruiting materials from stating "a preference for specific marital status" (e.g. "single person who enjoys travel" or "stable, married person preferred"), and employment applications cannot contain questions "pertaining solely to marital status . . . unless the employer can show a business necessity for the inquiry." Id. § 510.1. "Marital status" under the guidelines is defined as "the state of being married, in a domestic partnership, single, divorced, separated or widowed, and the usual conditions associated therewith, including pregnancy or parenthood." Id. at § 599.1; see also D.C. Code § 2-1401.02(17).

4. ***Transsexuality.*** Applicant who claimed that she had been denied employment based on her transsexuality stated a claim that she had been discriminated against "because of her sex" in violation of Title VII. Schroer v. Billington, 424 F. Supp. 2d 203 (D.D.C. 2006), later proceedings at 525 F. Supp. 2d 58, 62 (D.D.C. 2007) (denying defendant's second motion to dismiss on the ground that plaintiff's amended complaint stated a "sex stereotyping" claim under Title VII). But see Underwood v. Archer Mgmt. Servs. Inc., 857 F. Supp. 96, 97-98 (D.D.C. 1994) (transsexuality is not included in the Human Rights Act's definition of sex and, therefore, a plaintiff may not pursue a cause of action for discrimination based on transsexuality. A plaintiff fails to state a claim where she only alleges discrimination because of her "status as a transsexual" and "alleges no facts regarding discrimination because she is a woman.")

5. ***Family Responsibilities.*** The D.C. Human Rights Act prohibits employment discrimination on the basis of family responsibilities. D.C. Code § 2-1402.11. The Human Rights Act defines "family responsibilities" as "the state of being, or the potential to become, a contributor to the support of a person or persons in a dependent relationship, irrespective of their number, including the state of being the subject of an order of withholding or similar proceedings for the purpose of paying child support or a debt related to child support." D.C. Code § 2-1401.02(12).

C. Smoking

By statute, the District of Columbia prohibits employers from refusing to hire or employ an applicant and otherwise discriminating against an employee on the basis of the applicant's or employee's use of tobacco or tobacco products. D.C. Code § 7-1703.03(a) (2001). The statute explicitly does not prohibit employers from establishing permitted or required workplace smoking restrictions or from establishing tobacco-use restrictions that constitute bona fide occupational qualifications. Id. Violation of the statute creates a private cause of action for the aggrieved employee, who is entitled to recover damages that "include lost or back wages or salary." Id. at § (b-c).

By regulation, employers in the District of Columbia, subject to narrow enumerated exceptions, must adopt policies prohibiting smoking in any enclosed areas of employment. D.C. Mun. Regs. tit. 20 § 2101.5 (exceptions at D.C. Mun. Regs. tit. 20 § 2105. The employer may permit smoking in an outdoor area under its control, subject to the terms and conditions of any lease or contract between the owner and the tenant. D.C. Mun. Regs. tit. 20 § 2101.6.

D. Blogging

No reported cases.

E. Other

1. ***Obtaining Medical Treatment.*** The Court of Appeals has held, although not in an employment context, that the right to privacy includes the right to obtain medical treatment without publicity concerning that fact. Vassiliades v. Garfinckel's, 492 A.2d 580, 586–87 (D.C. 1985) (holding that physician's publicizing "before and after" photographs of plastic-surgery patient constitutes unlawful invasion of privacy). "[C]ertainly if there is any right of privacy at all, it should include the right to obtain medical treatment at home or in a hospital for an individual personal condition (at least if it is not contagious or dangerous to others) without personal publicity." Id. at 587-88 (quoting Barber v. Time, Inc., 159 S.W.2d 291, 295 (Mo. 1942)). This arguably has implications for an employer's treatment of private information concerning an employee's medical treatment.

2. ***Political Affiliation.*** The D.C. Human Rights Act prohibits employment discrimination on the basis of political affiliation. D.C. Code § 2-1402.11. Specifically, the Political Affiliation Guidelines of the District's Office of Human Rights and the District's Commission on Human Rights prohibit an employer other than a political organization from refusing to hire or discharging or otherwise discriminating against an employee because of the employee's "present or past political affiliation or lack of political affiliation." D.C. Mun. Regs. tit. 4 § 515.1. An employer is further prohibited from retaliating against an employee for failure to vote for a designated candidate and from requiring employees to contribute financial or other support for any political party or candidate. Id. at § 515.3.

3. ***Personal Appearance.*** The District of Columbia Human Rights Act prohibits employment discrimination on the basis of personal appearance. D.C. Code § 2-1402.11. "Personal appearance" is defined as "the outward

appearance of any person, irrespective of sex, with regard to bodily condition or characteristics, manner or style of dress, and manner or style of personal grooming, including, but not limited to, hair style and beards," but does "not relate... to the requirement of cleanliness, uniforms, or prescribed standards, when uniformly applied to a class of employees for a reasonable business purpose" or "when such bodily conditions or characteristics, style or manner of dress or personal grooming presents a danger to the health, welfare or safety of any individual." D.C. Code § 2-1401.02(22); D.C. Mun. Regs. tit. 4 § 599. Consistent with this prohibition, unless for a reasonable business purpose, an employer "shall not refuse to allow an employee to wear a hair or dress style symbolic of heritage, religion or race." Id. See also Turcios v. U.S. Servs. Indus., 680 A.2d 1023, 1027 (D.C. 1996) (employer uniformly applied its "no tail hairstyles" to employees at facility); Kennedy v. Dist. of Columbia, 654 A.2d 847 (D.C. 1994) (fire department's facial hair regulations discriminatorily applied to firefighter).

"However, an employer may prescribe standards of appearance or dress for personnel which serve a reasonable business purpose" (e.g., uniforms to identify employees) or which "prevent a danger to the health, welfare, or safety of employees or customers" (e.g., head and hand coverings for food service workers). D.C. Mun. Regs. tit. 4 §§ 513 ("Personal Appearance Guidelines"), 599 ("Definitions"). Where an employer prescribes standards or codes for dress and appearance, they "shall be applied equally to all employees performing the same kind of work." Id. at 506.6 ("Terms, Conditions, Rights, and Privileges of Employment").

An employee fails to make out a prima facie case of personal appearance discrimination where the comments about her appearance that she attributes to her supervisor were "stray comments" that do not reflect discriminatory animus and were also "facially complimentary" comments that "do not give rise to a reasonable inference of discrimination unless proffered with evidence tending to show that, in reality, the apparent compliments actually were snidely made, implying discriminatory animus." McManus v. MCI Commc'ns Corp., 748 A.2d 949, 952, 955 (D.C. 2000) (affirming summary judgment against African-American employee who "often came to work in African-styled attire and wore her hair with dreadlocks, braids, twists, and cornrows" and whose supervisor commented, among other things, that she "look[ed] like an African princess").

An employer discriminated against a plaintiff on the basis of personal appearance and constructively discharged the plaintiff where a supervisor frequently subjected plaintiff to derogatory comments about her appearance and behavior. Atlantic Richfield Co. v. D.C. Comm'n on Human Rights, 515 A.2d 1095, 1097 (D.C. 1986). The supervisor criticized plaintiff's "low cut and tight blouses" and made "many comments" about plaintiff's breasts and about her showing cleavage. The supervisor also "criticized the cost of [plaintiff's] clothes" and questioned plaintiff about her interaction with men who visited the office. Id. In addition, the supervisor told plaintiff that a company official described her behavior at a party as "resembl[ing] that of a prostitute." Id. The court held that plaintiff demonstrated under the burden-shifting approach of McDonnell Douglas Corp. v. Green, 411 U.S. 792 (1973), that the employer's explanation for its conduct was a pretext for discrimination because the employer did not have a uniformly applied standard of dress and because plaintiff's "appearance was similar to that of [her] coworkers." 515 A.2d at 1100. The court observed that the record demonstrated that the employer's conduct "manifest[ed] a preoccupation with [plaintiff's] physique and the cost of her clothes" and that plaintiff's "moral character was also called into question on account of [her employer's perception of] her appearance." Id.

In Underwood v. Archer Mgmt. Servs. Inc., 857 F. Supp. 96, 98–99 (D.D.C. 1994), the Federal District Court for the District of Columbia held that a transsexual plaintiff states a claim for relief where she alleges that employer discharged her because she "retains some masculine traits." Id.

The court in Natural Motion by Sandra, Inc. v. D.C. Comm'n on Human Rights, 687 A.2d 215 (D.C. 1997), affirmed the Commission's finding of liability and award of compensatory damages and medical expenses where the employer terminated an employee who "developed lesions, swelling and discoloration" on his leg from an AIDS-related illness. For three years prior to plaintiff's termination, his co-workers subjected him to derogatory remarks about his appearance, illness, and sexual orientation. Id. at 216, 218. The employer claimed that it properly terminated plaintiff due to plaintiff's absences and client complaints. However, the employer produced insufficient evidence in support of this reason, which the court deemed to be a pretext for discrimination. Id. at 218.

VI. RECORDS

The District of Columbia Freedom of Information Act ("FOIA") provides that, with limited specified exemptions, "[a]ny person has a right to inspect, and . . . to copy any public record of a public body . . . in accordance with reasonable rules . . . concerning the time and place of access." D.C. Code § 2-532(a) (2001). See Dunhill v. Director, D.C. Dept. of Transp., 416 A.2d 244, 246-47 (D.C. 1980); Hines v. D.C. Board of Parole, 567 A.2d 909 (D.C. 1989). Except for "information of which disclosure is authorized or mandated by other law," the Act exempts from disclosure "[i]nformation of a personal nature where the public disclosure thereof would constitute a clearly unwarranted invasion of personal privacy." D.C. Code § 2-534(a)(2). In determining whether disclosure would constitute such an invasion of privacy, "the public interest in disclosure" is balanced "against the privacy interest Congress and the Council of the District of Columbia intended the exemption to protect." Padou v. District of Columbia, 29 A.3d 973, 979-80 (D.C. 2011). **In the application of this rule, it may be necessary for documents to be redacted and produced in part, such as where a document contains both private and non-private information. District of Columbia v. Fraternal Order of Police Metropolitan Police Labor Committee, 33 A.3d 332, 347 (D.C. Cir. 2011) (directing District Court to undertake an in camera review of a sample of police trial board and EEO investigation files to determine whether redaction would render the documents "wholly unintelligible" and thus not subject to production).** The Act also exempts from disclosure, among other items, "[t]est questions and answers to be used in future license, employment or academic examinations, but not previously administered examinations or answers to questions thereon." Id. at § 2-534(a)(5). The Act's statutory exemptions "are to be narrowly construed, with ambiguities resolved in favor of disclosure." Riley v. Fenty, 7 A.3d 1014, 1018 (D.C. 2010) (quoting Washington Post v. Minority Bus. Opportunity Comm'n, 560 A.2d 517, 521 (D.C. 1989)).

A. Personnel Records

1. ***Private Employers.*** There is no statutory obligation that private employers grant employees access to their personnel files. However, employers are required to "secure all personnel files and other documents which contain information which is susceptible to use for a discriminatory purpose and shall allow access to the files only on a 'need to know' basis." D.C. Mun. Regs. tit. 4 § 506.10 (Terms, Conditions, Rights, and Privileges of Employment); see also supra I.A.2 (General Law of Privacy) and infra VI.D (Subpoenas/Search Warrants).

2. ***Public Employers.*** By statute, the District of Columbia is required to establish, maintain, and dispose of all official government personnel records "in a manner designed to ensure the greatest degree of applicant or employee privacy while providing adequate, necessary, and complete information for the District to carry out its responsibilities." D.C. Code § 1-631.01 (2001).

Disclosure of Personnel Information. District of Columbia policy is to make available upon request personnel information under its control to "appropriate personnel and law-enforcement authorities," except where "such disclosure would constitute an unwarranted invasion of personal privacy or is prohibited under law." D.C. Code § 1-631.03. A government employee's access or "control" over "documents created in the ordinary course of the government's business is secondary to that of his employer; he cannot on his own initiative remove government files and provide them to a third party," even if that party is a former employee of the government agency. Lowe v. Dist. of Columbia, 250 F.R.D. 36, 38–39 (D.D.C. 2008). However, where personal information about non-party employees may be relevant to the issues in a lawsuit, it may be disclosed subject to a protective order. See Huthnance v. Dist. of Columbia, 255 F.R.D. 285, 287–88 (D.D.C. 2008); Fonville v. Dist. of Columbia, 230 F.R.D. 38, 44–45 (D.D.C. 2005).

Employee's Access to Record. The official personnel record of a District employee shall be disclosed to the employee or any representative of his or her choice. All such disclosures shall be made in the presence of a representative of the agency having custody of the records. D.C. Code § 1-631.05(a)(1).

Information Not Disclosed to Employee. Information in an official personnel file may not be disclosed to an employee if it is (1) information received on a confidential basis under an agreement that the identity of the source of the information remain undisclosed (unless the identifying information is deleted in a manner to preclude the source's identity), (2) medical information which the employee's physician judges to be injurious to the employee's health if disclosed, (3) criminal investigative reports, (4) suitability inquiries and confidential questionnaires, or (5) test and examination materials under use for selection and promotion purposes. D.C. Code § 1-631.05(a)(2).

Employee's Right to Present Information. A District employee has the right "to present information immediately germane to any information contained in his or her official personnel record" and to seek to remove irrelevant, immaterial or untimely information from the record. D.C. Code § 1-631.05(b).

B. Medical Records.

"Pre-employment medical inquires, or inquires as to whether an applicant is disabled or to the severity of the disability, shall not be allowed . . . ." D.C. Mun. Regs. tit. 4 § 503.6. However, employers may proscribe standards for personal appearance. See id.; see also id. at § 513 (Personal Appearance Guidelines).

C. Criminal Records

The District of Columbia Freedom of Information Act exempts from disclosure "[i]nvestigatory records compiled for law-enforcement purposes" when producing such records would, among other things, "[c]onstitute an unwarranted invasion of privacy." D.C. Code § 2-534(a)(3). It is also unlawful in the District of Columbia for an employer to require an applicant or employee to produce his or her arrest record at his or her own expense. Arrest records that are permissibly requested "shall contain only listings of convictions and forfeitures of collateral that have occurred within 10 years of the time at which such record is requested." D.C. Code § 2-1402.66 (2001); See also D.C. Mun. Regs. tit. 4 § 503 (Prehire Inquiries).

The Director of the Department of Corrections is required to conduct on a biennial basis National Crime Information Center ("NCIC") criminal background investigations on all department employees, including non-probationary employees. The director may also conduct NCIC investigations at unspecified times at her or his discretion. D.C. Code § 24-211.41 (2001).

Additionally, the Mayor is authorized to conduct criminal background checks, including fingerprinting, of certain employees, applicants, and volunteers for positions that provide services to children. D.C. Code § 4-1501.05.

D. Subpoenas / Search Warrants

District of Columbia courts employ a traditional balancing test in determining whether to compel the disclosure of personnel records in response to a subpoena. In general, courts in the District of Columbia will only compel the subpoenaed disclosure of personnel records that are relevant to the underlying litigation – that is, "reasonably calculated to lead to the discovery of admissible evidence" under Fed. R. Civ. P. 26(b)(1). Washington v. Thurgood Marshall Academy, 230 F.R.D. 18, 24-25 (D.D.C. 2005); see also In the Matter of M.W.G., 427 A.2d 440, 442-43 (D.C. 1981). However, these courts also recognize a significant privacy interest in personnel records. Fonville v. Dist. of Columbia, 230 F.R.D. 38, 44-45 (D.D.C. 2005). Thus, a District of Columbia court will typically compel the disclosure only of that information in personnel records which a party cannot obtain by other means, and only subject to a protective order. Gilbey v. Dept. of the Interior, 1990 WL 174889, at *2 (D.D.C. Oct. 22, 1990); see Fonville, 230 F.R.D. at 44-45.

VII. ACTIONS SUBSEQUENT TO EMPLOYMENT

A. References

District of Columbia courts recognize a cause of action for retaliation arising from negative job references. Passer v. Am. Chem. Soc., 935 F.2d 322, 331 (D.C. Cir. 1991); Niedermeier v. Office of Max S. Baucus, 153 F. Supp. 2d 23, 31 (D.D.C. 2001). To state such a claim, a plaintiff must allege: (1) the nature of the references that he or she believes were disparaging or negative; (2) that these references were provided to a third party with which he or she had applied for a job; and (3) that the third party then denied him or her the job as a result of those references. Niedermeier, 153 F. Supp. 2d at 31. However, post-employment retaliation claims will not be recognized under the False Claims Act. United States ex rel. Head v. Kane Co., 798 F.Supp.2d 186, 209 (D.D.C. 2011) (finding that the False Claims Act contains more restrictive language than federal anti-discrimination statutes in regard to retaliation claims, and specifically is intended to limit such claims to retaliatory actions taken prior to the end of the worker's employment).

B. Non-Compete Agreements

Non-compete provisions in employment agreements and other covenants not to compete have been enforced in the District of Columbia for decades. Godfrey v. Roessle, 5 App. D.C. 299 (1895); Allison v. Seigle, 79 F.2d 170 (D.C. Cir. 1935). These restrictions are now analyzed under a reasonableness standard modeled on the Restatement (Second) of Contracts §§ 186-88. Deutsch v. Barsky, 795 A.2d 669, 676-77 (D.C. 2002); see Morgan Stanley DW Inc. v. Rothe, 150 F. Supp. 2d 67, 74 (D.D.C. 2001) (covenant not to compete enforceable as long as it not "an unconscionable contract provision"). This is "a fact intensive inquiry that depends on the totality of the circumstances." Deutsch, 795 A.2d at 677 (quoting Valley Med. Specialists v. Farber, 982 P.2d 1277, 1283 (Ariz. 1999)). In general, however, District of Columbia courts balance the "promisee's legitimate interest" in enforcement of the covenant against "the nature of the hardship" – and specifically the business hardship – claimed by the promisor and, to a lesser degree, the injury to the public in enforcing the covenant. Deutsch, 795 A.2d at 677-79.

A non-compete clause that "is reasonably limited as to time and territory and is not such as to constitute an unfair restraint of trade contrary to public policy, or to work an unfair hardship upon the restricted party, [] is a valid contractual obligation." Meyer v. Wineburgh, 110 F. Supp. 957, 959 (D.D.C. 1953). Thus, District of Columbia Courts have enforced covenants: (1) not to solicit customers of a former employer for one year and within a 100-mile radius, Morgan Stanley, 150 F. Supp. 2d at 74; (2) not to do business with the customers of a former employer for five years and within a 30-mile radius of any company office, Meyer, 110 F. Supp. at 959; and (3) not to operate a directly competing business within a ten-block radius during the lifetime of a former co-owner's business, Allison, 79 F.2d at 171. The District of Columbia Court of Appeals also rejected a facial challenge to a two-year, five-mile radius covenant not to compete among two dentists. Deutsch, 795 A.2d at 676-77. The United States Court of Appeals for the District of Columbia, however, refused to enforce a three-year covenant not to compete for the customers of a kitchen supply business within five states and the District of Columbia because of "the nature of the business, the character of the service performed by, and the station of the employee, in relation to [the] area in which the former employer seeks to be protected." Chemical Fireproofing Corp. v. Krouse, 155 F.2d 422, 423 (D.C. Cir. 1946).

District of Columbia courts have not hesitated to issue temporary restraining orders, preliminary injunctions, and other forms of equitable relief to enforce these non-compete covenants. See Morgan Stanley, 150 F. Supp. 2d at 74 (granting motion for restraining order enforcing non-compete clause and citing analogous examples). Particularly relevant to the question of equitable relief is whether the plaintiff will suffer irreparable harm "in the loss of its customers and by the possibly permanently damaged relationships with its customers." Id. at 78.

VIII. OTHER ISSUES

A. Statutes of Limitations

The District of Columbia statute of limitations does not contain an express provision for claims of invasion of privacy. However, "on the rationale that invasion of privacy is essentially a type of defamation," the statute's one-year limitations period for libel and slander has been applied to invasion of privacy claims in the District of Columbia. Grunseth v. Marriott Corp., 872 F. Supp. 1069, 1074-75 (D.D.C. 1995); see also Paul v. Judicial Watch, Inc., 543 F. Supp. 2d 1, 10 (D.D.C. 2008) (applying to invasion of privacy claims the one-year statute of limitations under D.C. Code § 12-301(4), which governs libel, slander, and similar intentional torts); Henderson v. MTV, 2006 WL 1193872, at *1, 34 Med. L. Rptr. 1725 (D.D.C. May 3, 2006) (applying one-year statute of limitations to false light claims); Nix v. Hoke, 139 F. Supp. 2d 125, 134 n.9 (D.D.C. 2001); Doe v. Southeastern Univ., 732 F. Supp. 7, 8 (D.D.C. 1990) ("Invasion of privacy is essentially a defamation type action."). But cf. Rochon v. FBI, 691 F. Supp. 1548, 1562-63 (D.D.C. 1988) (applying to plaintiff's common law claims, including invasion of privacy, the three-year default period for actions for which a limitation is not otherwise specifically prescribed). Whether the discovery rule applies to defamation and defamation-type claims remains an open question. See Maupin v. Haylock, 931 A.2d 1039 (D.C. 2007). But see Sykes v. U.S. Attorney for D.C., 770 F. Supp. 2d 152, 154-55 (D.D.C. 2011) (noting that the "District of Columbia applies the 'discovery rule' to determine when a tort action accrues," without distinguishing defamation actions).

Claims for negligent or intentional infliction of emotional distress, however, are subject to the three-year default statute of limitations period under District of Columbia law, unless they are "dependent" or "grounded in" other claims for which a limitations period is specifically prescribed. Mittleman v. U.S., 104 F.3d 410, 416 (D.C. Cir. 1997) (citing Saunders v. Nemati, 580 A.2d 660, 661-62 (D.C. 1990). In Mittleman, the Court of Appeals for the District of Columbia Circuit remanded a matter to the District Court with instructions for the District Court to determine whether the plaintiff's emotional distress claims were "independent enough of the false statements to be governed by a statute of limitations other than the one-year period for slander and libel. Mittleman, 104 F.3d at 416.

The statute of limitations for claims under the D.C. Human Rights Act is one year. See D.C. Code § 2-1403.16(a); Brown v. Children's Nat'l Med. Ctr., 773 F. Supp. 2d 125, 136-37 (D.D.C. 2011); Carter v. Dist. of Columbia, 980 A.2d 1217, 1223 (D.C. 2009). The statute of limitations is tolled by filing a complaint with the D.C. Office of Human Rights. D.C. Code § 2-1403.16(a); Brown, 773 F. Supp. 2d at 136-37.

B. Jurisdiction

The Superior Court of the District of Columbia has jurisdiction over any civil matter brought in the District of Columbia, provided exclusive jurisdiction over the matter is not vested in a Federal court. D.C. Code § 11-921(a-b).

With respect to claims alleging violations of the D.C. Human Rights Act, a complainant must choose initially to either pursue administrative remedies with the D.C. Office of Human Rights ("OHR") or to file suit. D.C. Code § 2-1403.16 (a); see also Adams v. District of Columbia, 783 F.Supp.2d 392, 395 (D.D.C. 2011). "The jurisdiction of the court and OHR are mutually exclusive in the first instance. Thus, where one opts to file with OHR, he or she generally may not also file a complaint in court." Brown v. Capitol Hill Club, 425 A.2d 1309, 1311 (D.C. 1981). However, "where the [OHR] has dismissed such complaint on the grounds of administrative convenience, or where the complainant has withdrawn a complaint, such person shall maintain all rights to bring suit as if no complaint had been filed." D.C. Code § 2-1403.16(a). A claim brought before the OHR must be investigated to determine whether there is probable cause to believe that the respondent has engaged in an unlawful discriminatory practice. D.C. Code § 2-1403.05(a-b). Should the OHR find no probable cause, the claimant may seek reconsideration and/or seek judicial review. Simpson v. D.C. Office of Human Rights, 597 A.2d 392, 397–99 (D.C. 1991). The courts also have jurisdiction to review a final agency decision. Id.

Whether claims are cognizable under the D.C. Human Rights Act turns "not on the place of employment but on where the events alleged to be discriminatory took place." Monteilth v. AFSCME, 982 A.2d 301, 303 (D.C. 2009) "It would not be enough to establish subject matter jurisdiction under the [D.C. Human Rights Act] simply to show that the company is headquartered here or has offices here. Either the [discriminatory] decision must be made, or its effects must be felt, or both must have occurred, in the District of Columbia." Id. at 304-05. **Thus, in Cole v. Boeing Co., 845 F.Supp.2d 277 (D.D.C. 2012), the court dismissed for lack of subject matter jurisdiction certain claims brought by a plaintiff under the D.C.**

Human Rights Act that arose from events alleged to have occurred after her employment was transferred to Virginia. Id. The court did, however, apply the D.C. Human Rights Act to other claims based on events that took place in the District of Columbia prior to the transfer, and held open the possibility that in future cases a claim involving both out-of-jurisdiction and within-jurisdiction events, if the events are sufficiently related, may allow the application of the Act to the entire claim including the out-of-jurisdiction events. Id. at 284 (referring to "three distinct phases" of alleged discrimination and noting that "there is little, if any, factual overlap between the hostile work environment and retaliation [Plaintiff] complains she suffered while in the District, and her later claims of discrimination in Virginia").

C. Worker's Compensation Exclusivity

"When a workplace injury occurs in the District, the [D.C. Worker's Compensation Act ("DCWCA")] by its sweeping terms of coverage almost always applies in its entirety." McGregor v. Grimes, 884 A.2d 605, 607 (D.C. 2005). With limited exceptions where both the employer and employee have limited contacts with the District and the employer has furnished insurance under the worker's compensation regime of another jurisdiction, the Act will apply. Id.; D.C. Code § 32-1503(a). Under the DCWCA, worker's compensation benefits are the exclusive remedy available for injuries or death arising out of or occurring in the course of employment. Doe v. United States, 797 F.Supp.2d 78, 81 (D.D.C. 2011); Vanzant v. Wash. Metro. Area Transit Auth., 557 F. Supp. 2d 113, 117 (D.D.C. 2008). "[T]he exclusivity provision generally bars a law suit by an injured employee against a fellow employee (as well as the employer)." McGregor, 884 A.2d at 606; see also Cruz v. Paige, 683 A.2d 1121 (D.C. 1996). Worker's compensation coverage extends to "claims for emotional distress or mental anguish where the underlying cause or tort is covered by the [DCWCA]," as well as to "injuries that are the result of willful and intentional conduct of either a fellow employer or a third party." Vanzant, 557 F. Supp. 2d at 117; Ramey v. Potomac Elec. Power Co., 468 F. Supp. 2d 51, 55–56 (D.D.C. 2006). However, "injuries" under the DCWCA do not include those arising from discrimination or sexual harassment. Harvey v. Strayer College, 911 F. Supp. 24, 27 (D.D.C. 1996) (citing Underwood v. Nat'l Credit Union Admin., 665 A.2d 621, 621 (D.C. 1995)); see Everson v. Medlantic Healthcare Group, 414 F. Supp. 2d 77, 86 (D.D.C. 2006) (finding a claim alleging injury due to a dangerous work condition precluded under the DCWCA to the extent it alleged injuries separate from the plaintiff's non-precluded hostile work environment claim). "The only injuries that fall outside the scope of the [DCWCA] are 'injuries specifically intended by the employer to be inflicted on the particular employee who is injured." Legesse v. Rite Aid Corp., 2005 U.S. Dist. LEXIS 29582 (D.D.C. Apr. 23, 2007); see also Doe, 797 F.Supp.2d at 82. So long as an employee is "entitled" to benefits under the DCWCA, he is subject to the exclusivity provisions. McGregor, 884 A.2d at 609.

D. Pleading Requirements

The District of Columbia Court of Appeals has held that a complaint must include "well-pleaded factual allegations" that "plausibly given rise to an entitlement for relief," construing Superior Court Rule 8(a) to be consistent with Federal Rule 8(a) as interpreted by the United States Supreme Court in Twombly and Iqbal. Mazza v. Housecraft LLC, 18 A.3d 786, 790-91 (D.C. 2011) (vacated as moot, but reasoning later adopted by Potomac Dev. Corp. v. District of Columbia, 28 A.3d 531, 544 n.4. (2011)). A claim will be found to have facial plausibility "when the plaintiff pleads factual content that allows the court to draw the reasonable inference that the defendant is liable for the misconduct alleged." Potomac, 28 A.3d at 543-44.

SURVEY OF FLORIDA EMPLOYMENT LIBEL LAW

Sanford L. Bohrer and Scott D. Ponce
Holland & Knight LLP
701 Brickell Avenue, Suite 3000
P.O. Box 015441
Miami, Florida 33131
Telephone: (305) 789-7678; Facsimile: (305) 789-7799

(With Developments Reported Through **November 1, 2012**)

GENERAL COMMENTS

None.

SIGNIFICANT DEVELOPMENTS SINCE THE 2012 *SURVEY*

There are no significant developments this year.

I. GENERAL LAW

A. General Employment Law

1. ***At Will Employment.*** Florida is an "employment at will" state, and with rare exceptions (e.g., whistleblower statutes, discrimination statutes), in the absence of a contract for a fixed term, an employer can terminate an employee without cause and suffer no consequences. See Bryant v. Shands Teaching Hosp. and Clinics, Inc., 479 So. 2d 165, 167 (Fla. 1st DCA 1985); Leonardi v. City of Hollywood, 715 So. 2d 1007, 1010 n.1 (Fla. 4th DCA 1998) (The general rule of at-will employment is that an employee can be discharged at any time, as long as he or she is not terminated for a reason prohibited by law, such as retaliation or unlawful discrimination); see also Kelly v. Gill, 544 So. 2d 1162, 1164 (Fla. 5th DCA 1989) ("Breach of an obligation of good faith and fair dealing has not been recognized in Florida as a viable cause of action, at least where a wrongful dismissal is claimed."); Snow v. Ruden McClosky, Smith, Schuster & Russell, P.A., 896 So. 2d 787, 791 (Fla. 2d DCA 2005) (the implied covenant is not an independent term within the parties' contract; thus, it cannot override an express contractual provision); Escarra v. Regions Bank, 2009 WL 4111131 (11th Cir. Fla. 2009); cf. Golden v. Complete Holdings, Inc., 818 F. Supp. 2d 1495, 1496-97 (M.D. Fla. 1993) (Arguing that a former employee was an at-will employee did not require dismissal of claims against employer for negligent misrepresentation, promissory estoppel, fraudulent misrepresentation, and outrageous conduct; at-will employment doctrine only applies to claims for breach of contract).

B. Elements of Libel Claim

1. ***Basic Elements.*** To recover for defamation, a plaintiff must prove the defendant communicated ("published") to a third person a false and defamatory and unprivileged statement of fact about the plaintiff. See Thomas v. Jacksonville Television, Inc., 699 So. 2d 800, 803 (Fla. 1st DCA 1997); Valencia v. Citibank Int'l, 728 So. 2d 330 (Fla. 3d DCA 1999), reh'g den. (April 14, 1999) (holding that Florida law does not provide an exception to the publication requirement of defamation). "The general rule in Florida is that allegedly defamatory words should be set out in the complaint for the purpose of fixing the character of the alleged libelous publication." See also Edward L. Nezelek, Inc. v. Sunbeam Television Corp., 413 So. 2d 51, 55 (Fla. 3d DCA 1982); Lipsig v. Ramlawi, 760 So. 2d 170, 184 (Fla. 3d DCA 2000) (quoting Nezelek, 413 So. 2d at 55); Cooper v. Miami Herald Publ'g Co., 31 So. 2d 382 (1947). "[W]hen the cause of action for defamation is based on oral statements, it is sufficient that the plaintiff set out the substance of the spoken words with sufficient particularity to enable the court to determine whether the publication was defamatory." Nezelek, 413 So. 2d at 55.

2. ***Fault.*** The level of fault that must be shown may depend on the plaintiff's private or public status and the private or public nature of the statement. A recent decision suggested the same rule should apply regardless of whether the defendant is a media defendant or not and held the plaintiff must plead fault. Log Creek, L.L.C. v. Kessler, 2010 WL 2426612 (N.D. Fla. June 3, 2010).

a. **Private Figure Plaintiff/Matter of Public Concern.** Since the United States Supreme Court's decision in Gertz v. Robert Welch, Inc., 418 U.S. 323 (1974), overruling Rosenbloom v. Metromedia, Inc., 403 U.S. 29 (1971), whether speech is matter of public concern has been relevant only in determining public figure status. See, e.g., Rety v. Green, 546 So. 2d 410, 425 (Fla. 3d DCA 1989), rev. den., 553 So. 2d 1165, 1166 (Fla. 1989). No published Florida decision addresses this issue in the employment context.

b. **Private Figure Plaintiff/Matter of Private Concern.** In Gertz v. Robert Welch, Inc., 418 U.S. 323 (1974), the Court held that as long as they did not impose liability without fault, the states could determine for themselves what standard of care is applicable in libel and slander actions brought by private figure plaintiffs against the press. In Miami Herald Publ'g Co. v. Ane, 458 So. 2d 239, 242 (Fla. 1984), the Florida Supreme Court held "it is sufficient that a private plaintiff prove negligence." The Florida Supreme Court noted there is no privilege "for a newspaper or a private person to defame a private person merely because the defamatory communication is directed to a matter of public or general concern." Id. These decisions arose in the media context. At least one court applying Florida law has required proof of fault outside the media context. Pica Servs., Inc. v. Behringer, 593 F. Supp. 113 (S.D. Fla. 1984).

c. **Public Figure Plaintiff/Matter of Public Concern.** When the subject matter of a public employee's speech is one of legitimate public concern, as opposed to one of personal concern, a public employee must be free to speak out on such an issue without fear of retaliatory dismissal, and statements by a public employee that are substantially correct may not be used as grounds for dismissal even though they may be critical in tone. Huerta v. Hillsborough Co., 720 So. 2d 276, 277 (Fla. 2d DCA 1998); Board of Regents v. Snyder, 826 So. 2d 382 (Fla. 2d DCA 2002). This constitutional protection does not apply to private employers.

3. ***Falsity.*** Article 1, Section 4 of the Florida Constitution provides that "[i]f the matter charged as defamatory is true and was published with good motives," the defendant "shall be acquitted or exonerated." No modern decision has elucidated the meaning of "good motives," but Florida's standard jury instructions include truth and good motives as a defense, subject to the proposition that the First Amendment may preclude any action for defamation without falsity. Florida Standard Jury Instructions, Instruction 405.9.b, Note 5. See also Zorc v. Jordan, 765 So. 2d 768 (Fla. 4th DCA 2000) ("A false statement of fact is absolutely necessary if there is to be recovery in a defamation action"). At least in matters which are not of public concern or do not involve public figures, the burden of proof of truth is on the defendant. Substantial truth of the allegedly defamatory statement is sufficient to maintain the affirmative defense. See Smith v. Cuban Am. Nat'l Found., 731 So. 2d 702 (Fla. 3d DCA 1999) (explaining that under the substantial truth doctrine a statement need not be "perfectly accurate if the 'gist' or the 'sting' of the statement is true"). On the other hand, some courts have characterized the burden of proof as on the plaintiff to prove falsity. Colodny v. Iverson, Yoakum, Papiano & Hatch, 936 F. Supp. 917, 923 (M.D. Fla. 1996) ("Just like the other elements, the element of 'falsity' is an essential part of the plaintiff's prima facie case of defamation"). See also Larkins v. The Bank, 2005 WL 1278877, * 5 (N.D. Fla. May 10, 2005) (where plaintiff's defamation claims were dismissed because plaintiff failed to allege the falsity of the publication). See Section I.B.1, supra.

4. ***Defamatory Statement of Fact.*** A statement may be deemed defamatory which "exposes a person to distrust, hatred, contempt, ridicule or obloquy or which causes such person to be avoided, or which has a tendency to injure such person in his office, occupation, business or employment." See Thomas v. Jacksonville Television, Inc. 699 So. 2d 800, 803 (Fla. 1st DCA 1997). The Florida Supreme Court recently decided that Florida recognizes libel by implication, adopting the principle that "if the defendant juxtaposes a series of facts so as to imply a defamatory connection between them, or creates a defamatory implication by omitting facts, he may be held responsible for the defamatory implication, unless it qualifies as an opinion, even though the particular facts are correct." Jews For Jesus, Inc. v. Rapp, 997 So. 2d 1098, 1108 (Fla. 2008) (quoting Prosser and Keeton on the Law of Torts § 116, at 117 (5th ed. Supp.1988)). A statement may also be deemed defamatory if it imputes to another characteristics or conditions incompatible with the proper exercise of one's business, trade or profession. See Randolph v. Beer, 695 So. 2d 401 (Fla. 5th DCA 1997); Thomas, 699 So. 2d at 800; Florida Standard Jury Instructions, MI 4.3. Florida follows federal law with regard to whether a statement is a statement of fact or opinion. See, e.g., Fla. Med. Ctr., Inc. v. New York Post Co., Inc., 568 So. 2d 454 (Fla. 4th DCA 1990). Where the facts on which the "opinion" are stated in the communication, the courts tend to protect the speech as "pure opinion." See Lipsig v. Ramlawi, 760 So. 2d 170, 183 (Fla. 3d DCA 2000); Zambrano v. Devanesan, 484 So. 2d 603 (Fla. 4th DCA 1986); Sullivan v. Barrett, 510 So. 2d 982 (Fla. 4th DCA 1987); Beck v. Lipkind, 681 So. 2d 794, 795 (Fla. 3d DCA 1996); Stembridge v. Mintz, 652 So. 2d 444 (Fla. 3d DCA 1995), disting'd in LRX, Inc. v. Horizon Assocs. Joint Venture ex rel. Horizon-ANF, Inc., 842 So. 2d 881, 886 (Fla. 4th DCA 2003) (noting that in Stembridge, all of the underlying facts were accurately disclosed, whereas in LRX, the underlying "facts" could be found to constitute material misstatements, and thus were not protected). A statement may be deemed defamatory if it "tends to subject one to hatred, distrust, ridicule, contempt or disgrace." See Thomas, 699 So. 2d at 803.

5. ***Of and Concerning Plaintiff.*** The statement must actually be about the plaintiff. Thus, where the statement is about a group of persons, the action can be maintained only if the group is sufficiently small or the circumstances otherwise give rise to the conclusion that the statement is about the plaintiff. See Thomas, 699 So. 2d at 800.

6. ***Publication.*** "Publication" requires that the statement be communicated to a third party. See Tishman-Speyer Equitable S. Fla. Venture v. Knight Invs., Inc., 591 So. 2d 213 (Fla. 4th DCA 1991). A letter sent to a party who has an interest in the matter is not publication. Id. A statement made to the person alleging the defamation is not publication. American Airlines v. Geddes, 960 So. 2d 830, 833 (Fla. 3d DCA 2007). It is not publication to make the statement to a corporate executive or managerial employee of a plaintiff corporation. See Advantage Personnel Agency, Inc.

v. Hicks & Grayson, Inc., 447 So. 2d 330 (Fla. 3d DCA 1984); American Airlines v. Geddes, 960 So. 2d 830, 833 (Fla. 3d DCA 2007) ("When the entity alleged to have committed the defamation is a corporation, the courts have held that statements made to corporate executive or managerial employees of that entity are, in effect, being made to the corporation itself, and thus lack the essential element of publication."). It is not publication to make the statement to a partner or co-venturer. See Campbell v. Jacksonville Kennel Club, Inc., 66 So. 2d 495 (Fla. 1953). Statements to a low-ranking employee of a plaintiff corporation may, however, constitute publication. See Advantage Personnel Agency, Inc., 447 So. 2d at 330. Statements to the plaintiff's attorney may also be publication, as the attorney cannot be considered the plaintiff's agent for all purposes. See Pledger v. Burnup & Sims, Inc., 432 So. 2d 1323 (Fla. 4th DCA 1983), rev. den., 446 So. 2d 99 (Fla. 1984). Statements made on a company website may constitute publication. Axiom Worldwide, Inc. v. Beccerra, 2009 WL 1347398, *7 (M.D. Fla. May 13, 2009). To plead a claim for defamation properly a plaintiff must specifically identify the persons to whom the allegedly defamatory comments were made. Jackson v. N. Broward County Hosp. Dist., 766 So. 2d 256 (Fla. 4th DCA 2000); Woodhull v. Mascarella, 2009 WL 1790383, *3 (N.D. Fla. June 24, 2009).

a. **Intracorporate Communication.** Where a corporation is the defendant, internal distribution of the defamatory statement to corporate employees or officers generally should not be regarded as publication to third persons, particularly where the internal publications are necessary to the operations of the corporation. Nevertheless, Florida courts have routinely treated such distributions to employees as publications to third persons. See Biggs v. Atlantic Coastline R.R., 66 F.2d 87 (5th Cir. 1933); accord S. Bell Tel. & Tel. Co. v. Barnes, 443 So. 2d 1085 (Fla. 3d DCA 1984); Glynn v. City of Kissimmee, 383 So. 2d 774 (Fla. 5th DCA 1980); Drennen Westinghouse Elec. Corp., 328 So. 2d 52 (Fla. 1st DCA 1976); Arison Shipping Co. v. Smith, 311 So. 2d 739 (Fla. 3d DCA 1975). ("[T]he qualified privilege attaching to business communications is lost when the scope of an intracorporate communication to those have corresponding interests and duties is exceeded."). See generally, Intra-corporate Communications: Sufficient Publication for Defamation of Mere Corporate Babbling, 7 Comm./Ent. 647 (1985).

In regards to workplace rumors, "[a]bsent evidence regarding [the source of the rumors], such rumors are insufficient" to establish that the corporation published the allegedly defamatory statement. Lopez v. Ingram Micro, Inc., 1997 WL 401585, *2 (S.D. Fla. 1997). See also Smith v. Anheuser-Busch Brewing Co., 346 So. 2d 125 (Fla. 1st DCA 1977) (holding that an allegedly defamatory statement addressed by a brewery manager, simultaneously and privately, to two employees, which sought to elicit an explanation concerning their alleged joint action in stealing beer, was not a publication.); see also Lopez, 1997 WL 401585 at *2 (communications made by investigators during their investigation of theft of property did not qualify as publication).

b. **Compelled Self-Defamation.** Under the doctrine of compelled self-defamation, a defendant will be liable for alleged defamatory statements made to the plaintiff in private if the plaintiff is compelled to republish the alleged defamatory statements to a third party, such as a prospective employer. Florida law, however, does not consider a compelled publication by the plaintiff to meet the publication requirement of defamation. See Valencia v. Citibank Int'l, 728 So. 2d 330 (Fla. 3d DCA 1999).

c. **Republication.** Republication of a statement initially published by another is a publication, even if the republisher explicitly refuses to vouch personally for its verity. See Lewis v. Evans, 406 So. 2d 489 (Fla. 2d DCA 1981). If republication is from a reliable source, such as a wire service, and the defendant has not been negligent, the defendant is not liable for the republication. See Nelson v. Associated Press, Inc., 667 F. Supp. 1468 (S.D. Fla. 1987); Layne v. Tribune Co., 146 So. 234 (Fla. 1933). A defendant who sends defamatory material only to the plaintiff, which the plaintiff subsequently publishes to third parties, is only liable if the plaintiff's republication is reasonably foreseeable. See Granda-Centeno v. Lara, 489 So. 2d 142 (Fla. 3d DCA 1986).

7. ***Statements Versus Conduct.*** By inference, it appears that the act of termination itself, even if wrongful, is not considered to be a defamation in Florida. Attendant statements, however, may enjoy only a qualified privilege which can be defeated. See Healy v. Suntrust Service Corp., 569 So. 2d 458 (Fla. 5th DCA 1990); see also Spears v. Albertson's , Inc., 848 So. 2d 1176, (Fla. 1st DCA 2003) ("A determination of whether . . . words constitute slander must be made by considering the context in which the words were spoken.")

8. ***Damages.*** The harm stemming from defamatory statement is measured as objectively interpreted by a "substantial and respectable" minority of the community. Jews For Jesus, Inc. v. Rapp, 997 So. 2d 1098 (Fla. 2008) (quoting and adopting Restatement (Second) of Torts, § 559, comment (e)). Recoverable damages include injury to reputation or health, for shame, humiliation, mental anguish, hurt feelings, aggravation or activation of disease or defect, medical expenses, and lost earnings and lost earning capacity. Florida Standard Jury Instructions, MI 4.4. A compensatory damage award in a Florida libel case may include recovery for direct or indirect pecuniary loss, mental suffering, and injury to reputation. See Miami Herald Publ'g Co. v. Brautigam, 127 So. 2d 718 (Fla. 3d DCA 1961) cert. den., 135 So. 2d 741 (Fla. 1961). Damages for pain and suffering apparently may be awarded even where there is no damage to reputation. Time, Inc. v. Firestone, 424 U.S. 448, 460 (1976). The Court in Miami Herald Publ'g Co. v. Ane, held that the Gertz First

Amendment requirement of "proof of some actual damage" is satisfied by proof of "mental anguish and personal humiliation." 423 So. 2d 376, 390 (Fla. 3d DCA 1982). This was specifically upheld in Miami Herald Publ'g Co. v. Ane, 458 So. 2d 239 (Fla. 1984). Prejudgment interest is not available on non-economic damages, such as the damages awarded to compensate harm to one's reputation. Lipsig v. Ramlawi, 760 So. 2d 170, 192 (Fla. 3d DCA 2000).

a. **Presumed Damages and Libel Per Se.** Florida had traditionally followed the majority view on libel per se and presumed damages until the Supreme Court's decision in Gertz v. Robert Welch, Inc., 418 U.S. 323 (1974). Subsequent to Gertz, the law in Florida regarding libel per se is that there is no liability without fault, at least in the media defendant context. See Mid-Florida Television Co. v. Boyles, 467 So. 2d 282 (Fla. 1985) (holding that "[l]ibel per se is dead") (Ehlrich, J. concurring). This rule continues as applied to alleged defamations involving matters of public concern. No Florida case has been decided after Dun & Bradstreet v. Greenmoss Builders, 472 U.S. 749 (1985), which squarely holds that presumed damages are now available in alleged defamations not involving matters of public concern. However, in Rety v. Green, 546 So. 2d 410, 425 (Fla. 3d DCA 1989), the court acknowledged the distinction between matters of public and private concern upon which the per se presumption of malice can be distinguished from Gertz. See also Fla. Med. Ctr. v. New York Post Co., 568 So. 2d 454, 458 (Fla. 4th DCA 1990) (emphasizing whether the matter was of public concern in analyzing "full constitutional protection" for statements of opinion). See also Johnson v. Clark, 484 F. Supp. 2d 1242, 1254 (M.D. Fla. 2007) ("in cases of 'per se' defamation brought by a private plaintiff against a non-media defendant, non-economic damages may be presumed without special proof."); NITV, L.L.C. v. Baker, 61 So. 3d 1249 (Fla. 4th DCA 2011) (approving substantial general damages award). Compare Log Creek v. Kessler, 2010 WL 2426612, at 8 (N.D. Fla. June 3, 2010) (no liability without fault); with Florida Jury Instruction 405.10.f, providing for nominal damages, and Note 7 thereto.

(1) **Employment-Related Criticism.** An employer can be held liable for defamation committed by its employees in the scope of their employer's apparent authority, even if their acts did not serve the employer's interest. Saadi v. Maroun, 2009 WL 1424184, *3 (M.D. Fla. May 20, 2009). See also I.B.8.a, supra.

(2) **Single Instance Rule.** The plaintiff is permitted to prove merely a general distribution of the libel; the extent of circulation only bears on damages. See Prosser, Law of Torts (4th ed. 1971) at 769. It does not affect the limitations period for commencing an action or the number of actions which may be commenced. See Fla. Stat. § 770.07 (2009). Thus, a plaintiff who sues a newspaper publisher in a given venue must recover all damages which he has suffered everywhere in that action notwithstanding that the newspaper may have been republished in different locations and at different times. See also Fla. Stat. § 770.05.

b. **Punitive Damages.** Punitive damages may be recovered. If the statement relates to a matter of public concern, in addition to the usual ill will, the plaintiff must show by clear and convincing evidence that the defendant knew the statement was false or had serious doubts as to its truth. Florida Standard Jury Instructions, MI 4.4. ("If the statement was on a matter of public concern, the standard of liability for punitive damages is both the First Amendment actual malice standard. . . . and express malice."); WalMart Stores, Inc. v. Kordon, 656 So. 2d 528 (Fla. 2d DCA 1995) (requiring that a party prove "willful, wanton and intentional misconduct" to support a claim of punitive damages), rev'd on other grounds, 666 So. 2d 140 (Fla. 1996); Rety v. Green, 546 So. 2d 410 (Fla. 3d DCA 1989) (awarding plaintiff $2,500,000 for punitive damages in egregious case of libel). For an employer to be held vicariously liable for punitive damages under a theory of respondent superior, there must be some fault on the employer's part, though not necessarily willful and wanton behavior, in addition to the employee's misconduct. Mercury Motors Express, Inc. v. Smith, 393 So. 2d 545 (Fla. 1981).

In the context of the internet, one Florida court held that the Florida statute requiring written notice by a plaintiff as a condition precedent to action for libel or slander did not apply to a defendant who was a private individual posting messages on an internet message board. Zelinka v. Americare Healthscan, Inc., 763 So. 2d 1173, 1174 (Fla. 4th DCA 2000). Florida Statute § 770.02 allows a media defendant to avoid punitive damages by the timely publication of a correction, apology, or retraction. The Zelinka court held that while an individual who maintains a web site and regularly publishes internet "magazines" on that site might be considered a "media defendant" who would be entitled to notice, a private individual that merely makes statements on a web site owned and operated by someone else would not be considered a media defendant. Id. In Alvi Armani Med., Inc. v. Hennessey, 629 F.Supp.2d 1302, 1307-08 (S.D. Fla. Dec. 9, 2008), the Court held that the "other medium" language in the Florida notice statute encompasses the internet.

II. PRIVILEGES AND DEFENSES

A. Scope of Privileges

Privileges can be either absolute, meaning no suit can be brought for such the statement at issue, or qualified, meaning suit can be maintained only upon a showing of common law express malice. Outside the employment context, Florida has a wide range of privileges relating to defamation claims.

1. ***Absolute Privilege.*** All letters, reports, and other oral or written communications made in connection with unemployment compensation proceedings that have been exchanged between employer and employee or sent from either of them to representatives of the State of Florida Division of Unemployment Compensation are absolutely privileged. Section 443.041(3), Fla. Stat. (2009); see also Feldman v. Glucroft, 522 So. 2d 798, 801 (Fla. 1988). Some other absolute privileges which might apply to the employment relationship are for statements made in the following contexts:

a. Judicial and quasi-judicial proceedings. See Kelly v. McNayr, 185 So. 2d 194 (Fla. 3d DCA 1966); Burton v. Salzberg, 725 So. 2d 450 (Fla. 3d DCA 1999); see also Stucchio v. Tincher, 726 So. 2d 372 (Fla. 5th DCA 1999) (holding that an absolute privilege exists if the statement was made "in connection with" or "in the course of" an existing judicial proceeding); Dadic v. Schneider, 722 So. 2d 921 (Fla. 4th DCA 1998) (finding that statements made by counsel during the course of a judicial proceeding to inform the court of the reasons for the motion were absolutely privileged); Delmonico v. Travnor, 50 So. 3d 4 (Fla. 4th DCA 2010), accepted for review, 47 So. 2d 1287 (Fla. 2010) (attorney's alleged statements to potential witnesses before their testimony were absolutely privileged); Gandy v. Trans World Computer Tech. Group, 787 So. 2d 116 (Fla. 2d DCA 2001) (holding that EEOC investigation was a quasi-judicial proceeding and statements material to the subject of the inquiry were absolutely privileged); Seidel v. Hill, 264 So. 2d 81 (Fla. 1st DCA 1972) (holding that workers compensation proceedings are quasi-judicial proceedings and the statements made therein are absolutely privileged); Perl v. Omni Int'l of Miami, Ltd., 439 So. 2d 316 (Fla. 3d DCA 1983) (affirming the dismissal of a slander claim where the communication was privileged pursuant to section 443.041(3) of the Florida Statutes). Reimnitz v. Source One Distributors, Inc., 2007 WL 1624 778, *5 (S,D, Fla. June 4, 2007) (holding that statements to the Florida Unemployment Commission are absolutely privileged); Compare Ball v. D'Lites Enterprises, Inc., 65 So. 3d 637 (Fla. 4th DCA 2011) (website statements about pending lawsuit not entitled to absolute immunity for statements made in connection with a judicial proceeding.)

b. Grievance. Tobkin v. Jarboe, 710 So. 2d 975, 977 (Fla. 1998) holds "that an individual who files a complaint against an attorney and makes no public announcement of the complaint, thereby allowing the grievance procedure to run its natural course, is afforded absolute immunity from a defamation action by the complained-against attorney. However, if, after filing a complaint, the complainant comments publicly or outside the grievance process, then the afforded immunity ceases to exist." The Fourth DCA limited this holding. In State v. Rutherford, 863 So. 2d 445, 445 (Fla. 4th DCA 2004) the court held that, "while Tobkin provides an absolute immunity against retaliatory civil lawsuits brought by attorneys who were the subject of bar complaints against the complainants, it does not go so far as to shield a complainant from an action by the State for abusing the process by filing a false complaint under penalties of perjury. To hold otherwise would render Rule 3-7.3(c), Rules Regulating The Florida Bar, meaningless. There would be no other reason for requiring the oath language if "penalties of perjury" did not mean that the complainant could be prosecuted for perjury for filing a false complaint. See also Magre v. Charles, 729 So. 2d 440 (Fla. 5th DCA 1999). But see, Fullerton v. Fla. Med. Assoc., Inc., 2006 WL 1888545 (Fla. 1st DCA 2006) (holding that medical peer review statute did not immunize association from doctors defamation action and that the Health Care Quality Improvement Act did not immunize association from doctor's defamation action).

c. Statements made by members of the executive branch, by federal officials **or public officials** in the course of their official duties. See Tucker v. Resha, 634 So. 2d 756 (Fla. 1st DCA 1994); Albritton v. Gandy, 531 So. 2d 381 (Fla. 1st DCA 1988); Florida State University Board of Trustees v. Monk, **68 So. 3d 316** (Fla. 1st DCA 2011); **Blake v. City of Port St. Lucie, 73 So. 3d 905 (Fla. 4th DCA 2011) (also holding statute granting qualified immunity to an employer does not abrogate absolute immunity under common law.)**

d. Statements contained in a Railway Labor Act Grievance Complaint when the statements relate to the cause of action. See Bell v. Gellert, 469 So. 2d 141 (Fla. 3d DCA 1985).

e. Statements made by state law enforcement officials when these officials are witnesses in criminal trials. See Lloyd v. Hines, 474 So. 2d 376 (Fla. 1st DCA 1985).

f. Statements made with the plaintiff's consent. (Consent may also be characterized as a defense separate from privilege.) See Litman v. Mass. Mut. Life Ins. Co., 739 F.2d 1549, 1560 (11th Cir. 1984); Lopez v. Ingram Micro, Inc., 1997 WL 401585, *2 (S.D. Fla. 1997); Charles v. State Dep't. of Children and Families, 141 So. 2d 1 (Fla. 4th DCA 2005) (also characterized as "invited defamation," which is a complete defense to an action or defamation). Although Florida has approved this general rule, it is couched in terms of a lack of a publication. Maine v. Allstate Ins. Co., 240 So. 2d 857 (Fla. Dist. Ct. 1970) ("[A] communication addressed to a third party, procured to be so addressed by the party libeled, does not amount to a publication.").

g. Statements made within the scope of the official duties of employees charged with supervisory responsibilities. See Skoblow v. Ameri-Manage Inc., 483 So. 2d 809 (Fla. 3d DCA 1986); Lopez v. Sch. Bd. of Palm Beach County, 1999 WL 1081263 (S.D. Fla. 1999).

h. Statements made by state bar employees, regardless of whether such statements were made with malice, where the statements were made in connection with their official duties during the course of bar disciplinary proceedings. Spano v. Hoffman, 968 So. 2d 674, 675 (Fla. 4th DCA 2007).

2. ***Qualified Privileges.*** The most important privilege in the employment context is the qualified privilege of an employer to communicate information about a former employee to a prospective employer, a privilege which is codified by statute. Fla. Stat. § 768.095 (2009). "There are many occasions recognized under common law as being privileged. Statements made by an employer or to an employer regarding an employee's or former employee's performance have long been recognized as a privileged occasion." See John Hancock Mut. Life Ins. Co. v. Zalay, 581 So. 2d 178 (Fla. 2d DCA 1991). See also Thomas v. Tampa Bay Downs, 761 So. 2d 401 (Fla. 2d DCA 2000); Linafelt v. Beverly Enters.-Fla. Inc., 745 So. 2d 386, 388 (Fla. 1st DCA 1999); Garcia v. Walder Elecs., 563 So. 2d 723 (Fla. 3d DCA 1990); Florida Standard Jury Instructions, MI 4.3. To overcome this well-established privilege, a claimant must establish that his or her employer acted with express malice or malice in fact, which means essentially an intent to harm the employee. See Nodar v. Galbreath, 462 So. 2d 803, 810 (Fla. 1984). This showing "is a very high standard for a plaintiff to meet," particularly because courts presume that statements subject to the qualified privilege were made in good faith. Shaw v. R.J. Reynolds Tobacco Co., 818 F. Supp. 1539, 1542 (M.D. Fla. 1993); see also Nodar, 462 So. 2d at 809 ("A communication made in good faith on any subject matter by one having an interest therein, or in reference with which he has a duty, is subject to a privilege if made to a person having a corresponding interest or duty."); Boehm v. Am. Bankers Ins. Group, 557 So. 2d 91 (Fla. 3d DCA 1990). **In the public employer context, this statutory qualified privilege does not abrogate the common law absolute privilege. Blake v. Port St. Lucie, 73 So. 3d 905 (Fla. 4th DCA 2011).**

Section 768.095 of the Florida Statutes provides immunity for employers disclosing information about former employees: "An employer who discloses information about a former employee's job performance to a prospective employer of the former employee upon request of the prospective employer or of the former employee is presumed to be acting in good faith, and unless lack of good faith is shown by clear and convincing evidence, is immune from civil liability for such disclosure or its consequences," as recognized in Linafelt, 745 So. 2d at 388.

The following types of statements are categorized as being qualifiedly privileged and might be applicable in the employment context:

a. Statements which are made during "pre-litigation settlement" negotiations. See Pledger v. Burnup & Sims, Inc., 432 So. 2d 1323 (Fla. 4th DCA 1983). The Eleventh Circuit stated that qualified immunity is not limited to pre -litigation negotiations. In Jackson v. BellSouth Telecommunications, 372 F.3d 1250, 1276 (11th Cir. 2004), the court stated that "while it is true that in Pledger a panel of Florida's Fourth District Court of Appeals found that statements made during settlement discussions *before* suit was filed were subject only to a qualified privilege, *Pledger* plainly did not hold that the absolute privilege was inapplicable to settlement negotiations during the course of ongoing litigation."

b. Irrelevant statements or writings which are made during judicial, legislative, or executive proceedings. See Urchisin v. Hauser, 221 So. 2d 752 (Fla. 4th DCA 1969), rev'd on other grounds, 231 So. 2d 6 (Fla. 1970). See also Larkins v. The Bank, 2005 WL 1278877, at *5 (N.D. Fla. May 10, 2005) (statements made in a complaint are "absolutely privileged, and cannot, under Florida law, support a claim for defamation").

c. Fair and accurate reports of court proceedings, government records, other official actions, and events of public interest. Florida law extends the fair report privilege to statements made in a variety of contexts. See Fridovich v. Fridovich, 598 So. 2d 65 (Fla. 1992) (statements made to state attorney investigators). The Eleventh Circuit has narrowed this proposition to a question of timing. In Green Leaf Nursery v. E.I. DuPont De Nemours and Co., 341 F.3d 1292, 1303 (11th Cir. (Fla.) 2003) the court noted that "[i]n *Fridovich,* the [court] held that, even though defamatory statements made in the course of judicial proceedings are absolutely privileged, defamatory statements made to the authorities *prior* to the institution of criminal charges were only entitled to a qualified immunity, which was sufficiently overcome by the egregious facts of the case." In Dupont, the court found that the defendant's alleged misconduct occurred *during* the litigation and was thus absolutely immune. Stucchio v. Tincher, 726 So. 2d 372 (Fla. 5th DCA 1999) (statement made by former employer in connection with a pending judicial proceeding); Rodriguez Diaz v. Abate, 598 So. 2d 197 (Fla. 3d DCA 1992) (statements made to police); Shiell v. Metropolis Co., 136 So. 537 (Fla. 1931) (statements made in court proceedings); Carson v. News-Journal Corp., 790 So. 2d 1120 (Fla. 2d DCA 2001), dismissed., 805 So. 2d 805 (Fla. 2002), cert. den., 122 S.Ct. 778 (2002) (statements filed with the Florida Bureau of Unemployment Compensation). To qualify for the fair reports privilege, a news report of a public document must convey the entire substance of the document, or any separable part thereof. Carson v. News-Journal Corp., 790 So. 2d at 1120; Shiell., 136 So. at 537 (Fla. 1931). The fair reports privilege "extends to the publication of the contents of official documents, as long as the account is reasonably accurate and fair." Rasmussen v. Collier County Publ'g Co., 946 So. 2d 567, 571 (Fla. 2d DCA 2006).

d. Defamatory statements made in NASD filing. Upon termination of the employment of a broker, a brokerage firm is required to file with the NASD a Uniform Notice of Termination for Securities Industry Regulation ("U-5 Form"). See NASD By-laws, Art. IV. § 3(a). Defamatory statements made on U-5 form filed with the NASD are entitled to a qualified privilege. See Eaton Vance Distribs. v. Ulrich, 692 So. 2d 915, 916 (Fla. 2d DCA), rev. den., 705 So. 2d 8 (Fla. 1997).

e. Voluntary testimony given before a legislative body. See Fiore v. Rogero, 144 So. 2d 99 (Fla. 2d DCA 1962).

f. Voluntary statements made by private individuals to police in furtherance of an investigation are clothed in a qualified privilege, Fridovich v. Fridovitch, 598 So. 2d 65 (Fla. 1992); Border Collie Rescue, Inc. v. Ryan, 418 F. Supp. 2d 1330 (M.D. Fla. 2006) (same).

g. Statements made regarding news of public interest or concern. See Jones, Varnum & Co. v. Townsend Administratix, 21 Fla. 431 (1885).

h. Statements directed at a government agency regarding a public issue. See Best Towing and Recovery, Inc. v. Beggs, 531 So. 2d 243 (Fla. 2d DCA 1988).

a. **Common Interest.** As stated above, matters in which the author and the audience share a common right, duty, or interest enjoy a qualified privilege. See Restatement (Second) of Torts § 596 (1998). See also Putnal v. Inman, 80 So. 316 (Fla. 1916) questioned by Caldwell v. Personal Fin. Co. of St. Petersburg, 46 So. 2d 726 (Fla. 1950) (holding that closely held credit reports are qualifiedly privileged); Abram v. Odham, 89 So. 2d 334 (Fla. 1956) (holding that statements delivered to a wide audience regarding political opinion polls are qualifiedly privileged).

b. **Duty.** See II.A.2, supra.

c. **Criticism of Public Employee.** See II.A.2, supra.

d. **Limitation on Qualified Privileges.**

(1) **Constitutional or Actual Malice.** Actual malice is a different type of malice than the common law malice that is an element of every common law cause of action for libel or slander. "Actual malice" is publication with knowledge of falsity or reckless disregard of the truth. Proof of constitutional malice is not required to defeat a qualified privilege.

(2) **Common Law Malice.** A qualified privilege may be defeated with evidence of common law malice. The "gravamen of express malice is the abuse of a privileged occasion by improper motives on the part of the speaker." Nodar v. Galbreath, 462 So. 2d 803, 811 n.8 (Fla. 1984). Malice may not be imputed. See Axelrod v. Califano, 357 So. 2d 1048 (Fla. 1st DCA 1978). See also, Salazar v. Telemundo Network Group, LLC., 2006 WL 1650725 (Fla. 11th Cir. Ct. 2006) (holding that "if the gist [of a statement] is substantially true, then minor inaccuracies are insufficient to show actual malice").

e. **Question of Fact or Law.** Under Florida law, the court, and not a jury, decides the issue of whether statements are privileged. See Nodar v. Galbreath, 462 So. 2d 803, 810 (Fla. 1984) ("Where the circumstances surrounding a defamatory communication are undisputed, or are so clear under the evidence as to be unquestionable, then the question of whether the occasion upon which they were spoken was privileged is a question of law to be decided by the court"); Abraham v. Baldwin, 52 Fla. 151, 42 So. 591 (1906) (for same proposition); John Hancock Mut. Life Ins. Co. v. Zalay, 581 So. 2d 178, 179 (Fla. 2d DCA), rev. den., 591 So. 2d 185 (Fla. 1991); Falic v. Legg Mason Wood Walker, Inc., 347 F. Supp. 2d 1260, 1264 (S.D. Fla. 2004) (for same proposition); Johnson v. Clark, 484 F. Supp. 2d 1242, 1247 (M.D. Fla. 2007) (for same proposition). The Fifth District has concluded that: "Whether the privilege exists or has been exceeded in some manner creates a mixed question of law and fact which normally should be determined by the trier of fact." Healy v. Suntrust Serv. Corp., 569 So. 2d 458 (Fla. 5th DCA 1990); Glynn v. City of Kissimmee, 383 So. 2d 774, 776 (Fla. 5th DCA 1980). In Healy and Glynn, the issue of whether allegedly slanderous statements were made to "too wide an audience" was held to be a question for the jury, even though the circumstances surrounding the statements were not in dispute.

f. **Burden of Proof.** Qualified privilege is an affirmative defense. See Linafelt v. Beverly Enters.-Fla. Inc., 662 So. 2d 986, 988 (Fla. 1st DCA 1995) (qualified privilege not considered on a motion to dismiss).

B. Standard Libel Defenses

1. ***Truth.*** There is some question as to whether truth is a portion of the plaintiff's case or a defense. Although Florida courts originally followed the traditional approach of placing the burden of proving the truth on the defendant (see, e.g., Fla. Publ'g Co. v. Lee, 80 So. 245 (Fla. 1918)), the U.S. Supreme Court has shifted the burden to the

plaintiff in cases involving matters of public concern. See Philadelphia Newspapers v. Hepps, 475 U.S. 767, 12 Media L. Rep. 1977 (1986). Three of Florida's five District Courts of Appeal anticipated Hepps by placing the burden of proving falsity on the plaintiff. See Applestein v. Knight Newspapers, Inc., 337 So. 2d 1005 (Fla. 3d DCA 1976); Delacruz v. Peninsula State Bank, 221 So. 2d 772 (Fla. 2d DCA 1969); Hawke v. Broward Nat'l Bank of Fort Lauderdale, 220 So. 2d 678 (Fla. 4th DCA 1969). Each one of these cases involved private figures. Other courts have held or suggested that in accordance with Article I, Section 4 of Florida's Constitution, truth is not a defense unless accompanied by good motives. See, e.g., Cape Publ'ns v. Reakes, 840 So. 2d 277, 279-280 (Fla. 5th DCA 2003); LRX, Inc. v. Horizon Assocs. Joint Venture, 842 So. 2d 881 (Fla. 4th DCA 2003).

2. ***Opinion.*** Statements of "pure opinion" are not actionable as libel. Beck v. Lipkind, 681 So. 2d 794, 795 (Fla. 3d DCA 1996) ("Opinions cannot be defamatory . . . . Pure opinion occurs when the defendant makes a comment or opinion based on facts which are set forth in the article or which are otherwise known or available to the reader or listener as a member of the public.") Palm Beach Newspapers, Inc. v. Early, 334 So. 2d 50 (Fla. 4th DCA 1976), cert. den., 354 So. 2d 351, 3 Media L. Rep. 2183 (Fla. 1977), cert. den., 439 U.S. 910 (1978); Magre v. Charles, 729 So. 2d 440 (Fla. 5th DCA 1999); see also, Fortson . Colangelo, 2006 WL 1589792 (S.D. Fla. 2006) (holding that a statement by the owner of a rival team calling player a "thug," as well as statements in a newspaper column, were protected opinion or rhetorical hyperbole, which was not actionable as defamatory). However, statements of mixed fact and opinion are actionable and require the issues to be determined by the jury. Milkovich v. Lorain Journal Co., 497 U.S. 1 (1990), analyzing statements in a newspaper column and finding them to "impute conduct incompatible with the plaintiff's lawful business," the court found the statements actionable. See Fla. Med. Ctr., Inc. v. New York Post Co., 568 So. 2d 454, 18 Media L. Rep. 1224, rev. den., 581 So. 2d 1309 (Fla. 1991). In determining whether the statement is one of pure or mixed opinion, the court "must examine the words used, together with the totality of the circumstances and the context, within which it was published." See Sullivan v. Barrett, 510 So. 2d 982, 984 (Fla. 4th DCA 1987). In Barrett, the court stated that a finding of pure opinion will usually result even when the facts upon which the speaker relied are presented along with the commentary. See Stembridge v. Mintz. 652 So. 2d 444 (Fla. 3d DCA 1995) (holding that a statement in a Bar Inquiry Form, which set forth the facts upon which the writer relied, was pure opinion). A speaker cannot invoke a "pure opinion" defense if the facts underlying the opinion are false or inaccurately presented. Lipsig v. Ramlawi, 760 So. 2d 170, 184 (Fla. 3d DCA 2000). "If the 'facts' upon which the opinion is based are stated in the article, but those 'facts' are either incomplete or incorrect, or the speaker's assessment of them is erroneous, the statement may imply a false assertion of fact." Johnson v. Clark, 484 F. Supp. 2d 1242, 1247 (M.D. Fla. 2007) ("A statement is not protected as pure opinion if it implies the existence of undisclosed defamatory facts as its basis.").

3. ***Consent.*** Consent is a defense to a defamation action. See Litman v. Mass. Mut. Life Ins. Co., 739 F.2d 1549, 1560 (11th Cir. 1984); Rosenberg v. American Bowling Congress, 589 F. Supp. 547, 551 (M.D. Fla. 1984); Charles v. State Dep't. of Children and Families, 941 So. 2d 1 (Fla. 4th DCA 2005).

4. ***Mitigation.*** There are no Florida decisions in the employment context.

III. RECURRING FACT PATTERNS

A. Statements in Personnel File

Typically, a statement contained in a personnel file is not held to give rise to a claim for defamation. See Cripe v. Board of Regents, 358 So. 2d 244 (Fla. 1st DCA 1978) (holding that evaluator was not liable for defamatory statements contained in a performance evaluation); Randolph v. Beer, 695 So. 2d 401 (Fla. 5th DCA 1997). A public employee who asserted that co-workers, while acting in the scope of employment, defamed him through the letter of dismissal placed in his personnel file did not state a claim for defamation. Perdomo v. Jackson Mem. Hosp., 443 So. 2d 298, 300 (Fla. 3d DCA 1983).

B. Performance Evaluations

See III.A, supra. Also, police lieutenants, acting within scope of their duties in filing reports charging a sergeant with misconduct, were absolutely immune from defamation liability. Forman v. Murphy, 501 So. 2d 640 (Fla. 4th DCA 1986).

C. References

See II.A.2, supra.

D. Intracorporate Communication

See I.B.6.a, supra. Allegations that an employer's manager falsely accused an employee of misconduct, with knowledge of the falsity of the accusation, and with express malice to defame employee to fellow employees, stated a cause of action for defamation. See Jackson v. BellSouth Mobility, Inc., 626 So. 2d 1085 (Fla. 4th DCA 1993).

E. Statements to Government Regulators

See II.A, supra.

F. Reports to Auditors and Insurers

See Wagner, Nugent et al. v. Flanagan, 629 So. 2d 113 (Fla. 1993) (suggesting that defamatory statements could be contained in a letter from the insured to the insurer).

G. Vicarious Liability of Employers for Statements Made by Employees

The Florida Supreme Court has held a corporation is liable for defamation committed by an agent or employee. See Baker v. Atlantic Coast Line R.R., 192 So. 606 (Fla. 1939); see also Kiwanis Club v. de Kalafe, 723 So. 2d 838 (Fla. 3d DCA 1998) (ruling that an organization cannot be held vicariously liable for defamation if its officers or representatives are not liable for defamation).

1. ***Scope of Employment.*** A public employer is only liable for statements made by its employees in the scope of their duties. See Kamenesh v. City of Miami, 772 F. Supp. 583, 595 n.17 (S.D. Fla. 1991).

a. **Blogging.** In Saadi v. Maroun, 2009 WL 1424184, *3 (M.D. Fla. May 20, 2009), the Court held that a triable issue of fact existed concerning the authorship of alleged libelous statements posted on defendant's blog.

2. ***Damages.*** A corporation cannot be held liable for punitive damages for the actions of its employees without a showing of independent fault on behalf of the corporation. See Mercury Motors v. Smith, 393 So. 2d 545 (Fla. 1981).

H. Internal Investigations

No Florida cases.

IV. OTHER ACTIONS BASED ON STATEMENTS

A. Negligent Hiring, Retention, and Supervision

Florida is an "employment at will" state, and with rare exceptions (e.g., discrimination statutes), in the absence of a contract for a fixed term, an employer can terminate an employee without cause and suffer no consequences. Thus, many of the recent decisions relating to employee testing come in the context of workers' compensation or unemployment compensation cases.

1. ***Elements.*** Florida recognizes the tort of negligent hiring, training, supervision, and retention of employees. In order to prevail on these claims, the plaintiff must prove that the employer owes a duty to the plaintiff and that the breach of the duty was the proximate cause of the plaintiff's injuries.

Negligent hiring occurs when the employer knew or should have known of the employee's unfitness prior to the hiring decision. See Garcia v. Duffy, 492 So. 2d 435, 438 (Fla. 2d DCA 1986); Sunshine Birds and Supplies, Inc. v. United States Fidelity and Guar. Co., 696 So. 2d 907, 911 n.7, 912 (Fla. 3d DCA 1997); State Farm Fire & Cas. Co. v. Compupay, Inc., 654 So. 2d 944 (Fla. 3d DCA 1995). Employers therefore have a duty to exercise the level of care which, under all the circumstances, the reasonably prudent person would exercise in choosing or retaining an employee for the particular duties to be performed. Tallahassee Furniture Co. v. Harrison, 583 So. 2d 744, 750 (Fla. 1st DCA 1991). An employer thus can be held responsible for an employee's intentional tort, even if it occurs outside the scope of the employee's employment, if the employer knew or should have known that the employee might injure others.

Negligent retention occurs when the employer becomes aware or should have become aware of the problems with an employee that indicated his unfitness and the employer fails to take any further action, such as investigation, discharge, or reassignment. See Garcia v. Duffy, 492 So. 2d 435, 438 (Fla. 2d DCA 1986); Lowe v. ENTCOM, Inc., 2005 WL 1667681, at *4 (M.D. Fla. July 14, 2005); Quezada v. Circle K Stores, Inc., 2005 WL 1633717, at *2 (M.D. Fla. July 2, 2005).

2. ***Defenses.*** Florida employers often find themselves defending the torts of negligent hiring, retention and supervision as companion claims to federal or Florida statutory employment discrimination claims, as these torts offer plaintiffs a way to avoid statutory damage caps. Several defenses to these claims, however, are available. First, Florida's well-established "impact rule" precludes negligence claims where there is no physical injury alleged. See Childress v. Prudential Ins. Co. of Am., 1994 WL 487574, 1994 U.S. Dist. LEXIS 20007 (M.D. Fla. 1994) (applying impact rule to

employment cases); Monzo v. Southland Corp., Case No. 95-2563-Civ-Hoeveler, 1998 U.S. Dist. LEXIS 16916 (S.D. Fla. 1998) (granting summary judgment on negligent retention and supervision claims because of lack of evidence of physical injuries).

Second, an employer is not held liable under these theories absent a separate tort committed by an employee. Walsingham v. Browning, 525 So. 2d 996, 996-97 (Fla. 1st DCA 1988) (holding that a predicate act must first be established against an employee through a "judicial determination" before the employer could be liable for negligent supervision); Texas Skaggs, Inc. v. Joannides, 372 So. 2d 985, 986 (Fla. 2d DCA 1979); cert. den., 381 So. 2d 767 (Fla. 1980) (vacating plaintiffs' jury award based on negligent training and retention by the employer because the plaintiffs failed to allege and prove that the supervised employee had committed a tort that had caused the plaintiffs' injury).

Third, these types of negligence claims against employers are arguably barred by the exclusivity provisions of Florida's Workers' Compensation laws, found in Section 440.11 of the Florida Statutes. See Byrd v. Richardson-Greenshields Sec., Inc., 552 So. 2d 1099, 1104 (Fla. 1989) (holding that Workers' Compensation is not the exclusive remedy for sexual harassment claims); Robertson v. Edison Bros. Stores, Inc., 1995 WL 356052, at *2, 1995 U.S. Dist. LEXIS 5683, 8 Fla. Law W. Fed. D 744 (M.D. Fla. 1995) (recognizing narrowness of exception created in Byrd and dismissing negligent retention claim); Hirsch v. Capital Bank, Case No. 97-05839, Dade County, Florida (Oct. 20, 1997) (dismissing with prejudice plaintiff's negligent retention and supervision claims as "barred by the exclusivity provisions of Florida's Workers' Compensation Law"). But see Vernon v. Medical Mngmt. Assoc. of Margate, 912 F. Supp. 1549, 1564 (S.D. Fla. 1996); Gomez v. Metro-Dade County, 801 F. Supp. 674, 683 (S.D. Fla. 1992); Watson v. Bally Mfg. Corp., 844 F. Supp. 1533, 1537 (S.D. Fla. 1993), aff'd, 84 F.3d 438 (11th Cir. Ct. 1996).

Fourth, claims against church defendants for negligent hiring, retention, or supervision of pastors who subject church members to criminal or inappropriate behavior are not necessarily barred by the First Amendment if a court's evaluation of the claim would create excessive entanglement between church and state. See, e.g., Doe v. Evans, 814 So. 2d 370 (Fla. 2002), and Malicki v. Doe, 814 So. 2d 347 (Fla. 2002) (barring negligent retention action on grounds that "a court's determination regarding whether the church defendant's conduct was 'reasonable' would necessarily entangle the court in issues of the church's religious law, practices, and policies"). **On the other hand, where a church pastor defames an ex-member to church members and ex-members, the First Amendment does not bar the claim. Bilberg v. Myers, 91 So. 2d 887 (Fla. 5th DCA 2012).**

B. Intentional Infliction of Emotional Distress

1. ***Elements.*** This tort is often a companion tort in employment actions designed to circumvent Federal and Florida statutory damage caps. Moreover, one commentator concluded after that by allowing a libel plaintiff to recover damages when his sole injury was emotional distress, the tort of libel and slander has been transformed into the tort of infliction of emotional distress. S. Stanley, Torts: A Change in the Nature of the Libel Action, 28 U. Fla. L. Rev. 1052 (1976). Reversing a Florida Supreme Court decision, the United States Supreme Court held that the First Amendment does not prohibit a state from allowing a defamation plaintiff to prevail where his only damage is emotional distress. See Time, Inc. v. Firestone, 424 U.S. 448 (1976). Subsequently, the Florida Supreme Court has reaffirmed this point of federal constitutional law, Miami Herald Publ'g Co. v. Ane, 458 So. 2d 239 (Fla. 1984), but the Florida court has never revisited the issue of whether the common law action requires proof of damage to reputation as is discussed above.

Because of the Firestone decision, it is important for counsel in libel and slander actions where no damage to reputation is alleged to be familiar with the rules applicable in actions for intentional infliction of emotional distress because the cause of action is more correctly characterized as such. To state a claim for intentional infliction of emotional distress, a plaintiff must allege four elements: (1) deliberate or reckless infliction of mental suffering; (2) by outrageous conduct; (3) which conduct must have caused suffering; and (4) the suffering must have been severe. See Hart v. U.S., 894 F.2d 1539 (11th Cir. 1990), cert. den., 498 U.S. 980 (1990).

2. ***Defenses.*** Conduct alleged may be characterized as insulting, disturbing and concerning but still not meet Florida's rigid standard of "extreme" and "outrageous." Metro. Life Ins. Co. v. McCarson, 467 So. 2d 277 (Fla. 1985) (recognizing the availability of tort of intentional infliction of emotional distress in Florida). In McCarson, the Florida Supreme Court approvingly cited comment d of the Restatement (Second) of Torts § 46, which explains that liability for intentional infliction of emotional distress "clearly does not extend to mere insults, indignities, threats, annoyances, petty oppressions, or other trivialities." The Southern of District of Florida has dismissed a claim for intentional infliction of emotional distress because the alleged conduct, "while inconsiderate and insulting, did not rise to the level of 'extreme' and 'outrageous.'" See Novoa v. The Southland Corp., Case No. 96-1332-Civ. Hoeveler, Order, Nov. 18, 1996; Lay v. Roux Labs., Inc., 379 So. 2d 451, 452 (Fla. 1st DCA 1980) (finding employer's threats to fire coupled with "humiliating language, vicious verbal attack [and] racial epithets" insufficient to meet Florida standard of "extreme" and "outrageous"); Ponton v. Scarfone, 468 So. 2d 1009, 1009-10 (Fla. 2d DCA 1985) (holding that even though plaintiff's allegation of sexual advance by former employer was "condemnable by civilized social standards, [it did] not ascend, or perhaps descend, to a level

permitting us to say that the benchmarks enunciated in Metropolitan have been met"), rev. den., 478 So. 2d 54 (Fla. 1985); Quezada v. Circle K Stores, Inc., 2005 WL 1633717, at *2 (M.D. Fla. July 2, 2005) (holding that employer's conduct was not sufficiently outrageous and extreme to support a claim for intentional infliction of emotional distress where employees contracted tuberculosis from infected co-worker and employer was aware that co-worker had tested positive for tuberculosis and had said nothing). The First DCA has noted, however, that Florida state court cases, such as Linafelt, were based only on claims of alleged acts of verbal abuse and were not also based on claims of alleged repeated acts of offensive physical contact in the workplace. Johnson v. Thigpen, 788 So. 2d 410, 413 (Fla. 1st DCA 2001). The court noted that federal courts interpreting Florida law have allowed claims for intentional infliction of emotional distress in the workplace to go forward in circumstances involving repeated verbal abuse coupled with repeated offensive physical contact. Id.

"Courts in Florida and in the Eleventh Circuit have been extremely reluctant to recognize outrageous conduct in the employment context." Blount v. Sterling Healthcare Group, Inc., 934 F. Supp. 1365, 1370-71 (S.D. Fla. 1996) (dismissing claim as not sufficiently outrageous where allegations included tight hugging, rubbing the plaintiff's breasts, massaging the back of her head, and other verbal harassment). See also Studstill v. Borg Warner Leasing, 806 F.2d 1005, 1008 (11th Cir. 1986) (holding that verbal sexual harassment, including dirty jokes, comments and invitations, was insufficient to support an intentional infliction of emotional distress claim); Watson v. Bally Manufacturing Corp., 844 F. Supp. 1533, 1537 (S.D. Fla. 1993), aff'd, 84 F.3d 438 (11th Cir. 1996) (holding that verbal sexual harassment did not rise to the level necessary to support the claim for intentional infliction of emotional distress); Hernandez v. Tallahassee Med. Ctr., 896 So. 2d 839, 841 (Fla. 1st DCA 2005) (holding that an employer's direction to its employee to report to work "right away", despite awareness that employee suffered epileptic seizures and should not drive, did not exceed all bounds of decency); Williams v. Worldwide Flight Serv., Inc., 877 So. 2d 869, 870 (Fla. 3d DCA 2004) (finding that supervisor's conduct of calling employee a "nigger" and "monkey" and threatening him with job termination was not so extreme or outrageous as to permit employee to recover for intentional infliction of emotional distress); Reed v. Georgia-Pacific Corp., 2006 WL 166534, *2 (M.D. Fla. 2006) (holding that employer's actions, such as discouraging Plaintiff from seeking medical attention for his on-the-job injury, pressuring Plaintiff not to report his injury, minimizing the injury, accompanying Plaintiff on his medical exams and requesting that Plaintiff be given over-the-counter medications, do not rise to the level of extreme and outrageous behavior.).

C. Interference with Economic Advantage

In Florida, a former employee can state a cause of action for intentional interference with an advantageous business relationship for communications between the former employer and prospective employers in certain narrow situations. The elements of this tort are (1) the existence of a business relationship not necessarily evidenced by an enforceable contract, (2) knowledge of relationship on the part of the defendant, (3) an intentional and unjustified interference with that relationship, and (4) damage as a result of the breach. See Nowik v. Mazda Motors of Am. (East) Inc., 523 So. 2d 769, 771 (Fla. 1st DCA 1988); Sloan v. Sax, 505 So. 2d 526, 527-28 (Fla. 3d DCA 1987) (listing five elements instead of four: "(4) by a third party; and (5) damages to the claimant caused by the interference."); Rudnick v. Sears, Roebuck and Co., 358 F. Supp. 2d 1201, 1205 (S.D. Fla. 2005) (also listing the five elements); see also Cox v. CSX Intermodal, Inc., 732 So. 2d 1092 (Fla. 1st DCA 1999), reh'g den., 744 So. 2d 453 (Fla. 1999) ("Generally, a tortious interference claim exists only against persons who are not parties to the contractual relationship. Further, an employee or representative of a contracting party must be considered as a party to the contractual relationship") (internal citations omitted). In Boehm v. Am. Bankers Ins. Group, 557 So. 2d 91 (Fla. 3d DCA 1990), the court ruled that a former employer's statements, made pursuant to a request by an executive search agent and pertaining to whether or not a former employee was a homosexual, were not actionable tortuous interference. But see Linafelt v. Beverly Enters.-Fla., Inc., 745 So. 2d 386, 388 (Fla. 1st DCA 1999) (noting superseding effect of Fla. Stat. § 768.095 (1997)).

Further, under Florida's economic loss rule, where a contract exists, the plaintiff may only bring a tort action "for either intentional or negligent acts considered to be independent from acts that breached the contract." HTP, Ltd. v. Lineas Aereas Costarricenses, S.A., 685 So. 2d 1238, 1239 (Fla. 1996) (emphasis added); Indemnity Ins. Co. of N. Am. v. Am. Aviation, Inc., 891 So. 2d 532, 537 (Fla. 2004). See also Shands Teaching Hosp. and Clinics, Inc. v. Beech St. Corp., 899 So. 2d 1222, 1229-1230 (Fla. 1st DCA 2005) (finding that a plaintiff can bring an action for tortious interference with an already established business relationship and contract where the defendant's fraudulent actions were the cause of the contract's breach). Even where a defendant "flagrantly, unjustifiably, and oppressively breaches a contract," there is no basis for recovery in negligence without a tort independent from the breach of contract. AFM Corp. v. S. Bell Tel. and Tel. Co., 515 So. 2d 180 (Fla. 1987). In Moransais v. Heathman, 744 So. 2d 973, 981 (Fla. 1999), the Florida Supreme Court curtailed what it characterized as the "unprincipled extension of the rule." The Court held that despite the existence of a contract between the parties, plaintiff's professional claim was not barred by the economic loss rule: "[T]he mere existence of a contract between the professional services corporation and a consumer does not eliminate the professional obligation of the professional who actually renders the service to the consumer or the common law action that a consumer may have against a professional provider.... We conclude that the principles underlying the economic loss rule are insufficient to preclude an action for professional malpractice under the circumstances presented here." Id.

When claims of intentional interference with business relations are based on alleged publication of false and defamatory statements, the claims are not separately viable. See Ford v. Rowland, 562 So. 2d 731, 735 (Fla. 5th DCA 1990), rev. den., 574 So. 2d 141, 142, 143 (Fla. 1990). In Seminole Tribe of Fla. v. Times Publ'g Co., the court dismissed for failure to state a claim a complaint based on publication of an investigative newspaper article, opining that "we question whether this common law cause of action could ever be stretched to cover a case involving news gathering and publication." 780 So. 2d 310, 318 (Fla. 4th DCA 2001). Moreover, such claims against a media defendant would be subject to Florida's pre-suit notice statute for defamation actions. Fla. Stat. 770.01 (2000). Finally, intentional interference actions will lie even where a party interferes with a contract that is terminable at will, unless the defendant's actions constituted lawful competition. See Perez v. Rivero, 534 So. 2d 914 (Fla. 3d DCA 1988).

D. Prima Facie Tort

Florida does not recognize this cause of action.

V. OTHER ISSUES

A. Statute of Limitations

The statute of limitations for defamation actions is two years. Fla. Stat. § 95.11(4)(g) (2001). The limitations period begins to run on the day of publication, regardless of when the plaintiff discovers the existence of the publication. See Wagner, Nugent, Johnson, Roth, Romano, Erikson & Kupfer, P.A. v. Flanagan, 629 So. 2d 113 (Fla. 1994). Florida law permits the legal representative to sue on behalf of the deceased plaintiff. See Fla. Stat. § 46.021 (providing that "no cause of action dies with the person").

B. Jurisdiction

Section 770.05 of the Florida Statutes provides that no person shall have more than one choice of venue for damages for any tort founded upon any single publication or utterance. Section 770.06 of the Florida Statutes operates to bar re-litigation of a judgment on the merits of an action based on such publication or utterance. Under Florida law, the tort of defamation is committed in the place where it is published for the purposes of determining jurisdiction. Casita L.P. v. Maplewood Equity Partners, L.P., 960 So. 2d 854, 857 (Fla. 3d DCA 2007). A telephonic, electronic, or written communication is deemed "published" in Florida, subjecting the publisher to long-arm jurisdiction under section 48.193(1)(b) of the Florida Statutes if the communication was made into this state by a person outside the state, even if the person has no other contacts with the state. Id. See also, Carida v. Holy Cross Hosp., 424 So. 2d 849 (Fla. 4th DCA 1982) (slanderous telephone calls into state can support a finding of tortuous act committed in Florida), *overruled on other grounds*, Doe v. Thompson, 620 So. 2d at 1004; Silver v. Levinson, 648 So. 2d 240 (Fla. 4th DCA 1994) (mailing of defamatory letter into Florida); Achievers Unlimited, Inc. v. Nutri Herb, Inc., 710 So. 2d 716(Fla. 4th DCA 1998) (defamatory statements over telephone to Florida residents by nonresident).

C. Worker's Compensation Exclusivity

See section IV.A.2, supra.

D. Pleading Requirements

It has been presumed that the pleading rules for employment related defamation are the same as for any other tort action. But see, Moore v. AS-Com Inc., 2006 WL 1037108 (M.D. Fla. 2006) (dealing with pleading a counterclaim for defamation in employment actions). However, in Diaz v. Kaplan Univ., the Court required a more descriptive recitation of the facts to support Plaintiff's claim of slander; requiring a level of detail in the allegations more akin to that required for pleading fraud. 567 F.Supp.2d 1394, 1405 (S.D. Fla. July 31, 2008) ("the plaintiff's allegations of 'using racially discriminatory and vulgar remarks,' while a conclusory description of inappropriate statements in a work environment, does not constitute slander."); see also Bell v. Novartis Pharmaceuticals Corp., 2008 WL 2694893 (M.D. Fla. July 3, 2008) (requiring a more detailed pleading of facts supporting defamation claim).

Generally, as with all other actions, the burden of proving the elements of the cause of action are with the plaintiff. On some issues, such as truth or falsity of the statement, however, there is some confusion.

SURVEY OF FLORIDA EMPLOYMENT PRIVACY LAW

Sanford L. Bohrer and Scott D. Ponce
Holland & Knight LLP
701 Brickell Avenue, Suite 3000
P.O. Box 015441
Miami, Florida 33131
Telephone: (305) 789-7678;
Facsimile: (305) 789-7799

(With Developments Reported Through **November 1, 2012**)

GENERAL COMMENTS

None.

SIGNIFICANT DEVELOPMENTS SINCE THE 2011 *SURVEY*

None.

I. GENERAL LAW OF PRIVACY

A. Legal Basis of Privacy Claims

Florida recognizes three variants of the invasion of privacy cause of action. Two common law theories of recovery are recognized - publication of private facts and intrusion upon seclusion. Heath v. Playboy Enters., Inc., 732 F. Supp. 1145, 1147-48 (S.D. Fla. 1990) (citations omitted). The third theory of recovery, appropriation for commercial benefit, is statutory in Florida. Fla. Stat. § 540.08 (1999). In 2008, the Florida Supreme Court declined to recognize the false light cause of action. Jews for Jesus, Inc. v. Rapp, 997 So.2d 1098 (Fla. 2008); Anderson v. Gannett Co. Inc., 994 So.2d 1048 (Fla. 2008). In addition, Florida intermediate appellate courts have indicated there might be a "relational" right of privacy, stating relatives of a deceased person might have a claim for invasion of privacy under appropriate circumstances. See Williams v. City of Minneola, 575 So. 2d 683, 689-90 (Fla. 5th DCA 1991), rev. den., 589 So. 2d 289 (Fla. 1991); Armstrong v. H&C Communications, Inc., 575 So. 2d 280, 282-82 (Fla. 5th DCA 1991), Loft v. Fuller, 408 So. 2d 619, 623-25 (Fla. 4th DCA 1982), rev. den., 419 So. 2d 1198 (Fla. 1982). But see Santiesteban v. Goodyear Tire & Rubber Co., 306 F.2d 9, 12-13 (5th Cir. 1962).

Article I, Section 23 of the Florida Constitution protects the private lives of citizens against intrusion by the government: "Every natural person has the right to be let alone and free from governmental intrusion into his private life except as otherwise provided herein." This section "provides a constitutional right of privacy broader in scope than the protection provided in the United States Constitution." See Berkeley v. Eisen, 699 So. 2d 789 (Fla. 4th DCA 1997); Beverly Enters.-Fla., Inc. v. Deutsch, 765 So. 2d 778 (Fla. 5th DCA 2000). This, however, does not give rise to a claim of "governmental intrusion." See Resha v. Tucker, 670 So. 2d 56 (Fla. 1996). In addition, information disclosed in public records and public meetings is unaffected by the constitutional provision, which says "This section shall not be construed to limit the public's right of access to public records and meetings as provided by law." Specifically, government agency personnel records not exempted by statute are not shielded from public access by this provision. See Michel v. Douglas, 464 So. 2d 545, 546 (Fla. 1985); Sun-Sentinel Co. v. United States Department of Homeland Security, 431 F. Supp. 2d 1258 (S.D. Fla. 2006) (mandating the disclosure of employee e-mails that are not exempt from disclosure). But see State v. City of Clearwater, 863 So. 2d 149 (Fla. 2003) (public employees' personal emails found on city's computer do not constitute public records and are exempt from disclosure).

B. Causes of Action

As noted above, Florida has one statutory theory of invasion of privacy and two common law theories. See Heath, 732 F. Supp. at 1145.

1. ***Misappropriation/Right of Publicity.*** Section 540.08 of the Florida Statutes prohibits the publication, display or other public use for "purposes of trade or for any commercial or advertising purpose" the name, photograph, or likeness of any natural person. See Heath, 732 F. Supp. at 1147-48 (citations omitted). There are exemptions, but none other than consent is applicable in the employment context. See Fla. Stat. § 540.08(3) (1999). The right of publicity may be defined as a celebrity's right to the exclusive use of his or her name and likeness, and it is assignable during the life of the celebrity. See Gridiron.com, Inc. v. Nat'l Football League Player's Assoc., 106 F. Supp. 2d 1309 (S.D. Fla. 2000).

2. ***False Light.*** Florida does not recognize this cause of action. Jews for Jesus, Inc. v. Rapp, 997 So.2d 1098 (Fla. 2008); Anderson v. Gannett Co. Inc., 994 So.2d 1048 (Fla. 2008); Straub v. Lehtinen, Vargas & Riedi, 7 So. 3d 649 (Fla. 4th DCA 2009).

3. ***Publication of Private Facts.*** The Florida Supreme Court recognized publication of private facts in Florida in Cape Publ'ns, Inc. v. Hitchner, 549 So. 2d 1374, 1377, (Fla. 1989) appeal dismissed, 493 U.S. 929 (1989), adopting the formulation contained in Section 652D of the Restatement (Second) of Torts (1977). The court said the elements can be summarized as 1) the publication, 2) of private facts, 3) that are offensive and 4) that are not of public concern.

In order to be actionable, the publication must be to the "public in general or to a large number of persons as distinguished from one individual or a few." Santiesteban v. Goodyear Tire & Rubber Co., 306 F. 2d 9, 11 (5th Cir. 1962). See also Steele v. Offshore Shipbuilding, Inc., 867 F.2d 1311, 1315 (11th Cir. 1989) (employees could not maintain invasion of privacy action for officer's sexually oriented joking because comments never made to more than a few people); Williams v. City of Minneola, 575 So. 2d 683, 689 (Fla. 5th DCA) (police officers' gratuitous display of photographs and videotape of autopsy since they were distributed to a few people and there was no substantial similarity that they would be publicly disseminated), review den., 589 So. 2d 289 (Fla. 1991); cf. Lewis v. Snap-On Tools Corp., 708 F. Supp. 1260, 1262 (M.D. Fla. 1989) (conclusory allegation that company disclosed private facts to a "large number of persons" did not meet requirement that publication be made to the general public in such a manner as to become outrageous and certain to become public knowledge); Smith v. Bendix Field Eng'g Corp., 123 Lab. Cas. P 57,080, 1992 WL 316313 (M.D. Fla. Jan. 29, 1992) (disclosure to "at least one of Plaintiff's employers" not sufficient publicity). In most cases, of course, publication by a medium will be sufficient to meet this element of the tort.

At least one court has found that ideas shared with a stranger outside the confines of one's home are not private. See Mills v. Wenner Media, LLC, 2005 WL 1126662, at*2, 33 Media L. Rep. 2022 (M.D. Fla. May 5, 2005). **But see Bilbreg v. Myers, 91 So.3d 887, 892 (Fla.5th DCA 2012), holding some disclosure is not enough to make it "public," citing Williams v. City of Minneola, supra.**

The operative private facts must be offensive and objectionable to a reasonable person of ordinary sensibilities. Consent is only relevant where a genuine issue exists as to either the plaintiff's public figure status or the legitimacy of the public concern (fourth element). See Heath, 732 F. Supp. at 1149. There are no Florida decisions on the issues of privileges and defenses relevant to the employment context. The damages recoverable by a plaintiff are those typical of any tort involving emotional harm. See Santiesetban, 306 F.2d at 9. Also, there are no special procedures applicable to this action. The statute of limitations is four years. Fla. Stat. § 95.11(3)(o).

In a recent decision of interest, an appellate court approved of a cause of action for publication of private facts against a radio station operator whose "disc jockey" disclosed private facts about the plaintiff whom the disc jockey had dated on and off over a 20-year period. Doe v. Beasley Broadcast Group, __ So. 3d, __, 2012 WL 4210455 (Fla. 2nd DCA 2012).

4. ***Intrusion.*** In Purrelli v. State Farm Fire and Cas. Co., 698 So. 2d 618, 620 (Fla. 2d DCA 1997), the Court held intrusion upon seclusion is the intentional intrusion "upon the solitude or seclusion of another," quoting from the Restatement (Second) of Torts § 652B (1977)). There is usually no intrusion upon seclusion when a plaintiff is in a public place, such as her workplace. See Benn v. Fla. E. Coast Ry. Co., 1999 WL 816811 (S.D. Fla. July 21, 1999). Although a number of decisions arise in the more typical physical trespass to property context (e.g., Thompson v. City of Jacksonville, 130 So. 2d 105 (Fla. 1st DCA 1961), questioned by Simpson v. City of Miami, 155 So. 2d 829 (Fla. 3d DCA 1963) (police officers negligently broke into and searched the plaintiff's premises), intrusion can include touching a person in an undesired or offensive manner. See State Farm Fire & Cas. Co. v. Compupay, Inc., 654 So. 2d 944, 948-49 (Fla. 3d DCA 1995); Stoddard v. Wohlfahrt, 573 So. 2d 1060 (Fla. 5th DCA 1991). See also Vernon v. Med. Mgmt. Assocs. of Margate, Inc., 912 F. Supp. 1549, 1561 (S.D. Fla. 1996) (holding that an alleged pattern of persistent verbal and physical sexual abuse, including "persistent touching, squeezing, fondling, hugging, blowing and tickling, along with the repetition of lewd and vulgar sexual remarks," by a doctor/supervisor against a receptionist was sufficient to state claim for intrusion upon physical solitude); Stockett v. Tolin, 791 F. Supp. 1536 (S.D. Fla. 1992) (finding an intrusion upon seclusion where an employee entered the ladies' room and committed a battery upon a coworker); and Liberti v. Walt Disney World Co., 912 F. Supp. 1494, 1506, (M.D. Fla. 1995) (employee plaintiffs alleging that employer used them as "bait" in order to catch fellow employee spying on them in the female employees dressing room stated claim for invasion of privacy/intrusion). But see Allstate Ins. Co. v. Ginsberg, 351 F.3d 473 (11th Cir. 2003) (pleadings of unwelcome conduct including touching in a sexual manner and sexually offensive comments do not state a cause of action for the Florida common law tort claim of invasion of privacy). **See also Watterson v. Smallwoods, Inc., ___ So. 3d ___, 2012 WL 1605423 (Fla. 4th DCA 2012) (citing Allstate).** Mere talk about such touching is not sufficient. Thus, "utterances, designed to induce [the plaintiff] to join with him in a sexual liaison . . . fall short of the mark." See Ponton v. Scarfone, 468 So. 2d 1009, 1010 (Fla. 2d DCA 1985). There are no Florida

decisions on the issue of damages relevant to the employment context and there are no special procedures applicable to this action. The statute of limitations is four years. Section 95.11(3)(o), Fla. Stat. (1999).

C. Other Privacy-related Actions

1. ***Intentional Infliction of Emotional Distress.*** This tort is often a companion tort in employment actions designed to get around Federal and Florida statutory damage caps. To state a claim for intentional infliction of emotional distress, a plaintiff must allege four elements: (1) deliberate or reckless infliction of mental suffering; (2) by outrageous conduct; (3) which conduct must have caused suffering; and (4) the suffering must have been severe. See Hart v. U.S., 894 F.2d 1539 (11th Cir. 1990), cert. den., 498 U.S. 980 (1990); See also Scelta v. Delicatessen Support Servs., 57 F. Supp. 2d 1327 (M.D. Fla. 1999). The Florida Supreme Court has modified the tort by requiring that the conduct be so extreme and outrageous as to transcend all bounds of decency and be regarded as appalling and intolerable in a civilized community. See Metro. Life Ins. Co. v. McCarson, 467 So. 2d 277 (Fla. 1985); Aguilera v. Inserv., Inc., 905 So. 2d 84, 92 (Fla. June 16, 2005); Williams v. S.E. Fla. Cable, Inc., 782 So. 2d 988 (Fla. 4th DCA 2001); House of God v. White, 2001 Fla. App. LEXIS 1061 (Fla. 4th DCA 2001). Conduct alleged may be characterized as insulting, disturbing and concerning but still not meet Florida's rigid standard of "extreme" and "outrageous." McCarson, 467at 277. ("Liability [for intentional infliction of emotional distress] clearly does not extend to mere insults, indignities, threats, annoyances, [or petty oppressions] . . ."). The Southern of District of Florida has dismissed a claim for intentional infliction of emotional distress because the alleged conduct, "while inconsiderate and insulting, did not rise to the level of 'extreme' and 'outrageous.'" See Novoa v. The Southland Corp., Case No. 96-1332-Civ. Hoeveler, Order, Nov. 18, 1996; Lay v. Roux Labs, Inc., 379 So. 2d 451, 452 (Fla. 1st DCA 1980) (finding employer's threats to fire coupled with "humiliating language, vicious verbal attack [and] racial epithets" insufficient to meet Florida standard of "extreme" and "outrageous"); Ponton v. Scarfone, 468 So. 2d 1009, 1009-10 (Fla. 2d DCA 1985) (holding that even though plaintiff's allegations of sexual advance by former employer was "condemnable by civilized social standards, [it did] does not ascend, or perhaps descend, to a level permitting us to say that the benchmarks enunciated in Metropolitan have been met"), rev. den., 478 So. 2d 54 (Fla. 1985).

"[C]ourts in Florida and in the Eleventh Circuit have been extremely reluctant to recognize outrageous conduct in the employment context." Blount v. Sterling Healthcare Group, Inc., 934 F. Supp. 1365, 1370-71 (S.D. Fla. 1996) (dismissing claim as not sufficiently outrageous where allegations included tight hugging, rubbing the plaintiff's breasts, massaging the back of her head, and other verbal harassment); see also Ball v. Heilig-meyers Furniture Co., No. 98-599-Civ-T-17A, 1999 WL 80355, *5 (M.D. Fla. Feb. 10, 1999) (store manager's verbal sexual comments and physical grabbing and rubbing against plaintiff employee was not sufficiently outrageous); Hag v. United Airlines, Inc., 1996 U.S. Dist. LEXIS 21043 (S.D. Fla. 1996) (employer did not "ratify" sexual comments of employees so as to be liable when no evidence existed that supervisors of employer adopted the comments made or otherwise benefited from the conduct); Studstill v. Borg Warner Leasing, 806 F.2d 1005, 1008 (11th Cir. 1986) (holding that verbal sexual harassment, including dirty jokes, comments and invitations, was insufficient to support an intentional infliction of emotional distress claim); Watson v. Bally Mfg. Corp., 844 F. Supp. 1533, 1537 (S.D. Fla. 1993), aff'd, 84 F.3d 438 (11th Cir. 1996) (holding that verbal sexual harassment did not rise to the level necessary to support the claim for intentional infliction of emotional distress); Hernandez v. Tallahassee Med. Ctr., 896 So. 2d 839, 841 (Fla. 1st DCA 2005) (holding that an employer's direction to its employee to report to work "right away", despite awareness that employee suffered epileptic seizures and should not drive, did not exceed all bounds of decency); Williams v. Worldwide Flight Serv., Inc., 877 So. 2d 869, 870 (Fla. 3d DCA 2004) (finding that supervisor's conduct of calling employee a "nigger" and "monkey" and threatening him with job termination was not so extreme or outrageous as to permit employee to recover for intentional infliction of emotional distress). But see Vernon v. Med. Mgmt. Assocs. of Margate, Inc., 912 F. Supp. 1549, 1551 (S.D. Fla. 1996) (an alleged pattern of persistent physical verbal and physical sexual abuse by doctor/supervisor against a receptionist was sufficient to allege the element of extreme and outrageous conduct for the intentional infliction of emotional distress claim) and Liberti v. Walt Disney World Co., 912 Supp. 1494, 1506-07 (M.D. Fla. 1995) (employee plaintiffs alleging that employer used them as "bait" in order to catch fellow employee spying on them in the female employees dressing room stated claim for invasion of privacy/intrusion). Byrd v. BT Foods, Inc., 948 So. 2d 921, 928 (Fla. 4th DCA 2007) (Teasing of HIV infected employee is not sufficiently outrageous). A recent decision has held that the employee can be compelled to arbitrate his claim. Xerox Corporation v. Smartech Document Management, 979 So. 2d 957 (Fla. 3d DCA 2007).

2. ***Interference With Prospective Economic Advantage.*** In Florida, a former employee can state a cause of action for intentional interference with an advantageous business relationship for communications with prospective employers in only very narrow situations. See, Section 768.095, Florida Statutes; Linafelt v. Beverly Enters.-Fla., Inc., 745 So. 2d 386 (Fla. 1st DCA 1999) (reversing directed verdict for employer and remanding for a new trial). The elements of this tort are (1) the existence of a business relationship not necessarily evidenced by an enforceable contract, (2) knowledge of relationship on the part of the defendant, (3) an intentional and unjustified interference with that relationship, and (4) damage as a result of the breach. See Nowik v. Mazda Motors of Am. (East) Inc., 523 So. 2d 769, 771 (Fla. 1st DCA 1988); Cox v. CSX Intermodal, Inc., 1999 Fla. App. LEXIS 162 (Fla. 1st DCA 1999). In Boehm v. Am. Bankers Ins. Group, 557 So. 2d 91

(Fla. 3d DCA 1990), the court ruled that a former employer's statements, made pursuant to a request by an executive search agent and pertaining to whether or not a former employee was a homosexual, were not actionable tortious interference.

3. ***Prima Facie Tort.*** Florida does not recognize this cause of action.

II. EMPLOYER TESTING OF EMPLOYEES

Florida is an "employment at will" state, and with rare exceptions (e.g., discrimination statutes), in the absence of a contract for a fixed term, an employer can terminate an employee without cause and suffer no consequences. Thus, many of the recent decisions relating to employee testing come in the context of workers' compensation or unemployment compensation cases. However, Florida recognizes the torts of negligent hiring, training, supervision, and retention of employees, and thus employer testing has become more commonplace.

A. Psychological or Personality Testing

1. ***Common Law and Statutes.*** Testing of employees or applicants through "pen and paper" methods is not restricted either by statute or case decision in Florida. However, such testing must not violate applicable discrimination laws, such as the Florida Civil Rights Act. Fla. Stat. Ch. 760 (1999).

2. ***Private Employers.*** There are no relevant decisions.

3. ***Public Employers.*** There are no relevant decisions.

B. Drug Testing

1. ***Common Law and Statutes.*** Florida has two separate drug-free workplace statutes. One applicable to public employers and employees, section 112.0455 Fla. Stat. (1999), and the other applicable to private employers and employees, section 440.101 Fla. Stat. (1999). There is no legal duty to test under either of the statutes. See 112.0455 (4) and § 440.102(2). Torres v. Eagle Technologies, Inc., 2010 WL 2243700 (M.D. Fla. 2010). Florida does, however, proscribe a mandatory program if employers wish to qualify for workers' compensation discounts and possibly deny medical and indemnity benefits under the workers' compensation statutes. Fla. Stat. §440.102 (2). Under the Statutory Drug Free Workplace Program, employers are eligible for a 5% discount in their workers' compensation insurance premiums if the drug-testing policy comports with the statutory criteria. *Id.* If an employers' drug testing policy does not comply with the Program, the employer may still implement it, however, the employer will not be eligible for the discount. Fla. Stat. § 440.102(7)(e) ("[t]his section . . . does not abrogate the right of an employer under state law to conduct drug tests, or to implement employee drug-testing programs; however, only those programs that meet the criteria outlined in this section qualify for reduced rates under section 627.0915 [of the Florida Statutes]"). However, an employer who implements a drug free workplace policy but not pursuant to 440.102, may enforce that policy and discharge a non-complying employee. Laquerre v. Palm Beach Newspapers, Inc., 20 So. 3d 392 (Fla. 4th DCA 2009).

Employers may conduct the following types of drug tests: 1) job applicant testing, 2) reasonable suspicion testing, 3) routine fitness for duty testing, and 4) follow up testing. See Fla. Stat. § 112.0455 (7) and § 440.102(4). Pre-offer applicant testing, however, can pose potential problems for the employer pursuant to the Americans with Disabilities Act. For public employees, the time spent on the drug test is deemed to be performed during work time for purposes of determining compensation and benefits. See Fla. Stat. § 112.0455 (8)(g). Moreover, Florida's constitution recognizes a right to privacy. Fla. Const. Art. I § 23. Nonetheless, no Florida case law addresses whether Florida citizens possess such a privacy right in the context of employee drug-testing. According to one court, an Ionscan test, using a variation of mass spectrometry, is not a drug test under the statute. Mitchell v. Department of Corrections, 675 So. 2d 162 (Fla. 4th DCA 1996). An appellate court decision has implied that an employee has no right to refuse to take a random drug test pursuant to a policy announced in the employer's handbook for its employees, but held that because the request to take the test was made after the employee had "clocked out," the refusal to take the test was not sufficient to deny him workers' compensation benefits. See Kirkland v. Unemployment Appeals Comm'n, 681 So. 2d 1211 (Fla. 5th DCA 1996).

2. ***Private Employers.*** Unemployment benefits can be denied in Florida if the employer's request for a urinalysis test is based on a reasonable suspicion of drug use and the employee refuses to submit to the urinalysis test. Fowler v. Unemployment Appeals Comm'n, 537 So. 2d 162 (Fla. 5th DCA 1989). But see Kirkland v. Unemployment Appeals Comm'n, 681 So. 2d 1211 (Fla. 5th DCA 1996) (holding that claimant was not unreasonable in refusing random drug test requested when he was off the clock).

3. ***Public Employers.*** Non-federal public employers that operate under a collective bargaining agreement must negotiate the implementation and requirements of drug testing programs. Section 440.102 (13), Fla. Stat.

(1999); see also Communications Workers of Am. v. City of Gainesville, 697 So. 2d 167, 168 (Fla. 1st DCA 1997). Drug testing of police officers observed purchasing drugs has been approved, but the Court noted the extraordinary circumstances and made it clear drug testing procedures must be worked out in the collective bargaining process in all but the most extraordinary case. See Fraternal Order of Police, Miami Lodge 20 v. City of Miami, 609 So. 2d 31 (Fla. 1992); City of Palm Bay v. Bauman, 475 So. 2d 1332 (Fla. 5th DCA 1985) (holding that reasonable suspicion, not probable cause, is the standard for drug tests for police officers and fire-fighters). Recently, in Baron v. City of Hollywood, 93 F. Supp. 2d 1337, the District Court for the Southern District of Florida held that the city's policy of requiring all applicants to submit to a drug test violated the Fourth Amendment. The statute defines drug test broadly, but a recent decision held that an Irons can test, a variation of mass spectrometry in which a sample is obtained by vacuuming the subject's shoulder area to the hands, front and back, is not covered by the statute, and thus can be conducted without "reasonable suspicion." The court held that a "drug test" under the statute is a test of body tissues or fluids, and the Irons can test only tested dust particles picked by the vacuum. See Mitchell v. Dep't of Corr., 675 So. 2d 162 (Fla. 4th DCA 1996).

C. Medical Testing

1. ***Common Law and Statutes.*** By statute, Florida law restricts the use of "genetic testing" in the insurance context, which has obvious implications for the workplace. Thus, in the absence of "a diagnosis of a condition related to genetic information, no health insurer . . . may cancel, limit, or deny coverage, or establish differentials in premium rates, based on such information." Fla. Stat. § 627.4301(2)(a) (1999). In addition, health insurers cannot "require or solicit genetic information, use genetic test results, or consider a person's decisions of actions relating to genetic testing in any manner for any insurance purpose." Fla. Stat. § 627.4301(2)(b) (1999). Florida law also restricts DNA testing, which is permitted only in three instances: (a) for purposes of criminal prosecution; (b) for purposes of determining paternity; and (3) only with the informed consent of the person to be tested, who has exclusive control over the results. Fla. Stat. § 760.40(2)(a) (1999). Florida permits testing of persons charged with or alleged by a petition for delinquency to have committed an offense which involves the transmission of body fluids, upon the request of the victim. The results are only disclosed to the individual charged with or adjudicated delinquent, the victim and to public health authorities only. Fla. Stat. § 960.003 (1999); see also Fosman v. State, 664 So. 2d 1163 (Fla. 4th DCA 1995).

Section 381.00 *et seq.* of the Florida Statutes contains a series of provisions governing HIV testing. Section 381. 004(3)(f) provides that, subject to certain exceptions not pertinent here, "the identity of any person upon whom [an HIV] test has been performed and [the] test results are confidential" and that "[n]o person who has obtained or has knowledge of a test result pursuant to [section 381.004] may disclose ××× the identity of any person upon whom a test is performed[ ] or the results of such a test in a manner which permits identification of the subject of the test" except as specifically authorized by law. In Florida Department of Corrections v. Abril, 969 So. 2d 201 (Fla. 2007), the Court found that the employee, using section 381.00 as the standard of care, had stated a cause of action for negligence against her employer based on her allegation that the laboratory, selected by the employer, faxed the results of her HIV test to unsecured fax machines and co-workers thus became aware of test results).

2. ***Private Employers.*** See II.C.1, supra. Also note that an employee's failure to disclose his HIV status to his employer, in order to protect his privacy, did not amount to misconduct warranting denial of unemployment compensation benefits. Hummer III v. Unemployment Appeals Comm'n, 573 So. 2d 135 (Fla. 5th DCA 1991).

3. ***Public Employers.*** See II.C.1, supra.

D. Polygraph Tests

Florida has no polygraph statutes applying to the employment relationship. Pre-employment agreements to submit to polygraph tests are enforceable. See Vaughan v. Shop & Go, Inc., 526 So. 2d 91, 93 (Fla. 4th DCA 1987). However, absent an agreement to undergo future polygraph testing, an employee cannot be denied unemployment compensation benefits for refusing to submit to polygraph testing. See Swops v. Fla. Indus. Comm'n Unemployment Compensation Bd. of Review, 159 So. 2d 653 (Fla. 3d DCA 1963); Farmer v. City of Fort Lauderdale, 427 So. 2d 187 (Fla. 4th DCA 1983). The Federal Employee Polygraph Protection Act of 1988 prohibits the use of polygraph devices by most private employers and expressly exempts public, governmental employers. Polkey v. Transtecs Corp., 404 F. 3d 1264, 1268-1269 (11th Cir. 2005) (EPPA even regulates federal defense contractors); see also, Richardson v. Dougherty County, Georgia, 2006 WL 1526064 *2 (11th Cir. 2006) (admitting affidavits mentioning results of polygraph as an explanation of investigation by Sheriff's office into allegations of sexual misconduct).

E. Fingerprinting

There are no reported decisions or statutes relevant to this issue in the employment context.

III. SEARCHES

There is no Florida statute, and almost no Florida case law, regarding workplace searches.

A. Employee's Person

Where employees were made aware that as a term of their employment they were subject to body searches, a "shakedown" search was not an invasion of an employee's privacy. See Clark v. State, 395 So. 2d 525, 529 (Fla. 1981).

1. ***Private Employers.*** There are no relevant decisions.

2. ***Public Employers.*** The plurality decision in O'Connor v. Ortega, 480 U.S. 709 (1987) seems to indicate that for the public employer, "probable cause" is not needed to conduct a workplace search. What is required is that the employer's conduct be reasonable, which is determined by balancing the employees' legitimate expectations of privacy against the government's need for supervision, control and efficient operation of the workplace. See Baseman v. State, 513 So. 2d 1101 (Fla. 2d DCA 1987).

B. Employee's Work Area

Whether an employee has a legitimate expectation and hence, a right of privacy in his or her workplace requires a determination based on the facts of the existence of a subjective and objective expectation of privacy. Kelly v. State, 77 So. 3d 818, 822 (Fla. 4th DCA 2012). A Florida appellate court has indicated, following the U.S. Supreme Court decision in O'Connor v. Ortega, 480 U.S. 709 (1987), that a search of a government employee's desk in violation of the government agency's own regulations violated his right of privacy. The decision indicates an acquiescence in the regulations may subject an employee to a search pursuant to them, but does not constitute an unconditional waiver of his constitutional rights. The decision was under the U.S. Constitution. See Bateman v. State, 513 So. 2d 1101 (Fla. 2d DCA 1987). One Florida court held that an employer's search of an employee's desk did not violate the Fourth Amendment. State v. Olsen, 745 So. 2d 454 (5th DCA 1999); see also Alexander v. State, 902 So. 2d 292, 293 (Fla. 3d DCA 2005). Most recently, a Florida appellate court held that in the circumstances in that case, a pastor had an expectation of privacy in his office and workplace computer and that his superiors could not consent to the search. State v. Young, 974 So. 2d 601 (Fla. 1 DCA 2008), rev. denied, 988 So.2d 623 (table), 2008 WL 2718908 (Fla. 2008). The evaluation is fact based, but, for example, where an employer has a clear policy allowing others to monitor a workplace computer, an employee using the computer has no reasonable expectation of privacy. Id.

C. Employee's Property

1. ***Private Employers***. In Thomas v. United Parcel Service, Inc., 864 So. 2d 567 (Fla. 2d DCA 2004), the Court determined that an employee's refusal to allow a search of his personal effects did not constitute misconduct that would bar unemployment compensation. The employee's refusal to allow the search of his bag could not be considered a violation of employment standards because the employer had failed to implement a policy regarding the search of workers and their personal effects. See III.A.-B, supra. An employee's refusal to permit a search of his briefcase in violation of a written company "Right to Search" policy did constitute misconduct that would bar unemployment compensation. Leedham v. State, 950 So. 2d 475 (Fla. 4 DCA 2007). **A recent decision held that discovery requests, including subpoenas, that implicate employees' privacy rights should not be litigated by their employer, but instead the employees themselves should be given the opportunity to assert their privacy rights. Wyndham Vacation Resorts v. Ocean Walk Condominium Association, 86 So. 3d 592 (Fla. 5th DCA 2012).**

2. ***Public Employers.*** See III.A.-B, supra.

IV. MONITORING OF EMPLOYEES

A. Telephones and Electronic Communications

1. ***Wiretapping.*** Section 934.03 of the Florida Statutes prohibits the interception, disclosure, or use of any wire, oral or electronic communication with any electronic, mechanical or other device. For the purposes of Section 934.03, the Court in State v. Inciarrano, 473 So. 2d 1272 (Fla. 1985) held that the legislature did not intend that every oral communication be free from interception without the consent of all parties; instead, the statute protects those oral communications uttered by an individual exhibiting an expectation of privacy, under circumstances reasonably justifying such an expectation. In Royal Health Care Servs., Inc. v. Jefferson-Pilot Life Ins. Co., 924 F.2d 215 (11th Cir. 1991), the Court, relying in part on a "business extension" exemption to the act and in part on the act's definition of the term "interception," construed the act as not prohibiting the recording of telephone calls in the ordinary course of business. See also United States v. Biro, 143 F.3d 1421 (11th Cir. 1998) (18 U.S.C. § 2512(2) proscribing sending, possession, or sale of wiretap devices for

surreptitious surveillance held not unconstitutionally vague as applied). Monitoring of non-emergency calls to and from a "911" call center was held lawful even though such monitoring is not an exception to the prohibitions in Chapter 934. Brillinger v. City of Lake Worth, 978 So. 2d 265 (Fla. 4 DCA 2008).

2. ***Electronic Communications.*** There are no statutes or reported decisions on this point in the employee context. Section 934.03(2)(d) of the Florida Statutes prohibits the interception, disclosure or use of any oral or electronic communication. The statute requires that both parties to the communication consent to the recording. The statute applies to information transmitted to a pager, State v. Jackson, 650 So. 2d 24 (Fla. 1995) and to cordless telephones, State v. Mozo, 655 So. 2d 1115 (Fla. 1995). There are various exceptions, statutory and case law, but most have no relationship to the employment context. In State v. Smith, 641 So. 2d 849 (Fla. 1994), the Florida Supreme Court held that section 934.03 does not prohibit the non-consensual recording of a person's voice under circumstances where the person whose voice is recorded does not have a "reasonable expectation of privacy." The Court reasoned that such a recording did not violate the Fourth Amendment to the United States Constitution (and the parallel provision of the Florida Constitution) – as interpreted by Katz v. United States, 389 U.S. 347 (1967), and subsequent decisions, and thus did not violate Chapter 934. This decision can be used to avoid the requirement that all parties to a communication must consent to an interception. One Florida appellate court has apparently used this approach. In Dep't of Agric. & Consumer Servs. v. Edwards, 654 So. 2d 628 (Fla. 1st DCA 1995), review den., 662 So. 2d 931 (Fla. 1995), the court held it was not a violation of Chapter 934 for a subordinate officer to record his conversation with supervising law enforcement officers because the fact that the supervising law enforcement officers had no subjective expectation of privacy in their statements, considering the number of officers present and the disciplinary nature of the interview. Id. at 633. See also Stevenson v. State, 667 So. 2d 410 (Fla. 1st DCA 1996) (holding Chapter 934 not violated by warrantless use of "bionic ears" to intercept from 50-to-75 feet oral solicitation of cocaine sale to defendant in van). But in Brandin v. State, 669 So. 2d 280, 282 (Fla. 1st DCA 1996), the same court declined to "accept the blanket proposition that under Chapter 934 the police [or presumably the media] are free to intercept communications on public streets without obtaining judicial assent." This statute does not apply to visual recording.

3. ***Other Electronic Monitoring.*** In O'Brien v. O'Brien, 899 So. 2d 1133 (Fla. 5th DCA 2005), the court affirmed the trial court's decision to classify certain electronic communications as inadmissible evidence during the parties' divorce proceedings because the wife had obtained the communications illegally. In O'Brien, unbeknownst to the husband, the wife secretly installed a spy ware program onto the husband's computer in order to monitor and record his Internet conversations and explorations. Id. at 1134. The husband had in fact been engaging in on-line chats with another woman, and the spy ware took snapshots of all that appeared on the computer screen, including conversations, instant messages, e-mails sent and received, and the websites visited. Id.

The court of appeals upheld the lower court's ruling, concluding that "because the spy ware installed by the [w]ife intercepted the electronic communication contemporaneously with transmission, copied it, and routed the copy to a file in the computer's hard drive, the electronic communications were [indeed] intercepted." Id. at 1137. By electronically monitoring her husband's computer and Internet usage, the wife was found to be in violation of Florida's Security of Communication Act, which was designed to allow persons to have an expectation of privacy within their conversations. Id. at 1136. Under Florida law, it is a violation of a person's right to privacy to engage in covert electronic monitoring.

B. Mail

There are no decisions or statutes relevant to this issue in the employment context.

C. Surveillance/Photographing

There are no statutes regarding surveillance in the employment context. The tort of intrusion has arisen in context of surveillance. See Wolfson v. Lewis, 924 F. Supp. 1413, 1434 (E.D. Pa. 1996). An employer's "shadowing" of a former employee was held insufficient to support an invasion of privacy claim in Catania v. E. Airlines, Inc., 381 So. 2d 265 (Fla. 3d DCA 1980), but the Court noted such a cause of action is proper if "the surveillance of the plaintiff by the defendant [is] shown to have been in a vicious and malicious manner, not reasonably linked to a legitimate purpose," citing Tucker v. Am. Employers' Ins. Co., 171 So. 2d 437 (Fla. 2d DCA 1965). In a later decision in the Tucker case, a different appellate court made clear that it was not addressing the issue of what level of conduct would be sufficient for a privacy cause of action. Tucker v. Am. Employers' Ins. Co., 218 So. 2d 221 (Fla. 4th DCA 1969). Tucker involved surveillance of a person making an insurance claim, not an employee. See also Liberti v. Walt Disney World Co., 912 F. Supp. 1494, 1506 (M.D. Fla. 1995) (employee plaintiffs alleging that employer used them as "bait" in order to catch fellow employee spying on them in the female employees dressing room stated claim for invasion of privacy/intrusion). In other states, however, courts have specifically held that employees lack reasonable expectations of privacy against disclosed, soundless video surveillance while in open, undifferentiated work area. See Vega-Rodriguez v. Puerto Rico Tel. Co., 110 F.3d 174 (1st Cir. 1997). Video surveillance alone, when no oral communication is captured, i.e. "intercepted," is not unlawful under Florida's interception statute, but can be the basis for an invasion of privacy claim. Minotty v. Baudo, 42 So. 3d 824 (Fla. 4th DCA 2010).

V. ACTIVITIES OUTSIDE THE WORKPLACE

A. Statute or Common Law

There are no statutes governing outside activities with the exception of local and state employment discrimination statutes. But see, Palm Bay v. Bauman, 475 So. 2d 1322 (Fla. 1985) (holding that the city had right to adopt a policy which prohibited police officers and fire fighters from using controlled substances at any time while they are employed, whether such use was on or off the job). On the other hand, it has been held that employer photographic surveillance of picketing employees constituted an unfair labor practice. School Board of Escambia County v. Public Employees Relations Commission, 350 So.2d 819 (Fla. 1st DCA 1977).

B. Employees' Personal Relationships

1. ***Romantic Relationships Between Employees.*** Anti-fraternization policies are not prohibited by statute or case law.

2. ***Sexual Orientation.*** While not recognized by the Florida Civil Rights Act (Section 760.01, et seq) as a cause of action, some county ordinances in Florida do prohibit discrimination in the workplace on the basis of sexual orientation. See e.g., Miami -Dade County, [Fla.] Human Rights Ordinance, ch. 11A, art. I, Section 11A-1 (1998); Broward County, Fla., Code of Ordinances, ch. 16 ½, art. I, Section 16 ½-2 (1998); Palm Beach. Co. Ord. § 2-262 (2005). See also Boehm v. Am. Bankers Ins. Group, 557 So. 2d 91 (Fla. 3d DCA 1990), superseded by statute on unrelated grounds, (statements to executive search agent by president of company that former employee was or might be a homosexual were not actionable tortious interference).

3. ***Marital Status.*** The Florida Civil Rights Act, unlike Title VII, includes a prohibition of discrimination on the basis of marital status. Fla. Stat. Chapter 760. So does the Florida Educational Equity Act, Section 1000.05(2), Florida Statutes. Additionally, some county ordinances in Florida also prohibit discrimination in the workplace on the basis of an individual's marital status. See e.g., Miami -Dade County, [Fla.] Human Rights Ordinance, ch. 11A, art. I, Section 11A-1 (2000); Broward County, Fla., Code of Ordinances, ch. 16 ½, art. I, Section 16 ½-2 (1999). The elements of a claim of marital discrimination are: (1) marital status; (2) performance of employment position in satisfactory manner; and (3) despite such performance, condition or privilege of employment affected by marital status. See Sanders v. Mayor's Jewelers, Inc., 942 F. Supp. 571 (S.D. Fla. 1996). However, the Act states that an employer is not prohibited from taking adverse employment action based upon a valid anti-nepotism policy. Fla. Stat. § 760.10(8)(d) (1999). Section 112.3135 of the Florida Statutes contains a restriction on employment of relatives in the chapter regarding public officers and employees. Recently, the Florida Supreme Court has held that the term "marital status" as used in section 760.10 means the state of being married, single divorced, widowed or separated and does not include the specific identity or actions of an individual's spouse. Donato v. Am. Tel. & Tel. Co., 767 So. 2d 1146 (Fla. 2000) (holding that Florida does not recognize a cause of action for "marital status" discrimination where the basis of the claim rests on the allegedly unlawful discharge of an employee for actions by the employee's spouse). See also Burke-Fowler v. Orange County, 390 F. Supp. 2d 1208 (M.D. Fla. June 30, 2005) (where no protection under Florida law existed for a plaintiff alleging that her termination was based on marital status discrimination because her husband was an inmate).

C. Smoking

Section 386.204 of the Florida Statutes prohibits any person from smoking inside an indoor workplace. Moreover, Section 633.34(6) mandates that a firefighter be a non-user of tobacco for at least one year prior to employment. Indeed, Florida's Constitutional right of privacy does not prohibit a municipality from requiring job applicants to refrain from using tobacco or tobacco products for one year before applying for, and as a condition for being considered for employment, even though the use of tobacco is not related to the job function sought by the applicant. City of N. Miami v. Kurtz, 653 So. 2d 1025 (Fla. 1995) (job applicants could return to smoking after being hired).

D. Blogging

No Florida statutes or cases have yet addressed this relatively novel activity.

VI. RECORDS

Florida's public records law, Chapter 119 of the Florida Statutes, sets forth the basic right of access to all governmentally held records in Florida. Exemptions to the public records law are found throughout the Florida Statutes, but are collected in Florida's Government in the Sunshine Manual and Public Records Law Manual published annually by the First Amendment Foundation (the "Manual"). The law applies to all state agencies and political subdivisions, but does not apply to the legislature. See Locke v. Hawkes, 595 So. 2d 32 (Fla. 1992). E-mail can be considered a public record. In re

Amendments to Rule of Judicial Administration 2.051 – Public Access to Judicial Records, 651 So. 2d 1185 (Fla. 1995). The general rule regarding personnel records of government employees is the same as for other public records: "unless the Legislature has expressly exempted an agency's personnel records from disclosure of authorized the agency to adopt rules limited access to such records, personnel records are subject to public inspection." Manual, 1997 Edition, p.88, see also Michel v. Douglas, 464 So. 2d 545 (Fla. 1985). There is no Florida statute providing for the giving of notice to individuals when information is collected about them in public records or to be discussed in public meetings. It has been held that public employers must provide their employees with the opportunity for a post-termination name clearing hearing when "stigmatizing" information is made part of the public records. See Buxton v. City of Plant City, Fla., 871 F.2d 1037 (11th Cir. 1989). One court has also held the public employer has an obligation to notify the discharged employee of the right to the name clearing hearing. See Garcia v. Walder Elecs., Inc., 563 So. 2d 723 (Fla. 3d DCA 1990), rev. den., 576 So. 2d 287 (Fla. 1990).

There are no statutory remedies against the government for unauthorized disclosures. There is no duty on a public agency to exclude from personnel records private information unrelated to the employee's job, and there is no cause of action by a public employee against a public employer which fails to do so. See Michel, 464 So. 2d at 545. An example of a statutory protection is Section 231.291(3)(a)3 of the Florida Statutes, which states that derogatory information about a public school employee may not be inspected until ten days after notice to the employee. But see Dade County Sch. Bd. v. Miami Herald, 443 So. 2d 268, 272 (Fla. 3d DCA 1983) (holding that school board's privacy-based reasons for exempting the personnel files of its teachers from public disclosure, deemed inadequate to overcome strong policy in favor of openness).

Public employers are not compelled to allow public access to an employee's personal emails. State v. City of Clearwater, 863 So. 2d at 149 (Fla. 2003). Even though personal emails may be sent from, received on or stored in a government computer system, that personal correspondence is not a matter of public record. One court has held that because the emails are not public records, there is no statutory duty to preserve them. Floeter v. City of Orlando, 2007 WL 486633 (M.D. Fla. 2007). Nondisclosure may not apply, however, to emails that the employee labels as "public."

A. Personnel Records

Court orders compelling discovery, *i.e.*, subpoenas, may impinge on constitutional rights, namely privacy. See Alterra Healthcare Corp. v. Estate of Shelley, 827 So. 2d 936, 941 (Fla. 2002). This is especially so because, "within the litigation process there is great potential for the invasion of privacy." Blood Serv., Inc. v. Rasmussen, 467 So. 2d 798, 790 (Fla. 3rd DCA 1985). For example, in CAC-Ramsay Health Plans, Inc. v. Johnson a former employee filing an employment discrimination suit against his former employer for wrongful termination, requested the wholesale production of files of all black and Hispanic employees as well as of employees discharged during a certain time period. 641 So. 2d 434 (Fla. 3rd DCA 1994). Florida's Third District Court of Appeal held that it was error for the trial court to have granted such a broad discovery request, reasoning that the personnel files contained confidential information of employees that were not even related to the case. Id. at 435.

The court sought to protect the personnel records and the privacy rights of non-party employees by limiting the discovery request to exclude private information such as social security numbers, home addresses, telephone numbers, background investigations, drug test results, and evaluations. Id. See also Thomas v. Smith, 882 So. 2d 1037 (Fla. 2d DCA 2004) (where the court held that taxpayers had an expectation of privacy in their social security numbers), and Seta Corp. of Boca, Inc. v. Attorney Gen., 756 So. 2d 1093 (Fla. 4th DCA 2000) (going so far as to quash completely, not merely limit, the lower court's order for personnel file production). The court ruled that on remand the trial court had to devise a discovery order that ensured the plaintiff would receive the information he was seeking while simultaneously safeguarding the employees' privacy, but was silent on whether the employer could assert the privacy rights of its employees in the first place. CAC-Ramsay Health Plans, Inc., 641 So. 2d at 436.

The Florida Supreme Court, in Alterra Healthcare Corp. v. Estate of Shelley, 827 So. 2d 936, (Fla. 2002), held that a private employer lacks standing to challenge a discovery request by asserting the privacy rights of his employees. In Alterra, the defendant nursing home objected to discovery request seeking employee personnel information on the basis that it violated the employees' constitutional rights to privacy. Id. at 939. The Florida Supreme Court noted that even where a "constitutional right to privacy is implicated, that right is a personal one, inuring solely to individuals." Id. at 941. The Florida Supreme Court recognized that while the employee's privacy rights may have been implicated, it was up to the employees, not the employer, to intervene in the action and claim such right. Id. at 945.

In State Farm Fire and Cas. Co. v. Sosnowski the Fifth District Court of Appeal upheld the lower court's initial protective order granting the parties permission to label certain records "confidential" so as to avoid their disclosure to other parties or witnesses. 830 So. 2d 886 (Fla. 5th DCA 2002). Specifically, the employer had labeled his employee records relating to evaluations "confidential" and the plaintiff was thereby foreclosed from sharing such information with other parties or witnesses. Id. The court upheld the discovery order not because State Farm was asserting the privacy rights of its employees, but because the plaintiff's arguments for setting aside the order were without merit. Id. at 888 n.2.

In Palm Beach Care Assoc., Inc. v. Mufti, 935 So. 2d 122 (Fla. 4th DCA 2006), the Fourth District Court of Appeal held that the trial court departed from the essential requirements of law when it granted former employee's motion to compel former employer to disclose allegedly confidential and patient data. The Court reasoned that the trial court failed to consider the former employer's objections to discovery which were based on privacy and privilege concerns.

B. Medical Records

Florida Statutes, Section 440.125 (1999), states that medical records of injured employees are not open to the public. However, where an employee is seeking workers compensation benefits for an injury allegedly sustained while on the job, there is no reasonable expectation of privacy in medical records as they relate to the treating physician, the employer, and its insurance carrier. See S & A Plumbing v. Kimes, 756 So. 2d 1037 (Fla. 1st DCA 2000); Nelson v. Labor Finders, Inc., 897 So. 2d 501 (Fla. 1st DCA 2005) (allowing review of medical records when employer raised fraud defense to workers' compensation claim); but see, Reed v. Georgia-Pacific Corp., 2006 WL 166534 *2 (M.D. Fla. 2006) (finding that the employer invaded Plaintiff's privacy when it entered the examining room during a medical examination against Plaintiff's will). Even in litigation relating to medical records, it has been held that a person's medical records implicate the right of privacy under Florida's constitution. McEnany v. Ryan, 44 So. 3d 245 (Fla. 4th DCA 2010).

C. Criminal Records

One Florida decision discussing an employer's investigation of the criminal background of a prospective employee found the employer not liable for negligent hiring or supervision where the employer could not legally obtain recorded information on previous arrests not resulting in convictions. Metro. Dade County v. Martino, 710 So. 2d 20, 21 (Fla. 3d DCA 1998).

D. Subpoenas / Search Warrants

If a third-party requests the inspection of the employer's records concerning an employee, then the employer can assert his own constitutional right to privacy. In such an instance, the inspection of employer records could only take place pursuant to a warrant or a subpoena. See Brock v. Emerson Elec. Co., 834 F. 2d 994 (11th Cir. 1987). In Brock, the Eleventh Circuit held that while the Occupational Safety and Health Act agency has a right to conduct reasonable inspections of an employer's documents, "it must delimit the confines of a search by designating the needed documents in a formal subpoena." Id. at 997. Furthermore, the Eleventh Circuit stated that the subpoenaed party had the right to obtain judicial review of the reasonableness of the demand prior to suffering penalties for refusing to comply. Id.

Florida has another statute, Fla. Stat. Section 240.253 (1993), to address the rights of university employees within the State of Florida. Fla. Stat. Section 240.253 states that these records are exempt from the provisions of Fla. Stat. Section 119.07(1), *i.e.*, Florida's public records law, and information contained in such records can only be released upon employee's written authorization or upon court order. A federal district court, having the occasion to address a document request for university employee records, ruled that while the Florida Statutes did not provide for notice to employees before disclosure, the court would grant such document request only upon notice to employees and upon confidentiality restrictions to be placed upon the records. See Alexander v. Herbert, 150 F.R.D. 690, 694 (M.D. Fla. 1993). The court's reason for doing so was that the court was "sensitive to the privacy concerns expressed by [d]efendants." Id.

VII. ACTIONS SUBSEQUENT TO EMPLOYMENT

A. References

See Section II.A.2 of the Survey of Florida Employment Libel Law dealing specifically with this topic. Additionally, there are no Florida cases or statutes addressing an employer's duty to warn, either by requested references or otherwise, other employers of an employee's negligent behavior or detrimental tendencies.

B. Non-Compete Agreements

In Florida, the validity of non-competition agreements entered into by employers and employees is governed by Florida Statutes Section 542.335 (2004). This statute requires a non-competition agreement to be: (1) reasonable in time; (2) reasonable in the area it covers; (3) reasonable as to the line of business; (4) justified by a legitimate business interest; and (5) not in violation of public policy. Post-employment restrictive covenant agreements continue to be valid if the appropriate facts are present. Environmental Services, Inc. v. Carter, 9 So.3d 1258 (Fla. 5th DCA 2009).

Under Section 542.335(1)(b)(2) of the Florida Statutes, confidential business information is considered a legitimate business interest that can be protected by a non-compete agreement. However, "information that is commonly known in the industry and not unique to the allegedly injured party is not confidential and is not entitled to protection." AutoNation, Inc. v. O'Brien, 347 F. Supp. 2d 1299, 1304 (S.D. Fla. 2004). In AutoNation the employee worked for the employer for a little over a year, during which time he signed two non-compete agreements. Id. at 1302. During that time, employee had access to AutoNation's Best Practices, which was derived from each AutoNation dealership and represents a compilation of the employer's best business strategies and techniques. Id. at 1305. Employee also had access to AutoNation's Peer Performance Reports, which included information regarding gross revenue, operating expenses, inventories, finances, and personnel summaries of AutoNation's dealerships. Id. The court found this information, along with information disclosed at AutoNation's Monthly Operating Review Meetings, and information on AutoNation's Deal Central website to be confidential and proprietary. Id.

The court determined that the evidence demonstrated that the employee was in a position to use the employer's confidential business information in a way that would irreparably harm the employer's business interests. Id. at 1306. The court granted a preliminary injunction against the employee finding that AutoNation established a legitimate business interest in enforcing the employee's non-compete agreement where the employee sought to work with a direct competitor of AutoNation. Id. at 1309.

A court may institute temporary and permanent injunctions, along with any other appropriate and effective remedy, in order to enforce a non-compete agreement. Fla. Stat. § 542.335(1)(j). A court will not fail to grant an injunction to the employer simply because the employer inadvertently predicates its request on the old statute governing non-compete agreements. See Am. Residential Serv. v. Event Tech. Serv., Inc., 715 So. 2d 1048, 1049 (Fla. 3rd DCA 1998) (stating that, if anything, by relying on the old statute the employer held itself to a higher standard that the one prescribed in § 542.335). In addition, a court may award attorney's fees and costs to the prevailing party in an action to enforce the non-compete agreement. Fla. Stat. § 542.335(1)(k). The court will grant an injunction where an employer shows that irreparable injury would result if the non-compete agreement is not enforced. See Fla. Stat. § 542.335(1)(j) (stating that the violation of an enforceable non-compete agreement creates a presumption of irreparable injury). At least one court held that the presumption of irreparable injury where a valid non-compete agreement is breached is a rebuttable presumption, not a conclusive one. Don King Prod. v. Chavez, 717 So. 2d 1094 (Fla. 4th DCA 1998).

Florida courts will not allow an employer to design an "after-the-fact" non-compete agreement by using the theory of threatened misappropriation to enjoin an employee from working for the employer of his or her choice. See Del Monte Fresh Produce Co. v. Dole Food Co., 148 F. Supp. 2d 1326, 1336 (S.D. Fla. 2001). In Del Monte, the employer, who had failed to have the employee sign a non-compete agreement, attempted to enjoin the employee from working for the employer's competitor through a theory of inevitable disclosure. Id. The employer claimed that the employee's work over sixteen years with employer involved confidential information and knowledge that could not be segregated in the employee's mind while he was working for the competitor, even if he intended to do so. Id. The court rejected that theory, stating that Florida had not adopted the threatened misappropriation doctrine, and that competition for business by a competitor is expected from former employees who are not bound by a non-compete agreement. Id. at 1337.

VIII. OTHER ISSUES

A. Statutes of Limitations

A four-year time statute applies to the various privacy torts. See Fla. Stat. § 95.11 (3) (2001) (four-year statute of limitations on most torts). In Putman Berkley Group Inc. v. Dinn, 734 So. 2d 532 (Fla. 4th DCA 1999), the Fourth District Court of Appeals held that the four-year limitations period to commence an action for misappropriation of likeness, under Section 540.08 of the Florida Statutes or common law invasion of privacy, accrues at the moment of first publication due to Florida Statutes Section 770.07 Single Instance or Single Publication Rule.

B. Jurisdiction

C. Worker's Compensation Exclusivity

D. Pleading Requirements

No Florida decision has applied any other special procedures to common law privacy actions.

SURVEY OF GEORGIA EMPLOYMENT LIBEL LAW

Peter C. Canfield, Russell A. Jones, and Melissa H. Alexander
Dow Lohnes PLLC
Six Concourse Parkway
Suite 1800
Atlanta, Georgia 30328
Telephone: (770) 901-8800; Facsimile: (770) 901-8874

(With Developments Reported Through **November 1, 2012**)

GENERAL COMMENTS

Under the Georgia Uniform Rules for Superior and State Courts, the filing of a motion by the defendant does not toll the time for filing an answer." Cato Oil & Grease Co. v. Lewis, 250 Ga. 24, 25, 295 S.E.2d 527, 528 (1982); Smith v. Local Union No. 1863, 260 Ga. App. 683, 684 n.4, 580 S.E.2d 566, 569 n.4 (2003). A defendant who files a motion to dismiss and no answer risks entry of a default judgment. As of July 1, 2009, the filing of a motion to dismiss in a Georgia civil action shall stay discovery for 90 days or until the ruling on such motion, whichever is sooner. If discovery is necessary to address defenses relating to jurisdiction, venue, service or joinder, limited discovery needed to respond to these defenses is permitted. See O.C.G.A. § 9-11-12(j).

SIGNIFICANT DEVELOPMENTS SINCE THE 2012 *SURVEY*

Nothing to report.

I. GENERAL LAW

A. General Employment Law

1. ***At Will Employment.*** There is no cause of action against an employer for discharge of an employee with no definite and certain contract of employment. Balmer v. Elan Corp., 278 Ga. 227, 228, 599 S.E.2d 158 (2004) ("Georgia follows the general rule that employment relationships supported by no consideration other than the performance of duties and the payment of wages are terminable at will by either the employer or the employee, absent a controlling agreement specifying the terms of such employment."); Borden v. Johnson, 196 Ga. App. 288, 290, 395 S.E.2d 628, 630 (1990) (holding that "unless our General Assembly has created a specific exception to O.C.G.A. § 37-7-1, an at-will employee has no viable state remedy in the form of a tort action for 'wrongful' discharge against his or her former employer"). The employer may discharge an at will employee with or without cause and regardless of its motives. Balmer, 278 Ga. at 228, 599 S.E.2d at 160; Troy v. Interfinancial, 171 Ga. App. 763, 320 S.E.2d 872 (1984). See O.C.G.A. § 34-7-1. In Brewer v. Metropolitan Atlanta Rapid Transit Auth., 204 Ga. App. 241, 241, 419 S.E.2d 60, 61 (1992), an employee alleged that the failure of his employer to follow its own rules and procedures violated his rights and that the acts of the employer in disciplining and discharging him damaged his reputation. The court rejected the claim and ruled that "[w]here a plaintiff's employment is terminable at will, the employer, with or without cause and regardless of its motives, may discharge the employee without liability . . . [and that] [d]amage to [plaintiff]'s reputation would be actionable only if it was the result of [his employer]'s non-privileged publication of false words regarding its disciplining of him or the termination of his employment." Id.

B. Elements of Libel Claim

1. ***Basic Elements.*** Libel is defined by statute in Georgia as "a false and malicious defamation of another, expressed in print, writing, pictures, or signs, tending to injure the reputation of the person and expose him to public hatred, contempt, or ridicule." O.C.G.A. § 51-5-1. A libel plaintiff must prove that defendant published the statement by communicating it to a third party. O.C.G.A. § 51-5-3. Slander or oral defamation consists in imputing to another: (1) a crime, (2) a contagious disorder, (3) improper business or professional behavior, or (4) uttering disparaging words from which flow special damages. O.C.G.A. § 51-5-4. A cause of action for libel or slander requires publication to a third party.

2. ***Fault.*** The level of fault to be established depends on plaintiff's public or private status. However, the Georgia courts have not distinguished between the level of fault required to establish a claim for libel concerning issues of public concern and issues of private concern.

a. **Private Figure Plaintiff/Matter of Public Concern.** "[U]nder Georgia law, a plaintiff alleging defamation relating to speech on a matter of public concern bears the burden of proving falsity." Adventure Outdoors, Inc. v. Bloomberg, 552 F.3d 1290, 1298 (11th Cir. 2008) (citing Mathis v. Cannon, 276 Ga. 16, 21, 573 S.E.2d

376, 380 (2002)). A private figure plaintiff need not prove that a defamatory statement was made with actual malice. He or she may recover if the defendant failed to use ordinary care to determine the truth or falsity of the statement. Diamond v. American Family Corp., 186 Ga. App. 681, 683-84, 368 S.E.2d 350, 353 (1988); Triangle Publications v. Chumley, 253 Ga. 179, 181, 317 S.E.2d 534, 536 (1984). There are no cases in Georgia that distinguish between the level of fault required for matters of public concern and matters of private concern, and the standard applied is ordinary care where the plaintiff is a private figure.

For decisions rejecting a plaintiff's public figure status, see Gettner v. Fitzgerald, 297 Ga. App. 258, 677 S.E.2d 149 (2009) (holding that creative director of advertising agency was not public figure in connection with allegedly false reports on his demotion in trade publication; "Although VNU's report may have appealed to its readers' 'morbid or prurient curiosity' about why Gettner was demoted, there is no evidence in the record that the issue . . . could have any substantial ramifications for anyone other than him and his immediate family."); Straw v. Chase Revel, Inc., 813 F.2d 356, 361, 13 Media L. Rep. 2269 (11th Cir. 1987) (publisher of magazine with limited circulation among a small sector of the business community not a public figure); Georgia Soc'y of Plastic Surgeons v. Anderson, 257 Ga. 710, 712, 363 S.E.2d 140, 142, 14 Media L. Rep. 2065, 2067 (1987) (plaintiff specialists held not to be limited purpose public figures because controversy (1) was "primarily a private struggle within the confines of the medical profession"; (2) was "chiefly of interest" to physicians who perform plastic surgery; and (3) had been "manifested, for the most part, . . . [in] publications whose circulation is generally confined to doctors"); Western Broadcasting v. Wright, 182 Ga. App. 359, 360, 356 S.E.2d 53, 54, 14 Media L. Rep. 1286, 1287 (1987) (attorney was not a limited purpose public figure with respect to a broadcast report of his trial since he did not avail himself of any opportunities to present his case to the media and did not make use of whatever notoriety was thrust upon him by the trial to influence a public issue); Sewell v. Eubanks, 181 Ga. App. 545, 546, 352 S.E.2d 802, 803 (1987) (plaintiff candidate for reelection to property association's board not a general or limited purpose public figure despite his position on the board; activity in such a "limited, private organization" held not to constitute a "public controversy").

b. **Private Figure Plaintiff/Matter of Private Concern.** "Malicious" as used in the statutory definition of libel has been interpreted to require statements indicative of common law malice, i.e., statements of a type that are deliberately calculated to injure. Schafer v. Time Inc., 142 F.3d 1361 (11th Cir. 1998), reh'g en banc denied 162 F.3d 1179 (11th Cir. 1998). Such malice may be presumed from the character of the defamatory statement. "Any statement can be malicious in the sense that it is of a type calculated to injure, regardless of how the writer feels toward the subject, if it suggests injurious (or, more plainly, bad) things about the subject to the ordinary reader." Id. See also Straw, 813 F.2d at 362 -63, 13 Media L. Rep. 2269 (common law malice can be inferred); Simon v. Shearson Lehman Bros., Inc., 895 F.2d 1304, 1320 (11th Cir. 1990) (under Georgia law, "common law malice is presumed from the character of the defamatory statement and has nothing to do with the defendant's state of mind"). "A private individual need not prove a defamatory statement was made with actual malice. He or she may recover if the broadcaster failed to use ordinary care to determine the truth or falsity of the statement." Diamond, 186 Ga. App. at 683-84, 368 S.E.2d at 353. "The standard of conduct required of a publisher in such a case 'will be defined by reference to the procedures a reasonable publisher in its position would have employed prior to publishing an item such as the one at issue.'" Gettner, 297 Ga. App. at 265, 677 S.E.2d at 155-56 (quoting Triangle Publications, 253 Ga. at 181, 317 S.E.2d at 536, 10 Media L. Rep. at 2078).

c. **Public Figure Plaintiff/Matter of Public Concern.** Both the Eleventh Circuit and Georgia courts have adopted a three-part test to determine if a plaintiff is a limited purpose public figure. Little v. Breland, 93 F.3d 755, 757 (11th Cir. 1996) (citing Silvester v. American Broadcasting Companies, Inc., 839 F.2d 1491 (11th Cir. 1988)), in which the Eleventh Circuit adopted the test set forth in Waldbaum v. Fairchild Publications, Inc., 627 F.2d 1287 (D.C. Cir. 1980); Mathis, 276 Ga. 16, 573 S.E.2d 376 (adopting Silvester test); Atlanta Humane Society v. Mills, 274 Ga.App. 159, 618 S.E.2d 18 (2005) (same); Atlanta Journal Constitution v. Jewell, 251 Ga. App. 808, 555 S.E.2d 175 (2001) (finding libel plaintiff to be a voluntary limited purpose public figure pursuant to Silvester and Waldbaum). Under this analysis, a court must (1) isolate the public controversy, (2) examine the plaintiff's involvement in the controversy, and (3) determine whether the alleged defamation was germane to the plaintiff's participation in the controversy. Id. When cases arise within the context of a labor dispute, plaintiffs may not avail themselves of Georgia's libel law and its remedies unless they can show that the allegedly libelous material was published with actual malice. Douglas v. Maddox, 233 Ga. App. 744, 505 S.E.2d 43, 136 Lab. Cas. ¶ 58,432 (requiring showing of actual malice in the circulation of flyers by the Teamsters accusing management of violation of the federal labor laws). One may obtain the status of "public figure" by position alone or by commanding a substantial amount of public interest. Williams v. Trust Co. of Georgia, 140 Ga. App. 49, 52, 230 S.E.2d 45, 48 (1976). An issue is of "public concern" if it is "being debated publicly and if it ha[s] foreseeable and substantial ramifications for nonparticipants. . . ." Riddle v. Golden Isle Broadcasting, 275 Ga.App. 701, 705, 621 S.E.2d 822, 826 (2005).

Georgia has recognized as "public figures" artists, athletes, business people, dilettantes, college athletic directors, basketball coaches, college deans, professional boxers, baseball players and professional wrestlers. Id. at 53. See also Jones v. Albany Herald Publishing Co., 290 Ga. App. 126, 658 S.E.2d 876 (2008) (holding public employee indicted for theft to be an involuntary limited purpose public figure); Bollea v. World Championship Wrestling, Inc., 271 Ga. App. 555, 557, 610 S.E.2d 92 (2005) (wrestler Hulk Hogan is a public figure); Atlanta Humane Society, 274 Ga.App. 159, 618 S.E.2d 18 (director of company that provided animal control services for county, who had spoken to media on behalf of company, was limited purpose public figure for purposes of controversy over company's performance of its contract with the county); Mathis, 276 Ga. 16, 573 S.E.2d 376 (corporate executive who helped county government develop a waste project and was involved in a county financial crisis regarding waste deliveries was found to be a limited purpose public figure); Sparks v. Peaster, 260 Ga. App. 232, 581 S.E.2d 579 (2003) (local activist a limited-purpose public figure by reason of his extensive participation in city affairs); Sonnenfeld v. Emory University, No. 1:98-cv-1555 (N.D. Ga. May 24, 2000) (a business school professor, who generated controversy by leaving one university to become dean of another, was a public figure); Blomberg v. Cox Enters., 228 Ga. App. 178, 491 S.E.2d 430 (1997) (Hall of Fame baseball player and his career consulting firm were public figures). In Riddle, 275 Ga.App. 701, 621 S.E.2d 822, the Court of Appeals held that a rapper, who had earned very little income from his music and was working as a banquet server, who had been the subject of only one newspaper article in a local paper, and of whom a rap radio station manager had never heard, was not a general purpose public figure.

To establish actual malice pursuant to the New York Times v. Sullivan, 376 U.S. 254, 84 S. Ct. 710 (1964) standard, there must be a showing by clear and convincing evidence that a false publication was made with a high degree of awareness of its probable falsity. Hemenway v. Blanchard, 163 Ga. App. 668, 672, 294 S.E.2d 603, 606 (1982); Lake Park Post, Inc. v. Farmer, 264 Ga. App. 299, 590 S.E.2d 254 (2004). This standard "is not measured by whether a reasonably prudent man would have published, or would have investigated before publishing. There must be sufficient evidence to permit the conclusion that the defendant in fact entertained serious doubts as to the truth of his publication." Id; see also Atlanta Humane Society, 274 Ga.App. 159 (holding libel defendant was entitled to rely upon television news report without having to investigate the underlying accuracy of the report). Even where a plaintiff produces evidence sufficient to create a fact issue regarding defendants' knowledge of the falsity of the statements, he falls short of the constitutional standard for establishing actual malice by clear and convincing evidence; and if the plaintiff fails to prove actual malice, summary judgment is the proper vehicle for constitutional protection. Smith v. Turner, 764 F. Supp. 632 (N.D. Ga. 1991) (former chairman of county board of tax assessors sued county commissioners over his ouster).

3. ***Falsity.*** Falsity is an essential element of a claim for libel. Savannah News-Press, Inc. v. Harley, 100 Ga. App. 387, 111 S.E.2d 259 (1959) (a petition which fails to allege falsity does not state a claim). Under Georgia law an omission of information from a statement admittedly published, or failure to make a written statement, even though the failure may have disparaged the plaintiff's reputation, cannot serve as the basis for a libel action. See Zielinski v. Clorox Co., 215 Ga. App. 97, 98, 450 S.E.2d 222, 225 (1994) (employer's failure to explain reasons for plaintiff's dismissal not actionable). Truth is recognized as an absolute defense both by state constitution, Ga. Const. 1983, Art. I., Sec. I, Par. VI, and statute, O.C.G.A. § 51-5-6. Substantial accuracy also has been held sufficient. Stange v. Cox Enters., 211 Ga. App. 731, 735, 440 S.E.2d 503, 507 (1994) ("minor factual errors which do not go to 'the substance, the gist, the sting' of the story" are not actionable) (quoting Masson v. New Yorker Magazine, 501 U.S. 496, 517, 111 S. Ct. 2419, 2433 (1991). See also Jaillett v. Georgia Television Co., 238 Ga. App. 885, 520 S.E.2d 721 (1999) (report on air conditioner repair substantially true: "a statement is not considered false unless it would have a different effect on the mind of the viewer from that which the pleaded truth would have produced"). Georgia law puts the burden of proving falsity on the plaintiff. Cox Enters. v. Thrasher, 264 Ga. 235, 442 S.E.2d 740, 22 Media L. Rep. 1799 (1994). Nor is there an obligation to publish the "whole truth." See McDonald v. Few, 270 Ga. App. 671, 672, 607 S.E.2d 265 (2004) ("The failure to include more information or the omission of information from a published statement does not constitute libel, even though it is not the whole truth.").

4. ***Defamatory Statement of Fact.*** A defamatory statement is one that tends to injure the reputation of the person and expose him to public hatred, contempt, or ridicule. O.C.G.A. § 51-5-1. Georgia law does not recognize "name-calling" as a tort. Bekele v. Ryals, 177 Ga. App. 445, 446, 339 S.E.2d 655, 656 (1986) (insulting racial epithets directed at plaintiff not actionable); Gast v. Brittain, 277 Ga. 340, 589 S.E.2d 63 (2003) (statement that plaintiff was "immoral" and did not live his life according to the ideals of the organization not actionable libel); Atlanta Humane Society, 274 Ga.App. 159, 618 S.E.2d 18 (statement that plaintiff was "evil" and not " 'worthy' to lick excrement from shoes" not actionable libel); Sonnenfeld v. Emory University, No. 1:98-cv-1555 (N.D. Ga. May 24, 2000) (holding statements that a professor was a "loner" and "was unwilling to invest in junior colleagues" to be opinions that "do not imply defamatory facts and, therefore, are not actionable"). See also Bennett v. Hendrix, 2009 U.S. App. LEXIS 6992, *37-40 (11th Cir. Mar. 31, 2009) (holding that speech in heat of political campaign may be "'vituperative, abusive and inexact,'" but nonetheless reversing dismissal of libel claim against county sheriff premised on campaign flyer that described plaintiff -- in support of sheriff's political opponent -- as a "convicted criminal" despite fact that charges against plaintiff had been dismissed; the assertion "is sufficiently factual to be susceptible to being proved true or false"); Evans v. The Sandersville Georgian, 296 Ga. App. 666, 669, 675 S.E.2d 574, 578 (2009) (finding that statements in letter to editor that a lawsuit was "frivolous" and "lame" were not defamatory because "'[t]he average reader, construing the statements in the context of the entire article,

would have taken the statements for what they were . . . subjective, hyperbolic opinion that cannot be proved to be true or false.'"); McCall v. Couture, 293 Ga. App. 305, 308, 666 S.E.2d 637 (2008) (holding that referring to treasurer as a "weak link" and stating that he should not be permitted to manage neighborhood association's finances were statements of opinion and not actionable); Bollea, 271 Ga. App. 555, 557, 610 S.E.2d 92 (holding that pre-scripted speech made in the "fictional context" of a pro wrestling telecast not libel because it could not reasonably be interpreted as a factual statement about plaintiff himself, as opposed to plaintiff's fictional wresting character); Bullock v. Jeon, 226 Ga. App. 875, 487 S.E.2d 692 (1997) (holding that the use of invectives a-h, s-o-b, and m-f did not impute a violation of any criminal law: "m-f' . . . is a degrading insult, but it has not been interpreted as an actual accusation that the object of the remark has committed an illegal sexual act . . . . No reasonable person exposed to [defendant's] invective, uttered as a parting shot after he had been ordered off the premises and immediately following an argument unrelated to sex, could have concluded that [defendant] was accusing [plaintiff] of having sexual intercourse with his own mother"); Blomberg, 228 Ga. App. 178, 491 S.E.2d 430, 25 Media L. Rep. 2342 (accusation that plaintiff was a "silver-tongued devil" not actionable); Jaillett v. Georgia Television Co., 238 Ga. App. 885, 520 S.E.2d 721 (1999) (use of the term "rip-off" not defamatory where in context it denoted a "bad deal," not "dishonest or shady practices"); Gordon Document Products, Inc. v. Service Technologies, Inc., 308 Ga. App. 445, 455, 708 S.E.2d 48, 57 (2011) (holding that statement that a company was "trying to beef up the company, so that they could make the books look good and sell it" is not defamatory because such statement is not, in and of itself, "damaging or derogatory.") An employer's use of the term "psycho" in a job reference constituted his own personal opinion about Plaintiff's personality. Pospicil v. The Buying Office, Inc., 71 F. Supp. 2d 1346, 1362 (N.D. Ga. 1999). Although there is no wholesale defamation exemption for anything capable of being labeled an opinion, the Georgia courts have held that the "expression of opinion on matters with respect to which reasonable men might entertain differing opinions is not [defamatory]." Id., citing, Webster v. Wilkins, 217 Ga. App. 194, 195, 456 S.E.2d 699 (1995) (reasonable persons could differ on their opinion of another person's personality, and moreover, cursing and name-calling do not constitute defamation per se). An inspection report that listed deficiencies in a contracted employee's work was held to contain non-actionable opinion. Davis v. Sherwin-Williams Co., 242 Ga. App. 907, 531 S.E.2d 764 (2000). A statement by a former supervisor in front of witnesses that plaintiff, an ex-employee, was not allowed on company property was held not to be defamatory. Lepard v. Robb, 201 Ga. App. 41, 410 S.E.2d 160 (1991). See also Information Sys. and Networks Corp. v. City of Atlanta, 281 F.3d 1220 (11th Cir. 2002) (commissioner's statement that he found plaintiff-vendor's performance to be inadequate is non-actionable opinion that is incapable of being proved false); Hylton v. American Ass'n for Voc. Instructional Materials, 214 Ga. App. 635, 639, 448 S.E.2d 741, 744 (1994) (statements indicating plaintiff had been placed on administrative leave not defamatory); Zielinski, 215 Ga. App. at 98, 450 S.E.2d at 225 ("bald announcement of [plaintiff's] termination carried no defamatory implication"). A posted notice intended for store employees stating that plaintiff "is not allowed in the store" did not support an action for defamation, where such words did not tend to injure plaintiff's reputation or expose her to "public hatred, contempt, or ridicule." Chance v. Munford, Inc., 178 Ga. App. 252, 342 S.E.2d 746 (1986). In Palombi v. Frito-Lay, Inc., 241 Ga. App. 154, 526 S.E.2d 375 (1999), the Court rejected the contention that a supervisor investigating allegations of theft defamed an accused employee by stating "we're going to get to the bottom of this." "By its inherent expression of ignorance of the facts, the phrase does not amount to a statement by the speaker that wrongdoing has occurred." Id. at 155, 526 S.E.2d at 377.

On the other hand, "[a]n opinion can constitute actionable defamation if the opinion can reasonably be interpreted, according to the context of the entire writing in which the opinion appears, to state or imply defamatory facts about the plaintiff that are capable of being proved false." Gast, 277 Ga. 340, 589 S.E.2d 63. For example, a statement that an individual is "greedy and selfish cannot be proved false and is therefore a matter of opinion" and cannot give rise to a slander or libel suit. Holsapple v. Smith, 267 Ga. App. 17, 599 S.E.2d 28, 33 (2004). But a statement that someone "screwed a client" and "intentionally messed things up" could be considered defamatory. Id. at 22 (in Bellemead, LLC v. Stoker, 280 Ga. 635, 631 S.E.2d 693 (2006), the Georgia Supreme Court rejected the test used by the Holsapple court). In Hayes Microcomputer Products, Inc. v. Franza, 268 Ga.App. 340, 601 S.E.2d 824 (2004), the court held it was for the jury to determine whether announcing that employees had been terminated "for cause" and for breaching their fiduciary duties could  be considered defamatory; see also Gettner v. Fitzgerald, 297 Ga. App. 258, 261-62, 677 S.E.2d 149, 154 (2009) (holding that a statement that an employee was demoted for unsatisfactory job performance could be proven false if plaintiff could demonstrate his demotion was "for other entirely different reasons."); Thoroughbred Legends v. Walt Disney Company, 2008 U.S. Dist. LEXIS 19960, *42-43 (N.D. Ga. Feb. 12, 2008) (denying motion to dismiss defamation claim arising out of fictionalized movie regarding famous racehorse, finding that movie's disclaimer, which appeared at end of credits and "passe [d] over the screen very quickly," was insufficient to require dismissal as matter of law); Smith v. Stewart, 291 Ga. App. 86, 660 S.E.2d 822 (2008), cert. denied (2008) (affirming denial of summary judgment in defamation case arising out of novel *The Red Hat Club,* notwithstanding that novel was presented as work of fiction and included various overtly farcical events in plot, because jury should decide whether plaintiff was defamed by disreputable conduct of character in novel whose backstory shared certain similarities with plaintiff's life); Harcrow v. Struhar, 236 Ga. App. 403, 511 S.E.2d 545 (1999)**, cert. denied (2012)** (flyer falsely stating that two neighbors are the "prime suspects" in an animal cruelty case in conjunction with statements implying their guilt is actionable, notwithstanding an attempted disclaimer stating "I'm not saying that they are responsible for this atrocious act."); see also Barnes v. Cumulus Media Partners, 2007 U.S. Dist. LEXIS 83761 (N.D. Ga.

Nov. 13, 2007) (false report that on-air radio personality was "fired" was sufficient to state a claim for defamation given that the pleadings set forth surrounding circumstances involving publicly-known dismissal of a different on-air personality for misconduct and evidence of special damages incurred by defendant); Schiefer v. Dep't. of Homeland Security, 2007 U.S. Dist. LEXIS 52259, *20 (S.D. Ga. July 19, 2007) (finding complaint stated claim for defamation because complaint alleged that circumstances of firing "'indicated much more than the fact of termination'").

5. ***Of and Concerning Plaintiff.*** "The defamatory words must refer to some ascertained or ascertainable person, and that person must be the plaintiff." Ledger-Enquirer Co. v. Brown, 214 Ga. 422, 423, 105 S.E.2d 229, 230 (1958). In Collins v. Creative Loafing, 264 Ga. App. 675, 592 S.E.2d 170 (2003), the plaintiff was a telemarketer who alleged that a caricature accompanying defendant's article was defamatory of her. In rejecting the claim, the court noted that, although both the plaintiff and the caricature "are female and have dark hair, bangs, and glasses," the plaintiff could not, as a matter of law, be considered the subject of the caricature: "The cartoon . . . is a gross exaggeration of the human face; the face has two antennae-like pencils sticking out of its head, four hands holding telephones to unseen ears, and a cigarette hanging out of a gaping mouth." Id. at 678. The caricature was unrecognizable as a real person, much less any particular person, and there was no evidence in the record that anyone associated the caricature with the plaintiff. Id. Similarly, the statements in a newsletter that the management of a resort facility "had received 'various threats' with regard to the serving of liquor, and that 'this harassment was instituted by persons who for their own selfish reasons wish to see Kingwood fail'" are not defamatory. The affidavits of witnesses that they knew the statement referred to plaintiffs were insufficient to create a jury issue, for the court found, "as a matter of law, the newsletter is not defamatory of [plaintiffs]." Fiske v. Stockton, 171 Ga. App. 601, 604, 320 S.E.2d 590, 593 (1984). See also Jaillett v. Georgia Television Co., 238 Ga. App. 885, 520 S.E.2d 721 (1999) (reference to "one man operations," even if disparaging, did not refer to plaintiff). However, in Davis v. Copelan, 215 Ga. App. 754, 763-64, 452 S.E.2d 194, 202 (1994), the court reversed summary judgment where nine of 29 discharged hospital employees brought an action for libel complaining of an editorial in a hospital newsletter characterizing those discharged as "criminals or suspected criminals." See also Southern Co. v. Hamburg, 220 Ga. App. 834, 839, 470 S.E.2d 467 (press release stating company was undertaking investigation into compliance with ethical standards taken together with subsequent press release stating investigation resulted in plaintiff's discharge authorizes jury finding that press releases impugned plaintiff's character), appeal after remand, 233 Ga. App. 135 (1998). Where a publication clearly separates defamatory allegations from the nondefamatory allegations made against the plaintiff, there is no defamation cause of action for the plaintiff. Gast v. Brittain, 277 Ga. 340, 341-42, 589 S.E.2d 63, 64 (2003).

6. ***Publication.*** Before there can be a recovery for libel there must be a publication to any person other than the party libeled. Sigmon v. Womack, 158 Ga. App. 47, 279 S.E.2d 254 (1981). Plaintiff has the burden to prove a publication of the libelous matter. Id. See also Cartwright v. Wilbanks, 247 Ga. App. 187, 541 S.E.2d 393 (2000) (no publication for report placed in teacher's personnel file); Carter v. Hubbard, 224 Ga. App. 375, 377, 480 S.E.2d 382, 384 (1997) (holding that the mere act of sending a letter to third parties who never read or received the letter did not constitute publication); Fly v. Kroger Co., 209 Ga. App. 75, 76, 432 S.E.2d 664, 665 (1993) (no publication where plaintiff "merely speculated that [other] employees had been gossiping about her"); Safety-Kleen Corp. v. Smith, 203 Ga. App. 514, 417 S.E.2d 171 (1992) (plaintiff believed former work colleagues made disparaging comments, but could not establish actual words uttered); Brewer v. MARTA, 204 Ga. App. 241, 419 S.E.2d 60 (1992) (discharge of employee is not in and of itself a defamatory publication); Otteni v. Hitachi America, Ltd., 678 F.2d 146, 147 (11th Cir. 1982) (sending a letter in response to demand for termination pay to former employee's attorney did not constitute publication). If there is no evidence that an allegedly defamatory letter was sent to anyone other than plaintiff himself, there is no publication. Chisolm v. Tippens, 289 Ga. App. 757, 658 S.E.2d 147 (2008).

a. **Intracorporate Communication.** "When the communication is intracorporate, or between members of unincorporated groups or associations, and is heard by one who, because of his/her duty or authority has reason to receive the information, there is no publication of the allegedly slanderous material." Kurtz v. Williams, 188 Ga. App. 14, 15, 371 S.E.2d 878, 880 (1988) (no publication where hospital superintendent advised other hospital officials of note alleging that plaintiff employee was having extramarital affair on the job); see also Stringfield v. IAP World Servs., Inc., No. CV 109-88, 2011 WL 1167133 (S.D. Ga. March 28, 2011) (granting motion for summary judgment in favor of defendant employer where plaintiff alleged claims of libel and slander and where the communication was received by employees with good reason to receive the information as a result of their positions within the company); Yancey v. Clark Atlanta University, 2010 WL1265181 *2-3 (N.D. Ga. 2010) (letter referencing a student doctor's "underdeveloped skills" fell within the intracorporate exception to the definition of publication where the letter was only sent to three members of the university administration). In the context of the termination of a plaintiff's employment, the Georgia Court of Appeals has written that "the relevant question is whether, because of their duty or authority, the persons attending the termination meeting had reason to receive the information disseminated during that meeting." McClesky v. Home Depot, Inc., 272 Ga. App. 469, 472, 612 S.E.2d 617 (2005); see also Scouten v. Amerisave Mortgage Corp., 283 Ga. 72, 656 S.E.2d 820 (2008) ("[N]ot all intracorporate statements come within the [intracorporate privilege] exception, only those statements received by one who because of his duty or authority has reason to receive the information."); Saye v. Deloitte & Touche, 295 Ga. App. 128, 133-34, 670 S.E.2d 818, 823-24 (2008) (rejecting argument that communications between accounting firm and audit client should be treated as "intracorporate communications" for purposes of publication), cert. denied (2009); Perry Golf Course Development v. Housing Authority of Atlanta, 294 Ga. App. 387, 394, 670 S.E.2d 171, 178 (2008) (error to dismiss defamation claim if allegations of complaint can be construed to allege defamatory statements "were made to a party not authorized to receive them"). In most cases applying the rule, intracorporate means among the officers or employees who have a direct duty and authority to know the information. See O'Neal v. Home Town Bank of Villa Rica, 237 Ga. App. 325, 334, 514 S.E.2d 669 (1999) ("Typically a handful of management employees have conferred about another employee to determine the course of action to take in response to allegations about the employee's conduct . . . . Application of the rule has never been extended to shareholders of a corporation"). See also Atlanta Multispecialty Surgical Associates, LLC v. DeKalb County Medical Center, 273 Ga. App. 355, 615 S.E.2d 166 (2005) (no publication where director of surgical department prepared flyer summarizing complaints of overcharging and distributed the flyers to those who shared responsibility for the department's programs); Nelson v. Glynn-Brunswick Hospital Authority, 257 Ga. App. 571, 571 S.E.2d 557 (2002) (no publication where lab results about an employee physician that suffered from an infectious disease were communicated between the lab technician, lab director, hospital administrator and other members of the hospital staff); Bates v. Variable Annuity Life Ins. Co., 200 F. Supp.2d 1375 (N.D. Ga. 2002) (no publication where allegedly defamatory e-mail describing reasons for plaintiff's termination was distributed by corporate manager to other corporate managers); Brewer v. Purvis, 816 F. Supp. 1560, 1579 (M.D. Ga. 1993) (no publication where alleged libel was disseminated by defendant school association to superintendent of school board), aff'd without op., 44 F.3d 1008 (11th Cir. 1995) (unpublished); Fly v. Kroger, 209 Ga. App. 75, 77, 432 S.E.2d 664, 666 (1993) (even assuming that defamatory statements had been made about plaintiff, employee's managers and union representative were persons with authority and duty to hear allegations of employee's improper conduct, and thus no publication occurred); Terrell v. Holmes, 226 Ga. App. 341, 487 S.E.2d 6 (1997) (no publication where vice-president for academic affairs of a university was consulted by president of the university regarding the termination of another vice-president); Ekokotu v. Pizza Hut, Inc., 205 Ga. App. 534, 536, 422 S.E.2d 903, 904-05 (1992) (no publication where sexual harassment allegations were revealed only to supervisors who needed to be informed of all factors involved in decision to terminate assistant manager); Lepard v. Robb, 201 Ga. App. 41, 410 S.E.2d 160 (1991) (no publication where supervisor sent employee a letter outlining reasons for employee's termination); Green v. Sun Trust Banks, Inc., 197 Ga. App. 804, 399 S.E.2d 712 (1990) (publication not shown where plaintiff could not specify which defendant used defamatory word and where, in any event, only plaintiff and speaker were present, and where other statements were intracorporate). But see Hayes Microcomputer Products, Inc. v. Franza, 268 Ga. App. 340, 601 S.E.2d 824 (2004) (holding that intracorporate communication privilege did not apply where the communication was made to "every employee with an email address," including employees with whom the plaintiffs had no relationship); Zielinski v. Clorox Co., 215 Ga. App. 97, 98, 450 S.E.2d 222, 225 (1994) (refusing to recognize as "intra-corporate communications" statements made at all-plant meeting to employees without duty or authority to hear about plaintiff's dismissal). Even statements made by non-employees are not "published" if made to a person in authority in the course of an employer's investigation of an employee's job performance. Luckey v. Gioia, 230 Ga. App. 431, 432, 496 S.E.2d 539 (1998) (no publication where doctor made allegation of unprofessional conduct to nurse's direct supervisor despite fact that doctor was independent contractor: "[t]o hold otherwise could impede legitimate inquiries by employers into employee conduct").

In Galardi v. Steele-Inman, 266 Ga. App. 515, 597 S.E.2d 571 (2004), the Court of Appeals held that the intracorporate communications doctrine could apply even where the speaker and the recipient of the message were not part of the same business entity. There, the operator of a beauty pageant made a statement to the promoter of the same pageant that one of the contestants was being disqualified and banned from the contest for allegedly interfering with the pageant voting. Although the operator and promoter were separate business enterprises, the court held that the two organizations "fully undertook together" the pageant and that the relevant communication between representatives of the two organizations was protected under the intracorporate privilege doctrine. Id. at 576.

b. **Compelled Self-Publication.** Georgia has recognized a claim for compelled self-publication only in a limited factual situation. In Colonial Stores v. Barrett, 73 Ga. App. 839, 38 S.E.2d 306 (1946), the employee had a cause of action when he was required by law to present a certificate stating that he had been discharged because of improper conduct. The court noted that the former employer knew that the certificate was required to be presented to the new employer under the requirements of the War Manpower Commission. Absent a legal requirement to publish information, no action for compelled self-publication has been found. Where a plaintiff employee herself informed a prospective employer that her previous employer had terminated her for "misappropriation of funds" there was no claim for libel because the employee libeled herself by her own voluntary actions. Sigmon v. Womack, 158 Ga. App. 47, 279 S.E.2d 254 (1981). Where alleged defamatory statements were published in documents submitted in a worker's compensation hearing, there was no claim for libel because plaintiff had subpoenaed the documents for use in the hearing and the libel was thus invited. Auer v. Black, 163 Ga. App. 787, 294 S.E.2d 616 (1982).

c. **Republication.** Repetition by a person of a libelous charge authored by another is libelous and renders the repeater liable in damages for its publication. Davis v. Macon Tel. Publishing Co., 93 Ga. App. 633, 640, 92 S.E.2d 619, 621 (1956) ("talebearers are as bad as talemakers"); Baskin v. Rogers, 229 Ga. App. 250, 252, 493 S.E.2d 728, 730 (1997) (repetition of slanderous rumor actionable). It is not the law in Georgia that if republication were a natural consequence of publication, then the original publisher would be held liable for damages accruing from republication. Peacock v. Retail Credit Co., 302 F. Supp. 418, 421 (N.D. Ga. 1969), aff'd, 429 F.2d 31 (5th Cir. 1970). Where no special damages are sought, and the original letter by the plaintiff's former employer regarding plaintiff's employment was not actionable, the employer could not be held liable for the republication of the letter in a political advertisement, unless the employer should have foreseen that the letter was intended for the use to which it was subsequently put by plaintiff's political opponent. Hughes v. Rhodes, 111 Ga. App. 389, 392-93, 141 S.E.2d 841, 844 (1965).

In McCandliss v. Cox Enterprises, 265 Ga.App. 377, 593 S.E.2d 856 (2004), the court rejected the argument that, when an article is published on a newspaper's website, the article is "republished" for statute of limitations purposes.

7. ***Statements versus Conduct.*** Georgia does not recognize defamation claims based on conduct or actions that are not expressed in print, writing, pictures, signs, or which are not orally spoken. O.C.G.A. §§ 51-5-1, 51-5-4. In Brewer v. MARTA, 204 Ga. App. 241, 419 S.E.2d 60 (1992), the court found that disciplining and discharging an at-will employee is not, as a matter of law, actionable. Damage to plaintiff's reputation is actionable only if the harm is a result of defendant's nonprivileged publication of false words regarding its disciplining of plaintiff or the termination of employment. There must be publication of defamatory information, and the firing of an individual does not fulfill that requirement. See Brewer, 816 F. Supp. at 1579 (summary judgment granted where plaintiff offered no authority to support allegation that he was defamed by defendant's recommendation that plaintiff be terminated), aff'd without op., 44 F.3d 1008 (unpublished). Where there was a large and prominently displayed sign at the entrance which advised all patrons that the store reserved the right to inspect all packages, and "store greeter" did that and nothing more – although, as viewed by plaintiff, she was neither discreet nor polite – her words and actions, even as interpreted by the plaintiff, amounted to nothing more than: "I'm going to check your boxes, it's my job," and no criminal offense was imputed to the plaintiff. Burrow v. K-Mart Corp., 166 Ga. App. 284, 304 S.E.2d 460 (1983).

8. ***Damages.*** Actual damages are not limited to pecuniary loss or loss of earning power, but include impairment of reputation and standing in the community, hurt feelings and mental distress. See, e.g., Straw v. Chase Revel, Inc., 813 F.2d 356, 360, 13 Media L. Rep. 2269 (11th Cir. 1987) (jury's award of compensatory damages for injury to plaintiff's reputation was supported by evidence that the plaintiff's company had grown slowly after the defamatory article was published and that as a result of the article the plaintiff suffered ridicule from colleagues); Riddle v. Golden Isles Broadcasting, 2008 Ga. App. LEXIS 791 (2008) (reversing trial court's order granting new trial and reinstating verdict of $100,000 where radio personality allegedly said rap musician was wanted for murder, a statement that "constituted slander per se"); Neely v. Strength, 291 Ga. App. 304, 661 S.E.2d 677 (2008) (affirming trial court's award of $500,000 for compensatory damages and $4 million for punitive damages against defaulting owner of radio station where station employee said plaintiff, a county sheriff, was a murderer and that drug dealers had paid for his membership in a country club); Barnes v. O'Connell, 300 Ga. App. 399, 400, 685 S.E.2d 344, 345-46 (2009) (affirming award of $175,000 to coin dealer accused of theft by defendant and rejecting argument that evidence of plaintiff's good reputation at trial refuted the presumption of injury to him). In Esenyie v. UDOFIA, 236 Ga. App. 155, 156, 511 S.E.2d 260, 261 (1999), the court affirmed a $3,000,000 compensatory damages award to plaintiffs accused of criminal acts by their church, noting that the trial court's order recited that "the court was absolutely stricken and impressed with the demeanor of each of the witnesses, the Plaintiffs, in describing what impact the Defendants' slander . . . has had on their lives."

a. **Presumed Damages and Libel Per Se.** Georgia law permits the recovery of presumed damages in cases of slander or libel per se. Floyd v. Atlanta Newspapers, Inc., 102 Ga. App. 840, 841, 117 S.E.2d 906, 908 (1960); Safety-Kleen Corporation v. Smith, 203 Ga. App. 514, 516, 417 S.E.2d 171, 174 (1992). In Stone v. McMichen, 186 Ga. App. 510, 511, 367 S.E.2d 839, 841 (1988), the court reaffirmed that "[a] charge that a person is guilty of a crime is libelous per se and requires no proof of special damages." To be actionable per se, the challenged statement must "charge the commission of a specific crime punishable by law," not just unethical behavior. Parks v. Multimedia Techs. Inc., 239 Ga. App. 282, 293, 520 S.E.2d 517, 527 (1999) (dismissing defamation claim based on allegation that plaintiff was "acting illegally in regards to the corporation that he was an officer and director in" because no proof of special damages); see also Ferman v. Bailey, 2008 Ga. App. LEXIS 766 (June 26, 2008) (statements accusing employee of filing a false police report were slanderous per se); McGee v. Gast, 257 Ga. App. 882, 572 S.E.2d 398 (2002) (statement that a Boy Scout volunteer was seen "committing illegal activities" held not to be slander per se because it did not specify the nature of the alleged crime); **Giles v. Heyward, 315 Ga.App. 409, 726 S.E.2d 434 (2012) (church member's accusations of adultery and theft against a deacon made during a church meeting were slander per se).** "Disparaging terms are slanderous per se only if the terms convey the impression that the crime in question is being charged, and also are couched in such language as might reasonably be expected to convey that meaning to any one who happened to hear the utterance." Lippy v. Benson, 276 Ga. App. 50, 622

S.E.2d 385 (2005) (quoting Bullock v. Jeon, 226 Ga.App. 875, 877, 487 S.E.2d 692 (1997)) (holding that defendant's statements to social worker that neighborhood children were left unsupervised and that father appeared to "enjoy" watching his sons play naked in his front yard failed to sufficiently allege elements of the crimes of cruelty to children, child molestation, child abandonment or reckless conduct and so did not constitute slander per se) (In Bellemead, LLC v. Stoker, 280 Ga. 635, 631 S.E.2d 693 (2006), the Georgia Supreme Court expressly disapproved of the test used by the Lippy court)). Moreover, "vague statements or even derogatory comments do not reach the point of becoming slander per se when a person cannot reasonably conclude from what is said that the comments are imputing a crime to the plaintiff." Taylor v. Calvary Baptist Temple, 279 Ga. App. 71, 74, 630 S.E.2d 604, 607 (2006) (holding that "telling a student to 'be safe,'" that a teacher's termination was "'for a reason,'" and advising students not to attend teacher's SAT prep courses following the teacher's termination "do not lead a reasonable person to consider [plaintiff] a child molester or one who contributes to a minor's delinquency").

In addition, "Statements that tend to injure one in his or her trade, occupation, or business have been held to be libelous per se, and one need not prove special damages in such instances." Southern Co. v. Hamburg, 220 Ga. App. 834, 840, 470 S.E.2d 467 (affirming the denial of a motion for j.n.o.v. and rejecting the argument that a jury award of $543,000 was not supported by evidence), appeal after remand, 233 Ga. App. 135 (1998); Chong v. ReeBaa Construction, 284 Ga. App. 830, 645 S.E.2d 47 (2007) (allegation that defendant published statement that plaintiff was a "liar" and "crook" in connection with construction project for which plaintiff served as general contractor constituted slander per se), rev'd on other grounds, 283 Ga. 222, 657 S.E.2d 826 (2008); Turnage v. Kasper, 307 Ga. App. 172, 184 S.E.2d 842, 854 (2011) (statement describing plaintiff as a "known drug dealer" constitutes slander per se). However, based on Gertz v. Robert Welch, Inc., 418 U.S. 323 (1974), Georgia courts have recognized that as a matter of constitutional law such damages cannot be recovered without clear and convincing evidence of actual malice. Heard v. Neighbor Newspapers, Inc., 193 Ga. App. 719, 389 S.E.2d 267, 268 (1989), ("[a] plaintiff who does not prove knowledge of falsity or reckless disregard for the truth is restricted to compensation for actual injury"); Williams v. Trust Co., 140 Ga. App. 49, 52, 230 S.E.2d 45, 48 (1976) ("states may not permit recovery of presumed or punitive damages . . . when liability is not based on a showing of knowledge of falsity or reckless disregard for the truth"). As yet, no reported Georgia cases have interpreted or applied Dun & Bradstreet, Inc. v. Greenmoss Builders, Inc., 472 U.S. 749 (1985).

(1) **Employment-Related Criticism.** "Statements which tend to injure one in his trade, occupation or business are libelous per se," and special damages need not be proven. John D. Robinson Corp. v. Southern Marine & Indus. Supply Co., 196 Ga. App. 402, 404, 395 S.E.2d 837, 839 (1990) (jury could find libel per se where letters to customers written by business competitor contained statements about plaintiff that were shown by evidence introduced to be false). See also Bellemead, LLC v. Stoker, 280 Ga. 635, 631 S.E.2d 693 (2006) (holding that statements that plaintiff, a developer, "isn't going to be selling lots here in Warner Robbins much longer" and that "he is probably going back to Valdosta," and that the prospective customer should do business with the defendant could not constitute libel per se because they did not, on their face, "cast aspersions on [plaintiff's] reputation because of the particular demands or qualifications of his profession"); Holsapple v. Smith, 267 Ga. App. 17, 599 S.E.2d 28, 33 (2004) (statement that plaintiff "screwed a client" and "intentionally messed things up" could be considered charge against plaintiff in her "trade, office, or profession") (in Bellemead, 280 Ga. 635, 631 S.E.2d 693, as explained below, the Georgia Supreme Court expressly disapproved of the test used by the Holsapple court); Stalvey v. Atlanta Business Chronicle, Inc., 202 Ga. App. 597, 414 S.E.2d 898, 20 Media L. Rep. 1389 (1992) (jury could find when reading the entire article that the statements attacked plaintiff's reputation as a property (apartment) manager). See also Strange v. Henderson, 223 Ga. App. 218, 220, 477 S.E.2d 330, 332 (1996) (holding a false accusation that the owner of rental property failed to insure or pay property taxes on such property could reasonably be construed to refer to one's "trade, profession, or business" and therefore, was actionable per se). Sherwood v. Boshears, 157 Ga. App. 542, 278 S.E.2d 124 (1981); Acrotube, Inc. v. J.K. Fin. Group, Inc., 653 F. Supp. 470 (N.D. Ga. 1987); but see Walker v. Walker, 293 Ga. App. 872, 877, 668 S.E.2d 330, 336 (2008) (affirming dismissal of defamation claim brought by father claiming he was defamed by wife's statements in connection with custody dispute because his pleadings did not allege that the statements were "in reference to his trade, office or occupation" and did not set out special damages). In Barnes v. Cumulus Media Partners, 2007 U.S. Dist. LEXIS 83761 (N.D. Ga. Nov. 13, 2007), the court held that publishing that the plaintiff "was fired" did not constitute slander per se, but that it could, depending on the circumstances, constitute slander per quod.

In Bellemead, 280 Ga. 635, 631 S.E.2d 693 (2006), the Georgia Supreme Court clarified the standard for determining whether a statement can constitute libel or slander per se. The court held that the *only* appropriate inquiry is whether the words at issue are "recognizable as injurious on their face" and "cast aspersions on [a person's] reputation because of the particular demands or qualifications of his profession." Furthermore, the court held that "it is inappropriate to rely on innuendo to determine if the words at issue constitute slander per se." Id. at 638-39, 631 S.E.2d at 696. The court held that the statements at issue could not meet this standard. Id. In so ruling, the court rejected a test previously employed by the Georgia Court of Appeals, under which statements could be considered libelous or slanderous per se if "the statements can reasonably be interpreted as stating or implying defamatory facts about plaintiff and, if so, whether the defamatory assertions are capable of being proved false." Id. (restating and rejecting test previously employed in Lippy, 276 Ga. App. 50, 622 S.E.2d 285; Holsapple, 267 Ga. App. 17, 622 S.E.2d 385; Stoker v. Bellemeade, LLC, 272 Ga.App. 817, 615 S.E.2d 1 (2005)).

(2) **Single Instance Rule.** Language imputing ignorance or a mistake on a single occasion that does not impute general ignorance or lack of skill is not libel per se. Holder Construction Co. v. Ed Smith & Sons, Inc., 124 Ga. App. 89, 182 S.E.2d 919 (1971); Crown Andersen Inc. v. Georgia Gulf Corp., 251 Ga. App. 551, 554 S.E.2d 518 (2001).

b. **Punitive Damages.** Punitive damages "may be awarded only in such tort actions in which it is proven by clear and convincing evidence that the defendant's actions showed willful misconduct, malice, fraud, wantonness, oppression, or that entire want of care which would raise the presumption of conscious indifference to consequences." O.C.G.A. § 51-12-5.1(b). If it is found that defendant's action or inaction was done with specific intent to cause harm, there is no limitation on the amount of punitive damages; otherwise the maximum punitive damage award is $250,000. O.C.G.A. §§ 51-12-5.1(f),(g). The Georgia Supreme Court has adopted "a bright line rule" requiring both a charge on specific intent to cause harm and a separate finding of specific intent to cause harm by the trier of fact in order to avoid the $250,000 cap on punitive damages. McDaniel v. Elliott, 269 Ga. 262, 497 S.E.2d 786 (1998), amended by, 98 Fulton County D. Rep. 1270 (Ga. 1998).

II. PRIVILEGES AND DEFENSES

A. Scope of Privileges

1. ***Absolute Privilege.*** Much of Georgia's law pertaining to absolute privileges has been codified in O.C.G.A. § 51-5-8, which protects publication of all charges, allegations and averments contained in regular pleadings filed in a court of competent jurisdiction. Hightower v. Kendall Co., 225 Ga. App. 71, 72, 483 S.E.2d 294 (1997); Jordan v. Burger King Corp., 124 Ga. App. 652, 185 S.E.2d 577 (1971). To the extent that an employee's claim is based upon his employer's written statement to the Department of Labor, the statements are "absolutely privileged" and cannot serve as "the subject matter or basis for any action for slander or libel in any court of the State of Georgia." Desmond v. Troncalli Mitsubishi, 243 Ga. App. 71, 75-76; 532 S.E.2d 463, 468 (2000). Cooper-Bridges v. Ingle, 268 Ga.App. 73, 601 S.E.2d 445 (2004); Comsouth Teleservices, Inc. v. Liggett, 243 Ga. App. 446, 448, 531 S.E.2d 190, 192 (2000) (statements to Department of Labor are absolutely privileged). Affidavits before a magistrate, made for the purpose of causing an arrest, are absolutely privileged. Watkins v. Laser/Print-Atlanta, Inc., 183 Ga. App. 172, 173, 358 S.E.2d 477, 478 (1987). Documents that are relevant and material to a lawsuit and that are attached to the complaint are absolutely privileged. Compare Garner v. Roberts, 238 Ga. App. 738, 520 S.E.2d 255 (1999) (privilege applied where dentist who sued for nonpayment of bill attached to the complaint a copy of the bill that included an itemized list of dental services rendered and the prices for those services) and Vito v. Paley, 269 Ga. App. 547, 604 S.E.2d 620 (2004) (privilege applied to medical expert's affidavit attached to medical malpractice complaint) with O'Neal v. Home Town Bank of Villa Rica, 237 Ga. App. 325, 334, 514 S.E.2d 669 (1999) (letter sent to shareholders quoting from answer to complaint filed in lawsuit not absolutely privileged because letter is itself not a pleading).

In addition, "[c]ommunications between an employer and the [Department of Labor] regarding a claim for unemployment benefits are 'absolutely privileged and shall not be made the subject matter or basis for any action for slander or libel in any court of the State of Georgia.'" Reid v. City of Albany, 276 Ga. App. 171, 173, 622 S.E.2d 875, 878 (2005). And, in Collins v. Onyx Waste Services of North America, LLC, 2005 U.S. Dist. LEXIS 38258 (M.D. Ga. Dec. 20, 2005), the court applied the absolute privilege of O.C.G.A. § 51-5-8 to statements the employer made to the Equal Employment Opportunity Commission during the investigation of a Title VII charge.

2. ***Qualified Privileges.*** Pursuant to O.C.G.A. § 51-5-7, the following are statutorily recognized qualified privileges: (1) statements made in good faith in the performance of a public duty; (2) statements made in good faith in the performance of a legal or moral private duty; (3) statements made with a good faith intent on the part of the speaker to protect his or her own interest in a matter in which it is concerned; (4) statements made in good faith as part of an act in furtherance of the right of free speech or the right to petition government in connection with an issue of public interest or concern; (5) fair and honest reports of the proceedings of legislative and judicial bodies; (6) fair and honest reports of court proceedings; (7) comments of counsel, fairly made, on the circumstances of that counsel's case, and the conduct of parties in connection therewith; (8) truthful reports of information received from an arresting officer or police authorities; and (9) comments upon the acts of public persons in their public capacity and with reference thereto. O.C.G.A. § 51-5-7(4) was adopted effective April 1, 1996 in conjunction with the passage of an anti-SLAPP (strategic litigation against public participation) statute, O.C.G.A. § 9-11-11.1. A company's letter to key customers informing them of legal action against two former employees who were believed to be soliciting customers was privileged as a measure to protect the company's

interests pursuant to O.C.G.A. § 51-5-7(3). Fine v. Communications Trends, Inc., 305 Ga. App. 298, 699 S.E.2d 623 (2010). The particular privilege under O.C.G.A. § 51-5-7 (3), although primarily applicable to claims of libel and slander, may also be asserted as a defense to a claim of tortious interference with contractual relations. Choice Hotels Int'l, Inc. v. Ocmulgee Fields, Inc., 222 Ga. App. 185, 474 S.E.2d 56, 59 (1996).

a. **Common Interest.** A police report made by a pharmacist regarding stolen pills, which included the results of an internal investigation in implicating an employee and a videotape in which the employee was seen taking painkillers off a shelf, pouring them into her hand, and making a motion toward her mouth was privileged because the report was made "in complete good faith" and in an effort to protect itself from theft. McIntyre v. Eckerd Corp., 2007 U.S. Dist. LEXIS 15806, *9 (N.D. Ga. March 5, 2007), aff'd, 251 Fed. App'x 621 (11th Cir. 2007). A letter sent by a wood-treating company in response to a competitor's advertisement that the company's products posed a health hazard, which letter accurately stated that a district court had issued a preliminary injunction against the competitor from making potentially misleading statements, was privileged because it was sent in good faith, in an attempt to support a legitimate business interest, was properly limited in scope, and was sent to the appropriate persons on a proper occasion. Hickson Corp v. Northern Crossarm Co., 357 F.3d 1256, 1262 (11th Cir. 2004). A report relayed from a lab technician to hospital administrators and employees stating that a hospital physician was suffering from an infectious disease was privileged since it was made with a good faith intent on the part of the hospital to protect its interest in the safety of its patients and its own corporate interests. Nelson v. Glynn-Brunswick Hospital Authority, 257 Ga. App. 571, 571 S.E.2d 557 (2002). An inspection report made by the defendant regarding work done by the plaintiff -- who used defendant's products -- was made with a good faith intent to protect its interest in a matter in which it was concerned. Davis v. Sherwin-Williams Co., 242 Ga. App. 907, 531 S.E.2d 764 (2000). A fax message from corporate headquarters' agent to affiliate shipping agent advising agent of plaintiff's financial status was privileged since the statements were made with a good faith intent on the part of the speaker to protect his interest in a matter in which he was concerned. Kitchen Hardware, Ltd. v. Kuehne & Nagel, Inc., 205 Ga. App. 94, 421 S.E.2d 550 (1992); Moulton v. VC3, 2000 U.S. Dist. LEXIS 19916, *24-25 (N.D. Ga. Nov. 7, 2000) (statement to police chief that "suspicious activity" on a computer network had been detected was privileged); Bates v. Variable Annuity Life Ins. Co., 200 F. Supp. 2d 1375 (N.D. Ga. 2002) (e-mail sent by corporate manager to other corporate managers detailing the reasons for plaintiff's termination was privileged because evidence showed that it was sent in good faith in a effort to uphold the company's legitimate business interests, was properly limited in scope, and was sent on a proper occasion and only to appropriate persons). A letter written by an agent of a condominium association, mailed to the homeowner-lessor of the condominium occupied by plaintiff was made only to one who had reason to receive the information which concerned her rental property and income and her duties and responsibilities to the condominium association and therefore did not constitute publication of the allegedly defamatory matter as required to state a cause of action for libel. Carter v. Willowrun Condominium Ass'n, 179 Ga. App. 257, 345 S.E.2d 924 (1986). Statements made in a letter written in the normal course of business in an effort to resolve a bona fide dispute between two parties concerning their respective rights clearly fall within the purview of O.C.G.A. § 51-5-7 (3). Layfield v. Turner Adv. Co., 181 Ga. App. 824, 354 S.E.2d 14 (1987). In McClesky v. Home Depot, 272 Ga. App. 469, 612 S.E.2d 617 (2005), the employer told a terminated employee's co-worker the reason for the employee's termination: that a background check had revealed that the employee had previously been convicted of several crimes under a previous alias and had failed to reveal that fact on his application. However, that background check later turned out to be erroneous. In finding that the privilege applied, the court held that "statements made in response to inquiries as to another person are deemed privileged when the inquirer is one naturally interested in his welfare." Id. at 473 (quoting Jones v. JC Penny Co., 164 Ga. App. 432, 433 (1982). The court noted that the employee to whom the information had been divulged was a friend of the plaintiff who worked closely with the plaintiff and whose work was affected by plaintiff's absence. The court further noted that the other employee initiated the inquiry about why the plaintiff was not at work and was told of the reasons in a private room and specifically instructed that the information was confidential. Id.

b. **Duty.** Statements made in good faith pursuant to a police investigation of a crime are made in the performance of public duty and therefore privileged. Cleveland v. Greengard, 162 Ga. App. 201, 201-02, 290 S.E.2d 545, 546 (1982). Similarly, internal corporate statements made in the course of an investigation are privileged. See Fisher v. J.C. Penney Co., 135 Ga. App. 913, 219 S.E.2d 626 (1975) (an employee is duty bound to report that a fellow employee had been arrested for shoplifting in one of the employer's stores, and a report thereof is therefore privileged); Meyer v. Ledford, 170 Ga. App. 245, 316 S.E.2d 804 (1984) (where a statement was given at the request of a superior officer in the course of an official investigation concerning improper conduct by a fire department official, it was privileged); Ass'n Services, Inc. v. Smith, 249 Ga. App. 629, 549 S.E.2d 454 (2001) (statements made by private investigator to worker's compensation insurance carrier were privileged); **Smith v. Lott, 730 S.E.2d 663, 669-70, 12 FCDR 2516 (Ga.App. 2012) (city manager's statements to an investigator regarding his concerns and objectives for an internal investigation, including claims of alleged malfeasance on part of plaintiff, were privileged).**

c. **Criticism of Public Employee.** Debate on public issues should be uninhibited, robust, and wide-open and may well include vehement, caustic, and sometimes unpleasantly sharp attacks on government and public officials. Morton v. Stewart, 153 Ga. App. 636, 266 S.E.2d 230 (1980). Lawton v. Georgia Television Co., 216 Ga. App. 768, 456 S.E.2d 274 (1995) (broadcast based on a National Guard report on the investigation of allegations of sexual harassment by an individual officer was within the conditional privileges of O.C.G.A. § 51-5-7); Jessup v. Rush, 271 Ga. App. 243, 609 S.E.2d 178 (2005) (letter questioning wisdom of hiring police officer who had allegedly broken up a family, been involved in a public confrontation with the "jealous husband" and improperly worn his uniform to subsequent court proceedings held privileged).

d. **Limitation on Qualified Privileges.** Unlike the absolute privileges, the qualified privileges are conditional and disappear in the face of malice – either constitutional or common law malice. In Quikrete Cos. v. Schelble, 186 Ga. App. 330, 331, 367 S.E.2d 114, 115 (1988), the court stated that Georgia law allows recovery if the privilege is used as a cloak for the venting of private malice. "Stated another way, good faith and good intentions are necessary and essential ingredients of a conditionally privileged communication." Cohen v. Hartlage, 179 Ga. App. 847, 849, 348 S.E.2d 331, 333 (1986). Pursuant to O.C.G.A. § 51-5-9, "In every case of privileged communications, if a privilege is used merely as a cloak for venting private malice and not bona fide in promotion of the object for which the privilege is granted, the party defamed shall have a right of action." Despite its language, Georgia courts applying O.C.G.A. § 51-5-9, in cases involving both private and public figure plaintiffs, have interpreted the statute using the New York Times Co. v. Sullivan standard of actual malice. Hammer v. Slater, 20 F.3d 1137, 1142 (11th Cir. 1994). Thus, while communications between an accounting firm and its audit client are privileged pursuant to a statutory privilege recognized at O.C.G.A. § 43-3-32, that privilege is not absolute and "turns on the issue of malice." Saye v. Deloitte & Touche, 295 Ga. App. 128, 132, 670 S.E.2d 818, 822 (2008), cert. denied (Ga. Mar. 9, 2009). Unsupported inferences or conjecture regarding a defendant's motivation do not suffice to show the malice required to pierce a qualified privilege, particularly where the defendant did not know the plaintiff prior to the challenged statement. Brewer v. Schacht, 235 Ga. App. 313, 317, 509 S.E.2d 378, 383 (1998).

(1) **Constitutional or Actual Malice.** Georgia courts have held that the privileges set forth in O.C.G.A. § 51-5-7 are vitiated by a showing of actual malice. To establish actual malice there must be a showing by clear and convincing evidence that a false publication was made with a high degree of awareness of its probable falsity. Hemenway v. Blanchard, 163 Ga. App. 668, 672, 294 S.E.2d 603, 606 (1982); Smith v. Turner, 764 F. Supp. 632 (N.D. Ga. 1991). In Hammer, 20 F.3d 1137, 22 Media L. Rep. 2233, the court noted that privilege was conditioned upon a showing of constitutional actual malice, rather than common law malice. See also Nelson v. Glynn-Brunswick Hospital Authority, 257 Ga. App. 571, 571 S.E.2d 557 (2002) (finding no actual malice on the part of defendant hospital authority and its administrators where they released a report stating that a hospital physician was suffering from an infectious disease because the administrators had a good relationship with the physician and did not criticize his abilities); Peeples v. Citizens & Southern Commercial Corp., 209 Ga. App. 157, 433 S.E.2d 319 (1993) (private figure plaintiff must demonstrate actual malice to rebut defendant's prima facie showing of privilege). In Cooper-Bridges v. Ingle, 268 Ga. App. 73, 601 S.E.2d 445 (2004), the plaintiff argued that the defendant's statement to the Department of Labor that plaintiff was fired for being intoxicated on the job was malicious because the defendant did not administer a sobriety test. The court rejected that argument, noting that the judgment that plaintiff was intoxicated was made by several police officers who were experienced in recognizing signs of intoxication. Therefore, plaintiff could not demonstrate that the statement was made with knowledge that it was false or in reckless disregard of whether it was false. See also Evans v. The Sandersville Georgian, 296 Ga. App. 666, 669, 675 S.E.2d 574, 578 (2009) (evidence showing that author of letter to editor "disliked [plaintiff's] family personally or politically . . . does not show actual malice in the *New York Times* sense."); but see Lake Park Post, Inc. v. Farmer, 264 Ga. App. 299, 590 S.E.2d 254 (2004) (finding actual malice existed in case where newspaper called police officer a "murderer" and claimed that he had beaten an unarmed suspect to death with his flashlight, even though the suspect was not resisting arrest, where videotape of the alleged incident – which was available to the defendants – showed that the suspect was resisting arrest and that the flashlight with which the police officer had supposedly beaten the suspect was attached to the police officer's belt during the entire incident).

(2) **Common Law Malice.** In order to prove malice sufficient to forfeit the statutory privilege, it must be shown that the defendant acted willfully, corruptly, or maliciously, and showing of mere negligence is insufficient to create an issue as to defendant's malice. Heard v. Neighbor Newspapers, Inc., 190 Ga. App. 756, 380 S.E.2d 279 (1989), rev'd on other grounds, 259 Ga. 458, 383 S.E.2d 553 (1989). There must be proof of malice and it may not be inferred. Cohen, 179 Ga. App. 847, 348 S.E.2d 331 (malice towards psychology intern could not be inferred from the direct evidence of his supervisor's controversy with colleagues over supervision of the intern).

e. **Question of Fact or Law.** Generally, the question of whether a communication was privileged is a question of fact as it relates to the issue of good faith of defendant. Southern Bus. Machs. of Savannah, Inc. v. Norwest Fin. Leasing, Inc., 194 Ga. App. 253, 390 S.E.2d 402 (1990); Kennedy v. Johnson, 205 Ga. App. 220, 421 S.E.2d 746 (1992). The question of privilege and good faith is generally one for the jury. Sweeney v. Athens Regional Medical Ctr., 709 F. Supp. 1563 (M.D. Ga. 1989); Zielinski v. Clorox Co., 270 Ga. 38, 40, 504 S.E.2d 683, 685 (1998). However, application of privilege is appropriate at summary judgment where plaintiff fails to submit evidence of malice to defeat the privilege. See Rabun v. McCoy, 273 Ga. App. 311, 615 S.E.2d 131 (2005); Morton, 153 Ga. App. 636, 266 S.E.2d 230.

f. **Burden of Proof.** Though the initial burden is on defendant to establish privilege and defendant's good faith, plaintiff's failure to establish evidence of malice will result in the entry of summary judgment. See Meyer, 170 Ga. App. 245, 316 S.E.2d 804 (where plaintiff charged malice, affidavits from each of the individual defendants indicating that they acted properly in the course of their duties and without malice toward plaintiff eliminated any genuine issue of material fact and placed the burden on plaintiff to come forward with showing of malice; where plaintiff failed to make such a showing, summary judgment against her was proper); Rabun, 273 Ga. App. 311, 615 S.E.2d 131 (holding that, where defendant submits actual evidence of lack of malice, plaintiff cannot rebut that showing with mere "conclusory allegations and speculation" but must present evidence sufficient to establish a jury issue). Plaintiff must carry his burden with respect to each statement that is challenged. Bigley v. Mosser, 235 Ga. App. 583, 509 S.E.2d 406 (1998) ("The success or failure of various claims will depend upon whether each particular statement was false and defamatory"). "'Whether a showing of actual malice [necessary to defeat privilege] has been made is an issue to be determined by the trial judge in the first instance, and thus is particularly appropriate for summary resolution.'" Fine v. Communications Trends, Inc., 305 Ga. App. 298, 699 S.E.2d 623 (2010) (internal punctuation omitted; quoting Rabun, 273 Ga. App. at 316, 615 S.E.2d at 138.

B. Standard Libel Defenses

1. ***Truth.*** Truth is recognized as an absolute defense both by state constitution, Ga. Const. 1983, Art. I., Sec. I, Par. VI, and statute, O.C.G.A. § 51-5-6. Substantial accuracy also has been held sufficient. Stange v. Cox Enters., 211 Ga. App. 731, 735, 440 S.E.2d 503, 507 (1994) ("minor factual errors which do not go to 'the substance, the gist, the sting' of the story" are not actionable) (quoting Masson v. New Yorker Magazine, 501 U.S. 496, 517, 111 S. Ct. 2419, 2433 (1991); Bates v. Variable Annuity Life Ins. Co., 200 F. Supp.2d 1375 (N.D. Ga. 2002) (e-mail detailing the reasons for plaintiff's termination was not actionable because the evidence showed that it was truthful); see also Speedway Grading Co. v. Gardner, 206 Ga. App. 439, 441, 425 S.E. 2d 676, 678 (1992) (truth can be proved as justification for statement); Stalvey v. Atlanta Business Chronicle, 202 Ga. App. 597, 414 S.E.2d 898, 20 Media L. Rep. 1389 (1992) (truthfulness of statement is question of fact for the jury). McDonald v. Few, 270 Ga. App. 671, 672, 607 S.E.2d 265 (2004) ("The failure to include more information or the omission of information from a published statement does not constitute libel, even though it is not the whole truth.").

In judging substantial truth, statements "cannot be considered in isolation to determine whether they are true or false." Estate of Richard Jewell v. The Atlanta Journal-Constitution, No. A11A0510, 2011 WL 2697045 (Ga. App. July 13, 2011) (affirming the dismissal of defamation claims premised on reporting about plaintiff's emergence as a suspect in a notorious crime, finding that the challenged statements could not be read as "an accusation . . . that Jewell planted the bomb," but rather would have been understood by a reasonable reader as a that was "preliminary in nature and published during the very early stages of an ongoing investigation").

2. ***Opinion.*** Although Georgia courts have long recognized the constitutionally based opinion privilege announced in Gertz v. Robert Welch, Inc., 418 U.S. 323, 1 Media L. Rep. 1633 (1974), no specific test has become well-established for distinguishing opinion from fact. In Brewer v. Purvis, 816 F. Supp. 1560, 1580 (M.D. Ga. 1993), aff'd without op., 44 F.3d 1008 (11th Cir. 1995) (unpublished), the court relied on Milkovich v. Lorain Journal Co., 497 U.S. 1 (1990), in holding that "some opinions are actionable under the law of defamation." The court interpreted Milkovich as creating a "two-pronged test" to determine whether an opinion was actionable: (1) could a reasonable fact finder conclude that a statement implied a defamatory assertion; and (2) if so, is the assertion "factual enough to be proved true or false." Id. at 1579-80. See also Gast v. Brittain, 277 Ga. 340, 589 S.E.2d 63, 64 (2003) ("An opinion can constitute actionable defamation if the opinion can reasonably be interpreted, according to the context of the entire writing in which the opinion appears, to state or imply defamatory facts about the plaintiff that are capable of being proved false."). The Brewer court concluded that statements by defendant that plaintiff football coach had "fouled up" and that plaintiff "should have known" about improper grade changes made for members of plaintiff's high school football team were potentially actionable. Brewer, 816 F. Supp. at 1580; see also Cassells v. Hill, No. 1:07-CV-2755-TCB, 2010 WL 4616573 (N.D. Ga. Nov. 8, 2010) (allegation that deputy sheriff approved improper overtime payments to subordinates without authorization of sheriff is potentially defamatory). But see Davis v. Sherwin-Williams Co., 242 Ga. App. 907, 531 S.E.2d 764 (2000) (an inspection report that listed deficiencies in work performed by a fired, contracted employee was held to be non-actionable opinion); Hoffmann-Pugh v. Ramsey, 193 F. Supp. 2d 1295 (N.D. Ga. 2002) (defendants' statements about their housekeeper could not support a libel claim as they were not defamatory, as understood by the average reader, and were non-actionable opinion); McCall v. Couture, 293 Ga. App. 305, 308, 666 S.E.2d 637, 640 (2008) (letter to homeowners association board describing board member as a "weak link" was "wholly subjective opinion" and not actionable); Barnes v. Cumulus Media Partners, 2007 U.S. Dist. LEXIS 83761 (N.D. Ga. Nov. 13, 2007) (finding comments by on-air radio show partners stating that former on-air personality was a "retard" and "captain back acne" were merely "hyperbolic and scatological language that is not

actionable"); Barna Log Homes of Georgia, Inc. v. Wischmann, No. A11A0680, 2011 WL 2697314 (Ga. App. July 13, 2011) (statements in email that builder's work was "sloppy" and buyer was "stunned" were based on disclosed facts; statements on website that builder was "grossly overcharging" and "did a poor job on the engineering overview" would not be taken by the reader as anything other than the wholly subjective opinion of one customer). In Jaillett v. Georgia Television Co., 238 Ga. App. 885, 520 S.E.2d 721 (1999), however, the court, citing pre- and post-Milkovich opinions, rejected defamation liability where the bases of an opinion were disclosed: "If an opinion is based on facts already disclosed in the communication, the expression of opinion implies nothing other than the speaker's subjective interpretation of the facts." But see Dominy v. Shumpert, 235 Ga. App. 500, 503, 510 S.E.2d 81, 85 (1998) (allegation that doctor's treatment of patient constituted "mismanagement" and that doctor was "incompetent to practice medicine in any capacity" held to be actionable statements of fact, though conditionally privileged because made in the performance of a public duty: "while undoubtedly [defendant's] professional opinion, [the statements] are also statements of ultimate fact that can be measured by the standard of medical care established [by statute]"); Infinite Energy, Inc. v. Pardue, 310 Ga. App. 355, 713 S.E.2d 456, 464 (2011) ("To the extent that Infinite Energy bases its defamation claim on published statements [contained in the defendant law firm's press release] that it deceived, cheated, and misled its customers by overcharging them, the claim is actionable," because market rates for natural gas are "quantifiable" so the challenged statements are "capable of being proved false.").

3. ***Consent.*** Where a libel is invited, there is no publication and hence no recovery is possible. Sophianopoulos v. McCormick, 192 Ga. App. 583, 584, 385 S.E.2d 682, 683 (1989) (no recovery for negative letters about plaintiff professor sent by chairman of academic department to the American Association of University Professors (AAUP), where plaintiff had requested AAUP assistance and knew request would occasion sending of unfavorable letters). "To constitute an invited libel '[i]t is enough that the complainant requests or consents to the presence of a third party and solicits the publication of matter which he knows or has reasonable cause to suspect will be unfavorable to him.'" Id. (quoting Stone v. Brooks, 253 Ga. 565, 565-66, 322 S.E.2d 728, 729 (1984); Georgia Power Co. v. Busbin, 249 Ga. 180, 289 S.E.2d 514 (1982)). See also Terrell v. Holmes, 226 Ga. App. 341, 487 S.E.2d 6 (1997) (where plaintiff informed employee of the remarks complained of and allowed employee to telephone defendant to intercede on plaintiff's behalf, "[t]he only rational conclusion to be drawn from the evidence is that [plaintiff] invited the publication"); Kenney v. Gilmore, 195 Ga. App. 407, 408, 393 S.E.2d 472, 473 (1990) (no publication where "the only communication of the challenged matter was between . . . a former employer, and . . . the agent of a prospective employer"; moreover, because plaintiff authorized the communication, "the alleged defamation might be deemed to have been 'invited'"). But see Turnage v. Kasper, 307 Ga. App. 172, 184, 704 S.E.2d 842, 854 (2011) (rejecting defense of "invited" libel where evidence did not support assertion that defendant's neighbors spoke to him for purposes of inviting slanderous statements about plaintiff at plaintiff's behest).

4. ***Mitigation.*** Either party to a Georgia libel action alleging libel by a newspaper or other print media may present evidence showing that the plaintiff did or did not make a written retraction demand within seven days prior to the filing of the action. If no written request for retraction was made, or if a written demand was made, timely honored within seven days of receipt and the alleged libelous matter was published without malice, then plaintiff is not entitled to punitive damages, and the defendant may plead the retraction in mitigation of damages. O.C.G.A. § 51-5-11; Stange v. Cox Enters. Inc., 211 Ga. App. 731, 440 S.E.2d 503 (1994). Similarly, a retraction demand timely honored within three days of receipt by a radio or television station may mitigate damages pursuant to O.C.G.A. § 51-5-12.

III. RECURRING FACT PATTERNS

A. Statements in Personnel File

If communicated improperly to a third party without justification or authority, false and defamatory statements in personnel files can be actionable as libel. See Garren v. Southland Corporation, 237 Ga. 484, 228 S.E.2d 870 (1976) (notation in personnel file that plaintiff was "discharged for shortages" held to be libelous); Yandle v. Mitchell Motors, Inc., 199 Ga. App. 211, 404 S.E.2d 313 (1991) (employer's failure to note, in employee's personnel file, illness of employee's child as the reason for poor job performance was held not actionable as libel); ITT Rayonier, Inc. v. McLaney, 204 Ga. App. 762, 765, 420 S.E.2d 610, 613 (1992) (supervisor's crude and profane expression of his opinion that employee's job performance was unsatisfactory did not constitute actionable defamation); Williams v. Cook, 192 Ga. App. 811, 386 S.E.2d 665 (1989) (anonymous letter alleging improper conduct used in the course of personnel deliberations concerning a transfer of plaintiff was not actionable); accord Kurtz v. Williams, 188 Ga. App. 14, 371 S.E.2d 878 (1998); Land v. Delta Airlines, Inc., 147 Ga. App. 738, 250 S.E.2d 188 (1978) (memo in personnel file explaining reasons for disciplinary action was conditionally privileged); Taylor v. St. Joseph Hospital, Inc., 136 Ga. App. 831, 222 S.E.2d 671 (1975) (alleged defamatory information in personnel file relating to unsatisfactory performance was privileged); LuAllen v. Home Mission Board, 125 Ga. App. 456, 188 S.E.2d 138 (1972) (no publication of alleged libelous matter maintained in personnel file); Kramer v. Kroger Co., 243 Ga. App. 883, 887, 534 S.E.2d 446 (2000) (statements in personnel file regarding alleged theft were not published to any third party and were not actionable);Cartwright v. Wilbanks, 247 Ga. App. 187, 541 S.E.2d 393 (2000) (a personnel report written by a supervisor with a duty to write the report is not published by placement in a personnel file);

Smith v. Lott, 730 S.E.2d 663, 669, 12 FCDR 2516 (Ga. App. 2012) (where an employment personnel report is written by a supervisor who has the duty to write the report and it is sent to the keeper of personnel records, there is no publication of that report).

B. Performance Evaluations

Reports prepared by immediate supervisor of employee evaluating her performance and intended for use within corporation are conditionally privileged. Further, there is no publication where the report is circulated only to those whose responsibility it would be to be cognizant of such facts. Land, 147 Ga. App. 738, 250 S.E.2d 188. "The publication of allegedly defamatory information in the course of an employer's investigation of an employee's job performance, when made to persons in authority, is not 'publication' within the meaning of O.C.G.A. § 51-5-1(b)," Kramer, 243 Ga. App. at 887, 534 S.E.2d 446, citing Luckey v. Gioia, 230 Ga. App. 431, 432, 496 S.E.2d 539 (1998); Lepard v. Robb, 201 Ga. App. 41, 410 S.E.2d 160 (1991) (publication of allegedly defamatory information in the course of an employer's investigation of an employee's job performance, when made to persons in authority, is not "publication" within the meaning of the law); Ekokotu v. Pizza Hut, Inc., 205 Ga. App. 534, 422 S.E.2d 903 (1992); Anderberg v. Georgia Electric Membership Corporation, 175 Ga. App. 14, 332 S.E.2d 326 (1985).

C. References

As a general rule, a communication in respect of the character or qualifications of an employee or former employee may be made to any person who has a legitimate interest in the subject matter thereof, such as a prospective employer. Land, 147 Ga. App. 738, 250 S.E.2d 188. See Khattab v. Morehouse School of Medicine, 2009 U.S. Dist. LEXIS 74418 (N.D. Ga. Aug. 20, 2009) (adopting magistrate judge's report and recommendation that where hospital resident was discharged for poor performance, statements made by hospital to other hospitals in which resident sought employment are not actionable unless statements are false); Kitchen Hardware, Ltd. v. Kuehne & Nagel, Inc., 205 Ga. App. 94, 421 S.E.2d 550 (1992) (a fax message from corporate headquarters' agent to affiliate shipping agent advising agent of plaintiff's financial status was privileged since the statements were made with a good faith intent on the part of the speaker to protect his interest in a matter in which he was concerned); Kenney, 195 Ga. App. 407, 393 S.E.2d 472 (where the challenged communication between the plaintiff's former employer and her prospective employer was accurate, and the former employer asserted that he bore no ill will toward the plaintiff, the trial court properly granted summary judgment to the defendant); Sophianopoulos, 192 Ga. App. 583, 385 S.E.2d 682 (where university professor sought assistance of a professional association in resolving a complaint with his superiors, and knew that they would respond with information unfavorable to him, professor's actions were sufficient to constitute an invited libel); Kenney, 195 Ga. App. 407, 393 S.E.2d 472 (where the only communication of allegedly libelous matter was between a former employer and the agent of a prospective employer, and where the former employee had expressly authorized such communication, there was no publication, in the sense contemplated in this statutory scheme); Jordan v. Hancock, 91 Ga. App. 467, 86 S.E.2d 11 (1955) (if reports of merchants made in good faith to each other in reference to the character and conduct of prospective employees are to be regarded as privileged communications, limitations of the rule under which such communications are privileged must be definitely defined; for the right to publish defamatory matters should, in the interest of society, be closely guarded, and the rule under which one claims the privilege to do so strictly construed); but see Lively v. McDaniel, 240 Ga. App. 132, 522 S.E.2d 711 (1999) (statements made by former employer about employee during telephone conversations with prospective were provably false and therefore actionable); Quikrete Cos. v. Schelble, 186 Ga. App. 330, 367 S.E.2d 114 (1988) (evidence created a question of fact with regard to defendant corporation's privilege and its "actual malice" in directing its attorney to forward to plaintiff and plaintiff's employer a letter seeking the return of any confidential commercial information which plaintiff may have taken with him upon his departure from the corporation); cf. McKenna Long Aldridge, LLP v. Keller, 267 Ga. App. 171, 598 S.E.2d 892 (2004) (dismissing plaintiff's claims of negligence, libel, and tortious interference with business relations against former employer's attorneys who sent demand letter to plaintiff's current employer on their client's behalf). Where parties enter into an agreement not to make disparaging statements about each other, the making of such statements, even if true, can constitute breach of the agreement.

D. Intracorporate Communication

In defamation cases involving an employer's disclosure to other employees of the reasons for a plaintiff's discharge, the general rule is that a qualified privilege exists where the disclosure is limited to those employees who have a need to know by virtue of the nature of their duties and other employees who are otherwise directly affected either by the discharged employee's termination or the investigation of the offense leading to termination. Scouten v. Amerisave Mortgage Corp., 283 Ga. 72, 656 S.E.2d 820 (2008) ("[N]ot all intracorporate statements come within the [intracorporate privilege] exception, only those statements received by one who because of his duty or authority has reason to receive the information."); Jones v. J.C. Penney Co., 164 Ga. App. 432, 297 S.E.2d 339 (1982); McClesky v. Home Depot, Inc., 272 Ga. App. 469, 612 S.E.2d 617 (2005) (telling plaintiff's close friend and co-worker of reasons for plaintiff's termination was a privileged communication);

Bates v. Variable Annuity Life Ins. Co., 200 F. Supp. 2d 1375 (N.D. Ga. 2002) (e-mail sent by corporate manager to other corporate managers detailing the reasons for plaintiff's termination was privileged because evidence showed that it was sent in good faith in a effort to uphold the company's legitimate business interests, was properly limited in scope, and was sent on a proper occasion and only to appropriate persons). A statement made by an employee in the course of his employment and concerning a matter directly related to the performance of his job does not constitute a publication sufficient to support an action for defamation. Griggs v. K-Mart Corp., 175 Ga. App., 726, 727, 334 S.E.2d 341, 342 (1985); Nelson v. Glynn-Brunswick Hospital Authority, 257 Ga. App. 571, 571 S.E.2d 557 (2002) (finding no publication and affirming dismissal of libel suit where plaintiff-physician's blood test results were communicated from the lab technician to the lab director, hospital administrator and other members of the hospital staff, including the Executive Committee); Land v. Delta Airlines, 147 Ga. App. 738, 250 S.E.2d 188 (1978) (reports prepared by immediate supervisor of employee evaluating her performance and intended for use within corporation were conditionally privileged); Lepard, 201 Ga. App. 41, 410 S.E.2d 160 (a communication made by one corporate agent to another is not publication in the legal sense). Ekokotu, 205 Ga. App. 534, 422 S.E.2d 903 (sexual harassment allegations during intracorporate investigation not actionable); Williams v. Cook, 192 Ga. App. 811, 386 S.E.2d 665 (1989) (hospital superintendent's disclosure of an anonymous letter regarding the conduct of an employee was privileged, where the letter was privately communicated only to persons who, by reason of their job functions, needed to be informed of all the factors involved in the deliberations concerning the employee's possible transfer); see also Pierre v. Cingular Wireless, 397 F. Supp. 2d 1364 (N.D. Ga. 2005) (rejecting invasion of privacy claim brought by plaintiff whose supervisor had allegedly encouraged another employee to report the employee's marijuana use to the employer's ethics hotline because "the complaint was [not] relayed to anyone outside of management who did not have a need to know" and "all discussions about the complaint [by the employer's management team] were privileged communications made in good faith to enforce [the employer's] policies and protect its interests"). But see Saye v. Deloitte & Touche, 295 Ga. App. 128, 133-34, 670 S.E.2d 818, 823-24 (2008) (rejecting argument that communications between accounting firm and audit client should be treated as "intracorporate communications" for purposes of publication), cert. denied (2009); Perry Golf Course Development v. Housing Authority of Atlanta, 294 Ga. App. 387, 394, 670 S.E.2d 171, 178 (2008) (error to dismiss defamation claim if allegations of complaint can be construed to allege defamatory statements "were made to a party not authorized to receive them"); Hayes Microcomputer Products, Inc. v. Franza, 268 Ga. App. 340, 601 S.E.2d 824 (2004) (holding that intracorporate communication privilege did not apply where communication was made to "every employee with an email address," including employees with whom the plaintiffs had no relationship); Duchess Chenilles, Inc. v. Masters, 84 Ga. App. 822, 67 S.E.2d 600 (1951) (statement alleging theft was made in the presence of police officers and also in the presence of three neighbors of the plaintiff, only one of whom was alleged to be an employee of the defendant). Being an employee or shareholder without more is not enough to support application of the "intracorporate rule." O'Neal v. Home Town Bank of Villa Rica, 237 Ga. App. 325, 334-35, 514 S.E.2d 669, 678 (1999).

In Galardi v. Steele-Inman, 266 Ga. App. 515, 597 S.E.2d 571 (2004), the Court of Appeals held that the intracorporate communications doctrine could apply even where the speaker and the recipient of the message were not part of the same business entity. There, the operator of a beauty pageant made a statement to the promoter of the same pageant that one of the contestants was being disqualified and banned from the contest for allegedly interfering with the pageant voting. Although the operator and promoter were separate business enterprises, the court held that the two organizations "fully undertook together" the pageant and that the relevant communication between representatives of the two organizations was protected under the intracorporate privilege doctrine. Id. at 520.

E. Statements to Government Regulators

Statements to government regulators should be absolutely protected under O.C.G.A. § 51-5-8 where associated with a judicial proceeding. See, e.g., Auer v. Black, 163 Ga. App. 787, 294 S.E.2d 616 (1982) (even if statements were libelous and were published in workers' compensation hearing, they were not actionable inasmuch as the document in which they appeared had been subpoenaed by plaintiff for use in the hearing); Cooper-Bridges v. Ingle, 268 Ga. App. 73, 601 S.E.2d 445 (2004) (statement to Department of Labor privileged). Further the qualified privileges of O.C.G.A. § 51-5-7 may be applicable to such statements.

F. Reports to Auditors and Insurers

Generally, statements to auditors and insurers will be privileged under O.C.G.A. § 51-5-7(3). Haezebrouck v. State Farm Mut. Auto. Inc. Co., 216 Ga. App. 809, 455 S.E.2d 842 (1995) (a report by a medical consultant to an insurance company was privileged since it was made in the performance of the consultant's private duty to the company. Even assuming the report contained libelous matter, such disclosure was not the "publication of libelous matter"); Willis v. United Family Life Ins., 226 Ga. App. 661, 487 S.E.2d 376 (1997) (letters sent by an insurance company to life insurance policy holders containing information which might, if not revealed, cause their coverage to lapse or be canceled, were privileged); but see Saye, 295 Ga. App. at 132, 670 S.E.2d at 822, cert. denied (2009) (letter written by accounting firm to its audit client advocating dismissal of an employee of client was only conditionally privileged and could be actionable if written with malice).

G. Vicarious Liability of Employers for Statements Made by Employees

1. ***Scope of Employment.*** As regards slander, a corporation is not liable for the slanderous utterances of an agent acting within the scope of his employment unless it affirmatively appears that the agent was expressly directed or authorized to slander the plaintiff. Burrow v. K-Mart Corp., 166 Ga. App. 284, 304 S.E.2d 460 (1983); see also B&F Sys., Inc. v. LeBlanc, Civil Action No. 7:07-CV-192(HL), 2011 WL 4103576, at *28 (M.D. Ga. Sept. 14, 2011) (finding that defendant not liable for slander where statements were made by defendants' employees that plaintiff had "gone belly up, was not reputable, and was not paying its bills" and where there was no evidence that defendants directed or authorized the unnamed employees to make the remarks); H&R Block Eastern Enters., Inc. v. Morris, 606 F.3d 1285 (11th Cir. 2010). "The doctrine of respondeat superior does not apply in slander cases, and a corporation is not liable for the slanderous utterances of an agent acting within the scope of his employment, unless it affirmatively appears that the agent was expressly directed or authorized to slander the plaintiff." Kramer v. Kroger Co., 243 Ga. App. 883, 886, 534 S.E.2d 446 (2000); Galardi, 266 Ga. App. at 517, 597 S.E.2d at 574 ("A corporation is not liable for the slanderous utterances of an agent acting within the scope of his employment, unless it affirmatively appears that the agent was expressly directed or authorized to slander the plaintiff. For liability to attach, the corporation must expressly order and direct the agent to say those very words."); Tronitec, Inc. v. Shealy, et al., 249 Ga. App. 442, 547 S.E.2d 749 (2001) (statement accusing former employees of stealing customer lists may be actionable); Anderson v. Housing Auth., 171 Ga. App. 841, 843, 321 S.E.2d 378, 380 (1984); Chambers v. Gap Stores, Inc., 180 Ga. App. 233, 348 S.E.2d 592 (1986); see also Ekokotu v. Pizza Hut, Inc., 205 Ga. App. 534, 422 S.E.2d 903 (1992); Safety-Kleen Corp. v. Smith, 203 Ga. App. 514, 417 S.E.2d 171 (1992); Fuhrman v. EDS Nanston, Inc., 225 Ga. App. 190, 483 S.E.2d 648 (1997). It must be proven that the corporation expressly ordered and directed the officer to say those very words. Gantt v. Patient Communications Sys., Inc., 200 Ga. App. 35, 406 S.E.2d 796 (1991); WMH, Inc. v. Thomas, 260 Ga. 654, 398 S.E.2d 196 (1990); Ray v. American Legion Auxiliary, 224 Ga. App. 565, 567, 481 S.E.2d 266 (1997) ("some authority exists for the proposition that discharge in the wake of alleged slander . . . fails to create an issue of fact regarding corporate ratification of slander"). "As a corporation can act only by or through its agents, and as there can be no agency to slander, it follows that a corporation cannot be guilty of slander; it has not the capacity for committing that wrong." Ray, 224 Ga. App. at 566, 481 S.E.2d at 267. Desmond v. Troncalli Mitsubishi, 243 Ga. App. 71, 75, 532 S.E.2d 463 (2000) (statements to customer that salesperson was fired for stealing were not authorized or ratified and thus not actionable). See also Church of God, Inc. v. Shaw, 194 Ga. App. 694, 695, 391 S.E.2d 666 (1990) (holding that "a corporation lacks the capacity to commit slander"). Just as Georgia law precludes a plaintiff from maintaining a direct action against a corporation for slander, it also bars plaintiff's separately labeled, but wholly derivative claim for respondeat superior. See Sweeney v. Athens Regional Medical Ctr., 709 F. Supp. 1563, 1581 (M.D. Ga. 1989) ("The court agrees that [under Georgia law] the doctrine of respondeat superior does not apply to actions for slander."); Lepard v. Robb, 201 Ga. App. 41, 42, 410 S.E.2d 160, 162 (1991) (ruling that "[t]he doctrine of respondeat superior does not apply in slander cases"). By contrast to slander, the rule regarding libel is that a corporation may commit libel under the usual rules of respondeat superior. Gantt, 200 Ga. App. 35, 406 S.E.2d 796; Kitchen Hardware, Ltd. v. Kuehne & Nagel, Inc., 205 Ga. App. 94, 421 S.E.2d 550 (1992). The principal is liable for the torts of his employee committed while acting within the scope of his employment. Mulherin v. Globe Oil Co., 173 Ga. App. 790, 791, 328 S.E.2d 406, 407-08 (1985); Davis v. Copelan, 215 Ga. App. 754, 764, 452 S.E.2d 194, 202 (1994) (jury issue whether president and CEO of hospital is acting within scope of employment in authoring editorial in hospital newsletter). Accordingly, if the employee is not liable, the employer cannot be vicariously liable. Dominy v. Shumpert, 235 Ga. App. 500, 506, 510 S.E.2d 81, 86 (1998).

a. **Blogging.** No reported cases.

2. ***Damages.*** The principal's liability is derivative of the employee's. Gardner v. Boatright, 216 Ga. App. 755, 756, 455 S.E.2d 847 (1995) (where claim against editor fails for lack of actual malice, derivative claim against corporate publisher also fails). In a libel case, "[e]ven the malicious intent of the employee is imputable to the employer." John D. Robinson Corp. v. Southern Marine & Indus. Supply Co., 196 Ga. App. 402, 405, 395 S.E.2d 837, 840 (1990); Macon Tel. Publishing Co. v. Elliott, 165 Ga. App. 719, 722, 302 S.E.2d 692, 695, 9 Media L. Rep. 2252, 2254 (1983) ("the rule in Georgia in libel is that the malicious conduct of an employee is imputed to the employer provided it is within the scope of his authority").

H. Internal Investigations

A police report made by a pharmacist regarding stolen pills, which included the results of an internal investigation in implicating an employee and a videotape in which the employee was seen taking painkillers off a shelf, pouring them into her hand, and making a motion toward her mouth was privileged because the report was made "in complete good faith" and in an effort to protect itself from theft. McIntyre v. Eckerd Corp., 2007 U.S. Dist. LEXIS 15806, *9 (N.D. Ga. March 5, 2007), aff'd, 251 Fed. Appx. 621 (11th Cir. 2007). In addition, in Pierre v. Cingular Wireless, 397 F. Supp. 2d 1364 (N.D. Ga. 2005), the court rejected an invasion of privacy claim brought by plaintiff whose supervisor had allegedly encouraged another employee to report the employee's marijuana use to the employer's ethics hotline. The court dismissed the claim on the grounds that "the complaint was [not] relayed to anyone outside of management who did not have a need to know" and "all discussions about the complaint [by the employer's management team] were privileged communications made in good faith to enforce [the employer's] policies and protect its interests." See also Doss v. City of Savannah, 290 Ga. App. 670, 676, 660 S.E.2d 457, 462 (2008) (affirming summary judgment on defamation claim based on memos between police chief and city human resources director, on the grounds that the memo "was internal and no evidence exists that it was published outside the City government"); **Smith v. Lott, 730 S.E.2d 663, 669, 12 FCDR 2516 (Ga.App. 2012) (city manager's statements to investigator regarding his concerns and objectives for an internal investigation, including claims of alleged malfeasance on part of plaintiff, were privileged).**

IV. OTHER ACTIONS BASED ON STATEMENTS

A. Negligent Hiring, Retention, and Supervision

A cause of action for negligence against an employer in Georgia may be stated if the employer, in the exercise of reasonable care, should have known of an employee's reputation or propensity to engage in criminal or tortious conduct, the harm resulting from such conduct was foreseeable, and the employee was hired with such knowledge or was continued in their employment. Middlebrooks v. Hillcrest Foods, Inc., 256 F.3d 1241 (11th Cir. 2001) (racial discrimination); H.J. Russell & Co. v. Jones, 250 Ga. App. 28, 550 S.E.2d 450 (2001) (sexual harassment); Coleman v. Housing Authority of Americus, 191 Ga. App. 166, 170, 381 S.E.2d 303 (1989) (reversing summary judgment for employer on claim for negligent hiring and retention of perpetrator of alleged sexual harassment); Cox v. Brazo, 165 Ga. App. 888, 889, 303 S.E.2d 71 (sexual harassment), aff'd, 251 Ga. 491, 307 S.E.2d 474 (1983); Rogers v. Carmike Cinemas, Inc., 211 Ga. App. 427, 439 S.E.2d 663 (1993) (sexual harassment); Pospicil v. The Buying Office, Inc., 71 F. Supp. 2d 1346, 1360-61 (N.D. Ga. 1999) (sexual harassment). The employer is not held to the standard that but for the fact that it hired the offending party, the harm would not have occurred; rather, the employer is liable only if the harm falls within the risk that is foreseeable given the employee's tendencies. Munroe v. Universal Health Servs., Inc., 277 Ga. 861, 596 S.E.2d 604 (2004); Poole v. North Georgia Conference of Methodist Church, Inc., 273 Ga. App. 536, 537, 615 S.E.2d 604 (2005) ("[A]bsent a causal connection between the employee's particular incompetency for the job and the injury sustained by the plaintiff, the defendant employer is not liable to the plaintiff for hiring an employee with that particular incompetency."); but see Govea v. City of Norcross, 271 Ga. App. 36, 49, 608 S.E.2d 677 (2004) (holding that jury could conclude that it was foreseeable that a police officer "with a history of inattentiveness and disregard for safety rules" might give his gun to a teenager). The underlying conduct of the employee must be intentional or reckless. Trimble v. Circuit City Stores, Inc., 220 Ga. App. 498, 501, 469 S.E.2d 776, 779 (1996). The appropriate standard of care in a negligent hiring or retention case is whether the employer knew or should have known that the employee was not suited for the particular employment because of a propensity to commit the acts complained of. **Dehaan v. Urology Center of Columbus, No. 4:12–CV–06 (CDL), 2012 WL 1300554, *3 (M.D. Ga. Apr. 16, 2012) (dismissing plaintiff's claims of negligent hiring and retention where plaintiff failed to allege facts showing that the alleged harasser had a propensity to scream, curse at, or berate his subordinates or that his employer knew or should have known about such propensity)**; Mangrum v. Republic Indus., 260 F. Supp. 2d 1229, 1256 (N.D. Ga. 2003) (granting summary judgment for defendant on negligent retention claim because plaintiff offered no evidence that the alleged harasser had a tendency to sexually harass women at all let alone in the workplace and, therefore, plaintiff failed to show that defendant employer knew or should have known of such tendencies); Heard v. Mitchell's Formal Wear, Inc., 249 Ga. App. 492, 549 S.E.2d 149 (2001) (evidence that employee had thrown things when he was upset and manager's statement that everyone knew that employee "panics and so forth when he is working" insufficient to put employer on notice that employee had violent propensities); Kemp v. Rouse-Atlanta, Inc., 207 Ga. App. 876, 429 S.E.2d 264 (1993) (summary judgment granted to employer of alleged improperly trained security guard because training would not have uncovered latent character defects for purposes of putting the employer on notice of violent propensities); see also Walter Champion Co. v. Dodson, 252 Ga. App. 62, 555 S.E.2d 519 (2001) (employer not liable for negligent retention because even if it knew about employee's prior attempted thefts, that knowledge did not make employee's subsequent act of violence foreseeable). A claim for negligence against an employer is dependent on the viability of the underlying tort. See, e.g., Wynn v. Paragon Sys., 301 F. Supp. 2d 1343, 1355 (S.D. Ga. 2004) (granting summary judgment on negligent retention claim given that the claim was derivative of plaintiff's hostile work environment claim, which was found to be meritless); Eckhardt v. Yerkes Regional Primate Ctr., 254 Ga. App. 38, 561 S.E.2d 164 (2002) (because plaintiffs' wrongful termination claim lacked merit given that Georgia law does not provide a public policy exception for whistleblowing by at-will employees, there was no underlying tort on which to base their claim of negligent retention); Sevcech v. Ingles Markets, Inc., 222 Ga. App. 221, 474 S.E.2d 4 (1996) (claims for slander, intentional infliction of emotional distress and negligence arising from allegations of shoplifting); Brown v. Colonial Stores, Inc., 110 Ga. App. 154, 159, 138 S.E.2d 62, 65 (1964) ("Since no actionable tort was committed [relating to an accusation of insufficient funds] such that the plaintiff might recover from the speaker, he cannot recover against the employer"); **Brathwaite v. Fulton-Dekalb Hosp. Auth., 729 S.E.2d 625, 631, 12 FCDR 2240 (Ga.App. 2012) (affirming summary judgment for defendant where plaintiff's claim for negligent hiring was based on defendant's alleged violation of the Georgia whistleblower statute but plaintiff's alleged whistleblowing complaints were not protected by**

the underlying statute). A plaintiff cannot evade the restrictions of the at-will employment doctrine or the requirements of defamation law merely by attaching a different label to his claim. Brewer v. Metropolitan Atlanta Rapid Transit Auth., 204 Ga. App. 241, 419 S.E.2d 60 (1992). See also Agee v. Huggins, 888 F. Supp. 1573, 1579 (N.D. Ga. 1995) (noting that plaintiff's claim for "breach of duty," libel and slander merely constituted "three separate counts of defamation"); Boyette v. American Int'l Adjustment Co., Inc., 1994 U.S. Dist. LEXIS 4594, 64 Fair Empl. Prac. Cas. (BNA) 675 (N.D. Ga. March 31, 1994) (ruling that "Georgia courts would apply the same rule [barring claims for 'wrongful termination' by at-will employees] to a state tort claim of 'negligent retention or supervision' [related to workplace discipline]"), aff'd without op., 56 F.3d 1391 (11th Cir. 1995).

B. Intentional Infliction of Emotional Distress

In order to prevail on a claim of intentional infliction of emotional distress under Georgia law, a plaintiff must show that (1) the conduct was intentional or reckless; (2) the conduct was extreme and outrageous; (3) there must be a causal connection between the wrongful conduct and the emotional distress; and (4) the emotional distress must be severe. Hendrix v. Phillips, 207 Ga. App. 394, 428 S.E.2d 91 (1993). Where a plaintiff establishes nothing more than isolated instances of conduct which amount simply to tasteless and rude social conduct, the conduct is not actionable. Metropolitan Atlanta Rapid Transit Authority v. Mosley, 280 Ga. App. 486, 634 S.E.2d 466 (2006) (holding crude and inappropriate conduct that lasted for a matter of seconds and was in public and not physically threatening is not actionable as intentional infliction of emotional distress); Perkins-Carrillo v. Systemax, Inc., 2006 U.S. Dist. LEXIS 39894, *64 (N.D. Ga. May 26, 2006) (insensitive and tasteless conduct involving employer phoning another company to verify employee's presence there and stating employee had family emergency, then hanging up the phone when employee picked it up is not sufficiently outrageous "to sustain a claim for intentional infliction of emotional distress"); Kornegay v. Mundy, 190 Ga. App. 433, 379 S.E.2d 14 (1989). "The law is clear that performance evaluations critical of an employee do not fall into the outrageous category even though (i) given in crude and obscene language, (ii) done with a smirk, (iii) conducted in a belittling, rude, and condescending manner to embarrass and humiliate the employee, (iv) given at a poor time, (v) tinged with the intent to retaliate for former conflicts, and (vi) constituting a false accusation of dishonesty or lack of integrity." Jarrard v. United Parcel Service, 242 Ga. App. 58, 60, 529 S.E.2d 144, 147 (2000); Harris v. Equifax, Inc., 2006 U.S. Dist. LEXIS 13499, *38-39 (N.D. Ga. Mar. 23, 2006) (dismissing as a matter of law plaintiff's claim for intentional infliction of emotional distress because plaintiff's stress from being yelled at by his supervisor and his anxiety and severe depression resulting from a change in supervision "is far less egregious than allegations in other cases" where courts have ruled those plaintiffs "could not sustain a IIED [intentional infliction of emotional distress] claim as a matter of law"). Also, "sharp or sloppy business practices, even if in breach of contract, are generally not considered as going beyond all reasonable bounds of decency as to be utterly intolerable in a civilized society." United Parcel Service v. Moore, 238 Ga. App. 376, 378, 519 S.E.2d 15 (1999) (conduct in stopping payment on a check not sufficiently outrageous and extreme to be tortious); see also Miraliakbari v. Pennicooke, 254 Ga. App. 156, 561 S.E.2d 483 (2002) (employer's refusal to allow employee to leave work or even to use the phone to attend to child who had been injured at school was not sufficiently outrageous to support claim). Defamatory or derogatory remarks regarding one's employment generally do not rise to the level of extreme and outrageous conduct required. Nicholson v. Windham, 257 Ga. App. 429, 571 S.E.2d 466 (2002) (asking employee to participate in employer's illegal activity and firing her for her refusal to do so sufficient to state a claim for intentional infliction of emotional distress); Everett v. Goodloe, 268 Ga. App. 536, 602 S.E.2d 284, (2004) (holding that defendant's exposing himself, forcing plaintiff to touch him, lunging at her, and grabbing plaintiff's breasts would normally constitute intentional infliction of emotional distress; however, given the prior relationship between plaintiff and defendant, it was not actionable and summary judgment was properly granted to defendant); Mangrum v. Republic Indus., Inc., 260 F. Supp. 2d 1229, 1256 (N.D. Ga. 2003) (holding that, where supervisor had engaged in a long pattern of sexual harassment, the only conduct that even arguably gave rise to a claim for intentional infliction of emotional distress was when supervisor exposed himself to the plaintiff); Board of Public Safety v. Jordan, 252 Ga. App. 577, 566 S.E.2d 837 (2001) (plaintiff's termination for social, economic, and/or political reasons was not sufficiently outrageous and egregious to constitute intentional infliction of emotional distress); Durley v. APAC, Inc., 236 F.3d 651 (11th Cir. 2000) (sex and disability discrimination was not extreme and outrageous conduct); Hodor v. GTE Mobilnet, Inc., 244 Ga. App. 297, 535 S.E.2d 300 (2000) (statements perceived by plaintiff as racial animus were not extreme and outrageous); Kramer v. Kroger Co., Inc., 243 Ga. App. 883, 888, 534 S.E.2d 446 (2000) (statement that plaintiff "could not be trusted with money" was not outrageous conduct); **Southland Propane, Inc. v. McWhorter, 312 Ga.App. 812, 819, 720 S.E.2d 270, 276-77 (2011) (accusations of misappropriating corporate funds and forgery, terminating plaintiff's employment, and then ordering plaintiff to leave the premises do not constitute extreme and outrageous conduct); Ghodrati v. Stearnes, 314 Ga.App. 321, 323-34, 723 S.E.2d 721, 723 (2012) (co-workers' calling employee by racist and derogatory names and posting inappropriate signs about employee on restroom door as well as in middle of workplace was not sufficiently extreme or outrageous to support a claim for intentional infliction of emotional distress against co-workers and employer);** but cf. Johns v. Ridley, 245 Ga. App. 710, 537 S.E.2d 746 (2000) (13 months of harassment created a jury issue as to outrageousness of the conduct), rev'd on other grounds, 274 Ga. 241, 552 S.E.2d 853 (2001) (ruling that the State Tort Claim Act barred the employee's suit against his supervisor because the Act exempts state officers and employees from liability for any torts committed while acting within the scope of their official duties or employment); **Patterson v. WMW, Inc., Civil Action File No. 1:11–CV–3172–WSD–SSC, 2012 WL 3261290, *12 (N.D. Ga. June 15, 2012) (holding that plaintiff's allegations that she was subjected to humiliating, derogatory, and abusive language throughout her employment, in front of co-workers and customers, because of her sex, satisfied the "extreme and outrageous" element of her intentional infliction of emotional distress claim)**. In addition, an employer is not liable on a claim for intentional infliction of emotional distress for acts of alleged sexual harassment where the alleged acts are not undertaken by the supervisor in furtherance of the employer's business and were outside the scope of the supervisor's employment, unless the employer ratifies the conduct by failing to correct harassment of which it has notice. Travis Pruitt & Assoc. , P.C. v. Hooper, 277 Ga. App. 1, 8, 625 S.E.2d 445, 452 (2005) (holding that employer's investigation of and response to allegation of sexual harassment was not extreme or outrageous conduct that would support a claim against the employer); Mears v. Gulfstream Aerospace Corp., 225 Ga. App. 636, 641, 484 S.E.2d 689 (1997) ("An employer cannot be vicariously liable for an employee's intentional harassment of another employee unless the employer ratifies the conduct."); B.C.B. Co., Inc. v. Troutman, 200 Ga. App. 671, 672, 409 S.E.2d 218 (1991); Favors v. Alco Mfg. Co., 186 Ga. App. 480, 482, 367 S.E.2d 328 (1988); **Cramer v. Bojangles' Restaurants, Inc., Civil Action No. 2:10–CV–0159–RWS–SSC, 2012 WL 716176, *17 (N.D. Ga. Feb. 8, 2012) (granting summary judgment for defendant employer on intentional infliction of emotional distress claim where, as soon as employer was put on notice of alleged sexual misconduct by plaintiff's supervisor, the employer investigated the allegations and terminated the supervisor)**; but see Ferman v. Bailey, 2008 Ga. App. LEXIS 766 (Ga. App. June 26, 2008) (holding that allegations that supervisor sexually assaulted and sexually harassed employee sufficient to support claim for intentional infliction of emotional distress). Similarly, frustration in the workplace resulting from a personality conflict among employees does not give rise to an action for intentional infliction of emotional distress. Id.; Moses v. Prudential Ins. Co. of America, 187 Ga. App. 222, 225, 369 S.E.2d 541 (1988) ("Liability for intentional infliction of emotional distress clearly does not extend to mere insults, indignities, threats, annoyances, petty oppressions or other trivialities"); Borden v. Johnson, 196 Ga. App. 288, 290-91, 395 S.E.2d 628, 630 (1990) (discharge on the basis of pregnancy does not support a claim for intentional infliction of emotional distress). An at-will employee can be terminated with or without cause and without regard to the motives of his employer. See Harris, 2006 U.S. Dist. LEXIS 13499, at *34-35 (N.D. Ga. Mar. 23, 2006) ("Georgia courts consistently hold that employment actions are insufficiently 'extreme' or 'outrageous' to support a claim for intentional infliction of emotional distress"); Phillips v. Pacific & Southern Co., 215 Ga. App. 513, 515, 451 S.E.2d 100 (1994) (claim by reporter who alleged intentional infliction of emotional distress against the television station which fired him because of his contract with a motion picture producer dismissed at summary judgment). See also Phinazee v. Interstate Nationalease, Inc., 237 Ga. App. 39, 514 S.E.2d 843 (1999) (discharge, absent an improper racial motive, will not give rise to a claim for intentional infliction of emotional distress nor will mere insults and indignities). In Peoples v. Guthrie, 199 Ga. App. 119, 404 S.E.2d 442 (1991), the plaintiff was accused in front of other employees of cheating on an examination given at her office. Although the accusation was intentional, it was not intended to harm the plaintiff, and therefore, the court held, plaintiff could not state a claim for intentional infliction of emotional distress. See also Scouten v. Amerisave Mortgage Corp., 284 Ga. App. 242, 244, 643 S.E.2d 759, 761 (2007) (disseminating information that employee had been terminated for theft not intentional infliction of emotional distress), rev'd on other grounds, 283 Ga. 72 (2008); Nelson v. Gwynn-Brunswick Hosp. Auth., 257 Ga. App. 571, 571 S.E.2d 557 (2002) (hospital's dissemination of information that doctor had tested positive for Hepatitis-C not intentional infliction because steps had been taken to protect doctor's privacy and information was only released to a small number of individuals); Hendrix, 207 Ga. App. at 396, 428 S.E.2d at 93 (element of intent lacking when defendant made a written apology and was formally reprimanded for his conduct after cursing plaintiff in a business meeting). In Moses, 187 Ga. App. 222, 225, 369 S.E.2d 541 (1988), the court found that a threat to an insurance salesman to stop soliciting former clients "or you are going to find your butt in court or your neck broken somewhere" did not support a claim for intentional infliction of emotional distress. 187 Ga. App. at 225. A false accusation of dishonesty or lack of integrity in connection with one's employment conduct is not intentional infliction of emotional distress. Peoples, 199 Ga. App. 119, 404 S.E.2d 442. In Bozeman v. Per-Se Technologies, Inc., 456 F. Supp. 2d 1292, 1344-45 (N.D. Ga. 2006), the court found that allegations of "numerous occasions" of "verbal abuse," including job threats and "at least two physical threats" were not sufficient to support an intentional infliction of emotional distress claim. However, activity that might not result in liability for intentional infliction of emotional distress if engaged in on a single occasion might result in such liability if engaged in repeatedly. Cummings v. Walsh Constr. Co., 561 F. Supp. 872, 882 (S.D. Ga. 1983) (repeated solicitations for sex, along with threats of discharge, may be actionable when a single request for sex would not have been). The conduct in question must be directed towards the plaintiff in order to be actionable. Tomczyk v. Rollins, 2009 U.S. Dist. LEXIS 33556 (N.D. Ga. Apr. 20, 2009) (with regard to plaintiff's claim for intentional infliction of emotional distress, excluding any evidence of similar acts allegedly committed by defendant against women other than plaintiff and evidence of defendant's alleged uses of racially offensive language other than in conversations with plaintiff); Wolff v. Middlebrooks, 256 Ga. App. 268 (2002) (defamatory comments made by former employer during a radio broadcast to thousands of listeners, and not directly to former employee, are not actionable as intentional infliction of emotional distress); Potts v. UAP-GA AG Chem., Inc., 256 Ga. App. 153, 567 S.E.2d 316 (2002) (misrepresentation by employer's branch manager to employee's physician cannot support recovery for intentional infliction of emotional distress as it was not directed at plaintiff); Jackson v. Nationwide Credit, Inc., 206 Ga. App. 810, 811, 426 S.E.2d 630 (1992) (upholding summary judgment for defendant when defendant's actions were directed against plaintiffs' employers, not plaintiffs). Plaintiff's burden of proof in an intentional infliction of emotional distress claim is a stringent one; plaintiff must show that the defendant's actions were so terrifying or insulting as naturally to humiliate, embarrass or frighten the plaintiff. Lewis v. Northside Hosp., Inc., 267 Ga. App. 288, 599 S.E.2d 267 (2004) (holding that the shove of a co-worker was not actionable where the severity of harm was small, the offending employee had no degree of control over the plaintiff, and there was no evidence that the employee believed the plaintiff would be especially vulnerable); Sossenko v. Michelin Tire Corp., 172 Ga. App. 771, 772, 324 S.E.2d 593 (1984) (statements and advice by members of his employer's personnel department regarding his job performance not sufficiently egregious to constitute intentional infliction of emotional distress); Farrell v. Time Service, Inc., 178 F. Supp. 2d 1295 (N.D. Ga. 2001) (employee's allegation that she was terminated solely on the basis of her pregnancy does not state a claim for intentional infliction of emotional distress). The alleged emotional distress must be so severe that no reasonable person could be expected to endure it. Mangrum, 260 F. Supp. 2d at 1256; Williams v. Voljavec, 202 Ga. App. 580, 415 S.E.2d 31 (1992); Perkins-Carrillo v. Systemax, Inc., 2006 U.S. Dist. LEXIS 39894, *65 (N.D. Ga. May 26, 2006) (plaintiff's claims of insomnia, anxiety, crying spells, occasional headaches, and "a tightening feeling in her chest" are not symptoms which "no reasonable man could be expected to endure") (internal citations omitted); Soloski v. Adams, 600 F. Supp. 2d 1276, 1322, 1371-72 (N.D. Ga. 2009) (granting summary judgment based on magistrate judge's recommendation that defendant university's decision that plaintiff dean of journalism college committed sexual harassment did not cause plaintiff severe emotional distress, even though plaintiff stated he experienced intense feelings of embarrassment and humiliation); Shaw v. ASB Greenworld, Inc. 2007 U.S. Dist. LEXIS 49249, *16-17 (M.D. Ga. July 9, 2007) (plaintiff's "hurt feelings" were not a severe reaction to conduct plaintiff described as "unpleasant").

A claim for intentional infliction of emotional distress will fail if it is held that the underlying libel claim based on the same facts fails. See Evans v. The Sandersville Georgian, 296 Ga. App. 666, 670, 675 S.E.2d 574, 578 (2009) (holding that because plaintiff failed to prove actual malice with regard to his libel claim based on newspaper's publication of letter to editor urging city council not to rehire plaintiff into police department, plaintiff's claim for intentional infliction of emotional distress must also fail).

C. Interference with Economic Advantage

In order to succeed on a claim for tortious interference with a contractual relationship or business relations, the plaintiff must establish "that by acting improperly and without privilege, purposefully and with malice and the intent to injure, the defendants induced a third party or parties not to enter into or continue a business relationship with the plaintiff that thereby caused financial injury." Taylor v. Calvary Baptist Temple, 279 Ga. App. 71, 72, 630 S.E.2d 604, 606 (2006). Hylton v. American Assoc. For Vocational Instructional Materials, Inc., 214 Ga. App. 635, 638, 448 S.E.2d 741 (1994) (identifying elements as (1) the existence of a contractual relationship; (2) interference with the relationship by one who is a stranger to the contract; and (3) resulting damage to the contractual relationship) (citing St. Mary's Hosp. of Athens v. Radiology Prof. Corp., 205 Ga. App. 121, 124, 421 S.E.2d 731 (1992)). The appellate courts are split on whether an at-will employee cannot sustain an interference with contract claim. Compare Culpepper v. Thompson, 254 Ga. App. 569, 571, 562 S.E.2d 837 (2002) (concluding that at-will employee "had no enforceable contract rights with which to interfere so as to give rise to a breach of contract and damages; thus, since the underlying contract could not be enforced by him as an employment at will, then, the tortious conduct of a third party does not give rise to an action for inducing a breach of the employment contract"), with Gunnells v. Marshburn, 259 Ga. App. 657, 659, 578 S.E.2d 273 (2003) ("[Plaintiff] correctly argues that the fact that employment is at will and that the employer is free from liability for discharging an employee does not carry with it immunity to a third person who, without justification, causes the discharge of the employee."); see also Rose v. Zurowski, 236 Ga. App. 157, 158-59, 511 S.E.2d 265, 267 (1999) (evidence of malice alone was insufficient to show tortious interference where employee divulged truthful information and personal opinions about co-employee's work); Moore v. Barge, 210 Ga. App. 552, 553, 436 S.E.2d 746 (1993). An essential element of tortious interference with business relations is that the alleged tortfeasor used wrongful means to induce a third party or parties not to enter into or continue a business relationship with the plaintiff. Camp v. Eichelkraut, 246 Ga. App. 275, 539 S.E.2d 588 (2000). "Such wrongful means generally involve predatory tactics such as physical violence, fraud or misrepresentation, defamation, use of confidential information, abusive civil suits, and unwarranted criminal prosecutions." American Buildings Co. v. Pascoe Building Sys., Inc., 260 Ga. 346, 349, 392 S.E.2d 860 (1990). Accord Tom's Amusement Company, Inc. v. Total Vending Svs., 243 Ga. App. 294, 296, 533 S.E.2d 413 (2000) (solicitation of competitor's employees to gain confidential information); Hickson Corp. v. Northern Crossarm Co., 357 F.3d 1256, 1262 (11th Cir. 2004) (affirming summary judgment for plaintiff on defendant's counterclaim for tortious interference with contract where plaintiff sent a letter to its customers in response to advertisements by defendant, a competitor of plaintiff, that questioned the safety of plaintiff's products and invited customers to switch to defendant's products). A person whose employment contract is at will has no cause of action for wrongful termination or tortious interference with the contract against one who has an absolute right to terminate that employee or against the employer itself. Ga. Power Co. v. Busbin, 242 Ga. 612, 613, 250 S.E.2d 442 (1978). Accordingly, a claim for tortious interference with a contract may be brought only when the interference is done by one who is a "stranger" to the contract. **Brathwaite v. Fulton-DeKalb Hosp. Authority, 729 S.E.2d 625, 12 FCDR 2240 (Ga.App. 2012) (cause of action existed where plaintiff alleged that her manager, before the manager was hired by defendant employer, solicited and obtained an agreement with the defendant's chief financial officer to terminate plaintiff after the manager was hired)**; Taylor, 279 Ga. App. at 73, 630 S.E.2d at 606 (rejecting claim against school by former teacher for allegedly interfering with teacher's attempts to continue teaching SAT prep course to students following the termination of his employment because the school was not a third party to the relationship between the former teacher and the school's students); Harrick v. National Collegiate Athletic Ass'n, 454 F. Supp. 2d 1255, 1260 (N.D. Ga. 2006) (holding that NCAA was not stranger to contract between college basketball coach and university athletic association, where coach's job responsibilities included compliance with NCAA regulations); Galardi v. Steele-Inman, 266 Ga. App. 515, 521 (2004) ("one must be a stranger to both the contract and the business relationship giving rise to and underpinning the contract"); Moore, 210 Ga. App. at 554. See also Culpepper, 254 Ga. App. 569, 562 S.E.2d 837 (defendant was in a privileged relationship with plaintiff's employer and therefore was not a stranger to the contract; moreover plaintiff's at will employment provides no basis for a claim for tortious interference with contract); Physician Specialists in Anesthesia, P.C. v. MacNeill, 246 Ga. App. 398, 539 S.E.2d 216 (2000) (physician shareholders were not strangers to the patient relationships of the corporation); Johnson v. Rogers, 214 Ga. App. 557, 559, 448 S.E.2d 710, 712 (1994) (no claim for tortious interference where defendants were not "intermeddlers acting both improperly and without privilege"). One is not a "stranger" to the contract just because one is not a party to the contract. Atlanta Mkt. Ctr. Mgmt. Co. v. McLane, 269 Ga. 604, 608, 503 S.E.2d 278 (1998) (listing examples of non-parties to contract that, nonetheless, are not "strangers" to the contract). Where a cause of action for tortious interference relies for proof of injury on asserted conduct which made the performance of the contract more difficult, the plaintiff must nevertheless still prove that the defendant directly and without authority maliciously induced adverse action by a third party with respect to claimant's contractual relationship with the third party. See St. Mary's Hosp. of Athens, Inc., 205 Ga. App. at 123, 421 S.E.2d at 734 (reversing denial of summary judgment for defendant for failure to prove the element of inducement of adverse action by a third party); Sandifer v. Long Investors, Inc., 211 Ga. App. 757, 760, 440 S.E.2d 479 (1994) (affirming summary judgment for defendant based on absence of a genuine issue of material fact regarding direct inducement of action by third party.) In Favors v. Alco Manufacturing Co., et al., 186 Ga. App. 480, 367 S.E.2d 328 (1988), the court held that where a plant manager discharged a female employee following her complaints of sexual harassment by a supervisor and the manager had authority to discharge the plaintiff, there was no claim against the manager for tortious interference with plaintiff's employment contract regardless of the manager's motives. Id. at 484. The privilege found under O.C.G.A. § 51-5-7(3), although primarily applicable to claims of libel and slander, may also be asserted as a defense to a claim of tortious interference with contractual relations. Choice Hotels International, Inc. v. Ocmulgee Fields, Inc., 222 Ga. App. 185, 188, 474 S.E.2d 56, 59; Moulton v. VC3, 2000 U.S. Dist. LEXIS 19916 (N. D. Ga. Nov. 7, 2000).

Furthermore, a plaintiff "must demonstrate that absent the interference, the prospective business relations were reasonably likely to develop." Looney v. M-Squared, Inc., 262 Ga.App. 499, 586 S.E.2d 44 (2003) (quotations and internal alterations omitted); see also Galardi, 266 Ga. App. at 577 (reversing judgment in favor of plaintiff because she failed to show direct evidence that defendants "interfered with her prospective business relations or that they had any contact with any entities which refused to hire" her).

A claim for interference with prospective economic advantage will fail if it is held that the underlying libel claim based on the same facts fails. See Evans v. The Sandersville Georgian, 296 Ga. App. 666, 670, 675 S.E.2d 574, 578 (2009) (holding that because plaintiff failed to prove actual malice with regard to his libel claim based on newspaper's publication of letter to editor urging city council not to rehire plaintiff into police department, plaintiff's claim for interference with prospective economic advantage must also fail).

D. Prima Facie Tort

Prima facie tort has never been recognized by the Georgia courts. Furthermore, the Georgia courts have on several occasions expressly stated that new tort actions will not be judicially created. See, e.g., Deacon v. Deacon, 122 Ga. App. 513, 177 S.E.2d 719, 720 (1970); Mauldin v. Sheffer, 113 Ga. App. 874, 880, 150 S.E.2d 150, 154 (1966) (holding that tort must arise from "either a duty imposed by a valid statutory enactment of the legislature or a duty imposed by a recognized common law principle declared in the reported decisions of the appellate courts of the State"). No decision of the Georgia courts has ever recognized an action for prima facie tort and the legislature has not seen fit to codify any such action. The Georgia Code does, however, provide for recovery of damages upon breach of a recognized legal duty. O.C.G.A. § 51-1-6. The Georgia courts have expressly held that this statute does not create a cause of action, but merely authorizes recovery of damages for a breach of legal duty that is recognized pursuant to statute or common law. City of Buford v. Ward, 212 Ga. App. 752, 755, 443 S.E.2d 279, 283 (1994).

V. OTHER ISSUES

A. Statute of Limitations

Georgia requires that an action for defamation be brought within one year from the date of the alleged defamatory communication. O.C.G.A. § 9-3-33. The one-year statute of limitations runs from the date of publication. Infinite Energy, Inc. v. Pardue, 310 Ga. App. 355, 713 S.E.2d 456, 464 (2011) (holding that complaint alleging slander was timely filed on the first anniversary of the date of publication and overruling Jacobs v. Shaw, 219 Ga. App. 425, 427-28, 465 S.E.2d 460, 463 (1995) and McCandliss v. Cox Enterprises, 265 Ga.App. 377, 593 S.E.2d 856 (2004) to the extent those cases conflict with the court's ruling); Brewer v. Purvis, 816 F. Supp. 1560, 1579 (M.D. Ga. 1993), aff'd without op., 44 F.3d 1008 (11th Cir. 1995) (unpublished); see also Brewer v. Schacht, 235 Ga. App. 313, 316, 509 S.E.2d 378, 382 (1998) (rejecting contention that cause of action did not arise until injury occurred); see also Torrance v. Morris Pub. Group LLC, 281 Ga. App. 563, 566-67, 636 S.E.2d 740, 743 (2006) (holding that one-year statute of limitations for defamation claim against individual who made statement to newspaper reporter began running on date last statement was made – and not on date articles were published – in absence of evidence that the reporter was acting as the individual's agent or servant in subsequent republication of the statements).

A two-year statute of limitations applies to intentional infliction of emotional distress claims, as opposed to the one-year statute of limitations on libel actions. See Henrickson v. Pain Control & Rehabilitation, 205 Ga. App. 843, 424 S.E.2d 27 (1992), rev'd on other grounds, 263 Ga. 331, 434 S.E.2d 51 (1993). The limitations period for a claim of intentional infliction of emotional distress begins to run when the alleged conduct "culminates in damage." Mears v. Gulfstream Aerospace Corp., 225 Ga. App. 636, 639, 484 S.E.2d 659 (1997). Where a claim for intentional infliction of emotional distress is premised on allegedly slanderous statements, the claim is subject to the one-year statute of limitations applicable to claims of defamation. Jahannes v. Mitchell, 220 Ga. App. 102, 469 S.E.2d 255 (1996); Davis v. Hospital Auth., 154 Ga. App. 654, 269 S.E.2d 867 (1980). However, the one-year statute of limitations does not apply to tortious interference with contract claims, "even if the interference allegedly was accomplished through defamation." McCandliss, 265 Ga. App. at 380, 593 S.E.2d at 859.

Georgia recognizes "that an individual has a valuable property right in his employment, trade or profession and that this property right is subject to a four-year statute of limitation;" as such, this limitations period applies to claims asserting tortious interference with employment. Lee v. Gore, 221 Ga. App. 632, 633, 472 S.E.2d 164 (1996). The four-year limitations period applies even where certain libel elements may exist if "the [employment] is the thing legally threatened, and the publication of the words is merely an instrument and incident of this result." Lee, 221 Ga. App. at 634-35 (quoting Dale v. City Plumbing, 112 Ga. App. 723, 728, 146 S.E.2d 349 (1965)); see also Brewer, 235 Ga. App. at 317 (finding that in a claim asserting tortious interference with employment contract, "the one year statute of limitations for defamation actions is inapplicable, even if the interference allegedly was accomplished through defamation"). A defamation plaintiff cannot extend the statute of limitations by belatedly characterizing his "defamation/false light" count as one for "injurious falsehood" to property. Douglas Asphalt Co. v. Qore, Inc., 2009 U.S. Dist. LEXIS 11002, *3 (N.D. Ga. Feb. 13, 2009) (finding plaintiff did not put defendants on notice of injurious falsehood claim and noting that even if Georgia recognized a claim for injurious falsehood, it is not "preordained" that a longer statute of limitations would apply), aff'd in part, rev'd in part, vacated in part, and remanded by Nos. 10-12695, 10-12827, 2011 WL 4357400 (11th Cir. Sept. 20, 2011) (noting that in the absence of Georgia courts' recognition of a cause of action for injurious falsehood, federal courts in the state have been "extremely reluctant" to allow such claims under Georgia law).

B. Jurisdiction

Georgia's long-arm statute permits the assertion of jurisdiction over an individual who (1) transacts any business within this state; (2) commits a tortious act or omission within the state, except "as to a cause of action for defamation of character arising from the act"; or (3) commits a tortious injury in Georgia caused by an act or omission outside of Georgia, if the tortfeasor regularly does or solicits business, or engages in any other persistent course of conduct in the state. O.C.G.A. §§ 9-10-91(1), (2), (3). Georgia courts have interpreted the long-arm statute as allowing a cause of action against a nonresident tortfeasor for defamation of character if the sufficient minimum contacts prescribed by the above provision exist. See Cassells v. Bradlee Management Serv., 161 Ga. App. 325, 327, 291 S.E.2d 48, 50, aff'd, 249 Ga. 614, 292 S.E.2d 717, 8 Media L. Rep. 1968 (1982); Hayes v. Irwin, 541 F. Supp. 397 (N.D. Ga. 1982), aff'd without op., 729 F.2d 1466 (11th Cir. 1984).

When a suit does not arise out of a person's contacts with Georgia, the state may exercise general jurisdiction based on the court's findings regarding factors such as regularly doing business in the state, deriving substantial revenue from goods or services in the state, having agents or employees in the state, maintaining an office in the state, and having subsidiaries or business affiliates in the state. See, e.g., Aero Toy Store v. Grieves, 279 Ga. App. 515, 521, 631 S.E.2d 734 (2006).

C. Worker's Compensation Exclusivity

An employee's rights against an employer to recover on account of any injuries by an accident arising out of and occurring in the course of employment are determinable solely under the Workers' Compensation Act, O.C.G.A. § 34-9-1 et seq. and are not determinable at common law. In other words, the Act is the employee's exclusive remedy. O.C.G.A. § 34-9-11; Mull v. Aetna Cas. & Sur. Co., 226 Ga. 462, 175 S.E.2d 552 (1970); Stebbins v. Georgia Veneer & Package Co., 51 Ga. App. 56, 179 S.E. 649 (1935).

To be compensable under the Act, the injury must consist of a physical injury or harm. See W. W. Fowler Oil Co. v. Hamby, 192 Ga. App. 422, 385 S.E.2d 106 (1989); Hanson Buick v. Chatham, 163 Ga. App. 127, 129, 292 S.E.2d 428 (1982). Thus, claims for intentional infliction of emotional distress, libel and slander, unconnected to any physical injury, do not fall under the Act because such torts cannot be considered physical injuries. See Oliver v. Wal-Mart Stores, 209 Ga. App. 703, 704, 434 S.E.2d 500, 501 (1993).

On the other hand, if an employee brings compensable claims for physical injury as well as related claims for non-physical injury, the claims for non-physical injury still fall within the purview of the Act and the Act remains the employee's exclusive remedy, even if the non-physical claims are not compensable. See Coca-Cola Co. v. Parker, 297 Ga. App. 481, 483, 677 S.E.2d 361, 363 (2008) (holding that Act was exclusive remedy covering plaintiff's claim for physical injury caused by fallen equipment, and plaintiff's claim for mental injury caused by supervisor's subsequent request that employee perform duties exceeding her physical restrictions was precluded by exclusivity provision of Act); Lewis v. Northside Hosp., Inc., 267 Ga. App. 288, 292, 599 S.E.2d 267, 270 (2004) (holding that Act was exclusive remedy covering plaintiff's claim for battery, even though plaintiff did not claim she was physically injured, and plaintiff's ancillary common law claims for mental damages were precluded by Act); Bryant v. Wal-Mart Stores, 203 Ga. App. 770, 771-72, 417 S.E.2d 688, 691 (1992) (holding that Act was exclusive remedy covering decedent's claim for false imprisonment and decedent's related claims for non-physical injuries to his peace, happiness and feelings were precluded by Act even if they were non-compensable under it). Mental injury is compensable under the Act only if it arises naturally and unavoidably from a discernible physical occurrence. See DeKalb County Bd. of Ed. v. Singleton, 294 Ga. App. 96, 99-100, 668 S.E.2d 767, 769-70 (2008).

D. Pleading Requirements

Under Georgia law, with respect to any type of action (not just libel cases), the filing of a motion to dismiss does not toll the time for filing an answer. Cato Oil & Grease Co. v. Lewis, 250 Ga. 24, 25, 295 S.E.2d 527, 528 (1982). Failure to set forth the libel in exact words is an amendable pleading defect. White v. Parks, 93 Ga. 633, 635, 20 S.E. 78 (1894). To succeed on a claim of libel by innuendo, a plaintiff must plead the covert meaning claimed, that the author intended the statements in the publication to be understood as such, and that the statements were so understood by those who read it. See Safety-Kleen Corp. v. Smith, 203 Ga. App. 514, 515, 417 S.E.2d 171 (1992) (a slander claim cannot survive absent "proof of the words actually spoken"); accord Griffin v. Branch, 116 Ga. App. 627, 632, 158 S.E.2d 452, 457 (1967); Jacobs v. Shaw, 219 Ga. App. 425, 427-28, 465 S.E.2d 460, 463 (1995) (dismissing a claim for alleged republication of slander because complaint only identified statements published prior to running of statute of limitation). But see Infinite Energy, Inc. v. Pardue, 310 Ga. App. 355, 713 S.E.2d 456, 464 (2011) (holding that complaint alleging slander was timely filed on the first anniversary of the date of publication and overruling Jacobs v. Shaw, 219 Ga. App. 425, 427-28, 465 S.E.2d 460, 463 (1995) and McCandliss v. Cox Enterprises, 265 Ga.App. 377, 593 S.E.2d 856 (2004) to the extent those cases conflict with the court's ruling).

Effective April 1, 1996, Georgia adopted an anti-SLAPP (strategic litigation against public participation) statute. O.C.G.A. § 9-11-11.1. The statute applies to any action that arises from an act that "could reasonably be construed as an act in furtherance of the right of free speech or the right to petition the government for redress of grievances . . . in connection with an issue of public interest or concern." O.C.G.A. § 9-11-11.1(b). The statute defines such an act to include "any written or oral statement, writing, or petition made in connection with an issue under consideration or review by a legislative, executive, or judicial body, or any other official proceeding authorized by law." O.C.G.A. § 9-11-11.1(c). **See, e.g., Jefferson v. Stripling, 728 S.E.2d 826, 12 FCDR 1952 (Ga. App. 2012) (complaints by opposing parties in estate property distribution dispute to state bar concerning attorney's alleged misconduct were within scope of anti-SLAPP statute).**

The statute requires a "written verification" sworn to by both the party and the attorney filing a complaint in any action covered by the law. O.C.G.A. § 9-11-11.1(b). In the verification, the party and the attorney must swear that after reasonable inquiry they believe (1) the action to be well grounded in fact and existing law or a good faith extension of existing law, (2) that the claim is not interposed for any improper purpose such as to suppress a person's or entity's right of free speech, and (3) that the action is not premised on a statement protected under a newly codified statutory privilege applying to "statements made in good faith as part of an act in furtherance of the right of free speech or the right to petition the government for redress of grievances . . . in connection with an issue of public interest or concern." O.C.G.A § 51-5-7(4).

See Davis v. Emmis Publishing Co., 244 Ga. App. 795, 536 S.E.2d 809 (2000) (failure to verify complaint in compliance with anti-SLAPP statute is an amendable defect, but statute limits time period in which amendment is allowed to ten days after omission is called to plaintiff's attention); Chatham Orthopaedic Surgery Center v. Georgia Alliance Community Hospitals, 262 Ga. App. 353, 358 (2003) (finding that failure to file a verification as required by statute is "a nonamendable defect requiring dismissal of the complaint with prejudice"); but see Land v. Boone, 265 Ga. App. 551, 555, 594 S.E.2d 741, 745 (2004) (dismissal under the statute is not an "adjudication on the merits" and "the suit can be refiled" with proper verification).

The statute authorizes an immediate legal challenge to a verified complaint. A defendant is entitled to move to strike the plaintiff's verification, and the defendant's motion must be heard within thirty days of service barring exigent circumstances. During the pendency of the motion, all discovery is stayed. See generally Providence Constr. Co. v. Bauer, 229 Ga. App. 679, 494 S.E.2d 527 (1997) (affirming dismissal of claim by developer seeking to enforce restrictive covenant prohibiting a development's current residents from opposing developer's rezoning efforts). "If the trial court makes a substantive, evidentiary determination that the verification is false because the claim infringes on the rights of free speech or petition as defined in the statute, then the court may dismiss the claim." Jenkins v. Anderson, 295 Ga. App. 537, 538, 672 S.E.2d 418, 420 (2009). In the event defendant's motion is successful, the law expressly authorizes the court to sanction the party that brought the claim or the party's attorney, or both, by ordering the payment of defendant's attorney's fees. Effective July 1, 1998, O.C.G.A. § 9-11-11.1 was amended to permit the recovery of attorney's fees even in the event a party bringing the SLAPP action dismisses it in response to a motion brought under the statute. See O.C.G.A. § 9-11-11.1(f) (permitting application for attorneys' fees "not later than 45 days after the final disposition"). If the action is found to have violated the anti-SLAPP statute, the entry of a sanction by the trial court is mandatory, not discretionary. Hagemann v. Berkman Wynhaven Associates, 290 Ga. App. 677, 660 S.E.2d 449 (2008) (expressly disapproving of any contrary implication in Walden v. Shelton, 270 Ga. App. 239, 606 S.E.2d 299 (2004)); Metzler v. Rowell, 248 Ga. App. 596, 547 S.E.2d 311 (2001) (affirming dismissal of complaint under O.C.G.A. § 9-11-11.1 and rejecting contention that privilege did not apply to claim for tortious interference with business relations); Denton v. Browns Mill Development Co., 275 Ga. 2, 6, 561 S.E.2d 431 (2002) (affirming trial court's dismissal of defamation claim, but reversing dismissal of trespass claim because the alleged trespass does not "qualify as an act in furtherance of the right of free speech or the right to petition the government."). Lovett v. Capital Principles, LLC, 300 Ga. App. 799, 686 S.E.2 411 (2009) (affirming dismissal of slander claim under O.C.G.A. § 9 -11-11.1 finding that school district's recommendations concerning plaintiff's implementation of a computer software system was an "official proceeding authorized by law" and rejecting claim that anti-SLAPP statute did not apply because the speech related to a commercial transaction).

In November 2003, the Georgia Court of Appeals ordered the dismissal of two related defamation claims under Georgia's anti-SLAPP statute finding that, notwithstanding the plaintiffs' compliance with the verification requirement imposed by the statute, the court was authorized by the statute to consider the substance of plaintiffs' lawsuits and conclude that they were without merit. Harkins v. Atlanta Humane Society, 264 Ga. App. 356, 590 S.E.2d 737 (2003); Atlanta Humane Society v. Mills, 264 Ga. App. 597, 591 S.E.2d 423 (2003). On consolidated appeal, the Georgia Supreme Court held that dismissal under the anti-SLAPP statute was proper only if the statements in question were made in furtherance of the right of free speech and the claim was not well-grounded, was interposed for an improper purpose, or defendant's statements were privileged as a matter of law. Atlanta Humane Soc'y v. Harkins, Atlanta Humane Soc'y v. Mills, 278 Ga. 451, 603 S.E.2d 289 (2004). Finding the appellate court's analysis incomplete under this standard, the Supreme Court remanded both cases for further examination. Id. at 452. On remand, the Court of Appeals determined that the employee whistleblower's statements to the media addressed matters of public concern and, being made in good faith, were privileged communications. Harkins v. Atlanta Humane Soc'y, 273 Ga. App. 489, 618 S.E.2d 16 (2005) (dismissing suit under anti-SLAPP statute). Cf. Georgia Community Support & Solutions, Inc. v. Berryhill, 275 Ga. App. 189, 620 S.E.2d 178 (2005) (finding plaintiff's claim sufficient under the same mode of analysis) (cert. granted Berryhill v. Georgia Community Support & Solutions, Inc., 2006 Ga. LEXIS 125 (Feb. 13, 2006)). The Court of Appeals did not even reach the anti-SLAPP issue in the companion case, concluding that the humane society was a governmental entity incapable of bringing the suit, that its director was a limited-purpose public figure, and that the statements did not indicate the malice necessary to succeed on the claim. Atlanta Humane Soc'y v. Mills, 274 Ga. App. 159, 618 S.E.2d 18 (2005).

In Berryhill v. Georgia Community Support & Solutions, Inc., 281 Ga. 439, 638 S.E.2d 278 (2006), the Georgia Supreme Court made clear the scope of Georgia's anti-SLAPP statute is limited by subsection (c), so its protections apply only to statements made in or in connection with official proceedings. Although generally limiting the scope of the statute, the Court did recognize that the protections of the anti-SLAPP statute extend beyond the participants in official proceedings and a statement is protected even if it merely "relate[s] to an official proceeding instigated by someone else." Additionally, the opinion suggests that a clear statement calling for initiation of official proceedings also might fall within the statute. Id. at 442.

SURVEY OF GEORGIA EMPLOYMENT PRIVACY LAW

Peter C. Canfield, Russell A. Jones, and Melissa H. Alexander
Dow Lohnes PLLC
Six Concourse Parkway
Suite 1800
Atlanta, Georgia 30328
Telephone: (770) 901-8800; Facsimile: (770) 901-8874

(With Developments Reported Through **November 1, 2012**)

GENERAL COMMENTS

Effective July 1, 1985, the Supreme Court of Georgia promulgated Uniform Rules for Superior and State Courts, replacing the various local rules that previously had been in effect.

Under Georgia procedure, "the filing of a motion by the defendant does not toll the time for filing an answer." Cato Oil & Grease Co. v. Lewis, 250 Ga. 24, 25, 295 S.E.2d 527, 528 (1982). A defendant who files a motion to dismiss and no answer risks entry of a default judgment. Effective July 1, 2009, the filing of a motion to dismiss in a Georgia civil action shall stay discovery for 90 days or until the ruling on such motion, whichever is sooner. If discovery is necessary to address defenses relating to jurisdiction, venue, service or joinder, limited discovery needed to respond to these defenses is permitted. See O.C.G.A. § 9-11-12(j).

SIGNIFICANT DEVELOPMENTS SINCE THE 2012 *SURVEY*

The Eleventh Circuit Court of Appeals recently addressed the effective date of Georgia's new Restrictive Covenant Act. In Becham v. Synthes USA, No. 11-14495, 2012 WL 1994604 (11th Cir. June 4, 2012), the Eleventh Circuit determined that restrictive covenants executed on or after May 11, 2011 are to be analyzed under the new statutory covenant law, codified at O.C.G.A. § 13-8-50 et seq. All other restrictive covenants executed before that date must be analyzed under Georgia's pre-existing common law rules regarding restrictive covenant enforceability.

I. GENERAL LAW OF PRIVACY

A. Legal Basis of Privacy Claims

Georgia has recognized a cause of action for invasion of privacy as a matter of common law since early in this century. Pavesich v. New England Life Ins. Co., 122 Ga. 190, 50 S.E. 68 (1905). The Supreme Court of Georgia has long held that "The right of privacy is embraced within the absolute rights of personal security and personal liberty." Georgia courts agree with Dean Prosser's view that invasion of privacy is in reality a complex of four separate but related torts: "(1) intrusion upon the plaintiff's seclusion or solitude, or into his private affairs; (2) public disclosure of embarrassing private facts about the plaintiff; (3) publicity which places the plaintiff in a false light in the public eye; (4) appropriation, for the defendant's advantage, of the plaintiff's name or likeness." Martin Luther King, Jr. Ctr. for Social Change, Inc. v. American Heritage Prod., Inc., 250 Ga. 135, 142, 296 S.E.2d 697, 702-03, 8 Media L. Rep. 2377, 2381 (1982) (quoting Cabaniss v. Hipsley, 114 Ga. App. 367, 370, 151 S.E.2d 496, 500 (1966)); Everett v. Goodloe, 268 Ga. App. 536, 602 S.E.2d 284 (2004); Troncalli v. Jones, 237 Ga. App. 10, 13, 514 S.E.2d 478, 482 (1999); Johns v. Ridley, 245 Ga. App. 710, 712, 537 S.E.2d 746, 749 (2000), rev'd on other grounds, 274 Ga. 241, 552 S.E.2d 853 (2001) (ruling that the State Tort Claim Act barred the employee's suit against his supervisor because the Act exempts state officers and employees from liability for any torts committed while acting within the scope of their official duties or employment); Hickson v. Home Fed., 805 F. Supp. 1567, 1573 (N.D. Ga. 1992), aff'd without op., 14 F.3d 59 (11th Cir. 1994); Perez v. Atlanta Check Cashers, Inc., 302 Ga. App. 864, 692 S.E.2d 670 (2010); Eason v. Marine Terminals Corp., 309 Ga. App. 669, 710 S.E.2d 867 (2011) (holding that employees' claim that their employers violated their right to privacy by posting their false positive drug test results was pre-empted by Labor Management Relations Act); **Simpson v. Certegy Check Servs., No. CV 510–079, 2012 WL 3552848, *4 (S.D. Ga. Aug. 14, 2012) (holding that claim for invasion of privacy/false light based on a consumer-reporting agency's disclosure of plaintiff's credit information to a third party requesting the information was pre-empted by the Fair Credit Reporting Act where such disclosure was not false or given with malicious or willful intent to damage plaintiff).**

B. Causes of Action

1. ***Misappropriation/Right of Publicity.*** The "right of publicity" was first identified by Georgia courts in Cabaniss v. Hipsley, 114 Ga. App. 367, 378, 151 S.E.2d 496 (1966). Georgia courts considered the issue more than half a century earlier in Pavesich v. New England Life Ins. Co., 122 Ga. 190, 50 S.E. 68 (1905), in which the court held: "The publication of a picture of a person, without his consent, as a part of an advertisement for the purpose of exploiting the

publisher's business, is a violation of privacy of the person whose picture is reproduced, and entitles him to recover without proof of special damage." 122 Ga. at 191, 50 S.E. at 68. **The right of publicity is recognized even post-mortem. See Bogart, LLC v. Ashley Furniture Indus., Inc., No. 3:10–CV–39 (CDL), 2012 WL 3745833, at *12 (M.D. Ga. Aug. 28, 2012) (("'the right of publicity survives the death of its owner and is inheritable and devisable'") (quoting Martin Luther King, Jr. Ctr., 250 Ga. at 140, 296 S.E.2d at 704)).**

The Supreme Court of Georgia has defined misappropriation as follows: "[T]he appropriation of another's name and likeness, whether such likeness be a photograph or sculpture without consent and for financial gain of the appropriator is a tort in Georgia, whether the person whose name and likeness is used is a private citizen, entertainer, or . . . a public figure . . . ." Martin Luther King, Jr. Ctr. v. American Heritage Prod., Inc., 250 Ga. 135, 143, 296 S.E.2d 697, 703 (1982); Whisper Wear, Inc. v. Morgan, 277 Ga. App. 607, 609, 627 S.E.2d 178, 180 (2006) ("This Court has recognized that the appropriation of another's identity, picture, papers, name or signature without consent and for financial gain is a tort for which an action lies on the theory that it constitutes an invasion of a property right, or an invasion of privacy."). However, "[p]ublication about a matter of public interest fails to state an invasion of privacy claim." Thoroughbred Legends, LLC v. Walt Disney Co., 2008 WL 616253, *10 (N.D. Ga. Feb. 12, 2008) (considering misappropriation claim under Georgia law and holding that First Amendment barred claim based upon a matter of public interest, even where the newsworthy event occurred in the past); Toffoloni v. LFP Publ'g Group, 572 F.3d 1201 (11th Cir. 2009) (reversing district court's holding that newsworthiness exception applied to plaintiff's right of publicity claim based on Hustler Magazine's publication of private nude photographs of professional wrestler Nancy Benoit in conjunction with article on her highly-publicized murder; article was merely incidental to photographs, photographs were not connected to incident of public concern, and just because a person is involuntarily involved in a newsworthy event does not mean all aspects of her life are newsworthy).

The measure of damages in a misappropriation case is the value of the benefit derived by the person appropriating the other's name and likeness. Alonso v. Parfet, 253 Ga. 749, 750, 325 S.E.2d 152 (1985); Martin Luther King, Jr. Ctr. v. American Heritage Prod., Inc., 250 Ga. 135, 142-43. Special damages need not be proven. Pavesich v. New England Life Ins. Co., 122 Ga. 190, 191. Punitive damages are not recoverable "unless a right to recover general, nominal or special damages is shown." Cabaniss v. Hipsley, 114 Ga. App. 367, 386, 151 S.E.2d 496 (1966).

In Rivell v. Private Healthcare Sys., Inc., 520 F.3d 1308 (11th Cir. 2008) (per curiam), the Eleventh Circuit (applying Georgia law) held that a claim for misappropriation is not preempted simply because a contract also applies to the conduct at issue. The court explained that when a party exceeds the scope of permission to use a person's name or likeness, this may form the basis of both a breach of contract claim and a claim for the tort of misappropriation. Id. The agreements at issue may be used to support an affirmative defense of consent to the misappropriation. Id.

In Gettner v. Fitzgerald, 297 Ga. App. 258, 267, 677 S.E.2d 149, 158 (2009), the Georgia Court of Appeals considered a claim for misappropriation in the employment context. The court held that summary judgment in favor of a defendant former employer was proper where the plaintiff former employee's misappropriation claim was based on the employer's failure to remove the employee's credentials and picture from its website following termination of employment. The court found that because there was no evidence that the employer benefited from the unauthorized use of the employee's credentials or image, the plaintiff failed to make out a prima facie case of misappropriation.

2. ***False Light.*** Georgia recognizes false light invasion of privacy as an independent cause of action. See Maples v. National Enquirer, 763 F. Supp. 1137 (N.D. Ga. 1990); Williams v. Church's Fried Chicken, Inc., 158 Ga. App. 26, 279 S.E.2d 465 (1981); Brown v. Capricorn Records, Inc., 136 Ga. App. 818, 222 S.E.2d 618 (1975); Cabaniss v. Hipsley, 114 Ga. App. 367, 378, 151 S.E.2d 496 (1966). To recover on a claim of false light invasion of privacy, a plaintiff must establish that the defendant disseminated to the public false information which depicts the plaintiff incorrectly and which, even if not defamatory in a strict sense, is so highly offensive to a reasonable person that it injures the plaintiff's reputation or sensibilities. See Collins v. Creative Loafing of Savannah, Inc., 264 Ga. App. 675, 592 S.E.2d 170 (2003) (finding no false light invasion of privacy claim based on caricature where no reasonable person would have believed that the caricature depicted plaintiff); Cabaniss, 114 Ga. at 376; Blakey v. Victory Equip. Sales, 259 Ga. App. 34, 576 S.E.2d 288 (2002) (holding that there was no publication, and therefore no claim for false light, where a credit reporting agency provided information to its clients about the plaintiff's credit problems); Ass'n Servs., Inc. v. Smith, 249 Ga. App. 629, 549 S.E.2d 454 (2001) (holding that the videotaping of the wrong employee by a private investigator looking into a workers' compensation claim did not amount to false light and, even if it did, it would not be "highly offensive to a reasonable person"); Zielinski v. Clorox Co., 215 Ga. App. 97, 450 S.E.2d 222 (1994), rev'd on other grounds, 270 Ga. 38, 504 S.E.2d 683 (1998), vacated in part by 235 Ga. App. 886, 510 S.E.2d 856 (1999); Ass'n Services, Inc. v. Smith, 249 Ga. App. 629, 549 S.E.2d 454 (2001) (surveillance videotape of plaintiff that was used in a worker's compensation investigation of plaintiff's sister was neither offensive nor disseminated to the public).

Also, the plaintiff in a false light case must establish that the information was in fact false. The court found in Pospicil v. The Buying Office, Inc., that the term "psycho," as used by a former employer in giving an employment reference, amounted to a personal opinion about Plaintiff's personality, not a clinical diagnosis of her mental stability, and as such, the statement could not be proven true or false and thus did not give rise to a false light action. 71 F. Supp. 2d 1346, 1362 (N.D. Ga. 1999) ("no reasonable person could conclude that [the employer's use of the term 'psycho'] which has become rather commonplace in our society, was highly offensive"); Bollea v. World Championship Wrestling, Inc., 271 Ga. App. 555, 557, 610 S.E.2d 92, 96-97 (2005) (holding that pre-scripted speech made in the "fictional context" of a pro wrestling telecast not false light invasion of privacy because it could not reasonably be interpreted as a factual statement about plaintiff himself, as opposed to plaintiff's fictional wrestling character).

No Georgia case has specifically addressed the method of calculating damages or the amount allowable on claims for false light invasion of privacy. Items of special damage must be specifically pled and proven. O.C.G.A. § 9-11-9 (g). Punitive damages may be awarded "only in such tort actions in which it is proven by clear and convincing evidence that the defendant's actions showed willful misconduct, malice, fraud, wantonness, oppression, or that entire want of care which would raise the presumption of conscious indifference to consequences." Multimedia WMAZ v. Kubach, 212 Ga. App. 707, 711, 443 S.E.2d 491 (1994); see also O.C.G.A. § 51-12-5.1(b).

The few Georgia cases concerning false light invasion of privacy in the employment context have been generally favorable to the employer. In Jackson v. Nationwide Credit, Inc., the court held that the action of a supervisor in escorting an employee out of the office upon the employee's dismissal was insufficient to rise to the level of false light invasion of privacy. 206 Ga. App. 810, 426 S.E.2d 630 (1992). In Zielinski, the plaintiff alleged that the employer made statements at an all-plant meeting implicating plaintiff in an embezzlement scheme to defraud the company. The court held that an employer is not liable for slanderous utterances of its agent, even one who acts within the scope of his employment, unless the company specifically told the agent what to say. 215 Ga. App. 97, 450 S.E.2d 222 (1994), rev'd on other grounds, 270 Ga. 38, 504 S.E.2d 683 (1998), vacated in part by 235 Ga. App. 886, 510 S.E.2d 856 (1999). Intracorporate communications to those who have a need to know the information will not support an action for false light invasion of privacy. Zielinski v. Clorox Co., 215 Ga. App. 97, 102, 450 S.E.2d 222 (1994), rev'd on other grounds, 270 Ga. 38, 504 S.E.2d 683 (1998), vacated in part by 235 Ga. App. 886, 510 S.E.2d 856 (1999). In most cases applying the rule, intra-corporate means among officers or employees who have a direct duty and authority to know the information. O'Neal v. Home Town Bank of Villa Rica, 237 Ga. App. 325, 334, 514 S.E.2d 669, 678 (1999) (refusing to extend intra-corporate rule to employees or shareholders); Hayes Microcomputer Products, Inc. v. Franza, 268 Ga. App. 340, 601 S.E.2d 824 (2004) (holding, in context of libel case, that intracorporate communication privilege did not apply where the communication was made to "every employee with an email address," including employees with whom the plaintiffs had no relationship). See also Nelson v. Glynn-Brunswick Hospital Authority, 257 Ga. App. 571, 571 S.E.2d 557 (2002) (no publication where lab results about an employee physician who suffered from an infectious disease were communicated between the lab technician, lab director, hospital administrator and other members of the hospital staff).

In Galardi v. Steele-Inman, 266 Ga. App. 515, 597 S.E.2d 571 (2004), the Court of Appeals, in the context of a libel/tortious interference case, held that the intracorporate communications doctrine could apply even where the speaker and the recipient of the message were not part of the same business entity. There, the operator of a beauty pageant made a statement to the promoter of the same pageant that one of the contestants was being disqualified and banned from the contest for allegedly interfering with the pageant voting. Although the operator and promoter were separate business enterprises, the court held that the two organizations "fully undertook together" the pageant and that the relevant communication between representatives of the two organizations was protected under the intracorporate privilege doctrine. Id. at 576.

3. ***Publication of Private Facts.*** Georgia has long recognized a cause of action for invasion of privacy based on the publication of private facts. Pavesich v. New England Life Ins. Co., 122 Ga. 190, 50 S.E. 68 (1905). Three elements are necessary for recovery under the theory of public disclosure of embarrassing private facts about the plaintiff: (1) there must be a public disclosure of the private facts; (2) the facts disclosed to the public must be private, secluded, or secret facts and not public facts; and (3) the matter made public must be offensive and objectionable to a reasonable man of ordinary sensibilities under the circumstances. Cabaniss v. Hipsley, 114 Ga. App. 367, 372, 151 S.E.2d 496 (1966); Zieve v. Hairston, 266 Ga. App. 753, 756, 598 S.E.2d 25 (2004). If the plaintiff disclosed the information to others, the information may no longer be considered "private." In Cummings v. Walsh Construction Co., the court held that the employee waived her right to privacy when she engaged in sexual intercourse with a supervisor and told others about it. 561 F. Supp. 872 (S.D. Ga. 1983); see also Canziani v. Visiting Nurse Health Systems, Inc., 271 Ga. App. 677, 610 S.E.2d 660 (2005) (affirming summary judgment for invasion of privacy claim based upon home care nurse's communications with insurance carrier, where plaintiff had signed a form giving the nurse permission to so communicate); Bradley v. Pfizer, Inc., No. 11-11132, 2011 WL 3962824 (11th Cir. Sept. 9, 2011) (applying Georgia law) (finding that employee's invasion of privacy claim failed where employee acknowledged that he had no expectation of privacy in any material placed on his company-issued laptop computer). The supervisor was found not liable for disclosing the same information to others. Id. In

Zieve, however, the court noted that this doctrine has its limits: "the scope of the waiver is related to and limited by the scope of the actions on which the waiver is based." Zieve, 266 Ga. App. at 757 (quoting Multimedia WMAZ, Inc. v. Kubach, 212 Ga. App. 707, 709, 443 S.E.2d 491 (1994)).

A plaintiff need not establish damage to reputation to recover general damages for wrongful publication of private facts. Multimedia WMAZ v. Kubach, 212 Ga. App. 707, 443 S.E.2d 491 (1994). General damages may be awarded based on evidence that "the defendant's actions cause [the plaintiff] severe mental distress with physical repercussions." Id., 212 Ga. App. at 712. Special damages, including lost wages, are recoverable for wrongful publication of private facts. Id. Punitive damages may be awarded "only in such tort action in which it is proven by clear and convincing evidence that the defendant's actions showed willful misconduct, malice, fraud, wantonness, oppression, or that entire want of care which would raise the presumption of conscious indifference to consequences." Id., 212 Ga. App. at 711.

In Pierre v. Cingular Wireless, 397 F. Supp. 2d 1364 (N.D. Ga. 2005), the court rejected a "public disclosure of embarrassing facts" claim brought by an employee whose supervisor had allegedly encouraged another employee to report the employee's marijuana use to the employer's ethics hotline. The court rejected the claim on the basis of its determination that "the complaint was [not] relayed to anyone outside of management who did not have a need to know" and that "all discussions about the complaint [by the employer's management team] were privileged communications made in good faith to enforce [the employer's] policies and protect its interests." Id. at 1383.

In Gettner v. Fitzgerald, 297 Ga. App. 258, 267, 677 S.E.2d 149, 158 (2009), the Georgia Court of Appeals held that summary judgment in favor of defendant former employer and its chief executive officer was proper where the employer's publication of allegedly embarrassing facts to a trade publication reporter regarding employee's demotion for "poor performance" was protected by the terms of a release given by employee to employer. The release, which was a condition of employee's receiving severance pay, stated that employee released employer and its officers from any known or unknown invasion of privacy claim.

4. ***Intrusion.*** In Georgia, intrusion is closely related to trespass; and with regard to trespass Georgia has stated that "[t]he right of enjoyment of private property being an absolute right of every citizen, every act of another which unlawfully interferes with such enjoyment is a tort for which an action shall lie." O.C.G.A. § 51-9-1. The connection between intrusion and trespass is reflected in cases such as Kobeck v. Nabisco, Inc., in which the court held that an employer's disclosure of its employee's attendance record was not an intrusion upon seclusion because it failed to reach the required physical level of intrusion like that of a trespass. 166 Ga. App. 652, 305 S.E.2d 183 (1983). Liability for intrusion, however, requires a greater showing of intent than trespass. The statute of limitations for intrusion is also only two years, where the limitations period for trespass is four years. O.C.G.A. § 9-3-30.

In Johnson v. Allen, 272 Ga. App. 861, 613 S.E.2d 657 (2005), the Court of Appeals held that a manager – and via the doctrine of respondeat superior, the employer – could be held liable for the tort of intrusion upon seclusion for installing a video camera in the women's restroom of the employer's facility. Although the cameras had been installed after rumors of drug use in the women's restroom, the court still held that the employer could be held liable. In so holding, the court noted that the cameras in Johnson had been installed in response to mere rumors – as opposed to specific facts – that drugs were being sold on the premises and that the monitoring had continued long after the rumors were received. The case was thus distinguishable from those holding that "a stall in a public restroom is not a private place when it is used for other than its intended purpose." Id. at 864, 613 S.E.2d at 661 (citing In re C.P., 274 Ga. 599, 600, 555 S.E.2d 426 (2001); Wylie v. State, 164 Ga. App. 174, 296 S.E.2d 743 (1982); Elmore v. Atlantic Zayre, 178 Ga. App. 25, 341 S.E.2d 905 (1986)).

The Georgia Supreme Court has held that an employer does not commit intrusion by warning an employee of the company's interest in her testimony in another matter; the company's interests were at stake and its actions were insufficient to rise to the level of an intrusion upon the employee's privacy. Yarbray v. Southern Ball Tel. & Tel. Co., 261 Ga. 703, 409 S.E.2d 835 (1991). The Georgia Supreme Court has recognized an extension of the tort beyond physical invasion to include prying and intrusion that would be offensive or objectionable to a reasonable person. Yarbray, 261 Ga. at 705. Thus, the tort of intrusion includes unauthorized surveillance, such as eavesdropping or wiretapping. Id. at n. 3; Ass'n Services, Inc. v. Smith, 249 Ga. App. 629, 549 S.E.2d 454 (2001) (affirming denial of summary judgment on claim of intrusion against private investigation firm that videotaped claimant at home and at work). However, no Georgia cases have recognized a cause of action for intrusion into "psychological sanctity" or an inner "sphere of privacy." Pospicil v. The Buying Office, Inc., 71 F. Supp. 2d 1346, 1361 (N.D. Ga. 1999) (sexual jokes, comments and innuendo insufficient to support plaintiff's claim for intrusion into her "psychological sanctity."); Johns v. Ridley, 245 Ga. App. 710, 712, 537 S.E.2d 746, 749 (2000) (supervisor's telephone calls to subordinate employee's home concerning work-related matters did not support claim of intrusion), rev'd on other grounds, 274 Ga. 241, 552 S.E.2d 853 (2001) (ruling that the State Tort Claim Act barred the employee's suit against his supervisor because the Act exempts state officers and employees from liability for any torts committed while acting within the scope of their official duties or employment); Sitton v. Print Direction, Inc., No.

A11A1055, 2011 WL 4469712 (Ga. Ct. App. Sept. 28, 2011) (holding that employer's review of employee's email on employee's laptop located in employer's office and used to conduct business for the employer was not such an unreasonable intrusion on employee's seclusion or solitude as to rise to the level of invasion of privacy).

Highly personal demands (including sexual demands) or questions by a person in authority may constitute an intrusion on a person's psychological solitude or integrity. In Simon v. Morehouse Sch. of Medicine, the court denied the employer's motion for summary judgment where the employee claimed intrusion based on her supervisors' alleged sexual harassment and physical assaults. 908 F. Supp. 959 (N.D. Ga. 1995). Similarly, the Georgia of Appeals upheld in Troncalli v. Jones, 237 Ga. App. 10, 13, 514 S.E.2d 478, 482 (1999), citing Yarbray, a jury verdict in favor of the plaintiff on a claim of intrusion where it was alleged that the defendant intentionally touched her breasts, made a threatening gesture and put his mouth on her neck at business-related functions. However, an employee's voluntary act of engaging in intercourse or other sexual conduct may negate an intrusion claim. See Cummings v. Walsh Constr. Co., 561 F. Supp. 872 (S.D. Ga. 1983) (female employee waived right to personal seclusion when she voluntarily engaged in sexual intercourse with a supervisor); Everett v. Goodloe, 268 Ga. App. 536, 602 S.E.2d 284 (2004) (affirming grant of defendant's motion for summary judgment where "a personal relationship between the parties preceded and existed contemporaneously with the alleged improper conduct"). But see Benedict v. State Farm Bank, FSB, 309 Ga. App. 133, 709 S.E.2d 314 (2011) (finding that plaintiff failed to state a claim of intrusion where plaintiff did not allege any conduct akin to surveillance, a physical trespass upon his property, or a physical touching of his person).

There is no reported case in Georgia on the availability of general or punitive damages for intrusion. Special damages must be specifically pled and proven. O.C.G.A. § 9-11-9(g).

C. Other Privacy-Related Actions

1. ***Intentional Infliction of Emotional Distress.*** Georgia has adopted the tort of intentional infliction of emotional distress as set forth in the Restatement (Second) of Torts. Bridges v. Winn-Dixie Atlanta, 176 Ga. App. 227, 230, 335 S.E.2d 445 (1985). Because at-will employees may be discharged without regard to the employer's motives, the discharge of an at-will employee alone is insufficient to support a claim of intentional infliction of emotional distress. Biven Software, Inc. v. Newman, 222 Ga. App. 112, 473 S.E.2d 527 (1996). See also Phinazee v. Interstate Nationalease, Inc., 237 Ga. App. 39, 514 S.E.2d 843 (1999) (discharge, absent an improper racial motive, will not give rise to a claim for intentional infliction of emotional distress nor will mere insults and indignities).

A claim for intentional infliction of emotional distress will fail if it is held that the underlying libel claim based on the same facts fails. See Evans v. The Sandersville Georgian, 296 Ga. App. 666, 670, 675 S.E.2d 574, 578 (2009) (holding that because plaintiff failed to prove actual malice with regard to his libel claim based on newspaper's publication of letter to editor urging city council not to rehire plaintiff into police department, plaintiff's claim for intentional infliction of emotional distress must also fail).

Employees have been able to recover where the employer falsely accused the employee of stealing money and threatened to have the police incarcerate her until she paid the shortage, Beavers v. Johnson, 112 Ga. App. 677, 680, 145 S.E.2d 776, 778 (1965); conspired with law enforcement officials to conduct intimidating termination interviews, Davis v. Copelan, 215 Ga. App. 754, 452 S.E.2d 194, 203 (1994); and forged the employee's name on a Medicaid form, Andress v. Augusta Nursing Facilities, Inc., 156 Ga. App. 775, 275 S.E.2d 368 (1980). "[C]ritical comments by an employer to its employee, even though belittling, rude, and given at a poor time when the employee is very vulnerable, do not make the employer liable." Potts v. UAP-GA Ag Chem., Inc., 256 Ga. App. 153, 567 S.E.2d 316 (2002) (comment to employee recently injured at work that employee did not have a valid worker's compensation claim not intentional infliction of emotional distress). However, "[i]t is firmly established that even malicious, willful or wanton conduct will not support a claim of intentional infliction of emotional distress if the conduct was not directed toward the plaintiff." Munoz v. American Lawyer Media, L.P., 236 Ga. App. 462, 465, 512 S.E.2d 347, 351 (1999); Tomczyk v. Rollins, 2009 WL 1044868, *3 (N.D. Ga. Apr. 20, 2009); Wolff v. Middlebrooks, 256 Ga. App. 268, 568 S.E.2d 88 (2002) (radio personality's on-air defamatory comment about plaintiff could not sustain claim for intentional infliction of emotional distress because the comments were directed at the station's listeners, not the plaintiff).

Substantive elements of intentional infliction of emotional distress are as follows:

Intentional or Reckless Conduct. In Georgia, the defendant's behavior must be "willful and wanton or intended to harm the plaintiff." Coleman v. Housing Auth., 191 Ga. App. 166, 170, 381 S.E.2d 303 (1989). See also Peoples v. Guthrie, 199 Ga. App. 119, 404 S.E.2d 442 (1991) (denying intentional infliction of emotional distress claim where plaintiff was accused in front of other employees of cheating on an examination given at her office; although the accusation was intentional, it was not intended to harm the plaintiff); Hendrix v. Phillips, 207 Ga. App. 394, 396, 428 S.E.2d 91 (1993) (element of intent lacking when defendant made a written apology and was formally reprimanded for his conduct after cursing at plaintiff in a business meeting); Nelson v. Gwynn-Brunswick Hosp. Auth., 257 Ga. App. 571, 571 S.E.2d 557 (2002) (hospital's dissemination of information that doctor had tested positive for Hepatitis-C not intentional infliction because steps had been taken to protect doctor's privacy and information was only released to a small number of individuals).

Extreme and Outrageous Conduct. Georgia courts are strict about the degree of extreme and outrageous conduct required to state a claim for intentional infliction of emotional distress. Moses v. Prudential Ins. Co., 187 Ga. App. 222, 369 S.E.2d 541 (1988). Georgia requires the conduct to be either "extreme and outrageous or so terrifying or so insulting as to naturally humiliate, embarrass, or frighten the plaintiff." Johnson v. MARTA, 207 Ga. App. 869, 873, 429 S.E.2d 285 (1993). See Harris v. Equifax, Inc., 2006 WL 819757, *11 (N.D. Ga. Mar. 23, 2006) ("Georgia courts consistently hold that employment actions are insufficiently 'extreme' or 'outrageous' to support a claim for intentional infliction of emotional distress"). Liability does not result from "mere insults, indignities, threats, annoyances, petty oppressions, or other trivialities." Moses, 187 Ga. App. at 225 (quoting Restatement (Second) of Torts, § 46(1), comment d). A false accusation of dishonesty or lack of integrity in connection with one's employment conduct does not constitute intentional infliction of emotional distress. People v. Guthrie, 199 Ga. App. 119, 404 S.E.2d 442 (1991). See also Sossenko v. Michelin Tire Corp., 172 Ga. App. 771, 772, 324 S.E.2d 593 (1984) (statements by members of employer's personnel department concerning dissatisfaction with plaintiff's job performance not sufficiently egregious to constitute intentional infliction of emotional distress). The conduct must be directed towards the plaintiff in order to be actionable. Jackson v. Nationwide Credit, Inc., 206 Ga. App. 810, 811, 426 S.E.2d 630 (1992) (upholding summary judgment for defendant when defendant's actions were directed against plaintiffs' employers, not plaintiffs); Wolff v. Middlebrooks, 256 Ga. App. 268, 568 S.E.2d 88 (2002) (radio personality's on-air defamatory comment about plaintiff could not sustain claim for intentional infliction of emotional distress because the comments were directed at the station's listeners, not the plaintiff). For a discussion of cases addressing various types of conduct alleged to be outrageous under Georgia law, see Price v. State Farm Mut. Auto Ins. Co., 878 F. Supp. 1567 (S.D. Ga. 1995); Jarrard v. United Parcel Service, 242 Ga. App. 58, 60, 529 S.E.2d 144, 147 (2000) (liability does not extend to harsh job evaluation or other "mere insults, indignities, threats, annoyances, petty oppressions, or other vicissitudes of daily living."); Johns v. Ridley, 245 Ga. App. 710, 537 S.E.2d 746 (2000) (affirming denial of summary judgment to defendant-employer where supervisor engaged in a 13 month course of conduct with 36 separate incidents of harassment and threats to subordinate employee), rev'd on other grounds, 274 Ga. 241, 552 S.E.2d 853 (2001); Nelson v. Gwynn-Brunswick Hosp. Auth., 257 Ga. App. 571, 571 S.E.2d 557 (2002) (hospital's dissemination of information that doctor had tested positive for Hepatitis-C not sufficiently outrageous to constitute intentional infliction because steps had been taken to protect doctor's privacy and information was only released to a small number of individuals); Miraliakbari v. Pennicooke, 254 Ga. App. 156, 561 S.E.2d 483 (2002) (employer's refusal to allow employee to leave work or even to use the phone to attend to child who had been injured at school was not sufficiently outrageous to support claim); Nicholson v. Windham, 257 Ga. App. 429, 571 S.E.2d 466 (2002) (asking employee to participate in employer's illegal activity and firing her for her refusal to do so sufficient to state a claim for intentional infliction of emotional distress); Mangrum v. Republic Indus., Inc., 260 F. Supp. 2d 1229, 1256 (N.D. Ga. 2003) (holding that, where supervisor had engaged in a long pattern of sexual harassment, the only conduct that even arguably gave rise to a claim for intentional infliction of emotional distress was when supervisor exposed himself to the plaintiff); Lewis v. Northside Hosp., Inc., 267 Ga. App. 288, 599 S.E.2d 267 (2004) (affirming summary judgment for defendant on plaintiff's claim stemming from an incident in which she was shoved by a co-worker because, *inter alia*, the relationship between plaintiff and her co-worker was not one in which the co-worker had control over the plaintiff); Travis Pruitt & Assoc. , P.C. v. Hooper, 277 Ga. App. 1, 8, 625 S.E.2d 445, 452 (2005) (employer's investigation of and response to sexual harassment allegation was not extreme or outrageous conduct that would support a claim for intentional infliction of emotional distress against the employer); Metropolitan Atlanta Rapid Transit Authority v. Mosley, 280 Ga. App. 486, 491-92, 634 S.E.2d 466, 470-71 (2006) (holding crude and inappropriate conduct that lasted for a matter of seconds, occurred in public, and was not physically threatening is not actionable as intentional infliction of emotional distress); Perkins-Carrillo v. Systemax, Inc., 2006 WL 1553957 (N.D. Ga. May 26, 2006) (insensitive and tasteless conduct involving employer phoning another company to verify employee's presence there and stating employee had family emergency, then hanging up the phone when employee picked it up is not sufficiently outrageous "to sustain a claim for intentional infliction of emotional distress"); Harris v. Equifax, Inc., 2006 WL 819575, *11 (N.D. Ga. Mar. 23, 2006) (dismissing as a matter of law plaintiff's claim for intentional infliction of emotional distress because plaintiff's stress from being yelled at by his supervisor and his anxiety and severe depression resulting from a change in supervision "is far less egregious than allegations in other cases" where courts have ruled those plaintiffs "could not sustain a IIED [intentional infliction of emotional distress] claim as a matter of law"); Bozeman v. Per-Se Technologies, Inc., 2006 456 F. Supp. 2d 1282, 1337 (N.D. Ga. Oct. 16, 2006) (holding that allegations of "verbal abuse . . . on numerous occasions, including, inter alia, threats to [plaintiff's] job, and at least two physical threats" could not support claim for intentional infliction of emotional distress); Williams v. ATC Group Services, Inc., 2006 WL 3191181, *11 (N.D. Ga. Oct. 30, 2006) (plaintiff who worked in a cubicle instead of an office, was paid $1.00 less than a co-worker, and did not have the word "manager" in his job description was not subject to outrageous conduct that would support a claim for intentional infliction of emotional distress); **Southland Propane, Inc. v. McWhorter, 312 Ga.App. 812, 819, 720 S.E.2d 270, 276-77 (2011) (an employer's accusations against plaintiff of misappropriating corporate funds and forgery, terminating plaintiff's**

employment, and then ordering plaintiff to leave the premises do not constitute extreme and outrageous conduct); Ghodrati v. Stearnes, 314 Ga.App. 321, 323-34, 723 S.E.2d 721, 723 (2012) (repeatedly calling plaintiff racist and derogatory names and posting inappropriate signs about plaintiff on employee restroom door and in the middle of the shop, although rude and tasteless, was not outrageous enough to support a claim). But see Woods v. Georgia Pacific Corp., 2007 WL 403582, *3 (S.D. Ga. Feb 1, 2007) (holding plaintiff subject to "humiliating and threatening sexual and racial comments" and the resulting adverse working conditions which led to "substantial emotional injury," pled enough facts to state a claim for intentional infliction of emotional distress); Ferman v. Bailey, 292 Ga. App. 288, 644 S.E.2d 285 (2008) (holding that allegations that supervisor sexually assaulted and sexually harassed employee sufficient to support claim for intentional infliction of emotional distress); Couick v. Morgan, No. 4:10-cv-153, 2010 WL 5158206 (S.D. Ga. Dec. 14, 2010) (denying defendant's motion for summary judgment on claim of intentional infliction of emotional dismiss where plaintiff alleged that defendants denied her FMLA leave, fired her in retaliation for making a complaint against her supervisor, and failed to address her supervisor's verbal abuse, which included berating her in front of coworkers, screaming at plaintiff over the phone, and otherwise acting unprofessionally).

Severe Emotional Distress. The plaintiff must also show that the defendant's actions were "extreme and outrageous or so terrifying or so insulting as to naturally humiliate, embarrass, or frighten the plaintiff." Johnson v. MARTA, 207 Ga. App. 869, 873, 429 S.E.2d 285. The alleged emotional distress must be so severe that no reasonable person could be expected to endure it. Mangrum, 260 F. Supp. 2d at 1256; Williams v. Voljavec, 202 Ga. App. 580, 415 S.E.2d 31 (1992). See Perkins-Carrillo, 2006 WL 1553957 (plaintiff's claims of insomnia, anxiety, crying spells, occasional headaches, and "a tightening feeling in her chest" are not symptoms which "no reasonable man could be expected to endure") (internal citations omitted); Soloski v. Adams, 600 F. Supp. 2d 1276, 1322, 1371-72 (N.D. Ga. 2009) (granting summary judgment based on magistrate judge's recommendation that defendant university's decision that plaintiff dean of journalism college committed sexual harassment did not cause plaintiff severe emotional distress, even though plaintiff stated he experienced intense feelings of embarrassment and humiliation); Shaw v. ASB Greenworld, Inc. 2007 WL 2044263, *7 (M.D. Ga. Jul 9, 2007) (plaintiff's "hurt feelings" were not a severe reaction to conduct plaintiff described as "unpleasant").

Causation. The plaintiff must establish "a causal connection between the wrongful conduct and the emotional distress." Bridges v. Winn-Dixie Atlanta, 176 Ga. App. 227, 230, 335 S.E.2d 445 (1985). See also Blockum v. Fieldale Farms Corp., 275 Ga. 798, 801, 573 S.E.2d 36 (2002) (holding that plaintiff's own statements to his physician regarding the alleged source of his symptoms was sufficient to create issue of fact as to causation).

2. ***Interference With Prospective Economic Advantage.*** Georgia courts have recognized the tort of interference with prospective economic advantage in connection with defamation claims. See, e.g., Hylton v. American Ass'n for Vocational Instructional Materials, Inc., 214 Ga. App. 635, 448 S.E.2d 741 (1994) (plaintiff-employee alleged tortious interference with contract of employment, but could not recover where he could not have shown damage to the contractual relationship and where alleged defamatory memorandum was never published; defendant showed that employer had voted not to renew plaintiff's employment contract before submission of allegedly defamatory memorandum by defendant to employer).

Elements of the tort of interference with contract in Georgia are as follows: (1) existence of a contractual relationship; (2) interference with the relationship by someone who is a stranger to the contract; and (3) resulting damage to the contractual relationship. Id. at 638. A cause of action may properly be brought by an at-will employee, but the employee must allege or present evidence of wrongful or improper actions in connection with the discharge. Rose v. Zurowski, 236 Ga. App. 157, 159, 511 S.E.2d 265, 267 (1999) ("Bad motive, a subjective prompter, does not poison the legitimacy of an act, which is measured objectively."); Palombi v. Frito-Lay, Inc., 241 Ga. App. 154, 157, 526 S.E.2d 375 (1999) (an employee's supervisor is not a stranger to an employment contract); Dong v. Shepeard Community Blood Ctr., 240 Ga. App. 137, 139, 522 S.E.2d 720, 722 (1999) (accord). The appellate courts are split on whether an at-will employee can sustain an interference with contract claim. Compare Culpepper v. Thompson, 254 Ga. App. 569, 571, 562 S.E.2d 837 (2002) (concluding that at-will employee "had no enforceable contract rights with which to interfere so as to give rise to a breach of contract and damages; thus, since the underlying contract could not be enforced by him as an employment at will, then, the tortious conduct of a third party does not give rise to an action for inducing a breach of the employment contract") with Gunnells v. Marshburn, 259 Ga. App. 657, 659, 578 S.E.2d 273 (2003) ("[Plaintiff] correctly argues that the fact that employment is at will and that the employer is free from liability for discharging an employee does not carry with it immunity to a third person who, without justification, causes the discharge of the employee.").

Elements of the tort of interference with prospective economic advantage, otherwise known as interference with business relations, are as follows: (1) the defendant acts improperly, without privilege; (2) defendant's behavior is malicious, purposeful, and undertaken with the intent to injure; (3) defendant induces a third party not to enter into or continue a business relationship with the plaintiff; and (4) plaintiff suffers a financial harm from defendant's actions. Hayes v. Irwin, 541 F. Supp. 397, 429 (N.D. Ga. 1982), aff'd without op., 729 F.2d 1466 (11th Cir. 1984). See also Taylor v.

Calvary Baptist Temple, 279 Ga. App. 71, 72, 630 S.E.2d 604 (2006). The court in Wood v. Archbold Medical Ctr., Inc. expanded on the meaning of "without privilege" by stating, "the requirement under a tortious interference with business relations claim that a defendant act without privilege refers to whether the defendant has a legitimate economic interest in the business relationship, not whether the defendant can assert some sort of federal or state immunity" [for actions taken]. 2006 WL 1805729, *6 (M.D. Ga. June 28, 2006). Furthermore, a plaintiff "must demonstrate that absent the interference, the prospective business relations were reasonably likely to develop." Looney v. M-Squared, Inc., 262 Ga. App. 499, 586 S.E.2d 44 (2003) (quotations and internal alterations omitted).

A claim for interference with prospective economic advantage will fail if it is held that the underlying libel claim based on the same facts fails. See Evans v. The Sandersville Georgian, 296 Ga. App. 666, 670, 675 S.E.2d 574, 578 (2009) (holding that because plaintiff failed to prove actual malice with regard to his libel claim based on newspaper's publication of letter to editor urging city council not to rehire plaintiff into police department, plaintiff's claim for interference with prospective economic advantage must also fail).

3. ***Prima Facie Tort.*** Prima facie tort has never been recognized by the Georgia courts. In fact, Georgia courts have on several occasions expressly stated that new tort actions will not be judicially created. See, e.g., Deacon v. Deacon, 122 Ga. App. 513, 177 S.E.2d 719, 720 (1970); Mauldin v. Sheffer, 113 Ga. App. 874, 879, 150 S.E.2d 150, 154 (1966). No decision of the Georgia courts has ever recognized an action for a prima facie tort and the Georgia legislature has not codified any such action.

II. EMPLOYER TESTING OF EMPLOYEES

A. Psychological or Personality Testing

1. ***Common Law and Statutes.*** No reported case or relevant statute.

2. ***Private Employers.*** Georgia does not require an employer to subject its employees to psychological or personality testing. To the contrary, where an employer does not force its employees to submit to psychological testing without their consent, but otherwise exercises ordinary care, the employer will not be found liable for negligent hiring and retention. In dicta, one court has questioned generalized testing. That court stated, "We know of no requirement of compulsory psychological periodic blanket testing and counseling of all of one's employees. In fact, were this to be done by employers, without the employees' consent, serious First Amendment individual rights of privacy and other employee constitutional and civil rights might be at issue." Southern Bell Tel. & Tel. Co. v. Sharara, 167 Ga. App. 665, 307 S.E.2d 129, 132 (1983).

On the other hand, where an employee claims his employer submitted him to psychological testing but cannot remember whether he was actually forced to do so, an invasion of privacy claim will not be upheld. Phillips v. DAP, Inc., 10 F. Supp. 2d 1334, aff'd without op., 165 F.3d 41 (11th Cir. 1998) (insufficient evidence of invasion of privacy where mentally retarded employee was taken by employer for psychological testing and later could not remember whether he had been forced to see the psychologist).

3. ***Public Employers.*** Law enforcement officers must submit to psychological evaluations for purposes of fitness for duty assessment, employment status, or duty assignment. The officer is entitled to a copy of the report. O.C.G.A. § 31-33-7.

B. Drug Testing

1. ***Common Law and Statutes.*** Georgia does not restrict the types of testing (e.g., for alcohol, drugs, etc.) or testing procedures (e.g., urine, breath, blood, etc.) employers may use. Random testing of employees is also not prohibited.

2. ***Private Employers.*** There is no legal obligation for employers to conduct drug tests, but those who adhere to the drug testing provisions of O.C.G.A § 34-9-415 are eligible for a five percent discount on their workers' compensation premiums. Conditions for obtaining the discount include requiring: applicants to submit to testing after receiving an offer of employment; employees to submit to "reasonable suspicion" testing; employees to submit to testing as part of a fitness for duty medical examination; and employees to submit to a test after a work-related injury. A written drug testing policy must also be provided to employees 60 days prior to its implementation. On-site testing is prohibited under these provisions. See Brown v. Allied Printing Ink Co., 241 Ga. App. 310, 526 S.E.2d 626 (1999) (affirming summary judgment in favor of employer regarding claims arising from positive random drug test); Stanford v. Paul W. Heard & Co., 240 Ga. App. 869, 525 S.E.2d 419 (1999) (affirming dismissal of claims of tortious interference with employment, intentional infliction of emotional distress and negligence arising from publication of positive drug test results); Marine Port Terminals, Inc. v. Dixon, 252 Ga. App. 340, 556 S.E.2d 246 (2001) (reversing grant of workers' compensation benefits to employee who

refused to submit to drug test where the administrative law judge had applied an improper analysis to the facts of the case and misconstrued the parties' burden of proof).

While the Georgia statutory provisions creating a workers' compensation discount do require that the employer keep the drug test results confidential, O.C.G.A. § 34-9-420, the Georgia Court of Appeals has limited the ability of employees to recover from their employers when the employer releases drug test information. In Foster v. Swinney, 263 Ga. App. 510, 588 S.E.2d 307 (Ga. App. 2003), the plaintiff was an employee who had failed an employer-mandated drug test. Subsequently, the employer contacted the employee's home and told the employee's 15 year-old stepson that the plaintiff had failed the drug test and had been fired. While noting Georgia's strong public policy in favor of the confidentiality of medical records, the 'Court of Appeals nonetheless affirmed the employer's motion to dismiss. The court noted that Georgia's prohibitions against the release of medical records only applied to situations in which the patient was seeking treatment, and that an employer-mandated drug test did not fall into this category. See also Gooden v. Carson, 2006 WL 1209923, *6 (N.D. Ga. April 26, 2006) ("Georgia law clearly states that the unauthorized disclosure of drug test results does not result in a state law claim for invasion of privacy.").

In Wilson v. Home Depot USA, Inc., 288 Ga. App. 582, 654 S.E.2d 408 (2007), the Georgia Court of Appeals considered an invasion of privacy claim brought by an employee who had been fired for failing a drug test. The employee alleged that the results of the positive test were improperly released to his ex-wife, who was also a manager of a different location. The plaintiff moved for summary judgment on the invasion of privacy claim, arguing that the dispositive issue was whether the employer's release of the drug test results to his ex-wife was privileged. The court denied that motion for summary judgment, holding that a genuine issue of fact existed as to whether the manager of another store was privileged to receive the information.

3. ***Public Employers.*** Public employers are generally more restricted than private employers with respect to drug testing employees. Courts have expressly acknowledged that certain drug tests by private employers are allowed in circumstances under which a public employer would be prevented from conducting them because of constitutional limitations on searches. See American Fed. of Gov't Employees v. Weinberger, 651 F. Supp. 726, 737 (S.D. Ga. 1986) (random urinalysis testing allowed for private employer but not public employer).

However, courts have upheld drug testing by public employers where there is a compelling state interest to conduct the test. In Georgia Dep't of Corrections v. Colbert, the Supreme Court of Georgia held that drug testing of prison employees was constitutional because the compelling state interest of preventing illegal drug use in prisons outweighed individual privacy concerns. 260 Ga. 255, 391 S.E.2d 759 (1990). Drug testing procedures were not to be left up to the discretion of the warden, however. Two years earlier, the Supreme Court likewise upheld the drug testing of police officers because the compelling state interest in protecting public safety outweighed individual privacy concerns. City of East Point v. Smith, 258 Ga. 111, 365 S.E.2d 432 (1988). The Court found that although urine testing may be considered intrusive and trigger state constitutional protection for the officers, such testing was reasonable under the circumstances; city officials also had no discretion over the testing, which was limited to marijuana use only. See also Allen v. Marietta Bd. of Lights and Water, Inc., 693 F. Supp. 1122, 1127 (N.D. Ga. 1987) (no violation of Fourth Amendment rights where "urinalyses were conducted solely to further employment-related objective and in a manner to minimize intrusion").

The Drug-Free Workplace Programs Act provides that a rebuttable presumption of drug use arises when an employee who is injured at work unjustifiably refuses to submit to a drug test. O.C.G.A. § 34-9-17(b)(3). The Georgia Supreme Court has held that the rebuttable presumption exists even if the employee did not have advance notice of the consequences for refusing to submit to the drug test. Georgia Self-Insurers Guaranty Trust Fund v. Thomas, 269 Ga. 560, 501 S.E.2d 818 (1998). However, an employer need not implement a certified drug-free workplace program to justify a discharge for a failed or refused drug test in violation of the employer's policy. Georgia-Pacific Corporation v. Ivey, 250 Ga. App. 181, 549 S.E.2d 471 (2001); accord Hearn v. The Board of Public Education, 191 F.3d 1329 (11th Cir. 1999).

Other statutory provisions affecting public employers are as follows: school bus drivers are subject to random testing for use of illegal drugs and to random testing for use of alcohol during the school day, O.C.G.A. § 20-2-1121; public employers must conduct random drug testing of state employees in jobs classified as "high risk," O.C.G.A. § 45-20-92; and all applicants for state employment must submit to drug testing according to federal workplace testing procedures, O.C.G.A. § 45-20-110 (1998).

C. Medical Testing

1. ***Common Law and Statutes.*** No reported case or relevant statute.

2. ***Private Employers.*** The Supreme Court of Georgia has held that workers' compensation does not shield a company doctor from malpractice liability, even though the company "controlled [the] practice of medicine and [the]

manner of treatment" that the doctor provided to employees. Davis v. Stover, 184 Ga. App. 560, 563, 362 S.E.2d 97 (1987), aff'd, 258 Ga. 156, 366 S.E.2d 670 (1988).

3. ***Public Employers.*** No reported case.

D. Polygraph Tests

Georgia delimits, but does not prohibit employers from conducting polygraph tests on their employees. O.C.G.A. § 51-1-37 authorizes the recovery of back wages against the examiner for the period of unemployment caused by a negligently-administered examination.

As with drug tests, public employers are generally more restricted in their use of polygraph tests than private employers. The Supreme Court of Georgia has held that a public employer may dismiss an employee for refusing to take a polygraph test so long as the employee was informed that (1) the questions will relate specifically and narrowly to the performance of official duties; (2) the answer cannot be used against the employee in any subsequent criminal proceeding; and (3) the penalty for refusal is dismissal. Moss v. Central State Hosp., 176 Ga. App. 116, 335 S.E.2d 456 (1985), rev'd on other grounds, 255 Ga. 403, 339 S.E.2d 226 (1986). See also Hester v. City of Milledgeville, 777 F.2d 1492 (11th Cir. 1985) (city may require firefighters or police officers to undergo polygraph testing without violating rights against self-incrimination if employees are not required to waive their constitutional rights and the test is not used as the only basis for discipline), reh'g en banc denied, 782 F.2d 180 (11th Cir. 1986).

E. Fingerprinting

Fingerprinting of employees is generally not prohibited, but an employer may not fingerprint employees in a discriminatory manner. See Bempah v. Kroger Co., 51 Fair. Empl. Prac. Cas. (BNA) 195 (S.D. Ga. 1989) (employer violated Title VII by singling out employee for fingerprinting because of his race during theft investigation).

Background investigations and fingerprinting are required for applicants in the following areas of employment: (1) teachers and educational administrators, O.C.G.A. § 20-2-211; (2) firefighters, O.C.G.A. § 25-4-8; (3) healthcare workers, O.C.G.A. § 31-7-259; (4) private investigators, O.C.G.A. § 43-38-6; (5) Department of Human Resources employees, O.C.G.A. § 49-2-14; and (6) day care employees, O.C.G.A. § 49-5-62.

III. SEARCHES

A. Employee's Person

1. ***Private Employers.*** There is no Fourth Amendment protection against searches conducted exclusively by a private employer. Bunn v. State, 153 Ga. App. 270, 265 S.E.2d 88 (1980).

2. ***Public Employers.*** The Fourth Amendment protection against unreasonable searches applies to public entities. Braddock v. State, 127 Ga. App. 513, 194 S.E.2d 317 (1972) (warrantless search and arrest by federal safety inspector upheld where employee did not have a reasonable expectation of privacy).

B. Employee's Work Area

A search warrant authorizing the search of a person and his property at his home will not be extended to allow a search of that person at his place of employment. State v. Dills, 237 Ga. App. 165, 167, 514 S.E.2d 917, 919 (1999) (upholding suppression of evidence seized during a search of a person at the construction site where he worked).

C. Employee's Property

1. ***Private Employers.*** While there are no reported cases directly on point, several cases have addressed the issue of the scope of an employee's reasonable expectation of privacy when *law enforcement*, rather than the private employer, conducts a search of the employee's property maintained at the workplace. See Tidwell v. State, 285 Ga. 103, 104-05, 674 S.E.2d 272, 273-74 (2009) (sheriff's search of defendant's personal locker located within defendant's personal sleeping quarters at defendant's place of employment not reasonable, because sheriff did not have search warrant, locker clearly could be locked, and permission to search was granted by co-worker without authority over plaintiff's locker or sleeping quarters); but see United States v. Sutton, 2009 WL 481411, *6-9 (M.D. Ga. Feb. 25, 2009) (FBI agents' search of lawyer's office reasonable because agents attended search protocol meeting prior to search, only minimal amount of evidence outside scope of warrant was seized, and such improperly seized evidence was not turned over to prosecution); United States v. Aguirre, 2008 WL 4790659, *14 (S.D. Ga. Nov. 3, 2008) (IRS agents' failure to include search protocol in warrant to search defendant's computers not fatal because, in affidavits, agents explained need to search computers and described techniques, and nothing in record suggested that information obtained from computers were used in investigation concerning case).

2. ***Public Employers.*** The Fourth Amendment protection against unreasonable searches applies to public entities. Braddock v. State, 127 Ga. App. 513, 194 S.E.2d 317 (1972) (warrantless search and arrest by federal safety inspector upheld where employee did not have a reasonable expectation of privacy).

IV. MONITORING OF EMPLOYEES

A. Telephone and Electronic Communications

It is unlawful under Georgia law for "any person in a clandestine manner intentionally to overhear, transmit, or record or attempt to overhear, transmit, or record the private conversation of another which shall originate in a private place." O.C.G.A. § 16-11-62(1). Georgia law, like federal law, prohibits only clandestine taping by persons who are not parties to the conversation. Therefore, as long as one party consents to the recording, the recording is lawful. O.C.G.A. § 16-11-66(a); Parrott v. Wilson, 707 F.2d 1262 (11th Cir. 1983); Mitchell v. State, 239 Ga. 3, 235 S.E.2d 509 (1977); Sheppard v. Reid, 198 Ga. App. 703, 402 S.E.2d 793 (1991); Perkins-Carrillo v. Systemax, Inc., 2006 WL 1553957 (N.D. Ga. May 26, 2006) (court granted employer summary judgment on federal and state wiretapping claims because plaintiff signed "Acknowledgement and Agreement" form allowing telephone calls to be monitored and recorded). Eavesdropping victims can bring civil actions under Georgia's eavesdropping act. Tapley v. Collins, 41 F. Supp. 2d 1366, 1369 (S.D. Ga. 1999), rev'd on other grounds, 211 F.3d 1210 (11th Cir. 2000); Barlow v. Barlow, 272 Ga. 102, 526 S.E.2d 857 (2000) (cordless telephone conversation protected under wiretapping statute); Bishop v. State, 241 Ga. App. 517, 526 S.E.2d 917 (1999) (parent's recording of telephone conversation of thirteen year old daughter violated statute).

1. ***Wiretapping.*** O.C.G.A. § 16-11-65 allows employers who meet certain licensing and other criteria, including the ability to show a "clear, apparent, and logically reasonable need for the use of equipment in connection with a legitimate business activity . . ., " to intercept telephonic communications for business service improvement; such conversations may not, however, be recorded. Georgia courts allow an employer to monitor its employees' telephone conversations where the employees were advised that monitoring was occurring and told that phones were for business use only. Jackson v. Nationwide Credit, Inc., 206 Ga. App. 810, 426 S.E.2d 630 (1992) (no intrusion upon seclusion for routine monitoring of telephone calls where employer provided appropriate notice); but see Anderson v. City of Columbus, 374 F. Supp. 2d 1240 (M.D. Ga. 2005) (denying summary judgment on claim under Georgia wiretapping statute where, although call -center employee had been told that incoming calls would be recorded, genuine issue of fact existed as to whether employee was aware of a "glitch" in the system under which anything said into telephone headset would be recorded, even after telephone call had ended).

2. ***Electronic Communications.*** It is unlawful under Georgia law "intentionally and secretly to intercept . . . the contents of a message sent by telephone, telegraph, letter, or by any other means of private communication," or to "divulge to any unauthorized person or authority the content or substance of any private message intercepted lawfully" under O.C.G.A. § 16-11-65 (allowing for interception of telephonic communications for business service improvement). O.C.G.A. § 16-11-62(4), (5); Conner v. Tate, 130 F. Supp. 2d 1370 (N.D. Ga. 2001) (dissemination of unlawfully accessed voicemail messages sufficient to state a claim under O.C.G.A. § 16-11-62 prohibiting transmission of private communications of others).

3. ***Other Electronic Monitoring.*** Georgia's "computer invasion of privacy" statute, O.C.G.A. 16-9-93(c), states that "any person who uses a computer or computer network with the intention of examining any employment, medical, salary, credit, or any other financial or personal data relating to any other person with knowledge that such examination is without authority shall be guilty of the crime of computer invasion of privacy." For employers, the key to this statute is that such access be "without authority." Jackson v. Nationwide Credit, Inc., 206 Ga. App. 810, 426 S.E.2d 630 (1992) (no intrusion upon seclusion for routine monitoring of telephone calls where employer provided appropriate notice); Sitton v. Print Direction, Inc., No. A11A1055, 2011 WL 4469712 (Ga. Ct. App. Sept. 28, 2011) (holding that employer's review of employee's email on employee's personal laptop computer located in employer's office and used to conduct business for the employer was not computer theft, computer trespass, or computer invasion of privacy; holding that employer's actions were not such an unreasonable intrusion on employee's seclusion or solitude as to rise to the level of invasion of privacy; holding that employer's retrieval of email from employee's personal laptop computer did not constitute unlawful eavesdropping or surveillance).

Georgia law makes it a crime to "disclose[] a number, code, password, or other means of access to a computer or computer network knowing that such disclosure is without authority and which results in damages (including the fair market value of any services used and victim expenditure) to the owner of the computer or computer network in excess of $500.00." O.C.G.A. 16-9-93(e). There are no reported cases applying O.C.G.A. § 16-9-93(c) or (e) to keystroke monitoring or internet usage monitoring by an employer.

B. Mail

It is unlawful under Georgia law "intentionally and secretly to intercept . . . the contents of a message sent by telephone, telegraph, letter, or by any other means of private communication". O.C.G.A. § 16-11-62(4), (5) (emphasis added). There are no reported cases.

C. Surveillance/Photographing

It is unlawful under Georgia law to "observe, photograph, or record the activities of another which occur in any private place and out of public view . . ." without the consent of all persons being observed. O.C.G.A. § 16-11-62(2). See In re Holloway, 266 Ga. 599, 469 S.E.2d 167 (1996) (State Bar proceeding against attorney who secretly videotaped his secretary in the bathroom). Private place is defined in O.C.G.A. § 16-11-60(3) as "a place where one is entitled reasonably to expect to be safe from casual or hostile . . . surveillance." See Snider v. State, 238 Ga. App. 55, 57, 516 S.E.2d 569, 571 (1999). It is not unlawful, however, to observe or photograph prison inmates, so long as such surveillance or photography does not take place while the prisoner is discussing his case with his attorney. O.C.G.A. § 16-11-62(2).

It is also unlawful under Georgia law to "go on or about the premises of another or any private place for the purpose of invading the privacy of others by eavesdropping upon their conversations or secretly observing their activities." O.C.G.A. § 16-11-62(3).

There is no immunity from invasion of privacy liability when an employer hires a third party to conduct surveillance of an injured employee at his home and the third party conducts the surveillance in an unreasonable manner. Ellenberg v. Pinkerton's Inc., 125 Ga. App. 648, 188 S.E.2d 911 (1972). In Ellenberg, the employee sued his employer for injuries he sustained at work. The employer hired a third party investigator to conduct surveillance on plaintiff. The investigator "conducted the surveillance in an open and notorious manner to the general alarm of the plaintiff, his family and neighbors; [and] the action of the defendant was well calculated to intimidate Ellenberg into dropping his action . . . ." Id. at 911. The court held that although the employer had a limited right to invade the employee's privacy, surveillance must be done "in a reasonable and proper manner and only in furtherance of its interest with regard to the suit against it." Id. at 914. The employer cannot relinquish its responsibility for a proper investigation by the use of a third party investigator. Cf. Ass'n Services, Inc. v. Smith, 249 Ga. App. 629, 549 S.E.2d 454 (2001) (issue of fact regarding videotaping at home and work for purposes of a worker's compensation investigation of injury).

One Georgia court has held that an employer is not liable for intrusion of privacy where it engages in surveillance of a restroom provided for its customers. Elmore v. Atlantic Zayre, Inc., 178 Ga. App. 25, 341 S.E.2d 905 (1986). In Elmore, a customer complained about homosexual activity in the bathroom stalls of defendant's retail facility. As a result of the defendant's observations, plaintiff was apprehended and charged with sodomy. The court held that because the employer "had an overriding responsibility to its patrons to keep th[e] restroom free of crime, safe, and available for its intended purpose," its intrusion into the plaintiff-customer's seclusion was not unreasonable. 341 S.E.2d at 906. This case was distinguished, however, in Johnson v. Allen, 272 Ga. App. 861, 613 S.E.2d 657 (2005). In Johnson, the court held that video monitoring of a private area was unlawful when done over a long period of time and in response to non-specific rumors, not in direct response to "specific information of illegal activity."

V. ACTIVITIES OUTSIDE THE WORKPLACE

A. Common Law or Statutes

Public employees, at least, have a right to privacy with respect to their statements outside of work. In Waters v. Chaffin, a police officer was disciplined for his off-duty criticism and ridicule of a superior officer. The court wrote that "everyone has a legitimate interest in maintaining a zone of privacy where he can speak about work without fear of censure." 684 F.2d 833, 837 (11th Cir. 1982). The police department failed to show that the speech "disrupt[ed] the officer's efficiency or the internal operation of the department" and that the speech was reasonably likely to harm its "efficiency, discipline, or harmony." Id. at 839-840. See also Local 491, International Brotherhood of Police Officers v. Gwinnett County, GA, 510 F. Supp. 2d 1271 (2007) (holding Defendant's questioning of police officers relating to their off-duty union activity in connection with an investigation into a different officer's on-duty disloyal statements was unconstitutional.

B. Employees' Personal Relationships

1. ***Romantic Relationships Between Employees.*** Investigation of a public employee's potential sexual misconduct does not automatically give rise to an invasion of privacy cause of action. "The right of privacy, protectable in tort, however, extends only to unnecessary public scrutiny. It does not protect legitimate inquiry into the operation of a government institution and those employed by it." Meyer v. Ledford, 170 Ga. App. 245, 316 S.E.2d 804, 807 (1984).

Furthermore, a private employee's voluntary act of engaging in intercourse or other sexual conduct may negate his or her privacy claims. See Cummings v. Walsh Constr. Co., 561 F. Supp. 872 (S.D. Ga. 1983) (female employee waived right to personal seclusion and private facts when she voluntarily engaged in sexual intercourse with a supervisor and then told others about it).

2. ***Sexual Orientation.*** There is no anti-discrimination statute in Georgia prohibiting employers from discriminating against individuals based on sexual orientation.

In Shahar v. Bowers, 114 F.3d 1097 (11th Cir. 1997), the Eleventh Circuit held that the Attorney General's Office did not violate a homosexual woman's constitutional right of intimate association when it revoked its offer of employment after learning of her "marriage" to another woman. According to the court, the government employer's interest in maintaining public confidence in the state's highest law enforcement office outweighed the plaintiff's interest in intimate association. Id. at 1110. One factor in the court's decision was the implicit conflict of interest that would arise from Ms. Shahar's employment with the Attorney General's Office, which had the duty of enforcing the Georgia law against sodomy.

However, the Georgia Supreme Court subsequently found the state sodomy law unconstitutional under the Georgia Constitution. Powell v. State, 270 Ga. 327, 510 S.E.2d 18 (1998). In Powell, a case which involved heterosexual activity, the court held that normal, consensual, private, adult sexual activity (but not incest or certain other unprotected sexual activity) was a protected right of privacy and the state could not justify its interference with that right. The effect of this holding on Shahar is unclear at this time, as the decision in Shahar was not based solely on the presumed constitutionality of the state sodomy law. One conceivable effect of Powell, however, is that sodomy may no longer be considered a violation of a state law that would trigger "for cause" termination in an employment agreement. See Glenn v. Brumby, 724 F. Supp. 1284 (N.D. Ga. 2010) (holding that Georgia General Assembly's Office of Legislative Counsel violated discharged transsexual employee's rights under the Equal Protection Clause).

3. ***Marital Status.*** There is no prohibition in Georgia against terminating an employee based on marital status. See Huiet v. Atlanta Gas Light Co., 70 Ga. App. 233, 28 S.E.2d 83 (1943) (contractual prohibition against marriage was not void as against public policy).

C. Smoking

Georgia has no legislation imposing general restrictions on smoking in public places. Smoking in certain public places, however, including enclosed elevators and daycare centers, which are clearly designated by no smoking signs, is prohibited. O.C.G.A. § 16-12-2.

D. Blogging

While no reported Georgia cases deal with employee blogging, Georgia is a strong at-will state. "The employer[,] with or without cause and regardless of its motives may discharge the employee without liability." Eckhardt v. Yerkes Regional Primate Center, 254 Ga. App. 38, 38, 561 S.E.2d 164, 165 (2002). Georgia courts have even rejected attempts to create a common-law exception to the at-will doctrine for "whisteblowing" employees. Id. (granting employer's motion to dismiss where plaintiffs alleged that they were terminated for internally reporting dangerous procedures).

VI. RECORDS

A. Personnel Records

Georgia law does not require employers to provide employees access to their personnel files. Employers must keep accurate records of the name, address, and occupation of each employee, daily and weekly hours worked, and the wages paid during each pay period; these records must be kept for at least one year. O.C.G.A. § 34-2-11.

Factors to consider in determining whether private information relating to a public employee should be disclosed includes the reliability of the information and its relevance to the public issue. Harris v. Cox Enters., Inc., 256 Ga. 299, 348 S.E.2d 448 (1986). The attendance records of an employee are not private or secret. In Kobeck v. Nabisco, Inc., 166 Ga. App. 652, 305 S.E.2d 183 (1983), the court suggested that the employer was privileged to disclose attendance records contained in the confidential personnel file of an employee to her husband. The statements regarding the employee's attendance were made in the performance of a private moral duty and information on attendance is not considered private or secret. Ultimately, however, the court avoided answering that question, holding that attendance records were not of such a "private nature" that their dissemination to plaintiff's husband could be said to invade plaintiff's privacy. Finally, the court held that release of employment records was not the kind of "physical intrusion" needed to sustain an intrusion into seclusion cause of action. The husband assumed his wife was having an affair after learning of her absences from work and committed suicide.

O.C.G.A. § 34-8-120(b) lays out an individual's right to privacy with respect to records held by the Department of Labor and outlines the situations where the right to privacy must yield to other considerations. As stated by the Supreme Court of Georgia in Athens Observer Inc. v. Anderson, 245 Ga. 63, 263 S.E.2d 128 (1980), "the right of privacy, protectable in tort, however extends only to unnecessary public scrutiny." Courts have upheld a state agency's release to the media, pursuant to the Georgia Public Records Act, of an investigatory report concerning employee sexual harassment. The report was held not to be a part of the employee's personnel file and even if it were, there was no prohibition against disclosing personnel files. The Act prohibits disclosure of information that would constitute an invasion of one's privacy, but the matter was deemed to be one of public importance. Fincher v. Georgia, 231 Ga. App. 49, 497 S.E.2d 632 (1998). **O.C.G.A. § 34-8-126 provides an exception to § 34-8-120(b) in that records may be made available in judicial proceedings where the "presiding officer" makes a finding in an order that "the need for the information or records in the proceeding outweighs any reasons for the privacy and confidentiality of the information or records." Ezzard v. Eatonton & Putnam Water & Sewer Authority, No. 5:11–CV–505 (CAR), 2012 WL 3901748, *2 (M.D.Ga. Sept. 7, 2012) (denying Georgia Department of Labor's motion to quash plaintiff's request for "[a]ny and all files and records pertaining to [plaintiff's] claim for unemployment compensation...including without limitations any and all hearing transcripts with exhibits, and any and all communications from the parties" where the judge determined that plaintiff's privacy would not be invaded since plaintiff was the one making the request).**

The Open Records Act, O.C.G.A. § 50-18-70 et seq., permits any citizen of Georgia to inspect public records of an agency, as defined in O.C.G.A. § 50-18-70(a), except those which are prohibited or exempted from public inspection by law or by court order. See Goddard v. City of Albany, 285 Ga. 882, 684 S.E.2d 635 (2009) (holding that the personnel records of municipal employees are not entitled to any blanket exemption from Georgia's Open Records Act); **Smith v. Lott, 730 S.E.2d 663, 669, 12 FCDR 2516 (Ga. App. 2012) (holding that city manager was not liable for defamation where he did not verbally disclose anything to plaintiff's prospective employer that the prospective employer did not already obtain through the Georgia Open Records Act).**

O.C.G.A. § 50-18-72 limits the disclosure of public records including the following: (1) medical records in which disclosure would result in an invasion of privacy; (2) confidential evaluations during the hiring process; (3) information collected related to the "suspension, firing, or investigation of complaints against public officers or employees until ten days after the same has been presented to the agency or an officer for action or the investigation is otherwise concluded . . .;" and (4) personal information on law enforcement officials.

The production of non-party employee payroll records has been held to raise fewer privacy concerns and protections than personnel records, especially if the payroll records are produced to counsel, who is prohibited by ethical and professional obligations from disseminating the information beyond the needs of the case, if identifying information in the payroll records is not likely to end up in the hands of identity theft predators, and if there is no evidence that the production is likely to harm the employer's competitive position in the marketplace. See Ojeda-Sanchez v. Bland Farms, LLC, 2009 WL 2365976, *2-3 (S.D. Ga. July 31, 2009).

B. Medical Records

O.C.G.A. § 50-18-72 limits the disclosure of public records, including medical records, in which disclosure would result in an invasion of privacy. The privilege of confidentiality of psychiatric records is particularly restrictive. See Sletto v. Hospital Authority, 239 Ga. App. 203, 521 S.E.2d 199 (1999) (holding that, where medical center erroneously released plaintiff's psychiatric records, jury issue existed as to whether center adequately controlled those records). The right of privacy in medical records may be waived in writing or to the extent that the medical information is at issue in any civil or criminal proceeding; however, a subpoena for medical records absent such waiver and without notice is improper. King v. State, 272 Ga. 788, 535 S.E.2d 492 (2000) (reversing DUI conviction based on medical records obtained by an ex parte subpoena to third party medical providers). In Karpowicz v. Hyles, 247 Ga. App. 292, 543 S.E.2d 51 (2000), the Georgia Court of Appeals affirmed the grant of summary judgment in favor of a lawyer on a claim of intrusion arising from the lawyer's subpoena for and use of psychiatric records for impeachment of a witness. The court ruled that the lawyer was authorized to presume that the hospital had not released privileged information.

When an employee submits a claim for workers' compensation, receives payment of weekly income benefits, or the employer has paid any medical expenses, the employee loses his physician privilege of confidentiality concerning any communications related to his claims, history, or treatment of the injury. O.C.G.A. § 34-9-207.

Georgia law does not require an employer to provide employees access to their medical files, but health care providers must provide a complete and current copy of the medical record, upon written request, to any person who has received health care services from the provider. O.C.G.A. § 31-33-2, § 31-33-1.

An employee that is subject to an employer's drug testing is not considered a "patient" of the employer or of the testing laboratory for purposes of Georgia statutes precluding the release of medical records. Foster v. Swinney, 263 Ga. App. 510, 588 S.E.2d 307 (2003).

In Harrison v. Benchmark Elec. Huntsville, Inc., 593 F.3d 1206 (11th Cir. 2010), the Eleventh Circuit explicitly recognized, for the first time, that a plaintiff has a private right of action under the ADA, 42 U.S.C. § 12112(d)(2), regarding the bar against pre-employment offer medical examinations or inquiries that relate to an applicant's disability status, irrespective of plaintiff's disability status.

C. Criminal Records

An employer who required applicant to disclose all criminal offenses, which information was then confirmed for accuracy and truthfulness by employer's security department, could not be held liable for negligent hiring or retention of applicant because employer conducted appropriate investigation and did not obtain any information of applicant's violent propensities. Southern Bell Tel. & Tel. Co. v. Sharara, 167 Ga. App. 665, 307 S.E.2d 129 (1983).

Certain convictions under Georgia's First Offender Program are not considered to be a conviction of a crime and may not be used to disqualify a person in any application for employment or appointment to office in either the public or private sector. O.C.G.A. § 42-8-63. See also Maddox v. Yellow Freight Systems, Inc., 243 Ga. App. 894, 534 S.E.2d 561 (2010) (holding there is no statutory cause of action for violation of O.C.G.A. § 42-8-63).

D. Subpoenas / Search Warrants

In King v. State, 272 Ga. 788, 535 S.E.2d 492 (2000), the Supreme Court held that an individual enjoys a constitutional right of privacy in his or her medical records. The court therefore quashed the prosecution's attempt to obtain a criminal defendant's medical records via an *ex parte* subpoena, on the grounds that the statute under which the subpoena was issued did not give the defendant notice of the subpoena or an opportunity to object before the records were produced. In Ellis v. State, 275 Ga. App. 881, 884, 622 S.E.2d 89, 91 (2005), the court held that an individual's medical records could be obtained via a search warrant, because the procedures for obtaining a search warrant adequately protected an individual's privacy rights.

VII. ACTIONS SUBSEQUENT TO EMPLOYMENT

A. References

"Georgia courts have long recognized that a prima facie privilege shields statements made concerning a current or former employee by a current or former employer to one, such as a prospective employer, who has a legitimate interest in such information." Kenney v. Gilmore, 195 Ga. App. 407, 409, 393 S.E.2d 472, 473 (1990). The privilege, however, is a qualified one and be overcome with a showing of actual malice. Id.

B. Non-Compete Agreements

The Georgia Constitution itself declares void all contracts "intended to have the effect of defeating or lessening competition." Ga. Const, Art. 3, § 6, ¶ 5(c)(1). "[A] restrictive covenant contained in an employment contract is considered to be in partial restraint of trade and will be upheld if the restraint imposed is not unreasonable, is founded on a valuable consideration, and is reasonably necessary to protect the interest of the party in whose favor it is imposed, and does not unduly prejudice the interests of the public." W.R. Grace & Co. v. Mouyal, 262 Ga. 464, 465, 422 S.E.2d 529, 531 (1992).

In 2009, the Georgia Legislature passed and Governor Perdue signed House Bill 173 to establish new rules for the temporal and geographic scope of non-compete agreements, the types of activities that can be prohibited, and the categories of employees who can be bound by such prohibitions, and to allow courts to "blue pencil," or strike out unreasonable portions of, non-compete agreements. **This legislation was intended to replace the complicated common law rules regarding the enforceability of restrictive covenants in Georgia at that time. The effective date of the 2009 legislation was made expressly contingent upon the passage of an amendment to the Georgia Constitution which would give power to the General Assembly to authorize contracts in the restraint of trade. That amendment was adopted in November 2010. See Ga. Const. Art. 3, § 6, ¶ 5(c). Due to controversy regarding the effective date of House Bill 173, however, on May 11, 2011, Governor Nathan Deal signed House Bill 30, codified as O.C.G.A. §§ 13-8-50 et seq., which substantially reenacted House Bill 173, with minor changes, and attempted to clear up confusion regarding the statute's effective date. In a recent Eleventh Circuit case, Becham v. Synthes USA, No. 11-14495, 2012 WL 1994604, (11th Cir. June 4, 2012), the court squarely addressed the new law's effective date and concluded that restrictive covenants entered into on or after May 11, 2011 are controlled by the new Restrictive Covenant Act. All other restrictive covenants entered into prior to that date are controlled by Georgia's pre-existing common law regarding the enforceability of restrictive**

covenants. Id. at *4. There have been no reported cases analyzing restrictive covenants under the new Restrictive Covenant Act.

Under Georgia's restrictive covenant statute, the "legitimate business interests" that an employer may protect through restrictive covenants are defined to include, without limitation, trade secrets, other valuable confidential information, substantial relationships with customers and vendors, customer good will, and extraordinary or specialized training. O.C.G.A. § 13-8-51(9). Further, the statute authorizes judicial modification – or "blue-penciling" – of an otherwise overly broad covenant "so long as the modification does not render the covenant more restrictive with regard to the employee than as originally drafted by the parties." O.C.G.A. § 13-8-53(d). The statute also provides guidance regarding the permissible time limits of restrictive covenants. Employment covenants of two years or less are presumed reasonable, while covenants of more than two years are presumed unreasonable. O.C.G.A. § 13-8-57(b). The statute also makes clear that nondisclosure covenants need not have a time limit in order to be enforceable, but rather that confidential information may be protected for as long as it remains confidential or a trade secret. O.C.G.A. § 13-8-53(e).

Under Georgia's common law, courts have adopted a three-part test as a "tool" for determining whether non-compete agreements are reasonable. Non-compete agreements will be upheld if they are reasonably limited as to (1) time; (2) the scope of conduct prohibited; and (3) the geographic area to which they apply. Watson v. Waffle House, Inc., 253 Ga. 671, 324 S.E.2d 175 (1985). Few Georgia courts have overturned covenants because they were unreasonable as to time, and covenants as long as five years – a time period longer than the employee was employed – have been upheld. Smith v. HBT, Inc., 213 Ga. App. 560, 563, 445 S.E.2d 315, 318 (1994) (upholding five year restrictive covenant where employee had only been employed by employer for four years); see also Mathis v. Orkin Exterminating Co., 254 Ga. App. 335, 562 S.E. 213 (2002) (upholding two year non-compete agreement). But an agreement that is unclear or uncertain as to time will not be enforced. Keuhn v. Selton Ass'n, Inc., 242 Ga. App. 662, 530 S.E.2d 787 (2000). A non-compete agreement may only prohibit an employee from performing the same or similar work as that which he or she performed for the employer. Covenants in which employees have been prohibited from working for a competitor 'in any capacity" will be struck down. Howard Schultz & Assocs., Inc. v. Broniec, 239 Ga. 181, 236 S.E.2d 265 (1977); Fleury v. AFAB, Inc., 205 Ga. App. 642, 423 S.E.2d 49 (1992); Gandolfo's Deli Boys LLC v. Holman, 490 F. Supp. 2d 1353 (N.D. Ga. 2007); Stultz v. Safety and Compliance Management, Inc., 285 Ga. App. 799, 648 S.E.2d 129 (2007); **Fantastic Sams Salons Corp. v. Maxie Enters., Inc., No. 3:11–CV–22 (CDL), 2012 WL 210889 (M.D.Ga. Jan. 24, 2012).** The geographic area in which an employee is prohibited from competing must also be clearly defined and reasonably limited. Georgia courts have held that employees may only be prohibited from competing in the areas in which they actually performed work for their employer. Wiley v. Royal Cup, Inc., 258 Ga. 357, 370 S.E.2d 744 (1988). This is to be distinguished from the area in which the *employer* does business. Id. See Impreglon, Inc. v. Newco Enterprises, Inc., 508 F. Supp. 2d 1222 (2007); Beacon Security Technology, Inc. v. Beasley, 648 S.E.2d 440 (Ga. App. 2007). See also Gandolfo's Deli Boys, LLC v. Hollman, 490 F. Supp. 2d 1353, 1358 (N.D. Ga. 2007) (holding that an overbroad territorial restriction, which is "capable of changing and expanding during the life of the agreement" is invalid); Tucker v. EBSCO Industries, Inc., 2007 WL 397065 (N. D. Ga. Feb 1, 2007) (holding unreasonable a restrictive covenant containing a vague description of the territory covered in the agreement, which was also "unreasonably broad in scope because it seeks to limit plaintiff from soliciting or servicing 'any customer or account of the type sold or serviced by [defendant]"); Onbrand Media v. Codex Consulting, Inc., 301 Ga. App. 141, 687 S.E.2d 168 (2009) (holding that the non-compete provisions in a non-disclosure agreement were unenforceable because they contained no territorial limits or limits on the scope of restricted activity); **Crump Ins. Servs. v. All Risks, Ltd., 315 Ga.App. 490, 727 S.E.2d 131 (2012) (holding unreasonable a non-compete that was not limited geographically and prohibited former employees from accepting business from certain customers for two years, regardless of whether the employees had worked directly with the customers)**. However, a non-compete agreement that lacks a geographic restriction may be upheld if the employee is only prohibited from soliciting business with those customers with whom he or she actually had contact while working for the employer. W.R. Grace & Co. v. Mouyal, 262 Ga. 464, 422 S.E.2d 529 (1992) (upholding customer non -solicitation agreement without geographic restrictions). See also Palmer & Cay of Georgia v. Lockton Cos., Inc., 280 Ga. 479, 484, 629 S.E.2d 800, 804 (2006), rev'g 273 Ga. App. 511, 615 S.E.2d 752 (2005), on remand, 284 Ga. App. 196, 643 S.E.2d 746 (2007) (holding reasonable a non-solicitation agreement prohibiting, for a two-year period, solicitation of any customers the former employee personally served at any time during his employment at the company);

The consideration that must be given to support a restrictive covenant is merely formal. The prospect of employment or, in the case of a current employee, continued employment, will suffice. Thomas v. Coastal Indus. Svcs., 214 Ga. 832, 108 S.E.2d 328 (1959).

Georgia courts recognize several different kinds of employer interest sufficient to justify covenants not to compete. Customer relationships, the company's investment in training its employees and the company's corporate goodwill are all interests sufficient to justify post-employment non-compete agreements. W.R. Grace, 262 Ga. at 466, 422 S.E.2d 529 ("[An] employer has a protectible interest in the customer relationships its former employee established and/or nurtured while employed by the employer and is entitled to protect itself from the risk that the former employee might appropriate customers by taking unfair advantage of the contacts developed while working for the employer."); Habif, Arogeti & Wynne, P.C. v. Baggett, 231 Ga. App. 289, 498 S.E.2d 346 (1998); Pierce v. Industrial Boiler Co., 252 Ga. 558, 559 , 315 S.E.2d 423 (1984) (upholding covenant not to compete because it protected "the employer's legitimate interest in the investment of time and money in developing the employee's skills"); Reardigan v. Shaw Industries, Inc., 238 Ga. App. 142, 144, 518 S.E.2d 144 (1999) (upholding salesman's restrictive covenant because the restrictive covenant was a "legitimate protection of the employer's investment in customer relations and good will"); SmallBizPros v. Court, 414 F. Supp. 2d 1245, 1249-50 (M.D. Ga. 2006) (holding reasonable a non-compete agreement restricting Defendants from engaging as owners or managers in the operation of a business providing bookkeeping or income tax preparation services within the franchise territory since the restrictions "do not altogether prevent Defendants from doing accounting work . . . in such a business that is owned and managed by someone else as long as they do not divert customers").

VIII. OTHER ISSUES

A. Statute of Limitations

The statute of limitation for "[a]ctions for injuries to the person . . . [is] two years after the right of action accrues, except for injuries to the reputation, which shall be brought within one year after the right of action accrues." O.C.G.A. § 9-3 -33. Georgia courts have recognized that in false light cases, the interest at stake is an individual's reputation, therefore, the one-year statute of limitations applies. Brewer v. Rogers, 211 Ga. App. 343, 350, 439 S.E.2d 77 (1993) (quoting Cabaniss v. Hipsley, 114 Ga. App. 367, 370, 151 S.E.2d 496, 500 (1966)). In invasion of privacy cases other than false light cases, Georgia courts have applied the two-year statute of limitations applicable to claims for injuries to the person. Hudson v. Montcalm Pub. Corp., 190 Ga. App. 629, 379 S.E.2d 572 (1989) (publication of private facts); Jones v. Hudgins, 163 Ga. App. 793, 796, 295 S.E.2d 119, 121 (1982) (misappropriation); Summers v. Bailey, 55 F.3d 1564 n.3 (11th Cir. 1995) (invasion of privacy claim alleging intrusion). In cases involving the publication of private facts, the statute begins on the date the information is released, not on the date that the plaintiff discovers its release. Sletto v. Hospital Authority, 239 Ga. App. 203, 521 S.E.2d 199 (1999).

A two-year statute of limitations period generally applies to intentional infliction of emotional distress claims. See Henrickson v. Pain Control & Rehabilitation, 205 Ga. App. 843, 424 S.E.2d 27 (1992), rev'd on other grounds, 263 Ga. 331, 434 S.E.2d 51 (1993).

Georgia recognizes "that an individual has a valuable property right in his employment, trade or profession and that this property right is subject to a four-year statute of limitation;" as such, this limitations period applies to claims asserting tortious interference with employment. Lee v. Gore, 221 Ga. App. 632, 633, 472 S.E.2d 164 (1996). The four-year limitations period applies even where certain libel elements may exist if "the [employment] is the thing legally threatened, and the publication of the words is merely an instrument and incident of this result." Lee v. Gore, 221 Ga. App. at 634-35 (quoting Dale v. City Plumbing, 112 Ga. App. 723, 728, 146 S.E.2d 349 (1965)); see also Brewer v. Schacht, 235 Ga. App. 313, 317, 509 S.E.2d 378, 383 (1998) (finding that in a claim asserting tortious interference with employment contract, "the one year statute of limitations for defamation actions is inapplicable, even if the interference allegedly was accomplished through defamation."); see also McCandliss v. Cox Enters., 265 Ga. App. 377, 380, 593 S.E.2d 856 (2004) (holding that the one-year statute of limitations does not apply to tortious interference with contract claims, "even if the interference allegedly was accomplished through defamation").

Georgia courts have not extended the continuing tort doctrine to torts concerning invasion of privacy. Rivell v. Private Health Care Systems, Inc., No. CV 106–176, 2012 WL 3308901, *5 (S.D.Ga Aug. 13, 2012).

B. Jurisdiction

Georgia's long-arm statute permits the assertion of jurisdiction over an out-of-state person who (1) transacts any business within this state; (2) commits a tortious act or omission within the state, except as to a cause of action for defamation of character arising from the act; or (3) commits a tortious injury in Georgia caused by an act or omission outside of Georgia, if the tortfeasor regularly does or solicits business, or engages in any other persistent course of conduct in the state. O.C.G.A. §§ 9-10-91(1), (2), (3). When a suit does not arise out of a person's contacts with Georgia, the state may exercise general jurisdiction based on the court's findings regarding factors such as regularly doing business in the state, deriving substantial revenue from goods or services in the state, having agents or employees in the state, maintaining an office in the state, and having subsidiaries or business affiliates in the state. See, e.g., Aero Toy Store v. Grieves, 279 Ga. App. 515, 521, 631 S.E.2d 734 (2006); **Thomas v. Strange Engineering, Inc., No. CV 111–074, 2012 WL 993244, *4 (S.D. Ga. Mar. 22, 2012) (defendant's shipping of a product to Georgia and deriving revenue from the sale of that product satisfied the requirements of O.C.G.A. § 9-10-91(1)).**

C. Worker's Compensation Exclusivity

An employee's rights against an employer to recover on account of any injuries by an accident arising out of and occurring in the course of employment are determinable solely under the Workers' Compensation Act, O.C.G.A. § 34-9-1 et seq. and are not determinable at common law. In other words, the Act is the employee's exclusive remedy. O.C.G.A. § 34-9-11; Mull v. Aetna Cas. & Sur. Co., 226 Ga. 462, 175 S.E.2d 552 (1970); Stebbins v. Georgia Veneer & Package Co., 51 Ga. App. 56, 179 S.E. 649 (1935).

To be compensable under the Act, the injury must consist of a physical injury or harm. See W. W. Fowler Oil Co. v. Hamby, 192 Ga. App. 422, 385 S.E.2d 106 (1989); Hanson Buick v. Chatham, 163 Ga. App. 127, 129, 292 S.E.2d 428 (1982). Thus, a claim for intentional infliction of emotional distress, unconnected to any physical injury, does not fall under the Act because such a tort cannot be considered a physical injury. See Oliver v. Wal-Mart Stores, 209 Ga. App. 703, 704, 434 S.E.2d 500, 501 (1993).

On the other hand, if an employee brings compensable claims for physical injury as well as related claims for non-physical injury, the claims for non-physical injury still fall within the purview of the Act and the Act remains the employee's exclusive remedy, even if the non-physical claims are not compensable. See Coca-Cola Co. v. Parker, 297 Ga. App. 481, 483, 677 S.E.2d 361, 363 (2008) (holding that Act was exclusive remedy covering plaintiff's claim for physical injury caused by fallen equipment, and plaintiff's claim for mental injury caused by supervisor's subsequent request that employee perform duties exceeding her physical restrictions was precluded by exclusivity provision of Act); Lewis v. Northside Hosp., Inc., 267 Ga. App. 288, 292, 599 S.E.2d 267, 270 (2004) (holding that Act was exclusive remedy covering plaintiff's claim for battery, even though plaintiff did not claim she was physically injured, and plaintiff's ancillary common law claims for mental damages were precluded by Act); Bryant v. Wal-Mart Stores, 203 Ga. App. 770, 771-72, 417 S.E.2d 688, 691 (1992) (holding that Act was exclusive remedy covering decedent's claim for false imprisonment and decedent's related claims for non-physical injuries to his peace, happiness and feelings were precluded by Act even if they were non-compensable under it). Mental injury is compensable under the Act only if it arises naturally and unavoidably from a discernible physical occurrence. See DeKalb County Bd. of Ed. v. Singleton, 294 Ga. App. 96, 99-100, 668 S.E.2d 767, 769-70 (2008).

D. Pleading Requirements

No reported case beyond what has already been discussed.

SURVEY OF HAWAI'I EMPLOYMENT LIBEL LAW

Jeffrey S. Portnoy, Peter W. Olson, and Elijah Yip
Cades Schutte LLP
1000 Bishop Street
Honolulu, Hawai'i 96813
Telephone: (808) 521-9200; Facsimile: (808) 521-9210

(With Developments Reported Through **November 1, 2012**)

GENERAL COMMENTS

The state court system in Hawai'i has two trial levels, the circuit court and the district court. By statute, the civil jurisdiction of the district courts is limited to claims where the amount in controversy does not exceed $20,000. In addition, the district courts do not have jurisdiction over libel claims. H.R.S. § 604-5(d). As a practical matter, therefore, most employment-related lawsuits are filed in the state circuit courts. Decisions of the circuit and district courts are generally unreported and unpublished. Hawai'i has two appellate court levels, the Hawai'i Supreme Court and the Hawai'i Intermediate Court of Appeals ("ICA"). The ICA has initial jurisdiction over all appeals, subject to certain circumstances where an application for transfer to the supreme court may be sought under H.R.S. § 604-58. Under H.R.S. § 604-59, review may be sought of the ICA's decision by application to the supreme court for a writ of certiorari.

SIGNIFICANT DEVELOPMENTS SINCE THE 2012 *SURVEY*

None.

I. GENERAL LAW

A. General Employment Law

1. ***At Will Employment.*** An employment contract of indefinite duration is terminable at the will of either party, for any reason or no reason. Parnar v. Americana Hotels, Inc., 65 Haw. 370, 652 P.2d 625 (Haw. 1982) see also Shoppe v Gucci America, Inc. 94 Haw. 368, 14 P.3d 1049 (Haw. 2000) (in the absence of a written employment agreement, a collective bargaining agreement, or a statutorily conferred right, employment is at will and may be terminated at the will of either party for any reason or no reason). An employer may nevertheless be held liable in tort to an at will employee where the discharge of that employee violates a clear mandate of public policy. Parnar, 65 Haw. at 380, 652 P.2d at 631. Although the court in Parnar declined to recognize a bad faith exception to the at will employment doctrine, the court alternatively held that the plaintiff could allege a retaliatory discharge in violation of a clear mandate of public policy. Id. In Parnar, the plaintiff alleged that she was discharged in order to prevent her testimony before a grand jury investigating alleged price-fixing by her employer; the court determined that the clear mandate of public policy was "easily discern[ed] in the antitrust laws." Id. The nature of the at-will employment relationship does not impose a duty upon the employer to terminate in good faith. Catron v. Tokio Marine Management, Inc., 90 Haw. 407, 978 P.2d 845 (Haw. 1999).

As a general rule, the common law remedy for wrongful discharge is precluded only when a statutory provision relied upon as a bar to the discharge expressly, or by necessary implication, provides a sufficient remedy for wrongful discharge in itself, making the creation of an additional common law remedy unnecessary. Smith v. Chaney Brooks Realty, Inc., 10 Haw. App. 250, 865 P.2d 170 (Haw. Ct. App. 1994) (H.R.S. § 388(1), regulating employee wages and hours, established clear mandate of public policy to protect at will employee from being discharged for asserting rights accorded her by its provisions, and does not itself provide a sufficient remedy for such a discharge), distinguishing Lapinad v. Pacific Oldsmobile-GMC, Inc., 679 F. Supp. 991 (D. Haw. 1991) (Hawai'i 's employment discrimination statute, H.R.S. § 378-2, afforded sufficient remedy for wrongful discharge, thus barring the employee's common law action).

In Kinoshita v. Canadian Pacific Airlines, Ltd., 68 Haw. 594, 724 P.2d 110 (Haw. 1986), the court also held that if an employer promulgates rules that provide for "specific treatment in specific situations and an employee is induced thereby to remain on the job and not actively seek other employment," those promises constitute an implied and enforceable contract for employment, regardless of a preexisting at will employment arrangement. See also Calleon v. Miyagi, 76 Haw. 310, 876 P.2d 1278 (Haw. 1984), citing Kinoshita, 68 Haw. 594, 724 P.2d 110 (Haw. 1986). Thus, an employer may create an implied contract for employment by promulgating employee rules for "specific treatment in specific situations" in employee manuals and handbooks. See Calleon, 76 Haw. at 317, 876 P.2d at 1287, and Kinoshita, 68 Haw. at 603, 724 P.2d at 117. Disclaimers in an employee handbook do not per se preclude a claim for breach of an implied contract of employment; such disclaimers may be vitiated if (1) they are not clear, conspicuous, and understandable; (2) contradict language in the employment manual or handbook; or (3) contradict subsequent oral or written statements by the employer. Gonsalves v. Nissan Motor Corp. in Hawaii, Ltd., 100 Haw. 149, 58 P.3d 1196 (2002) (finding employee handbook did not unfairly induce the plaintiff to rely on it and thus did not create implied contract of employment); Ricasa v. Hilton Hotels Corp., 107 Haw. 507, 115 P.3d 686, 2005 WL 1714376 (2005) (unpublished summary disposition order) (reversing summary judgment entered in favor of defendant employer based on disclaimer in employee handbook; there were genuine issues of material fact whether plaintiff's termination was a retaliatory action based on his report of unlawful workplace harassment).

B. Elements of Libel Claim

1. ***Basic Elements.*** To prove defamation, a plaintiff must establish four elements: (a) a false and defamatory statement concerning another; (b) an unprivileged publication to a third party; (c) fault amounting at least to negligence on the part of the publisher (actual malice where the plaintiff is a public figure); and (d) either actionability of the statement irrespective of special harm or the existence of special harm caused by the publication. Gonsalves v. Nissan Motor Corp. in Hawaii, Ltd., 100 Haw. 149, 171, 58 P.3d 1196, 1218 (2002); Beamer v. Nishiki, 66 Haw. 572, 578, 670 P.2d 1264, 1271 (Haw. 1983); Dunlea v. Dappen, 83 Haw. 28, 36, 924 P.2d 196, 204 (Haw. 1996); Gold v. Harrison, 88 Haw. 94, 100, 962 P.2d 353, 359, 26 Media L. Rep. (BNA) 2313, 2317 (Haw. 1998). A complainant pursuing a state law defamation claim predicated on a statement made during the course of a labor dispute must prove: (1) that the allegedly defamatory statement asserts a fact or implies an assertion of an objective fact; (2) that the factual assertion is false; and (3) that the speaker published the challenged statement with actual malice. Steam Press Holdings, Inc. v. Hawaii Teamsters and Allied Workers Union, Local 996, 302 F.3d 998 (9th Cir. 2002), citing Linn v. United Plant Guard Workder, Local 114, 383 U.S. (1966). Whether a defendant's statement was defamatory is a question of fact, whereby the fact finder must determine if the communication "tends to harm the reputation of another as to lower him in the estimation of the community or deter third persons from associating or dealing with him." Beamer, 66 Haw. at 580, 670 P.2d at 1271, citing Kahanamoku v. Advertiser Publishing Co., Ltd., 26 Haw. 500 (Haw. 1922). Whether a communication is defamatory "depends among other factors, upon the temper of the times, the current of contemporary public opinions, with the result that words, harmless in one age, in one community, may be highly damaging to reputation at another time or in a different place." Id. An allegedly defamatory statement is to be read as a whole to determine its defamatory impact. Id.

2. ***Fault.***

a. **Private Figure Plaintiff/Matter of Public Concern.** A negligence standard of liability governs private individual defamation actions. Aku v. Lewis, 52 Haw. 366, 477 P.2d 162 (Haw. 1970); see also Cahill v. Hawaiian Paradise Corp., 56 Haw. 522, 536, 543 P.2d 1356, 1366 (Haw. 1975). Thus an employee who alleged that his employer had wrongfully accused him of stealing, and thereby defamed him, was required to prove that his employer acted at least negligently. See Vlasaty v. The Pacific Club, 4 Haw. App. 556, 560, 670 P.2d 827, 831 (Haw. Ct. App. 1983). There is little developed case law on the private/public figure distinction. In Kroll Associates v. City and County of Honolulu, 833 F. Supp. 802 (D. Haw. 1993), the court held that an investigative firm hired by the defendant city to investigate corruption within the city's municipal bus system was neither a general purpose nor a limited purpose public figure. With regard to the latter issue, the court adopted the two-step analysis from Gertz v. Robert Welch Inc., 418 U.S. 323 (1974), but found the plaintiff had not voluntarily thrust itself into a political controversy over the payment of a bill for the firm's services.

b. **Private Figure Plaintiff/Matter of Private Concern.** No reported cases deal precisely with private figure plaintiffs and matters of private concern. However, in a defamation action by an employee claiming that his employer's reference to him during staff meetings as an "old man" thereby "lowered him in the eyes of others," the court held that the test for harm to reputation "is an objective one." Howard v. Daiichiya-Love's Bakery, 714 F. Supp. 1108, 1114 (D. Haw. 1989). Thus, "more than" the plaintiff's subjective humiliation was required as a matter of law to recover damages for defamation. Id.

c. **Public Figure Plaintiff/Matter of Public Concern.** In a public figure defamation action regarding a matter of public concern, actual malice must be shown with clear and convincing clarity. Fong v. Merena, 66 Haw. 72, 655 P.2d 875 (Haw. 1982). Under the "actual malice" standard, public figures who bring defamation action must prove that the publisher of the defamatory statement acted with knowledge of its falsity or reckless disregard of the truth. Rodriguez v. Nishiki, 65 Haw. 430, 653 P.2d 1145 (1982).

3. ***Falsity.*** Truth is a complete defense to a claim for defamation. Wilson v. Freitas, 121 Hawai'i 120, 214 P.3d 1110 (Haw. App. 2009); Gonsalves v. Nissan Motor Corp. in Hawaii, Ltd., 100 Haw. 149, 173, 58 P.3d 1196, 1120 (2002); Waterhouse v. Spreckels, 5 Haw. 246 (1884); Wright v. Hilo Tribune-Herald, Ltd., 31 Haw. 128 (1929). Old Hawaii case law holds that the burden of proving truth is on the defendant, and plaintiff need not allege falsity. Kahanamoku v. Advertiser Publishing Co., 25 Haw. 701 (1920). The evidence must establish substantial truth in its entirety. Wright v. Hilo Tribune Herald, Ltd., 31 Haw. 128 (1929). In Beamer v. Nishiki, 66 Haw. 572, 670 P.2d 1264 (1983), the Hawaii Supreme Court held that on a motion for summary judgment, a public figure plaintiff has the burden of proving a false and defamatory statement. In Freitas, the court cited Philadelphia Newspapers Inc. v. Hepps , 475 U.S. 767 (1986) for the proposition that where the publication at issue involves a matter of public concern, a private-figure plaintiff in a defamation

action must bear the burden of showing that speech at issue is false before recovering damages from a media defendant. Freitas, 121 Hawai'i at 128, 214 P.3d at 1119. A public official plaintiff has the burden at trial of piercing the defendant's First Amendment protection by showing knowledge of falsity or reckless disregard of the truth. Tagawa v. Maui Pub. Co., 49 Haw. 675, 427 P.2d 79 (1967). In a post-Hepps case decided by the United States District Court for the District of Hawaii, the court held Hepps requires the plaintiff to prove falsity. Basilius v. Honolulu Publishing Co., 711 F. Supp. 548 (D. Haw. 1989); see also In re UPI, 16 Media L. Rep. 2401 (D.D.C. 1989).

4. ***Defamatory Statement of Fact.*** In Steam Press Holdings, Inc. v. Hawaii Teamsters and Allied Workers Union, Local 996, 302 F.3d 998 (9th Cir. 2002), the Ninth Circuit Court of Appeals reversed a judgment in favor of the employer plaintiff on a claim for defamation against the defendant union and its president because it held that the challenged statements, i.e., that the employer was "making money" and "hiding money", did not state or imply the assertion of an objective fact. Rather, the totality of the circumstances compelled the conclusion that the union president was making a "call to arms" to the union's membership, and was not asserting an objective, verifiable fact. In Wright v. Hilo-Tribune Herald, Ltd., 31 Haw. 128 (Haw. 1929), the court held that the publication of an untrue and defamatory statement of fact against a public servant was not privileged. The court explicitly adopted the rule that "[t]he right to comment or criticize does not extend to, or justify, allegations of fact of a defamatory character. If the publication is not a comment or criticism, but a statement of fact, the rules to be applied to the nature of recovery are those applicable to any other case of defamation; if defamatory and false, it is actionable, although made in good faith, without malice, and under the honest belief that it is true. Probable cause for making it is not a factor to be considered in determining whether it is privileged or not. Where the accusation is defamatory, the damage does not result from the criticism based upon the facts but from the false accusation that the facts exist for which the criticism was made." Wright, 31 Haw. at 143, quoting 36 C.J.S., § 289.

5. ***Of and Concerning Plaintiff.*** The First Amendment requires proof that the challenged statement be "of and concerning" the complainant. Steam Press Holdings, Inc. v. Hawaii Teamsters and Allied Workers Union, Local 996, 302 F.3d 998, 1004 (9th Cir. 2002). In Cahill v. Hawaiian Paradise Park Corp., 56 Haw. 522, 543 P.2d 1356 (Haw. 1975), a media libel case, the court found that although one of the named plaintiffs, Timothy Cahill, was not explicitly mentioned in a radio broadcast, the term "Cahill family" as used by defendants was "reasonably susceptible of a meaning which include[d] Timothy as well as the members of the family mentioned by name in the broadcast." Cahill, 56 Haw. at 528, 543 P.2d at 1361. Although defamatory material need not mention the plaintiff by name, it must refer to the plaintiff by "clear implication." Thompson v. Saint Louis School, No. 28856, 2011 WL 661818, at *7 (App. Feb. 24, 2011). In Thompson, the Intermediate Court of Appeals stated in dicta that a claim for defamation brought against the school by the parents of an expelled student was not viable where it was based on a letter that the school issued to parents to discuss the subject of lying. The letter did not mention the expelled student, and even under a strained reading, the letter did not clearly implicate him where it did not accuse any particular individual of lying and spoke about lying in general terms.

6. ***Publication.*** An actionable defamation requires publication by the employer. Vlasaty v. Pacific Club, 4 Haw. App. 556, 560, 670 P.2d 827, 831 (Haw. Ct. App. 1983). Publication means a communication by the employer to some third party other than the employee defamed. Vlasaty, 4 Haw. App. at 560, 670 P.2d at 831, citing Runnels v. Okamoto, 56 Haw. 1, 525 P.2d 1125 (Haw. 1974); Gonsalves v. Nissan Motor Corp. in Hawaii, Ltd., 100 Haw. 149, 58 P.3d 1196 (2002).

a. **Intracorporate Communication.** The court in Kainz v. Lussier, 4 Haw. App. 400, 667 P.2d 797 (Haw. Ct. App. 1983), held that allegedly defamatory letters written by defendant to corporate shareholders were qualifiedly privileged as they were written and sent "in the discharge of his private legal duty as corporate secretary and director to investigate and report to the shareholders on the affairs of [the corporation] and the progress of a project [that the corporation] was undertaking." Kainz, 4 Haw. App. at 404, 667 P.2d at 801. A qualified privilege arises when (1) the author of a defamatory statement reasonably acts in the discharge of some public or private duty, legal, moral, or social and (2) where the publication concerns a subject matter in which the author and the recipients of the publication have a correlative interest or duty. Id. The qualified privilege is conditional and it must be exercised (1) in a reasonable manner and (2) for a proper purpose. Id., at 405, 667 P.2d at 802. The qualified privilege may be abused by (1) excessive publication, (2) use of the occasion for an improper purpose, or (3) lack of belief or grounds for belief in the truth of what is said. Id. See also II.A.2, infra.

b. **Compelled Self-Publication.** In Gonsalves v. Nissan Motor Corp. in Hawaii, Ltd., 100 Haw. 149, 58 P.3d 1196 (2002), the Hawaii Supreme Court expressly rejected a claim of defamation by compelled self-publication. In a matter of first impression, the court rejected compelled self-publication on policy grounds, holding that it would give the plaintiff a disincentive to mitigate damages and because it conflicts with the doctrine of at-will employment.

c. **Republication.** A republication of defamatory material is a new and separate tort. Hoke v. Paul, 65 Haw. 478, 483, 653 P.2d 1155, 1160 (Haw. 1982); Gonsalves v. Nissan Motor Corp. in Hawaii, Ltd., 100 Haw. 149, 172, 58 P.3d 1196, 1119 (2002). The republication of libelous matter contained in the pleadings or other papers in civil actions prior to hearing is an adoption and endorsement of such libelous matter by the one republishing it and such republication is not privileged. Murphy v Maui Publishing Co., Ltd., 23 Haw. 804, 811 (Haw. 1917). No cases on foreseeable republication by others.

7. ***Statements versus Conduct.*** In Courtney v. Canyon Television and Appliance Rental, Inc., 899 F.2d 845 (9th Cir. 1990), the plaintiff, who had been employed as a store manager for defendant, alleged that the new manager defamed him by making a count of cash and inventory of store merchandise in front of customers upon plaintiff's dismissal. Courtney, 899 F.2d 845. The court first assumed arguendo "that the cash count and inventory procedures were false and defamatory 'statements,'" then turned to the issue of privilege. Id. The court recognized that the otherwise reasonable action of performing a cash count and merchandise inventory "may not be privileged" if done "in an obvious manner in front of customers," who "clearly [have no] 'interest or duty' in this aspect of Canyon's business affairs." Nevertheless, the court concluded that the "assumed false and defamatory statements were privileged" on the basis that plaintiff presented "neither allegations nor evidence suggesting that the cash account and inventory could have been done in a less public manner." Id. [emphasis added]. Thus one could infer that such actions constitute sufficient "statements" for the purpose of alleging "actionable" defamation. See also Beamer v. Nishiki, 66 Haw. 572, 578, 670 P.2d 1264, 1271 (Haw. 1983) (to prove defamation, "a plaintiff must establish . . . actionability of the statement irrespective of special harm or the existence of special harm caused by the publication").

8. ***Damages.*** A plaintiff in a defamation action may recover general, compensatory, and special damages. The general damages which the law presumes to result from the publication of defamatory matter arise by inference of law, and they are not required to be proved by direct evidence. Van Poole v. Nippu Jiji Co., Ltd., 34 Haw. 354, 357 (Haw. 1937). The term "general damages" always connotes "compensatory damages" and is sometimes synonymous with "actual damages." Id. A libel plaintiff claiming loss of earnings must show that the defamation was "material element or substantial cause" or the actual economic damage. Jenkins v. Liberty Newspaper Ltd. Partnership, 89 Haw. 254, 269, 971 P.2d 1089, 1104, 27 Media L. Rep. (BNA) 1513, 1526 (Haw. 1999).

When the defamatory language is libelous per se, general damages are such as naturally, proximately and necessarily result from the publication complained of and include those which will compensate the person defamed for the injury to his reputation, business and feelings which the defamatory publication caused. Id. Where the defamatory charge complained of is actionable per se the plaintiff is prima facie entitled, without any direct evidence of general damages, to recover compensatory damage, and is not required to introduce evidence of actual damages to entitle him to recover substantial damages. Van Poole, 34 Haw. at 361; Steam Press Holdings, Inc., et al. v. Hawaii Teamsters and Allied Workers, Local 996, Civ. No. 99-00187 HG, 2001 WL 1715894 (D. Haw. Sept. 28, 2001) (holding that statements which defame the plaintiff in connection with his business or occupation are libel per se), rev'd on other grounds, 302 F.3d 998 (9th Cir. 2002). If the words are actionable per se such damages may be presumed without proof of special damages. Id.

The court in Van Poole also took note of appropriate circumstances for awarding nominal damages to a defamation plaintiff, without explicitly deciding whether the defendant in that case was entitled as of right to an instruction on nominal damages: "[I]n libel and slander where it appears that 'there is no ill will or malice on the part of defendant, and no special damages, actual injury, or pecuniary loss, . . . or where the evidence is such as would justify a plea of justification, an award for nominal damages only may be justified.'" Van Poole v. Nippu Jiji Co., Ltd., 34 Haw. at 354 (Haw. 1937).

a. **Presumed Damages and Libel Per Se.** A finding that the publication is libelous per se presumes general damages to the injured party; thus, special damages need not be shown. Kahanamoku v. Advertiser Publishing Co., 25 Haw. 701, 709 (Haw. 1920). See also Russell v. American Guild of Variety Artists, 53 Haw. 456, 458, 497 P.2d 40, 42 (Haw. 1972). The plaintiff may also recover punitive damages if the defendant acted with "actual malice." Russell, 53 Haw. at 458, 497 P.2d at 42. Under Hawai'i law, the following classes of libel are libel per se: (1) statements which impute to a person the commission of a crime; (2) statements which have a tendency to injure him in his office, profession, calling or trade; and (3) statements which hold him up to scorn and ridicule and to feelings of contempt or execration, impair him in the enjoyment of society and injure those imperfect rights of friendly intercourse and mutual benevolence which man has with respect to man. Partington v. Bugliosi, 825 F. Supp. 906, 915 (D. Haw. 1993), citing Butler v. United States, 365 F. Supp. 1035, 1044 (D. Haw. 1983). See also Russell v. American Guild of Variety Artists, 53 Haw. 456, 497 P.2d 40 (Haw. 1972). Racial epithets do not constitute defamation per se. Dowkin v. Honolulu Police Dep't, Civil NO. 10-00087 SOM/LEK, 2010 WL 4961135, at *10 (D. Haw. Nov. 30, 2010).

(1) **Employment-Related Criticism.** A complainant pursuing a state law defamation claim predicated on a statement made during the course of a labor dispute must prove: (1) that the allegedly defamatory statement asserts a fact or implies an assertion of an objective fact; (2) that the factual assertion is false; and (3) that the speaker published the challenged statement with actual malice. Steam Press Holdings, Inc. v. Hawaii Teamsters and

Allied Workers Union, Local 996, 302 F.3d 998 (9th Cir. 2002), citing Linn v. United Plant Guard Workder, Local 114, 383 U.S. (1966).

(2) **Single Instance Rule.** No reported cases.

b. **Punitive Damages.** Punitive damages may be awarded only in cases where the wrongdoer has acted wantonly, oppressively, or with such malice as implies a spirit of mischief or criminal indifference to civil obligations, or where there has been some willful misconduct or that entire want of care which would raise the presumption of a conscious indifference to consequences. Masaki v. General Motors Corp., 71 Haw. 1, 780 P.2d 566 (Haw. 1989). An award of punitive damages must be proven by clear and convincing evidence. Id. In Mehau v. Gannet Pacific Corp., 66 Haw. 133, 658 P.2d 312 9 Media L. Rep. (BNA) 1337 (Haw. 1983), public figure plaintiffs in a defamation action were required to show "actual malice" by each of the multiple defendants under a clear and convincing standard of proof in order to recover punitive damages. See also Iddings v. Mee-Lee, 82 Haw. 1, 14, 919 P.2d 263, 276 (Haw. 1996), citing Mehau, 66 Haw. at 146, 780 P.2d at 322, 9 Media L. Rep. (BNA) at 1341; Steam Press Holdings, Inc., et al. v. Hawaii Teamsters and Allied Workers, Local 996, Civ. No. 99-00187 HG, 2001 WL 11715894 (D. Haw. Sept. 28, 2001) (denying plaintiff's request for award of punitive damages where the compensatory damages awarded by the court adequately reflected the unlawful nature of the defendant union's conduct) rev'd on other grounds, 302 F.3d 998 (9th Cir. 2002). In Lauer v. Young Men's Christian Association of Honolulu, 57 Haw. 390, 557 P.2d 1334 (Haw. 1976), the court held that as a matter of public policy, the City and County of Honolulu, as a municipal corporation, should not be held liable for punitive damages in a defamatory action even if plaintiff could show actual malice by the city's agent. Lauer, 57 Haw. at 402-3, 557 P.2d at 1341-2.

II. PRIVILEGES AND DEFENSES

A. Scope of Privileges

1. ***Absolute Privilege.*** Hawaii courts apply an absolute litigation privilege in defamation actions for words and writings that are material and pertinent to judicial proceedings. Matsuura v. E.I. du Pont de Nemours & Co., 102 Hawai'i 149, 154, 73 P.3d 687, 692 (2003). Communications regarding alleged unethical conduct of a member of the bar to the Chief Justice of Hawai'i , the committee established pursuant to Rule 16 of the Supreme Court of the State of Hawai'i , or the Committee on Legal Ethics of the Bar Association of Hawai'i are absolutely privileged. Wong v. Schorr, 51 Haw. 608, 466 P.2d 441 (Haw. 1970). An attorney is absolutely privileged to publish defamatory matter concerning another in communications preliminary to, in the institution of, during the course of, and/or as a part of a judicial proceeding in which he participates as counsel, if the defamatory matter has some relation to the proceeding. Hall v. State of Hawai'i , 7 Haw. App. 274, 285, 756 P.2d 1048, 1056 (Haw. Ct. App. 1988). However, the privilege is not limited to attorneys. Roberts v. City & County of Honolulu, Civ. No. 07-00391 DAE-KSC, 2008 WL 4107983, at *6 (D. Haw. Sept. 3, 2008). In an unpublished memorandum opinion, the Ninth Circuit Court of Appeals held that an employer is absolutely privileged to make statements in judicial and administrative proceedings related to the employee's misconduct and termination, when the employee presented no evidence that the statements were made outside the context of the employer's investigation and grievance procedure required by the collective bargaining agreement. Park v. Young Brothers, Ltd., 114 Fed. Appx. 344, 345 (9th Cir. 2004).

2. ***Qualified Privileges.*** A qualified privileged occasion arises when the author of the defamatory statement reasonably acts in the discharge of some public or private duty (legal, oral, or social), and where the publication concerns subject matter in which the author has an interest, and the recipients of the publication have a corresponding interest or duty. Aku v. Lewis, 52 Haw. 366, 371, 477 P.2d 162, 166 (Haw. 1970). A qualified privilege is conditional and is lost if it is abused. Vlasaty v. The Pacific Club, 4 Haw. App. 556, 564, 670 P.2d 827, 833 (Haw. Ct. App. 1983). A qualified privilege may be abused by the use of words not reasonably necessary to protect the particular interest for which the privilege is given. Aku, 52 Haw. at 371, 477 P.2d at 166.. Non-judicial government officials, acting in the performance of their public duties, are protected against liability for defamation claims by a conditional or qualified privilege. Towse v. State, 64 Haw. 624, 647 P.2d 696 (Haw. 1982). To overcome that privilege, the plaintiff prove malice by clear and convincing evidence. Id. See also I.B.6(a), supra.

a. **Common Interest.** The interest or duty of the recipients is essential to the privilege. Aku v. Lewis, 52 Haw. 366, 371, 477 P.2d 162, 166 (Haw. 1970). If the person or persons to whom the communication is addressed have no recognized interest in the statement, there is no privilege. Id. In claiming such privilege, it is essential that the author of the defamatory matter and the recipients have a common interest and the communication is of a type reasonably deemed to protect or further that interest. Vlasaty v. The Pacific Club, 4 Haw. App. 556, 561, 670 P.2d 827, 832 (Haw. App. Ct. 1983), citing Kainz v. Lussier, 4 Haw. App. 400, 667 P.2d 797 (Haw. Ct. App. 1983); see also Lauer v. Young Men's Christian Ass'n, 57 Haw. 390, 557 P.2d 1334 (Haw. 1976) (a qualifiedly privileged occasion arises when the author of the defamatory statement reasonably acts in the discharge of some public or private duty, legal, moral, or social, and where the publication concerns subject matter in which the author has an interest and the recipients of the publication a corresponding interest or duty). An example of common interest in Hawai'i law was found where an employer communicated that an employee had improperly received disability and unemployment benefits to its insurance carrier. Uema v. Nippon Express Hawaii, Inc., 26 F. Supp. 2d 1241, 1249 (D. Haw. 1998). In Uema, the common interest was based on promoting their business relationship. Id.

b. **Duty.** A qualified privileged occasion arises when the author of the defamatory statement reasonably acts in the discharge of some public or private duty (legal, oral, or social), and where the publication concerns subject matter in which the author has an interest and the recipients of the publication have a corresponding interest or duty. Aku v. Lewis, 52 Haw. 366, 371, 477 P.2d 162, 166 (Haw. 1970).

c. **Criticism of Public Employee.** The doctrine of privilege "give[s] immunity to commentators upon, and critics of, proven or admitted official conduct and acts so long as their comments and criticisms, though unreasonable and harmful, are made in good faith and are not inspired by actual malice." Wright v. Hilo-Tribune Herald, 31 Haw. 128, 139 (Haw. 1929). However, in Wright the court declined to extend the privilege to commentators of an untrue and defamatory statement of fact regarding a superintending nurse at a county hospital. Id.

d. **Limitation on Qualified Privileges.** Under Hawai'i law, qualified privileges are limited in terms of abuse rather than malice. See Vlasaty v. The Pacific Club, 4 Haw. App. 556, 564, 670 P.2d 827, 833 (Haw. Ct. App. 1983). Thus, a qualified privilege is lost if abused in any of the following ways: (1) excessive publication; (2) use of the occasion for an improper purpose; or (3) lack of belief or grounds for belief in the truth of what is said. Kainz v. Lussier, 4 Haw. App. 400, 405, 667 P.2d 797, 802 (Haw. Ct. App. 1983); see Ragasa v. County of Kauai, 2006 WL 753021 (D. Haw. May 22, 2006) (holding plaintiffs had created triable issue of fact as to whether defendants abused common interest privilege).

(1) **Constitutional or Actual Malice.** The word "malice" as used in the context of an abuse of a qualified privilege is not given the same meaning as that attributed to it in the constitutional privilege area. Russell v. American Guild of Variety Artists, 53 Haw. 456, 462, 497 P.2d 40, 45 at n. 4 (Haw. 1972). Constitutional or actual malice constitutes knowledge that the communication was false or with reckless disregard of whether it was false or not. Id. See also Tagawa v. Maui Publishing Co., Ltd., 50 Haw. 648, 652, 448 P.2d 337, 340 (Haw. 1968). In actual malice defamation actions, the question to be resolved at summary judgment is whether there is a genuine issue of material fact from which a jury reasonably could find actual malice with convincing clarity. Jenkins v. Liberty Newspaper Ltd. Partnership, 89 Haw. 254, 259, 971 P.2d 1089, 1093, 27 Media L. Rep. (BNA) 1513, 1516 (Haw. 1999), quoting Mehau v. Gannett Pacific Corp., 66 Haw. 133, 145, 658 P.2d 312, 321, 9 Media L. Rep. (BNA) 1337, 1341 (Haw. 1983). Neither an investigatory failure nor a mistaken report, without a high degree of awareness of the probable falsity, raises the issue of actual malice. See Jenkins, 89 Haw. at 262, 971 P.2d at 1097, 27 Media L. Rep. (BNA) at 1520 (mistaken report) and Tagawa v. Maui Publishing Co., Ltd., 50 Haw. 648, 652, 448. P.2d 337 (1968) (investigatory failure).

(2) **Common Law Malice.** In the context of the qualified privilege case, the malice test is an objective one. In Aku v. Lewis, 52 Haw. 366, 477 P.2d 162 (Haw. 1970), the court observed that the term "malice" had acquired a plethora of definitions; later in Russell v. American Guild of Variety Artists the court adopted Prosser's definition of the term, that is, the defendant asserting a qualified privilege is required to show that he acted "as a reasonable [person] under the circumstances, with due regard to the strength of his belief, the grounds that he [had] to support it, and the importance of conveying that information." Russell, 53 Haw. at 462, 497 P.2d at 45 n.4.

e. **Question of Fact or Law.** Whether a communication is privileged is a question of law to be determined by the court. Kainz v. Lussier, 4 Haw. App. at 404, 667 P.2d at 801 (Haw. Ct. App. 1983). The question whether the qualified privilege was abused is one of fact for the trier of fact to decide. Id. at 405, 667 P.2d at 802. Because a qualified privilege may be lost if abused, a finding of qualified privilege alone is insufficient to grant summary judgment. Uema v. Nippon Express Hawaii, Inc., 26 F. Supp. 2d 1241, 1249 (D. Haw. 1998) (summary judgment for employer was improper where court found that questions of potential abuse of privilege remained, e.g., whether statement was true and made in good faith). In Black v. Correa, 2008 WL 3845230 (D. Haw. Aug. 18, 2008), the district court held that the facts put forth by the plaintiff were sufficient to create a triable issue of fact on the malice issue.

f. **Burden of Proof.** No reported cases address the burden of proof with respect to qualified privileges.

B. Standard Libel Defenses

1. ***Truth.*** Truth is a complete defense. Wilson v. Freitas, 121 Hawai'i at 128, 214 P.3d at 1119; Gonsalves v. Nissan Motor Corp. in Hawaii, Ltd., 100 Haw. 149, 58 P.3d 1196 (2002). In civil cases for libel and slander, "the law has been settled everywhere that the truth, when pleaded and proved, is a defense, whether the damages claimed are general or special, and however malicious the publication may have been." Waterhouse v. Spreckels, 5 Haw. 246, 248 (Haw.

1884). However, the defendant cannot justify the defamatory publication "by showing that some part of it, divisible from the rest, was true." Wright v. Hilo Tribune-Herald, Ltd., 31 Haw. 128, 131-32, (Haw. 1929). As the court expounds in Wright, "[i]t is essential. . .in order to constitute a complete defense, that the evidence relied on establishes the truth of the defamatory matter in its entirety and not that it establish only a part of it." Wright v. Hilo Tribune-Herald, Ltd., 31 Haw. 128, 131-32, (Haw. 1929).

2. ***Opinion.*** No employment cases, but in Partington v. Bugliosi, 825 F. Supp. 906 (D. Haw. 1993), a federal district court noted that there is "a dearth of case law on the distinction between statements of fact and expressions of opinion" in Hawai'i . Partington, 825 F. Supp. at 919. Perhaps the closest a Hawaii appellate court has come to recognizing protection for opinion is the Intermediate Court of Appeals' holding that a statement in a magazine that it was "widely accepted as fact" that the plaintiff was the suspected serial killer "was a statement of the author's opinion that was not susceptible of being proved true or false." Wilson v. Freitas, 121 Hawai'i at 128, 214 P.3d at 1119. The test for distinguishing a statement of fact from an expression of opinion in federal defamation cases, as mandated by Gertz v. Robert Welch Inc., 418 U.S. 323 (1974), is as follows: "(1) whether the words can be understood in a defamatory sense in light of the facts surrounding the publication, including the medium by which and the audience to which the statement is disseminated; (2) whether the context in which the statements were made . . . would lead the audience to anticipate persuasive speech such as 'epithets, fiery rhetoric, or hyperbole'; and (3) whether the language used is the kind generated in a 'spirited legal dispute.'" Id. See also Gold v. Harrison, 88 Haw. 94, 962 P.2d 353, 26 Media L. Rep. (BNA) 2313 (Haw. 1998) (rhetorical hyperbole case; adopted Milkovich standard to determine whether a statement is false and defamatory), citing Milkovich v. Lorain Journal Co., 497 U.S. 1, 16 (1989).

3. ***Consent.*** No current case law. The position previously taken by courts in Hawai'i regarding public servants is that although they, like candidates for public office, consent to their position, they are not required to sacrifice the loss of their reputation to "every member of the public, whenever an untrue charge of disgraceful conduct is made against them, if only his accuser honestly believes the charge upon reasonable ground." Wright v. Hilo Tribune-Herald 31 Haw. 128 (Haw. 1929). As the court in Wright concluded, "to sanction such a doctrine would do the public more harm than good." Wright, 31 Haw. at 141.

4. ***Mitigation.*** Retraction of a defamatory publication is a partial defense to a libel claim and may show mitigation of damages, but it cannot, by itself, defeat the underlying claim. Partington v. Bugliosi, 825 F. Supp. 906, 913 (D. Haw. 1993).

III. RECURRING FACT PATTERNS

A. Statements in Personnel File

No reported cases.

B. Performance Evaluations

No reported cases specifically involving performance evaluation. However, in Brown v. Chinen, 2008 WL 2073496 (D. Haw. May 14, 2008), the district court granted motions to dismiss as to a complaint by a former archeologist hired by the State of Hawaii Historic Preservation Division. The plaintiff alleged his contract with the State was not renewed because, among other things, of defamatory statements made by his former supervisor. In analyzing whether the alleged defamatory statements implicated a liberty interest sufficient to support the plaintiff's First Amendment retaliation claim under 42 U.S.C. § 1983, the court held that the statements complained of did not "rise to the level of defamatory statements that cause a stigma of moral turpitude" on the plaintiff.

C. References

In 1998 the Hawai'i legislature passed H.R.S. § 663-1.95, providing qualified immunity to employers who give references about former employees. Specifically, H.R.S. § 663-1.95(a) provides that an employer that gives to a prospective employer information or opinion about a current or former employee's job performance is presumed to be acting in good faith and shall have a qualified immunity from civil liability for disclosing the information and for the consequences of the disclosure. Subsection (b) provides that the good faith presumption under subsection (a) shall be rebuttable upon a showing by a preponderance of the evidence that the information or opinion disclosed was either (1) knowingly false, or (2) knowingly misleading. H.R.S. § 663-1.95(b). In granting summary judgment to the defendant employer, the district court held that speculation by the plaintiff that his former employer made defamatory statements to prospective employers in retaliation for plaintiff having filed an employment discrimination charge, preventing the plaintiff from obtaining offers of employment, was insufficient to support the plaintiff's defamation claim. Chenoweth v. Maui Chem. and Paper Products, Inc., 2008 WL 4107906 (D. Haw. Sept. 3, 2008).

D. Intracorporate Communications

See I.B.6.a, supra.

E. Statements to Government Regulators

No reported cases.

F. Reports to Auditors and Insurers

In Runnels v. Okamoto, 56 Haw. 1, 525 P.2d 1125 (Haw. 1974), the court held that city council members who received copies of an allegedly defamatory audit prepared by a city council auditor had not participated in the publication of the defamation, and were therefore improperly charged in the lawsuit. Runnels, 56 Haw. at 5, 525 P.2d at 1128. The court concluded that "[w]hile everyone who participates in the publication of defamatory remarks may be properly charged with having published them, the mere acceptance of such remarks as true cannot constitute publication, regardless of how much weight that acceptance may lend to their apparent validity." Id. As to the city council auditor, the court affirmed that the doctrine of "absolute immunity" no longer shields such nonjudicial government officers or employees from liability for his tortious acts. Id. at 4, 525 P.2d at 1128, aff'g Medeiros v. Kondo, 55 Haw. 499, 522 P.2d 1269 (Haw. 1974). However, a plaintiff must show that such nonjudicial government officers acted with malice in order to prevail over a defendant's motion for summary judgment. Runnels v. Okamoto, 56 Haw. 1, 5, 525 P.2d 1125, 1129 (Haw. 1974).

G. Vicarious Liability of Employers for Statements Made by Employees

1. ***Scope of Employment.*** An employer may be liable for compensatory damages for the defamatory acts of an employee if the employee was acting within the scope and course of his employment. Hoke v. Paul, 65 Haw. 478, 479, 653 P.2d 1155, 1157 (Haw. 1982), citing Kahanamoku v. Advertiser Publishing Co., Ltd., 26 Haw. 500 (1922); but cf. Ragasa v. County of Kauai, 2006 WL 753021 (D. Haw. May 22, 2006) (holding a municipality cannot be held liable for the tortious acts of government employees, including defamation claims, under a theory of respondeat superior). Conduct is within the scope of employment if (1) it is of the kind a person is employed to perform, (2) it occurs substantially within the authorized time and space limits, and (3) it is actuated at least in part by a purpose to serve the employer. Mehau v. Reed, 76 Haw. 101, 113, 869 P.2d 1320, 1332 (Haw. 1994). In Vlasaty v. The Pacific Club, 4 Haw. App. 556, 562, 670 P.2d 827, 832 (Haw. Ct. App. 1983), defendants argued that plaintiff's testimony regarding allegedly defamatory statements made by the defendant club's then-president was inadmissible as hearsay. Id. The court held that the statements made by the club's supervisory employees, and testified to by plaintiff, regarding the president's alleged defamation were uttered by the employees within the scope of their employment, and were, therefore, admissible under Rule 803(a)(2)(b) of the Hawai'i Rules of Evidence as vicarious admissions against the club. Id.; cf. Steam Press Holdings, Inc., et al. v. Hawaii Teamsters and Allied Workers, Local 996, Civ. No. 99-00187 HG, 2001 WL 1715894 (D. Haw. Sept. 28, 2001) (union official could not be held individually liable for false statements made during labor negotiations, but union was held liable), rev'd on other grounds, 302 F.3d 998 (9th Cir. 2002).

a. **Blogging.** In Konop v. Hawaiian Airlines, Inc., 302 F.3d 868 (9th Cir. 2002), an airline pilot who maintained a secure website where he posted bulletin boards critical of his employer, various officers of the company and his union, brought suit against his employer alleging that the employer violated the Wiretap Act, Stored Communications Act, and the Railway Labor Act when a vice president of the company gained access to the website under false pretenses and disclosed its contents. The Ninth Circuit Court of Appeals reversed a summary judgment entered by the trial court in favor of the employer and allowed the employee to go forward with certain claims. In Mesa Airlines, Inc. v. Uslan, 2007 WL 1821298 (D. Ariz. Jun. 25, 2007), a federal district court in Arizona held that personal jurisdiction was lacking in Arizona with respect to a lawsuit filed against an airline pilot that lived in Hawaii and maintained a website that was critical of a Phoenix-based airline. The lawsuit made claims for trademark infringement, unfair competition, false advertising and defamation, but the court did not reach the merits of those claims because it concluded that personal jurisdiction was lacking.

2. ***Damages.*** An employer may be liable for compensatory damages for the defamatory acts of an employee if the employee was acting within the scope and course of his employment. Hoke v. Paul, 65 Haw. 478, 479, 653 P.2d 1155, 1157 (Haw. 1982), citing Kahanamoku v. Advertiser Publishing Co., Ltd., 26 Haw. 500 (1922).

H. Internal Investigations

There are no reported cases involving libel claims, however, in Gonsalves v. Nissan Motor Corp. in Hawaii, Ltd., 100 Haw. 149, 58 P.3d 1196 (2002), the court held that a company vice president's statement to a former employee made in connection with an investigation of a co-worker's sexual harassment complaint, telling the employee he would not lose his job and did not need an attorney, were contrary to public policy and thus were not enforceable on the basis of promissory estoppel after the former employee was fired by the company.

IV. OTHER ACTIONS BASED ON STATEMENTS

A. Negligent Hiring, Retention, and Supervision

In Shaw v. North American Title Co., 76 Haw. 323, 876 P.2d 1291 (Haw. 1994), the plaintiff alleged, among other claims, negligent supervision or hiring of employees by North American Title Company ("NATCO") which resulted in damages to plaintiff's credit rating as well as emotional distress. The plaintiff claimed that by reissuing checks and sending them directly to his creditors, NATCO had foreclosed plaintiff's ability to negotiate payment with his creditors in exchange for deletion of negative entries in his credit reports. Id. at 326, 876 P.2d at 1295. The court held that plaintiff had thereby alleged a prima facie case that NATCO committed a "tortious act within [Hawai'i]" sufficient to satisfy that provision of Hawai'i 's long arm statute. Id. at 329, 876 P.2d at 1298, citing H.R.S. § 634-35(a).

Relying on cases that had applied the so-called "effects test" "in the defamation context in which the communication itself is tortious," the court concluded that the plaintiff sufficiently demonstrated that NATCO had "arguably 'targeted' Shaw in Hawai'i when it reissued checks directly to Shaw's creditors (against Shaw's specific instructions) rather than giving the reissued checks to Shaw." Id. at 332, 876 P.2d at 1300, citing Calder v. Jones, 465 U.S. 783 (1984) (endorsing the "effects test" of jurisdiction in situations involving tortious acts) and Brainerd v. University of Alberta, 873 F.2d 1257 (9th Cir. 1989) (assertion of jurisdiction under "effects test" comports with due process).

B. Intentional Infliction of Emotional Distress

In order to show intentional infliction of emotional distress in Hawai'i , a plaintiff must prove (1) that the act allegedly causing the harm was intentional or reckless; (2) that the act was outrageous; and (3) that the act caused (4) extreme emotional distress to another. Hac v. University of Hawaii, 102 P.2d 92, 73 P.3d 46 (2003); Nagata v. Quest Diagnostics Inc., 303 F. Supp.2d 1121 (D. Haw. 2004) (denying defendant's motion for summary judgment on claims for intentional infliction of emotional distress arising from an error in drug testing); Stallings v. Walmart, Inc., 123 Fed. Appx. 273, 274 (9th Cir. 2004) (unpublished opinion affirming the district court's grant of summary judgment to defendant on plaintiff's IIED claim). Bodily injury, while compensable, is not necessary to establish severe emotional distress. Id. See also Courtney v. Canyon Television and Appliance Rental, Inc., 899 F.2d 845 (9th Cir. 1990); Dunlea v. Dappen, 83 Haw. 28, 924 P.2d 196 (Haw. 1996). In Courtney, the plaintiff, who had been employed as a store manager for the defendant, alleged that the new manager defamed him by making a count of cash and inventory of store merchandise in front of customers upon plaintiff's dismissal. The Ninth Circuit concluded that the plaintiff's claim for intentional infliction of emotional distress arising from his allegations of defamation and wrongful discharge was barred by Hawai'i 's workers' compensation statute. Id. at 851. But see Kahale v. ADT Automotive Services, Inc., 2 F. Supp. 2d 1295 (D. Haw. 1998) (Hawai'i Supreme Court now recognizes that claims based on alleged intentional conduct of an employer are not barred by Hawai'i 's workers' compensation statute, therefore Courtney case no longer good law), citing Furukawa v. Honolulu Zoological Society, 85 Haw. 7, 18, 936 P.2d 643 (1997). Nevertheless, the court asserted that plaintiff would still not prevail even if such a claim were not barred under the statute, since plaintiff had "failed to provide that [the employer's] conduct was 'unreasonable' . . . or that [the employer] should have expected the acts surrounding [the] discharge to result in emotional distress." Id., citing Lapinad v. Pacific Oldsmobile-GMC, 679 F. Supp. 991, 996 (D. Haw. 1988). The court declared that "[d]ischarge, without evidence of more, does not create a case for emotional distress." Id.; see also Ross v. Stoufer Hotel Co. (Hawaii) Ltd., 76 Haw. 454, 879 P.2d 1037 (Haw. 1994) (holding employer could not be held liable for intentional infliction of emotional distress arising out of discharge of employee because he married fellow employee in the same department, absent evidence the employer acted unreasonably in the course of discharging the employee); Catron v. Tokio Marine Management, Inc., 90 Haw. 407, 978 P.2d 845 (Haw. 1999) (holding there is no duty to terminate an at-will employee in good faith); Soone v. Kyo-ya Company, Ltd., 353 F. Supp. 2d 1107, 1117 (D. Haw. 2005) (holding employer could not be held liable for intentional infliction of emotional distress when one of its agents informs the employee's union representative that the employee is fired).

C. Interference with Economic Advantage

Hawaii's equivalent to an action based on interference with economic advantage in the employment defamation context is the tort for interference with prospective contractual relations. A plaintiff must allege six elements to state such a claim: (1) a prospective contractual relationship existed between the plaintiff and a third party; (2) the defendant knew of this relationship; (3) the defendant intentionally interfered with the plaintiff's prospective contract; (4) the defendant acted without proper justification; (5) the defendant's interference caused the third party to fail to consummate the prospective contract with the plaintiff; and (6) the defendant's interference caused damages to the plaintiff. Kutcher v. Zimmerman, 87 Haw. App. 394, 406, 957 P.2d 1076 (Haw. Ct. App. 1998). In Kutcher, the court held that, as part of his prima facie case, a plaintiff must plead and prove that the interference was without proper justification. Id. To satisfy this element of the tort, the plaintiff may show that the defendant acted without proper justification where the interference was "tortious, illegal, or unconstitutional[,] and/or involved violations of statutes, regulations, or recognized common-law rules[,]" including the common law rules for defamation. Id. The court specifically concluded that "the privilege of communicating truthful information" may be raised as a defense to this tort. Id.

The plaintiff in Kutcher was being considered for employment by Avis Rent-a-Car ("Avis") on the island of Maui. Id. at 397. Avis required that he undergo a drug screening test as a condition of prospective employment. In bringing an action for interference with prospective contractual relations, the plaintiff alleged that a communication between a clinic lab employee and an Avis district manager regarding his behavior while at the clinic for the mandatory drug screening test constituted a "tortious and improper interference" with his "'business relationship' with Avis." Id. The court ultimately held that "under the circumstances of this case," the clinic lab employee's communication of information to the district manager at Avis was privileged because it was truthful," and therefore affirmed the lower court's grant of summary judgment in favor of the defendant clinic lab employee. Id.

D. Prima Facie Tort

In Kutcher v. Zimmerman, 87 Haw. App. 394, 957 P.2d 1076 (Haw. Ct. App. 1998), the court declined to follow the approach taken in the first Restatement of Torts § 766, which treats intentional interference with prospective contractual relations as a prima facie tort, subject to proof of a "privilege" as an affirmative defense. Id. at 401. Under that approach, "the plaintiff must prove only that the defendant intentionally interfered with his [or her] prospective contractual relations and caused him [or her] injury." Id. The burden then shifts to the defendant "to demonstrate as an affirmative defense that under the circumstances, his [or her] conduct, otherwise culpable, was justified and therefore privileged." Id. Rather, as discussed above, the court in Kutcher declared that in Hawai'i , the plaintiff must plead and prove that the defendant acted without proper justification as a part of his prima facie case. Id. at 406.

V. OTHER ISSUES

A. Statute of Limitations

Under H.R.S. § 657-4 (2001), all actions for libel or slander shall be commenced within two years after the cause of action accrued, and not after. A claim for defamation accrues when the plaintiff discovers or reasonably should have discovered the publication of the defamation. Hoke v. Paul, 65 Haw. 478, 483, 653 P.2d 1155, 1159 (Haw. 1982); Shipley v. Hawaii, 2006 WL 2474059 (D. Haw. Aug. 24, 2006) (dismissing employment defamation claims because more than two years elapsed since the plaintiff discovered or reasonably should have discovered of the alleged defamatory statements). In Bauernfiend v. AOAO Kihei Beach Condominiums, 99 Haw. 281, 54 P.3d 452 (2002), the Hawaii Supreme Court held that a personal injury action filed on the second anniversary of the plaintiff's alleged injury was timely filed, and overruled a footnote in Hoke v. Paul that suggested a different method of computing the limitations period. In Roberts v. City and County of Honolulu, 2008 WL 4107983 (D. Haw. Sept. 3, 2008), the district court held plaintiff's defamation claim was time-barred by the two-year statute of limitations. The plaintiff admitted she was aware of an alleged defamatory email more than two years before she filed suit, but argued her claim was not stale because she was unaware of the identity of the author of the email. The court rejected that argument, holding that her cause of action for defamation accrued when she discovered the publication; there was no independent requirement that she know the identity of the author, and the plaintiff did not offer evidence that the identity of the author was no discoverable with reasonable diligence.

B. Jurisdiction

The state court system in Hawai'i has two trial levels, the circuit court and the district court. Under H.R.S. § 604-5 (d), district courts do not have jurisdiction over actions for libel, slander, or defamation of character. H.R.S. § 604-5(d) (2001).

C. Worker's Compensation Exclusivity

Hawai'i's workers' compensation law covers employees who suffer "personal injury either by accident arising out of and in the course of the employment or by disease proximately caused by or resulting from the nature of the employment[.]" H.R.S. § 386-3. The rights and remedies made available under the workers' compensation statute "shall exclude all other liability of the employer to the employee . . . on account of the injury[.]" H.R.S. § 386-5. However, the exclusivity of remedies under the workers' compensation law does not apply to "sexual harassment or sexual assault and infliction of emotional distress or invasion of privacy related thereto[.]" Id. A civil action asserting such claims is allowed. Id. The Hawai'i Supreme Court has also recognized an exception to the exclusivity bar for claims based on alleged intentional conduct of an employee, such as emotional distress incident to employment discrimination, as in Furukawa v. Honolulu Zoological Society, 85 Hawai'i 7, 936 P.2d 643 (1997). The Hawai'i Supreme Court reasoned that claims based on intentional conduct are not "accidents" within the meaning of the workers' compensation statute. See id. at 18, 936 P.2d 654;

see also Kahale v. ADT Automotive Services, Inc., 2 F. Supp. 2d 1295 (D. Haw. 1998) (following Furukawa and holding that claim for intentional infliction of emotional distress in a Title VII discriminatory discharge action was not barred by workers' compensation statute). Claims for negligent infliction of emotional distress, however, are barred. Marshall v. Univ. of Haw., 9 Haw. App. 21, 821 P.2d 937 (1991).

D. Pleading Requirements

Hawai'i is a "notice pleading" jurisdiction, requiring only a short and plain statement of the claim. The state court rules of civil procedure track the counterpart federal rules almost verbatim. In a defamation action in Hawai'i , the plaintiff must plead and prove four elements: (a) a false and defamatory statement concerning another; (b) an unprivileged publication to a third party; (c) fault amounting at least to negligence on the part of the publisher [actual malice where the plaintiff is a public figure]; and (d) either actionability of the statement irrespective of special harm or the existence of special harm caused by the publication. Gold v. Harrison, 88 Haw. 94, 100, 962 P.2d 353, 359, 26 Media L. Rep. (BNA) 2313, 2317 (Haw. 1998), citing Beamer v. Nishiki, 66 Haw. 572, 578-79, 670 P.2d 1264, 1271 (1983) (quoting Restatement (Second) of Torts § 558 (1977)).

SURVEY OF HAWAI'I EMPLOYMENT PRIVACY LAW

Paul Alston, Esq. and Mei-Fei Kuo, Esq.
Alston Hunt Floyd & Ing
1001 Bishop Street
Pacific Tower, Suite 1800
Honolulu, Hawai'i 96813
Telephone: (808) 524-1800; Facsimile: (808) 524-4591

(With Developments Reported Through **November 1, 2012**)

GENERAL COMMENTS

According to the Ninth Circuit, Hawai'i courts tend to look to California law in the absence of Hawaiian authority. Locricchio v. Legal Services Corp., 833 F.2d 1352, 1357 (9th Cir. 1987) (citing In re Pago Pago Aircrash, 525 F.Supp. 1007, 1021 (C.D. Cal. 1981)). Lawyers – especially those from California – accept this proposition at their peril. While the Hawai'i Supreme Court often adopts rules established in Restatements, its supposed reliance on California law is more imagined than real.

The Hawai'i Supreme Court has defined the reaches of the right to privacy in Brende v. Hara, 113 Hawai'i 424, 153 P.3d 1109 (2007). The Court explained that the right of privacy found in Article I, Section 6 of the Hawai'i Constitution is designed to include information found in employment records in the recognition that:

> [T]he dissemination of private and personal matters, be it true, embarrassing or not, can cause mental pain and distress far greater than bodily injury. . . . [The right to privacy] can be used to protect an individual from invasion of the individual's private affairs, public disclosure of embarrassing facts, and publicity placing the individual in a false light. . .includ[ing] the right of an individual to tell the world to "mind your own business."

Id. at 430, 153 P.3d at 1115.

SIGNIFICANT DEVELOPMENTS SINCE THE 2012 *SURVEY*

None.

I. GENERAL LAW OF PRIVACY

A. Legal Basis of Privacy Claims

Unlike the federal Constitution, the Hawai'i Constitution includes a separate and distinct right to privacy, embodied in Article I, Section 6 of the Hawai'i Constitution, which provides that "the right of the people to privacy is recognized and shall not be infringed without the showing of a compelling state interest."

Since the 1978 Constitutional Convention, which amended the Hawai'i Constitution to include Section 6, the Supreme Court of Hawai'i has held that the right of privacy under Section 6 protects at least two kinds of individual privacy interests: the interest in avoiding disclosure of personal matters and the interest in freely making certain kinds of intimate personal decisions. See, e.g., Nakano v. Matayoshi, 68 Haw. 140, 147-48, 706 P.2d 814, 818-19 (1985); State v. Mueller, 66 Haw. 616, 627-28, 671 P.2d 1351, 1358-59 (1983). The assembly adopting Section 6 reported that "[p]rivacy as used in this sense concerns the possible abuses in the use of highly personal and intimate information in the hands of government and private parties . . . ." Comm. of the Whole Rep. No. 15, in Proceedings of the Constitutional Convention of Hawai'i of 1978, Vol. I, at 1024.

The Supreme Court has further noted that Section 6 affords much greater privacy rights than the federal right to privacy, and therefore, the Court is "free to give broader privacy protection than that given by the federal constitution." State v. Kam, 69 Haw. 483, 748 P.2d 372 (1988). Indeed, the Hawai'i Supreme Court in Brende v. Hara, 113 Hawai'i 424, 153 P.3d 1109 (2007), has further clarified Section 6's privacy right as a right designed to preclude the dissemination of information that could be construed as embarrassing or causing mental distress.

Likewise, Article I, Section 7 of the Hawai'i Constitution, on its face, affords greater protection than its federal counterpart, the Fourth Amendment to the United States Constitution. Section 7 provides:

The right of the people to be secure in their persons, houses, papers, and effects against unreasonable searches, seizures and invasions of privacy shall not be violated; and no warrants shall issue, but upon probable cause, supported by oath or affirmation, and particularly describing the place to be searched and the persons or things to be seized or the communications to be intercepted.

The Supreme Court, however, has rejected two challenges to drug screening by agencies of the City of Honolulu on grounds that such testing violates Article I, Section 7. See, e.g., McCloskey v. Honolulu Police Dep't, 71 Haw. 568, 799 P.2d 953, 5 IER Cas. (BNA) 1577 (1990); Doe v. City & County of Honolulu, 8 Haw. App. 571, 816 P.2d 306, 6 IER Cas. (BNA) 1406 (1991).

Hawai'i's Employment Practices Act, HRS Chapter 378, similarly provides broader privacy protections than its federal counterpart, Title VII (42 U.S.C.A. § 200e(b)), in that, unlike federal law, the State of Hawai'i extends its employment discrimination prohibitions to all employers, not just those with fifteen or more employees. Haw. Rev. Stat. Ann. § 378-1 (2006) (defining "employer" as any person . . . having one or more employees, but . . . not . . . the United States."). Cf. 42 U.S.C.A. § 200e(b) (West 1994). Hawai'i Revised Statutes § 378-2 makes it an unlawful to discriminate in hiring, employment, or discharge "because of race, sex, **including gender identity or expression**, sexual orientation, age, religion, color, ancestry, disability, marital status, or arrest and court record, **or domestic or sexual violence victim status if the domestic or sexual violence victim provides notice to the victim's employer of such status or the employer has actual knowledge of such status**" or to "use any form of application for employment or to make any inquiry in connection with prospective employment, that expresses, directly or indirectly, any limitation, specification, or discrimination. . . ." Haw. Rev. Stat. Ann. § 378-2 (**2011**). Chapter 378 includes within the definition of "because of sex,"

> pregnancy, childbirth, or related medical conditions; and women affected by pregnancy, childbirth or related medical conditions shall be treated the same for all employment-related purposes, including receipt of benefits under fringe benefit programs, as other individuals not so affected but similar in their ability or inability to work.

Haw. Rev. Stat. Ann. § 378-1 (2006).

Hawai'i Revised Statutes § 378-2, related to Hawai'i's Employment Practices Act, was amended in 2011 to state that it is unlawful to discriminate in the employment realm based on "gender identity or expression" and "domestic or sexual violence victim status". As amended, HRS § 378-2 makes it an unlawful to discriminate in hiring, employment, or discharge "because of race, sex, including gender identity or expression, sexual orientation, age, religion, color, ancestry, disability, marital status, or arrest and court record, or domestic or sexual violence victim status if the domestic or sexual violence victim provides notice to the victim's employer of such status or the employer has actual knowledge of such status" or to "use any form of application for employment or to make any inquiry in connection with prospective employment, that expresses, directly or indirectly, any limitation, specification, or discrimination. . . ." Haw. Rev. Stat. Ann. § 378-2 (2011).

Section 378-3 allows, however, (1) religious organizations to give preference to individuals in the same religion or denomination and to make hiring decisions "calculated to promote the religious principles for which the organization is established or maintained;" (2) the department of education or private schools to consider criminal convictions in determining whether a prospective employee is suited to working in close proximity to children; and (3) financial institutions to deny employment to, or discharge from employment, any person who has been convicted of any crime of dishonesty or breach of trust. Haw. Rev. Stat. Ann. §§ 378-3(5), (8), (9) (2006).

Employers may inquire into and consider a prospective employee's criminal background for up to 10 years prior (except for incarcerations), provided that the conviction record bears a rational relationship to the duties and responsibilities of the position, and the consideration takes place only after the prospective employee has received a conditional offer of employment. Haw. Rev. Stat. Ann. § 378-2.5 (2006).

In Wright v. Home Depot U.S.A., Inc., 111 Hawai'i 401, 142 P.3d 265 (2006), plaintiff-employee argued that his termination for a prior conviction for the use of a controlled substance was wrongful and discriminatory. In Wright, plaintiff appealed the trial court's granting of defendant-employer's motion to dismiss and contended that Haw. Rev. Stat. Ann. § 378-2.5 does not apply because his conviction occurred prior to his employment. Plaintiff also argued that even if Haw. Rev. Stat. Ann. §378-2.5 applied, his prior conviction was not rationally related to his employment. Id. at 407, 142 P.3d at 271. Conversely, defendant argued that: "(1) the expressed terms of the statute do not prohibit consideration of a current employee's conviction that occurred prior to his employment with the employer; and (2) [the employee's] prior conviction was rationally related to his duties and responsibilities at Home Depot." Id. at 409, 142 P.3d at 273.

The Supreme Court of Hawai'i disagreed with Plaintiff's arguments and held that under the plain meaning of the terms of Haw. Rev. Stat. Ann. § 378-2.5, an employer may "'inquire about and consider an individual's criminal conviction record' in the context of 'hiring, termination, or the terms, conditions, or privileges of employment' as long as 'the conviction bears a rational relationship to the duties and responsibilities of the position.'" Id. at 410, 142 P.3d at 274. As the Court explained, "by limiting [Haw. Rev. Stat. Ann. § 378-2.5(a)] to only prospective employees...the phrase 'termination, or the terms, conditions, or privileges of employment' would be rendered superfluous." Id. at 410, 142 P.3d at 273-74 (citing In re City and County of Honolulu Corp. Counsel, 54 Haw. 356, 373, 507 P.2d 169, 178 (1973)).

While the Wright Court agreed with the employer's interpretation of Haw. Rev. Stat. Ann. §378-2.5, the Court ultimately held that by taking the plaintiff's allegations as true and viewing the complaint in the light most favorable to the non-moving party, "[plaintiff had] sufficiently alleged a claim against Home Depot for violations of Haw. Rev. Stat. Ann. § 378-2." Id. at 412, 142 P.3d at 276. The Court further explained, "whether, on an ongoing basis, [plaintiff] will be able to demonstrate that his prior conviction does not bear a rational relationship to his employment is an issue within the province of the trier of fact and not a proper issue to be determined by this court as a matter of law on a motion to dismiss." Id.

Moreover, an inquiry into and consideration of a prospective employee's conviction record may occur only after the applicant has received a conditional job offer. Haw. Rev. Stat. Ann. § 378-2.5(d) (2006). The limitation to the most recent ten-year period, excluding the period of incarceration, does not apply to employers who are expressly permitted to inquire into an individual's criminal history for employment purposes pursuant to any federal or state law other than subsection (a). Id. The statute sets forth a non-exclusive list of employers who are expressly permitted to make such an inquiry. Haw. Rev. Stat. Ann. §§ 378-2.5(d)(1)-(18) (2006). Additionally, Section 378-3 does not prevent employers from refusing to hire, or from discharging, any employee for reasons relating to the ability of the individual to perform the work in question. Haw. Rev. Stat. Ann. § 378-3(3) (2006).

In addition to providing a cause of action for unlawful discrimination, Chapter 378 provides a private cause of action to employees for, among others offenses, sexual harassment, infliction of emotional distress, or invasion of privacy related thereto. Haw. Rev. Stat. Ann. § 378-3(10) (2006). Victims of sexual harassment or sexual assault and infliction of emotional distress or invasion of privacy related thereto need not file discrimination complaints with the Hawai'i Civil Rights Commission before proceeding to trial. B.K.B. v. Maui Police Dep't, 276 F.3d 1091, 1103, 87 Fair Empl. Prac. Cas. (BNA) 1306, 82 Empl. Prac. Dec. (CCH) P40, 914 (D. Haw. 2002) (quoting Haw. Rev. Stat. § 378-3(10)).

It is unlawful for an employer to prohibit an employee from "expressing breast milk during any meal period or other break period required by law to be provided by the employer or required by collective bargaining agreement." Haw. Rev. Stat. Ann. § 378-10 (2006).

Moreover, Section 378-26.5 of the Employment Practices Act makes it unlawful for any employer to, among others, (1) require a lie detector test as a condition of employment or continued employment; (2) terminate or otherwise discriminate for refusing to submit to a lie detector test; or (3) ask an employee or prospective employee to submit to a lie detector test unless the employee or prospective employee is informed both orally and in writing that the test is voluntary and that refusal will not result in termination of the employee or jeopardize the prospective employee's chance of a job. Haw. Rev. Stat. Ann. § 378-26.5(1)-(3) (2006). Section 378-26.5 does not apply, however, to lie detector tests administered by any law enforcement agency; the United States and any subdivision thereof; or to psychological tests administered by a law enforcement agency to determine the suitability of a candidate for employment with the law enforcement agency. Haw. Rev. Stat. Ann. § 378-27(3)-(5) (2006).

Chapter 92F, the Uniform Information Practices Act, allows public access to government records and processes, "tempered by a recognition of the right of the people to privacy," as embodied in Hawai'i Constitution. Haw. Rev. Stat. Ann. § 92F-2 (2006).

Sections 92F-13 and 92F-14 exemplify the competing interests at work under this Chapter. Section 93F-13, for example, excludes from disclosure "[g]overnment records which, if disclosed, would constitute a clearly unwarranted invasion of personal privacy." Haw. Rev. Stat. Ann. § 92F-13 (2006). Section 92F- 14(b) identifies information relating to medical, psychiatric, or psychological history, and information in an agency's personnel file as types of information in which an individual has a significant privacy interest, but excludes information related to employment misconduct that results in an employee's suspension or discharge. Haw. Rev. Stat. Ann. § 92F-14(b)(4)(B) (2006). Section 92F-14(a), likewise, provides that the "disclosure of a government record shall not constitute a clearly unwarranted invasion of personal privacy if the public interest in disclosure outweighs the privacy interest in the individual." Haw. Rev. Stat. Ann. § 92F-14(a) (2006).

Haw. Rev. Stat. Ann § 92F-12(9), amended by 2007 Hawai'i Act 14, H.B. 1393 (2007) also prohibits governmental agencies from disclosing an individual's social security number and home address in certified payroll records on public works contracts. Additionally, Haw. Rev. Stat. § 92F-14(b)(9) (2006) provides that an individual has a significant privacy interest in his or her social security number.

B. Causes of Action

1. ***Misappropriation/Right of Publicity.*** The Supreme Court of Hawai'i, in the case of Fergerstrom v. Hawaiian Ocean View Estates, 50 Haw. 374, 378, 441 P.2d 141 (1968), recognized the cause of action for

misappropriation of a person's name or picture for commercial purposes for the first time. In Fergerstrom, employees of the defendant construction corporation took pictures of one of the plaintiffs and of the house plaintiffs purchased from the defendant at various stages of construction. The defendant used the photographs and the plaintiffs' name in sales brochures, advertisements, publications, and television commercials. The Supreme Court upheld plaintiffs' claims against defendant for invasion of privacy, although Hawai'i law had not previously recognized the tort.

The Court declined to decide, however, whether other causes of action commonly included under a general right of privacy would receive similar protection, noting that "these issues remain to be resolved in subsequent cases raising them, preferably after a trial on the merits." Fergerstrom, 50 Haw. at 378, 441 P.2d at 144.

Hawai'i Revised Statutes §§ 657-7 and 662-4 limit the period for claims of misappropriation and other torts to two years, except in the case of a medical tort claim, when the limitation of action provisions set forth in section 657-7.3 shall apply.

2. ***False Light.*** In Chung v. McCabe Hamilton & Renny Co., Ltd., 109 Hawai'i 520, 128 P.3d 833 (2006), a union member filed an action against the employer and certain employees alleging various tort causes of action, including false light invasion of privacy. The employer argued that the false light invasion of privacy claim was preempted by the National Labor Relations Act ("NLRA") and the circuit court agreed in dismissing the claim against the employer. On appeal, the Hawai'i Supreme Court held that the false light invasion of privacy claim was not preempted by the NLRA and, therefore, reversed dismissal of the claim. Id. at 534-35, 128 P.3d at 847-48. The Hawai'i Supreme Court further recognized that to establish a claim for false light invasion of privacy in Hawai'i, "the plaintiff must show that defendant had 'knowledge of . . . or reckless disregard as to the falsity of the publicized matter and the false light in which [the plaintiff] would be placed[,] . . . which would be 'highly offensive to a reasonable person. . .' " Id. (citing Restatement (Second) of Torts § 652E (1991)).

In Shipley v. Hawai'i, 2007 U.S. Dist. LEXIS 4548 (D. Haw. 2007), a public school teacher brought a false light claim against the Hawai'i Department of Education after administrators allegedly placed in her permanent personnel file a record of a grievance the teacher had filed against a school administrator. The grievance record, the plaintiff asserted, followed her from school to school as the teacher changed jobs and caused various administrators to retaliate against her. The U.S. District Court dismissed the claim, finding that the plaintiff failed to meet the standard stated in Chung v. McCabe, *supra*. First, the plaintiff put forward no evidence that the "publicized matter" – the grievance record in her file -- was "false." Second, there was no evidence that the defendants had knowledge of or reckless disregard as to the falsity of the McKinley grievance record. Third, the plaintiff put forth no evidence that any of the defendants "published" the allegedly defamatory grievance record. Shipley, 2007 U.S. Dist. LEXIS 4548 at *40.

Likewise, in Farmer v. Hickam Federal Credit Union, 2010 Haw. App. LEXIS 39 (2010), reprinted at 122 Hawai'i 201, 224 P.3d 455 (2010), the Hawaii Intermediate Court of Appeals upheld a circuit court's dismissal of a false light claim brought by a former credit union employee. The claim involved an auditor's report finding that the plaintiff had made more than one hundred loans that appeared to violate the credit union's loan policies. Id., 2010 Haw. App. LEXIS 39 at *2. Among other claims, the plaintiff brought a false light claim, alleging that the credit union created a false impression in the eyes of other credit union employees that the plaintiff was incompetent and making bad decisions. Id. at *35. In its memorandum opinion, the Court stated that "it is not an invasion of the right of privacy ... to communicate a fact ... to a single person or even a small group of persons." Id. at *34. Thus, the plaintiff's complaint failed to allege a sufficient degree of publicity to sustain his false light claim. Id.

A false light claim also may be defeated by a qualified privilege. That is to say, conduct which otherwise would be actionable may escape liability because the defendant is acting in furtherance of some duty that is entitled to protection, "even at the expense of uncompensated harm to the plaintiff's reputation." Russell v. American Guild of Variety Artists, 53 Hawai'i 456, 460, 497 P.2d 40, 43 (1972); see also Roberts v. City & County of Honolulu, 2008 U.S. Dist. LEXIS 16068 (D. Haw. Mar. 3, 2008). This qualified privilege may arise when the author of a defamatory statement reasonably acts to discharge a public or private duty, and where the publication concerns subject matter in which the author of the publication shares a corresponding interest with the publication's recipients. Russell, 53 Haw. at 460, 497 P.2d at 43. In Russell, the plaintiff was an entertainer who brought a libel claim against an entertainers' guild and the guild's Honolulu agent after the Honolulu agent wrote a letter to the plaintiff's booking agent erroneously stating that the plaintiff had been confined to a state mental institution for one year. Id. at 457, 497 P.2d at 41. The Hawaii Supreme Court ruled that the letter was libelous per se because the letter suggested the plaintiff was unfit to perform the duties of her employment as an entertainer. Id. at 458, 497 P.2d at 42. But the Court also found that the Honolulu guild agent shared a common interest in the plaintiff with the letter's recipient, and there was substantial evidence to support the trial court's findings that the Honolulu guild agent made his erroneous statements in good faith and without malice. Id. at 465, 497 P.2d at 16. On these grounds, the Court affirmed the lower court's finding that the Honolulu guild agent had a qualified privilege.

3. ***Publication of Private Facts.*** The tort of unfair publicity is actionable if the plaintiff demonstrates that the defendant engaged in (1) public disclosure (2) of a private fact regarding the plaintiff (3) which would be offensive and objectionable to a reasonable person, and (4) which is not of legitimate public concern. Black v. City and County of Honolulu, 112 F. Supp. 2d 1041, 1054, 79 Empl. Prac. Dec. (CCH) P40,319 (D. Haw. 2000). In Black, an employee of the Honolulu Police Department ("HPD") filed a sexual harassment complaint. As part of its investigation, HPD's Internal Affairs department ("IA") prepared a confidential report on the plaintiff's complaint. The plaintiff claimed that HPD disclosed private facts about her to the public when HPD gave the local media access to the IA report.

The plaintiff moved for summary judgment on her unfair publicity claim. While the plaintiff successfully established that the IA report had been released, no one could identify the person responsible for the disclosure despite a six-month internal HPD investigation. Although there was conjecture that the IA report was released by someone in HPD, there was no substantial evidence to support the conclusion. Therefore, the Black court concluded that the plaintiff failed to provide enough evidence to demonstrate, as a matter of law, that HPD was liable for the tort of unfair publicity.

4. ***Intrusion.*** A defendant is liable in tort "for intrusion into another's seclusion if the defendant intentionally intrudes, physically or otherwise, upon the solitude or seclusion of another, or upon the private concerns of another, and the intrusion would be highly offensive to a reasonable person." Black v. City and County of Honolulu, 112 F. Supp. 2d 1041,1052-53, 79 Empl. Prac. Dec. P40319 (D. Haw. 2000)(citing Restatement (Second) of Torts § 652B (1976)). In Black, the plaintiff, while an employee of the Honolulu Police Department ("HPD"), allegedly was harassed by her supervising officer. After the plaintiff filed a complaint with HPD's Internal Affairs department ("IA"), she claimed, among other things, that she was the subject of "Operation Foxtrot", a twenty-four hour a day surveillance operation that lasted approximately one week, and that HPD placed a "wire trap" on her pager. These activities, according to the plaintiff, infringed on her right to privacy.

While recognizing that covert surveillance activities such as Operation Foxtrot implicate the privacy interests of individuals in their persons, the Black court declined to decide the plaintiff's claim as a matter of law, noting that two issues remained unresolved: (1) whether the surveillance was "highly offensive" to a reasonable person, and (2) whether the plaintiff waived her privacy rights. Similarly, while recognizing that a trapping of a personal pager without a valid warrant would appear to be a per se violation of a person's right to privacy, the court declined to grant the plaintiff's motion for summary judgment because a question of fact existed regarding whether the pager belonged to the plaintiff or HPD.

C. Other Privacy-related Actions

1. **Intentional Infliction of Emotional Distress.** Under prior Hawai'i law, an employee was relegated to seeking compensation under Hawai'i's workers' compensation statute for an employer's intentional infliction of emotional distress. See Marshall v. University of Hawai'i, 9 Haw. App. 21, 821 P.2d 937 (1991) (plaintiff's intentional infliction of emotional distress claims were barred by the exclusivity provision of the workers' compensation statute). However, the legislature amended Haw. Rev. Stat. § 386-5 in 1992 to specifically exclude claims for sexual harassment or sexual assault and infliction of emotional distress or invasion of privacy related thereto, from the exclusivity provision of the workers' compensation statute.

Consistent with the 1992 amendments, courts interpreting Hawai'i's workers' compensation statute have held that a plaintiff may pursue a civil action for intentional infliction of emotional distress against the plaintiff's employer. See, e.g., Morishige v. Spencecliff Corp., 720 F. Supp. 829, 837, 119 Lab. Cas. P56657, 4 IER Cases (BNA) 1271 (D. Haw. 1989) (intentional infliction of emotional distress claims against the employee's supervisors individually are not preempted by the workers' compensation statute); Bragalone v. Kona Coast Resort Joint Venture, 866 F. Supp. 1285, 1294, 66 Fair Empl. Prac. Cas. (BNA) 65 (D. Haw. 1994) (employee's intentional infliction of emotional distress claim against employer was not barred by the workers' compensation statute); Furukawa v. Honolulu Zoological Soc'y, 85 Hawai'i 7, 936 P.2d 643, 70 Empl. Prac. Dec. (CCH) P44679, reconsideration denied, 85 Hawai'i 196, 940 P.2d 403 (1997) (the trial court improperly excluded evidence of plaintiff's intentional infliction of emotional distress claim because Haw. Rev. Stat. § 386-5 did not bar claims brought by an employee against his or her employer for emotional distress); Takaki v. Allied Machinery Corp., 87 Hawai'i 57, 68, 951 P.2d 507, 518, 13 IER Cases (BNA) 1256 (App. 1998) (a plaintiff was allowed to pursue his claim for intentional infliction of emotional distress caused by his wrongful termination). Similarly, a plaintiff's claim for negligent infliction of emotional distress related to sexual harassment is not barred by the workers' compensation statute. Nelson v. University of Hawai'i, 97 Hawai'i 376, 395, 38 P.3d 95, 114 (2001).

Previously, Hawai'i appellate courts held that to prevail on an intentional infliction of emotional distress claim, the plaintiff had to prove: "(1) that the act allegedly causing the harm was intentional; (2) that the act was unreasonable; and (3) that the actor should have recognized that the act was likely to result in illness." Marshall v. University of Hawai'i, 9 Haw. App. at 38, 821 P.2d at 947. In 2003, however, the Hawai'i Supreme Court abrogated its prior decisions and held that the likelihood of illness is no longer a necessary element of the tort. Hac v. University of Hawai'i, 102 Hawai'i

92, 73 P.3d 46 (2003). The result is that, in order to prevail on an IIED claim under Hawai'i law, the plaintiff must prove: (a) that the conduct allegedly causing the harm was intentional or reckless; (b) that the conduct was outrageous; (c) causation; and (d) extreme emotional distress. Nagata v. Quest Diagnostics Inc., 303 F. Supp. 2d 1121, 1125-26 (D. Haw. 2004) (citing Hac v. University of Hawai'i, 102 Hawai'i 92, 73 P.3d 46 (2003)); Snyder v. Phelps, 131 S. Ct. 1207, 1215, 179 L. Ed. 2d 172 (2011). With respect to the first element, the plaintiff must prove that the defendant's conduct was "reckless". Nagata, at 1126. "Recklessness requires that the defendant must know, or have reason to know, the facts which create the risk." Id. (citations omitted). Damages for emotional distress in the employment context are recoverable under a contract only if the alleged conduct (1) violates a duty that is independently recognized by principles of tort law and (2) transcends the breach of the contract. Burlington Ins. Co. v. Oceanic Design & Constr., Inc., 383 F.3d 940, 954 (9th Cir. 2004) (citing Francis v. Lee Enters., Inc., 89 Hawai'i 234, 971 P.2d 707, 708 (1999)) (construing Hawai'i law).

"Severe emotional distress" is defined as "mental suffering, mental anguish, mental or nervous shock", and includes "all highly unpleasant mental reactions, such as fright, horror, grief, shame, humiliation, embarrassment, anger, chagrin, disappointment, worry and nausea." Hac, 102 Hawai'i at 106, 73 P.3d at 60 (quoting Restatement (Second) of Torts § 46). "The intensity and the duration of the distress are factors to be considered in determining its severity." Id. (quoting Restatement, supra, § 46). Hence, while bodily injury is compensable, it is not necessary to establish severe emotional distress. Id. The actor's intentional conduct, however, must have actually caused the plaintiff to suffer severe emotional distress. Id. (citing Restatement, supra, § 46 cmt. k). Whether the defendant's actions are unreasonable or outrageous is for the court in the first instance, although where reasonable persons may differ on that question it should be left to the jury. Shoppe v. Gucci America, Inc., 94 Hawai'i 368, 387, 14 P.3d 1049, 1068 (2000) (citing Wong v. Panis, 7 Haw. App. 414, 421, 772 P.2d 695, 700 (1989) & Restatement (Second) of Torts § 46 cmt. h)).

While the standard appears to be rather straight-forward, courts have applied it with somewhat mixed results. For example, in Bragalone a former employee asserted an intentional infliction of emotional distress claim, among others, against her former employer and manager. Bragalone v. Kona Coast Resort Joint Venture, 866 F. Supp. 1285, 66 Fair Empl. Prac. Cas. (BNA) 65 (D. Haw. 1994). She alleged that the manger interrupted her whenever she spoke, yelled at her, changed his instructions to her, told her she could quit if she was unhappy, gave her conflicting work instructions, and told her not to question the manager's actions. The court opined that, while the manger's comments were "certainly distasteful", they did not rise to the level of outrageousness necessary to maintain a claim under Hawai'i law. Id. at 1295. Accordingly, the court granted summary judgment in favor of the defendants on plaintiff's intentional infliction of emotional distress claim.

In Takaki, an employee sued his employer and its president for wrongful discharge, intentional infliction of emotional distress and racial discrimination. According to the plaintiff, "quite often" "his immediate supervisor" called him a "lousy f—king Jap." Takaki, 87 Hawai'i at 68, 951 P.2d at 518. The defendants claimed that the plaintiff's termination "hardly rose to the level of outrageousness and/or unreasonable conduct" sufficient to support an emotional distress claim. The Hawai'i Supreme Court disagreed. It therefore vacated the award of summary judgment and remanded the case, concluding that reasonable minds may differ on whether the termination, which was allegedly motivated by race, was unreasonable or outrageous. Id. at 69, 951 P.2d at 519.

Nearly three years after Takaki was decided, the Hawai'i Supreme Court affirmed the trial court's entry of summary judgment on a plaintiff's intentional infliction of emotional distress claim in Shoppe. The plaintiff in Shoppe brought claims against her employer and district manager for age discrimination, breach of employment contract, fraud, and intentional or negligent infliction of emotional distress. She claimed that her manager shouted at her and was abusive towards her, which resulted in a significant rise in her blood pressure and difficulty sleeping. The plaintiff described a "vicious verbal attack" in which the manager allegedly yelled, "You have to start doing your job" and slammed down the phone when plaintiff inquired why the manager was being rude. Shoppe, 94 Hawai'i at 387, 14 P.3d at 1068. In addition, the plaintiff claimed that her manager singled her out on three or four occasions and directed her to wear more makeup because the store was "aiming for a much younger look." Id. at 387, 14 P.3d at 1068. She was also allegedly chastised in front of other employees about her attire and need to comb her hair. Id. at 387, 14 P.3d at 1068. The Supreme Court opined that, while the plaintiff "may have resented the tone and substance" of the manager's criticisms, the court could "hardly classify such remarks as 'outrageous' or 'beyond the bounds of decency.'" Id. at 387, 14 P.3d at 1068.

In Mukaida, the plaintiff alleged a host of tort and statutory claims against her employer and a co-worker with whom she had a sexual relationship. Mukaida v. Hawaii, 159 F. Supp.2d. 1211 (D. Hawai'i 2001). In her complaint, she alleged, among others, claims for battery, assault and emotional distress. While conceding that she had a consensual sexual relationship with her co-worker, the plaintiff claimed to have been subjected to the unwelcomed sexual requests, advances and contact of her co-worker after the relationship ended. Without specifically describing the facts that supported the plaintiff's intentional infliction of emotional distress claim, the court denied summary judgment in favor of the defendants on the emotional distress claim because genuine issues of material fact existed regarding the assault and battery claims. Mukaida, 159 F. Supp. 2d at 1239-40.

In Nagata, the plaintiff-employee provided a urine sample to his employer pursuant to the employer's drug-testing policy. Nagata, 303 F. Supp. 2d at 1124. The lab tested the sample and reported that the sample was inconsistent with human urine. Id. The employer subsequently terminated the employee. Two years later, the lab informed the testing physician that it "did not measure the creatinine concentration of specimens to at least one decimal place" during the period in which the employee's urine sample had been analyzed. Id. As a result, the lab did not know whether the employee's urine sample actually met the Department of Health and Human Services' criteria for determining whether a specimen was substituted. Id. The lab therefore canceled the employee's test and instructed the testing physician to inform the employer that "any personnel action taken with respect to the donor on the basis of the canceled test no longer has a basis in DOT regulations." Id. The employer notified the employee of the lab's error and offered him re-employment. Id.

The employee sued the lab on various tort theories, including intentional infliction of emotional distress ("IIED"). All of his claims were dismissed except for the IIED claim. The lab moved for summary judgment on the remaining claim. The Nagata court denied the lab's motion for summary judgment, concluding that: (a) a jury could find that the lab had reason to know that a high degree of risk existed that its delay in disclosure would cause serious harm to the employee, and that the lab disregarded that risk (Id. at 1127); (b) a genuine issue of material fact existed regarding whether the lab's delayed disclosure rose to the level of outrageous conduct (Id. at 1128 (citing Restatement (Second) of Torts § 46, cmt. d)); (c) the evidence, when viewed in a light most favorable to the employee, might establish that the employee's emotional distress, which may have been triggered by the loss of his job, continued as a result of the lab's alleged withholding of information from him (Id. at 1129); and (d) the employee's claim that he contemplated suicide and suffered from depression, substance abuse, shame, and confusion, were symptoms of severe emotional distress recognized by the Hawai'i Supreme Court. Id. (citing Hac v. University of Hawaii, 102 Hawai'i 92, 73 P.3d 46 (2003)).

Hawai'i Revised Statutes §§ 657-7 and 662-4 set the limitations period for claims of misappropriation and other torts at two years, except in the case of a medical tort claim, when the limitation of action provisions set forth in section 657-7.3 applies.

2. ***Interference With Prospective Economic Advantage.*** Two cases have identified the requisite elements of tortious interference with a prospective economic advantage, with one difference. In Kutcher v. Zimmerman, 87 Hawai'i 394, 957 P.2d 1076 (App. 1998), the court held that the requisite elements are: (1) a prospective contractual relationship between the plaintiff and a third-party; (2) knowledge by the defendant of the existence of the relationship; (3) intentional acts by the defendant designed to disrupt the relationship; (4) the defendant acted without proper justification; (5) subsequent breach of the contract by a third-party; and (6) damages proximately caused by the defendants acts. Id. at 405, 957 P.2d at 1087. In Locricchio v. Legal Services Corp., 833 F.2d 1352, 1357 (9th Cir. 1987), the court held that the elements of tortious interference with a prospective economic advantage are those listed above, excluding the fourth listed element. Id. at 1357. The Locricchio Court also noted that the prospective economic relationship need not take the form of an offer, but there must be specific facts proving the possibility of future association. Id. See also Hawaii Medical Ass'n v. Hawaii Medical Service Ass'n, Inc., 113 Hawaii 77, 116, fn. 33, 148 P.3d 1179, 1218, fn. 33 (2006) (citing Restatement (Second) of Torts § 766B).

In Kutcher, the court identified the privileges set forth in §§ 768 through 773 of the Restatement (Second) of Torts as "proper justification" defenses available to defendants. Kutcher, 87 Hawai'i at 408, 957 P.2d at 1090, 13 IER Cas. 1753. These defenses include truth of the statements asserted by defendant allegedly designed to interfere with plaintiff's prospective advantage, and that the allegedly tortious acts were done pursuant to industry standard or custom. Kutcher, 87 Hawai'i at 411, 957 P.2d at 1093-94.

The plaintiff in Kutcher was a prospective employee of Avis Rent-a-Car ("Avis"). As a part of the application process, Avis required Kutcher to submit to a drug screening test at Clinical Laboratories of Hawai'i ("CLH") in Kahului, Maui. At the Kahului lab, Kutcher became angry and argumentative with one of the lab's employees after she informed him that he would have to submit a second sample for testing. Kutcher advised the employee that he intended to go to CLH's Wailuku lab for testing because he did not think he was being treated fairly. When Kutcher failed to appear at the Wailuku lab, defendant, an employee of the Wailuku lab, telephoned Avis and reported that Kutcher had not appeared for his drug screening test and that he had become angry and rude with the Kahului lab employee. Avis subsequently decided not to offer Kutcher a position with Avis, due in part to his failure to complete the drug screening test, and in part because of Avis's concern for Kutcher's ability to interact with others.

Kutcher sued both the Wailuku lab employee who had placed the phone call to Avis, and the Kahului lab employee who had relayed the information about Kutcher's conduct to her. The court granted both defendants' motions for summary judgment, finding that Kutcher had submitted no evidence that the Kahului employee intentionally interfered with his relationship with Avis, and that the Wailuku employee's actions were properly justified, given that her statements to Avis were true, and that it was CLH policy to advise its customers when their employees failed to submit themselves for a drug screening test. Kutcher, 87 Hawai'i at 411, 957 P.2d at 1093-94, 13 IER Cas. 1753.

Likewise, in Locricchio, the court found that defendant, Legal Services Corporation ("LSC") did not intentionally interfere with plaintiff's prospective economic advantage. Locrichhio, 833 F.2d at 1357. In Locricchio, plaintiff was the executive director of the Legal Aid Society of Hawai'i ("LASH"), funded largely in part by LSC. Locricchio had a contract with LASH until 1980, stating that LASH could terminate his employment only for cause. In 1978, LASH began investigating whether Locricchio had misappropriated any of LASH's funds, and held hearings to review the charges against him.

Before the end of LASH's hearings, a director of LSC advised the LASH Board of Directors that it would have to terminate Locricchio as a condition to further funding. Thereafter, the hearing officer issued his findings of fact, which criticized Locricchio for fiscal abuses. The LASH Board voted unanimously to terminate Locricchio's employment contract.

Locricchio filed suit against LSC alleging interference with contract, interference with prospective economic advantage, defamation, and intentional infliction of emotional distress. Although after his firing from LASH Locricchio had difficulty finding employment in the legal services community, the court found that Locricchio,

> failed to show any specific potential relationship with these employers that would have inured to his economic benefit but for LSC's wrongful interference. . . . While Locricchio amply showed that LSC's action in firing him hindered his ability to obtain gainful employment elsewhere, he failed to prove that this inability was a direct result of LSC's wrongful interference with his employment endeavors.

Locricchio, 833 F.2d at 1357-58. Nonetheless, the court held that LSC had interfered with Locricchio's contract with LASH when it directed LASH's Board to terminate him. The court based its ruling on LSC's failure to comply with the Legal Services Corporation Act which requires LSC to attempt to achieve compliance with the Act first "through informal consultation with the recipient [LASH][;]" which it had not done. Id. at 1356 (citing 45 C.F.R. § 1618.5(a) (1986)).

Tort claims in Hawai'i, such as intentional interference with economic advantage, are governed by a two-year statute of limitations. See Haw. Rev. Stat. Ann. § 657-7 (2006); Haw. Rev. Stat. Ann. § 662-4 (2006).

3. ***Prima Facie Tort.*** No reported cases.

4. **Invasion of Privacy.**In Kamaka v. Goodsill Anderson Quinn & Stifel, 117 Hawai'i 92, 176 P.3d 91 (2008), a terminated attorney brought suit against her former law firm and asserted inter alia claims for negligent investigation and invasion of privacy. The terminated employee argued that the circuit court erred in dismissing her negligent investigation claim because Haw. Rev. Stat. § 386-3, related to injuries covered by the Workers' Compensation Law, provides for compensation where an employee suffers "personal injury either by accident arising out of and in the course of employment." Id. at 108-109, 176 P.3d at 107-108. The employer argued that an employee is barred by the exclusivity provision of Hawai'i's Workers' Compensation Law, under Haw. Rev. Stat. § 386-5, which precludes an employee from asserting other claims for liability and negligence against his or her employer. Id. The Hawai'i Supreme Court upheld the dismissal of the negligent investigation claim and explained that Haw. Rev. Stat. § 386-5 provides for an "exclusiveness or right to compensation" related to workers' compensation claims. Id. at 109, 176 P.3d at 108. However, the Hawai'i Supreme Court recognized that Haw. Rev. Stat. § 386-5 "unambiguously provides that claims for infliction of emotional distress or invasion of privacy are not subject to the exclusivity provision when such claims arise from claims for sexual harassment or sexual assault, in which case a civil action may be brought." Id.

II. EMPLOYER TESTING OF EMPLOYEES

A. Psychological or Personality Testing

No reported cases.

B. Drug Testing

1. ***Common Law and Statutes.*** Chapter 329B of the Hawai'i Revised Statutes prescribes the standard method in the State of Hawai'i for substance abuse screening to ensure the privacy rights of the persons tested and that reliable and accurate results are achieved. Any person or agency who willfully and knowingly violates any provision of Chapter 329B may be fined not less than $1,000 and not more than $10,000 for each violation, plus reasonable costs and attorney's fees. Haw. Rev. Stat. Ann. § 329B-7 (2006). Injunctive relief may also be granted against any party proposing to commit any act in violation of Chapter 329B. Haw. Rev. Stat. Ann. § 329B-7 (2006).

2. ***Private Employers.*** A federal district court, construing Hawai'i law, ruled that an employee who was terminated after failing his employer-mandated drug test may maintain an action for intentional infliction of emotional distress against the laboratory that conducted the test for failure to follow proper testing procedures. Nagata v. Quest

Diagnostics Inc., 303 F.Supp.2d 1121 (D. Haw. 2004). In Nagata, the plaintiff-employee provided a urine sample to his employer pursuant to the employer's drug-testing policy. Id. at 1123. The lab tested the sample and reported that the sample was inconsistent with human urine. Id. The employer subsequently terminated the employee.

Two years later, the lab informed the testing physician that it "did not measure the creatinine concentration of specimens to at least one decimal place" during the period in which the employee's urine sample had been analyzed. Id. As a result, the lab did not know whether the employee's urine sample actually met the Department of Health and Human Services' criteria for determining whether a specimen was substituted. Id. The lab therefore canceled the employee's test and instructed the testing physician to inform the employer that "any personnel action taken with respect to the donor on the basis of the canceled test no longer has a basis in DOT regulations." Id. The employer notified the employee of the lab's error and offered him re-employment. Id.

The employee sued the lab on various tort theories, including intentional infliction of emotional distress ("IIED"). All of his claims were dismissed except for the IIED claim. The lab moved for summary judgment on the remaining claim. The court denied the motion. To prevail on an IIED claim under Hawai'i law, the plaintiff must prove: (a) that the conduct alleged causing the harm was intentional or reckless; (b) that the conduct was outrageous; (c) causation; and (d) extreme emotional distress. Id. at 125-26 (citing Hac, 102 Hawai'i 92, 73 P.3d 46). After noting the recent change in Hawai'i law on the elements required to make out a prima facie IIED claim, the Nagata court held that the scope of the first element now requires proof that the defendant's conduct was "reckless" (i.e., that the defendant "know, or have reason to know, the facts which create the risk"). Id. at 1126 (citations omitted).

The Nagata court denied the lab's motion for summary judgment, concluding that: (a) a jury could find that the lab had reason to know that a high degree of risk existed, that its delay in disclosure would cause serious harm to the employee, and that the lab disregarded that risk (Id. at 1127); (b) a genuine issue of material fact existed regarding whether the lab's delayed disclosure rose to the level of outrageous conduct (Id. at 1128 (citing Restatement (Second) of Torts § 46, cmt. d)); (c) the evidence, when viewed in a light most favorable to the employee, might establish that the employee's emotional distress, which may have been triggered by the loss of his job, continued as a result of the lab's alleged withholding of information from him (Id. at 1129); and (d) the employee's claim the he contemplated suicide and suffered from depression, substance abuse, shame, and confusion, were symptoms of severe emotional distress recognized by the Hawai'i Supreme Court. Id. (citing Hac, 102 Hawai'i 92, 73 P.3d 46).

3. ***Public Employers.*** The Hawai'i Supreme Court has twice rejected challenges to the constitutionality of drug testing of public employees. In McCloskey v. Honolulu Police Dep't, 71 Haw. 568, 799 P.2d 953, 5 IER Cas. (BNA) 1577 (1990), the Honolulu Police Department ("HPD") required plaintiff-police officer to submit a urine sample for testing for the presence of marijuana and cocaine only. The officer was permitted to produce her urine sample in the privacy of a bathroom stall with no visual observation or monitoring. Under HPD's drug screening program, the samples were identified only by a control number, HPD utilized a strict chain of custody procedure and confirmatory tests to prevent false reports of the presence of illegal drugs, and kept all test results confidential. In addition, an agreement between HPD and the police officers' union prohibited the test results from being used for criminal charges.

The plaintiff in McCloskey refused to submit to a drug test and filed suit against HPD, alleging that the drug screening tests violated her right to privacy under Sections 6 and 7 of the Hawai'i Constitution. The Supreme Court of Hawai'i declined to decide whether compelled urinalysis testing might implicate a right to privacy under the state constitution, because it held, instead, that the HPD testing program was the necessary means to the compelling state interests of (1) insuring that individual police officers are able to perform their duties safely; (2) protecting the public safety; and (3) preserving HPD's integrity and ability to perform its job effectively. McCloskey, 71 Haw. at 575-76, 799 P.2d at 957, 5 IER Cas. 1577. The Court also concluded that, "a police officer, by reason of the employment as a police officer, has a diminished expectation of privacy." McCloskey, 71 Haw. at 579, 799 P.2d at 959, 5 IER Cas. 1577.

Similarly, in Doe v. City & County of Honolulu, 8 Haw. App. 571, 816 P.2d 306, 6 IER Cas. (BNA) 1406 (1991), plaintiff-fire fighter challenged the constitutionality of drug screening by the Honolulu Fire Department ("HFD") under both the United States and Hawai'i Constitutions. The HFD screening program provided for drug screening (1) on a "regular or frequent basis;" (2) as a part of a fire fighter's annual or pre-entry medical examination; (3) as a part of "probationary requirements;" or (4) on a "reasonable suspicion" basis. Doe, 8 Haw. App. at 575, 816 P.2d at 316, 6 IER Cas. 1406. The appellate court, likewise, found that fire fighters, as with police officers, have a diminished expectation of privacy. Doe, 8 Haw. App. at 584-85, 816 P.2d at 314-15.

The Doe Court upheld the constitutionality of the search under Section 7 of the Hawai'i Constitution, concluding that the search was reasonable and did not infringe upon plaintiff's Section 7 rights. Doe, 8 Haw. App. at 591, 816 P.2d at 317-18, 6 IER Cas. 1406. The court further held that the search did not violate plaintiff's right to privacy under Section 6 because the City of Honolulu had a compelling interest relating to the safety of fire fighters and the public they served, and because the City's compelling interest outweighed the fire fighter's privacy concerns. Doe, 8 Haw. App. at 593, 816 P.2d at 318-19, 6 IER Cas. 1406.

Constitutional causes of action, such as those asserted in McCloskey and Doe, are governed by a six-year limitations period under Haw. Rev. Stat.. § 657-1. Tamura v. FAA, 675 F. Supp. 1221, 1224 (D. Haw. 1987). See Haw. Rev. Stat. Ann. § 657-1 (2006). However, suits brought under 42 U.S.C. § 1981 are governed by the two-year limitations period under Haw. Rev. Stat.§ 657-7. Lesane v. Hawaiian Airlines, 75 F. Supp. 2d 1113 (D. Haw. 1999). Similarly, actions brought pursuant to 42 U.S.C. 1983 are governed by the forum state's statute of limitations for personal injury actions. See Wilson v. Garcia, 471 U.S. 261, aff'd, 471 U.S. 261 (1985); Knox v. Davis, 260 F.3d 1009 (9th Cir. 2001). In Hawai'i, personal injury actions must be brought within two years. See Haw. Rev. Stat. Ann. § 657-7 (2006). Claims for sexual harassment or sexual assault and infliction of emotional distress or invasion of privacy related thereto are governed by Haw. Rev. Stat. § 657-7. B.K.B. v. Maui Police Dep't, 276 F.3d 1091, 1103, 87 Fair Empl. Prac. Cas. (BNA) 1306, 82 Empl. Prac. Dec. (CCH) P40,914 (D. Haw. 2002).

C. Medical Testing

No reported cases.

D. Polygraph Tests

Section 378-26.5 of the Employment Practices Act makes it unlawful for any employer to, among others, (1) require a lie detector test as a condition of employment or continued employment; (2) terminate or otherwise discriminate for refusing to submit to a lie detector test; or (3) ask an employee or prospective employee to submit to a lie detector test unless the employee or prospective employee is informed both orally and in writing that the test is voluntary and that refusal will not result in termination of the employee or jeopardize the prospective employee's chance of a job. Haw. Rev. Stat. Ann. § 378-26.5(1)-(3) (2006). Section 378-26.5 does not apply, however, to lie detector tests administered by any law enforcement agency; the United States and any subdivision thereof; or to psychological tests administered by a law enforcement agency to determine the suitability of a candidate for employment with the law enforcement agency. Haw. Rev. Stat. Ann. § 378-27(3)-(5) (2006). No cases have been reported under this statute.

E. Fingerprinting

No reported cases.

III. SEARCHES

A. Employee's Person

There are no reported cases directly addressing an employer's right to search an employee's person. However, in Doe v. City and County of Honolulu, 8 Haw. App. 571, 861 P.2d 306 (1991), the Hawai'i Supreme Court held that "[w]here a type of public employment requires employees to comply with rules and regulations bearing upon their health and fitness, 'the expectations of privacy of [these] employees are diminished[.]' " Id. at 584, 816 P.2d at 314 (quoting Skinner v. Railway Labor Executives' Association, 489 U.S. 602, 627, 109 S.Ct. 1402, 1418 (1989)). There, the Hawai'i Supreme Court concluded that because the applicable regulations require all fire fighters, including the plaintiff, to undergo annual physical examinations, which include the drawing of blood and collection of urine, such a collection process "is not a basis for any privacy intrusion objection." Id.

In State v. Bonnell, 75 Haw. 124, 856 P.2d 1265 (1993), the Hawai'i Supreme Court held that an employer may not give "third-party consent" to search an employee's person because "such a notion is utterly repugnant to the constitutional right against unreasonable searches, seizures, and invasions of privacy codified in article I, section 7" of the Hawai'i Constitution. Id. at 148-48, 856 P.2d at 1278.

B. Employee's Work Area

Under Hawai'i law, a person with a possessory interest, such as a tenant, may have a protected privacy interest in the premises he or she occupies. State v. Vinuya, 96 Hawai'i 472, 32 P.3d 116 (2001). In Vinuya, the defendant was convicted of assault, carrying or use of a firearm in the commission of a separate felony, place to keep a firearm, prohibited possession of a firearm, and possession of a prohibited firearm. Id. at 476, 32 P.3d at 120. The conviction was based on a sawed-off shotgun that was found in the defendant's locked bedroom at his mother's house during a warrantless search. Id., 96 Hawai'i at 477, 32 P.3d at 121. On appeal, the defendant argued that the conviction must be reversed because the warrantless search was constitutionally impermissible. Id., 96 Hawai'i at 478, 32 P.3d at 122. Specifically, the defendant argued that his mother's consent to search his locked bedroom was invalid. Id., 96 Hawai'i at 479, 32 P.3d at 123.

In concluding that the search was constitutionally impermissible, the Hawai'i Supreme Court noted that a person may have a protected privacy interest in the office he or she occupied while employed by another, so long as the facts show that the person had a reasonable expectation of privacy. Id., 96 Hawai'i at 482, 32 P.3d at 126 (citing Mancusi v. DeForte, 392 U.S. 364 (1968)). The Vinuya court was buttressed by its prior decisions in State v. Bonnell, 75 Haw. 124, 142-43, 856 P.2d 1265, 1275-76 (1993) (holding that a person can have a reasonable expectation of privacy in an employee break room, apart from the common area of the post office) and State v. Matias, 51 Haw. 62, 66, 451 P.2d 257, 260 (1969) (relying on Mancusi for the proposition that the defendant was not required to hold title to the place searched in order to challenge the search of the bedroom he had occupied as an overnight guest). Vinuya, 96 Hawai'i at 482, 32 P.3d at 126.

Although Vinuya involves a governmental search and seizure, it is significant in the employment context for several reasons. First, it makes it abundantly clear that a person with a possessory interest in property, such as a tenant, may have a reasonable expectation of privacy in the premises. Id., at 483, 32 P.3d at 127. Second, a person occupying the premises without the "benefit of any formal possessory interest in the premises have a reasonable expectation of privacy of 'essentially the same dimensions' as the owner or lessee of the premises." Id., 96 Hawai'i at 483, 32 P.3d at 127 (citations omitted). A tacit agreement of exclusive control over the premises may be sufficient to give rise to a protected privacy interest. Id., 96 Hawai'i at 483, 32 P.3d at 127 (citations omitted). Third, dictum in Vinuya suggests that the payment of rent in exchange for the right of possession is not required for a protected privacy interest to arise. Id., 96 Hawai'i at 483, 32 P.3d at 127 (citation omitted). Fourth, it appears to be irrelevant whether the claimant had permanent or temporary possession of the premises at time of the search. Id., 96 Hawai'i at 483, 32 P.3d at 127 (citation omitted). This rationale, coupled with the court's recognition that a person may have a protected privacy interest in the office he or she occupied while employed by another, provide compelling reasons for concluding that an employee may have a reasonable expectation of privacy in his or her work area while employed by another, at least with respect to governmental searches.

Vinuya is consistent with other state and federal cases recognizing a person's protected privacy interest. E.g., State v. Biggar, 68 Haw. 404, 407, 716 P.2d 493, 495 (1986) (stating that a person has a reasonable expectation of privacy inside a closed toilet stall); State v. Lo, 66 Haw. 653, 675 P.2d 754, 760 (1983) (stating that a hotel room ostensibly serving as someone's temporary abode is a "private place" and a person is entitled to privacy therein); Mancusi v. DeForte, 392 U.S. 364, 88 S. Ct. 2120 (1968) (holding that "a union employee had a legitimate expectation of privacy . . . in the contents of records that he stored in an office that he shared with several other union officials"); O'Connor v. Ortega, 480 U.S. 709, 107 S. Ct. 1492 (1987) (recognizing that an employee "had a reasonable expectation of privacy in his desk and file cabinets"); U.S. v. Ziegler, 474 F.3d 1184 (9th Cir. 2007) (stating that a person has a reasonable expectation of privacy in his office).

A person does not, however, have a reasonable expectation of privacy in a private viewing booth containing a "glory hole" which allows observation into the booth by adjoining booth users. State v. Lawson, 103 Hawai'i 11, 78 P.3d 1159 (App. 2003). In Lawson, a patron of a pornographic video rental business entered the premises carrying a glass pipe. Id., at 17, 78 P.3d at 1165. An employee of the establishment suspected that the pipe might be used for illegal purposes and notified police officials after the patron entered a private viewing booth containing a "glory hole." Id. The glory hole is designed to allow individuals in adjacent booths to interact sexually with one another, as well as to permit voyeurism, exhibitionism and fellatio. Id. Peering through the glory hole, the police officers observed the patron using the glass pipe and a lighter. Id. One of the officers also noticed that the patron's pants were down to his thighs. Id.

On appeal, the defendant contended that "he exhibited a subjective expectation of privacy when he 'specifically chose to conduct his actions in a private, closed, locked video booth in a private business that dealt exclusively in pornographic materials, not in a public park or on the street.'" Id., at 21, 78 P.3d at 1169. He further argued that "the nature of his activities 'concerned matters that are inherently private' and 'it is reasonable to infer that an individual who chooses to watch pornography with his pants down around his thighs while attempting to use drugs has a subjective expectation of privacy in such actions.'" Id. The appellate court disagreed. Id.

Analogizing cases involving privacy interests in public restroom stalls, the Hawai'i Intermediate Court of Appeals stated that a "defendant only has the right to reasonably expect to enjoy such privacy as the design of the stall afforded." Id., at 21-22, 78 P.3d at 1169-70 (citation omitted). Bathroom stalls, for example, do not afford complete privacy to the extent that a person's activities are performed beneath the partition and can be viewed by one using the common area of the restroom. Id. (citations omitted). The court therefore affirmed the conviction. To the extent Lawson relies on cases involving a person's privacy interest in public restroom stalls, it appears to represent a slight retreat from the Hawai'i Supreme Court's holding in State v. Biggar, 68 Haw. 404, 407, 716 P.2d 493, 495 (1986) (holding that a person's reasonable expectation of privacy inside a closed stall was violated by a police detective standing on the adjacent toilet and peering over the partition). But see Janra Enterprises, Inc. v. City and County of Honolulu, 107 Hawai'i 314, 322, 113 P.3d 190,198 (2005) (holding that viewing adult material in an enclosed panoram booth on commercial premises is not protected by the fundamental right of privacy enshrined in article I, section 6 of the Hawai'i Constitution).

Recognizing Hawai'i's temperate climate and the "social function" garages play in our island life, the Hawai'i Supreme Court held that a person may have a reasonable expectation of privacy in a washroom located within a garage of a home he was visiting. State of Hawai'i v. Cuntapay, 104 Hawai'i 109, 85 P.3d 634 (2004). In Cuntapay, police officers approached the garage area of a residence and observed seven to ten adult males seated around a table in the garage. Id., at 110-11, 85 P.2d at 635-36. As the officers approached, the defendant walked away from the table and into a washroom located in the garage area. Id., at 111, 85 P.3d at 636. The door to the washroom was open. Id. As the defendant walked away from the officer, he had a small black object in his right hand. Id. The officer observed the defendant walk into the washroom and reach behind a washing machine. Id. After doing so, the defendant left the washroom and walked towards the officer. Id. The officer then reached behind the washing machine and discovered a magnetic box that was slightly opened. Id. A plastic bag protruded from the box with a rock-like substance within it. Id. The defendant was placed under arrest. Id.

The Cuntapay court held that the defendant had a reasonable expectation of privacy in the washroom. It reasoned that, "in light of our temperate climate, garages play a social function in our island life and often are gathering places for social activities hosted by the homedweller." Id. at 117, 85 P.3d at 642. The court concluded that "our society would view [the defendant's] expectation of privacy in the washroom within a garage as reasonable." Id.

C. Employee's Property

An addressee has both a possessory and a privacy interest in a mailed package. United States v. Hernandez, 313 F.3d 1206, 1209 (9th Cir. 2002). The recipient of a mailed item also has a reasonable expectation that the mail will not be detained by postal employees beyond the normal delivery date and time. Id. at 1210. Similarly, one who voluntarily deposits mail in the United States mail for delivery retains a limited possessory interest in the mailed item. Id. at 1209. However, there can be no reasonable expectation that postal service employees will not handle the package or that they will not view its exterior. Id. at 1209-10.

Likewise, in United States v. Sheldon, 351 F. Supp. 2d 1040, 1043 (D. Haw. 2004), a federal judge recognized that both a sender and the addressee have privacy interests in mailed packages. Generally, a third party who is neither the sender nor the addressee of a mailed package does not share this privacy interest. Id. at 1043. Nevertheless, where a party claims to own a parcel addressed to someone else and acts in a manner consistent with ownership, the party may have a privacy interest in the mailed parcel. Id. at 1044. To determine whether an individual has a privacy interest in an object, the court considers several facts, including (1) the individual's claim of ownership, (2) exercise of control and supervision over the parcel, (3) any measures taken by the individual to insure privacy, and (4) whether the type of container used demonstrates a privacy interest in the contents. Id. at 1044 (citations omitted).

IV. MONITORING OF EMPLOYEES

A. Telephones and Electronic Communications

1. ***Wiretapping.*** Haw. Rev. Stat. Ann. §§ 803-41 through -48 (2006) prohibits interception, use, gaining access, or using a mobile tracking device. This statute tracks the federal electronic eavesdropping statute. A single party to the communication may consent to and authorize the tap. However, the one-party consent exception does not apply to installation of a recording device in a "private place" to be used outside the place, without the consent of the person(s) entitled to privacy therein. Haw. Rev. Stat. § 803-42(b)(3) (2006); State v. Lo, 66 Haw. 653, 675 P.2d 754 (1983). But see State v. Lee, 67 Haw. 307, 310, 686 P.2d 816, 818, reconsideration denied, 67 Haw. 684, 744 P.2d 780 (1984) (a person is entitled to no greater protection against the use of recorded conversations merely because the conversations occurred in the person's office, even if the office could be considered a private place; the legislature did not intend to prohibit the installation or use of recording devices in private places).

In 1995, the Disciplinary Board rescinded a prior determination that all non-consensual tape recordings by an attorney are unethical, although it noted that a lawyer's creation and/or use of such tape recordings, in some circumstances, may still violate the rules of professional conduct. See Office of Disciplinary Counsel, Formal Opinion No. 30 (Nov. 30 1988), Modification of Formal Opinion No. 30 (Jul. 27, 1995).

There are no reported cases involving the legality of wiretapping in the private sector. The Supreme Court of Hawaii has held, however, that a warrant is not required to record a conversation when the state obtains the consent of one of the parties to the conversation. State v. Okubo, 67 Haw. 197, 199-200, 682 P.2d 79, 80-81, aff'd, 67 Haw. 197, 682 P.2d 79 (1984).

2. ***Electronic Communications.*** The wire-tapping, without a valid warrant, of a personal pager may constitute a per se violation of an individual's right to privacy. See Black v. City and County of Honolulu, 112 F. Supp. 2d 1041, 1054, 79 Empl. Prac. Dec. P40319 (D. Haw. 2000). In Black, an employee of the Honolulu Police

Department ("HPD") filed a sexual harassment complaint with HPD's Internal Affairs department ("IA"). Id. at 1046. Thereafter, the plaintiff was allegedly subjected to various retaliatory acts which, according to the plaintiff, included the placement of a "wire trap" on her pager. Id. In her lawsuit, the plaintiff contended that HPD's use of a "wire trap" on her pager without first obtaining a warrant violated her right to privacy. Id. at 1054.

In its opinion, the Black court noted that, pursuant to Article I, Section 6 of the Hawai'i Constitution, individuals in Hawai'i have a reasonable expectation of privacy with respect to the outgoing telephone numbers they call and the incoming telephone numbers they receive on their private telephone lines. Black, 112 F. Supp. 2d at 1054 (citing State v. Rothman, 70 Haw. 546, 556, 779 P.2d 1, 7 (1989)). Because HPD failed to first obtain a warrant before installing the "wire trap" on the plaintiff's pager, the court stated that HPD's use of the device would appear to be a per se violation of the plaintiff's right to privacy. However, the court refused to grant summary judgment in favor of the plaintiff because the evidence conflicted regarding the ownership of the pager. Id. HPD claimed that it issued the pager to the plaintiff. The plaintiff, in contrast, claimed that she replaced the HPD-issued pager with her own after the HPD-issued pager had broken. The Black court concluded that if the wire-trapping involved the HPD-issued pager instead of the plaintiff's personal pager, then the plaintiff could not claim that she had a reasonable expectation of privacy. Id.

B. Mail

Although there are no cases in Hawai'i directly addressing employer monitoring of an employee's mail, an addressee has both a possessory and a privacy interest in a mailed package. United States v. Hernandez, 313 F.3d 1206, 1209 (9th Cir. 2002). The recipient of a mailed item also has a reasonable expectation that the mail will not be detained by postal employees beyond the normal delivery date and time. Id. at 1210. Similarly, one who voluntarily deposits mail in the United States mail for delivery retains a limited possessory interest in the mailed item. Id. at 1209. However, there can be no reasonable expectation that postal service employees will not handle the package or that they will not view its exterior. Id. at 1209-10.

Likewise, in United States v. Sheldon, 351 F. Supp. 2d 1040, 1043 (D. Haw. 2004), the District Court of Hawai`i recognized that both a sender and the addressee have privacy interests in mailed packages. Generally, a third party who is neither the sender nor the addressee of a mailed package does not share this privacy interest. Id. at 1043. Nevertheless, where a party claims to own a parcel addressed to someone else and acts in a manner consistent with ownership, the party may have a privacy interest in the mailed parcel. Id. at 1044. To determine whether an individual has a privacy interest in an object, the court considers several facts, including (1) the individual's claim of ownership, (2) exercise of control and supervision over the parcel, (3) any measures taken by the individual to insure privacy, and (4) whether the type of container used demonstrates a privacy interest in the contents. Id. at 1044 (citations omitted).

C. Surveillance/Photographing

Under Hawai'i law, covert surveillance implicates the privacy interests of individuals in their persons. Black v. City and County of Honolulu, 112 F. Supp. 2d 1041, 1053 (D. Haw. 2000). An employer's liability in tort for its surveillance activities turns on two issues: (1) whether the surveillance was "highly offensive" to a reasonable person, and (2) whether it was conducted without the employee's consent. Id. The offensiveness of an intrusion is examined under an objective standard and is factually dependent. Id. In addition, a plaintiff will not be deemed to have consented to the surveillance absent evidence of a clear, unequivocal decision to waive the right to privacy or other conduct indicating that the plaintiff should be estopped from asserting a right of privacy. Id. at 1053-54.

The Black case involved alleged incidences of sexual harassment involving employees of the Honolulu Police Department ("HPD"). After filing a complaint with HPD's Internal Affairs department ("IA"), the plaintiff alleged that she became the subject of "Operation Foxtrot", a round-the-clock surveillance operation that lasted approximately one week. Id. at 1046. The impetus for Operation Foxtrot was disputed. Id. at 1053. While the plaintiff contended that the surveillance was intended to harass her, HPD and its police chief alleged that the operation was aimed at protecting the plaintiff in light of the threatening notes, calls, and pages the plaintiff received. Id.

According to the court, whether Operation Foxtrot was "highly offensive" required the resolution of two questions. First, would a reasonable person find the surveillance operation highly offensive given threats of the kind the plaintiff received? Second, would a reasonable person find the operation highly offensive if the person was not given prior notice of the operation? Because both of these inquiries involved factual questions, the court denied the plaintiff's motion for summary judgment.

The court, however, reached a different conclusion with respect to HPD's contention that the plaintiff consented to the surveillance or otherwise waived her right to privacy when she discovered HPD's surveillance efforts. Although a right to privacy may be waived or lost through a course of conduct estopping its assertion if the complaining party displays a clear, unequivocal, and decisive act of waiver, courts indulge in every reasonable presumption against waiver of fundamental constitutional rights. Id. at 1053-54 (citations omitted). The burden of proof rests on the party claiming waiver. Id. (citations omitted). Although question of waiver is usually a question of fact, where the evidence is undisputed, the question becomes one of law. Id. at 1054 (citation omitted). In Black, the court opined that the plaintiff did not abandon her right to privacy merely by being friendly to the officers who kept the plaintiff under surveillance. At best, the plaintiff was trying to make an uncomfortable situation less awkward. Thus, the court concluded, the defendants' waiver and consent argument failed as a matter of law. Id.

D. Other Electronic Monitoring.

No reported cases.

V. ACTIVITIES OUTSIDE THE WORKPLACE

A. Statute or Common Law

Hawai'i Revised Statutes Chapter 378, the Employment Practices Act, makes it an unlawful discriminatory practice to refuse to hire or to employ, or to bar or discharge from employment, any individual because of race, sex, sexual orientation, religion, color, ancestry, disability, marital status, or arrest and court records. Haw. Rev. Stat. Ann. § 378-2 (2006). As stated in IA supra, Chapter 378 covers all employers, not just those with fifteen or more employees like its federal counterpart, Title VII. See 42 U.S.C.A. § 2000e(b). Chapter 378 also includes within the definition of "because of sex,"

> pregnancy, childbirth, or related medical conditions; and women affected by pregnancy, childbirth or related medical conditions shall be treated the same for all employment-related purposes, including receive of benefits under fringe benefit programs, as other individuals not so affected but similar in their ability or inability to work.

Haw. Rev. Stat. Ann. § 378-1 (2006). Consequently, an employer cannot lawfully inquire, either directly or indirectly, into whether a job applicant is pregnant. Sam Teague, Ltd. v. Hawai'i Civil Rights Comm'n, 89 Hawai'i 269, 279 971 P.2d 1104, 1114 (1999). Moreover, the Hawai'i Supreme Court, in Sam Teague, Ltd., held that defendant employer's termination of plaintiff following her maternity leave constituted illegal sex discrimination under Haw. Rev. Stat. § 378-2. In this case, defendant had a "no extended leave" policy during an employee's first year of employment. Id. at 273, 971 P.2d at 1108. After plaintiff took maternity leave during her first year of employment, defendant terminated plaintiff based on her violation of the no-leave policy. Id. at 274, 971 P.2d at 1109. The Court determined, however, that because no-leave policies, such as the one at issue, have a disparate impact on women, given that "pregnancy and childbirth are . . . phenomena shared only by women, and only female employees are susceptible to employment losses tied to either," such policies constitute sex discrimination under Haw. Rev. Stat. § 378-2. Id. at 277, 971 P.2d at 1112.

Section 378-3 allows, however, (1) religious organizations to give preference to individuals in the same religion or denomination and to make hiring decisions "calculated to promote the religious principles for which the organization is established or maintained;" (2) the department of education or private schools to consider criminal convictions in determining whether a prospective employee is suited to working in close proximity to children; and (3) financial institutions to deny employment to, or discharge from employment, any person who has been convicted of any crime of dishonesty or breach of trust. Haw. Rev. Stat. Ann. §§ 378-3(5), (8), (9) (2006).

Employers may inquire into and consider a prospective employee's criminal background for up to 10 years prior (except for incarcerations), provided that the conviction record bears a rational relationship to the duties and responsibilities of the position, and the consideration takes place only after the prospective employee has received a conditional offer of employment. Haw. Rev. Stat. Ann. § 378-2.5 (2006). Haw. Rev. Stat. Ann. § 378-2.5 (2006). However, an inquiry into and consideration of a prospective employee's conviction record may occur only after the applicant has received a conditional job offer. Id. § 378-2.5(b) (2006). The limitation to the most recent ten-year period, excluding the period of incarceration, does not apply to employers who are expressly permitted to inquire into an individual's criminal history for employment purposes pursuant to any federal or state law other than subsection (a). The statute sets forth a non-exclusive list of employers who are expressly permitted make such an inquiry. Id. §§ 378-2.5(d)(1)-(17) (2006). Additionally, Section 378-3 does not prevent employers from refusing to hire, or from discharging, any employee for reasons relating to the ability of the individual to perform the work in question. Haw. Rev. Stat. Ann. § 378-3(3) (2006).

In Kinoshita v. Canadian Pacific Airlines, Ltd., 803 F.2d 471, 42 Empl. Prac. Dec. (CCH) P36814, 1 IER Cas. 971 (9th Cir. 1986), for example, defendant airlines discharged two employees after they were arrested for conspiracy to promote cocaine. The employees sued the airlines for breach of contract and for violation of § 378-2, alleging that defendant unlawfully discharged them because of their court or arrest record. Id. at 473. The court in Kinoshita ruled that defendant did not violate Haw. Rev. Stat. § 378-2 when it discharged the plaintiffs because the discharges were not based on the "mere fact" of the plaintiffs' arrest and court record, but were instead due to the perception that plaintiffs were involved in drug-related activity. Id.at 475, 42 Empl. Prac. Dec. (CCH) P36814, 1 IER Cas. 971.

In order to establish a claim of discrimination under Chapter 378, a plaintiff must show disparate, discriminatory treatment by his employer from that treatment of "similarly situated" co-employees. Furukawa v. Honolulu Zoological Soc'y, 85 Haw. 7, 13, 936 P.2d 643, 649, 70 Empl. Prac. Dec. (CCH) P44679 (1997) reconsideration denied, 85 Hawai'i 196, 940 P.2d 403 (1997). In other words, a plaintiff must prove that his or her employer "is treating 'some people less favorably than others because of [a characteristic protected under Chapter 378].'" Id. In Furukawa, the Supreme Court concluded that, "[g] enerally, similarly situated employees are those who are subject to the same policies and subordinate to the same decision-maker as the plaintiff." Id.

A plaintiff alleging discrimination under § 378-2 must prove, therefore, that all "relevant aspects" of his or her employment situation are similar to those employees with whom he or she seeks to compare his or her treatment. Those "relevant aspects" include: (1) the level of authority of the employee; (2) whether the employee evaluates other employees in the course of his or her duties; and (3) whether the employee is responsible for enforcement of the company's sexual harassment policy. Furukawa, 85 Hawai'i at 13, 936 P.2d at 649, 70 Empl. Prac. Dec. (CCH) P44679 (citing Pierce v. Commonwealth Life Ins., Co., 40 F.3d 796, 802 (6th Cir. 1994)). The Furukawa Court rejected, as excessively narrow, defendant's contention that, in order to establish a prima facie case, a discrimination plaintiff must compare his treatment to a fellow employee similarly situated in all respects, including that the fellow employee have the same supervisor, be subjected to the same standards, and engage in the same conduct as the plaintiff, without differentiating or mitigating circumstances that would distinguish the conduct or the employer's treatment. Furukawa, 85 Hawai'i at 13, 936 P.2d at 647, 70 Empl. Prac. Dec. (CCH) P44679.

Once a plaintiff establishes a prima facie case that his or her employer discriminated against him or her on the basis of a protected characteristic, the burden of production then shifts to the defendant-employer to rebut the presumption that the employer unlawfully discriminated against the employee, by offering a legitimate, nondiscriminatory explanation for the adverse employment action. Finally, if the defendant successfully rebuts the presumption of discrimination, the burden shifts back to the plaintiff to show that the defendant's explanation is pretextual. Furukawa, 85 Hawai'i at 12, 936 P.2d at 648, 70 Empl. Prac. Dec. (CCH) P44679

In addition to these types of claims of unlawful discrimination, Chapter 378 provides a private cause of action to employees for, among others offenses, sexual harassment, sexual assault, infliction of emotional distress, or invasion of privacy related thereto. Haw. Rev. Stat. Ann. § 378-3(10) (2006).

The two-year limitations period set forth in Haw. Rev. Stat. § 657-7 governs discrimination claims brought under Chapter 378. Lesane v. Hawaiian Airlines, 75 F. Supp. 2d 1113, 1120 (D. Haw. 1999); Linville v. Hawai'i, 874 F. Supp. 1095, 1104 (D. Haw. 1994). See Haw. Rev. Stat. Ann. § 657-7 (2006).

B. Employees' Personal Relationships

1. ***Romantic Relationships Between Employees.*** No reported cases.

2. ***Sexual Orientation.*** See Haw. Rev. Stat. Ann. Ch. 378. No reported cases.

3. ***Marital Status.*** Under Haw. Rev. Stat. Ann. § 378-2 (2006), it is unlawful to refuse to hire or to terminate married persons working for the same employer, unless such termination is related to the employee's qualifications or job performance. Ross v. Stouffer Hotel Co., 72 Haw. 350, 816 P.2d 302, 58 Empl. Prac. Dec. (CCH) P41529, 72 Fair Empl. Prac. Cas. (BNA) 1611 (Haw. 1991) remanded, Ross v. Stouffer Hotel Co., 76 Haw. 454, 879 P.2d 1037, 72 Fair Empl. Prac. Cas. (BNA) 1616 (Haw. 1994). In Ross, Amfac Hotels and Resorts ("Amfac") hired plaintiff, Ross, and his live-in girlfriend, Treffry, as massage therapists in August, 1986. Id.at 456, 879 P.2d at 1039. Both Ross and Treffry worked at the Amfac's Poipu Beach Fitness Center. In August, 1987, Ross and Treffry married.

A couple of weeks later, Stouffer Hotels ("Stouffer") acquired the hotel at which Ross and Treffry worked from Amfac. Ross and Treffry thereafter became aware that Stouffer had a policy which prohibited two "direct relatives" from working in the same department. The policy required one of the relatives to transfer or resign, if the two became married after being hired by the same department.

Stouffer informed Ross and Treffry that one of them would need to either apply for a transfer to another department or resign, and if they were unable to make such decision, Stouffer's management would be obligated to terminate the employment of the less senior employee, in this case, Ross. Stouffer subsequently discharged Ross after neither he nor Treffry applied for a transfer or resigned.

Ross then filed suit against Stouffer, alleging, among other counts, wrongful discharge in violation of Hawai'i Revised Statute § 378-2, on grounds that Stouffer had discriminated against him because of his marital status. The Supreme Court of Hawai'i rejected Stouffer's argument that it had discharged Ross not because of his marital status, but because of whom he married. The court held,

It makes no sense, therefore, to conclude, as the dissent does, that an employer who discriminates based on the "identity and occupation" of a person's spouse is not also discriminating against that person because he or she is married. An employer can't do one without the other. Stated otherwise, a no-spouse policy, by definition, applies only to the class of married persons. Consequently, when an employer discharges and employee pursuant to such a policy, it necessarily discriminates "because of . . . [the employee's] marital status[.]" HRS § 378-2. The facts of this case make the point.

Ross, 76 Haw. at 458, 879 P.2d at 1041, 72 Fair Empl. Prac. Cas. 1615.

The two-year limitations period set forth in Haw. Rev. Stat. § 657-7 governs discrimination claims brought under Chapter 378. Lesane v. Hawaiian Airlines, 75 F. Supp. 2d 1113 (D. Haw. 1999); Linville v. Hawai'i, 874 F. Supp. 1095, 1104 (D. Haw. 1994). See Haw. Rev. Stat. Ann. § 657-7 (2006).

C. Smoking

No reported cases.

D. Blogging

No reported cases.

VI. RECORDS

A. Personnel Records

Chapter 92F of the Hawai'i Revised Statutes requires governmental agencies to open their records to public disclosure, provided that the need for such disclosure outweighs any invasion of personal privacy. See Haw. Rev. Stat. Ann. § 92F et seq. (2006). See also I.A, supra. In State of Hawai'i Org. of Police Officers v. Society of Prof'l Journalists-University of Hawai'i Chapter, 83 Hawai'i 378, 927 P.2d 386, 154 L.R.R.M. 2373 (1996), the police officers' union and four unnamed police officers sued to enjoin the City of Honolulu and the Honolulu Police Department from disclosing the disciplinary records contained in the personnel files of the four plaintiff-police officers to the defendant. Although Haw. Rev. Stat. § 92F-14(b) classifies personnel records as information in which an individual has a significant privacy interest, Haw. Rev. Stat. § 92F-14(b)(4) excludes information contained in a personnel file related to employment misconduct that results in an employee's suspension or discharge. The plaintiffs alleged, therefore, that Haw. Rev. Stat. § 92F-14(b)(4) effected an unconstitutional invasion of the police officers' right to privacy in violation of Article I, Section 6 of the Hawai'i Constitution. See I.A, supra for the substantive text of Haw. Rev. Stat. § 92F-14(b)(4) and Section 6.

The Supreme Court held that plaintiffs failed to overcome the presumption that the legislature had achieved a balance between the competing interests of individual privacy and public access to government records in accordance with the mandate of Article I, Section 6 of the Hawai'i Constitution. The Court also concluded that "information regarding a police officer's misconduct in the course of his or her duties as a police officer is not within the protection of Hawai'i's constitutional right to privacy. State of Hawai'i Org. of Police Officers, 83 Hawai'i at 396-97, 927 P.2d at 404-05, 154 L.R.R.M. 2373. See also State v. Mallan, 86 Hawai'i Haw. 440, 443 n.4, 950 P.2d 178, 181 n.4 (1998) (the state Constitution protects medical, financial, educational and employment records).

The Supreme Court has also determined that Article I, Section 6 of the Hawai'i Constitution does not protect the financial records of certain state employees from disclosure. In Nakano v. Matayoshi, 68 Haw. 140, 706 P.2d 814 (1985), plaintiffs challenged, as an unconstitutional invasion of privacy, and a denial of equal protection and due process of law, Section 20-91.1 of the Hawai'i County Code which compelled "regulatory employees" of the County to submit disclosures of their income and financial interests biennially to the County Board of Ethics.

Section 2-9.1 of the Hawai'i County Code was enacted pursuant to Article XIV of the Hawai'i Constitution, which directs "each political subdivision [to] adopt a code of ethics which shall apply to appointed and elected officers and employees" and "include . . . provisions on gifts, confidential information, use of position, contracts with government agencies. . . . " It further mandates that non-elected "public officials having significant discretionary or fiscal powers . . . shall make confidential financial disclosures." "[A]n employee of the State or any of its political subdivisions may [not] reasonably expect that his [or her] interest in avoiding disclosure of his [or her] financial affairs is protected to the same extent as that of other citizens." Nakano, 68 Haw. at 148, 706 P.2d at 819.

All constitutional causes of action are governed by a six-year limitations period under HRS § 657-1. Tamura v. Federal Aviation Administration, 675 F. Supp. 1221, 1224-25 (D. Haw. 1987). See Haw. Rev. Stat. Ann. § 657-1 (2006).

B. Medical Records

Under prior Hawai'i law, entities—including employers—were precluded from using or disclosing certain "protected health information" except as authorized by Haw. Rev. Stat. Ann. § 323C-21(a) et seq. The 2001 legislature, however, repealed the statute. After a series of information briefings in January 2001, and careful review of the dissenting report, the 2001 legislature found little support for a medical privacy law in light of the adoption of federal rules and regulations on medical privacy by the United States Department of Health and Human Services. The legislature also cited a lack of evidence of widespread abuse in Hawai'i to support its repeal of the Act. Act 244, Session Laws of Hawai`i 2001. However, the Hawai'i Supreme Court has recognized that the state Constitution protects medical, financial, educational and employment records. State v. Mallan, 86 Hawai'i 440, 443 n.4, 950 P.2d 178, 181 n.4 (1998).

C. Criminal Records

No reported cases.

D. Subpoenas / Search Warrants

Subpoenas are governed by Rule 45 of the Hawai'i Rules of Civil Procedure. They are issued by the clerk of the court in which the action is pending. Haw. R. Civ. P. 45(a). A subpoena may require a person to give testimony or require the production of documentary evidence. Id. Upon motion made at or before the time specified in the subpoena, a party or person may ask the court to (1) quash or modify the subpoena if it is unreasonable and oppressive or (2) condition denial of the motion upon the advancement by the person on whose behalf the subpoena is issued of the reasonable cost of producing the documentary evidence. Id. 45(b). An order quashing or enforcing a subpoena will be disturbed on appeal only if it is plainly arbitrary and without support in the record. Powers v. Shaw, 1 Haw. App. 374, 619 P.2d 1098 (1980).

A person responding to a subpoena for the production of documents must produce the documents as they are kept in the usual course of business or must organize and label them to correspond with the categories in the demand. Haw. R. Civ. P. 45(3)(1). When subpoenaed information is withheld on a claim that it is privileged or subject to protection as trial preparation materials, the claim must be made expressly and be supported by a description of the nature of the documents, communications, or things not produced that is sufficient to enable the demanding party to contest the claim. Haw. R. Civ. P. 45(e)(2). The failure, without adequate excuse, to obey a subpoena may be deemed a contempt of the court. Haw. R. Civ. P. 45(f).

VII. Actions Subsequent to Employment

A. References

No reported cases.

B. Non-Compete Agreements

As a general rule, "[e]very contract, combination in the form of a trust or otherwise, or conspiracy, in restraint of trade or commerce in the State, or in any section of this State is illegal." Haw. Rev. Stat. § 480-4(a). Nevertheless, restrictive covenants or agreements ancillary to a legitimate purpose not violative of [Chapter 480] are permitted, unless the effect may be substantially to lessen competition or to tend to create a monopoly in any line of commerce in any section of the State." Haw. Rev. Stat. Ann. § 480-4(c) (2006).

The restrictive covenants and agreements enumerated under Section 480-4(c) are not exclusive in their respective fields. Technicolor, Inc. v. Traeger, 57 Haw. 113, 121, 551 P.2d 163, 170 (1976). Courts are therefore authorized to analyze all restrictive covenants that are not listed as "per se violations" and determine their validity in similar fashion as federal courts would in interpreting Section 1 of the Sherman Act. Id. at 121-22, 551 P.2d at 170.

Consistent with federal law, Hawai'i courts apply a "rule of reason" test to determine the validity of restrictive covenants that are not classified as "per se violations". Technicolor, 57 Haw. at 122, 551 P.2d at 170. A restrictive covenant is "not reasonable", and is hence invalid, if:

> (i) it is greater than required for the protection of the person for whose benefit it is imposed; (ii) it imposes undue hardship on the person restricted; or (iii) its benefit to the covenantee is outweighed by injury to the public.

Id. "In making this analysis, the court must examine such factors as geographical scope, length of time, and breadth of the restriction placed on a given activity." Id.

Where a non-compete agreement does not preclude a person from working for a competitor, but only from assisting the competitor, for a period of two years, in selling specific products to specifically described customers, the agreement is not impermissibly broad. UARCO Inc. v. Lam, 18 F. Supp. 2d 1116, 1121-22 (D. Haw. 1998) (construing Hawai'i law). Similarly, a confidentiality clause that precludes a former employee from disclosing and using confidential information and trade secrets only for as long as the information was kept secret, is not impermissibly broad. Id. at 1122.

Under Hawai'i law, covenants not to compete are not assignable. Id. However, a successor corporation possesses all of the obligations and rights of its predecessor following a merger. Id. Thus, covenants not to compete are enforceable by a successor corporation that carries on the employer's business following a merger. Id.

VIII. OTHER ISSUES

A. Statutes of Limitations

Chapter 657 of the Hawai'i Revised Statutes sets forth the limitations periods applicable to causes of action in the State of Hawai'i. Hawai'i Revised Statutes §§ 657-7 and 662-4 govern the limitations period for tort claims. Section 657-7 provides,

> Actions for the recovery or compensation for damage or injury to persons or property shall be instituted within two years after the cause of action accrued, and not after, except [if plaintiff is under a legal disability].

Haw. Rev. Stat. Ann. § 657-7 (2006). Section 662-4 states,

> A tort claim against the State shall be forever barred unless action is begun within two years after the claim accrues, except in the case of a medical tort claim when the limitation of action provisions set forth in section 657-7.3 shall apply.

Haw. Rev. Stat. Ann. § 662-4 (2006). The two-year limitations period set forth in § 657-7 also governs discrimination claims brought under Chapter 378. Lesane v. Hawaiian Airlines, 75 F. Supp. 2d 1113, 1120 (D. Haw. 1999); Linville v. Hawai'i, 874 F. Supp. 1095, 1104 (D. Haw. 1994).

Courts have applied the six-year limitations period under Haw. Rev. Stat.. § 657-1 to constitutional claims. See, e.g., Tamura v. Federal Aviation Administration, 675 F. Supp. 1221, 1224 (D. Haw. 1987). However, suits brought under 42 U.S.C. § 1981 are governed by the two-year limitations period under Haw. Rev. Stat. § 657-7. Lesane v. Hawaiian Airlines, 75 F. Supp. 2d 1113, 1120 (D. Haw. 1999). Similarly, actions brought pursuant to 42 U.S.C. 1983 are governed by the forum state's statute of limitations for personal injury actions. See Wilson v. Garcia, 471 U.S. 261, 275 (1985); Knox v. Davis, 260 F.3d 1009 (9th Cir. 2001). In Hawai'i, personal injury actions must be brought within two years. See Haw. Rev. Stat. Ann. § 657-7 (2006).

Although the statute of limitations requires that claims be filed "within" a specified time after the cause of action accrued "and not after", a claim is timely if it is filed on the anniversary that the cause of action accrued. Bauernfiend v. AOAO Kihei Beach Condominiums, 99 Hawai'i 281, 284, 54 P.3d 452, 455 (2002) (overruling Hoke v. Paul, 65 Haw. 478, 653 P.2d 1155 (1982)). In Bauernfiend, the plaintiff alleged that she suffered physical injuries and severe emotional distress as the result of an "out-of-control ride" in the elevator of the condominium building where she resided. Id. at 282, 54 P.3d at 453. Although the plaintiff's claim was governed by a two-year statute of limitations, she filed her complaint on the second anniversary of her alleged injury. Id. Relying on a footnote in Hoke v. Paul, 65 Haw. 478, 653 P.2d 1155 (1982), the defendant contended that the plaintiff's claim was untimely because the complaint was not filed "within" two years after the cause of action of accrued. The Hawai'i Supreme Court disagreed and remanded the case for further proceedings. Id. at 284, 54 P.3d at 455.

B. Jurisdiction

Workers' compensation claims arising out of Haw. Rev. Stat. Chapter 386, Hawai`i's Workers' Compensation Act, are in the original jurisdiction of the Director of the Department of Labor and Industrial Relations ("DLIR"). Haw. Rev. Stat. § 386-73 (2010) states in relevant part that "the director of labor and industrial relations shall have original jurisdiction over all controversies and disputes arising under this chapter . . [and the] decisions of the director shall be enforceable by the circuit court as provided in section 386-91." However, there is a "right of appeal from the decisions of the director to the appellate board and thence to the intermediate appellate court". Id.

Employment related disputes arising out of common law tort or contract are in the subject matter jurisdiction of the circuit courts. In Hough v. Pacific Ins. Co., Ltd., 83 Haw. 457, 927 P.2d 858 (1996), the Hawaii Supreme Court recognized that Hawai`i's Workers' Compensation Act, which provided original jurisdiction to Director of DLIR over all controversies and disputes arising under Workers' Compensation Act, does not deprive circuit court of subject matter jurisdiction over employee's common-law tort claims not based on original work injury. Id. at 466, 927 P.2d at 867.

C. Worker's Compensation Exclusivity

The Workers' Compensation Act in Hawai`i is governed by Haw. Rev. Stat. Chapter 386. Haw. Rev. Stat. § 386-5 provides for the exclusiveness of right to compensation as follows:

> The rights and remedies herein granted to an employee or the employee's dependents on account of a work injury suffered by the employee shall exclude all other liability of the employer to the employee, the employee's legal representative, spouse, dependents, next of kin, or anyone else entitled to recover damages from the employer, at common law or otherwise, on account of the injury, except for sexual harassment or sexual assault and infliction of emotional distress or invasion of privacy related thereto, in which case a civil action may also be brought.

See also Estate of Coates v. Pacific Engineering, 71 Haw. 358, 362, 791 P.2d 1257, 1259-60 (1990) ("The Hawaii State Legislature, by enacting the exclusivity provision, intended that our Workers' Compensation system be the exclusive remedy for work-related injuries and deaths.").

Haw. Rev. Stat. § 386-1 defines "work injury" as "a personal injury suffered under the conditions specified in section 386-3," that is, one "arising out of and in the course of the employment." "Employment," in turn, "means any service performed by an individual for another person under any contract of hire or apprenticeship, express or implied, oral or written, whether lawfully or unlawfully entered into." Haw. Rev. Stat. § 386-1.

In Tate v. GTE Hawaiian Telephone Co., 77 Hawai'i .100, 881 P.2d 1246 (1994), the Hawai`i Supreme Court clarified the nature and scope of coverage under the Hawai'i workers' compensation law by explaining the test used to determine when an injury is a "work injury" and, thus, compensable under Haw. Rev. Stat. Chapter 386.

> For an injury to be compensable under a workers' compensation statute, there must be a requisite nexus between the employment and the injury. The nexus requirement is articulated in Hawai'i, as in the majority of jurisdictions, on the basis that, to be compensable, an injury must arise out of and in the course of employment.

Id. at 103, 881 P.2d at 1249. Furthermore, the court explained that "[a]n injury is said to arise in the course of the employment when it takes place within the period of employment, at a place where the employee may reasonably be, and while he or she is fulfilling his or her duties or engaged in doing something incidental thereto." Id. at 103-04, 881 P.2d at 1249-50.

D. Pleading Requirements

Hawai'i is a "notice pleading" state, requiring only a "short and plain statement of the claim" and a demand for relief. See Haw. R. Civ. P. 8(a). No technical forms of pleading are required. Haw. R. Civ. P. 8(e). Special damages, however, must be plead with specificity. Haw. R. Civ. P. 9(g).

SURVEY OF IDAHO EMPLOYMENT LIBEL LAW

Debora K. Kristensen
Givens Pursley LLP
601 West Bannock Street
Boise, Idaho 83701
www.givenspursley.com
Telephone: (208) 388-1200; Facsimile: (208) 388-1300

(With Developments Reported Through **November 1, 2012)**

GENERAL COMMENTS

The State of Idaho is divided into seven judicial districts, with each district court maintaining a separate magistrate division. Idaho's appellate system consists of two courts: the Court of Appeals (4 judges) and the Supreme Court (5 justices). Decisions concerning defamation issues generally are appealed directly to, and retained by, the Idaho Supreme Court, although the Court has the discretion to assign such matters to the Court of Appeals. Idaho courts are likely to follow the restatement of the law, and in particular the Restatement (Second) of Torts in the absence of pertinent Idaho statutory or case law. **The Idaho state court system is increasingly moving towards on-line access to its dockets. For more information go to www.idcourts.us/repository/start.do.**

If you are involved in a case in federal court in Idaho, be certain to obtain a copy of the Local Federal Rules of Procedure. They are very detailed and impose many time limits with respect to discovery and other procedural matters, including the disclosure of witness lists and exhibits thirty days before trial. In addition, be prepared to file all materials electronically through the court's Electronic Case Filing ("ECF") system. For more information about the federal court's local rules and ECF system, go to its website at www.id.uscourts.gov.

SIGNIFICANT DEVELOPMENTS SINCE THE 2012 *SURVEY*

In Noak v. Idaho Department of Corrections, 152 Idaho 305, 271 P.3d 703 (2012), the medical director of the Idaho Department of Corrections ("IDOC") was replaced following an investigation into his alleged battery of a patient. An employee of the IDOC, Richard Haas, wrote a letter to the Idaho Board of Medicine ("IBOM") notifying it of the occurrence, although the IBOM took no action against the physician, Dr. John Noak. After his firing, Noak brought an action against various parties, including Haas, for defamation and intentional infliction of emotional distress based on the letter he sent to the IBOM. At trial, Haas relied on the statutory privilege afforded communications under Idaho Code § 54-1818, which requires licensed physicians and surgeons to report other physicians to the IBOM if they possess "knowledge of a violation" that would subject such physician to discipline under Idaho Code § 54-1814. Specifically, section 54-1818 provides that "no person shall be civilly liable for communications, reports or acts of any kind made, given or handled under the provisions of this act." The trial court agreed with Haas and granted his summary judgment dismissing Noak's claims. On appeal, Noak argued that the absolute immunity of section 54-1818 only applied to physicians and surgeons, not laypersons such as Haas. The Idaho Supreme Court disagreed with Noak, finding that the statute's use of "'No person' means 'no person.'" Noak, 152 Idaho at ___, 271 P.2d at 711. Accordingly, "Because Haas' letter to IBOM was a communication within the meaning of I.C. § 54-1818, any claims based upon the letter, including the defamation claim and the infliction of emotional distress claim, are barred by that statute's immunity provision." Id.

I. GENERAL LAW

A. General Employment Law

1. ***At Will Employment***. Employment in Idaho is presumed to be at-will. **Bollinger v. Fall River Rural Electric Cooperative, Inc., 152 Idaho 632, ___, 272 P.3d 1263, 1269 (2012) ("Employment in Idaho is presumed to be at will unless the employee is hired pursuant to a contract that states a fixed term or limits the reasons for discharge. In the absence of an express contract, a limitation to the at-will employment presumption may be implied where the circumstances surrounding the employment relationship could cause a reasonable person to conclude that the parties intended a limitation on discharge");** Wesco Autobody Supply, Inc. v. Ernest, 149 Idaho 881, 891, 243 P.3d 1069, 1079 (2010) (same); Jenkins v. Boise Cascade Corp, 141 Idaho, 233, 240 108 P.3d 380, 387 (2005) (same); Thomas, M.D. v. Medical Center Physicians, P.A., 138 Idaho 200, 61 P.3d 557, 563 (2002) ("Unless an employee is hired pursuant to a contract which specifies the duration of the employment, or limits the reasons why the employee may be discharged, the employee is 'at-will.'"); see also Thomas v. Ballou-Lattimer Drug Co., 92 Idaho 337, 341, 442 P.2d 747, 751 (1965). There is no cause of action for the mere discharge of an at-will employee. Van v. Portneuf Medical Center, 147 Idaho 552, 212 P.3d

982, 991 (2009) ("Generally, an employer may discharge an at-will employee at any time for any reason without incurring liability"); Mitchell v. Zilog, Inc., 125 Idaho 709, 712, 874 P.2d 520 (1994) ("Either party may terminate the relationship at any time for any reason without incurring liability"); Metcalf v. Intermountain Gas Co., 116 Idaho 622, 624, 778 P.2d 744, 746 (1989) (same); Jenkins, 141 Idaho at 240 (same).

A terminated at-will employee may bring an action for wrongful discharge if the motivation for the discharge contravenes public policy. See Van, 147 Idaho 552, 212 P.3d at 991 ("the right to discharge an at-will employee is limited by considerations of public policy, such as when the motivation for the firing contravenes public policy"); Thomas, M.D., 138 Idaho 200, 61 P.3d at 565; Roberts v. Bd. of Trustees, Pocatello, Sch. Dist. No. 25, 134 Idaho 890, 11 P.3d 1108 (2000) (school board exceeded its authority by firing employee without providing her a meaningful opportunity to be heard in a fair and impartial manner, as required by statute); Metcalf, 116 Idaho at 625-26; MacNeil v. Minidoka Memorial Hospital, 108 Idaho 588, 589, 701 P.2d 208, 209 (1985). An employee who reports wrongful conduct to superiors within the company is protected to the same extent as an employee who reports the wrongful conduct to an outside entity. Thomas, M.D., 138 Idaho 200, 61 P.3d at 565 (physician employee obtained whistleblower status by reporting to employer the falsification of medical records and performance of unnecessary operations by a fellow doctor).

"The public policy exception has been held to protect employees who refuse to commit unlawful acts, who perform important public obligations, or who exercise certain legal rights or privileges." Crea v. FMC Corp., 135 Idaho 175, 16 P.3d 272, 275 (2000) (employee alleged that he was fired because he uncovered and disclosed to his employer documents indicating that employer had caused serious contamination in ground water). See also Van, 147 Idaho 552, 212 P.3d at 991 ("The public policy exception to the employment at-will doctrine has been held to protect employees who refuse to commit unlawful acts, who perform important public obligations, or who exercise certain legal rights and privileges"). However, Idaho courts construe the public policy exception to at-will employment very narrowly. See Edmondson v. Shearer Lumber Products, 139 Idaho 172, 177-178, 75 P.3d 733, 738-739 (2003) (refusing to extend the public policy exception to support free speech absent state action or to support an employee's right to engage in political activities); McKay v. Ireland Bank, 138 Idaho 185, 59 P.3d 990, 995 (2002) (refusing to extend the public policy exception to protect an employee's right to run for political office). "Once the court defines the public policy, the question of whether the public policy was violated is one for the jury." Van, 147 Idaho 552, 212 P.3d at 991.

Also, a terminated at-will employee may bring a defamation action against a former employer if he is able to demonstrate each of the elements of a defamation claim. See, e.g., Arnold v. Diet Center, Inc., 113 Idaho 581, 746 P.2d 1040 (Ct. App. 1987).

B. Elements of Libel Claim

1. ***Basic Elements***. A defamation plaintiff "must prove that the defendant: (1) communicated information concerning the plaintiff to others; (2) that the information was defamatory; and (3) that the plaintiff was damaged because of the communication." Clark v. Spokesman Review, 144 Idaho 427, 163 P.2d 216, 219 (2007). See also Weitz v. Green, 148 Idaho 851, 230 P.3d 743, 754 (2010) (citing elements of claim from Clark); Swisher v. Collins, 2008 WL 687305 *28 (D.Idaho March 10, 2008) ("A claim for defamation requires evidence of the following: 1. That the [defendant] published or communicated . . . a statement or statements about the [plaintiff]; 2. That the statements were false in a material respect; 3. That the [defendant] knew of the falsity of the statements, or acted with a reckless disregard for their truth; 4. That the statements reflected adversely upon the [plaintiff's] character, integrity, good name and standing in the community in that the statements impugned his credit worthiness; 5. That the defamatory statements caused damage to the [plaintiff]; and 6. The nature and extent of the damages, and the dollar amounts thereof." (citing Eggleston v. Klemp, Case. No. CV 06-218-N-EJL, 2007 WL 1468686 * 2 (D.Idaho May 18, 2007)). Moreover, Jury Instruction 4.82 of the model Idaho Jury Instructions (2003 ed.) ("IDJI 2d") provides that a plaintiff has the burden of proving each of the following in a defamation action: (1) the defendant communicated information concerning the plaintiff to others; and (2) the information impugned the honesty, integrity, virtue or reputation of the plaintiff or exposed the plaintiff to public hatred, contempt or ridicule; and (3) the information was false; and (4) the defendant knew it was false, or reasonably should have known that it was false; and (5) the plaintiff suffered actual injury because of the defamation; and (6) the amount of damages suffered by the plaintiff. IDJI 2d 4.82 and comments thereto. See Eggleston v. Klemp, 2007 WL 1468686 (D. Idaho, May 18, 2007); Student Loan Fund of Idaho, Inc. v. Duerner, 131 Idaho 45, 52, 951 P.2d 1272, 1279 (1997). Libel is defined in Idaho's criminal statutes as: "A malicious defamation . . . tending to blacken the memory of one who is dead, or to impeach the honesty, integrity, virtue or reputation, or publish the natural or alleged defects of one who is alive, and thereby to expose him to public hatred, contempt or ridicule." Idaho Code § 18-4801. Idaho courts have used this definition in civil libel cases. See Sweeney v. Capital News Pub. Co., 37 F. Supp. 355, 356 (D. Idaho 1941).

2. ***Fault.*** The level of fault, if any, that must be shown depends on the plaintiff's private or public figure status and the private or public nature of the defendant's statement.

a. **Private Figure Plaintiff/Matter of Public Concern.** While there are no cases in the employment context, the Idaho Supreme Court has held that in defamation actions involving private figures and matters of public concern, the plaintiff has the burden of proof in demonstrating that the complained of statement is false and made with fault. Wiemer v. Rankin, 117 Idaho 566, 570, 790 P.2d 347, 351-52, 17 Media L. Rep. 1753 (1990). The Court in Wiemer did not specifically identify what level of fault would be required in such circumstances, stating only that plaintiff "would be entitled to recover damages for any actual injury he may have sustained without proving actual malice on [defendant's] part." Id. at 574, 790 P.2d at 355. In so doing, the Court referred to former model Idaho Jury Instruction 480-4, which assumed that Idaho would adopt a negligence standard in these cases. See also IDJI 2d 4.82-4. To date, however, no Idaho court has decided what level of fault is required. Thus, the Idaho courts could conceivably conclude that an intermediate level of fault between actual malice and negligence applies.

b. **Private Figure Plaintiff/Matter of Private Concern.** No appellate court in Idaho has decided what level of fault, if any, must be shown in the context of a private figure in a matter of private concern. The model Idaho Jury Instructions, cited with approval in Wiemer, assume that Idaho courts would adopt a negligence standard. See also IDJI 2d 4.82 and comments thereto. Perhaps based on this assumption, at least one state court has incorrectly concluded that Idaho has adopted the negligence standard in cases involving private figures and matters of private concern. See The Gazette, Inc. v. Harris, 325 S.E.2d 713, 11 Media L. Rep. 1609 (Va. 1985).

c. **Public Figure Plaintiff/Matter of Public Concern.** The federal constitutional standard of actual malice from New York Times v. Sullivan, 376 U.S. 254 (1964) will apply in defamation actions involving public figures and matters of public concern. Clark v. Spokesman Review, 163 P.2d at 219; Bandelin v. Pietsch, 98 Idaho 337, 563 P.2d 395, 2 Media L. Rep. 1600, cert. denied, 434 U.S. 891 (1977). See also Worrell-Payne v. Gannett Co., 2002 WL 31246121, *3 (9th Cir. 2002) (unpublished decision) (finding no evidence of actual malice sufficient to avoid summary judgment). While acknowledging that malice is defined as knowledge of falsity or reckless disregard of the truth, the Idaho Supreme Court has noted that the "essence" of actual malice is "a knowing state of mind on the part of the publisher." Bandelin, 98 Idaho at 342, 563 P.2d at 400. See also Clark, 163 P.2d at 219-220 ("In a defamation action, actual malice is knowledge of falsity or reckless disregard of truth" and this must be demonstrated by clear and convincing evidence); Wiemer, 117 Idaho at 576, 790 P.2d at 357 (in analyzing actual malice, court must "determine whether there is sufficient evidence to permit the conclusion that [defendant] in fact entertained serious doubts as to the truth of his statements or that subjectively [defendant] had a high degree of awareness of the probable falsity of the statements").

3. ***Falsity.*** If a statement is proven to be true, it is not defamatory. Steele v. Spokesman-Review, 138 Idaho 249, 61 P.3d 606, 609-610 (2003); Worrell-Payne, 2002 WL 31246121 at *3. When the defamatory statement involves a matter of public concern, the additional burden of pleading and proving falsity will lie with the plaintiff. Clark, 163 P.2d at 219; Wiemer v. Rankin, 117 Idaho 566, 570, 790 P.2d 347, 351-52, 17 Media L. Rep. 1753 (1990); Worrell-Payne, 2002 WL 31246121 at *1 (9th Cir. 2002) (unpublished decision) (placing burden upon the plaintiff to show falsity of statements). In cases involving matters of private concern, the common law rule applies which places on the defendant the burden of proving the truth of the statement as an affirmative defense. Baker v. Burlington Northern, Inc., 99 Idaho 688, 690, 587 P.2d 829, 4 Media L. Rep. 2240 (1978). However, the current model jury instructions place the burden of proof on the plaintiff to prove the allegedly defamatory statement is false. See IDJI 2d 4.82 and comments thereto. See Vanderford Co., Inc. v. Knudson, 144 Idaho 547, 165 P.3d 261, 271 (2007), dismissing slander of title action because "The publication of the notice of *lis pendens* is not defamatory. It merely informs the public that the property is involved in litigation."

4. ***Defamatory Statement of Fact.*** Only statements of fact are properly the basis for an action sounding in defamation. Wiemer v. Rankin, 117 Idaho at 572, 790 P.2d at 352; Cerda v. Saint Alphonsus Regional Medical Center, 2007 WL 2384381 *3. "A statement that is incapable of being disproved does not constitute an assertion of fact; it is a 'pure' opinion. A pure opinion is not actionable." Worrell-Payne v. Gannett Co., Inc., 134 F.Supp.2d 1167, 1172, 29 Media L. Rep. 1205, 1208 (D. Idaho 2000), aff'd, 2002 WL 31246121 (9th Cir. 2002) (unpublished decision). Additionally, an omission is not a statement of fact. McPheters v. Maile, 138 Idaho 391, 64 P.3d 317 (2003).

5. ***Of and Concerning Plaintiff.*** No cases, although Idaho R. Civ. P. 9(i) requires all complaints for libel and slander to state that the defamatory matter was "published or spoken concerning the plaintiff."

6. ***Publication.*** As with the other common law elements of defamation, publication is assumed to be an element of a prima facie claim for defamation in Idaho, although no Idaho court has specifically stated as much. See I.B.1, supra. But see Idaho Code § 18-4805 (criminal libel statute provides that "[t]o sustain a charge of publishing a libel, it is not needful that the words or things complained of should have been read or seen by another. It is enough that the accused knowingly parted with the immediate custody of the libel under circumstances which exposed it to be read or seen by any other person than himself").

a. **Intracorporate Communication.** Without specifically finding that publication was made when an employer internally disclosed the reasons for an employee's termination, such a finding was implied in Arnold v. Diet Center, Inc., 113 Idaho 581, 585-86, 746 P.2d 1040 (Ct. App. 1987). The court found that such a statement may be defamatory, but was protected by a qualified privilege. Id.

b. **Compelled Self-Publication.** There are no reported Idaho cases on compelled self-publication. However, a footnote in Arnold, 113 Idaho 581, 586, n. 2, 746 P.2d at 1045 n.2, observes that "the only other evidence [other than privileged communications between employees] offered suggests that [plaintiff] alone published the reason for his termination to third parties." In light of this evidence, the Court affirmed the dismissal of the plaintiff's defamation claim, suggesting that a compelled self-defamation claim would not be recognized in Idaho.

c. **Republication.** Idaho criminal libel statutes (which have never been considered by an Idaho court) expressly provide for republication liability. Idaho Code § 18-4806. Such liability is also implied in the civil context through the state's retraction statute (Idaho Code § 6-712) and the adoption of the Uniform Single Publication Act (Idaho Code § 6-702). No Idaho court has squarely addressed the issue of liability of the original author of the republished material vis-a-vis the responsibility of the republisher. But see Barlow v. International Harvester Co., 95 Idaho 881, 522 P.2d 1102 (1974) (judgment against employer based on slanderous statements made by employees upheld on agency principles).

7. ***Statements versus Conduct.*** Something that is defamatory ordinarily must be either oral or written. See, e.g., Idaho Code § 18-4801 (criminal libel is malicious defamation expressed in writing); Idaho Code §§ 6-701-714 (civil provision). Doing of a lawful act in a lawful manner will not subject the actor to liability for defamation, despite the fact that said act "may indirectly injure some one." Barton v. Rogers, 21 Idaho 609, 618, 123 P. 478 (1912). See also Gardner v. Hollifield, 96 Idaho 609, 613-14, 533 P.2d 730 (1975), appeal after remand, 97 Idaho 607, 549 P.2d 266 (1976). The Idaho Supreme Court recently held that an attorney's statements and conduct made during the course of his/her representation of a client in litigation were protected from civil liability under the litigation privilege. Taylor v. McNichols, 149 Idaho 826, 243 P.3d 642 (2010).

8. ***Damages.*** A defamation plaintiff must plead special damages unless the claim falls into one of the categories of defamation per se, in which case damages are presumed. Yoakum v. Hartford Fire Ins. Co., 129 Idaho 171, 180, 923 P.2d 416, 425 (1996). See also Barlow, 95 Idaho at 890, 522 P.2d at 1111; Weeks v. M-P Publications, Inc., 95 Idaho 634, 516 P.2d 193, 195 (1973); Browder v. Cook, 59 F. Supp. 225, 231 (D. Idaho 1944); Sweeney v. Capital News Pub. Co., 37 F. Supp. 355, 357 (D. Idaho 1941); Jenness v. Co-Operative Publishing Co., 36 Idaho 697, 703, 213 P. 351 (1923). However, presumed damages will not be allowed in cases involving statements of public concern unless the plaintiff establishes that the defendant acted with actual malice. Wiemer, 117 Idaho 566, 573-74, 790 P.2d 347, 354-55 (1990). An individual or corporate plaintiff in a defamation per se case is entitled, absent truth or privilege, to "substantial damages without proving actual damages" in an amount the jury considers just and proper in view of all the circumstances. Barlow, 95 Idaho at 896-97, 522 P.2d at 1117-18 (sustaining large "general damages" award in absence of proof of special damages).

a. **Presumed Damages and Libel Per Se.** Adopting the approach of the Restatement (Second) of Torts, the Idaho Supreme Court has recognized four categories of statements as constituting defamation per se: statements which impute to the plaintiff (1) a criminal offense (see Barlow, 95 Idaho at 891, 522 P.2d 1112 (statement that plaintiff was "thief" and had "stolen" money); Dayton v. Drumheller, 32 Idaho 283, 287, 182 P. 102, 103 (1919) (charge of arson)); (2) a loathsome disease; (3) a matter incompatible with his trade, business, profession, or office (see Dwyer v. Libert, 30 Idaho 576, 582-83, 167 P. 651 (1917) (charge that plaintiff, a patrolman, lied in a serious business transaction)); or (4) serious sexual misconduct. Yoakum v. Hartford Fire Ins. Co., 129 Idaho at 180, 923 P.2d at 425 (relying on Restatement (Second) of Torts §§ 570-574 (1977)). See'also Barlow v. International Harvester Co., 95 Idaho at 890, 522 P.2d at 1111. Moreover, a defamatory utterance regarding a corporation is defamatory per se when it "assails its management or credit and inflicts injury on its business." Barlow, 95 Idaho at 890, 522 P.2d at 1111 (citing Restatement (Second) of Torts §§ 561, 573 (1938)).

"In Idaho, if the language at issue is plain and unambiguous, it is a question of law for the court to determine if the alleged defamatory publication amounts to libel per se." Two Jinn, Inc. v. Green, 2007 WL 1381804 *4 (D.Idaho, March 7, 2007) (citing S.N.Weeks v. M-P Publications, Inc., 95 Idaho 634, 636, 516 P.2d 193, 195 (1973)).

(1) **Employment-Related Criticism.** Statements critical of a public official's performance of her official duties (i.e., she engaged in "nepotism," frequent "absenteeism" and "mismanagement") have been held to be non-actionable. Worrell-Payne v. Gannett Co., 2002 W.L. 31246121, **2-4 (9th Cir. 2002) (unpublished decision).

(2) **Single Instance Rule.** No cases.

b. **Punitive Damages.** In Idaho, a claimant must prove, by clear and convincing evidence, oppressive, fraudulent, malicious or outrageous conduct by the party whom the claim for punitive damages is asserted. See I.C. § 6-1604; I.R.C.P. 9(g). Punitive damages are an "extraordinary remedy" and are to be used to punish and deter a defendant where his conduct is wanton, malicious, gross or outrageous, or where facts imply malice and oppression. See I. C. § 6-1601(9); Linscott v. Rainier Nat. Life Ins. Co., 100 Idaho 854, 857, 606 P.2d 958 (1980). Accordingly, Idaho courts have held that punitive damages "should only be awarded in the most unusual and compelling circumstances." O'Neil v. Vasseur, 118 Idaho 257, 265, 796 Idaho 134 (1990). See, e.g., Barlow, 95 Idaho at 897-98 (award of punitive damages for slander and tortious interference with contract affirmed against individual and corporate defendants). Punitive damages will not be allowed in cases involving statements of public concern unless the plaintiff establishes that the defendant acted with actual malice. Wiemer v. Rankin, 117 Idaho 566, 573-74, 790 P.2d 347, 354-55 (1990) (citing Gertz v. Robert Welch, Inc., 418 U.S. 323, 347-50 (1974)).

Idaho law specifically provides that punitive damages may not be alleged in the prayer of a complaint. Idaho Code § 6-1604(2). Rather, the plaintiff must bring a pre-trial motion to amend the complaint to include a punitive damages claim once adequate discovery has been conducted to demonstrate that there is a "reasonable likelihood of proving facts at trial sufficient to support an award of punitive damages." Idaho Code § 6-1604(2). Punitive damages are capped at an amount equal to the greater of $250,000 or an amount equal to three times the compensatory damages in the judgment. Idaho Code § 6-1604(3). If the case is tried to a jury, the jury shall not be informed of this limitation.

II. PRIVILEGES AND DEFENSES

A. Scope of Privileges

Where there are no statutes or cases on point, Idaho courts routinely follow the Restatement (Second) of Torts in dealing with issues of privilege in the defamation context. A number of statutory privileges are set forth in Idaho Code § 6-710 (privileged broadcasts) and § 6-713 (privileged publication by a newspaper); however these specifically apply only to members of the media.

1. ***Absolute Privilege.*** Truth is a complete defense to a defamation action. Baker v. Burlington Northern, Inc., 99 Idaho 688, 690, 587 P.2d 829, 4 Media L. Rep. 2240 (1978); see also Hemingway v. Fritz, 96 Idaho 364, 366, 529 P.2d 264 (1974) (defendant's alleged malicious motivation in publishing material is irrelevant if the material is true). But, "it is not necessary for the defendant to prove the literal truth of his statement in every detail, rather it is sufficient for a complete defense if the substance or gist of the slanderous or libelous statement is true." Baker, 99 Idaho at 690. See also Steele v. Spokesman-Review, 138 Idaho 249, 61 P.3d at 609-610 ("'[S]o long as the substance, the gist, the sting of the allegedly libelous charge be justified,' minor inaccuracies do not amount to falsity."); Worrell-Payne v. Gannett Co., 2002 WL 31246121, *3 (9th Cir. 2002) (unpublished decision) (holding "substance or gist" of statements were true). Thus, an employer was absolutely privileged from defamation liability where it informed employee and his supervisors that employee was terminated for failing to disclose his true criminal history on his job application. Baker, 99 Idaho at 690.

Idaho has also recognized an absolute privilege against liability for defamatory statements made during or for a judicial or other "proceeding of a judicial nature before a court or official clothed with judicial or quasi judicial power." See Weitz v. Green, 148 Idaho 851, 230 P.3d 743, 754-55 (2010) (extending absolute privilege against civil actions for defamation afforded to defamatory matter published in due course of a judicial proceeding to claims for slander of title) (overruling Weaver v. Stafford, 134 Idaho 691, 701, 8 P.3d 1234, 1244 (2000)); (Richeson v. Kessler, 73 Idaho 548, 551-52, 255 P.2d 707 (1953) (statements in letter to District Judge by attorney expressing objections to brief could not be basis for defamation claim); Overman v. Klein, 103 Idaho 795, 799, 654 P.2d 888 (1982) (statements of witnesses in judicial proceedings are absolutely protected, provided they are "relevant to the court's inquiry"). The absolute privilege also attaches to written statements submitted to judicial or quasi-judicial bodies, even if the statement is part of a preliminary or proposed judicial proceeding. Malmin v. Engler, 124 Idaho 733, 737, 864 P.2d 179 (Ct. App. 1993) (citing Restatement (Second) of Torts § 586 (1977)). In Taylor v. McNichols, 149 Idaho 826, 243 P.3d 642, the Idaho Supreme Court "held that the "litigation privilege is an absolute privilege, which only applies when a specific condition precedent is met, namely, that an attorney is acting within the scope of his employment, and not solely for his personal interests." Id. at 841, 243 P.3d at 657. In so finding, the Court held for the first time that both defamatory statements and conduct of attorneys made in the course of his/her representation of a client fall within the litigation privilege. Id. at 841, 243 P.3d at 657.

2. ***Qualified Privileges.*** A person who makes a defamatory statement will not be subject to liability if a qualified, or conditional, privilege attaches. Idaho recognizes several such privileges.

a. **Common Interest.** Idaho recognizes a conditional or qualified privilege that protects the publisher of defamatory material from liability if the publication is made to one who shares a common interest, as for example, a business relationship. Barlow v. International Harvester Co., 95 Idaho 881, 522 P.2d 1102, 1112-13 (1974). See also Cerda v. Saint Alphonsus Regional Medical Center, 2007 WL 2384381 *6 (former employer's reference to prospective employer of its former employee is within the common interest privilege); Gough v. Tribune-Journal Co., 75 Idaho 502, 509, 275 P.2d 663, 666-67 (1954) (citizens' letter criticizing budget proposed by county commissioners and urging commissioners' recall was protected by common interest privilege since sent to other taxpayers who had "common interests"); Arnold v. Diet Center, Inc., 113 Idaho 581, 585, 746 P.2d 1040 (Ct. App. 1987) (employer was found to have a "legitimate interest" in informing one of its workers about the reasons for another worker's termination and, therefore, was protected by the qualified privileged).

b. **Duty.** Statements made in the performance of official duties are covered by a qualified privilege. See Gardner v. Hollifield, 96 Idaho 609, 533 P.2d 730 (1975), appeal after remand, 97 Idaho 607, 613-14, 549 P.2d 266 (1976) (statements made by a school superintendent to members of the board of trustees of a school district concerning the competency of a school teacher were deemed to be conditionally privileged from defamation liability).

c. **Criticism of Public Employee.** A qualified privilege protects criticism of a public employee or official. See Dwyer v. Libert, 30 Idaho 576, 583, 167 P. 651 (1917) (a formal complaint filed with a mayor and city council, which resulted in the termination of a police officer, was protected by a qualified privilege from defamation liability). See also Gough, 75 Idaho at 509, 275 P.2d at 666-67 (arguably applying this privilege). In most cases, because the plaintiff will be a public figure and the statements will pertain to a matter of public concern, the plaintiff will also have the heavy burden of showing actual malice. See Worrell-Payne v. Gannett Co., 2002 WL 31246121, **2-3 (9th Cir. 2002) (unpublished decision) (statements critical of public official's performance of her official duties as Executive Director of the Boise City/Ada County Housing Authority [*i.e.*, she engaged in "nepotism," frequent "absenteeism" and "mismanagement"] held non-actionable).

d. **Limitation on Qualified Privileges.** "A conditional privilege may be lost when a speaker on an otherwise privileged occasion publishes false and defamatory matter concerning another which either (a) he in fact does not believe to be true or (b) has no reasonable grounds for believing it to be true." Gardner, 97 Idaho 607, 549 P.2d at 269. See also Cerda, 2007 WL 2384381 *6; Barlow, 95 Idaho at 892, 522 P.2d at 1113; Gough, 75 Idaho at 510, 275 P.2d at 667-68; Arnold, 113 Idaho at 585-86, 746 P.2d at 1044-45.

(1) **Constitutional or Actual Malice.** Proof of constitutional malice would defeat a qualified privilege. "Reckless disregard" for the truth, the constitutional standard for actual malice, means that the defendant "entertained serious doubts as to [the] truth of the publication" or "had a high degree of awareness of [its] probable falsity." See Olson v. EG & G Idaho, Inc., 134 Idaho 778, 9 P.3d 1244, 1246 (2000) (noting that "focus will be on whether the evidence indicates that [defendant] purposely avoided the truth"); Wiemer v. Rankin, 117 Idaho 566, 575-76, 790 P.2d 347, 357 (1990).

(2) **Common Law Malice.** Common law malice, sometimes referred to as "express malice" or "malice in fact," is defined as "the publication of defamatory matter in bad faith, without belief in the truth of the matter published, or with reckless disregard of the truth or falsity of the matter." Barlow, 95 Idaho at 892, 522 P.2d at 1113. Proof of common law malice would defeat a qualified privilege.

(3) **Other Limitations on Qualified Privileges.** No reported cases.

e. **Question of Fact or Law.** "[T]he question of whether the communications arose 'in the due course of a judicial proceeding' and were 'reasonably related to that judicial proceeding' [and, therefore, are conditionally privileged] are questions of fact." Swisher v. Collins, 2008 WL 687305 *29 (D.Idaho March 10, 2008). But, the determination of whether an allegedly defamatory statement is privileged is a question of law. Barlow v. International Harvester Co., 95 Idaho at 892, 522 P.2d at 1113; Cerda, 2007 WL 2384381 * 6. The determination of whether a privileged statement has been abused, and therefore lost, is a question of fact. Id. See also Browder v. Cook, 59 F. Supp. 225, 232 (D. Idaho 1944). "The Court may take the question of malice from the jury only if there is no evidence of malice and the undisputed facts admit only one conclusion." Cerda v. Saint Alphonsus Regional Medical Center, 2007 WL 2384381 *6 (citing Barlow, 522 P.2d at 1113).

f. **Burden of Proof.** A qualified privilege is an affirmative defense that must be plead by the defendant. State v. Sheridan, 14 Idaho 222, 93 P.656, 660 (1908) ("[w]here the article published is libelous per se, the truth of the article or the motive which prompted its publication are matters of defense"). Once the defendant proves that the statement made was privileged, the burden is on the plaintiff to show malice or other grounds for setting aside the privilege. See Gardner v. Hollifield, 96 Idaho at 612 n.2, 533 P.2d 730 ("[i]f the defendant asserts the defense of conditional privilege, it is open to the plaintiff to prove abuse of the privilege, the burden being upon him to do so"); Arnold v. Diet Center, Inc., 113 Idaho at 585-86, 746 P.2d 1040 (statement found to be protected by qualified privilege because plaintiff failed "to show that the statements by [defendant] were made in bad faith, without belief in the truth of the matter communicated or with a reckless disregard of the truth or falsity of the matter").

B. Standard Libel Defenses

1. ***Truth.*** At common law, truth was an affirmative defense to a defamation action, and that rule continues to be Idaho law with regard to cases involving matters of private concern. See I.B.3, supra. In cases involving matters of public concern, however, the burden of proving falsity now rests with plaintiff. Id. Idaho courts have recognized the concept of substantial truth, holding "[i]n a slander or libel suit it is not necessary for the defendant to prove the literal truth of his statement in every detail, rather it is sufficient for a complete defense if the substance or gist of the slanderous or libelous statement is true." Baker v. Burlington Northern, Inc., 99 Idaho 688, 690, 587 P.2d 829, 4 Media L. Rep. 2240 (1978). See II.A.1, supra.

2. ***Opinion.*** Only statements alleging fact are properly the basis of an action sounding in defamation. Wiemer v. Rankin, 117 Idaho 566, 572, 790 P.2d 347, 352 (1990) (citing Gertz v. Robert Welch, Inc., 418 U.S. 323, 339-40 (1974)); Worrell-Payne v. Gannett Co., 134 F.Supp.2d 1167, 1172, 29 Media L. Rep. 1205, 1208 (D. Idaho 2000) ("A statement that is incapable of being disproved does not constitute an assertion of fact; it is a 'pure' opinion. A pure opinion is not actionable") (citations omitted). Statements of opinion are constitutionally protected and, therefore, not actionable. Idaho State Bar v. Topp, 129 Idaho 414, 416, 925 P.2d 1113 (1996) (citing Milkovich v. Lorain Journal Co., 497 U.S. 1, 19 (1990)). In determining whether a statement is an assertion of fact or opinion, "the important consideration . . . is not whether the particular statement fits into one category or another, but whether the particular article provided sufficient information upon which the reader could make an independent judgment for himself." Idaho State Bar, 129 Idaho at 416 (citing Wiemer, 117 Idaho at 572, 790 P.2d at 353). Thus, statements which otherwise appear to be opinion will nonetheless be treated as assertions of fact "if the speaker implies that he is privy to undisclosed facts and that he has 'private first hand knowledge which substantiates the assertions made.'" Id. (an attorney's statement that a judge's ruling was motivated by political concerns "went beyond the realm of pure 'opinion'"); Worrell-Payne, 134 F.Supp.2d at 1172, 29 Media L. Rep. at 1208 ("A statement of opinion based on fully disclosed facts can be punished only if the stated facts are themselves false and demeaning"). See also Wiemer, 117 Idaho at 572, 790 P.2d at 353 (statement that evidence in apparent suicide was "overwhelming" that victim did not shoot herself was a statement of fact, not opinion).

3. ***Consent.*** A plaintiff who consents to defamatory statements cannot bring suit for defamation. See Dwyer v. Libert, 30 Idaho 576, 584, 167 P. 651 (1917) (recognizing consent as privilege to defamation, but refusing to recognize such under facts of case).

4. ***Mitigation.*** A failure to mitigate damages is an affirmative defense under I.R.C.P. 8(c). Taylor v. Browning, 129 Idaho 483, 492, 927 P.2d 873, 882 (1996).

III. RECURRING FACT PATTERNS

A. Statements in Personnel File

School district employees have a statutory right to access information contained in their personnel files, with the exception of recommendation letters. Idaho Code § 33-518. However, Idaho law does not generally require that employers allow employees access to employment files. While certain information is required to be maintained under federal law, employers are free to adopt any recordkeeping policy they wish, so long as appropriate records are kept, and for privacy reasons, the information is kept confidential. While there are no Idaho cases directly on point, defamation actions based on statements in personnel files may be subject to a defense based on the common interest privilege (see II.A.2.a, supra) and opinion. See II.B.2, supra.

B. Performance Evaluations

There are no Idaho cases directly on point. However, defamation actions based on performance evaluations may be subject to a defense based on the common interest privilege (see II.A.2.a, supra) and opinion. See II.B.2, supra.

In a somewhat related vein, the Idaho Supreme Court held that I.C. § 39-1392c provides immunity "from liability or action for money damages or other legal or equitable relief" to those who provide information or opinions to any health care organization and those health care organizations that receive or rely upon such information. Harrison v. Binnion, 147 Idaho 645, 649, 214 P.3d 631, 635 (Idaho July 7, 2009). But, the Court held that I.C. § 39-1392c did not grant immunity for credentialing decisions based on that information, because to do so "would be an expansion of that statute beyond its wording." Id.

C. References

Idaho Code Section 44-201 provides, "An employer who in good faith provides information about the job performance, professional conduct, or evaluation of a former or current employee to a prospective employer of that employee, at the request of the prospective employer of that employee, or at the request of the current or former employee, may not be held civilly liable for the disclosure or the consequences of providing the information." Idaho Code § 44-201(2). The statute creates a "rebuttable presumption that an employer is acting in good faith when the employer provides information about the job performance, professional conduct, or evaluation of a former or current employee to a prospective employer," which may only be overcome by clear and convincing evidence that the employer disclosed information with actual malice or "deliberate intent to mislead." Id. To date, no appellate court in Idaho has applied and interpreted this statute.

While there are no reported cases applying I.C. § 44-201, the issue of liability associated with providing references for former employees recently was addressed in Cerda v. Saint Alphonsus Regional Medical Center, 2007 WL 2384381 (D.Idaho August 17, 2007). In Cerda, plaintiff was employed as a dispatcher and EMT for ground transport with a hospital's Life Flight Department until her termination pursuant to a Reduction-in-Force. When plaintiff applied for other positions, her former supervisor at the hospital reported that she had "dependability issues." These issues were related to the end of plaintiff's employment when she started missing work shifts due to an illness. Plaintiff sued the hospital (her former employer) for defamation, intentional infliction of emotional distress, negligent infliction of emotional distress and breach of the implied covenant of good faith and fair dealing based on its reference. The hospital moved for summary judgment on all claims and the trial court, applying Idaho law, held: (1) the hospital's statement to plaintiff's prospective employers that she had "dependability issues" was a statement of fact, not opinion; (2) a question of fact existed as to the truthfulness of such statement; and (3) although protected by the common interest privilege, a question of fact existed as to whether the hospital acted with malice in making such statement. Id. at * 3-6. Accordingly, the court denied the hospital's motion for summary judgment on plaintiff's defamation claim. The court did, however, grant the hospital's motion for summary on plaintiff's intentional infliction of emotional distress claim, finding that the hospital's "comments to prospective employers, and the Defendants' other actions in relation to [plaintiff's] employment do not rise to the level of extreme conduct such that a reasonable member of the community would deem it outrageous or beyond all possible bounds of decency." Id. at *7. Similarly, the court granted the hospital's motion for summary judgment on plaintiff's negligent infliction of emotional distress and breach of the implied covenant of good faith and fair dealing claims. Id. at *8-9.

D. Intracorporate Communication

A qualified privilege will generally attach to the dissemination of statements within a corporation in furtherance of the corporation's operations and interest. See Arnold v. Diet Center, Inc., 113 Idaho 581, 585, 746 P.2d 1040, 1044-45 (Ct. App. 1987) (citing Restatement (Second) of Torts § 596 (1976)). In Arnold, a terminated employee claimed his former employer invaded his right to privacy and defamed him by publishing the fact that he was terminated due to a breach of the employer's confidentiality agreement. The Court of Appeals found that the employer had a legitimate interest in stressing to its employees the importance of complying with their confidentiality agreement, and thus, that the employer's communication was protected by a qualified privilege. Id. at 585, 746 P.2d at 1044. The Court of Appeals also found that there was no showing of any abuse by the employer that would cause it to lose its qualified privilege. Id.

In Peterson v. Hewlett-Packard Co., 358 F.3d 599 (9th Cir. 2004), an employee was discharged for insubordination, for refusing to take down posters in his work area that cited scriptural passages criticizing homosexuals. The Ninth Circuit Court of Appeals upheld the termination, holding that the company's decision was not based upon animus against the employee's religion but rather the company's policies against harassment and towards encouraging diversity and tolerance. Id. at 605.

E. Statements to Government Regulators

In Nampa Charter School, Inc. v. DeLaPaz, 140 Idaho 23, 89 P.3d 863 (2004), a charter school sued a former employee and her spouse for claims including slander and libel, based upon criticisms voiced by them about deficiencies in the school's special education program. The Court upheld the dismissal of the charter school's claims, holding that the charter school should be treated as a governmental entity and, therefore, that the school could not maintain an action for libel and slander against private individuals speaking on a matter of public concern. Id.

In Smith v. Mitton, 140 Idaho 893, 104 P.3d 367 (2004) (a non-defamation case), a city employee was terminated after voicing concerns to his co-workers, his supervisor, the City Administrator and the City's insurance agent about a waste of public funds and the Mayor's conflict of interest related to the City of Burley's new health insurance plan. He also wrote a letter to the Idaho Department of Insurance, which upset the Mayor and the employee's supervisor. The employee sued the City for violation of the Idaho Whistleblower Act. I. C. § 6-2104. The City took the position that the employee was fired because of a negative attitude and not for implicating a waste of public funds or questioning the legality of requested tasks at work. However, the Idaho Supreme Court affirmed the trial court's conclusion "that the evidence presented was adequate to support a reasonable jury's finding of a violation of the Whistleblower Statute." Id. at 373. Accordingly, the Supreme Court affirmed the trial court's award of lost wages, attorneys fees and costs. Id. at 377.

In Van v. Portneuf Medical Center, 147 Idaho 552, 212 P.3d 982 (2009), the former director of maintenance for a medical center's helicopter program brought a wrongful termination and breach of contact action against the medical center after he was fired, alleging that his termination was the result of his reporting numerous perceived violations of state and federal law with respect to the helicopters' maintenance. Van claimed that his termination violated Idaho's Whistleblower Act (I.C. § 6-2104) and, as such, contravened public policy so as to support his cause of action for wrongful termination of his at-will employment. The medical center moved for summary judgment on all claims, and the trial court granted the motion. On appeal, the Idaho Supreme Court reversed in part, and affirmed in part, holding that Van's statutory whistleblower claim was not governed by the Idaho Tort Claims Act and, therefore, not subject to its notice requirements. The Court also held that the Whistleblower Act could not be "used to establish the public policy upon which a breach of at-will employment contract claim is based." Van, 147 Idaho 552, 212 P.3d at 991.

Statements made by government regulations should be subject to a qualified privilege. See II.A.2., supra. An absolute privilege attaches to written statements submitted to judicial or quasi-judicial bodies, even if such statements are part of preliminary proceedings. Malmin v. Engler, 124 Idaho 733, 737, 864 P.2d 179 (Ct. App. 1993) (citing Restatement (Second) of Torts § 586 (1977)). **And, an absolute statutory privilege attached to any person making a communication to the Idaho Board of Medicine within the meaning of Idaho Code § 54-1818. See Noak v. Idaho Department of Correction, 152 Idaho at __, 271 P.3d at 711.**

F. Reports to Auditors and Insurers

There are no reported cases in Idaho, although such reports should be subject to a qualified privilege. See II.A.2, supra. An absolute privilege attaches to written statements submitted to judicial or quasi-judicial bodies, even if such statements are part of preliminary proceedings. Malmin, 124 Idaho at 737, 864 P.2d 179 (citing Restatement (Second) of Torts § 586 (1977)).

G. Vicarious Liability of Employers for Statements Made by Employees

1. ***Scope of Employment.*** An employer may be held vicariously liable for defamatory statements made by an employee if the employee was acting within the scope of his employment at the time the statements were made. Barlow v. International Harvester Co., 95 Idaho 881, 889, 522 P.2d 1102, 1110 (1974). See generally Finholt v. Cresto, 143 Idaho 894, 155 P.3d 695, 698 (2007); Podolan v. Idaho Legal Aid Serv., Inc., 123 Idaho 937, 944, 854 P.2d 280, 287 (Ct. App. 1993); Smith v. Thompson, 103 Idaho 909, 911, 655 P.2d 116, 118 (Ct. App. 1982). But see Brown v. City of Pocatello, 148 Idaho 802, 229 P.3d 1164, 1173 (2010) ("As a general rule, a principal is not liable for the negligence of an independent contractor in performing the contracted services"). The scope of one's employment encompasses those acts which are so closely connected with what the employee is supposed to do, and so fairly and reasonably incident to it, that they may be regarded as methods of carrying out the objectives of the employer. Podolan, 123 Idaho at 944, 854 P.2d at 287. "In general, the [employee's] conduct is within the scope of his employment if it is of the kind which he is employed to perform, occurs substantially within the authorized limits of time and space, and is actuated, at least in part, by a purpose to serve the [employer]." Id. But, an employer will generally not be liable for intentional torts of its employees because such acts are not within the scope of their employment. See Smith, 103 Idaho at 911, 655 P.2d at 118 (employer not liable for employee's burning of a house because such act is not within scope of employment). The Idaho Supreme Court clarified the definition of "scope of employment" as "if the employee's purpose is purely personal, it does not matter that the employee is using the employer's tools or driving the employer's vehicle or some other activity that merely resembles his or her employment. The employee must be engaged in some type of work that is assigned to him or her in the general sense of doing something to serve the employer." Richard J. and Esther E. Wooley Trust v. Debest Plumbing, Inc., 133 Idaho 180, 184, 983 P.2d 834, 838 (1999). Indeed, after reviewing relevant case law the court held that "serving the 'master'" is central to finding that an employee's conduct is within the scope of employment. Id. See Thompson v. Clear Spring Goods, Inc., 148 Idaho 697, 228 P.3d 378, 380 (2010) (in worker's compensation context, Court held that injuries suffered by employee when she left work during shift to move her car did not arise "out of and in the course of her employment"); (Rausch v. Pocatello Lumber Co., Inc., 135 Idaho 80, 14 P.3d 1074, 1079 (Idaho Ct. App. 2000) (employee's "horseplay," "pranks" and "joking" not within scope of employment). Whether an employee is acting within the scope of his employment when he sends a potentially defamatory message is a question of fact. See Truckstop.Net LLC v. Sprint Communications Co., 537 F.Supp.2d 1126, 1140 (D.Idaho 2008).

In Finholt, the Idaho Supreme Court was asked to extend the reach of an employer's responsibility in a tort case by adopting exceptions traditionally seen in workers compensation cases. The Court noted that under the "coming and going" rule applied in workers compensation cases, "an employee is not within the course and scope of his employment on his way to work and from work." Finholt, 155 P.3d at 699. An exception thereto exists for the "traveling employee" whereby "'employees whose work entails travel away from the employer's premises' and are required 'to maintain [themselves] while traveling'" will give rise to an employer's coverage of the employee while on the trip. Id. The Court did not reach the question of whether to apply the traveling employee exception to tort claims "because the theory would not apply to the facts presented by this case." Id.

a. **Blogging.** No reported cases.

2. ***Damages.*** An employer who is held vicariously liable for an employee's defamation is responsible for the compensatory damage award. See Barlow, 95 Idaho at 897, 522 P.2d at 1118. And, punitive damages may be assessed against the corporation where management has "participated in or authorized or ratified" the employee's acts. Id., 95 Idaho at 897-98, 522 P.2d at 1118-19 ("corporate liability for punitive damages may arise where there is participation in the alleged tortious conduct by a 'managing and policy-making agent' as well as by a corporation director or officer").

H. Internal Investigations. No reported cases.

IV. OTHER ACTIONS BASED ON STATEMENTS

A. Negligent Hiring, Retention, and Supervision

If a supervisor knows or should know that a supervisee is likely to cause bodily harm to others if not controlled, the supervisor is under a duty to exercise reasonable care to control the supervisee so that he/she will not injure third persons. Rausch, 14 P.3d at 1080 ("[a] negligent supervision claim is not based upon imputed or vicarious liability but upon the employer's own negligence in failing to exercise due care to protect third parties from the foreseeable tortious acts of an employee"); Podolan v. Idaho Legal Aid Serv., Inc., 123 Idaho 937, 946, 854 P.2d 280, 289 (citing Sterling v. Bloom, 111 Idaho 211, 225, 723 P.2d 755, 769 (1986); Litchfield v. Nelson, 122 Idaho 416, 420, 835 P.2d 651, 655 (Ct. App. 1992)); Hei v. Holzer, 139 Idaho 81, 88, 73 P.3d 94, 101 (2003). This duty arises out of the supervisor's relationship to the supervisee, and not the supervisor's direct relationship with the endangered persons. Podolan, 123 Idaho at 946, 854 P.2d at 289; Sterling, 111 Idaho at 22, 723 P.2d at 769. "[N]egligent supervision liability encompasses conduct of the employee that is *outside* the scope of employment, at least if the employee is on the employer's premises or using an instrument or property of the employer." Rausch, 14 P.3d at 1080 (emphasis in original).

Although the Idaho Tort Claims Act states that governmental entities and their employees, while acting within the course and scope of their employment, are not liable for any claims arising out of assault and battery, the act does not foreclose the assertion of negligence claims. See Kessler v. Barowsky, 129 Idaho 647, 931 P.2d 641 (1997) (involving negligent supervision claim brought against law enforcement officials); Doe v. Durtschi, 110 Idaho 466, 716 P.2d 1238 (1986) (involving negligent hiring and retaining claim brought against school district). However, in Hunter v. State of Idaho, et al., 138 Idaho 44, 57 P.3d 755 (2001), the employer was not liable for negligent supervision, where an employee murdered another former employee outside of the workplace.

B. Intentional Infliction of Emotional Distress

In order to recover for intentional infliction of emotional distress, the plaintiff must prove that: (1) the defendant's conduct was intentional or reckless; (2) the defendant's conduct was extreme and outrageous; (3) there was a causal connection between the wrongful conduct and the emotional distress; and (4) the emotional distress was severe. **Bollinger v. Fall River Rural Electric Cooperative, Inc., 152 Idaho at __, 272 P.3d at 1274.** See also Mortensen v. Stewart Title Guaranty Co., 149 Idaho 437, 235 P.3d 387 , 396 (2010); Johnson v. McPhee, 147 Idaho 455, 464, 210 P.3d 563, 572 (2009); Yeargin v. Landry, 2008 WL 314414 * 6 (D.Idaho Feb. 4, 2008); Muffley v. Gem County, 2008 WL 110970 *2 (D.Idaho January 8, 2008); McKinley v. Guaranty National Insurance Co., 144 Idaho 247, 159 P.3d 884, 891 (2007); Nation v. State of Idaho, 144 Idaho 177, 158 P.3d 953, 968 (2007); Cerda v. Saint Alphonsus Regional Medical Center , 2007 WL 2384381 *7; Alderson v. Bonner, 142 Idaho 733, 132 P.3d 1261 (2006); Spence v. Howell, 126 Idaho 763, 774, 890 P.2d 714, 725 (1995) (citing Curtis v. Firth, 123 Idaho 598, 601, 850 P.2d 749, 752 (1993)); Brown v. Matthews Mortuary, Inc., 118 Idaho 830, 834, 801 P.2d 37 (1990). And, Idaho courts have long acknowledged that only "very extreme conduct" will support an award of damages. Hatfield v. Max Rouse & Sons Northwest, 100 Idaho 840, 850, 606 P.2d 944 (1980). "To qualify as 'extreme and outrageous' the defendant's conduct must be more than merely objectionable or unreasonable." Alderson v. Bonner, 132 P.3d at 1268. "To be actionable, the conduct must be so extreme as to 'arouse an average member of the community to resentment against the defendant' and 'must be more than unreasonable, unkind, or unfair.'" Mortensen, 235 P.3d at 397 (citing 86 C.J.S. *Torts* § 74 (2009)) (held that "[m]erely exercising a legal right does not satisfy the outrageousness element of an emotional distress claim"). See also Johnson, 210 P.3d at 572. "Whether a plaintiff has suffered the requisite severe distress is ordinarily a question for the jury, but Idaho appellate courts have not hesitated to hold the evidence insufficient as a matter of law when it clearly did not describe mental turmoil of sufficient gravity." Alderson, 132 P.3d at 1269. See also

Weinstein v. Prudential Property and Casualty Ins. Co., 149 Idaho 299, 233 P.3d 1221 (2010) ("The intensity and duration of the distress are factors to be considered in determining its severity. Severe distress must be proved; but in many cases the extreme and outrageous character of the defendant's conduct is in itself important evidence that the distress has existed"). Unlike a claim for negligent infliction of emotional distress, a claim for intentional infliction of emotional distress does not require a showing of physical injury or manifestation. Curtis, 123 Idaho at 601, 850 P.2d at 752. Because this tort frequently involves a series of acts over time, the concept of continuing tort may apply, holding the statute of limitations in abeyance until all of the tortious acts cease. Id. at 604, 850 P.2d at 755.

In Zaleha v. Rosholt, Robertson & Tucker, Chtd., 131 Idaho 254, 953 P.2d 1363 (1998), the Idaho Supreme Court addressed the issue of causation in an intentional infliction of emotional distress claim. In Zaleha, plaintiff sued her husband's former employer for intentional infliction of emotional distress, alleging that the employer had caused her husband severe emotional distress by the manner in which they dismissed him from his employment and that this, in turn, inflicted severe emotional distress upon her. In upholding the trial court's dismissal of plaintiff's claims, the Idaho Supreme Court noted that "defendants did not direct any of their conduct toward [plaintiff]. If she suffered injury, it was indirect injury based on her emotional reaction to the conduct of the defendants toward [her husband]." Accordingly, the Court held that "the connection between the defendants' conduct and any injury [plaintiff] suffered is too tenuous to impose a duty on the defendants." Id. at 256.

Where a claim for intentional infliction of emotional distress arises out of alleged false speech, defenses to defamation may apply. In Steele v. Spokesman-Review, 138 Idaho 249, 61 P.3d 606 (2003), the Idaho Supreme Court concluded that statements published by a newspaper article were either true or, if false, not material deviations from the truth. Steele, 138 Idaho 249, 61 P.3d at 610. The Court further concluded that since the plaintiff was a public figure and failed to show a false statement made with malice, his claim for intentional infliction of emotional distress failed, as a matter of law. Id.

C. Interference with Economic Advantage

Idaho recognizes a cause of action for tortious interference with economic advantage. In order to establish a prima facie case, the plaintiff must prove: (1) the existence of a valid economic expectancy; (2) knowledge of the expectancy on the part of the interferer; (3) intentional interference inducing termination of the expectancy; (4) the interference was wrongful by some measure beyond the fact of the interference itself (i.e., that the defendant interfered for an improper purpose or improper means); and (5) resulting damage to the plaintiff whose expectancy has been disrupted. Wesco Autobody Supply, Inc. v. Ernest, 149 Idaho 881, 893, 243 P.3d 1069, 1081 (2010). See also Highland Enterprises, Inc. v. Barker, 133 Idaho 330, 338, 986 P.2d 996, 1004 (1999) (same); Cantwell v. Boise, 146 Idaho 127, 137-138, 191 P.3d 205, 215-216 (2009) ("To establish a claim for intentional interference with a prospective economic advantage, Cantwell must show (1) the existence of a valid economic expectancy, (2) knowledge of the expectancy on the part of the interferer, (3) intentional interference inducing termination of the expectancy, (4) the interference was wrongful by some measure beyond the fact of the interference itself, and (5) resulting damage to the plaintiff whose expectancy has been disrupted"); (Justmed, Inc. v. Byce, 2007 WL 2479887 * 12 (D.Idaho, Aug. 29, 2007); Rudd v. Mingo Tribal Preservation Trust, 2007 WL 1455878 *6 (D.Idaho, March 29, 2007); Downey Chiropractic Clinic v. Nampa Restaurant Corp., 127 Idaho 283, 285-86, 900 P.2d 191, 193-94 (1995) (citing Idaho First Nat'l Bank v. Bliss Valley Foods, Inc., 121 Idaho 266, 286, 824 P.2d 841, 861 (1991)). The knowledge element is "satisfied by actual knowledge of the prospective [economic advantage] or by knowledge of facts which would lead a reasonable person to believe that such interest exists." Highland Enterprises, 133 Idaho at 338-39, 986 P.2d at 1004-05. In proving the intent element, the plaintiff may show that the interference is intentional if the actor desires to bring it about or if he knows that the interference is certain or substantially certain to occur as a result of his action. Id. at 340, 986 P.2d at 1006. The wrongfulness element may be shown by proving that either: "(1) [t]he defendant had an improper purpose or objective to harm the plaintiff; or (2) [t]he defendant used a wrongful means to cause injury to the prospective business relationship." Downey, 127 Idaho at 286, 900 P.2d at 194. Once the plaintiff has established a prima facie claim, the burden shifts to the defendant to establish a privilege. Yoakum v. Hartford Fire Ins. Co., 129 Idaho 171, 178-79, 923 P.2d 416, 423-24 (1996); Idaho First Nat'l Bank, 121 Idaho at 286, 824 P.2d at 861.

Additionally, a claim for tortious interference can be based on interference with a contract. The plaintiff must show: (1) the existence of a contract; (2) knowledge of the contract on the part of the defendant; (3) an intentional interference by the defendant that causes a breach of the contract; and (4) injury to the plaintiff as a result of the breach. Northwest Bec-Corp v. Home Living Service, 136 Idaho 835, 841, 41 P.3d 263, 269 (2002). See also Rudd, 2007 WL 1455878 * 4; Thirsty's L.L.C. v. Tolerico, 143 Idaho 48, 137 P.3d 435, 437 (2006). However, it is clearly established in Idaho that an employer cannot be held liable for tortious interference with its own employment contracts. Thomas, M.D. v. Medical Center Physicians, P.A., 138 Idaho 200, 61 P.3d 557, 564 (2002).

Liability under these tort theories is not unlimited. In Zaleha v. Rosholt, Robertson & Tucker, Chtd., 131 Idaho 254, 953 P.2d 1363 (1998) for example, the plaintiff sued her husband's former employer for interference with economic advantage, alleging that the employer's dismissal of her husband "intentionally interfered with her employment at a real estate brokerage." Zaleha, 131 Idaho at 255. The Idaho Supreme Court dismissed her claim, holding that "the connection between the defendants' conduct and any injury [plaintiff] suffered is too tenuous to impose a duty on the defendants." Id. at 256.

D. Prima Facie Tort

No cases.

V. OTHER ISSUES

A. Statute of Limitations

In Idaho, the statute of limitations for libel and slander is two years. See Idaho Code § 5-219. Idaho Code § 6-702 codifies the single publication rule, which provides that a plaintiff shall have no more than one cause of action for libel or slander or invasion of privacy or another tort founded upon any single publication or utterance. "Accrual of a cause of action occurs, and therefore the statute of limitations begins to run, 'when the wrongful act or omission results in damages. The cause of action accrues even though the full extent of the injury is not then known or predictable.'" McCabe v. Craven, 145 Idaho 954, 188 P.3d 896, 898 (2008) (citing Wallace v. Kato, 549 U.S. 384, 127 S.Ct. 1091, 1095 (2007)).

B. Notice of Tort Claim

Before suing a State of Idaho employee for alleged defamatory statements made in the course and scope of his public employment, the plaintiff must file a notice of tort claim with the Secretary of State. Anderson v. Spalding, 137 Idaho 509, 50 P.3d 1004, 1013 (2002). See also Driggers v. Grafe, 148 Idaho 295, 221 P.3d 521, 523 (2009) ("failure to comply with the notice requirement bars a suit regardless of how legitimate it might be"); Swisher v. Collins, 2008 WL 687305 at * 30 (defamation claim against state employees barred under I.C. § 6-905 for failure to file notice of claim); Gibson v. Ada County, 142 Idaho 746, 133 P.3d 1211, 1217 (2006) ("Prior to bringing a suit for tort against a political subdivision or their employee for any act or omission arising out the scope of employment, a party must file a notice of the claim with the secretary or clerk of the political subdivision. I.C. §§ 6-906, 6-908 (2003). The notice must be filed within 180 days of when the claim arose or reasonably should have been discovered, whichever is later. I.C. §§ 6-906, 6-908"). In addition, defamation claims against federal agencies cannot be asserted under the Federal Tort Claims Act. Swisher v. Collins, 2008 WL 687305 * 28.

In Hoffer v. City of Boise, 151 Idaho 400, 257 P.3d 1226 (2011), the Idaho Supreme Court clarified that "the plain language of I.C. § 6-904(3) [Idaho Tort Claim Act] exempts governmental entities from liability for tortious interference with contract rights and defamation." 257 P.3d at 1229. Such immunity does not apply to governmental employees, however, if an allegation of malice and/or criminal intent is made by the plaintiff. Id.

In Van v. Portneuf Medical Center, 147 Idaho 552, 212 P.3d 982 (2009), the Idaho Supreme Court held that a claim made pursuant to Idaho's Whistleblower Act (I.C. § 6-2101 *et seq.*) was not governed by the Idaho Tort Claims Act and, therefore, not subject to its notice requirements.

C. Jurisdiction

Long-arm jurisdiction is governed by Idaho Code § 5-514. See Smalley v. Kaiser, 130 Idaho 909, 912, 950 P.2d 1248, 1251 (In order for an Idaho court to exert jurisdiction over an out-of-state defendant, the Supreme Court of Idaho has imposed a two-part test. First, the act giving rise to the cause of action must fall within Idaho's long-arm statute and second, the constitutional standards of due process must be met."). Although no defamation claim has dealt with this issue, foreign defendants who libel or slander an Idaho plaintiff in Idaho would arguably be subject to Idaho's jurisdiction under Idaho Code § 5-514(b) (long arm jurisdiction applies to anyone who commits "tortious act within this state"). See also Houghton Farms, Inc. v. Johnson, 119 Idaho 72, 803 P.2d 978 (1990) (adopting the approach of Burger King Corp. v. Rudzewicz, 471 U.S. 462 (1985)); Schneider v. Sverdsten Logging Co., 104 Idaho 210, 657 P.2d 1078 (1983) (fact that injury occurred in Idaho in an allegedly tortious manner sufficient to invoke jurisdiction under Idaho Code § 5-514(b)).

D. Worker's Compensation Exclusivity

The Idaho Worker's Compensation Act provides employees a definite remedy for injuries arising out of and in the course of employment. I.C. § 72-201. "This relief is provided 'to the exclusion of every other remedy, proceeding, or compensation, except as it is otherwise provided in the worker's compensation scheme." Blake v. Starr, 146 Idaho 847, 849, 203 P.3d 1246, 1248 (2009) (finding contractor exempt from liability under I.C. § 72-209(3) in suit brought by subcontractor injured on the job). **"'[A] person injured in the course of employment has *only* one claim against the employer, and that**

claim is under the Worker's Compensation Act, not a tort action.'" Gerdon v. Rydalch, 153 Idaho 237, 280 P.3d 740, 745 (2012) (citing Hansen v. Estate of Harvey, 119 Idaho 333, 336, 806 P.2d 426, 429 (1991)).

E. Pleading Requirements

Idaho is a notice pleading state. A pleading which sets forth a claim for relief must contain: "(1) if the court has limited jurisdiction, a short and plain statement of the grounds upon which the court's jurisdiction depends, (2) a short and plain statement of the claims showing that the pleader is entitled to relief, and (3) a demand for judgment for the relief to which the pleader deems himself or herself entitled." See Idaho Code § 5-335. See also I.R.C.P. 8(a)(1); Mortensen, 149 Idaho at 443, 235 P.3d at 393 ("The key to a valid pleading is that it must put the opposing party on notice of the claims against it"). In libel and slander actions, "it is not necessary to state in the complaint any extrinsic facts for the purpose of showing the application to the plaintiff of the defamatory matter out of which the cause of action arose; but it is sufficient to state, generally, that the same was published or spoken concerning the plaintiff." Idaho R. Civ. P. 9(i). If the action is for recovery due to personal injury, the claim for relief should not specify the amount of damages claimed, but rather should contain a general allegation of damage and state that the damages claimed are within the jurisdictional limits of the court. See Idaho Code § 5-335; Idaho R. Civ. P. 9(g). Idaho Code § 6-1603 limits noneconomic damages for "personal injury" to $250,000; provided, however, that the cap shall increase or decrease in accordance with the percentage increase or decrease of the average annual wage as computed pursuant to Idaho Code § 72-409(2). Idaho law specifically provides that punitive damages may not be alleged in the prayer of the Complaint. See Idaho Code § 6-1604(2). Rather, the plaintiff must bring a pre-trial motion to amend the Complaint to include a punitive damages claim once adequate discovery has been conducted to demonstrate that there is a "reasonable likelihood of proving facts at trial sufficient to support an award of punitive damages." Idaho Code § 6-1604(2). No judgment for punitive damages shall exceed the greater of two hundred fifty thousand ($250,000) or an amount which is three (3) times the compensatory damages contained in such judgment. I.C. § 6-1604(3). If a case is tried to a jury, the jury shall not be informed of this limitation. I.C. § 6-1604(3).

The Idaho Supreme Court has established a schedule of filing fees for all pleadings, along with designated categories of pleadings. These categories and corresponding fees should be indicated on the first page of each pleading.

SURVEY OF IDAHO EMPLOYMENT PRIVACY LAW

Debora K Kristensen
Givens Pursley, LLP
601 West Bannock Street
Boise, Idaho 83701
www.givenspursley.com
Telephone: (208) 388-1200; Facsimile: (208) 388-1300

(With Developments Reported Through **November 1, 2012**)

GENERAL COMMENTS

The state of Idaho is divided into seven judicial districts, with each district court maintaining a separate magistrate division. Idaho's appellate system consists of two courts: the Court of Appeals(4 judges sit with no less than a 3-judge panel) and the Supreme Court (5 justices). Idaho courts are likely to follow the restatement of the law, and in particular the Restatement (Second) of Torts, in the absence of pertinent Idaho statutory or case law. **The Idaho state court system is increasingly moving towards on-line access to its dockets. For more information go to www.idcourts.us/repository/ start.d.**

The Idaho Rules of Civil Procedure, specifically Rule 26(b)(4), deal with trial preparation and experts. Subsection (A)(i) was revised concerning discovery of facts known and opinions held by experts expected to testify, otherwise discoverable under provisions of subsection (b)(1) of the rule and acquired or developed in anticipation of litigation or for trial, may now be obtained by interrogatory and/or deposition including the following: "A complete statement of all opinions to be expressed and the basis and reasons therefore; the data or other information considered by the witness in forming the opinions; any exhibits to be used as a summary of or support for the opinions; any qualifications of the witness, including a list of all publications authored by the witness within the preceding ten years; the compensation to be paid for the testimony; and a listing of any other cases in which the witness has testified as an expert at trial or by deposition within the preceding four years."

If you are involved in a case in federal court in Idaho, be certain to obtain a copy of the Local Federal Rules of Procedure. They are very detailed and impose many time limits with respect to discovery and other procedural mattes, including the disclosure of witness lists and exhibits thirty days before trial. In addition, be prepared to file all material electronically through the court's Electronic Case Filing ("ECF") system. For more information about the federal court's local rules and ECF system, go to its website at www.id.uscourts.gov.

SIGNIFICANT DEVELOPMENTS SINCE THE 2012 SURVEY

In Bollinger v. Fall River Rural Electric Cooperative, Inc., 152 Idaho ___, 272 P.3d 1263 (2012), a long-time at -will employee was terminated as part of a larger reduction in workforce. On the day of her termination, the employee was given a severance agreement to take home and review, escorted to her office and told to gather her personal items. She was given thirty minutes to do so and two supervisors helped her box her belongings. The employee sued the employer for breach of express and implied contract, retaliatory discharge and wrongful termination, and negligent and intentional infliction of emotional distress. The trial court granted summary judgment to the employer on all claims, and the employee appealed. On appeal, the Idaho Supreme Court affirmed the dismissal of all of the employee's claims, reiterating that "employment in Idaho is presumed to be at will unless the employee is hired pursuant to a contract that states a fixed term or limits the reasons for discharge." Id., 152 Idaho at __, 272 P.3d at 1269. As to the intentional infliction of emotional distress claim, the Court noted that such a claim required action that was more than "unjustifiable, but rather must rise to the level of 'atrocious' behavior 'beyond all possible bounds of decency.'" Id., 512 Idaho at ___, 272 P.3d at 1274. In this case, the Court found that "Bollinger was an at-will employee, so the simple fact that she was discharged without cause cannot constitute extreme and outrageous behavior. Further, although Bollinger's discharge was abrupt and the time she was given to pack her office relatively rushed, such conduct is not atrocious or beyond all possible bounds of decency. In fact, escorting an employee who has just been terminated from the building in a timely fashion is an acceptable means to minimize disruption in the workplace." Accordingly, the Court affirmed the trial court's dismissal of all of the employee's claims.

I. GENERAL LAW OF PRIVACY

A. Legal Basis of Privacy Claims

The Idaho Supreme Court recognized the right to privacy, and adopted Dean Prosser's approach to the tort of invasion of privacy, in Peterson v. Idaho First Nat'l Bank, 83 Idaho 578, 367 P.2d 284 (1961). The Court identified four categories of invasion of privacy: (1) intrusion upon the plaintiff's seclusion or solitude, or into his private affairs; (2) public disclosure of embarrassing facts about the plaintiff; (3) publicity which places the plaintiff in a false light in the public eye; and (4) appropriation, for the defendant's advantage, of the plaintiff's name or likeness. Id. at 583, 367 P.2d at 287 (citing Privacy, William L. Prosser, 48 CAL. L. REV. 383, 389 (1960)). See also Hoskins v. Howard, 132 Idaho 311, 971 P.2d 1135 (1998); Baker v. Burlington Northern, Inc., 99 Idaho 688, 691, 587 P.2d 829, 832 (1978); Nation v. State, Dept. of Correction, 144 Idaho 177, 158 P.3d 953 (2007). There are no statutes in Idaho which give rise to a civil cause of action for invasion of privacy, and the Idaho courts consideration of the issue is not rooted in a constitutional analysis. Rather, such an analysis is solely based on Dean Prosser's thesis.

The Ninth Circuit Court of Appeals has decided two Idaho cases that could have implications for employers with respect to assertions of religious rights and sexual orientation.

In Olsen v. Idaho State Board of Medicine, et al., 363 F.3d 916 (9th Cir. 2004), the Ninth Circuit Court of Appeals addressed Idaho's Free Exercise of Religion Act, I.C. § 73-402(2). In Olsen, the plaintiff alleged that the Idaho Board of Medicine had wrongfully denied the reinstatement of her physician's assistant license because of her Mormon religion, in violation of the Free Exercise of Religion Act. The court held that the Free Exercise of Religion Act did not apply retroactively to a claim of religious discrimination alleged by a physician's assistant, where the alleged incidents occurred prior to February 1, 2001, the enactment date of the Act. Id. at 930.

In Peterson v. Hewlett-Packard Co., 358 F.3d 599 (9th Cir. 2004), an employee was discharged for insubordination, for refusing to take down posters in his work area that cited scriptural passages criticizing homosexuals. Hewlett-Packard argued that the employee's posters violated the company's workplace diversity campaign, which was intended to promote tolerance in the workplace. The Ninth Circuit Court of Appeals upheld the termination at the summary judgment stage, holding that the termination decision was not disparate treatment on the basis of the employee's religion. Id. at 605. In so holding, the court concluded that the company was not impermissibly restricting the employee's religious beliefs but rather was merely enforcing its policies against harassment and toward diversity and tolerance in the workplace. Id.

B. Causes of Action

1. ***Misappropriation/Right of Publicity.*** The tort of misappropriation was first adopted by the Idaho Supreme Court in 1961, and requires that a plaintiff demonstrate that an aspect of his or her identity, name or likeness was appropriated by the defendant for his or her own advantage. Peterson v. Idaho First Nat'l Bank, supra. Since 1961, however, no reported Idaho cases have considered this tort.

2. ***False Light.*** The tort of false light requires some public disclosure of a falsity or fiction concerning the plaintiff. Baker v. Burlington Northern, Inc., 99 Idaho at 691, 587 P.2d at 832 (citations omitted); Peterson, 83 Idaho at 583, 367 P.2d at 287. Indeed, although the Court in Hoskins v. Howard, supra, noted that the "precise elements of this cause of action are unclear," quoting Baker, 99 Idaho at 691, 587 P.2d at 832, it did reaffirm that there must be some "public disclosure of falsity or fiction concerning the plaintiff." In Holbrook v. Chase, 12 Media L. Rep. 1732, 1736 (Idaho 4th Dist. 1985), the court held that when a false light claim "rests upon the same acts as the libel and slander claims, it is subject to the same immunities and defenses as the libel and slander" claims. More than an immaterial deviation from the truth is required. "Where the publication is free from material falsehood, recovery under this cause of action may not be had." Steele v. Spokesman-Review, 138 Idaho 249, 61 P.3d 606, 610, 31 Media L. Rep. 1412 (2002). The Court in Clark v. Spokesman-Review,144 Idaho 427, 163 P.3d 216, 35 Media L. Rep. 1737 (2007) adopted the same test for false light that was illustrated in Baker. Then the Clark court explained that "[w]hen a communication is constitutionally privileged, a plaintiff must prove actual malice by clear and convincing evidence on his invasion of privacy claims." Id., 144 Idaho at 433, 163 P.3d at 222.

3. ***Publication of Private Facts.*** To state a claim for invasion of privacy through publication of private facts claims, a plaintiff must plead: (1) public disclosure; (2) of private, not public, facts; and (3) the matter publicized was highly offensive to a reasonable person. See Baker v. Burlington Northern, Inc., 99 Idaho at 691, 587 P.2d at 832 (setting forth elements of claim); Peterson, 83 Idaho at 583, 367 P.2d at 287; Taylor v. K.T.V.B., Inc., 96 Idaho 202, 525 P.2d 984 (1974). A claim for publication of private facts does not require that the matter disclosed be false. Baker, 99 Idaho at 691, 587 P.2d at 832; Peterson, 83 Idaho at 583, 367 P.2d at 287. See also Uranga v. Federated Publications, Inc., 138 Idaho 550, 67 P.3d 29, 32-33, 31 Media L. Rep. 1536 (2003) (claim based upon newspaper's publication of embarrassing private facts). In Hoskins v. Howard, supra, the Idaho Supreme Court reiterated that, to establish a claim for public disclosure of private facts, "the areas intruded upon must be, and be entitled to be, private." Id. at 317. See also Nation v. State, Dept. of Correction, supra (applying the same three part test from Baker). The Court further explained, "for a conversation to be entitled to privacy, the speaker must have a subjective expectation that the conversation will remain private. That expectation must also be one which society is willing to accept as reasonable. In other words, the expectation of privacy must be objectively reasonable under the circumstances." Id. Applying this standard and rejecting the majority of courts who have

held that cordless telephone users have no reasonable expectation of privacy, the Court held that a material issue of fact existed as to whether plaintiffs' had a legitimate expectation that their cordless telephone conversation would remain private. Id. In cases involving speech by the press, the interests of the plaintiff in his privacy are balanced against the interest of the press in reporting information contained in records open to the public. Uranga, 138 Idaho at 555, 67 P.3d at 34.

4. ***Intrusion.*** Idaho courts have held that "liability for a claim of invasion of privacy by intrusion requires: (1) an intentional intrusion by the defendant; (2) into a matter, which the plaintiff has a right to keep private; (3) by the use of a method, which is objectionable to the reasonable person." Jensen v. State, 139 Idaho 57, 62, 72 P.3d 897, 902 (2003) (citations omitted). "There is liability for such an intrusion if it would be highly offensive to a reasonable person. An intrusion may occur without a physical invasion, for example, as by eavesdropping by means of wire-tapping, or by persistent and unwanted phone calling. Clearly, however, there must be something in the nature of a prying or intrusion. Also, that which is intruded into must be, and be entitled to be, private." O'Neil v. Schuckardt, 112 Idaho 472, 477, 733 P.2d 693, 698 (1986), appeal after remand, 116 Idaho 507, 777 P.2d 729 (1989). In Hoskins v. Howard, 132 Idaho 311, 971 P.2d 1135 (1998), the Idaho Supreme Court reiterated that "[t]o be actionable, the prying or intrusion into the plaintiff's private affairs must be of a type which is offensive to a reasonable person" and "the areas intruded upon must be, and be entitled to be, private." Id. at 132 Idaho at 317, 971 P.2d at 1147. Based on this finding, the Court held that a material issue of fact existed as to whether plaintiffs had a legitimate expectation that their cordless telephone conversation would remain private. See also Uranga v. Federated Publications, Inc., supra (2003) (holding that a plaintiff does not have a legitimate expectation of privacy in a statement about his sexuality contained in a 40-year-old public court record); Alderson v. Bonner, 142 Idaho 733, 132 P.3d 1261 (Ct. App. 2006) (holding there was sufficient evidence to allow the jury to decide if a videotaper invaded privacy of young woman by intruding upon her seclusion or solitude or into her private affairs).

C. Other Privacy-related Actions

Unless specifically exempted, any injury arising out of and in the course of employment must be submitted to worker's compensation. The Idaho Supreme Court has noted that an employee's state tort claims against his or her employer are "abolished under I.C. § 72-209, which abolishes all such claims in favor of exclusive liability and jurisdiction under the Worker's Compensation Act. DeMoss v. City of Coeur d'Alene, 118 Idaho 176, 795 P.2d 875 (1990) (intentional infliction of emotional distress claim dismissed). See also Yeend v. UPS, Inc., 104 Idaho 333, 659 P.2d 87 (1982) (emotional distress as a result of fall at work does not give rise to liability for tort of intentional infliction of emotional distress because such claim is compensable only under the worker's compensation scheme).

1. ***Intentional Infliction of Emotional Distress.*** In order to recover for intentional infliction of emotional distress, the plaintiff must prove that: (1) the defendant's conduct was intentional or reckless; (2) the defendant's conduct was extreme and outrageous; (3) there was a causal connection between the wrongful conduct and the emotional distress; and (4) the emotional distress was severe. **Bollinger v. Fall River Rural Electric Cooperative, Inc., 152 Idaho at __, 272 P.3d at 1274**; Spence v. Howell, 126 Idaho 763, 774, 890 P.2d 714, 725 (1995) (citing Curtis v. Firth, 123 Idaho 598, 601, 850 P.2d 749, 752 (1993)). See also Mortensen v. Stewart Title Guaranty Co., 149 Idaho 437, 235 P.3d 387, 396 (2010); Johnson v. McPhee, 147 Idaho 455, 464, 210 P.3d 563, 572 (2009); Estate of Becker v. Callahan, 140 Idaho 522, 527, 96 P.3d 623, 628 (2004) (evidence did not establish extreme or outrageous conduct in attorney's drafting of a will). This four- part test was affirmed by the Idaho Supreme Court in McKinley v. Guaranty Nat. Ins. Co., 144 Idaho 247, 159 P.3d 884 (2007). The McKinley court explained that "[t]he district court acts as a gatekeeper for IIED claims, weeding out weak causes of action." Id., 159 P.3d at 891. In McKinley the court dismissed the IIED claim because there was no evidence that the defendant automobile liability insurer acted intentionally or recklessly in investigating plaintiff's accident.

Idaho courts have long acknowledged that only "very extreme conduct" will support an award of damages. Hatfield v. Max Rouse & Sons Northwest, 100 Idaho 840, 850, 606 P.2d 944 (1980). See also Brown v. Matthews Mortuary, Inc., 118 Idaho 830, 834, 801 P.2d 37, 41 (1990) (the loss of a corpse was not extreme or outrageous). "To be actionable, the conduct must be so extreme as to 'arouse an average member of the community to resentment against the defendant' and 'must be more than unreasonable, unkind, or unfair." Mortensen, 235 P.3d at 397 (citing 86 C.J.S. Torts § 74 (2009)) (held that "[m]erely exercising a legal right does not satisfy the outrageousness element of an emotional distress claim"). See also Johnson, 210 P.3d at 572. Also, unlike a claim for negligent infliction of emotional distress, a claim for intentional infliction of emotional distress does not require a showing of physical injury or manifestation. Curtis, 123 Idaho at 601, 850 P.2d at 752. Because this tort frequently involves a series of acts over time, the concept of continuing tort may apply, holding the statute of limitations in abeyance until all of the tortious acts cease. Id. at 604, 850 P.2d at 755.

In Zaleha v. Rosholt, Robertson & Tucker, Chtd., 131 Idaho 254, 953 P.2d 1363 (1998), the Idaho Supreme Court addressed the issue of causation in an intentional infliction of emotional distress claim. In Zaleha, plaintiff sued her husband's former employer for intentional infliction of emotional distress, alleging that the employer had caused her husband severe emotional distress by the manner in which they dismissed him from his employment and that this, in turn, inflicted severe emotional distress upon on her. In upholding the trial court's dismissal of plaintiff's claims, the Idaho Supreme Court noted that "defendants did not direct any of their conduct toward [plaintiff]. If she suffered injury, it was indirect injury based on her emotional reaction to the conduct of the defendants toward [her husband]." Accordingly, the Court held that "the connection between the defendants' conduct and any injury [plaintiff] suffered is too tenuous to impose a duty on the defendants." Id. at 256, 953 P.2d at 1365.

In Steele v. Spokesman-Review, 138 Idaho 249, 61 P.3d 606 (2002), the Idaho Supreme Court concluded that alleged statements published by the defendant in a newspaper article were either true or, if false, not material deviations from the truth. Id. at 253, 61 P.3d at 610. The Court further concluded that since the plaintiff was a public figure and failed to show a false statement made with malice, his claim for intentional infliction of emotional distress failed, as a matter of law. Id.

2. ***Interference With Prospective Economic Advantage.*** Idaho recognizes a cause of action for tortious interference with economic advantage. In Zaleha v. Rosholt-Robertson & Tucker, Chtd., supra, for example, the plaintiff also sued her husband's former employer for interference with economic advantage, alleging that the employer's dismissal of her husband "intentionally interfered with her employment at a real estate brokerage." Id. at 255, 61 P.2d at 1364. The Idaho Supreme Court dismissed her claim, holding that the connection between the defendants' conduct and any injury [plaintiff] suffered is too tenuous to impose a duty on the defendants." Id. at 256, 61 P.2d at 1364.

In order to establish a prima facie case of intentional interference with a prospective economic advantage, the plaintiff must prove: (1) the existence of a valid economic expectancy; (2) knowledge of the expectancy on the part of the interferer; (3) intentional interference inducing termination of the expectancy; (4) the interference was wrongful by some measure beyond the fact of the interference itself (i.e., that the defendant interfered for an improper purpose or improper means); and (5) resulting damage to the plaintiff whose expectancy has been disrupted. See Wesco Autobody Supply, Inc. v. Ernest, 149 Idaho 881, 893, 243 P.3d 1069, 1081 (2010). See also Highland Enterprises, Inc. v. Barker, 133 Idaho 330, 338, 986 P.2d 996, 1004 (1999) (citations omitted); Downey Chiropractic Clinic v. Nampa Restaurant Corp., 127 Idaho 283, 285-86, 900 P.2d 191, 193-94 (1995) (citing Idaho First Nat'l Bank v. Bliss Valley Foods, Inc., 121 Idaho 266, 286, 824 P.2d 841, 861 (1991)). The knowledge element is "satisfied by actual knowledge of the prospective [economic advantage] or by knowledge of facts which would lead a reasonable person to believe that such interest exists." Highland Enterprises, 133 Idaho at 338-39, 986 P.2d at 1004-05. See also Wesco, 149 Idaho at 894, 243 P.3d at 1082. In proving the intent element, the plaintiff may show that the interference is intentional if the actor desires to bring it about or if he knows that the interference is certain or substantially certain to occur as a result of his action. Wesco, 149 Idaho at 894, 243 P.3d at 1082. The wrongfulness element may be shown by proving that either: "(1) [t]he defendant had an improper purpose or objective to harm the plaintiff; or (2) [t]he defendant used a wrongful means to cause injury to the prospective business relationship." Wesco, 149 Idaho at 893, 243 P.3d at 1081. "[A]n enforceable contract need not be shown to exist, just a valid exonomic expectancy." Id. Once the plaintiff has established a prima facie claim, the burden shifts to the defendant to establish a privilege. Yoakum v. Hartford Fire Ins. Co., 129 Idaho 171, 178-79, 923 P.2d 416, 423-24 (1996); Idaho First Nat'l Bank, 121 Idaho at 286, 824 P.2d at 861.

A claim for tortious interference also can be based on interference with a contract. The plaintiff must show: (1) the existence of a contract; (2) knowledge of the contract on the part of the defendant; (3) an intentional interference by the defendant that causes a breach of the contract; and (4) injury to the plaintiff as a result of the breach. Northwest Bec-Corp v. Home Living Service, 136 Idaho 835, 841, 41 P.3d 263, 269 (2002). See also Thirsty's L.L.C. v. Tolerico, 143 Idaho 48, 137 P.3d 435, 437 (2006) (citing Barlow v. Int'l Harvester Co., 95 Idaho 881, 893, 522 P.2d 1102, 1115 (1974)). However, it is clearly established in Idaho that an employer cannot be held liable for tortious interference with its own employment contracts. Thomas v. Medical Center Physicians, P.A., 138 Idaho 200, 207, 61 P.3d 557, 564 (2002).

3. **Prima Facie Tort.** No cases directly on point.

II. EMPLOYER TESTING OF EMPLOYEES

A. Psychological or Personality Testing

No applicable statutes or case law.

B. Drug Testing

1. ***Common Law and Statutes.*** The Idaho Employer Alcohol and Drug-Free Workplace Act allows private employers to test employees and prospective employees for the presence of drugs as a condition of hiring or continued employment, provided the employer satisfies all of the act's requirements. See I.C. §§ 72-1701 - 72-1717. One of the requirements under the act is that the employer provide a written policy on drug testing, which states the type of tests an employee may be subject to, and that a violation of the policy may result in termination of employment. See I.C. § 72-1705.

For example, in Smith v. Zero Defects, Inc., 132 Idaho 881, 980 P.2d 545 (1999), a private employer instituted a zero tolerance drug policy, a violation of which was upheld as "misconduct" sufficient to disqualify an employee from receiving unemployment compensation. The act also details the procedure for collecting samples and testing employees for drugs. See I.C. § 72-1704.

The Federal Drug-Free Workplace Act of 1988 applies to most federal contractors and grantees of federal agencies and requires them to provide a drug-free workplace. See 41 U.S.C. § 701 et seq.

2. ***Private Employers***. If an employee is fired for using drugs during his day off, it is necessary that the company policy make it clear that drugs cannot be used outside of work. See Merriott v. Shearer Lumber Products, 127 Idaho 620, 903 P.2d 1317 (1995) (employee tested positive for marijuana and admitted use on day off). The Merriott court stated that because the employer failed to communicate its expectations they could not require the employee to "comply with its uncommunicated expectations." Id. at 622, 903 P.2d at 1320. In Merriott the key question was if the employee was fired for misconduct in relation to eligibly of unemployment benefits. The employer's compliance with the Idaho Employer Alcohol and Drug-Free Workplace Act (the act) was not raised in the Merriott, and the court found that the employee was not fired for misconduct and was eligible for unemployment benefits. Id.

However, it is important to note that just because an employer does not comply with the act it does not mean that an employee that is discharged for drug use will be eligible for unemployment benefits. Desilet v. Glass Doctor, 142 Idaho 655, 132 P.3d 412, 415-16 (2006). "The Act establishes drug and alcohol testing guidelines. Compliance with the Act, however, is voluntary and if complied with, provides the benefit that an employee who is discharged for failing a drug test, will be deemed to have committed misconduct under the employment as defined in I.C. § 72-1366." Id.

3. ***Public Employers.*** Public entities may conduct drug testing of employees under the Idaho Private Employer Alcohol and Drug-Free Workplace Act. See I.C. § 72-1715.

C. Medical Testing

1. ***Common Law and Statutes.*** No applicable Idaho statutes or case law. However, Idaho employers are subject to the provisions of the Idaho Human Rights Act, I.C. § 67-5901, et seq., and the Americans with Disabilities Act of 1990 ("ADA"), 42 U.S.C. § 12101, et seq. The ADA allows employers to make an offer of employment conditioned on the results of a medical examination. However, such an offer must meet the following requirements: (1) the examination must be given to all entering employees, not just those whom the employer may believe are disabled; (2) the results must be kept confidential; and (3) such an examination may not be used to discriminate against individuals with disabilities, unless the results make the individuals unqualified for the particular job. 42 U.S.C. § 12112(d)(3). A physical examination includes any kind of medical or psychological test that is done for the purpose of measuring biological condition or response. After a worker is employed, a physical examination can be required only if it is job-related and consistent with business necessity. 42 U.S.C. § 12112 (d)(4)(A).

2. ***Private Employers.*** No cases.

3. ***Public Employers.*** No cases.

D. Polygraph Tests

The Idaho Code prohibits employers, other than law enforcement agencies, from requiring as a condition of employment or continuation of employment that a person take a polygraph test or any form of a lie detector test. See I.C. §§ 44-903 and 44-904.

E. Fingerprinting

No cases.

III. SEARCHES

The only Idaho cases dealing with searches are those in the criminal context. These cases hold that a person's legitimate and reasonable expectation of privacy, as it relates to warrantless police searches, is protected by the Fourth Amendment of the United States Constitution and Article 1, Section 17 of the Idaho Constitution. State v. Limberhand, 117 Idaho 456, 459, 788 P.2d 857, 860 (Ct. App. 1990). In considering this issue a court must determine whether "an actual, subjective expectation of privacy" was manifested, and whether that expectation, when viewed objectively, "was justified under the circumstances." Id. The crossover impact of these cases upon civil privacy claims is yet to be determined, but one likely application is the determination as to in what physical areas or environments one might have a "reasonable expectation of privacy." Employers providing prior notice, through an employee policy, may have greater rights to require searches than other employers who have not given notice. Thus, an employer intending to preserve the right to search their premises should institute a policy detailing that such searches may take place and, therefore, an employee should not retain any expectation that areas within the workplace are private.

While Idaho courts are at liberty to find greater protection under Article 1, Section 17 of the Idaho Constitution than is afforded under the Fourth Amendment of the United States Constitution, it is not likely that they will because the Idaho Supreme Court has instructed that "such consistency makes sense to the police and the public." State v. Donato, 135 Idaho 469, 471, 20 P.3d 5, 7 (2001) (citing State v. Charpentier, 131 Idaho 649, 653, 962 P.2d 1033, 1037 (1998)).

A. Employee's Person

No cases.

B. Employee's Work Area

There are no Idaho cases or statutes on point. However, if the employer is a governmental entity, a search is subject to the constraints of the Fourth Amendment of the United States Constitution, guaranteeing freedom from unreasonable searches and seizures. If the employee has a reasonable expectation of privacy in the area to be searched, the Fourth Amendment requires a two-step balancing test to evaluate whether the search was (1) justified at its inception and (2) permissible in scope. A search is justified if there are reasonable grounds for suspecting that the search will turn up evidence that the employee is guilty of work-related misconduct, or if the search is necessary for a noninvestigatory work related purpose such as to retrieve a file. The search is reasonable in scope if the measures used are reasonably related to the objectives of the search, and not excessively intrusive, considering the nature of the misconduct being investigated. See, e.g., O'Connor v. Ortega, 480 U.S. 709 (1987).

Private employers generally have greater leeway to search the property they make available for their employee's daily use. See, e.g., State v. Johnson, 110 Idaho 516, 716 P.2d 1288 (1986) (search by landlord did not implicate Fourth Amendment or Idaho Constitution because there was no state action); State v. Crawford, 110 Idaho 577, 716 P.2d 1349 (Ct. App. 1986) (even if a search is wrongful, if it is done by a private party there is no Fourth Amendment or Idaho Constitution protection).

C. Employee's Property

No cases.

IV. MONITORING OF EMPLOYEES

A. Telephones and Electronic Communications

1. ***Wiretapping.*** The Idaho Code prohibits the unauthorized interception of any wire, electronic or oral communication. See I.C. § 18-6702(1). However, a person may intercept a wire, electronic or oral communication if one of the parties to the communication gave prior consent to such interception. See I.C. § 18-6702(2)(d). Unauthorized wiretapping may give rise to a claim for intrusion. See, e.g., O'Neil v. Schuckardt, 112 Idaho 472, 477, 733 P.2d 693, 698 (1986). For example, in Hoskins v. Howard, 132 Idaho 311, 971 P.2d 1135 (1998), the Idaho Supreme Court found that cordless telephone conversations are protected wire communications under the Idaho Communications Security Act, I.C. § 18 -6701 et seq., and interception of such communications could form the basis of intrusion and public disclosure of embarrassing private facts claims. Moreover, such an interception is considered a felony subject to five years in prison or a fine not to exceed $5,000, or by both fine and imprisonment. I.C. § 18-6702. Idaho Code § 18-6709 also provides a private right of action for the recovery of (1) actual damages "but not less than liquidated damages computed at the rate of one hundred dollars ($100) a day for each day of violation or one thousand dollars ($1,000), whichever is higher"; (2) punitive damages; and (3) costs and attorneys fees. The "discovery exception," which tolls a statute of limitations under certain circumstances until the violation is discovered, does not apply to the three-year statute of limitations applicable to claims under the Idaho Communications Secrecy Act. Knudsen v. Agee, 128 Idaho 776, 779, 918 P.2d 1221, 1224 (1996).

Employers in Idaho are also subject to the provisions of the federal wiretap act, which prohibits the interception of oral communications. See 18 U.S.C. §§ 2510 - 2522 (1988) (the Omnibus Crime Control and Safe Streets Act). There are numerous exceptions to this prohibition. For example, the act prohibits content monitoring. Thus, an employer can monitor the fact that a phone call is made without violating the act, so long as content is not monitored. In addition, if one party consents to the interception of the communication, no violation occurs. 18 U.S.C. § 2511(2)(d). Indeed, consent will be implied when one of the parties to the communication records the conversation.

2. ***Electronic Communications.*** There are no cases directly on point. However, as discussed above, a person may not intercept a wire, electronic or oral communication unless he/she obtained the consent of one of the parties to the communication prior to the interception. See I.C. § 18-6702(2)(c) and (d); 18 U.S.C. § 2511(2)(d).

3. ***Other Electronic Monitoring.*** No cases.

B. Mail

The Idaho Code prohibits a person from opening sealed mail not addressed to such person unless the person was authorized to do so either by the writer or by the person to whom it was addressed. See I.C. § 18-6718.

C. Surveillance/Photographing

There are no reported cases alleging a civil cause of action for an employer's use of surveillance photography. Idaho Code § 18-6609 defines and criminalizes the act of "video voyeurism."

V. ACTIVITIES OUTSIDE THE WORKPLACE

A. Statute or Common Law

As discussed above, Idaho has enacted the Idaho Employer Alcohol and Drug-Free Workplace Act which case law interpretation of could allow employers to regulate employees drug use outside of the workplace according to written company policy. The Ninth Circuit Court of Appeals has interpreted Idaho's Free Exercise of Religion Act, I.C.§73-402(2). In Olsen v. Idaho State Board of Medicine, 363 F.3d 916 (9th Cir. 2004), the court held that the Free Exercise of Religion Act did not apply retroactively to a claim of religious discrimination alleged by a physician's assistant, where the alleged incidents occurred prior to February 1, 2001, the enactment date of the Act.

Additionally, the Idaho Supreme Court has refused to hold an employer liable for negligent supervision based on off-duty conduct, where an employee raped and murdered another former employee outside of the workplace. Hunter v.State, Dept. of Corrections, Div. of Probation & Parole, 138 Idaho 44, 57 P.3d 755 (2001) (holding that car wash business could not be held liable for negligent supervision of a felon who, in off-the-job conduct, raped and murdered a former female co-worker). For purposes of determining ineligibility for unemployment insurance benefits due to a termination for misconduct, an employer's rule governing off-duty conduct must have a reasonable relationship to the employer's interests. O'Neal v. Employment Sec. Agency, 89 Idaho 313, 317, 404 P.2d 600, 602 (1965) (denial of benefits where postal employee admitted firing due to violation of postal regulation forbidding infamous, dishonest, immoral or notoriously disgraceful conduct). The O'Neal court also stated that, "An employer, be he public or private, has the right to expect his employees to refrain from acts which would bring dishonor on the business name or the institution." 89 Idaho at 319, 404 P.2d at 603-04. The Idaho courts tend to have a strong preference to true at-will employment. See Edmondson v. Shearer Lumber Products, 139 Idaho 172, 75 P.3d 733 (2003) (employee who was fired for attending meetings and expressing views that that were contrary to his employer had no claim for wrongful discharge).

B. Employees' Personal Relationships

1. ***Romantic Relationships Between Employees.*** No cases.

2. ***Sexual Orientation.*** In Peterson v. Hewlett-Packard Co., 358 F.3d 599 (9th Cir. 2004), the Ninth Circuit Court of Appeals upheld the termination of an employee who was discharged for insubordination, for refusing to take down posters in his work area that cited scriptural passages criticizing homosexuals. In reaching this conclusion, the court held that the company was not impermissibly restricting the employee's religious beliefs but rather was merely enforcing its policies against harassment and towards diversity and tolerance in the workplace. Id. at 605.

3. ***Marital Status.*** No cases. The Commission on Human Rights Statute does not include marital status just race, color, religion, sex or national origin; with age also included in certain sections. See I.C. § 67-5909.

C. Smoking

No applicable statutes or cases for private sector work places, although bills have been introduced in the Idaho legislature that would prohibit employers from regulating an employee's use of any "lawful product" or participation in any "lawful activity" during non-work hours. See, e.g., Colo. Rev. Stat. § 24-34-402.5 (1991); Nev. Rev. Stat. Ann. § 613.333 (1991); N.D. Cen. Code § 14-02.4-09 (1991). While these bills have not passed, attempts to introduce such a provision in the future are almost certain.

In 1985, Idaho adopted the Clean Indoor Air Act. I.C. § 39-5501 et seq. This Act was designed to protect "the public health, comfort and environment, the health of employees who work at public places and the rights of nonsmokers to breathe clean air by prohibiting smoking in public places and at public meetings." I.C. § 39-5501. "Public places" is defined expansively to mean enclosed indoor areas used by the general public, including restaurants, retail stores, public conveyances, and hospitals. The Act prohibits smoking in public places or public meetings except in designated smoking areas, but where such areas are designated, good faith efforts must be made to minimize the effect of smoke in adjacent nonsmoking areas. Idaho Code § 39-5503 has a detailed list of places, such as bars, which may designate the entire building as a smoking area. The Idaho legislature amended I.C. § 39-5503 to remove bowling alleys as a designated place. 2007 Idaho Laws Ch. 272.

D. Blogging

No cases.

VI. RECORDS

A. Personnel Records

School district employees have a statutory right to access information contained in their personnel files, with the exception of recommendation letters. I.C. § 33-518. However, Idaho law does not generally require that employers allow employees access to employment files. While certain information is required to be maintained under federal law, employers are free to adopt any recordkeeping policy they wish, so long as appropriate records are kept, and for privacy reasons, the information is kept confidential. However, the names and salary information of public employees may be disclosed pursuant to Idaho's public records statute. I.C. §§ 9-338 and 9-340C. See Magic Valley Newspapers, Inc. v. Magic Valley Regional Medical Center, 138 Idaho 143, 145-146, 59 P.3d 314, 316-317 (2002). In addition, there is a presumption that "all public records are open unless expressly provided otherwise by statute." Federated Publications, Inc. v. Boise City, 128 Idaho 459, 463, 915 P.2d 21, 25, 24 Media L. Rep. 2139 (1996) (the names and resumes of the applicants for city council position were not exempt from disclosure). See also Dalton v. Idaho Dairy Products Commission, 107 Idaho 6, 684 P.2d 983 (1984) (disclosure of names and addresses of state dairy farmers was mandated under statute providing for disclosure of public records). In Nation v. State, Dept. of Correction, 144 Idaho 177, 158 P.3d 953 (2007) the court determined that the Idaho Public Records Act does not create a statutory duty on the Department of Corrections to prevent disclosure of state corrections officers' personal records from disclosure. Thus, the release to the county sheriff of unredacted worker compensation forms did not create a cause of action under the theory of negligence per se against the Department. Id., 158 P.3d at 965.

The scope of what is open to public disclosure under the Idaho Public Records Act was examined in Cowles Pub. Co. v. Kootenai County Bd. of County Com'rs, 144 Idaho 259, 159 P.3d 896, 35 Media L. Rep. 2107 (2007) where the court was asked to determine if emails between the female manager of a juvenile education and training court and her supervisor, the county prosecutor, were public records open to disclosure. The female manager first argued that the emails were personal emails and therefore not a public record under the act. However, the court rejected this argument holding the emails are a public record pursuant to I.C. § 9-338(13) because "they relate to the public's business and were prepared, owned and used by the County." Id., 159 P.3d at 901. However, the court felt is necessary to qualify this decision by stating "that the emails at issue are part of a series of on-going correspondence between two county employees – the county prosecutor and his subordinate." Id. The female manager next argued that even if the emails were a public record they are exempt from disclosure as a personnel record under I.C. § 9-340C(1). However, the court held that this correspondence is not the type that the legislature intended to exempt from disclosure. The court stated that these emails were not personnel correspondence and thus not exempt from disclosure. Id., 159 P.3d at 902.

In a 2011 high-profile case, a trial court ruled that the personnel file of a deceased University of Idaho professor could be released to the public under Idaho's Public Records Act. Second District Judge John R. Stegner ruled that the definition of "former public official" does include one who is dead, but then applied a balancing test and ordered disclosure of the records, determining that the public's right to know outweighed the privacy right of the "former public official" under I.C. § 9-340C. In this case, the professor was accused of shooting and killing a female graduate student before killing himself. See Regents of the University of Idaho v. TPC Holdings, Inc, Case No. CV-2011-916, Declaratory Judgment (Second Judicial District, Idaho, Oct. 7, 2011).

In Arnold v. Diet Center, Inc., 113 Idaho 581, 746 P.2d 1040 (Ct. App. 1987), a terminated employee claimed his former employer invaded his right to privacy and defamed him by publishing the fact that he was terminated due to a breach of the employer's confidentiality agreement. The Court of Appeals found that the employer had a legitimate interest in stressing to its employees the importance of complying with their confidentiality agreement, and thus, that the employer's communication was protected by a qualified privilege. Id. at 585, 746 P.2d at 1044. The Court of Appeals also found that there was no showing of any abuse by the employer that would cause it to lose its qualified privilege. Id.

B. Medical Records

Idaho Code § 39-1392b provides that all medical records shall be confidential and privileged subject to limited exceptions set forth in I.C. § 39-1392e. Medical records are specifically exempt from the requirements of the Idaho Public Records Act. I.C. § 9-340C(13).

While there are no state statutes dealing with an employer's responsibility in maintaining such records, given the clear legislative intent that medical records be treated as confidential, employers should take all reasonable steps to maintain their confidentiality. Moreover, employers may be required to maintain the confidentiality of their employee's medical records under federal law. See, e.g., 42 U.S.C. § 12112(d)(3)(B) (ADA requires that employers maintain the confidentiality of an applicant's or employee's occupational injury or workers' compensation claim).

C. Criminal Records

In Baker v. Burlington Northern, Inc., 99 Idaho 688, 587 P.2d 829, 4 Media L. Rep. 2240 (1978), the Court held that there was no invasion of an employee's privacy when his employer truthfully disclosed his criminal record. The employee alleged that the employer's disclosure of his criminal record constituted public disclosure of private embarrassing facts. In its opinion, the Court discussed Cox Broadcasting Corp. v. Cohn, 420 U.S. 469 (1975), and the public benefit arising out of the publication of the true contents of public records, especially records revealing recent criminal activity. Baker, 99 Idaho at 692, 587 P.2d at 833. The Court found that the employer's disclosure of the employee's recent criminal activity was a disclosure of public, not private, facts. Id.

Similarly, in Uranga v. Federated Publications, Inc., 138 Idaho 550, 67 P.3d 29, 31 Media L. Rep. 1536 (2003), the Idaho Supreme Court upheld the right of the press to publish reports of old criminal activity, without risk of an unlawful invasion of privacy. In that case, a newspaper accurately published a 40-year old, sworn, handwritten statement given to police and placed in a court file, which stated that the plaintiff engaged in homosexual activity. Uranga, 138 Idaho 550, 67 P.3d at 32.

D. Subpoenas / Search Warrants

No cases.

VII. ACTIONS SUBSEQUENT TO EMPLOYMENT

A. References

No cases.

B. Non-Compete Agreements

The Idaho Court of Appeals has stated that, "the general rule is that a non-compete agreement is enforceable if it is supported by consideration, ancillary to a lawful contract, reasonable and consistent with public policy." McCandless v. Carpenter, 123 Idaho 386, 390, 848 P.2d 444, 448 (Ct. App. 1993) (signed non-compete agreement is held to be invalid due to a lack of consideration to support specific performance). "The Idaho Supreme Court has held that noncompete agreements are enforceable in a variety of contexts including the sale of a business, employment relationships, principal-agent relationship where agent forfeited commissions because of competitive activity, and the sale of a franchise." Id. at 391, 848 P.2d at 449.

However, the Idaho Supreme Court has seemed to examine non-compete provisions contained in employment contracts with a higher level of suspicion. The Court has said they are "disfavored" and "strictly construed against the employer." Intermountain Eye and Laser Centers, P.L.L.C. v. Miller, 142 Idaho 218, 224, 127 P.3d 121, 127 (2005) (citations omitted) (a restriction on ophthalmologist's ability to engage in the "practice of medicine," is outside the scope of a legitimate business interest). If the non-compete provision is more restrictive then necessary to protect a legitimate business interest, or is harsh on the employee, or injures the public the provision will be found to be unreasonable and not enforced. Id.

In Freiburger v. J-U-B Engineers, Inc., 141 Idaho 415, 111 P.3d 100 (2005), the Idaho Supreme Court ruled that a non-competition clause in an employment contract was unreasonable and greater than necessary The district court, on summary judgment, declined to strike the offending language in the unreasonable and overbroad covenant in order to make it reasonable stating that they would have to "rewrite" the entire covenant to make it reasonable.

The language that the court struggled with was not the covenant not to compete as much as it was the anti-piracy portion of the agreement. The Idaho Supreme Court held that the employer had a legitimate business interest, but that the core language of the covenant bothered them. That language read as follows:

> . . . I agree that for a period of two years following any date of termination of my employment with J-U-B, I would not attempt to take, take or join with anyone to take, (without the consent of J-U-B) any of past or present clients or projects or any pending clients or projects, for which J-U-B has or would be providing professional services. . . . (Emphasis theirs.)

Id. at 106.

The above is standard language, and typical language found in many employment agreements. The Idaho Supreme Court found that the covenant as described is clearly an overbroad means of protecting J-U-B's legitimate business interest. The court found that J-U-B has actively operated throughout the Northwest Region for nearly 30 years and clearly has a large client base both past and present, yet the covenant prohibits the employee from taking any of this large group of clients regardless of whether the employee helped to develop J-U-B's goodwill effort toward that client. The court found since the covenant included past clients or projects, without any meaningful limitation, it is an overbroad means of protecting the employer's interest in the goodwill the employee helped to develop.

The Idaho Supreme Court then went on and ruled that judicial modification of the covenant was not appropriate because it is "so lacking in the essential terms which would protect the employee" such that the trial court is no longer modifying, but rewriting the covenant.

The Freiburger case gives a good overview of the law in Idaho concerning covenants not to compete, but more pointedly gives the drafter of such employee agreements some insight into how restrictive and narrow the Idaho Supreme Court's view is of such matters.

In response to the above case and attitude as expressed by the Idaho Supreme Court, in 2008 the Idaho Legislature adopted I.C. §§ 44-2701 to 44-2704 wherein it is statutorily decreed that "a key employee or key independent contractor may enter into a written agreement or covenant that protects the employer's legitimate business interests and prohibits the key employee or key independent contractor from engaging in employment or a line of business that is in direct competition with the employer's business after termination of employment, and the same shall be enforceable, if the agreement or covenant is reasonable as to its duration, geographical area, type of employment or line of business, and does not impose a greater restraint than is reasonably necessary to protect the employer's legitimate business interests."

The statutory provisions define with specificity who is a "key employee" or "key independent contractor" and also defines a "legitimate business interest" as including what is historically protected by covenants not to compete, including employer's goodwill, technologies, marketing information, customer lists, etc. See I.C. § 44-2702(2).

Also, I.C. § 44-2703 specifically directs a court to modify an agreement or covenant that is deemed to be "unreasonable in any respect." Id.

Finally, I.C. § 44-2704, states that the covenant not to compete is to be limited to 18 months and is given a rebuttable presumption of reasonableness during said time period. The geographical area of a proposed covenant not to compete is restricted to areas "in which the key employee or key independent contractor provided services or had a significant presence or influence." There is no such restriction as to time or geography when trade secrets or other proprietary information is involved.

The statute also declares that there shall be a "rebuttable presumption that an employee or independent contractor who is among the highest paid five percent (5%) of the employer's employees or independent contractors is a 'key employee' or a 'key independent contractor'."

VIII. OTHER ISSUES

A. Statutes of Limitations

In Idaho, the statute of limitations for personal injury actions is two years. See I.C. § 5-219.

B. Jurisdiction

There are no applicable statutes or case law in regard to jurisdiction.

C. Worker's Compensation Exclusivity

While the exclusivity provision of the Idaho's Workers' Compensation Act provides that the liability of the employer under the Act shall be exclusive and in place of all other liability of the employer to the employee **(see, e.g., Gerdon v. Rydalch, 153 Idaho 237, 280 P.3d 740, 745 (2012) (citing Hansen v. Estate of Harvey, 119 Idaho 333, 336, 806 P.2d 426,**

429 (1991) ("'[A] person injured in the course of employment has *only* one claim against the employer, and that claim is under the Worker's Compensation Act, not a tort action'"), the exclusiveness of an injured employee's remedy is not absolute; circumstances may arise where an injured employee may seek redress in an Idaho forum other than the Industrial Commission where an alleged injury occurs in the course and scope of employment, but the injury is not compensable under the Act. See I.C. §§ 72-209(1), 72-211; Roe v. Albertson's Inc., 112 P.3d 812, 141 Idaho 524 (2005). By interpretation, a cause of action that would not be exclusive is an invasion of privacy claim against the employer because such an "injury" is not contemplated by I.C. § 72-101 et. seq.

D. Pleading Requirements

In Idaho, a pleading which sets forth a claim for relief must contain: "(1) if the court has limited jurisdiction, a short and plain statement of the grounds upon which the court's jurisdiction depends, (2) a short and plain statement of the claims showing that the pleader is entitled to relief, and (3) a demand for judgment for the relief to which the pleader deems himself or herself entitled." See I.C. § 5-335. See also I.R.C.P. 8(a)(1); Mortensen, 149 Idaho at 443, 235 P.3d at 393 ("The key to a valid pleading is that it must put the opposing party on notice of the claims against it"). If the action is for recovery due to personal injury, the claim for relief should not specify the amount of damages claimed, but rather should contain a general allegation of damage and state that the damages claimed are within the jurisdictional limits of the court. See I.C. § 5-335; I.R.C.P. 9(g). Idaho Code § 6-1603 limits noneconomic damages for "personal injury" to $250,000; provided, however, that the cap shall increase or decrease in accordance with the percentage increase or decrease of the average annual wage as computed pursuant to I.C. § 72-409(2). Idaho law specifically provides that punitive damages may not be alleged in the prayer of the Complaint. See I.C. § 6-1604(2). Rather, the plaintiff must bring a pre-trial motion to amend the Complaint to include a punitive damages claim once adequate discovery has been conducted to demonstrate that there is a "reasonable likelihood of proving facts at trial sufficient to support an award of punitive damages." Id. No judgment for punitive damages shall exceed the greater of $250,000 or an amount which is three times the compensatory damages contained in such judgment. I.C. § 6-1604(3). If the case is tried to a jury, the jury shall not be informed of this limitation. The limitations on noneconomic damages contained in I.C. § 6-1603 are not applicable to punitive damages.

The Idaho Supreme Court has established a schedule of filing fees for all pleadings, along with designated categories of pleadings. These categories and corresponding fees should be indicated on the first page of each pleading.

SURVEY OF ILLINOIS EMPLOYMENT LIBEL LAW

Richard J. O'Brien, Paul E. Veith, Eric S. Mattson, Linda R. Friedlieb, and Joseph C. Cooper
Sidley Austin LLP
One South Dearborn Street
Chicago, Illinois 60603
Telephone: (312) 853-7000; Facsimile: (312) 853-7036

(With Developments Reported Through **November 1, 2012**)

GENERAL COMMENTS

The Illinois Appellate Court is divided into five districts. When a conflict arises among the districts (and in the absence of controlling authority from the Illinois Supreme Court), "the circuit court is bound by the decisions of the appellate court of the district in which it sits." Aleckson v. Round Lake Park, 176 Ill. 2d 82, 92, 679 N.E.2d 1224, 1229, 223 Ill. Dec. 451, 456 (1997). Cf. id. at 94-95, 679 N.E.2d at 1229-30, 223 Ill. Dec. at 456-57 (Harrison, J., specially concurring) (arguing that "[b]ecause there is only one appellate court, a decision by any division of that court is binding precedent on all circuit courts throughout the state, regardless of locale"; contending that circuit courts should follow "most recent appellate court decision on point").

Beginning on July 1, 2011, Illinois stopped publishing official case reporters and switched to a "public domain" system of citing cases. See Ill. S. Ct. R. 6. In state court, briefs must cite the official reporter for earlier cases and use the public-domain citation for opinions released on and after July 1, 2011. See id. The commentary to Ill. S. Ct. R. 6 provides examples of the correct citation format for public-domain citations.

SIGNIFICANT DEVELOPMENTS SINCE THE 2012 *SURVEY*

The Illinois Supreme Court held that the Illinois Citizen Participation Act, Illinois's "anti-SLAPP" statute, requires defendants to show that a complaint is "*solely* based on, relating to, or in response to . . . [the defendants'] acts in furtherance of [the defendant's] rights of petition, speech or association, or to otherwise participate in government." Sandholm v. Kuecker, 2012 IL 111443, ¶ 45, 962 N.E.2d 418, 433, 356 Ill. Dec. 733, 749. Only if defendants satisfy this burden does the burden shift to the plaintiff to provide "clear and convincing evidence that defendants' acts are not immunized from liability under the Act." Id. (holding that defendants failed to meet their burden because plaintiff sought damages for "personal harm to his reputation from defendants' alleged defamatory and tortious acts," made to the media and the school board during a campaign to have plaintiff removed from his position as a teacher and basketball coach). Sandholm significantly curtailed the scope of the Act.

A string of decisions have applied the Sandholm principles to motions to dismiss under the Act. See, e.g., Cartwright v. Cooney, No. 10 CV 1691, 2012 WL 1021816, at *7 (N.D. Ill. Mar. 26, 2012) (declining to dismiss claims based on statements in online comments, in a complaint to the Illinois Attorney Registration and Disciplinary Commission, and in an *ex parte* memorandum to a judge in related litigation, even though defendant may have been "attempting to procure a favorable result with the ARDC or [the judge]"); Hammons v. Soc'y of Permanent Cosmetic Prof'ls, 2012 IL App (1st) 102644, 967 N.E.2d 405, 359 Ill. Dec. 675, 40 Media L. Rep. 1608 (declining to dismiss claims based on statements alleging plaintiff's lack of professional competence, which defendants posted on their blog/ message board and restated at public conferences); August v. Hanlon, 2012 IL App (2d) 111252, ¶ 38. See also Trudeau v. Consumeraffairs.com, Inc., No. 10 C 7193, 2011 WL 3898041, at *6 (N.D. Ill. Sept. 6, 2011) (declining to dismiss claims based on statements in online article because "no reasonable person would consider the article to have been an act of participation in the government process").

Separately, in Tunca v. Painter, 2012 IL App (1st) 093384, ¶ 74, 965 N.E.2d 1237, 1262, 358 Ill. Dec. 758, 783, the court adopted "the modern rule . . . under which a defamer is liable for damages caused by repetitions that were reasonably foreseeable, or the natural and probable consequence of his original statement." Id. (holding that defendants could be liable for disparaging plaintiff's professional competence "in the presence of other doctors and medical personnel at the hospital where plaintiff practices" because the statements "subsequently became widespread throughout the hospital").

In the "fact vs. opinion" area, Pitale v. Holestine, No. 11 C 00921, 2012 WL 638755, at *7 (N.D. Ill. Feb. 27, 2012), considered the literary and social context of an allegedly defamatory blog post to determine whether the post constituted a fact or opinion under the four-part test discussed at II.B.2, infra. The court found that statements on the blog, as compared with an "online encyclopedia," presented a "closer question" under the "literary and social context" factor. Id. Ultimately, the court held that the statements were factual because they provided a "factual background

on [the plaintiff] and describe[d] his history," noting that "even when statements appear on part of a website that is used to express opinion, statements will not be considered opinions when they imply actual facts." Id.

Where a plaintiff petitions to discover an anonymous defendant's identity and the plaintiff fails to make allegations that would overcome a motion to dismiss, the court will deny the petition. Stone v. Paddock Publ'ns, 2011 IL App (1st) 093386, ¶ 18, 961 N.E.2d 380, 389, 356 Ill. Dec. 284, 293, 39 Media L. Rep. 2697. An anonymous defendant is "not required to file [a motion to dismiss], but rather, it remains the petitioner's burden to show that the discovery is necessary, *i.e.*, that petitioner can allege facts supporting a cause of action." Id.

I. GENERAL LAW

A. General Employment Law

1. ***At Will Employment.*** At-will employees may be discharged for any reason or for no reason, unless the discharge violates clearly mandated public policy. See Interstate Scaffolding, Inc. v. Illinois Workers' Compensation Comm'n, 236 Ill. 2d 132, 149, 923 N.E.2d 266, 276, 337 Ill. Dec. 707, 717 (2010). For example, if an employee is fired for filing a worker's compensation claim, he may bring a claim for retaliatory discharge. Kelsay v. Motorola, Inc., 74 Ill. 2d 172, 384 N.E.2d 353, 23 Ill. Dec. 559 (1978); see also Grabs v. Safeway, Inc., 395 Ill. App. 3d 286, 291, 917 N.E.2d 122, 126, 334 Ill. Dec. 525, 529 (1st Dist. 2009).

B. Elements of Libel Claim

1. ***Basic Elements.*** Illinois has eliminated the separate torts of libel and slander in favor of a single tort for defamation. Bryson v. News America Pubs., Inc., 174 Ill. 2d 77, 89, 672 N.E.2d 1207, 1215, 220 Ill. Dec. 195, 203, 25 Media L. Rep. 1321 (1996); see also Naleway v. Agnich, 386 Ill. App. 3d 635, 643-45, 897 N.E. 2d 902, 912-13, 325 Ill. Dec. 363, 373-74 (2d Dist. 2008) (describing the evolution of Illinois defamation law). "To state a defamation claim, a plaintiff must present facts showing that the defendant made a false statement about the plaintiff, that the defendant made an unprivileged publication of that statement to a third party, and that this publication caused damages." Green v. Rogers, 234 Ill. 2d 478, 491, 917 N.E.2d 450, 458, 334 Ill. Dec. 624, 633 (2009); see also Madison v. Frazier, 539 F.3d 646, 653 (7th Cir. 2008) (same).

2. ***Fault.***

a. **Private Figure Plaintiff/Matter of Public Concern.** A private figure plaintiff need not prove actual malice, even where the defamatory statements relate to matters of public concern. Troman v. Wood, 62 Ill. 2d 184, 198, 340 N.E.2d 292, 299 (1975). Instead, "recovery may be had upon proof that the publication was false, and that the defendant knew it to be false, or, believing it to be true, lacked reasonable grounds for that belief." Id. The Illinois Appellate Court has likewise held that a private figure plaintiff may recover actual damages upon a showing that the defendant was negligent. Rosner v. Field Enters., Inc., 205 Ill. App. 3d 769, 804, 564 N.E.2d 131, 152, 151 Ill. Dec. 154, 175 (1st Dist. 1990). See also Owens v. CBS, Inc., 173 Ill. App. 3d 977, 994, 527 N.E.2d 1296, 1308, 123 Ill. Dec. 521, 533 (5th Dist. 1988) (applying negligence standard to report that plaintiff's neighbor had accused her of sending an assassination threat to the President); Dawson v. New York Life Ins. Co., 135 F.3d 1158, 1162 (7th Cir. 1998) ("In Illinois, a plaintiff can prevail on a defamation claim by showing that the defendant acted negligently in making the defamatory statement."). But see Colson v. Stieg, 89 Ill. 2d 205, 433 N.E.2d 246, 60 Ill. Dec. 449 (1982) (actual malice standard applied where assistant professor claimed that he was defamed by chairman of department during personnel committee meeting).

b. **Private Figure Plaintiff/Matter of Private Concern.** To recover actual damages, "proof of negligence is sufficient where a private plaintiff is involved and no common law privilege is applicable." Rosner, 205 Ill. App. 3d at 815, 564 N.E.2d at 159, 151 Ill. Dec. at 182; see also Imperial Apparel, Ltd. v. Cosmo's Designer Direct, Inc., 227 Ill. 2d 381, 394-95, 882 N.E.2d 1011, 1020, 317 Ill. Dec. 855, 864, 36 Media L. Rep. 1335 (2008).

c. **Public Figure Plaintiff/Matter of Public Concern.** The actual malice standard applies where the allegedly defamatory statement concerns a public figure plaintiff on a matter of public concern. See, e.g., Matchett v. Chicago Bar Ass'n, 125 Ill. App. 3d 1004, 1011, 467 N.E.2d 271, 277, 81 Ill. Dec. 571, 577 (1st Dist. 1984); Madison v. Frazier, 539 F.3d 646, 657 (7th Cir. 2008). In such cases, plaintiff must prove that the defendant made the defamatory statement with knowledge that it was false or with reckless disregard of whether it was false or not. Id. The Seventh Circuit has summarized the "reckless disregard" prong of the actual malice standard as follows: "The plaintiff must demonstrate that the author in fact entertained serious doubts as to the truth of his publication, . . . or acted with a high degree of awareness of . . . probable falsity, or, while suspecting falsity, deliberately avoided taking steps that would have confirmed the suspicion." J.H. Desnick, M.D., Eye Serv., Ltd. v. ABC, 233 F.3d 514, 517, 29 Media L. Rep. 1053 (7th Cir. 2000) (internal quotation marks and citations omitted). Furthermore, "a failure to investigate before publishing, even when a reasonably prudent person would have done so, is not sufficient to establish reckless disregard." Madison, 539 F.3d at 658 (citing Harte-Hanks Communications, Inc. v. Connaughton, 491 U.S. 657, 666-67, 109 S. Ct. 2678 (1989)). Although actual malice may not be proven through a mere failure to investigate, it may be shown, under appropriate circumstances, by "a failure to inquire into the truth of one's own inference" if "there is substantial reason to doubt the truth of that inference." Edwards v. Paddock Pubs., Inc., 327 Ill. App. 3d 553, 556, 763 N.E.2d 328, 337, 261 Ill. Dec. 358, 367, 30 Media L. Rep. 1142 (1st Dist. 2001).

"A limited public figure is one who would otherwise be a private figure but who has thrust himself into a public controversy." American Hardware Mfrs. Ass'n v. Reed Elsevier, Inc., No. 03 CV 9421, 2010 WL 55657, at *9 (N.D. Ill. Jan. 4, 2010). "In assessing whether a figure is a limited public figure, Illinois courts look to whether (1) there is a public controversy, (2) the plaintiff played a meaningful role in the controversy, and (3) the allegedly defamatory story is germane to the plaintiff's role in the controversy." Id. "The plaintiff must have been a public figure before the allegedly defamatory statements occurred." Id. Further, evidence that plaintiffs are known or well-regarded within a particular industry does not, by itself, make them limited public figures. Id. Union leaders who are involved in a controversy of interest to union members should be considered limited purpose public figures. See Dubinsky v. United Airlines Master Executive Council, 303 Ill. App. 3d 317, 336-37, 708 N.E.2d 441, 455-56, 236 Ill. Dec. 855, 869-70 (1st Dist. 1999).

3. ***Falsity.*** The Illinois Constitution provides that "[i]n trials for libel, both civil and criminal, the truth, when published with good motives and for justifiable ends, shall be a sufficient defense." Ill. Const. art. I, § 4. The Illinois Supreme Court long ago held that this provision conflicts with the First Amendment when the "actual malice" standard is involved (Farnsworth v. Tribune Co., 43 Ill. 2d 286, 290, 253 N.E.2d 408, 410 (1969)), and more recently has held unequivocally that "falsity is an element of the plaintiff's defamation claim." Voyles v. Sandia Mortgage Corp., 196 Ill. 2d 288, 299, 751 N.E.2d 1126, 1133, 256 Ill. Dec. 289, 296 (2001). Accord, Green v. Rogers, 234 Ill. 2d 478, 491, 917 N.E.2d 450, 459, 334 Ill. Dec. 624, 633 (2009) (listing as an element of a defamation claim "that the defendant made a false statement about the plaintiff"). Thus, truthful statements cannot give rise to defamation liability. Parker v. Bank of Marion, 296 Ill. App. 3d 1035, 1038, 695 N.E.2d 1370, 1372, 231 Ill. Dec. 251, 253 (5th Dist. 1998) (upholding directed verdict in favor of defendants where statement that plaintiff was "fired for touching women" was true, even though plaintiff denied that touching was sexual in nature). See also II.B.1 infra.

4. ***Defamatory Statement of Fact.*** "A defamatory statement is a statement that harms a person's reputation to the extent it lowers the person in the eyes of the community or deters the community from associating with her or him." Green, 234 Ill. 2d at 491, 917 N.E.2d at 459, 334 Ill. Dec. at 633. Put differently, "[a] statement is 'defamatory' if it impeaches a person's integrity, virtue, human decency or reputation and thereby lowers that person in the estimation of the community or deters a third party from dealing with that person." Girsberger v. Kresz, 261 Ill. App. 3d 398, 412, 633 N.E.2d 781, 792-93, 198 Ill. Dec. 940, 951-52 (1st Dist. 1993). See also Moore v. People for the Ethical Treatment of Animals, Inc., 402 Ill. App. 3d 62, 68, 932 N.E.2d 448, 454-55, 342 Ill. Dec. 321, 327-28 (1st Dist. 2010); Knafel v. Chicago Sun-Times, Inc., 413 F.3d 637, 639 (7th Cir. 2005).

In contrast to factual statements, "statements of opinion generally are not actionable… Only if a statement of opinion is actually a false assertion of fact can it constitute defamation." Earl v. H.D. Smith Wholesale Drug Co., No. 08-3224, 2009 WL 1871929, at *2 (C.D. Ill. June 23, 2009). The more vague and general an opinion, the less likely it is to be actionable. Id. (noting that some words are so broad that they lack the detail and precise meaning necessary to be considered defamatory). "Statements that do not contain factual assertions are protected under the first amendment and may not form the basis of a defamation action." Moore, 402 Ill. App. 3d at 68, 932 N.E.2d at 455, 342 Ill. Dec. at 328. See also II.B.2. infra.

Illinois follows the traditional approach of classifying defamatory statements as per se or per quod. Thomas v. Fuerst, 345 Ill. App. 3d 929, 934, 803 N.E.2d 619, 623, 281 Ill. Dec. 215, 219 (1st Dist. 2004); Madison v. Frazier, 539 F.3d 646, 653 (7th Cir. 2008).

A statement is defamatory per se if it is "so obviously and naturally harmful to the person to whom it refers that a showing of special damages is unnecessary." Owen v. Carr, 113 Ill. 2d 273, 277, 497 N.E.2d 1145, 1147, 100 Ill. Dec. 783, 785 (1986); see also Knafel, 413 F.3d at 639.

More specifically, a statement is defamatory per se if it imputes the commission of a criminal offense, imputes infection with a loathsome communicable disease, imputes an inability to perform or lack of integrity in the discharge of duties of office or employment, or prejudices a party or imputes lack of ability in her trade, profession or business. Green, 234 Ill. 2d at 491-92, 917 N.E.2d at 459, 334 Ill. Dec. at 634. In addition to these common law categories, the Slander and Libel Act, 740 Ill. Comp. Stat. 145/1 et seq., provides that accusations of fornication, adultery and false swearing are defamatory per se. The judge, not the jury, determines whether a statement falls into a defamatory per se category. Darovec Marketing Group, Inc. v. Bio-Genics, Inc., 42 F. Supp. 2d 810, 816 (N.D. Ill. 1999).

The cases finding a statement to be defamatory per se are as broad in scope as the categories themselves. See, e.g., Maxon v. Ottawa Pub. Co., 402 Ill. App. 3d 704, 716, 929 N.E.2d 666, 677, 341 Ill. Dec. 12, 23 (3d Dist. 2010) (statements that plaintiff paid a bribe to obtain a favorable ruling on a zoning matter); Missner v. Clifford, 393 Ill. App. 3d 751, 760, 914 N.E.2d 540, 549, 333 Ill. Dec. 121, 130 (1st Dist. 2009) (accusations of forgery and extortion); Myers v. Telegraph, 332 Ill. App. 3d 917, 922, 773 N.E.2d 192, 197-98, 265 Ill. Dec. 830, 835-36 (5th Dist. 2002) (accusation that plaintiff had pleaded guilty to a felony rather than a misdemeanor); Giant Screen Sports v. Canadian Imperial Bank of Commerce, 553 F.3d 527, 532 (7th Cir. 2009) (statements that implied plaintiff was unable to uphold its contractual obligations); Hale v. Pace, No. 09 C 5131, 2011 WL 1303369, at *15 (N.D. Ill. Mar. 31, 2011) (statements to police officers that plaintiff refused to pay bus fare); Moriarty v. Dyson, Inc., No. 09 C 2777, 2010 WL 2745969, at *4 (N.D. Ill. July 8, 2010) (statements that plaintiff engaged in a sexual relationship with co-workers); Fishering v. City of Chicago, No. 07 C 6650, 2008 WL 834436, at *4 (N.D. Ill. Mar. 27, 2008) (statements that plaintiff had "skipped town," had taken money, and was being pursued by police). An accusation of criminal conduct is defamatory per se only if the charged offense is "indictable, involve[s] moral turpitude, and [is] punishable by a term of imprisonment." Neuros Co. v. KTurbo, Inc., No. 08-cv-5939, 2011 WL 1692170, at *12 (N.D. Ill. May 3, 2011).

When a statement imputes an inability to perform the duties of employment or a lack of integrity, the plaintiff must show that the statements relate to him in his professional capacity, not to his personal character. Cody v. Harris, 409 F.3d 853, 857-58 (7th Cir. 2005) (employer's false accusations that former employee posted pornographic images on employer's website in retaliation for firing were not defamatory per se because the statements addressed employee's personal integrity, not his skills as a sales manager); Cunningham v. UTI Integrated Logistics, Inc., Civil No. 09-1019, 2010 WL 1558718, at *4 (S.D. Ill. April 19, 2010) (finding that statements that warehouse employee made racist remarks and physically intimidated co-workers related to his personal character, not his job); Brown v. GC Am., Inc., No. 05 C 3810, 2005 WL 3077608, at *5-9 (N.D. Ill. Nov. 15, 2005) (dismissing defamation per se claim based on statement that employee "had a strike against him" for engaging in a public altercation with a co-worker and an incorrect statement that a previously resolved sexual harassment claim was still pending; statements did not address employee's ability to do his job).

A statement will not be treated as defamatory per se (and therefore not actionable, unless it is defamatory per quod) if it is reasonably capable of an innocent construction. Anderson v. Vanden Dorpel, 172 Ill. 2d 399, 412, 667 N.E.2d 1296, 1301, 217 Ill. Dec. 720, 725 (1996); see also Tuite v. Corbitt, 224 Ill. 2d 490, 507, 866 N.E.2d 114, 125, 310 Ill. Dec. 303, 314, 35 Media L. Rep. 1193 (2007). The innocent construction rule provides that "'a written or oral statement is to be considered in context, with the words and the implications therefrom given their natural and obvious meaning; if, as so construed, the statement may reasonably be innocently interpreted or reasonably be interpreted as referring to someone other than the plaintiff it cannot be actionable per se.'" Anderson, 172 Ill. 2d at 412, 667 N.E.2d at 1302, 217 Ill. Dec. at 726 (quoting Chapski v. Copley Press, 92 Ill. 2d 344, 442 N.E.2d 195, 65 Ill. Dec. 884, 8 Media L. Rep. 2403 (1982)). In other words, "a statement reasonably capable of a nondefamatory interpretation, given its verbal or literary context, should be so interpreted." Leyshon v. Diehl Controls, Inc., 407 Ill. App. 3d 1, 6, 946 N.E.2d 864, 871, 349 Ill. Dec. 368, 375 (1st Dist. 2010). The innocent construction rule is a question of law and its application should be determined by the court. J. Maki Constr. Co. v. Chicago Reg'l Council of Carpenters, 379 Ill. App. 3d 189, 203, 882 N.E.2d 1173, 1186, 318 Ill. Dec. 50, 63 (2d Dist. 2008).

If a statement is reasonably capable of an innocent construction, the court should find that it is not actionable; the court is not supposed to "balance" different reasonable constructions. Green v. Rogers, 234 Ill. 2d 478, 500, 917 N.E.2d 450, 463, 334 Ill. Dec. 624, 637 (2009). At the same time, the court should not "strain to interpret allegedly defamatory words in their mildest and most inoffensive sense in order to hold them nonlibelous under the innocent construction rule." Bryson v. News America Pubs., Inc., 174 Ill. 2d 77, 93, 672 N.E.2d 1207, 1217, 220 Ill. Dec. 195, 205, 25 Media L. Rep. 1321 (1996) (declining to construe "slut" to mean "bully"). "[T]he Illinois courts have firmly emphasized that '[o]nly *reasonable* innocent constructions will remove an allegedly defamatory statement from the per se category.'" Republic Tobacco Corp. v. North Atl. Trading Co., 381 F.3d 717, 727 (7th Cir. 2004).

The innocent construction rule is regularly applied in the employment context. A wide variety of negative statements about employees have been held to be capable of an innocent construction and therefore not actionable. In a leading case on the subject, the Illinois Supreme Court upheld the dismissal of a defamation claim where the employer stated that the employee did not get along with co-workers and did not follow up on assignments, reasoning that the statements could be construed to mean that "plaintiff did not fit in with the organization of the employer making the assessment and failed to perform well in that particular job setting, and not as a comment on her ability to perform in other, future positions." Anderson, 172 Ill. 2d at 412, 667 N.E.2d at 1301, 217 Ill. Dec. at 725. See also Valentine v. North Am. Co. for Life & Health Ins., 60 Ill. 2d 168, 171, 328 N.E.2d 265, 267 (1974) (former employer's statement that insurance salesman was "a lousy agent" could be innocently construed to mean that "plaintiff did not properly or satisfactorily represent the company and that there had been a 'lousy' or generally unsatisfactory agency relationship"); Dunlap v. Alcuin Montessori School, 298 Ill. App. 3d 329, 339, 698 N.E.2d 574, 581, 232 Ill. Dec. 483, 490 (1st Dist. 1998) (school board's statement that there had been "virtually a total breakdown of trust and confidence between [plaintiff, the former school principal,] and the Board" held capable of innocent construction); Quinn v. Jewel Food Stores, Inc., 276 Ill. App. 3d 861, 868-69, 658 N.E.2d 1225, 1232, 213 Ill. Dec. 204, 211 (1st Dist. 1995) (statements in employer's evaluation form that plaintiff was "very aggressive, to the point of being cocky . . . could be a problem!" and "[a] con artist! Watch out for the bullshit!" were capable of innocent construction); Taradash v. Adelet/Scott-Fetzer Co., 260 Ill. App. 3d 313, 317-18, 628 N.E.2d 884, 887, 195 Ill. Dec. 420, 423 (1st Dist. 1993) (employer's statement that employee was terminated for "lack of performance" could be innocently construed); Skopp v. First Federal Savings of Wilmette, 189 Ill. App. 3d 440, 444-46, 545 N.E.2d 356, 359-60, 136 Ill. Dec. 832, 835-36 (1st Dist. 1989) (employer's statement that former employee was terminated "for cause" capable of innocent construction); Pruitt v. Chow, 742 F.2d 1104, 1107-08 (7th Cir. 1984); Van Vliet v. Cole Taylor Bank, No. 10 CV 3221, 2011 WL 148059, at *6 (N.D. Ill. Jan. 18, 2011) (finding employer's statements that plaintiff retained marketable securities as collateral without reflecting those securities on a collateral summary report capable of innocent construction because they could be construed to mean that "the Plaintiff had performance failures in this particular job; rather than having a general inability to perform in other, future positions"); Bishop v. ABN-AMRO Servs. Co., No. 02 C 7330, 2003 U.S. Dist. LEXIS 12368, at *9 (N.D. Ill. July 16, 2003) (statements about employee's unsatisfactory audit, failure to make corrections, and termination could be innocently construed as referring to the performance standards of one employer, and not the employee's general ability); Hach v. Laidlaw Transit, Inc., No. 02 C 996, 2002 WL 31496240, at *3 (N.D. Ill. Nov. 7, 2002) (statements criticizing manager's performance were subject to innocent construction because they were "context-specific" and did not suggest "a general inability to perform comparable work in some other setting").

The innocent construction rule is not a panacea for defendants, however. Other negative statements — which are occasionally hard to distinguish from those that have been innocently construed — have been held to fall outside the rule. See, e.g., Tuite, 224 Ill. 2d at 513, 866 N.E.2d at 128, 310 Ill. Dec. at 317 (holding that implications that plaintiff bribed officials on behalf of the mob in a book about corruption would not be innocently construed by the average reader); Swick v. Liautaud, 169 Ill. 2d 504, 518, 662 N.E.2d 1238, 1245, 215 Ill. Dec. 98, 105 (1996) (accusations that employee was an industrial spy who lied to, stole from and tried to deceive management were defamatory per se and were not susceptible to innocent construction); Leyshon v. Diehl Controls, Inc., 407 Ill. App. 3d 1, 7, 946 N.E.2d 864, 872, 349 Ill. Dec. 368, 376 (1st Dist. 2010) (finding employer's statement that plaintiff was terminated "for cause under the terms of [the plaintiff's] employment agreement" to be incapable of innocent construction when the employment agreement stated that "[c]ause shall include gross negligence, gross neglect of duties, gross insubordination and willful violation of any law applicable to the conduct of the Company's business and affairs"); Gardner v. Senior Living Sys., Inc., 314 Ill. App. 3d 114, 118-19, 731 N.E.2d 350, 354-55, 246 Ill. Dec. 822, 826-27 (1st Dist. 2000) (statements that plaintiff took former employer's software and never returned it held to be defamatory per se because they imputed the commission of a crime); Dubinsky v. United Airlines Master Executive Council, 303 Ill. App. 3d 317, 325-27, 708 N.E.2d 441, 448-49, 236 Ill. Dec. 855, 862-63 (1st Dist. 1999) (statement that "I believe that Federal laws have been broken" and accusation that plaintiffs could face prosecution under RICO held to be defamatory and not susceptible to innocent construction; but subsequent statement regarding same controversy that "whether or not RICO or other federal laws apply will be decided in civil court or by the Justice Department" and that "RICO was specifically written for such questions as bribery, money offered to influence negotiations, mail fraud, laundering money, embezzlement of union funds, collusion, conspiracy, kickbacks, enterprise to dominate labor unions, etc." were capable of innocent construction and therefore not actionable); Becker v. Zellner, 292 Ill. App. 3d 116, 125-26, 684 N.E.2d 1378, 1386, 226 Ill. Dec. 175, 183 (2d Dist. 1997) (employer's statements that plaintiff paralegals were "devious" and that they produced "worthless" work product were slander per se and not capable of innocent construction); Powell v. XO Servs, Inc., 781 F. Supp. 2d 706, 713-15 (N.D. Ill. 2011) (finding accusations that plaintiff engaged in a pattern of lying and authorizing false documents as imputing a want of integrity or ability and therefore incapable of innocent construction); Horton v. Nat'l City Mortg. Services Co., No. 09-1391, 2010 WL 1253994, at *5 (C.D. Ill. Mar. 24 2010) (placing appraiser on a "do not use" list and writing in all capital letters that her appraisals would not be accepted was defamatory per se and incapable of innocent construction); Wachter v. Indian Prairie Sch. Dist., No. 05 C 3898, 2006 WL 305882, at *4 (N.D. Ill. Feb. 1, 2006) (statements in a school board member's Notice of Remedy that employee engaged in "inappropriate personal contact and interaction with students," such as "suggestive and inappropriate physical contact," and had partially undressed in the school building to show a tattoo were not capable of innocent construction); Eberhardt v. Morgan Stanley Dean Witter Trust FSB, No. 00 C 3303, 2001 WL 111024, at *4 (N.D. Ill. Feb. 2, 2001) (e-mail sent by defendant's agent to other employees "warning" them not to conduct business with plaintiffs and stating that plaintiffs were not authorized to administer estate planning program was defamatory per se and not capable of innocent construction); Levitt v. S.C. Food Serv., Inc., 820 F. Supp. 366, 367 (N.D. Ill. 1993) (former employee's statement in resume that "'[n]ew management led to the dismissal of non-Oriental employees'" was defamatory per se and could not be innocently construed).

As these cases illustrate, it can be difficult to predict whether a particular statement will be given an innocent construction. More than twenty years ago, the Illinois Supreme Court acknowledged that the innocent construction rule "has spawned a morass of case law in which consistency and harmony have long ago disappeared," Mittelman v. Witous, 135 Ill. 2d 220, 232, 552 N.E.2d 973, 978, 142 Ill. Dec. 232, 237 (1989), and the case law has not gotten much clearer since then. In general, it appears that specific statements about specific incidents are more likely to be held actionable than general statements about the plaintiff's performance. Beyond that, however, the cases are decided on their facts, and the outcomes are sometimes irreconcilable.

The innocent construction rule does not apply to actions for defamation per quod. Id. at 232-33, 552 N.E.2d at 979, 142 Ill. Dec. at 238. A statement constitutes defamation per quod if "(1) the defamatory character of the statement is not apparent on its face, and extrinsic facts are required to explain its defamatory meaning; or (2) the defamatory character of the statement is apparent on its face, but the statement does not fit within any of the recognized defamation per se categories." Equis Corp. v. Staubach Co., No. 99 C 7046, 2000 WL 283982, at *2 (N.D. Ill. March 13, 2000); see also Cunningham v. UTI Integrated Logistics, Inc., No. 09-1019, 2010 WL 1558718, at *4 (S.D. Ill. April 19, 2010). "When a defamation claim is one for defamation per quod ... a plaintiff must show special damages, i.e., actual damages of a pecuniary nature, to succeed." Hukic v. Aurora Loan Services, 588 F.3d 420, 438 (7th Cir. 2009); see also Moore v. People for the Ethical Treatment of Animals, Inc., 402 Ill. App. 3d 62, 68, 932 N.E.2d 448, 455, 342 Ill. Dec. 321, 328 (1st Dist. 2010).

"Special damages" are actual damage to the plaintiff's reputation and pecuniary loss resulting from the defamatory statement. Bryson v. News Am. Pubs., Inc., 174 Ill. 2d 77, 104, 672 N.E.2d 1207, 1222, 220 Ill. Dec. 195, 210, 25 Media L. Rep. 1321 (1996). Special damages must be pleaded with particularity; it is not sufficient to allege general damage to health or reputation, economic loss, or emotional distress. Kurczaba v. Pollock, 318 Ill. App. 3d 686, 694-95, 742 N.E.2d 425, 433-34, 252 Ill. Dec. 175, 183-84 (1st Dist. 2000). See also Salamone v. Hollinger Int'l, Inc., 347 Ill. App. 3d 837, 842-44, 807 N.E.2d 1086, 1091-93, 283 Ill. Dec. 245, 250-52 (1st Dist. 2004) (holding that allegations of humiliation, embarrassment, harm to reputation and that unspecified customers stopped patronizing plaintiff's store were insufficiently specific); Lott v. Levitt, 556 F.3d 564, 570 (7th Cir. 2009) (finding claims of "substantial reputational and monetary damages" without any explanation of how the allegedly defamatory statements caused the harm were insufficient). Pleading damages with particularity is required in federal court as well. Hukic, 588 F.3d at 438.

Per quod claims have traditionally required plaintiffs to plead and prove extrinsic facts that show the defamatory nature of a statement which is not actionable on its face. See Cunningham, 2010 WL 1558718, at *5. In Bryson, the Illinois Supreme Court recognized a new type of defamation per quod arising when the allegedly defamatory statement does not fall into one of the traditional per se categories and does not involve extrinsic circumstances, but nevertheless is defamatory "on its face." Bryson, 174 Ill. 2d at 103, 672 N.E.2d at 1221, 220 Ill. Dec. at 209. The Supreme Court's characterization of such a claim as a per quod claim is curious. The gravamen of a traditional per quod claim is the *absence* of defamatory meaning on the face of a challenged statement. It is not clear whether the type of defamation per quod recognized in Bryson will be subject to the innocent construction rule. And some courts still appear to require extrinsic evidence to prove the statement at issue is defamatory. See, e.g., Myers v. Levy, 348 Ill. App. 3d 906, 914, 808 N.E.2d 1139, 1147, 283 Ill. Dec. 851, 859 (2d Dist. 2004) ("A claim for defamation per quod requires the plaintiff to allege . . . extrinsic facts to establish that the statement is defamatory.").

5. ***Of and Concerning Plaintiff.*** If a defamatory statement does not refer to the plaintiff, the plaintiff has no cause of action. See, e.g., Aroonsakul v. Shannon, 279 Ill. App. 3d 345, 350, 664 N.E.2d 1094, 1098, 216 Ill. Dec. 166, 170 (2d Dist. 1996); Dry Enters., Inc. v. Sunjut AS, No. 07 C 1657, 2008 WL 904902, at *7 (N.D. Ill. Mar. 31, 2008). Where the plaintiff is not specifically named in the defamatory statement, Illinois law requires that the complaint allege facts sufficient to show that people other than the parties "must have reasonably understood" to whom the statement was referring. Muzikowski v. Paramount Pictures Corp., 322 F.3d 918, 925 (7th Cir. 2003). However, this heightened pleading requirement does not apply in federal court. Id. at 926.

In Illinois state court, the judge determines in the first instance whether a statement can be understood as referring to plaintiff. Aroonsakul, 279 Ill. App. at 350, 664 N.E.2d at 1098, 216 Ill. Dec. at 170. In making this assessment, the innocent construction rule applies. See I.B.4, supra; Bryson, 174 Ill. 2d at 90 & 96-99, 672 N.E.2d at 1215 & 1218-19, 220 Ill. Dec. at 203 & 206-07. If a statement may reasonably be thought to refer to someone other than the plaintiff, then the plaintiff cannot state a claim for defamation *per se*. Solaia Tech., LLC v. Specialty Publ'g Co., 221 Ill. 2d 558, 580, 852 N.E.2d 825, 839, 304 Ill. Dec. 369, 383 (2006) (citing Chapski v. Copley Press, 92 Ill. 2d 344, 352, 442 N.E.2d 195, 65 Ill. Dec. 884 (1982)).

6. ***Publication.*** Publication is an essential element of a defamation claim. "In the law of defamation, the word 'published' just means that the defamatory statement was made to someone other than the plaintiff." Kamelgard v. Macura, 585 F.3d 334, 342 (7th Cir. 2009). See, e.g., Cianci v. Pettibone Corp., 298 Ill. App. 3d 419, 427, 698 N.E.2d 674, 680, 232 Ill. Dec. 583, 589 (1st Dist. 1998) (no publication where plaintiff alleged that other employees knew of her suspension and firing, but failed to show that defendant had told them); Adams v. Pull'r Holding Co., LLC., No. 09 C 7170, 2010 WL 1611078, at *5 (N.D. Ill. Apr. 20, 2010) (dismissing defamation claims where plaintiff failed to specifically identify the persons or entities to whom the allegedly defamatory statements were published); Storch v. West Town Refrigeration

Corp., No. 04 C 3656, 2006 WL 2176025, at *15-16 (N.D. Ill. July 31, 2006) (granting summary judgment where plaintiff's evidence that defendant made defamatory statement was inadmissible hearsay); Cole v. Chicago Tribune Co., No. 96 C 3320, 2000 WL 656644, at *13 (N.D. Ill. May 23, 2000) (granting summary judgment on defamation claim where employee could not show that employer made statements to third party).

a. **Intracorporate Communication.** Intracorporate communications may satisfy the publication requirement for a defamation claim. Anderson v. Beach, 386 Ill. App. 3d 246, 249, 897 N.E.2d 361, 365, 325 Ill. Dec. 113, 117 (1st Dist. 2008); Popko v. Continental Cas. Co., 355 Ill. App. 3d 257, 262, 823 N.E.2d 184, 189, 291 Ill. Dec. 174, 179 (1st Dist. 2005) (holding that memo from manager to his supervisor recommending that subordinate be fired was published when it was sent to the supervisor); Gibson v. Philip Morris, Inc., 292 Ill. App. 3d 267, 274-76, 685 N.E.2d 638, 644-45, 226 Ill. Dec. 383, 389-90 (5th Dist. 1997) (recognizing that "there is no statement of law in Illinois that corporate internal communications are not publications," implicitly rejecting the view that intracorporate communications do not constitute publication); Harrel v. Dillards Dept. Stores, Inc., 268 Ill. App. 3d 537, 543, 644 N.E.2d 448, 452, 205 Ill. Dec. 892, 896 (5th Dist. 1994) (expressly leaving open the question of whether statements or opinions exchanged between employees conducting an internal investigation have been "published," but noting in dictum that a statement would "[u]nquestionably" be considered published if it were made to a person not involved in the investigation); Gehrls v. Gooch, 2010 WL 1849400, at *2 -3 (N.D. Ill. May 7, 2010) (finding that a personnel report in plaintiff's file stating she engaged in "inappropriate intimate conduct" satisfied the publication requirement); Parish v. Motorola, Inc., No. 06 C 1690, 2007 WL 967914, at *4 (N.D. Ill. Mar. 29, 2007) (holding that "statements can be 'published,' for defamation purposes, when they are set forth in an interoffice document, presumably including a performance evaluation"), aff'd, 270 Fed. Appx. 431 (7th Cir. 2008); Jones v. Britt Airways, Inc., 622 F. Supp. 389, 391 (N.D. Ill. 1985) (expressly rejecting argument that intracorporate publications are not considered published for purposes of defamation law); but see Davis v. John Crane, Inc., 261 Ill. App. 3d 419, 421, 430, 633 N.E.2d 929, 931, 937, 199 Ill. Dec. 133, 135, 141 (1st Dist. 1994) (holding that a statement was not published where a management official, in the presence of another manager, read a prepared statement indicating that an employee was being fired for "violation of company policy in the area of drugs").

b. **Compelled Self-Publication.** Illinois has rejected the theory of compelled self-publication. According to the Illinois Appellate Court, recognizing such a theory would discourage plaintiffs from mitigating their damages, unduly burden free speech, and unreasonably broaden the scope of potential liability for defamation. Harrel v. Dillards Dept. Stores, Inc., 268 Ill. App. 3d 537, 547, 644 N.E.2d 448, 455, 205 Ill. Dec. 892, 899 (5th Dist. 1994). Accord, Emery v. N.E. Ill. Reg'l Commuter R.R. Corp., 377 Ill. App. 3d 1013, 1026-29, 880 N.E.2d 1002, 1012-15, 317 Ill. Dec. 10, 20–23 (1st Dist. 2007) (noting that such a theory also conflicts with the doctrine of employment at will).

c. **Republication.** Repeating a defamatory statement exposes the republisher to liability, even if the republisher attributes the statement to a third person. Hale v. Scott, 371 F.3d 917, 919 (7th Cir. 2004); Catalano v. Pechous, 83 Ill. 2d 146, 168, 419 N.E.2d 350, 361, 50 Ill. Dec. 242, 253, 6 Media L. Rep. 2511 (1980). But see Harrison v. Addington, 2011 IL App (3d) 100810, ¶¶ 39-40, 955 N.E.2d 700, 707, 353 Ill. Dec. 233, 240 (finding that defendant did not make defamatory statement because he "merely made the truthful statement regarding what [another defendant] had alleged"). However, the person who repeats the statement cannot be held liable unless he acted with the requisite degree of fault. Thus, if the actual malice standard applies, the plaintiff must show that the republisher acted with knowledge of falsity or reckless disregard of truth or falsity, even where the original speaker acted with actual malice. Catalano, 83 Ill. 2d at 168, 419 N.E.2d at 361, 50 Ill. Dec. at 253.

On the issue of whether a speaker can be held liable for foreseeable republications by others, the Seventh Circuit has held that a credit reporting agency could not be held liable for the republication of one of its credit reports unless it authorized the republication. Oberman v. Dun & Bradstreet, 586 F.2d 1173, 4 Media L. Rep. 2137 (7th Cir. 1978). Citing a century-old decision of the Illinois Appellate Court, the Seventh Circuit said that "'no liability attaches to the author of the libel for . . . reproduction, unless it is made by his authority or consent, either express or implied.'" Id. at 1175 (quoting Clifford v. Cochrane, 10 Ill. App. 570 (1882)). The court left open the possibility that an Illinois court facing the issue today might decide that a speaker is liable for the unauthorized republication of his statement if it is the "natural or probable consequence" of the original publication. Id. **Picking up on this cue, the Illinois Appellate Court distinguished Oberman as a federal case that "had to follow Clifford" under federalism principles, whereas "unlike the federal court, this court is not bound to follow the decision in Clifford" – a decision "entered by another appellate court." Tunca v. Painter, 2012 IL App (1st) 093384, ¶ 74, 965 N.E.2d 1237, 1260, 358 Ill. Dec. 758, 781. The court adopted "the modern rule . . . under which a defamer is liable for damages caused by repetitions that were reasonably foreseeable, or the natural and probable consequence of his original statement." Id. at ¶ 74, 965 N.E. 2d at 1262, 358 Ill. Dec. at 783. The court held that the defendants could be liable for making allegedly false allegations about the plaintiff's professional competence "in the presence of other doctors and medical personnel at the hospital where plaintiff practices" because the statements "subsequently became widespread throughout the hospital" and because other doctors stopped**

referring patients to plaintiff after hearing the statements being repeated. Id. at ¶ 75, 965 N.E. 2d at 1263, 358 Ill. Dec. at 784.

7. ***Statements versus Conduct.*** Defamation claims generally must be supported by actual statements. Actions such as using security guards to escort a terminated employee from the workplace are not sufficient to support a claim for defamation. Davis v. John Crane, Inc., 261 Ill. App. 3d 419, 432, 633 N.E.2d 929, 938, 199 Ill. Dec. 133, 142 (1st Dist. 1994); Dubrovin v. Marshall Field's & Co. Employee's Credit Union, 180 Ill. App. 3d 992, 996-97, 536 N.E.2d 800, 803, 129 Ill. Dec. 750, 753 (1st Dist. 1989) (rejecting defamation claim where employer (1) asked terminated employee to clean out his desk, leave behind certain personal belongings, and return office keys, (2) escorted employee to exit, requesting the return of a building pass en route, and (3) had security guard inspect employee's personal belongings).

8. ***Damages.*** In general, Illinois follows the damages rules in the Restatement (Second) of Torts. Damages are not limited to out-of-pocket loss, but instead may include compensation for "impairment of reputation and standing in the community, personal humiliation, and mental anguish and suffering." Owens v. CBS, 173 Ill. App. 3d 977, 996-97, 527 N.E.2d 1296, 1309, 123 Ill. Dec. 521, 534 (5th Dist. 1988). Although such an award must be "supported by competent evidence," plaintiffs are not required to present evidence "which assigns an actual dollar value to the injury." Id. In addition, a plaintiff may be entitled to special damages such as lost wages or other pecuniary loss. Gibson v. Philip Morris, Inc., 292 Ill. App. 3d 267, 278-79, 685 N.E.2d 638, 647, 226 Ill. Dec. 383, 392 (5th Dist. 1997).

a. **Presumed Damages and Libel Per Se.** A plaintiff may recover presumed damages if the defamatory statement falls into one of the defamation per se categories. Mittelman v. Witous, 135 Ill. 2d 220, 230-31, 552 N.E.2d 973, 978, 142 Ill. Dec. 232, 237 (1989). The plaintiff in such cases may also be required to plead and prove "actual malice." Id. at 235, 552 N.E.2d at 980, 142 Ill. Dec. at 239; Republic Tobacco Corp. v. North Atl. Trading Co., 381 F.3d 717, 733 (7th Cir. 2004). Presumed damages are "'an estimate, however rough, of the probable extent of actual loss a person had suffered and would suffer in the future, even though the loss could not be identified in terms of advantageous relationships lost, either from a monetary or enjoyment-of-life standpoint.'" Brown & Williamson Tobacco Corp. v. Jacobson, 827 F.2d 1119, 1138, 14 Media L. Rep. 1497 (7th Cir. 1987) (quoting Prosser & Keeton on Torts § 116A, at 843 (5th ed. 1984)). Determining the amount of presumed damages is "a very inexact and somewhat arbitrary process." Id. at 1142.

The Seventh Circuit has observed that "presumed damages are speculative in nature," and has cautioned that courts must "protect[] a defamation defendant from being subjected to an astronomical award based upon a jury's guess about the plaintiff's unproven harm." Republic Tobacco Corp., 381 F.3d at 734. In one case, the court reduced the trial court's award of $3.36 million in presumed damages – a number that had already been reduced from the jury's award of $8.4 million – to $1 million, a number that the court considered "more appropriate" than the higher figures. Id. "Presumed damages serve a compensatory function – when such an award is given in a substantial amount to a party who has not demonstrated evidence of concrete loss, it becomes questionable whether the award is serving a different purpose." Id. For similar reasons, the Seventh Circuit held in another case that a successful defamation plaintiff was entitled to $1 million in presumed damages, even though the plaintiff had asked for $7 million in presumed damages, the jury had awarded $3 million, and the district court had reduced the award to a dollar. Brown & Williamson, 827 F.2d at 1139-42.

Because presumed damages are allowed in defamation per se cases, plaintiffs are not required to show that they suffered any reputational damage whatsoever. Hollymatic Corp. v. Daniels Food Equip., Inc., 39 F. Supp. 2d 1115, 1121 (N.D. Ill. 1999). However, the *amount* of damages is an evidentiary issue, Camphausen v. Schweitzer, 10 C 3605, 2010 WL 4539452 (N.D. Ill. Nov. 3, 2010), and the absence of evidence of harm could lead to reduced damages. In Bonkowski v. Z Transp., Inc., No. 00 C 5396, 2004 WL 524723, at *4 (N.D. Ill. March 5, 2004), the plaintiff truck driver in an unopposed bench trial sought compensatory damages of $110,700 and punitive damages of $332,100 for defendant's statement that the plaintiff had stolen a truck. Id. at *4. The court described the requested damages as "grossly inflated" and found that "the actual damage to Plaintiff's reputation from the slanderous statements is small." Id. The court awarded $3,300, or one month's earnings, in compensatory damages, and declined to award punitive damages. Id.

In contrast to claims for defamation per se, in claims for defamation per quod damages "must be alleged and proved." Adams v. Sussman & Hertzberg, Ltd., 292 Ill. App. 3d 30, 46 n.3, 684 N.E.2d 935, 947 n.3, 225 Ill. Dec. 944, 956 n.3 (1st Dist. 1997); see also Hukic v. Aurora Loan Services, 588 F.3d 420, 438 (7th Cir. 2009) (describing special damages as "actual damages of a pecuniary nature").

(1) **Employment-Related Criticism.** Attacks on an employee's performance amount to defamation per se where they "impute inability to perform or want of integrity in the discharge of duties of office or employment" or "prejudice a party, or impute lack of ability, in his trade, profession or business." Mittelman v. Witous, 135 Ill. 2d 220, 238-39, 552 N.E.2d 973, 982, 142 Ill. Dec. 232, 241 (1989) (allowing plaintiff, an attorney, to proceed with claim against partner at former law firm where partner accused plaintiff of spending three years prosecuting a case despite knowledge that claims were barred by statute of limitations). See also Lyssenko v. Int'l Titanium Powder, LLC, No. 07 CC

6678, 2010 WL 2925879, at *2 (N.D. Ill. July 23, 2010) (assuming on a motion to dismiss that statements that employee had "violat[ed] his employment conditions," "remov[ed] and/or destr[oyed]" records, and engaged in "protracted hostility towards other [ ] employees" at a board meeting could be defamatory per se); but see Maag v. Illinois Coalition for Jobs, Growth, & Prosperity, 368 Ill. App. 3d 844, 850, 858 N.E.2d 967, 973, 306 Ill. Dec. 909, 915 (5th Dist. 2006) (holding that criticism of a judge's rulings that did not touch on his private life or suggest a corrupt motive could not support claim for defamation per se because the criticism did not address his integrity or ability as a jurist); Cody v. Harris, 409 F.3d 853, 856-58 (7th Cir. 2005) (employer's false accusations that former employee posted pornographic images on employer's website in retaliation for firing were not defamation per se because the statements addressed employee's personal integrity, not his ability to perform his job as a sales manager); De La Rama v. Illinois Dept. of Human Servs., No. 05 C 5163, 2007 WL 54060, at *9 (N.D. Ill. Jan. 5, 2007) (holding that statements about employee's unauthorized absences were not defamatory as they "related only to [the plaintiff's] failure to follow hospital procedures for obtaining a leave of absence, not to her ability to fulfill her duties as a nurse").

(2) **Single Instance Rule.** In Mittelman, the Illinois Supreme Court rejected the single instance rule and the "now-discredited" line of Illinois cases that applied it. 135 Ill. 2d at 247, 552 N.E.2d at 986, 142 Ill. Dec. at 245. Previous cases had held that "criticism of an individual's conduct only in a particular instance was nonactionable." Id. These cases, the court said, "ignore reality" because "a charge that someone lied to his constituency or mishandled an important case could have devastating consequences for the person so maligned." Id.

b. **Punitive Damages.** Private plaintiffs suing over defamatory statements involving a "purely private matter" do not have to prove actual malice to recover punitive damages. Imperial Apparel, Ltd. v. Cosmo's Designer Direct, Inc., 227 Ill. 2d 381, 395, 882 N.E.2d 1011, 1020, 317 Ill. Dec. 855, 864, 36 Media L. Rep. 1335 (2008). Defendants may nevertheless present "facts tending to show that there was no actual malice in mitigation of the damages, even though evidence of such facts cannot have the effect of withdrawing the question of exemplary damages from the jury." Camphausen, 2010 WL 4539452, at *4.

The appropriate amount of punitive damages generally depends on three factors: "(1) the nature and enormity of the wrong, (2) the financial status of the defendant, and (3) the potential liability of the defendant resulting from multiple claims." Republic Tobacco Corp. v. North Atl. Trading Co., 381 F.3d 717, 735 (7th Cir. 2004) (internal quotations omitted); see also Slovinski v. Elliot, 237 Ill. 2d 51, 58, 927 N.E.2d 1221, 1225, 340 Ill. Dec. 210, 214 (2010). These factors are not exclusive; the court has discretion to consider the unique facts of each case. Black v. Iovino, 219 Ill. App. 3d 378, 393, 580 N.E.2d 139, 149 (1st Dist. 1991). While the jury generally sets the amount of any punitive damages, the court may remit the damages if the jury's verdict is unsupported by evidence. Slovinski, 237 Ill. 2d at 64, 927 N.E.2d at 1228, 340 Ill. Dec. at 217. In Slovinski, the Illinois Supreme Court upheld the remittance of $2 million in punitive damages to $81,600 (equal to the compensatory damages award) in a defamation case where the plaintiff failed to prove willful premeditation, plaintiff's primary argument in favor of large punitive damages. 237 Ill. 2d at 64, 927 N.E.2d at 1228, 340 Ill. Dec. at 217. The court also took into account the facts that the defamatory statement was made only once, the scope of the audience was limited, and the harm was limited. Id.

II. PRIVILEGES AND DEFENSES

A. Scope of Privileges

1. ***Absolute Privilege.*** Statements made in the course of judicial proceedings or quasi-judicial proceedings, along with statements that are "necessarily preliminary" to such proceedings, are protected by an absolute privilege. See, e.g., Lykowski v. Bergman, 299 Ill. App. 3d 157, 165, 700 N.E.2d 1064, 1071, 233 Ill. Dec. 356, 363 (1st Dist. 1998); Jones v. Countrywide Home Loans, Inc., No. 09 C 4313, 2010 WL 551418, at *9 (N.D. Ill. Feb. 11, 2010). The absolute privilege also extends to statements made in the course of legislative proceedings. Mihailovic v. Soldato, No. 03 C 6675, 2004 WL 528010, at *6 (N.D. Ill. Mar. 17, 2004). The privilege applies "no matter how false or outrageous" the statements may be. Lykowski, 299 Ill. App. 3d at 165, 700 N.E.2d at 1071, 233 Ill. Dec. at 363. The party claiming an absolute privilege must present sufficient evidence of the factual basis for applying it. Medow v. Flavin, 336 Ill. App. 3d 20, 34, 782 N.E.2d 733, 745, 270 Ill. Dec. 174, 186 (1st Dist. 2002). The privilege has been applied to protect communications among attorneys and their clients or potential clients, opposing counsel, and attorneys for co-plaintiffs or co-defendants. Thompson v. Frank, 313 Ill. App. 3d 661, 664, 730 N.E.2d 143, 146, 246 Ill. Dec. 463, 466 (3d Dist. 2000); Popp v. O'Neil, 313 Ill. App. 3d 638, 730 N.E.2d 506, 246 Ill. Dec. 481 (2d Dist. 2000); **Sheikh v. Lichtman, No. 11 C 2334, 2012 WL 1378668, at *9 (N.D. Ill. April 19, 2012) (applying the privilege to a part-time attorney retained by a city).** An Illinois court has also applied the privilege to statements in letters from a litigant soliciting information from third parties. Vasarhelyi v. Vasarhelyi, No. 09 C 2240, 2010 WL 1474652, at *3-4 (N.D. Ill. Apr. 19, 2010).

Illinois follows sections 587 and 588 of the Restatement (Second) of Torts (1977), which provide a broad definition of "judicial proceeding" and require that the statement bear only a minimal relationship to the issues in the proceeding. "The privilege will attach even where the defamatory statement is not confined to specific issues related to the litigation, and all doubts should be resolved in favor of a finding of pertinency." Malevitis v. Friedman, 323 Ill. App. 3d 1129, 753 N.E.2d 404, 407, 257 Ill. Dec. 209 (1st Dist. 2001). Thus, the privilege has been applied in a variety of contexts beyond court pleadings and in-court statements: (1) testimony at a disciplinary proceeding before a local board of police and fire commissioners, Hartlep v. Torres, 324 Ill. App. 3d 817, 756 N.E.2d 371, 258 Ill. Dec. 389 (1st Dist. 2001); (2) police officers' statements during an internal investigation into misconduct, where internal regulations required officers to report perceived misconduct, Busch v. Bates, 323 Ill. App. 3d 823, 753 N.E.2d 1184, 1192-93, 257 Ill. Dec. 558 (5th Dist. 2001); (3) statements to the Illinois Attorney Registration and Disciplinary Commission, Lykowski, 299 Ill. App. 3d at 165, 700 N.E.2d at 1071, 233 Ill. Dec. at 363, (4) an employer's report to police that plaintiff had threatened, harassed and assaulted a co-worker, Layne v. Builders Plumbing Supply Co., 210 Ill. App. 3d 966, 969, 569 N.E.2d 1104, 1106, 155 Ill. Dec. 493, 495 (2d Dist. 1991); (5) statements during a meeting about pending litigation attended by officers and board members of a bank and their attorneys, Skopp v. First Fed. Savings of Wilmette, 189 Ill. App. 3d 440, 447-48, 545 N.E.2d 356, 360-61, 136 Ill. Dec. 832, 836-37 (1st Dist. 1989); (6) statements in a demand letter written by an attorney inviting cooperation and resolution of a dispute prior to formal litigation, Simon v. Oltmann, No. 98 C 1759, No. 99 C 1055 (Consolidated), 2001 WL 1035719, at *8-9 (N.D. Ill. Aug. 31, 2001); (7) a memorandum to a bankruptcy trustee alleging dishonest and unethical conduct by a law firm, Edelman, Combs & Latturner v. Hinshaw & Culbertson, 338 Ill. App. 3d 156, 165-66, 788 N.E.2d 740, 749, 273 Ill. Dec. 149, 158 (1st Dist. 2003); (8) a letter from a principal to his employer accusing a teacher of offering bribes to parents in exchange for favorable testimony in an upcoming trial, Marchioni v. Board of Ed. of City of Chicago, 341 F. Supp. 2d 1036, 1051-52 (N.D. Ill. 2005); (9) testimony of an expert witness at a deposition, MacGregor v. Rutberg, 478 F.3d 790, 792 (7th Cir. 2007) (declining to create an "expert witness exception" to the Illinois doctrine of testimonial immunity); **(10) information in a report provided by a court-appointed psychological evaluator, Cooney v. Rossiter, 2012 IL App (1st) 102129, 2012 WL 3326350 (1st Dist. Aug. 10, 2012);** (11) material produced in response to a subpoena, U.S. Dept. of Educ. v. NCAA, 481 F.3d 936, 939 (7th Cir. 2007); (12) statements made by an employer's attorney to a former employee's husband about anticipated litigation, Lewis v. School Dist. # 70, 523 F.3d 730, 745-46 (7th Cir. 2008); and (13) statements in a review sent to the Illinois Department of Human Rights and the Equal Employment Opportunity Commission, Kronenberg v. Baker & McKenzie LLP, 692 F. Supp. 2d 994, 997 (N.D. Ill. 2010).

Whether a proceeding is "quasi-judicial" depends on the nature of the proceeding and the powers and duties of the body conducting the proceeding. Zych v. Tucker, 363 Ill. App. 3d 831, 835, 884 N.E.2d 1004, 1008, 300 Ill. Dec. 561, 565 (1st Dist. 2006). Six powers have been identified as indicating that a body is quasi-judicial rather than merely administrative: (1) the power to exercise judgment and discretion; (2) the power to hear and determine or to ascertain facts and decide; (3) the power to make binding orders and judgments; (4) the power to affect the personal or property rights of private persons; (5) the power to examine witnesses, compel the attendance of witnesses, and conduct a hearing; and (6) the power to enforce decisions or impose penalties. Id. All six powers need not be present for a body to qualify as "quasi-judicial." Id. Quasi-judicial proceedings include arbitration hearings regarding the termination of an employee. Bushell v. Caterpillar, Inc., 291 Ill. App. 3d 559, 683 N.E.2d 1286, 225 Ill. Dec. 623 (3d Dist. 1997). Statements at such proceedings are protected by an absolute privilege.

Legislative hearings include hearings, for example, of a park district board. Mihailovic v. Soldato, No. 03 C 6675, 2004 WL 528010, at *6 (N.D. Ill. March 17, 2004). The privilege extends to statements made by public and private figures as long as the statement is arguably related to the legislative proceeding. Krueger v. Lewis, 359 Ill. App. 3d 515, 521-24, 834 N.E.2d 457, 464-66, 295 Ill. Dec. 876 (1st Dist. 2005) (applying privilege to audience member's accusations of bribery at a village board meeting); Mihailovic, 2004 WL 528010, at *6 (noting that the absolute privilege extends to statements made by private as well as public officials because "[c]itizens ought not to be chilled from making public comments to legislative bodies by fear of being subjected to suit for defamation"). There is no requirement that the statement be made under oath or that the person appear at the meeting pursuant to a subpoena. Krueger, 359 Ill. App. 3d at 522-23, 834 N.E.2d at 465, 295 Ill. Dec. 876.

The absolute privilege, while broad, is not without limits. The privilege will not necessarily apply to communications by or to those with no role in the judicial or legislative process, even if the comments relate to the protected subject matter. Fonseca v. Nelson, No. 08-CV-0435, 2009 WL 78144, at *6 (S.D. Ill. Jan. 12, 2009) (holding that prosecutor's statements to the press were not entitled to absolute immunity because they had no functional tie to the judicial process); Fox v. Tomczak, No. 04 C 7309, 2006 WL 1157466, at *7 (N.D. Ill. Apr. 26, 2006) (same); **August v. Hanlon, 2012 IL App (2d) 111252, ¶ 38, 2012 WL 3893213, at *38 (same).** In addition, defamatory language in a proposed amended complaint may not be privileged if it is filed without leave of court. Kurczaba v. Pollock, 318 Ill. App. 3d 686, 702-06, 742 N.E.2d 425, 439-42, 252 Ill. Dec. 175, 189-92 (1st Dist. 2000).

The Seventh Circuit has held that public officials who make statements "within the scope of their authority" may be protected against defamation claims by an absolute privilege or immunity. Klug v. Chicago School Reform Bd. of Trustees, 197 F.3d 853, 861 (7th Cir. 1999). Under this rule, a public school official's assertion that plaintiff was "not qualified for her high school position" was held to be protected. Id. Accord, Hanania v. Loren-Maltese, 319 F. Supp. 2d 814, 838-39 (N.D. Ill 2004) (holding that town president was protected by absolute privilege if her allegedly defamatory statements were "within the scope of her duties" and that "[a]n official's unworthy purpose or corrupt motive does not invalidate her immunity"). However, when a police officer revealed a letter complaining of a coworker's misconduct to officers outside her chain of command, she was not acting in the scope of her official duties. Anderson v. Beach, 386 Ill. App. 3d 246, 250, 897 N.E.2d 361, 366, 325 Ill. Dec. 113, 118 (1st Dist. 2008). "The relevant inquiry is whether the allegedly defamatory statement of the government official was reasonably related to his or her public duties." Capeheart v. Northeastern Illinois University, No. 08 CV 1423, 2010 WL 894052, at *3 (N.D. Ill. March 9, 2010).

Statements made under a duty to report misconduct may also be protected by absolute privilege, regardless of whether those statements were made during an investigation. In Goldberg v. Brooks, 409 Ill. App. 3d 106, 948 N.E.2d 1108, 350 Ill. Dec. 601 (1st Dist. 2011), a teacher's assistant complained to the principal that the plaintiff, a bus driver, drove her outside of the bus's normal route against her will. Id. at 107-08, 948 N.E.2d at 1111, 350 Ill. Dec. at 604. The principal also received a complaint from a parent, stating that the plaintiff yelled at her child and another student for crossing in front of the bus too slowly. Id. at 108, 948 N.E.2d at 1111, 350 Ill. Dec. at 604. The principal reported these incidents to the plaintiff's employer. Id. The court held that absolute privilege protected both the teacher's assistant's statements to the principal and the principal's subsequent statements to the plaintiff's employer. Id. at 112-13, 948 N.E.2d at 1115, 350 Ill. Dec. at 608. According to the court, the teacher's assistant's statements were protected because she was "under a duty to report misconduct." Id. at 112, 948 N.E.2d at 1115, 350 Ill. Dec. at 608. And the principal's statements were protected because the principal made them while exercising the duties of her position. Id.

In addition, Illinois law provides that a "local public entity is not liable for injury caused by any action of its employees that is libelous or slanderous or for the provision of information either orally, in writing, by computer or any other electronic transmission, or in a book or other form of library material." 745 Ill. Comp. Stat. 10/2-107. The statute lists the types of entities which qualify as "local public entities," including traditional city and township organizations and not-for-profit corporations conducting public business. 745 Ill. Comp. Stat. 10/1-206; see also SMJ Towing, Inc. v. Village of Midlothian, No. 05 C 3020, 2005 WL 3455856, at *5-7 (N.D. Ill. Dec. 16, 2005) (dismissing defamation claim against village because it was a protected local public entity under the Illinois Tort Immunity Act); Hood v. Illinois High Sch. Assoc., 359 Ill. App. 3d 1065, 835 N.E.2d 938, 296 Ill. Dec. 585 (2d Dist. 2005) (rejecting high school association's "local public entity" defense because the association was a statewide voluntary organization, not a local non-profit as required by the statute). The statutory privilege also protects employees of local public entities for statements they make within the scope of their authority. 745 Ill. Comp. Stat. 10/2-210.

The College Campus Press Act provides additional protection to state-sponsored institutions of higher learning for statements made by students in campus media. 110 Ill. Comp. Stat. 13/1-97. This statute provides immunity to the institution from lawsuits "arising from expression actually made in campus media, with the exception of the institution's own expression." 110 Ill. Comp. Stat. 13/35.

The absolute privilege is an affirmative defense. Malevitis v. Friedman, 323 Ill. App. 3d 1129, 753 N.E.2d 404, 406, 257 Ill. Dec. 209 (1st Dist. 2001). Whether the privilege applies is a question of law for the court. Bushell v. Caterpillar, Inc., 291 Ill. App. 3d 559, 561, 683 N.E.2d 1286, 1288, 225 Ill. Dec. 623, 625 (3d Dist. 1997). The privilege may be lost, however, if the privileged statement is forwarded to a third party who is not within the privilege. Lykowski v. Bergman, 299 Ill. App. 3d 157, 166-67, 700 N.E.2d 1064, 1071-72, 233 Ill. Dec. 356, 363-64 (1st Dist. 1998).

Privileges that bar defamation actions also bar other claims based on the same conduct. Mihailovic v. Soldato, No. 03 C 6675, 2004 WL 528010, at *7 (N.D. Ill. Mar. 17, 2004) (including conspiracy and intentional interference with business relations).

2. ***Qualified Privileges.*** In Kuwik v. Starmark Star Marketing and Administration, Inc., 156 Ill. 2d 16, 619 N.E.2d 129, 188 Ill. Dec. 765 (1993), the Illinois Supreme Court adopted the approach to qualified privileges described in the Restatement (Second) of Torts. Under the Restatement, "a court looks only to the occasion itself for the communication and determines as a matter of law and general policy whether the occasion created some recognized duty or interest to make the communication so as to make it privileged." Id. at 27, 619 N.E.2d at 134, 188 Ill. Dec. at 770. The defendant bears the burden of showing that the privilege applies. Id. A qualified privilege arises where the allegedly defamatory statement concerns (1) an interest of the speaker, (2) an interest of the recipient of the statement or some other third party, or (3) an interest of the public. Id. at 29, 619 N.E.2d at 135, 188 Ill. Dec. at 771.

Once the defendant has shown a qualified privilege, the burden shifts to the plaintiff to show an abuse of that privilege. Before Kuwik, abuse of the privilege required a showing of constitutional actual malice, i.e., a showing that the defendant spoke with knowledge of falsity or reckless disregard of truth or falsity. But Kuwik "expand[ed] the definition of abuse of a qualified privilege." 156 Ill. 2d at 30, 619 N.E.2d at 135, 188 Ill. Dec. at 771. "We now hold that to prove an abuse of the qualified privilege, the plaintiff must show a direct intention to injure another, or a reckless disregard of the defamed party's rights and of the consequences that may result to him." Id. (internal quotation marks and brackets omitted). "Thus, an abuse of a qualified privilege may consist of any reckless act which shows a disregard for the defamed party's rights, including the failure to properly investigate the truth of the matter, limit the scope of the material, or send the material to only the proper parties." Id. at 30, 619 N.E.2d at 136, 188 Ill. Dec. at 772.

A qualified privilege will usually protect employers when they conduct internal investigations or evaluate their employees. Popko v. Continental Cas. Co., 355 Ill. App. 3d 257, 264, 832 N.E.2d 184, 190, 291 Ill. Dec. 174, 180 (1st Dist. 2005) ("a corporation has an unquestionable interest in investigating and correcting a situation where one of its employees may be engaged in suspicious conduct within the company"). See, e.g., Anderson v. Beach, 386 Ill. App. 3d 246, 252, 897 N.E.2d 361, 366, 325 Ill. Dec. 113, 118 (1st Dist. 2008) (holding a letter describing an officer's concern for the safety, well-being, and reputation of women working with a coworker accused of misconduct was conditionally privileged); Vickers v. Abbott Labs., 308 Ill. App. 3d 393, 719 N.E.2d 1101, 241 Ill. Dec. 698 (1st Dist. 1999) (qualified privilege protected statements made during course of employer's sexual harassment investigation; upholding summary judgment in favor of defendants); Turner v. Fletcher, 302 Ill. App. 3d 1051, 706 N.E.2d 514, 235 Ill. Dec. 959 (4th Dist. 1999) (qualified privilege protected physician's evaluation of plaintiff as unfit to work as a police officer; upholding dismissal of claims); Smock v. Nolan, 361 F.3d 367, 372 (7th Cir. 2004) (administrator of a polygraph exam protected by qualified privilege in reporting the results to his Illinois State Police supervisors); Haywood v. Lucent Techs., Inc., 323 F.3d 524, 533 (7th Cir. 2003) (qualified privilege protected communications from management employees to security that former employee was unstable and that security should call police if she appeared on company premises); McDermott v. Cont'l/Midland, Inc., No. 02 C 8063, 2003 WL 223440, at *3-4 (N.D. Ill. Jan. 31, 2003) (qualified privilege protects statements by personnel director to employee's supervisor articulating reasons for employee's termination); Trask v. Gen. Elec. Co., 207 F. Supp. 2d 843, 847-48 (N.D. Ill. 2002) (qualified privilege protects forwarding of employee termination letter from human resources department to manager); Locsmondy v. Arrow Pneumatics, No. 99 C 6463, 2001 WL 109810, at *8 (N.D. Ill. Feb. 5, 2001) (corporate president's memorandum describing sexual harassment complaints against CEO was subject to qualified privilege).

When a qualified privilege applies to the defendant's statements, a trial is necessary if there is a question of fact as to whether the privilege has been abused. Turner, 302 Ill. App. 3d at 1057, 706 N.E.2d at 518, 235 Ill. Dec. at 963; Medallion Prods., Inc. v. McAlister, No. 06 C 2597, 2008 WL 5046055, at *17 (N.D. Ill. Nov. 20, 2008) ("[T]he Court may not take this determination out of the hands of the jury unless the evidence in the record unequivocally demonstrates the absence of abuse.").

To survive a motion to dismiss based on a qualified privilege, a plaintiff must plead that the defendant acted with intent to harm or with recklessness as to the plaintiff's rights. See Horton v. Nat'l City Mortg. Services Co., No. 09-1391, 2010 WL 1253994, at *6 (C.D. Ill. Mar. 24, 2010) (holding that complaint pleaded abuse of privilege where plaintiff pleaded failure to investigate the allegedly defamatory statements); United Labs., Inc. v. Savaiano, No. 06 C 1442, 2007 WL 4557095, at *9 (N.D. Ill. Dec. 21, 2007) (holding that even if a qualified privilege applied, plaintiffs' allegations that defendants acted with "intent to harm" was sufficient to survive a motion to dismiss). Nevertheless, a defendant can prevail on a motion to dismiss "if the pleadings and attached exhibits present no genuine issue of material fact." Turner, 302 Ill. App. 3d at 1057, 706 N.E.2d at 518, 235 Ill. Dec. at 963 (upholding dismissal of claims where attachments to complaint did not support conclusory allegation that defendant "knew" that plaintiff "was in fact psychologically fit" for duty). Summary judgment is even more likely. See Vickers, 308 Ill. App. 3d 393, 719 N.E.2d 1101, 241 Ill. Dec. 698; Naeemullah v. Citicorp Servs., Inc., 78 F. Supp. 2d 783, 793 (N.D. Ill. 1999).

In addition to the common law privilege, a statutory privilege applies to communications from employers made in connection with the administration of the Unemployment Insurance Act, "unless they are false in fact and malicious in intent." 820 Ill. Comp. Stat. 405/1900.1. Federal labor law may also preempt state defamation law and provide a privilege for certain communications within labor unions. Sullivan v. Conway, 157 F.3d 1092, 1099 (7th Cir. 1998). However, that privilege may be defeated "if the speaker had made an unflattering statement that he did not believe to be true or had been indifferent to whether it was true or false." Starr v. Int'l Brotherhood of Elec. Workers, No. 03 C 1760, 2003 WL 23509646, at *5 (N.D. Ill. Dec. 17, 2003).

The Illinois Medical Studies Act protects information used during "internal quality control" or "in the course of medical study" where it is aimed at "reducing morbidity or mortality" or "improving patient care." 735 Ill. Comp. Stat. 5/8-2101. In Kopolovic v. Shah, 2012 IL App (2d) 110383, ¶ 36, 967 N.E.2d 368, 381, 359 Ill. Dec. 638, 652, the court held that the Act did not immunize a doctor from defamation liability for challenging plaintiff's medical ethics in a memorandum to hospital directors. The court characterized the Act as creating an "evidentiary privilege" as opposed to "immunity from liability," noting that the privilege is "aimed at shielding . . . sensitive information within the Act's scope from discovery or use at trial." Id. at ¶ 33, 967 N.E. 2d at 380, 359 Ill. Dec. at 650.

A fair report privilege protects defendants who accurately convey the contents of an official proceeding, even if that account repeats defamatory material from the proceeding. Eubanks v. Nw. Herald Newspapers, 397 Ill. App. 3d 746, 750, 922 N.E.2d 1196, 1200 (2d Dist. 2010) (newspaper protected where it accurately conveyed information from an official police bulletin later found to have erroneously named the plaintiff); Fedders Corp. v. Elite Classics, 279 F. Supp. 2d 965, 970-71 (S.D. Ill. 2003) (holding that a press release describing a complaint filed in court could be privileged); **Hill v. Schmidt, 2012 IL App (5th) 110324, ¶ 20, 969 N.E.2d 563, 569, 360 Ill. Dec. 753, 759 (holding that the privilege protected a reporter who accurately conveyed a story from a prosecutor, even though he later published a different version of the story that was based on another source). But see August v. Hanlon, 2012 IL App (2d) 111252, ¶ 38, 2012 WL 3893213, at *38 (holding that the fair report privilege does not protect an attorney who makes defamatory statements to a reporter, even if the privilege "might arguably apply to the newspaper that published the article upon which plaintiff's complaint is based").** The fair report privilege has two requirements: (1) the report must relate what happened in an official proceeding or report, and (2) the report must be complete and accurate or a fair abridgement of the proceeding. Solaia Tech., LLC v. Specialty Publ'g Co., 221 Ill. 2d 558, 587-88, 852 N.E.2d 825, 843, 304 Ill. Dec 369, 387 (2006). A person may not confer the fair report privilege on himself by filing a defamatory lawsuit and then reporting to others what is contained in the complaint, nor may the privilege be conferred upon another person through collusion. Id. at 588, 852 N.E.2d at 844, 304 Ill. Dec. at 388.

a. **Common Interest.** A common interest between the speaker and the recipient of a statement will bring the statement within the scope of the privilege. See, e.g., Cianci v. Pettibone Corp., 298 Ill. App. 3d 419, 426, 698 N.E.2d 674, 679-80, 232 Ill. Dec. 583, 588-89 (1st Dist. 1998) (holding that employer's statements about terminated employee's misuse of courier service were privileged); DePinto v. Sherwin-Williams Co., 776 F. Supp. 2d 796, 810 (N.D. Ill. 2011) (finding paint manufacturer to be protected by qualified privilege when its employees made statements about the quality of the plaintiff's work to a developer who had an exclusive contract to use the manufacturer's products); LaScola v. US Sprint Communications, 739 F. Supp. 431, 437-38 (N.D. Ill. 1990) (employer had qualified privilege to tell customer that former sales representative was fired for disclosing confidential customer information), aff'd, 946 F.2d 559 (7th Cir. 1991).

b. **Duty.** Where the defendant has a duty to speak, his statements will be protected by a qualified privilege. Courts typically find that managers and executives have a duty to discuss the performance and possible malfeasance of employees. See, e.g., Harrel v. Dillards Dept. Stores, Inc., 268 Ill. App. 3d 537, 542-43, 644 N.E.2d 448, 455, 205 Ill. Dec. 892, 899 (5th Dist. 1994) (managers had privilege to discuss allegations against employee who was terminated for dishonesty and possible theft); Davis v. John Crane, Inc., 261 Ill. App. 3d 419, 430, 633 N.E.2d 929, 937, 199 Ill. Dec. 133, 141 (1st Dist. 1994) (vice president of human resources had duty to enforce company's employment policies and work rules, including anti-drug policy); Miller v. Danville Elks Lodge, 211 Ill. App. 3d 145, 154, 569 N.E.2d 1160, 1165-66, 155 Ill. Dec. 549, 554-55 (4th Dist. 1991) (qualified privilege applied where club manager had duty to report employee's alleged misuse of petty cash fund); Sullivan v. Conway, 157 F.3d 1092, 1098 (7th Cir. 1998) (union officials had duty to discuss qualifications of union lawyer); Bogosian v. Board of Educ. of Community School Dist. 200, 134 F. Supp. 2d 952, 958 (N.D. Ill. 2001) (teacher had statutory duty to report reasonable suspicions of child abuse to school principal); Naeemullah v. Citicorp Servs., Inc., 78 F. Supp. 2d 783, 793 (N.D. Ill. 1999) (supervisor had an interest — even a duty — to make statements regarding employee's job performance).

c. **Criticism of Public Employee.** The Illinois Appellate Court has followed the Restatement (Second) of Torts § 598, cmt. e (1977), which provides that "a defamatory publication made by a citizen to a public officer concerning the work of a subordinate under his control or supervision is conditionally privileged." Turner v. Fletcher, 302 Ill. App. 3d 1051, 1056, 706 N.E.2d 514, 518, 235 Ill. Dec. 959, 963 (4th Dist. 1999).

If the criticism is made by the government or one of its employees, the statements may be protected by the Illinois Local Governmental and Governmental Employees Tort Immunity Act, 745 Ill. Comp. Stat. 10/1-101 et seq. Under the Act, local public entities "are not liable for injury caused by any action of its employees that is libelous or slanderous." Id. § 2-107; see Hutchins v. Harrison, No. 08 C 5366, 2009 WL 1139121, at *2 (N.D. Ill. Apr. 28, 2009) (noting defendants, a county corrections captain and county superintendent, properly invoked the Act).

d. **Limitation on Qualified Privileges.**

(1) **Constitutional or Actual Malice.** Under the Illinois Supreme Court's ruling in Kuwik, a showing of actual malice defeats a qualified privilege. See Harrel v. Dillards Dept. Stores, Inc., 268 Ill. App. 3d 537, 544, 644 N.E.2d 448, 452-54, 205 Ill. Dec. 892, 896-98 (5th Dist. 1994). Lower courts have acknowledged that Kuwik expanded the definition of abuse of the privilege beyond actual malice to include "any reckless acts leading to the defamation." Vickers v. Abbot Lab., 308 Ill. App. 3d 393, 404, 719 N.E.2d 1101, 1110, 241 Ill. Dec. 698, 707 (1st Dist. 1999); Awalt v. Allied Sec., Remedial Constr. Servs., L.P., No. Civ. 04-126, 2006 WL 181681, at *5-6 (S.D. Ill. Jan. 17, 2006).

(2) **Common Law Malice.** A showing of evil intent, ill will, or spite may overcome a qualified privilege. See Harrel, 268 Ill. App. 3d at 544, 644 N.E.2d at 452, 205 Ill. Dec. at 896 (stating that such a showing must be made to overcome privilege, but apparently confusing common law malice with actual malice).

e. **Question of Fact or Law.** The existence of a qualified privilege is determined by the court as a matter of law. Kuwik, 156 Ill. 2d at 27, 619 N.E.2d at 134, 188 Ill. Dec. at 770. But whether the privilege has been abused may present a question of fact. Id. at 31-32, 619 N.E.2d at 136, 188 Ill. Dec. at 772.

f. **Burden of Proof.** The defendant has the burden of showing that his statements were made under circumstances that give rise to a privilege. Id. at 27, 619 N.E.2d at 134, 188 Ill. Dec. at 770. Once a court has determined that a statement is privileged, the plaintiff must show that "there was a direct intention to injure or a reckless disregard of plaintiff's rights by the defendant." Harrel, 268 Ill. App. 3d at 545, 644 N.E.2d at 453, 205 Ill. Dec. at 897. At the summary judgment stage, "once a defendant has established a qualified privilege, the plaintiff must come forward with actual evidence creating an issue of fact" regarding abuse of the privilege. Vickers, 308 Ill. App. 3d at 404, 719 N.E.2d at 1110, 241 Ill. Dec. at 707.

B. Standard Libel Defenses

1. ***Truth***. The plaintiff bears the burden of proving falsity. See I.B.3, supra. But if the defendant seeks to establish truth as a defense, he "need only demonstrate the truth of the 'gist' or 'sting' of the defamatory material. Only 'substantial truth' is required for this defense, which may be raised by a motion to dismiss." Lemons v. Chronicle Pub. Co., 253 Ill. App. 3d 888, 890, 625 N.E.2d 789, 791, 192 Ill. Dec. 634, 636, 22 Media L. Rep. 1222 (4th Dist. 1993); see also Haynes v. Alfred A. Knopf, Inc., 8 F.3d 1222, 1227-29, 21 Media L. Rep. 2161 (7th Cir. 1993). Inaccurate items of secondary importance are not actionable, particularly if they do no more harm to the plaintiff's reputation than substantially true statements. See Global Relief Found., Inc. v. New York Times Co., 390 F.3d 973, 987 (7th Cir. 2004).

While substantial truth is sometimes a jury question, it can be decided as a matter of law if no reasonable jury could fail to find the statement substantially true. Id. at 986-87; Clarage v. Kuzma, 342 Ill. App. 3d 573, 795 N.E.2d 348, 355, 276 Ill. Dec. 995, 1002 (3d Dist. 2003). See, e.g., Moore v. People for the Ethical Treatment of Animals, Inc., 402 Ill. App. 3d 62, 71, 932 N.E.2d 448, 457, 342 Ill. Dec. 321, 330 (1st Dist. 2010) (1st Dist. 2010) (finding that statement that defendant placed a shock collar around a dog's genitals was substantially true where defendant admitted to placing a shock collar around the dog's hindquarters); J. Maki Constr. Co. v. Chicago Reg'l Council of Carpenters, 379 Ill. App. 3d 189, 203, 882 N.E.2d 1173, 1186, 318 Ill. Dec. 50, 63 (2d Dist. 2008) (holding that no reasonable jury could find that substantial truth had not been established when the word "conviction" was used to refer to disciplinary action regarding internal union charges); Harrison v. Chicago Sun-Times, Inc., 341 Ill. App. 3d 555, 563, 793 N.E.2d 760, 767, 276 Ill. Dec. 1, 8 (1st Dist. 2003) (finding report that plaintiff was charged with kidnapping to be substantially true when plaintiff was charged with wrongful removal under federal and international child abduction laws); Wynne v. Loyola Univ. of Chicago, 318 Ill. App. 3d 443, 451-52, 741 N.E.2d 669, 675-76, 251 Ill. Dec. 782, 788-89 (1st Dist. 2000) (upholding summary judgment in favor of defendants where memorandum describing plaintiff's history of psychiatric problems, plaintiff's history of fertility problems, and plaintiff's conversations about and responses to those problems was substantially true). But see Parker v. House O'Lite Corp., 324 Ill. App. 3d 1014, 756 N.E.2d 286, 258 Ill. Dec. 304 (1st Dist. 2001) (reversing summary judgment in favor of defendant on issue of substantial truth); Phillips v. Quality Terminal Servs., LLC, No. 08-cv-6633, 2009 WL 4674051, at *8 (N.D. Ill. Dec. 4, 2009) (finding question of fact about the substantial truth of employer's statement that plaintiff failed a drug test where plaintiff alleged the results were incorrect).

2. ***Opinion.*** Illinois has not provided special protection for expressions of opinion beyond that contained in the First Amendment. Bryson v. News Am. Pubs., Inc., 174 Ill. 2d 77, 99-102, 672 N.E.2d 1207, 1219-21, 220 Ill. Dec. 195, 207-09, 25 Media L. Rep. 1321 (1996) (discussing Milkovich v. Lorain Journal Co., 497 U.S. 1, 110 S. Ct. 2695, 111 L. Ed. 2d 1 (1990)); Kolegas v. Heftel Broadcasting Corp., 154 Ill. 2d 1, 14-15, 607 N.E.2d 201, 208, 180 Ill. Dec. 307, 314, 20 Media L. Rep. 2105 (1992) (citing Milkovich for the proposition that "only those statements that cannot reasonably be interpreted as stating actual facts are protected under the first amendment") (internal quotations and brackets omitted). "The mere fact that a statement of fact is couched in the rhetorical hyperbole of an opinion does not render it nonactionable. The test is whether the statement can be reasonably interpreted as stating actual fact." Maxon v. Ottawa Pub. Co., 402 Ill. App. 3d 704, 716, 929 N.E.2d 666, 677, 341 Ill. Dec. 12, 23 (3d Dist. 2010).

Whether a statement is fact or opinion is a question of law. Kronenberg v. Baker & McKenzie LLP, 692 F. Supp. 2d 994, 998 (N.D. Ill. 2010). The court should consider "(1) whether the statement has a precise core of meaning for which a consensus of understanding exists, or conversely, whether the statement is indefinite and ambiguous; (2) whether the statement is verifiable; i.e. capable of being objectively characterized as true or false; (3) whether the literary context of the statement would influence the average reader's readiness to infer that a particular statement has factual content; and (4) whether the broader social context or setting in which the statement appears signals a usage as either fact or opinion." Drury

v. Sanofi-Synthelabo Inc., 292 F. Supp. 2d 1068, 1070 (N.D. Ill. 2003) (quoting Haywood v. Lucent Techs., Inc., 169 F. Supp. 2d 890, 915 (N.D. Ill. 2001)); see also Solaia Tech., LLC v. Specialty Pub. Co., 221 Ill. 2d 558, 581, 852 N.E.2d 825, 840, 304 Ill. Dec. 369 (2006). "If it is plain that the speaker is expressing a subjective view, an interpretation, a theory, conjecture, or surmise, rather than claiming to be in possession of objectively verifiable facts, the statement is not actionable." Giant Screen Sports v. Canadian Imperial Bank of Commerce, 553 F.3d 527, 534-35 (7th Cir. 2009). See also Maag v. Ill. Coalition for Jobs, Growth, & Prosperity, 368 Ill. App. 3d 844, 851, 858 N.E.2d 967, 974, 306 Ill. Dec. 909, 916 (5th Dist. 2006) (holding that critical statements about judge in campaign flyer were protected as opinion in part because they were made in the context of a heated election campaign where "[e]xaggerated rhetoric is commonplace").

The opinion defense arises regularly in the employment context. See, e.g., Rose v. Hollinger Int'l, Inc., 383 Ill. App. 3d 8, 11-19, 889 N.E.2d 644, 647-54, 321 Ill. Dec. 379, 382-89 (1st Dist. 2008) (finding a statement that a former employee damaged company's finances to be nonactionable opinion because readers would not know precisely which finances were damaged and because the statement was not objectively verifiable); J. Maki Constr. Co. v. Chicago Reg'l Council of Carpenters, 379 Ill. App. 3d 189, 200-02, 882 N.E.2d 1173, 1183-85, 318 Ill. Dec. 50, 60-62 (2d Dist. 2008) (holding that union pamphlets stating that plaintiff's houses were "crappy" constituted nonactionable opinion because the word "crappy" is vague and not verifiable); Green v. Trinity Int'l Univ., 344 Ill. App. 3d 1079, 1093, 801 N.E.2d 1208, 1220, 280 Ill. Dec. 263, 275 (2d Dist. 2003) (holding that statements that plaintiff professor acted rudely and unprofessionally constituted non-actionable opinion because "[w]hat is considered rude or unprofessional differs from person to person"); Lifton v. Board of Educ. of City of Chicago, 416 F.3d 571, 579 (7th Cir. 2005) (principal's statements that teacher was "lazy," "unstable," and "resting on her laurels" were not actionable because, to constitute defamation, the statement must be objectively verifiable); Kougias v. Ill. Dept. of Human Servs., No. 07 C 4481, 2011 WL 1004278, at *9 (N.D. Ill. Mar. 16, 2011) (co-worker's comments to plaintiff that she was unfit to be a psychiatrist were "nothing more than an irrational argumentative characterization not worthy of serious consideration").

Where a statement has a factual core, it is not opinion. See, e.g., Maxon, 402 Ill. App. 3d at 716, 929 N.E.2d at 677, 341 Ill. Dec. at 23 ("Statements that someone has committed bribery in order to obtain a favorable ruling on a zoning matter are, unlike calling someone a 'world class crook,' 'a traitor,' or characterizing a negotiating position as 'blackmail,' not generally taken as mere hyperbole."); Stavros v. Marrese, 323 Ill. App. 3d 1052, 753 N.E.2d 1013, 1018, 257 Ill. Dec. 387 (1st Dist. 2001) (holding that accusation of "extortion" was "objectively verifiable and therefore actionable"); Lyssenko v. Int'l Titanium Powder, LLC, No. 07 C 6678, 2008 WL 8625903, at *4 (N.D. Ill. May 6, 2008) (holding that statement that plaintiff had "burned bridges" was factual because it "suggests that the plaintiff engaged in specific conduct that had an identifiable result, namely, the destruction of his relationships with individuals within the government"); SMJ Towing, Inc. v. Village of Midlothian, No. 05 C 3020, 2005 WL 3455856, at *6 (N.D. Ill. Dec. 16, 2005) (holding that statement that "SMJ was involved in the illegal drug trade" was not a protected opinion because it is precise, readily understood, and verifiable); Quiroz v. Hartgrove Hosp., No. 97 C 6515, 1999 WL 281343, at *15-16, 75 Empl. Prac. Dec. (CCH) ¶ 45,833 (N.D. Ill. Mar. 24, 1999) (calling plaintiff an adulteress and a prostitute who tried to extort money from defendant were verifiable facts, but statements that plaintiff was "incompetent" and "stupid," in absence of specific examples, "are not capable of being proven true or false as they are inherently subjective"). Simply including language such as "we believe" or "in my opinion" does not transform an otherwise actionable factual statement into a non-actionable opinion. Flori v. Thornton, No. 06-3021, 2006 WL 1686166, at *2 (C.D. Ill. June 19, 2006). And a statement is not necessarily hyperbolic opinion just because it is published on the Internet. Maxon, 402 Ill. App. 3d at 716, 929 N.E.2d at 677, 341 Ill. Dec. at 23; **Pitale v. Holestine, No. 11 C 00921, 2012 WL 638755, at *7 (N.D. Ill. Feb. 27, 2012) (finding that statements on blogs present a "close[] question" under the "literary and social context" factor, but holding that the statements were factual because they provided a "factual background on [the plaintiff] and describe[d] his history").**

The opinion defense can provide a strong basis for obtaining dismissal of defamation claims based on evaluations of employees. Generalized labels placed on an employee (such as "incompetent") are likely to be considered protected opinions, especially when they are not accompanied by specific examples of misfeasance. See, e.g., Wynne v. Loyola Univ. of Chicago, 318 Ill. App. 3d 443, 452-53, 741 N.E.2d 669, 676, 251 Ill. Dec. 782, 789 (1st Dist. 2000) (characterizations of plaintiff's behavior as "bizarre," "inappropriate" and "uniformly unpleasant" were protectable statements of opinion); Hopewell v. Vitullo, 299 Ill. App. 3d 513, 701 N.E.2d 99, 233 Ill. Dec. 456 (1st Dist. 1998); Quinn v. Jewel Food Stores, Inc., 276 Ill. App. 3d 861, 866-67, 658 N.E.2d 1225, 1231, 213 Ill. Dec. 204, 210 (1st Dist. 1995) (statements in employer's evaluation form that plaintiff was "cocky," a "con artist" and warning to "[w]atch out for the bullshit!" were not statements of fact, but were instead "characterizations and opinions formed based on [employer's] interview with plaintiff"); Sullivan v. Conway, 157 F.3d 1092, 1097 (7th Cir. 1998) (calling plaintiff a "very poor lawyer" was not actionable because it was "an opinion that is so difficult to verify or refute that it cannot feasibly be made a subject of inquiry by a jury"); Kronenberg v. Baker & McKenzie LLP, 692 F. Supp. 2d 994, 998 (N.D. Ill. 2010) (finding that ratings such as "meets expectations" and comments like plaintiff "has difficulty working with others to whom he reports," "has not allowed proper supervision of the matters on which he is working," and "has failed to work together with other attorneys in the practice group" were non-verifiable opinions); Brown v. GC America, Inc., No. 05 C 3810, 2005 WL 3077608, at *8-9 (N.D. Ill. Nov. 15, 2005) (dismissing defamation complaint because statements that employee was incompetent, lacked ability to teach, should be fired, and was responsible for the company's shortcomings were protected statements of opinion); Drury v. Sanofi-Synthelabo Inc., 292 F. Supp. 2d 1068, 1070 (N.D. Ill. 2003) (supervisor's characterizations of plaintiff as a "cancer" on the team were "vague expressions of sentiments, not statements of verifiable fact"); Hach v. Laidlaw Transit, Inc., No. 02 C 996, 2002 WL 31496240, at *4-5 (N.D. Ill. Nov. 7, 2002) (statements that executive's attitude was "that of a victim" and "not that of a winner" and that he should be terminated due to his "failing management" were statements of opinion); Toyos v. Northwestern Univ., No. 01 C 5407, 2002 WL 252731, at *3 (N.D. Ill. Feb. 21, 2002) (recommending former employee "with some reservations" held not actionable because the recommendation was an opinion, not an "objectively verifiable" assertion).

However, the opinion defense is not absolute and certain statements in the employment context may be held to be actionable statements of fact. See Dubinsky v. United Airlines Master Executive Council, 303 Ill. App. 3d 317, 325-28, 708 N.E.2d 441, 448-50, 236 Ill. Dec. 855, 862-64 (1st Dist. 1999) (statement that "I believe that Federal laws have been broken" held to be an actionable statement of fact, while statements that "whether or not RICO or other federal laws apply will be decided in civil court or by the Justice Department," that plaintiffs engaged in "collusion" and a "conspiracy," and that one plaintiff was a "crook" were non-actionable opinions; also analyzing the fact/opinion distinction for other statements); Gehrls v. Gooch, No. 09 C 6338, 2010 WL 1849400, at *3 (N.D. Ill. May 7, 2010) (declining to dismiss complaint based on report in personnel file that accused plaintiff of engaging in "inappropriate intimate conduct" in the galley of a plane while working, while recognizing that "there likely will be an issue as to whether the statement" is constitutionally protected opinion).

3. ***Consent.*** Plaintiff's consent to the publication of defamatory material results in a qualified privilege. See Millsaps v. Bankers Life Co., 35 Ill. App. 3d 735, 743, 342 N.E.2d 329, 335 (2d Dist. 1976) (where plaintiff authorized his physician to provide report to insurance company, report was conditionally privileged because doctor "did only what plaintiff authorized him to do"); Judge v. Rockford Mem. Hosp., 17 Ill. App. 2d 365, 377, 150 N.E.2d 202, 207 (2d Dist. 1958) ("Generally, where alleged defamatory material is published privately and confidentially in response to an inquiry made by the party allegedly defamed or his authorized agent, it is qualifiedly privileged if it does not go beyond the scope of the inquiry.").

4. ***Mitigation.*** Although there is scant case law on the subject, a plaintiff's provocation of a defamatory statement and a defendant's retraction of a defamatory statement may reduce the damages to which a plaintiff would otherwise be entitled. Fleming v. Kane County, 636 F. Supp. 742, 749 (N.D. Ill. 1986). One court held that plaintiffs' failure to request a retraction, failure to publish information to counteract the defamatory statements, and refusal to cooperate with defendants before the defamatory statements were published may be relevant to a mitigation defense. J.H. Desnick, M.D., Eye Servs., Ltd. v. ABC, No. 93 C 6534, 1999 WL 51796, at *2, 27 Media L. Rep. 1689 (N.D. Ill. Jan. 29, 1999) (denying plaintiffs' motion for summary judgment on defendants' affirmative defense of mitigation of damages). The effect of such a defense is generally a jury question. Id.

III. RECURRING FACT PATTERNS

A. Statements in Personnel File

Depending on the circumstances, statements in a personnel file may not be considered "published." Pandya v. Hoerchler, 256 Ill. App. 3d 669, 673, 628 N.E.2d 1040, 1043, 195 Ill. Dec. 576, 579 (1st Dist. 1993). But see Gehrls v. Gooch, No. 09 C 6338, 2010 WL 1849400, at *3 (N.D. Ill. May 7, 2010) (declining to dismiss complaint based on summary report placed in personnel file). They may also be protected by a qualified privilege. See II.A.2, supra.

B. Performance Evaluations

Statements in performance evaluations may be considered non-verifiable opinions rather than statements of fact. See II.B.2, supra; see also Quinn v. Jewel Food Stores, Inc., 276 Ill. App. 3d 861, 866-67, 658 N.E.2d 1225, 1231, 213 Ill. Dec. 204, 210 (1st Dist. 1995); Naeemullah v. Citicorp Servs., Inc., 78 F. Supp. 2d 783, 793 (N.D. Ill. 1999); Kronenberg v. Baker & McKenzie LLP, 692 F. Supp. 2d 994, 998 (N.D. Ill. 2010). However, performance reviews may be considered published. Kronenberg, 692 F. Supp. 2d at 997 (publication of review internally at law firm constituted publication). They are also likely to be protected by a qualified privilege. See II.A.2, supra.

C. References

The innocent construction rule can provide strong grounds for challenging defamation claims based on negative references. See I.B.4, supra. While there is no bright-line test, and while the courts do not always apply the rule consistently, the rule generally applies where a negative reference can reasonably be construed to mean that the employee did not work out well in a particular position. See, e.g., Anderson v. Vanden Dorpel, 172 Ill. 2d 399, 413, 667 N.E.2d 1296, 1302, 217 Ill. Dec.

720, 726 (1996) (statements that employee "failed to follow up on assignments" could be construed to mean that employee "did not fit in" at employer, rather than a comment on employee's ability to perform in other jobs).

In contrast, if a reference clearly indicates that the employee was not fit to perform his job and would not be qualified to perform similar jobs, the innocent construction rule will not bar a defamation claim. See, e.g., Stratman v. Brent, 291 Ill. App. 3d 123, 135, 683 N.E.2d 951, 959, 225 Ill. Dec. 448, 456 (2d Dist. 1997) (innocent construction rule did not apply where police chief said that former police officer was given nickname which designates a person who is mentally disturbed, was a loner with a negative attitude, and was incapable of handling stress; that police chief sought a reason to fire plaintiff, was relieved when he resigned, and would not recommend him for employment with other law enforcement agencies; and that other officers would "mutiny" if plaintiff were rehired).

A qualified privilege may apply to references regarding former employees. See, e.g., Quinn v. Jewel Food Stores, Inc., 276 Ill. App. 3d 861, 870-72, 658 N.E.2d 1225, 1233-34, 213 Ill. Dec. 204, 212-13 (1st Dist. 1995); Skopp v. First Federal Savings of Wilmette, 189 Ill. App. 3d 440, 444-46, 545 N.E.2d 356, 359-60, 136 Ill. Dec. 832, 835-36 (1st Dist. 1989). Moreover, the Illinois Employment Record Disclosure Act, 745 Ill. Comp. Stat. 46/10, provides that an employer cannot be held liable for responding to an inquiry from a prospective employer with "truthful written or verbal information, or information that it believes in good faith is truthful, about a current or former employee's job performance."

D. Intracorporate Communication

A qualified privilege generally protects intracorporate communications which are made in furtherance of the business of the employer, such as statements made during an internal investigation. See, e.g., Popko v. Continental Cas. Co., 355 Ill. App. 3d 257, 264, 823 N.E.2d 184, 190, 291 Ill. Dec. 174, 180 (1st Dist. 2005). See also II.A.2, supra.

E. Statements to Government Regulators

Statements to police or to judicial or quasi-judicial bodies may be protected by an absolute privilege. See Lykowski v. Bergman, 299 Ill. App. 3d 157, 165, 700 N.E.2d 1064, 1071, 233 Ill. Dec. 356, 363 (1st Dist. 1998) (statements to Illinois Attorney Registration and Disciplinary Commission); Kronenberg v. Baker & McKenzie LLP, 692 F. Supp. 2d 994, 997 (N.D. Ill. 2010) (statements to Illinois Department of Human Rights and Equal Employment Opportunity Commission). See also II.A.1, supra.

G. Reports to Auditors and Insurers

No reported cases.

H. Vicarious Liability of Employers for Statements Made by Employees

1. ***Scope of Employment.*** An employer may be liable for defamatory statements made by an employee or agent only if the statements are within the scope of employment or agency or, as to those hearing or reading the statement, within the employee's apparent authority. Restatement (Second) of Agency § 247 (1957). See also Reed v. Northwestern Pub. Co., 124 Ill. 2d 495, 517, 530 N.E.2d 474, 484, 125 Ill. Dec. 316, 325, 11 Media L. Rep. 1382 (1988) ("a corporation is jointly and severally liable for libelous statements actionable against its employee when the employee is acting within the scope of his employment"); Chisholm v. Foothill Capital Corp., 3 F. Supp. 2d 925, 938 (N.D. Ill. 1998). "An employee's action falls within the scope of employment if '(a) it is of the kind he is employed to perform; (b) it occurs substantially within the authorized time and space limits; (c) it is actuated, at least in part, by a purpose to serve the master.'" Taboas v. Mlynczak, 149 F.3d 576, 582-83 (7th Cir. 1998) (quoting Restatement (Second) of Agency § 228; holding that employees' statements about supervisor's "perceived misfeasance" were within scope of employment).

An employer will not be held liable for defamatory statements made by an independent contractor. See Miles v. WTMX Radio, No. 02 C 427, 2002 WL 31103471, at *4 (N.D. Ill. Sept. 18, 2002). Nor will an employer be held liable if its employees act out of personal motives rather than acting as part of their official duties. Emery v. N.E. Ill. Reg'l Commuter R.R. Corp., No. 02 C 9303, 2003 WL 22176077, at *8 (N.D. Ill. Sept. 18, 2003) (dismissing defamation claim against employer where plaintiff alleged that other employees' statements "'were not made within the scope of their official duties, but for personal motives'").

a. **Blogging.** No reported cases.

2. ***Damages.*** See generally I.B.8, supra.

H. Internal Investigations

Illinois courts have extended a qualified privilege to employees who make statements during internal investigations when the employee is under some obligation to make the report. A statement is protected by a qualified privileged when the defendant (1) makes it in good faith; (2) makes it with an interest or duty to be upheld; (3) limits it in scope to that purpose; (4) makes it on a proper occasion; and (5) publishes it in a proper manner and only to proper parties. Larson v. Decatur Memorial Hosp., 236 Ill. App. 3d 796, 602 N.E.2d 864, 176 Ill. Dec. 918 (4th Dist. 1992) (holding that employer could not be held liable for comments that plaintiff sold and used marijuana because such statements were made as part of a legitimate internal investigation and, hence, subject to a qualified privilege); see also Ptasznik v. St. Joseph Hosp., 464 F.3d 691 (7th Cir. 2006) (finding no liability for statements in emails and documents created during employer's internal investigation); Smock v. Nolan, 361 F.3d 367 (7th Cir. 2004) (holding polygraph examiner's statements protected by a qualified privilege where examiner had duty to report results of police officer's polygraph examination); Naeemullah v. Citicorp Services, Inc., 78 F. Supp. 2d 783 (N.D. Ill. 1999). See also II.A.2, supra.

When a party has a legal obligation to submit the results of an internal investigation, statements made in the investigation may be absolutely privileged. Busch v. Bates, 323 Ill. App. 3d 823, 753 N.E.2d 1184, 257 Ill. Dec. 558 (5th Dist. 2001) (holding that internal investigation report that state police officers were legally required to file could not be the basis of a defamation action).

IV. OTHER ACTIONS BASED ON STATEMENTS

A. Negligent Hiring, Retention, and Supervision

1. ***Elements.*** An employer may be liable for the negligent hiring or retention of unfit employees. Van Horne v. Muller, 185 Ill. 2d 299, 310, 705 N.E.2d 898, 904, 235 Ill. Dec. 715, 721 (1998). To state a cause of action under these theories, a plaintiff must allege "(1) that the employer knew or should have known that the employee had a particular unfitness for the position so as to create a danger of harm to third persons; (2) that such particular unfitness was known or should have been known at the time of the employee's hiring or retention; and (3) that this particular unfitness proximately caused the plaintiff's injury." Id. at 311, 705 N.E.2d at 904, 235 Ill. Dec. at 721; Doe v. Brouillette, 389 Ill. App. 3d 595, 605-06, 906 N.E.2d 105, 115, 329 Ill. Dec. 260, 270 (1st Dist. 2009). A plaintiff may also state a claim for negligent supervision by alleging that (1) the employer had a duty to supervise the employee, (2) the employer was negligent in supervising the employee, and (3) the negligence caused injury to the plaintiff. Van Horne v. Muller, 294 Ill. App. 3d 649, 657, 691 N.E.2d 74, 79, 229 Ill. Dec. 138, 143 (1st Dist. 1998), rev'd on other grounds, 185 Ill. 2d 299, 705 N.E.2d 898, 235 Ill. Dec. 715 (1998).

2. ***Claims Based on Statements.*** The Illinois Supreme Court has rejected a speech-based claim for negligent hiring and retention of an employee, but reserved the question of whether such a claim might ever be recognized. Van Horne v. Muller, 185 Ill. 2d 299, 705 N.E.2d 898, 235 Ill. Dec. 715 (1998). The case involved a disk jockey who was hired in spite of (or perhaps because of) a history of pulling outrageous stunts, such as prompting listeners to storm a university library by announcing that $500 was hidden in a book. Id. at 309, 705 N.E.2d at 904, 235 Ill. Dec. at 721. The court held that plaintiff had failed to allege "a sufficient nexus between the particular alleged unfitness of [the disk jockey] and the injury suffered by plaintiff." Id. at 313, 705 N.E.2d at 905, 235 Ill. Dec. at 722. Specifically, the court held that the plaintiff alleged that the disk jockey had engaged in "offensive and outrageous conduct" before being hired, but this history "does not establish that he had a propensity to make false, defamatory statements." Id. at 314, 705 N.E.2d at 906, 235 Ill. Dec. at 723. The court cautioned that it was not deciding whether it would ever recognize a claim for negligent hiring or retention based on an employee's defamatory statements. Id. at 312, 705 N.E.2d at 905, 235 Ill. Dec. at 722.

B. Intentional Infliction of Emotional Distress

1. ***Elements.*** To state a claim for intentional infliction of emotional distress, a plaintiff must allege that (1) defendant engaged in extreme and outrageous conduct, (2) defendant intended or expected that the conduct would cause severe emotional distress, and (3) the conduct caused severe emotional distress. Doe v. Calumet City, 161 Ill. 2d 374, 392, 641 N.E.2d 498, 506, 204 Ill. Dec. 274, 282 (1994); see also Thomas v. Fuerst, 345 Ill. App. 3d 929, 935, 803 N.E.2d 619, 625, 281 Ill. Dec. 215, 221 (1st Dist. 2004); Swearnigen-El v. Cook County Sheriff's Dept., 602 F.3d 852, 863-64 (7th Cir. 2010).

To satisfy the first element, the conduct must be "'so outrageous in character, and so extreme in degree, as to go beyond all possible bounds of decency.'" Public Fin. Corp. v. Davis, 66 Ill. 2d 85, 90, 360 N.E.2d 765, 767, 4 Ill. Dec. 652, 654 (1976) (quoting Restatement (Second) of Torts § 46, comment d (1965)); Hukic v. Aurora Loan Servs., 588 F.3d 420, 438 (7th Cir. 2009). "Whether conduct is extreme and outrageous is evaluated on an objective standard based on all the facts and circumstances." Thomas, 345 Ill. App. 3d at 935, 803 N.E.2d at 625, 281 Ill. Dec. at 221.

The Illinois Appellate Court has recognized that "courts often hesitate to find that a plaintiff has stated a claim for intentional infliction of emotional distress in employment situations." Vickers v. Abbott Labs., 308 Ill. App. 3d 393, 410, 719 N.E.2d 1101, 1115, 241 Ill. Dec. 698, 712 (1st Dist. 1999) (upholding summary judgment against plaintiff who claimed to have suffered severe emotional distress as a result of a sexual harassment investigation). "This trend reflects a concern that everyday job stresses should not give rise to a cause of action for intentional infliction of emotional distress." Id. Accord, Van Stan v. Fancy Colours & Co., 125 F.3d 563, 567-68 (7th Cir. 1997). Liability does not extend to "mere insults, indignities, threats, annoyances, petty oppressions or trivialities." Atlas v. City of North Chicago, No. 03 C 4814, 2004 WL 816456, at *3 (N.D. Ill. Mar. 12, 2004) (quoting Public Fin. Corp. v. Davis, 66 Ill. 2d 85, 89-90, 4 Ill. Dec. 652, 654, 360 N.E.2d 765, 767 (1976)).

Gould v. Barrett, No. 99 C 7661, 2002 WL 485342, at *7-9 (N.D. Ill. Mar. 29, 2002), provides an example of these principles in action. There, the court held that even where an employer reprimanded an employee, excluded her, failed to notify her of policy changes, ignored her concerns for personal safety, and generally made it difficult for her to continue working, a claim for intentional infliction of emotional distress would not succeed. Id. at *5-6. "While it is clear that [the employer's] reaction to [employee's] situation and subsequent conduct may have been hard-hearted, unenlightened, and reminiscent of the Charles Dickens character Ebenezer Scrooge prior to his eventual transformation, the Court holds that, as a matter of law, Illinois law requires more in order to establish extreme and outrageous character in the employment context." Id. at *9. For other examples of these principles in particular cases, see Wynne v. Loyola Univ. of Chicago, 318 Ill. App. 3d 443, 454, 741 N.E.2d 669, 677-78, 251 Ill. Dec. 782, 790-91 (1st Dist. 2000) (upholding summary judgment in favor of an employer and co-workers when plaintiff claimed that defendants published a memorandum critical of plaintiff, refused to transfer plaintiff to another position, and appointed a department head whom plaintiff disliked); Swearnigen-El, 602 F.3d at 864 (7th Cir. 2010) (evidence about de-deputization, transfer, and suspension pending investigation was not sufficiently "extreme and outrageous" to survive summary judgment); Lifton v. Board of Educ. of City of Chicago, 416 F.3d 571, 579 (7th Cir. 2005) (finding that allegations that the principal and Board of Education issued a warning, broadcast the Board meeting where it was discussed on television, threatened plaintiff with discharge, monitored her parent-teacher conferences, and asked for her lesson plans could not be characterized as so extreme and outrageous as to give rise to liability); and Thompson-Adams v. Renzenberger, Inc., No. 10 C 54, 2010 WL 1229380, at *3 (N.D. Ill. March 25, 2010) (allegations of sexual harassment insufficiently outrageous to state a claim).

2. ***Claims Based on Statements.*** Speech-based claims for intentional infliction of emotional distress are generally not viable after the defamation claim is dismissed. See, e.g., Layne v. Builders Plumbing Supply Co., 210 Ill. App. 3d 966, 973, 569 N.E.2d 1104, 1109, 155 Ill. Dec. 493, 498 (2d Dist. 1991); Pruitt v. Chow, 742 F.2d 1104, 1109 (7th Cir. 1984). In particular, false allegations of misconduct at work typically do not rise to the level of extreme or outrageous conduct. Earl v. H.D. Smith Wholesale Drug Co., No. 08-3224, 2009 WL 1871929, at *4 (C.D. Ill. June 23, 2009). However, Illinois has not adopted a per se rule to this effect, and one court, in a 2-1 decision, found that excessive publication of a true statement (that plaintiff was "fired for touching women") could form the basis for an emotional distress claim, even though the defamation claim was deficient. Parker v. Bank of Marion, 296 Ill. App. 3d 1035, 1039-40, 695 N.E.2d 1370, 1372-73, 231 Ill. Dec. 251, 253-54 (5th Dist. 1998).

C. Interference with Economic Advantage

1. ***Elements.*** To state a claim for interference with prospective economic advantage, a plaintiff must allege: "(1) a reasonable expectancy of entering into a valid business relationship, (2) the defendant's knowledge of the expectancy, (3) an intentional and unjustified interference by the defendant that induced or caused a breach or termination of the expectancy, and (4) damage to the plaintiff resulting from the defendant's interference." Anderson v. Vanden Dorpel, 172 Ill. 2d 399, 406-07, 667 N.E.2d 1296, 1299, 217 Ill. Dec. 720, 723 (1996). At-will employees must plead tortious interference with a prospective business expectancy, rather than tortious interference with contractual relations. Atanus v. American Airlines, Inc., No. 1-09-2380, 2010 WL 2486746, at *4 (Ill. App. 1st Dist. June 18, 2010).

2. ***Claims Based on Statements.*** Speech-based claims for intentional interference with prospective economic relations may founder on the first element, a reasonable expectancy of entering into a business relationship. See, e.g., Anderson, 172 Ill. 2d at 407-11, 667 N.E.2d at 1299-1301, 217 Ill. Dec. at 723-25. Although there may be cases where a job applicant can satisfy this element without having an offer in hand, allegations that plaintiff had positive interviews with a prospective employer and that she was the "leading candidate" for the job do not. Id. In upholding the dismissal of such a claim, the Illinois Supreme Court indicated that it was concerned that allowing plaintiff's claim to proceed would mean that "anyone supplying a negative reference to a prospective employer might conceivably find himself or herself subject to an action for intentional interference with prospective economic advantage." Id. at 411, 667 N.E.2d at 1301, 217 Ill. Dec. at 725. Accord Walker v. Braes Feed Ingredients, Inc., No. 02 C 9236, 2003 WL 1956162, at *2-4 (N.D. Ill. Apr. 23, 2003). Further, one cannot have a reasonable expectation of keeping a job if one is acting improperly. Atanus, 2010 WL 2486746, at *5 (employee who was literally working for two employers simultaneously (during the same hours) had no reasonable expectation of keeping the positions).

Provision of true information is not tortious interference. Id. ("where a business entity provides accurate and proper reports to another entity in a reasonable business transaction, providing those reports should not constitute intentional interference"). See also Voyles v. Sandia Mortgage Corp., 196 Ill. 2d 288, 300-01, 751 N.E.2d 1126, 1133-34, 256 Ill. Dec. 289, 296-97 (2001) (holding that because allegedly defamatory reports were accurate, there was no "intentional" or "unjustified" interference with any business expectancy); Hukic v. Aurora Loan Servs., 588 F.3d 420, 433 (7th Cir. 2009) (finding no unjustified interference by lenders where they accurately reported plaintiff's default). Tortious interference claims are also subject to the same privilege rules that limit defamation claims. See Wilton Partners III LLC v. Gallagher, No. 03 C 1519, 2003 WL 22880834, at *3 (N.D. Ill. Dec. 5, 2003) (noting that "an absolute litigation privilege" protects statements spoken or written as part of legal proceedings "so long as the communication at issue pertains to the pending litigation").

Internal investigations resulting in disciplinary action against or termination of an employee are unlikely to create a valid tortious interference claim, as "a corporate employer cannot interfere with its own business relationship with its employees." Vickers v. Abbott Labs., 308 Ill. App. 3d 393, 411, 719 N.E.2d 1101, 1116, 241 Ill. Dec. 698, 713 (1st Dist. 1999).

D. Prima Facie Tort

Illinois does not recognize a prima facie tort as a separate tort. Credit Ins. Consultants, Inc. v. Republic Fin. Servs., Inc., No. 92 C 8320, 1993 WL 388659, at *11 n.9 (N.D. Ill. Sept. 23, 1993); Barry Gilberg, Ltd. v. Craftex Corp., 665 F. Supp. 585, 596-97 (N.D. Ill. 1987).

V. OTHER ISSUES

A. Statute of Limitations

The statute of limitations for defamation is one year. 735 Ill. Comp. Stat. 5/13-201. "The cause of action generally accrues on the date the defamatory material is published to a third party." Naeemullah v. Citicorp Servs., Inc., 78 F. Supp. 2d 783, 791 (N.D. Ill. 1999). If the defamatory statement "was 'hidden, inherently undiscoverable, or inherently unknowable,' Illinois courts apply the 'discovery rule' such that the statute of limitations does not accrue until the plaintiff knew or should have known of the defamatory report." Hukic v. Aurora Loan Servs., 588 F.3d 420, 435 (7th Cir. 2009) (quoting Blair v. Nev. Landing P'ship, 369 Ill. App. 3d 318, 326, 859 N.E.2d 1188, 1195, 307 Ill. Dec. 511, 518 (2d Dist. 2006)); Yano v. City Colleges of Chicago, No. 08 C 4492, 2010 WL 4705149, at *2 (N.D. Ill. Nov. 10, 2010) (applying discovery rule to an e-mail because the plaintiff learned of the injury only after the defendants produced the e-mail); see also Tom Olesker's Exciting World of Fashion, Inc. v. Dun & Bradstreet, Inc., 61 Ill. 2d 129, 136, 334 N.E.2d 160, 164 (1975). However, if the injury itself is known, the statute of limitations is not tolled merely because the plaintiff was unaware of the specific identities of those who made the defamatory statements. Peal v. Lee, 403 Ill. App. 3d 197, 208, 933 N.E.2d 450, 462, 342 Ill. Dec. 864 (1st Dist. 2010) (citing Guebard v. Jabaay, 65 Ill. App. 3d 255, 258, 381 N.E.2d 1164, 21 Ill. Dec. 620 (1978)).

With regard to minors, Illinois has a tolling statute that tolls the statute of limitations of specified claims until two years after the person turns eighteen. 735 Ill. Comp. Stat. 5/13-211. Defamation claims are covered by this statute. See Yano, 2010 WL 4705149, at *2.

Illinois has adopted the Uniform Single Publication Act, 740 Ill. Comp. Stat. 165/1, so that, in general, "the subsequent distribution of existing copies of an original publication neither creates a fresh cause of action nor tolls the applicable statute of limitations." Founding Church of Scientology v. American Med. Ass'n, 60 Ill. App. 3d 586, 588-89, 377 N.E.2d 158, 160, 18 Ill. Dec. 5, 7 (1st Dist. 1978). See also Hukic, 588 F.3d at 436 (under the Act, "the cause of action accrues on the single date of first publication"). But see id. at 436-37 (predicting the Illinois Supreme Court would not apply the single publication rule to multiple credit reports over a period of years). The test for determining whether a later distribution of defamatory material creates a new cause of action is "whether a defendant consciously republishes the statement." Dubinsky v. United Airlines Master Exec. Council, 303 Ill. App. 3d 317, 333, 708 N.E.2d 441, 454, 236 Ill. Dec. 855, 868 (1st Dist. 1999).

Allegations of additional defamatory statements in an amended complaint generally do not "relate back" to the original complaint for purposes of the statute of limitations. Kakuris v. Klein, 88 Ill. App. 3d 597, 601-03, 410 N.E.2d 984, 987-89, 43 Ill. Dec. 851, 854-56 (1st Dist. 1980). Defamation claims asserted as counterclaims are also not barred by the statute of limitations, "as long as the plaintiff's claim arose before the cause of action brought as a counterclaim was barred." Benitez v. American Standard Circuits, Inc., No. 08 CV 1998, 2009 WL 742686, at *6 (N.D. Ill. March 18, 2009).

B. Jurisdiction

The Illinois long-arm statute permits Illinois courts to exercise jurisdiction to the fullest extent permitted by constitutional requirements. 735 Ill. Comp. Stat. 5/2-209(c). Thus, publication of a defamatory statement in Illinois may subject the defendant to jurisdiction in Illinois courts. See, e.g., Keeton v. Hustler Magazine, Inc., 465 U.S. 770, 104 S. Ct.

1473, 79 L. Ed. 2d 790, 10 Media L. Rep. 1405 (1984). Further, publication of defamatory statements on a website directed toward Illinois may subject the defendant to jurisdiction in Illinois courts. Tamburo v. Dworkin, 601 F.3d 693, 706 (7th Cir. 2010) ("although they acted from points outside the forum state, these defendants specifically aimed their tortious conduct at [plaintiff] and his business in Illinois with the knowledge that he lived, worked, and would suffer the 'brunt of the injury' there"). Publication of a defamatory statement in Illinois does not subject the defendant to jurisdiction in Illinois if the requirements of the Due Process Clause have not been satisfied. Hanson v. Ahmed, 387 Ill. App. 3d 941, 889 N.E.2d 740, 744, 321 Ill. Dec. 475, 479 (1st Dist. 2008) (no jurisdiction over Missouri resident for statements made telephonically in Missouri to an insurance company in Illinois regarding a claim submitted by an Illinois resident).

C. Worker's Compensation Exclusivity

The Illinois Workers Compensation Act, 820 Ill. Comp. Stat. 305/1 et seq., provides the exclusive remedy for accidental injuries in the workplace. Richardson v. County of Cook, 250 Ill. App. 3d 544, 547, 621 N.E.2d 114, 117, 190 Ill. Dec. 245, 248 (1st Dist. 1993). An employee may overcome the preemption of the Act by demonstrating "(1) that the injury was not accidental; (2) that the injury did not arise from his or her employment; (3) that the injury was not received during the course of employment; or (4) that the injury was not compensable under the act." Id. (quoting Meerbrey v. Marshall Field and Co., Inc., 139 Ill. 2d 455, 463, 564 N.E.2d 1222, 1226, 151 Ill. Dec. 560, 564 (1990)). Worker's compensation exclusivity provisions do not bar claims for injuries that the employer or the employer's alter ego intentionally inflict on the employee. Meerbrey, 139 Ill. 2d at 463, 564 N.E.2d at 1226, 151 Ill. Dec. at 564.

D. Pleading Requirements

Defamation claims must set forth the allegedly defamatory words "clearly and with particularity." Krueger v. Lewis, 342 Ill. App. 3d 467, 470, 794 N.E.2d 970, 972, 276 Ill. Dec. 720, 722 (1st Dist. 2003); O'Donnell v. Field Enters., Inc., 145 Ill. App. 3d 1032, 1042, 491 N.E.2d 1212, 1219, 96 Ill. Dec. 752, 759, 12 Media L. Rep. 1927 (1st Dist. 1986). The exact words do not necessarily have to be alleged, but plaintiff must identify "a precise and particular account of the statements that defendant allegedly made." Green v. Rogers, 234 Ill. 2d 478, 493, 917 N.E.2d 450, 460, 334 Ill. Dec. 624, 634 (2009). If the plaintiff makes allegations "on information and belief," then the basis for that information and belief must also be identified. Id. at 495, 917 N.E.2d at 462, 334 Ill. Dec. at 635. See also Moore v. People for the Ethical Treatment of Animals, Inc., 402 Ill. App. 3d 62, 74, 932 N.E.2d 448, 459, 342 Ill. Dec. 321, 332 (1st Dist. 2010) (finding pleading insufficient where plaintiffs "fail to mention when these statements were made to neighbors, to which neighbors the statements were made, and what exactly was said to the neighbors"); Lykowski v. Bergman, 299 Ill. App. 3d 157, 163-64, 700 N.E.2d 1064, 1069, 233 Ill. Dec. 356, 361 (1st Dist. 1998) (upholding dismissal where complaint alleged that defendant accused plaintiff of "certain unethical acts and improper conduct" and sent letter accusing plaintiff of being a "liar" and "guilty of unethical and improper conduct"). Moreover, although Illinois courts have generally abolished the distinction between libel and slander, the in haec verba requirement is applied less stringently in the slander context, where verbatim statements are more difficult to reproduce. See Mittelman v. Witous, 135 Ill. 2d 220, 230-31, 552 N.E.2d 973, 978, 142 Ill. Dec. 232, 237 (1989) (dictum).

Due to the regime of notice pleading, federal courts generally do not adhere to the in haec verba requirement as rigorously as state courts. Gehrls v. Gooch, No. 09 C 6338, 2010 WL 1849400, at *3 (N.D. Ill. May 7, 2010). Thus, in federal court, "an employee can state an actionable claim of defamation if he alleges the basic substance of the alleged defamatory statement, and the defaming statement need not be quoted verbatim." Russo v. Nike, Inc., No. 99 C 2726, 2000 WL 347777, at *4 (N.D. Ill. Mar. 28, 2000). But see Carpenter v. Aspen Research Advisers, No. 10 C 6823, 2011 WL 1297733, at *3 (N.D. Ill. Apr. 5, 2011) (dismissing defamation claim for lack of specificity regarding date, time, and nature of alleged defamatory statements); Adams v. Pull'r Holding Co., LLC., No. 09 C 7170, 2010 WL 1611078, at *5 (N.D. Ill. Apr. 20, 2010) (dismissing defamation claims where plaintiff pleaded "only the most general allegations that plaintiff made false and damaging statements to unnamed third parties related to his termination," which were insufficient to put the defendant on notice).

When a plaintiff is required to plead constitutional "actual malice," some courts have held that the complaint must contain "specific allegations from which actual malice may reasonably be inferred." Lykowski, 299 Ill. App. 3d at 164, 700 N.E.2d at 1070, 233 Ill. Dec. at 362. "[B]are allegations" of actual malice are not sufficient. Id. Accord Mittelman, 135 Ill. 2d at 238, 552 N.E.2d at 981-82, 142 Ill. Dec. at 240-41. Other courts, however, have found that boilerplate allegations of the elements of actual malice are sufficient. See, e.g., Colson v. Stieg, 89 Ill. 2d 205, 215-16, 433 N.E.2d 246, 250-51, 60 Ill. Dec. 449, 453-54 (1982); Krueger v. Lewis, 342 Ill. App. 3d 467, 472-73, 794 N.E.2d 970, 974, 276 Ill. Dec. 720, 724 (1st Dist. 2003); Marczak v. Drexel Nat'l Bank, 186 Ill. App. 3d 640, 646-47, 542 N.E.2d 787, 791, 134 Ill. Dec. 441, 445 (1st Dist. 1989).

When a plaintiff seeks damages for defamation per quod, plaintiff must plead special damages with specificity. Thomas v. Fuerst, 345 Ill. App. 3d 929, 933, 803 N.E.2d 619, 623, 281 Ill. Dec. 215, 219 (1st Dist. 2004) (citing Bryson v. News Am. Pubs., Inc., 174 Ill. 2d 77, 103, 672 N.E.2d 1207, 220 Ill. Dec. 195 (1996)).

Where a plaintiff petitions to discover an anonymous defendant's identity under Illinois Supreme Court Rule 224 (Ill. S. Ct. R. 224), and the plaintiff fails to provide "allegations sufficient to overcome" a motion to dismiss, the court will not grant the petition. Stone v. Paddock Publ'ns, 2011 IL App (1st) 093386, ¶ 18, 961 N.E.2d 380, 389, 356 Ill. Dec. 284, 293, 39 Media L. Rep. 2697 ("if a petitioner cannot satisfy the [motion to dismiss] standard, it is clear that the unidentified individual is not responsible for damages and the proposed discovery is not 'necessary'"). Stone clarified that an anonymous individual need not move to dismiss, "but rather, it remains the petitioner's burden to show that the discovery is necessary, *i.e.*, that petitioner can allege facts supporting a cause of action." Id.

E. Procedural Grounds for Dismissal

The Citizen Participation Act, popularly known as an anti-SLAPP ("strategic lawsuits against public participation") statute, creates a basis for dismissal of a defamation suit early in the litigation. 735 Ill. Comp. Stat. 110/1 et seq. The Act provides for the dismissal of claims based on statements that were made in furtherance of the defendant's constitutional rights to petition, speech, or association, or to otherwise participate in government. Id. §§ 110/15, 110/20(c).

The Illinois Supreme Court has significantly curtailed the scope of the Act. In Sandholm v. Kuecker, 2012 IL 111443, ¶ 48, 962 N.E. 2d 418, 430, 356 Ill. Dec. 733, 745, the court warned of the "particular danger" of construing the Act "too broadly," noting that the Act seeks to "strike a balance between the rights of persons to file lawsuits for injury and the constitutional rights of persons to petition, speak freely, associate freely, and otherwise participate in government." The court held that defendants invoking the Act must show that the complaint is "*solely* based on, relating to, or in response to . . . [the defendants'] acts in furtherance of [the defendant's] rights of petition, speech or association, or to otherwise participate in government." Id. at ¶ 45, 962 N.E. 2d at 433, 356 Ill. Dec. at 749. Only if the defendants satisfy this burden does the burden shift to the plaintiff to provide "clear and convincing evidence that defendants' acts are not immunized from liability under the Act." Id. (holding that defendants failed to carry their burden because plaintiff genuinely sought damages for "personal harm to his reputation from defendants' alleged defamatory and tortious acts," made to various media and to the school board during a campaign to have plaintiff removed from his position as a teacher and basketball coach). See also Wright Development Group, LLC v. Walsh, 238 Ill. 2d 620, 635, 939 N.E.2d 389, 398, 345 Ill. Dec. 546 (2010) (finding statements made to a reporter inside an alderman's office while the alderman's staff was mingling nearby to be "in furtherance of" the defendant's right to free speech and therefore protected by the Act).

Illinois courts have not concluded that "seeking a person's removal from a job is an action genuinely aimed at procuring favorable government action under all circumstances." Chi v. Loyola Univ. Med. Ctr., 787 F. Supp. 2d 797, 811 (N.D. Ill. 2011). In Chi, the court stated that the "submission of a routine employee evaluation form" was "a far cry" from advocacy, ultimately finding that the evaluation was not protected. Id. at 811-12.

A motion to dismiss pursuant to the Act is supposed to be given expedited consideration, at least in state court. Any such motion must be heard and ruled upon within 90 days after notice is given to the opposing party. 735 Ill. Comp. Stat. 110/20(a). If the motion is denied or the trial court fails to rule within 90 days, movants are afforded expedited appeals, again at least in state court. Id. Another procedural benefit for defendants is that discovery is suspended pending a ruling on the motion. Id. § 110/20(b). Prevailing movants are entitled to attorneys' fees and costs. Id. § 110/25. The substance of the Act applies in federal court because it creates a "substantive affirmative defense to plaintiff's complaint," even though it also provides a procedure to enforce this defense. Trudeau v. Consumeraffairs.com, Inc., No. 10 C 7193, 2011 WL 3898041, at *5 (N.D. Ill. Sept. 6, 2011).

SURVEY OF ILLINOIS EMPLOYMENT PRIVACY LAW

Richard J. O'Brien, Paul E. Veith, Eric S. Mattson, Linda R. Friedlieb, and Joseph C. Cooper
Sidley Austin LLP
One South Dearborn Street
Chicago, Illinois 60603
Telephone: (312) 853-7000; Facsimile: (312) 853-7036

(With Developments Reported Through **November 1, 2012**)

GENERAL COMMENTS

The Illinois Appellate Court is divided into five districts. When a conflict arises among the districts (and in the absence of controlling authority from the Illinois Supreme Court), "the circuit court is bound by the decisions of the appellate court of the district in which it sits." Aleckson v. Round Lake Park, 176 Ill. 2d 82, 92, 679 N.E.2d 1224, 1229, 223 Ill. Dec. 451, 456 (1997). Cf. id. at 94-95, 679 N.E.2d at 1229-30, 223 Ill. Dec. at 456-57 (Harrison, J., specially concurring) (arguing that "[b]ecause there is only one appellate court, a decision by any division of that court is binding precedent on all circuit courts throughout the state, regardless of locale"; contending that circuit courts should follow "most recent appellate court decision on point").

Beginning on July 1, 2011, Illinois stopped publishing official case reporters and switched to a "public domain" system of citing cases. See Ill. S. Ct. R. 6. In state court, briefs must cite the official reporter for earlier cases and use the public-domain citation for opinions released on and after July 1, 2011. See id. The commentary to Ill. S. Ct. R. 6 provides examples of the correct citation format for public-domain citations.

SIGNIFICANT DEVELOPMENTS SINCE THE 2012 *SURVEY*

The Seventh Circuit struck down the Illinois Eavesdropping Act as violating the First Amendment to the extent that it forbids people from making non-consensual recordings of police officers doing their jobs in public. ACLU v. Alvarez, 679 F.3d 583 (7th Cir. 2012). The court held that, as applied to the ACLU's plans to record police officers, the Act "likely violates the First Amendment's free-speech and free-press guarantees." Id. at 587. The court noted that "this case has nothing to do with private conversations or surreptitious interceptions." Id. at 606.

In Carroll v. Merrill Lynch, No. 12-1076 (7th Cir. Oct. 16, 2012), the Seventh Circuit held that the fear of crime exemption to the Illinois Eavesdropping Act requires only "reasonable suspicion" that a party to the recorded conversation is committing or may commit a crime, and that the exemption applies to "any crime." Id. at 14-15 (exempting from the Act defendant's recording of a threatening late-night phone call to his home where defendant's wife recorded the conversation for fear that plaintiff might "throw a brick" through a window; in addition, the threatening call itself may have been criminal under Illinois law).

For the first time, the Illinois Supreme Court recognized the tort of intrusion upon seclusion. Lawlor v. North American Corp., 2012 IL 112530, ¶ 35 (upholding jury verdict finding that employer intruded upon former employee's seclusion during an investigation into whether employee violated her non-competition agreement).

The Illinois Supreme Court also held that the fact that a plaintiff commits an illegal act in private rather than in public does not implicate the privacy clause in the Illinois Constitution; to trigger that clause, the plaintiff must allege that government agents or actions invaded his privacy. Illinois v. Hollins, 2012 IL 112754, 971 N.E.2d 504 (rejecting criminal defendant's argument that "the 'zone of privacy' afforded by the privacy clause protects his right to record his legal, consensual sexual encounter" with a 17-year-old girl).

In Goldstein v. Colborne Acquisition Co., No. 10 C 6861, 2012 U.S. Dist. LEXIS 75743 (N.D. Ill. June 1, 2012), the court found unreasonable a group of employees' subjective expectations of privacy in electronic communications, including e-mails to their attorneys that were sent from their work accounts. Id. at *16. Thus, the employees waived the attorney-client privilege when they used their work e-mail accounts to respond to a discovery request. Id.

Under certain circumstances, an employer may access without permission an employee's personal Facebook and Twitter accounts to promote the employer's business without violating the Illinois Right of Publicity Act or committing an "intrusion upon seclusion" tort. Maremont v. Susan Fredman Design Group, Ltd., No. 10 C 7811, 2011 U.S. Dist. LEXIS 140446, at *18-21 (N.D. Ill. Dec. 7, 2011). In Maremont, an employee had used her Facebook and Twitter accounts to promote her employer's business. Id. at *4-7. When the employee was injured and became unable to continue posting, her employer began posting under her accounts without her permission, via other employees who acted as "guest bloggers." Id. The court granted summary judgment to the employer on the Right of Publicity claim

because the employee could not show that her employer appropriated her likeness; the employer's "guest bloggers" did not pass themselves off as the employee. Id. Likewise, the court granted summary judgment on the "intrusion upon seclusion" claim because the employee failed to show that the employer intruded upon any private information in her accounts, as she already had made the information accessible to the public. Id.

In Best v. Berard, 776 F. Supp. 2d 752, 758-59, 40 Media L. Rep. 1867 (N.D. Ill. 2011), the court expanded the "non-commercial" exemption to Right of Publicity claims "with an eye toward avoiding a First Amendment violation." Id. The court held that, under the exemption, a party may use a plaintiff's identity "in an entertainment program that conveys truthful footage of an arrest" because information about arrests "rises to the level of public concern." Id. at 757-59.

Blogging and posting Wikipedia entries about a former colleague may form the basis of a false light invasion of privacy claim where the post or entry is not mere opinion and is not "capable of an innocent construction." Pitale v. Holestine, No. 11 C 00921, 2012 U.S. Dist. LEXIS 24631, at *15-17, *23-24 (N.D. Ill. Feb. 27, 2012) (denying motion to dismiss where false light claim was based on blog posts and Wikipedia entries that implied former boss's professional irresponsibility).

To meet the first element of an intrusion upon seclusion claim, a plaintiff must establish that, at the time of the alleged intrusion, the plaintiff was "in a place a reasonable person would believe to be secluded." Webb v. CBS Broad., Inc., No. 08 C 6241, 2011 U.S. Dist. LEXIS 103601, at *10, 39 Media L. Rep. 2385 (N.D. Ill. Sept. 13, 2011). In Webb, the court granted summary judgment in favor of defendants, who broadcast images of plaintiffs and their children in the back yard of a family member, because the yard was in plain view of the street, even though defendants used a zoom lens to capture plaintiffs' activities. Id. at *12.

I. GENERAL LAW OF PRIVACY

A. Legal Basis of Privacy Claims

The Illinois Constitution provides, "The People shall have the right to be secure in their persons, houses, papers and other possessions against unreasonable searches, seizures, invasions of privacy or interceptions of communications by eavesdropping devices or other means." Ill. Const. art. I § 6. This provision "goes beyond federal constitutional guarantees by expressly recognizing a 'zone of personal privacy.'" Burger v. Lutheran General Hosp., 198 Ill. 2d 21, 759 N.E.2d 533, 259 Ill. Dec. 753 (2001), quoting Kunkel v. Walton, 179 Ill. 2d 519, 537 (1997). But the provision applies only to state action, not to private individuals or employers. Kelly v. Franco, 72 Ill. App. 3d 642, 644-46, 391 N.E.2d 54, 56-57, 28 Ill. Dec. 855, 857-58 (1st Dist. 1979); Bianco v. ABC, 470 F. Supp. 182, 187 (N.D. Ill. 1979). It does not create a private right of action, at least where a statute already provides an adequate remedy. Farrar v. City of Chicago, No. 00 C 1675, 2001 WL 184979, at *2 (N.D. Ill. Feb. 22, 2001). **The mere fact that a plaintiff commits an illegal act in private rather than in public does not implicate the privacy clause; rather, the plaintiff must allege that government agents or actions invaded his privacy. Illinois v. Hollins, 2012 IL 112754, 971 N.E.2d 504, 361 Ill. Dec. 402.**

The Illinois Supreme Court recognized a cause of action for invasion of privacy in 1970 in Leopold v. Levin, 45 Ill. 2d 434, 259 N.E.2d 250 (1970), although the tort was first recognized by an intermediate appellate court in Illinois nearly two decades earlier in Eick v. Perk Dog Food Co., 347 Ill. App. 293, 106 N.E.2d 742 (1st Dist. 1952). In Leopold, plaintiff Nathan Leopold — half of the notorious "Leopold and Loeb" duo who kidnapped and murdered a 14-year-old boy, Bobby Franks, in 1924 — sued an author over his fictionalized account of the murder. The court rejected Leopold's claim for invasion of privacy, holding that First Amendment principles and other considerations barred the claim. At the same time, the court agreed that "there should be recognition of a right of privacy, a right many years ago described in a limited fashion by Judge Cooley with utter simplicity as the right 'to be let alone.'" Id. at 440, 259 N.E.2d at 254. The court continued, "Privacy is one of the sensitive and necessary human values and undeniably there are circumstances under which it should enjoy the protection of law." Id. at 440-41, 259 N.E.2d at 254.

Additionally, the Illinois General Assembly has created certain statutory causes of action for invasion of privacy. For example, the Illinois Right to Privacy in the Workplace Act allows employees to sue employers for discriminating against them based on their consumption of lawful products such as tobacco. 820 Ill. Comp. Stat. 55/15. Before filing a lawsuit under the Act, an employee must first exhaust administrative remedies. Hampton v. Village of Washburn, 317 Ill. App. 3d 439, 442-44, 739 N.E.2d 1019, 1021-23, 251 Ill. Dec. 86, 88-90 (4th Dist. 2000).

B. Causes of Action

1. ***Misappropriation/Right of Publicity.*** An Illinois court first recognized a cause of action for invasion of privacy in Eick v. Perk Dog Food Co., 347 Ill. App. 293, 106 N.E.2d 742 (1st Dist. 1952). In its advertising, a dog food company portrayed a blind girl as a prospective donee of a "Master Eye Dog," and the girl sued for invasion of

privacy. The court allowed plaintiff to proceed with a claim for "defendants' unauthorized use of her picture for advertising purposes." Id. at 306, 106 N.E.2d at 748.

The common law right of publicity has been supplanted by the Illinois Right of Publicity Act, 765 Ill. Comp. Stat. 1075/1 et seq. See id. § 60. The Act prohibits the unauthorized use of another person's identity for commercial purposes. Id. § 30. "Identity" includes a person's name, signature, photo, image, likeness, voice, or any other characteristic that a reasonable viewer or listener identifies with that person. Id. § 5. Notably, the Act applies only when the identity is used for "commercial purposes," which is defined as the public use of the identity in connection with the sale, advertising, or promotion of goods or services, or for fundraising. Id. The Act expressly permits the use of another person's identity in non-commercial activities such as news, artistic works, public affairs, or sports broadcasts. Id. § 35(b); Collier v. Murphy, No. 02 C 2121, 2003 WL 1606637, at *2-3, 31 Media L. Rep. 2159, 2161-62 (N.D. Ill. Mar. 26, 2003) (holding that Right of Publicity Act did not apply to alleged cartoon impersonation of plaintiff in a television show); Cummings v. ESPN Classic, Inc., No. 08-cv-0718, 2009 WL 650559, at *2 (S.D. Ill. Mar. 9, 2009) (finding that ESPN's broadcast of a boxing match without boxer's permission fell under the Right of Publicity Act's non-commercial purpose exception). **In Best v. Berard, 776 F. Supp. 2d 752, 758, 40 Media L. Rep. 1867 (N.D. Ill. 2011), the court dismissed a Right of Publicity claim because the depiction of plaintiff's arrest "and its surrounding circumstances – including the computer screen shots giving information about prior arrests or citations – conveyed truthful information on matters of public concern protected by the First Amendment." Id.**

Violators of the Act are liable for the greater of (1) actual damages, the profits derived from the unauthorized use, or both, or (2) $1,000. 765 Ill. Comp. Stat. 1075/40.

Although the Right of Publicity Act does not expressly provide a statute of limitations, Illinois courts have adopted the one-year limitations period that applied to the analogous common-law tort. Blair v. Nevada Landing P'ship, RBG, LP, 369 Ill. App. 3d 318, 323, 859 N.E.2d 1188, 1192, 307 Ill. Dec. 511, 515 (2d Dist. 2006). The use of an employee's likeness in different mediums over a period of time for a single purpose is considered a single act for the purpose of determining when a cause of action accrued. Id. at 324, 859 N.E.2d at 1193, 307 Ill. Dec. at 516. See also Maremont v. Susan Fredman Design Group, Ltd., No. 10 C 7811, 2011 U.S. Dist. LEXIS 26441, at *13, 39 Media L. Rep. 1992 (N.D. Ill. Mar. 15, 2011) (holding that defendant's repeated use of its employee's Facebook and Twitter accounts to impersonate the employee while she recovered from injuries constituted a continuing violation for purposes of determining when a cause of action accrued). A republication of the likeness that has been altered to reach a new audience or promote a different product could constitute a new cause of action. Blair, 369 Ill. App. 3d at 325, 859 N.E.2d at 1199, 307 Ill. Dec. at 517.

Because recovery for misappropriation is designed to protect against the commercial use of a person's identity without consent, the harm is the use itself, and no further damages are required. Petty v. Chrysler Corp., 343 Ill. App. 3d 815, 826, 799 N.E.2d 432, 441-42, 278 Ill. Dec. 714, 723-24 (1st Dist. 2003). Nominal damages will be assumed. Id. Accordingly, plaintiffs may recover for misappropriation under the Act even if their identities had no intrinsic commercial value prior to the defendant's use. Villalovos v. Sundance Assocs., Inc., No. 01 C 8468, 2003 U.S. Dist. LEXIS 387, at *15 (N.D. Ill. Jan. 13, 2003). Damages for mental distress are also recoverable. Petty, 343 Ill. App. 3d at 828, 799 N.E.2d at 443, 278 Ill. Dec. at 725. However, a plaintiff may not recover punitive damages in the absence of "malice or reckless disregard" on the part of the defendant. Id. at 828-29, 799 N.E.2d at 443-44, 278 Ill. Dec. at 725-26. Under the Right of Publicity Act, punitive damages may be awarded for willful violations, and the court may award the prevailing party reasonable attorneys' fees, costs, and litigation expenses. 765 Ill. Comp. Stat. 1075/40(b) & 55.

The Right of Publicity Act is not preempted by the federal Copyright Act. See Toney v. L'Oreal U.S.A., Inc., 406 F.3d 905 (7th Cir. 2005); Brown v. ACMI Pop Division, 375 Ill. App. 3d 276, 873 N.E.2d 954, 963, 314 Ill. Dec. 24, 33 (1st Dist. 2007). The Copyright Act and the Right of Publicity Act protect different interests and regulate different conduct. Toney, 406 F.3d at 910. The Right of Publicity Act protects the interest in the commercial value and use of a person's identity or persona; the Copyright Act, in contrast, protects fixed, tangible works. Id. at 909-10. According to the Seventh Circuit, the Right of Publicity Act does not interfere with the Copyright Act because a person's identity "is an amorphous concept that is not protected by copyright law; thus, the state law protecting it is not preempted." Id. at 910 (finding no preemption of model's claim for use of her photograph on a product label, despite defendants' ownership of copyright in the photograph, because the harm was the message of endorsement and loss of control of the commercial value of her identity).

2. ***False Light.*** Relying on the approach taken by the Restatement (Second) of Torts, Illinois courts have recognized a cause of action for false light invasion of privacy. See, e.g., Lovgren v. Citizens First Nat'l Bank of Princeton, 126 Ill. 2d 411, 418, 534 N.E.2d 987, 989, 128 Ill. Dec. 542, 544 (1989); Aroonsakul v. Shannon, 279 Ill. App. 3d 345, 664 N.E.2d 1094, 216 Ill. Dec. 166 (2d Dist. 1996). A plaintiff must allege that (1) the defendant publicized a matter concerning the plaintiff that placed the plaintiff in a false light, (2) the false light in which the plaintiff is placed "would be

highly offensive to a reasonable person," and (3) the defendant knew of the falsity or acted with reckless disregard of truth or falsity. Lovgren, 126 Ill. 2d at 418, 534 N.E.2d at 989, 128 Ill. Dec. at 544, quoting Restatement (Second) of Torts § 652E (1977). Accord Dubinsky v. United Airlines Master Executive Council, 303 Ill. App. 3d 317, 330, 708 N.E.2d 441, 451, 236 Ill. Dec. 855, 865 (1st Dist. 1999); Satkar Hospitality, Inc. v. Cook County Bd. of Review, No. 10 C 6682, 2011 U.S. Dist. LEXIS 35930, at *10-11 (N.D. Ill. Apr. 4, 2011); Moriarty v. Dyson, Inc., No. 09 C 2777, 2010 WL 2745969, at *4 (N.D. Ill. July 8, 2010). **Blog posts and Wikipedia entries implying professional irresponsibility may be considered "highly offensive" to a reasonable person. Pitale v. Holestine, No. 11 C 00921, 2012 U.S. Dist. LEXIS 24631, at *15-17, *23-24 (N.D. Ill. Feb. 27, 2012).**

Corporations may not sue for false light invasion of privacy under Illinois law, as they have no right of privacy. Oberweis Dairy, Inc. v. Democratic Cong. Campaign Comm., Inc., No. 08 C 4345, 2009 WL 635457, at *2 (N.D. Ill. Mar. 11, 2009).

False light and defamation are similar in many respects. While plaintiffs may proceed under both causes of action, recovery is permitted only under one claim or the other, not both. Myers v. Levy, 348 Ill. App. 3d 906, 915, 808 N.E.2d 1139, 1148, 283 Ill. Dec. 851, 860 (2d Dist. 2004); Myers v. Telegraph, 332 Ill. App. 3d 917, 926, 773 N.E.2d 192, 201, 265 Ill. Dec. 830, 839 (5th Dist. 2002). The similarity between the causes of action means that dismissal of a defamation claim often results in dismissal of a false light claim based on the same facts. See, e.g., Eubanks v. Nw. Herald Newspapers, 397 Ill. App. 3d 746, 750-51, 922 N.E. 2d 1196, 1200-01, 337 Ill. Dec. 619, 623-24, 38 Media L. Rep. 1413 (2d. Dist. 2010); Camphausen v. Schweitzer, No. 10 C 3605, 2011 WL 4496091, at *4 (N.D. Ill. Sept. 27, 2011).

One difference between the two torts is that the publicity requirement of a false light claim is more stringent than the publication requirement for a defamation claim. Barrett v. Fonorow, 343 Ill. App. 3d 1184, 1192, 799 N.E.2d 916, 923, 279 Ill. Dec. 113, 120 (2d Dist. 2003). To satisfy the publicity requirement of false light, the matter must be "made public, by communicating it to the public at large, or to so many persons that the matter must be regarded as substantially certain to become one of public knowledge." Id. (quoting Restatement (Second) of Torts § 652D cmt. a (1977)). The courts are split on how broad the disclosure must be, specifically whether the "special relationship" standard applicable in public disclosure of private facts cases also applies in false light cases. In public disclosure of private facts cases, the disclosure requirement "may be satisfied by proof that the plaintiff has a special relationship with the 'public' to whom the information is disclosed." Miller v. Motorola, 202 Ill. App. 3d 976, 980-81, 560 N.E.2d 900, 903, 148 Ill. Dec. 303, 306 (1st. Dist. 1990); see also I.B.3, infra. The rationale behind this standard is that the disclosure of sensitive or embarrassing information to those who stand in a special relationship to the plaintiff could be just as harmful as disclosure to the larger public. Id.

Courts have applied the special relationship standard to false light claims, but not always consistently. Some courts have applied the standard broadly. See Moriarty, 2010 WL 2745969, at *4 ("[I]n Illinois a statement need not be disclosed to the public at large if it was published to a 'public' with whom plaintiff had a special relationship."); Hernandez v. Dart, 635 F. Supp. 2d 798, 811-12 (citing Miller for proposition that disclosure to a small group of people satisfies the public disclosure element); Duncan v. Peterson, 359 Ill. App. 3d 1034, 1048-49, 835 N.E.2d 411, 423-24, 296 Ill. Dec. 377, 389-90 (2d Dist. 2005) (finding a special relationship between a pastor and three former church leaders who had recently left the pastor's church); Poulos v. Lutheran Social Servs., 312 Ill. App. 3d 731, 739-40, 728 N.E.2d 547, 555-56, 245 Ill. Dec. 465, 473-74 (1st Dist. 2000) (holding that plaintiff had a special relationship with his employer); Herion v. Village of Bensenville, No. 00 01026, 2000 WL 1648937 (N.D. Ill. Nov. 1, 2000) (allowing false light claim to survive a motion to dismiss based on statements made to law enforcement and city officials regarding plaintiff officer).

Other courts in Illinois apply the special relationship test for false light claims in a more restrictive manner, and limit or even deny its applicability to workplace communications. In Davis v. Jewish Vocational Serv., 2010 WL 1172537, at *5-6 (N.D. Ill. Mar. 17, 2010), the plaintiff alleged that employees of an employment placement service "recklessly informed one another that he had a felony conviction, which was untrue." Id. at *5. The plaintiff claimed that the "special relationship" between plaintiff and the employees responsible for his placement and supervision satisfied the "before the public" element of a false light claim. Id. "In the absence of a superseding decision by the Illinois Supreme Court," the court applied the special relationship test but relied on Seventh Circuit precedent to ascertain whether the plaintiff's allegations satisfied the test. Id. The court quoted Frobose v. American Savings & Loan Ass'n of Danville, 152 F.3d 602, 618 (7th Cir. 1998), "that 'communications and actions between and among the employees, officers, and directors of the association, who by virtue of their positions would have a natural interest in, if not a responsibility to know about, the matters communicated' do not support a false light claim," and rejected the plaintiff's false light claim. Id. See also Walker v. Braes Feed Ingredients, Inc., No. 02 C 9236, 2003 U.S. Dist. LEXIS 6873 (N.D. Ill. Apr. 23, 2003) (dismissing false light claim based on former employer's disclosure of false information to a prospective employer, with whom plaintiff had a "minimal and attenuated" relationship, because tie was insufficient to establish a special relationship).

Claims based on language critical of the plaintiff, but not clearly true or false, will not support a claim for false light. Salamone v. Hollinger Int'l, Inc., 347 Ill. App. 3d 837, 844, 807 N.E.2d 1086, 1093, 283 Ill. Dec. 245, 252 (1st Dist. 2004); **Pitale, 2012 U.S. Dist. LEXIS 24631, at *24 (dismissing claims based on "mere assertions of opinion").** Nor may claims for false light be based on what is *not* said. Green v. Trinity Int'l Univ., 344 Ill. App. 3d 1079, 1090-91, 801 N.E.2d 1208, 1218, 280 Ill. Dec. 263, 273 (2d Dist. 2003) (university's letter to students and faculty informing them of plaintiff's dismissal, which did not include language typically used to report the dismissal of employees who have not committed an act of moral turpitude, did not portray plaintiff in a false light). If a statement is protected by the First Amendment, it cannot serve as the basis for a false light claim. Imperial Apparel, Ltd. v. Cosmo's Designer Direct, Inc., 227 Ill. 2d 381, 393, 882 N.E.2d 1011, 1019, 317 Ill. Dec. 855, 863, 36 Media L. Rep. 1335 (2008). **Statements capable of an "innocent construction" are not actionable. Pitale, 2012 U.S. Dist. LEXIS 24631, at *8-17.**

3. ***Publication of Private Facts.*** To state a claim for public disclosure of private facts, plaintiff must allege that (1) defendant publicized a matter concerning the private life of the plaintiff, (2) the matter would be "highly offensive to a reasonable person," and (3) the matter "is not of legitimate concern to the public." Roehrborn v. Lambert, 277 Ill. App. 3d 181, 184, 660 N.E.2d 180, 182, 213 Ill. Dec. 923, 925 (1st Dist. 1995) (quoting Restatement (Second) of Torts § 652D (1977)). False statements are not actionable under this tort. Villalovos v. Sundance Assocs., Inc., No. 01 C 8468, 2003 U.S. Dist. LEXIS 387, at *8-9, 31 Media L. Rep. 1274 (N.D. Ill. Jan. 13, 2003).

A plaintiff cannot state a claim without showing that the facts involved were truly private. See Feltman v. Blatt, Hasenmiller, Leibsker & Moore, LLC, No. 06 C 2379, 2008 WL 5211024 (N.D. Ill. Dec. 11, 2008) (holding disclosure of plaintiff's Social Security number could not constitute a claim because Social Security numbers are not private facts under Illinois law). The publication of an aggregation of publicly available facts, however, may constitute a violation. Best v. Malec, No. 09 C 7749, 2010 WL 2364412, at *5 (N.D. Ill. June 11, 2010) (refusing to dismiss a publication of private facts claim because the aggregation of public facts such as "name, age, height, weight and driver's license number" could be classified as "facially compromising**"). Cf. Best v. Berard, 837 F. Supp. 2d 933, 937-38, 40 Media L. Rep. 1873 (N.D. Ill. 2011) (granting summary judgment in favor of defendants for same private-facts claim where reality television show disclosed plaintiff's date of birth, height, weight, telephone number, driver's license number, and arrest history, because height and weight are not protected medical information, the telephone number was no longer current and therefore not private, a driver's license is publicly available information, and the "'the right . . . to prevent the publicizing of one's criminal history' is 'now defunct'" (quoting Doe v. City of Chicago, 360 F.3d 667, 672 (7th Cir. 2004));** Cooney v. Chicago Pub. Sch., 407 Ill. App. 3d, 358, 367, 943 N.E.2d 23, 32, 347 Ill. Dec. 733 (1st Dist. 2010) (upholding dismissal of publication of private facts claim where defendant sent 1,750 former employees a list containing every other former employee's name, address, Social Security number, marital status, medical and dental insurers, and health insurance plan information). Disclosure of embarrassing facts will not create a right to sue when the plaintiff has not kept the facts secret. Wynne v. Loyola Univ. of Chicago, 318 Ill. App. 3d 443, 453, 741 N.E.2d 669, 677, 251 Ill. Dec. 782, 790 (1st Dist. 2000) (report about plaintiff's personal life not actionable where plaintiff had disclosed those facts to co-workers). For example, one court found that disclosing that the plaintiff had been involved with a married man was not actionable because plaintiff and her paramour were "open about their romantic relationship." Chisholm v. Foothill Capital Corp., 3 F. Supp. 2d 925, 940 (N.D. Ill. 1998).

With regard to the "offensiveness" element of a private facts claim, one court has held that an employer's unauthorized disclosure of an employee's mastectomy to other employees could be considered "highly offensive to a reasonable person." Miller, 202 Ill. App. 3d at 981, 560 N.E.2d at 903, 148 Ill. Dec. at 306. Another court has stated in dicta that disclosing that someone is gay "is not a legitimate public concern and disclosure could be highly offensive." Doe v. Templeton, No. 03 C 5076, 2004 WL 1882436, at *3 (N.D. Ill. Aug. 6, 2004).

The "publication" element of the tort is not satisfied unless (1) "'the matter is made public, by communicating it to the public at large, or to so many persons that the matter must be regarded as substantially certain to become one of public knowledge,'" or (2) "'a special relationship exists between the plaintiff and the 'public' to whom the information has been disclosed [such that] the disclosure may be just as devastating to the [plaintiff].'" Beverly v. Reinert, 239 Ill. App. 3d 91, 97, 606 N.E.2d 621, 625, 179 Ill. Dec. 789, 793 (2d Dist. 1992) (quoting Restatement § 652D, cmt. a and Miller, 202 Ill. App. 3d at 980, 560 N.E.2d at 903, 148 Ill. Dec. at 306, respectively).

Under the "special relationship" standard, publication to fellow employees, club members, parishioners, or relatives may qualify as a "publication." Doe v. TCF Bank Illinois, 302 Ill. App. 3d 839, 841, 707 N.E.2d 220, 221, 236 Ill. Dec. 375, 376 (1st Dist. 1999); Miller, 202 Ill. App. 3d at 981, 560 N.E.2d at 903, 148 Ill. Dec. at 306; see also Browning v. AT&T, 682 F. Supp. 2d 832, 841 (N.D. Ill. 2009) (denying dismissal where plaintiff alleged information was published to business acquaintances and friends); Johnson v. Kmart Corp., 311 Ill. App. 3d 573, 580, 723 N.E.2d 1192, 1197, 243 Ill. Dec. 591, 596 (1st Dist. 2000) (stating that employers should be included in the group of individuals with whom a plaintiff may have a special relationship for purposes of satisfying the "publication" element of the tort). But see Walker v. Braes Feed

Ingredients, Inc., No. 02 C 9236, 2003 U.S. Dist. LEXIS 6873 (N.D. Ill. Apr. 23, 2003) (holding that a special relationship does not exist between an applicant and a prospective employer).

Incidental publication to a small group of strangers with no particular interest in the matter does not qualify as a publication. Beverly, 239 Ill. App. 3d at 100, 606 N.E.2d at 626, 179 Ill. Dec. at 794 (possibility that clerical staff in law office saw letter containing "private facts" did not constitute "publication"). In Karraker v. Rent-A-Center, Inc., 316 F. Supp. 2d 675 (C.D. Ill. 2004), rev'd on other grounds, 411 F.3d 831 (7th Cir. 2005), an employee stated a claim for public disclosure of private facts by alleging that the manner in which his personality test results were copied, stored, and mailed revealed intimate facts about him. However, the court ultimately granted summary judgment in favor of defendants because the "mere possibility that someone might have seen the communication at issue is insufficient as a matter of law to sustain this claim." Id. at 683.

The publication element is also not met if "the recipient of the information has a 'natural and proper interest' in the information." TCF Bank Illinois, 302 Ill. App. 3d at 842-43, 707 N.E.2d at 222, 236 Ill. Dec. at 377 (holding that plaintiff's spouse had a "natural and proper interest" in learning the extent of plaintiff's credit card debt). In the employment context, an employee is permitted to consult with co-workers about the private life of another if it is within the scope of his employment, giving him a proper interest in the subject. Shockley v. Svoboda, 342 F.3d 736, 739-40 (7th Cir. 2003) (holding that defendant did not invade plaintiff's privacy when defendant shared his suspicions with other professors about a possible affair between plaintiff and a student because he was acting within the scope of his employment in reporting activity that may expose university to a lawsuit). Employers will not be liable for providing law enforcement with confidential information about an employee who is the subject of an investigation, even if the employee is wrongly accused. Price v. Campbell, 314 F. Supp. 2d 793, 796 (N.D. Ill. 2004) (holding that a law enforcement officer had a legitimate interest in the identity and location of an employee being investigated for a crime; allowing employer to reveal employee's confidential personnel file and work schedule without incurring liability, even though the basis for investigation was later found to be groundless).

Harm or damages from a publication of private facts may include damages for emotional distress. Rowe v. UniCare Life & Health Ins. Co., No. 09 C 2286, 2010 WL 86391, at *9 (N.D. Ill. Jan. 5, 2010).

An employer is not liable under the doctrine of *respondeat superior* for an employee's release of confidential information when no reasonable person would conclude that the release of information was the type of conduct that the employee was employed to perform. Bagent v. Blessing Care Corp., 224 Ill. 2d 154,171, 862 N.E.2d 985, 995-96, 308 Ill. Dec. 782, 792-93 (2007) (holding that hospital was not liable for employee's disclosure, in violation of hospital policy, of patient's pregnancy to patient's sister).

4. ***Intrusion.*** **For the first time, the Illinois Supreme Court recognized the tort of intrusion upon seclusion. Lawlor v. North American Corp. of Illinois, 2012 IL 112530, ¶ 35.** Previously, the Illinois Appellate Court had recognized a cause of action for intrusion upon seclusion. Burns v. Masterbrand Cabinets, Inc., 369 Ill. App. 3d 1006, 874 N.E.2d 72, 314 Ill. Dec. 162 (4th Dist. 2007); Johnson v. Kmart Corp., 311 Ill. App. 3d 573, 578, 723 N.E.2d 1192, 1196, 243 Ill. Dec. 591, 595 (1st Dist. 2000); Benitez v. KFC Nat'l Mgmt. Co., 305 Ill. App. 3d 1027, 1033-34, 714 N.E.2d 1002, 1007, 239 Ill. Dec. 705, 710 (2d Dist. 1999); Davis v. Temple, 284 Ill. App. 3d 983, 991-95, 673 N.E.2d 737, 742-44, 220 Ill. Dec. 593, 598-600 (5th Dist. 1996); Melvin v. Burling, 141 Ill. App. 3d 786, 490 N.E.2d 1011, 95 Ill. Dec. 919 (3d Dist. 1986).

"In an intrusion upon seclusion claim, the injury must occur from the prying itself, not publication." Harman v. Gist, No. 02 C 6112, 2003 WL 22053591, at *7 (N.D. Ill. Sept. 2, 2003); **Lawlor, 2012 IL 112530, ¶ 33 (upholding jury verdict finding that employer intruded upon employee's seclusion during an investigation into whether employee violated her non-competition agreement).** See also Browning v. AT&T Corp., 682 F. Supp. 2d 832, 838 (N.D. Ill. 2009) (finding no harm on an intrusion clam where the damages stemmed not from defendant's examination of personal information, but from the provision of that personal information to third parties).

To state a claim for intrusion upon seclusion, a plaintiff must allege facts supporting four elements: "(a) that the defendant intruded or pried into the plaintiff's seclusion without authorization, (b) that the intrusion would have been offensive or objectionable to a reasonable person, (c) that the matter upon which the intrusion occurred was private, and (d) that the intrusion caused anguish and suffering." Benitez, 305 Ill. App. 3d at 1037, 714 N.E.2d at 1009, 239 Ill. Dec. at 712. Cf. Schmidt v. Ameritech, 329 Ill. App. 3d 1020, 1030-31, 768 N.E.2d 303, 312, 263 Ill. Dec. 543, 552 (1st Dist. 2002) (finding that in order to prove element (b), the plaintiff must demonstrate that the intrusion is not merely offensive, but highly offensive to a reasonable person; reversing $5,160,000 verdict in favor of plaintiff where defendant employer reviewed plaintiff's telephone records to determine that he lied about his whereabouts).

To satisfy the first element, a plaintiff must establish that, at the time of the alleged intrusion, the plaintiff was "in a place a reasonable person would believe to be secluded." Webb v. CBS Broad., Inc., No. 08 C 6241,

2011 U.S. Dist. LEXIS 103601, at *10, 39 Media L. Rep. 2385 (N.D. Ill. Sept. 13, 2011). In Webb, the court granted summary judgment in favor of defendants, who broadcast images of plaintiffs and their children in the back yard of a family member who was a "person of interest" in a criminal investigation. The plaintiffs' activities "were in plain view, and thus not secluded." Id. at *12. The court noted that the yard was exposed to "many vantage points," and that the video footage, which defendants filmed from a neighbor's house, "could have been made from the public sidewalk or public street"). Id.

Authorization to examine private information may be made implicitly or by statute, precluding an intrusion claim. See Bassett v. I.C. Sys., Inc., No. 09 C 0301, 2010 WL 2179175, at *9 (N.D. Ill. June 1, 2010) (finding that phone calls made by a debt collector in order to collect a debt, when plaintiff did not tell the collector to stop calling him, were not unauthorized); Belleville v. Cottrell, Inc., No. 09-cv-962, 2010 WL 1251442, at *5 (S.D. Ill. Mar. 24, 2010) (finding no intrusion where Missouri's worker's compensation law authorizes access to medical information); Browning, 682 F. Supp. 2d at 837-38 (holding that defendant was authorized by federal statute to look into plaintiff's records to protect its monetary interest).

A prerequisite for an intrusion upon seclusion claim is that the plaintiff must "attempt[] to keep private facts private." Carroll v. Merrill Lynch, No. 07 C 1575, 2011 U.S. Dist. LEXIS 51311, at *69 (N.D. Ill. May 31, 2011) (quoting Acosta v. Scott LLC, 377 F. Supp. 2d 647, 650 (N.D. Ill. 2005)). In Carroll, the plaintiff sued after the defendant recorded and distributed a telephone conversation with the plaintiff without her permission. Id. at *67. The court held that the plaintiff "had no reasonable expectation of privacy in the contents of the conversation" because she openly discussed it with others and posted details of it on the Internet. Id. at *69. **An intrusion into the home is per se an intrusion upon a private matter. Jackson v. Bank of N.Y., No. 11-cv-6410, 2012 U.S. Dist. LEXIS 89258, at *15 (N.D. Ill. June 28, 2012).**

Although expectations of privacy are not as strong in the workplace as in the home, an employee may have a great enough expectation of privacy to permit a claim for intrusion upon seclusion. Acosta v. Scott Labor LLC, 377 F. Supp. 2d 647, 650 (N.D. Ill. 2005). Whether a workplace activity is private must be assessed in the full context of the employment relationship. Id. at 651. Factors to consider include (a) whether the employee has exclusive use over the workspace, (b) the extent to which others may access the workspace, and (c) whether the employee had notice that the workspace was subject to intrusions. Id. (finding no intrusion upon seclusion when employee was secretly videotaped in a shared work area because the activities were not private). See also Lee v. Northwestern University, No. 10 C 1157, 2010 WL 2757550, at *5 (N.D. Ill. July 13, 2010) (refusing to dismiss complaint that employer intruded upon the privacy of a campus police officer by searching his personal laptop, journals, CDs, and voice recorder, because those items "could contain highly personal information"); Horgan v. Simmons, 704 F. Supp. 2d 814, 822 (N.D. Ill. 2010) (finding that an employer's questioning about an employee's HIV status "fails to establish a sufficient 'prying' into a zone of solitude necessary to establish a claim under the tort").

Plaintiffs may seek both compensatory and punitive damages for intrusion upon seclusion claims. **Lawlor v. North American Corp., 2012 IL 112530, ¶ 35 (upholding award of punitive damages against employer for the authorized acts of its agent, but limiting award to an amount equal to compensatory award because there was no evidence of a premeditated scheme to harm employee, the acts in question were part of a legitimate investigation into employee's possible violation of her noncompetition agreement, and the relevant information was not distributed outside the company).**

C. Other Privacy-Related Actions

1. ***Intentional Infliction of Emotional Distress.*** To state a claim for intentional infliction of emotional distress, a plaintiff must allege that (1) defendant engaged in extreme and outrageous conduct, (2) defendant intended or expected that the conduct would cause severe emotional distress, and (3) the conduct caused severe emotional distress. Wilson v. Norfolk & Western Ry. Co., 187 Ill. 2d 369, 383-84, 718 N.E.2d 172, 180, 240 Ill. Dec. 691, 699 (1999).

To satisfy the first element, the conduct must be "'so outrageous in character, and so extreme in degree, as to go beyond all possible bounds of decency.'" Public Finance Corp. v. Davis, 66 Ill. 2d 85, 90, 360 N.E.2d 765, 767, 4 Ill. Dec. 652, 654 (1976) (quoting Restatement (Second) of Torts § 46, cmt. d (1965)). See also Wynne v. Loyola Univ. of Chicago, 318 Ill. App. 3d 443, 454, 741 N.E.2d 669, 677, 251 Ill. Dec. 782, 790 (1st Dist. 2000) (upholding summary judgment for defendant where defendant's conduct – publishing memorandum containing embarrassing facts about plaintiff, refusing to transfer plaintiff to another position, and appointing a department head whom plaintiff disliked – was not sufficiently extreme); Franciski v. Univ. of Chicago Hosps., 338 F.3d 765 (7th Cir. 2003) (rejecting claim that hospital intentionally inflicted emotional distress by removing parents of young patient and limiting their visits after repeated episodes of yelling, cursing, and other inappropriate behavior). The distress suffered "must be so severe that no reasonable person could be expected to endure it." Thomas v. Fuerst, 345 Ill. App. 3d 929, 936, 803 N.E.2d 619, 625, 281 Ill. Dec. 215, 221 (1st Dist. 2004). "'Mere insults, indignities, threats, annoyances, petty oppressions, or trivialities' do not qualify as extreme and outrageous conduct." Best v. Malec, No. 09 C 7749, 2010 WL 2364412, at *6 (N.D. Ill. June 11, 2010) (quoting Kolegas v. Heftel Broad. Corp., 154 Ill. 2d 1, 20-21, 607 N.E.2d 201, 211 (1992)).

The Illinois Appellate Court has recognized that "courts often hesitate to find that a plaintiff has stated a claim for intentional infliction of emotional distress in employment situations." Vickers v. Abbott Labs., 308 Ill. App. 3d 393, 410, 719 N.E.2d 1101, 1115, 241 Ill. Dec. 698, 712 (1st Dist. 1999). See also McCammon-Chase v. Circle Family Care, Inc., No. 09 C 7450, 2010 WL 2925893, at *7 (N.D. Ill. July 23, 2010) ("In the employment setting, though, the conduct alleged must be particularly outrageous"). "This trend reflects a concern that everyday job stresses should not give rise to a cause of action for intentional infliction of emotional distress." Vickers, 308 Ill. App. 3d at 410, 719 N.E.2d at 1115, 241 Ill. Dec. at 712. The rationale is that "if everyday job stresses resulting from discipline, personality conflicts, job transfers, or even terminations could give rise to a cause of action for intentional infliction of emotional distress, nearly every employee would have a cause of action." Raab v. County of Jo Daviess, 08 C 50087, 2010 U.S. Dist. LEXIS 79003, at *18 (N.D. Ill. Aug. 5, 2010) (quoting Graham v. Commonwealth Edison Co., 318 Ill. App. 3d 736, 742 N.E.2d 858, 867, 252 Ill. Dec. 320 (1st Dist. 2000)). One court has held that "when a plaintiff is suing her employer for intentional infliction of emotional distress, the 'showing of extreme and outrageous behavior is more strictly applied.'" Gould v. Barrett, No. 99 C 7661, 2002 U.S. Dist. LEXIS 5454, at *21-22 (N.D. Ill. Mar. 29, 2002). The court held that even where an employer reprimands an employee, excludes her, fails to notify her of policy changes, ignores her concerns for personal safety, and generally makes it difficult for her to continue working, a claim for intentional infliction of emotional distress will not succeed. Id. at *26-27. "While it is clear that [the employer's] reaction to [the employee's] situation and subsequent conduct may have been hard-hearted, unenlightened, and reminiscent of the Charles Dickens character Ebenezer Scrooge prior to his eventual transformation, the Court holds that, as a matter of law, Illinois law requires more in order to establish extreme and outrageous character in the employment context." Id. at *28.

Firing an employee, even on pretextual grounds, is not by itself extreme and outrageous conduct, even if the motive was illegal discrimination. Lawrence v. E. Cent. Ill. Area Agency on Aging, No. 10-CV-1240, 2011 U.S. Dist. LEXIS 29963, at *19 (C.D. Ill. Feb. 22, 2011) ("We cannot subject employers to intentional infliction of emotional distress claims each time they decide to discharge an employee – even an employee with severe emotional problems – unless their conduct is truly egregious"). Other cases rejecting emotional distress claims in the employment context include Swearnigen-El v. Cook County Sheriff's Dept., 602 F.3d 852, 864 (7th Cir. 2010) (finding that employee's demotion, transfer, and suspension without pay pending a hearing did not rise to "extreme" levels because the evidence in the investigation supported the actions taken); Chi v. Loyola Univ. Med. Ctr., No. 10 C 6292, 2011 U.S. Dist. LEXIS 55743, at *21-22 (N.D. Ill. May 24, 2011) (finding allegations that employer reprimanded employee undeservedly, placed him on probation without identifying specific deficiencies, and interfered with his professional development, if true, reflected an unpleasant work environment but did not support a cause of action for intentional infliction of emotional distress); Carroll v. Merrill Lynch, No. 07 C 1575, 2011 U.S. Dist. LEXIS 51311, at *71 (N.D. Ill. May 13, 2011) (finding that recording plaintiff's telephone conversation and replaying that conversation back to plaintiff's managers knowing it would lead to plaintiff's termination was insufficient to support an emotional distress claim); Pratt v. McAnarney, No. 08-3144, 2010 WL 2594745, at *7 (C.D. Ill. June 25, 2010) ("There is nothing 'extreme or outrageous' about Defendant investigating Plaintiff's claims, requesting Plaintiff's cooperation in the investigation, and then disciplining Plaintiff when, due to her insubordination, the investigation ended up taking several days longer than it should have and revealed that Plaintiff's allegations were untruthful."); **Ulm v. Mem'l Med. Ctr., 2012 IL App (4th) 110421, ¶¶ 45-46, 964 N.E.2d 632, 643, 357 Ill. Dec. 953, 964 (holding that retaliation against employee "did not meet the standard of 'extreme and outrageous' conduct" where employee refused to certify the accuracy of employer's medical records out of concern that certification would be illegal, even though employer addressed employee in an "openly hostile" manner, informed co-workers that she would be fired, relocated her twice, reassigned her secretary, told her that her "education was useless," gave her remedial work, and ultimately discharged her).** But see Graham v. Commonwealth Edison Co., 318 Ill. App. 3d 736, 742 N.E.2d 858, 252 Ill. Dec. 320 (1st Dist. 2000) (alleged sham investigation of employee deemed sufficiently outrageous to support claim for intentional infliction of emotional distress); Lee v. Northwestern Univ., No. 10 C 1157, 2010 WL 2757550, at *4 (N.D. Ill. July 13, 2010) (refusing to dismiss claim based on search of employee's laptop, journals, and CDs found in locker, finding that factual development was necessary to "assess whether Northwestern engaged in conduct that exceeded the bounds of decency"); Moriarty v. Dyson, Inc., No. 09 C 2777, 2010 WL 2745969, at *5 (N.D. Ill. July 8, 2010) ("Plaintiff has alleged that defendant informed her co-workers that she was having sexual relations with two other employees including the president of the company, and that the president was terminated as a result. The statements were made by persons with authority over plaintiff and continued over an extended period of time. If untrue, they could easily cause a woman with ordinary morals and sensibility to perceive them to be sufficiently offensive and sinister to rise to the level of extreme and outrageous behavior."); Fleszar v. Am. Med. Ass'n, No. 09-cv-2247, 2010 WL 1005030, at *9 (N.D. Ill. Mar. 11, 2010) (allegations that employer "repeatedly engaged in extreme and outrageous conduct toward her, including a colleague's yelling at her to get out of his office, an acting director's referring to [her] work areas as the 'low rent district,' suggesting she tampered with documents, and being escorted from her office in front of her coworkers" were sufficient to survive motion to dismiss).

When assessing the outrageousness of emotionally damaging conduct, the relative power of the parties should be considered. See Fox v. Hayes, 600 F.3d 819, 842 (7th Cir. 2010). "The more control defendant has over the plaintiff, the more likely that defendant's conduct will be deemed outrageous." Atlas v. City of North Chicago, No. 03 C 4814, 2004 WL 816456, at *4 (N.D. Ill. Mar. 12, 2004). **See also O'Connell v. Cont'l Elec. Constr. Co., No. 11 C 2291, 2011 U.S. Dist. LEXIS 119921, at *14-15 (N.D. Ill. Oct. 17, 2011) (holding that supervisor's removal of employee's anti-anxiety medication from employee's desk drawer "may properly be deemed 'extreme and outrageous' conduct," particularly in light of supervisor's position of authority and knowledge of employee's "fragile mental state" following diagnosis of severe anxiety and depression and treatment for cancer).**

Emotional distress claims are sometimes barred by Illinois statutes. For example, the Illinois Workers Compensation Act, 820 Ill. Comp. Stat. 305/1 et seq., bars recovery for emotional distress from accidental injuries arising out of and in the course of employment. See VIII.C, infra. **The Act does not bar emotional distress claims that allege intentional conduct. Green v. Casey's Retail Co., No. 11-1103, 2012 U.S. Dist. LEXIS 9316, at *10 (S.D. Ill. Jan. 26, 2012).**

The Illinois Human Rights Act, 775 Ill. Comp. Stat. 5/2-102; 775 Ill. Comp. Stat. 5/8-111, gives the Illinois Human Rights Commission exclusive jurisdiction over civil rights violations. As a result, the Act preempts tort claims, including claims for intentional infliction of emotional distress, that are "inextricably linked" to allegations of sexual harassment or other civil rights violations if there is no independent legal basis for the claim. Geise v. Phoenix Co., 159 Ill. 2d 507, 516, 639 N.E.2d 1273, 1277-77, 203 Ill. Dec. 454, 458 (Ill. 1994). Claims are "inextricably linked" to a claim arising under the Act if the Act furnishes the legal duty that the defendant allegedly breached. Naeem v. McKesson Drug Co., 444 F.3d 593, 603-04 (7th Cir. 2006). See also Quantock v. Shared Mktg. Servs., Inc., 312 F.3d 899, 905 (7th Cir. 2002) (claim for intentional infliction of emotional distress preempted when "supported by factual allegations identical to those set forth in [plaintiff's] Title VII sexual harassment claim"); Johnson v. Bristol-Myers Squibb Co., No. 10 C 1553, 2010 U.S. Dist. LEXIS 105116, at *19 (N.D. Ill. Oct. 1, 2010) (finding claim for intentional infliction of emotional distress arising out of workplace sexual assault preempted by the Human Rights Act); Hubbard v. Dollar Tree Stores, Inc., No. 04 C 0012, 2005 WL 589005, at *5-6 (N.D. Ill. Mar. 9, 2005) (emotional distress claim preempted by Human Rights Act because pregnancy discrimination and emotional distress claims rested on the same facts); **Onafuye v. JP Morgan Chase NA, No. 09 C 5100, 2012 U.S. Dist. LEXIS 14338, at *28 (N.D. Ill. Feb. 7, 2012) (finding emotional distress claim preempted where distress resulted from alleged discrimination)**. Torts that do not depend on a civil rights violation are not preempted. See, e.g., Zuidema v. Raymond Christopher, Inc., No. 11-cv-306, 2011 U.S. Dist. LEXIS 71052, at *16 (N.D. Ill. June 30, 2011) (finding that battery claim was not preempted); Lee, 2010 WL 2757550, at *4 (finding personal property claims for search of laptop, journals and CDs "arguably separate" from discrimination claims).

2. ***Interference With Prospective Economic Advantage.*** To state a claim for interference with prospective economic advantage, a plaintiff must allege: "(1) a reasonable expectancy of entering into a valid business relationship, (2) the defendant's knowledge of the expectancy, (3) an intentional and unjustified interference by the defendant that induced or caused a breach or termination of the expectancy, and (4) damage to the plaintiff resulting from the defendant's interference." Anderson v. Vanden Dorpel, 172 Ill. 2d 399, 406-07, 667 N.E.2d 1296, 1299, 217 Ill. Dec. 720, 723 (1996). Illinois courts look to the Restatement (Second) of Torts § 772 (1999) for guidance on interference claims. Atanus v. American Airlines, Inc., 403 Ill. App. 3d 549, 554-55, 932 N.E.2d 1044, 1049, 342 Ill. Dec. 583, 588 (1st Dist. 2010).

An interference claim can be pursued only against a third party to the relationship. Ali v. Shaw, 481 F.3d 942, 946 (7th Cir. 2007) (finding that an employer cannot tortiously interfere with its own relationship). Therefore, tortious interference claims are appropriate only in "cases of outsiders intermeddling maliciously in the contracts or affairs of other parties." Id. at 945 (quoting Fellhauer v. City of Geneva, 142 Ill. 2d 495, 568 N.E.2d 870, 154 Ill. Dec. 649 (Ill. 1991)). As a result, employees cannot sue their former employers for tortious interference for being fired. Gehrls v. Gooch, No. 09 C 6338, 2010 WL 1849400, at *4 (N.D. Ill. May 7, 2010); Kronenberg v. Baker & McKenzie LLP, 692 F. Supp. 2d 994, 1000 (N.D. Ill. 2010).

On the other hand, an employee can sue a supervisor or fellow employee for tortious interference for misusing authority to harm the employee. Thakkar v. Station Operators Inc., 697 F. Supp. 2d 908, 930 (N.D. Ill. 2010). **An affirmative defense to an interference claim is that the defendant acted "to protect an interest which the law deems to be of equal or greater value" as compared with the plaintiff's rights. Center for Dermatology & Skin Cancer Ltd. v. Humana Ins. Co., No. 11 C 6837, 2012 U.S. Dist. LEXIS 17707, at *9-10 (N.D. Ill. Feb. 8, 2012) (quoting HPI Health Care Servs., Inc. v. Mt. Vernon Hosp., Inc., 131 Ill. 2d 145, 157, 545 N.E.2d 672, 677, 137 Ill. Dec. 19, 24 (1989)).** Further, "giving proper and accurate reports" is not an unjustified interference. Atanus, 2010 WL 2486746, at *5 (holding that employer who gave second employer time records showing the employee was supposed to be on both jobs at the same time was not liable).

3. ***Prima Facie Tort.*** Illinois does not recognize a prima facie tort as a separate tort. Barry Gilberg, Ltd. v. Craftex Corp., 665 F. Supp. 585, 596-97 (N.D. Ill. 1987).

II. EMPLOYER TESTING OF EMPLOYEES

A. Psychological or Personality Testing

1. ***Common Law and Statutes.*** See II.A.2-3, infra. The Americans With Disabilities Act, 42 U.S.C. § 12101 et seq., prohibits employers from conducting pre-employment medical tests as a condition of employment. See Karraker v. Rent-A-Center, Inc., 411 F.3d 831, 834 (7th Cir. 2005). "Psychological tests that are 'designed to identify a mental disorder or impairment' qualify as medical examinations, but psychological tests 'that measure personality traits such as honesty, preferences, and habits' do not." Id. at 835 (citation omitted). If a psychological test is used only to identify personality traits, but also has the capacity to test for mental disorders, the test is impermissible if it has the effect of screening out candidates with mental disorders. Id. at 835-37.

2. ***Private Employers.*** Under the Illinois Human Rights Act, 775 Ill. Comp. Stat. 5/2-103, employers may require applicants to submit to pre-employment psychological examinations to determine whether they can perform the necessary activities and to ascertain the nature of accommodation that may be needed to enable applicants to perform acceptably. See 56 Ill. Admin. Code § 2500.60(b). Such tests may not be used to disqualify applicants on the basis of the risk of future injury, and the results of pre-employment examinations must be made available to applicants on request. Id.

An employer may not require applicants to list all of their disabling conditions. However, applicants may be required to disclose mental disabilities which may impair their ability to perform their duties. Id. § 2500.60(a)

3. ***Public Employers.*** Agencies that wish to perform pre-employment psychological or personality testing must submit their proposed programs for approval to the Director of the Department of Central Management Services. 80 Ill. Admin. Code § 302.105(a). Applicants who submit to psychological testing are not necessarily entitled to review their test results. See Roulette v. Dept. of Cent. Mgmt. Serv., 141 Ill. App. 3d 394, 490 N.E.2d 60, 95 Ill. Dec. 587 (1st Dist. 1986). Moreover, the dissemination of the results of such tests to other employees may not give rise to a claim for intentional infliction of emotional distress, even where the results reflect poorly on the employee. Lundy v. City of Calumet City, 209 Ill. App. 3d 790, 567 N.E.2d 1101, 153 Ill. Dec. 874 (1st Dist. 1991). Constitutional issues may also be implicated by the administration of psychological tests by public employers. Greenawalt v. Ind. Dept. of Corr., 397 F.3d 587, 592 (7th Cir. 2005) ("Perhaps it could even be argued that the administration by public officers of a particularly intrusive, and gratuitously humiliating, psychological test is a deprivation, without due process of law, of an interest in privacy that is an aspect of the liberty protected by the due process clauses of the Fifth and Fourteenth Amendments").

B. Drug Testing

1. ***Common Law and Statutes.*** See II.B.2-3, infra.

2. ***Private Employers.*** The Illinois Human Rights Act is agnostic on the question of drug testing. 775 Ill. Comp. Stat. 5/2-104(C)(4) ("Nothing in this Act shall be construed to encourage, prohibit, or authorize the conducting of drug testing for the illegal use of drugs by job applicants or employees or making employment decisions based on such test results"). Nevertheless, the Act provides that employers may prohibit the use of alcohol and illegal drugs at the workplace and require that employees not be under the influence of alcohol or illegal drugs at work. Id. § 2-104(C)(3)(a)-(b). The Act also permits employers to administer drug tests to employees who have completed or are in the midst of a drug rehabilitation program. Id. § 2-104(C)(2). A drug test itself is not an adverse employment action "unless it 'is not performed in a routine fashion following the regular and legitimate practices of the employer, but [rather] is conducted in a manner that harasses or humiliates employees.'" Ames v. Home Depot U.S.A., Inc., No. 08 CV 6060, 2009 WL 4673859, at *11 (N.D. Ill. Dec. 2, 2009).

3. ***Public Employers.*** The United States Supreme Court has upheld warrantless drug testing programs for government employees in sensitive positions. National Treasury Employees Union v. Von Raab , 489 U.S. 656, 109 S. Ct. 1384, 103 L. Ed. 2d 685 (1989); Skinner v. Railway Labor Executives Ass'n, 489 U.S. 602, 109 S. Ct. 1402, 103 L. Ed. 2d 639 (1989). The Seventh Circuit has also upheld random, warrantless drug testing where safety concerns are implicated, upholding such testing of operators of dump trucks and other heavy equipment because a public employer "has a compelling interest in ensuring that its employees who regularly drive large equipment are not impaired by drugs or alcohol." Krieg v. Seybold, 481 F.3d 512, 520 (7th Cir. 2007).

In Illinois, public agencies that wish to perform pre-employment drug testing must submit their proposed programs for approval to the Director of the Department of Central Management Services. 80 Ill. Admin. Code § 302.105(a).

Under the Illinois Drug Free Workplace Act, state grantees and contractors must certify that they will provide a drug-free workplace. 30 Ill. Comp. Stat. 580/1 et seq.

C. Medical Testing

1. ***Common Law and Statutes.*** The Genetic Information Privacy Act, 410 Ill. Comp. Stat. 513/1 et seq., provides that an employer may not release genetic testing information to anyone other than (1) the employee or his authorized representative, (2) a person "designated in a specific written legally effective release of the test results" executed by the employee or his authorized representative, or (3) representatives of health care facilities or providers under certain specified circumstances. Id. §§ 25-30. An employer may not solicit, request, or require genetic testing or genetic information of an individual or their family members as a condition of employment, preemployment application, labor organization membership, or licensure. Id. § 25(c)(1). The Act creates a private right of action. Id. § 40. If the unauthorized disclosure was negligent, the plaintiff may recover $1,000 or actual damages, whichever is greater. Id. § 40(a)(1). If the unauthorized disclosure was intentional or reckless, the plaintiff may recover $5,000 or actual damages, whichever is greater. Id. § 40(a)(2). In addition, successful plaintiffs are entitled to recover attorneys' fees and may obtain an injunction where appropriate. Id. § 40(a)(3)-(4).

The AIDS Confidentiality Act, 410 Ill. Comp. Stat. 305/1 et seq., generally forbids disclosure of a request for or results of HIV testing to anyone other than the subject of the test or their legally authorized representative. Id. § 305/9. The Act creates a private right of action and permits the recovery of either actual damages or liquidated damages ($2,000 for negligent violations, $10,000 for reckless or intentional violations). Id. § 13. The Act also gives successful plaintiffs the right to recover attorneys' fees. Id. However, the Act does not permit the recovery of punitive damages. Doe v. Chand, 335 Ill. App. 3d 809, 819, 781 N.E.2d 340, 349, 269 Ill. Dec. 543, 552 (5th Dist. 2002).

2. ***Private Employers.*** Employers "may require all applicants who have been found otherwise qualified for selection to submit to pre-employment physical or psychological examinations, for the purpose of determining whether such applicants are capable of acceptably performing the activities necessary to the job or training at issue." 56 Ill. Admin. Code § 2500.60(b). Such tests may not be used to disqualify applicants on the basis of the risk of future injury, and the results of pre-employment examinations must be made available to applicants on request. Id. An employer may not require applicants to list all of their medical conditions, but applicants may be required to disclose physical disabilities which impair their ability to perform the particular duties acceptably. Id. § 2500.60(a).

3. ***Public Employers.*** State agencies that wish to perform pre-employment medical testing must submit their proposed programs for approval to the Director of the Department of Central Management Services. 80 Ill. Admin. Code § 302.105(a).

A federal district court found that a Chicago police officer's Fourth Amendment rights were violated when a physician working for the City of Chicago forced him to submit to a blood test. Krocka v. Bransfield, 969 F. Supp. 1073, 1093 (N.D. Ill. 1997). The physician was trying to determine whether the officer was taking an anti-depressant drug. Id. at 1092. A jury awarded the officer $200 in damages. Krocka v. City of Chicago, 203 F.3d 507, 511 (7th Cir. 2000).

D. Polygraph Tests

The federal Employee Polygraph Protection Act prohibits most polygraph testing by private employers. 29 U.S.C. §§ 2001-2009. In Veazey v. Communications & Cable of Chicago, Inc., 194 F.3d 850, 854-60 (7th Cir. 1999), the Seventh Circuit traced the history and rationale of the Act and discussed the academic studies that have cast doubt on the reliability of polygraph tests. The specific issue in Veazey dealt with the scope of the phrase "lie detector" in the Act, 29 U.S.C. § 2001(3). Id. at 853. The plaintiff claimed that his former employer violated the Act when it fired him for refusing to record an offensive message during an investigation into whether the employee had left the message on the voice mail of another employee. Id. The majority opinion agreed that "simply using a tape recorder to compare voice samples would not violate the [Act]," but found that the employer may have intended to subject the recording to a voice stress analyzer to determine whether the employee was telling the truth. Id. at 858-59 & n.8. "Accordingly," the majority said, "a tape recorder, when used in conjunction with one of the devices enumerated in the statute or a similar device, may fit within the definition of a 'lie detector' under the [Act]." Id. at 859.

In the limited cases where polygraph testing is permitted, both the federal act and the Illinois Detection of Deception Examiners Act forbid polygraph examiners from inquiring into certain subject areas during employment-related examinations: (1) religious beliefs or affiliations, (2) beliefs regarding racial issues, (3) political beliefs or affiliations, (4) beliefs, affiliations or lawful activities regarding labor unions, and (5) sexual preferences or activity. 29 U.S.C. § 2007(b)(1)(C); 225 Ill. Comp. Stat. 430/14.1. These limitations do not apply if the subject area is "directly related to employment." Id.

Polygraph tests are not admissible in Illinois administrative hearings, even if the subject has agreed to submit to the polygraph examination. Kaske v. City of Rockford, 96 Ill. 2d 298, 70 Ill. Dec. 841, 450 N.E.2d 314 (1983) (finding that it was error to use the results of a polygraph examination at a police officer's disciplinary hearing); see also 50 Ill. Comp. Stat. 725/3.11 (expressly protecting peace officers from being subject to polygraph examinations or disciplinary action for refusing to submit to such examination).

In theory, widespread disclosure of polygraph results could give rise to a cause of action for public disclosure of private facts. But in Roehrborn v. Lambert, 277 Ill. App. 3d 181, 660 N.E.2d 180, 213 Ill. Dec. 923 (1st Dist. 1995), the court affirmed the dismissal of a privacy claim where the defendant gave plaintiff's polygraph and psychological test results only to the administrator of a police training program. This disclosure, the court held, did not satisfy the requirement that defendant give "publicity" to the private fact — a standard that requires more than mere publication to a third person. Id. at 184-85, 660 N.E.2d at 182-83, 213 Ill. Dec. at 925-26.

Public agencies that wish to perform pre-employment polygraph testing must submit their proposed programs for approval to the Director of the Department of Central Management Services. 80 Ill. Admin. Code § 302.105(a).

E. Fingerprinting

In Young v. Chicago Housing Authority, 350 Ill. App. 287, 112 N.E.2d 719 (1st Dist. 1953), the Illinois Appellate Court upheld the Chicago Housing Authority's practice of fingerprinting employees. The court stated that "[n]o stigma is attached to fingerprinting" and that "[i]t is widely accepted and used as a method of determining employee fitness." Id. at 291, 112 N.E.2d at 721.

III. SEARCHES

A. Employee's Person

1. ***Private Employers.*** In Toothman v. Hardee's Food Systems, Inc., 304 Ill. App. 3d 521, 710 N.E.2d 880, 238 Ill. Dec. 83 (5th Dist. 1999), the Illinois Appellate Court upheld a jury verdict in favor of plaintiffs after the managers of a fast-food restaurant strip-searched four employees in an effort to find $50 that was missing from the store safe. (It later turned out that no money was missing.) While the managers testified that they merely required the plaintiffs to empty their pockets and take off their shoes and socks, the plaintiffs testified that they were taken to a small, windowless, locked room and ordered to strip down to their underwear. The Appellate Court agreed that plaintiffs' claims against their employer were not barred by the exclusive remedy provisions of the Workers' Compensation Act, 820 Ill. Comp. Stat. 305/1 et seq. Id. at 525-34, 710 N.E.2d at 883-89, 238 Ill. Dec. at 86-92. Based on theories of false imprisonment, assault, and battery, the Appellate Court upheld compensatory damages of $25,000 for each plaintiff against all defendants, $200,000 in punitive damages for each plaintiff against the employer, and $375 and $50 in punitive damages for each plaintiff against the managers who conducted the search. Id. at 525 & 535, 710 N.E.2d at 883 & 889, 238 Ill. Dec. at 86 & 91.

2. ***Public Employers.*** The Seventh Circuit has held that the doctrine of qualified immunity may protect warrantless strip searches of correctional officers. Scoby v. Neal, 981 F.2d 286 (7th Cir. 1992).

B. Employee's Work Area

Employees may bring an "intrusion on seclusion" claim if their work areas are searched without consent. See I.B.4, supra. At a minimum, however, the search would have to cause "anguish and suffering" to the employee. See Hoth v. American States Ins. Co., 735 F. Supp. 290 (N.D. Ill. 1990) (dismissing claim for invasion of privacy based on a private employer's search of employee's office, including locked file cabinet and desk, because plaintiff claimed only that he lost his job as a result, not that he felt "anguish and suffering"). See also O'Donnell v. CBS, Inc., 782 F.2d 1414, 1420, 12 Media L. Rep. 1697 (7th Cir. 1986) (upholding summary judgment in favor of employer where employee claimed that employer ordered his secretary to search his private files). But see Lee v. Northwestern University, No. 10 C 1157, 2010 WL 2757550, at *5 (N.D. Ill. July 13, 2010) (refusing to dismiss intrusion claim based upon search of contents of locker, including laptop and journals, as opposed to search of locker itself).

Where public employers are involved, Fourth Amendment concerns are implicated. See City of Ontario v. Quon, 130 S. Ct. 2619, 2628 (2010) ("Individuals do not lose Fourth Amendment rights merely because they work for the government instead of a private employer"). However, neither a warrant nor probable cause is required to search an employee's work area (or communications) if a the search is "reasonable," i.e., "it is 'justified at its inception'" and "'the measures adopted are reasonably related to the objectives of the search and not excessively intrusive in light of' the circumstances giving rise to the search." Quon, 130 S. Ct. at 2630. In general, the search must be designed to retrieve government property or investigate work-related misconduct. Gossmeyer v. McDonald, 128 F.3d 481, 490 (7th Cir. 1997) (upholding dismissal of claims of child protection investigator whose files were searched for child pornography based on anonymous tip from co-worker). See also Chicago Fire Fighters Union v. City of Chicago, 717 F. Supp. 1314 (N.D. Ill. 1989) (holding that fire department's policy of conducting unannounced, warrantless searches of lockers did not violate firefighters' Fourth Amendment rights); Maes v. Folberg, 504 F. Supp. 2d 339, 351 (N.D. Ill. 2007) (finding that employee had a reasonable expectation of privacy in her workplace computer and that there were no allegations of misconduct or other justification for the search).

C. Employee's Property

1. ***Private Employers.*** A private employer does not have authority to consent to a government search of employees' living quarters, even where the living quarters are provided by the employer. Illinois Migrant Council v. Pilliod, 540 F.2d 1062, 1069 (7th Cir. 1976).

2. ***Public Employers.*** An absolute immunity may bar invasion of privacy claims against certain government employees. Morton v. Hartigan, 145 Ill. App. 3d 417, 427, 495 N.E.2d 1159, 1165-66, 99 Ill. Dec. 424, 430-31 (1st Dist. 1986) (upholding dismissal of invasion of privacy claim against manager in Attorney General's office where manager searched employee's desk and briefcase to recover a public document).

IV. MONITORING OF EMPLOYEES

A. Telephones and Electronic Communications

The Illinois Eavesdropping Act, 720 Ill. Comp. Stat. 5/14-1 et seq., generally forbids the use of an "eavesdropping device" to hear, record, or intercept the conversations or electronic communications of others without their consent. "[T]here is no indication in the Act that it applies only to conversations when there is an objective expectation of privacy. To the contrary, the plain language of the statute provides that the Act applies to any conversation between two or more individuals regardless of whether any party has an objective or subjective expectation of privacy." Plock v. Bd. of Educ. of Freeport Sch. Dist. No. 145, 396 Ill. App. 3d 960, 968, 920 N.E.2d 1087, 1094, 336 Ill. Dec. 497, 504 (2d Dist. 2009) (holding that a school district's proposed policy of audio-taping special education classrooms violated the Act). The Act applies to conversations that take place in both public and private settings. Id.

A person may "impliedly consent" to the monitoring of his communications for purposes of the Act. Illinois v. Ceja, 204 Ill. 2d 332, 349-50, 789 N.E.2d 1228, 1241, 273 Ill. Dec. 796, 809 (Ill. 2003). "The circumstances relevant to an implication of consent will vary from case to case, but will ordinarily include language or acts that tend to prove that a party knows of, or assents to, encroachments on the routine expectation that conversations are private." Id. Consent may be inferred from the lack of objection to the taping. Locsmondy v. Arrow Pneumatics, No. 99 C 6463, 2001 WL 109810, at *8 (N.D. Ill. Feb. 5, 2001); **Poris v. Lake Holiday Property Owners Ass'n, Inc., 2012 IL App (3d) 110131, ¶ 41, 965 N.E.2d 464, 472, 358 Ill. Dec. 393, 401 ("When an individual is told that his conversation is being recorded and, nevertheless, knowingly engages in conversation, there is no eavesdropping violation"), petition for leave to appeal granted, 968 N.E.2d 1072, 360 Ill.Dec. 319 (2012).** When the evidence is conflicting, determining consent may require an evidentiary hearing. Independent Trust Corp. v. Hurwick, 351 Ill. App. 3d 941, 953, 814 N.E.2d 895, 905, 286 Ill. Dec. 669, 679 (1st Dist. 2004).

The exclusionary rule of the Act applies only to state law claims; whether recordings may be used to prosecute claims under federal law is governed by the more liberal "one party consent" standard in 18 U.S.C. § 2511 et seq. Electronic surveillance evidence gathered "pursuant to federal law, but in violation of the [state] eavesdropping statute, is not inadmissible absent evidence of collusion between federal and state agents to avoid the requirements of state law." Illinois v. Coleman, 227 Ill. 2d 426, 439, 882 N.E.2d 1025, 1032, 317 Ill. Dec. 869, 876 (2008).

The Seventh Circuit struck down the Illinois Eavesdropping Act as violating the First Amendment to the extent that it forbids people from making non-consensual recordings of police officers doing their jobs in public. ACLU v. Alvarez, 679 F.3d 583 (7th Cir. 2012). The court held that, as applied to the ACLU's plans to record police officers, the Act "likely violates the First Amendment's free-speech and free-press guarantees." Id. at 587. The court noted that "this case has nothing to do with private conversations or surreptitious interceptions." Id. at 606.

The Act provides numerous but mostly narrow exemptions. 720 Ill. Comp. Stat. 5/14-3. **In Carroll v. Merrill Lynch, No. 12-1076 (7th Cir. Oct. 16, 2012), the Seventh Circuit held that the fear of crime exemption requires only a "reasonable suspicion" that a party to the recorded conversation is committing or may commit a crime, and further held that the exemption applies to "any crime." Id. at 14-15.**

Violation of the Act is a Class 4 felony (for a first offense) or a Class 3 felony (for any subsequent offense). Id. § 14-4. A corporation commits a felony when a "high managerial agent," acting in the scope of employment, violates the Act. Id. § 5/5-4(a)(2); Morris v. Ameritech Ill., 337 Ill. App. 3d 40, 46, 785 N.E.2d 62, 67, 271 Ill. Dec. 411, 416 (1st Dist. 2003).

Parties to conversations that were either recorded or overheard in violation of the Act may be entitled to injunctive relief, actual damages, and punitive damages. 720 Ill. Comp. Stat. 5/14-6. See also Vasquez v. City of Woodstock, 242 Ill. App. 3d 766, 611 N.E.2d 44, 183 Ill. Dec. 191 (2d Dist. 1993) (upholding injunction barring defendant, which allegedly recorded telephone conversations of police department personnel in violation of the Act, from listening to, replaying, erasing, editing, destroying or altering tapes of conversations). The statute of limitations for a claim under the Act is five years. McDonald's Corp. v. Levine, 108 Ill. App. 3d 732, 737-39, 439 N.E.2d 475, 479-80, 64 Ill. Dec. 224, 228-29 (2d Dist. 1982).

The Act provides for liability against eavesdroppers and their "principals." See 720 Ill. Comp. Stat. 5/14-6. "Principal" includes anyone who "[k]nowingly employs another who illegally uses an eavesdropping device in the course of such employment." Id. § 14-1(c)(1). An employer cannot be held liable under this provision merely because its employees violate the Act in the course of their employment. Cebula v. General Elec. Co., 614 F. Supp. 260, 267 (N.D. Ill. 1985). Instead, the term "knowingly" generally means that a supervisor must know of or direct the unlawful eavesdropping. Morris, 337 Ill. App. 3d at 47, 785 N.E.2d at 67, 271 Ill. Dec. at 416. Accord Cebula, 614 F. Supp. at 267-68.

Recording co-workers without consent constitutes legitimate grounds for termination of an employee. Johnson v. Jung, Nos. 02 C 5221, 04 C 6158, 2009 WL 3156743, at *9 (N.D. Ill. Sept. 28, 2009). An employee whose telephone conversations are surreptitiously recorded may also have a claim for intrusion on seclusion. See I.B.4, supra; Amati v. City of Woodstock, 829 F. Supp. 998, 1009-11 (N.D. Ill. 1993).

1. ***Wiretapping.*** In addition to the Illinois Eavesdropping Act, federal law provides a potential remedy for employees when employers record their telephone calls without their knowledge or consent. 18 U.S.C. § 2510 et seq. The statute, however, exempts monitoring of communications occurring in the ordinary course of an employer's business. 18 U.S.C. § 2510(a)(i); see also Grey v. Kirkland & Ellis, LLP, Nos. 07 C 975, 07 C 978, 07 C 979, 2010 WL 3526478, at *1 n.3 (N.D. Ill. Sept. 2, 2010) (noting that the exemption would only apply to a work telephone). In Amati v. City of Woodstock, 176 F.3d 952 (7th Cir. 1999), the Seventh Circuit upheld a jury verdict in favor of the employer under the federal eavesdropping law, where employees' calls on a supposedly "untapped" police department line were recorded. The recording of such calls, the Seventh Circuit held, was "regrettable," but nevertheless fell within a statutory exclusion for eavesdropping "by an investigative or law enforcement officer in the ordinary course of his duties." Id. at 954-56 (quoting 18 U.S.C. § 2510 (5)(a)(ii)). The Seventh Circuit has also ruled that the federal eavesdropping law does not apply to municipalities. Abbott v. Village of Winthrop Harbor, 205 F.3d 976, 983 (7th Cir. 2000).

2. ***Electronic Communications.*** The Illinois Eavesdropping Act forbids the surreptitious interception of "electronic communications," a term that is defined broadly enough to encompass e-mail and other electronic communications. 720 Ill. Comp. Stat. 5/14-1(e). In contrast to other provisions of the Act, the interception of an "electronic communication" is forbidden only when "the sending and receiving parties intend the electronic communication to be private." Id. (emphasis added). See generally Hurst v. Bd. of the Fire & Police Comm'n of Clinton, 2011 IL App (4th) 100964, ¶ 19, 952 N.E.2d 1246, 1251, 352 Ill. Dec. 20, 25.

In Hurst, the plaintiff, a police officer, alleged that his chief of police violated the Illinois Eavesdropping Act when he obtained evidence of the plaintiff viewing pornography on a city-owned terminal in his vehicle while on duty. Id. at ¶¶ 19-21, 952 N.E.2d at 1251, 352 Ill. Dec. at 25. The court found that the images were "not electronic communications according to the statute" because nothing in the record suggested "the sending parties of the various pornographic images intended to keep them private." Id. The court went on to state that the "plaintiff had no reasonable expectation of privacy or confidentiality" with regard to the device because the police department's Policy and Procedures Manual disclosed that messages sent on the mobile data terminal were retrievable. Id.

Shefts v. Petrakis, 758 F. Supp. 2d 620 (C.D. Ill. 2010), illustrates the implied consent rule in the context of mobile e-mail devices provided by an employer. The defendants, concerned that the plaintiff was sexually harassing company employees and violating his fiduciary duties, secretly arranged to have his e-mails routed to a separate account for monitoring. The defendants also monitored plaintiff's text messages. Id. at 625-26. In response to plaintiff's claim that they had violated the Illinois Eavesdropping Act, the defendants maintained that plaintiff "could not have had a reasonable expectation of privacy in his communications sent and received by him on equipment connected to [the company's] information systems." Id. at 632-33. The court agreed. It held that whether plaintiff had a reasonable expectation of privacy depended on "whether [the company] had a policy in place regarding the monitoring of such systems, as well as whether [plaintiff] was aware that [defendant] or others at [the company] may be monitoring his activities." Id. Because the employee manual stated that "all communications sent and received on [company] equipment were subject to monitoring by Company officials," and because plaintiff had recently been appointed as the company's "security liaison," the court held that he had no reasonable expectation of privacy after the manual went into effect. Id. at 634-35.

Similarly, in Goldstein v. Colborne Acquisition Co., No. 10 C 6861, 2012 U.S. Dist. LEXIS 75743 (N.D. Ill. June 1, 2012), the court found unreasonable a group of employees' subjective expectations of privacy in electronic

communications, including e-mails to their attorneys. Id. at *16. As a result, the employees waived the attorney-client privilege when they used their work emails to respond to a discovery request. Id. The court considered four factors in determining whether the employees' "belief of confidentiality" was reasonable: "(1) whether the corporation banned personal or objectionable use of company computer or e-mail; (2) whether the company monitored the use of the employee's computer or e-mail; (3) whether third parties had a right of access to the computer or e-mail; and (4) whether the corporation notified the employee, or whether the employee was aware, of use and monitoring policies." Id. at *9, *12-13. Although the company did not monitor e-mails and did not ban personal e-mails outside business hours, it did ban objectionable e-mails and had reserved the right to "access and disclose all messages sent over its electronic mail system, for any purpose." Id. at *13-14.

Applying Fourth Amendment principles, the Seventh Circuit has stated in dicta that an employer's reservation of the right to inspect its computers "destroyed any reasonable expectation of privacy" that an employee may have. Muick v. Glenayre Elecs., 280 F.3d 741, 743 (7th Cir. 2002). The court observed: "[T]he abuse of access to workplace computers is so common (workers being prone to use them as media of gossip, titillation, and other entertainment and distraction) that reserving a right of inspection is so far from being unreasonable that the failure to do so might well be thought irresponsible." Id.

3. ***Other Electronic Monitoring.*** No statutes or reported cases.

B. Mail

No statutes or reported cases.

C. Surveillance/Photographing

"Courts have consistently held that videotaping a work area or office in an attempt to monitor workplace conduct is not a violation of privacy," in part because "employment is not inherently private as a matter of law." Acosta v. Scott Labor LLC, 377 F. Supp. 2d 647, 651 & 652 (N.D. Ill. 2005). Depending on the circumstances, however, video surveillance in the workplace may lead to a claim for intrusion upon seclusion. See I.B.4, supra; see also Brazinski v. Amoco Petroleum Additives Co., 6 F.3d 1176, 1182-84 (7th Cir. 1993) (court assumed — but did not hold — that plaintiff, a contractor, had a privacy claim where company placed video camera inside company locker room, but upheld summary judgment in favor of company because plaintiff failed to present evidence that she had actually been videotaped or even used locker room while camera was in place). Cf. Thornton v. Univ. Civil Serv. Merit Board, 154 Ill. App. 3d 1016, 1020-21, 507 N.E.2d 1262, 1265 -66, 107 Ill. Dec. 893, 896-97 (5th Dist. 1987) (upholding use of videotape in civil service hearing showing that plaintiff was gambling at work because plaintiff did not have a reasonable expectation of privacy). Whether a workplace is considered private will depend on the employee's expectation of privacy in the area and the employment relationship. Acosta, 377 F. Supp. 2d at 650-51. An employer may, however, use surveillance to "test the bona fides of a employee's workers' compensation claim." Casanova v. American Airlines, Inc., 616 F.3d 695, 698 (7th Cir. 2010).

The Illinois Appellate Court has upheld a trial judge's finding against four employees for spying on fellow employees through a hole in the ceiling of the women's bathroom. Benitez v. KFC Nat'l Mgmt. Co., 305 Ill. App. 3d 1027, 714 N.E.2d 1002, 239 Ill. Dec. 705 (2d Dist. 1999). But in an unpublished and non-precedential portion of the opinion, the court upheld the dismissal of the claims against the employer on the ground that the claims were barred by the exclusivity provisions of the Workers' Compensation Act, 820 Ill. Comp. Stat. 305/1 et seq.

It is unlawful to videotape or transmit live video of a person without consent in the person's home or in a restroom, tanning bed, tanning salon, locker room, changing room, or hotel room. 720 Ill. Comp. Stat. 5/26-4. The knowing dissemination of videotapes, photographs, film, or live video taken in violation of the statute is a felony.

If a workplace is unionized, the use of hidden surveillance cameras in the workplace is a mandatory subject of collective bargaining. National Steel Corp. v. NLRB, 324 F.3d 928 (7th Cir. 2003).

D. Workplace Behavior

The Nursing Mothers in the Workplace Act, 820 Ill. Comp. Stat. 260/1 et seq., requires employers with more than five employees to provide unpaid break time for nursing mothers to allow them to express milk, unless the break would "unduly disrupt the employer's operations." Id. § 10. The Act also requires employers to make reasonable efforts to provide private areas for nursing. The Right to Breastfeed Act requires that both private and public places permit a mother to breastfeed, "irrespective of whether the nipple of the mother's breast is uncovered during or incidental to the breastfeeding." 740 Ill. Comp. Stat. 137/1 et seq. The Act creates a private right of action for equitable relief and attorneys' fees and costs. Id. § 15.

Employers may not prohibit employees from speaking their native languages at work when discussing matters unrelated to the duties of their employment. 755 Ill. Comp. Stat. 5/2-102(A-5). Restricting this behavior is a violation of an employee's civil rights. Id.

V. ACTIVITIES OUTSIDE THE WORKPLACE

A. Statute or Common Law

The limitations on employers' ability to regulate the activities of employees outside the workplace are generally rooted in statute, not the common law.

Employees may be restricted by contract from disseminating private or confidential information about their employer, even after they leave their job. Coady v. Harpo, Inc., 308 Ill. App. 3d 153, 160-62, 719 N.E.2d 244, 250-51, 241 Ill. Dec. 383, 389-90 (1st Dist. 1999) (upholding contractual provision forbidding employee from publicizing information about her former employer, Oprah Winfrey). See also VII.B, infra.

B. Employees' Personal Relationships

1. ***Romantic Relationships Between Employees.*** Few cases have addressed the question of whether and to what extent an employer may regulate romantic relationships between employees. However, no Illinois statute protects the privacy of such relationships, and one court has found that firing an employee because of her romantic relationship with a co-employee probably does not violate Illinois public policy. Talley v. Washington Inventory Serv., No. 93 C 1653, 1993 WL 169276, 1993 U.S. Dist. LEXIS 6831 (N.D. Ill. 1993) (dismissing retaliatory discharge claim where former employee asserted that she was fired for dating fellow employee whom she later married), aff'd, 37 F.3d 310 (7th Cir. 1994). With regard to employees who have an extramarital affair with another employee, an Illinois court has held that the employer cannot be held vicariously liable in an alienation-of-affections action when the conduct was not within the scope of employment. Hargan v. Sw. Elec. Coop., Inc., 311 Ill. App. 3d 1029, 1033, 725 N.E.2d 807, 810, 244 Ill. Dec. 334, 337 (5th Dist. 2000).

2. ***Sexual Orientation.*** The Illinois Human Rights Act forbids employers from discriminating on the basis of sexual orientation. 775 Ill. Comp. Stat. 5/1-102.

3. ***Marital Status.*** The Illinois Human Rights Act forbids employers from discriminating on the basis of marital status, i.e., "the legal status of being married, single, separated, divorced or widowed." 775 Ill. Comp. Stat. 5/1-103 (J); id. §1-103(Q); id. § 2-102(A). In Boaden v. Dep't of Law Enforcement, 171 Ill. 2d 230, 664 N.E.2d 61, 215 Ill. Dec. 664 (1996), the Illinois Supreme Court held that the Act does not prohibit discrimination based on the identity of an employee's spouse. Thus, the court held that the Illinois State Police could enforce a "no spouse" policy that prohibited married couples from working on the same shift in the same patrol area. Id.

C. Smoking

The Illinois Right to Privacy in the Workplace Act generally prohibits employers from regulating employees' use of "lawful products" away from work during non-work hours. 820 Ill. Comp. Stat. 55/5(a). Among the products covered by the Act are tobacco, alcohol, food, and over-the-counter and prescription drugs. 56 Ill. Admin. Code § 360.110(g). The Act provides an exception where the employer is a non-profit organization (such as the American Lung Association) that discourages the use of a lawful product. 820 Ill. Comp. Stat. 55/5(b). The Act also allows employers to impose higher health insurance premiums on smokers, as long as the higher premiums reflect the actual cost to the employer and the employer explains the higher rates to its employees. Id. § 5(c)).

D. Blogging

Under certain circumstances, an employer may access without permission an employee's personal Facebook and Twitter accounts to promote the employer's business without violating the Illinois Right of Publicity Act or intruding upon the employee's seclusion. Maremont v. Susan Fredman Design Group, Ltd., No. 10 C 7811, 2011 U.S. Dist. LEXIS 140446, at *18-21 (N.D. Ill. Dec. 7, 2011). In Maremont, an employee previously used her Facebook and Twitter accounts to promote her employer's business. Id. at *4-7. When the employee was injured and became unable to continue posting, her employer began posting under her personal accounts without her permission, via other employees who acted as "guest bloggers." Id. The court granted summary judgment in favor of the employer on both the Right of Publicity and intrusion on seclusion claims. Id. (holding that employee could not demonstrate either the "appropriation" element under the Right of Publicity claim or that she had "attempted to keep private facts private" under the intrusion upon seclusion claim). The court's holding on the Right of Publicity claim depended heavily on the specific nature of the Twitter posts, which explained the guest blogging arrangement, and the employee's own Twitter and Facebook posts upon her return, which linked to the same company blog and thanked the guest bloggers. Id. at

***18-19. The court also noted that the employee stored passwords to the accounts on a work server, posted about work from her personal Twitter and Facebook accounts with links to the company blog, and advertised the personal accounts in her work e-mails. Id. at *5, *19-21.**

Blog posts and Wikipedia entries about a former colleague may form the basis of a false light invasion of privacy claim, where the blog post or Wikipedia entry is not mere opinion and is not "capable of an innocent construction." Pitale v. Holestine, No. 11 C 00921, 2012 U.S. Dist. LEXIS 24631, at *15-17, *23-24 (N.D. Ill. Feb. 27, 2012).

VI. RECORDS

A. Personnel Records

The Illinois Personnel Record Review Act, 820 Ill. Comp. Stat. 40/0.01 et seq., permits employees to review their personnel records, provides criteria for the review, details what information may not be contained in personnel records, and provides penalties for violations. In general, the Act requires employers with five or more employees (excluding the employer's family members) to permit employees or their representatives to inspect and copy their own personnel records. Id. §§ 1-2; Cothran v. Northwestern Medical Faculty Foundation, No. 09 C 7367, 2010 WL 1335006, at *3 (N.D. Ill. Mar. 30, 2010). In construing the Act, the Illinois Appellate Court has recognized that "[t]here is a strong public policy to provide the employee rights of access to this vital data without undue burden." Landwer v. Scitex Am. Corp., 238 Ill. App. 3d 403, 407, 606 N.E.2d 485, 488, 179 Ill. Dec. 653, 656 (1st Dist. 1992).

Under the Act, employers are prohibited from publicly divulging any disciplinary action taken against an employee without first providing the employee with written notice. 820 Ill. Comp. Stat. 40/7. This provision applies both to written records and verbal statements conveying information in the records. Bogosian v. Bd. of Educ. of Cmty. Sch. Dist. 200, 134 F. Supp. 2d 952, 960-62 (N.D. Ill. 2001). The disciplinary actions contemplated by the section are not limited to dismissals and other formal actions, but also include other actions relating to the discipline of an employee. Id. Finally, an employee's public disclosure of the facts relating to a disciplinary action does not constitute a waiver of the employee's right to notice under this section. Id.

The Act prohibits employers from maintaining files on non-employment activities such as the employee's political activities. Id. § 9. The prohibition does not apply to activities at work or during working hours which "interfere with the performance of the employee's duties or the duties of other employees or activities." Id. It also does not apply to an employee's criminal conduct or to conduct which "may reasonably be expected to harm the employer's property, operations or business, or could by the employee's action cause the employer financial liability." Id.

Under section 10 of the Act, an employee's right to inspect his personnel records does not apply to:

1. Letters of reference;

2. Any portion of a test document, except a cumulative test score (see Kopchar v. City of Chicago, 395 Ill. App. 3d 762, 771, 919 N.E.2d 76, 84, 335 Ill. Dec. 555, 563 (1st Dist. 2009) (holding that City complied with the Act by providing plaintiff with nothing more than a cumulative test score); Roulette v. Department of Central Management Services, 141 Ill. App. 3d 394, 490 N.E.2d 60, 95 Ill. Dec. 587 (1st Dist. 1986) (public employer can refuse a job applicant access to evaluation material));

3. Planning materials relating to the employer's staffing decisions, unless (a) they affect only one employee, (b) they are used to determine an individual employee's qualifications for employment, promotion, transfer or raise, or (c) they are used to determine whether an employee should be discharged or disciplined;

4. Personal information about third parties that would constitute a clearly unwarranted invasion of privacy;

5. An employer that does not maintain any personnel records;

6. Records of a claim between the employer and employee that may be discovered in a judicial proceeding; or

7. Records of the employer's investigation into an employee's criminal conduct or other misbehavior, unless the employer takes adverse action against the employee based on information in the records.

The act is administered by the Illinois Department of Labor, but it also provides a private cause of action for damages under certain circumstances. 820 Ill. Comp. Stat. 40/12. The employee must exhaust administrative remedies before filing suit. Anderson v. Bd. of Educ., 169 F. Supp. 2d 864, 868-70 (N.D. Ill. 2001); Hefley v. Davis, No. 08 CV 172, 2008 WL 5114647, at *3 (N.D. Ill. Dec. 2, 2008).

B. Medical Records

The Seventh Circuit has found that employees have a "'substantial' right in the confidentiality of medical information that can be overcome only by a sufficiently strong state interest." Denius v. Dunlap, 209 F.3d 944, 956 (7th Cir. 2000). See also Denius v. Dunlap, 330 F.3d 919, 928 (7th Cir. 2003) (upholding judgment in favor of plaintiff). Furthermore, the Illinois Supreme Court has recognized that "'the confidentiality of personal medical information is, without question, at the core of what society regards as a fundamental component of individual privacy.'" Burger v. Lutheran Gen. Hosp., 198 Ill. 2d 21, 759 N.E.2d 533, 259 Ill. Dec. 753 (2001), quoting Kunkel v. Walton, 179 Ill. 2d 519, 537 (1997). See also 735 Ill. Comp. Stat. 5/8-802 (codifying physician-patient privilege). **But protected medical information does not include "every piece of information that might be disclosed about a person's body." Best v. Berard, 837 F. Supp. 2d 933, 937-38, 40 Media L. Rep. 1873 (N.D. Ill. 2011) (holding that plaintiff did not have a privacy interest in height and weight, which defendants disclosed on a reality television show, because these statistics did not amount to "medical information").**

The Mental Health and Developmental Disabilities Confidentiality Act, 740 Ill. Comp. Stat. 110/1 et seq., generally prohibits access to psychiatric or other mental health records. See generally Norskog v. Pfiel, 197 Ill. 2d 60, 755 N.E.2d 1, 257 Ill. Dec. 899 (2001); Quigg v. Walgreen Co., 388 Ill. App. 3d 696, 905 N.E.2d 293, 328 Ill. Dec. 759 (2d Dist. 2009). The Act also protects parties outside the mental health provider-recipient relationship (such as family members) who may be harmed by disclosure of these materials. Quigg, 388 Ill. App. 3d at 702, 905 N.E.2d at 298, 328 Ill. Dec. at 764.

The Act provides only limited protection for the results of psychological "fitness exams" conducted on police officers. According to the Illinois Appellate Court, police officers have no reasonable expectation that the results of these exams will be kept confidential from their superiors. Sangirardi v. Village of Stickney, 342 Ill. App. 3d 1, 16, 793 N.E.2d, 787, 799, 276 Ill. Dec. 28, 40 (1st Dist. 2003). But see McGreal v. Ostrov, 368 F.3d 657, 688-90 (7th Cir. 2004) (observing that the Act "contains no disclosure exception for police departments"; distinguishing Sangirardi and holding that plaintiff was "entitled to have a jury hear his claim and determine whether the defendants reasonably ordered the [psychological] exam and whether the disclosure and republication exceeded the scope necessary to determine fitness for duty").

The Illinois Right to Privacy in the Workplace Act, 820 Ill. Comp. Stat. 55/10, prohibits employers from inquiring into whether a "prospective employee has ever filed a claim for benefits under the Workers' Compensation Act or Workers' Occupational Diseases Act." Narrowly construing the statute, the Seventh Circuit held that employers are permitted to ask prospective employees about prior workplace injuries and the treatment sought for those injuries, even though such inquiries will give employers a good idea of who has filed workers' compensation claims. Carter v. Tennant Co., 383 F.3d 673, 682-83 (7th Cir. 2004) (dismissing employee's suit for retaliatory discharge and violation of the Act because questions about prior injuries were permissible and employee failed to answer them truthfully).

Private employers must give job applicants access to the results of pre-employment physical or psychological examinations. 56 Ill. Admin. Code § 2500.60(b).

C. Criminal Records

The Illinois Human Rights Act prohibits employers from inquiring into an employee's or prospective employee's arrest record. 775 Ill. Comp. Stat. 5/2-103; DeMyrick v. Guest Quarters Suite Hotels, 944 F. Supp. 661, 668-69 (N.D. Ill. 1996). But see Oden v. Cahill, 79 Ill. App. 3d 768, 398 N.E.2d 1061, 35 Ill. Dec. 111 (1st Dist. 1979) (rejecting job applicant's claim for back pay and other relief even though her employer, the Chicago Police Department, committed "wholly improper" violation of this provision, thereby delaying plaintiff's hiring). Employers may ask about criminal convictions, and they may ask about particular incidents that formed the basis for an employee's arrest. See 775 Ill. Comp. Stat. 5/2-103; Beard v. Sprint Spectrum, LP, 833 N.E.2d 449, 295 Ill. Dec. 616 (3d Dist. 2005) (intent of law is to "prevent inquiry into mere charges or allegations of criminal behavior but to allow inquiry where criminal conduct has been proven"). **See also Stratton v. Merrill Lynch Pierce Fenner & Smith, Inc., No. 11 C 8011, 2012 U.S. Dist. LEXIS 60426, at *14 (Apr. 25, 2012) (holding that section 5/2-103 "explicitly allows inquiry into convictions").** Conviction records are publicly available pursuant to the Illinois Uniform Conviction Information Act. 20 Ill. Comp. Stat. 2635/1 et seq. However, employers may not ask applicants if they have had criminal records expunged or sealed, and employment applications must explicitly inform applicants that they are not obliged to disclose expunged or sealed records. 20 Ill. Comp. Stat. 2630/12(a); 705 Ill. Comp. Stat. 405/5-915(8)(a) (provisions do not apply to law enforcement agencies or prosecutors' offices). Even if an employer is aware of an expunged or sealed record, it may not consider the record in making employment decisions. Id.

The Illinois Health Care Worker Background Check Act requires health care employers to conduct a criminal history check for most workers who provide patients with direct contact health care services. 225 Ill. Comp. Stat. 46/1 et seq. The Act permits employers to fire any employee whose record reveals a conviction for any of numerous offenses, including sexual assault, abuse or neglect of a patient, theft, trespassing, or possession of illegal substances.

D. Subpoenas / Search Warrants

An employer in the Northern District of Illinois cannot serve a subpoena on an e-mail provider or telephone company to obtain all of an employee's e-mails or text messages, even if the request is limited to information transmitted using workplace technology. Special Mkts. Ins. Consultants, Inc. v. Lynch, No. 11 C 9181, 2012 U.S. Dist. LEXIS 61088, at *6-12 (N.D. Ill May 2, 2012) (holding that "dragnet subpoenas" violate the Stored Communications Act, 18 U.S.C. § 2701 et seq., and that such subpoenas "are not consistent with the Supreme Court's measured approach" to privacy rights in technology). The court noted that employers can serve employees with document requests for e-mails and text messages pursuant to discovery rules. Id. at *10-11.

VII. ACTIONS SUBSEQUENT TO EMPLOYMENT

A. References

No Illinois court has imposed an affirmative duty on employers to provide references for former employees absent a contract requiring them to do so. Sinio v. McDonald's Corp., No. 04 C 4161, 2005 U.S. Dist. LEXIS 11660 (N.D. Ill. May 16, 2005) (former employer's failure to return phone calls from prospective employer is not sufficient to sustain a claim for intentional interference with prospective economic advantage); Arado v. Gen. Fire Extinguisher Corp., 626 F. Supp. 506, 511 (N.D. Ill. 1985) (no recovery available for claim that employer wrote a negative reference letter). Employers also cannot be held liable for responding to an inquiry from a prospective employer with "truthful written or verbal information, or information that it believes in good faith is truthful, about a current or former employee's job performance." Employment Record Disclosure Act, 745 Ill. Comp. Stat. 46/10. If a reference is provided, a cause of action for defamation may be maintained if the usual requirements for such a claim are met. Arado, 626 F. Supp. at 511 (absent defamation, "Illinois does not recognize a tort of injury to business reputation where oral or written statements call into question one's qualifications or competence to perform his or her work").

Illinois state courts have not yet decided what obligations former employers may have to disclose adverse information to prospective employers. Neptuno Treuhand-UND Ver Waltungsgesellschaft MBH v. Arbor, 295 Ill. App. 3d 567, 577, 692 N.E.2d 812, 820, 229 Ill. Dec. 823, 831 (1st Dist. 1998) ("Illinois has not recognized a cause of action for 'negligent referral' and this is certainly not the case to decide the issue"); but see Doe-2 v. McLean County Unit Dist. No. 5 Bd. of Dir., 593 F.3d 507, 516 (7th Cir. 2010) (interpreting Neptuno as holding that "[a] referring employer may be liable for failing to disclose a former employee's misconduct, if the employer has a special or fiduciary duty to the plaintiff that raises a duty to speak"). However, a federal court in Illinois has held that a Section 1983 action may lie against a public entity that refused to disclose to a prospective employer its knowledge of a former employee's criminal record, at least when the non-disclosure resulted from a custom or policy. Sassak v. City of Park Ridge, 431 F. Supp. 2d 810, 814-818 (N.D. Ill. 2006).

B. Non-Compete Agreements

Before considering whether to enforce a non-compete agreement, a court must first determine that it constitutes a valid contract. Millard Maint. Serv. Co. v. Bernero, 207 Ill. App. 3d 736, 744, 566 N.E.2d 379, 384, 152 Ill. Dec. 692, 697 (1st Dist. 1990). To be valid, the agreement must be ancillary to another contract and supported by consideration. Id. Continued employment for a substantial period of time is an adequate form of consideration. Id.

"Generally, Illinois disfavors non-compete provisions in employee contracts." Viad Corp. v. Houghton, No. 08-CV-6706, 2010 WL 748089, at *4 (N.D. Ill. Feb. 26, 2010). Consequently, "restrictive covenants are to be strictly construed." Citadel Inv. Group, LLC v. Teza Tech. LLC, 398 Ill. App. 3d 724, 736, 924 N.E.2d 95, 106, 338 Ill. Dec. 235, 246 (1st Dist. 2010); see also Alliance 3PL Corp. v. New Prime, Inc., 614 F.3d 703, 706 (7th Cir. 2010) ("Illinois understands non-compete clauses to cover no more than the reasonable import of their language and does not allow expansive readings of restrictive covenants, because more competition often serves the public interest in low prices").

To be enforceable, a non-compete agreement must be reasonable in scope as to duration, geographic area, and activity. Dryvit Sys., Inc. v. Rushing, 132 Ill. App. 3d 9, 13, 477 N.E.2d 35, 38, 87 Ill. Dec. 434, 437 (1st Dist. 1985). The scope of a non-compete agreement is reasonable if it does not injure the public, cause undue hardship to the employee, or exceed the scope necessary to protect the legitimate business interests of the employer. Id.

In assessing whether the territorial scope of a non-compete agreement is reasonable, courts "generally look to whether the restricted area is coextensive with the area in which the employer is doing business," in order to ensure that the employee is only "excluded from doing business in the territorial zone in which the relationships with the employer's customers could have been established in ways that could be detrimental in the hands of a competitor." Cambridge Eng'g, Inc. v. Mercury Partners 90 BI, Inc., 378 Ill. App. 3d 437, 448, 879 N.E.2d 512, 523, 316 Ill. Dec. 445, 456 (1st Dist. 2007) (finding a ban on conducting business throughout Canada was overly broad given the employer's limited business there). Non

-compete agreements that contain no geographic constraints are too broad and far-reaching to be enforceable. Del Monte Fresh Produce, N.A., Inc. v. Chiquita Brands Int'l Inc., 616 F. Supp. 2d 805, 817 (N.D. Ill. 2009). And blanket prohibitions on the types of employment a former employee may pursue may render a non-compete agreement unenforceable. Integrated Genomics, Inc. v. Kyrpides, No. 06 C 6706, 2010 WL 375672, at *9 (N.D. Ill. Jan. 26, 2010); Del Monte, 616 F. Supp. 2d at 818 (finding a restriction on the former employee "'being connected in any manner with' an entity that bought fruit, vegetables, or other produce from Del Monte" too restrictive). **See also Triumph Packaging Group v. Ward, 834 F. Supp. 2d 796, 814-15 (N.D. Ill. 2011) (finding non-compete clause "extremely overbroad and likely unenforceable" where clause prohibited employment in any area where Triumph engaged in business or had plans to engage in business (roughly half of the United States); had a duration of at least 24 months; and prohibited former employee from "working in any capacity, or associating in any way, with any of Triumph's competitors").**

Upon finding a non-compete clause overly restrictive, Illinois courts are reluctant, as a matter of public policy, to reform the contract, opting instead to invalidate the contract altogether. Integrated Genomics, 2010 WL 375672, at *9 (N.D. Ill. Jan. 26, 2010); Cambridge Eng'g, 378 Ill. App. 3d at 456, 879 N.E.2d at 529, 316 Ill. Dec. at 462; Del Monte, 616 F. Supp. 2d at 818 (finding a non-compete agreement with overly restrictive geographic and activity provisions "unsalvageable"). Courts may rely upon their equitable powers to extend the duration of a covenant not to compete when an employee violates the terms of the agreement. Mintel Int'l Group, Ltd. v. Neergheen, No. 08-cv-3939, 2010 WL 145786, at *10 (N.D. Ill. Jan. 12, 2010) (extending the duration of a covenant not to compete but limiting the scope of the "blanket agreement"). But see Peerless Indus. v. Crimson AV, LLC, No. 11 C 1768, 2011 U.S. Dist. LEXIS 62407, at *17 (N.D. Ill. June 10, 2011) (stating that Illinois courts have been reluctant to extend the time period for a non-compete provision) (citing Citadel Inv. Group, LLC v. Teza Techs. LLC, 398 Ill. App. 3d 724, 734-36, 924 N.E.2d 95, 104-06, 338 Ill. Dec. 235 (1st Dist. 2010)).

VIII. OTHER ISSUES

A. Statutes of Limitations

Illinois has adopted a one-year statute of limitations for privacy torts involving the publication of information: false light invasion of privacy, public disclosure of private facts, and misappropriation of the likeness of another. 735 Ill. Comp. Stat. 5/13-201. This statute does not apply to a claim for intrusion upon seclusion, which does not involve publication. Benitez v. KFC Nat'l Mgmt. Co., 305 Ill. App. 3d 1027, 1032-35, 714 N.E.2d 1002, 1006-08, 239 Ill. Dec. 705, 709-11 (2d Dist. 1999). **Accord Jackson v. Bank of N.Y., No. 11-cv-6410, 2012 U.S. Dist. LEXIS 89258, at *13-14 (N.D. Ill. June 28, 2012).** The statute also does not apply to claims for intentional infliction of emotional distress, which are governed by a two-year limitations period. See Suppressed v. Suppressed, 206 Ill. App. 3d 918, 926, 565 N.E.2d 101, 106, 151 Ill. Dec. 830, 835 (1st Dist. 1990). **But see Pennington v. Bd. of Educ., No. 11 C 3890, 2012 U.S. Dist. LEXIS 26772, at *2, *6 (N.D. Ill. Mar. 1, 2012) (applying 745 Ill. Comp. Stat. 10/8-101(a), which imposes a one-year statute of limitations for civil actions against local entities and their employees, to emotional distress claim).** The statute of limitations for a claim under the Illinois Eavesdropping Act is five years. McDonald's Corp. v. Levine, 108 Ill. App. 3d 732, 737-39, 439 N.E.2d 475, 479-80, 64 Ill. Dec. 224, 228-29 (2d Dist. 1982). Illinois also imposes a five-year statute of limitations on tortious interference claims. Leonel & Noel Corp. v. Cerveceria Centro Americana, 758 F. Supp. 2d 596, 605 (N.D. Ill. 2010) (citing 735 Ill. Comp. Stat. 5/13-205).

B. Jurisdiction

The Illinois long-arm statute permits Illinois courts to exercise jurisdiction to the fullest extent permitted by constitutional requirements. 735 Ill. Comp. Stat. 5/2-209(c).

C. Worker's Compensation Exclusivity

The Illinois Workers Compensation Act, 820 Ill. Comp. Stat. 305/1 et seq., provides the exclusive remedy for accidental injuries in the workplace. Richardson v. County of Cook, 250 Ill. App. 3d 544, 547, 621 N.E.2d 114, 117, 190 Ill. Dec. 245, 248 (1st Dist. 1993). An employee may overcome the preemption of the Act by demonstrating either "(1) that the injury was not accidental; (2) that the injury did not arise from his or her employment; (3) that the injury was not received during the course of employment; or (4) that the injury was not compensable under the act." Id. (quoting Meerbrey v. Marshall Field & Co., 139 Ill. 2d 455, 463, 564 N.E.2d 1222, 1226, 151 Ill. Dec. 560, 564 (1990). The Act's exclusivity provisions do not bar claims for injuries which the employer or the employer's alter ego intentionally inflicts upon the employee. Meerbrey, 139 Ill. 2d at 463. **See also Escobedo v. Shirdi, No. 10 C 6598, 2012 U.S. Dist. LEXIS 32461, at *2 (N.D. Ill. Mar. 12, 2012).** "However it is not sufficient that a supervisory employee acted within the scope of his or her employment in committing the act; rather, it must constitute the act of the employer itself or its alter ego in order to avoid preemption." Sarate v. Loop Transfer Inc., No. 95 C 5671, 1997 WL 543068, at *6 (N.D. Ill. Aug. 28, 1997). "To determine whether an individual is acting as the alter ego of a defendant, a court must consider factors such as: (1) the employee's dominance in the company; (2) whether the individual has an ownership interest in the company; and (3) whether the individual 'speaks for the company' in that he has 'final decision making authority.'" Thompson-Adams v. Renzenberger, Inc., No. 10 C 54, 2010 WL 1229380, at *2 (N.D. Ill. March 25, 2010).

An accidental injury has been defined as "an injury which is traceable to a definite time, place and cause, and occurs in the course of employment unexpectedly and without affirmative act or design of the employee." Benitez v. Am. Standard Circuits, Inc., No. 08 CV 1998, 2009 WL 742686, at *5 (N.D. Ill. March 18, 2009) (quoting McPherson v. City of Waukegan, 379 F.3d 430, 442 (7th Cir. 2004)). However, intentional torts committed by coworkers are considered "accidental" under the Act unless the employer "commanded or expressly authorized" the torts. Id. at *5.

D. Pleading Requirements

Privacy claims are not held to any higher standard than other tort claims. However, Illinois state courts require "fact pleading," so plaintiffs must provide more detail in their complaints than is required in federal court. See, e.g., Winfrey v. Chicago Park Dist., 274 Ill. App. 3d 939, 943, 654 N.E.2d 508, 512, 211 Ill. Dec. 46, 50 (1st Dist. 1995).

SURVEY OF INDIANA EMPLOYMENT LIBEL LAW

Richard P. Winegardner
Barnes & Thornburg LLP
11 South Meridian Street
Indianapolis, Indiana 46204-3535
Telephone: (317) 231-7512; Facsimile: (317) 231-7433

(With Developments Reported Through **November 1, 2012**)

GENERAL COMMENTS

Recently there has been a noticeable trend reflecting a significant increase in defamation claims arising out of the employment relationship. Generally, a defamation action requires proof of publication or communication of defamatory words to a person or persons other than the individual who has allegedly been defamed. The courts recognize two defenses to a claim for defamation, either that the statement was true or that the statement was privileged.

Indiana's trial level courts for civil litigation are Circuit and Superior courts, organized by county. Indiana's intermediate court, the Court of Appeals, is comprised of five districts, three of which receive cases from particular geographical regions of the state. The Supreme Court of Indiana is the state's highest judicial body.

SIGNIFICANT DEVELOPMENTS SINCE THE 2012 *SURVEY*

In Gagan v. Yast, the Indiana Court of Appeals elaborated on the qualified privilege as it applies to attorney-client communications concerning attorney disclosures required under Indiana Rule of Professional Conduct 1.7. 966 N.E.2d 177 (Ind. Ct. App. 2012) transfer denied, 971 N.E.2d 1214 (Ind. 2012). In Gagan, the plaintiff shareholders sued the defendant attorney regarding statements made during a phone call in which the attorney withdrew his representation due to a conflict of interest. Id. at 181. Under Indiana Rule of Professional Conduct 1.7, the defendant had a duty to disclose the nature of the conflict, the reasons for the conflict, and the fact that the defendant's professional judgment could be affected by the conflict. Id. at 185. Pursuant to this duty, the defendant explained to his clients his concern that the plaintiffs had improperly withdrew millions of dollars from a corporation in which he was a shareholder. Id. at 181. The plaintiffs alleged this statement was defamatory and sued. In affirming summary judgment in favor of the defendant attorney, the Indiana Court of Appeals concluded that the defendant had both a common interest with the plaintiffs and a duty to communicate the conflict of interest under the rules of professional conduct. Id. at 184-185. Consequently, the defendant was protected by the qualified privilege even if the remarks could be considered defamatory. Id.

I. GENERAL LAW

A. General Employment Law

1. ***At Will Employment.*** Indiana adheres to the doctrine of employment-at-will, with limited exceptions. The Indiana Supreme Court has reaffirmed the "vitality of the employment-at-will doctrine in Indiana" in holding that adequate independent consideration is generally necessary to convert an at-will relationship into an employment relationship requiring an employer to discharge an employee for good cause. Orr v. Westminster Vill. N., Inc., 689 N.E.2d 712, 722 (Ind. 1997); see also McCalment v. Eli Lilly & Co., 860 N.E.2d. 884, 891-93 (Ind. Ct. App. 2007). Generally, if there is no definite or ascertainable term of employment, then the employment is at-will, and is presumptively terminable at any time, with or without cause, by either party. Wior v. Anchor Indus., Inc., 669 N.E.2d 172, 175 (Ind. 1996); McClanahan v. Remington Freight Lines, Inc., 517 N.E.2d 390, 392 (Ind. 1988). However, if the parties have entered into a contract for a definite or ascertainable term, and the employer has not reserved the right to terminate the employment relationship before the conclusion of the contract, then the employer generally may not terminate the employment relationship before the end of the specified term, except for cause or by mutual agreement. See Trinity Baptist Church v. Howard, 869 N.E.2d 1225, 1228-30 (Ind. Ct. App. 2007); Markley Enters., Inc. v. Grover, 716 N.E.2d 559, 564 (Ind. Ct. App. 1999); Orr, 689 N.E.2d at 717; Morgan Drive Away, Inc. v. Brant, 489 N.E.2d 933, 934 (Ind. 1986). The Indiana Supreme Court has recognized three limited exceptions, or put more simply, three ways to avoid or rebut the presumption of employment-at-will. First, if an employee establishes that the employee has provided "adequate independent consideration" in support of the employment contract, the Court assumes the parties intended to establish a relationship in which the employer may terminate the employee for good cause only. See Orr, 689 N.E.2d at 718 (Ind. 1997); see also Romack v. Pub. Serv. Co., 511 N.E.2d 1024, 1026 (Ind. 1987) (adopting in substantial part and incorporating Romack v. Pub. Serv. Co., 499 N.E.2d 768, 777 (Ind. Ct. App. 1986) (Conover, J., dissenting)). Second, the Indiana Supreme Court has recognized the use of the doctrine of promissory estoppel in claims for damages resulting from detrimental reliance on a promise of employment. An employee can effectively invoke

the doctrine of promissory estoppel by asserting and demonstrating that the employer: 1) made a promise to the employee, 2) that the employee relied on that promise to his detriment, and 3) and that the promise otherwise fits within the test for promissory estoppel. See Orr, 689 N.E.2d at 718; see also Jarboe v. Landmark Cmty.Newspapers, 644 N.E.2d 118, 121 (Ind. 1994). Finally, the Court has recognized a public policy exception to the general rule of employment-at-will when an employer discharges an employee for exercising a statutory right, performing a statutory duty, or refusing to act illegally. See Meyers v. Meyers, 861 N.E.2d 704, 706-707 (Ind. 2007); McGarrity v. Berlin Metal, Inc., 774 N.E.2d 71 (Ind. Ct. App. 2002); McClanahan v. Remington Freight Lines, 517 N.E.2d 390, 392-93 (Ind. 1988); Campbell v. Eli Lilly & Co., 413 N.E.2d 1054, 1061 (Ind. 1980); Frampton v. Cent. Ind. Gas Co., 297 N.E.2d 425, 428 (Ind. 1973); see also Hamann v. Gates Chevrolet, Inc., 910 F.2d 1417, 1418 (7th Cir. 1990) (interpreting Indiana law). The plaintiff must base his retaliatory or wrongful discharge case on a statute or regulation, not on a generalized violation of public policy. See Wior v. Anchor Indus., Inc., 669 N.E.2d 172, 177 & n.5 (Ind. 1996); Campbell v. Eli Lilly & Co., 413 N.E.2d 1054, 1061 (Ind. 1980); Hamblen v. Danners, Inc., 478 N.E.2d 926, 929 (Ind. Ct. App. 1985).

B. Elements of Libel Claim

1. ***Basic Elements.*** Libel is malicious defamation expressed in writing. See Olsson v. Ind. Univ. Bd. of Trs., 571 N.E.2d 585, 587 (Ind. Ct. App. 1991). The basic elements of a defamation claim are: 1) communication with defamatory imputation, 2) publication, 3) malice, and 4) damages. Dugan v. Mittal Steel USA Inc., 929 N.E. 2d 184, 186 (Ind. 2010); Melton v. Ousley, 925 N.E. 2d 430, 437 (Ind. Ct. App. 2010); Kelley v. Tanoos, 865 N.E.2d 593, 597 (Ind. 2007); Trail v. Boys & Girls Clubs of N.W. Indiana, 845 N.E.2d 130, 136 (Ind. 2006); Schrader v. Eli Lilly & Co., 639 N.E.2d 258, 261 (Ind. 1994); Haegert v. McMullan, 953 N.E.2d 1223, 1230 (Ind. Ct. App. 2011); Turner v. Boy Scouts of America, 856 N.E.2d 106, 111 (Ind. Ct. App. 2006); Shepard v. Shurz Commc'n, 847 N.E.2d 219, 224 (Ind. Ct. App. 2006). See also Containment Tech. Group v. American Soc'y of Health Sys. Pharmacists, No. 1:07-cv-0997-DFH-TAB, 2009 WL 838549, at *9 (S.D. Ind. Mar. 26, 2009); Purdue Employees, Fed. Credit Union v. Van Houten, No. 4:08-CV-45-AS-APR, 2008 U.S. Dist. LEXIS 73258, at *12 (N.D. Ind. Sept. 24, 2008) Smith v. Biomet, Inc., No. 3:01-CV-753 PS, 2005 U.S. Dist. LEXIS 5251, at *32 (N.D. Ind. Mar. 24, 2005). To maintain an action for defamation, the plaintiff must show that the alleged defamatory matter was published – *i.e.* communicated -- to a third person or persons. Bals v. Verduzco, 600 N.E.2d 1353, 1354 (Ind. 1992); Mart v. Hess, 703 N.E.2d 190, 194 (Ind. Ct. App. 1998); Smith v. Biomet, No. 3:01-CV-753, 2005 U.S. Dist. LEXIS 5251, at *33 (N.D. Ind. Mar. 24, 2005). When the plaintiff is a public figure or if the statement involves a public matter, the plaintiff must prove actual malice. See generally I.B.2, infra. A statement may be defamatory if it harms a person's reputation by lowering the person in the community's estimation or deterring third persons from dealing or associating with the person. See Dugan, 929 N.E. 2d at 186; K.D. T.N. v. B.D., 929 N.E. 2d 863, 875 (Ind. Ct. App. 2010); Rambo v. Cohen, 587 N.E.2d 140, 145 (Ind. Ct. App. 1992); Powers v. Gastineau, 568 N.E.2d 1020, 1023 (Ind. Ct. App. 1991); Near E. Side Cmty. Org. v. Hair, 555 N.E.2d 1324, 1330 (Ind. Ct. App. 1990).

2. ***Fault.*** In matters involving public figures or matters of public concern, Indiana has adopted the St. Amant definition of actual malice, holding that the plaintiff must establish that at the time of publication the defendant in fact entertained serious doubt as to the truth of the statement. See Love v. Rehfus, 946 N.E.2d 1, 15-16 (Ind. 2011); Journal-Gazette Co. v. Bandido's, Inc., 712 N.E.2d 446, 456, 27 Media L. Rep. 2089, 2103 (Ind. 1999), cert. denied, 120 S. Ct. 499, 145 L. Ed. 2d 385 (U.S. 1999); CanaRx Services, Inc. v. Lin Television Corp., No. 1:07-cv-1482-LJM-JMS, 2008 U.S. Dist LEXIS 42236, at *22 (S.D. Ind. May 29, 2008) (Television news station did not act maliciously in broadcasting a news report since the reporter, who conducted months of research, entertained no doubt about the truth of the story); See also Amcoat Techs., Inc. v. Sobieray, No. 1:03-CV-1564-RLY-TAB, 2005 U.S. Dist. LEXIS 8217, at *20 n.5 (S.D. Ind. Feb. 4, 2005) ("the requirement that actual malice be shown in matters of public or general concern really amounts to a requirement that the communicator have knowledge of the falsity or have demonstrated reckless disregard of whether the published statement was true or false") (quoting Bandido's); Beauchamp v. City of Noblesville, 320 F.3d 733, 746 (7th Cir. 2003). Mere evidence of factual error, failure to investigate, or ill will does not, standing alone, constitute actual malice. See Shine v. Loomis, 836 N.E.2d 952, 958-60 (Ind. Ct. App. 2006) (reckless disregard for truth requires more than a departure from reasonably prudent conduct); Amcoat, 2005 U.S. Dist. LEXIS 8217, at *21 ("though Sobieray may have intended that his letter have a negative effect on . . . Amcoat, it did not contain an inaccurate defamatory statement and therefore no proof of actual malice exists"); Chester v. Indianapolis Newspapers, Inc., 553 N.E.2d 137, 140, 17 Media L. Rep. 1903 (Ind. Ct. App. 1990) (negligently interpreting public records, failing to search other records or misconstruing comment from person interviewed for story inadequate to establish malice); Aafco Heating & Air Conditioning Co. v. Northwest Publ'ns, Inc., 162 Ind. App. 671, 321 N.E.2d 580, 591, 1 Media L. Rep. 1683 (Ind. Ct. App. 1974), cert. denied, 424 U.S. 913 (1976) (stating that mere failure to examine a public report or the misinterpretation of the conclusion of the report would not support an inference of actual malice). See also Beauchamp v. City of Noblesville, 320 F.3d 733, 746 (7th Cir. 2003) (stating that reckless conduct is not measured by whether a reasonably prudent person would have investigated before publishing); Chang v. Michiana Telecasting Corp., 900 F.2d 1085, 1089 (7th Cir. 1990) (failing to verify all information from a tipster when what was verified checked out is not malice, nor is failing to confirm the information from a second source; fact that reporter's notes were missing did

not support inference of actual malice); Containment Tech. Group v. American Soc'y of Health Sys. Pharmacists, No. 1:07-cv -0997-DFH-TAB, 2009 WL 838549, at *14, *16 (S.D. Ind. Mar. 26, 2009) ("lack of peer review of the final version is not a sign of recklessness" when normal practice of peer review was followed for initial manuscripts and "[b]ad but honest science is not actionable as defamation"); Schaefer v. Newton, 868 F. Supp. 246, 253 (S.D. Ind. 1994) (stating that references made to plaintiff in book about serial killers were neither fabricated nor so inherently improbable to preclude summary judgment on grounds of absence of actual malice); Fazekas v. Crain Consumer Group Div. of Crain Communications, Inc., 583 F. Supp. 110, 114, 10 Media L. Rep. 1513 (S.D. Ind. 1984) (holding that a claim that defendant "should have been aware that a controversy was brewing" about the subject of the article at most stated a claim of negligence and was inadequate to prove malice); Fadell v. Minneapolis Star & Tribune Co. 425 F. Supp. 1075, 1084, 2 Media L. Rep. 1961 (N.D. Ind. 1976), aff'd. 557 F.2d 107, 2 Media L. Rep. 2198 (7th Cir. 1977), cert. denied 434 U.S. 966, 2 Media L. Rep. 2198 (1977) (stating that factual error and failure to independently investigate article submitted by experienced reporter would not support an inference of actual malice). Indirect evidence, however, can be used to establish malice. Ratcliff v. Barnes, 750 N.E.2d 433, 437-38 (Ind. Ct. App. 2001) (evidence that employee, who named a fellow employee as the "perpetrator" behind the theft of county property, knew of the policy allowing employees to take such property home was sufficient to establish actual malice when coupled with evidence that statement was made in retaliation for a previous statement made by the other employee).

a. **Private Figure Plaintiff/Matter of Public Concern.** The Indiana Supreme Court has affirmed the actual malice standard in matters of public or general concern for private plaintiffs and expressly rejected the Gertz negligence standard. See Journal-Gazette Co. v. Bandido's, Inc., 712 N.E.2d 446, 452, 27 Media L. Rep. 2089, 2099 (Ind. 1999), cert. denied, 120 S. Ct. 499, 145 L. Ed. 2d 385 (U.S. 1999); Poyser v. Peerless, 775 N.E.2d 1101, 1107 (Ind. Ct. App. 2002); Henrichs v. Pivarnik, 588 N.E.2d 537, 542 (Ind. Ct. App. 1992) ("it makes no sense to draw the distinction between 'public' officials or figures and 'private' individuals in terms of defining the constitutional guarantees of free speech and press"); Beauchamp v. City of Noblesville, 320 F.3d 733, 746 (7th Cir. 2003). Topics which qualify as matters of public concern have been liberally extended to all matters which "affect our efforts to live and work together in a free society" and to include subjects relating to "truth, science, morality and arts in general as well as responsible governments." Aafco Heating & Air Conditioning Co. v. Northwest Publ'ns, Inc., 162 Ind. App. 671, 680, 321 N.E.2d 580, 586, 590, 1 Media L. Rep. 1683 (Ind. Ct. App. 1974), cert. denied, 424 U.S. 913 (1976). See also Filippo v. Lee Publications, Inc., 485 F. Supp.2d 969, 973-74 (N.D. Ind. 2007) (a matter of general or public interest is one in which the public's primary interest is in the event and its focus is on the conduct of the participant and the content, effect, and significance of the conduct); Moore v. Univ. of Notre Dame, 968 F. Supp. 1330, 1338 n.11 (N.D. Ind. 1997) (the public interest is necessarily broad and cover a panoply of topics). The Aafco standard applies equally to media and non-media defendants. See Conwell v. Beatty, 667 N.E.2d 768, 774 (Ind. Ct. App. 1996); Near E. Side Cmty. Org. v. Hair, 555 N.E.2d 1324, 1329 (Ind. Ct. App. 1990). A plaintiff cannot avoid this "general or public interest" standard by claiming that the allegedly defamatory statement was made by the defendant as a competitor who sought to gain commercial advantage. Woods v. Evansville Press, 791 F.2d 480, 484, 12 Media L. Rep. 2179 (7th Cir. 1986).

Examples of matters found to be "of public concern:" **Comments by a firefighter in a private email" regarding the efficiency and financial stability of a township's fire department, Love v. Rehfus, 946 N.E.2d 1, 10 (Ind. 2011); Statements made by the chair of a union's bargaining committee regarding her employer's tax abatements and bargaining position; Brandom v. Coupled Products, LLC, No. 92A03-1112-PL-542 2012 Ind. App. Lexis 476 at **2-13 (Ind. Ct. App., Sep. 21, 2012);** A local newspaper article regarding the quality of plaintiff's property tax assessments, the property tax system, and the way in which the county spends its funds, Nexus Group, Inc. v. Heritage Appraisal Serv., 942 N.E.2d 119, 122 (Ind. Ct. App. 2011); a letter sent to numerous county auditors in Indiana claiming that the plaintiff misappropriated the property tax software it was selling to the counties, Nikish Software Corp. v. Manatron, Inc., 801 F. Supp. 2d 791, 798-799 (S.D. Ind. 2011); a local newspaper article regarding plaintiff's arrest for rape and other crimes, Beauchamp v. City of Noblesville, 320 F.3d 733, 746 (7th Cir. 2003); a local newspaper column regarding a plaintiff's purchase and operation of a local TV station, Woods v. Evansville Press, 791 F.2d 480, 12 Media L. Rep. 2179 (7th Cir. 1986); a narrative commentary, in a telecast, dealing with treatment of African Americans in movies, Perry v. Columbia Broad. Sys., Inc., 499 F.2d 797 (7th Cir. 1974), cert. denied, 419 U.S. 883 (1974); a letter sent to parents from school administration relating to the termination of an elementary school teacher, Poyser v. Peerless, 775 N.E.2d 1101, 1107 (Ind. Ct. App. 2002); a news release regarding hospital's improved ability to provide quality healthcare at reasonable costs, St. Margaret Mercy Healthcare Ctrs., Inc. v. Ho, 663 N.E.2d 1220, 1224 (Ind. Ct. App. 1996); a community meeting addressing issues of quality education and housing, Near E. Side Cmty. Org. v. Hair, 555 N.E.2d 1324 (Ind. Ct. App. 1990); an article concerning a plaintiff, who had been featured in a nationally known adult magazine and had also participated as a celebrity at an internationally known auto race, who was involved in an investigation concerning alleged police and prosecutorial corruption, Cochran v. Indianapolis Newspapers, Inc., 175 Ind. App. 548, 372 N.E.2d 1211, 3 Media L. Rep. 2131 (Ind. Ct. App. 1978); an article concerning a private individual who appeared voluntarily before a grand jury and talked to reporters concerning activities of her son who was under grand jury investigation, id.; a series of articles about an electrical fire at the home of a local resident which caused the death of two young children, Aafco, 162 Ind. App. at 680, 321 N.E.2d at 584, 1

Media L. Rep. 1683; a statement by a police chief concerning the police department's patrol of a city park and the circumstances surrounding an arrest; Davis v. City of Greenwood, IP 00-057-C-M/S, 2000 U.S. Dist. LEXIS 20550 at *36 (S.D. Ind. Nov. 17, 2000); a statement by one county employee concerning possible misuse of county property by another county employee, Ratcliff v. Barnes, 750 N.E.2d 433, 437-38 (Ind. Ct. App. 2001); statements concerning alleged research improprieties by a M.D.; Jindal v. Univ. Transplant Assoc., Inc., IP-00-678-C-M/F, 2002 U.S. Dist LEXIS 12416 (S.D. Ind. March 7, 2002); a discussion of the safety of medical devices, Containment Tech. Group v. American Soc'y of Health Sys. Pharmacists, No. 1:07-cv-0997-DFH-TAB, 2009 WL 838549, at *13 (S.D. Ind. Mar. 26, 2009); a discussion concerning the management of a sewer plant, St. John v. Town of Ellettsville, 46 F. Supp.2d 834, 849 (S.D. Ind. 1999); and a series of articles about the drunk driving arrest of a vice-chairman of a local drug free task force, Filippo, 485 F. Supp. 2d at 471.

b. **Private Figure Plaintiff/Matter of Private Concern.** Private plaintiffs are required to prove common law malice when the matter is a private concern. See Schrader v. Eli Lilly & Co., 639 N.E.2d 258, 262 (Ind. 1994); Owens v. Schoenberger, 681 N.E.2d 760, 763 (Ind. Ct. App. 1997); Street v. Shoe Carnival, Inc., 660 N.E.2d 1054, 1058 (Ind. Ct. App. 1996). Indiana courts have held that a public school principal is not a "public official," and therefore the "actual malice" standard does not apply when the matter at issue is not a public concern. Beeching v. Levee, 764 N.E.2d 669, 677 (Ind. Ct. App. 2002). Common law malice generally requires an intent to commit a wrongful act without justification or excuse. See Davidson v. Cincinnati Ins. Co., 572 N.E.2d 502, 507 (Ind. Ct. App. 1991) (citing with approval definitions of malice contained in Webster's Third New International Dictionary and Black's Law Dictionary). The Indiana Supreme Court, however, has not been able to reach a consensus on the exact standard to apply in a private figure/private concern case. See Journal-Gazette v. Bandido's Inc., 712 N.E.2d 446 (Ind. 1999) (2-1-2 opinion where concurring justice indicated in dicta that negligence standard would apply while the two dissenting justices opined that strict liability standard would apply against non -media defendants). A federal court, citing this uncertainty, did not include malice as an element of a defamation claim where the plaintiff was a private figure and the alleged defamatory statement was not a matter of public concern. Biomet, Inc. v. Smith, 238 F. Supp. 2d 1036, 1046 (N.D. Ind. 2002). But see Chang v. Michiana Telecasting Corp., 900 F.2d 1085, 1087 (7th Cir. 1990) (despite "[s]kepticism among Indiana judges," the Seventh Circuit applied the actual malice standard to a private-figure plaintiff because "[t]he Supreme Court of Indiana has had ample opportunity to express a different view and so far has elected not to do so").

c. **Public Figure Plaintiff/Matter of Public Concern.** The Indiana Supreme Court has expressly adopted the Rosenbloom standard, 403 U.S. 75, 85 (1971), which shifts the focus of the New York Times privilege from the plaintiff's status to the newsworthiness of the statements published. See Journal-Gazette v. Bandido's, Inc., 712 N.E.2d 446, 452, 27 Media L. Rep. 2089, 2099 (Ind. 1999), cert. denied, 120 S. Ct. 499, 145 L. Ed. 2d 385 (U.S. 1999). Regardless, numerous individuals and occupations have be found to be public figures including judges, Heeb v. Smith, 613 N.E.2d 416, 419 (Ind. Ct. App. 1993); Henrichs v. Pivarnik, 588 N.E.2d 537, 542, 20 Media L. Rep. 1787 (Ind. Ct. App. 1992), sheriffs and township tax assessors, Indianapolis Newspapers, Inc. v. Fields, 259 N.E.2d 651 (Ind. App. 1970), cert. denied, 400 U.S. 930 (1970); see also Fadell v. Minneapolis Star & Tribune Co., Inc., 425 F. Supp. 1075, 2 Media L. Rep. 1961 (N.D. Ind. 1976), aff'd, 557 F.2d 107, 2 Media L. Rep. 2198 (7th Cir. 1977), cert. denied 434 U.S. 966, 2 Media L. Rep. 2198 (1977), and county surveyors. Isgrigg v. Cosmos Broad. Corp., 30 Media L. Rep. 1331 (S.D. Ind. 2002). Indiana courts have further held that a former "Playmate" and "Miss Hurst Golden Shifter," who had appeared at the Indianapolis '500' auto race, was a public figure, Cochran v. Indianapolis Newspapers, Inc., 175 Ind. App. 548, 372 N.E.2d 1211, 1219, 3 Media L. Rep. 2131 (Ind. Ct. App. 1978), as were policemen and firemen running for election, Republican volunteer workers and precinct delegates, a university professor who was both a noted author and former state legislator, and a college basketball coach. See Aafco Heating & Air Conditioning Co. v. Northwest Publ'ns, Inc., 162 Ind. App. 671, 321 N.E.2d 580, 1 Media L. Rep. 1683 (Ind. Ct. App. 1974), cert. denied, 424 U.S. 913 (U.S. 1976). In addition, a convicted double murderer who had made public statements about being a serial killer was found to be a public figure on the subject of serial murders. See Schaefer v. Newton, 868 F. Supp. 246, 252 (S.D. Ind. 1994), aff'd without opinion, 57 F.3d 1073 (7th Cir. 1995).

A public figure is required to prove actual malice in a suit for defamation. See Conwell v. Beatty 667 N.E.2d 768, 775 (Ind. Ct. App. 1996); Henrichs v. Pivarnik, 588 N.E.2d 537, 542 , 20 Media L. Rep. 1787 (Ind. Ct. App. 1992); Cochran v. Indianapolis Newspaper, 175 Ind. App. 548, 372 N.E.2d 1211, 1219, 3 Media L. Rep. 2131 (Ind. Ct. App. 1978).

3. ***Falsity.*** In a claim for defamation, the statement must be both false and defamatory. Melton v. Ousley, 925 N.E. 2d 430, 437 (Ind. Ct. App. 2010); Eversole v. Spurlino Materials of Indianapolis, LLC, 804 F. Supp. 2d 922, 937 (S.D. Ind. 2011) (company not liable for defamation because statements distributed to employees claiming that the plaintiff had never complained directly to management regarding discrimination and that the lawsuit continued to cost the company money to defend were true); W.S.K. v. M.H.S.B., 922 N.E. 2d 671, 693 (Ind. Ct. App. 2010) (hospital not liable for defamation based on its publication of the reasons for its denial of a physician's hospital privileges application where the assertions were truthful); McKeighen v. Daviess County Fair Board, 918 N.E. 2d 717, 724 (Ind. Ct. App. 2009) (county fair board not liable for defaming derby participant even when it accused the participant of deception by using a prohibited model car because the participant did not establish that the accusation was false); Lessley v. City of Madison, 654 F. Supp. 2d 877,

912 (S.D. Ind. 2009) (statement made by mayor and city attorney that a female motorist possessed marijuana was true and did not amount to defamation). "The United States Constitution requires a false statement of fact in order to impose liability for defamation." Heeb v. Smith, 613 N.E.2d 416, 420, 21 Media L. Rep. 1558, 1561 (Ind. Ct. App. 1993); see also Cortez v. Jo-Ann Stores, Inc., 827 N.E.2d 1223, at *11 n.3 (Ind. Ct. App. 2005) ("true statements never give rise to liability for defamation"). The plaintiff has the burden of pleading and proving that the statement complained of was false in some material respect. See Indianapolis Newspapers, Inc. v. Fields, 259 N.E.2d 651, 670 (Ind. App. 1970), cert. denied, 400 U.S. 930 (1970). Moreover, for cases governed by the actual malice standard, the plaintiff has the burden of proving that the defendant made the statement with knowledge of its falsity or with reckless disregard for the truth. Shine v. Loomis, 836 N.E.2d 952, 958-60 (Ind. Ct. App. 2006) (reckless disregard for truth requires more than a departure from reasonably prudent conduct). See also Schaefer v. Newton, 868 F. Supp. 246, 252 (S.D. Ind. 1994), aff'd without opinion, 57 F.3d 1073 (7th Cir. 1995); Heeb v. Smith, 613 N.E.2d 416, 21 Media L. Rep. 1558 (Ind. App. 1993). In addition, a plaintiff who has fostered or allowed a false statement to circulate publicly may be estopped from proving its falsity. See Perry v. Columbia Broad. Sys., Inc., 499 F.2d 797, 799-800 (7th Cir. 1974), cert. denied 419 U.S. 883 (1974). Once the plaintiff has met his initial burden, however, the defendant bears the burden of proving truth. See Near E. Side Cmty. Org. v. Hair, 555 N.E.2d 1324, 1330 (Ind. App. 1990); see also II.B.1, infra. Notably, Indiana does not recognize a tort based on disclosure of truthful but private facts. See Doe v. Methodist Hosp., 690 N.E.2d 681, 693, 26 Media L. Rep. 1289 (Ind. 1997); Meury v. Eagle-Union Cmty. Sch. Corp., 714 N.E.2d 233, 242 (Ind. Ct. App. 1999).

4. ***Defamatory Statement of Fact.*** Whether a particular statement constitutes fact or opinion for libel purposes is initially a question of law for the court, Kelley v. Tanoos, 865 N.E.2d 593, 596 (Ind. 2007); Rambo v. Cohen, 587 N.E.2d 140, 147 (Ind. Ct. App. 1992); Milkovich v. Lorain Journal Co., 497 U.S.1, 110 S.Ct. 2695, 111 L. Ed.2 1 (1990), as is the question of whether a statement could possess a defamatory meaning or implication, Baker v. Tremco Inc., 917 N.E. 2d 650, 657 (Ind. 2009); Journal-Gazette v. Bandido's, 712 N.E.2d 446, 457, 27 Media L. Rep. 2089, 2104 (Ind. 1999), cert. denied, 120 S. Ct. 499, 145 L. Ed. 2d 385 (1999); Melton v. Ousley, 925 N.E. 2d 430, 439 (Ind. Ct. App. 2010). See also Woods v. Evansville Press, 791 F.2d 480, 486, 12 Media L. Rep. 2179 (7th Cir. 1986); Blubaugh v. Am. Contract Bridge League, No. IP 01-358-C H/K, 2004 U.S. Dist LEXIS 3178, at *35, 2004-1 Trade Cas. (CCH) P74,322 (S.D. Ind. Feb. 18, 2004) (holding that a prediction that an outcome would be a "slam dunk" was "too vague to be falsified" and thus could not have a defamatory meaning), aff'd, 117 Fed. Appx. 475 (7th Cir. 2004), reh'g, en banc, denied, 2004 U.S. App. LEXIS 27009 (7th Cir. Dec. 17, 2005), and cert. denied, 2005 U.S. LEXIS 3641 (U.S. Apr. 25, 2005); Sanderson v. Ind. Soft Water Servs., No. IP 00-0459-C H/K, 2004 U.S. Dist. LEXIS 15671, at *20-21, 2004-2 Trade Cas. (CCH) P74,545 (S.D. Ind. July 23, 2004) (statements not actionable because "many are not statements of fact at all and thus cannot be provable as true or false"). If a statement is ambiguous in that it is reasonably susceptible to either a defamatory or non-defamatory interpretation, the jury must determine how a reasonable person would construe the statement. Collins, 703 F. Supp. 2d 862, 874 (N.D. Ind. 2010); Shepard v. Shurz Commc'n, 847 N.E.2d 219, 225 n. 4 (Ind. Ct. App. 2006) ("When a statement is capable of either a defamatory or non-defamatory interpretation, the determination is a question of fact for the jury."); Schrader v. Eli Lilly & Co., 621 N.E.2d 635, 640 (Ind. Ct. App. 1993), overruled on other grounds, 639 N.E.2d 258 (Ind. 1994) ("unless [the statement] is free from reasonable doubt, it is for the jury to determine the meaning and construction of the alleged defamatory language").

While statements must be given their natural and ordinary meaning in the context and under the circumstances in which they were made, Schrader v. Eli Lilly & Co., 639 N.E.2d 258, 263 (Ind. 1994) (holding that posted notices could not have been understood by company outsiders as being damaging to plaintiffs' reputations), the defamatory nature of a communication must generally appear without resort to extrinsic facts or circumstances. Branham v. Celadon Trucking Servs., Inc., 744 N.E.2d 514, 522 (Ind. Ct. App. 2001); **Martino v. Western & Southern Financial Group, 3:08-CV-308-TLS, 2012 WL 876749, at *13 (N.D. Ind. March 13, 2012) (a letter to the Indiana Department of Insurance stating that a former employee failed to provide documentation establishing his employment eligibility does not, on its face, impute criminal conduct or professional misconduct and is not defamatory and therefore cannot support a claim of defamation per se)**. And, when determining whether a statement has a defamatory interpretation, a court may not intrude upon ecclesiastical debates. Indiana Area Found. of United Methodist Church, Inc. v. Snyder, 953 N.E.2d 1174, 1180 (Ind. Ct. App. 2011) (the First Amendment effectively prohibits civil tribunals from reviewing statements made by officials of a religious organization which set forth in ecclesiastical terms the reasons for the pastoral employee's termination). Assertions that an allegedly defamatory statement is barred by the First Amendment because consideration of the comments would necessarily require the court's entanglement into religious doctrine, however, do not divest a court of subject matter jurisdiction. West v. Wadlington, 933 N.E.2d 1274, 1276 (Ind. 2010).

Statements about another person's attitudes, beliefs, and personality traits are typically protected opinions, not defamatory statements of fact. Eversole v. Spurlino Materials of Indianapolis, LLC, 804 F. Supp. 2d 922, 937 (S.D. Ind. 2011) (statement made in company memorandum that some workers "have made the workplace unpleasant" is a vague, unverifiable statement of opinion which cannot amount to actionable defamation); McClain v. TP Orthodontics, No. 3:07-cv-

113-JVB, 2009 U.S. Dist. LEXIS 66679 (N.D. Ind. July 30, 2009) (statement that person "wasn't a good mother" cannot be proved true or false and thus is not defamatory); Filippo v. Lee Publications, Inc., 485 F. Supp.2d 969, 980 (N.D. Ind. 2007); Newman v. Jewish Community Center Ass'n of Indianapolis, Inc., 875 N.E.2d 729, 740 (Ind. Ct. App. 2007) (statements that person was "demanding" and "very argumentative" do not have defamatory imputation); N. Ind. Pub. Serv. Co. v. Dabagia, 721 N.E.2d 294, 303 (Ind. Ct. App. 1999) (racial slurs and epithets are defamatory in nature only if the plaintiff can show that the words were intended and understood to be a statement about a subject that was defamatory in itself or that lowered the subject in the eyes of the community); Rosa v. Valparaiso Community Schools, No. 2:04-cv-190, 2006 WL 487880 (N.D. Ind. Feb. 27, 2006) (calling someone the "N" word is not defamatory); Gatto v. St. Richard Sch., Inc., 774 N.E.2d 914 (Ind. Ct. App. 2002) (vague and neutral statement regarding an employee is not susceptible to defamatory meaning); Lovings v. Thomas, 805 N.E.2d 442, 449 (Ind. Ct. App. 2004) (statement that plaintiff was "causing a problem" does not imply person is engaged in a criminal act); Assocs. Fin. Servs. Co. v. Bowman, Heintz, Boscia & Vician, No. IP 99-1725-C M/S, 2004 U.S. Dist. LEXIS 6520 at **66-71 (S.D. Ind. March 31, 2004) (allegation that defendant made comments which left a negative impression is inactionable "slander in the air" in the absence of evidence establishing exactly what the defendant said). But cf. Powers v. Gastineau, 568 N.E.2d 1020, 1027 (Ind. Ct. App. 1991) (holding it was a fact question whether calling someone a "lunatic" was capable of defamatory interpretation); Near E. Side Cmty. Org. v. Hair, 555 N.E.2d 1324, 1329-30 (Ind. Ct. App. 1990) (declining to follow Illinois case holding that "slum lord" and "slum landlord" are capable of innocent construction).

The positioning of true statements and headlines may create a false implication or impression, and the defense of truth "must extend to the innuendo, the libelous implications and insinuations, as well as to the direct accusations in the statement." Cochran v. Indianapolis Newspapers, Inc., 175 Ind. App. 548, 372 N.E.2d 1211, 1217, 3 Media L. Rep. 2131 (Ind. Ct. App. 1978). In Indiana, implications may, as a matter of law, be capable of a defamatory interpretation. See id.; Owens v. Schoenberger, 681 N.E.2d 760, 766 (Ind. Ct. App. 1997). Indiana generally does not recognize libel by omission. To recover, the plaintiff must show "what has been omitted has made a material assertion of fact untrue." Heeb v. Smith, 613 N.E.2d 416, 423, 21 Media L. Rep. 1558, 1563 (Ind. Ct. App. 1993).

5. ***Of and Concerning Plaintiff.*** Indiana follows the general rule that defamatory words are not actionable "unless they refer to some ascertained or ascertainable person, and that person must be the plaintiff." Schrader v. Eli Lilly & Co., 639 N.E.2d 258, 261 (Ind. 1994). For example, in Furno v. Citizens Ins. Co. of Am., 590 N.E.2d 1137, 1141 (Ind. Ct. App. 1992), the court held that a general statement about the chiropractic profession was not sufficient to impute that the defendant was unfit in his profession. See also Containment Tech. Group v. American Soc'y of Health Sys. Pharmacists, No. 1:07-cv-0997-DFH-TAB, 2009 WL 838549, at *11 (S.D. Ind. Mar. 26, 2009) (statements that do not refer to the plaintiff "standing alone" cannot be defamatory); Sanderson, No. IP 00-0459-C H/K, 2004 U.S. Dist. LEXIS 15671, at **22-25 (Indiana has not recognized the group libel theory).

6. ***Publication.*** In an action for defamation, the plaintiff must show that the defamatory matter was "published," that is, communicated to a third person or persons. See Schrader v. Eli Lilly & Co., 639 N.E.2d 258, 261 (Ind. 1994); Bals v. Verduzco, 600 N.E.2d 1353, 1354 (Ind. 1992); Haegert v. McMullan, 953 N.E.2d 1223, 1231 (Ind. Ct. App. 2011). Publication to an agent of the plaintiff acting on the plaintiff's behest does not fulfill the publication requirement. See Melton v. Ousley, 925 N.E. 2d 430, 439 (Ind. Ct. App. 2010) (statements in a letter to a golf professional's attorney were tantamount to statements to the professional himself and did not meet the requirements for publication); Moreno-Nicholas v. City of Indianapolis, 2000 U.S. Dist. LEXIS 16668, at *25, 84 Fair Empl. Prac. Cas. (BNA) 1388 (S.D. Ind. Oct. 26, 2000) (communicating defamatory statements to the plaintiff's agent is "tantamount to a publication to the Plaintiff himself, and as such does not fulfill the publication requirement"); Delval v. PPG Indus., Inc., 590 N.E.2d 1078, 1081 (Ind. Ct. App. 1992) (holding that mental health professionals were acting on the plaintiff's behalf and, therefore, communications with the health professionals did not constitute publication); Brockman v. Detroit Diesel Allison Div. of Gen. Motors Corp., 174 Ind. App. 240, 244, 366 N.E.2d 1201, 1201 (Ind. Ct. App. 1977) (holding that statements made at a grievance meeting were not published because the union was acting to resolve the grievance filed by the plaintiff). Furthermore, the defendant must actually participate in the publication. Turner v. Boy Scouts of America, 856 N.E.2d 106, 111-12 (Ind. Ct. App. 2006) (defendant's receipt of alleged defamatory information from a third person did not constitute publication); Thompson v. Huntington, 69 F. Supp. 2d 1071 (S.D. Ind. 1999) (rudeness or passive involvement in exchange does not constitute publication); Glasscock v. Corliss, 823 N.E.2d 748, 753 n.3 (Ind. Ct. App. 2005) (one defendant's silence, even while another defendant called plaintiff a thief, was held not defamatory because silence lacked the element of publication).

a. **Intracorporate Communication.** The Indiana Supreme Court has held that employee evaluation information communicated intracompany to management personnel may be considered published for purposes of a defamation action. See Trail v. Boys & Girls Clubs of N.W. Indiana, 845 N.E.2d 130, 136 (Ind. 2006); Schrader v. Eli Lilly & Co., 639 N.E.2d 258, 262 (Ind. 1994) (stating slide presentation to employees and notices on company bulletin boards constitute publication).

b. **Compelled Self-Publication.** Indiana has not recognized a cause of action for defamation based on self-publication. See Sarratore v. Longview Van Corp., 666 F. Supp. 1257, 1263-64 (N.D. Ind. 1987) (discussing Indiana law).

c. **Republication.** Every repetition or republication of a defamatory statement or article is a publication itself and a new and distinct libel. See Sourbier v. Brown, 123 N.E. 802, 804 (Ind. 1919); Weenig v. Wood, 169 Ind. App. 413, 349 N.E.2d 235, 246 (Ind. Ct. App. 1976). The originator of a defamatory statement is liable for any republication which is the natural consequence of his actions, but not from the independent and unauthorized actions of another. See Powers v. Gastineau, 568 N.E.2d 1020, 1024 (Ind. Ct. App. 1991); see also Smith v. Biomet, Inc., No. 3:01-CV-753 PS, 2005 U.S. Dist. LEXIS 5251, at *42-43 (N.D. Ind. Mar. 24, 2005) (rejecting Biomet's argument that it was "merely a republisher of the statement," and holding that, because Biomet had altered the original statement, its liability in this case derived from its own actions). In cases governed by the actual malice standard "when liability depends on mental states," a republisher must be shown to have known that the original statement was untrue or shown to have had reason to doubt the original statement. Chang v. Michiana Telecasting Corp., 900 F.2d 1085, 1090 (7th Cir. 1990) (interpreting Indiana law).

7. ***Statements versus Conduct.*** Indiana courts have not specifically addressed the issue of whether conduct or actions, rather than verbal statements, constitute defamation. However, in Kolczynski v. Maxton Motors, Inc., 538 N.E.2d 275, 276 (Ind. Ct. App. 1989), the Court of Appeals held that an employer's conduct of having a key made for plaintiff's car and searching the car for stolen property does not constitute slander. Additionally, the Indiana Supreme Court has noted in dicta that "in order to impose liability for defamation, the United States Constitution requires a false *statement* of fact." See Journal-Gazette v. Bandido's, 712 N.E.2d 446, 457, 27 Media L. Rep. 2089, 2104 (Ind. 1999), cert. denied, 120 S. Ct. 499, 145 L. Ed. 2d 385 (1999) (emphasis added); Cf. Branham v. Celadon Trucking Servs., Inc., 744 N.E.2d 514, 522 (Ind. Ct. App. 2001) (photograph does not constitute a defamatory communication because it truthfully represents what the subject of the photo was doing).

8. ***Damages.*** Indiana law recognizes two components of actual damages. General damages are those which the law presumes to be the natural, proximate and necessary result of the publication, including injury to plaintiff's reputation, standing in the community, personal humiliation and mental anguish and suffering. Special damages are those which are pecuniary in nature and are not assumed to be necessary or inevitable but must be shown by allegation and specific proof to have been actually incurred as a natural and proximate result of the defamatory statement. See Indianapolis Newspapers, Inc. v. Fields, 259 N.E.2d 651, 667 (Ind. 1970), cert. denied, 400 U.S. 930 (1970); Lovings v. Thomas, 805 N.E.2d 442, 448 (Ind. Ct. App. 2004); Lessley v. City of Madison, 654 F. Supp. 2d 877, 912 (S.D. Ind. 2009). Damages for emotional distress and bodily harm may be awarded in a defamation action as "parasitic damages, viable only when attached to normal (i.e., pecuniary) special damages." Rambo v. Cohen, 587 N.E.2d 140, 146 (Ind. Ct. App. 1992). Nominal damages may be awarded when the insignificant character of the defamatory matter or the plaintiff's bad character leads the jury to believe that no substantial harm has been done. See Briggs v. Clinton County Bank & Trust Co., 452 N.E.2d 989, 999 (Ind. Ct. App. 1983); Elliott v. Roach,, 409 N.E.2d 661, 684, 78 Ind. Dec. 50, 66-68 (Ind. Ct. App. 1980). Due to Indiana's Aafco decision requiring private individuals who bring an action involving an event of public interest to prove actual malice, Indiana courts have not directly addressed the "actual damages" rule of Gertz, although Indiana courts in dicta have indicated that "proof of 'actual injury'" may now be required to recover general compensatory damages. See Elliott v. Roach, 409 N.E.2d 661, 685, 78 Ind. Dec. 50, 72-74 (Ind. Ct. App. 1980). Indiana courts have also allowed private figure plaintiffs to enjoin a defendant from making slanderous statements of a primarily private concern upon a showing of malice and irreparable injury. Barlow v. Sipes, 744 N.E.2d 1, 7-10 (Ind. Ct. App. 2001) (plaintiff is entitled to a preliminary injunction because a dollar amount could not be placed on either the economic or reputational injuries sustained as a result of the defamation).

a. **Presumed Damages and Libel Per Se.** A statement is defamatory per se if the defamatory nature of the words is apparent on their face, without resorting to extrinsic facts. Dugan v. Mittal Steel USA Inc., 929 N.E. 2d 184 (Ind. 2010); N. Ind. Pub. Serv. Co. v. Dabagia, 721 N.E.2d 294, 303 (Ind. Ct. App. 1999). See also Kelley v. Tanoos, 865 N.E.2d 593, 596 (Ind. 2007) (examples of slanderous statements that are defamatory per se are those that impute criminal conduct, a loathsome disease, misconduct in a trade, profession or business, or sexual misconduct); Trail v. Boys & Girls Clubs of N.W. Indiana, 845 N.E.2d 130, 137 (Ind. 2006); Nikish Software Corp. v. Manatron, Inc., 801 F. Supp. 2d 791, 798 (S.D. Ind. 2011) (a letter sent to plaintiff's potential customers alleging that plaintiff illegally obtained its products imputes misconduct in the plaintiff's trade and therefore is defamatory per se); Davis v. Genova Products, Inc., No. 4:07 cv 40, 2008 U.S. Dist. LEXIS 2865, at *8 (N.D. Ind. January 11, 2008) (fabricated claims of sexual misconduct and sexual harassment impute criminal and sexual misconduct and thus are defamatory per se). See also I.B.8.a(1), infra. Once a court determines that a communication is defamatory per se, the plaintiff is entitled to damages without further proof because the law presumes the plaintiff's reputation has been damaged. See Dugan, 929 N.E. 2d at 186; Baker v. Tremco Inc., 917 N.E. 2d 650, 657 (Ind. 2009); Kelley, 865 N.E.2d at 597; Collins v. Purdue University, 703 F. Supp. 2d 862, 874 (N.D. Ind. 2010); Lessley v. City of Madison, 654 F. Supp. 2d 877, 911 (S.D. Ind. 2009) at 911. In response to the Gertz decision, however, a plaintiff must prove malice in order to sustain presumed damages when the matter is of public concern. See Journal-Gazette

v. Bandido's, 712 N.E.2d 446, 457, 27 Media L. Rep. 2089, 2104 (Ind. 1999), cert. denied, 120 S. Ct. 499, 145 L. Ed. 2d 385 (1999); Aafco Heating & Air Conditioning Co. v. Northwest Publ'ns, Inc., 162 Ind. App. 671, 679, 321 N.E.2d 580, 586 (Ind. Ct. App. 1974), cert. denied, 424 U.S. 913 (1976); Chang v. Michiana Telecasting Corp., 900 F.2d 1085, 1087 (7th Cir. 1990), 14 Media L. Rep. 1889 (N.D. Ind. 1987). If malice is proved, presumed damages (including punitive damages) may be awarded for statements that are defamatory per se, even in the absence of actual damages. See Smith v. Biomet, Inc., No. 3:01-CV-753 PS, 2005 U.S. Dist. LEXIS 5251, at *44 (N.D. Ind. Mar. 24, 2005) (in upholding $400,000 verdict, court finds "[w]hen a communication is defamatory per se, 'the law presumes the plaintiff's reputation has been damaged, and the jury may award a substantial sum for this presumed harm, even without proof of actual harm'") (quoting Rambo v. Cohen, 587 N.E.2d 140, 145 (Ind. Ct. App. 1992); Henrichs v. Pivarnik, 588 N.E.2d 537, 545, 20 Media L. Rep. 1787 (Ind. Ct. App. 1992)).

(1) **Employment-Related Criticism.** A statement constitutes libel per se if it attacks a person's honesty and integrity in his trade, business, profession, office or occupation. See Dugan v. Mittal Steel USA Inc., 929 N.E. 2d 184, 186 (Ind. 2010); Kelley v. Tanoos, 865 N.E.2d 593, 596 (Ind. 2007); Bell v. Clark, 653 N.E.2d 483, 490 (Ind. Ct. App. 1995), aff'd by, 670 N.E.2d 1290 (Ind. 1996) (holding that a letter to limited partners stating that general partner took inappropriate loans from partnership was libel per se); Weenig v. Wood, 349 N.E.2d 235, 246 (Ind. Ct. App. 1976) (accusation that employee embezzled funds was defamation per se); see also Glasscock v. Corliss, 823 N.E.2d 748 (Ind. Ct. App. 2005) (statements were defamatory per se because, in context, defendants' statements at a company meeting accused plaintiff of a crime and also implied misconduct by plaintiff in her occupation). But see Baker v. Tremco Inc., 917 N.E. 2d 650, 657 (Ind. 2009) (statement by an employer's representative that a former employee had engaged in inappropriate sales practices was too vague to amount to defamation per se).

(2) **Single Instance Rule.** No cases reported regarding the single instance rule.

b. **Punitive Damages.** Punitive damages may be assessed only where libelous statements are published with actual malice. See Smith v. Biomet, Inc., No. 3:01-CV-753 PS, 2005 U.S. Dist. LEXIS 5251, at *45 (N.D. Ind. Mar. 24, 2005) (finding jury's award of compensatory and punitive damages appropriate where the defamatory statement was found to have been made with knowledge that it was false). Common law or "presumed malice" does not entitle a plaintiff to punitive damages. See Street v. Shoe Carnival, Inc., 660 N.E.2d 1054, 1060 (Ind. Ct. App. 1996); Harper v. Goodin, 409 N.E.2d 1129, 1135, 78 Ind. Dec. 182 (Ind. Ct. App. 1980). Under Ind. Code § 34-51-3-2, clear and convincing evidence is required to support an award of punitive damages. A court may award punitive damages in the absence of compensatory damages where the statement is defamatory per se. See Henrichs v. Pivarnik, 588 N.E.2d 537, 545, 20 Media L. Rep. 1787 (Ind. Ct. App. 1992). But see Street v. Shoe Carnival, Inc., 660 N.E.2d 1054 (Ind. Ct. App. 1996) (holding that compensatory damages are a prerequisite to recovery of punitive damages). Punitive damages are particularly appropriate where the wrongdoer occupies a position of trust. See Bell v. Clark, 653 N.E.2d 483, 490 (Ind. Ct. App. 1995), aff'd by, 670 N.E.2d 1290 (Ind. 1996). Other factors courts have considered when determining whether punitive damages should be awarded are: "(1) the degree of reprehensibility of the defendant's conduct; (2) the ratio of the award to the actual harm inflicted on the plaintiff; and (3) the comparison of the award and civil penalties authorized or imposed in comparable cases." Coachmen Indus., Inc. v. Dunn, 719 N.E.2d 1271, 1278 (Ind. Ct. App. 1999).

II. PRIVILEGES AND DEFENSES

A. Scope of Privileges

1. ***Absolute Privilege.*** In Near E. Side Cmty. Org. v. Hair, 555 N.E.2d 1324, 1331 (Ind. Ct. App. 1990), the court observed that "[t]he First Amendment does not offer absolute immunity for libelous and damaging falsehoods." While Indiana has not recognized an absolute privilege for the media, Indiana courts have recognized absolute common law privileges for communications to school authorities raising complaints against educators, statements made by legislators which relate to official business and statements contained in pleadings filed during court proceedings and made by judges, attorneys, parties, and witnesses so long as they are relevant to the proceedings. See Hartman v. Keri, 883 N.E.2d774, 777 (Ind. 2008); PNC Bank, N.A. v. OCMC, Inc., 2010 U.S. Dist. LEXIS 98368 (S.D. Ind. Ind. Sept. 20, 2010) (absolute privilege applies to statements made in judicial pleadings unless comments are "entirely disconnected with the litigation."); Miller v. Reinert, 839 N.E.2d 731 (Ind. Ct. App. 2006), reh'g denied (2006) (libel complaint dismissed as it was based entirely upon statements made in an appellate brief to the court). This absolute judicial privilege has been applied to probation officers assisting a juvenile court in placing children with foster families, as well as to case workers who assisted the juvenile court with the care and custody of children. H.B. v. State, 713 N.E.2d 300, 302-03 (Ind. Ct. App. 1999). The absolute privilege further extends to communications made prior or subsequent to a judicial proceeding, provided that the communication is related to the proceeding, made in good faith and in contemplation of a proceeding before the trial court or on appeal. See Coachmen Indus., Inc. v. Dunn, 719 N.E.2d 1271, 1276 (Ind. Ct. App. 1999); Van Eaton v. Fink, 697 N.E.2d 490, 495 (Ind. Ct. App. 1998). It is a question of law whether statements in pleadings are pertinent and relevant. See Trotter v. Ind. Waste Sys., 632 N.E.2d 1159, 1162 (Ind. Ct. App. 1994); Chrysler Motors Corp. v. Graham, 631 N.E.2d 7, 9 (Ind. Ct.

App. 1994). See also Badger v. Greater Clark County Sch., No. 4:03-CV-00101-SEB-WGH, 2005 U.S. Dist. LEXIS 4277, at *34-35 (S.D. Ind. Feb. 15, 2005) ("[T]he privilege is withdrawn only when the statements are so palpably irrelevant to the subject matter of the controversy that no reasonable person could doubt its irrelevancy and impropriety."). Statements made in pleadings which are mailed to third parties in an attempt to gain leverage and/or cause economic damages, however, are not entitled to an absolute privilege. Assocs. Fin. Servs. Co. v. Bowman, Heintz, Boscia & Vician, IP 99-1725-C-M/S, 2001 U.S. Dist. LEXIS 7874 at *26-28 (S.D. Ind. April 25, 2001). Neither are statements made in trial preparation material such as survey questionnaires. See Raybestos Prods. Co. v. Younger, 54 F.3d 1234 (7th Cir. 1995). In contrast, a prosecutor enjoys absolute immunity from liability when his or her statement to the press informs the public about a case pending in his or her office. Fermaglich v. Indiana, No. IP01-1859-C-T/K, 2004 U.S. Dist. LEXIS 24539, at *72 (S.D. Ind. Sept. 29, 2004). The same rule immunizes the Indiana attorney general. Am. Dry Cleaning & Laundry v. State, 725 N.E.2d 96, 99 (Ind. Ct. App. 2000).

This immunity extends not only to court actions but also administrative enforcement proceedings. Kirk v. City of Kokomo, 772 F.Supp.2d 983, 993-994 (S.D. Ind. 2011) (defendants were immune for statements included in the charging documents filed in and used to initiate administrative proceeding with the Kokomo Board of Works and Safety); E.L.C. Elec., Inc. v. Ind. Dept. of Labor, 825 N.E.2d 16, 23 (Ind. Ct. App. 2005) (Department of Labor entitled to absolute immunity from company on its defamation claim because its employees' actions were done pursuant to their duties of inspection and enforcement of the Common Construction Wage Act); Crenshaw v. Baynerd, 180 F.3d 866, 868 (7th Cir. 1999) (statements by the commissioners of the Indiana Civil Rights Commission are absolutely privileged).

A federal court in Indiana has held that Section 5318(g) of the Amunzio-Wyle Anti-Money Laundering Act, 31 U.S.C. § 5318(g), provides absolute immunity to financial institutions which report suspicious activities to law enforcement. Gregory v. Bank One, 200 F. Supp. 2d 1000 (S.D. Ind. 2002) (holding that bank could assert immunity in lawsuit brought by former teller without having to disclose whether report was in fact made).

One who consents to publications which could constitute a defamatory statement, such as one who agrees to submit his conduct to investigation knowing that its results will be published, is barred from recovery, if the publication does not exceed the consent. See Eitler v. St. Joseph Reg'l Med. Ctr. South-Bend Campus, Inc., 789 N.E.2d 497, 500 (Ind. Ct. App. 2003) (affirming summary judgment because signed employee evaluation authorization/release form was explicit consent to publication that plaintiff had reason to know might be defamatory), transfer denied by 812 N.E.2d 803 (Ind. 2004); Brockman v. Detroit Diesel Allison Div. of Gen. Motors Corp., 174 Ind. App. 240, 245, 366 N.E.2d 1201, 1204 (Ind. Ct. App. 1977). The privilege conferred by the consent of the subject of the defamatory statement is absolute and evidence of alleged malice does not defeat an absolute privilege. See Eitler, 789 N.E.2d at 500-01; Ernst v. Ind. Bell Tel. Co., 475 N.E.2d 351, 356 (Ind. Ct. App. 1985).

2. ***Qualified Privileges.***

a. **Common Interest.** Indiana recognizes the common law qualified privileges relating to statements "made in good faith on any subject matter in which the party making the communication has an interest or in reference to which he has a duty, either public or private, either legal, moral, or social, if made to a person having a corresponding interest or duty." Williams v. Tharp, 914 N.E. 2d 756, 762 (Ind. 2009); Trail v. Boys & Girls Clubs of N.W. Indiana, 845 N.E.2d 130, 136 (Ind. 2006); Schrader v. Eli Lilly & Co., 639 N.E.2d 258, 262 (Ind. 1994); **Gagan v. Yast, 966 N.E.2d 177, 184 (Ind. Ct. App. 2012) (privilege applies to attorney's communication to his clients about conflict of interest issues)**. The existence of a qualified privilege does not change the actionable nature of the words spoken, but rather rebuts the element of malice implied by law for the making of a defamatory statement. Cortez v. Jo-Ann Stores, Inc., 827 N.E.2d 1223 (Ind. Ct. App. 2005). This privilege "is intended to facilitate 'full and unrestricted communication on matters in which the parties have a common interest or duty.'" Kelley v. Tanoos, 865 N.E.2d 593, 598 (Ind. 2007), quoting Chambers v. American Trans Air, Inc. 577 N.E.2d 612, 615 (Ind. Ct. App. 1991), trans. denied. As such, the qualified privilege protects communications made in connection with membership qualifications, employment references, intracompany communications, and the extension of credit. Dugan v. Mittal Steel USA Inc., 929 N.E. 2d 184, 188 (Ind. 2010) (supervisor's statements to chief of security that an employee was stealing time and attempting to defraud the company were protected by the common interest privilege); Newman v. Jewish Community Center Ass'n of Indianapolis, Inc., 875 N.E.2d 729, 735 (Ind. Ct. App. 2007) at 741 (common interest privilege applies to intra-organizational communications regarding volunteers). See also Biomet, Inc. v. Smith, 238 F. Supp. 2d 1036, 1048 (N.D. Ind. 2002) (Indiana courts have applied this privilege to communications between employers and employees, business partners, members of fraternal organizations, creditors and credit agencies and between a school and its parents); Bochenek v. Walgreen Co., 18 F. Supp. 2d 965, 972 (N.D. Ind. 1998) (qualified privilege protected employer's statements to employees that former manager had been caught stealing); Blubaugh v. Am. Contract Bridge League, No. IP 01-358-C H/K, 2004 U.S Dist LEXIS 3178, at *25 (S.D. Ind. Feb. 18, 2004) (noting that statements made in the context of fraternal associations or societies can be protected by qualified privilege), aff'd, 117 Fed. Appx. 475 (7th Cir. 2004), reh'g, en banc, denied, 2004 U.S. App. LEXIS 27009 (7th Cir. Dec. 17, 2005), cert. denied, 2005

U.S. LEXIS 3641 (U.S. Apr. 25, 2005). Communications between parents and school concerning the school's administrators and faculty are also qualifiedly privileged. Gatto v. St. Richard Sch., Inc., 774 N.E.2d 914 (Ind. Ct. App. 2002).

So to are statements made among employees while investigating a possible criminal action, 929 N.E.2d at 188; Conwell v. Beatty, 667 N.E.2d 768, 779 (Ind. Ct. App. 1996); K -Mart Corp. v. Brzezinski, 540 N.E.2d 1276, 1282 (Ind. Ct. App. 1989), cert. denied, reh'g denied, 545 N.E.2d 842 (Ind. Ct. App. 1989); Dietz v. Finlay Fine Jewelry Corp., 754 N.E.2d 958, 969 (Ind. Ct. App. 2001); and personnel evaluation information; Bals v. Verduzco, 600 N.E.2d 1353, 1356 (Ind. 1993); Trail, 845 N.E.2d at 137 (allowing employer to give prospective employers negative report about employee); **Williams v. Lovchik, 830 F.Supp.2d 604, 615 (S.D. Ind. 2011) (qualified privilege protects statements contained in a personnel evaluation which were communicated in good faith)**; Haegert v. McMullan, 953 N.E.2d 1223, 1232 (Ind. Ct. App. 2011) (statements placed in personnel file by persons who accused employee of sexual harassment protected by qualified privilege); Grimes v. Union Planters Bank, No. 1:02-cv-1573-JDT-TAB, 2004 U.S. Dist. LEXIS 21665 (S.D. Ind. Aug. 30, 2004) ("[i]ntracompany communications regarding the fitness of an employee are protected by the qualified privilege in order to accommodate the important role of free and open intracompany communications and legitimate human resource and management needs"); Van De Leuv v. Methodist Hosp. of Ind., Inc., 642 N.E.2d 531, 536 (Ind. Ct. App. 1994) (stating that an employee reference given by a former employer to a prospective employer is protected by the qualified privilege); Chambers, 577 N.E.2d at 615 (Ind. Ct. App. 1991) (recognizing qualified privilege for statements made by former employer to prospective employer of job applicant); Olsson v. Ind. Univ. Bd. of Trs., 571 N.E.2d 585 (Ind. Ct. App. 1991) (holding that university had qualified privilege to send letter to school administrators describing student-teacher as "marginal"). The Indiana legislature has codified this latter privilege, establishing that a prior employer is immune for job reference information given. Ind. Code § 22-5-3-1 ("employer that discloses information about a current or former employee is immune from civil liability for the disclosure and the consequences proximately caused by the disclosure, unless it is proven by a preponderance of the evidence that the information disclosed was known to be false at the time the disclosure was made"). Indeed, Ind. Code § 22-5-3-1 has been found to "expresses the legislature's approval of a free flow of information between a former and prospective employer." Eitler v. St. Joseph Reg'l Med. Ctr. South-Bend Campus, Inc., 789 N.E.2d 497, 503 (Ind. Ct. App. 2003), transfer denied by 812 N.E.2d 803 (Ind. 2004).

Indiana courts have also held that statements published during the course of a labor controversy otherwise subject to the jurisdiction of the NLRB are qualifiedly privileged and are actionable only if made with actual malice and the plaintiff can prove the alleged defamatory statement caused him damage. See Brockman v. Detroit Diesel Allison Div. of Gen. Motors Corp., 174 Ind. App. 240, 247, 366 N.E.2d 1201, 1205 (Ind. Ct. App. 1977); Indep. Workers of Noble County, Inc. v. Int'l Bhd. of Elec. Workers, 273 F. Supp. 313, 321-22 (N.D. Ind. 1967). The privilege also applies to statements made to the Indiana Employment Security Division relating to a claim of unemployment compensation. See Ind. Code § 22-4-17-9; Lawson v. Howmet Aluminum Corp., 449 N.E.2d 1172, 1175 (Ind. Ct. App. 1983); Knight v. Baker, 173 Ind. App. 314, 363 N.E.2d 1048, 1051 (Ind. Ct. App. 1977).

b. **Duty.** See II.A.2.a, supra. The privilege arises not just from a common interest a defendant migh share with others; it also arises when the defendant has a "duty" to speak. Thus, communications made to law enforcement officials have been held to be qualifiedly privileged so as to encourage private individuals to assist law enforcement with investigations and in the apprehension of criminals. Williams v. Tharp, 914 N.E. 2d 756, 762 (Ind. 2009); Kelley v. Tanoos, 865 N.E.2d 593, 600 (Ind. 2007); Holcomb v. Walter's Dimmick Petroleum, Inc., 858 N.E.2d 103, 106-107 (Ind. 2006), quoting Conn v. Paul Harris Stores, 439 N.E.2d 195, 198-99 (Ind. Ct. App. 1982), trans. denied ("Liability will not be imposed when the defendant does nothing more than detail his version of the facts to a policeman and ask for his assistance, leaving to the officer to determine what is the appropriate response, at least where his representation of the facts does not prevent the intelligent exercise of the officer's discretion."). Further, "[j]ust as statements to law enforcement further a public interest, similar statements made to a private citizen may further the same interest." Kelley v. Tanoos, 865 N.E.2d 593, 600 (Ind. 2007). In Puckett v. McKinney, 175 Ind. App. 673, 677, 373 N.E. 2d 909, 911 (Ind. Ct. App. 1978), the court found the privilege applied to comments about a teacher because the principal had a duty to evaluate teachers and make recommendations to the school board regarding continued employment. See also Badger v. Greater Clark County Sch., No. 4:03-CV-00101-SEB-WGH, 2005 U.S. Dist. LEXIS 4277, at *33 (S.D. Ind. Feb. 15, 2005) ("Certainly, a school board has an interest and a duty to provide and maintain qualified personnel within the school corporation; thus, communications between and among school board members relating to school personnel is protected by the qualified privilege unless that privilege has been forfeited"). Moreover, because an employer has a duty to respond when an employee initiates a grievance process, any response provided is privileged. Farr v. St. Francis Hospital & Health Centers. 570 F.3d 829, 834 (7th Cir. 2009). In addition, Ind. Code § 34-30-15-15 (formerly § 34-4-12.6-3) provides that all communications of health care providers to a peer review committee are privileged. See Mulder v. Vankerson, 637 N.E.2d 1335, 1338 (Ind. Ct. App. 1994). Also privileged are comments by a legal assistant made in the course of fulfilling her duty under Ind. Professional Conduct Rule 3.4 to report falsified evidence submitted to the court by the attorney she works for, Van Eaton v. Fink, 697 N.E.2d 490, 496 (Ind. Ct. App. 1998), **and statements by a lawyer pursuant to his duty to raise conflict of interest issues under Ind.**

Professional Conduct Rule 1.7. Gagan v. Yast, 966 N.E.2d 177, 184 (Ind. Ct. App. 2012). However, a lawyer employed to represent a limited partnership does not have a duty to inform the limited partners of his opinion that the general partner has engaged in unacceptable conduct. See Bell v. Clark, 670 N.E.2d 1290, 1293 (Ind. 1996).

c. **Criticism of Public Employee.** Indiana recognizes a qualified privilege of fair comment applying to comments about public officials and their conduct and the fair and accurate reporting of public proceedings. See Aafco Heating & Air Conditioning Co. v. Northwest Publ'ns, Inc., 321 N.E.2d 580, 583-84, 1 Media L. Rep. 1683 (Ind. Ct. App. 1974), cert. denied, 424 U.S. 913 (1976); Henderson v. Evansville Press, Inc., 127 Ind. App. 592, 600, 142 N.E.2d 920, 923-24 (Ind. Ct. App. 1957).

d. **Limitation on Qualified Privileges.** The Indiana Supreme Court recognized the common law qualified privilege can be overcome by establishing malice/abuse in Indianapolis Horse Patrol, Inc. v. Ward, 247 Ind. 519, 525, 217 N.E.2d 626, 629 (Ind. 1966) (privilege lost upon showing of actual malice). Malice, in turn, can be shown by the abuse of the privilege. Williams v. Tharp, 914 N.E. 2d 756, 762 (Ind. 2009). And abuse occurs when "(1) the communicator was primarily motivated by ill will in making the statement; (2) there was excessive publication of the defamatory statements; or (3) the statement was made without belief or grounds for belief in its truth." Williams, 914 N.E. 2d at 762-64 (qualified privilege can be lost when citizen reported wrongdoing to police knowing that the information was false); Dietz v. Finlay Fine Jewelry Corp., 754 N.E.2d 958, 969 (Ind. Ct. App. 2001) (qualified privilege lost when security manager accused employee of theft of jewelry and giving customer unauthorized discount when manager only had reason to believe that employee had provided an unauthorized discount; in addition, qualified privilege was lost when interview was held in the presence of another employee whose duties were unrelated to the investigation); Mayne v. Fort Wayne Cardiology, No. 1:06-CV-288, 2007 U.S. Dist. LEXIS 81704, at *50 (N.D. Ind. November 2, 2007) (qualified privilege lost when plaintiff submitted evidence that statements given in performance review and other employment records were deliberately false); Cortez v. Jo-Ann Stores, Inc., 827 N.E.2d 1223 (Ind. Ct. App. 2005). The qualified privilege will also be lost if the communication did not further the "common interest" shared by the speaker and the recipient. Kelley v. Tanoos, 865 N.E.2d 593, 599 (Ind. 2007). Depending on the "common interest" at issue, however, the plaintiff may be required to show that the defendant actually knew his statement was false in order to invalidate the qualified privilege. Williams, 914 N.E.2d at 765-66 (the common interest of encouraging citizens to report suspected criminal activity mandates that the plaintiff establish that the reporter knew his statement was false).

(1) **Constitutional or Actual Malice.** The qualified privilege to publish statements concerning matters of public concern or interest does not apply if the statements are made with actual malice. Poyser v. Peerless, 775 N.E.2d 1101, 1107 (Ind. Ct. App. 2002); see also I.B.2.a, supra; Near E. Side Cmty. Org. v. Hair, 555 N.E.2d 1324, 1330-31 (Ind. Ct. App. 1990); Woods v. Evansville Press Co., Inc., No. EV 81-263-C, 1985 U.S. Dist. LEXIS 23754, 11 Media L. Rep. 2201 (S.D. Ind. April 17, 1985), aff'd, 791 F.2d 480, 487 (7th Cir. 1986); Gaus v. County of Wells, 620 F. Supp. 1462, 1472 (N.D. Ind. 1985). Consequently, a qualified privilege "may be defeated by a showing of 'actual' or 'express' malice, that is, the statements exceed the scope of the purposes for which the privilege exists." Burks v. Rushmore, 569 N.E.2d 714, 716 (Ind. Ct. App. 1991). To overcome the defense of privilege, however, the plaintiff must prove defendant's actual malice by clear and convincing evidence. See Heeb v. Smith, 21 Media L. Rep. 1558, 613 N.E.2d 416 (Ind. Ct. App. 1993). See also Containment Tech. Group v. American Soc'y of Health Sys. Pharmacists, No. 1:07-cv-0997-DFH-TAB, 2009 WL 838549, at *14 (S.D. Ind. Mar. 26, 2009); Cain v. Elgin, Joliet & E. Ry. Co., No. 2:04-CV-347, 2006 WL 163010 at *18 (N.D. Ind. Jan. 19, 2006); Fazekas v. Crain Communications, 583 F. Supp. 110, 112, 10 Media L. Rep. 1513 (S.D. Ind. 1984).

(2) **Common Law Malice.** Indiana courts have not made a clear distinction between actual malice and common law malice when discussing the limitations on the qualified privilege. However, a qualified privilege may be lost upon proof that the speaker was primarily motivated by ill will. See II.2.d, supra. An employer's failure to conduct an adequate investigation prior to publishing derogatory statements about an employee may also constitute "malice." Tacket v. Gen. Motors Corp, 836 F.2d 1042, 1047 (7th Cir. 1987), rev'd on other grounds, 93 F.3d 332 (7th Cir. 1996) (interpreting Indiana law).

(3) **Other Limitations on Qualified Privileges.** The qualified privilege does not apply if it is abused by excessive publication of the defamatory statement. See Schrader v. Eli Lilly & Co., 639 N.E.2d 258, 262 (Ind. 1994). This limitation also covers "publication to inappropriate parties." Id. Indiana courts examine the entire context of the situation to determine what constitutes "excessive publication." See id. In Schrader, for example, making an allegedly defamatory statement available to approximately 1,500 employees did not constitute "excessive publication" because each employee had a common interest in the communication. Id. On the other hand, the qualified privilege did not apply when an allegedly defamatory statement was publicized by former employer to plaintiff's former customer when plaintiff was no longer employed by employer and plaintiff had ceased to have business relationship with former customer. Biomet, Inc. v. Smith, 238 F. Supp. 2d. 1036, 1048 (N.D. Ind. 2002).

e. **Question of Fact or Law.** It is a question of law whether a qualified privilege exists, unless facts giving rise to the privilege are disputed. See Bals v. Verduzco, 600 N.E.2d 1353, 1356 (Ind. 1992); Owens v. Schoenberger, 681 N.E.2d 760, 764 (Ind. Ct. App. 1997); Conwell v. Beatty, 667 N.E.2d 768, 779 (Ind. Ct. App. 1996). Once a factual dispute is shown, however, "a trier of fact may determine [whether] the privilege was abused by use of the occasion for an improper purpose or by lack of belief or grounds for belief in the truth of what is said." K-Mart Corp. v. Brzezinski, 540 N.E.2d 1276, 1282 (Ind. Ct. App. 1989), reh'g denied, 545 N.E.2d 842 (Ind. Ct. App. 1989).

f. **Burden of Proof.** The defendant has the burden of showing that his/her statements are protected by a qualified privilege. Once he or she does so, the burden shifts to the plaintiff to prove the privilege was lost through malice or abuse. "A claimant can do this by proving an absence of good faith, or excessive publication, or that the statement was made without belief or grounds for belief in its truth." Trail v. Boys & Girls Clubs of N.W. Indiana, 845 N.E.2d 130 (Ind. 2006). Bald accusations by a plaintiff without evidentiary support are insufficient to meet this burden. Pierce v. Bank One-Franklin, 618 N.E.2d 16, 20 (Ind. Ct. App. 1993) (plaintiff's unsupported assertions of bad faith and excessive publication failed as a mischaracterization of the record); Chambers v. Am. TransAir, Inc., 577 N.E.2d 612, 616 (Ind. Ct. App. 1991) (plaintiff failed to establish that the defamatory statements were primarily motivated by ill will). **Equally insufficient are allegations that a defendant acted in bad faith because it was a business competitor with adversarial interests. Nexus Group, Inc. v. Heritage Appraisal Serv., 942 N.E.2d 119, 123 (Ind. Ct. App. 2011).** Even evidence that the defendant harbored a general ill will towards the plaintiff is not enough; the plaintiff must establish that the defendant's malice relates to the actual publication of the defamatory statement. Williams v. Tharp, 914 N.E. 2d 756, 762 (Ind. 2009); Schrader v. Eli Lilly & Co., 639 N.E.2d 258, 262 (Ind. 1994); Bals v. Verduzco, 600 N.E.2d 1353, 1354 (Ind. 1992); Cortez v. Jo-Ann Stores, Inc., 827 N.E.2d 1223 (Ind. Ct. App. 2005). **Malice can be shown, however, through evidence that the speaker knew the statement was false or entertained serious doubts as to its truth. Brandom v. Coupled Products, LLC, No. 92A03-1112-PL-542 2012 Ind. App. Lexis 476 at **15-21 (Ind. Ct. App., Sep. 21, 2012) (statement made by chair of bargaining committee may have been made with malice when she told a newspaper that her employer was seeking specific concessions which the employer had not, in fact, sought).** The plaintiff can also meet his/her burden of defeating the qualified privilege by showing that the defamatory statements went beyond the group interest or if publication was made to persons who have no reason to receive the information. Burks v. Rushmore, 569 N.E.2d 714, 717 (Ind. Ct. App. 1991). Notably, the standards of proof remain the same regardless of whether the plaintiff is an individual or a corporation. Amcoat Techs., Inc. v. Sobieray, No. 1:03-CV-1564-RLY-TAB, 2005 U.S. Dist. LEXIS 8217, at *14 n.4 (S.D. Ind. Feb. 4, 2005) (that plaintiff was a corporation did not change the standards for proving it had been defamed).

B. Standard Libel Defenses

1. ***Truth***. Truth is a complete defense in a civil action for libel. Palmer v. Adams, 137 Ind. 72, 74, 36 N.E. 695, 695 (Ind. 1894); Melton v. Ousley, 925 N.E. 2d 430, 437 (Ind. Ct. App. 2010); Eversole v. Spurlino Materials of Indianapolis, LLC, 804 F. Supp. 2d 922, 937 (S.D. Ind. 2011) (true statements never give rise to liability for defamation). Simply put, a "person cannot be liable for defamation if the alleged statement is true." Norris v. Bd. of Educ., 797 F. Supp. 1452, 1463 (S.D. Ind. 1992). Indiana courts also recognize the defense of substantial truth. See Heeb v. Smith, 613 N.E.2d 416, 420, 21 Media L. Rep. 1558 (Ind. Ct. App. 1993). Indeed, "[t]o establish truth as a defense in a defamation action . . . it is not necessary to establish the literal truth of the article; rather, only 'substantial truth' is required for this defense." Vachet v. Cent. Newspapers, Inc., 816 F.2d 313, 316, 13 Media L. Rep. 2337, 2339 (7th Cir. 1987). Showing that the "gist" of the statement is true, therefore, is sufficient to defeat a defamation claim. See Heeb, 613 N.E.2d at 421; Vachet., 816 F.2d at 316; CanaRx Services, Inc. v. Lin Television Corp., No. 1:07-cv-1482-LJM-JMS, 2008 U.S. Dist LEXIS 42236, at *17 (S.D. Ind. May 29, 2008) ("Truth is a defense to defamation, but the literal truth is not required…it is enough that the 'gist' or the 'sting' of the statement is true."). The test to determine if a statement is substantially true is "whether any inaccuracies caused the statement to produce a different effect on the audience than would have been produced had the literal truth been spoken." Heeb, 613 N.E.2d at 421. For example, in Assocs. Corp., the court held that although a letter regarding the plaintiff's termination was partially inaccurate regarding the identity of the plaintiff's supervisor, the letter was true because the only implication that could be drawn was that the plaintiff was dishonest and was being fired for her dishonesty, which was true. Assocs. Corp. v. Smithley, 621 N.E.2d 1116, 1120 (Ind. Ct. App. 1993). Similarly, writing letters attempting to lower the esteem of a company, but doing so without making false or inaccurate statements, has been held non-defamatory. See Amcoat Techs., Inc. v. Sobieray, No. 1:03-CV-1564-RLY-TAB, 2005 U.S. Dist. LEXIS 8217 at *19-20 (S.D. Ind. Feb. 4, 2005) ("[W]hile there is no denying that Sobieray was attempting to lower the esteem of Amcoat in the eyes of [others], he was doing so utilizing the truth about his and others' experiences . . . ."). Cf. Smith v. Biomet, Inc., No. 3:01-CV-753 PS, 2005 U.S. Dist. LEXIS 5251, at *37 (N.D. Ind. Mar. 24, 2005) (holding that the truth defense was unavailable to Biomet, because there was "some evidence that Biomet substantially changed the gist of Smith's alleged statement ... by making the threat more serious and imminent"). Truth is a defense that the defendant bears the burden of proving. See Near E. Side Cmty. Org. v. Hair, 555 N.E.2d 1324, 1330 (Ind. Ct. App. 1990).

2. ***Opinion.*** Indiana courts have held that the Milkovich standard, 497 U.S. 1 (1990), applies to statements of opinion. See McQueen v. Fayette County Sch. Corp., 711 N.E.2d 62, 66 (Ind. Ct. App. 1999). As a result, Indiana law no longer recognizes an absolute privilege for all "opinions." See id. Rather than asking courts to distinguish "truth" from "opinion," the dispositive question is "whether a reasonable fact finder could conclude that the statement implies facts which may be proven true or false." Id. This legal test does not depend on whether the statement implies underlying facts but whether the statement implies objectively verifiable or testable facts. Filippo v. Lee Publications, Inc., 485 F.Supp. 2d 969, 980 (N.D. Ind. 2007). See also, Eversole v. Spurlino Materials of Indianapolis, LLC, 804 F. Supp. 2d 922, 937 (S.D. Ind. 2011) (vague, unverifiable statements of opinion cannot amount to actionable defamation); Sims v. Humane Soc. of St. Joseph County Indiana Inc., 758 F. Supp. 2d 737, 748 (N.D. Ind. 2010) (statement that plaintiffs provided "minimal care" to their pets was a protected opinion that cannot constitute defamation because it was inherently subjective and not objectively verifiable or testable for truth); Sanderson v. Ind. Soft Water Servs., No. IP 00-0459-C H/K, 2004 U.S. Dist. LEXIS 15671, at *20-21, 2004-2 Trade Cas. (CCH) P74,545 (S.D. Ind. July 23, 2004) (finding that statements were not actionable because "many are not statements of fact at all and thus cannot be provable as true or false"); United Consumers Club, Inc. v. Bledsoe, No. 2:97-cv-276, 2006 U.S. Dist. LEXIS 52778 (N.D. Ind. July 17, 2006) (statement that membership in a consumer club were low because of a lack of savings is protected as an opinion as it was not objectively verifiable.). In addition, a parody which clearly indicates to its audience that the piece does not purport to be a statement of fact but rather is an expression of criticism or opinion is not defamatory. Hamilton v. Prewett, 860 N.E.2d 1234, 1244 (Ind. Ct. App. 2007).

3. ***Consent.*** One who consents to a publication which could constitute a defamatory statement, such as one who agrees to submit his conduct to investigation knowing that its results will be published, is barred from recovery so long as the publication does not exceed the consent. See Eitler v. St. Joseph Reg'l Med. Ctr. South-Bend Campus, Inc., 789 N.E.2d 497, 500-01 (Ind. Ct. App. 2003), transfer denied by 812 N.E.2d 803 (Ind. 2004); Brockman v. Detroit Diesel Allison Div. of Gen. Motors Corp., 174 Ind. App. 240, 245, 366 N.E.2d 1201, 1204 (Ind. Ct. App. 1977). The privilege conferred by the consent of the subject of the defamatory statement is absolute and evidence of alleged malice does not defeat an absolute privilege. See Eitler, 789 N.E.2d at 500; Ernst v. Ind. Bell Tel. Co., 475 N.E.2d 351, 355 (Ind. Ct. App. 1985). See II.A.1, supra.

4. ***Mitigation.*** In defense of a claim for defamation, a defendant may allege mitigating circumstances to reduce damages. Ind. Code. § 34-15-1-2 (1998). A plaintiff who claims damages resulting from the wrongful act of another has a duty under the law to use reasonable diligence to mitigate to avoid or minimize those damages. An injured plaintiff may not sit idly by when presented with an opportunity to reduce his damages. Defendant has the burden of proving the damages claimed by a plaintiff could have mitigated. Indiana law reflects the historic rule that matters in mitigation could be proved under a plea of justification or general denial. Elliott v. Roach, 409 N.E.2d 661, 681, 78 Ind. Dec. 50 (Ind. Ct. App. 1980); Tracy v. Hacket, 19 Ind. App. 133, 49 N.E. 185 (Ind. 1898).

III. RECURRING FACT PATTERNS

A. Statements in Personnel File

Statements or information contained in an employee's personnel file may be protected by a qualified privilege if communicated in good faith. See Bals v. Verduzco, 600 N.E.2d 1353, 1356 (Ind. 1992); Haegert v. McMullan, 953 N.E.2d 1223, 1232 (Ind. Ct. App. 2011).

B. Performance Evaluations

The qualified privilege is available to protect personnel evaluation information communicated in good faith. See Bals v. Verduzco, 600 N.E.2d 1353, 1356 (Ind. 1992); **Williams v. Lovchik, 830 F.Supp.2d 604, 615 (S.D. Ind. 2011) (qualified privilege protects statements contained in a personnel evaluation which were communicated in good faith).** Evaluations of an employee based on personal observations and interactions of the employee made in good faith by a supervisor or employer fall within the protection of the privilege. See Olsson v. Ind. Univ. Bd. of Trs., 571 N.E.2d 585, 587 (Ind. Ct. App. 1991) (communications concerning the qualifications of a school teacher, including a letter evaluating the performance of a student teacher were privileged); see also Badger v. Greater Clark County Sch., No. 4:03-CV-00101-SEB-WGH, 2005 U.S. Dist. LEXIS 4277, at *33 (S.D. Ind. Feb. 15, 2005) ("Certainly, a school board has an interest and a duty to provide and maintain qualified personnel within the school corporation; thus, communications between and among school board members relating to school personnel is protected by the qualified privilege unless that privilege has been forfeited.").

C. References

The qualified privilege is available to protect references communicated in good faith. See Bals v. Verduzco, 600 N.E.2d 1353, 1356 (Ind. 1993); Van De Leuv v. Methodist Hosp. of Ind., Inc., 642 N.E.2d 531, 536 (Ind. Ct. App. 1994) (stating that an employee reference given by a former employer to a prospective employer is protected by the qualified privilege); Chambers v. Am. Trans Air, Inc., 577 N.E.2d 612 (Ind. Ct. App. 1991) (recognizing qualified privilege for statements made by former employer to prospective employer of job applicant); Olsson v. Ind. Univ. Bd. of Trs., 571 N.E.2d 585 (Ind. Ct. App. 1991) (holding that university had qualified privilege to send letter to school administrators describing student-teacher as "marginal"). In Assocs. Corp., the court held that although a letter regarding the plaintiff's termination was partially inaccurate regarding the identity of the plaintiff's supervisor, the letter was true because the only implication that could be drawn was that the plaintiff was dishonest and was being fired for her dishonesty, which was true. 621 N.E.2d at 1119. The Indiana legislature has codified this privilege, establishing that a prior employer is immune for job reference information given if the reference does not contain intentionally false information. Ind. Code § 22-5-3-1 ("employer that discloses information about a current or former employee is immune from civil liability for the disclosure and the consequences proximately caused by the disclosure, unless it is proven by a preponderance of the evidence that the information disclosed was known to be false at the time the disclosure was made"). In contrast, the Indiana Supreme Court has held that one who knowingly supplies false information in response to an employment inquiry is liable for any physical injury that flows from such false information. Passmore v. Multi-Mgmt. Servs., Inc., 810 N.E.2d 1022 (Ind. 2004) (adopting Restatement (Second) of Torts § 310). In cases of such affirmative misrepresentations, it is no defense that the supplier of the information did not intend for harm to occur. Id. at 1025. In the same case, however, the Indiana Supreme Court refused to impose liability for negligence in supplying employment recommendations and thereby rejected Restatement (Second) of Torts § 311. Id. at 1026-27. A plaintiff who signs a release consenting to "any defamation and/or blacklisting that might arise" from her former supervisor's completion of new employer's evaluation form is barred from bringing suit even if the information given is intentionally false. Eitler v. St. Joseph Reg'l Med. Ctr. South-Bend Campus, Inc., 789 N.E.2d 497, 501 (Ind. Ct. App. 2003), transfer denied by 812 N.E.2d 803 (Ind. 2004). The court found that plaintiff who signed a release form authorizing her former employer to complete an employment evaluation form for her new employer consented to any defamation that might arise from the former employer's completion of the evaluation. Id. at 500-01. The evaluation form contained a clause releasing all parties from any and all liability for furnishing and receiving the information. Id. The court held that the employee's explicit consent to the publication of defamatory matter created an absolute privilege where employer's publication was within scope of employee's consent. Id. at 501.

D. Intracorporate Communication

Indiana recognizes that defamatory statements are not actionable due to qualified privilege if a need exists for full and unrestricted intracorporate communication on a subject which both parties have a common interest or duty. Schrader v. Eli Lilly & Co., 639 N.E.2d 258, 262 (Ind. 1994) (intracompany communications regarding the fitness of an employee are protected by the qualified privilege, in order to accommodate the important role of free and open intracompany communications and legitimate human resource management needs). Thus, the privilege has been applied to protect communications made between co-employees about another employee when relevant to the employment. Burks v. Rushmore, 569 N.E.2d 714, 717 (Ind. Ct. App. 1991) (intracompany "communications [which] concerned corresponding duties, fell within the group employment interest, were used for a proper purpose, and were made to persons who had legitimate employment reasons to receive the information" fell within the protection of the qualified privilege).

E. Statements to Government Regulators

Statements made to the Indiana Employment Security Division relating to a claim of unemployment compensation are protected by a qualified privilege under Ind. Code § 22-4-17-9. Ernst v. Ind. Bell Tel. Co., 475 N.E.2d 351 (Ind. Ct. App. 1985); Lawson v. Howmet Aluminum Corp., 449 N.E.2d 1172 (Ind. Ct. App. 1983). In contrast, statements made in administrative enforcement proceedings are absolutely privileged. Kirk v. City of Kokomo, 772 F.Supp.2d 983, 993-994 (S.D. Ind. 2011) (defendants were immune for statements included in the charging documents filed in and used to initiate administrative proceeding with the Kokomo Board of Works and Safety); Gregory v. Bank One, IP00-0545-C-H/F (S.D. Ind. May 14, 2002) (Section 5318(g) of the Amunzio-Wyle Anti-Money Laundering Act, 31 U.S.C. § 5318(g), provides absolute immunity to financial institutions which report suspicious activities to law enforcement and bank does not even need to disclose whether a report was made in order to assert this immunity).

F. Reports to Auditors and Insurers

Indiana's unfair competition act provides that publication of any statement, assertion, or representation with respect to any person in the conduct of his insurance business which is untrue, deceptive, or misleading is expressly in violation of Ind. Code § 27-4-1-4 (2002). This act, however, has not effectively eliminated the affirmative defense of truth to an action for defamation. Gibraltar Mut. Ins. Co. v. Hoosier Ins. Co., 486 N.E.2d 548, 553 (Ind. Ct. App. 1985).

G. Vicarious Liability of Employers for Statements Made by Employees

1. ***Scope of Employment.*** An employer will not be held liable for publication of a defamatory statement by his agent or servant unless the agent or servant acted within the scope of his employment. Tacket v. Delco Remy Div. of Gen. Motors, 678 F. Supp. 1387, 1393 (S.D. Ind. 1987) rev'd on other grounds, 93 F.3d 332 (7th Cir. 1996).

Moreover, an Indiana federal court has suggested that a principal may not be held liable for the defamatory statements of an independent contractor unless malice can be imputed to the principal itself. Blubaugh v. Am. Contract Bridge League, No. IP 01-358-C H/K, 2004 U.S. Dist LEXIS 3178, at *37 (S.D. Ind. Feb. 18, 2004), aff'd, 117 Fed. Appx. 475 (7th Cir. 2004), reh'g, en banc, denied, 2004 U.S. App. LEXIS 27009 (7th Cir. Dec. 17, 2005), cert. denied, 2005 U.S. LEXIS 3641 (U.S. Apr. 25, 2005). **See also Brock v. U.S. Steel Corp., 2:09-CV-00344, 2011 WL 3443954, at *9 (N.D. Ind. Aug. 8, 2011) (in order for a corporation to be held liable for an intentional tort like defamation which was committed by its employee, the plaintiff must show "the individual who committed the tort was acting pursuant to a policy or decision made through the corporation's regular decision-making channels" and that the plaintiff's injury was the intended product of that policy or decision).**

In determining whether the agent or servant is acting within the scope of his employment or agency, the court will consider his actual authority, his apparent authority and any inherent authority. Assocs. Fin. Servs. Co. v. Bowman, Heintz, Boscia & Vician, No. IP 99-1725-C M/S, 2004 U.S. Dist. LEXIS 6520 at ** 45-63 (S.D. Ind. March 31, 2004). Indiana courts have held that a principal would be held liable for any defamatory statements made by its agent who had apparent authority to make statements on the principal's behalf. Big Wheel Rests., Inc. v. Bronstein, 302 N.E.2d 876, 879 (Ind. Ct. App. 1973); see also Smith v. Biomet, Inc., No. 3:01-CV-753 PS, 2005 U.S. Dist. LEXIS 5251, at *40-42 (N.D. Ind. Mar. 24, 2005). However, employers may not be held liable for subsequent statements by an agent or servant that distort original truthful statements, because such subsequent distortions constitute misinterpretations, not repetitions. Biomet, 2005 U.S. Dist. LEXIS 5251, at *38; Tacket, 678 F. Supp. at 1394. In addition, an employer is not vicariously liable for rumors circulating among employees prior to any statements on the matter by the employer's authorized agent. Tacket, 678 F. Supp. at 1397.

Governmental entities are also subject to liability for torts committed by their agents or employees (including defamation) unless one of the immunity provisions of the Indiana Tort Claims Act applies. Ind. Code § 34-13-3-3 (Indiana Tort Claims Act, formerly § 34-4-16.5-3). See also Celebration Fireworks, Inc. v. Smith, 682 N.E.2d 569, 571 (Ind. Ct. App. 1997), rev'd on other grounds, 727 N.E.2d 450, 454 (Ind. 2000); Scott v. City of Seymour, 659 N.E.2d 585, 588 (Ind. Ct. App. 1995). A government employee acting within the scope of his duties and in the performance of a discretionary function enjoys immunity from damages for unintentional injuries. Ind. Code § 34-13-3-3 & 5; Bushong v. Williamson, 790 N.E.2d 467, 472-73 (Ind. 2003); Campbell v. Town of Austin, No. NA 01-222-C H/K, 2004 U.S. Dist. LEXIS 1925 at ** 21-23 (S.D. Ind. Feb. 9, 2004). A tort claim against a political subdivision is barred unless notice is filed with "the governing body of that political subdivision . . . within 180 days after the loss occurs." Celebration Fireworks, Inc. v. Smith, 682 N.E.2d 569, 572 (Ind. Ct. App. 1997), rev'd on other grounds, 727 N.E.2d 450, 454 (Ind. 2000). This notice requirement applies not only to suits against political subdivisions but also to suits against employees of political subdivisions. See Meury v. Eagle-Union Cmty. Sch. Corp., 714 N.E.2d 233, 241 (Ind. Ct. App. 1999); Celebration Fireworks, Inc. v. Smith, 682 N.E.2d 569, 571 (Ind. Ct. App. 1997), rev'd on other grounds, 727 N.E.2d 450, 454 (Ind. 2000); VanValkenburg v. Warner, 602 N.E.2d 1046, 1048 (Ind. Ct. App. 1992), transfer denied. However, notice is required only if the act or omission causing the plaintiff's loss is within the scope of the defendant's employment. VanValkenburg, 602 N.E.2d at 1049. An employee cannot be said to be acting within the scope of his employment, "where the act is done on the employee's own initiative and not in the service of the employer." Id. (quoting Shelby v. Truck & Bus Group Div. of Gen. Motors Corp., 533 N.E.2d 1296, 1298 (Ind. Ct. App. 1989)).

a. **Blogging.** The Indiana Court of Appeals has found that a blogger who wrote a parody concerning an owner of a water conditioning business was not liable for defamation as a person reading the website as a whole could not reasonably believe that the claims made therein to be true. Hamilton v. Prewett, 860 N.E.2d 1234, 1243-47 (Ind. Ct. App. 2007) (noting that the website had a disclaimer which stated that the character described in the website was fictional and that the description of the character was so exaggerated and distorted that a reasonable person would not believe that the content was meant to be a statement of fact). The court cautioned, however, that "[a] defendant who couches a defamatory imputation of fact in humor cannot simply avoid liability by dressing his wolfish words in humorous sheep's clothing. " Id. at 1245. **See also Sharkey v. Cochran, 1:09-cv-517-JMS-DKL, 2012 U.S. Dist. LEXIS 38273 (Mar. 21, 2012) (plaintiff could pursue claim against a blogger who referred to him as a "sociopath", a "charlatan of the lowest degree", a "sexist pig", and "a man who seeks to prey upon those who he perceives as weaker").**

Of course, one problem in pursuing those who use wolfish words in a blog is that the writer often chooses to remain anonymous. The Indiana Court of Appeals has nevertheless determined that a news organization cannot be compelled to disclose the identity of a blogger unless the plaintiff first provides prima facie evidence on every element of his/her claim which is not dependent on the identity of the blogger. In re Indiana Newspapers, Inc., 936 N.E.2d 534, 537 (Ind. Ct. App. 2012). Because the actual malice element is dependent on the identity of the blogger, however, a would be plaintiff does not need to submit evidence of malice before seeking to compel the name of a blogger. Id. at 552.

2. ***Damages.*** See I.B.8.a.-b, supra.

H. Internal Investigations

The qualified privilege applies to internal investigations regarding employee misconduct. Burks v. Rushmore, 569 N.E.2d 714, 716 (Ind. Ct. App. 1991). Consequently, an employer is protected by the qualified privilege with regard to allegedly defamatory statements made during the course of an employer's investigation into employee misconduct. Kolczynski v. Maxton Motors, Inc., 538 N.E.2d 275, 276 (Ind. Ct. App. 1989), trans. denied. This privilege is lost, however, if a defamatory statement is made in the presence of employees who are not necessary to the investigation. Dietz v. Finlay Fine Jewelry Corp., 754 N.E.2d 958, 969 (Ind. Ct. App. 2001).

IV. OTHER ACTIONS BASED ON STATEMENTS

A. Negligent Hiring, Retention, and Supervision

Indiana follows the Restatement of Agency § 213 in determining the existence of negligent hiring. Baugher v. Hattersley, 436 N.E.2d 126, 128 (Ind. Ct. App. 1982). The Restatement (Second) of Torts provides that: A person conducting an activity through servants or other agents is subject to liability for harm resulting from his conduct if he is negligent or reckless: (b) in the employment of improper persons or instrumentalities in work involving risk of harm to others; . . . (d) in permitting, or failing to prevent, negligent or other tortious conduct by persons, whether or not his servants or agents, upon premises or with instrumentalities under his control.

In the case of independent contractors, the rule in Indiana is that a principal is not liable for the negligence of an independent contractor, except for the following five recognized exceptions, collectively known as "non-delegable duties": (1) where the contract requires the performance of intrinsically dangerous work; (2) where the principal is by law or contract charged with performing the specific duty; (3) where the act will create a nuisance; (4) where the act to be performed will probably cause injury to others unless due precaution is taken; and (5) where the act to be performed is illegal. Bagley v. Insight Communications Co., 658 N.E.2d 584, 586, 11 I.E.R. Cas. (BNA) 372 (Ind. 1995). An employer of an independent contractor may be subject to liability for personal injuries caused by the employer's failure to exercise reasonable care to employ a competent and careful contractor when one of the five exceptions is applicable. Id. at 587; see also PSI Energy, Inc. v. Roberts, 829 N.E.2d 943, 950-54 (Ind. 2005) (discussing Bagley and the general state of Indiana law with respect to negligent hiring claims in the context of independent contractors).

To establish negligent retention in Indiana, plaintiff must establish that the employer negligently retained an employee that the employer knew was in the habit of misconducting himself in a manner which was dangerous to others. See Levinson v. Citizens Nat'l Bank, 644 N.E.2d 1264, 1269 (Ind. Ct. App. 1994); Frye v. Am. Painting Co., 642 N.E.2d 995, 998 (Ind. Ct. App. 1994) (reversing summary judgment where the employee had history of violence including burglary, theft and arson, employer knew of at least one criminal incident and continued to employ the employee, and employee subsequently burglarized and set fire to customer's home). Indiana does not recognize the tort of negligent supervision. Terrell v. Rowsey, 647 N.E.2d 662, 665 (Ind. Ct. App. 1995); Gossage v. Little Caesar Enters., Inc., 698 F. Supp. 160, 162 (S.D. Ind. 1988).

B. Intentional Infliction of Emotional Distress

Under Indiana law, the tort of intentional infliction of emotional distress is defined as "extreme and outrageous conduct intentionally or recklessly caus[ing] severe emotional distress to another . . . ." Cullison v. Medley, 570 N.E.2d 27, 31 (Ind. 1991); City of Anderson v. Weatherford, 714 N.E.2d 181, 184 (Ind. Ct. App. 1999); Conwell v. Beatty, 667 N.E.2d 768, 776 (Ind. Ct. App. 1996); see also Beauchamp v. City of Noblesville, 320 F.3d 733, 747 (7th Cir. 2003). As a result of the Indiana Supreme Court's decision in Cullison, Indiana recognizes intentional infliction of emotional distress (IIED) as an independent tort, and a predicate or host tort is no longer necessary to assert a separate claim based on intentional infliction. However, "[t]he requirements to prove the tort are 'rigorous.'" Cordell v. Ancilla Domini Sisters, Inc., No. 3:02 CV 0835 AS, 2004 U.S. Dist. LEXIS 26366, at *53 (N.D. Ind. Dec. 13, 2004); see also Bullock-Banks v. Am. Water Works Serv. Co., No. 1:03-cv-01459-DFH-TAB, 2005 U.S. Dist. LEXIS 11775, at *28 (S.D. Ind. May 12, 2005) ("Under Indiana law, a claim for intentional infliction of emotional distress requires evidence that the defendant's action was taken with intent to harm and was so outrageous as to be beyond the bounds of decency."). **In response to a claim that the conduct was outrageous, the defendant may take advantage of the same qualified privilege available to defamation defendants. Williams v. Tharp, 914 N.E.2d 756, 769 (Ind. 2009).** Furthermore, to establish a cognizable claim of intentional infliction of emotional distress plaintiff must show that defendant intended to cause plaintiff emotional harm. See Cullison, 570 N.E.2d at 31 (no intent to cause emotional harm where the defendant was berated, called a "pervert" and implicitly threatened with a gun); Cordell, 2004 U.S. Dist. LEXIS 26366, at *53 (listing the elements of the tort and expressly noting that "[i]t is the intent to harm one emotionally that constitutes the basis for the tort of intentional infliction of emotional distress").

An employee's or agent's "tortious intent will be imputed to an employer that is a legal entity or artificial person [for intentional torts] where either 1) the corporation is the tortfeasor's alter ego or 2) the corporation has substituted its will for that of the individual who committed the tortious acts." Coble v. Joseph Motors, Inc., 695 N.E.2d 129, 134 (Ind. Ct. App. 1998) (affirming summary judgment where there was no evidence of the employer's intent to cause emotional harm to the plaintiff); **Brock v. U.S. Steel Corp., 2:09-CV-00344, 2011 WL 3443954, at *9 (N.D. Ind. Aug. 8, 2011) (a corporation is chargeable with tortious intent when "the individual who committed the tort was acting pursuant to a policy or decision made through the corporation's regular decision-making channels by those with authority to do so.") Moreover, the plaintiff must show that his injury was the intended product of the policy or decision pursuant to which he claims the employee was acting. Id.**

Under the Indiana Tort Claims Act, individual members of a board, committee, commission, authority or other instrumentality of a government entity, who act in their official capacity and within the scope of their employment, may not be individually named as a party in a civil action. See Ind. Code § 34-13-3-5(a); see also Badger v. Greater Clark County Sch., No. 4:03-CV-00101-SEB-WGH, 2005 U.S. Dist. LEXIS 10816, at *7-8 (S.D. Ind. June 1, 2005) (holding that Badger's attempt to hold school board members individually liable for state-law tort claims of defamation and intentional infliction of emotional distress was not permitted by the Indiana Tort Claims Act, which "expressly forecloses liability on the part of the individual board members in their personal capacity in such situations").

C. Interference with Economic Advantage

It is well settled that intentional interference with a contract may be an actionable tort. Bochnowski v. Peoples Fed. Sav. & Loan Ass'n, 571 N.E.2d 282, 284 (Ind. 1991). To maintain an action for tortious interference with a contract, plaintiff must prove five essential elements: 1) the existence of a valid and enforceable contract; 2) knowledge of the contract's existence; 3) that the defendant intentionally induced the alleged breach; 4) absence of justification; and 5) damages proximately caused by the wrongful inducement of the breach. Winkler v. V.G. Reed & Sons, Inc., 638 N.E.2d 1228, 1235 (Ind. 1994); Billmoria Computer Sys. v. Am. Online, Inc., 829 N.E.2d 150, 156 (Ind. Ct. App. 2005); Davis, 2008 U.S. Dist. LEXIS 2865, at *6; White v. Local Union No. 1111, No. 1:03-cv-0815-DFH-TAB, 2005 U.S. Dist. LEXIS 1647, at *34 (S.D. Ind. Jan. 20, 2005). A claim for tortious interference with an employment relationship can be asserted even if the employee is terminable at will. However, the plaintiff must be prepared to show that the defendant interferer acted intentionally and without a legitimate business purpose. White, 2005 U.S. Dist. LEXIS 1647, at *34-35; Bochnowski, 571 N.E.2d at 285. Where a third party's conduct substantially and materially impairs the execution of an employment contract, frustrating the employee's expectations and making performance more burdensome, the inducement of breach element of a claim for tortious interference with a contractual relationship is satisfied. Levee, 729 N.E.2d at 222.

In ascertaining whether a defendant's conduct in intentionally interfering with a contract is warranted, factors to consider are: (1) the nature of the defendant's conduct; (2) the defendant's motive; (3) the interests of the plaintiff with which the defendant's conduct interferes; (4) the interests sought to be advanced by the defendant; (5) the social interests in protecting the freedom of action of the defendant and the contractual interests of the plaintiff; (6) the proximity or remoteness of the defendant's conduct to the interference; and (7) the relations between the parties. Levee v. Beeching, 729 N.E.2d 215, 221 (Ind. Ct. App. 2000). In examining the factors for justification, "[t]he weight to be given each consideration may differ from case to case, but the overriding question is whether the defendant's conduct has been fair and reasonable under the circumstances." Billmoria Computer Sys. v. Am. Online, Inc., 829 N.E.2d 150, 156 (Ind. Ct. App. 2005) (finding the "absence of justification" element "is established only if the interferer acted intentionally, without a legitimate business purpose, and the breach is malicious and exclusively directed the injury and damages of another"). The existence of a legitimate reason for the defendant's actions, therefore, provides the necessary justification to avoid liability. Melton v. Ousley, 925 N.E.2d 430, 441-42 (Ind. Ct. App. 2010) (since the PGA set up a procedure where a member could ask the organization to investigate another member's classification, defendant had the appropriate justification when he asked for just such an investigation).

Indiana also recognizes the tort of tortious interference with a business relationship. The elements of this tort are: (1) the existence of a valid relationship; (2) the defendant's knowledge of the existence of the relationship (3) the defendant's intentional interference with that relationship (4) the absence of justification; and (5) damages resulting from defendant's wrongful interference with the relationship. See Levee v. Beeching, 729 N.E.2d 215, 222-23 (Ind. Ct. App. 2000). The plaintiff must also prove that the defendant acted illegally in achieving its end. See Brazauskas v. Fort Wayne-South Bend Diocese, Inc., 796 N.E.2d 286, 291 (Ind. 2003) (tortious interference with a business relationship requires some independent illegal action); Smith v. Bioment, Inc., No. 3:01-CV-753 PS, 2005 U.S. Dist. LEXIS 5251, at *16 (N.D. Ind. Mar. 24, 2005) (holding that Bioment's interactions with Smith's customers (including defaming him) did not rise to the level of tortious interference, as they met neither the absence of justification nor the illegality of conduct requirements).

D. Prima Facie Tort

The doctrine of a prima facie tort has some recognition in New York, which recognizes a claim for the infliction of intentional harm even though the act resulting in harm is otherwise lawful. However, Indiana rejects this concept. See Frampton v. Cent. Ind. Gas Co., 297 N.E.2d 425 (Ind. 1973); Jones v. Lathrop-Moyer Co., 99 Ind. App. 127, 190 N.E. 883, 885 (Ind. Ct. App. 1934); see also Campbell v. Town of Austin, No. NA 01-222-C H/K, 2004 U.S. Dist. LEXIS 1925 (S.D. Ind. Feb. 9, 2004).

V. OTHER ISSUES

A. Statute of Limitations

Generally, a two-year statute of limitations applies to defamation claims. Ind. Code § 34-11-2-4 (formerly I.C. § 34-1-2-2). Indiana law generally provides that "a cause of action accrues, and thus the statute of limitations begins to run, when the resultant damage of a negligent act is 'susceptible of ascertainment.'" Wehling v. Citizens Nat'l Bank, 586 N.E.2d 840, 842 (Ind. 1992); see also Martin v. Richey, 711 N.E.2d 1273, 1284 (Ind. 1999). Prior to the Wehling decision, Indiana courts had held that the statute of limitations began to run when the defamatory statement was discovered or should have been discovered (at least in the case where the statements were published in a circumstance where they were likely to be kept secret from the injured party). Burks v. Rushmore, 534 N.E.2d 1101, 1004 (Ind. 1989). Now, under Wehling, the trigger arguably is not the discovery of the defamatory statement but when the damage from the defamatory statement is capable of ascertainment. 586 N.E.2d at 842. Nevertheless, the clock will run when litigation on claims arising out of the same actions or events is pending. See Wood v. Marion County Sheriff, No. 1:02-CV-1450 RLY-TAB, 2004 U.S. Dist. LEXIS 27705 (S.D. Ind. Sept. 21, 2004) (barring plaintiff from adding a defamation claim to his preexisting complaint where litigation already has been pending for more than two years).

Pursuant to the Indiana Tort Claims Act, Ind. Code § 34-13-3-3 (formerly § 34-4-16.5-3), a tort claim against a political subdivision is barred unless notice is filed with "the governing body of that political subdivision . . . within 180 days after the loss occurs." Celebration Fireworks, Inc. v. Smith, 727 N.E.2d 450, 451-52 (Ind. 2000). The tort claim notice must be issued, in writing, within 180 days to preserve any potential tort claim against a governmental entity for torts committed by its agencies or employees. Celebration Fireworks, Inc. v. Smith, 682 N.E.2d 569, 571 (Ind. Ct. App. 1997), rev'd on other grounds, 727 N.E.2d 450, 454 (Ind. 2000); Scott v. City of Seymour, 659 N.E.2d 585, 588 (Ind. Ct. App. 1995).

B. Jurisdiction

Under Indiana law, jurisdiction is presumed and need not be alleged. Thus, a challenge to jurisdiction must be established by a preponderance of the evidence unless lack of jurisdiction is apparent on the face of the complaint. Fidelity Fin. Servs., Inc. v. West, 640 N.E.2d 394, 396 (Ind. Ct. App. 1994); Lee v. Goshen Rubber Co., 635 N.E.2d 214, 215 (Ind. Ct. App. 1994). Since Indiana follows the minimum contacts rule, the defendant must establish, in order to meet this burden of proof, that he lacks such minimum contacts with the forum state that the maintenance of a defamation lawsuit in Indiana would offend "traditional notions of fair play and substantial justice." Noble Roman's Inc. v. French Baguette LLC, 684 F. Supp. 2d 1065, 1070 (S.D. Ind. 2010) (citations omitted); Gaus v. County of Wells, 620 F. Supp. 1462 (N.D. Ind. 1985). Such fair play is not offended when a party who enters into a multi-year agreement with an Indiana franchisor is sued by that franchisor in Indiana. Noble Romans, 684 F.Supp. 2d at 1070-71. Consequently, an Indiana-based court has personal jurisdiction over a defamation action concerning allegedly defamatory statements about the Indiana-based franchisor which were made on the franchisee owner's Florida-based website. Id. Even if personal jurisdiction does not exist, a defendant who seeks affirmative relief in the form of summary judgment waives its objections to personal jurisdiction. Glasscock v. Corliss, 823 N.E.2d 748, 755 (Ind. Ct. App. 2005).

In defamation actions where there is no disagreement between the laws of the states involved, the law of the forum state applies. Schaefer v. Newton, 868 F. Supp. 246, 252, 22 Media L. Rep. 2239 (S.D. Ind. 1994). When there is a dispute over choice of law, however, Indiana applies a modified version of the "most significant contacts" choice of law test. Containment Tech. Group v. American Soc'y of Health Sys. Pharmacists, No. 1:07-cv-0997-DFH-TAB, 2009 WL 838549, at * 6 (S.D. Ind. Mar. 26, 2008) (disagreement over whether to apply Indiana's or Maryland's anti-SLAPP statute). Where the alleged defamation occurred in a published report that reached readers in many states, the court will typically look to the state where the injury to the plaintiff's reputation occurred. Id. at *7, *8 ("Since the alleged injury here would have been felt most severely in Indiana, Indiana law governs the dispute."). Indiana courts will not apply the theory of depecage (by which different states' laws may be applied to different issues, claims, and defenses in the same case) when ruling on choice of law issues. Id. at *8 (court found that "[b]ecause the defamation claim is properly heard under Indiana law, the anti-SLAPP defense under Indiana law also applies" and thus declined to apply Indiana law to the defamation claim and Maryland law to the anti-SLAPP defense.)

With respect to cases raising both state and federal claims, federal courts will often exercise supplemental jurisdiction over state-law tort claims, including defamation. See, e.g., Mossman v. Dental Enters., No. 3:05-CV-007 RM, 2005 U.S. Dist. LEXIS 8656 (N.D. Ind. May 9, 2005) (granting supplemental jurisdiction for plaintiff's Title VII and state defamation claims). Certain federal statutes, however, may pre-empt state law defamation claims. Dixon v. Borgarner Diversified Transmission Prods., Inc., No. 1:03-cv-00945-SEB-VSS, 2005 U.S. Dist. LEXIS 4273 (S.D. Ind. Mar. 15, 2005) (discussing the circumstances under which section 301 of the federal Labor Management Relations Act preempts state law tort claims); White v. Local Union No. 1111, No. 1:03-cv-0815-DFH-TAB, 2005 U.S. Dist. LEXIS 1647, at *32 (S.D. Ind. Jan. 20, 2005) (finding that plaintiff's tortious interference claim was not preempted by section 301 of the federal Labor Management Relations Act); Purdue Employees, Fed. Credit Union v. Van Houten, No. 4:08-CV-45-AS-APR, 2008 U.S. Dist. LEXIS 73258, at *11 (N.D. Ind. Sept. 24, 2008) ("[I]n all instances not involving intent to injure consumers, the [Fair Credit Reporting Act] preempts state law defamation claims."). State statutes have also been held to divest courts of subject matter jurisdiction over defamation claims. Popovich v. Danielson, 896 N.E.2d 1196, 1203 (Ind. Ct. App. 2008) (defamation claim based on statements made in medical records dismissed for failure to follow Medical Malpractice Act procedures where determining whether statements made in medical records are false required questioning a doctor's "exercise of professional expertise, skill, or judgment").

C. Workers' Compensation Exclusivity

Indiana's Workers' Compensation Act does not bar a defamation claim when a plaintiff makes no mention of any physical injury, disability, or impairment. Hart v. Webster, 894 N.E.2d 1032, 1037 (Ind. Ct. App. 2008) (defamation claim was dismissed in error when plaintiff claimed damages to "personal and business reputation, humiliation, and emotional injuries").

D. Pleading Requirements

Ind. Code §§ 34-15-1-1 and -2 set out the rules of pleading libel and slander in Indiana. The Indiana Supreme Court made clear in Trail v. Boys & Girls Clubs of N.W. Indiana, 845 N.E.2d 130 (Ind. 2006) that a plaintiff desiring to withstand a 12(b)(6) motion to dismiss must include the allegedly defamatory statement in its judicial complaint. Mere allegations regarding the substance or effect of the defamatory words, therefore, are not sufficient. Trail, 845 N.E.2d at 136-138 (holding that "permitting defamation actions to proceed without the inclusion of the alleged statement would sanction claims brought by individuals who allege nothing more than that someone must have said something defamatory about them, or else they would not have been terminated or unable to secure new employment while many of these individuals might have an actual grievance, merely making such an accusation does not establish a claim sufficiently to permit courts to determine its legal legitimacy"); Branaman v. Hinkle, 137 Ind. 496, 37 N.E. 546 (1894); Newman v. Jewish Community Center Ass'n of Indianapolis, Inc., 875 N.E.2d 729, 735-36, 742 (Ind. Ct. App. 2007) (complaint must identify both the specific defamatory statement and the speaker); Purdue Employees, Fed. Credit Union v. Van Houten, No. 4:08-CV-45-AS-APR, 2008 U.S. Dist. LEXIS 73258, at *13 (N.D. Ind. Sept. 24, 2008) ("[l]eaving this Court to guess the content of [the defendant's] statements is not sufficient to survive a motion to dismiss"); Cowgill v. Whitewater Publ'g, No. 1:08-cv-0258-JMS-DFH, 2008 U.S. Dist. LEXIS 42235, at *3-5 (S.D. Ind. May 29, 2008) (plaintiff who only alleged that false and misleading statements were made about her and communicated to others failed to plead with the required particularity); Farr v. St. Francis Hosp. & Health Ctr., No. 1:06-cv-779 SEB-JMS, 2007 U.S. Dist. LEXIS 72532 at *11 (S.D. Ind. Sept. 26 2007) (complaint was deficient as it failed to reference "the number of speakers or statements made, to whom the statements were made, or when or in what context the statements were made."); Assocs. Fin. Servs. Co. v. Bowman, Heintz, Boscia & Vician, No. IP 99-1725-C M/S, 2004 U.S. Dist. LEXIS 6520 (S.D. Ind. March 31, 2004) (plaintiff "must plead the words used" in order to state a claim for defamation). A plaintiff who fails to properly plead a cognizable claim for defamation in the complaint may not then reference specific facts for the first time in his response brief in opposition to summary judgment. Zisis v. St. Joseph Township, 979 F. Supp. 806, 815 (N.D. Ind. 1997) (defendants entitled to summary judgment on claim of defamation to the extent that it existed).

Not all federal courts, however, follow Indiana's specific pleading requirements. See U.S. Rail Corp. v. Sturch, No. 1:08-cv-585-WTL-DML, 2009 WL 564235, at *3 (S.D. Ind. Mar. 5, 2009) ("While notice pleading is sufficient for a claim of defamation, and thus the Plaintiffs were not necessarily required to set out the 'who, what, when, and where' of the alleged defamatory statements, they were required to provide enough information to give the Defendants fair notice of what statements the defamation claim refers to."); Magarl, L.L.C. v. Crane Co., No. IP 02-0478-C-T/L, 1:03-CV-01255-JDT-TWL, 2004 U.S. Dist. LEXIS 24283 (S.D. Ind. Sept. 29, 2004) (rejecting the proposition that a complaint for defamation must plead the specified words alleged to be defamatory, and further rejecting argument that the complaint must allege the time and the place of the defamation; "even if Indiana has a heightened pleading standard for defamation claims, Watts' [counter-]claim is brought in federal court where notice pleading applies," and "federal judges are forbidden to supplement federal rules by requiring heightened pleading claims not listed in Rule 9"). It is unclear what, if any effect, the Supreme Court's decision in Iqbal will have on these holdings. Ashcroft v. Iqbal, 129 S. Ct. 1937, 173 L.E.2d 868 (2009).

Truth as a defense is preserved only when affirmatively pled. Elliott v. Roach, 409 N.E. 2d 661, 681, 78 Ind. Dec. 50 (Ind. Ct. App. 1980); Ind. Code § 34-15-1-2 (2005). See I.B.1, supra.

SURVEY OF INDIANA EMPLOYMENT PRIVACY LAW

Jeffery M. Mallamad and Christopher R. Taylor
Bingham Greenebaum Doll LLP
2700 Market Tower
10 West Market Street
Indianapolis, Indiana 46204
Telephone: (317) 635-8900; Facsimile: (317) 236-9907

(With Developments Reported Through **November 1, 2012**)

GENERAL COMMENTS

None.

SIGNIFICANT DEVELOPMENTS SINCE THE 2012 *SURVEY*

None.

I. GENERAL LAW OF PRIVACY

A. Legal Basis of Privacy Claims

1. ***Constitutional Law.*** Article I, Section 11 of the Indiana Constitution provides that citizens have the right "to be secure in their persons, houses, papers, and effects, against unreasonable search or seizure . . . and no warrant shall issue, but upon probable cause, supported by oath or affirmation, and particularly describing the place to be searched and the person or thing to be seized." This language is nearly identical to the Fourth Amendment's search and seizure provision. The Indiana Supreme Court, however, has interpreted Article I, Section 11 as providing an independent prohibition against unreasonable searches and seizures. Peterson v. State, 674 N.E.2d 528, 533 (Ind. 1996). Moreover, Indiana's search and seizure analysis differs from federal Fourth Amendment analysis in that Indiana employs a one-part "reasonableness" inquiry; the reasonableness of the official act or behavior determines whether there has been a violation under the Indiana Constitution. Id.; Litchfield v. State, 824 N.E.2d 356, 360 (Ind. 2005) (the totality of the circumstances requires consideration of both the degree of intrusion into the subject's ordinary activities and the basis upon which the government actor selected the subject of the search). Persons who have ownership, control, possession, or interest in either the premises searched or the property seized have standing under this Article. Peterson, 674 N.E.2d at 534. A public employer who executes an unreasonable search and seizure of an employee or the employee's property may be liable under this section.

Article I, Section 11 protects persons from official, but not private, acts. Moran v. State, 644 N.E.2d 536, 540 (Ind. 1994). Searches that are performed pursuant to Article I, Section 11 are deemed official and usually require a warrant to be reasonable. This is not, however, a hard and fast rule. See Linke v. Northwestern School Corp., 763 N.E.2d 972, 977-79 (Ind. 2002) (Article I, Section 11 search (drug testing) of students by administrators was constitutional and did not require individualized suspicion but consideration of the totality of the circumstances balancing the privacy interests of the students against the school corporation's interests; law enforcement functions in an adversarial manner, but school authorities and pupils have a non-adversarial commonality of interest). Finally, only actions taken by public employers (not private employers) may be declared unlawful under Article I, Section 11. Knotts v. State, 187 N.E.2d 571, 574 (Ind. 1963).

Neither the Indiana Supreme Court nor the Indiana Court of Appeals has specifically addressed whether a party may sue for damages resulting from a violation of Article I, Section 11, but based on the decision in Cantrell v. Morris, 849 N.E.2d 488, 492 (Ind. 2006), it is doubtful such a private right of action would be recognized. In Cantrell, the Indiana Supreme Court held that a terminated public employee has no private right of action for damages under Article I, Section 9 of the Indiana Constitution, reasoning that there is no need to create a separate cause of action under the Indiana Constitution where existing tort law protects the constitutional right sought to be vindicated. Id. Subsequent Indiana federal courts have explicitly extended the Cantrell holding to claims under Article I, Section 11. See, e.g. Branson v. Newburgh Police Dep't, 849 F.Supp.2d 802, 812 (S.D. Ind. 2011).

There is no state equivalent to 42 U.S.C. § 1983 or Bivens v. Six Unknown Named Agents of Federal Bureau of Narcotics, 403 U.S. 388 (1971). Further, Indiana does not recognize common law claims against private employers arising directly under the Indiana Constitution. See Bailey v. Washington Theatre Co., 34 N.E.2d 17, 19-20 (Ind. 1941).

Article I, Section 10 of the Indiana Constitution provides: "In all prosecutions for libel, the truth of the matters alleged to be libellous [*sic*] may be given in justification." Generally, if the substance of the alleged libel can be proven true there can be no liability. Palmer v. Adams, 36 N.E. 695, 695 (Ind. 1894); Branham v. Celadon Trucking Servs.,

Inc., 744 N.E.2d 514, 522 (Ind. Ct. App. 2001) (noting that true statements never give rise to liability for defamation), transfer denied, 753 N.E.2d 16 (Ind. 2001). This constitutional provision has been cited as potentially precluding a public disclosure of private facts invasion of privacy claim. Doe v. Methodist Hosp., 690 N.E.2d 681, 693 (Ind. 1997).

In 2005, the Indiana Supreme Court vacated a Court of Appeals decision that held privacy is a core state constitutional right. Clinic for Women, Inc. v. Brizzi, 837 N.E. 2d 973 (Ind. 2005). The court held that it was unnecessary to determine whether there is any right to privacy or abortion provided or protected by Indiana's Constitution because the plaintiffs failed to overcome their initial burden in challenging the facial validity of the statute in question, and the statute did not impermissibly impinge upon any right to privacy or right to abortion that might exist. Id. at 978.

2. ***Statutory Law.*** It is a Class A misdemeanor under Indiana Code § 35-46-1-15.1 to violate certain court orders (e.g., protective orders, no-contact orders, temporary restraining orders) and a Class D felony if there has been a prior violation of the statute.

3. ***Common Law.*** Indiana recognizes the tort of invasion of privacy. See generally Doe v. Methodist Hosp., 690 N.E.2d 681 (Ind. 1997); Cullison v. Medley, 570 N.E.2d 27 (Ind. 1991); State ex rel. Mavity v. Tyndall, 66 N.E.2d 755 (Ind. 1946). The tort is similar to defamation, but reaches different interests. Newman v. Jewish Cmty. Ctr. Ass'n, 875 N.E.2d 729, 743 (Ind. App. 2007). Defamation reaches injury to reputation, while privacy actions involve injuries to emotions and mental suffering. Id. The general tort of invasion of privacy is comprised of four distinct sub-torts: (1) intrusion upon seclusion; (2) appropriation of likeness; (3) public disclosure of private facts; and (4) false-light publicity. Id. at 736; Munsell v. Hambright, 776 N.E.2d 1272, 1282 (Ind. App. 2002). However, the Indiana Supreme Court has ruled, in a plurality opinion, that a tort claim for invasion of privacy based on public disclosure of private facts is not recognized in Indiana. Doe, 690 N.E.2d at 693 (per Shepard, C.J., with one Justice concurring and three Justices concurring in the result). See also Felsher v. Univ. of Evansville, 755 N.E.2d 589, 593 (Ind. 2001) (acknowledging rejection of public disclosure branch of invasion of privacy tort); Munsell, 776 N.E.2d at 1282 ("there is some uncertainty with regard to whether all of the sub-torts are recognized under Indiana law"); Greenawalt v. Indiana Dept. of Corrections, 397 F.3d 587, 591 (7th Cir. 2005) (Indiana has thus far refused to recognize the public disclosure of private information branch of the invasion of privacy tort). In addition, corporations cannot maintain actions for invasion of privacy. Felsher, 755 N.E.2d at 594 (university whose name and abbreviation was used by a professor for website and e-mail addresses did not have an appropriation of a name or likeness claim against the professor).

B. Causes of Action

1. ***Misappropriation/Right of Publicity.*** The tort of invasion of privacy by misappropriation of name or likeness occurs where the defendant appropriates the plaintiff's name or likeness for the defendant's benefit or advantage. Creel v. I.C.E. & Assocs., Inc., 771 N.E.2d 1276, 1280 n.3 (Ind. App. 2002). The phrase "name or likeness" is commonly used in the context of misappropriation, and embraces the concept of a person's character, which is legally protected against appropriation by another for his or her own use or benefit. Felsher, 755 N.E.2d at 593-94. However, a person who enters a business or calling which gives the public a legitimate interest in his character, activities, and affairs may waive his or her right of privacy with respect to appropriation of his or her image. Continental Optical Co. v. Reed, 86 N.E.2d 306, 309 (Ind. App. 1949) Furthermore, certain photographs that are considered newsworthy or of public interest may receive First Amendment protection that exempts the user of those photographs from liability for the tort of appropriation. Time, Inc. v. Sand Creek Partners, L.P., 825 F. Supp. 210, 212 (S.D. Ind. 1993) (newsworthiness of public concert photographs of a well-known musician and a popular actress outweighed any privacy rights the musician or actress may have had in those photographs).

By statute, Indiana also protects the right of publicity. Ind. Code § 32-6-1-1, et seq. "Right of publicity" means a personality's property interest in the personality's name, voice, signature, photograph, image, likeness, distinctive appearance, gesture, or mannerism. Ind. Code § 32-36-1-7. A person may not use an aspect of a personality's right of publicity for a commercial purpose during the personality's lifetime or for 100 years after the date of the personality's death without having obtained previous written consent from a person. Ind. Code § 32-36-1-8(a).

2. ***False Light.*** One who gives publicity to a matter concerning another that places the other before the public in a false light is subject to liability to the other for invasion of his or her privacy if (a) the false light in which the other was placed would be highly offensive to a reasonable person, and (b) the actor had knowledge of or acted in reckless disregard as to the falsity of the publicized matter and the false light in which the other would be placed. Lovings v. Thomas, 805 N.E.2d 442, 446 (Ind. App. 2004) (affirming summary judgment for defendant where defendant merely informed manager of convention that plaintiff was "causing a problem up by our booth, and I would like him removed"; comment was not communicated to public at large or even to substantial number of people). "Publicity," for purposes of an invasion of privacy claim regarding false-light publicity, occurs when the matter is made public, by communicating it to the public at large, or to so many persons that the matter must be regarded as substantially certain to become one of public knowledge. Id. The difference is not one of means of communication, which may be oral, written, or by any other means, but it is one of a

communication that reaches, or is sure to reach, the public. Id. Since the tort of false light invasion of privacy was first recognized in Indiana in the case of State ex rel. Mavity v. Tyndall, 66 N.E.2d 755 (Ind. 1946), however, plaintiffs have not succeeded on the claim in any reported cases. See, e.g. Sims v. Humane Soc'y of St. Joseph County, 758 F.Supp.2d 737, 748-49 (N.D. Ind. 2010) (false light claim dismissed for failure to state a claim where allegedly false information was only communicated to one or two people, not the public at large); Collins v. Purdue Univ., 703 F.Supp.2d 862, 876-77 (N.D. Ind. 2010) (false light claim dismissed on motion for judgment on the pleadings where newspaper published no false information about plaintiff); Miller v. Javitch, Block & Rathbone, LLP, 397 F. Supp. 2d 991, 1005-06 (N.D. Ind. 2005); Branham v. Celadon Trucking Services, Inc., 744 N.E.2d 514, 524-25 (Ind. App. 2001); Furno v. Citizens Ins. Co., 590 N.E.2d 1137, 1141 (Ind. App. 1992); Near East Side Community Org. v. Hair, 555 N.E.2d 1324, 1335 (Ind. App. 1990).

3. ***Publication of Private Facts.*** "Public disclosure of private facts" occurs when a person gives publicity to a matter that concerns the private life of another, a matter that would be highly offensive to a reasonable person, and that is not of legitimate public concern. Munsell v. Hambright, 776 N.E.2d 1272, 1282 (Ind. App. 2002). A communication to a single person or to a or to a small group of persons is not actionable because the publicity element requires communication to the public at large or to so many persons that the matter is substantially certain to become one of public knowledge. Id.

As stated above, however, the Indiana Supreme Court has suggested, in a plurality opinion, that a tort claim for invasion of privacy based on public disclosure of private facts is not recognized in Indiana. Doe v. Methodist Hosp., 690 N.E.2d 681, 693 (Ind. 1997) (per Shepard, C.J., with one Justice concurring and three Justices concurring in the result); see also Felsher v. Univ. of Evansville, 755 N.E.2d 589, 593 (Ind. 2001) (acknowledging rejection of public disclosure branch of invasion of privacy tort); Greenawalt v. Indiana Dept. of Corrections, 397 F.3d 587, 591 (7th Cir. 2005) (Indiana has thus far refused to recognize the public disclosure of private information branch of the invasion of privacy tort).

4. ***Intrusion.*** When the invasion of a plaintiff's right to privacy takes the form of intrusion, a plaintiff must demonstrate that there was an intrusion upon his or her physical solitude or seclusion, as by invading his or her home or other quarters, or conducting an illegal search. Munsell, 776 N.E.2d at 1283; Creel v. I.C.E. & Assocs., Inc., 771 N.E.2d 1276, 1280 (Ind. App. 2002); Branham, 744 N.E.2d at 524 (plaintiff employee who was photographed while sleeping in public break room as another employee posed next to him in underwear did not have a claim for intrusion because incident took place in a setting open to all employees). To rise to the level of tortious conduct, the intrusion must be something which would be offensive or objectionable to a reasonable person. Creel, 771 N.E.2d at 1280. Indiana courts have narrowly defined the tort of invasion of privacy by intrusion. In Cullison v. Medley, 570 N.E.2d 27, 31 (Ind. 1991), the Indiana Supreme Court stated that the tort requires intrusion into the plaintiff's private "physical" space. There have been no cases in Indiana in which a claim of intrusion was proven without physical contact or invasion of the plaintiff's physical space such as the plaintiff's home. See, e.g., Curry v. Whitaker, 943 N.E.2d 354, 358-59 (Ind. App. 2011) (homeowners' intrusion claim failed where neighbors' surveillance cameras were only aimed at the parties' common yard and the exterior of homeowners' property, and not at the interior of homeowners' home); Ledbetter v. Ross, 725 N.E.2d 120, 123 (Ind. App. 2000) (holding that a single telephone call, involving no threats or abusive language, cannot as a matter of law be the basis for the tort of invasion of privacy by intrusion); Terrell v. Rowsey, 647 N.E.2d 662, 667 (Ind. App. 1995) (determining that there was no actionable intrusion where defendant opened the plaintiff's car door while plaintiff sat in the car, reached behind the driver's seat, and grabbed an empty beer bottle, without making physical contact with the plaintiff); Cullison v. Medley, 570 N.E.2d 27, 31 (Ind. 1991) (concluding that, while invasion of the plaintiff's home could constitute a claim for invasion of privacy, harassment of the plaintiff in a restaurant or on the public street outside his home could not). An intrusion claim may be waived by the plaintiff's conduct. Moffett v. Gene B. Glick Co., 621 F. Supp. 244, 283 (N.D. Ind. 1985) (holding that intrusion claim based on racial slurs directed at employee was waived when the employee discussed the employee's interracial relationship at work thus making what was formerly private a topic of office conversation), overruled on other grounds by Reeder-Baker v. Lincoln Nat'l Corp., 644 F. Supp. 983 (N.D. Ind. 1986).

C. Other Privacy-related Actions

1. *Intentional Infliction of Emotional Distress.*

a. **Generally**. The tort of intentional infliction of emotional distress was first recognized as a separate cause of action without the need for an accompanying tort in Cullison v. Medley, 570 N.E.2d 27 (Ind. 1991). In Cullison, the Indiana Supreme Court defined the tort as occurring where "one who by extreme and outrageous conduct intentionally or recklessly causes severe emotional distress to another." Lindsey v. DeGroot, 898 N.E.2d 1251, 1264 (Ind. App. 2009). The elements of the tort, then, are that the defendant: (1) engages in extreme and outrageous conduct; (2) which intentionally or recklessly; (3) causes; (4) severe emotional distress to another. Id. The requirements to prove the tort are rigorous. Id. As noted in many Indiana state and federal cases, conduct is extreme and outrageous:

> only where the conduct has been so outrageous in character, and so extreme in degree, as to go beyond all possible bounds of decency, and to be regarded as atrocious, and utterly intolerable in a civilized community. Generally, the case is one in which the recitation of the facts to an average member of the community would arouse his resentment against the actor, and lead him to exclaim, "Outrageous!"

Conwell v. Beatty, 667 N.E.2d 768, 777 (Ind. App. 1996) (quoting Restatement (Second) of Torts § 46 (1965)). "The law does not provide a remedy for every annoyance that occurs in everyday life. Many things which are distressing or may be lacking in propriety or good taste are not actionable." Branham v. Celadon Trucking Servs., Inc., 744 N.E.2d 514, 518 (Ind. App. 2001). Intentional infliction of emotional distress is only found "where conduct exceeds all bounds usually tolerated by a decent society and causes mental distress of a very serious kind." Lachenman v. Stice, 838 N.E.2d 451, 457 (Ind. App. 2005).

What constitutes "extreme and outrageous" conduct depends, in part, upon prevailing cultural norms and values. Bradley v. Hall, 720 N.E.2d 747, 753 (Ind. App. 1999). But in the appropriate case, the question of whether the defendant's conduct was extreme and outrageous can be decided as a matter of law. See, e.g., Haegert v. McMullan, 953 N.E.2d 1223, 1235-36 (Ind. App. 2011) (no outrageous conduct where supervisory professor filed sexual harassment complaint against subordinate professor in accordance with her responsibilities and because she believed the university's zero tolerance policy had been violated); York v. Frederick, 947 N.E.2d 969, 976 (Ind. App. 2011) (funeral home's conduct in forcing casket into a vault that was too small, and in burying vault even though it could not be properly sealed, did not constitute outrageous conduct, as required to establish a claim for intentional infliction of emotional distress); Keri v. Bd. of Trustees of Purdue Univ., 458 F.3d 620, 651 (7th Cir. 2006) (no extreme and outrageous conduct where university terminated professor's employment after investigating reports of inappropriate behavior with his students and unsatisfactory teaching and determining those reports were credible); Lachenman, 838 N.E.2d at 457 (no extreme and outrageous conduct where defendant failed to control a dog that attacked and killed plaintiff's dog); but cf. Tucker v. Roman Catholic Diocese of Lafayette, Indiana, 837 N.E.2d 596, 602 (Ind. App. 2005) (Catholic priest's molestation of child is extreme and outrageous conduct); Bradley, 720 N.E.2d at 753 (fact issue existed as to whether supervisor engaged in extreme and outrageous conduct by allegedly shouting at employee, criticizing her work in front of other employees, inquiring about her menopause and whether her husband was sexually impotent because of his diabetes, and misrepresenting employer's intentions regarding eliminating her position).

For purposes of an intentional infliction of emotional distress claim, a defendant acts "intentionally" when his specific intent is to cause emotional distress or when he is substantially certain that his acts will cause emotional distress. Bradley v. Hall, 720 N.E.2d 747, 752 n.6 (Ind. App. 1999). A defendant acts "recklessly" if he acts in deliberate disregard of a high degree of probability that the emotional distress will follow. Id.

b. **Specific to Employers**. Under traditional agency law, employers generally are not liable for the intentional torts of their employees because such intentional torts are considered outside the scope of employment. Baker v. Westinghouse Elec. Corp., 637 N.E.2d 1271, 1275 (Ind. 1994) Accordingly, Indiana courts have consistently rejected attempts by employees to hold employers vicariously liable for the intentional torts of supervisors, managers, or coworkers. Id.; Foshee v. Shoney's Inc., 637 N.E.2d 1277, 1281 (Ind. 1994); Perry v. Stitzer Buick GMC, Inc., 637 N.E.2d 1282, 1287 (Ind. 1994); Eichstadt v. Frisch's Restaurants, Inc., 879 N.E.2d 1207, ___ (Ind. App. 2008). The tort of intentional infliction of emotional distress is no exception. Holbrook v. Lobdell-Emery Mfg. Co., 219 F.3d 598, 600-02 (7th Cir. 2000).

Before an injury can be said to have been intended by an employer, two requirements must be met. Eichstadt, 879 N.E.2d at 1210. First, the employer itself—and not one of the employer's employees—must have harbored the intent. Id. Second, the employer must have intended the injury or had actual knowledge that an injury was certain to occur. Id. at 1210-11. Tortious intent will be imputed to an employer that is a legal entity where either (1) the legal entity is the tortfeasor's alter ego, or (2) the legal entity has substituted its will for that of the tortfeasor. Id. at 1211. To prevail on an alter ego theory, the employee must show that both ownership and control of the employer are in the tortfeasor's hands. Id. Under the substitution of will theory, an employer is chargeable with tortious intent when the tortfeasor was acting pursuant to a policy or decision made through the employer's regular decision-making channels by those with the authority to do so, and injury to the employee must be shown to have been the intended product of the policy or decision at issue. Id.

2. ***Interference with Prospective Economic Advantage.*** Indiana recognizes the tort of interference with contract consisting of the following elements: existence of a valid and enforceable contract; defendant's knowledge of the contract; defendant's intentional inducement of breach of contract; the absence of justification; and damages resulting from defendant's wrongful inducement of the breach. Winkler v. V.G. Reed & Sons, 638 N.E.2d 1228, 1235 (Ind. 1994). This cause of action has been used by business competitors in situations where one company has interfered with the contracts of another or where a former employee has been hired and uses the knowledge he or she gained from a previous employer to

attempt to gain the previous employer's business. The action may be maintained in an at-will relationship. Bochnowski v. Peoples Fed. Sav. & Loan Ass'n, 571 N.E.2d 282 (Ind. 1991).

The elements of a related but separate claim, tortious interference with a business relationship, are: (1) the existence of a valid relationship, (2) the defendant's knowledge of that relationship, (3) intentional interference with that relationship, (4) illegal conduct by the defendant, (5) lack of justification, and (6) damage caused by the interference. Felsher v. Univ. of Evansville, 755 N.E. 2d 589, 598 n.21 (Ind. 2001); Levee v. Beeching, 729 N.E.2d 215, 222 (Ind. Ct. App. 2000) (holding that illegal conduct must be shown but a valid contract need not exist).

3. ***Prima Facie Tort.*** Indiana does not recognize a cause of action for prima facie tort. Soltes v. School City of East Chicago, 344 N.E.2d 865, 867 n. 2 (Ind. App. 1976); Campbell v. Town of Austin, 2004 U.S. Dist. LEXIS 1925, *24 (S.D. Ind. February 9, 2004).

II. EMPLOYER TESTING OF EMPLOYEES

Employees challenging an employer's testing program often bring a claim based on the Fourth Amendment. The constitutional restraints, however, apply to nongovernmental entities only if there is a sufficient governmental nexus. Shelley v. Kraemer, 334 U.S. 1 (1948). This governmental nexus can be satisfied where the private entity "entangles the government by using a governmental agency as part of its testing program, where the private entity is performing a governmental function, or where the entity's actions are so highly regulated that its actions are essentially state-compelled. Leland B. Cross, Jr. & Douglas C. Haney, Legal Issues Involved in Private Sector Medical Testing of Job Applicants and Employees, 20 Ind. L. Rev. 517, 519 (1987).

Though not liable under the Fourth Amendment, a private employer may be subjected to claims under common law for invasion of privacy, intentional infliction of emotional distress, assault and battery, or false arrest or imprisonment when a mandatory medical testing program is instituted. Cross, supra at 521-22. A testing program which restricts testing to applicants who have received a conditional offer of employment and current employees in specific contexts that provide a reasonable basis for testing, such as for jobs requiring heavy lifting or other work-related matters, are resistant to liability. Id. Further, because employee testing affects the terms and conditions of employment, the testing described in the following sections may be subject to collective bargaining for employees represented by a union. See Colgate-Palmolive Co., 323 N.L.R.B. 515 (1997) (installation of surveillance cameras was found to be tantamount to physical examinations, drug/alcohol testing requirements, and polygraph testing, all of which the Board has found to be mandatory subjects of bargaining).

A. Psychological or Personality Testing

1. ***Common Law and Statutes.*** No Indiana statute specifically regulates the use of psychological or personality tests on employees, nor has the use of such tests been the subject of a reported decision by an Indiana state court. Because certain types of psychological tests may be considered medical examinations, their use by employers may be limited by the Americans with Disabilities Act (ADA), 42 U.S.C. § 12101 et seq. In general, a psychological examination is medical for purposes of the ADA if it would provide evidence that would lead to identifying a mental disorder or impairment. See Equal Employment Opportunity Commission, Enforcement Guidance: Disability-related Inquiries and Medical Examinations Under the Americans with Disabilities Act (ADA) (July 27, 2000). In contrast, tests designed to measure only such things as honesty, tastes, and habits are not medical. Id.

Psychological and personality tests that attempt to gauge an applicant's emotional stability and opinions regarding such areas as sex, family life, religion, racial attitudes, and ideology seek information of a highly private nature may give rise to state law privacy related claims. In Greenawalt v. Indiana Dept. of Corrections, 397 F.3d 587 (7th Cir. 2005), the Seventh Circuit rejected a Fourth Amendment unreasonable search claim by an employee of the Indiana Department of Corrections who was required to submit to a psychological examination to keep her job. In doing so, however, the court noted that states are free to protect privacy more comprehensively than the Fourth Amendment commands and identified several potential Indiana state law privacy claims the employee might be able to bring. The court was clear, however, that the Fourth Amendment does not expand accordion-like to fill what may be a gap in the privacy law of a particular state. Id. at 591-92 (alternatively suggesting that the due process clause of the Fifth and Fourteenth Amendments might protect a liberty interest in nondisclosure of private information based on Whalen v. Roe, 429 U.S. 589, 600 (1977)).

B. Drug Testing

1. ***Common Law and Statutes.*** A 1992 Seventh Circuit decision concurred with other circuits that federal rather than state law governs employees regardless of whether the collective bargaining agreement expressly mentioned drug tests. In re Amoco Petroleum Additives Co., 964 F.2d 706, 710 (7th Cir. 1992).

2. ***Private Employers.*** Indiana's Controlled Substances Act prohibits the possession and distribution of certain drugs. There are no Indiana statutes, however, specifically regulating drug testing for private employees. Indiana's Employment Discrimination Against Disabled Persons Act, Indiana Code § 22-9-5 et seq., does not prohibit testing to determine the illegal use of drugs and gives an employer the right to prohibit the illegal use of drugs and alcohol at work. See Ind. Code § 22-9-5-6 and -24. The Act also requires that employees not be under the influence of drugs or alcohol at the workplace and that employees' behavior conform to the requirements of the Drug-Free Workplace Act of 1988. The Act neither prohibits nor encourages employers under the jurisdiction of the Department of Transportation to conduct the drug testing of employees or applicants whose position involves safety sensitive duties. See Atkins v. Board of Sch. Comm'rs, 830 F. Supp. 1169, 1175-77 (S.D. Ind. 1993) (holding that school bus drivers can be required to submit to physical examinations, including drug tests, at the request of their employer regardless of whether employer has a suspicion of drug or alcohol use where the employment contract incorporates Indiana Code § 22-9.1-3-4 along with the requirement providing for unscheduled physical exams).

Generally, drug testing on reasonable suspicion has been upheld in virtually all jurisdictions. Under Indiana Code § 22-9-5-6, it is not a violation for an employer to adopt or administer reasonable policies, including drug testing, to ensure that employees who have either successfully completed or are currently participating in a drug rehabilitation program are not using illegal drugs. Again, this section does not encourage, prohibit, or authorize testing for the illegal use of drugs.

There is no invasion of a Constitutional right of privacy by a private employer where an employee has (1) notice of the employer's drug testing policy, (2) there was no state action involved, and (3) the policy supported the removal of drug abusers from the private sector workplace. Butler v. Review Bd. of the Ind. Dep't of Employment & Training Servs., 633 N.E.2d 310, 313 (Ind. App. 1994). Where a state prosecutor receives a tip that an employee has tested positive on an employer-mandated drug test, a prosecutor acting without a grand jury must first seek leave of court before issuing a subpoena duces tecum to a third party for the production of the results of the drug test. Oman v. Indiana, 737 N.E.2d 1131, 1146-47 (Ind. 2000) (holding that employer drug test may be used in a criminal prosecution against the employee only if obtained through a valid legal process externally initiated from the employment setting). An employee positive test result cannot form the sole relevant initial evidence for charging criminal conduct. Id.; see also State v. Gunn, 741 N.E.2d 787 (Ind. App. 2001).

When a collective bargaining agreement exists, federal law may preempt claims related to drug-testing. Jobes v. Tokheim Corp., 657 N.E.2d 145, 146, 149 (Ind. App. 1995) (preempting defamation and invasion of privacy action against former employer who terminated employee for testing positive for illegal drugs based on drug-test administered after accident).

3. ***Public Employers.*** Public employees in Indiana may be subject to drug testing if it is reasonable, the need is compelling, and a testing policy is in existence before any actual testing takes place. Miller v. Vanderburgh County, 610 N.E.2d 858, 863 n.4 (Ind. App. 1993); see also Skinner v. Railway Labor Executives' Ass'n, 489 U.S. 602 (1989) (testing program justified by health and safety concerns); Aguilera v. City of East Chicago, 768 N.E.2d 978, 985-86 (Ind. App. 2002) (citing Oman and upholding a city requirement that an employee submit to mandatory testing as a condition of continued employment after a random test of that employee tested positive for cocaine). The government may depart from the usual warrant and probable cause requirements of the Fourth Amendment when the affected employees are engaged in safety sensitive tasks. Aguilera, 768 N.E.2d at 985.

Despite the constitutionality of drug tests administered to public employees, the results of a compulsory drug test obtained pursuant to a government employer's work place drug testing policy may not be used as evidence in the subsequent criminal prosecution of the employee. State v. Gunn, 735 N.E.2d 304, 305 (Ind. 2000), aff'd and explained on reh'g, 741 N.E.2d 787 (Ind. App. 2001). The use of that policy to pursue criminal prosecutions against employees is a violation of those employees' Fourth Amendment rights absent a special need other than crime detection that justifies the Fourth Amendment intrusion. Id. at 307-08.

C. Medical Testing

1. ***Common Law and Statutes.*** Indiana's Employment Discrimination Against Disabled Persons Act, Indiana Code § 22-9-5-20, prohibits an employer, employment agency, or labor organization with six or more employees from conducting a medical examination or making inquiries of a job applicant as to whether the applicant is an individual with a disability or as to the nature or severity of a disability. Employers in industries affecting commerce who have fifteen or more employees would also be covered by the federal Americans with Disabilities Act (ADA).

An employer may require a medical examination after a conditional offer of employment has been made. Ind. Code § 22-9-5-20. The employer may condition employment on the results if: (a) all similarly situated new employees are subjected to the examination regardless of disability; and (b) information obtained is maintained on separate forms and in separate medical files and is treated as a confidential medical record. Id. The need for the medical examination must be shown to be job related and consistent with business necessity. Id. An employer is not prohibited from making pre-employment inquiries into the ability of an applicant to perform job related functions. Id.

An employer may prohibit the use of illegal drugs and alcohol at the workplace. Ind. Code § 22-9-5-24. The statute, however, neither specifically prohibits nor authorizes an employer to test a job applicant or an employee for the illegal use of drugs or to make employment decisions based on those results. Ind. Code § 22-9-5-24(c). Testing for the illegal use of drugs is not considered a medical examination according to Ind. Admin. Code tit. 910 r. 3-3-15.

HIV/AIDS/Hepatitis B Testing. An HIV test may not be administered without the consent of the individual being tested, unless there is a court order based on clear and convincing evidence of a serious and present health threat to others. Ind. Code § 16-41-6-1.

A person may not disclose nor be compelled to disclose by subpoena or otherwise information involving a communicable disease unless: (i) the disclosure is made for statistical purposes and does not identify the individual; (ii) all individuals identified in the statistical information give their consent; or (iii) in response to public health laws designed to protect the health or life of a named party. Ind. Code § 16-41-8-1(b)(1-3). Intentional, knowing, or reckless disclosure of this protected information is a Class A misdemeanor. Ind. Code § 16-41-8-1(c). If an individual has been charged with a potential disease causing offense, a prosecuting attorney can seek access the individual's medical information, as well as the medical information on another person if it would be relevant to the individual's defense, by filing a petition for release of the medical information with the court. Ind. Code § 16-41-8-4 (adopted by Pub. Law 2009-125, § 2).

Indiana Code § 16-41-7-1 is Indiana's "duty to warn" statute for persons (carriers) who have AIDS, HIV or Hepatitis B. Indiana provides immunity to persons who have reasonable cause and in good faith report to a health officer a carrier who is a serious danger to the health of others as defined in Indiana Code § 16-41-7-2(a), has engaged in noncompliant behavior, or is suspected of being a person at risk. Ind. Code § 16-41-7-2(b). Lack of good faith or knowingly or recklessly making a false report subjects the individual making the report to civil and criminal actions. Ind. Code § 16-41-7-2 (c, d).

2. ***Private Employers***. Private employers may require employees returning from disability leave or other medically related absences to submit to a medical examination before returning to work. In Place v. Abbott Labs., 215 F.3d 803, 809 (7th Cir. 2000), Abbott required any employee who had been out on disability leave for at least five days to coordinate their return to work with the company's health department. Although an independent medical examination was not required of every employee who wished to return to work from a disability leave, the policy did state that these examinations would be performed when the health department thought they were warranted. Id. Plaintiff argued that she was being discriminated against by the company when it required her to submit to a psychological evaluation before returning to work. Id. The court held that this type of examination was not discriminatory under the circumstances and that employers have the right to determine whether employees on disability leaves are mentally and physically ready to return to the work place. Id. at 809-10.

D. Polygraph Testing

There are no Indiana statutes specifically regulating the use of employee polygraph testing. See Greenawalt v. Indiana Dept. of Corrections, 397 F.3d 587, 592 (7th Cir. 2005) (noting that there are no Indiana cases that hold that requiring a public employee to take a lie-detector test without good cause is an invasion of privacy). The federal Employee Polygraph Protection Act of 1988, 29 U.S.C. §§ 2001-2007, prohibits the use of polygraph testing by private employers except under certain conditions (including ongoing investigations, security services employers, and employers who manufacture, distribute, or dispense controlled substances). Violation of this statute may subject an employer to a civil penalty up to $10,000. The statue also creates a private right of action in favor of the affected employee or prospective employee.

E. Fingerprinting

No Indiana statute regulates the fingerprinting of employees in general, although employees of certain entities may be required to provide fingerprints in order to facilitate a criminal background check authorized by statute. See Ind. Code §§ 4-30-6-4 (vendors, retailers and employees of state lottery commission); 20-26-5-10 (employees and contractors of school corporations); 25-30-1-11 (employees of licensed private detectives). Indiana courts have not addressed the use of such a test that is not expressly authorized by statute.

III. SEARCHES

A. Employee's Person

Because there is no specific statutory law relevant to employee searches, an employee would likely have to assert an invasion of privacy claim. Thus, searching an employee or his or her work area is permissible as long as it does not become a wrongful intrusion into one's private activities, in such manner as to outrage or cause mental suffering, shame, or humiliation to a person of ordinary sensibility. Continental Optical Co. v. Reed, 86 N.E.2d 306, 308 (Ind. 1949). In other words, a search of a locker or car may be permissible, while a strip search clearly would not be. An employee does not have a right to be free from an invasion of privacy, only a right to be free from unreasonable invasions of privacy. Terrell v. Rowsey, 647 N.E.2d 662, 664 (Ind. App. 1995) (employer's action of opening car door and removing paper sack containing beer bottle would not offend a person of ordinary sensibility as plaintiff was on his employer's property and he admitted to drinking alcohol and, in addition, employer acted out of responsibility for worker safety through a minimal intrusion). Public employees may be afforded additional constitutional protections.

B. Employee's Work Area

Employees may have a legitimate expectation of privacy in their offices, desks and files depending upon factors such as access, company policy, and whether these areas lock. The United States Supreme Court has held that a search of an employee's office will be justified when there are reasonable grounds for suspecting that the search will turn up evidence of employee misconduct. O'Connor v. Ortega, 480 U.S. 709 (1987).

C. Employee's Property

The Court of Appeals has held that an employer's search of an employee's vehicle, while on company property, did not offend a person of ordinary sensibility when the employer detected the odor of an alcoholic beverage and opened the vehicle door approximately six inches to investigate the vehicle and its occupant. Terrell, 647 N.E.2d at 664. The court cited the employer's responsibility for the safety of other employees, as well as the minimal nature of the intrusion in upholding summary judgment in favor of the employer. Id. at 667; but see id. at 667-69 (Sullivan, J, dissenting) (citing contrary case law from other jurisdictions regarding searches).

IV. MONITORING OF EMPLOYEES

No cases have interpreted Indiana common law in the area of employment monitoring. However, an employer who utilizes monitoring of employees should consider providing all employees with a surveillance policy in writing, educate all employees on the monitoring policy, and establish a legitimate business purpose for the monitoring.

A. Telephones and Electronic Communications

Indiana Code § 35-33.5-5-6 provides civil and criminal immunity to telephone or telegraph companies or other persons who provide information in accordance with law enforcement procedures. Indiana Code § 35-33.5-1 is the criminal statute for wiretapping by law enforcement agencies.

The Electronic Communications Privacy Act of 1986, 18 U.S.C. § 2510 et seq., covers all monitoring of telephone calls and voice-mail messages and may apply to e-mail communications. The Seventh Circuit has held that the act does not apply to municipalities. See Abbott v. Village of Winthrop Harbor, 205 F.3d 976, 980-81 (7th Cir. 2000) (holding that the Act applies only to "persons, a definition that unequivocally excludes local government entities). The Act provides for three (3) exceptions: (1) consent of parties; (2) monitoring of lines by providers of service; and (3) interception in the ordinary course of business. Any monitoring of personal telephone calls should be avoided.

1. ***Wiretapping.*** Intercepting telephone communications by a person other than the sender or receiver of the communication, without consent, violates the Indiana wiretapping statute. Dommer v. Dommer, 829 N.E.2d 125, 141-42 (Ind. App. 2005) (noting that Indiana's wiretapping statute largely stands on its own from the federal Wiretapping Act). The victim of such an interception has a civil cause of action against the offender and may recover actual damages or a set amount of liquidated damages. The knowing or intentional offender also commits a Class C felony.

In Emerson v. Markle, 539 N.E.2d 35, 39 (Ind. App. 1989), the court held that a union representative violated the federal wiretapping statute by directing a teacher to tape record a private conversation with the school's principal where: the union representative was not a party to the conversation, the conversation was taped for the purpose of committing a tortious, criminal or otherwise injurious act, and the principal had a reasonable expectation of privacy with respect to what was said. In this case the union representative had a history of making threatening comments to the principal, the principal's standard practice was to conduct teacher evaluations with his door closed and the union representative later broadcast the record to numerous parties in an attempt to get the principal fired. Id. at 37-39.

2. ***Electronic Communications.*** Neither Indiana statutes nor Indiana courts have addressed an employer's monitoring of employee electronic mail (e-mail). Employees may believe that e-mail messages are private. Generally, an employee maintains a protectable interest in things he or she owns or in items that the employee has an objectively reasonable expectation of privacy in. Therefore, every employer should consider establishing and publishing a

formal policy on e-mail use which specifies that employee e-mail communications are the property of the business. This should eliminate an employee's reasonable expectation of privacy in any such communications.

3. ***Other Electronic Monitoring.*** No relevant cases.

B. Mail

Indiana does not have any laws regarding an employer's monitoring of employee mail, nor have reported cases addressed this issue.

C. Surveillance/Photographing

There are no reported Indiana cases challenging an employer's video surveillance of an employee as an invasion of privacy, but Indiana courts have declared such video monitoring, in the context of criminal search and seizure law, a violation of a reasonable expectation of privacy. State v. Thomas, 642 N.E.2d 240, 244-45 (Ind. App. 1994). In determining the reasonableness of a person's expectation of privacy, the court considered: (1) the surreptitious means by which the video surveillance was accomplished, including the location of the equipment and the method utilized to install it; and, (2) the degree of intrusion inherent in the continuous nature of video surveillance. Id. at 244. The court also considered the ownership and possession of the searched area and posited that a person may have a subjective expectation of privacy that becomes objectively reasonable in an area of his or her workplace. Id. at 246. The court ultimately held that the covert video surveillance violated the employee's reasonable expectations of privacy and constituted an illegal warrantless search, but limited this holding to warrantless video surveillance for law enforcement reasons. Id. at 247; cf. Creel v. I.C.E. & Assoc., 771 N.E.2d 1276, 1280-81 (Ind. App. 2002) (no invasion of privacy where plaintiffs were secretly videotaped during church services because plaintiffs had no reasonable expectation of privacy in their activities).

Monitoring must serve a legitimate business purpose and should only be done in areas provided for business or where employees could not reasonably expect to be left alone. Based on Thomas, employees should be notified that they are subject to visual monitoring and the purpose of the monitoring.

V. ACTIVITIES OUTSIDE THE WORKPLACE

A. Statutes or Common Law

In the context of public employment, a non-policy-making, non-confidential public employee cannot be terminated on the sole basis of political beliefs. McDermott v. Bicanic, 550 N.E.2d 93 (Ind. App. 1990). A policy-making employee may under certain circumstances be terminated based on political affiliation. Id. at 94. The employer must demonstrate that party affiliation is an appropriate requirement for the public office involved. Id.

Generally, an at-will employee can be discharged by a private employer unless there is relevant case law or statutory law preventing such termination. See Orr v. Westminster Village North, 689 N.E.2d 712, 717 (Ind. 1997). One such statute is the Indiana law that protects an employee's beliefs as they relate to abortions. No hospital or other person may discriminate against or discipline a person because of the person's moral beliefs concerning abortion. Ind. Code § 16-34-1-6. Another statute is the Smoker's Rights Law that makes it unlawful for an employer to require, as a condition of employment, that an employee or prospective employee refrain from the off-duty use of tobacco products. Ind. Code § 22-5-4-1. Local ordinances may also apply that expand the protections afforded employees by state and federal law.

B. Employees' Personal Relationships

1. ***Romantic Relationships Between Employees.*** There are no reported Indiana cases concerning protections afforded to employees with regard to romantic relationships, although there are cases with facts that include office romances. See Thayer v. Vaughn, 798 N.E.2d 249, 256 (Ind. App. 2003) (accepting assessment by a business that an employee's consensual affair with a co-owner of the business had a negative impact on the office work environment and declining to sit as a "super-personnel department that re-examines an entity's business decisions"). Employers may consider adopting a written policy addressing this issue to avoid potential future liability under Title VII.

2. ***Sexual Orientation.*** Indiana does not recognize sexual orientation as a protected classification and, therefore, affords no legal remedy for discrimination. Homosexuality does not deprive one from protection under Title VII and is irrelevant to the analysis. Vandeeventer v. Wabash Nat. Corp., 887 F.Supp. 1178 (N.D. Ind. 1995). Moreover, homosexuality, bisexuality, transvestism, transsexualism, and sexual behavior disorders are not considered disabilities under Indiana's Employment Discrimination Against Disabled Persons Act. Ind. Code § 22-9-5-6. A number of localities, however, have ordinances that prohibit discrimination based on sexual orientation and other circumstances not covered by state and federal law.

In Cornell v. Hamilton, 791 N.E.2d 214 (Ind. App 2003), an openly homosexual State employee challenged the denial of her request for leave time (based on the death of her partner's father) under the Indiana constitution's privileges and immunities clause. Such leave time was available to married couples. The court of appeals affirmed summary judgment for the State, holding that the employee was not similarly situated to other married employees in the privileged class. Id. at 220. The court of appeals questioned whether the particular classification based on marital status remained rational, but because the employee conceded that the policy was rationally related to marriage, the close question of whether, in this age of changing family relationships, the policy's distinction based on marital status is rational was not before the court. The only question was whether the privilege was equally available to all persons similarly situated.

3. ***Marital Status.*** Indiana Code § 20-28-10-12 prohibits the enforcement of any rule or regulation concerning the employment of teachers that discriminates in any manner on the basis of marital status. Discrimination resulting from an individual's marital status violates the intent of Congress to do away with disparate employment practices among men and women and, accordingly, falls within the category of sex as set forth in the provisions of the Civil Rights Act. Meier v. Evansville-Vanderburgh School Corp., 416 F.Supp. 748, 750 (S.D. Ind. 1976).

C. Smoking

An employer may not require an employee, or prospective employee, to refrain from using tobacco products outside the course of employment. Ind. Code § 22-5-4-1. Likewise, an employer may not discriminate against an employee with respect to compensation, benefits, or terms of employment based on tobacco usage outside the course of employment. Id. The prohibitions do not apply to religious organizations, churches, or schools or business conducted by these entities. Ind. Code § 22-5-4-4. See Best Lock Corp. V. Review Bd. of Ind. Dept. of Employment and Training Serv., 572 N.E.2d 520 (Ind. App. 1991) (employer's rule prohibiting smoking both on and off-duty did not bear a sufficient relation to a legitimate business interest of the company).

D. Blogging

No reported cases.

VI. RECORDS

A. Personnel Records

Private employees have no right by statute or common law to review their personnel files. Many employers in Indiana, however, allow review with a supervisor present. It is advisable to establish a written policy covering such review as indiscriminate disclosure of employee records may give rise to an invasion of privacy claim.

Upon written request from an employee who has been discharged or has voluntarily quit, Indiana Code § 22-6-3-1 states that an employer must provide a written statement setting forth the nature and character of service rendered by such employee, the length of employment and a truthful statement of the reason the employee quit or was discharged. This provision applies to all employers who require prospective employees to provide a written recommendation or application showing qualifications or experience for employment.

With regard to public employees, public records generally must be available for inspection and copying. Ind. Code § 5-14-3-3. Certain records, however, including personnel files of public employees and files of applicants for public employment, are excluded (with some broad exceptions) from the disclosure requirement. Ind. Code § 5-14-3-4(b)(8); see South Bend Tribune v. South Bend Community Sch. Corp., 740 N.E.2d 937 (Ind. App. 2000) (noting that candidates for the position of Superintendent of Schools are applicants for public employment within the meaning of the statute and, thus, fall squarely within the exception). A public agency must make available to the public information about a public employee that is related to a final disciplinary action, the status of formal charges, and general information such as name, compensation, educational background and the employee's job description. Ind. Code § 5-14-3-4(b)(8). Furthermore, public employees must have access to their own personnel files. Id.

If a state agency maintains a personnel information system, it must maintain and use that personnel information only as it is relevant and necessary to accomplish a purpose of the agency. Ind. Code § 4-1-6-2. Unlike private employers, the state agency must also segregate confidential information from that which is a matter of public record. Id.

Public employees, officials, or employees or officers of public agency contractors or subcontractors who intentionally, knowingly, or recklessly disclose or fail to protect information *classified as confidential by state statute* commit a Class A misdemeanor. Ind. Code § 5-14-3-10(a). An unintentional and unknowing disclosure of confidential or erroneous information in response to a request made under § 5-14-3-3(d) is immune from liability, as are disclosures in reliance on advisory opinions of the public access counselor. Ind. Code § 5-14-3-10(c) (addressing requests for records which are maintained in electronic data storage systems).

Records that *may not be disclosed* include: (1) those declared confidential by state statute, (2) those declared confidential by rule adopted by a public agency under specific authority to classify public records as confidential granted to the public agency by statute, and (3) those required to be kept confidential by federal law. Other specific records that cannot be disclosed are grade transcripts and license examination scores obtained as part of a licensure process, or patient medical records and charts created by a provider unless the patient gives written consent under Indiana Code 16-39.

B. Medical Records

Indiana Code § 16-41-8-1 prohibits a person from disclosing or being compelled to disclose medical or epidemiological information involving a communicable disease or other disease that is a health danger. This information can be released under the following circumstances: (1) for statistical purposes if the identity of the individual is not revealed; (2) with the written consent of all individuals identified in the information released; (3) to enforce public health and delinquency laws and laws prohibiting the transfer of contaminated body fluids; and (4) to protect the health or life of a named party. Id.

A patient's mental health records are confidential and generally may be disclosed only with the patient's consent. Mental health records may be released without the patient's consent under certain limited circumstances. In general, the recipients must be either involved in the delivery or acquisition of health care services, medical research, state data collection or general law enforcement, or they must be individuals involved in appropriate court proceedings. Ind. Code § 16-39-2-6. Indiana Code § 16-39-4-5(c)(2) covers release of certain other records, including substance abuse treatment, upon the patient's written consent to an insurer. Mental health records are not discoverable or admissible in legal proceedings without consent of the patient, except as provided in Ind. Code § 16-39-2-8. Munsell v. Hambright, 776 N.E.2d 1272, 1278 (Ind. App. 2002) (holding that attorney was not justified in sending subpoenas instead of following statute to obtain records).

Pursuant to Indiana Code § 16-39-5-2, insurance companies issuing policies for accident and sickness insurance can obtain health information and medical records with a written consent from the insured. Records can be used for legitimate business purposes (including submission of claims for payment to third parties, collection of accounts, litigation defense and the like). Ind. Code § 16-39-5-3.

With a court order, Indiana Code § 27-2-19-8 allows a law enforcement agency, insurer or governmental agency which is investigating a fraudulent claim for insurance coverage to obtain the claimant's medical records from any other law enforcement agency, insurer or governmental agency without a prior authorization or release from claimant if there is a reasonable belief that a request for authorization or release would hinder the fraud investigation.

Medical and psychological records kept by a state agency shall, upon written authorization of the patient, be released to a physician or psychologist designated by the patient. The nature and source of the information must be disclosed, as well as the names and addresses of any recipients of personal or confidential information about the patient, along with the nature and purpose of the disclosure. Ind. Code § 4-1-6-3.

C. Criminal Records

Indiana law provides that law enforcement agencies shall release or allow inspection of a limited criminal history to employers if the subject of the request has applied for employment. Ind. Code § 10-13-3-27. Limited criminal history means information with respect to any arrest or criminal charge, which must include a disposition. Ind. Code § 10-13-3-11. However, if the event occurred less than one (1) year before the date of the request, it shall be considered a limited criminal history even if no disposition has been entered. Id.

Pursuant to Indiana Code § 5-14-3-5, certain information concerning any person who is arrested, summoned or jailed for an offense must be made available for inspection and copying, including: (a) name, age and address; (b) information concerning the criminal charges; (c) circumstances of the arrest or issuance of the summons; (d) the investigating agency and officer; (e) the reason person was jailed; and (f) the amount of bond.

Health care facilities and other entities in the business of contracting to provide nurse's aides or other unlicensed employees to another health facility must apply within three (3) business days from the date a person is employed as a nurse's aide or other unlicensed employee for a copy of the person's limited criminal history from the Indiana central repository for criminal history information. Ind. Code § 16-28-13 et seq.

D. Confidential Financial Information

A public employer may not require an employee to provide authorization for the release of a virtually limitless range of confidential financial information as a condition to continued employment. Denius v. Dunlap, 209 F.3d 944, 958 (7th Cir.

2000). The court therefore held that a sweeping disclosure requirement, lacking any safeguards against misuse or further disclosure, and supported by no justification infringed the plaintiff's right of privacy concerning confidential information. Id. (public employer provided no justification for requiring this type of confidential financial information, did not indicate how it would use the information it gathered and did not guarantee the confidentiality of the information).

E. Subpoenas / Search Warrants

In Rios v. Indiana University, the district court addressed a former employee's emergency motion to quash third party subpoenas that were sent to prospective new employers by the employee's former employer. 2005 U.S. Dist. LEXIS 15454, *4 (N.D. Ind. July 28, 2005). Recognizing the former employee's desire to keep employment negotiations as confidential as possible so as to not interfere with employment negotiations, the district court nonetheless held that the former employee had a duty to supplement her initial disclosures and discovery responses under F.R.C.P. 26(a) and (e). Id. at 5, 6. Accordingly, the third party subpoenas, requesting production of documents such as completed employment applications, were permissible and the emergency motion to quash was denied. Id. at 87.

Indiana does not have any laws regarding third parties' ability to obtain search warrants for employee records or workspaces, nor have reported cases addressed this issue.

VII. ACTIONS SUBSEQUENT TO EMPLOYMENT

A. References

Blacklisting. An employee who has been discharged and is later prevented by his or her former employer from obtaining subsequent employment may seek penal damages against the former employer in a civil action. Ind. Code § 22-5-3-1(a). The employer can also be found guilty of a Class C infraction. Id. An essential element of this claim is that the former employer prevented the discharged employee from obtaining employment. Hull v. Central Transport, Inc., 628 F. Supp. 784, 793 (N.D. Ind. 1986). Thus an employee must allege, at least, that the employee tried to obtain subsequent employment and was unable to do so because of the blacklisting by the former employer. Id. Ind. Code § 22-5-3-1(a), however, does not prohibit a person from providing a truthful written statement of the reasons for an employee's discharge to any person to whom the employee has applied for employment. Id. Furthermore, the statute grants an employer immunity from civil liability for disclosing information about a current or former employee, unless a preponderance of the evidence shows that the information was known to be false at the time it was disclosed. Ind. Code § 22-5-3-1(b). See Steele v. McDonalds Corp., 686 N.E.2d 137 (Ind. App. 1997) (addressing truthful disclosure by former employer who called a former employee's present employer noting employee's status as a convicted felon and reason for termination). Indiana Code § 22-6-3-1 requires employers, upon written request of a former employee, to provide a service letter to the former employee. Under Ind. Code § 22-5-3-1, a truthful statement of the reasons for the discharge may be provided to a prospective employer who inquires about a former employee. Unless the information disclosed was known to be false at the time of disclosure, an employer is immune from civil liability for the disclosure and its consequences.

A common law qualified privilege has also been recognized regarding a former employer's statements to a prospective employer in the context of a defamation action. Chambers v. America Trans Air, Inc., 577 N.E.2d 612, 615 (Ind. App. 1991). In Chambers, the court stated that there is a self-evident social utility in free and open communications between former and prospective employers concerning an employee reference. Id. at 616. The privilege may be lost if the alleged defamatory communications are motivated by ill will, excessively publicized, or made without a belief or grounds for belief in their truth. Id.

Indiana Code § 22-5-3-2 prohibits an employer from preventing a former employee by any means whatever from obtaining future employment. Employers who violate this provision are liable for both compensatory and exemplary damages. Id. This statue was enacted in 1889 in response to the blacklisting practices of railroads. However, the statutory language is much more expansive than that, covering any railway company or any other company, partnership, limited liability company or corporation. Ind. Code § 22-5-3-2. Indiana Code § 22-5-3-2 was not cited in a reported decision for over ninety years; however, in 1998, a federal district court held that an employer violated the statute by maintaining an unsuccessful lawsuit against a former employee to enforce a covenant not to compete and enjoin the employee from obtaining employment with a competitor. Bridgestone/Firestone, Inc. v. Lockhart, 5 F. Supp.2d 667, 687-88 (S.D. Ind. 1998).

The Bridgestone/Firestone court distinguished Indiana Code § 22-5-3-2 from Section 1 of the statute, which requires proof that the employee was actually prevented from obtaining other employment, and held that an unsuccessful lawsuit seeking an injunction against employment is an attempt by words or writing, or any other means whatever to prevent a former employee from obtaining employment. Id. at 688. The court awarded compensatory damages but denied exemplary damages because the employer had a reasonable basis in law for bringing the suit, and the court interpreted Indiana law to require proof of malice before punitive damages could be awarded. Id.

After issuing its decision in Bridgestone/Firestone, the court became aware of Wabash R. Co. v. Young, 69 N.E. 1003 (Ind. 1904), which held that Indiana Code § 22-5-3-2 does not protect employees who voluntarily terminate their employment. Based upon its review of more recent Indiana Supreme Court precedent interpreting this constitutional provision, the Bridgestone/Firestone court declined to follow Wabash and held that Indiana Code § 22-5-3-2 does apply to employees who voluntarily quit or resign their employment. Bridgestone/Firestone, 5 F. Supp. 2d at 687 n.13. The Indiana Court of Appeals, however, has affirmed that Wabash remains the law in Indiana. Burk v. Heritage Food Service Equipment, Inc., 737 N.E.2d 803, 818 (Ind. App. 2000). In Burk, the Court of Appeals acknowledged that the constitutional provision on which Wabash was based no longer requires that the title of the act express the entire subject of the act. Nevertheless, the Burk court held that despite this change in the constitutional provision as well as our supreme court's subsequent, less restrictive interpretation of Article IV, Section 19, we are still obliged to follow the precedent established by our Supreme Court. Burk, 737 N.E.2d at 818. Accordingly, Indiana Code § 22-5-3-2 does not protect employees who voluntarily terminate their employment.

Finally, Indiana courts do have jurisdiction to hear blacklisting claims involving religious employees, but a religious employer will be entitled to summary judgment if the court must interpret and analyze church doctrine in determining the blacklisting claim. Brazauskas v. Fort Wayne-South Bend Diocese, Inc., 796 N.E.2d 286 (Ind. 2003) (applying federal Constitutional law interpreting the First Amendment's Free Exercise Clause).

B. Non-Compete Agreements

Employee non-compete agreements are enforceable in Indiana, but are not generally favored because such agreements are in restraint of trade. Oxford Financial Group, Ltd. v. Evans, 795 N.E.2d 1135, 1143 (Ind. App. 2003) (any ambiguity in a non-compete agreement is construed against the drafter seeking to restrain trade). Non-compete clauses are enforced only if reasonable with respect to the legitimate interests of the employer, restrictions on the employee and the public interest. Vukovich v. Coleman, 789 N.E.2d 520, 525 (Ind. App. 2003). A covenant not to compete must be reasonable with respect to time, geography and types of activity prohibited. Id. (a covenant not to compete without a geographic limitation is presumptively void).

VIII. OTHER ISSUES

A. Statutes of Limitations

Actions based on injuries to a person's property, person or character must be commenced within two years of the accrual of the cause of action. Ind. Code § 34-11-2-4. Actions based on the terms, conditions and privileges of employment not covered by a written contract must be brought within two (2) years of the date of the act or omission. Ind. Code § 34-11-2 -1. Actions against the State of Indiana relating to the terms, conditions and privileges of employment must be brought within two (2) years of the date of the act or omission. Ind. Code § 34-11-2-2.

Actions for contracts not in writing must be commenced within six (6) years after the cause of action has accrued. Ind. Code § 34-11-2-7. Actions upon promissory notes, bills of exchange and other written contracts for the payment of money executed after August 31, 1982, must be brought within six (6) years after the cause of action accrues. Ind. Code § 34-11-2-9. Actions upon most other written contracts must be brought within ten (10) years of the accrual of the action. Ind. Code § 34-11-2-11.

Actions for treble damages are governed by a two (2) year statute of limitations. Browning v. Walters, 616 N.E.2d 1040, 1046 (Ind. App. 1993) (holding that treble damages were punitive in nature and therefore subject to the two year statute of limitations applicable to forfeiture of statutory penalties (now Ind. Code § 34-11-2-4)).

B. Jurisdiction

An employee who has both state and federal claims may assert both claims in the same cause of action or choose to ignore the federal causes of action and pursue only the state causes of action. Fields v. Cummins Employees Fed. Credit Union, 540 N.E.2d 631, 639 (Ind. App. 1989), overruled on other grounds by Wine-Settergren v. Lamey, 716 N.E.2d 381 (Ind. 1999). The remedies available for state common law torts may be broader because the remedies available under Title VII are capped. Further, state law claims may allow a plaintiff to sue additional parties such as individuals who may not be liable under federal laws.

C. Worker's Compensation Exclusivity

The exclusivity provision of the Worker's Compensation Act, Indiana Code § 22-3-2-6, applies when physical injury is present, but not when injuries are only emotional and the injuries do not prevent the employee from working. Perry v. Stizer Buick GMC, 637 N.E.2d 1282, 1288-89 (Ind. 1994) (discharged employee's claims for assault, slander, and battery were not barred by the exclusivity provision of the Worker's Compensation Act because the resulting injuries were not physical, nor did they involve a disability or impairment that prevented the employee from working); Dietz v. Finlay Fine Jewelry Corp., 754 N.E.2d 958, 965 (Ind. App. 2001) (injuries were not personal injuries under the Worker's Compensation Act).

Lawson v. Raney Mfg., 678 N.E.2d 122 (Ind. App. 1997), overruled in part on other grounds by GKN Co. v. Magness, 744 N.E.2d 397, 404 (Ind. 2001), further reinforced that the Worker's Compensation Act was the exclusive remedy for employment related injuries which occur by accident. Id. at 125. GKN Co. clarified that an employer bears the burden of proving that the employee's claim falls within the scope of the Worker's Compensation Act unless the complaint demonstrates the existence of an employment relationship. In Sims v. United States Fid. & Guar. Co., 782 N.E.2d 345 (Ind. 2003), the Indiana Supreme Court held that Ind. Code § 22-3-4-12.1, which grants the Indiana Workers Compensation Board exclusive jurisdiction to determine whether an insurer has committed an independent tort in adjusting or settling a worker's claim, is constitutional and does not offend the open courts provision of Article I, Section 12 of the Indiana Constitution or the right to a trial by jury as expressed in Article I, Section 20.

D. Pleading Requirements

Indiana is a notice pleading state, although certain claims by trial rule or case law (ex. fraud and defamation) must include specificity.

SURVEY OF IOWA EMPLOYMENT LIBEL LAW

Michael A. Giudicessi and Angela J. Morales
Faegre Baker Daniels LLP
Suite 3100, 801 Grand Avenue
Des Moines, Iowa 50309
Telephone: (515) 248-9000 / (800) 228-0836
Facsimile: (515) 248-9010

William J. Hunnicutt
Wells Fargo & Company
800 Walnut Street/MAC N0001-10A
Des Moines, Iowa 50309
Telephone: (515) 557-1287
Facsimile: (515) 327-4253

(With Developments Reported Through **November 1, 2012**)

GENERAL COMMENTS

Iowa has a unified trial court system whereby original jurisdiction for claims in excess of $5,000 rests in the district court. Claims for damages of $5,000 or less must be brought in the small claims court. Iowa Code § 631.1 (2011). Appeals from final decisions of the district court may be made as a matter of right to the Iowa Supreme Court. The Iowa Supreme Court may refer the case to the Iowa Court of Appeals for appellate review or retain jurisdiction over the appeal. If a case is referred to the Iowa Court of Appeals, the Supreme Court may choose to review it on an application for further review. The general standard of appellate review in civil cases is on error for cases at law and de novo for cases in equity. Libel cases generally are deemed cases at law where review is on errors assigned. See Anderson v. Low Rent Hous. Comm'n, 304 N.W.2d 239, 7 Media L. Rep. 1726 (Iowa 1981). Certain issues, such as those implicating constitutional questions, are subject to de novo review. Id. at 246.

Increasingly, the case law of defamation in Iowa is evolving from employment cases, often where defamation is an additional count in a case stemming from an alleged wrongful termination. These cases sometimes rely on defamation standards set in cases involving media defendants. The courts do not always note, however, the distinctions between media and non-media defendants. In Brase v. Mosley, No. 00-0568, 2002 WL 31525366, at *4 (Iowa Ct. App. Nov. 15, 2002) (citations omitted), the Iowa Court of Appeals stated that the definition of actual malice set forth in New York Times v. Sullivan, 376 U.S. 254, 1 Media L. Rep. 1527 (1964) ("a statement made with knowledge that it is false or made with reckless disregard for its truth or falsity") applies to both media and non-media defendants in cases involving defamation claims by public figures or officials.

SIGNIFICANT DEVELOPMENTS SINCE THE 2012 *SURVEY*

None.

I. GENERAL LAW

A. General Employment Law

1. ***At Will Employment.*** Employment in Iowa is presumed to be at-will. Berg v. Norand Corp., 169 F.3d 1140, 1146 (8th Cir.), cert. denied, 120 S. Ct. 174 (1999); Jones v. Lake Park Care Ctr., Inc., 569 N.W.2d 369, 374 (Iowa 1997); Anderson v. Douglas & Lomason Co., 540 N.W.2d 277, 281 (Iowa 1995). In the absence of a valid employment contract, an employer may discharge an employee at any time, for any reason, or no reason at all. Phipps v. IASD Health Serv. Corp., 558 N.W.2d 198, 202 (Iowa 1997); Huegerich v. IBP, Inc., 547 N.W.2d 216, 219 (Iowa 1996). Iowa permits claims for wrongful discharge under two narrow exceptions to the employment at-will doctrine: (a) when the discharge clearly violates a "well recognized and defined public policy of the state," Huegerich, 547 N.W.2d at 220 (quoting Springer v. Weeks & Leo Co., Inc., 429 N.W.2d 558, 560 (Iowa 1988)); Davis v. Horton, 661 N.W.2d 533, 535–36 (Iowa 2003); Ballalatak v. All Iowa Agric. Ass'n, 781 N.W.2d 272, 275 (Iowa 2010), and (b) where a unilateral or implied contract is entered through an employer's handbook or policy manual. Phipps, 558 N.W.2d at 202. Because Iowa courts have recognized these exceptions, "the traditional doctrine of permitting termination 'at any time, for any reason, or no reason at all' is now more properly stated as permitting 'termination at any time for any lawful reason.'" Revell v. Maytag Corp., 430 F. Supp. 2d 873, 883 (S.D. Iowa 2006) (citing Fitzgerald v. Salsbury Chem., Inc., 613 N.W.2d 275, 281 (Iowa 2000) (emphasis in original)); see also Boyle v. Alum-Line, Inc., 710 N.W.2d 741, 749 (Iowa 2006) (clarifying "any reason" language by striking a jury's factual finding that an employer who terminated an at-will employee complaining of sexual harassment by her male co-workers was acting in a way "reasonably calculated to stop the sexual harassment"). Iowa courts "have consistently refused to adopt a covenant of good faith and fair dealing with respect to at-will employment relationships." Revell, 430 F. Supp. 2d at 883 (citation omitted).

An employer may be subject to tort liability for the retaliatory discharge of an employee when the discharge violates a well recognized and defined public policy of Iowa. Lara v. Thomas, 512 N.W.2d 777, 782 (Iowa 1994); see Webner v. Titan Distrib., Inc., 267 F.3d 828, 835–37 (8th Cir. 2001) (citations omitted) (discussing elements of retaliatory discharge and when emotional distress damages are available for a retaliation claim under Iowa law); Harvey v. Care Initiatives, Inc., 634 N.W.2d 681, 686 (Iowa 2001) (holding there is no clear public policy that proscribes the discharge of an independent contractor in retaliation for the reporting of a health care facility violation); McMahon v. Mid-America Constr. Co., No. 99-1741, 2000 WL 1587952, at *2–5 (Iowa Ct. App. Oct. 25, 2000) (citing Fitzgerald v. Salsbury Chem., Inc., 613 N.W.2d 275, 283 (Iowa 2000)) (declining to decide whether an employer's refusal to rehire an employee in retaliation for the filing of a workers' compensation claim constitutes a cause of action because plaintiff had failed to provide substantial evidence the protected activity was a determining factor in the employer's refusal to rehire, but noting the Iowa Supreme Court has "warned against broad application of the public policy exception"); Thomas v. Union Pac. R.R. Co., No. 44-99-cv-20188, 2001 WL 741739, at *2–4 (S.D. Iowa May 23, 2001) (holding the public policy underlying Iowa Code § 730.2 does not create an exception to the employment at will doctrine where plaintiffs allege wrongful failure to rehire); Napreljac v. Monarch Mfg. Co., No. 4-02-CV-10075, 2003 WL 21976024, at *7–8 (S.D. Iowa May 27, 2003); Shoop v. Drake Univ., No. 03-0700, 672 N.W.2d 335, 2003 WL 22455652, at *1 (Oct. 29, 2003); Boyle v. Alum-Line, Inc., 710 N.W.2d 741, 750–52 (Iowa 2006) (holding that a trial court cannot dismiss a retaliatory discharge claim without making "findings concerning the elements of plaintiff's case"); Brenneman v. Famous Dave's of America, Inc., 410 F. Supp. 2d 828, 845 (S.D. Iowa 2006) (detailing the elements to be proved by a plaintiff asserting a retaliatory discharge claim against her employer); see also Clark v. Eagle Ottawa, LLC, No. 06-CV-2028-LRR, 2007 U.S. Dist. LEXIS 12061, at *15–16 (N.D. Iowa Feb. 20, 2007) (finding that "Plaintiff cannot avail himself of the protections of Iowa's public policy exceptions to the at-will employment doctrine, unless he has alleged that he is an at-will employee"); Carter v. Racing Assoc. of Central Iowa, No. 08-1900, 2009 WL 4241860, at *2 (Iowa Ct. App. Nov. 25, 2009) (discussing elements of wrongful discharge in violation of public policy claim and discussing when a public policy is sufficient to warrant an exception to the at-will doctrine); Ballalatak, 781 N.W.2d 272, 278 (holding the public policy found in Iowa's workers' compensation statute strongly protects injured employees, but does not extend to coworkers or supervisors who internally express concerns regarding compliance with the workers compensation statutes as it relates to another employee); **Dorshkind v. Oak Park Place of Dubuque II, L.L.C., No. 11-2100, 2012 WL 4900430 (Iowa Ct. App. Oct. 17, 2012) (distinguishing Ballalatak and holding Iowa statute concerning assisted-living and dementia care programs could support a public policy claim for internal whistle-blowing);** Berry v. Liberty Holdings, Inc., 803 N.W.2d 106, 112 (Iowa 2011) (vacating the decision of the Court of Appeals and finding Iowa's comparative fault statute, Iowa Code Chapter 668, does not contain a clearly defined and well-recognized public policy); **see generally Anderson v. Bristol, Inc., 847 F. Supp. 2d 1128, 1137-38 (S.D. Iowa 2012) (citing Iowa cases, including Fitzgerald, 613 N.W.2d at 282, and discussing standards to determine when a statute can be the source of a well recognized and clearly defined public policy).**

A claim for wrongful discharge in violation of public policy may be precluded or preempted when the public policy asserted underlies a statute. Lucht v. Encompass Corp., 491 F. Supp. 2d 856, 867 (S.D. Iowa 2007) (holding "the identical factual basis and the comprehensive remedies available under the FMLA militate on both legal bases against permitting the wrongful discharge claim to proceed"); see also Hussaini v. Gelita USA, Inc., 749 F. Supp. 2d 909, 921 (N.D. Iowa 2010) (holding the plaintiff's wrongful discharge claim was preempted by the NLRA because it involved conduct actually or arguably prohibited by the NLRA); Nuss v. Cent. Iowa Binding Corp., 284 F. Supp. 2d 1187, 1203 (S.D. Iowa 2003) (holding that plaintiff's common law wrongful discharge claim was preempted by the ICRA because the claim was not separate and independent of plaintiff's discrimination claims); Smidt v. Porter, 695 N.W.2d 9, 17 (Iowa 2005) (holding that plaintiff's common law wrongful discharge claim was preempted by the ICRA because the operative facts giving rise to her wrongful discharge claim were the same ones forming her statutory pregnancy discrimination claims); Truckenmiller v. Burgess Health Ctr., 814 F.Supp.2d 894, 912 (N.D. Iowa 2011) (same); **Barucic v. Titan Tire Corp., 839 F.Supp.2d 1038, 1050 (S.D. Iowa 2012) (discussing preemption by ICRA); Anderson, 847 F. Supp. 2d at 1136-37 (S.D. Iowa 2012) (discussing preemption by FMLA).**

In addition to the requirement that the claimed public policy must be well recognized and clearly defined, the employee must establish that he/she engaged in the protected activity and that there is a causal connection between the protected activity and the termination. Gosa v. Nu-World Amaranth, Inc., No. 10-CV-2074-LRR, 2012 WL 463023, at *4–8 (N.D. Iowa Feb. 11, 2012) (holding employees had not engaged in protected conduct and had failed to demonstrate causation); Barucic v. Titan Tire Corp., 839 F.Supp.2d 1038, 1050 (S.D. Iowa 2012) (holding plaintiff failed to show causation between his alleged protected activity and termination); Red Hat v. CRST Van Expedited, Inc., No. 11-CV-41, 2012 WL 4903341, at *17 (N.D. Iowa Oct. 16, 2012) (dismissing public policy claim premised on protected activity of spouse).

"The timing of an adverse employment action may offer circumstantial evidence of a retaliatory motive, but a mere coincidence in timing is not sufficient in itself to establish causation for a retaliatory discharge claim. The timing of events must be fairly close to create an inference of an employer's improper motive." In re Colombo, 325 B.R. 587, 597 (N.D. Iowa 2005) (citation omitted); Deleon v. Iowa Select Farms, Inc., No. 04-1332, 2005 WL 1225440, at *3 (Iowa Ct. App. May 25, 2005) (holding that retaliatory discharge claim failed as a matter of law because there was insufficient evidence that filing of workers' compensation claim was the "determinative factor" in the decision to terminate plaintiff); **see also Johnson v. Dollar General, No. C11-3038-MWB, 2012 WL 3072997, at *28-29 (N.D. Iowa July 30, 2012) (discussing causal connection)**. Evidence concerning the employer's justification for the termination decision is also relevant to the issue of causation. See Raymond v. U.S.A. Healthcare Center-Fort Dodge, LLC, 468 F. Supp. 2d 1047, 1059–62 (N.D. Iowa 2006) (holding that a reasonable fact finder could find employee's filing of her worker's compensation claim was the determinative factor in her discharge based on her evidence of differential treatment of similarly situated employees).

The public policy exception to the employment at-will doctrine is not limited to the "mandates of specific statutes," but rather courts "may imply a prohibition against termination if the policy basis for so doing clearly appears from other sources." Davis, 661 N.W.2d at 536 (citing Borschel v. City of Perry, 512 N.W.2d 565, 568 (Iowa 1994)); see also Jasper v. H. Nizam, Inc., 764 N.W.2d 751, 767–68 (Iowa 2009) (finding a public policy for adequate staffing at daycare centers based on the standards for protection of children in Chapter 237A and the staff ratio requirements of the Iowa Administrative Code). However, when considering a potential public policy exception, the courts "proceed cautiously and will only extend such recognition to those policies that are well recognized and clearly defined." Davis, 661 N.W.2d at 536 (citation omitted); see Lloyd v. Drake Univ., 686 N.W.2d 225, 228–31 (Iowa 2004) (rejecting wrongful discharge claim premised on argument that plaintiff's termination from defendant-employer for upholding the criminal laws violated public policy because the asserted public policy "is far too generalized" and "is neither clearly defined nor well recognized"). In Obrecht v. Electrolux Home Prods., Inc., No. C04-3089-MWB, 2005 WL 578477, at *4–7 (N.D. Iowa Mar. 9, 2005) (citing Springer v. Weeks & Leo Co., 429 N.W.2d 558 (Iowa 1988)), after noting that the Iowa Supreme Court has recognized a retaliatory discharge claim based on the filing of a workers' compensation claim, the Northern District of Iowa held that any settlement agreement provision that condones such a prohibited discharge is void.

An implied contract of employment can arise from an employee handbook or policy if it is sufficiently definite in its terms to create an offer, it is communicated to and accepted by the employee so as to create an acceptance, and the employee provides consideration. Jones, 569 N.W.2d at 375; McBride v. City of Sioux City, 444 N.W.2d 85, 91 (Iowa 1989); see also Curtis v. Rockwell Collins, Inc., No. 00-0593, 2001 WL 194824, at *2 (Iowa Ct. App. Feb. 28, 2001) (holding terms in handbook were not sufficiently definite to create contract of employment); Bradshaw v. Brown Group, Inc., 258 F.3d 847, 850–51 (8th Cir. 2001) (applying Iowa law and holding manual was not sufficiently definite to create unilateral contract of employment); Fesler v. Whelen Eng'g. Co., 794 F.Supp.2d 994 (S.D. Iowa 2011) (same); Poeckes v. City of Orange City, No. 04-0991, 2005 WL 2508379, at *2 (Iowa Ct. App. Oct. 12, 2005) (discussing requirement that the handbook be communicated to employee and distinguishing Anderson v. Douglas & Lomason Co., 540 N.W.2d 277 (Iowa 1995)). The party asserting that a unilateral contract exists bears the burden of proving its existence. Anderson v. Douglas & Lomason Co., 540 N.W.2d 277, 281 (Iowa 1995). If an employee signs an acknowledgement memorializing at-will status, the courts will generally not find an implied contract arising from an employment handbook. Berg, 169 F.3d at 1146. If the employee handbook or policy specifically and unambiguously disclaims the existence of an employment contract, courts will not find an implied contract arising from the employment handbook or policy. Allen v. Hon Indus., Inc., No. 00-2017, 2001 WL 1659240, at *2 (Iowa Ct. App. Dec. 28, 2001); Olson v. Ballantine, 695 N.W.2d 43, 2004 WL 2578958, at *2 (Iowa Ct. App. Nov. 15, 2004); Leclere v. Big Lot Stores, Inc., No. 06-CV-1018-LRR, 2006 U.S. Dist. LEXIS 86167, at *14–20 (N.D. Iowa Nov. 27, 2006) (finding that "no reasonable employee would understand the Handbook to create a unilateral contract" in light of the comprehensive disclaimers that were "clear in their terms and unambiguous in their scope"); Meier v. Family Dollar Services, Inc., 443 F. Supp. 2d 1036, 1050–51 (N.D. Iowa 2006) (finding employee remained at-will and that handbook did not create a unilateral contract because of employer's prominent, unambiguous disclaimer).

B. Elements of Libel Claim

1. ***Basic Elements.*** Libel in Iowa is a publication of false material, expressed either in printing or in writing, or by signs and pictures, tending to injure the reputation or good name of another person or to expose the person to public hatred, contempt or ridicule or to injure the person in the maintenance of the person's business. Kerndt v. Rolling Hills Nat'l Bank, 558 N.W.2d 410, 418 (Iowa 1997); Ideal Instruments, Inc. v. Rivard Instruments, Inc., 434 F. Supp. 2d 598, 625 (N.D. Iowa 2006) (also assuming Iowa state courts would recognize defamation claims premised on allegations of patent infringement or trade libel); Lyons v. Midwest Glazing L.L.C., 235 F. Supp. 2d 1030, 1043 (N.D. Iowa 2002) (citations omitted); King v. Sioux City Radiological Group, P.C., 985 F. Supp. 869, 877 (N.D. Iowa 1997); Thomas v. St. Luke's Health Sys., Inc., 869 F. Supp. 1413, 1442 (N.D. Iowa 1994), aff'd, 61 F.3d 908 (8th Cir. 1995). To establish a prima facie case of defamation, a plaintiff must demonstrate that the defendant "(a) published a statement that was (b) defamatory and (c) of and concerning the plaintiff." Taggart v. Drake Univ., 549 N.W.2d 796, 802 (Iowa 1996); Dillon v. Ruperto, No. 09-0600, 2010 WL 2383517, at *7 (Iowa Ct. App. June 16, 2010); Brase v. Mosley, No. 00-0568, 2002 WL 31525366, at *5–6 (Iowa Ct. App. Nov. 15, 2002); Kent v. Iowa, 651 F. Supp. 2d 910, 962–64 (S.D. Iowa 2009); Mechdyne v. Garwood, 707 F. Supp. 2d 864 (S.D. Iowa 2009); Brass v. City of Manly, No. C02-3004-PAZ, 2003 WL 1907158, at *10 (N.D. Iowa Apr. 17, 2003); Morris v. Am. Freightways, Inc., No. 4:01-CV-40475, 2003 WL 472510, at *2 (S.D. Iowa Feb. 20, 2003); see also Malone v. Des Moines Area Cmty. Coll., No. 4:04-CV-40103, 2005 WL 290008, at *10 (S.D. Iowa Jan. 26, 2005) (citations omitted)

(listing elements that non-public plaintiff must prove when the statements are not libel per se as follows: "(1) that Defendants made the statements about Plaintiff; (2) the statements were false; (3) Defendants made the statements with malice; (4) Defendants communicated the statements to a party other than Plaintiff; and (5) a reasonable person would understand the statements to be an expression that would tend to injure a person's reputation, expose them to public hatred, contempt, or ridicule, or injure Plaintiff in the maintenance of his business"). The plaintiff's petition must state the defamatory sense in which such statement was used. Iowa Code § 659.1. See V.C, infra.

With respect to due process constitutional claims, in Mercer v. City of Cedar Rapids, 308 F.3d. 840, 849 (8th Cir. 2002), the Court held that comments made to the press after a police officer's termination "did not infringe a constitutionally recognized liberty interest" as they were limited to plaintiff's "ability to perform her job and the impact of her actions on the workplace." Therefore, the Court did not need to consider whether the "post-termination comments were the sort of random and unpredictable deprivation for which a post-deprivation tort action for slander satisfies the requirements of the Due Process Clause." Id. (citation omitted); see also Malone, 2005 WL 290008, at *11 (discussing standards, stating that "unsatisfactory performance or general misconduct are insufficient to create such a stigma that implicates an employee's liberty interest in his reputation," and rejecting argument that plaintiff's Fourteenth Amendment liberty interest was implicated by alleged statements); **Mills v. State of Iowa, No. 3:10-CV-112, 2012 WL 4514686, at *17-20 (S.D. Iowa Oct. 3. 2012) (generally holding same);** Brass v. City of Manly, No. C02-3004-PAZ, 2003 WL 1907158, at *9–10 (N.D. Iowa Apr. 17, 2003) (stating that former police chief had not been "accused of dishonesty, immorality, criminality, racism or the like" and therefore could not establish that any liberty interest had been impinged); see generally Mills v. Iowa Bd. of Regents, 770 F. Supp. 2d 986, 1001 (S.D. Iowa 2011) (discussing due process and terminated employee's allegation he was entitled to name-clearing hearing); Christiansen v. West Branch Comm. Sch. Dist., No. 10-CV-131, 2011 WL 1230274, at *11–12 (N.D. Iowa Mar. 28, 2011) (discussing employee's substantive due process claim).

2. ***Fault.*** The level of fault a plaintiff must demonstrate depends on whether the plaintiff is a private individual, a public official or, for purposes of certain damage claims, whether the statement relates to a matter of public concern. See generally Brase v. Mosley, No. 00-0568, 2002 WL 31525366, at *4 (Iowa Ct. App. Nov. 15, 2002) (citations omitted) (stating that the definition of actual malice set forth in New York Times applies to both media and non-media defendants in cases involving defamation claims by public figures or officials). The issue of the plaintiff's status as a private individual or a public figure is a question of law to be resolved by the trial court. Anderson v. Low Rent Hous. Comm'n, 304 N.W.2d 239, 245, 7 Media L. Rep. 1726, 1728 (Iowa 1981). Such a finding by the trial court is subject to de novo review. Id.; Brase v. Mosley, No. 00-0568, 2002 WL 31525366, at *8 (Iowa Ct. App. Nov. 15, 2002) (stating that appellate review of public figure status implicates federal constitutional law, therefore, review is de novo).

a. **Private Figure Plaintiff/Matter of Public Concern.** A public concern encompasses "those controversies raising issues that might reasonably be expected to have impact beyond parties directly enmeshed in the particular controversy." Jones v. Palmer Commc'ns, Inc., 440 N.W.2d 884, 900, 16 Media L. Rep. 2137, 2148 (Iowa 1989) (citing In re IBP Confidential Bus. Documents Litig., 797 F.2d 632, 644, 13 Media L. Rep. 1113, 1122 (8th Cir. 1986)). In Jones, a case involving a private figure plaintiff, the Court declined to extend full constitutional protection to issues of public concern. The Court adopted a standard analogous to a professional malpractice standard of negligence in a case involving a fire fighter whose employment was terminated. However, the Court said that punitive damages could not be awarded in cases involving issues of public concern without clear and convincing proof of actual malice. Id., 16 Media L. Rep. at 2147–48. Iowa courts have held the following are matters of public concern: controversies relating to government agencies and programs, see, e.g., Jones v. Palmer Commc'ns, Inc., 440 N.W.2d 884, 16 Media L. Rep. 1726 (Iowa 1981); Haas v. Evening Democrat Co., 252 Iowa 517, 107 N.W.2d 444 (1961); public records, Howard v. Des Moines Register & Tribune Co., 283 N.W.2d 289, 5 Media L. Rep. 1667 (Iowa 1979); conduct of public officials in discharge of their official duties, McCarney v. Des Moines Register & Tribune Co., 239 N.W.2d 152 (Iowa 1976); issues of public notoriety or matters that have become public knowledge, see, e.g., Bremer v. Journal-Tribune Publ'g Co., 247 Iowa 817, 76 N.W.2d 762 (Iowa 1956) (finding body of local missing boy). The Court found no valid public interest or concern in the following cases: bidding for vacant public land before a televised session of the Des Moines City Council, Rees v. O'Malley, 461 N.W.2d 833 (Iowa 1990); investigation of bank shortage, Brown v. First Nat'l Bank of Mason City, 193 N.W.2d 547 (Iowa 1972). In addition, the Court has held that simple newsworthiness will not by itself generate a valid public concern. Jones v. Palmer Commc'ns, Inc., 440 N.W.2d 884, 900, 16 Media L. Rep. 2137, 2148 (Iowa 1989).

b. **Private Figure Plaintiff/Matter of Private Concern.** A plaintiff alleging defamation ordinarily must prove that the statements at issue were made with malice, were false and caused damage. Kerndt v. Rolling Hills Nat'l Bank, 558 N.W.2d 410, 418 (Iowa 1997) (citing Jenkins v. Wal-Mart Stores, Inc., 910 F. Supp. 1399, 1425 (N.D. Iowa 1995)); Malone v. Des Moines Area Cmty. Coll., No. 4:04-CV-40103, 2005 WL 290008, at*10 (S.D. Iowa Jan. 26, 2005) (discussing elements plaintiff must prove when statements are not libel per se). If the statements are determined to be defamatory per se, malice is presumed. Vinson v. Linn-Mar Cmty. Sch. Dist., 360 N.W.2d 108, 117 (Iowa 1984); see also Harrington v. Wilber, 353 F. Supp. 2d 1033, 1039 (S.D. Iowa 2005) (citations omitted) (stating that defamatory per se statements "'are actionable in and of themselves without proof of malice, falsity or damage. In actions based on language not libelous per se, all of these elements must be proved . . . .'"). See discussion of Schlegel v. Ottumwa Courier, 585 N.W.2d 217, 27 Media L. Rep. 1178 (Iowa 1998) in I.B.8.a, infra, with respect to issue of defamation per se and presumed damages.

c. **Public Figure Plaintiff/Matter of Public Concern.** There are two types of public figures: those who through fame and notoriety are public figures for all purposes, and those who inject themselves or are drawn into a particular public controversy and thereby become public persons for matters which are of public concern. Anderson v. Low Rent Hous. Comm'n, 304 N.W.2d 239, 245, 7 Media L. Rep. 1726, 1727 (Iowa 1981) (citing Gertz v. Robert Welch, Inc., 418 U.S. 323, 94 S. Ct. 2997, 41 L. Ed. 2d 789, 1 Media L. Rep. 1633 (U.S. 1974)). Whether or not a person is a public figure is a matter of law for the court to decide. Brase v. Mosley, No. 00-0568, 2002 WL 31525366, at *7–8 (Iowa Ct. App. Nov. 15, 2002) (citation omitted). In Brase, 2002 WL 31525366, at *3, at the time allegedly defamatory statements were made to a local newspaper regarding the plaintiff's ownership of "drug houses," the plaintiff was running for city council in a campaign based upon raising public awareness of the need to save old buildings. The Iowa Court of Appeals concluded that the plaintiff was a limited purpose public figure and that recovery required proof of New York Times actual malice. Id. In Kiesau v. Bantz, 686 N.W.2d 164, 178 (Iowa 2004) (citations omitted), the Iowa Supreme Court noted that it had "previously rejected the expansive view that all government employees are public officials as inconsistent with the plain meaning of the standards announced by the Supreme Court," and held that "a low ranking deputy sheriff" is not a public official.

Public figures alleging defamation must demonstrate New York Times "actual malice" by clear and convincing evidence. Jones v. Palmer Commc'ns, Inc., 440 N.W.2d 884, 895, 16 Media L. Rep. 2137, 2143 (Iowa 1989); Anderson, 304 N.W.2d at 247; Blessum v. Howard County Bd. of Supervisors, 295 N.W.2d 836, 843 (Iowa 1980); see also Campbell v. Citizens For An Honest Gov't, 255 F.3d 560, 569–76, 29 Media L. Rep. 2155, 2160–65 (8th Cir. 2001) (applying federal law, examining evidence, and concluding public figure law enforcement plaintiffs had not met burden of proving by clear and convincing evidence that the defendants acted with actual malice). See II.A.2.d. (1), infra. Recently, the Supreme Court of Iowa expressly adopted the principle of defamation by implication and extended the theory to public figure suits. Stevens v. Iowa Newspapers, Inc., 728 N.W.2d 823, 827–29, 35 Media L. Rep. 1385 (Iowa 2007) (citation omitted) (stating that "defamation by implication arises, not from what is stated, but from what is implied when a defendant (1) juxtaposes a series of facts so as to imply a defamatory connection between them, or (2) creates a defamatory implication by omitting facts . . . even though the particular facts are correct").

3. ***Falsity.*** Generally, to support a claim for defamation, the plaintiff must establish the statement was false. Huegerich v. IBP, Inc., 547 N.W.2d 216, 221 (Iowa 1996) (citing Restatement (Second) of Torts, § 558 (1977)); see also Mercer v. City of Cedar Rapids, 308 F.3d 840, 848 (8th Cir. 2002) (citations omitted) (stating rule that "[i]f the accusation is general and implies the commission of unspecified misconduct of a particular type, the statement is true if the plaintiff committed any misconduct of that type"); Campbell v. Citizens For An Honest Gov't, 255 F.3d 560, 567–69, 29 Media L. Rep. 2155, 2159–60 (8th Cir. 2001) (applying federal law and examining whether public figure law enforcement plaintiffs had met burden of proving the falsity of the statements); **Home Show Tours, Inc. v. Quad City Virtual, Inc., 827 F.Supp.2d 924, 941-44 (S.D. Iowa 2011) (holding libel claims failed because statements were not false)**. However, a finding that a statement is "libelous per se relieves the plaintiff of the obligation to prove that the statements were false." King v. Sioux City Radiological Group, P.C., 985 F. Supp. 869, 878 (N.D. Iowa 1977) (citing Lara v. Thomas, 512 N.W.2d 777, 785 (Iowa 1994); Vinson v. Linn-Mar Cmty. Sch. Dist., 360 N.W.2d 108, 115–16 (Iowa 1984)); see also Harrington v. Wilber, 353 F. Supp. 2d 1033, 1039 (S.D. Iowa 2005) (citations omitted) (stating that defamatory per se statements "'are actionable in and of themselves without proof of malice, falsity or damage. In actions based on language not libelous per se, all of these elements must be proved . . . .'"). See Part II.B.1, infra. In Morris v. Am. Freightways, Inc., No. 4:01-CV-40475, 2003 WL 472510 (S.D. Iowa Feb. 20, 2003), plaintiff employee was terminated because his employer suspected him of dishonesty. The employee brought a defamation suit against his former employer alleging that the reason for his termination was being circulated by his former co-workers. Id. at *1. The Court held that the plaintiff's defamation claim failed because the truth of the allegedly defamatory statements concerning the reason for his termination was not disputed as the plaintiff conceded he was terminated for suspicion of dishonesty. Id. at *3.

However, the Supreme Court of Iowa recently adopted the principle of defamation by implication, which "arises, not from what is stated, but from what is implied when a defendant (1) juxtaposes a series of facts so as to imply a defamatory connection between them, or (2) creates a defamatory implication by omitting facts . . . even though the particular facts are correct." Stevens v. Iowa Newspapers, Inc., 728 N.W.2d 823, 827–29, 35 Media L. Rep. 1385 (Iowa 2007) (citation omitted). "Otherwise, by a careful choice of words in juxtaposition of statements in a publication, a potential defendant may make statements that are true yet just as damaging as if they were actually false." Id. at 828.

4. ***Defamatory Statement of Fact.*** As discussed in I.B.1, supra, defamatory language must, when given its ordinary meaning, "impute to the person assailed some act or attribute tending to expose him to public hatred or ridicule." Quinn v. Prudential Ins. Co., 116 Iowa 522, 90 N.W. 349 (1902); see Stevens v. Iowa Newspapers, Inc., 728

N.W.2d 823, 832, 35 Media L. Rep. 1385 (Iowa 2007) (holding that statement that plaintiff had made "near libelous characterizations" is "so nebulous it is incapable, as a matter of law, of bearing a defamatory meaning"); Lloyd v. Drake Univ., 686 N.W.2d 225, 232 (Iowa 2004) (holding that statements in report of a panel organized by plaintiff's former employer to study an allegedly racially motivated incident involving plaintiff-former security guard could not "reasonably be interpreted as suggesting [plaintiff] was a racist"); Godfredsen v. Lutheran Bhd., No. 0-431, 2000 WL 1675869, at *4 (Iowa Ct. App. Nov. 8, 2000) (finding that employer's statements to its insureds regarding former agent could reasonably be understood as defamatory because at a minimum they contained negative imputations regarding agent's work and potentially even accused agent of a criminal offense); Park v. Hill, 380 F. Supp. 2d 1002, 1016–17 (N.D. Iowa 2005) (holding that statement was not defamatory where the factual inference lacked any tendency to injure plaintiff's reputation or expose him to "public hatred, contempt or ridicule," or to injure him in the maintenance of his business); **see also Home Show Tours, Inc. v. Quad City Virtual, Inc., 827 F.Supp.2d 924, 942-43 (S.D. Iowa 2011) (citing Yates v. Iowa West Racing Ass'n, 721 N.W.2d 762, 771-72 (Iowa 2006)) (discussing the "four-factor test for the trial court to use in determining whether the challenged statement is defamatory")**. "It is for the court to determine whether words are capable of a defamatory meaning and for the jury to determine whether they were so understood." Kiner v. Reliance Ins. Co., 463 N.W.2d 9, 14 (Iowa 1990) (citing Brown v. First Nat'l Bank, 193 N.W.2d 547, 552 (Iowa 1972)); **see Home Show Tours, Inc., 827 F.Supp.2d 924 at 942-43 (citing Yates, 721 N.W.2d at 771-72) (stating court should not indulge far-fetched interpretations but rather should construe the statements as they would be understood by the common or average mind);** Kerndt v. Rolling Hills Nat'l Bank, 558 N.W.2d 410 (Iowa 1997); Wilson v. IBP, Inc., 558 N.W.2d 132 (Iowa 1996); Lowe v. Todd's Flying Serv., Inc., No. 99-0708, 2001 WL 58113, at *4 (Iowa Ct. App. Jan. 24, 2001) (noting that if a statement is susceptible to more than one possible meaning the jury must decide if it is defamatory, but affirming summary judgment dismissing libel claim because the statements were not libel per se and former employer failed to establish any harm); Brass v. City of Manly, No. C02-3004-PAZ, 2003 WL 1907158, at *32 (N.D. Iowa Apr. 17, 2003).

5. ***Of and Concerning Plaintiff.*** To establish a case of defamation, a plaintiff must establish the statement in question was of and concerning him or her. Taggart v. Drake Univ., 549 N.W.2d 796, 802 (Iowa 1996); Huegerich v. IBP, Inc., 547 N.W.2d 216, 221 (Iowa 1996) (citing Restatement (Second) of Torts, § 558 (1977)); see also Yates v. Iowa West Racing Ass'n, No. 04-0434, 2005 WL 2509688, at *4 n.3 (Iowa Ct. App. Oct. 12, 2005) (noting that statement at issue did not identify the plaintiffs and holding it "cannot constitute slander"). However, the alleged defamatory publication need not mention the plaintiff by name; a publication may be libelous if it could reasonably be held to be "of or concerning" the plaintiff. Shaw Cleaners & Dyers v. Des Moines Dress Club, 215 Iowa 1130, 245 N.W. 231 (1932); see generally Mercer v. City of Cedar Rapids, 308 F.3d 840, 847–48 (8th Cir. 2002). In Ball v. Taylor, 416 F.3d 915, 917–18 (8th Cir. 2005), the Eighth Circuit held that when an employer made statements at a press conference that union employees had filed fraudulent disability claims, those statements "could reasonably be understood to be of and concerning each employee," even though the employer did not state the names of the employees individually. Because the employer referred to the employees as a group, and then disseminated copies of the complaint identifying the employees, a conclusion could be drawn that those statements "specifically referenced each of the employees." Id. Thus, the Eighth Circuit "need not predict whether the Iowa Supreme Court would adopt" the group defamation doctrine (which generally provides "that a plaintiff's membership in a defamed group does not give rise to an individual cause of action for defamation") because an exception to the doctrine was applicable even if the doctrine was accepted by Iowa courts and that exception is consistent with Iowa law. Id. After remand, the jury awarded damages to the 20 plaintiffs remaining in the case. The U.S. District Court granted the defendant judgment as a matter of law on the ground there was insufficient proof at trial that the statements were "of and concerning each remaining plaintiff." The Eighth Circuit affirmed in a second appeal, stating the plaintiffs "presented insufficient evidence 'to establish that anyone in Taylor's audience understood the individual plaintiffs to be the object of his statements.'" Brummett et al. v. Taylor, 569 F.3d 890, 892 (8th Cir. 2009). In Reeder v. Carroll, 759 F. Supp. 2d 1064, 1082–84 (N.D. Iowa 2010), a federal court discussed Ball and concluded that "regardless of whether the Iowa Supreme Court would adopt the [group defamation] doctrine [it] has interpreted the third element [of a defamation claim] in a manner consistent with the group defamation exception.'" The Reeder Court concluded statements referring to "this group" failed because "nothing suggests that 'the circumstances of the publication reasonably give rise to the conclusion that there is a particular reference to'" plaintiff. Id.

6. ***Publication.*** In order to prevail on a libel claim, the plaintiff must prove the alleged defamatory statements were published. Huegerich v. IBP, Inc., 547 N.W.2d 216, 221 (Iowa 1996) (citing Belcher v. Little, 315 N.W.2d 734, 737 (Iowa 1982)); Marks v. Estate of Hartgerink, 528 N.W.2d 539, 545 (Iowa 1995) (citing Royston v. Vander Linden, 197 Iowa 536, 536, 197 N.W. 435, 436 (1924)); see also Cedar Rapids Lodge & Suites, LLC v. JFS Dev., Inc., No. 09-CV-175, 2011 WL 149964, at *2 (N.D. Iowa Jan. 18, 2011) (granting summary judgment dismissal of defamation claim because evidence did not establish triable issue of publication); Reeder v. Carroll, 759 F. Supp. 2d 1064, 1081–82 (N.D. Iowa 2010) (granting summary judgment dismissal of defamation and false light claims based on letters for which there was insufficient evidence that the defendant was the writer or publisher). "It is elementary one cannot be liable for slander by the use of defamatory language which is heard only by the party to whom the words refer." Marks, 528 N.W.2d at 545 (citing Royston,

197 Iowa at 536, 197 N.W. at 436); see also Jenkins v. Wal-Mart Stores, Inc., 910 F. Supp. 1399, 1425 (N.D. Iowa 1995); Davenport v. City of Corning, No. 06-1156, 2007 WL 3085797, at *5–6 (Iowa Ct. App. Oct. 24, 2007) (holding that defendant's communication of defamatory statements to private investigators hired by plaintiff in response to "artful questions from the investigators designed to" induce him to say something defamatory about the plaintiff were not "published"). In addition, Iowa courts have held that every publication or repetition of a defamatory matter constitutes a separate and independent claim from the original publication. Kiner v. Reliance Ins. Co., 463 N.W.2d 9, 14 (Iowa 1990) (citing Bond v. Lotz, 214 Iowa 683, 687, 243 N.W. 586, 587 (1932)). Generally speaking, when an allegedly defamed party is responsible for showing the libelous language to others, the element of publication is not satisfied. See Huegerich, 547 N.W.2d at 221; Suntken v. Den Ouden, 548 N.W.2d 164 (Iowa Ct. App. 1964). See I.6.b. infra.

a. **Intracorporate Communication.** The Iowa Supreme Court has declined to determine whether intra-office defamation meets the standard of publication. In Taggart v. Drake Univ., 549 N.W.2d 796, 803 (Iowa 1996), the Court recognized that there are two lines of cases in other jurisdictions on the subject—one that holds that intra-office statements do not amount to publication and one that holds that such statements are published but are subject to a qualified privilege. The Court stated that it "need not and do[es] not opt for either line of cases because plaintiff loses either way." In dicta, the United States District Court for the Northern District of Iowa hints that such internal communications may not meet the standard of publication. See King v. Sioux City Radiological Group, P.C., 985 F. Supp. 869, 877 n. 3 (N.D. Iowa 1997). See Part III.D, infra.

b. **Compelled Self-Publication.** Iowa courts have recognized that self-publication by the plaintiff may support a defamation action where the plaintiff is under a strong compulsion to do so. See Thomas v. St. Luke's Health Sys., Inc., 869 F. Supp. 1413, 1444 (N.D. Iowa 1994), aff'd, 61 F.3d 908 (8th Cir. 1995) (citing Belcher v. Little, 315 N.W.2d 734, 738 (Iowa 1982)); Suntken v. Den Ouden, 548 N.W.2d 164, 167 (Iowa Ct. App. 1996). "What constitutes strong compulsion must of necessity be decided by the finder of fact under the circumstances in each case when substantial evidence of such compulsion is introduced." Id. (citing Belcher, 315 N.W.2d at 738); Hofer v. Catfish Bend Casinos, No. 03-2061, 2004 WL 1813097, at *1 (Iowa Ct. App. Aug. 11, 2004) (affirming summary judgment dismissal of libel claim because, "[a] lthough compulsion is a question for the fact-finder," there was no genuine issue of material fact with respect to whether plaintiff had disclosed under compulsion to his friends the contents of a letter from defendant-casino excluding him from casino property, because his disclosure to acquaintances was made merely because they "were asking him why he was no longer coming to the casino"). In Ollie v. Titan Tire Corp., No. 4-00-CV-10457, 2002 U.S. Dist. LEXIS 12949, at *15 (S.D. Iowa Mar. 6, 2002), aff'd, 336 F.3d 680 (8th Cir. 2003), the plaintiff asserted that publication of allegedly defamatory statements occurred when he was compelled to disclose the alleged basis for his termination when applying for unemployment benefits and filing charges with the Iowa Civil Rights Commission and the Equal Employment Opportunity Commission. The Court stated that despite a "relatively liberal view of publication," employers "are not without protection." Id. at *16 (citing Theisen v. Covenant Med. Ctr., 636 N.W.2d 74, 83 (Iowa 2001)). Therein, the Court concluded that the defendant was protected by a qualified privilege. Id. at *17; see also Theisen v. Covenant Med. Ctr., Inc., 636 N.W.2d 74 (Iowa 2001) (addressing the nexus between doctrines of qualified immunity and compelled self-publication, and recognizing "a qualified privilege for statements made by employers to employees concerning the reasons for an employee's discharge regardless of whether the employer or employee publishes the statement"); Wright v. Keokuk County Health Ctr., 399 F. Supp. 2d 938, 958 (S.D. Iowa 2005) (granting qualified privilege to employer for statements regarding employee termination despite foreseeability that employee would feel compelled to repeat them in future job interviews); Thompto v. Coborn's, Inc., 871 F. Supp. 1097, 1128 (N.D. Iowa 1994) (stating that if the publication by the defendant was subject to a qualified privilege, that privilege would extend to any self-republication).

c. **Republication.** Individuals who make libelous statements are liable for damages resulting from the repetition or republication of such statements, when such repetition or republication could reasonably be foreseen. Thomas v. St. Luke's Health Sys., Inc., 869 F. Supp. 1413, 1442 (N.D. Iowa 1994), aff'd, 61 F.3d 908 (8th Cir. 1995) (citing Brown v. First Nat'l Bank of Mason City, 193 N.W.2d 547, 554 (Iowa 1972)). Iowa courts have not yet dealt with the independent liability of a republisher.

An employer or corporation may be held liable for defamation by an employee if the defamatory statement was published by a fellow employee who was acting within the scope of his or her employment. Huegerich v. IBP, Inc., 547 N.W.2d 216, 221 (Iowa 1996) (citing Vowles v. Yakish, 191 Iowa 368, 371–72, 179 N.W. 117, 119 (1920)). See III.G.1 infra.

7. ***Statements versus Conduct.*** In Theisen v. Covenant Med. Ctr, Inc., 636 N.W.2d 74 (Iowa 2001), the Iowa Court addressed dramatic pantomime and noted "[p]roof that a terminated employee was simply escorted from the place of employment, without words or other conduct, has been held insufficient as a matter of law to establish a claim of defamation by dramatic pantomime." Id. (citing Bolton v. Dep't of Human Servs., 540 N.W.2d 523, 525 (Minn. 1995)). The Court further stated "such incidents are part of the everyday work environment," and that there could be no "publication" if no

one had actually seen the plaintiff being escorted from the building. Id. See also Huegerich v. IBP, Inc., 547 N.W.2d 216, 221, 223 (Iowa 1996) (noting that "courts have reached different results on whether the act of terminating an employee is defamatory" and "whether an investigation by an employer into a suspected crime of an employee constitutes a defamatory publication," and holding that actions of management in conducting random drug search and subsequently discharging employee were insufficient to constitute a defamatory publication).

8. ***Damages.*** Before a plaintiff can make a recovery in a defamation action, he or she must prove some sort of "cognizable injury, such as injury to reputation" to recover actual damages. Johnson v. Nickerson, 542 N.W.2d 506, 513 (Iowa 1996); see also Graves v. Iowa Lakes Cmty. Coll., 639 N.W.2d 22, 26 (Iowa 2002) (noting there can be no recovery in a defamation action if there is no injury.); **Home Show Tours, Inc. v. Quad City Virtual, Inc., 827 F.Supp.2d 924, 941–44 (S.D. Iowa 2011) (holding plaintiff failed to prove damages as, *inter alia*, it failed to identify any specific individual that had not hired it as a result of the alleged libelous statements)**; Sykes v. Hengel, 394 F. Supp. 2d 1062, 1072 (S.D. Iowa 2005) (citing Kiesau v. Bantz, 686 N.W.2d 164 (Iowa 2004)) (holding that because statement was not libelous per se Plaintiff must "prove some cognizable injury to his reputation," and evidence of hurt feelings "is not enough to defeat summary judgment in an action for libel per quod"); see generally Bruning v. Carroll Cmty. Sch. Dist., No. C04-3091-MWB, 2006 WL 1234822, at *44 (N.D. Iowa May 3, 2006) ("[W]ords are defamatory per se only if they are of such a nature, whether true or not, that the court can presume as a matter of law that their publication will have defamatory effect."). Under Iowa law, a corporation may recover damages for injury to its reputation as well as recovery of lost profits. Lundell Mfg. Co. v. Am. Broad. Cos., 98 F.3d 351, 364, 25 Media L. Rep. 1001, 1011 (8th Cir. 1996).

a. **Presumed Damages and Libel Per Se.** Iowa courts have said defamation per se is actionable without proof of harm. See Godfredsen v. Lutheran Bhd., No. 0-431, 2000 WL 1675869, at *4 (Iowa Ct. App. Nov. 8, 2000) (citing Wilson v. IBP, Inc., 558 N.W.2d 132, 139 (Iowa 1996)); Lara v. Thomas, 512 N.W.2d 777, 786 (Iowa 1994) (citing Rees v. O'Malley, 461 N.W.2d 833, 839 (Iowa 1990)) (stating that recovery is limited to those damages which are "the natural and probable consequences of the publication," including recovery for emotional distress and resulting bodily harm); Brown v. First Nat'l Bank of Mason City, 193 N.W.2d 547, 555 (Iowa 1972) (The jury must be presented with evidence upon which the consequences may be judged, such as the nature of the plaintiff's reputation before the publication and the extent of publication.); Gries v. Akal Security, Inc., No. 06-CV-33-LRR, 2007 U.S. Dist. LEXIS 71902, at *110 (S.D. Iowa Aug. 27, 2007); Harrington v. Wilber, 353 F. Supp. 2d 1033, 1039 (S.D. Iowa 2005) (citations omitted) (stating that defamatory per se statements "'are actionable in and of themselves without proof of malice, falsity or damage. In actions based on language not libelous per se, all of these elements must be proved . . . .'"); see generally Barreca v. Nickolas, 683 N.W.2d 111, 116 (Iowa 2004) (discussing slander per se); Kent v. Iowa, 651 F. Supp. 2d 910, 963–64 (S.D. Iowa 2009) (discussing elements of slander per se in the context of an employee making accusations of sexual harassment); Mechdyne Corp. v. Garwood, 707 F. Supp. 2d 864 (S.D. Iowa 2009) (discussing elements of libel per se versus libel per quod); Bruning v. Carroll Cmty. Sch. Dist., No. C04-3091-MWB, 2006 WL 1234022, at *44 (N.D. Iowa May 3, 2006) (citing Kiesau v. Bantz, 686 N.W.2d 164, 175 (Iowa 2004)) ("[A]n attack on the integrity and moral character of a party is [defamatory] per se."); Wright v. Keokuk County Health Ctr., 399 F. Supp. 2d 938, 949 (S.D. Iowa 2005) (discussing slander per se in the general category of "incompetence in occupation"); Park v. Hill, 380 F. Supp. 2d 1002, 1016 (N.D. Iowa 2005) (discussing defamation per se). **However, an Iowa case has stated "while statements that are libelous per se require no proof of damages, in order for the fact finder to determine the extent of the injury, there must be evidence of reputation and the extent of publication." RC & CA Doghouse, L.L.C. v. Riccadonna, No. 11-1400, 2012 WL 2407383, at *9–10 (Iowa Ct. App. June 27, 2012) (citing Rees, 461 N.W.2d at 839) (noting oral testimony, including testimony regarding embarrassment, and upholding $5,000 reputational damages award)**.

In Schlegel v. Ottumwa Courier, 585 N.W.2d 217, 27 Media L. Rep. 1178 (Iowa 1998), a defamation case against a *media* defendant, the Iowa Supreme Court ruled that a plaintiff must prove reputational harm "to recover 'parasitic' damages such as emotional distress and humiliation." See also Bradbery v. Dubuque County, No. 99-1881, 2001 WL 23144, at *3 (Iowa Ct. App. Jan. 10, 2001) (recognizing that Schlegel overruled Jones v. Palmer Commc'ns, Inc., 440 N.W.2d 884 (Iowa 1989) on this issue). In Kiesau v. Bantz, 686 N.W.2d 164, 178 (Iowa 2004) (citing Schlegel, 585 N.W.2d at 222–23), a defamation case against a *non-media* defendant, the Court stated: "Once the jury found the altered photograph was libelous per se, the law conclusively presumed the existence of damages to [plaintiff's] reputation from the publication and allowed the jury to award substantial damages without proving actual damage to her reputation. In addition to damages to [plaintiff's] reputation, she is also entitled to damages for the actual injury inflicted by the libelous statement including personal humiliation, mental anguish and suffering, and the out-of-pocket costs for treating those conditions."

(1) **Employment-Related Criticism.** Statements that reflect on an employee's capacity or fitness to perform his or her business, trade, profession or office have been held defamatory per se. Huegerich v. IBP, Inc., 547 N.W.2d 216, 221 (Iowa 1996) (employer's inquiries as to whether employee has a drug problem can be defamatory per se because imputation of substance abuse clearly reflects on employee's capacity and fitness to perform his or her duties); Lara v. Thomas, 512 N.W.2d 777, 785 (Iowa 1994) (employer's imputation of employee's substance abuse found

reflective on employee's abilities to perform the duties of veterinary assistant and held to be defamatory per se); White & Johnson, P.C. v. Bayne, No. 3-211/02-0757, 2003 WL 21696938, at *4 (Iowa Ct. App. July 23, 2003) (holding statement that "challenged plaintiffs' skill in their profession and the occupation by which they earn a living" was defamatory per se); Gries v. Akal Security, Inc., No. 06-CV-33-LRR, 2007 U.S. Dist. LEXIS 71902, at *110 (S.D. Iowa Aug. 27, 2007) (holding that alleged defamatory statements that plaintiff aggressively pushed a coworker qualify as defamation per se because they affect plaintiff's reputation in his business); Wright v. Keokuk County Health Ctr., 399 F. Supp. 2d 938, 951–52 (S.D. Iowa 2005) (finding that employee's alleged misuse of company credit card and tax identification number "reflect on his integrity, trustworthiness, and fitness . . . for his job duties" and are therefore slander per se); Smith v. Iowa Jewish Senior Life Ctr., 161 F. Supp. 2d 991, 999 (S.D. Iowa 2001) (applying Iowa law and holding as slanderous per se statement by former employer's attorney to husband of current employer that employee was suing former employer for sex discrimination but that the former employer's position was that she was fired for falsifying records); King v. Sioux City Radiological Group, P.C., 985 F. Supp. 869, 878 (N.D. Iowa 1997) (statement that hospital's director of radiology was not competent in his employment and a liar was libelous per se); Jenkins v. Wal-Mart Stores, Inc., 910 F. Supp. 1399, 1426 (N.D. Iowa 1995) (alleged statements by former department store employee's supervisor regarding employee's alleged theft of television set from store were defamatory per se); see also Kiesau v. Bantz, 686 N.W.2d 164, 178 (Iowa 2004) (holding there was substantial evidence to support finding that altered photograph showing plaintiff-officer "standing with her K-9 dog in front of her sheriff's vehicle in uniform with her breasts exposed" was libelous per se as photograph "could be reasonably understood to attack the integrity and moral character" of plaintiff); Harrington v. Wilber, 353 F. Supp. 2d 1033, 1040 (S.D. Iowa 2005) (discussing defamatory per se statements and holding that accusation that plaintiff was a murderer was defamatory per se); see generally Barreca v. Nickolas, 683 N.W.2d 111, 116 (Iowa 2004) (citations omitted) (discussing general categories of slander per se statements); **Home Show Tours, Inc. v. Quad City Virtual, Inc., 827 F.Supp.2d 924, 941 (S.D. Iowa 2011) (same)**; Iowa Protection & Advocacy Servs., Inc. v. Tanager Place, No. C-04-0069, 2005 WL 2035225, at *4 (N.D. Iowa Aug. 24, 2005) (emphasis added) (citations omitted) (holding that "to prove defamation per se it is sufficient to show [the] statements *affected* [the plaintiff's] business or attacked its integrity or moral character"). But see generally Sykes v. Hengel, 394 F. Supp. 2d 1062, 1075 (S.D. Iowa 2005) (stating that "[w]hile a businessperson may feel bruised by statements suggesting business failure on his watch, accurate statements of the condition of the company during that period do not support a cause of action on this theory of liability," and holding that statements at issue did not constitute libel per se as a matter of law). "'An attack on the integrity and moral character of a party'" is also libelous per se. Sykes, 394 F. Supp. 2d at 1072 (citing Vinson v. Linn-Mar Cmty. Sch. Dist., 360 N.W.2d 108, 115–16 (Iowa 1985)); Kono v. Meeker, 743 N.W.2d 872 (Iowa Ct. App. 2007) (citing Vinson v. Linn-Mar Cmty. Sch. Dist., 360 N.W.2d 108, 115–16 (Iowa 1985)).

"If a statement is clear and unambiguous, the issue of whether the statement is libelous per se is for the court," and if "the court determines a statement is libelous per se as a matter of law, the burden shifts to the defendant to prove the statement was used and understood in a different sense." Kiesau v. Bantz, 686 N.W.2d 164, 175 (Iowa 2004) (citations omitted); Iowa Protection & Advocacy Servs., Inc., 2005 WL 2035225, at *4 (citing Vinson, 360 N.W.2d at 116); **see also Home Show Tours, Inc., 827 F.Supp.2d at 941**. "If the language can reasonably be construed as having two meanings, then it is up to the jury to decide whether the statement is libelous per se." Kiesau, 686 N.W.2d at 175 (citation omitted); Iowa Protection & Advocacy Servs., Inc., 2005 WL 2035225, at *5; see also Harrington, 353 F. Supp. 2d at 1040 (citations omitted) ("The determinative rule is: 'If the language is capable of two meanings including the one ascribed by the complainant, it is for the jury to say whether such meaning was the one conveyed.'"). "In determining whether language is libelous per se, it must be viewed stripped of any pleaded innuendo. . . . Words which are libelous per se do not need an innuendo, and, conversely, words which need an innuendo are not libelous per se." Sykes, 394 F. Supp. 2d at 1072 (citations and internal quotation marks omitted). A statement is libelous per quod "if it is necessary to refer to facts or circumstances beyond the words actually used to establish the defamation." Id. (citing Johnson v. Nickerson, 542 N.W.2d 506, 510 (Iowa 1996)) (internal quotation marks omitted).

Any employer that attempts to "blacklist" a discharged or former employee or prevent such former employee from obtaining other employment shall be liable for treble damages. Iowa Code § 730.2; see also Iowa Code § 730.1 (damages and serious misdemeanor); see generally Iowa Code § 730.3 (simple misdemeanor for false charges concerning honesty); Thomas v. Union Pac. R.R. Co., No. 44-99-cv-20188, 2001 WL 741739, at *2–4 (S.D. Iowa May 23, 2001) (holding the public policy underlying Iowa Code § 730.2 does not create an exception to the employment at-will doctrine where plaintiffs allege wrongful failure to rehire). In Glenn v. Diabetes Treatment Ctrs., 116 F. Supp. 2d 1098, 1103–04 (S.D. Iowa 2000), the Court discussed generally the elements of civil blacklisting and noted the dearth of Iowa case law interpreting Iowa's statute. In granting summary judgment for the employer, the Court predicted that the Iowa Supreme Court would require that the alleged blacklisting be intentional, because "without the element of intent, a former employer could conceivably be exposed to treble damages for a mistake in providing information about a former employee to a prospective employer." The Court of Appeals of Iowa discussed the application of Iowa Code § 730.2 in Conrad v. Iowa Central Community College, 756 N.W.2d 48, 2008 WL 2746324, at *3–5 (Iowa Ct. App. July 16, 2008) (unpublished). Specifically, the Court stated § 730.2 "applies to 'any discharged employee' and also to 'any employee who may have *voluntarily* left said company's service.'" Id. at *4 (emphasis added). Furthermore, citing language directly from the statute, the Court held that section 730.2 does not apply to individuals, but only to companies, partnerships, or corporations. Id. at *5. Thus, the employee had no blacklisting claim against the president of Iowa Central Community College individually, but did have a claim against Iowa Central Community College because the president "acted with the authority of [Iowa Central Community College]." Id.

(2) **Single Instance Rule.** Iowa courts have not recognized the "single instance rule."

b. **Punitive Damages.** Actual damages are a prerequisite to a claim for punitive damages. Schlegel v. Ottumwa Courier, 585 N.W.2d 217, 226, 27 Media L. Rep. 1178 (Iowa 1998) (citation omitted); see Brase v. Mosley, No. 00-0568, 2002 WL 31525366, at *5 (Iowa Ct. App. Nov. 15, 2002) (citation omitted); see also Caveman Adventures UN, Ltd. v. Press Citizen Co., Inc., 633 N.W.2d 757, 29 Media L. Rep. 2297 (Iowa 2001) (reversing punitive damage award for lack of actual malice); White & Johnson, P.C. v. Bayne, No. 3-211/02-0757, 2003 WL 21696938, at *6 (Iowa Ct. App. July 23, 2003) (citing Schlegel, 585 N.W.2d at 221–26) (vacating punitive damage award in favor of plaintiff who was not awarded compensatory damages for defamation claim as "lack of a damage award can be evidence of a lack of actual damages," and affirming punitive damages award in favor of other plaintiffs who had been awarded compensatory damages); C Plus Northwest, Inc. v. DeGroot, 534 F. Supp. 2d 937, 945 (S.D. Iowa 2008) (citing Schlegel). Generally, Iowa Code Chapter 668A controls recovery of punitive damages. In libel cases, the plaintiff, whether a private or public figure, must prove actual malice by clear and convincing evidence to recover such damages. See Wilson v. IBP, Inc., 558 N.W.2d 132, 140–41 (Iowa 1996); Lara v. Thomas, 512 N.W.2d 777, 786 (Iowa 1994); Thomas v. St. Luke's Health Sys., Inc., 869 F. Supp. 1413, 1442 (N.D. Iowa 1994), aff'd, 61 F.3d 908 (8th Cir. 1995); see also Caveman Adventures UN, Ltd. v. Press-Citizen Co., 633 N.W.2d 757, 761–62, 29 Media L. Rep. 2297, 2299–2301 (Iowa 2001) (citing Jones v. Palmer Commc'ns, Inc., 440 N.W.2d 884, 891 (Iowa 1989)) (noting that "punitive damages may not be recovered in defamation actions against media publishers or broadcasters unless actual malice is established" and holding after discussion of actual malice standard in context of commercial speech that there was insufficient evidence to show the media defendant acted with reckless disregard for the truth or with knowledge of the falsity of the advertisement); see generally Cawthorn v. Catholic Health Initiatives Iowa Corp., 743 N.W.2d 525, 528–29 (Iowa 2007) (discussing punitive damages generally). In general, "[a]wards will be tested with a view of the extent and nature of outrageous conduct, the amount necessary for future deterrence, and with deference to the relationship between the punitive award and plaintiff's injury, as reflected in any award for compensatory damages." Wilson, 558 N.W.2d at 147 (quoting Ezzone v. Riccardi, 525 N.W.2d 388, 399 (Iowa 1994) (citing Honda Motor Co., Ltd. v. Oberg, 512 U.S. 415, 114 S. Ct. 2331, 129 L. Ed. 2d 336 (U.S. Or. 1994))); **RC & CA Doghouse, L.L.C. v. Riccadonna, No. 11-1400, 2012 WL 2407383, at *10–11 (Iowa Ct. App. June 27, 2012) (generally discussing standards for punitive damages).** See II.A.2.d.(1), infra; I.B.2.a, supra. Punitive damages, of course, are subject to other state and federal constitution considerations.

II. PRIVILEGES AND DEFENSES

A. Scope of Privileges

1. ***Absolute Privilege.*** Iowa law recognizes an absolute privilege for defamatory statements made during a judicial proceeding. Kennedy v. Zimmerman, 601 N.W.2d 61, 64, 28 Media L. Rep. 1188, 1190 (Iowa 1999); Spencer v. Spencer, 479 N.W.2d 293, 295 (Iowa 1991); Beeck v. Kapalis, 302 N.W.2d 90, 97 (Iowa 1981); McFarland v. McFarland, Nos. C08-4047, C09-4047, 2011 WL 4402356, at *12–16 (N.D. Iowa Sept. 20, 2011) (discussing absolute privilege under Iowa law for statements in judicial proceeding, and predicting Iowa Supreme Court would apply privilege to *witnesses* pursuant to Restatement (Second) of Torts § 588); McFarland v. McFarland, No. C08-4047, 2010 WL 2899013, at *9 (N.D. Iowa July 26, 2010) (finding affidavit submitted to the court in a child custody and property distribution dispute was "made as part of a judicial proceeding" and thus protected by an absolute privilege); Mechdyne Corp. v. Garwood, 707 F. Supp. 2d 864 (S.D. Iowa 2009) (finding "litigation letters exchanged between counsel . . . are privileged and cannot form the basis of a defamation claim."). But see Kennedy v. Zimmerman, 601 N.W.2d 61, 65–66, 28 Media L. Rep. 1188, 1190–92 (Iowa 1999) (statements made to a reporter about judicial proceedings were not privileged because they were not in the course of a judicial proceeding); Rees v. O'Malley, 461 N.W.2d 833, 837 (Iowa 1990) (statements made during an open session of governmental body were not privileged); Cowman v. LaVine, 234 N.W.2d 114, 124 (Iowa 1975) (statements made at city council meeting by councilman about assistant police chief were not subject to absolute privilege); White & Johnson, P.C. v. Bayne, No. 3-211/02-0757, 2003 WL 21696938, at *3–4 (Iowa Ct. App. July 23, 2003) (holding that absolute judicial privilege did not apply to document entitled "Pretrial Brief" because document was mailed to plaintiff and third-parties prior to the commencement of litigation, "the document was not a pleading" nor something the court requested be filed, and the document was sent to persons not connected to the future litigation); Harrington v. Wilber, 353 F. Supp. 2d 1033, 1043–44 (S.D. Iowa 2005) (rejecting application of absolute prosecutorial immunity privilege to statements made by prosecutor at press conference); Smith v. Iowa Jewish Senior Life Ctr., 161 F. Supp. 2d 991, 999-1000 (S.D. Iowa 2001) (statement by former employer's attorney to husband of current employer, in response to his inquiry regarding employee's lawsuit against

former employer, was not protected by the judicial proceeding privilege because the current employer's husband "was not an attorney and did not have permission" to call on employee's behalf). "Judicial proceedings" include administrative proceedings. Tallman v. Hanssen, 427 N.W.2d 868, 869–70 (Iowa 1988) (workers' compensation hearing held to be judicial proceeding entitled to absolute privilege); see also Yates v. Iowa West Racing Ass'n, No. 04-0434, 2005 WL 2509688, at *3–4 (Iowa Ct. App. Oct. 12, 2005) (holding that "under the facts of the present case" the Iowa Racing and Gaming Commission "was acting in a judicial capacity" and thus statements made by attorney at meeting were protected by an absolute privilege); Wright v. Keokuk County Health Ctr., 399 F. Supp. 2d 938, 950–51 (S.D. Iowa 2005) (extending absolute privilege to unemployment insurance appeal that functioned as a judicial proceeding). In addition, communications preliminary to a judicial proceeding may be protected by the privilege. See Northrup v. Lewis, No. 7-209, 2007 Iowa Ct. App. LEXIS 505, at *4–6 (Iowa Ct. App. Apr. 25, 2007) (holding that "communication between two attorneys about a legal matter on behalf of their clients, and which was preliminary to judicial proceedings, was subject to an absolute privilege"); McFarland, 2011 WL 4402356, at *14 (stating Restatement (Second) of Torts § 588 applies to communications made "preliminary to" or "during" a judicial proceeding).

See generally Johnson v. Arden, 614 F.3d 785, 792 (8th Cir. 2010) (finding the Communications Decency Act of 1996, 47 U.S.C. § 230(c)(1) and (e)(3), provides internet service providers "with federal immunity against state tort defamation actions that would make service providers liable for information originating with third party users of the service . . . ."); Nieman v. Firstar Bank, No. C03-4113-MWB, 2005 WL 2346998, at *4–6 (N.D. Iowa Sep. 26, 2005) (holding that federal statute covering financial institutions conferred unqualified immunity on defendant national bank from liability for employee's defamation claim asserted in connection with defendant's involvement in criminal investigation of plaintiff's suspected wrongdoing); Graham v. Contract Transp., Inc., 4:98-cv-90546, 2001 WL 740118, at *6 (S.D. Iowa Apr. 24, 2001) (declining to decide whether drug testing services company was entitled to an absolute privilege based upon its argument an absolute privilege attached because of its duty to publish drug test results under Department of Transportation testing guidelines, but noting the defendant had made a "strong case" for its applicability).

2. ***Qualified Privileges.*** No liability can be imposed for a publication that is subject to a qualified privilege so long as the privilege is not abused. King v. Sioux City Radiological Group, P.C., 985 F. Supp. 869, 878–79 (N.D. Iowa 1997) (citing Taggart v. Drake Univ., 549 N.W.2d 796, 803 (Iowa 1996); Marks v. Estate of Hartgerink, 528 N.W.2d 539, 545 (Iowa 1995); Vojak v. Jensen, 161 N.W.2d 100, 105 (Iowa 1968); see also Theisen v. Covenant Med. Ctr., Inc., 636 N.W.2d 74 (Iowa 2001) (recognizing "a qualified privilege for statements made by employers to employees concerning the reasons for an employee's discharge regardless of whether the employer or employee publishes the statement"); Dillon v. Ruperto, No. 09-0600, 2010 WL 2383517, at *7 (Iowa Ct. App. June 16, 2010) (discussing limited privilege in the context of termination letter); Smith v. Des Moines Public Sch., 259 F.3d 942, 948 (8th Cir. 2001) (citing Vojak v. Jenson, 161 N.W.2d 100, 105 (Iowa 1968)) (applying qualified privilege to remarks made in open session of school board meeting because they concerned the termination of an administrator); Kent v. Iowa, 651 F. Supp. 2d 910, 966–68 (S.D. Iowa 2009) (discussing whether qualified privilege was abused and whether defendant acted with actual malice); Mechdyne Corp. v. Garwood, 707 F. Supp. 2d 864 (S.D. Iowa 2009) (discussing same); Smith v. Iowa Jewish Senior Life Ctr., 161 F. Supp. 2d 991, 1000 (S.D. Iowa 2001) (citing Lara v. Thomas, 512 N.W.2d 777, 786 (Iowa 1994)) (applying Iowa law and noting that a "person's past employer and current employer have [an] interest in whether that person is a good employee," but denying summary judgment because actual malice defeats the privilege). The elements of a qualified privilege in Iowa have traditionally been the following: (1) the statement was made in good faith; (2) the defendant had an interest to uphold; (3) the scope of the statement was limited to the identified purpose; and (4) the statement was published on a proper occasion, in a proper manner, and only to proper parties. Winckel v. Von Maur, Inc., 652 N.W.2d 453 (Iowa 2002); Theisen v. Covenant Med. Ctr., Inc., 636 N.W.2d 74, 84 (Iowa 2001); Vojak v. Jensen, 161 N.W.2d 100, 105 (Iowa 1968); Murken v. Sibbel, No. 00-1239, 2001 WL 1451051, at *3 (Iowa Ct. App. Nov. 16, 2001) (citing Marks v. Estate of Hartgerink, 528 N.W.2d 539 (Iowa 1995)); Morris v. Am. Freightways, Inc., No. 4:01-CV-40475, 2003 WL 472510, at *4 (S.D. Iowa Feb. 20, 2003); Lyons v. Midwest Glazing, L.L.C., 235 F. Supp. 2d 1030, 1046 (N.D. Iowa 2002) (citations omitted); Mercer v. City of Cedar Rapids, 104 F. Supp. 2d 1130, 1167–68 (N.D. Iowa 2000) (citations omitted); see also Long v. Lauffer, No. 09-1916, 797 N.W.2d 621 (Table), 2011 WL 222530, at *9–10 (Iowa Ct. App. Jan. 20, 2011) (qualified privilege applied to statements in 911 call alleging plaintiff had fired gun because caller had interest in upholding his safety and communicated statements in good faith and only to law enforcement); Boykin v. Alliant Energy Corp., No. C04-3093-PAZ, 2006 WL 220156, at *14 (N.D. Iowa Jan. 30, 2006) (finding statements privileged even if untrue because they were not made with "reckless disregard for the truth"); Ollie v. Titan Tire Corp., No. 4-00-CV-10457, 2002 U.S. Dist. LEXIS 12949, at *16–17 (S.D. Iowa Mar. 6, 2002), aff'd, 336 F.3d 680 (8th Cir. 2003). However, in Barreca v. Nickolas, 683 N.W.2d 111, 118 (Iowa 2004) (citations omitted), the Iowa Supreme Court noted that "the parties dispute whether [defendant-alderman's] statement [at a city council meeting] was made in good faith, published on a proper occasion, in a proper manner, and only to proper parties," and stated that "[a]lthough the parties continue to frame the issue in this way, we do not," because the court's "task is simply to determine whether the occasion of the . . . statement was qualifiedly privileged . . . ." See also Olson v. Ballantine, 695 N.W.2d 43, 2004 WL 2578958, at *3 (Iowa Ct. App. Nov. 15, 2004) (noting that under Barreca, instead of the three-prong test, "the court's task

now is simply to determine whether the occasion of the statement was qualifiedly privileged"); Sykes v. Hengel, 394 F. Supp. 2d 1062, 1077 (S.D. Iowa 2005) (citation omitted) (stating that "'a court looks only to the occasion itself for the communication and determines as a matter of law and general policy whether the occasion created some recognized duty or interest' in making the communication privileged"); but see Long, 2011 WL 222530, at *9–10 (evaluating whether qualified privileged applied but not discussing in terms of whether the *occasion* of the statement was privileged). In Park v. Hill, 380 F. Supp. 2d 1002, 1017–28 (N.D. Iowa 2005), a federal district court sitting in Iowa extensively discussed the Iowa Supreme Court's eschewing of the multi-element test and adoption of the "privileged occasions" test in Barreca. The Park Court noted that Barreca examined "prior precedents to determine the circumstances in which persons . . . were entitled to a qualified privilege." The Court stated in Park that "even in the absence of similar cases, [it] is not without guidance" because the Barreca Court relied on the Restatement (Second) of Torts § 593 for its adoption of the "privileged occasions" test. That Restatement section refers to §§ 594 to 598A, which describe specific "privileged occasions." The Park Court stated that "[i]t follows from the adoption of § 593 in Barreca that the Iowa Supreme Court would also look to these sections of the Restatement for the description of specific 'privileged occasions.'" The Park Court specifically and extensively discussed two of those sections, which address the "protection of the publisher's interest" occasion and the "common interest" occasion. See also Gries v. Akal Security, Inc., No. 06-CV-33-LRR, 2007 U.S. Dist. LEXIS 71902, at *114 (S.D. Iowa Aug. 27, 2007) (noting that the "Restatement instructs courts to consider a list of factors to determine which occasions give rise to a qualified privilege," including "(1) protection of the publisher's interest, (2) protection of the interest of the recipient or third party, (3) common interest, (4) family relationships, and (5) communication to those who may act in the public interest"). Other subsequent federal district court decisions have noted that the Barreca Court adopted a privileged "occasions" test. See Sykes, 394 F. Supp. 2d at 1076–77 (holding memorandum to corporate unit holders regarding reasons for president's termination and financial status of corporation was privileged because defendants had a duty to keep unit holders apprised and unit holders had an interest in the information) (also citing Theisen v. Covenant Med. Ctr., 636 N.W.2d 74, 85 (Iowa 2001) and noting that in "'the employment context, the qualified privileged is the only effective means of preventing every termination decision from automatically becoming a case of defamation'"); Gries, 2007 U.S. Dist. LEXIS 71902, at *115–17 (holding that the "occasions" of employer's communications to a business partner were privileged because they were in furtherance of the common interest of "jointly investigating employee misconduct and were concerned with ensuring the safety of . . . employees," and stating that the purpose of the qualified privilege to allow unrestricted communication regarding a matter in which parties have a duty or interest "would be thwarted if employers were not allowed to investigate alleged altercations between their employees"); see also Reeder v. Carroll, 759 F. Supp. 2d 1064, 1077–78, 1084–90 (N.D. Iowa 2010) (discussing Barreca, analyzing applicability of qualified privilege under Restatement's "privileged occasions" test, and concluding qualified privilege, as well as statutory immunity under physician licensing and mandatory reporting statute, applied to physician's letter to licensing board).

Whether the privilege is available is a matter of law for the court to decide, and issues of fact that may defeat the privilege are questions for the jury. Godfredsen v. Lutheran Bhd., No. 0-431, 2000 WL 1675869, at *4 (Iowa Ct. App. Nov. 8, 2000) (citing Brown v. First Nat'l Bank, 193 N.W.2d 547, 553 (Iowa 1972); Higgins v. Gordon Jewelry Corp., 433 N.W.2d 306, 309 (Iowa Ct. App. 1988)) (also noting differences of opinion on proper role of court and jury in ascertaining the presence of good faith); see also Reeder, 759 F. Supp. 2d at 1084–90 (granting summary judgment dismissal because evidence insufficient as a matter of law to establish actual malice); Olson v. Ballentine, 695 N.W.2d 43, 2004 WL 2578958, at *4 (Iowa Ct. App. Nov. 15, 2004) (unpublished) (reversing summary judgment of slander claim because of fact issue as to whether former employer had abused qualified privilege). See II.A.2(e), infra.

Iowa Code § 96.11(6)(b)(2) confers a privilege for written or verbal statements made to Job Service or to a person administering employment security laws. However, immunity from liability for libel or slander is conferred only so long as the person is not acting with malice. But see Haldeman v. Total Petroleum, Inc., 376 N.W.2d 98, 102–03 (Iowa 1985) (applying provisions of Iowa Code § 96.11(6)(b)(2) in 1985, before the addition to the statutory language conferring the privilege of the words "unless the report or statement is made with malice" in 1988, and concluding the legislature intended to create absolute immunity because of the absence of "qualifying language, such as 'in the absence of malice'"). Iowa Code § 730.5(12)(b) provides that a "cause of action for defamation, libel, slander, or damage to reputation shall not arise against an employer establishing a program of drug or alcohol testing" unless the employer discloses the test results to a third-party, the "test results disclosed incorrectly indicate the presence of alcohol or drugs," and the "employer negligently discloses the results."

a. **Common Interest.** A qualified privilege traditionally was recognized for communications made in good faith between individuals with common interests. Taggart v. Drake Univ., 549 N.W.2d 796, 803–04 (Iowa 1996) (alleged defamatory statements occurred during annual evaluation by department chair of plaintiff, and department chair was required to pass judgment based on his academic experience and observations); Bitner v. Ottumwa Cmty. Sch. Dist., 549 N.W.2d 295, 300 (Iowa 1996) (statements made in the course of investigation of shortage of school funds were protected by qualified privilege where business manager learned of possible problems with certain checks relating to plaintiff's school); Haldeman v. Total Petroleum, Inc., 376 N.W.2d 98, 103 (Iowa 1985) (job reference given by former employer to prospective employer that employee had been discharged due to former employer's policy of discharging all employees on a shift on which cash shortage occurs was subject to qualified privilege); Godfredsen v. Lutheran Bhd., No. 0-431, 2000 WL 1675869, at *5 (Iowa Ct. App. Nov. 8, 2000) (employer's communications with its insureds regarding its former agent served a common interest); Malone v. Des Moines Area Cmty. Coll., No. 4:04-CV-40103, 2005 WL 290008 (S.D. Iowa Jan. 26, 2005) (holding employer was "subject to the qualified immunity insofar as the alleged defamatory statements were made during the investigation of the sexual harassment complaints made against Plaintiff"); Graham v. Contract Transp., Inc., No. 4-98-CV-90546, 2001 WL 740118, at *5 (S.D. Iowa Apr. 24, 2001) (holding former employer had a qualified privilege to release positive drug test results to plaintiff's prospective employers because the statements were made in good faith, the former employer had an interest and duty to report the results by virtue of federal law, and the prospective employers had a corresponding interest and duty); see also Long v. Lauffer, No. 09-1916, 797 N.W.2d 621 (Table), 2011 WL 222530, at *9–10 (Iowa Ct. App. Jan. 20, 2011). But see Brown v. First Nat'l Bank of Mason City, 193 N.W.2d 547, 552–53 (Iowa 1972) (bank president's communication to newspaper regarding bank shortage was not subject to qualified privilege because general public had no valid interest); see also Kliebenstein v. Iowa Conf. of the United Methodist Church, 663 N.W.2d 404, 406–07 (Iowa 2003) (stating that communications between members of religious organizations are qualifiedly privileged as long as the communication are in furtherance of their common purpose or interest), cert. denied, 124 S. Ct. 450 (2003). In Park v. Hill, 380 F. Supp. 2d 1002, 1020–25 (N.D. Iowa 2005), a federal district court sitting in Iowa extensively discussed the Restatement's "protection of the publisher's interest" privileged occasion and the "common interest" privileged occasion. See also Reeder v. Carroll, 759 F. Supp. 2d 1064, 1085–87 (N.D. Iowa 2010) (holding post-Barreca that the "occasion" of statements to licensing board reporting concerns about plaintiff-physician's patient care were qualifiedly privileged because they were in furtherance of the publisher's interest in complying with his mandatory reporting obligation and the interest of the board and public in ensuring competent medical care); Gries v. Akal Security, Inc., No. 06-CV-33-LRR, 2007 U.S. Dist. LEXIS 71902, at *115–17 (S.D. Iowa Aug. 27, 2007) (holding post-Barreca that the "occasions" of employer's communications to a business partner were privileged because they were in furtherance of the common interest of "jointly investigating employee misconduct and were concerned with ensuring the safety of . . . employees").

b. **Duty.** A qualified privilege also traditionally could arise from the necessity of full and unrestricted communication concerning a matter in which the parties have a duty. Bitner v. Ottumwa Community Sch. Dist., 549 N.W.2d 295, 303 (Iowa 1996) (certified public accountants were protected by qualified privilege with respect to statements made in audit of school activity fund controlled by plaintiff); Iowa Code § 272C.8 (an individual shall not be liable for filing complaint or report with peer review committee or licensing board unless made with malice); see also Reeder v. Carroll, 759 F. Supp. 2d 1064, 1084–87 (N.D. Iowa 2010) (physician mandatory reporting duty); Graham v. Contract Transp., Inc., 4:98-cv-90546, 2001 WL 740118, at *5 (S.D. Iowa Apr. 24, 2001) (holding former employer had a qualified privilege to release positive drug test results to plaintiff's prospective employers because the statements were made in good faith, the former employer had an interest and duty to report the results by virtue of federal law, and the prospective employers had a corresponding interest and duty).

c. **Criticism of Public Employee.** The qualified privilege of fair comment and criticism applies to public officials. See Anderson v. Low Rent Hous. Comm'n, 304 N.W.2d 239, 246–47, 7 Media L. Rep. 1726, 1727–28 (Iowa 1981); Haas v. Evening Democrat Co., 252 Iowa 517, 107 N.W.2d 444 (1961); Salinger v. Cowles, 195 Iowa 873, 191 N.W. 167 (1922); Cherry v. Des Moines Leader, 114 Iowa 298, 86 N.W. 323 (1901). See generally I.B.1, supra.

d. **Limitation on Qualified Privileges.** Traditionally, for a qualified privilege to attach, the communication had to be in good faith, concerning a subject matter in which the speaker has a duty, right, interest or obligation, and to a listener who has a corresponding duty, right, interest or obligation. Taggart v. Drake Univ., 549 N.W.2d 796, 803 (Iowa 1996) (citing Brown v. First Nat'l Bank of Mason City, 193 N.W.2d 547, 552 (Iowa 1972)); see also Lyons v. Midwest Glazing, L.L.C., 235 F. Supp. 2d 1030, 1046–47 (N.D. Iowa 2002) (citations omitted). However, if the statement is not made in good faith, the privilege does not attach. Lara v. Thomas, 512 N.W.2d 777, 786 (Iowa 1994); Hadleman v. Total Petroleum, Inc., 376 N.W.2d 98, 104 (Iowa 1985); Murken v. Sibbel, 00-1239, 2001 WL 1451051, at *3 (Iowa Ct. App. Nov. 16, 2001); Godfredsen v. Lutheran Bhd., No. 0-431, 2000 WL 1675869, at *5 n.4 (Iowa Ct. App. Nov. 8, 2000) (noting there is no Iowa authority defining good faith in the context of qualified privilege).

Generally no qualified privilege attaches to statements made to the public unless the public is a proper party to the communication, i.e., "the general public has a valid interest in the matter giving rise to the allegedly defamatory publication." Mercer v. City of Cedar Rapids, 104 F. Supp. 2d 1130, 1168 (N.D. Iowa 2000). Compare Park v. Hill, 380 F. Supp. 2d 1002, 1020–26 (N.D. Iowa 2005) (discussing the Restatement's "publisher's interest" and "common interest" privileged occasions and limitations on the permitted recipients of the statements). Applying this analysis, in Mercer the Court held that the qualified privilege was available in the context of a Chief of Police's statements to the public concerning the termination of a police officer. See Mercer v. City of Cedar Rapids, 129 F. Supp. 2d 1226, 1241 (N.D. Iowa 2001) (deferring to court's earlier finding in summary judgment that there was sufficient evidence to find actual malice and upholding jury's finding that the privilege had been lost because of the presence of actual malice), aff'd in part and rev'd in part, 308 F.3d 840 (8th Cir. 2002) (affirming holding that chief's "public comments about a public employee's termination" were protected by a qualified privilege but reversing district court conclusion that there was sufficient evidence of actual malice to support the defamation claim, because while evidence of anger may be relevant to the "ill will that defeats a claim of qualified privilege under state law," it was irrelevant to existence of constitutional actual malice which was required therein as plaintiff was a public figure); see also Bradbery v. Dubuque County, No. 99-1881, 2001 WL 23144, at *3 (Iowa Ct. App. Jan. 10, 2001) (holding that public official's telling broadcaster of crime program that defendant was "wanted" supported a qualified privilege defense because official was acting within scope of his duties by protecting public, there was a "valid public interest in the dissemination of the information," and the range was reasonable given the broadcast area); Harrington v. Wilber, 353 F. Supp. 2d 1033, 1045 (S.D. Iowa 2005) (holding that qualified privilege applied to prosecutor's press release, which included accusations that plaintiff was a murder). Generally, "members of subordinate legislative bodies . . . are entitled to a qualified privilege for statements made in the performance of their official duties 'upon any subject matter pertinent and relevant' to the occasion." Barreca v. Nickolas, 683 N.W.2d 111, 118 (Iowa 2004) (citations omitted). In the Barreca case, a city alderman was held to have a qualified privilege when addressing the city council with respect to "a complaint about alleged indecent and illegal conduct at a local business." See id. at 119; see also Olson v. Ballantine, 695 N.W.2d 43, 2004 WL 2578958, at *3 (Iowa Ct. App. Nov. 15, 2004) (unpublished) (holding that "statements made by county employees to their Board of Supervisors about activities that occurred in a county facility calls for application of a qualified privilege"); Wright v. Keokuk County Health Ctr., 399 F. Supp. 2d 938, 955–56 (S.D. Iowa 2005) (denying a qualified privilege defense for detailed disclosure constituting slander made to a former employee who held the position currently held by the plaintiff or to a former boss at a different company).

A qualified privilege is not available for statements made with actual malice. Winckel v. Von Maur, Inc., 652 N.W.2d 453, 459 (Iowa 2002); Lyons, 235 F. Supp. 2d at 1046 (citations omitted); see also Olson, 2004 WL 2578958, at *4 (reversing summary judgment of slander claim because there was a genuine issue of material fact as to whether former employer had abused the qualified privilege). Iowa courts previously held that as used in the common law context, actual malice "depend[s] on the motive for the statement" and "requires proof that the statement was made with malice in fact, ill-will or wrongful motive." Lyons, 235 F. Supp. 2d at 1046 (citations omitted). However, the Iowa Supreme Court recently abandoned the previous common law standard requiring proof of improper purpose and instead adopted the New York Times standard of actual malice for purposes of defeating a common law qualified privilege, which "occurs when a statement is made with the knowledge that it is false or with reckless disregard for its truth or falsity." See Barreca, 683 N.W.2d at 120–23; see also Park v. Hill, 380 F. Supp. 2d at 1018 (stating that in Barreca "the Iowa Supreme Court changed—or fixed once and for all—the definition of 'actual malice' for purposes of determining whether a 'qualified privilege' had been abused"); Sykes v. Hengel, 394 F. Supp. 2d 1062, 1077–78 (S.D. Iowa 2005) (citation omitted) (stating as well that on a summary judgment motion "the Court must decide as a matter of law if there is a genuine issue of material fact whether the Defendants 'entertained serious doubts about the truth'" of the statements at issue).

(1) **Constitutional or Actual Malice.** "Actual malice" under New York Times Co. v. Sullivan, focuses on the "defendant's attitude toward the truth of the statements, rather than on the defendant's attitude toward the plaintiff." King v. Sioux City Radiological Group, P.C., 985 F. Supp. 869, 880 n. 6 (N.D. Iowa 1997) (citing Price v. Viking Penguin, Inc., 881 F.2d 1426, 1433, 16 Media L. Rep. 2169, 2173 (8th Cir. 1989)); see also Mercer v. City of Cedar Rapids, 308 F.3d 840, 849 (8th Cir. 2002) (contrasting actual malice for qualified privilege and First Amendment purposes, and stating that as a matter of law plaintiff had failed to prove the actual malice necessary to impose liability in a public figure case because while evidence of anger may be relevant to the "ill will that defeats a claim of qualified privilege under state law," it was irrelevant to existence of constitutional actual malice); compare Reeder v. Carroll, 759 F. Supp. 2d 1064, 1088 n.10 (N.D. Iowa 2010) (citing Barreca and stating that, despite abandonment of "improper purpose" definition, Barreca court stated that evidence of ill-will "may be admissible if it is 'probative to show knowledge of falsity or reckless disregard for the truth'"). The New York Times actual malice standard is subjective and thus the question is whether the defendant "in fact entertained serious doubts as to the truth of his publication." Caveman Adventures UN, Ltd. v. Press-Citizen Co., 633 N.W.2d 757, 762, 29 Media L. Rep. 2297, 2301 (Iowa 2001) (quoting St. Amant v. Thompson, 390 U.S. 727, 731 (1968)). The standard requires a "high degree of awareness of . . . probable falsity." Id.; 29 Media L. Rep. at 2301 (quoting Garrison v. Louisiana, 379 U.S. 64, 74 (1964)). Further, the Iowa Supreme Court has recognized that whether there was actual malice "must be judged within the context in which the challenged statements were published." Id.; 29 Media L. Rep. at 2300. A private figure plaintiff seeking punitive damages must prove actual malice. See I.B.8.b, supra. While in the past, cases reviewing whether a qualified privilege has been waived typically have not used the actual malice standard, see generally Caveman Adventures UN, Ltd., 633 N.W.2d at 761; 29 Media L. Rep. at 2300 (citing Vojak v. Jensen, 161 N.W.2d 100, 107 (Iowa 1968); Vinson v. Linn-Mar Cmty. Sch. Dist., 360 N.W.2d 108 (Iowa 1984)) (stating that Iowa's common-law definition of actual malice differs from New York Times actual malice and has been described as "statements made with 'ill-will, hatred or desire to do another harm,'" and noting the application of the New York Times standard in Vinson in the determination whether punitive damages were available under Gertz), as noted in Part II.A.2.d(2), infra, the Iowa Supreme Court recently adopted the New York Times standard of actual malice for purposes of defeating a common law qualified privilege. See

Barreca v. Nickolas, 683 N.W.2d 111, 121–23 (Iowa 2004) (quoting St. Amant v. Thompson, 390 U.S. 727, 732 (emphasis added)) (applying New York Times standard of actual malice and stating that defendant "published the allegation to the public with no basis other than an anonymous and uncorroborated tip. Although a failure to investigate, standing alone, ordinarily will not establish a knowing or reckless disregard for truth, '[p]rofessions of good faith will be unlikely to prove persuasive . . . where a story is . . . based wholly on an unverified anonymous telephone call.'"); see also Reeder v. Carroll, 759 F. Supp. 2d 1064, 1078, 1087–90 (N.D. Iowa 2010) (discussing actual malice standard under Barreca and plaintiff's arguments based on *alleged* lack of investigation, history of animosity, financial stake and fact licensing board ultimately dismissed charges against plaintiff-physician, and concluding as a matter of law defendant did not act with actual malice in relaying concerns to board about plaintiff's patient care because, *inter alia*, board had concluded after four-year investigation that there was probable cause to file charges).

(2) **Common Law Malice.** Prior to the 2004 Iowa Supreme Court Barreca v. Nickolas, 683 N.W.2d 111 (Iowa 2004) case, Iowa courts frequently referred to "actual malice" but actually applied a "common law malice" standard. See generally Winckel v. Von Maur, Inc., 652 N.W.2d 453, 459 (Iowa 2002). Under the "common law malice" standard, a qualified privilege could be lost if the plaintiff proved the alleged defamatory statement was made with malice in fact, ill-will, hatred, the desire to do harm or a wrongful motive. Taggart v. Drake Univ., 549 N.W.2d 796, 804 (Iowa 1996); Marks v. Estate of Hartgerink, 528 N.W.2d 539, 546 (Iowa 1995); Haldeman v. Total Petroleum, Inc., 376 N.W.2d 98, 103–04 (Iowa 1985); Murken v. Sibbel, No. 00-1239, 2001 WL 1451051, at *3 (Iowa Ct. App. Nov. 16, 2001); see Smith v. Des Moines Pub. Sch., 259 F.3d 942, 948–49 (8th Cir. 2001); Lyons v. Midwest Glazing, L.L.C., 235 F. Supp. 2d 1030, 1046 (N.D. Iowa 2002) (citations omitted) ("The qualified privilege is lost if the statements are not made in good faith or made with actual malice."). Absent that "common law" or motivational malice, a qualified privilege would stand even if the alleged defamatory statements were false. Marks, 528 N.W.2d at 546; Lyons, 235 F. Supp. 2d at 1046 (citations omitted); see Park v. Hill, 380 F. Supp. 2d 1002, 1019 (N.D. Iowa 2005) (citation omitted) (stating that "[n]otwithstanding that the standard for 'actual malice'" changed in Barreca, "it appears that the law in Iowa continues to be that, in the absence of actual malice, '[e]ven untrue statements may be qualifiedly privileged'"). In Winckel v. Von Maur, Inc., 652 N.W.2d 453, 459 (Iowa 2002), the Iowa Supreme Court held that "actual malice" precluding the application of the qualified privilege meant "statements made with ill-will, hatred, or desire to do another harm." The Court noted that even if the New York Times standard of actual malice is met, it does not automatically follow that the qualified privilege cannot attach. Rather, the final determination must be made under the Iowa standard of "actual malice." Id. at 460 n.1.

However, in 2004, in Barreca v. Nickolas, 683 N.W.2d 111, 120–23 (Iowa 2004), the Iowa Supreme Court appeared to have discarded the old common law improper purpose definition of actual malice when it held that in determining whether a defendant has abused a qualified privilege a plaintiff must prove the New York Times standard of actual malice. See also Olson v. Ballantine, 695 N.W.2d 43, 2004 WL 2578958, at *3 (Iowa Ct. App. Nov. 15, 2004) (citing Barreca, 683 N.W.2d at 123). The Iowa Supreme Court acknowledged in Barreca that the wrongful motive definition of actual malice had been "long but somewhat inconsistently applied." For example, in Winckel v. Von Maur, 652 N.W.2d 453, 459–60 (Iowa 2002) the Court defined actual malice as ill-will, hatred or desire to do another harm, but in Taggart v. Drake Univ., 549 N.W.2d 796, 804 (Iowa 1996), the Court stated that actual malice also occurs "when a statement is made with knowledge that it is false or with reckless disregard for its truth or falsity." See Barreca, 683 N.W.2d at 120 ("Because Taggart was not decided upon First Amendment grounds, reference to the New York Times definition of actual malice in Taggart was improper.").

The Court in Barreca stated several grounds for abandoning the common law definition of actual malice. First, "because the purpose of a common law privilege is to protect speech that furthers interests to which the law attaches special importance, it should not matter whether the speaker acts out of ill will if the speech furthers those interests, as long as the speaker does not know the statements are false, and does not recklessly disregard indications of their falsity." The second reason is simplicity. "Constitutional and common law privileges often coexist in the same case, and the existence of more than one definition of malice can only bewilder juries (and possibly the judges and lawyers who try to explain the differences to them)." Id. at 122. However, the Court further stated that evidence of a defendant's ill-will towards the plaintiff is not necessarily inadmissible, as "it may be probative to show knowledge of falsity or reckless disregard of the truth." Id. at 123 n.8.

Post-Barreca decisions have applied the New York Times standard to determine whether the common law qualified privilege has been abused. See, e.g., Gries v. Akal Security, Inc., No. 06-CV-33-LRR, 2007 U.S. Dist. LEXIS 71902, at *118–21 (S.D. Iowa Aug. 27, 2007) (holding as a matter of law that employer did not abuse its qualified privilege "by way of excessive publication, nor did it act with actual malice," and stating that although employer's investigation of employee misconduct "may not have been the best way to investigate the matter" employee has not shown that defendant entertained serious doubts about the truth of statements made during the investigation); Sykes v. Hengel, 394 F. Supp. 2d 1062, 1078 (S.D. Iowa 2005) (noting that while plaintiff's evidence "may tend to suggest motive, it does not tend to show that the Defendants entertained serious doubts about the truthfulness of the statements" and granting summary judgment dismissal of defamation claim).

e. **Question of Fact or Law.** Availability of privilege is a question of law for the court. Barreca v. Nickolas, 683 N.W.2d 111, 118 (Iowa 2004); Marks v. Estate of Hartgerink, 528 N.W.2d 539, 546 (Iowa 1995); Vinson v. Linn-Mar Community Sch. Dist., 360 N.W.2d 108, 116 (Iowa 1984); Brown v. First Nat'l Bank of Mason City, 193 N.W.2d 547, 551 (Iowa 1972); King v. Sioux City Radiological Group, P.C., 985 F. Supp. 869, 880 (N.D. Iowa 1997); Jenkins v. Wal-Mart Stores, Inc., 910 F. Supp. 1399, 1427 (N.D. Iowa 1995); see also Mercer v. City of Cedar Rapids, 308 F.3d 840, 849 (8th Cir. 2002) (citation omitted) (stating the "[constitutional] question whether the evidence in the record in a defamation case is sufficient to support a finding of actual malice is a question of law"). If the occasion of the statement "was . . . privileged, it must then be determined whether that privilege was abused. Generally, the former question is for the judge; the latter for the jury." Barreca v. Nickolas, 683 N.W.2d 111, 118 (Iowa 2004) (citations omitted). But see generally Park v. Hill, 380 F. Supp. 2d 1002, 1026–28 (N.D. Iowa 2005) (granting summary judgment dismissal of defamation claim because plaintiff had not generated a genuine issue of material fact that defendant had actual malice); Sykes v. Hengel, 394 F. Supp. 2d 1062, 1079 (S.D. Iowa 2005) (holding that plaintiff did not make "the requisite showing that Defendants abused [the] privilege to defeat summary judgment").

f. **Burden of Proof.** The burden is on the defendant to prove the existence of a qualified privilege. Lara v. Thomas, 512 N.W.2d 777, 785 (Iowa 1994); Rees v. O'Malley, 461 N.W.2d 833, 837 (Iowa 1990); Wright v. Keokuk County Health Ctr., 399 F. Supp. 2d 938, 953 (S.D. Iowa 2005); King v. Sioux City Radiological Group, P.C., 985 F. Supp. 869, 880 (N.D. Iowa 1997); Jenkins v. Wal-Mart Stores, Inc., 910 F. Supp. 1399, 1427 (N.D. Iowa 1995). In addition, a qualified privilege is an affirmative defense which must be pleaded. Taggart v. Drake Univ., 549 N.W.2d 796, 803 (Iowa 1996); Vinson v. Linn-Mar Cmty. Sch. Dist., 360 N.W.2d 108, 116 (Iowa 1984); King, 985 F. Supp. at 880. Once statements are found to be protected by a qualified privilege, the burden shifts to plaintiff to show actual malice. Murken, 2001 WL 1451051, at *3.

B. Standard Libel Defenses

1. ***Truth.*** Truth, as well as "substantial truth," serves as a complete defense to a libel action. Wilson v. IBP, Inc., 558 N.W.2d 132, 140–41 (Iowa 1996) (citing Behr v. Meredith Corp., 414 N.W.2d 339 (Iowa 1987)); Wunschel v. City of Ida Grove, No. 01-1129, 2002 WL 1332621 (Iowa Ct. App. June 19, 2002); Mechdyne Corp. v. Garwood, 707 F. Supp. 2d 864 (S.D. Iowa 2009); Morris v. Am. Freightways, Inc., No. 4:01-CV-40475, 2003 WL 472510, at *3 (S.D. Iowa Feb. 20, 2003) (citations omitted); King v. Sioux City Radiological Group, P.C., 985 F. Supp. 869, 878 (N.D. Iowa 1997) (citing Huegerich v. IBP, Inc., 547 N.W.2d 216, 221 (Iowa 1996)); see also Godfredsen v. Lutheran Bhd., No. 01-1711, 674 N.W.2d 682, 2003 WL 22701336, at *3–4 (Iowa Ct. App. Nov. 17, 2003) (unpublished) (holding that evidence supported jury instruction on affirmative defense of truth). "In order to prevail on a defamation claim, a plaintiff must ordinarily prove that the statements . . . were false," but statements that are defamatory per se "are actionable without proof of . . . falsity." Thomas v. St. Luke's Health Sys., Inc., 869 F. Supp. 1413, 1442 (N.D. Iowa 1994), aff'd, 61 F.3d 908 (8th Cir. 1995) (citations omitted); see also Mercer v. City of Cedar Rapids, 308 F.3d 840, 848 (8th Cir. 2002) (citations omitted) (holding district court's treatment of truth as an affirmative defense was error because the statement was not slanderous per se and thus plaintiff must prove falsity); Harrington v. Wilber, 353 F. Supp. 2d 1033, 1039 (S.D. Iowa 2005) (citations omitted) (stating that defamatory per se statements "'are actionable in and of themselves without proof of malice, falsity or damage. In actions based on language not libelous per se, all of these elements must be proved . . . .'"). "However, the truth of the libelous statements remains as an absolute defense to liability for those statements" if "the defendant has properly pleaded and ultimately proves the affirmative defense of 'truth.'" King, 985 F. Supp. at 878 (citations omitted). See I.B.3, supra.

"It is no longer necessary for a libel defendant to establish the literal truth of the publication in every detail as long as the 'sting' or 'gist' of the defamatory charge is substantially true." Behr, 414 N.W.2d at 342 (quoting Vachet v. Central Newspapers, Inc., 816 F.2d 313, 316, 13 Media L. Rep. 2337, 2339 (7th Cir. 1987)); Stevens v. Iowa Newspapers, Inc., 711 N.W.2d 732, 2006 WL 126626, at *6; 34 Media L. Rep. 1430 (Iowa Ct. App. Jan. 19, 2006); **Home Show Tours, Inc. v. Quad City Virtual, Inc., 827 F.Supp.2d 924, 942-43 (S.D. Iowa 2011) (citing Restatement (Second) of Torts § 581A, comment f) ("'It is not necessary to establish the literal truth of the precise statement made. Slight inaccuracies of expression are immaterial provided the defamatory charge is true in substance.'")**; Bruning v. Carroll Cmty. Sch. Dist., No. C04-3091-MWB, 2006 WL 1234822, at *46 (N.D. Iowa May 3, 2006); Iowa Protection & Advocacy Servs., Inc. v. Tanager Place, No. C-04-0069, 2005 WL 2035225, at *6 (N.D. Iowa Aug. 24, 2005) (citations and internal quotation marks omitted) (stating that the "gist or sting of the defamatory charge . . . is the heart of the matter in question" and the "[Iowa Supreme Court] determine[s] the gist or sting by look[ing] at the highlight of the [publication], the pertinent angle of it, and not to items of secondary importance which are inoffensive details, immaterial to the truth of the defamatory statement"); Wright v. Keokuk County Health Ctr., 399 F. Supp. 2d 938, 957 (S.D. Iowa 2005); see generally Mercer, 308 F.3d at 848 (citations omitted) (stating rule that "if the accusation is general and implies the commission of unspecified misconduct of a particular type, the statement is true if the plaintiff committed any misconduct of that type"). While the court may decide whether the statement has the sting or gist of the defamatory charge as a matter of law when the underlying facts are undisputed, when the underlying facts are disputed the question must be submitted to the jury. Smith v. Des Moines Public Sch., 259 F.3d 942, 947–48 (8th Cir. 2001) (applying Iowa case law). It has also been noted that the "Iowa Supreme Court has repeatedly held that in mounting a truth defense the defendant carries 'the burden of proving the truth of the statements *in the sense imputed to them by the plaintiff.*'" Iowa Protection & Advocacy Servs., Inc., 2005 WL 2035225, at *6 (citations omitted) (denying summary judgment where the parties did not agree how to interpret the statements at issue and defendants did not contend the statements were true in the sense the plaintiff imputed to them).

Recently, the Supreme Court of Iowa expressly adopted the principle of defamation by implication which "arises, not from what is stated, but from what is implied when a defendant (1) juxtaposes a series of facts so as to imply a defamatory connection between them, or (2) creates a defamatory implication by omitting facts . . . even though the particular facts are correct." Stevens v. Iowa Newspapers, Inc., 728 N.W.2d 823, 827–29, 35 Media L. Rep. 1385 (Iowa 2007) (citation omitted) (also extending the theory to public figure suits). Compare Milkovich v. Lorain Journal Co., 497 U.S. 1, 17 Media L. Rep. 2009 (1990) (discussing statement in Philadelphia Newspapers, Inc. v. Hepps, 475 U.S. 767 that "'the common-law presumption that defamatory speech is false cannot stand when a plaintiff seeks damages against a media defendant for speech of public concern'"). In Stevens, a departing sports writer for a newspaper claimed that the columnist responding to his final column had defamed him by alleging that he made factual errors in his work and rarely attended the events that he covered throughout his career at the paper. The Court held that though the statements might have been literally true, they carried an underlying implication that was just as damaging as if they were actually false, because they omitted the fact that attendance was not a requirement of a sports columnist. Id. at 831. The Court then held that a reasonable jury could find by clear and convincing evidence that the statement regarding attendance at events was false in its implication and was made with reckless disregard for the truth under the New York Times standard for public figures. Id.

Article I, § 7 of the Iowa Constitution provides that "[i]n all prosecutions or indictments for libel, the truth may be given in evidence to the jury and if it appears to the jury that the matter charged as libelous was true, and was published for good motives and for justifiable ends, the party shall be acquitted."

2. ***Opinion.*** Opinion is absolutely protected under the First Amendment. Jones v. Palmer Commc'ns, Inc., 440 N.W.2d 884, 891, 16 Media L. Rep. 1667, 2140 (Iowa 1989); see generally Harrington v. Wilber, 353 F. Supp. 2d 1033, 1042 (S.D. Iowa 2005) (citation omitted) ("[W]hile 'pure' opinions are wholly protected by the First Amendment, a statement that 'may . . . imply a false assertion of fact' is actionable."); Iowa Protection & Advocacy Servs., Inc. v. Tanager Place, No. C-04-0069, 2005 WL 2035225, at *7–8 (N.D. Iowa Aug. 24, 2005) (citations omitted) (same) (holding that defendant's statement "clearly implied she knew some undisclosed facts to support [her] conclusion" and thus statement was actionable "even though she prefaced it with cautionary language"). However, in Jones, the Court was careful to distinguish fact from opinion by stating that if the allegedly defamatory material is "precise and easy to verify" it likely is fact rather than opinion. See also Harrington, 353 F. Supp. 2d at 1041–43 (citations omitted) (indicating that "'the statement must be taken as part of a whole, including the tone of the broadcast and the use of cautionary language'" and stating that Iowa courts use the following factors in determining whether a statement is fact or opinion: "the precision and specificity of the statement," "the verifiability of the statement," "the literary context in which the statement was made," the social context, and the public context or political arena in which the statement was made); Bruning v. Carroll Cmty. Sch. Dist., No. C04-3091-MWB, 2006 WL 1234822, at *53 (N.D. Iowa May 3, 2006) (explaining the three factors in the context of alleged defamation by police against juveniles accused of sexual harassment); Ideal Instruments, Inc. v. Rivard Instruments, Inc., 434 F. Supp. 2d 598, 624 (N.D. Iowa 2006) (rejecting "opinion" argument and holding that from the alleged statements "an intention to assert, as a fact, that [plaintiff] was conducting its business improperly, can reasonably be inferred"); Iowa Protection & Advocacy Servs., Inc., 2005 WL 2035225, at *7 (citations omitted) (considering whether statements made to a newspaper reporter were fact or opinion, balancing factors, and concluding "[u]nder the totality of the circumstances" that although the context of a newsworthy event weighs in favor of a finding of opinion, the precision and verifiability of the statements at issue weighed more heavily towards a finding that the statements were of fact); see generally Delaney v. Int'l Union Local No. 94, 675 N.W.2d 832, 844 (Iowa 2004) (citation omitted) (concluding that non-union members' defamation claims against a union were preempted by federal labor law, and noting that "[b]ecause cartoons use 'hyperbole, exaggeration and caricature to communicate their messages to the reader . . . [o]ne cannot reasonably interpret a cartoon as literally depicting an actual event or situation'"). "Whether a statement is an opinion or fact is an issue for the court to decide." Iowa Protection & Advocacy Servs., Inc., 2005 WL 2035225, at *7 (citing Secrist v. Harkin, 874 F.2d 1244, 1248 (8th Cir. 1989)); Bruning, 2006 WL 1234822, at *52 ("[I]n the context of the First Amendment, whether a statement is one of fact or opinion is a question of law to be decided by the court.").

In 1901, the Iowa Supreme Court held that comment or criticism of public officials' performance of duties is protected under the qualified fair comment privilege. Cherry v. Des Moines Leader, 114 Iowa 298, 86 N.W. 323 (1901). Because the Cherry case was based on Iowa constitutional and common law provisions, it takes on renewed importance in light of the Milkovich ruling. In Jones v. Palmer Commc'ns, Inc., 440 N.W.2d 884, 16 Media L. Rep. 1667 (Iowa 1989), the Court said Cherry's protection was "now affected by constitutional interpretations which provide absolute protection for statements of opinion." However, Jones is a pre-Milkovich case. See Mercer v. City of Cedar Rapids, 129 F. Supp. 2d 1226, 1237 (N.D. Iowa 2001) (quoting Lundell Mfg. v. Am. Broad. Co., 98 F.3d 351, 359 (8th Cir. 1996)) (examining authorities regarding opinion, noting that because there was a jury question regarding the defamatory nature of the statements at issue "there necessarily was a jury question as to whether [employer's] statements were reasonably capable of defamatory meaning, that is whether they 'impl[ied] an assertion of fact' that was false," finding there was sufficient evidence to uphold jury's finding that the statements were false assertions of fact, and thus rejecting employer's argument that the statements were protected opinion), aff'd in part and rev'd in part, 308 F.3d 840 (8th Cir. 2002) (holding it was not necessary to decide falsity issue because defamation claim failed on actual malice grounds); see also Harrington, 353 F. Supp. 2d at 1041–43 (applying both Jones and Milkovich); Iowa Protection & Advocacy Servs., Inc., 2005 WL 2035225, at *7–8 (citing to both Jones and Milkovich). In a post-Milkovich case, Kiesau v. Bantz, 686 N.W.2d 164, 177 (Iowa 2004), the Iowa Supreme Court did not cite to Milkovich when discussing opinion. Therein, the Court applied the factors outlined in Jones v. Palmer Commc'ns, Inc. and held that a photograph of a fellow officer altered by a deputy sheriff so that in the photograph it appeared that the officer's breasts were exposed was not opinion, because the photograph's representation of the officer was precise, specific, easily verifiable, and the deputy sheriff "did not publish the altered photograph in any political context" and sent the photograph to fellow employees "without any disclaimer" and sometimes anonymously. Id. (also holding that jury instructions adequately incorporated concept of parody, which requires a jury finding that "the altered photograph could not reasonably be understood as describing actual facts" about plaintiff); see also Kliebenstein v. Iowa Conference of the United Methodist Church, 663 N.W.2d 404 (Iowa 2003) (not citing Milkovich or discussing issue of whether a statement that attributed the "spirit of Satan" to the plaintiff was capable of defamatory meaning, but sending defamation claim back to trial court, thereby indicating Court thought there was a triable issue), cert. denied, 124 S. Ct. 450 (2003); **Lange v. Diercks, 808 N.W.2d 754, No. 11-0191, 2011 WL 5515152, at *11 (Iowa Ct. App. Nov. 9, 2011) (unpublished) (finding that Iowa's Student Free Expression Law, Iowa Code § 280.22, which prohibits libelous material in student publications, should be read to include the affirmative defense of parody and stating "[d]isregarding an affirmative defense like parody for purposes of determining acceptable expression under the statute would place an entire form of expression—which may provide valuable learning opportunities and which is often legitimately used in the mass media everyday—beyond students' reach").** In a recent Iowa Court of Appeals decision, Bowles v. McGivern, No. 03-0143, 680 N.W.2d 378, 2004 WL 239864, at *2 (Iowa Ct. App. Feb. 11, 2004) (unpublished) (citation omitted), the Court applied Jones v. Palmer Commc'ns, Inc. and held that a statement by an alderman at a city council meeting that one of his constituents was a "freaking crazy woman" constituted nonactionable opinion, because "crazy" is "commonly used to express an opinion that someone is unusual, impractical, erratic, or unsound" and the setting in which the comment was made "supports the conclusion that his words were mere name-calling." See generally Stephenson v. Wellmark, Inc., No. 04-1547, 2005 WL 1398167, at *3 (Iowa Ct. App. June 15, 2005) (affirming summary judgment dismissal of plaintiff's defamation suit against her former employer based on statements made by coworkers regarding her termination and noting that statements of coworker "fail to show he had personal knowledge of the reason for the firing; rather he was only speculating and it would be difficult to find the statement slanderous").

More recently, in Yates v. Iowa West Racing Assn., 721 N.W.2d 762 (Iowa 2006), the Iowa Supreme Court extensively discussed the law concerning opinions. The Court recognized that Milkovich "rejected the dichotomy between fact and opinion as the framework of analysis," but held that its previous test for discerning fact from opinion is very similar to the test used in Milkovich to identify protected statements: "We therefore will employ the four-factor test we adopted in Palmer Communications (the Janklow v. Newsweek standards) to identify protected opinion under the Milkovich framework of analysis." See Reeder v. Carroll, 759 F. Supp. 2d 1064, 1079–80 (N.D. Iowa 2010) (discussing Janklow/Yates factors and concluding statement at issue was nonactionable opinion). Thus, the Iowa court has arguably continued to protect opinion under Milkovich even though Milkovich stated that opinion is not protectable speech based on that characterization alone.

3. ***Consent.*** **In an unpublished Iowa Court of Appeals decision in which the court determined that Iowa's Student Free Expression Law, Iowa Code § 280.22, which prohibits libelous material in student publications, should consider affirmative defenses to libel, the Court specifically stated that "consent should be considered." Lange v. Diercks, No. 11-0191, 808 N.W.2d 754, 2011 WL 5515152, at *11 (Iowa Ct. App. Nov. 9, 2011) (unpublished).** In Graham v. Contract Transp., Inc., 4:98-cv-90546, 2001 WL 740118, at *7 (S.D. Iowa Apr. 24, 2001), the Court stated that consent is a complete defense to a defamation claim and held that plaintiff's defamation claim was precluded by the releases he signed authorizing the publication of his drug test results to prospective employers.

4. ***Mitigation.*** No Iowa cases have addressed mitigating circumstances on the part of a defendant.

III. RECURRING FACT PATTERNS

A. Statements in Personnel File

One Iowa case has stated that statements contained in personnel files are generally protected by a qualified privilege. Taggart v. Drake Univ., 549 N.W.2d 796, 803–04 (Iowa 1996) (holding performance evaluation of faculty member protected by a qualified privilege).

B. Performance Evaluations

In Taggart v. Drake Univ., 549 N.W.2d 796, 803–04 (Iowa 1996) the Court found that the performance evaluations of the plaintiff were protected by a qualified privilege.

See generally Lloyd v. Drake Univ., 686 N.W.2d 225, 232 (Iowa 2004) (holding that statements in report of a panel organized by plaintiff's former employer to study an allegedly-racially motivated incident involving plaintiff-former security guard could not "reasonably be interpreted as suggesting [plaintiff] was a racist"); Olson v. Ballantine, 695 N.W.2d 43, 2004 WL 2578958, at *3–4 (Iowa Ct. App. Nov. 15, 2004) (unpublished) (holding that statements made by co-worker regarding plaintiff's alleged inappropriate conduct at work were subject to a qualified privilege but fact issues concerning actual malice precluded summary judgment).

C. References

An employer or an employer's representative who acts reasonably in providing work-related information about a current or former employee of the employer is immune from civil liability. Iowa Code § 91B.2; see Lowe v. Todd's Flying Serv., Inc., No. 99-0708, 2001 WL 58113, at *3 (Iowa Ct. App. Jan. 24, 2001) (noting argument of former employee that release he signed in application for prospective employer releasing former employers from liability for furnishing information is against public policy and beyond the legislature's intent in § 91B.2, but declining to address issue because it was not properly preserved); Graham v. Contract Transp., Inc., 4:98-cv-90546, 2001 WL 740118, at *5–7 (S.D. Iowa Apr. 24, 2001) (holding former employer immunized from liability for release of positive drug test results to plaintiff's prospective employers because there was no evidence it had acted unreasonably under Iowa Code § 91B.2; and holding that plaintiff's defamation claim was precluded by the releases he signed authorizing the publication of his drug test results to prospective employers because the releases specifically named the former employer as a party to be released); see also II.A.2, supra; Haldeman v. Total Petroleum, Inc., 376 N.W.2d 98, 103 (Iowa 1985) (holding statements made by former employer of terminated gas station cashier to prospective employer protected by qualified privilege); Sawheny v. Pioneer Hi-Bred Int'l, Inc., 93 F.3d 1401, 1410–11 (8th Cir. 1996) (statements to a foreign government about a former employer protected by qualified privilege under Iowa law); Smith v. Iowa Jewish Senior Life Ctr., 161 F. Supp. 2d 991, 1000 (S.D. Iowa 2001) (citing Lara v. Thomas, 512 N.W.2d 777, 786 (Iowa 1994)) (applying Iowa law and noting that a "person's past employer and current employer have [an] interest in whether that person is a good employee" and thus holding the privilege applicable to statement by former employer's attorney to husband of current employer, but denying summary judgment because actual malice defeats the privilege). In Hlubek v. Pelecky, 701 N.W.2d 93, 99–101 (Iowa 2005), the Iowa Supreme Court discussed applicable standards under Iowa Code § 91B.2. The Court held that the statutory immunity provided by § 91B.2 applied to the plaintiff's interference with contract and with prospective business relationship claims because the plaintiff had presented no evidence that his former employer acted unreasonably in providing a reference to his prospective employer.

Any employer that attempts to "blacklist" a discharged or former employee or prevent such former employee from obtaining other employment shall be liable for treble damages. Iowa Code § 730.2. The Court of Appeals of Iowa discussed the application of Iowa Code § 730.2 in Conrad v. Iowa Central Community College, 756 N.W.2d 48, 2008 WL 2746324, at *3–5 (Iowa Ct. App. July 16, 2008) (unpublished). Specifically, the Court stated section 730.2 "applies to 'any discharged employee' and also to 'any employee who may have *voluntarily* left said company's service.'" Id. at *4 (emphasis added). Furthermore, citing language directly from the statute, the Court held that section 730.2 does not apply to individuals, but only to companies, partnerships, or corporations. Id. at *5. Thus, the employee had no blacklisting claim against the president of Iowa Central Community College individually, but did have a claim against Iowa Central Community College because the president "acted with the authority of [Iowa Central Community College]." Id. See also I.B.8(a)(1), supra.

In addition, Iowa Code § 730.1 provides: "If any person agent, company, or corporation, after having discharged any employee from service, shall prevent or attempt to prevent, by word or writing of any kind, such discharged employee from obtaining employment . . . except by furnishing in writing on request a truthful statement as to the cause of the person's discharge, such person, agent, company, or corporation shall be guilty of a serious misdemeanor and shall be liable for all damages sustained by any such person." See generally Iowa Code § 730.3 (providing that false statement without probable cause reporting that any employee "has received any money or thing of value for the transportation of persons or property or for other service for which the person has not accounted" or reporting that any employee "refused to collect any money or ticket for transportation of persons or property or other service when it was their duty so to do" is a simple misdemeanor).

Iowa Code § 730.5(12)(b) provides that a "cause of action for defamation, libel, slander, or damage to reputation shall not arise against an employer establishing a program of drug or alcohol testing" unless the employer discloses the test results to a third-party, the "test results disclosed incorrectly indicate the presence of alcohol or drugs," and the "employer negligently discloses the results."

D. Intracorporate Communication

Even if they are considered "published," communications within an entity may be subject to a qualified privilege. See Benishek v. Cody, 441 N.W.2d 399, 402 (Iowa Ct. App. 1989) (holding accusations of embezzlement made to plaintiff and co-worker protected by qualified privilege); Jenkins v. Wal-Mart Stores, Inc., 910 F. Supp. 1399, 1425–27 (N.D. Iowa 1995) (holding that allegations of theft made in intra-corporate setting are protected by qualified privilege but that fact question existed regarding whether statements were made in good faith); Thomas v. St. Lukes Health Sys., Inc., 869 F. Supp. 1413, 1441–45 (N.D. Iowa 1994), aff'd, 61 F.3d 908 (8th Cir. 1995) (holding that intra-corporate communications concerning plaintiff's possible drug use were protected by qualified privilege but that fact question existed regarding whether defamatory statements were made in good faith); see generally Malone v. Des Moines Area Cmty. Coll., No. 4:04-CV-40103, 2005 WL 290008, at *12 (S.D. Iowa Jan. 26, 2005) (holding that statements "made during the investigation of the sexual harassment complaints made against Plaintiff" were subject to a qualified privilege). Regarding the issue of whether intracorporate communications are considered "published," see the discussion of Taggart v. Drake Univ., 549 N.W.2d 796, 802–04 (Iowa 1996) in I.B.6(a), supra. See also King v. Sioux City Radiological Group, P.C., 985 F. Supp. 869, 977–81 (N.D. Iowa 1997) (holding that fact question existed whether defamatory statements were made in bad faith vitiating qualified privilege and noting that parties failed to raise issue of whether statements made in intra-corporate communications are considered published); see generally Gries v. Akal Security, Inc., No. 06-CV-33-LRR, 2007 U.S. Dist. LEXIS 71902, at *110–11 & n.17 (S.D. Iowa Aug. 27, 2007) (stating in dicta that court has "serious doubts" that statements during investigation of employee misconduct were published to third parties).

E. Statements to Government Regulators

Statements made during and in preparation for judicial proceedings, including administrative proceedings, are protected by absolute privilege. Spencer v Spencer, 479 N.W.2d 293, 295 (Iowa 1991); Beeck v. Kapalis, 302 N.W.2d 90, 97 (Iowa 1981); Tallman v. Hanssen, 427 N.W.2d 868, 869–70 (Iowa 1988). See II.A, supra. Iowa Code § 96.11(6)(b)(2) confers a privilege for written or verbal statements made to job service or to a person administering employment security laws. However, immunity from liability for libel or slander is conferred only so long as the person is not acting with malice. But see Haldeman v. Total Petroleum, Inc., 376 N.W.2d 98, 102–03 (Iowa 1985) (applying provisions of Iowa Code § 96.11 (6)(b)(2) in 1985, before the addition to the statutory language conferring the privilege of the words "unless the report or statement is made with malice" in 1988, and concluding the legislature intended to create absolute immunity because of the absence of "qualifying language, such as 'in the absence of malice'"). Statements made in "good faith" by an employer in cooperation with state investigators seeking to establish the basis for an employee's termination, including the provision of records to civil rights investigators, are subject to qualified privilege. Thompto v. Coborn's Inc., 871 F. Supp. 1097, 1127 (N.D. Iowa 1994); see also Sawheny v. Pioneer Hi-Bred Int'l, Inc., 93 F.3d 1401, 1410 (8th Cir. 1996) (cloaking statements to foreign regulators with qualified privilege); see generally Clay v. HyVee, Inc., No. 07-1858, 2008 WL 5412076 (Iowa Ct. App. Dec. 31, 2008) (unpublished) (customer could not maintain libel claim against store employees who reported suspected criminal activity because even though the employees violated company policy and negligently investigated potential fraudulent procurement of prescription drugs, there was no evidence the statements were made with a high degree of probable falsity, and thus applicable privileges were not lost); Reeder v. Carroll, 759 F. Supp. 2d 1064, 1084–87 (N.D. Iowa 2010) (concluding qualified privilege, as well as statutory immunity under physician licensing and mandatory reporting statute, applied to letter to licensing board reporting concerns about plaintiff-physician's patient care); Nieman v. Firstar Bank, No. C03-4113-MWB, 2005 WL 2346998, at *4–6 (N.D. Iowa Sep. 26, 2005) (holding that federal statute covering financial institutions conferred unqualified immunity on defendant national bank from liability for employee's defamation claim asserted in connection with defendant's involvement in criminal investigation of employee's suspected wrongdoing).

F. Reports to Auditors and Insurers

Statements made to auditors and insurers are generally protected by qualified privilege. Bitner v. Ottumwa Cmty. Sch. Dist., 549 N.W.2d 295, 301 (Iowa 1996) (holding statements made to auditing firm investigating school principal's handling of school district funds were protected by qualified privilege); see Sunley v. Metro. Life Ins. Co., 132 Iowa 123, 109 N.W. 463, 464 (1906) (holding statement made by an employer to an employee's surety protected by qualified privilege).

G. Vicarious Liability of Employers for Statements Made by Employees

1. ***Scope of Employment.*** Employers are liable for defamatory statements made by employees when acting within the scope of their employment. Vowles v. Yakish, 179 N.W. 117, 120–21 (Iowa 1920) (holding employer insurance company not liable for slanderous statements made by employee adjuster outside the scope of his employment); see Huegerich v. IBP, Inc., 547 N.W.2d 216, 221 (Iowa 1996) (stating an employer may be held liable for defamation if defamatory statement published while employee is acting within the scope of his or her employment); Iowa Protection & Advocacy Servs., Inc. v. Tanager Place, No. C-04-0069, 2005 WL 2035225, at *3 (N.D. Iowa Aug. 24, 2005) (same); Stueckrath v. Bankers Trust Co., No. 6-931, 2007 Iowa Ct. App. LEXIS 76, at *13–14 (Iowa Ct. App. Jan. 31, 2007) (holding that alleged defamatory statement by coworker was not imputable to employer because it was made in a social setting in the context of casual conversation and not made within the scope of her employment); see also Lyons v. Midwest Glazing, L.L.C., 235 F. Supp. 2d 1030, 1044 (N.D. Iowa 2002); Smith v. Iowa Jewish Senior Life Ctr., 161 F. Supp. 2d 991, 999 (S.D. Iowa 2001) (applying Iowa law in context of defamation claim and attributing the statements of employer's attorney to employer because attorney was acting in his capacity as employer's attorney at the time). In Morris v. Am. Freightways, Inc., No. 4:01-CV-40475, 2003 WL 472510 (S.D. Iowa Feb. 20, 2003), the Court stated that the following test is to be applied in determining whether an employer is liable for the defamatory statements of an employee: "(a) Was the person who uttered the slanderous words an authorized agent of the corporation? (b) If so, was he at the time acting within the scope of his employment? and (c) Was the language charged used in the actual performance of his duties touching on the matter in question?" Id. at *11 (quoting Vowles v. Yakish, 191 Iowa 368, 179 N.W. 117, 118–19 (Iowa 1920)).

In Lyons v. Midwest Glazing, L.L.C., 235 F. Supp. 2d 1030, 1044–45 (N.D. Iowa 2002) (citing Godar v. Edwards, 588 N.W.2d 701 (Iowa 1999)), the Court discussed the "scope of employment" element of respondeat superior liability under Iowa law and stated that "for an act to be within the scope of employment the conduct complained of 'must be of the same general nature as that authorized or incidental to the conduct authorized.'" Id.; see also Fisher v. Elec. Data Sys., 278 F. Supp. 2d 980, 996 (S.D. Iowa 2003) (quoting Godar v. Edwards, 588 N.W.2d 701, 705 (Iowa 1999)) (stating same). If the employees' conduct "is so unlike that authorized that it is 'substantially different'" the employer is not vicariously liable. Lyons, 235 F. Supp. 2d at 1044 (citation omitted). Therein, the Court held that the defamatory statements at issue "were a substantial deviation from [the employees'] duties" at the defendant employer and were "not 'necessary to accomplish the purpose of the employment'" and thus were not made in the scope of employment. Id. at 1045–47. See also Stephenson v. Wellmark, Inc., No. 04-1547, 705 N.W.2d 106, 2005 WL 1398167, at *2–3 (Iowa Ct. App. June 15, 2005) (unpublished) (citation omitted) (affirming summary judgment dismissal of plaintiff's defamation suit against her former employer based on statements made by coworkers regarding her termination because plaintiff did not demonstrate "a genuine issue of fact about whether the individuals were acting within the scope of their employment" when making the alleged defamatory statements).

See generally Stueckrath v. Bankers Trust Co., No. 6-931, 2007 Iowa Ct. App. LEXIS 76, at *12–13 (Iowa Ct. App. Jan. 31, 2007) (analyzing whether employee's out of court statement that coworkers spread rumors about the plaintiff was admissible as an admission by a party-opponent, and holding that standard governing whether a statement by a third person can constitute an admission by a party-opponent was "clearly" not met as to the individual defendant-coworkers); Kent v. Iowa, 651 F. Supp. 2d 910, 956–57 (S.D. Iowa 2009) (discussing state workers individual liability for slander claim and whether defendant was acting within scope of employment for purposes of sovereign immunity); Ideal Instruments, Inc. v. Rivard Instruments, Inc., 434 F. Supp. 2d 598, 623–24 (N.D. Iowa 2006) (addressing individual liability of corporate officers for the intentional tort of defamation made while acting within as well as outside the scope of their employment); Sykes v. Hengel, 394 F. Supp. 2d 1062, 1078 (S.D. Iowa 2005) (addressing personal liability of individual defendants for actions taken as board managers and agents of limited liability company).

a. **Blogging.** There are no reported Iowa decisions discussing blogging in this context. **See generally S.J.W. v. Lee's Summit R-7 Sch. Dist., 696 F.3d 771 (8th Cir. 2012) (reversing Western District of Missouri order granting preliminary injunction to students asserting constitutional claims for suspension based on blogging); State of Iowa v. Runge, No. 11-0778, 2012 WL 5356174, at *4 (Iowa Ct. App. Oct. 31, 2012) (discussing whether criminal defendant's blog comments were properly considered in sentencing decision).**

2. ***Damages.*** There have been no reported defamation decisions specifically addressing the measure of damages in a vicarious liability context.

H. Internal Investigations

Statements that reflect on an employee's capacity or fitness to perform his or her business, trade, profession or office have been held defamatory per se. See, e.g., King v. Sioux City Radiological Group, P.C., 985 F. Supp. 869, 878 (N.D. Iowa 1997) (statement that hospital's director of radiology was not competent in his employment and a liar was libelous per se); Jenkins v. Wal-Mart Stores, Inc., 910 F. Supp. 1399, 1426 (N.D. Iowa 1995) (alleged statements by former department store employee's supervisor regarding employee's alleged theft of television set from store were defamatory per se). Accusations of certain criminal activity are also defamatory per se. Thomas v. St. Luke's Health Sys, Inc., 869 F. Supp. 1413, 1442 (N.D. Iowa 1994) (citations omitted), aff'd, 61 F.3d 908 (8th Cir. 1995). Thus, statements accusing employees of certain misconduct, like possessing illegal drugs, constitute defamation per se. See Huegerich v. IBP, Inc., 547 N.W.2d 216, 221 (Iowa 1996) (employer's inquiries as to whether employee has a drug problem can be defamatory per se because imputation of substance abuse clearly reflects on employee's capacity and fitness to perform his or her duties). Even if defamatory per se, the plaintiff still has the burden of proving the element of publication. Id. at 221, 223 (noting that "courts have reached different results on whether the act of terminating an employee is defamatory" and "whether an investigation by an employer into a suspected crime of an employee constitutes a defamatory publication," and holding that actions of management in conducting random drug search and subsequently discharging employee were insufficient to constitute a defamatory publication). See III.D, supra, discussing "Intracorporate Communication."

Statements made during internal investigations may be subject to a qualified privilege if the privilege is not abused. See, e.g., Theisen v. Covenant Med. Ctr., Inc., 636 N.W.2d 74, 84 (Iowa 2001) (holding employer's accusation employee had sent an obscene voice mail to a co-worker "easily falls within the criteria necessary to establish a qualified privilege as a matter of law" as employer had an "undisputed interest in the subject of the statement" made during a sexual harassment investigation and the statement was made during a "closed-door meeting" with employee's supervisor and the director of employee services, "a proper time and place to discuss such an accusation with limited parties"); Bitner v. Ottumwa Cmty. Sch. Dist., 549 N.W.2d 295, 300–03 (Iowa 1996); Malone v. Des Moines Area Cmty. Coll., No. 4:04-CV-40103, 2005 WL 290008 (S.D. Iowa Jan. 26, 2005) (holding employer was "subject to the qualified immunity insofar as the alleged defamatory statements were made during the investigation of the sexual harassment complaints made against Plaintiff"); see also Gries v. Akal Security, Inc., No. 06-CV-33-LRR, 2007 U.S. Dist. LEXIS 71902, at *115–17 (S.D. Iowa Aug. 27, 2007) (holding post-Barreca that the "occasions" of employer's communications to a business partner were privileged because they were in furtherance of the common interest of "jointly investigating employee misconduct and were concerned with ensuring the safety of . . . employees," and stating that the purpose of the qualified privilege to allow unrestricted communication regarding a matter in which parties have a duty or interest "would be thwarted if employers were not allowed to investigate alleged altercations between their employees"). See II.A.2, supra, "Qualified Privilege." See also Wright v. Keokuk County Health Ctr., 399 F. Supp. 2d 938, 953–56 (S.D. Iowa 2005), which discussed whether the privilege applied to an employer's statement to various individuals that plaintiff was being investigated and ultimately terminated for misusing company funds. The Court in Wright concluded, *inter alia*, that while there was a fact issue whether the disclosure to plaintiff's direct reports was an appropriate occasion, similar statements made to an employee responsible for accounts payable and human resources were privileged as "discussing the situation with her was a reasonable and necessary part" of the investigation. Id.; see also Thomas, 869 F. Supp. at 1444 (concluding employer only repeated patient's allegation that employee used cocaine "within the appropriate managerial sphere . . . or to persons outside of that sphere who could advise them as to the appropriate manner in which to handle the allegations"). A qualified privilege is lost if the statement is made with the knowledge that it is false or with reckless disregard for its truth or falsity." See Barreca v. Nickolas, 683 N.W.2d 111, 120–23 (Iowa 2004); see also Gries, 2007 U.S. Dist. LEXIS 71902, at *118–21 (holding as a matter of law that employer did not abuse its qualified privilege "by way of excessive publication, nor did it act with actual malice," and stating that although employer's investigation of employee misconduct "may not have been the best way to investigate the matter" employee has not shown that defendant entertained serious doubts about the truth of statements made during the investigation); Wright, 399 F. Supp. 2d at 956 n.8 (noting defendant's argument that the absence of actual malice was demonstrated by the fact they conducted a bona fide investigation, but declining to address argument because defendant misstated the actual malice standard); Jenkins v. Wal-Mart Stores, Inc., 910 F. Supp. 1399, 1425–27 (N.D. Iowa 1995) (analyzing whether qualified privilege was lost under former "ill-will/wrongful motive" standard for determining whether privilege abused, and holding that there were fact issues regarding whether allegations of employee theft were made in good faith because they were based on uncorroborated allegations of manager); Thomas, 869 F. Supp. at 1444–45 (stating that "defendants had a legitimate concern about allegations that a rehabilitation technician had himself been using illegal drugs and . . . they conducted a reasonable investigation of those allegations," and concluding that employer had not abused privilege under previous "ill-will" standard). See generally Iowa Code § 91B.2 (conferring immunity from civil liability where employer provides work-related information about an employee upon employee's request or authorization, unless the employer "acted unreasonably in providing the work-related information"); Graham v. Contract Transp., Inc., 220 F.3d 910, 914 (8th Cir. 2000) (discussing whether a defamation claim was preempted by federal law and contrasting statements made during an employer's investigation of employee misconduct with those made after the investigation had been completed).

While Iowa courts have recognized the tort of negligent hiring, including negligent supervision and retention, D.R.R. v. English Enters, 356 N.W.2d 580, 583 (Iowa Ct. App. 1984), they have rejected claims premised on negligent investigation. See Theisen, 636 N.W.2d at 81–83 (rejecting terminated employee's claim of negligent investigation against employer for firing him after another employee accused him of leaving an obscene message without first conducting a reasonable investigation); see also Huegerich v. IBP, Inc., 547 N.W.2d 216, 220 (Iowa 1996) (rejecting negligent discharge as an exception to employment at-will doctrine). The Iowa Supreme Court has stated that "an employer has no duty to conduct a reasonable investigation in favor of an at-will employee." Theisen, 636 N.W.2d at 83 (also rejecting employee's argument that, even if employer was not compelled to investigate before firing him for sexual harassment, once employer undertook an investigation it had a duty to conduct the investigation with reasonable care, and holding that Restatement sections relied on by employee were inapposite as, *inter alia*, duty in sexual harassment investigation is to the alleged victim and the plaintiff/alleged harasser had not suffered any physical harm). See IV.A, infra, regarding "Negligent Hiring, Retention, and Supervision."

General criticism of an employee generally is not considered sufficient to establish the outrageous conduct element of an intentional infliction of emotional distress claim. Northrup v. Farmland Indus., Inc., 372 N.W.2d 193 (Iowa 1985). In many cases, claims for intentional infliction of emotional distress based on criticisms and accusations of misconduct are dismissed on summary judgment as not constituting conduct qualifying as outrageous under the stringent proof standard. See Cheek v. ABC Bev. Mfrs., Inc., No. 05-1962, 2006 WL 2560890, at *3–4 (Iowa Ct. App. Sept. 7, 2006) (unpublished) (finding that employer's filing of police report and participation in employee's criminal prosecution, even if done with malicious intent, could not establish outrageous conduct); Benishek v. Cody, 441 N.W.2d 399, 402 (Iowa Ct. App. 1989) (holding employer's accusation that employee had embezzled was not outrageous); Napreljac v. John Q. Hammons Hotels, Inc., 461 F. Supp. 2d 981, 1042 (S.D. Iowa 2006) (holding that the alleged conduct was not sufficiently outrageous even if the employer knew that the accident report, which formed the basis for termination of the employee, was both false and manufactured by other employees); Thomas v. St. Luke's Health Sys, Inc., 869 F. Supp. 1413, 1441 (N.D. Iowa 1994) (holding employer's actions in taking reasonable steps to investigate accusations by patient that employee was using cocaine were not outrageous as a matter of law), aff'd, 61 F.3d 908 (8th Cir. 1995). See also the discussion in Wright v. Keokuk County Health Ctr., 399 F. Supp. 2d 938, 946 (S.D. Iowa 2005) (citations omitted) comparing Iowa cases and noting that although "Iowa courts have found an employer's treatment of an employee rises to the level of outrageous when it entails an extensive campaign of harassment and baseless accusations," Iowa courts have held that conduct such as seeking criminal charges through proper procedures or accusing an employee of embezzlement are not sufficiently outrageous.

See also IV.C, infra, regarding "Interference With Economic Advantage"; Godfredsen v. Lutheran Bhd., No. 0-431, 2000 WL 1675869, at *6 (Iowa Ct. App. Nov. 8, 2000) (stating in context of interference claim that employer "had a legitimate business interest in communicating with its insureds to retain their business and investigate [its former agent's] potential breach of restrictive covenants").

Under Iowa law an employer cannot require, request, administer, or threaten an employee to take a polygraph examination as a condition of employment, promotion, change in status of employment, or as an express or implied condition of a benefit or privilege of employment. Iowa Code § 730.4; Wilcox v. Hy-Vee Food Stores, Inc., 458 N.W.2d 870 (Iowa 1990). The statute does not apply to the state or a political subdivision when it is selecting a candidate for employment as a peace officer, corrections officer, or positions with law enforcement agencies of political subdivisions in which employees have "direct access to prisoner funds, any other cash assets, and confidential information." Iowa Code § 730.4(3). Polygraph examinations administered by the government must adhere to the published anti-discrimination policy of the government entity conducting the examination. Iowa Code § 730.4(3)(b). In Theisen v. Covenant Med. Ctr., Inc., 636 N.W.2d 74 (Iowa 2001), the Court rejected a discharged employee's claim that his termination for refusing to submit to a voice print analysis violated the public policy embodied in Iowa Code § 730.4. The Court noted that "the plain language of section 730.4 pertains to devices, such as polygraphs, that purport to measure the truth or veracity of an employee's statement," and the "statute does not, by its terms, prohibit lawful tests or procedures used by an employer in the identification of employees suspected of workplace crime." Id.

Iowa Code § 730.5 governs drug testing of employees and applicants by private employers. See the "Drug Testing" section in Part II.B of the Privacy outline.

Although beyond the scope of this outline, it is generally noted that internal investigations may implicate the privacy interests of employees. See, e.g., Pulla v. Amoco Oil Co., 882 F. Supp. 836 (S.D. Iowa 1994) (considering a privacy claim in the context of a co-employee's improper review of the plaintiff's credit card records to verify that plaintiff had indeed been sick on the days he used sick leave), aff'd in relevant part, 72 F.3d 648, 661 (8th Cir. 1995); O'Bryan v. KTIV Television, 868 F. Supp. 1146, 1158 (N.D. Iowa 1994) (holding there was no intrusion cause of action for an employer's search and examination of the contents of an employee's desk and office for employer-owned documents without the employee's knowledge because the employee did not have a reasonable expectation of privacy in his desk or office area), aff'd in relevant part, 64 F.3d 1188 (8th Cir. 1995).

IV. OTHER ACTIONS BASED ON STATEMENTS

With respect to the issue of preemption of defamation and related claims by federal labor law, federal cases discussing the issue include, Graham v. Contract Transp., Inc., 220 F.3d 910, 913–14 (8th Cir. 2000) (holding union member's defamation claim not preempted under federal labor law); compare Gore v. Trans World Airlines, 210 F.3d 944 (8th Cir. 2000); Johnson v. Anheuser Busch, Inc., 876 F.2d 620 (8th Cir. 1989). For an Iowa state case discussing the issue, see Delaney v. Int'l Union Local No. 94, 675 N.W.2d 832, 842–46 (Iowa 2004) (holding federal labor law and supremacy clause preempted non-union members' defamation and related claims against a union, and stating "a state law defamation claim is *not* preempted if the plaintiff shows the defendant made a false statement of fact with 'actual malice,' i.e. with a knowing or reckless disregard of the truth," "courts ought not become the grammar police and thereby chill free speech in this context," and drawings in that case resembling cartoons "cannot reasonably be taken at face value"). For cases discussing whether defamation and related claims are preempted by other federal laws, see Chapman v. LabOne, 390 F.3d 620, 627–29 (8th Cir. 2004) (federal laws regulating the drug testing of railroad employees); Mathis v. Henderson, 243 F.3d 446, 449–51 (8th Cir. 2001) (Title VII); Murray v. Solidarity of Labor Org. Int'l Union Benefit Fund, 172 F. Supp. 2d 1134 (N.D. Iowa 2001) (ERISA).

A. Negligent Hiring, Retention, and Supervision

Iowa courts have recognized the tort of negligent hiring, including negligent supervision and retention. D.R.R. v. English Enters, 356 N.W.2d 580, 583 (Iowa Ct. App. 1984). Compare Theisen v. Covenant Med. Ctr., Inc., 636 N.W.2d 74 (Iowa 2001) (rejecting terminated employee's claim of negligent investigation against employer for firing him after another employee accused him of leaving an obscene message without first conducting a reasonable investigation); Huegerich v. IBP, Inc., 547 N.W.2d 216, 220 (Iowa 1996) (rejecting negligent discharge as an exception to employment at-will doctrine). Such a cause of action will exist only "when the employer owes a special duty to the injured party." Godar v. Edwards, 588 N.W.2d 701, 708–09 (Iowa 1999). Such a duty may arise when an employee "because of their employment, may pose a threat of injury to the public." Fredricksburg Farmers Coop. v. Stanley and Elwood Farms, No. 00-0278, 2001 WL 1580488, at *2 (Iowa Ct. App. Dec. 12, 2001); Godar, 588 N.W.2d at 709. An employer is liable "only if all the requirements of an action of tort for negligence exist." Fredricksburg, 2001 WL 1580488, at *2. An employer will not be held liable when it had no actual knowledge or suspicions of the inappropriate behavior. Id. at 709–10 (finding school district not liable under negligent hiring, supervision and retention theories for sexual abuse perpetrated on student by district employee). In Schoff v. Combined Ins. Co., 604 N.W.2d 43, 52–53 (Iowa 1999), the Iowa Supreme Court concluded that an employer cannot be held liable for negligent supervision or training where the conduct that purportedly would have been avoided through proper supervision or training is not actionable in and of itself. See Cubit v. Mahaska County, 677 N.W.2d 777, 784–85 (Iowa 2004) (internal quotations omitted) (citing Schoff for rule that a "claim of negligent supervision must include as an element an underlying tort or wrongful act committed by the employee"). Compare Stockton Realty Co. v. Muscatine Cnty. Solid Waste Mgmt. Agency, No. 03-1331, 2004 WL 1902518, at *8 (Iowa Ct. App. Aug. 26, 2004) (citation omitted) (stating that the "tort of negligent supervision is aimed at the independent negligent action, or personal fault, of the principal," and "the wrongful act of the agent, while a factual cause of a plaintiff's damages, is not in and of itself the breach which legally caused those damages; it is a breach by the principal of its own duty to use reasonable care in supervising the agent"). In Schoff, a management employee was accused of negligent misrepresentation, a cause of action that was inapplicable under the factual circumstance. See also Doe v. Hartz, 52 F. Supp. 2d 1027, 1073 (N.D. Iowa 1999) (denying defendants' motions to dismiss negligent supervision claims, resulting from priest's alleged assault on parishioner, because priest/employee may pose threat against public and sufficient evidence may exist that employer knew or should have known of priest's potential to injure the parishioner). The Iowa Supreme Court has also noted that although a "necessary element of a claim for negligent supervision or retention is an underlying tort or wrongful act committed by the employee," "the cause of action arises from the employer's own tortious conduct" and the "'underlying tort or wrongful conduct is simply a link in the causal chain leading to compensable damages.'" IMT Ins. Co. v. Crestmoor Golf Club, 702 N.W.2d 492, 496 (Iowa 2005) (citations omitted).

Negligent retention occurs when an employee of the defendant commits an underlying tort or wrongful act that caused a compensable injury and the negligent retention of the employee caused the injury. Kiesau v. Bantz, 686 N.W.2d 164, 172 (Iowa 2004). In such a lawsuit, the plaintiff must prove "a case within a case." Id. In Wilson v. Cintas Corporation, 760 N.W.2d 211 (Iowa Ct. App. 2008), plaintiff brought an emotional distress and negligent retention suit against his employer for the repeated taunts and slurs spoken by a co-worker. The appeals court affirmed summary judgment for the employer on the grounds that the alleged ongoing verbal harassment was not itself actionable so no underlying tort or wrongful act supported the claim of emotional harm.

The Iowa Supreme Court enunciated the elements of a negligent supervision claim as follows: "(1) the employer knew, or in the exercise of ordinary care should have known, of its employee's unfitness at the time the employee engaged in wrongful or tortious conduct; (2) through the negligent . . . supervision of the employee, the employee's incompetence, unfitness, or dangerous characteristics proximately caused injuries to the plaintiff; and (3) there is some employment or agency relationship between the employee and the defendant employer." Estate of Harris v. Papa John's Pizza, 679 N.W.2d 673, 680 (Iowa 2004) (citations omitted); see also Walderbach v. Archdiocese of Dubuque, Inc., 730 N.W.2d 198, 200–01 (Iowa 2007) (dismissing negligent supervision claim on summary judgment because evidence that the archdiocese knew of the abuse was merely speculative and evidence was insufficient to show an employer/employee relationship between archdiocese and priest who allegedly abused plaintiff); McGraw v. Wachovia Securities, LLC., No. 08-CV-2064, 2009 WL 2949290, at*6

(N.D. Iowa Sept. 10, 2009) (discussing elements of negligent supervision claim and noting "liability in a negligent supervision claim arises from the employer's conduct . . . not the employee's conduct.").

In Piper v. Jerry's Homes, No. 0102018, 671 N.W.2d 531, 2003 WL 22199580, at *4 (Iowa Ct. App. Sept. 24, 2003), the plaintiff asserted a negligent hiring claim and urged the Court to adopt Restatement (Second) of Torts § 411, which "subjects an employer to liability for physical harm to a third person that results from the employer's 'failure to exercise reasonable care to employ a competent and careful contractor to do work which will involve a risk of physical harm unless it is skillfully and carefully done . . . .'" Id. (citation omitted). Section 411 imposes liability on a general contractor for the incompetence or carelessness of a subcontractor if the general contractor "had reason to know, at the time the subcontractor was selected, that the subcontractor was incompetent or careless in the particular way that injured the plaintiff." Id. (citation omitted). In Piper, the Court found it unnecessary to determine if § 411 should be adopted, because the plaintiff did not meet its requirements. Id. In 2011, the Iowa Court of Appeals decided to adopt § 411, finding it to be "an appropriate guide to determine whether a duty exists when a person is injured by an independent contractor that was negligently selected by the employer." Jones v. Schneider Nat'l, Inc., 797 N.W.2d 611, 614 (Iowa Ct. App. 2011) (noting the Iowa Supreme Court's reliance on Restatement principles on similar issues). In recognizing § 411, the Court of Appeals reaffirmed the requirement that a plaintiff bringing a negligent hiring claim must show "'the employer knew, or in the exercise of reasonable care should have known, of...unfitness at the time of hiring.'" Id. at 617 (citing Godar, 588 N.W.2d at 708). The Court of Appeals declined to extend the protection to employees of an independent contractor, interpreting the phrase "third parties" in § 411 did not include employees of an independent contractor. Id. at 615-16 (citation omitted) (noting a majority of jurisdictions have determined that employers of independent contractors are not vicariously liable to the employees of an independent contractor and finding the purposes of § 411 were satisfied by the receipt of workers' compensation benefits); **see Kelly v. Riser, Inc., No. 11-1898, 2012 WL 5356104, at *6-7 (Iowa Ct. App. Oct. 31, 2012) (applying Jones and § 411, and holding that negligent hiring claim of independent contractor's employee failed)**.

In Graves v. Iowa Lakes Cmty. Coll., the Iowa Supreme Court declined to extend the cause of action for negligent supervision beyond injuries inflicted upon third parties to non-physical injuries suffered by fellow employees. Graves v. Iowa Lakes Cmty. Coll., 639 N.W.2d 22, 25 (Iowa 2002) (noting that while there is authority supporting the extension of the action to fellow employees, such cases have not extended the action in the absence of physical injury). However, the Iowa Supreme Court recently overruled Graves "to the extent [it] holds a negligent hiring, supervision, or retention claim requires physical injury." See Kiesau v. Bantz, 686 N.W.2d 164, 173 (Iowa 2004). Moreover, with respect to the issue of fellow employees, the Iowa Supreme Court recently stated in the Papa John's Pizza case, discussed infra, that it disagreed with a characterization that Graves "constitutes a 'favorable comment' upon the possibility of extending the tort to cover fellow employees in a case . . . wherein the fellow employee suffered a physical injury." Estate of Harris v. Papa John's Pizza, 679 N.W.2d 673, 680 (Iowa 2004). Rather, the Court stated that in Graves it had "not comment[ed] favorably upon the fact other courts had extended the tort" to actions asserted by fellow employees incurring physical injury, but rather the Court "simply recognized three other courts had so extended it." Id.

In that case, Estate of Harris v. Papa John's Pizza, 679 N.W.2d 673, 681–82 (Iowa 2004), the Iowa Supreme Court held that a negligent supervision claim asserted by the estate of an employee was preempted by the exclusivity provision of the Iowa Workers' Compensation Act. Therein, the negligent supervision claim was asserted against the defendant-employer by the estate of an employee for a "chest shot" inflicted by a fellow employee leading to plaintiff's death. Prior to the Papa John's Pizza case, no Iowa case appeared to have considered whether an employee could maintain a negligent hiring, retention, or supervision suit against his/her employer in light of the exclusive remedy provisions of the Iowa Workers' Compensation statute. With respect to the issue of intentional torts, in holding that the negligent supervision claim premised upon a "chest shot" that led to the employee's death was preempted by the Iowa Workers' Compensation Act, the Pappa John's Pizza Court also noted that "there is an insufficient showing in the record that the Nelson standard has been satisfied." Papa John's Pizza, 679 N.W.2d at 681 (citation omitted). In that regard, the Court had cited language from Nelson that "[u] nless the employer has commanded or expressly authorized the assault, it cannot be assumed to be intentional from his standpoint any more than from the standpoint of any third person." Id. (citing Nelson v. Winnebago Indus., Inc., 619 N.W.2d 385 (Iowa 2000)). See generally Phillips v. Swift & Co., 137 F. Supp. 2d 1126, 1131–40 (S.D. Iowa 2001) (in context of breach of fiduciary duty claim discussing generally the exclusivity of Iowa Worker's Compensation Act, noting that it is "now fairly safe to say that intentional torts are outside the scope" of the Act but "which intentional torts are outside the scope, or at least to what extent they are outside the scope is not clear," and reconciling various cases); Beard v. Flying J, Inc., 266 F.3d 792, 802–03 (8th Cir. 2001) (citing Nelson v. Winnebago Indus., Inc., 619 N.W.2d 385 (Iowa 2000)) (concluding that Nelson Court had not meant to abandon general rule that intentional torts are not preempted by workers' compensation law, and holding battery claim of former employee against supervisor was not preempted). See V.C, infra.

The Iowa Workers' Compensation statute, however, permits an employee to sue a co-worker where that co-worker was guilty of "gross negligence amounting to such lack of care as to amount to wanton neglect for the safety of another." Iowa Code § 85.20; see LaFleur v. Campos, No. 6-700, 2006 Iowa Ct. App. LEXIS 1797, at *2–3 (Iowa Ct. App. Nov. 30,

2006); Judge v. Clark, No. 6-251, 2006 Iowa Ct. App. LEXIS 1296, at *15–18 (Iowa Ct. App. Nov. 16, 2006). To meet this standard of gross negligence, there must be knowledge on the part of the co-employee of the danger, and knowledge that injury is a probable rather than possible result of the danger and a conscious failure on the part of the co-employee to avoid the peril. See Thompson v. Bohlken, 312 N.W.2d 501, 503 (Iowa 1981); see also Nelson v. Winnebago Indus., Inc., 619 N.W.2d 385, 390–91 (Iowa 2000) (revisiting Thompson and applying its principles in suit against co-employees); Walker v. Ceco Concrete Constr., L.L.C., 149 F. Supp. 2d 849, 853–54 (S.D. Iowa 2001) (citing Walker v. Mlakar, 489 N.W.2d 401, 405–06 (Iowa 1992)) (applying Iowa Code § 85.20 in the construction context and noting "Iowa courts' reluctance to find co-employee liability in admittedly dangerous, industrial working conditions absent some showing that the co-employee actually knew of the perilous condition and yet allowed work to proceed"). In Jones v. Schneider Nat'l, Inc., 797 N.W.2d 611, 615–16 (Iowa Ct. App. 2011), the Court of Appeals adopted Restatement (Second) of Torts § 411, imposing a standard of care upon employers hiring independent contractors, and distinguishing an employer of an independent contractor from other third parties permitted by the Workers' Compensation statute to be sued for gross negligence. (citation omitted) (noting the cost of workers' compensation insurance likely had been passed on to the employer from the independent contractor).

Claims for negligent hiring or supervision may be preempted by other statutes as well. See, e.g., Estate of Fischer v. Dyno Oil, Inc., No. 11-0452, 814 N.W.2d 622, 2012 WL 642884, at *2–3 (Iowa Ct. App. Feb. 29, 2012) (finding that the Iowa Dram Shop Act preempted negligent supervision and training claim).

B. Intentional Infliction of Emotional Distress

Iowa law has recognized claims for intentional infliction of emotional distress where there is: (1) outrageous conduct by the defendant, (2) an intent by the defendant to cause emotional distress or reckless disregard for the probability of such causation, (3) the suffering by plaintiff of severe or extreme emotional distress and (4) actual and proximate causation of the emotional distress by the defendant's outrageous conduct. See Zuhdija Napreljac v. John Q. Hammons Hotels, Inc., 461 F. Supp. 2d 981, 1039 (S.D. Iowa 2006); Doe v. Hartz, 52 F. Supp. 2d 1027, 1068 (N.D. Iowa 1999); Hanson v. Hancock County Mem'l Hosp., 938 F. Supp. 1419 (N.D. Iowa 1996); Nelson v. J.C. Penney Co., Inc., 75 F.3d 343 (8th Cir. 1996); Amsden v. Grinnell Mut. Reins. Co., 203 N.W.2d 252, 255 (Iowa 1972); Ette v. Linn-Mar Cmty. Sch. Dist., 656 N.W.2d 62, 70 (Iowa 2002) (citation omitted); Fisher v. Elec. Data Sys., 278 F. Supp. 2d 980 (S.D. Iowa 2003) (citation omitted); Martinez v. Cole Sewell Corp., 233 F. Supp. 2d 1097, 1138, (N.D. Iowa 2002) (citation omitted); Barreca v. Nickolas, 683 N.W.2d 111, 123–24 (Iowa 2004) (citation omitted); Schuller v. Great-West Life & Annuity Ins. Co., No. C-04-62-LRR, 2005 WL 2257634, at *57 (N.D. Iowa Sept. 15, 2005) (citation omitted); Peterson v. Prosser, No. C08-4005, 2010 WL 797130, at *15 (N.D. Iowa Mar. 4, 2010) (citation omitted); McFarland v. McFarland, 684 F. Supp. 2d 1073, 1089 (N.D. Iowa 2010); Becker v. Longinaker, No. 09-0833, 2010 WL 1578400, at *15 (Iowa Ct. App. Apr. 21, 2010)**; Graves v. City of Waterloo, No. C10-2014, 2011 WL 5563546, at *5 (N.D. Iowa, Nov. 15, 2011) (discussing evidence admissible to show extreme emotional distress)**.

Iowa courts impose strict proof requirements regarding whether the alleged conduct could reasonably be regarded as outrageous and to qualify as such, "the conduct must be extremely egregious; mere insult, bad manners, or hurt feelings are insufficient." Taggart v. Drake Univ., 549 N.W.2d 796, 803 (Iowa 1996). It is for the court to determine in the first instance whether the defendants' conduct may reasonably be regarded as so extreme and outrageous as to permit recovery. Hartz, 52 F. Supp. 2d at 1068 (quoting Hanson, 938 F. Supp. at 1440). Iowa courts define "outrageous conduct" to mean conduct so extreme "as to go beyond all possible bounds of decency and to be regarded as atrocious and utterly intolerable in a civilized community." Vaughn v. AG Processing, Inc., 459 N.W.2d 627 (Iowa 1990); Harsha v. State Sav. Bank, 346 N.W.2d 791 (Iowa 1984); Vinson v. Linn-Mar Cmty. Sch. Dist., 360 N.W.2d 108 (Iowa 1984); Ette, 656 N.W.2d at 70–71 & n.1 (citation omitted); Schuller v. Great-West Life & Annuity Ins. Co., No. C-04-62-LRR, 2005 WL 2257634, at *57 (N.D. Iowa Sept. 15, 2005) (citations omitted); see Frederick v. Simpson College, 149 F. Supp. 2d 826, 842 (S.D. Iowa 2001) (applying Iowa law and holding professor's conduct towards student did not constitute outrageous conduct because plaintiff was an adult student and professor's behavior did not rise to the level of outrageous under Iowa law despite the fact it was offensive and disgusting); Chapman v. LabOne, 460 F. Supp. 2d 989, 1006 (S.D. Iowa 2006) (finding as a matter of law that laboratory's communication of allegedly false failed drug test result to employer did not rise to the level of atrocious and utterly intolerable); McFarland v. McFarland, 684 F. Supp. 2d 1073, 1091–92 (N.D. Iowa 2010) (finding allegations that a wife "sent an email . . . to over 300 households . . . falsely accus[ing]" husband of physical abuse and submitted affidavits with false information with the "purpose of assisting [wife] in wrongfully denying [husband] custody" of their children constituted outrageous conduct sufficient for a claim of intentional infliction of emotional distress to survive a motion to dismiss); **see also Koeppel v. Speirs, 808 N.W.2d 177, 185 n.2 (Iowa 2011) (noting that while "the act of intentionally placing an inoperable camera . . . into a private area may not support the intrusion element of the invasion of privacy, it could give rise to the tort of intentional infliction of emotional distress")**. An absolute privilege bars claims of intentional infliction of emotional distress based on statements made during a judicial proceeding. See McFarland v. McFarland, Nos. C08-4047, C09-4047, 2011 WL 4402356, at *4, 15, 16 (N.D. Iowa Sept. 20, 2011) (granting summary judgment dismissal of claims based on alleged defamatory statements made during prior judicial proceeding, and holding absolute privilege barred both the defamation claims and related claims based on the statements, including intentional infliction of emotional distress claim). "Outrageous conduct does not extend to mere insults, indignities, threats, annoyances, petty oppressions, hurt feelings, bad manners or other trivialities which a reasonable person could be expected to endure." Blasen v. Welu, No. LACV 053658, 2004 WL 3488071, at *2 (Iowa Dist. Ct. Nov. 1, 2004). General criticism of an employee generally is not considered outrageous conduct. Northrup v. Farmland Indus., Inc., 372 N.W.2d 193 (Iowa 1985). This is true even where a supervisor "engaged in a deliberate campaign to badger and harass" the plaintiff/employee. Vinson, 360 N.W.2d at 119.; but see Wright v. Keokuk County Health Ctr., 399 F. Supp. 2d 938, 946 (S.D. Iowa 2005) (comparing Iowa cases and citing Blong v. Snyder, 361 N.W.2d 312, 315–17 (Iowa Ct. App. 1984) for proposition that "Iowa courts have found an employer's treatment of an employee rises to the level of outrageous when it entails an extensive campaign of harassment and baseless accusations"). The ongoing, repetitive nature of the conduct does not elevate verbal abuse by a co-worker into outrageous conduct. Wilson v. Cintas Corporation, 760 N.W.2d 211, 2008 WL 5235514, at *3 (Iowa Ct. App. 2008). In most cases, the Iowa Supreme Court has sustained motions for summary judgment dismissing the intentional infliction counts based on statements made by an employer or supervisor as not constituting conduct qualifying as outrageous under the stringent proof standard. Taggart, 549 N.W.2d at 802; see generally Cheek v. ABC Bev. Mfrs., Inc., No. 05-1962, 2006 WL 2560890, at *3–4 (Iowa Ct. App. Sept. 7, 2006) (unpublished) (finding that employer's filing of police report and participation in employee's criminal prosecution, even if done with malicious intent, could not establish outrageous conduct); Zuhdija Napreljac v. John Q. Hammons Hotels, Inc., 461 F. Supp. 2d 981, 1042 (S.D. Iowa 2006) (holding that the alleged conduct was not sufficiently outrageous even if the employer knew that the accident report, which formed the basis for termination of the employee, was both false and manufactured by other employees); Benishek v. Cody, 441 N.W.2d 399, 402 (Iowa Ct. App. 1989) (holding employer's accusation that employee had embezzled was not outrageous).

As to the second element, a person's conduct is reckless if they know with a high degree of probability that emotional distress will result and they act with deliberate disregard of that probability. See Cutler v. Klass, Whicher & Mishne, 473 N.W.2d 178 (Iowa 1991); M.H. v. State, 385 N.W.2d 533 (Iowa 1986); Meyer v. Nottger, 241 N.W.2d 911 (Iowa 1976).

The third element, extreme or severe emotional distress, can be established by direct and clear evidence of either "a notably distressful mental reaction" or physical symptoms of the distress. Sheridan v. City of Des Moines, No. 4:00-cv-90024, 2001 WL 901267, at *8–9 (S.D. Iowa Aug. 8, 2001) (citing Steckelberg v. Randolph, 448 N.W.2d 458, 462 (Iowa 1989)); see Barreca, 683 N.W.2d at 124 (citations omitted) (holding that (1) plaintiff-dance club "as a limited liability company, certainly cannot suffer emotional distress," and (2) evidence of humiliation, stress, embarrassment, and loss of sleep plaintiff-club owner alleged to have suffered "does not amount to 'severe or extreme emotional distress'"); Carlson v. SCI Iowa Funeral Servs., Inc., No. 02-1853, 674 N.W.2d 682, 2003 WL 22807406, at *3 (Iowa Ct. App. Nov. 26, 2003) (unpublished) (affirming dismissal of intentional infliction of emotional distress claims by plaintiffs who had not sought medical treatment and whose distress consisted of "hurt and frustration and anger," but reversing dismissal of claims by plaintiffs who had consulted physicians); Blasen v. Welu, 2004 WL 3488071, at *2 (holding loss of appetite and sleeplessness were insufficient).

In many cases, employee claims for intentional infliction of emotional distress have been preempted by the Iowa Civil Rights Act ("ICRA"). Napreljac v. Monarch Mfg. Co., No. 4-02-CV-10075, 2003 WL 21976024, at *8 (S.D. Iowa May 27, 2003) (holding that plaintiff's intentional infliction of emotional distress claim based on disability discrimination and preempted by the ICRA); Martinez, 233 F. Supp. 2d at 1138 (holding plaintiff's intentional infliction of emotional distress claim based on disability and national origin discrimination was preempted by ICRA); Greenland v. Fairtron Corp., 500 N.W.2d 36, 38 (Iowa 1993) (holding plaintiff's intentional infliction of emotional distress claim was preempted by the ICRA because "[d]iscrimination through sexual harassment is the [alleged] 'outrageous conduct'"); Channon v. United Parcel Serv., Inc., 629 N.W.2d 835, 858 (Iowa 2001) (affirming the validity of Greenland and holding the Iowa Civil Rights Act preempted plaintiff's emotional distress claim because it was based on allegations of discrimination); but see Grimm v. U.S. West Commc'ns, Inc., 644 N.W.2d 8 (Iowa 2002) (holding plaintiff pled facts sufficient to survive a pre-answer motion to dismiss arguing that her intentional infliction of emotional distress claim was preempted by the federal Labor Management Relations Act and the Iowa Civil Rights Act and that it was premature for the court to consider defendants' argument that the claim was preempted by Iowa's Workers' Compensations statute).

Statutory preemption of common law tort claims, including intentional infliction of emotional distress, "occurs unless the claims are separate and independent, and therefore incidental, causes of action. The claims are not separate and independent when, under the facts of the case, success in the [common law claims] . . . requires proof of discrimination." Fisher, 278 F.Supp.2d at 995 (quoting Greenland, 500 N.W.2d at 38). In Fisher, the Court stated that "proof of discrimination is not essential to [plaintiff's] emotional distress claim to the extent it arises from . . . alleged assault and battery." Id.; see also Garrison v. Kemin Industries, No. 22825-8-III, 2005 WL 852533 (S.D. Iowa Apr. 11, 2005) (finding that a public policy claim identical to plaintiff's statutory claims in an age discrimination case were preempted). For a discussion concerning the interaction of the intentional infliction of emotional distress tort with other laws, see **Minor v. State, 819 N.W.2d 383 (Iowa**

2012) (holding that state employee was immune from liability, under the Iowa Tort Claims Act, for intentional infliction of emotional distress claim asserted against her on the basis of alleged misrepresentations); Chapman v. LabOne, 390 F.3d 620, 627–29 (8th Cir. 2004) (holding that common law claims, including intentional infliction of emotional distress, asserted by railroad employee terminated for a failed drug test *against the testing laboratory* were not preempted by federal laws regulating the drug testing of railroad employees and reversing Chapman v. LabOne, 252 F. Supp. 2d 814, 819 (S.D. Iowa 2003) which held the claims were preempted); Brown v. Quik Trip Corp., 641 N.W.2d 725, 727–29 (Iowa 2002) (holding that a purely mental injury is compensable under the workers' compensation statute if medical and legal causation are established, and stating that the general test for legal causation is "whether the claimant's stress was 'of greater magnitude than the day-to-day mental stresses experienced by other workers employed in the same or similar jobs, regardless of their employer'"); **Johnson v. Dollar General, No. C11-3038-MWB, 2012 WL 3072997, at *30 (N.D. Iowa July 30, 2012) (stating plaintiff "concedes that he does not have an intentional infliction of emotional distress claim, because of the effect of the Iowa Workers Compensation Act on a claim for emotional distress arising out of a work situation")**. See V.C, infra.

Iowa generally does not recognize negligent infliction of emotional distress as an independent ground for liability, but rather as an element of damages which may accompany another tort. See Doe v. Cherwitz, 518 N.W.2d 362 (Iowa 1994); Niblo v. Parr Mfg., Inc., 445 N.W.2d 351 (Iowa 1989); see also Carlson v. SCI Iowa Funeral Servs., Inc., No. 02-1853, 674 N.W.2d 682, 2003 WL 22807406, at *5–6 (Iowa Ct. App. Nov. 26, 2003) (unpublished) (reversing summary judgment dismissal of negligent infliction of emotional distress claim because, while "[d]amages for emotional distress in a negligence action are normally denied absent a claim of physical injury," an "exception exists . . . where the nature of the relationship between the parties is such that there arises a duty to exercise ordinary care to avoid causing emotional harm" and there was a fact question concerning the existence of a contract for funeral services between plaintiff and defendant).

C. Interference with Economic Advantage

Iowa recognizes the tort of intentional interference with prospective economic advantage, also referred to as prospective business relations. A claim for interference with prospective economic advantage requires a showing of intentional and improper interference and that the defendant's sole or predominant purpose was to financially harm or destroy the plaintiff. Conrad v. Iowa Central Community College, 756 N.W.2d 48, 2008 WL 2746324 (Iowa Ct. App. July 16, 2008) (unpublished); Brown v. Kerkhoff, 504 F. Supp. 2d 464, 551–53 (S.D. Iowa 2007); Corcoran v. Land O' Lakes, Inc., 39 F. Supp. 2d 1139, 1150 (N.D. Iowa 1999); Compiano v. Hawkeye Bank & Tr. of Des Moines, 588 N.W.2d 462, 464 (Iowa 1999); Tredrea v. Anesthesia & Analgesia, P.C., 584 N.W.2d 276, 283 (Iowa 1998); Willey v. Riley, 541 N.W.2d 521, 527 (Iowa 1995); Economy Roofing & Insulating Co. v. Zumaris, 538 N.W.2d 641, 651–52 (Iowa 1995); Nesler v. Fisher & Co., Inc., 452 N.W.2d 191, 199 (Iowa 1990); Dillon v. Ruperto, No. 09-0600, 2010 WL 2383517, at *4–7 (Iowa Ct. App. June 16, 2010) (discussing tortious interference with prospective business and when a qualified privilege is applicable); D & E Sanitation Co. v. City of Hawarden, No. 98-1841, 2000 WL 328022, at *3 (Iowa Ct. App. Mar. 29, 2000); Ideal Instruments, Inc. v. Rivard Instruments, Inc., 434 F. Supp. 2d 598, 626–27 (N.D. Iowa 2006); GE Capital Corp. v. Commercial Servs. Group, Inc., 485 F. Supp. 2d 1015, 1025–27 (N.D. Iowa 2007); see also Chapman v. LabOne, 460 F. Supp. 2d 989, 1005 (S.D. Iowa 2006 (dismissing interference claims because there was no evidence laboratory acted to intentionally interfere with employee's relationship with employer when disclosing results of drug test to employer); Ideal Instruments, Inc., 434 F. Supp. 2d at 627 (finding that statements made about competitor could be defamatory and thus "reasonably impl[ied] an intent to injure or destroy [competitor's] business"); Godfredsen v. Lutheran Bhd., No. 0-431, 2000 WL 1675869, at *6 (Iowa Ct. App. Nov. 8, 2000) (stating employer "had a legitimate business interest in communicating with its insureds to retain their business and investigate [its former agent's] potential breach of restrictive covenants" and therefore holding as a matter of law agent could not prove employer's sole or predominate purpose was to financially injure or destroy him); Educ. Tech., Ltd. v. Meinhard, 99-0689, 2001 WL 488088, at *6–7 (Iowa Ct. App. May 9, 2001) (examining whether evidence supported finding of a predominant purpose to destroy or injure); Lake Panorama Serv. Corp. v. Cent. Iowa Energy Coop., 636 N.W.2d 747 (Iowa 2001) (unreleased) (distinguishing facts from prior cases as "[o]rdinarily the parties are business competitors," but here the two parties' relationship was "by design, one of cooperation rather than competition," and holding there was insufficient evidence to support jury's finding of a predominant purpose to financially destroy or injure a competitor); EFCO Corp. v. Symons Corp., 219 F.3d 734 (8th Cir. 2000); Glenn v. Diabetes Treatment Ctrs., 116 F. Supp. 2d 1098, 1106 (S.D. Iowa 2000); Jennings v. Mid-American Energy Co., 282 F. Supp. 2d 954, 964 (S.D. Iowa 2003) (citation omitted). "[P]laintiffs who allege tortious interference with prospective business relations are held to a strict standard of substantial proof 'that the defendant acted with a predominantly improper purpose.'" Jennings, 282 F. Supp. at 964 (quoting Hoefer v. Wisc. Educ. Assoc. Ins. Tr., 470 N.W.2d 336, 341 (Iowa 1991)); see also Tompkins Lawncare, Inc. v. Buchholz, 697 N.W.2d 126, 2005 WL 597016, at *1–3 (Iowa Ct. App. Mar. 16, 2005) (affirming jury verdict of liability and damages for intentional interference with plaintiff's prospective business advantage); **Home Show Tours, Inc. v. Quad City Virtual, Inc., 827 F.Supp.2d 924, 947–48 (S.D. Iowa 2011) (dismissing claim for interference with prospective business relations for failure to raise inference of either improper purpose or damages)**. If a defendant acts for more than one purpose, the improper purpose must dominate for liability to attach. Corcoran, 39 F. Supp. 2d at 1150–51; Compiano, 588 N.W.2d at 464; Tredrea, 584 N.W.2d at 283; Willey, 541 N.W.2d at 526–27. An "alleged interference is not improper if: a) the relation concerns a matter involved in the competition between the actor and the other, and b) the actor does not employ wrongful means, and c) his action does not create or continue an unlawful restraint of trade, and d) his purpose is at least in part to advance his interest in competing with the other." Chem. Methods, Ltd. v. Cue, No. 04-1518, 2005 WL 1750406, at *2–3 (Iowa Ct. App. July 27, 2005) (citations omitted) (stating also that "wrongful means . . . generally encompasses bribery, fraud, misrepresentation, deceit, and misuse of confidential information"). A contract need not exist, but prospective economic advantage must be reasonably likely and the defendant must have knowledge of the expectation. Nesler, 452 N.W.2d at 191; see Keegan v. City of Blue Grass, No. 03-0194, at *3–4 (Iowa Ct. App. Jan. 28, 2004) (citation omitted) (holding that "a defendant must have *actual* knowledge of the prospective business relationship"); see also Chem. Methods, Ltd., 2005 WL 1750406, at *2 (citation omitted) (stating that "cases involving interference with at-will contracts are more akin to interference with a prospective contractual relation because the alleged interference only damages a future expectancy, not a legal right"); Gray v. Harding, No. 11-0018, 2011 WL 4578481, at *13 (Iowa Ct. App. Oct. 5, 2011) (affirming summary judgment in a tortious interference with at-will employment claim and requiring the plaintiff to demonstrate the sole or predominant purpose of the defendant was to injure or financially destroy the plaintiff); Moore Dev., Ltd. v. M.G. Midwest, Inc., No. C06-1014, 2007 U.S. Dist. LEXIS 59067, at *30 (N.D. Iowa Aug. 13, 2007) (holding plaintiff did not identify a prospective business relationship by merely asserting it had "several inquiries" from potential tenants). The interference must have either caused a third party not to enter into or continue a business relationship or prevented plaintiff from entering into or continuing a business relationship. Willey, 541 N.W.2d at 527; Nesler, 452 N.W.2d at 198–99; see generally Kluver v. Hy-Vee Food Stores, Inc., No. 03-0729, 2003 WL 23008787, at *2 n.2 (Iowa Ct. App. Dec. 24, 2003) (citing Harbit v. Voss Petroleum, Inc., 553 N.W.2d 329, 331 (Iowa 1996)) (stating in dicta that tortious interference claim against supervisor for interference with plaintiff's employment relationship would fail because it "can be committed only by a third party not a party to a contract"); Conrad v. Iowa Central Community College, 756 N.W.2d 48, 2008 WL 2746324 (Iowa Ct. App. July 16, 2008) (unpublished). The plaintiff must suffer an actual loss or damage as a result of the interference. Speculative or nominal damages, or the threat of future harm, are insufficient to state a cause of action. Willey, 541 N.W.2d at 527; Harsha v. State Sav. Bank, 346 N.W.2d 791, 800 (Iowa 1984); Stoller Fisheries, Inc. v. Am. Title Ins. Co., 258 N.W.2d 336, 341 (Iowa 1977). An absolute privilege bars tortious interference claims based on statements made during judicial proceedings. See McFarland v. McFarland, Nos. C08-4047, C09-4047, 2011 WL 4402356, at *4, 15, 16 (N.D. Iowa Sept. 20, 2011) (granting summary judgment dismissal of claims based on alleged defamatory statements made during prior judicial proceeding, and holding absolute privilege barred both the defamation claims and related claims based on the statements, including tortious interference claim). Iowa also recognizes justification as an affirmative defense to a claim for interference with prospective economic advantage. Locksley v. Anesthesiologists of Cedar Rapids, P.C., 333 N.W.2d 451 (Iowa 1983); Bump v. Stewart, Wimer & Bump, P.C., 336 N.W.2d 731, 737 (Iowa 1983).

An employee's claim for intentional interference with business relations can only be sustained against a supervisor or agent of the employer if the supervisor or agent exceeded his or her qualified privilege. See, e.g., Sykes v. Hengel, 394 F. Supp. 2d 1062, 1079 (S.D. Iowa 2005) (quoting Jones v. Lake Park Care Ctr., Inc., 569 N.W.2d 369, 376–77 (Iowa 1997)) (stating in context of interference with an existing contract that "'[o]nly a third-party, separate from the contracting parties, can be liable for such a tort. A director or officer acts as an agent of the corporation when acting in good faith to protect the interests of the corporation.'"); Dillon v. Ruperto, No. 09-0600, 2010 WL 2383517, at *5–6 (Iowa Ct. App. June 16, 2010) (discussing when scope of qualified privilege is exceeded by agent of corporation). **Compare Rusch v. Midwest Indus. Inc, No. 10-CV-4110-DEO, 2012 WL 1564704, at *4–7, n. 11 (N.D. Iowa May 1, 2012) (noting that the "qualified immunity [of a supervisor/employee] appears to be built into the basic elements necessary to sustain an intentional interference with prospective business relations claim" because both require a showing that the interference was improper, and further stating "this Court can think of no reason" why the defense of qualified immunity would be limited to interference with contract claims and not be applicable to interference with prospective business relations claims as well).**

Some employee claims for intentional interference with prospective economic advantage, like intentional infliction of emotional distress, may be preempted by statute. But see Chapman v. LabOne, 390 F.3d 620, 627–29 (8th Cir. 2004) (holding that common law claims, including tortious interference with business relationships, asserted by railroad employee terminated for a failed drug test *against the testing laboratory* were not preempted by federal laws regulating the drug testing of railroad employees and reversing Chapman v. LabOne, 252 F. Supp. 2d 814, 819 (S.D. Iowa 2003) which held the claims were preempted).

Iowa has also recognized the tort of intentional interference with *existing* contractual relationships which has a lower burden than intentional interference with a *prospective* business advantage. See Brown v. Kerkhoff, 504 F. Supp. 2d 464, 551–53 (S.D. Iowa 2007); GE Capital Corp. v. Commercial Servs. Group, Inc., 485 F. Supp. 2d 1015, 1027 (N.D. Iowa 2007) (holding that tortious interference with an *existing* contract requires a showing that the interference was "improper," while tortious interference with a *prospective* contract requires higher, specific showing that the predominate or sole purpose of the interference was to "financially injure or destroy the claimant"); see also Green v. Racing Ass'n of Cent. Iowa, 713 N.W.2d

234, 243 (Iowa 2006) (stating the five necessary elements for an intentional inference with contract claim under Iowa law); Books Are Fun, Ltd. v. Rosebrough, No. 4:05-CV-00644-JEG, 2006 U.S. Dist. LEXIS 64196, at *20–48 (S.D. Iowa Sept. 6, 2006) (analyzing both intentional interference for existing contracts and prospective business advantage); Brown v. Kerkoff, No. 4:06-CV-00342-JEG, 2007 U.S. Dist. LEXIS 62458, at *234–40 (S.D. Iowa Aug. 23, 2007) (same); Midwest Motorsports P'ship v. Hardcore Racing Engines, Inc., No. 6-742, 2007 Iowa Ct. App. LEXIS 537, at *6–11 (Iowa Ct. App. Apr. 25, 2007) (same); Kent v. Iowa, 651 F. Supp. 2d 910, 958–63 (S.D. Iowa 2009) (discussing elements of tortious interference with a contract) (citations omitted); Mechdyne Corp. v. Garwood, 707 F. Supp. 2d 864 (S.D. Iowa 2009) (discussing elements of intentional interference with an existing contract).

D. Prima Facie Tort

Iowa has not recognized prima facie tort as a cause of action. See French v. Foods, Inc., 495 N.W.2d 768, 772 (Iowa 1993) (declining to establish prima facie tort cause of action). Iowa has recognized that negligence per se will exist only upon violation of a statute which lays down "a rule of conduct specifically designed for the safety and protection of a certain class of persons" such as an OSHA regulation or the "rules of the road" for drivers. See, e.g., Wiersgalla v. Garrett, 486 N.W.2d 290, 292 (Iowa 1992). While Iowa statutorily has recognized a cause of action for defamation, see Iowa Code Chap. 659, that statute is one of general applicability and not designed for protection of a particular class of persons. Accordingly, strong argument can be made that a cause of action for negligence per se does not arise from the publication of defamatory matter in violation of Iowa Code Chap. 659. See generally Nash v. Schultz, 417 N.W.2d 241, 242–43 (Iowa Ct. App. 1987). Further, application of the negligence per se doctrine likely would be violative of state and federal constitutional safeguards that limit defamation claims of public officials and public figures and that impose the actual malice standard for most punitive damage claims in defamation cases.

V. OTHER ISSUES

A. Statute of Limitations

The statute of limitations for defamation actions is two years from the date of publication. Iowa Code § 614.1(2); see generally Crouse v. Iowa Orthopedic Ctr., No. 03-1626, 2005 WL 1224577, at *4–6 (Iowa Ct. App. May 25, 2005) (citation omitted) (affirming dismissal of defamation claim on statute of limitations grounds and stating that claim accrued "when the defendants performed their last allegedly . . . defamatory act" to plaintiff's damage). Iowa courts have not discussed adoption of the "single publication" rule; instead every publication or repetition of defamatory matter constitutes a separate and independent claim from the original publication. Kiner v. Reliance Ins. Co., 463 N.W.2d 9 (Iowa 1990). In Stites v. Ogden Newspapers, Inc., No. 00-1975, 2002 WL 663621, at *2 (Iowa Ct. App. Apr. 24, 2002), the Iowa Court of Appeals rejected application of the discovery rule in defamation actions and held that the statutory limitations period begins to run on the date of publication and not on the date the injured party learns of it. See also Davenport v. City of Corning, No. 06-1156, 2007 WL 3085797, at *6 (Iowa Ct. App. Oct. 24, 2007); see generally Scott v. Gen. Cas. Ins. Co., 662 N.W.2d 373, No. 01-0338, 2003 WL 288959, at *2–3 (Iowa Ct. App. Feb. 12, 2003) (applying the two-year statute of limitations in Iowa Code § 614.1 (2) to plaintiff's defamation, bad faith, and breach of fiduciary duty claims, and holding that there was no fraudulent concealment and that the continuous treatment doctrine did not apply).

B. Jurisdiction

The Eighth Circuit upheld a decision from the Southern District of Iowa that dismissed a libel claim for lack of personal jurisdiction over the defendant. Hicklin Eng'g, Inc. v. Aidco, Inc., 959 F.2d 738 (8th Cir. 1992). The defendant was a Michigan corporation that had allegedly sent correspondence containing defamatory statements to several of plaintiff's customers. The Court noted that none of the correspondence was published in or targeted at Iowa and the Court determined it was not sufficient to bestow personal jurisdiction. Hicklin Eng'g, 959 F.2d at 739. See also Ideal Instruments, Inc. v. Rivard Instruments, Inc., 434 F. Supp. 2d 598, 633–37 (N.D. Iowa 2006) (addressing *forum non conveniens* challenge); **High Plains Const., Inc. v. Gay, 831 F. Supp. 2d 1089, 1096 (S.D. Iowa 2011) (holding contacts sufficient to support specific personal jurisdiction over intentional interference with contractual relations claim premised on slanderous statements); Fraserside IP L.L.C. v. Netvertising Ltd., No. C11-3034, 2012 WL 4762125 (N.D. Iowa Oct. 5, 2012) (discussing personal jurisdiction standards within context of defendant's internet contacts with Iowa in copyright infringement case). See generally Minor v. State, 819 N.W.2d 383 (Iowa 2012) (holding court lacked subject matter jurisdiction over intentional infliction of emotional distress claim due to plaintiff's failure to satisfy administrative exhaustion requirements under the Iowa Tort Claims Act).**

C. Worker's Compensation Exclusivity

Intentional torts are generally outside the exclusivity of the act, although "'[u]nless the employer has commanded or expressly authorized the [intentional tort], it cannot be said to be intentional from his standpoint any more than from the standpoint of any third person,'" See Nelson v. Winnebago Indus., Inc., 619 N.W.2d 385, 387-88 (Iowa 2000) (citation omitted). In addition, injuries that fall outside the workers' compensation statute are also outside the exclusivity of the act. See id. (stating that Wilson v. IBP, Inc., 558 N.W.2d 132 (Iowa 1996) held that "a former employee's suit for slander was not preempted by workers' compensation because the Workers' Compensation Act provided no adequate remedy for that tort"). Employment libel claims regularly proceed to trial and appeal without dismissal based on worker's compensation act preemption. Compare Graves v. City of Durant, No. C09-0061, 2010 WL 785850, at *17 (N.D. Iowa Mar. 5, 2010) (Iowa Civil Right Act does not preempt workplace libel lawsuit because defamation claim is not "wholly intertwined" with discrimination claims). See IV.A, supra; IV.B, supra.

D. Pleading Requirements

A plaintiff's petition must set forth specifically the statements that are allegedly defamatory and the defamatory sense in which they were used. Nelson v. Melvin, 236 Iowa 604, 19 N.W.2d 685, 689 (Iowa 1945); Asay v. Hallmark Cards, Inc., 594 F.2d 692, 698–99 (8th Cir. 1979); see also Iowa Code § 659.1. Defamation is "not a favored cause of action and must always be specifically alleged." Cimijotti v. Paulsen, 219 F. Supp. 621, 622 (N.D. Iowa 1963). A plaintiff must prove his/her case "in the statements alleged as no other statements may be used to prove defamation." Id. Nevertheless, in a recent Iowa Supreme Court case, Lloyd v. Drake Univ., 686 N.W.2d 225, 232–33 (Iowa 2004), the Court appeared to move toward accepting mere notice pleading in a defamation case. In Lloyd, the Court noted that the lower court had dismissed plaintiff's defamation claim "rel[ying], in part, upon the common-law pleading rule as adopted in Nelson v. Melvin, which required that a plaintiff's petition in a defamation action set forth the defamatory words relied upon with particularity," and "*[n]otwithstanding the fact that we have long since adopted notice pleading in this state*, on appeal [plaintiff] does not challenge the continuing validity of the common-law rule." Id. (emphasis added). The Court "decline[d] the defendant's invitation to . . . affirm dismissal of th[e] case upon the old common-law pleading rule stated in Nelson." Id. at 232. In Stevens v. Iowa Newspapers, Inc., 728 N.W.2d 823, 827 n. 1, 35 Media L. Rep. 1385 (Iowa 2007), the Iowa Supreme Court rejected the argument that the plaintiff could not maintain a suit on a defamation by implication theory because he did not expressly plead it, stating that "it is clear under notice pleading that a specific theory of a claim need not be alleged." "[T]o state a claim for defamation in federal court, a plaintiff need only comply with Federal Rule of Civil Procedure 8(a)(2), which requires only a short and plain statement of the claim showing that the plaintiff is entitled to relief." Cedar Rapids Lodge & Suites, LLC. v. JFS Dev., Inc., No. 09-CV-175, 2010 WL 2836949 (N.D. Iowa July 19, 2010).

It has been stated in the summary judgment context that plaintiffs must "identify the defamatory statements with . . . specificity. . ." and "[w]here plaintiff does not allege essential content and context regarding the claimed defamation, [the defendant] cannot adequately defend on the basis of qualified privilege." Morris v. Am. Freightways, Inc., No. 4:01-CV-40475, 2003 WL 472510, at *4 (S.D. Iowa Feb. 20, 2003) (citation omitted); see also Brass v. City of Manly, No. C02-3004-PAZ, 2003 WL 1907158, at *33 (N.D. Iowa Apr. 17, 2003) (dismissing defamation claim on summary judgment because there was no evidence of any potential defamatory statement in the record and stating that because plaintiff had failed to "identify with any particularity" the allegedly defamatory communications, it was impossible to determine whether qualified privilege applies); see generally Donnell v. Cedar Rapids, 437 F. Supp. 2d 904 (N.D. Iowa 2006) (denying summary judgment motion in employment defamation case "where the timing of the termination is suspicious"); Malone v. Des Moines Area Cmty. Coll., No. 4:04-CV-40103, 2005 WL 290008, at *12 (S.D. Iowa Jan. 26, 2005) (granting summary judgment of defamation claim and noting that Plaintiff "fails to even specify the statements allegedly defaming his character").

A libel defendant's answer must assert the affirmative defenses of truth or privilege. King v. Sioux City Radiological Group, P.C., 985 F. Supp. 869, 878–80 (N.D. Iowa 1997) (citing Spencer v. Spencer, 479 N.W.2d 293, 296 (Iowa 1991); Cowman v. LaVine, 234 N.W.2d 114 (Iowa 1975); Taggart v. Drake Univ., 549 N.W.2d 796, 803 (Iowa 1996); Vinson v. Linn-Mar Cmty. Sch. Dist., 360 N.W.2d 108, 116 (Iowa 1984)).

SURVEY OF IOWA EMPLOYMENT PRIVACY LAW

Michael A. Giudicessi and Angela J. Morales
Faegre Baker Daniels LLP
Suite 3100, 801 Grand Avenue
Des Moines, Iowa 50309
Telephone: (515) 248-9000 / (800) 228-0836)
Facsimile: (515) 248-9010

William J. Hunnicutt
Wells Fargo & Company
7000 Vista Drive/MAC N8235-048
Des Moines, Iowa 50266
Telephone: (515) 327-4360
Facsimile: (515) 327-4253

(With Developments Reported Through **November 1, 2012**)

GENERAL COMMENTS

Iowa has a unified trial court system whereby original jurisdiction for claims in excess of $5,000 rests in the district court. Claims for damages of $5,000 or less must be brought in the small claims court. Iowa Code § 631.1 (2011). Appeals from final decisions of the district court may be made as a matter of right to the Iowa Supreme Court. The Iowa Supreme Court may refer the case to the Iowa Court of Appeals for appellate review or retain jurisdiction over the appeal. If a case is referred to the Iowa Court of Appeals, the Supreme Court may choose to review it on an application for further review. The general standard of appellate review in civil cases is on error for cases at law and de novo for cases in equity.

SIGNIFICANT DEVELOPMENTS SINCE THE 2012 *SURVEY*

The Iowa Supreme Court recently considered an intrusion on seclusion claim in the context of electronic surveillance in the workplace. The Court held that "an electronic invasion occurs under the intrusion on solitude or seclusion component of the tort of invasion of privacy when the plaintiff establishes by a preponderance of the evidence that the electronic device or equipment used by a defendant *could have* invaded privacy in some way." Koeppel v. Speirs, 808 N.W.2d 177, 184-86 (Iowa 2011) (emphasis added) (also generally discussing the tort of intrusion on seclusion). The Court further noted that "harm from intrusion arises when a plaintiff reasonably believes an intrusion has occurred." Id. at 185.

I. GENERAL LAW OF PRIVACY

A. Legal Basis of Privacy Claims

The Iowa Constitution provides that "[t]he right of the people to be secure in their persons, houses, papers and effects, against unreasonable seizures and searches shall not be violated . . . ." Iowa Const. art. 1, § 8. Iowa does not have a statutorily created invasion of privacy tort. The 2004 legislature enacted, however, a criminal provision, which provides that "[a] person who knowingly views, photographs, or films another person, for the purpose of arousing or gratifying the sexual desire of any person, commits invasion of privacy" where the non-consenting subject is in a full or partial state of nudity. See Iowa Code § 709.21. The right to privacy at common law has been recognized and described by the Iowa Supreme Court as "the right of an individual to be let alone, to live a life of seclusion, to be free from unwanted publicity." Bremmer v. Journal-Tribune Publ'g Co., 247 Iowa 817, 821, 76 N.W.2d 762, 764 (1956); see also Davenport v. City of Corning, 742 N.W.2d 605 (Iowa Ct. App. 2007). One court has rejected a plaintiff's claim that her right to privacy is a property interest entitled to due process protection. Hanson v. Hancock County Mem'l Hosp., 938 F. Supp. 1419, 1432 (N.D. Iowa 1996). Compare Mercer v. City of Cedar Rapids, 308 F.3d 840, 845–46 (8th Cir. 2002) (holding comments made to press after a police officer's discharge "did not infringe a constitutionally recognized liberty interest" as they were limited to plaintiff's "ability to perform her job and the impact of her actions on the workplace").

B. Causes of Action

The Iowa Supreme Court has recognized the four privacy-related actions by direct citation to the Restatement (Second) of Torts § 652A. See Stessman v. Am. Black Hawk Broad. Co., 416 N.W.2d 685, 686–87, 14 Media L. Rep. 2073, 2074 (Iowa 1987); Anderson v. Low Rent Hous. Comm'n, 304 N.W.2d 239, 248, 7 Media L. Rep. 1726, 1730 (Iowa), cert. denied, 454 U.S. 1086 (1981); Howard v. Des Moines Register and Tribune Co., 283 N.W.2d 289, 291, 5 Media L. Rep. 1667, 1667–68 (Iowa 1979), cert. denied, 445 U.S. 904 (1980); Winegard v. Larsen, 260 N.W.2d 816, 818 (Iowa 1977); Yoder v. Smith, 253 Iowa 505, 507, 112 N.W.2d 862, 863–64 (1962); see also In re Marriage of Tigges, 758 N.W.2d 824, 829 (Iowa 2008); Coplin v. Fairfield Pub. Access Television Comm., 111 F.3d 1395, 1403, 25 Media L. Rep. 1737, 1742 (8th Cir. 1997). See also Hill v. MCI Worldcom Commc'ns, Inc., 141 F. Supp. 2d 1205, 1213–15 (S.D. Iowa 2001) (addressing whether state law privacy claims were limited by defendant telephone company's limitation of liability section in its federally filed tariff pursuant to Communications Act, and holding plaintiff's damages requests were not barred because defendant's tariff did not address the charges related to maintaining the confidentiality of customer account information). All injuries to person or reputation in Iowa are subject to a two-year statute of limitations. Iowa Code § 614.1(2). The statute is generally subject to tolling for claims by minors to provide one year from reaching the age of majority. Id. § 614.8(2); see also id. § 614.8(1) (extending statute of limitations for "persons with mental illness").

1. ***Misappropriation/Right of Publicity.*** Iowa has recognized the tort of misappropriation and has cited with approval its elements as set forth in the Restatement (Second) of Torts § 652C. Stessman v. Am. Black Hawk Broad. Co., 416 N.W.2d 685, 686 (Iowa 1987); Winegard v. Larsen, 260 N.W.2d 816, 822 (Iowa 1977). There are no reported Iowa decisions, however, considering the misappropriation tort or applying its elements.

2. ***False Light.*** Iowa recognizes the tort of false light. Chapman v. LabOne, 460 F. Supp. 2d 989, 1006 (S.D. Iowa 2006); Kiesau v. Bantz, 686 N.W.2d 164 (Iowa 2004); Jones v. Palmer Commc'ns, Inc., 440 N.W.2d 884, 894, 16 Media L. Rep. 2137, 2143 (Iowa 1989), overruled on other grounds by Schlegel v. Ottumwa Courier, 515 N.W.2d 217, 224 (Iowa 1998); Anderson v. Low Rent Hous. Comm'n, 304 N.W.2d 239, 248, 7 Media L. Rep. 1726, 1730 (Iowa 1981); Winegard v. Larsen, 260 N.W.2d 816, 823 (Iowa 1977). Iowa has adopted the elements as set forth in the Restatement (Second) of Torts § 652E. Anderson, 304 N.W.2d at 248, 7 Media L. Rep. at 1730; Winegard, 260 N.W.2d at 823; McFarland v. McFarland, 684 F. Supp. 2d 1073, 1092 (N.D. Iowa 2010).

To succeed on a false light claim, a plaintiff must prove that: (1) there was an untruthful publication which places the person before the public in a manner that would be highly offensive to a reasonable person; and (2) the actor had knowledge of or acted in reckless disregard as to the falsity of the publicized matter and the false light in which the other would be placed. Kiesau, 686 N.W.2d at 179; Anderson, 304 N.W.2d at 248, 7 Media L. Rep. at 1730; Winegard, 260 N.W.2d at 823; McFarland, 684 F. Supp. 2d at 1092; see also **Home Show Tours, Inc. v. Quad City Virtual, Inc., 827 F.Supp.2d 924, 944–45 (S.D. Iowa 2011) (holding that plaintiff failed to show genuine issue of material fact as to either falsity or damages)**; Reeder v. Carroll, 759 F. Supp. 2d 1064, 1082–84 (N.D. Iowa 2010) (concurrently analyzing defamation and false light claims, and concluding regardless of whether the Iowa Supreme Court would adopt the group defamation doctrine, claims premised on statements about "this group" failed because "nothing suggests that 'the circumstances of the publication reasonably give rise to the conclusion that there is a particular reference'" to plaintiff). Publicity in an invasion of privacy claim "'means that the matter is made public, by communicating it to the public at large, or to so many persons that the matter must be regarded as substantially certain to become one of public knowledge. . .'" Chapman, 460 F. Supp. 2d at 1006–07 (quoting Restatement (Second) of Torts, § 652D) (holding laboratory's disclosure of drug test results to employer did not meet "publicity" requirement, even if coworkers deduced from employee's termination that he had failed the test); see McFarland 684 F. Supp. 2d at 1092 (noting that Iowa has not addressed what is "sufficient to meet the publicity" standard but finding an email sent to over 300 households was "sufficiently broad, at the motion to dismiss stage . . . to satisfy the publicity element."). The publication, even if deliberately false, must be material and substantial to be actionable under the false light theory. Winegard, 260 N.W.2d at 823. "The essential element of untruthfulness differentiates 'false light' from the other forms of invasion of privacy and many times affords an alternate remedy for defamation . . . ." Anderson, 304 N.W.2d at 248, 7 Media L. Rep. at 1730; Reeder, 759 F. Supp. 2d at 1079; **see also Home Show Tours, Inc., 827 F.Supp.2d at 945 (citing Winegard, 260 N.W.2d at 823) ("The tort of false light 'overlaps the law of defamation,' . . . and therefore requires proof of untruthfulness, however the plaintiff need not prove that he was defamed . . . . 'Even when deliberately false statements are made, they are not actionable under the false light theory unless they are material and substantial.'")**. A false light claim, however, is subject to the same constitutional restraints as defamation cases, and a plaintiff cannot evade defamation standards by pleading false light as an alternative theory. Jones, 440 N.W.2d at 894, 16 Media L. Rep. at 2143; see also Bradbery v. Dubuque County, No. 99-1881, 2001 WL 23144, at *4 (Iowa Ct. App. Jan. 10, 2001) (citing Berry v. Nat'l Broad. Co., 480 F.2d 428, 431 (8th Cir. 1973)) (noting that false light and defamation are alternate claims and a plaintiff cannot recover under both), cert. dismissed, 418 U.S. 911 (1974)). Compare Kish v. Iowa Cent. Cmty. Coll., 142 F. Supp. 2d 1084, 1100 (N.D. Iowa 2001) (citing Anderson, 304 N.W.2d at 248) (noting that a plaintiff is not required to prove defamation in order to recover for false light claim); Kiesau v. Bantz, 686 N.W.2d 164, 179 (Iowa 2004) (affirming jury verdict in favor of plaintiff on a claim for defamation and false light invasion of privacy and noting that all of the damages awarded by the jury regarding the invasion of privacy claim were the same damages she was allowed to recover under her defamation claim); McFarland v. McFarland, Nos. C08-4047, C-09-4047, 2011 WL 4402356, at *4, 15, 16 (N.D. Iowa Sep. 20, 2011) (granting summary judgment dismissal of claims based on alleged defamatory statements made during prior judicial proceeding, and holding absolute privilege barred both the defamation claims and related claims based on the statements, including invasion of privacy-false light claim). In a false light action in the employment context, the court affirmed a jury verdict in favor of the plaintiff, a former sheriff's deputy, and against a former co-worker who circulated via email a photograph of the plaintiff that was altered to make it appear as if the plaintiff had exposed her breasts in the photograph. Kiesau, 686 N.W.2d at 179. In another false light action brought in the employment context, the court affirmed a jury verdict for the plaintiff where the plaintiff's former employer made false statements to the media concerning the reasons for the plaintiff's termination. Anderson, 304 N.W.2d at 249–52, 7 Media L. Rep. at 1730–32.

The right of privacy may be lost by express or implied waiver by the complaining party. Id. at 249, 7 Media L. Rep. at 1731. Such waiver, however, must be shown with evidence of conduct clearly indicating that the plaintiff voluntarily and intentionally acquiesced in the falsity. Id., 7 Media L. Rep. at 1731. Consent is an affirmative defense to an invasion of privacy claim "so long as the publication does not exceed the scope of consent." Id. at 251, 7 Media L. Rep. at 1732.

In Reeder, the Northern District of Iowa Court concurrently analyzed the applicability of the qualified privilege to libel and false light claims based on concerns reported to a licensing board about plaintiff-physician's patient care. The Court concluded the qualified privilege and statutory immunity provided for in the physician licensing and mandatory reporting statute applied to the statements, and found the defendant had not acted with actual malice. 759 F. Supp. 2d at 1064, 1084–90 (N.D. Iowa 2010).

In Kish, 142 F. Supp. 2d at 1100, the Court predicted, in light of the adoption by the Iowa Supreme Court of the Restatement's privacy principles, the proper measure of damages for a false light claim under Iowa law is embodied in Restatement (Second) of Torts § 652H (including damages from harm to party's interest in privacy, mental distress normally resulting from an invasion, and special damage). **See also Home Show Tours, Inc., 827 F.Supp.2d at 945**. General damages and damages for loss of reputation are not compensable under an invasion of privacy claim. Kiesau, 686 N.W.2d at 179. "Iowa Courts do not permit a plaintiff to recover on both a defamation theory and on a false light invasion of privacy theory." Mills v. Iowa Bd. Of Regents, 770 F. Supp. 2d 986, 998–99 (S.D. Iowa 2011) (internal citations omitted).

3. ***Publication of Private Facts.*** Iowa has recognized the tort of publication of private facts and has adopted its elements as set forth in the Restatement (Second) of Torts § 652D. Howard v. Des Moines Register & Tribune Co., 283 N.W.2d 289, 5 Media L. Rep. 1667 (Iowa 1979); Winegard v. Larsen, 260 N.W.2d 816, 823 (Iowa 1977); Yoder v. Smith, 253 Iowa 505, 112 N.W.2d 862 (1962); see also Coplin v. Fairfield Pub. Access TV Comm., 111 F.3d 1395, 1403–06 (8th Cir. 1997) (stating that Iowa recognizes a tort for invasion of privacy and analyzing the interrelationship between that tort and the First Amendment). The disclosure must be public and must involve facts concerning the private life of the plaintiff. Howard, 283 N.W.2d at 298, 5 Media L. Rep. at 1673; Winegard, 260 N.W.2d at 823; see also Hill v. MCI Worldcom Commc'ns, Inc., 141 F. Supp. 2d 1205, 1210–13 (S.D. Iowa 2001) (addressing whether defendant telephone company's disclosure to plaintiff's ex-husband of numbers she had called can satisfy the publication element, examining Iowa case law, holding that an exception to the widespread publicity requirement if there is a confidential relationship is consistent with Iowa law and in particular with language in Yoder v. Smith, 112 N.W.2d 862, 864 (Iowa 1962), and declining to follow Hanson v. Hancock County Mem'l Hosp., 938 F. Supp. 1419, 1437–38 (N.D. Iowa 1996) to the extent it suggests the contrary). The disclosure must not be a matter of legitimate public concern. Howard, 283 N.W.2d at 298, 5 Media L. Rep. at 1673. There is no liability where the defendant gives further publicity to information that is already public, such as that disclosed in public records. Howard, 283 N.W.2d at 298, 5 Media L. Rep. at 1673; Winegard, 260 N.W.2d at 823. In a private facts case brought in the employment context, the court held that a creditor's letter to an employer requesting that it garnish an employee's wages to collect a debt was not an invasion of privacy. Yoder, 253 Iowa at 510, 112 N.W.2d at 865 ("[A] creditor has a right to take reasonable action to pursue his debtor and persuade payment, although the steps taken may result in some invasion of the debtor's privacy."). In Hill, 141 F. Supp. 2d at 1213, the Court denied defendant telephone company's motion to dismiss because the disclosure to Plaintiff's ex-husband, who had previously stalked Plaintiff, of numbers Plaintiff had called would be highly offensive and even potentially dangerous to a reasonable person and the information was not of a legitimate concern to her ex-husband. In Evans v. Benson, 731 N.W.2d 395, 397 (Iowa 2007), the Supreme Court of Iowa held that a former employee could not prevail on claims of invasion of privacy and negligent disclosure of confidential medical records against his health care provider where the disclosure to his employer was not the proximate cause of his termination. Id. (finding that employee had already been recommended for termination before the nurse's telephone call to warn manager of employee's intention to harm him).

4. ***Intrusion.*** Iowa has recognized the tort of intrusion on seclusion and has adopted its elements as set forth in the Restatement (Second) of Torts § 652B. Stessman v. Am. Black Hawk Broad. Co., 416 N.W.2d 685, 687, 14 Media L. Rep. 2073, 2074 (Iowa 1987); Lamberto v. Brown, 326 N.W.2d 305, 309, 8 Media L. Rep. 2525, 2528–29 (Iowa 1982); Winegard v. Larsen, 260 N.W.2d 816, 823 (Iowa 1978); In re Marriage of Tigges, 758 N.W.2d 824, 829 (Iowa 2008); **Koeppel v. Speirs, 808 N.W.2d 177, 180-81 (Iowa 2011);** see also Tinius v. Carroll County Sheriff Dep't, 321 F. Supp. 2d 1064, 1082 (N.D. Iowa 2004); Luken v. Edwards, No. C10-4097-MWB, 2011 WL 1655902, at *5 (N.D. Iowa May 3, 2011); Powell v. Yellow Book USA, Inc., 445 F.3d 1074, 1080 (8th Cir. 2006). One who intentionally intrudes upon the solitude or seclusion of another is liable if the intrusion would be highly offensive to a reasonable person. Hill v. McKinley, 311 F.3d 899, 905–06 (8th Cir. 2002); Tinius, 321 F. Supp. 2d at 1082; Stessman, 416 N.W.2d at 687, 14 Media L. Rep. at 2074; Lamberto, 326 N.W.2d at 309, 8 Media L. Rep. at 2528–29; Winegard, 260 N.W.2d at 822; In re Marriage of Tigges, 758 N.W.2d at 829; see also Hill v. MCI Worldcom Commc'ns, Inc., 141 F. Supp. 2d 1205, 1209–10 (S.D. Iowa 2001) (noting that Iowa has not addressed the issue but concluding after an examination of relevant Iowa case law that under Iowa law defendant telephone company's disclosure to plaintiff's ex-husband of numbers she had called, "properly obtained information," does not support a claim for intrusion); Luken, 2011 WL 1655902, at *5–6 (finding in the context of a ruling on a motion to dismiss that defendant's repeated interceptions of private and confidential telephone conversations between plaintiff and his attorney about plaintiff and defendant's divorce, if true, would satisfy both the intrusion and "highly offensive

to a reasonable person" elements of the claim). Publication is not an element of the intrusion tort. Tinius, 321 F. Supp. 2d at 1082 n.3 (citing Restatement (Second) of Torts § 652B); Lamberto, 326 N.W.2d at 309, 8 Media L. Rep. at 2529. The intrusion must be intentional and must intrude upon the seclusion that the plaintiff has maintained about his or her person or affairs. Stessman, 416 N.W.2d at 687, 14 Media L. Rep. at 2074; Winegard, 260 N.W.2d at 822; see also O'Bryan v. KTIV Television, 868 F. Supp. 1146, 1158 (N.D. Iowa 1994), aff'd in relevant part, 64 F.3d 1188 (8th Cir. 1995); Davenport v. City of Corning, No. 06-1156, 2007 WL 3085797, at *8–9 (Iowa Ct. App. Oct. 24, 2007) (holding that summary judgment was not proper on plaintiff's claim that defendant had continuously driven by and looked at him in his house, but affirming dismissal of claim based on drive-bys at plaintiff's public place of business even if the drive-bys were persistent and harassing, because the frequency and persistence of the conduct goes to whether the conduct would be highly offensive to an ordinary reasonable person and does not alter the requirement that the plaintiff have been "in a private place when the conduct occurred"); In re Marriage of Tigges, 758 N.W.2d at 829–30 (holding that a husband's installation of motion-sensitive cameras in a bedroom he shared with his wife constituted intrusion on seclusion because wife had reasonable expectation of privacy in the marital bedroom); Luken, 2011 WL 1655902, at *5 (denying defendant's motion to dismiss plaintiff's claim of intrusion upon seclusion in part because plaintiff's allegation in her amended complaint that defendant repeatedly listened to private and confidential telephone calls between plaintiff and his attorney about plaintiff and defendant's divorce established the intrusion element of the claim). At least one court has stated that an intrusion cannot occur unless the "actor believes, or is substantially certain that he lacks the necessary legal or personal permission to commit the intrusive act." Tinius, 321 F. Supp. 2d at 1084 (internal marks omitted).

The Iowa Supreme Court, in Koeppel v. Speirs, 808 N.W.2d 177, 184-86 (Iowa 2011), held that a plaintiff does not have to show an electronic device actually recorded images or sounds in order to recover under a claim for intrusion. In that case, the plaintiff-employee had discovered a video camera concealed in the workplace bathroom and the parties disputed the proof necessary to demonstrate that an act of intrusion occurred and whether or not it was necessary to prove that the employer had actually recorded or viewed images on the video camera. The Court ultimately held that "an electronic invasion occurs under the intrusion on solitude or seclusion component of the tort of invasion of privacy when the plaintiff establishes by a preponderance of the evidence that the electronic device or equipment used by a defendant *could have* invaded privacy in some way." Although there must be "proof the equipment is functional," the "equipment does not need to be operational at the time it is discovered" but rather the fact finder need only conclude the equipment "could have been operational so as to invade the plaintiff's privacy." Id. at 184-86 (emphasis added) (also generally discussing the tort of intrusion on seclusion).

Although "[i]t is axiomatic that there can be no tort if there is no injury," "the act of intrusion is complete once it is discovered by the plaintiff because acquisition of information is not a requirement" and the "harm from intrusion arises when the plaintiff reasonably believes an intrusion has occurred." Koeppel, 808 N.W.2d at 185; see also In re Marriage of Tigges, 758 N.W.2d 824, 830 (Iowa 2008) (noting that lack of embarrassing content or of extensive publication do not defeat an intrusion claim because "The wrongdoing of the conduct springs not from the specific nature of the recorded activities, but instead from the fact [the] activities were recorded without [Plaintiff's] knowledge and consent at a time and place and under circumstances in which she had a reasonable expectation of privacy."). With regard to the degree of injury necessary to recover and damages recoverable under an intrusion claim, see also Hill, 311 F.3d at 906 (explaining that the Iowa Supreme Court has not explained the standards in any great detail but affirming plaintiff's verdict where law enforcement officers removed clothing of female plaintiff, strapped her to restraining board in county jail, and carried her down hallway uncovered); Hanson v. Hancock County Mem'l Hosp., 938 F. Supp. 1419, 1436 (N.D. Iowa 1996); Powell, 445 F.3d at 1080 (noting that acts by a co-worker such as "spiking drinks, stealing pens, taking papers from a desk, and reading someone's email" might give rise to an intrusion of privacy claim if the plaintiff had provided sufficient evidence to show the actions actually occurred); Pulla v. Amoco Oil Co., 882 F. Supp. 836, 869 (S.D. Iowa 1994), aff'd in relevant part, 72 F.3d 648 (8th Cir. 1995) (opining that the proper standard for damages in a privacy case is found in the Restatement (Second) of Torts § 652H, which provides that damages are recoverable for emotional distress or public humiliation if the damages were actually suffered, are of a kind that normally result from such an invasion of privacy, and are normal and reasonable in their extent; and holding damages need not be extreme or heightened for a plaintiff to recover); Pulla v. Amoco Oil Co., 72 F.3d 648, 661 (8th Cir. 1995) (holding award of punitive damages was excessive because Amoco's conduct, *inter alia*, was isolated and it was not a company practice or policy to invade employee privacy in such a manner); Hill, 311 F.3d at 906 (analyzing the award of special damages on an invasion of privacy claim, citing Restatement (Second) of Torts § 652H(c), and affirming jury verdict in plaintiff's favor for physical injury caused by the invasion of privacy).

In an intrusion case brought in the employment context, the court held there was no cause of action for an employer's search and examination of the contents of an employee's desk and office for employer-owned documents without the employee's knowledge because the employee did not have a reasonable expectation of privacy in his desk or office area. O'Bryan, 868 F. Supp. at 1158; see also Wilson v. City of Des Moines, 442 F.3d 637, 643 (8th Cir. 2006) (holding that an employee could not allege invasion of privacy as to her private sexual behavior when she exhibited similar behaviors in the workplace probative of welcomeness — a defense to her sexual harassment claim). In another intrusion case, the court considered a privacy claim in the context of a co-employee's improper review of the plaintiff's credit card records to verify that plaintiff had indeed been sick on the days he used sick leave. Pulla v. Amoco Oil Co., 882 F. Supp. 836 (S.D. Iowa 1994), aff'd in relevant part, 72 F.3d 648, 661 (8th Cir. 1995). In affirming the jury's verdict against Amoco, the court held that an employer's objectives or interests are not a complete defense to a privacy claim, but must be balanced against the degree of intrusion caused by the conduct. Id. at 866–67; see generally Tinius, 321 F. Supp. 2d at 1083 (explaining that the Iowa courts have not articulated the elements of the claim but granting summary judgment to sheriff deputies who assisted medical personnel in obtaining a urine sample from plaintiff who appeared under the influence of contraband on the ground that the deputies were acting within their community caretaking functions). The court found that it was reasonable for the jury to find Amoco's conduct was highly intrusive on the employee's privacy and was highly offensive to a reasonable person.

In Luken, 2011 WL 1655902, at *6–8, the United States District Court for the Northern District of Iowa granted defendant's motion to dismiss with respect to plaintiff's asserted claim of "invasion of attorney-client privilege." The Court refused to adopt plaintiff's legal theory, noting the absence of any authority that a claim of invasion of attorney-client privilege "comports with Iowa law, or that Iowa courts would adopt it if given the opportunity." Id. at *8.

C. Other Privacy-related Actions

1. ***Intentional Infliction of Emotional Distress.*** Iowa law has recognized claims for intentional infliction of emotional distress where there is: (1) outrageous conduct by the defendant; (2) an intent by the defendant to cause emotional distress or reckless disregard for the probability of such causation; (3) the suffering by plaintiff of severe or extreme emotional distress; and (4) actual and proximate causation of the emotional distress by the defendant's outrageous conduct. See Zuhdija Napreljac v. John Q. Hammons Hotels, Inc., 461 F. Supp. 2d 981, 1039 (S.D. Iowa 2006); Cole v. Wells Fargo Bank, 437 F.Supp.2d 974, 981–82 (S.D. Iowa 2006); Gauthier v. Waterloo Cmty. Sch. Dist., 2006 WL 463512, at *3 (N.D. Iowa Feb. 24, 2006); Wright v. Keokuk County Health Ctr., 399 F. Supp. 2d 938, 946 (S.D. Iowa 2005); Schuller v. Great-West Life & Annuity Ins. Co., 2005 WL 2257634, at *57 (N.D. Iowa Sept. 15, 2005); Eckles v. City of Corydon, 341 F.3d 762, 770 (8th Cir. 2003); Nelson v. J.C. Penney Co., Inc., 75 F.3d 343 (8th Cir.), cert. denied, 519 U.S. 813 (1996); Tinius v. Carroll County Sheriff Dep't, 321 F. Supp. 2d 1064, 1081 (N.D. Iowa 2004); Lawyer v. City of Council Bluffs, 240 F. Supp. 2d 941, 955 (S.D. Iowa 2002); Doe v. Hartz, 52 F. Supp. 2d 1027, 1068 (N.D. Iowa 1999); Hanson v. Hancock County Mem'l Hosp., 938 F. Supp. 1419 (N.D. Iowa 1996); Ette v. Linn-Mar Cmty. Sch. Dist., 656 N.W.2d 62, 70 (Iowa 2002); Amsden v. Grinnell Mut. Reinsurance Co., 203 N.W.2d 252, 255 (Iowa 1972); **Graves v. City of Waterloo, No. C10-2014, 2011 WL 5563546, at *5 (N.D. Iowa, Nov. 15, 2011) (discussing evidence admissible to show extreme emotional distress)**.

"It is for the court to determine in the first instance whether the defendants' conduct may reasonably be regarded as so extreme and outrageous as to permit recovery." Hartz, 52 F. Supp. 2d at 1068 (quoting Hanson, 938 F. Supp. at 1440). Iowa courts impose strict proof requirements regarding whether the alleged conduct could reasonably be regarded as outrageous, and to qualify as such, "the conduct must be extremely egregious; mere insult, bad manners, or hurt feelings are insufficient." Taggart v. Drake Univ., 549 N.W.2d 796, 802 (Iowa 1996). Iowa courts define "outrageous conduct" to mean conduct so extreme "as to go beyond all possible bounds of decency and to be regarded as atrocious and utterly intolerable in a civilized community." Vaughn v. Ag Processing, Inc., 459 N.W.2d 627 (Iowa 1990); Blasen v. Welu, No. LACV 053658, 2004 WL 3488071, at *2 (Iowa Dist. Ct. Nov. 1, 2004) (citing Mills v. Guthrie County Rural Elec. Coop. Ass'n, 454 N.W.2d 846, 850 (Iowa 1990)); see also **Koeppel v. Speirs, 808 N.W.2d 177, 185 n.2 (Iowa 2011) (noting that while "the act of intentionally placing an inoperable camera . . . into a private area may not support the intrusion element of the invasion of privacy, it could give rise to the tort of intentional infliction of emotional distress")**; Lawyer, 240 F. Supp. 2d at 955 (applying Iowa law and holding that officer's statutorily authorized use of force cannot amount to outrageous conduct outside the bounds of decency); Frederick v. Simpson Coll., 149 F. Supp. 2d 826, 842 (S.D. Iowa 2001) (applying Iowa law and holding professor's conduct towards student did not constitute outrageous conduct because plaintiff was an adult student and professor's behavior did not rise to the level of outrageous under Iowa law despite the fact it was offensive and disgusting); Carlson v. SCI Iowa Funeral Servs., 674 N.W.2d 682, at *3 (Iowa Ct. App. 2003) (unpublished table decision) (concluding that wrongful embalming of plaintiffs' parent could amount to extreme and outrageous conduct and reversing motion for summary judgment); Vinson v. Linn-Mar Cmty. Sch. Dist., 360 N.W.2d 108 (Iowa 1984); Harsha v. State Sav. Bank, 346 N.W.2d 791 (Iowa 1984); Cheek v. ABC Bev. Mfrs., Inc., No. 05-1962, 2006 WL 2560890, at *3–4 (Iowa Ct. App. Sept. 7, 2006) (unpublished) (finding that employer's filing of police report and participation in employee's criminal prosecution, even if done with malicious intent, could not establish outrageous conduct); Chapman v. LabOne, 460 F. Supp. 2d 989, 1006 (S.D. Iowa 2006) (finding as a matter of law that laboratory's communication of allegedly false failed drug test result to employer did not rise to the level of atrocious and utterly intolerable). An absolute privilege bars claims of intentional infliction of emotional distress based on statements made during a judicial proceeding. See McFarland v. McFarland, Nos. C08-4047, C09-4047, 2011 WL 4402356, at *4, 15, 16 (N.D. Iowa Sept. 20, 2011) (granting summary judgment dismissal of claims based on alleged defamatory statements made during prior judicial proceeding, and holding absolute privilege barred both the defamation claims and related claims based on the statements, including intentional infliction of emotional distress claim). "Outrageous conduct does not extend to mere insults, indignities, threats, annoyances, petty oppressions, hurt feelings, bad manners or other trivialities which a reasonable person could be expected to endure." Blasen, 2004 WL 3488071, at *2. General criticism of an employee generally is not considered outrageous conduct. Northrup v. Farmland Indus., Inc., 372 N.W.2d 193 (Iowa 1985). This is true even where a supervisor "engaged in a deliberate campaign to badger and harass" the plaintiff/employee. Vinson v. Linn-Mar Cmty. Sch. Dist., 360 N.W.2d 108, 119 (Iowa 1984); but see Wright v. Keokuk County Health Ctr., 399 F. Supp. 2d 938, 946 (S.D. Iowa 2005) (comparing Iowa cases and citing Blong v. Snyder, 361 N.W.2d 312, 315–17 (Iowa Ct. App. 1984) for proposition that "Iowa courts have found an employer's treatment of an employee rises to the level of outrageous when it entails an extensive campaign of harassment and baseless accusations"). In Zuhdija Napreljac v. John Q. Hammons Hotels, Inc., 461 F. Supp. 2d 981, 1042 (S.D. Iowa 2006), a federal court held that the alleged conduct was not sufficiently outrageous, even if the employer knew that the accident report (which formed the basis for termination of the employee) was both false and manufactured by other employees. In most cases, the Iowa Supreme Court has affirmed motions for summary judgment dismissing the intentional infliction counts based on statements made by an employer or supervisor as not constituting conduct qualifying as outrageous under the stringent proof standard. Id. One court described Iowa's standards for showing sufficiently outrageous conduct as "a high hurdle" and noted that "few cases can be located where an Iowa court actually held the conduct alleged was sufficiently outrageous." Wright, 399 F. Supp. 2d at 946 (finding that employer's communications with other employees about plaintiff's alleged misuse of the company credit card did not rise to the level of outrageous conduct); see also Benishek v. Cody, 441 N.W.2d 399, 402 (Iowa Ct. App. 1989) (holding employer's accusation that employee had embezzled was not outrageous).

A person's conduct is reckless if he/she knows with a high degree of probability that emotional distress will result and acts with deliberate disregard of that probability. See Cutler v. Klass, Whicher & Mishne, 473 N.W.2d 178 (Iowa 1991); M.H. By and Through Callahan v. State, 385 N.W.2d 533 (Iowa 1986); Meyer v. Nottger, 241 N.W.2d 911 (Iowa 1976). Extreme or severe emotional distress is required and can be established by direct and clear evidence of either "a notably distressful mental reaction" or physical symptoms of the distress. Barreca v. Nickolas, 683 N.W.2d 111, 124 (Iowa 2004) (stating that humiliation, embarrassment, stress, and loss of sleep did not amount to severe or extreme emotional distress); Carlson, 674 N.W.2d 682, at *3; Ellis Yacht Club, Inc. v. River Moon, L.L.C., No. 00-1341, 2002 WL 31640600, at *4 (Iowa Ct. App. Nov. 25, 2002) (stating that "[a] plaintiff must show more than that he felt bad or was disappointed," summarizing cases, and reversing plaintiff's verdict on the ground that there was no evidence showing that plaintiff underwent medical or psychiatric care or took medications or suffered physical manifestations of her emotional distress); Sheridan v. City of Des Moines, No. 4:00-CV-90024, 2001 WL 901267, at *8–9 (S.D. Iowa Aug. 8, 2001) (citing Steckelberg v. Randolph, 448 N.W.2d 458, 462 (Iowa 1989)); see also Blasen, 2004 WL 3488071, at *2 (holding loss of appetite and sleeplessness were insufficient). A fictitious entity, such as a limited liability company, cannot suffer emotional distress as a matter of law. Barreca, 683 N.W.2d at 124.

The Iowa Supreme Court has held that where a plaintiff alleges the employer's outrageous conduct giving rise to emotional distress is discrimination, the emotional distress claim is preempted by the Iowa Civil Rights Act. Greenland v. Fairtron Corp., 500 N.W.2d 36, 38 (Iowa 1993); see Cole v. Wells Fargo Bank, 437 F.Supp.2d 974, 785 (S.D. Iowa 2006) (finding plaintiff's emotional distress claims preempted by her disability and religious discrimination claims under the Iowa Civil Rights Act); Gauthier v. Waterloo Cmty. Sch. Dist., No. Civ. 4-02-CV-10075, 2006 WL 463512, at *4 (N.D. Iowa Feb. 24, 2006) (finding plaintiff's distress claim preempted by her disability discrimination claim under the Iowa Civil Rights Act); Napreljac v. Monarch Mfg. Co., No. Civ. 4-02-CV-10075, 2003 WL 21976024, at *8 (S.D. Iowa May 27, 2003) (holding that Iowa Civil Rights Act preempted intentional infliction of emotional distress claim because it was based on disability discrimination); Martinez v. Cole Sewell Corp., 233 F. Supp. 2d 1097, 1140 (N.D. Iowa 2002) (holding that Iowa Civil Rights Act preempted intentional infliction of emotional distress claim because claim was based on disability and national origin discrimination); Channon v. United Parcel Serv., Inc., 629 N.W.2d 835, 858 (Iowa 2001) (affirming the validity of Greenland and holding the Iowa Civil Rights Act preempted plaintiff's emotional distress claim because it was based on allegations of sex discrimination); see also Grimm v. U.S. West Commc'ns, Inc., 644 N.W.2d 8 (Iowa 2002) (holding plaintiff pled facts sufficient to survive a pre-answer motion to dismiss arguing that her intentional infliction of emotional distress claim was preempted by the federal Labor Management Relations Act and the Iowa Civil Rights Act and that it was premature for the court to consider defendants' argument that the claim was preempted by Iowa's workers' compensation statute); compare Fisher v. Elec. Data. Sys., 278 F. Supp. 2d 980, 995 (S.D. Iowa 2003) (holding that Iowa Civil Rights Act did not preempt intentional infliction of emotional distress claim to the extent that the claim arose out of an assault and battery separate from defendant's discriminatory conduct); Weems v. Federated Mut. Ins. Co., 220 F. Supp. 2d 979, 995 (N.D. Iowa 2002) (holding that Iowa Civil Rights Act did not preempt intentional infliction of emotional distress claim where factual basis of claim involved strip-search of employee by supervisor looking for concealed recording device).

In addition, § 301 of the Labor Management Relations Act, 29 U.S.C. § 185, preempts an intentional inflection of emotional distress claim to the extent that the claim depends upon the interpretation of a collective bargaining agreement. Madren v. Super Value, Inc., 183 F. Supp. 2d 1138, 1144 (S.D. Iowa 2002). In Delaney v. Int'l Union UAW Local No. 94, 675 N.W.2d 832, 846 (Iowa 2004), the court held that non-union workers' intentional infliction of emotional distress action arising out of union publications regarding "scabs" was preempted by federal labor law and the Supremacy Clause of the United States Constitution to the extent the claim alleged no tortious conduct other than speech. For discussion concerning the interaction of the intentional infliction of emotional distress tort with other laws, see **Minor v. State, 819 N.W.2d 383 (Iowa 2012) (holding that state employee was immune from liability under the Iowa Tort Claims Act for intentional infliction of emotional distress claim asserted against her on the basis of alleged misrepresentations)**; Chapman v. LabOne, 390 F.3d 620, 627–29 (8th Cir. 2004) (holding that common law claims, including intentional infliction of emotional distress and invasion of privacy, asserted by railroad employee terminated for a failed drug test *against the testing laboratory* were not preempted by federal laws regulating the drug testing of railroad employees and reversing Chapman v. LabOne, 252 F. Supp. 2d 814, 819 (S.D. Iowa 2003) which held the claims were preempted); Brown v. Quik Trip Corp., 641 N.W.2d 725, 727–29 (Iowa 2002) (holding that a purely mental injury is compensable under the workers' compensation statute if medical and legal causation are established, and stating that the general test for legal causation is "whether the claimant's stress was 'of greater magnitude than the day-to-day mental stresses experienced by other workers employed in the same or similar jobs, regardless of their employer'"); **Johnson v. Dollar General, No. C11-3038-MWB, 2012 WL 3072997, at *30 (N.D. Iowa July 30, 2012) (stating that plaintiff "concedes that he does not have an intentional infliction of emotional distress claim, because of the effect of the Iowa Workers Compensation Act on a claim for emotional distress arising out of a work situation")**.

Iowa does not recognize negligent infliction of emotional distress as an independent ground for liability absent physical harm except where (1) the defendant breached a duty of care "not to cause emotional distress to those who witness conduct that causes serious harm to a close relative," or (2) "the nature of the relationship between the plaintiff and the defendant is such that it supports the imposition of a duty of care on the defendant to avoid causing emotional harm to the plaintiff." Clark v. Estate of Rice, 653 N.W.2d 166, 170–71 (Iowa 2002); see also Carlson, 674 N.W. 2d 612, at *3–4. Iowa also recognizes the negligent infliction of emotional distress as an element of damages which may accompany another tort. See Doe v. Cherwitz, 518 N.W.2d 362 (Iowa 1994); Niblo v. Parr Mfg., Inc., 445 N.W.2d 351 (Iowa 1989).

2. ***Interference With Prospective Economic Advantage***. Iowa recognizes the tort of intentional interference with prospective economic advantage, also referred to as prospective business advantage. A claim for interference with prospective economic advantage requires a showing of intentional and improper interference and that the defendant's sole or predominant purpose was to financially harm or destroy the plaintiff. Conrad v. Iowa Central Community College, 756 N.W.2d 48 (Iowa. App. 2008); Brown v. Kerkhoff, 504 F. Supp. 2d 464, 551–53 (S.D. Iowa 2007); GE Capital Corp. v. Commercial Servs. Group, Inc., 485 F. Supp. 2d 1015, 1025–27 (N.D. Iowa 2007); EFCO Corp. v. Symons Corp., 219 F.3d 734 (8th Cir. 2000); Ideal Instruments, Inc. v. Rivard Instruments, Inc., 434 F. Supp. 2d 598, 626–27 (N.D. Iowa 2006); Jennings v. Mid-Am. Energy Co., 282 F. Supp. 2d 954 (S.D. Iowa 2003); Glenn v. Diabetes Treatment Centers, 116 F. Supp. 2d 1098, 1106 (S.D. Iowa 2000); Corcoran v. Land O' Lakes, Inc., 39 F. Supp. 2d 1139, 1150 (N.D. Iowa 1999); The New Uchtorff Cos,. Inc. v. Johnson Mfg., No. 99-1763, 2004 WL 899636, at *4 (Iowa Ct. App. Apr. 28, 2004); Lorenzen-Steffen Ins. Agency v. United Fire & Cas. Co., 666 N.W.2d 619 (Iowa Ct. App. 2003) (unpublished table decision); Graves v. Iowa Lakes Cmty. Coll., 639 N.W.2d 22, 25 (Iowa 2002); Educational Tech., Ltd. v. Meinhard, No. 99-0689, 2001 WL 488088, at *6–7 (Iowa Ct. App. May 9, 2001); Godfredsen v. Lutheran Bhd., 2000 WL 1675869, at *6 (Iowa Ct. App. Nov. 8, 2000); D & E Sanitation Co. v. City of Hawarden, No. 98-1841, 2000 WL 328022, at *3 (Iowa Ct. App. Mar. 29, 2000); Compiano v. Hawkeye Bank & Trust, 588 N.W.2d 462, 464 (Iowa 1999); Tredrea v. Anesthesia & Analgesia, P.C., 584 N.W.2d 276, 283 (Iowa 1998); Willey v. Riley, 541 N.W.2d 521, 527 (Iowa 1995); Economy Roofing & Insulating Co. v. Zumaris, 538 N.W.2d 641, 651–52 (Iowa 1995); Nesler v. Fisher & Co., Inc., 452 N.W.2d 191, 199 (Iowa 1990); see also Tompkins Lawncare, Inc. v. Buchholz, No. 03-1284, 2005 WL 597016, at *2 (Iowa Ct. App. Mar. 16, 2005); Chapman v. LabOne, 460 F. Supp. 2d 989, 1005 (S.D. Iowa 2006) (dismissing interference claims because there was no evidence laboratory acted to intentionally interfere with employee's relationship with employer when disclosing results of drug test to employer); **Home Show Tours, Inc. v. Quad City Virtual, Inc., 827 F.Supp.2d 924, 947–48 (S.D. Iowa 2011) (dismissing claim for interference with prospective business relations for failure to raise inference of either improper purpose or damages)**. "[T]he predominant purpose of the defendant's conduct must be to financially injure or destroy the plaintiff's business." Chemical Methods, Ltd. v. Cue, No. 04-1518, 2005 WL 1750406, at *2 (Iowa Ct. App. July 27, 2005) (citing Willey, 541 N.W.2d at 526–27); see also Ideal Instruments, Inc., 434 F. Supp. 2d at 627 (finding that statements made about competitor could be defamatory and thus "reasonably impl[ied] an intent to injure or destroy [competitor's] business"). If a defendant acts for more than one purpose, the improper purpose must dominate for liability to attach. Corcoran, 39 F. Supp. 2d at 1150–51; Compiano, 588 N.W.2d at 464; Tredrea, 584 N.W.2d at 283; Willey, 541 N.W.2d at 526–27. An "alleged interference is not improper if: a) the relation concerns a matter involved in the competition between the actor and the other; b) the actor does not employ wrongful means; c) his action does not create or continue an unlawful restraint of trade; and d)

his purpose is at least in part to advance his interest in competing with the other." Chem. Methods, Ltd., 2005 WL 1750406, at *2–3 (citations omitted) (stating also that "wrongful means . . . generally encompasses bribery, fraud, misrepresentation, deceit, and misuse of confidential information"); see also GE Capital Corp. v. Commercial Servs. Group, Inc., 485 F. Supp. 2d 1015, 1028 (N.D. Iowa 2007). A contract need not exist, but prospective economic advantage must be reasonably likely and the defendant must have knowledge of the expectation. See Keegan v. City of Blue Grass, No. 03-0194, 2004 WL 139069 (Iowa Ct. App. Jan. 28, 2004) (reversing district court judgment where plaintiff did not show defendants had knowledge of the prospective economic advantage); Nesler, 452 N.W.2d at 191; see also King v. Sioux City Radiological Group, P.C., 985 F. Supp. 869, 882 (N.D. Iowa 1997); Moore Dev., Ltd. v. M.G. Midwest, Inc., No. C06-1014, 2007 U.S. Dist. LEXIS 59067, at *30 (N.D. Iowa Aug. 13, 2007) (holding plaintiff did not identify a prospective business relationship by merely asserting it had "several inquiries" from potential tenants). The interference must have either caused a third party not to enter into or continue a business relationship or prevented plaintiff from entering into or continuing a business relationship. Willey, 541 N.W.2d at 527; Nesler, 452 N.W.2d at 198–99; Conrad v. Iowa Central Community College, 756 N.W.2d 48 (Iowa Ct. App. 2008). The plaintiff must suffer an actual loss or damage as a result of the interference. Speculative or nominal damages, or the threat of future harm, are insufficient to state a cause of action. Jennings, 2003 WL 22176002, at *9; Willey, 541 N.W.2d at 527; Harsha v. State Sav. Bank, 346 N.W.2d 791, 800 (Iowa 1984); Stoller Fisheries, Inc. v. Am. Title Ins. Co., 258 N.W.2d 336, 341 (Iowa 1977). An absolute privilege bars tortious interference claims based on statements made during judicial proceedings. See McFarland v. McFarland, Nos. C08-4047, C09-4047, 2011 WL 4402356, at *4, 15, 16 (N.D. Iowa Sept. 20, 2011) (granting summary judgment dismissal of claims based on alleged defamatory statements made during prior judicial proceeding, and holding absolute privilege barred both the defamation claims and related claims based on the statements, including tortious interference claim). Iowa recognizes justification as an affirmative defense to claims for interference with prospective economic advantage. Locksley v. Anesthesiologists of Cedar Rapids, P.C., 333 N.W.2d 451 (Iowa 1983); Bump v. Stewart, Wimer & Bump, P.C., 336 N.W.2d 731, 737 (Iowa 1983).

In Kern v. Palmer College of Chiropractic, 757 N.W.2d 651, 663-64 (Iowa 2008), the Court held that conduct that fraudulently induces the plaintiff to engage in a course of conduct resulting in his termination supports a tortious interference claim. Cases have indicated that interference with an at-will employment relationship is analogous to interference with a prospective business advantage. King, 985 F. Supp. at 884, (citing RTL Distrib., Inc. v. Double S Batteries, Inc., 545 N.W.2d 587, 590 (Iowa Ct. App. 1996)); see also Chem. Methods, Ltd., 2005 WL 1750406, at *2 (citation omitted) (stating that "cases involving interference with at-will contracts are more akin to interference with a prospective contractual relation because the alleged interference only damages a future expectancy, not a legal right"); Gray v. Harding, No. 11-0018, 2011 WL 4578481, at *13 (Iowa Ct. App. Oct. 5, 2011) (affirming summary judgment on tortious interference with at-will employment claim requiring the plaintiff to show the sole or predominant purpose of the defendant was to injure or financially destroy the plaintiff).

An employee's claim for intentional interference with business relations can only be sustained against a supervisor or agent of the employer if the supervisor or agent exceeded his or her qualified privilege. See, e.g., Sykes v. Hengel, 394 F. Supp. 2d 1062, 1079 (S.D. Iowa 2005) (quoting Jones v. Lake Park Care Ctr., Inc., 569 N.W.2d 369, 376–77 (Iowa 1997)) (stating in context of interference with an existing contract that "'[o]nly a third-party, separate from the contracting parties, can be liable for such a tort. A director or officer acts as an agent of the corporation when acting in good faith to protect the interests of the corporation.'"); Dillon v. Ruperto, No. 09-0600, 2010 WL 2383517, at *5–6 (Iowa Ct. App. June 16, 2010) (discussing when scope of qualified privilege is exceeded by agent of corporation). **Compare Rusch v. Midwest Indus. Inc, No. 10-CV-4110-DEO, 2012 WL 1564704, at *4–7, n.11 (N.D. Iowa May 1, 2012) (noting that the "qualified immunity [of a supervisor/employee] appears to be built into the basic elements necessary to sustain an intentional interference with prospective business relations claim" because both torts require a showing that the interference was improper).**

Some employee claims for intentional interference with prospective economic advantage, like intentional infliction of emotional distress, may be preempted by statute. But see Chapman v. LabOne, 390 F.3d 620, 627–29 (8th Cir. 2004) (holding that common law claims, including tortious interference with business relationships and invasion of privacy, asserted by railroad employee terminated for a failed drug test *against the testing laboratory* were not preempted by federal laws regulating the drug testing of railroad employees and reversing Chapman v. LabOne, 252 F. Supp. 2d 814, 819 (S.D. Iowa 2003) which held the claims were preempted).

Iowa has also recognized the tort of intentional interference with *existing* contractual relationships, which has a lower burden than intentional interference with a *prospective* business advantage. See Kern v. Palmer College of Chiropractic, 757 N.W.2d 651, 662 (Iowa 2008); Brown v. Kerkhoff, 504 F. Supp. 2d 464, 551–53 (S.D. Iowa 2007); GE Capital Corp. v. Commercial Servs. Group, Inc., 485 F. Supp. 2d 1015, 1027 (N.D. Iowa 2007) (holding that tortious interference with an *existing* contract requires a showing that the interference was "improper," while tortious interference with a *prospective* contract requires higher, specific showing that the predominate or sole purpose of the interference was to "financially injure or destroy the claimant"); see also Green v. Racing Ass'n of Cent. Iowa, 713 N.W.2d 234, 243 (Iowa 2006) (stating the five necessary elements for an intentional inference with contract claim under Iowa law); Books Are Fun, Ltd. v. Rosebrough, No. 4:05-CV-00644-JEG, 2006 U.S. Dist. LEXIS 64196, at *20–48 (S.D. Iowa Sept. 6, 2006) (analyzing both intentional interference for existing contracts and prospective business advantage claims); Brown v. Kerkoff, No. 4:06-CV-00342-JEG, 2007 U.S. Dist. LEXIS 62458, at *234–40 (S.D. Iowa Aug. 23, 2007) (same); Midwest Motorsports P'ship v. Hardcore Racing Engines, Inc., No. 6-742, 2007 Iowa App. LEXIS 537, at *6–11 (Iowa Ct. App. Apr. 25, 2007) (same).

3. ***Prima Facie Tort.*** Iowa has not recognized prima facie tort. See French v. Foods, Inc., 495 N.W.2d 768, 772 (Iowa 1993). However, in Doe v. Iowa Health System, 766 N.W.2d 787 (Iowa 2009), the court analyzed a pure negligence claim based on an alleged breach by an employer of its duty to preserve medical records as confidential pursuant to statute.

II. EMPLOYER TESTING OF EMPLOYEES

Iowa recognizes the tort of negligent hiring, including negligent supervision and retention. Godar v. Edwards, 588 N.W.2d 701, 709 (Iowa 1999); D.R.R. v. English Enters, 356 N.W.2d 580, 583 (Iowa Ct. App. 1984); Fredricksburg Farmers Coop. v. Stanley and Elwood Farms, No. 00-0278, 2001 WL 1580488, at *2 (Iowa Ct. App. Dec. 12, 2001); see also Kiesau v. Bantz, 686 N.W.2d 164, 173 (Iowa 2004) (overruling Graves v. Iowa Lakes Cmty Coll., 639 N.W.2d 22 (Iowa 2002) "to the extent [it] holds a negligent, hiring, supervision, or retention claim requires physical injury"); but see Huegerich v. IBP, Inc., 547 N.W.2d 216, 220 (Iowa 1996) (rejecting negligent discharge as an exception to employment at-will doctrine). "A cause of action based on negligent hiring, supervision, or retention allows an injured party to recover where the employee's conduct is outside the scope of employment because the employer's own wrongful conduct has facilitated in some manner the tortious acts or wrongful conduct of the employee." Kiesau, 686 N.W.2d at 172; see also IMT Ins. Co. v. Crestmoor Golf Club, 702 N.W.2d 492, 496 (Iowa 2005) (citation omitted). A claim for negligent supervision must include as an element an underlying tort or wrong committed by the employee. See Cubit v. Mahaska County, 677 N.W.2d 777, 785 (Iowa 2004); see also Schoff v. Combined Ins. Co., 604 N.W.2d 43, 52–53 (Iowa 1999) (holding that an employer cannot be held liable for negligent supervision or training where the conduct that purportedly would have been avoided through proper supervision or training is not actionable in and of itself). Such a cause of action will exist only "when the employer owes a special duty to the injured party." Godar, 588 N.W.2d at 708–09. Such a duty may arise when an employee "because of their employment, may pose a threat of injury to the public." Id. at 709. An employer is liable "only if all the requirements of an action of tort for negligence exist." Fredricksburg Farmers Coop., 2001 WL 1580488, at *2. The Iowa Supreme Court noted that although a "necessary element of a claim for negligent supervision or retention is an underlying tort or wrongful act committed by the employee," "the cause of action arises from the employer's own tortious conduct" and the "'underlying tort or wrongful conduct is simply a link in the causal chain leading to compensable damages.'" IMT Ins. Co., 702 N.W.2d at 496 (citations omitted). Since the recognition of this tort in Iowa there have been no decisions specifically considering an employer's pre-hiring duty of care, including testing or investigation. But see generally Schoff, 604 N.W.2d at 52–53 (rejecting negligent training and supervision claim premised on alleged misrepresentations made to plaintiff by supervisor during job interview because supervisor's conduct was not actionable); Piper v. Jerry's Homes, No. 0102018, 671 N.W.2d 531, 2003 WL 22199580, at *4 (Iowa Ct. App. Sept. 24, 2003). See generally Theisen v. Covenant Med. Ctr., Inc., 636 N.W.2d 74 (Iowa 2001) (rejecting terminated employee's claim of negligent investigation against employer for firing him after another employee accused him of leaving an obscene message without first conducting a reasonable investigation). The Iowa Court of Appeals has also found that an employer in a company administratively dissolved by the Secretary of State has no duty of care for negligent hiring and supervision of an employee. Johnson v. Sherman, No. 05-1264, 2006 WL 1896291, at *2 (Iowa Ct. App. July 12, 2006) (finding that employer of dissolved coach company owed no duty for negligent hiring or supervision of employee who shot citizens with gun from company safe). The Iowa Court of Appeals adopted Restatement (Second) of Torts § 411, finding it to be "an appropriate guide to determine whether a duty exists when a person is injured by an independent contractor that was negligently selected by the employer." Jones v. Schneider Nat'l, Inc., 797 N.W.2d 611, 614 (Iowa Ct. App. 2011) (noting the Iowa Supreme Court's reliance on Restatement principles on similar issues). In recognizing § 411, the Court of Appeals reaffirmed the requirement that a plaintiff bringing a negligent hiring claim must show "'the employer knew, or in the exercise of reasonable care should have known, of …unfitness at the time of hiring."' Id. at 617 (citing Godar, 588 N.W.2d at 708). The Court of Appeals declined to extend protection to employees of an independent contractor, interpreting the phrase "third parties" in § 411 did not include employees of an independent contractor. Id. at 615-16 (citation omitted) (noting a majority of jurisdictions have determined that employers of independent contractors are not vicariously liable to the employees of an independent contractor and finding the purposes of § 411 were satisfied by the receipt of workers' compensation benefits); **see Kelly v. Riser, Inc., No. 11-1898, 2012 WL 5356104, at *6-7 (Iowa Ct. App. Oct. 31, 2012 (applying Jones and § 411, and holding negligent hiring claim of independent contractor's employee failed)**. For a discussion concerning preemption of negligent supervision claims by the Iowa Workers' Compensation Act, see Survey of Iowa Employment Libel Law, Part IV.A. **Claims for negligent hiring or supervision may be preempted by other statutes as well. See, e.g., Estate of Fischer v. Dyno Oil, Inc., No. 11-0452, 814 N.W.2d 622, 2012 WL 642884, at *2–3 (Iowa Ct. App. Feb. 29, 2012) (finding that the Iowa Dram Shop Act preempted negligent supervision and training claim).**

A. Psychological or Personality Testing

1. ***Common Law and Statutes.*** Apart from concerns such tests raise under anti-discrimination statutes (including restrictions thereunder concerning disability-related inquiries), Iowa law generally does not prohibit psychological or personality testing of employees or prospective employees. The Iowa Civil Rights Act, however, prohibits employment discrimination based on age, race, creed, color, sex, sexual orientation, gender identity, national origin, religion, or disability. Iowa Code § 216.6 (amended 2007). Accordingly, an employer cannot test an employee or applicant to reveal the presence of a protected status. Iowa law also provides that a person in possession of psychological testing material shall not disclose the material to any person, including the individual who is a subject of the test. Iowa Code § 228.9. A subject of the test, however, can request in writing that the material be disclosed to a licensed psychologist. Id.

2. ***Private Employers.*** As discussed above, Iowa law generally does not regulate psychological or personality testing of employees or applicants.

3. ***Public Employers.*** Cognitive and psychological examinations administered by or on behalf of a government body for law enforcement officer candidates are confidential to the extent that their disclosure could reasonably be believed by the custodian of the records to interfere with the accomplishment of the objectives for which they are administered. Iowa Code § 22.7(19).

B. Drug Testing

1. ***Common Law and Statutes.*** Iowa Code § 730.5 governs drug testing of employees and applicants by private employers. See Eaton v. Iowa Employment Appeal Bd., 602 N.W.2d 553 (Iowa 1999) (discussing Iowa Code § 730.5 "as it existed in 1996 and 1997"); see also Harrison v. Iowa Employment Appeal Bd., 659 N.W.2d 581, 588–89 (Iowa 2003) (discussing Iowa Code § 730.5, stating that the statute is "designed to ensure accurate testing and to protect employees from unfair and unwarranted discipline," and holding that former employee was not disqualified from unemployment benefits based on an initial positive drug test result where the employer failed to substantially comply with the procedural safeguards set forth in the Iowa Code); Artistic Solid Waste Sys., Inc. v. Employment Appeal Bd., No. 00-2018, 2002 WL 663625, at *2–3 (Iowa Ct. App. Apr. 24, 2002) (discussing Iowa Code § 730.5 and whether former employee was disqualified from unemployment benefits based on initial positive drug test result) (Note that this case relies on Eaton, which interpreted the statute as it existed before the 1998 amendments). The statute was substantially revised in 1998. See also 2004 Iowa Acts (80 G.A.) S.F. 2173 (2004 revisions to statute establishing procedures for taking oral fluid tests and for determining what constitutes a positive test result with regard to oral fluid tests). However, "section 730.5 'does not apply to drug tests conducted on employees required to be tested pursuant to federal statutes, federal regulations, or orders issued pursuant to federal law." See Welcher v. American Ordnance, No. 04-1045, 2006 WL 126631, at *6 (Iowa Ct. App. Jan. 19, 2006); Iowa Code § 730.5(2); see also Iowa Code § 730.5(8)(e)..

Iowa Code § 730.5(12)(b) provides that a "cause of action for defamation, libel, slander, or damage to reputation shall not arise against an employer establishing a program of drug or alcohol testing" unless the employer discloses the test results to a third-party, the "test results disclosed incorrectly indicate the presence of alcohol or drugs," and the "employer negligently discloses the results."

2. ***Private Employers.*** Iowa law permits private employers to conduct statutorily specified forms of drug and/or alcohol tests of employees in certain circumstances, including, for example, based on "reasonable suspicion," during rehabilitation, or following certain accidents. Employers also can test applicants for the presence of alcohol and/or drugs. Before any testing is conducted, however, employers must adopt a written policy that meets the strict requirements of the statute and must conduct supervisors' training. Employers can terminate employees or refuse to hire applicants for a positive test result under many circumstances, even if it is a first offense. "[A] discharge from employment may be based on an employee drug-testing program only if that program is being carried out in compliance with the governing statutory law." McVey v. Nat'l Org. Serv., Inc., 719 N.W.2d 801, 803–04 (Iowa 2006) (citation omitted) (holding that fact issue regarding whether terminated employee had received the drug-testing policy precluded summary judgment); see Iowa Code § 730.5(9); **see also Skipton v. S & J Tube, Inc., No. 11-1902, 2012 WL 3860446 (Iowa Ct. App. Sept. 6, 2012).** The statute also imposes strict requirements on employers to maintain the confidentiality of test information. All communications and records concerning drug and/or alcohol testing of employees or applicants are confidential and can be disclosed only under limited circumstances. Records can be released to an employee or applicant upon request. See, e.g., Smith v. CRST, Inc., No. C05-0051, 2006 WL 1750972, at *8 (N.D. Iowa June 26, 2006) (holding that an employer releasing false drug test information about a former applicant to another employer acted in good faith and without knowledge of the misinformation and therefore remained immune from civil liability under Iowa Code section 91B.2(1)). The records may be disclosed in certain circumstances, including, for example, in an administrative or judicial proceeding under workers' compensation or unemployment compensation law, or where action is taken against the employer based on a test result. Test results cannot be used as evidence in a criminal investigation against an employee, but may be disclosed to federal or state agencies as required

by law or to a treatment facility. In affirming summary judgment, the Eighth Circuit predicted that Iowa courts would hold that an employee cannot maintain a cause of action based upon the employer's reliance on a drug test that does not comport with United States Department of Transportation regulations as grounds to terminate the employee. The Court noted that under these facts the employee can claim, at most, negligent discharge which expressly has been rejected as a cause of action in Iowa. Graham v. Contract Transp., Inc., 220 F.3d 910, 912 (8th Cir. 2000). In Graham v. Contract Transp., Inc., No. 4-98-CV-90546, 2001 WL 740118, at *7 (S.D. Iowa Apr. 24, 2001), the Southern District of Iowa held that plaintiff's defamation claim was precluded by the releases he signed authorizing the publication of his drug test results to prospective employers, and the court rejected the argument that Aid Ins. Co. v. Davis Co., 426 N.W.2d 631, 633 (Iowa 1988), invalidated the releases because the releases in Graham specifically named the former employer as a party to be released. In Sims v. NCI Holding Corporation, 759 N.W.2d 333 (Iowa 2009), Iowa's drug testing statute was described as promoting drug-free workplace efforts by employers. Therefore, the Court established a liberal test of substantial compliance, thereby restricting the causes of action an employee could sustain for drug testing statute violations. Id. at 338.

3. ***Public Employers.*** Iowa's drug testing law does not apply to public employers. In McDonell v. Hunter, 809 F.2d 1302, 1310 (8th Cir. 1987), the Eighth Circuit upheld an Iowa Department of Corrections policy that requires corrections officers to submit to random urinalyses for drug and alcohol, finding that corrections officers have a lessened privacy expectation.

In Crisman v. Eckert, No. 6-1002, 2007 Iowa Ct. App. LEXIS 234, at *8–13 (Iowa Ct. App. Feb. 28, 2007), the Iowa Court of Appeals upheld the termination of a city employee who failed a drug test. After applying contract principles, including the doctrine of acquiescence, to interpret an agreement between the city and employee, the Court determined the employee had agreed to take a drug test in order to return to work. Id. (finding that by taking the drug test instead of in some manner protesting or seeking clarification, employee acquiesced to the employer's interpretation of what was required of him to show he was "fit for duty").

C. Medical Testing

1. ***Common Law and Statutes.*** The Iowa Constitution provides that "The right of the people to be secure in their persons, houses, papers and effects, against unreasonable seizures and searches shall not be violated . . . ." Iowa Const. Art. 1, § 8. There are no reported cases, however, wherein a court has considered whether a medical test given by an employer is violative of this provision. Iowa also has specific statutory provisions governing medical testing. See, e.g., Iowa Code § 139A.19 (providing that if a healthcare provider sustains an exposure to an individual, the individual to whom the health care provider was exposed is required to consent to testing to determine if the individual has a contagious or infectious disease and is deemed to consent to the notification of the healthcare provider of the results of the test), amended by H.F. 467, 84th G.A. § 20 (Iowa 2011); Iowa Code § 141A.8 (providing that if a care provider sustains a significant exposure to an individual, the individual to whom the care provider was exposed is required to consent to a test to determine the presence of HIV infection), repealed by H.F. 467, 84th G.A. § 32 (Iowa 2011), which expands chapter 139A to include HIV, § 18. In addition, medical testing raises concerns under anti-discrimination statutes, including restrictions concerning disability -related inquiries.

2. ***Private Employers.*** Iowa law prohibits an employer from requesting or requiring as a condition of employment that an employee or prospective employee submit to a test for the presence of HIV and from taking any action affecting the terms, conditions, or privileges of employment solely as a result of the employee obtaining an HIV test. Iowa Code § 216.6(1)(d). The statute similarly prohibits employers and unions or employment agencies from agreeing to allow such testing. The prohibition does not apply, however, if the state epidemiologist determines and the director of public health declares that a person with a condition related to AIDS poses a significant risk of transmission of the virus to other persons in a specific occupation. Information related to any HIV test is a confidential record and can only be disclosed under specifically delineated circumstances. Iowa Code § 141A.9(1). Such information "may be shared between employees of the department who shall use the information collected only for the purposes of carrying out their official duties in preventing the spread of the disease or the spread of other reportable diseases." Id. § 141A.9(7). Similarly, a person cannot be required to submit to an HIV test in connection with an application for insurance without a written release. Iowa Code § 505.16. An employer also is prohibited from requesting, requiring, or administering a genetic test to a person as a condition of employment or pre-employment application. Iowa Code § 729.6. An employer cannot affect the terms, conditions, or privileges of employment or pre-employment application based on the person's obtainment of a genetic test. Similarly, an employer cannot enter into an agreement with a union or employment agency which provides any pay or benefit in return for taking a genetic test. Iowa Code § 729.6(6). An employer cannot discharge, discipline, or discriminate against a person who, acting in good faith, filed a complaint or testified in regard to a violation of this statute. Id. § 729.6(7). The statute excludes an employee who requests a genetic test and who provides written and informed consent for the purpose of investigating a workers' compensation claim or in determining the employee's susceptibility to toxic substances in the workplace, provided the employer takes no adverse employment action in connection with the test. Id. §729.6(9).

3. ***Public Employers.*** Iowa's statutes governing HIV testing and genetic testing apply to public employers.

D. Polygraph Tests

Under Iowa law an employer cannot require, request, administer, or threaten an employee to take a polygraph examination as a condition of employment, promotion, change in status of employment, or as an express or implied condition of a benefit or privilege of employment. Iowa Code § 730.4; Wilcox v. Hy-Vee Food Stores, Inc., 458 N.W.2d 870 (Iowa 1990). A violation of this statute gives rise to a private cause of action. Wilcox, 458 N.W.2d at 872. An employee, acting in good faith, cannot be discharged, disciplined, or discriminated against for filing a complaint or testifying in regard to violation of this statute. Iowa Code § 730.4(4). The statute does not apply to the state or a political subdivision when it is selecting a candidate for employment as a peace officer, corrections officer, or positions with law enforcement agencies of political subdivisions in which employees have "direct access to prisoner funds, any other cash assets, and confidential information." Iowa Code § 730.4(3). Under an Iowa Attorney General's formal opinion, the terms "peace officer" and "corrections officer" do not include civil employees at a county jail such as janitors, maintenance workers, secretaries, clerks, or interns. Op. Att'y Gen. No. 94-9-2 (1994). Polygraph examinations administered by the government must adhere to the published anti-discrimination policy of the government entity conducting the examination. Iowa Code § 730.4(3)(b). In a case that pre-dates the enactment of Iowa's polygraph statute, the Iowa Supreme Court held that a city auto mechanic's termination for refusing to submit to a polygraph test was improper. City of Sioux City v. Fairbanks, 287 N.W.2d 579 (Iowa 1980). In so holding, the Court opined that a public employee reasonably may be expected to answer questions concerning work-related conduct or his competence to continue in his employment, but cannot be required to take a polygraph test absent "proper authorization or pre -employment notice." Id. at 581. The Court expressly omitted policeman and firemen from this prohibition because of the nature and duty of their employment. In Mennen v. Easter Stores, 951 F. Supp. 838 (N.D. Iowa 1997), the court engaged in a lengthy analysis of a claim under the federal Employee Polygraph Protection Act. Because it found the defendant liable under the federal act, it limited its analysis of Iowa law to the observation that Iowa's polygraph statute provides no greater relief than the federal act. Id. at 858 n.24. In Theisen v. Covenant Med. Ctr., Inc., 636 N.W.2d 74 (Iowa 2001), the Court rejected a discharged employee's claim that his termination for refusing to submit to a voice print analysis violated the public policy embodied in Iowa Code § 730.4. The Court noted that "the plain language of section 730.4 pertains to devices, such as polygraphs, that purport to measure the truth or veracity of an employee's statement," and the "statute does not, by its terms, prohibit lawful tests or procedures used by an employer in the identification of employees suspected of workplace crime." Id.

E. Fingerprinting

Iowa law does not regulate the fingerprinting of employees or applicants. One court has concluded that Iowa Code § 730.4, which regulates the use of polygraph examinations, does not prohibit an employer from using fingerprints. See Theisen v. Covenant Med. Ctr., Inc., 636 N.W.2d 74, 80 (Iowa 2001) (stating that the polygraph statute "clearly places limits on the testing or analysis to which an employer can be subjected, but it does not prohibit an employer from using identification techniques such as comparison of photographs, fingerprints or voice prints" and that "[t]he statute does not . . . prohibit lawful tests or procedures used by an employer in the identification of employees suspected of workplace crime").

III. SEARCHES

The Iowa Constitution provides that "The right of the people to be secure in their persons, houses, papers and effects, against unreasonable seizures and searches shall not be violated . . . ." Iowa Const. art. 1, § 8.

A. Employee's Person

1. ***Private Employers.*** No reported cases discuss a private employer's ability or inability to search an employee's person. One court has concluded that an employer's search of an employee's person and subsequent discharge for possession of prohibited substances did not, standing alone, amount to a defamatory publication. Huegerich v. IBP, Inc., 547 N.W.2d 216 (Iowa 1996). Another court has concluded that a supervisor's partial strip search of an employee, under the threat of termination for noncompliance, to disprove the presence of a suspected recording device did not amount to outrageous conduct as a matter of law and could not support a claim for intentional infliction of emotional distress. Weems v. Federated Mut. Ins. Co., 220 F. Supp. 2d 979, 998–99 (N.D. Iowa 2002).

2. ***Public Employers.*** The Eighth Circuit upheld an Iowa Department of Corrections policy that requires corrections officers to consent to certain searches as a condition of employment, on the basis that correctional officers' expectation of privacy are diminished while they are within the prison. McDonell v. Hunter, 809 F.2d 1302, 1306 (8th Cir. 1987). Accordingly, strip searches were found to be permissible if they were based on reasonable and individualized suspicion. The court similarly upheld the requirement that corrections officers submit to random urinalyses for drug and alcohol testing. The court reiterated, however, that a government employer cannot require its employees to consent to an unreasonable search as a condition of employment. Id. at 1310.

B. Employee's Work Area

In O'Bryan v. KTIV Television, 868 F. Supp. 1146, 1158 (N.D. Iowa 1994), aff'd in relevant part, 64 F.3d 1188 (8th Cir. 1995), the court granted summary judgment in favor of an employer who searched and examined the contents of an employee's desk and office for employer-owned documents without the employee's knowledge. The court reasoned that summary judgment was proper because, among other things, the employee did not have a reasonable expectation of privacy in his desk or office area. O'Bryan, 868 F. Supp. at 1158. See also Smith v. CRST, Inc., No. C05-0051, 2006 WL 1750972, at *3 (N.D. Iowa June 26, 2006) (noting that when a prospective employer requested information about a former applicant for a semi-truck position, the former employer's response could include information gathered from a vehicle search).

C. Employee's Property

1. ***Private Employers.*** No reported cases discuss a private employer's search of an employee's property.

2. ***Public Employers.*** In McDonell v. Hunter, 809 F.2d 1302, 1306 (8th Cir. 1987), the court upheld an Iowa Department of Corrections policy that subjected employees' automobiles to random searches. The court reiterated, however, that a government employer cannot require its employees to consent to an unreasonable search as a condition of employment. Id. at 1310. In True v. Nebraska, 612 F.3d 676, 682 (8th Cir. 2010), a case arising under federal law, the court said, "[I]t is reasonable . . . to search by 'systematic random selection,' employee vehicles in prison parking lots to which inmates have unsupervised access."

IV. MONITORING OF EMPLOYEES

A. Telephones and Electronic Communications

Iowa law prohibits tapping into or connecting a listening or recording device to any telephone or other communication wire, or listening to, recording, or otherwise intercepting a conversation or communication of any kind. Iowa Code § 727.8. The statute provides, however, that a sender or recipient of a communication, or one who is openly present and participating in or listening to a communication, may record the communication. Thus one party to a communication may record it, without court order, regardless of whether other parties to the communication consent. State v. Reid, 394 N.W.2d 399, 405 (Iowa 1986); see also Reed v. Cedar County, No. 05-CV-64-LRR, 2007 U.S. Dist. LEXIS 9915, at *12–13 (N.D. Iowa Feb. 12, 2007) (finding plaintiff did not violate Iowa or federal law by recording conversation in which she participated). The Iowa Supreme Court has rejected a constitutional challenge to this statute. See State v. Philpott, 702 N.W.2d 500, 503 (Iowa 2005). Iowa's Interception of Communications statute prohibits a person from intercepting a wire communication or oral communication by use of an electronic, mechanical, or other device. Iowa Code § 808B.2. The statute also prohibits the procurement of another to engage in such interception or the use or disclosure of information that was illegally intercepted. This statute no longer contains a sunset provision. In Hall v. Iowa Merit Employment Comm'n, 380 N.W.2d 710, 713–15 (Iowa 1986), the Iowa Supreme Court found a public employee's act of illegally recording employee conversations to which she was not a party and without the employees' consent and her subsequent guilty plea to the same were not separate acts of misconduct under the state merit system.

1. ***Wiretapping.*** Wiretapping falls within scope of prohibitions noted above. In Iowa Beta Chapter of Phi Delta Phi Fraternity v. State of Iowa, 763 N.W.2d 250 (Iowa 2009), a fraternity sued after the University of Iowa used the content of intercepted electronic communications to the organization regarding a hazing incident. The Supreme Court found the fraternity had standing to pursue a claim under Iowa Code § 808B.8, in part because the intercepted communication related to fraternity business and its content was used to discipline the fraternity as a whole. Id. at 260. Further, the Court said fraternity members had a privacy expectation as to the intercepted communications, which occurred during confidential business meetings in the fraternity that were tape recorded clandestinely by a member. Finally, the Court found the acts of making the recordings in this case could be deemed willful, but declared that "mere listening to the intercepted communication is not a use under the Iowa statute." Id. at 265. Instead, a person "must actively use the intercepted communication for civil liability to attach." Id. In this case, the Court imposed liquidated damages of $73,200, or $100 per day for 732 days, measured by the time between the date the communication was intercepted and the last date upon which the university used it. Id. at 268. **See generally Luken v. Edwards, No. C10-4097-MWB, 2011 WL 1655902, at *5 (N.D. Iowa May 3, 2011), 2012 WL 5332193 (N.D. Iowa Oct. 26, 2012) (discussing federal wiretapping laws).**

2. ***Electronic Communications.*** Electronic communications fall within scope of prohibition noted above.

3. ***Other Electronic Monitoring.*** There are no reported Iowa cases discussing any other forms of electronic monitoring.

B. Mail

Iowa law contains no provisions related to opening another person's mail, nor are there any reported cases considering the improper opening of mail in the employment context. Federal law, however, prohibits a person from taking mail addressed to another before it has been delivered with the intent "to obstruct the correspondence, or to pry into the business or secrets of another." See 18 U.S.C. § 1702.

C. Surveillance/Photographing

The Iowa Supreme Court held that a plaintiff-employee did not have to show that a camera hidden in a workplace bathroom actually recorded images of her in order to sustain a claim for intrusion, but had to show merely that it *could have* recorded those images. Koeppel v. Speirs, 808 N.W.2d 177 (Iowa 2011) (finding that, although the hidden camera and monitor produced only "snowy, grainy, foggy" images when the police investigated the plaintiff's complaint, plaintiff's claim should not have been dismissed because there was evidence the camera was capable of operation that "would lead a reasonable person to believe his or her privacy had been invaded"). See I.B.4, supra.

In addition to the potential application of the common law of intrusion, the 2004 legislature enacted a criminal provision which provides that "[a] person who knowingly views, photographs, or films another person, for the purpose of arousing or gratifying the sexual desire of any person, commits invasion of privacy" where the non-consenting subject is in a full or partial state of nudity. See Iowa Code § 709.21. Stalking, which is defined as engaging in a course of conduct directed at a specific person that would cause a reasonable person to fear bodily injury or death, is a felony under Iowa law. Iowa Code § 708.11. Installation and use of hidden surveillance cameras in the workplace is a mandatory subject of bargaining under federal labor law. Colgate-Palmolive Co., 323 N.L.R.B. 515, 1997 WL 202232 (NLRB 1997). See generally State v. Walker, 804 N.W.2d 284, 294 (Iowa 2011) (discussing videotaped surveillance within context of statutory right in Iowa Code § 804.20 for an inmate to consult "alone and in private" with his/her attorney, and stating that "private" means "'withdrawn from company or observation'" and "[p]ersons visually monitored by a security camera are not 'withdrawn from . . . observation'").

V. ACTIVITIES OUTSIDE THE WORKPLACE

A. Statute or Common Law

The Iowa Civil Rights Act prohibits employment discrimination based on age, race, creed, color, sex, sexual orientation, gender identity, national origin, religion, or disability. Iowa Code § 216.6. "Although the text of the Iowa Civil Rights Act does not require accommodation of employee's religious practices, the Iowa Supreme Court has read into Iowa Code section 216.6(1)(a) the duty to accommodate . . . in the alleged religious discrimination context." Cole v. Wells Fargo Bank, 437 F.Supp.2d 974, 983 n.8 (S.D. Iowa 2006) (holding that plaintiff's religious discrimination claim arising from her employer's refusal to allow her to change her schedule so she could attend religious services should be decided as an Iowa Civil Rights Act claim rather than an individual tort claim); see also Powell v. Yellow Book USA, Inc., 445 F.3d 1074 (8th Cir. 2006) (noting that "an employer has no legal obligation to suppress any and all religious expression merely because it annoys a single employee"). Elected or appointed public officials are subject to the state's nepotism policy, which prohibits such officials from appointing relatives to serve as the official's deputy, clerk, or helper without the approval of the public body responsible for approving the official's bond. Iowa Code § 71.1. Police officers may engage in off-duty employment, provided the employment is "wholly consistent with public duties" and neither interferes with nor is required by official duties. Borlin v. Civil Serv. Comm'n, 338 N.W.2d 146, 149 (Iowa 1983); State v. Hinshaw, 197 Iowa 1265, 198 N.W. 634, 637 (1924). A city, however, may prohibit its officers from engaging in any off-duty employment. Borlin, 338 N.W.2d at 149 (citing Jurgens v. Davenport R.I. & N.W. Ry. Co., 249 Iowa 711, 716, 88 N.W.2d 797, 801 (1958)). Further, police officers and firefighters are subject to suspension for misconduct off-duty. Kline v. Civil Serv. Comm'n, No. 02-1643, 2003 WL 22087588, at *3 (Iowa Ct. App. Sep. 10, 2003) (holding that officer's actions of throwing dice while in uniform and on-duty and drinking to excess while off-duty were appropriate bases for disciplinary action); Butler v. Civil Serv. Comm'n, Nos. 0-628/99-1999, 2000 WL 1827714, at *4 (Iowa Ct. App. Dec. 13, 2000) (citing Iowa Code § 400.19); Millsap v. Cedar Rapids Civil Serv. Comm'n, 249 N.W.2d 679, 687 (Iowa 1997)); see also Dolan v. Civil Serv. Comm'n, 634 N.W.2d 657 (Iowa 2001); **Rosdail v. Civil Serv. Comm'n of Cedar Rapids, No. 11-0514, 2011 WL 6764957 (Iowa Ct. App. Dec. 21, 2011).**

B. Employees' Personal Relationships

1. ***Romantic Relationships Between Employees.*** Iowa law does not prohibit private employers from placing restrictions on the personal relationships of its employees. In Born v. Blockbuster Videos, Inc., 941 F. Supp. 868 (S. D. Iowa 1996), the court held that state and federal provisions which protect a person's privacy apply to state action only and that plaintiffs' discharge for violating company policy prohibiting dating among supervisors and subordinates did not violate public policy, as plaintiffs were unable to cite any authority that private limitations on association fell within the public policy exception to the employment at-will doctrine. In Mercer v. City of Cedar Rapids, 104 F. Supp. 2d 1130, 1178–79 (N.D. Iowa

2000), aff'd in relevant part, 308 F.3d 840 (8th Cir. 2002), the Court held that, as a matter of law, a police officer could not maintain an action for wrongful discharge in violation of public policy when the discharge was based upon her consensual personal relationship with another member of the police department. Although the Court recognized, without holding, that a person employed in the private sector might have such a cause of action based upon intrusion, police officers appropriately are subject to more stringent rules and regulations. Accordingly, "inquiries into the nature of a police officer's off-duty relationship with a superior officer, and even termination of a police officer because of an off-duty relationship with a superior officer that the police officer described as 'romantic' would not be 'highly offensive to a reasonable person,' even in the absence of a non-fraternization rule or regulation." Mercer, 104 F. Supp. 2d at 1179. In affirming the decision on appeal, the Eighth Circuit stated that it agreed "with the district court that no well-recognized and clear Iowa public policy protects an at-will employee's privacy interest in a romantic relationship with a co-worker, especially when the employer concludes that the relationship has adversely affected the workplace." Mercer, 308 F.3d at 846.

2. ***Sexual Orientation.*** The Iowa Code provides that "[p]ersons within the state of Iowa have the right to be free from any violence, or intimidation by threat of violence, committed against their persons or property because of their . . . sexual orientation." Iowa Code § 729A.1. In addition, the Code provides that a victim of such violence or intimidation who has suffered physical, emotional, or financial harm may bring a civil action for injunctive relief, general and special damages, reasonable attorneys' fees, and costs. Iowa Code § 729A.5. The Iowa Civil Rights Act specifically prohibits discrimination based on "sexual orientation" and "gender identity." Iowa Code § 216.6 (amended in 2007 to add "sexual orientation" and "gender identity" as protected classes); see also Seim v. Three Eagles Communications, Inc., No. 09-CV-3071, 2011 WL 2149061, at *3–5 (N.D. Iowa June 1, 2011) (denying defendant's motion for summary with respect to plaintiff's claims of sexual orientation/same-sex sexual discrimination, noting among other things that the Iowa Civil Rights Act defines at Iowa Code § 216.2(14) "sexual orientation" to mean "actual or perceived heterosexuality, homosexuality, or bisexuality"). Before sexual orientation was added as a protected class, in Grimm v. U.S. West Commc'ns, Inc., 644 N.W.2d 8 (Iowa 2002), the plaintiff brought an action against her former employer and supervisor alleging, inter alia, intentional infliction of emotional distress. The defendants argued that the emotional distress claim was a disguised sexual orientation discrimination claim and was thereby preempted by the Iowa Civil Rights Act "even though the statute does not apply to sexual orientation." Id. at 16–17 (citation omitted). The Iowa Supreme Court reversed the district court's dismissal of the action on procedural grounds, holding that plaintiff had pled sufficient facts to survive a pre-answer motion to dismiss. Id. at 17. Some municipal ordinances also prohibit discrimination based on sexual orientation. See, e.g., Des Moines, Iowa, Code § 62-71 (prohibiting discrimination in employment based on sexual orientation); Iowa City, Iowa, Code § 2-3-1 (prohibiting discrimination in employment based on sexual orientation); Davenport, Iowa, Code § 2.58.100 (prohibiting discrimination in employment based on sexual orientation).

3. ***Marital Status.*** An executive order signed September 14, 1999, providing that individuals shall not be denied access to state employment opportunities because of marital status was struck down in December 2000 by a state trial judge. See King v. Vilsack, No. CE 040318 (Iowa Dist. Ct., Dec. 7, 2000) (declaring Exec. Order No. 7 (Sept. 14, 1999) unconstitutional). Iowa law does not specifically prohibit employment discrimination based on marital status in private employment. In Baker v. City of Iowa City, 750 N.W.2d 93 (Iowa 2008), however, the Iowa Supreme Court held that the Iowa Civil Rights Act leaves room for local governments to enact ordinances that prohibit discrimination in employment on the basis of marital status. The Iowa Code does prohibit discrimination on the basis of marital status in the granting of licenses to enter certain professions. Iowa Code § 147.3. Such professions include the practice of medicine and surgery, podiatry, osteopathy, osteopathic medicine and surgery, psychology, chiropractic, physical therapy, nursing, dentistry, dental hygiene, optometry, speech pathology, audiology, occupational therapy, respiratory care, pharmacy, cosmetology, barbering, social work, dietetics, marital and family therapy or mental health counseling, massage therapy, mortuary science, acupuncture, and the practice as a physician assistant. Iowa Code § 147.2, **amended by S.F. 364, 84th G.A. § 1101 (Iowa 2012) (expanding list of professions)**. In Varnum v. Brien, 763 N.W.2d 862 (Iowa 2009), the Iowa Supreme Court recognized the validity of same sex marriages. As a result, any rights accorded or protected due to marital status must be equal irrespective of whether the spouses are a heterosexual or a same-sex couple.

C. Smoking

In 2008 the Iowa legislature enacted the Smokefree Air Act. Iowa Code §142D.1 (2008). The Smokefree Air Act prohibits smoking in all "public places" and "all enclosed areas within places of employment." Iowa Code §142D.3 (2008). Public places include enclosed areas to which the public is invited or to which the public is permitted, including common areas. Iowa Code §142D.2(16) (2008). Places of employment include any area under the control of an employer, including company vehicles, and all areas that an employee frequents during the course of employment or while volunteering. Iowa Code §142D.2(13) (2008). While places of employment that are outdoors are exempt from the Smokefree Air Act, employers may voluntary declare the entire area as a nonsmoking place. Iowa Code §142D.4(6) (2008); Iowa Code §142D.5(1) (2008).

D. Blogging

There are no reported Iowa decisions discussing blogging in the employment privacy context. **See generally S.J.W. v. Lee's Summit R-7 Sch. Dist., 696 F.3d 771 (8th Cir. 2012) (reversing Western District of Missouri order granting preliminary injunction to students asserting constitutional claims for suspension based on blogging); State of Iowa v. Runge, No. 11-0778, 2012 WL 5356174, at *4 (Iowa Ct. App. Oct. 31, 2012) (discussing whether criminal defendant's blog comments were properly considered in sentencing decision).**

VI. RECORDS

The Iowa child support recovery unit maintains a centralized employee registry database for newly hired and rehired private and public employees. Employers must report the employee's name, address, social security number, date of birth and the date, if any, the employee qualifies for dependent health care coverage. Iowa Code § 252G.3. The registry records are confidential and may be accessed only by certain state agencies which administer the child support enforcement program, determine eligibility for entitlement payments, and recoup debts owed to the state. Iowa Code §§ 22.7(28), 252G.5. If a public body negligently releases a record covered by a confidential exemption, there is no private cause of action for damages from the release. Marcus v. Young, 538 N.W.2d. 285 (Iowa 1995); Eickmayer v. State, 666 N.W.2d 620 (Iowa Ct. App. 2003) (unpublished table decision).

The Iowa Public Information Board Act, passed in 2012 and effective July 1, 2013, creates a public information board to investigate and administer complaints under Iowa's open meetings act and public records act, Iowa Code Chapters 21 and 22. 2012 Iowa Legis. Serv. Ch. 1115 (S.F. 430).

A. Personnel Records

Employees have access to and are permitted to obtain a copy of their personnel file maintained by the employer, including performance evaluations, disciplinary records, and other information concerning employee-employer relations. Iowa Code § 91B.1. An employer need not, however, provide access to written employment references. The employer and employee must agree on the time the employee may have access to the file, and an employer representative may be present. The employer may charge the employee a reasonable fee for each copy made. Former employees, however, do not have a right to copy their personnel files; one court has ruled that the statute applies only to current employees. Muller v. Hotsy Corp., 917 F. Supp. 1389, 1422 (N.D. Iowa 1996); **Dunn v. Dubuque Glass Co., No. 11-CV-1001-LRR, 2012 WL 1564700, at *12 (N.D. Iowa May 1, 2012).** Iowa Code § 91B.2 grants current and former employers civil immunity in the disclosure of work-related information to employees or their prospective employers as long as the employers act reasonably. See Smith v. CRST, Inc., No. C05-0051, 2006 WL 1750972, at *6 (N.D. Iowa June 26, 2006) (citing section 91B.2 and granting immunity to a former employer providing records on a former applicant to a new employer).

Personal information in confidential personnel files of government bodies are confidential and exempt from disclosure under Iowa's public records act. Iowa Code § 22.7(11). The legislature amended that provision in 2011 by, *inter alia*, delineating specific items of information that are subject to disclosure as public records, including the individual's name, dates of employment, educational background, compensation, positions held, names of previous employers and employment history, and the "fact that the individual was discharged as the result of a final disciplinary action." See S.F. 289, 84th G.A. § 10 (Iowa 2011). In a case prior to the 2011 amendment, the Iowa Supreme Court held records concerning individual public employees' salaries, use of vacation, and use of sick leave are not exempt from disclosure so long as such records do not reveal personal medical conditions or professional evaluations. Clymer v. City of Cedar Rapids, 601 N.W.2d 42, 48, 27 Media L. Rep. 2622, 2626–27 (Iowa 1999). In a recent case, the Iowa Court of Appeals discussed prior Iowa Supreme Court precedent interpreting the provision and stated that "evaluations of job performance are clearly 'confidential under Iowa law'" and, while in circumstances in which the information "'falls somewhere in between'" what is clearly confidential and what is clearly subject to disclosure courts apply a balancing test that weighs the public's need to know against individual privacy interests, the discipline reports at issue in that case were "job performance records that are clearly confidential under Iowa law" and thus no balancing test was required. ACLU Foundation of Iowa v. Records Custodian, No. 11-0095, 2011 WL 4950199, at *1–3 (Iowa Ct. App. Oct. 19, 2011) (discussing Clymer v. City of Cedar Rapids, 601 N.W.2d 42 (Iowa 1999)), **aff'd, 818 N.W.2d 231 (Iowa 2012)**; DeLaMater v. Marion Civil Serv. Comm'n, 554 N.W.2d 875 (Iowa 1996); In re Des Moines Indep. Cmty. Sch. Disc. Pub. Records, 487 N.W.2d 666 (Iowa 1992)); compare Shannon v. Koehler, No. 08-4059, 2010 WL 3943661, at *3–5 (N.D. Iowa Oct. 6, 2010) (stating that, because Iowa Code section 22.7(11) was "unclear" as to whether the personnel file of former law enforcement officer at issue in that case was subject to privacy exemption, the "fact specific, balancing test should be applied," and ultimately affirming as not clearly erroneous magistrate judge's denial of motion to quash subpoena although "I personally would have granted" the motion to quash). In that case, the Court of Appeals also noted the 2011 amendment, which "clarifies the legislature's intent" by identifying as an exemption from the confidentiality requirement applicable to personnel records only a "*single* form of disciplinary action—an action that results in discharge," and the Court stated "the absence of an exemption [from the confidentiality requirement] for *all* disciplinary actions reflects the legislature's intent to retain the confidentiality of the type of information [discipline reports] sought in this case." ACLU Foundation of Iowa, 2011 WL 4950199, at *3. **The Iowa Supreme Court ultimately affirmed the Court of Appeals and held that "[u]nder our prior caselaw and that of other jurisdictions, we can easily conclude that the plain language of the statute supports the exemption in this case. Accordingly, it is unnecessary to apply a balancing test." ACLU Foundation of Iowa, Inc. v. Records Custodian, 818 N.W.2d 231, 235-36 (Iowa 2012).**

In a case involving a private employer's inadvertent disclosure of employee information, including social security numbers, the Iowa Court of Appeals found that no public policy protects an employee from discharge "for her actions to protect her right to privacy and to protect her social security number." Schmit v. Iowa Machine Shed Co., No. 6-691/05-1927, 2006 WL 2872944 (Iowa Ct. App. Oct. 11, 2006).

B. Medical Records

Hospital records, medical records, and professional counselor records held by government bodies are subject to confidentiality provisions of Iowa's public records act. Iowa Code § 22.7(2). Further, Iowa Code § 228.2 proscribes the disclosure of mental health information and prescribes the procedures to be used when such information is disclosed pursuant to five narrow exceptions: voluntary disclosure, administrative disclosure, compulsory disclosure, disclosure for claims administration and peer review, and disclosure to family members. Iowa Code § 228.9 generally prohibits the disclosure of psychological test material but permits the individual who is the subject of the test to authorize disclosure to a licensed psychologist. In Doe v. Central Iowa Health System, 766 N.W.2d 787, 790 (Iowa 2009), the Court assumed without deciding that Iowa Code Chapter 228 created a private cause of action for a plaintiff suing for release of his medical information. Iowa Code § 139A.3 provides that a healthcare provider or public, private, or hospital clinical laboratory attending a person infected with a reportable disease must obtain certain personal information from the person and report that information to the Iowa Department of Public Health and that such report shall be confidential and not accessible to the public. The Iowa Code further provides that reports to the Department of Public Health which include the identity of persons infected with a sexually transmitted disease shall be confidential only to the extent necessary to prevent the identification of such persons named in the reports. Iowa Code § 139A.30. The Supreme Court of Iowa has held that a former employee could not prevail on claims of invasion of privacy and negligent disclosure of confidential medical records against his health care provider where the disclosure to his employer was not the proximate cause of his termination. Evans v. Benson, 731 N.W.2d 395, 397 (Iowa 2007) (finding that employee had already been recommended for termination before the nurse's telephone call to warn manager of employee's intention to harm him). In Doe v. Central Iowa Health System, 766 N.W.2d 787, 792, n2 (Iowa 2009), the Court reviewed a claim based on negligent release of medical information by an employer and noted the plaintiff "never alleged a common law cause of action such as invasion of privacy." The Court affirmed entry of a post-verdict motion for the employer based on plaintiff's failure to show causation of his claimed emotional injury by negligent disclosure of medical records.

C. Criminal Records

Criminal identification files of law enforcement agencies are subject to the confidentiality provisions of Iowa's public records act. Iowa Code § 22.7(9). Records of current and prior arrests and criminal history files, however, are public records. Id. See Judicial Branch, State Ct. Admin'r v. Iowa Dist. Ct. for Linn County, 800 N.W.2d 569, 579 (Iowa 2011) (recognizing Iowa Code § 22.7(9) and holding Iowa Code Section 692.17(1), the Criminal History Data Act, does not require criminal cases that end in dismissal to be removed from the computerized ICIS docket or the Iowa Court online website). See also Iowa Code Chapters 692 and 907.

D. Subpoenas / Search Warrants

Iowa imposes no procedures or deadlines for service of a subpoena that apply specially to employees. But see generally Iowa Code §§ 622.70–71A (discussing witness compensation applicable to officers, peace officers, public officials, and volunteer fire fighters). Courts are, however, sensitive to quashing third-party subpoenas that implicate private employee information.

Rule 1.1701 of the Iowa Rules of Civil Procedure does not state a specific minimum time period between service of the subpoena and the date of the testimony or production. Rule 1.1701(2) states that a reasonable time must be given or the subpoena will be quashed. See generally Iowa. R. Civ. P. 1.1701(6). The attorney or party responsible for the issuing of a subpoena must take reasonable steps to avoid imposing undue burden or expense on the person subject to the subpoena. Iowa R. Civ. P. 1.1701(2)(a). An unduly burdensome subpoena will be modified or quashed by the court. Iowa R. Civ. P. 1.1701 (2)(c)(1) (noting the following as additional grounds for quashing or modifying a subpoena: the subpoena requires disclosure of privileged or protected matter, requires a non-party to travel beyond specified limits, or does not allow a reasonable time for compliance). If demanded, non-parties who are subpoenaed are entitled to receive in advance their witness fees and traveling fees to and from the court. Iowa Code § 622.74. Upon application, the clerk of court may issue a subpoena. Iowa

Code § 622.63. The subpoenaed party must object in writing to a subpoena to produce documents within 14 days of service, or before the time specified in the subpoena for compliance if such is less than 14 days. Iowa R. Civ. P. 1.1701(2)(b). If objection is made, the subpoenaing party is not entitled to inspection and copying of the documents in the absence of a court order, and a motion to compel can be filed at any time. Id. A motion to compel or motion to quash a subpoena should be filed with the court that issued it. Iowa R. Civ. P. 1.1701(2)(b), 2(c). If a motion to compel is filed, a motion to quash and alternative motion for protective order can be filed immediately along with a resistance to the motion to compel. See generally Iowa R. Civ. P. 1.504 (protective orders), 1.517 (motions to compel). See Iowa Code chapter 622 for additional provisions regarding subpoenas.

There is little Iowa authority addressing search warrants in the employment context, and this is particularly so with respect to warrants that seek to search employee files or workspace. See generally In re Inspection of Titan Tire, 637 N.W.2d 135 (Iowa 2001) (discussing employer's motion to quash state OSHA agency's administrative inspection warrant to conduct safety inspection at plant).

VII. ACTIONS SUBSEQUENT TO EMPLOYMENT

A. References

An employer or an employer's representative who acts reasonably in providing work-related information about a current or former employee of the employer is immune from civil liability. Iowa Code § 91B.2(1) (2010); see Hlubek v. Pelecky, 701 N.W.2d 93, 99 (Iowa 2005) (discussing applicable standards under Iowa Code § 91B.2 and holding that statute immunized defendant from liability for tortious interference claims); Lowe v. Todd's Flying Serv., Inc., No. 99-0708, 2001 WL 58113, at *3 (Iowa Ct. App. Jan. 24, 2001) (noting argument of former employee that release he signed in application for prospective employer releasing former employers from liability for furnishing information is against public policy and beyond the legislature's intent in § 91B.2, but declining to address issue because it was not properly preserved); Graham v. Contract Transp., Inc., 4-98-CV-90546, 2001 WL 740118, at *5–7 (S.D. Iowa Apr. 24, 2001) (holding in defamation action that former employer was immunized from liability for release of positive drug test results to plaintiff's prospective employers because there was no evidence it had acted unreasonably under Iowa Code § 91B.2; and holding that plaintiff's defamation claim was precluded by the releases he signed authorizing the publication of his drug test results to prospective employers because the releases specifically named the former employer as a party to be released); see also Haldeman v. Total Petroleum, Inc., 376 N.W.2d 98, 103 (Iowa 1985) (holding in defamation action that job reference statements made by former employer of terminated gas station cashier to prospective employer were protected by qualified privilege). An employer acts unreasonably if the information provided violates the employee's civil rights; is knowingly provided to a person with no legitimate interest in the work-related information; or the information does not pertain to the inquiry made, is provided with malice, or is provided without a good-faith belief in its truth. Iowa Code § 91B.2(2).

Any employer that attempts to "blacklist" a discharged or former employee or prevent such former employee from obtaining other employment shall be liable for treble damages. Iowa Code § 730.2; Conrad v. Iowa Central Community College , 756 N.W.2d 48 (Iowa Ct. App. 2008) (holding that the plain language of Iowa Code §730.2 indicates that it applies to both those employees who were discharged and to those who voluntarily left the employer's service). In addition, Iowa Code § 730.1 makes blacklisting a crime by providing: "If any person agent, company, or corporation, after having discharged any employee from service, shall prevent or attempt to prevent, by word or writing of any kind, such discharged employee from obtaining employment . . . except by furnishing in writing on request a truthful statement as to the cause of the person's discharge, such person, agent, company, or corporation shall be guilty of a serious misdemeanor and shall be liable for all damages sustained by any such person." See generally Iowa Code § 730.3.

Iowa Code § 730.5(12)(b) provides that a "cause of action for defamation, libel, slander, or damage to reputation shall not arise against an employer establishing a program of drug or alcohol testing" unless the employer discloses the test results to a third-party, the "test results disclosed incorrectly indicate the presence of alcohol or drugs," and the "employer negligently discloses the results."

B. Non-Compete Agreements

"Covenants not to compete, as a general rule, are enforceable in Iowa." Orkin Exterminating Co. v. Burnett, 146 N.W.2d 320, 324 (Iowa 1966); see also Cogley Clinic v. Martini, 112 N.W.2d 678, 681 (Iowa 1962). Continued employment for an indefinite period of time is sufficient consideration for a non-compete agreement. Phone Connection, Inc. v. Harbst, 494 N.W.2d 445, 449 (Iowa Ct. App. 1992) (citations omitted); Pro Edge, L.P. v. Gue, 374 F. Supp. 2d 711, 741 (N.D. Iowa 2005) (citation omitted). The "restriction placed on the employee must be no greater than necessary to protect the employer and may not create hardships on the employee out of proportion to the benefits the employer may be expected to gain."

Moore Bus. Forms, Inc. v. Wilson, 953 F. Supp. 1056, 1064 (N.D. Iowa 1996) (citation omitted). "The Iowa Supreme Court has determined that restrictive covenants are enforceable in the franchisor-franchisee context as well as the employer-employee context." Am. Express Fin. Advisors, Inc. v. Yantis, 358 F. Supp. 2d 818, 829 (N.D. Iowa 2005) (finding that a non-compete agreement between American Express and one of its former financial advisor employees was enforceable despite the franchisee's claim that he was acting as an independent businessman) (citing Casey's Gen. Stores, Inc. v. Campbell Oil Co., 441 N.W.2d 758 (Iowa 1989)). The Iowa courts use a three-part test to determine whether a non-compete agreement is enforceable: "(1) Is the restriction reasonably necessary for the protection of the employer's business; (2) is it unreasonably restrictive of the employee's rights; and (3) is it prejudicial to the public interest?" Lamp v. Am. Prosthetics, Inc., 379 N.W.2d 909, 910 (Iowa 1986) (citations omitted); see also Am. Express Fin. Advisors, Inc., 358 F. Supp. 2d at 829; Pro Edge, 374 F. Supp. 2d at 739; AMPC, Inc. v. Meyer, No. 02-0602, 2003 WL 21459665, at *2 (Iowa Ct. App. June 25, 2003) (citation omitted); White Pigeon Agency, Inc. v. Madden, No. 00-1189, 2001 WL 855366, at *4 (Iowa Ct. App. July 31, 2001) (citation omitted); Revere Transducers, Inc. v. Deere & Co., 595 N.W.2d 751, 760–61 (Iowa 1999) (citing Lamp, 379 N.W.2d at 909); Dan's Overhead Doors & More, Inc. v. Wennermark, No. 7-271, 2007 Iowa Ct. App. LEXIS 589, at *7–10 (Iowa Ct. App. May 23, 2007) (finding restrictive covenant was not reasonably necessary to protect employer's business where, *inter alia*, former employees did not possess "unique or extraordinary skills," and covenant was not reasonably necessary to protect employer's investment in employee training where there was no evidence of a direct loss of customers); Thrasher v. Grip-Tite Mfg. Co., Inc., 535 F. Supp. 2d 937, 943 (S.D. Iowa 2008). The Iowa courts "apply a reasonableness standard in maintaining a proper balance between the interests of the employer and the employee." AMPC, Inc., 2003 WL 21459665, at *2 (citation omitted). **The same three-part test is applied to both employer-employee agreements and agreements between business owners, however, agreements "between owners as ancillary to a purchase agreement are viewed with more indulgence." Sutton v. Iowa Trenchless, L.C., 808 N.W.2d 744, 749 (Iowa Ct. App. 2011).** In determining whether to enforce a covenant, courts consider "a variety of factors, including an employee's close proximity to customers and access to peculiar knowledge gained through employment that provides a means to pirate the customer, the nature of the business to be protected and the occupation to be restrained, the employee's access to information peculiar to the employer's business, the opportunity to take some part of the employer's goodwill, the reasonable expectations that some of the employer's customers will follow the employee to the new employment, and general matters of basic fairness." Moore Bus. Forms, Inc., 953 F. Supp. at 1064 (citations omitted); see also Dental East, P.C. v. Westercamp, 423 N.W.2d 553, 555 (Iowa Ct. App. 1988); Am. Express Fin. Advisors, Inc. v. Yantis, 358 F. Supp. 2d 818, 829 (N.D. Iowa 2005); Pro Edge, L.P. v. Gue, 374 F. Supp. 2d 711, 739 (N.D. Iowa 2005). With respect to the first prong, the employer bears the initial burden of showing that the covenant is reasonably necessary. Dental East, P.C., 423 N.W.2d at 555 (citations omitted). The second prong of the test considers the time and geographic restrictions. See Revere Transducers, Inc., 595 N.W.2d at 761 (citation omitted) ("We have stated that '[c]ovenants not to compete are unreasonably restrictive unless they are tightly limited as to both time and area.'"); see also Pro Edge, 374 F. Supp. 2d at 740 (noting that plaintiff's business of embryo transfer of livestock is a very specialized field for which a non-compete agreement with a 250-mile radius was reasonable and "adequately tailored to protect the customer base the plaintiffs have established"). It has been noted that "the duration of a restrictive covenant typically ranges from two to three years" and covenants "beyond five years have not been enforced." Phone Connection, Inc., 494 N.W.2d at 449–50 (citations omitted); see also Uncle B's Bakery, Inc. v. O'Rourke, 920 F. Supp. 1405, 1433 (N.D. Iowa 1996) (citations omitted) (stating that a five-year time period "is at the very limits of what Iowa courts have found enforceable"). In determining whether the time restriction is valid, at least one court has considered "relative youth and significant investment in development of [the employer's] unique processes." Uncle B's Bakery, Inc., 920 F. Supp. at 1433. "The restrictive covenant must bear some relation to the activities of the employee. It must not restrain his activities in a territory into which his former work had not taken him or given him the opportunity to enjoy undue advantage in later competition with his employer." Baker v. Starkey, 144 N.W.2d 889, 895 (Iowa 1966) (citation omitted). A restriction based on customers instead of geography has been upheld. See Moore Bus. Forms, Inc., 953 F. Supp. at 1068 (partially enforcing a covenant barring a former employee from selling to his former customers). With respect to the third prong, it has been held that a covenant was not prejudicial to the public interest because there were other competitors in the area to serve the public. Phone Connection, Inc., 494 N.W.2d at 449. In Board of Regents v. Warren, 760 N.W.2d 209, 2008 WL 5003750 (Iowa Ct. App. 2008), the Court of Appeals affirmed the district court's refusal to enforce a non-competition covenant against a physician because the public interest in health care would suffer if the doctor was not allowed to practice in an underserved county. In many cases, companies will seek injunctive relief to enforce their non-compete agreements and must therefore demonstrate a threat of irreparable harm. Iowa courts have found that "mere violation of a valid covenant not to compete supports an inference of the existence of a threat of irreparable harm." Pro Edge, 374 F. Supp. 2d at 749 (holding that the possibility of harm increases where the "largest and most premiere customers are located within the restricted area"); see also Am. Express Fin. Advisors, 358 F. Supp. 2d at 835 (finding that a former employee pirating financial advising customers would likely lead to irreparable harm unless the court granted injunctive relief).

VIII. OTHER ISSUES

A. Statutes of Limitations

Privacy claims, as injuries to person or reputation, are subject to the Iowa two-year statute of limitations. Iowa Code § 614.1(2). In Re Marriage of Tigges, 758 N.W.2d 824, 830 (Iowa 2008). The statute is subject to tolling for claims by minors. Iowa Code § 614.8(2); see also id. § 614.8(1) (extending statute of limitations for "persons with mental illness").

B. Jurisdiction

Absent applicability of a collective bargaining agreement or an arbitration clause, jurisdiction over an employment privacy claim would rest in the District Court.

C. Worker's Compensation Exclusivity

Iowa cases have proceeded with consideration of employee privacy claims based on the notion they are not preempted by the Iowa worker's compensation statute. See also discussion in Survey of Iowa Employment Libel Law, Part V.C.

D. Pleading Requirements

Each averment of a pleading shall be simple, concise, and direct. No technical forms of pleading are required. A party may set forth alternative theories of recovery and may state as many separate claims or defenses as it has regardless of consistency and whether based in law or equity. Iowa Rule of Civil Procedure 1.402. The Iowa Court of Appeals affirmed denial of an employee's motion to amend her petition to add a false light invasion of privacy claim against her employer, because the new claim would substantially change the issues and prejudice the defendants' preparation for trial. Cheek v. ABC Bev. Mfrs., Inc., No. 05-1962, 2006 WL 2560890, at *1–2 (Iowa Ct. App. Sept. 7, 2006) (unpublished) (employee's petition to amend came nearly three weeks after the close of pleadings and less than six weeks before trial).

SURVEY OF KANSAS EMPLOYMENT LIBEL LAW

David C. Vogel, Angela M. Tsevis, and Janelle L. Williams
Lathrop & Gage LLP
2345 Grand Boulevard
Kansas City, Missouri 64108
Telephone (816) 292-2000; Facsimile (816) 292-2001

(With Developments Reported Through **November 1, 2012**)

GENERAL COMMENTS

Kansas has two courts of precedent, the Supreme Court and the intermediate Court of Appeals, both of which are reported by the Kansas Supreme Court Reporter of Decisions. Cases from such courts are reported in the Kansas Reports and the Kansas Court of Appeals Reports, respectively. Parallel citations to these Kansas cases appear in the Pacific Reporter.

SIGNIFICANT DEVELOPMENTS SINCE THE 2012 *SURVEY*

None.

I. GENERAL LAW

A. General Employment Law

1. ***At Will Employment.*** Kansas remains an "employment at will" jurisdiction, meaning that absent an express or implied employment contract, "employees or employers may terminate an employment relationship at any time, for any reason." Campbell v. Husky Hogs, L.L.C., 255 P.3d 1 (Kan. 2011); Hughes v. Keath, 328 F. Supp. 2d 1161, 1164 (D. Kan 2004) (applying Kansas law). This general rule is subject to exceptions where the termination is deemed to be in contravention of a public policy of the state. See Ortega v. IBP. Inc., 255 Kan. 513, 874 P.2d 1188 (1994); Hysten v. Burlington Northern Santa Fe Ry. Co., 277 Kan. 551, 85 P.3d 1183 (2004); Wells v. Accredo Health Group, Inc., 2006 WL 1913140, *3 (D. Kan. 2006) (applying Kansas law)("Absent a clear mandate of public policy . . . plaintiff cannot establish a retaliatory discharge case."). To establish an exception to the at will rule, an employee "must show . . . that no alternative state or federal remedy exists." Lasley v. Hershey Foods Corp., 35 F. Supp. 2d 1319 (D. Kan. 1999) (applying Kansas law); Flenker v. Willamette Industries, Inc., 266 Kan. 198, 967 P.2d 295 (1999).

B. Elements of Libel Claim

1. ***Basic Elements.*** Under Kansas law, the tort of defamation includes both slander and libel. Batt v. Globe Eng'g Co., 13 Kan. App. 2d 500, 774 P.2d 371 (1989). "[T]he elements of the tort of defamation are: (1) false and defamatory words, (2) communicated to a third person, (3) which result in harm to the reputation of the person defamed." McCauley v. Raytheon Travel Air Co., 152 F. Supp. 2d 1276, 1276 (D. Kan. 2001); see also Lloyd v. Quorum Health Resources, 77 P.3d 993, 1000 (Kan. 2003); Folkers v. Am. Massage Therapy Ass'n Inc., 2004 U.S. Dist. LEXIS 2156 (D. Kan.) (applying Kansas law). "Under Kansas law, defamatory words are those which tend to diminish the esteem, respect, goodwill, or confidence in which the plaintiff is held, or to excite adverse, derogatory, or unpleasant feelings or opinion against her." Heckman v. Zurich Holding Co. of America, 2007 U.S. Dist. LEXIS 14720 (D. Kan) at *23 (citing Woodmont Corp. v. Rockwoods Ctr. P'ship, 811 F. Supp. 1478, 1487 (D. Kan. 1993)). The Kansas Court of Appeals has held that Kansas no longer draws the traditional *per se*/*per quod* distinctions for defamation claims, stating that, "any plaintiff in a defamation action must allege and prove actual damages and may no longer rely on the theory of presumed damages." Zoeller v. American Family Mut. Ins. Co., 17 Kan.App.2d 223, 229 (1992). However, the Federal District Court for the District of Kansas recently recognized a defamation *per se* claim, which does not require proof of special damages. See Heckman v. Zurich Holding Co. of America, 2007 U.S. Dist. LEXIS 14720 (D. Kan.). Additionally, "[w]hen a plaintiff's reputation is so diminished at the time of publication of the allegedly defamatory material that only nominal damages at most could be awarded because the person's reputation was not capable of sustaining further harm, the plaintiff is deemed libel-proof as a matter of law and is not permitted to burden a defendant with a trial." Lamb v. Rizzo, 391 F.3d 1133, 1137 (10th Cir. 2005) (holding Kansas Supreme Court would adopt libel-proof plaintiff doctrine).

2. ***Fault.***

a. **Private Figure Plaintiff/Matter of Public Concern.** The Kansas Supreme Court has indicated in dicta that regardless of the status of the plaintiff, actual malice on the part of the defendant is required in any case involving matters of public concern. Knudsen v. Kansas Gas and Electric Co., 248 Kan. 469, 807 P.2d 71 (1991). In Bosley v. Home Box Office, Inc., 59 F. Supp. 2d 1147 (D. Kan. 1999), a federal district court applying Kansas law held that a broadcast by a cable television network of footage from "an anti-drug protest designed to combat the selling of illegal drugs" was a newsworthy event that involved a matter of public concern, and although the court did not reach the question whether the plaintiff was a public figure, it held that he could not recover unless he could demonstrate the publication was made with actual malice.

b. **Private Figure Plaintiff/Matter of Private Concern.** In defamation cases involving private figures and matters of private concern, negligence is the apparent standard of liability in Kansas. Sellars v. Stauffer Communications, Inc., 9 Kan. App. 2d 573, 684 P.2d 450 (1984), aff'd, 236 Kan. 697, 695 P.2d 812 (1985).

c. **Public Figure Plaintiff/Matter of Public Concern.** Where the plaintiff is a public figure, Kansas adopts the precedent of the United States Supreme Court and holds that a plaintiff must prove the defendant acted with actual malice, i.e., knowledge of or reckless disregard as to the falsity of the publication at issue. See, e.g., Redmond v. Sun Publishing Co., 239 Kan. 30, 716 P.2d 168 (1986); Hein v. Lacy, 228 Kan. 249, 616 P.2d 277 (1980); Busey v. Bd. of County Commr's of Shawnee County, 116 P.3d 55, *5 (Kan. App. 2005) (applying actual malice standard in invasion of privacy action).

3. ***Falsity.*** As discussed below, truth is a complete privilege to a defamation claim. In addition, "where the . . . statements are substantially true, there is no liability . . . ." Ruebke v. Globe Communications Corp., 241 Kan. 595, 738 P.2d 1246 (1987) (emphasis added). Although some cases refer to truth as a defense available to defendants, Id., Kansas courts generally seem to place the burden of proving falsity on the plaintiff. Munsell v. Ideal Food Stores, 208 Kan. 909, 494 P.2d 1063 (1972).

4. ***Defamatory Statement of Fact.*** No cases.

5. ***Of and Concerning Plaintiff.*** To be actionable, the alleged defamatory publication must be about and concerning the plaintiff. Hanrahan v. Horn, 232 Kan. 531, 657 P.2d 561 (1983). The language of the defamatory statement should be such that those who hear or read it should, in light of the surrounding circumstances, be able to understand that it referred to the plaintiff. State v. Mayberry, 33 Kan. 441, 6 P. 553 (1885).

6. ***Publication.***

a. **Intracorporate Communication.** "Remarks made in the course and scope of employment by one corporate employee and communicated to a second corporate employee concerning the job performance of a third employee constitute publication for the purposes of a defamation action against a corporate employer." Luttrell v. United Telephone System, Inc., 9 Kan. App. 2d 620, 683 P.2d 1292 (1984), aff'd, 236 Kan. 710, 695 P.2d 1279 (1985).

b. **Compelled Self-Publication.** Courts applying Kansas law have held that otherwise "voluntary" statements which a former employee makes to potential employers regarding the reason for his or her discharge by a previous employer constitute communication by the former employer. Polson v. Davis, 635 F. Supp. 1130 (D. Kan. 1986) (applying Kansas law), aff'd, 895 F.2d 705 (10th Cir. 1990). "Although a plaintiff's truly voluntary communication of a defamatory statement bars all recovery, a coerced repetition of the defamatory statement by the plaintiff has no such effect." Id. Where a terminated plaintiff seeks reemployment, she is "effectively coerced" into repeating the allegedly defamatory reasons for her termination; if she does not seek reemployment, she has failed to mitigate her damages, but by seeking such employment, she must either repeat the reasons for leaving her previous job or lie to her potential employers. Id. See also Booth v. Electronic Data Systems Corp., 799 F. Supp. 1086 (D. Kan. 1992) (applying Kansas law and holding that "voluntary statements to potential future employers made by the plaintiff/employee constitute publication by the defendant for purposes of sustaining a defamation claim").

A plaintiff must apparently specifically plead compelled self-publication in her complaint in order to make a viable claim on this issue. In Gearhart v. Sears, Roebuck & Co., 27 F. Supp. 2d 1263 (D. Kan. 1998) (applying Kansas law), the court granted the employer's motion for summary judgment despite the plaintiff's claim that she suffered damages after relaying the reasons for her termination to a potential employer at a job fair. The court held that the harm came "from [the plaintiff's] own statement" and that the plaintiff's failure to plead any harm resulting from her own compelled statements was irrelevant as such statements were not set out in her complaint.

c. **Republication.** "When [a] third person . . . communicates the original defamatory statement to a fourth person, it is called republication or repetition. Republication of a libel is a separate tort which creates a separate basis of liability against the republisher. The original publisher may also be liable for republication if repetition by third persons was reasonably expected as the natural and probable consequence of the original publication." Wright v. Bachmurski, 29 Kan. App. 2d 595, 601, 29 P.3d 979 (2001) (internal citations omitted).

7. ***Statements versus Conduct.*** The Tenth Circuit, applying Kansas law, addressed this distinction in Hall v. Hercules, Inc., 494 F.2d 420 (10th Cir. 1974), in which an employee alleged that his employer's multiple requests that the employee come to company offices to be questioned about a bomb threat in view of other employees constituted slander. Although the court did not specifically address the issue whether an employer's conduct can constitute defamation, it held that the company's action toward the plaintiff "was well within" an employer's privilege to interrogate employees in the course of an investigation into criminal conduct. Id. Finding no evidence of actual malice, the court affirmed the district court's entry of judgment notwithstanding the verdict in the employer's favor. Id.

8. ***Damages.*** A plaintiff who pleads that his or her reputation has been injured due to an allegedly defamatory publication is apparently entitled to damages for pecuniary losses as well as general compensatory damages for mental distress provided the plaintiff can show injury to reputation. Gobin v. Globe Publishing Co., 232 Kan. 1, 649 P.2d 1239 (1982); Gomez v. Hug, 7 Kan. App. 2d 603, 645 P.2d 916 (1982). A plaintiff must specifically set forth the nature of any punitive damages in the complaint. Kan. Stat. Ann. § 60-209(g). The total amount of noneconomic or general damages recoverable by a party from all defendants may not exceed $250,000. Kan. Stat. Ann. § 60-19a02.

A handful of recent cases applying Kansas law have held that in order to avoid summary judgment, a plaintiff must provide evidence supporting an allegation that his reputation was damaged as a result of the alleged defamation, and a mere allegation in the plaintiff's pleading is insufficient. See Bosley v. Home Box Office, Inc., 59 F. Supp. 2d 1147 (D. Kan. 1999) (applying Kansas law); Dominguez v. Davidson, 266 Kan. 926, 974 P.2d 112 (1999) (employer and supervisor entitled to summary judgment on defamation claims where "record is devoid of evidence of such a nature that would show how plaintiff's reputation in the community of his residence has been affected," letter to employer stating that plaintiff's "family and friends believe [employer] treated him unfairly" does not qualify as evidence of damage to reputation). See also Hall v. Kansas Farm Bureau, 50 P.3d 495, 504 (Kan. 2002) ("[d]amages recoverable for defamation, whether per se or not, [cannot] be presumed but must be proven"); McCauley v. Raytheon Travel Air. Co., 152 F. Supp. 2d 1267, 1277 (D. Kan. 2001) (plaintiff must provide evidence which links false statement to inability to gain employment). "Under Kansas law, damages to reputation are not presumed and must be proved regardless of the type of libel or slander. Smith v. Associates Ltd. Partnership, 225 F. Supp. 2d 1293, 1303 (D. Kan. 2002). However, "[i]njuries to one's sensitivities is not enough to support a claim for defamation; a plaintiff must show how his or her true reputation in the community of his or her residence has been affected." Id. **Debord v. Mercy Health System of Kansas, 2012 WL 941387, *12 (D. Kan. March 20, 2012) ("A victim's own observations may be suitable as proof of harm to his reputation for defamation cases in Kansas, but they must raise a reasonable inference that the damage was caused by the plaintiff's statements.").**

In St. Catherine Hospital v. Rodriguez, 25 Kan. App. 2d 763, 971 P.2d 754 (1998), the court dismissed a doctor's claim that his reputation had been damaged by plaintiff. The physician had failed to controvert facts alleging "that his true representation in the community was not affected" by the statements. Although the plaintiff claimed that the number of referrals from other doctors to his department had dropped, thus proving damage to his reputation, the court noted that he did not dispute the hospital's contentions that no physician or hospital administrator had told him they had less respect for his abilities, no other physician had seen a copy of the report, and no one in the general public had indicated a loss of respect for him. The plaintiff did not identify any witness who would testify that the plaintiff's reputation had been damaged, and although a party opposing summary judgment "is not required to prove its case," the party "must set forth specific facts showing that there is a specific issue for trial."

Even "unquestionably thin" evidence as to damage to a plaintiff's reputation, however, may stave off summary judgment. The Kansas Supreme Court has held that a plaintiff's interrogatory responses stating that a decrease in requests for his professional participation in events followed the defendants' statements, along with deposition testimony from an acquaintance and a former colleague that they considered the plaintiff "in a questionable light" or were "concerned about [the plaintiff's] practice" after reading the statements, is sufficient to avoid the entry of summary judgment. Moran v. State of Kansas, 267 Kan. 583, 985 P.2d 127 (1999). See also Edwards & Assocs. v. Black & Veatch, 84 F. Supp. 2d 1182, 1203 (D. Kan. 2000) (noting that plaintiff's "weak" evidence of damage to reputation, consisting primarily of an affidavit that since the alleged defamation there had been a "virtual absence" of request for services, was enough to prevent summary judgment).

a. **Presumed Damages and Libel Per Se.** The Court of Appeals of Kansas has held that Kansas has abrogated the distinction between the two types of defamation and now requires every plaintiff to "show how his or her true reputation in the community of his or her residence has been affected." Lindemuth v. Goodyear Tire and Rubber Co., 19 Kan. App. 2d 95, 864 P.2d 744 (1993). See also Zoeller v. American Family Mut. Ins. Co., 17 Kan.App.2d 223, 229 (1992). However, a plaintiff need not present expert testimony proving that he suffered "quantifiable monetary loss" in the form of actual damages in order to recover. Moran v. State of Kansas, 267 Kan. 583 (1999). Despite the holding from the Court of Appeals of Kansas that defamation *per se* is no longer a cognizable claim, the Federal District Court for the District of Kansas recently permitted such a claim, holding that, "statements which impute plaintiff's unfitness for her trade or profession" are defamatory *per se* and do not require proof of special damages. Heckman v. Zurich Holding Co. of America, 2007 U.S. Dist. LEXIS 14720 (D. Kan) at *25.

(1) **Employment-Related Criticism.** A federal district court applying Kansas law has held that a statement that a former city employee was terminated for "unprofessional conduct" "directly impugns plaintiff's fitness for her profession" and therefore could constitute libel per se. Polson v. Davis, 635 F. Supp. 1130 (D. Kan. 1986), aff'd, 895 F.2d 705 (10th Cir. 1990). A statement in a service letter that a plaintiff was terminated "due to his lack of availability for work," however, "can in no way be viewed as libelous *per se*" despite the plaintiff's argument that it implied he was "tardy, continually absent, lazy, incompetent, or otherwise in violation of the work ethic." Richters v. Rollins Protective Service Co., 442 F. Supp. 941 (D. Kan. 1977) (applying Kansas law).

(2) **Single Instance Rule.** While Kansas courts have never considered the single publication rule, two federal courts have predicted the state would apply it. Rinsley v. Brandt, 446 F. Supp. 850 (D. Kan. 1977); Fouts v. Fawcett Publications, 116 F. Supp. 535 (D. Conn. 1953). See also Wright v. Bachmurski, 29 P.3d 979 (Kan. Ct. App. 2001) (court of appeals discussed defendants' assertion of single publication rule, yet found it inapplicable to specific facts of case).

b. **Punitive Damages.** If a plaintiff is able to prove actual malice on the part of the defendant, punitive damages are available. Gobin v. Globe Publishing Co., 216 Kan. 223, 531 P.2d 76 (1975). A federal court interpreting Kansas law has held that a plaintiff also must show entitlement to compensatory damages for punitive damages to be available. Mid-America Food Services v. ARA Services, 578 F.2d 691 (8th Cir. 1978). The nature of such damages must be specifically stated in the complaint, but no dollar amount shall be set forth. Kan. Stat. Ann. § 60-209(g). Under Kansas law, a jury determines whether punitive damages should be awarded, while the court determines the amount. A statutory cap precludes any punitive damage award from exceeding the lesser of 1) the defendant's annual gross income or 2) $5 million, unless the profitability of the defendant's misconduct exceeds the limitation and in that case the limitation shall be 1 ½ times the amount of profit gained by the defendant's misconduct.

II. PRIVILEGES AND DEFENSES

A. Scope of Privileges

1. ***Absolute Privilege.*** "An absolute privilege in defamation actions is recognized 'in cases where the public service or the administration of justice requires complete immunity, as in legislative, executive, or judicial proceedings, the occasion for the immunity being not so much for those engaged as for the promotion of the public welfare.'" Polson v. Davis, 635 F. Supp. 1130 (1986) (quoting Bradford v. Mahan, 219 Kan. 450, 454, 548 P.2d 1223, 1228 (1976)), aff'd, 895 F.2d 705 (10th Cir. 1990). Kansas state courts construe the absolute privilege narrowly. Id. "The standard [for absolute privilege] is whether the communication [i]s relevant to an issue involved in the judicial proceeding." Bethea v. Wells Fargo Bank, N.A., 2010 WL 4868180, *8 (D. Kan. November 23, 2010) (applying Kansas law).

However, it appears that the absolute privilege would apply to statements made by employers in the context of resolving a grievance filed by an employee pursuant to a collective bargaining agreement as a matter of federal labor law. See General Motors Corp. v. Mendicki, 367 F.2d 66 (10th Cir. 1966) ("statements made either by representatives of management or by representatives of an employee at a conference and bargaining session having for its purpose the adjustment of a grievance of the employee or other peaceable disposition of such grievance are unqualifiedly privileged"); Hasten v. Phillips Petroleum Co., 640 F.2d 274 (10th Cir. 1981)(written discharge notice to employee within scope of absolute privilege where notice "was a part of the entire proceeding contemplated by the provisions of the agreement for the grievance machinery"). But see Munsell v. Ideal Food Stores, 208 Kan. 909, 494 P.2d 1063 (1972) (communication by employer of reasons for former employee's discharge to employee's union "was qualifiedly or conditionally privileged").

Moreover, "statements made in quasi-judicial proceedings before an administrative body" such as those made in a state unemployment compensation hearing, also "are absolutely privileged and cannot serve as a basis for a defamation action." Batt v. Globe Engineering Co., 13 Kan. App. 2d 500, 774 P.2d 371 (1989). See also Wilkinson v. Shoney's, 4 P.3d 1149, 1169 (Kan. 2000) (noting that statements at quasi-judicial proceedings are absolutely privileged).

2. ***Qualified Privileges.***

a. **Common Interest.** Kansas courts have applied a qualified privilege to a broad array of employment related communications. Numerous cases set forth the general rule that "[a] communication is qualifiedly privileged if it is made in good faith on any subject matter in which the person communicating has an interest . . . if it is made to a person having a corresponding interest . . . ." Lutrell v. United Telephone Service, Inc., 9 Kan. App. 2d 620, 683 P.2d 1292 (1984), aff'd, 236 Kan. 710, 695 P.2d 1279 (1985). "The essential elements of a qualifiedly privileged communication are good faith, an interest to be upheld, a statement limited in its scope to the upholding of such interest and publication in a proper manner only to proper parties." Naab v. Inland Container Corp., 877 F. Supp. 546 (D. Kan. 1994) (applying Kansas law). In Moreland v. Perkins, Smart, & Boyd, Inc., 240 P.3d 601 (Kan. Ct. App. 2010), the court held that an employer's statements, contained in a mandatory disclosure form, regarding the reasons for an employee's termination were entitled to a qualified privilege.

b. **Duty.** The qualified privilege set forth above applies with equal force when the communication at issue is between actors with corresponding duties in the subject matter. See Lutrell v. United Telephone Service, Inc., 9 Kan. App. 2d 620, 683 P.2d 1292 (1984), aff'd, 236 Kan. 710, 695 P.2d 1279 (1985) (communication is qualifiedly privileged where the subject matter of the communication is one in which the speaker has a duty "if it is made to a person having a corresponding . . . duty"); see also Lloyd v. Quorum Health Resources, 77 P.3d 993, 1000-01. The elements of the qualified privilege are identical to those set forth in Section II(A)(2)(a).

c. **Criticism of Public Employee**. Both Gomez v. Hug, 7 Kan. App. 2d 603, 645 P.2d 916 (1982) and Polson v. Davis, 635 F. Supp. 1130 (D. Kan. 1986), aff'd, 895 F.2d 705 (10th Cir. 1990) involve defamation claims by employees of governmental entities, but neither case suggests that the qualified privilege regarding employment communications is expanded or limited in this context. In Conway v. City of Wichita, 1996 U.S. Dist. LEXIS 19626 (D. Kan.), the court found that the qualified privilege protected the defendants, yet reiterated the privilege would have been removed had the communication been made with actual malice.

In Moran v. State of Kansas, 267 Kan. 583, 985 P.2d 127 (1999), the Kansas Supreme Court stated that government employees are not immune from liability for claims of defamation under the "discretionary function exception" of K.S.A. 1998 Supp. 75-6104(e) where they act with actual malice.

d. **Limitation on Qualified Privileges.**

(1) **Constitutional or Actual Malice.** The qualified privilege may be overcome if the statement was made with actual malice, in that the speaker "acted with knowledge of falsity or reckless disregard for the truth." Lutrell v. United Telephone Service, Inc., 9 Kan. App. 2d 620, 683 P.2d 1292 (1984), aff'd, 236 Kan. 710, 695 P.2d 1279 (1985). It is the employee's burden to "present extrinsic proof of actual malice." Batt v. Globe Engineering Co., 13 Kan. App. 2d 500, 774 P.2d 371 (1989). See also Donnell v. HCA Health Services of Kansas, Inc., 29 Kan. App. 2d 426, 433, 28 P.3d 420 (2001) (holding that K.S.A. 65-422 grants immunity in the peer review process by hospitals of staff physicians so long as "the actions by the peer review group were taken in good faith and without malice"); Davis v. Hildyard, 113 P.3d 827, 830-31 (Kan. App. 2005) (same).

In any event, the privilege is not overcome merely by an employer's failure to conduct an investigation to determine the truth or falsity of the allegedly defamatory statement so long as "there are no circumstances that are reasonably sufficient to put the defendant on notice that an imputation, which he reasonably believes to be true, is false." Dobbyn v. Nelson, 2 Kan. App. 2d 358, 579 P.2d 721 (1978) (quoting 50 Am. Jur. 2d, Libel and Slander § 198). Moreover, a claim that an employer acted with malice in making statements about the reasons for an employee's termination may be "negated" where the employer conducts an investigation into the alleged conduct at issue. See Dominguez v. Davidson, 266 Kan. 926, 974 P.2d 112 (1999).

Kansas courts have expressed reticence to grant summary judgment where a defendant's intent is at issue for purposes of determining actual malice. "A court should be cautious in granting a motion for summary judgment when resolution of the dispositive issue necessitates a determination of the state of mind of one or both of the parties." Smith v. Farha, 266 Kan. 991, 974 P.2d 563 (1999) (internal citations and quotations omitted). In Smith, the Kansas Supreme Court reversed a district court's grant of summary judgment for a member of a hospital's quality assurance committee, holding that a defendant in a defamation case is not entitled to summary judgment merely because he asserts that he published the statements at issue with a belief that they were true. In addition, the court noted that the defendant had failed to address the issues of malice or good faith in the uncontroverted facts of his summary judgment motion. See also Koehler v. Hunter Care Centers, Inc., 6 F. Supp. 2d 1237 (D. Kan. 1998) (applying Kansas law) (holding that genuine issue of material fact as to whether hospital acted in good faith in making statements to board of nursing regarding former employee precluded summary judgment on issue of malice). "Courts should be cautious when granting summary judgment on issues which necessitate a determination of a party's state of mind." Hill v. Perrone, 42 P.3d 210, 214 (Kan. App. 2002).

(2) **Common Law Malice.** No reported cases in Kansas suggest a plaintiff employee must show common law malice on the part of an employer to overcome a qualified privilege.

e. **Question of Fact or Law.** "It is the court's responsibility to make the initial determination that a statement is capable of a defamatory meaning." Hobson v. Coastal Corp., 962 F. Supp. 1407 (D. Kan.

1997) (applying Kansas law). "In performing this function, the court must consider all the circumstances surrounding the communication." Id. (citing Restatement (Second) of Torts § 614 cmt. a (1989)).

"The determination of whether a conditional privilege exists is a matter of law for the court when the facts upon which such a determination must stand are undisputed." Dobbyn v. Nelson, 2 Kan. App. 2d 358, 579 P.2d 721 (1978). Whether the speaker acted with actual malice is generally a question of fact for a jury, although the issue may be resolved on summary judgment "[i]f the plaintiff fails to offer clear and convincing evidence of an extrinsic character to prove actual malice on the part of the defendant." Naab v. Inland Container Corp., 877 F. Supp. 546 (D. Kan. 1994) (quoting Knudsen v. Kansas Gas & Elec. Co., 248 Kan. 469, 807 P.2d 71 (1991)).

f. **Burden of Proof.** It is apparently an employer's burden to raise the existence of a privilege. See Edwards & Assocs. v. Black & Veatch, L.L.P., 84 F. Supp. 2d 1182 (D. Kan. 2000) ("the qualified privilege defense is an affirmative one, and as such, must be preserved in the answer to a complaint or, at the very least, in the pretrial order"). In any event, it is a plaintiff employee's burden to plead and prove the existence of actual malice in order to overcome the privilege. Polson v. Davis, 635 F. Supp. 1130 (D. Kan. 1986) (applying Kansas law), aff'd, 895 f.2d 705 (10th Cir. 1990). Moreover, a plaintiff "must also present sufficient evidence for a reasonable factfinder to find that the statement is false" even at the summary judgment stage. Hobson v. Coastal Corp., 962 F. Supp. 1407 (D. Kan. 1997) (applying Kansas law).

B. Standard Libel Defenses

1. ***Truth.*** Truth continues to be a valid defense to a defamation action under Kansas law. Castleberry v. Boeing Co., 880 F. Supp. 1435 (D. Kan. 1995) (applying Kansas law). As discussed above in Section I(B)(3), substantial truth also entitles the publisher to a privilege defense.

2. ***Opinion.*** Courts interpreting Kansas law have adopted broad privileges for statements of opinion. Rinsley v. Brandt, 700 F.2d 1304 (10th Cir. 1983); Hein v. Lacy, 228 Kan. 249, 616 P.2d 277 (1980). No employment defamation cases appear to analyze the opinion defense.

3. ***Consent.*** At least one case suggests that in addition to the qualified privilege applicable to employment references (now codified by statute, see Section III(C)), a plaintiff may be barred from recovering for an allegedly defamatory employment reference because of the employee's actual or implied consent to the communication. See Turner v. Halliburton Co., 240 Kan. 1, 722 P.2d at 1106 (1986). See also Munsell v. Ideal Food Stores, 208 Kan. 909, 494 P.2d 1063 (1972) ("where a plaintiff voluntarily participates in the publication of a defamatory statement . . . the defamation is deemed to be the result of his own voluntary act.").

4. ***Mitigation.*** No reported Kansas case involves mitigation of damages in the employment context. Under common law, however, a retraction of or apology following the statement may allow a defendant to mitigate damages. Sweaney v. United Loan & Finance Co., 205 Kan. 66, 468 P.2d 124 (1970).

III. RECURRING FACT PATTERNS

A. Statements in Personnel File

In Polson v. Davis, 635 F. Supp. 1130 (D. Kan. 1986), aff'd, 895 F.2d 705 (10th Cir. 1990), a federal district court addressed whether a notice of termination placed in an employee's personnel file which stated she had been terminated for "unprofessional conduct" could constitute defamation under Kansas law. Although the statement was protected by qualified privilege, plaintiff's assertions that the publisher of the statement "told her he would ruin her reputation and that she would never again function as a professional in the community" created a triable issue as to whether the defendant made the statement with actual malice, thereby defeating the privilege. Id. Thus, the court denied defendant's motion for summary judgment on plaintiff's defamation claim.

In Bell v. Bd. of County Comm'rs, 2004 U.S. Dist. LEXIS 5100 (D. Kan.), a federal district court considered whether placing a termination letter in an employee's personnel file constituted "publication" for First Amendment liberty interest purposes. Although the statements made in the termination letter were shielded from disclosure by Kansas' Open Records Act, the employee handbook provided county commissioners and department heads with access to all personnel files. Id. at *52. Following Tenth Circuit guidance, the United States District Court for the District of Kansas held that "the alleged stigmatizing statement was made and published in the course of plaintiff's termination." Accordingly, the court denied defendant's motion for summary judgment. Id. at *53.

B. Performance Evaluations

"Kansas law recognizes defamation claims in the context of statements by managerial employees concerning an employee's job performance." Arnold v. Air Midwest, Inc., 877 F. Supp. 1452 (D. Kan. 1995) (applying Kansas law), aff'd,

100 F.3d 857 (10th Cir. 1996). The qualified privilege is available to employers defending against defamation claims from employees arising from comments about the job performance of those employees. "By virtue of the qualified privilege, the employer who is evaluating . . . an employee in good faith and within the bounds of the employment relationship is protected from the threat of defamation suits by the enhanced burden of proof which the plaintiff would have to bear." Lutrell v. United Telephone Service, Inc., 9 Kan. App. 2d 620, 683 P.2d 1292 (1984), aff'd, 236 Kan. 710, 695 P.2d 1279 (1985). In Naab v. Inland Container Corp., 877 F. Supp. 546 (D. Kan. 1994) (applying Kansas law), a plaintiff employee could not show actual malice in a supervisor's performance appraisal when he admitted that the supervisor "carefully and conscientiously prepared the performance appraisal."

In the context of medical professionals, K.S.A. 65-442 "provides for a qualified privilege from liability for those statements made by any member of a medical staff committee, such as a peer review committee, in the furtherance of his or her duties, provided that those statements were made in good faith and without malice." Smith v. Farha, 266 Kan. 991, 974 P.2d 563 (1999). See also Donnell v. HCA Health Servs. of State, 28 P.3d 420 (Kan. App. 2001) (defendant immune from liability where peer review proceedings were conducted without bad faith or malice); Davis v. Hildyard, 113 P.3d 827, 830-31 (Kan. Ct. App. 2005) (same).

C. References

For many years, the common law qualified privilege protected statements made by a plaintiff's former employer to potential employers. See Turner v. Halliburton Co., 240 Kan. 1, 722 P.2d 1106 (1986); Hobson v. Coastal Corp., 962 F. Supp. 1407 (D. Kan. 1997) (applying Kansas law) (employer "is qualifiedly privileged to discuss a former employee's employment history with other prospective employers"). In 1995, the Kansas Legislature codified this principle by enacting Kan. Stat. Ann. 44-119a(a), which states in pertinent part that an employer "who discloses information about a current or former employee to a prospective employer of the employee shall be qualifiedly immune from civil liability." The statute provides absolute immunity to an employer who releases information about an employee's date of employment, pay level, job description and duties and wage history. Kan. Stat. Ann. 44-119a(b). Moreover, a current or former employer also may be protected by absolute liability from disclosing written evaluations of the employee and whether the employee's termination was voluntary and the reasons for it, so long as the employer is responding in writing to a written request from a prospective employer. Kan. Stat. Ann. 44-119a(c).

D. Intracorporate Communication

As set forth generally above, statements in the employment context may be qualifiedly privileged so long as they are made in good faith, on a subject matter in which the publisher has an interest, do not exceed the scope of the interest to be upheld, and are published "in a proper manner only to proper parties." See, e.g., Castleberry v. Boeing Co., 880 F. Supp. 1435 (D. Kan. 1995) (applying Kansas law). In Castleberry, for example, the court held that an employer's statements to several management employees about the reasons for the termination of two other management employees were protected by the qualified privilege. Id. at 1443-44. The Kansas Court of Appeals has set forth this position in more expansive language, declaring that statements by an employee's supervisor "regarding business or employment made in good faith to other . . . managerial employees were protected by a qualified privilege." Batt v. Globe Engineering Co., 13 Kan. App. 2d 500, 774 P.2d 371 (1989) (plaintiff's defamation claim based on contents of employee separation notice). **See also Haggins v. Liberti, 2011 WL 6740542, *9 (D. Kan. December 22, 2011) (Kansas law affords a qualified privilege to employers who make limited publication of defamatory material for good faith business purposes, even if the information is inaccurate).**

E. Statements to Government Regulators

"Statements made in quasi-judicial proceedings before an administrative body" such as those made in a state unemployment compensation hearing, also "are absolutely privileged and cannot serve as a basis for a defamation action." Batt v. Globe Engineering Co., 13 Kan. App. 2d 500, 774 P.2d 371 (1989). Wilkinson v. Shoney's, 4 P.3d 1149, 1169 (Kan. 2000) (noting that statements at quasi-judicial proceedings are absolutely privileged); Jarvis v. Drake, 250 Kan. 645, 830 P.2d 23 (1992) (attorney discipline proceedings); Clear Water Truck Co. v. M. Bruenger & Co., Inc., 214 Kan. 139, 519 P.2d 682 (1974) (Interstate Commerce Commission). But see Moreland v. Perkins, Smart, & Boyd, Inc., 240 P.3d 601 (Kan. Ct. App. 2010) (statements by employer in a Form U-5 submitted to the Financial Industry Regulatory Authority indicating reasons for employee's termination were entitled to qualified privilege only, and not absolute privilege, under Kansas statutory and common law).

F. Reports to Auditors and Insurers

No reported Kansas case involves reports to auditors or insurers.

G. Vicarious Liability of Employers for Statements Made by Employees

1. ***Scope of Employment.*** "A corporation may be liable for the defamatory utterances of its agent which are made within the scope of his authority." Nat'l Motor Club of America v. Auto Club of America, 2003 WL 715902, *4 (D. Kan. 2003); see also Lutrell v. United Telephone Service, Inc., 9 Kan. App. 2d 620, 683 P.2d 1292 (1984), aff'd, 236 Kan. 710, 695 P.2d 1279 (1985). A union, however, is not vicariously liable for the statements of a plaintiff's coworkers who happen to be union members so long as the coworkers "were not representatives or agents of the union." Witt v. Roadway Express, 880 F. Supp. 1455 (D. Kan. 1995)

a. **Blogging.** No reported Kansas case involves the issue of employers' liability for comments on employees' blogs.

2. ***Damages.*** No reported Kansas case involves the issue of damages in a vicarious liability context.

H. Internal Investigations

In Kansas, the qualified privilege protects employers conducting internal investigations to an extent. "[T]he employer who is evaluating or investigating an employee in good faith and within the bounds of the employment relationship is protected from the threat of defamation suits…." Lutrell v. United Telephone Service, Inc., 9 Kan. App. 2d 620, 683 P.2d 1292 (1984), aff'd, 236 Kan. 710, 695 P.2d 1279 (1985). The employee bears an enhanced burden of proof to overcome the privilege. See II.A.2.d.(1), supra.

IV. OTHER ACTIONS BASED ON STATEMENTS

A. Negligent Hiring, Retention and Supervision

"Kansas law recognizes a claim by non-employee third parties for negligent supervision and retention." Bryan v. Eichenwald, 2001 U.S. Dist. LEXIS 9920 (D. Kan.), at *22 (citing Kan. State Bank & Trust Co. v. Specialized Transp. Serv., Inc., 819 P.2d 587, 598 (1991)); Dolquist v. Heartland Presbytery, 2004 U.S. Dist. LEXIS 469 (D. Kan.) (applying Kansas law) (also suggesting that Kansas courts may recognize a claim for *intentional* failure to supervise). Liability "lies when an employer has reason to believe that undue risk of harm exists as a result of the employment of the alleged tortfeasor." Bryan, 2001 U.S. Dist. LEXIS, at *22. "A claim for negligent supervision requires that any harm sustained by the plaintiff was foreseeable by the employer." Id. For this claim to go forward, a plaintiff must show that an employee committed the underlying tort (in this case, defamation). Initially, the plaintiff must show that an employee's statements to fellow employees were "false, were understood in a defamatory sense, and harmed plaintiff's reputation." Id. Furthermore, the plaintiff must show that such statements were uttered "while acting in the course of employment, that the statements were made while on [the employer's] premises or that there exists a nexus between the uttered statements and [the employer's] operations." Bryan, at *26. In Bryan, the plaintiff contended that Nordstrom, Inc. was aware of defamatory statements made by an employee about the plaintiff to fellow employees. The court denied summary judgment finding there was a genuine issue regarding whether Nordstrom had knowledge that the employee was "telling other employees that plaintiff was a 'stalker.'" Id. at *25. As a consequence, "a reasonable fact finder could conclude that Nordstrom should have foreseen that plaintiff's reputation would be injured by such statements." Id.

B. Intentional Infliction of Emotional Distress

Nothing in Kansas law suggests that defamation law somehow precludes an intentional infliction of emotional distress claim. See Pfannenstiel v. Osborne Publishing Co., 939 F. Supp. 1497 (D. Kan. 1996) (analyzing intentional infliction claim under Kansas law arising from allegedly defamatory publication). At least one Kansas appellate decision has allowed an employee to go forward with an emotional distress claim despite the fact that he could not withstand summary judgment on a slander claim based on verbal insults by his employer. Gomez v. Hug, 7 Kan. App. 2d 603, 645 P.2d 916 (1982)

C. Interference with Economic Advantage

In cases where a former employee seeks to recover against his former employer for the giving of a poor reference, employees have supplemented their defamation claims with a claim of "tortious interference with a prospective business advantage or relationship." Turner v. Halliburton Co., 240 Kan. 1, 722 P.2d 1106 (1986). Such a claim, however, is protected by the same privilege as allegedly defamatory statements, as well as others including "justification." Id. Again, a plaintiff may only overcome these privileges by proving actual malice. Id. See also Booth v. Electronic Data Systems Corp., 799 F. Supp. 1086 (D. Kan. 1992) (applying Kansas law) (holding that "the qualified privilege that applies to the defendant as to the defamation claim also applies to the tortious interference claim"). In addition, a plaintiff cannot avoid the one-year statute of limitations for defamation claims by terming his claim one for tortious interference. "[C]ertain tortious interference actions can arise from facts separate from a defamation, but when both causes of action arise from the defamatory act, [a plaintiff] should not be able to circumvent the statute of limitations by merely terming the claim tortious interference when in essence it is one of defamation, subject to a one year limitation of action. In such a situation, we will look to the gravamen of the action, not to the label applied to it by" the plaintiff. Taylor v. International Union of Electronic, Salaried, Machine and Furniture Workers, 25 Kan. App. 2d 671, 968 P.2d 685 (1998). See also Sports Unlimited, Inc. v. Lankford Enterprises, 93 F. Supp. 2d 1164, 1168 (D. Kan. 2000) (stating that because plaintiff's claim was solely based on defamatory statements, it was a defamation claim barred by the statute of limitations).

The Court of Appeals of Kansas considered and rejected an argument that the state should recognize the tort of business disparagement. St. Catherine Hospital v. Rodriguez, 25 Kan. App. 2d 763, 971 P.2d 754 (1998).

D. Prima Facie Tort

No reported Kansas case involves a prima facie tort claim based on statements.

V. OTHER ISSUES

A. Statute of Limitations.

By statute, a plaintiff must bring a defamation action under Kansas law within one year of the publication of the allegedly defamatory statement. K.S.A. 60-514 (cited in Logan v. United States, 272 F.Supp.2d 1182, 1187 (D. Kan. 2003)). A plaintiff will not be allowed to avoid this limitation period by characterizing his claim in a manner that avoids the statutory bar. See Taylor v. International Union of Electronic, Salaried, Machine and Furniture Workers, 25 Kan. App. 2d 671, 968 P.2d 685 (1998).

However, at least one federal district court applying Kansas law has expressed a belief that Kansas courts would hold the statute in an employment defamation case is not triggered until the employee discovers the publication at issue. Hobson v. Coastal Corp., 962 F. Supp. 1407 (D. Kan. 1997). "Like a credit reporting case, publication of defamatory material in an employment history case is also likely to go undiscovered until long after the statute of limitations has run." Id. See also Deghand v. Wal-Mart Stores, Inc., 904 F. Supp. 1218 (D. Kan. 1995) (noting that plaintiff may amend complaint to add claim based on allegedly defamatory publication by employer where plaintiff did not have actual knowledge of publication for more than fifteen months). But see Geolas v. Boy Scouts of America, 23 F. Supp. 2d 1254 (D. Kan. 1998) ("normal discovery accrual rule does not apply to claims of defamation. . . . statute of limitations commences to run from the date the allegedly defamatory statement is uttered or published; it is immaterial when [the plaintiff] contends that he actually learned of" it).

Additionally, when a plaintiff brings claims requiring administrative exhaustion together with a defamation claim, "the pursuit of administrative review as to the former will not toll the statute of limitations as to the latter." Doerge v. Crum's Enterprises, Inc., 2007 U.S. Dist. LEXIS 39868 (D. Kan.) at *21.

B. Jurisdiction.

Employment contracts containing arbitration clauses may require arbitration of defamation or other tort claims arising out of the employment relationship. See Kenney v. Hallmark Cards, Inc., 2009 WL 102682, *3 (applying Kansas law) (employer's dispute resolution program created a contractual duty of arbitration).

C. Worker's Compensation Exclusivity

"The exclusive remedy provision of the [Kansas] Worker's Compensation Act…bars an employee or his dependents from bringing a common-law action against the employer to recover damages resulting from injuries sustained by the employee in the course of his employment." Frye v. Mel Hambelton Ford, Inc., 793 P.2d 1271, *3 (Kan. App. 1990) (citing Fritzon v. City of Manhattan, 215 Kan. 810, 813, 528 P.2d 1193 (1974)). However, the Kansas Court of Appeals recognized in dicta that "torts which result in no physical injury, such as false imprisonment, *libel*, malicious prosecution, invasion of right of privacy, fraud, deceit, and intentional infliction of emotional distress are not subject to the exclusive remedy provisions in workers compensation acts." Frye, 793 P.2d 1271, *4 (emphasis added) (citing 2A Larson's Workmen's Compensation Law § 68.30, p. 13-85).

D. Pleading Requirements.

"To effectively plead a defamation claim under Kansas law, a plaintiff must set forth the alleged defamatory words published, the names of those persons to whom they were published and the time and place of their publication." Marten v. Yellow Freight System, Inc., 993 F. Supp. 822. 829 (D. Kan. 1998). To set out a claim of defamation, a plaintiff must include in the complaint the words alleged to be defamatory, the persons to whom they were communicated, and the time and place of publication. Schulze v. Coykendall, 218 Kan. 653, 545 P.2d 392 (1976). The plaintiff may plead generally that the defamatory publication was of and concerning the plaintiff. Kan. Stat. Ann. § 60-209(j). The defendant must challenge this element in its answer, and bears the burden of controverting it. Id.

In a federal diversity case, the sufficiency of a complaint alleging defamation under Kansas law is judged under Fed.R. Civ. P. 8(a). "'In the context of a defamation claim, rule 8(a) requires that the complaint provide sufficient notice of the communications complained of to allow [the defendant] to defend itself.'" Lewis v. Herman's Excavating, Inc., 2000 U.S. Dist. LEXIS 19053, at *11-12 (D. Kan. Nov. 2, 2000) (citing McGeorge v. Continental Airlines, Inc., 871 F.2d 952, 955 (10th Cir. 1989)). "There is a significant exception to the general rule of liberally construing a complaint in applying rule 12(b)(6): when the complaint attempts to state a 'traditionally disfavored' cause of action, such as defamation, courts have construed the complaint by a stricter standard." Id. (citing 5A Wright & Miller § 1357). See also Fisher v. Lynch, 531 F. Supp. 2d 1253, 1271 (D. Kan. 2008) (noting the heightened pleading standard involved with defamation claims). The court may allow a plaintiff to amend a complaint containing an insufficiently pled claim of defamation in the face of a motion to dismiss. See, e.g., Auld v. Value Place Prop. Mgmt. LLC, 2010 U.S. Dist. LEXIS 14907, *18 (D. Kan. Feb. 19, 2010) (although the plaintiff failed to identify with the necessary specificity which defendant made the allegedly defamatory statements, or to whom and specifically when the statements were made, because this deficiency was procedural rather than substantive, the plaintiff was allowed to amend his complaint "to allege additional clarifying facts" involving his defamation claim).

SURVEY OF KANSAS EMPLOYMENT PRIVACY LAW

Michael W. Merriam
700 SW Jackson -- Roof Garden Suite
Topeka, Kansas 66603
Telephone: (785) 233-3700; Facsimile: (785) 234-8997
Daren Bruschi, Research Assistant

(With Developments Reported Through **November 1, 2012**)

GENERAL COMMENTS

Kansas has two courts of precedent, the Supreme Court and the intermediate Court of Appeals, both of which are reported by the Kansas Supreme Court Reporter of Decisions. Cases from such courts are reported in the Kansas Reports and the Kansas Court of Appeals Reports, respectively. Parallel citations to these Kansas cases appear in the Pacific Reporter.

SIGNIFICANT DEVELOPMENTS SINCE THE 2012 *SURVEY*

None.

I. GENERAL LAW OF PRIVACY

A. Legal Basis of Privacy Claims

Kansas was among the first states to recognize an action for invasion of privacy in Kunz v. Allen, 102 Kan. 883, 172 P. 532 (1918), in a case which would be considered a misappropriation case today. All four traditional branches of the privacy torts as defined by the Restatement (Second) of Torts § 652A-E are recognized in Kansas. Froelich v. Adair, 213 Kan. 357, 516 P.2d 993 (1973); Dotson v. McLaughlin, 216 Kan. 201, 531 P.2d 1(1975); Rawlins v. Hutchinson Publishing Co., 218 Kan. 295, 543 P.2d 988 (1975). See also Ali v. Douglas Cable Communications, 929 F. Supp. 1362 (D. Kan. 1996); Bryan v. Eichenwald, 2001 U.S. Dist. Lexis 9920 (D. Kan. Nov. 21, 2001); Watson v. City of Kansas City, 2001 U.S. Dist. Lexis 22548 (D. Kan. Nov. 21, 2001). Adopting the Restatement (Second) of Torts § 652A, the court recognizes invasion of privacy where there is: (1) unreasonable intrusion upon the seclusion of another; (2) appropriation of another's name or likeness; (3)unreasonable publicity given to another's private life; or (4) publicity that unreasonably places another in a false light before the public." Finlay v. Finlay, 18 Kan. App. 2d 479, 856 P.2d 183 (1993). See also Blackwell v. Harris Chemical North America, Inc., 11 F. Supp.2d 1302 (D.Kan. 1998). In its criminal law, Kansas defines eavesdropping and breach of privacy, criminal false communication, and unauthorized disclosure of tax returns to be Class A non-person misdemeanors. See K.S.A. 21-6101 (eavesdropping and breach of privacy), 21-6103 (criminal false communication) 21-6104 (tax disclosure). Maliciously exposing a convicted or charged person and criminal disclosure of a warrant are defined as Class B non-person misdemeanors. See K.S.A. 21-6105 (exposure of convicted or charged person), 21-5906 (warrant). There are no constitutional provisions regarding privacy claims. However, see generally II.A.2, infra. An employee survived summary judgment on an invasion of privacy claim based on coercive sexual demands of a highly offensive and intrusive nature in Greenhorn v. Marriott International, Inc., 258 F. Supp.2d 1249 (D. Kan. 2003). In Lindenmuth v. Goodyear Tire & Rubber, Inc., 19 Kan.App.2d 95, 864 P.2d 744 (1993), under the facts, the Court refused to find state law claims of intentional infliction of emotional distress, defamation and tortuous interference with contract to be preempted by the Labor Management Relations Act of 1947.

B. Causes of Action

1. ***Misappropriation/Right of Publicity.*** Kansas has recognized this tort specifically in Johnson v. Boeing Airplane Co., 175 Kan. 275, 262 P.2d 808 (1953), although it was not so designated. But in a similar employment context claim, the tort was so designated. Dry v. Boeing, 2002 US Dist. Lexis 23288 (D. Kan). In Froelich v. Adair, 213 Kan. 357, 516 P.2d 993, Restatement (Second) of Torts §§ 652A-E, and specifically § 652C, were adopted as the law of this state. Kansas has long recognized common law claims to trade names and consequent protection of commercial activity. American Fence Co. v. Gestes, 190 Kan. 393, 375 P.2d 775 (1962). Kansas statutes commercially protect trademarks and trade names, K.S.A. 81-201 et seq. Elements from the Restatement (Second) of Torts § 652C include (1) appropriation of plaintiff's identity or persona, (2) for the use or benefit of defendant. Kansas follows the Restatement elements and requires that a person's name or image was used in public context, without his authorization, to benefit defendant commercially. In both Kunz v. Allen, 102 Kan. 883, 172 P. 532 (1918) and Johnson v. Boeing, the use of plaintiff's identity was clearly for the commercial advantage of the defendant. Burden of proof requires the general tort liability standard of preponderance of the evidence. The statute of limitations for misappropriation/right of publicity is the same as that for all general torts in Kansas, two years. K.S.A. 60-513(a)(4).

2. ***False Light.*** Kansas has specifically adopted the Restatement (Second) of Torts definitions, including false light invasion of privacy. Froelich v. Adair, 213 Kan. 357, 516 P.2d 933 (1973); Ratts v. Bd of County Commissioners, 141 F. Supp. 2d 1289, 1323 (2001); Rinsley v. Frydman, 221 Kan. 297, 559 P.2d 334 (1977). No Kansas case has substantively developed the false light tort; however, a U.S. District Court applying Kansas law has discussed the tort at length. Rinsley v. Brandt, 446 F. Supp. 850 (D. Kan. 1977). See also Pfannenstiel v. Osborne Publishing Co., 939 F. Supp. 1497 (D. Kan. 1996). Substantive elements include (1) a statement that is false (2) communicated to third parties (3) which is offensive to a reasonable person. Some degree of fault on the part of the defendant must also be shown, ranging from negligence for private parties to constitutional or actual malice for public officials/figures. It would appear that simple negligence, as contrasted with the Restatement requirement of actual knowledge or reckless disregard of falsity, will be adequate at least with private figure plaintiffs. Rinsley v. Brandt, supra. No damages may be presumed, but must be established by proof and the former presumption accompanying libel per se has been abolished. Gobin v. Globe Publishing Co. 216 Kan. 223, 531 P.2d 76 (1975). A public figure must prove actual malice by clear and convincing evidence. Ruebke v. Globe Communications Corp., 241 Kan. 595, 738 P. 2d 1246 (1987). Although the libel-proof plaintiff doctrine had only been acknowledged but never used, The 10th Circuit Court adopted the doctrine for cases where "the plaintiff had already suffered from a lowered reputation in the community because of the plaintiff's prior convictions for the crime alleged in the publication or for a similar crime." Lamb v. Rizzo 391 F.3d 1133 (2004). The defamation statute of limitation in Kansas in one year. K.S.A. 60-514. A federal district court has held that the general tort liability statute of two years under K.S.A. 60-513(a)(4) applies to false light invasion of privacy actions, even though undistinguishable from defamation. Rinsley v. Brandt, supra. See I.B.1, supra. However, this was addressed in Castleberry v. Boeing Corp., 8807 F. Supp. 1435 (D. Kan 1995) where the court noted that the injury being claimed distinguishes these two torts. The injury in defamation actions is damage to the reputation whereas the injury in false light actions is mental distress. See also Byers v. Synder, 44 Kan. App. 2d 380, 396 (Kan. Ct. App. 2010) (observing Kansas courts generally treat false light and defamation as the same tort). In Lloyd v. Quorum Health Resources, LLC, 31 Kan. App. 2d 943 (77 P.3d 993 2003), the Court applied a qualified privilege based on a hospital administrator's duty to bring allegations of hostile work environment against a physician with hospital privileges to the attention of the hospital's Board of Trustees. The physician produced no evidence of common law malice. The Court also refused to apply peer review privileges or medical staff bylaw procedures to what was essentially a Title VII claim investigated by the Board.

3. ***Publication of Private Facts.*** Kansas has specifically recognized the tort of publicity given to private life from the Restatement (Second) of Torts § 652D. Munsell v. Ideal Food Stores, 208 Kan. 909, 494 P.2d 1063 (1972).See also I.A, supra, Ali v. Douglas Cable Communications, 929 F. Supp. 1362 (D. Kan. 1996); Watson v. City of Kansas City, 2001 U.S. Dist. Lexis 10575 (D. Kan. 2001). Carson v. Lynch Multimedia Corp., 123 F. Supp. 2d 1254 (D. Kan. 2000) states that in Dominguez v. Davidson, 266 Kan. 926, 937, 974 P.2d 112 (1999), "the Kansas Supreme Court adopted the definition of publicity set by this Court in Ali....". [Examined, in Frye v. IBP, Inc., 15 F. Supp. 2d 1032, 1040 (D. Kan. 1998)]. Kansas has adopted § 652D of the Restatement (Second) of Torts, which states, "[o]ne who gives publicity to a matter concerning the private life of another is subject to liability to the other for invasion of his privacy, if the matter is of a kind that (a) would be highly offensive to a reasonable person, and (b) is not of legitimate concern to the public," Werner v. Kliewer, 238 Kan. 289, 710 P.2d 1250 (1985). The general tort statute of limitations in Kansas is two years. K.S.A. 60-513(a)(4).

4. ***Intrusion.*** The intrusion prong of the invasion of privacy tort has been specifically recognized in Kansas. Froelich v. Adair, 213 Kan. 357, 516 P.2d 993 (1973); Dotson v. McLaughlin, 216 Kan. 201, 531 P.2d 1 (1975); Moore v. R.Z. Sims Chevrolet-Subaru, Inc., 241 Kan. 542, 738 P.2d 852 (1987). See also Ali v. Douglas Cable Communications, 929 F. Supp. 1362 (D. Kan. 1996); Blackwell v. Harris Chemical North America, Inc., 11 F.Supp.2d 1302 (D.Kan. 1998). Kansas has specifically adopted the Restatement (Second) of Torts § 652B in Froelich v. Adair, supra. Section 652 B, entitled "Intrusion Upon Seclusion" states, "One who intentionally intrudes, physically or otherwise, upon the solitude or seclusion of another, or his private affairs or concerns, is subject to liability to the other for invasion of his privacy, if the intrusion would be highly offensive to a reasonable man." In this case of first impression, the court recognized the intrusion upon seclusion right where a private defamation defendant surreptitiously obtained hair samples from the hospital room of the defamation plaintiff's alleged homosexual lover. The court noted that publication-oriented privileges which apply in other defamation and invasion of privacy actions which include publication as an element of the tort, do not apply in intrusion cases. In Froelich v. Werbin, 219 Kan. 461, 548 P.2d 482 (1976), the court held that the intrusion, physical or otherwise, upon the solitude or seclusion of another or his private affairs or concerns is subject to liability if the intrusion would be highly offensive to a reasonable man, and if the interference with the seclusion is a substantial one. See I.B.1, supra. In Nicholas v. Nicholas, 277 Kan. 171, 83 P.3d 214 (2004), the court held an invasion of privacy cause of action upon seclusion does not survive the death of the plaintiff.

C. Other Privacy-Related Actions

1. ***Intentional Infliction of Emotional Distress.*** Intentional infliction of emotional distress has been recognized in Kansas as the tort of "outrage." In Bradshaw v. Swaggerty, 1 Kan. App. 2d 213, 563 P.2d 511 (1977), the

Kansas court adopted the Restatement (Second) of Torts § 46(1). It has been followed in numerous cases since then, although no Kansas decision has ever found conduct to be sufficiently outrageous to constitute a violation of this tort. In Valadez v. Emmis Communications, 290 Kan. 472 (2010) the court explained that conduct that rises to this level must transcend a certain amount of criticism, rough language, and occasional acts that are inconsiderate and unkind. The law will not intervene where one's feelings are merely hurt. The conduct must be outrageous to a point past the bounds of decency and is utterly intolerable in a civilized society. However, in the debtor-creditor field, the Kansas court is more lenient. See Dotson v. McLaughlin, 216 Kan. 201, 531 P.2d 1 (1975) and Dawson v. Associates Financial Services Co., 215 Kan. 814, 529 P.2d 104 (1974). Distinguished by Holdren v. General Motors Corp., 31 F. Supp.2d 1279, 1283 (D. Kan. Oct. 19, 1998). See Roberts v. Saylor, 230 Kan. 289, 637 P.2d 1175 (1981) for the most complete discussion of the tort. Kansas has set a very high standard for the tort of outrage. Butler v. City of Prairie Village, 974 F. Supp. 1386 (D. Kan. 1997); affirmed in part, reversed in part, by Butler v. City of Prairie Village, 172 F.3d 736 (10th Cir., Apr. 6, 1999). Lange v. Showbiz Pizza Time, Inc., 12 F. Supp.2d 1150 (D. Kan. 1998) Gerharrt v. Sears, Roebuck & Co., Inc., 27 F. Supp.2d 1263, 1278 (D. Kan. Oct 19, 1998). The four elements of intentional infliction of emotional distress (the tort of "outrage") include: (1) conduct of a defendant must be intentional or in reckless disregard of plaintiff; (2) conduct must be extreme and outrageous; (3) there must be a causal connection between defendant's conduct and plaintiff's mental distress, and (4) plaintiff's mental distress must be severe and extreme. Wilkerson v. P.I.A. Topeka, Inc., 900 F. Supp. 1418, 1423 (D. Kan. 1995) (citing Taiwo v. Vu, 249 Kan. 585, 592, 822 P.2d 1024 (1991)). Distinguished, Holdren v. General Motors Corp., 31 F. Supp. 2d 1279, 1284 (D. Kan. Oct. 19, 1998); Tran v. Standard Motor Products, Inc., 10 F. Supp. 2d 1199, 1213 (D. Kan. May 29, 1998); Smith v. Welch, 967 P.2d 727, 732, 265 Kan. 868, 874 (Kan. Sept. 18, 1998); Miller v. Sloan, Listrom Eisenbarth, Sloan & Glassman, 267 Kan. 245, 978 P.2d 922 (1999) discussed, Green v. City of Wichita, 47 F. Supp. 2d 1273, 1280. See also Pfannenstiel v. Osborne Publishing Co., 939 F. Supp. 1497 (D. Kan. 1996); Gillum v. Federal Home Loan Bank of Topeka, 970 F. Supp. 843 (D. Kan. 1997); Bailey v. Federal Home Loan Bank of Topeka, 1998 WL 982900, #1 (D. Kan. Sept. 23, 1998); Blackwell v. Harris Chemical North America, Inc., 11 F.Supp.2d 1302 (D. Kan. 1998); Marten v. Yellow Freight System, Inc., 993 F. Supp. 822 (D. Kan. 1998). White v. Dunlop, et al., 175 F. Supp. 2d 1281 (D. Kan. 2001). No Kansas cases discuss what privileges are available. The statute of limitations is two years. K.S.A. 60-513(a)(4). See I.B.1, supra. The federal court held that Kansas would not recognize independent causes of action for intentional infliction of emotional distress or negligent hiring, supervision and retention where the employee's claim was for hostile work environment harassment and pregnancy discrimination. Lawyer v. Eck and Eck Machine Co. Inc. 197 F. Supp. 2d 1267 (D. Kan. 2002). See also Carraway v. Cracker Barrel Old Country Store, 2003 U.S. Dist. Lexis 12326 (D. Kan); Greenhorn, supra.

2. ***Interference With Prospective Economic Advantage.*** Kansas has explicitly accepted tortious interference with a prospective business advantage. Turner v. Halliburton Co., 240 Kan. 1, 722 P.2d 1106 (1986) Reebles, Inc., v. Bank of America, 25 P.3d 871 (Kan. Ct. App. 2001). See also Classic Communications v. Rural Telephone Serv., 956 F. Supp. 910 (D. Kan. 1997), reconsideration denied, 1997 WL 231087; United Wats, Inc. v. Cincinnati Ins. Co., 971 F. Supp. 1375 (D. Kan. 1997). The five elements of tortious interference with a prospective business advantage include; (1) the existence of a business relationship or expectancy with the probability of plaintiff receiving future economic benefit; (2) knowledge by defendant of the relationship or expectancy; (3) that, except for the conduct of the defendant, plaintiff was reasonably certain to have continued the relationship or realized the expectancy; (4) intentional misconduct by defendant, and (5) plaintiff's damages are a direct or proximate cause of defendant's misconduct. Turner v. Halliburton Co., supra. See also Pfannenstiel v. Osborne Publishing Co., 939 F. Supp. 1497 (D. Kan. 1996); Gillum v. Federal Home Loan Bank of Topeka, 970 F. Supp. 843 (D. Kan. 1997); Altrutech, Inc. v. Hooper Holmes, Inc., 6 F.Supp.2d 1269 (D.Kan. 1998); Classic Communications v. Rural Telephone Serv., 956 F.Supp. 910 (D.Kan. 1997), reconsideration denied 1997 WL 231087; United Wats, Inc. v. Cincinnati, Ins. Co., 971 F.Supp. 1375 (D.Kan. 1997); Burcham v. Unison Bancorp, Inc., 276 Kan 393, 77 P.3d 130, 151 (2003). Justification is the most common affirmative defense to an action for tortious interference with a prospective economic advantage. This defense comes into play only after the tortious interference has occurred. Justification denotes the presence of exceptional circumstances which show that no tort has been committed and to imply a lawful excuse which excludes actual or legal malice. Justification can depend on the circumstances in each case, including the nature of the interferer's conduct, the character of the expectancy with which the conduct interfered, the relationship between the parties, the interest sought to be advanced by the interferer, and the social desirability of protecting the expectancy or the interferer's freedom of action. Turner v. Halliburton Co., supra. Another defense includes the lack of actual malice by the defendant. The plaintiff must prove actual malice by the defendant in a tortious interference with prospective economic advantage. Absent actual malice, a qualified privilege exists for the defendant. See Turner v. Halliburton Co., supra. A U.S. District Court applying Kansas law found that a qualified privilege existed for a high school principal to advise or induce a school district to terminate a teacher's contract. Schartz v. Unified School Dist. No. 512, 953 F. Supp. 1208 (D. Kan. 1997). The Tenth Circuit Court of Appeals, applying Kansas law, stated that the plaintiff has the burden of overcoming a justification or privilege. DP-TEK v. AT&T Global Information Solutions Co., 100 F.3d 828 (10th Cir. 1996). See I.B.1, supra. The Court in Sports Unlimited, Inc. v. Lakeford Enterprises, Inc., 275 F.3d 996 (CA 10, 2002) applied the one-year statute of limitations for Kansas defamation actions to a claim for tortious interference with contract and tortious interference with prospective business advantage because the claims were based on a competitor's allegedly defamatory statements.

3. ***Prima Facie Tort.*** Not recognized in Kansas. No Kansas cases.

II. EMPLOYER TESTING OF EMPLOYEES

A. Psychological or Personality Testing

1. ***Common Law and Statutes.*** K.S.A. 74-5323 provides that the confidential relations and communications between a licensed psychologist and the psychologist's client shall be privileged.

K.S.A. 65-5602 provides that a patient of a treatment facility has a privilege to prevent treatment or ancillary personnel from disclosing that the patient has been or is currently receiving treatment or from disclosing confidential communications made in the diagnosis or treatment of the patient's mental, alcoholic, drug dependency or emotional condition. Court stated that records in issue were not subject to the provisions of K.S.A. 65-5602(a) because plaintiff had not been a patient of the witness and did not receive treatment from the witness' facility. Ali v. Douglas Cable Communs., 890 F. Supp. 993 (D. Kan. 1995).

K.S.A. 59-2979 states that disclosure of records pertaining to the treatment for mentally ill persons shall be privileged and shall not be disclosed except under the following conditions: upon written consent, upon the order of any court, upon the request from an attorney representing the patient, or former patient, upon request by any state or national accreditation agency for scholarly study, except that such agency shall not further disclose this information to any person not otherwise authorized by law to receive such information. Willful violation of this section is a class C misdemeanor.

2. ***Private Employers.*** Although Kansas law does not specifically address psychological or personality testing by private employers, the Kansas Bill of Rights could be viewed as containing an implicit right of privacy. Specifically, Section 1 (equal rights and natural rights of life, liberty and the pursuit of happiness), Section 7 (religious liberty), Section 10 (right to fair trial), Section 11 (free speech) and Section 15 (search and seizure) could be used to establish and argue a right of privacy by private employees. However, a Kansas court has held that the conduct of a private individual acting under no authority from the state is not included in the proscription of the Fourth Amendment or the Kansas Bill of Rights. State v. Miesbauer, 232 Kan. 291, 654 P.2d 934 (1982). See also II.A.1, supra.

3. ***Public Employers.*** See II.A.1, supra.

B. Drug Testing

1. ***Common Law and Statutes.*** K.S.A. 59-29b79 states that alcoholism and substance abuse treatment records are privileged to the patient and shall not be disclosed, except upon consent, bona fide medical emergency, medical research and court order. The information furnished for medical research shall not be published in a way which may disclose the patient's name or other identifying information. Willful violation is a class C misdemeanor.

2. ***Private Employers.*** K.S.A. 44-706(b)(2) allows for disqualification for unemployment compensation benefits if the employee fails or refuses to submit to a chemical test administered pursuant to a pre-existing employee existence program or as a condition of further employment. The test must meet the standards of the Drug Free Workplace Act, 41 U.S.C. 701 *et seq.* Otherwise, the termination of an employee as a result of failing a drug test does not preclude the former employee from receiving unemployment compensation. Discussed, Pouncil v. Kansas Employment Sec. Bd. Of Review, 970 P.2d 547, 551, 25 Kan.App.2d 740 (Kan.App. Dec 18, 1998) aff'd 268 Kan. 470, 997 P.2d 715, 2000 Kan. Lexis 17, Unemployment Ins. Rep. (CCH) P8259 (2000). National Gypsum v. State Employment Sec., 244 Kan. 678,772 P.2d 786 (1989). See II.A.2 and II.B.1, supra, and V.A, infra. In Bracken v. Dixon Industries, Inc., 272 Kan. 1272, 38 P.3d 679 (2002), the court affirmed summary judgment to an employer against a claim of retaliatory discharge arising from a proposed workers compensation claim, where the discharge was due to a drug test failure without any causal connection to the workers compensation claim. In Foos v. Terminix, 89 P.3d 546, 277 Kan. 687 (2004), the court held K.S.A. 1999 Supp. 44-501(d)(2) mandates that probable cause "arise, exist, or occur contemporaneous" with the collection of the blood alcohol test to be admissible in a workers compensation hearing.

3. ***Public Employers.*** K.S.A. 75-4362 provides that the director of the division of personnel services of the department of administration shall have the authority to implement a drug screening program for the following state employees: governor, lieutenant governor, and attorney general. Also subject to the drug screening program are job applicants for safety sensitive positions in the state government including law enforcement officers, state corrections officers, positions with the state schools for the blind, the state schools for the deaf, the state veteran's home, the heads of state agencies appointed by the governor, and employees on the governor's staff. Except in limited circumstances, the results of such test shall be confidential and not disclosed publicly.

In 2002, the legislature repealed a law that provided that the director of the division of personnel services of the department of administration may establish and implement an alcohol and drug testing program for employees of mental health institutions. 2002 Kan. Laws ch. 111, § 2 (repealing K.S.A. 75-4363).

No employee can be terminated solely due to a failed test under K.S.A 75-4362 so long as the individual has not previously had a valid positive test result and the individual undergoes a drug evaluation and successfully completes any education or drug treatment program recommended by the evaluation.

C. Medical Testing

See II.A-B, supra, and VI.B, infra.

D. Polygraph Tests

Kansas has recognized that courts in other jurisdictions have allowed an employee's claim for retaliatory discharge because the employer punished the employee for refusing to take a polygraph examination. Morriss v. Coleman Co. Inc., 241 Kan. 501, 738 P.2d 841 (1987); Wilkinson v. Shoney's, Inc., 269 Kan. 194 (2001); Buckley v. Keebler Co., 153 F.3d 726 (10th Cir. (Kan.) May 29, 1998); (ex) Rodriguez v. I.B.P., Inc., 153 F.3d 728 (10th Cir. (Kan.) Jul. 20, 1998) aff'd 243 F.3d 1221 (2001) U.S. App. Lexis 3904, 2001 Colo, J. C.A.R. 1341, 49 Fed Serv. 3d (Callaghan) 1222 (10th Cir. Kan. 2001); petition for cert filed Aug. 28, 2001. This type of retaliatory discharge claim has not, however, been specifically adopted in Kansas. In criminal proceedings, the results of a polygraph test are inadmissible unless stipulated by both parties. State v. Ulland, 24 Kan. App. 2d 249, 943 P.2d 947 (1997). State v. Lumley, 977 P.2d 914, 267 Kan. 4 (Kan. Apr. 16, 1999); State V. Wakefield, 977 P.2d 941, 267 Kan. 116 (Kan. Apr. 16, 1999).

E. Fingerprinting

Fingerprinting by employers is generally allowed. See Atchison, Topeka, and Sante Fe Railway Co. v. Lopez, 216 Kan. 108, 531 P.2d 455 (1975). Candidates for the office of sheriff must be fingerprinted. K.S.A. 19-826(b). See also Chamberlain v. Buhrman, 250 Kan. 277, 825 P.2d 168 (1992). Generally, K.S.A. 21-2501 allows the fingerprinting of certain criminals by law enforcement agencies.

III. SEARCHES

A. Employee's Person

See II.A.2, supra, and III.B-C, infra.

B. Employee's Work Area

An employee's work site can be searched by the employer and officials from the Occupational Safety and Health Administration (OSHA) for safety purposes. Martin v. Gard, 811 F.Supp. 616 (D.Kan. 1993). See also III.C, infra.

C. Employee's Property

1. ***Private Employers.*** In a federal case, an employee refused to let his employer search his vehicle before leaving the warehouse. In doing so, the employee prevented the alleged tort of invasion of privacy by intrusion upon seclusion and therefore failed in his argument for damages. Gretencord v. Ford Motor Co., 538 F.Supp. 331 (1982). Fry v. I.B.P., Inc., 15 F.Supp.2d 1032, 1043 (D. Kan. 1998). Nonetheless, this case illustrates that such searches may be permissible in certain situations. Id. See II.A.2, supra. An employer can authorize a search by law enforcement officers of common storage areas and offices used for business purposes. However, this court also held that a search warrant for an employee's private desk, credenza and file cabinet, all of which did not contain any property or documents related to company operations, was impermissibly overbroad. State v. Gordon, 221 Kan. 253, 559 P.2d 312 (1977), State v. Wakefield, 267 Kan. 116, 977 P.2d 941 (1999). See also III.B, supra.

2. ***Public Employers.*** See III.A-C.1, supra.

IV. MONITORING OF EMPLOYEES

A. Telephones and Electronic Communications

Eavesdropping is a recognized offense in Kansas. K.S.A. 21-6101. Eavesdropping is surreptitiously listening or observing the private conversations or personal conduct of other persons in a private place, or using a recording or amplifying device outside such a place, or intercepting telephone or electronic communications. Eavesdropping is a Class A non-person misdemeanor. Kansas also recognizes "Breach of Privacy" which is, without authority, intercepting a message by electronic communications, or letter, or divulging the contents of such a message knowing it was illegally intercepted. Breach of privacy is a Class A non-person misdemeanor. K.S.A. 21-6101. Kansas requires the consent of one party. See State v. Hruska, 219 Kan. 233, 547 P.2d 732 (1976) although the telephone company is specifically authorized to monitor any phone from which it reasonably believes illegal calls are being placed; State v. Bowman National Security Agency, Inc., 231 Kan. 631, 647 P.2d 1288 (1982); State v. Roudybush, 235 Kan. 834, 686 P.2d 100 (1984). However, in Ali v. Douglas Cable Communications, 929 F.Supp. 1362 (D.Kan. 1996) the court held that the employer properly monitored the employee's telephone calls and that the employees cannot reasonably claim any offensive intrusion by the monitoring or recording of their business calls at the work place since such calls were made for the benefit of their employer.

Kansas recognizes "stalking," which is defined as the intentional, reckless and repeated following or harassment of another person and making a credible threat with the intent to place such person in reasonable fear for such person's safety. K.S.A. 21-5427. This statute was held constitutional in State v. Whitesell, 270 Kan. 259, 13 P.3d 887 (2000). Surveillance is allowed in areas of open, public nature such as a security personnel locker area at a community college. Such surveillance does not violate any constitutional rights, federal or state laws. Thompson v. Johnson County Community College, 930 F. Supp. 501 (D. Kan. 1996), affirmed 108 F.3d 1388 (10th Cir. Kan. 1997). See also IV.A, supra. However, photographing a person in a "private place" with a hidden camera is eavesdropping within the meaning of K.S.A. 21-6101. See State v. Martin, 232 Kan. 778, 658 P.2d 1024 (1983).

1. ***Wiretapping.*** The interception of a wire, oral or electronic communication is allowed in certain situations by investigative or law enforcement officers and agencies having responsibility to investigate certain criminal offenses, a laundry list which is found in K.S.A. 22-2515. An application must be made to a judge of competent jurisdiction by the attorney general, district attorney, or county attorney before such interception may occur. K.S.A. 22-2515. See also K.S.A. 22-2516.

As applied to governmental functions, the unlawful disclosure of an authorized interception of wire, oral or electronic communications is a recognized offense in Kansas. K.S.A. 21-5923. It is unlawful to communicate to any person or make public in any way, except as provided by law, the existence of an application or order for such interception issued pursuant to K.S.A. 22-2516, or any resulting investigation with the intent to obstruct or prevent the authorized interception. Unlawful disclosure of authorized interception of wire, oral or electronic communications is a severity level 10, nonperson felony.

2. ***Electronic Communications.*** See IV.A and IV.A.1, supra.

3. ***Other Electronic Monitoring.*** An offender under house arrest may be subject to electronic monitoring which can include an active or passive global positioning system capable of tracking the offender's movements, a remote alcohol monitoring device, or a radio frequency device capable of monitoring an individual's location. See K.S.A. 21-6609.

B. Mail

See IV.A, supra.

C. Surveillance/Photographing

None.

V. ACTIVITIES OUTSIDE THE WORKPLACE

A. Statute or Common Law

K.S.A. 44-706(b) provides that alcohol or drug use by employees while off duty is not evidence of "misconduct" for the purpose of terminating unemployment benefits. See also II.B.2, supra.

B. Employees' Personal Relationships

1. ***Romantic Relationships Between Employees.*** See V.B.3, infra.

2. ***Sexual Orientation.*** See V.B.3, infra.

3. ***Marital Status.*** K.S.A. 65-6410 states that persons licensed under the marriage and family therapist act, along with employees and associates of such person, shall not be required to disclose any information which they received unless required by other state law, present danger to the health or safety of an individual, required pursuant to a civil or criminal proceeding, or all family members receiving therapy agree to waiver of the privilege.

Marriage is defined as a "civil contract between two parties who are of the opposite sex." All other marriages are declared as contrary to the public policy of Kansas and are void. K.S.A. 23-2501. In In re Estate of Gardiner, 273 Kan. 191, 42 P.3d 120 (2002), the court held "persons of the opposite sex" means a biological gender from birth, and therefore a post-operative male-to-female transsexual is not a woman (and thus vice versa) under Kansas marriage statutes. In 2005, Kansas voters approved a constitutional amendment banning same-sex marriages.

C. Smoking

Smoking in public places or at public meetings is prohibited. Smoking is not allowed in elevators, school buses, public means of transportation, and any other place prohibited by the fire marshal or other law, ordinance or regulation. K.S.A. 21-6110. "Public place" is defined as "enclosed indoor areas open to the public or used by the general public including but not limited to: Restaurants, retail stores, public means of transportation, passenger elevators, health care institutions or any other place where health care services are provided to the public, educational facilities, libraries, courtrooms, state, county or municipal buildings, restrooms, grocery stores, school buses, museums, theaters, auditoriums, arenas and recreational facilities." K.S.A. 21-46109. Public meetings include all meetings open to the public. Employers with an enclosed space as the place of employment are required to provide a smoke-free work place. These employers must adopt and maintain a written smoking policy that prohibits smoking without exception in all areas of the place of employment. K.S.A. 21-6110 (b). Any person found guilty of smoking in violation of this law is guilty of a misdemeanor punishable by fine of not more than $100 for the first violation and not more than $500 for the third violation. K.S.A. 21-6112.

D. Blogging

Kansas law has not addressed blogging. No cases or statutes.

VI. RECORDS

Through the Kansas Open Records Act (KORA), Kansas allows many records to be open to the public. K.S.A. 45-215 *et seq.* Records not required to be open are found in a laundry list within KORA. See K.S.A. 45-221. The public records required to be open are not restricted to just written information. Burroughs v. Thomas, 23 Kan. App. 2d 769, 937 P.2d 12 (1997), review denied.

K.S.A. 45-230 defines unlawful use of names derived from public records by stating, "No person shall knowingly sell, give or receive, for the purpose of selling or offering for sale any property or service to persons listed therein, any list of names and addresses contained in or derived from public records . . . ."

Six exceptions enumerated in K.S.A. 45-230 include:

(1) Names and addresses obtained from division of vehicles under K.S.A. 74-2012 (but this statute has further restrictions);

(2) names and addresses of persons licensed or registered to practice a profession may be given or sold to and received by an organization composed of such persons for membership or informational purposes related to the practice of the profession;

(3) names and addresses of persons applying for licenses, certificates, registrations, or permits to practice a profession shall be sold or given to, and received by, organizations providing professional or vocational educational materials or courses to such persons for the purpose of providing information about the availability of such materials and courses;

(4) names and addresses and other information from voter registration lists may be compiled, used, sold and received by any person, as defined in K.S.A. 2011 Supp. 21-5111, solely for political campaign or election purposes;

(5) names and addresses from the public records of postsecondary institutions as defined in K.S.A. 74-3201b may be given to, and received and disseminated by such institution's separately incorporated affiliates and supporting organizations for use in the furtherance of the purposes and programs of such institutions and such affiliates and supporting organizations;

(6) to the extent otherwise authorized by law.

A person who knowingly violates this section is subject to a civil penalty in an action brought by a district attorney in a sum set by the court not to exceed $500.

A. Personnel Records

K.S.A. 44-406 states that private employment agencies shall maintain a register with the name and address of every person who shall make application for employment, and the name and nature of employment wanted. The register may be inspected by the secretary of human resources or persons designated by the secretary.

K.S.A. 44-119a provides for "qualified immunity" from civil liability for an employer's disclosure of information about a former or current employee to a prospective employer. "Absolute" immunity from civil liability is provided for such disclosure of (1) date of employment; (2) pay level; (3) job description and duties; and (4) wage history; as well as written responses to written requests for prior employee evaluations and whether the employee was voluntarily or involuntarily terminated and the reasons therefore. As of yet, no Kansas cases have interpreted the meaning of "qualified" and "absolute" immunity.

K.S.A. 21-6105 provides one definition of criminal false communication as recklessly circulating or causing to be circulated any false report, statement, or rumor with the intent to injure the financial standing of the bank, financial or business institution or the financial standing of any individual within the state. Violation is a class A nonperson misdemeanor.

K.S.A. 45-221(a)(4), a provision in the Kansas Open Records Act, exempts from disclosure "personnel records, performance ratings or individually identifiable records pertaining to employees or applicants for employment, except that this exemption shall not apply to the names, positions, salaries *or actual compensation employment contracts or employment-related contracts or agreements* and lengths of service of officers and employees of public agencies once they are employed as such" and K.S.A. 45-217(b) defines "clearly unwarranted invasion of personal privacy" to mean "revealing information that would be highly offensive to a reasonable person, including information that may pose a risk to a person or property and is not of legitimate concern to the public."

B. Medical Records

K.S.A. 60-427 allows a patient to claim the physician-patient privilege if a judge finds that: (1) the communication was confidential between the physician and patient; (2) the patient or the physician reasonably believed the communication necessary or helpful to enable the physician to make a diagnosis of the condition of the patient or to prescribe or render treatment therefore; (3) the witness (i) is the holder of the privilege, (ii) at the time of the communication was the physician or a person to whom disclosure was made because reasonably necessary for the transmission of the communication or for the accomplishment of the purpose for which it was transmitted, or (iii) is any other person who obtained knowledge or possession of the communication as the result of an intentional breach of the physician's duty of nondisclosure by the physician or the physician's agent or servant; and (4) the claimant is the holder of the privilege or a person authorized to claim the privilege for the holder of such privilege. Id. Although the hospital or physician, as compared to the patient, is not the holder of such privilege, such hospital or physician, absent statutory authority, shall not reveal, ex parte, information subject to such privilege without knowledge or consent of the patient privilege holder. Wesley Medical Center v. Clark, 234 Kan. 13, 669 P.2d 209 (1983). Superceded by statute/Rule stated in Fretz v. Keltner, 109 F.R.D. 303, 309 (D. Kan. Dec. 3, 1985). Physician-patient privilege may apply even when the patient is unconscious or unaware of the physician's presence and does not consent or actually objects to being treated. State v. Pitchford, 10 Kan. App. 2d 293, 697 P.2d 896 (1985). The court also held there is no physician-patient privilege when the examining doctor is disinterested, meaning the doctor examines a person with no intention of offering treatment or advice. Id. See also II.A.1, supra, regarding psychologist-client privilege.

K.S.A. 65-4922(g) provides that reports of a health care provider or a medical care facility agent or employee who is directly involved in the delivery of health care services or has knowledge that a health care provider has acted below the applicable standard of care that has reasonable probability of causing injury to a patient, or has acted in a way that may be grounds for disciplinary action by the appropriate licensing agency are confidential. See also K.S.A. 65-4925.

K.S.A. 65-4915 provides that health care providers' peer review committee records are privileged and shall not be subject to discovery, subpoena or other means of legal compulsion for their release to any person or entity or for admission in evidence of any judicial or administrative proceeding. A hospital, in advancing a counterclaim for services, did not waive the peer review privilege pursuant to K.S.A. 65-4915. Herbstreith v. Bakker, 249 Kan. 67, 815 P.2d 102 (1991). See also II.A.1 and II.B, supra. But in Adams v. St. Francis Medical Center, 264 Kan. 144, 955 P.2d 1169 (1998), the Court required discovery disclosure of relevant facts in such records based upon a balancing of the plaintiff's need for the information against the need for peer review confidentiality. Malice in a peer review session may negate the privilege. Davis v. Hildyard, 34 Kan. App. 2d 22, 113 P.3d 827 (2005).

K.S.A. 65-6002 provides that physician reports to the secretary of health and environment of any person that is suffering from, or has died from AIDS, or that relates to HIV shall be confidential and shall not be disclosed or made public except in the following situations: (1) if the person cannot be identified and the disclosure is for statistical purposes; (2) upon written consent; (3) if disclosure is necessary to protect the public health; (4) for medical emergency, and (5) if required in a court proceeding involving a minor and the information is disclosed in camera. However, coroner's records are not exempt from public disclosure. Burroughs v. Thomas, 23 Kan. App. 2d 769, 937 P.2d 12 (1997), review denied.

K.S.A. 65-5601 *et seq.* provides for confidentiality of patients in treatment facilities (mental health related) and a privilege against disclosure. A variety of exceptions to the privilege (e.g., court orders, necessary treatment communication) exist.

A coroner's autopsy and investigation records are not considered medical records under the Kansas Open Records Act and must be disclosed. Burroughs v. Thomas, 23 Kan. App. 2d 769, 937 P.2d 12 (1997).

C. Criminal Records

K.S.A. 21-6105 defines unjustifiably exposing a convicted or charged person, as unjustifiably communicating or threatening to communicate to another any oral or written statement that any person has been charged with or convicted of a felony, with intent to interfere with the employment or business of the person so charged or convicted. Violation is a class B nonperson misdemeanor. This does not apply to any person or organization supplying this information to another person or organization requesting the information.

K.S.A. 22-4710 states that it is unlawful for any employer or prospective employer to require a person to inspect or challenge any criminal history record relating to such person for the purpose of obtaining a copy of the criminal history record in order to qualify for employment. Violation is a class A misdemeanor. Notwithstanding the above, an employer may require a job applicant or prospective job applicant or prospective independent contractor to sign a release allowing the employer to access such person's criminal history record information for purposes of determining the applicant's fitness for employment. An employer is not liable for an employment decision based upon knowledge of such criminal record history information so long as the information reasonably bears upon the applicant's trustworthiness or the safety and well-being of the employer or the employer's customers. Id. In Wichita Eagle v. Simmons, 274 Kan. 194, 50 P.3d 66,, the Kansas Supreme Court required a variety of records on "supervised persons" (parolees) to be subject to disclosure under KORA. However, the availability of medical records on parolees pertaining to drug and alcohol treatment is limited based on federal HIPPA requirements. Kan. Att'y Gen. Op. No. 2011-005 (March 7, 2011).

D. Subpoenas / Search Warrants

A subpoena for records in an action in which the business is not a party shall inform that the person may serve upon the attorney designated in the subpoena written objection within 14 days after the service of the subpoena. If such objection is made, the business records need not be produced except pursuant to an order of the court upon motion with notice to the person to whom the subpoena was directed. K.S.A. § 60-245a.

Courts have recognized that employees may have an objectively reasonable expectation of privacy in their workspaces or parts thereof. United States v. Higgins, 282 F.3d 1261, 1270 (10th Cir.2002); See O'Connor v. Ortega, 480 U.S. 709, 715-19, 107 S.Ct. 1492, 94 L.Ed.2d 714 (1987). Employees' expectations of privacy in the workplace are decided on a case-by-case basis. See O'Connor v. Ortega, 480 U.S. at 718, 107 S.Ct. 1492. Such expectations "may be reduced by virtue of actual office practices and procedures, or by legitimate regulation." *Id.* at 717. The courts may consider additional factors including: " '(1) the employee's relationship to the item seized; (2) whether the item was in the immediate control of the employee when it was seized; and (3) whether the employee took actions to maintain his privacy in the item.' " United States v. Angevine, 281 F.3d 1130, 1134 (10th Cir. 2002) U.S. v. Cooper, 283 F.Supp.2d 1215 (D.Kan. 2003).

VII. ACTIONS SUBSEQUENT TO EMPLOYMENT

A. References.

No Kansas cases.

B. Non-Compete Agreements.

There are four factors in determining whether to enforce a covenant not to compete. In addition to questioning the reasonableness of the time and territory restrictions in the covenant, a court considers whether the contract protects a legitimate business interest, imposes an undue burden on the employee, or injures the public. Only a legitimate business interest may be protected by a non-competition covenant. If the sole purpose is to avoid ordinary competition, it is unreasonable and unenforceable. Legally sufficient interests in the setting of an employment agreement include trade secrets and customer contacts or relationships. Allen, Gibbs & Houlik, L.C. v. Ristow, 32 Kan. App. 2d 1051, 94 P.3d 724 (2004).

VIII. PROCEDURAL ISSUES

A. Statutes of Limitations

See I.B.1-4 and VII.A, supra.

B. Pleading Requirements

Any pleading which sets forth a claim for relief shall contain "a short and plain statement of the claim showing that the pleader is entitled to relief and . . . a demand for judgment for the relief to which the pleader deems such pleader's self entitled." K.S.A. 60-208. Any pleading demanding relief in excess of $75,000 shall set forth only that the amount sought as damages is in excess of $75,000, without demanding any specific amount of money, except for contract actions. Pleadings which demand damages in the amount of $75,000 or less shall specify the amount of damages sought to be recovered. Id. See also I.B.1, supra, regarding claims for punitive damages. Any pleading containing averments of fraud or mistake shall be stated with particularity. However, malice, intent, knowledge and other conditions of the mind may be generally stated. K.S.A. 60-209. In actions for libel and slander, the plaintiff need not state in the petition any extrinsic facts to show how the defamatory statement applied to such plaintiff. Id. However, it has been held that a plaintiff claiming defamation must allege the exact words published, to whom such word were published, and when and where such words were published. Schulze v. Coykendall, 218 Kan. 653 (1976).

SURVEY OF KENTUCKY EMPLOYMENT LIBEL LAW

Deborah H. Patterson
Wyatt Tarrant & Combs, LLP
2800 PNC Plaza
500 W. Jefferson St.
Louisville, KY 40202
Telephone (502) 589-5235; Facsimile (502) 589-0309
dpatterson@wyattfirm.com

(With Developments Reported Through **November 1, 2012**)

GENERAL COMMENTS

In Kentucky, circuit courts are the trial courts of general jurisdiction, with a right of appeal to the Court of Appeals. Until 1976, the Court of Appeals was Kentucky's highest court. In 1976, the Kentucky Supreme Court, which may grant discretionary review from the Court of Appeals, was created.

Effective January 1, 2005, the Kentucky Civil Rules were amended to require the citation format outlined in *The Bluebook: A Uniform System of Citation* ("the Bluebook"). Formerly, Kentucky courts did not follow the standard Bluebook system of citation. See 2004 Ky. Ct. Order 5 (amending Ky. R. Civ. Pro. 76.12).

By order of the Kentucky Supreme Court, effective January 1, 2007:

> Opinions that are not to be published shall not be cited or used as binding precedent in any other case in any court of this state; however, unpublished Kentucky appellate decisions, rendered after January 1, 2003, may be cited for consideration by the court if there is no published opinion that would adequately address the issue before the court. Opinions cited for consideration by the court shall be set out as an unpublished decision in the filed document and a copy of the entire decision shall be tendered along with the document to the court and all parties to the action.

See 2006 Ky. Ct. order 17.

SIGNIFICANT DEVELOPMENTS SINCE THE 2012 *SURVEY*

None.

I. GENERAL LAW

A. General Employment Law

1. ***At Will Employment.*** Kentucky has long followed the basic rule that employment for an indefinite period of time is terminable at will by either party, without notice or cause. Commonwealth v. Solly, 253 S.W.3d 537 (Ky. 2008) Wymer v. JH Properties, Inc., 50 S.W.3d 195 (Ky. 2001); Firestone Textile Co. Div., see also Firestone Tire and Rubber Co. v. Meadows, 666 S.W.2d 730 (Ky. 1983); Miller v. N.W. Ritter Lumber Co., 33 Ky. L. Rptr. 698, 110 S.W. 869 (Ky. 1908); see also Prod. Oil Co. v. Johnson, 313 S.W.2d 411 (Ky. 1958); Gambrel v. United Mine Workers, 249 S.W.2d 158,160 (Ky. 1952); Louisville & N.R. Co. v. Wells, 160 S.W.2d 16, 18 (Ky. 1942). An at will employment relationship can be modified only if the employer clearly states an intention to do so. Worden v. Louisville and Jefferson County Metro. Sewer Dist., 847 F. Supp. 75, 77 (W.D. Ky. 1994); see also Shah v. Am. Synthetic Rubber Corp., 655 S.W.2d 489, 492 (Ky. 1983).

Kentucky recognizes two limited public policy exceptions to the at will doctrine which prohibit the discharge of an at will employee (1) for failing or refusing to violate the law in the course of employment and (2) for exercising a right conferred by the Constitution or statute. Gryzb v. Evans, 700 S.W.2d 399, 402 (Ky. 1985)/; See also Firestone Textile Co. Div., Firestone Tire and Rubber Co. v. Meadows, 666 S.W.2d 730, 733 (Ky. 1983); First Prop. Mgmt. Corp. v. Zarebidaki, 867 S.W.2d 185 (Ky. 1993); Pari-Mutuel Clerks Union of Kentucky, Local 541 v. Kentucky Jockey Club, 551 S.W.2d 801 (Ky. 1977).

B. Elements of Libel Claim

1. ***Basic Elements.*** "Libel is the publication of a written, defamatory, and unprivileged statement." McCall v. Courier-Journal and Louisville Times Co., 623 S.W.2d 882, 884, 7 Media L. Rep. 2118, 2119 (Ky. 1981). A

defamation claim requires four elements: "(1) defamatory language; (2) about the plaintiff; (3) which is published; and (4) which causes injury to reputation." Columbia Sussex Corp. v. Hay, 627 S.W.2d 270, 273, 7 Media L. Rep. 2424 (Ky. Ct. App. 1981); see also Gahafer v. Ford Motor Co., 328 F.3d 859 (6th Cir. 2003); CMI, Inc. v. Intoximeters, Inc., 918 F. Supp. 1068, 1083 (W.D. Ky. 1995). In determining if a writing is defamatory, the court will evaluate whether the writing tends to "(1) bring a person into public hatred, contempt or ridicule; (2) cause him to be shunned or avoided; or (3) injures him in his business or occupation." McCall, 623 S.W.2d at 884. In other words, language will be considered defamatory when it "tends so to harm the reputation of another as to lower him in the estimation of the community or to deter third persons from associating or dealing with him." Stringer v. Wal-Mart Stores, Inc., et al., 151 S.W.3d 781, 793 (Ky. 2004). The writing must be analyzed in its entirety with the probable effect on the average reader considered. McCall, 623 S.W. 2d at 884. Additionally, the statement must be false. CMI, 918 F. Supp. at 1083. Rumors and innuendo are not enough to constitute defamation. Brett v. Media Operations, Inc., Brett v. Media Gen. Operations, Inc., 326 S.W.3d 452, 459 (Ky Ct. App. 2010). Brett v. Media Gen. Operations, Inc., 326 S.W. 3d 452, 459 (Ky Ct. App. 2010).

Kentucky courts divide libel and slander into two categories: those that are actionable per se and those that are actionable per quod. See CMI, 918 F. Supp. at 1083; see also Hill v. Evans, 258 S.W.2d 917 (Ky. 1953). Defamatory words that are actionable per se are those that "tend to expose the plaintiff to public hatred, ridicule, contempt or disgrace, or to induce an evil opinion of him in the minds of right thinking people and to deprive him of their friendship, intercourse and society." Digest Pub. Co. v. Perry Pub. Co., 284 S.W.2d 832, 834 (Ky. 1955). **Allegations of criminal behavior or unfitness to perform a job are actionable per se and "proof of context indicating malice is not required." Harstad v. Whiteman, 338 S.W.3d 804, 810 (Ky. App. 2011). Words are also actionable per se if they impute the sexual misconduct or immorality to an individual such as portraying that he or she is sexually promiscuous, engaging in adultery, or precipitating a sexually transmitted disease. Jones v. Dirty World Entm't Recordings, LLC, 840 F.Supp. 1008 (E.D. Ky. 2012).** To be actionable per se, it is not necessary that words imply or impute a crime, or involve immoral conduct. Id.; see also Columbia Sussex Corp. v. Hay, 627 S.W.2d 270, 270, 7 Media L. Rep. 2424 (Ky. Ct. App. 1981). Potentially nondefamatory words may rise to the level of libel per se when reviewed with other statements and taken in context. Marcus & Millichap Real Estate Investment Brokerage Co., 395 F. Supp. 2d 541, 555 (W.D. Ky. 2005). Words may be actionable per quod even if they are not defamatory in themselves if the plaintiff can prove special damages caused by the words. CMI, 918 F. Supp. at 1083. In order to assess a statement's meaning, courts examine extrinsic circumstances surrounding the words. Id.

2. ***Fault.***

a. **Private Figure Plaintiff/Matter of Public Concern**. Although Kentucky has yet to distinguish clearly between public and private concerns, courts have described the standard of recovery for private figures. "[A] private plaintiff may recover on a showing of simple negligence, measured by what a reasonably prudent person would or would not have done under the same or similar circumstances. " McCall v. Courier-Journal and Louisville Times Co., 623 S.W.2d 882, 886, 7 Media L. Rep. 2118 (Ky. 1981). At least in the case of a media defendant, this is true even where the defamatory statements were matters of public concern. Yancey v. Hamilton, 786 S.W.2d 854, 859, 17 Media L. Rep. 1012 (Ky. 1989).

b. **Private Figure Plaintiff/Matter of Private Concern.** See I.B.2.a, supra.

c. **Public Figure Plaintiff/Matter of Public Concern.** It is clear that the constitutional protection of political speech requires public officials, who bring defamation lawsuits against critics of their official conduct, to meet a higher standard of proof than ordinary citizens if they are to prevail. See also Welch v. American Publ'g Co. of Ky., 3 S.W.3d 724, 726 (Ky. 1999). A defamatory statement about a public figure is actionable only if it was made with actual malice, *i.e.*, with knowledge that it was false or with reckless disregard of its truth or falsity. Id. at 727.

Although it is the role of the trial judge to determine whether an individual can be considered a public figure, if the facts influencing this decision are in dispute, the jury is to resolve the facts. Yancey v. Hamilton, 786 S.W.2d 854, 859, 17 Media L. Rep. 1012 (Ky. 1989). To determine if an individual is a public figure, the court "must first look to a point in time before the defamatory statements generated their own controversy and ask: (1) in what particular and identifiable public controversy; (2) did [the individual] by some voluntary act involve himself to the extent that he either assumed a role of public prominence, or was in a position to influence others or the outcome of the controversy, and (3) did [the individual] enjoy regular and continuing access to the media?" Warford v. Lexington Herald-Leader Co., 789 S.W.2d 758, 766, 17 Media L. Rep. 1785 (Ky. 1990). Additionally, the court should evaluate the "nature and extent" of the individual's role in the controversy. Id. at 767. Applying these standards, the Warford court concluded that a collegiate assistant basketball coach was not a public figure. Id. at 771.

If a private individual voluntarily injects himself into a public controversy or concern, he may become a limited purpose public figure and be required to meet the actual malice standard of New York Times Co. v. Sullivan, 376 U.S. 254, 1 Media L. Rep. 1527 (1964); See Yancey v. Hamilton, 786 S.W.2d at 859. However, the mere fact that a person was arrested on a matter of public concern is not alone sufficient to change the status of a private individual to a limited purpose public figure. Yancey, 786 S.W.2d at 859. In an unpublished decision, Johnson v. E.W. Scripps Co., 2003 WL 1342961 (Ky. Ct. App. Feb. 28, 2003), the Kentucky Court of Appeals held that an individual who had grown to prominence based on his real estate activities and interaction with city government qualified as a limited purpose public figure. (This is an unreported case and cannot be cited as authority in any Kentucky court but may be considered by the court). The Court of Appeals has also found an individual to be a public figure where, by virtue of his status as a high ranking official in the local school system and his membership on the Board of Education, he voluntarily involved himself in an area of controversy and interest to the general public. McFadden v. Cape Publications, Inc., 2003 WL 22061569 (Ky. Ct. App. Sept. 5, 2003). (This is an unreported case and cannot be cited as authority in any Kentucky court but may be considered by the court.) A federal district court recently held that even a so-called "involuntary public figure" must voluntarily assume the risk of publicity through some action or failure to act. Trover v. Paxton Media Group, No. 4:05CV-014-H, 2007 WL 4302088, at *3-6 (W.D. Ky. Dec. 5, 2007) (This is an unreported case and cannot be cited as authority in any Kentucky court but may be considered by the court). That court rejected as "rather expansive" the D.C. Circuit's view of involuntary public figures in Dameron v. Wash. Magazine, Inc., 779 F.2d 736, 742-43 (D.C. Cir. 1985), which did not impose a voluntariness requirement, relying instead on the Fourth Circuit's narrower definition in Wells v. Liddy, 186 F.3d 505, 539-40 (4th Cir. 1999). Trover, 2007 WL 4302088, at 3-6.

Actual malice is a false statement made with the knowledge that it was false or published with reckless disregard for the truth. Sparks v. Boone, 560 S.W.2d 236 (Ky. Ct. App. 1977). "Actual malice entails more than mere negligence." Welch v. American Publ'g Co. of Ky., 3 S.W. 3d 724, 727 (Ky. 1999). With a media defendant, "[a]ctual malice cannot be based solely on expert evidence that [the media outlet] deviated from accepted journalistic practices." Ky. Kingdom Amusement Co. v. Belo Ky., Inc. d/b/a WHAS-TV, 179 S.W.3d 785, 792 (Ky. 2005). However, a journalism expert's testimony may assist the fact-finder in understanding the circumstantial evidence of the case; therefore, the Kentucky Supreme Court held that a trial court did not commit error in admitting the testimony of an expert. Id. In Ball v. E.W. Scripps Co., 801 S.W.2d 684, 18 Media L. Rep. 1545 (Ky. 1990), the Kentucky Supreme Court reversed the Court of Appeals and reinstated a jury's finding of actual malice in the publication of a series of stories critical of a county prosecutor. The court held that the record provided evidence sufficient for a jury to have found that the publication was made with actual malice, including the way the articles were laid out and the failure to make any retraction. Id. In Warford v. Lexington Herald-Leader Co., 789 S.W.2d 758, 17 Media L. Rep. 1785 (Ky. 1990), the Kentucky Supreme Court held that the evidence could support a finding of actual malice since it was clear that the newspaper must have entertained serious doubts as to the truth of the published allegation. The court noted that a finding of actual malice could be supported by the minimal efforts made to verify the source's credibility, by the fact that the paper knew of the potential harm the publication could cause the plaintiff but did not heighten its investigative efforts accordingly, and by the evidence demonstrating the paper was committed to running the story regardless of the truth. Id. A court recently noted, in dictum, that "[i]n defamation cases where the defendant is an institution rather than an individual, the plaintiff is required to prove that the individual responsible for the statement's publication acted with the requisite state of mind, i.e. actual malice." Gen. Drivers, Warehousemen and Helpers Local Union No. 89 v. Winstead, No. 3:03-CV-791-S, 2007 WL 4300633, at *4 (W.D. Ky. Dec. 4, 2007) (This is an unreported case and cannot be cited as authority in any Kentucky court but may be considered by the court). However, in Welch, 3 S.W.3d at 729, the Kentucky Supreme Court ruled that a newspaper's failure to investigate the accuracy of statements in a political ad prior to publication was not enough to support a finding of actual malice. Welch was distinguished from Warford because it involved a political advertisement rather than an investigative news story. Id. In an unpublished decision, Seaman v. Musselman, 2003 WL 21512489 (Ky. Ct. App. July 3, 2003), the Kentucky Court of Appeals found that the failure to investigate was not enough to support a finding of actual malice in a case involving a satirical news article. (This is an unreported case and cannot be cited as authority in any Kentucky court but may be considered by the court.)

3. ***Falsity.*** To maintain an action for libel, the published statements must be false. See CMI, Inc. v. Intoximeters, Inc., 918 F. Supp. 1068, 1083 (W.D. Ky. 1995); see also Wolff v. Benovitz, 192 S.W.2d 730, 733, (Ky. 1945) ("[n]o one can be heard to complain in a civil action that the truth was published of him"). Plaintiffs must present evidence that the allegedly defamatory language is not true in order to demonstrate a claim for defamation. Fieldturf, Inc. v. Southwest Recreational Indus., Inc., 235 F. Supp. 2d 708, 735 (E.D. Ky. 2002), *vacated in part on other grounds by* Fieldturf, Inc. v. Southwest Recreational Indus., Inc., 357 F.3d 1266 (Fed. Cir. 2004). Furthermore, it has long been the rule that "in an action for libel, pleading and proof of the truth of the written statements is always a complete defense, although the publication may be inspired by malice or ill will and be libelous per se." Pennington v. Little, 99 S.W.2d 776, 777 (Ky. 1936); see also Buchholtz v. Dugan, 977 S.W.2d 24, 27 (Ky. Ct. App. 1998). A substantially true statement is not false and not actionable. Bell v. Courier-Journal & Louisville Times Co., 402 S.W.2d 84 (Ky. 1966). A statement is substantially true when the

inaccuracy does not appreciably affect the defamatory result. Pearce v. Courier-Journal, 683 S.W.2d 633, 11 Media L. Rep. 1498 (Ky. Ct. App. 1985). However, the doctrine of "substantial truth" relates only to incidental information and not to the essential content of a defamatory communication. Ky. Kingdom Amusement Co. v. Belo Ky., Inc., 179 S.W.3d 785, 791 (Ky. 2005).

4. ***Defamatory Statement of Fact.*** Kentucky common law recognized that an expression of opinion can amount to defamation, McGowan v. Manifee, 23 Ky. (7 T.B. Mon.) 314 (Ky. 1828), but the Kentucky Court of Appeals has applied the Gertz view that a statement of opinion based on disclosed true facts is absolutely privileged. Haynes v. McConnell, 642 S.W.2d 902 (Ky. Ct. App. 1982). With respect to the fact-opinion distinction, the Kentucky Supreme Court has adopted and followed the Restatement (Second) of Torts approach. A statement in the form of an opinion "is actionable only if it implies the allegation of undisclosed defamatory fact as the basis for the opinion." Restatement (Second) of Torts § 566 (1977); see also Yancey v. Hamilton, 786 S.W.2d 854, 857, 17 Media L. Rep. 1012 (Ky. 1989) (rejecting the four-part test set out in Ollman v. Evans, 750 F.2d 970, 11 Media L. Rep. 1433 (D.C. Cir. 1984), in favor of the Restatement (Second) of Torts approach). The Kentucky Supreme Court, in Welch v. American Publ'g Co. of Ky., 3 S.W.3d 724, 730 (Ky. 1999), held that the terms "[b]roke" and "[s]quandered" were "generalized rhetoric bandied about in a political campaign [and] not the language upon which a defamation lawsuit should be based, but instead is political opinion solidly protected by the First Amendment." The Kentucky Constitution expressly recognizes the inherent and inalienable right "of freely communicating . . . thoughts and opinions." Ky. Const. § 1. It has been suggested that this section may provide an additional independent basis for the application of the Gertz view of opinion. Haynes, 642 S.W.2d at 905. In Marshall v. Welch, 2004 WL 1857190 (Ky. Ct. App., 2004), the Kentucky Court of Appeals held that the natural meaning of the word "bizarre" is not necessarily characterized as slanderous or defamatory. (This is an unreported case and cannot be cited as authority in any Kentucky court but may be considered by the court.)

5. ***Of and Concerning Plaintiff.*** A statement can be defamatory even if the plaintiff is not specifically named. However, the plaintiff must be living; an action for defamation does not survive the death of the party defamed. KRS 411.140; Mineer v. Williams, 82 F. Supp. 2d 702, 704 (E.D. Ky. 2000). The statement does not lose its defamatory nature by failing to name its subject as long as his/her identity is recognizable by friends and acquaintances. E.W. Scripps Co. v. Cholmondelay, 569 S.W.2d 700, 702, 3 Media L. Rep. 2462 (Ky. Ct. App. 1978). The fact that a person or corporation has been inaccurately designated in a defamatory publication is immaterial if the words are readily comprehended to apply to the plaintiff. Axton Fisher Tobacco Co. v. Evening Post Co., 183 S.W. 269, 274 (Ky. 1916); see also Louisville Times Co. v. Emrich, 66 S.W.2d 73 (Ky. 1933).

Although difficult to prove, a defamation claim can arise from a statement directed at an entire class. "To defame a class, the statement must be applicable to every member of the class, and if the words used contain no reflection upon any particular individual, no averment can make them defamatory." Kentucky Fried Chicken of Bowling Green, Inc. v. Sanders, 563 S.W.2d 8, 9, 3 Media L. Rep. 2054 (Ky. 1978). Additionally, the court held that, "as the size of the class increases it becomes more and more difficult for one to show that he was the one at whom the statement was directed." Id. at 9. If the class is relatively small, however, any member of the class can sue if defamatory imputations were made against the whole class. Columbia Sussex Corp. v. Hay, 627 S.W.2d 270, 275, 7 Media L. Rep. 2424 (Ky. Ct. App. 1981). In group libel situations, a plaintiff cannot collect damages unless the libelous statements are applicable to every member of the class, not merely to an aggregate body of persons. O'Brien v. Williamson Daily News, 735 F. Supp. 218, 222, 18 Media L. Rep. 1037 (E.D. Ky. 1990), aff'd., 931 F.2d 893 (6th Cir. 1991).

6. ***Publication.*** "Absent publication, there can be no libel." Caslin v. General Elec. Co., 608 S.W.2d 69, 70 (Ky. Ct. App. 1980). A statement can be published without mentioning the plaintiff's name. Vanover v. Wells, 94 S.W.2d 999, 1001 (Ky. 1936) (citing Justice v. Wellman, 260 Ky. 479, 86 S.W.2d 132 (Ky. 1935)).

a. **Intracorporate Communication.** In Biber v. Duplicator Sales & Service, Inc., 155 S.W.3d 732 (Ky. Ct. App. 2004), the Kentucky Court of Appeals held that communications within an entity should be considered a publication under defamation law. Therefore, such statements are not protected by the intra-corporate immunity rule and are actionable under defamation law.

b. **Compelled Self-Publication.** No reported cases.

c. **Republication.** One who repeats a slander is liable. Evans v. Smith, 21 Ky. (T.B. Mon.) 363 (Ky. 1827); Nicholson v. Rust, 21 Ky. L. Rptr. 645, 52 S.W. 933 (Ky. 1899). "An unauthorized repetition or successive publication of libelous matter affords in itself a right of action." Gearhart v. WSAZ, Inc., 150 F. Supp. 98, 109 (E.D. Ky. 1957), aff'd sub nom. WSAZ, Inc. v. Lyons, 254 F.2d 242 (6th Cir. 1958). The mere act of editing a website to add unrelated content or making mere technical changes to a website does not constitute republication of unrelated defamatory material; however, where substantive material is added to a website and that material is related to defamatory material already posted, a republication has occurred and the statute of limitations is restarted. Davis v. Mitan, 347 B.R. 607, 612 (W.D. Ky. 2006). Applying this rule, a federal district court predicted that under Kentucky law a later article's mere reference and a website's hyperlink to a previously published alleged defamatory article did not constitute republication. Salyer v. The Southern Poverty Law Center, 701 F. Supp. 2d 912, 916-18 (W.D. Ky. 2009). Nor did republication occur by mailing a copy of the defamatory article that was part of the original printing. Id. at 919-20.

7. ***Statements versus Conduct.*** No reported cases.

8. ***Damages.*** An explanation of various damage awards was clearly articulated in Columbia Sussex Corp. v. Hay, 627 S.W.2d 270, 274, 7 Media L. Rep. 2424 (Ky. Ct. App. 1981). In Columbia Sussex, the Kentucky Court of Appeals stated, "[d]efamation damages are categorized into compensatory (general and special) and punitive. Special damages are those beyond mere embarrassment which support actual economic loss; general damages relate to humiliation, mental anguish, etc." Id. at 274.

a. **Presumed Damages and Libel Per Se.** Words which are libelous per se are "by themselves regarded [as] sufficient evidence of pecuniary loss, and no evidence other than their use is required to show pecuniary loss." Compton v. Wilkins, 176 S.W. 36, 38 (Ky. 1915). Published words are actionable per se if they directly tend to prejudice or injure anyone in his profession, trade or business, Tucker v. Kilgore, 388 S.W.2d 112 (Ky. 1964), or if they tend to bring the plaintiff into contempt, ridicule or disgrace. Gearhart v. WSAZ, Inc., 150 F. Supp. 98 (E.D. Ky. 1957), aff'd sub nom. WSAZ, Inc. v. Lyons, 254 F.2d 242 (6th Cir. 1958). Words are measured by their natural effect on the mind of the average lay person. Id. Defamatory words determined to be libel per se are actionable on their face since injury to reputation is presumed. Stringer v. Wal-Mart Stores, Inc., et al., 151 S.W.3d 781, 794 (Ky. 2004).

(1) **Employment-Related Criticism.** In Columbia Sussex Corp. v. Hay, 627 S.W.2d 270, 7 Media L. Rep. 2424 (Ky. Ct. App. 1981), the President and General Manager of a hotel required employees to take a polygraph test after a robbery at the hotel. While informing the hotel manager that all the employees were required to take the polygraph test, the President said, in the presence of others, that he suspected either the hotel manager or one of the employees to be responsible for the robbery. The court concluded that the words were slanderous per se and that injury to reputation could be presumed. Id. In Gahafer v. Ford Motor Co., 328 F.3d 859 (6th Cir. 2003), the Sixth Circuit Court of Appeals determined that a supervisor's outburst accusing the plaintiff of spending too much time on a project was not equivalent to an accusation of "unfitness, incompetence or lack of qualification," and therefore did not amount to slander per se under Kentucky law. Id. at 862, 863. However, an employer's false accusation of theft by an employee is actionable per se regardless of the amount of money involved or whether such an accusation is general or specific. Stringer v. Wal-Mart Stores, Inc., et al., 151 S.W.3d 781(Ky. 2004). An employer's allegation of a "sexual liaison" with a co-worker and of the misappropriation of company funds by its employee was likewise found to be libelous per se by the Kentucky Court of Appeals. Disabled Am. Veterans Dept. of Ky., Inc. v. Crabb, 182 S.W.3d 541 (Ky. Ct. App. 2005). However, the Kentucky Court of Appeals held that while statements of habitual tardiness in the employee's trade or profession would be defamatory per se in the normal defamation case, because the statements occurred in the context of a labor dispute, the employee must prove special damages. Gilliam v. Pikeville United Methodist Hospital of Kentucky, Inc., 215 S.W.3d 56 (Ky. Ct. App. 2006). In determining that the federal case law regarding the National Labor Relations Act preempts the presumption of damages in cases of libel per se, the court relied on the United States Supreme Court's opinion in Linn v. United Plant Guard Workers of America, Local 114, 383 U.S. 53 (1966). Id. See also II.A.2.a. and III, infra.

(2) **Single Instance Rule.** Although a Kentucky state court has not yet directly addressed this issue, a federal district court predicted that Kentucky would adopted the "single publication rule." Mitan v. Davis, 243 F. Supp. 2d 719, 722 (W.D. Ky. 2003). Under this rule, "any one edition of a book or newspaper, or any one radio or television broadcast, exhibition or a motion picture or similar aggregate communication is a single publication." Id. (quoting Restatement (Second) of Torts § 557A (1977)). "As a result, the aggregate communication can give rise to only one action in any one jurisdiction where the dissemination occurred and only one statute of limitations, which begins to run when 'the finished product was released by the publisher for sale in accord with trade practice.'" Id. (quoting Zuck v. Interstate Publishing Corp., 317 F.2d 727, 730 (2d Cir. 1963)). "A republication occurs when a defamatory article is placed in a new form (paperback as opposed to hardcover) or edited in a new form." Id. (citing Firth v. State, 184 Misc.2d 105, 706 N.Y.S. 2d 835, 841 (N.Y.Ct.Cl. 2000)). The court reasoned that a Kentucky court examining the issue today would adopt the rule because (1) Kentucky courts have frequently looked to the Restatement of Torts in ascertaining tort liability, (2) the single publication rule is widely accepted in other jurisdictions, (3) several well-respected commentators on Kentucky law have treated the single publication rule as prevailing, and (4) the single publication rule is much better equipped to handle aggregate communication. Id.

b. **Punitive Damages.** The recovery of punitive damages in a libel action is affected by both case law and statute in Kentucky. Unfortunately, those authorities offer conflicting views on the proper standards of recovery. Where actual malice and also the malice and oppression required by Kentucky's punitive damages statute, KRS 411.184, are proven by clear and convincing evidence, punitive damages are recoverable. Ky. Kingdom Amusement Co. v. Belo Ky., Inc., 179 S.W.3d 785 (Ky. 2005).

(1) **Case law requirements.** The leading case addressing the issue of punitive damages in Kentucky is Columbia Sussex Corp. v. Hay, 627 S.W.2d 270, 7 Media L. Rep. 2424 (Ky. Ct. App. 1981). In Columbia Sussex, the court held that because "a showing of special damages is mandatory to create a prima facie action for slander, such necessarily is a prerequisite to an award of punitive damages." Id. at 274. "With slander per se, however, the representation of special damages is optional; it is required neither for a prima facie case nor for the recovery of punitive damages." Id. at 274 (citing Taylor v. Moseley, 170 Ky. 592, (Ky. 1916)). The court specifically pointed out the distinction between this case and Gertz v. Robert Welch, Inc., 418 U.S. 323, 342, 1 Media L. Rep. 1633 (1974). Id. at 276. Gertz involved a media defendant whom the Court guarded from strict liability by requiring the showing of actual malice before punitive damages could be awarded. Because Columbia Sussex involved a private plaintiff and a private defendant, the Kentucky Supreme Court concluded that the interest in protecting uninhibited reporting by the press was absent. Id. In such a case, malice does not have to be shown before punitive damages will be awarded Id. at 277.

(2) **Statutory requirements.**

(a) **Defendants generally.** Since Columbia Sussex, the Kentucky legislature has enacted a punitive damages statute. KRS 411.184(2) requires plaintiffs in all cases in which punitive damages are sought to prove "by clear and convincing evidence, that the defendant from whom such damages are sought acted toward the plaintiff with oppression, fraud or malice." KRS 411.184(1)(c) defines malice as "conduct which is specifically intended by the defendant to cause tangible or intangible injury to the plaintiff or conduct that is carried out by the defendant both with a flagrant indifference to the rights of the plaintiff and with a subjective awareness that such conduct will result in human death or bodily harm." Although this statute appears to conflict with the rule announced in Columbia Sussex, the Kentucky Supreme Court has held KRS 411.184(1)(c) unconstitutional. See Williams v. Wilson, 972 S.W.2d 260 (Ky. 1998). Furthermore, the court held that the constitutionality of KRS 411.184(2) was not properly before the court and specifically withheld judgment of the constitutionality of that provision. Id. Since Williams, the Kentucky Supreme Court has not addressed the constitutionality of KRS 411.184 but has applied the statute in allowing an award of punitive damages in a defamation case involving a public figure. Ky. Kingdom Amusement Co. v. Belo Ky., Inc., 179 S.W.3d 785, (Ky. 2005). See Farmland Mut. Ins. Co. v. Johnson, 36 S.W.3d 368, 381-382 (Ky. 2000).

(b) **Media defendants**. With media defendants, Kentucky requires the plaintiff first make a sufficient demand for a correction of the alleged defamatory statement and be denied such correction before the plaintiff is entitled to punitive damages.

In libel actions against a newspaper, magazine, or periodical, KRS 411.051 (1) provides:

> In any action for damages for the publication of a defamatory statement in a newspaper, magazine, or periodical, the defendant shall be liable for actual damages sustained by plaintiff. The defendant may plead the publication of a correction in mitigation of damages. Punitive damages may be recovered only if the plaintiff shall allege and prove publication with legal malice and that the newspaper, magazine, or periodical failed to make conspicuous and timely publication of a correction after receiving a sufficient demand for correction.

In instances involving radio or television broadcasting stations, KRS 411.061(1) provides:

> In any action against a radio or television broadcasting station for damages for the publication of a defamatory statement by a visual or sound radio broadcast, the plaintiff shall recover no more than special damages unless he shall allege and prove that he made a sufficient demand for correction and that the radio or television broadcasting station, failed to make conspicuous and timely publication of said correction.

II. PRIVILEGES AND DEFENSES

A. Scope of Privileges

1. ***Absolute Privilege.*** The cases in which an absolute privilege applies are strictly limited to judicial and legislative proceedings, matters involving military affairs, and communications made in the discharge of a duty under

express authority of law by or to heads of executive departments of the state. Begley v. Louisville Times Co., 272 Ky. 805, (Ky. 1938); Tanner v. Stevenson, 138 Ky. 578, (Ky. 1910). The privilege as to judicial proceedings extends to all pleadings, motions, affidavits, and other such papers. Hayes v. Rodgers, 447 S.W.2d 597 (Ky. 1969). Legislative immunity applies not only to speech and debate but also to voting, reporting and every act or execution of legislative duties. Wiggins v. Stuart, 671 S.W.2d 262 (Ky. Ct. App. 1984). **This absolute privilege is not restricted to the state legislature, but also extends to members of secondary legislative bodies. Smith v. Martin, 331 S.W.3d 637, 640–41 (Ky. App. 2011) (noting that under KRS 83A.060(15) "members of secondary legislative bodies, such as city councils, acquired an absolute privilege from liability for statements" made during a debate before a formal meeting of the assembly). The court stated that this privilege is "to be liberally construed and extends broadly to the publication of defamatory matter while performing legislative duties."** The scope of absolute privilege covers administrative bodies in the exercise of quasi-judicial powers which they are required by statute to exercise provided the defamatory communication is pertinent to the inquiry under investigation. Pearce v. Courier-Journal, 683 S.W.2d 633, 11 Media L. Rep. 1498 (Ky. Ct. App. 1985); McAlister & Co. v. Jenkins, 214 Ky. 802, 284 S.W. 88 (Ky. 1926). The absolute privilege applies only to heads of executive departments of state; it does not apply to heads of local government. Haynes v. McConnell, 642 S.W.2d 902 (Ky. Ct. App. 1982); Lanier v. Higgins, 623 S.W.2d 914 (Ky. Ct. App. 1981). The privilege conferred upon the reporting of judicial and administrative proceedings of public concern relates equally to actions founded upon the tort of invasion of the right of privacy. Pearce v. Courier-Journal, 683 S.W.2d 633, 11 Media L. Rep. 1498 (Ky. Ct. App. 1985).

A Kentucky Court of Appeals has reiterated a two-pronged test for determining whether the judicial proceedings privilege applies to a particular statement. This test was previously set forth in the Sixth Circuit case of General Electric Co. v. Sargent & Lundy, 916 F.2d 1119, 1127 (6th Cir. 1990). First, the statement must be made "preliminary to a proposed judicial proceeding, or in the institution of, or during the course and as a part of a judicial proceeding." Rogers v. Luttrell, 144 S.W.3d 841 (Ky. Ct. App. 2004). Second, the statement must have "some relation to a proceeding that is contemplated in good faith." Id. So long as a statement is found to fall under the judicial proceeding privilege, it is absolutely privileged regardless of whether the statement may be false or alleged with malice. Imboden v. Phelps, 2003 WL 21833358 (Ky. Ct. App. 2003). (This is an unreported case and cannot be cited as authority in any Kentucky court but may be considered by the court.)

2. ***Qualified Privileges.*** The doctrine of qualified privilege exists when the libel or slander is made in good faith without actual malice, with reasonable or probable grounds to believe it to be true, and upon a subject matter in which the author of the communication has an interest, or in reference to which he or she has a duty, to a person having a corresponding interest or duty. Louisville Times Co. v. Lyttle, 257 Ky. 132, 77 S.W.2d 432 (Ky. 1934). However, a qualified privilege "means nothing more than the occasion of making it rebut the prima facie inference of malice arising from the publication of matter prejudicial to the character of the plaintiff, and throws upon him the onus of proving malice in fact." Evening Post Co. v. Richardson, 113 Ky. 641, 68 S.W. 665 (Ky. 1902). All qualified privileges "must be exercised in a reasonable manner and for a proper purpose." Stringer v. Wal-Mart Stores, Inc., et al., 151 S.W.3d 781, 797 (Ky. 2004). Whether a communication is privileged is a question of law for the court. Caslin v. General Elec. Co., 608 S.W.2d 69, 71 (Ky. Ct. App. 1980); Landrum v. Braun, 978 S.W.2d 756 (Ky. 1998). **Whether a privilege may be waived or abused is an issue to be determined by the jury. Harstad v. Whiteman, 338 S.W.3d 804, 812 (Ky. App. 2011).** Further, under Kentucky law, a "factfinder may infer malice solely from falsity." Hodges v. Ford Motor Co., 272 Fed.Appx. 451, 2008 WL 897893, at *6 (6th Cir. Apr. 1, 2008).

a. **Common Interest.** One situation where a qualified privilege exists is where "the communication is one in which the party has an interest[,] it is made to another having a corresponding interest, [and] made in good faith and without actual malice." Baker v. Clark, 186 Ky. 816, 218 S.W. 280, 285 (Ky. 1920) (internal quotes omitted). Because under Church doctrine a Jewish individual was required to report to his rabbi the unorthodox preparation of food he witnessed, a qualified privilege applied. Wolff v. Benovitz, 301 Ky. 661, 192 S.W.2d 730 (Ky. 1945). "[T]he qualified privilege afforded to defamatory statements made in the course of church related matters" is recognized in Kentucky. Cargill v. Greater Salem Baptist Church, 215 S.W.3d 63 (Ky. Ct. App. 2006). Likewise, a qualified privilege attached when allegations of immoral conduct by a teacher were discussed at a meeting of a Parent-Teacher Association even though the remarks were libelous per se. Thompson v. Bridges, 209 Ky. 710, 273 S.W. 529 (Ky. 1925). A common interest also created a qualified privilege precluding liability in a case where a man shared with his neighbor the name of the individual he thought was responsible for setting their homes on fire. Edwards v. Kevil, 133 Ky. 392, 118 S.W. 273 (Ky. 1909). In contrast, statements by managers of a delivery service to contract employees regarding alleged theft by another contract employee did not fall within the protection of qualified privilege, because the contractors did not need to know about the conduct of another contractor, and the managers could not believe in good faith that they had a duty to discuss the matter with the contractors. Bertram v. Fed. Express Corp., No. 05-28-C, 2008 WL 170063, at *5 (W.D. Ky. Jan. 17, 2008) (This is an unreported case and cannot be cited as authority in any Kentucky court but may be considered by the court). Nevertheless, employers are liable for defamatory statements made by agents and servants acting within the scope of their authority regardless of the employer's knowledge of or approval of the statement. Dossett v. New York Min. & Mfg. Co., 451 S.W.2d 843 (Ky. 1970). In the employment context, written communications concerning an employee's performance appraisal are privileged communications. Louisville & N.R. Co. v. Marshall, 586 S.W.2d 274 (Ky. Ct. App. 1979); Caslin v. General Elec. Co., 608 S.W.2d 69 (Ky. Ct. App. 1980); Wyant v. SCM Corp., 692 S.W.2d 814 (Ky. Ct. App. 1985); Stewart v. Pantry, Inc., 715 F. Supp. 1361, 1366-67 (W.D. Ky. 1988). See also Rich for Rich v. Kentucky Country Day, Inc., 793 S.W.2d 832, 838 (Ky. Ct. App. 1990); Columbia Sussex Corp. v. Hay, 627 S.W.2d 270, 275-76, 7 Media L. Rep. 2424 (Ky. Ct. App. 1981); Dossett v. New York Min. & Mfg. Co., 451 S.W.2d 843 (Ky. 1970).

b. **Duty.** Communications required for the common protection of society are privileged if made without malice. Nix v. Caldwell, 81 Ky. 293 (1883). Consequently, charges that a schoolteacher "has no education and don't [sic] do her duty at school" were not actionable when made in a letter written to the state department of education and in good faith with reasonable and probable grounds for believing them to be true. Johnson v. Langley, 247 Ky. 387, (Ky. 1933). In Bonham v. Dotson, 216 Ky. 660, (Ky. 1926), a letter from a school trustee to the state superintendent of schools which asserted a building contractor's incompetency was also qualifiedly privileged if not false and malicious. When a college student was dismissed for indecently exposing himself in the window of his dormitory room, letters from the college president to the student's father explaining the reasons for dismissal were privileged as pursuant to the president's duty. Baskett v. Crossfield, 190 Ky. 751, 228 S.W. 673 (Ky. 1920). Reporting information about a crime, when done with probable cause, has long been privileged in Kentucky. Evans v. Sir Pizza, No. 09-86-KSF, 2010 WL 2365331, at *4 (E.D. Ky. Jun 11, 2010) (citing Grimes v. Coyle, 45 Ky. (6th B.Monroe) 301 (1845)). However, no privilege attached to an accusation of guilt of a crime made to a police officer executing a related search warrant after it had been issued. Rutherford v. Church, 243 Ky. 501, 49 S.W.2d 326 (Ky. 1932). In an unpublished decision, McGurl v. Friends School, Inc., 2002-CA-115-MR, 2003 WL 1343248 (Feb. 14, 2003), the court stated that "[a] qualified privilege exists where there is a duty to publish the information in question." Because a parent volunteering at a school had a duty to communicate threats to school administrators, and a school administrator had a duty to communicate threats to school counsel and to the police, the court in that case found that a qualified privilege did exist. Id. (This is an unreported case and cannot be cited as authority in any Kentucky court but may be considered by the court.) The Kentucky Supreme Court also found that an "absolute privilege" protects those who are required by law to publish defamatory material, except persons "who, with a malicious purpose and under no legal compulsion to do so, creates defamatory material with the expectation that it would be published." Hill v. Kentucky Lottery Comm'n., 327 S.W.3d 412, 425 (Ky. 2010). Recently, the Kentucky Court of Appeals found that a plaintiff failed in his burden to show that a statement made provided during quasi-judicial/administrative proceedings were made for an improper purpose. Hawkins v. Miller, 301 S.W.3d 507, 509 (Ky. Ct. App. 2009).

c. **Criticism of Public Employee.** "Comment on and criticism of the acts and conduct of public men are privileged, if fair and reasonable and made in good faith. The right to criticize, however, does not embrace the right to make false statements of fact." Democrat Pub. Co. v. Harvey, 181 Ky. 730, 205 S.W. 908 (Ky. 1918). Accordingly, a defamatory question asked of the plaintiff, a city employee, by the city manager in an investigatory meeting was not actionable. Stewart v. Williams, 309 Ky. 706, 218 S.W.2d 948 (Ky. 1949).

d. **Limitation on Qualified Privileges.** Sustaining a claim of qualified privilege requires (1) that the defamatory communication be made in good faith, without malice, in answer to an inquiry, and in the reasonable protection of the defendant's own interest or performance of a duty to society; (2) that the defendant honestly believes the communication to be true; (3) that reasonable or probable grounds for the suspicion are known to the defendant; (4) that the communication, if made in answer to an inquiry, does not go further than to truly state the facts upon which the suspicion is grounded, and to satisfy the inquirer that there are reasons for the suspicion. Miller v. Howe, 245 Ky. 568, 53 S.W.2d 938, 939 (Ky. 1932). However, the Miller court noted that the requirements were not to be applied rigidly, because there are cases that should be privileged although all four requirements are not specifically met. See id. Because Kentucky law permits the inference of malice from the mere falsity of a statement, a dispute over the truth or falsity of a defamatory statement requires the court leave the question of whether actual malice exists to the jury as well, even where qualified privilege applies and no other evidence of malice is produced. Hodges v. Ford Motor Co., 272 Fed.Appx. 451, 2008 WL 897893, at *5-6 (6th Cir. Apr. 1, 2008) (not selected for publication in the Federal Reporter). **But see Harstad v. Whiteman, 338 S.W.3d 804, 813 (Ky. App. 2011) (noting that falsity alone did not allow the court to reasonably conclude that the statements were maliciously uttered as opposed to being the product of mistaken observation).**

(1) **Constitutional or Actual Malice.** Constitutional malice is not required to defeat a qualified privilege. See, e.g., Pearce v. Courier-Journal & Louisville Times Co., 683 S.W.2d 633, 11 Media L. Rep. 1498 (Ky. App. 1985). **But see Toler v. Sud-Chemie, Inc., 2011 WL 744515 (Ky. App.) (qualified privilege is overcome by proof of "actual malice," not "malice in fact").**

(2) **Common Law Malice**. In Pearce v. Courier-Journal & Louisville Times Co., 683 S.W.2d 633, 11 Media L. Rep. 1498 (Ky. App. 1985), the Kentucky Court of Appeals held that a qualified privilege

could be defeated by showing that a publication was "made solely for the purpose of causing harm to the person defamed." Id. **But see Toler, 2011 WL 744515.**

(3) **Other Limitations on Qualified Privileges.** A defendant loses the privilege if he or she acts maliciously or in excess of the privilege. Baker v. Clark, 186 Ky. 816, 218 S.W. 280 (Ky. 1920). Exercising an otherwise qualified privilege in an unreasonable manner or for an improper purpose, as when an individual member of a large organization is singled out and exposed to public scorn, defeats the privilege. The defamatory matter published must bear upon the interest entitled to protection in order for the privilege to attach. Tucker v. Kilgore, 388 S.W.2d 112 (Ky. 1964). Excessive publication will defeat the privilege as well. Rutherford v. Church, 243 Ky. 501, 49 S.W.2d 326 (Ky. 1932); Conner v. Taylor, 233 Ky. 706, 26 S.W.2d 561 (Ky. 1930).

e. **Question of Fact or Law.** The question of the existence of privilege is a matter of law for the court's determination. Caslin v. General Elec. Co., 608 S.W.2d 69 (Ky. Ct. App. 1980); see also Landrum v. Braun, 978 S.W.2d 756 (Ky. Ct. App. 1998). The Kentucky Court of Appeals in Columbia Sussex Corp., Inc. v. Hay, 627 S.W.2d 270, 7 Media L. Rep. 2424 (Ky. Ct. App. 1981) ruled that the jury must be given an opportunity to judge a defense of privilege. **Whether a privilege may be waived or abused is an issue to be determined by the jury. Harstad v. Whiteman, 338 S.W.3d 804, 812 (Ky. App. 2011).**

f. **Burden of Proof.** The standard of proof for a public figure plaintiff is clear and convincing evidence. Warford v. Lexington Herald-Leader Co., 789 S.W.2d 758, 771, 17 Media L. Rep. 1785 (Ky. 1990). Where privilege is at issue, the plaintiff has the burden to defeat the defense by showing either that there was no privilege under the circumstances or that it had been abused. Columbia Sussex Corp., Inc. v. Hay, 627 S.W.2d 270, 7 Media L. Rep. 2424 (Ky. Ct. App. 1981). **However, under Kentucky law, "[a] fact finder may infer malice solely from falsity." Hodges v. Ford Motor Co., No. 06-6223, 2008 WL 897893, at *6 (6th Cir. Apr. 1, 2008) (unreported). But see Harstad v. Whiteman, 338 S.W.3d 804, 813 (Ky. App. 2011) (noting that falsity alone did not allow the court to reasonably conclude that the statements were maliciously uttered as opposed to being the product of mistaken observation).** Where qualified privilege is pleaded, the burden of proving actual malice is on the plaintiff who must show that publication was induced by a malicious motive. Weinstein v. Rhorer, 240 Ky. 679, 42 S.W.2d 892 (Ky. 1931); Tanner v. Stevenson, 138 Ky. 578, 128 S.W. 878 (Ky. 1910).

B. Standard Libel Defenses

1. ***Truth.*** In Kentucky "truth is a complete defense and thus a defendant able to prove the truth of the defamatory statement at issue cannot be held liable for defamation." Stringer v. Wal-Mart Stores, Inc., 151 S.W.3d 781, 795-96 (Ky. 2004). Substantial truth is a complete defense to a libel action, even though the publication may have been inspired by malice or ill will and is libelous per se. Buchholtz v. Dugan, 977 S.W.2d 24, 27 (Ky. Ct. App. 1998). A statement is substantially true when the inaccuracy in the reportage does not appreciably affect the defamatory result. Pearce v. Courier-Journal & Louisville Times Co., 683 S.W.2d 633, 11 Media L. Rep. 1498 (Ky. App. 1985). But see Kentucky Kingdom Amusement v. Belo Kentucky, Inc., 179 S.W.3d 785, 791-92 (Ky. 2005) (holding that the "substantially true" analysis relates only to incidental information and not essential content). One court has suggested that the truth defense does not have constitutional origins, but could be abolished by statute. Pennington v. Little, 266 Ky. 750, 99 S.W.2d 776 (Ky. 1936). The defendant's belief as to the truth of a defamatory statement and the defendant's intent to injure the plaintiff are both irrelevant when the statement made by the defendant is true. Louisville Press Co. v. Tennelly, 105 Ky. 365, 49 S.W. 15 (Ky. 1899). The party asserting this defense has the burden of proof in establishing the truth or privileged nature of the statement. Randy's Body Shop, Inc. v. Kentucky Farm Bureau, 2002-CA-1614-MR, 2004 WL 405742 (Ky. Ct. App., March 5, 2004). (This is an unreported case and cannot be cited as authority in any Kentucky court but may be considered by the court.)

2. ***Opinion.*** Kentucky common law recognized that an expression of opinion can amount to defamation, McGowan v. Manifee, 23 Ky. (7 T.B. Mon.) 314 (Ky. 1828), but the Kentucky Court of Appeals has applied the Gertz view that a statement of opinion based on disclosed true facts is absolutely privileged. Haynes v. McConnell, 642 S.W.2d 902 (Ky. Ct. App. 1982). With respect to the fact-opinion distinction, the Kentucky Supreme Court has adopted and followed the Restatement (Second) of Torts approach. A statement in the form of an opinion "is actionable only if it implies the allegation of undisclosed defamatory fact as the basis for the opinion." See Restatement (Second) of Torts § 566 (1977). See also Yancey v. Hamilton, 786 S.W.2d 854, 857, 17 Media L. Rep. 1012 (Ky. 1989) (rejecting the four-part test set out in Ollman v. Evans, 750 F.2d 970, 11 Media L. Rep. 1433 (D.C. Cir. 1984), in favor of the Restatement (Second) of Torts approach). In Ball v. E.W. Scripps Co., 801 S.W.2d 684, 18 Media L. Rep. 1545 (Ky. 1990), the Kentucky Supreme Court held that a number of statements were fact rather than opinion under this standard. The Kentucky Constitution expressly recognizes the inherent and inalienable right "of freely communicating . . . thoughts and opinions." Ky. Const. § 1. It has been suggested that this section may provide an additional independent basis for the application of the Gertz view of opinion. Haynes v. McConnell, 642 S.W.2d 902 (Ky. Ct. App. 1982). In Rich for Rich v. Kentucky Country Day, Inc., 793 S.W.2d

832 (Ky. Ct. App. 1990), the Court of Appeals found that statements by a teacher that a student was lazy or irresponsible were pure opinion. In Schroering v. Courier-Journal & Louisville Times Co., No. 95-CA-520-MR (Ky. App. Apr. 26, 1996), mot. for discretionary review, No. 96-SC-000468 (Ky. 1996), a defeated district judge candidate sued a newspaper for an endorsement editorial which relayed statements of attorneys and judges concerning the candidate's competency. Relying on Milkovich v. Lorain Journal Co., 497 U.S. 1 (1990), the Kentucky Court of Appeals found that the statements were the personal opinions of the persons interviewed and could not be proven false. Thus, the article was not defamatory. (This is an unreported case and cannot be cited as authority in any Kentucky court).

In addition, in the employment context, the Kentucky Court of Appeals affirmed summary judgment in favor of an employer in a defamation action based on an internal audit report concerning a dismissed employee. Because the opinion expressed in the report that the employee had violated company policy and penal statutes were based upon disclosed true facts, the report was "pure opinion" and absolutely privileged. Buchholtz v. Dugan, 977 S.W.2d 24, 28 (Ky. Ct. App. 1998).

3. ***Consent.*** In Stewart v. Pantry, Inc., 715 F. Supp. 1361 (W.D. Ky. 1988), the plaintiffs claimed they were defamed when their employer sent the results of their polygraph examinations (which indicated dishonesty) to the plaintiffs' supervisors and the company's risk management department. The court rejected plaintiffs' defamation claim because the plaintiffs had signed consent forms for the tests and authorized communication of the results to the employer. Id. at 1366-67. The Kentucky Court of Appeals has followed Section 583 of the Restatement (Second) of Torts in addressing the consent defense. Nichols v. Pikeville United Methodist Hospital of Kentucky, Inc., No. 2002-CA-1117-MR, 2003 WL 22799493 (Ky. Ct. App. 2003). Section 583 provides that "the consent of another to the publication of defamatory matter concerning him is a complete defense to his action for defamation." In order for a consent to be valid, it is not necessary for the consenting individual to know that the matter to be published is defamatory in nature. Id. Rather, it is enough that an individual has reason to know that the published material may be defamatory. Id. In such a case, the individual, by consenting, takes the risk that the information published may, in fact, be defamatory. Id. Moreover, so long as there is consent to the publication of the allegedly defamatory statements, the presence or absence of good faith on the part of the defamer is immaterial in determining whether the consent is valid. Id.

4. ***Mitigation.*** "Parties, when sued for [defamation], may admit the publication, and plead any matter in mitigation of damages, and to rebut the presumption of malice." Evening Post Co. v. Hunter, 18 Ky. L. Rptr. 726, 38 S.W. 487 (Ky. 1896). Damages have been mitigated based on evidence of a general rumor, belief, or suspicion that the plaintiff was guilty of the acts charged in the defamation, Calloway v. Middleton 9 Ky. (2 A.K. Marsh) 372 (Ky. 1820); evidence that the defendant did not originate the defamatory charge, Evans v. Smith, 21 Ky. (5 T.B. Mon) 363 (Ky. 1827); evidence of the general bad character or reputation of the plaintiff, Eastland v. Caldwell, 5 Ky. (2 Bibb) 21 (Ky. 1810); evidence that the defendant stated his disbelief in the truth of the statement, Nicholson v. Merritt, 109 Ky. 369, 59 S.W. 25 (Ky. 1900); and evidence that the defamatory language was used in the heat of a political campaign and in retaliation for charges previously made by the plaintiff, Deitchman v. Bowles, 166 Ky. 285, 179 S.W. 249 (Ky. 1915). However, evidence that the defamation occurred while the defendant was angry or in the heat of passion will not mitigate damages. Vest v. Norman, 1 Ky. L. Rptr. 317 (Ky. 1880) (anger is not a mitigating circumstance); Schwarz v. Griffith's Ex'r., 7 Ky. L. Rptr. 532 (Ky. 1886) (heat of passion is not a mitigating circumstance).

III. RECURRING FACT PATTERNS

A. Statements in Personnel File

Kentucky courts have previously found Internal reports regarding an employee's work performance as not published if the employer does not share them with anyone outside the employer. Wyant v. SCM Corp., 692 S.W.2d 814, 816 (Ky. Ct. App. 1985). The more current view is that such internal reports are published but enjoy a qualified privilege. Biber, et al. v. Duplicator Sales & Service, Inc., 155 S.W.3d 732 (Ky. Ct. App. 2004).

B. Performance Evaluations

Written statements in a performance evaluation do not subject the employer to liability for libel. In Caslin v. General Elec. Co., 608 S.W.2d 69 (Ky. Ct. App. 1980), a former employee brought a libel action against his former employer alleging that statements in his performance evaluation were defamatory. The court, in upholding summary judgment for the employer, stated, "these reports are communications within the employing company which are necessary to its functioning and, therefore, do not incur a liability to appellant." Id. at 70 (citing Dossett v. New York Min. & Mfg. Co., 451 S.W.2d 843 (Ky. 1970)). In Louisville & Nashville R. Co. v. Marshall, 586 S.W.2d 274 (Ky. Ct. App. 1979), an employee filed a libel action against his employer due to statements written by a supervisor evaluating the employee's work performance. A collective bargaining agreement was in operation at the time the evaluation was written. In reversing the jury's award for the employee, the court held that "under the circumstances of this case, the communications complained of as libelous by the appellee were, in fact, privileged communications under the terms of the collective bargaining agreement." Id. at 283-84.

C. References

In Holdaway Drugs, Inc. v. Braden, 582 S.W.2d 646 (Ky. 1979), a drugstore employee was terminated because the drugstore owner believed he was stealing drugs. When he applied for a new job with a life insurance company, the drugstore owner was contacted and asked various questions regarding his former employee. The drugstore owner informed the company that the applicant was suspected of stealing narcotics and the life insurance company chose not to hire the former employee. Id. at 648. The court held that the jury should be instructed that the drugstore owner was not liable for any damages resulting from the statements he made to the life insurance company unless the jury concluded the drugstore owner acted with actual malice. Id. at 650.

D. Intracorporate Communication

In the past, some Kentucky courts have found intracorporate communications to be protected from liability in defamation actions. See Wyant v. SCM Corp., 692 S.W.2d 814, 826 (Ky.Ct. App. 1985). However, in Biber, et al. v. Duplicator Sales & Service, Inc., 155 S.W.3d 732 (Ky. Ct. App. 2004), the Kentucky Court of Appeals rejected this privilege. The Court in Biber held that alleged statements made between officers or employees of a corporation are actionable under defamation law. The plaintiff in Biber owned a corporation which contracted with Duplicator Sales & Service, Inc. In his lawsuit, the plaintiff claimed that the president and one of the managers of Duplicator made slanderous statements about him to other employees of Duplicator. The defendants argued that the intra-corporate immunity rule shielded them from liability for defamation. However, the Court rejected this argument finding "no reason to insulate a corporation, its officers, or employees from liability for defamation simply because the statements were made exclusively to corporate officers or employees." Id. at 737.

E. Statements to Government Regulators

In Matthews v. Holland, 912 S.W.2d 459 (Ky. Ct. App. 1995), a former elementary school principal brought a libel action against the superintendent for forwarding her performance evaluations to the Kentucky Professional Standards Board. The court concluded the superintendent was statutorily required to forward the evaluations and therefore was entitled to absolute immunity while acting under the express authority of the law. Id. at 461. Likewise, letters solicited by Kentucky Board of Medical Licensure regarding a physician are protected by a qualified privilege. Shure v. Ford, No. 2011-CA-000144, 2012 WL 1657133 (Ky. Ct. App. May 11, 2012).

F. Reports to Auditors and Insurers

No reported cases.

G. Vicarious Liability of Employers for Statements Made by Employees

1. ***Scope of Employment.*** An employer may be held responsible for defamatory remarks made by an employee acting within the scope of his employment. For example, in Dossett v. New York Min. & Mfg. Co., 451 S.W.2d 843 (Ky. 1970), a plant manager suspected an employee of stealing copper wire. When the plant manager advised his supervisor of the situation, the supervisor instructed the plant manager to fire the employee. The employee, in alleging he was slandered, claimed that the plant manager fired him in front of several other employees and that the plant manager accused him of being a thief. The Kentucky Supreme Court held that because the plant manager was authorized to discharge the plaintiff by his employer, the act of discharging the plaintiff was done within the manager's scope of employment and the employer could be held liable for any slander he committed during the discharge. Id. at 846; cf. Disabled Am. Veterans Dept. of Ky., Inc. v. Crabb, 182 S.W.3d 541 (Ky. Ct. App. 2005) (declining to find vicarious liability for supervisor's libelous comments made to employee during termination of employee). A federal court case laid out the four factors Kentucky courts use to determine whether a particular employee action was within the scope of employment: (1) whether the conduct was similar to that which the employee was hired to perform; (2) whether the action occurred substantially within the authorized special and temporal limits of employment; (3) whether the action was in furtherance of the employer's business; and (4) whether the conduct, though unauthorized, was expectable in view of the employee's duties. Booker v. GTE.NET, LLC, 214 F.Supp.2d 746, 749 (E.D. Ky. 2002). In Booker, employees used the name and created an e-mail account for another employee in order to send a "rude and critical" e-mail to a customer. Id. at 747. After an investigation by her employer revealed her innocence, the plaintiff sued her employer under a vicarious liability/respondeat superior theory for the acts of the employees responsible for creating the fake e-mail address and sending the offensive letter. Id. at 748. Using the four factors, the court determined that the employees' acts were not within their scope of employment. Id. at 750. The Sixth Circuit affirmed the Booker decision and included a discussion of the above four factors in its opinion. Booker v. GTE.NET, LLC, 350 F.3d 515 (6th Cir. 2003). Kentucky law recognizes the rule of franchisor vicarious liability whereby "the franchisor is vicariously liable for the tortious conduct of the franchisee when it, in fact, has control or right of control over the daily operation of the specific aspect of the franchisee's business that is alleged to have caused the harm." Papa John's

Intern., Inc. v. McCoy, 244 S.W.3d 44, 56 (Ky. 2008). In Papa John's, the Kentucky Supreme Court concluded that the pizza deliveryman's act of making allegedly false statements to police officers was an independent course of conduct that did not serve any purpose of his employer [franchisee, RWT]. Id. The court further noted, "Papa John's, the franchisor, had no control over the franchisee's [RWT's] employee's isolated and allegedly intentional, tortious conduct." Id.

a. **Blogging.** No reported cases.

2. ***Damages.*** See, III.G.1, infra.

H. Internal Investigations

Under Kentucky law, an employer enjoys a qualified privilege to prepare and maintain documents relating to employees' work performance and to internal investigations. See Caslin v. General Elec. Co., 608 S.W.2d 69, 70 (Ky. Ct. App. 1980); see also Stewart v. Pantry, Inc., 715 F. Supp. 1361, 1367 (W.D. Ky. 1988) (communications regarding employee's performance, termination and results of polygraph examinations did not result in liability for defamation and were privileged under Kentucky law); Columbia Sussex Corp. v. Hay, 627 S.W.2d 270, 275, 7 Media L. Rep. 2424 (Ky. Ct. App. 1981) (privilege covers communications regarding ongoing investigations within organization).

IV. OTHER ACTIONS BASED ON STATEMENTS

A. Negligent Hiring, Retention, and Supervision

Kentucky has acknowledged the viability of claims for negligent hiring and retention. In Oakley v. Flor-Shin, Inc. 964 S.W.2d 438 (Ky. Ct. App. 1998), a K-mart employee was sexually assaulted by an employee of a company that contracted with K-mart to clean floors. The female employee brought an action against the floor cleaner's employer alleging negligent hiring and retention. The court agreed that the established law in this Commonwealth recognizes that an employer can be held liable when its failure to exercise ordinary care in hiring or retaining an employee creates a foreseeable risk of harm to a third person. Id. at 442. In Ten Broeck Dupont, Inc. v. Brooks, 283 S.W. 3d 705 (Ky. 2009), the Kentucky Supreme Court held that "[i]n order for an employer to be held liable for negligent hiring or retention the employee must have committed a tort." The tort may either be intentional or negligent. Id. at 727. Kentucky law recognizes the tort of negligent supervision adopted from the Restatement (Second) of Agency § 213. Booker v. GTE.NET LLC, 350 F.3d 515, 517 (6th. Cir. 2003) (citing Smith v. Isaacs, 777 S.W.2d. 912, 914 (Ky. 1989). "[A]n employer can be held liable for negligent supervision only if he or she knew or had reason to know of the risk that the employment created. Id. (See Restatement (Second) of Agency § 213 (1958) (Comment & Illustrations)).

B. Intentional Infliction of Emotional Distress

In Kroger Co. v. Willgruber, 920 S.W.2d 61 (Ky. 1996), and later in Stringer v. Wal-Mart Stores, Inc., et al., 151 S.W.3d 781 (Ky. 2004), the Kentucky Supreme Court reaffirmed the elements of proof necessary to prevail on a claim of intentional infliction of emotional distress: (1) the wrongdoer's conduct must be intentional or reckless; (2) the conduct must be outrageous and intolerable in that it offends the generally accepted standards of decency and morality; (3) there must be a causal connection between the wrongdoer's conduct and the emotional distress; and (4) the emotional distress must be severe. Kroger Co., 920 S.W.2d at 65.

The tort of intentional infliction of emotional distress does not provide a cause of action for "petty insults, unkind words and minor indignities." Id. See Craft v. Rice, 671 S.W.2d 247, 251 (Ky. 1984) (adopting the Restatement (Second) of Torts § 46 version of the tort). Although an employee can bring an action for intentional infliction of emotional distress against her employer, the employer's conduct must be "so extreme in degree, as to go beyond all possible bounds of decency, and to be regarded as atrocious, and utterly intolerable in a civilized community." Bednarek v. United Food and Commercial Workers Intern. Union, Local Union 227, 780 S.W.2d 630, 632 (Ky. Ct. App. 1989) (quoting Restatement (Second) of Torts § 46, comment d (1965)). The Kentucky Supreme Court has stressed that "major outrage is essential" to the tort of intentional infliction of emotional distress. Stringer v. Wal-Mart Stores, Inc., et al., 151 S.W.3d 781 (Ky. 2004). An employer's alleged actions of forcing an employee to falsify employment records, and then terminating him for falsifying such records, did not rise to level of outrageousness needed to sustain a claim for intentional infliction of emotional distress under Kentucky law. Sacharnoski v. Capital Consol., Inc., 187 F. Supp.2d 843 (W. D. Ky. 2002). The fact that an employee was discharged does not, without more, create a claim of outrage. See Hines v. Elf Atochem North America, Inc., 813 F. Supp. 550, 553 (W.D. Ky. 1993); see also Stewart v. Pantry, Inc., 715 F. Supp. 1361, 1364-65 (W.D. Ky. 1988). Nor can an employee state a claim for intentional infliction of emotional distress where the employer investigated the employee for wrongdoing and disciplined the employee based on the results of the investigation. There can be no liability where the actor merely exercises legal rights in a permissible way. Wells v. Huish Detergents, Inc., 19 Fed. Appx. 168 (6th Cir. 2001) (unpublished decision).

C. Interference with Economic Advantage

Kentucky adheres to the view of the Restatement (Second) of Torts § 766 (1977) so as to impose liability upon one who, without privilege to do so, induces or otherwise causes a third person not to enter into or continue a business relationship with another and causes harm thereby. Carmichael-Lynch-Nolan Advertising Agency, Inc. v. Bennett & Associates, 561 S.W.2d 99 (Ky. Ct. App. 1977). See CMI, Inc. v. Intoximeters, Inc., 918 F. Supp. 1068 (W.D. Ky. 1995); see also Nat'l Collegiate Athletic Ass'n By and Through Bellarmine College v. Hornung, 754 S.W.2d 855 (Ky. 1988); Burchett v. General Tel. Co. of the South, 699 F. Supp. 114, 117 (E.D. Ky. 1988) (finding that plaintiff failed to show the required element of malice to support his claim that his former employer's policy of preventing former employees from working on its property interfered with his prospective contractual relations). To successfully support a claim for interference with economic advantage, plaintiffs must demonstrate: (1) the existence of a valid business relationship or expectancy; (2) defendant's knowledge of the relationship or expectancy; (3) defendant's intentional interference with that relationship or expectancy; (4) an improper motive; (5) causation; and (6) special damages. Fieldturf, Inc. v. Southwest Recreational Indus., Inc., 235 F. Supp. 2d 708, 735 (E.D. Ky. 2002), *vacated in part on other grounds by* Fieldturf, Inc. v. Southwest Recreational Indus., Inc., 357 F.3d 1266 (Fed. Cir. 2004). Tortious interference claims based on a supervisor's interference with an employee's employment contract can be difficult to prove because a company acts through its agents and only a third party can interfere with existing contractual relations. McCarthy v. KFC Corp., 607 F.Supp. 343 (W.D. Ky. 1985). The applicable statute of limitations for an interference claim is five years. KRS 413.120(7); Ritchie v. United Mine Workers of America, 410 F.2d 827 (6th Cir. 1969).

D. Prima Facie Tort

No reported cases.

V. OTHER ISSUES

A. Statute of Limitations

Actions for both libel and slander must be brought within one year after the cause of action accrues. KRS 413.140 (1)(d). The statute of limitations begins to run upon the publication of the allegedly defamatory matter that causes the defamation or injury. Caslin v. General Elec. Co., 608 S.W.2d 69 (Ky. Ct. App. 1980). Pursuant to the single publication rule, a libel action accrues on the date that the allegedly defamatory statements were first published. Mitan v. Davis, 243 F. Supp. 2d 719, 724 (W.D. Ky. 2003). See Nichols v. Lebanon Enterprise Newspaper, No. 2008-CA-002063 (Ky. App. Nov. 20, 2009) (rejecting claim that "continuing and accumulating harm caused by a libelous publication has no statute of limitations") (unpublished).

B. Jurisdiction

Venue of a prosecution for libel lies in the county in which the person libeled and complaining resides, as well as in the county where the newspaper was printed and issued. Shields v. Commonwealth, 55 S.W. 881 (Ky. Ct. App. 1900). The United States district court in Kentucky adopted the effects test of the single publication rule, a "special mode of analysis for personal jurisdiction issues where defamation…is concerned." Jones v. Dirty World Entm't Recordings, LLC, 766 F.Supp. 828, 834 (E.D. Ky. 2011). Although defendants knew that the plaintiff worked in Ohio but were unaware that she lived in Kentucky, personal jurisdiction in Kentucky was still valid, because it was foreseeable that someone employed in Southern Ohio would live in Northern Kentucky. Id. This was enough to give the "State a legitimate interest in holding [the defendant] answerable on a claim related to those activities." Id. at 835, quoting Keeton v. Hustler Magazine, Inc., 465 U.S. 770, 776 (1984). This satisfies the fair warning requirement for personal jurisdiction—that individuals must be fairly warned that "a particular activity may subject them to jurisdiction of a foreign court." Hinners v. Robey, 336 S.W.3d 891 (Ky. 2011), quoting Shaffer v. Heitner, 433 U.S. 186, 218 (1977).

C. Worker's Compensation Exclusivity

The Kentucky Workers Compensation System is the exclusive venue for the recovery of damages resulting from a workplace injury or death. KRS §342.690.

D. Pleading Requirements

"A petition to recover damages for slander or libel states no cause of action unless it sets out the alleged slanderous or libelous words." Schulten v. Bavarian Brewing Co., 96 Ky. 224, 28 S.W. 504 (Ky. 1894). A court has granted summary judgment in defendants' favor when the plaintiff failed to describe the alleged defamatory statements, state where they were published or indicate how the defendants were responsible for them. Brett v. Media General Operations, Inc., 326 S.W.3d 452 (Ky. Ct. App. 2010).

SURVEY OF KENTUCKY EMPLOYMENT PRIVACY LAW

Jon L. Fleischaker
Ashley C. Pack
Dinsmore & Shohl LLP
101 South Fifth Street, Suite 2500
Louisville, KY 40202
Telephone: (502) 540-2300 Facsimile: (502) 581-8111
ashley.pack@dinslaw.com

(With Developments Reported Through **November 1, 2012**)

GENERAL COMMENTS

In Kentucky, circuit courts are the trial courts of general jurisdiction, with a right of appeal to the Court of Appeals. Until 1976, the Court of Appeals was Kentucky's highest court. In 1976, the Kentucky Supreme Court, which may grant discretionary review from the Court of Appeals, was created.

Effective January 1, 2005, the Kentucky Rules of Civil Procedure (CR 76.12(4)) were amended to require the citation format outlined in *The Bluebook: A Uniform System of Citation* ("the Bluebook"). Formerly, Kentucky courts did not follow the standard Bluebook system of citation.

Finally, as a practical matter, there are not many reported Kentucky cases in the area of employment privacy. Kentucky courts, however, generally follow the positions of the Restatement (Second) of Torts in most areas.

SIGNIFICANT DEVELOPMENTS SINCE THE 2012 *SURVEY*

None.

I. GENERAL LAW OF PRIVACY

A. Legal Basis of Privacy Claims

Invasion of privacy is a common law cause of action that was first recognized as a separate tort in 1927. Brents v. Morgan , 221 Ky. 765, 299 S.W. 967 (Ky. 1927). See also Foster-Milburn Co. v. Chinn, 134 Ky. 424, 120 S.W. 364, 366 (Ky. 1909). In 1981, the Kentucky Supreme Court adopted the Restatement version of the tort, as stated in the Restatement (Second) of Torts § 652A (1976). McCall v. Courier-Journal & Louisville Times Co., 623 S.W.2d 882, 7 Media L. Rep. 2118 (Ky. 1981), cert. denied, 465 U.S. 975, 102 S. Ct. 2239 (1982). As with defamation claims in Kentucky, common law claims for invasion of privacy terminate upon the death of the potential plaintiff. Montgomery v. Montgomery, 60 S.W.3d 524, 30 Media L. Rptr. 1045 (Ky. 2001). See also Mineer v. Williams, 82 F. Supp. 2d 702, 28 Media L. Rptr. 1577 (E.D. Ky. 2000). Furthermore, in order to assert a claim for invasion of privacy, a plaintiff must have had an actual and reasonable expectation of privacy. Warinner v. North Am. Sec. Solutions, Inc., No. 3:05-CV-244-S, 2008 WL 2355727, at *3 (W.D. Ky. June 5, 2008) (holding that employees who engaged in drug activity while on the worksite and in other public places did not have a reasonable expectation of privacy).

B. Causes of Action

1. ***Misappropriation/Right of Publicity.*** The tort of invasion by appropriation was actually recognized in Kentucky before Kentucky common law accepted invasion of privacy as a separate tort. Foster-Milburn Co. v. Chinn, 134 Ky. 424, 120 S.W. 364 (Ky. 1909). As noted in I.A., supra, however, Kentucky has since adopted the Restatement position on invasion of privacy, including the tort of misappropriation or right of publicity. McCall v. Courier-Journal & Louisville Times Co., 623 S.W.2d 882 (Ky. 1981).

In Cheatham v. Paisano Publications, 891 F. Supp. 381 (W.D. Ky. 1995), the court analyzed Kentucky law, in light of the Restatement, and held that the elements of a misappropriation claim are: a) plaintiff must prove that he or she has a property interest in plaintiff's likeness, design, or image by proving that the image has commercial value from which the plaintiff intended to profit; and b) defendant deprived plaintiff of the commercial benefit of the image by appropriating it for defendant's own commercial gain.

The plaintiff must have developed a notoriety strong enough to have commercial value within some identifiable group or area. Commercial value may be established by proof of: 1) the distinctiveness of the identity or image, and 2) the degree of recognition among those receiving the publicity. Id. at 387.

In addition to the common law claim, Kentucky also has a statute which addresses commercial use of the names and likenesses of public figures. KRS § 391.170 states:

> (1) The general assembly recognizes that a person has property rights in his name and likeness which are entitled to protection from commercial exploitation. The general assembly further recognizes that although the traditional right of privacy terminates upon death of the person asserting it, the right of publicity, which is a right of protection from appropriation of some element of an individual's personality for commercial exploitation, does not terminate upon death.
>
> (2) The name or likeness of a person who is a public figure shall not be used for commercial profit for a period of fifty (50) years from the date of his death without the written consent of the executor or administrator of his estate.

2. ***False Light.*** Kentucky has accepted "false light" as a branch of the tort of invasion of privacy. McCall, 623 S.W.2d at 887. The elements of false light invasion of privacy are: a) publicity of a fairly broad nature by the defendant that places the plaintiff in a false position before the public; b) the false light in which the plaintiff was placed would be highly offensive to a reasonable person; and c) the publisher had knowledge of, or acted in reckless disregard as to the falsity of the publicized matter and the false light in which the other was placed. Id. at 888. See also Stewart v. Pantry, Inc., 715 F. Supp. 1361, 1369 (W.D. Ky. 1988); and Lopez v. Oklahoma Hearst-Argyle Television, Inc., 2006 U.S. Dist. LEXIS 10892, at *22-23 (E.D. Ky. Mar. 14, 2006). Furthermore, a false light privacy claim requires that the allegedly untruthful statements be capable of reference to a certain individual, not just to members of a group in general. O'Brien v. Williamson Daily News, 735 F. Supp. 218, 223 (E.D. Ky. 1990), aff'd, 931 F.2d 893 (6th Cir. 1991). Additionally, to be actionable, the statements complained of must be in writing and must be publicized to the public. See Rufra v. United States Bankcorp, Inc., No. 3:05CV-594-H, 2006 WL 2178278, at *6, 2006 U.S. Dist. LEXIS 53215, at *17-18 (W.D. Ky. July 28, 2006). An internal memorandum about the plaintiff cannot create a false light claim. Wymer v. JH Prop., Inc., No. 1998-CA-00986-MR, 1999 WL 731591, at *5, 1999 Ky. App. LEXIS 115 (Ky. Ct. App. Sept. 17, 1999), aff'd in relevant part, 50 S.W.3d 195, 200 (Ky. 2001). While the truth is not a complete defense to a false light claim, it is a defense insofar as the publisher knows the statement to be true, because the publisher could not have acted in reckless disregard as to a statement's falsity if he or she knew it to be true. See Flege v. Williamstown Indep. Sch., No. 06-47-DLB, 2007 WL 679022, at *21 (E.D. Ky. Mar. 1, 2007).

3. ***Publication of Private Facts.*** In adopting the Restatement, Kentucky recognized the publication of private facts as an actionable invasion of privacy. McCall, 623 S.W.2d at 887. The elements of the tort of publication of private facts are: a) the matter publicized is of a kind that would be highly offensive to a reasonable person; and b) the matter publicized is not of legitimate concern to the public. McSurely v. McClellan, 753 F.2d 88, 112 (D.C. Cir. 1985) (interpreting Kentucky law). While some "public" disclosure is required for publication, the court in McSurely found the size of the public to be irrelevant. The court held that publication of humiliating facts to one person, the husband of the subject, was sufficient because he was "the most significant possible audience" for that particular information. Id. at 113. However, Ghassomians v. Ashland Independent School Dist., 55 F. Supp.2d 675, 693 (E.D. Ky. 1998) held that a communication to a single person or small group of people does not constitute "publicity," while publication to a crowd or through the mass media does. In Ghassomians, the defendant found the plaintiff's diary, read it, and then gave copies to one other person. This was insufficient to be considered "publication" of private matters. The court specifically refused to consider whether the simple act of disclosure satisfied "publicity" when the information was not obtained in a tortious manner. See also Beaven v. U.S. Dep't. of Justice, No. 03-84-JBC, 2007 WL 1032301 (E.D. Ky. Mar. 30, 2007) (holding that, even if a failure to keep a folder of confidential information secure could be considered a communication, because the information was only seen by a small group of people, this was not "publicity").

Publication of facts that are of public interest or that have become part of some public record cannot form the basis of a claim of publication of private facts. See Sellers v. Henry, 329 S.W.2d 214 (Ky. 1959) (publication of photo of young girl's mutilated body after automobile accident); Bell v. Courier-Journal & Louisville Times Co., 402 S.W.2d 84 (Ky. 1966) (publication by newspaper of fact that judge was delinquent in the payment of taxes, as disclosed in public records). Furthermore, the right to privacy in facts ends upon their publication by the individual or with the individual's consent. Brents v. Morgan, 221 Ky. 765, 299 S.W. 967, 970 (Ky. 1927).

4. ***Intrusion.*** As with the other three types of invasion of privacy, Kentucky has adopted intrusion as a tort. McCall, 623 S.W.2d at 887. The elements of tortious intrusion are: a) an intentional interference with the solitude or seclusion of another or his private affairs or concerns; and b) said interference would be highly offensive to a reasonable person. McSurely, 753 F.2d at 112. See also Douglas v. Stokes, 149 Ky. 506, 149 S.W. 849 (Ky. 1912); Smith v. Bob Smith Chevrolet, Inc., 275 F. Supp. 2d 808, 822 (W.D. Ky. 2003); Johns v. Firstar Bank, NA, Nos. 2004-CA-001558-MR, 2004-CA

-001709-MR, 2006 WL 741107, 2006 Ky. App. LEXIS 85 (Ky. Ct. App. Mar. 24, 2006) (claim brought was intrusion, but the case generally discusses the tort of invasion of privacy in Kentucky and the different causes of action encompassed thereby).

Additionally, the tort requires acts of an invasive nature. Merely making a request for medical records is not an intrusion upon seclusion because it is not an invasive action. See Mullins v. Gooch, No. 2005-CA-002480-MR, 2006 WL 3759463 (Ky. Ct. App. Dec. 22, 2006). See also Beaven v. U.S. Dept. of Justice, No. 03-84-JBC, 2007 WL 1032301 at *21 (E.D. Ky. Mar. 30, 2007) (*"Disclosure* of private information is distinct from an intentional *intrusion* into private matters."); Warinner v. North Am. Sec. Solutions, Inc., 2008 WL 2355727, at *3 (W.D. Ky. June 5, 2008). Furthermore, a person invading a person's privacy by intrusion need not intend to do so, they need only intend to engage in the intrusive activity. Barbo v. Kroger Co., No: 3:07-CV-14-S, 2007 WL 2350179, at *3 (W.D. Ky. Aug. 13, 2007).

C. Other Privacy-Related Actions

1. ***Intentional Infliction of Emotional Distress/Outrage.*** The Kentucky Supreme Court has recognized a separate cause of action for emotional distress due to intentional and unlawful interference with one's rights, regardless of whether such interference causes bodily injury, and has held that the applicable statute of limitations is five years. Craft v. Rice, 671 S.W.2d 247 (Ky. 1984).

The elements of the tort are: 1) the defendant's conduct must be intentional or reckless; 2) the conduct in question must be outrageous and intolerable in that it offends generally accepted standards of decency and morality; 3) there must be a causal relationship between the conduct in question and the emotional distress; and 4) the emotional distress must be severe. Id. at 249; see also Kroger Co. v. Willgruber, 920 S.W.2d 61, 65-67 (Ky. 1996) (defendant-employer's conduct constituted "the very essence of the tort of outrage" including "a plan of attempted fraud, deceit, slander, and interference with contractual rights, all carefully orchestrated in an attempt to bring Willgruber to his knees."); Stringer v. Wal-Mart Stores, Inc., 151 S.W.3d 781, 788 (Ky. 2004). Embedded in these elements is "a duty to refrain from intentional and reckless conduct." McDonald's Corp. v. Ogborn, 309 S.W.3d 274, 294, 2009 Ky. App. LEXIS 236 (2009). Although this cause of action is more commonly sustained by acts of commission, acts of omission have been held sufficient. Id. For example, where an employer intentionally failed to warn or train its employees about a hoax in order to protect its reputation, it was liable for intentional infliction of emotional distress. Id.

The requisite intent is the intent to cause emotional distress in the victim. Haggard v. Martin, No. 3:01-CV-614-H, 2002 WL 753230 (W.D. Ky. Apr. 25, 2002); see also Brewer v. Hillard, 15 S.W.3d 1, 8 (Ky. Ct. App. 1999) (same-sex sexual harassment case in which the plaintiff also claimed intentional infliction of emotional distress by the harassing supervisor). This cause of action was meant to be a "gap filler" and where there is no evidence that the conduct was intended only to cause extreme emotional distress, and the conduct amounts to the commission of a traditional tort for which recovery for emotional distress is allowed, there cannot be a cause of action for outrage. Bennett v. Malcomb, 2010 Ky. App. LEXIS 148 (2010).

Generally, in order to be successful in establishing intentional infliction of emotional distress, the defendant's conduct must have been "a deviation from all reasonable bounds of decency and . . . utterly intolerable in a civilized community." Humana of Kentucky, Inc. v. Seitz, 796 S.W.2d 1, 2-3 (Ky. 1990) (not intentional infliction of emotional distress where a hospital employee ordered the plaintiff to "shut up" during the course of her labor and delivery of a stillborn infant then informed her that the infant would be disposed of at the hospital); see also Warinner v. North Am. Sec. Solutions, Inc., No. 3:05-CV-244-S, 2008 WL 2355727, at *4 (W.D. Ky. June 5, 2008) (holding that an employer conducting an undercover investigation into possible violations of its drug policy does not rise to the level of intentional infliction of emotional distress/outrage). However, a defendant need not have intended to inflict emotional distress, but only intended to engage in that activity that did so. Barbo v. Kroger Co., No. 3:07-CV-14-S; 2007 WL 2350179, at *3 (W.D. Ky. Aug. 13, 2007). In Morris v. Oldham County Fiscal Court, 201 F.3d 784 (6th Cir. 2000), the Court of Appeals for the Sixth Circuit held that a supervisor's conduct did not rise to the level of outrageousness necessary for recovery, although it included giving the employee "the finger," making harassing telephone calls, and throwing roofing nails on the driveway of the employee's home. Id. at 795; see also Wells v. Huish Detergents, Inc., No. 00-5203, 19 Fed. App'x. 168, 2001 WL 873745 (6th Cir. July 24, 2001) (holding that an employer's investigation and discipline of an employee for wrongdoing did not amount to intentional infliction of emotional distress, even assuming that employer unlawfully terminated the employee for pursuing a workers' compensation benefits claim).

Following Humana, supra, the burden has remained high for a plaintiff bringing a claim for intentional infliction of emotional distress. Most plaintiffs cannot prevail. See generally Hall v. Consol of Kentucky, Inc., 162 Fed. Appx. 587 (6th Cir. 2006) (general claims of wrongful discharge in violation of public policy did not rise to the level of outrage); Hackworth v. Guyan Heavy Equip., Inc., 613 F. Supp. 2d 908, 915–16 (E.D. Ky. May 11, 2009) (employer's use of ex-employee's name when doing business with employee's former customers would not constitute outrage), Dillard v.

Marathon Ashland Petroleum LLC, No. 3:05CV-340-H, 2006 WL 1868498, at *1-2, 2006 U.S. Dist. LEXIS 45522 (W.D. Ky. June 30, 2006) (being singled out for certain types of duties, taunts by co-workers and other types of retaliation by co-workers does not rise to the level of outrage). The burden includes an additional element when the tortious conduct is related to speech about a public figure. In Divita v. Zeigler, No. 2005-CA-001343-MR, 2007 WL 29390 (Ky. Ct. App. Jan. 5, 2007), the Kentucky Court of Appeals adopted the limited holding of Hustler Magazine v. Falwell, 485 U.S. 46, 108 S. Ct. 876, 14 Media L. Rep. 2281 (1988) (holding that public figures may not recover for the tort of intentional infliction of emotional distress by reason of publications unless the publication contains a false statement, or one made with "actual malice," i.e. with knowledge of the falsity or with reckless disregard of its truthfulness). In Divita, Plaintiff and public television figure Darcie Divita was found to bear the burden of proving by clear and convincing evidence that the defendant radio host's comments about her were made with actual malice.

Bringing an intentional infliction of emotional distress claim in the employment context can present additional challenges when the plaintiff asserts multiple causes of action against an employer in the same case. For example, in Wilson v. Lowe's Home Ctr., 75 S.W.3d 229 (Ky. Ct. App. 2002), the Kentucky Court of Appeals held that an employee's allegations that he was subjected to racial remarks on a daily basis by his co-workers and supervisors for a period of approximately seven years were sufficient to establish a claim for intentional infliction of emotional distress against his employer and managers. However, the Court of Appeals also recognized that an employee's intentional infliction of emotional distress claim against employer was subsumed by the employee's civil rights claim against the employer. However, the employee's intentional infliction of emotional distress claims against his managers were not so subsumed. Id. at 238-9. The Court of Appeals recently affirmed that an employee's statutory disability discrimination claim against her employer preempted her common law claim of intentional infliction of emotional distress/outrageous conduct against her employer. Kroger Co. v. Buckley, 113 S.W.3d 644 (Ky. Ct. App. 2003); see also Burkhart v. Comty. Serv. Project, Inc., 2006 U.S. Dist. LEXIS 34182 (E.D. Ky. May 26, 2006); Miller v. Sola Int'l, Inc., No. 05-34-DLB, 2006 WL 1717052, 2006 U.S. Dist. LEXIS 44533 (E.D. Ky. June 19, 2006) (intentional infliction of emotional distress/outrage claim failed because it rested on the merits of the plaintiff's FMLA retaliation claim, which also failed).

2. ***Interference With Prospective Economic Advantage.*** Kentucky has adopted intentional interference with prospective contractual relations as set out in the Restatement (Second) of Torts § 766B (1979). Cullen v. South East Coal Co., 685 S.W.2d 187 (Ky. Ct. App. 1983). The court held:

> One who intentionally and improperly interferes with another's prospective contractual relation (except a contract to marry) is subject to liability to the other for the pecuniary harm resulting from the loss of the benefits of the relation, whether the interference consists of
>
> (a) inducing or otherwise causing a third party not to enter into or to continue the prospective relation; or
>
> (b) preventing the other from acquiring or continuing the prospective relation.

Id. at 189-90. The determination of "improper interference" requires consideration of the actor's motive, the interest being advanced or protected, the nature of the conduct, the means of interference, and whether or not the interference was based upon malice. Id. at 190. See also Manhattan Assoc., Inc. v. Rider, No. 3:02CV-265-S, 2002 WL 1774056 (W.D. Ky. Aug. 1, 2002) (holding that because the noncompete and nonsolicitation clauses in defendant's employment agreement were not enforceable, defendant's conduct in contacting and soliciting plaintiff's customers was not conduct that was "improper"); National Collegiate Athletic Ass'n v. Hornung, 754 S.W.2d 855 (Ky. 1988) (holding no liability where party is acting in good faith, without malice, to assert his own legally protected interest).

In Ashland, Inc. v. Windward Petroleum, Inc., No. 04-554-JBC, 2006 WL 1913364, 2006 U.S. Dist. LEXIS 49709 (E.D. Ky. July 11, 2006), the United States District Court for the Eastern District of Kentucky acknowledged a distinction between intentional interference with prospective economic advantage, and interference with advantageous business relationships. Id. at *23-24. The court said that the former tort cannot be maintained if the "only alleged interference is with an existing contract." Id. Alternatively, according to the court, "interference with advantageous business relationship is the proper cause of action to bring against a party who interfered with a plaintiff's relationship with its longstanding customers." Id. (The opinion cites no Kentucky decisions relating to interference with advantageous business relationships.)

The statute of limitations for an interference claim is five years. See Wiliams v. Owensboro Bd. of Educ., No. 4:07-CV-149-R, 2009 WL 248426 (W.D. Ky. Feb. 3, 2009), at *3. For a detailed discussion of the statute of limitations issue, see § VIII.A., infra.

3. ***Prima Facie Tort.*** No reported decisions.

II. EMPLOYER TESTING OF EMPLOYEES

A. Psychological or Personality Testing

1. ***Common Law and Statutes.*** No statutes specifically address psychological or personality testing in an employment context. For the single reported case on this issue, see II.A.3, infra.

2. ***Private Employers.*** No reported decisions.

3. ***Public Employers.*** One Kentucky decision acknowledged that police officers for the Urban County Government were screened through such methods as testing, psychiatric evaluations, and polygraph examinations, though the court cited no statute or other authority for the proposition that this practice is acceptable. Lexington-Fayette Urban County Gov't v. Middleton, 555 S.W.2d 613, 620 (Ky. Ct. App. 1977).

B. Drug Testing

1. ***Common Law and Statutes.*** Kentucky Administrative Regulations require public school bus drivers to submit to drug tests following any accident resulting in bodily injury or $1,000.00 or more in property damage. 702 Ky. Admin. Reg. 5:080 § 2(2) (b). The constitutionality of this regulation was challenged, inter alia, on the grounds that the drug tests constitute an unreasonable search and seizure. The Kentucky Court of Appeals upheld the regulation, stating that the government has a compelling need to discover drug and alcohol use when the safety of children is involved, in this case, the drug and alcohol use of a public school bus driver. Cornette v. Commonwealth of Kentucky, 899 S.W.2d 502 (Ky. Ct. App. 1995).

Additionally, KRS § 15.382 requires that law enforcement officers certified under KRS § 15.380 through § 15.404 must meet certain qualifications at the time of their certification. Among those qualifications is the requirement that the candidate "[h]ave passed a drug screening test administered or approved by the council by administrative regulation." It is important to note, however, that this provision governs tests administered prior to certification, not testing during employment.

2. ***Private Employers.*** In Smith v. Kentucky Unemployment Ins. Comm'n, 906 S.W.2d 362 (Ky. Ct. App. 1995), the Court of Appeals implicitly supported the use of drug testing by private employers. The decision upheld the claimant's disqualification from receiving unemployment benefits for misconduct, stating that testing positive for marijuana could be grounds for termination for misconduct if the employer has a known policy of keeping a drug-free workplace. In Shrout v. The TFE Group, 161 S.W.3d 351 (Ky. Ct. App. 2005), a truck driver who was terminated after a false positive drug test brought suit against his employer, alleging wrongful discharge in violation of public policy and defamation. The defamation claim was based on the employer's disclosure of the positive test results to potential employers. The plaintiff argued that since the test was flawed, his employer was not allowed to disclose the results to potential employers. Id. at 355. The Kentucky Court of Appeals held that the plaintiff stated a cause of action for defamation that was sufficient to survive a motion to dismiss.

3. ***Public Employers.*** See II.B.1, supra; Under Cornette, supra, mandatory drug testing of public school bus drivers is permitted. Also, the Kentucky Court of Appeals affirmed the dismissal of a Kentucky Transportation Cabinet employee who tested positive for marijuana during random drug testing implemented as part of the Cabinet's zero tolerance policy for drug use. Mollette v. Ky. Personnel Bd., 997 S.W.2d 492 (Ky. Ct. App. 1999). The Court further held that the records of the laboratory that conducted the testing were admissible under the business exception rule to hearsay, KRE 803(6), and that these records can be relied upon as the sole basis for discharge with no other evidence that the employee had used drugs or had exhibited drug induced behavior. Id. The Kentucky Court of Appeals recently affirmed that even though a positive drug test was the fruit of a reversed Civil Service Commission decision, the test was conducted pursuant to a valid and enforceable order, and the plaintiff was subject to punishment for a positive drug test. In Relford v. Lexington-Fayette Urban County Gov't Civil Serv. Comm'n, No. 2002-CA-000045-MR, 2003 WL 21126798 (Ky. Ct. App. May 16, 2003), the plaintiff was employed as a civil service employee of the Lexington Fayette Urban County Government (LFUCG) as an electrician. After the plaintiff was arrested for possession of drug paraphernalia, his employer served him with a Notification of Reasonable Cause Testing, which required him to undergo a drug test. The notification incorrectly stated that the plaintiff had been charged with possession of drug paraphernalia and possession of a controlled substance. Plaintiff protested that he should not be subject to drug testing because the reasonable cause notice was inaccurate. His employer disagreed, and moved to terminate him for failing to take the test. Due to the deficiencies in the notice, the LFUCG Civil Service Commission ordered that the plaintiff's termination should be reduced to a suspension, and ordered him into a drug treatment program that included drug testing. Plaintiff later tested positive for cocaine. After the Circuit Court held that the Civil Service Commission's original decision was incorrect, plaintiff moved to dismiss his positive drug test because it

was the fruit of a reversed Civil Service Commission decision. The Court of Appeals upheld the Circuit Court's reliance on KRS 67A.290, which states that the enforcement of the Commission's order is not suspended pending appeal. Therefore, plaintiff's drug test came as a result of a valid and enforceable order, and the plaintiff was subject to punishment for the positive result. The Sixth Circuit later held in a case brought by the same plaintiff in federal court that the county did not violate the employee's Fourth Amendment right to be free from unreasonable search and seizure when it mandated his participation in a substance abuse program and subjected him to random drug testing following his first positive drug test. Relford v. Lexington-Fayette Urban County Gov't, 390 F.3d 452 (6th Cir. 2004), cert. denied, 544 U.S. 1049, 125 S. Ct. 2300 (U.S. 2005).

In another case brought in federal court, the District Court for the Eastern District of Kentucky held that there is no general Fourth Amendment prohibition against suspicionless and random drug testing. Crager v. Board of Ed. of Knott County, Kentucky, 313 F. Supp. 2d 690 (E.D. Ky. 2004). In that case, a tenured teacher of the Knott County school systems objected to the random drug testing of teachers. The district court noted, in upholding the right of the school board to randomly drug test the teachers, that the Sixth Circuit previously upheld a drug testing policy in Tennessee that provided for the suspicionless testing of teachers because they are in safety sensitive positions, and given the highly regulated nature of their profession, suspicionless drug testing of teachers is not unreasonable under the Fourth Amendment. Id. at 693-97 (citing Knox County Educ. Assoc. v. Knox County Bd. of Educ., 158 F.3d 361 (6th Cir. 1998)).

C. Medical Testing

1. ***Common Law and Statutes.*** No statutes specifically address medical testing of employees. However, KRS§ 207.140(1) allows employers to make "any preemployment inquiry about the existence of an applicant's disability and about the extent to which that disability has been overcome by treatment, medication, appliances, or other rehabilitation." Employers should be aware, however, that while this statute is still in effect, it seems to be inconsistent with the mandates of the Americans with Disabilities Act, 42 U.S.C. § 12101-12183. Additionally, KRS § 15.382, noted in II.B., supra, also requires that persons seeking certification for certain law enforcement positions:

> (10) Have passed a medical examination as defined by the council by administrative regulation to determine if he can perform peace officer duties as determined by a validated job task analysis. However, if the employing agency has its own validated job task analysis, the person shall pass the medical examination, appropriate to the agency's job task analysis, of the employing agency. All agencies shall certify passing medical examination results to the council, which shall accept them as complying with KRS 15.315 to 15.510.

This provision governs tests administered as requirements for certification, not those required during employment.

2. ***Private Employers.*** Case law indicates an implicit approval of preemployment medical testing. For instance, in Honaker v. Duro Bag Mfg. Co., 851 S.W.2d 481 (Ky. 1993), the plaintiff applied for employment with Duro. The employment application included a consent to a preemployment physical and drug and alcohol screening that was signed by the plaintiff. Honaker knew he would be unable to pass a physical due to a previous back injury so he had his cousin appear and take the physical for him. The court held that the physical was a condition precedent to employment, and as plaintiff had not himself passed the exam, he was not eligible for workers' compensation benefits when he aggravated the previous injury while on the job. This decision, however, should be viewed with caution in light of the fact that the events in question all occurred prior to the passage of the Americans with Disabilities Act, 42 U.S.C. § 12101 et. seq.

3. ***Public Employers.*** No reported decisions.

D. Polygraph Tests

While no Kentucky statutes discuss the universal administration of polygraph tests by employers, KRS Title III, Chapter 15, which regulates the Department of Law and law enforcement agencies, states that an agency may, at its own expense, administer its own physical agility, polygraph, psychological, medical, and drug screen tests, as well as additional tests. See KRS § 15.384(2).

There are several decisions in Kentucky relating to the use of a polygraph examination. However, these decisions should be utilized with caution in that they all predate the Employee Polygraph Protection Act of 1988, 29 U.S.C. § 2001-2009.

In Douthitt v. Kentucky Unemployment Ins. Comm'n, 676 S.W.2d 472 (Ky. Ct. App. 1984), the Court of Appeals held that it is unreasonable for an employer to require employees to submit to polygraph tests for the purposes of *unemployment compensation benefits only*. The court refused to issue any opinion as to the use of the exams for other purposes. Id. at 475.

Two years before Douthitt, however, the same court stated that an employer could use a polygraph exam as part of a reasonable investigation into a robbery where the employer has reason to believe that an employee may have been involved in the crime. Furthermore, the threat of termination upon refusal to submit to the exam does not constitute coercion that would vitiate the consent, nor can submitting to the test under those same circumstances give rise to a claim for false imprisonment. Columbia Sussex Corp., Inc. v. Hay, 627 S.W.2d 270 (Ky. Ct. App. 1981).

Finally, in Stewart v. Pantry, Inc., 715 F. Supp. 1361 (W.D. Ky. 1988), the District Court held that a claim for wrongful discharge cannot be based on the fact that the employer dismissed an at-will employee after the employee failed a polygraph examination, nor does the use of a polygraph constitute extreme or outrageous conduct sufficient to establish a claim of intentional infliction of emotional distress. Also, consent to the test, even when obtained through the threat of dismissal for failure to comply, will preclude a claim for invasion of privacy and for defamation based on communication of the results to the employee's supervisors.

E. Fingerprinting

KRS § 15.382, as noted in II.B. and II.C, supra, also requires that law enforcement officers seeking certification for employment must be fingerprinted for a criminal background check. See KRS § 15.382(5).

III. SEARCHES

A. Employee's Person

1. ***Private Employers.*** No reported decisions.

2. ***Public Employers.*** No reported decisions; however, of course, a public employer remains bound by the due process requirements of the Fourth Amendment.

B. Employee's Work Area

No reported decisions in Kentucky.

C. Employee's Property

1. ***Private Employers.*** No reported decisions.

2. ***Public Employers.*** No reported decisions, but see O'Connor v. Ortega, 480 U.S. 709, 107 S. Ct. 1492 (1987) (discussing a search of a public employee's office and the reasonable expectation of privacy in that space).

IV. MONITORING OF EMPLOYEES

A. Telephones and Electronic Communications

1. ***Wiretapping.*** Kentucky statutes make it a crime to eavesdrop through the use of electronic or other means, or to possess or install eavesdropping devices. KRS §§ 526.010, .020, .030, and .040. Installation of eavesdropping devices are class D felonies. KRS § 526.010, .020, .030. Possession of an eavesdropping device is a class A misdemeanor. KRS § 526.040. KRS § 526.060 provides that it is a Class A misdemeanor for anyone that obtains information during the course of his or her employment with a communications common carrier to divulge that information. However, pursuant to KRS § 526.010, if one party to the communication consents to recording, amplification, or transmission, there is no violation. There are no Kentucky cases regarding wiretapping in the context of employment.

There is, however, a Sixth Circuit decision based upon the federal wiretapping statute, 18 U.S.C. § 2510-2522, which prohibits the unauthorized recording, disclosure or use of electronically intercepted communications. Dorris v. Absher, 179 F.3d 420 (6th Cir. 1999) (originating in Tennessee). In Dorris, the Sixth Circuit held as a matter of first impression that passively listening to an illegally intercepted communication, without more, does not constitute a "use" of that information and, therefore, cannot constitute a violation of the federal statute. Also as a matter of first impression, the Court of Appeals held that the district court has the discretion to decide whether to award damages at all, and, if damages are awarded, to assess the statutory damage award of $10,000 for each individual violation.

2. ***Electronic Communications.*** There are no statutes in Kentucky that directly address electronic communications of employees. The Kentucky Court of Appeals decided a case involving postings by employees on an intra-office electronic bulletin board. In the case of Jones v. Lexington H-L Serv., Inc., No. 2003-CA-002072-MR, 2004 WL 2914880 (Ky. Ct. App. Dec. 17, 2004), employees of the company had posted remarks on an electronic bulletin board

regarding another employee. The employee filed an action alleging, among other things, invasion of privacy. The Court of Appeals dismissed the invasion of privacy claim because there was no evidence that the quotes on the bulletin board purported to seriously attribute qualities to any of the persons whose names appeared in the file.

The case of Warshak v. United States, 490 F.3d 455 (6th Cir. 2007), in which the Sixth Circuit held that individuals have a reasonable expectation of privacy in e-mail messages stored with, sent, or received through commercial internet service providers, was vacated in July 2008. Following an en banc rehearing, the court vacated the prior opinion because the original claims were not ripe for review. Warshak v. United States, 532 F.3d 521, 526 (6th Cir. 2008).

3. ***Other Electronic Monitoring***. No reported decisions.

B. Mail

KRS § 526.050 provides that opening, reading, or otherwise tampering with sealed private communications, or obtaining from an employee, officer or representative of a communications common carrier information with respect to the contents or nature of a communication, is a Class A misdemeanor.

KRS § 438.210 imposes a fine of up to $500 and/or imprisonment for not more than one year for any person who willfully and maliciously prevents, obstructs or delays the sending of any message.

KRS § 514.140 makes it a Class D felony to seal, conceal, damage or destroy any mail matter of another. There are no reported decisions.

C. Surveillance/Photographing

The main decision in Kentucky dealing with the photographing of employees is Thomas v. General Elec. Co., 207 F. Supp. 792 (W.D. Ky. 1962), in which the employer notified employees that it would be photographing them at scheduled times and locations for the purposes of safety and efficiency reviews. The employer proceeded with the photographing despite the fact that one employee, the plaintiff, objected. The court held that an employer may photograph employees in the workplace for the purposes improving safety, efficiency, and productivity. Such photographing does not constitute an invasion of the employee's privacy so long as the employer's sole purpose is related to the work environment. Id. at 799. Henry v. Metrop. Sewer Dist., 922 F.2d 332 (6th Cir. 1990), is a case involving a public employer in Kentucky that hired a private investigation firm to perform undercover surveillance of employees in a successful attempt to uncover drug trafficking and use. The Court held that such actions did not constitute an invasion of privacy and affirmed the summary judgment on this count. Id. at 340. Henry, supra, has not received favorable treatment in subsequent cases: it has been disagreed with, called into doubt and has not been followed in numerous instances.

While Kentucky courts have approved of undercover surveillance of employees in certain situations, such surveillance must be performed within the bounds of reason. In Kroger Co. v. Willgruber, 920 S.W.2d 61 (Ky. 1996), an employer was found liable for the intentional infliction of emotional distress upon a former employee, in part because the employer wrongfully and deceitfully persuaded a disability carrier to conduct surveillance on the ex-employee in an attempt to delay his receipt of disability benefits in order to "economically compel him to sign the documents releasing Kroger from liability." Id. at 67. For more on intentional infliction of emotional distress in Kentucky, see VII.A, infra.

In Stringer v. Wal-Mart Stores, Inc., 151 S.W.3d 781 (Ky. 2004), the Kentucky Supreme Court affirmed part of a Court of Appeals decision that reversed a $20 million verdict in favor of former Wal-Mart employees who were fired for eating "claims candy," *i.e.,* candy from open or torn bags removed from the store's shelves that had been taken to the store's "claims area" to be processed by a claims clerk and then either discarded or returned. The employees claimed, in part, that Wal-Mart invaded their privacy and violated Kentucky's anti-eavesdropping statute (KRS § 526.030) by using a video camera with audio capabilities to film the claims area. The Court of Appeals found, however, that Wal-Mart did not invade the employees' privacy because it did not have any intent to eavesdrop. The Kentucky Supreme Court did not address the intent issue, but instead affirmed the court's decision on the basis that the employees failed to prove any damages as a result of the recorded conversations. Accordingly, the court found that Wal-Mart was entitled to a directed verdict on the invasion of privacy issue.

V. ACTIVITIES OUTSIDE THE WORKPLACE

A. Statute or Common Law

Pertinent statutes are discussed below in the individual sections to which they apply.

B. Employees' Personal Relationships

1. ***Romantic Relationships Between Employees.*** Nothing in Kentucky statutory or common law restricts the right of employers to establish and enforce anti-fraternization policies for their at-will employees. Therefore, discharge for engaging in such forbidden relationships will not give rise to a claim for wrongful termination. Grzyb v. Evans, 700 S.W.2d 399 (Ky. 1985).

2. ***Sexual Orientation.*** KRS § 344.300(1) provides,

> Cities and counties are authorized to adopt and enforce ordinances, orders, and resolutions prohibiting all forms of discrimination, including discrimination on the basis of race, color, religion, disability, familial status, or national origin, sex, or age, and to prescribe penalties for violations thereof, such penalties being in addition to the remedial orders and enforcement herein authorized.

In Hyman v. City of Louisville, 132 F. Supp. 2d 528 (W.D. Ky. 2001), vacated on grounds that plaintiff lacked standing, 53 Fed. Appx. 740 (6th Cir. 2002), the District Court for the Western District of Kentucky upheld a city ordinance which prohibited employment discrimination on basis of gender identity or sexual orientation and prohibited publication of an employment advertisement expressing gender identity or sexual orientation preference. A physician challenged the ordinance, claiming the advertisement for employment posted by him which indicated preference as to sexual orientation for prospective employees was protected speech within the First Amendment. See also Rogers v. Fiscal Court of Jefferson County, 48 S.W.3d 28 (Ky. Ct. App. 2001).

3. ***Marital Status.*** A Kentucky statute governing education reform contain an anti-nepotism provision whereby relatives, including spouses, of school district employees are precluded from serving as members of the school board. KRS § 160.180. The Kentucky Supreme Court upheld the statute as constitutional, though the decision did not specifically address any possible privacy implications. Chapman v. Gorman, 839 S.W.2d 232 (Ky. 1992). The Kentucky Supreme Court reversed a decision of the Kentucky Court of Appeals that held that the inclusion of "aunts" and "uncles" in KRS 160.180(1) violated the equal protection clause of the Fourteenth Amendment and was therefore unconstitutional. Commonwealth v. Crutchfield, 157 S.W.3d 621 (Ky. 2005). In reversing the Court of Appeals, the Kentucky Supreme Court noted that there only had to be a rational basis for including aunts and uncles, but not nieces and nephews, in the statute, and held that the inclusion of aunts and uncles in the definition of relative undoubtedly furthered the goal of eliminating nepotism, which was the purpose of the statute. Id. at 625.

Also, in an unpublished decision out of the Eastern District of Kentucky, the Sixth Circuit held that a job related anti-spouse policy that prevents spouses from working in the same area for legitimate business reasons cannot form the basis of a claim for sex discrimination. Mahoney v. Dayton Walther Corp., 861 F.2d 721 (TABLE), No. 87-6222, 1998 WL 114790, 1988 U.S. App. LEXIS 14628 (6th Cir. Oct. 31, 1988). In Littlejohn v. Rose, 768 F.2d 765 (6th Cir. 1985), cert. denied, 475 U.S. 1045, 106 S. Ct. 1260 (U.S. 1986), the Court held that the decision by school officials to decline to offer reemployment to a teacher would violate the teacher's constitutional right to privacy if based on the teacher's involvement in divorce proceedings.

C. Smoking

Kentucky civil rights statutes include provisions which make it unlawful for an employer to refuse to hire, or to discharge, any individual on the grounds that the person is a smoker or a nonsmoker, so long as the individual complies with any workplace policy concerning smoking. KRS § 344.040(1).

It is also unlawful for an employer to deprive an employee of opportunities or to negatively affect the employee's status because the individual is a smoker or nonsmoker. KRS § 344.040(2).

Furthermore, it is unlawful for an employer to require as a condition of employment that an employee or applicant abstain from using tobacco products outside the course of employment, as long as the individual complies with workplace smoking policies. KRS § 344.040(3).

There are no reported decisions on point.

D. Blogging

A recent decision in the Western District of Kentucky addressed the liability of a nursing student who blogged about her clinical rotations. In Yoder v. Univ. of Louisville, No. 3:09-CV-205-S, 2009 WL 2406235 (W.D. Ky. Aug. 3, 2009), the university claimed that the student violated the nursing school's confidentiality and professionalism policies by posting a blog entry about watching a mother give birth. The court held that the student's posting did not violate the school's confidentiality policy because it did not contain identifying details about the mother. Id. at *6. The court also found no violation of the school's professionalism requirement because the student posted the entry in a personal rather than a professional capacity. Id. at *7.

VI. RECORDS

The Kentucky Open Records Act, KRS § 61.878, generally provides for "free and open examination of public records." See also Kentucky Bd. of Examiners of Psychologists v. Courier-Journal & Louisville Times Co., 826 S.W.2d 324, 20 Media L. Rep. 1692 (Ky. 1992). However, the statute expressly provides for an exception where the records contain personal information, the disclosure of which would constitute a clearly unwarranted invasion of privacy. KRS § 61.878(1)(a).

A. Personnel Records

The Open Records Act contains a provision that any public employee must be allowed to inspect his or her personnel file and to copy any documents that relate to him or her. KRS § 61.878(3). There is no similar provision for the employees of private entities.

In one personnel records case, a local human rights commission sought to view the personnel records of employees of a local school board for the purpose of investigating a claim of sex discrimination. The Kentucky Court of Appeals held that full disclosure of the records was not required under the Open Records Act. The personnel records contained, among other things, highly personal and confidential information, such as the facts surrounding sex offenses committed against a member of an employee's family. As this information did not bear on the underlying discrimination claim, the Court ordered the Lexington-Fayette Urban County Human Rights Commission to specify the information sought, thereby permitting the board to "sanitize" the records of any unnecessary data before turning them over. Bd. of Educ. of Fayette County v. Lexington-Fayette Urban County Human Rights Comm'n., 625 S.W.2d 109 (Ky. Ct. App. 1981).

In Zink v. Commonwealth Dep't. of Workers' Claims, 902 S.W.2d 825 (Ky. Ct. App. 1994), an attorney sought access to injury report forms that were filed with the department as part of the workers' compensation process so that he could utilize the reports in marketing and solicitation. The Kentucky Court of Appeals held that the records were exempt from the Open Records Act under the invasion of privacy provision because they contained such private information as the employee's name, address, telephone number, date of birth, social security number, marital status, pay rate, and number of dependents.

In another Open Records Act case, Kentucky Bd. of Examiners of Psychologists v. Courier-Journal & Louisville Times Co., 826 S.W.2d 324 (Ky. 1992), a newspaper brought an action to gain full access to records of complaints filed by clients alleging sexual misconduct by a psychologist. The Board of Examiners turned over certain of its records, but withheld the actual investigation file from inspection. The Kentucky Supreme Court applied the privacy exemption, noting the highly personal (to the psychologist's clients) nature of the sexual allegations and stated that the use of the privacy exemption requires a "case-specific approach" that balances the privacy interest against the public's right to know.

However, in Palmer v. Driggers, 60 S.W.3d 591, 30 Media L. Rep. 1079 (Ky. Ct. App. 2001), the Kentucky Court of Appeals held that the personal privacy exemption did not preclude a newspaper from gaining access to a complaint against a police officer for actions of misconduct while on duty. The Court held that the public had a significant interest in the actions of its police officers and the information was only embarrassing or humiliating to the police officers or his fellow officers, not innocent, private citizens. See also Cape Publications v. City of Louisville, 191 S.W.3d 10, 13 (Ky. Ct. App. 2006) (release of performance evaluations of public parks employees to the media, with private personal information redacted, was appropriate), and Arend v. Bd. of Educ. of Bullitt County, No. 2005-CA-001372-MR, 2007 WL 625079 (Ky.Ct.App. Mar. 2, 2007) (the contents of a teacher's private reprimand, which included the findings of an investigation that the teacher had engaged in sexual harassment and conduct unbecoming a teacher, did not contain personal information, but matters of professional misconduct not exempt from the Open Records Act).

In another Open Records Act case, the Kentucky Court of Appeals found that videotape recordings that were taken of a teacher's classroom with the teacher's knowledge were "education records." The Kentucky Family Educational Rights Act prohibits disclosure of education records without parental or student consent, but also provides an exception that allows for disclosure to teachers with a legitimate educational interest. The Kentucky Court of Appeals held that the teacher's request should not be considered as being made by a member of the public, but instead should be judged in light of her position as a teacher. Since she was in the classroom whenever the videotapes were made, there was no confidentiality issue. Therefore, the Court of Appeals reversed and remanded for a determination of whether the plaintiff had a legitimate educational interest in viewing the tapes. Medley v. Board of Education, Shelby County, 168 S.W.3d 398 (Ky. Ct. App. 2004).

Another issue with personnel files is whether or not they are subject to discovery. While there is little case law on point, one decision out of the Eastern District of Kentucky adopted the Sixth Circuit's "liberal view of discovery when determining whether personnel files should be disclosed." Griffith v. Wal-Mart Stores, Inc., 163 F.R.D. 4, 5 (E.D. Ky. 1995). Therefore, in a discriminatory discharge case, the managerial personnel files sought were discoverable, even though no pattern or practice of discrimination was alleged. Id.

In another recent opinion, the Kentucky Court of Appeals found that public records protected by the attorney-client privilege were excludable from the disclosure requirements of the Open Records Act. In Hahn v. Univ. of Louisville, 80 S.W.3d 771 (Ky. Ct. App. 2001), an employee of the University of Louisville made an open records request to the University relating primarily to her employment records. At the time of the request, the employee had claims pending in litigation against the University. The Court held that the attorney-client privilege provided in the Rules of Civil Procedure together with the Open Records Act's proviso that "no court shall authorize the inspection by any party of any materials pertaining to civil litigation beyond that which is provided in the Rules of Civil Procedure governing pretrial discovery" governed this question. Accordingly, the Court upheld the University's decision not to disclose the records. The Court also rejected the employee's claim that state employees have a special right of access trumping the attorney-client privilege. Id.

B. Medical Records

The Kentucky Supreme Court held that when a plaintiff sought medical benefits that were provided by workers' compensation law, he became subject to the provisions of the Kentucky Workers' Compensation Act, which requires that an employee who reports a work-related injury must execute a waiver of privilege and the doctor must provide the employer with any information relating to the injury or disease for which the employee claims compensation. Melo v. Barnett, 157 S.W.3d 596, 597 (Ky. 2005). In that case, the plaintiff sued a doctor for informing the plaintiff's employer that he had HIV, and the Kentucky Supreme Court held that the claimant consented to the disclosure of his HIV status as a condition of receiving benefits. Id. at 599. See also Mount v. U.S. Postal Service, 79 F.3d 531 (6th Cir. (Ky.)1996) (disclosure of medical records to Postal Service employees responsible for making employment and disciplinary decisions does not violate the Privacy Act, 5 U.S.C. § 552).

C. Criminal Records

There are only two Kentucky decisions concerning criminal records in an employment context.

In the first, Dep't of Corr. v. Courier-Journal & Louisville Times, 914 S.W.2d 349 (Ky. Ct. App. 1996), the Kentucky Court of Appeals held that the job assignments and disciplinary records of prison inmates are subject to inspection under the Open Records Act.

The second is a negligent hiring case in which the Court of Appeals acknowledged the possibility that the employer should have known of the criminal propensities of the employee in question "had it conducted a criminal background check pursuant to its established policy." Oakley v. Flor-Shin, Inc., 964 S.W.2d 438, 442 (Ky. Ct. App. 1998).

There are also several statutes relating to mandatory criminal background investigations. For instance, Kentucky statutes require a criminal record check for every applicant for employment at a school or child-care center if the job would place the applicant in a position to supervise or discipline minors. KRS § 17.165 and KRS § 160.380. Kentucky statutes also require local boards of education to perform a criminal records check on all public school volunteers who will have contact with or supervisory responsibility for children at the school site or on school-sponsored trips. KRS § 161.148(4).

Also, the State Lottery Corporation must perform a background investigation on any person desiring to be an employee or vendor of the corporation. KRS § 154A.080.

Likewise, prospective employees of a private provider of adult correctional facilities will be subject to a thorough background investigation, including criminal, medical, and employment history. KRS § 197.510(17).

Additionally, KRS § 238.525(5) requires that any applicant for a charitable gaming license shall be subject to a state and national criminal history background check prior to licensure.

Finally, KRS § 15.382 requires that all persons seeking certification to become an officer of the law as defined in § 15.380 through § 15.404 shall be subject to a background check.

D. Subpoenas / Search Warrants

KRS § 336.060 gives authority to the commissioner of the Department of Labor, in conducting an investigation or hearing, to issue subpoenas to compel the attendance of witnesses and the production of books, papers and records competent and relevant to a matter under investigation by that department. KRS § 337.425 gives authority to the Executive Director of the Office of Workplace Standards to enter a place of employment of any employer to inspect and copy payrolls and other employment records. In addition, it also allows the executive director, or his authorized representative to examine witnesses or require by subpoena any witnesses or documentary evidence relating to the subject matter of any investigation.

In the case of Cabe v. Kitchen, 415 S.W.2d 96 (Ky. 1967), the Kentucky Court of Appeals, at the time the highest state court, recognized the right of the Commissioner of the Kentucky Department of Labor to subpoena payroll records from businesses. However, there are no other reported decisions in Kentucky that discuss the issue of subpoenaing employee records.

There are no reported decisions in Kentucky on search warrants served on employers seeking to search employees' files or workspace.

VII. ACTIONS SUBSEQUENT TO EMPLOYMENT

A. References

No reported decisions in Kentucky.

B. Non-Compete Agreements

There are no statutes that specifically address the legality of non-compete agreements in employment contracts. However, the Kentucky Court of Appeals upheld a covenant not-to-compete, saying that such a covenant is reasonable if "on consideration and circumstances of the particular case, the restriction is such only as to afford fair protection to the interests of the covenantee and is not so large as to interfere with the public interests or impose undue hardship on the party restricted." Cent. Adjustment Bureau, Inc. v. Ingram Assoc., Inc., 622 S.W.2d 681 (Ky. Ct. App. 1981) (quoting Hammons v. Big Sandy Claims Services, Inc., 567 S.W.2d 313 (Ky. Ct. App. 1978)).

In addition, the Sixth Circuit recognized that Kentucky courts have acknowledged that non-competition clauses play a critical role in business and are favored as long as they are reasonable in geographic scope and duration. Managed Health Care Associates, Inc. v. Kethan, 209 F.3d 923 (6th Cir. 2000). Additionally, the Sixth Circuit stated in that case that it believed that the Kentucky Supreme Court would conclude that non-competition clauses are assignable and upheld a non-competition clause in an employment contract where the employer assigned the employee's non-competition agreement to its successor. Id. at 930.

VIII. OTHER ISSUES

A. Statutes of Limitations

There is no statute or case which specifies a statute of limitations for any of the above causes of action for invasion of privacy. Generally, however, the statute of limitations for other actions sounding in tort is one year. Furthermore, at least one Kentucky court has stated that because the torts of false light, invasion of privacy and defamation are so closely related, the procedural requirements of one of the causes of action are applicable to the other as well. White v. Manchester Enter., Inc., 871 F. Supp. 934, 938, 23 Media L. Rep. 1309 (E.D. Ky. 1994). See also Mineer v. Williams, 82 F.Supp.2d 702, 28 Media L.Rptr. 1577 (E.D. Ky. 2000). This may be taken as an indication that the statute of limitations for libel and slander will also apply to false light actions. The statute of limitations for defamation actions is one year. KRS § 413.140(1)(d).

The statute of limitations for intentional interference with an economic advantage is five years, although it is unclear which Kentucky statute applies to the claim. In Williams v. Owensboro Bd. of Educ., No. 4:07-CV-149-R, 2009 WL 248426 (W.D. Ky. Feb. 3, 2009), the Western District of Kentucky examined two potential options: KRS § 413.120(4), which applies to the destruction of property interests, and KRS § 413.120(7), which is a "catch-all" statute of limitations. The court did not reach the question of which statute applies to interference claims because both statutes impose the same five-year limitations period. Id. at *3.

There is no clear statement, either in the statutes or case law, of what statute of limitations applies to actions for negligent hiring (which was recognized as actionable in Oakley v. Flor-Shin, Inc., 964 S.W.2d 438 (Ky. Ct. App. 1998), also cited in § VI.C, supra).

B. Jurisdiction

No reported decisions specifically address jurisdictional issues in employment privacy cases.

C. Workers' Compensation Exclusivity

Workers' compensation is the exclusive remedy for workers who suffer injuries arising out of and in the course of employment. KRS § 342.690(1). Covered injuries can include emotional distress suffered as a result of a work-related event. See Meade v. Arnold, 63 F. Supp. 2d. 913, No. 08-84-ART, 2009 WL 2240396 (E.D. Ky. Jul. 27, 2009), at *3. Therefore, workers' compensation benefits may supersede employees' tort claims for intentional infliction of emotional distress.

Plaintiffs may be able to bring tort claims in lieu of workers' compensation claims under three circumstances: (1) if the plaintiff has opted out of the workers' compensation system, see KRS § 342.395(1); (2) if the employer "deliberate[ly] inten[ded]" to cause the plaintiff's injury, KRS § 342.610(4); or (3) if the plaintiff's injury resulted from the "willful and unprovoked physical aggression" of another employee, officer, or director, KRS § 342.690(1). Kentucky courts interpret the "deliberate intention" exception narrowly. See, e.g., Rainer v. Union Carbide Corp., 402 F.3d 608, 615 (6th Cir. 2005) (stating that to achieve "deliberate intent" under Kentucky law, an employer must have "determined to injure an employee and used some means appropriate to that end, and there must be a specific intent.")

D. Pleading Requirements

Pleading requirements are: (a) a short and plain statement of the claim showing that the pleader is entitled to relief and (b) a demand for judgment for the relief to which he deems himself entitled. Relief in the alternative or of several different types may be demanded. CR 8.01(1). Only averments of fraud or mistake need be stated with particularity. Averments of malice, intent, knowledge, or other conditions of mind may be made generally. CR 9.02.

Unpublished opinions may not be cited as binding authority in Kentucky. However, CR 76.28(4)(c) now permits that unpublished decisions rendered after January 1, 2003, may be cited for consideration by the court if there is no published opinion that would adequately address the issue before the court. Opinions cited for consideration by the court shall be set out as an unpublished decision in the filed document and a copy of the entire decision shall be tendered along with the document to the court and all parties to the action.

Pursuant to a 2006 amendment to Federal Rules of Appellate Procedure Rule 32.1, Sixth Circuit Rule 28(g) (formally Sixth Circuit Rule 24(c)) now permits the citation of cases issued on or after January 1, 2007 and designated as "unpublished," "not for publication," "non-precedential," "not precedent," or the like. Previously, the citation of unpublished decisions was disfavored except for the purpose of establishing res judicata, estoppel, the law of the case, or in the event that a party believed an unpublished decision to have precedential value and that no published opinions would serve as well.

SURVEY OF LOUISIANA EMPLOYMENT LIBEL LAW

Mary Ellen Roy, David Korn and Dan Zimmerman
Phelps Dunbar LLP
One Canal Place, Suite 2000
365 Canal Street
New Orleans, Louisiana 70130-6534
Telephone: (504) 566-1311; Facsimile: (504) 568-9130

(With Developments Reported Through **November 1, 2012**)

GENERAL COMMENTS

Unlike the other 49 states, Louisiana follows the Civil Code (which outsiders often refer to as the "Napoleonic Code"). Defamation claims fall within La. Civil Code article 2315, the general tort codal article. As in other jurisdictions, Louisiana courts generally follow judicial precedent but they typically refer to it as "jurisprudence" or "juridical authority" rather than "case law." While in theory Louisiana courts do not subscribe to the "common law," in practice, the Louisiana Supreme Court has adopted certain common law concepts such as causes of action for intentional interference with contract and intentional (or negligent) infliction of emotional distress.

The general Louisiana trial courts are called district courts. The intermediate appellate court is the Court of Appeal (not Court of Appeals), which is divided into five circuits. The state Supreme Court hears few direct appeals in civil cases, choosing whether or not to accept cases on supervisory writs. Intermediate interlocutory review is more readily available in Louisiana than in many jurisdictions, however, as aggrieved parties may file writs seeking review with the Court of Appeal and the Supreme Court on interlocutory issues.

Louisiana has adopted a public domain citation format that requires all cases published after December 31, 1993 to be cited in the following format when cited in court papers: Fitzgerald v. Tucker, 98-2313 (La. 6/29/99), 737 So.2d 706.

SIGNIFICANT DEVELOPMENTS SINCE THE 2012 *SURVEY*

None.

I. GENERAL LAW

A. General Employment Law

1. ***At Will Employment.*** In Louisiana, there are two types of contracts for hire: the limited duration contract and the terminable at-will contract. May v. Harris Management Corp., 928 So.2d 140, 148 (La.App. 1st Cir. 2005). An employee in Louisiana can be terminated at will if the term of the employment is unspecified or indefinite. May, 928 So.2d at 147-48; Williams v. Delta Haven, Inc., 416 So.2d 637 (La.App. 2d Cir. 1982); La. Civ. Code arts. 2024, 2746, 2747, and 2749. An employer is free to terminate with or without cause, even if the employment contract is in writing, so long as it has no definite term. La. Civ. Code arts. 2746, 2747 and 2024; Williams, 416 So.2d at 638. An employment contract cannot be binding for more than ten years. Deus v. Allstate Ins. Co., 15 F.3d 506 (5th Cir.), cert. denied, 513 U.S. 1014 (1994). The principle of at-will employment in Louisiana is sufficiently strong that even if a decision to terminate is based upon false or negligently-gathered information, an employer still has the right to fire with impunity. Johnson v. Delchamps, Inc., 897 F.2d 808 (5th Cir. 1990) (discharge upheld even when based upon negligently administered polygraph test); Herbert v. Placed Refining Co., 564 So.2d 371 (La. App. 1 Cir. 1990) (discharge upheld even when based upon negligently tested urine sample). But see, Bains v. YMCA, 969 So.2d 646 (La.App. 4th Cir. 2007) (employment at will doctrine did not preclude applicant from stating cause of action for detrimental reliance).

An employer can terminate an employee who has a limited-duration employment contract for cause. See Certified Security Systems, Inc. v. Yuspeh, 713 So.2d 558 (La.App. 4th Cir. 1998) (employee deliberately concealed financial condition of company from its board); Campbell v. Elcom, Inc., 728 So.2d 1035 (La.App. 2d Cir. 1999) (supervisor did not operate within budget and disregarded need for prior approval of overtime); cf. Prevost v. Eye Care and Surgery Center, 635 So.2d 765 (La.App. 1st Cir.), writ denied, 639 So.2d 1168 (La. 1994) (physician not accepting new insurance scheme not cause for termination).

Employment can never be terminated for discriminatory reasons in violation of federal or state anti-discrimination laws. In Louisiana, an employer cannot discriminate on the basis of age, race, color, religion, sex and/or national origin. La. R.S. 23:312, 23:332 et seq. See also Seagrave v. Dean, 908 So.2d 41, 44-45 (La.App. 1st Cir. 2005), writ denied, 925 So.2d 543 (La.) cert. denied, 549 U.S. 822 (2006).

B. Elements of Libel Claim

1. ***Basic Elements.*** The basic elements of a defamation claim in Louisiana are: (1) a false and defamatory statement concerning another; (2) an unprivileged publication to a third party; (3) fault on the part of the publisher; and (4) resulting injury. Kennedy v. Sheriff of East Baton Rouge, 935 So.2d 669, 674 (La. 2006). As a matter of state law, these elements must be proven by the plaintiff by a preponderance of the evidence. Brown v. Connor, 860 So.2d 27, 30 (La.App. 5th Cir. 2003). Generally, defamation is not actionable as a constitutional tort, but evidence of such actions can "be a link in a chain showing a deprivation of liberty or property without due process." See Cousin v. Small, 2001 WL 617455, 2001 U.S. Dist. LEXIS 7903, at *24 (E.D. La.), aff'd, 325 F.3d 627 (5th Cir.), cert. denied, 540 U.S. 826 (2003).

2. ***Fault.*** Whether a plaintiff must prove "actual malice" or some lesser degree of fault depends on whether the plaintiff is a private individual or public figure and on whether a qualified privilege applies. When words are defamatory per se, that is, when the words themselves expressly or implicitly accuse another of criminal conduct or by their very nature tend to injure one's personal or professional reputation, without considering extrinsic facts or circumstances (and if the plaintiff is a private person and no qualified privilege applies), fault is presumed, and the burden shifts to the defendant to rebut the presumption. Kennedy v. Sheriff of East Baton Rouge, 935 So.2d 669, 675 (La. 2006). If the lawsuit involves a matter of public concern, however, the burden does not shift, and the plaintiff must prove fault, whether the defendant is a media defendant or not. Kennedy, 935 So.2d 669 at 678, citing Gertz v. Robert Welch, Inc., 418 U.S. 323, 344-47, 1 Media L. Rep. 1633 (1974).

a. **Private Figure Plaintiff/Matter of Public Concern.** In dicta in Kennedy v. Sheriff of East Baton Rouge, 935 So.2d 669, 679-81 (La. 2006), the Louisiana Supreme Court purported to decide that the fault standard applicable in cases concerning defamation of a private individual involving a matter of public concern and a non-media defendant is the malice standard articulated in Costello v. Hardy, 864 So.2d 129 (La. 2004), rather than the actual malice standard set forth in New York Times v. Sullivan, 376 U.S. 254, 1 Media L. Rep. 1527 (1964). In Kennedy, however, the Court applied the actual malice standard because a conditional privilege was involved. Kennedy, 935 So.2d at 688. Previously, the Louisiana Supreme Court had expressly left the question of the appropriate fault standard in such circumstances open, choosing instead to decide the cases on other issues. See Trentecosta v. Beck, 703 So.2d 552, 560 (La. 1997) (concluding that it was unnecessary to determine whether the "actual malice" standard or some lesser degree of fault should apply when a private individual is injured by a *non-media defendant* about a matter of public concern because the plaintiff established the defendant's liability even under the actual malice standard); see also Sassone v. Elder, 626 So.2d 345, 352 n.10, 22 Media L. Rep. 1049 (La. 1993) (noting that it would not address whether the actual malice standard applies in actions by private individuals against *media defendants* in matters of public concern because it held that there was no defamatory statement made). The Louisiana Supreme Court has suggested that a different fault standard may be applicable to media defendants as compared to non-media defendants. Trentecosta, 703 So.2d at 560 n.11; but see Kennedy, 935 So.2d at 677-78 (Gertz and Philadelphia Newspaper holdings should apply to media and non-media defendants, as a matter of state law). The malice standard described by the Louisiana Supreme Court in Costello and Kennedy is whether there is "a lack of reasonable belief in the truth of the statement giving rise to the defamation." Kennedy, 935 So.2d at 680; Costello, 864 So.2d at 143.

b. **Private Figure Plaintiff/Matter of Private Concern.** In cases of a private figure plaintiff and a matter of private concern, fault is otherwise known as malice, and the Louisiana Supreme Court has described malice as whether there is "a lack of reasonable belief in the truth of the statement giving rise to the defamation." Kennedy, 935 So.2d at 680; Costello, 864 So.2d at 143.

c. **Public Figure Plaintiff/Matter of Public Concern.** As the Louisiana Supreme Court has acknowledged, while the fault standard applicable to defamation cases brought by private figure plaintiffs is determined by state law, for a public figure, "the law of libel and slander has been delineated by federal constitutional law." Romero v. Thomson Newspapers (Wisconsin), Inc., 648 So.2d 866, 869, 870 (La. 1995), 23 Media L. Rep. 1528, cert. denied, 515 U.S. 1131 (1995); see also Kennedy v. Sheriff of East Baton Rouge, 935 So.2d 669, 675 (La. 2006). Accordingly, a public figure or public official plaintiff must meet the New York Times Co. v. Sullivan, 376 U.S. 254, 1 Media L. Rep. 1527 (1964), standard to recover damages for defamation. The public figure or public official "must establish by clear and convincing evidence that the defamatory statement was made with actual malice, that is, 'with knowledge that it was false or with reckless disregard of whether it was false or not.'" Davis v. Borskey, 660 So.2d 17, 23 (La. 1995) (quoting New York Times, 376 U.S. at 279-80). Where the public official plaintiff is seeking damages against his government employer, the employer may not rely on worker's compensation as a bar to the action since defamation suits allege no "physical injury." City of Nachitoches v. Employers Reinsurance Corp., 819 So.2d 413 (La.App. 3d Cir. 2002).

"'The 'public official' designation applies at the very least to those among the hierarchy of government employees who have, or appear to have, substantial responsibility for or control over the conduct of governmental affairs.'" Davis, 660 So.2d at 21 n.6 (quoting Rosenblatt v. Baer, 383 U.S. 75, 85-86, 1 Media L. Rep. 1558 (1966)) (holding that plaintiff, purchasing agent for a state university, was a "public official" for purposes of defamation action against director of university student union and state after state investigator released a report based on allegations that plaintiff was involved in wrongdoing in solicitation of bids). See also Anders v. Andrus, 773 So.2d 289 (La.App. 3d Cir. 2000), writ denied, 788 So.2d 427 (La. 2001) (police officer is a public official). But see Fitzgerald v. Tucker, 715 So.2d 1281 , (La.App. 3d Cir. 1998) (holding that the Administrative Director of Louisiana State Board for Certification of Substance Abuse Counselors was not a "public official" because her job was not a "high level" government position and "would not be viewed by the public as a job which gave her great control over governmental affairs"), rev'd on other grounds, 737 So.2d 706 (La. 1999) (finding it unnecessary to address whether plaintiff was a public official).

"A public figure is a non-public official who is intimately involved in the resolution of important public questions or who by reason of his fame shapes events in areas of concern to society at large." Trentecosta v. Beck, 703 So.2d 552, 560, 560 n.8 (La. 1997) (citing Curtis Publishing Co. v. Butts, 388 U.S. 130, 164, 1 Medial L. Rep. 1568 (1967)); Kennedy, 935 So.2d at 676 n. 4. See also Folse v. Delgado Community College, 776 F. Supp. 1133 (E.D. La. 1991) (holding that former head basketball coach of community college was not a public figure, explaining, "Not to belittle Delgado (i.e., a small, community junior college in the city of New Orleans with largely local student body), but the defendants' suggestion that even the title 'head' coach bestowed on an employee of such an institution could imbue a person with the miasma 'public figure' status borders on specious"); Thompson v. Emmis Television Broadcasting, 894 So.2d 480 (La.App. 4th Cir.), writ denied 899 So.2d 580 (La. 2005) (finding that a church pastor "made himself a public figure through his political activism and his position in the community"). Whether an individual is a public figure is a matter of law for the Court to decide. Broussard v. Kaplan, 604 So.2d 77, 83 (La.App. 3d Cir. 1992).

3. ***Falsity.*** Generally, the plaintiff must prove falsity by a preponderance of the evidence. Sommer v. State Dep't of Transportation and Development, 758 So.2d 923 (La.App. 4th Cir.), writ denied, 772 So.2d 122 (La. 2000). In a case involving a statement that is defamatory per se (when the plaintiff is a private person and no qualified privilege applies), falsity is presumed but may be rebutted by the defendant. Kennedy v. Sheriff of East Baton Rouge, 935 So.2d 669, 675 (La. 2006); DiLeo v. Davis, 1995 WL 143531, *7 n.4, 1995 U.S. Dist. LEXIS 4118, 23 Media L. Rep. 1756 (E.D. La.). When the plaintiff is a public figure, the plaintiff must prove falsity by clear and convincing evidence. Kennedy, 935 So.2d 669 at 675. Likewise, when a matter of public concern is involved, the plaintiff, whether a private or public figure, bears the burden of proving falsity, regardless of whether the defendant is a member of the media or not. Kennedy, 935 So.2d at 678, citing Philadelphia Newspapers, Inc. v. Hepps, 475 U.S. 767 (1986); Romero v. Thomson Newspapers (Wisconsin), Inc., 648 So.2d 866, 870 (La.), cert. denied, 515 U.S. 1131 (1995).

The truth or falsity of a statement must be looked at in the context in which it was said. Christian v. Fontenot, 672 So.2d 436, 443 (La.App. 2d Cir.), writ denied, 679 So.2d 105 (La. 1996); see also Cyprien v. Board of Supervisors, 5 So.3d 862 (La. 2009) (in light of undisputed fact that plaintiff provided resume with incorrect information, factual dispute over whether plaintiff also provided copy of his resume with correct information not significant).

Repeating allegations made by others that plaintiff embezzled, stole, and misappropriated church funds was not false because the allegations had, in fact, been made. Thompson v. Emmis Television Broadcasting, 894 So.2d 480 (La.App. 4 Cir.), writ denied, 899 So.2d 580 (La. 2005).

4. ***Defamatory Statement of Fact.*** "A communication is defamatory if it tends to harm the reputation of another so as to lower the person in the estimation of the community, deter others from associating or dealing with the person, or otherwise expose the person to contempt or ridicule." Kennedy v. Sheriff of East Baton Rouge, 935 So.2d 669, 674 (La. 2006). "However, the intent and meaning of the alleged defamatory statement must be gathered from the context as well as the words, and all parts of the statement and the circumstances of its publication must be considered to derive the true meaning." Fourcade v. City of Gretna, 598 So.2d 415, 419 (La.App. 5th Cir. 1992); see also Cooksey v. Stewart, 938 So.2d 1206 (La.App. 2d Cir. 2006). The question of whether a statement is capable of particular meaning and whether that meaning is defamatory is a question of law for the court. Sassone v. Elder, 626 So.2d 345, 352, 22 Media L. Rep. 1049 (La. 1993); Heine v. Reed, 28 So.3d 529, 534 (La.App. 4th Cir. 2009), writ denied, 31 So.3d 365 (La. 2010). "The question for the court in determining whether words have a defamatory meaning is whether a third person hearing the communication would have reasonably understood the communication, taken in context, as intended in a defamatory sense." Davis v. Borskey, 660 So.2d 17, 22 (La. 1995). Words that do not harm the reputation of the plaintiff, although unflattering, are not defamatory; "casual remarks made in informal conversation" do not constitute defamation. Harris v. State Farm Fire & Casualty Co., 2000 WL 33282467, 2000 U.S. Dist. LEXIS 19904 (W.D. La.) (statements made in company meetings that plaintiff employee "will never move up" and "sings too much" are not defamatory); Heine, 28 So.3d at 536 (description of plaintiff as "prissy . . . heavily bedecked in gold with a head of very badly dyed brown hair," was "unkind and insensitive," but not defamatory).

Louisiana law distinguishes between words that, taken in context, are defamatory and words that are defamatory per se without reference to their context. A communication is defamatory per se if the words "expressly or implicitly accuse another of criminal conduct, or which by their very nature tend to injure one's personal or professional reputation, without considering extrinsic facts or circumstances," Kennedy, 935 So.2d at 676. Compare Manale v. City of New Orleans, 673 F.2d 122, 125 (5th Cir. 1982) (holding that fellow police officer's calling plaintiff "a little fruit" and "gay" at police roll call were defamatory per se under Louisiana law); Rachal v. State Dep't of Wildlife and Fisheries, 918 So.2d 570, 575 (La.App. 3d Cir. 2005) (false accusation that plaintiff was seen having sex with a co-worker in employer's vehicle was defamation per se); and Smith v. Atkins, 622 So.2d 795, 799-800 (La.App. 4th Cir. 1993) (holding that law professor's calling female student a "slut" was defamatory per se), with Matherne v. Response Instrument Services & Engineering Corp., 533 So.2d 1011 (La.App. 1st Cir. 1988), writ denied, 537 So.2d 1166 (La. 1989) (corporate director's statements to effect that he believed the plaintiff co-director and a former employee were "emotionally involved" were not defamatory per se because the mere statement that the two had an emotional relationship "does not in itself impute any immorality on the part of either party or lower their reputations in the community"). Words that impute criminal activity to the plaintiff are defamatory *per se*. Tonubbee v. River Parishes Guide, 702 So.2d 971, 974 (La.App. 5th Cir. 1997), 26 Media L. Rep. 1348, writ denied, 709 So.2d 747 (La.), cert. denied, 525 U.S. 858 (1998); see also Heflin v. Sabine Association of Retarded Citizens, 685 So.2d 665 (La.App. 3d Cir. 1996), (employer's accusation of theft defamatory per se since theft is a crime). A television news report that repeated allegations made by others that plaintiff had embezzled, stolen, and misappropriated church funds was not defamatory per se. Thompson v. Emmis Television Broadcasting, 894 So.2d 480 (La.App. 4th Cir.), writ denied, 899 So.2d 580 (La. 2005).

If a statement is defamatory per se, falsity and malice are presumed and the defendant bears the burden of rebutting the presumption. Kennedy, 935 So.2d at 675; Maggio v. Liztech Jewelry, 912 F. Supp. 216, 219 (E.D. La. 1996). If allegedly defamatory statements are "technically inaccurate," they are not defamatory unless the difference between the inaccurate statement and the truth would damage the plaintiff's reputation. Bernofsky v. Administrators of Tulane Educational Fund, 2000 WL 422394, 2000 U.S. Dist. LEXIS 5561 (E.D. La.), aff'd, 253 F.3d 700 (5th Cir.), cert. denied, 534 U.S. 1036 (2001).

5. ***Of and Concerning Plaintiff.*** The defamatory statements must concern an identifiable plaintiff. Sassone v. Elder, 626 So.2d 345, 355, 22 Media L. Rep. 1049 (La. 1993). See also McConathy v. Ungar, 765 So.2d 1214 (La.App. 2d Cir.), writ denied, 774 So.2d 982 (La. 2000). Statements about a group or a class generally are not actionable unless the group is so small that the words could be understood to have personal reference and application to that group so that each member is defamed as an individual. See Bujol v. Ward, 778 So.2d 1175, 1180 (La.App. 5th Cir.), writ denied, 791 So.2d 117 (La. 2001). Statements about a deceased person are not actionable. Gugliuzza v. K.C.M.C., Inc., 606 So.2d 790, 20 Media L. Rep. 1866 (La. 1992); Johnson v. KTBS, Inc., 889 So.2d 329 (La.App. 2d Cir. 2004). Defamatory statements about a business, however, may be of and concerning the owner of that business, if the business is the alter ego of the owner. See Gorman v. Swaggart, 524 So.2d 915, 919-20, 15 Media L. Rep. 2107 (La.App. 4th Cir.), writ denied, 530 So.2d 571 (La. 1988), cert. denied, 489 U.S. 1017 (1989).

6. ***Publication.*** Publication requires that statements be made to a person other than the one defamed. Kennedy v. Sheriff of East Baton Rouge, 935 So.2d 669, 674 (La. 2006). Silence in response to a request for a reference does not amount to defamation because "a defamatory action requires communication of defamatory words." Bernofsky v. Administrators of Tulane Educational Fund, 2000 WL 422394, 2000 U.S. Dist. LEXIS 5561 (E.D. La.), aff'd, 253 F.3d 700 (5th Cir.), cert. denied, 534 U.S. 1036 (2001).

a. **Intra-corporate Communication.** Louisiana has accepted the intra-corporate nonpublication rule holding that an intra-corporate communication among officers or agents of the same corporation and in relation to their duties for the corporation is merely a communication of the corporation itself; it cannot be construed as being a communication to a third party for the purpose of satisfying the publication requirement. Espree v. Tobacco Plus, Inc., 772 So.2d 389, 392 (La.App. 3d Cir. 2000); Brunet v. Fullmer, 777 So.2d 1240, 1242 (La.App. 4th Cir. 1/10/01), (by analogy, under agency principles communications between insurance adjuster and insurer constitute intra-corporate communications even when the adjuster is employed by another company); Commercial Union Insurance Co. v. Melikyan, 424 So.2d 1114 (La.App. 1st Cir. 1982) (statements between employees, made within the course and scope of their employment, are not statements communicated or publicized to third persons). But see Barber v. Marine Drilling, 2002 WL 237848, 2002 U.S. Dist. LEXIS 2821 (E.D. La.) (statements that fall outside of the course and scope of employment may not be protected as privileged intra-corporate communications).

Some courts, however, have held that publication did take place under these circumstances, but then applied qualified privilege as an affirmative defense. Cashio v. Holt, 425 So.2d 820, 822 (La.App. 5th Cir. 1982), writ denied, 430 So.2d 94 (La. 1983) (publication only to managers enjoyed qualified privilege); Martin v. Lincoln General

Hospital, 588 So.2d 1329, 1330 (La.App. 2d Cir. 1991), writ denied, 592 So.2d 1302 (La. 1992) (publication to auditor who conveyed information to Board of Directors had qualified privilege).

b. **Self-Publication and Compelled Self-Publication.** There is no publication if the only communication to third persons is made by the plaintiff; it is essential that the allegedly defamatory statement be made by the defendant. Gilliland v. Feibleman's Inc., 161 La. 24, 108 So. 112 (La. 1926); see also Hoover v. Livingston Bank, 451 So.2d 3 (La.App. 1st Cir. 1984) (defamation action dismissed where only publication occurred when plaintiff informed prospective employer of the alleged defamatory statement); Cashio v. Holt, 425 So.2d 820, 822 (La.App. 5th Cir. 1982), writ denied, 430 So.2d 94 (La. 1983) (fired employee's dissemination of his termination letter not publication); Bellard v. Gautreaux, 2011 WL 1103320 (M.D. La. 3/22/11) (no "publication" shown "when plaintiff self-publicizes to prospective employers"). However, one Louisiana appellate court, in dicta, recognized that a plaintiff's relating the allegedly defamatory statement to third persons would be sufficient for publication if the plaintiff had good reason to tell each person. Fourcade v. City of Gretna, 598 So.2d 415 (La.App. 5th Cir. 1992).

c. **Republication.** A person is responsible for all natural and probable republications of their original statement. Atwood v. Grand Casinos of Louisiana, Inc., 887 So.2d 634, 638 (La.App. 3d Cir. 2004). Thus, those who repeat a defamatory statement may be liable, even if they believe the statement to be true. Fourcade v. City of Gretna, 598 So.2d 415 (La.App. 5th Cir. 1992). Each subsequent publication is considered to be a new tort. Neyrey v. Lebrun, 309 So.2d 722 (La.App. 4th Cir. 1975).

7. ***Statements versus Conduct.*** The act of terminating a person's employment is not in itself actionable as a communication of words or statements concerning the employee. Hicks v. Stone, 425 So.2d 807, 813 (La.App. 1st Cir. 1982), writ denied, 429 So.2d 129 (La. 1983); Guillory v. State Farm Ins. Co., 662 So. 2d 104, 112 (La.App. 4th Cir. 1995) (placing employee on loss control program could not form basis for defamation suit).

8. ***Damages.*** Louisiana allows recovery of general (non-pecuniary) damages, even absent a claim for special damages (such as loss of income). Bell v. Rogers, 698 So.2d 749, 754 (La.App. 2d Cir. 1997). General damages include injury to reputation, personal humiliation, embarrassment, mental anguish, anxiety and hurt feelings, each of which is a separate element of damage. Costello v. Hardy, 864 So.2d 129, 141 (La. 2004). Even without claiming special damages, and with little or no effect on the plaintiff's reputation, the plaintiff may recover damages for embarrassment, anxiety, humiliation or hurt feelings. Bell, 698 So.2d at 754-55. At least one court has held that a plaintiff's spouse may recover for loss of consortium so long as the defamed plaintiff was alive at the time of the defamatory statement. See Maurice v. Snell, 632 So.2d 393, 396 (La.App. 4th Cir.), writ denied, 637 So.2d 507 (La. 1994). However, the general rule in Louisiana is that a plaintiff cannot recover for defamatory statements made about another even when the statement inflicts indirect injury upon the plaintiff. Johnson v. KTBS, Inc., 889 So.2d 329 (La.App. 2 Cir. 2004), writ denied 896 So.2d 68 (La. 2005); McBeth v. United Press International, Inc., 505 F.2d 959 (5th Cir. 1974).

Any injury for which damages are sought must be proved by "competent evidence," and plaintiff must show a "but for" link between the defamatory statement and the injury. Bell, 698 So.2d at 755. However, it is not required to establish the actual pecuniary valve of the injury. Lege v. White, 619 So. 2d 190, 191 (La.App. 3d Cir. 1993).

Except for a few aberrations, until the mid-1990s, general damage awards had not exceeded $10,000. See Lege; Melancon v. Hyatt Corp., 589 So.2d 1186 (La.App. 4th Cir. 1991), writ denied, 592 So.2d 411 (La. 1992) (reducing a jury award of $45,000 for mental pain and suffering, $22,500 for embarrassment and humiliation, $22,500 for loss of reputation and $25,000 for spouse's loss of consortium to a lump sum of $10,000 for mental pain and suffering, loss of reputation, embarrassment and humiliation, and $5,000 for loss of consortium, while allowing the $87,000 award for lost wages to stand). But see McHale v. Lake Charles American Press, 390 So.2d 556, 6 Media L. Rep. 2478 (La.App. 3d Cir. 1980), cert. denied, 452 U.S. 941 (1981) (newspaper editorial justified $150,000 in general damages for damage to reputation and mental anguish suffered by plaintiff, who was the target of the editorial).

Recently, the amounts awarded have increased substantially. In Sommer v. State Dep't of Transportation and Development, 758 So.2d 923 (La.App. 4th Cir.), writ denied, 772 So.2d 122 (La. 2000), the Court of Appeal affirmed as amended a general damage award of $1,000,000.00 and an award of $471,529.00 in lost income resulting from an alleged conspiracy to defame the plaintiff with her new employer. See also Steed v. St. Paul's United Methodist Church, 728 So.2d 931 (La.App. 2d Cir.), writ denied, 740 So.2d 1290 (La. 1999) (upholding award of $90,000 in general damages to minister who a church employee falsely accused of sexual harassment); Trentecosta v. Beck, 714 So.2d 721 (La.App. 4th Cir.), writ denied, 726 So.2d 28 (La. 1998) ($50,000 awarded for a police officer's statement, published in a newspaper article, that accused the plaintiff of bilking money from charities while running a bingo hall); DiLeo v. Davis, 1995 WL 143531, *7 n.4, 1995 U.S. Dist. LEXIS 4118, 23 Media L. Rep. 1756 (E.D. La.) ($2 million jury verdict for general damages remitted to $500,000).

a. **Presumed Damages and Libel Per Se.** A statement is defamatory per se if, by its very nature, it injures the plaintiff's personal or professional reputation. Costello v. Hardy, 864 So.2d 129 (La. 2004); Cangelosi v. Schwegmann Brothers Giant Supermarkets, 390 So.2d 196 (La. 1980). This includes impliedly or explicitly accusing someone of criminal conduct. Martin v. Markley, 11 So.2d 593 (La. 1942).

"The element of injury may . . . be presumed or inferred from the publication of words which are defamatory per se." Bell v. Rogers, 698 So.2d 749, 754 (La.App. 2d Cir. 1997); see also Vincent v. Miller, 867 So.2d 780, 782 (La.App. 3d Cir. 2004). The status of this holding in the wake cases such as Gertz v. Robert Welch, Inc., 418 U.S. 323, 1 Media L. Rep. 1633 (1974), and Philadelphia Newspapers, Inc. v. Hepps, 475 U.S. 767 (1986), is unclear. Trahan, one of the few cases even to acknowledge Gertz when discussing presumed damages, did not find anything within the Supreme Court holding that contradicted established Louisiana law. Trahan seemed to differentiate between injury to reputation, which could be presumed upon publication of language that is defamatory per se, and general damages, which must be proved by competent evidence (although no proof of the specific dollar value of these damages is required). Trahan, 368 So.2d at 185.

In addition, the Louisiana Supreme Court recognized that a private figure plaintiff claiming that he was defamed by a factual misstatement involving a public issue is required to show actual malice to recover presumed damages. Romero v. Thomson Newspapers (Wisconsin), Inc., 648 So.2d 866, 870 (La.), cert. denied, 515 U.S. 1131 (1995).

(1) Employment-Related Criticism. Statements regarding employment-related criticisms are treated as any other statement and can be considered defamation per se, if, for example, the statement imputes the commission of a crime to the plaintiff. Williams v. Touro Infirmary, 578 So.2d 1006, 1009 (La.App. 4th Cir. 1991); see also Sommer v. State Dep't of Transportation and Development, 758 So.2d 923 (La.App. 4th Cir.), writ denied, 772 So.2d 122 (La. 2000) (written statements made by one employer to another wrongfully asserting fraudulent behavior by employee relating to use of sick leave held defamatory); Doe v. Grant, 839 So.2d 408 (La.App. 4th Cir.), writ denied, 842 So.2d 1102 (La. 2003) (despite criticism that was per se defamatory, disclosure of summary suspension of physician was necessary to ensure public safety and to ensure that hospital staff was aware that hospital privileges had been suspended and thus was privileged). If an employer provides accurate information about a current or former employee's job performance or reasons for separation to a prospective, current or former employer, that employer is immune from civil liability and other consequences of such disclosure, provided that such employer is not acting in bad faith. La. R.S. 23:291(A). Furthermore, any prospective employer who reasonably relies upon information pertaining to an employee's job performance or reasons for separation, disclosed by a former employer, shall be immune from civil liability. La. R.S. 23:291(B).

(2) Single Instance Rule. Louisiana courts have not addressed the "single instance rule."

b. **Punitive Damages.** Punitive damages are not recoverable in Louisiana unless specifically allowed for by statute. Punitive damages were briefly available in defamation cases, but only between 1976 and 1980. Ciecierski v. Avondale Shipyards, Inc., 572 So.2d 834 (La.App. 4th Cir. 1990), writ denied, 574 So.2d 1256 (La. 1991).

c. **Injunctive relief.** Injunctions against making defamatory statements are not allowed. Greenberg v. DeSalvo, 254 La. 1019, 229 So.2d 83, 86 (1969), cert. denied, 397 U.S. 1075 (1970); Vartech Systems, Inc. v. Hayden, 971 So.2d 247, 261 (La.App. 1st Cir. 2006) (overturning injunction against former employees who were subject to non-compete clause).

II. PRIVILEGES AND DEFENSES

A. Scope of Privileges

1. ***Absolute Privileges.*** "An absolute privilege protects a speaker without reference to his notion of the truth or falsity of the statement." Zuber v. Buie, 849 So.2d 559 (La.App. 1st Cir.), writ denied, 855 So.2d 318 (La. 2003). Under the Louisiana Constitution, legislators speaking within the "legitimate legislative sphere" have an absolute privilege that they may raise as an affirmative defense to a defamation claim. La. Const. art. III, § 8; Copsey v. Baer, 593 So.2d 685, 688 (La.App. 1st Cir. 1991), writ denied, 594 So.2d 876 (La. 1992). There is also an absolute privilege for witnesses who give testimony, short of perjury, in judicial and quasi-judicial proceedings. Smolensky v. McDaniel, 144 F.Supp.2d 611 (E.D. La. 2001). Louisiana law grants an absolute privilege to non-litigant witnesses in a judicial proceeding when their testimony is pertinent and material to the proceeding. Zuber. Attorneys and parties to a suit do not enjoy this absolute privilege, but may be protected by the qualified privilege discussed infra. There is an absolute privilege for statements made in complaints filed in bar disciplinary matters. The Louisiana Supreme Court publically reprimanded an attorney who filed a defamation suit against a former client based on statements made in a bar complaint. In re Raspanti, 8 So.3d 526 (La. 2009).

An employer enjoys "unqualified" immunity from defamation suits by employees that are based upon the employer's release of negative evaluations and investigations to the employee's union. Rougeau v. Firestone Tire & Rubber Co., 274 So.2d 454, 457 n.1 (La.App. 3d Cir. 1973).

2. ***Qualified Privileges.*** Under certain circumstances, an employer is entitled to a qualified privilege defense in a defamation action brought by an employee. Espree v. Tobacco Plus, Inc., 772 So.2d 389 (La.App. 3d Cir. 2000); Duplessis v. Warren Petroleum, Inc., 672 So.2d 1019 (La.App. 4th Cir. 1996). A person may enjoy a qualified or conditional privilege from defamatory statements if (1) made in good faith, (2) on a subject in which the person communicating has an interest or owes a duty and (3) to a person with a corresponding interest or duty. Bell v. Rogers, 698 So.2d 749 (La.App. 2d Cir. 1997); see also Aranyosi v. Delchamps, Inc., 739 So.2d 911 (La.App. 1st Cir. 1999), writ denied, 750 So.2d 198 (La. 1999) (statements made to police officers in the course of police investigation enjoy qualified privilege); Ruffin v. Wal-Mart Stores Inc., 818 So.2d 965, 968 (La.App. 1st Cir. 2002) (employers enjoy a qualified privilege for communications to and from the Department of Employment Security); Doe v. Grant, 839 So.2d 408 (La.App. 4th Cir.), writ denied, 842 So.2d 1102 (La. 2003) (qualified privilege applies to defamation claims arising out of physician peer review process); Roux v. Pflueger, 16 So.3d 590 (La.App. 4th Cir. 2009) (qualified privilege applies to church financial committee's letter to church official with duty to investigate church's finances).

With regard to the employer/employee relationship, an employer has a right to investigate the suspected wrongdoings of its employees without becoming liable for defamation, even if others become aware of its investigation. An employer's communications regarding a subject in which they have an interest or a duty are not considered published when made in good faith. City of Natchitoches v. Employers Reinsurance Corp., 819 So.2d 413 (La.App. 3d Cir. 2002). But see Melancon v. Hyatt Corp., 589 So.2d 1186 (La.App. 4 Cir. 1991) (privilege does not extend so far as to allow communication of employer's reason for terminating employee to any and all other employees).

Statements made in the course of a judicial proceeding are subject to a qualified privilege with respect to a defamation claim if the statements are (1) material to the proceeding, (2) are made with probable cause and (3) without malice. Costello v. Hardy, 864 So.2d 129 (La. 2004); Rogers v. Ash Grove Cement Co., 799 So.2d 841, 846 (La.App. 2d Cir. 2001) (attorneys are entitled to a qualified privilege where statements made in court are material to the proceeding). One Louisiana Court has extended the privilege to cover a complaint letter written by a client that allegedly defamed the client's attorney. See Pecantte-Brown v. Collins, 2008 WL 5158893, 2008 La. App. Unpub. LEXIS 594 (La. App. 3d Cir.), writ denied, 3 So.3d 490 (La. 2009).

a. **Common Interest.** A qualified privilege attaches to statements made on a subject in which the speaker has an interest or duty to another person with a corresponding interest or duty. Bell v. Rogers, 698 So.2d 749 (La.App. 2d Cir. 1997) (qualified privilege attached to written report stating that nurse had misappropriated hospital property). Likewise, statements made during the investigation of possible wrongdoing by an employee are privileged if made in good faith. Kelly v. West Cash & Carry Building Materials Store, 745 So.2d 743 (La.App. 4th Cir. 1999); Espree v. Tobacco Plus, Inc., 772 So.2d 389 (La.App. 3d Cir. 2000). For example, a statement by a city councilman in an open meeting that the city's financial officer was stealing funds and should be fired was conditionally qualified and could not be used as a basis for a defamation action against the city because it related to investigation of a matter in which the city had an interest. City of Natchitoches v. Employers Reinsurance Corp., 819 So.2d 413, 420 (La.App. 3 Cir, 2002). This is true even if third persons become aware of the investigation and subsequent discharge of an employee. Wright v. Dollar General Corp., 602 So.2d 772, 775 (La.App. 2d Cir.), writ denied, 606 So.2d 538 (La. 1992) (statement made by employer to law enforcement officials in the course of investigation of criminal activity is privileged and provides no basis for defamation suit even assuming the accuracy of plaintiff's allegations). A director's statement that might otherwise be defamatory, made to employees of corporation who had interest in co-director's ability to manage, was privileged. Matherne v. Response Instrument Service & Engineering Corp., 533 So.2d 1011 (La.App. 1st Cir. 1988), writ denied, 537 So.2d 1166 (La. 1989). Similarly, comments made among subordinate and supervisors about business-related actions taken by another employer were held to be privileged. Ward v. Sears, Roebuck, & Co., 339 So.2d 1255 (La.App. 1st Cir. 1976). Finally, under the common interest test, an attorney has a qualified privilege for defamatory statements made in a judicial pleading while representing his or her client. Lentini v. Northwest Louisiana Legal Services, Inc., 841 So.2d 1017 (La.App. 2d Cir.,), writ denied, 845 So.2d 1052 (La. 2003)

b. **Duty.** Statements made in the discharge of a duty to the public are entitled to a qualified privilege from liability for defamation. Jones v. Wesley, 424 So.2d 1109 (La.App. 1st Cir. 1982) (director of local government agency had duty to report possible wrongdoing of employee to district attorney's office). Similarly, a report of drug use by an employee at the workplace made by a law enforcement agent to an employer is subject to the qualified privilege. Smith v. Placid Oil Co., 393 So.2d 266 (La.App. 1st Cir. 1980), writ denied, 398 So.2d 533 (La. 1981). Statements by an employer to the Louisiana Office of Employment Security, which administers unemployment compensation benefits, enjoy a qualified privilege. Melder v. Sears, Roebuck and Co., 731 So.2d 991, 999 (La.App. 4th Cir. 1999). Employees had duty to report their concerns to law enforcement when they believed customers had stolen merchandise from employer's store. Simon v. Variety Wholesalers, Inc., 788 So.2d 544 (La.App. 1st Cir.), writ denied, 802 So.2d 617 (La. 2001).

c. **Criticism of Public Employee.** Defamation law in Louisiana allows far greater latitude in criticism of public officials than private individuals. State v. Moses, 655 So.2d 779 (La.App. 4th Cir. 1995). Public officials must show "actual malice" in a defamation claim against an employer. Louisiana courts determine the status of "public official" by whether the public has an independent interest in the qualifications and performance of the person who holds the position beyond the public interest in the qualifications and performance of all public employees. State v. Defley, 395 So.2d 759 (La. 1981); Landrum v. Board of Comm'rs, 685 So.2d 382 (La.App. 4th Cir. 1996) (terminated police officer deemed to be a "public official"). "Actual malice" must be proved by clear and convincing evidence. City of Natchitoches v. Employers Reinsurance Corp., 819 So.2d 413 (La.App. 3d Cir. 2002). However, a public employee who is neither a "public official" nor a "public figure" is not limited by the actual malice test. Foote v. Sarafyan, 432 So.2d 877 (La.App. 4th Cir. 1982), writ denied, 440 So.2d 736, 737 (La. 1983) (university professors are not public officials); Fitzgerald v. Tucker, 737 So.2d 706 (La. 1999); but see Hicks v. Stone, 425 So.2d 807 (La.App. 1st Cir. 1982), writ denied, 429 So.2d 129 (La. 1983) (dean of university is public official and required to prove actual malice).

d. **Limitation on Qualified Privileges.**

(1) **Constitutional or Actual Malice.** A defendant who publishes a defamatory statement under circumstances that give rise to a qualified privilege is still subject to liability if the plaintiff can show that the defendant (1) knew the matter to be false or (2) acted in reckless disregard as to its truth or falsity. Trentecosta v. Beck, 703 So.2d 552, 562-64 (La. 1998). Because plaintiffs who are public figures and public officers must prove "actual malice with regard to the falsity of the statement, such proof also proves the lack of any reasonable grounds for belief in the truth of the statement, which is the equivalent of proving the defendant's abuse of any privilege urged as a defense." Id. at 562-63. As the Louisiana Supreme Court has reasoned, "[a]rguably, conditional privileges therefore have lost their significance under the current state of the law which requires the offended person to prove the publisher's fault with regard to the falsity of the statement, at least when proof of actual malice is required as an element of the cause of action." Id. at 563.

(2) **Common Law Malice.** The qualified privilege rebuts the plaintiff's allegations of malice and places the burden on the plaintiff to establish malice or lack of good faith. Clements v. Ryan, 382 So.2d 279, 282 (La.App. 4th Cir. 1980). Good faith or lack of malice does not mean lack of hostility or ill feeling; it means that the person making the statement must have reasonable grounds for believing that it is true and he must honestly believe that it is true. Steed v. St. Paul's United Methodist Church, 728 So.2d 931 (La.App. 2d Cir.), writ denied, 740 So.2d 1290 (La. 1999); Rouly v. Enserch Corp., 835 F.2d 1127, 1130 (5th Cir. 1988) (former employee plaintiff presented no evidence that malice or lack of good faith motivated statements made within company walls; reference to plaintiff as "S.O.B." did not show malice). See also Sommer v. State Dep't of Transportation and Development, 758 So.2d 923, 942 (La.App. 4th Cir.), writ denied, 772 So.2d 122 (La. 2000) (employer acted in bad faith because it did not have a reasonable belief that the plaintiff's actions were fraudulent or illegal); Fourcade v. City of Gretna, 598 So.2d 415, 422 (La.App. 5th Cir. 1992) (statements made by police academy director to cadet's friends and father that conveyed impression that cadet was kicked out of the academy for using steroids were not protected by a qualified privilege because the statements "were not made in the interest of the academy or in good faith," reasoning that because the director "refused to allow [plaintiff] to exonerate himself from the unsubstantiated accusation, . . . it [could not] be said that the interview was conducted for investigative purpose or in good faith"); Connor v. Scroggs, 821 So.2d 542, 551-52 (La.App. 2d Cir. 2002) (allegations of molestation by young child were "unreliable and untruthful" and parents acted in bad faith by expressing those allegations to other persons).

e. **Question of Fact or Law.** If the facts supporting a claim of privilege are in dispute, whether a statement is privileged is a question of fact for the jury; "when the facts are not disputed," the issue of whether a privilege attaches in the first place "is purely one of law." State v. Lambert, 178 So. 508, 510 (La. 1938). But, "Louisiana law invests a jury with the responsibility of deciding if the qualified privilege . . . has been abused." Doe v. Doe, 941 F.2d 280, 291 (5th Cir.), reh'g granted in part and denied in part, 949 F.2d 736 (5th Cir. 1991). See also Smith v. Our Lady of the Lake Hospital, Inc., 639 So.2d 730 (La. 1994) (whether a conditional privilege exists is generally determined by the court as a matter of law, but determining abuse of a conditional privilege is a fact question for the jury); Bradford v. Judson, 12 So.3d 974 (La.App. 2d Cir. 2009) (reversing district court's grant of summary judgment and special motion to strike because of factual disputes relating to whether qualified privilege was abused).

f. **Burden of Proof.** The qualified privilege is an affirmative defense that the defendant bears the burden of proving and must specifically plead. La. Code Civ. Proc. art. 1005; Douglas v. Thomas, 728 So.2d 560, 563 n. 6 (La.App. 2d Cir.), writ denied, 741 So.2d 661 (La. 1999); Sommer v. State Dep't of Transportation and Development, 758 So.2d 923, 942 (La.App. 4th Cir.), writ denied, 772 So.2d 122 (La. 2000); Melancon v. Hyatt Corp., 589 So.2d 1186, 1189 (La.App. 4th Cir. 1991), writ denied, 592 So.2d 411 (La. 1992). If the defendant proves that a qualified privilege exists, the plaintiff bears the burden of proving malice or lack of good faith to rebut the privilege. Rouly v. Enserch Corp., 835 F.2d 1127, 1130 (5th Cir. 1988) (former employee plaintiff did not present enough evidence to negate former employer's good faith concerning statements made by company employees within company walls). In other words, "[i]n effect, assertion of a qualified privilege constitutes a rebuttal of the allegation of malice." Boyd v. Community Center Credit Corp., 359 So.2d 1048, 1050 (La.App. 4th Cir. 1978) (where former employer was required to furnish information concerning plaintiff employee's termination to the Department of Employment Security and did so in a reasonable, relevant, and non-malicious manner, the communication, if defamatory at all, was conditionally privileged).

B. Standard Libel Defenses

1. ***Truth.*** Truth is an absolute defense to defamation. La. R.S. 13:3602; Moore v. Cabaniss, 699 So.2d 1143, 1146 (La.App. 2d Cir. 1997), writ denied, 705 So.2d 1108 (La. 1998). "It is not necessary to prove the truth of every unimportant detail in [the defamatory statement], but it is sufficient to prove that the charges therein are substantially true." Otero v. Ewing, 115 So. 633, 636 (La. 1927); see also Bernofsky v. Administrators of Tulane Educational Fund, 2000 WL 422394, 2000 U.S. Dist. LEXIS 5561 (E.D. La.) (statements that plaintiff had sued department head "personally" and "no longer had any research funds to support his position" were substantially true because plaintiff's previous suit had targeted the department head and plaintiff's research funds were insufficient to fund his position); Romero v. Thomson Newspapers (Wisconsin), Inc., 648 So.2d 866 (La.), cert. denied, 515 U.S. 1131 (1995) (characterizing doctor as "nearing retirement" substantially true, despite his actually having a "limited, semi-retired practice"); Rosen v. Capital City Press, 314 So.2d 511 (La.App. 1st Cir. 1975) (newspaper reporting plaintiff's arrest for narcotics dealing was substantially true even though plaintiff was dealing central nervous system stimulants).

2. ***Opinion.*** The Louisiana Supreme Court, relying on Gertz v. Robert Welch, Inc., 418 U.S. 323 (1974), has concluded "that the First Amendment freedoms . . . afford, at the very least, a defense against defamation actions for expressions of opinion . . . ." Mashburn v. Collin, 355 So.2d 879, 885, 3 Media L. Rep. 1673 (La. 1977). "Although difficult to state in abstract terms, as a practical matter, the crucial difference between statement of fact and opinion depends upon whether ordinary persons hearing or reading the matter complained of would be likely to understand it as an expression of the speaker's or writer's opinion, or as a statement of existing fact." Id. If an opinion gives rise to false factual inferences, the defendant will be liable only if the statement was made with "knowing or reckless falsity." Id. As later explained by the Louisiana Supreme Court, "if the opinion does not involve an express or implied assertion of fact there can be no liability, because without an assertion of fact there can be no falsity. And even if the opinion creates an inference that certain facts exist, the factual assertion must be defamatory in order to be actionable, as defamatory words are another essential element of any defamation claim." Bussie v. Lowenthal, 535 So.2d 378, 381 (La. 1988); see also Singleton v. St. Charles Parish, 833 So.2d 486 (La.App. 5th Cir. 2002), writ denied, 839 So.2d 44 (La. 2003) ("a pure statement of opinion, which does not express or imply the existence of underlying facts, usually is not actionable in defamation because falsity is an indispensable element of a defamation claim and a purely subjective statement can be neither true nor false"). The question whether a statement is one of fact or opinion depends upon the circumstances in which the statement was made, and the reasonable inferences which may be drawn from a statement of opinion will vary depending upon the circumstances of the case. Fitzgerald v. Tucker, 737 So.2d 706 (La. 1999); see Greene v. Department of Corrections, 21 So.3d 348,(La.App. 1st Cir. 2009) (employer calling employee "pathological liar" was opinion).

3. ***Consent.*** There are no reported cases in Louisiana that recognize consent as a defense to defamation.

4. ***Mitigation.*** Mitigating circumstances can be offered to reduce damages, but not liability. For example, mitigating factors could include: a retraction of a defamatory statement by a publisher, Francis v. Lake Charles American Press, 265 So.2d 206 (La. 1972); utterances against a person while in a state of great excitement, Gladney v. deBretton, 49 So.2d 18 (La. 1950); apology, Chretien v. F.W. Woolworth Co., 160 So.2d 854 (La.App. 4th Cir.), writ denied, 163 So.2d 356 (La. 1964); and an absence of malice, Clement v. His Creditors, 37 La. Ann. 692 (La. 1885).

III. RECURRING FACT PATTERNS

A. Statements in Personnel File

Statements contained within an employee's personnel file will generally not satisfy the publication requirement for defamation actions, provided they are made in the course and scope of employment and not publicized to third parties who have no interest in the information. Melder v. Sears, Roebuck and Co., 731 So.2d 991 (La.App. 4th Cir. 1999) (placing reason for leaving in file of employee who was discharged for theft, although later exonerated, not considered publication); Marshall v. Circle K Corp., 715 F. Supp. 1341, 1343 (M.D. La. 1989), aff'd, 896 F.2d 550 (5th Cir. 1990) ("statements between employees, made within the course and scope of their employment, are not statements communicated or publicized to third persons so as to constitute a publication."); Doe v. Grant, 839 So.2d 408 (La.App. 4th Cir.), writ denied, 842 So.2d 1102 (La. 2003) (results of hospital peer review process entered into plaintiff's personnel file to ensure the safety of patients in addition to placing the nurses on notice that plaintiff's privileges had been suspended were not "published" for defamation purposes). See also III.B, infra, for a further discussion of employers' qualified privilege for communications made in good faith concerning work related matters.

Personnel and payroll records which stated that the plaintiff deprived the company of funds and was discharged for misconduct are factual statements which carry no derogatory connotation. Magnano v. BellSouth Telecommunications, Inc., 1992 WL 365029, 1992 U.S. Dist. LEXIS 17857 (E.D. La.).

B. Performance Evaluations

Internal communications by employees to superiors regarding work related matters, particularly the job performance of any employee, are entitled to a qualified privilege when made in good faith to the proper parties. Ward v. Sears, Roebuck & Co., 339 So.2d 1255 (La.App. 1st Cir. 1976); Aronzon v. Southwest Airlines, 2004 WL 57079, 2004 U.S. Dist. LEXIS 249 (E.D. La.); Mbarika v. Board of Supervisors, 992 So.2d 551 (La.App. 1st Cir. 2008) (university department chair's "good faith assessment of a faculty member's performance in the annual performance evaluation process is clearly entitled to a conditional privilege"). Additionally, "statements between employees, made within the course and scope of their employment, are not statements communicated or publicized to third persons so as to constitute a publication." Marshall v. Circle K Corp., 715 F. Supp. 1341, 1343 (M.D. La. 1989), aff'd, 896 F.2d 550 (5th Cir.1990). Statements between faculty members in the context of personnel decisions, including statements about a plaintiff's qualifications and how she conducted her job duties, were not published. Marino v. Louisiana State University Board of Supervisors, 1998 WL 560290, 1998 U.S. Dist. LEXIS 13836 (E.D. La. 8/27/98). Statements made between employees of the hospital within the course and scope of their employment, regarding the suspension of another employee in a peer review process, cannot be considered published. Doe v. Grant, 839 So.2d 408 (La.App. 4th Cir.), writ denied, 842 So.2d 1102 (La. 2003). However, statements that the plaintiff had not answered questions correctly during her interview, made by two of defendant's other employees for the purpose of making a decision about whether to award plaintiff a promotion, may not be entitled to a qualified privilege. Motton v. Lockheed Martin Corp., 1996 WL 267989, 1996 U.S. Dist. LEXIS 7128 (E.D. La. 8/27/96).

C. References

By statute, Louisiana provides an employer with immunity from civil liability for references made upon request by a prospective employer about a current or former employee, as long as the employer provides accurate information in good faith about the employee's job performance or reasons for separation. La. R.S. 23:291. An employer is considered in bad faith if it is found that "the information disclosed was knowingly false and deliberately misleading." Id. Louisiana law also protects a prospective employer who reasonably relies on the information pertaining to an employee's job performance or reasons for separation, which has been disclosed by a former employee. In such instances, a prospective employer will be immune from civil liability for negligent hiring, negligent retention and other causes of action related to the hiring of the employee, unless further investigation is required by law. La. R.S. 23:291. Chapman v. Ebeling, 945 So.2d 222, 228 (La.App. 2d Cir. 2006) (prior employer's statement of plaintiff's professional weaknesses, including emotional outbursts, not actionable when communicated in response to reference check by prospective employer).

D. Intra-corporate Communication

Some courts have held that intra-corporate communications do not satisfy the "publication" element of a defamation claim because "an intra-corporate communication, among officers or agents of the same corporation, and in relation to their duties for the corporation, is merely a communication of the corporation itself" and, hence, cannot be construed as being a "communication to a third party." Commercial Union Ins. Co. v. Melikyan, 424 So.2d 1114, 1115 (La.App. 1st Cir. 1982). See also Brunet v. Fullmer, 777 So.2d 1240, 1242 (La.App. 4th Cir. 2001) (extending the rule of Melikyan to communications between insurer and insurance adjuster even when the adjuster is employed by another company and is only an agent of insurer); Cangelosi v. Schwegmann Brothers Giant Supermarkets, 390 So.2d 196 (La. 1980). Other courts have held that such communications are protected by a qualified or conditional privilege when they are between appropriate persons within an employer's walls, concerning allegations of conduct by an employee that bears on the employer's interest, and which are made in good faith. Martin v. Lincoln General Hospital, 588 So.2d 1329, 1333 (La.App. 2d Cir. 1991), writ denied, 592 So.2d 1302 (La. 1992) (account supervisor's statements to hospital auditor protected by qualified privilege).

E. Statements Regarding Reasons for Termination

Generally, statements regarding reasons for an employee's termination, made within the course and scope of employment, are not considered statements communicated or publicized to third persons so as to constitute publication. Triplett v. Belle of Orleans, L.L.C., 2000 WL 264002, 2000 U.S. Dist. LEXIS 3362 (E.D. La. 3/8/00); Mitchell v. Tracer Construction Co., 256 F.Supp.2d 520 (M.D. La. 2003) (statement to plaintiff that plaintiff was terminated for violating company rules was not "published" because it was a true statement, made only to plaintiff). However, a communication about the reason for an employee's termination to any other employees is not privileged just because the other employees may have an interest in knowing. Melancon v. Hyatt Corp., 589 So.2d 1186, 1188 (La.App. 4th Cir. 1991), writ denied, 592 So.2d 411 (La. 1992) (indiscriminate publication among employees such as cafeteria workers not privileged).

F. Statements Made During An Investigation

When an employer undertakes an investigation of employee misconduct, related statements are protected by a qualified privilege if they are made in good faith and on a subject about which the communicator and receiver have a corresponding interest and duty. "Such a privilege arises from the social necessity of permitting free and unrestricted communication concerning matters in which the parties have a common duty or interest, and acts to protect good faith communicators from liability if the statement later turns out to be inaccurate." Hines v. Arkansas Louisiana Gas Co., 613 So.2d 646, 655 (La.App. 2d Cir.), writ denied, 617 So.2d 932 (La. 1993) (defendant owed a duty to investigate allegations of sexual harassment and its employees had a legitimate interest in knowing what activities could result in their termination). Thus, "an employer has a right to investigate suspected wrongdoing of its employees without, for that reason, becoming liable for defamation when others become aware of the investigation." Espree v. Tobacco Plus, Inc., 772 So.2d 389 (La.App. 3d Cir. 2000) (communications regarding investigation of employee's wrongdoing with other persons having an interest and a duty to receive such communications are conditionally privileged, and there can be no finding of defamation because the privileged communication is not a publication of defamatory words).

G. Statements to Government Regulators and Law Enforcement

Communications between an employer and state agencies, such as the Office of Employment Security, are subject to a qualified privilege. See Wright v. Bennett, 924 So.2d 178 (La.App. 1st Cir. 2005) (Department of Employment Security); Eschete v. Hildebrand, 930 So.2d 196 (La.App. 5th Cir. 2006) (workers compensation). Responses to inquiries from the Louisiana Department of Labor and the United States Equal Employment Opportunity Commission are also protected by the qualified privilege. Triplett v. Belle of Orleans, L.L.C., 2000 WL 264002, 2000 U.S. Dist. LEXIS 3362 (E.D. La. 3/8/00); Smolensky v. McDaniel, 144 F. Supp. 2d. 611, 618-19 (E.D. La. 2001).

Even inaccurate reporting of criminal conduct is not considered malice when there is no intent to mislead. "The public has an interest in possible criminal activity being brought to the attention of the proper authorities, and remarks made in good faith setting forth well-founded charges are clearly privileged." Kelly v. West Cash & Carry Building Materials Store, 745 So.2d 743, 753 (La.App. 4th Cir. 1999).

H. Reports to Auditors and Insurers

Statements made by an employee to an auditor are protected by a qualified privilege. Martin v. Lincoln General Hospital, 588 So.2d 1329 (La.App. 2d Cir. 1991), writ denied, 592 So.2d 1302 (La. 1992) (statements made about hospital employee to hospital auditor were protected by qualified privilege in employee's defamation action because statements were made in good faith in response to auditor's questions). Statements made by an insurance adjuster to an insurer are privileged intra-corporate communications. See Brunet v. Fullmer, 777 So.2d 1240, 1242 (La.App. 4th Cir. 2001) ("for the business of insurance adjusting to be carried out properly, an adjuster must be able to express his opinion frankly to the insurer, without fear of retribution").

I. Vicarious Liability of Employers for Statements Made by Employees

Once an employee-employer relationship and a tortious or negligent act by the employee have been established, an employer may be found liable for an employee who makes defamatory statements in the course and scope of his employment. Atwood v. Grand Casinos of Louisiana, Inc., 819 So.2d 440 (La.App. 3d Cir. 2002); Manale v. City of New Orleans, 673 F.2d 122 (5th Cir. 1982). The Court of Appeal upheld the State's liability for defamatory statements made by its employees and a contract attorney under a "conspiracy" theory. See Sommer v. State Dep't of Transportation and Development, 758 So.2d 923 (La.App. 4th Cir.), writ denied, 772 So.2d 122 (La. 2000) (evidence supported a finding that the defendants conspired to defame the plaintiff with her new employer and, as co-conspirators, the State, its employees and its attorney were held solidarily liable). The employer will also be liable if he has authorized or ratified the remarks. Trentecosta v. Beck, 703 So.2d 552, 560 (La. 1997); Ardoyno v. Ungar, 352 So.2d 320, 321 (La.App. 4th Cir. 1977), writ denied, 354 So.2d 210 (La. 1978). Moreover, although the tort of defamation is an individual tort that does not ordinarily give rise to solidary liability, it could give rise to solidary liability when defamatory statements are made in the course and scope of employment and were authorized or ratified by the employer. Atwood, 819 So.2d at 443.

1. ***Scope of Employment.*** The factors to consider in determining whether statements were made within the scope and course of employment are "whether [employee's] conduct (1) was 'primarily employment rooted'; (2) was reasonably incidental to the performance of employment duties; (3) occurred on the employment premises; and (4) occurred during working hours." Manale v. City of New Orleans, 673 F.2d 122, 126 (5th Cir. 1982) (finding solidary liability where the defamatory statements were made while on duty, despite supervisor's warnings to stop). Another formulation of the test is whether the employee's acts were "so closely connected in time, place and causation to his employment duties as to be regarded as a risk of harm fairly attributable to employer's business, as compared with conduct motivated by purely

personal considerations entirely extraneous to the employer's interest." Bennett v. Corroon and Black Corp., 517 So.2d 1245, 1248 (La.App. 4th Cir. 1987), writ denied, 520 So.2d 425 (La. 1988) (finding the posting of obscene cartoons, with the plaintiff's name attached, in a men's restroom to be outside the scope of employment). See also La. Civ. Code art. 2320 ("Masters and employers are answerable for the damage occasioned by their servants and overseers, in the exercise of the functions in which they are employed . . . [R]esponsibility only attaches, when the masters or employers . . . might have prevented the act which caused the damage, and have not done it."); Bell v. Rogers, 698 So.2d 749, 756 (La.App. 2d Cir. 1997) (investigation into nurse's overpayment was within course and scope of employment of hospital officials conducting the investigation); Bordelon v. Stafford, 1 So.3d 697 (La.App. 3d Cir. 2008) (rejecting argument that statement made by employee in violation of employer's policies can never be within course and scope of employment).

a. **Blogging.** There are no reported cases in Louisiana regarding employer liability for employees' blogs.

2. ***Damages.*** An employer and employee are jointly and solidarily liable for damages if the employer is found vicariously liable for her employee's speech. La. R.S. 9:3921. If there is a settlement between the employee and the plaintiff, the employer will not be allowed to seek indemnification or contribution from the employee. Id.

J. Internal Investigations

A conditional privilege exists when a "communication is made (a) in good faith, (b) on any subject matter in which the person communicating has an interest or in reference to which he has a duty, (c) to a person having a corresponding interest or duty." Rachal v. State, 918 So.2d 570 (La.App. 3d Cir. 2005). The qualified privilege "can include communication regarding an employee's conduct if it 'bears on the employer's interest.'" Wingrave v. Hebert, 964 So.2d 385 (La.App. 4th Cir. 2007).

However, no privilege applied where supervisor provided document to fellow employees of state agency, detailing anonymous telephone call he allegedly had received, asserting that other employees had engaged in sexual act in employees' truck in public place. The employees who defendant "told about the complaint were his subordinates and did not have a corresponding interest or duty regarding the complaint; therefore, no privilege existed." Rachal.

IV. OTHER ACTIONS BASED ON STATEMENTS

A. Negligent Hiring, Retention, and Supervision

To state a claim for negligent hiring or retention, a plaintiff is required to prove that an employment relationship existed, that the employee was incompetent, that the employer knew or should have known of the employee's incompetence, that the employee was negligent on the occasion giving rise to the plaintiff's injuries, and that the employer's negligence was a cause in fact and a legal cause of the harm to plaintiff. Harris v. Pizza Hut, Inc., 455 So.2d 1364, 1370 (La. 1984). Compare Harrington v. Board of Elementary and Secondary Education, 714 So.2d 845 (La.App. 4th Cir.), writ denied, 728 So.2d 1287 (La. 1998) (university negligent for hiring director without inquiring about his criminal history when student is raped) and Smith v. Orkin Exterminating Co., Inc., 540 So.2d 363 (La.App. 1st Cir. 1989) (employer liable for negligent administration of annual polygraph test after employee assaulted customer) with Lou-Con, Inc. v. Gulf Building Services, Inc., 287 So.2d 192 (La.App. 4th Cir.1973), writ denied, 290 So.2d 899, 901 (La. 1974) (employer's background check with local authorities of employee who committed theft and arson was reasonable even though employer did not check with federal authorities) and Kelley v. Dyson, 10 So.3d 283 (La.App. 5th Cir. 2009) (employer not liable for negligent retention of employee who assaulted fellow employee after work and off the jobsite).

Louisiana's worker's compensation statute, La. R.S. 23:1032, has been held to bar negligence claims by an employee against an employer. See Vallery v. Southern Baptist Hospital, 630 So.2d 861, 863 (La.App. 4th Cir. 1993), writ denied, 634 So.2d 860 (La. 1994) (exclusive remedy provision of Louisiana worker's compensation statute precluded employee's claim of negligent infliction of emotional distress.

A claim for negligent hiring of a physician falls within the definition of "malpractice" and must be presented to a medical review panel. La. R.S. 40:1299.41(A)(13).

B. Intentional Infliction of Emotional Distress

1. ***Elements.*** A plaintiff must establish "(1) that the conduct of the defendant was extreme and outrageous; (2) that the emotional distress suffered by the plaintiff was severe; and (3) that the defendant desired to inflict severe emotional distress or knew that severe emotional distress would be certain or substantially certain to result from his conduct." White v. Monsanto Co., 585 So.2d 1205, 1209-10 (La. 1991). The conduct "must be so outrageous in character, and so extreme in degree, as to go beyond all possible bounds of decency, and to be regarded as atrocious and utterly

intolerable in a civilized community." Id. at 1209. The defendant must intend to cause severe emotional distress, not just humiliation or embarrassment. Id. at 1210.

2. ***Relationship to Employment Law.*** The extreme and outrageous character of the conduct "may arise from an abuse by the actor of a position, or a relation with the other, which gives him actual or apparent authority over the other, or power to affect his interest." White v. Monsanto Co., 585 So.2d 1205, 1210 (La. 1991) Claims for intentional infliction of emotional distress commonly arise from the workplace; however, harsh words arising out of "disciplinary action and conflict in a pressure-packed workplace environment," are subject to a qualified privilege. Id. Further, an "at will" employee has no cause of action for intentional infliction of emotional distress arising out of a wrongful termination, because the employee has no reasonable expectation of guaranteed employment. Stevenson v. Lavalco, Inc., 669 So.2d 608 (La.App. 2d Cir.), writ denied, 673 So.2d 611 (La. 1996). Recognition of a cause of action for intentional infliction of emotional distress in a workplace environment has usually been limited to cases involving a pattern of deliberate, repeated harassment over a period of time. See Alcorn v. City of Baton Rouge, 898 So.2d 385 (La.App. 1st Cir. 2004), writ denied, 899 So.2d 12 (La. 2005); Almerico v. Dale, 927 So.2d 586, 592-93 (La.App. 5th Cir. 2006).

C. Interference with Contract

Stating that it was not its "intention, however, to adopt whole and undigested the fully expanded common law doctrine of interference with contract," the Louisiana Supreme Court recognized a limited cause of action for tortious or intentional interference with contract to enforce a "corporate officer's duty to refrain from intentional and unjustified interference with the contractual relation between his employer and a third person." 9 to 5 Fashions, Inc. v. Spurney, 538 So.2d 228, 234 (La. 1989).

The elements were originally stated as: "1) the existence of a contract or legally protected interest between the plaintiff and the corporation; 2) the corporate officer's knowledge of the contract; 3) the officer's intentional inducement or causation of the corporation to breach the contract or his intentional rendition of its performance impossible or more burdensome; 4) absence of justification on the part of the officer; and 5) causation of damages to the plaintiff by the breach of contract or difficulty of its performance brought about by the officer." Id. Louisiana courts are divided regarding whether and to what extent to extend the cause of action to other fact situations. Compare Yoes v. Shell Oil Co., 657 So.2d 241, 251 (La.App. 5th Cir.), writ denied, 663 So.2d 714 (La. 1995) (stating that no court has expanded 9 to 5 Fashions beyond the elements set forth in that decision) with Communication & Information Resources, Inc. v. Expressions Acquisition Corp., 675 So.2d 1164 (La.App. 5th Cir. 1996) (expanding cause of action to member of Board of Directors).

The theory has not been extended, however, to allow a cause of action against a corporate entity defendant. Technical Control Systems, Inc. v. Green, 809 So.2d 1204 (La.App. 3d Cir. 2002). In Scheffler v. Adams & Reese LLP, 950 So.2d 641, 644 (La. 2/22/07), the Louisiana Supreme Court rejected an intentional interference with contract claim against a law firm, holding that "no cause of action will exist between co-counsel based on the theory that co-counsel have a fiduciary duty to protect one another's prospective interests in a fee."

Employment-at-will is not a legally protected interest sufficient to raise a claim under this cause of action. Durand v. McGaw, 635 So.2d 409, 411 (La.App. 4th Cir.), writ denied, 640 So.2d 1318 (La. 1994). A similar "invasion of business interest" claim requires a showing that the defendant had improperly and maliciously influenced others not to deal with the plaintiff. Christian v. Fontenot, 672 So.2d 436, 445 (La.App. 2d Cir.), writ denied, 697 So.2d 105 (La. 1996). Louisiana does not recognize the tort of negligent interference with a contract. Colbert v. B.F. Carvin Construction Co., 600 So.2d 719 (La.App. 5th Cir.), writ denied, 604 So.2d 1311 (La. 1992).

D. Prima Facie Tort

Louisiana does not recognize prima facie tort.

V. Other Issues

A. Statute of Limitations

The statute of limitation (in Louisiana called the "prescriptive period") for all torts in Louisiana, including defamation, is one year from the date of injury or from the date that the damages occurred. La. Civ. Code art. 3492; Rozas v. Department of Health and Human Resources, 522 So.2d 1195, 1196 (La.App. 4th Cir.), writ denied, 523 So.2d 1338 (La. 1988). Under the policy of *contra non valentum*, this prescriptive period will not run during the time when the plaintiff is ignorant of the facts upon which his claim is based. This tolling of the prescriptive period will not occur if the plaintiff had "constructive notice" of the alleged defamatory statement involved, or if "reasonable diligence" would have revealed the relevant facts. Rozas (a readily available evaluation and a decision based upon that evaluation should have alerted the plaintiff to negative statements about his work contained in that evaluation). Once a year has passed, the burden of proof is on the plaintiff to show why the prescriptive period should be suspended (why his ignorance was reasonable). Velez v. Carbovelt, 779 So.2d 12, 14 (La.App. 1st Cir. 2000).

A defamation suit arising out of a judicial proceeding may not be brought, and the prescriptive period will not begin to run, until the proceeding is concluded. Ortiz v. Barriffe, 523 So.2d 896 (La.App. 4th Cir.), writ denied, 531 So.2d 273 (La. 1988); see also Nolan v. Jefferson Parish Hospital Service District, 790 So.2d 725 (La.App. 5th Cir. 2001) (same for defamation action arising out of unemployment compensation administrative proceedings). But see James v. Clark, 767 So.2d 962 (La.App. 1st Cir. 2000) (prescriptive period is not suspended for attorney to pursue defamation action against opposing attorney for statements made during litigation).

Louisiana applies continuing violation analysis to claims for intentional infliction of emotional distress alleging a repeated pattern of harassment over a period of time, meaning that "prescription does not commence until the last act occurs or the conduct is abated." Bustamento v. Tucker, 607 So.2d 532, 539 n. 9 (La. 1992).

Prescription must be pled specifically prior to submission of a case for a decision. Steed v. St. Paul's United Methodist Church, 728 So.2d 931 (La.App. 2d Cir.), writ denied, 740 So.2d 1290 (La. 1999).

B. Jurisdiction

Committing an act of defamation in the state is sufficient to satisfy the minimum contacts requirement of Louisiana's "Long-Arm" Statute. La. R.S. 13:3201. Jones v. Davis, 233 So.2d 310, 318-20 (La.App. 2d Cir.), writ refused, 235 So.2d 101 (La. 1970). Defamatory statements made outside the state also allow for the exercise of "Long Arm" jurisdiction when statements are made to individuals in Louisiana and their effects are aimed at a Louisiana resident and felt within the state. Carlisle v. Sotirin, 2005 WL 78938, 2005 U.S. Dist. LEXIS 490 (E.D. La. 1/11/05), citing Calder v. Jones, 465 U.S 783 (1984). At least one court has interpreted Louisiana law so as to allow personal jurisdiction to be established over a Texas-based newspaper, based on the newspaper's distribution in Louisiana. Buckley v. Beaumont Enterprise, 232 F.Supp. 986 (E.D. La. 1964); see also Golino v. Curtis Publishing Co., 248 F.Supp. 576, 579 (E.D. La. 1965); aff'd, 383 F.2d 586 (5th Cir. 1967) (distribution of one percent of the circulation of a national magazine suffices to establish personal jurisdiction). Venue is proper in Louisiana where the defamation occurred, or where damages were suffered by the plaintiff, La. Code Civ. Proc. art. 74, including any jurisdiction in which the defamatory statement was circulated. Walker v. Associated Press, 162 So.2d 437 (La.App. 2d Cir.), writ refused, 164 So.2d 360 (La. 1964). See also Cyprien v. Board of Supervisors, 950 So.2d 41 (La.App. 4th Cir. 2007) (venue proper in Orleans Parish because athletic director participated by telephone from New Orleans in hearing on coach's Oklahoma unemployment claim in which allegedly defamatory statements were made by athletic director).

C. Worker's Compensation Exclusivity

Although the Louisiana's Worker's Compensation Act provides the exclusive remedy for a compensable injury arising from the employment relationship, there may be liability in tort when the employee's injury is not a compensable injury. Conner v. Naylor Indus. Services, Inc., 579 So.2d 1226, 1227 (La. App. 3d Cir. 1991) (citing Spillman v. South Central Bell Telephone Co., 518 So.2d 994, 994 (La. 1998). Thus, because a defamation lawsuit is not a "suit seeking damages for physical injury or mental injury caused by a physical injury arising out of a work-related accident," a defamation claimant is not limited to recovery through worker's compensation. City of Natchitoches v. Employers Reinsurance Corp., 819 So.2d 413, 420 (La.App. 3d Cir. 2002) (citing Espree v. Tobacco Plus, Inc., 772 So.2d 389, 391 (La.App. 3d Cir. 2000).

D. Pleading Requirements

A properly plead petition must contain specific factual details, and not just general conclusions of fact or law. Badeaux v. Southwest Computer Bureau, Inc., 929 So.2d 1211 (La. 2006). See Badon v. Koppenol, 424 So.2d 1237 (La.App. 1st Cir. 1982) (plaintiff did not state a cause of action with general allegation that the defendants had given false and malicious testimony concerning plaintiff's duties as a police officer, without alleging the basis for this conclusion). A plaintiff alleging a cause of action for defamation must set forth in the petition with reasonable specificity the defamatory statements published by the defendant. Fitzgerald v. Tucker, 737 So.2d 706, 713 (La. 1999). The plaintiff cannot expand the petition at trial to include additional defamatory statements unless she adduces such evidence without objection and it is not pertinent to any other issue. Id. at 715. The petition must also allege fault and damages, but need not quote the allegedly defamatory words verbatim, so long as the petition alleges a state of facts or condition of things which would show fault. Badeaux, 929 So.2d at 1218. The plaintiff in a defamation suit must name the individual offenders and allege separate acts of defamation as to each, including specific defamatory statements. Id. In federal court, the defamation plaintiff "at a minimum . . . needs to identify . . . the alleged defamatory statements, the maker of the statements, the date the statements were made or published, and the third parties to whom the statements were made or otherwise published." Scott v. Houma-Terrebonne Housing Authority, 2002 WL 31007412, 2002 U.S. Dist. LEXIS 16719 (E.D. La. 9/6/02).

Qualified privileges are affirmative defenses, and as such must be specifically pled in the answer. Costello v. Hardy, 864 So.2d 129, 142 n. 13 (La. 2004); Douglas v. Thomas, 728 So.2d 560, 563 n. 6 (La.App. 2d Cir.), writ denied, 741 So.2d 661 (La. 1999).

Summary Judgment. Although summary judgment is seldom appropriate for determinations based on subjective facts of motive, intent, good faith, knowledge or malice, "summary judgment may be granted on subjective intent issues when no issue of material fact exists concerning the pertinent intent." Jones v. Estate of Santiago, 870 So.2d 1002 (La. 2004). Louisiana courts have evidenced a strong preference for dealing with defamation cases through summary judgment proceedings because of the possible chilling effect that the threat of litigation could have on First Amendment freedoms. See Sassone v. Elder, 626 So.2d 345 (La. 1993); Romero v. Thomson Newspapers, 648 So.2d 866, 870 (La.), cert. denied, 515 U.S. 1131 (1995). This preference may or may not exist for non-media defendants. Compare Bell v. Rogers, 698 So.2d 749, 753 (La.App. 2d Cir. 1997) ("defamation claims are inordinately susceptible to summary adjudication . . . regardless of whether the defendant is or is not a member of the news media") with Guilbeaux v. Times of Acadiana, Inc., 693 So.2d 1183, 1188 (La.App. 3d Cir.), writ denied, 701 So.2d 1327 (La. 1997) (preference applies to media defendants).

If the defendant negates an essential element of the plaintiff's claim or affirmatively shows that there is no evidence in the record to establish an essential element of plaintiff's case, Motton v. Lockheed Martin Corp., 703 So.2d 202, 206 (La.App. 4th Cir. 1997), the summary judgment motion will "test the evidentiary strength of the plaintiff's case to determine whether the plaintiff will likely be able to prove his or her factual assertions with convincing clarity at trial." Bell, 698 So.2d at 753.

Special Motion to Strike (anti-SLAPP statute). The Louisiana anti-SLAPP statute, La. Code Civ. Proc. art. 971, provides that a "cause of action against a person arising from any act of that person in furtherance of the person's right of petition or free speech under the United States or Louisiana Constitution in connection with a public issue shall be subject to a special motion to strike, unless the plaintiff has established a probability of success on the claim. In making its determination, the court shall consider the pleadings and supporting and opposing affidavits stating the facts upon which the liability or defense is based." La. Code Civ. Proc. art. 971(A)(1)(2). The statute provides for a stay of discovery while a special motion to strike is pending, unless the plaintiff shows good cause and receives a court order allowing "specified discovery" to be conducted. La. Code Civ. Proc. art. 971(D).

In Lee v. Pennington, 830 So.2d 1037 (La.App. 4th Cir. 2002), writ denied, 836 So.2d 52 (La. 2003), the Court upheld the statute against constitutional equal protection and due process challenges. In addition, the Court held that the "language of the statute is clear that attorney fees must be awarded to a prevailing defendant" on a special motion to strike. La. Code Civ. Proc. art. 971(B). In 2004, the Louisiana legislature amended the anti-SLAPP statute to require that any prevailing party, not just a prevailing defendant, be awarded reasonable attorneys' fees and costs. La. Code Civ. Proc. art. 971(B).

After first ruling otherwise, on reconsideration a U.S. District Court concluded that a special motion to strike may be used to strike individual causes of action in a lawsuit. A request for injunctive relief, however, is merely a remedy, not a "cause of action," and, thus, is not subject to a special motion to strike. Louisiana Crisis Assistance Center v. Marzano-Lesnevich, 2012 WL 2717075 (E.D. La. 7/9/12).

In Thomas v. City of Monroe, 833 So.2d 1282 (La.App. 2d Cir. 2002), the Court of Appeal applied article 971, to dismiss a defamation claim. See also Thompson v. Emmis Television Broadcasting, 894 So.2d 480 (La.App. 4th Cir.), writ denied 899 So.2d 580 (La. 2005) (affirming dismissal of defamation claim under anti-SLAPP statute because plaintiff had not established a probability of success).

A town is a "person" within the meaning of La. Code Civ. Proc. art. 971 and may file a motion to strike. Hunt v. Town of Llano, 930 So.2d 251 (La.App. 3d Cir. 2006).

Denial of an article 971 motion in a federal court proceedings is an "immediately-appealable collateral order." Henry v. Lake Charles American Press, LLC, 566 F.3d 164, 37 Media L. Rep. 1641 (2009).

SURVEY OF LOUISIANA EMPLOYMENT PRIVACY LAW

Mary Ellen Roy, David Korn and Dan Zimmerman
Phelps Dunbar LLP
One Canal Place, Suite 2000
365 Canal Street
New Orleans, Louisiana 70130-6534
Telephone: (504) 566-1311; Facsimile: (504) 568-9130;

(With Developments Reported Through **November 1, 2012**)

GENERAL COMMENTS

Unlike the other 49 states, Louisiana follows the Civil Code (which outsiders often refer to as the "Napoleonic Code"). Invasion of privacy claims fall within La. Civil Code article 2315, the general tort codal article. As in other jurisdictions, Louisiana courts follow judicial precedent but they typically refer to it as "jurisprudence" or "juridical authority" rather than "case law." While in theory Louisiana courts do not subscribe to the "common law," in practice the Louisiana Supreme Court has adopted certain common law concepts such as causes of action for intentional interference with contract and intentional (or negligent) infliction of emotional distress and even, at times, the Restatement (Second) of Torts, such as for privacy actions.

The general Louisiana trial courts are called district courts. The intermediate appellate court is the Court of Appeal, which is divided into five circuits. The state Supreme Court hears few direct appeals in civil cases, choosing whether or not to accept cases on supervisory writs. Interlocutory review is more readily available in Louisiana than in many jurisdictions, as aggrieved parties may file writs seeking review with the Court of Appeal and the Supreme Court on interlocutory issues.

Louisiana has adopted a public domain citation format that requires all cases published after December 21, 1993 to be in the following format when cited in court papers: Fitzgerald v. Tucker, 98-2313 (La. 6/29/99), 737 So.2d 706.

SIGNIFICANT DEVELOPMENTS SINCE THE 2012 *SURVEY*

None.

I. GENERAL LAW OF PRIVACY

A. Legal Basis of Privacy Claims

1. ***Constitutional Law.*** The Louisiana Constitution provides protection against unreasonable searches and seizures which is similar to the U.S. Constitution, and also offers an explicit prohibition against "invasion of privacy." Article 1 § 5. This provision has been construed to provide broader protection than the federal constitution against governmental invasions of privacy. State v. Vikesdal, 688 So.2d 685 (La.App. 2d Cir. 1997); Zaffuto v. City of Hammond, 308 F.3d 485, 491 (5th Cir. 2002) ("question of whether a federal constitutional right to privacy claim has been violated is a distinct question from whether . . . a state common law right to privacy has been violated"; constitutional privacy right includes 4th amendment privacy interest in wire communications and 14th amendment protection of the individual interest in avoiding disclosure of personal matters). Article 1, §7 of the Louisiana Constitution protects freedom of speech and of the press, but also states that every "person may speak, write, and publish his sentiments on any subject, but is responsible for abuse of that freedom." State constitutional privacy claims are not actionable when the defendant is a private party. Hennig v. Alltel Communications, Inc., 903 So.2d 1137, 1140 (La.App. 5th Cir. 2005).

2. ***Statutory and Common Law.*** Private rights of action for invasion of privacy arise from case law interpreting La. Civil Code art. 2315, the Civil Code article establishing general tort liability. See Daly v. Reed, 669 So.2d 1293 (La.App. 4th Cir. 1996), citing Jaubert v. Crowley Post-Signal, Inc., 375 So.2d 1386, 5 Media L. Rep. 2084 (La. 1979). The right to privacy is typically characterized as "the right to be let alone." Tate v. Woman's Hospital Foundation, 56 So.3d 194, 198 (La. 2011). The right to privacy may be invaded in four distinct ways: by appropriating an individual's name or likeness, by unreasonably intruding on physical solitude or seclusion, by publicity which unreasonably places a person in a false light before the public, and by unreasonable public disclosure of embarrassing private facts. Jaubert. In Louisiana, "Courts have indicated a right to privacy in favor of corporations." DROR International, LP v. Thundervision, LLC, 2010 WL 2219352 (Bkrtcy. E.D. La. 2010).

B. Causes of Action

1. ***Misappropriation/Right of Publicity.*** Louisiana recognizes a cause of action for the misappropriation of an individual's name or likeness or an aspect of his personality for the defendant's own use or benefit.

McAndrews v. Roy, 131 So.2d 256 (La.App. 1st Cir. 1961) (publication of "before" and "after" pictures of plaintiff in an advertisement of the defendant's physical improvement course constituted an actionable invasion of privacy); Tooley v. Canal Motors, Inc., 296 So.2d 453 (La.App. 4th Cir. 1974) (continued use of a name also belonging to plaintiff in an advertisement, after notice to defendant that use of the name caused confusion disrupting plaintiff's business, was actionable). It is not necessary that the use or benefit be commercial or pecuniary in nature, but, mere publication by a newspaper does not constitute use or benefit on the part of the publisher. Jaubert v. Crowley Post-Signal, Inc., 375 So.2d 1386, 1388, 5 Media L. Rep. 2084 (La. 1979). Consent is a defense. Slocum v. Sears Roebuck & Co., 542 So.2d 777 (La.App. 3d Cir. 1989) (plaintiff impliedly consented to use of child's pictures for Sears' photography studio display). However, consent did not excuse the use of photographs ten years after the plaintiff gave consent in McAndrews, supra.

2. ***False Light.*** Louisiana law recognizes a claim for "publicity that unreasonably places the plaintiff in a false light before the public." Jaubert; Simpson v. Perry, 887 So.2d 14, 16 (La.App. 1st Cir. 2004). False light is an unreasonable invasion of the plaintiff's "right to an inviolate personality," with publicity of a public display that affronts the private self because it is both unreasonable and false. Easter Seal Society v. Playboy Enterprises, Inc., 530 So.2d 643, 646, 15 Media L. Rep. 2384 (La.App. 4th Cir.), writ denied, 532 So.2d 1390 (La. 1988). In analyzing a claim for false light invasion of privacy, the three elements to be considered are a privacy interest, falsity, and unreasonable conduct. Simpson.

A plaintiff has no expectation of privacy in a public place such as a public sidewalk or a truancy center. Stern v. Doe, 806 So.2d 98, 101 (La.App. 4th Cir. 2001), 30 Media L. Rep. 1793. The material need not be defamatory, but only false and objectionable to a reasonable person under the circumstances. Jaubert; Stern, 806 So.2d at 102 (broadcast of plaintiff's arrest and the contents of his pocket (including condom) was not "highly offensive" to a reasonable person). However, a finding that the publication of information was true eliminates the plaintiff's claim under a false light theory. Lemke v. Keiser & Auzenne, L.L.C., 922 So.2d 690 (La.App. 3d Cir. 2006). The reasonableness of the defendant's conduct is measured by balancing the plaintiff's interest in protecting his privacy and the defendant's interest in pursuing his course of conduct. Klump v. Schwegmann Brothers Giant Supermarkets, Inc., 376 So.2d 514, 515 (La.App. 4th Cir. 1979), writ denied, 378 So.2d 1391 (La. 1980). The public's interest in disclosure of the challenged material is not a relevant factor. Doe v. Doe, 941 F.2d 280, 19 Media L. Rep. 1705 (5th Cir.), rehearing granted in part and denied in part, 949 F.2d 736 (5th Cir. 1991). There is no requirement of malicious intent. Spears v. McCormick & Co., Inc., 520 So.2d 805, 810 (La.App. 3d Cir. 1987), writ denied, 522 So.2d 563 (La. 1988). To "be placed in a false light, a plaintiff has to be identified in some way to have a privacy interest." Godfrey v. AAB Amusement Co., Inc., 2005 WL 2467773 at *11, 2005 U.S. Dist. Lexis 44966 (W.D.La.).

A qualified privilege exists for statements made by an employer in good faith, on a subject in which the employer has an interest or duty, to one who has a corresponding interest or duty. Wright v. Bennett, 924 So.2d 178(La.App. 1st Cir. 2005). Employers have an interest and a duty to investigate employee misconduct. Smith v. Arkansas Louisiana Gas Co., 645 So.2d 785 (La.App. 2d Cir. 1994), writ denied, 650 So.2d 1179 (La. 1995) (investigation of sexual harassment claims); Klump (investigation of theft claims). "Good faith" requires having "reasonable grounds for believing that the statement is correct." Hines, 613 So.2d at 656. False light invasion of privacy claims arising out of alleged instance of medical malpractice fall under the Louisiana Medical Malpractice Act, La. R.S. 40:1299.41 et seq., which requires review by medical review panel prior to suit. Dading v. Goodyear Tire & Rubber Co., 2005 WL 2037450, 2005 U.S. Dist. LEXIS 17836 (E.D. La.).

3. ***Publication of Private Facts.*** The publication of private facts claim requires public disclosure of private facts which are true, but embarrassing or painful to the plaintiff, Jaubert v. Crowley Post-Signal, Inc., 375 So.2d 1386, 1390, n.6, 5 Media L. Rep. 2084 (La. 1979), and which are not of legitimate public concern. Romero v. Thomson Newspapers (Wisconsin), Inc., 648 So.2d 866, 870 (La. 1995), 23 Media L. Rep. 1528, cert. denied, 515 U.S. 1131 (1995). The publicity must involve private facts, otherwise "a person's conduct may be the cause of another person's embarrassment, discomfiture, or monetary loss, but it will not constitute a 'legal cause'" of invasion of privacy. Jaubert, 375 So.2d at 1388 (anything visible in a public place is not considered a private fact); Spears v. McCormick & Co., Inc., 520 So.2d 805, 810 (La.App. 3d Cir. 1987), writ denied, 522 So.2d 563 (La. 1988). The passage of significant amounts of time may convert facts which were once a matter of public record, such as a prior conviction, into private facts. Roshto v. Hebert, 439 So.2d 428, 9 Media L. Rep. 2417 (La. 1983). The reasonableness of the defendant's conduct is measured by balancing the plaintiff's interest in protecting his privacy and the defendant's interest in pursuing his course of conduct. Jaubert, 375 So.2d at 1389; Sapia v. Regency Motors, Inc., 276 F.3d 747, 751-52 (5th Cir. 2002). "The right of privacy is limited by society's right to be informed about legitimate subjects of public interest." Tonubbee v. River Parishes Guide, 702 So.2d 971 (La.App. 5th Cir. 1997), writ denied, 709 So.2d 747 (La. 1998), cert. denied, 525 U.S. 858 (1998); see also Kyle v. Perrilloux, 868 So.2d 27 (La.App. 1st Cir. 2003). A telephone company's release of phone records to customer's spouse is not unreasonable. Hennig v. Alltel Communications, Inc., 903 So.2d 1137, 1141 (La.App. 5th Cir. 2005). Allegation that employer released confidential medical information to employee's prospective mortgage lender, stating that the employee "had been on extended sick leave [and] had undergone eye surgery" and that there was concern whether the employee "intended to return to

work" was sufficient to survive an exception of no cause of action (Louisiana's equivalent to motion to dismiss for failure to state a claim). Fox v. City of Alexandria, 971 So.2d 468 (La.App. 3d Cir. 2007).

A qualified privilege exists for statements made by an employer in good faith, on a subject in which the employer has an interest or duty, to one who has a corresponding interest or duty. Wright v. Bennett, 924 So.2d 178(La.App. 1st Cir. 2005). This privilege does not protect an employer's public disclosure of embarrassing private facts to anyone beyond those persons who have a legitimate need to know. Wright; see also Landrum v. Board of Comm'rs, 685 So.2d 382 (La.App. 4th Cir. 1996) (employer's public disclosure of results of employee's drug test was not privileged). However, no basis for a claim lies in disclosure of facts which are readily accessible to the public. Aucoin v. Kennedy, 355 F.Supp.2d 830 (E.D. La. 2004).

4. ***Intrusion.*** The right of privacy protects against "unreasonable intrusion into [a plaintiff's] seclusion or solitude, or into his private affairs. Angelo Iafrate Construction, LLC v. State ex rel. Dep't of Transportation and Development, 879 So.2d 250 (La.App. 1st Cir. 2004). This includes "the right to be free of unwarranted intrusion into [one's] own quarters." Parish National Bank v. Lane, 397 So.2d 1282, 1286 (La. 1981). Only an unreasonable intrusion which "seriously interferes" with the plaintiff's privacy interest is actionable. Parish National Bank, 397 So.2d at 1286; see also Zellinger v. Amalgamated Clothing, 683 So.2d 726, 732 (La.App. 2d Cir. 1996) (on rehearing) (late night, threatening phone calls could be actionable intrusion). The intrusion must be of a situation or activity which is private; "an invasion does not occur when an individual makes a photograph of a public sight which any one is free to see." Jaubert v. Crowley Post-Signal, Inc., 375 So.2d 1386, 1388, 5 Media L. Rep. 2084 (La. 1979).

The reasonableness of the defendant's conduct is measured by balancing the plaintiff's interest in protecting his privacy and the defendant's interest in pursuing his course of conduct. Hennig v. Alltel Communications, Inc., 903 So.2d 1137, 1141 (La.App. 5th Cir. 2005); Zaffuto v. City of Hammond, 308 F.3d 485 (5th Cir. 2002) (defendant had no legitimate interest in tape-recording and disclosing private telephone conversation between government employee and wife); Troyer v. Boomtown, LLC, 2004 WL 2984364, 2004 U.S. Dist. LEXIS 25618 (E.D. La.). The reasonableness of the defendant's intrusion may be justified by legal authorization or by circumstance. St. Julien v. South Central Bell Tel. Co., 433 So.2d 847 (La.App. 3d Cir. 1983). Even an illegal trespass might be reasonable if done for humanitarian motives. Love v. Southern Bell Tel. & Tel. Co., 263 So.2d 460 (La.App. 1st Cir.), writ denied , 266 So.2d 429 (La. 1972).

However, an employer was held liable for breaking into an employee's house for the purpose of gathering information regarding his drinking. Love, supra. Terminating employees for refusal to sign a consent form for a polygraph test was not actionable, however. Ballaron v. Equitable Shipyards, Inc., 521 So.2d 481 (La.App. 4th Cir.), writ denied, 522 So.2d 571 (La. 1988). Moreover, it was reasonable for a school board, during wartime, to inquire into teacher's use of afterschool time, Reed v. Orleans Parish School Board, 21 So.2d 895 (La.App. Orleans 1945), and for a school board to require employees to undergo medical examinations by a physician of the employee's choice and to report the result to school officials. Pitcher v. Iberia Parish School Board, 280 So.2d 603 (La.App. 3d Cir.), writ denied, 283 So.2d 496 (La. 1973), cert. denied, 416 U.S. 904 (1974).

There is no cause of action for a consented-to intrusion. Tate v. Woman's Hospital Foundation, 56 So.3d 194, 197-98 (La. 2011). Terminating employees for refusal to sign a consent form for a polygraph test was not actionable. Ballaron v. Equitable Shipyards, Inc., 521 So.2d 481 (La.App. 4th Cir.), writ denied, 522 So.2d 571 (La. 1988). The threat of terminating at-will employment did not vitiate consent to an intrusion. Tate. Moreover, it was reasonable for a school board, during wartime, to inquire into teacher's use of afterschool time, Reed v. Orleans Parish School Board, 21 So.2d 895 (La.App. Orleans 1945), and for a school board to require employees to undergo medical examinations by a physician of the employee's choice and to report the result to school officials. Pitcher v. Iberia Parish School Board, 280 So.2d 603 (La.App. 3d Cir.), writ denied, 283 So.2d 496 (La. 1973), cert. denied, 416 U.S. 904 (1974).

C. Privileges and Defenses

1. ***Private Employers.*** In general, the right to privacy can be lost by express or implied waiver, consent, or by certain actions that prevent its assertion. East Baton Rouge Consolidated Special Service Fire Protection Dist. v. Crossen, 892 So.2d 666 (La.App. 5th Cir. 2004); Parish National Bank v. Lane, 397 So.2d 1282 (La. 1981); St. Julien v. South Central Bell Tel. Co., 433 So.2d 847 (La.App. 3d Cir. 1983).

As with defamation cases, a qualified privilege may apply to invasions of privacy claims arising in an employment context. See Smith v. Arkansas Louisiana Gas Co., 645 So.2d 785 (La.App. 2d Cir. 1994) (qualified privilege for statements made during investigation of employee).

2. ***Public Employers.*** A public employee's expectations of privacy can be reduced by an employer's practices and procedures. Leckelt v. Board of Comm'rs, 714 F.Supp. 1377 (E.D. La. 1989), aff'd, 909 F.2d 820 (5th Cir.

1990) (nurse had a significantly diminished expectation of privacy in the results of his HIV-antibody test given that hospital required its employees to report exposure to infectious diseases and to undergo serological testing where necessary).

D. Other Privacy-related Actions

1. *Intentional Infliction of Emotional Distress*

a. **Elements.** A plaintiff must establish "(1) that the conduct of the defendant was extreme and outrageous; (2) that the emotional distress suffered by the plaintiff was severe; and (3) that the defendant desired to inflict severe emotional distress or knew that severe emotional distress would be certain or substantially certain to result from his conduct." White v. Monsanto Co., 585 So.2d 1205, 1209-10 (La. 1991); see also Nicholas v. Allstate Ins. Co., 765 So.2d 1017 (La. 2000). The conduct "must be so outrageous in character, and so extreme in degree, as to go beyond all possible bounds of decency, and to be regarded as atrocious and utterly intolerable in a civilized community." White, 585 So.2d at 1209. The defendant must intend to cause severe emotional distress, not just humiliation or embarrassment. Id. at 1210. Moreover, due to the inherent adversarial nature of litigation, the "emotional distress" suffered by a party as a result of non-privileged testimony given at trial is not actionable. Coutee v. Beurlot, 964 So.2d 304 (La. 2007).

b. **Relationship to Employment Law.** The extreme and outrageous character of the conduct "may arise from an abuse by the actor of a position, or a relation with the other, which gives him actual or apparent authority over the other, or power to affect his interest." Singleton v. St. Charles Parish, 833 So.2d 486, 493 (La.App. 5th Cir. 2002), writ denied, 839 So.2d 44 (La. 2003). Claims for intentional infliction of emotional distress commonly arise from the workplace; harsh words arising out of "disciplinary action and conflict in a pressure-packed workplace environment," however, are subject to a qualified privilege. Id.; see also Murray v. City of Baton Rouge, 2007 WL 2377333, 2007 La.App. Unpub. Lexis 64 (La.App. 1st Cir.), (supervisor's actions in pointing finger at employee while criticizing her performance and failing to give her an access key were not actionable as intentional infliction of emotional distress). The "jurisprudence has limited the cause of action to cases which involve a pattern of deliberate, repeated harassment over a period of time. The distress suffered by the employee must be more than a reasonable person could be expected to endure." Nicholas v. Allstate Ins. Co., 765 So.2d 1017, 1026 (La. 8/31/00). Further, an "at will" employee has no cause of action for intentional infliction of emotional distress arising out of a wrongful termination, because the employee has no reasonable expectation of guaranteed employment. Stevenson v. Lavalco, Inc., 669 So.2d 608 (La.App. 2d Cir.), writ denied, 673 So.2d 611 (La. 1996).

A report of suspected criminal activity in the workplace, "made in good faith and founded upon reasonable suspicion, cannot constitute 'extreme and outrageous' conduct" as is necessary to state a claim for intentional infliction of emotional distress. Cook v. American Gateway Bank, 49 So.3d 23, 2010 WL 3517946 (La.App. 1st Cir. 2010).

2. *Interference with Contract*

a. **Elements.** Stating that it was not its "intention, however, to adopt whole and undigested the fully expanded common law doctrine of interference with contract," the Louisiana Supreme Court recognized a limited cause of action for tortious or intentional interference with contract to enforce only a "corporate officer's duty to refrain from intentional and unjustified interference with the contractual relation between his employer and a third person." 9 to 5 Fashions, Inc. v. Spurney, 538 So.2d 228, 234 (La. 1989).

The plaintiff must establish: "(1) the existence of a contract or a legally protected interest between the plaintiff and the corporation; (2) the corporate officer's knowledge of the contract; (3) the officer's intentional inducement or causation of the corporation to breach the contract or his intentional rendition of its performance impossible or more burdensome; (4) absence of justification on the part of the officer; (5) causation of damages to the plaintiff by the breach of contract or difficulty of its performance brought about by the officer." Id. Louisiana courts are divided regarding whether and to what extent to extend the cause of action to other fact situations. Compare Yoes v. Shell Oil Co., 657 So.2d 241, 251 (La.App. 5th Cir.), writ denied, 663 So.2d 714 (La. 1995) (stating that no court has expanded 9 to 5 Fashions beyond the elements set forth in that decision) with Communication & Information Resources, Inc. v. Expressions Acquisition Corp., 675 So.2d 1164 (La.App. 5th Cir. 1996) (expanding cause of action to member of Board of Directors).

Louisiana courts have not recognized a cause of action for intentional interference with a proposed contract. Lilawanti Enterprises, Inc. v. Walden Book Co., Inc., 670 So.2d 558, 559 (La.App. 4th Cir. 1996). Also, Louisiana courts have not recognized a cause of action for negligent interference with contractual relations of a third party. Hennig v. Alltel Communications, Inc., 903 So.2d 1137, 1141 (La.App. 5th Cir. 2005).

b. **Relationship to Employment Law.** Louisiana courts have refused to recognize broad claims for tortious interference with employment contracts. See Lynn v. Berg Mechanical, Inc., 582 So.2d 902 (La.App. 2d Cir. 1991) (corporate officer's termination of plaintiff's employment contract with company did not constitute tortious interference with contract); Durand v. McGaw, 635 So.2d 409 (La.App. 4th Cir.), writ denied, 640 So.2d 1318 (La. 1994) (defendant's complaints to plaintiff's employer and interference with plaintiff's employment contract not actionable); MD Care, Inc. v. Angelo, 672 So.2d 969 (La.App. 4th Cir.), writ denied, 673 So.2d 1039 (La. 1996) (prior employer's claim against employee's present employer for luring employee away not actionable). See also Favrot v. Favrot, 68 So.3d 1099 (La.App. 4th Cir. 2/9/11) (an "at-will employee simply has no legally protected interest in his employment necessary for a claim for tortious interference with a contract"). One court, however, has recognized a claim for tortious interference with contract by an employee against his employer's lessor for denying the employee access to his place of employment. Neel v. Citrus Lands, Inc., 629 So.2d 1299 (La.App. 4th Cir. 1993).

3. ***Prima Facie Tort.*** Louisiana does not recognize prima facie tort.

II. EMPLOYER TESTING OF EMPLOYEES

A. Psychological or Personality Testing

There are no Louisiana statutes or authorities that prohibit or regulate psychological or personality testing of employees by employers. Louisiana courts have declined to require employers to conduct psychological testing upon employees and workers absent some law, regulation, or hiring policy to the contrary. See Trinity Universal Ins. Co. v. Lyons, 896 So.2d 298, 300 (La.App. 3d Cir. 2005) (rejecting plaintiff's argument that city should be held liable for its failure to require psychological testing of volunteers); Smith v. Lafayette Parish Sheriff's Dep't, 874 So.2d 863, 867 (La.App. 3d Cir. 2004) (rejecting rape victim's claim that sheriff's department should have used psychological testing; the court found that because there were no regulations or hiring procedures regarding law enforcement employees, the hiring policy was within the sheriff's discretion).

B. Drug Testing

1. ***Common Law and Statutes.*** La. R.S. 49:1001, et seq., sets forth the criteria and procedures for drug testing by private and public employers. La. R.S. 49:1015 sets forth additional criteria and procedures for drug testing of a public employee. La. R.S. 23:1081(7) specifically allows drug testing by a private employer immediately after an alleged job accident; if the employee refuses, the employee is presumed to have been intoxicated at the time of the accident. The results of an employer-administered drug test are admissible evidence when testing is done by the employer pursuant to a written and promulgated substance abuse rule or policy established by the employer. La. R.S. 23:1081(8).

2. ***Private Employers.*** While private employers are subject to La. R.S. 49:1001, et seq., restrictions imposed by the Fourth Amendment of the United States Constitution do not apply to a private employer's random drug testing program. Chiles Offshore, Inc. v. Administrator, Dep't of Employment Security, 551 So.2d 849, 851 (La.App. 3d Cir. 1989) (employee's refusal to participate in drug screening test is misconduct and grounds for termination). All drug testing of individuals in Louisiana must be performed by SAMSHA Certified (National Institute on Drug Abuse) or CAP-FUDT-Certified (College of American Pathologist Forensic Urine Drug Testing) Laboratories if: (1) mandatory or discretionary consequences will be rendered to the individual as a result of the testing; and (2) drug testing is performed for any or all of the following classes of drugs: marijuana, opioids, cocaine, amphetamines and phencyclidine. La. R.S. 49:1005(A). The statute sets forth rights and responsibilities for both the employee and employer. For example, all information, interviews, reports, statements, memoranda, or test results received by the employer through its drug testing program are confidential communications and may not be used or received in evidence, obtained in discovery, or disclosed in any public or private proceedings, except in an administrative or disciplinary proceeding or hearing, or civil litigation where drug use by the tested individual is relevant. La. R.S. 49:1012(A). Any employee confirmed positive has the right to access his records relating to the drug testing by making written request within seven days. La. R.S. 49:1011(A). In addition, no cause of action for defamation of character, libel, slander, or damage to reputation or privacy arises in favor of any person against an employer or testing entity who has established a program of drug or alcohol testing in accordance with the Act, except under limited circumstances. La. R.S. 49:1012(B).

3. ***Public Employers.*** Under specified circumstances, La. R.S. 49:1015 allows drug testing by public employers following an accident, as a prerequisite to hiring, and randomly for safety-sensitive or security-sensitive jobs. Drug testing is allowed following an accident during the course and scope of employment under circumstances which result in a reasonable suspicion that drugs are being used. Drug testing may be performed only pursuant to a written policy. Any public employee who operates or maintains a public vehicle or supervises one who does must be drug tested as a condition of hiring and randomly throughout employment. "As a condition of hiring" applies to promotions as well as new hires. McKendall v. City of New Orleans, 1993 WL 85954, *4, 1993 U.S. Dist. LEXIS 3538 (E.D. La.) (employee promoted to a safety-sensitive position was required to be drug tested as condition of promotion). Moreover, a public employer may order an employee to submit to drug testing on the basis of individualized suspicion under certain circumstances, i.e., tip from a reliable informant, degree of corroboration, and other facts. George v. Department of Fire, 637 So.2d 1097, 1101 (La.App.

4th Cir. 1994). Unlike a private employer, a public employer's policy that requires a public employee to submit to drug testing after an accident without the requirement of reasonable suspicion that drugs are being used violates the Fourth Amendment. United Teachers of New Orleans v. Orleans Parish School Board, 142 F.3d 853 (5th Cir. 1998). In United Teachers of New Orleans, the Court determined that the Orleans Parish School Board's drug policy which required drug testing after an accident violated the Fourth Amendment inasmuch as no special needs exception to the requirement of individualized suspicion of wrongdoing applied.

C. Medical Testing

No public or private employer can require an employee or prospective employee to pay for a medical exam required by an employer. However, an employer may seek reimbursement from an employee who terminates his employment sooner than ninety working days after hire for a reason other than either a substantial change made to his employment by the employer or, if the employee fails to report to work, provided an employee is compensated at a rate not less than one dollar above the existing federal minimum wage and is not a part-time or seasonal employee. La. R.S. 23:897; La. R.S. 23:634(B).

Louisiana limits genetic testing in the workplace and prohibits employers from discriminating against any employee on the basis of protected genetic information. La. R.S. 23:368-369. "La. R.S. 23:368 was intended to prohibit an employer from using genetic information for discriminatory purposes, but was not intended to create a general prohibition of the use of genetic testing by an employee in a non-discriminatory context." Tate v. Woman's Hospital Foundation, 56 So.3d 194, 198 n.3 (La. 2011). An employer can require protected genetic information from an employee who has received a conditional offer of employment if (1) the information is used exclusively to determine if further medical testing is needed to diagnose a current medical condition, (2) such medical condition could prevent the applicant from performing essential functions of the job, and (3) the information is kept confidential. La. R.S. 23:368(E)(1). Genetic monitoring of biological effects of toxic substances in the workplace is permitted but only under certain circumstances. La. R.S. 23:368(E)(3). Employers must post a notice from the Louisiana Workforce Commission informing employees of limits on protected genetic information. La. R.S. 23:369.

Louisiana's worker's compensation law provides that an employee claiming worker's compensation must submit to a medical examination by a qualified medical practitioner provided and paid for by the employer. La. R.S. 23:1121. See also Smith v. Southern Holding, Inc., 839 So.2d 5 (La. 2003) (La. R.S. 23:1121(B) gives an injured employee an absolute right to select one physician in any field without the approval of the employer). The employer must give a copy of the medical report to the employee within six days of the employer's receipt of such report. La. R.S. 23:1122. If the employee refuses to submit to or otherwise obstructs the medical examination, workers' compensation can be suspended until the medical examination takes place. La. R.S. 23:1124. However, before the suspension of the claimant's compensation, a judicial determination must be made to determine the reasonableness of the requested medical examination. Atwell v. First General Services, 951 So.2d 348, 356 (La.App. 1st Cir. 2006). Whether or not an employee is injured, whenever an employee submits to a medical exam at the request of an employer, an employee shall be given a copy of the report within 30 days from the date the requestor receives the report. La. R.S. 23:1125.

D. Polygraph Tests

Polygraph examiners must inform examinees that his or her participation is voluntary and that refusal to submit to a polygraph shall not be an inference of guilt, nor shall it be a cause or justification for termination of employment within the meaning of any law relating to unemployment compensation. La. R.S. 37:2848. There are otherwise no Louisiana laws addressing the legality of polygraph tests.

Louisiana courts have held that civil service employees may be ordered to take polygraph examinations; employees who refuse or fail to do so can be suspended or discharged. See Evans v. DeRidder Municipal Fire and Police Civil Service Board, 815 So.2d 61, 66-67 (La. 2002), cert. denied, 537 U.S.1108 (2003); Jones v. Department of Public Safety and Corrections, 923 So.2d 699 (La.App. 1st Cir. 2005,. But see Jackson v. Department of Health and Hospitals, 752 So.2d 357, 363 (La.App. 1st Cir. 2000) (severe mitigating circumstances justified employee's refusal to take polygraph exam). The Civil Service Commission, however, is not bound by the results of a polygraph examination; rather, the Commission can weigh a positive or negative reading similar to any other evidence. See Harrell v. Department of Health and Hospitals, 48 So.3d 297, 206 (La.App. 1st Cir. 2010).

E. Fingerprinting

No public or private employer can require an employee or prospective employee to pay for fingerprinting required by an employer. However, an employer may seek reimbursement from an employee who terminates his employment sooner than ninety working days after hire for a reason other than either a substantial change made to his employment by the employer or if the employee fails to report to work, provided an employee is compensated at a rate not less than one dollar above the existing federal minimum wage and is not a part-time or seasonal employee. La. R.S. 23:897; La. R.S. 23:634(B).

III. SEARCHES

A. Employee's Person

Article 1, Section 5, of the Louisiana Constitution, protects an individual's right of privacy from unreasonable searches, seizures, and invasions of privacy. Louisiana courts recognize a cause of action for violation of an individual's right to privacy. State v. Vikesdal, 688 So.2d 685 (La.App. 2d Cir. 1997); Zaffuto v. City of Hammond, 308 F.3d 485, 491 (5th Cir. 2002) ("The question of whether a federal constitutional right to privacy has been violated is a distinct question from whether . . . a state common law right to privacy has been violated"); constitutional privacy right includes Fourth Amendment privacy interest in wire communication and Fourteenth Amendment protection of the individual interest in avoiding disclosure of personal matters). See also Pack v. Wise, 155 So.2d 909 (La.App. 3d Cir.), writ refused, 157 So.2d 231 (La. 1963).

1. ***Private Employers.*** Louisiana courts have not addressed the issue of a "search" of an employee's person by a private employer. However, the right of privacy protects against "unreasonable intrusion into [a plaintiff's] seclusion or solitude or into his private affairs." Angelo Iafrate Construction, LLC v. State ex rel. Dep't of Transportation and Development, 879 So.2d 250 (La.App. 1st Cir. 2004); see also Broderick v. Department of Environmental Quality, 761 So.2d 713 (La.App. 1st Cir.), writ denied, 768 So.2d 1284 (La. 2000). This includes "the right to be free of unwanted intrusion into [one's] own quarters." Parish National Bank v. Lane, 397 So.2d 1282, 1286 (La. 1981). Only an unreasonable intrusion which "seriously interferes" with the plaintiff's privacy interest is actionable. Parish National Bank, 397 So.2d at 1286; see also Zellinger v. Amalgamated Clothing, 683 So.2d 726, 732 (La.App. 2d Cir. 1996) (on rehearing) (late night, threatening phone calls could be actionable intrusion). To the extent that a search of an employee's person is unreasonable, employers may be subject to liability under a tort theory of intrusion.

2. ***Public Employers.*** Whether a search is intrusive must be viewed in the context of the individual's legitimate expectation of privacy. Anderson v. Dep't of Public Safety and Corrections, 985 So.2d 160, 164 (La.App. 1st Cir. 2008). The test for determining the legitimacy of an expectation of privacy involves both subjective and objective considerations.. The individual must have a subjective expectation of privacy and the expectation must be "one that society is prepared to recognize as 'reasonable.'" Id., quoting Katz v. U.S., 389 U.S. 347, 361 (1967). The legitimacy of public employer searches depends on the employees' reasonable expectations of privacy which is based on the particular confines of the facilities where they are employed. See Anderson. See also Leckelt v. Board of Comm'rs, 714 F.Supp. 1377 (E.D. La. 1989), aff'd, 909 F.2d 820 (5th Cir. 1990) (nurse had significantly diminished expectation of privacy in the results of his HIV -antibody test given that the hospital required its employees to report exposure to infectious diseases and to undergo serological testing where necessary).

B. Employee's Work Area

A public employer is subject to the restraints of the Fourth Amendment if it conducts a search of an employee's work space. Varnado v. Department of Employment and Training, 687 So.2d 1013, 1023 (La.App. 1st Cir. 1996), writ denied, 692 So.2d 394 (La. 1997) (worker's compensation hearing officers had a reasonable expectation of privacy in their offices, desks and filing cabinets and search of same without reasonable grounds to conclude that search would reveal any employee misconduct was unreasonable); see also Razor v. New Orleans Dep't of Police, 926 So.2d 1 (La.App. 4th Cir. 2006) (search of police officer's car (and home) pursuant to warrant). However, a public employee does not have as high an expectation of privacy as a private citizen. Compare Anderson v. Department of Public Safety and Corrections, 985 So.2d 160 (La.App. 1st Cir. 2008) (courts have repeatedly recognized that employees of incarceration facilities have diminished expectations of privacy while within the confines of facilities requiring the implementation of extreme security measures), with Saacks v. City of New Orleans, 687 So.2d 432 (La.App. 4th Cir. 1996), writ denied, 693 So.2d 769 (La.), cert. denied, 522 U.S. 914 (1997) (permitting evidence seized from search of office to be introduced at civil service hearing on termination of police officer); Williams v. Collins, 728 F.2d 721 (5th Cir. 1984) (employee had no reasonable expectation of privacy in his government-furnished desk); State v. Lambright, 525 So.2d 84 (La.App. 3d Cir.), writ denied, 530 So.2d 83 (La. 1988) (search of a former employee's desk after he had been terminated and had apparently removed all of his personal belongings did not violate the right to privacy of the defendant). A warrantless search of employee's work areas by public employer to investigate employee misconduct without individualized suspicion is reasonable when: (a) privacy interests are minimal, (b) there is a furtherance of an important governmental interest by the intrusion, (c) the search is justified at its inception, and (d) the search is permissible in its scope. State v. Ziegler, 637 So.2d 109 (La. 1994).

C. Employee's Property

1. ***Private Employers.*** Engaging the service of a locksmith to enter an employee's home in furtherance of the employer's intent and designed to prove plaintiff's unworthiness as a supervisory employee was

unreasonable. Love v. Southern Bell Tel. and Tel. Co., 263 So.2d 460, 466 (La.App. 1st Cir.), writ denied, 266 So.2d 429 (La. 1972).

2. ***Public Employers.*** Louisiana courts have not addressed intrusions onto the private property of public employees.

D. Employee's Electronic Communications and Files

See section IV.A., infra.

IV. MONITORING OF EMPLOYEES

A. Telephone and Electronic Communications

1. ***Wiretapping.*** Interception and disclosure of wire or oral communication is illegal, unless the person intercepting the communication is a party to the communication or one of the parties has given prior consent to the interception. La. R.S. 15:1303. There is no exception to the Electronic Surveillance Act for spouses. See Kirkland v. Franco, 92 F.Supp.2d 578, 581 (E.D. La. 2000).

The Louisiana eavesdropping statute does not require an element of criminal willfulness or intent for civil liability to attach. Keller v. Aymond, 722 So.2d 1224 (La.App. 3d Cir. 1998), writ denied, 742 So.2d 551, 552 (La.), cert. denied, 528 U.S. 963 (1999); Johnson v. Aymond, 709 So.2d 1072 (La.App. 3d Cir.), writ denied, 720 So.2d 1214 (La. 1998). Thus, one party's consent of audio-taping of conversations is legal under Louisiana law as long as the taping is not done for the purpose of committing any criminal or tortious act. See Brown v. Brown, 877 So.2d 1228 (La.App. 2 Cir. 2004) (Wife's secretly-recorded telephone conversations with husband on her own telephone were not illegally intercepted since the calls were recorded by a party to the conversation). In Briggs v. American Air Filter Co., Inc., 630 F.2d 414 (5th Cir. 1980), the court held that an employer may monitor and record phone calls if the employer has particular suspicions that an employee is disclosing trade secrets. The "ordinary course of business" exception was applicable in Briggs because the intercepted call was a business, not a personal call, and the act of listening was limited in purpose and time and was not part of a general practice of surreptitious monitoring. In Benoit v. Roche, 657 So.2d 574 (La.App. 3d Cir. 1995), the court concluded that genuine issues of material fact existed regarding whether an employer may have invaded the privacy of its employees and violated the Louisiana electronic surveillance act by secretly placing an electronic surveillance device in the employee breakroom and by monitoring employees' telephone calls. A party can record a conversation they are not a party to and not be in violation of La. R.S. 15:1303 if: (a) the person recording (hearer) is in a place they have a right to be and hear unaided by a mechanical device, and (b) the recording device could record no more than the hearer could hear unaided. State v. Smith, 848 So.2d 650 (La.App. 4th Cir. 2003).

2. ***Electronic Communications.*** The federal Electronic Communications Privacy Act of 1986 ("ECPA") governs electronic communications. 18 U.S.C. §§ 2510, et seq. Under the ECPA, consent of one party to the e-mail is sufficient for its interception (as long as it is not for criminal or tortious purposes) and e-mail can be read by an employer if the e-mail is generated through an employer-owned system. An employer's right to access personal messages may also turn on the court's interpretation of an employer's actions as intercepting the message versus merely accessing stored data. Steve Jackson Games, Inc. v. United States Secret Service, 36 F.3d 457 (5th Cir. 1994) (ECPA's prohibition on interception requires simultaneous transmission and acquisition of electronic communication and does not apply to stored e-mail).

Louisiana's Electronic Surveillance Act, La. R.S. 15:1302, et seq., prohibits interception only of "wire or oral communications" and does not expressly prohibit interception of "electronic communications." Becker v. Toca, 2008 WL 4443050, *6, 2008 U.S. Dist. LEXIS 89123 (E.D. La. 9/26/08).

3. ***Other Electronic Monitoring.*** Louisiana courts have not addressed other types of electronic monitoring.

B. Mail

An individual cannot have a reasonable expectation of privacy in mail which is sent to him at his place of employment through his employer's mail system. Wheeler v. King, 1991 WL 195488, 1991 U.S. Dist. LEXIS 13679 (E.D. La. 9/20/01).

C. Surveillance/Photographing

La. R.S. 14:284 makes it unlawful to spy through windows or doors on the premises of another for the purpose of invading the privacy of that person without the consent of the person spied upon. It is not necessary that the "Peeping Tom" be upon the premises of the person being spied upon.

However, surveillance of an employee's home by an employer while the employee was on sick leave was not deemed to be an invasion of privacy, since the employee left the house in open view. Claverie v. Louisiana State University Medical Center, 553 So.2d 482 (La.App. 1st Cir. 1989); see also Ryan v. Kelmar & Assocs., Inc., 2009 WL 348764, at *2 (5th Cir.) (use of readily-available, consumer-grade "zoom" technology from a public road and parking lot to conduct surveillance of allegedly-injured employee working in his yard was not a violation of employee's reasonable expectation of privacy). An employer is not liable for the torts of an independent contractor investigator videotaping an employee claiming an injury. Singletary v. Fridley, 762 So.2d 692 (La.App. 1st Cir.), writ denied, 769 So.2d 545 (La. 2000). But see Souder v. Pendleton Detectives, Inc., 88 So.2d 716 (La.App. 1st Cir. 1956) (petition filed by workers' compensation claimant and wife for invasion of right of privacy sufficiently alleged cause of action on theory that defendant's or worker's compensation insurer and its investigating agent, a detective agency, might have violated Louisiana's Peeping Tom Statute by trespassing on the property of claimant and wife and peeking into their windows). Videotape of alleged injured employee doing physical activity is not in violation of La. R.S. 15:1303(A)(4), if there is no audio.

It was reasonable for an employer to direct that a former employee of a store be kept under video surveillance while in the store, where all customers are subject to monitoring. Melder v. Sears, Roebuck and Co., 731 So.2d 991 (La.App. 4th Cir. 1999).

V. ACTIVITIES OUTSIDE THE WORKPLACE

A. Statute or Common Law

There are no Louisiana statutes regarding an employee's activities outside the workplace.

B. Employees' Personal Relationships

1. ***Romantic Relationships Between Employees.*** Termination of an employee who violated anti-fraternization policy of company has been upheld. Smith v. Wal-Mart Stores, 891 F.2d 1177 (5th Cir. 1990) (no finding of sexual discrimination in administration of policy). Such policies have been held legal for private employers of at-will employees. Watkins v. United Parcel Service, Inc., 797 F. Supp. 1349 (S.D. Miss.), aff'd, 979 F.2d 1535 (5th Cir. 1992) (no invasion of privacy because plaintiff did not show bad faith or other reckless prying by defendant).

2. ***Sexual Orientation.*** Discharge from employment for an employee's homosexual status is not prohibited by Title VII. Blum v. Gulf Oil Corp., 597 F.2d 936 (5th Cir. 1979). No Louisiana statutes prohibit discrimination based on sexual orientation; certain city and municipal ordinances, however, do prohibit such discrimination. Louisiana does not prohibit discrimination based on crossdressing or gender identity. Oiler v. Winn-Dixie Louisiana, Inc., 2002 WL 31098541, 2002 U.S. Dist. LEXIS 17417 (E.D. La. 9/16/02) ("sex" in Title VII context means only biological sex and not sexual preference).

3. ***Marital Status.*** There is no Louisiana statute that prohibits discrimination on the basis of marital status. In Durham v. Louisiana State Racing Comm'n, 458 So.2d 1292, 1294 (La. 1984), the Court explained: "Married persons have not historically suffered from discrimination or needed protection from the majority." An employee who did not disclose that he had been married and divorced had his employment contract terminated by the Archdiocese of New Orleans because his lifestyle was contrary to their teachings. The appellate court upheld the termination, reasoning that the plaintiff had not acted in good faith. Bischoff v. Brothers of the Sacred Heart, 416 So.2d 348 (La.App. 4th Cir. 1982). However, dicta in another federal appellate court decision indicates that the Court would disapprove of employment discrimination based on marital status. See Willingham v. Macon Tel. Publishing Co., 507 F.2d 1084 (5th Cir. 1975) ("a line must be drawn between distinctions grounded on such fundamental rights as the right to have children or to marry and those interfering with the manner in which an employer exercises his judgment as to the way to operate a business"). The same court, however, has not recognized a Title VII claim for an adverse employment decision based on marital status as a "sex plus" claim if the same restrictions applied to men as to women. Loper v. American Airlines, Inc., 582 F.2d 956 (5th Cir. 1978); see also Cooper v. Delta Air Lines, Inc., 274 F.Supp. 781 (E.D. La. 1967) ("no-marriage" rule does not discriminate on the basis of sex if all employees impacted by rule are of the same sex).

Louisiana has the authority to suspend any state license, certification, registration, etc., to engage in a profession, business, occupation, or industry for nonpayment of child support. La. R.S. 9:315.40, et seq.

4. ***Standards of Conduct.*** Termination of an employee who violated a private elementary school's standard of conduct policy has been upheld. LaCross v. Cornerstone Christian Academy, 896 So.2d 105 (La.App. 3d Cir. 2004). In LaCross, a discharged teacher brought a breach of contract action against a private school alleging that the school wrongfully terminated her employment due to allegedly lying on the employment application with regard to her use of alcohol. During the application process, LaCross completed a job application and indicated that she did not use alcoholic

beverages. When she was informed that she had been hired as a teacher, she went to happy hour and consumed four or five beers to celebrate. The next day, a third party informed the school that LaCross cursed, drank alcohol to the point that she made a public spectacle, and went out drinking with a man who was not her husband. When the school confronted LaCross about the allegations, she admitted that she had been out drinking, and confirmed the essential elements of the report. Following the confrontation, the school concluded that LaCross clearly lied on her employment application and violated the school's standard of personal holiness. Shortly thereafter, LaCross' employment was terminated. The Court upheld the termination on the basis that the employer might never have offered employment to LaCross had it known that her standards of conduct did not comply with the standards of conduct that were central to the mission of the academy.

C. Smoking

La. R.S. 23:966 makes it unlawful for an employer to discriminate against a employee on the basis of his/her being either a smoker or a non-smoker, as long as an employee complies with all applicable laws and workplace policies on smoking. The provision sets forth a statutory fine for employers who violate the smoking discrimination law.

D. Blogging

There are no Louisiana statutes regarding blogging. Likewise, there are no reported cases involving blogging in the employment context. However, one Louisiana court has been called upon to consider evidence of information on a web blog in a divorce action. The court did not find the information contained in the blog to be persuasive because, inter alia, the statements were neither relevant nor made under oath. See Steinbach v. Steinbach, 957 So.2d 291, 299-300 (La.App. 3d Cir. 2007).

VI. RECORDS

A. Personnel Records

There is no general statutory law in Louisiana concerning the maintenance, contents, or dissemination of an employer's personnel file on an employee. However, custom, which can have the force of law, dictates that employers have the right to maintain personnel files on their employees and control the contents of those files. See Doe v. Entergy Services, Inc., 608 So.2d 684, 687 (La.App. 4th Cir. 1992), writ denied, 613 So.2d 978 (La.), cert. denied, 510 U.S. 816 (1993).

La. R.S. 44:11 in the Louisiana Public Records law governs disclosure of personnel records of public employees. Certain items in the personnel records of public employees are deemed confidential: 1) the home address and telephone number, if the employee has requested that they be confidential; 2) Social security numbers, and the name and account number of any financial institution to which the employee's wages or salary are directly deposited by electronic means (except where such information is required to be disclosed pursuant to any other provision of law, such as child support enforcement, health insurance, and retirement reporting); and 3) medical records claim forms, insurance applications, requests for the payment of benefits, and all other health records of public employees and their dependents. See City of Baton Rouge/ Parish of East Baton Rouge v. Capital City Press, LLC, 4 So.3d 807 (La.App. 1st Cir. 2008), writ dismissed, 998 So.2d 99, 100 (La. 2009) (internal affairs records on police officers were subject to public records request, except for matters deemed confidential); but see East Bank Fire Protection District v. Crossen, 892 So.2d 666 (La.App. 5th Cir. 2004), writ denied, 897 So.2d 608 (La. 2005) (assistant fire chief's personnel records exempt from public records law).

Workers exposed to toxic substances are entitled to obtain information from the records of an employer concerning the nature of those substances and their consequential adverse health effects. See La. R.S. 23:1016(A).

B. Medical Records

Access to an employee's medical records is generally subject to regulations adopted under the Health Insurance Portability and Accountability Act ("HIPAA"), Pub.L. No. 104-191, 110 Stat. 1936 (1996). See 45 C.F.R. §§ 160 and 164. HIPAA contains specific procedural requirements that must be followed when attempting to obtain medical information by way of subpoena. 45 C.F.R. § 164.512e. To the extent that state law is contrary to HIPAA regulations, HIPAA will preempt the state law. La. R.S. 13:3715.1 provides the mechanism for obtaining medical or hospital records on an individual from a healthcare provider. This statute generally states that medical records of an employee can be obtained via subpoena after certain formalities have been observed. A warrant is required to search an individual's pharmaceutical prescriptions and medical records for criminal investigative purposes. State v. Skinner, 10 So.3d 1212, 1218 (La. 2009).

Workers compensation claims have their own rules regarding privacy and access to information. La. R.S. 23:1125 provides that whenever an employee who is being treated by his choice of medical provider and submits to any type of medical examination at the request of the employer, or the employer's insurer or representative, and the requester receives a medical report, such employee or his representative shall be entitled to a copy of the written report of the results of the examination within 30 days from the date the requester receives the report.

The statute further provides that whenever an employee has accepted medical treatment by a healthcare provider referred by the employer, the employer's insurer, or the representative of either, the employee shall be entitled to receive a copy of any medical records of the medical provider that are in the possession of the employer or its insurer within 30 days from the date of written demand. See La. R.S. 23:1125(B). Such written report or records shall be furnished to the employee or his representatives at no cost to the employee. See La. R.S. 23:1125(C).

C. Criminal Records

There is no general statutory law in Louisiana addressing criminal records in the possession of employers. La. R.S. 40:1300.52 provides for mandatory criminal background checks on licensed ambulance personnel and non-licensed healthcare providers of nursing care health related services, medic services, and supportive assistance prior to any employer making an offer to employ or to contract with such individuals.

D. Subpoenas / Search Warrants

Claims for federal constitutional invasion of privacy require balancing privacy interests against the interest in complying with a valid subpoena. Dyess v. Louisiana State University Board of Supervisors, 2005 WL 2060915, 2005 U.S. Dist. LEXIS 18314 (E.D. La.) (plaintiff's privacy interest in avoiding disclosure of educational records outweighed by University's interest in complying with valid subpoena).

There is no general statutory law in Louisiana addressing a litigant's ability to subpoena an employee's personnel records. However, La. Code Civ. Proc. art. 1354 provides the procedural mechanism that is used to obtain a personnel file via a subpoena duces tecum. A subpoena may be used to order a person to produce at trial, deposition, or hearing "books, papers, documents, any other tangible things, or electronically stored information in his possession or under his control, if a reasonably accurate description thereof is given." This procedural mechanism may be used to obtain the personnel file of private employees.

VII. ACTIONS SUBSEQUENT TO EMPLOYMENT

A. References

La. R.S. 23:291 concerns the disclosure of employment-related information. Under the statute, employers who provide accurate information, whether verbal or written, about a current or former employee's job performance and reasons for separation are afforded a qualified privilege. The privileged is negated, however, when the employer acts in bad faith; a showing by the preponderance of the evidence that the information disclosed was knowingly false and deliberately misleading will prove bad faith. See La. R.S. 23:291(A); Livingston v. Gaviolo, 2006 WL 37029, *4, 2006 U.S. Dist. LEXIS 948 (W.D. La.) (qualified immunity for claim of defamation).

A prospective employer who reasonably relies on information about an employee's job performance or reasons for separation is immune from civil liability for negligent hiring, negligent retention and other similar causes of action unless further investigation, including but not limited to a criminal background check, is required by law. See La. R.S. 23:291(B)

B. Non-Compete Agreements

1. *Scope of Prohibition in the Employment Context.* Louisiana has long had a strong public policy disfavoring non-competition agreements between employers and employees. See SWAT 24 Shreveport Bossier, Inc. v. Bond, 808 So.2d 294, 298 (La. 2001). Louisiana's first non-compete statute basically nullified any provision in which an employee agreed not to compete with his employer after the conclusion of his employment. See 1934 La. Acts No. 133. In enacting Act 133, the legislature adopted the public policy previously articulated by Louisiana courts in striking down such agreements. The current version of the law is contained in La. R.S. 23:921. After numerous revisions, the current version of La. R.S. 23:921(A) provides that every contract or agreement, or provision thereof, which restrains an individual from exercising a lawful profession, trade or business is null and void, unless such contract or agreement is specifically permitted by or meets one of the exceptions provided under some other sub-section of La. R.S. 23:921.

In the employment context, the statute provides, in pertinent part, that: "Any person, including a corporation and the individual shareholders of such corporation, who is employed as an agent, servant or employee may agree with his employer to refrain from carrying on or engaging in a business similar to that of the employer and/or from soliciting customers of the employer within a specified parish or parishes, municipality or municipalities, or parts thereof, so long as the employer carries on a like business therein, not to exceed a period of two years from termination of employment. La. R.S.

23:921(C). For purposes of subsection (C), a person who becomes employed by a competing business, regardless of whether or not that person is an owner or equity interest holder of that competing business, may be deemed to be carrying on or engaging in a business similar to that of the party having a contractual right to prevent that person from competing. See La. R.S. 23:921(D). The statute also contains non-compete provisions that apply to persons who sell the goodwill of a business, independent contractors, partners, corporate shareholders, limited liability companies, franchisees, franchisors and computer programmers. See La. R.S. 23:921(B), (C), (E), (F), (G), (J), (K) and (L). If it is determined that members of the agreement were engaged in ultra vires acts, an agreement may be null and void. See La. R.S. 23:921(H).

2. ***Damages.*** La. R.S.23:921(H) sets forth the relief available to an employer for the breach of an enforceable non-compete agreement, including damages for the loss sustained, the profit of which he has been deprived and injunctive relief. The employer is not required to prove irreparable injury in order to obtain injunctive relief. Vartech Systems, Inc. v. Hayden, 951 So.2d 247, 255 (La.App. 1st Cir. 2006). Employers are not entitled to liquidated damages. G.T. Michelli Co., Inc. v. McKey, 599 So.2d 355 (La.App. 1st Cir. 1992); see also Kimball v. Anesthesia Specialists of Baton Rouge, Inc., 809 So.2d 405, 415 (La.App. 1st Cir. 2001).

3. ***Geographic and Temporal Scope.*** Non-competes are strictly construed against the party seeking enforcement. SWAT 24 Shreveport Bossier, Inc. v. Bond, 808 So.2d 294, 298 (La. 2001). The statute expressly provides that a non-compete or non-solicitation provision must specifically delineate the "parish or parishes, municipality or municipalities, or parts thereof" in which the employee is prohibited from competing or soliciting. The geographic limitation must be express and clearly discernable. Hose Specialty & Supply Management Co., Inc. v. Guccione, 865 So.2d 183, 184 (La.App. 5th Cir. 2003). The statute also indicates that the term of the non-compete or non-solicitation provision may not exceed two years beyond the employee's termination of employment. La. R.S. 23:921(C). Some courts have required that the non-compete or non-solicitation provision at issue strictly comport with the statutory requirements regarding geographic and temporal scope. See Turner Professional Services, Ltd. v. Broussard, 762 So.2d 184, 186 (La.App. 1st Cir. 2000); Team Environmental Services, Inc. v. Addison, 2 F.3d 124, 127 (5th Cir. 1993). Other courts have reformed overbroad provisions where the agreement at issue contained a severability clause. See Dixie Parking Service, Inc. v. Hargrove, 691 So.2d 1316, 1321 (La.App. 4th Cir. 1997); Henderson Implement Co., Inc. v. Langley, 707 So.2d 482, 486 (La.App. 3d Cir. 1998).

4. ***Definition of Employer's Business.*** La. R.S.23:921 does not require a definition of the employer's business for the agreement to be valid; however, if the agreement contains a definition of the employer's business, it cannot be overly broad such that it prevents former employees from engaging in more activities than were performed for the former employer. Baton Rouge Computer Sales, Inc. v. Miller-Conrad, 767 So.2d 763, 764-65 (La.App. 1st Cir. 2000). The employee must be carrying on or engaging in the employee's own business; an agreement that restrains an employee from carrying on or engaging in a competing business as the employee of another would be null and void. Vartech Systems, Inc. v. Hayden, 951 So.2d 247, 256 (La.App. 1st Cir. 2006).

5. ***Choice of Law and/or Choice of Forum Provisions.*** La. R.S. 23:921(A)(2) precludes the enforcement of a choice of law and/or a choice of forum provision unless said provision is expressly, knowingly and voluntarily agreed to and ratified by the employee after the occurrence of the incident which is the subject of the civil or administrative proceeding.

6. ***Actions by Employees or Former Employees.*** Employers who attempt to enforce an overbroad non-compete or non-solicitation agreement against their former employees may possibly be subject to a claim under the Louisiana Unfair Trade Practices and Consumer Protection Law "LUTPA"), La. R.S. 51:1401 et seq. In Gearheard v. DePuy Orthopaedics, Inc., 2000 WL 533352, 2000 U.S. Dist. LEXIS 6473 (E.D. La.), the court addressed the remedies available to an employee or independent contractor when his employer has attempted to bind him to an unenforceable covenant not to compete, holding that such employee or independent contractor could bring claims for damages under a tort cause of action, i.e., intentional interference with contractual relations, as well as under the LUTPA. See Id. at **3-6.

VIII. OTHER ISSUES

A. Statutes of Limitations

The statute of limitation (in Louisiana called the "prescriptive period") for any invasion of privacy claim is the basic tort limitation of one year from the date injury or damage is sustained. La. Civil Code art. 3492; see Sharif v. Metropolitan Convention & Visitors Bureau, Inc., 2009 WL 701731, 2009 U.S. Dist Lexis 25975 (E.D. La.). The continued distribution of material supporting an invasion of privacy claim may constitute a continuing tort, and prescription would then be measured from the date of the last act. Fontaine v. Roman Catholic Church, 625 So.2d 548, 555 (La.App. 4th Cir. 1993), writ denied, 630 So.2d 787 (La. 1994). The doctrine of contra non valentem may toll the prescriptive period for invasion of privacy claims when the cause of action is not known or reasonably knowable by the plaintiff. Id. (victim of sexual abuse was unaware of his damages until one year before suit).

B. Jurisdiction

An invasion of privacy claim is a delictual action under Louisiana Civil Code article 2315 which may be filed and adjudicated in Louisiana state courts. Federal courts would have supplemental jurisdiction over a pendant invasion of privacy claim under 28 U.S.C.A. § 1367; a federal court. however, may decline to exercise supplemental jurisdiction if the claim raises a novel or complex issue of state law or substantially predominates over the claim over which the court has original jurisdiction, the federal court has dismissed all claims over which it had original jurisdiction, or there are some other compelling reasons for declining jurisdiction. 29 U.S.C.A 1367(c).

C. Worker's Compensation Exclusivity

Generally, when a worker seeks to recover from his employer for injuries suffered during the course and scope of employment, the Louisiana Worker's Compensation Act, La. R.S. 23:1032, provides immunity from civil liability in favor of an employer. Cole v. State Dep't of Public Safety & Corrections, 825 So.2d 1134, 1138 (La. 2002). The "intentional act" loophole is the only exception to the Worker's Compensation Act and courts interpret this exception narrowly. Bridges v. Carl E. Woodward, Inc., 663 So.2d 458 (La.App. 4th Cir. 1995). To obtain a judicial remedy for employer invasions of privacy, the employee must show that the invasion was intentional and that the employer was substantially certain that he would injure the employee by the invasion. Broussard v. Smith, 999 So.2d 1171 (La.App. 3d Cir. 2008). Lesser degrees of certainty such as "reasonably foreseeable" and "should have known" do not constitute an "intentional act" as required to recover outside the Worker's Compensation Act. Adams v. Time Saver Stores, Inc., 615 So.2d 460, 461-62 (La.App. 4th Cir. 1993). Accordingly, an employee must meet a strict evidentiary burden of persuasion to show that an employer invasion of privacy claim is compensable outside of the Worker's Compensation Act. Id.

D. Pleading Requirements

Louisiana has fact pleadings. Invasion of privacy is defined as an unreasonable intrusion into a person's seclusion or solitude or into his private affairs. Moore v. Cabaniss, 699 So.2d 1143 (La.App. 2d Cir. 1997), writ denied, 705 So.2d 1108 (La. 1998). A cause of action for invasion of privacy is properly pled when the petition alleges facts sufficient to show that the essential elements of the tort of invasion of privacy have been established. Green v. Alaska National Ins. Co., 759 So.2d 165 (La.App. 4th Cir. 2000).

E. Special Motion to Strike (anti-SLAPP statute)

The Louisiana anti-SLAPP statute, La. Code Civ. Proc. art. 971, provides that a "cause of action against a person arising from any act of that person in furtherance of the person's right of petition or free speech under the United States or Louisiana Constitution in connection with a public issue shall be subject to a special motion to strike, unless the plaintiff has established a probability of success on the claim. In making its determination, the court shall consider the pleadings and supporting and opposing affidavits stating the facts upon which the liability or defense is based." La. Code Civ. Proc. art. 971 (A)(1)(2). The statute provides for a stay of discovery while a special motion to strike is pending, unless the plaintiff shows good cause and receives a court order allowing "specified discovery" to be conducted. La. Code Civ. Proc. art. 971(D).

In Stern v. Doe, 806 So.2d 98 (La.App. 4th Cir. 2001), 30 Media L. Rep. 1793, the Court of Appeal applied the statute for the first time to dismiss an invasion of privacy claim. In Lee v. Pennington, 830 So.2d 1037 (La.App. 4th Cir. 2002), writ denied, 836 So.2d 52 (La. 2003), the Court upheld the statute against constitutional equal protection and due process challenges. In addition, the Court held that the "language of the statute is clear that attorney fees must be awarded to a prevailing defendant" on a special motion to strike. La. Code Civ. Proc. art. 971(B). In 2004, the Louisiana legislature amended the anti-SLAPP statute to require that any prevailing party, not just a prevailing defendant, be awarded reasonable attorneys' fees and costs. La. Code Civ. Proc. art. 971(B).

After first ruling otherwise, on reconsideration a U.S. District Court concluded that a special motion to strike may be used to strike individual causes of action in a lawsuit. A request for injunctive relief, however, is merely a remedy, not a "cause of action," and, thus, is not subject to a special motion to strike. Louisiana Crisis Assistance Center v. Marzano-Lesnevich, 2012 WL 2717075 (E.D. La. July 9, 2012).

A town is a "person" within the meaning of La. Code Civ. Proc. art. 971 and may file a motion to strike. Hunt v. Town of New Llano, 930 So.2d 251 (La.App. 3d Cir. 2006).

Denial of an article 971 motion in a federal court proceedings is an "immediately-appealable collateral order." Henry v. Lake Charles American Press, LLC, 566 F.3d 164, 37 Media L. Rep. 1641 (2009).

SURVEY OF MAINE EMPLOYMENT LIBEL LAW

Geoffrey K. Cummings, Esq.
Matthew J. LaMourie, Esq.
Preti, Flaherty, Beliveau & Pachios LLP
One City Center
P. O. Box 9546
Portland, Maine 04112-9546
Telephone: (207) 791-3000; Facsimile: (207) 791-3111

(With Developments Reported Through **November 1, 2012**)

GENERAL COMMENTS

The Maine court system includes two levels of trial courts, the District Court and the Superior Court. The Superior Court has original jurisdiction over all civil actions, unless otherwise specified by statute. Bench and jury trials are available in the Superior Court. All trials in the District Court are bench trials. Appeals from both the District and Superior Courts are to the Maine Supreme Judicial Court, commonly known as the Law Court when sitting in its capacity as an appellate court. Unless otherwise specified by statute, any civil matter may also be brought in the District Court provided that no equitable relief is demanded. Maine has no intermediate level appeals tribunal.

The only officially reported decisions in Maine are those of the Maine Supreme Judicial Court appearing in the Maine Reporter through 1965 and thereafter in the Atlantic Reporter. Maine's judicial system initiated a new citation form as of January 1, 1997. In addition to citations to the Atlantic Reporter, state courts require citation to the calendar year of the opinion, followed by a sequential number assigned to the opinion. Each paragraph in the opinion is preceded by a paragraph number, which is required for pinpoint citations. (e.g., Vogt v. Churchill, 1997 ME 7, ¶ 1, 687 A.2d 961).). These sequential numbers and paragraph numbers appear on all opinions issued after January 1, 1997.

Maine's Supreme Judicial Court, or the Law Court, has handed down only a limited number of cases involving employment defamation. Accordingly, most of the law of employment defamation must be distilled from more generalized defamation cases.

SIGNIFICANT DEVELOPMENTS SINCE THE 2012 *SURVEY*

None.

I. GENERAL LAW

A. General Employment Law

1. ***At Will Employment.*** The Maine Supreme Court has firmly upheld the doctrine of employment at will. Bard v. Bath Iron Works Corp., 590 A.2d 152 (Me. 1991). An employment contract of indefinite duration, with one exception, may be terminated at will by either party. Terrio v. Millinocket Community Hosp., 379 A.2d 135 (Me. 1977). The exception is that parties to an employment contract of indefinite duration may enter into an employment contract terminable only pursuant to its express terms, such as "for cause," by clearly and unambiguously stating their intentions to do so. Larrabee v. Penobscot Frozen Foods, Inc., 486 A.2d 97 (Me. 1984). Such a contract must expressly restrict an employer's common law rights to discharge an employee at will and clearly limit the employer to the specified methods of terminating the employment. Written or oral language that merely implies that discharge will be for cause only is not sufficient to bind an employer. Libby v. Calais Regional Hosp., 554 A.2d 1181 (Me. 1989).

The Maine Supreme Court has refused to recognize the tort of wrongful discharge. Bard v. Bath Iron Works Corp., 590 A.2d 152 (Me. 1991). However, the Court has not ruled out the possible recognition of such a cause of action when a discharge of an employee contravenes some strong public policy. Larrabee v. Penobscot Frozen Foods, Inc., 486 A.2d 97 (Me. 1984). A more recent federal district decision notes that courts in Maine have "declined to entertain wrongful discharge claims when they are brought by at-will employees." Learnard v. The Inhabitants of the Town of Van Buren, 182 F. Supp. 2d 115, 127-128 (D. Me. 2002)

B. Elements of Defamation Claim

1. ***Basic Elements.*** In setting forth the elements of a defamation claim the Maine Supreme Court consistently follows the Restatement (Second) of Torts § 558 (1977). Those elements are: (a) a false and defamatory statement concerning another; (b) an unprivileged publication to a third party; (c) fault amounting at least to negligence on the

part of the publisher; and (d) either actionability of the statement irrespective of special harm or the existence of special harm caused by the publication. Lester v. Powers, 596 A.2d 65 (Me. 1991); Rippett v. Bemis, 672 A.2d 82 (Me. 1996); Morgan v. Kooistra, 2008 ME 26, ¶ 26, 941 A.2d 447, 455. Defamatory meaning is widely construed by the state courts: "A statement is defamatory if it tends so to harm the reputation of another as to lower him in the estimation of the community or to deter third persons from associating or dealing with him." Rippett, 672 A.2d at 86, citing Bakal v. Weare, 583 A.2d 1028, 1029 (Me. 1990). The breadth of this reading is often cited by trial judges as a basis for denying dismissal or summary judgment motions for defendants. Haworth v. Feigon, 623 A.2d 150, 156 (Me. 1993) (holding that when statements are ambiguous and capable of equally conflicting interpretations they should be submitted to the jury). The Law Court has adopted the definition of "special harm" set forth in the Restatement (Second) of Torts §575 comment b (1977). Withers v. Hackett, 1998 ME 164, ¶ 8, 714 A.2d 798, 801 ("special harm" is the loss of something having economic or pecuniary value).

2. ***Fault.*** There are no reported cases distinguishing between issues of public and private concern. A different standard is applied in cases involving public figures or officials and those involving private figure plaintiffs. The Maine Supreme Court had adopted the analysis in Rosenblatt v. Baer, 383 U.S. 75 (1966) that the definition of public official generally turns on whether the plaintiff has "substantial responsibility for or control over the conduct of governmental affairs." Persons considered to be public officials or public figures include: all officers of law enforcement, from ordinary patrolmen to chief of police, Roche v. Egan, 433 A.2d 757 (Me. 1981); and department heads of state government bureaus, Michaud v. Inhabitants of the Town of Livermore Falls, 381 A.2d 1110 (Me. 1978). The Supreme Judicial Court in Roche v. Egan, 433 A.2d at 762, also noted in dicta that the Supreme Court has "stopped short of the conclusion that all public employees are public officials." Id., citing Hutchinson v. Proxmire, 443 U.S. 111 (1979). Persons found *not* to be public officials or public figures include: public school teachers, True v. Ladner, 513 A.2d 257 (Me. 1986) (holding that teachers are not "public officials" because they usually do not exercise "substantial administrative or policy making responsibilities"); craftsmen who are recipients of media coverage, Haworth v. Feigon, 623 A.2d 150, 158 (Me. 1993) (plaintiff lacked the kind of fame that would allow media access to rebut defamatory statements); the teacher of a student to be featured on a television show, Ramirez v. Rogers, 540 A.2d 475 (Me. 1988) (requiring relationship between defamatory statement and reason for fame or notoriety); and a neighborhood pediatrician, Saunders v. VanPelt, 497 A.2d 1121 (Me. 1985).

Maine courts have followed the standard New York Times definition of "actual malice" in defamation actions involving public officials and public figures. Absent evidence of "convincing clarity" that the defendant knew statements to be untrue or acted with "reckless disregard of truth," statements made regarding the character and conduct of a public official are not actionable. Michaud v. Inhabitants of the Town of Livermore Falls, 381 A.2d 1110 (Me. 1978); Haworth v. Feigon, 623 A.2d 150, 158 (Me. 1993); Roche v. Egan, 433 A.2d 757 (Me. 1981); True v. Ladner, 513 A.2d 257 (Me. 1986). The standard of actual malice focuses on defendant's attitude toward truth or falsity of the publication rather than on defendant's ill will or animosity against plaintiff. Tucci v. Guy Gannett Publishing Co., 464 A.2d 161, 9 Media L. Rep. 2344 (Me. 1983). Worth noting is that some lower courts have had difficulty understanding the distinction between New York Times actual malice and common-law malice, and have been persuaded by plaintiffs' counsel at trial to adopt a non-libel definition of actual malice: "[Actual] malice exists where the defendant's tortious conduct is motivated by ill will towards the plaintiff." Tuttle v. Raymond, 494 A.2d 1353, 1361 (Me. 1985). See also Boivin v. Jones Vining, 578 A.2d 187, 189 (Me. 1990).

a. **Private Figure Plaintiff/Matter of Public Concern.** In a case involving a private figure plaintiff concerning a matter of public importance, the Law Court accepted the assumption of parties and of the trial court that negligence was a proper basis of liability for such a case. Hudson v. Guy Gannett Broadcasting Co., 521 A.2d 714, 13 Media L. Rep. 2189 (Me. 1987). The court did not suggest that the assumption below was correct or that it was incorrect but citing Gertz v. Robert Welch, Inc., 418 U.S. 323 (1974) noted that, in private figure defamation cases, the state was free to apply any basis of liability except liability without fault. The private figure involved in Hudson was an employee at a paper mill who was fired for drinking alcohol on the job. His firing was included in a news report stating that twelve employees were fired for drug use, but no names were given. See also Galarneau v. Merrill Lynch, 504 F.3d 189 (1st Cir. 2007).

b. **Private Figure Plaintiff/Matter of Private Concern.** The Law Court has not specifically held what level of fault must be shown in the context of a private figure in a matter of private concern. However, in a private figure/private concern case, the court rejected the argument that the jury should have been instructed that the plaintiff had to prove by clear and convincing evidence that the defamatory statements were false and made with actual malice. Instead, it held that "the trial justice correctly applied common law defamation principles." Ramirez v. Rogers, 540 A.2d 475 (Me. 1988).

c. **Public Figure Plaintiff/Matter of Public Concern.** The federal constitutional standard set forth in New York Times v. Sullivan, 376 U.S. 254 (1964), i.e., actual malice, will apply in such cases in Maine. See, e.g., Gautschi v. Maisel, 565 A.2d 1009 (Me. 1989); Lester v. Powers, 596 A.2d 65 (Me. 1991). The plaintiffs in both these cases were professors at private colleges.

3. ***Falsity.*** When the facts in a published report are true and do not reasonably support false inferences, summary judgment shall be entered for the defendant. Loe v. Town of Thomaston, 600 A.2d 1090 (Me. 1991). If claimant was in fact a criminal accomplice, a question of fact, this would serve as a defense to a police officer who publicly accused the claimant of criminal complicity. Rippett v. Bemis, 672 A.2d 82 (Me. 1996). Maine has adopted the defense of substantial truth, following the Restatement (Second) of Torts § 581A (1977). McCullough v. Visiting Nurse Association of Southern Maine, 1997 ME 55, 691 A.2d 1201. In applying the doctrine, the court asked whether an accurate statement would have been less damaging than the one which was published. McCullough, 1997 ME at ¶ 10.

4. ***Defamatory Statement of Fact.*** Maine's common law of defamation does not allow recovery for statements of opinion alone. Lester v. Powers, 596 A.2d 65 (Me. 1991). The standard for determining whether a statement expresses "fact" or "opinion" looks to the totality of the circumstances. The Court has held that a comment is opinion if it is clear from the surrounding circumstances that the maker of the statement did not intend to state an objective fact, but instead intended to make a personal observation of the facts. Caron v. Bangor Publishing Co., 470 A.2d 782, 10 Media L. Rep. 1365 (Me. 1984). A statement of opinion may be actionable if it implies the existence of undisclosed defamatory facts. Lester, supra. An example of this is contained in True v. Ladner, where a school superintendent told another school district that a teacher they were considering for hire was not a good teacher. The statements made suggested that the superintendent had personally reviewed the teacher, when, in fact, he had not. True v. Ladner, 513 A.2d 257, 262 (Me. 1986). There does not appear to be any different treatment for libel as opposed to slander.

5. ***Of and Concerning Plaintiff.*** In order for written or spoken defamation to be actionable, it must be "of and concerning" the plaintiff. Robinson v. Guy Gannett Publishing Company, 297 F. Supp. 722 (D. Me. 1969); See also Hudson v. Guy Gannett Broadcasting Co., 521 A.2d 714, 13 Media L. Rep. 2189 (Me. 1987) (leaving "of and concerning" question for jury determination). There is no case law in Maine that suggests that corporate officers may recover for defamatory statements about corporations, but there is one case that allows an officer and the corporation to recover when both have been defamed by a statement. Vahlsing Christina Corp. v. Stanley, 487 A.2d 264 (Me. 1985).

6. ***Publication.*** A defamation plaintiff must prove that the allegedly defamatory statement was published to a third party. Bakal v. Weare, 583 A.2d 1028 (Me. 1990).

a. **Intracorporate Communication.** The Maine Supreme Court has held that intracorporate communications constitute publication. Heselton v. Wilder, 496 A.2d 1063 (Me. 1985). The Court has generally followed the Restatement (Second) of Torts § 577 (1977) and recognizes that, although such communications are publications, they may be protected by a qualified privilege. Staples v. Bangor Hydro-Electric Co., 629 A.2d 601 (Me. 1993). The Maine Supreme Court has found that a supervisor's communications of allegations that a plaintiff took money from a cash register to persons in the employer's loss prevention department constituted a publication. Heselton, supra. The Court has also found that a department director's statement to a director of personnel was a publication. Staples, supra.

b. **Compelled Self-Publication.** Maine has not explicitly adopted the doctrine of defamation by compelled self-publication. In one case, the Maine Supreme Court avoided the issue by finding that even if it were to adopt the doctrine, the defendant was protected by a conditional privilege. Cole v. Chandler, 2000 ME 104, 752 A.2d 1189. The Maine Federal District Court previously held that the Maine Supreme Court, given the opportunity, would adopt the theory and, accordingly, ruled in favor of a plaintiff seeking to recover in accordance with that doctrine. Carey v. Mt. Desert Island Hosp., 910 F. Supp. 7 (D. Me. 1995). However, a self-compelled publication to a pastor regarding termination does not qualify "within the narrow confines of Carey." Smith v. Heritage Salmon, Inc., 180 F. Supp 2d 208, 222 (D. Me. 2002).

c. **Republication.** No cases directly addressing this issue have come before the Law Court. However, in Bedard v. Greene, et al., 409 A.2d 676 (Me. 1979), the court affirmed the dismissal of a third-party complaint after a libel defendant sought contribution against two other persons who had allegedly repeated the defamatory statements. The court held that because the action was based on defendant's intentional publication of defamatory matter, defendant, as an intentional tortfeasor, could not shift through contribution any part of a potential judgment to others.

7. ***Statements versus Conduct.*** No reported cases distinguish between defamation claims based on statements and those based on conduct.

8. ***Damages.*** Compensatory damages in libel and slander actions may include elements of mental suffering, humiliation, embarrassment, effect upon reputation and loss of social standing, so far as they have been proved or may reasonably be presumed. Saunders v. VanPelt, 497 A.2d 1121 (Me. 1985); Gautschi v. Maisel, 565 A.2d 1009 (Me. 1989). The emotional distress and punitive damages resulting from defamation are distinct from those resulting from related but different tortious conduct. Such damages may be subject to separate calculations by a jury. Withers v. Hackett, 1999 ME 117, ¶ 8, 734 A.2d 189, 191. Where defamatory statements were slanderous per se, plaintiff could recover compensatory damages without proof of special damages. Saunders, supra; Springer v. Seaman, 658 F. Supp. 1502 (D. Me. 1987); Ramirez

v. Rogers, 540 A.2d 475 1364 (Me. 1988); Haworth v. Feigon, 623 A.2d 150 (Me. 1993); Galarneau v. Merrill Lynch, 504 F.3d 189 (1st Cir. 2007). The evidence of plaintiff's mental suffering could support a substantial award in an action for slander per se. Marston v. Newavom, 629 A.2d 587 (Me. 1993). In Packard v. Central Maine Power Co., 477 A.2d 264 (Me. 1984), the Maine Supreme Court seemed to adopt Prosser's analysis that claims for "humiliation, wrath or sorrow" were "parasitic" damages requiring proof of damage to reputation as a condition of recovery. See William L. Prosser, et al., Prosser and Keeton on the Law of Torts § 111 (4th ed. 19771). However, Packard was decided at a time when Maine still required physical manifestations or similar objective proof of injury before emotional distress damages could be recovered. The significance of the holding in Packard is, therefore, in doubt.

a. **Presumed Damages and Libel Per Se.** In an action for slander per se a private figure/ private concern plaintiff need not prove special damages or actual malice to recover a substantial amount and the jury assessment will be held excessive only if it is not rationally supportable. Saunders v. VanPelt, 497 A.2d 1121 (Me. 1985); Ramirez v. Rogers, 540 A.2d 475 (Me. 1988); Gautschi v. Maisel, 565 A.2d 1009 (Me. 1989). A claimant may recover compensatory damages without proving special harm if false statements have been made relating to a profession, occupation or official station in which the plaintiff is employed. Haworth v. Feigon, 623 A.2d 150 (Me. 1993); Cookson v. Brewer School Department, 2009 ME 57, 974 A.2d 276; Galarneau v. Merrill Lynch, 504 F.3d 189 (1st Cir. 2007).

(1) **Employment-Related Criticism.** Defamatory words relating to a profession or occupation are slanderous per se. Saunders v. VanPelt, 497 A.2d 1121 (Me. 1985); Galarneau v. Merrill Lynch, 504 F.3d 189 (1st Cir. 2007).

(2) **Single Instance Rule.** Under the "single instance rule," when a statement relates to only one instance of business or professional misconduct, presumed damages are not available and the plaintiff must prove special damages. The Maine Supreme Judicial Court has not yet had the occasion to consider the rule.

b. **Punitive Damages.** Principles of tort law in Maine, when overlaid against libel law, seem to indicate that the recovery of punitive damages requires both actual and common-law malice. When actual malice is established by clear and convincing proof, a jury may award punitive damages. Awards of punitive damages have been reversed because plaintiff proved merely reckless disregard, but not actual ill will, by the defendant. Staples v. Bangor Hydro -Electric Co., 629 A.2d 601 (Me. 1989). Compare Tuttle v. Raymond, 494 A.2d 1353 (Me. 1985) (non-libel case establishing requirement if "ill will or spite" for recovery of punitive damages). Prior to Staples, supra, in a private figure, non-public concern slander case, Maine ruled that ill will alone, regardless of "actual malice," permitted punitive damages. Ramirez v. Rogers, 540 A.2d 475 (Me. 1988). The defendant's wealth or lack thereof may be considered by the jury when determining whether punitive damages should be awarded. Saunders v. VanPelt, 497 A.2d 1121 (Me. 1985). See also Galarneau v. Merrill Lynch, 504 F.3d 189 (1st Cir. 2007) (evidence at trial insufficient to support showing of malice necessary for punitive liability).

II. PRIVILEGES AND DEFENSES

A. Scope of Privileges

1. ***Absolute Privilege.***

a. **Judicial Proceedings.** Allegedly libelous statements contained in court pleadings, made by an attorney, which are relevant to the judicial proceedings at hand, are absolutely privileged. Dineen v. Daughan, 381 A.2d 663 (Me. 1978); Vogt v. Churchill, 1997 ME 5, 687 A.2d 961; Simon v. Navon, 951 F. Supp. 279 (D. Me. 1997); F.D.I.C. v. S. Prawer & Co., 829 F. Supp. 439 (D. Me. 1993). However, excessive publication about, but not necessary to, pending litigation is not privileged and may be actionable. Vahlsing Christina Corp. v. Stanley, 487 A.2d 264 (Me. 1985). The Law Court has also recognized a privilege, without specifying whether it is absolute or qualified, that allows counsel to make inquiries and develop evidence relating to a legal proceeding. Tanguay v. Asen,1998 ME 277, 722 A.2d 49.

b. **Quasi-Judicial Proceedings**. Decisions which are quasi-judicial in nature and made by public authorities in the exercise of their lawfully conferred functions are absolutely privileged. Rodway v. Wiswall, 267 A.2d 374 (Me. 1970); Baker v. Charles, 919 F. Supp. 41 (Me. 1996) (privilege may attach to communications with regulatory agencies).

2. ***Qualified Privileges.*** The Maine Supreme Judicial Court has recognized the conditional privileges set out in the Restatement (Second) of Torts §§ 593-598A (1977). Saunders v. VanPelt, 497 A.2d 1121, 1125 (Me. 1985). In Lester v. Powers, 596 A.2d 65 (Me. 1991) the Maine Supreme Court offers an extensive discussion of conditional privileges and their relationship to nonactionable opinion. The Court relies heavily on the Restatement (Second) of Torts §§ 594-598 (1977) in holding that "any situation in which an important interest of the recipient will be furthered by frank communication

may give rise to a conditional privilege." The defendant has the burden of proving the circumstances necessary for the existence of a conditional privilege. It is for the court to determine whether matters give rise to a conditional privilege. If the circumstances are disputed it is for the jury to determine what the circumstances were in fact. If a privilege exists, the plaintiff must then show the loss of the conditional privilege through its abuse. Saunders v. VanPelt, 497 A.2d 1121 (Me. 1985); Springer v. Seaman, 658 F. Supp. 1502 (D. Me. 1987); Rippett v. Bemis, 672 A.2d 82 (Me. 1996); Galarneau v. Merrill Lynch, 504 F.3d 189 (1st Cir. 2007). Another similar discussion of conditional privileges and their potential abuse may be found in Cole v. Chandler, 2000 ME 104, 752 A.2d 1189 (conditional privilege arises in any situation in which an important interest of the recipient of a defamatory statement will be advanced by frank communication). Conditional privilege is also at issue in a case involving a claim of defamation arising out of bingo games. Rice v. Alley, 2002 ME 43, 791 A.2d 932. The Court held that allegedly defamatory statements made about a member of the Elk's Ladies Auxiliary at a meeting were conditionally privileged and that there was insufficient evidence to show that the privilege had been abused. Id.

a. **Common Interest.** The Maine Supreme Court has affirmed the existence of a qualified privilege with respect to matters in which persons having a common interest in a particular subject matter correctly or reasonably believe that there is information that another sharing the common interest is entitled to know. The Court has adopted the privilege as set forth in the Restatement (Second) of Torts § 596 (1977). Staples v. Bangor Hydro-Electric Co., 629 A.2d 601 (Me. 1993).

b. **Duty.** The Maine Supreme Court has held that a public employee is entitled to a conditional privilege if the challenged statement was "required or permitted in the performance of his official duties." Morgan v. Kooistra, 2008 ME 26, ¶ 33, 941 A.2d 447, 456 (quoting Restatement (Second) of Torts § 598A (1977)).

c. **Criticism of Public Employee.** Maine courts have not specifically recognized a qualified privilege based on a right to criticize a public employee. Roche v. Egan, 433 A.2d 757 (Me. 1981). The Maine Supreme Court held that it was harmless error for the trial justice to have refused to instruct a jury on the privileges of a person living in a community to make statements to a police officer (about another police officer) for the purpose of protecting one's property and to communicate to a police officer for the purpose of aiding in the detection of a crime (by another police officer). The court reasoned that, since the jury would be instructed that the defendants could be held liable only if it were shown that they acted "with reckless disregard to the truth," that instruction would obviate the need for any further instructions on the common law conditional privileges. Given the opportunity to recognize a qualified privilege for statements that constitute a criticism of a public employee, we believe the Maine Supreme Court would readily adopt it.

d. **Limitation on Qualified Privileges.**

(1) **Constitutional or Actual Malice.** Maine courts recognize that a conditional privilege is lost if a jury finds that a defendant knew his statement to be false or recklessly disregarded its truth or falsity, i. e., entertained a high degree of awareness of probable falsity or serious doubt as to the truth of the statement. Staples v. Bangor Hydro-Electric Co., 629 A.2d 601 (Me. 1993); Cole v. Chandler, 2000 ME 104, 752 A.2d 1189; Galarneau v. Merrill Lynch, 504 F.3d 189 (1st Cir. 2007); Morgan v. Kooistra, 2008 ME 26, ¶ 33, 941 A.2d 447, 456. In Staples the jury found that a supervisor's accusations of computer sabotage against plaintiff, with no proof, met this standard.

(2) **Common Law Malice.** The Maine courts also recognize the existence of a limitation of qualified privileges when a jury finds that a defendant acted with common malice, i.e., "entirely out of ill will" toward a plaintiff. Staples v. Bangor Hydro-Electric Co., 629 A.2d 601 (Me. 1993). An example of this kind of malice was found in a case where the owner of a gymnastics school claimed that a rival owner abused the students. This statement was made when the defendant discovered that a student of the rival school was going to appear on television. Ramirez v. Rogers, 540 A.2d 475 (Me. 1988).

e. **Question of Fact or Law.** Whether a conditional privilege arises in a given circumstance is a question of law. Morgan v. Kooistra, 2008 ME 26, ¶ 33, 941 A.2d 447, 456; Cole v. Chandler, 2000 ME 104, 752 A.2d 1189. Whether a conditional privilege has been abused is a question of fact. Morgan, supra.

f. **Burden of Proof.** After the issue has been "properly raised," a defendant has the burden of proving the circumstances necessary for the existence of a conditional privilege. Saunders v. VanPelt, 497 A.2d 1121 (Me. 1985). When the privilege has been established, it becomes the plaintiff's burden to show the loss of the privilege through its abuse. Id., Gautschi v. Maisel, 565 A.2d 1009 (Me. 1989). Cole v. Chandler, 2000 ME 104, 752 A.2d 1189

B. Standard Libel Defenses

1. ***Truth.*** Truth has long been a defense to defamation claims, but it must be pleaded affirmatively and then proven by a defendant. Boulet v. Beals, 177 A.2d 665 (Me. 1962). However, in cases where the plaintiff is a public

figure or a media defendant is involved, it is the plaintiff's burden to prove by clear and convincing evidence that the defamatory statements were false and made with actual malice. Ramirez v. Rogers, 540 A.2d 475 (Me. 1985). It is not necessary to establish the literal truth of the statement made. Minor inaccuracies of expression are immaterial provided that the defamatory charge is true in substance. McCullough v. Visiting Nurse Service of Southern Maine, Inc., 1997 ME 55, 691 A.2d 1201 (statement that employee was terminated for "several incidents" when, in fact, she was only terminated for two, held substantially true). Another example of truth as a defense can be found in a case where an employee of a company that sold meat told a customer that a rival seller had been dismissed from his previous position because of cheating customers. This statement was found to be true and thus was a valid defense. Picard v. Brennan, 307 A.2d 833 (Me. 1973).

2. ***Opinion.*** A statement is not actionable if it is clear the maker did not intend to state an objective fact, but rather to present an interpretation of the facts. Fortier v. International Broth. Of Elec. Workers, Local 2327, 605 A.2d 79 (Me. 1992). The Maine Supreme Judicial Court has noted that its analysis of opinion privilege is consistent with that set forth by the U.S. Supreme Court in Milkovich v. Lorain Journal Co., 497 U.S. 1 (1990). A statement ostensibly in the form of an opinion is actionable if it implies the allegation of undisclosed defamatory facts as the basis for the opinion. True v. Ladner, 513 A.2d 257 (Me. 1986). The distinction between a statement of fact and a statement of opinion depends on whether ordinary persons hearing or reading the matter complained of would be likely to understand it as an expression of the speaker's or writer's opinion or as a statement of existing fact. Caron v. Bangor Publishing Co., 470 A.2d 782, 10 Media L. Rep. 1365 (Me. 1984)(statement by newspaper columnist that overweight policeman was not "an effective cop on the beat or a tribute to his uniform" held to be opinion). The determination of whether an allegedly defamatory statement is an expression of fact or opinion is a question of law. Id. The Maine Supreme Court has relied on Gertz v. Robert Welch, Inc., 418 U. S. 323 (1974) in explaining the rationale for the opinion privilege. Caron v. Bangor Publishing Co., supra. Once it is determined that a defendant is entitled to a conditional privilege, the burden shifts to the plaintiff to prove that the defendant abused the privilege. Cole v. Chandler, supra.

3. ***Consent.*** No reported Maine Supreme Court cases address consent.

4. ***Mitigation.*** In the only modern case addressing mitigation, it was held that provocation, though no excuse for defamation, should be considered as a mitigating factor when assessing punitive damages. Farrell v. Kramer, 193 A.2d 560 (Me. 1963). A retraction statue, 14 M.R.S.A. § 153 (1994) provides that:

> the defendant in an action for libel may prove in mitigation of damages that the charge was made by mistake or through error or by inadvertence and that he has in writing, within a reasonable time after the publication of the charge, retracted the charge and denied its truth as publicly and as fully as he made the charge. He may prove in mitigation of damages that the plaintiff failed to notify the defendant of the libel in a timely fashion and by that the defendant was therefore unable to lessen damage to the plaintiff's reputation. He may prove in mitigation of damages that the plaintiff has already recovered or has brought action for damages for, or has received or has agreed to receive compensation for, substantially the same libel.

A plaintiff need not request a retraction as a prerequisite to instituting a libel action.

C. Additional Defenses

The Maine Supreme Court has recognized the exclusivity provision of the Maine Workers' Compensation Act as a partial defense to a defamation claim brought against fellow employees. Cole v. Chandler, 2000 ME 104, 752 A.2d 1189. The Court recognized the defense as applicable to those portions of the claim which sought recovery for personal injuries, which the Court defined as "mental or physical injuries." Those remaining portions of the claim that sought damages for injuries for economic wellbeing were not subject to the defense offered by the exclusivity provision, but were potentially subject to conditional defamation privileges.

The Court has also recognized that immunity provisions set forth in the Maine Tort Claims Act, 14 M.R.S.A. 8101, *et seq.*, may be the basis of total immunity or a limitation on liability for defamation claims. Morgan v. Kooistra, 2008 ME 26, ¶ 20, 941 A.2d 447, 453-54. The Maine Tort Claims Act may also form the basis for immunity for a claim of interference with a contractual relationship brought by a municipal employee against the city manager. Quintal v. City of Hallowell, 2008 ME 155, ¶¶ 33-36, 956 A.2d 88, 96-97.

Similarly, the Maine Supreme Court found that the discretionary function immunity provisions of the Maine Tort Claims Act mandated dismissal of an action brought by a discharged local police officer alleging slander per se, invasion of privacy, and negligent infliction of emotional distress against the local county sheriff. Hilderbrand v. Washington County Commissioners, 2011 ME 132, 33 A.3d 425.

The First Circuit Court of Appeals has ruled that Maine's anti-SLAPP statute, 14 M.R.S.A. § 556, may provide substantive defenses to claims of defamation and interference with an advantageous contractual relationship in the employment context. Godin v. Schencks, 629 F.3d 79 (1st Cir. 2010). A discharged school employee brought a § 1983 due process claim against her former employer, as well as the defamation and interference claims against three fellow school employees. The District Court ruled that Maine's anti-SLAPP statute did not apply in federal court proceedings, setting up the interlocutory appeal to the First Circuit. That Court held that the statute did apply, and that the substantive legal defenses available under it should be considered by the District Court upon remand.

III. RECURRING FACT PATTERNS

A. Statements in Personnel File

There are no reported cases in Maine in which a defamation claim is based on statements contained in a personnel file

B. Performance Evaluations

The Maine Legislature has enacted statutes which provide immunity to "any person acting without malice" and to physicians and other health care providers for making reports or other information available to peer review committees or other review or accrediting entities. 24 M.R.S.A. § 2511 (1997) or 32 M.R.S.A. § 3293 (1997). The Maine Supreme Judicial Court has recognized that a performance evaluation of an associate professor requested by a college tenure committee from a former student could be the basis for a defamation claim, but that it was subject to the conditional privilege which attaches to those situations where society has an interest in promoting free, but not absolutely unfettered, speech. Lester v. Powers, 596 A.2d 65 (Me. 1991). See also Onat v. Penobscot Bay Medical Center, 574 A.2d 872 (Me. 1990) (defendants entitled to conditional privilege for critical statements about physician made in course of peer review process; court did not reach physicians' additional defense of statutory immunity under 24 M.R.S.A. § 2511 (1997) or 32 M.R.S.A. § 3293 (1997)); Gautschi v. Maisel, 565 A.2d 1009 (Me. 1989) (tenure committee member entitled to conditional privilege for negative comments concerning fellow professor).

C. References

The Maine Legislature has enacted a statute which appears to provide immunity to employers who disclose information about a former employee's job performance or work record to a prospective employer, unless lack of good faith is shown by clear and convincing evidence. To date, there are no reported cases interpreting the statute. The statute includes a proviso indicating that it is not in derogation of any claims or protections previously existing under state law, thus leaving the effectiveness of the immunity suggested by the statute in doubt. 26 M.R.S.A. § 598. The Maine Supreme Judicial Court has recognized that an adverse job reference about a teacher given by a school superintendent can be the basis for a defamation claim, subject to a conditional privilege. True v. Ladner, 513 A.2d 257 (Me. 1986).

D. Intracorporate Communication

The Maine Supreme Court has held that intracorporate communications constitute publication. Heselton v. Wilder, 496 A.2d 1063 (Me. 1985). The Court has generally followed the Restatement (Second) of Torts § 577 (1977) and recognizes that, although such communications are publications, they may be protected by qualified privilege. Staples v. Bangor Hydro-Electric Co., 629 A.2d 601 (Me. 1993).

E. Statements to Government Regulators

Maine's unemployment compensation statutes provide that any information transmitted to the Bureau of Employment Security, to the Unemployment Insurance Commission, to any of their duly authorized representatives in the course of pursuing or opposing an unemployment insurance claim is "absolutely privileged" and may not be made the subject matter or basis of any defamation action. 26 M.R.S.A. § 1047. See also III.B, supra.

F. Reports to Auditors and Insurers

Absent "fraud, malice or bad faith," no civil liability attaches for any tort against a person who reports suspected "fraudulent insurance acts" when such reports are made to certain authorized agencies. 24-A M.R.S.A. § 2187.

G. Vicarious Liability of Employers for Statements Made by Employees

1. ***Scope of Employment.*** An employer may be held liable for an employee's defamation committed during the course of his employment under the doctrine of respondeat superior. Rippett v. Bemis, 672 A.2d 82 (Me. 1996).

a. **Blogging.** There are no Maine cases addressing blogging.

2. ***Damages.*** There are no reported cases in Maine addressing the issue of liability for damages in claims based on vicarious liability. Based on Rippett, supra, although recovery of damages was not specifically discussed, an employer would be held responsible for any compensatory damages that were awarded.

H. Internal Investigations.

There are no Maine cases addressing potential employer liability for libel based on internal investigations.

IV. OTHER ACTIONS BASED ON STATEMENTS

A. Negligent Hiring, Retention, and Supervision

Maine recognizes the torts of negligent hiring, retention, and supervision. See, e.g., Dexter v. Town of Norway, 1998 ME 195, 715 A.2d 169; Swanson v. Roman Catholic Bishop of Portland, 1997 ME 63, 692 A.2d 441. There are no reported cases interrelating such torts to defamation claims.

B. Intentional Infliction of Emotional Distress

The tort of intentional infliction of emotional distress has been recognized as separate and distinct from defamation, even though the emotional distress was caused by the slanderous statements. Calvert v. Corthell, 599 A.2d 69 (Me. 1991). The tort of negligent infliction of emotional distress, however, is subsumed within a claim for defamation when based on the slanderous statements. Packard v. Central Maine Power Co., 477 A.2d 264 (Me. 1984).

The Maine Supreme Court has recognized the exclusivity provision of the Maine Workers' Compensation Act as a defense to claims seeking damages brought by fellow employees for intentional infliction of emotional distress. Cole v. Chandler, 2000 ME 104, 752 A.2d 1189. The Court noted that the exclusivity provision was intended to provide immunity from all work-related claims for personal injuries, which include both mental and physical injuries, against employers or fellow employees. Because the claims for intentional infliction of emotional distress sought recovery only for mental injuries, the Court reasoned that the exclusivity provision would apply.

C. Interference with Economic Advantage

The Maine Supreme Judicial Court has held that where claims of defamation, interference with economic advantage, and intentional infliction of emotional distress all arose from the same statements, all such torts were also subject to a conditional privilege. Onat v. Penobscot Bay Medical Center, 574 A.2d 872 (Me. 1990). The Maine Supreme Court dealt with the issue once again in a more recent case. Cole, supra. A discharged employee brought actions seeking recovery from two former fellow employees for, among other things, interference with an advantageous economic relationship, i.e., his employment relationship. The Court recognized the exclusivity provision of the Maine Workers' Compensation Act as a defense to those portions of the claims seeking recovery for personal injuries, which the Court defined as "mental or physical injuries." Those portions of the claims that sought damages for injuries to economic wellbeing were not subject to the protections afforded by the exclusivity provision. The Court held that those latter portions were, however, subject to the conditional privilege afforded defamation defendants under Maine law, provided any such privilege was not abused.

The First Circuit Court of Appeals affirmed the District Court's denial of a claim for an unreasonable/ unconstitutional deprivation of freedom from government interference with the plaintiff's private employment. Mead v. Independence Association, 684 F.3d 226 (1st Cir. 2012). A discharged employee of a state regulated private operator of assisted living facilities brought an action against her employer and the two state employees responsible for an inspection report that allegedly contributed to the employer's decision to terminate the plaintiff. The Court found that the employer was a nonstate actor immune from liability for unconstitutional actions. The Court also upheld the dismissal of the claims against the two state employees, holding that the complaint did not allege facts that would support a claim for unreasonable government interference with plaintiff's private employment or a claim for unconstitutional stigmatization.

D. Prima Facie Tort

There are no reported cases in Maine addressing prima facie tort.

V. OTHER ISSUES

A. Statute of Limitations

Maine applies a two-year statute of limitations for both libel and slander. 14 M.R.S.A. § 753 (1964). See also Small v. Inhabitants of the City of Belfast, 547 F. Supp. 761 (D. Me. 1982); Franklin v. Erickson, 128 Me. 181, 146 A. 437 (Me. 1929).

B. Jurisdiction

The Maine Supreme Court has held that in instances when a denied motion for summary judgment was based on issues of privilege and/or immunity, the Supreme Court will review such denials "based on judicially created exceptions to the final judgment rule." Morgan v. Kooistra, 2008 ME 26, ¶ 18, 941 A.2d 447, 453.

There are no statutes addressing the issue of jurisdiction in defamation cases.

C. Worker's Compensation Exclusivity

The exclusivity provision of the Maine Workers' Compensation Act may be found at 39-A M.R.S.A. § 204. The Maine Supreme Judicial Court has recognized the statute as a defense to portions, but not all, of the damages sought in a claim against fellow employees for defamation and other employment-related torts. Cole v. Chandler, 2000 ME 024, 752 A.2d 1189. The Court recognized the exclusivity provision as a defense to those portions of the claim seeking recovery for personal injuries, which the Court defined as "mental or physical injuries." Those portions of the claim that sought damages for injuries to economic wellbeing were not subject to the protections afforded by the exclusivity provision. See also II.C, infra.

D. Pleading Requirements

Although a libel defendant is entitled to know precisely what statement is attributed to him, and the words must be proved strictly as alleged, Picard v. Brennan, 307 A.2d 833 (Me. 1973), there are no reported appellate decisions in which a dismissal has been granted based on a failure of the plaintiff to allege the exact words. Affirmative defenses, including privilege, must be pleaded affirmatively. Boulet v. Beals, 177 A.2d 665 (Me. 1962).

SURVEY OF MAINE EMPLOYMENT PRIVACY LAW

Geoffrey K. Cummings, Esq.
Matthew J. LaMourie, Esq.
Preti, Flaherty, Beliveau & Pachios LLP
One City Center
P. O. Box 9546
Portland, Maine 04112-9546
Telephone: (207) 791-3000; Facsimile: (207) 791-3111

(With Developments Reported Through **November 1, 2012**)

GENERAL COMMENTS

The Maine court system includes two levels of trial courts, the District Court and the Superior Court. The Superior Court has original jurisdiction over all civil actions, unless otherwise specified by statute. Bench and jury trials are available in the Superior Court. All trials in the District Court are bench trials. Appeals from both the District and Superior Courts are to the Maine Supreme Judicial Court, commonly known as the Law Court when sitting in its capacity as an appellate court. Unless otherwise specified by statute, any civil matter may also be brought in the District Court provided that no equitable relief is demanded. Maine has no intermediate level appeals tribunal.

The only officially reported decisions in Maine are those of the Maine Supreme Judicial Court appearing in the Maine Reporter through 1965 and thereafter in the Atlantic Reporter. Maine's judicial system initiated a new citation form as of January 1, 1997. In addition to citations to the Atlantic Reporter, state courts require citation to the calendar year of the opinion, followed by a sequential number assigned to the opinion. Each paragraph in the opinion is preceded by a paragraph number, which is required for pinpoint citations. (e.g., Vogt v. Churchill, 1997 ME 7, ¶ 1, 687 A.2d 961).). These sequential numbers and paragraph numbers appear on all opinions issued after January 1, 1997.

SIGNIFICANT DEVELOPMENTS SINCE THE 2012 *SURVEY*

None.

I. GENERAL LAW OF PRIVACY

A. Legal Basis of Privacy Claims

Civil privacy claims in the State of Maine are based on common law. Maine has recognized the tort of invasion of privacy as it is set forth in § 652A of the Restatement (Second) of Torts. Nelson v. Maine Times, 373 A.2d 1221 (Me. 1977). Accordingly, an invasion of privacy occurs when an individual has (1) appropriated another individual's name or likeness for the individual's benefit, (2) placed another individual in a false light in the public eye, (3) publicly disclosed private facts, or (4) intruded upon another individual's physical and mental solitude or seclusion. Id.; see also Loe v. Town of Thomaston, 600 A.2d 1090 (Me. 1991). Invasion of privacy is an intentional tort. Maine Mut. Fire Ins. Co. v. Gervaise, 1998 ME 197, 715 A.2d 938.

Maine has a criminal statute that provides criminal penalties for certain violations of privacy. The statute reads as follows:

> 1. A person is guilty of violation of privacy if, except in the execution of a public duty or as authorized by law, that person intentionally:
>
> A. Commits a civil trespass on property with the intent to overhear or observe any person in a private place;
>
> B. Installs or uses in a private place without the consent of the person or persons entitled to privacy in that place, any device for observing, photographing, recording, amplifying or broadcasting sounds or events in that place;
>
> C. Installs or uses outside a private place without the consent of the person or persons entitled to privacy therein, any device for hearing, recording, amplifying or broadcasting sounds originating in that place that would not ordinarily be audible or comprehensible outside that place; or

D. Engages in visual surveillance in a public place by means of mechanical or electronic equipment with the intent to observe or photograph, or record, amplify or broadcast an image of any portion of the body of another person present in that place when that portion of the body is in fact concealed from public view under clothing and a reasonable person would expect it to be safe from surveillance.

1-A. It is a defense to a prosecution under subsection 1, paragraph D that the person subject to surveillance had in fact attained 14 years of age and had consented to the visual surveillance.

2. As used in this section "private place" means a place where one may reasonably expect to be safe from surveillance but does not include a place to which the public or a substantial group has access.

3. Violation of privacy is a Class D crime.

17-A M.R.S.A. § 511. The statute provides for no private cause of action. A comment by the drafting committee indicates that the statute is intended to prevent seeing or hearing things that are justifiably expected to be private. The definition of "private place" as set forth in subsection 2 obviously limits the application of the statute. There have been no reported cases brought under the statute.

B. Causes of Action

1. ***Misappropriation/Right of Publicity.*** Maine has recognized the tort of invasion of privacy by appropriation of name or likeness, as set forth in the Restatement (Second) of Torts:

> One who appropriates to his own use or benefit the name or likeness of another is subject to liability to the other for invasion of his privacy.

Nelson v. Maine Times, 373 A.2d 1221 (Me. 1977) (quoting Restatement (Second) of Torts § 652C (1976)).

We believe the Maine Supreme Court, given the opportunity, would apply Maine's six-year statute of limitations, 14 M.R.S.A. § 752, to a cause of action for invasion of privacy based on misappropriation. But see I.B.2, infra.

2. ***False Light.*** Maine has recognized the tort of invasion of privacy as a result of publicity that unreasonably places the other in a false light before the public. Nelson v. Maine Times, 373 A.2d 1221 (Me. 1977); Cole v. Chandler, 2000 ME 204, 752 A.2d 1189. The Court has adopted the tort as set forth in the Restatement (Second) of Torts:

> One who gives publicity to a matter concerning another that places the other before the public in a false light is subject to liability to the other for invasion of his privacy, if (a) the false light in which the other was placed would be highly offensive to a reasonable person, and (b) the actor had knowledge of or acted in reckless disregard as to the falsity of the publicized matter and the false light in which the other would be placed.

Restatement (Second) of Torts § 652E (1977).

The Maine Supreme Court has recognized the Maine Workers' Compensation Act as a defense to portions, but not all, of the damages sought in a claim for invasion of privacy based on publicity which places the plaintiff in a false light in the public eye. Cole v. Chandler, 2000 ME 204, 752 A.2d 1189. A discharged employee brought actions seeking recovery from two former fellow employees for, among other things, false light invasion of privacy. The Court recognized the exclusivity provision of the Workers' Compensation Act as a defense to those portions of the claim seeking recovery for personal injuries, which the Court defined as "mental or physical injuries." Those portions of the claim that sought damages for injuries to economic wellbeing were not subject to the protections afforded by the exclusivity provision. See also VII.A and B, infra.

In a civil rights case brought by a physician, the First Circuit upheld the decision of the Maine Federal District Court, which determined that Maine's Supreme Judicial Court, given the opportunity, would apply a two-year statute of limitations to "false light" actions. The Court reasoned that a "false light" action would, in many cases, coincide with a defamation action. Maine's two-year statute of limitations, 14 M.R.S.A. § 753, applies to actions for "assault and battery, false imprisonment, and slander and libel." The First Circuit held that applying the six-year statute of limitations to false light cases would defeat "the obvious legislative intent to impose a relatively short period of limitations for the bringing of defamation actions." Gashgai v. Leibowitz, 703 F.2d 10, 13 (1st Cir. 1983).

3. ***Publication of Private Facts.*** Maine recognizes the tort of invasion of privacy as a result of unreasonable publicity given to the other's private life, as the tort is stated in § 652D of the Restatement (Second) of Torts:

> One who gives publicity to a matter concerning the private life of another is subject to liability to the other for invasion of his privacy, if the matter publicized is of a kind that (a) would be highly offensive to a reasonable person, and (b) is not of legitimate concern to the public.

Nelson v. Maine Times, 373 A.2d 1221 (Me. 1977) (quoting Restatement (Second) of Torts § 652D (1976)).

The Maine Supreme Court has ruled that the release by a town of the details of a municipal employee's resignation and settlement did not constitute the tort of invasion of privacy by publication of private facts. Loe v. Town of Thomaston, 600 A.2d 1090 (Me. 1991).

The First Circuit has upheld a Maine Federal District Court decision in which it was ruled that an employee who was denied immediate payment of his benefits upon retiring could not prevail on a claim of invasion of privacy through publication of private facts when officers of the retirement plan sent a letter to the attorney of the employee's former wife stating that the employee had recently terminated his employment and that the officers were concerned about making any distribution of the retirement account before having definite assurance that the former wife had no claim or rights to any of the proceeds. Lodge v. Shell Oil Co., 747 F.2d 16 (1st Cir. 1984).

We believe the Maine Supreme Court, given the opportunity, would apply Maine's six-year statute of limitations, 14 M.R.S.A. § 752, to a cause of action for invasion of privacy based on publication of private facts. But see I.B.2, supra.

4. ***Intrusion.*** The Maine Supreme Judicial Court has recognized the tort of invasion of privacy as a result of unreasonable intrusion upon the solitude of another, as set forth in § 652B of the Restatement (Second) of Torts:

> One who intentionally intrudes, physically or otherwise, upon the solitude or seclusion of another or his private affairs or concerns, is subject to liability to the other for invasion of his privacy, if the intrusion would be highly offensive to a reasonable person.

Nelson v. Maine Times, 373 A.2d 1221 (Me. 1977) (quoting Restatement (Second) of Torts, § 652B (1976)).

The Maine Supreme Court has ruled that the release by a town of the details of a municipal employee's resignation and settlement did not constitute the tort of invasion of privacy by publication of private facts or by intrusion. Loe v. Town of Thomaston, 600 A.2d 1090 (Me. 1991).

We believe the Maine Supreme Court, given the opportunity, would apply Maine's six-year statute of limitations, 14 M.R.S.A. § 752, to a cause of action for intrusion of privacy by intrusion. But see I.B.2, supra.

C. Other Privacy-Related Actions

1. ***Intentional Infliction of Emotional Distress.*** Maine recognizes the tort of intentional infliction of emotional distress in an employment environment. Staples v. Bangor Hydro-Electric Co., 461 A.2d 499 (Me. 1989). The action raised counts for wrongful discharge, deprivation of due process, defamation, and intentional infliction of emotional distress. The Court analyzed the wrongful discharge and intentional infliction of emotional distress counts separately. With respect to the wrongful discharge claim the Court found that Maine's doctrine of employee-at-will controlled. With respect to the emotional distress claim, the Court found no evidence that the employer's conduct was "so extreme and outrageous as to exceed 'all possible bounds of decency' and must be regarded as 'atrocious, and utterly intolerable in a civilized community.'" Id. at 501 (citing Vicnire v. Ford Motor Credit Co., 401 A.2d 148, 154 (Me. 1979) (quoting Restatement (Second) of Torts § 46, comment d)(1965)). Plaintiff's potential remedies included compensatory as well as punitive damages. The Court noted no particular privileges or defenses in viewing the intentional infliction of emotional distress claim separately and freestanding from all others.

In a more recent case, the Maine Supreme Court recognized the exclusivity provision of the Maine Workers' Compensation Act as a defense to claims seeking damages brought by fellow employees for intentional infliction of emotional distress. Cole v. Chandler, 2000 ME 204, 752 A.2d 1189. The Court noted that the exclusivity provision was intended to provide immunity from all work-related claims for personal injuries, which include both mental and physical injuries, against employers or fellow employees. Because the claim for intentional infliction of emotional distress sought recovery only for mental injuries, the Court reasoned that the exclusivity provision would apply.

2. ***Interference With Prospective Economic Advantage.*** Maine recognizes the cause of action for tortious interference with an employment contract. Global v. Minette-Mills, Inc., 638 A.2d 712 (Me. 1994). A former employee alleged that he had been discharged as a result of actions taken by two employees of another company. The action sought damages based on multiple theories, including tortious interference with an advantageous business relationship. The Court held that a party could recover damages for tortious interference with a contract if a defendant, by fraud or intimidation, procured the breach of a contract that would have continued but for such wrongful interference. Id. at 716 (citing C. N. Brown Co. v. Gillin, 569 A.2d 1206, 1210 (Me. 1990)). The Court ruled that compensatory and punitive damages were recoverable against both the employing entity and the two employees. The Court did not identify any particular privileges or defenses that might be available in such a case.

The Maine Supreme Court dealt with the issue once again in a more recent case. Cole, supra. A discharged employee brought actions seeking recovery from two former fellow employees for, among other things, interference with an advantageous economic relationship, i.e., his employment relationship. The Court recognized the exclusivity provision of the Maine Workers' Compensation Act as a defense to those portions of the claim seeking recovery for personal injuries, which the Court defined as "mental or physical injuries." Those portions of the claim that sought damages for injuries to economic wellbeing were not subject to the protections afforded by the exclusivity provision. The Court held that those latter portions were, however, subject to the conditional privilege afforded defamation defendants under Maine law, provided any such privilege was not abused.

3. ***Prima Facie Tort.*** There are no reported cases in Maine addressing prima facie tort.

II. EMPLOYER TESTING OF EMPLOYEES

In cases involving employer testing, Maine courts have not made any distinction between private and public employers.

A. Psychological or Personality Testing

On only one occasion has the Maine Supreme Judicial Court discussed the issue of psychological testing. Maine Human Rights Commission v. City of Auburn, 425 A.2d 990 (Me. 1981). In that case, the Court held that, following a finding of unlawful sex discrimination in the recruitment of police officers by the city, it was premature for the trial court to have ordered the immediate hiring of two female applicants, without either requiring the applicants to pass agility and psychological tests required of all applicants or determining that the tests were not free of any unlawfully discriminatory features or consequences. One of the issues dealt with by the Court was whether the city could establish that the psychological test had any relationship to the applicants' ability to perform the functions of the job. The Maine Human Rights Act, 5 M.R.S.A. § 4551, et seq., prohibits discrimination in the employment of disabled employees. A provision limits the use of "medical examinations," but makes no specific mention of psychological testing. 5 M.R.S.A. § 4572. The limitations on "medical examinations," which are not defined, may very well also apply to psychological or personality examinations, since the Act refers to "physical or mental" disability. 5 M.R.S.A. § 4571. See II.C, infra. There are no other statutes or cases that suggest any limits or restrictions on the use of psychological or personality testing by an employer, whether public or private.

B. Drug Testing

Drug testing in Maine is strictly governed and strictly limited by a series of complex statutes. 26 M.R.S.A. § 681, et seq. The statutes essentially bar all substance abuse testing of applicants or employees except in those businesses that have established a substance abuse testing program that has been submitted to and been approved by the Office of Substance Abuse of the State of Maine. Such programs are subject to numerous requirements and limitations. Statutes prohibit an employer from requiring, requesting, or even suggesting that any applicant or employee take a drug test unless all requirements of the statutes have been met. In addition, the statutes prohibit an employer from requiring, requesting, or suggesting that an employee or applicant waive that employee's or applicant's rights as established by the statutes. A confidentiality provision mandates that, unless the employee or applicant consents, all information obtained by the employer during the testing process be kept confidential. 26 M.R.S.A. § 685. Breach of the confidentiality provisions may result in a penalty of up to $1,000 for the first offense and up to $2,000 for the second offense. 26 M.R.S.A. § 689. The statutory definition of "employer" includes both public and private entities, so there is no differentiation between each class of employer. 26 M.R.S.A. § 682

C. Medical Testing

Limitations on medical testing may be found in the Maine Human Rights Act. 5 M.R.S.A. § 4551, et seq. An employer, whether public or private, may not require a medical examination of an applicant unless and until an offer of employment has been made to the individual and all entering employees are subjected to the same examination regardless of the possible existence of a disability. 5 M.R.S.A. § 4572. The statute further provides that information obtained regarding the medical condition or history of an applicant is to be collected and maintained on separate forms and in separate medical files and must be treated as a confidential medical record, with certain specific exceptions. Id. Similarly, an employer may not require a medical examination of an employee unless the examination or inquiry is shown to be job related and consistent with business necessity. Id. The Maine Supreme Judicial Court has noted without comment that all applicants for police officer positions were required to take and pass a medical examination before being allowed to take written and oral examinations. Maine Human Rights Commission v. City of Auburn, 425 A.2d 990 (Me. 1981). See II.A, supra. There is no suggestion in the decision that there is anything inappropriate about medical testing, other than the limitations set forth in the Maine Human Rights Act. The subsection of the Act cited above which mandates that a medical examination be given only after an offer of employment has been made was enacted in 1995, and thus after the court's decision in Maine Human Rights Commission v. City of Auburn, supra.

D. Polygraph Tests

The Maine Legislature has enacted statutes prohibiting an employer from requiring, requesting, or suggesting that any applicant for employment submit to a polygraph examination as a condition of obtaining employment. 32 M.R.S.A. § 7166. Similarly, no employer may require, request, or suggest that any current employee submit to a polygraph examination as a condition of employment, administer, or cause to be administered to an employee any such examination, or use or refer to results of such examination for any employment purposes. Id. The statute exempts law enforcement agencies from its prohibitions. It also allows an employee to voluntarily request a polygraph examination in connection with his employment, and allows an employer to use or refer to the results of an examination so requested, provided that the results may not be used against the employee by the employer for any purpose. Id. There are no recorded cases citing the statute. In an employment defamation case, the Maine Supreme Judicial Court held that it was reversible error for the trial court to have admitted evidence of the plaintiff's willingness to take a lie detector test. Heselton v. Wilder, 496 A.2d 1063 (Me. 1985).

E. Fingerprinting

Teachers and other educational personnel are required, at the time they seek certification or renewal of their certification, to submit fingerprints to the Department of Education. The fingerprints would then be utilized for the purpose of conducting state and national criminal history record checks. 20-A M.R.S.A. § 6103. Any subject of such a federal or state criminal record check may obtain a copy of the results of the check by following the appropriate federal or state procedures. Id. School bus operators are not subject to the fingerprinting requirements. 29-A M.R.S.A. § 2303. There are no other statutes or cases concerning or limiting fingerprinting in an employment context.

III. SEARCHES

Article I, Section 5 of the Constitution of the State of Maine prohibits unreasonable searches and seizures of individuals and their "houses, papers, and possessions." There are, however, no statutory provisions specifically dealing with searches in the workplace.

A. Employee's Person

1. ***Private Employers.*** There are no statutory or constitutional provisions governing searches of employees by private employers. The Maine Supreme Judicial Court has not had the occasion to deal with the issue. We believe that any lawsuit based on an employer's search of an employee's person would be based on the tort of invasion of privacy by intrusion. See I.B.4, supra. Private employers have the ability to expand the scope of what constitutes a reasonable intrusion by putting employees on notice that they are subject to searches.

2. ***Public Employers.*** Public employers would be governed by Article I, Section 5 of the Constitution of the State of Maine as well as the parallel provisions set forth in the Fourth Amendment of the U.S. Constitution. There are no reported Maine cases addressing a public employee's rights with respect to a search of his or her person.

B. Employee's Work Area

1. ***Private Employers.*** There are no statutory or constitutional provisions concerning searches of a private employee's work area. We believe that any such claims would be based on a cause of action for invasion of privacy by intrusion. In a criminal case involving the seizure of items from a safe, the Maine Supreme Judicial Court focused on the legitimate expectations of privacy with respect to the safe and its contents. State v. Sweatt, 427 A.2d 940 (Me. 1981). In a footnote, the court cited United States v. Torch, 609 F.2d 1088 (4th Cir. 1979) (employee lacked standing to suppress evidence seized from his employer's warehouse in a case where the employee was absent during the search, had no financial interest in the employer company or in the premises, had no area of the warehouse set aside for his own use, and had no right to exclude persons from the premises). Sweatt, 427 A.2d at 945, n.2.

2. ***Public Employers.*** Searches of a public employee's work area would be subject to Article I, Section 5 of the Constitution of the State of Maine. See III.A.2, supra. The constitutionality of a public employer's search of an employee's workplace would be determined by federal precedent. The two relevant factors to be considered are the employee's reasonable expectation of privacy and the reasonableness of the employer's search. Both factors may have different standards, depending on what is being searched. For example, the employee's reasonable expectation of privacy may be lower and the employer's search may be more reasonable when the subject of the search is the employee's office, in contrast to the employee's desk, briefcase, or file cabinets. O'Connor v. Ortega, 580 U.S. 709 (1987).

C. Employee's Property

1. ***Private Employers.*** We believe the analysis of searches of a private employee's property would parallel that set forth above with respect to a private employee's person. See III.A.1, supra.

2. ***Public Employers.*** We believe the analysis of searches of a public employee's property would parallel that set forth above with respect to a public employee's person. See III.A.2, supra.

IV. MONITORING OF EMPLOYEES

A. Telephones and Electronic Communications

Maine statutes prevent the "interception" of any wire or oral communication without the consent of either the sender or receiver of that communication. 15 M.R.S.A. § 710 provides that anyone who intercepts a wire or communication without consent is guilty of a class C crime. In a non-employment context, the Maine Supreme Judicial Court has held that consent for interception of a communication may be conferred from surrounding circumstances indicating that a party willingly agreed to surveillance. State v. Keahling, 601 A.2d 620 (Me. 1991) (citing Griggs-Ryan v. Smith, 904 F.2d 112 (1st Cir. 1990)). The court held that, in the absence of any objection on the part of either participant in a telephone conversation, consent to the recording could be inferred from a statement by the mother of one of the individuals that she would record their conversation if they continued to talk. Accordingly, an employer who makes it clear, as a condition of employment, that an employee's e-mail or telephone conversations are subject to monitoring should be able to avoid any argument that it has violated the interception statute. Violators of the intercept statute are subject to an action seeking actual damages, but not less than $100 per day for each day of violation, as well as reasonable attorney's fees. 15 M.R.S.A. § 711.

1. ***Wiretapping.*** The statute described above applies to any oral communication or any communication made in whole or in part through the use of facilities for transmission of communications by the aid of wire, cable, or other like connection. Accordingly, the statute applies to tapping of telephone conversations. See also Williams v. Poulos, 801 F. Supp. 867 (D. Me. 1992).

2. ***Electronic Communications.*** See IV.A, supra. The statute applies to electronic communications. In United States v. Bunnell, 2002 WL 981457 (D. Me.), the Maine Federal District Court found that where the use of a computer had been assigned at-large to all employees and where the employee was aware that the computer would be accessed by other employees and the employer, the employee's expectation of privacy was not reasonable. The Maine Supreme Judicial Court has suggested that disclosure of a memo to an employee from his personal attorney would normally be subject to attorney/client privilege, but that was stored on a company computer, might constitute an ethical violation if such disclosure took place prior to some form of judicial review. Fibre Materials, Inc. v. Maurice Subilia, 2009 ME 71, 974 A.2d 918.

3. ***Other Electronic Monitoring.*** There are no reported Maine cases addressing other forms of electronic monitoring.

B. Mail

There are no statutes or case law concerning an employee's right of privacy with respect to mail received in the workplace. We believe the courts in Maine would rely on common law causes of action, such as a claim for invasion of privacy for unreasonable intrusion upon the seclusion of another. See I.A.4, supra. Article 1, Section 5 of the Maine Constitution provides that "people shall be secure in their persons, houses, papers and possessions from all unreasonable searches."

C. Surveillance/Photographing

There are no Maine cases or statutes concerning surveillance or photography in an employment context. However, the rules promulgated by the Maine Workers' Compensation Board contain specific provisions concerning the discovery by a plaintiff of surveillance information. Rules and Regulations, Maine Workers' Compensation Board, Ch. 12, Section 14 (1998). Implicit in the provision is the fact that such surveillance or photographing is permitted. Surveillance of employees who have reported work-related injuries by their employer's workers' compensation insurance carrier is not uncommon in Maine. It is believed that any cause of action for an invasion of privacy through surveillance or photography would be based on common law principles defining the invasion of privacy by either unreasonable intrusion or appropriation of one's name or likeness. See I.B.1. and 4, supra.

V. ACTIVITIES OUTSIDE THE WORKPLACE

A. Statute or Common Law

There are no statutory provisions concerning an employee's privacy rights relating to activities outside the workplace. Any causes of action for breach of such rights would have to be derived from common law such as invasions of privacy on either intrusion or publication of private facts theories.

B. Employees' Personal Relationships

1. ***Romantic Relationships Between Employees.*** There are no protections for employees who choose to enter into romantic relationships with other employees. In an action against a county sheriff brought by a deputy who was discharged from his probationary position, it was held that there was no "clearly established" constitutional right to privacy in the deputy's co-habitation relationship with a girlfriend. Struck v. Hackett, 668 A.2d 411 (Me. 1995). The Maine Supreme Judicial Court relied on the U.S. Supreme Court analysis of the "freedom of intimate association" as set forth in Roberts v. United States Jaycees, 468 U.S. 609 (1984) (freedom of association under First Amendment of U.S. Constitution extends to marriages). Accordingly, public employers may be limited in taking employment related actions against an employee based solely on his or her marriage to a co-employee. Private employers would appear to have no such limitations. The Maine Human Rights Act provides protection from discrimination to a number of classes of individuals. 5 M.R.S.A. §§ 4571 and 4572. The statute does not extend protection to individuals based on their marital status or romantic relationships. The Maine Supreme Judicial Court has firmly upheld the doctrine of employee-at-will. Bard v. Bath Iron Works Corp., 590 A.2d 152 (Me. 1991).

2. ***Sexual Orientation.*** Effective 8 November 2005, sexual orientation was added to the list of characteristics afforded protection under the Maine Human Rights Act, 5 M.R.S.A. § 4551, et seq. Several Maine municipalities, including the City of Portland, also have passed ordinances prohibiting discrimination against employees based on sexual orientation. In Higgins v. New Balance Athletic Shoe, Inc., 194 F.3d 252 (1st Cir. 1999) the Court dismissed an employee's claim of sexual harassment, discrimination based on sexual orientation and hostile work environment stating that a claim of sexual harassment exists only where there is discrimination based on sex such that members of one sex are exposed to disadvantageous terms or conditions of employment, not merely when there is workplace harassment involving sexual matters.

3. ***Marital Status***. See V.B.1, supra.

C. Smoking

An employer is prohibited from requiring, as a condition of employment, that any employee or applicant refrain from using tobacco products outside the course of that employment. The statute also prohibits discrimination against an employee with respect to that individual's compensation, terms, conditions, or privileges of employment for using tobacco products outside the course of employment, as long as the employee complies with any workplace policy concerning the use of tobacco. 26 M.R.S.A. § 597.

D. Blogging.

There are no reported Maine cases addressing blogging.

VI. RECORDS

A. Personnel Records

An employee or former employee has the statutory right, upon written request, to review and copy the employee's personnel file. 26 M.R.S.A. § 631. The statute defines a personnel file as including, but not limited to, employee evaluations and reports relating to the employee's character, credit, work habits, compensation and benefits, and non-privileged medical records or nurses' notes relating to the employee. The Maine Supreme Court has expanded what is available as part of a personnel record. Harding v. Wal-Mart, 2001 ME 13, 765 A.2d 73. The Court said that investigative files concerning employee misconduct are records related to "character" and "work habits." Therefore, unless the Legislature acts to specifically exempt those files, they are part of the personnel file of the employee and access must be granted. Failure to provide an employee access, within ten days of the receipt of the request, subjects the employer to a civil fine. Id.

Amendments to the statute enacted by the Legislature in 1999 require that an employer "take adequate steps to ensure the integrity and confidentiality" of personnel records. The statute was previously silent as to confidentiality. The 1999 amendments also specifically allow the maintenance of personnel files in paper, microfiche, or electronic form, provided the employer makes available the equipment necessary to permit review and copying of non-paper records.

Portions of the personnel records, including medical information, of various categories of public employees are made confidential by statute. 5 M.R.S.A. § 7070 (certain personnel and medical records of state employees are confidential and not open to public inspection); 20-A M.R.S.A. § 6101 (certain personnel and medical records of school employees confidential and not open to public inspection); 30-A M.R.S.A. § 503 (certain personnel and medical records of county employees confidential and not open to public inspection); 30-A M.R.S.A. § 2702 (certain personnel and medical records of municipal employees confidential and not open to public inspection). Statutory provisions also allow the inspection and review of personnel files and medical information in the possession of the various categories of public employers. 5 M.R.S.A. § 7071 (state employees); 20-A M.R.S.A. § 6102 (school employees); 30-A M.R.S.A. § 503 (county employees); 30-A M.R.S.A. § 2702 (municipal employees).

B. Medical Records

See VI.A, supra. Also, records relating to the referral or medical treatment of a state employee in the state's employee assistance program are confidential. 5 M.R.S.A. § 957.

C. Criminal Records

There are no statutes or reported cases limiting an employer's reliance upon the criminal record of an applicant or employee. A school must maintain the confidentiality of any criminal records it obtains concerning its employees. 20-A M.R.S.A. § 6103.

D. Subpoenas / Search Warrants

There are no reported Maine cases addressing privacy issues relating to subpoenas.

VII. ACTIONS SUBSEQUENT TO EMPLOYMENT

A. References

There are no reported Maine cases concerning actions brought subsequent to employment that arise out of references. The Maine Legislature has enacted a statute which appears to provide immunity to employers who disclose information about a former employee's job performance or work record to a prospective employer, unless lack of good faith is shown by clear and convincing evidence. The statute includes a proviso indicating that it is not in derogation of any claims or protections previously existing under state law, thus leaving the effectiveness of the immunity suggested by the statute in doubt. 26 M.R.S.A. § 598.

B. Non-Compete Agreements

The Maine Supreme Judicial Court has held that non-competition agreements are contrary to public policy and will be enforced only to the extent they are reasonable in protecting the business interests at issue. Chapman & Drake v. Harrington, 545 A.2d 645 (Me. 1988). The reasonableness of a non-competition agreement is a question of law, to be determined by the courts based on the facts as to its duration, geographic area, and the interests sought to be protected. Id. Despite the Maine Supreme Court's stated limitations on enforcing such agreements, it has not hesitated to do so when faced with the appropriate facts. Id.; Brignull v. Albert, 666 A.2d 82 (Me. 1995).

VIII. OTHER ISSUES

A. Statutes of Limitations

We believe Maine would apply its general statute of limitations of six years to breach of privacy claims. 14 M.R.S.A. § 752. However, the Maine Federal District Court, with the affirmance of the First Circuit Court of Appeals, has applied Maine's two-year statute of limitations, 14 M.R.S.A. § 753, to a false light invasion of privacy claim. Gashgai v. Leibowitz, 703 F.2d 10 (1st Cir. 1983). See I.B.2, supra. Litigants should be warned that a state or federal court in Maine might extend the ruling of Gashgai to other privacy claims and apply a two-year statute of limitations.

B. Jurisdiction

There are no Maine statutes or cases specifically addressing the issue of jurisdiction in employment privacy cases. Such matters may be brought in either the District Court or the Superior Court.

C. Worker's Compensation Exclusivity

The exclusivity provision of the Maine Workers' Compensation Act may be found at 39-A M.R.S.A. § 104. The Maine Supreme Court has recognized the Maine Workers' Compensation Act as a defense to portions, but not all, of the damages sought in a claim for invasion of privacy based on publicity which places the plaintiff in a false light in the public eye. Cole v. Chandler, 2000 ME 204, 752 A.2d 1189. See I.B.2, infra.

D. Pleading Requirements

There are no particular pleading requirements set forth for breach of privacy or other privacy related causes of action. Maine is a "notice pleading" jurisdiction. Notice-pleading simply requires that a defendant be provided with fair notice of the claim against him, and is sufficiently performed by a rather generalized statement. Richards v. Soucy, 610 A.2d 268 (Me. 1992) (citation omitted). Affirmative defenses must be plead affirmatively. Dougherty v. Oliviero, 427 A.2d 487 (Me. 1981) (citing M.R. Civ. P. 8(c)).

SURVEY OF MARYLAND EMPLOYMENT LIBEL LAW

Gary B. Eidelman
Heather R. Pruger
Saul Ewing LLP
500 East Pratt Street
Baltimore, Maryland 21202
Telephone: (410) 332-8975; Facsimile: (410) 332-8976

(With Developments Reported Through **November 1, 2012**)

GENERAL COMMENTS

Maryland has a long history of common law based case law relating to defamation. Cases are reported in the Maryland Reports for the highest appellate court in Maryland and the Maryland Appellate Reports for the intermediate appellate court. All federal cases cited in the survey arose from the District of Maryland.

SIGNIFICANT DEVELOPMENTS SINCE THE 2012 *SURVEY*

None.

I. GENERAL LAW

A. General Employment Law

1. ***At-Will Employment.*** Maryland adheres to the doctrine of at-will employment. Unless otherwise agreed, employment is for an indefinite duration and can be legally terminated at the pleasure of either party at any time, for any reason, even a reason that is arbitrary, capricious, or fundamentally unfair. Suburban Hosp., Inc. v. Dwiggins, 324 Md. 294, 300, 310, 596 A.2d 1069, 1077 (1991) (declining to "impose a general requirement of good faith and fair dealing in at-will employment situations"); Adler v. Am. Std. Corp., 291 Md. 31, 35, 432 A.2d 464, 467 (1981); Deutsch v. Chesapeake Ctr., 27 F. Supp. 2d 642, 644 (D. Md. 1998). Maryland, however, recognizes the tort of wrongful discharge and protects employees where the employer's motivation for discharge contravenes "some clear mandate of public policy." Adler, 291 Md. at 31, 432 A.2d at 473. **The tort of abusive discharge is one of limited scope. Goode v. American Veterans, Inc., Civ. No. 8:11-cv-02414, 2012 WL 2276760, at *5 (D. Md. June 15, 2012).** The complaining party "must plead with particularity the source of the public policy" allegedly violated by the termination. Porterfield v. Mascari II, Inc., 374 Md. 402, 429, 823 A.2d 590, 606 (2003) (holding that Maryland does not recognize a general right to consult with an attorney concerning matters of personal importance as a "clear mandate of public policy," and dismissing an employee's allegation of wrongful discharge for failure to state a claim where she alleged that she was discharged for expressing an intent to seek legal advice prior to responding to an unfavorable work evaluation); Wholey v. Sears Roebuck, 370 Md. 38, 43, 803 A.2d 482, 484 (2002) (explaining that public policy protects employees from termination on the basis of their reports to law enforcement concerning suspected criminal activity, but "does not extend to protect termination of an employee for reporting suspected wrongdoing in the workplace when merely reported to employee's supervisor"); Miller v. US Foodservice, Inc., 405 F. Supp. 2d 607, 610-13 (D. Md. 2005) (employees responding to inquiries from the government in response to an ongoing criminal investigation are protected from wrongful discharge to the same degree as employees who report a suspected crime and thereby initiate the criminal investigation); King v. Marriott Int'l, Inc., 160 Md. App. 689, 707, 866 A.2d 895, 905-06 (2005) (explaining that public policy does not support a fiduciary's claim of wrongful discharge for making "an internal complaint of corporate wrongdoing to co-workers or supervisors," and does not protect "a person who objects, internal to employment, to proposed action on the ground that the person suspects a violation of fiduciary duty"); Kramer v. Mayor and City of Baltimore, 124 Md. App. 616, 634, 723 A.2d 529, 538 (1999) (explaining that a City's Charter, which is not state wide, "do not rise to the level of a "public policy" of this State"). The Maryland Court of Appeals expanded the tort of wrongful discharge in the case of Insignia Residential Corp. v. Ashton, 359 Md. 560, 573, 755 A.2d 1080, 1087 (2000). The Court held that an at-will employee may bring a wrongful discharge claim for refusing to submit to her supervisors' sexual advances, conduct which the Court held constitutes prostitution in violation of a clear mandate of public policy. In holding that such a cause of action exists, the Court recognized as rising to the level of public policy the history of efforts in Maryland to control prostitution and the social problems generated by prostitution. In the same year, the Court further expanded the tort in Griesi v. Atl. Gen. Hosp. Corp., 360 Md. 1, 16, 756 A.2d 548, 556 (2000), holding that a job seeker could sue his or her potential employer for damages if the employer negligently misrepresented a material fact during the pre-hire process, even if the position sought was one for at-will employment. The Court held that a "special relationship" may develop out of extensive interviews and pre-hire negotiations between an employer and interviewee. In such cases, an employer owes a duty to convey accurate information to its prospective hire about material facts.

B. Elements of Libel Claim

1. ***Basic Elements.*** The requisite elements of a prima facie case of employment defamation are as follows:

(1) The alleged defamatory statement or action must expose a person to public scorn, hatred, contempt, or ridicule; or the statement must have imputed to the employee a lack of capacity or qualification to properly fulfill the duties and responsibilities of his job or occupation. Mareck v. Johns Hopkins Univ., 60 Md. App. 217, 222, 482 A.2d 17, 20 (1984), cert. denied, 302 Md. 288, 487 A.2d 292 (1985); Thacker v. City of Hyattsville, 135 Md. App. 268, 762 A.2d 172 (2000) cert. denied, 363 Md. 206, 768 A.2d 55 (2001); Nistico v. Mosler Safe Co., 43 Md. App. 361, 367, 405 A.2d 340, 343 (1979); Mates v. N. Am. Vaccine, Inc., 53 F. Supp. 2d 814 (D. Md. 1999); Dobkin v. Johns Hopkins Univ., 172 F.3d 43 (4th Cir.), cert. denied, 528 U.S. 875 (1999); Severn Marketing Assoc's, Inc. v. Doolin, Civ. No. 09-3295, 2010 WL 3834994, *6 (D. Md. Sept. 29, 2010).

(2) The alleged defamatory statement or action is false and the employer (or its declaring agent) either knew that the statement was false, acted in reckless disregard of the truth or falsity of the statement, or acted negligently in failing to ascertain the truth or falsity of the statement. Reuber v. Food Chem. News, Inc., 899 F.2d 271, 272, 278-80 (4th Cir. 1990); Agora, Inc., v. Axxess, Inc., 90 F. Supp. 2d 697, 701 (D. Md. 2000); Doolin, 2010 WL 3834994 at *6. There is no defamation under Maryland law where an employer produces and disseminates documents accusing the employee of failing to comport his appearance with regulations to the extent that no false statement was made about the employee and the employee violated rules, regardless of the employee's contention that rules or their application violated his constitutional rights. Booth v. Maryland, 207 F. Supp. 2d 394 (D. Md. 2002), aff'd in part, rev'd in part, 327 F.3d 377 (4th Cir. 2003).

(3) The alleged defamation was communicated by the employer (or its declaring agent) by words or actions to a third party who reasonably recognized the communication to be defamatory. De Leon v. St. Joseph Hosp. Inc., 871 F.2d 1229, 1236-37 (4th Cir. 1989); Doolin, 2010 WL 3834994 at *6.

(4) The employer made the statement with malice; that is, with knowledge of falsity or reckless disregard of the truth, or otherwise abused a qualified privilege to make the defamatory communication (assuming that this privilege was raised by the employer and found applicable by the court). Reuber, 899 F.2d at 279-80.

(5) The employee was actually damaged by the defamation. Id.; Doolin, 2010 WL 3834994 at *6.

2. ***Fault.*** In Maryland, proof of fault is based on a standard of negligence. Jacron Sales Co. v. Sindorf, 276 Md. 580, 350 A.2d 688 (1976). Applying the standard established by the Supreme Court in Gertz v. Robert Welch, Inc., 418 U.S. 323, 348-50 (1974), the Court of Special Appeals held that, while private employers are not generally liable for their employees' defamatory communications, a private employer may be held liable for such communications upon proof of the employer's negligence. Bagwell v. Peninsula Reg'l Med. Ctr., 106 Md. App. 470, 511, 665 A.2d 297, 317 (1995), cert. denied, 341 Md. 172, 669 A.2d 1360 (1996).

a. **Private Figure Plaintiff/Matter of Public Concern.** One who publishes a false and defamatory communication concerning a private person in relation to a private or public matter is subject to liability if the employer (or its declaring agent) negligently failed to ascertain the falsity of the defamatory statement. Metromedia, Inc. v. Hillman, 285 Md. 161, 170-72, 400 A.2d 1117, 1122-23 (1979).

b. **Private Figure Plaintiff/Matter of Private Concern.** One who publishes a false and defamatory communication concerning a private person in relation to a private or public matter, is subject to liability, if the employer (or its declaring agent) negligently failed to ascertain the falsity of the defamatory statement. Metromedia, 285 Md. at 170-72, 400 A.2d at 1122-23.

c. **Public Figure Plaintiff/Matter of Public Concern.** The federal constitutional standard from New York Times Co. v. Sullivan, 376 U.S. 254 (1964)—actual malice—applies to Maryland defamation actions involving public figures and matters of public concern. Snyder v. Phelps, 580 F.3d 206, 218 (4th Cir. 2009), aff'd, 131 S. Ct. 1207, 1215-19 (2011) (discussing the ill-defined boundaries of the public concern test). If the alleged defamation relates to private matters not concerning or affecting a public figure in a public capacity, however, the negligence standard will apply. Jacron, 276 Md. 580, 350 A.2d 688. See Snyder, 580 F.3d at 218; Carroll v. City of Westminster, 52 F. Supp. 2d 546 (D. Md. 1999), aff'd, 233 F.3d 208 (4th Cir. 2000).

3. ***Falsity.*** The plaintiff bears the burden of pleading and proving falsity. Jacron, 276 Md. at 600, 350 A.2d at 700. In actions governed by a negligence standard, the plaintiff must prove falsity of an alleged defamatory statement by a preponderance of the evidence. Id. Where an actual malice standard is applied, however, a plaintiff must prove falsity by clear and convincing evidence. Batson v. Shiflett, 325 Md. 684, 722, 602 A.2d 1191 (1992). A statement is not false unless the truth would have a different effect on the mind of the reader. Biospherics, Inc. v. Forbes, Inc., 151 F.3d 180, 185 (4th Cir. 1999). See also McReady v. O'Malley, 804 F. Supp. 2d 427, 442-44 (D. Md. 2011) (dismissing an employee's defamation claim where he failed to provide any evidence that the statements made by his former employer were false); Davidson-Nadwodny v. Wal-Mart Assoc., Inc., Civ. No. CCB-07-2595, 2008 WL 2415035 (D. Md. June 3, 2008) (dismissing an employee's claim that her employer defamed her by referencing her complaints of sexual harassment because the employer's statements were true).

4. ***Defamatory Statement of Fact.*** A defamatory statement is one "spoken of a person in his office, trade, profession or business which tends to expose him to the hazard of losing his office, or which charges him with fraud, indirect dealings or incapacity. . . . The words must go so far as to impute some incapacity or lack of due qualification to fill the position." Fennell v. G.A.C. Fin. Corp., 242 Md. 209, 219, 218 A.2d 492, 497 (1966). See also Nistico, 43 Md. App. at 367, 405 A.2d at 343 (holding that a statement is defamatory if "it implies [an employee] was untrustworthy and not a fit person to perform the type of work in which he specialized"). While a statement need not be one of pure "fact" to form the basis for a defamation claim, such a claim cannot be based on statements of "loose, figurative, or hyperbolic language" or "exaggerated rhetoric" which a person could not reasonably believe asserted actual fact. Snyder, 580 F.3d at 219-21. A statement of opinion is also insufficient. McReady, 804 F.Supp.2d at 441. In other words, a statement "that adversely affects [an employee's] fitness for the proper conduct of his business . . . [is] actionable per se at common law." Hearst Corp. v. Hughes, 297 Md. 112, 118, 466 A.2d 486 (1983). "[T]he words must go so far as to impute to him some incapacity or lack of due qualification to fill the position." Foley v. Hoffman, 188 Md. 273, 284, 52 A.2d 476, 481 (1947) (quoting Sillars v. Collier, 23 N.E. 723 (Mass. 1890)). The defamatory statement must be such that, "if true, would disqualify him or render him less fit properly to fulfill the duties incident to the special character assumed." Kilgour v. Evening Star Newspaper Co., 96 Md. 16, 29, 53 A. 716, 719 (1902). E.g., Murray v. U. Food and Comm'l Worker's Union, Local 400, 229 F. Supp. 2d 465, 477-78 (D. Md. 2002), aff'd, 100 Fed. Appx. 165, *11 (4th Cir. June 9, 2004) (affirmance unpublished) (dismissing a union organizer's defamation claim based on statements made by the union regarding the organizer's alleged incapacity to perform his occupation because the union made the statement without malice and under a good faith belief that the statement was true, and the organizer suffered no actual harm).

5. ***Of and Concerning Plaintiff.*** A plaintiff alleging defamation must prove that the contested statement was "of and concerning him or her." AIDS Counseling and Testing Ctrs. v. Group W TV, 903 F.2d 1000, 1005 (4th Cir. 1990). Whether a statement refers to the plaintiff is a question of fact and depends on whether the statement was reasonably understood by readers or listeners to refer to the plaintiff. Goldsborough v. Orem & Johnson, 103 Md. 671, 682, 64 A. 36 (1906); Snyder, 580 F.3d at 222-26.

6. ***Publication.*** A plaintiff alleging defamation must allege and prove that the purportedly defamatory statement was intentionally published to a third party. Mareck v. Johns Hopkins Univ., 60 Md. App. 217, 223, 482 A.2d 17, 20, cert. denied, 302 Md. 288, 487 A.2d 292 (1985). In the employment context, publication generally occurs when an employer or its agent conveys a defamatory communication to a third person who understands its defamatory meaning. Id. Where, however, an employee lacks any evidence that his employer took affirmative steps to publish allegedly defamatory statements outside of the company, the employee's claim is without merit. Kerr v. The Johns Hopkins Univ., Civ. No. L-10-3294, 2011 WL 4072437, *6 (D. Md. Sept. 12, 2011). See also Baker v. Kent County Bd. of Educ., Civ. No. RDB-07-824, 2007 WL 2694210 (D. Md. Sept. 10, 2007) (holding that plaintiff failed to establish a prima facie case of defamation where she alleged only that the Assistant Superintendent and members of the Board of Education "assisted and/or acquiesced" in the publication of alleged defamatory statements); Silvera v. Home Depot U.S.A., Inc., 189 F. Supp. 2d 304 (D. Md. 2002) (holding that hearsay deposition testimony concerning publication of a defamatory statement could not support allegations of defamation); Samuels v. Tschechtelin, 135 Md. App. 483, 531, 763 A.2d 209, 235 (2000) ("The terminated employee must show that his former employer has published false statements about him.").

a. **Intracorporate Communication.** Publication by an agent of a corporation can occur by a defamatory communication made among employees, whether within or outside of the corporation. Gambrill v. Schooley, 93 Md. 48, 60-61, 48 A. 730, 731 (1901) (holding that publication occurred when a stenographer recorded the employer's libelous letter). In Maryland, however, employers are not liable for publication of defamatory statements by an employee who is not acting as the employer's agent, Reaves v. Westinghouse Elec. Corp., 683 F. Supp. 521, 526 (D. Md. 1988), absent negligence on the employer's part, see I.B.2, supra.

b. **Compelled Self-Publication.** The tort of compelled self-publication is not recognized in Maryland. Accordingly, employers are not liable for compelled self-publication. De Leon v. St. Joseph Hosp., Inc., 871 F.2d 1229 (4th Cir. 1989).

c. **Republication.** One who republishes a defamatory statement adopts it as his own, and is liable in equal measure to the victim. Woodruff v. Trepel, 125 Md. App. 381, 399, 725 A.2d 612, 621 (1999); Helinski v. Rosenberg, 90 Md. App. 158, 164-65, 600 A.2d 882, 885-86, rev'd on other grounds, 328 Md. 664, 616 A.2d 866 (1992). The original publisher is liable for republication by others if republication was foreseeable as natural and probable; foreseeability is a jury question. Shepard v. Nabb, 84 Md. App. 687, 581 A.2d 839 (1990).

7. ***Statements versus Conduct.*** Actionable defamation may occur either by words or actions. Caldor, Inc. v. Bowden, 330 Md. 632, 655, 625 A.2d 959, 970 (1993) (holding that parading an employee through store in handcuffs could reasonably give rise to defamatory meaning); Gen. Motors Corp. v. Piskor, 277 Md. 165, 171 n.2, 352 A.2d 810, 815 n.2 (1976) (finding defamation where a plant guard forcibly detained an employee in full view of potentially thousands of employees, thereby reasonably and falsely inferring the employee's theft). But see Mates v. N. Am. Vaccine, Inc., 53 F. Supp. 2d 814 (D. Md. 1999) (finding no defamation where a press release published on an Internet web site was simply an announcement). There is no "defamation by arrest" cause of action in Maryland. Thacker v. City of Hyattsville, 135 Md. App. 268, 762 A.2d 172 (2000).

8. ***Damages.*** There is no presumption that a defamed employee has suffered damages. Rather, damages must be alleged in the complaint with particularity, and must be proven. Mareck, 60 Md. App. at 223, 482 A.2d at 21. In order for a defamation claim to succeed, the plaintiff must show that he or she has sustained actual injury. Quality Sys., Inc. v. Warman, 132 F. Supp. 2d 349 (D. Md. 2001); Brown v. Prince George's Hosp., Civ. No. RWT-09-295, 2011 WL 2413344, *6 (D. Md. June 9, 2011) (granting summary judgment against an employee who failed to present any evidence to support her assertions that she suffered $340,000 in back pay and $1 million in future losses, but was unable to identify any positions for which she was not selected as a result of the alleged defamation).

Damages are allowed only where actual injury has been established, which can include "impairment of reputation and standing in the community, personal humiliation and mental anguish and suffering." Jacron, 276 Md. at 587, 350 A.2d at 692. Damages for actual injury are not limited to out-of-pocket loss. Nistico, 43 Md. App. at 368 n.2, 405 A.2d at 344 n.2. Damages for loss of consortium based on defamation can also be recovered, even in the absence of physical injury arising from the defamation. Exxon Corp. USA v. Schoene, 67 Md. App. 412, 508 A.2d 142 (1986). Any failure to allege and prove actual injury should result in a judgment in favor of the defendant, even if the plaintiff otherwise establishes that he was defamed. Nistico, 43 Md. App. at 368 n.2, 405 A.2d at 344 n.2. That said, upon a showing of actual injury and clear and convincing evidence of malice, prospective, presumed, and/or punitive damages may also be permitted. See I.B.8.b, infra.

While Maryland has a statutory damages cap that generally limits recovery of damages in tort claims for all non-economic compensatory damages, Maryland courts have held that the cap does not apply to cases involving intentional torts. See Md. Code Ann., Cts. & Jud. Proc. § 11-108 (**2011**) (establishing caps for non-economic compensatory damages based on the date of accrual of the action); Muenstermann by Muenstermann v. U.S., 787 F. Supp. 499, 528 (D. Md. 1992) (explaining that the compensatory damages cap applies only to causes of action in which the negligent acts occurred within the period capped by the statute); Lawson v. U.S., 454 F. Supp. 2d 373, 429 n.56 (D. Md. 2006) (clarifying that the statutory compensatory damage cap applies to causes of action based on when the negligent or defamatory act occurred, and not when the cause of action was discovered). While Maryland courts have not addressed whether the statutory cap applies in defamation cases, they have consistently held the cap to be inapplicable to intentional tort claims, specifically including intentional infliction of emotional distress. See Snyder v. Phelps, 533 F. Supp. 2d 567, 586 (D. Md. 2008), rev'd on other grounds, 580 F.3d 206 (4th Cir. 2009), aff'd 131 S. Ct. 1207 (2011) ("[T]he Maryland statutory cap on noneconomic damages does not apply to intentional acts such as intentional infliction of emotional distress."); Cole v. Sullivan, 110 Md. App. 79, 676 A.2d 85 (Md. Spec. App. 1996) (holding that Maryland's statutory cap on economic damages "does not apply to intentional torts, whether or not personal bodily injuries are involved"). Additionally, the cap does not apply to economic or punitive damages.

a. **Presumed Damages and Libel Per Se.** Words or conduct amount to defamation per se if their injurious character is a self-evident fact of common knowledge. Shapiro v. Massengill, 105 Md. App. 743, 661 A.2d 202 (1995) cert. denied, 341 Md. 28, 668 A.2d 36 (1995). Statements made by an employer or its agents that convey the notion that the employee does not possess the honesty or capacity to perform the responsibilities of his trade, profession, or business are defamatory per se. Id. Carter v. Aramark Sports and Entm't Servs., Inc., 153 Md. App. 210, 238, 835 A.2d 262, 278 (2003), cert denied, 380 Md. 231, 844 A.2d 427 (2004) ("The allegation that a person is a thief constitutes defamation per se.") In such instances, there is no constitutional bar to presumed damages. Gooch v. Md. Mech. Sys., 81 Md. App. 376, 393 -94, 567 A.2d 954, 962, cert denied, 319 Md. 484, 573 A.2d 807 (1990).

If a statement is defamatory per se, and the plaintiff can show actual malice by clear and convincing evidence, damages are presumed. McReady v. O'Malley, 804 F. Supp. 2d 427, 441 (D. Md. 2011). See also Hanlon v. Davis, 76 Md. App. 339, 545 A.2d 72 (1988) (explaining that a trier of fact is constitutionally barred from awarding damages based on a presumption of damages in a negligent defamation case, but that damages may be awarded on the basis of this presumption where there is clear and convincing evidence of malice). If, however, a statement is defamatory per se, and the defendant was negligent in making the false statement, plaintiff must prove that he suffered actual damages. McReady, 804 F. Supp. 2d at 441. In actions for negligent defamation per se, a plaintiff's recovery is limited to actual damages only, which may include out-of-pocket losses, impairment of reputation and standing in the community, personal humiliation, or emotional distress. Hanlon, 76 Md. App. 339, 545 A.2d 72; Murray v. United Food & Comm'l Workers Union, 100 Fed. Appx. 165, *11 (4th Cir. June 9, 2004) (unpublished). It is an open question in Maryland whether this rule applies for defamation per quod. Hearst, 297 Md. at 112, 466 A.2d at 486.

(1) **Employment-Related Criticism.** An employer's statements that criticize an employee's conduct do not qualify as defamation per se unless those comments impute fraud, dishonesty, incompetency, incapacity, or unfitness in the performance of the employee's trade. Fennell, 242 Md. at 219, 218 A.2d at 497; Adler, 538 F. Supp. at 572. In the context of words used to explain the reason for an employee's discharge or rejection from a job and the related adverse action, Maryland courts have distinguished between defamatory statements an employee was unfit for his occupation, Wilson v. Cotterman, 65 Md. 190, 197, 3 A. 890, 891 (1886), and non-defamatory statements such as day-to-day observations and criticisms regarding employee performance, Leese v. Baltimore County , 64 Md. App. 442, 497 A.2d 159, cert. denied, 305 Md. 106, 501 A.2d 845 (1985). While a former employer's conversations with a prospective employer are conditionally privileged, that privilege may be overcome by proof of malice. Deutsch v. Chesapeake Ctr., 27 F. Supp. 2d 642, 645 (D. Md. 1998). See also II.A.2, infra. Thus, a former employer's statements to a prospective employer that an individual was "evasive, secretive, dishonest, dishonorable, and perhaps even a criminal," if proven false, amount to defamation per se, although they remain subject to the extent that there was a reasonable necessity for the prospective employer to be informed of the circumstances and reasons underlying the former employee's discharge. Szot v. Allstate Ins., 161 F. Supp. 2d 596 (D. Md. 2001).

(2) **Single Instance Rule.** There is no "single instance rule" recognized in Maryland.

b. **Punitive Damages.** Punitive damages are not available in defamation cases unless the plaintiff can plead and prove actual malice (defined as conduct motivated by ill-will, fraud, intent to injure, or the like) by clear and convincing evidence. Tierco Md., Inc. v. Williams, 381 Md. 378, 414 n.29, 849 A.2d 504, 526 n.29 (2004) (recognizing that "evidence of racial animus, if properly linked to the causes of action pled, may be relevant to establish actual malice for the purpose of the punitive damages claim"); Shapiro v. Massengill, 105 Md. App. 743, 661 A.2d 202, cert. denied, 341 Md. 28, 668 A.2d 36 (1995) (noting that private plaintiffs must meet the New York Times actual malice standard to recover punitive damages). In a defamation action, "punitive damages are not recoverable based on ill will, spite, or intent to injure; instead, to recover punitive damages, the plaintiff must establish that the defamatory falsehood was made with actual knowledge that it was false." Id. This standard applies regardless of the type of plaintiff or defendant involved. Shapiro, 105 Md. App. at 743, 661 A.2d at 202. A punitive damage award may be made in the discretion of the jury, provided that at least nominal compensatory damages have been awarded. IBEW, Local 1805 v. Mayo, 281 Md. 475, 379 A.2d 1223 (1977). See also Caldor, Inc. v. Bowden, 330 Md. 632, 662, 625 A.2d 959, 973 (1993) (recognizing that there must be an award of compensatory damages for each count which forms the foundation for an award of punitive damages). Punitive damages can be assessed against the employer of a reporter for defamatory publication by its employee even though the employer did not authorize, approve, or ratify the defamatory publication. Embrey v. Holly, 293 Md. 128, 442 A.2d 966 (1982).

II. PRIVILEGES AND DEFENSES

A. Scope of Privileges

1. ***Absolute Privileges.*** An absolute privilege exists for defamatory statements made in the course of judicial proceedings by judges, parties, and witnesses even if the statements have no relation to judicial proceeding. Elliott v. Evans, 942 F. Supp. 238, 243 (1996). See also Gill v. Ripley, 352 Md. 754, 761-62, 724 A.2d 88, 92 (1999) (recognizing that prosecutors have absolute immunity with respect to claims arising from their role in the judicial process); Woodruff v. Trepel, 125 Md. App. 381, 394, 725 A.2d 612, 618 (1999) (holding that a letter to plaintiff's attorney regarding client's custody matters covered by the judicial proceeding privilege). But see Classen Immunotherapies, Inc. v. King Pharm., Inc., 403 F.

Supp. 2d 451, 460 (D. Md. 2005) (recognizing that statements made in an extrajudicial publication, such as a press release which relates to the litigation, are not protected by the litigation privilege). There is a sufficient nexus between a judicial proceeding and the settlement of that proceeding, including the negotiations leading to that settlement, the settlement agreement, and the implementation of that settlement agreement, to extend the absolute judicial privilege to settlement related documents published during the course of a judicial proceeding to parties to the litigation or to potential litigants on the same subject matter. Sodergren v. The Johns Hopkins Univ. Applied Physics Lab., 138 Md. App. 686, 773 A.2d 592 (2001).

A similar absolute privilege applies to all stages of administrative proceedings which afford due process safeguards similar to those of judicial proceedings. Booth v. Total Health Care, Inc., 880 F. Supp. 414, 416 (D. Md. 1994) (holding that statements made in formal response to a complaint filed with Maryland Human Relations Commission are absolutely privileged). Whether absolute privilege attaches to an administrative hearing is decided on a case-by-case basis. Offen v. Brenner, 402 Md. 191, 200, 935 A.2d 719 (2007) (explaining that whether privilege for statements made during an administrative proceeding is absolute or conditional depends on (1) whether the importance of the public function outweighs need to protect individual reputation; and (2) whether the proceeding provides adversarial safeguards akin to judicial trials; nature of allegedly defamed person's position relevant but not determinative; absolute privilege applies to administrative hearings concerning, e.g., allegations of medical incompetence; child abuse; abuse of public authority).

Defamation suits and any claims "arising out of" defamatory acts are specifically excluded under the Federal Tort Claims Act ("FTCA"), 28 U.S.C. § 2680(h), rendering the government immune from defamation-type claims. Popovic v. United States, 175 F.3d 1015 (4th Cir. Apr. 20, 1999) (unpublished table decision) (holding that the government retains its sovereign immunity against claims of defamation, libel, and slander); Talbert v. United States, 932 F.2d 1064, 1067 (4th Cir. 1991) (explaining that a federal employee's claim for negligent record-keeping was barred by the libel and slander exception of the FTCA)); Beckwith v. Hart, 263 F. Supp. 2d 1018, 1021 (D. Md. 2003) (citing 28 U.S.C. § 2680(h) and holding that inmates' claim against Bureau of Federal Prisons employee for libel and slander was specifically exempted from the Federal Tort Claims Act).

A federal or state employee who makes false statements in the course of his discretionary acts within scope of his duties is absolutely immune under federal common law from defamation action under state tort laws. McReady v. O'Malley, 804 F. Supp. 2d 427, 444 (D. Md. 2011); Burgoyne v. Brooks, 76 Md. App. 222, 544 A.2d (1988). See also Md. Code Ann., Cts. & Jud. Proc. § 5-522(b) (2011) (articulating state immunity). To the extent a defamatory statement is made negligently, rather than intentionally, the common law public official immunity additionally applies. Lee v. Cline, 384 Md. 245, 258, 863 A.2d 297, 305 (2004). See also Houghton v. Forrest, 412 Md. 578, 585-86, 989 A.2d 223, 227-28 (2010) (declining to deviate from the rule that common law public official immunity does not extend to public officials who commit intentional torts including defamation).

Consent to publication also provides absolute privilege if the person knows the statement's contents, or that the statement may contain defamatory material. Bagwell v. Peninsula Reg'l Med. Ctr., 106 Md. App. 470, 511, 665 A.2d 297, 317 (1995), cert. denied, 341 Md. 172, 669 A.2d 1360 (1996).

2. ***Qualified Privileges.*** It is well established in Maryland that communications arising out of the employer-employee relationship enjoy a qualified privilege. McReady v. O'Malley, 804 F. Supp. 2d 427, 444 (D. Md. 2011); Happy 40, Inc. v. Miller, 63 Md. App. 24, 31, 491 A.2d 1210, 1214, cert. denied, 304 Md. 299, 498 A.2d 1185 (1985); Stevenson v. Baltimore Baseball Club, Inc., 250 Md. 482, 243 A.2d 533 (1968), overruled on other grounds, Marchesi v. Franchino, 283 Md. 131, 387 A.2d 1129 (1978). A privileged communication is "one made, in good faith, upon any subject-matter in which the party communicating has an interest or in reference to which he has, or honestly believes he has, a duty, to a person having a corresponding interest or duty, and which without the occasion upon which it is made would be defamatory and actionable." Bavington v. Robinson, 124 Md. 85, 89-90, 91 A. 777, 778 (1914) (emphasis added). See also Blankson-Arkoful v. Sunrise Sr. Living Servs., Inc., Civ. No. 10-1913, 2011 WL 4793215, *2 (4th Cir. Oct. 11, 2011) (unpublished) (recognizing that no liability attaches to an otherwise defamatory statement that is made "in good faith, [and] in 'furtherance of some interest of social importance, which is entitled protection'"); Higginbotham v. Pub. Serv. Comm'n of Md., 412 Md. 112, 129-31, 985 A.2d 1183, 1192-93 (2009) (articulating that the State's employees are immune from liability in tort for defamatory actions committed (1) within the scope of their employment, and (2) without malice or gross negligence); Carter v. Aramark Sports and Entm't Servs., Inc., 153 Md. App. 210, 238, 835 A.2d 262, 278 (2003), cert. denied, 380 Md. 231, 844 A.2d 427 (2004). See also Montgomery Investigative Servs., Ltd. v. Horne, 173 Md. App. 193, 206, 918 A.2d 526, 533 (2007) (qualified privilege exists where employer has a legitimate business interest in checking the criminal backgrounds of its employees and extends to the company that provides such background checks to the employer); McDermott v. Hughley, 317 Md. 12, 30, 561 A.2d 1038, 1047 (1989) (holding that statements regarding employee's examination made by psychologist under contract to employer enjoyed qualified privilege); Gen. Motors Corp. v. Piskor, 277 Md. 165, 172-73, 352 A.2d 810, 815-16 (1976) (holding that statements accusing auto assembly plant employee of theft enjoy

conditional privilege); Hanrahan v. Kelly, 269 Md. 21, 36-37, 305 A.2d 151, 160-61 (1973) (holding that a letter charging a partner with impropriety was privileged).

A conditional privilege applies to statements made by a speaker with a legitimate interest in the statement, or that shares a common interest with the recipient. Seneschal v. AM Broadband, LLC, Civ. No. 08-2171, 2010 WL 3522436, *10 (D. Md. Sept. 8, 2010) (recognizing the qualified immunity where an individual publishes a statement in good faith in furtherance of interests shared with others, particularly in the employee-employer relationship); Mazer v. Safeway, Inc., 398 F. Supp. 2d 412, 429-30 (D. Md. 2005) (holding that a former employer was privileged to send an employee's new employer a letter notifying it that the employee had misappropriated confidential information in violation of the Maryland Uniform Trade Secrets Act, where no malice was shown); Peurifoy v. Cong. Motors, Inc., 254 Md. 501, 514, 255 A.2d 332, 339 (1969) (holding that a car dealership's statement charging an employee with mismanagement enjoyed privilege); Henthorn v. W. Md. Ry., 226 Md. 499, 508, 174 A.2d 175, 179-80 (1961) (holding that a statement accusing railroad employee of theft enjoyed qualified privilege); Carroll v. City of Westminster, 52 F. Supp. 2d 546 (D. Md. 1999), aff'd, 233 F.3d 208 (4th Cir. 2000) (holding that statements made by a police officer regarding the outcome of a drug test and reason for plaintiff's termination were privileged because the defendant's statement related to a violation of the law); Deutsch v. Chesapeake Ctr., 27 F. Supp. 2d 642, 645 (D. Md. 1998) (holding that a former employer's statements to a prospective employer were conditionally privileged and protected without proof of malice); Dobkin v. Johns Hopkins Univ., 173 F.3d 43 (4th Cir.), cert. denied, 528 U.S. 875 (1999) (holding that statements made about the plaintiff's medical health, psychological state and alleged sexual harassment were not defamatory).

A person is protected against civil liability for defamation where, in good faith, he publishes a statement in furtherance of his own legitimate interests, or those shared in common with the recipient or third parties or where his declaration would be of interest to the public in general. See Ransom v. Balt. Co., 111 F. Supp. 2d 704, 711-12 (D. Md. 2000) ("Maryland law recognizes a common law privilege for a defamatory statement if 'publication of the utterance advances social policies of greater importance than the vindication of a plaintiff's reputational interest.'"); Simon v. Union Hosp. of Cecil County, Inc., 15 F. Supp. 2d. 787, 795 (D. Md. 1998), rev'd in part on other grounds, 199 F.3d 1328 (4th Cir. Oct. 20, 1999) (unpublished). An employer's statements that a former employee was "evasive, secretive, dishonest, dishonorable, and perhaps even a criminal," if proven false, amounted to defamation *per se,* however, the former employer enjoyed a qualified privilege in that the statements were not communicated beyond those reasonably necessary to be informed of the circumstances and reasons underlying the former employee's discharge. Szot v. Allstate Ins., 161 F. Supp. 2d 596 (D. Md. 2001). See, e.g., Carter v. Morgan, 34 Fed. Appx. 427 (4th Cir. Apr. 25, 2002) (table case) (holding that a qualified privilege precluded liability on the basis of a statement that would otherwise qualify as defamatory that was made by the president of the company to another employee who was responsible for scheduling and hiring employees, there was no evidence of malice). A qualified privilege is conditioned upon the absence of malice, and can be forfeited if abused. Spence v. NCI Info. Sys., Inc., Civ. No. 05-3127, 2009 WL 524739, *6 (D. Md. Feb. 27, 2009). See also Orrison v. Vance, 262 Md. 285, 292, 277 A.2d 573, 576 (1971) (if the qualified privilege is "not exercised in a reasonable manner and for a proper purpose," the speaker will "forfeit his immunity").

In addition to the common law privilege, Maryland employers also enjoy a statutory qualified privilege to convey information, as long as disclosed in good faith, about employees or former employees about the job performance or the reason for termination of employment of an employee or former employee of the employer: (1) to a prospective employer at the request of the prospective employer, the employee, or former employee; or (2) if requested or required by a federal, state or industry regulatory authority, or if the information is disclosed in a report, filing, or other document required by law, rule, order, or regulation of the regulatory authority. Md. Code Ann., Cts. & Jud. Proc. § 5-423 (**2011**). There is a presumption that the employer acted in good faith in disclosing such information unless it is shown by clear and convincing evidence that the employer: (1) acted with actual malice; or (2) intentionally or recklessly disclosed false information. Id.

a. **Common Interest.** See II A.2, supra. Statements made pursuant to a common interest are protected by a qualified privilege. Carter, 153 Md. App. at 239-40, 835 A.2d at 278 ("An occasion is conditionally privileged when the circumstances are such as to lead any one of several persons having a common interest in a particular subject matter correctly or reasonably to believe that facts exist which another sharing such common interest is entitled to know."). Members of identifiable groups that share similar goals or values usually have common interests. Id. For example, there is a common interest between a former employer and a new employer concerning statements made by a former employee to the new employer concerning his knowledge of his prior employer's confidential information and, as such, possible violations of the Maryland Uniform Trade Secrets Act. Mazer v. Safeway, Inc., 398 F. Supp. 2d 412, 429-30 (D. Md. 2005) (recognizing the existence of common interests where a former employer had an interest in protecting its proprietary information and the new employer could have faced potential liability if confidential information was disclosed to it by its new employee). Similarly, there is a common interest between franchisor and franchisee concerning statements made by the franchisee about its former employee to the franchisor in connection with the former employee's application to own and operate a franchise. Darvish v. Gohari, 130 Md. App. 265, 274-75, 745 A.2d 1134, 1139-40 (2000), aff'd, 363 Md. 42,

767 A.2d 321 (2001). There is also a common interest between any person making a report of child abuse or neglect and the public when reporter of statement exercises good faith in making report of suspected child abuse. Rite-Aid Corp. v. Hagley, 374 Md. 665, 687-692, 824 A.2d 107, 120-123 (2003). See also Carter, 153 Md. App. at 239-40, 835 A.2d at 279 (holding that supplier and director had common interest privilege to communicate with respect to allegations that usher for baseball team was a thief, thus precluding liability of supplier or director for defamation).

However, the common interest privilege is generally lost upon a showing of malice, i.e., knowing falsity or reckless disregard for the truth. Carter, 153 Md. App. 210, 239-40, 835 A.2d 262, 278 ("The privilege does not arise in the first place unless the communication relates in some degree to the common interest, and once the privilege arises it is lost if it is abused by malice or excessive publication.").

b. **Duty.** See II.A.2, supra. Statements made pursuant to a duty are protected by a qualified privilege. Alford v. Genesis Healthcare, Civ. No. RDB-05-3278, 2007 WL 1073725, *5 (D. Md. Apr. 9, 2007) (unpublished) (holding that a qualified privilege exists protects a nursing director's statutorily-mandated report to the Maryland Board of Nursing concerning a subordinate nurse's actions that she suspected to be grounds for disciplinary actions) (unpublished); Smith v. Danielczyk, 400 Md. 98, 928 A.2d 795, 812, 816 (2007) (holding that a qualified privilege protected police officers' otherwise defamatory statements about fellow officers made in an application for a search warrant where the communication was required or permitted in the performance of their official duties); Larsen v. Chinwuba, 377 Md. 92, 103-07, 832 A.2d 193, 199-202 (2003) (holding that the statutory immunity protected the insurance Commissioner's allegedly defamatory statements in letters sent to a Health Maintenance Organization because the statements were made during the regular course of business, related entirely to the operations of the Insurance Administration, and were incidental to the business of managing the Administration).

c. **Criticism of Public Employee.** See II A.2, supra. Statements criticizing public employee are protected by a qualified privilege. An absolute privilege defense will apply to a defamation action involving communications made by students and parents to public school authorities about the perceived misconduct of a public school teacher and coach. Reichardt v. Flynn, 374 Md. 361, 823 A.2d 566 (2003). In Reichardt v. Flynn, the court held that strong public interest favored the ability of students and parents to report teacher's alleged sexual misconduct without fear of liability for defamation, as teacher had received adequate procedural safeguards in that teacher had the opportunity to appeal superintendent's discipline to the County Board of Education and if unsuccessful, to the State Board of Education, which would be subject to judicial review. Id. These procedural safeguards were designed to minimize the occurrence of defamatory statements in school administration proceedings. Id. However, to the extent that a public employee's employer makes statements that "(1) placed a stigma on [her] reputation; (2) were made public by the employer; (3) were made in conjunction with [her] termination or demotion; and (4) were false," the public employee may establish a constitutional liberty interest claim for defamation. Hamilton v. Mayor & City Council of Balt., 807 F. Supp. 2d 331, 357 (D. Md. 2011).

d. **Limitation on Qualified Privileges.** A plaintiff can overcome the qualified privilege for communications arising out of employment relations by proving that the employer made the defamatory statements with reckless disregard for their truth, or with actual malice. De Leon v. St. Joseph Hosp., Inc., 871 F.2d 1229 (4th Cir. 1989). The privilege can also be lost if the plaintiff demonstrates that the publication was made for a purpose other than to further the social interest entitled to protection. McDermott v. Hughley, 317 Md. 12, 29, 561 A.2d 1038, 1047 (1989). An employer does not abuse its conditional privilege by voluntarily responding to questions from employees concerning its reasons for discharging a fellow employee; in responding to such inquiries, an employer is given great latitude concerning the scope of its remarks. Rabinowitz v. Oates, 955 F. Supp. 485, 489 (D. Md. 1996); Happy 40, Inc. v. Miller, 63 Md. App. 24, 491 A.2d 1210, cert. denied, 304 Md. 299, 498 A.2d 1185 (1985). The qualified privilege arising from an employment relationship continues to exist even after the person defamed is no longer an employee. Exxon Corp. v. Schoene, 67 Md. App. 412, 508 A.2d 142 (1986).

(1) **Constitutional or Actual Malice.** Actual malice requires that the employer either had "knowledge of falsity or reckless disregard for truth." Marchesi v. Franchino, 283 Md. 131, 139, 387 A.2d 1129, 1133 (1978). A jury may reasonably infer malice from the specificity and inflammatory nature of the alleged statements or from the employer's concession that, if made, the statements were false. Simon, 15 F. Supp. 2d 787, rev'd in part on other grounds, 199 F.3d 1328 (4th Cir. Oct. 20, 1999) (unpublished). Reckless disregard of the truth means that the employer had a high degree of awareness of probable falsity. De Leon, 871 F.2d 1229. Negligence on the part of the employer is not enough to constitute "reckless disregard," Jacron Sales Co. v. Sindorf, 276 Md. 580, 599, 350 A.2d 688, 699 (1976), nor is a claim that different information beneficial to the employee was available only if the employer had conducted a better or more thorough investigation, De Leon, 871 F.2d at 1235 n.10. See also Mazer v. Safeway, Inc., 398 F. Supp. 2d 412, 430-31 (D. Md. 2005) (holding that a former employer did not act with reckless disregard for the truth where it sent a letter to a former employee's new employer concerning employee's "possible" misappropriation of proprietary information, based on its own internal investigation); Murray v. U. Food and Comm'l Worker's Union, Local 400, 229 F. Supp. 2d 465, 477-78 (D. Md.

2002), aff'd, 100 Fed. Appx. 165, *11 (4th Cir. 2004) (table) (finding that union organizer's defamation claim failed where statements made by the union were based on the union's good faith belief that its statements were true, the statements were not made with malice, and the organizer presented no evidence of damages); Henry v. Nat'l Ass'n of Air Traffic Specialists, Inc., 836 F. Supp. 1204, 1212 (D. Md. 1993) (articulating that plaintiff must prove that defendants made each statement with knowledge that it was false or with reckless disregard of its falsity); Woodruff v. Trepel, 125 Md. App. 381, 402, 725 A.2d 612, 623 (1999) (malice may be a reckless disregard for the truth, the use of unnecessarily abusive language or other circumstances which would support a conclusion that the defendant acted in an ill-tempered manner or was motivated by ill-will). Evidence of an employer's insensitivity to the impact of its statements, departure from journalistic standards, publishers' motive of profit, or a conscious decision not to investigate even when a source's veracity is unknown, is relevant but insufficient to provide actual malice. Reuber v. Food Chem. News, Inc., 925 F.2d 703, 714-17 (4th Cir. 1991); Nat'l Life Ins. v. Phillips Publ'g Inc., 793 F. Supp. 627 (D. Md. 1992). See also Johnson v. Toys R US-Delaware, Inc., 95 Fed. Appx. 1, *7-8 (4th Cir. Feb. 23, 2004) (table case) (holding that statements made by a store employee were not made with malice and therefore did not constitute defamation when the employee deactivated gift cards purchased by customer based upon suspicion that the cards were stolen and instructed third-party administrator to inform anyone using the cards that they had been reported stolen).

(2) **Common Law Malice.** The common law standard for malice requires that a plaintiff prove spite or ill-will, i.e., that the publication was made solely for the purpose of causing harm to the subject of the publication. Horning v. Hardy, 36 Md. App. 419, 425, 373 A.2d 1273, 1277 (1977); Kapiloff v. Dunn, 27 Md. App. 514, 343 A.2d 251 (1975).

e. **Question of Fact or Law.** The determination of whether a publication is susceptible to a defamatory meaning, and the determination of whether the words are actually defamatory is made by the jury. Montgomery Investigative Servs., Ltd. v. Horne, 173 Md. App. 193, 223, 918 A.2d 526, 543 (2007); Chesapeake Publ'g Corp. v. Williams, 339 Md. 285, 295, 661 A.2d 1169, 1174 (1995).

f. **Burden of Proof.** The burden of overcoming any qualified privilege rests on the plaintiff. Anderson v. Liberty Lobby, Inc., 477 U.S. 242, 249-52 (1986); De Leon, 871 F.2d at 1233 n.7. **Maryland law will presume that an employer acted in good faith absent clear and convincing evidence that the employer acted with actual malice or intentionally or recklessly disclosed false information about the employee. Hermina v. Safeway, Inc., Civ. No. WMN-11-1523, 2012 WL 12759, at *6 (D. Md. Jan 3, 2012) (citing Md. Code Ann., Cts. & Jud. Proc. § 5-423).**

B. Standard Libel Defenses

1. ***Truth.*** At common law, truth was an affirmative defense to a defamation action. Now, the plaintiff has the burden of pleading and proving falsity. Batson v. Shiflett, 325 Md. 684, 722, 726, 602 A.2d 1191 (1992). See Carroll v. City of Westminster, 52 F. Supp. 2d 546 (D. Md. 1999), aff'd 233 F.3d 208 (4th Cir. 2000) (dismissing a defamation claim because the information was true); Hart v. Bon Secours Baltimore Health Sys., Civ. No. 08-2516, 2010 WL 3245427, * 7 (D. Md. Aug. 17, 2010) (holding that an employee could not maintain an action against her employer where she could not meet her burden of proving the falsity of her employer's alleged defamatory statement); Machie v. Manger, Civ. No. 09-2196, 2010 WL 2132223, *6 (D. Md. May 25, 2010) (holding that an employee could not maintain an action on the basis of defamatory statements that he was charged with a crime when he was in fact charged with the crime, even if the charge had been made erroneously); **Hermina, 2012 WL 12759 at *7 (holding that a claim for defamation could not be maintained on the basis of an employer's statement that a loss prevention investigation occurred because the statement was factually true and did not identify plaintiff as the subject of the investigation).**

2. ***Opinion.*** There is no wholesale privilege for statements asserted as opinion. While expression of opinion may imply assertion of fact, the dispositive question is whether a reasonable fact finder could conclude that a statement implies objective facts. Crowley v. Fox Broad. Co., 851 F. Supp. 700 (D. Md. 1994). In determining whether a defamatory statement is opinion or fact, Maryland courts will consider: (a) whether the challenged statement can be objectively characterized as true or false; and (b) the language of statement, the specific context of the statement, and the broader social context in which the statement appeared. Henry, 836 F. Supp. at 1215 (holding that allegedly defamatory letters constituted protected opinions because they failed to meet second prong, especially in their broader context of a labor dispute); Biospherics, Inc. v. Forbes, Inc., 151 F.3d 180, 183 (4th Cir. 1999) (commenting that if a defendant's words cannot be categorized as either true or false, they cannot be defamatory). But see Batson, 325 Md. at 723-25, 602 A.2d at 1211 (holding that statements made in the context of a heated labor dispute that plaintiff may have been responsible for misuse of union funds implied objective facts and as a result were not protected as opinion). See also Hughley v. McDermott, 72 Md. App. 391, 530 A.2d 13 (1987), aff'd on other grounds, 317 Md. 12, 561 A.2d 1038 (1989) (without expressly adopting the Restatement (Second) of Torts § 566, holding that statements couched as expressions of opinion consisting of "calculated untruths" were actionable). If a statement is substantially true, minor inaccuracies therein will not give rise to a defamation

claim. Dobkin v. Johns Hopkins Univ., 173 F.3d 43 (4th Cir.), cert. denied, 528 U.S. 875 (1999). See also Polanco v. Fager, 886 F.2d 66, 69 (4th Cir. 1989) (articulating that the doctrine of fair comment applies if the facts upon which a comment is based are set out, or are so referred to as to be clearly recognizable and easily accessible, and are either true or privileged); A.S. Abell Co. v. Kirby, 227 Md. 267, 270-84, 176 A.2d 340 (1961); Thacker, 135 Md. App. at 268, 762 A.2d at 172 (recognizing that when a defendant bases his expression of a derogatory opinion on the existence of alleged facts that he does not state, but that are assumed to be true by both parties to the communication, he is not subject to liability whether the assumed facts are defamatory or not, if the communication does not give rise to the reasonable inference that it is also based on other facts that are defamatory).

3. ***Consent.*** Consent to publication also provides absolute privilege if a person knows the statement's contents or knows that the statement may contain defamatory material. Bagwell v. Peninsula Reg'l Med. Ctr., 106 Md. App. 470, 511, 665 A.2d 297, 317 (1995), cert. denied, 341 Md. 172, 669 A.2d 1360 (1996). A plaintiff who consents to a defamatory statement cannot bring suit for defamation. McDermott v. Hughley, 317 Md. 12, 27, 561 A.2d 1038, 1046 (1989); Restatement (Second) of Torts § 583 (1997) (articulating that consent is an absolute defense to a claim of defamation). See also Carroll, 52 F. Supp. 2d at 566 ("Consent is an absolute defense to defamation.").

4. ***Mitigation.*** An employer may offer proof of mitigating circumstances including the source of his information and grounds for his belief. See generally Stanley Mazaroff, Maryland Employment Law § 5 (1990).

5. ***Prior Notice Requirement.*** The Local Government Tort Claims Act requires submission of an administrative notice within 180 days after the alleged injury. Luy v. Balt. Police Dep't, 326 F. Supp. 2d 682 (D. Md. 2004) (citing Md. Code Ann., Cts. & Jud. Proc. § 5-304(a)) (dismissing plaintiff's defamation claim for failure to provide prior notice of his claim to the Baltimore City Solicitor, as required by Maryland statute when seeking unliquidated damages from a local government or its employees).

III. RECURRING FACT PATTERNS

A. Statements in Personnel File

Employers have a qualified privilege, based on common interest and duty, to make statements in a personnel file. See II.A.2, supra. Sciolino v. City of Newport News, Virginia, 480 F.3d 642, 650 (4th Cir. 2007) (dismissing a police officer's assertion of a due process claim based on the termination letter placed into his personnel file which accused him of deliberately destroying city property, because he failed to show either that (1) his former employer had a practice of releasing personnel files to all inquiring employers, or (2) his former employer would have released his personnel file to an employer to which he intended to apply).

B. Performance Evaluations

Employers have a qualified privilege, based on common interest and duty, to make statements in performance evaluations. See II.A.2, supra.

C. References

Employers have a qualified privilege based on common interest and duty, to make statements in making references. See II.A.2, supra. A qualified privilege exists as to disclosures about job performance or reasons for termination of an employee or former employee to a prospective employer upon request, or if disclosure is required by law or industry regulation; this privilege is lost upon a showing of ill will or knowledge of falsity. Md. Code Ann., Cts. & Jud. Proc., § 5-423. See Spence v. NCI Info. Sys., Inc., Civ. No. 05-3127, 2009 WL 524739, *8 (D. Md. Feb. 27, 2009) (holding that a supervisor's negative assessment of former employee's interpersonal skills to a prospective employer was subject to a conditional privilege). In adult dependent care programs, Md. Code Ann., Health-Gen. § 19-1911 (Repl. Vol. 1996), recognizes that an employer providing a reference is to be presumed to be acting in good faith and will not be held liable for disclosing any information about the job performance or the reason for termination of an employee or former employee with respect to criminal history records and background checks. Lowery v. Smithsburg Emergency Med. Serv., 173 Md. App 662, 688-89, 920 A.2d 546, 561 (2007).

D. Intracorporate Communication

Intracorporate communications have a qualified privilege based on common interest and duty. See I.B.6.a, supra.

E. Statements to Government Regulators

An employer's statements made in response to a government agency investigation of a claim or complaint by an employee outside of a formal adjudicatory hearing to a government agency are subject to the qualified privilege for communications arising out of employer/employee relations. Offen v. Brenner, 334 Fed. Appx. 578, *3 (4th Cir. June 9, 2009) (table). This includes where an employer provides defamatory information about an employee in response to a request by the Equal Employment Opportunity Commission, Maryland Human Relations Commission, a county or local human relations commission, the National Labor Relations Board, Occupational Safety and Health Administration, or any other administrative agency, as long as the defamatory statement is not made with knowledge of its falsity or reckless disregard of the truth. See generally Stanley Mazaroff, Maryland Employment Law, § 5.02[7][c] (1990).

Information provided by an employer under oath at a formal administrative hearing may be absolutely privileged depending on: (1) the nature of the public function of the proceeding; and (2) the adequacy of the procedural safeguards which minimize the occurrence of defamatory statements. Gersh v. Ambrose, 291 Md. 188, 197, 434 A.2d 547, 551-52 (1981). Factors used in considering whether the procedural standards adequately protect against defamatory statements include whether a legally cognizable tribunal was administering the proceedings; whether the public hearing was adversarial in nature; whether the witnesses were sworn in and subject to cross examination; and whether the employee had an opportunity to present his or her side of the story. McDermott, 317 Md. at 26, 561 A.2d at 1045 (1989). See also II.A.1, supra.

F. Reports to Auditors and Insurers

There are no cases in Maryland concerning defamation contained in reports to auditors and/or insurers, although such reports would likely be subject to a qualified privilege. See II.A.2, supra. An absolute privilege attaches to statements submitted to judicial and quasi-judicial bodies, even if the statement is part of a preliminary investigation. Gersh, 291 Md. at 197, 434 A.2d at 551-52.

G. Vicarious Liability of Employers for Statements Made by Employees

1. ***Scope of Employment.*** Employers are liable for defamatory statements/conduct of its employees where an employee was acting within the scope of his or her employment. Restatement (Second) of Torts § 409 (1979). Vicarious liability does not, however, apply to defamatory statements made by employee to a third person when the statement was made outside the scope of the employee's employment or during the course of during an internal investigation conducted on the employer's behalf. Reaves v. Westinghouse Elec. Corp., 683 F. Supp. 521 (D. Md. 1988). **In order to impose vicarious liability, the defamatory statement made by an employee must be made to a third person who is not him or herself an agent or employee. Mwabira-Simera v. Thompson Hospitality Services, LLP, Civ. No. WMN-11-2989, 2012 WL 959383, at *4 (D. Md. Mar. 20, 2012).**

a. **Blogging.** There are currently no cases in Maryland.

2. ***Damages.*** While compensatory damages can be recovered, Maryland courts have rejected the criteria set for by the Restatement (Second) of Torts § 409 (1979) for allowing punitive damages against the employer. Embrey v. Holly, 293 Md. 128, 442 A.2d 966 (1982).

H. Internal Investigations

Under Maryland law, an employer is vicariously liable for defamatory statements made by an employee conducting an internal investigation because such statements fall within the scope of employment. Reaves, 683 F. Supp. at 526. At the same time, an employee being interviewed in an internal investigation as a potential participant in the alleged wrongdoing is speaking in a personal capacity, and therefore an employer cannot be held vicariously liable for defamatory statements made by the employee in this context. Id. However, the employee being interviewed may be subject to personal liability for defamatory statements regarding fellow employees. Id. Statements made in the course of an internal investigation may also fall within the qualified privilege provided by the employer-employee relationship. See, e.g., Szot v. Allstate Ins., 161 F. Supp. 2d 596, 607 (D. Md. 2001) (holding that communications dealing directly with a subject matter of mutual interest to the communicator and recipient for a reasonable employment-related purpose are privileged). Moreover, an internal investigation found to be negligently conducted cannot form the basis of a finding of malice required to bring a successful defamation claim. Reaves, 683 F. Supp. at 536 n.6.

IV. OTHER ACTIONS BASED ON STATEMENTS

A. Negligent Hiring, Retention, and Supervision

The elements of negligent hiring are: (a) the employer owed a duty to the plaintiff to use reasonable care in selecting its employees; (b) the employer breached its duty of care in selecting the employee, i.e., the employer's acts of omission or commission in selecting the employee were not reasonably prudent under the circumstances; (c) the employer's failure to exercise reasonable care was a proximate cause of injury to the plaintiff [(1) if the employer exercised reasonable care, it would have discovered or properly considered information that would have precluded a reasonable employer from hiring or retaining the employee; and (2) because the employee was placed in a position to cause the injury to the plaintiff]; and (d) the plaintiff has suffered damages. There is a rebuttable presumption that an employer has used due care in hiring an employee. Horridge v. St. Mary's Cnty. Dep't of Soc. Servs., 382 Md. 170, 854 A.2d 1232 (2004). An employer cannot be held negligent for failure to discover, for example, an employee's prior questionable but non-criminal relationships. Latty v. St. Joseph's Soc. of the Sacred Heart, Inc., 198 Md. App. 254, 272-74, 17 A.3d 155, 165-66 (2011) (holding that a religious society committed no actionable negligence in hiring a priest who had previously breached his vow of celibacy and had taken "advantage of his position of power" over an organist, commenting that "[i]f we were to hold that the society was negligent in this case, it would have the effect of requiring all employers to become entangled in their employees' relationships and to monitor them").

Maryland law recognizes that an employer can be found liable for negligent hiring of an independent contractor as well. See Schramm v. Foster, 341 F. Supp. 2d 536, 551-52 (D. Md. 2004) (holding that an independent contractor, a third party company that provided shipping services, was required to use reasonable care in selecting the truckers it maintained to serve as carriers).

B. Intentional Infliction of Emotional Distress

Claims for intentional infliction of emotion distress are subject to a "very high" pleading standard in Maryland, and are only "rarely viable." Rollins v. Verizon Md., Inc., Civ. No. RDB-09-2379, 2010 WL 4449361, *8 (D. Md. Nov. 5, 2010). While individual employees may be liable under this tort, liability cannot attach to an employer under a respondeat superior theory. Bishop v. Bd. of Educ. of Calvert Cnty., Civ. No. DKC-11-1100, 2011 WL 2651246, *9 (D. Md. July 5, 2011) (collecting Maryland authority in support of the proposition that liability for intentional infliction of emotional distress cannot extend to a school board "because an intentional tortious action constitutes an abandonment of employment and is not 'done in furtherance of the beneficent purposes of the educational system'").

The elements of intentional infliction of emotional distress are: (a) the conduct must be intentional or reckless; (b) the conduct must be extreme and outrageous; (c) there must be a causal connection between the wrongful conduct and emotional distress; and (d) the emotional distress must be severe. Harris v. Jones, 281 Md. 560, 566, 380 A.2d 611, 614 (1977); Johnson v. MV Trans. Inc., 716 F. Supp. 2d 410, 414 (D. Md. 2010); Snyder v. Phelps, 131 S. Ct. 1207, 1215 (2011). The essential element of this tort is extreme and outrageous conduct. Mere insults, indignities, threats, annoyances and petty oppressions or other trivialities do not constitute extreme and outrageous conduct. Harris, 281 Md. at 567, 380 A.2d at 614 (quoting Restatement (Second) of Torts § 46 cmt. d (1965)). The Maryland Court of Appeals has emphasized that the tort of intentional infliction of emotional distress "is to be used sparingly and only for opprobrious behavior that includes truly outrageous conduct." Ky. Fried Chicken Nat'l Mgmt. Co. v. Weathersby, 326 Md. 663, 670, 607 A.2d 8 (1992) (citing Batson v. Shiflett, 325 Md. 684, 734-35, 602 A.2d 1191 (1992)). Liability for this tort has been found "only where the conduct has been so outrageous in character, and so extreme in degree, as to go beyond all possible bounds of decency, and to be regarded as atrocious, and utterly intolerable in a civilized community." Ky. Fried Chicken Nat'l Mgmt. Co., 326 Md. at 670, 607 A.2d 8 (quoting Restatement (Second) of Torts § 46 comment d (1965)). Gantt v. Security USA, Inc., 356 F.3d 547, 557 (4th Cir. 2004), cert. denied, 543 U.S. 814 (security guard who was kidnapped from work, then raped and tortured, can take an intentional infliction of emotional distress claim to trial alleging her employer, despite a protective order, placed her in danger when she was assigned to an isolated location where she feared for her life).

The Maryland Court of Special Appeals has stated that extreme and outrageous conduct for the purpose of this tort exists "only if 'the average member of the community must regard the defendant's conduct . . . as being a complete denial of the plaintiff's dignity as a person.'" Leese v. Balt. City, 64 Md. App. 442, 469-70, 497 A.2d 159, 173, cert. denied, 305 Md. 106, 501 A.2d 845 (1985) (quoting Dick v. Mercantile-Safe Deposit & Tr. Co., 63 Md. App. 270, 276, 492 A.2d 674, 677 (1985)). Thus, rough language, abusive outbursts, or occasional inconsiderate or unkind acts are not enough to constitute outrageousness. Rollins, 2010 WL 4449361, *8 (dismissing a former employee's claim for intentional infliction of emotional distress arising from her supervisor's harassing behavior, commenting that "poor behavior at the workplace rarely rises to the level of extreme and outrageous conduct). Similarly, adverse employment actions involving demotions, failure to promote, discipline and discharge will not, standing alone, satisfy this standard. Id.; Beye v. Bureau of Nat'l Affairs, 59 Md. App. 642, 477 A.2d 1197, cert. denied, 301 Md. 639, 484 A.2d 274 (1984). In addition to extreme and outrageous conduct, an employee seeking to assert a claim under this tort must allege that he or she is suffering an "emotional response to the defendant's conduct" that is so severe that it disrupts the employee's ability to function on a daily basis. Bishop, 2011 WL 2651246, *10.

C. Interference with Economic Advantage

The elements of interference with economic advantage are: (a) the existence of an employment contract or reasonable expectation of a continuing or future employment relationship or benefit; (b) knowledge of this contract or expectation by the defendant; (c) intentional interference with the plaintiff's employment contract or expectation by, the defendant acting as a third party, without legal justification and for the defendant's own benefit or to injure the plaintiff; and (d) actual damages to the plaintiff. Wrongful or malicious interference with economic relations includes acts of defamation. Carter v. Aramark Sports and Entm't Servs., Inc., 153 Md. App. 210, 242, 835 A.2d 262, 281 (2003), cert. denied, 380 Md. 231, 844 A.2d 427 (2004). Unless the plaintiff can show that a defendant acted fraudulently or intentionally concealed the termination of a contract, the statute of limitations for a claim for interference with economic advantage begins tolling on the date that the contract is terminated. Dual Inc. v. Lockheed Martin Corp., 383 Md. 151, 168-70, 857 A.2d 1095, 1104-06 (2004).

Despite the fact that the broad principles of this tort have long been recognized, there is a dearth of reported case law in Maryland applying these principles to employment cases. But see Fowler v. Printers II, 89 Md. App. 448, 598 A.2d 794 (1991). The employee has the burden of proving the existence of the employment contract, knowledge of this contract, interference by the defendant, and actual damages. Once the employee meets this burden, the burden shifts to the defendant to justify the interference. Fitzgerald v. Penthouse Int'l Ltd., 525 F. Supp. 585, 603 (D. Md. 1981), rev'd in part on other grounds, 691 F.2d 666 (4th Cir. 1982), cert. denied, 460 U.S. 1024 (1983). See W. Prosser, The Law of Torts § 129 at 943 (4th Ed. 1971) ("[T]he defendant may show that the interference is privileged by reason of the interests furthered by his conduct, but the burden rests upon him to do so.). The question of privilege is as broad as the catalog of possible interests involved, and it must be considered in light of the means adopted and the relations between the parties."

D. Prima Facie Tort

No cases.

V. OTHER ISSUES

A. Statute of Limitations

There is a one-year statute of limitations for a defamation action. Md. Code Ann., Cts & Jud. Proc., § 5-105. The statute generally commences to run when a statement is published. Luy v. Baltimore Police Dept., 326 F. Supp. 2d 682, 691 (D. Md. 2004), aff'd, 120 Fed. Appx. 465 (4th Cir. 2005) (table) (applying Md. law and citing Bagwell v. Peninsula Reg'l Med. Ctr., 106 Md. App. 470, *cert. den.*, 341 Md. 172, 669 A.2d 1360 (1996)). See also Vaeth v. Mayor & City Council of Balt. City, Civ. No. WDQ-11-182, 2011 WL 4711904, *4 (Oct. 4, 2011) (granting motion to dismiss defamation claim brought on the basis of allegations of undated statements that "must have been made" more than one year prior to plaintiff's filing of the lawsuit); Brown v. Prince George's Hosp., Civ. No. RWT-09-295, 2011 WL 2413344, *4 (D. Md. June 9, 2011) (granting summary judgment dismissing all defamation claims brought on the basis of communications made more than one year prior to plaintiff's filing of the lawsuit); Johnson v. MV Trans., Inc., 716 F. Supp. 2d 410 (D. Md. 2010) (dismissing defamation claim where alleged defamatory statements were made on July 18, 2006 and action was filed on July 27, 2007).

However, the discovery rule applies to defamation and, as a result, the statute of limitations begins to run when the person defamed knew or should have known that he was injured by the false statement. Shepard v. Nabb, 84 Md. App. 687, 581 A.2d 839 (1990); Sears, Roebuck & Co. v. Ulman, 287 Md. 397, 412 A.2d 1240 (1980). **See, e.g., Gainsburg v. Steben & Co., Inc., 838 F.Supp.2d 339 (D. Md. 2011) (holding that defamation claim was barred by statute of limitations when plaintiff learned of defamatory statement on June 23, 2009 and filed claim on August 31, 2011).**

Additionally, note that to the extent another cause of action is based on defamatory statements, the statute of limitations associated with the other cause of action may apply. See, e.g., Richardson v. Selective Ins. Grp., Inc., Civ. No. 06-2594, 2007 WL 1657423, *5-6 (D. Md. May 31, 2007) (statute of limitations for tortious interference with economic advantage claim based on defamatory references to prospective employers is three years rather than the one year statute of limitations applicable to an action for libel or slander).

B. Jurisdiction

As a tort claim, an action for defamation must be brought in the jurisdiction in which the statement was published to third parties. McGaw v. Biovail Pharm., Inc., 300 F. Supp. 2d 371, 374 (D. Md. 2004). However, sending allegedly defamatory statements into Maryland by telephone or letter from outside the State does not, without more, permit the exercise of personal jurisdiction under Maryland long-arm statute. See Dring v. Sullivan, 423 F. Supp.2d 540 (D. Md. 2006) (holding that an out-of-state defendant's allegedly defamatory contact with Maryland plaintiff through an e-mail message distributed via a listserv was insufficient to subject defendant to personal jurisdiction in defamation action filed in Maryland); Zinz v. Evans, Mitchell Indus., 22 Md. App. 126, 324 A.2d 140, cert. denied, 272 Md. 751, 324 A.2d 140 (1974).

However, Maryland courts may lack subject matter jurisdiction over certain defamation actions, due to statutory exemption of certain agencies or preemption. See, e.g., Beckwith v. Hart, 263 F. Supp. 2d 1018, 1021 (D. Md. 2003) (citing 28 U.S.C. § 2680(h) and dismissing inmates' claims against the Bureau of Federal Prisons for lack of jurisdiction pursuant to the Federal Tort Claims Act's exemptions); Talbert v. United States, 932 F.2d 1064, 1067 (4th Cir. 1991) (holding that a federal employee's claim for negligent record-keeping was barred by the libel and slander exception of the FTCA). See also Ali v. Giant Food LLC, 595 F. Supp. 2d 618 (D. Md. 2009) (dismissing an employee's defamation claim against his former employer's loss control manager as the employer belonged to a union and his defamation claims were preempted by the Labor Management Relations Act).

C. Worker's Compensation Exclusivity

Generally under Maryland law, an injured employee's remedy under the worker's compensation statute is the exclusive remedy against the employer for causes of action sounding in tort. Md. Code Ann., Lab. & Empl. § 9-509 (2008); Knoche v. Cox, 282 Md. 447, 453 (1978) ("aside from the exceptions created by the Worker's Compensation Act itself, the operation of the law is exclusive of all other remedy and liability, as to both employer and employee who come within its purview"). However, non-physical torts, such as defamation, do not fall within the ambit of the Workers' Compensation Act and are not subject to the exclusivity provision of the Act. Le v. Federated Dep't Stores, Inc., 80 Md. App. 89. 93, 560 A.2d 42, 44 (1989) (holding that an employee's false arrest, defamation, and intentional infliction of emotional distress claims against employer were not precluded by the Workers' Compensation Act). Furthermore, damages caused by defamation are not compensable under Workers' Compensation Act. Tynes v. Shoney's Inc., 867 F. Supp. 330 (D. Md. 1994).

D. Pleading Requirements

In order for a complaint to withstand a motion to dismiss, it must allege: (1) a false and defamatory communication; (a) which the maker knows is false and knows that it defames the other, or (b) that the makers acted in reckless disregard of these matters, or (c) that the maker has acted negligently in failing to ascertain them, and (2) that the statement was one which appears on its face to be defamatory, such as a statement that one is a thief, or that the explicit extrinsic facts and innuendo make the statement defamatory; and (3) allegations of damages with some particularity. Metromedia, Inc. v. Hillman , 285 Md. 161, 172, 400 A.2d 1117, 1123 (1979) (quoted in Nistico v. Mosler Safe Co., 43 Md. App. 361, 365-66, 405 A.2d 340, 343 (1979)). See Carroll v. City of Westminster, 52 F. Supp. 2d 546 (D. Md. 1999), aff'd, 233 F.3d 208 (4th Cir. 2000). If the words are not defamatory per se, the plaintiff must also set forth in his complaint explicit extrinsic facts which demonstrate the defamatory meaning of the statement. Schoonfield v. Balt. Mayor & City Council, 399 F. Supp. 1068, 1090 n.29 (D. Md. 1975), aff'd, 544 F.2d 515 (4th Cir. 1976). If the complaint facially shows that it is subject to the employer's qualified privilege for communications arising out of the employment relationship, the complaint must further contain factual allegations of malice to survive a motion to dismiss. Id. Compare Talley v. Farrell, 156 F. Supp. 2d 534 (D. Md. 2001) (declining to dismiss plaintiff's complaint where plaintiff alleged that statements "were part of an orchestrated attempt to create a hostile environment for [him] and poison the pool of officers from whom a trial board would be drawn to hear the complaint against [him]") with Deutsch v. Chesapeake Ctr., 27 F. Supp. 2d 642, 645 (D. Md. 1998) (denying defamation claim for failure to establish malice by clear and convincing evidence). A complaint must go beyond pleading "bare assertions 'devoid of further factual enhancement,' which are not entitled to an assumption of truth." Nemet Chevrolet, LTD v. Consumeraffairs.com, Inc., 591 F.3d 250, 260 (4th Cir. 2009). Rather, a complaint must include sufficient facts to allow the court to infer more than "the mere possibility" of defamation, and must "nudge" its claims "across the line from the conceivable to plausible." Doolin, 2010 WL 3834994 at *6 (finding that a complaint stated a plausible claim of defamation where it alleged facts that defendant had communicated to third parties that plaintiff had engaged in or intended to engage in illegal conduct); Altevogt v. Kirwan, Civ. No. WDQ-11-1061, 2011 WL 3648382, *3 (D. Md. Aug. 11, 2011) (dismissing a complaint for defamation where the employee relied only on conclusory allegations, and failed to "identif[y] the third party the defamatory remark was made to, state the content of the remark, or allege what employment this prevented him from obtaining"); **Artis v. U.S. Foodservices, Inc., Civ. No. ELH-11-3406, 2012 WL 2126532, at *10 (D. Md. June 12, 2012) (dismissing a complaint for failure to state a claim of defamation where plaintiff's complaint was "devoid of a single factual allegation" to support the bald allegation that plaintiff had been "personally attacked, harass[ed], and false[ly] accuse[d] by [former employer] for years.").**

Although summary judgment is generally considered inappropriate before adequate time for discovery has taken place, the Fourth Circuit has emphasized that it, like other reviewing courts, places great weight on the Rule 56(f) Affidavit, believing that "[a] party may not simply assert in its brief that discovery was necessary and thereby overturn summary judgment when it failed to comply with the requirement of Rule 56(f) to set out reasons for the need for discovery in an Affidavit." Paukstis v. Kenwood Golf and Country Club, Inc., 241 F. Supp. 2d. 551, 561-62 (D. Md. 2003) (citing Evans v. Techs. Applications and Serv. Co., 80 F.3d. 954, 961 (4th Cir. 1996)). A claimant had a duty to undertake some factual investigation, such as providing affidavits from those who allegedly overheard the supposed defamatory statements. Id.

SURVEY OF MARYLAND EMPLOYMENT PRIVACY LAW

David A. Grant
Baker & Hostetler LLP
1050 Connecticut Avenue, N.W.
Suite 1100
Washington, D.C. 20036
Telephone: (202) 861-1500; Facsimile (202) 861-1783

(With Developments Reported Through **November 1, 2012**)

GENERAL COMMENTS

None.

SIGNIFICANT DEVELOPMENTS SINCE THE 2012 *SURVEY*

Maryland became the first state to enact legislation prohibiting employers from requesting or requiring an employee or applicant to disclose any user name, password, or other means for accessing a personal account or service. See HB 964, SB 433 (to be codified at Md. Code Ann., Lab. & Empl. § 3-712). Employers are also prohibited from taking, or threatening to take, disciplinary action or from refusing to hire a job applicant for failure to disclose such information. The legislation became effective on October 1, 2012. By its terms, then, Maryland law now protects employee access to personal social media accounts like Facebook and Twitter. The legislation, however, does not bar employers from gaining access to employee's non-personal accounts and, information stored on company internal computer systems. The legislation also does not condone the downloading by employees of employer proprietary or financial information, particularly if such conduct might lead to violations of securities or financial law or regulatory requirements. There is no explicit enforcement mechanism.

Additional legislation passed by the Maryland legislature now also prohibits "a labor organization from being compelled to disclose, under certain circumstances, certain communications or information received or acquired in confidence while acting in a representative capacity concerning an employee grievance." HB 1042, SB 797 (to be codified at Md. Code Ann., Cts. & Jud. Proc. § 9-124). The legislation became effective October 1, 2012, but does not apply to any collective-bargaining agreement in effect as of October 1, 2012 or to any communication received by a labor organization before October 1, 2012. There are a number of specified exceptions to the relevant non-disclosure requirements, especially in the context of a criminal proceeding or when the union believes disclosure is necessary to prevent certain death or substantial bodily harm. Further, the facts underlying the protected communication are not privileged or otherwise protected.

In an interesting case at the cross-section of new technology and federal criminal law, United States District Court Judge Robert Titus concluded that the application of a federal stalking statute to Twitter and blog postings constituted an impermissible content-based restriction on free speech "because it limits speech on the basis of whether that speech is emotionally distressing…." U.S. v. Cassidy, 814 F.Supp.2d 574, 584 (D. Md. 2011).

I. GENERAL LAW OF PRIVACY

A. Legal Basis of Privacy Claims

Invasion of privacy claims are based upon the common law and state constitution of Maryland. The Court of Appeals of Maryland recognized the invasion of privacy tort in Carr v. Watkins, 227 Md. 578, 586-88, 177 A.2d 841, 845-46 (1962). Recent cases affirm that Maryland recognizes the four different types of invasion of privacy set out in the Restatement (Second) of Torts § 652A(2) (1977). See Bailer v. Erie Ins. Exch., 344 Md. 515, 525-26, 687 A.2d 1375, 1380 (1997); Allen v. Bethlehem Steel Corp., 76 Md. App. 642, 647-48, 547 A.2d 1105, 1108, cert. denied, 314 Md. 458, 550 A.2d 1168 (1988). In Kessler v. Equity Management, Inc., 82 Md. App. 577, 572 A.2d 1144 (1990), the court explained that, under the Maryland constitution, civil liability exists for persons who violate others' constitutionally protected rights of privacy. See also Wholey v. Sears Roebuck Co., 370 Md. 38, 43, 803 A.2d 482, 484 (2002) (recognizing common law public policy exception to the employment-at-will doctrine protecting an employee from termination "based upon the reporting of suspected criminal activities to the appropriate law enforcement authorities"). But see Terry v. Legato Sys., Inc. 241 F. Supp. 2d 566, 569-70 (D. Md. 2003) ("internal reporting of suspected unlawful conduct is not a public policy that has been recognized in Maryland as a basis for a wrongful discharge claim"); Porterfield v. Mascari II, Inc., 374 Md. 402, 823 A.2d 590 (2003) (no violation of Maryland public policy "when an employer fires an at-will employee for stating her intent to seek advice from legal counsel before responding to an adverse employment evaluation."); Luy v. Balt. Police Dep't, 326 F. Supp.

2d 682, 691-92 (D. Md. 2004) (discussing claim for violation of Maryland public policy when identified policies could be vindicated by federal statutory remedies).

B. Causes of Action

The statute of limitations applied to all four forms of the invasion of privacy tort is three years. See Allen v. Bethlehem Steel Corp., 76 Md. App. 642, 649, 547 A.2d 1105, 1108 (citing Md. Code Ann., Courts § 5-101 (1957)), cert. denied, 314 Md. 458, 550 A.2d 1168 (1988). A forum-selection clause generally will be honored. See Berry v. Soul Circus, Inc., 189 F. Supp. 2d 290 (D. Md. 2002).

1. ***Misappropriation/Right of Publicity***. The use of another's name or likeness to advertise a business or product, or for "similar commercial purposes," may constitute an invasion of privacy. See Lawrence v. A.S. Abell Co., 299 Md. 697, 702-703, 475 A.2d 448, 451, 10 Media L. Rep. 2001 (1984). Only the appropriation of the "commercial or other values associated with the name or the likeness" of an individual is an invasion of privacy. The mere "incidental use" of an individual's identity does not constitute an invasion of privacy. Id. ("The value of the plaintiff's name is not appropriated by mere mention of it, . . . nor is [it] appropriated when it is published for purposes other than taking advantage of his reputation, prestige, or other value associated with him, for purposes of publicity." (quoting Restatement (Second) of Torts § 652C cmt. d)); LTVN Holdings, LLC v. Odeh, 2010 WL 2612690 at **5-6 (D. Md. June 25, 2010) (dismissing invasion of privacy claim on grounds of "incidental use").

2. ***False Light***. A claim for false light invasion of privacy is established where one party places another before the public in a false light, which would be "highly offensive to a reasonable person." See Bagwell v. Peninsula Reg'l Med. Center, 106 Md. App. 470, 513-14, 665 A.2d 297, 318 (1995) (quoting Restatement (Second) of Torts § 652E), cert. denied, 341 Md. 172, 669 A.2d 1360 (1996)). Recovery is permitted only where the facts publicized are not true, see id. at 514, and where the false light is communicated to the "public at large, or to so many persons that the matter must be regarded as substantially certain to become one of public knowledge," Cambridge Title Co. v. Transamerica Title Ins. Co., 817 F. Supp. 1263, 1278 (D. Md. 1992) (quoting Restatement (Second) of Torts § 652D cmt. a), aff'd, 989 F.2d 491 (4th Cir. 1993). See also Furman v. Sheppard, 130 Md. App. 67, 77, 744 A.2d 583, 587-88 (2000) (truth is a complete defense to a false light claim); Ostrzenski v. Seigel, 3 F. Supp. 2d, 648, 653 (D. Md. 1998) ("[t]he gist of the tort is a publication by the defendant that unreasonably places the plaintiff in a false and offensive light before the public"), aff'd, 177 F.3d 245 (4th Cir. 1999); Dobkin v. Johns Hopkins Univ., Civ. A. No. HAR 93-2228, 1996 U.S. Dist. LEXIS 6445, at *37 (D. Md. Apr. 17, 1996) ("In Maryland, the elements of a claim of false light invasion of privacy are: (1) publicity in a false light before the public; (2) which a reasonable person would find highly offensive; and (3) that the actor had knowledge of or acted in reckless disregard of the publicized matter placing plaintiff in a false light"), aff'd, 172 F.3d 43, Nos. 96-1715, 1716 1999 WL 22901, 1999 U.S. App. LEXIS 725 (4th Cir. Jan. 21, 1999) (unpublished disposition), cert. denied, 528 U.S. 875 (1999), accord Campbell v. Lyon, 26 Fed. Appx. 183, 188, No. 00-2275, 2001 U.S. App. LEXIS 27328 (4th Cir. Dec. 27, 2001), 2001 WL 1658895 (unpublished), Hovatter v. Logan Widdowson, 2004 U.S. Dist. LEXIS 18646 at ** 30-31 (D. Md. Sept. 15, 2004); Mazer v. Safeway, Inc., 2005 U.S. Dist. LEXIS 25802 at ** 49-52 (D. Md. Oct. 22, 2005); S. Volkswagen, Inc. v. Centrix Fin., LLC, 357 F. Supp. 2d 837, 845-46 (D. Md. 2005), (distinguishing false light claim from defamation or publicity claims). Holland v. Psychological Assessment Resources, Inc., 482 F. Supp. 2d, 667, 681 (D. Md. 2007) (reiterating elements of false light cause of action and dismissing claim when the truth of all the statements on which the false light claim was undisputed); Alford v. Genesis Healthcare, 2007 U.S. Dist. LEXIS 26196, at ** 17-19 (D. Md. Apr. 9, 2007) (granting summary judgment on false light claim where statement was protected by a conditional or qualified privilege). Spence v. NCI Information Systems, Inc., 2009 U.S. Dist. LEXIS 16415 at *23 (D. Md. Feb. 27, 2009) (same). Henderson v. Claire's Stores, Inc., 607 F. Supp.2d 725, 733 (D. Md. 2009) (granting summary judgment on false light claim when there was no evidence that statements were made to the public at large and at most statements were "within earshot of a small group of individuals who may or may not have heard part or all of … [the] statements"). **Byington *v. NBRS* Financial Bank, 2012 WL 4846757 (D. Md. Oct. 10, 2012) (alleged false accusation of "check kiting" against a former employee and her accompanying compelled self-publication of the accusation "does not reach the level of publicity required to state a plausible false light claim because she only communicated this information to a small group of potential employers").**

Publicity of matters of general public interest, or of matters relating to public officials or public figures, may constitute an invasion of privacy if done with malice, which is found where the party acted with knowledge of falsity or reckless disregard for the truth. See Harnish v. Herald-Mail Co., 264 Md. 326, 337, 286 A.2d 146, 152 (1972).

Where plaintiff alleged only that defendant appointed to conduct physician peer review had falsely misrepresented that he had no conflicts of interest with plaintiff, court granted motion to dismiss false light claim on grounds that allegedly false statement "is not even mildly offensive, let alone 'highly offensive' as required by Maryland law." Ostrzenski, 3 F. Supp. 2d at 653.

In Simon v. Union Hosp., Inc., 15 F. Supp. 2d 787, 797 (D. Md. 1998), aff'd in relevant part, 199 F.3d 1328, No. 98-2138, 1999 WL 957744, 2 1999 U.S. App. LEXIS 26453 (4th Cir. Oct. 20, 1999), the federal district court held that the Maryland common law qualified privilege which protects allegedly defamatory statements which the defendant publishes "'in furtherance of his own legitimate interests, or those shared in common with the recipient or third parties, or where his declaration would be of interest to the public in general,'" applied equally to the plaintiff's false light claim. Id. at 795 (quoting Marchesi v. Franchino, 283 Md. 131, 387 A.2d 1129 (1978)). Thus, because the plaintiff failed to show that his former employer acted with actual malice when it reported to the National Physician's Data Bank that the plaintiff was being suspended for apparent violations of billing practices, his claim was dismissed. See also Sodergren v. Johns Hopkins Univ. Applied Physics Lab., 138 Md. App. 686, 694-705, 773 A.2d 592, 597-604 (2001) (applying absolute judicial privilege to bar, inter alia, false light claims based upon dissemination of letters of apology as part of litigation settlement). Reichardt v. Flynn, 374 Md. 361, 823 A.2d 566 (2003) (absolute privilege applied to communications made during course of internal investigation by public school system of alleged misconduct of teacher and coach); Mazer v. Safeway, Inc., supra, 2005 U.S. Dist. LEXIS 25802 at ** 49-52 (D. Md. Oct. 27, 2005) (conditional privilege applies to employer's statements alleging misappropriation of confidential company information and granting summary judgment).

Under Maryland law, a claim for false light or invasion of privacy defamation does not survive an individual's death. See Coppinger v. Schantag, 2006 U.S. Dist. LEXIS 222 (D. Md. Jan. 5, 2006).

3. ***Publication of Private Facts***. Publicity of private matters is an invasion of privacy if the publicity would be highly offensive to a reasonable person, and the matter publicized is not of legitimate public concern. See Bilney v. The Evening Star Newspaper Co., 43 Md. App. 560, 406 A.2d 652, 5 Media L. Rep. 1931 (1979) (quoting Restatement (Second) of Torts § 652D); Reuber v. Food Chem. News, Inc., 925 F.2d 703, 719, 18 Media L. Rep. 1689 (4th Cir. 1991), cert. denied, 501 U.S. 1212 (1991). The standard of reasonableness may differ in the employment context, where an employer may have a legitimate interest in a private matter where a member of the public would not. See Household Fin. Corp. v. Bridge, 252 Md. 531, 539, 250 A.2d 878, 883 (1969) (stating that an employer, unlike the general public, may have a legitimate interest in the debts owed by an employee) (quoting Patton v. Jacobs, 118 Ind. App. 358, 365, 78 N.E.2d 789, 791-792 (1948)).

The publicity must be a public disclosure, not a private communication, in order to constitute unreasonable publicity of an individual's private life. See Household Fin. Corp., 252 Md. at 542-43. The facts disclosed must be private and otherwise unavailable to the public, and may trigger liability even if true. See Hollander v. Lubow, 277 Md. 47, 57-58, 351 A.2d 421, 426-27 (quoting W. Prosser, The Law of Torts, 809-811, 814 (4th ed. 1971)), cert. denied, 426 U.S. 936 (1976). See also Furman v. Sheppard, 130 Md. App. 67, 77, 744 A.2d 583, 588 (2000) (affirming grant of dismissal on private facts claim where the pictures of plaintiff taken by private investigator would have been admissible in personal injury suit and were taken while plaintiff was on a yacht in navigable water in open view to the public); Taylor v. NationsBank, N.A., 128 Md. App. 414, 738 A.2d 893 (1999), aff'd in relevant part, 365 Md. 166, 776 A.2d 645 (2001) (rejecting plaintiff's private facts claim based upon bank's revelation of unlisted phone number to plaintiff's employer because (1) the unlisted number "does not achieve the level of a private fact that, if revealed, could cause a reasonable person the kind of mental distress that resembles the distress suffered by victims of defamation," and (2) "revelation to a single person" does not satisfy the "publicity" requirement of the tort); Interphase Garment Solutions, LLC v. Fox Television Studios, Inc., 566 F. Supp.2d 460, 467 (D. Md. 2008) (rejecting plaintiff's invasion of privacy claim because public court documents are not private facts); Campbell v. Lyon, 26 Fed. Appx. 183, 188, No. 00-2275, 2001 U.S. App. LEXIS 27328 (4th Cir. Dec. 27, 2001), 2001 WL 1658895 (unpublished) (confirming absence of liability when the defendant merely gives further publicity to information about the plaintiff that is already public) (citation and quotation omitted). But see Talley v. Farrell, 156 F. Supp. 2d 534 (D. Md. 2001) (rejecting police psychologist's motion to dismiss when employee alleged that psychologist revealed certain statements made by employee "in the context of a routine counseling session" to members of police department's Internal Affairs Division.), appeal dismissed, 43 Fed. Appx. 657, 2002 WL 1932402 (4th Cir. 2002) (unpublished).

Even where there is a legitimate public interest, there are limits as to what private facts may be publicized. A balancing is required in order to determine if the public interest outweighs the privacy interests of the individual. See Bilney v. The Evening Star Newspaper Co., 43 Md. App. 560, 572-73, 406 A.2d 652, 660 (1979) ("Some reasonable proportion is also to be maintained between the event or activity that makes the individual a public figure and the private facts to which publicity is given.") (quoting Restatement (Second) of Torts § 652D cmt. h).

An insurer may have a duty to defend an employer against a claim for "false light" under an insurance policy encompassing "[o]ral or written publication of material that violates a person's right of privacy." Applied Signal & Image Technology v. Harleysville Mutual Ins. Co., 252 F. Supp. 2d 215, 216-19 (D. Md. 2003).

4. ***Intrusion***. An intentional intrusion into the private affairs or seclusion of another, which would offend a reasonable person, constitutes a tortious invasion of privacy. See Bailer v. Erie Ins. Exch., 344 Md. 515, 526, 687

A.2d 1375, 1380-81 (Md. 1997) (quoting Restatement (Second) of Torts § 652B); Hollander v. Lubow, 277 Md. 47, 56-57, 351 A.2d 421, 426 (1976) (quoting William Prosser, The Law of Torts, 807-08 (4th ed. 1971)), cert. denied, 426 U.S. 936 (1976); McCauley v. Suls, 123 Md. App. 179, 190, 716 A.2d 1129, 1134 (1998) ("Wrongful intrusion requires an intentional act"); Mitchell v. Baltimore Sun Co., 164 Md. App. 497, 883 A.2d 1008 (2005), cert. denied, 889 A.2d 418 (2006). The intentional act must be one of intrusion or prying, see id. at 57 (quoting William Prosser, The Law of Torts, 807-808 (4th ed. 1971)), and must be an intrusion into a "private place or . . . a private seclusion that the plaintiff has thrown about his person or affairs" in order to trigger liability, see Pemberton v. Bethlehem Steel Corp., 66 Md. App. 133, 163, 502 A.2d 1101, 1116 (quoting Restatement (Second) of Torts § 652B cmt. c), cert. denied, 306 Md. 289, 508 A.2d 488, cert. denied, 479 U.S. 984 (1986). Accord Trundle v. Homeside Lending, Inc., 162 F. Supp. 2d 396 (D. Md. 2001). There is no liability for observing a plaintiff in a public place because the plaintiff is not then in seclusion. Furman v. Sheppard, 130 Md. App. 67, 73, 744 A.2d 583, 586 (2000) (internal citations omitted).

C. Other Privacy-Related Actions

1. *Intentional Infliction of Emotional Distress*

a. **Elements.** Maryland has recognized the tort of intentional infliction of emotional distress since the case of Harris v. Jones, 281 Md. 560, 380 A.2d 611 (1977). See generally Lasater v. Guttman, 2010 WL 3528859 at *9 (Md. Sept. 13, 2010) (noting that "[i]n the 30 years since the Court of Appeals recognized the tort ... it has upheld such claims only four times") (citing cases). For a plaintiff to recover for intentional infliction of emotional distress, he or she must satisfy following elements: (1) conduct must be intentional or reckless; (2) conduct must be extreme and outrageous; (3) there must be causal connection between wrongful conduct and emotional distress; and (4) emotional distress must be severe. Penhollow v. Bd. of Comm'rs for Cecil County, 116 Md. App. 265, 695 A.2d 1268 (1997); Doe v. Doe, 122 Md. App. 295, 335, 712 A.2d 132, 152 (1998), rev'd on other grounds, 358 Md. 113, 747 A.2d 617 (2000); Gantt v. Sec., USA, Inc., 356 F.3d 547, 552-53 (4th Cir.), cert. denied, 125 S.Ct. 51 (2004); Park v. Miller, 2004 U.S. Dist. LEXIS 21690 at * 14 (D. Md. Oct. 28, 2004) (stressing that "[t]o qualify as severe emotional distress, the plaintiff must have suffered a severely disabling emotional response to the defendant's conduct . . . which must be pled with specific facts regarding the nature, intensity, and duration of the alleged emotional trauma.") (quotations and citations omitted); McKenzie v. Comcast Cable Communs., Inc., 2005 U.S. Dist. LEXIS 23520 at ** 37-38 (D. Md. July 21, 2005) (reiterating that, under Maryland law, tort of intentional infliction of emotional distress is rarely viable) (quotation and citation omitted); Valderrama v. Honeywell Technology Solutions, Inc., 473 F. Supp. 2d 658, 666 & n.20 (D. Md. 2007) ("[t]he tort is reserved for only a disabling emotional response, for wounds that are incapable of healing themselves") (citations and quotations omitted); Takacs v. Fiore, 473 F. Supp. 2d 647, 656 (D. Md. 2007) (claim dismissed when, among other things, individual "was unable to work" and "her daily functioning was adequate"); Knox v. State Farm & Cas. Co., 2005 U.S. Dist. LEXIS 8113 at ** 8-11 (D. Md. May 5, 2005) (stressing that Maryland does not recognize a cause of action for negligent infliction of emotional distress.) Accord, Jacobsen v. Towers, Perrin, Forster & Crosby, Inc., 2006 U.S. Dist. LEXIS 79924 at ** 14-18 (D. Md. Oct. 31, 2006).

For conduct to meet the test of "outrageousness," it must be "so extreme in degree, as to go beyond all possible bounds of decency, and to be regarded as atrocious, and utterly intolerable in a civilized community." Whether the conduct complained of meets this test is, in the first instance, for the court to determine; in addressing that question, the court must consider not only the conduct itself but also the "personality of the individual to whom the misconduct is directed." This high standard of culpability exists to screen out claims amounting to "mere insults, indignities, threats, annoyances, petty oppressions, or other trivialities" that simply must be endured as part of life." Batson v. Shiflett, 325 Md. 684, 734, 602 A.2d 1191 (1992) [citations omitted]. See also Simon v. Union Hosp. Inc., 15 F. Supp. 2d 787, 799 (D. Md. 1998) ("Maryland courts are reluctant to mete out recovery under the tort of intentional infliction of emotional distress"), aff'd in relevant part, 199 F.3d 1328, No. 98-2138, 1999 WL 957744, 1999 U.S. App. LEXIS 26453 (4th Cir. October 20, 1999); Estate of Alcalde v. Deaton Specialty Hosp. Home, Inc., 133 F. Supp. 2d 702, 712 (D. Md. 2001). Silvera v. Home Depot U.S.A., Inc., 189 F. Supp. 2d 304, 311-12 (D. Md. 2002) (stressing that intentional infliction tort is "reserved for those wounds that are truly severe and incapable of healing themselves") (quotation and citation omitted). Baltimore-Clark v. Kinko's Inc., 270 F. Supp. 2d 695, 701 (D. Md. 2003) (emphasizing difficulty of satisfying elements of intentional infliction claim); Clark v. Dep't of Pub. Safety & Corr. Servs, 247 F. Supp. 773, 778 (D. Md. 2003). Waldrop v. Science Applications Int'l Corp., 2010 WL 2773571 at *3 (D. Md. Jul. 13, 2010) (no prima facie case of "outrageousness" despite supervisor's numerous inappropriate remarks relating to national origin, selection of individual for "additional training in the English language," embarrassment of individual being forced to wear "blue gilded sunglasses at staff meeting ... for being 3-5 minutes late for the meeting," and refusal of supervisor to communicate with individual). **Robinson v. Darcars of New Carrollton, Inc., 2012 WL 993405 at *3-4 (D. Md. March 22, 2012) (use of racial slur "nigger" in front of several African-American employees and pulling of employee's hair not sufficiently "extreme and outrageous").**

A Maryland court will also consider (a) the actor's knowledge that the other is peculiarly susceptible to emotional distress, (b) the setting of the conduct, especially where the actor (such as an employer) is in a peculiar position to harass the plaintiff, and (c) the personality of the individual to whom the misconduct is directed. Weathersby v. Kentucky Fried Chicken Nat'l Mgmt. Co., 86 Md. App. 533, 587 A.2d 569 (1991) (recognizing Montgomery County Code provision that bars employment discrimination based on sexual orientation), rev'd on other grounds, 326 Md. 663, 607 A.2d 8 (1992). Ford v. Douglas, 144 Md. App. 620, 799 A.2d 448, 452 (2002) (reiterating totality of circumstances analysis, including consideration of conduct that might also be encompassed within separate cause of action for battery). See Green v. Wills Group, Inc., 161 F. Supp. 2d 618, 624 (D. Md. 2001) (rejecting intentional infliction claim when, among other things, plaintiff was an "active participant" in taped conversations that were integral to her claim and "was heard laughing multiple times.")

b. **Relationship to Employment Law.** In one privacy-related case, a Maryland court held in favor of an employee who claimed intentional infliction of emotional distress based on her employer's constructively discharging her for failure to take a polygraph test. Moniodis v. Cook, 64 Md. App. 1, 494 A. 2d 212, cert. denied, 304 Md. 631, 500 A. 2d 649 (1985). The court upheld the plaintiff's common law claims even though there was a Maryland statute banning employers from making hiring decisions based on refusals to take polygraph tests, because the statute provided no private right of action, and therefore the court was not convinced that the plaintiff had a sufficient legal remedy without the availability of common law claims. In general, however, Maryland courts have expressed an unwillingness to allow claims of intentional infliction of emotional distress where other claims — statutory or common law — are more appropriate. See Miller v. Ratner, 114 Md. App. 18, 688 A.2d 976 (1996) (denying an employee's intentional infliction of emotional distress claim on the basis that "One cannot sue to recover for injuries arising from [an action that is legally acceptable] by simply casting the defendant's conduct as a breach of contract, or negligence, or some other intentional tort."), cert. denied, 345 Md. 458, 693 A.2d 355 (1997). In Simon v. Union Hosp., Inc., 15 F. Supp. 2d 787, 799-800 (D. Md. 1998), the court dismissed a former employee's claim for intentional infliction of emotional distress finding that the evidence that plaintiff "is under tremendous stress, requires counseling, is often depressed, despondent and unable to sleep" failed to demonstrate that his emotional response is "so severe that 'no reasonable man . . . should be expected to endure it'") (citation omitted) (alteration in original), aff'd in relevant part, 199 F.3d 1328, No. 98-2138, 1999 WL 957744, 2 1999 U.S. App. LEXIS 26453 (4th Cir. October 20, 1999); see also Thacker v. City of Hyattsville, 135 Md. App. 268, 315-16, 762 A.2d 172, 197 (2000), cert. denied, 363 Md. 206, 768 A.2d 55 (2001) (upholding trial court's dismissal of employee's intentional infliction claim against arresting officer and city officials because employee failed to prove his distress was severe where he continued his employment at the site where he had been arrested and pursued his normal life activities); Manikhi v. Mass Transit Admin., 360 Md. 333, 758 A.2d 95 (2000) (rejecting former employee's claim for intentional infliction of emotional distress because allegation that she was forced "to seek medical treatment" as a result of the alleged harassing behavior of co-worker was insufficient to demonstrate the severe emotional distress necessary); Harley v. Suburban Hospital, Inc., 2004 U.S. Dist. LEXIS 7809 at ** 15-18 (D. Md. Apr. 30, 2004); aff'd per curiam, 122 Fed. Appx. 39, 2005 U.S. App. LEXIS 2708 (January 21, 2005). As inappropriate as workplace harassment is, such behavior almost never rises to the level of outrageousness, and almost never results in such severely debilitating emotional trauma, as to reach the high threshold invariably applicable to a claim of intentional infliction of emotional distress under Maryland law. Arbabi v. Fred Meyers, Inc., 205 F. Supp. 2d 462, 466 (D. Md. 2002); Alston v. Baltimore Gas & Elec. Co., Civil Action No. CCB-07-2237, 2008 WL 5428126 at *7 (D. Md. Dec. 31, 2008) (stating that poor behavior at the workplace rarely rises to the level of outrageous required for a claim of intentional infliction of emotional distress).

2. ***Interference With Prospective Economic Advantage.*** Maryland recognizes the torts of intentional interference with existing contractual relationships, and intentional interference with potential contractual relationships. See Fowler v. Printers II, 89 Md. App. 448, 598 A.2d 794 (1991), cert. denied, 325 Md. 619, 602 A.2d 710 (1992), Sharrow v. State Farm Mut. Auto Ins. Co., 306 Md. 754, 511 A.2d 492 (1986); accord, Mona Elec. Group, Inc. v. Truland Serv Corp., 56 Fed. Appx. 108, 110, 2003 U.S. App. LEXIS 83 (4th Cir. Jan. 6, 2003) (unpublished) ("[p]ursuant to Maryland law, tortious interference with contract and tortious interference with prospective contracts falling under the single tort of tortious interference with economic relations"). Intentional interference with contractual or economic relations is shown when there is: (1) a contract or a legally protected expectation between the plaintiff and a third party; (2) that the defendant knows about; (3) and the defendant intentionally interferes with the contract or expectation for the defendant's own benefit or to injure the plaintiff; (4) without justification; (5) resulting in actual damages to the plaintiff. Bagwell v. Peninsula Reg'l Med. Ctr., 106 Md. App. 470, 665 A.2d 297 (1995), cert. denied, 341 Md. 172, 669 A.2d 1360 (1996); Prudential Real Estate Affiliates, Inc. v. Long & Foster Real Estate, Inc., 208 F.3d 210 (table), 2000 WL 248170, 2000 U.S. App. LEXIS 3394 (4th Cir. Mar. 6, 2000) (same). havePower, LLC v. Gen. Elec. Co., 183 F. Supp. 2d 779, 784-85 (D. Md. 2002); MCS Services, Inc. v. Jones, 2010 WL 3895380 at **5-6 (D. Md. Oct. 1, 2010) (denying motion to dismiss in the wake of allegations that third party hired former employee, accepted confidential trade secrets of former employee's employer, and then used this information to intimidate customers to cease doing business with former employee's employer). In the case of interference with at will employment relationships, a plaintiff must show an additional element: that the defendant used wrongful means in interfering with the contract. Fowler, supra, Waterfall Farm Sys., Inc. v. Craig, 914 F. Supp. 1213 (D. Md. 1995), Macklin v. Logan, 334 Md. 287, 639 A.2d. 112 (1994). See Lofton v. TLC Laser Eye Ctrs., Inc., No. Civ. CCB-00-1667, 2001 WL

121809, 2001 U.S. Dist. LEXIS 1476 (D. Md. Feb. 8, 2001) ("there is no malicious or wrongful interference, particularly with an at-will contract . . . where TLC is acting to enforce a colorable, even if ultimately unenforceable, contractual right"); Ancora Capital &. Mgmt. Group, LLC v. Corporate Mailing Servs. Inc., 214 F. Supp. 2d 493, 500 (D. Md. 2002) ("trading on the goodwill" of former at-will employee may constitute "wrongful means" that justifies pursuit of tortious interference claim).

As a matter of law, a party to a contract and/or his agents cannot tortiously "interfere" with his or her own contract; the party can, at most, breach it. Natural Design, Inc. v. The Rouse Co., 302 Md. 47, 71, 48 A.2d 663 (1984); Clark v. Dep't of Public Safety and Corr. Servs, 247 F. Supp. 773, 777-78 (D. Md. 2003); Baron Fin. Corp. v. Natanzon, 2006 U.S. Dist. LEXIS 46854 at ** 7-8 (D. Md. July 11, 2006).

3. ***Prima Facie Tort.*** Maryland does not recognize a cause of action for prima facie tort.

II. EMPLOYER TESTING OF EMPLOYEES

A. Psychological or Personality Testing

Although Maryland has no law regarding psychological or personality testing of employees, Maryland does prohibit employers from requiring applicants to answer questions regarding physical, psychiatric, or psychological disability, illness, handicap or treatment unless the disability, illness, handicap or treatment "has a direct, material, and timely relationship to the capacity or fitness of the applicant to perform the job properly." Md. Code Ann., Lab. & Empl. § 3-701.

B. Drug Testing

If an employer has a legitimate business reason, it may require an employee, a prospective employee or a contractor to be tested for the use or abuse of any controlled dangerous substance or alcohol. Md. Code Ann., Health-Gen. § 17-214 Provided the employer has a legitimate business reason, the employer must have the specimen, which may be blood, urine or hair (and, beginning on October 1, 2003, saliva), with some restrictions listed in the statute, tested by a laboratory approved under the statute. Md. Code Ann., Health-Gen. § 17-214(b) (as amended by 2003 Md. Laws 88). At the time of the testing and if the person tested requests, the employer must inform the employee of the name and address of the laboratory that will test the employee's specimen. Id. at § 17-214(b)(1)(ii).

Upon receiving and confirming a positive test result, the employer must provide the employee with: (i) a copy of the laboratory test indicating the test results, (ii) a copy of the employer's written policy on the use or abuse of controlled dangerous substances or alcohol by employees, contractors, or other persons, (iii) if applicable, written notice of the employer's intent to take disciplinary action, terminate employment, or change the conditions of continued employment and, (iv) a statement or copy of the provisions set forth in the statute's subsection on verification of test result. Id. at § 17-214(c)(1). The employer must provide this information to the employee in person or by certified mail within thirty days from the date the test was performed. Id. at § 17-214(c)(2). In addition, the person required to submit to the job related alcohol and controlled dangerous substance test may request that another approved laboratory perform an independent test on the same sample, provided the employee pays the cost of the test. Id. at § 17-214(e) (as recodified by Md. Laws 2001 ch. 615).

Recognizing the intrusive nature of alcohol and drug testing, Maryland has attempted to limit the scope of information the employer may receive from the test. Id. at § 17-214(i) (as recodified by Md. Laws 2001 ch. 615). According to the statute, the laboratory, physician or any other person, in the course of obtaining information for or as a result of the job related alcohol and controlled dangerous substance test, may not reveal to the employer: (i) the use of a non-prescription drug, excluding alcohol, that is not prohibited under the laws of the State, or (ii) the use of a medically prescribed drug, unless the person being tested is unable to establish that the drug was medically prescribed under the laws of the state. Id. However, the prohibitions of disclosure do not apply to the extent they conflict with the Federal Commercial Motor Vehicle Safety Act of 1986 and the Federal Motor Carrier Safety Regulations. Id.

In Carroll v. City of Westminster, 52 F. Supp. 2d 546 (D. Md. 1999), aff'd, 233 F.3d 208 (4th Cir. 2000), the federal district court rejected a challenge to the constitutionality of the defendant police department's drug testing policy. Under the policy, all newly-hired police officers were required to sign a drug test waiver which provided that:

> As a condition of employment with the Westminster Police Department, the undersigned employee agree's [sic] that the Police Department may at anytime [sic], with or without cause, require tests relating to the use of any drugs; such tests to include, but not be limited to chemical tests, urinalysis, polygraph, etc.; within the condition as a perquisite [sic] to employment with the Westminster Police Department.

Following his termination for failing a drug test, the plaintiff brought a 42 U.S.C. § 1983 action alleging that the defendants violated his Fourth Amendment rights by subjecting him to urinalysis pursuant to an unconstitutional policy and by performing drug testing on him without his knowledge. The court rejected the plaintiff's claims holding that, "Westminster's substantial interests in insuring that its police officers are drug free clearly justifies departure from the warrant or individualized suspicion requirement necessary to conduct a Fourth Amendment search." Id. at 558. Additionally, the court found that the defendants had a proper basis for the test based upon individualized suspicion, and that "[s]igning that waiver constituted sufficient notice to Carroll that his urine could be tested at any time." Id. at 560.

C. Medical Testing

Maryland does not prohibit an employer from having a physician conduct a proper medical evaluation on an applicant to assess his or her ability to perform the job. Md. Code Ann., Lab. & Empl. § 3-701(a). In hiring an employee, an employer may base its hiring decisions on physical or mental qualifications that are "bona fide occupational qualification[s] reasonably necessary to the performance of the normal operation of that particular business or enterprise." Md. Code Ann., art. 49B, § 12; Balt. and Ohio R. Co. v. Bowen, 60 Md. App. 299, 482 A.2d 921 (1983); Jana Guy, The Developing Law on Equal Employment Opportunity for the Handicapped, 7 U. Balt. L. Rev. 183 (1978). Conversely, it is an unlawful employment practice for an employer to fail to refuse to hire or to discharge any individual because of a physical or mental handicap "unrelated in nature or extent so as to reasonably preclude the performance of the employment." Md. Code Ann., art. 49B, § 12.

In interviewing or testing an employee, an employer may not require a prospective employee to answer an oral or written question that relates to a physical, psychiatric, or psychological disability, illness, handicap, or treatment unless the disability, illness, handicap, or treatment has a direct, material, and timely relationship to the capacity or fitness of the applicant to perform the job properly. Md. Code Ann., Lab. & Empl. § 3-701(b) If the employer violates this section, an applicant for employment has two choices: the applicant may submit to the Commissioner of Labor and Employment a written complaint, or the applicant may bring an action for injunctive relief, damages, or other relief. Md. Code Ann., Lab. & Empl. § 3-701(c).

D. Polygraph Tests

Employers may not require or demand, as a condition of employment, prospective employment, or continued employment, that an individual submit to a lie detector test or other similar test which includes a polygraph test. Md. Code Ann., Lab. & Empl. §§ 3-702. However, the statute creates an exception to this prohibited activity for certain law enforcement officers and correctional officers. Md. Code Ann., Lab. & Empl. §§ 3-702(b)(2), (3). Insuring that the employee or prospective employee is aware of this law, Maryland law requires an employer to set out the following notice in bold-faced upper case type in its employment application: "Under Maryland law, an employer may not require or demand, as a condition of employment, prospective employment, or continued employment, that an individual submit to or take a lie detector or similar test. An employer who violated this law is guilty of a misdemeanor and subject to a fine not exceeding $100." Md. Code Ann., Lab. & Empl. § 3-702(d)(1). In addition, the application must provide a space for the applicant to sign the document, acknowledging receipt of the notice, and the applicant must sign the notice. Md. Code Ann., Lab. & Empl. § 3-702(d)(2), (e).

If the employer violates the statute, the District Court of Maryland, interpreting Maryland law, has held that no private right of action for damages exists arising from the mere violation of the statute. Johnson v. United Parcel Servs., Inc. 722 F. Supp. 1282, 1283 (D. Md. 1989), aff'd, 927 F.2d 596 (4th Cir. 1991). As the Court of Special Appeals held in Weathersby v. Kentucky Fried Chicken National Management Co., the statute is sufficiently written to provide aggrieved persons with an adequate remedy for an employer's violation of the statute. Weathersby v. Kentucky Fried Chicken Nat'l Mgmt. Co., 86 Md. App. 533, 546 (1991), rev'd on other grounds, 326 Md. 663, 607 A.2d 8 (1992). Upon an employer's violation of the statute, an employee or prospective employee may submit a written complaint to the Commissioner of Labor and Industry. Md. Code Ann., Lab. & Empl. § 3-702(f). If the Commissioner of Labor and Industry determines that an employer has violated the statute, the commissioner may attempt to resolve the situation through mediation, or request that the Attorney General bring an action on behalf of the employee seeking injunctive relief and monetary damages. Md. Code Ann., Lab. & Empl. § 3-702(g).

E. Fingerprinting

Although Maryland law does not prohibit private employers from fingerprinting an employee or prospective employee, in some cases, Maryland law requires employers and employees to be fingerprinted as part of a criminal history records check. For example, prospective employees of certain private child care facilities must undergo a criminal history records check. Md. Code Ann., Fam. Law § 5-561, 562 (subject to technical amendments, effective January 1, 2006). As a condition of a criminal history records check, a prospective employee or employee must submit to the appropriate agency a complete set of legible fingerprints. In another example, employers of Adult Dependent Care Programs may require criminal history records checks which includes the fingerprinting of employees. Md. Code Ann., Health-Gen. § 19-1901.

III. SEARCHES

A. Employee's Person

Although there are no reported cases regarding employer searches of employees' persons, Maryland case law suggests that an employee's right of privacy at work may be limited when the employer has made clear that it reserves the right to search the workplace. Faulkner v. State, 317 Md. 441, 564 A.2d 785 (1989). In United States v. Simons, 206 F.3d 392, 398 (4th Cir. 2000), aff'd, 5 Fed. Appx. 332, No. 00-4571, 2001 WL 265182 (4th Cir. Mar. 19, 2001), cert. denied, 122 S. Ct. 292 (2001) the United States Court of Appeals for the Fourth Circuit held that remote, warrantless searches of defendant's office computer by his public employer, and employer's entry into defendant's office to retrieve his hard drive "did not violate his Fourth Amendment rights."

B. Employee's Work Area

Although there are no reported cases regarding employer searches of employees' work areas, Maryland case law suggests that an employee's right of privacy at work may be limited when the employer has made clear that it reserves the right to search the workplace. Faulkner v. State, 317 Md. 441, 564 A.2d 785 (1989).

C. Employee's Property

An employee may not have a reasonable expectation of privacy in property stored at work, when the employer has made clear that it reserves the right to search the workplace. Faulkner v. State, 317 Md. 441, 564 A.2d 785 (1989) (employer justified in searching employees' lockers).

On a related note, one court held that an employee who is terminated for refusing to invade another's private property may maintain a cause of action for wrongful discharge in violation of public policy. Kessler v. Equity Mgmt. Inc., 82 Md. App. 577, 572 A.2d 1144 (1990) (". . . the constitutionally protected right of privacy, the right to be free of others' snooping, spying, rummaging, or searching through one's personal and private papers, is such a fundamental right that no employer may require an employee to violate it as a condition of employment").

IV. MONITORING OF EMPLOYEES

A. Telephones and Electronic Communications

1. ***Wiretapping.*** Intentionally intercepting the telephone conversation of an employee is a felony, unless the employer is a party to the conversation and has obtained prior consent from all persons involved in the conversation. Md. Code Ann., Cts. & Jud. Proc. §§ 10-402 and 10-410; see also Perry v. State, 357 Md. 37, 741 A.2d 1162 (1999) (paragraph c(3) of section 10-402 is the only provision that would allow a private person, not acting as a government agent in conformance with a court order, or as an employee of a communications company, to intercept a wire communication). Violation of this statute carries a maximum penalty of 5 years imprisonment and/or a fine of $100,000. Notably, the National Labor Relations Act does not exempt an employee from prosecution for violations of the wiretapping act, even if the employee's wiretapping activity was arguably for the purpose of concerted activity. Petric v. State of Md., 66 Md. App. 470, 504 A.2d 1168, cert. denied, 306 Md. 289, 508 A.2d 489 (1986). See also O'Shea v. Teamsters Local 639, 2006 U.S. Dist. LEXIS 12325 at * 4 (D. Md. March 23, 2006) (no breach of Union's duty of fair representation and upholding arbitration award terminating employment of individual who secretly taped conversations with Company officials in violation of Paragraph (c)(3) of Section 10-402). For a recent discussion of the Maryland Wiretap Act, see Schmerling v. Injured Workers' Insurance Fund, 368 Md. 434, 448-50, 454, 795 A.2d 715, 723, 726 (Md. 2002) ("add-on" monitoring and recording equipment ostensibly utilized to evaluate and improve customer service nonetheless did not fall within statutory "telephone exemption" and constituted prohibited intercepting device).

2. ***Electronic Communications.*** Intentionally intercepting the electronic communication of an employee is a felony, unless the employer is a party to the communication and has obtained prior consent from all persons involved in the conversation. Md. Code Ann., Cts. & Jud. Proc. § 10-402. Violation of this statute is a felony that carries a maximum penalty of 5 years imprisonment and/or a fine of $100,000.

3. ***Other Electronic Monitoring.*** There are no officially reported Maryland cases specifically addressing employer monitoring of employee computer keystroking.

B. Mail

The Maryland law prohibits the taking and breaking open of "any letter whatsoever" by anyone who is not the intended recipient, unless the intended recipient has given permission, was repealed in 2002. Md. Legis. Acts 2002, Ch. 26 §

1 (repealing Md. Code Ann., art. 27, § 354). There currently has been no reenactment of this section or the enactment of a section covering the same subject matter. There is no specific law governing employers.

C. Surveillance/ Photographing

Surveillance, depending on how it is conducted, may constitute an invasion of privacy. Pemberton v. Bethlehem Steel Corp., 66 Md. App. 133, 502 A.2d 1101, cert. denied, 306 Md. 289, 508 A.2d 488, cert. denied, 479 U.S. 984 (1986). If it is conducted in a reasonable and non-obtrusive manner, it is not actionable. Id. at 164, 1117. In Furman v. Sheppard, 130 Md. App. 67, 744 A.2d 583 (2000), the Maryland Court of Special Appeals rejected the plaintiffs' argument that a private investigator's videotaping of them at a private yacht club constituted an invasion of privacy because the investigator, although trespassing while conducting the surveillance, observed the plaintiffs in a public waterway in full view of other boaters.

An employee who seeks to hold his employer liable for surveillance must prove that (1) the employer intentionally intruded upon his solitude or seclusion or private affairs; and (2) this intrusion is highly offensive to a reasonable person. Pemberton, 306 Md. at 163, 508 A.2d at 1116.

Md. Code Ann. art. 27, § 597C regulating visual surveillance in bathrooms or restrooms in retail stores was repealed in 2001 (Md. Legis. Acts 2001, c.10).

V. ACTIVITIES OUTSIDE THE WORKPLACE

A. Statute or Common Law

Under Maryland's "Fair Employment Practices Act," an employer cannot discharge, refuse to hire, or otherwise discriminate against an employee because of the employee's religious activities during non-working hours. See Md. Code Ann., State Gov. § 20-606(a) (prohibiting employment discrimination based on race, color, religion, sex, age, disability, national origin, marital status, sexual orientation, genetic information, refusal to submit to a genetic test or make available the results of a genetic test). See generally Shabazz v. Bob Evans Farms, Inc., 163 Md. App. 602, 881 A.2d 1212, cert. denied, 390 Md. 92, 887 A.2d 656 (2005). **Taylor v. Giant of Maryland, LLC, 423 Md. 628, 650, 33 A.3d 445, 458 (2011) (sex discrimination and retaliation claims were not preempted by Section 301 of the Labor-Management Relations Act, as amended, when employer's action did not turn on meaning and interpretation of collective-bargaining agreement, but on employer's "design in invoking" the agreement).** Agreements to arbitrate statutory employment discrimination claims are enforceable under appropriate circumstances. See Holloman v. Circuit City Stores, Inc., 391 Md. 580, 588-98, 894 A.2d 547, 551-58 (Md. 2006). In addition, employers in the executive branch of state government cannot lawfully regulate off-duty conduct by discriminating on the basis of political affiliation. See Md. Code Ann., State Pers. & Pens. § 5-208(b) (1997). Unlike some jurisdictions, Maryland does not have a broad "Legal Activities Law" that prohibits discrimination against employees who engage in lawful activities that an employer finds objectionable.

However, certain public employers may regulate off-duty conduct of public servants. For example, officers in the Department of Safety and Correctional Services must adhere to the Department's rules on personal conduct at all times, whether on or off-duty. See Dep't of Pub. Safety & Corr. Servs. v. Howard, 339 Md. 357, 663 A.2d 74 (1995) (observing that a violation of a rule applying to on and off-duty personal conduct can constitute removal "for cause"); see also Warner v. Town of Ocean City, 81 Md. App. 176, 567 A.2d 160 (1989) (considering propriety of administrative sanctions against a police officer who violated a department rule that pertained to on and off-duty conduct); Beeler v. Behan, 55 Md. App. 517, 464 A.2d 1091 (rejecting police officer's contention that he could not be disciplined for publicly criticizing the police department while off-duty), cert. denied, 298 Md. 243, 468 A.2d 624 (1983). See also Bruns v. Pomerleau, 319 F. Supp. 58 (D. Md. 1970) (police department could not refuse to hire a nudist).

Effective October 1, 2011, Maryland joined several other states that regulate and restrict an employer's use of credit history. See Maryland Job Applicant Fairness Act, HB 87, SB 132 (to be codified at Md. Code Ann., Lab. & Empl. § 3-711 (2011 Supp.)). The Act generally precludes employers (with certain narrowly defined exceptions) from using an applicant's or employee's credit history to: 1) deny employment to an applicant; 2) discharge an employee; or 3) determine compensation or terms and conditions of employment. (An employer may require and use credit report and credit history for other purposes after an offer of employment has been made.) There are certain positions for which an employer may request and use credit information if the employer has a "bona fide purpose" disclosed in writing to the applicant or employee that is "substantially job-related." Such positions include: 1) managerial positions that involve setting the direction or control of a business department, division, or unit; 2) positions that involve access to personal information, except for personal information customarily provided in a retail transaction; 3) positions that involve a fiduciary responsibility to the employer such as wiring payments, collecting debts, transferring money, or entering into contracts; 4) positions that will be provided with an expense account or corporate debit or credit card; and 5) positions with access to trade secrets or confidential business information. The Maryland Commission of Labor and Industry has the authority to administer and enforce the provisions of the Act and to issue civil money penalties for violations of the Act.

B. Employees' Personal Relationships

1. ***Romantic Relationships Between Employees.*** Personnel policies that prohibit romantic relationships between employees appear to be valid in Maryland because there is no law proscribing such policies. See, e.g., Prestianni v. United Parcel Servs., Inc., 149 F.3d 1170 (Table), No. 96-2783, 1998 WL 276455 (4th Cir. May 27, 1998) (upholding employee's discharge based on failure to comply with company manual that discouraged romantic relationships between supervisors and subordinates). On the other hand, the state's highest court declared that it is illegal for an employer to discriminate against employees who are involved in interracial relationships. Gutwein v. Easton Publ'g Co., 272 Md. 563, 325 A.2d 740 (1974) (finding racial discrimination in violation of Fair Employment Practice Act when an employer terminated a white employee because of the employee's relationship with his African American fiancee), cert. denied, 420 U.S. 991 (1975). Gutwein suggests that an employer cannot enforce a non-fraternization policy if the policy bans only relationships between co-workers of different races, religions, or national origins.

2. ***Sexual Orientation.*** On May 15, 2001, Maryland Governor Parris Glendening signed the Antidiscrimination Act of 2001, which amends the Maryland Fair Employment Practices Act to prohibit discrimination in employment on the basis of sexual orientation. 2001 Md. Laws, ch. 340. Baltimore City and three of the state's counties provide protection from employment discrimination based on sexual orientation. See Baltimore, Md., Code art. 4, § 10 (Supp. 1995); Howard County, Md., Code § 12.208 (1998); Montgomery County, Md., Code § 27-19 (Supp. 1998); Prince George's County, Md., Code §§ 2-186, 2-222 (1995) Under state law, a person who is subjected to an unlawful employment practice under a county code may, within 2 years, bring and maintain a civil action against the person who committed the alleged discriminatory act. Md. Code Ann., State Gov. § 20-1202. See also Tyma v. Montgomery County, 2002 WL 1307482 (Md. June 4, 2002) (discussing benefits for same-sex partners in the workplace).

3. ***Marital Status.*** Employers may not fire, refuse to hire or discriminate against an employee on the basis of marital status. Md. Code Ann., State Gov. § 20-6-6(a); see also Md. Comm'n on Human Relations v. Balt. Gas & Elec. Co., 296 Md. 46, 459 A.2d 205 (1983). Nonetheless, an employer can implement an anti-nepotism policy if the policy protects business interests and is based upon "relational," rather than "marital," status. See id. (discussing an administrative agency's ruling that an employer's refusal to hire employee's close relative was based on "relational status" and, hence, not illegal).

C. Smoking

The Code of Maryland Regulations (COMAR) prohibits smoking in enclosed workplaces even if an employee is off-duty while on the business premises. Md. Regs. Code tit. 9, § 12.23, 01 (Supp. 1997). The Court of Appeals rejected an argument that the workplace smoking prohibition violates state privacy rights. Fogle v. H & G Rests. Inc., 337 Md. 224, 654 A.2d 441 (1995). Consequently, employers must ban smoking in indoor work areas, employee lounges, employee cafeterias, and other workplace environments, even if an employee visits those areas while off-duty. Md. Regs. Code tit. 9, § 12.23. Technically, the statute enables employers to regulate off-duty conduct because employers can refuse to create designated smoking areas for employees who wish to smoke on business premises during work breaks. See Md. Regs. Code tit. 9, § 12.23 ("employer may permit smoking in a designated smoking area . . ."). See generally 2002 Md. AG LEXIS 15 (Opinion No. 02-016) (9/23/02) (providing useful background and synthesis of Maryland smoking regulations).

D. Blogging

The Maryland Court of Appeals has established a five-factor test to determine when Maryland trial courts should order disclosure of identifying information from Internet forum participants known only by their pseudonyms or usernames. Independent Newspapers, Inc. v. Brodie, 407 Md. 415, 966 A.2d 432 (2009). The court's decision, among other things, contains a helpful and detailed description of "blogs" and communications that can occur on blogs. 407 Md. at 423-24, 966 A.2d at 437-38. See also Harden v. Wicomico County, 2011 WL 2489414 (4th Cir. June 23, 2011) (not officially reported) (employee who, among other things, posted information on his online blog about county employee's alleged sexual harassment of other employees did not engage in protected oppositional activity under Title VII of the Civil Rights Act of 1964; "County's interest in protecting confidential, sensitive records" outweighed individual's interest in exposing alleged harassment).

VI. RECORDS

A. Personnel Records

Maryland has no statute regarding personnel records of private employers. Custodians of public records may provide personnel records only to the person in interest or their elected or appointed supervisor. Md. Code Ann., State Gov't § 10-616.

Effective January 1, 2008, Maryland law requires that all businesses take steps to ensure the privacy of the personal information furnished by all individuals, including employees and applicants for employment. Md. Code Ann., Com. Law §14-3501 (2008). The Personal Information Protection Act (the "Act") imposes two new obligations on Maryland businesses: (1) They must implement and maintain reasonable security procedures and practices to protect all personal information provided, such as social security numbers, driver's license numbers, individual tax identification numbers, or financial account numbers; and (2) they must notify state residents if there is a security breach involving the individual's personal information being held by the business. The Act also covers information maintained by a third-party in requiring the business to ensure that any outside service provider they use also follows its own reasonable security procedures and practices to protect personal information. Violations of the Act are considered unfair or deceptive trade practices under Maryland law. Potential penalties for unfair or deceptive trade practices include: $1,000 for the initial violation, $5,000 fine for subsequent violations, and misdemeanor criminal charges with carrying up to a $1,000 fine and/or one year imprisonment. Md. Code Ann., Com. Law § 13-411.

Effective October 1, 2008, Maryland law requires that Maryland employers record employees' racial classifications and gender. The stated purpose underlying this requirement is to permit the Maryland Commissioner of Labor to study wage disparity issues. This data collection requirement expires on December 31, 2013. Md. Code Ann., Lab. & Empl. § 3-305(a)(3), (4).

B. Medical Records

Employers are prohibited from requiring applicants to answer questions regarding physical, psychiatric, or psychological disability, illness, handicap or treatment unless the disability, illness, handicap or treatment "has a direct, material, and timely relationship to the capacity or fitness of the applicant to perform the job properly." Md. Code Ann., Lab. & Empl., § 3-701. Employers also may not discriminate against employees on the basis of information gained through participation of the employee in group medical coverage. Md. Code Ann., Lab. & Empl. § 5-604.

Furthermore, Maryland law restricts the disclosure of records pertaining to an employee's medical history, mental health, or use of drugs or alcohol. Md. Code Ann., Health-Gen. § 4-301-4-306 (restricting the disclosure of medical records); Md. Code Ann., Health-Gen. § 4-307 (restricting the disclosure of mental health records); Md. Code Ann., Health-Gen. § 8-601 (restricting the disclosure of alcohol and drug abuse records).

C. Criminal Records

An employer may not require a job applicant to disclose, in an application or interview, information concerning a criminal conviction that has been expunged or pardoned. Md. Code Crim. Proc. § 10-109. However, this requirement may not apply to employees who are required to carry firearms. 71 Op. Atty Gen. Md. 242 (1986).

D. Subpoenas

Maryland does not have special statutory authority governing the use or application of subpoenas in the employment context. See generally Md. Code Ann., Rule 2-510 (Circuit Court Rules). Subpoenas for employer documentation from governmental agencies will generally be upheld in the face of privacy considerations as long as "the inquiry is within the authority of the agency, the demand is not too indefinite and the information sought is reasonably relevant." United States v. Morton Salt Co., 338 U.S. 632, 653 (1950); **EEOC v. Randstad, 605 F.3d 433, 451-52 (4th Cir. 2012) (rejecting argument that compliance with subpoena would be "unduly burdensome" when an affidavit from Director of IT Applications stated that it would take three employees at least 40 hours each, at a total estimated labor cost of $14,000 to $19,000, to gather the requested information; employer's business operation under these circumstances was not "threaten[ed] or seriously disrupt[ed]")**; see, e.g., Reich v. Nat'l Eng'g & Contracting Co., 13 F.3d 93, 98 (4th Cir. 1993) (enforcing OSHA subpoenas for OSHA Form 200's containing log and summary of all serious occupational injuries and illnesses over five-year period, but recognizing employer's privacy interest in information contained in that form and requiring OSHA to return or destroy copies at conclusion of agency's investigation); Marshall v. Stevens People & Friends for Freedom, 669 F.2d 171, 177-78 (4th Cir. 1981) (quashing on First Amendment grounds subpoenas from Secretary of Labor seeking disclosure of names of employer's non-supervisory employees associated with committees opposing unionization in connection with governmental investigation under Labor-Management Reporting and Disclosure Act, but enforcing subpoena seeking information that would disclose committee's financial contacts with employer and other organizations opposing unionization). But see Equitable Trust Co. v. Md. Comm'n on Human Rel., 287 Md. 80, 411 A.2d 86 (1979) (declining to enforce Commission subpoena when complaint underlying subpoena did not meet requirements of relevant statute); Lubin v. Agora, Inc., 389 Md. 1, 882 A.2d 833 (2005) (subpoenas of potential violations of Maryland securities laws seeking identities of subscribers to company whose business included publishing investment newsletters was overbroad and barred under First Amendment). In re Grand Jury, John Doe No. G.J. 2005-2; United States v. Under Seal, 478 F.3d 581 (4th Cir. 2007) (affirming decision of district court to quash subpoena issued by grand jury seeking production of documents regarding a city police department's internal investigation of one of its officers for alleged use of excessive force when city properly claimed that subpoenas unduly burdened confidentiality of its investigations and potential violation of cooperating officers' rights against self-incrimination).

VII. ACTIONS SUBSEQUENT TO EMPLOYMENT

A. References

Maryland recognizes a conditional privilege for "[c]ommunications arising out of the employer-employee relationship," both at common law and by statute. Gohari v. Darvish, 363 Md. 42, 56, 767 A.2d 321, 328 (2001); Md. Code Ann., Cts. & Jud. Proc. § 5-423. See generally Kerr v. Johns Hopkins University, 2011 WL 4072437 at *6 (D. Md. Sept 12, 2011). To this end, an employer in good faith may not be held liable for disclosing any information about the job performance or the reason for termination of employment of an employee or a former employee either (1) to a prospective employer of the employee or former employee at the request of the prospective employer, the employee, or former employee or (2) if requested by a federal, state or industry regulatory authority or if the information is disclosed in a document required by law. Md. Code Ann., Cts & Jud. Proc. § 5-423(a)(1), (2). An employer who discloses such information is presumed to be acting in good faith unless it is shown by clear and convincing evidence that the employer (1) acted with actual malice toward the employee or former employee; or (2) intentionally or recklessly disclosed false information about this employee or former employee. Md. Code Ann., Cts. & Jud. Proc. § 5-423(b)(1), (2). See generally Deutsch v. Chesapeake Ctr., 27 F. Supp. 2d 642 (D. Md. 1998). Montgomery Investigative Services, Ltd. v. Horne, 173 Md. App. 193, 918 A.2d 526 (Md. App.), cert. denied, 399 Md. 596, 965 A.2d 635 (2007); Spence v. NCI Information Systems, Inc., 2009 U.S. Dist. LEXIS 16415 at ** 16 -23 (D. Md. Feb. 27, 2009).

B. Non-Compete Agreements

There is no Maryland statute that generally governs or regulates the enforceability of non-compete agreements. The Maryland Uniform Trade Secrets Act provides statutory remedies for misappropriation of a trade secret. Md. Code Ann., Commercial Law §§ 11-1201-1209. See generally Lejeune v. Coin Acceptors, Inc., 381 Md. 288, 848 A.2d 451 (2004). Minter v. Wells Fargo Bank, N.A., 258 F.R.D. 118 (D. Md. 2009) (refusing to seal documents that did not contain highly "sensitive" information of a personal and commercial nature or confidential trade secrets).

Although the enforceability of a particular restrictive covenant in a specific case will turn on the facts, the policy of Maryland to permit reasonable restrictive covenants in connection with employment agreements is firmly rooted in Maryland common law. MCS Servs. v. Coronel, 2008 MDBT 3; 2008 Md. Cir. Ct. LEXIS 3 (Md. Cir. Ct. 2008). Maryland courts have adopted generally-recognized common-law principles restricting these agreements. To this end, "Maryland follows the general rule that restrictive covenants may be applied and enforced only against those employees who provide unique services, or to prevent the future misuse of trade secrets, routes or lists of clients, or solicitation of customers." E.g., Becker v. Bailey, 228 Md. 93, 97, 299 A.2d 835, 838 (1973); Ruhl v. F.A. Bartlett Tree Expert. Co., 245 Md. 118, 127, 225 A.2d 288, 293 (Md. 1967). See generally Brian Malsberger, Covenants Not to Compete: A State-by-State Survey 1741-83 (4th ed. 2004); Stanley Mazaroff and Todd Horn, Maryland Employment Law § 3.07 (2d ed. 2005).

Where a non-compete agreement is enforceable, its duration and geographic area must be "only so broad and is reasonably necessary to protect the employer's business . . ." and must not "impose undue hardship on the employee or the public," Intelus Corp. v. Barton, 7 F. Supp. 2d 635, 641 (D. Md. 1998). "Maryland courts have consistently upheld noncompete covenants for up to 2 years after employment has been terminated." Brian Malsberger, supra, 1749-50 (citing cases). See generally PADCO Advisors, Inc. v. Omdahl, 179 F. Supp. 2d 600, 606-07 (D. Md. 2002). Wachovia Ins. Servs., Inc. v. Hinds, 2007 U.S. Dist. LEXIS 82103 (D. Md. Aug. 31, 2007) (granting motion for preliminary injunction for breach of restrictive covenants against soliciting or diverting relevant business for period extending eighteen months after termination of employment); **Ohio Learning Centers, LLC v. Sylvan Learning, Inc., 2012 WL 1067668 at 11-12 (D. Md. March 27, 2012) (upholding non-competition covenant of two years duration and five-mile geographic radius related to offering of certain individualized educational services);** Teksystems, Inc. v. Bolton, Inc., 2010 WL 447782 at **3-6 (D. Md. Feb. 4, 2010) (upholding 18-month restriction prohibiting individual from working within 50-mile radius of his former office in light of employer's legitimate business interests and employee's senior managerial position and subject-matter expertise). But see MCS Services, Inc. v. Jones, supra, 2010 WL 3895380 at **3-5 (D. Md. Oct. 1, 2010) (striking down covenant that literally interpreted would prevent former employee "from working in any capacity for a competitor" even if the position was unrelated to his previous job responsibilities. SNS One, Inc. v. Hage, 2011 WL 2746713 at *4 (D. Md. July 11, 2011) (striking down non-competition covenant with no limitation "as to the types of competitors to whom it applies" and when there were "no specific facts to support an industry-wide restriction"). The enforceability of relevant restrictions is determined on a case-by-case basis based upon the totality of the circumstances. E.g., Becker v. Bailey, supra, 268 Md. at 97, 299 A.2d at 838. Maryland courts have severed unreasonable restrictions unless "the pivotal terms of the agreement are sufficiently ambiguous." Stanley Mazaroff and Todd Horn, supra, § 3.07; see Holloway v. Faw, Casson & Co., 78 Md. App.

205, 552 A.2d 1311 (1989), aff'd in part and rev'd in part, 572 A.2d 510, 511 (Md. 1990); Deutsche Post Global Mail, Ltd. v. Conrad, 292 F. Supp. 2d 748, 757-58 (D. Md. 2003), aff'd mem., 116 Fed. Appx. 435, 2005 U.S. App. LEXIS 24249 (4th Cir. 2004).

Under appropriate circumstances, non-compete agreements will be enforced through injunctive relief. E.g., Deurelias v. City Baking Co., 155 Md. 280, 287, 141 A. 542, 547 (1928). Employers may also receive actual, liquidated, and compensatory damages, depending upon the circumstances. See, e.g., Planmastics, Inc. v. Showers, 137 F. Supp. 2d 616, 624 (D. Md. 2001) (delineating three-part test for recovery of lost profits), aff'd, 30 Fed. Appx. 117, 2002 U.S. App. LEXIS 3315 (4th Cir. 2002) (unpublished); Holloway v. Faw, Casson & Co., supra, 572 A.2d at 511 (liquidated damages awarded but no injunction); Tuttle v. Riggs-Warfield-Roloson, Inc., 251 Md. 45, 246 A.2d 588 (1965) (compensatory damages). But see Willard Packaging Co. v. Javier, 169 Md. App. 109, 136, 899 A.2d 940, 955-56 (2006) ("absent a rational relationship to anticipated actual damage, the liquidated damage amount was a de facto unenforceable penalty").

VIII. OTHER ISSUES

A. Statutes of Limitations

The statute of limitations applied to all four forms of the invasion of privacy tort is three years. See Allen v. Bethlehem Steel Corp., 76 Md. App. 642, 649, 547 A.2d 1105, 1108 (citing Md. Code Ann., Courts § 5-101 (1957)), cert. denied, 314 Md. 458, 550 A.2d 1168 (1988). The statute of limitations for intentional infliction of emotional distress and interference with contractual relations is three years. Md. Code Ann., Cts. & Jud. Proc. § 5-101; see Ford v. Douglas, supra, 144 Md. App. 620, 623, 799 A.2d 448, 450-51 (2002) (discussing statutes of limitation and limiting one-year statute to action for "assault, libel, or slander"). Accord Richardson v. Selective Ins. Group, Inc., 2007 U.S. Dist. LEXIS 40811, at ** 15-19 (D. Md. May 31, 2007). See generally Tobacco Technologies, Inc. v. Taiga International N.V., 626 F. Supp. 2d 537 (D. Md. 2009) ("[p]ursuant to Maryland's discovery rule, the three-year statute of limitations begins to run from the moment a plaintiff in fact knew or reasonably should have known of the wrong") (quotations and citations omitted).

B. Jurisdiction

Maryland has a long-arm statute that has been construed as co-extensive with the Due Process Clause of the United States Constitution. Md. Code Ann., Cts. & Jud. Proc. § 6-103; see, e.g., Carefirst of Maryland, Inc. v. Carefirst Pregnancy Centers, Inc., 334 F.3d 390, 396-97 (4th Cir. 2003); Mackey v. Compass Mktg., Inc., 391 Md. 117, 892 A.2d 479 (Md. 2006). The long-arm statute, among other things, provides that a Maryland court may exercise jurisdiction over a person outside the state who "causes tortious injury in the State by an act or omission in the State." (Md. Code Ann., Cts. & Jud. Proc. § 6-103 (b)(3)) or who "causes tortious injury in the State or outside of the State by an act or omission outside the State if he regularly … engages in any other persistent course of conduct in the State." Md. Code Ann., Cts. & Jud. Proc. § 6-103(b)(4). Personal jurisdiction was not present in an invasion of privacy claim, therefore, when the defendants' only contacts in Maryland "were the occasional placement of telephone orders for, and the consequent receipt of, investigative services from Maryland." Stover v. O'Connell Assocs., Inc., 84 F.3d 132, 137 (4th Cir. 1996); Janoska v. D.C. Development, LLC, 2010 WL 419386 at **3-4 (D. Md. Jan. 29, 2010) (no statutory immunity for owner of land on which ski slope employee was injured when employee was employed by owner's subcontractor, not by owner itself); cf. Snyder v. Phelps, 2006 U.S. Dist. LEXIS 79020 (D. Md. Oct. 30, 2006) (staging protests at funeral in Maryland and publishing allegedly defamatory information on the Internet were sufficient contacts for purposes of exercise of personal jurisdiction over intrusion claim), rev'd on other grounds, ____ U.S. _____, 131 S. Ct. 1207 (2011), Chambers v. Chambers, 2011 WL 3512140 (D. Md. Aug. 8, 2011) (personal jurisdiction exists over persons intentionally directing electronic activity into Maryland with the purpose of causing injury to a Maryland resident). See generally CoStar Realty Information, Inc. v. Field, 612 F. Supp. 2d 660 (D. Md. 2009) (discussing exercise of personal jurisdiction and Maryland case law and noting, among other things, that challenges to personal jurisdiction may be waived by either express or implied consent).

C. Worker's Compensation Exclusivity

Except for specified intentional conduct, the Maryland Workers' Compensation Act provides the exclusive remedy against an employer for injuries sustained by an employee in the course of employment. Md. Code Ann., Lab. & Empl. § 9-509(a), (b); see, e.g., Hill v. Knapp, 396 Md. 700, 711, 914 A.2d 1993, 1199 (2007); Suburban Hospital v. Kirson, 362 Md. 140, 145-46, 763 A.2d 105, 205 (2000); **McCulllough v. Liberty Heights Health & Rehabilitation Center, 830 F.Supp.2d 94, 99-100 (D. Md. 2011);** but see Ruffin Hotel Corp. of Md., Inc. v. Gasper, 418 Md. 594, 617, 17 A.3d 676, 689 (2011) (Maryland Workers Compensation Act does not preempt claim for negligent hiring or negligent retention "whenever such a claim is asserted by an employee against his or her employer as a result of intentional and unlawful misconduct of a fellow employee"); The Great Atlantic & Pacific Tea Co. v. Imbraguglio, 346 Md. 573, 583, 697 A.2d 885, 890 (1997) ("[t]he Act neither excuses third parties for their own negligence nor limits their liability"); Athas v. Hill, 300 Md. 133, 149, 476 A.2d 710, 718 (1984) (although the Act does not generally preclude tort action between co-employees, "supervisory employees cannot be held liable for negligently performing the employer's nondelegable duties"); Cleaning Authority, Inc. v. Neubert, 2010 WL 3516939 at *5 (D. Md. Sept. 7, 2010) (declining to exercise jurisdiction over individual defendant, inter alia, based upon "a person electronically receiving information via the Internet from Maryland) (emphasis in the original). To fall outside the ambit of the exclusive remedy provisions of the Maryland Workers' Compensation Act, an employee must prove that an injury was "the result of the deliberate intent of the employer." Md. Code Ann., Lab. & Empl. § 9-509(d); see Gantt v. Security, USA, Inc., 356 F.3d 547, 554-55 (4th Cir.), cert. denied, 543 U.S. 814 (2004) (proof of an employer's "willful, wanton, or reckless conduct," does not suffice; the intentional tort exception requires proof of the employer's "actual, specific and deliberate intent to injure the employee"). An employee's emotional distress claim that she was intentionally given an undesirable work assignment while she feared for her life was not barred by the exclusivity requirements of the statute, although assault, battery, and kidnapping claims were so barred since there was no evidence that an employer acted with the specific intent to impose these injuries upon her. See Id.

D. Pleading Requirements

Allegations of intentional infliction of emotional distress must be plead with specificity; notice pleading is not enough. Leese v. Balt. City, 64 Md. App. 442, 497 A.2d 159, cert. denied, 305 Md. 106, 501 A.2d 845 (1985), Harris v. Jones, 281 Md. 560, 572, 380 A.2d 611, 617 (1977); Arbabi v. Fred Meyers, Inc., 205 F. Supp. 2d 462, 466 (D. Md. 2002) (quotation and citations omitted).

SURVEY OF MASSACHUSETTS EMPLOYMENT LIBEL LAW

Robert A. Bertsche
Prince Lobel Tye LLP
100 Cambridge Street
Boston, Massachusetts 02114
Telephone: (617) 456-8018; Facsimile: (617) 456-8100
rbertsche@PrinceLobel.com

(With Developments Reported Through **November 1, 2012**)

SIGNIFICANT DEVELOPMENTS SINCE THE 2012 *SURVEY*

Watch your language when you cross the border into Massachusetts. What seemed a novel notion just a few years ago – that a true statement could subject a speaker to defamation liability – has become an accepted part of Massachusetts law as expounded by the state and federal courts. In Coughlin v. Town of Arlington, No. 10-102013-MLW, 2011 WL 6370932 (D. Mass. Dec. 19, 2011), the federal district court rejected a magistrate judge's recommended dismissal of a defamation claim based on publication of the two plaintiffs' email communications, "the truth of which is not challenged." That is because, as the state Appeals Court reminded us this year, in this Commonwealth, even a truthful statement about someone can subject you to damages, if the statement is harmful to reputation and made with spite or ill will. In an "unpublished" decision – one of many this year – the Appeals Court addressed the libel claim brought by a municipal employee against a School Committee member who sent an accurate email to other committee members noting that the employee had previously sued the city and won. The Appeals Court affirmed summary judgment for the city – not on the grounds that the email was true, but rather on the grounds that, because the email was true, the plaintiff could not prevail without a showing of "actual malice," which had not been shown. Caputo v. City of Haverhill, No. 11-P-1321, 82 Mass. App. Ct. 1109, 971 N.E.2d 337, 2012 WL 3076542, *2 (Mass. App. Ct. July 31, 2012) (unpublished) (also finding, as an alternative basis for judgment, that the email was not defamatory). See also Barrows v. Wareham Fire Dist., 82 Mass. App. Ct. 623, 628 n.6, -- N.E.2d -- (2012) ("*In most cases* the statement must be false" (emphasis added)) (dictum). The astute reader will note that the facts of Coughlin and Caputo are eerily similar to those of the long-running federal court battle of Noonan v. Staples, 556 F.3d 20 (1st Cir. 2009), reh'g denied, 561 F.3d 4 (1st Cir. 2009); see also Noonan v. Staples, Inc., 707 F. Supp. 2d 85, 88-89, 92 (D. Mass. 2010), in which the constitutionality of the "truthful libel" statute, Mass. Gen. Laws c. 231, § 92, was broached but ultimately not decided. *(Memo to employers wishing to avoid this unsettled area of law: Don't send emails about terminated employees!)*

We were also reminded this year that whether an individual's defamatory statement to a police officer is fully privileged depends on a fine distinction under Massachusetts law: whether the statement was a voluntary and unsolicited report made by a complainant acting on his or her own initiative (in which case only a conditional privilege applies) or whether instead it was a statement made as the initial step toward a proposed criminal proceeding. In 1991, the Supreme Judicial Court said the line was to be drawn on a case-by-case basis, balancing an individual's right to reputation against society's right to secure the testimony of a witness unburdened by fear of civil liability. Correllas v. Viveiros, 410 Mass. 314, 322-23 (1991). Twenty-one years later, the question arose again, not once but twice. The First Circuit Court of Appeals sidestepped it, determining that whatever the extent of privilege, it had not been abused under the facts of that case. Jones v. Scotti, No. 11-2213, 2012 WL 4373655 (1st Cir. Sept. 26, 2012) (unpublished). And a federal district court, applying Massachusetts law, ruled that the question – whether a police chief's report to state troopers was part of an investigation or, as plaintiff alleged, part of a gratuitous "smear campaign" – warranted discovery, thereby precluding the 12(b)(6) dismissal advocated by the defendant. Piccone v. Bartels, No. 11-10143-MLW, 2012 WL 45921770 (D. Mass. Sept. 29, 2012).

In yet another "unpublished" decision pursuant to Appeals Court Rule 1:28 (such summary decisions may be cited for their persuasive value but not as binding precedent; the growing number appears due to record filings at the Appeals Court amidst budget cuts), the Appeals Court affirmed, on non-constitutional grounds, what the U.S. Supreme Court had declared as a constitutional matter in Hustler v. Falwell, 485 U.S. 46 (1988): that where an intentional infliction of emotional distress claim is based on a published statement, it cannot succeed if the statement was not a defamatory falsehood. Boyle v. Cape Cod Times, No. 11-P-196, 81 Mass. App. Ct. 1107, 959 N.E.2d 457, 2012 WL 28661, *2 n.3 (Mass. App. Ct. Jan. 6, 2012). As a matter of law, the Court held, such a statement is not "extreme and outrageous," "beyond all possible bounds of decency," or "utterly intolerable in a civilized community." Id.

The Appeals Court established this year that the Massachusetts Tort Claims Act, Mass. Gen. Laws c. 258, §§ 2, 10(c), categorically bars all claims against public employers that arise out of libel or slander uttered by a public

employee. On the heels of a Superior Court judge's suggestion that the Act – which bars claims against public employers that arise out of an employee's "intentional tort, including ... libel [and] slander" – might permit private-figure claims based on *negligent* defamation, see Haney v. City of Boston, 2012 WL 3144816 (Mass. Super. Ct. July 30, 2012), the Appeals Court ruled otherwise in a separate case. In Barrows v. Wareham Fire Dist., 82 Mass. App. Ct. 623, 627-30, -- N.E.2d -- (2012), the Appeals Court explained that "the gravamen of the tort of defamation does not lie in the nature or degree of the misconduct but in its outcome, i.e., the injury to the reputation of the plaintiff." This "unique characteristic" of the defamation tort justified the Legislature's inclusion of libel and slander in a list of "intentional" torts for purposes of the tort claims exemption. Id.

I. GENERAL LAW

A. General Employment Law

1. ***At Will Employment.*** Under Massachusetts law, unless provided otherwise by an applicable express or implied employment contract, all employees are at-will. Either the employer or employee may terminate the employment relationship at any time, with or without notice, for any reason or no reason at all, except for any reason prohibited by statute, common law, or public policy. Wright v. Shriners Hosp. for Crippled Children, 412 Mass. 469, 472, 589 N.E.2d 1241, 1244 (1992); Jackson v. Action for Boston Community Development, Inc., 403 Mass. 8, 9, 525 N.E.2d 411 (1988). A consequence of the at-will employment doctrine is that, absent a statutory or contractual provision or official workplace rule that provides an assurance of continued employment, a public employee has no property interest in her position. Gomez v. Rivera Rodriguez, 344 F.3d 103, 111 (1st Cir. 2003)

There are three exceptions to the employment-at-will doctrine in Massachusetts. First, an employee may not be fired on account of his or her age, race, color, religious creed, national origin, sex, sexual orientation, handicap, ancestry, genetic information, military service, or in retaliation for the employee's opposition to such discriminatory practices. Mass. G.L. c.151B; see also Title VII, 42 U.S.C. §2000e-2(a)(1). Cf. Godfrey v. Globe Newspaper Co., 457 Mass. 113, 928 N.E.2d 327 (2010) (rejecting handicapped employee's claim that he was denied a "reasonable accommodation" to enable him to continue his work, and affirming employee's termination because he was not a "qualified" handicapped person). An employer or other person may also be liable to a former employee under G.L. c.151B, §§ 4(4) and 4(4A) "for retaliatory or interfering conduct that occurs after the employment relationship has terminated." Psy-Ed Corp. v. Klein, 459 Mass. 697, 699, 947 N.E.2d 520, 525 (2011).

Second, an employee may not be terminated for reasons that violate public policy. This doctrine has been interpreted to mean that an employer may not terminate an employee "for asserting a legally guaranteed right (e.g., filing workers' compensation claim), for doing what the law requires (e.g., serving on a jury) or for refusing to do what which the law forbids (e.g., committing perjury)." Wright, 412 Mass. at 472; see also King v. Driscoll, 418 Mass. 576, 638 N.E.2d 488 (1994). The doctrine also may include certain situations where an employer terminates an employee for "whistle-blowing." However, the "whistle-blowing" doctrine has been interpreted narrowly. Flesner v. Technical Communications Corp., 410 Mass. 805, 575 N.E.2d 1107 (1991); Shea v. Emmanuel College, 425 Mass. 761, 682 N.E.2d 1348 (1997). Public employers in Massachusetts are subject to more rigid whistle-blower rules. By statute, Mass. G.L. c.149, §185, government employers may not retaliate against employees who disclose or threaten to disclose a policy or practice of the employer that the employee reasonably believes violates a law or a rule, or that the employee reasonably believes poses a risk to public health, safety, or the environment.

Third, employers may not terminate employees in order to deprive them of compensation that they have already earned, including commissions which employees have already earned but have not yet been paid. Fortune v. National Cash Register Co., 373 Mass. 96, 364 N.E.2d 1251 (1977). This theory of liability is a subset of the doctrine that "[e]very contract in Massachusetts is subject, to some extent, to an implied covenant of good faith and fair dealing." Ayash v. Dana-Farber Cancer Institute, et al., 443 Mass. 367, 385, 822 N.E.2d 667, 683-84 (2005).

B. Elements of Libel Claim

1. ***Basic Elements.*** "To prevail on a claim of defamation, a plaintiff must establish that the defendant was at fault for the publication of a false statement regarding the plaintiff, capable of damaging the plaintiff's reputation in the community, which either caused economic loss or is actionable without proof of economic loss." White v. Blue Cross & Blue Shield of Massachusetts, Inc., 442 Mass. 64, 66, 809 N.E.2d 1034, 1036 (2004); see also Dragonas v. School Comm. of Melrose, 64 Mass. App. Ct. 429, 437, 833 N.E.2d 679 (2005); **O'Brien v. Chretien, No. 11-P-2092, 82 Mass. App. Ct. 1117, 976 N.E.2d 214, 2012 WL 5193373 (Mass. App. Ct. Oct. 23, 2012) (unpublished);** Noonan v. Staples, Inc., 707 F. Supp. 2d 85, 89 (D. Mass. 2010). Defamation in writing "or some other equivalent medium" is libel; oral defamation is slander. Ravnikar v. Bogojavlensky, 438 Mass. 627, 629, 782 N.E.2d 508, 510 (2003); McAvoy v. Shufrin, 401 Mass. 593, 595, 518 N.E.2d 513 (1988) (libel); Ellis v. Safety Ins. Co., 41 Mass. App. Ct. 630, 635, 672 N.E.2d 979 (1996). See also

Noonan, 707 F. Supp. 2d 85, 89 (D. Mass. 2010) ("'Libel and slander ... are two kinds of defamation'"), quoting LeBeau v. Town of Spencer, 167 F. Supp. 2d 449, 456 (D. Mass. 2001). The elements of the two torts are identical, except that in certain cases a slander plaintiff must allege and prove special damages as a prerequisite to recovery on the merits. Ravnikar, 438 Mass. at 630, 782 N.E.2d at 511. See, e.g., Haddad v. Wal-Mart Stores, Inc., 455 Mass. 91, 92 n.2, 914 N.E.2d 59, 62 n.2 (2009) (noting that jury found no liability on slander claim because plaintiff suffered no damages from the statement). See also V.D, infra. (In Noonan v. Staples, Inc., 556 F.3d 20, 25 (1st Cir. 2009), the Court of Appeals mistakenly identified five elements to a *libel* claim: "(1) that the defendant published a written statement; (2) of and concerning the plaintiff; that was both (3) defamatory, and (4) false; and (5) either caused economic loss, or is actionable without proof of economic loss." Because libel – written defamation – is always "actionable without proof of economic loss," see discussion of fourth element in this section, infra, the fifth of Noonan's five asserted elements of *libel* is unnecessary and redundant.)

In every case, the plaintiff must show the following. First, that the communication was "published" to a third party. White, 442 Mass. at 66, 809 N.E.2d at 1036; Yohe v. Nugent, 321 F.3d 35, 40 (1st Cir. 2003) ("the statement must have been to at least one other individual other than the one defamed"). **In Anjomi v. Kalai, 828 F. Supp. 2d 410, 414-15 (D. Mass. 2011), the federal district court, applying Massachusetts law, dismissed a defamation claim based on a letter shared only with the plaintiff and the plaintiff's wife.**

Second, plaintiff must show that the communication was of or about the plaintiff. Ravnikar, 438 Mass. at 629, 782 N.E.2d at 510; New England Tractor-Trailer Training of Connecticut, Inc. v. Globe Newspaper Co., 395 Mass. 471, 477, 480 N.E.2d 1005 (1985). See I.B.5, infra.

Third, plaintiff must show that the communication was defamatory, that is, that it "would tend to hold the plaintiff up to scorn, hatred, ridicule or contempt, in the minds of any considerable and respectable segment in the community." Phelan v. May Dep't Stores Co. et al., 443 Mass. 52, 56, 819 N.E.2d 550, 553 (2004), quoting Stone v. Essex County Newspapers, Inc., 367 Mass, 849, 853, 330 N.E.2d 161 (1975).

Fourth, plaintiff must show that the statement "either caused the plaintiff economic loss ... or is actionable without proof of economic loss." Ravnikar v. Bogojavlensky, 438 Mass. 627, 629-30, 782 N.E.2d 508, 510-11 (2003); North Shore Pharmacy Services, Inc. v. Breslin Consulting Assocs., 491 F. Supp. 2d 111, 128 (D. Mass. 2007). This formulation is awkward, since libel – written words – is always "actionable without proof of economic loss," Ravnikar, 438 Mass. at 630, 782 N.E.2d at 511. So, for libel, the exception swallows the rule. Thus only plaintiffs claiming slander – oral words – are required to show that the statement caused them economic loss. Other statements that are actionable without proof of economic loss are oral statements that (1) charge the plaintiff with a crime; (2) allege that the plaintiff has certain diseases; or, notably for this outline, (3) "may prejudice the plaintiff's profession or business." Ravnikar, 438 Mass. at 630, 782 N.E.2d at 511; North Shore Pharmacy Services, 491 F. Supp. 2d at 128; Phelan v. May Dep't Stores Co., 443 Mass. 52, 55-56, 819 N.E.2d 550 (2004).

Fifth, the plaintiff must allege, and in most if not all cases prove, that the communication was false. Murphy v. Boston Herald, 449 Mass. 42, 51 n.10, 865 N.E.2d 746, 754 n.10, 35 Media L. Rep. 1865 (2007) (proof by a preponderance of the evidence). But see McMann v. Doe, 2006 U.S. Dist. LEXIS 80112 (D. Mass. Oct 31, 2006) (Tauro, J.) (stating in dictum that where the comments are not of public concern, plaintiff no longer bears the burden of proving falsity). See I.B.3, infra.

Sixth, the plaintiff must show that the defendant was at fault in making the statement. Ravnikar, 438 Mass. at 627, 630, 782 N.E. 2d at 510-11; Jones v. Taibbi, 400 Mass. 786, 797, 512 N.E.2d 260 (1987)**; Jones v. Scotti, No. 08-10583-LTS, 2012 WL 4373655, *4 (1st Cir. Sept. 26, 2012) (unpublished).** The requisite level of fault is "actual malice" in the case of a public-official or public-figure plaintiff, negligence in the case of a private-figure plaintiff. Stone, 367 Mass. at 857-58, 860, 330 N.E.2d 161; **Jones, supra, at *4.** See I.B.2, infra.

Finally, the statement is not actionable if it is immunized by an absolute or qualified (conditional) privilege, unless the qualified privilege is abused. See, e.g., Bratt v. International Business Machines Corp., 392 Mass. 508, 467 N.E.2d 126 (1984) (discussing employer's business-interest and common-interest conditional privileges); **Jones v. Scotti, supra, at *4.** See II.A, infra.

One final introductory note: Pertinent to this survey of defamation law in the *employment* setting is the question whether individual non-media defendants are entitled to the same degree of First Amendment solicitude as the institutional media when sued for libel. The federal district court in Massachusetts has rejected the media/non-media distinction, at least as applied to the determinations of whether a statement is one of public concern and is protected opinion. McMann v. Doe, 460 F. Supp. 2d 259, 269 n. 62 (D. Mass. 2006). A Superior Court decision, by contrast, justified its refusal to dismiss an employment-related libel claim by noting that the case "does not involve a defamation claim against the news media" and that "courts have been more favorably inclined to protect the interests of the press and news media than other private or public plaintiffs." Moriarty v. Sullivan, 21 Mass. L. Rep. 254, 2006 Mass. Super. LEXIS 328, *9 n.7 (Hampden Super. Ct. May 16, 2006).

2. ***Fault***. Whether a plaintiff is a private figure or a public figure or public official is a distinction "of profound consequence" in a libel case, "as it determines whether a plaintiff need prove only negligence on the defendant's part or must show actual malice." Mandel v. Boston Phoenix, 492 F. Supp. 2d 26 n.1 (D. Mass. 2007). "Where facts are undisputed, the status of a libel plaintiff is a question of law for the judge." Astra USA, Inc. v. Bildman, 455 Mass. 116, 144, 914 N.E.2d 36, 57 (2009), cert. denied, 130 S. Ct. 3276, 176 L. Ed. 2d 1183 (2010), citing Bowman v. Heller, 420 Mass. 517, 522, 651 N.E.2d 369, cert. denied, 516 U.S. 1032 (1995). See also Stone v. Essex County Newspapers, Inc., 367 Mass. 849, 862-63, 330 N.E.2d 161 (1975) (plaintiff's status is a question of law to be determined by the court "whenever (a) all of the facts bearing thereon are uncontested or agreed by the parties, (b) the case is tried before a judge without a jury, or (c) all of the facts bearing thereon are specially found and reported by the jury by way of answers to special questions submitted to them"). In all other cases, it is a "question for the jury to answer after instructions by the judge on the applicable law and on what facts must be found to constitute the plaintiff a public official or a public figure." Stone, 367 Mass. at 863. The First Circuit Court of Appeals, in a case arising under Massachusetts law, appears to give the judge even greater leeway, holding that "the question of whether a defamation plaintiff is a public figure is properly resolved by the court, not a jury, regardless of the contestability of the predicate facts." Pendleton v. City of Haverhill, 156 F.3d 57, 26 Media L. Rep. 2281 (1st Cir. 1998). The determination "must be supported by evidence sufficiently powerful to establish 'the actual truth of the proposition to be proved' – the familiar standard of proof by a preponderance of the evidence." Mandel v. Boston Phoenix, 492 F. Supp. 2d 26 (D. Mass. 2007). On appeal, "[i]n the absence of disputed material facts, the question whether a person is a public official is one of law," reviewed de novo. Lane v. MPG Newspapers, 438 Mass. 476, 479, 781 N.E.2d 800, 803, 31 Media L. Rep. 1279 (2003).

The required showing of fault does not depend on whether the subject matter is of public or merely private concern, except that even a private-figure plaintiff may not recover presumed damages in a public-concern libel case without a showing of New York Times actual malice. Galarneau v. Merrill Lynch, Pierce, Fenner & Smith Inc., 504 F.3d 189, 198-99 (1st Cir. 2007). Moreover, if allegedly libelous statements are published in the context of a "labor dispute," as defined in 29 U.S.C. § 152(9), a plaintiff must prove actual malice as a condition of any recovery. Tosti v. Ayik, 386 Mass. 721, 723-25, 437 N.E.2d 1062 (1982) cert. denied, 484 U.S. 964 (1982). That requirement is one imposed by federal labor law. The term "labor dispute" is to be "broadly and liberally construed." Netherwood v. Am. Fed'n of State, County and Mun. Employees, Local 1725, 53 Mass. App. Ct. 11, 22-23, 757 N.E. 2d 257, 267 (2001), quoting Tosti, 386 Mass. at 723, 437 N.E. 2d 1062 (1982).

a. **Private Figure Plaintiff/Matter of Public Concern.** Private persons may recover in defamation merely "on proof of negligent publication of a defamatory falsehood." Stone, 367 Mass. 849, 857-59, 330 N.E.2d 161 (1975) (emphasis in original); see also Gertz v. Robert Welch, Inc., 418 U.S. 323, 1 Media L. Rep. 1633 (1974). Although Stone involved a media defendant, its holding that the negligence standard applies in a private-figure plaintiff case does not appear to depend upon whether the defendant is part of the media. Gilbert v. Bernard, 4 Mass. L. Rep. 143, 1995 WL 809550 at *2, 1995 Mass. Super. LEXIS 566 (Mass. Super. Ct. 1995); see also Astra USA, Inc. v. Bildman, 455 Mass. 116, 144, 914 N.E.2d 36, 57 (2009) (dictum), cert. denied, 130 S. Ct. 3276, 176 L. Ed. 2d 1183 (2010).

In defamation cases arising out of the employment setting, plaintiffs are often private persons – even though the question of the plaintiff's status is frequently not reached. In Draghetti v. Chmielewski, 416 Mass. 808, 626 N.E.2d 862, 22 Media L. Rep. 1456 (1994), a police officer sued the police chief for defamation, and won a $50,000 jury verdict. On appeal, the defendant argued for the first time that plaintiff was a public figure, required to prove actual malice pursuant to New York Times Co. v. Sullivan, 376 U.S. 265, 279-80, 1 Media L. Rep. 1527 (1964). The Supreme Judicial Court suggested that plaintiff was indeed a public official, citing Fleming v. Benzaquin, 390 Mass. 175, 189, 454 N.E.2d 95 (1983) – subsequently, in Rotkiewicz v. Sadowsky, 431 Mass. 748, 730 N.E. 2d 282 (2000), the court so held – but ruled that the argument had been waived. Draghetti, 416 Mass. at 815. See also Galarneau v. Merrill Lynch, Pierce, Fenner & Smith Inc., 504 F.3d 189 (1st Cir. 2007) (declining to apply heightened standard of review on appeal where defendants had not argued to trial court that plaintiff was public figure, that allegedly defamatory statement involved a matter of public concern, that "clear and convincing" quantum of proof applied, or even that the First Amendment placed any limit on the law to be applied to plaintiff's defamation claim).

Among the plaintiffs that Massachusetts courts have recognized as private figures, required to show negligence in order to prove their defamation claim, are a corporation that is a wholesaler of alcoholic beverages, Dexter's Hearthside Restaurant, Inc. v. Whitehall Co., 24 Mass. App. Ct. 217 (1987), 221, 508 N.E.2d 113, 14 Media L. Rep. 1664, rev. denied, 400 Mass. 1104, 511 N.E.2d 620 (1987); the proprietor of a youth hostel, Shaari v. Harvard Student Agencies, Inc., 427 Mass. 129, 691 N.E.2d 925, 26 Media L. Rep. 1730 (1998); the husband of a former state court judge, Milgroom v. News Group Boston, Inc., 412 Mass. 9, 12, 586 N.E.2d 985, 988, 20 Media L Rep. 1097 (1992); a private career

-training school for the tractor-trailer industry, New England Tractor-Trailer Training of Connecticut, Inc. v. Globe Newspaper Co., 395 Mass. 471, 477 n.4, 480 N.E.2d 1005 (1985); an employee of a city water department, in connection with statements not relating to his job performance, Tartaglia v. Townsend, 19 Mass. App. Ct. 693, 696, 477 N.E.2d 1005 (1985); and a veterinary doctor working at a private animal hospital, Reilly v. Associated Press, 59 Mass. App. Ct. 764, 769 n.3, 797 N.E.2d 1204 (2003).

In a private-figure libel case against the media, it was negligent for a reporter not to first contact a "willing source to clarify certain statements" before publishing them, and not to alert readers "that there were disputed facts." Reilly v. Associated Press, 59 Mass. App. Ct. 764, 779, 797 N.E.2d 1204 (2003). If a defendant has negligently failed to anticipate that a reasonable third party would interpret the defendant's defamatory statement as referring to the plaintiff, that is a sufficient showing of fault to permit the claim to proceed. Stanton v. Metro Corp., 438 F.3d 119, 131-32, 34 Media L. Rep. 1321 (1st Cir. 2006).

Where the speech at issue is a matter of public concern, even a private-figure plaintiff must show both falsity and actual damages. McMann v. Doe, 2006 U.S. Dist. LEXIS 80112, * 23 (D. Mass. Oct. 31, 2006). Determining whether speech is a matter of public concern requires "examining the whole record to learn the comments' content, form, and context," including the speaker's "subjective intent to create a public discourse." Id. at n.58 (finding that website comments about a real estate developer, anonymously posted, were of public concern). "Only a relatively small section of the populace need be concerned for a matter to count as a public concern." Id. In Astra USA, Inc. v. Bildman, the Supreme Judicial Court concluded with "little difficulty" that "the issue of widespread sexual harassment at a publicly traded company employing 1,000 people" was a matter of "general concern," noting that the issue of workplace harassment is the focus of considerable state and federal regulation, as well as a matter of "frequent and often heated public debate." 455 Mass. 116, 144-45, 914 N.E.2d 36, 57-58 (2009), cert. denied, 130 S. Ct. 3276, 176 L. Ed. 2d 1183 (2010). Using the terms "public concern," "general concern," and "general interest" interchangeably, the court added that such a dispute also reflected "other issues of general interest, such as corporate integrity, corporate governance, and corporate financial controls, among others, all of which have attracted much recent media attention." 455 Mass. at 144 n.43, 914 N.E.2d at 57 n.43.

Note to the unwary: A defendant who does not timely argue that an issue is of public concern, or that constitutional protections should apply, may have waived those protections, at least in a case involving a private-figure plaintiff. See, e.g., Noonan v. Staples, Inc., 556 F.3d 20, 28 n.7 (declining to consider the constitutional issues because they were "not raised" in defendant's initial appellate brief and were "not developed" on panel rehearing), reh'g and reh'g *en banc* denied, 561 F.3d 4 (1st Cir. 2009) (holding that "the fact that the issue raises constitutional concerns does not save the waiver"). By contrast, a plaintiff will not be barred from arguing for a negligence standard simply because he did not explicitly assert on summary judgment that he was a private figure. Astra USA, Inc. v. Bildman, 455 Mass. 116, 143 n.41, 914 N.E.2d 36, 56 n.41 (2009), cert. denied, 130 S. Ct. 3276, 176 L. Ed. 2d 1183 (2010).

b. **Private Figure Plaintiff/Matter of Private Concern.** See I.B.2.a, supra. Massachusetts state court decisions have indicated that the fault standard that must be shown by a private-figure plaintiff is no different when the communication is of purely private concern, than when it is of public concern. Stone v. Essex County Newspapers, Inc., 367 Mass. 849, 858-59 n.6, 330 N.E.2d 161 (1975) ("no plaintiff, whether a public or private person, can now recover in a defamation action without proving at least negligence in the publication of the falsehood"); New England Tractor-Trailer Training of Connecticut, Inc. v. Globe Newspaper Co., 395 Mass. 471, 477 n.4, 480 N.E.2d 1005 (1985) ("We view the fault requirement of Gertz to be intact regardless whether the private parties are suing on matters of public or private concern"). See also Astra USA, Inc. v. Bildman, 455 Mass. 116, 144, 914 N.E.2d 36, 57 (2009) (noting in dictum that whether the dispute is a public or private one, private-figure libel plaintiffs may not prevail absent "proof of negligent publication of a defamatory falsehood"), cert. denied, 130 S. Ct. 3276, 176 L. Ed. 2d 1183 (2010). But federal court decisions applying Massachusetts law have been less adamant on this point. For example, the First Circuit Court of Appeals declared in Noonan v. Staples, Inc., 561 F.3d 4, 7 (1st Cir. 2009), an employment libel case, that "as to matters of private concern, the First Amendment does 'not necessarily force any change in at least some of the features of the common-law landscape'" quoting Phila. Newspapers v. Hepps, 475 U.S. 767, 775, 106 S. Ct. 1558 (1986). That is because there is "'reduced constitutional value of speech involving no matters of public concern.'" See Noonan, 561 F.3d at 7, quoting Dun & Bradstreet, 472 U.S. at 761. See also Levinsky's, Inc. v. Wal-Mart Stores, Inc., 127 F.3d 122, 128 & n.4, 26 Media L. Rep. 1161 (1st Cir. 1997) (suggesting that liability without fault is not constitutionally proscribed in a private figure/private concern/nonmedia case). In Andresen v. Diorio, 2003 U.S. App. LEXIS 23071, *20-21 (1st Cir. Nov. 12, 2003), the First Circuit Court of Appeals said that it remained "formally unsettled" whether a plaintiff suing a non-media, non-public-figure defendant in a case involving a matter of private concern, must establish negligence. Nevertheless, the Court said that "Massachusetts, apparently assuming that such a constitutional requirement exists, has already reshaped its own defamation law to require negligence" even in such a case. Id.

c. **Public Figure Plaintiff/Matter of Public Concern.** A public official is someone whose position "would invite public scrutiny and discussion of the person holding it, entirely apart from the scrutiny and discussion occasioned by the particular charges in controversy." Stone v. Essex County Newspapers, Inc., 367 Mass. at 864, citing Rosenblatt v. Baer, 383 U.S. 75, 86-87 (1966) n.13. A public figure is someone who has either "achieved such pervasive fame or notoriety that he becomes a public figure for all purposes and in all contexts . . . or . . . voluntarily injects himself or is drawn into a particular public controversy and thereby becomes a public figure for a limited range of issues." Stone, 367 Mass. at 866, citing Gertz v. Robert Welch, Inc., 418 U.S. 323, 1 Media L. Rep. 1633 (1974). See also Lane v. MPG Newspapers, 438 Mass. 476, 478 n.4, 781 N.E.2d 800, 803 n.4, 31.Media L. Rep. 1279 (2003) ("Public figures are persons who, while not public officials, occupy a sufficiently prominent place in public affairs to be held to the same requirements as public officials in actions for defamation").

Not all government employees are "public officials"; the designation is reserved for those who have, or appear to the public as having, substantial responsibility for the conduct of public affairs. Stone v. Essex County Newspapers, Inc. 367 Mass. 849, 858, 330 N.E.2d 161 (1975); Kassel v. Gannett Co., Inc., 875 F.2d 935, 16 Media L. Rep. 1814 (1st Cir. 1989); Rotkiewicz v. Sadowsky, 431 Mass. 748, 752-53, 730 N.E.2d 282 (2000). The relevant considerations include "whether the person's position is one that invites public scrutiny and discussion apart from that brought on by the controversy at issue," "the employee's remuneration and duties, his or her participation in decisions on public issues, the impact of the government position on everyday life, the potential for social harm from abuse of the government position, and the employee's access to the press." Netherwood v. Am. Fed'n of State, County and Munic. Employees, Local 1725, 53 Mass. App. Ct. 11, 16, 757 N.E. 2d 257, 262-63 (2001); see also Rotkiewicz, 431 Mass. at 753. Courts making this assessment must consider whether the employee's position in government "has such apparent importance that the public has an independent interest in the qualifications and performance of the person that holds it, beyond the general interest in the qualifications and performance of all government employees." Rotkiewicz v. Sadowsky, 431 Mass. 748, 752-53, 730 N.E.2d 282 (2000) (police officer is a "public official" in defamation action based on statements relating to his official conduct), quoting Rosenblatt v. Baer, 383 U.S. 75, 86 (1966). Other relevant considerations are the employee's ability to set policy guidelines that are of importance to public debate, the impact of the government position on everyday life, the potential for social harm from abuse of the government position, and the employee's access to the press. Id., citing Gertz v. Robert Welch, Inc., 418 U.S. at 344.

Whether a plaintiff is a "limited purpose public figure" is determined by applying the two-part test first set out in Geertz, 418 U.S. at 351, see also Lluberes v. Uncommon Prod'ns, LLC, 663 F.3d 6, 13 (1st Cir. 2011), and followed in Jones v. Taibbi, 400 Mass. 786, 797-98, 512 N.E.2d 260 (1987). Astra USA, Inc. v. Bildman, 455 Mass. 116, 143-44, 914 N.E.2d 36, 56-57 (2009), cert. denied, 130 S. Ct. 3276, 176 L. Ed. 2d 1183 (2010), citing Bowman v. Heller, 420 Mass. 517, 524 n.7, 651 N.E.2d 369, cert. denied, 516 U.S. 1032, 116 S. Ct. 682, 133 L.Ed.2d 530 (1995). First, the allegedly defamatory statements must involve a matter of "public controversy." Astra USA, Inc., 455 Mass. at 144, 914 N.E.2d at 57 (noting that alleged harassment at defendant publicly traded corporation had become a matter of "national and international discourse about permissible conduct in the workplace"). Second, the "nature and extent of [the plaintiff's] participation in the controversy" must be examined. Id., 455 Mass. at 144 & n.44, 914 N.E.2d at 57 & n.44. In Astra USA, where a c.e.o. had injected himself into a "central role" in the controversy of sexual harassment at his publicly traded company, and had "'access to the channels of effective communication' that most private individuals do not enjoy," the court deemed him a limited purpose public figure for purposes of his libel claim against the company. 455 Mass. at 145, 914 N.E.2d at 58 (noting that c.e.o. "was neither a victim nor an unwitting participant in the broad media coverage of his dispute" with the company), quoting Gertz, 418 U.S. at 344, 94 S. Ct. 2997. Note that it is not enough that a plaintiff may have defended himself after being defamed; rather, the court will look for evidence that a plaintiff affirmatively sought to influence public opinion or himself initiated the controversy that later engulfed him. Astra USA, 455 Mass. at 145 & n.45, 914 N.E.2d at 58 & n.45. See also Tripoli v. Boston Herald-Traveler Corp., 359 Mass. 150, 156, 268 N.E.2d 350 (1971) (plaintiff who "palpably engineered efforts to project himself into the public limelight" is a limited purpose public figure).

Public-figure or public-official plaintiffs are relatively rare in employment defamation cases, which often turn on issues of conditional privilege rather than fault. But see Astra USA, Inc. v. Bildman, 455 Mass. 116, 143-44, 914 N.E.2d 36, 56-57 (2009) (affirming trial court's finding that c.e.o. who injected himself into public limelight in order to criticize company's sexual harassment investigation was a "limited purpose public figure" required to offer "clear and convincing proof . . . that the statement was made with knowledge of its falsehood or with reckless disregard for whether it was false"), cert. denied, 130 S. Ct. 3276, 176 L. Ed. 2d 1183 (2010). See also McNulty v. Kessler, 3 Mass. L. Rptr. 457 (Super. Ct. 1995) (20-year high school principal was public official); Puccia v. Edwards, 10 Mass. L. Rptr. 185, 1999 WL 513895, 1999 Mass. Super. LEXIS 253 (Super. Ct. 1999) ("political appointee at a public agency with a high public profile" is public official).

If the plaintiff is a public figure or public official, and – in the case of a public official – the alleged defamation is based on criticism "relating to" the plaintiff's "official conduct," Lane v. MPG Newspapers, 438 Mass. 476,

479, 781 N.E.2d 800, 803, 31 Media L. Rep. 1279 (2003); Dixon v. International Br'hood of Police Officers, 504 F.3d 73 (1st Cir. 2007), then that plaintiff may not prevail absent proof of "actual malice." Stone v. Essex County Newspapers, Inc., 367 Mass. 849, 862-67, 330 N.E.2d 161 (1975); Murphy v. Boston Herald, Inc., 449 Mass. 42, 48, 865 N.E.2d 746, 752, 35 Media L. Rep. 1865 (2007). "Actual malice," in such a context, means "that the statement was made with knowledge of its falsehood or with reckless disregard for whether it was false." Astra USA, 455 Mass. at 143, 914 N.E.2d at 56-57. Such proof must be shown "not merely by the fair preponderance of the evidence, but by 'clear and convincing proof.'" Stone, 367 Mass. at 870, quoting Gertz v. Robert Welch, Inc., 418 U.S. 323, 342, 1 Media L. Rep. 1633 (1974), New York Times, 376 U.S. at 285-86; Astra USA, 455 Mass. at 143, 914 N.E.2d at 56-57. See also Murphy, 449 Mass. at 48, 865 N.E.2d at 752 (2007) ("clear and convincing evidence").

With respect to public-official plaintiffs, the actual malice standard "only applies to comments 'relating to … official conduct,' New York Times Co., 376 U.S. at 279-80, but that limitation has been broadly construed to reach 'anything which might touch on … [the] official's fitness for office.' Garrison v. Louisiana, 379 U.S. 64 (1964)." Dixon v. International Br'hood of Police Officers, 504 F.3d 73 (1st Cir. 2007). Because "[s]o many things can 'touch on' someone's 'fitness for office,'" the restriction rarely comes into play. Id. A charge of criminal conduct against an official or candidate would always satisfy that condition. Lane, 438 Mass. at 484, 781 N.E.2d at 807. Moreover, the standard applies even where "'an official's private reputation, as well as his public reputation, is harmed.'" Id., quoting Garrison, 379 U.S. at 77.

The U.S. Supreme Court has recognized that the phrase "actual malice" may have been an unfortunate shorthand label for what is more clearly described as "publication of a statement with knowledge of falsity or reckless disregard as to truth or falsity." Masson v. New Yorker Magazine, 501 U.S. 496, 511, 18 Media L. Rep. 2241 (1991). The term "actual malice" is especially likely to cause confusion with respect to employment defamation cases in Massachusetts, because so many pre-New York Times cases in Massachusetts – **and even the occasional modern one, see Barrows v. Wareham Fire Dist., 82 Mass. App. Ct. 623, 631, -- N.E.2d -- (2012)** – use the term "actual malice" to refer to spite, hatred, or ill will, sufficient to cause loss or abuse of an employer's conditional business-interest or common-interest privilege. The problem is that this so-called brand of "actual malice" – spite, ill will, ulterior motive – consists of precisely the factors that are insufficient under New York Times and Stone to permit a public-figure or public-official plaintiff to prevail. (To try to reduce the confusion somewhat, unless otherwise noted, this outline uses the term "actual malice" only in its constitutional sense.)

The Supreme Judicial Court has defined "actual malice" – the constitutional kind – as a showing that the defendant published the false and defamatory statement "'with knowledge that it was false or with reckless disregard of whether it was false or not.'" Murphy v. Boston Herald, 449 Mass. 42, 48, 865 N.E.2d 746, 752, 35 Media L. Rep. 1865 (2007), quoting King v. Globe Newspaper Co., 400 Mass. 705, 719, 512 N.E.2d 241, 14 Media L. Rep. 1811 (1987), cert. denied, 485 U.S. 962 (1988). Otherwise put, a jury must determine whether the defendants "published each statement either knowing that it was not, or entertaining serious doubts that it was, true." Murphy, 449 Mass. at 57, 865 N.E.2d at 758. The test is entirely subjective, Stone, 367 Mass. at 867; King, 400 Mass. at 719, and demands substantially more than mere negligence, Murphy, 449 Mass. at 48, 865 N.E.2d at 752. It requires a showing – by clear and convincing proof – that the author or speaker of a statement "entertained serious doubts about the truth of his or her statement." King, 400 Mass. at 720; Murphy, 449 Mass. at 48, 57, 865 N.E.2d at 752, 759 (jury must determine that defendant "actually knew" the statements were false or had "serious, unresolved doubts as to their accuracy"); Rotkiewicz v. Sadowsky, 431 Mass. 748, 755, 730 N.E.2d 282 (2000) ("inquiry is a subjective one as to the defendant's attitude toward the truth or falsity of the statement rather than the defendant's attitude toward the plaintiff"). Even a corporate defendant "is capable of possessing the subjective state of mind required for a determination of 'actual malice.'" Murphy, 449 Mass. at 64 n.22, 65-66, 865 N.E.2d at 762 n.22, 764 (imputing to employer the state of mind of an employee acting within the scope of his employment). The question is not whether a reasonably prudent person would have investigated before making the statement at issue, but rather whether there is enough evidence that the defendant, at the time s/he made the statement, subjectively entertained serious doubts as to the statement's truth. Judd, 27 Mass. App. Ct. at 175-76; Callahan v. Westinghouse Broadcasting Co., Inc., 372 Mass. 582, 588 n.3, 363 N.E.2d 240, 2 Media L. Rep. 2226 (1977); Lyons v. New Mass Media, Inc., 390 Mass. 51, 55, 453 N.E.2d 451 (1983); Berard v. Town of Millville, 113 F. Supp. 2d 197 (D. Mass. 2000).

A defendant's testimony that he believed the statements were true when he published them is not enough to ensure a favorable verdict. Murphy v. Boston Herald, 449 Mass. 42, 49, 865 N.E.2d 746, 753, 35 Media L. Rep. 1865 (2007). "Exactly how much evidence is sufficient, as a matter of constitutional law, to establish actual malice is determined on a case-by-case basis." Murphy, 449 Mass. at 48-49, 865 N.E.2d at 752-53. The reviewing court "must examine the content of the statements, and the circumstances under which they were made, to see 'whether they are of a character which the principles of the First Amendment … protect.'" Id. at 49, 865 N.E.2d at 753.

3. ***Falsity.*** Truth is, in most cases, an absolute defense to a defamation claim. Ravnikar v. Bogojavlensky, 438 Mass. 627 , 629 n.3, 782 N.E.2d 508, 510 n.3 (2003); Milgroom v. News Group Boston, Inc., 412 Mass.

9, 12-13, 586 N.E.2d 985, 20 Media L. Rep. 1097 (1992); **Barrows v. Wareham Fire Dist., 82 Mass. App. Ct. 623, 628 n.6, -- N.E.2d -- (2012).** Whether it is a defense in all cases, however, is put in question by an 1855 statute whose constitutionality has been questioned. The statute, Mass. Gen. Laws c. 231, § 92, provides that in a libel case, "the truth shall be a justification *unless* [']actual malice['] is proved." (Emphasis added.) As used in the statute, "actual malice" means "malevolent intent or motive," not constitutional malice, and courts have repeatedly so ruled. See Gilbert v. Bernard, 4 Mass. L. Rptr. 143, 1995 WL 809550, 1995 Mass. Super. LEXIS 566 (Super. Ct. 1995); see also Noonan v. Staples, Inc., 707 F. Supp. 2d 85, 91 (D. Mass. 2010) (noting that a finding of malice "is at least plausible" where the defamatory true statement was made by a supervisor about an employee who had caused the employer "a great deal of expense" and the supervisor "some personal inconvenience").)

For decades, courts had chipped away at this "defamatory truth" statute, Mass. Gen. Laws c. 231, § 92, on constitutional grounds. The Supreme Judicial Court in Materia v. Huff, 394 Mass. 328, 333 n.6, 475 N.E.2d 1212 (1985), held that the statute was unconstitutional as applied to cases brought by public figures. Thirteen years later, in Shaari v. Harvard Student Agencies, Inc., 427 Mass. 129, 691 N.E.2d 925, 26 Media L. Rep. 1730 (1998), the same court held that the statute cannot apply in a private-figure case against the media involving a matter of public concern. 427 Mass. at 134. But the narrowness of the Shaari ruling left the statute untouched with respect to libel claims brought by private figures against non-media defendants and/or not involving a matter of public concern. See Noonan v. Staples, Inc., 556 F.3d 20, 28 (1st Cir. 2009). (A Superior Court ruled in 1995 that the statute would also be unconstitutional if applied in a private-figure *non-media* case involving a matter of public concern, but the trial court's decision was never brought up on appeal. See Gilbert v. Bernard, 4 Mass. L. Rptr. 143, 1995 WL 809550, *2 n.3, 1995 Mass. Super. LEXIS 566 (Super. Ct. 1995) ("Gertz rendered M.G.L. c. 231, § 92 unconstitutional because that statute permits recovery in the absence of any falsehood if the statement at issue is defamatory and the defendant acted malevolently."), citing Stone v. Essex County Newspapers, Inc., 367 Mass. 849, 858, 860 (1975) ("private persons ... may recover compensation on proof of negligent publication of a defamatory *falsehood*" (emphasis added)).)

Since 1998, Massachusetts state and federal appellate courts have expressly avoided opining on whether the statute would be unconstitutional if applied in the private-figure, public-concern context, but nevertheless have treated the exception as an established one in the law. The Supreme Judicial Court stated in 2003 that "Massachusetts, by statute, allows a plaintiff to recover for a truthful defamatory statement if it was published in writing (or its equivalent) and with actual malice," although it did acknowledge that the "scope of the statute ... is limited by the provisions of the First Amendment to the United States Constitution." Ravnikar v. Bogojavlensky, 438 Mass. 627, 629 n.3, 782 N.E.2d 508, 510 n.3 (2003), citing Mass. Gen. Laws c. 231, § 92. (Because Ravnikar involved slander rather than libel, the statute did not apply; therefore, the reference to it was academic.) The very next year, the court repeated the same acknowledgment in dictum. See White v. Blue Cross and Blue Shield of Massachusetts, Inc., 442 Mass. 64, 66 n.4 (2004). The First Circuit Court of Appeals volunteered in 2006 that because a private-figure plaintiff's defamation claim was based on "allegedly false statement," the court would not consider "whether she could recover on a lesser showing" than falsity. Stanton v. Metro Corp., 438 F.3d 119, 131 n.10, 34 Media L. Rep. 1321 (1st Cir. 2006). **In Coughlin v. Town of Arlington, No. 10-102013-MLW, 2011 WL 6370932 (D. Mass. Dec. 19, 2011), the federal district court rejected a magistrate judge's recommended dismissal of a defamation claim based on publication of the two plaintiffs' email communications, "the truth of which is not challenged." And in 2012, the state Appeals Court, citing White, ruled that a libel plaintiff suing over a *true* statement could not recover – not because the statement was true, but because "a showing of actual malice was required and none is shown here." Caputo v. City of Haverhill, No. 11-P-1321, 82 Mass. App. Ct. 1109, 971 N.E.2d 337, 2012 WL 3076542 (Mass. App. Ct. July 31, 2012) (unpublished). See also Barrows v. Wareham Fire Dist., 82 Mass. App. Ct. 623, 628 n.6, -- N.E.2d -- (2012) ("*In most cases* the statement must be false" (emphasis added)), citing Bander v. Metropolitan Life Ins. Co., 313 Mass. 337, 342, 47 N.E.2d 595 (1943) and Mass. Gen. Laws c. 231, § 92.**

It appeared that the issue would come to a head in 2009, in a case involving an employee who sued for defamation after his employer sent an email stating that he was fired for "stealing from" the company (a fact which the court deemed to be substantially true). In a companion case, the First Circuit Court of Appeals had left open the possibility (but had not squarely decided) that, in this non-media setting involving a matter of purely private interest, Mass. Gen. Laws c. 231, § 92, might allow the employee to recover damages. See Noonan v. Staples, Inc., 556 F.3d 20 (1st Cir. 2009), reh'g denied, 561 F.3d 4 (1st Cir. 2009). Then, in a closely related second case, the employer defended against the employee's defamation claims by mounting a "frontal assault" on the constitutionality of the statute. Noonan v. Staples, Inc., 707 F. Supp. 2d 85, 88-89, 92 (D. Mass. 2010). But when Judge Young issued an opinion indicating that he would rule imminently on the constitutionality of the statute, the plaintiff peremptorily mooted the issue by dismissing all of his claims. As a result, the constitutionality of the "defamatory truth" statute has not been determined in the context of a private figure suing over a matter of private concern.

By far the more typical defamation case involves an alleged falsehood, and Massachusetts law is clear that the plaintiff bears the burden of alleging falsity in all such cases. McAvoy v. Shufrin, 401 Mass. 593, 597, 518

N.E.2d 513, 14 Media L. Rep. 2298 (1988). The plaintiff also bears the burden of proving falsity, at least in cases against media defendants on a matter of public concern. Murphy v. Boston Herald, 449 Mass. 42, 51, 865 N.E.2d 746, 754, 35 Media L. Rep. 1865 (2007); Friedman v. Boston Broadcasters, Inc., 402 Mass. 376, 381, 522 N.E.2d 959 (1988); Reilly v. Associated Press, 59 Mass. App. Ct. 764, 769, 797 N.E.2d 1204 (2003). Although the Supreme Judicial Court has not addressed the burden of proving falsity in cases not involving media defendants or matters of public concern, one well-reasoned Superior Court decision concludes that the burden remains with the plaintiff at all times. Gilbert v. Bernard, 4 Mass. L. Rptr. 143, 1995 WL 809550, 1995 Mass. Super. LEXIS 566 (Super. Ct. 1995), citing Stone v. Essex County Newspapers, Inc., 367 Mass. 849, 858, 330 N.E.2d 161 (1975) (requiring that a private person prove a "defamatory falsehood," not merely a "defamatory statement"). But see McAvoy, 401 Mass. at 597 ("while the plaintiff bears the burden of alleging the falsity of the libel, it is up to the defendant to prove truth as an affirmative defense"); Miller v. Tope, No. 02-11151-DPW, 2003 U.S. Dist. LEXIS 21211, *51 (D. Mass. Nov. 24, 2003) (same, citing McAvoy).

On appeal, the jury's finding of falsity receives no special scrutiny; the finding "is subject to our traditional standard of review of any jury's finding of fact, that is, whether the finding has a basis in the evidence and reasonable inferences that could be drawn therefrom." Murphy v. Boston Herald, 449 Mass. 42, 51, 865 N.E.2d 746, 754, 35 Media L. Rep. 1865 (2007).

4. ***Defamatory Statement of Fact.*** To be actionable, a communication must be both defamatory in meaning and factual in nature. (This section deals with what it means for a statement to be "defamatory." As to the fact-opinion distinction and use of rhetorical hyperbole and the like, see II.B.2, infra.) Under Massachusetts law, a statement is defamatory "if it 'may reasonably be read [or "understood," see Noonan v. Staples, Inc., 707 F. Supp. 2d 85, 89 (D. Mass. 2010)] as discrediting [the plaintiff] in the minds of any considerable and respectable class of the community.'" Noonan v. Staples, Inc., 556 F.3d 20, 25 (1st Cir. 2009), quoting Disend v. Meadowbrook Sch., 33 Mass. App. Ct. 674, 604 N.E.2d 54, 55 (1992). A defamatory communication consists of words which "would tend to hold the plaintiff up to scorn, hatred, ridicule or contempt, in the minds of any considerable and respectable segment in the community." Phelan v. May Dep't Stores Co., 443 Mass. 52, 819 N.E.2d 550, 553 (2004)(internal quotations omitted); Stanton v. Metro Corp., 438 F.3d 119, 125 (1st Cir. 2006); Draghetti v. Chmielewski, 416 Mass. 808, 811, 626 N.E.2d 862 (1994); **Barrows v. Wareham Fire Dist., 82 Mass. App. Ct. 623, 628, -- N.E.2d -- (2012)**. For purposes of determining whether a statement is defamatory, the test appears to be not whether the statement has injured the plaintiff's reputation in the community, but rather whether it "could" do so. Ravnikar v. Bogojavlensky, 438 Mass. 627, 629-30, 782 N.W.2d 508, 510 (2003). See also North Shore Pharmacy Services, Inc. v. Breslin Consulting Assocs., 491 F. Supp. 2d 111, 128 (D. Mass. 2007). "Statements about a person's vocational reputation . . . are particularly likely to be defamatory." DelloRusso, 47 Mass. App. Ct. at 478, 714 N.E.2d at 364. "A court may dismiss written defamation claims, i.e., libel claims, if the communication is 'incapable of a defamatory meaning.'" Amrak Prod'ns, Inc. v. Morton, et al., 410 F.3d 69, 72 (1st Cir. 2005), quoting Brauer v. Globe Newspaper Co., 351 Mass. 53, 217 N.E.2d 736, 738 (Mass. 1966) (quoting, in turn, Muchnick v. Post Publ'g Co., 332 Mass. 304, 125 N.E.2d 137, 138 (Mass. 1955)). However, if the court answers this "threshold question" by deciding that the communication is "'reasonably susceptible of a defamatory meaning,'" then "the ultimate issue of whether the article is defamatory is not the court's to decide." Stanton v. Metro Corp., 438 F.3d at 124-25 quoting Amrak, 410 F.3d at 72, and Phelan, 443 Mass. at 56-57, 819 N.E.2d at 554 (Mass. 2004).

"In deciding whether a statement is defamatory, both the context in which and the circumstances under which the statement was made are important considerations." Vranos v. Skinner, 77 Mass. App. Ct. 280, 296, 930 N.E.2d 156, 169 (Mass. App. Ct. 2010) (holding that it was not defamation for hospital supervisor to tell physicians that "if [they] knew" what he knew, they would "understand" reasons for colleague's summary suspension pursuant to a hospital rule permitting such suspension under certain circumstances), citing Restatement (2d) of Torts § 563, comments d, e. The common knowledge and understanding of the recipients of the communication also matter. See Dexter's Hearthside Restaurant, Inc. v. Whitehall Co., 24 Mass. App. Ct. 217, 219, 508 N.E.2d 113, 14 Media L. Rep. 1664 (1987) (readers of delinquent accounts list published by state Alcoholic Beverages Control Commission understand the purpose of the list); DelloRusso v. Monteiro, 47 Mass. App. Ct. 475, 477, 714 N.E.2d 362, 364 (1999) (holding that a typist who claims libel based on a negative reference is defamed if the content of the reference holds her up to scorn and discredit in her community of government agencies that employ typists). A statement will be actionable even if the plaintiff's reputation is not damaged, or the plaintiff is not held up to ridicule, "in the *community at large* or among *all* reasonable people," and even if a "numerical majority" of the audience would arrive at a non-defamatory interpretation, so long as a "considerable and respectable class of people" would find it defamatory. Stanton v. Metro Corp., 438 F.3d 119, 127, 34 Media L. Rep. 1321 (1st Cir. 2006) (italics added).

Libel – written words – is actionable whether the defamation is on its face (per se) or contextual (per quod), New England Tractor-Trailer Training of Connecticut, Inc. v. Globe Newspaper Co., 395 Mass. 471, 480 N.E.2d 1005 (1985), and whether or not there is proof of economic loss, Ravnikar v. Bogojavlensky, 438 Mass. 627, 630, 782 N.E.2d 508, 511 (2003); see also North Shore Pharmacy Services, Inc. v. Breslin Consulting Assocs., 491 F. Supp. 111, 128 (D. Mass. 2007). In a slander – spoken words – case, however, the plaintiff must allege and prove special damages as part of its prima facie case unless the words spoken fall into certain limited categories historically referred to as constituting slander per se. Alba v. Sampson, 44 Mass. App. Ct. 311, 312, 690 N.E.2d 1240 (1998). See also Psy-Ed Corp. v. Klein, 459 Mass. 697, 704 n.18, 947 N.E.2d 520, 528 n.18 (2011); Ravnikar, 438 Mass. at 630. (As if only to confuse matters, "per se" in the slander context has a different meaning than it does in the libel context. The distinction between "libel per se" and "libel per quod" no longer has any practical significance.)

Spoken words (or, apparently, defamatory conduct, see Phelan v. May Dep't Stores co. et al., 443 Mass. 52, 56, 819 N.E.2d 550, 554 (2004)), are actionable without proof of economic loss if "they charge the plaintiff with a crime, or state that he is suffering from certain diseases, or prejudice him in his office, profession or business or may probably tend to do so." Lynch v. Lyons, 303 Mass. 116, 118-19, 20 N.E.2d 953 (1939); Ravnikar, 438 Mass. at 630, 782 N.E.2d at 511; Phelan, 443 Mass. at 56, 819 N.E.2d at 554. See also North Shore Pharmacy Services, Inc. v. Breslin Consulting Assocs., 491 F. Supp. 2d 111, 128 (D. Mass. 2007), quoting Restatement (Second) of Torts § 561(a), comment b to clause a ("a corporation may maintain an action for defamatory words that discredit it and tend to cause loss to it in the conduct of its business, without proof of special harm resulting to it"). If the slander does not affect the plaintiff "in his trade or profession," and does not fall in one of the other slander per se categories, it is not actionable per se, and therefore special damages must be shown. Bander v. Metropolitan Life Ins. Co., 313 Mass. 337, 345-46, 47 N.E.2d 595 (1943). The requirement of special damages rarely comes into play in employment slander actions, because a statement injuring someone's professional reputation constitutes slander per se. Id. However, it was not slander per se for a manager to say at a staff meeting that it was "a disgrace" to have the plaintiff in the office, id., or for a higher-ranked employee to call a subordinate a "fucking asshole" and accuse him of a mean before-hours office prank, saying, "You're going to jail," Alba v. Sampson, 44 Mass. App. Ct. 311, 312-13, 690 N.E.2d 1240 (1998). Such words "can only be construed as words of general disparagement directed at [plaintiff] as an individual as opposed to his professional accountant position, because they "did not impute some lack of an essential qualification 'demanded of a person in the lines of endeavor pursued by [the plaintiff],'" Alba, 44 Mass. App. Ct. at 313, quoting Lynch v. Lyons, 303 Mass. 116, 119, 20 N.E.2d 953 (1939), or "serious and willful misconduct in office or in business," Alba, 44 Mass. App. Ct. at 313; Mayo v. Dalbar, Inc., 2002 WL 1020725, *4-5, 14 Mass L. Rptr. 493 (Mass. Super April 19, 2002) (finding no evidence in record that statement to security personnel that "plaintiff should be denied access to the building" prejudiced plaintiff in her profession or tended to do so).

As to what diseases rise to the level of supporting a slander per se claim, there are few Massachusetts cases. In Ravnikar v. Bogojavlensky, 438 Mass. 627, 630-31 & n.5, 782 N.E.2d 508, 511 & n.5 (2003), plaintiff alleged that it was slander per se for defendant to say she was dying of cancer, not because cancer was such a disease (she conceded she had suffered cancer in the past, though she said she had been successfully treated), but because the comment that she was "dying" could prejudice her medical practice. The Court agreed, noting that to say a physician is dying of cancer "creates an inference that that physician lacks a necessary professional characteristic," and will tend to discourage potential plaintiffs; hence, the slanderous statement is actionable without proof of economic damage. 438 Mass. at 631-32, 782 N.E.2d at 511-12.

A statement "'fairly imputing immorality'" is defamatory, without regard to how direct or explicit the statement may be in definitively ascribing to the plaintiff any certain "'indiscretions,'" "promiscuous conduct," or "'want of chastity.'" Stanton v. Metro Corp., 438 F.3d 119, 131, 34 Media L. Rep. 1321 (1st Cir. 2006), quoting Thayer v. Worcester Post Co., 284 Mass. 160, 162, 187 N.E. 292, 293 (Mass. 1933). Whether it is defamatory under Massachusetts law to call someone a homosexual appears to be an unresolved question. In Albright v. Morton, et al., 321 F. Supp. 2d 130 (D. Mass. 2004), the United States District Court in Massachusetts (Gertner, J.) ruled that in light of recent federal and state supreme court decisions on homosexuality, see Lawrence v. Texas, 539 U.S. 558 (2003) (invalidating state statute criminalizing same-sex sexual conduct) and Goodridge v. Dep't of Public Health, 440 Mass. 309, 798 N.E.2d 941 (2003) (requiring that the state legislature permit same-sex marriage), a statement identifying an individual as homosexual is not defamatory *per se* under Massachusetts law. Although the First Circuit Court of Appeals affirmed the district court's dismissal of the complaint, it did so on other grounds, expressly declining to address this question. Amrak Prod'ns, Inc. v. Morton, et al., 410 F.3d 69, 73 (2004).

It is defamatory to accuse an individual, either directly or by insinuation, of being a criminal or participating in a criminal act. Phelan v. May Dep't Stores Co. et al., 443 Mass. 52, 56, 819 N.E.2d 550, 554 (2004) ("the imputation of a crime is defamatory per se, requiring no proof of special damages" in a defamation-by-conduct case); Noonan v. Staples, Inc., 707 F. Supp. 2d 85, 90 (D. Mass. 2010) (accusation of "stealing" is "a classic defamatory statement if untrue"); Arsenault v. Allegheny Airlines, Inc., 485 F. Supp. 1373, 1378 (D. Mass. 1980), aff'd, 636 F.2d 1199 (1st Cir. 1980). It is also defamatory to accuse a person of intending to commit a criminal act. Draghetti v. Chmielewski, 416 Mass. 808, 812, 626 N.E.2d 862, 22 Media L. Rep. 1456 (1994); Reilly v. Associated Press, 59 Mass. App. Ct. 764, 778, 797 N.E.2d 1204 (2003). An employer's statement to an employee, in the presence of a third party, that it "has strong evidence you are involved in a car theft" constitutes slander. Lyons v. National Car Rental Systems, Inc., 30 F.3d 240, 243 (1st Cir. 1994); see also Galvin v. New York, N. H. & H. R. Co, 341 Mass. 293, 295, 168 N.E.2d 262 (1960) (defamatory to yell to plaintiff, within hearing of onlookers, "Why don't you take the stuff out of your car that you stole during the night and have this over with?"); Masso v. United Parcel Service, 884 F. Supp. 610, 621 (D. Mass. 1995) (defamatory to accuse employee of taking kickbacks);

Whitcomb v. Hearst Corp., 329 Mass. 193, 107 N.E.2d 295 (1952) (defamatory to say plaintiff was convicted of theft by military court and sentenced to hard labor). A defendant need not expressly accuse the plaintiff of criminal activity for the statement to be actionable; defamatory meaning can be established by implication or context, and a facially non-defamatory statement can become actionable by reason of the surrounding facts. See Ball v. Wal-Mart, Inc., 102 F. Supp. 2d 44, 49-50 (D. Mass. 2000) (store employee's statement, "Well, what do we have here," while searching plaintiff's bags, could reasonably be construed as an accusation of shoplifting).

While conceding that "a false accusation of commission of a crime is defamatory *per se,*" the federal district court, applying Massachusetts law, said that principle does not apply to a statement in a "neutral" police log indicating that plaintiff engaged in "violation of a by-law or an ordinance." In context, the court said, "[t]he statement is most reasonably interpreted as merely a nearly contemporaneous recording of police activity and the general type and level of infraction being violated." Fitzgerald v. Town of Kingston, 13 F. Supp. 2d 119, 126 (D. Mass. 1998).

"Statements suggesting that one lacks a necessary professional characteristic are defamatory." Reilly v. Associated Press, 59 Mass. App. Ct. 764, 778, 797 N.E.2d 1204 (2003); North Shore Pharmacy Services, Inc. v. Breslin Consulting Assocs., 491 F. Supp. 2d 111, 127 (D. Mass. 2007). Even absent allegations of dishonesty or specific misconduct, "[s]tatements about a person's vocational reputation . . . are particularly likely to be defamatory." DelloRusso v. Monteiro, 47 Mass. App. Ct. 475, 478, 714 N.E.2d 362, 364 (1999). Thus, "to charge that a judge is biased or unfair, or otherwise cannot be trusted to administer justice according to the law, is to strip away the qualities for which the office is respected and held to be legitimate," thereby anchoring a libel claim. Murphy v. Boston Herald, 449 Mass. 42, 51 n.9, 865 N.E.2d 746, 754 n.9, 35 Media L. Rep. 1865 (2007).

Defamation can also occur by implication, suggestion, innuendo, or insinuation. Reilly v. Associated Press, 59 Mass. App. Ct. 764, 774, 797 N.E.2d 1204 (2003). One Superior Court decision said that a supervisor's derogatory comments about the plaintiff's management skills during daily conference calls, and his screaming of obscenities in her direction, "may be indicative of her skills as a manager," and thus might constitute defamatory statements of fact. Martin-Kirkland v. United Parcel Service, Inc., No. 03-4520-H, 21 Mass. L. Rep. 66, 2006 Mass. Super. LEXIS 193, *32-33 (Middlesex Super. Ct. Apr. 11, 2006) (denying defendant's summary judgment motion). Even if no wrongdoing or bad character is imputed, the plaintiff may be defamed by an inference "which might be drawn by a considerable and respectable segment of the community." Smith v. Suburban Restaurants, Inc., 374 Mass. 528, 530, 373 N.E.2d 215 (1978), quoted in Noonan v. Staples, Inc., 556 F.3d 20, 25-26 (1st Cir. 2009); Goss v. Needham Co-operative Bank, 312 Mass. 309, 310, 44 N.E.2d 690 (1942).

Merely saying that an employee was suspended or demoted is not defamatory, regardless of any inferences that may be drawn from the announcement. Kersey v. Dennison Mfg. Co., Inc., 1992 WL 71390, at *4, No. 89-2650-MA (D. Mass. Feb. 21, 1992). It was not defamatory to state, accurately, that a contract with the plaintiff had been terminated "for cause," and that plaintiff's building project "had to be modified to meet the building code." **ARCADD, Inc. v. Patterson, 80 Mass. App. Ct. 1111, 955 N.E.2d 933, 2011 WL 4972132, *1 (Oct. 20, 2011) (unpublished). A business owner was not defamed by saying that his bookkeeper quit when in fact she was fired, or by the allegedly false statement that he could not be reached for comment. Boyle v. Cape Cod Times, No. 11-P-196, 81 Mass. App. Ct. 1107, 959 N.E.2d 457, 2012 WL 28661, *2 (Mass. App. Ct. Jan. 6, 2012) (unpublished).**

Nor can there be defamation by omission: a plaintiff cannot succeed on a libel claim on the grounds that he was not listed by the company as one of its "key employees." Paren v. Craigie, 2006 U.S. Dist. LEXIS 43288, *38 (D. Mass. June 15, 2006) (Neiman, C.M.J.) (calling plaintiff's allegation one of "tortured logic"). But see Ford v. Warner-Lambert Co., 1987 WL 9905 at *4, 1987 U.S. Dist. LEXIS 3087, No. CA 86-0770-C (D. Mass. April 8, 1987) (letter stating that employee was suspended due to account shortages may be defamatory, because it may reflect on plaintiff's honesty, credit and business character). Nor is it defamatory to state that plaintiff, at his performance evaluation, received a "poor review." Mathias v. Beatrice Foods Co., 23 Mass. App. Ct. 915, 917, 500 N.E.2d 812 (1986).

The threshold question on a motion to dismiss -- whether a statement is reasonably susceptible of a defamatory meaning -- is a question of law for the court. Phelan v. May Dep't Stores Co., 443 Mass. 52, 56, 819 N.E.2d 550, 554 (2004); Foley v. Lowell Sun Publishing Co., 404 Mass. 9, 11 (1989); **Boyle v. Cape Cod Times, No. 11-P-196, 81 Mass. App. Ct. 1107, 959 N.E.2d 457, 2012 WL 28661 (Mass. App. Ct. Jan. 6, 2012) (unpublished);** Albright v. Morton, 410 F.3d 69, 72 (1st Cir. 2005). Often such a question can be answered by resorting to prior case law or a standard reference work. Noonan v. Staples, Inc., 707 F. Supp. 2d 85, 90-91 (D. Mass. 2010); Millar Elevator Serv. Co. v. Liatsis, No. 9804547D, 12 Mass. L. Rptr. 559, 2000 WL 33171009, *6 (Mass. Super. Nov. 28, 2000). (The *American Heritage Dictionary* was the reference of choice in both Liatsis (2d College ed. 1985) and Noonan (4th College ed. 2002).) "The communication 'must be interpreted reasonably.'" Albright, 410 F.3d at 72, quoting Foley, 533 N.E.2d at 197; Noonan, 707 F. Supp. 2d at 91 (applying a word's "commonly understood meaning"); **Boyle, 2012 WL 28661 at *2 n.4 (examining**

statement's "potential to discredit [plaintiff] in the mind of a reasonable reader"). "Context matters," Albright, 410 F.3d at 72-73; the court must "examine the statement in its totality in the context in which it was uttered or published," and cannot examine "merely a particular phrase or sentence," id. at 73, quoting Myers v. Boston Magazine Co., 380 Mass. 336, 403 N.E.2d 376, 379 (1980).

If the words at issue are incapable of a defamatory meaning, then the claim cannot succeed. Nolan v. Krajcik, 384 F. Supp. 2d 447, 474 (D. Mass. 2005). Where any defamatory tendency of a communication is "somewhat amorphous, . . . rather than specific and significant," then the issue of defamatory meaning should not go to the jury. Tartaglia v. Townsend, 19 Mass. App. Ct. 693, 698-99, 477 N.E.2d 178 (1985); see also Cole v. Westinghouse Broad. Co., 386 Mass. 303, 312, 435 N.E.2d 1021, 1027 (Mass. 1982) (where meaning of statements "is imprecise and open to speculation," the statements "cannot be proved false" and therefore "cannot be held libelous"). But if a statement is susceptible of defamatory and non-defamatory meanings, it presents a question for the trier of fact "and cannot be ruled non-libelous as a matter of law." Smith, 374 Mass. at 530; see also Phelan v. May Dep't Stores Co. et al., 443 Mass. 52, 57, 819 N.E.2d 550, 554 (2004); Stanton v. Metro Corp., 438 F.3d 119, 124-25 (1st Cir. 2006).

Massachusetts has not explicitly recognized the so-called "incremental harm doctrine" that forms a part of the common law libel tort in many other states. Where it is recognized, the doctrine "reasons that when unchallenged or nonactionable parts of a particular publication are damaging, another statement, though maliciously false, might be nonactionable on the grounds that it causes no harm beyond the harm caused by the remainder of the publication." Church of Scientology Intern. v. Time Warner, Inc., 932 F. Supp. 589, 593 (S.D.N.Y. 1996), quoted in Noonan v. Staples, Inc., 707 F. Supp. 2d 85, 90 (D. Mass. 2010). One might reasonably anticipate that Massachusetts state courts would adopt the incremental harm doctrine, since they have adopted the closely related concepts of the "libel-proof plaintiff," see Jackson v. Longcope, 394 Mass. 577 (1985) (no liability where plaintiff's reputation was already so poor that it could not have suffered further from the publication of even false and libelous statements) and "substantial truth," see Noonan v. Staples, 556 F.3d 20, 28 (1st Cir. 2009), citing Murphy v. Boston Herald, Inc., 449 Mass. 42 (2007) and Jones v. Taibbi, 400 Mass. 786 (1987) (holding that only "substantial truth" of publication is required to satisfy the truth defense to defamation). In Vranos v. Skinner, 77 Mass. App. Ct. 280, 297, 930 N.E.2d 156, 169 (Mass. App. Ct. 2010), the Appeals Court affirmed summary judgment for a libel defendant partly on the grounds that a supervisor's statement about the plaintiff "added nothing to whatever defamatory sting flowed" from the fact that the plaintiff had been suspended (which suspension could not create a defamation claim because it was privileged by the Massachusetts peer review statute), citing Howell v. Enterprise Pub. Co., 455 Mass. 641, 667, 920 N.E.2d 1 (2010) ("in context, the additional characterization did not convey a substantially greater defamatory sting than the [privileged] testimony and images entered in evidence at the hearing"). However, neither the Supreme Judicial Court nor any lower state court in Massachusetts has ever explicitly acknowledged the doctrine, and the federal district court has shied away from it on those grounds. See Noonan, 707 F. Supp. 2d at 90; see also Mandel v. Boston Phoenix, Inc., 456 F.3d 198, 210 n.6 (1st Cir. 2006) (noting that the "question of whether the incremental harm doctrine is part and parcel of Massachusetts law" is "apparently open").

5. ***Of and Concerning Plaintiff.*** Defamatory words are "of and concerning" plaintiff if "the plaintiff can show that either the defendant intended its words to refer to the plaintiff and that they were so understood, or that the defendant's words reasonably could be interpreted to refer to the plaintiff and that the defendant was negligent in publishing them in such a way that they could be so understood." New England Tractor-Trailer Training of Conn., Inc. v. Globe Newspaper Co., 395 Mass. 471, 483, 480 N.E.2d 1005 (1985); Eyal v. Helen Broadcasting Corp., 411 Mass. 426, 429-30, 583 N.E.2d 228, 19 Media L. Rep. 1989 (1991); Driscoll v. Board of Trustees of Milton Academy, 70 Mass. App. Ct. 285, 298, 873 N.E.2d 1177 (2007); Reilly v. Associated Press, 59 Mass. App. Ct. 764, 777, 797 N.E.2d 1204 (2003); North Shore Pharmacy Services, Inc. v. Breslin Consulting Assocs., 491 F. Supp. 2d 111, 127-28 (D. Mass. 2007). Instead of requiring that the statement be "of and concerning the plaintiff," one federal district court has substituted a more vernacular formulation: that the statement "was about, and concerned, the plaintiff." See Noonan v. Staples, Inc., 707 F. Supp. 2d 85, 89 (2010).

"While the plaintiff need not prove that the defendant 'aimed' at the plaintiff, he...must prove that the defendant was negligent in writing or saying words which reasonably could be understood to 'hit' the plaintiff." Reilly, 59 Mass. App. Ct. at 777 (private-figure libel case), quoting New England Tractor-Trailer, 395 Mass. at 478. Driscoll v. Board of Trustees of Milton Academy, 70 Mass. App. Ct. 285, 298, 873 N.E.2d 1177 (2007) involved a school's statement to parents about several sexual encounters on campus, one involving five students (including the identified plaintiff, who was disciplined), and two others involving four unnamed students identified only as "those we have already disciplined." Because the school had "listed the number of participants in each incident so that it is clear that not every boy involved in the [five-boy] incident participated in the [other two] incidents," the court ruled that it would not be "reasonable" to conclude that the discussion of the other two incidents was "of and concerning" the plaintiff.

A for-profit corporation has a defamation cause of action against one who publishes matter that "tends to prejudice it in the conduct of its business or to deter others from dealing with it…." North Shore Pharmacy Services, Inc. v. Breslin Consulting Assocs., 491 F. Supp. 2d 111, 127 (D. Mass. 2007), quoting Restatement (Second) of Torts § 561(a). See also Eyal v. Helen Broad. Corp., 411 Mass. 426, 433, 583 N.E.2d 228, 232 (1991) (statement holding corporation up to disdain or disfavor in community is capable of being found defamatory). Indeed, in 2010 a jury awarded $149,000 to an Ohio -based debt collection firm libeled by a website created and controlled by a dissatisfied customer. The jury ruled that the company was a limited-purpose public figure, but that the website comments were published with actual malice. Cadle Co. v. Schlichtmann et al., No. ESCV2005-00603 (Mass. Super. Ct. July 6, 2010), *notice of appeal filed Oct. 7, 2010*; see also Massachusetts Lawyers Weekly, July 5, 2010.

As a general rule, "[a]n officer of a corporation may not recover damages for a libel published about the corporation." Dexter's Hearthside Restaurant, Inc. v. Whitehall Co., 24 Mass. App. Ct. 217, 218, 508 N.E.2d 113, 14 Media L. Rep. 1664 (1987); Gilbert Shoe Co. v. Rumpf Publishing Co., 112 F. Supp. 228, 229 (D. Mass. 1953). See also ELM Medical Laboratory, Inc. v. RKO General, Inc., 403 Mass. 779, 784-85, 532 N.E.2d 675 (1989) (same). (However, such an officer can, of course, recover damages from a corporation that defames him. See, e.g., Astra USA, Inc. v. Bildman, 455 Mass. 116, 914 N.E.2d 36 (2009) (holding that c.e.o. was limited purpose public figure), cert. denied, 130 S. Ct. 3276, 176 L. Ed. 2d 1183 (2010).) Conversely, a defamatory statement about the owner of a corporation is not, without more, "of and concerning" the corporation. Eyal, 411 Mass. at 426. A statement that "Scientologists" or "someone like a Scientologist" stole a person's filing fee could not reasonably be understood as being "of and concerning" the plaintiff corporation. Church of Scientology v. Flynn, 578 F. Supp. 266 (D. Mass. 1984). However, "a corporation may be defamed by communications defamatory of its officers and agents that also 'reflect discredit upon the method by which the corporation conducts its business.'" North Shore Pharmacy Services, 491 F. Supp. 2d at 128 (where corporation was a "one-man operation," allowing jury to decide whether corporation was defamed by comments about its owner), quoting Restatement (Second) of Torts § 561 (a), comment (b) to clause (a).

6. ***Publication.*** The plaintiff must establish that a defamatory statement was communicated, orally or in writing, to a third-party recipient. Ravnikar v. Bogojavlensky, 438 Mass. 627, 629, 782 N.E.2d 508, 510 (2003); Hiles v. Episcopal Diocese of Mass., 437 Mass. 505, 519, 773 N.E.2d 929, 940 (2002). See also Noonan v. Staples, Inc., 556 F.3d 20, 25 n.2 (1st Cir. 2009) (noting that publication "'requires that the defendant communicate the defamatory statement to a third party'"), quoting White v. Blue Cross & Blue Shield of Mass., Inc., 442 Mass. 64, 809 N.E.2d 1034, 1036 (2004). Communicative physical conduct in the presence of third parties can constitute publication for purposes of a defamation claim. Vranos v. Skinner, 77 Mass. App. Ct. 280, 295, 930 N.E.2d 156, 168-69 (Mass. App. Ct. 2010) ("defamation, broadly viewed, arises out of communications, not from the particular form the communications take"); Phelan v. May Dep't Stores Co., 60 Mass. App. Ct. 843, 849-50, 806 N.E.2d 939, 945-46, aff'd, 443 Mass. 52, 819 N.E.2d 550 (2004) (finding the plaintiff's testimony that his co-workers witnessed a security guard escorting him throughout his workplace over a period of several hours was sufficient evidence of "publication" of a defamatory statement). The recipients must include someone other than the person defamed. Bouley v. City of New Bedford, et al., 2005 U.S. Dist. LEXIS 30922, *18 (D. Mass. Dec. 5, 2005) (no "publication" where notice of trespass and notice putting plaintiff on administrative leave were communicated only to plaintiff, who in turn communicated them to the press). Publication to one other person is enough, Phelan, 443 Mass. at 56, 819 N.E.2d at 554, even if that person was in a position to know the statement was not true. Shafir v. Steele, 431 Mass. 365, 727 N.E.2d 1140 (2000). A plaintiff-employee cannot recover, for example, for even scathing criticism uttered in the context of a private one-on-one performance evaluation. See Comerford v. West End Street Railway, 164 Mass. 13, 15, 41 N.E. 59 (1895) (no recovery for plaintiff berated by employer when no one else was present). "A libelous remark is published if (1) the defendant (or his agent) prepared, composes and writes the remark; (2) hands or causes the writing to be delivered to some third persons; and (3) the third person reads and understands the contents (or the defendant reads the writing to some third person who listens and understands)." Arsenault, 485 F. Supp. at 1379. A plaintiff must have personal knowledge or specific facts establishing that there has been publication. See Barthelmes v. Martineau, 2000 WL 1269666, *7, 2000 Mass. Super. LEXIS 252, No. CA 982378A (Mass. Super. Ct. May 22, 2000) (plaintiff's affidavits based only "on information and belief" are insufficient to establish unprivileged publication); see also Beriont v. Reichlen, 2000 WL 33170693, *3, No. 994486 (Mass. Super. Ct. Nov. 6, 2000) (alleging that defamatory statement "could have been overheard" is not sufficient to withstand summary judgment).

a. **Intracorporate Communication.** Massachusetts has expressly rejected the proposition that an intracorporate communication – a communication between and among officers and agents of the same corporation in reference to the corporation's business – does not qualify as a "publication" for purposes of libel law. Bander v. Metropolitan Life Ins. Co., 313 Mass. 337, 348-49, 47 N.E.2d 595 (1943); Lyons v. National Car Rental Sys., 30 F.3d 240, 244 (1st Cir. 1994); Arsenault v. Allegheny Airlines, Inc., 485 F. Supp. 1373, 1379 (D. Mass. 1980), aff'd, 636 F.2d 1199 (1st Cir. 1980), cert. denied, 454 U.S. 821 (1981). **(In a different context, the Appeals Court has held that the confidentiality clause of a high school coach's settlement agreement does not bar disclosure of the agreement to the school superintendent and**

school committee members. Caputo v. City of Haverhill, No. 11-P-1321, 82 Mass. App. Ct. 1109, 971 N.E.2d 337, 2012 WL 3076542, *1 (Mass. App. Ct. July 31, 2012).) However, in federal cases involving public employees claiming a violation of due process, a communication between employer and employee in a single system of public employment does not constitute "public dissemination" sufficient to establish a constitutional tort. See Burton v. Town of Littleton, et al., 426 F.3d 9, 15-18 (1st Cir. 2005), quoting Ratliff v. City of Milwaukee, 795 F.2d 612, 626-27 (7th Cir. 1986) ("In a common law defamation action, any publication of false and defamatory material might be sufficient, but in the context of the liberty interest protected by the *Fourteenth Amendment*, [plaintiff] was required to show broader publication."). See generally IV.F, infra.

b. **Compelled Self-Publication.** In White v. Blue Cross & Blue Shield of Massachusetts, 442 Mass. 64, 65, 809 N.E.2d 1034, 1035 (2004), the Supreme Judicial Court rejected the doctrine of compelled self-publication. The Court affirmed the dismissal of a defamation claim in which the plaintiff alleged that his employer's stated reasons for his termination were false and defamatory, and that he would be compelled to "publish" these statements in discussions with prospective employers. Id. The Court reasoned that because the employee's real concern was his termination and the reasons for it, not the communication of these reasons to him, the employee should look to other principles of employment law for relief – not the law of defamation. White, 442 Mass. at 68, 809 N.E.2d at 1037. The plaintiff could also bring a claim for defamation or intentional interference with advantageous business relations against the source of the defamatory allegations – here, a corporation that accused the plaintiff of disclosing the terms of a confidential financial settlement. White, 442 Mass. at 72, 809 N.E.2d at 1040.

c. **Republication.** In general, the republisher of a defamatory statement "'is subject to liability as if he had originally published it.'" Miller v. Tope, No. 02-11151-DPW, 2003 U.S. Dist. LEXIS 21211 at *34 (D. Mass. Nov. 24, 2003), quoting Restatement (Second) of Torts § 578 (1977). See Flynn v. Associated Press, 401 Mass. 776, 780 n.5, 519 N.E.2d 1304, 15 Media L. Rep. 1265 (1988); Dulgarian v. Stone, 420 Mass. 843, 849, 652 N.E.2d 603 (1995); Jones v. Taibbi, 400 Mass. 786, 792, 512 N.E.2d 260, 14 Media L. Rep. 1864 (1987). Thus, a supervisor can be liable for defamation if he attaches, to his personnel evaluation regarding the plaintiff, a letter written by another supervisor that contains false and defamatory factual allegations. Miller, 2003 U.S. Dist. LEXIS 21211 at *34. "Liability for a defamatory statement may not be avoided 'merely [by] adding a truthful preface that someone else has so stated.'" Jones, 400 Mass. at 792, quoting Ricci v. Venture Magazine, Inc. 574 F. Supp. 1563, 1572, 10 Media L. Rep. 1016 (D. Mass. 1983).

Republication of a statement by the original speaker may create a new cause of action. In Kalter v. Wood, 67 Mass. App. Ct. 584, 855 N.E.2d 421 (2006), for example, the defendant sent an identical letter, complaining about inappropriate touching by a doctor, to local police, to the state Division of Professional Licensure, and to her medical insurance carrier, Blue Cross Blue Shield of Massachusetts. The court ruled that the publications to government agencies would have been immunized by the Anti-SLAPP statute's protection for petitioning activity, G.L. c.231, § 59H, but that the identical letter to the insurance carrier was not. See also Esserian v. Harvard University, 2005 Mass. Super. LEXIS 251, *5 (May 4, 2005) (Brassard, J.)

As to a speaker's liability for foreseeable republications by others, the Supreme Judicial Court recently reached back to a couple of 19th century cases in order to hold that "[a]n original publisher of defamatory material is liable for subsequent republication where 'the repetition was authorized or intended by the original defamer, or the repetition was reasonably to be expected.'" Murphy v. Boston Herald, 449 Mass. 42, 44, 865 N.E.2d 746, 764, 35 Media L. Rep. 1865 (2007), quoting Restatement (Second) of Torts § 576 (1977) and citing Burt v. Advertiser Newspaper Co., 154 Mass. 238, 247, 28 N.E. 1 (1891) and Miller v. Butler, 60 Mass. 71, 6 Cush. 71, 74 (1850). It is not clear, however, how broadly that holding will be applied, as Murphy involved a newspaper reporter's liability for statements that he published – with actual malice, as the jury found – and that were subsequently republished in the same newspaper (itself a co-defendant) by other reporters who "were authorized (and even encouraged) to do so." 449 Mass. at 65, 865 N.E,2d at 764. Indeed, one of the cases relied upon specifically limits the liability of a defendant for republication by others, noting, "Wrongful acts of independent third persons, not actually intended by the defendant, are not regarded by the law as natural consequences of his wrong, and he is not bound to anticipate the general probability of such acts, any more than a particular act by this or that individual." Burt v. Advertiser Newspaper Co., 154 Mass. 238, 247, 28 N.E. 1 (1891) (Holmes, J.). Similarly, the federal district court in Massachusetts has held that where a defendant's statement about the plaintiff is republished in the press, liability against the defendant will hinge on whether the defendant is "responsible for its publication." Nolan v. Krajcik, 384 F. Supp. 2d 447, 474 (D. Mass. 2005). At least one Massachusetts Superior Court seems to indicate that the employer will not be liable for in-house gossip, so long as there is no showing that the gossip originated with a supervisory of management employee. Godfrey v. Boston Globe Newspaper Co., No. 05-0337-E, 21 Mass. L. Rep. 695, 2006 Mass. Super. LEXIS 625, *14-16 (Suffolk Super. Ct. Nov. 2, 2006) (dismissing terminated employee's defamation claim that by posting his picture at its security station the employer "generated a story around the workplace that he stone from the company" and finding there was "no competent evidence in the summary judgment record that such statements came from those with authority to speak for the [employer]").

A different issue is presented when republication of the defamatory statement occurs not by a third party but by the plaintiff himself. In that context, the 2007 Murphy decision's reliance on the 157-year-old precedent of Miller v. Butler is troubling. Miller involved a private letter mailed by the two defendants to the plaintiff himself, who then circulated it to others. The court held the two letter-writers responsible on the grounds that such further circulation by the plaintiff was somehow the "natural and probable ... tendency and consequences" of the defendants' own acts. Miller, 60 Mass. at 74. That 1850 ruling seems inconsistent with the Massachusetts Appeals Court's 1994 decision in O'Connell v. Bank of Boston, 37 Mass. App. Ct. 416, 422 & n.3, 640 N.E.2d 513 (1994), rev. denied, 419 Mass. 1104, 646 N.E.2d 409 (1995), dismissing claims of a plaintiff who "republished" the defamatory statements to her fiancé. As the Appeals Court held in O'Connell, "This was tantamount to publication by the plaintiff, not the [employer]." In 2005, the Massachusetts federal district court case had reached a similar conclusion in a case where the plaintiff "republished" the defamatory statements to the press. Bouley v. City of New Bedford, et al., 2005 U.S. Dist. LEXIS 30922 (D. Mass. Dec. 5, 2005).

7. ***Statements versus Conduct.*** Massachusetts has not recognized the doctrine of "defamation by conduct," whereby conduct is deemed defamatory even though the statement communicated by the conduct is not actually verbalized – or, at least, so the Supreme Judicial Court declared in Astra USA, Inc. v. Bildman, 455 Mass. 116, 143 n.42, 914 N.E.2d 36, 56 n.42 (2009) (dictum), **cert. denied, 130 S. Ct. 3276, 176 L. Ed. 2d 1183 (2010)**. The Astra USA opinion made no mention of the Court's clear statement, only five years earlier, that defamation *can* arise from a defendant's physical actions, even in the absence of any spoken or written communication. Phelan v. May Dep't Stores Co. et al., 443 Mass. 52, 57, 819 N.E.2d 550, 554 (2004) ("Although not explicitly recognized in prior Massachusetts case law, we conclude that defamatory publication *may* result from the physical actions of a defendant, in the absence of written or spoken communication."). However, where the conduct is "ambiguous and open to various interpretations," lacking "a specific, obvious meaning," then it is for the jury to decide "whether such communication was understood" by third parties "as having a defamatory meaning." Id., 443 Mass. at 58, 819 N.E.2d at 555 (noting that a security guard's escorting of plaintiff employee for several hours during the workday, and relocating him to various conference rooms, "did not necessarily convey" criminal wrongdoing by the employee, particularly in the absence of any "chasing, grabbing, restraining, or searching"). Plaintiff bears the burden of proving defamatory meaning under such circumstances. See also Petsch-Schmid v. Boston Edison Co., 914 F. Supp. 697, 705-06 (D. Mass. 1996) (allowing terminated employee's claim to proceed to trial where "it is possible that the escort may have been conducted in such a manner as to communicate a defamatory statement to other employees about the plaintiff."); Ball v. Wal- Mart, Inc., 102 F. Supp. 2d 44, 49-50 (D. Mass. 2000) (store employee's facially non-defamatory conduct, in combination with his statements, could reasonably be construed as an accusation of larceny).

8. ***Damages.*** The Massachusetts rules regarding the damages that are available in a defamation action, and under what circumstances, are a complex web of common law, statute, and constitutional law. The overarching rule, however, is easily stated: "A plaintiff in a successful defamation case is entitled ... to fair compensation for actual damages, including emotional distress and harm to reputation (and any special damages that have been pleaded and proved)." Ayash v. Dana-Farber Cancer Inst., 443 Mass. 367, 404-05, 822 N.E.2d 667, cert. denied sub nom. Globe Newspaper Co. v. Ayash, 546 U.S. 927 (2005). Increasingly, particularly in cases involving internet postings, one sees plaintiffs asking courts to order defendants to take down a web site or refrain from future disparagement. As stated in one persuasive Superior Court ruling, "the Court must tread cautiously where the relief sought constitutes a prior restraint on another's right to free speech because 'our law thinks it is better to let the defamed plaintiff take his damages for what they are worth than to entrust a single judge (or even a jury) with the power to put a sharp check on the spread of the possible truth.'" Haddad v. Nordgren Memorial Chapel, Inc., No. 04-0390-A, 20 Mass. L. Rep. 230, 2005 Mass. Super. LEXIS 558, *6-7, 2005 WL 3605475 (Worcester Super. Ct. Nov. 9, 2005) (noting also that defendants' claim of anticipated business harm is merely speculative, whereas defendant's "irreparable harm is the impairment of his First Amendment right to free speech" which, "even if only a temporary loss, is not redressable by monetary damages"), quoting Krebiozen Research Found. v. Beacon Press, 334 Mass. 86, 93, 134 N.E.2d 1 (1956).

A successful defamation plaintiff is entitled to actual compensatory damages. Shafir v. Steele, 431 Mass. 365, 373, 727 N.E.2d 1140, 1146 (2000); Stone v. Essex County Newspapers, Inc. 367 Mass. 849, 860, 330 N.E.2d 161 (1975). Actual compensatory damages under Massachusetts law may be divided into two subcategories – "general" damages and "special" damages – and the conditions for recovery vary from one to the other. Fiori v. Truck Drivers, Local 170, 354 F.3d 84, 87 (1st Cir. 2004). General damages, when proved, are available in all cases of libel and slander per se (see I.B.4, supra), Ravnikar v. Bogojavlensky, 438 Mass. 627, 630, 782 N.E.2d 508, 511 (2003), citing Shafir v. Steele, 431 Mass. at 373; Restatement (2d) of Torts §622 comment b, §623 comment a (1977). But see Martinez v. New Eng. Med. Ctr. Hosp. Inc., 307 F. Supp. 2d 257, 269 (D. Mass. 2004) (concluding that defamation claim failed where "no real employment prospect" was lost on account of purportedly defamatory statement). Special damages apparently may be recovered only when they have been specifically alleged in the complaint. Stone, 367 Mass. at 860; Tosti v. Ayik, 394 Mass. 482, 497, 437 N.E.2d 1062 (1987).

General damages are those naturally and necessarily expected to result from the defamatory publication. Muchnick v. Post Publishing Co., 332 Mass. 304, 308, 125 N.E.2d 137 (1955). With respect to individuals they include, in all cases, compensation for harm to the plaintiff's reputation and standing in the community, and for plaintiff's personal humiliation, mental anguish, and mental suffering. Shafir v. Steele, 431 Mass. 365, 373, 727 N.E.2d 1140, 1146 (2000); Ravnikar v. Bogojavlensky, 438 Mass. 627, 630, 782 N.E.2d 508, 511 (2003) (noting that in cases of libel and slander per se, "a plaintiff may recover noneconomic losses, including emotional injury and damage to reputation"). A plaintiff is entitled to recover damages for "the pain and suffering which the defamatory statement was ... a substantial factor in producing." Murphy v. Boston Herald, 449 Mass. 42, 67, 865 N.E.2d 746, 765, 35 Media L. Rep. 1865 (2007) (adding that "[m]ental or physical pain and suffering produced by some other event, act, or omission" may not be recovered). Mental distress caused by seeing family members suffer as a result of a defamatory attack is also recoverable. Murphy, 449 Mass. at 67, 865 N.E.2d at 765 (holding that jury properly could consider plaintiff's emotional distress as a result of watching his daughter suffer from fear and trauma in the aftermath of publication of defamatory article). A corporation may recover for damage to its reputation "'for conducting its affairs honestly or competently,'" North Shore Pharmacy Services, Inc. v. Breslin Consulting Assocs., 491 F. Supp. 111, 128 (D. Mass. 2007), but not for mental suffering. Id., 24 Mass. App. Ct. at 220.

General damages may also include the lost wages and other consequences directly resulting from the loss of employment with the defendant, Bander, 313 Mass. at 346, if the claim is for a defamation relating to the plaintiff's profession or employment, Muchnick, 332 Mass. at 308. In such a case, however, general damages do *not* include damages resulting from an inability to obtain new employment, because such damages do not flow directly and necessarily from the defamation. Id. Instead, those would be classified as special damages: damages that are naturally, but not necessarily, caused by the defamation. Craig v. Proctor, 229 Mass. 339, 343, 118 N.E. 647 (1918); Lewis v. Vallis, 356 Mass. 662, 665, 255 N.E.2d 337 (1970). Similarly, damages resulting from the refusal of third parties to hire the plaintiff, because of the defamation, are special damages. See Bander, 313 Mass. at 346 (holding that no such damages were proved). (Muddying the waters somewhat, the Court of Appeals has also used the phrase "special damages" in dictum to refer to those compensatory damages that constitute "economic loss." Jourjine v. Nokia Corp., 312 Fed. Appx. 344, 345 n.5 (1st Cir. 2009) (unpublished, *per curiam*), citing Ravnikar v. Bogojavlensky, 438 Mass. 627, 630, 782 N.E.2d 508, 511 (2003) (holding that defamation that does not cause "special damages" is not actionable unless it is either slander *per se* or libel).)

The distinction between general and special damages under Massachusetts law is important for two reasons. First, as stated above, in all defamation cases special damages apparently cannot be recovered unless alleged in the complaint. Muchnick, 332 Mass. at 308. Second, as discussed at I.B.1, supra, and at V.C, infra, in some cases slander is not actionable at all unless special damages are alleged and proved.

The actual compensatory damages available to a successful plaintiff typically include compensation for "'impairment of reputation and standing in the community, personal humiliation, and mental anguish and suffering.'" Stone v. Essex County Newspapers, Inc., 367 Mass. 849, 861, 330 N.E.2d 161 (1975), quoting Gertz v. Robert Welch, Inc., 418 U.S. 323, 349-50, 1 Media L. Rep. 1633 (1974). Where there is no evidence that words, even if ridiculing the plaintiffs, did so "in the minds of any considerable and respectable segment of the community," and plaintiffs admit that no one viewed them in a negative light because of the comments, plaintiffs' damages are "suspect at best." Schultz v. Kelly, 188 F. Supp. 2d 38, 59 (D. Mass. 2002). See also Fuentes v. Hampden County Sheriff's Dep't, 429 F. Supp. 2d 253 (D. Mass. 2006) (dismissing claim on summary judgment because plaintiff "could not name a single individual who believed that his reputation had been damaged"). All such awards "'must be supported by competent evidence concerning the injury,'" but there is no requirement of evidence "'which assigns an actual dollar value to the injury.'" Stone, 367 Mass. at 861, quoting Gertz, 418 U.S. at 349-50. To obtain damages for mental suffering, it was enough that one plaintiff alleged she felt "bludgeoned" and "stunn[ed]," and experienced "outrage" and "anger." Shafir v. Steele, 431 Mass. 365, 373, 727 N.E.2d 1140, 1146 (2000). "Compensatory damages must be calculated to compensate the plaintiff for her losses, based with reasonable certainty on the evidence, only for harm caused by the wrongful conduct." Ayash v. Dana-Farber Cancer Institute, et al., 443 Mass. 367, 405, 822 N.E.2d 667, 697, 33 Media L. Rep. 1513 (2005). The Supreme Judicial Court has held that in defamation cases trial and appellate courts "have a special duty of vigilance in charging juries and reviewing verdicts to see that damages are no more than compensatory." Stone, 367 Mass. at 861. Appellate judges "have a special duty in reviewing verdicts in defamation cases, 'because of constitutional considerations, and the potential difficulties in assessing fair compensation.'" Ayash, 443 Mass. at 404, 822 N.E.2d at 697, quoting Stone, 367 Mass. at 861. Nonetheless, the First Circuit Court of Appeals, called upon to review the district court's denial of remittitur following a $100,000 New Hampshire jury verdict for defamation, false imprisonment, and allied claims, held that the award was "not so grossly excessive that justice would be denied" by letting it stand, as the plaintiff had suffered "intangible losses." Forgie-Buccioni v. Hannaford Bros., Inc., 413 F.3d 175, 183 (1st Cir. 2005). An employee who succeeds in a defamation case against an employer may also be entitled to wages, pension, stock, and medical benefits lost as a result of the defamation, but only for so long as, based on competent evidence, it appears that the inability to obtain new employment was due to the defamation. Tosti II, 394 Mass. at 496-98; Tosti v. Ayik, 400 Mass. 224, 227-28, 508 N.E.2d 1368 ("Tosti III"), cert. denied, 484 U.S. 964 (1987). Such a plaintiff also "must make a good faith effort to mitigate damages by seeking other comparable employment." Tosti III, 400 Mass. at 227. A plaintiff may recover for time lost from employment in order to investigate the defamatory communication, even though his wages were not docked. Elmer v. Fessenden, 154 Mass. 427, 428-29, 28 N.E. 299 (1891); see also Harby v. Prince, 355 Mass. 572, 574, 246 N.E.2d 422 (1969) (attorney may recover for time spent responding to defamatory attacks).

Nominal damages of, say, one dollar may be awarded either by the plaintiff's preference – where the plaintiff, in essence, seeks only vindication and not a substantial monetary award – or by jury verdict, perhaps where the jury considers a plaintiff libel-proof or the defamation trivial, R. Smolla, Law of Defamation § 9.02 (1993), either on its own or in relation to other damages awarded to the plaintiff. See, e.g., Tuli v. Brigham & Women's Hosp., 656 F.3d 33, 44 (affirming jury's $1 slander award, which was atop $1.6 million award on hostile work environment and retaliation claims). The Supreme Judicial Court has acknowledged that "a libel plaintiff who cannot prove damages is normally entitled to an award of nominal damages if he establishes that he was libeled." Jackson v. Longcope, 394 Mass. 577, 579, 476 N.E.2d 617, 11 Media L. Rep. 2282 (1985); accord Ravnikar v. Bogojavlensky, 438 Mass. 627, 630, 782 N.E.2d 508, 511 (2003) ("An undamaged plaintiff may recover nominal damages."); Shafir v. Steele, 431 Mass. 365, 373, 727 N.E.2d 1140 (2000); North Shore Pharmacy Services, Inc. v. Breslin Consulting Assocs., 491 F. Supp. 111, 128 (D. Mass. 2007). See also Restatement (2d) of Torts, § 623 (special note on remedies for defamation other than damages), cited in Ravnikar, 438 Mass. at 630, 782 N.E.2d at 511. Nevertheless, "a libel-proof plaintiff is not entitled to burden a defendant with a trial in which the most favorable result the plaintiff could achieve is an award of nominal damages." Jackson, 394 Mass. at 580. And a plaintiff's failure to request a nominal damages instruction at trial, or to object to the absence of one, amounts to waiver of the point. Jourjine v. Nokia Corp., 312 Fed. Appx. 344, 345 (1st Cir. 2009) (unpublished, *per curiam*). See also Lakian v. Globe Newspaper Co., 399 Mass. 379, 383-84, 504 N.E.2d 1046, 1048-49 (1987) (holding that failure to award nominal damages, when not objected to, is not reversible error).

a. **Presumed Damages and Libel Per Se.** The Supreme Judicial Court, citing Gertz v. Robert Welch, Inc., 418 U.S. 323, 349 (1974), has noted that a defamation plaintiff suing over a matter of public concern may not recover presumed damages unless constitutional actual malice is proved. Stone v. Essex County Newspapers, Inc., 367 Mass. 849, 858, 330 N.E.2d 161 (1975). Indeed, the Court has gone further, saying as a blanket matter, in a case of public concern in which plaintiff's public or private status had not yet been determined, that "the plaintiff's recovery is limited to actual damages." Id. at 860. The Court subsequently declined to decide whether constitutional principles forbid a public figure, even one who proves actual malice, from recovering presumed damages altogether. Lakian v. Globe Newspaper Co., 399 Mass. 379, 382, 504 N.E.2d 1046, 13 Media L. Rep. 2368 (1987). As to whether presumed damages are available in a private figure's defamation action involving a matter of *private* concern, the Appeals Court has said, in dictum, that such damages are allowed. Dexter's Hearthside Restaurant, Inc. v. Whitehall Co., 24 Mass. App. Ct. 217, 221, 508 N.E.2d 113, 14 Media L. Rep. 1664 (1987), rev. denied, 400 Mass. 1104, 511 N.E.2d 620 (1987). However, there is some tension between that Appeals Court ruling and the Supreme Judicial Court's rejection of the public concern/private concern distinction that underpinned the Supreme Court's allowance of presumed damages in private-figure, private-concern cases. See New England Tractor-Trailer Training of Connecticut, Inc. v. Globe Newspaper Co., 395 Mass. 471, 477 n.4, 480 N.E.2d 1005 (1985); compare Dun & Bradstreet, Inc. v. Greenmoss Builders, Inc., 472 U.S. 749, 763, 11 Media L. Rep. 2417 (1985). It may be that, presented with the question, the SJC would prohibit presumed damages altogether. See J. Nolan, 37 Mass. Practice Series, Tort Law §128 ("The old rule of 'presumed damages' is no longer constitutionally acceptable").

(1) **Employment-Related Criticism.** Under Massachusetts law, all libel claims are actionable, whether or not special damages are alleged or can be proved (although special damages are not recoverable unless alleged and proved). Stone v. Essex County Newspapers, Inc., 367 Mass. 849, 853, 860, 330 N.E.2d 161 (1975) (rejecting doctrine of libel per se). Slander, however, is actionable only if it falls within the three categories of slander per se, see V.C, infra, or if special damages are alleged and proved. Lynch v. Lyons, 303 Mass. at 118-19. One of the three categories – a communication that "prejudice[s] [the plaintiff] in his office, profession or business or may probably tend to do so," Lynch, 303 Mass. at 119 – is of direct relevance to employment defamation cases. It has been narrowly construed, and called a "narrow exception." See Alba v. Sampson, 44 Mass. App. Ct. 311, 312-13, 690 N.E.2d 1240 (1998), rev. denied, 695 N.E.2d 667 (1998). It might not matter that there is no evidence that the slander was heard or believed by any co-worker. See Smiddy v. Pearlstein, 201 Mass. 246, 87 N.E. 572 (1909) (where the defamation charge is one of crime, "[i]t is not essential to the plaintiff's case that the persons who heard the charges should have believed them to be true. The injury to the reputation is not the sole element of damage . . . . The jury have the right to consider the mental suffering of the plaintiff"). Words of "general disparagement," as opposed to those relating to the plaintiff's job conduct, fall outside the "office, profession or business" exception. Alba, 44 Mass. App. Ct. at 312-13. It follows that, by analogy, *written* words of "general disparagement," while actionable, do not support wrongful-termination or lost-wage damages unless such damages – which would be "special damages" in that context, because they do not flow directly *and necessarily* from the defamatory communication, Muchnick, 332 Mass. at 308, see also I.B.8, supra – were specially pleaded and proved.

(2) **Single Instance Rule.** Massachusetts has not adopted a "single instance rule" such as that adopted in New York as a limitation on that state's "defamation per se" doctrine.

b. **Punitive Damages.** Neither punitive damages nor exemplary damages are available in a defamation action in Massachusetts. That principle is established both by statute and by common law. G.L. c. 231, § 93; Ravnikar v. Bogojavlensky, 438 Mass. 627, 630 n.4, 782 N.E.2d 508, 511 n.4 (2003); Stone v. Essex County Newspapers, Inc., 367 Mass. 849, 860, 861, 330 N.E.2d 161 (1975). Trial and appellate courts must scrutinize jury awards for signs of impermissible punitive considerations. See Tosti v. Ayik, 394 Mass. 482, 495, 499, 476 N.E.2d 928 (1985); Stone, 367 Mass. at 860; see also Fiori v. Truck Drivers, Local 170, 354 F.3d 84, 88-89 (1st Cir. 2004).

II. PRIVILEGES AND DEFENSES

A. Scope of Privileges

1. ***Absolute Privilege.*** Where an absolute privilege exists, it "provides a complete defense to slander and libel suits, immunizing the defendant from all liability even if the defamatory statement is uttered maliciously or in bad faith." Ezekiel v. Jones Motor Co., Inc., 374 Mass. 382, 385, 372 N.E.2d 1281 (1978). See also Zajac v. Zajac, 2007 Mass. Super. LEXIS 336, *12 (Worc. Super. Ct. Aug. 17, 2007). "Generally, the recognition of an absolute privilege in defamation cases is limited to cases in which public policy or the administration of justice requires complete immunity from the threat of defamation suits." Ezekiel, 374 Mass. at 385. The rationale behind the absolute privilege is to ensure that a party's or witness's "full disclosure" in a judicial proceeding "should not be hampered by fear of an action for defamation." Restatement (Second) of Torts § 588 comment a (1977), quoted in Fisher v. Lint, 69 Mass. App. Ct. 360, 366, 868 N.E.2d 161, 167 (2007). Whether an absolute privilege applies is decided "on a case-by-case basis, after a fact-specific analysis, with a proper consideration of the balance between a plaintiff's right to seek legal redress for injuries suffered and the public policy supporting the application of such a strong protection from the burdens of litigation." Fisher v. Lint, 69 Mass. App. Ct. 360, 365-66, 868 N.E.2d 161, 167 (2007). When it applies, it extends broadly, barring all causes of action arising out of the privileged conduct. Fisher, 69 Mass. App. Ct. at 370, 868 N.E.2d at 170; Correllas, 410 Mass. at 321; Doe v. Nutter, McClennen & Fish, 41 Mass. App. Ct. 137, 140, 668 N.E.2d 1329 (1996).

The absolute privilege extends to statements made in the course of judicial proceedings and which pertain to those proceedings, Correllas v. Viveiros, 410 Mass. 314, 319, 572 N.E.2d 7 (1991) (criminal proceedings); Sadlowski v. Benoit, 24 Mass. L. Rep. 207, 208 Mass. Super. LEXIS 191 (Mass. Super. June 24, 2008) (same); Aborn v. Lipson, 357 Mass. 71, 72-73, 256 N.E.2d 442 (1970) (civil proceedings); DelloRusso v. Monteiro, 47 Mass. App. Ct. 475, 479 n.3, 714 N.E.2d 362, 365 n.3 (1999) (witness testimony in judicial proceeding; "statement made in course of criminal investigation;" dictum), including the filing of a memorandum of lis pendens in connection with litigation affecting the title to real estate, Powell v. Stevens, 69 Mass. App. Ct. 87, 866 N.E.2d 918 (2007) (noting that the lis pendens "is in effect a republication of the proceedings in [a pending litigation] and is, therefore, accorded the same absolute privilege as any other publication in that action") and statements made in bankruptcy filings, Paren v. Craigie, 2006 U.S. Dist. LEXIS 43288, *38 (D. Mass.) (noting "the absolute privilege from defamation offered to statements made in judicial filings"). The privilege also covers statements made "preliminary to a proposed or contemplated judicial proceeding as long as they bear some relation to the proceeding." Fisher v. Lint, 69 Mass. App. Ct. 360, 366, 868 N.E.2d 161, 167-68 (2007). See also Lovitz v. Brown, No. 06-12245, 2007 U.S. Dist. LEXIS 28998, *1-2 (D. Mass. April 20, 2007) ("statements by a party, counsel or witness in the institution of, or during the course of, a judicial proceeding are absolutely privileged provided such statements relate to that proceeding"); Motzkin v. Trustees of Boston University, 938 F. Supp. 983, 1000 (D. Mass. 1996); Zajac v. Zajac, 2007 Mass. Super. LEXIS 336, *11 (Mass. Super. Ct. Aug. 16, 2007) (statements made during divorce proceedings in probate court); Eberle v. DiViacchi, 5 Mass. L. Rptr. 213, 214; 1996 WL 218210, No. CA 95-0055-B (Mass. Super. Ct. Mar. 29, 1996) (applying absolute privilege to expert witness affidavit filed in opposition to post-dismissal motion for fees); Hartford v. Hartford, 60 Mass. App. Ct. 446, 451-52, 803 N.E.2d 334 (2004); Knapp v. Neptune Towers Associates, No. 04-4211-BLS1, 23 Mass. L. Rep. 4, 2007 Mass. Super. LEXIS 307 (Suffolk Super. Ct. Aug. 2, 2007) (bringing of complaint is absolutely privileged).

Even statements made outside the courtroom, and made by a private investigator acting as the attorney's agent, fall within the privilege if they pertain to the proceeding. Leavitt v. Bickerton, 855 F. Supp. 455 (D. Mass. 1994). So do statements written by an attorney in the context of (and threatening) the institution of a civil action. Doe v. Nutter, McClennen & Fish, 41 Mass. App. Ct. 137, 140-41, 668 N.E.2d 1329 (1996) (Chapter 93A demand letter). Also covered by the absolute privilege are "statements made to police or prosecutors prior to trial . . . if they are made in the context of a proposed judicial proceeding." Correllas, 410 Mass. at 321; Fiske v. Town of North Attleboro, No. 04-04764, 22 Mass. L. Rep. 242, 2007 Mass. Super. LEXIS 69, *31-32 (Middlesex Super. Ct. Feb. 14, 2007); Zajac, 2007 Mass. Super. LEXIS 336 at *11, quoting Correllas; Burke v. Town of Walpole, et al., 405 F.3d 66, 94 (1st Cir. 2005), quoting O'Connell v. Bank of

Boston, 37 Mass. App. Ct. 416, 421, 640 N.E.2d 513 (1994), rev. denied, 419 Mass. 1104, 646 N.E.2d 409 (1995) (swearing out of criminal complaint is absolutely privileged).

However, the absolute privilege in connection with judicial proceedings has its limitations. The privilege is available "only when the challenged remarks are relevant or pertinent to the judicial proceedings," and "may be lost by unnecessary or unreasonable publication to one for whom the occasion is not privileged." Sullivan v. Birmingham, 11 Mass. App. Ct. 359, 362, 416 N.E.2d 528 (1981) (suggesting that attorneys might be liable for defamation based on pleadings filed in court if they had directly communicated with the news media on such matters). Indeed, in Davidson v. Cao, 211 F. Supp. 2d 264, 275 (D. Mass. 2002), the federal district court denied a motion to dismiss a libel claim again a party that not only filed a claim containing allegedly false assertions (an act the court conceded was privileged), but also discussed with the press the lawsuit's allegations and "affirmatively and unnecessarily disseminated the complaint containing the false statements to the press." The court distinguished out-of-state cases that extend the litigation privilege to distributing a complaint to the media, noting that "[a]llowing defamation suits for communications to the news media will not generally inhibit parties or their attorneys from fully investigating their claims." Id., quoting Sullivan, 416 N.E.2d at 531 & n.19. When applied to pre-litigation communications, the privilege does not necessarily apply when the party or attorney making the statement did not "seriously contemplate[] a judicial proceeding in good faith," Smith v. Suburban Restaurants, Inc., 374 Mass. 528, 531, 373 N.E.2d 215 (1978); Visnick v. Marriott International, Inc., No. 02-0681-C, 22 Mass. L. Rep. 727, 2007 Mass. Super. LEXIS 311 (Middlesex Super. Ct. Aug. 6, 2007), or where "an attorney's defamatory letter serves only to threaten litigation in order to deter the recipient from engaging in certain conduct." Axton-Cross Co., Inc. v. Blanchette, 2 Mass. L. Rptr. 646, 648, 1994 WL 879570, 1994 Mass. Super. LEXIS 398 (Super. Ct. 1994); see also Sriberg, 370 Mass. at 109, 345 N.E.2d at 884 (in pre-litigation context, privilege does not apply "where there is not serious consideration of suit"). A Superior Court judge declined to apply the absolute privilege where he concluded that the defendant had not met her burden of showing that the statements in question – contained in a demand letter sent by the defendant herself, not by counsel – were made at a time when "litigation was seriously considered and contemplated in good faith." Visnick, 2007 Mass. Super. LEXIS 311 at *11-17. The decision indicates that litigants seeking to prove applicability of the privilege in doubtful cases may be well advised to submit an affidavit from counsel indicating that they sought legal advice and explaining, if necessary, any lag time between the making of the statements and the actual bringing of the proceeding.

The absolute privilege applies to statements made under oath by a witness to a legislative committee, so long as the committee is acting within its jurisdiction and the words spoken are pertinent to the matter under investigation. Sheppard v. Bryant, 191 Mass. 591, 78 N.E. 394 (1906). It also applies to "statements of a quasi-judicial officer made in the exercise of his duties." Lovitz v. Brown, No. 06-12245, 2007 U.S. Dist. LEXIS 28998, *2 (D. Mass. April 20, 2007). The Massachusetts Appeals Court applied the privilege to the trial board of the State Police after finding that the board was a "formal administrative proceeding ... analogous to a military court martial board," recorded, with adversarial format, with witnesses testifying under oath and under the threat of perjury, and decisions required to be supported by "substantial evidence" and subject to appeal to court. "In short," the court held, "the State police trial board possesses the authority and provides the procedural protections that differentiates a quasi judicial board from one that merely performs an administrative function." Fisher v. Lint, 69 Mass. App. Ct. 360, 367-69, 868 N.E.2d 161, 168-70 (2007). The absolute privilege also covers sworn statements made in unemployment compensation proceedings. Petsch-Schmid v. Boston Edison Co., 914 F. Supp. 697, 705 (D. Mass. 1996); see also Andresen v. Diorio, 349 F.3d 8, 16 (1st Cir. 2003) (dicta); G.L. c.151A, §46; and statements submitted in other administrative agency hearings, Stepanischen v. Merchants Despatch Transp. Corp., 722 F.2d 922, 932 (1st Cir. 1983).

In some cases, whether an absolute or conditional privilege applies will depend on the particular circumstances. Thus, while statements made to police or prosecutors in the context of a contemplated legal proceeding are absolutely privileged, only a conditional privilege applies where "the defendants went to the police, or communicated with others, on their own initiative and published an accusation which might otherwise never have been known." Correllas v. Viveiros, 410 Mass. 314, 322, 572 N.E.2d 7 (1991); see also Zajac v. Zajac, 2007 Mass. Super. LEXIS 336, *11-12 (Worc. Super. Ct. Aug. 16, 2007). "'The key to understanding these cases lies in the fact that, when the defendants made the allegedly defamatory statements, no criminal action or judicial proceeding was then being contemplated or proposed.'" Zajac, 2007 Mass. Super. LEXIS 336 at *12, quoting Correllas, 410 Mass. at 323. Borderline cases must be decided on their facts, in order to "balance the right of a plaintiff to preserve his or her reputation from defamatory accusations, with the right of society to secure the testimony of a witness in proposed and in actual judicial proceedings without the party or witness laboring under the threat of a civil law suit." Correllas, 410 Mass. at 323; see also Disend v. Meadowbrook School, 33 Mass. App. Ct. 674, 677, 604 N.E.2d 54 (1992); compare Seelig v. Harvard Coop. Soc'y, 355 Mass. 532, 538, 246 N.E.2d 642 (1969) (only *after trial* does court determine that allegedly slanderous statements were privileged because made as part of a police officer's investigation). **In one such case, the federal district court denied a motion to dismiss on the grounds that it could not be determined, at that stage of the proceedings, whether a police chief's report to a state trooper was part of an investigation or, as plaintiff contended, part of a gratuitous "smear campaign." Piccone v. Bartels, No. 11-10143-**

MLW, 2012 WL 4592770 (D. Mass. Sept. 29, 2012). In another such case, a libel plaintiff argued for a conditional privilege because the defendant had made an unsolicited report to police at a time when no criminal proceeding had begun. The federal district court, applying Massachusetts law, applied an absolute privilege "because it was a statement made to law enforcement about a violation of criminal law," but on appeal, in an unpublished decision, the Court of Appeals sidestepped the question, saying that even under a qualified privilege no action would lie. Jones v. Scotti, No. 11-2213, 2012 WL 4373655 *3-4 (1st Cir. Sept. 26, 2012) (unpublished), aff'g on other grounds 2011 WL 4381919 (D. Mass. Sept. 13, 2011).

A claim of libel may also be affected by statutory privileges conferred on certain employers. For example, under Massachusetts law, a public employer is not liable for negligence claims if they are based upon "the exercise or performance or the failure to exercise a discretionary function or duty" on the part of an employee acting within the scope of his employment, "whether or not the discretion is abused." Mass. Gen. Laws c. 258, § 10(b). Similarly, because "the limited waiver of governmental immunity under the Massachusetts Tort Claims Act does 'not apply to ... any claim arising out of an intentional tort, including ... libel, slander, ... [or] invasion of privacy,'" Mass. Gen. Laws c. 258, § 10(c), a municipality cannot be sued for libel or invasion of privacy. **Barrows v. Wareham Fire Dist., 82 Mass. App. Ct. 623, 630, -- N.E.2d -- (2012). See III.G, infra.** (Note, however, that the statute does not bar such a claim against an individual public official. Anzalone v. Administrative Office of Trial Court, 457 Mass. 647, 660-61, 932 N.E.2d 785-86 (Aug. 30, 2010), citing South Boston Betterment Trust Corp. v. Boston Redevelopment Auth., 438 Mass. 57, 69, 777 N.E.2d 812 (2002).) An employee's claims for defamation against an employer are outside the purview of the Massachusetts Workers' Compensation Act, G.L. c.152, § 24, and thus not barred by that statute's exclusivity provisions. Foley v. Polaroid Corp., 381 Mass. 545, 551-52, 413 N.E.2d 711, 715 (1980), cited in Fleming v. National Union Fire Ins. Co., et al., 445 Mass. 381, 388 n.8, 837 N.E.2d 1113, 1120 n.8 (2005).

In Fisher v. Lint, 69 Mass. App. Ct. 360, 361 n.3, 868 N.E.2d 161, 164 n.3 (2007), the Massachusetts Appeals Court assumed, without deciding, that denial of a pretrial motion based on an absolute privilege is immediately appealable under the doctrine of present execution, thereby giving the appellate court jurisdiction to also decide ancillary issues, citing Fabre v. Walton, 436 Mass. 517, 521-22, 781 N.E.2d 780 (2002) (denial of anti-SLAPP special motion to dismiss immediately appealable) and Brum v. Dartmouth, 428 Mass. 684, 688, 704 N.E.2d 1147 (1999) (ancillary issues).

2. ***Qualified Privileges.*** In many cases alleging defamation by an employer, an employee will not have particular difficulty making out a case on each of the traditional elements of a libel or slander claim. If one supervisor tells another supervisor, after an incomplete investigation, that the plaintiff was suspended due to allegations of theft, and it turns out that the allegations are not true, all the elements will likely be satisfied: (1) negligent (2) publication of a (3) false and (4) defamatory (5) statement of fact (6) concerning the plaintiff. For that reason, the employer's qualified privilege is of utmost importance in employment defamation cases. By invoking that privilege, employers can sometimes obtain summary judgment, a directed verdict, or success at trial on libel or slander claims that would otherwise form the foundation for an award of damages to the plaintiff.

Privileges, whether qualified or absolute, reflect the recognition "that, on certain occasions and for certain purposes, the importance of free communication outweighs the interest in protecting reputation." Barrows v. Wareham Fire Dist., 82 Mass. App. Ct. 623, 631, -- N.E.2d -- (2012), citing Restatement (2d) of Torts, ch. 25, topic 3 scope note, at 258 (1964). In general, a speaker enjoys a qualified (or "conditional") privilege under any of several circumstances. First, the qualified privilege applies where the communication is elicited by the plaintiff, as for example where the plaintiff requests disclosure of the reasons she was not hired. DelloRusso v. Monteiro, 47 Mass. App. Ct. 475, 478-79, 714 N.E.2d 362, 364-65 (1999). (See discussion, infra, this section, "Consent." See also II.B.3, infra.) Second, the qualified privilege applies where the employer's statement "is reasonably necessary to serve the employer's legitimate interest in the fitness of an employee to perform his or her job." Bratt v. International Business Machines Corp., 392 Mass. 508, 512-13, 467 N.E.2d 126 (1984). (See discussion, infra, this section, "Business Interest.") Third, the qualified privilege applies to "[c]ommunications between those having a common interest in the substance of the communications," so long as the communication is "reasonably calculated" to protect that common interest. Johnson v. Educational Testing Service, 754 F.2d 20, 26 (1st Cir. (1984)), cert. denied, 472 U.S. 1029 (1985). See II.A.2.a, infra. Fourth, the qualified privilege applies to the communication of information pursuant to a legal duty. Dexter's Hearthside Restaurant, Inc. v. Whitehall Co., 24 Mass. App. Ct. 217, 222, 508 N.E.2d 113, 14 Media L. Rep. 1664 (1987), rev. denied, 400 Mass. 1104, 511 N.E.2d 620 (1987). See II.A.2.b, infra. (This four-part division of the qualified privilege under Massachusetts law is necessarily arbitrary; cases listed below under one heading can sometimes be classified under another as well, and the bases for the court's decisions tend to blur together at the edges. Nevertheless, the division of cases into (1) consent, (2) business interest, (3) common interest, and (4) duty may be of some aid in analysis.) The qualified privilege is defeated, and thereby lost, if abused. See II.A.2.f, infra.

Massachusetts also recognizes the "fair report" doctrine, which protects "fair and accurate reports of official actions and statements." See generally Howell v. Enterprise Publishing Co., LLC, 455 Mass. 641, 650-670, 920 N.E.2d 1, 13

-27 (2010). Although the fair report doctrine typically arises in the context of defamation claims against the news media, Massachusetts courts appear to have left open the possibility that it could also serve to protect a non-media defendant in a libel case. Where it applies, the privilege is not absolute; it is defeated by a showing "'that the publisher does not give a fair and accurate report of the official statement [or action], or malice.'" Howell, 455 Mass. 641, 651 n.8, 920 N.E.2d 1, 14 n.8, quoting Yohe v. Nugent, 321 F.3d 35, 44 (1st Cir. 2003). Because it operates somewhat differently than other privileges under Massachusetts law, it is discussed separately in this outline, as a sub-category of the truth defense. See II.B.1, infra.

a. **Common Interest.** Massachusetts recognizes that an employer is protected by a conditional privilege to publish defamatory material "if the publisher and the recipient share a common interest 'and the communication is of a kind reasonably calculated to protect or further it.'" Sklar v. Beth Israel Deaconess Medical Center, 59 Mass. App. Ct. 550, 558, 797 N.E.2d 381 (2003), quoting Sheehan v. Tobin, 326 Mass. 185, 190-91, 93 N.E.2d 524 (1950); Cornwell v. Dairy Farmers of America, Inc., 369 F. Supp. 2d 87, 111 (D. Mass. 2005) (applying the privilege to statements about an employee's job performance and conduct made to the employee's supervisor, department head or others who should be informed provided "the publication is reasonably necessary to serve the employer's legitimate interest in the fitness of an employee to perform his or her job," quoting McCone v. New Eng. Tel. & Tel. Co., 393 Mass. 231, 235, 471 N.E.2d 47, 51 (1984)). The federal district court has described it as "'a conditional common law privilege'" when "'the publisher and recipient share some legitimate mutual interest "reasonably calculated" to be served by the communication.'" Singh v. Blue Cross/Blue Shield, 2002 WL 1941472, *18, No. 01-2586 (1st Cir. Aug. 27, 2002) (finding allegedly defamatory "peer review" conducted to establish eligibility as approved provider is shielded by privilege).

The Appeals Court applied the common interest privilege to a communication between a school principal and parents regarding information about a teacher who would be leading their children on a field trip overseas. Dragonas v. School Committee of Melrose, 64 Mass. App. Ct. 429, 438, 833 N.E.2d 679, 687 (2005). See also Fuentes v. Hampden County Sheriff's Dep't., 2004 U.S. Dist. LEXIS 12053, at *7 (D. Mass. June 25, 2004); Sklar, 59 Mass. App. Ct. at 558 (applying privilege to hospital's transmission to licensing board of an audit report criticizing occupational therapist's professional practices). An employee of one company was privileged to make disparaging comments about the performance of an employee of another company with which the first company had a business relationship "insofar as the comments are relevant to that relationship." Humphrey v. National Semiconductor Corp., 18 Mass. App. Ct. 132, 133-34, 463 N.E.2d 1197 (1984), rev. denied, 469 N.E.2d 830 (1984) (noting that the case presents "a particularly obvious example of the common interest qualified privilege"); Cornwell, 369 F. Supp. 2d at 111; Winsmann v. Choate Health Mgmt., Inc., 2002 WL 1290202, *11 (Mass. Super. April 26, 2002) (statement regarding unprofessional incident between co-workers was privileged because information was connected to common enterprise of training professionals though providing services to patients); Garrity v. John Hancock Mut. Life Ins. Co., 2002 U.S. Dist. LEXIS 8343, *4 (D. Mass. May 7, 2002) (supervisors' statements to former co-workers that employees were terminated for sending and receiving "sexually lewd, harassing [and] defamatory" and "sexually explicit" emails are privileged communications). Likewise, an employer was privileged to make defamatory statements about its sales representative to a client, where the employer and the client shared an interest in having the best possible representative servicing the client and in not violating industry agreements in their dealings with her. Cluff v. O'Halloran, 2000 WL 33115601, *7-*8, No. CA 99-0428A (Mass. Super. Ct. Dec. 22, 2000). A labor union's officers were also entitled to the protection of the common interest privilege from defamation claims based on information they disseminated to union members through the union's official journal. Sheehan v. Tobin, 326 Mass. 185, 191, 93 N.E.2d 524 (1950) (remanding case for jury determination as to whether privilege was abused). See also Catrone v. Thoroughbred Racing Associations, 929 F.2d 881, 887-91 (1st Cir. 1991) (reports to members of trade association shielded by qualified privilege) (applying Massachusetts law). An employer was privileged to tell a manager that if the terminated plaintiff-employee returned to the workplace, she should be asked to leave, failing which police should be called. Sellig v. Visiting Nurse & Community Health, Inc., 10 Mass. L. Rptr. 231, 1999 WL 515795, at *9, 1999 Mass. Super. LEXIS 243 (Super. Ct. 1999) ("An employer has an interest in keeping trespassers off its premises, including but not limited to suspended employees, especially given that an employer may have some legal obligations to protect its employees from workplace threats and troubles").

A police chief is not entitled, under the common interest privilege, to share defamatory information about a police officer with the local newspaper. Draghetti v. Chmielewski, 416 Mass. 808, 814, 626 N.E.2d 862, 22 Media L. Rep. 1456 (Mass. 1994). "Such a distortion of the meaning of the 'common interest' privilege would create a privilege for virtually all newsworthy statements." Id. But see Burke v. Town of Walpole, et al., 405 F.3d 66, 94 (1st Cir. 2005) (distinguishing Draghetti on grounds that it concerned statements not made "during the original investigation" to "persons concerned with the investigation," and concluding that Massachusetts would recognize a conditional privilege founded on the police chief's "duty" to appear before a meeting of citizens concerned about a violent crime).

b. **Duty.** "Statements made by public officials while performing their official duties are conditionally privileged," if not absolutely so, because "[t]he threat of defamation suits may deter public officials from complying with their official duties when those duties include the need to make statements on important public issues."

Mulgrew v. Taunton, 410 Mass. 631, 635, 574 N.E.2d 389 (1991), **quoted in Barrows v. Wareham Fire Dist., 82 Mass. App. Ct. 623, 630-31, -- N.E.2d -- (2012) (finding a privilege where alleged defamation uttered by city's water superintendent was made in his official capacity, and "the public clearly had an interest in both the issues being investigated and the content of the allegations").** The Supreme Judicial Court has twice sidestepped the question of whether that privilege might in fact be an absolute one. Mulgrew, 410 Mass. at 635; Vigoda v. Barton, 348 Mass. 478, 484, 204 N.E.2d 441 (1965) (executive officials). **See Barrows, 82 Mass. App. Ct. at 630 n.10 (noting that "thus far the court has determined it unnecessary to consider the application of an absolute privilege because the conduct it has considered has been well within the limits of a conditional privilege").** Applying the privilege, the Supreme Judicial Court held that a police chief's statements critical of a police officer, made to the city council's committee on police and licenses, were qualifiedly privileged. Mulgrew v. City of Taunton, 410 Mass. 631, 574 N.E.2d 389 (1991) (noting that police chief was acting "in the exercise of his official duties" when addressing the council). The First Circuit significantly extended that privilege in 2005, holding that a police chief invited to a meeting of citizens concerned about a violent crime, and who attended "in his official capacity," is conditionally privileged to discuss the status of the investigation with the citizens' group. Burke v. Town of Walpole, et al., 405 F.3d 66, 94 (1st Cir. 2005). Communications to police in the course of the investigation of a crime are also shielded by at least a qualified privilege. Hutchinson v. New England Telephone & Telegraph Co., 350 Mass. 188, 214 N.E.2d 57 (1966); **Jones v. Scotti, No. 11-2213, 2012 WL 4373655 *3-4 (1st Cir. Sept. 26, 2012) (unpublished);** see also Correllas v. Viveiros, 410 Mass. 314, 572 N.E.2d 7 (1991) (certain statements to police may be absolutely privileged). But see Draghetti v. Chmielewski, 416 Mass. 808, 814, 626 N.E.2d 862, 22 Media L. Rep. 1456 (1994) (because "a police chief has no official duty to report internal investigations to the press," his doing so is not protected by the qualified privilege).

Even a private individual who is under a legal duty to communicate information alleged to be defamatory is protected by a qualified privilege. Dexter's Hearthside Restaurant, Inc. v. Whitehall Co., 24 Mass. App. Ct. 217, 222, 508 N.E.2d 113, 14 Media L. Rep. 1664 (1987), rev. denied, 400 Mass. 1104, 511 N.E.2d 620 (1987). The privilege was applied in Dexter's to shield a wholesaler of alcoholic beverages obliged by state law to report customers whose accounts were more than sixty days delinquent. The Appeals Court recited the Restatement (Second) of Torts § 595, comment f, for the proposition that a "legal duty imposed for the protection of a particular . . . class of persons carries with it either an absolute or conditional privilege" – conditional in the case of a private citizen – "to make such defamatory imputations of another as are reasonably necessary to the performance of the legal duty." Dexter's, 24 Mass. App. Ct. at 222.

Under Massachusetts law, a public employer is not liable for negligence claims if they are based upon "the exercise or performance or the failure to exercise a discretionary function or duty" on the part of an employee acting within the scope of his employment, "whether or not the discretion is abused." Mass. Gen. Laws c. 258, § 10(b).

c. **Consent.** The Appeals Court has described the defense of "consent" as being in the nature of a qualified privilege, applicable only where the speaker has a "good faith belief" in the truth of the communication. DelloRusso v. Monteiro, 47 Mass. App. Ct. 475, 478-79, 714 N.E.2d 362, 364-65 (1999). Two decided cases illustrate the principle. In Burns v. Barry, 353 Mass. 115, 118, 228 N.E.2d 728 (1967), the Supreme Judicial Court affirmed a directed verdict against a plaintiff who arranged to have a friend pose as a prospective employer, in order to learn why plaintiff was denied registration as an engineer. The response was defamatory, so the plaintiff sued. As the lower court held, "If there was a wrong here, it was one invited and procured by the plaintiff himself and it would constitute great inequity to allow him to recover on the basis of it." Id. Similarly, in DelloRusso, a former public school clerk-typist sought to be rehired for that position. After being denied, she asked the state Department of Personnel Administration to uncover the reason. The Appeals Court held that because she "started the chain of inquiry," she could not sue for libel based on the answer that was received. 47 Mass. App. Ct. at 478, 714 N.E.2d at 364-65. See also Restatement (Second) of Torts §583 comment d ("one who agrees to submit his conduct to investigation knowing that its results will be published, consents to the publication of the honest findings of the investigators"). Similarly, in Beriont v. Reichlen, 2000 WL 33170693, *3, No. 994486 (Mass. Super. Ct. Nov. 6, 2000), an employee asked the employer to investigate allegedly defamatory statements by a fellow employee. Finding that the employer conducted the investigation at the plaintiff's specific request, and therefore in its own legitimate interest, the court held that statements made during that investigation are not actionable, noting "the plaintiff cannot be permitted to invite an investigation – and then claim harm when that investigation is conducted."

The federal district court in Massachusetts has observed, similarly, that "where an employer makes a defamatory statement about a former employee in providing a recommendation, at the former employee's request, to a prospective employer," the conditional privilege applies. Miller v. Tope, No. 02-11151-DPW, 2003 U.S. Dist. LEXIS 21211 (D. Mass. Nov. 24, 2003).

The settlement of a dispute between employer and employee may also give rise to the qualified privilege of consent. In Cignetti v. Healy, 89 F. Supp. 2d 106, 126 (D. Mass. 2000), a firefighter, while denying any wrongdoing, agreed to settle a dispute involving charges submitted by his supervisor to the Chief of the fire department.

Under the settlement, the employee accepted a three-day suspension and a letter of reprimand. The employee later sued, in part over an allegedly defamatory general order informing personnel of the plaintiff's misconduct and the disciplinary action taken against him. In granting summary judgment for the defendant on the libel count, the court held that, in agreeing to the settlement, the plaintiff in fact admitted to the underlying charges and, therefore, the defendant had not abused his privilege by publishing the general order. Id.

The qualified privilege of consent is abused if the person publishing the defamatory material does not have "a good faith . . . belief that it was true." Cignetti, 89 F. Supp. 2d at 126. In DelloRusso, it was not abuse of the privilege to give an incomplete reason why the plaintiff was not hired, so long as the defendants honestly believed the reason they gave was valid. Moreover, such "honest belief" in the truth of the material communicated "presupposes a modicum of effort to verify the facts, if 'verification is practical and the matter is sufficiently weighty to call for safeguards against error.'" 47 Mass. App. Ct. at 479, 714 N.E.2d at 365, quoting Mendez v. M.S. Walker, Inc., 26 Mass. App. Ct. 431, 433-34, 528 N.E.2d 891 (1988). (This "presupposition" suggests that the burden of overcoming the qualified privilege – while described as "actual malice" – is in fact something less than the "actual malice" standard that must be met by public officials or public figures who bring a libel claim. See Stone v. Essex County Newspapers, Inc., 367 Mass. 849, 862-67, 330 N.E.2d 161 (1975); compare DelloRusso and Mendez with St. Amant v. Thompson, 390 U.S. 727, 733 (1968) ("[f]ailure to investigate does not in itself establish bad faith").) It appears that the qualified privilege of consent might also be defeated by a showing of common-law malice, DelloRusso v. Monteiro, 47 Mass. App. Ct. 475, 478 n.4, 714 N.E.2d 362, 365 n.4 (1999), and presumably by reckless overpublication as well. See II.A.2.d, infra.

d. **Business Interest.** The employer's qualified privilege applies where the employer's allegedly defamatory statement "is reasonably necessary to serve the employer's legitimate interest in the fitness of an employee to perform his or her job." Bratt v. International Business Machines Corp., 392 Mass. 508, 509, 512-13, 467 N.E.2d 126 (1984) (applying conditional privilege to libel claim based on personnel director's distribution of memoranda discussing plaintiff-employee's apparent paranoia and mental problems); Sensing v. Outback Steakhouse of Florida, Inc., (D. Mass. 2008); Carmack v. National Railroad Passenger Corp., 486 F. Supp. 2d 58 (D. Mass. 2007); Arnold v. CVS Pharmacy, 2008 U.S. Dist. LEXIS 52851 (D. Mass. July 8, 2008); Broomes v. Blue Cross Blue Shield of Mass., 2008 Mass. Super. LEXIS 58, *18-19 (Mass. Super. Jan 4. 2008); Cornwell v. Dairy Farmers of America, Inc., 369 F. Supp. 2d 87, 111 (D. Mass. 2005). "The privilege serves the important purpose of promoting the free flow of information in the workplace." Broomes, 2008 Mass. Super. LEXIS at *18. The privilege applies in a variety of circumstances. Vanguri v. FMR Corp., No. 10-P-494, 78 Mass. App. Ct. 1130, 941 N.E.2d 1149, 2011 WL 677388, *2 (Mass. App. Ct. Feb. 28, 2011) (unpublished) (conditional privilege to disclose defamatory information about employee's performance to other subsidiaries of parent company); Sklar v. Beth Israel Deaconess Medical Center, 59 Mass. App. Ct. 550, 558, 797 N.E.2d 381 (2003) (hospital's transmission to licensing board of an audit report criticizing plaintiff's professional practices; the privilege applies if the "publisher" is "a supervisor, executive, or a corporate officer and the information is reasonably related to the employer's legitimate business interest) (internal quotations omitted); Cluff v. O'Halloran, 2000 WL 33115601, *7 No. CA 99-0428A (Mass. Super. Ct. Dec. 22, 2000) (privilege applies even where parties dispute whether plaintiff was an employee or independent contractor); Bratt, 392 Mass. at 509 (internal company memoranda regarding employee's workplace conduct); Straitt v. Telos Corp., No. 94-10578-NG, slip op. at 21-22 (D. Mass. Oct. 24, 1996) (employer's sending of e-mails regarding plaintiff's mental stability); Carozza v. Blue Cross Blue Shield of Massachusetts, Inc., 2001 WL 1517584, *13, 14 Mass. L. Rptr. 88 (Mass. Super. 2001) (communications concerning possibility that plaintiff might be dangerous). It has also been applied to intra-company statements investigating alleged sexual misconduct by an employee, and discussing the employee's emotional stress. Foley v. Polaroid Corp., 400 Mass. 82, 94-96, 508 N.E.2d 72 (1987). An employer has been found to possess a legitimate interest to inform employees of misconduct of fellow employees in an effort to prevent recurrence of bad acts. Garrity v. John Hancock Mutual Life Insur. Co., 2002 WL 974676, *4, 18 IER Cases 981, No. CA 00-12143-RWZ (D. Mass. May 7, 2002) (finding employer's dissemination of information concerning plaintiffs' termination for sending and receiving sexually explicit e-mails was privileged and rejecting plaintiff's argument that no business purpose was served by dissemination to all employees, including those who worked in different departments); LeBlanc v. Digital Equipment Corp., No. 91-40152, 1996 Mass. Super. LEXIS 582, *14-17 (Worcester Super. Ct. March 25, 1996) (noting that "intracompany communications" in the course of a theft investigation and afterwards, to inform those in terminated employee's department that he would no longer be working there, and to let workers know that the company's rules had been enforced, particularly where the terminated employee was a supervisor, are conditionally privileged).

In investigation cases, the privilege protects even statements made by a fellow employee during an investigation conducted at plaintiff's request. See Beriont v. Reichlen, 2000 WL 33170693, 3, No. 994486 (Mass. Super. Ct. Nov. 6, 2000); Williams v. Brigham & Women's Hospital, Inc., 2002 WL 532979, *6, 14 Mass. L. Rptr. 438 (Mass. Super. Ct. [date] 2002) (applying conditional privilege to statements made to investigators and supervisory personnel) regarding employee's alleged check-cashing scheme.

The conditional "business interest" privilege also operates to protect an employer's limited publication of a letter suspending plaintiff's employment, even assuming such publication is defamatory. Goldhor v. Hampshire College, 25 Mass. App. Ct. 716, 724, 521 N.E.2d 1381 (1988). Retaining suspension and termination notices in an employee's personnel file, in compliance with Massachusetts law, also falls under the business interest privilege. Khalil v. Museum of Science, 2000 WL 1372485, *4, 2000 Mass. Super. LEXIS 386, No. CA-97-01811F (Mass. Super. Ct. Aug. 18, 2000). Similarly, the privilege shielded supervisory employees who, in a letter to the appointing authority, said the plaintiff lacked "the necessary psychological and physiological skills necessary to perform effectively as a firefighter." Judd v. McCormack, 27 Mass. App. Ct. 167, 173, 535 N.E.2d 1284 (1989). But see Draghetti v. Chmielewski, 416 Mass. 808, 813-14, 626 N.E.2d 862, 22 Media L. Rep. 1456 (1994) (privilege does not apply to police chief's criticism of police officer in the media; privilege is limited to instances where information is "published to a narrow group who shared an interest in the communication"). The conditional privilege has also been applied to a company's internal reporting procedure under an anti-harassment and anti-discrimination policy. Such a reporting mandate furthers the legitimate business interest of eliminating potentially costly civil harassment or discrimination suits. Barthelmes v. Martineau, 2000 WL 1269666, *8 Mass. Super. LEXIS 252 No. CA982378A (Mass. Super. Ct. May 22, 2000). See also Martins v. Boston Public Health Comm'n, 51 Mass. App. Ct. 1110, 727 N.E.2d 758 (2001).

Finally, the privilege also applies to information provided to protect or further a legitimate business interest of recipients. Flotech, Inc. v. E.I. Du Pont de Nemours & Co., 814 F.2d 775, 778, 14 Media L. Rep. 1135 (1st Cir. 1987) (shielding company's statement to customers that its own product had proven ineffective for its intended purpose); In re Retailers Commercial Agency, Inc., 342 Mass. 515, 519-20, 174 N.E.2d 376 (1961) (credit reports to subscribers are conditionally privileged). Some courts assert the qualified privilege in even broader terms, without reference to the need for a legitimate business interest. See Cignetti v. Healy, et al, 89 F. Supp. 2d 106, 126 (D. Mass. 2000) ("Statements made within the context of an employment relationship by and to a plaintiff's supervisor or co-workers are conditionally privileged if the speaker reasonably believed that his statements were true and acted in good faith. . . . To overcome that privilege, the burden is on the plaintiff to show abuse of the privilege or that the statements at issue were made with malice").

e. **Criticism of Public Employee.** There are no reported Massachusetts cases establishing a qualified privilege on the part of citizens to criticize a public employee. However, statements made by public officials while performing their official duties are at least conditionally privileged. Mulgrew v. City of Taunton, 410 Mass. 631, 635, 574 N.E.2d 389 (1991); **Barrows v. Wareham Fire Dist., 82 Mass. App. Ct. 623, 630-31, -- N.E.2d -- (2012). See II.A.2.b, supra.**

f. **Limitation on Qualified Privileges.** In general, the conditional privilege is abused, and therefore lost, if "'defamatory material is published for some purpose other than that for which the particular privilege is given.'" Catrone v. Thoroughbred Racing Assocs. of N. Am., 929 F.2d 881, 890 (1st Cir. 1991), quoting Sheehan v. Tobin, 326 Mass. 185, 190, 93 N.E.2d 524 (1950). More specifically, an employer's "conditional privilege is lost if the defendant (1) knew the information was false, (2) had no reason to believe it to be true, or (3) recklessly published the information unnecessarily, unreasonably, or excessively." Dragonas v. School Committee of Melrose, 64 Mass. App. Ct. 429, 438, 833 N.E.2d 679, 687 (2005) (quoting Sklar v. Beth Israel Deaconess Med. Ctr., 59 Mass. App. Ct. 550, 558 (2003)); **Jones v. Scotti, No. 11-2213, 2012 WL 4373655, *4 (1st Cir. Sept. 26, 2012) (unpublished).** "Recklessness causing the loss of a conditional privilege could be shown, among other ways, by a failure to verify information in circumstances where verification was practical and the matter was sufficiently weighty to call for safeguards against error." Vanguri v. FMR Corp., No. 10-P-494, 78 Mass. App. Ct. 1130, 941 N.E.2d 1149, 2011 WL 677388, *2 (unpublished), citing Mendez v. M.S. Walker, Inc., 26 Mass. App. Ct. 431, 432-34, 528 N.E.2d 891 (1988). The standard appears to be a somewhat more indulgent variation of the constitutional actual malice standard: as the Appeals Court put it in Sklar, knowledge of the falsity, or lack of any reason to believe in the truth, of the information conveyed. See II.A.2.f.(1), infra. It is also lost if the employer recklessly overpublished the defamatory allegation. See II.A.2.f.(3), infra. **"A conditional privilege may thus be recklessly abused and lost whether the fault lies in the misconduct of determining the truth of the material published or in the misconduct of unnecessarily, unreasonably, or excessively publishing the material." Barrows v. Wareham Fire Dist., 82 Mass. App. Ct. 623, 631, -- N.E.2d -- (2012).** Finally, the Appeals Court in Dragonas stated that, despite rumors of its demise, a fourth manner of extinguishing the conditional privilege remains extant: "if the plaintiff proves the defendant acted out of malice," by which the court is referring to common-law malice, derived from "some base ulterior motive." Dragonas, 64 Mass. App. Ct. at 438-39, 833 N.E.2d 679, 687-88, quoting Dexter's Hearthside Restaurant, Inc. v. Whitehall Co., 24 Mass. App. Ct. 217, 223, 508 N.E.2d 113 (1987). See II.A.2.f.(2), infra.

Though Mendez speaks in terms of recklessness, it appears to apply something close to a negligence standard, and it has been criticized. As one commentator has noted, "It is difficult to reconcile Mendez with prior decisions of the Supreme Judicial Court." J. Conroy, "Defamation in the Workplace: The Law of Massachusetts," Mass. L. Rev. 84, 91 (Summer 1989). Nevertheless, the Mendez standard was repeated and applied in a 2011 Appeals Court rescript opinion holding that a company acted recklessly, and thereby lost the conditional privilege, where it had erroneously published an "ineligible for rehire" designation in its internal personnel database. The opinion rested on the court's balancing of interests: While "[o]nly a modicum of effort was required" to ensure accuracy of the designation, "the potential harm to [the employee] flowing from an incorrect designation ... (loss of future job prospects [at the parent company]) was significant." Vanguri v. FMR Corp., No. 10-P-494, 78 Mass. App. Ct. 1130, 941 N.E.2d 1149, 2011 WL 677388, *2 (unpublished) (vacating summary judgment for employer and holding that whether conditional privilege was abused was a jury question), citing Mendez, 26 Mass. App. Ct. at 432-34. The Supreme Judicial Court has not yet weighed in on this question.

"[W]hatever the manner of abuse, recklessness, at least, should be required" before the privilege is lost. Bratt v. International Business Machines Corp., 392 Mass. 508, 515, 467 N.E.2d 126 (1984); **Barrows v. Wareham Fire Dist., 82 Mass. App. Ct. 623, 631, -- N.E.2d -- (2012) ("recklessness is the minimum degree of misconduct required to forfeit a conditional privilege"); Jones v. Scotti, No. 11-2213, 2012 WL 4373655, *4 (1st Cir. Sept. 26, 2012) (unpublished).** See Tuli v. Brigham & Women's Hosp., 656 F.3d 33, 44 (1st Cir. 2011) (affirming jury's damages award against supervisor on slander claim, noting that in light of all the evidence, supervisor's false and defamatory statement to hospital credentials committee "could rationally be attributed by the jury to recklessness or worse").

(1) **Constitutional or Actual Malice.** An employer loses the qualified privilege if it published a defamatory statement with knowledge that it was false or in reckless disregard of the truth – the constitutional "actual malice" standard. Tosti v. Ayik, 386 Mass. 721, 726, 437 N.E.2d 1062 (1982); Dexter's Hearthside Restaurant, Inc. v. Whitehall Co., 24 Mass. App. Ct. 217, 223, 508 N.E.2d 113, 14 Media L. Rep. 1664 (1987), rev. denied, 400 Mass. 1104, 511 N.E.2d 620 (1987). **See also Barrows v. Wareham Fire Dist., 82 Mass. App. Ct. 623, 631, -- N.E.2d -- (2012).** The privilege may also be lost based on something less: if the defendant "had no reason to believe it to be true." Sklar v. Beth Israel Deaconess Medical Center, 59 Mass. App. Ct. 550, 558, 797 N.E.2d 381 (2003). See also Vanguri v. FMR Corp., No. 10-P-494, 78 Mass. App. Ct. 1130, 941 N.E.2d 1149, 2011 WL 677388, *2 (Mass. App. Ct. Feb. 28, 2011) (unpublished) ("conditional privilege would be lost on a showing that [individual defendant] '(1) knew the information was false, (2) had no reason to believe it to be true, or (3) recklessly published the information unnecessarily, unreasonably, or excessively,'" quoting Dragonas v. School Comm. of Melrose, 64 Mass. App. Ct. 429, 438, 833 N.E.2d 679 (2005), quoting from Sklar, 59 Mass. App. Ct. at 558). "Simple negligence, want of sound judgment, or hasty action will not cause loss of the privilege." Dexter's, 24 Mass. App. Ct. at 223; **Jones v. Scotti, No. 11-2213, 2012 WL 4373655, *4 (1st Cir. Sept. 26, 2012) (unpublished) (more than negligence must be shown);** Winsmann v. Choate Health Mgmt., Inc., 2002 WL 1290202, *11 (Mass. Super. Ct. April 26, 2002). In **Jones, the First Circuit reasoned that where there were only "minor discrepancies" between the parties' versions of the truth, the plaintiff could not show that the defendant abused a conditional privilege by uttering a statement that he "either knew or should have known ... to be false." 2012 WL 4373655 at *4-5.** Similarly, in Saxonis v. City of Lynn et al., 62 Mass. App. Ct. 916, 817 N.E.2d 793 (2004), the Appeals Court found no abuse of the privilege where plaintiff "has shown no reasonable expectation of proving her conclusory allegations that the [hiring] meeting was a pretext for [defendants] to subject her to a barrage of false accusations rather than a legitimate interview." Nonetheless, the Appeals Court has indicated that "actual malice," as used in this context under Massachusetts law, may describe something less than the constitutional "actual malice" standard that must be met by public officials or public figures who bring a libel claim. While the Supreme Court held in St. Amant v. Thompson, 390 U.S. 727, 733 (1968), that failure to investigate is *not* equivalent to actual malice, the Appeals Court in Sklar suggested that failure to do any investigation at all into the statement's truth might cause an employer to lose the privilege. 59 Mass. App. Ct. at 558 (privilege lost if employer had "no reason to believe it to be true"). Conversely, the ability to demonstrate that a thorough investigation was undertaken may ward off a finding that the privilege was abused. **For instance, in Barrows v. Wareham Fire Dist., 82 Mass. App. Ct. 623, 632, -- N.E.2d -- (2012), the Appeals Court affirmed summary judgment for a defendant city official on the grounds that, because the defendant had engaged in a three-month investigation prior to making the official statement alleged to be defamatory, the plaintiff could not show abuse of the conditional privilege.**

(2) **Common Law Malice.** The Appeals Court, ending any uncertainty that may have existed on this point, established in 2005 that a showing of common-law malice will defeat the conditional privilege. Dragonas v. School Committee of Melrose, et al., 64 Mass. App. Ct. 429, 438, 833 N.E.2d 679, 687 (2005); Noonan v. Staples, Inc., 556 F.3d 20, 31 (1st Cir. 2009) (privilege overcome by a showing of "malice," defined as "base ulterior motive," including "intention to injure another"), quoting Dragonas, 833 N.E.2d at 687. **See also Barrows v. Wareham Fire Dist., 82 Mass. App. Ct. 623, 631, 632 & n.12, -- N.E.2d -- (2012) (using, in dictum, the term "actual malice," but in a context suggesting that the intended meaning is "bad faith," "animus," or "malice" in fact, not constitutional malice).** "Malice, in this sense, occurs when the 'defamatory words, although spoken on a privileged occasion, were not spoken pursuant to the right and duty which created the privilege but were spoken out of some base ulterior motive.' Dexter's Hearthside Restaurant, Inc. v. Whitehall Co., 24 Mass. App. Ct. 217, 223, 508 N.E.2d 113 (1987). This 'may consist either in a direct intention to injure another,' Bratt v. International Bus. Machs. Corp., 392 Mass. 508, 514, 467 N.E.2d 126 (1984) ... or an 'intent to abuse the occasion [giving rise to the privilege] by resorting to it "as a pretence," ... or "reckless disregard" of

the rights of another.' Ezekiel v. Jones Motor Co., 374 Mass. 382, 390, 372 N.E.2d 1281 (1978)." Dragonas, 42 Mass. App. Ct. at 438-39, 833 N.E.2d at 687-88. The Supreme Judicial Court had previously held, and other courts have repeated, that an employer may lose the qualified privilege when the defamatory statements are made with "malice in fact." Bratt v. International Business Machines Corp., 392 Mass. 508, 512 & n.9, 467 N.E.2d 126 (1984). Dragonas opens the door for plaintiffs to defeat summary judgment by assembling facts that would lead to an inference of spite or ill will. To be sure, its facts are somewhat extreme. The Appeals Court cautioned that it will not be enough for a plaintiff to show that a defendant "merely disliked" the plaintiff or that "animosity was part of the defendant's motivation." 64 Mass. App. Ct. at 439, 833 N.E.2d at 688. Rather, there must be a showing that the publication "is not made chiefly for the purpose of furthering the interest which is entitled to protection." Id. Still, the case recognizes a jury question as to common-law malice based on a school principal's intemperate comments to parents whose children were to accompany the plaintiff teacher on an overseas field trip. The court notes that the principal described the teacher to parents as someone who might "rip your face off," and that the teacher had accused the principal of sexual harassment. It notes that there was an "ongoing antagonistic relationship" between the two. 64 Mass. App. Ct. at 440, 833 N.E.2d at 688. See also Ezekiel v. Jones Motor Co., 374 Mass. at 391-92 (extrinsic evidence of the history of the employment relationship is relevant in determining whether the defendant possessed an improper motive). Based on such evidence from which common-law malice can be inferred, the court not only allowed the defamation claim to go to the jury, but also denied summary judgment on plaintiff's age discrimination claim, holding that the principal's behavior "raised triable issues" regarding whether a performance evaluation of the teacher was not conducted in good faith and was instead a pretext for discrimination. Dragonas, 64 Mass. App. Ct. at 444, 833 N.E.2d at 691. **See also Coughlin v. Town of Arlington, No. 10-102013-MLW, 2011 WL 6370932 (D. Mass. Dec. 19, 2011) (denying motion to dismiss because plaintiffs had sufficiently pleaded that defendants had disclosed defamatory information in order to further a "retaliatory campaign" against them);** Martin-Kirkland v. United Parcel Service, Inc., No. 03-4520-H, 21 Mass. L. Rep. 66, 2006 Mass. Super. LEXIS 193, *33 (Middlesex Super. Ct. Apr. 11, 2006) (denying summary judgment for defendants because, despite existence of the conditional privilege, supervisor allegedly criticized plaintiff "with the intent to injure her management authority and to demean her, using her work performance as a mere pretext" – an allegation sufficient to create a question of fact as to whether supervisor was driven by malice, defeating the privilege for the supervisor defendant and (by respondeat superior) the employer defendant as well).

In an unpublished opinion two years before Sklar, the Appeals Court in dictum appeared to confine the limitation to a statement that "resulted from an expressly malicious motive," Martins v. Boston Public Health Comm'n, 51 Mass. App. Ct. 758, 747 N.E.2d 758 (2001), quoting Bratt, 392 Mass. at 517. Where it has been invoked, "[m] alice has been stated to require evidence of 'an improper motive,' Hartmann v. Boston Herald-Traveler Corp., 323 Mass. 56, 65, 80 N.E.2d 16 (1948), or an intent to abuse the occasion by resorting to it 'as a pretence,' Remington v. Congdon, [2 Pick. 310,] 315; 19 Mass. 310 (1824), or 'reckless disregard' of the rights of another, Retailers Commercial Agency, Inc., petitioner, 342 Mass. at 521." Ezekiel v. Jones Motor Co., Inc., 374 Mass. 382, 390, 372 N.E.2d 1281 (1978). The "ill will" may establish abuse of the conditional privilege only if it is "sufficiently tied to the defamatory statement." Miller v. Tope, 2003 U.S. Dist. LEXIS 21211 at *47 (D. Mass. Nov. 24, 2003). A jury could find "malice in fact" when an employee was interrogated in the manner of "an inquisition" in which "accusations and threats were made" and "there was no attempt to determine the facts objectively." Lyons, 30 F.3d at 245. The "malice in fact" exception to the qualified privilege has been particularly applied in cases where there is evidence that the statement was made to retaliate against an employee who had filed claims or charges against the employer. It will also apply where the alleged defamer was a rival of the plaintiff or had an ax to grind against the plaintiff. See, e.g., Bander v. Metropolitan Life Ins. Co., 313 Mass. 337, 344, 47 N.E.2d 595 (1943) (retaliation); Grindall v. First National Stores, Inc., 330 Mass. 557, 559, 116 N.E.2d 687 (1953) (dislike); Childs v. Erhard, 226 Mass. 454, 457, 115 N.E. 924 (1917) (rivalry).

(3) **Other Limitations on Qualified Privileges.** Finally, the qualified privilege is also lost if there has been "'unnecessary, unreasonable or excessive publication,' provided the plaintiff proves that the defendant acted 'recklessly.'" **Barrows v. Wareham Fire Dist., 82 Mass. App. Ct. 623, 631, -- N.E.2d -- (2012), quoting Bratt v. International Business Machines Corp., 392 Mass. 508, 513-17, 467 N.E.2d 126 (1984).** That includes an instance where the employer communicates the statement to persons who had no business need to know the information communicated – that is, "to others, as to whom the occasion is not privileged." Galvin v. New York, N.H. & H.R.R., 341 Mass. 293, 297, 168 N.E.2d 262 (1960), **quoted in Barrows, 82 Mass. App. Ct. at 631.** The conduct must amount to "reckless overpublication" in order to defeat the privilege. Phelan v. May Dep't Stores Co., 60 Mass. App. Ct. 843, 850, 806 N.E.2d 939, 946 (2004); Burke v. Town of Walpole, 405 F.3d 66, 95 (1st Cir. 2005) (referring to "unnecessary, unreasonable or excessive publication" coupled with evidence that the defendant "published the defamatory information recklessly"). **Thus, it was not overpublication to accuse an employee in the presence of his immediate supervisor or union representatives, or to do so publicly when the employee himself requested that a hearing be open to the public. Barrows, 82 Mass. App. Ct. at 632.** See also Cornwell v. Dairy Farmers of America, Inc., 369 F. Supp. 2d 87, 112 (D. Mass. 2005) (no loss of privilege in absence of evidence that alleged defamation was published only "to persons within [employer] who would naturally receive such information, and to [plaintiff's outside] supervisor ... who would normally be

the one to receive the information"). The clearest case on this subject suggests that the privilege is not lost unless the employer *knows* it is publishing excessively; even publication that is "unnecessary, unreasonable or excessive" will not abrogate the privilege unless the employer was reckless. Bratt, 392 Mass. 508, 513-17, 467 N.E.2d 126 (1984); Foley v. Polaroid Corp., 400 Mass. 82, 95, 508 N.E.2d 72 (1987); Mulgrew v. City of Taunton, 410 Mass. 631, 634, 574 N.E.2d 389 (1991); Sklar v. Beth Israel Deaconess Medical Center, 59 Mass. App. Ct. 550, 558 (2003) (privilege lost if employer "recklessly published the information unnecessarily, unreasonably, or excessively").

In Noonan v. Staples, Inc., 556 F.3d 20, 31 (1st Cir. 2009), where the record failed to establish that a privileged communication was made "only to those inside the 'narrow group who shared an interest in the communication,'" summary judgment was denied due to excessive publication sufficient to not only overcome the employer's conditional privilege but also to satisfy the common-law "actual malice" exception of the Massachusetts truth-but-malice statute, Mass. G. L. c. 231, § 92. The Court also suggested that summary judgment may be particularly difficult to achieve in such circumstances. It noted that when assessing whether there has been either abuse of the conditional privilege or common-law malice under the statute, if the plaintiff has presented evidence "beyond conclusory allegations or mere speculation" such that "motive and intent play a leading role" in the analysis, then summary judgment should not be granted. Id., quoting Barss v. Tosches, 785 F.2d 20, 22 (1st Cir. 1986). However, summary judgment was allowed where the undisputed record showed that the libel defendant's statement to police was an "eminently reasonable" report of a serious threat. **Jones v. Scotti, No. 11 -2213, 2012 WL 4373655, *5 (1st Cir. Sept. 26, 2012) (unpublished) (adding that use of a "formal, signed statement" evidenced that complainant "was not acting frivolously or recklessly").**

g. **Question of Fact or Law.** Whether a communication is subject to the qualified privilege is a matter of law to be determined by the judge. Joyce v. Globe Newspaper Co., 355 Mass. 492, 498, 245 N.E.2d 822 (1969); Sheehan v. Tobin, 326 Mass. 185, 194, 93 N.E.2d 524 (1950). Whether the privilege has been abused is a question of fact for the jury "if there is a basis for divergent views." Joyce, 355 Mass. at 498-99; Lewis v. Vallis, 356 Mass. 663, 666, 255 N.E.2d 337 (1970).

h. **Burden of Proof.** The defendant has the burden of proving the existence of circumstances giving rise to the qualified privilege. Humphrey v. National Semiconductor Corp., 18 Mass. App. Ct. 132, 134, 463 N.E.2d 1197 (1984), rev. denied, 393 Mass 1101, 469 N.E.2d 830 (1984); Zajac v. Zajac, 2007 Mass. Super. LEXIS 336, *12 (Mass. Super. Ct. Aug. 16, 2007) (denying motion to dismiss where, "liberally construing the pleadings," court finds that plaintiff "has alleged facts sufficient to conclude" that conditional privilege does not apply). The burden then shifts to the plaintiff to prove that the privilege was abused. Foley v. Polaroid Corp., 400 Mass. 82, 95, 508 N.E.2d 72 (1987); Vanguri v. FMR Corp., No. 10-P-494, 78 Mass. App. Ct. 1130, 941 N.E.2d 1149, 2011 WL 677388, *2 (unpublished). See also Cornwell v. Dairy Farmers of America, Inc., 369 F. Supp. 2d 87, 112 (D. Mass. 2005) (noting that burden is on employee to show that privilege has been abused). The First Circuit has twice asserted (arguably in dicta) that, on a motion for summary judgment, the plaintiff "'bears the burden of establishing abuse of the conditional privilege by clear and convincing evidence.'" Singh v. Blue Cross/Blue Shield, 308 F.3d 25, 47 (1st Cir. 2002), quoting Catrone v. Thoroughbred Racing Ass'ns of N. Am., Inc., 929 F.2d 881, 889 (1st Cir. 1991); see also Elicier v. Toys 'R' Us, Inc., 130 F. Supp. 2d 307, 310 (D. Mass. 2001), although the basis in Massachusetts law for applying the "clear and convincing" standard in this context is not readily apparent.

B. Standard Libel Defenses

1. ***Truth.*** With one (increasingly significant) exception, discussed below, a statement is not actionable if it is true or substantially true. Milgroom v. News Group Boston, Inc., 412 Mass. 9, 12-13, 586 N.E.2d 985, 20 Media L. Rep. 1097 (1992); Reilly v. Assoc. Press, 59 Mass. App. Ct. 764, 770, 797 N.E.2d 1204 (2003) ("when a statement is substantially true, a minor inaccuracy will not support a defamation claim"), cited in Noonan v. Staples, Inc., 707 F.3d 85, 90 (D. Mass. 2010); Nolan v. Krajcik, 384 F. Supp. 2d 447, 473 (D. Mass. 2005); Smith v. City of Boston, 2004 U.S. Dist. LEXIS 13062, *26 (D. Mass. July 13, 2004). While "truth" is frequently discussed as a defense, the Supreme Judicial Court has held that it is the plaintiff's burden to prove falsity – indeed, the absence of substantial truth – by a preponderance of the evidence. Murphy v. Boston Herald, 449 Mass. 42, 51 n.10, 865 N.E.2d 746, 754 n.10, 35 Media L. Rep. 1865 (2007). Falsity means "a 'material change in the meaning conveyed by the statement,'" Murphy, 449 Mass. at 56-57, 865 N.E.2d at 758, quoting Masson v. New Yorker Magazine, Inc., 501 U.S. 496, 517 (1991).

Truth is a straightforward inquiry under Massachusetts law, and a statement that is literally true is not rendered false by the context. Thus, for example, where a company issued a true statement that an employee did not comply with its travel and expense policy, there is no jury question on the issue of truth even if the employee asserts that he was acting in the company's best interest, that he was engaging in behavior widespread within the company, or that the company was treating his transgression with such unprecedented gravity as to suggest he had engaged in criminal or unethical behavior. Noonan v. Staples, Inc., 556 F.3d 20, 26-27 (1st Cir. 2009) (distinguishing the "simpler" "truth-or-falsity inquiry" from the court's inquiries into whether a statement is "defamatory" or is "of and concerning" a particular plaintiff, both of which are determined in light of the context and circumstances). To establish the defense of truth, the truth of the underlying defamation must be shown; a defendant normally cannot escape liability merely by attributing defamatory statements to a third party. Jones v. Taibbi, 400 Mass. 786, 794, 512 N.E.2d 260, 14 Media L. Rep. 1844 (1987). But see Howell v. Enterprise Publishing Co., LLC, 455 Mass. 641, 920 N.E.2d 1 (2010) (applying "fair report" privilege to protect news media against liability for fair and accurate reports of official governmental actions and statements).

The statement need not be true in all technical particulars. Rather, to avoid liability, a defendant need only show that the statement is "substantially true." Milgroom, 412 Mass. at 12-13; Murphy, 449 Mass. at 50-51, 865 N.E.2d at 754 ("minor inaccuracies will not constitute falsity if the substance of the alleged libelous matter is true"); Reilly v. Associated Press, 59 Mass. App. Ct. 764, 770, 797 N.E.2d 1204 (2003) ("when a statement is substantially true, a minor inaccuracy will not support a defamation claim"); **Boyle v. Cape Cod Times, No. 11-P-196, 81 Mass. App. Ct. 1107, 959 N.E.2d 457, 2012 WL 28661, *2 (2012) (unpublished). Thus, in Boyle, the Appeals Court affirmed summary judgment based on substantial truth despite two "minor factual discrepancies": first, defendant's accusation that plaintiff owed his employees $33,000, compared to plaintiff's admission that he owed money and that employees were claiming $20,000; and second, defendant's charge that plaintiff operated his business "illegally," compared to plaintiff's version: that although he lacked a license, he had verbal authorization to operate without one.** See also Noonan v. Staples, Inc., 556 F.3d at 28 n.5 (whether employer's investigation of plaintiff's misconduct was "thorough," as it was characterized in employer's e-mail to staff, was a "minor detail [that] does not deprive the e-mail of its substantially true character").

Truth is determined by looking at the statement as a whole. Dulgarian, 420 Mass. at 848. Accordingly, where an employee is fired for conduct she admits is true, the employer ordinarily will not be held liable for disclosing that conduct to others as the reason for plaintiff's termination. Fiorillo v. May Department Stores, 11 Mass. L. Rptr. 478, 2000 WL 804649, *5, 2000 Mass. Super. LEXIS 123 (Mass. Super. Ct. 2000) (statements that the plaintiff violated company policy were substantially true and, therefore, cannot form the basis of liability). The same result obtains if it can be shown that the employer's allegedly defamatory reason for an employee's termination is in fact true. See, e.g., Mulvihill v. Top-Flite Golf Co., 2003 U.S. App. LEXIS 13440, *34, n.5 (1st Cir. 2003) (stating in dictum that if plaintiff contravened employer's sexual harassment policy, it is not defamatory to tell co-workers he was guilty of sexual harassment); Cluff v. O'Halloran, 2000 WL 33115601, No. 99-0428A *8 (Mass. Super. Ct. Dec. 22, 2000) (informing customers that independent contractor violated franchise agreement is not defamatory if the statement is true). But see Noonan v. Staples, Inc., 556 F.3d 20, 28-31 (1st Cir. 2009) (suggesting that a true report of an employee's discharge may under certain circumstances constitute defamation under Massachusetts law), discussed below.

"Massachusetts has not recognized the neutral reporting privilege." Reilly v. Associated Press, 59 Mass. App. Ct. 764, 770, 797 N.E.2d 1204 (2003) (noting that defendant may be liable for quoted defamatory falsehoods, if published with the requisite fault). It has, however, recognized the "fair report" doctrine, which protects "fair and accurate reports of official actions and statements," though not ordinarily in the non-media context. See generally Howell v. Enterprise Publishing Co., LLC, 455 Mass. 641, 650-670, 920 N.E.2d 1, 13-27 (2010). Where it applies, the privilege is not absolute; it is defeated by a showing "'that the publisher does not give a fair and accurate report of the official statement [or action], or malice.'" Howell, 455 Mass. 641, 651 n.8, 920 N.E.2d 1, 14 n.8, quoting Yohe v. Nugent, 321 F.3d 35, 44 (1st Cir. 2003). The defense of truth may also be established by applying collateral estoppel principles where the subject matter of the alleged defamation was litigated in a prior action, and the truth of the allegations necessarily determined. Hoult v. Hoult, 157 F.3d 29, 33 (1st Cir. 1998); Noonan v. Staples, Inc., 707 F. Supp. 2d 85, 90 (D. Mass. 2010), citing Grella v. Salem Five Cent Sav. Bank, 42 F.3d 26, 30 (1st Cir. 1994).

Although a defendant may assert a statement's truth as an "absolute defense" to a defamation claim, see Massachusetts School of Law at Andover, Inc. v. American Bar Association, 142 F.3d 26, 42 (1st Cir. 1998), citing Bander v. Metropolitan Life Ins. Co., 313 Mass. 337, 47 N.E.2d 595, 598 (1943), in fact the First Circuit Court of Appeals has recognized the possibility of "a narrow exception to this defense" when applying Massachusetts law. See Noonan v. Staples, Inc., 556 F.3d 20, 28-31 (1st Cir. 2009), citing White v. Blue Cross & Blue Shield of Mass., Inc., 442 Mass. 64, 66 n.4, 809 N.E.2d 1034, 1036 n.4 (2004) and Conroy v. Fall River Herald News Publ'g Co., 306 Mass. 488, 492, 28 N.E.2d 729, 731-32 (1940). The "exception" arises from an 1855 statute, last revised in 1902, that purports to permit liability for truthful defamatory statements under certain circumstances. See Mass. Gen. Laws c. 231, § 92 ("The defendant in an action for writing or for publishing a libel may introduce in evidence the truth of the matter contained in the publication charged as libelous; and the truth shall be a justification *unless actual malice is proved*.") (emphasis added); see also Perry v. Hearst Corp., 334 F.2d 800, 801 (1st Cir. 1964) ("truth is not a defense if the publication was made with actual malice," citing G.L. c. 231, § 92). The Massachusetts Supreme Judicial Court has made clear that the statute is unconstitutional as applied to cases involving public-figure or public-official plaintiffs, or matters of public concern – at least when a media defendant is involved (and, the court suggested, probably even as to nonmedia defendants as well). Shaari v. Harvard Student Agencies, Inc., 427 Mass. 129, 131-34, 691 N.E.2d 925, 26 Media L. Rep. 1730 (1998); see also White, 442 Mass. at 66 n.4 (observing that statute allows recovery for a "truthful defamatory statement published in writing (or its equivalent) with actual malice ... except as confined by the requirements of the First Amendment to the United States Constitution"); Noonan, 556 F.3d at 28 n.7 ("[t]his exception to the truth defense is not constitutional when applied to matters of public concern"); **Coughlin v. Town of Arlington, No. 10-102013-MLW, 2011 WL 6370932, *14 n.17 (D. Mass. Dec. 19, 2011) (noting that "if the matter is of public concern, truth remains a defense to a claim of defamation," but then saying that the defense was waived because not raised).** But the Shaari opinion fails to reach a small class of cases: those involving private-figure plaintiffs and matters of private concern. The employment defamation dispute of Noonan v. Staples, Inc., 556 F.3d 20 (1st Cir. 2009) arguably presented such a case, and has left this small area of Massachusetts law quite a muddle. In Noonan, the First Circuit Court of Appeals proceeded to apply G.L. c. 231, § 92 to the facts at hand without any nod to its possible unconstitutionality, because, according to the Court, the defendant had waived the constitutionality argument. 556 F.3d at 28 n.7. (When the question later arose squarely in a companion case in the federal district court, that court pronounced the constitutional inquiry "a matter of profound importance" – and failed to reach an answer before the case settled. See Noonan v. Staples, Inc., 707 F. Supp. 2d 85, 92 (D. Mass. 2010).)

In applying the 1855 statute, the Court of Appeals had accepted defendants' erroneous argument that "actual malice," as used in the statute, had the modern meaning of "constitutional malice," or reckless disregard of the truth. Noonan, 539 F.3d 1, 9-10 (1st Cir. 2008), opinion withdrawn on rehearing, 556 F.3d 20 (1st Cir. 2009). On rehearing, however, the Court corrected that error, concluding, in accord with state court cases, that in fact the ancient statute's reference to "actual malice" means common-law malice, defined as "ill will" or "malevolent intent." 556 F.3d at 28-30. See also Gilbert v. Bernard, 4 Mass. L. Rptr. 143, 1995 WL 809550, 1995 Mass. Super. LEXIS 566 (Super. Ct. 1995) ("malevolent intent or motive"), citing Fay v. Harrington, 176 Mass. 270, 274, 57 N.E. 369 (1900); Perry, 334 F.2d at 801 (declining to define "malice" as used in the statute, but citing to Bander v. Metropolitan Life Ins. Co., 313 Mass. 337, 344 (1943) and suggesting that "ill will" is intended). See also Noonan v. Staples, Inc., 707 F. Supp. 2d 85, 92 (D. Mass. 2010) (holding that jury could impute such malice where the supervisor who made the challenged statement had been personally inconvenienced, and the employer put to considerable expense, by the plaintiff). Then, finding that there was evidence sufficient for a jury to conclude that the defendant employer made the statement in question out of ill will (by singling out one employee "in order to humiliate him," and excessively publishing the defamatory statement to an unnecessarily large group of employees), the Court of Appeals reversed the trial court's dismissal of the defamation claim and remanded the case for trial, 556 F.3d at 30-31, 36, after which the jury in October 2009 handed up a general verdict for the employer.

2. ***Opinion.*** "[D]efamation requires, among other elements, the existence of a false 'statement' about 'the plaintiff.'" Paren v. Craigie, et al., 2006 U.S. Dist. LEXIS 43288, *38 (D. Mass. June 15, 2006) (Neiman, C.M.J.). The determination whether a statement is one "of fact or opinion, or a combination of both," is "critical." Driscoll v. Board of Trustees of Milton Academy, 70 Mass. App. Ct. 285, 296, 873 N.E.2d 1177 (2007). Statements of fact may be actionable, but statements of pure opinion are constitutionally protected. Driscoll, 70 Mass. App. Ct. at 296; North Shore Pharmacy Services, Inc., et al. v. Breslin Assocs. Consulting, 491 F. Supp. 2d 111, 126 (D. Mass. 2007); Woods v. Baystate Health System, 2005 U.S. Dist. LEXIS 12465 (D. Mass. June 15, 2005). Also protected are opinions based on disclosed or assumed nondefamatory facts, """no matter how unjustified and unreasonable the opinion may be or how derogatory it is.""" **Piccone v. Bartels, No. 11-10143-MLW, 2012 WL 4592770 (D. Mass. Sept. 29, 2012),** quoting National Association of Gov't Employees, Inc. v. Central Broadcasting Corp., 379 Mass. 220, 226-28, 396 N.E.2d 996 (1979), quoting Restatement of Torts (2d) § 566 (1977). See also Miller v. Tope, No. 02-11151-DPW, 2003 U.S. Dist. LEXIS 21211, at *29-30 (D. Mass. Nov. 24, 2003), quoting Lyons v. Globe Newspaper Co., 415 Mass. 258, 267, 612 N.E.2d 1158, 21 Media L. Rep. 1977 (1993). The mere expression of opinion based on disclosed non-defamatory facts cannot be the basis of a defamation claim. Driscoll, 70 Mass. App. Ct. at 296-97.

However, "only pure opinion, as opposed to 'an expression of opinion that implies a false assertion of fact,'" is entitled to protection from liability. North Shore Pharmacy Services, Inc., et al. v. Breslin Assocs. Consulting, 491 F. Supp. 2d 111, 126 (D. Mass. 2007), quoting Reilly v. Associated Press, 59 Mass. App. Ct. 764, 770, 797 N.E.2d 1204, 1210-11 (2003). "Therefore, 'a cause of action for defamation may still be sustained where an opinion "implies the allegation of undisclosed defamatory facts as the basis for the opinion."'" North Shore Pharmacy Services, 491 F. Supp. 2d at 126, quoting Yohe v. Nugent, 321 F.3d 35, 41 (1st Cir. 2003); Fuentes v. Hampden County Sheriff's Dep't., 2004 U.S. Dist. LEXIS 12053, *9 (D. Mass. June 25, 2004) ("While statements of opinion are generally not actionable as defamation, such statements may be actionable if they imply that undisclosed defamatory facts are the basis for the opinion."). In drawing the distinction, courts focus on "whether the assertion can be proven false." Driscoll v. Board of Trustees of Milton Academy, 70 Mass. App. Ct. 285, 296 n.10, 873 N.E.2d 1177 (2007). "'[A]ccusations which can be proved true or false at trial' are statements of fact." North Shore Pharmacy Services, 491 F. Supp. 2d at 127 quoting Lyons v. New Mass Media, Inc., 390 Mass. 51, 60, 453 N.E.2d 451, 458 (1993). Communications may be actionable if they imply the existence of false and defamatory facts, or if they "can be said to be more than expressions of opinion . . . and to impute to [the plaintiff] as a fact wrongful or reprehensible conduct of the type which the . . . decisions . . . treat as actionable." Tartaglia v. Townsend, 19 Mass. App. Ct. 693, 696, 477 N.E.2d 178 (1985). See I.B.4, supra.

In deciding whether a statement is opinion or fact, a court must examine the statement in its totality and in context; consider all the words used; give weight to cautionary terms; and consider all the surrounding circumstances, including the medium by which the statement is disseminated and the audience to which it is published. Driscoll, 70 Mass. App. Ct. at 297. **For example, in Piccone v. Bartels, No. 11-10143-MLW, 2012 WL 4592770 (D. Mass. Sept. 29, 2012), the court denied a motion to dismiss a libel claim over a police chief's statement that the plaintiff "may know" the location of her fugitive relatives, even though the chief also stated that he "could not provide any specific information" to that effect. The court said the statement could plausibly be understood as implying that the chief had a factual basis which he could not disclose due to legal impediments. Id.**

Whether a statement is construed as fact or opinion may also depend on the capacity or position of the speaker. See Reilly v. Associated Press, 59 Mass. App. Ct. 764, 771, 793 N.E.2d 1204 (2003) (statements that veterinarian gave "sloppy," "lazy" treatment would be recognized by reasonable reader as "generalizations uttered by a distraught pet owner"). A statement is an opinion if it is "quintessentially subjective," where the meaning is imprecise and open to speculation such that it cannot be proved true or false. Cluff v. O'Halloran, 2000 WL 33115601, *6 (Mass. Super. Ct. Dec. 22, 2000) (calling an employee "incompetent" is "imprecise, inherently subjective, and not readily capable of being proven true or false"); Welch v. Tellabs Operations, Inc., 2001 WL 1525828, *1, 14 Mass. L. Rptr. 44 (Mass. Super. Ct. Sept. 24, 2001) (because opinions are inherently subjective, the fact that employer's opinion concerning the plaintiff was not shared by all supervisors did not give rise to a defamation claim).

In employment cases, the following phrases have been held to be non-actionable opinion: a performance evaluation that plaintiff "has not shown the necessary psychological and physiological skills necessary to perform effectively as a firefighter," and an instructor's conclusion that "if you put a chain around him and drag him around, he might make a good man in 100 years," Judd v. McCormack, 27 Mass. App. Ct. 167, 169, 170, 174-75, 535 N.E.2d 1284 (1989) (applying conditional privilege to claim for intentional interference with advantageous relations, and finding no abuse of the privilege); abusive taunts, including calling an age discrimination plaintiff a member of the "Geritol generation," Galdauckas v. Interstate Hotels Corp. No. 16, 901 F. Supp. 454, 471 (D. Mass. 1995); an in-house memo accusing plaintiff of providing "lack of proper management" and having an "unfortunate habit of procrastination," Kersey v. Dennison Manufacturing Co., Inc., 1992 WL 71390, *5 (D. Mass. Feb. 21, 1992); Beriont v. Reichlen, 2000 WL 33170693, *3 No. 994486 (Mass. Super. Ct. Nov. 6, 2000) (not "defamation per se" to accuse plaintiff of moving equipment from one company laboratory to another, because the accusation of "theft," taken in context, neither imputes criminal conduct nor affects the plaintiff's business or professional reputation). An employee's allegation at a press conference that her supervisor was "a racist and a harasser," which in context did not imply any undisclosed defamatory facts, Puccia v. Edwards, 10 Mass. L. Rptr. 185, 1999 WL 513895, 1999 Mass. Super. LEXIS 253 (Mass. Super. Ct. 1999); a former employer's response to a prospective employer's reference form, in which the employer checked off "poor" in rating the employee's "emotional stability," Bianchi v. Commonwealth Childcare Corp. et al., 2000 WL 1508175, No. 97-2023-B (Mass. Super. Ct. 2000) (the concept of "emotional stability" is a "phrase in use in everyday speech in a colloquial sense and not as a specific term of art" and "calls for a wide range of subjective judgment" and "was clearly a matter of opinion and not a statement of fact"); a voicemail from a supervisor to plaintiff's co-workers describing plaintiff as ill-prepared and disorganized, Scott v. Sulzer Carbomedics, Inc., 141 F. Supp. 2d 154, 178-79 (D. Mass. 2001) ("'disorganized and ill-prepared' are broad descriptive terms susceptible to varying interpretations").

But a supervisor's statement to a hospital credentials committee "that he had been told that between 20 and 30 nurses no longer wanted to work ... in the operating room" with the plaintiff neurosurgeon is a factual assertion. Tuli v. Brigham & Women's Hosp., 656 F.3d 33, 44 (1st Cir. 2011). So are allegations that a medical auditor "did not have a background doing audits" and that his work "contained numerous errors" are assertions of fact; they are sufficient to support a slander claim, as is the assertion that the auditor is of questionable ethics because he "disseminated confidential information," which is an opinion based on an allegedly defamatory fact. North Shore Pharmacy Services, Inc. v. Breslin Associates Consulting LLC, 491 F. Supp. 2d 111, 127 (D. Mass. 2007). Statements that a veterinarian played golf and lied about it, instead of treating a sick animal that later died, are factual and capable of being proved false. Reilly v. Associated Press, 59 Mass. App. Ct. 764, 772, 797 N.E.2d 1204 (2003). A Superior Court drew the same conclusion as to a warning in a doctor's personnel file that another complaint "of this nature" would cause his removal from the defendant hospital's services. Jaraki v Quinlan, 1994 WL 879877, 1994 Mass. Super. LEXIS 180 (Mass. Super. Ct. June 30, 1994).

3. ***Consent.*** The Supreme Judicial Court has been reluctant to assume that a plaintiff's voluntary submission to an investigation or grievance procedure constitutes consent to the publication of an unprivileged defamation. See Ezekiel v. Jones Motor Co., 374 Mass. 382, 389, 372 N.E.2d 1281 (1978) (not relying on consent); cf. Remington v. Congdon, 2 Pick. 310, 314-15 (1824) (finding consent to investigation). The Appeals Court, however, has recognized that a

plaintiff who requests disclosure of "the reasons behind a failure to hire or behind a disciplinary action" has consented to a publication even if it turns out to be defamatory. Under such circumstances, the defendant has a qualified privilege so long as he or she believed that the defamatory material was true. DelloRusso v. Monteiro, 47 Mass. App. Ct. 475, 478-79, 714 N.E.2d 362, 364-65 (1999). As expressed by one commentator, "After asking for a reference from her former boss or supervisor or listing him as a reference in her application, a plaintiff is poorly positioned to complain when the result is not to her liking." J. Conroy, "Defamation in the Workplace: The Law of Massachusetts," in Mass. L. Rev. (Summer 1989) 84, 88, citing Childs v. Erhard, 226 Mass. 454, 456, 115 N.E. 924 (1917). See II.A.2.a, supra. If the defamation is volunteered by the plaintiff, its repetition by another is not actionable. Billings v. Fairbanks, 136 Mass. 177, 178 (1883).

An employee may consent to a potentially defamatory reference, and thereby lose the right to sue over it, by providing a signed authorization and release. Miller v. Tope, No. 02-11151-DPW, 2003 U.S. Dist. LEXIS 21211, *37-38 (D. Mass. Nov. 24, 2003). Because the authorization and release in Miller was contingent on the employer providing the information "in good faith and without malice," it appears to have added little to the defendant's protections under the conditional business interest privilege (see II.A.2.b and II.A.2.f, infra) – except that it extended the protections beyond defamation claims, and provided a qualified defense to other tort claims that the court suggested would not be covered by the common-law privilege. Miller, 2003 U.S. Dist. LEXIS 21211 at *45 & n.30. But see Correllas v. Viveiros, 410 Mass. 314, 324, 527 N.E.2d 7 (1991) (holding that conditional privilege also applies to claims for intentional infliction of emotional distress); Thomas v. Sears, Roebuck & Co., 144 F.3d 31, 34 (1st Cir. 1998) (holding that conditional privilege also applies to claims for intentional interference with contract); see also IV.B and IV.C, infra.

4. ***Mitigation***. A jury may consider the retraction of a libelous statement "as a factor in mitigating damages." Ayash v. Dana-Farber Cancer Institute, et al., 443 Mass. 367, 407 n.38, 822 N.E.2d 667, 699 n.38, 33 Media L. Rep. 1513 (2005). See also Whitcomb v. Hearst Corp., 329 Mass. 193, 203, 107 N.E.2d 295 (1952); G.L. c. 231, § 93. In Whitcomb, the Supreme Judicial Court approved of a jury instruction authorizing jurors to "determine to what extent any retraction that was published minimized or mitigated the damages which [the plaintiff] sustained. It is within your province to say that the retractions, the corrections, the apologies mitigated his damages entirely, down to a nominal degree. It is within your province to say that the retractions, corrections, the apologies, mitigated it in no degree. Or you can say that it mitigated it to some extent, you determining the amount of it." 392 Mass. at 202-03. See also Tartaglia v. Townsend, 19 Mass. App. Ct. 693, 697 n.5, 477 N.E.2d 178 (1985) (post-publication efforts to correct inaccuracies, and publication of corrections commensurate with the original publication, "may shed some light on whether the inaccuracies . . . were intentional or inadvertent").

III. RECURRING FACT PATTERNS

A. Statements in Personnel File

Massachusetts employers must permit current and former employees to review their personnel record and to obtain a copy upon written request. G.L. c. 149, § 52C. "Personnel record" is "a record kept by an employer that identifies an employee, to the extent that the record is used or has been used, or may affect or be used relative to that employee's qualifications for employment, promotion, transfer, additional compensation or disciplinary action." Id. An employer of 20 or more employees must include in the file "all employee performance evaluations, including . . . employee evaluation documents"; "written warnings of substandard performance"; "copies of dated termination notices"; and "other documents relating to disciplinary action." Id. An employee who disagrees with information contained in his or her personnel record may submit a written statement explaining his or her position; the statement then becomes part of the personnel record and must be included whenever the record is provided to a third party. Alternatively, an employee and employer may agree to remove or correct information contained in the personnel record. Finally, if the employer includes in the personnel record "any information which such employer knew or should have known to be false, then the employee shall have remedy through the collective bargaining agreement, other personnel procedures or judicial process to have such information expunged." Id. The employee may also have a claim for publication of a libel, if the false material was defamatory and of and concerning the plaintiff.

Negative statements contained in an employee's personnel file typically fall within the employer's qualified privilege, and cannot form the basis of a defamation claim if created in accordance with the employer's policies, and not "recklessly published to outsiders." Galdauckas v. Interstate Hotels Corp. No. 16, 901 F. Supp. 454, 470-71 (D. Mass. 1995). See also Jaraki v. Quinlan, 1994 WL 879877 at *5, 1994 Mass. Super. LEXIS 180 (Mass. Super. Ct. 1994) (derogatory letter that was part of personnel record was not actionable because opinion, and if factual would be protected by the qualified privilege unless actual malice were shown). For that reason, "courts applying Massachusetts law have routinely rejected claims of defamation based upon internal business communications and statements made in the workplace, including statements contained in an employee's personnel file." Paren v. Craigie, et al., 2006 U.S. Dist. LEXIS 43288, *42 (D. Mass. June 15, 2006) (Neiman, C.M.J.). The First Circuit Court of Appeals held in Thomas v. Sears, Roebuck & Co., 144 F.3d 31,

34 (1st Cir. 1998) that internal company feedback and deficiency memoranda, which included a comment that the plaintiff was disloyal and a troublemaker, were privileged. See also Galdauckas, 901 F. Supp. at 471 (holding that defamatory statement in personnel file was conditionally privileged). In Paren, the federal district court held that an ex-c.e.o.'s statement about an employee was conditionally privileged even though it was made after the c.e.o. had left the company, because it was made "in furtherance of the company's on-going business interests." Paren, supra at *42.

B. Performance Evaluations

Standing alone, an unfavorable performance evaluation is not sufficient to stake a defamation claim. McCone v. New England Telephone & Telegraph Co., 393 Mass. 231, 235-36, 471 N.E.2d 47 (1984), cited in Paren v. Craigie, et al., 2006 U.S. Dist. LEXIS 43288, *42 (D. Mass. June 15, 2006) (Neiman, C.M.J.). Appraisals of character and health are also conditionally privileged, so long as they reasonably relate to employment. Bratt v. International Business Machines Corp., 392 Mass. 508, 509, 516-17, 467 N.E.2d 126 (1984). So are comments contained in a company's "internal company feedback and deficiency memoranda." Thomas v. Sears, Roebuck & Co., 144 F.3d 31, 34 (1st Cir. 1998); see also Molinar v. Western Electric Co., 525 F.2d 521, 531-32 (1st Cir. 1975) ("unsatisfactory" rating on "Termination of Employment" form routinely distributed to company divisions is conditionally privileged), cert. denied, 424 U.S. 978 (1976). That is true even when the evaluative comments are "harsh and tasteless." Judd v. McCormack, 27 Mass. App. Ct. 167, 170, 175, 535 N.E.2d 1284 (1989) (noting that comment regarding firefighter, that "if you put a chain around him and drag him around, he might make a good man in 100 years" is "impolite bluntness" but not malice sufficient to abrogate the conditional privilege). In addition to the protection afforded internal performance reviews, "an employee of a company enjoys a qualified privilege to make disparaging comments about the performance of an employee of another company with which the first has a business relationship in so far as the comments are relevant to that relationship." Humphrey v. National Semiconductor Corp., 18 Mass. App. Ct. 132, 133, 463 N.E.2d 1197, rev. denied, 393 Mass. 1102, 469 N.E.2d 830 (1984).

C. References

The defenses of opinion and conditional privilege are frequently used against claims of defamation arising out of letters of reference and evaluations for prospective employers or licensing boards. See, e.g., Miller v. Tope, No. 02-11151-DPW, 2003 U.S. Dist. LEXIS 21211 (D. Mass. Nov. 24, 2003). In Miller, involving a physician-plaintiff, the court found that an evaluation form containing a five-point scale assessing such characteristics as "Clinical Knowledge," "Character and ethics," and "Cooperativeness" was protected opinion. Id. at *12, *33 ("'to permit such claims in this environment would cast an appalling chill over candor in medical education,'" quoting Baldwin v. Univ. of Texas Med. Branch at Galveston, 945 F. Supp. 1022 (S.D. Tex. 1996), aff'd, 122 F.3d 1066 (5th Cir. 1997)). See also Bianchi v. Commonwealth Childcare Corp. et al., 2000 WL 1508175 (Mass. Super. Ct. 2000) (former employer's response to a prospective employer's reference form, in which the employer checked off "poor" in rating the employee's "emotional stability," was held to be a non-actionable statement of opinion, as well as conditionally privileged). In Welch v. Tellabs Operations, Inc., the court protected a reference -- containing a comment that an employee was ineligible for rehire "due to a lack of motivation" -- as non-defamatory opinion, without relying on the conditional privilege. No. 00617E 2001 WL 1525828, *1, 14 Mass. L. Rptr. 44 (Mass. Super. Ct. Sept. 24, 2001). The court noted that references are based on opinions and the recipient of an employee reference assumes that non-defamatory facts exist to support the reference. Id. Therefore, the reasoning goes, references cannot give rise to claims for undisclosed defamatory facts. **See also O'Brien v. Chretien, No. 11-P-2092, 82 Mass. App. Ct. 1117, 976 N.E.2d 214, 2012 WL 5193373 (Mass. App. Ct. Oct. 23, 2012) (unpublished) (denying motion for judgment notwithstanding the verdict following jury award for plaintiff against former employer).**

In Miller v. Tope, supra, the federal district court also invoked the conditional "business interest" privilege, which applies when an employer "makes an allegedly defamatory statement about a former employee;" see also Arsenault v. Allegheny Airlines, Inc., 485 F. Supp. 1373 (D. Mass. 1980), aff'd, 636 F.2d 1199 (1st Cir. 1980), cert. denied, 454 U.S. 821 (1981), and also applies "where an employer makes a defamatory statement about a former employee in providing a recommendation, at the former employee's request, to a prospective employer"; see also Doane v. Grew, 220 Mass. 171, 107 N.E. 620 (1915). "[L]etters of reference or evaluation" are clearly within the ambit of the qualified privilege. Dexter's Hearthside Restaurant, Inc. v. Whitehall Co., 24 Mass. App. Ct. 217, 222, 508 N.E.2d 113, 14 Media L. Rep. 1664, rev. denied, 400 Mass. 1104, 511 N.E.2d 620 (1987). So is an employer's inquiry to an employee's previous employer relating to the quality of the employee's job performance. Terravecchia v. Fleet Bank, No. 2004-3086F, 22 Mass. L. Rep. 314, 2007 Mass. Super. LEXIS 88, *12-13 (Mass. Super. Ct. March 21, 2007) (relying on conditional privilege to grant summary judgment to defendant employer in defamation claim where employee failed to allege recklessness). However, a rogue supervisor's acts of providing defamatory bad references to third parties will not render the supervisor's employer liable where the supervisor was not acting within the course of his employment because only the company's human resources department had authority to provide references. Feehily v. Muzi Motors, Inc., 79 Mass. App. Ct. 1116 (2011) (unpublished disposition pursuant to Rule 1:28). Finally, while it may seem obvious, the federal district court in Massachusetts has observed that a terminated employee cannot make out a defamation claim based only on her "concern" about what her former employer would say "if a reference called." Rather, a defamation plaintiff must be able to identify "actual specific defamatory statements" allegedly made by the defendant, as well as "particular injury suffered as a result" of such statements. Anthony v. Busby, et al., 2005 U.S. Dist. LEXIS 33070 (D. Mass. Dec. 15, 2005) (Zobel, J.).

D. Intracorporate Communication

In Massachusetts, intracorporate communications qualify as "publications," see I.B.6(a), supra, but routinely fall within the qualified privilege. See Bander v. Metropolitan Life Ins. Co., 313 Mass. 337, 348-50, 47 N.E.2d 595 (1943). Two exceptions to that general rule are the twin defamation cases brought by an employee, the first over an email his company sent to some 1,500 employees, explaining that the employee was fired for violating the employer's expense policies, and the second over the statement made in a conference call of company managers that the employee had "never denied stealing" from the company. The courts sidestepped the question of conditional privilege, suggesting in the first case that either the company's excessive publication of the email, or the fact that it was published with common-law malice, robbed it of any conditional privilege, Noonan v. Staples, Inc. ("Noonan I"), No. 06-CV-10716, 2007 WL 6064454, 1-2 (D. Mass. June 28, 2007) (dictum; excessive publication), aff'd in part and rev'd in part, on other grounds, 556 F.3d 20, 31 (1st Cir. 2009) (common-law malice, defined as "base ulterior motive," including "intention to injure another"). The only reported opinion in the second case did not explicitly address the conditional privilege, but applied collateral estoppel principles to establish that there had been no malice. Noonan v. Staples, Inc. ("Noonan II"), 707 F. Supp. 2d 85, 88 (D. Mass. 2010). See also Tuli v. Brigham & Women's Hosp., 656 F.3d 33 (1st Cir. 2011) (affirming $20,000 jury award on intentional interference claim against supervisor who, in presentation to credentials committee, overstated complaints about employee's work and failed to disclose his own biases based on employee's claims against him).

E. Statements to Government Regulators

The publication of defamatory material to the state unemployment office is absolutely privileged. G.L. c. 151A, § 46; Arsenault v. Allegheny Airlines, Inc., 485 F. Supp. 1373, 1379 (D. Mass. 1980), aff'd, 636 F.2d 1199 (1st Cir. 1980), cert. denied, 454 U.S. 821 (1981). So are statements to police that are made in the context of a contemplated criminal proceeding. Correllas v. Viveiros, 410 Mass. 314, 320-21, 572 N.E.2d 7 (1991).

A police chief's statements to the municipal appointing authority regarding the qualifications of a police recruit were protected by a qualified privilege. Judd v. McCormack, 27 Mass. App. Ct. 167, 173, 535 N.E.2d 1284 (1989); see also Mulgrew v. Taunton, 410 Mass. 631, 635, 574 N.E.2d 389 (1991) (police chief's statements to city council's committee on police and licenses, made in his official capacity and in the exercise of official duties, are subject to conditional privilege). The qualified privilege also protects those whose statements to the State Department of Personnel Administration, regarding reasons why the plaintiff was not hired, were made in response to the plaintiff's request. DelloRusso v. Monteiro, 47 Mass. App. Ct. 475, 478-79, 714 N.E.2d 362, 364-65 (1999). A similar principle appears to have animated the state Appeals Court when it granted a judgment notwithstanding the verdict to a union sued for libel after complaining to the school superintendent about a manager's conduct. Netherwood v. Am. Fed'n of State, County and Mun. Employees, Local 1725, 53 Mass. App. Ct. 11, 23, 757 N.E.2d 257, 267 (2001) (noting that "the intention of the defendant local was to give notice to and provide the superintendent an opportunity to conduct a non-public investigation into charges which school department employees were making against a school department supervisor concerning employment issues").

Where a hospital supervisor filed a complaint with licensing authorities about the performance of an occupational therapist on her staff, the employee's claim of defamation was dismissed even though the reviewing board suggested that the claim was "frivolous." Sklar v. Beth Israel Deaconess Med. Ctr., 59 Mass. App. Ct. 550, 558 (2003). The complaint to the professional board had been based on, and included a copy of, the hospital's peer audit which had led to the employee's dismissal.

Additionally, a public schoolteacher was barred from proceeding with a Section 1983 claim alleging injury to her constitutional liberty interest as a result of alleged defamatory statements made to the state commissioner of education in connection with the termination of her employment. Burton v. Town of Littleton, 426 F.3d 9, 14-19 (1st Cir. 2005) (holding that a school superintendent's allegedly false and defamatory statement to the commissioner, recounting that the teacher's employment was terminated because she hit a student, was not sufficiently disseminated to the public to trigger constitutional liberty protections because it was part of a personnel document and not a public record, and under state law could not be publicly disclosed). The opinion also notes, importantly for the purposes of this survey, that the degree of "dissemination" required to establish a constitutional infringement of plaintiff's liberty interest is higher than the mere "publication" sufficient to support a common-law defamation claim.

Note that in certain cases, statements to government regulators may be protected as exercise of the defendant's right of petition, defined broadly in the Massachusetts Anti-SLAPP Act, G.L. c. 231, § 59H. See, e.g., Kalter v. Wood, 67 Mass. App. Ct. 584, 855 N.E.2d 421 (2006) (assuming, without deciding, that letter to police and to local licensing authority were exercises of right of petition, but that grievance letter to medical insurance carrier heavily regulated by the state was not). See also Sklar v. Beth Israel Deaconess Med. Ctr., 59 Mass. App. Ct. 550, 558 n.10 (2003) (dismissing plaintiff's defamation claim on other grounds, and therefore declining to rule on defendant's claim that hospital's reporting of negative peer audit to licensing authorities was protected under the Anti-SLAPP Act); but see Moriarty v. Mayor of Holyoke, 71 Mass. App. Ct. 442 (Mass. App. Ct. 2008) (holding that protections of Anti-SLAPP statute do not extend to government workers acting on behalf of the government, not as private citizens).

F. Reports to Auditors and Insurers

The proceedings, reports, and records of medical peer review committees, which hospitals are statutorily mandated to establish, are confidential and may not be introduced in court, and those who participate in good faith in the peer review proceedings are immunized from liability by statute. Mass. Gen. Laws c. 111, § 203(c), 204(a). For that reason, a medical center's letter summarily suspending a physician's privileges, which was part of the peer review process, cannot form the basis of a defamation claim. Vranos v. Skinner, 77 Mass. App. Ct. 280, 293, 930 N.E.2d 156, 167 (Mass. App. Ct. 2010). Nor can such a claim proceed based on the fact of suspension itself, because a trial on such a claim would be "fundamentally antithetical" to the peer review statute, and the unavailability at trail of documents explaining the suspension might create "erratic results." Id., 77 Mass. App. Ct. at 295-96, 930 N.E.2d at 168-69.

G. Vicarious Liability of Employers for Statements Made by Employees

1. ***Scope of Employment.*** If a defamatory statement is made by employees in the course of their employment, the employer will be subject to liability. Galvin v. New York, New Haven & Hartford Railroad, 341 Mass. 293, 296, 168 N.E.2d 262 (1960). The employer may also be liable for an employee's actions outside the scope of employment if the employer ratifies the actions. Pinshaw v. Metropolitan Dist. Comm'n, 33 Mass. App. Ct. 733, 735, 604 N.E.2d 1321 (1992), quoted in Feehily v. Muzi Motors, Inc., 79 Mass. App. Ct. 1116 (2011) (unpublished disposition pursuant to Rule 1:28). See, e.g., Murphy v. Boston Herald, 449 Mass. 42, 64 n.22, 865 N.E.2d 746, 763 n.22, 35 Media L. Rep. (2007) ("Where an article is written within the scope of a reporter's employment, his 'state of mind' may be imputed to his employer for purposes of liability"); Stone v. Essex County Newspapers, Inc., 367 Mass. 849, 868, 330 N.E.2d 161 (1975); cf. Netherwood v. American Fed'n of State, County and Municipal Employees, Local 1725, 53 Mass. App. Ct. 11, 22, 757 N.E.2d 257, 267 (2001) (suggesting that because business agent was authorized by union to send allegedly defamatory letter, union could be liable). A newspaper was found liable for its employee's statements on a television talk show, where the appearance was made with the approval and encouragement of his editors, and the discussion was about articles the employee published in the newspaper. Murphy, 449 Mass. at 69, 865 N.E.2d at 766 (Mass. 2007).

An agent's conduct is within the scope of employment under Massachusetts law if (1) "it is of the kind he is employed to perform"; (2) "it occurs substantially within the authorized time and space limits"; and (3) "it is motivated, at least in part, by a purpose to serve the employer." Worcester Ins. Co. v. Fells Acres Day Sch., Inc., 408 Mass. 393, 404, 558 N.E.2d 958 (1990), quoted in Feehily v. Muzi Motors, Inc., 79 Mass. App. Ct. 1116 (2011) (unpublished disposition pursuant to Rule 1:28); Kelly v. United States, 924 F.2d 355, 357 (1st Cir. 1991), quoted in Strunk v. Odyssey Consulting Group, Ltd., No. 10-12174-DJC, 2011 WL 3567025, *4 (D. Mass. Aug. 11, 2011); see also Operation Rescue National v. United States, 975 F. Supp. 92 (D. Mass. 1997), aff'd on other grounds, 147 F.3d 68 (1st Cir. 1998); Arsenault v. Allegheny Airlines, Inc., 485 F. Supp. 1373, 1378 n.5 (D. Mass. 1980), aff'd, 636 F.2d 1199 (1st Cir. 1980), cert. denied, 454 U.S. 821 (1981). As to prong one, an individual supervisor who badmouths a former employee to prospective employers is not engaged in conduct "of the kind he is employed to perform" where an employee handbook specifically limited reference inquiries to the company's human resources department. Feehily v. Muzi Motors, Inc., 79 Mass. App. Ct. 1116 (2011) (unpublished disposition pursuant to Rule 1:28). As to prongs two and three, an employee normally is acting within the scope of employment unless he "acts from purely personal motives ... in no way connected with the employer's interest." Pinshaw v. Metro Dist. Comm'n, 402 Mass. 687, 694-95, 524 N.E.2d 1351 (1988), quoted in Strunk, supra at *4. Employees who had authority to fire an employee acted within the scope of their employment when they told the plaintiff the grounds for their wanting to discharge him. Ezekiel v. Jones Motor Co., Inc., 374 Mass. 382, 391, 372 N.E.2d 1281 (1978). See also Bander, 313 Mass. at 348 (employer liable when employee acting under apparent authority).

An individual supervisor – like the individual publisher of a newspaper – will not be liable for the statements of employees absent evidence that the supervisor had "control over or knowledge of the contents" of the defamatory communication "or of the editorial process." Reilly v. Associated Press, 59 Mass. App. Ct. 764, 764 n.1, 797 N.E.2d 1204, 1204 n.1 (2003); see also Burns v. Potter, 334 F. Supp. 2d 13, (D. Mass. 2004) (finding U.S. Postmaster General could not be held liable for alleged defamation by local postmaster); Smith v. City of Boston, et al., 2004 U.S. Dist. LEXIS 13062, *24-25 (D. Mass. July 13, 2004) (commissioner of inspectional services not liable for alleged defamation by unnamed "city official" in newspaper article, particularly where there is no evidence that commissioner spoke to the newspaper or directed the information to be released).

Under the Federal Tort Claims Act (FTCA), 28 U.S.C. §§ 1346(b), 2671-2680, as amended in 1988 by the Westfall Act, see 28 U.S.C. §§ 2679(b)(1) and 2679(d), federal employees are absolutely immune from common law tort suits for acts they committed within the scope of their employment. Strunk v. Odyssey Consulting Group, Ltd., No. 10-12174-DJC, 2011 WL 3567025, *3 (D. Mass. Aug. 11, 2011). Once the Attorney General certifies that conduct occurred within the scope of a federal employee's employment, the United States is substituted as defendant – a substitution that is conclusive for purposes of removal but otherwise subject to substantive challenge. Id. (holding that plaintiff failed to meet burden of proving that federal employee's statements were made outside course of employment, and therefore also failed in his challenge to government's certification and substitution as defendant), citing Davric Me. Corp. v. United States Postal Serv., 238 F.3d 58, 65 (1st Cir. 2001). Although in many cases such suits may still proceed against the federal government, the Westfall Act contains exceptions (at 28 U.S.C. § 2680(h)) that "preserve[] the United States' sovereign immunity from suits for defamation and other specified torts," including tortious interference with advantageous or contractual relations, and therefore such tort claims must be dismissed entirely. Strunk, 2011 WL 3567025, at *3, *6; see also Davric, 238 F.3d at 64; **Radakovic v. U.S. Office of Personnel Management, 2012 WL 1900037 (D. Mass. May 23, 2012) (libel and slander claims not recognized under FTCA); see also Barrows v. Wareham Fire Dist., 82 Mass. App. Ct. 623, 630 n.9, -- N.E.2d -- (2012) (noting that FTCA exempts "all varieties of slander and libel from suit").** Similarly, the Massachusetts Tort Claims Act, Mass. Gen. Laws c. 258, § 2, allows claims against public employers for the "negligent or wrongful acts or omissions of their employees acting within the scope of their employment," but expressly exempts "any claim arising out of an intentional tort, including … libel [and] slander…," Mass. Gen. Laws c. 258, § 10(c). **In Barrows, 82 Mass. App. Ct. at 630, the Appeals Court rejected an argument that a defamation claim based upon a public employee's merely "reckless," rather than "intentional," conduct would not fall into the exemption. That is because "the nature of the wrong in a defamation of a private party is unrelated to the defendant's intentions or his degree of malice"; "[i]ntent is presumed, or, at a minimum, responsibility and liability is imputed as if intent was manifest, even when publication is negligently or carelessly effectuated." Id., citing In re Pereira, 44 B.R. 248, 252 (Bankr. D. Mass. 1984). (The Appeals Court's ruling appears to put the kibosh to a detailed Superior Court analysis only three months earlier, which had held that a private-figure libel claim against a municipality could proceed because it was grounded in negligence and therefore not an "intentional" tort. See Haney v. City of Boston, 2012 WL 3144816 (Mass. Super. Ct. July 30, 2012).)**

Municipalities cannot be held liable for constitutional torts under 42 U.S.C. §1983 based upon the theory of respondeat superior. A municipality may be sued only for its own unconstitutional or illegal policies. Berard v. Town of Millville, 113 F. Supp. 2d 197 (D. Mass. 2000) (no municipal liability under §1983 for allegedly defamatory statements of police chief where complaint did not allege the existence of any relevant custom or policy of town). A plaintiff must show that "the action that is alleged to be unconstitutional implements or executes a policy statement, ordinance, regulation, or decision officially adopted and promulgated by the [municipality's] officers [or is] pursuant to governmental 'custom.'" Id., quoting Monell v. Dept. of Social Services, 436 U.S. 658, 690 (1978).

a. **Blogging.** In its first encounter with the doctrine of third-party immunity under Section 230 of the Communications Decency Act (CDA), 47 U.S.C. § 230, the First Circuit Court of Appeals joined other circuits that have construed the Act "broadly," and had "no trouble" determining that operators of the Raging Bull web site were immune from liability for posts to its message board. Universal Communication Systems, Inc., et al. v. Lycos, Inc., et al., 478 F.3d 413, 35 Media L. Rep. 1417 (1st Cir. 2007). Section 230(c) of the Communications Decency Act does not, however, prevent a jury from considering comments by third parties, posted on a libel defendant's website, when assessing damages resulting from the defamatory statement on the site. Murphy v. Boston Herald, 449 Mass. 42, 67 n.24, 865 N.E.2d 746, 765 n.24, 35 Media L. Rep. 1865 (2007).

Anonymous internet speech received notable protection from the federal district court in Massachusetts, which recognized that the issue was one of First Amendment dimension. In McMann v. Doe, 2006 U.S. Dist. LEXIS 80112 (D. Mass. Oct. 31, 2006), Judge Tauro offered two independent bases for dismissing the claim of a Massachusetts real estate developer concerned about a website named after him (www.paulmcmann.com) and containing sparse but ominous comment: that McMann "turned lives upside down," that others should "be afraid, be very afraid," and that further specific facts would be forthcoming. Addressing an issue of first impression in the First Circuit, the court ruled that in a non-federal question case against an anonymous defendant, diversity of parties cannot be presumed. 2006 U.S. Dist. LEXIS 80112 at *10-11. (It so ruled despite the 1988 amendment of the removal statute, allowing removal of cases where some defendants are sued under fictitious names.) Lack of jurisdiction, however, did not prevent the court from opining that even if there were jurisdiction, the plaintiff's claim would not survive summary judgment because the speech at issue did not state or imply false facts. 2006 U.S. Dist. LEXIS 80112 at *26.

2. ***Damages.*** See III.G.1, supra. The above-cited cases presume that an employer held vicariously liable for an employee's defamation is responsible for the damages awarded. Punitive damages are unavailable under Massachusetts law. G.L. c. 231, § 93; Stone v. Essex County Newspapers, Inc., 367 Mass. 849, 860, 861, 330 N.E.2d 161 (1975). See I.B.8.b, supra.

H. Internal Investigations

Statements made in the context of an internal investigation or a disciplinary hearing are protected by a conditional privilege. LeBoeuf v. Stevens, No. 97-1133A, 11 Mass. L. Rep. 585, 2000 Mass. Super. LEXIS 107 (Worcester Super. Ct. April 6, 2000). See also LeBlanc v. Digital Equipment Corp., No. 91-40152, 1996 Mass. Super. LEXIS 582, *14-17 (Worcester Super. Ct. March 25, 1996) (noting that "intracompany communications" in the course of a theft investigation and afterwards, to inform those in terminated employee's department that he would no longer be working there, and to let workers know that the company's rules had been enforced, particularly where the terminated employee was a supervisor, are conditionally privileged). In investigation cases, the privilege protects even statements made by a fellow employee during the investigation conducted at plaintiff's request. See Beriont v. Reichlen, 2000 WL 33170693, 3, No. 994486 (Mass. Super. Ct. Nov. 6, 2000) ("The protection afforded the employer must necessarily extend to the employees being interviewed directly by the employer in the context of the plaintiff's request for an investigation"); Williams v. Brigham & Women's Hospital, Inc., 2002 WL 532979, *6, 14 Mass. L. Rptr. 438 (Mass. Super. 2002) (applying conditional privilege to statements regarding employee's alleged check-cashing scheme made to investigators and supervisory personnel because employer had legitimate interest in determining whether one of its employees was involved in passing fraudulent checks).

In Cornwell v. Dairy Farmers of America, Inc., 369 F. Supp. 2d 87 (D. Mass. 2005), an employee of a food brokerage reported to her supervisor, as well as to supervisors at the food manufacturer with which her brokerage did business, that a salesman for the manufacturer had made certain specific inappropriate and sexually suggestive comments. She repeated her comments in the course of an internal investigation by the manufacturer, which resulted in the salesman's termination. After the salesman sued for defamation, the federal district court dismissed his claims on summary judgment, finding that the brokerage employee's comments were conditionally privileged under the business interest and common interest privileges. Id. at 110-112. A police officer suing for defamation over a union president's allegations that she lied during an internal investigation must show actual malice in order to prevail, because she is a public official and the allegations relate to her official conduct. Dixon v. International Br'hood of Police Officers, No. 06-1210 et seq., 2007 U.S. App. LEXIS 22891 (1st Cir. Sept. 28, 2007).

The Supreme Judicial Court affirmed dismissal of an Episcopal priest's defamation claims arising out of a parishioner's allegations, made to the church's Bishop, that the priest had engaged in a sexual relationship with her. The court ruled that the claim was barred by the Constitutional right to free exercise of religion, because it "touches the core of the church-minister relationship" and because the "First Amendment's protection of internal religious disciplinary proceedings would be meaningless if a parishioner's accusation that was used to initiate those proceedings could be tested in a civil court." Hiles v. Episcopal Diocese of Massachusetts, et al., 437 Mass. 505, 511-15, 773 N.E.2d 929, 935-38 (2002). **A police chief's directive that a police officer not discuss a pending internal investigation of that officer was not a violation of the officer's First Amendment rights, where it was narrowly drawn and a rational measure to protect the integrity of the investigation. Jones v. Scotti, No. 11-2213, 2012 WL 4373655 (1st Cir. Sept. 26, 2012) (unpublished).**

IV. OTHER ACTIONS BASED ON STATEMENTS

A. Negligent Hiring, Retention, and Supervision

Massachusetts recognizes a cause of action for negligent hiring or negligent retention of an employee by an employer. Carson v. Canning, 180 Mass. 461, 62 N.E. 964 (1902). In Carson, a plaintiff was allowed to recover in negligence against a pawn broker whose manager absconded with pledged property. The theory of recovery was that "the manager was an unfit person for his trust and that the defendant could and would have found that out if he had used ordinary care." Foster v. The Loft, Inc., 26 Mass. App. Ct. 289, 290, 526 N.E.2d 1309, rev. granted, 403 Mass. 1102, 529 N.E.2d 1345 (1988). Under this doctrine, "an employer whose employees are brought in contact with members of the public in the course of the employer's business has a duty to exercise reasonable care in the selection and retention of his employees." Foster, 26 Mass. App. Ct. at 290; Doyle v. Hasbro, Inc., 884 F. Supp. 35, 42 (D. Mass. 1995). An employer must use due care to avoid selecting or retaining an employee who he should know "is a person unworthy, by habits, temperament, or nature, to deal with the persons invited to the premises by the employer." Annotation, Liability of Employer, Other Than Carrier, For a Personal Assault Upon Customer, Patron, or Other Invitee, 34 A.L.R.2d 372, 390 (1954), quoted in Foster, 26 Mass. App. Ct. at 291. Knowledge of "past acts of impropriety, violence or disorder" by the employee is generally sufficient to forewarn a propensity for assault, for example, "although not every infirmity of character, such, for example, as dishonesty or querulousness, will lead to such result." Id.

"'Negligent retention . . . occurs when, during the course of employment, the employer becomes aware or should have become aware of problems with an employee that indicated his unfitness, and the employer fails to take further action such as investigating, discharge or reassignment.'" Foster, 26 Mass. App. Ct. at 291, quoting Garcia v. Duffy, 492 So. 2d 435, 438-39 (Fla. Dist. Ct. App. 1986). This liability is independent of any liability on the part of the employer under the principles of respondeat superior. Foster, 26 Mass. App. Ct. at 291 n.4. But see Ball v. Wal-Mart, Inc., 102 F. Supp. 2d 44, 54 (D. Mass. 2000) (claim of negligent retention fails where plaintiff has submitted no evidence to suggest that Wal-Mart knew or had reason to know of any condition which rendered the retained employee unfit).

Massachusetts courts have declined to extend the tort to cover: claims of negligent supervision based on allegations that employees extorted kickbacks from a trucking company, Doyle v. Hasbro, Inc., 884 F. Supp. 35, 42 (D. Mass. 1995); "negligent discharge" of an employee who had allegedly received negligent supervision and training, Schnurbush v. Boston Gas Co., No. 91-15, slip op. at 9 (Essex Super. Ct. Nov. 25, 1992) (Flannery, J.), aff'd without opinion, 36 Mass. App. Ct. 1112, 633 N.E.2d 444 (1994); and a claim of negligent investigation of theft allegations against an employee, O'Connell v. Bank of Boston, 37 Mass. App. Ct. 416, 419, 640 N.E.2d 513 (1994), rev. denied, 419 Mass. 1104, 646 N.E.2d 409 (1995) (dismissing on the grounds that the employer owed its former employee no duty regarding the investigation). The Appeals Court in O'Connell also held that to the extent the investigated employee suffers an injury, that injury is compensable under the doctrine of malicious prosecution. 37 Mass. App. Ct. at 419-420.

The Massachusetts Workers' Compensation Act bars common law claims for personal injuries that are based on an employer's negligent hiring, retention, or supervision of a co-worker or employee. Green v. Wyman-Gordon Co., 422 Mass. 551, 664 N.E.2d 808 (1996); Clarke v. Kentucky Fried Chicken of California, Inc., 57 F.3d 21, 28-29 (1st Cir. 1995); Galdauckas v. Interstate Hotels Corp. No. 16, 901 F. Supp. 454, 469-70 (D. Mass. 1995); Choroszy v. Wentworth Inst. of Tech., 915 F. Supp. 446, 452-53 (D. Mass. 1996); Ruffino v. State Street Bank & Trust Co., 908 F. Supp. 1019, 1052 (D. Mass. 1995).

Claims for municipal liability under the Federal Civil Rights Act can succeed only if the plaintiff can show that the municipality itself has caused a constitutional violation by "the existence of a policy or custom [that caused the plaintiff's injury] and a causal link between that policy and the constitutional harm" suffered by the plaintiff. Nolan v. Krajcik, 384 F. Supp. 2d 447, 471 (D. Mass. 2005). See also III.G.1, supra. A lack of police training may support §1983 liability "only where the failure to train amounts to deliberate indifference to the rights of persons with whom the police come into contact." Id., quoting Canton v. Harris, 489 U.S. 378, 388 (1989).

B. Intentional Infliction of Emotional Distress

To prevail on a claim for intentional infliction of emotional distress, "a plaintiff must show (1) that the defendant intended to cause, or should have known that his conduct would cause, emotional distress; (2) that the defendant's conduct was extreme and outrageous; (3) that the defendant's conduct caused the plaintiff's distress; and (4) that the plaintiff suffered severe distress." Sena v. Commonwealth, 417 Mass. 250, 263-64, 629 N.E.2d 986, 993 (1994), quoted in North Shore Pharmacy Services, Inc., et al. v. Breslin Assocs. Consulting, 491 F. Supp. 2d 111, 132 (D. Mass. 2007). **Where such a claim is based on the publication of statements that are not actionably false and defamatory, then, as a matter of law, "the defendants' conduct in publishing the statements was not 'extreme and outrageous,' 'beyond all possible bounds of decency,' or 'utterly intolerable in a civilized community.'" Boyle v. Cape Cod Times, No. 11-P-96, 81 Mass. App. Ct. 1107, 959 N.E.2d 457, 2012 WL 28661, *2 n.3 (Jan. 6, 2012), citing Howell v. Enterprise Publishing Co., LLC, 455 Mass. 641, 672 (2010).** The tort is not limited to cases involving bodily harm, North Shore Pharmacy Services, 491 F. Supp. 2d 111, 134, citing Migliori v. Airborne Freight Corp., 426 Mass. 629, 632 n.2, 690 N.E.2d 413, 415 n.2 (1998).

The threshold for an intentional infliction claim is "quite demanding." Miller v. Tope, No. 02-11151-DPW, 2003 U.S. Dist. LEXIS 21211, 60-61 (D. Mass. Nov. 24, 2003) (holding that more than "mere insults, indignities, threats" must be shown, and even tortious or criminal intent alone is not sufficient). "[I]nsults and criticisms are not considered tortious conduct," Testaverde v. Massachusetts Teachers Ass'n, No. 97-P-2092, slip op. at 6 (Mass. App. Ct. April 24, 2000), and "an atrocity is something more than a faulty evaluation," Chakrabarti v. Cohen, 31 F.3d 1, 6 (1st Cir. 1994). Summary judgment may be granted for the defendant where these elements cannot be met as a matter of law. See Bianchi v. Commonwealth Childcare Corp., et al., 2000 WL 1508175 (Mass. Super. Ct. 2000) (former employer's response to a prospective employer's reference form, in which the employer checked off "poor" in rating the employee's "emotional stability," cannot be held to be so extreme and outrageous as to be beyond all possible bounds of decency and utterly intolerable in a civilized society); Panse v. Norman, 2005 U.S. Dist. LEXIS 20272 (D. Mass. 2005) (not enough that defendants may not have fully executed their duties to plaintiff and may have had improper motive). **Still, even the high threshold was met by a claim that an employer accessed and disseminated personal emails between two employees that contained details of their sexual relationship, with the result that they suffered mental anguish and severe psychological injuries. Coughlin v. Town of Arlington, No. 10-102013-MLW, 2011 WL 6370932, *16-17 (D. Mass. Dec. 19, 2011) (denying motion to dismiss).**

In those rare cases where plaintiff has submitted sufficient admissible evidence to warrant jury findings "both that the defendants' conduct was extreme and outrageous and that it had a 'severe and traumatic effect upon [plaintiff's] emotional tranquility,'" then summary judgment should not be allowed. Tech Plus, Inc. v. Ansel, 59 Mass. App. Ct. 12, 26, 793 N.E.2d

1256, 1268 (2003) (allowing intentional infliction claim to go forward where defendant said plaintiff was anti-Semitic and had persecuted defendant because of his Jewish heritage). In North Shore Pharmacy Services, Inc., et al. v. Breslin Assocs. Consulting, 491 F. Supp. 2d 111, 132-33 (D. Mass. 2007), the federal district court allowed an intentional infliction claim to proceed to trial where it was founded on "a pattern of conduct amounting to a concerted effort to drive [the plaintiff] out of business" by taking steps "designed to destroy plaintiff's reputation and business prospects," including by disparaging the plaintiff to his client. (One can imagine that the court's finding of "extreme and outrageous" conduct in North Shore Pharmacy Services may have been influenced by the fact that after bringing his claim, the plaintiff had committed suicide, allegedly as a result of the defendant's harassment.)

To state a claim for negligent infliction of emotional distress, a plaintiff must show: (1) negligence; (2) emotional distress; (3) causation; (4) physical harm manifested by objective symptomatology; and (5) that a reasonable person would have suffered emotional distress under the circumstances of the case. Sullivan v. Boston Gas Co., 414 Mass. 129, 132-33, 605 N.E.2d 805 (1993), quoting Payton v. Abbott Labs, 386 Mass. 540, 547 (1982). For such a claim to proceed to trial, "it is fundamentally necessary that the defendants have failed without excuse to fulfill a [tort-based] duty of care that was owed." Lovitz v. Brown, No. 06-12245, 2007 U.S. Dist. LEXIS 28998, *2-3 (D. Mass. April 20, 2007). The claim also requires "some objective evidence of physical harm." Lane v. MPG Newspapers, 438 Mass. 476, 478 n.5, 781 N.E.2d 800, 803 n.5, 31 Media L. Rep. 1279 (2003). To show physical harm, plaintiff must show at least "objective corroboration of the emotional distress alleged," Payton, 386 Mass. at 547, and may need expert testimony, Sullivan, 414 Mass. at 137. A plaintiff (herself a physician) defeated defendant's summary judgment motion by proffering an affidavit stating symptoms induced by the stress she suffered. Miller v. Tope, No. 02-11151-DPW, 2003 U.S. Dist. LEXIS 21211, *59-60 (D. Mass. Nov. 24, 2003). Damages for negligent infliction of emotional distress may be limited to what a "reasonable" person would have experienced under the circumstances. North Shore Pharmacy Services, Inc., et al. v. Breslin Assocs. Consulting, 491 F. Supp. 2d 111, 133 n.11 (D. Mass. 2007).

Claims for intentional infliction of emotional distress, when asserted by an employee against an employer, are typically barred by the exclusivity provision of the Massachusetts Workers' Compensation Act, G.L. c. 152, § 24. Andresen v. Diorio, 349 F.3d 8, 15-16 (1st Cir. 2003); Foley v. Polaroid Corp., 381 Mass. 545, 413 N.E.2d 711 (1980); Green v. Wyman-Gordon Co., 422 Mass. 551, 558 (1996) (exclusivity provision bars claims for intentional and negligent infliction); Doe v. Purity Supreme, 422 Mass. 563, 664 N.E.2d 815 (1996). But see Bowman, 420 Mass. 517 (workers' compensation bar not raised or discussed). Claims for negligent infliction of emotional distress are similarly barred. Green, 422 Mass. at 558-61; Winsmann v. Choate Health Management, Inc., 8 Mass. L. Rptr. 480, 1998 WL 282901, 1998 Mass. Super. LEXIS 93 (Super. Ct. 1998) (dismissing negligent infliction claim). However, post-termination misconduct by an employer against its discharged employee is not subject to the bar. Mello v. Stop & Shop Cos., 402 Mass. 555, 524 N.E.2d 105 (1988). Also, a direct suit against a co-worker or supervisor who intentionally inflicted emotional distress, while acting outside the scope of employment, may proceed. O'Connell v. Chasdi, 400 Mass. 686, 690, 511 N.E.2d 349 (1987).

Where a defamation claim is barred by a conditional privilege, so is a claim for intentional infliction of emotional distress. Howell v. Enterprise Publishing Co., LLC, 455 Mass. 641, 672 (2010); Correllas v. Viveiros, 410 Mass. 314, 324, 572 N.E.2d 7 (1991) ("A privilege which protected an individual from liability for defamation would be of little value if the individual were subject to liability under a different theory of tort"); Meltzer v. Grant, 193 F. Supp.2d 373, 377-381 (D. Mass. 2002) (applying Massachusetts law). Cf. Zajac v. Zajac, 2007 Mass. Super. LEXIS 336, *12-14 (Worc. Super. Ct. Aug. 16, 2007) (denying motion to dismiss claims of intentional and negligent infliction of emotional distress based on wife's report to police of claims that her husband acted abusively; court refused to dismiss defamation claims based on the same conduct, finding that the wife's report was only conditionally privileged and that the husband had sufficiently alleged facts to defeat the privilege). Similarly, a public official cannot succeed on a claim of intentional infliction of emotional distress based on a publication, without a showing of constitutional malice. See Lane v. MPG Newspapers, 438 Mass. 476, 478 n.5, 781 N.E.2d 800, 803 n.5, 31 Media L. Rep. 1279 (2003), citing Hustler Magazine, Inc. v. Falwell, 485 U.S. 46, 56 (1988).). By statute, the Commonwealth of Massachusetts is immune from being sued in the state courts for intentional infliction of emotional distress, Mass. G.L. c. 258, § 10(c), **even though the tort can be proved by "reckless" or "wanton" misconduct. Barrows v. Wareham Fire Dist., 82 Mass. App. Ct. 623, 627 n.3, -- N.E.2d – (2012), citing Tilton v. Franklin, 24 Mass. App. Ct. 110, 112, 506 N.E.2d 897 (1987)**. However, the statute does not bar such a claim against an individual public official. Anzalone v. Administrative Office of Trial Court, 457 Mass. 647, 660, 932 N.E.2d 774, 785 (2010), citing South Boston Betterment Trust Corp. v. Boston Redevelopment Auth., 438 Mass. 57, 69, 777 N.E.2d 812 (2002).

C. Interference with Economic Advantage

To succeed on an employment-based claim for intentional interference with advantageous relations in Massachusetts, a plaintiff must show that "(1) she had an advantageous employment relationship with her employer; (2) the defendant knowingly induced the employer to break that relationship; (3) the defendant's interference, in addition to being intentional, was improper in motive or means; and (4) the employee was harmed by the defendant's actions." Weber v.

Community Teamwork, Inc., 434 Mass. 761, 781, 752 N.E.2d 700 (2001); Anzalone v. Administrative Office of Trial Court, 457 Mass. 647, 660, 932 N.E.2d 774, 785 (2010); Ayash v. Dana-Farber Cancer Institute, et al., 443 Mass. 367, 394, 822 N.E.2d 667, 690, 33 Media L. Rep. 1513 (2005); Sklar v. Beth Israel Deaconess Medical Center, 59 Mass. App. Ct. 550, 554 (2003). See also Tuli v. Brigham & Women's Hosp., 656 F.3d 33, 43 (2011) ("Under Massachusetts law, the elements are a known advantageous relationship such as employment…; deliberate interference, improper in motive or means; and resulting economic harm."); North Shore Pharmacy Services, Inc., et al. v. Breslin Assocs. Consulting, 491 F. Supp. 2d 111. 129 (D. Mass. 2007). The same elements apply when the claim is one for tortious interference with contract. Psy-Ed Corp. v. Klein, 459 Mass. 697, 715, 716, 947 N.E.2d 520, 536, 537 (2011) (noting also that party cannot tortiously interfere with a contract to which he is a party); G.S. Enters., Inc. v. Falmouth Marine, Inc., 410 Mass. 262, 272, 571 N.E.2d 1363 (1991). **"Defamation constitutes improper means." O'Brien v. Chretien, No. 11-P-2092, 82 Mass. App. Ct. 1117, 976 N.E.2d 214 (Mass. App. Ct. Oct. 23, 2012) (unpublished),** citing Cavicchi v. Koski, 67 Mass. App. Ct. 654, 658, 855 N.Ed. 2d 1137 (2006).

An important additional requirement applies "in the employment and discharge context" when the defendant is a corporate official acting in the scope of his corporate responsibilities. There, unlike in other tortious interference cases, under Massachusetts law "a plaintiff has a heightened burden of showing the improper motive or means constituted 'actual malice,' that is, 'a spiteful, malignant purpose, unrelated to the legitimate corporate interest,'" Psy-Ed Corp. v. Klein, 459 Mass. 697, 716, 947 N.E.2d 520, 536 (2011), and was the "'controlling factor' in the defendant's interference." Sklar, 59 Mass. App. Ct. at 554, citing Weber v. Cmty. Teamwork, Inc., 434 Mass. 761, 752 N.E.2d 700, 716 (2001); Tuli, 656 F.3d at 43 & n.8. That is because a supervisor, acting in the context of his or her employment, is otherwise privileged to interfere with an employee's advantageous relationship. Sklar, 59 Mass. App. Ct. at 554. Note that although they use the term "actual malice," the courts in Ayash, Sklar, and Weber are in fact referring not to constitutional "actual malice" as defined in New York Times Co. v. Sullivan, 376 U.S. 254, 279-80, 1 Media L. Rep. 1527 (1964), but instead to "malevolence," Ayash, 443 Mass. at 395, or "a 'spiteful, malignant purpose, unrelated to the legitimate corporate interest' of the employer," Weber, 434 Mass. at 782, and Ayash, 443 Mass. at 395, both quoting Boothby v. Texon, Inc., 414 Mass. 468, 487, 608 N.E.2d 1028 (1993); see also Tuli, 656 F.3d at 43, quoting King v. Driscoll, 418 Mass. 576, 638 N.E.2d 488, 494-95 (1994); Anzalone, supra, citing Sereni v. Star Sportswear Mfg. Corp., 24 Mass. App. Ct. 428, 433, 509 N.E.2d 1203 (1987), "or put differently, was personally hostile or harbored ill will toward the plaintiff," Sklar, 59 Mass. App. Ct. at 554-55. See also Brisson v. City of New Bedford, et al., 2005 U.S. Dist. LEXIS 26280, *35-36 (D. Mass. Oct. 31, 2005) ("The requisite 'malice' in this context is 'a spiteful, malignant purpose, unrelated to the legitimate corporate interest of the employer.'"). The additional level of protection provided by the malice/ill will requirement "seeks to protect a corporate official's freedom of action," Alba v. Simpson, 44 Mass. App. Ct. 311, 314, 690 N.E.2d 1240, aff'd, 427 Mass. 1104 (1998), since a supervisor, "in the context of his or her employment, is privileged to interfere with the employee's advantageous relationship." Sklar, 59 Mass. App. Ct. at 554. See also Beriont v. Reichlen, 2000 WL 33170693, *4 (Mass. Super. Ct. Nov. 6, 2000). Such ill will is demonstrated where a supervisor screamed at and insulted the plaintiff employee daily, O'Brien v. New England Tel. & Tel. Co., 422 Mass. 686, 690, 664 N.E.2d 843 (1996), threatened physical violence against and publicly slandered the plaintiff, Clement v. Rev-Lyn Constr. Co., 40 Mass. App. Ct. 322, 325, 663 N.E.2d 1235 (1996), or gave contradictory accounts about plaintiff's performance and demonstrated ill will toward her, Miller v. Tope, No. 02-11151-DPW, 2003 U.S. Dist. LEXIS 21211, *39-50, 62 (D. Mass. Nov. 24, 2003). Malice can also be proved by inference, but only if plaintiff can produce admissible evidence to show more than mere adverse impact, as well as a link between the defendant's conduct and the evidence of hostility or spite. Sklar, 59 Mass. App. Ct. at 555, 556. A complaint that merely invokes such phrases as "unconscionable," "irreparable harm," and "wrongful interference," without more, is not enough, because "[a]n act or omission may be wrongful, and a delay may be unconscionable, without necessarily being malicious"). Anzalone v. Administrative Office of Trial Court, 457 Mass. 647, 660-61, 932 N.E.2d 774, 785-86 (2010). Similarly, "personal dislike alone will not warrant an inference of the requisite ill will." King v. Driscoll, 418 Mass. 576, 587 (1994), and "a reasonable measure undertaken on behalf of the company by a supervisor" will not be "tainted merely because the supervisor also disliked the employee," Tuli v. Brigham & Women's Hosp., 656 F.3d 33, 43 (1st Cir. 2011), discussing Boothby v. Texon, Inc., 414 Mass. 468, 608 N.E.2d 1028, 1040 (1993). A "negligent, sloppy, or callous investigation" does not necessarily lead to an inference of the necessary spite or personal hostility. Sklar, 59 Mass. App. Ct. at 556, nor does a course of action that is "ill considered or short sighted," Psy-Ed Corp. v. Klein, 459 Mass. 697, 719, 947 N.E.2d 520, 538-39 (2011); but see Tuli, 656 F.3d at 44 (holding that Weber v. Cmty. Teamwork, Inc., 434 Mass 761, 752 N.E.2d 700, 715-16 (2001) "did not say and could not mean that improper business behavior is inherently non-malicious and can never amount to wrongful interference").

In a non-supervisory context, where a defendant's defamation of the plaintiff has caused the breach of contract or severing of advantageous relations, the necessary "improper means" has been shown. United Truck Leasing Corp., 406 Mass. at 817; Cavicchi v. Koski, 67 Mass. App. Ct. 654, 658, 855 N.E.2d 1137 (2006). See also Testaverde v. Massachusetts Teachers Ass'n, No. 97-P-2092, slip op. at 11, 49 Mass. App. Ct. 1106 (Mass. App. Ct. April 24, 2000) (unpublished). Likewise where plaintiff alleged that defendants not only defamed and refused to deal with the plaintiff, but also took steps to affirmatively preclude a third party from continuing to work with the plaintiff. North Shore Pharmacy Services, Inc., et al. v. Breslin Assocs. Consulting, 491 F. Supp. 2d 111, 129-30 (D. Mass. 2007) (noting that mere refusal to deal would not be enough).

The fourth prong – a showing of actual harm caused by the defendant's actions – requires "actual pecuniary loss as a result of the defendants' actions," and a showing of emotional distress and reputational harm is not enough. Tech Plus, Inc. v. Ansel, 59 Mass. App. Ct. 12, 19, 793 N.E.2d 1256, 1263 (2003) (affirming defendants' judgment notwithstanding the verdict on claims of intentional interference with existing and prospective business relations); see also Tuli v. Brigham & Women's Hosp., 656 F.3d 33, 44 (1st Cir. 2011) (affirming $20,000 jury verdict on intentional interference claim, where economic harm flowed from supervisor's failure to give plaintiff a performance evaluation; award corresponds to minimum percentage raise in base salary received by employees who received an evaluation); North Shore Pharmacy Services, Inc., et al. v. Breslin Assocs. Consulting, 491 F. Supp. 2d 111, 129-30 (D. Mass. 2007) (allowing claim to proceed where plaintiff alleged that future contract work was lost as a result of defendants' actions). This element of the claim will not be satisfied where the defendant merely made a complaint that led to an investigation that ultimately led to firing of the plaintiff. Netherwood v. Am. Fed'n of State, County and Munic. Employees, Local 1725, 53 Mass. App. Ct. 11, 22, 757 N.E.2d 257, 266 (2001) (noting that there were too many "significant intervening events" to permit a finding that actual harm "directly and proximately" resulted from the alleged defamation).

Where a conditional privilege applies, it bars not only defamation claims but also claims for intentional interference with contractual or advantageous relations, Thomas v. Sears, Roebuck & Co., 144 F.3d 31, 34 (1st Cir. 1998), unless plaintiff can establish that the defendants "acted 'out of a spiteful, malignant purpose that has no connection to the legitimate business interests of the employer.'" Cornwell v. Dairy Farmers of America, Inc., 369 F. Supp. 2d 87, 113 (D. Mass. 2005), quoting Petsch-Schmid v. Boston Edison Co., 914 F. Supp. 697, 706 (D. Mass. 1996). A claim of intentional interference with contract that depends entirely on allegations of defamation must be dismissed if the underlying defamation claim is dismissed. Fitzgerald v. Town of Kingston, 13 F. Supp. 2d 119, 127 (D. Mass. 1998); see also Cluff v. O'Halloran, 2000 WL 33115601, *9 (Mass. Super. Ct. Dec. 22, 2000) (granting summary judgment on interference claim where plaintiff failed to prove defamation or that defendant "acted for a spiteful purpose unrelated to her legitimate business interest"); Amrak Prod'ns, Inc. v. Morton, et al., 410 F.3d 69, 73 (1st Cir. 2005). By statute, G. L. c. 258, § 10(c), the Commonwealth of Massachusetts and state entities are immune from being sued in the state courts for interference with advantageous or contractual relations. Anzalone v. Administrative Office of Trial Court, 457 Mass. 647, 660-61, 932 N.E.2d 774, 785-86 (2010) (noting that AOTC, as a state entity, is immune). However, the statute does not bar such a claim against an individual public official. Id., citing South Boston Betterment Trust Corp. v. Boston Redevelopment Auth., 438 Mass. 57, 69, 777 N.E.2d 812 (2002).

D. Prima Facie Tort

Massachusetts does not appear to have recognized or discussed the doctrine of prima facie tort in any published decision.

E. Consumer Protection Act

The Massachusetts Consumer Protection Act, Gen. Laws c. 93A, § 11, does not apply to acts arising out of the employment relationship, Psy-Ed Corp. v. Klein, 459 Mass. 697, 704 n.18, 719, 947 N.E.2d 520, 528 n.18, 539 (2011), nor does it apply in a dispute between two joint venturers, Cavicchi v. Koski, 67 Mass. App. Ct. 654, 662, 855 N.E.2d 1137 (2006). Even where the claim does not arise out of the employment Relationship, the showing of a "loss of money or property" required as an element of a cause of action under § 11 is not demonstrated by a temporary loss of reputation unaccompanied by any "tangible economic harm or pecuniary loss as a result of the defendants' actions." Tech Plus, Inc. v. Ansel, 59 Mass. App. Ct. 12, 20-21, 793 N.E.2d 1256, 1264 (2003). However, such loss is sufficiently shown where a party "was forced to incur attorney's fees and other costs in defending ... a lawsuit" brought "to obtain commercial advantage." North Shore Pharmacy Services, Inc., et al. v. Breslin Assocs. Consulting, 491 F. Supp. 2d 111, 131-32 (D. Mass. 2007) (declining to grant summary judgment for defendant on Chapter 93A claim that "rests on ... claims for abuse of process, defamation and tortious interference"), quoting Tech Plus, 59 Mass. App. Ct. at 21, 793 N.E.2d at 1264 and Fafard Real Estate & Dev. Corp. v. Metro-Boston Broad., Inc., 345 F. Supp. 2d 147, 154 (D. Mass. 2004). Having dismissed a defamation claim, the First Circuit Court of Appeals had no trouble dismissing a "derivative" Chapter 93A claim arising out of the same facts. Amrak Prod'ns, Inc. v. Morton, et al., 410 F.3d 69, 73 (1st Cir. 2005).

F. Constitutional Defamation

The First Circuit Court of Appeals has recognized that a public employee may, under certain circumstances, have a cause of action against his employer if "the stigma surrounding [the employee's] termination foreclosed his opportunity to obtain other employment, thereby depriving him of a liberty interest and triggering the procedural due process requirements of the Fourteenth Amendment." Ortega-Rosario v. Alvarado-Ortiz, et al., 917 F.2d 71, 74 (1st Cir. 1990). Neither employment termination nor defamation, standing alone, will create a deprivation of liberty such as to invoke the right to a name-clearing hearing. Id.; see also Monahan v. Romney, 625 F.3d 42, 47-48 (1st Cir. 2010) (no deprivation of constitutionally protected liberty interest if alleged defamation did not occur in the course of employment termination), cert. denied, 131 S. Ct. 2895, 179 L. Ed. 2d 1190 (2011), citing Lyons v. Sullivan, 602 F.2d 7, 11 (1st Cir. 1979). Merely placing a pejorative memorandum in a public employee's personnel file is insufficient to trigger such protections; rather, the false and defamatory charges must have been "disseminated by the employer" and must "stigmatize the employee so that the employee's freedom to obtain alternative employment is significantly impaired." Id.

However, "'where a public-sector employer creates and disseminates a false and defamatory impression about an employee in connection with the employee's discharge,' the *Due Process Clause* 'requires the employer to provide the employee with an opportunity to dispute the defamatory allegations,' and the employer's failure to do so is actionable under §1983." Burton v. Town of Littleton, et al., 426 F.3d 9, 15 (1st Cir. 2005), quoting Wojcik v. Mass. State Lottery Comm'n, 300 F.3d 92, 103 (1st Cir. 2002). The federal district court found Due Process requirements satisfied where the plaintiff, ex-chair of the state Civil Service Commission, was afforded pre-deprivation process in the form of an extended conversation with the Governor and was entitled to adequate post-deprivation remedies under Massachusetts law. See Monahan v. Romney, 625 F.3d 42, 46 n.3 (1st Cir. 2010) (affirming district court on other grounds), cert. denied, 131 S. Ct. 2895, 179 L. Ed. 2d 1190 (2011). Wojcik establishes that such a claim exists only if the charge would "seriously damage" the employee's standing; its truth is disputed by the employee; it was made intentionally and "in a formal setting," and not merely as the result of unauthorized leaks; it was made in conjunction with "an alteration of the employee's legal status, such as the termination of his employment"; and the employee requested, but was denied, a name-clearing hearing. Id. (finding no deprivation where publication was a misinterpretation by media of employer's accurate statements).

Attempts to apply this constitutional theory to private employers have generally failed. The First Circuit Court of Appeals affirmed the summary judgment dismissal of a federal civil rights claim, under 42 U.S.C. §1983, against a police officer whose disparaging remarks about the plaintiff, published in a local newspaper, allegedly caused the plaintiff to be terminated from his job working for a private-sector employer. Pendleton v. City of Haverhill, 156 F.3d 57, 62-63, 26 Media L. Rep. 2281, 2283-84 (1st Cir. 1998).

In a Bivens action against a defendant federal official, an allegation that a third party discharged the plaintiff as a result of the defendant's defamatory statements to the press does not state a viable constitutional claim. Aversa v. United States, 99 F.3d 1200, 1216, 25 Media L. Rep. 1033, 1045 (1st Cir. 1996). Rather, "in order to state a cognizable claim that defamation together with loss of employment worked a deprivation of a constitutionally-protected liberty interest, a plaintiff must allege that the loss of employment resulted from some further action by the defendant in addition to the defamation. Where it is the defendant who terminated the plaintiff, the further action is the termination." Aversa, 99 F.3d at 1216. In Davric Maine Corp. v. United States Postal Service, 238 F.3d 58, 68 (1st Cir. 2001), the First Circuit held that defamation alone cannot constitute a constitutional tort under Bivens.

V. OTHER ISSUES

A. Statute of Limitations

The Massachusetts statute of limitations for both libel and slander actions is three years. G.L. c. 260, § 4. That limitations period, of course, controls in the federal as well as state courts. McAvey v. Emergency Fleet Corp., 15 F.2d 405, 406 (D. Mass. 1926). Absence from the state tolls the statutory period. G.L. c. 260, § 9. The general rule in libel actions is that "the cause of action accrues, and the statute of limitations begins to run, on publication of the defamatory statement." Flynn v. Associated Press, 401 Mass. 776, 780, 519 N.E.2d 1304, 15 Media L. Rep. 1265 (1988); Esserian v. Harvard University, 2005 Mass. Super. LEXIS 251, *4 (May 4, 2005) (Brassard, J.); Smith v. City of Boston, et al., 2004 U.S. Dist. LEXIS 13062, *26 (D. Mass. July 13, 2004). "Once the defendant pleads the statute of limitations ... and establishes that the action was brought more than three years from the date of the injury, the burden of proving facts that take the case outside the impact of the statute falls to the plaintiff." Darviris v. Petros, 59 Mass. App. Ct. 323, 326, 795 N.E.2d 1196 (2003), quoting Riley v. Presnell, 409 Mass. 239, 243-44, 565 N.E.2d 780 (1991), and quoted in Esserian, 2005 Mass. Super. LEXIS 251 at *4. The Massachusetts "discovery rule" provides that certain causes of action based on "inherently unknowable wrongs do not accrue until the plaintiff learns, or reasonably should have learned, that he has been harmed by the defendant's conduct." Flynn., 401 Mass. at 781; see also Esserian, 2005 Mass. Super. LEXIS 251 at *6. However, a plaintiff "need not apprehend the full extent or nature of an injury in order for a cause of action to accrue." Silvestris v. Tantasqua Reg'l Sch. Distr., 446 Mass. 756, 766 (2006); the limitations period begins to run on the date when the plaintiff is aware of defamatory statements that had caused her possible damage, even if she did not know at that time the full extent of the damage they caused, Vanguri v. FMR Corp., 78 Mass. App. Ct. 1130, 941 N.E.2d 1149, 2011 WL 677388, *1 (Mass. App. Ct. Feb. 28, 2011) (unpublished). The discovery rule "does not apply to a public libel printed in a newspaper widely available to the public, including the plaintiff." Flynn, 401 Mass. at 781-82 & n.7 (suggesting that the outcome might be different if the alleged defamation had been confidential or concealed from the plaintiff). See also Catrone v. Thoroughbred Racing Associations of North America, Inc., 929 F.2d 881, 885-87 (1st Cir. 1991) (declining to apply Massachusetts discovery rule to reports that, while not generally distributed, were "widely disseminated" in the relevant community and could have been discovered during the limitations period had the plaintiff exercised "some diligence").

Massachusetts utilizes a "functional approach" to choice of law issues. New England Telephone & Telegraph Co. v. Gourdeau Construction Co., 419 Mass. 658, 647 N.E.2d 42 (1995); see also Nierman v. Hyatt Corp., 59 Mass. App. Ct. 844, 845, 798 N.E.2d 329, 330 (2003), aff'd 441 Mass. 693, 695, 808 N.E.2d 290 (2004). Accordingly, it applied the one-year statutes of limitations of Texas and New York to bar a libel claim brought in Massachusetts, a state with "no relationship to the occurrence, no relationship to the defendants, and virtually no relationship to the plaintiff." Stanley v. CF-VH Associates, Inc. 956 F. Supp. 55, 58 (D. Mass. 1997).

The continuing presence of a negative performance evaluation in a plaintiff-employee's personnel file did not give rise to a "continuing violation" such as to toll a plaintiff's federal Civil Rights Act claim. Underwood v. Digital Equipment Corp., Inc., 576 F. Supp. 213, 216 (D. Mass. 1983) (continuing effects of an earlier action do not create a continuing violation). Presumably, an effort to extend the 3-year defamation statute on such grounds would meet the same fate.

B. Jurisdiction

Personal jurisdiction. Courts in Massachusetts lacked personal jurisdiction over a claim brought against a California defendant based on comments he made during a telephone conversation initiated by a Massachusetts reporter. Ticketmaster-New York, Inc. v. Alioto, 26 F.3d 201, 22 Media L. Rep. 1682 (1st Cir. 1994) (deciding case on federal constitutional grounds and side-stepping Massachusetts long-arm statute, G.L. c. 233A, § 3). But a Massachusetts court had personal jurisdiction over an out-of-state defendant who, personally and as officer of an out-of-state corporation, sent allegedly defamatory emails about a Massachusetts resident to a list of recipients including some from Massachusetts. Hebb v. Greens Worldwide, Inc., No. 06-4368, 2007 Mass. Super. LEXIS 388 (Suffolk Super. Ct. Sept. 17, 2007) (act outside Massachusetts causing injury in Massachusetts is sufficient to create personal jurisdiction under G.L. c. 233A, § 3(d)). In Abiomed, Inc. v. Turnbull, 379 F. Supp. 2d 90 (D. Mass. 2005), the federal district court in Massachusetts concluded that it had personal jurisdiction over an Ohio resident who owns no property in Massachusetts, on the basis of several hundred email messages posted on a Yahoo.com electronic message board dedicated to discussion of the plaintiff, a Massachusetts company and a competitor of the defendant's employer.

Choice of law. Where an alleged libel is published and distributed in Massachusetts, Massachusetts law applies. Church of Scientology v. Flynn, 578 F. Supp. 266, 267 (D. Mass. 1984); Loeb v. Globe Newspaper Co., 489 F. Supp. 481 (D. Mass. 1980). However, the law of another jurisdiction – including its limitations period – may be applied when that jurisdiction has the "most significant relationship to the occurrence and to the parties." New England Telephone & Telegraph Co. v. Gourdeau Construction Co., Inc., 419 Mass. 647, 664, 647 N.E.2d 42 (1995). Massachusetts utilizes a "functional approach" to choice of law issues. New England Telephone & Telegraph Co. v. Gourdeau Construction Co., 419 Mass. 658, 647 N.E.2d 42 (1995); see also Nierman v. Hyatt Corp., 59 Mass. App. Ct. 844, 845, 798 N.E.2d 329, 330 (2003), aff'd 441 Mass. 693, 695, 808 N.E.2d 290 (2004). In defamation and other tort actions, Massachusetts "does not strictly adhere to the rule of *lex loci delicti* and, instead, employs a more flexible approach." Davidson v. Cao, 211 F. Supp.2d 264, 273 (D. Mass. 2002). Where a publication occurs in several states, unless another state has a more significant relationship to the claim, "the law of the state where the defamed person was domiciled" -- or where a defamed corporation had its principal place of business – "at the time of publication applies 'if the matter complained of was published in that state.'" Id., citing Restatement (2d) of Conflicts of Laws § 150(2) and comment b (1971). If that state has "little connection to a multistate defamation claim," then "concerns" arise. Davidson, 211 F. Supp. 2d at 274, citing Keeton v. Hustler Magazine, Inc., 828 F.2d 64, 66 (1st Cir. 1987). Where one of several libel defendants resides abroad (but the other three reside or have a principal place of business in Massachusetts), Massachusetts law applied even as to the foreign defendant, both because of the Commonwealth's legitimate interests in protecting the reputations of its medical community (of which the foreign defendant was a part), and to support both "[u]niformity of result" and ease of determining and applying the law. Davidson, 211 F. Supp. 2d at 274.

Where alleged defamatory comments were made by faculty at a Minnesota public university to a Massachusetts licensing board, regarding a plaintiff domiciled in Massachusetts, the court applied Massachusetts law. Miller v. Tope, No. 02-11151-DPW, 2003 U.S. Dist. LEXIS 21211, *22 n.21, *29 n.24 (D. Mass. Nov. 24, 2003). The court relied on the Restatement (2d) of Conflicts § 145, and noted that despite Minnesota law relating to official immunity, "Minnesota has a less significant interest than Massachusetts which will be enforcing its policy against libel because both the injury and injury-causing conduct occurred" in Massachusetts. Id., also citing Restatement (2d) of Conflicts § 163 ("the rule of liability of the state of injury should usually be applied unless the policy underlying the rule of non-liability is a strong one, as would probably be true if the conduct was required as opposed to being only privileged").

Subject matter jurisdiction. **For the federal court to dismiss a diversity claim for failure to meet the $75,000 amount-in-controversy requirement, "the sum claimed by the plaintiff controls if the claim is apparently made in good faith. It must appear to a legal certainty that the claim is really for less than the jurisdictional amount to justify dismissal." Piccone v. Bartels, No. 11-10143-MLW, 2012 WL 4592770 (D. Mass. Sept. 29, 2012) (Magistrate's report**

and recommendation), quoting Spielman v. Genzyme Corp., 251 F.3d 1, 5 (1st Cir. 2001), quoting St. Paul Mercury Indemnity Co. v. Red Cab Co., 303 U.S. 283, 288 (1938). In Piccone, the federal magistrate noted that "courts in defamation cases have often awarded sums far in excess of $75,000," 2012 WL at *5, citing Murphy v. Boston Herald, Inc., 449 Mass. 42, 865 N.E.2d 746, 751 (Mass. 2007) (trial court award of $2.1 million), and Tosti v. Ayik, 400 Mass. 224, 508 N.E.2d 1368, 1369 (Mass. 1987) (finding that award of $275,000 for defamation and tortious interference with employment relationship was not excessive).

The First Amendment prohibits civil courts from intervening in disputes concerning religious doctrine, discipline, faith, or internal organization. In Hiles v. Episcopal Diocese of Massachusetts, the court considered a letter accusing a priest of an improper sexual relationship. 437 Mass. 505, 514, 773 N.E.2d 929 (2002). Because the claim arose out of the "church-minister" relationship in the church discipline context, it fell within the category of religious belief, a matter the Church is entitled to decide free from governmental intrusion. Id.

Preemption. The federal Employee Retirement Income Security Act (ERISA), 29 U.S.C. §§ 1001-1461, preempted state-law defamation claims based on statements that the court ruled were inseparably linked to defendant company's adoption of a plan governed by ERISA. Fairneny v. Savogran Co., 422 Mass. 469, 476, 664 N.E.2d 5 (1996). Where a plaintiff's defamation claims against fellow employees were not limited to specific grievance proceedings and did not require interpretation of the collective bargaining agreement, they were not preempted by Section 301 of the Labor Management Relations Act, 29 U.S.C. § 185. Naitram v. Local 2222 of the Int'l Brotherhood of Electrical Workers, 982 F. Supp. 83 (D. Mass. 1997); but see Rogers v. NStar Electric, et al., 389 F. Supp. 2d 100 (D. Mass. 2005) (noting that defamation claim against employer was governed by CBA, which may define scope of the employer's conditional privilege, but that defamation claim against fellow employee was not so governed absent company rules under the CBA that create a privilege for co-worker). State-law preemption occurs "if a court, in passing upon the claim, would be required to interpret the collective bargaining agreement. In practice, this test boils down to whether the asserted state-law claim plausibly can be said to depend upon the meaning of one or more provisions within the collective bargaining agreement." Flibotte v. Pennsylvania Truck Lines, Inc., 131 F.3d 21, 26 (1st Cir. 1997), citing Lingle v. Norge Div. of Magic Chef, Inc., 486 U.S. 399, 405-06 (1988). A state law claim "depends" on interpretation of a collective bargaining agreement if it alleges a breach of duties arising under that agreement or if its resolution "arguably hinges upon an interpretation of the collective bargaining agreement." Flibotte, 131 F.3d at 26, quoted in Rogers, 389 F. Supp. 2d at 106.

C. Workers' Compensation Exclusivity

The waiver provision in the Massachusetts workers' compensation statute, Mass. G.L. c. 152, § 24, does not bar defamation claims, even if they are related to employment. Andresen v. Diorio, 349 F.3d 8 (1st Cir. Mass. 2003); Foley v. Polaroid Corp., 381 Mass. 545, 551-2, 413 N.E.2d 711, 715 (1980) ("Foley I") (noting that bar also does not apply to claims for malicious prosecution and violation of civil rights); Fleming v. National Union Fire Ins. Co., et al., 445 Mass. 381, 388 n.8, 837 N.E.2d 1113, 1120 n.8 (2005). See, e.g., Arnold v. CVS Pharm., 2008 U.S. Dist. LEXIS 52851, *24 (D. Mass. July 8, 2008) (dismissing emotional distress claim based on workers' compensation exclusivity, and defamation claim on other grounds). The workers' compensation statute applies when an employee "receives a personal injury arising out of and in the course of his employment," G.L. c. 152, § 26. Massachusetts courts construe it to bar any claim of intentional and negligent infliction of emotional distress, simple negligence, and loss of consortium that arises out of the employment relationship, "regardless of whether it occurs during the precise period of employment." Andresen, 349 F.3d at 16. **(The statute does not bar claims against an individual for acts committed outside the scope of employment. Coughlin v. Town of Arlington, No. 10-102013-MLW, 2011 WL 6370932, *17 (D. Mass. Dec. 19, 2011)).**

But it is established that "injury to … reputation is not the type of personal injury contemplated by" the statute, because workers' compensation is aimed at compensating for the inability to earn wages, or for loss of support flowing from wages. Foley I, 381 Mass. at 551-52. See also Dorn v. Astra USA, 975 F. Supp. 388 (D. Mass. 1997) (workers' compensation act "does not cover injuries from common law torts such as defamation [], which are intended to protect against harm other than injury to mind or body"), citing Green v. Wyman-Gordon Co., 422 Mass. 551, 560, 664 N.E2d 808, 814 (1996). As explained in Foley I, "The act has been interpreted to encompass physical and mental injuries arising out of employment, whereas the gist of an action for defamation is injury to reputation, irrespective of any physical or mental harm." While recognizing "the conceptual problem inherent in the employee's including physical and mental injury as elements of damage in the defamation claim," nonetheless the Supreme Judicial Court held that "to block the main thrust of this action because of peripheral items of damages, when a compensation claim could not purport to give relief for the main wrong of injury to reputation, would be incongruous, and outside the obvious intent of the exclusiveness clause." 381 Mass. at 552. Therefore, a plaintiff "may recover for emotional injuries sustained in connection with claims," like defamation, "that are not barred by the exclusivity provisions of the workers' compensation act." Wyman-Gordon, 422 Mass. at 560-61, citing Flesner v. Technical Communications Corp., 410 Mass. 805, 814 n.9, 575 N.E.2d 1107 (1991); Foley v. Polaroid Corp., 400 Mass. 82, 93, 508 N.E.2d 72 (1987) ("Foley II"); Foley I, 381 Mass. at 552. In other words, despite the bar to stand-alone claims of infliction of emotional distress, "emotional distress damages are not barred where the underlying claim is not barred," such as in defamation claims, where "physical or mental harm is incidental, and is not an indispensable ingredient" of the claim. Wyman-Gordon, 442 Mass. at 561, quoting Foley I, 381 Mass. at 552. On the other hand, where "mental harm is the essence of the [claim]," it is an indispensable ingredient, and the claim is barred. Wyman-Gordon, 442 Mass. at 561. **Similar reasoning led the Supreme Judicial Court to deny accidental disability retirement benefits to a Superior Court judge who alleged he was disabled due to posttraumatic stress disorder and physical ailments resulting from a newspaper's publication of defamatory articles about him. The Court ruled that the judge's disabling injuries were not sustained "while in the performance of" his judicial duties -- a "much more restrictive" standard than that of the workers' compensation statute. Murphy v. Contributory Retirement Appeal Bd., 463 Mass. 333, 346-352, 974 N.E.2d 46, 57-61 (2012).**

D. Pleading Requirements

Must defamation plaintiffs set forth their claims with a higher degree of specificity than plaintiffs alleging other claims? We recently declared in this outline that "[t]he days of strict pleading requirements for defamation claims – if, indeed, such days ever existed – are now past," but we may have spoken too quickly. In McCarthy v. City of Newburyport, 252 Fed. Appx. 328, 334, 2007 U.S. App. LEXIS 25450, *11-12 (1st Cir. Oct. 31, 2007) (unpublished), the Court of Appeals, applying Massachusetts law, granted summary judgment to a city and its police chief when it found that the plaintiff, a police officer, failed to allege "(1) the basis of the libel or slander claim, along with the precise wording of at least one sentence of the statement at issue; (2) the means and approximate dates of publication; and (3) the falsity of those statements." The ruling relies on Dorn v. Astra USA, 975 F. Supp. 388 (D. Mass. 1997), despite the First Circuit's later ruling in Andresen v. Diorio, 349 F.3d 8, 17 (1st Cir. 2003) that federal, not state, pleading standards apply in federal court and that a defamation plaintiff need only comply with the notice pleading requirements of Fed. R. Civ. P. Rule 8. See also Bleau v. Greater Lynn Mental Health & Retardation Ass'n, 371 F. Supp. 2d 1, 2-4 (D. Mass. 2005) (concluding that Andresen effectively overturned two prior district court cases – Chiara v. Dizaglio, 81 F. Supp. 2d 242 (D. Mass. 2000) and Dorn – that had applied a heightened pleading standard for defamation claims). In McCarthy, the Court of Appeals mentions neither Andresen nor the 2007 decision of the federal district court sitting in Massachusetts, which declared in North Shore Pharmacy Services, 491 F. Supp. 2d 124 (D. Mass. 2007) that "plaintiffs are not required to set forth the alleged defamatory statements verbatim." The district court in North Shore Pharmacy Services had said the plaintiff need only "set forth such allegations in support of its defamation claim that were sufficient to give the [defendants] 'fair notice' of its claim and the grounds upon which it rests." Id., quoting Swierkiewicz v. Sorema N.A., 534 U.S. 506, 512, 122 S. Ct. 992, 998, 152 L. E. 2d 1 (2002).

Similar confusion reigns with respect to the pleading standard in state court. The consensus of authority appears to indicate that state courts require only the notice pleading requirements of Rule 8, or perhaps a slightly higher degree of particularity. The state Appeals Court noted that it is not necessary, even in cases of slander, to set out the false statements allegedly made by the defendant; it is enough that the "tenor and substance" of the words used is alleged. Cavicchi v. Koski, 67 Mass. App. Ct. 654, 660 n.9855 N.E.2d 1137 (2006), rejecting and overruling Lee v. Kane, 72 Mass. 495, 6 Gray 495, 496 (1856). Superior Court cases are all over the map. One judge roundly dismissed suggestions of a heightened pleading standard, stating instead that the "traditional standard governing rule 12(b)(6) motions set forth in Nader v. Citron, 372 Mass. 96, 98, 360 N.E.2d 870 (1977)" would apply. Moriarty v. Sullivan, No. 2004-010, 21 Mass. L. Rep. 254, 2006 Mass. Super. LEXIS 328, *7-10 (Hampden Super. Ct. May 16, 2006) (Sweeney, J.). Another said the typical standard applies so long as defamatory statements are set out with particularity. Endodontic Assoc. of Lexington, Inc. v. Johnston-Neeser, No. 05-3319, 20 Mass. L. Rep. 677, 2006 Mass. Super. LEXIS 145, *15-19 (Middlesex Super. Ct. March 16, 2006). **Most recently, in Haney v. City of Boston, No. 11-2668-C, 2012 WL 3144816 (Mass. Super. Ct. July 30, 2012), one Superior Court declared that "[i]n Massachusetts, there is a heightened pleading standard required for defamation," but as authority it relied on two federal cases: Dorn, 975 F. Supp. at 396, and Bleau, 371 F. Supp. 2d at 2, which stated in dicta that "Dorn's discussion of Massachusetts' pleading requirements in defamation cases is still correct."**

At the very least, it is clear that at the trial stage, if not before, there must be evidence of the exact words uttered by a libel defendant. Paren v. Craigie, et al., 2006 U.S. Dist. LEXIS 43288, 45-46 (D. Mass. June 15, 2006) (Neiman, C.M.J.) (noting that a defendant "is entitled to knowledge of the precise language challenged as defamatory," quoting Phantom Touring, Inc. v. Affiliated Publications, 953 F.2d 724, 728 n.6 (1st Cir. 1992). A federal district court judge dismissed a defamation claim that "failed to describe any relevant communication(s) by defendants, whether superficially defamatory or not." Acciavatti v. Professional Services Group, Inc., 982 F. Supp. 69, 77 (D. Mass. 1977). The court declined to allow a motion for a more definite statement: "Use of such a motion is proper where the pleading 'is so vague or ambiguous that a party cannot reasonably be required to frame a responsive pleading' even though the complaint evidences all necessary elements of the claim. Fed. R. Civ. P. 12(e). Conversely, it is not proper where, as here, the complainant has altogether omitted one or some of these elements from the complaint." Id., 982 F. Supp. at 77-78. See also White v. Spence, 5 Mass. App. Ct. 679, 685, 369 N.E.2d 731 (1977); Senay v. Meehan, 5 Mass. App. Ct. 854, 855, 364 N.E.2d 1085 (1977) (permitting defendants to move pursuant to Mass. R. Civ. P. 12(e) for a more definite statement of the "defamatory statements" referred to in the complaint); Panse v. Norman, 2005 U.S. Dist. LEXIS 20272, *8 (D. Mass. 2005) (dismissing claim that "failed to identify any specific defamatory statements or the author of any such statements, much less a causal relationship between the statements and [plaintiff's] alleged injury"); but see Davidson, 211 F. Supp. 2d at 276 (noting that "courts" consistently refuse to require plaintiffs to set forth allegedly defamatory statements *en haec verbis*," quoting Barber v. Nationwide Communications, Inc., 1995 WL 940517 at *3 (N.D. Tex. 1995)). Where a discharged employee sought to bring a defamation claim against her employer, the Supreme Judicial Court permitted her the opportunity to replead her claims in light of the court's ruling. Madsen v. Erwin, 395 Mass. 715, 726-27, 481 N.E.2d 1160 (1985).

Plaintiff bears the burden of alleging falsity in the complaint. McAvoy v. Shufrin, 401 Mass. 593, 597, 518 N.E.2d 513, 14 Media L. Rep. 2298 (1988). Plaintiff apparently must also allege special damages, else such damages may not be recovered; that rule appears to apply to both slander and libel actions. Stone v. Essex County Newspapers, Inc., 367 Mass. 849, 860, 330 N.E.2d 161 (1975); Tosti v. Ayik, 394 Mass. 482, 497, 476 N.E.2d 928 (1985). As to qualified privilege, defendant bears the burden of showing facts to create the privilege, after which plaintiff bears the burden of proving that the privilege has been abused. Therefore, plaintiff need not plead facts sufficient to overcome the qualified privilege. Chan v. Immunetics, Inc., 9 Mass. L. Rptr. 719, 1999 WL 218490 at *4-5, 1999 Mass. Super. LEXIS 120 (Mass. Super. Ct. 1999).

Slander actions are subject to an additional, harsher, requirement: The plaintiff in a slander action must allege special damages in order to survive a motion to dismiss, and must prove such damages in order to recover at all on the claim, unless the spoken words fall into one of the three categories known as "slander per se." Sharratt v. Housing Innovations, Inc., 365 Mass. 141, 147 n.1, 310 N.E.2d 343 (1974); Ravnikar v. Bogojavlensky, 438 Mass. 627, 630, 782 N.E.2d 508, 511 (2003). See, e.g., Haddad v. Wal-Mart Stores, Inc., 455 Mass. 91, 92 n.2, 914 N.E.2d 59, 62 n.2 (2009) (noting that jury found no liability on slander claim because plaintiff had suffered no damages as a result). An oral communication is slander per se if it charges the plaintiff with a crime, states that the plaintiff is suffering from certain diseases, or "prejudice[s] him in his office, profession, or business or may probably tend to do so." Lynch v. Lyons, 303 Mass. 116, 119, 20 N.E.2d 953 (1939).

E. Motions to Dismiss and for Summary Judgment

Because the existence of the employer's conditional or qualified privilege, and whether it has been abused, are fact-specific questions, it is unlikely that a motion to dismiss on conditional privilege grounds will be successful. See **Piccone v. Bartels, No. 11-10413-MLW, 2012 WL 4592770 (D. Mass. Sept. 29, 2012) ("facts often need to be developed in discovery to determine whether the defendant's statements are protected by an absolute or conditional privilege");** Disend v. Meadowbrook School, 33 Mass. App. Ct. 674, 666-67 (1992); Winsmann v. Choate Health Management, Inc., 8 Mass. L. Rep. 480, 1998 WL 282901, 1998 Mass. Super. LEXIS 93 (Mass. Super. Ct. 1998) (motion to dismiss is "not the proper vehicle to attack the plaintiff's defamation claims" based on qualified privilege); Chan v. Immunetics, Inc., 9 Mass. L. Rep. 719, 1999 WL 218490 at *5, 1999 Mass. Super. LEXIS 120 (Super. Ct. 1999) (same); Berard v. Town of Millville, 113 F. Supp. 2d 197 (D. Mass. 2000) (same). By contrast, however, an absolute privilege may well justify a motion to dismiss, and denial of a motion on those grounds will assumably be immediately appealable. See, e.g., Fisher v. Lint, 69 Mass. App. Ct. 360, 361 n.3, 868 N.E.2d 161, 164 n.3 (2007). And where a defamation claim is truly frivolous on its face, a court will allow a motion to dismiss, and may even impose sanctions on the plaintiff. See Dace v. Commonwealth of Mass./Univ. of Mass. Dartmouth, et al., 11 Mass. L. Rptr. 208, 1999 WL 1487590, *4, 1999 Mass. Super. LEXIS 555 (Mass. Super. Ct. 1999) (statements made by executive director to a tenured professor were pure opinion and, therefore, not actionable -- "[w] ere that not clear from the outset, a minimum of legal research would have revealed it"; motion to dismiss allowed and attorneys' fees awarded against the plaintiff).

In 2008, the Supreme Judicial Court adopted the strict interpretation of Mass. R. Civ. P. 12(b)(6) that was previously applied at the federal level to Fed. R. Civ. P. 12(b)(6)) in Bell Atl. Corp. v. Twombly, 550 U.S. 544, 555, 127 S. Ct. 1955, 167 L.Ed.2d 929 (2007). See Iannacchino v. Ford Motor Co., 451 Mass. 623, 636, 888 N.E.2d 879 (2008). Under that standard, a complaint "does not need detailed factual allegations," but must contain "more than labels and conclusions," and factual allegations must "raise a right to relief above the speculative level . . . [based on the assumption that all the allegations in the complaint are true [even if doubtful in fact] . . . ." Bell Atl. Corp., 550 U.S. at 555, as quoted in Anzalone v. Administrative Office of Trial Court, 457 Mass. 647, 661, 932 N.E.2d 774, 786 (2010). Whether that stricter interpretation also applies to motions for judgment on the pleadings – described by one court as "a motion to dismiss incorporated in the answer," Noonan v. Staples, Inc., 707 F. Supp. 2d 85, 88 (D. Mass. 2010) – remains to be seen.

Under the federal rules, "[w]hether a complaint should survive a motion to dismiss depends upon whether the pleading satisfies the 'plausibility' standard." Strunk v. Odyssey Consulting Group, Ltd., No. 10-12174-DJC, 2011 WL 3567025, *1 (D. Mass. Aug. 11, 2011), citing both Ashcroft v. Iqbal, 129 S. Ct. 1937, 1949-50, 173 L. Ed. 2d 868 (2009), and Bell Atl. Corp., supra; **see also Piccone v. Bartels, No. 11-10143-MLW, 2012 WL 4592770, *1 (D. Mass. Sept. 29, 2012).** To determine plausibility, "the court should first identify and disregard conclusory allegations." Strunk, 2011 WL 3567025 at *1, citing Ocasio-Hernandez v. Fortuno-Burset, 640 F.3d 1, 12 (1st Cir. 2011) ("A plaintiff is not entitled to 'proceed perforce' by virtue of allegations that merely parrot the elements of the cause of action."). Even "seemingly incredible" "[n]on-conclusory factual allegations" must be treated as true, and assessed "to determine whether they '"allow the court to draw the reasonable inference that the defendant is liable for the misconduct alleged."'" Strunk, 2011 WL 3567025 at *1 (quoting Ocasio-Hernandez, 640 F.3d at 12 (quoting Iqbal, 129 S. Ct. at 1949, 1951)). See also Noonan, 707 F. Supp. 2d at 88-89 (holding that if a complaint "alleges facts that would 'plausibly' entitle [the plaintiff] to relief," the claim ought not to be dismissed). Under the federal standard, motions to dismiss and motions for judgment on the pleadings "'are ordinarily accorded much the same treatment.'" Id. at 88-89 (quoting Aponte –Torres v. Univ. of Puerto Rico, 445 F.3d 50, 54 (1st Cir. 2006)).

In deciding a motion to dismiss under Rule 12(b)(6), the court will "take the well-pleaded allegations in the complaint as true and ... make all reasonable inferences in favor of the plaintiff." Fisher v. Lint, 69 Mass. App. Ct. 360, 365, 868 N.E.2d 161, 167 (2007); Harvard Law Sch. Coalition for Civil Rights v. President & Fellows of Harvard College, 413 Mass. 66, 68, 595 N.E.2d 316 (1992); **Piccone v. Bartels, No. 11-10143-MLW, 2012 WL 4592770, *1 (D. Mass. Sept. 29, 2012).** See also Zajac v. Zajac, 2007 Mass. Super. LEXIS 336, *4 (Worc. Super. Ct. Aug. 17, 2007) (denying motion to dismiss where plaintiff alleged sufficient facts to permit a finding that conditional privilege does not apply). Under the pre-Iannacchino standard, dismissal will be ordered only "when it appears certain 'that the plaintiff can prove no set of facts in support of his claim which would entitle him to relief,'" Fisher, supra, quoting Nader v. Citron, 372 Mass. 96. 98, 360 N.E.2d 870 (1977). The motion will be denied if it appears plaintiff is entitled "'to any form of relief, even though ... the theory on which he seems to rely may not be appropriate.'" Zajac, supra at *4-5, quoting Nader, 372 Mass. at 104. Still, even pre-Iannacchino, the court's indulgence will only go so far. One federal district court dismissed a claim, without prejudice, for failure to meet the requirements of Fed. R. Civ. P. 8(a)(2), holding that "a plaintiff's obligation to provide the 'grounds' of his 'entitle[ment] to relief' requires more than labels and conclusions, and a formulaic recitation of the elements of a cause of action will not do." Beetz v. Ambrosi, No. 07-CV-10323-RGS, 2007 U.S. Dist. LEXIS 51671 (D. Mass. 2007) (noting that "[t]he 'liberal' notice pleading regime of Rule 8 may not now be as liberal as it once was").

A court addressing a motion to dismiss may consider "documents that are central to plaintiffs' claims or sufficiently referenced" in the complant without converting the motion into one for summary judgment. **Piccone v. Bartels, No. 11-10413-MLW, 2012 WL 4592770, *1 (D. Mass. Sept. 29, 2012). This includes not only exhibits attached to the complaint,** Davidson v. Cao, 211 F. Supp.2d 264, 267 n.2 (D. Mass. 2002), but also any document incorporated by reference or specifically referenced in (even if not physically attached to) the Complaint. **Piccone, 2012 WL 4592770, *1;** Moriarty v. Sullivan, No. 2004-010, 21 Mass. L. Rep. 254, 2006 Mass. Super. LEXIS 328, *3 n.3 (Hampden Super. Ct. May 16, 2006); Desrochers v. TIAX, LLC, 2003 Mass. Super. LEXIS 138 at *8 n.2, 10 (Middlesex Super. Ct. May 1, 2003) (incorporated by reference); Rogers v. NStar Electric, et al., 389 F. Supp. 2d 100, 105 n.3 (D. Mass. 2005) (specifically referenced). The Superior Court in Desrochers repeated that "'when ... a complainant's factual allegations are expressly linked – and admittedly dependent upon – a document (the authenticity of which is not challenged), that document effectively merges into the pleadings and the trial court can review it in deciding a motion to dismiss under Rule 12(b)(6).'" Desrochers, 2003 Mass. Super. LEXIS 138, at *10, quoting Edwin v. Blenwood Associates, Inc., 9 F. Supp. 2d 70, 72 (D. Mass. 1998); see also Albright v. Morton, 321 F. Supp. 2d 130, 134 n.2 (D. Mass. 2004), aff'd, 410 F.3d 69 (1st Cir. 2005). Finally, the court may also take judicial notice of other court documents whose authenticity is not challenged, Desrochers, 2003 Mass. Super. LEXIS 138, at *9-10, and of prior proceedings and rulings in the same court, Noonan v. Staples, Inc., 707 F. Supp. 2d 85, 89 (D. Mass. 2010). On appeal, courts will apply *de novo* review to the grant of a motion to dismiss, "accepting all factual allegations in the complaint as true and drawing all reasonable inferences favorable to the appellant." Amrak Prod'ns, Inc. v. Morton, et al., 410 F.3d 69, 72 (1st Cir. 2005); Stanton v. Metro Corp., 438 F.3d 119, 123, 34 Med. L. Rep. 1321 (1st Cir. 2006) (referring to "well-pleaded" factual allegations); Fisher v. Lint, 69 Mass. App. Ct. 360, 365, 868 N.E.2d 161, 167 (2007).

Practitioners should keep in mind the increasing use of special motions to dismiss under the Massachusetts Anti-SLAPP Act, Mass. Gen. Laws c. 231, § 59H, which under certain circumstances provides for dismissal of claims based on a party's exercise of its right of petition, as defined broadly in that statute. See, e.g., Cormier v. MacDow, No. 06-4015, 22 Mass. L. Rep. 739, 2007 Mass. Super. LEXIS 323 (Middlesex Super. Ct. Aug. 15, 2007) (allowing special motion to dismiss defamation claims that arose entirely from defendants' petitioning activities, where plaintiff could not demonstrate by a preponderance of the evidence that the petitioning activities were devoid of any reasonable factual support or any arguable basis in law). To succeed on a special motion to dismiss, the moving party must demonstrate that the claim against it is "based on" that party's exercise of its right of petition, and has no substantial basis other than or in addition to those petitioning activities. Duracraft Corp. v. Holmes Products Corp., 427 Mass. 156, 167-68, 691 N.E.2d 935 (1998); Fustolo v. Hollander, 455 Mass. 861, 865, 920 N.E.2d 837, 840 (2010); Moriarty v. Mayor of Holyoke, 71 Mass. App. Ct. 442, 833 N.E.2d 311 (2008). To trigger the statute, the petitioning activities must be such that the movant is "seeking redress of a grievance of his own," not merely expressing such a concern on behalf of others. Fustolo, 455 Mass. at 865-69, 920 N.E.2d at 840-43 (holding that reporter's articles on a subject of concern to her do not constitute the requisite petitioning, because reporter was not "seeking redress of a grievance of [her] own"). Whether the movant was paid by her employer to perform her petitioning activities is not dispositive, because "speech may constitute protected petitioning activity even if it 'involves a commercial motive.'" Id., 455 Mass. at 869-70, 920 N.E.2d at 843-44, quoting North Am. Expositions Co. Ltd. Partnership v. Corcoran, 452 Mass. 852, 863, 898 N.E.2d 831 (2009). Once the initial two-part showing is made, the burden shifts to the non-movant to show both that the movant's exercise of its right of petition was devoid of any reasonable factual support or any arguable basis in law, and that the movant's acts caused actual injury to the non-movant. Gen. Laws c. 231, § 59H. A trial court's denial of a special motion to dismiss is subject to interlocutory appellate review for abuse of discretion or other error of law. Cadle Co. v. Schlichtmann, 448 Mass. 242, 250, 859 N.E.2d 858 (2007); Kalter v. Wood, 67 Mass. App. Ct. 584, 586, 855 N.E.2d 421 (2006). See also Fustolo, 455 Mass. at 864, 920 N.E.2d at 840.

Dismissal under Mass. R. Civ. P. 8(a), which requires that the complaint contain a "short and plain" statement of the facts and claims, is permissible where a judge has found that the complaint "fails adequately to inform the defendants of the precise nature of the claims against them, and the grounds therefore." Driscoll v. Board of Trustees of Milton Academy, 70 Mass. App. Ct. 285, 299, 873 N.E.2d 1177 (2007). However, a rare partial dissent in the Driscoll case admonished that "'dismissals on the basis of pleadings, before facts have been found, are discouraged.'" 70 Mass. App. Ct. at 301 (Mills, J., dissenting in part), quoting Gennari v. Revere, 23 Mass. App. Ct. 979, 979, 503 N.E.2d 1331 (1987).

"Summary judgment procedures are especially favored in defamation cases" in Massachusetts. King v. Globe Newspaper Co., 400 Mass. 705, 708, 512 N.E.2d 241, 14 Media L. Rep. 1811 (1987), cert. denied, 485 U.S. 940 and 962 (1988). This rule, originally developed in the media libel context, has been applied in employment cases as well. See, e.g., Testaverde v. Massachusetts Teachers Ass'n, No. 97-P-2092, slip op. at 2 (Mass. App. Ct. April 24, 2000) (summary judgment "frequently favored" in defamation cases). That is because "[a]llowing a trial to take place in a meritless case 'would put an unjustified and serious damper on freedom of expression.'" Appleby v. Daily Hampshire Gazette, 395 Mass. 32, 37, 478 N.E.2d 721, 11 Media L. Rep. 2372 (1985), quoting National Ass'n of Gov't Employees, Inc. v. Central Broadcasting Corp., 379 Mass. 220, 233, 396 N.E.2d 996, 5 Media L. Rep. 2078 (1979), cert. denied, 446 U.S. 935 (1980). "Even if a defendant in a libel case is ultimately successful at trial, the costs of litigation may induce an unnecessary and undesirable self-censorship." King v. Globe, 400 Mass. at 708. Those costs may also undermine and chill the free communication of business information, necessary for the effective functioning of the workplace, that the employer's conditional privilege is intended to protect. Bratt v. International Business Machines Corp., 392 Mass. 508, 512-13, 467 N.E.2d 126 (1984).

"Generally, under Massachusetts law, summary judgment for a libel defendant is appropriate if 'the publication is not reasonably capable of any defamatory meaning, and cannot reasonably be understood in any defamatory sense,'" Noonan v. Staples, Inc., 556 F.3d 20, 25-26 (1st Cir. 2009), quoting Sharratt v. Housing Innovations, Inc., 365 Mass. 141, 143, 310 N.E.2d 343, 345 (1974) and King v. Northeastern Publ'g Co., 294 Mass. 369, 370-71, 2 N.E.2d 486, 487 (1936). Where undisputed facts are sufficient to warrant summary judgment, a plaintiff's request for additional discovery will not defeat summary judgment. Barthelmes v. Martineau, 2000 WL 1269666, *4, 2000 Mass. Super. LEXIS 252 (Mass. Super. Ct. 2000) (employees' motion under Rule 56(f) and motion to extend the tracking order were denied where additional information could not refute the employer's conditional privilege).

Nevertheless, defendants moving for summary judgment in defamation cases must still meet the usual summary judgment burdens. Miller v. Tope, No. 02-11151-DPW, 2003 U.S. Dist. LEXIS 21211 at *48 n.32 (D. Mass. Nov. 24, 2003); **see also Barrows v. Wareham Fire Dist., 82 Mass. App. Ct. 623, -- N.E.2d – (2012) (movant must affirmatively demonstrate absence of a triable issue").** Summary judgment will frequently be inappropriate because the issue of actual malice (important to showing abuse of a qualified privilege) involves a determination of state of mind. Miller, 2003 U.S. Dist. LEXIS 21211 at *48 n.32 ("plaintiff is entitled to a jury trial if there is some indication from which an inference of malice could be drawn"). While the federal court has inherent power to grant summary judgment even in the absence of a motion, it is unlikely to do so unless the defending party has been given advance notice that it might do so. See, e.g., Baltodano v. Merck, Sharp & Dohme (I.A.) Corp., 637 F.3d 38, 43-44 (1st Cir. 2011); North Shore Pharmacy Services, Inc., et al. v. Breslin Assocs. Consulting, 491 F. Supp. 2d 111, 123 n.6 (D. Mass. 2007).

The familiar standard applies in employment libel cases: "The party moving for summary judgment in a case in which the opposing party will have the burden of proof at trial is entitled to summary judgment if he demonstrates ... that the party opposing the motion has no reasonable expectation of proving an essential element of that party's case." Ravnikar v. Bogojavlensky, 438 Mass. 627, 629, 782 N.E.2d 508, 510 (2003). **See also ARCADD, Inc. v. Patterson, 80 Mass. App. Ct. 1111 955 N.E.2d 933, 2011 WL 4972132, *2 (Oct. 20, 2011) (unpublished) (granting summary judgment for defendant where plaintiff "did not provide anything that could contravene the reasonable inferences that the statements were nonactionable opinions or shielded by conditional privilege"),** citing Kourouvacilis v. General Motors Corp., 410 Mass. 706, 716 (1991). **In that regard, it may behoove a defendant to move to strike plaintiffs' affidavits submitted in an attempt to create a material issue of fact as to elements including falsity, defamatory meaning, and fault. ARCADD, 2011 WL 4972132, *2 & n.4 (noting that "plaintiffs' failure sufficiently to address" such motion was a "significant**

misstep"). On appeal of summary judgment, the court takes the facts in the light most favorable to the non-movant, Howell v. Enterprise Publishing Co., LLC, 455 Mass. 641, 643 n.3, 920 N.E.2d 1, 8 n.3 (2010), and makes an independent examination of the record as a whole, Reilly v. Associated Press, 59 Mass. App. Ct. 764, 765, 797 N.E.2d 1204 (2003); **ARCADD, 2011 WL 4972132, *2 n.3 (de novo review on appeal);** Baltodano v. Merck, Sharp & Dohme (I.A.) Corp., 637 F.3d 38, 41 (1st Cir. 2011) (same). **Still, a well-reasoned lower court decision "provides a helpful analysis and makes [the appellate court's] review more efficient." Boyle v. Cape Cod Times, No. 11-P-196, 81 Mass. App. Ct. 1107, 959 N.E.2d 457, 2012 WL 28661, *2 n.2 (Jan. 6, 2012) (unpublished).**

In the Massachusetts Superior Courts, a party moving for summary judgment must comply with the "anti-ferreting" rule set out in Superior Court Rule 9A(b)(5), requiring parties concisely to state and respond to the material undisputed facts and legal elements governing the claim. A non-movant's failure to comply permits the court to take as admitted those facts asserted by the moving party that are not disputed in accordance with the rule. Dziamba v. Warner & Stackpole LLP, 56 Mass. App. Ct. 397, 398-401, 778 N.E.2d 927, 929-31 (2002).

F. Discovery and Trial

Where plaintiff's status as a public or private figure has not been determined prior to trial, it behooves a "reasonably prudent plaintiff" to put forward a case establishing actual malice as well as negligence; failure to do so may result in waiver of the actual malice defense. Dixon v. International Br'hood of Police Officers, Nos. 06-1210 et al., 2007 U.S. App. LEXIS 22891 (1st Cir. Sept. 28, 2007). The value of a special jury questionnaire to a "well-managed" libel trial was highlighted by the Supreme Judicial Court when it noted that the questionnaire permits the appellate court "to track the jury's reasoning process" and, when appropriate, to "preserve the verdict" even if it is found on appeal that some of the statements found actionable by the jury were not libelous as a matter of law. Murphy v. Boston Herald, Inc., 449 Mass. 42, 46 n.3, 865 N.E.2d 746, 751 n.3, 35 Media L. Rep. 1865 (2007).

In assessing damages, a jury was properly permitted to consider hate mail sent to the plaintiff following the defendant's defamatory publication. Murphy, 449 Mass. at 66, 865 N.E.2d at 764.

A Massachusetts statute provides that proceedings, reports, and records of a medical peer review committee shall be confidential and not subject to discovery, unless the peer review activities were not undertaken in good faith. G.L. c. 111, §§ 204(a)-(b), 205(b). In Vranos v. Franklin Medical Center, et al., 448 Mass. 425, 862 N.E.2d 11 (2007), the Supreme Judicial Court held that a hospital's communications to medical credentialing organizations were mandated by law and public policy and do not waive the statutory privilege. Moreover, the court held, the statute's exception for activities not undertaken in good faith is a narrow one. To invoke the privilege as a grounds for permitting discovery into peer review proceedings, a litigant must produce evidence, not mere suspicion or speculation, that "the medical review process itself ... was infected with lack of good faith." 448 Mass. at 435, 438, 862 N.E.2d at 18-19, 21, citing Pardo v. General Hosp. Corp., 446 Mass. 1, 12, 841 N.E.2d 692 (2006). Because peer review documents are inadmissible in judicial proceedings, a medical center's letter summarily suspending a physician's privileges, which was part of the peer review process, cannot form the basis of a defamation claim. Vranos v. Skinner, 77 Mass. App. Ct. 280, 293, 930 N.E.2d 156, 167 (Mass. App. Ct. 2010).

G. Appeal

On appeal of a jury verdict finding "actual malice" in the publication of a false and defamatory statement against a public figure or public official, the reviewing court must conduct an "independent examination" of the sufficiency of the record evidence for that finding. Murphy v. Boston Herald, 449 Mass. 42, 49, 57, 865 N.E.2d 746, 753, 758-59, 35 Media L. Rep. 1865 (2007), citing Bose Corp. v. Consumers Union of U.S., Inc., 466 U.S. 485, 499-501, 508-09 n.27 (1984) and McAvoy v. Shufrin, 401 Mass. 593, 596-97, 518 N.E.2d 513 (1988). See also Mandel v. Boston Phoenix, Inc., 456 F.3d 198, 208 (1st Cir. 2006) ("purely factual determinations [such as credibility calls] remain subject to the usual degree of deference"). "Although the independent examination is not 'de novo' in the literal sense, see Bose Corp., supra at 514 n.31, core First Amendment values require a searching reassessment of the factual record in full, to ensure that all inferences underlying the jury's ultimate determinations are legitimate and provide clear and convincing evidence of actual malice." Murphy, 449 Mass. at 50, 865 N.E.2d at 753-54. Nevertheless, "[d]eterminations of credibility under the Bose standard remain the province of the jury." Id., 449 Mass. at 55, 865 N.E.2d at 757.

By contrast, the jury's finding of falsity receives no special scrutiny; the finding "is subject to our traditional standard of review of any jury's finding of fact, that is, whether the finding has a basis in the evidence and reasonable inferences that could be drawn therefrom." Murphy, 449 Mass. at 51, 865 N.E.2d at 754.

H. Res Judicata

State law requires a plaintiff to first present a timely complaint of discrimination to the Massachusetts Commission Against Discrimination before suing in court, just as federal law requires administrative exhaustion at the Equal Employment

Opportunity Commission. Mass. Gen. Laws c.151B, §9; Martins v. Boston Public Health Comm'n, 77 Fed. Appx. 4, 2003 U.S. App. LEXIS 20589, *4 (1st Cir. Oct. 7, 2003). Plaintiffs who split their claims by filing discrimination charges at the MCAD while concurrently filing common-law claims (say, for defamation) in court do so at their peril. In Martins, 2003 U.S. App. LEXIS 20589, *3-4, the First Circuit Court of Appeals held that *res judicata* precluded a plaintiff from litigating his Title VII retaliation claim in federal court. It noted that he had the opportunity to bring that claim in a prior state-court action alleging defamation.

Collateral estoppel will apply to establish the truth of a defamatory statement where that issue was litigated in a prior action, and the truth of the allegations necessarily determined. Hoult v. Hoult, 157 F.3d 29, 33 (1st Cir. 1998); Noonan v. Staples, Inc., 707 F. Supp. 2d 85, 90 (D. Mass. 2010) (barring relitigation of decided issues of truth and common-law malice), citing Grella v. Salem Five Cent Sav. Bank, 42 F.3d 26, 30 (1st Cir. 1994).

I. Insurance Coverage

In Employers Reinsurance Corp. v. Globe Newspaper Co., Inc., 560 F.3d 93, 96, 37 Media L. Rep. 1536 (1st Cir. 2009), the Court of Appeals vacated a federal district court ruling that invoked the "known loss" doctrine to bar insurance coverage for a libel claim that led to a $2.1 million jury verdict against a newspaper. The coverage case arose because, when applying for a new insurance policy, the newspaper did not specifically disclose a demand letter that it had received months earlier, and which had not ripened into litigation at the time of obtaining the policy. The First Circuit ruled that the known loss doctrine was inapplicable, because it only applies if the insured knew, at the time of obtaining the insurance coverage, "'that a specific loss has already happened or is *substantially certain* to happen,'" quoting U.S. Liab. Ins. Co. v. Selman, 70 F.3d 684, 690 (1st Cir. 1995). Although the ruling was a victory for the insured, the Court of Appeals noted that the policy included a "prior acts endorsement" containing two coverage conditions – that the insured had no "notice or knowledge" of the claim when the policy went into effect, and that the insured had no other available insurance applicable to the claim – that may or may not have been fulfilled. Noting that "[t]his case is not about principle but about money," the Court urged both sides to consider settlement. 560 F.3d at 98.

Does a media insurer owe a duty to a libel plaintiff to negotiate a prompt settlement following the plaintiff's win at trial, even if the case is being appealed? In an important decision involving the state consumer protection act, the federal district court in Massachusetts made it clear that the answer is quite fact-specific. Mutual Ins. Co., Ltd. v. Murphy, 630 F. Supp. 2d 158 (D. Mass. 2009). The issue arose in a final chapter of Judge Ernest Murphy's state-court libel battle against the *Boston Herald*, which had led to a $2 million verdict in his favor. Upset that he did not receive payment until two years later when the award was affirmed on appeal, Judge Murphy sued the *Herald*'s insurer for treble damages under the Massachusetts statute governing unfair claim settlement practices. The district court (Saris, J.) held that whether the insurer owed a duty to the libel plaintiff turned on whether the insurance company retained, and exercised, control over defense and settlement of the claim. 630 F. Supp. 2d at 165. After closely examining the terms of the insurance policy, the insurer's role in the litigation and appeal, and the insured's conduct of the case, the court granted summary judgment for the insurance company. It relied particularly on the facts that the policy was a "hybrid" of a liability policy and an indemnity policy; that the policy gave to the insured the burden of defense and choice of counsel; that the insurer was not required to (and did not) assume charge of defense or settlement, and in fact could not impose a settlement without the insured's consent; and that the insured controlled the litigation strategy and never asked the insurer's permission to settle. 630 F. Supp. 2d at 162-170.

The Court of Appeals, applying Massachusetts law, addressed the scope of the "personal injury" coverage of a commercial general liability insurance policy in Great American Ins. Co. v. Riso, Inc., 479 F.3d 158 (1st Cir. 2007). The coverage purported to extend to "oral or written publication of material that slanders or libels a person or organization or disparages a person's or organization's goods, products or services…." Clearly it applies to claims of libel, slander, and product disparagement – but does it also apply to other claims alleging damage due in part to disparaging communications about the insured? In Great American, the Court of Appeals struggled with the Massachusetts Supreme Judicial Court's decision in Boston Symphony Orchestra, Inc. v. Commercial Union Ins. Co., 406 Mass. 7, 545 N.E.2d 1156, 1158 (Mass. 1989), which broadly construed similar language and extended coverage to a breach of contract claim alleging that the insured's breach had damaged the reputation of the plaintiff in the underlying case. The Court of Appeals distinguished BSO as involving a lawsuit that "could be seen, by a stretch, as one for defamation sailing under a foreign flag," and chose to read the SJC's ruling "modestly," as had the Massachusetts Appeals Court in New England Tea & Coffee Co. v. Fireman's Fund Ins. Co., 54 Mass. App. Ct. 903, 763 N.E.2d 103, 104 (Mass. App. Ct. 2002). Accordingly, the First Circuit in Great American read the personal injury clause as inapplicable to an antitrust claim which, though it included allegations that the insured company had disparaged its competitors, was brought not by the disparaged competitors but rather by a customer that asserted it was harmed by the anticompetitive conduct. 479 F.3d at 161-63.

A homeowner's insurance policy clause providing coverage for "bodily injury" did not apply to claims of defamation and intentional infliction of emotional distress against the insured, because "bodily injury" requires physical injury. Allstate Ins. Co. v. Diamant, 401 Mass. 654, 518 N.E.2d 1154 (1988). An allegation that the manner of an employee's termination – abrupt, instructed to leave all personal belongings behind, escorted out by a police detail – resulted in damage to the employee's reputation, was not sufficient to trigger insurance coverage under a policy covering "personal injury," defined as "injury, other than bodily injury, arising out of ... oral or written publication of material that slanders or libels a person ..." New England Tea & Coffee Co. v. Fireman's Fund Ins. Co., 54 Mass. App. Ct. 903, 763 N.E.2d 103 (2002). Where an insurance policy excludes coverage for "personal injury sustained . . . as a result of an offense directly or indirectly related" to the employment of the person alleging injury, it may exclude coverage for claims alleging even post-employment defamations by the employer. Parish of Christ Church v. Church Ins. Co., 166 F.3d 419 (1st Cir. 1999). But a significantly narrower exclusion for "personal injury" to a person arising out of any "employment-related practices, policies, acts or omissions, such as coercion, demotion, evaluation, reassignment, decipline [*sic*], defamation, harassment, humiliation, discrimination directed at that person," applicable "whether the Insured may be liable as an employer or in any other capacity," was found to be "inherently ambiguous" as applied to a former employee's claim for malicious prosecution against the insured. Therefore, construing ambiguities against the insurer, the court ruled that the insurer had breached its duty to defend, and was liable for all defense costs and the entire resulting judgment. Peterborough Oil Co., Inc. v. Clark, et al., 2005 U.S. Dist. LEXIS 27973 (D. Mass. Oct. 28, 2005). In dictum, the opinion notes that a post-termination defamation claim, such as the one lodged in Parish of Christ Church, will not necessarily be excluded. 2005 U.S. Dist. LEXIS 27973 at *29.

An insurance policy coverage exclusion for employment-related practices was held to be ambiguous, and therefore inapplicable, to a claim against an employer for malicious prosecution of its former employee. The decision suggests that post-employment defamation will not necessarily be considered to be employment-related and therefore excluded from coverage. Peterborough Oil Co., Inc. v. Clark, 2005 U.S. Dist. LEXIS 27973, *28 (D. Mass. Oct. 31, 2005) (Saylor, J.).

SURVEY OF MASSACHUSETTS EMPLOYMENT PRIVACY LAW

Jenny K. Cooper
Carolyn B. French
Bingham McCutchen LLP
1 Federal Street
Boston, Massachusetts 02130
Telephone: (617) 951-8000; Facsimile: (617) 951-8736

Elizabeth A. Ritvo
Brown Rudnick LLP
One Financial Center
Boston, Massachusetts 02111
Telephone: (617) 856-8200; Facsimile: (617) 856-8201

(With Developments Reported Through **November 1, 2012**)

GENERAL COMMENTS

The highest court in the Commonwealth of Massachusetts is the Supreme Judicial Court. The appellate court below the Supreme Judicial Court is the Appeals Court. At the trial level are the Superior Courts and the District Courts. The Superior Court has exclusive jurisdiction over statutory actions for invasion of privacy under MASS. GEN. LAWS ch. 214, §1B and §3A. The District Court, however, may decide a claim "which would normally fall within the exclusive jurisdiction of the Superior Court as long as at least one other claim in the same action is within the traditional jurisdiction of the District Court." Ravnikar v. Bogojavlensky, 438 Mass. 627, 634, 782 N.E.2d 508, 514 (2003). Additionally, such claims would still be subject to traditional remand and removal procedures. Id.

SIGNIFICANT DEVELOPMENTS SINCE THE 2012 *SURVEY*

In Amato v. District Attorney for Cape and Islands Dist., 80 Mass. App. Ct. 230, 240, 952 N.E.2d 400, 409 (2011), the Appeals Court held that §1B provides a right of action for intrusion upon seclusion.

I. GENERAL LAW OF PRIVACY

A. Legal Basis of Privacy Claims

1. ***Constitution.*** Article 14 of the Massachusetts Declaration of Rights, a part of the Massachusetts Constitution, affirms the right of all persons to be free from unreasonable searches and seizures. It is identical in substance to the Fourth Amendment to the federal Constitution, and also only extends to state action. See Folmsbee v. Tech Tool Grinding & Supply, 417 Mass. 388, 391, 630 N.E.2d 586, 588-89 (1994). However, the Supreme Judicial Court has interpreted the protections of the Massachusetts provision as being more extensive than those under the Fourth Amendment. See Commonwealth v. Lyles, 453 Mass. 811, 812, 905 N.E.2d 1106, 1108 (2009); Commonwealth v. Phillips, 452 Mass. 617, 624, 897 N.E.2d 31, 39 (2008).

2. ***Statutes.*** The Massachusetts Right of Privacy statute, MASS. GEN. LAWS ch. 214, § 1B provides that "A person shall have a right against unreasonable, substantial or serious interference with his privacy." The statute gives the Superior Court jurisdiction over claims to enforce this right through equitable relief and damages. The statute applies to both state and private actors. See Bally v. Northeastern Univ., 403 Mass. 713, 717 n.3, 532 N.E.2d 49, 51 n.3 (1989). It applies only to persons; a corporation does not have a right of privacy under MASS. GEN. LAWS ch. 214, § 1B. Warner-Lambert Co. v. Execuquest Corp., 427 Mass. 46, 50-51, 691 N.E.2d 545, 548 (1998).

According to the Supreme Judicial Court, to give rise to a cause of action under Chapter 214, the conduct involved must be unreasonable, and it must also be either substantial *or* serious. Schlesinger v. Merrill Lynch, Pierce, Fenner & Smith, Inc., 409 Mass. 514, 517-18, 567 N.E.2d 912, 914 (1991) ("The [privacy] statute obviously was not intended to prohibit serious or substantial interferences which are reasonable or justified ... Likewise, we doubt that the Legislature intended to commit scarce judicial resources to preventing an interference which could be characterized as unreasonable, but which is only trivial or insubstantial."). See also O'Connor v. Police Comm'r, 408 Mass. 324, 330, 557 N.E.2d 1146, 1150 (1990).

The Massachusetts Civil Rights Act, MASS. GEN. LAWS ch. 12, §§ 11H, 11I, permits the Attorney General or any aggrieved party to bring a civil action against one, who through threats, intimidation or coercion, has interfered with another's exercise of his or her rights under federal or Massachusetts law. Claims under the Civil Rights Act may be brought against entities such as corporations, societies, associations and partnerships. Sarvis v. Boston Safe Deposit & Trust Co., 47 Mass. App. Ct. 86, 95, 711 N.E.2d 911, 920 (1999); Commonwealth v. Elm Med. Labs., 33 Mass. App. Ct. at 77, 596 N.E.2d at 379. Unlike the federal Civil Rights Act, 42 U.S.C. 1983, there is no requirement of state action. See Bally v. Northeastern Univ., 403 Mass. 713, 717 n.3, 532 N.E.2d 49, 51 n.3; Commonwealth v. Elm Med. Labs., 33 Mass. App. Ct. 71, 77, 596 N.E.2d 376, 379 (1992). Indeed, the court in Sarvis implicitly questioned whether Massachusetts Civil Rights Act claims may be brought against the state or its political subdivisions. 47 Mass. App. Ct. at 96 n.10, 711 N.E. 2d at 920.

The Massachusetts Public Records Law, MASS. GEN. LAWS ch. 4, § 7, Twenty-sixth, defines public records as any documentary materials made or received by a public entity that do not fall within one of the statute's enumerated exemptions. This provision is similar to the federal Freedom of Information Act (FOIA), 5 U.S.C. 552, and courts have looked to federal case law under FOIA to interpret it. See, e.g., Wakefield Teachers Ass'n v. Sch. Comm., 431 Mass. 792, 793, 731 N.E.2d 63, 64 (2000); Globe Newspaper Co. v. Boston Retirement Bd., 388 Mass. 427, 432-34, 433 n.11, 446 N.E.2d 1051, 1054-56 n.11 (1983). MASS. GEN. LAWS ch. 4, § 7, Twenty-sixth (c) includes, among the exempted materials, "personnel and medical files or information; also any other materials or data relating to a specifically named individual, the disclosure of which may constitute an unwarranted invasion of personal privacy." MASS. GEN. LAWS ch. 4, § 7, Twenty-sixth (a), (c). The clause, "disclosure of which may constitute an unwarranted invasion of personal privacy," has been interpreted to modify the phrase "also any other materials or data relating to a specifically named individual," but not the phrase "personnel and medical files or information." Globe, 388 Mass. at 431, 446 N.E.2d at 1054; see also VI.A.B., infra. The types of personal information which the privacy exemption is designed to protect include marital status, legitimacy of children, identity of fathers of children, medical condition, welfare payments, alcoholic consumption, family fights (and) reputation. Attorney Gen. v. Assistant Comm'r. of Real Prop. Dept., 380 Mass. 623, 626 n.2, 404 N.E.2d 1254, 1256 n.2 (1980) (citation omitted).

The privacy exemption of the Public Records Law sets a more rigorous prohibition against disclosure than does MASS. GEN. LAWS ch. 214, §1B's proscription against "unreasonable, substantial or serious interference with one's privacy." Globe Newspaper Co. v. Dist. Attorney for the Middle Dist., 439 Mass. 374, 788 N.E.2d 513 (2003). Thus, there may be circumstances in which publishing a document that is exempt from the Public Records Law under the privacy exemption does not amount to a §1B privacy invasion. See generally Howell v. Enterprise Pub. Co., LLC, 72 Mass. App. Ct. at 751-52, 893 N.E.2d at 1282-83, 36 Media L. Rep. 2313, rev'd in part on other grounds, 455 Mass. 641, 920 N.E.2d 1, 38 Media L. Rep. 1141 (2010).

The identity of doctors who treat public employees is not exempt under the "personnel and medical files or information" exemption. See The Patriot Ledger v. Masterson, 25 Mass. L. Rep. 261, No. 106511, 2009 Mass. Super. LEXIS 62 (Mass. Super. Ct. 2009).

Pursuant to the Massachusetts Inspection of Public Records Law, MASS. GEN. LAWS ch. 66, §10, the custodian of any public record shall permit any person to inspect and receive a copy of such record within ten days of request. See Globe Newspaper Co. v. Comm'r of Educ., 439 Mass. 124, 125, 786 N.E.2d 328, 329 (2003) (rebuttable presumption, that the release of public records within ten days of the receipt of a request to inspect or copy is reasonable, may be overcome by a requestor who can demonstrate a compelling need for earlier disclosure). In any court proceeding under the statute, there shall be a presumption that the record sought is public, and the burden shall be on the custodian to prove with specificity the exemption which applies. MASS. GEN. LAWS ch. 66, §10(c) (West Supp. 2000). Exempted from this disclosure requirement are, among other things, home addresses and telephone numbers of employees of the public safety or criminal justice system, except in cases involving disclosure to an employee organization or to a criminal justice agency. MASS. GEN. LAWS ch. 66, §10(d) (West Supp. 2001).

3. ***Common Law.*** Prior to the enactment of MASS. GEN. LAWS ch. 214, §1B, the Supreme Judicial Court consistently declined to recognize the existence of a common law invasion of privacy action. See Tower v. Hirschhorn, 397 Mass. 581, 585 n.4, 492 N.E.2d 728, 732 n.4 (1986); Alberts v. Devine, 395 Mass. 59, 70, 479 N.E.2d 113, 120-21 (1985).

Massachusetts has not recognized the tort of negligent invasion of privacy, but it has not foreclosed the possibility of doing so. See Barnes v. Town of Webster, No. 04-2420, 2005 Mass. Super. LEXIS 480, at *2-3 (Mass. Super. Ct. Oct. 6, 2005).

B. Causes of Action

1. ***Misappropriation/Right of Publicity.*** The use of another's name, portrait or picture for advertising purposes or for the purposes of trade without that individual's written consent is actionable. MASS. GEN. LAWS ch. 214, §3A. The Superior Court may order injunctive relief and damages, including treble damages, for knowing violations. Massachusetts courts have looked to the Restatement (Second) of Torts §652C (1981) in interpreting the provisions of MASS. GEN. LAWS ch. 214, §3A. See Tropeano v. Atl. Monthly Co., 379 Mass. 745, 400 N.E.2d 847, 5 Media L. Rep. 2526 (1980). An incidental use of a person's picture, not done deliberately to exploit the value of the picture for advertising or trade, is not actionable. Tropeano, 379 Mass. at 750-51, 400 N.E.2d at 851, 5 Media L. Rep. 2526 (1980). See also Draghetti v. Chmielewski, 416 Mass. 808, 811-12, 626 N.E.2d 862, 866, 22 Media L. Rep. 1456 (1994) (following Tropeano, 379 Mass. at 750-51); Jodoin v. Baystate Health Systems, Inc., No. 08-40037, 2010 U.S. Dist. LEXIS 29931, at *94 (D. Mass. Mar. 29, 2010).

In Jodoin, the plaintiff sued her employer for using a photograph of a group of Baystate Health employees, including the plaintiff, in a mailing that informed residents in the area of the company's new address. Jodoin v. Baystate

Health Systems, Inc., No. 08-40037, 2010 U.S. Dist. LEXIS 29931, at *94 (D. Mass. Mar. 29, 2010). The court granted summary judgment for the employer, finding that even if the plaintiff had established that her image was used for trade or advertising purposes, she had failed to provide any evidence that her employer benefitted financially from using her image. Id. In addition, the plaintiff had failed to demonstrate that her employer's use of her image caused her harm. Id. at *95. The plaintiff did not complain about the use of her image until she was terminated. Id.

An action against an employer for misappropriation of an employee's name or likeness is judged by the same standard of proof applied in Tropeano. Zereski v. Am. Postal Workers Union, No. 97-1567, 1998 Mass. Super. LEXIS 507, at *18 (Mass. Super. Ct. Aug. 13, 1998). In Zereski, the court denied an employee's claim that the use of her name in a union newsletter for the purpose of effecting a change in union leadership constituted a violation under MASS. GEN. LAWS ch. 214, §3A. Id. The claim failed because the employee did not allege that the defendants used her name in order to promote themselves or their product or that they were motivated by financial gain or desire for publicity as required by the statute. Id.

Appropriation of another's name or likeness for commercial purposes may also give rise to a claim under the Right of Privacy Act, MASS. GEN. LAWS ch. 214, §3A (1989). See Shepard's Pharmacy, Inc. v. Stop & Shop Co., 37 Mass. App. Ct. 516, 523, 640 N.E.2d 1112, 1116 (1994) (involving pharmacy chain which prematurely announced that individual pharmacist would be joining chain in advertisement featuring pharmacist's likeness).

2. ***False Light.*** Massachusetts has not recognized the tort of false light invasion of privacy, although it has not firmly closed the door on doing so. See Ayash v. Dana-Farber Cancer Inst., 443 Mass. 367, 382 n.16, 882 N.E.2d 667, 682 n.16 (2005); Lucas v. City of Boston, No. 07-cv-10979-DPW, 2009 U.S. Dist. LEXIS 55621, at *93 (D. Mass. June 19, 2009); Brauer v. Globe Newspaper Co., 351 Mass. 53, 217 N.E.2d 179 (1966); Yovino v. Fish, 27 Mass. App. Ct. 442, 450, 539 N.E.2d 548, 553 (1989).

3. ***Publication of Private Facts.*** Massachusetts' Right of Privacy statute, MASS. GEN. LAWS ch. 214, §1B prohibits "unreasonable, substantial or serious interference" with one's privacy. The Supreme Judicial Court has interpreted §1B as prohibiting "disclosure of facts about an individual that are of a highly personal or intimate nature when there exists no legitimate countervailing interest." Bratt v. Int'l Bus. Mach., 392 Mass. 508, 518, 467 N.E.2d 126, 133-34 (1984). It has also noted that the statute is analogous to the Restatement's Publicity Given to Private Life tort, Restatement (Second) of Torts § 652D (1977). Bratt, 392 Mass. 508, 519 n.15, 467 N.E.2d 126, 129 n.15 (1984); Ayash v. Dana-Farber Cancer Inst., No. CIV.A. 96-0565E, 1997 WL 438769, at *2 (Mass. Super. Ct. July 9, 1997), partially rev'd on other grounds, 443 Mass. 367, 882 N.E.2d 667 (2005). The Restatement, however, defines publicity as being communicated to the public at large, while MASS. GEN. LAWS ch. 214, § 1B does not require such widespread publicity for an action to lie. Ayash, 1997 WL 438769, at *2 (quoting Restatement (Second) of Torts §652D, cmt. d); Peckham v. Boston Herald, Inc., 48 Mass. App. Ct. 282, 286, 719 N.E.2d 888, 891 (1999).

In fact, Massachusetts courts have held that intra-corporate disclosures can constitute unwarranted invasions of privacy under MASS. GEN. LAWS ch. 214,§ 1B. Oropallo v. Brenner, 25 Mass. L. Rep. 147, 150, No. 105683, 2009 Mass. Super. LEXIS 13, at *15 (Mass. Super. Ct. Jan. 14, 2009); Williams v. Commonwealth Limousine Serv., Inc., No. 98-4351, 1999 Mass. Super. LEXIS 17, at *4 (Mass. Super. Ct. Jan. 22, 1999).

The tort has been described as the spreading of the details of life before the public gaze in a manner highly offensive to the ordinary reasonable person. Ayash, 443 Mass. at 382, 882 N.E.2d at 682 (quoting Restatement (Second) of Torts § 652D, cmt. b). When the subject-matter of the publicity is of legitimate public concern, there is no invasion of privacy. Id.

Under the Massachusetts Right of Privacy statute, MASS. GEN. LAWS ch. 214, §1B, disclosure of statements restricted to issues regarding the plaintiff's fitness [as a potential employee] does not constitute an unreasonable interference with plaintiff's privacy. Martinez v. New England Med. Ctr. Hosps., Inc., 307 F. Supp. 2d 257, 267 (D. Mass. 2004). Where the plaintiff's employer disclosed to plaintiff's friend, who was posing as a prospective employer, the reasons for plaintiff's termination, the plaintiff's plans to move out of state, and the plaintiff's absenteeism, such disclosure related only to issues of the plaintiff's job performance, and thus were not facts of a highly personal or intimate nature. Id.

Disclosure of information limited to professional conduct in a matter that is already the focus of a high degree of public scrutiny was of legitimate public concern and did not create an action under MASS. GEN. LAWS c. 214, §1B. Ayash v. Dana-Farber Cancer Inst., 443 Mass. 367, 384-85, 822 N.E.2d 667, 683 (2005). Where the plaintiff's employer identified plaintiff as the subject of a confidential peer review action and possibly leaked documents implicating plaintiff's fault in a medical malpractice investigation, the disclosures were only part of a matter of intense public interest and not of an exceedingly personal or intimate nature. Id. at 385.

Information gathered by the public school system and its employees regarding a teacher's erratic behavior and the discussion of that information was related to a legitimate business (or academic) interest in workplace safety and student and employee well-being, and was not an actionable tort of publication of private facts. Bouley v. City of New Bedford, et al., No. 00-cv-12580-RGS, 2005 U.S. Dist. LEXIS 30922, at *22 (D. Mass. Dec. 5, 2005), citing Bratt v. Int'l Bus. Mach., 392 Mass. 508, 510, 467 N.E.2d 126, 129 (1984).

An employer may not unreasonably interfere with an employee's right to privacy by disclosing the employee's personal information if there is no countervailing legitimate business interest which justifies the disclosure. Oropallo, 2009 Mass. Super. LEXIS 13, at *15; Williams v. Commonwealth Limousine Serv., Inc., No. 98-4351, 1999 Mass. Super. LEXIS 17, at *4 (Mass. Super. Ct. Jan. 22, 1999); Zereski v. Am. Postal Workers Union, No. 97-1567, 1998 Mass. Super. LEXIS 507, at *18 (Mass. Super. Ct. Aug. 13, 1998). In Oropallo, the court denied a motion for summary judgment by an employer who claimed it had a legitimate business interest in circulating a confidential memorandum alluding to a former employee's sexual affair with a co-worker. Oropallo, 2009 Mass. Super. LEXIS 13, at *16. The court could not determine as a matter of law that the employer's interest in the sexual relationships between co-workers outweighed the employee's privacy interest in her personal relationships. Id. at *15-16. In Zereski, an employee alleged that her employer invaded her privacy by disclosing the contents of her personnel records, which allegedly contained derogatory and vulgar statements made about her by her supervisor. The court denied a motion to dismiss, finding that a jury issue existed as to whether the employer, a union that published the remarks in its newsletter in an effort to oust the supervisor from union office, had a legitimate business purpose in publishing the statements. Zereski, 1998 Mass. Super. LEXIS 507, at *24. In Williams, the court denied an employer's motion to dismiss an employee's invasion of privacy claim where the employer had posted the employee's termination letter in the office. 1999 Mass. Super. LEXIS 17, at *2. While the court in Williams reasoned that informing subordinates of a co-worker's performance problems could constitute an unprivileged invasion of privacy, it also noted that deterrent and informational objectives, both offered in defense by the employer, could constitute legitimate business interests. Id. at *3.

Where, on an acknowledged recorded line, two supervisors discussed whether to grant an employee a day off and how to get her to resign, there was no actionable invasion of privacy where conversation did not involve any personal or intimate facts about either supervisor and the employer had a legitimate business interest in recording this conversation. Peters v. Equiserve, No. 05-1052, 2006 Mass. Super. LEXIS 110, at *17-18 (Mass. Super. Ct. Feb. 24, 2006).

4. ***Intrusion.*** The Supreme Judicial Court has not determined whether intrusion on seclusion is actionable under the Right of Privacy statute, MASS. GEN. LAWS ch. 214, §1B. **However, the Appeals Court has held that §1B does indeed provide such a right of action. Amato v. District Attorney for Cape and Islands Dist., 80 Mass. App. Ct. 230, 240, 952 N.E.2d 400, 409 (2011).** See also Cook v. WHDH-TV, Inc., 8 Mass. L. Rep. No. 17, 392 (Mass. Super. Ct. March 4, 1998) (citation omitted) (holding that the rigid application of invasion of privacy tort law to invasions occurring in public places ought not deprive [the plaintiff] of the judgment of a jury of his peers as to whether defendants unreasonably and substantially or seriously invaded his privacy). See also Guertin v. McAvoy, No. 04-2004, 2005 Mass. Super. LEXIS 143, at *27 (Mass. Super. Ct. Mar. 9, 2005) (court did not rule out the possibility of the Supreme Judicial Court recognizing a MASS. GEN. LAWS. ch. 214, §1B claim based on intrusion on seclusion).

Repeated, harassing phone calls and visits to public officials at home and work constitute an invasion of privacy. See Town of Brookline v. Goldstein, 388 Mass. 443, 449-50, 447 N.E.2d 641, 645 (1983).

Acts of sexual harassment may also give rise to successful claims for invasion of privacy under MASS. GEN. LAWS ch. 214, §1B. See, e.g., Melnychenko v. 84 Lumber Co., 424 Mass. 285, 287 n.4, 290-91, 676 N.E.2d 45, 46 n. 4, 48 (1997) (where a supervisor was found to have violated employee's privacy rights by grabbing the plaintiffs in private areas, exposing himself to them, soliciting sexual acts, making allegations about their sexual conduct to others in person as well as over an office announcement system, and performing other crude acts).

C. Other Privacy-Related Actions

1. ***Intentional Infliction of Emotional Distress.*** Massachusetts Workers Compensation law provides the exclusive remedy for claims of intentional infliction of emotional distress in relation to personnel matters where the employee has not previously given notice to his employer reserving his common law rights. MASS. GEN. LAWS ch. 152 § 24; St. Arnaud v. Chapdelaine Truck Ctr., Inc., 836 F. Supp. 41 (D. Mass. 1993); Brown v. Nutter, McClennen & Fish, 45 Mass. App. Ct. 212, 215 (1998) ("emotional distress of the type alleged here is a personal injury compensable under the act"); Mathias v. Beatrice Foods Corp., 23 Mass. App. Ct. 915, 916, 500 N.E.2d 812, 814 (1986).

A plaintiff bringing a claim for intentional infliction of emotional distress must show: (1) that the actor intended to inflict emotional distress or that he knew or should have known that emotional distress was the likely result of his conduct; (2) that the conduct was extreme and outrageous, was beyond all possible bounds of decency and was utterly intolerable in a civilized community; (3) that the actions of the defendant were the cause of the plaintiff's distress; and (4) that the emotional distress sustained by the plaintiff was severe and of a nature that no reasonable man could be expected to endure it. Agis v. Howard Johnson Co., 371 Mass. 140, 144-45, 355 N.E.2d 315, 318-19 (1976) (involving restaurant owner who began randomly discharging employees upon suspicion of employee theft). See also Santiago v. City of Lowell, et al., No. 05-12196-RWZ, 2006 U.S. Dist. LEXIS 32040, at *4-5 (D. Mass. May 19, 2006) (holding that firing, vilifying, on-the-job harassment, and taking steps to maximize plaintiff's shame in the eyes of coworkers constitute elements required to establish claim of intentional infliction of emotional distress). An employee may assert a claim for intentional infliction of emotional distress based on postemployment actions taken by his former employer. See, e.g., Du v. Sunol Molecular Corp., No. 09-11797, 2010 U.S. Dist. LEXIS 67355, at *3 (D. Mass. July 7, 2010) (court allowed an employee's claim for intentional infliction of emotional distress based on allegations that his former employer filed postemployment lawsuits against him in several jurisdictions in retaliation for reporting problems with a clinical trial to the federal government).

Courts have recognized certain exceptions to the rule that the Workers Compensation law provides the exclusive remedy for claims of intentional infliction of emotional distress in relation to workplace injury. A plaintiff may claim damages for emotional distress where the mental injury is not an essential element of the tort. Thus, a plaintiff may not be barred from her mental distress that resulted from invasion of privacy and other torts. Zereski v. Am. Postal Workers Union, No. 97-1567, 1998 Mass. Super. LEXIS 507, at *21 (Mass. Super. Ct. August 14, 1998). Also, an employee alleging emotional distress as a result of discrimination may recover for the injury under the Massachusetts Employment Discrimination Statute (MASS. GEN. LAWS ch. 15, § 1B(4)) even where common law claims for such harm would be barred by worker's compensation laws. DeBarboza v. Cablevision, Inc., No. 98-4244-E, 1999 Mass. Super. LEXIS 43, at *6 (Mass. Super. Ct. Jan. 1999). An employee may recover for emotional distress from a fellow employee, even a superior, if the offending co-worker's actions were beyond the scope of employment and did not further the employer's interest. Brown v. Nutter, McClennan & Fish, 45 Mass. App. Ct. 212, 216, 696 N.E.2d 953, 956 (1998). However, an employee may not recover for emotional distress from a fellow employee if the offending co-worker acted at least partially for a job-related purpose. Id. at 218, 696 N.E.2d at 957. See also Evans v. TJ Maxx, Marmaxx, Inc., No. MICV2003-04501-A, 2005 Mass. Super. LEXIS 41 (Mass. Super. Ct. Feb. 15, 2005) (holding that a superior acted sufficiently within the scope of employment to bar recovery when superior threatened plaintiff with demotion, cited him for minor infractions beyond the purview of his job responsibilities, and made statements to other co-workers that he would like to beat up plaintiff because of his sexual orientation); Martin-Kirkland v. United Parcel Serv., et al., No. 03-4520-H, 2006 Mass. Super. LEXIS 193, at *20, 21 (Mass. Super. Ct. April 11, 2006), aff'd, 2008 Mass. App. Unpub. LEXIS 179 (Mass. App. Ct. 2008) (supervisor's complaints to others about employee's lack of production sufficiently related to the supervisor's position).

Even though a city assessor had filed a state whistleblower suit claiming that she had been wrongfully discharged in retaliation for refusing to undervalue certain property, she could also assert claims against city officials for violations of her civil rights, defamation, and infliction of emotional distress. A state employee who institutes an action under MASS. GEN. LAWS ch. 149, § 185(d) waives all rights and remedies arising out of retaliatory action, but does not waive claims which are substantially separate from and independent of the cause of action to recover for the retaliatory action. LePage v. Cent. Mass. Reg'l Planning Comm'n, 25 Mass. L. Rep. 326, 328, No. 106420, 2009 Mass. Super. LEXIS 82, at *7 (Mass. Super. Ct. Mar. 4, 2009), aff'd 78 Mass. App. Ct. 1119 (2011); Haddad v. Scanlon, No. 99-180, 1999 Mass. Super. LEXIS 272, at *10 (Mass. Super. Ct. July 16, 1999).

The social-worker-client privilege was not waived when a plaintiff claimed emotional distress damages based upon hostile work environment, not psychic injury or psychic disorder. Myers v. Tom Foolerys, Inc., No. WCV98-353A, 1999 Mass. Super. LEXIS 405, at *5-6 (Mass. Super. Ct. Sept. 29, 1999). In order to overcome the privilege, the defendant who seeks production of documents protected by the social-worker-client privilege must demonstrate that the plaintiff is seeking recovery for something other than garden-variety claims of emotional distress (i.e., claiming damages for psychic injury or psychiatric disorder.) Id. (followed by Sorenson v. H&R Block, Inc., No. 99-10268-DPW, 2000 U.S. Dist. LEXIS 16250, at *4 (D. Mass. Nov. 2, 2000)).

An employer was not liable for intentional infliction of emotional distress where the employer questioned an employee in the presence of others regarding a misappropriation of funds and where the employer's questioning allegedly took place in a locked office. See Nault v. UPS, No. 98-1542, 2001 Mass. Super. LEXIS 115, at *10 (Mass. Super. Ct. Feb. 26, 2001).

Allegations that the employee had a poor performance record, ordering the employee to leave the premises within five minutes, and not letting the employee return to work for four days did not rise to the level of extreme and outrageous conduct needed for an emotional distress claim. Terravecchia v. Fleet Bank, et al., No. 2004-3086F, 2007 Mass. Super. LEXIS 88 (Mass. Super. Ct. Mar. 21, 2007).

An employee's claim against the City of Peabody for intentional infliction of emotional distress was barred by the Massachusetts Tort Claims Act, MASS. GEN. LAWS ch. 258, § 10(c). See Howcroft v. City of Peabody, 51 Mass. App. Ct. 573, 597, 747 N.E.2d 729, 742-48 (2001). The employee's claims for intentional infliction of emotional distress against other city employees in their individual capacities were not barred by governmental immunity. Id. at 596.

A plaintiff employee's intentional infliction of emotional distress suit against a private investigator who had reported her alleged involvement in a check forging scheme to her employer survived the investigator's motion for summary judgment. Genuine issues of fact remained as to whether the investigator's conduct was extreme and outrageous. Williams v. Brigham & Women's Hosp., Inc., No. 001546A, 2002 WL 532979, at *10-11 (Mass. Super. Ct. Jan. 8, 2002). However, the counts alleging intentional infliction of emotional distress on the part of her employer were dismissed. Id.

2. ***Interference with Prospective Economic Advantage.*** Massachusetts recognizes the tort of interference with an advantageous business relationship. To establish intentional interference with contractual or business relations, the plaintiffs must show (1) the existence of a contract or a business relationship which contemplated economic benefit; (2) the defendant's knowledge of the contract or business relationship; (3) the defendant's intentional interference with the contract or business relationship for an improper purpose or by improper means; and (4) damages. Swanset Dev. Corp. v. Taunton, 423 Mass. 390, 397, 668 N.E.2d 333, 338 (1996). See also Doyle v. Hasbro, Inc., 103 F.3d 186 (1st Cir. 1996). Generally, an employer may not be liable for interference with its own employment relationship with an employee. Labor and Employment in Massachusetts, 18-5(c), 18-39 (citing Appley v. Locke, 396 Mass. 540, 543, 487 N.E.2d 501, 503 (1986); Gram v. Liberty Mut. Ins. Co., 384 Mass. 659, 663 n.3, 429 N.E.2d 21, 24 n.3 (1981); Vigoda v. Barton, 338 Mass. 302, 304, 155 N.E.2d 409, 411 (1959)); Bennett v. City of Holyoke, 230 F. Supp. 2d 207 (D. Mass. 2002), aff'd on other grounds, 362 F.3d 1 (1st Cir. 2004). However, the Supreme Judicial Court upheld a jury verdict against a supervisor who interfered with an employee's employment relationship by way of abusive behavior and denial of training and work where it found malice and absence of any relation between the conduct and legitimate business interests. See O'Brien v. New England Tel. & Tel. Co., 422 Mass. 686, 664 N.E.2d 843 (1996). Cf. Ossinger v. City of Newton, 26 Mass. App. Ct. 831, 837, 533 N.E.2d 228, 232 (1989) (upholding a directed verdict for a mayor who discharged an at-will city employee suspected of larceny because of the lack of evidence of any bad faith or "invidious motive" on the part of the mayor).

In the employment and discharge context, an employee who claims interference with contractual relations must meet a heightened standard and prove that the company's official acted with actual malice, and thus for a purpose unrelated to any legitimate corporate interest. In this context, courts have construed the term "company official" expansively, to include high level corporate officers, directors involved in management, and supervisors who are not corporate officers, as long as the employee was under their supervision. See Blackstone v. Cashman, 448 Mass. 255, 266 (2007). However, evidence of mere dislike, such as derogatory comments about an employee's clothes and background, is insufficient proof that the supervisor acted with malice in securing the employee's discharge. Alba v. Sampson, 44 Mass. App. Ct. 311, 315-16, 690 N.E.2d 1240, 1243-44 (1998). Actual malice requires "a spiteful malignant purpose unrelated to the legitimate interest." Psy-Ed Corp. v. Klein, 459 Mass. 697, 716 (2011) (quoting Blackstone v. Cashman, 448 Mass. 255, 260-61 (2007)); Terravecchia v. Fleet Bank, 2004-3086F, 22 Mass. L. Rep. 314, 2007 Mass. Super. LEXIS 88, at *14 (Mass. Super. Ct. Mar. 21, 2007) . The actual malice standard is intended to prove improper motive or means on the part of a corporate official and as such, the burden is placed on the plaintiff claiming interference with contractual relations; it is not a defense that must be proved by a defendant. Blackstone, 448 Mass. at 261. In LeGoff v. Trustees of Boston Univ., 23 F. Supp. 2d 120, 129 (D. Mass. 1998), the court noted that Massachusetts courts have expanded the definition of malice to include intentional discrimination. Id. at 130. However, in an action where a white male alleged that he was denied a tenure track position at a university because the university wanted to fill the position with a minority candidate, the President and Provost of the University did not necessarily act with actual malice. Edsall v. Assumption Coll., 367 F. Supp. 2d 72, 84-85 (D. Mass. 2005).

A plaintiff may show actual malice by inference, however a plaintiff will not succeed by merely showing an adverse impact with what the court calls "a laundry list" of facts which may or may not indicate that the defendant acted out of actual malice. Terravecchia, 2007 Mass. Super. LEXIS 88, at *15.

A supervisor did not act with actual malice when the record demonstrated that he consulted with other company executives, consulted with human resources to insure that termination was consistent with company policy and treatment of other employees, and consulted corporate counsel. Valls v. Geon Engineered Films, Inc., No. 03-2496-C, 2005 Mass. Super. LEXIS 101, at *17 (Mass. Super. Ct. March 24, 2005).

A police officer asserted a triable claim for intentional interference with contractual relations against his supervisor and fellow police officers where he alleged that the defendants retaliated against him for complaining that other police were smoking in violation of a statute restricting smoking in public buildings. Howcroft v. City of Peabody, 51 Mass. App. Ct. 573, 597, 747 N.E.2d 729, 747-48 (2001).

An employee's claim for malicious interference with his employment agreement must fail where the employee failed to perform his job responsibilities and advanced his own interests over those of the company and where he failed to establish that the employer acted with malice in terminating his employment. Pulsifer v. Bitflow, Inc., No. 97-4508, 2001 Mass. Super. LEXIS 30, at *23, *53 (Mass. Super. Ct. Jan. 6, 2001).

In Zimmerman v. Direct Fed. Credit Union, 121 F. Supp. 2d 133, 137 (D. Mass. 2000), aff'd, 262 F.3d 70 (1st Cir. 2001), the court upheld a jury verdict for intentional interference with contractual relations where the plaintiff alleged that the defendant coworker unlawfully retaliated against her after she brought a complaint for discrimination.

In Shafir v. Steele, 431 Mass. 365, 27 N.E.2d 1140 (2000), the Court expressly recognized for the first time in Massachusetts the tort of intentional interference with a party's own performance of a contract with a third party. Thus, when a plaintiff breaches a contract with a third party due to interference by the defendant, the plaintiff may sue the defendant. The court adopted Restatement (Second) of Torts § 766A.

3. ***Prima Facie Tort.*** No Massachusetts cases on point.

II. EMPLOYER TESTING OF EMPLOYEES

A. Psychological or Personality Testing

1. ***Common Law and Statutes.*** At least one court has interpreted the statutory restrictions on employer-required, preemployment medical examinations, MASS. GEN. LAWS ch. 151B, § 4(16), as extending to psychological exams. White v. City of Boston, No. CIV. A. 95-6483F, 1997 WL 416586, at *2 (Mass. Super. Ct. July 22, 1997), aff'd, 428 Mass. 250 (1998). The prohibition does not extend, however, to situations where a former employee is seeking re-employment with the same employer. White, 1997 WL 416586 at *3.

2. ***Private Employers.*** An employee's civil rights under the Massachusetts Civil Rights Act, MASS. GEN. LAWS ch. 12, §§ 11H, 11I, were not violated when his employer threatened to dismiss him if he did not submit to psychological testing. Vaughan v. XRE/ADC Corp., No. C.A. 95-6187E, 1996 WL 1185094 (Mass. Super. Ct. June 5, 1996). The court relied on a lack of any physical intimidation or reasonable fear of injury, as well as plaintiff's status as an at-will employee. Cf. Cort v. Bristol-Myers Co., 385 Mass. 300, 311, 431 N.E.2d 908, 914 (1982) (considering plaintiff's claim that employer's questionnaire was prohibited because it could be used as the basis of a comprehensive psychiatric evaluation, but rejecting that claim because plaintiff produced no evidence that it was so used). Additionally, a Massachusetts federal district court refused to recognize an invasion of privacy claim when an employee's supervisor merely suggested a psychological exam, no exam ever took place, no results were disclosed, and the proposed exam was reasonable. Carmack v. Nat'l R.R. Passenger Corp., 486 F. Supp. 2d 58, 80-82 (D. Mass. 2007).

Under the First Amendment, the court did not have jurisdiction to determine whether a church conference's conditions to reinstatement of a minister, including the conference's ability to review records of medical and psychological examinations of the minister that it required, constituted an invasion of privacy. Callahan v. First Congregational Church of Haverhill, 441 Mass. 699, 715, 808 N.E.2d 301, 313 (2004).

3. ***Public Employers.*** An oral examination to evaluate the personality of a civil servant is appropriate for determining the employee's merit for promotion purposes. McDowell v. Hurley, 291 Mass. 258, 260, 197 N.E. 25 (1935). While the statute interpreted by McDowell is no longer in effect, the principle involved continues to be relevant given the existence of similar current statutes. See, e.g., MASS. GEN. LAWS ch. 31, §16 (civil service examinations fairly test the knowledge, skills and abilities); Id. §22 (allowing applicants to request review of whether exam fairly tested fitness for duties of position); Id. §24 (allowing appeal on grounds that exam did not fairly test fitness for duties of position); Id. §10 (permitting alternative departmental promotional exams, including competitive exams). The First Circuit found that the federal constitution was not offended by a school superintendent's demand that a tenured teacher undergo a psychiatric evaluation, where mental instability of the teacher to the degree suggested might have constituted a ground for dismissal of a tenured teacher under Massachusetts law. Lyons v. Sullivan, 602 F.2d 7, 10 (1st Cir. 1979).

Psychological fitness screening is required for one seeking appointment as a police officer. See Lambley v. Kameny, 43 Mass. App. Ct. 277, 278, 682 N.E.2d 907, 908 (1997). See also Archer v. Town of Saugus, No. 90-3605-S, 1994 WL 878769 (Mass. Super. Ct. Nov. 18, 1994) (a condition of plaintiff's appointment as a police officer was that he undergo a police department-sponsored and Department of Personnel Administration-approved psychological examination, the results of which, in case of failure, are subject to review and may be appealed).

B. Drug Testing

Drug testing cases generally involve urinalyses randomly conducted by employers. The Supreme Judicial Court has recognized mandatory urinalyses as involving a significant invasion of privacy. Webster v. Motorola, Inc., 418 Mass. 425,

431, 637 N.E.2d 203, 207 (1994), (quoting Folmsbee v. Tech Tool Grinding & Supply, 417 Mass. 388, 392, 630 N.E.2d 586, 589 (1994)). Accord O'Connor v. Police Comm'r, 408 Mass. 324, 328, 557 N.E.2d 1146, 1150 (1990); Horsemen's Benevolent and Protective Ass'n v. State Racing Comm'n, 403 Mass. 692, 704, 532 N.E.2d 644, 652 (1989). The basis for this is the holding that urination is inherently a private activity. Webster, 418 Mass. at 431, 637 N.E.2d at 207 (quoting Folmsbee, 417 Mass. at 393, 630 N.E.2d at 590); Accord Horsemen's, 403 Mass. at 699, 532 N.E.2d at 648. Furthermore, individuals have a privacy interest in information detectable through urinalysis. Webster, 418 Mass. at 431, 637 N.E.2d at 207. See also Horsemen's, 403 Mass. at 700, 532 N.E.2d at 649 (noting that urinalyses may disclose other personal information, such as pregnancy, use of medication or birth control, and presence of disease). Additionally, to the extent that it may be requested to rebut an initial positive test result, information concerning an employee's medical conditions is also within the realm of one's privacy interest. Webster, 418 Mass. at 431, 637 N.E.2d at 207. See also Horsemen's, 403 Mass. at 700, 532 N.E.2d at 649.

With regard to requiring drivers to take drug tests, the federal Omnibus Transportation Employee Testing Act of 1991 preempted any claims under the Massachusetts Constitution or Massachusetts General Laws. Keaveney, et al. v. Town of Brookline, et al., 937 F. Supp. 975, 983 (D. Mass. 1996) (holding that employees who engaged in interstate commerce by driving vehicles for their employer, and were forced to take drug tests, could not recover damages).

1. ***Common Law and Statutes.*** Massachusetts has no drug testing statute. Rather, drug testing policies in the private sector are challenged through actions under the Right of Privacy Law, MASS. GEN. LAWS ch. 214, § 1B (1989), and the Civil Rights Law, see I.A, supra. Public sector drug testing is challenged through claims under these statutes as well as Article 14 of the Massachusetts Declaration of Rights. See I.A, supra.

2. ***Private Employers.*** Civil Rights Act, MASS. GEN. LAWS ch. 12, §§11H, 11I. Massachusetts courts have declined to extend Chapter 12's protection in instances where drug testing was not directed at a specific person or class of persons. See, e.g., Webster v. Motorola, Inc., 418 Mass. 425, 430, 637 N.E.2d 203, 206 (1994). Prior cases, where relief was awarded under Chapter 12, involved physical confrontation or threats to contract rights. See, e.g., Webster, 418 Mass. at 430, 639 N.E.2d at 206 (denying Article 14 claim of plaintiffs who allegedly were threatened with the loss of their at -will positions because "[n]o physical confrontation is alleged[,]" and because plaintiffs had no contractual right to their positions).

Right of Privacy Statute, MASS. GEN. LAWS ch. 214, § 1B. To determine whether an employer's drug testing policy violates its employee's rights under MASS. GEN. LAWS ch. 214, § 1B, the employee's interest in privacy must be balanced against the employer's competing interest in determining whether its employees are using drugs. Webster, 418 Mass. at 431, 637 N.E.2d at 207. See also O'Connor v. Police Comm'r, 408 Mass. 324, 330, 557 N.E.2d 1146, 1150 (1990); Folmsbee v. Tech Tool Grinding & Supply, Inc., 417 Mass. 388, 392, 630 N.E.2d 586, 589 (1994) (stating that "the employer's legitimate interest in determining the employee's effectiveness in their jobs should be balanced against the seriousness of the intrusion on the employee's privacy" (quoting Bratt v. Int'l Bus. Mach., 392 Mass. 508, 519 n.15, 467 N.E.2d 126, 129 n.15)); Webster, 418 Mass. at 431, 637 N.E.2d at 207 (holding that "private employers are not subject to the more stringent requirements of probable cause that govern public employers") (quoting Folmsbee, 417 Mass. at 393 n.7, 630 N.E.2d at 589)); Accord Horsemen's Benevolent and Protective Ass'n v. State Racing Comm'n, 403 Mass. 692, 706; 532 N.E.2d 644, 652 (1989).

The employee's privacy interests are balanced against such factors as the impact that an employee's health can have on the employee's performance, the nature of the business involved, and the employee's duties. See Webster v. Motorola, 418 Mass. 425, 432, 637 N.E.2d 203, 208 (1994). Employers also have an interest in creating a safe, drug-free workplace. See Webster, 418 Mass. at 433, 637 N.E. 2d at 209. An employer's legitimate concerns extend to the safety of the employer, the employees (see Folmsbee v. Tech Tool Grinding & Supply Co., Inc., 417 Mass. 388, 393, 630 N.E.2d 586, 590 (1994)), the customers, and the public. See Webster, 418 Mass. at 434, 637 N.E.2d at 209; Folmsbee, 417 Mass. at 393, 630 N.E.2d at 590. In Folmsbee, for example, the Supreme Judicial Court was influenced by the fact that the employer's business required "extreme alertness and precision." 417 Mass. at 393.

In Webster, 418 Mass. at 434, 637 N.E.2d at 209, an employer's testing was considered reasonable where the employee "was not observed while urinating, and was not visually inspected during the procedure, the information reported to the employer was limited, the results were independently verified first, and the methods used were highly accurate." Accord Folmsbee v. Tech Tool Grinding & Supply, Inc., 417 Mass. 388, 630 N.E.2d 586 (1994) (employer provided thirty days' advance notice of testing and promised retesting and drug counseling at company expense for anyone who tested positive, and employees were tested by an experienced facility through procedures designed to minimize intrusiveness).

The post-accident drug testing of an employee was found justified by an employer's legitimate business interest where the employee's work was sufficiently dangerous that he risked serious injury to himself, to others, or to the machine if he were to use the machine while under the influence of drugs, and where the urine test was used solely for detection of controlled substances. Harrison v. Eldim, Inc., No. 99-404F, 2000 Mass. Super. LEXIS 33, at *7 (Mass. Super. Ct. Feb. 16, 2000). The general interest of all businesses in protecting the safety of their employees and providing them a drug-free environment in which to work is not itself sufficient to justify requiring an employee to submit to urinalysis. Id. An employer need not have a drug problem in the workplace before he can institute drug testing to prevent such a problem. Id. at *10.

The Supreme Judicial Court has reserved the question of whether the Right of Privacy Statute reaches attempts to interfere with a person's privacy. Folmsbee, 417 Mass. at 392, 630 N.E.2d at 590 (involving a plaintiff discharged for refusing to submit to an employer's mandatory drug test). Accord Bally v. Northeastern Univ., 403 Mass. 713, 721 n.5, 532 N.E.2d 49, 53 n.5 (1989); Cort v. Bristol-Myers, 385 Mass. 300, 311 n.1, 431 N.E.2d 908, 914 n.1 (1982) (involving plaintiffs who refused to answer questions they deemed personal on a mandatory questionnaire, and were later discharged).

3. ***Public Employers.*** In addition to the statutes discussed in II.B, supra, public employees may invoke Article 14 of the Massachusetts Declaration of Rights in challenging drug testing practices. In evaluating alleged Article 14 violations, courts balance the governmental need for the search against the search's intrusiveness into a person's reasonably expected privacy. O'Connor v. Police Comm'r, 408 Mass. 324, 328, 557 N.E.2d 1146, 1150 (1990). See also Horsemen's Benevolent and Protective Ass'n v. State Racing Comm'n, 403 Mass. 692, 704, 532 N.E.2d 644, 651 (1989). See, e.g., Guiney v. Police Comm'r, 411 Mass. 328, 330, 582 N.E.2d 523, 524 (1991) (holding that the government must make a strong factual showing that a substantial public need exists for the imposition of such a process applicable to all police officers, which cannot rely upon unsubstantiated justifications or the mere presence of a nationwide drug problem).

In Guiney, the police department's random, nonconsensual drug testing program was found to violate Article 14 in part because "[t]here [was] nothing in the record to indicate that there has been any problem, or any public perception of a problem, arising from the illicit use of drugs by Boston police officers." Moreover, the court found no showing of how random drug testing by urinalysis will provide information that is needed to identify officers whose on-duty performance was affected by illicit drug use. 411 Mass. at 330, 582 N.E.2d at 526. Cf. Horsemen's, 403 Mass. at 706, 532 N.E.2d at 652 (holding that random urinalysis of licensees violates Article 14 where there is no probable cause, where the agency has not advanced a substantiated, compelling justification, and where a positive test result does not necessarily indicate drug impairment at the time of the test).

In contrast to this line of precedent stands Bennett v. Mass. Bay Transp. Auth., No. CIV.A. 93-1409-E, 1998 WL 52250 (Mass. Super. Ct. Jan. 28, 1998), in which the lower court upheld random urinalyses for public transit employees. Distinguishing Guiney v. Police Comm'r, 411 Mass. 328, 582 N.E.2d 523 (1991), the Superior Court noted evidence in the record of an actual drug problem among MBTA employees, a public perception of such a problem, the unique way that urinalyses will allow for the identification of vehicle operators under the influence of drugs, and a well-defined group of safety-sensitive employees. See Bennett, 1998 WL 52250, at *11, *12. See also O'Connor v. Police Comm'r, 408 Mass. 324, 557 N.E.2d 1146 (1990) allowing consensual drug testing of police cadets in light of the government's concerns of public confidence, difficulty of discerning drug use, the impairment such use causes in "perception, judgment, physical fitness, and integrity," and the irreconcilability of drug use with law enforcement. O'Connor, 408 Mass. at 328-29, 557 N.E.2d at 1149. Consensual drug testing does not violate Article 14, unless it is unreasonably required. See O'Connor, 408 Mass. at 329, 557 N.E.2d at 1150.

The First Circuit has also upheld random urinalysis for state public transit employees. O'Brien v. Mass. Bay Transp. Auth., 162 F.3d 40, 45 (1st Cir. 1998) (finding that the federal Omnibus Transportation Employee Testing Act, which requires random drug and alcohol screening for employee's performing safety-sensitive functions, preempts Article 14 of the Massachusetts Declaration of Rights). The court here ruled that acceptance of significant federal funding obliges MBTA authorities to abide by the federal statute. Id.

In Byrne v. Mass. Bay Transp. Auth., 196 F. Supp. 2d 77 (D. Mass. 2002), the United States District Court for the District of Massachusetts noted that the balancing test to be used in evaluating the propriety of a drug testing policy under MASS. GEN. LAWS ch. 214 § 1B is very similar to the balancing approach applied in the Fourth Amendment analysis. Id. at 85. It then found that since the drug testing policy employed by the MBTA did not violate the Fourth Amendment, it was unlikely that the policy would be found to be an unreasonable, substantial, or serious interference with the plaintiff's privacy in violation of § 1B. Id. at 85-86.

Individual government officials are immune from personal liability under Article 14, the Civil Rights Act, MASS. GEN. LAWS ch. 12 §§ 11H, 11I, and the Right of Privacy statute in connection with their development of drug testing programs. Duarte v. Healy, 405 Mass. 43, 537 N.E.2d 1230 (1989) (involving municipal officers who developed a drug testing policy for firefighting recruits).

C. Medical Testing

1. ***Common Law and Statutes.*** Mandatory medical testing may be challenged by private sector employees through actions under the Right of Privacy statute, MASS. GEN. LAWS ch. 214, § 1B, and the Civil Rights Act. See I.A, supra. In the public sector, medical testing may additionally be challenged under Article 14 of the Massachusetts Declaration of Rights. See I.A, supra. Medical testing may also implicate the other statutes discussed below.

Testing Regarding Disabilities. The Massachusetts Anti-Discrimination Statute, MASS. GEN. LAWS ch. 151B, prohibits an employer from making a pre-employment inquiry about whether the applicant is handicapped or about the nature or severity of the handicap. An employer may condition an offer of employment on the results of a medical examination conducted solely for the purpose of determining whether the employee, with a reasonable accommodation, is capable of performing the essential functions of the job. MASS. GEN. LAWS ch. 151B, § 4(16). Chapter 151B was largely patterned after the federal Rehabilitation Act, 29 U.S.C. 794, and courts interpreting the disability-testing restrictions under Massachusetts law have looked to federal decisions under both the Rehabilitation Act and the American with Disabilities Act, 42 U.S.C. 12112. See White v. City of Boston, No. CIV.A. 95-6483F, 1997 WL 416586 (Mass. Super. Ct. July 22, 1997); Talbert Trading Co. v. Mass. Comm'n Against Discrimination, 37 Mass. App. Ct. 56, 60, 636 N.E.2d 1351, 1353 (1994), rev'd on other grounds, City of New Bedford v. Mass. Comm'n Against Discrimination, 440 Mass. 450, 463, 799 N.E.2d 578, 588 (2003). The restrictions on employer-required medical exams do not apply where a former employee is seeking re-employment with the same employer. White, 1997 WL 416586, at *3 (noting that, in such situations, there is no danger of an exam revealing disabilities that were previously hidden). An employer may also consider how an employee's disability may affect the safety and welfare of other employees. Talbert, 37 Mass. App. Ct. at 61 n.3, 632 N.E.2d at 1355 n.3.

AIDS/HIV Testing. Massachusetts law prohibits HIV testing, disclosure of HIV test results, and identification of the subject of an HIV test without the subject's prior informed and written consent. MASS. GEN. LAWS ch. 111, § 70F. No employer may require an HIV test as a condition of employment. Id.

Genetic Testing. Pursuant to MASS. GEN. LAWS ch. 151B, § 4(19)(a), Massachusetts employers may not consider genetic information in making decisions about current or prospective employees. Id. Employers may not terminate or refuse to hire a person based on genetic information, may not require disclosure of genetic information or require genetic testing as a condition of employment, offer a person an inducement to undergo a genetic test or to disclose genetic information, question a person about genetic information or previous genetic testing, or otherwise seek, receive, or maintain genetic information for non-medical purposes. Id.

2. ***Private Employers.*** See II.B.2,C.1, supra.

3. ***Public Employers.*** The Civil Service administrator may establish physical requirements as prerequisites for appointment to any civil service position; provided, however, that no applicant shall be discriminated against because he previously suffered from cancer if he is otherwise physically qualified and he signs a waiver of rights to disability benefits with respect to said cancer. MASS. GEN. LAWS ch. 31, § 21. First-time applicants may be required to undergo physical examinations prior to appointment, while applicants for promotion may be required to submit certificates of physical fitness from physicians. Id. Those failing to meet the requirements will not be disqualified if they can prove that the failure resulted from an injury sustained on the job which does not prevent them from performing the duties required. Id. Disabled veterans may be required to present a certificate from a physician stating that the disability does not prevent them from performing the required duties. MASS. GEN. LAWS ch. 31, § 26. See also II.B.3, C.1, supra.

D. Polygraph Tests

An employer is prohibited from requesting or requiring that an employee or applicant for employment take a lie-detector test. MASS. GEN. LAWS ch. 149, § 19B(2). No waiver of this prohibition by an employee or applicant will be effective. MASS. GEN. LAWS ch. 149, § 19B(3). All employment applications must inform applicants of the statutory prohibition, and employers are prohibited from penalizing those who refuse to take such a test. MASS. GEN. LAWS ch. 149, § 19B(2). The statute does not apply to tests administered by law enforcement agencies as part of criminal investigations. A law enforcement officer who is the subject of a criminal investigation may be required to undergo a lie detector test. Baker v. City of Lawrence, 379 Mass. 322, 409 N.E.2d 710 (1979). The exception allowing law enforcement employers to administer polygraph or lie detector tests to employees as part of criminal investigations under MASS. GEN. LAWS ch. 149, § 19(B)(2) also applies where the conduct complained of, if true, would constitute a crime even though criminal prosecution was not possible at the time of the administration of the polygraph. Furtado v. Town of Plymouth, 451 Mass. 529, 538, 888 N.E.2d 357, 364 (2008).

Where an enforcement agency is conducting an investigation into a crime alleged to have been committed by a person in connection with the duties of his employment, and where the employee refuses, or indicates hesitation, to take a polygraph test, the employer may then request that the employee do so, with implied job sanctions if the employee finally declines. Bellin v. Kelley, 48 Mass. App. Ct. 573, 581, 724 N.E.2d 319, 325 (2000), aff'd, 435 Mass. 261, 755 N.E.2d 1274 (2001). An employer who violates the statute is subject to criminal penalties, MASS. GEN. LAWS ch. 149, § 9B(1), (3), and an aggrieved individual may bring a civil action for injunctive relief and damages, MASS. GEN. LAWS ch. 149, § 19B(4).

Because the Massachusetts polygraph statute is generally more restrictive than the federal equivalent, the former will control in most cases. 1 Employee Privacy Law 6:38, at 107 (citing 29 U.S.C. 2002, 2006(d), (e), (f)). However, while the Federal Act prohibits even the use or reliance on polygraph test results in connection with employment by private sector employers in most situations, the state statute does not contain such a prohibition. Id. In such situations, then, the federal act would control. See also II.A, supra.

E. Fingerprinting

No statutes or reported cases deal directly with the issue of fingerprinting in the employment context. State regulations require or allow fingerprinting for admittance to certain professions. See, e.g., 205 MASS. CODE REGS. 2.17 (1993) (applicants for license as horse racing trainer); 205 MASS. CODE REGS. 4.25 (1993) (licensed horse racing participants); 205 MASS. CODE REGS. 5.04 (1996) (application to become special state police officer); 205 MASS. CODE REGS. 3.02 (1996) (permitting Boxing Commission to require fingerprints from boxing license applicants); 205 MASS. CODE REGS. 12.202 (1996) (application to become securities broker-dealer).

III. SEARCHES

A. Employee's Person

1. ***Private Employers.*** No Massachusetts cases on point.

2. ***Public Employers.*** In Fusaro v. Blakely, 40 Mass. App. Ct. 120, 661 N.E.2d 1399 (Mass. App. Ct. 1996), the court upheld a verdict finding federal and Massachusetts civil rights violations by hospital and police officers who investigated an employee on suspicion of drug crimes. In the course of their employment and in furtherance of the hospital's interest, the officers searched the clothes, person, and car of the suspect and pharmacy technician, threatened to have him fired, and used other coercive investigative tactics. Id. In the context of a motion to suppress evidence seized by United States postal inspectors from mail carrier's person and vehicle, the court held that the employee must freely and voluntarily give officers permission to search. United States v. Gunning, 405 F. Supp. 2d 79, 81-82 (D. Mass. 2005). Consent is not freely given if a reasonable person would have believed that his consent was required by investigating officers. Id. at 82.

B. Employee's Work Area

An employee's invasion of privacy claim against her employer, a private university, for allegedly inspecting her computer and paper files while she was out of work due to illness, was dismissed because files were the employer's property and the employee had little, if any, privacy interest in them. Battenfield v. Harvard Univ., No. 91-5089F, 1993 Mass. Super. LEXIS 253 (Mass. Super. Ct. Aug. 31, 1993). See also Nadal-Ginard v. Children's Hosp. Corp., No. 94-3782-E, 1995 Mass. Super. LEXIS 383, at *13-14 (Mass. Super. Ct. Dec. 1, 1998), where the court, without comment on the issue, found for a former employer on a former employee's Chapter 214, §1B claim arising from the employers allegedly allowing a search of the employee's office upon suspicion of embezzlement, citing, inter alia, Bratt v. Int'l Bus. Mach. Corp., 392 Mass. 508, 521, 467 N.E.2d 126, 135 (1984) (requiring the court to balance the employer's legitimate business interest in obtaining and publishing the information against the substantiality of the intrusion on the employee's privacy).

C. Employee's Property

1. ***Private Employers.*** A search of an employee's belongings by a special police officer who was working as a security guard for a private employer did not violate the employee's Fourth Amendment rights, because it was a legitimate and reasonable means of protecting the employer's property. See Commonwealth v. Leone, 386 Mass. 329, 435 N.E.2d 1036 (1982). Cf. Commonwealth v. Pasqualino, No. 94-0177, 1995 WL 808969 (Mass. Super. Ct. Feb. 9, 1995) (approving the procedures used in search of home of employee suspected of stealing from employer, where the search was conducted pursuant to a warrant by police accompanied by other company employees).

2. ***Public Employers.*** In Fusaro v. Blakely, 40 Mass. App. Ct. 120, 661 N.E.2d 1399 (1996), the court upheld a verdict finding federal and Massachusetts civil rights violations by hospital and police officers who investigated an employee on suspicion of drug crimes. In the course of their employment and in furtherance of the hospital's interest, the officers searched the clothes, person, and car of the suspect and pharmacy technician, threatened to have him fired, and used other coercive investigative tactics. Id.

In the context of a motion to suppress evidence seized by United States postal inspectors from mail carrier's person and vehicle, employee must freely and voluntarily give permission for search. United States v. Gunning, 405 F. Supp. 2d 79, 81-82 2005 (D. Mass. 2005). Consent is not freely given if a reasonable person would have believed that his consent was required by investigating officers. Id. at 82.

IV. MONITORING OF EMPLOYEES

A. Telephones and Electronic Communications

1. ***Wiretapping.*** Massachusetts is an all-party consent state. The Massachusetts Wiretap Act codified by MASS. GEN. LAWS ch. 272, §99 et. seq., prohibits the interception of wire and oral communications by private individuals in the absence of consent by all parties. In order to prove a violation of the Massachusetts Wiretapping Statute, the plaintiff has the burden of establishing by a fair preponderance of the evidence: (1) an unlawful recording; (2) knowing use or disclosure of the unlawful recording within the three year statute of limitations; and (3) in order to recover punitive damages, actual damage. Birbiglia v. St. Vincent Hosp., No. 91-1280, 1994 WL 878836, at *9 (Mass. Super. Ct., Dec. 29, 1994), aff'd, 427 Mass. 80 (1998). Certain interceptions are exempt, including office intercommunication systems used in the ordinary course of business, MASS. GEN. LAWS ch. 272, § 99(D)(1). Violators of the statute are subject to both criminal penalties, § 99(C)(1), and civil remedies, § 99(Q).

The Massachusetts statute is at least as protective of individual rights as the Federal statute, 18 U.S.C. 2510 -20, which requires only one party's consent. O'Sullivan v. NYNEX Corp., 426 Mass. 261, 264, 264 n.5, 687 N.E.2d 1241, 1244 (1997), citing United States v. McKinnon, 721 F.2d 19 (1st Cir. 1983); Commonwealth v. Vitello, 367 Mass. 224, 247, 251, 327 N.E.2d 819, 833, 836 (1975). Given the similarities between federal and state wiretap statutes, Massachusetts courts may look to federal court interpretations of the federal statute in interpreting the Massachusetts law. See Crosland v. Horgan, 401 Mass. 271, 275, 516 N.E.2d 147, 149 (1987).

One exception to Wiretap Act requirements is the use of an intercom in the ordinary course of business. MASS. GEN. LAWS ch. 272, § 99(D). See Commonwealth v. Pierce, 66 Mass. App. Ct. 283, 286, 846 N.E.2d 1189, 1192 (2006) (Court did not suppress evidence obtained when officers overheard men in custody over the police station intercommunication system. The intercom was used for station security in the ordinary course of business of the police department).

In the employment context, monitoring business calls is legal, but eavesdropping on private calls is illegal unless there is a legitimate business purpose for the employer to monitor an employee's conversation. O'Sullivan v. NYNEX Corp., 426 Mass. 261, 266, 687 N.E.2d 1241, 1245 (1997) (citation omitted) (involving suit under Wiretap Act by customers who feared they were recorded by phone company's system for monitoring employee solicitation calls, a system of which employees were aware). Accord Crosland v. Horgan, 401 Mass. 271, 275, 516 N.E.2d 147, 149 (1987). The employer would need to hang up the extension telephone as soon as he or she established that the call made by the employee was personal rather than business. O'Sullivan v. NYNEX Corp., No. CIV.A. 6600-D, 1996 WL 560274, at *7 (Mass. Super. Ct. Sept. 26, 1996), aff'd, 426 Mass. 261, 687 N.E.2d 1241 (1997). In light of the statutory purpose of protection from invasions of privacy, neither the concept of legitimate business purpose nor ordinary course of business can be expanded to mean anything that interests a company. Crosland, 401 Mass. at 275, 516 N.E.2d at 150.

In O'Sullivan, the court concluded that NYNEX's monitoring was consistent with accepted business practices, and was necessary for quality control, proper supervision of employees, and ensuring compliance with telecommunications statutes. O'Sullivan v. NYNEX Corp., 426 Mass. 261, 267, 687 N.E.2d 1241, 1245 (1997). In Crosland v. Horgan, 401 Mass. 271, 516 N.E.2d 147 (1987), the court found that a jury could reasonably conclude that it was within the normal course of business for a hospital supervisor to eavesdrop on a conversation between two other hospital employees for the purpose of catching one of them making a bomb threat. The eavesdropping was done at the direction of a police officer and with the consent of one of the employees. In Peters v. Equiserve, et al., compliance with regulations and quality control were deemed legitimate business purposes. 2006 Mass. Super. LEXIS 110, at *13 (Mass. Super. Ct. Feb. 24, 2006).

Declining to impose a strict, literal reading of the Wiretap Act, MASS. GEN. LAWS ch. 272, § 97(A), the court in Dillon v. Mass. Bay Transp. Auth., 49 Mass. App. Ct. 309, 729 N.E.2d 329 (2000) review denied, 432 Mass. 1105, 733 N.E.2d 1067 (2002), found that the MBTA's recording of its employee's telephone conversations did not violate the Act, even though the recording equipment was not purchased from a common carrier and thus was not narrowly included within the common carrier exception to the Act. The Act's "ordinary course of business" requirement was deemed satisfied by the employer's claim that the equipment aided its review of reporting and investigation procedures for accidents.

In Commonwealth v. Brown, No. 92-7600, 1993 Mass. Super. LEXIS 337 (Mass. Super. Ct. Dec. 15, 1994), disclosure of wiretap information was allowed pursuant to the statute's law enforcement exception contained in MASS. GEN. LAWS ch. 272, § 99D(2)(a). The Commonwealth did not violate the Wiretapping Law by revealing wiretap information to officials of the telephone company, even though those officials were also the defendant's employers. "[T]he police only disclosed information to [New England Telephone] in order to facilitate the ongoing investigation [regarding drug crimes]." Brown, 1993 Mass. Super. LEXIS, at *6.

In Benson v. Norwood Dodge Sales, Inc., No. 0000049, 2000 Mass. Super. LEXIS 421, at *15 (Mass. Super. Ct. Aug. 14, 2000), the court declined to dismiss a claim for violation of the Wiretap Act where the employer allegedly installed video and audio devices and intercepted the plaintiff's oral communications without her consent. The court rejected the argument that the Wiretap Act does not provide a civil remedy. Id. at *14 (citing MASS. GEN. LAWS ch. 272, § 99Q).

2. ***Electronic Communications***. The Massachusetts Wiretap Act, codified by MASS. GEN. LAWS ch. 272, § 99 et. seq., prohibits the interception of wire and oral communications by private individuals in the absence of consent by all parties, and is at least as protective of individual rights as the Federal statute, 18 U.S.C. 2510-20, which requires only one-party consent. O'Sullivan v. NYNEX Corp., 426 Mass. 261, 264, 264 n.5, 687 N.E.2d 1241, 1244 n.5 (1997), citing United States v. McKinnon, 721 F.2d 19 (1st Cir. 1983); Commonwealth v. Vitello, 367 Mass. 224, 247, 251, 327 N.E.2d 819, 833, 836 (1975). Given similarities between federal and state wiretap statutes, Massachusetts courts may look to federal court interpretations of the federal statute in interpreting the Massachusetts law. See Crosland v. Horgan, 401 Mass. 271, 275, 516 N.E.2d 147, 149 (1987). The Wiretap Act of 1968, 18 U.S.C. 2510-2522, specifies, *inter alia*, the conditions under which law enforcement officers can intercept wire communications.

In Restuccia v. Burk Tech., Inc. No. 95-2125, 1996 Mass. Super. LEXIS 367 (Mass. Super. Ct. Aug. 13, 1996), the court found that an employer's practice of backing up all computer files, including e-mail, fell within the statute's exception for systems used in the ordinary course of business, and was therefore a permissible interception. Further, it dismissed the plaintiff's argument that an employer's reading of his employee's e-mail constituted an interception under the statute. Nevertheless, the court denied the defendant's motion for summary judgment on the plaintiff's invasion of privacy claim, reasoning that "[t]here remain genuine issues of material fact on the issue of whether plaintiffs had a reasonable expectation of privacy in their e-mail messages and whether [the employer's] reading of the e-mail messages constituted an unreasonable, substantial or serious interference with plaintiff's privacy." Id. at *9. Burk Technology subsequently successfully defended the suit. The employer did not have a written e-mail policy. However, testimony showed that the employees had sufficient technical knowledge to know that their e-mail was not private.

However, the United States District Court for the District of Massachusetts has held that the reading of e-mails after they have been transmitted to the recipient does not constitute interception within the [Massachusetts] wiretap statute. Garrity v. John Hancock Mut. Life Ins. Co., No. CIV.A. 0012143-RWZ, 2002 WL 974676, at *3 (D. Mass. 2002). See MASS. GEN. LAWS ch. 272, § 99. The plaintiffs in Garrity were fired for violating their employer's e-mail policy. That policy prohibited messages that are defamatory, abusive, obscene, profane, sexually oriented, threatening or racially offensive. Id. at *1. It also reserved to the company the right to access all e-mail files. Id. The plaintiff's claims of invasion of privacy, violation on the Massachusetts wiretap statute, violation of public policy, ERISA, and defamation all failed. Id. at *2-4.

An employee's use of company laptop computer to retrieve private, password protected, personal e-mails did not constitute the employee's waiver of attorney-client privilege where copies of e-mails were automatically stored in the company's temporary computer files and where employee was unaware of such temporary storage. Nat'l Econ. Research Ass'n v. Evans, No. 04-2618-BLS2, 2006 Mass. Super. LEXIS 371, at *13 (Mass. Super. Ct. Aug. 2, 2006).

In a summary judgment decision, a Superior Court judge found that, given the substantial privacy interest in e-mail, opening another's e-mail may constitute an invasion of privacy. Tamm v. Hartford Ins., No. 02-0541BLS2, 2003 Mass. Super. LEXIS 214 (Mass. Super. Ct. July 10, 2003). Here, an employer accused a consultant of reading or opening privileged e-mails and then forwarding those messages to third parties.

3. ***Other Electronic Monitoring*** No Massachusetts cases on point.

B. Mail

In LaFleur v. Bird-Johnson Co., No. 001060A, 1994 WL 878831, at *2-3 (Mass. Super. Ct. Nov. 3, 1994), the lower court rejected an employee's claim that her statutory privacy rights were violated by her employer when a company security guard opened personal mail addressed to her and sent to her office. The mail revealed the employee's status as a cross-dresser, as well as her depression and suicidal tendencies. The court weighed the employer's interest against the seriousness of the intrusion, as prescribed in O'Connor v. Police Comm'r., 408 Mass. 324, 330, 557 N.E.2d 1146, 1150 (1990). Since the employer, a defense contractor, was acting in compliance with federal security requirements regarding the handling of mail, the court found that the employer's legitimate security interest outweighed the potential invasion of the employee's privacy. LaFleur, 1994 WL 878831, at *2. The court also found the potential intrusion on the employee's privacy to be small, as there was no evidence that the letter was viewed by employees other than the security guard. Id. at *3.

C. Surveillance/Photographing

Aside from a statute prohibiting the use of two-way mirrors, video cameras, and similar devices in the dressing rooms of retail clothing stores, MASS. GEN. LAWS ch. 93, § 89, Massachusetts statutes are silent on the issue of surveillance of employees. In Clermont v. Sheraton Boston Corp., No. 930909F, 1993 WL 818763 (Mass. Super. Ct. Dec. 17, 1993), employees were allowed to seek damages for emotional distress under MASS. GEN. LAWS ch. 214, § 1B, where the employer hotel maintained a hidden camera in the men's locker room. (The cameras, which recorded semi-nude employees, were installed by the hotel management upon suspicion of drug dealing in the locker room. The case settled prior to trial). However, in Nelson v. Salem State College, an employee had no reasonable expectation of privacy in her workplace area which was open to the public and visible to passersby through its windows. 446 Mass. 525, 534-35, 845 N.E.2d 338, 347 (2006). Other employees were not liable for invasion of privacy under MASS. GEN. LAWS ch. 214, § 1B where they had placed a surveillance camera in an area where they thought criminal activity was taking place and where the camera recorded the plaintiff employee in states of undress (when she believed she was not visible to the public.) Id.

In a 1969 opinion, in response to a question from the Massachusetts House of Representatives, the Supreme Judicial Court found unconstitutionally broad a bill that would prohibit employers from using any surveillance or monitoring device without giving notice to and gaining consent from their employees. In re Opinion of Justices, 356 Mass. 756, 250 N.E.2d 448 (1969). In 1970, the Supreme Judicial Court found unconstitutionally broad and vague a bill that would have prohibited employers from using monitoring devices in factories for the purpose of conducting studies, in the absence of notice to and consent from their employees. Opinion of Justices, 358 Mass. 827, 260 N.E.2d 740 (1970).

An employer's violation of a privacy statute, which results in resignation of an employee, could contravene public policy and warrant the imposition of liability on the employer for constructive discharge. O'Donnell v. Miller, No. 98-01139, 1999 Mass. Super. LEXIS 554, *11 (Mass. Super. Ct. Dec. 2, 1999) (quoting Cort v. Bristol-Myers Co., 385 Mass. 300, 431 N.E.2d 908 (1982)). (Employee quit after discovering employer had secretly installed a video camera in the bathroom because of suspected vandalism.)

Police may use employer's surveillance video footage as evidence. Commonwealth v. Rivera, 445 Mass. 119, 124, 833 N.E.2d 1113, 1118 (2005). The police had no part in the making, inducing, soliciting, or otherwise encouraging the making of the surveillance tape. Id. The court also stressed the fact that the crime caught on the tape, murder, was of grave public concern. Id. Given these two factors, the police did not violate the Massachusetts Wiretap statute by using an employer's surveillance footage to elicit an admission from a defendant. Id.

V. ACTIVITIES OUTSIDE THE WORKPLACE

A. Statute or Common Law

Challenges to employer conduct in this area have been brought through actions under the Right to Privacy law and the Civil Rights law, see I.A, supra.

The Supreme Judicial Court rejected a claim by Boston police officers that a questionnaire relating to officers' off-duty activities, distributed as part of a departmental investigation into allegations of inappropriate and possibly unlawful conduct by officers, violated officers' right to privacy under Chapter 214. Broderick v. Police Comm'r, 368 Mass. 33, 330 N.E.2d 199 (1975). However, an inquiry into private affairs must bear a sufficiently rational connection to the officer's position in the governmental service, in the sense that the questions must be reasonably related to the officer's ability and fitness to perform his official duties. Id. at 42-43.

In Cort v. Bristol-Meyers Co., 385 Mass. 300, 306-10, 431 N.E.2d 908, 911-13 (1982), the court declined to hold a former employer liable for discharging employees who refused to provide certain personal information on a company questionnaire. "[R]estrictions on the authority of public employers seeking information from public employees are greater than those imposed on private employers." Cort, 385 Mass. at 307, 431 N.E.2d at 911. However, a private employer could be liable for firing an employee for failure to respond to questions which constitute an invasion of privacy as described in MASS. GEN. LAWS ch. 214. See Cort, 385 Mass. at 306-307, 431 N.E.2d at 911.

In French v. UPS, the court found that it was not an invasion of privacy under MASS. GEN. LAWS ch. 214, § 1B for a supervisor to disclose to his employer or for a company to seek further information regarding a drinking incident which occurred at the plaintiff employee's home while his supervisor and another employee were present and which involved a fourth company employee. 2 F. Supp. 2d 128 (D. Mass. 1998). In these circumstances, the fact that another employee drank too much while at the plaintiff's home was not a fact private to the plaintiff. Id. Because all the employees involved held supervisory positions at the company, the court also found there were legitimate business reasons for the employer, UPS, to seek information about the incident, including concerns about the soundness of judgment exercised by its supervisory employees regarding alcohol abuse generally and in a particular setting where all participants were UPS employees. Id. Any questioning of the plaintiff about facts known to others was at most deemed a de minimus intrusion into the plaintiff's privacy and not actionable under the statute. Id.

Employers may not discharge or reduce the wages of an employee for giving or withholding a vote. MASS. GEN. LAWS ch. 56, § 33. An employer also may not attempt to influence a voter to give or withhold his vote by promising higher wages or threatening to discharge him or lower his wages. Id. Also, supervisors in manufacturing, mechanical or mercantile establishment[s] may not prevent any employee eligible to vote from taking leave from work during the period of two hours after the opening of the polls, if the employee requests such leave. MASS. GEN. LAWS ch. 149, § 178. Those who violate the statute may be fined up to five hundred dollars. See Id. § 180.

In Pereira v. Comm'r of Soc. Serv., the Supreme Judicial Court held that a public employer did not violate the First Amendment when it fired an employee who made a racist comment at a private dinner. 432 Mass. 251, 733 N.E.2d 112 (2000). The event was unrelated to her employment. Id. In balancing the interests, the Court found that the plaintiff's interest in telling the racist joke was relatively insubstantial, and that the Department of Social Services' interest in preventing such expression at a political event, where there was little likelihood of privacy, was sufficient to justify her dismissal. Id. The Court recognized that the plaintiff's joke could potentially undermine DSS relations with its clients and the larger community where trust and confidence can be essential. Id.

B. Employee's Personal Relationships

1. ***Romantic Relationships Between Employees.*** The balancing test set forth in Bratt v. Int'l Bus. Mach., 392 Mass. 508, 467 N.E.2d 126 (1984), see II.B.2, supra, has been applied to situations involving intra-office romances. In McNulty v. Kessler, the investigation by supervisors and co-workers regarding the existence of a romantic relationship between a high school principal and his secretary, was found not to be an unreasonable invasion of privacy under MASS. GEN. LAWS ch. 214, § 1B. No. 914375, 1995 WL 809931 (Mass. Super. Ct. April 3, 1995). Disclosures about the principal occurred in the context of inquiry about the principal's performance of his duties and were limited to matters relating to his fitness to serve as a high school principal. Id.

An employer did not violate its at-will employee's civil rights by discharging him because of his romantic involvement with his supervisor. See Gladstone v. Cmty. Newsdealers, Inc., No. 94-02678, 1995 Mass. Super. LEXIS 819 (Mass. Super. Ct. Jan. 12, 1995).

Other challenges to terminations of romantically-involved co-workers under the Massachusetts Employment Discrimination Statute (MASS. GEN. LAWS ch. 151B, § 4) and the Massachusetts Civil Rights Act (MASS. GEN. LAWS ch. 12, §§ 11H, 11I) have also failed. Similarly, at-will employees failed to state a claim under the Massachusetts Civil Rights Act (MCRA), MASS. GEN. LAWS ch. 12, §§ 11H-I, where they were terminated for co-habitating, conduct deemed by the employer to violate its family values philosophy. Johnson v. ADESA Auctions Corp., No. 965264, 1998 Mass. Super. LEXIS 489, at *7-9 (Mass. Super. Ct. July 21, 1998). Although the court, citing LaSota v. Town of Topsfield, 979 F. Supp. 45 (D. Mass. 1997), held that the couple had a right to associate intimately without interference, it found that the employer did not violate such right to associate with threats, intimidation or coercion. Johnson, 1998 Mass. Super. LEXIS, at *6. Stating that at-will employees could be terminated for no reason or any reason at all, the court concluded the plaintiff's termination did not result in the loss of contract rights and thus did not constitute a threat or violation of the plaintiff's constitutional rights with intimidation or coercion. Id. at *8.

2. ***Sexual Orientation.*** Massachusetts Employment Discrimination Law prohibits those employing more than five employees from discriminating on the basis of sexual orientation, unless based on a bona fide occupational qualification. MASS. GEN. LAWS ch. 151B, § 4. Exempted from this provision, however, are religious organizations motivated by the desire to promote religious principles. See id.

While Massachusetts courts have not addressed the privacy issues regarding the solicitation of information about sexual orientation in the employment context, their decisions on other privacy-related employment matters involving sexual orientation have produced mixed results. Compare Weise v. Courier Corp., No. 92-8084B, 1994 WL 879681, at *2 (Mass. Super. Ct. March 10, 1994), aff'd, 39 Mass. App. Ct. 1120, 659 N.E.2d 290 (1995) (holding that merely asking a question about one's sexual orientation does not support an inference of improper motive in action for intentional interference with advantageous relations, where supervisor asked discharged bisexual employee's co-worker if discharged employee was gay or had AIDS); LaFleur v. Bird-Johnson, No. 00-1060A, 1994 WL 878831, at *3-6 (Mass. Super. Ct. Nov. 3, 1994) (rejecting employee's claims that anti-gay derision was pervasive and severe enough to constitute sexual orientation discrimination or sexual harassment); Sch. Comm. v. Civil Serv. Comm'n, 43 Mass. App. Ct. 486, 684 N.E.2d 620 (1997) (upholding Commission's more lenient treatment of school custodian arrested for publicly engaging in homosexual act with another adult while off-duty, agreeing that conduct was not related to and did not impair efficiency of work, and there was no danger to children).

A *prima facie* case for sexual orientation discrimination under MASS. GEN. LAWS. ch. 151B, § 4 can be established by imposition of different work rules and assignments, along with pervasive intimidation. Vera v. Faust, 26 M.D.L.R. 341, 2004 Mass. Comm. Discrim. LEXIS 76, at *24-25 (Mass. Comm. Discrim. 2004). Both coworkers and employers can be held liable for such discrimination. Id. MASS. GEN. LAWS. ch. 151B, § 4 also creates liability for aiding and abetting sexual orientation discrimination. 2004 Mass. Comm. Discrim. LEXIS 76 at *28-29. Complainant must show wholly individual and distinct wrong from main claim, as well as intent to discriminate. Id. MASS. GEN. LAWS. ch. 151B, § 4 also prohibits retaliation against persons who have opposed practices forbidden under Chapter 151 or who have filed a complaint of discrimination. 2004 Mass. Comm. Discrim. LEXIS 76 at *31. A *prima facie* case for aiding and abetting consists of proof that the complainant 1) engaged in protected activity, 2) was aware that she had engaged in protected activity, 3) was subjected to adverse employment action by respondent, and 4) can show a causal connection between the protected activity and the adverse employment action. Id.

Although discrimination claims must be filed with the Massachusetts Commission Against Discrimination within six months of the occurrence of the alleged discriminatory event, where the alleged discrimination forms "a pattern of behavior," the continuing violation doctrine applies. Pelletier v. Town of Somerset, 458 Mass. 504, 520 (2010). In Pelletier v. Town of Somerset, a plaintiff alleging discrimination on the basis of gender and sexual orientation could seek damages outside the usual statute of limitations period "if the alleged events are part of an ongoing pattern of discrimination, and there is a discrete violation within the statute of limitations period to anchor the earlier claims." Id.

3. ***Marital Status.*** One court found an invasion of privacy action to lie where a supervisor inquired about the marital status and plans to have children of a female employee who, unbeknownst to the supervisor, was unable to bear children. See Finney v. Madico, Inc., No. 93-6579, 1994 WL 879530 (Mass. Super. Ct. June 24, 1994), rev'd on other grounds, 42 Mass. App. Ct. 46, 674 N.E.2d 655, appeal denied, 424 Mass. 1107, 678 N.E.2d 1134 (1997). See also Delmonte v. Laidlaw Envtl. Serv., 46 F. Supp. 2d 89, 93 (D. Mass. 1999).

4. ***Sexual Activity.*** In Cronin v. Town of Amesbury, 895 F. Supp. 375, 384-85 (D. Mass. 1995), aff'd on other grounds, 81 F.3d 257 (1st Cir. 1996), the court concluded that a public employer may discipline a tenured public employee for private activities reasonably related to the fitness of the employee to perform in his position, and that while a public employee has a constitutionally protected liberty interest in his private sexual activities, this interest must be balanced against the public employer's justifiable concerns about the conduct's impact upon the employee's effectiveness. The court recognized one such case in Spartaro v. Commonwealth, No. ESCV200402281, 2007 WL 738486 (Mass. Super. Ct. Jan. 4, 2007), holding that the reasonableness of a Department of Social Services' investigation, regarding whether its employee previously violated a prohibition on romantic relationships between social workers and their clients, was a question for the finder of fact at trial.

C. Smoking

Massachusetts has abolished smoking in most workplaces by statute. MASS. GEN. LAWS ch. 270, § 22. Smoking is prohibited in indoor as well as enclosed outdoor areas. Id. It is the employer's responsibility to prevent smoking in areas that are either indoors or enclosed and under its control. Id. Certain establishments, such as smoking bars and membership clubs, are specifically exempted from the non-smoking statute. Id. at 22(c). Regulations adopted by local boards prohibiting smoking in establishments exempted under MASS. GEN. LAWS. ch. 270, § 22 are not pre-empted by that law. Am. Lith. Naturalization Club v. Bd. of Health of Athol, 446 Mass. 310, 321, 844 N.E. 2d 231, 240 (2006). M. G. L. c. 270, 22(j) expressly allows smoking regulations by municipalities and their boards which were stricter than those created by the statute. Am. Lith. Naturalization Club, 446 Mass. at 320, 844 N.E.2d at 240.

Some municipalities in Massachusetts passed ordinances prohibiting or restricting smoking in the workplace prior to the enactment of MASS. GEN. LAWS ch. 270, § 22. See, e.g., Cambridge Ordinance Number 1046 (prohibiting smoking in workplace covering more than 1500 square feet); Newton Ordinance Number S-72 (requiring employers to have smoking policies and respond to employee complaints); Brookline Town Bylaws, Article XLII (same). Municipal ordinances stricter than the newly-adopted state law remain in force. See Tri-Nel Mgmt., Inc. v. Board of Health of Barnstable, 433 Mass. 217, 741 N.E.2d 37 (2001) (state statute establishing minimum statewide restrictions on smoking in restaurants to protect and accommodate nonsmoking public did not preempt town from enacting regulation which imposed absolute ban on smoking in all food service establishments, lounges and bars).

In some cases, Massachusetts has recognized the propriety of employer regulations banning tobacco use by employees outside the workplace as well. Massachusetts prohibits on-duty or off-duty tobacco use by police officers and firefighters appointed since January 1, 1998. MASS. GEN. LAWS ch. 41, § 101A. Those who do smoke may be discharged.

See id.; Town of Plymouth v. Civil Serv. Comm'n, 426 Mass. 1, 686 N.E.2d 188 (1997) (holding the statute constitutional in light of the rational connection between the law and its legitimate public purpose, the reduction of the risk of hypertension and heart disease, and thus the state's liability for disability benefits). Where the employer prohibited its employees from smoking tobacco, whether or not during work hours or in the workplace, where the employer required the plaintiff to submit to nicotine testing after he was hired and where the employee was fired for testing positive for nicotine, a federal court found that the employee stated a plausible privacy interest under Mass. Gen. Laws Ch. 214 §1B to be balanced against the employer's stated interest in having a healthy workforce and lower health care costs. Rodrigues v. Scotts Co., LLC, No. 07-10104-GAO, 2008 WL 251971 (D. Mass. Jan. 30, 2008).

D. Blogging

No Massachusetts cases on point.

VI. RECORDS

A. Personnel Records

Employee Privacy Interest in Personnel Records. Individuals have a heightened expectation of privacy in personnel records and release of information from a personnel file can be a substantial interference with a right to privacy. Bratt v. Int'l Bus. Mach. Corp., 392 Mass. 508, 467 N.E.2d 126 (1984). To determine whether the release of such information constitutes an unreasonable interference with an employee's right of privacy, courts will balance the employer's legitimate interest in determining the employee's effectiveness in his job against the seriousness of the intrusion on the employee's privacy. Id. Pursuant to MASS. GEN. LAWS ch. 149 § 52C, an employer must notify an employee within ten days of its placing negative information in an employee's personnel records. See also Fitzgerald v. Morrison, No. 00-2247B, 2002 WL 389872 (Mass. Super. Ct. Jan. 10, 2002). Upon written request, an employee must be allowed to examine and copy his own personnel record. MASS. GEN. LAWS ch. 149, § 52C. If an employer has placed in a personnel record information which he knew or should have known to be false, then the employee may have a remedy through the collective bargaining agreement, other personnel procedures or judicial process to have such information expunged. Id. Employers of twenty or more employees must keep the complete record of each employee until three years after the employee is terminated or until final disposition of any action brought by an employee against his employer. See id. The statute does not apply to private university faculty members who are tenured, on tenure track, or in similar positions. Id. Those who violate the statute may be fined between five hundred and twenty-five hundred dollars. See id.

Massachusetts General Laws ch. 149, § 52C does not provide a private cause of action where an employer has failed to provide employees with copies of their personnel files; it grants enforcement rights only to the Attorney General. Kessler v. Cambridge Health Alliance, 62 Mass. App. Ct. 589, 595, 818 N.E.2d 582, 586-87 (2004); Estate of Talarico v. City of Cambridge, No. 97-02240, 1999 Mass. Super. LEXIS 12, at *4-6 (Mass. Super. Ct. Jan. 19, 1999).

Dissemination of Public Employee Personnel Records. The definition of public records set forth in the Massachusetts Public Records Law, MASS. GEN. LAWS ch. 4, § 7(26), and the public inspection requirements set forth in MASS. GEN. LAWS ch. 66, § 10 are generally viewed in tandem. See, e.g., Teachers Ass'n v. Sch. Comm., 431 Mass. 792, 801, 731 N.E.2d 63, 69 (2000); Pottle v. Sch. Comm., 395 Mass. 861, 482 N.E.2d 813, 12 Media L. Rep. 1336 (1985); Globe Newspaper Co. v. Boston Retirement Bd., 388 Mass. 427, 446 N.E.2d 1051, 9 Media L. Rep. 2309 (1983); Hastings & Sims Publg. Co. v. City Treasurer, 374 Mass. 812, 375 N.E.2d 299 (1978); Worcester Telegram & Gazette Corp. v. Chief of Police of Worcester, 58 Mass. App. Ct. 1, 787 N.E.2d 602 (2003), appeal denied, 440 Mass. 1103, 795 N.E.2d 574 (2003). There is a presumption in favor of disclosure and the government bears the burden to demonstrate that a document is exempt from disclosure. Pottle, 395 Mass. at 865, 482 N.E.2d at 816-17 (citing MASS. GEN. LAWS ch. 66, § 10(c)); accord Atty Gen. v. Sch. Comm. of Northampton, 375 Mass. 127, 131, 375 N.E.2d 1188, 1191 (1978); Hastings, at 374 Mass. at 817. The seriousness of any invasion of privacy is balanced against the public right to know. Pottle, 395 Mass. 482 N.E.2d 813, 12 Media L. Rep. 1336 (quoting Atty Gen. v. Collector of Lynn, 377 Mass. 151, 156, 385 N.E.2d 505, 4 Media L. Rep. 2563 (1979)).

Those employed in the public sector have diminished expectations of privacy, Pottle, 395 Mass. 861, 866, 482 N.E.2d 813, 12 Media L. Rep. 1336; accord Hastings & Sims Publg. Co. v. City Treasurer, 374 Mass. 812, 818–19, 375 N.E.2d 299 (1978); Globe Newspaper Co. v. Boston Retirement Bd., 388 Mass. 427, 436 n.15, 446 N.E.2d 1051 (1983), and have long been subject to restrictions and regulations not affecting private employees. Hastings, 374 Mass. at 818, 375 N.E. 2d at 304. Names and home addresses are not intimate details of a highly personal nature, because they are available from other sources. Pottle, 395 Mass. 861, 866, 482 N.E.2d 813, 12 Media L. Rep. 1336. See Hastings 374 Mass. 812, 817, 375 N.E.2d 299.

Municipal employees' names and payroll records are not exempt from disclosure. See, e.g., Pottle, 395 Mass. 861, 864-65, 866, 482 N.E.2d 813, 12 Media L. Rep. 1336 (1985) (requiring release of teachers' names, titles and addresses to educators union); Hastings, 374 Mass. at 818, 375 N.E.2d at 303 (requiring release of police officers' names and salaries). Public records subject to disclosure include certified payroll records of public works contractors and subcontractors submitted to the state pursuant to MASS. GEN. LAWS ch. 149, §§ 44E, 44F. Information such as social security number, date of birth, unusual reason for a deduction, i.e., child support, may be redacted from public records but information such as name, address, classification, hours worked, base pay and regular deductions must be made available. See Advisory from the Office of the Attorney General's Fair Labor and Business Practices Division, excerpted in Labor and Employment in Massachusetts App. F, at F-10-11. See Atty Gen. v. Sch. Comm., 375 Mass. 127, 132, 375 N.E.2d 1188, 1191 (1978) (requiring disclosure of the identities of certain candidates for the position of superintendent of schools).

In Globe Newspaper Co. v. Exec. Office of Admin. & Fin., No. 011-1184, 2011 Mass. Super. LEXIS 130 (Mass. Super. Ct. Apr. 25, 2011), the court denied a preliminary injunction requesting disclosure of the names and other identifying information of public employees that had been redacted from previously produced copies of separation, settlement and severance agreements, finding that the personnel and privacy exemptions could be implicated and requiring a fuller record in order to balance the public interest in disclosure against the interests of individual public employees.

The Public Records Law does not require disclosure of medical and personnel information where the files on information sought were of a personal nature and related to a particular individual. Globe Newspaper Co. v. Boston Retirement Bd., 388 Mass. 427, 437, 446 N.E.2d 1051 (1983). Such information is absolutely exempt from mandatory disclosure. Globe, 388 Mass. at 434-35, 435 n.13, 446 N.E.2d at 1056, n.13. Information which does not permit the identification of any individual, including statistical information compiled from medical records, is not exempt. Globe, 388 Mass. at 435, n.14, 446 N.E.2d at 1056 n.14 (1983).

In Wakefield Teachers Ass'n v. Sch. Comm., the Supreme Judicial Court found that disciplinary reports were subject to Public Record Law exemption for personnel or medical files. 431 Mass. 792, 731 N.E.2d 63 (2000). The Court's analysis was not affected by whether the public employee's name had been redacted from the report. See id. The privacy exemption creates two categories: (1) personnel and medical files or information; and (2) other materials or data relating to a specifically named individual, the disclosure of which may constitute an unwarranted invasion of privacy. Id. at 796-97. Personnel and medical files or information exemption clause is not modified by the phrase "relating to a specifically named individual, the disclosure of which may constitute an unwarranted invasion of privacy." Id. at 797. Determination of whether such information is personnel or medical information does not depend on the physical location of the information, but whether the information is of a personal nature and relates to a particular individual. Id. "Personnel and medical files or information" is a category of information that falls outside the definition of "public records." Geier v. Town of Barre, 25 Mass. L. Rep. 121, 123, No. 105679, 2009 Mass. Super. LEXIS 8, at *5 (Mass. Super. Ct. Jan. 9, 2009).

Ruling in another round of the public records dispute between the Worcester Telegram & Gazette and the Worcester police concerning access to a police department internal affairs file, the Massachusetts Appeals Court found that the personnel file or information exemption under the Public Records law did not extend to officers' reports, witness interview summaries or an internal affairs report compiled during an investigation of a citizen complaint. Worcester Telegram & Gazette Corp. v. Chief of Police of Worcester, 58 Mass. App. Ct. 1, 787 N.E.2d 602 (2003), appeal denied, 440 Mass. 1103, 795 N.E.2d 574 (2003). The court distinguished these non-exempt materials from a disciplinary decision or report which is exempt as a personnel file or information. See id. As the police department did not argue that these materials were also exempt under the privacy or the investigatory exemptions, the court did not address whether those exemptions would apply to the documents in question. See id. The court also stated that the personnel file or information exemption was not dependent on whether the same information was available through alternative sources and noted that the same information could simultaneously be contained in a public record and in exempt personnel file or information. See id. The court noted that the legislative term "personnel [file] or information" derives its meaning from the nature or character of the document, not from its label or its repository. Id. at 8, citing Worcester Telegram & Gazette Corp. v. Chief of Police of Worcester, 436 Mass. 378, 764 N.E.2d 847 (2002) (Worcester I).

The court in Geier v. Town of Barre declined to recognize a private right of action based on an employee's claim that her personnel records were "absolutely exempt from disclosure." No. 105679, 2009 Mass. Super. LEXIS 8, at *5 (Mass. Super. Ct. Jan. 9, 2009). The court noted that in Globe, 388 Mass. 427, the Supreme Judicial Court had "assumed" the Public Records Law did not necessarily preclude agencies from releasing personnel files in their discretion. Geier, 2009 Mass. Super. LEXIS 8, at *6-7. The court declined to interpret Wakefield Teachers Ass'n, 431 Mass. 792, as holding that all such records be exempt from disclosure in all circumstances. Geier, 2009 Mass. Super. LEXIS 8, at *8-9.

The personnel records of persons who hold honorary positions are available to the public under MASS. GEN. LAWS ch. 66, § 10. See Cape Cod Times v. Sheriff of Barnstable County, 443 Mass. 587, 594, 823 N.E.2d 375, 381 (2005). In Cape Cod Times, the court ordered the sheriff to disclose the names and addresses of those who held the honorary title of reserve deputy sheriff because the sheriff appointed reserve deputy sheriffs as a public official acting in his official capacity, even though the reserve deputy sheriff position was predominantly funded by a private association. See id. at 593, 823 N.E. 2d at 380-81.

No claim for invasion of privacy was found where a private university supervisor disseminated information regarding an employee's salary, job description and thesis proposal to other university personnel. See Battenfield v. Harvard Univ., No. 91-5089F, 1993 WL 878 920 (Mass. Super. Ct. Aug. 31, 1993). Such information was not intimate or highly personal, and the dissemination was related to the university's legitimate interest in evaluating the employee's professional and academic fitness. See id.

Disclosure to the broad public is not a requirement for a valid invasion of privacy claim; the disclosure of private facts about an employee between coworkers can be sufficient publication under the Massachusetts Right of Privacy statute. Bennett v. City of Holyoke, 230 F. Supp. 2d 207 (D. Mass. 2002), aff'd on other grounds, 362 F.3d 1 (1st Cir. 2004). Here, a police sergeant brought an invasion of privacy claim against the chief of police who provided the sergeant's personnel files, including information on domestic disputes between the sergeant and his wife, to a union officer ostensibly to undermine the sergeant's prospect for promotion. See id. On summary judgment, the court found that the disclosure of past altercations of a private or intimate nature, such domestic disputes, which are not public knowledge, may be invasive of privacy. See id.

Credit Reports. Use of credit reports for purposes of employment, promotion, reassignment or retention is regulated by statute. MASS. GEN. LAWS ch. 93 § 50. A credit reporting agency may furnish credit reports to one whom it believes will use the report for employment purposes, see MASS. GEN. LAWS ch. 93, § 51, although it may not include stale information relative to bankruptcies, suits and judgments, paid tax liens, accounts placed for collection, criminal records, and other matters. See MASS. GEN. LAWS ch. 93, § 52(b). A reporting agency must notify a consumer when and to whom it provides public records which may adversely impact the consumer's ability to gain employment, and it must maintain procedures ensuring that such information is complete and up to date. MASS. GEN. LAWS ch. 93, § 60. An agency providing reports for employment purposes shall enter into an agreement with the user requiring that written notice be given to employees before a credit report is requested. Id. Notice in employment manuals is sufficient for current employees. See id. If employment is denied or terminated because of information in a credit report, the employer must notify the consumer within ten days of the decision. MASS. GEN. LAWS ch. 93, § 62.

B. Medical Records

Employer Solicitation of Information. There is a strong public policy in Massachusetts that favors confidentiality as to medical data about a person's body. Globe Newspaper Co. v. Chief Medical Examiner, 404 Mass. 132, 135, 533 N.E.2d 1356, 1358, 16 Media L. Rep. 1996 (1989); see, e.g., MASS. GEN. LAWS ch. 111, § 70(E) (guaranteeing confidentiality of patient records and communications in medical facilities, and right to privacy during medical treatment or care); MASS. GEN. LAWS ch. 111E, § 18 (guaranteeing confidentiality of information regarding treatment at drug rehabilitation facilities in absence of judicial order or specific consent by patient); MASS. GEN. LAWS ch. 111, § 70F (requiring consent for disclosure of HIV testing information); MASS. GEN. LAWS ch. 111, § 119 (requiring confidentiality of records regarding morbidity reports and venereal disease, except upon judicial order to one entitled by virtue of his official duties); MASS. GEN. LAWS ch. 111, § 110B (restricting disclosure of reports regarding Reyes Syndrome); MASS. GEN. LAWS ch. 111D, § 6 (requiring confidentiality of reports of infectious diseases); cf. MASS. GEN. LAWS ch. 233, § 20B (establishing privilege with respect to communications between psychotherapist and patient); II.C, supra.

As discussed in II.C, supra, the Massachusetts Employment Discrimination Statute prohibits an employer from making a preemployment inquiry of an applicant as to whether the applicant is a handicapped individual or as to the nature or severity of the handicap. MASS. GEN. LAWS ch. 151B, § 4(16). Employers may request such information for affirmative action purposes, see MASS. GEN. LAWS ch. 151B, § 4(16), provided that: the information is only desired for affirmative action purposes; disclosure by the employee is voluntary; refusal to disclose does not result in any adverse consequences; and the information will be maintained as confidential. See Mass. Comm'n Against Discrimination Handicapped Regulations pt. VII, cited in Labor and Employment in Massachusetts, 1-4(d), at 1-37, 1-38. The employer must inform the applicant of these protections. Id.

An employer may not discharge or refuse to hire an individual for failing to provide information regarding admission to a mental health facility, unless based on a bona fide occupational qualification, as long as the individual has been discharged and his mental competence for the job can be proven by a psychiatrist's certificate. See MASS. GEN. LAWS ch. 151B, § 4(9A).

Whether the employee has or has not yet specifically requested to return to work, an employer has a legitimate interest in ascertaining a disabled employee's prospect for return. Pyrcz v. Branford Coll., No. 981365, 1999 Mass. Super. LEXIS 323, at *15 (Mass. Super. Ct. July 26, 1999) (employee was discharged from his job after suffering a nervous breakdown and undergoing subsequent medical treatment). There is an obvious need to know how long the employee is likely to be out, whether there will be restrictions on his activities when he returns, etc. Id. Thus, an employer does not unreasonably interfere with its disabled employee's privacy merely by inquiring about such subjects. See id.

Employer Dissemination of Information. Disclosure of private facts about an employee including medical information among other employees in the same corporation can constitute sufficient publication under MASS. GEN. LAWS ch. 214, § 1B. Bratt v. Int'l Bus. Mach. Corp., 392 Mass. 508, 467 N.E.2d 126 (1984). But see Hughes v. City of Malden, No. CA 92-0356F, 1994 WL 902951, at *3 (Mass. Super. Ct. Nov. 4, 1994) (holding that supervisor's mention of employee's depressed mental state as reason for employee's sick leave request in internal memo to personnel office simply does not rise to the level of an unreasonable or serious interference with a person's privacy under MASS. GEN. LAWS ch. 214).

Summary judgment was denied where the court found that a reasonable jury could conclude that the defendant, Chief of Police for the City of Holyoke, violated the Massachusetts Right of Privacy statute by distributing the plaintiff officer's psychiatric evaluation to officers who were not the plaintiff's supervisors and by publicly posting at the police department a doctor's note concerning the plaintiff. Wagner v. City of Holyoke, 241 F. Supp. 2d 78, 100 (D. Mass. 2003).

In the context of disclosure to management of an employee's medical information by the company doctor, the court balanced the degree of intrusion on privacy and the public interest in maintaining doctor-patient confidentiality against the employer's interest in the information. Bratt v. Int'l Bus. Mach., 392 Mass. 508, 467 N.E.2d 126 (1984). The employer's interest must be substantial and valid to outweigh the interest of the employee. Id. In Gauthier v. Police Comm'r, 408 Mass. 335, 557 N.E.2d 1374 (1990), a police cadet supervisor's act of informing cadets via publication about another cadet's dismissal for testing positive for drugs did not constitute a violation of the Massachusetts Right of Privacy Statute, MASS. GEN. LAWS ch. 214B, § 1B. The court balanced the police department's legitimate interest in deterring drug use by cadets against the diminished expectation of privacy of police cadets. Gauthier, 408 Mass. at 339, 557 N.E.2d at 1376.

It was not an invasion of privacy where an employer disclosed to a vendor with whom the former employee had worked that the employee had a child with a medical condition, where employer did not explain the nature of the child's condition, and where employee had resigned because employer could not accommodate employee's need for a flex time schedule to care for her child. Hansen v. J.L. Hammett Int'l, Inc., No. A98-00849, 1999 Mass. Super. LEXIS 424, at *9 (Mass. Super. Ct. Sept. 2, 1999). Although recognizing that disclosure of a family member's medical condition could constitute an invasion of privacy, the court found in the factual circumstances of this case that such disclosure did not constitute an unreasonable and substantial or serious invasion of privacy. See id. Furthermore, the employer disclosed the information concerning the plaintiff's sudden departure from employment in order to maintain good relations with the vendor. Id. at *10.

A plaintiff's employer could not be liable under the Massachusetts Civil Rights Act for the alleged unlawful seizure of the plaintiff by police where the employer reported the plaintiff's allegedly threatening comments and a physician's interpretation of those comments to police. Andresen v. Diorio, 349 F.3d 8, 14 (1st Cir. 2003). Absent serious fault and even if the information turns out to be false, the employer, similar to other bystanders, has a state law privilege to supply information to police, "and the civil right statute must be read conformably." Id. at 11.

An employer did not invade an employee's privacy when it posted the employee's medical appointment on a computer calendar that was visible to other employees. See Jodoin v. Baystate Health Systems, Inc., No. 08-40037, 2010 U.S. Dist. LEXIS 29931, at *96 (D. Mass. Mar. 29, 2010). Specifically, the plaintiff alleged that her employer published the notation "NJ disability meeting" and the date and location of the meeting on an openly available computer calendar. See id. The court found that even if people associated the notation with the plaintiff, the employer did not publish any private information that would lead people to believe that the notation referred to the plaintiff's disability or to deduce the nature of her disability. See id.

C. Criminal Records

In connection with hiring or any other employment matters, an employer may not request, record or penalize an individual for not providing any information regarding: an arrest, detention or criminal disposition not resulting in conviction; a first conviction for any of certain common misdemeanors enumerated in the statute; or a misdemeanor for which conviction or release from incarceration occurred more than five years earlier. MASS. GEN. LAWS ch. 151B, § 4(9). No person who withholds such information shall be guilty of perjury or giving false statements. Id.

Employers may not request on initial job applications the individual's criminal offender record information ("CORI") unless such information is required for a particular position by federal or state law or regulation. See MASS. GEN. LAWS ch. 151B § 4 (9½). The Act also does not prevent use of such information in employment decisions, if obtained from a source other than the applicant, as long as the employer did not specifically request that type of information. See id.

In 2012, the Commonwealth created a new database for CORI, which is accessible to employers. MASS. GEN. LAWS ch. 6 § 172. Effective in May 2012, in connection with an employment decision, an employer in possession of an applicant's criminal history record, whether obtained from the Commonwealth or any other source, must provide the applicant with a copy of such record prior to questioning the applicant about his criminal history or if the employer makes an adverse decision to the applicant based on his criminal history. MASS. GEN. LAWS. Ch. 6 §172(c).

D. Subpoenas / Search Warrants

Subpoenas. There is no general exemption for employee records under Massachusetts law. Mass. R. Civ. P. 45; see generally MASS. GEN. LAWS ch. 233. However, MASS. GEN. LAWS ch. 111, § 204(a) immunizes records of medical peer review committees from judicial and administrative subpoenas.

Search Warrants. No Massachusetts cases on point

VII. ACTIONS SUBSEQUENT TO EMPLOYMENT

A. References

A reference that includes a false statement can subject an employer to an action for defamation or intentional interference with advantageous relations. See St. Clair v. Trs. of Boston Univ., 25 Mass. App. Ct. 662, 662-63, 521 N.E.2d 1044, 1045 (1988). Where an employer obtains and discloses personal information concerning an employee, legitimate countervailing business interests may render disclosure of personal information reasonable and not actionable under MASS. GEN. LAWS ch. 214, § 1B. See Bratt v. Int'l Bus. Mach. Corp., 392 Mass. 508, 520, 467 N.E.2d 126, 129 (1984)

B. Non-Compete Agreements

Non-compete agreements are generally enforceable to the extent that they are reasonable and necessary to protect the legitimate business interests of the employer. E.g., Marine Contractors Co. v. Hurley, 365 Mass. 280, 287, 310 N.E.2d 915, 920 (1974); All Stainless, Inc. v. Colby, 364 Mass. 773, 778, 308 N.E.2d 481, 485 (1974). Massachusetts courts protect three employer interests: (1) the protection of trade secrets (Analogic Corp. v. Data Translation, Inc., 371 Mass. 643, 358 N.E.2d 804 (1973)); (2) confidential information (Novelty Bias Binding Co. v. Shevrin, 342 Mass. 714, 175 N.E.2d 374 (1973)); and (3) good will of the employer (New England Tree Expert Co. v. Russell, 306 Mass. 504, 28 N.E.2d 997 (1940)). If any or all of these factors are present in the case, absent other reasons in equity for non-enforcement, a non-compete agreement is enforceable. New England Canteen Serv. v. Ashley, 372 Mass. 671, 674, 363 N.E.2d 526 (1977). However, a non-compete agreement, even if it protects a legitimate business interest of the employer, will only be enforced to the extent that it is reasonable. See All Stainless, 364 Mass. at 778, 308 N.E.2d at 485. A non-compete agreement is reasonable if (1) it is supported by consideration, (2) it is reasonably limited in all circumstances, including time and space, and (3) it is otherwise consonant with public policy. See Bowne of Boston, Inc. v. Levine, No. 97-5789A, 1997 Mass. Super. LEXIS 69, at *5 (Mass. Super. Ct. Nov. 25, 1997). Continued employment alone may be sufficient consideration to support non-competition and other restrictive covenants. See Optos, Inc. v. Topcon Med. Sys., Inc., No. 10-12016-DJC, 2011 U.S. Dist. LEXIS 22263 (D. Mass. 2011); EMC Corp. v. Donatelli, 25 Mass. L. Rep. 399, 402, No. 107135, 2009 Mass. Super. LEXIS 120, at *16-17 (Mass. Super. Ct. May 5, 2009).

Where the potential for damage caused by an employee's knowledge of any confidential information would expire with the passage of time, a provision isolating the employee from competition "so long as he lives" was unreasonable. Kroeger v. Stop & Shop Cos., Inc., 13 Mass. App. Ct. 310, 318, 432 N.E.2d 566, 571 (1982).

Restraints upon a former executive's competitive activity may range beyond the precise geographical area where the former executive conducted business for his or her employer. See Kroeger, 13 Mass. App. Ct. at 317, 432 N.E.2d at 570. However, a provision that restricted a key executive from working in the United States was unenforceable as to states in which the employer had never conducted business and where the employer had no plans to conduct business. See id. at 317, 432 at N.E.2d at 571.

Although in most circumstances a two year restriction on competition is reasonable, it may not be reasonable when the time of employment is only slightly greater than a year. Ikon Office Solutions, 59 F. Supp. 2d at 129.

Non-compete agreements that restrict the geographic area of a physician's practice after employment are unenforceable by statute. See MASS. GEN. LAWS ch. 112, § 12X. Provisions that provide for compensation in the event that an employed physician accept employment within a specified geographic area are also unenforceable under this section. See id.; Falmouth Ob-Gyn Assocs., Inc. v. Abisla, 417 Mass. 176, 182, 629 N.E.2d 291, 294 (1994).

Non-compete agreements under Massachusetts law can be enforced in states that have statutory provisions against such agreements. See EMC Corp., 2009 Mass. Super LEXIS 120, at *10 (enforcing a non-compete agreement under Massachusetts law despite the fact that the defendant had moved to California, which has a statutory provision barring the enforcement of non-compete agreements).

VIII. OTHER ISSUES

A. Statutes of Limitations

Actions under the Right to Privacy law and other statutes that do not set forth limitation periods but provide a vehicle for the maintenance of tort actions are governed by MASS. GEN. LAWS ch. 260, § 2A, which requires actions to be brought within three years after the cause of action accrues, subject to any statutorily provided tolling provisions. 2 Mass. Jur. 17:26 at 123; see also Finney v. Madico, 42 Mass. App. Ct. 46, 52, 674 N.E.2d 655, 658 (1997). There is a three-year limitations period under the Civil Rights Law. MASS. GEN. LAWS ch. 260, § 5B.

B. Jurisdiction

MASS. GEN. LAWS ch. 214, § 1B gives the Superior Court jurisdiction to enforce the right of a person against unreasonable, substantial or serious interference with his privacy through equitable relief and damages.

C. Worker's Compensation Exclusivity

Massachusetts Workers Compensation law provides the exclusive remedy for claims of personal injury, including mental or emotional injury, where such injury is an element of the tort, by an employee where the employee has not previously given notice to his employer reserving his common law rights. See MASS. GEN. LAWS ch. 152 § 24; Saab v. Mass. CVS Pharm., LLC, 452 Mass. 564, 566-67, 896 N.E.2d 615, 618 (2008) ("The act 'was designed to replace tort actions,' Alves's Case, 451 Mass. 171, 177 n.9, 884 N.E.2d 468 (2008), by providing 'a uniform, statutory remedy for injured workers, in contrast to a piecemeal, tort-based system.' Green v. Wyman-Gordon Co., 422 Mass. 551, 559-560, 664 N.E.2d 808 (1996).").

D. Pleading Requirements

Massachusetts courts have not fully developed the requirements for pleadings and the range of defenses with respect to invasion of privacy actions. See Haggerty v. Globe Newspaper Co., 383 Mass. 406, 408, 419 N.E.2d 844, 845, 7 Media L. Rep. 615 (1981).

E. Privacy of Employee Personal Identifying Information

Massachusetts General Laws ch. 93H and 93I, and the accompanying regulations, 201 MASS. CODE REGS. 17.00 – 17.05, require businesses that own, license, store, or maintain personal identifying information relating to customers or employees who are Massachusetts residents to safeguard such information, and to implement written information security programs for doing so. The regulations also require businesses that store customer and employee personal identifying information electronically to establish and maintain a computer security system to protect against unauthorized access to or use of such information. See 201 MASS. CODE REGS. at 17.04. A business that owns or licenses personal identifying information that knows or has reason to know of a data security breach or unauthorized use of such information, is required to provide written notice "as soon as practicable and without unreasonable delay" to the impacted individual, the Attorney General, and the Director of the Office of Consumer Affairs and Business Regulation. Mass. Gen. L. ch. 93H, §3(b). A business that maintains or stores, but does not license or own such information, is required to provide notice to the affected individual and to the owner or licensor of such information, and to cooperate with the owner or licensor following the incident. Mass. Gen. L. ch. 93H, §3(a). Additional information regarding notification requirements in the event of a data security breach or unauthorized use of personal identifying information can be found in the statute. See Mass. Gen. L. ch. 93H, §3.

F. Harassment Prevention Orders

The Commonwealth of Massachusetts has a harassment prevention statute, under which a private citizen may obtain a harassment prevention order against another person, regardless of whether they have a familial relationship or a substantially similar relationship. See Mass. Gen. L. ch. 258E, § 3(a). Actionable harassment includes (1) three or more acts of "willful and malicious" conduct committed "with the intent to cause fear, intimidation, abuse or damage to property and that does in fact cause fear, intimidation, abuse or damage to property" or (2) a forceful or threatening act that causes another person to involuntarily engage in sexual relations or other related crimes, as specified by the statute. See id. § 1. "Willful and malicious conduct" includes cruelty, revenge, or hostility. See id. A harassment prevention order is valid for up to one year from the date that it is entered. See id. § 3(d). The proceedings by which the court determines whether to grant a prevention order are civil in nature, but violations of these orders are criminal offenses. See id. § 4. The complainant may ask the court to require the harasser to, among other things, stay away from the victim's place of employment. See id. § 3(a).

SURVEY OF MICHIGAN EMPLOYMENT LIBEL LAW

Adam S. Forman, David G. King, and Christopher M. Trebilcock
Miller, Canfield, Paddock and Stone, P.L.C.
150 W. Jefferson, Suite 2500
Detroit, Michigan 48226
Telephone: (313) 963-6420; Facsimile: (313) 496-7500

(With Developments Reported Through **November 1, 2012**)

GENERAL COMMENTS

While this outline uses standard citation format, the Michigan courts have adopted their own citation form: All cases must contain a citation to the appropriate official Michigan reporter as well as a parallel citation to West's Northwest reporter, separated by a semi-colon. Case names must be italicized, not underlined. The reporter abbreviations must not contain any periods as part of the citation.

Example: Smith v Jones, 123 Mich 456; 333 NW2d 444 (1985).

Not: Smith v. Jones, 123 Mich. 456, 333 N.W.2d 444 (1985).

For general citation rules, see Michigan Uniform System of Citation, Administrative Order No. 2006-3. For other matters, refer to A Uniform System of Citation, 13th ed., for guidance, but conform citations to Michigan citation style.

SIGNIFICANT DEVELOPMENTS SINCE THE 2012 *SURVEY*

None.

I. GENERAL LAW

A. General Employment Law

1. ***At Will Employment.*** In Michigan an employment relationship for an indefinite period is presumed to be terminable at will, i.e. by either party at any time, for any reason or no reason. Rood v. General Dynamics Corp., 444 Mich. 107, 116, 507 N.W.2d 591 (1993); Lynas v. Maxwell Farms, 279 Mich. 684, 273 N.W. 315 (1937). The presumption of employment at will is overcome with proof of either a contract provision for a definite term of employment, or one that forbids discharge absent just cause. Lytle v. Malady, 458 Mich. 153, 579 N.W.2d 906 (1998). To overcome this presumption, a party lacking proof of a definite term of employment must present sufficient evidence of either (a) a provision forbidding discharge absent just cause, through an explicit or implied-in-fact promise from the employer (the "contract theory" of Touissaint v. Blue Cross & Blue Shield of Michigan, 408 Mich. 579, 292 N.W.2d 880 (1980)) or (b) a legitimate expectation of job security instilled by employer policies and procedures applicable to the workforce as a whole (the "legitimate expectations" prong of Touissaint). The breach of an agreement to hire an employee as an at-will employee can only result in nominal damages. Franzel v. Kerr Mfg. Co., 234 Mich. App. 600, 600 NW2d 66 (1999).

"Even in an at-will employment relationship, 'some grounds for discharging an employee are so contrary to public policy as to be actionable.'" Hein v. All America Plywood Co., 232 F.3d 482, 486 (6th Cir. 2000); quoting, Suchodolski v. Mich. Consol. Gas Co., 412 Mich. 692, 316 N.W.2d 710, 711 (1982).

Michigan permits claims of wrongful discharge. See Hill v. Pharmacia & Upjohn Co., 2001 US Dist LEXIS 5752 (W.D. Mich. Apr. 30, 2001).

Oral statements may be sufficient to overcome the presumption of at-will employment if the statements are clear and unequivocal, and would permit a reasonable person to find that a reasonable promisee would interpret the statements made as a promise of termination only for just cause. Branham v. Thomas M. Cooley Law Sch., 2010 WL 3505930 (W.D. Mich. Sept 7, 2010) (unpublished) (citing Rowe v. Montgomery Ward & Co., 437 Mich. 627, 473 N.W.2d 268 (1991)), aff'd, 689 F.3d 558 (6th Cir. 2012); Mt. Tai Asset Mgmt. Corp. v. Metro Equity Group, LLC., 2011 WL 65863 (E.D. Mich. Jan. 11, 2011) (unpublished).

B. Basic Elements of a Libel Claim

1. ***Basic Elements.*** Defamation consists of "(1) a false and defamatory statement concerning the plaintiff, (2) an unprivileged publication to a third party, (3) fault amounting to at least negligence on the part of the publisher, and (4) either actionability of the statement irrespective of special harm, or the existence of special harm caused by the

publication." Rouch (II) v. Enquirer & News, 440 Mich. 238, 251, 487 N.W.2d 205, 20 Media L. Rep. 2265 (1992) (on remand), cert denied, 507 U.S. 967, 113 S. Ct. 1401, 122 L. Ed. 774 2d (1993). See also Dadd v. Mount Hope Church, 486 Mich. 857, 780 N.W.2d 763 (2010).

2. ***Fault.***

a. **Private Figure Plaintiff/Matter of Public Concern.** Michigan requires that a private figure plaintiff show at least negligence on the part of an employer who makes an allegedly defamatory statement. M.C.L. § 609.2911; Rouch (I) v. Enquirer & News of Battle Creek, 427 Mich. 157, 398 N.W.2d 245, 13 Media L. Rep. 2201 (1986) (affirming and remanding). Even if a plaintiff is a private figure, if allegedly defamatory statements involve a matter of public concern, the plaintiff bears the burden of proving the falsity of the allegedly defamatory statements. Williams v. Detroit Bd. of Educ., 523 F. Supp. 2d 602 (E.D. Mich. 2007) (citing Rouch (I), supra) (appellate history omitted).

b. **Private Figure Plaintiff/Matter of Private Concern.** As with statements involving matters of public concern, Michigan requires that a private figure plaintiff show at least negligence on the part of an employer when the employer's allegedly defamatory statements deal with a matter of private concern. M.C.L. § 600.2911.

c. **Public Figure Plaintiff/Matter of Public Concern.** Michigan applies the federal constitutional standard from New York Times v. Sullivan, 376 U.S. 254, 84 S. Ct. 710. 11 L. Ed. 2d 686 (1964) — actual malice — to cases involving public officials. Postill v. Booth Newspapers, 118 Mich. App. 608, 325 N.W.2d 511 (1982). Determining whether a person is a public figure in a defamation claim is a question of law to be answered by the trial court. Bufalino v. Detroit Magazine, Inc., 433 Mich. 766, 449 N.W.2d 410 (1989). An action for libel or slander of a public figure shall not be brought unless the statement was published "with knowledge that it was false or with reckless disregard of whether or not it was false." M.C.L. § 600.2911(6). See also Tomkiewicz v. The Detroit News, Inc., 246 Mich. App. 662, 635 N.W.2d 36 (2001). "Reckless disregard for truth is not established merely by showing that the statements were made with preconceived objectives or insufficient investigation. Further, reckless disregard is measured by whether the publisher entertained serious doubts concerning the truth of the statements published." Mino v. Clio Sch. Dist., 255 Mich. App. 60, 661 N.W.2d 586 (2003). A city manager was found to be a public figure that had to prove by clear and convincing evidence that a publication is a defamatory falsehood made with actual malice. Collins v. Ham, 2008 WL 2437259, at *8 (Mich. Ct. App. June 17, 2008) (unpublished). A public school principal is a public figure to the extent that a defamation claim against the principal involves communications relating to the principal's conduct as a principal. Williams v. Detroit Bd. of Educ., 523 F. Supp. 2d 602, 610 (E.D. Mich. 2007); see also, Schmidli v. City of Fraser, 784 F. Supp. 2d 794 (E.D. Mich. 2011) (library director is a public official because she had control over how the library could best serve the public). The controversy over a principal's alleged misappropriation of funds at a public school is a matter of public concern. Williams v. Detroit Bd. of Educ., 306 F. App'x 934 (6th Cir. 2009).

3. ***Falsity.*** The plaintiff in a defamation action must prove falsity as an element of his or her claim. See In re Chmura, 464 Mich. 58, 72, 626 N.W.2d 876, 886 (2001); Peterfish v. Frantz, 168 Mich. App. 43, 52-53, 424 N.W.2d 25 (1988) (involving a public official plaintiff); Rouch (I) v. Enquirer & News of Battle Creek, 427 Mich. 157, 398 N.W.2d 245, 13 Media L Rep 2201 (1986) (affirming and remanding); Locricchio v. Evening News Ass'n, 438 Mich. 84, 476 N.W.2d 112, 19 Media L. Rep. 1065 (1991), cert denied, 503 U.S. 907, 112 S. Ct. 1267 (1992). See also Patillo v. Equitable Life Assurance Soc'y of the United States, 199 Mich. App. 450, 502 N.W.2d 696 (1992) (although plaintiff stormed out of the employer's office when accused of insubordination, this was insufficient to prove that the plaintiff was in fact insubordinate); Baggs v. Eagle-Pitcher Industries, Inc., 957 F.2d 268 (6th Cir. 1992) (applying Michigan law) (no defamation claim even assuming defendant had said that all of the plaintiffs who refused the company drug test used illegal drugs, where eight of the ten plaintiffs admitted to using illegal drugs); Smith v. Anonymous Joint Enterprise, 2011 WL 744943 (Mich. App. Mar. 3, 2011) (statements in investigation report regarding public employee were matters of opinion and not thus not false). In Richards v. Sandusky Cmty Schs, 102 F. Supp. 2d 753 (E.D. Mich. 2000), plaintiff brought a defamation claim when her former employer provided her prospective employer with a copy of a disciplinary letter plaintiff had received. The court found that plaintiff failed to prove that anything in the letter was false (and that plaintiff signed an authorization allowing the release of the letter). See also McMillan v. Nowicki, 2005 Mich. App. LEXIS 787 (Mar 22, 2005) (unpublished) (summary disposition affirmed where none of the challenged statements were objectively provable as false, rather they were merely defendant's opinions of plaintiff's work performance on a particular project based on defendant's personal observations) See Pedell v. Heartland Health Care Ctr., 2007 Mich. App. LEXIS 773 (Mar. 20, 2007) (unpublished) (where there was no dispute regarding what was said, Plaintiff testified that he did not know whether any disparaging remarks were made about him and Plaintiff himself disclosed his change in employment status to various individuals and firms who contacted him to do work as an expert witness, court held that plaintiff could not sue in defamation for disclosure of a true fact that plaintiff himself disclosed many times.) See Collins v. Ham, 2008 WL 2437259, *8 (Mich. Ct. App. June 17, 2008) (unpublished) (holding that there was no genuine issue of material fact as to the accuracy of defendant's communications where city council's attorney made statements at public hearing that she had not heard from plaintiff and did not know

whether plaintiff would be attending hearing because evidence established that city council's attorney sent letter to plaintiff asking plaintiff to clarify whether he would be attending public hearing and that there was no indication that plaintiff had responded to the letter). See also Williams v. Detroit Bd. of Educ., 306 F. App'x 934 (6th Cir. 2009) (affirming the lower court's grant of summary judgment because the plaintiff –principal failed to create a genuine issue of material fact about the falsity of defendants' statements); Schmidli v. City of Fraser, 784 F. Supp. 2d. 794 (E.D. Mich. 2011) (director admitted that statements in memo city officials sent to city council regarding staff complaints were true); Heffelfinger v. Bad Axe Pub. Schs., 2011 WL 118772 (Mich. Ct. App. Jan. 13, 2011) (unpublished) (statements made about former teacher were substantially true).

4. ***Defamatory Statement of Fact.*** A statement will be defamatory in Michigan "if it tends to so harm the reputation of another so as to lower him in the estimation of the community or to deter third persons from associating or dealing with him." Rouch (II) v. Enquirer & News, 440 Mich. 238, 251, 487 N.W.2d 205, 20 Media L. Rep. 2265 (1992) (on remand), cert. denied, 507 U.S. 967, 113 S. Ct. 1401, 122 L. Ed. 2d 774 (1993); Baggs v. Eagle-Pitcher Indus., Inc., 957 F.2d 268 (6th Cir. 1992) (applying Michigan law). For example, statements indicating that an employee was discharged "for cause" may be held defamatory if the communication proves unprivileged. DeFlaviis v. Lord and Taylor, 223 Mich. App. 432, 566 N.W.2d 661 (1997). However, a statement of pure opinion is not actionable unless "it implies the allegation of undisclosed defamatory facts as the basis for the opinion." Fisher v. Detroit Free Press, 158 Mich. App. 409, 413, 404 N.W.2d 765, leave denied, 428 Mich. 914 (1987). Furthermore, personal criticism in and of itself is not defamatory. Berlin v. Superintendent of Pub. Instruction, 181 Mich. App. 154, 164-65, 448 N.W.2d 764 (1989); Nuyen v. Slater, 372 Mich. 654, 662, 127 N.W.2d 369 (1964). Courts must use an objective standard in determining whether a statement is defamatory. Fisher, 158 Mich. App. at 412 ("the meaning of a statement is that meaning which, under the circumstances, a reasonable person who sees the statement reasonably understands to be the meaning intended"); Bethea v. Applebee's Int'l, 2000 U.S. Dist. LEXIS 1456 (W.D. Mich. Jan. 31, 2000) (unpublished) (statement by defendant's representative denying charges by plaintiff and other picketers that Applebee's engaged in discrimination were not, when considered in context, capable of a defamatory meaning); Wojnaroski v. Grot, 2006 Mich. App. LEXIS 482 (Feb. 23, 2006) (unpublished) (statement by defendant employer that plaintiff former employee had been terminated for "misconduct" was not defamatory since the term "misconduct", as used in this case, could not reasonably be construed as implying that plaintiff had engaged in illegal activity and plaintiff presented no evidence to support that the term was intended to be understood in that sense); Meier v. Detroit Diesel Corp., 2006 Mich. App. LEXIS 2412 (Mar. 22, 2005) (unpublished) (plaintiff did not properly plead a defamation claim since he failed to identify any specific words or statements in the evaluation or emails that he believed to defame him); Pedell v. Heartland Health Care Ctr., 2007 Mich. App. LEXIS 773 (Mar. 20, 2007) (unpublished) (where there was no dispute regarding what was said, Plaintiff testified that he did not know whether any disparaging remarks were made about him and Plaintiff himself disclosed his change in employment status to various individuals and firms who contacted him to do work as an expert witness, court held that plaintiff could not sue in defamation for disclosure of a true fact that plaintiff himself disclosed many times.); Henderson v. Walled Lake Consol Schs., 469 F.3d 479 (6th Cir. 2006) (summary judgment granted as to slander claim where court held that the employer can be liable in *respondeat superior* only if the individual's slanderous statement was made while he was engaged in his employer's work *and* was acting within the scope of his authority (quoting Dortman v. ACO Hardware, Inc., 405 F. Supp. 2d. 812 (E.D. Mich. 2005)). Further, an employer is not liable for a defamatory statement, even though made in the workplace, if the statement was not made in relation to a matter about which the employee's duties required him to act.); Dubuc v. El-Magrabi, 2010 WL 3564838, at *4 (Mich. App. Sept. 14, 2010) (unpublished) (independent medical examiner's report on plaintiff seeking disability benefits was not defamatory since purpose was to substantiate plaintiff's disability claim), rev'd in part, 489 Mich. 869, 795 N.W.2d 593 (Apr. 6, 2011).

5. ***Of and Concerning Plaintiff.*** To be defamatory, the statement must be "of and concerning plaintiff." Hodgins Kennels, Inc. v. Durbin, 170 Mich. App. 474, 480-81, 429 N.W.2d 189 (1988), rev'd on other grounds, 432 Mich. 894, 438 N.W.2d 247 (1989). The court must determine whether the communication could reasonably be understood to involve the plaintiff, but, if it was in fact understood in that manner is an issue for the jury. Hodgins, 170 Mich. App. at 480; Linbaugh v. Sheraton Mich. Co., 198 Mich. App. 335, 337-38, 497 N.W.2d 585 (1993) (summary disposition improper where a jury, by use of "extrinsic facts," could determine that a female employee was the character depicted in a sexually explicit cartoon); **Nicklas v. Green, Green & Adams, P.C., 2012 WL 2126066 (Mich. App. June 12, 2012) (e-mail communication concerned the heart program in general as opposed to the plaintiff).**

6. ***Publication.*** Generally, any publication must be made by the offending party to someone in addition to the person defamed. Smith v. Fergan, 181 Mich. App. 594, 596, 450 N.W.2d 110 (1989) (publication requirement satisfied when an alleged defamatory statement was made to two employees, each accused of theft); Reed v. Mercy Health Servs., 1999 WL 33435072 (Mich. Ct. App. Oct. 12, 1999) (affirming the lower court's grant of summary judgment, which held that suspending plaintiff's employment pending investigation of an embezzlement charge was not publication). Allegation that defamatory statements were made public by publication on an internet page satisfies the requirement that the publication element of defamation be pleaded with specificity. Ben-Tech Indus Automation v. Oakland Univ., 2005 Mich.

App. LEXIS 32 (Jan 11, 2005) (unpublished); McMillan v. Nowicki, 2005 Mich. App. LEXIS 787 (Mar. 22, 2005) (unpublished) (Defendant's alleged defamatory comments to a reference checker not actionable where the plaintiff hired the reference checker to solicit a reference from defendant, knowing that defendant did not have entirely positive things to say about him, thus consenting to any publication to the reference checker; and no one else saw the report); Forth v. Kroger Co., 2010 WL 3937314 (E.D. Mich. Oct. 5, 2010) (plaintiff failed to establish facts necessary that company representatives were responsible for spreading rumor that he was terminated for alleged theft); **Nicklas v. Green, Green & Adams, P.C., 2012 WL 2126066 (Mich. App. June 12, 2012) (plaintiff failed to show that letter prepared by doctor was shared with others in the hospital).**

a. **Intracorporate Communication.** Michigan common law does not distinguish between intercompany and intracompany disclosure. Rather, "where the qualified privilege applies, it shields the individual who releases the information to a prospective employer, or a different department within the same employer . . . ." Murdock v. Higgings, 454 Mich. 46, n 14, 559 N.W.2d 639 (1997) (citing Bacon v. Mich. Cent R.R. Co., 66 Mich. 166, 21 N.W. 324 (1884)); see e.g., Whiting v. Allstate Ins. Co., 433 Fed.App'x 395 (6th Cir. Aug. 8, 2011) (unpublished) (applying qualified privilege to communications in a discharge letter and those between in-house counsel and company investigator and human resource manager).

b. **Compelled Self-Publication.** Michigan courts generally do not recognize defamation claims based on "compelled self-publication," a theory which places liability on a former employer for the plaintiff's own disclosure of the employer's defamatory statements to a prospective employer, because it arises from the single case of Grist v. Upjohn Co., 16 Mich. App. 452, 168 N.W.2d 389 (1969). See, Forth v. Kroger Co., 2010 WL 3937314, at *5 (E.D. Mich. Oct. 5, 2010) (unpublished) (recognizing that this theory of recovery is suspect under Michigan law). In Michigan, a plaintiff cannot prevail on a defamation claim unless someone other than the plaintiff published the statements to a prospective employer. Merritt v. Detroit Mem'l Hosp., 81 Mich. App. 279, 286, 265 N.W.2d 124 (1978) (in the absence of publication by someone other than the plaintiff "the trial court found that plaintiff and no one else disclosed the reasons for her termination," and as such the plaintiff's claim must fail). See III.A, infra.

c. **Republication.** No reported cases address this topic in the labor and employment field.

7. ***Statements versus Conduct.*** Generally, a defamation claim requires that a statement be either written or oral. However, Michigan courts have allowed libel claims based on pictures, rather thaen written words. Linebaugh v. Sheraton Mich. Corp., 198 Mich. App. 335, 497 N.W.2d 585 (1993), leave denied, 444 Mich. 942, 512 N.W.2d 847 (1994) (court allowed a claim for defamation based on the distribution of a sexually suggestive cartoon alleging sexual relations between plaintiff and a male employee). Furthermore, slander, which is generally defined as offensive oral communication, has also been held actionable through the use of conduct or gestures. Bonkowski v. Arlan's Dep't Store, 383 Mich. 90, 97, 174 N.W.2d 765 (1970) (court held that the actions of a store security guard, searching plaintiff within the view of other patrons, was sufficient for a defamation claim).

8. ***Damages.*** One element of defamation requires that a plaintiff show damages either due to the nature of the defamation, defamation per se, or defamation per quod. Postill v. Booth Newspapers, 118 Mich. App. 608, 618, 325 N.W.2d 511 (1982). Plaintiff must establish specific harm, such as loss of income related to the defamatory statements, in order to collect damages for defamation per quod. Sias v. General Motors Corp., 372 Mich. 542, 550-51, 127 N.W.2d 357 (1964). See Meier v. Detroit Diesel Corp., 2006 Mich. App. LEXIS 2412 (Mar. 22, 2005) (unpublished) (plaintiff failed to plead appropriate damages and merely speculated that he was denied a raise due to a negative evaluation and that the evaluation would be on file and would hurt him in the event that a potential employer contacted defendant former employer).

a. **Presumed Damages and Libel Per Se.** According to M.C.L. § 600.2911(1); M.S.A. 27A.2911(1), if defamatory words are defamatory per se, then they "are actionable in themselves." This means that "the court will presume without proof that [plaintiff's] reputation has thereby been impaired." Mains v. Whiting, 87 Mich. 172, 181, 49 N.W. 559 (1891). Michigan recognizes defamation per se in four instances: (1) statements accusing the plaintiff of committing a crime; (2) statements indicating that the plaintiff is infected with a contagious disease; (3) statements that harm the plaintiff in their employment or profession; (4) and statements imputing to the plaintiff a lack of chastity. Newman v. Stein, 75 Mich. 402, 403, 42 N.W. 956 (1889); see also, Colista v. Thomas, 241 Mich. App. 529, 616 N.W.2d 249 (2000); **Williams v. New World Commc'ns of Detroit, Inc., 2012 WL 555776, *8 at n. 2 (Mich. App. Feb. 1, 2012); and** Ogle v. Hocker, 430 Fed.App'x 373 (6th Cir. May 27, 2011) (unpublished) (words imputing a lack of chastity are per se defamatory).

"Words charging the commission of a crime are defamatory per se, and hence, injury to the reputation of the person defamed is presumed to the extent that the failure to prove damages is not a ground for dismissal." Tomkiewicz v. The Detroit News, Inc., 246 Mich. App. 662, 635 N.W.2d 36 (2001) (quoting Burden v. Elias Bros. Big Boy Rests., 240 Mich. App. 723, 727-28, 613 N.W.2d 378 (2000)).

Where defendant former employee published on the internet an academic paper that "suggested" criminal wrongdoing by plaintiff former employer, the circuit court erred in dismissing plaintiff's defamation claim for failure to prove special damages, because special damages need not be proven when the defendant's words impute the commission of a crime by the plaintiff. Ben-Tech Indus. Automation v. Oakland Univ., 2005 Mich. App. LEXIS 32 (Jan. 11, 2005) (unpublished).

Where defendant employer told employees that plaintiff former employee had been terminated for "misconduct", the court held that the statement was not defamatory since the term "misconduct", as used in this case, could not reasonably be construed as implying that plaintiff had engaged in criminal activity and plaintiff presented no evidence to support that the term was intended to be understood in that sense. Wojnaroski v. Grot, 2006 Mich. App. LEXIS 482 (Feb. 23, 2006) (unpublished).

Defamation with respect to professional standing is not libel per se. Where a former employee sued a former co-worker and their former employer, the Michigan Court of Appeals held that "Because the statute allows recovery only for actual damages for defamation regarding one's profession; the statute lists per se actions separately under a different subsection; and this Court in Glazer, supra indicated actual damages must be proven, plaintiffs [are] required to show actual damages." Gafka v. Ahern, 2005 Mich. App. LEXIS 1738 (July 19, 2005) (unpublished).

Where defendants, several Department of Education employees, allegedly identified plaintiff school teacher as having a criminal conviction in correspondence sent to school district pursuant to school safety legislation, the court held that because a false accusation of a criminal conviction could harm plaintiff's employment, the plaintiff had alleged libel per se. Frohriep v. Flanagan, 278 Mich. App. 665, 754 N.W.2d 912 (2008), rev'd in part on other grounds, 483 Mich. 920, 763 N.W.2d 279 (2009).

Not every type of defamatory statement is actionable. "If a statement cannot be reasonably interpreted as stating actual facts about the plaintiff, it is protected by the First Amendment. Parodies, political cartoons, and satires are generally entitled to protection. Where the words are no more than rhetorical hyperbole or 'a vigorous epithet' they are not considered actionable." Harrison v. Great Lakes Bev. Co., 2001 Mich. App. LEXIS 2357 (2001) (unpublished) (quoting Ireland v. Edwards, 230 Mich. App. 607, 584 N.W.2d 632 (1998)). See Johnson v. Millennium Treatment Servs., 2007 Mich. App. LEXIS 1198 (May 1, 2007) (unpublished).

(1) **Employment-Related Criticism.** Under Michigan law an employer has the qualified privilege to defame an employee by making statements to other employees whose duties interest them in the subject matter. Forth v. Kroger Co., 2010 WL 3937314, at * 4 (E.D. Mich. Oct. 5, 2010) (unpublished) (quoting Gonyea v. Motor Parts Fed. Credit Union, 192 Mich. App. 74, 480 N.W.2d 297 (1991)). Michigan courts recognize as per se defamatory statements by an employer that accuse an employee of theft. Shannon v. Taylor AMC/Jeep, Inc., 168 Mich. App. 415, 418, 425 N.W.2d 165 (1988) (if false, statements to defendant's customers that plaintiff was discharged for stealing constituted slander per se since it was injurious to the employee in his profession or employment). However, courts have also found actionable per se defamatory statements that, if true, would not amount to a crime. Croton v. Gillis, 104 Mich. App. 104, 108 -09, 304 N.W.2d 820 (1981) (employer's statements that plaintiff was discharged due to his attitude and inability to work with other officers was sufficient for a claim of defamation per se).

(2) **Single Instance Rule.** No cases address this topic in the employment context.

b. **Punitive Damages.** Punitive damages are available to a plaintiff in defamation action against media defendants and only if "the defendant acted with common-law malice – in the sense of ill will or bad faith – in publishing the libel." Peisner v. Detroit Free Press, 421 Mich. 125, 136, 364 N.W.2d 600 (1984). While styled as "punitive damages," they may not be awarded to actually punish the defendant, but rather to compensate the plaintiff for additional emotional distress. In Peisner, the court determined that it would be reversible error for the court to instruct a jury that "actual malice" – i.e. knowledge of falsity or reckless disregard for the truth – would be sufficient for an award of punitive damages. Id. A plaintiff seeking punitive damages must give "notice to defendant to publish a retraction" and provide "a reasonable time to do so." M.C.L. § 2911(2)(b). Failure to do so may limit plaintiff's right to punitive damages. Various Mkts., Inc. v. The Chase Manhattan Bank, 908 F. Supp. 459, 469 (E.D. Mich. 1995).

II. PRIVILEGES AND DEFENSES

A. Scope of Privileges

1. ***Absolute Privilege.*** Employers have an absolute privilege against liability for defamatory statements made during judicial proceedings and administrative hearings. Harrison v. Arrow Metal Prods. Corp., 20 Mich. App. 590, 610, 174 N.W.2d 875 (1969) (citing Timmis v. Bennett, 352 Mich. 355, 362-63, 89 N.W.2d 748 (1958)). Specifically, Michigan employers are protected by M.C.L. § 421.11(b) regarding any statements made during grievance

proceedings dictated by a collective bargaining agreement, Fulghum v. United Parcel Serv., 424 Mich. 89, 98-102, 378 N.W.2d 472 (1985) (Levin, J., concurring), and for any statements made to Michigan Unemployment Insurance Agency ("MUIA") in the course of its administrative functions. Sias v. General Motors Corp., 372 Mich. 542, 548, 127 N.W.2d 357 (1964). See also Mero v. U.S. Figure Skating Ass'n., 2006 U.S. Dist. LEXIS 4854 (E.D. Mich. Jan. 20, 2006) (unpublished) (defendant figure skating association is not entitled to absolute privilege since its grievance proceedings do not fall under the scope of a public judicial, legislative, or military proceedings); Slomka v. City of Hamtramck Hous. Comm'n, 2007 Mich. App. LEXIS 2579 (Nov. 15, 2007) (unpublished) (statements made by employer in a judicial pleading, as long as relevant, material and pertinent to the issue, are absolutely privileged regardless of falsity or malice on the part of the author). Privilege extends to information and testimony produced pursuant to a subpoena but does not extend to affidavits prepared prior to the commencement of a suit. Ellis v. Kaye-Kibbey, 581 F. Supp. 2d 861, 881 (W.D. Mich. 2008) (defendant entitled to absolute privilege for providing information in response to a subpoena but not entitled to absolute privilege where a suit had not yet commenced).

A second absolute privilege arises from consent. MUIA records and determinations may not be used in judicial or administrative proceedings unless the MUIA is a party. Harrison v. Arrow Metal Prods. Corp., 20 Mich. App. 590, 615, 174 N.W.2d 875 (1969) ("If the employee consents to publication, it is absolutely privileged"); see also Merritt v. Detroit Mem'l Hosp., 81 Mich. App. 279, 286, 265 N.W.2d 124 (1978) (plaintiff failed to object to publication of statements to union representatives at a grievance proceeding, and thus consented); Hollowell v. Career Decisions, Inc., 100 Mich. App. 561, 574-75, 298 N.W.2d 915 (1980) (court treated plaintiff's request that management review a poor evaluation from a superior as consent to publication of the defamatory statements). If an employer has an absolute privilege, that statement is not actionable even though it is false and maliciously published. Harrison, 20 Mich. App. at 610 (citing Lawrence v. Fox, 357 Mich. 134, 137, 97 N.W.2d 719 (1959)).

A third absolute privilege arises from immunity granted to judges, legislators, and executive officials acting within the scope of their authority under the Governmental Tort Liability Act (GTLA), M.C.L. § 691.1407(5). **With some noted exceptions, a governmental agency is immune from tort liability if the governmental agency is engaged in the exercise or discharge of a governmental function. MCL § 691.1407(1). The elective or highest appointive executive official of all levels of government is also immune from tort liability for injuries to persons or damages to property if he or she is acting within the scope of his or her executive authority. MCL § 691.1407(5). Lower-ranking governmental employees or officials may also be immune for tort liability, but the test differs depending on whether the alleged tort is intentional or negligence. The test for the latter is whether: (a) the employee is acting or reasonably believes he or she is acting within the scope of his or her authority; (b) the governmental agency is engaged in the exercise or discharge or a governmental function; and (c) the employee's conduct does not amount to gross negligence that is the proximate cause of the injury or damage. MCL § 691.1407(2). For the former, the test is whether the acts: (a) were undertaken during the course of employment and the employee was acting, or reasonably believed that he was acting, within the scope of his authority; (b) were undertaken in good faith, or were not undertaken with malice; and (c) the acts were discretionary, as opposed to ministerial. MCL § 691.1407(3) and Odom v Wayne County, 482 Mich 459, 479-480; 760 NW2d 217 (2008).** See Brown v. Mayor of Detroit, 271 Mich. App. 692, 723 N.W.2d (2006) (defendant was acting within the scope of his authority as the Mayor of Detroit when he answered questions from news reporters regarding plaintiff's termination as Deputy Chief Officer, and was therefore entitled to absolute immunity under the GTLA), rev'd in part on other grounds, 478 Mich. 589, 734 N.W.2d 514,(2007); Cluley v. Lansing Bd. Of Water and Light, 2006 Mich. App. LEXIS 607 (Mar. 7, 2006) (unpublished) (court found that the defendant public entity, could lawfully investigate and take disciplinary measures against an employee through its general manager and thus, the trial court did not err in finding that the BWL was absolutely immune from liability because it was engaged in a governmental function); Heffelfinger v. Bad Axe Pub. Schs., 2011 WL 118772 (Mich. Ct. App. Jan. 13, 2001) (unpublished) (superintendent had absolute immunity when he reported plaintiff's alleged misconduct to the school board and then repeated the allegations at an open board meeting). **Estill v. Davis, 2012 WL 1697023 (Mich. Ct. App. May 15, 2012) (school board member was not entitled to immunity because statements were not made within his authority per bylaws).** The statutory fair reporting privilege, M.C.L. § 600.2911(3), however, does not preclude a defamation claim against an employer who has created a public record which is then used in a news report. Williams v. Detroit Bd. of Educ., 523 F. Supp. 2d 602 (E.D. Mich. 2007) (statutory fair reporting privilege did not preclude defamation claim brought by plaintiff against his former employer where newspapers published the contents of an audit report created by former employer as part of an investigation into plaintiff's alleged misappropriation of school funds and equipment).

2. ***Qualified Privileges.*** In Michigan, an employer will not be libel for a defamatory statement if a qualified privilege is applicable. Dadd v. Mount Hope Church, 486 Mich. 857, 860-862, 780 N.W.2d 763 (2010).

a. **Common Interest.** Michigan has long recognized a qualified privilege for those with an interest in the employment relationship. Bacon v. Mich. Cent. R.R. Co., 66 Mich. 166, 33 N.W. 181 (1887) ("It extends to all communications made bona fide upon any subject matter in which the party communicating has an interest, or in reference to which he has a duty, to a person having a corresponding interest or duty"). Thus, an employer has a qualified privilege when making statements to other employees whose duties interest them in the subject matter. Gonyea v. Motor Parts Fed. Credit Union, 192 Mich. App. 74, 78-79, 480 N.W.2d 297 (1991). See also **Osak v Univ of Mich, 2012 WL 5061640 (Mich App. Oct. 18, 2012) (unpublished) (supervisor's letter to human resources department stating that plaintiff was "let go for falsification of data" was qualifiedly privileged);** Wojnaroski v. Grot, 2006 Mich. App. LEXIS 482 (Feb. 23, 2006) (unpublished) (qualified privilege existed where statements regarding plaintiff's termination for poor performance was made by the president of an organization to its members at a general meeting); Roberts v. Trinity Health-Mich., 2006 Mich. App. LEXIS 3429 (Nov 21, 2006) (unpublished) (employer's statements were qualifiedly privileged as statements made from an employer to a prospective employer are privileged unless made with malice, i.e., the employer knew that the statements were false or made without regard for their truthfulness. Whiting v. Allstate Ins. Co., 433 F. App'x 395 (6th Cir. 2011) (unpublished) (supervisors' statements about plaintiff's violation of company's Code of Ethics were qualifiedly privileged); Forth v. Kroger Co., 2010 WL 3937314 (E.D. Mich. Oct. 5, 2010) (statements made by supervisors to plaintiff and union supervisors were subject to conditional privilege), aff'd 471 F. App'x 484 (6th Cir. 2012). However, the qualified privilege generally extends only to personnel with a genuine interest, such as supervisory personnel. Sias v. General Motors Corp., 372 Mich. 542, 548, 127 N.W.2d 357 (1964) (no qualified privilege when statements about the reasons for plaintiff's termination were made to fellow employees with no supervisory authority); Patillo v. Equitable Life Assurance Soc'y of the United States, 199 Mich. App. 450, 455, 502 N.W.2d 696 (1992) (no qualified privilege when statements regarding the plaintiff's termination for insubordination were made to fellow employees with no interest in why plaintiff was terminated, and not limited to "supervisors, personnel department representatives or other company officials").

b. **Duty.** If an employer has a duty to report or discuss an employee's performance, that employer is also protected by a qualified privilege. Crawford v. TRW, Inc., 815 F. Supp. 1028 (E.D. Mich. 1993) (summary judgment granted to employer when plaintiff failed to show actual malice, and where employer posted letters regarding the settlement of plaintiff's grievance as required by the union's collective bargaining agreement as a way of informing union members about union business).

c. **Criticism of Public Employee.** A qualified privilege protects criticism of a public employee if that employee's "position is of such apparent importance that the public has an independent interest in her qualifications and in her performance of her duties beyond the general public interest in the qualifications and performance of all public employees." Peterfish v. Frantz, 168 Mich. App. 43, 48, 424 N.W.2d 25 (1988) (defendant protected by qualified privilege since plaintiff had significant control over many aspects of the local construction trade sufficient to classify her as a public official). Alleged defamatory statements regarding school superintendent are subject to a qualified immunity – requiring a plaintiff to prove that defendant made statements with actual malice. Kefgen v. Davidson, 241 Mich. App. 611, 617 N.W.2d 351 (2000). Except for an individual government employee afforded absolute immunity under the GTLA, an individual government employee who commits an intentional tort is not shielded by the GTLA if it is alleged that the employee committed an intentional tort for which liability was imposed on government employees before July 7, 1986. Frohriep v. Flanagan, 278 Mich. App. 665, 754 N.W.2d 912 (2008), rev'd in part on other grounds, 483 Mich. 920, 763 N.W.2d 279 (2009). However, a low-level government employee has common-law qualified immunity from intentional tort liability when the government employee: (1) acted in the course of his or her employment, and acted, or reasonably believed that he or she acted, within the scope of his or her employment; (2) acted in good faith; and (3) performed discretionary, as opposed to ministerial acts. Frohriep v. Flanagan, 278 Mich. App. 665, 754 N.W.2d 912 (2008), rev'd in part on other grounds, 483 Mich. 920, 763 N.W.2d 279 (2009).

d. **Limitation on Qualified Privileges.** If an employer either exceeds the scope of the qualified privilege or acts with "actual malice," then the qualified privilege may be lost. Bacon v. Mich. Cent. R.R. Co., 66 Mich. 166, 171, 33 N.W. 181 (1887) (it is a question of "actual malice" whether the true reasons for an employee's discharge was communicated to other employees).

(1) **Constitutional or Actual Malice.** Michigan courts have adopted the constitutional, or "actual malice" standard promulgated by the Supreme Court. New York Times v. Sullivan, 376 U.S. 254, 280, 84 S.Ct 710, 11 L. Ed. 2d 686 (1964). Accordingly, in order to prove "actual malice" the plaintiff must show that the defendant acted "with knowledge that [the statement at issue] was false or with reckless disregard of whether it was false or not." Wynn v. Cole, 91 Mich. App. 517, 523-24, 284 N.W.2d 144 (1979) (the court rejected the use of the common law malice standard in favor of "actual malice"). See also Tomkiewicz v. The Detroit News, Inc., 246 Mich. App. 662, 667, 635 N.W.2d 36, 41 (2001) ("It is well established that the United States Constitution affords a qualified privilege protecting the making of defamatory statements concerning public officials when the statements relate to the official's conduct in office"); Collins v. Detroit Free Press, 245 Mich. App. 27, 627 N.W.2d 5, 29 Media L. Rep. 1857 (2001) ("When a case involves a public figure, the plaintiff is required to show actual malice, not mere negligence"); Roberts v. Trinity Health-Mich., 2006 Mich. App. LEXIS 3429 (Nov 21, 2006) (unpublished) (employer's statements were qualifiedly privileged as statements made from an employer to a prospective employer are privileged unless made with malice, i.e., the employer knew that the

statements were false or made without regard for their truthfulness. In Frohriep v. Flanagan, 278 Mich. App. 665, 754 N.W.2d 912 (2008), rev'd in part on other grounds, 483 Mich. 920, 763 N.W.2d 279 (2009), a school teacher alleged that he was wrongly identified as having a criminal conviction in correspondence sent by Michigan Department of Education, but failed to overcome qualified privilege by showing that alleged libelous publication was made with actual malice because mere showing that statements are made with preconceived objectives or insufficient investigation is insufficient to show reckless disregard. Use of information and memorandums placed in an employee's personnel file, subject to a Freedom of Information Act (FOIA) request, when not prepared by the defendant may or may not constitute reckless disregard underlying actual malice. Smith v. Anonymous Joint Enter., 487 Mich. 102, 793 N.W.2d 533 (2010). In Smith, the Michigan Supreme Court applied the constitutional actual malice standard enunciated by the United States Supreme Court and found, in the particular facts of that case, sufficient evidence of actual malice existed for two of the three defendants.

(2) **Common Law Malice.** Common law malice requires a showing of ill will, spite or malice in fact. Apostle v. Booth Newspapers, Inc., 572 F. Supp. 897 (W.D. Mich. 1983). Michigan courts have rejected this standard, and instead have adopted the actual malice standard for plaintiffs challenging an employer's claim of qualified privilege. Wynn v. Cole, 91 Mich. App. 517, 523-24, 284 N.W.2d 144 (1979).

e. **Question of Fact or Law.** Determining whether any privilege exists, either qualified or absolute, is a question of law for the court. Lawrence v. Fox, 357 Mich. 134, 140-41, 97 N.W.2d 719 (1959); Shannon v. Taylor AMC/Jeep, Inc., 168 Mich. App. 415, 425 N.W.2d 165 (1988). If, however, there is a dispute regarding the facts which give rise to a claimed privilege, it is a question of fact for the jury to decide. Lawrence, 357 Mich. at 141. See Trs of the Painters Union Deposit Fund v. Interior/Exterior Specialists Co., 2007 US Dist LEXIS 21590 (E.D. Mich. Mar. 27, 2007) (unpublished) (summary judgment denied as question of fact existed as to whether or not the union's statements were made with malice or reckless disregard for truth).

f. **Burden of Proof.** In a defamation claim the employer/defendant bears the initial burden of proving a privilege exists. Lawrence, 357 Mich. at 140-41. Thereafter, "[a] plaintiff may overcome a qualified privilege only by showing that the statement was uttered with actual malice, i.e., with knowledge of its falsity or reckless disregard of the truth." Smith v. Fergan, 181 Mich. App. 594, 595, 450 N.W.2d 3 (1989) (citing Peterfish v. Frantz, 168 Mich. App. 43, 53, 424 N.W.2d 25 (1988)) (no reckless disregard of truth or falsity when an employer merely questioned one employee in the presence of another employee to determine if either had taken missing money).

B. Standard Libel Defenses

1. ***Truth.*** As set forth in I.B.3, falsity is an element of the prima facie case and must be proven by the plaintiff. See, e.g., Peterfish v. Frantz, 168 Mich. App. 43, 52-53, 424 N.W.2d 25 (1988) (involving a public figure); Rouch (I) v. Enquirer & News of Battle Creek, 427 Mich. 157, 398 N.W.2d 245, 13 Media L. Rep. 2201 (1986) (defamation claim based on a speech addressing public concern); Locricchio v. Evening News Ass'n, 438 Mich. 84, 476 N.W.2d 112, 19 Media L. Rep. 1065 (1991), cert. denied, 503 U.S. 907, 112 S. Ct. 1267, 117 L. Ed. 2d 495 (1992). In other words, if plaintiff fails to prove falsity, then he cannot make out a prima facie case of defamation. This had led some courts in the employment context to state (albeit incorrectly) that truth is a defense to a defamation claim. Baggs v. Eagle-Pitcher Indus., Inc., 957 F.2d 268, 273 (6th Cir. 1992) (citing Cochrane v. Wittbold, 359 Mich. 402, 102 N.W.2d 459, 463 (1960)). See also Steiger v. Montmorency Area Rural Cmty. Hous., 2006 Mich. App. LEXIS 358 (Feb. 14, 2006) (unpublished) (summary disposition affirmed where statement by defendant employer accusing plaintiff employee of embezzling funds were held to be true since no genuine factual dispute that plaintiff had embezzled funds existed). See Pedell v. Heartland Health Care Ctr., 2007 Mich. App. LEXIS 773 (Mar. 20, 2007) (unpublished) (where there was no dispute regarding what was said, plaintiff testified that he did not know whether any disparaging remarks were made about him and plaintiff himself disclosed his change in employment status to various individuals and firms who contacted him to do work as an expert witness, court held that plaintiff could not sue in defamation for disclosure of a true fact that plaintiff himself disclosed many times).

Substantial Truth. Michigan recognizes the concept of "substantial truth," protecting statements that, for the most part, are true. Koniak v. Heritage Newspapers, Inc., 198 Mich. App. 577, 499 N.W.2d 346 (1993), appeal denied, 444 Mich. 856, 508 N.W.2d 500 (1993). To determine whether something is substantially true, courts look to the effect the defendant's statement has on the person who hears or reads it. Id. See also In re Chmura, 464 Mich. 58, 75, 626 N.W.2d 876, 888 (2001); Rouch (II) v. Enquirer & News, 440 Mich. 238, 251, 487 N.W.2d 205, 20 Media L. Rep. 2265 (1992) (on remand), cert. denied, 507 U.S. 967 (1993) ("The common law has never required defendants to prove that a publication is literally and absolutely accurate in every minute detail"); McCracken v. Evening News Ass'n, 3 Mich. App. 32, 40, 141 N.W.2d 694 (1966) (holding that a libel claim cannot be based on "an inaccuracy that does not alter the complexion of the affair and would have no different effect on the reader than that which the literal truth would produce"); McAllister v. Detroit Free Press Co., 85 Mich. 453, 460-61, 48 N.W. 612 (1891) ("[A] slight inaccuracy in one of its details will not prevent the defendant's succeeding, provided the inaccuracy in no way alters the complexion of the affair, and would have no different effect on the reader than that which the literal truth would produce . . ."); Orr v. Argus-Press Co., 586 F.2d 1108, 1112 (6th Cir. 1978), cert. denied, 440 U.S. 960, 99 S. Ct. 1502, 59 L. Ed. 2d 773 (1979) (applying Michigan law, holding "it is not essential that the literal truth be established in every detail as long as the article contains the gist of the truth as ordinarily understood"). Cf. Hawkins v. Mercy Health Servs., Inc., 230 Mich. App. 315, 538 N.W.2d 725 (1998) (failing to state, in a press release, the reason the plaintiff nurse was discharged altered the gist or sting of the article from that which would have been created by a statement accurately identifying the reason underlying the discharge). See Roberts v. Trinity Health-Michigan, 2006 Mich. App. LEXIS 3429 (Nov 21, 2006) (unpublished) (employer's statements were qualifiedly privileged as statements made from an employer to a prospective employer are privileged unless made with malice, i.e., the employer knew that the statements were false or made without regard for their truthfulness. Heffelfinger v. Bad Axe Pub. Schs., 2011 WL 118772 (Mich. Ct. App. Jan. 13, 2011) (unpublished) (school superintendent's statements about the school's band director to a parent were attributable to the band director and thus substantially true). Matters of public record are evaluated under the substantial truth standard, even if inaccuracies exist in the public record. McIntoshi v. Detroit News, Inc., 2009 WL 153360 (Mich. Ct. App. Jan. 22, 2009) (unpublished).

In In re Chmura, 464 Mich. 58, 76, 626 N.W.2d 876 (2001), the Court concluded that in analyzing whether a judicial candidate has violated Canon 7(B)(1)(d), the Court must decide whether the communication is substantially true. "If so, the judicial candidate will not be in violation of the canon. However, if 'the substance, the gist, the sting' of the communication is false, then it can be said that the judicial candidate 'used or participated in the use of a false communication.' Once this has been determined, the inquiry then turns to whether a judicial candidate's communication was made knowingly or with reckless disregard. If it was, the candidate has acted in violation of Canon 7 (B)(1)(d)." Id.

Substantial truth is an absolute defense to a defamation claim. Taylor v. Am. Plastic Toys, Inc., 2002 Mich. App. LEXIS 452 (Mar. 19, 2002) (unpublished) (quoting Collins v. Detroit Free Press Inc., 245 Mich. App. 27, 627 N.W.2d 5 (2001)).

Where defendant county prosecutor (and former employer) made public statements accusing plaintiff former assistant prosecutor of dishonesty, professional misconduct, and potential criminal activity, the doctrine of substantial truth entitled defendant to summary judgment where the court found that though plaintiff was neither prosecuted for the alleged criminal activity nor formally punished by the bar for professional misconduct, the substance of the underlying actions giving rise to the defamatory statements was true, and this satisfied the requirement of substantial truth. Phillips v. Ingham County, 371 F. Supp. 2d 918 (W.D. Mich. 2005).

2. ***Opinion.*** Michigan holds that a statement of opinion is not actionable unless "it implies the allegation of undisclosed defamatory facts as the basis for the opinion." Fisher v. Detroit Free Press, Inc., 158 Mich. App. 409, 413, 404 N.W.2d 765 (1987).

"A statement of opinion is protected as long as the opinion 'does not contain a provably false factual connotation'." In re Chmura 464 Mich. at 73, 626 N.W.2d 876, quoting Milkovich v. Lorain Journal Co., 497 U.S. 1, 20, 110 S. Ct. 2695, 111 L. Ed. 2d 1 (1990). See also Erwin v. The Detroit News Inc., 29 Media L. Rep. 1863 (Mich. Ct. App. Feb. 6, 2001); Brooks v. Gill Indus., Inc., 2008 Mich. App. LEXIS 887 (May 1, 2008) (unpublished) (holding that "whether the phrase 'coon hunting' could be considered a racial epithet is a matter of opinion depending on whether one deems the phrase offensive" and that "[t]he characterization of language as offensive is subjective and cannot be provable as false."); Mathis v. Controlled Temperature, Inc., 2008 Mich. App. LEXIS 626 (Mar. 31, 2008) (unpublished) (holding that the phrase "unfavorable employment" merely expressed an opinion regarding plaintiff's work performance and that because it could not be reasonably interpreted as stating actual facts about plaintiff, it was not actionable as a matter of law); Meisner & Assoc., P.C. v. Stamper & Co., 2009 WL 211900 (Mich. Ct. App. Jan. 29, 2009) (unpublished) (finding that an e-mail containing a cost comparison of law firms hourly rates and stating that plaintiff's bills were "exorbitant" and "inflated" was a matter of opinion coupled with factual information regarding other area attorney fees).

3. ***Consent.*** An employer has an absolute defense if a plaintiff consents to a defamatory statement. Harrison v. Arrow Metal Prods. Corp., 20 Mich. App. 590, 615, 174 N.W.2d 875 (1970) ("If the employee consents to publication, it is absolutely privileged"); Merritt v. Detroit Mem'l Hosp., 81 Mich. App. 279, 265 N.W.2d 124 (1978) (publication of allegedly defamatory statements to plaintiff's representatives at a grievance proceeding was privileged since they were there at her request, and she failed to object); Hollowell v. Career Decisions, Inc., 100 Mich. App. 561, 298 N.W.2d 915 (1980) (Plaintiff found to have consented to the allegedly defamatory statements by her supervisor, since she requested the board of directors address her supervisor's complaints about her performance). Discharged plaintiff may not sue for defamation in conjunction with termination when plaintiff signed a release absolving employer-defendant of liability related to termination. Colluci v. Eklund, 240 Mich. App. 654, 613 N.W.2d 402 (2000). A communication is privileged if (1) there was either express or implied consent to the publication; (2) the statements were relevant to the purpose for which consent was given and (3) the publication of the statements was limited to those with a legitimate interest in their content. Ramsay v.

Speedway SuperAmerica, L.L.C., 2008 WL 3541206, *4-5 (Mich. Ct. App. Aug. 14, 2008) (unpublished) (release unambiguously permitted defendant to make communications and absolved defendant from liability attendant thereto). A release contained in an employment application is a form of contract, subject to contract principles applicable to third-party beneficiaries where a non-party seeks to enforce the release. Mathis v. Controlled Temperature, Inc., 2008 Mich. App. LEXIS 626 (Mar. 31, 2008) (unpublished). An individual need not have approved or even been aware of the exact contents of a defamatory statement in order to have met the definition of consent. Romero v. Buhimschi, 2009 WL 92226 (E.D. Mich. Jan. 14, 2009) (unpublished), aff'd 396 F. App'x 224 (6th Cir. 2010). The same defense applies to a student who consents to an otherwise defamatory statement by his or her collegiate coach, thereby protecting the coach. Heike v. Guevara, 2010 WL 538300, at *5 (E.D. Mich. Feb. 9, 2010) (unpublished).

4. ***Mitigation.*** Michigan's defamation statute, M.C.L. § 600.2911, recognizes situations where a defamation defendant may mitigate his damages. In the case of punitive and exemplary damages, a defendant may present evidence of retraction or correction of the defamatory statement to reduce damages. M.C.L. § 600.2911(2)(b). Furthermore, a slander defendant can prove mitigating circumstances by revealing his sources and the grounds for believing these sources. M.C.L. § 600.2911(3).

III. RECURRING FACT PATTERNS

A. Statements in Personnel File

In 1996, Michigan adopted a qualified immunity statute. M.C.L. § 423.452. According to this statute "[a]n employer may disclose to an employee or that individual's prospective employer information relating to the individual's job performance that is documented in the individual's personnel file upon the request of the individual or his or her prospective employer." Id. An employer is immune from "civil liability" for information disclosed under this statute, unless the employer knew disclosed information was false or misleading/reckless disregard for truth . . . [no mention of malice] or disclosure was specifically prohibited by state or federal statute. Id.

"Under Michigan law, 'if either the employer or the employee *knowingly* places in the personnel record information which is false, then the employer or employee, whichever is appropriate, shall have remedy through legal action to have that information expunged'" pursuant to M.C.L. § 423.505. Furby v. White, 7 F. App'x 306 (6th Cir. 2001), cert. denied, 534 U.S. 828, 122 S. Ct. 69, 151 L. Ed. 2d 35 (2001). "Violation of this provision creates a cause of action under which the aggrieved party may seek compliance with [Michigan's Bullard-Plawecki Employee Right to Know Act]." Id. at 30. Use of information and memorandums placed in an employee's personnel file, subject to a Freedom of Information Act (FOIA) request, when not prepared by the defendant may or may not constitute reckless disregard underlying actual malice. Smith v. Anonymous Joint Enter., 487 Mich. 102, 793 N.W.2d 533 (2010).

B. Performance Evaluations

Although there are no reported Michigan case on non-governmental employers, performance evaluations may be treated as a qualified privilege if they satisfy the requirements of limited scope and disclosure. See II.A.2, supra. Governmental immunity protects the evaluation of a governmental employee's performance and the subsequent documentation. Dean v. City of Bay City, 2009 WL 1439002, at *15-16 (Mich. Ct. App. May 21, 2009) (unpublished).

C. References

Michigan does recognize a qualified privilege "to divulge information regarding a former employee to a prospective employer." Gonyea v. Motor Parts Fed. Credit Union, 192 Mich. App. 74, 79, 480 N.W.2d 297 (1991), citing Moore v. St. Joseph Nursing Home, Inc., 184 Mich. App. 766, 768, 459 N.W.2d 100 (1990); Lawrence v. Syms Corp., 969 F. Supp. 1014 (E.D. Mich. 1997); Wynn v. Cole, 68 Mich. App. 706, 243 N.W.2d 923 (1976); Dalton v. Herbruck Egg Sales, 164 Mich. App. 543, 548, 417 N.W.2d 496 (1987) (informing potential employer that plaintiff is unreliable). In 1996, Michigan adopted a qualified immunity statute. M.C.L. § 423.452. Under this new statute, an employer is immune from civil liability, when it discloses to prospective employers information contained in the subject employee's personnel file, but will still lose that immunity on a showing of actual malice. Id.

D. Intracorporate Communication

Michigan common law does not distinguish between intercompany and intracompany disclosure. Rather, "where the qualified privilege applies, it shields the individual who releases the information to a prospective employer, or a different department within the same employer . . . ." Murdock v. Higgins, 454 Mich. 46, 58 & n. 14, 559 N.W.2d 639 (1997) (citing Bacon v. Mich. Cent. R.R. Co., 66 Mich. 166, 33 N.W. 181 (1887)).

E. Statements to Government Regulators

Michigan employers are protected by absolute privilege under M.C.L. § 421.11(b) for any statements made to the Michigan Unemployment Insurance Agency in the course of its administrative functions. Sias v. General Motors Corp., 372 Mich. 542, 548, 127 N.W.2d 357 (1964); Poledna v. Bendix Aviation Corp., 360 Mich. 129, 103 N.W.2d 789 (1960). Furthermore, employers have an absolute privilege against liability for defamatory statements made during judicial proceedings and administrative hearings. Harrison v. Arrow Metal Prods. Corp., 20 Mich. App. 590, 610, 174 N.W.2d 875 (1969), citing Timmis v. Bennett, 352 Mich. 355, 362-63, 89 N.W.2d 748 (1958). "Private figure defamation plaintiffs are only constitutionally required to prove ordinary negligence in order to establish defamation in cases involving the right to petition the government." J & J Construction Co. v. Bricklayers and Allied Craftsmen, 468 Mich. 722, 664 N.W.2d 728 (2003).

F. Reports to Auditors and Insurers

When an auditor is summoned to investigate a matter by an employer, statements made to the auditor regarding suspicions about a particular employee's involvement are privileged if those statements are in aid of the investigation. Johnson v. Gerasimos, 247 Mich. 248, 250, 225 N.W. 636 (1929) (employer was not liable when it informed an independent auditor that it suspected plaintiff of being behind a $25,000 shortfall, since the auditor was brought in to investigate this shortfall).

G. Vicarious Liability of Employer for Statements Made by Employees

1. ***Scope of Employment.*** An employer may be held vicariously liable for its employee's defamatory statements made while acting in their official capacities. Poledna, 360 Mich. at 139-40; Grist v. The Upjohn Co., 368 Mich. 578, 583, 118 N.W.2d 985 (1962) (corporation held liable for supervisor's statements that plaintiff was a poor worker). However, an employer will be dismissed as a defendant if its agent was acting outside of their scope of employment. Linebaugh v. Sheraton Mich. Corp., 198 Mich. App. 335, 341, 497 N.W.2d 585 (1993) (refusing to hold employer liable for defendant employees' circulation of a cartoon showing plaintiff in a sexually compromising position with another co-worker). But see Wright v. Micro Electronics Inc., 2008 Mich. App. LEXIS 558 (Mar. 18, 2008) (unpublished), rev'd on other grounds, 482 Mich. 882, 752 N.W.2d 466 (2008) (holding that it was reversible error for the trial court to focus only on whether employee who posted allegedly defamatory photographs had been acting in the scope of his employment duties because a question of fact existed as to whether defendant could have been liable under doctrine of respondeat superior because it either intended the employee's conduct or consequences, or because its own negligent or reckless conduct permitted the displays).

a. **Blogging.** No Michigan cases addressing this fact pattern.

2. ***Damages.*** No Michigan cases addressing this fact pattern.

H. Internal Investigations

No Michigan cases addressing this fact pattern.

I. Other

Judge may be suspended by Judicial Tenure Commission for use of defamatory statements in campaign materials, but "the determination of whether a candidate recklessly disregarded the truth or falsity of a public communication is an objective one. We reject as inappropriate the subjective 'actual malice' standard employed in defamation cases." *In re* Chmura, 461 Mich. 517, 608 N.W.2d 31 (2000).

IV. OTHER ACTIONS BASED ON STATEMENTS

A. Negligent Hiring, Retention and Supervision

Where employees have contact with the public in the regular course of business, Michigan law imposes on the employer a duty to exercise reasonable care to avoid selecting or retaining one whom the employer "knows or should know is a person unworthy, by habits, temperament, or nature to deal with" the public. Hersh v. Kentfield Builders, 385 Mich. 410, 189 N.W.2d 286 (1971). If the employer has learned of past acts of "impropriety, violence or disorder" on the part of the applicant/employee, that is generally sufficient to put the employer on notice that the employee may eventually commit an assault. Id. The employer's duty, however, does not extend to performing an in-depth background check of an employee/ applicant, where the employer has no knowledge of the individual's propensity for violence. Tyus v. Booth, 64 Mich. App. 88, 235 N.W.2d 69 (1975). Moreover, there is no common-law claim for negligent retention relating to workplace sexual harassment. McClements v. Ford Motor Co., 473 Mich. 373, 702 N.W.2d 166 (2005). **And, Michigan law requires an**

allegation of physical, not economic, injury to support a claim of negligent hiring/retention. Travis v. ADT Sec. Services, Inc., --- F. Supp.2d ---, 2012 WL 3516548, *6-7 (E.D. Mich. 2012). Finally, Michigan courts hold that the exclusive remedy provisions of Michigan's Worker's Disability Compensation Act of 1969, M.C.L. § 418.131 et seq, bar negligent hiring lawsuits brought by other employees. Downer v. Detroit Receiving Hosp., 191 Mich. App. 232, 477 N.W.2d 146 (1991).

B. Intentional Infliction of Emotional Distress

1. ***Elements.*** While the Michigan Supreme Court has never expressly adopted this tort, it has set forth the elements of this tort as follows: (a) extreme and outrageous conduct; (b) intent or recklessness; (c) causation; and (d) severe emotional distress. Roberts v. Auto-Owners Ins. Co., 422 Mich. 594, 374 N.W.2d 905 (1985). The Michigan Supreme Court has left undisturbed Court of Appeals cases applying this tort in both the employment and non-employment settings.

2. ***Relationship to Employment Law.*** To establish the prima facie case for this tort, an employee must allege conduct "so outrageous in character, and so extreme in degree, as to go beyond all possible bounds of decency, and to be regarded as atrocious, and utterly intolerable in a civilized community." Roberts, 422 Mich. at 603, 374 N.W.2d at 908. Liability does not extend to mere insults, indignities, threats, annoyances, petty oppressions or other trivialities. Id.; Graham v. Ford, 237 Mich. App. 670, 604 N.W.2d 713 (1999).

There are few instances where an employee has successfully established the prima facie case in the employment setting. See Linebaugh v. Sheraton Mich. Corp., 198 Mich. App. 335, 497 N.W.2d 585 (1993) (plaintiff stated a valid cause of action against a fellow employee for a cartoon depicting the plaintiff in a sexual encounter but summary judgment was appropriate in favor of the employer because the employee's acts were outside the scope of employment); Pratt v. Brown Machine Co., 855 F.2d 1225 (6th Cir. 1988) (company properly liable where it made plaintiff beg to have his job back and apologize for threatening a supervisor that had admitted to placing nearly 100 obscene phone calls to plaintiff's wife over the course of 18 months). But see Khalifa v. Henry Ford Hosp., 156 Mich. App. 485, 401 N.W.2d 884 (1986) (summary judgment awarded to employer); Meek v. Mich. Bell Tel. Co., 193 Mich. App. 340, 483 N.W.2d 407 (1991) (same); Ledl v. Quik Pik Food Stores, Inc., 133 Mich. App. 583, 349 N.W.2d 529 (1984) (same); Trudeau v. Fisher Body Div., Gen. Motors Corp., 168 Mich. App. 14, 423 N.W.2d 592 (1988) (same); Mauro v. Borgess Med. Ctr., 886 F. Supp. 1349 (W.D. Mich. 1995) (same).

Damages for the intentional infliction of emotional distress are not recoverable in an action for breach of an employment contract. Khalifa v. Henry Ford Hosp., 156 Mich. App. 485, 401 N.W.2d 884 (1986); Stopczynski v. Ford Motor Co., 200 Mich. App. 190, 503 N.W.2d 912 (1993). Since a school board was privileged to evaluate a teacher's classroom performance under the collective bargaining agreement, the board could not be liable for intentional infliction of emotional distress even though the board knew that the evaluation process would likely cause the teacher emotional distress. Sankar v. Detroit Bd. of Educ., 160 Mich. App. 470, 409 N.W.2d 213 (1987).

A claim of intentional infliction of emotional distress is an intentional tort. An employer is not liable for its employees' intentional torts committed outside the scope of employment. Salinas v. Genesys Health Sys., 263 Mich. App. 315, 317-18, 688 N.W.2d 112 (2004). An intentional tort is not normally within the scope of an employee's employment. McClements v. Ford Motor Co., 473 Mich. 373, 381, 702 N.W.2d 166 (2005).

The statute of limitations for the tort of intentional infliction of emotional distress is three years from when the action accrues. Nelson v. Ho, 222 Mich. App. 74, 564 N.W.2d 482 (1997); M.C.L. § 600.5805.

C. Interference With Prospective Economic Advantage

Michigan recognizes two torts addressing the interference of an economic or employment relationship.

Tortious Interference With Contractual Relationship. This tort applies to existing contractual relationships. To state a valid cause of action, a plaintiff must show: i) a valid contract existed; (ii) the contract was breached; (iii) a third party instigated the breach; and (iv) the breach was not justified. Northern Plumbing & Heating, Inc. v. Henderson Bros., Inc., 83 Mich. App. 84, 268 N.W.2d 296 (1978).

Tortious Interference With an Advantageous Business Relationship. This tort applies to expectations of economic gain. To state a valid cause of action, a plaintiff must show: (i) the existence of a valid business relationship or expectancy, which need not be evidenced by an enforceable contract; (ii) knowledge of the relationship or expectancy on the part of the interferer, a third party; (iii) an intentional interference that induces or causes the breach or termination of the relationship or expectancy; and (iv) resulting damage to the party whose relationship or expectancy has been disrupted. Id. See also **Cedroni Assoc, Inc v Tomblinson, Harburn Associates, Architects & Planners, Inc, 492 Mich 40, --- NW2d --- (2012);**

Roberts v. Trinity Health-Mich., 2006 Mich. App. LEXIS 3429 (Nov. 21, 2006) (summary disposition granted where plaintiff could not show that even if the employer's statements were false, they were still qualifiedly privileged as statements made from an employer to a prospective employer because the statements with made with malice, i.e., the employer knew that the statements were false or were made without regard for their truthfulness. Further, the plaintiff failed to raise a genuine issue of material fact as to whether the employer intentionally interfered with his business relationship with a prospective employer because the employer did not affirmatively act to interfere with plaintiff's relationship with the prospective employer.)

With either tort, the plaintiff must allege that the defendant intentionally committed a per se wrongful act or maliciously committed a lawful act that was unjustified in law to invade the contractual rights or business relationship of another. Feaheny v. Caldwell, 175 Mich. App. 291, 437 N.W.2d 358 (1989) (citing Formall, Inc. v. Cmty. Nat'l Bank of Pontiac, 166 Mich. App. 772, 421 N.W.2d 289 (1988)). Stated differently, the plaintiff must allege that the interferer did something illegal, unethical or fraudulent. Frohriep v. Flanagan, 278 Mich. App. 665, 754 N.W.2d 912 (2008), rev'd in part on other grounds, 483 Mich. 920, 763 N.W.2d 279 (2009).

Michigan courts are split over whether at-will employment contracts provide sufficient expectancy on the part of the employee to support these causes of action. Cf Tash v. Houston, 74 Mich. App. 566, 254 N.W.2d 579 (1977) (at-will employee had sufficient interest in continued employment to be protected from illegal interference by third parties); Dzierwa v. Mich. Oil Co., 152 Mich. App. 281, 393 N.W.2d 610 (1986) (no tortious interference cause of action can arise from the termination of an at-will employment contract). The recent trend appears to endorse the theory that an at-will employee has sufficient interest in continued employment to support these causes of action. See Feaheny v. Caldwell, 175 Mich. App. 291, 437 N.W.2d 358 (1989) (noting the split between Tash and Dzierwa and concluding that at-will employees may sue for tortious interference); Patillo v. Equitable Life Assurance Soc'y, 199 Mich. App. 450, 502 N.W.2d 696 (1992) (at-will employment relationship provides a basis for an action of tortious interference with contract).

Commonly an issue in tortious interference cases is whether the interfering party is actually a third-party for the purposes of the relationship. A corporate agent who dismisses an employee may be considered a third party to the contract if that agent was acting out of self-interest rather than in the interest of the corporation. Tash v. Houston, 74 Mich. App. 566, 254 N.W.2d 579 (1977) (employer's agents are privileged when acting on behalf of the corporation but lose that privilege when acting strictly for personal motives); see also Stack v. Marcum, 147 Mich. App. 756, 382 N.W.2d 743 (1985) (it is a question of fact for the jury to decide if an agent of the organization acted on his own behalf or the organization's behalf when he terminated an employee). But see Feaheny v. Caldwell 175 Mich. App. 291, 437 N.W.2d 358 (1989) (because no evidence existed that five corporate officers were acting outside the scope of their employment when they dismissed an employee, defendants are not liable as a matter of law for tortiously interfering with the employee's economic expectations); Dzierwa v. Mich. Oil Co., 152 Mich. App. 281, 393 N.W.2d 610 (1986) (since defendant was president, controlling shareholder, and chief executive officer of corporation as well as being the supervisor of the dismissed employee, plaintiff could not show that the defendant was acting outside the scope of his employment when he dismissed the employee); Reed v. Mich. Metro Girl Scout Council, 201 Mich. App. 10, 13, 506 N.W.2d 231 (1993) (corporate agents are not liable for tortious interference with the corporation's contracts unless they acted solely for their own benefit with no benefit to the corporation).

The statute of limitations for tortiously interfering with an employment contract is 3 years. M.C.L. § 600.5805.

C. Prima Facie Tort

Michigan does not recognize prima facie tort.

V. OTHER ISSUES

A. Statute of Limitations

Michigan has a one-year statute of limitations period for all defamation claims, whether slander or libel. MCL 600.5805(9).

B. Jurisdiction

Defendant may not rely upon Federal Airline Deregulation Act to preempt plaintiff's defamation suit because defamation is too tenuous, remote or peripheral to the statute. Thomas v. United Parcel Serv., 241 Mich. App. 171, 182, 614 N.W.2d 707 (2000).

C. Worker's Compensation Exclusivity

Michigan has an exclusive provision for suits against the employer for a personal injury or occupational disease. M.C.L. § 418.131(1). The only exception to the exclusive remedy is when the issue surrounds an intentional tort. Id. If an intentional tort creates mental or nervous injuries, these injuries may fall under the Worker's Compensation exclusion. Slayton v. Mich. Host, Inc., 122 Mich. App. 411, 416, 332 N.W.2d 498 (1983); Gray v. Morley, 460 Mich. 738, 596 N.W.2d 922 (1999). Intentional torts that do not implicate the hazards of the workplace, including defamation, fall within the exclusive remedy exception. Cavalier Mfg. v. Employers Ins. of Wausau, 211 Mich. App. 330, 339, 535 N.W.2d 583 (1995). Whether the facts alleged by plaintiff are sufficient to constitute an intentional tort triggering M.C.L. § 418.131(1)'s exclusivity provision is a question of law. Fries v. Mavrick Metal Stamping, Inc., 285 Mich. App. 706, 777 N.W.2d 205 (2009).

D. Pleading Requirements

For a claim to succeed, the elements of defamation must be pleaded with specificity, and must include "the defamatory words complained of, the connection of the defamatory words with plaintiff, and the publication of the alleged defamatory words." Ledl v. Quik Pik Stores, 133 Mich. App. 583, 589-90, 349 NW2d 529 (1984). "[A] plaintiff must 'allege where, when, [and] to whom the statement was published." Sault Ste Marie Tribe of Chippewa Indians v. Hamilton, 2010 WL 299483, at *3 (W.D. Mich. Jan. 20, 2010) (unpublished) (citing Hernden v. Consumers Power Co., 72 Mich. App. 349, 356, 249 N.W.2d 419, 422 (1976)).

SURVEY OF MICHIGAN EMPLOYMENT PRIVACY LAW

Herschel P. Fink
Cameron J. Evans
Honigman Miller Schwartz and Cohn LLP.
2290 First National Building
660 Woodward Ave.
Detroit, Michigan 48226-3507
Telephone: (313) 465-7000; Facsimile: (313) 465-8000

(With Developments Reported Through **November 1, 2012**)

GENERAL COMMENTS

All cases referenced in court documents must contain a citation to the appropriate official Michigan reporter as well as a parallel citation to West's Northwest reporter. These citations must be separated by a semi-colon and, more significantly, must not contain any periods as part of the citation.

Example: *Smith v Jones*, 123 Mich 456; 333 NW2d 444 (1985).

Not: *Smith v. Jones*, 123 Mich. 456, 333 N.W.2d 444 (1985).

For general citation rules, see Michigan Uniform System of Citation, AO 2006-3, amended by AO 1987-2 and AO 2001-5 *available at* http://coa.courts.mi.gov/rules/documents/9michiganuniformsystemofcitation.pdf. For other matters, refer to The Bluebook: A Uniform System of Citation, 19th ed., for guidance, but conform citations to Michigan citation style.

SIGNIFICANT DEVELOPMENTS SINCE THE 2012 SURVEY

None.

I. GENERAL LAW OF PRIVACY

A. Legal Basis of Privacy Claims

1. ***Constitutional Law.*** Unlike some states, the Michigan Constitution does not contain a provision explicitly recognizing an individual's right to privacy. As with the United States Constitution, courts have instead implied a right of privacy from certain provisions in the Michigan Constitution, such as the right to be free from unlawful searches and seizures.

2. ***Statutory Law.*** Michigan has adopted a few statutory schemes designed to protect an employee's privacy. These schemes are often backstopped by complementary federal statutes that ensure a base level of protection for each employee, and questions occasionally arise concerning conflicts between these state and federal statutes over which provisions of each apply.

3. ***Common Law.*** Michigan employees most often turn to the common law when seeking to assert a privacy right against an employer. Michigan recognizes the four traditional branches of the invasion-of-privacy tort: (1) misappropriation of identity; (2) false light; (3) publication of private facts; and (4) intrusion-into-seclusion.

B. Causes of Action

1. ***Misappropriation/Right of Publicity.*** Michigan first recognized the misappropriation/right of publicity cause of action in Pallas v. Crowley, Milner & Co., 322 Mich. 411, 33 N.W.2d 911 (1948) (stating the general rule that a person who unreasonably and seriously interferes with another's interest in not having his affairs known to others or his likeness exhibited to the public is liable to the other). In Beaumont v. Brown, 401 Mich. 80, 257 N.W.2d 522 (1977), the Michigan Supreme Court explicitly recognized a right of privacy in Michigan and included in that right a cause of action where there is appropriation, for the defendant's advantage, of the plaintiff's "name or likeness." While a Michigan court has yet to identify the specific elements of the misappropriation/right of publicity cause of action, one Michigan court held that a singer could state a claim for misappropriation of her voice only if she had a "distinctive and widely known voice," or if she was "renown in . . . [her] genre and location." Edwards v. Church of God in Christ, No. 220348, 2002 WL 393577, at *2 (Mich. App. Mar. 8, 2002) (holding plaintiff could not state a claim for misappropriation of her voice because she was "unknown" to the public.) In the most comprehensive discussion of the misappropriation/right of publicity tort by a court applying Michigan law, the Sixth Circuit held that a cause of action arises even if the defendant uses only an identifying characteristic of the plaintiff rather than the plaintiff's exact name or likeness. See Carson v. Here's Johnny Portable Toilets,

Inc., 698 F.2d 831 (6th Cir. 1983). The Sixth Circuit subsequently held "[a] right of publicity claim is similar to a false advertising claim in that it grants a celebrity the right to protect an economic interest . . . [h]owever, a right of publicity claim does differ from a false advertising claim in one crucial respect; a right of publicity claim does not require any evidence that a consumer is likely to be confused." Parks v. LaFace Records, 329 F.3d 437, 460 (6th Cir. 2003). The court in Parks held that all "a plaintiff must prove in a right of publicity action is that she has a pecuniary interest in her identity, and that her identity has been commercially exploited by a defendant."

In Ruffin-Steinback v. dePasse, 82 F. Supp. 2d 723, 729 (E.D. Mich. 2000), the court noted the lack of Michigan authority addressing the misappropriation/right of publicity tort. Relying on the RESTATEMENT (THIRD) OF UNFAIR COMPETITION 47 (1995) and authority from other jurisdictions, the court determined that Michigan **law** would limit the scope of the tort to instances where an individual's name or likeness was used "for the purposes of trade" rather than in news reporting, commentary, entertainment, works of fiction or nonfiction, or in advertising that is incidental to such uses. Id. at 729-730. Further, the Sixth Circuit determined that Michigan **law** would recognize a right of publicity and would find that the right of publicity survived death. Herman Miller, Inc. v. Palazzetti Imps. & Exps., Inc., 270 F.3d 298, 325 (6th Cir. 2001) (reasoning right of publicity protects the pecuniary right and interest in the commercial exploitation of one's identity and thus it is a property right that survives death).

In Battaglieri v. Mackinac Ctr. for Pub. Policy, 261 Mich. App. 296, 303, 680 N.W.2d 915, 920 (2004), the Michigan Court of Appeals ruled that the plaintiff's claim for misappropriation was ultimately barred by the First Amendment. In Battaglieri, an educational research public interest group used comments made by the head of the Michigan Education Association in a fundraising letter sent by the research group to its members. Id. at 298-299, 917-919. The head of the Michigan Educational Association sued, claiming the interest group misappropriated his identity for commercial purposes. Id. at 300, 919. Although the fundraising letter contained a commercial aspect, the court held that the primary thrust of the letter was to inform the public on, and advocate for, certain educational issues. Id. at 302, 920. Because the letter involved "discourse on matters of public interest," the Michigan Court of Appeals held that the First Amendment barred the plaintiff's misappropriation claims. Id. at 303, 920-921.

The statute of limitations for misappropriation actions in Michigan is three years. MCLA 600.5805(10).

2. ***False Light.*** Michigan recognizes a cause of action for false light invasion of privacy. To maintain such an action, a plaintiff must show that the defendant "broadcast to the public in general, or to a large number of people, information that was unreasonable and highly objectionable by attributing to the plaintiff characteristics, conduct, or beliefs that were false and placed the plaintiff in a false position." Porter v. City of Royal Oak, 214 Mich. App. 478, 487, 542 N.W.2d 905, 909 (1995) (quoting Duran v. Detroit News, Inc, 200 Mich. App. 622, 631-632, 504 N.W.2d 715, 721 (1993)). Summary judgment is appropriate where the defendant's actions neither attributed false characteristics to the plaintiff nor placed the plaintiff in a false position. See Duran, 200 Mich. App. at 632, 504 N.W.2d at 721; see also Neal v. Electronic Arts, Inc., 374 F. Supp. 2d. 574, 579 (W.D. Mich. 2005) (holding that the accidental use of African American plaintiff's likeness to represent a Caucasian player with the same name in a video game was not highly offensive). Michigan courts have also granted summary judgment in favor of the defendant when the plaintiff failed to establish that there was publication to a large group of people. See Ledl v. Quik Pik Food Stores, Inc., 133 Mich. App. 583, 592, 349 N.W.2d 529, 533 (1984); Dzierwa v. Mich. Oil Co., 152 Mich. App. 281, 288, 393 N.W.2d 610, 614 (1986). Finally, Michigan courts have found that the same First Amendment protection that applies to libel actions may bar or limit pursuit of a false light privacy claim. For example, if the plaintiff is deemed to be a "public official," the plaintiff must also prove that the defendant acted with "actual malice" (i.e., that it made the publication with knowledge of its falsity or through reckless disregard for the truth). Battaglieri, 261 Mich. App. at 296 (finding plaintiff's false light claim failed because plaintiff, a public figure, was unable to present any evidence that defendant published the comments with actual malice).

The statute of limitations for false light actions is three years. MCLA 600.5805(10); Derderian v. Genesys Health Care Sys., 263 Mich. App. 364, 386, 689 N.W.2d 145, 169 (2004).

3. ***Publication of Private or Embarrassing Facts.*** Michigan recognizes the tort of publication of private facts. To sustain a cause of action, the plaintiff must establish (1) a disclosure of information, (2) that is highly offensive to a reasonable person, and (3) is of no legitimate concern to the public. Smith v. Calvary Christian Church, 233 Mich. App. 96, 113-114, 592 N.W.2d 713, 721 (1998), rev'd on other grounds, 462 Mich. 679, 614 N.W.2d 590 (2000). The information published must concern the individual's private life and must not have been a matter of public record or otherwise exposed to the public eye. Ledsinger v. Burmeister, 114 Mich. App. 12, 24, 318 N.W.2d 558, 563 (1982) (summary judgment appropriate where epithet, while offensive, only revealed plaintiff's race, a matter already known to the public); Ruffin-Steinback, 82 F. Supp. 2d at 734 (no liability where defendant publicized information about plaintiff that was already public). On the other hand, where a plaintiff shares the information with only a select number of close friends, the

information is not properly considered public. Stratton v. Krywko, Nos. 248669, 248676 2005 WL 27522, at *15 (Mich. App. Jan. 6, 2005).

The statute of limitations is three years. MCLA 600.5805(10).

4. ***Intrusion.*** Michigan recognizes the intrusion-into-seclusion branch of the invasion of privacy tort. To prove this cause of action, the plaintiff must establish: (1) the existence of a secret and private subject matter; (2) a right possessed by the plaintiff to keep the subject matter private; and (3) the defendant using a method objectionable to the reasonable man to obtain the information. Lansing Ass'n. of Sch. v. Lansing Sch. Dist. Bd. of Educ., 216 Mich. App. 79, 87, 549 N.W.2d 15, 20 (1996), rev'd on other grounds sub. nom., Bradley v. Saranac Cmty. Schs. Bd. of Educ., 455 Mich. 285, 565 N.W.2d 650 (1997); Begin v. Mich. Bell Tel. Co., Nos. 279891, 284114, 2009 WL 1835091 (Mich. App. June 25, 2009) (to the extent that personnel and pension information regarding plaintiff concerned a secret and private subject matter, defendant obtained the information because of the relationship as a former employer, not by some method objectionable to a reasonable person).

The right to be free from this type of invasion of privacy is not absolute. Michigan courts have held that the right to privacy does not extend so far as to subvert rights that spring from other relationships, such as that between an employer and an employee. Saldana v. Kelsey-Hayes Co., 178 Mich. App. 230, 234, 443 N.W.2d 382, 384 (1989) (holding employer is permitted to monitor employee at home if employee is suspected of work-related disability fraud); see also Baum v. Springport Tel. Co., No. 227098, 2002 WL 551094, at *21 (Mich. App. Apr.12, 2002) (employee's intrusion claim failed because employee and supervisor were "close friends" who regularly discussed personal matters such that supervisor's questions to employee about an extramarital affair were not objectively unreasonable); Morrissey v. Nextel Retail Stores L.L.C., Nos. 277893, 279153, 2009 WL 387750 (Mich. App. Feb. 17, 2009) (where employer received and paid employee's cellular phone bills, employer did not obtain information from those billing statements in a manner that offends an ordinary person of ordinary sensibilities). But see Dalley v. Dykema Gossett, PLLC, 287 Mich. App. 296, 788 N.W.2d 679 (2010) (holding plaintiff stated a claim for intrusion upon seclusion where defendants, pursuant to a temporary restraining order, entered plaintiff's apartment and copied all of plaintiff's computer records, because TRO authorized neither access to apartment nor copying of computer records unrelated to lawsuit).

Furthermore, an employee's solitude was not violated where an employer released non-personal employee information such as the employee's name and address. Tobin v. Mich. Civil Serv. Comm'n., 416 Mich. 661, 672, 331 N.W.2d 184, 187 (1982); Herald Co. v. City of Bay City, 463 Mich. 111, 124, 614 N.W.2d 873, 879 (2000) (requiring public employer to release employment applications under a Freedom of Information Act request because such applications did not reveal any "intimate or embarrassing details of an individual's private life"). But see Mich. Fed. of Teachers & Sch. Related Personnel, AFT, AFL-CIO, v. Univ. of Mich., 481 Mich. 657, 665, n. 16; 753 N.W.2d 28, 34, n.16 (2008) (noting public employer is not required to release such information under FOIA statute).

The statute of limitations is three years. MCLA 600.5805(10).

C. Other Privacy-Related Actions

1. ***Intentional Infliction of Emotional Distress.***

a. **Elements.** Although the Michigan Supreme Court has never expressly adopted this tort, the Court has recognized the elements as follows: (a) extreme and outrageous conduct; (b) intent or recklessness; (c) causation; and (d) severe emotional distress. Roberts v. Auto-Owners Ins. Co., 422 Mich. 594, 602, 374 N.W.2d 905, 908 (1985).

b. **Relationship to Employment Law.** To establish the prima facie case for intentional infliction of emotional distress, the employee must allege conduct "so outrageous in character, and so extreme in degree, as to go beyond all possible bounds of decency, and to be regarded as atrocious and utterly intolerable in a civilized community." Roberts, 422 Mich. at 603, 374 N.W.2d at 908. Liability does not extend to mere insults, indignities, threats, annoyances, petty oppressions, or other trivialities. Id. at 603, 374 N.W.2d at 908-909.

There are only a few instances where an employee has successfully established, or at least successfully pleaded, this type of claim in the employment setting. See Pratt v. Brown Machine Co., 855 F.2d 1225 (6th Cir. 1988) (company liable where it made plaintiff beg to have his job back and apologize for threatening a supervisor that had admitted to placing nearly 100 obscene phone calls to plaintiff's wife over the course of 18 months); Linebaugh v. Sheraton Mich. Corp., 198 Mich. App. 335, 497 N.W.2d 585 (1993) (plaintiff stated a valid cause of action against a fellow employee for a cartoon depicting the plaintiff in a sexual encounter but summary judgment was appropriate in favor of the employer because the employee's acts were outside the scope of employment). On the other hand, such claims are usually dismissed prior to trial. See Khalifa v. Henry Ford Hosp., 156 Mich. App. 485, 401 N.W.2d 884 (1986) (summary judgment awarded to employer); Meek v. Mich. Bell Tel. Co., 193 Mich. App. 340, 483 N.W.2d 407 (1992) (same); Ledl v. Quik Pik Food Stores, Inc., 133 Mich. App. 583, 349 N.W.2d 529 (1984) (same); Trudeau v. Fisher Body Div., General Motors Corp., 168 Mich. App. 14, 423 N.W.2d 592 (1988) (same); Mauro v. Borgess Med. Cent., 886 F. Supp. 1349 (W.D. Mich. 1995) (same).

The statute of limitations for the tort of intentional infliction of emotional distress is three years. MCLA 600.5805(10); Nelson v. Ho, 222 Mich. App. 74, 84, 564 N.W.2d 482, 487 (1997).

2. ***Interference With Prospective Economic Advantage.*** Michigan recognizes two torts addressing the interference of an economic or employment relationship.

Tortious Interference With Contractual Relationship. This tort applies to existing contractual relationships. To state a valid cause of action, a plaintiff must show: (i) a valid contract existed; (ii) the contract was breached; (iii) a third party instigated the breach; and (iv) the breach was not justified. See N. Plumbing & Heating, Inc. v. Henderson Bros., Inc., 83 Mich. App. 84, 92, 268 N.W.2d 296, 298 (1978); Health Call of Detroit v. Atrium Home & Health Care Services, Inc., 268 Mich. App. 83, 706 N.W.2d 843 (2005).

Tortious Interference With an Advantageous Business Relationship. This tort applies to expectations of economic gain. To state a valid cause of action, a plaintiff must show: (i) the existence of a valid business relationship or expectancy, which need not be evidenced by an enforceable contract; (ii) knowledge of the relationship or expectancy on the part of the interferer; (iii) an intentional interference that induces or causes the breach or termination of the relationship or expectancy, and (iv) resulting damage to the party whose relationship or expectancy has been disrupted. N. Plumbing & Heating, at 88, 297.

With either tort, the plaintiff must allege that the defendant intentionally committed a per se wrongful act or maliciously committed a lawful act (that was unjustified in law) to invade the contractual rights or business relationship of another. See Feaheny v. Caldwell, 175 Mich. App. 291, 437 N.W.2d 358 (1989), overruled in part on other grounds Health Call of Detroit (citing Formall, Inc. v. Cmty. Nat'l Bank of Pontiac, 166 Mich. App. 772, 421 N.W.2d 289 (1988)). If defendant's conduct was not wrongful per se, the plaintiff must establish specific, affirmative acts that corroborate the unlawful purpose of the interference. CMI Internat'l., Inc. v. Intermet Internat'l. Corp., 251 Mich. App. 125, 131, 649 N.W.2d 808, 812 (2002) (citing Feldnan v. Green, 138 Mich. App. 360, 369-370, 360 N.W.2d 881, 886 (1984)); Badiee v. Brighton Area Schs., 265 Mich. App. 343, 69 N.W.2d 521 (2005).

Michigan endorses the theory that an at-will employee has sufficient interest in continued employment to support these causes of action. See McDonald Ford, Inc. v. All American Ford, Inc., No. 239085, 2003 WL 21299922, at *3 (Mich. App. June 5, 2003) (at-will employment relationship provides a basis for an action of tortious interference with contract); Feaheny, supra (noting Michigan court split and concluding that at-will employees may sue for tortious interference); Patillo v. Equitable Life Assurance Soc'y. of U.S., 199 Mich. App. 450, 502 N.W.2d 696 (1992) (at-will employment relationship provides a basis for an action of tortious interference with contract); Prysak v. R.L. Polk Co., 193 Mich. App. 1, 483 N.W.2d 629 (1992) (same); Health Call, 268 Mich. App. 83, 706 N.W.2d 843 (same); Everton v. Williams, 270 Mich. App. 348, 715 N.W.2d 320 (2006) (same).

The cause of action for tortious interference with a contract does not apply to the employer-employee relationship. Carlson v. Westbrooke Services Corp., 815 F. Supp. 1019, 1024-1025 (E.D. Mich. 1992). Thus, one common issue in these cases is whether the interfering party is actually a third-party for the purposes of the relationship. A corporate agent who dismisses an employee may be considered a third party to the contract if the agent was acting out of self-interest rather than in the interest of the corporation. See Tash v. Houston, 74 Mich. App. 566, 254 N.W.2d 579 (employer's agents are privileged when acting on behalf of employer, but lose privilege when acting strictly for personal motives); see also Stack v. Marcum, 147 Mich. App. 756, 382 N.W.2d 743 (1985) (holding question of fact existed whether agent acted on his own, or employer's, behalf when discharging employee); but see Feaheny,175 Mich. App. 291, 437 N.W.2d 358 (granting summary judgment because, as a matter of law, employees were not acting outside scope of employment); Dzierwa v. Mich. Oil Co., 152 Mich. App. 281, 393 N.W.2d 610 (1986) (granting summary judgment because individual who was president, controlling shareholder, and CEO of corporation as well as the supervisor of plaintiff, was not acting outside the scope of employment when he dismissed plaintiff).

Another issue that commonly arises in a tortious interference case is whether the plaintiff has presented sufficient evidence of damages resulting from the termination of the at-will employment contract. Claims for damages arising out of or related to the termination of an at-will contract were long considered speculative, therefore, in the absence of a tangible basis for ascertaining such damages, only nominal damages may be sought. Feahany, 175 Mich. App. 291, 437 N.W.2d 358. More recently, Michigan courts have emphasized that recovery of damages based on interference with an at-will contract (even the at-will employment contract) is not limited to nominal damages as a matter of law. Health Call, 268 Mich. App. 83, 706 N.W.2d 843 (overruling Feahany's limit of recovery to nominal damages for all actions arising out of or related to the termination of at-will contracts); see also Everton, 270 Mich. App. 348, 715 N.W.2d 320 (holding that Health Call applied to at-will employment contracts).

The statute of limitations for tortious interference with an employment contract is three years. MCLA 600.5805(10).

3. ***Prima Facie Tort.*** Michigan does not recognize a prima facie invasion of privacy tort.

II. EMPLOYER TESTING OF EMPLOYEES

A. Psychological or Personality Testing

1. ***Common Law and Statutes.*** Michigan courts have yet to address the privacy issues surrounding psychological or personality testing of employees from a common law tort perspective.

2. ***Private Employers.*** There are no Michigan cases addressing personality or psychological testing of employees by private employers.

3. ***Public Employers.*** There are no Michigan cases addressing personality or psychological testing of employees by public employers.

B. Drug Testing

1. ***Common Law and Statutes.*** There is no statute in Michigan specifically governing when employers may require employees to submit to drug tests.

The Michigan Persons with Disabilities Civil Rights Act, MCLA 37.1202 et seq. ("PWDCRA"), does not expressly prohibit an employer from requiring employees to undergo drug testing, although it is possible a court could interpret testing for illegal substances as being prohibited by the PWDCRA's ban on making employment decisions based on the results of "physical examinations." MCLA 37.1202(1)(d)-(e).

Michigan recognizes the four traditional branches of the invasion of privacy tort. See I.B, supra. Of those, two are relevant to the issue of drug testing.

Intrusion. Mandatory workplace urine testing is most likely an intrusion into privacy that a reasonable person would find objectionable. Baggs v. Eagle-Picher Indus. Inc., 957 F.2d 268, 274 (6th Cir. 1992). An employer may nonetheless require its employees to undergo drug testing, provided that the purpose of the drug testing is to obtain work-related information about an employee. Id. at 275. In Baggs, the employer determined that a number of employees were coming to work under the influence of illegal drugs or using and/or selling illegal drugs at work. To combat the problem, the employer issued a new drug policy to its employees, prohibiting working under the influence of illegal drugs and making a drug test at management's request a "condition of employment." Id. at 270. The Sixth Circuit Court of Appeals upheld management's use of the drug tests, stating that a Michigan employer "may use intrusive and even objectionable means to obtain employment-related information about an employee. There is no dispute that the information [employer] sought, whether employees were reporting to work with drugs in their systems, was related to plaintiff's employment." Id. at 275; see also DiTomaso v. Electronic Data Sys., No. 87-cv-60320AA, 1988 WL 156317 (E.D. Mich. Oct. 7, 1988) (upholding drug testing of employer's security personnel).

Public Disclosure of Embarrassing Facts. A reasonable person would likely find it objectionable to have the results of an employer-mandated drug test made public. Baggs, 957 F.2d at 273. Where an employee voluntarily makes the results public, however, the employer may comment publicly on the matter. Id. Furthermore, widespread press coverage of drug tests at an employer's plant may create a situation of public concern about which the employer had a right to comment. Id.; see also DiTomaso, 1988 WL 156317 (granting summary judgment to employer where employees failed to identify any person informed of the drug test results by the employer).

2. ***Private Employers.*** Michigan has no constitutional or statutory provisions restricting employers from requiring employees to submit to drug testing. Thus, private-sector employees in Michigan usually challenge employer-mandated drug testing through the traditional common law tort remedies.

3. ***Public Employers.*** The Michigan Supreme Court held that a county may require a prospective highway employee to undergo drug testing because the duties of the job required the employee to operate heavy machinery. Middlebrooks v. Wayne County, 446 Mich. 151, 521 N.W.2d 774 (1994). Relying on the reasoning in both Skinner v. Railway Labor Executives' Ass'n, 489 U.S. 609 (1989) and Nat'l Treasury Employees Union v. Von Raab, 489 U.S. 656 (1989), the Michigan Supreme Court first determined that the drug testing did not violate the Fourth Amendment to the

United States Constitution because, as in those cases, the job position at issue was one where "momentary lapse[s] of attention" could result in serious injury. Middlebrooks, 446 Mich. at 163, 521 N.W.2d at 780. Thus, the state's interest in promoting safety through drug testing outweighed any expectation of privacy the employee might have. Id. The Court also concluded that the drug-testing scheme did not violate the Michigan Constitution, since the employee had a reduced expectation of privacy arising from the fact that he was applying for a position that involved the use of dangerous equipment. Id. at 166, 521 N.W.2d at 782.

4. ***Medical Marihuana.*** **The Sixth Circuit has held that the Michigan Medical Marihuana Act, MCLA § 333.26421, et. seq., does not attempt to regulate the private environment and therefore bestows no employment rights on individuals employed by private employers. Casias v. Wal-Mart Stores, Inc., No. 11-1227, __ F.3d __ (6th Cir. 2012).** See also U.S. v. Mich. Dept. of Cmty. Health, No. 1:10-mc-109, 2011 WL 2412602 (W.D. Mich. June 9, 2011) (holding that the Michigan Medical Marihuana Act provides only limited affirmative defenses to state actions, including criminal prosecutions and grants and revocations of professional licenses).

C. Medical Testing

1. ***Common Law and Statutes.*** Michigan law generally permits employers to require medical or physical testing of employees, provided such tests are designed to evaluate the employee's ability to perform a specific job skill. However, mandatory blood draws for the purpose of general health screening violate an employee's Fourth Amendment rights. See Anderson v. City of Taylor, No. 04-74345, 2005 WL 1984438 (E.D. Mich. Aug. 11, 2005). Employees have also challenged these tests under the Michigan Persons with Disabilities Civil Rights Act ("PWDCRA"), MCLA 37.1101 et seq. Under the PWDCRA, an employer may not decline to hire an employee based on a disability unrelated to job performance. The PWDCRA permits employers to test prospective employees to ensure that any disability is not job related.

In Wilks v. Taylor Sch. Dist., 174 Mich. App. 232, 435 N.W.2d 436 (1988), the Michigan Court of Appeals upheld the use of a physical examination to determine if a prospective bus driver's back injury would affect her ability to carry out her job. The employer's doctor recommended against hiring the employee because of her medical condition. Id. at 234, 437. The employee did not challenge the examination. Rather, the employee challenged the results of the examination, claiming that her disability was unrelated to her job duties and that the PWDCRA prevented the employer from refusing to hire her. Id. at 236, 438. The Michigan Court of Appeals upheld the examination but remanded the case, noting that, once it was determined that an employee has a disability, the burden of proof shifts to the employer to justify its actions by showing that either (1) the employee's condition would interfere with her job duties, or (2) hiring the employee would pose a safety hazard. Id. at 241, 440; see also Dauten v. Muskegon Cty., 128 Mich. App. 435, 340 N.W.2d 117 (1983) (affirming employer's decision not to hire a lifeguard after results of a medical examination revealed employee had back condition that could affect her ability to carry out her job duties); Hamilton v. Consumers Energy Co., No. 266866, 2006 WL 2271055 (Mich. App. Aug. 8, 2006) (upholding employer's denial of promotion because employee had suffered a back injury affecting ability to perform part of the job).

HIV/AIDS Testing and Disclosure. Michigan law requires that anyone performing an HIV-related test first receive the written, informed consent of the person being tested. MCLA 333.5133 et seq. In the only case addressing employee AIDS testing, the Michigan Supreme Court held that a food service employer has a right under the public health code to require an employee suspected of having AIDS to undergo AIDS-related testing before assigning that employee to work in a capacity where an opportunistic infection would be transmitted through food. Sanchez v. Lagoudakis, 458 Mich. 704, 581 N.W.2d 257 (1998) (reasoning possibility that unbeknownst to employee or employer, employee may have one of the opportunistic diseases associated with AIDs, which might be spread by food handling). The Michigan Supreme Court noted, however, that its holding was limited to the food service industry. Id.

With respect to the disclosure of HIV/AIDS-related information, all reports, records, and data pertaining to the testing, care, treatment, reporting or notification, and research of the HIV infection are deemed confidential under Michigan law. MCLA 333.5131(1). Any person who discloses this information, except as specifically authorized by statute is guilty of a misdemeanor punishable by imprisonment for not more than one year and a fine of up to $5,000. MCLA 333.5131(8). An employer is liable for a violation of this statute unless it "had in effect at the time of the violation reasonable precautions designed to prevent the violation." Id.

Genetic Testing. Michigan law prohibits private and public employers from discriminating against an employee or applicant on the basis of genetic information unrelated to the ability to perform duties of the particular job or position. MCLA 37.1201(b). Under this amendment to the PWDCRA, it is unlawful for an employer to require employees or applicants for employment to submit to genetic testing or provide genetic information as a condition of employment or promotion. Michigan employers are also prohibited from accessing genetic information concerning an employee or applicant unless voluntarily provided to the employer by the employee or applicant. If genetic information concerning the employee or applicant *is* voluntarily disclosed, the employer is allowed to take action (perhaps even adverse action, like termination of employment) to protect the employee's health and safety if relevant to job performance.

The Genetic Information Nondiscrimination Act ("GINA"), 42 U.S.C. § 2000ff-1 et seq., does not preempt more protective state laws. Although GINA is similar to Michigan law in that it prohibits employers from discrimination on these bases, Michigan law lacks GINA's safe harbor provisions regarding employer acquisition of genetic information, as well as certain confidentiality measures required where an employer is allowed to possess genetic information. In this respect, Michigan employers must fully understand their obligations under Michigan law.

2. ***Private Employers.*** Michigan courts have yet to address a claim by a Michigan **private** employee that medical examinations ordered by a private employer constitute an invasion of privacy.

3. ***Public Employers.*** Michigan courts have yet to address a claim by a Michigan public employee that medical examinations ordered by a public employer constitute an invasion of privacy. But see II.C.1(a), supra.

D. Polygraph Tests

The Michigan Polygraph Protection Act of 1981, MCLA 37.201 et seq., ("Polygraph Protection Act"), applies to all Michigan employers (including employment agencies) and prohibits employers from: (1) requiring applicants or employees to take a polygraph examination; (2) threatening to administer such an examination; or (3) requiring an applicant or employee to waive his or her right to decline a polygraph examination. MCLA 37.203(1).

The Polygraph Protection Act allows, however, prospective employees to *voluntarily* request a polygraph to clear their name. MCLA 37.203(2). This provision appears to conflict with the federal Employee Polygraph Protection Act of 1988 (EPPA), which bans all use of polygraph tests (even those apparently requested by an employee), unless the employer's activity falls within certain exemptions. To date, no court has addressed this potential conflict. However, the legislative history of the Polygraph Protection Act indicates that "[i]f the employee wishes to clear him or herself, that option is still available." S. Rep. No. 284, 100th Cong. 2d Sess. 47, reprinted in 4 U.S.C.C.A.N. 734 (1988).

A Michigan employee may bring a civil suit for injunctive relief, money damages, or both, against an employer who violates the state Polygraph Protection Act. Damages include attorney's fees and "damages for injury or loss" caused by the alleged violation, including damages equal to twice the amount of any lost wages if the employee is discharged in violation of the state act. MCLA 37.207(1)-(3). A violation of the Polygraph Protection Act is a misdemeanor that can result in a $1,000 fine, 90 days in jail, or both. MCLA 37.208.

The Employee Polygraph Protection Act does not preempt a more restrictive provision of any state statute, local ordinance or negotiated collective bargaining agreement. 29 U.S.C. § 2009. Although Michigan's act is generally more restrictive than the federal act, there are a number of places where the federal act backstops the less restrictive portions of the Michigan act. For example, while the Michigan act prohibits an employer from requesting, requiring, administering or causing to be administered a polygraph examination, the federal act also prohibits an employer from *indirectly suggesting* that an applicant or employee take such an examination. 29 U.S.C. § 2002(1). The federal act also prohibits an employer from using or inquiring about the results of a polygraph examination the applicant or employee has already taken, 29 U.S.C. § 2002 (2), and *expressly* prohibits an employer from discharging, disciplining, discrimination against, denying a promotion to, or threatening an employee for refusing to take a polygraph test. 29 U.S.C. § 2002(3). The Michigan act could be read to imply these restrictions through the prohibition on employer-administered polygraph tests. Finally, the federal act prohibits adverse action against an employee because he or she filed a complaint under the act, testified or was about to testify in a proceeding under that act, or otherwise exercised his or her rights under that act. 29 U.S.C. § 2002(4).

E. Fingerprinting

While there are no cases regarding an employee's privacy when fingerprinted by an employer, there are Michigan statutes specifically requiring employers and potential employers to fingerprint. For example, licensed professional investigators are required to fingerprint all prospective employees. MCLA 338.837(5)(b). Furthermore, Michigan mandates fingerprinting (and background checks) of all prospective employees who would directly provide security through the employer's business and prohibits the employment of anyone as a direct provider of security before such fingerprints have been submitted to the department of the State Police. MCLA 338.1068(2), (3).

III. SEARCHES

A. Employee's Person

1. ***Private Employers.*** Although there are no Michigan cases addressing physical searches of an employee's person, a Michigan court held that an employer has the right to interrogate an employee about suspected

illegal conduct. See Earp v. City of Detroit, 16 Mich. App. 271, 167 N.W.2d 841 (1969) (rejecting employee's intrusion-into-seclusion claim because (1) employer had a right to investigate possible illegal conduct by employee; (2) the nature of the information sought was of public concern; and (3) employer did not publicize results of investigation).

2. ***Public Employers.*** The Michigan cases involving public employers generally concern correctional facilities and their employees. Boyd v. Civil Serv. Comm'n., 220 Mich. App. 226, 237-239, 559 N.W.2d 342, 347-348 (1996), upheld the strip search of a state prison employee for alleged possession of a controlled substance because prisons require heightened security and the employee had received mail at the prison that included instructions on smuggling controlled substances. Similarly, Esson v. Dep't. of Corrections, No. 196012, 1997 WL 33343723 (Mich. App. Oct. 7, 1997), upheld the strip search of a corrections officer because the officer was reportedly selling drugs and sex to inmates. In both cases, the department's internal manual gave notice of the possibility of strip searches. Although these cases are instructive on searches of an employee's person within a correctional department, it is unlikely to be helpful for general public employers, because significant penal interests carried substantially more weight in Boyd and Esson than traditional interests of public employers.

B. Employee's Work Area

1. ***Private Employers.*** No reported cases.

2. ***Public Employers.*** There are few cases addressing a public employers' search of an employee's workspace. The Michigan Court of Appeals has held that a deputy sheriff had no reasonable expectation of privacy in the office he shared with two other deputies, and thus had no grounds to object to the seizure of work-related papers from his desk. People v. Duvall, 170 Mich. App. 701, 706, 428 N.W.2d 746, 749 (1988). Relying on the principles discussed in Duvall, People v. Powell, 235 Mich. App. 557, 599 N.W.2d 499 (1999), held that a graduate student did not have a reasonable expectation of privacy in a restricted-access research laboratory where he worked. In other cases, courts have considered the search of an employee's office by a supervisor justified where the search is for noninvestigatory, work-related purposes or where there are reasonable grounds for suspecting such a search will produce evidence that the employee is guilty of work-related misconduct. John Doe (1-3) v. Dearborn Public Schs., No. 06-CV-12369-DT, 2008 WL 896066 at *5 (E.D. Mich. Mar. 31, 2008). **In denying a motion for a temporary restraining order, the United District Court for the Eastern District of Michigan held that the special needs doctrine applied to searches of public employees' workspaces during investigations of misconduct, even when the materials obtained were personal and from a locked safe. James v. Hampton, No. 12-10273, 2012 WL 176187 (E.D. Mich. Jan 22, 2012).**

C. Employee's Property

1. ***Private Employers.*** An independent computer consultant stated a valid cause of action against a law firm, its attorneys and agents for trespass by entering the consultant's home to secure private information on his computer under false pretenses. Dalley v. Dykema Gossett, PLLC, 287 Mich. App. 296, 788 N.W.2d 679 (2010).

2. ***Public Employers.*** In Shealy v. Caldwell, 16 Fed.Appx. 388, 400 (6th Cir. 2001), the Sixth Circuit found that a public employer may have violated the Fourth Amendment of the United States Constitution when directing a police officer to perform a warrantless search of the plaintiff-employee's purse. The court held that the plaintiff-employee had a reasonable expectation of privacy in her purse and determined that an issue of fact existed over whether the warrantless search was unreasonable. Id.

IV. MONITORING OF EMPLOYEES

A. Telephones and Electronic Communications

1. ***Wiretapping.*** The Michigan wiretapping statute prohibits the willful use of a "device" by a third party to eavesdrop on a private conversation *without the consent of all the parties to the conversation.* MCLA 750.539(c). Michigan courts have interpreted this statute to allow a *participant* in a private conversation to record the conversation without the other party's consent. Sullivan v. Gray, 117 Mich. App. 476, 481, 324 N.W.2d 58, 60 (1982). However, a participant *may not allow a third party* to record a private conversation on behalf of the participant. Dickerson v. Raphael, 222 Mich. App. 185, 198, 564 N.W.2d 85, 91 (1997), rev'd on other grounds 461 Mich. 851, 601 N.W.2d 108 (1999). A party who violates the statute is guilty of a felony punishable by imprisonment of up to 2 years and a fine of up to $2,000.00. MCLA 750.539(c). The Act also provides civil remedies against the eavesdropper including actual and punitive damages. MCLA 750.539(h).

The statute also prohibits the installation of a device, or its use, in any "private place," without consent, for the purposes of "observing, . . . photographing, or eavesdropping upon the sounds or events in that place." MCLA 750.539d (a). "Eavesdropping" is defined as overhearing, recording, amplifying, or transmitting any part of a private conversation.

MCLA 750.539a(2). "Private place" is defined as a place where a person has a reasonable expectation of safety from "casual or hostile intrusion or surveillance but [it] does not include a place to which the public or substantial group of the public has access." MCLA 750.539a(1). Even though conversations on cordless telephones can be inadvertently intercepted by others, a person using a cordless telephone still has an expectation of privacy with respect to such a conversation and a person who intentionally intercepts such a conversation violates the Act. See People v. Stone, 463 Mich. 558, 566, 621 N.W.2d 702, 706 (2001).

Unlike the federal wiretapping statute, 18 U.S.C. § 2510 et seq., the Michigan statute *does not* have an exception allowing the monitoring of communications conducted within the ordinary course of the employer's business. Thus, it is unclear whether Michigan employers who want to monitor employee telephone calls for quality control assurances can legally do so under this Act. To date, no Michigan court has directly addressed this issue. However, in Kiessel v. Oltersdort, No. 1:09-cv-179, 2010 WL 4878806 (W.D. Nov. 23, 2010), **aff'd on other grounds, 459 F. Appx. 910 (6th Cir. 2012)**, the court, evaluating a motion for summary judgment under both the federal and Michigan statutes, found that labeling employees' phones with a "private out" line creates an expectation of privacy, and is sufficient to preclude summary judgment in the employer's favor under the ordinary course of business exception, even if the employer published a policy stating that employee calls would be monitored. Id. at *3.

2. ***Electronic Communications.*** The Michigan wiretapping statute defines "eavesdropping" broadly to include the transmission of any part of the "private discourse of others without the permission of all persons engaged in the discourse." MCLA 750.539a(2). It is possible a Michigan court could interpret this definition to include e-mail.

In Combs v. Int'l Union, et al, No. 03-cv-71060-DT, 2004 WL 1585297, at *3 (E.D. Mich. Mar. 17, 2004), an employer reviewed the e-mail accounts of all of its employees at a particular plant, and suspended 12 employees for sending sexually suggestive material. The federal district court ruled that the suspensions did not violate a collective bargaining agreement when they were issued pursuant to the employer's computer use policy. Id. at *8. Additionally, the court held that the company could monitor e-mail transmissions and note-logs without prior notice to users. Id.

In 2008, the Michigan Court of Appeals considered the privacy implications of an alleged leak to local press of a city attorney's e-mails. Hoff v. Spoelstra, Nos. 272898, 275979, 276054, 276257, 2008 WL 2668298 at *9 (Mich. App. July 8, 2008). The city's information system policy stated that e-mails were considered public property, could be subject to FOIA disclosure, and thus the employee user should not expect any privacy regarding e-mail messages. Id. The city attorney thus had no reasonable expectation of privacy in e-mails in the city's computer system and recovery from the city manager and a city commissioner for intrusion upon seclusion and public disclosure of private facts based on the leak was barred. Id.

In Howell Educ. Association, MEA/NEA v. Howell Bd. of Educ., 287 Mich. App. 228, 789 N.W.2d 495 (2010), the Michigan Court of Appeals held that a school employee's e-mails regarding union matters were not public records subject to production pursuant to a Freedom of Information Act request.

3. ***Other Electronic Monitoring.*** No Michigan court has addressed the privacy issues associated with electronic communications such as the monitoring of employees' key strokes, or the monitoring of employees signing on or off of an electronic network. However, in Bailey v. Bailey, No. 07-11672, 2008 WL 324156 (E.D. Mich. Feb. 6, 2008), the court addressed whether an ex-husband's use of key-logging software to obtain the password to his ex-wife's e-mail account violated Michigan's wiretapping law. The court held that the statute did not apply because the pressing of keys by the ex-wife was not a conversation upon which the ex-husband could eavesdrop. The mere pressing of keys to enter passwords or messages did not give him access to her direct and private dialogue with another party because there was none at that time. It is likely Michigan courts would apply similar reasoning to an employer's use of a key logger to monitor employees.

B. Mail

No Michigan statutes or cases address the privacy issues surrounding use of the mail in the employment setting.

C. Surveillance/Photographing

Statute. Under Michigan law it is a felony for any person to install "in any private place, without the consent of the person or persons entitled to privacy in that place, any device for observing, . . . photographing, or eavesdropping upon the sounds or events in that place." MCLA 750.539d; see also MCLA 750.539i (providing that in either a civil or criminal case, installing a surveillance device in a private area is prima facie evidence of violation of the statute); but see MCLA 750.539g (c) (providing an exception to liability for "surveillance by an employee safeguarding property owned by, or in the custody of, his or her employer on his or her employer's property"); MCLA 750.539a(3) (defining surveillance as the act of secretly observing the activities of another person for the purpose of spying upon and invading the privacy of that person).

At least one court has held that an employer's bathroom can be a "private place" within the meaning of the statute. See People v. Abate, 105 Mich. App. 274, 306 N.W.2d 476 (1981) (holding that customer had sufficient expectation of privacy in employer's bathroom to make employer's use of two-way mirrors a violation of the statute). While Abate concerned a customer's expectation of privacy rather than an employee's, a court could conceivably extend the holding to a case involving employees. Thus, an employer must exercise care in installing surveillance devices in any area that could be considered a "private place."

Common Law. An employer may engage in surveillance of an employee provided that the reason for the surveillance is to obtain work-related information. See Saldana v. Kelsey-Hayes Co., 178 Mich. App. 230, 443 N.W.2d 382 (1989). In Saldana, an employee was allegedly injured in an on-the-job accident. Id. at 232, 383. Suspecting that the employee might be malingering, the employer hired a private investigator to observe the employee at home in an attempt to discern the extent of the employee's injuries. Id. As part of that surveillance, the investigator photographed the employee from a distance. Id. When the employer fired the employee based on the investigation, the employee filed an intrusion-into-seclusion claim. Id. at 233, 383. The court noted that the employer's duty to refrain from intruding upon the employee's private affairs is not absolute in nature, but rather is defined by those rights that arise as part of the business relationship between the employer and employee. Id. at 234, 384 (citing Lewis v. Dayton Hudson Corp., 128 Mich. App. 165, 169, 339 N.W.2d 857 (1983)). Thus, the employer had the right to investigate an employee suspected of committing fraud. More importantly, the court found that the employee had a reduced expectation of privacy, even at home, when the subject matter of the investigation was work-related. Id.

An employer's surveillance ability is not without limit. Applying Michigan law in Brannum v. Overton Cty. School Bd., 516 F. 3d 489 (6th Cir. 2008), the Sixth Circuit held the surveillance of a middle school locker room via video was inherently intrusive and significantly invaded students' reasonable expectation of privacy when in that locker room. Shortly after the Sixth Circuit's Brannum decision, a Michigan court held that as public employees, teachers had a clearly established right to be free from unreasonable searches by their public employer, and thus any video recording of their offices was impermissible. John Doe (1-3), No. 06-CV-12369-DT, 2008 WL 896066 (E.D. Mich. Mar. 31, 2008) (reasoning that Brannum could be applied to school employees, as well as students).

Michigan courts have also addressed the surveillance of customers by employers. While these cases do not directly relate to employee privacy, the courts utilize a very similar analysis, weighing the privacy expectations of the customer against the need for surveillance by the employer. See, e.g., Lewis, 128 Mich. App. at 172, 339 N.W.2d at 860 (employer justified in using two-way mirrors in dressing rooms to monitor customers because employer had a legitimate interest in preventing theft while customers had reduced expectation of privacy because signs placed them on notice that their activities might be monitored); but see Harkey v. Abate, 131 Mich. App. 177, 346 N.W.2d 74 (1983) (customer stated a prima facie case for invasion of privacy where employer installed see-through panels in the ceiling of the women's bathroom, even though the customer could not prove that the employer actually viewed the customer through the panels).

V. ACTIVITIES OUTSIDE THE WORKPLACE

A. Statute or Common Law

There are no Michigan statutes addressing the ability of employers to regulate the activity of employees outside the workplace.

The case law recognizes some limited power to regulate such conduct as it pertains to employment-related matters. For example, while Michigan recognizes a public-policy exception to the at-will doctrine, the Michigan Court of Appeals has held that an employer does not violate public policy by dismissing an employee for threatening to disseminate unflattering information about a customer. See Prysak v. R.L. Polk Co., 193 Mich. App. 1, 483 N.W.2d 629 (1992) (holding that a private employer is not required to recognize an employee's First Amendment rights of freedom of association and free speech).

B. Employees' Personal Relationships

1. ***Romantic Relationships Between Employees.*** There is no Michigan authority addressing when an employer may regulate romantic relationships between employees. Interpreting the United States Constitution, Michigan federal courts have disagreed over whether an employee has a protectable privacy interest in his or her romantic relationships. Compare Briggs v. N. Muskegon Police Dept., 563 F. Supp. 585 (W.D. Mich. 1983) (holding that public employer violated employee's constitutional rights when it dismissed him for cohabitating with a married woman that was not his wife) with Mercure v. Van Buren Twp., 81 F. Supp. 2d 814 (E.D. Mich. 2000) (holding public employee did not have a protectable privacy interest in his romantic relationship with a fellow employee's estranged wife).

2. ***Sexual Orientation.*** Under Michigan's civil rights statute, the Elliot-Larsen Civil Rights Act, an employer may not discriminate against an employee because of sex. MCLA 37.2102(1). The statute defines discrimination "because of sex" to include sexual harassment that creates an "intimidating, hostile or offense employment . . . environment." MCLA 37.2103(i)(iii). To date, Michigan courts have held that the statute does not prohibit an employer from making employment decisions based on sexual orientation. See Barbour v. Dep't of Soc. Servs., 198 Mich. App. 183, 497 N.W.2d 216 (1993); see also Mack v. City of Detroit, 467 Mich. 186, 196 (2002) (noting that Michigan's Elliot-Larsen Civil Rights Act does not protect citizens from discrimination based on sexual orientation).

The Michigan Supreme Court has held that the marriage amendment to the Michigan Constitution allows employers to discriminate on the basis of sexual orientation with respect to the provision of employment benefits. Mich. Const. Art. 1, § 25; National Pride at Work, Inc. v. Governor of Mich., 481 Mich. 56, 748 N.W.2d 524 (2008) (holding that the state constitution prohibits public employers from extending benefits to an employee's same sex domestic partner). The marriage amendment states: "the union of one man and one woman in marriage shall be the only agreement recognized as a marriage or similar union for any purpose." Mich. Const. Art. 1. § 25. The Court held that the state provision of employment-related benefits constituted a form of recognition of a union similar to marriage that was prohibited by the amendment. National Pride at Work, Inc., 481 Mich. 56, 748 N.W.2d 524. Moreover, the Court found a legitimate governmental interest existed in favoring the institution of marriage; thus, the amendment's prevention of the employee benefit provision did not violate the equal protection provisions of the state constitution.

3. ***Marital Status.*** The Elliot-Larsen Civil Rights Act also prohibits an employer from discriminating against an individual because of marital status. MCLA 37.2202(1)(a). While the Act does not define "marital status," the Michigan Supreme Court affirmed that the term means "whether a person is married," and held that an employer did not violate the Act where it refused to renew an employee's contract after the employee carried on a well-known affair. Veenstra v. Washtenaw Country Club, 466 Mich. 155, 167-168, 645 N.W.2d 643, 650 (2002); see also Mich. Const. Art. 1. § 25 (defining marriage). According to the Michigan Supreme Court, the civil rights statute protects an employee's "status" rather than an employee's "conduct." Veenstra, at 156, 644. The Michigan Supreme Court held that the employee could only prevail by presenting evidence that his employer dismissed him because he was getting a divorce (i.e., changing his marital status). Id. at 167, 650. See also Russ v. City of Troy, No. 217921, 2001 WL 689537 (Mich. App. Apr. 6, 2001) (defendant's "stray remark" that the plaintiff would not be promoted unless he was married was sufficient evidence of marital status discrimination to create a triable issue of fact regarding what the defendant's true motivations were in not promoting the plaintiff). Moreover, an employer does not violate the statute by refusing to hire a prospective employee based on the company's anti-nepotism policy. See Whirlpool Corp. v. Mich. Civil Rights Comm., 425 Mich. 527, 390 N.W.2d 625 (1986).

C. Smoking

Smoking became generally prohibited in work places in 2010. See MCLA 333.12601, et seq. Addiction to nicotine is not considered a disability for the purposes of the Michigan Persons with Disabilities Civil Rights Act ("MPDCRA"), MCLA 37.1101 et seq., and an employer may discharge an employee for smoking without violating that Act.

D. Blogging and Use of Social Media

In Bennett v. Detroit Police Chief, 274 Mich. App. 307, 309, 732 N.W.2d 164, 166 (2007), a police officer was suspended and eventually terminated for maintaining a website containing several blogs critical of the Mayor of Detroit and the chief of police. Governmental immunity protected both the city employees and the municipality from any liability stemming from the termination. Id. at 320, 172. Further, because blogging shares many characteristics with e-mail, courts will probably treat blogs like Combs v. Int'l Union, No. 03-cv-71060-DT, 2004 WL 1585297 (E.D. Mich. Mar. 17, 2004), treated e-mail.

There are no Michigan cases addressing privacy issues related to blogging encouraged by an employer.

From 2010 through 2011, the National Labor Relations Board ("NLRB") has taken administrative action against both unionized and non-unionized employers that take disciplinary action against employees who engage in concerted activity under the National Labor Relations Act. Activity is concerted when it is "engaged in with or on the authority of other employees, and not solely by and on behalf of the employee himself." JT's Porch Saloon & Eatery Ltd., No. 13-CA-46689, 2011 WL 2960964 (NLRB 2011) (holding that a bartender's Facebook posting complaining about the employer's tipping policy was not concerted because it did not attempt to mobilize employees and was simply an individual gripe). See also Lee Enterprises, Inc. d/b/a Arizona Daily Star, No. 28-CA-23267, 2011 WL 1825089 (NLRB 2011) (holding that a non-union newspaper reporter who insulted rival news reporting agencies on a twitter account promoted by his employer did not engage in concerted activity, as his speech did not involve terms and conditions of employment), but see Karl Knauz BMW, Knauz Auto Group, No. 13-CA-046452 (NLRB 2011) (finding that a non-unionized auto dealership wrongfully discharged employee who complained on Facebook that low quality food being served by the employer during a sales event would impact his sales commissions).

These new NLRB cases may create separate causes of action under Michigan law. In Garavaglia v. Centra, Inc., 211 Mich. App. 625, 536 N.W.2d 805 (1995), the court held that an employee who is terminated in contravention of the NLRA may pursue a wrongful discharge claim based on Michigan's public policy exemption to at-will employment. The Michigan Court of Appeals has limited, however, the Garavaglia decision to cases where the employer did not assert NLRA preemption as an affirmative defense. See Calabrese v. Tendercare of Michigan, Inc., 262 Mich. App. 256, 685 N.W.2d 313 (2004) (holding that the NLRA preempts separate Michigan causes of action).

VI. RECORDS

A. Personnel Records

Under the Bullard-Plawecki Employee Right to Know Act, MCLA 423.501 et seq., an employee has the right to review, copy, and file a response to any personnel record. An employee may also request the removal or correction of any personnel record. The Act applies to any Michigan employer, public or private, that employs four or more people.

The Act defines "personnel record" broadly to include any record that identifies the employee and is related in some way to the employee's employment. MCLA 423.501(2)(c). See, e.g., Mich. Prof'l. Employees Soc'y. v. Dep't . of Natural Res., 192 Mich. App. 483, 482 N.W.2d 460 (1992) (holding that handwritten notes taken during an employee interview were "personnel records" since they identified the employee and were used in a promotion decision); but see Muskovitz v. Lubbers, 182 Mich. App. 489, 452 N.W.2d 854 (1990) (holding that confidential peer review evaluations were not "personnel records" insofar as those records revealed the identity of the person who prepared them).

Under the Act, an employer may not release an employee's personnel records without written notice to the employee. However, an employee's ability to collect monetary damages from a violation of the Act is limited by a strict causation analysis. See McManamon v. Redford Charter Twp., 273 Mich. App. 131, 730 N.W.2d. 757 (2007). Furthermore, except when ordered to produce an employee's personnel records as part of a legal action or arbitration, an employer must delete from any disclosure all disciplinary reports, letters of reprimand, or other records of disciplinary action that are more than four years old. See MCLA 423.506; see also MCLA 423.452 (employer who discloses job performance information of an individual to a prospective employer is presumed to be acting in good faith and immune from civil liability for the disclosure).

An employer may not keep a record of an employee's associations, political activities, publications, or communications of non-employment activities unless permission is given by the employee. MCLA 423.508(1). This prohibition does not apply if the employee engages in such activities on the employer's premises or during the employee's work hours in such a manner as to interfere with the performance of the employee's duties. Id.

Finally, if the employer is a public entity, it may be required to turn over personnel-related records under Michigan's Freedom of Information Act. MCLA 15.231 et seq.; see also Kent County Deputy Sheriff's Ass'n. v. Kent County Sheriff, 463 Mich. 353, 616 N.W.2d 677 (2000) (public employer did not have to release under FOIA copies of reports that formed the basis for disciplinary decisions against two employees); Great Lakes Media, Inc. v. City of Pontiac, Nos. 208306, 208320, 2000 WL 33419383 (Mich. App. May 19, 2000) (FOIA required police department to release records pertaining to its internal investigation of excessive use of force by three police officers). See also VI.D. infra.

B. Medical Records

Medical records in an employee's file are not considered "personnel records" if those records are available to the employee from the doctor or facility that created them. MCLA 423.501(2)(c)(iii).

As noted in II.C., supra, there are other limitations on an employer's capacity to utilize or divulge an employee's medical records, pursuant to MCL 333.5131.

C. Criminal Records

Under the Bullard-Plawecki Employee Right to Know Act, MCLA 423.501 et seq., if an employer has reasonable cause to believe that an employee is engaging in criminal activity that may affect the employer, the employer may keep a separate file of information relating to its investigation of the employee. Upon completion of the investigation or after 2 years, whichever comes first, the employer must notify the employee that an investigation is or was being conducted into the employee's possible criminal activity. If, at the end of the investigation, no disciplinary action is taken against the employee, the employer must destroy the report. MCLA 423.509(1).

D. Subpoenas / Search Warrants

Pursuant to the Bullard-Plawecki Employee Right to Know Act, MCLA 423.501 et seq., an employer may not release an employee's personnel records without written notice to the employee. However, an employee's ability to collect monetary damages from violation of the Act is limited by a strict causation analysis. See McManamon v. Redford Charter Twp., 273 Mich. App. 131, 730 N.W.2d 757 (2007).

Michigan law does not provide any further protection to employees if their employer discloses their personnel records in accordance with a valid subpoena. Bradley v. Saranac Cmty Schs. Bd. of Ed., 455 Mich. 285, 565 N.W.2d 650 (1997) (holding personnel records of public school teachers and administrators subject to disclosure because not of a personal nature to be exempt from disclosure under Michigan's FOIA law). In the case of public employees, employee information may be disclosed in response to a FOIA request. Tobin v. Mich. Civil Serv. Comm'n., 416 Mich. 661, 664, 331 N.W.2d 184, 185 (1982); But see Mich. Fed'n of Teachers v. Univ. of Mich. 481 Mich. 657, 753 N.W.2d 28 (2008) (split decision holding that home addresses and telephone numbers of employees of a state university were not subject to disclosure under Michigan's FOIA law because revelation of such information would divulge little or nothing about a governmental agency's conduct). Further, the common law does not protect the disclosure of salary information disclosed under a FOIA request. Health Cent. v. Comm'r. of Ins., 152 Mich. App. 336, 393 N.W.2d 625 (1986).

E. Social Security Numbers

Michigan law generally prohibits disclosure of or requirement to disclose the full Social Security number of an employee, MCLA 445.81, et seq.

VII. ACTIONS SUBSEQUENT TO EMPLOYMENT

A. References

The Bullard-Plawecki Employee Right to Know Act, MCLA 423.501 et seq., does not require employee references supplied to an employer to be turned over to an employee if the identity of the person making the reference would be disclosed. Redacted or rearranged versions of reference documents from which the source of the reference cannot be determined must be supplied to an employee if requested. See, e.g., Mich. Prof'l. Employees Soc'y. v. Dep't of Natural Res., 192 Mich. App. 483, 482 N.W.2d 460 (1992) (holding that handwritten notes taken from oral references over the telephone constitute "employee references" for purposes of the Act); see also Muskovitz v. Lubbers, 182 Mich. App. 489, 452 N.W.2d 854 (1990) (holding that confidential peer review evaluations were "employee references" and could not be revealed if the identity of the person who prepared them could not be hidden).

B. Non-Compete Agreements

A contract that seeks to prevent the disclosure or use of confidential information is not an illegal restraint of trade. See Glucol Mfg. Co. v. Schulist, 239 Mich. 70, 214 N.W. 152 (1927). However, information that a former employee gains through a third party after the employee's termination is not subject to the agreement. See Frontier Corp. v. Telco Commc'ns Group, Inc., 965 F. Supp. 1200, 1210 (S.D. Ind. 1997) (applying Michigan substantive law).

VIII. OTHER ISSUES

A. Statute of Limitations

As noted, the statute of limitations for all tort actions covered in this outline is three years from the accrual of the injury to the employee. MCLA 600.5805(10).

Under the Bullard-Plawecki Employee Right to Know Act, an employee may sue his or her employer for any violations of the statute which occur during the employment relationship. The statute appears to indicate that the employee does not have a cause of action against his or her employer for violations of this Act once the employment relationship has been severed. See MCLA 423.511.

The statute of limitations for actions brought by an employee under the Michigan Persons with Disabilities Civil Rights Act, the Polygraph Protection Act, as well as the Michigan wiretapping statute is three years. MCLA 600.5805(10).

B. Jurisdiction

The Michigan court system is divided into judicial circuits along county lines. The circuit courts are the trial courts of general jurisdiction and have original jurisdiction in all civil cases involving more than $25,000. The district courts have exclusive jurisdiction of all civil litigation up to $25,000. The Michigan Court of Appeals is the intermediate appellate court.

Appellants appeal final judgments of the circuit courts to court of appeals as of right, and interlocutory orders by leave. Appellants appeal by leave from the court of appeals to the supreme court.

C. Worker's Compensation Exclusivity

Pursuant to the Worker's Disability Compensation Act ("WDCA"), the exclusive remedy provision applies when an employee is injured by the negligent acts of his employer or co-employee. MCLA 418.301(1); MCLA 418.131(1). The Bureau of Worker's Compensation has exclusive subject matter over worker's compensation claims. MCLA 418.841(1). The WDCA applies to all public employers and most private employers, subject to certain exceptions pertaining to agricultural employers. MCLA 418.115. The single exception to the exclusive remedy provision applies if the injurious act constituted an intentional tort. MCLA 418.131(1). An intentional tort is committed where the employer specifically intends to injure the employee and is successful in doing so. Id. An employer is deemed to have intended injury if the employer had actual knowledge an injury was certain to occur and willfully disregarded that knowledge. Id.

Liability for an employee's actions can be attributed to a corporate employer only when the acting employee is (1) in a supervisory or managerial capacity and (2) commits an intentional tort. Travis v. Dreis & Krump Mfg. Co., 453 Mich. 149, 551 N.W.2d 132 (1996); Oldham v. Blue Cross & Blue Shield of Mich., No. 196747, 1999 WL 33441287 (Mich. App. June 8, 1999) (Plaintiff did not survive summary judgment on claim against employer based on invasion of privacy committed by other employees within the scope of their employment; the WDCA is the sole remedy for such an employee and the co-employee's action did not constitute an intentional tort).

D. Pleading Requirements

As noted in IV.B.2, supra, to establish a prima facie case of interference with prospective economic advantage against an agent of a corporation, the employee must plead that the agent was acting outside the scope of his or her duties when terminating the employee.

SURVEY OF MINNESOTA EMPLOYMENT LIBEL LAW

Steven R. Anderson, Kathlyn E. Noecker,
John P. Borger, Daniel G. Prokott, and Leita Walker
Faegre Baker Daniels LLP
2200 Wells Fargo Center
90 South Seventh Street
Minneapolis, Minnesota 55402
Telephone: (612) 766-7000
Facsimile: (612) 766-1600
http://www.faegrebd.com

Daniel Oberdorfer
Christina A. Sans
Leonard, Street and Deinard
150 South Fifth Street, Suite 2300
Minneapolis, Minnesota 55402
Telephone: (612) 335-1832;
Facsimile: (612) 335-1657
http://www.leonard.com

(With Developments Reported Through **November 1, 2012**)

GENERAL COMMENTS

None.

SIGNIFICANT DEVELOPMENTS SINCE THE 2012 *SURVEY*

None.

I. GENERAL LAW

A. General Employment Law

1. ***At-Will Employment***. Minnesota is an at-will employment state. Pine River State Bank v. Mettille, 333 N.W.2d 622, 115 L.R.R.M. (BNA) 4493 (Minn. 1983). Minnesota, however, recognizes numerous exceptions to employment at-will. These include federal anti-discrimination laws and the Minnesota Human Rights Act, Minn. Stat. § 363.01 et seq.; the Minnesota equal pay for equal work law, Minn. Stat. § 181.66; the Minnesota age discrimination statute, Minn. Stat. § 181.81; the Minnesota whistleblower law, Minn. Stat. § 181.932 (see also Anderson-Johanningmeier v. Mid-Minnesota Women's Ctr., Inc., 637 N.W.2d 270 (Minn. 2002); Phipps v. Clark Oil & Refining Corp., 408 N.W.2d 569 (Minn. 1987) (public policy exception)); Minnesota's statute on the use of lawful substances, Minn. Stat. § 181.950; Minnesota's drug or alcohol testing statute, Minn. Stat. § 181.94; Minnesota's workers' compensation statute's retaliation provision, Minn. Stat. § 176.82; and Minnesota's jury duty statute, Minn. Stat. § 593.50. Another exception exists in the case of oral promises: "An oral promise to modify particular terms of at-will employment can become part of the employment agreement if the requirements for the formation of a unilateral contract are met: communication of a definite offer and acceptance for valuable consideration." Hayes v. K-Mart Corp., 665 N.W.2d 550, 553 (Minn. Ct. App. 2003) ("manager's promise of a pay raise was a term of employment suitable for inclusion in a unilateral employment contract" and as such "K-Mart's failure to grant Hayes the promised pay raise violated her employment agreement and gave her good cause to quit"), rev. denied (Minn. Sept. 24, 2003). Minnesota also recognizes that employment handbooks in some circumstances may contractually alter employment at will. See, e.g., Pine River, 333 N.W.2d at 626–27; Lee v. Fresenius Med. Care, Inc., 741 N.W.2d 117, 123 (Minn. 2007) (concluding that employer's employee handbook constituted an enforceable employment contract where employee signed an acknowledgment that she received the handbook and continued on the job for almost two years thereafter); Alexandria Hous. & Redevelopment Auth. v. Rost, 756 N.W.2d 896, 904-07 (Minn. Ct. App. 2008) (holding that employee handbook did not great a unilateral contract because none of the provisions in it were definitive enough to establish an enforceable contractual right to not be terminated except for cause and because the handbook included a disclaimer expressing the employer's intent to retain the at-will nature of the employment); Le v. City of Maplewood, No. A06-1684, 2007 Minn. App. LEXIS 818, at *7 (Minn. Ct. App. 2007) (unpublished opinion) (holding that although "an at-will employment relationship may be modified by an employer's policy manual or handbook if a unilateral contract on the terms defined in the policy manual or handbook has been formed, [where a policy manual] contains both the for-cause language and the disclaimer, the disclaimer prevents the formation of a unilateral contract"). But see Chambers v. Metro. Prop. & Cas. Ins. Co., 351 F.3d 848, 854 (8th Cir. 2003) (employee unable as a matter of law to sue on employer's prior employment policies where employer retained the right to modify and supersede such policies and the employee did not rely on them); Borgersen v. Cardiovascular Sys., 729 N.W.2d 619 (Minn. Ct. App. 2007) (a cover letter containing an at-will employment clause was inadmissible extrinsic evidence where a fully integrated employment agreement contained a for-cause provision); Johnson v. U.S. Bancorp, 2003 WL 22015838, at *3 (Minn. Ct. App. Aug. 26, 2003) (unpublished) ("Minnesota courts have consistently held that if an employee handbook clearly states that its language is not intended to create a contract, the handbook does not alter the status of at-will employees."). In addition, Minnesota recognizes tort exceptions to the at-will doctrine. See IV, infra.

B. Elements of Libel Claim

1. ***Basic Elements.*** In Minnesota, the elements of a defamation action are (1) a false and defamatory statement about the plaintiff, (2) in an unprivileged publication to a third party, (3) that harmed the plaintiff's reputation in the community. Pope v. ESA Servs., 406 F.3d 1001, 1011 (8th Cir. 2005), **overruled on other grounds by Torgerson v. City of Rochester, 643 F.3d 1031 (8th Cir. 2011)**; Weinberger v. Maplewood Review, 668 N.W.2d 667, 673 (Minn. 2003); Stuempges v. Parke, Davis & Co., 297 N.W.2d 252, 255 (Minn. 1980) (slightly different articulation of elements); Dunn v. Nat'l Bev. Corp., 729 N.W.2d 637 (Minn. Ct. App. 2007), aff'd 745 N.W.2d 549. The common law action is based in part upon the Restatement (Second) of Torts § 559 (1977) (a defamatory statement tends to "harm the reputation of another as to lower him in the estimation of the community or to deter third persons from associating or dealing with him"). In analyzing a defamation claim, context must be considered. Aviation Charter, Inc. v. Aviation Research Group/US, 416 F.3d 864, 868 (8th Cir. 2005).

2. ***Fault.*** Whether plaintiff is a private individual, a public official, or public figure is a matter of law. Jadwin v. Minneapolis Star & Tribune Co., 367 N.W.2d 476, 483, 11 Media L. Rep. (BNA) 1905 (Minn. 1985). Minnesota affords to non-media defendants the same First Amendment protection for criticism of public officials that it grants to the mass media. Britton v. Koep, 470 N.W.2d 518, 521, 19 Media L. Rep. (BNA) 1208 (Minn. 1991). Speech by non-media defendants, made through the news media, is subject to the same legal standards as speech by media defendants. Richie v. Paramount Pictures Corp., 544 N.W.2d 21, 26 n.5 (Minn. 1996).

a. **Private Figure Plaintiff/Matter of Public Concern.** Speech about matters of public concern, like that about public conduct of public officials, is given greater constitutional protection than speech involving strictly private matters. Diesen v. Hessburg, 455 N.W.2d 446, 17 Media L. Rep. (BNA) 1849 (Minn. 1990). In cases involving issues of public concern, private figure plaintiffs may not recover presumed or punitive damages absent a showing of actual malice. Jacobson v. Rochester Commc'ns Corp., 410 N.W.2d 830, 836 n.7, 14 Media L. Rep. (BNA) 1786 (Minn. 1987). A public figure may not prove falsity by implication. Honan v. County of Cottonwood, No. A04-1636, 2005 WL 2077277, *5 (Minn. Ct. App. Aug. 30, 2005); Schlieman v. Gannett Minn. Broad. Inc., 637 N.W.2d 297, 302–03 (Minn. Ct. App. 2001).

b. **Private Figure Plaintiff/Matter of Private Concern.** Private plaintiff/private issue defamation actions are analyzed under Minnesota common law, i.e. strict liability. Weissman v. Sri Lanka Curry House, Inc., 469 N.W.2d 471 (Minn. Ct. App. 1991); see also Bradley v. Hubbard Broad., 471 N.W.2d 670 (Minn. Ct. App. 1991).

c. **Public Figure Plaintiff/Matter of Public Concern.** Public officials must prove actual malice if the statements involve matters of public concern. Britton v. Koep, 470 N.W.2d 518, 521, 19 Media L. Rep. (BNA) 1208 (Minn. 1991); McDevitt v. Tilson, 453 N.W.2d 53, 17 Media L. Rep. (BNA) 2156 (Minn. Ct. App. 1990); see also Burgoon v. Delahunt, No. C8-00-882, 29 Media L. Rep. (BNA) 1148, 2000 WL 1780285, at *2 (Minn. Ct. App. Dec. 5, 2000) (statements about candidate for county board). A public figure is (1) someone who is in the position to resolve public issues, has control over conduct of governmental affairs, or in the qualifications and performance of whom the public has an interest beyond the interest in government employees generally, or (2) someone who has a role of special prominence in the affairs of society or has thrust him or herself to the forefront of a controversy to influence its resolution. McDevitt, 453 N.W.2d 53; see also Peterson v. Dakota County, 428 F. Supp. 2d 974 (D. Minn. 2006) (finding county social worker is a public figure because his/her position includes job duties that could affect or disrupt the lives of county residents), aff'd 479 F.3d 555 (8th Cir. 2007); Britton, 470 N.W.2d at 521 (probation officer is a public figure because he/she has significant authority in the performance of governmental duties). An otherwise private figure may become a limited purpose public figure upon a determination of the following (1) a public controversy existed; (2) the defendant had a purposeful or prominent role in that controversy; and (3) the allegedly defamatory statement was related to the controversy. **Stepnes v. Ritschel, 663 F.3d 952, 964 (8th Cir. 2011) (developer who sought media coverage by using a public relations firm to "shape the message" was a limited-purpose public figure)**; Metge v. Cent. Neighborhood Improvement Ass'n, 649 N.W.2d 488, 496 (Minn. Ct. App. 2002) (former executive director of neighborhood improvement association was limited public figure regarding controversy over her job duties); Chafoulias v. Peterson, 668 N.W.2d 642 (Minn. 2003), reh'g granted and modified, (Sept. 17, 2003) (as to media defendant, hotel owner making public statements in response to sexual harassment allegations was limited purpose public figure; as to individual defendant, state supreme court reversed appeals court that plaintiff was limited purpose public figure and remanded to examine whether individual defendant created the public controversy and whether plaintiff voluntarily injected himself into the public controversy).

3. ***Falsity.*** Minnesota courts have placed the burden of establishing each element of the claim, including falsity, on the plaintiff. Ferrell v. Cross, 557 N.W.2d 560, 565 (Minn. 1997); Rouse v. Dunkley & Bennett, P.A., 520 N.W.2d 406 (Minn. 1994); Benson v. Nw. Airlines, 561 N.W.2d 530 (Minn. Ct. App. 1997); see also Jeffries v. Metro-

Mark, Inc., 45 F.3d 258, 261 (8th Cir. 1995); Stringer v. Stan Koch & Sons Trucking, No. Civ. 04-3843, 2006 WL 212190 (D. Minn. Jan. 27, 2006) (mere conclusory allegations of falsity were insufficient to withstand a motion for summary judgment). In employment cases, truth is a defense only when the underlying implication of the statement is true, and not merely when the statement is "verbally accurate." Phipps v. Clark Oil & Refining Corp., 408 N.W.2d 569 (Minn. 1987); see also II.B.1, infra. It is possible for the presentation and arrangement of true statements, or the omission of certain facts from an otherwise true statement, to give a false implication and thereby provide a basis for a claim of defamation by implication. Toney v. WCCO TV, 85 F.3d 383, 387, 24 Media L. Rep. (BNA) 1993 (8th Cir. 1996); Phipps, 408 N.W.2d at 573; Karnes v. Milo Beauty & Barber Supply Co., 441 N.W.2d 565, 568 (Minn. Ct. App. 1989); Carter v. Peace Officers Std. & Training Bd., 558 N.W.2d 267, 273 (Minn. Ct. App. 1997).

4. ***Defamatory Statement of Fact.*** Words are defamatory to the plaintiff if they "tend to injure the plaintiff's reputation and expose the plaintiff to public hatred, contempt, ridicule, or degradation." Church of Scientology v. Minnesota State Medical Ass'n Foundation, 264 N.W.2d 152, 155, 3 Media L. Rep. (BNA) 2177 (Minn. 1978). Statements may be divided into three types: (1) statements that are defamatory on their face; (2) statements that can either be defamatory or not, depending on additional circumstances or facts; and (3) statements that cannot possibly have a defamatory meaning. Church of Scientology, 264 N.W.2d at 155. The question whether a particular statement is capable of defamatory meaning is a question of law. Phipps v. Clark Oil & Refining Corp., 408 N.W.2d 569, 573 (Minn. 1987). The question whether the statements were, in fact, understood to be defamatory is a question of fact. Utecht v. Shopko Dep't Store, 324 N.W.2d 652, 653 (Minn. 1982); see also Hammond v. Northland Counseling Ctr., No. Civ. 05-96-353, 1998 WL 315333 (D. Minn. Feb. 27, 1998). The factfinder is to decide "whether a reasonable person would believe the statement to be defamatory." Anderson v. Kammeier, 262 N.W.2d 366, 372 (Minn. 1977); see also II.B.2, infra. However, a court may decide as a matter of law that the statement is not susceptible to a defamatory meaning. See Landers v. AMTRAK, 345 F.3d 669, 672–73 (8th Cir. 2003) (applying Minnesota law) ("Declaring that an employee has performed satisfactorily cannot harm his reputation and therefore is not defamatory. ... [I]mpact on reputation is the relevant defamation inquiry, not whether [plaintiff's] satisfactory job performance ratings resulted in his termination because other employees were rated more highly."); Bauer v. Ford Motor Credit Co., 140 F. Supp. 2d 1019, 1021–23 (D. Minn. 2001) (action dismissed on summary judgment where plaintiffs failed to present evidence that anyone lowered their opinion of plaintiffs), vacated on other grounds, 149 F. Supp. 2d 1106 (D. Minn. 2001). The burden is on the plaintiff to present evidence specifically outlining the alleged defamation. Robertson v. Fed. Express Corp., No. 02-4161, 2004 WL 1278929, at *5 (D. Minn. June 5, 2004).

5. ***Of and Concerning Plaintiff.*** A plaintiff must show that the alleged defamatory remark could be understood to refer to him or her. Covey v. Detroit Lakes Printing Co., Div. of Forum Pub. Co., 490 N.W.2d 138, 143, 20 Media L. Rep. (BNA) 1671 (Minn. Ct. App. 1992). A statement defames plaintiff only if it actually refers to plaintiff, Brill v. Minnesota Mines, 200 Minn. 454, 274 N.W. 631, 112 A.L.R. 173 (1937), or if it is reasonably understood given the facts and circumstances of publication, to refer to plaintiff, even if it does not name plaintiff, Dressel v. Shipman, 57 Minn. 23, 58 N.W. 684 (1894). The statement must be identifiably about the plaintiff and not generally about things connected with the plaintiff. Geraci v. Eckankar, 526 N.W.2d 391, 397 (Minn. Ct. App. 1995) (supervisor's comments to job applicant about departing employee not identifiably about the plaintiff, thus not defamatory); Huyen v. Driscoll, 479 N.W.2d 76, 79 (Minn. Ct. App. 1991) (comments criticizing public agency not defamatory of agency's director); see also Davis v. Walt Disney Co., No. Civ. 04-1729, 2004 WL 1895234, at *7 (D. Minn. Aug. 23, 2004) (fictitious movie with some similarities in character names as plaintiff not of and concerning plaintiff). Similarly, statements concerning a group or class cannot defame an individual member of that group or class unless the group is so small that the statements can reasonably be understood to refer specifically to the plaintiff, or unless the circumstances of publication reasonably support the conclusion that the statement refers to the plaintiff in particular. See Schuster v. U. S. News & World Report, Inc., 459 F. Supp. 973, 4 Media L. Rep. (BNA) 1911 (D. Minn. 1978), aff'd, 602 F.2d 850 (8th Cir. 1979).

6. ***Publication***. A statement "must be communicated to someone other than the plaintiff" to be defamatory. Stuempges v. Parke, Davis & Co., 297 N.W.2d 252, 255 (Minn. 1980); see also Griffin v. Pinkerton's, Inc., 173 F.3d 661, 665 (8th Cir. 1999). A defamatory communication may be a simple oral assertion. Bohdan v. Alltool Mfg., Co., 411 N.W.2d 902, 907 (Minn. Ct. App. 1987). A defamation claim cannot be based solely on an action, such as escorting an employee off the premises, rather than upon a statement. Bolton v. Dept. of Human Servs., 540 N.W.2d 523 (Minn. 1995) ("Minnesota has never recognized defamation by conduct alone."). An employee's defamation claim may not survive summary judgment when the only evidence of the alleged defamatory statement is inadmissible hearsay. Bersch v. Rgnonti & Assocs., 584 N.W.2d 783 (Minn. Ct. App. 1998); see also Anderson v. Indep. Sch. Dist., 357 F.3d 806, 809–10 (8th Cir. 2004) (applying Minnesota law) (testimony by person who "overheard" allegedly defamatory statement but could not conclusively identify the speaker fails to establish publication by the defendant). In the employment context, courts will look to see whether an employer had reasonable grounds to make a defamatory statement; whether an investigation to determine truthfulness was conducted is a factor used to determine reasonableness. Brown v. Westaff (USA), Inc., 301 F. Supp. 2d 1011, 1021 (D. Minn. 2004) (finding privileged occasion and absence of malice as a matter of law).

a. **Intracorporate Communication.** A statement published only within a corporation is sufficient for maintaining a defamation action. Wirig v. Kinney Shoe Corp., 461 N.W.2d 374 (Minn. 1990) (theft allegations at meeting of managerial and non-managerial employees); Frankson v. Design Space Int'l, 394 N.W.2d 140, 143 (Minn. 1986); Karnes v. Milo Beauty & Barber Supply Co., 441 N.W.2d 565 (Minn. Ct. App. 1989); Harvet v. Unity Medical Center, Inc., 428 N.W.2d 574, 578 (Minn. Ct. App. 1988).

b. **Compelled Self-Publication.** Minnesota recognizes a narrow compelled self-publication doctrine to be rarely applied. Belde v. Ferguson Enters., 2005 U.S. Dist. LEXIS 18770, *16 (D. Minn. Aug. 31, 2005) (subjective feeling of compulsion was not enough to defeat motion for summary judgment); Lewis v. Equitable Life Assurance Soc., 389 N.W.2d 876 (Minn. 1986); Schackmann v. Cathedral High Sch., 2005 Minn. App. Unpub. LEXIS 240, *11 (Minn. Ct. App. Aug. 30, 2005) (acknowledging that on proper facts doctrine might extend beyond employment setting and apply to withdrawals from school); Keuchle v. Life's Companion P.C.A., Inc., 653 N.W.2d 214, 219–20 (Minn. Ct. App. 2002). Compelled self-publication occurs when the "defamed person was in some way compelled to communicate the defamatory statement to a third person" and it was "foreseeable to the defendant that the defamed person would be so compelled." Lewis, 389 N.W.2d at 886; see also Minnwest Bank Cent. v. Flagship Props. LLC, 689 N.W.2d 295, 301 (Minn. Ct. App. 2004). This can occur when an employer provides a defamatory reason to the employee for the employee's termination of employment. See, e.g., LeBaron v. Speedway SuperAmerica LLC, No. Civ. 05-1822, 2007 WL 107726 at *7–8 (D. Minn. Jan. 10, 2007). Employees should not have to lie to prospective employers regarding the reason their employment terminated. Lewis, 389 N.W.2d at 888; see also Keenan v. Computer Assocs. Int'l, 13 F.3d 1266 (8th Cir. 1994); Keuchle, 653 N.W.2d at 219–20 ("Because respondent believed that potential employers knew or would find out about the statement, she was compelled to self-publish so that she could defend her professional reputation."). The doctrine of compelled self-publication as it relates to separation from employment is limited to defamation actions and does not support a claim alleging violation of a due process or other liberty interest. Phillips v. State, 725 N.W. 2d 778, 785 (Minn. Ct. App. 2007). The burden is on plaintiff to show publication occurred and was compelled. Pope v. ESA Servs., 406 F.3d 1001, 1012 (8th Cir. 2005) (no compelled self-publication where employee made only vague references to a few job opportunities that were allegedly lost due to his forced publication of statement), **overruled on other grounds by Torgerson v. City of Rochester, 643 F.3d 1031 (8th Cir. 2011)**; Anderson v. Indep. Sch. Dist., 357 F.3d 806, 809–10 (8th Cir. 2004) (applying Minnesota law) (no compelled self-publication where employee received suspension letter and republished it to third parties to explain the injustice done to him); Franzwa v. City of Hackensack, 567 F. Supp. 2d 1097 (D. Minn. 2008) (suggesting the compelled self-publication doctrine is inapplicable where plaintiff felt he was forced to bring suit to address the allegedly false statements and thereby publish them; Smith v. DataCard Corp., 9 F. Supp. 2d 1067 (D. Minn. 1998) (no self-publication where plaintiff failed to provide evidence of job interviews, applications or rejection letters); Groeneweg v. Interstate Enters., 2005 Minn. App. LEXIS 405, *17 (Minn. Ct. App. Apr. 19, 2005) (no material issue of fact raised by plaintiff's speculation that she may be forced to self-publish statements in future); Lindgren v. Harmon Glass Co., 489 N.W.2d 804 (Minn. Ct. App. 1992) (no compelled self- defamation where plaintiff believed statement to be true). An employer may have statutory protection against this sort of claim, see III.A, infra. **In addition, an employer's communication to an employee of the reason for discharge may be qualifiedly privileged. See Sherman v. Rinchem Co., Inc., 687 F.3d 996, 1007-10 (8th Cir. 2012).**

c. **Republication.** One who merely delivers or transmits defamatory material previously published by another will be considered to have published the material only if he knew, or had reason to know, that the material was false and defamatory, Church of Scientology v. Minnesota State Medical Ass'n Foundation, 264 N.W.2d 152, 3 Media L. Rep. (BNA) 2177 (Minn. 1978), or if he espoused or concurred with the defamatory statement, Stock v. Heiner, 696 F. Supp. 1253 (D. Minn. 1988). In Longbehn v. City of Moose Lake, 2005 Minn. App. LEXIS 509 (Minn. Ct. App. May 17, 2005), the Court of Appeals affirmed summary judgment for a defendant who truthfully reported the fact that others in community referred to the plaintiff as "Pat the Pedophile;" the court did not address the truth of whether plaintiff was a pedophile (community comments were enough to affect the plaintiff's credibility as a police officer), and did not explicitly address the element of publication. Cf. Lewis v. St. Cloud State Univ., 693 N.W.2d 466, 471–72 (Minn. Ct. App. 2005) (state university cannot be held liable for defamatory material published in student-run newspaper where both state university's internal policies and First Amendment considerations precluded control over newspaper content).

7. ***Statements versus Conduct.*** Conduct alone may be insufficient to support a defamation claim against an employer. Bolton v. Dept. of Human Servs., 540 N.W.2d 523 (Minn. 1995) (act of merely escorting terminated employee off premises is insufficient). The Bolton court, however, found that "words and conduct may support each other's meanings in the defamatory context." Id. at 525–26; see also Svendsen v. State Bank of Duluth, 64 Minn. 40, 65 N.W. 1086 (1896) (conduct accompanied by written words sufficient for defamation action).

8. ***Damages.*** Except in cases of defamation per se, the plaintiff generally must be able to plead and prove specific actual damages (such as damage to his or her reputation or loss of standing in the community) to recover

damages in a defamation case. Lewis v. Equitable Life Assurance Soc., 389 N.W.2d 876, 886 (Minn. 1986); Stuempges v. Parke, Davis & Co., 297 N.W.2d 252, 255 (Minn. 1980); Jerdee v. Steve's Shoes, Inc., No. Civ. C2-46-208, 1996 WL 469495, 1996 Minn. App. LEXIS 990 (Minn. Ct. App. Aug. 20, 1996); Schoenhals v. Mains, 504 N.W.2d 233, 235–36 (Minn. Ct. App. 1993); McGrath v. TCF Bank Sav., FSB, 502 N.W.2d 801, 808 (Minn. Ct. App. 1993); Woodburn v. St. Paul Pathology, P.A., Nos. Civ. C7-93-125, Civ. C9-93-126, 1993 WL 267495, *5, 1993 Minn. App. LEXIS 732 (Minn. Ct. App. July 20, 1993); Grufman v. Jensen, Durfee & Assoc., No. Civ. C6-92-1272, 1993 WL 600, at *1, 1992 Minn. App. LEXIS 1298 (Minn. Ct. App. Jan. 5, 1993); Hunt v. Univ. of Minnesota, 465 N.W.2d 88, 93 (Minn. Ct. App. 1991). Actual damages (also called "special" damages) are recoverable only upon proof of actual injury supported by competent evidence. Jadwin v. Minneapolis Star & Tribune Co., 367 N.W.2d 476, 492, 11 Media L. Rep. (BNA) 1905 (Minn. 1985). A plaintiff may recover compensatory damages, including loss of earning capacity. Lewis v. Equitable Life Assurance Soc., 389 N.W.2d 876, 891 (Minn. 1986). A defamed person may also seek compensation for emotional distress as an element of damages, Bradley v. Hubbard Broad., 471 N.W.2d 670 (Minn. Ct. App. 1991), but emotional distress by itself is insufficient to meet the harm to reputation requirement, Richie v. Paramount Pictures Corp., 544 N.W.2d 21, 24 Media L. Rep. (BNA) 1897 (Minn. 1996) (media defendant). A plaintiff is not entitled to an award of attorneys' fees under the private attorney general statute because the outcome of the claim affects only the parties, not the public. Burtch v. Oakland Park, Inc., Nos. A05-1585, A05-1589, A05-1587, A05-1588, 2006 WL 1806196 (Minn. Ct. App. July 3, 2006).

a. **Presumed Damages and Libel Per Se**. Slander is actionable without proof of special damages only if it falls into one of the categories of defamation per se. See Longbehn v. Schoenrock, 727 N.W.2d 153, 162 (Minn. Ct. App. 2007) ("[I]n the absence of proof, general damages for defamation per se are limited to harm that 'would normally be assumed to flow from a defamatory publication of the nature involved.'" (quoting Restatements (Second) of Torts §621 cmt. a (1977)); Stuempges, 297 N.W.2d at 259. The following have been held to be defamatory per se: (1) statements accusing plaintiffs of committing a crime, see, e.g., Stokes v. CBS, 25 F. Supp. 2d 992, 999 (D. Minn. 1998) (murder); Hammersten v. Reiling, 262 Minn. 200, 115 N.W.2d 259 (1962) (accepting a bribe); Becker v. Alloy Hardfacing & Eng'g Co., 390 N.W.2d 374 (Minn. Ct. App. 1986) (stealing a car), aff'd in part, rev'd in part, 401 N.W.2d 655 (Minn. 1987); Karnes v. Milo Beauty & Barber Supply Co., 441 N.W.2d 565 (Minn. Ct. App. 1989) (implication that store manager was stealing or allowing stealing); (2) statements affecting plaintiffs in their business, trade or profession, see, e.g., Chambers v. Travelers Cos., Inc. 764 F. Supp. 2d 1071, 1083 (D. Minn. 2011)**, aff'd on other grounds, 668 F.3d 559 (8th Cir. 2012)**; Lewis v. Equitable Life Assurance Soc., 389 N.W.2d 876 (Minn. 1986) (discharged for "gross insubordination"); Nat'l Recruiters, Inc. v. Cashman, 323 N.W.2d 736 (Minn. 1982) ("nothing but a god damn loser"); Stuempges v. Parke, Davis & Co., 297 N.W.2d 252 (Minn. 1980) ("poor salesman who was not industrious, was hard to motivate and could not sell"); Kovatovich v. K-Mart Corp., 88 F. Supp. 2d 975 (D. Minn. 1999) (employee discharged for breaching duty of confidentiality); (3) statements imputing sexual misconduct, see Longbehn, 727 N.W.2d at 162 (recognizing the availability of general damages for defamation per se where plaintiff was referred to as "Pat the Pedophile"); Morey v. Barnes, 212 Minn. 153, 2 N.W.2d 829 (1942); (4) statements tending directly to affect a corporation's credit, property or business, see Advanced Training Sys. v. Caswell Equip. Co., 352 N.W.2d 1 (Minn. 1984); and (5) statements that tend to injure a corporation's credit, property, or business, Thomas & Betts Corp. v. Leger, 2004 Minn. App. LEXIS 1322, *26 (Minn. Ct. App. Nov. 24, 2004).

(1) **Employment-Related Criticism.** General disparagement does not qualify as defamation per se, but if the statement relates to the person "in his professional capacity and not merely as an individual without regard to his profession" it can be defamatory per se. Anderson v. Kammeier, 262 N.W.2d 366, 372 (Minn. 1977). Therefore, the employer was not entitled to summary judgment on defamation per se where the statements related to the way the employee conducted herself as an employee. O'Brien v. A.B.P. Midwest, Inc., 814 F. Supp. 766, 773–74 (D. Minn. 1992); Beek v. Nelson, 147 N.W. 668, 669 (Minn. 1914) (statement that plaintiff had "never done a decent or responsible thing for St. Paul" negatively affected plaintiff in his employment as a public works employee for the city). To constitute defamation per se, the words must be "particularly harmful" to the person in his/her business. Merely stating the individual "has been fired" does not constitute defamation per se because the fact does not necessarily injure or discredit the discharged employee. Jones v. Keith, No. Civ. 00-2741, 2002 WL 273141 (D. Minn. Feb. 25, 2002).

(2) **Single Instance Rule.** No reported cases.

b. **Punitive Damages.** In Minnesota, punitive damages generally are recoverable pursuant to Minn. Stat. § 549.20. Plaintiff must show by "clear and convincing evidence that the acts of the defendant show deliberate disregard [as defined in the statute] for the rights and safety of others." Minn. Stat. § 549.20(1)(a). The statute sets out eight factors which are to be considered in a claim for punitive damages. See Bradley v. Hubbard Broad., 471 N.W.2d 670 (Minn. Ct. App. 1991). Plaintiffs may not include a plea for punitive damages in their complaint; rather a plaintiff must move to amend, alleging the legal basis for the punitive damages claim and supporting it with "affidavits showing the factual basis for the claim." Minn. Stat. § 549.191; see also Hern v. Bankers Life Cas. Co., 133 F. Supp. 2d 1130, 1135 (D. Minn. 2001) (stating that "[u]nder Section 549.191, a plaintiff who seeks to assert a punitive damage claim must first obtain leave of the

Court to do so, based upon a prima facie showing of entitlement."). The statute now provides for bifurcation of the compensatory and punitive phases of the trial on the request of either party. Minnesota does not require a private plaintiff suing a nonmedia defendant as to a matter not of public concern to prove actual malice as a condition to recovering punitive damages. See Becker v. Alloy Hardfacing & Engineering Co., 390 N.W.2d 374 (Minn. Ct. App. 1986) aff'd in part, rev'd in part, 401 N.W.2d 655 (Minn. 1987) (relying on Minn. Stat. § 549.20(l)); see also Ulrich v. City of Crosby, 848 F. Supp. 861 (D. Minn. 1994); Hammond v. Northland Counseling Center, Inc., No. Civ. 05-96-3553, 1998 WL 315333 (D. Minn. Feb. 27, 1998). In cases of defamation per se, punitive damages are recoverable without proof of actual damages. Nat'l Recruiters, Inc. v. Cashman, 323 N.W.2d 736 (Minn. 1982); Stuempges v. Parke, Davis & Co., 297 N.W.2d 252, 259 (Minn. 1980); Northfield Nat'l Bank v. Associated Milk Producers, 390 N.W.2d 289, 298 (Minn. Ct. App. 1986).

II. PRIVILEGES AND DEFENSES

A. Scope of Privileges

1. ***Absolute Privilege.*** Defamatory statements may be protected by absolute privilege if the statement is (1) made by a judge, judicial officer, attorney or witness; (2) made at a judicial or quasi-judicial proceeding; and (3) the statement at issue is relevant to the subject matter of the litigation. Mahoney & Hagberg v. Newgard, 729 N.W.2d 302, 306 (Minn. 2007). Disclosure of personnel data pursuant to the Minnesota Government Data Practices Act is also absolutely privileged from actions for defamation. Doku v. Hennepin Health Care Sys., No. Civ. 09-353, 2009 U.S. Dist. LEXIS 47894, *8–9 (D. Minn. June 4, 2009) (citing Fieno v. State, 567 N.W.2d 739, 741 (Minn. Ct. App. 1997)).

An absolute privilege shields even intentionally false and malicious statements. Zutz v. Nelson, 788 N.W.2d 58, 62 (Minn. 2010); Matthis v. Kennedy, 243 Minn. 219, 223, 67 N.W.2d 413, 416 (1954); LeBaron v. Minnesota Bd. of Pub. Defense, 499 N.W.2d 39 (Minn. Ct. App. 1993). Statements made in the course of judicial, quasi-judicial, legislative or official proceedings are absolutely privileged provided that the statements have some relation to the judicial proceedings. See, e.g., Mahoney & Hagberg v. Newgard, 729 N.W.2d 302, 306 (Minn. 2007) (statements made in affidavit); Jenson v. Olson, 273 Minn. 390, 141 N.W.2d 488 (1965) (statements made in civil service hearing); Carradine v. State, 511 N.W.2d 733 (Minn. 1994) (statements made in an arrest report); Matthis v. Kennedy, 243 Minn. 219, 67 N.W.2d 413 (1954) (probate court proceeding); Peterson v. Steenerson, 113 Minn. 87, 129 N.W. 147 (1910) (legislative proceedings); Cole v. Star Tribune, 581 N.W.2d 364, 371 (Minn. Ct. App. 1998) (correspondence or statement to Board of Pardons "possibly pertinent" to proceedings); Kittler v. Eckberg, Lammers, Briggs, Wolff & Vierling, 535 N.W.2d 653 (Minn. Ct. App. 1995) (attorney solicitation letter); Dorn v. Peterson, 512 N.W.2d 902 (Minn. Ct. App. 1994) (presentation of the employer's position in an unemployment compensation proceeding, including internal corporate communications in preparation for the proceeding); LeBaron v. Minnesota Bd. of Pub. Defense, 499 N.W.2d 39 (Minn. Ct. App. 1993) (district public defender was under statutory obligation to report to State Public Defender reasons for terminating assistant public defender); McIntire v. State, 458 N.W.2d 714 (Minn. Ct. App. 1990) (communication among state agencies about reason for employee's discharge); Freier v. Indep. Sch. Dist., 356 N.W.2d 724 (Minn. Ct. App. 1984) (statements made in statutorily required public school board's hearing and in statutorily required written decision and order to discharge teacher); see also Willis v. Centennial Mortgage & Funding, Inc., No. Civ. 03-3641, 2004 WL 229076, at *7 (D. Minn. Feb. 2, 2004) (statements in connection with Department of Commerce proceeding); Pinto v. Internationale Set, Inc., 650 F. Supp. 306 (D. Minn. 1986) (attorney's demand letter); Taylor v. West Pub. Co., 548 F. Supp. 61 (D. Minn. 1982) (verbatim publication of judicial opinion), aff'd, 693 F.2d 837 (8th Cir. 1982). **The Minnesota Court of Appeals held that a company's letter to shareholders discussing a former director's lawsuit against the company and explaining that the company had filed breach of fiduciary duty counterclaims was absolutely privileged under the judicial proceedings privilege. Phillippi v. Cedar Creek Gas Co., No. A11-573, 2011 WL5829344, at *5-7 (Minn. Ct. App. Nov. 21, 2011) (unpublished decision).**

The republication of absolutely privileged statements may not be protected, at least in situations where the absolutely privileged statement is not a matter of public record. Bol v. Cole, 561 N.W.2d 143, 149 (Minn. 1997) (no absolute privilege for psychologist who allegedly defamed third party in child abuse report made pursuant to the Health Records Act when those statements were released to the child patient's mother); McDevitt v. Tilson, 453 N.W.2d 53, 17 Media L. Rep. (BNA) 2156 (Minn. Ct. App. 1990) (no privilege where a statement, though arguably required by law to be published, could have properly been kept confidential by invocation of the attorney-client privilege or Minnesota Government Data Practices Act). A statement to the news media by a private attorney concerning an ongoing court action may not be absolutely privileged. Chafoulias v. Peterson, No. Civ. C2-01-1617, 2003 WL 23025097, at *3–4 (Minn. Ct. App. Dec. 30, 2003) (unpublished opinion).

Whether the allegedly defamatory statements were made before a judicial tribunal is a question of law. McIntire v. State, 458 N.W.2d 714 (Minn. Ct. App. 1990) (employer required by law to report reason for employee's discharge); Rutherford v. County of Kandiyohi, 449 N.W.2d 457 (Minn. Ct. App. 1989) (notice of termination of probation officer was public document under MGDPA); McGaa v. Glumack, 441 N.W.2d 823 (Minn. Ct. App. 1989) (material submitted by airports commission pursuant to request from governor); Grossman v. School Bd., 389 N.W.2d 532 (Minn. Ct. App. 1986) (statute required publication of school board proceedings); Freier v. Independent School Dist., 356 N.W.2d 724 (Minn. Ct. App. 1984) (statute required public hearing of school board and written decision and order to discharge teacher); see also Jenson, 141 N.W.2d at 488. The question of whether a statement relates to the subject matter of litigation before a judicial tribunal is also a question of law. Matthis v. Kennedy, 243 Minn. 219, 67 N.W.2d 413 (1954).

2. ***Qualified Privileges***. A common law qualified or conditional privilege protects statements made in good faith and without malice, based upon reasonable belief, upon a proper occasion, for a proper purpose, to proper parties, and to uphold a proper interest. Zutz v. Nelson, 788 N.W.2d 58 (Minn. 2010) (members of watershed district board were protected by a qualified privilege, rather than an absolute privilege, against defamation suits for statements made when performing a legislative function on behalf of the district); Landers v. AMTRAK, 345 F.3d 669, 672–73 (8th Cir. 2003) (applying Minnesota law; holding that employee performance ratings were subject to qualified privilege); Nelson v. Wachovia Securities, LLC, 646 F. Supp. 2d 1066, 1074 (D. Minn. 2009) (statements made by regional president and senior employee relations consultant in connection with an internal employment investigation regarding the employee's threatening and violent treatment of his branch manager were qualifiedly privileged since they reflected the reasonable good faith belief of the president and consultant); Guzhagin v. State Farm Mut. Auto. Ins. Co., 566 F. Supp. 2d 962 (D. Minn. 2008) (insurance company's statement to its insureds about why it had denied coverage enjoyed qualified privilege); Cardiac Pacemakers, Inc. v. Aspen II Holding Co., 413 F. Supp. 2d 1016 (D. Minn. 2006) (company's letter to customers explaining the purpose of its lawsuit enjoyed qualified privilege); Anderson v. U. S. Bancorp, No. Civ. 03-5234, 2006 WL 2130440 (D. Minn. July 28, 2006) (statement to employee explaining the reason for employee's termination was subject to qualified privilege); Whyte v. Am. Bd. of Physical Med. & Rehab., 2005 U.S. Dist. LEXIS 6481, *23–24 (D. Minn. 2005) (certifying board with professional duty to report physician misconduct enjoys qualified privilege); Thompson v. Olsten Kimberly Qualitycare, Inc., 33 F. Supp. 2d 806, 815 (D. Minn. 1999) (employer's report to State nursing board protected by privilege); Roberts v. Bd. of Trs of the Minn. State Colleges & Univers., Nos. A03-528, A03-1053, 2004 Minn. App. LEXIS 306 (Minn. Ct. App. April 6, 2004) (unpublished opinion) (response to student inquiry about reasons for a professor's suspension was a proper occasion); Cook v. Callaway, 2002 WL 31369152, at *3 (Minn. Ct. App. Oct. 22, 2002) (unpublished opinion) (statement by a city police officer and licensed inspector to a liquor license applicant regarding an employee's drug sales on the job were protected by qualified privilege and plaintiff did not defeat the privilege by showing malice); but see Bahr v. Boise Cascade Corp., 766 N.W.2d 910, 920–22 (Minn. 2009) (holding that evidence was sufficient to create jury question on issue of malice where defendant referred to plaintiff as a "lazy, fat f***er," complained about his work ethic in harassment complaint, stated he needed a "wake up call," and possibly made a statement knowing it was false); Krutchen v. Zayo Bandwidth Northeast, LLC, 591 F. Supp. 2d 1002, 1020 (D. Minn. 2008) (denying motion to dismiss; holding that employee had alleged sufficient facts to state a claim that employer published false facts with malice when he alleged that employer made the statements as part of its "manufacture of a pretextual reason" for employee's termination); Chafoulias v. Peterson, No. Civ. C2-01-1617, 2003 WL 23025097, at *3–4 (Minn. Ct. App. Dec. 30, 2003) (unpublished opinion) ("bald" accusations of wrongdoing made by an attorney to a TV reporter in response to comments by an opposing party not made upon a proper occasion); Keuchle v. Life's Companion P.C.A., Inc., 653 N.W.2d 214, 220 (Minn. Ct. App. 2002) (while investigatory statements are generally privileged, here the investigation was not thorough, the employer failed to interview the employee and ignored statement by supervisor directly involved in incident; "[b]ecause of the cursory nature of [the employer's] actions," the employer is not entitled to a privilege). Minnesota also has a statute protecting "speech or lawful conduct that is genuinely aimed at procuring favorable government action." Minn. Stat. § 554.01 *et. seq.* (commonly called the anti-SLAPP or Strategic Lawsuit Against Public Participation statute). In Freeman v. Swift, 776 N.W.2d 485, 488-92 (Minn. Ct. App. 2009), the Minnesota Court of Appeals held a defendant was not immune from liability for defamation under the anti-SLAPP statute because the statements in question were aimed at audiences not connected to the public issue and therefore not aimed at procuring favorable government action.

a. **Common Interest.** Minnesota recognizes a common interest privilege. Cohen v. Beachside Two-I Homeowners' Ass'n, No. Civ. 05-706, 2006 WL 1795140 (D. Minn. June 29, 2006) (qualified privilege protects communication from a homeowners' association to its members based upon their common interest in the financial status of the community). Although most Minnesota cases do not utilize the phraseology, "common interest," statements made about the character of employees or the reasons for discharge or discipline, made upon a proper occasion, for a proper purpose are qualifiedly privileged. **Chambers v. Travelers Cos., Inc., 668 F.3d 559, 564-65 (8th Cir. 2012)**; Stuempges v. Parke, Davis & Co., 297 N.W.2d 252 (Minn. 1980); Frankson v. Design Space Int'l, 394 N.W.2d 140 (Minn. 1986); McBride v. Sears, Roebuck & Co., 306 Minn. 93, 235 N.W.2d 371 (1975); Mangan v. Cline, 411 N.W.2d 9 (Minn. Ct. App. 1987); Harvet v. Unity Med. Ctr., Inc., 428 N.W.2d 574 (Minn. Ct. App. 1988); Kletschka v. Abbott-Nw. Hosp., Inc., 417 N.W.2d 752 (Minn. Ct. App. 1988); Lee v. Metropolitan Airport Comm'n, 428 N.W.2d 815 (Minn. Ct. App. 1988); Karnes v. Milo Beauty & Barber Supply Co., 441 N.W.2d 565 (Minn. Ct. App. 1989); Clough v. Ertz, 442 N.W.2d 798 (Minn. Ct. App.

1989); Gunnufson v. Onan Corp., 450 N.W.2d 179 (Minn. Ct. App. 1990); Graham v. Special School Dist. No. 1, 462 N.W.2d 78 (Minn. Ct. App. 1990) aff'd in part, rev'd in part, 472 N.W.2d 114 (Minn. 1991); McIntire v. State, 458 N.W.2d 714 (Minn. Ct. App. 1990); Hunt v. Univ. of Minnesota, 465 N.W.2d 88, 65 Ed. Law Rep. 525 (Minn. Ct. App. 1991) (privilege recognized even though comments were made by a peer rather than a supervisor); Wilson v. Weight Watchers of Upper Midwest, Inc., 474 N.W.2d 380 (Minn. Ct. App. 1991) (comments regarding employee's possible alcohol problem); Eldeeb v. University of Minn., 864 F. Supp. 905 (D. Minn. 1994) (recommendation of nonpromotion) , aff'd, 60 F.3d 423 (8th Cir. 1995); Thompson v. Campbell, 845 F. Supp. 665, 69 Fair Empl. Prac. Cas. (BNA) 727 (D. Minn. 1994) (explanation to employees of reason for fellow employee's discharge); Ewald v. Wal-Mart Stores, 139 F.3d 619 (8th Cir. 1998) (same); Conerly v. CVN Cos., 785 F. Supp. 801 (D. Minn. 1992), aff'd 34 F.3d 1070 (8th Cir. 1994); Pfluger v. Southview Chevrolet Co., 967 F.2d 1218, 1219 (8th Cir. 1992) (terminated employee told he was a "thief, liar, defrauder and cheat"); Rudebeck v. Paulson, 612 N.W.2d 450 (Minn. Ct. App. 2000) (statements made in the course of sexual harassment investigation); McClure v. Am. Family Mutual Ins. Co., 223 F.3d 845, 853 (8th Cir. 2000) (terminated employees engaged in "disloyal and disruptive activity" and "conduct unacceptable by any business standard"); Somers v. City of Minneapolis, 245 F.3d 782, 788 (8th Cir. 2001) (statements in a civil service hearing notice and subsequent termination decision); Dynamic Air, Inc. v. Boccard S.A., No. Civ. 01-2148, 2003 WL 22097789, at *4–5 (D. Minn. Sept. 4, 2003) (email statement made in connection with requested technical assistance were protected by a qualified privilege as the statements were made "upon a proper occasion" and with a "proper motive"); but see Wirig v. Kinney Shoe Corp., 461 N.W.2d 374 (Minn. 1990) (no qualified privilege where defamatory statements made without reasonable or probable grounds); Kovatovich v. K-Mart Corp., 88 F. Supp. 2d 975 (D. Minn. 1999) (no qualified privilege where defamatory statements made relying entirely upon hearsay without verification); Brown v. Westaff (USA), Inc., 301 F. Supp. 2d 1011, 1020–21 (D. Minn. 2004) (defendant entitled to qualified privilege where statements were based on information supervisor had available even though he "could have conducted a more thorough investigation").

b. **Duty.** See II.A.1, supra. In addition, statements made in the public interest may be qualifiedly privileged. See P.G. v. Ramsey County, 141 F. Supp. 2d 1220, 1227 (D. Minn. 2001) (providing that statements in a psychologist's letter recommending supervised visitation in a parental rights termination proceeding were privileged, and stating that the public has a strong public interest in encouraging a psychologist to accurately assess patients); Bol v. Cole, 561 N.W.2d 143, 150 (Minn. 1997) ("strong public interest in reporting child abuse and protecting children from further abuse" gave psychologist a qualified privilege when disclosing information to parent of child patient).

c. **Criticism of Public Employee.** Statements commenting on the conduct of public officials may be qualifiedly privileged. Diesen v. Hessburg, 455 N.W.2d 446, 17 Media L. Rep. (BNA) 1849 (Minn. 1990); Friedell v. Blakely Printing Co., 163 Minn. 226, 203 N.W. 974 (1925). Not all public employees are public officials. LeDoux v. Nw. Publ'g, 521 N.W.2d 59 (Minn. Ct. App. 1994).

d. **Limitation on Qualified Privileges.** A qualified privilege is defeated by a showing that the defendant acted with ill will and improper motives, or causelessly and wantonly for the purpose of injuring the plaintiff. Bauer v. State, 511 N.W. 2d 447 (Minn. 1994).

(1) **Constitutional or Actual Malice.** Minnesota distinguishes between the malice required for overcoming a qualified privilege, referred to as "common law malice," and the constitutional standard set forth by the U.S. Supreme Court. While constitutional malice focuses on "the defendant's attitude toward the truth of what he has said," common law malice focuses on the defendant's "attitude toward the plaintiff." Stuempges v. Parke, Davis & Co., 297 N.W.2d 252, 258 (Minn. 1980); see also Chambers v. Travelers Cos., Inc. 764 F. Supp. 2d 1071, 1083 (D. Minn. 2011).

(2) **Common Law Malice.** Common law malice may be shown by evidence of personal ill feeling, exaggerated language, or excessive publication. Watson v. Ceridian Corp., No. A03-853, 2003 Minn. App. LEXIS 1537, at *23–24 (Minn. Ct. App. Dec. 30, 2003) (mere speculation about ill will is insufficient to survive summary judgment); Mercure v. West Publ'g Corp., No. A03-823, 2003 WL 23024519, at *5 (Minn. Ct. App. Dec. 30, 2003) (evidence that supervisor yelled at plaintiff on one occasion is insufficient to prove statements were made with ill will); Dorn v. Peterson, 512 N.W.2d 902 (Minn. Ct. App. 1994) (subjective assessment that defendant did not like plaintiffs is insufficient to establish common law malice). **Although abuse of the privilege is a jury issue, "pointing merely to instances in which [a defendant] might have better conducted the investigation does not provide a basis for a reasonable jury to [find actual malice]." Chambers v. Travelers Cos., Inc., 668 F.3d 559, 565 (8th Cir. 2012). The United States District Court for the District of Minnesota determined that a supervisor's "somewhat exaggerated" report to the police that the plaintiff stole scrap items from inside the company was not necessarily protected by a qualified privilege because the supervisor may have acted out of actual malice, and therefore denied summary judgment. Walker v. Wanner Eng'g, Inc., No. 11-671, ____ F.Supp. 2d ____, 2012 WL 2126037, *4 (D. Minn. June 12, 2012).**

e. **Question of Fact or Law.** The question of whether a privilege exists is a question of law. Lewis v. Equitable Life Assurance Soc., 389 N.W.2d 876, 889 (Minn. 1986). However, in determining whether an employer is protected by a qualified privilege, the issue of whether the employer had reasonable or probable cause to make the allegedly defamatory statement becomes a question of fact if the evidence permits more than one conclusion. Palmisano v. Allina Health Sys., 190 F.3d 881 (8th Cir. 1999). The existence of common law malice is usually a question of fact. Whyte v. Am. Bd. of Physical Med. & Rehab., 2005 U.S. Dist. LEXIS 6481, *24 (D. Minn. Apr. 4, 2005) (summary judgment granted where record devoid of evidence of ill will or improper motive); Stuempges v. Parke, Davis & Co., 297 N.W.2d 252, 257, 24 A.L.R.4th 132 (Minn. 1980); but see Ewald v. Wal-Mart Stores, 139 F.3d 619 (8th Cir. 1998) (affirming summary judgment for employer whose statements to store managers were based on reasonable belief that employee was involved in theft). The question of whether the privilege was abused is a jury question. Dunn v. Nat'l Bev. Corp., 729 N.W.2d 637 (Minn. Ct. App. June 19, 2007) citing Lewis v. Equitable Life Assurance Soc., 389 N.W.2d 876, 890 (Minn. 1986).

f. **Burden of Proof.** The defendant bears the burden of establishing the existence of a privilege. Stuempges v. Parke, Davis & Co., 297 N.W.2d 252, 257, 24 A.L.R.4th 132 (Minn. 1980). Once the employer has established a qualified privilege, the burden shifts to the employee to prove common law malice. Keenan v. Computer Assocs. Int'l, 13 F.3d 1266, 1270 (8th Cir. 1994).

B. Standard Libel Defenses

1. ***Truth.*** Truth is a complete defense to a claim of defamation. Graning v. Sherburne County, 172 F.3d 611 (8th Cir. 1999); Stuempges v. Parke, Davis & Co., 297 N.W.2d 252, 255 (Minn. 1980); Gillson v. State, Dep't of Natural Resources, 492 N.W.2d 835 (Minn. 1992); Jones v. Minneapolis Public Schools, 2003 WL 1962062, at *5–6 (Minn. Ct. App. Apr. 29, 2003). (Actually, it is no longer accurate to refer to truth as a "defense." All defamation plaintiffs in Minnesota bear the burden of providing falsity, see I.B.3, supra). If a statement is true in substance, inaccuracies of expression or detail are immaterial. Oaks Gallery & Country Store-Winona, Inc. v. Lee Enters., 613 N.W.2d 800, 803–04 (Minn. Ct. App.); Jadwin v. Minneapolis Star & Tribune Co., 390 N.W.2d 437, 13 Media L. Rep. (BNA) 1126 (Minn. Ct. App. 1986). Minor inaccuracies in an allegedly defamatory statement will not satisfy plaintiffs' burden of proving falsity. Benson v. Nw. Airlines, 561 N.W.2d 530 (Minn. Ct. App. 1997). In nonconstitutional cases, truth is a defense only when the underlying implication of the statement is true, and not merely when the statement is "verbally accurate." See Whyte v. Am. Bd. of Physical Med. & Rehab., 2005 U.S. Dist. LEXIS 6481, *20–21 (D. Minn. Apr. 4, 2005) (Minnesota law recognizes a defamation claim based on innuendo); Phipps v. Clark Oil & Refining Corp., 408 N.W.2d 569 (Minn. 1987). Statement that employee was being investigated is not defamatory because it was true. Roberts v. Bd. of Trs of the Minn. State Colleges & Univers., No. A03-528, A03-1053, 2004 Minn. App. LEXIS 306 (Minn. Ct. App. Apr. 6, 2004) (unpublished opinion); but see Pope v. ESA Servs., 406 F.3d 1001, 1011 (8th Cir. 2005) (statement that "we believe you took money," even though plaintiff admitted he took money to pay expenses, not necessarily true as a matter of law because the underlying statement may imply the plaintiff committed theft), **overruled on other grounds by Torgerson v. City of Rochester, 643 F.3d 1031 (8th Cir. 2011).**

2. ***Opinion.*** After Milkovich v. Lorain Journal Co., 497 U.S. 1 (1990), the Minnesota Court of Appeals has stated that defamation claims by a private plaintiff concerning private issues should be analyzed under state common law principles which do not distinguish between fact and opinion. Bradley v. Hubbard Broad., 471 N.W.2d 670, 674, (Minn. Ct. App. 1991); Weissman v. Sri Lanka Curry House, Inc., 469 N.W.2d 471 (Minn. Ct. App. 1991). Even so, Minnesota courts continue to recognize the four-factor test used prior to Milkovich in determining which statements are actionable as defamatory statements of fact. See Marchant Inv. & Mgmt. Co., Inc. v. St. Anthony W. Neighborhood Org., 694 N.W.2d 92, 96 (Minn. Ct. App. 2005) (noting that pre-Milkovich test "remains instructive" and expressly citing and following post-Milkovich factors distilled from various federal court cases, including broad context, use of figurative or hyperbolic language and reasonable expectations of audience); Geraci v. Eckankar, 526 N.W.2d 391, 397 (Minn. Ct. App. 1995). In addition, statements which cannot be reasonably interpreted as stating facts are not actionable as a matter of law. McGrath v. TCF Bank Sav., FSB, 502 N.W.2d 801, 808 (Minn. Ct. App. 1993), modified on other grounds, 509 N.W.2d 365 (Minn. 1993); **Chambers v. Travelers Cos., Inc., 668 F.3d 559, 565 (8th Cir. 2012) (statement to employee that she was being terminated for "continuing issues" cannot support a defamation claim because it is "insufficiently precise and cannot be proven false");** Pearson v. City of Big Lake, 689 F. Supp. 2d 1163, 1190-91 (D. Minn. 2010) (police chief's comments that sergeant had "personality conflicts" and that all of his problems had to do with two sergeants were not actionable because none of his alleged statements were verifiably untrue); see also Stolarczyk v. Spherion Corp., No. 08-CV-4678, 2009 U.S. Dist. LEXIS 19641 (D. Minn. Mar. 11, 2009) (statement classifying as a "weapon" an eleven-inch knife employee kept in her desk for purported purpose of cutting her lunch was not actionable); Benfield, Inc. v. Moline, No. Civ. 04-3513, 2006 WL 452903 (D. Minn. Feb. 22, 2006) (statements questioning an employee's integrity and referring to employee in stating "I don't deal with terrorists," were not actionable); Thompson v. Campbell, 845 F. Supp. 665, 686 (D. Minn. 1994) ("complainer" and "troublemaker" not actionable); Bebo v. Delander, 632 N.W.2d 732, 739 (Minn. Ct. App.

2001) ("a--hole," "c---sucker" and plaintiff was going to "f--- [others] over" not actionable); Lund v. Chicago & Northwestern Transp. Co., 467 N.W.2d 366 (Minn. Ct. App. 1991) ("brownnose," "shitheads," and "favoritism" not actionable); **Gacek v. Owens & Minor Distribution, Inc., 666 F.3d 1142, 1147-48 (8th Cir. 2012) (defendant's statement that plaintiff caused a co-worker's suicide is not actionable because it was speculation and not an expression of objectively verifiable facts);** but see Weissman v. Sri Lanka Curry House, Inc., 469 N.W.2d 471, 6 IER Cases 713 (Minn. Ct. App. 1991) ("dishonest" is actionable).

3. ***Consent.*** Statements made with plaintiff's consent are not actionable. See, e.g., Utecht v. Shopko Dep't Store, 324 N.W.2d 652 (Minn. 1982) (customer who asked store to block use of his lost charge card barred from seeking damages for injuries resulting from publicly posted signs admonishing clerks not to accept his charge card); Anderson v. Kammeier, 262 N.W.2d 366, 372 n.4 (Minn. 1977). When a union employee grieves a termination and the allegedly defamatory statements are repeated in a union hearing, consent is inferred. Otto v. Charles T. Miller Hospital, 262 Minn. 408, 115 N.W.2d 36 (Minn. 1962).

4. ***Mitigation.*** No reported cases.

III. RECURRING FACT PATTERNS

A. Statements in Personnel File

Minnesota Statute § 181.962 protects against defamation actions by employees pursuant to a review of their personnel records. The statute defines a "personnel record," provides certain exclusions, and outlines the procedure for review and the legal remedies for violations. The statute states that if an employee disputes specific information in the employee's personnel file, (1) the employer may agree to remove or revise the disputed information; or (2) the employee may submit a written statement explaining the employee's position, which should be included in the personnel record. Once an employee has exercised the right to review and been given the opportunity to challenge the contents of the personnel record, defamation actions based on the contents of the record or their communication are barred, whether the contents were communicated by the employer or by the employee, unless the employer has refused to comply with the provisions for revising the record or has communicated the contents of the record without including the employee's statement challenging the accuracy of the record. Minn. Stat. § 181.962, subd. 2.

B. Performance Evaluations

Employment performance evaluations are a proper occasion to allow a qualified privilege. See, e.g., Ulrich v. City of Crosby, 848 F. Supp. 861, 870–71 (D. Minn. 1994); Clough v. Ertz, 442 N.W.2d 798, 804 (Minn. Ct. App. 1989); Kletschka v. Abbott-Northwestern Hospital, Inc., 417 N.W.2d 752, 755, 51 Fair Empl. Prac. Cas. (BNA) 1094 (Minn. Ct. App. 1988); see also Fieno v. State, 567 N.W.2d 739 (Minn. Ct. App. 1997) (absolute privilege for reprimand and performance evaluation in public employee's personnel file). But see Landers v. AMTRAK, No. Civ. 00-2233, 2001 WL 1690061 (D. Minn. Dec. 28, 2001) (privilege may have been lost by showing of actual malice based on contradictions between supervisor and other witness testimony regarding performance evaluation; also holding that numeric performance ratings were not mere opinion but were factually based), aff'd on other grounds, 345 F.3d 669 (8th Cir. 2003).

C. References

Minn. Stat. § 181.967 provides employers with a qualified statutory privilege for giving job references. The statute provides that "no action may be maintained against an employer by an employee or former employee" for the disclosure of information pursuant to the statute unless the employee or former employee demonstrates by clear and convincing evidence that (1) the information was false and defamatory and (2) the employer "knew or should have known the information was false and acted with malicious intent to injure the employee or former employee." The privilege applies if a private employer discloses the following information without written authorization of the employee: dates of employment, compensation and wage history, job description and duties, employer-provided training and education, and "acts of violence, theft, harassment, or illegal conduct documented in the personnel record that resulted in disciplinary action or resignation and the employee's written response, if any, contained in the employee's personnel record." With respect to the latter information, the disclosure must be in writing and a copy must be sent contemporaneously by regular mail to the employee's last known address. With written authorization of the current or former employee, the privilege also applies if the employer discloses, in writing (with a copy to the employee or former employee), the following: written employee evaluations conducted before the employee's separation and the employee's written response, if any; written disciplinary actions in the five years before the authorization, and the employee's written response, if any, and written reasons for separation. The law expressly states it does not affect the availability of common law limitations on liability. It also does not apply to actions involving alleged violations of the Minnesota Human Rights Act or other statutes, and does not diminish rights under a collective bargaining agreement. The statute addresses public employers separately.

Before the passage of Minn. Stat. § 181.967 in 2004, courts held that employee references may be qualifiedly privileged. See, e.g., Eldeeb v. University of Minn., 864 F. Supp. 905, 913 (D. Minn. 1994), aff'd, 60 F.3d 423 (8th Cir. 1995); Stuempges v. Parke, Davis & Co., 297 N.W.2d 252, 257, 24 A.L.R.4th 132 (Minn. 1980).

D. Intracorporate Communication

Intracorporate communications may be qualifiedly privileged. See II.A.2.a, supra.

E. Statements to Government Regulators

Statutorily required statements may be absolutely privileged. See II.A.1, supra.

F. Reports to Auditors and Insurers

No reported cases.

G. Vicarious Liability of Employers for Statements Made by Employees

1. ***Scope of Employment.*** Employers may be held liable for their employees' defamatory statements to another employee only if the defamation occurred in the scope of the employee's duties, even if the defamation occurred on the employer's premises while the employee was working. O'Brien v. A.B.P. Midwest, Inc., 814 F. Supp. 766, 772, 127 Lab. Cas. (CCH) P57666 (D. Minn. 1992); Oslin v. State, 543 N.W.2d 408, 413–14 (Minn. Ct. App. 1996) (no defamation claim against employer for statements made by employees outside the scope of speakers' employment). An employee acts within the scope of his or her employment only when doing the actual tasks for which he or she has been employed, or those things that are "reasonably incidental" to that employment, and only when the conduct occurs "within work-related limits of time and place." See Carradine v. State, 494 N.W.2d 77 (Minn. Ct. App. 1992), aff'd in part, rev'd in part, remanded, 511 N.W.2d 733 (Minn. 1994); Marston v. Minneapolis Clinic of Psychiatry & Neurology, Ltd., 329 N.W.2d 306, 311 (Minn. 1982); Semrad v. Edina Realty, Inc., 470 N.W.2d 135, 143 (Minn. Ct. App. 1991), aff'd in part, rev'd in part, 493 N.W.2d 528 (Minn. 1992). The employer can escape liability by quickly taking remedial action to limit the agent's "authority" for and avoid ratification of the defamatory statement. See Semrad, 470 N.W.2d at 144–45.

a. **Blogging.** No reported cases.

2. ***Damages.*** No reported cases.

H. Internal Investigations

Statements made during the course of an employer's internal investigation or based on information learned during such an internal investigation may be qualifiedly privileged. See Palmisano v. Allina Health Sys., 190 F.3d 881, 886 (8th Cir. 1999) (recognizing that employer was entitled to a qualified privilege where employer conducted a thorough investigation and then made statements to the press that were supported by the results of that investigation); see also II.A.2.a, supra. Generally, management statements to other employees made in the course of investigating or punishing an employee or about reasons for an employee's termination of employment are qualifiedly privileged. See Ewald v. Wal-Mart Stores, 139 F.3d 619, 623 (8th Cir. 1998); McBride v. Sears, Roebuck & Co., 235 N.W.2d 371, 374 (Minn. 1975); Thompson v. Campbell, 845 F. Supp. 665, 680-81 (D. Minn. 1994). In order to be privileged, however, any statements must be made in good faith. See, e.g., Wirig v. Kinney Shoe Corp., 461 N.W.2d 374, 380 (Minn. 1990) (finding no qualified privilege where accused employee was not questioned and no investigation was conducted); Keuchle v. Life's Companion P.C.A., Inc., 653 N.W.2d 214, 220 (Minn. Ct. App. 2002) (finding no privilege where employer failed to conduct a thorough investigation, failed to interview the plaintiff, and ignored information learned during the investigation); Cox v. Crown CoCo, 544 N.W.2d 490, 498 (Minn. Ct. App. 1996) (concluding there were no reasonable or probable grounds for the defamatory statements because the employer did not investigate her suspicions or confront the employee with her accusations before she made the defamatory statements).

IV. OTHER ACTIONS BASED ON STATEMENTS

Minnesota recognizes numerous tort exceptions to employment at will, including the following.

A. Negligent Hiring, Retention, and Supervision

Minnesota has adopted separate torts for negligent hiring, negligent retention, and negligent supervision of employees. Liability may be imposed on an employer for its own negligence when it places a person with known propensities which should have been discovered through reasonable inquiry into a position in which, because of the circumstances of employment, it should have been foreseeable that the individual posed a threat of injury to others. Ponticas v. K.M.S. Invs.,

331 N.W.2d 907 (Minn. 1983); Hines v. Aandahl Constr. Co., LLC, No. A05-1634, 2006 WL 2598031 (Minn. Ct. App. Sept. 12, 2006) (employer was liable under theory of negligent hiring for failing to conduct a background check or drug test on employee housepainter where employer was aware of employee's history of chemical dependency and criminal activity). An employer may be liable under a negligent retention theory if it breaches its duty to refrain from retaining employees with known dangerous proclivities. Yunker v. Honeywell, Inc., 496 N.W.2d 419, 423 (Minn. Ct. App. 1993). Unlike in their decisions on negligent hiring and retention claims, the Minnesota courts have held that the tort of negligent supervision addresses only conduct of employees "while on the employer's premises or while using the employer's chattels." Semrad v. Edina Realty, Inc., 493 N.W.2d 528, 534 (Minn. 1992). These torts may be limited to circumstances involving a threat of physical injury or actual physical injury. Agcountry Farm Credit Servs., FLCA v. Oelke, No. A04-2096, 2005 WL 1950153 (Minn. Ct. App. Aug. 16, 2005) (refusing to recognize a negligent supervision cause of action without a showing of physical harm); Benson v. Nw. Airlines, 561 N.W.2d 530, 540 (Minn. Ct. App. 1997) (negligent hiring and retention); Bruchas v. Preventive Care, Inc., 553 N.W.2d 440, 442–43 (Minn. Ct. App. 1996) (negligent retention and supervision). Courts lack jurisdiction over negligent hiring claims brought against a church based on a pastor's alleged behavior because evaluation of such claims would require a court to examine the church's doctrine governing who is qualified to be a pastor, thereby making such claims precluded by the Establishment Clause of the First Amendment. J.M. v. Minn. Dist. Council of the Assemblies of God, 658 N.W.2d 589, 594–95 (Minn. Ct. App. 2003). Courts do not lack jurisdiction over negligent retention or negligent supervision claims brought against a church based on a pastor's alleged behavior because evaluation of such claims can be accomplished using neutral standards and without regard to religious doctrines. Id. at 597 (negligent retention); Odenthal v. Minn. Conf. of Seventh-Day Adventists, 657 N.W.2d 569, 574–76 (Minn. Ct. App. 2003) (negligent retention and negligent supervision). The Minnesota Human Rights Act preempts a negligent hiring, retention or supervision claim when the factual basis and injuries supporting that claim also would establish a violation of the MHRA and the obligations the defendant owes the plaintiff, as a practical matter, are the same under the claim and the MHRA. Springer v. McLane Co., Inc., 692 F. Supp. 2d 1050, 1059 (D. Minn. 2010).

B. Intentional Infliction of Emotional Distress

Minnesota recognizes the tort of intentional infliction of emotional distress in egregious cases. The plaintiff must show: (1) he or she was subjected to extreme and outrageous conduct; (2) the conduct was intentional or reckless; (3) the conduct caused emotional distress; and (4) the emotional distress was severe. Hubbard v. United Press Int'l, Inc., 330 N.W.2d 428, 439 (Minn. 1983). The conduct must be "so atrocious that it passes the boundaries of decency and is utterly intolerable to the civilized community." Id. (citing Haagenson v. National Farmers Union Property & Casualty Co., 277 N.W.2d 648, 652 (Minn. 1979) (citing Restatement Second Torts § 46)); see also Hill v. Scott, 349 F.3d 1068, 1075 (8th Cir. 2003) (allegation that police said "f__ you" and made a racist slur to plaintiff in the course of an arrest is insufficient to constitute extreme and outrageous conduct); Onyiah v. St. Cloud State Univ., 655 F. Supp. 2d 948, 970-71 (D. Minn. 2009) (plaintiff professor's portrayal of an "unfriendly and contentious work place" involving allegations that individual defendants encouraged students to harass the plaintiff in class and file false accusations against him with the university, among other allegations of harassment, did not rise to the egregious level of conduct required for an IIED claim); Langeslag v. KYMN, Inc., 664 N.W.2d 860, 866–70 (Minn. 2003) (the following do not meet the extreme and outrageous standard: allegedly filing false police reports on employer, threatening to sue employer, and directing vulgar language at employer; testimony by plaintiff regarding his emotional distress, coupled with ambiguous medical records, are insufficient to satisfy the extreme emotional distress requirement, absent medical testimony). Although rare, plaintiffs have been successful in recovering damages for intentional infliction of emotional distress in the employment context where the behavior of a boss was sufficiently egregious. See, e.g., Wenigar v. Johnson, 712 N.W.2d 190 (Minn. Ct. App. 2006) (affirming district court ruling finding sole proprietor liable for IIED where a developmentally disabled former employee was diagnosed with post-traumatic stress disorder as a result of abusive behavior by his sole proprietor boss).

C. Interference with Economic Advantage

At-will employees may pursue claims for tortious interference with contract in connection with their employment. Nordling v. N. State Power Co., 478 N.W.2d 498, 505, 7 IER Cases 10 (Minn. 1991). The elements of a claim for tortious interference with contract are: (1) the existence of a contractual employment relationship; (2) defendant's knowledge of the contract; (3) intentional procurement of breach of the contract; (4) lack of justification; and (5) damages caused by the breach. Kjesbo v. Ricks, 517 N.W.2d 585, 588 (Minn. 1994); see also Kallok v. Medtronic, Inc., 573 N.W.2d 356 (Minn. 1998) (non-compete agreement). A tortious interference claim cannot lie if the contract is not breached. Bebo v. Delander, 632 N.W.2d 732, 738 (Minn. Ct. App. 2001). A company officer, agent or employee is privileged to interfere with another's employment contract with the company "if the individual acts in good faith, whether competently or not, believing that his actions are in furtherance of the company's business." Dobesh v. CBS Broad., Inc., No. A03-978, 2004 WL 771725, at *6 (Minn. Ct. App. April 13, 2004) (quoting Nordling, 478 N.W.2d at 505); Guercio v. Prod. Automation Corp., 664 N.W.2d 379, 389–90 (Minn. Ct. App. 2003) (same).

In Minnesota, the special rules of defamation law may apply to a tortious interference with contract claim. *See, e.g.*, Beverly Hills Foodland v. United Food & Commercial Workers Union, Local 655, 39 F.3d 191 (8th Cir. 1994) (holding that plaintiff alleging tortious interference must satisfy the standard applicable to defamation claims where the tortious interference claim is based upon the same conduct or statements as a claim for defamation); Pearson v. City of Big Lake, 689 F. Supp. 2d 1163, 1191 (D. Minn. 2010) (holding that the plaintiff's tortious interference claim failed when it was based on a police chief's allegedly defamatory statements and was therefore duplicative of the plaintiff's defamation claim); St. Croix Printing Equip., Inc. v. Sexton, No. Civ. 06-4273, 2008 WL 3412090, *3 (D. Minn. Aug. 8, 2008) (casting doubt on whether a party can claim both tortious interference and defamation arising out of the same allegedly false statements); Johnson v. Columbia Broad. Sys., Inc., No. Civ. 3-95-624, slip op. at 3 (D. Minn. June 24, 1997) (holding that where plaintiff can sue in defamation he cannot avoid defamation standards by bringing tortious interference with contract claim); cf. Wild v. Rarig, 302 Minn. 419, 234 N.W.2d 775, 793 (Minn. 1975) (observing that "regardless of what the suit is labeled, the thing done to cause any damage to [the plaintiff] eventually stems from and grew out of the defamation"). **The truth of a statement may be a defense to a tortious interference with contract claim. Moore v. Hoff, No. A11-1923, N.W.2d, 2012 WL3553180, at *4 (Minn. Ct. App. Aug. 20, 2012).**

D. Prima Facie Tort

Minnesota has not accepted the doctrine of prima facie tort. See Price v. Viking Press, Inc., 625 F. Supp. 641, 651, 12 Media L. Rep. 1689 (D. Minn. 1985); Kjesbo v. Ricks, 517 N.W.2d 585, 588 (Minn. 1994).

V. OTHER ISSUES

A. Statute of Limitations

The statute of limitations for libel and slander is two years. Minn. Stat. § 541.07, subd. 1. The limitations period begins to run when the defamatory statement is published. Wild v. Rarig, 302 Minn. 419, 234 N.W.2d 775 (1975); see also Ericson v. Hallaway, No. A07-1047, 2008 Minn. App. Unpub. LEXIS 1010, *31-*34 (Minn. Ct. App. Aug. 26, 2008) (district court did not err in considering allegedly defamatory e-mails that were sent outside the statute of limitations period where the e-mails were part of a continuing violation and therefore not barred by the statute of limitations). Minnesota has adopted the "single publication rule." Church of Scientology v. Minnesota State Med. Ass'n Found., 264 N.W.2d 152, 3 Media L. Rep. (BNA) 2177 (Minn. 1978). The single publication rule also applies to compelled self-publication. Johnson v. Overnite Transp. Co., 19 F.3d 392, 128 Lab. Cas. (CCH) P57688, 9 I.E.R. Cas. (BNA) 466 (8th Cir. 1994). Unless resulting from fraudulent concealment, plaintiff's lack of knowledge of the defamatory publication does not toll the statute. McGaa v. Glumack, 441 N.W.2d 823 (Minn. Ct. App. 1989). The statute of limitations does not apply to the offering of evidence of defamatory statements to prove a claim for punitive damages. See Advanced Training Sys. v. Caswell Equip. Co., 352 N.W.2d 1 (Minn. 1984). The statute of limitations for the intentional infliction of emotional distress is two years. Larson v. New Richland Care Ctr., 538 N.W.2d 915, 920 (Minn. Ct. App. 1995), rev. granted, 1995 Minn. LEXIS 1074 (Minn. Dec. 20, 1995), grant of rev. vacated, 1997 Minn. LEXIS 181 (Minn. Mar. 4, 1997); Christenson v. Argonaut Ins. Cos., 380 N.W.2d 515, 518 (Minn. Ct. App. 1986); Krause v. Farber, 379 N.W.2d 93, 97 (Minn. Ct. App. 1985). The statute of limitations for negligent infliction of emotional distress is six years, but if the claim is based upon a predicate tort (such as defamation) that is subject to a shorter limitations period, the shorter period also bars the negligent infliction claim. Jones v. Indep. Sch. Dist. No. 720, 2003 WL 1702000, at *3 (Minn. Ct. App. April 1, 2003), following Wallin v. Minnesota Dep't of Corrections, 598 N.W.2d 393, 406 (Minn. Ct. App. 1999).

B. Jurisdiction

Minnesota's long arm statute provides for personal jurisdiction over nonresidents who commit acts outside the state which cause injury or property damage in Minnesota. Effective August 1, 2008, the Minnesota Legislature repealed a provision in the long arm statute that created an exception for matters which lie in defamation. 2008 Minn. Laws c. 185, § 1 (eff. Aug. 1, 2008) (repealing Minn. Stat. § 543.19(1)(d)(3)). See also Griffis v. Luban, 646 N.W.2d 527 (Minn. 2002) (holding that an Alabama court lacked jurisdiction over a Minnesota resident where the alleged defamatory statements about the plaintiff, a resident of Alabama, were posted on the internet by a Minnesota resident because the evidence failed to show that the Minnesota resident's statements were "expressly aimed" at the state of Alabama).

Courts lack jurisdiction over defamation claims against churches if resolution would require unconstitutional inquiry into religious matters. Compare Black v. Snyder, 471 N.W.2d 715, 56 Fair Empl. Prac. Cas. (BNA) 539, 58 Empl. Prac. Dec. (CCH) P41365 (Minn. Ct. App. 1991) (reasons given for discharge were essentially "ecclesiastical concern" and therefore beyond court scrutiny) with Geraci v. Eckankar, 526 N.W.2d 391, 396 (Minn. Ct. App. 1995) (employee's claims could be resolved by "neutral methods of proof" and were therefore appropriate for review).

Absent a writ of certiorari, courts also lack jurisdiction over defamation claims arising out of a quasi-judicial decision of an administrative or executive body to terminate an employee's employment. See Grundtner v. Univ. of Minn., 730 N.W. 2d 323, 331–32 (Minn. Ct. App. 2007) (affirming summary judgment for lack of subject matter jurisdiction where plaintiff's defamation claim against university necessarily related to plaintiff's discharge).

A defamation claim against a supervisor based on alleged oral or written statements made by the supervisor in the context of a disciplinary or grievance-arbitration procedure established by a collective bargaining agreement are preempted by Section 301 of the Labor Management Relations Act. Karnewie-Tuah v. Frazier, 757 N.W.2d 714, 722-23 (Minn. Ct. App. 2008).

C. Worker's Compensation Exclusivity

Minn. Stat. § 176.021, subd. 1, requires employers to "pay compensation in every case of personal injury or death of an employee arising out of or in the course of employment without regard to the question of negligence." As a result, "[i]f an employee suffers a personal injury or death arising out of and in the course of her employment, the [Minnesota Workers' Compensation] Act provides the employee's exclusive remedy." McGowan v. Our Savior's Lutheran Church, 527 N.W.2d 830, 833 (Minn. 1995) (citing Minn. Stat. § 176.031). "Where the Act provides the employee's exclusive remedy, the district courts have no jurisdiction." Id. (citing Huhn v. Foley Bros., 22 N.W.2d 3 (Minn. 1946)). "Under this scheme, an employee is precluded from bringing a tort action for damages against the employer." Stringer v. Minn. Vikings Football Club, LLC, 705 N.W.2d 746, 754 (Minn. 2005). However, "[t]ort claims against an employer or its insurer are not barred by exclusivity provisions of the Workers' Compensation Act if the injuries claimed or the damages sought did not arise out of and in the course of employment." Markgraf v. Douglas Corp., 468 N.W.2d 80, 83 (Minn. Ct. App. 1991) (quoting Kaluza v. Home Ins. Co., 403 N.W.2d 230, 236 (Minn. 1987)); see also Walker v. Minnesota Mining & Mfg. Co., 2000 WL 520254, *3 (Minn. Ct. App. May 2, 2000) (unpublished) (recognizing that a defamation claim that is distinct from an employee's original workplace injury is not preempted by the Minnesota Workers' Compensation Act).

The Act also contains certain exceptions to coverage. For example, "[t]he Act excludes from coverage injuries 'caused by the act of a third person or fellow employee intended to injure the employee because of personal reasons, and not directed against the employee as an employee, or because of the employment.'" McGowan, 527 N.W.2d at 833 (quoting Minn. Stat. § 176.011, subd. 16). "This is referred to as the assault exception." Meintsma v. Loram Maintenance of Way, Inc., 684 N.W.2d 434, 439 (Minn. 2004). "Cases involving the assault exception usually fall into one of three categories: (1) those that are noncompensable under the Act because the assailant was motivated by personal animosity toward his victim, arising from circumstances wholly unconnected with the employment; (2) those that are compensable under the Act because the provocation or motivation for the assault arises solely out of the activity of the victim as an employee; and (3) those that are compensable under the Act because they are neither directed against the victim as an employee nor for reasons personal to the employee." Id. (quoting McGowan, 527 N.W.2d at 831). The Minnesota Supreme Court has "narrowly construed the assault exception." Id.

The Minnesota Supreme Court has also recognized an "intentional injury exception." Gunderson v. Harrington, 632 N.W.2d 695, 702 (Minn. 2001). "In order to satisfy the intentional injury exception, the employee must demonstrate that the employer harbored a conscious and deliberate intent to injure him or her." Meintsma, 684 N.W.2d at 440; see also Gunderson, 632 N.W.2d at 703. Such intent "may not be inferred from mere negligence, though it be gross." Meintsma, 684 N.W.2d at 440 (quoting Breimhorst v. Beckman, 35 N.W.2d 719, 730 (Minn. 1949)). Also, "an employer's knowledge of a substantial certainty of injury to an employee does not trigger the intentional injury exception." Id.; Gunderson, 632 N.W.2d at 703.

D. Pleading Requirements

A complaint must allege all three elements of a defamation cause of action. Foley v. WCCO Television, Inc., 449 N.W.2d 497, 500, 17 Media L. Rep. (BNA) 1233 (Minn. Ct. App. 1989), cert. denied, 497 U.S. 1038 (1990). The complaint must provide specificity regarding the allegedly defamatory statement. Pope v. ESA Servs., 406 F.3d 1001, 1011 (8th Cir. 2005), **overruled on other grounds by Torgerson v. City of Rochester, 643 F.3d 1031 (8th Cir. 2011)**; Wikstrom v. Little Earth of United Tribes Housing Corp, No A06-1023, 2007 WL 1746908 (Minn. Ct. App. June 19, 2007) (affirming summary judgment for defendants where plaintiff's complaint included only vague allegations that defendants made false and libelous statements about plaintiff and that plaintiff would be forced to inform potential employers about the circumstances of her termination.); Stepnes v. Tennessen, No. Civ. 04-68, 2006 WL 2375645 (D. Minn. Aug. 16, 2006) (dismissing claim where plaintiff failed to identify with sufficient specificity a defamatory comment made by the defendant); Fearing v. St. Paul Police Dep't, 2005 U.S. Dist. LEXIS 6785, *16 (D. Minn. Apr. 20, 2005) (alleging defamation per se does not relieve the plaintiff from the burden to plead the defamatory statement specifically); Moreno v. Crookston Times Printing Co., 610 N.W.2d 321, 326–27 (Minn. 2000); American Book Co. v. Kingdom Pub. Co., 71 Minn. 363, 73 N.W. 1089, 1090 (1898). The exact language of an allegedly defamatory oral statement need not necessarily be repeated in the complaint. Fjelsta v. Zogg Dermatology PLC, No. Civ. 04-1717, 2006 WL 475283 (D. Minn. Feb. 28, 2006) (allegation that employer held a staff meeting to explain that employee was terminated for "endangering patients" was sufficiently specific to withstand a motion to dismiss); Thompson v. Campbell, 845 F. Supp. 665, 679, 69 Fair Empl. Prac. Cas. (BNA) 727 (D. Minn. 1994); Schibursky v. IBM, 820 F. Supp. 1169, 1181, 61 Fair Empl. Prac. Cas. (BNA) 1520, 64 Empl. Prac. Dec. (CCH) P42965 (D. Minn. 1993); McKenzie v. Rider Bennett, LLP, No. Civ. 05-1265, 2006 WL 839498 (D. Minn. March 28, 2006) (dismissing claim where plaintiff did not set forth with specificity which defendant allegedly made the defamatory statement, to whom it was made, or where). However, general statements about the alleged defamatory reasons for an employee's discharge will not withstand summary judgment. See Pope, 406 F.3d at 1011 (generally alleging that statements were made to plaintiff's co-workers that plaintiff was discharged for "timecard fraud" does not satisfy specificity requirement).

SURVEY OF MINNESOTA EMPLOYMENT PRIVACY LAW

Steven R. Anderson, Kathlyn E. Noecker,
John P. Borger, Daniel G. Prokott,
Leita Walker, and David Merritt
Faegre & Benson, L.L.P.
2200 Wells Fargo Center
90 South Seventh Street
Minneapolis, Minnesota 55402
Telephone: (612) 766-7000
Facsimile: (612) 766-1600
http://www.faegre.com

Daniel Oberdorfer
Leonard, Street and Deinard
150 South Fifth Street, Suite 2300
Minneapolis, Minnesota 55402
Telephone: (612) 335-1832;
Facsimile: (612) 335-1657
http://www.leonard.com

(With Developments Reported Through **October 1, 2012**)

GENERAL COMMENTS

None.

SIGNIFICANT DEVELOPMENTS SINCE THE 2012 *SURVEY*

None.

I. GENERAL LAW OF PRIVACY

A. Legal Basis of Privacy Claims

The Minnesota Supreme Court recognized a cause of action for tortious invasion of privacy in 1998. Lake v. Wal-Mart Stores, Inc., 582 N.W.2d 231, 26 Media L. Rep. 2175 (Minn. 1998). Prior decisions had refused to recognize the tort. See, e.g., Richie v. Paramount Pictures Corp., 544 N.W.2d 21, 24 Media L. Rep. 1897 (Minn. 1996); Hendry v. Conner, 303 Minn. 317, 226 N.W.2d 921 (1975). The Lake decision involved a claim by customers of Wal-Mart who brought a roll of film for development at the store. One of the photographs was a picture of the plaintiffs naked in the shower. The plaintiffs alleged that the store misappropriated the image, and that one or more copies of the photograph were circulating in the community. The court in Lake relied on the Restatement (Second) of Torts' definition of the cause of action, observing that the vast majority of jurisdictions now recognize some form of right to privacy. A dissent observed that the Minnesota Legislature should determine whether to adopt the tort because it is not rooted in the Constitution.

In 1999, the Minnesota Court of Appeals ruled that judicial recognition of the invasion of privacy tort would apply retroactively to conduct that occurred before the Lake decision. Summers v. R&D Agency, Inc., 593 N.W.2d 241 (Minn. Ct. App. 1999). In 2003, the Minnesota Supreme Court held that to state a claim for publication of private facts under the tort, a plaintiff must allege that "the matter is made public, by communicating it to the public at large, or to so many persons that the matter must be regarded as substantially certain to become one of public knowledge." Bodah v. Lakeville Motor Express, Inc., 663 N.W.2d 550, 557, 31 Media L. Rep. 1884 (Minn. 2003) (granting summary judgment to defendant); see also C.L.D. v. Wal-Mart Stores, Inc., 79 F. Supp. 2d 1080 (D. Minn. 1999) (granting summary judgment to defendant). Consent is an absolute defense to an invasion of privacy claim. See Anderson v. Mayo Clinic, No. A07-2071, 2008 WL 3836744 (Minn. Ct. App. Aug. 19, 2008) (unpublished) (citing Restatement (Second) of Torts § 625F (2008)). In Anderson, the Minnesota Court of Appeals reversed the district court's denial of the Mayo Clinic's motion for judgment on the pleadings, holding that a one-page document signed by the plaintiff authorizing the Mayo Clinic to disclose plaintiff's name and details regarding her condition and surgical treatments to "media representatives selected by Mayo Clinic" and others barred plaintiff's invasion of privacy claim. 2008 WL 3836744 at *4.

The Fair Credit Reporting Act preempts claims of invasion of privacy for certain claims except as to disclosures made with malice or willful intent to injure. Olwell v. Med. Info. Bureau, No. 01-1481, 2003 WL 79035 (D. Minn. Jan. 7, 2003) (noting the FCRA preempts invasion of privacy and other claims except as to "false information" furnished with malice or willful intent to injure). But see Nanstad v. N. States Power Co., No. 06-3087, 2007 WL 474966, at *6 (D. Minn. Feb. 9, 2007) (claim of publication of private information was not based on the collective bargaining agreement and thus not preempted by the Labor Management Relations Act).

B. Causes of Action

1. ***Misappropriation/Right of Publicity***. The Lake decision refers to the Restatement (Second) of Torts in adopting a cause of action for "appropriation." Lake, 582 N.W.2d at 235. The court stated that "appropriation

protects an individual's identity and is committed when one appropriates to his own use or benefit the name or likeness of another." Id. at 233 (quoting Restatement (Second) of Torts § 652E (1977)); see also Gregerson v. Vilana Financial, Inc., No. 06-1164 ADM/AJB, 2008 WL 451060, *10 (D. Minn. Feb. 15, 2008) (dismissing defendants' counterclaim of appropriation after a court trial, holding that defendants failed to establish a causal connection between plaintiff's use of defendants' name and defendant's owner's picture on plaintiff's website and an increase in traffic on plaintiff's website); Faegre & Benson, LLP v. Purdy, 447 F. Supp. 2d 1008, 1017–18 (D. Minn. 2006) (granting plaintiffs' motion for summary judgment that defendant illegally appropriated the names of plaintiffs by posting statements of support for defendant and falsely attributing them to plaintiffs and by demanding payment to remove the false postings); Ott v. Target Corp., 153 F. Supp. 2d 1055, 1074 (D. Minn. 2001) (finding under a summary judgment analysis that a retailer using a doll manufacturer's mark and likeness on goods produced by another manufacturer may have violated the doll manufacturer's right of publicity and leaving the final determination to the jury).

In 2010, the District of Minnesota engaged in extensive analysis of the interplay between the right of publicity, the First Amendment, and the Copyright and Lanham acts in a case involving NFL promotional videos that included game footage. Dryer v. Nat'l Football League, 689 F. Supp. 2d 1113 (D. Minn. 2010). The court in Dryer denied the NFL's motion for judgment on the pleadings in a putative class action brought by former professional football players, holding that the films at issue were commercial speech and that the "constitutional protection to be afforded the films may not outweigh Plaintiffs' interests in their own identities. Id. at 1121.

2. ***False Light***. Minnesota continues to decline to recognize the tort of false light publicity. See, e.g., Verona v. U.S. Bancorp, No. 7:09-CV-057-BR, 2011 WL 1252935 at *11 (E.D.N.C. Mar. 29, 2011) (applying Minnesota law); Leino v. Nelson, No. 00-CV-2202, 2001 WL 1141817, at *3 (D. Minn. Aug. 23, 2001); see also Parniani v. Cardinal Health, Inc., No. 06-2514, 2007 U.S. Dist. LEXIS 58377, at *18 (D. Minn. June 29, 2007) (claim of publication of private information was not based on the collective bargaining agreement and thus not preempted by the Labor Management Relations Act). The Lake decision explained that the court is "concerned that claims under false light are similar to claims of defamation, and to the extent that false light is more expansive than defamation, tension between this tort and the First Amendment is increased." 582 N.W.2d at 235–36.

3. ***Publication of Private Facts***. The Lake decision adopted the tort of publication of private facts. It defined this tort as "an invasion of privacy when one 'gives publicity to a matter concerning the private life of another . . . if the matter publicized is of a kind that (a) would be highly offensive to a reasonable person, and (b) is not of legitimate concern to the public." 582 N.W.2d at 233 (quoting Restatement (Second) of Torts § 652D (1977)); see also Lindgren v. Camphill Village Minnesota, Inc., No. Civ.00-2771, 2002 WL 1332796, at *12–13 (D. Minn. June 13, 2002) ("[I]t is not enough for the matter publicized to be subjectively offensive. Plaintiffs must show that the letters could be 'highly offensive to a reasonable person.'"); Leino, 2001 WL 1141817, at *3 (stating that the publication must be of private facts, not "public facts relating to [plaintiff's] professional life"); Phillips v. Grendahl, No. 00-1382, 2001 WL 1618593, at *2 (D. Minn. May 3, 2001) ("The request of a parent to obtain information on a future son-in-law from an investigative service may not be a genteel approach, but given concerns and lack of available alternative sources from which to garner information, the request does not become 'highly offensive.'"), aff'd in part, rev'd in part, 312 F.3d 357 (8th Cir. 2002); C.L.D. v. Wal-Mart Stores, Inc., 79 F. Supp. 2d 1080 (D. Minn. 1999); Lehman v. Zumbrota-Mazeppa Pub. Sch., No. A04-1226, 2005 WL 894756 (Minn. Ct. App. Apr. 19, 2005) (no claim for publication of private facts when school district published letter from former principal's doctor concerning his medical condition because appellant had already disclosed to the press that he was on medical leave related to stress and depression); Danforth v. Star Tribune Holdings Corp., No. A10-128, 2010 WL 4286242 at *5 (Minn. App. Nov. 2, 2010) (unpublished) (convicted sex-offender did not suffer an invasion of privacy by newspaper's publication of facts concerning his various criminal proceedings because (a) those facts were already in the public court record and (b) they fell within the realm of legitimate public concern.) The plaintiff carries the burden to prove "publicity" of private facts has occurred. Bodah v. Lakeville Motor Express, Inc., 663 N.W.2d 550, 555, 31 Media L. Rep. 1884 (Minn. 2003). In Bauer v. Ford Motor Credit Co., the court found that defendants had only contacted four close neighbors or relatives and one employer regarding collection of plaintiffs' alleged debt and therefore concluded that plaintiffs failed to satisfy the publication requirement. 140 F. Supp. 2d 1019, 1023–24 (D. Minn. 2001), judgment vacated in part, 149 F. Supp. 2d 1106 (D. Minn. 2001). It stated that plaintiffs could not rely on publication via the small town gossip mill because this approach would "would effectively eviscerate the requirement that the defendant be the one to have publicized the private information" and then "almost any form of gossip would be actionable regardless of the discretion taken in its initial communication." Id. at 1024 (citation omitted).

In Bodah, 663 N.W.2d 550, 31 Media L. Rep. 1884, the Minnesota Supreme Court adopted the Restatement (Second) of Torts' definition of publicity, that the "matter is made public by communicating it to the public at large, or to so many persons that the matter must be regarded as substantially certain to become one of public knowledge." Id. at 557; see also Phillips v. Grendahl, 312 F.3d 357, 372 (8th Cir. 2002) (dissemination to two people insufficient to meet publicity requirement); Olwell v. Medical Info. Bureau, 2003 WL 79035, No. Civ. 01-1481 JRT/FLN (D. Minn. Jan. 7, 2003) (disclosure of information by medical bureau to three insurance companies insufficient to meet publicity requirement); Yath v. Fairview Clinics, N.P., 767 N.W.2d 34 (Minn. Ct. App. 2009) (publication of personal medical information on Web site constituted publication to the public at large and therefore satisfied requirement of publicity regardless of the number of persons that actually viewed the website); Hanson v. Friends of Minn. Sinfonia, No. A03-1061, 2004 WL 1244229, at *6–7 (Minn. Ct. App. June 8, 2004) (reading a letter to a group of musicians in which the conductor rescinds an offer of work to one musician due to her health is not an invasion of this musician's privacy when this group of musicians has legitimate concern about the recovery and possible return of this musician, it was a limited audience and the information in the letter was limited); Robins v. Conseco Finance Loan Co., 656 N.W.2d 241, 245–56 (Minn. Ct. App. 2003) (disclosure of consumer report to one person insufficient to meet publicity requirement). In so doing, the Bodah court rejected the Minnesota Court of Appeals' formulation that would impose liability for egregious but limited disclosures of private information. The court suggested the tort is limited to cases in which the claimant's "private persona" has been violated through dissemination to the public at large. In Bodah, the court granted summary judgment to an employer who sent a fax listing 204 employee social security numbers to sixteen trucking terminals in six states. The Court rejected as "mere speculation" an allegation that the social security numbers were still being shared or were generally accessible.

4. ***Intrusion***. Minnesota recognizes the tort of intrusion. The Lake decision states that "[i]ntrusion upon seclusion occurs when one 'intentionally intrudes, physically or otherwise, upon the solitude or seclusion of another or his private affairs or concerns . . . if the intrusion would be highly offensive to a reasonable person.'" 582 N.W.2d at 233 (quoting Restatement (Second) of Torts § 652C (1977)); see also Osborne v. Minn. Recovery Bureau, Inc., No. 04-1167, 2006 WL 1314420, at *7 (D. Minn. May 12, 2006) (applying three factors: (1) intrusion, (2) that is highly offensive to a reasonable person; (3) into some matter into which a person has a legitimate expectation of privacy (citing Phillips v. Grendahl, 312 F.3d 357, 371 (8th Cir. 2002))); Parniani v. Cardinal Health, Inc., No. 06-2514, 2007 U.S. Dist. LEXIS 58377, at *18 (D. Minn. June 29, 2007) (motion to dismiss granted where plaintiff failed to make allegations about the nature of the intrusion, or show how it was unreasonable).

Factors to be examined by the court in its preliminary determination of the "highly offensive" element include: (1) the degree of intrusion; (2) the context, conduct, and circumstances surrounding the intrusion, including the number and frequency of the intrusive contacts; (3) the intruder's motives and objectives; (4) the setting into which the person intrudes; and (5) the expectations of those whose privacy is invaded. See Bauer v. Ford Motor Credit Co., 149 F. Supp. 2d 1106, 1109 (D. Minn. 2001). In Bauer, the plaintiffs moved for reconsideration on their intrusion upon seclusion claim, arguing that the court had failed to "properly account" for the number of contacts by defendants regarding collection of plaintiffs' alleged debt. 149 F. Supp. 2d at 1109. The court concluded under a summary judgment analysis that "where defendants received multiple and highly reliable confirmations of the inaccuracy of its records, the court must agree that a reasonable person could regard defendants' continued persistence, culminating in a repossession attempt at plaintiffs' home, as 'highly offensive' conduct." Id. at 1111; but see Carlson v. First Revenue Assurance, No. Civ. 02-209, 2002 WL 31866305 (D. Minn. Dec. 19, 2002) (as a matter of law six "dunning" letters not offensive, and noting unlike in Bauer, where numerous people told defendant that plaintiff owed no debt, here only plaintiff made such a claim). A sexual assault may constitute an intrusion upon seclusion. Birth v. Myles, No. 09-3386 DWF/JSM, 2010 WL 5067488 (D. Minn. Dec. 6, 2010) (defendant's motion for summary judgment denied where defendant shoved his knee into plaintiff's groin while trying to kiss her). A debt collector's abusive phone calls may also constitute an intrusion upon seclusion. Erickson v. Messerli & Kramer P.A., No. 09-3044 DWF/JJG, 2011 WL 1869044 at *10 (D. Minn. May 16, 2011). In Groeneweg v. Interstate Enterprises, Inc., No. A05-205, 2005 WL 894768 (Minn. Ct. App. Apr. 19, 2005), the court held the presence of fellow employees at a meeting in which the termination of appellant's employment was discussed did not amount to a claim for intrusion upon seclusion. In Swarthout v. Mutual Service Life Ins. Co., a life insurance company altered the insured's form for release of medical information, presented the altered release to various entities as if it had been signed by the insured and took medical information illicitly obtained with the altered release and posted it on an insurance database used by other insurance companies. 632 N.W.2d 741, 745 (Minn. Ct. App. 2001). The court determined that "the altering of [the insured's] release and the illicit obtaining, conveying, and publicizing of his private medical information" could be considered highly offensive. Id. But see Phillips v. Grendahl, 312 F.3d 357, 372 (8th Cir. 2002) (disclosure of skeletal consumer report not highly offensive); Simons v. Con-Way Central Express, Inc., No. Civ.02-3629, 2003 WL 22848939, at * 3 (D. Minn. Nov. 17, 2003) (finding that when an employee voluntarily disclosed his medical condition to his concerned supervisor behind closed doors in the supervisor's office it did not constitute an intrusion upon seclusion); Olwell v. Med. Info. Bureau, Civ. 01-1481, 2003 WL 79035 (D. Minn. Jan. 7, 2003) (plaintiff did not have a reasonable expectation of privacy in the data disclosed by medical bureau to three insurance companies because he explicitly authorized its disclosure); Jaramillo v. Weaver, No. A06-2343, 2007 WL 4303775 (Minn. Ct. App. Dec. 11, 2007) (unpublished) (affirming dismissal of complaint for failure to state a claim upon which relief may be granted where defendant, who was the mother of a fugitive staying with plaintiff as a houseguest, contacted plaintiff by telephone and mail in order to communicate with her son because there was no claim that defendant sought to engage plaintiff in conversation about his private family affairs and the contact was not highly offensive); Lehman v. Zumbrota-Mazeppa Pub. Sch., No. A04-1226, 2005 WL 894756 (Minn. Ct. App. Apr. 19, 2005) (school district's public disclosure of doctor's letter supporting former principal's request for medical leave was not an intrusion upon seclusion because former principal voluntarily provided the letter to the school district). In Walker v. Minnesota Mining, Manufacturing Co., the court held that a counselor's actions in acquiring patient medical records, accompanying patient to treatment appointments and sharing medical information with patient's supervisor at 3M were "petty and totally unworthy of a professional," but were not highly offensive. No. C4-99-1715, 2000 WL 520254, at *7 (Minn. Ct. App. 2000). It concluded that "[c]ourts are not empowered to fashion and enforce remedies for callous, boorish, or petty behaviors." Id.

In Summers v. R&D Agency, Inc., the Court of Appeals held that an intrusion claim applied retroactively to conduct occurring prior to the Lake decision. 593 N.W.2d 241 (Minn. Ct. App. 1999); see also Nelson v. Dicke, CIV.00-285, 2002 WL 511449, at *9 (D. Minn. Mar. 31, 2002) (holding that plaintiff's intrusion claim, based on a body cavity search conducted by prison officials, failed on official immunity grounds because there was no evidence that prison officials acted willfully or maliciously). The United States District Court has noted that surveillance of public activities is generally not a basis for a claim of intrusion into seclusion. Manion v. Nagin, No. Civ. 00-238, 2003 WL 21459680 (D. Minn. June 20, 2003); Seivers v. City of Minneapolis, No. 09-816 DSD/SER, 2011 WL 284486 at *6 (D. Minn. Jan. 25, 2011) (summary judgment for defendant because Minnesota courts have never recognized a cause of action for invasion of privacy in the context of police conduct, particularly where the contested events occurred in public); see also In re Nw. Airlines Privacy Litig., No. Civ.04-126, 2004 WL 1278459, at * 5 (D. Minn. June 6, 2004) (finding that an airlines' motives in releasing passenger name records, including name, flight number, credit card data, hotel reservation, car rental and traveling companions, to a government agency "in the wake of a terrorist attack that called into question the security of the nation's transportation system cannot be questioned" and the passengers did not have a claim for intrusion upon seclusion for this disclosure as they had voluntarily provided the information to the airline, their expectations of privacy were low and the disclosure was not highly offensive to a reasonable person). But see Milke v. Milke, No. 03-CV-6203, 2004 WL 2801585 (D. Minn. June 14, 2004) (summary judgment for plaintiff whose spouse surreptitiously tape recorded her phone conversations without her permission prior to divorce).

C. Other Privacy-related Actions

Minnesota recognizes numerous tort exceptions to employment at will, including the following.

1. ***Intentional Infliction of Emotional Distress.*** Minnesota recognizes the tort of intentional infliction of emotional distress in egregious cases. The plaintiff must show: (1) he or she was subjected to extreme and outrageous conduct; (2) the conduct was intentional or reckless; (3) the conduct caused emotional distress; and (4) the emotional distress was severe. Hubbard v. United Press Int'l, Inc., 330 N.W.2d 428 (Minn. 1983); see also Burt v. Yanisch, No. A03-1843, 2004 WL 1827866, at *6 (Minn. App. Aug. 17, 2004). The conduct must be "so atrocious that it passes the boundaries of decency and is utterly intolerable to the civilized community." See, e.g., Winspear v. Cmty. Dev. Inc., 553 F. Supp. 2d 1105, 1110 (D. Minn. 2008); Lindgren v. Camphill Village Minn., Inc., No. Civ.00-2771, 2002 WL 1332796, at *13 –14 (D. Minn. June 13, 2002); Boyer v. KRS Computer & Bus. Sch., No. Civ.00-1039, 2001 WL 1090237, at *2 (D. Minn. Sept. 17, 2001); Langeslag v. KYMN Inc., 664 N.W.2d 860, 865–68 (Minn. 2003) (false police reports, threats to sue and workplace arguments were insufficient to be extreme and outrageous conduct); Wenigar v. Johnson, 712 N.W.2d 190 (Minn. Ct. App. 2006) (harassment of person disabled as a result of a low IQ and lack of formal education constituted outrageous conduct); Walker v. Minn. Mining & Mfg. Co., No. C4-99-1715, 2000 WL 520254, at *6 (Minn. Ct. App. 2000). Testimony from individual making the claim and inconclusive medical records are insufficient to establish severe emotional distress. Langeslag, 664 N.W.2d at 868–70; Grosenick v. SmithKline Beecham Corp., No. 03-CV-2607, 2005 WL 1719117 (D. Minn. July 22, 2005) (requiring employee to work with supervisor about whom she made meritless sexual harassment claims does not constitute intentional infliction of emotional distress); Longbehn v. City of Moose Lake, No. A04-1214, 2005 WL 1153625 (Minn. Ct. App. May 17, 2005) (statements about job performance between an employer and an employee are not extreme and outrageous as a matter of law). But see Navarre v. S. Washington County Sch., 652 N.W.2d 9 (Minn. 2002) (in a claim under the Minnesota Data Practices Act, which permits recovery as a result of "any damage" caused by a violation of the Act, plaintiff's testimony that she was "extremely upset" and afraid to go outside is sufficient, even absent verifiable medical or psychological evidence).

2. ***Interference With Prospective Economic Advantage.*** At-will employees may pursue claims for tortious interference with contract in connection with their employment. Nordling v. N. States Power Co., 478 N.W.2d 498, 505 (Minn. 1991). The elements of a claim for tortious interference with contract are: (1) the existence of a contractual employment relationship; (2) defendant's knowledge of the contract; (3) intentional procurement of breach of the contract; (4) lack of justification; and (5) damages caused by the breach. Kresko v. Rulli, 432 N.W.2d 764, 769 (Minn. Ct. App. 1988); Walker, 2000 WL 520254, at *6; see also Peterson v. County of Dakota, 479 F.3d 555, 559–60 (8th Cir. 2007)

(Minnesota law does not permit an employee to a bring tortious interference claim against her union where the union declined to take the employee's grievance to arbitration); Lussier v. Wal-Mart Stores, Inc., No. 06-1395, 2007 U.S. Dist. LEXIS 63525, at * 14 (D. Minn. Aug. 28, 2007) (granting summary judgment for defendants in regards to plaintiff's claim of tortious interference with contract because plaintiff's termination was justified based upon his inappropriate work attire and plaintiff failed to present any evidence of bad motive); Hern v. Bankers Life Casualty Co., 133 F. Supp. 2d 1130, 1138-39 (D. Minn. 2001) (finding that plaintiff failed to state a claim for interference because plaintiff contends that the company's officer interfered with the contract between plaintiff and the company and as a general rule "a party to a contract cannot interfere with its own contract"); Hawkins v. DeRuyter, No. A03-1176, 2004 WL 1328008, at *2 (Minn. Ct. App. June 15, 2004) (tortious interference with contract claim is properly dismissed because appellant voluntarily left his position and cannot prove that he was constructively discharged and as such cannot prove third element of claim).

3. ***Prima Facie Tort***. Minnesota has not accepted the doctrine of prima facie tort. See Keckhafer v. Prudential Ins. Co., No. Civ.01-1017, 2002 WL 31185866, at *9 (D. Minn. Oct. 1, 2002); Price v. Viking Press, Inc., 625 F. Supp. 641, 651, 12 Media L. Rep, 1689 (D. Minn. 1985); New Creative Enters., Inc. v. Dick Hume & Assocs., Inc., No. C1-92-1423, 1992 Minn. App. LEXIS 1310 (Minn. Ct. App. Jan. 12, 1993), rev. denied, 1993 Minn. LEXIS 191 (Minn. 1993).

II. EMPLOYER TESTING OF EMPLOYEES

Minnesota recognizes the tort of negligent hiring. Ponticas v. K.M.S. Investments, 331 N.W.2d 907, 38 A.L.R.4th 225 (Minn. 1983). Employers, therefore, have a duty to exercise reasonable care in hiring applicants who may pose a threat of injury to others. Id. at 911; see also Yunker v. Honeywell, Inc., 496 N.W.2d 419, 8 IER Cases 513 (Minn. Ct. App. 1993). Negligent hiring occurs when the employer knew or should have known of the employee's unfitness prior to the hiring decision. The factual inquiry focuses on the inadequacy of the pre-employment investigation of the employee's background. Ponticas, 331 N.W.2d at 911. To set forth a legally sufficient claim for negligent hiring or negligent supervision, the complaint must allege actual physical injury or that the employee posed a threat of physical injury. Johnson v. Peterson, 734 N.W.2d 275, 277–78 (Minn. Ct. App. 2007). Minnesota does not recognize a claim for negligent training. Id.

A. Psychological or Personality Testing

1. ***Common Law and Statutes***. The Minnesota Human Rights Act permits preemployment testing of applicants if the tests (a) measure only essential job-related abilities; (b) are required of all applicants for the position regardless of ability (except tests permitted by the state workers' compensation statute) and (c) accurately measure the applicants' aptitude, achievement level, or whatever factors they purport to measure rather than reflecting the applicant's impaired sensory, manual or speaking skills (except when those are skills the test purports to measure). Minn. Stat. § 363A.20, subd. 8(a)(3). No reported Minnesota cases have interpreted this statute or determined how it would apply to psychological or personality testing. In addition, the MHRA's limitations on medical examinations will restrict psychological or personality tests deemed to be medical examinations. See II.C, infra. The Minnesota Human Rights Act does not prohibit testing of current employees except to the extent the test may be a medical examination or may be discriminatory. Minn. Stat. § 363A.20, subd. 8(a)(2) and 363A.08, subds. 1–8.

2. ***Private Employers***. The MHRA applies to all employers with one or more employees residing or working in Minnesota. Minn. Stat. § 363A.03, subds. 16, 30.

3. ***Public Employers***. The MHRA applies to all employers with one or more employees residing or working in Minnesota. Minn. Stat. § 363A.03, subds. 16, 30.

B. Drug Testing

1. ***Common Law and Statutes***. Minnesota enacted comprehensive legislation on employee drug and alcohol testing in 1987. Minnesota's Act permits drug and alcohol testing of applicants and employees under strictly prescribed conditions. The Act creates a private cause of action for violations of its provisions. Inquiries about drug and alcohol use are governed generally by the Minnesota Human Rights Act.

The Minnesota Drug and Alcohol Testing in the Workplace Act. The Act prescribes certain minimum statutory conditions that employers must meet if they want to test for drug and alcohol use among their employees. Even when these conditions are met, the Act closely regulates the conditions of testing and the circumstances under which employers make take disciplinary action, including discharge.

The Act prohibits drug or alcohol testing unless it is "pursuant to a written drug and alcohol testing policy that contains the minimum [statutory] information . . . ." Minn. Stat. § 181.951, subd. 1(b). An employer must distribute copies of the drug and alcohol testing policy ("DATP") to potential test subjects and post notice of implementation of a

DATP before testing any employee or applicant. Minn. Stat. § 181.952, subd. 2. A DATP must set forth the employees or job applicants subject to testing; the circumstances under which the employer may require drug or alcohol testing; the right of an employee or job applicant to refuse to undergo drug and alcohol testing and the consequences of refusal (which may include discharge or, in the case of an applicant, rejection of their application); any disciplinary or other adverse personnel action that may be taken based on a confirmatory test verifying a positive test result on an initial screening test; the right of an employee or job applicant to explain a positive test result on a confirmatory test or request and pay for a confirmatory re-test; and any other appeal procedures that may be available. See Minn. Stat. § 181.952, subd. 1; but see Belde v. Ferguson Enterprises, Inc., No. 04-4575, 2005 U.S. Dist. LEXIS 18770 (D. Minn. Aug. 31, 2005) (regarding employees covered by the federal Department of Transportation regulations, some DOT regulations preempt notice, random testing, and employment termination provisions of the Minnesota Drug and Alcohol Testing in the Workplace Act), aff'd, 2006 U.S. App. LEXIS 21147 (8th Cir. Aug. 18, 2006).

The second fundamental statutory condition of testing is that employers may only use approved laboratories to perform chemical testing. Minn. Stat. § 181.951, subd. 1(b). Drug testing laboratories must be: certified by the National Institute on Drug Abuse, in accord with guidelines for testing published in the Federal Register; accredited by the College of American Pathologists under its forensic urine drug testing laboratory program; or licensed to test for drugs in accord with the laws enacted by the state of New York. See Minn. Stat. § 181.953, subd. 1(a). For alcohol testing, laboratories must be: accredited by the College of American Pathologists under its laboratory accreditation program; or licensed to test for drug and alcohol in accord with laws enacted by the state of New York. See Minn. Stat. § 181.953, subd. 1(b). The Act expressly prohibits employers from using "a testing laboratory owned and operated by the employer . . . ." Minn. Stat. § 181.953, subd. 4. Thus, the employer may not use its own facilities and personnel to test samples. A testing laboratory is not strictly liable for errors in testing procedure. Baker v. Abo, 2003 WL 21639151, No. Civ. 01-1248 JRT/JSM (D. Minn. July 2, 2003) (summary judgment granted to defendant on strict liability and, where no proof of causation existed, on negligence theories).

The third fundamental, statutory condition of testing is that the employer must provide the employee or applicant with a form to acknowledge that the employee or applicant employee or applicant has seen the employer's DATP. The employer must provide applicants or employees who test positive additional written notice of their right to explain the positive test or request a confirmatory retest. Minn. Stat. § 181.953, subd. 6(b).

Permissible Testing. An employer may request or require a job applicant to undergo drug and alcohol testing provided a job offer has been made to the applicant and the same test is requested or required of all job applicants conditionally offered employment for that position. Minn. Stat. § 181.951, subd. 2 (emphasis added). Within three working days of receipt of the test result the Company must give written notice to the applicant of the test result and of the applicant' right to a copy of the test result report. Minn. Stat. § 181.953, subd. 7. If an applicant's confirmed test result is positive, this written notice must also inform the applicant that the positive test result on the initial screening test already has been confirmed by a statutorily prescribed confirmatory test, that he or she: (1) may submit additional information to explain the original positive test result, within three working days; and (2) may request a confirmatory re-test of the original sample, provided the request is made in writing and within five working days. Upon receipt of this notification, the applicant has five working days to demand, in writing, a retest at his or her own expense, to be conducted by the same laboratory or another licensed laboratory using the same threshold detection level. Minn. Stat. § 181.953, subds. 7, 9. If the employee demands retesting, the employer must, within three working days, "notify the original testing laboratory that the employee or job applicant has requested the laboratory to conduct the confirmatory retest or transfer the sample to another [licensed] laboratory . . . to conduct the confirmatory retest." Minn. Stat. § 181.953, subd. 9.

The Act specifically prohibits testing on an "arbitrary and capricious" basis, Minn. Stat. § 181.951, subd. 1 (c), and more generally prohibits testing of current employees, except under the following four circumstances: (1) at random of employees in "safety-sensitive positions"; (2) as part of a routine physical examination: (3) upon reasonable suspicion that the employee is under the influence of drugs or alcohol, has violated written work rules prohibiting the use, possession, sale, or transfer or drugs or alcohol while on the employer's premises or operating the employer's equipment, has sustained or caused a personal injury, or has caused or been involved in a work-related accident; and (4) to ensure the maintenance of sobriety following referral for chemical dependency treatment or evaluation. Minn. Stat. § 181.951, subds. 3-6; see Belsky v. Worldwide Parts & Accessories Corp., 2006 U.S. Dist. LEXIS 14758 (D. Minn. March 17, 2006) (granting plaintiff's motion for partial summary judgment and holding that damages for emotional distress are available for violations of the Minnesota Drug and Alcohol Testing in the Workplace Act, where defendant employer asked plaintiff to take a drug test before extending a job offer); Law Enforcement Labor Services v. Sherburne County, 695 N.W.2d 630 (Minn. Ct. App. May 3, 2005) (County's establishment of a random drug-testing policy for employees in safety-sensitive positions, as authorized by the Minnesota Drug and Alcohol Testing in the Workplace Act, was an inherent managerial right and was not subject to collective bargaining, under Public Employment Labor Relations Act, but implementation of provisions of policy that were not inextricably intertwined with policy's establishment were subject to collective bargaining).

Discipline and Discharge of Employees. Employees may not be disciplined in any fashion, or requested to undergo rehabilitation, because of a positive test result from an initial screening test that has not been verified by a confirmatory test. Minn. Stat. § 181.953, subd. 10(a). The Act contains certain disclosure requirements pertaining to employees. Whether an employee tests positive within three working days of receipt of the test result, the Company must give written notice to the employee of the test result and of the employee's right to a copy of the test result report. Minn. Stat. § 181.953, subd. 7. If an employee's confirmed test result is positive, this written notice must additionally inform the employee that he or she: (1) may submit information to explain the original positive test result, within three working days; (2) may request a confirmatory retest of the original sample, at his or her own expense, provided the request is made in writing and within five working days; (3) will not be subject to any adverse personnel action if the confirmatory retest does not confirm the original positive test result; (4) will not be discharged because of the original positive result, provided (a) he or she has not had a confirmed positive result on a test previously requested by the Company and (b) he or she agrees to participate in, and successfully completes, a counseling or rehabilitation program, whichever is more appropriate, as determined by the Company; (5) will not be unlawfully discriminated against based on medical information previously revealed; and (6) may have access to information contained in his or her personnel file relating to positive test result reports and other information acquired in, and conclusions drawn from, the testing process. Minn. Stat. § 181.953, subd. 7, 9, 10. Pending confirmation of test results (and, if applicable, reconfirmation of test results at the employee's request), the Company has the right to "temporarily suspend or transfer" the tested employee, provided "the employer believes that [the suspension or transfer] is reasonably necessary to protect the health or safety" of any person. Minn. Stat. § 181.953, subd. 10(c). An employee who is transferred must receive the same rate of pay in the new position. An employee who is suspended pending test results is entitled to back pay if the final test result does not end up positive. Id. The Act also prohibits discharge based solely upon a first confirmed positive test result, unless the employer has first given the employee an opportunity to participate in, at the employee's own expense or pursuant to coverage under an employee benefit plan, either a drug or alcohol counseling or rehabilitation program, whichever is more appropriate, as determined by the employer after consultation with a certified chemical use counselor or a physician trained in the diagnosis and treatment of chemical dependency; and the employee has either refused to participate in the counseling or rehabilitation program or has failed to successfully complete the program, as evidenced by withdrawal from the program before its completion or by a positive test result on a confirmatory test after completion of the program. Minn. Stat. § 181.953, subd. 10(b); Malkowski v. City of Mahtomedi, No. A04-1221, 2005 WL 894746 (Minn. Ct. App. June 14, 2005) (in an unemployment case, the Court of Appeals held that a city did not violate policy of reinstating employees who fail drug tests if they successfully complete treatment where employee voluntarily withdrew from treatment but offered to return); Wehlage v. ING Bank, FSB, No. 07-CV-1852, 2008 WL 4838718 (D. Minn. Nov. 5, 2008) (employer could not terminate employee for first failed drug test without offering him the opportunity to participate in a treatment program regardless of employee's prior voluntary participation in a treatment program). This does not prohibit employers from discharging employees who have engaged in drug- or alcohol-related conduct that, standing alone, would constitute sufficient grounds for discharge, even if the conduct came to light in connection with the employee's first positive test result. See Hanson v. City of Hawley, 2006 WL 1148125 (Minn. Ct. App. June 28, 2006) (unpublished) (holding that the Minnesota Drug and Alcohol Testing in the Workplace Act did not govern the defendant employer's decision to terminate an employee after a positive breath test where employee acknowledged violating the employer's no tolerance alcohol policy); In re Copeland, 455 N.W.2d 503, 506–07 (Minn. Ct. App. 1990); City of Minneapolis v. Johnson, 450 N.W.2d 156, 160 (Minn. Ct. App. 1990).

Costs of Testing and Treatment. Except for re-testing of confirmed positive test results, the employer may not request or require applicants or employees to pay for the costs of drug or alcohol testing. Minn. Stat. § 181.953, subd. 4. Employees may be required to pay for the cost of the statutorily prescribed treatment or rehabilitation unless an employee benefit plan covers the expense of a counseling or rehabilitation program. Minn. Stat. § 181.953, subd. 10(b)(1).

The Act requires that employers establish "reliable chain of custody procedures" to ensure proper handling and identification of samples to be tested. See Minn. Stat. § 181.953, subd. 5.

The two-year statute of limitations under Minn. Stat. § 541.07, subd. 1. applies to a wrongful termination action under the Minnesota Drug and Alcohol Testing in the Workplace Act. Sipe v. STS Mfg., Inc., 2012 WL 4475853 (Minn. App. Sept. 25, 2012).

2. ***Private Employers***. Minnesota's Drug and Alcohol Testing in the Workplace Act applies to both private and public employers. Minn. Stat. § 181.950, subd. 7. For private employers, test results are private and confidential, and may not be disclosed to any third party, including prospective employers and even governmental agencies, without the test subject's written permission. Minn. Stat. § 181.954, subd. 2. The Act does, however, provide exceptions for: (1) use of positive test results in arbitral, administrative, and judicial proceedings, provided that the information is relevant to the proceeding; (2) disclosure to federal agencies as required by law or federal governmental contract; and (3) disclosure to substance abuse treatment facilities for the purpose of evaluation or treatment. Minn. Stat. § 181.954, subd. 3.

3. ***Public Employers***. Minnesota's Drug and Alcohol Testing in the Workplace Act applies to both private and public employers. Minn. Stat. § 181.950, subd. 7. With respect to public employees, the test results and related information are classified as "private information" under the Minnesota Government Data Practices Act. Minn. Stat. § 181.954, subd. 2. A violation of these provisions is actionable at law, pursuant to Minn. Stat. § 181.956. An employee must be given access to information in the employee's personnel file relating to positive test result reports and other information acquired in the drug and alcohol testing process, including whatever conclusions were drawn and actions were taken based on the reports or other acquired information. Minn. Stat. § 181.953, subd. 10(e).

C. Medical Testing

1. ***Common Law and Statutes***. The MHRA restricts the use of medical inquiries or examinations more extensively than the ADA. Under the MHRA, an employer may not request or require a job applicant to undergo a medical examination unless the employer has made a conditional job offer. Even then, the employer may test only for essential job-related abilities, and the employer must require applicants within the same job category to be examined without regard to disability. Minn. Stat. § 363A.20, subd. 8(a)(1). An employer also may not inquire into medical conditions by requiring or requesting an applicant to furnish medical information before an offer has been made, nor may the employer attempt to obtain such information from another source. Minn. Stat. § 363A.08, subd. 4. The statute also requires employers to notify applicants within ten days if medical information adversely affects a hiring decision. Minn. Stat. § 363A.20, subd. 8 (c). See also II.A, supra.

Employers may not ask overly broad questions about the applicant's prior health. Huisenga v. Opus Corporation, 494 N.W.2d 469, 473 (Minn. 1992). An employer may ask applicants whether they can perform any or all job functions, as long the employer asks all applicants in the job category. Minn. Stat. § 363A.20, subd. 8(1). Employers may not ask applicants whether they can perform major life activities unless the questions relate specifically to the ability to perform job functions. Huisenga, 494 N.W.2d at 473. An employer may also ask about an applicant's prior attendance record, but the employer may not ask about prior worker's compensation claims. Id.

Because medical examinations under the MHRA are limited to testing only for essential job-related abilities, the medical information that an employer may request from an offeree is restricted to information related to the applicant's abilities to perform the essential functions of the job. Minn. Stat. § 363A.20, subd. 8(1). There is no limit to the number of medical examinations an employer may require. Hauglid v. Commissioner, No. C4-95-1589, 1996 WL 104778, 1996 Minn. App. LEXIS 282 (Minn. Ct. App. 1996) (unpublished), rev. denied, 1996 Minn. LEXIS 344 (Minn. 1996).

An employer can only perform a physical examination or inquiry upon a current employee under the MHRA with the consent of the employee. Even with consent, such tests may be used only to gain medical information in order to assess continuing ability to perform the job; determine employee health plan eligibility; complying with other federal, state or local law; explore the possibility of reasonable accommodations for the employee; or any other legitimate business reason not otherwise prohibited by law. Minn. Stat. § 363A.20, subd. 8(2).

Under the Minnesota Workers' Compensation statute, an injured employee must submit to examination by the employer's physician, if requested by the employer, and at reasonable times thereafter at the employer's request. An employee may refuse to submit to such an examination, but the refusal to comply with any reasonable request for examination may cause the suspension of the right to compensation. Minn. Stat. § 176.155, subd. 1.

2. ***Private Employers***. The MHRA and the state workers' compensation statute apply to all private employers. Minn. Stat. § 363A.03, subds. 16, 30; Minn. Stat. § 176.011, subd. 10.

3. ***Public Employers***. The MHRA applies to the state, and its departments, agencies and subdivisions. Minn. Stat. § 363A.03, subds. 16, 30; Kalia v. St. Cloud State University, 539 N.W.2d 828 (Minn. Ct. App. 1995). The state workers' compensation law applies to public employers. Minn. Stat. § 176.011, subd. 10.

D. Polygraph Tests

Minnesota's polygraph law forbids employees from directly or indirectly soliciting or requiring "a polygraph, voice stress analysis, or any test purporting to test the honesty of any employee or prospective employee." Minn. Stat. § 181.75. The statute prohibits any use of physiological tests of an employee's honesty. Alexander v. Eilers, 422 N.W.2d 312, 315, 3 IER Cases 535 (Minn. Ct. App. 1988). Other kinds of testing or evaluation (personal judgments, psychological tests or written questionnaires) are not prohibited by this statute. State by Spannaus v. Century Camera, Inc., 309 N.W.2d 735, 30 Empl. Prac. Dec. ¶ 33,008, 23 A.L.R.4th 171 (Minn. 1981). Violations of the act are misdemeanors, but in addition, an employee may bring a private action for damages resulting from violations. See Kamrath v. Suburban National Bank, 363 N.W.2d 108 (Minn. Ct. App. 1985) (jury awarded $60,000 in damages for a bank teller's emotional distress because he was asked to take a polygraph after the employer learned money was missing). Although police are permitted to use polygraphs as part of criminal investigations, even when those overlap with employment investigations, see Alexander, 422 N.W.2d at 315, employers may not use police to conduct polygraph examinations that are not part of a criminal investigation, Hanson v. Brothers and One, Inc., 491 N.W.2d 292, 295, 7 IER Cases 1325, 1327 (Minn. Ct. App. 1992). An employee can waive the protection provided by Minnesota's law by volunteering to submit to a polygraph exam. Lee v. Metropolitan Airport Commission, 428 N.W.2d 815, 823, 3 IER Cases 1152 (Minn. Ct. App. 1988). Minn. Stat. § 181.76 (1973) forbids the disclosure of either the fact that an employee took a polygraph test, or the results of the test; violation of the statute is a misdemeanor. Although the statute forbidding employer polygraphing provides for a private right of action, the statute forbidding disclosure is strictly a criminal statute. Jeffers v. Convoy Co., 636 F. Supp. 1337, 1341, 105 Lab. Cas. ¶ 55,664, 1 IER Cases 919 (D. Minn. 1986).

E. Fingerprinting

Fingerprinting may be required in connection with background checks or certain positions or licenses. See e.g., Minn. Stat. §§ 122A.18, subd. 8 (teachers); 299C.68 (apartment manager); 299L.02, subd. 5 (gambling enforcement); 326.336, subd. 1 (private detective): 349A.02, subd. 6 (lottery).

III. SEARCHES

A. Employee's Person

1. ***Private Employers***. Although there are no reported cases relevant to this issue in an employment context, the Minnesota Supreme Court's recent decision recognizing a tort for invasion of privacy may have a bearing. See Lake v. Wal-Mart Stores, Inc., 582 N.W.2d 231, 26 Media L. Rep. 2175 (Minn. 1998). See I, supra.

2. ***Public Employers***. A constitutional prohibition against workplace searches and seizures applies only to those cases where some state action is involved. The traditional Fourth Amendment test requires the court to balance the public employer's need for the search against the employee's right to be free from unreasonable searches. To determine whether a search is "reasonable," the court balances the employee's "legitimate expectation of privacy" against the promotion of a legitimate governmental interest. A legitimate expectation of privacy requires both an actual subjective expectation and societal acceptance of that expectation as reasonable. McDonell v. Hunter, 809 F.2d 1302, 1306, 55 USLW 2392, 1 IER Cases 1297 (8th Cir. 1987). Based on both the federal Constitution and the Minnesota Constitution, "[a] union acting as an exclusive bargaining agent, may validly consent to drug testing on behalf of the employees it represents," and "unless union employees can demonstrate a breach of their union's duty of fair representation, they are bound by that consent." Geffre v. Metropolitan Council, 2001 WL 1143174, at *2-3 (D. Minn. 2001) (slip copy).

B. Employee's Work Area

There are no reported cases relevant to this issue in an employment context. See I, supra.

C. Employee's Property

1. ***Private Employers***. An employee has no duty to permit an employer to search his car or home or to answer any questions about property found there. Cherveny v. 10,000 Auto Parts, 353 N.W.2d 685 (Minn. Ct. App. 1984). Once an employee consents to answer the employer's questions, the employee has a duty to answer truthfully. Id. at 688.

2. ***Public Employers***. See III.A.2, supra.

IV. MONITORING OF EMPLOYEES

A. Telephones and Electronic Communications

The Minnesota Privacy of Communications Act forbids the interception of any wire, electronic, or oral communication, or the disclosure of the contents of any communication, where the person making the disclosure knows or has reason to know that the information was obtained in violation of the Act. Minn. Stat. § 626A.02, subd. 1(a)–(d). Minn. Stat. § 626A.01, subd. 3, defines "wire communication" as:

> any aural transfer made in whole or in part through the use of facilities for the transmission of communications by the aide of wire, cable, or other like connection between the point of origin and the point of reception, including the use of such connection in a switching station. "Wire communication" includes any electronic storage of the communication.

Minn. Stat. § 626A.01, subd. 14 defines "electronic communication" as:

> a transfer of signs, signals, writing, images, sounds, data, or intelligence of any nature transmitted in whole or in part by wire, radio, electromagnetic, photoelectronic, or photooptical system that does not include: (1) a wire or aural communication; (ii) a communication made through a tone-only paging device; or (iii) a communication from a tracking device.

Minn. Stat. § 626A.01, subd. 16 defines "electronic communications system" as:

> a wire, radio, electromagnetic, photo-optical, or photoelectronic facility for the transmission of electronic communications, and a computer facility or related electronic equipment for the electronic storage of communications.

The Act does not prohibit interception where either the interceptor is a party to the communication, or one party to the communication has given consent. See Department of Human Rights v. Spiten, 424 N.W.2d 815, 820 (Minn. Ct. App. 1988); **Weesner v. U.S. Bancorp, 2011 WL 4471765 (D. Minn. Sept. 26, 2011) (recognizing the admissibility of a surreptitious recording of a workplace conversation by an employee).** This exemption does not apply where the interception is done for "the purpose of committing any criminal or tortious act in violation of the constitution or laws of the United States or of any state." Minn. Stat. § 626A.02, subd. 2(d). **A co-owner of a company may not be privileged to secretly monitor his co-owner's company email where the company lacked an email policy and did not monitor other employee's email. Gates v. Wheeler, No. A09-2355, 2010 WL 4721331 (Minn. App. Nov. 23, 2010) (unpublished) (upholding a temporary injunction)**; see also Milke v. Milke, No. 03-CV-6203, 2004 U.S. Dist. LEXIS 11199 (D. Minn. June 14, 2004) (both the Minnesota Privacy of Communication Act, Minn. Stat. § 626A.02, subd. 1(a)–(d) and Title III, 18 U.S.C.S. § 2511(1)(a)–(d) explicitly recognized a cause of action where a husband tapped his own phone to intercept and record his wife's conversations without her knowledge or consent). The use of devices "specifically designed to only record conversations to which the operator of the device is a party" is not an "interception" according to the law. Minn. Stat. § 626A.01, subd. 5 and 6(c). Violation of the Act is a felony punishable by a five year sentence and a $20,000 fine. Some first-time offenses are treated as misdemeanors. Minn. Stat. § 626A.02, subd. 4(b). A city or county attorney may bring a civil action in circumstances involving satellite and radio communications. Available remedies include injunctive relief and a mandatory civil fine for second-time violators. Minn. Stat. § 626A.13 provides for a private cause of action. Remedies include equitable relief, treble disgorgement of profits, punitive damages, and attorney's fees. Minn. Stat. § 626A.13, subds. 1-3. The Act has a two-year statute of limitations, dating from the discovery of the violation. Minn. Stat. § 626A.13, subd. 5. The Courts have held that "pen registers," which keep track of numbers dialed but do not record the contents of conversations, are not prohibited by the statute. State v. Cook, 498 N.W.2d 17 (Minn. 1993). Minnesota law protects communications whether or not those communications take place over a system which "affects interstate or foreign commerce." Any communications transmitted by a "wire cable, or other like connection," or any electronic communications "transmitted in whole or in part by a wire, radio, electromagnetic, photoelectronic, or photo-optical system" of almost any kind, are protected—including, internal voice mail or e-mail messages. Minn. Stat. § 626A.01, subds. 3, 14. In addition to the above, the Minnesota Lawyers Professional Responsibility Board has determined it is professional misconduct for a lawyer, in connection with the lawyer's professional activities, to record a conversation without the knowledge of all parties to the conversation except in limited circumstances. Opinion 18. The opinion does not prohibit a lawyer from giving advice about the legality of recording a conversation. There are no reported cases relevant to this issue in an employment context.

B. Mail

There are no reported cases relevant to this issue in an employment context.

C. Surveillance/Photographing

Minnesota's criminal code provides that "[a] person who enters upon another's property and surreptitiously gazes, stares, or peeps in the window of a house or place of dwelling of another with intent to intrude upon or interfere with the privacy of a member of the household is guilty of a misdemeanor." Minn. Stat. § 609.746, subd. 1. See Manion v. Nagin, 2003 WL 2145960, No. Civ. 00-238 ADM/RLE (D. Minn. June 20, 2003) (surveillance of public activities is generally not a basis for a claim of intrusion into seclusion); State v. Morris, 644 N.W.2d 114 (Minn. App. 2002) (exception to the state privacy statute, which allows videotaping of premises in commercial establishments as long as the owner has posted conspicuous signs warning that the premises were under surveillance, does not apply to a non-employee defendant who concealed a video camera in his bag and used it to surreptitiously tape females in a department store).

V. ACTIVITIES OUTSIDE THE WORKPLACE

A. Statute or Common Law

The Minnesota Court of Appeals has held that an employer is not responsible for a supervisor's allegedly harassing comment made at a social gathering outside the workplace and not sponsored by the employer. Thomas v. Coleman Enters., No. C6-99-1327, 2000 WL 385479 (Minn. Ct. App. 2000) (stating alleged remark was inadmissible).

B. Employees' Personal Relationships

1. Romantic Relationships Between Employees. The Minnesota Human Rights Act prohibits discrimination on the basis of marital status. Minn. Stat. § 363A.08. "Marital status" discrimination includes an adverse employment action because the employee is living with a person of the opposite sex without being married. State by McClure v. Sports & Health Club, Inc., 370 N.W.2d 844 (Minn. 1985); State by Johnson v. Porter Farms, Inc., 382 N.W.2d 543 (Minn. Ct. App. 1986); see also Marty v. Digital Equip. Corp., 345 N.W.2d 773 (Minn. 1984) (employee dating another employee); State by Cooper v. Mower County Social Servs., 434 N.W.2d 494 (Minn. Ct. App. 1989) (employee discharged for pregnancy outside of marriage). The statute also prohibits adverse action based on the identity or situation of a person's spouse or ex-spouse. Minn. Stat. § 363A.03; see also Johnson v. Schrunk, Nos. C5-95-970, C6-95-959, 1995 Minn. App. LEXIS 1553 (Minn. Ct. App. 1995) (employee fired after stating intent to divorce employer's daughter), rev. denied, 1996 Minn. LEXIS 153 (Minn. 1996); Counters v. Farmland Indus., Inc., No. C3-88-1158, 1988 WL 134800 (Minn. Ct. App. 1988) (employee discharged because wife did not move with him upon transfer). But see Jacques v. Real Estate Equities, Inc., No. C9-91-641, 1991 WL 198451 (Minn. Ct. App. 1991) (employee fired for turmoil caused by affairs that led to divorce, not for divorce); State by Johnson v. Floyd Wild, Inc., 384 N.W.2d 185, 188 (Minn. Ct. App. 1986) (employee discharged after announcing divorce plans but before marital status changed). The statute does not protect against discrimination based on the "political status" of one's spouse. Cybyske v. Indep. Sch. Dist. No. 196, 347 N.W.2d 256 (Minn. 1984).

2. ***Sexual Orientation***. Minnesota prohibits discrimination based upon sexual orientation, which includes living arrangements and other aspects of off-duty romance. Minn. Stat. § 363A.03, subd. 44 ("'Sexual orientation' means having or being perceived as having an emotional, physical, or sexual attachment to another person without regard to the sex of that person or having or being perceived as having an orientation for such attachment, or having or being perceived as having a self-image or identity not traditionally associated with one's biological maleness or femaleness."); see also id. § 363A.08; Sundberg v. High-Tech Inst., Inc., No. 03-CV- 3270, 2005 WL 174841 (D. Minn. Jan. 26, 2005) (rude inquiry by supervisor into employee's sexual orientation does not create hostile work environment); Goins v. W. Group, 635 N.W.2d 717, 720 (Minn. 2001) ("We hold that an employer's designation of employee restroom use based on biological gender is not sexual orientation discrimination in violation of the MHRA."); Doe v. City of Minneapolis, No. C2-02-817, 2002 WL 31819236 (Minn. Ct. App. Dec. 17, 2002) (official immunity protects police officials who assigned transgendered officer to a shift with no unisex bathroom). The statutory prohibition against discrimination based on sexual orientation does not apply to religious or fraternal organizations with respect to qualifications of employees based on sexual orientation provided sexual orientation is a bona fide occupational qualification, or to nonpublic service organizations whose primary function is providing occasional service to minors with respect to qualifications of employees or volunteers based on sexual orientation. Minn. Stat. § 363A.20, subds. 2–3; see also Lussier v. Wal-Mart Stores, No. 06-1395, 2007 U.S. Dist. LEXIS 63525, at *25–26 (D. Minn. Aug. 28, 2007) (Minnesota law prohibits any person from intentionally aiding, abetting, inciting, compelling or coercing an employer to engage in sexual orientation discrimination or to intentionally attempt to do so (citing Minn. Stat. §§ 363A.08 (2); 363A.14 (1), (2))); Doe v. Lutheran High School of Greater Minneapolis, 702 N.W.2d 322 (Minn. Ct. App. Aug. 23, 2005) (former employee's claim that he was discharged as campus pastor and secular teacher at religious high school based on his sexual orientation, in violation of the Minnesota Human Rights Act, required the court to analyze and apply church doctrine, and thus, consideration of claim was prohibited by the entanglement clause of the First Amendment); Thorson v. Billy Graham Evangelistic Assoc., 687 N.W.2d 652 (Minn. Ct. App. 2004) (state law exemption from sexual orientation discrimination prohibition for "secular business activities of a religious organization" applies not to the job responsibilities of a particular employee but to the mission of the organization).

3. ***Marital Status***. The prohibition of discrimination based upon marital status limits the use of anti-nepotism rules to those situations where the marital status functions as a bona fide occupational qualification. Kraft, Inc. v. State of Minnesota, 284 N.W.2d 386 (Minn. 1979); Belton-Kocher v. St. Paul Sch. Dist., No. C4-97-1497, 1998 WL 88197 at *4, (Minn. Ct. App. 1998) (affirming denial of summary judgment). The requirement that a job candidate not be married to his or her would-be supervisor may be a bona fide occupational qualification. Belton-Kocher v. St. Paul Sch. Dist., 610 N.W.2d 374 (Minn. Ct. App. 2000) (appeal after trial), rev. denied, 2000 Minn. LEXIS 430 (Minn. 2000); see also Savoren v. LSI Corp. of America, Inc., No. AO8-0674, 2009 WL 483069 (Minn. Ct. App. Feb. 24, 2009) (district court properly

granted summary judgment to employer where only evidence to support employee's claim of marital status discrimination was the fact that the employee was married to another employee who was also terminated).

C. Smoking

Minnesota law prohibits employers from refusing to hire a job applicant or disciplining or discharging an employee because the applicant or employee engages in or has engaged in the use or enjoyment of lawful consumable products which occurs off the employer's premises during nonworking hours. Minn. Stat. § 181.938, subd. 2. "Lawful consumable products" means products whose use or enjoyment is lawful and which are consumed during use or enjoyment, such as food, alcoholic or nonalcoholic beverages, and tobacco. Minn. Stat. § 181.938, subd. 2.

The statute does, however, contain four exceptions:

1. Where the employer's restriction relates to a bona fide occupational requirement and is reasonably related to employment activities or responsibilities of an employee or group of employees, or is necessary to avoid an actual or apparent conflict of interest with any responsibilities owed the employer by the employee, Minn. Stat. § 181.938, subd. 3(a);

2. Where the employer refuses to hire an applicant or discipline or discharge an employee who refuses or fails to comply with the conditions established by a chemical dependency treatment or aftercare program, Minn. Stat. § 181.938, subd. 3(b);

3. Where the employer offers, imposes, or has in effect a health or life insurance plan that distinguishes between employees based on use of lawful consumable products, provided that where different premium rates are charged to employees, the rates reflect the actual difference in cost to the employer, Minn. Stat.§ 181.938, subd. 3(c); and

4. Where the employer refuses to hire an applicant or disciplines or discharges an employee based on his or her past or present job performance, Minn. Stat. § 181.938, subd. 3(d).

Remedies for violating the statute are a civil action for damages for lost wages and benefits, and attorney's fees and court costs if the plaintiff prevails. Minn. Stat. § 181.938, subd. 4.

D. Blogging

No reported Minnesota cases

VI. RECORDS

A. Personnel Records

1. ***Review of Personnel Record***. The Minnesota Personnel Record Review and Access Act gives employees and former employees access to their "personnel records." See Minn. Stat. § 181.960, et seq.; see also Dahnke v. Hub City North Central, 2001 WL 118520, at *5 (Minn. Ct. App. 2001) (unpublished opinion) ("An employer must provide an employee who is separated from employment with a copy of the employees [sic] personnel record on request."). The statute lists what is included in a "personnel record" and what is not included, establishes inspection and copying procedures, provides for challenges to the information and outlines the legal remedies for violations. The statute requires that certain items, such as the application, wage history, performance evaluations, and leave records be included in employee files and be accessible to employees under specific conditions. However, "[w]ritten documents by a supervisor that are kept within the supervisors [sic] possession are not part of the personnel file." Dahnke, 2001 WL 118520, at *5.

When an employee makes a written request, the employer must provide the opportunity to review the personnel records. Minn. Stat. § 181.961, subd. 1. The employer must comply with the written review request within seven working days if the personnel record is located in Minnesota, and within fourteen working days if the personnel record is located elsewhere. Minn. Stat. § 181.961, subd. 2. The record must be available for review during the employer's normal hours of operation at the employee's place of employment or other reasonably nearby location. The employer may require that the review take place in the presence of the employer or the employer's designee. The employer must provide a copy of the record to the employee after the review, if the employee requests it. The record need not be made available during the employee's working hours. See id. Information that was omitted from the record provided to the employee for review may not be used by the employer in an administrative, judicial or quasi-judicial proceeding unless the employer did not intentionally omit the information and the employee is given a reasonable opportunity to review the omitted information prior to its use. Minn. Stat. § 181.963. If an employer violates a provision of this law, the employee may bring an action to compel compliance and for actual damages plus costs. Minn. Stat. § 181.965, subd. 1; Fiebelkorn v. IKON Office Solutions, Inc., 668 N.W.2d 1178, 1190-91 (D. Minn. 2009). A lawsuit under the statute that does not make a claim for actual damages may be dismissed for failure to state a claim. Brustad v. Rosas, 1999 WL 1256352, 1999 Minn. App. LEXIS 1384 (Minn. Ct. App., Dec. 28, 1999), rev. denied, 2000 Minn. LEXIS 199 (Minn. 2000). An employer may not retaliate against an employee for asserting rights or remedies under this law. Minn. Stat. § 181.964. For a violation of the retaliation section, an employee may recover actual damages, back pay, reinstatement, equitable relief, plus reasonable attorney fees. Minn. Stat. § 181.965, subds. 1, 2. Section 181.962 indicates that employee access to "written comments or data of a personal nature about a person other than the employee" may be prohibited "if disclosure of the information would constitute an intrusion upon the other person's privacy." Minn. Stat. § 181.960, subds. 4, 6. An employer is only required to provide an employee the opportunity to review personnel records every six months, except that upon separation from employment, a former employee may make a written request to review his or her personnel record "once each year after separation for as long as the personnel record is maintained." Minn. Stat. § 181.961, subd. 1.

All employers, as defined under Minn. Stat. § 181.960, subd. 3 (any employer with 20 or more employees, excluding state agencies, statewide systems, political subdivisions or advisory boards subject to Minn. Stat. Ch. 13), must provide written notice to each job applicant upon hire of the rights and remedies provided in the Personnel Record Review and Access Act. "Written notice" is not specifically defined. The remedies available for violations of the Personnel Record Review and Access Act include compelled compliance, recovery of actual damages plus costs, and, in cases of retaliation for asserting one's rights, the right to recover back pay, reinstatement, other make-whole and equitable relief, and reasonable attorney fees. See Minn. Stat. § 181.965.

2. ***Private Employers Disclosing Employee Information***. Under Minn. Stat. § 181.967, a private employer cannot be held liable for disclosing particular types of information about a current or former employee to a prospective employer or employment agency unless the employee demonstrates by clear and convincing evidence that (a) the information was false and defamatory; and (b) the employer knew or should have known the information was false and acted with malicious intent to injure the employee. Minn. Stat. § 181.967. This standard applies only to disclosure by a private employer to a prospective employer or employment agency of the following information about an employee (whether the employee is a current or former employee) in response to a request for such information: (1) the dates of employment, (2) compensation and wage history, (3) job description and duties, (4) training and education provided by the employer, (5) acts of violence, theft, harassment, or illegal conduct documented in the personnel record that resulted in disciplinary action or resignation and the employee's written response, if any, contained in the employee's personnel record. Disclosure of information in category (5) must be disclosed in writing, with a copy sent contemporaneously by mail to the employee's last known address.

Minn. Stat. § 181.967 also provides protection for an employer if the employer discloses certain types of information or documents pertaining to an employee after obtaining the written authorization of the current or former employee for such disclosure. The disclosures subject to the law's protections, provided there is prior written authorization, include: (a) written employee evaluations conducted before the employee's separation from the employer and the employee's response, if any; (b) written disciplinary warnings and actions in the five years before the date of the authorization and the employee's written response, if any; and (c) written reasons for separation from employment. An employer must contemporaneously provide the employee or former employee with a copy of the information disclosed and inform the employee to whom the information was disclosed.

3. ***Public Employers Disclosing Employee Information***. The liability protection established for private employees under Minn. Stat. § 181.967, subd. 2, also applies to the disclosure of all public personnel data and to the following private personnel data (as defined by Minn. Stat. § 13.43) by a public employer if the current or former employee gives written consent to the release of the private data: (a) written employee evaluations conducted before the employee's separation from the employer, and the employee's written response, if any, contained in the employee's personnel record; and (b) written reasons for separation from employment. Minn. Stat. § 181.967, subd. 4.

In Navarre v. South Washington County Schools, a teacher who was placed on paid leave of absence and then reassigned sued her school district and local newspaper for, among other claims, violation of the Minnesota Government Data Practices Act ("MGDPA"), which applies only to public employers. 633 N.W.2d 40, 46–48 (Minn. Ct. App. 2001). In granting a new trial, the appeals court determined that when an individual alleges a violation of the MGDPA for the release of private personnel data the court must first decide "whether the information released qualifies as private personnel data within the meaning of the act." Id. at 45. It cited to MGDPA's classification system as providing that information regarding the "existence and status of any complaints or charges against an employee, regardless of whether the complaint or charge resulted in a disciplinary action" is public; while the details of an existing complaint or charge are nonpublic unless there has been a "final disposition of any disciplinary action." Id. at 50; see also Anderson v. Indep. School District No. 97, 2002 WL 31163596 (D. Minn. Sept. 25, 2002).

In International Brotherhood of Electrical Workers, Local No. 292 v. City of St. Cloud, a labor union brought an action to seek payroll records of a city contractor under the Minnesota Government Data Practices Act (MGDPA). 750 N.W.2d 307, 310-311 (Minn. Ct. App. 2007). The court held that the union qualified as a "person" under the statute and was thus able to request the records. Id. at 715. It further noted that the statute's legislative history suggests that the law was intended to expand a union's ability to access personnel data; still, the court denied access here because the union failed to request the contested data properly. Id. at 715-16.

In State v. Novicky, the court denied appellant's request for an in camera review of personnel records of a police officer. No. A07-0170, 2008 WL 1747805, *8 (Minn. Ct. App. 2008). The court held that an officer's personnel documents regarding the existence or status of complaints against him are protected by the MGDPA and thus are not discoverable. Id. at *8. Additionally, the court noted that because the district court had reviewed the documents, it did not abuse its discretion in deciding to exclude them from the record. Id. at *9. Similarly, in State v. Anderson, a criminal defendant requested an in camera review of personnel records of a county employee with whom the defendant had corresponded while previously in jail. No. A07-0292, 2008 WL 2649273, *1 (Minn. Ct. App. 2008). The court held that the lower court did not abuse its discretion in declining to conduct the review on the grounds that the defendant had not made a "plausible showing" that the file would contain information favorable to him. Id. at *8.

B. Medical Records

Information obtained regarding the medical condition or history of an applicant or employee must be collected and maintained on separate forms and in separate medical files and treated as a confidential medical record. Minn. Stat. § 363A.20, subd. 8(a)(1)(iv). Records maintained under the MHRA pertaining to requests for accommodation must be retained for one year from the date of making the record or the date of the personnel action, whichever occurs later. Supervisors and managers may be informed regarding restrictions on and accommodations for the work or duties of the employee. Minn. Stat. § 363A.20, subd. 8(a)(1)(iv). First aid safety personnel may be informed if a disability might require emergency treatment. Id. Government officials investigating compliance with the MHRA must be provided relevant information. Id. Information may be released for purposes mandated by local, state, or federal law, provided that the results of the examination are used only in accordance with the law. Id.

C. Criminal Records

A public employer may not refuse to hire an applicant on the basis of a criminal record unless the crime relates directly to the position. Even if the position and the crime are directly related to each other, a convicted individual must be permitted to show evidence of rehabilitation and present fitness for the job. Minn. Stat. § 364.03, subd. 3. If a public employer refuses to hire an applicant because of a prior conviction for a crime, the employer must notify the person in writing of the following: (1) the grounds and reason for denial; (2) the complaint and grievance procedure; (3) the earliest date for reapplication; and (4) that all competent evidence of rehabilitation presented will be considered upon reapplication. The same rules apply to the issuing of professional licenses. Minn. Stat. § 364.04 forbids state employers from releasing arrest records where there is no valid conviction, the conviction has been annulled, or the conviction was for a misdemeanor without a jail sentence. Some public employers are permitted or required to do criminal background checks on applicants. The Minnesota Child Protection Background Check Act allows, but does not require, a children's service provider to obtain criminal conviction data on applicants. Minn. Stat. § 299C.62. Home care providers and their employees who have direct contact with clients must disclose all criminal conviction as part of the state licensing process. Minn. Stat. § 144A.46, subd. 5. Applicants seeking employment in a school district must provide a criminal history consent form. A school district may then hire a person pending the background check but may terminate that person based on the results of the check. The school district "is not liable for failing to hire or for terminating an individual's employment based on the result of a background check under this section." Minn. Stat. § 123B.03, subd. 2. Similarly, the Board of Teaching and the State Board of Education must do a criminal background history check on all applicants for initial licenses within their jurisdictions. Minn. Stat. § 122A.18. A property manager or person applying to be a property manager who has or would have the means, within the scope of the individual's duties, to enter tenants' rental dwelling units, must go through a criminal background check. The owner must refuse to hire or must discharge the manager if the manager has been convicted of a "background check crime," which includes felonies such as murder, homicide, robbery, and assault, and non-felonies such as harassment and stalking. Minn. Stat. § 299C.66, et seq.

D. Subpoenas / Search Warrants

Minn. R. Civ. Pro. 45 provides a court with subpoena power to require the production of, among other things, documents and tangible evidence. While Rule 34 provides for the inspection and copying of documents from named parties to an action, Rule 45 allows a party to obtain material for inspection and copying from non-parties. In this regard, under Rule 45.02, a subpoena may command the person to whom it is directed to produce the books, papers, documents or tangible things designated therein. Generally, a Rule 45 subpoena should be used only if the documents are unavailable from the opposing party or not otherwise available through the requestor's own efforts.

Under Rule 45.02, a party must either produce the evidence requested or: (1) seek to quash or modify the subpoena if it is unreasonable or oppressive, or (2) condition denial of the motion upon the advancement by the person in whose behalf the subpoena is issued of the reasonable cost of producing the books, papers, documents, or tangible things. Such a motion must be made promptly or at or before the time specified in the subpoena for compliance. A subpoena may be opposed for a number of reasons including privilege, undue burden, or irrelevancy under Rule 26. See David F. Herr & Roger S. Haydock, Minnesota Practice Series: Civil Rules Annotated, 45.02, at 419 (4th ed. 2003). But see Baskerville v. Baskerville, 246 Minn. 496, 75 N.W.2d 762 (1956) (where nonprivileged evidence is relevant and essential to the fair adjudication of the issue, the protective powers of the court should be exercised not to exclude the evidence absolutely but to admit it with protective safeguards). Furthermore, certain information sought from non-parties may be more limited than information sought from parties under Rule 34 and a non-party may successfully claim privacy rights or confidentiality interests outweigh a party's need for the information. Herr & Haydock, supra, 45.02, at 420. But see Baskerville, 246 Minn. 496, 75 N.W.2d 762 (there is usually no absolute protection against disclosure of trade secrets and practices on the ground that their revelation might result in giving information to a competitor, when if the evidence is not admitted, the issue cannot be fairly tried).

Non-party subpoenas for the production of documents are not intended to put the person subpoenaed to his own expense of producing or compiling such information. Rule 45.06 provides for the reimbursement or advancement of expenses to a complying non-party. See Bowman v. Bowman, 493 N.W.2d 141 (Minn. Ct. App. 1992) (decision to award expenses to non-party witness is not discretionary; witness who is not a party and is required to give testimony or produce documents relating to witness' profession, business or trade is entitled to reasonable expenses as a matter of law).

VII. ACTIONS SUBSEQUENT TO EMPLOYMENT

A. References

Under Minn. Stat. § 181.967, a private employer cannot be held liable for disclosing particular types of reference information about a current or former employee to a prospective employer or employment agency unless the employee demonstrates by clear and convincing evidence that (a) the information was false and defamatory; and (b) the employer know or should have known the information was false and acted with malicious intent to injure the current or former employee. Similar protections exist for public employers that disclose particular types on information about a current or former employee. Prior to the new law's passage, courts held that employee references may be qualifiedly privileged. See, e.g., Eldeeb v. University of Minnesota, 864 F. Supp. 905, 913 (D. Minn. 1994), aff'd, 60 F.3d 423 (8th Cir. 1995); Stuempges v. Parke, Davis & Co., 297 N.W.2d 252, 257, 24 A.L.R.4th 132 (Minn. 1980).

B. Non-Compete Agreements

The general rule under Minnesota law is that non-compete agreements are looked upon with disfavor. Covenants not to compete are agreements in partial restraint of trade, limiting the right of a party to work and earn a living. Therefore, such contracts are scrutinized with care. Freeman v. Duluth Clinic, Inc., 334 N.W.2d 626, 630 (Minn. 1983) (citing National Recruiters, Inc. v. Cashman, 323 N.W.2d 736, 740 (Minn. 1982); Bennett v. Storz Broadcasting Co., 270 Minn. 525, 533, 134 N.W.2d 892, 898 (1965)). However, covenants will be enforced if designed to protect legitimate interests, which include:

(1) Protection of customer goodwill by preventing solicitation of former customers. Medtronic, Inc. v. Gibbons, 527 F. Supp. 1085 (D. Minn. 1981) (a 360-day restriction on attempting "to divert any Company business by influencing customers with whom I or my subordinates were connected the last year of my employment" was reasonable) aff'd, 684 F.2d 565 (8th Cir. 1982); Davies & Davies Agency, Inc. v. Davies, 298 N.W.2d 127 (Minn. 1980) (concluding that the agency's actual need for protection was limited to prohibiting its former employees from actively soliciting business from agency customers); Walker Employment Service, Inc. v. Parkhurst, 300 Minn. 264, 271–72, 219 N.W.2d 437 (1974) (covenant was not unduly restrictive because it was intended to protect employer's confidential relationships with its customers).

(2) Protection of confidential information acquired during the course of employment. Cherne Industrial, Inc. v. Grounds & Associates, Inc., 278 N.W.2d 81, 92 (Minn. 1979) (irreparable harm may be inferred from a threat of disclosure of confidential information); Webb Publishing Co. v. Fosshage, 426 N.W.2d 445, 450 (Minn. Ct. App. 1988) (a restriction prohibiting contact with all customers, not just those with whom the departing employee had personal contact, may be justified if the departing employee had access to information on those customers that would aid her in soliciting their business). But see Jim W. Miller Const., Inc. v. Schaefer, 298

N.W.2d 455, 459 (Minn. 1980) (refusing to enforce a restrictive covenant because the techniques involved were "skillful variations of general processes known to the particular trade," and the knowledge acquired was generally available to the public from a variety of sources).

However, "punishing" the employee is not a legitimate reason. Eutectic Welding Alloys Corp. v. West, 281 Minn. 13, 160 N.W.2d 566, 571 (1968) ("Restrictive covenants that serve primarily to prevent an employee from working for others or for himself in the same competitive field so as to discourage him from terminating his employment constitute a form of industrial peonage without redeeming virtue in the American enterprise system.").

Furthermore, a restrictive covenant must be supported by adequate and independent consideration. Crop Insurance Service Co. v. Bredeson, 437 N.W.2d 698, 702 (Minn. App. 1989) (citing National Recruiters v. Cashman, 323 N.W.2d 736 (Minn. 1982) (holding that if an employee enters into the non-competition agreement "at the inception of the employment relationship," no additional consideration is necessary to support the agreement)). Executing the agreement on the first day of employment may be too late. Sanborn Mfg. Co. v. Currie, 500 N.W.2d 161 (Minn. Ct. App. 1993) (consideration was lacking where employee was presented with non-competition agreement on his first day of work and the consideration offered was identical to the compensation package he had already accepted); Drummond American LLC v. Share Corp., 2010 WL 3167326 (D. Minn. July 23, 2010) (holding that the employer did not establish a non-competition agreement was supported by adequate consideration because the employer failed to inform the employee that he would be required to sign a non-competition agreement before he accepted employment, even though there was no dispute that the employee signed the agreement before employment commenced). Independent consideration is required if the covenant is made after employment has begun. Freeman v. Duluth Clinic, 334 N.W.2d 626, 630 (Minn. 1983) (covenant that is not made ancillary to the initial employment contract must be supported by independent consideration); **C.H. Robinson Worldwide, Inc. v. Rodriguez, 2012 WL 4856245 (D. Minn. Oct. 12, 2012) (same)**. In Witzke v. Mesabi Rehabilitation Services Inc., the Minnesota Court of Appeals held that restrictive covenants included in an employment agreement signed approximately eight months after employment commenced were supported by adequate consideration because the employee not only continued employment for seventeen years, but was also professionally supported by the employer and advanced within it both in salary and position. No. A07-0421, 2008 WL 314535 (Minn. Ct. App. Feb. 5, 2008) (unpublished).

Restrictions imposed on the employee must be reasonable to be enforceable. The test for determining whether a restrictive covenant is reasonable is whether the restriction is narrowly tailored. Bennett v. Stortz Broadcasting Co., 270 Minn. 525, 134 N.W.2d 892 (1965) ("The test . . . is whether or not the restraint is necessary for the protection of the business or goodwill of the employer, and if so, whether the stipulation has imposed upon the employee any greater restraint than is reasonably necessary to protect the employer's business."). Relevant factors include the nature and character of the employment, the time for which the restriction is imposed, and the territorial extent of the locality to which the prohibition extends. Id. Under the "blue pencil doctrine," the court has discretion to modify the agreement so as to render it reasonable and enforceable. Bess v. Bothman, 257 N.W.2d 791, 794–95 (Minn. 1977); Dynamic Air, Inc. v. Bloch, 502 N.W.2d 796, 800 (Minn. Ct. App. 1993).

Defenses to the enforcement of a non-compete agreement include an employer's breach of contract or wrongful termination. Hruska v. Chandler Associates, Inc., 372 N.W.2d 709, 715–16 (Minn. 1985) (holding that a contractual provision (such as a covenant not to compete) may be unenforceable because one party's breach entitled the other to rescind the entire contract); Webb Publishing Co. v. Fosshage, 426 N.W.2d 445, 449 (Minn. Ct. App. 1988). Similarly, expiration of the underlying agreement will prohibit enforcement. In Burke v. Fine, 608 N. W. 2d 909 (Minn. Ct. App. 2000), the court held that an employee hired pursuant to a two-year employment contract with a non-compete agreement who continued working for the employer after the two-year period ended could not be held to the agreement.

VIII. OTHER ISSUES

A. Statutes of Limitations

The limitations period under the Minnesota Human Rights Act is one year from the date of the discriminatory practice. Minn. Stat. § 363A.28, subd. 3. The limitations period for recovery of wages is two years, except that it is three years if nonpayment is willful. Minn. Stat. § 541.07, subd. 5. The limitations period for libel, slander, assault, battery, false imprisonment or other intentional tort resulting in personal injury is two years. Minn. Stat. § 541.07, subd. 1. The two-year statute applies to claims for intentional infliction of emotional distress. Id.; Larson v. New Richland Care Center, 538 N.W.2d 915, 920 (Minn. Ct. App. 1995), rev. granted (Minn. 1995), rev. denied (Minn. 1997), abrogated on other grounds by Gordon v. Microsoft Corp., 645 N.W.2d 393, 399 n.5 (Minn. 2002); Christenson v. Argonaut Ins. Cos., 380 N.W.2d 515, 518 (Minn. Ct. App. 1986), rev. denied (Minn. 1986); Krause v. Farber, 379 N.W.2d 93, 97 (Minn. Ct. App. 1985), rev. denied. The United States District Court has held the two-year statute of limitations applies to intrusion into seclusion claims. Manion v. Nagin, No. Civ. 00-238, 2003 WL 21459680, (D. Minn. June 20, 2003). **The two-year statute of limitations**

under Minn. Stat. § 541.07, subd. 1. applies to a wrongful termination action under the Minnesota Drug and Alcohol Testing in the Workplace Act. Sipe v. STS Mfg., Inc., 2012 WL 4475853 (Minn. App. Sept. 25, 2012). The limitations period for contract claims generally is six years. Minn. Stat. § 541.05, subd. 1. The limitations period for statutory and negligent personal injuries is generally six years. Minn. Stat. § 541.05, subd. 2. However, a claim for negligent infliction of emotional distress is time-barred if it is dependent upon a failed defamation claim or other time-barred tort. Wallin v. Minn. Dep't of Corrections, 598 N.W.2d 393, 406 (Minn. Ct. App. 1999), rev. denied (Minn. Oct. 21, 1999).

B. Jurisdiction

Minnesota's long arm statute provides for personal jurisdiction over nonresidents who commit acts outside the state which cause injury or property damage in Minnesota. Effective August 1, 2008, the Minnesota Legislature repealed a provision in the long arm statute that created an exception for matters which lie in privacy. 2008 Minn. Laws c. 185, § 1 (eff. Aug. 1, 2008) (repealing Minn. Stat. § 543.19(1)(d)(3)); see also Biopolymer Eng'g, Inc. v. Immunocorp, Civ. No. 05-536 (JNE/SRN), 2009 WL 1255452, at *21 n.8 (D. Minn. 2009) (noting that "[f]or actions arising on or after August 1, 2008, [Minnesota's long arm statute], does not except causes of action for defamation or privacy.").

C. Worker's Compensation Exclusivity

Minn. Stat. § 176.021, subd. 1, requires employers to "pay compensation in every case of personal injury or death of an employee arising out of or in the course of employment without regard to the question of negligence." As a result, "[i]f an employee suffers a personal injury or death arising out of and in the course of her employment, the [Minnesota Workers' Compensation] Act provides the employee's exclusive remedy." McGowan v. Our Savior's Lutheran Church, 527 N.W.2d 830, 833 (Minn. 1995) (citing Minn. Stat. § 176.031). "Where the Act provides the employee's exclusive remedy, the district courts have no jurisdiction." Id. (citing Huhn v. Foley Bros., 22 N.W.2d 3 (Minn. 1946)). "Under this scheme, an employee is precluded from bringing a tort action for damages against the employer." Stringer v. Minn. Vikings Football Club, LLC, 705 N.W.2d 746, 754 (Minn. 2005). However, "[t]ort claims against an employer or its insurer are not barred by exclusivity provisions of the Workers' Compensation Act if the injuries claimed or the damages sought did not arise out of and in the course of employment." Markgraf v. Douglas Corp., 468 N.W.2d 80, 83 (Minn. Ct. App. 1991) (quoting Kaluza v. Home Ins. Co., 403 N.W.2d 230, 236 (Minn. 1987)).

The Act also contains certain exceptions to coverage. For example, "[t]he Act excludes from coverage injuries 'caused by the act of a third person or fellow employee intended to injure the employee because of personal reasons, and not directed against the employee as an employee, or because of the employment.'" McGowan, 527 N.W.2d at 833 (quoting Minn. Stat. § 176.011, subd. 16). "This is referred to as the assault exception." Meintsma v. Loram Maintenance of Way, Inc., 684 N.W.2d 434, 439 (Minn. 2004). "Cases involving the assault exception usually fall into one of three categories: (1) those that are noncompensable under the Act because the assailant was motivated by personal animosity toward his victim, arising from circumstances wholly unconnected with the employment; (2) those that are compensable under the Act because the provocation or motivation for the assault arises solely out of the activity of the victim as an employee; and (3) those that are compensable under the Act because they are neither directed against the victim as an employee nor for reasons personal to the employee." Id. (quoting McGowan, 527 N.W.2d at 831). The Minnesota Supreme Court has "narrowly construed the assault exception." Id. In Klaahsen v. APCOA/Standard Parking, Inc., No. Civ. 02-620, 2002 WL 1397041, *5–6 (D. Minn. June 26, 2002), the district court dismissed the plaintiff-employee's common law claims of assault, battery, intentional infliction of emotional distress, reckless infliction of emotional distress, and invasion of privacy for lack of subject matter jurisdiction on the grounds that the claims were preempted by the Workers' Compensation Act where the facts underlying the claims made clear that the conduct, alleged hazing of the plaintiff-employee, arose from circumstances related to the employment. See also Fu v. Owens, No. 08-620, 2009 WL 1178541, *4 (D. Minn. May 1, 2009) (where the only contact between the plaintiff-employee and co-worker with whom she was involved in an altercation was employment-related, co-worker's animosity toward plaintiff necessarily arose in the employment context and therefore plaintiff's claims for assault, battery, false imprisonment, negligent and intentional infliction of emotional distress, and negligent hiring, supervision, and retention, as well as her husband's claim for loss of consortium, were preempted by the Act and dismissed).

The Minnesota Supreme Court has also recognized an "intentional injury exception." Gunderson v. Harrington, 632 N.W.2d 695, 702 (Minn. 2001). "In order to satisfy the intentional injury exception, the employee must demonstrate that the employer harbored a conscious and deliberate intent to injure him or her." Meintsma, 684 N.W.2d at 440; see also Gunderson, 632 N.W.2d at 703. Such intent "may not be inferred from mere negligence, though it be gross." Meintsma, 684 N.W.2d at 440 (quoting Breimhorst v. Beckman, 35 N.W.2d 719, 730 (Minn. 1949)). Also, "an employer's knowledge of a substantial certainty of injury to an employee does not trigger the intentional injury exception." Id.; Gunderson, 632 N.W.2d at 703.

Minn. Stat. § 176.061, subd. 5(e) provides that "A coemployee working for the same employer is not liable for a personal injury incurred by another employee unless the injury resulted from the gross negligence of the coemployee or was intentionally inflicted by the coemployee." "The term 'coemployee' includes a corporate officer, general supervisor, or foreman." Stringer, 705 N.W.2d at 754. In other words, to maintain a tort action against coemployees, a plaintiff "must demonstrate that they either intentionally inflicted the injury or that the injury resulted from gross negligence." Meintsma, 684 N.W.2d at 440. "[T]o establish a gross negligence claim against a coemployee, the injured employee must show: 1. the coemployee had a personal duty toward the employee, the breach of which resulted in the employee's injury, and that the activity causing the injury was not part of the coemployee's general administrative responsibilities; and 2. the injury arose from gross negligence on the part of the coemployee." Stringer, 705 N.W.2d at 754. To establish an intentional injury claim against a coemployee, a plaintiff must demonstrate "an intent to cause injury." Meintsma, 684 N.W.2d at 441. "In other words, a defendant must consciously and deliberately intend to cause an injury, not just intend to do the act." Id.

D. Pleading Requirements

Pleadings must be simple, concise and direct; no technical form of pleading is required. See Minn. R. Civ. P. 8.05.

SURVEY OF MISSISSIPPI EMPLOYMENT LIBEL LAW

John C. Henegan, Alison Tasma Vance, and W. Mackin Johnson
Butler, Snow, O'Mara, Stevens & Cannada, PLLC
P.O. Box 6010
Ridgeland, MS 39158-6010
Telephone: (601) 948-5711; Facsimile: (601) 985-4500

(With Developments Reported Through **November 1, 2012**)

GENERAL COMMENTS

None.

SIGNIFICANT DEVELOPMENTS SINCE THE 2012 *SURVEY*

None.

I. GENERAL LAW

A. General Employment Law

1. ***At-Will Employment.*** Mississippi follows the employment-at-will doctrine. Perry v. Sears, Roebuck & Co., 508 So. 2d 1086, 1088 (Miss. 1987). Where no employment contract for a definite term exists, an employee may quit or be terminated from his job for good reason, bad or wrong reason, or no reason at all. McArn v. Allied Bruce-Terminix Co., 626 So. 2d 603, 606 (Miss. 1993). See also Slatery v. Northeast Miss. Contract Procurement, Inc., 747 So. 2d 257 (Miss. 1999; Shaw v. Burchfield, 481 So. 2d 247, 253-54 (Miss. 1985); Kelly v. Mississippi Valley Gas Co., 397 So. 2d 874, 874-75 (Miss. 1981). Unless forbidden by an employment contract, an employer may discharge an employee for any reason, except reasons independently declared legally impermissible. Shaw, 481 So. 2d at 254. Thus, the statutorily created duties to deal in good faith arising, for example, under the UCC, or the common law implied covenant of good faith and fair dealing do not govern the employment relationship. Hartle v. Packard Elec., 626 So. 2d 106, 110 (Miss. 1993) (citing Perry, 508 So. 2d at 1089). See also Lippincott v. Mississippi Bureau of Narcotics, 856 So. 2d 456, 467-68 (Miss. Ct. App. 2003); Young v. North Mississippi Medical Center, 783 So. 2d 661 (Miss. Ct. App. 2001). The court may refuse to enforce a signed non-compete agreement if the employee's termination was arbitrary, capricious or in bad faith. Empiregas, Inc. of Kosciusko v. Bain, 599 So. 2d 971, 975 (Miss. 1992).

The due process laws do not protect Mississippi at-will employees. A protected property interest in employment exists only where the employee has an express or implied right to continued employment. Davis v. Biloxi Pub. Sch. Dist., 937 So.2d 459 (Miss. Ct. App. 2005); Brandon v. Claiborne County, 828 So. 2d 202, 207 (Miss. Ct. App. 2001) (quoting White v. Mississippi State Oil & Gas Bd., 650 F.2d 540, 541-42 (5th Cir. 1981)). **On the other hand, Mississippi law does protect an at-will employee against a negligence claim for failure to do his or her job. Willis v. Rehab Solutions, PLLC., 82 So. 3d 583, 589-90 (Miss. 2012)**

Mississippi recognizes a "handbook" exception to the employment-at-will rule. In Bobbitt v. Orchard, Ltd., 603 So. 2d 356 (Miss. 1992), the Mississippi Supreme Court held that the employer created an enforceable promise when it disseminated an employee handbook with a progressive disciplinary system. The court found that a termination that violated the stated disciplinary system was unlawful since the handbook did not include a disclaimer or contractual provision preserving the employer's right to terminate employment at will. Bobbitt, 603 So. 2d at 362. Mississippi courts consistently refuses to apply that exception when the document upon which the employee relies contains a disclaimer preserving the at-will employment relationship. See, e.g., Byrd v. Imperial Palace of Mississippi, 807 So. 2d 433, 438 (Miss. 2001) (holding that even though the employee handbook provided for a grievance procedure for terminated employees, a disclaimer in the handbook, which provided that the employment relationship was at-will and that employees could be terminated at any time, did not fit the Bobbitt exception); Lee v. Golden Triangle Planning & Dev. Dist., Inc., 797 So. 2d 845, 848 (Miss. 2001) (where there is something in the employee handbook disclaiming an employment contract, an at-will employment arrangement stays intact); Smith v. Magnolia Lady, Inc., 925, So. 2d 898, 902-3 (Miss. Ct. App. 2006) (at-will employment status upheld when employment application and handbook contained disclaimers); Senseney v. Miss. Power Co., 914 So. 2d 1225, 1229 (Miss. Ct. App. 2005) (Bobbit exception is inapplicable when employment application contains at-will disclaimer that does not appear in employee handbook).

The Mississippi Supreme Court recognizes two narrow public policy exceptions to the employment-at-will doctrine. An employee may bringing a tort claim against his employer if he is discharged for either: (1) refusing to participate in an illegal act, or (2) reporting an illegal act committed by his employer to his employer or a third party. McArn v. Allied Bruce-Terminix Co., 626 So. 2d 603 (Miss. 1993). See also Heartsouth, PLLC v. Boyd, 865 So. 2d 1095, 1108-09 (Miss. 2003); Paracelsus Health Care Corp. v. Willard, 754 So. 2d 437, 442-43 (Miss. Ct. App. 1999). The McArn exception requires that the acts complained of warrant criminal penalties, as opposed to mere civil penalties, but the exception does not require an already committed crime. Hammons v. Fleetwood Homes of Miss., Inc., 907 So. 2d 357, 360 (Miss. Ct. App. 2004). An employee's good faith belief that the employer engaged in illegal activity is insufficient by itself to invoke the public policy exception; rather, the activity reported must, in fact, be illegal. Wheeler v. BL Dev. Corp., 415 F.3d 399, 404 (5th Cir. 2005). See also King v. Newton County Bd. of Suprs, 144 Fed. Appx. 381, 385 (5th Cir. 2005) (whistleblower exception does not apply when plaintiff fails to demonstrate act complained of was illegal). In DeCarlo v. Bonus Stores, Inc., 989 So.2d 351 (Miss. July 17, 2008), the Mississippi Supreme Court answered two certified questions from the United States Court of Appeals for the Fifth Circuit. First, the Mississippi Supreme Court held that state law permits a retaliatory discharge claim for discharge in retaliation for reporting a co-employee's illegal acts that relate to the employer's business. Id. at 357. Second, the Mississippi Supreme Court held that Mississippi does not allow for individual liability for retaliatory discharge even if the individual defendant's participation in the discharge was in the course and scope of his employment. Id.

B. Elements of Libel Claim

1. ***Basic Elements.*** To establish a claim for defamation, an ordinary plaintiff must show: (1) a false and defamatory statement concerning the plaintiff; (2) an unprivileged publication to a third party; (3) fault amounting at least to negligence on the part of the publisher; and (4) either actionability of the statement irrespective of special harm or the existence of special harm caused by the publication. Armistead v. Minor, 815 So. 2d 1189, 1193 (Miss. 2002); Franklin v. Thompson, 722 So. 2d 688, 692 (Miss. 1998); Moon v. Condere Corp., 690 So. 2d 1191, 1195 (Miss. 1997) (citing Blake v. Gannett Co., 529 So. 2d 595, 602, 15 Media L. Rep. 1561 (Miss. 1988)), rev'd on other grounds by Condere Corp. v. Moon, 880 So. 2d 1038 (Miss. 2005).

2. ***Fault.***

a. **Private Figure Plaintiff/Matter of Public Concern.** In Brewer v. Memphis Publishing Co., 626 F.2d 1238, 1245-47, 6 Media L. Rep. 2025 (5th Cir. 1980), the majority concluded that as a result of Gertz v. Robert Welch, Inc., 418 U.S. 323, 345, 1 Media L. Rep. 1633 (1974), Mississippi would adopt a negligence standard in private figure/matter of public concern defamation cases. In a special concurrence, Judge Godbold criticized the majority's discussion of Gertz as little more than hypothetical because the federal constitutional issues were resolved against the plaintiffs, thereby obviating the need for resolution of state law issues not previously addressed by the Mississippi Supreme Court. Id. at 1260. Nonetheless, the Mississippi Supreme Court has since cited portions of the state law discussion in Brewer with approval. Fulton v. Mississippi Publishers Corp., 498 So. 2d 1215, 1217, 13 Media L. Rep. 1746 (Miss. 1986).

b. **Private Figure Plaintiff/Matter of Private Concern.** If the subject matter of the defamation is not a matter of public concern, a private individual, even if a vortex or quasi public figure, need not prove actual malice. See Sartain v. White, 588 So. 2d 204, 213 (Miss. 1991); Staheli v. Smith, 548 So. 2d 1299 (Miss. 1989). Instead, the private plaintiff need only prove negligence. Boone v. Wal-Mart Stores, Inc., 680 So. 2d 844, 846 (Miss. 1996).

c. **Public Figure Plaintiff/Matter of Public Concern.** Public figures are generally those who have assumed prominent roles in societal affairs. Some occupy positions of such persuasive power and influence that they are deemed public figures for all purposes. More commonly, those classed as public figures have thrust themselves to the forefront of particular public controversies in order to influence the resolution of the issues involved. Blake v. Gannett Co., 529 So. 2d 595, 601 (Miss. 1988) (quoting Gertz v. Robert Welch, Inc. 418 U.S. 323, 345 (1974)). Where the plaintiff is a public figure, the law prohibits him from recovering damages unless he proves that the statement was made with actual malice - that is, with knowledge that it was false or with reckless disregard of whether it was false. Moon v. Condere Corp., 690 So. 2d 1191, 1195 (Miss. 1997) (citations omitted). The plaintiff must prove actual malice by clear and convincing evidence. Armistead v. Minor, 815 So. 2d 1189, 1193 (Miss. 2002); Gulf Publ'g Co. v. Lee , 434 So. 2d 687, 696, 9 Media L. Rep. 1865 (Miss. 1983).

Mississippi law also recognizes that when a private figure injects herself into a matter of legitimate public interest she becomes a vortex or quasi public figure. Ferguson v. Watkins, 448 So. 2d 271, 277 (Miss. 1984). The Mississippi Supreme Court noted two ways where a person might become a public figure for the purposes of the constitutional or actual malice standard of New York Times Co. v. Sullivan, 376 U.S. 254, 1 Media L. Rep. 1527 (1964): (1) by occupying positions of such persuasive power and influence that they are deemed public figures for all purposes, and (2) more commonly, those that have thrust themselves to the forefront of a particular public controversy in order to influence the resolution of the issues involved. Newson v. Henry, 443 So. 2d 817, 822, 10 Media L. Rep. 1421 (Miss. 1983) (citing Gertz, 418 U.S. 323,). In order to be a vortex public figure, the individual must comment on matters of public concern, and not merely on her private affairs, Ferguson, 448 So. 2d at 277, or matters of legitimate public interest. Staheli v. Smith, 548 So. 2d 1299, 1304 (Miss. 1989). When deciding whether a particular debate involves a matter of public concern, the court examines the expression's content, form, and context as revealed by the whole record. Id. (following Dun & Bradstreet, Inc. v. Greenmoss Builders, Inc. 472 U.S. 749, 11 Media L. Rep. 2417 (1985)). A quasi or vortex public figure must prove actual malice when he brings a defamation action arising from the matter of legitimate public interest. Ferguson, 448 So. 2d at 277-78. See also Moon v. Condere Corp., 690 So. 2d 1191, 1196 (Miss. 1997); Eason v. Federal Broadcasting Co., 697 So. 2d 435, 438, 25 Media L. Rep. 2372 (Miss. 1997).

Cases that found that the plaintiff was a vortex public figure: Simmons Law Group, P.A. v. Corporate Management, Inc., 42 So. 3d 511 (Miss. 2010) (private hospital and nursing home administrator was a vortex public figure required to prove actual malice); Ferguson, 448 So. 2d at 277 (three physicians who operated emergency room in public hospital were vortex public figures); Griffin v. Delta Democrat Times Publ'g Co., 815 So. 2d 1246, 1248-49 (Miss. Ct. App. 2002) (legal counsel for Board of Supervisors who an article allegedly misquoted regarding a municipal judge's unethical conduct; the legal counsel was found to be a public figure because the issue was a matter of public concern and the attorney had voluntarily involved himself in the matter's resolution). Cases holding that the plaintiff was not a vortex public figure: Eason, 697 So. 2d at 438 (criminal defendant does not become a vortex public figure); Sartain v. White, 588 So. 2d 204, 213 (Miss. 1991) (accusations that plaintiff is a murderer, robber, or terrorist would generally would be a matter of public concern, but in context of family neighborhood dispute are not of public concern); Staheli, 548 So. 2d at 1304-05 (whether public university professor was entitled to tenure or pay raise was not a matter of public concern). Once a person becomes a public figure, he or she remains a public figure with respect to the event or events that made him or her a public figure in the first place. He or she may in time become a private figure, but only with respect to the events of his or her life occurring when he or she leaves public life. Newson, 1443 So. 2d at 823.

3. ***Falsity.*** The threshold question in any defamation action is whether the published statements are false. McCullough v. Cook, 679 So. 2d 627, 631 (Miss. 1996) (citing Blake, 529 So. 2d at 602). A statement may be literally true, but material omissions from the true facts can create a defamatory impression and therefore be actionable. McCullough, 679 So. 2d at 632 (Miss. 1996). Nonetheless, the statement must not be literally true to be nonactionable; substantial truth is a complete defense to a defamation claim. Blake, 529 So. 2d at 603. As the United States Supreme Court noted, "[m]inor inaccuracies do not amount to falsity so long as the substance, the gist, the sting, of the libelous charge be justified. Put another way, the statement is not considered false, unless it would have a different effect on the mind of the reader from that which the pleaded truth would have produced." Armistead v. Minor, 815 So. 2d 1180, 1194 (Miss. 2002) (quoting Masson v. New Yorker Magazine, Inc., 501 U.S. 496, 517 (1991)).

4. ***Defamatory Statement of Fact.*** A communication is defamatory "which tends to injure one's reputation, and thereby expose him to public hatred, contempt or ridicule, degrade him in society, lessen him in public esteem or lower him in the confidence of the community . . . ." Gulf Publ'g Co. v. Lee , 434 So. 2d 687, 695, 9 Media L. Rep. 1865 (Miss. 1983); see also Manasco v. Walley, 216 Miss. 614, 63 So. 2d 91 (Miss. 1953). Ferguson v. Watkins, 448 So. 2d 271, 275 (Miss. 1984)(notes that the defamation must be clear and unmistakable from the words themselves and not be the product of any innuendo, speculation or conjecture). See also Gales v. CBS Broadcasting, Inc., 269 F. Supp. 2d 772, 777, 31 Media L. Rep. 2367 (S.D. Miss. 2003); Jernigan v. Humphrey, 815 So. 2d 1149, 1155 (Miss. 2002); accord Baugh v. Baugh, 512 So. 2d 1283, 1285 (Miss. 1987) (slander claim). In 1996, the Mississippi Supreme Court applied Milkovich v. Lorain Journal Co., 497 U.S. 1, 17 Media L. Rep. 2009 (1990), in Roussel v. Robbins, 688 So. 2d 714, 723 (Miss. 1996), noting that the Milkovich court rejected the constitutional distinction between opinion and fact. Id. at 723 (citing Keohane v. Wilkerson, 859 P.2d 291, 21 Media L. Rep. 1417 (Colo. Ct. App. 1993), aff'd, 882 P.2d 1293 (Colo. 1994)). Thus, after Milkovich, whether a statement is characterized as a fact or opinion is no longer a relevant inquiry in determining whether it may be constitutionally privileged. Rather, the relevant inquiry is whether the statement could be reasonably understood as declaring or implying a provable assertion of fact. Id. (quoting Keohane, 859 P.2d at 296). See Hudson v. Palmer, 977 So. 2d 369 (Miss. Ct. App. 2007) (reporter's relay of information from sheriff's department to business owner could not be reasonably understood to imply that plaintiff committed a crime); Smith v. White, 799 So. 2d 83 (Miss. 2001) (upon discovery of document tampering, employer's statement that employee had a key to office where documents were maintained was not slander per se); Speed v. Scott, 787 So. 2d 626 (Miss. Ct. App. 2001) (merely accusing one of being a thief is insufficient to establish that the statement is actionable per se; the seriousness of the alleged offense is determinative. For example, accusing one of stealing a pencil or something of minimal value is not actionable per se); cf. McFadden v. United States Fidelity & Guar. Co. 766 So. 2d 20 (Miss. Ct. App. 2000) (remarks that a doctor is crackpot and quack are defamatory as they attack one's capability in his trade or profession).

5. ***Of and Concerning Plaintiff.*** "[T]he words employed must have clearly been directed toward the plaintiff." Ferguson v. Watkins, 448 So. 2d 271, 275 (Miss. 1984); see Gales , 269 F. Supp. 2d at 777 (statement about large jury verdicts rendered in county not of or concerning jurors who rendered multi-million dollar damages verdict where

no juror or jury verdict was mentioned by name); Downtown Grill, Inc. v. Connell, 721 So. 2d 1113 (Miss. 1998) (parents may not recover for statements about their son); Mitchell v. Random House, Inc., 865 F.2d 664, 671, 16 Media L. Rep. 1207 (5th Cir. 1989) (sister may not recover for statements concerning her brother); Wilson v. Retail Credit Co., 325 F. Supp. 460, 463 n.5 (S.D. Miss. 1971), aff'd, 457 F.2d 1406 (5th Cir. 1972) (credit report about a wife does not create a libel claim by her husband).

6. ***Publication.*** The allegedly defamatory statement must be published, i.e., spoken or made in writing, to someone other than the plaintiff or her agent. Kirk Jewelers v. Bynum, 75 So. 2d 463 (Miss. 1954). "There is no publication if the defendant spoke the words with the reasonable expectation that they would not be overheard by a third party. . .". The test of publication is: were the words spoken in such a tone or manner and under such circumstances that the defendants had a reasonable expectation that no one would hear the words except the plaintiff? Smith v. Jones, 335 So. 2d 896, 897 (Miss. 1976); Sullivan v. Metropolitan Cas. Ins. Co., 256 F. 726 (5th Cir. 1919) (casualty insurer's letter to its insured explaining why insured's claim was denied, and the letter's delivery through insurer's local attorney who saw the letter's contents, is not a publication).

a. **Intra-corporate Communication.** An intra-corporate communication does not constitute a publication to a third party, at least where the statement is made by a corporate officer or employee within the course and scope of her duties to another officer or employee who is also acting within her duties. Cartwright-Caps Co. v. Fischel & Kaufman, 113 Miss. 359, 74 So. 278, 279 (1917) (a corporation's letter addressed to one of its customers which was dictated by the company's president to his stenographer is not a publication in the absence of any repetition by the officer or the stenographer to others outside the company or the addressee). But see Benson v. Hall, 339 So. 2d 570, 573 (Miss. 1976) (distinguishing between whether defamation was published as opposed to whether privilege applied; holding that statements in letter criticizing plaintiff's job performance was protected by privilege because it was only published to other members of University where plaintiff worked).

b. **Compelled Self-Publication.** This issue has not been addressed in Mississippi.

c. **Republication.** A person who repeats a defamatory statement that had been made by someone outside the jurisdiction of the court will be liable for the republication. Scott v. Peebles, 10 Miss. (2 S. & M.) 546 (1844). The author of a defamation is liable for any secondary publication which is the natural consequence of the author's original action. Newson v. Henry, 443 So. 2d 817, 821, 10 Media L. Rep. 1421 (Miss. 1983). A newspaper is not liable for the republication of statements which it is required by law to publish. Grantham v. Wilkes, 135 Miss. 777, 100 So. 673 (1924).

7. ***Statements versus Conduct.*** This issue has not been addressed in Mississippi.

8. ***Damages.*** The Mississippi Supreme Court has not discussed Gertz v. Robert Welch, Inc. , 418 U.S. 323 (1974), or Dun & Bradstreet, Inc. v. Greenmoss Builders, Inc., 472 U.S. 749 (1985), and how, if at all, those cases might affect the damages in defamation actions in Mississippi. Damages in libel actions must be based on proof of injury to reputation; it is insufficient to impose damages simply because of the humiliation or mental or emotional distress suffered by the plaintiff. Garziano v. E.I. du Pont de Nemours & Co., 818 F.2d 380, 395 (5th Cir. 1987) (citing Forman v. Mississippi Publishers Corp., 195 Miss. 90, 14 So. 2d 344, 347 (1943)).

Miss. Code Ann. § 11-1-60(2)(b) provides that in any civil action filed on or after September 1, 2004, other than for an injury based on malpractice against a health care provider, in the event the trier of fact finds the defendant liable, they shall not award the plaintiff more than One Million Dollars ($1,000,000.00) for noneconomic damages. "Noneconomic damages" are defined as "subjective, nonpecuniary damages arising from death, pain, suffering, inconvenience, mental anguish, worry, emotional distress, loss of society and companionship, loss of consortium, bystander injury, physical impairment, disfigurement, injury to reputation, humiliation, embarrassment, loss of the enjoyment of life, hedonic damages, other nonpecuniary damages, and any other theory of damages such as fear of loss, illness or injury." The statute specifically provides that "[t]he term noneconomic damages' shall not include punitive or exemplary damages." Miss. Code Ann. §11-1-60(1)(a).

a. **Presumed Damages and Libel Per Se.** Damages in actions involving slander per se are presumed. McCrory Corp. v. Istre, 252 Miss. 679, 173 So. 2d 640 (1965). To recover damages in actions involving slander per quod, special damages must be proved. Baugh v. Baugh, 512 So. 2d 1283, 1285 (Miss. 1987). "Slander requires proof of special harm unless statements were actionable per se." Speed v. Scott, 787 So. 2d 626, 632 (Miss. 2001). The court identified five categories of slander in Mississippi for which no special harm need be shown:

> (1) Words imputing the guilt or commission of some criminal offense involving moral turpitude and infamous punishment, (2) Words imputing the existence of some

> contagious disease, (3) Words imputing unfitness in an officer who holds an office of profit or employment, either in respect of morals or inability to discharge the duties thereof, (4) Words imputing a want of integrity or capacity, whether mental or pecuniary, in the conduct of a profession, trade or business; and in some other jurisdictions (5) words imputing to a female a want of chastity.

Speed, 787 So. 2d at 632 (quoting W.T. Farley, Inc. v. Bufkin, 159 Miss. 350, 132 So. 86, 87 (1931)). In Speed, the Mississippi Supreme Court defined special harm as the loss of something having economic or pecuniary value. "The limitation [that arose centuries ago] has persisted in the requirement that special harm, to serve as the foundation of an action for slander that is not actionable *per se*, must be temporal, material, pecuniary or economic in character." Speed, 787 So. 2d at 632 (quoting RESTATEMENT (SECOND) OF TORTS § 575 cmt. b. (1977)).

(1) **Employment-Related Criticism.** There are no Mississippi cases.

(2) **Single Instance Rule.** There are no Mississippi cases.

b. **Punitive Damages.** Punitive damages are recoverable where malice is shown. Montgomery & Ward Co. v. Skinner, 200 Miss. 44, 25 So. 2d 572 (1946). Statements made intemperately or in anger are insufficient by themselves to constitute malice if the defendant honestly believes the plaintiff's conduct to be as described. Arnold v. Quillian, 262 So. 2d 414, 415 (Miss. 1972). Mississippi allows punitive damages in the absence of actual damages where the defamation complained of was actionable per se and the plaintiff proved constitutional or actual malice. Newson v. Henry, 443 So. 2d 817, 824 (Miss. 1983). The court upheld punitive damages in the absence of actual malice where the subject matter of the statements was not a matter of public concern. Sartain v. White, 588 So. 2d 204, 213 (Miss. 1991).

In 1993, the State Legislature adopted Miss. Code § 11-1-65 (Supp. 1999), which regulates punitive damages. When initially adopted, the statute established the procedure for trying cases involving punitive damages, setting out the role for the trial court and the jury as well as listing the criteria a jury should consider before awarding punitive damages. The statute provided for a bifurcated proceeding, mandating that the issue of punitive damages not arise unless and until the trial court rendered a compensatory damages award f . As initially adopted, Section 11-1-65 expressly did not apply to defamation claims.

In 2002, the State Legislature amended the statute and adopted monetary capsthat limited awards based on a schedule related to a defendant's net worth. Miss. Code § 11-1-65(3) (Rev. 2002). In 2004, the State Legislature reduced the caps for defendants with a net worth under $750 million. Miss. Code § 11-1-65(3) (Rev. 2004). The 2004 amendment also made the entire statute applicable to defamation claims. Miss. Code § 11-1-65(3) (Rev. 2004).

II. PRIVILEGES AND DEFENSES

A. Scope of Privileges

1. ***Absolute Privilege.*** The Mississippi Supreme Court defined an absolutely privileged communication as one made in the interest of the public service or the due administration of justice, and it is practically limited to legislative and judicial proceedings and other state actions. Grantham v. Wilkes, 135 Miss. 777, 100 So. 673, 673 (1924) (quoting 17 R.C.L. 330); see Eason v. Federal Broadcasting Co., 697 So. 2d 435, 437 (Miss. 1997) (absolute privilege is practically limited to legislative and judicial proceedings and other state acts, including communications made in the discharge of a duty under express authority of law); Hardtner v. Salloum, 148 Miss. 346, 114 So. 621, 623-24 (1927) (adding military proceedings to the absolute privilege afforded legislative and judicial proceedings). Several Mississippi decisions refer to an absolute privilege for pleadings submitted in judicial proceedings if the publication is pertinent or relevant to the proceedings. See, e.g., Ladner v. Arrington, 374 So. 2d 831, 833 (Miss. 1979); Dethlefs v. Beau Maison Dev. Corp., 511 So. 2d 112, 117-18 (Miss. 1987) (lis pendens filings absolutely privileged as party had a justifiable claim); Lenoir v. Tannehill, 660 F. Supp. 42, 44 (S.D. Miss. 1986). The matter to which the privilege does not extend must be so palpably wanting in relation to the subject-matter of the controversy that no reasonable man can doubt its irrelevancy and impropriety. Hardtner, 114 So. 2d at 624. In Mallette v. Church of God International, 789 So. 2d 120 (Miss. 2001), the court affirmed the dismissal of a minister's defamation claim arising from a parishioner's letter written to a church based on absolute immunity from judicial review, citing the United States Constitution as authority for the proposition that "a civil court is forbidden . . . from becoming involved in ecclesiastical disputes." The court also applied a qualified privilege analysis, noting that the alleged defamatory information was limited to those with a common interest and was not disseminated beyond the closed hearing. Mallette, 789 So. 2d at 124.

2. ***Qualified Privileges.***

a. **Common Interest.** A communication made in good faith and on a subject matter in which the person making it has an interest or duty to make, is privileged if made to a person or persons having a corresponding interest or duty, even though communication contains matters that without this privilege would be slanderous, provided the statement is made without malice and in good faith. Eckman v. Cooper Tire & Rubber Co., 893 So. 2d 1049, 1052 (Miss. 2005) (quoting Smith v. White, 799 So. 2d 83, 86 (Miss. 2001)). An employer enjoys a qualified privilege when commenting on personnel matters to those who have a legitimate and direct interest in the communication's subject matter. Bulloch v. City of Pascagoula, 574 So. 2d 637, 642 (Miss. 1990) (citing Benson v. Hall, 339 So. 2d 570, 572 (Miss. 1976)). Examples where the qualified privilege has been upheld are: (1) employer's report to its employees concerning grounds for co-employee's discharge, Raiola v. Chevron U.S.A., Inc., 872 So. 2d 79, 85 (Miss. Ct. App. 2004); (2) employer's disclosure to fellow employees and independent contractors that a resigning employee was infected with a highly contagious disease, Grice v. FedEx Ground Package Sys., Inc., 925 So. 2d 907, 912 (Miss. Ct. App. 2006); (3) university department head's letter to university president regarding employee's job performance, Staheli v. Smith, 548 So. 2d 1299, 1305-06 (Miss. 1989); (4) employer's statement to insurance company on proof of loss form regarding employee's indictment for embezzlement, Funderburk v. Johnson, 935 So. 2d 1084, 1105-06 (Miss. Ct. App. Mar. 28, 2006); (5) individual's report to District Attorney that a co-worker failed a drug test, Brisco v. LeTourneau Techs., Inc., No. 5:07CV99, 2008 WL 4793791 (S.D. Miss. Oct. 27, 2008). See alsoClark v. Luvel Dairy Products, Inc., 821 So. 2d 827, 832 (Miss. Ct. App. 2001) (employer's communications regarding potential theft by employee protected by qualified privilege when publication limited to employee suspected, deputy sheriff, and key management personnel). Mississippi statute also provides a qualified privilege from defamation actions brought by employees against employers who establish a drug and alcohol testing program that meets the statute's criteria. Miss. Code § 71-7-25 (1972).

b. **Duty.** Mississippi recognizes a qualified privilege for statements made concerning any subject matter where the speaker has a duty in that subject. The duty is not a legal one, but only a moral or social duty of imperfect obligation. Grantham v. Wilkes, 135 Miss. 777, 100 So. 673, 673 (1924). In Hayden v. Foryt, 407 So. 2d 535, 539 (Miss. 1982), the Mississippi Supreme Court recognized that a chief anesthetist, who was under a duty to report on the actions of his subordinates, made the reports under a qualified privilege.

c. **Criticism of Public Employee.** If the an employer criticizes his public employee, then such criticism enjoys the same privilege afforded to all employers. See II. A. 2. a, supra. Additionally, if the public employee is a public figure, then a plaintiff must prove actual malice before recovering in an action for defamation. See I.B.2.c, supra. The court stated that only higher level, decision-making public employees are public officials. Staheli, 548 So. 2d at 1304. The following plaintiffs were classified as public officials: (1) county attorney and city police chief, Henry v. Collins, 380 U.S. 356 (1965); (2) city policeman, Pride v. Quitman County Voters League, 226 So. 2d 735, 737 (Miss. 1969); (3) school principal, Reaves v. Foster, 200 So. 2d 453, 458 (Miss. 1967).

d. **Limitation on Qualified Privileges.**

(1) **Constitutional or Actual Malice.** Once the court determines that the occasion for the publication of a defamatory statement involves a qualified privilege, a good faith presumption arises. The plaintiff must prove bad faith, actual malice, or abuse of the privilege through excess publication. See, e.g., Barmada v. Pridjian, 989 So. 2d 359 (Miss. Aug. 14, 2008) ("[w]here qualified privilege exists, a presumption of good faith arises" and "[a] plaintiff must present affirmative evidence demonstrating actual malice to defeat the qualified privilege."); Eckman v. Cooper Tire & Rubber Co., 893 So. 2d 1049, 1052 (Miss. 2005) (if the publication is subject to qualified privilege, liability for defamation may still attach upon a finding of malice, defined as knowledge of falsity or reckless disregard as to truth or falsity). Certain conduct will not serve as evidence of bad faith or actual malice. For example, an employee's dismissal following an investigation is not evidence of actual malice. Garziano v. E.I. du Pont, 818 F. 2d 380, 389 (5th Cir. 1987). Examples where the qualified privilege has been destroyed are: (a) making a statement with knowledge of its falsity, Smith v. White, 799 So. 2d 83, 87 (Miss. 2001); (b) law enforcement official's report to those outside the law enforcement sector which included matters beyond the facts of the arrest and the crime charged and included statements regarding the suspect's guilt, Krebs v. McNeal, 222 Miss. 560, 76 So. 2d 693 (1955); (c) employer's statements to employees made in presence of third persons who had no interest in matters regarding misplaced store monies, Montgomery Ward & Co. v Skinner, 200 Miss. 44, 25 So. 2d 572 (1946).

(2) **Common Law Malice.** Common law malice or malice in fact relates to the state or condition of the person's mind who speaks the defamatory words and includes intention to injure, hatred, ill will, or where the speaker in fact knew that the statements were false, or she spoke recklessly without knowing or caring whether the statements are true. Southwest Drug Stores of Miss., Inc. v. Garner, 195 So. 2d 837, 839-40 (Miss. 1967) (a store employee exceeded qualified privilege by accusing a customer of stealing store merchandise in the presence of others outside the store; malice in fact could be inferred from accusation).

(3) **Other Limitations on Qualified Privileges.** A qualified privilege does not protect a defamatory statement where excessive publication occurs to persons not within the circle of those people who have

a legitimate and direct interest in the communication's subject matter. Garziano v. E.I. Dupont de Nemours & Co., 818 F.2d 380, 391-92 (5th Cir. 1987) (applying Mississippi law). In Staheli v. Smith, 548 So. 2d 1299, 1395-96 (Miss. 1989), a University professor who was denied tenure sued the Dean for defamation based on comments and writings the Dean made during the tenure process. The court found no publication outside the circle because the faculty senate were included in the tenure process and the plaintiff brought the senate inside the circle when he appealed the chancellor's decision. Id.; see also Eckman v. Cooper Tire & Rubber Co., 893 So. 2d 1049, 1052 (Miss. 2005) (alleged defamatory statement was not excessively published and thus did not lose qualified privilege when the only people to read or hear the remarks were the plaintiff/surgeon's own employees, the employer asked to pay the surgeon's bill, and the physician asked to review the bill for employer).

e. **Question of Fact or Law.** The Fifth Circuit stated that "[a]lthough a question concerning a defendant's abuse of its qualified privilege may, in the proper case, be for the jury, if only one conclusion can be drawn from the facts, the courts may summarily dispose of the issue." Esmark Apparel, Inc. v. James, 10 F.3d 1156, 1163 (5th Cir. 1994) (citing RESTATEMENT (SECOND) OF TORTS § 619 (1977)).

f. **Burden of Proof.** When a qualified privilege exists, malice is not implied. The plaintiff must prove bad faith, actual malice, or abuse of the privilege through excess publication. Garziano, 818 F.2d at 388. Once the court determines that the occasion of an alleged defamatory statement falls under a qualified privileged, a presumption of good faith arises, which the plaintiff must rebut in order to recover. Esmark Apparel, Inc., 10 F.3d at 1162.

When the statement is capable of defamatory and nondefamatory meanings, the plaintiff must show that it was reasonably and properly understood to have a defamatory meaning. The jury, and not the hearer of the words, determines whether the words were slanderous. Smith v. White, 799 So. 2d 83, 87-88 (Miss. 2001); Montgomery Ward & Co. v. Skinner, 200 Miss. 44, 25 So. 2d 572 (1946); Taylor v. Standard Oil Co., 184 Miss. 392, 186 So. 294 (1939).

B. Standard Libel Defenses

1. ***Truth.*** Truth is a complete defense to an action for libel. Raiola v. Chevron U.S.A., Inc., 872 So. 2d 79, 86 (Miss. Ct. App. 2004); McCullough v. Cook, 679 So. 2d 627, 631 (Miss. 1996) (citations omitted). Although typically referred to as a defense, in actuality, the plaintiff bears the burden of proving the falsity of the alleged defamatory statement. Eckman, 893 So. 2d at 1053; Blake v. Gannett Co., 529 So. 2d 595, 603, 15 Media L. Rep. 1561 (Miss. 1988) (following Philadelphia Newspapers, Inc. v. Hepps, 475 U.S. 767, 12 Media L. Rep. 1977 (1986)). If the published statement is substantially true, the statement is not defamatory. Armistead v. Minor, 815 So. 2d 1189, 1194 (Miss. 2002); Blake , 529 So. 2d at 603. The statement's truth can be established through the principle of collateral estoppel. Raiola, 872 So. 2d at 86 (Mississippi Employment Security Commission ruling given preclusive effect).

2. ***Opinion.*** The Mississippi Supreme Court in Roussel v. Robbins, 688 So. 2d 714, 723 (Miss. 1996) applied the Milkovich v. Lorain Journal Co., 497 U.S. 1, 17 Media L. Rep. 2009 (1990)analysis in a defamation action between private individuals, holding that the relevant inquiry is whether the statement could reasonably be understood as declaring or implying a provable assertion of fact. Id. at 723. The Mississippi Supreme Court has since followed Roussel and applied its test in a public official defamation action brought against a public law enforcement officer. Franklin v. Thompson, 722 So. 2d 688, 693 (Miss. 1998). In Franklin, 722 So. 2d at 693, the Mississippi Supreme Court held that an opinion is actionable as defamation if a statement's substance or gist could reasonably be interpreted as declaring or implying an assertion of fact. See also Hamilton v. Hammons, 792 So. 2d 956 (Miss. 2001) (opinions based on disclosed, truthful, non-defamatory facts do not rise to level of actionable opinion as a matter of law).

3. ***Consent.*** This issue has not been expressly addressed in Mississippi. See Kirk Jewelers, Inc. v. Bynum, 75 So. 2d 463 (Miss. 1954) (slanderous publication to plaintiff or his agent representing him in the matter discussed and invited by the plaintiff or by his authorized agent will not support action for slander).

4. ***Libel-Proof Plaintiff Doctrine.*** In Armistead v. Minor, 815 So. 2d 1189, 1193-94 (Miss. 2002), the court stated that, "The libel-proof plaintiff doctrine reasons that when a particular plaintiff's reputation for a particular trait is sufficiently bad, further statements regarding that trait even if false and made with malice, are not actionable because, as a matter of law, the plaintiff cannot be damaged in his reputation as to that trait." Armistead, 815 So. 2d at 1193 (internal citations and quotations omitted). In Armistead, the Mississippi Supreme Court found that the libel-proof doctrine looks at the plaintiff's current reputation, which requires consideration of credibility issues. Therefore, the court held that summary judgment is not appropriate in applying the libel-proof doctrine. Armistead, 815 So. 2d 1193-94.

5. ***Mitigation.*** The Mississippi Supreme Court has allowed testimony relating to the plaintiff's general reputation for honesty and fair dealing to be heard on the mitigation of damages issue. Wells v. Branscome, 74 So. 2d

743, 745 (Miss. 1954). Since damages are based on harm to reputation, the quality of the plaintiff's reputation before the alleged defamation is relevant to the issue of damages. Id.

III. RECURRING FACT PATTERNS

A. Statements in Personnel File

In Staheli v. Smith, 548 So. 2d 1299 (Miss. 1989), a qualified privilege protected a state university dean's statements evaluating a professor for tenure and a pay raise. A state governmental official is protected from liability for damages for breach of a legal duty unless: (1) the duty is ministerial in nature, or (2) the duty involves the use of discretion and the official substantially exceeds his authority causing harm, or (3) he commits an intentional tort. Id. at 1305 (quoting McFadden v. State, 542 So. 2d 871, 877 (Miss. 1989)). As school's dean, Smith's statements regarding the professor's qualifications for tenure were privileged, because the duty was not ministerial; Smith did not intentionally make false statements; and Smith did not exceed the scope of his authority in performing the discretionary duty of commenting on the qualifications of professors for tenure. Staheli, 548 So. 2d at 1305. Because Smith's statements were made only to persons involved in making tenure decisions, and were made without malice, the statements were privileged. Staheli at 1306. See also Eckman v. Cooper Tire & Rubber Co., 893 So. 2d 1049, 1053 (Miss. 2005).

B. Performance Evaluations

Statements made in performance evaluations enjoy a qualified privilege when communicated only to persons who have an interest in the communication's subject matter. See II.A.2.a, supra. In Staheli, 548 So. 2d at 1305-06, the Mississippi Supreme Court applied the privilege finding that a university dean did not abuse the privilege when making comments regarding a professor applying for tenure. See III. A, supra.

C. References

No Mississippi cases have addressed this issue.

D. Intracorporate Communication

See I.B.6.a, supra.

E. Statements to Government Regulators

Communications made to the Mississippi Employment Security Commission by private employers concerning employees in the performance of their jobs shall be absolutely privileged and shall not be made the subject matter or basis of any suit for slander or libel in any Mississippi court unless the same be false in fact and maliciously written, sent, delivered, or made for the purposes of causing a denial of benefits under this chapter. Miss. Code § 71-5-131 (1972). See Raiola v. Chevron U.S.A., Inc., 872 So. 2d 7985 (Miss. 2004). In McGinty v. Acuity Specialty Prods. Group, Inc., No. 3:07CV715, 2009 WL 161827 (S.D. Miss. Jan. 22, 2009), the employer terminated the plaintiff after he failed to disclose a conflict of interest, submitted false expense reports, and made improper payments to family members. Id. at *1. The court ruled that the employer's communications regarding the plaintiff's termination to the Mississippi Employment Security Commission fell under the absolute privilege in MISS. CODE ANN. § 71-5-131 (2008) and were not proven to be false or malicious. Id. at *4.

F. Reports to Auditors and Insurers

In Miley v. Foster, 90 So. 2d 172 (Miss. 1956), the Mississippi Supreme Court found that a letter written by an insurance underwriter to a local insurance agent regarding the insured's credit rating was not defamatory. Even if the letter had been defamatory, because both the underwriter and the agent had an interest in the subject matter, the communication enjoyed a qualified privilege, which could be overcome only by a showing of malice. Miley, 90 So. 2d at 174. See also Funderburk v. Johnson, 935 So. 2d 1084 (Miss. Ct. App. 2006) (holding that Chief Financial Officer's statements on proof of loss form submitted to employer's insurance company were the subject of a qualified privilege).

G. Vicarious Liability of Employers for Statements Made by Employees

1. ***Scope of Employment.*** Mississippi follows the doctrine of respondeat superior. An employer may be vicariously liable for the negligent acts and intentional torts of its employee if the acts of the employee are (a) within the course and scope of employment and (b) in the furtherance of the employer's business. See J. Jackson & M. Miller, 1 Encyclopedia of Mississippi Law § 4.8, at pp. 170-72 (2001). In Milner Hotels, Inc. v. Dougherty, 195 Miss. 718, 15 So. 2d 358, 359-60 (1943), the court appears to suggest in dictum that a hotel employer can be held vicariously liable for the defamatory statements made by its manager employee to a hotel guest. The appellate court, however, did not discuss the

respondeat superior doctrine as applied to defamation claims, and it affirmed the judgment on other grounds. The appellate court did rule, however, that the hotel guest's claim brought under the Mississippi Actionable Words Statute, see Miss. Code § 95-1-1 (1972), could only be brought against the hotel manager and could not be maintained against the defendant hotel. Milner Hotels, Inc., 15 So. 2d at 359-60; see Dixie Fire Ins. Co. v. Betty, 101 Miss. 880, 58 So. 705 (1912). In Brisco v. LeTourneau Techs., Inc., No. 5:07CV99, 2008 WL 4793791 (S.D. Miss. Oct. 27, 2008), the court rejected the plaintiff's defamation claim. Id. at *7. After the plaintiff tested positive for drugs in an employee drug test, she claimed her employer disclosed the false results to individuals who were not designated to receive the results. Id. at *5. The court ruled the plaintiff's claim that the results were false and released to unnamed individuals failed to state the "substance or nature" of a defamatory statement, if any at all. Id. First, the plaintiff failed to prove the results were false. Id. at *5. In addition, since several co-workers testified that they learned of the failed drug test either directly or indirectly from the plaintiff herself, the court held the plaintiff failed to prove that defamatory statements were made by other employees "acting within the scope of their employment." Id. at *5-6. The court recognized that "the fact that a rumor is widespread proves nothing about its origin" especially when others testified the plaintiff disclosed the information herself. Id. at *7. Furthermore, the court ruled that one disclosure by a co-worker to the district attorney's office regarding a criminal proceeding fell under qualified privilege since the statement was made in "good faith in the prosecution of any inquiry regarding a crime which has been committed, and for the purpose of detecting and bringing to justice the criminal." Id. at *6.

Different respondeat superior rules apply to public entities and their employees under the State Sovereign Immunity Act, Miss. Code § 11-46-1 (1972). In McGehee v. DePoyster, 708 So. 2d 77 (Miss. 1998), a school principal brought a defamation action against the school district's superintendent in both his individual and official capacities. The Mississippi Supreme Court noted that under the state's sovereign immunity statute, Miss. Code §§ 11-46-5(2), 11-46-7(2) (Supp. 1997), "a governmental employee's conduct that constitutes libel, slander, [or] defamation are by statute outside the scope and course of employment of the employee." McGehee, 708 So. 2d at 80. The court also found that the defendant school superintendent's statements were not privileged because he stepped outside of the scope and course of his employment when he talked to the media rather than resolving the situation internally. Id. at 80-81.

a. **Blogging.** No Mississippi cases have addressed this issue.

2. ***Damages.*** No Mississippi cases have addressed this issue.

H. Internal Investigations

No Mississippi cases have addressed this issue.

IV. OTHER ACTIONS BASED ON STATEMENTS

A. Negligent Hiring, Retention, and Supervision

Mississippi recognizes a cause of action for negligent hiring, retention, supervision and training. Taylor v. Singing River Hosp. Sys., 704 So. 2d 75, 78-79 n.3 (Miss. 1997) (hospital did not its breach duty to use reasonable care in retaining competent physician when a credential that the hospital failed to verify was not one required by hospital or law and hospital had no reason to question physician's truthfulness or competence); Johnson v. Mississippi Dep't of Corrections, 682 So. 2d 367, 370 (Miss. 1996) (state agency has right to dismiss person when retention would be negligent); Patton v. Southern States Transp., Inc., 932 F. Supp. 795, 801 (S.D. Miss. 1996) (employer may be liable for negligent hiring of person with propensity for violence). In order to prevail on a negligent hiring and retention claim, a plaintiff must prove (1) that the employer knew or should have known of some incompetence on the employee's part, and (2) that the employer failed to do anything about it. Raiola v. Chevron U.S.A., Inc., 872 So. 2d 7985 (Miss. 2004). See also Holmes v. Campbell Properties, Inc., 2010 WL 1962479 (Miss. Ct. App. 2010) (holding that "specific evidence of an employer's actual or constructive knowledge of its employee's dangerous or violent tendencies is necessary in order to create a genuine issue of material fact on an improper training or supervision theory of liability."). In Campbell v. Jackson Bus. Forms Co., 841 F. Supp. 772, 774-75 (S.D. Miss. 1994), the plaintiff, defendant's former employee , brought a claim against her former employer for negligent supervision of a co-employee. The court held the negligent supervision claim was barred by the exclusive remedy provision of the Mississippi Workers' Compensation Act, Miss. Code § 71-3-9 (Rev. 1989). Campbell, 841 F. Supp. at 774-75. The court also dismissed the negligent supervision claim on the grounds that it was duplicative of the plaintiff's claim for sexual harassment under Title VII, which was time-barred. Id.

B. Intentional Infliction of Emotional Distress

The Mississippi Court of Appeals recognizes that damages are typically not recoverable in employment disputes involving intentional infliction of emotional distress claims. Clark v. Luvel Dairy Prods., Inc., 821 So. 2d 827, 830-31 (Miss. Ct. App. 2001) (citing Pegues v. Emerson Elec. Co., 913 F. Supp. 976, 982 (N.D. Miss. 1996)). The court of appeals further stated, "[r]ather, [o]nly in the most unusual cases does the conduct move out of the realm of an ordinary employment dispute into the classification of extreme and outrageous, as required for the tort of intentional infliction of emotional distress." Clark, 821 So. 2d at 831 (citing Prunty v. Arkansas Freightways, Inc., 16 F.3d 649 (5th Cir. 1994) (internal citations omitted)). But see Jones v. Fluor Daniel Services Corp., 959 So. 2d 1044 (Miss. 2007) (holding that plaintiffs' allegations of racial slurs in the workplace, segregation of employees by race and division of labor according to race were sufficient to defeat summary judgment on their intentional infliction of emotional distress claim).

C. Interference With Economic Advantage

The elements of a tortious interference with business relations claim are: (1) the acts were intentional and willful; (2) the acts were calculated to cause damage to the plaintiffs in their lawful business; (3) the acts were done with the unlawful purpose of causing damage and loss, without right or justifiable cause on the part of the defendant (which constitutes malice); and (4) actual damage and loss resulted. Cooper Tire & Rubber Co. v. Farese, 423 F.3d 446, 458-59 (5th Cir. 2005); Wong v. Stripling, 700 So. 2d 296, 303 (Miss. 1997); see also Gasparrini v. Bredemeier, 802 So. 2d 1062, 1067 (Miss. Ct. App. 2001) (holding that in order to succeed on a claim for tortious interference, a plaintiff must prove by a preponderance of the evidence the four elements of tortious interference with business relations). In Wong, 700 So. 2d at 303, the plaintiff alleged that his dismissal from the defendant hospital would deter other hospitals from hiring him. The court held while his dismissal could potentially serve as a basis for a revocation elsewhere, "[it] is not probative at all of the defendants' willful intent to interfere in those other business relationships." Id. In Raiola v. Chevron U.S.A., Inc., 872 So. 2d 79, 86 (Miss. Ct. App. 2004), the plaintiff argued that two individual co-employees tortuously interfered with his employment contract when they reported to their employer that the plaintiff was not working the number of hours he reported on his time sheets. The court held that in the absence of bad faith, "co-employees are privileged to interfere with [their employer's] contractual relationship with [a co-employee] if they occupy a position of responsibility with the company." Raiola, 872 So. 2d at 86.

D. Prima Facie Tort

No Mississippi cases have addressed this issue.

V. OTHER ISSUES

A. Statute of Limitations

Mississippi has a one-year statute of limitations for defamation actions. Miss. Code § 15-1-35 (1972). Ordinarily, the statute of limitations begins to run from the date of publication of the allegedly libelous statement to a third person. Staheli v. Smith, 548 So. 2d 1299, 1302 (Miss. 1989); see also McCorkle v. McCorkle, 811 So. 2d 258, 265 (Miss. Ct. App. 2001) ("Generally, an action for libel or defamation accrues at the time of the first publication for public consumption."). Where the nature of the publication is secretive and inherently undiscoverable, however, the statute does not begin to run until the plaintiff knew or, in the exercise of reasonable diligence, should have known, of the alleged defamation. Staheli, 548 So. 2d at 1303. But cf. Hudson v. Palmer, 977 So. 2d 369, 379 (Miss. Ct. App. 2007) (filing a police incident report is not so secret or inherently undiscoverable so as to delay accrual of a defamation cause of action).

Defamation suits against employees of public entities are governed by the Mississippi Tort Claims Act, Miss. Code § 11-46-1 et seq. (1972). The statute of limitations under the MTCA is one year. Miss. Code § 11-46-11 (1972). The discovery rule adopted in Staheli, supra, does not apply to a defamation claim arising under the MTCA, Miss. Code § 11-46-1 et seq., (1972), because the limitations provision of the MTCA does not use the same language found in Section 15-1-35. Ellisville State Sch. v. Merrill, 732 So. 2d 198 (Miss. 1999). The MTCA sets accrual on the date that the alleged wrongful conduct occurs; the State Legislature did not intend to subordinate the MTCA statute of limitations to other statutes of limitations.

Under Mississippi Rule of Civil Procedure 9(h), "[w]hen a party is ignorant of the name of an opposing party and so alleges in his pleading, the opposing party may be designated by any name, and when his true name is discovered the process and all pleadings and proceedings in the action may be amended by substituting the true name and giving proper notice to the opposing party." Also, Rule 15(c)(2) states that, "[a]n amendment pursuant to Rule 9(h) is not an amendment changing the party against whom a claim is asserted and such amendment relates back to the date of the original pleading."

In reference to the relation-back doctrine, the Mississippi Court of Appeals stated of Rule 9(h) that, "[i]t is a principle of general application, though, that ignorance of the opposing party for fictitious party practice extends beyond mere lack of knowledge of the opposing party's name. *Even if the plaintiff knows the true name of the person, he is still ignorant of his name if he lacks knowledge of the facts giving him a cause of action against that person.*" Gasparrini v. Bredemeier, 802 So. 2d 1062, 1065-66 (Miss. Ct. App. 2001) (emphasis in original). But the court of appeals explained that the relation back privilege provided under Rule 15(c)(2) requires the plaintiff to actually exercise a reasonably diligent inquiry into the identity of the fictitious party. Id. at 1066, quoting Doe v. Mississippi Blood Servs., Inc., 704 So. 2d 1016, 1019 (Miss. 1997).

B. Jurisdiction

Mississippi's long-arm statute reaches "[a]ny nonresident person, firm, general or limited partnership, or any foreign or other corporation not qualified under the Constitution and laws of this state as to doing business herein, who shall make a contract with a resident of this state to be performed in whole or in part by any party in this state, or who shall commit a tort in whole or in part in this state against a resident or nonresident of this state, or who shall do any business or perform any character of work or service in this state, shall by such act or acts be deemed to be doing business in Mississippi and shall thereby be subjected to the jurisdiction of the courts of this state." Service of summons and process upon the defendant shall be had or made as is provided by the Mississippi Rules of Civil Procedure. Miss. Code § 13-3-57 (Supp. 1994). The Mississippi Supreme Court has not provided an authoritative interpretation of the Mississippi long-arm statute in a defamation action. See Breckenridge v. Time, Inc., 253 Miss. 835, 179 So. 2d 781 (1965) (dismissing defamation action against media defendant on federal constitutional due process grounds. However, defamatory information published on an Internet website has been found to satisfy the tort prong of the Mississippi long-arm statute. Lofton v. Turbine Design, Inc., 100 F. Supp. 2d 404, 409 (N.D. Miss. 2000) (dismissing defamation action against non-resident corporation upon constitutional analysis). The federal courts of Mississippi have found that a nonresident media defendant's activities were sufficient to subject it to personal jurisdiction in Mississippi in Mize v. Harvey Shapiro Enterprises, Inc., 714 F. Supp. 220, 16 Media L. Rep. 2347 (N.D. Miss. 1989); Mitchell v. Random House, Inc., 703 F. Supp. 1250, 15 Media L. Rep. 2033 (S.D. Miss. 1988); Casano v. WDSU-TV, Inc., 313 F. Supp. 1130 (S.D. Miss. 1970); and Edwards v. Associated Press, 512 F.2d 258 (5th Cir. 1975). A single defamatory telephone call by a nonresident to a resident of the state has been found sufficient to establish personal jurisdiction over the nonresident under Mississippi's long-arm statute. Brown v. Flowers Indus., Inc., 688 F. 2d 328 (5th Cir. 1982).

C. Worker's Compensation Exclusivity

The Mississippi Workers' Compensation Act provides in part that "[t]he liability of an employer to pay compensation shall be exclusive and in place of all other liability of such employer to the employee...." Miss.Code Ann. § 71-3-9 (Rev. 2000). Based on the statutory requirement that the injury be accidental, the Mississippi Supreme Court has held that the statute does not bar an employee from pursuing a common law remedy against an employer for the employer's willful or malicious conduct. See Royal Oil Co. v. Wells, 500 So. 2d 439, 442 (Miss. 1986). No Mississippi case has addressed whether a libel claim is barred by the Act's exclusivity provisions.

D. Pleading Requirements

Plaintiffs must plead the exact words or synonymous words that constitute the alleged defamation. Holland v. Kennedy, 548 So. 2d 982, 986 (Miss. 1989); accord Lenoir v. Tannehill, 660 F. Supp. 42, 44 (S.D. Miss. 1986). In Mitchell v. Random House, Inc., 703 F. Supp. 1250, 15 Media L. Rep. 2033 (S.D. Miss. 1988), aff'd, 865 F.2d 664, 16 Media L. Rep. 1207 (5th Cir. 1989), the court noted that the nature of a libel action lends itself to judicial scrutiny in the early stages of a defamation lawsuit and granted the media defendants' motion to dismiss. See also Chalk v. Bertholf, 2007 WL 2038342, at *6 (Miss. Ct. App. 2007) (dismissing complaint because "the complaint failed to specify which of the twelve plaintiffs was slandered by which of the two defendants," and because "the complaint failed to set forth the statements, paraphrased or verbatim, that constituted slander."). **Prior to filing suit, a plaintiff must give at least ten (10) days notice that "identif [ies] the alleged false and defamatory statements with sufficient particularity to enable the broadcaster to investigate the allegations and issue a retraction, if necessary." Hudson v. WLOX, Inc.,2012 Miss. App. LEXIS 264, *11, 40 Media L. Rep. 1838 (Miss. Ct. App. May 8, 2012) (citing Miss. Code Ann. § 95-1-5).**

In cases involving slander per quod, special damages must be pled with particularity. Baugh v. Baugh, 512 So. 2d 1283, 1285 (Miss. 1987); see Barton v. Barnett, 226 F. Supp. 375, 377 (N.D. Miss. 1964).

SURVEY OF MISSISSIPPI EMPLOYMENT PRIVACY LAW

G. Todd Butler
Krissy M. Casey
Phelps Dunbar, L.L.P.
Post Office Box 16114
Jackson, Mississippi 39236
Telephone (601) 352-2300; Telecopier (601) 360-9777

(With Developments Reported Through **November 1, 2012**)

GENERAL COMMENTS

This is a digest of opinions of the Mississippi Supreme Court, the Mississippi Court of Appeals, the United States Fifth Circuit Court of Appeals, and the United States District Courts for the Northern and Southern Districts of Mississippi. Opinions of Mississippi trial courts are not officially reported.

SIGNIFICANT DEVELOPMENTS SINCE THE 2012 *SURVEY*

None.

I. GENERAL LAW OF PRIVACY

A. Legal Basis of Privacy Claims

The right of privacy, "whether perceived as emanating from the common law or natural law, is given constitutional standing by Article 3, § 32 of the Mississippi Constitution of 1890." In Re Brown, 478 So.2d 1033, 1040 (Miss. 1985) (affirming privacy right of sole surviving murder witness to refuse blood transfusion). That provision of our Bill of Rights states: "The enumeration of rights in this constitution shall not be construed to deny and impair others retained by, and inherent in, the people." It has not been held to create a private right of action for privacy invasion. See Cooper v. Drexel Chemical Co., 949 F. Supp. 1275, 1282 (N.D. Miss. 1996) (holding no private right of action exists under Article 7, § 191, which instructs the Legislature to protect corporate employees from interference with their social, civil, or political rights) and Kenyatta v. Moore, 623 F. Supp. 220, 224 (S.D. Miss. 1985) ("No private cause of action and damage remedy has ever been implied from the Mississippi Constitution.")

Mississippi has recognized common law privacy claims in the employment context. Our common law of privacy sprang full grown from the seminal article by Samuel B. Warren and Louis D. Brandeis, *The Right to Privacy*, 4 Harvard L. Rev. 193 (1890). See Martin v. Dorton, 50 So.2d 391, 392 (Miss. 1951) and In Re Brown, 478 So.2d 1033, 1039 (Miss. 1985). Our courts have adopted the formulations expressed in the Restatement (Second) of Torts, § 652 (1977), and in Prosser & Keeton, The Law of Torts § 118 (5th Ed. 1984). See Deaton v. Delta Democrat Publishing Company, 326 So.2d 471, 473 (Miss. 1976); Burris v. South Central Bell Tel. Co., 540 F. Supp. 905, 909 (S.D. Miss. 1982); Candebat v. Flanagan, 487 So.2d 207, 209 (Miss. 1986); Prescott v. Bay St. Louis Newspapers, Inc., 497 So.2d 77, 79 (Miss. 1986) (noting that Mississippi had neither adopted nor rejected the "false light" branch of privacy law); Bussen v. South Central Bell Telephone Co., 682 F. Supp. 319, 324 (S.D. Miss. 1987) (same); Mitchell v. Random House, Inc., 703 F. Supp. 1250, 1259-60 (S.D. Miss. 1988), affirmed, 865 F.2d 664, 671-72 (1989) (doubting that Mississippi had yet authorized "false light" privacy claims); Mize v. Harvey Shapiro Enterprises, Inc., 714 F. Supp. 220, 225 (N.D. Miss. 1989) (same); Young v. Jackson, 572 So.2d 378, 382 (Miss. 1990) (ruling that Mississippi had adopted Restatement § 652 false light claim in Prescott); Watkins v. United Parcel Service, Inc., 797 F. Supp. 1349, 1359 (S.D. Miss. 1992), affirmed, 979 F.2d 1535 (5th Cir. 1992); Glasgow v. Sherwin-Williams Co., 901 F. Supp. 1185, 1192 (N. D. Miss. 1995), affirmed, 146 F.3d 867 (5th Cir. 1998); Malloy v. Sears, Roebuck and Company, 1997 WL 170313 (N.D. Miss. 1997); White v. Interstate Brake Products, Inc., 1997 WL 332066 (N.D. Miss. 1997), appeal dismissed, 141 F.3d 1164 (5th Cir. 1998); Cook v. Mardi Gras Casino Corporation, 697 So.2d 378, 382 (Miss. 1997) (reaffirming false light holding of Young v. Jackson); Davis v. Smart Corporation, 1997 WL 786763 (N.D. Miss. 1997); Gray v. City of Olive Branch, 1998 WL 211766 (N.D. Miss. 1998); Hogue v. Roberts, 1998 WL 433947 (N.D. Miss. 1998).

B. Causes of Action

Mississippi courts have recognized four distinct theories of the common law tort of invasion of privacy:

(1) the intentional intrusion upon the solitude or seclusion of another;

(2) the appropriation of another's identity for an un-permitted use;

(3) the public disclosure of private facts; or

(4) holding another to the public eye in a false light.

Gales v. CBS Broadcasting, Inc., 269 F.Supp.2d 772, 783 (S.D. MS 2003), citing Deaton v. Delta Democrat Publ'g Co., 326 So.2d 471, 473 (Miss. 1976). However, our courts did not publish an opinion applying our privacy law to an employment case until 1990. In all invasion of privacy actions, a plaintiff "must show some bad faith or utterly reckless prying . . . ." Plaxico v. Michael, 735 So. 2d 1036, 1039 (Miss. 1999). The entire body of Mississippi employment privacy law consists of less than a dozen cases.

When an invasion of privacy claim accrues is important for limitation-period purposes. In Hudson v. Palmer, 977 So. 2d 369 (Miss. Ct. App. 2008), a patron of an automobile repair shop sued the shop owner and an employee on several bases, including invasion of privacy, after they filed a police complaint alleging disturbance of the peace. Though the patron claimed he did not become aware of the alleged untrue statements made to the police until he was arrested, the Court held that the patron's claim accrued at the time the statements were made, not at the time of the arrest.

1. ***Misappropriation/Right of Publicity.*** This cause of action was adopted in Candebat v. Flanagan, 487 So.2d 207, 209 (Miss. 1986), but there is no published opinion in the employment context. "The appropriation of another's identity for an unpermitted use" is actionable, and emotional distress damages may be recovered, without regard to whether the plaintiff's likeness, name or other personal, identifying information has, or was misappropriated for, market value, 487 So.2d at 212, apparently modifying the "property right" slant of Restatement (Second) of Torts § 652C. In Harbin v. Jennings, 734 So.2d 269 (Miss. App. 1999), the court reversed, for inadequate proof, an award of emotional distress damages in favor of a high school student whose graduation photo was appropriated for commercial purposes by the photographer and by a frame manufacturer, without consent. The court remanded the case with instructions to permit the jury to consider nominal damages instead, on the theory that actual injury is not essential to establish intentional tort, and that nominal damages may be awarded where no actual injury is proven.

2. ***False Light.*** Since Young v. Jackson, 572 So.2d 378, 382 (Miss. 1990), this branch of the privacy tort has been held to have been adopted in Prescott v. Bay St. Louis Newspapers, Inc., 497 So.2d 77, 79 (Miss. 1986), which described the essential elements of the claim, quoting Restatement (Second) of Torts § 652E (1976) --

One who gives publicity to a matter concerning another that places the other before the public in a false light is subject to liability to the other for invasion of his privacy, if

(a) the false light in which the other was placed would be highly offensive to a reasonable person, and

(b) the actor had knowledge or acted in reckless disregard as to the falsity of the publicized matter and the false light in which the other would be placed.

The court noted that "it is essential to the rule stated in this section that the matter published concerning the plaintiff is not true," but the falsity need not be defamatory. 497 So.2d at 79. See Gray v. City of Olive Branch, 1998 WL 211766 (N.D. Miss.) (suggesting that recovery may be had only when the publication is not defamatory); Hayne v. The Innocence Project, 2011 WL 198128, 10 (S.D. Miss.) (stating that truth is an absolute defense).

In Fairley v. ESPN, Inc., 2012 WL 3000671 (S.D. Miss. 2012), the court explained that "Mississippi law is undeveloped and uncertain as to whether, or under what specific circumstances the source of alleged defamation might be liable for rebroadcast of his statements, and thus as to whether a rebroadcast of his original statements commences the statute of limitations to run anew."

3. ***Publication of Private Facts.*** In Young v. Jackson, 572 So.2d 378, 382 (Miss. 1990), the Mississippi Supreme Court adopted the "precise statement" of this claim set forth in Restatement (Second) of Torts § 652D (1977) --

> One who gives publicity to a matter concerning the private life of another is subject to liability to the other for invasion of his privacy, if the matter publicized is of a kind that
>
> (a) would be highly offensive to a reasonable person, and
>
> (b) is not of legitimate concern to the public.

The Court found that the plaintiff's partial hysterectomy was a matter which she had the right to keep private, and the disclosure of which would be highly offensive, but that managers and co-workers had a legitimate interest in knowing that the plaintiff, a nuclear plant worker, had collapsed on the job from the after-effects of her partial hysterectomy, rather than from irradiation. Consequently, the privilege defense was sustained.

4. ***Intrusion.*** In Watkins v. United Parcel Service, 797 F. Supp. 1349, 1359 (S.D. Miss. 1992), the court first applied to the employment context the "intentional intrusion upon the seclusion of another" branch of privacy tort law, as expressed in Prosser, Handbook of the Law on Torts § 117 (4th Ed. 1971) and adopted by the Mississippi Supreme Court in Deaton v. Delta Democrat Publishing Company, 326 So.2d 471, 473 (Miss. 1976). Granting summary judgment for the defense, the Watkins court held that the plaintiff could not establish that his employer's interference with his work-related sexual relationship with a co-worker "would be highly offensive to the ordinary, reasonable man, as a result of conduct to which the reasonable man would strongly object." Further, the plaintiff failed to establish "some bad faith or utterly reckless prying" which is essential to recovery under this branch of the tort. The court in Glasgow v. Sherman-Williams Co., 901 F. Supp. 1185, 1192 (N.D. Miss. 1995) reached the same result in applying the same test to an employer which advised plaintiff's co-workers not to associate with him after his discharge. A broad band of privileged intrusions may be inferred from Plaxico v. Michael, 735 So.2d 1036 (Miss. 1999), which upheld dismissal as a matter of law of an intrusion claim brought by the lesbian lover of the defendant's former wife. The former husband was held justified in peeking through a bedroom window to photograph plaintiff nude in his former wife's bed in support of his position in his child support and custody dispute with his former wife.

C. Other Privacy-Related Actions

Mississippi law permits employees to recover for intentional and negligent infliction of emotional distress, and for malicious interference with existing contracts and reasonably anticipated economic relationships, but those claims have not been confused with privacy law, nor have they been permitted to "end-run" the presumption in favor of freely terminable employment relationships.

1. ***Intentional Infliction of Emotional Distress.*** Most claims for intentional infliction of emotional distress arising from an employment dispute have failed on one or both of two grounds. The tort is likened to "menace," one of the intentional torts enumerated in the one year limitation statute, Miss. Code Ann. § 15-1-35. See Guthrie v. J.C. Penney Co., 803 F.2d 202 (5th Cir. 1986); King v. Otasco, Inc., 861 F.2d 438, 442 (5th Cir. 1988); City of Mound Bayou v. Johnson, 562 So.2d 1212, 1219 n. 7 (Miss. 1990) (endorsing Erie-guess of Fifth Circuit in King v. Otasco); Watkins v. United States Parcel Service, Inc., 797 F. Supp 1349, 1361 (S.D. Miss. 1992); Campbell v. Jackson Business Forms Co., 841 F. Supp. 772, 774 (S.D. Miss. 1994); Malloy v. Sears, Roebuck and Company, 1997 WL 170313 (N.D. Miss. 1997); Norman v. Lipscomb Oil Company, 1998 WL 378390 (N.D. Miss. 1998); Toler v. City of Greenville, 1997 WL 332168 (N.D. Miss. 1997). But see Nichols v. Tri-State Brick and Tile, 608 So.2d 324, 333 (Miss. 1992) (rejecting §15-1-35's application to intentional torts not fairly analogous to those listed in statute) and see Norman v. Bucklew, 684 So.2d 1246, 1256 (Miss. 1996) (stating, in apparent agreement with the parties, and without citation to prior decisions, that three-year bar of Miss. Code Ann. § 15-1-49 governs combined claims of negligent and/or intentional infliction of emotional distress). An ambiguous claim for "outrageous conduct" will be deemed a claim for intentional infliction of emotional distress, since the two labels have become synonymous. Donald v. Amoco Production Co., 735 So.2d 161, 179 (Miss. 1999). And, because Mississippi adheres to the Restatement (Second) of Torts § 46, comment *d*, our courts do not permit recovery for the emotional wounds of ordinary employment disputes. See Nuwer v. Mariner Post-Acute Network, 332 F.3d 310, 316 (5th Cir. 2003). Therefore, the mere fact that an employee was terminated, while unpleasant, is not conduct that constitutes intentional infliction of emotional distress. Pipkin v. Piper Impact, Inc., 2003 WL 21683552 *3 (5th Cir. July 18, 2003). In fact, the Mississippi Supreme Court quoted the Fifth Circuit Court of Appeals and stated, "'[o]nly in the most unusual cases does the conduct move out of the realm of an ordinary employment dispute into the classification of extreme and outrageous, as required for the tort of intentional infliction of emotional distress.'" Raiola v. Chevon U.S.A., Inc., 872 So.2d 79, 85 (Miss. 2004), quoting Prunty v. Arkansas Freightways, inc., 16 F.3d 649, 654 (5th Cir. 1994). This precludes recovery even by plaintiffs who have been fired because they were wrongly accused of sex harassment. Glasgow v. Sherwin-Williams Co., 901 F. Supp. 1185, 1191-92 (N.D. Miss. 1995). It also precludes recovery by an employee fired, but never prosecuted, for stealing and selling the employer's ice cream. Clark v. Luvel Dairy Products, Inc., 2001 WL 1122021 (Miss. App. Sept. 25, 2001). A Fifth Circuit opinion held that an employee may not recover for intentional infliction of emotional distress against her employer for co-employee's sexual harassment. Under Mississippi law, an employer must ratify or authorize an employee's intentional conduct before he is liable. Hatley v. Hilton Hotels Corp., 308 F.3d 473, 475 (5th Cir. 2002). However, Mississippi courts have entertained plaintiffs' claims for intentional infliction of emotional distress despite the employers' argument that workers' compensation was the exclusive remedy where the injury resulted from willful and intentional acts of supervisor or co-employee acting in furtherance of defendant's business. Blailock v. O'Bannon, 795 So.2d 533 (Miss. 2001) and Davis v. Pioneer, Inc., WL 1554503 (Miss. App. July 16, 2002). Employer liability in negligence was found where an

employee committed the torts of invasion of privacy and extreme and outrageous conduct. American Guarantee and Liability Insurance Company v. 1906 Company, 273 F.3d 605, 615 (5th Cir. 2001).

In Grice v. FedEx Ground Package System, Inc., 925 So.2d 907 (Miss. App. Apr. 4, 2006), the Court recognized that an employer could not be held liable to a contract employee for intentional infliction of emotional distress because "liability for intentional infliction of emotional distress does not extend to mere threats." Instead, actionable conduct has been described as behavior that is "malicious, intentional, wanton, grossly careless, indifferent or reckless." Leaf River Forest Products, Inc. v. Ferguson, 662 So. 2d 648, 659 (Miss. 1995).

2. ***Interference With Prospective Economic Advantage.*** The Supreme Court of Mississippi recognizes the tort in the at-will employment context. See Levens v. Campbell, 733 So.2d 753, 760-61 (Miss. 1999) and Morrison v. Mississippi Enterprise for Technology, 798 So.2d 567, 574-75 (Miss. Ct. App. 2001). Though the tort is recognized in Mississippi, see Cenac v. Murry, 609 So.2d 1257 (Miss. 1992), Par Industries, Inc. v. Target Container Co., 708 So.2d 44 (Miss. 1998), our courts require "hard proof" of actual damages proximately caused by the defendant's wrong. See Fred's Stores of Mississippi v. M & H Drugs, Inc., 725 So.2d 902 (Miss. 1998) and Gasparrini v. Bredemeier, 802 So.2d 1062 (Miss. App. 2001). Employers are liable where their employee tortiously interferes with another's business relations. *Progressive Casualty Ins. v. All Care, Inc.*, 2005 WL 1384232 (Miss. App.). Negligent interference does not create a claim. King's Daughters and Sons Circle Number Two of Greenville v. Delta Regional Medical Center, 2003 WL 21386133 *6 (Miss. Ct. App. June 17, 2003). A supervisor can be held liable for this tort to an employee that he/she supervises if the supervisor intermeddles in the employee's employment relationship "*without sufficient reason*." Sago v. Wal-Mart Stores, Inc., 2003 WL 22076954 (S.D. Miss. Sept. 2, 2003).

Because Mississippi law treats a claim for unlawful interference with employment as a claim for tortious interference with a contract, "[t]he plaintiff must prove that 'the contract would have been performed but for the alleged interference.'" McKlemurry v. Thomas, 2011 WL 3625188, 7 (S.D. Miss. 2011).

3. ***Prima Facie Tort.*** The "prima facie tort" doctrine of other jurisdictions has not been applied to Mississippi employment disputes, and the narrower, UCC-inspired duty of good faith and fair dealing has been held inapplicable to Mississippi employment relationships. Hartle v. Packard Electric, 626 So.2d 106 (Miss. 1993). An ambiguous claim for "outrageous conduct" will be deemed a claim for intentional infliction of emotional distress, since the two labels have become synonymous. Donald v. Amoco Production Co., 735 So.2d 161, 179 (Miss. 1999).

II. EMPLOYER TESTING OF EMPLOYEES

No published Mississippi judicial decision applies our privacy common law to employer testing of employees. However, Mississippi statutes do impose modest regulations. Those are found in Miss. Code § 71-7-1. One Mississippi federal district court has emphasized that "provisions of that statute are voluntary, and employers are not required to comply with them. Moreover, an employer need not opt out of the statute, but must, instead, affirmatively elect to follow it. Where an employer does not affirmatively elect to conduct an employee drug and alcohol testing policy pursuant to the statute, 'the rights and obligations of the employer and its employees and job applicants will not in any way be subject to or affected by the provisions of [the statute], but will instead be governed by applicable principles of contract and common law.'" See Brisco v. LeTourneau Tech., Inc., 2008 WL 4793791 (S.D. Miss. 2008) (citations omitted)

A. Psychological or Personality Testing

1. ***Common Law and Statutes.*** No cases.

2. ***Private Employers.*** No cases.

3. ***Public Employers.*** No cases.

B. Drug Testing

1. ***Common Law and Statutes.*** Pursuant to statute, Mississippi employers may have vigorous drug and alcohol testing programs in place. See Tyson Foods, Inc. v. Hilliard, 772 So.2d 1103, 1107 (Miss. Ct. App. 2000). In 1991, the Mississippi Legislature passed a curious drug and alcohol testing statute which governs testing of public employees but which governs testing of private employees only if the employer elects coverage by written notice to employees. Regardless of the employer's election, the Act does not apply to drug testing which is governed by federal statutes and regulations. A plaintiff must first exhaust "all applicable grievance procedures and arbitration proceeding requirements." The action must be filed within one year after completion of any required grievance procedures. The Act limits monetary damages. Miss. Code Ann. § 71-7-1 et seq.

An employee may be justifiably discharged for refusal to submit to a properly required drug test. See Tyson Foods, Inc. v. Hilliard, 772 So.2d 1103, 1107 (Miss. Ct. App. 2000); Miss. Code Ann. § 71-7-13(7). However, a discharge for willful misconduct must be based not on mere refusal to take a test, but on "a confirmed positive drug and alcohol test." See Tyson Foods, Inc. v. Hilliard, 772 So.2d 1103, 1107 (Miss. Ct. App. 2000); Miss. Code Ann. § 71-7-13(3).

The Mississippi Workers' Compensation Law, Miss. Code Ann. § 71-3-121, requires the Commissioner of Insurance to promulgate rules requiring insured employers to adopt written safety plans which address drug and alcohol testing in accordance with the drug and alcohol testing statute.

2. ***Private Employers.*** The Mississippi drug and alcohol testing law covers only those private employers who elect coverage by written, thirty-day advance notice to their employees. Miss. Code Ann. § 71-7-27. A private employer's written policy must list all drugs the employer could test and describe each by brand name, common name, or chemical name. Miss. Code Ann. § 71-7-3(1)(i).

3. ***Public Employers.*** As originally enacted, the Mississippi drug and alcohol testing law did not permit public agencies to avoid coverage. Miss. Code Ann. § 71-7-3(7). A 2002 revision of the Mississippi drug and alcohol testing law by the Mississippi legislature was apparently intended to make compliance with the statute voluntary for public employers. A typographic error in the revised language, however, resulted in the legislation only applying to "alcohol testing" rather than the intended "drug and alcohol testing." The Mississippi Legislature corrected the error in April 2004, such that the statute clearly applies to both alcohol and drug testing. Miss. Code Ann. § 71-7-3(1). The only public sector employees who can be tested are those employed in law enforcement or public health and safety positions. Miss. Code Ann. § 71-7-7(2).

C. Medical Testing

1. ***Common law and statutes.*** No cases.

2. ***Private Employers.*** No cases.

3. ***Public Employers.*** No cases.

D. Polygraph Tests

Mississippi statutes do not forbid employers from subjecting employees to polygraph testing, nor do they authorize civil actions by employees who have been subjected to testing. The Mississippi Polygraph Examiners Law, Miss. Code Ann. § 73-29-1 et seq., provides licensing and professional standards for polygraph examiners.

E. Fingerprinting

Mississippi does not forbid or regulate collection or dissemination of fingerprint data generally. Rather, specific statutes address problems peculiar to certain law enforcement missions. Without a court order, the public (employers included) does not have access to fingerprints of juvenile offenders kept by law enforcement agencies. Miss. Code Ann. § 43-21-261.

The Mississippi Department of Information Technology Services cannot release law enforcement fingerprint data to the extent that the prints indicate "involvement of the individual in the criminal justice system." Miss. Code Ann. § 45-27-3 (d)(ii). However, certain employer entities which provide child services are permitted and required to obtain criminal history records of current and prospective employees and volunteers. Miss. Code Ann. § 45-31-12 (repealed 2000)(similar provisions in Miss. Code Ann. § 45-33-21 et. seq). And, sex offenders are required to register with the county of residence. That information is available to the public through the county sheriff's office and now through a state-administered web site. Miss. Code Ann. § 45-33-49.

III. SEARCHES

Nothing in the Mississippi Constitution of 1890, the Mississippi Code, or Mississippi common law specifically regulates searches of private employees by private employers. Mississippi's common law of privacy is conceptually applicable, but there is no reported decision. Public employers are subject to constitutional search and seizure limitations, of course.

A. Employee's Person

1. ***Private Employers.*** No cases.

2. ***Public Employers.*** Article 3, § 23 of the Mississippi Constitution of 1890 prohibits the State to conduct unreasonable searches and seizures. Its application to public employment has not been discussed in any published opinion.

B. Employee's Work Area

No cases.

C. Employee's Property

1. ***Private Employers.*** No cases.

2. ***Public Employers.*** No cases.

IV. RESTRICTING EMPLOYEE'S PROPERTY – Miss. Code Ann. § 45-9-55

As of July 2006, both public and private employers are prohibited from establishing, maintaining, or enforcing any policy or rule that has the effect of prohibiting a person from transporting or storing a firearm in a locked vehicle in any parking lot, parking garage, or other designated parking area. Miss. Code Ann. § **45-9-55** (2006 Miss. Laws Ch. 450 (H.B. 1141)). Exceptions: 1. A private employer may prohibit an employee from transporting or storing a firearm in a vehicle in a parking lot, parking garage, or other parking area the employer provides for employees to which access is restricted or limited through the use of a gate, security system or other means of restricting general public access onto the property; 2. This prohibition does not apply to vehicles owned or leased by the employer and used by the employee in the course of business; 3. This prohibition does not apply where the possession of a firearm is prohibited by state or federal law. Id.

This section also provides additional protection to employers in that it exempts both public and private employers from liability for damages resulting from or arising out of an occurrence involving the transportation, storage, possession or use of a firearm covered by Section 45-9-55. Id.

V. MONITORING OF EMPLOYEES

A. Telephones and Electronic Communications

Mississippi statutes do not address employer interception of employees' communications and the matter has not produced a published Mississippi court opinion. The issue was raised in Hogue v. Roberts, 1998 WL 433947 (N.D. Miss. 1998), but avoided by the court's summary judgment, the plaintiff having been unable to offer any proof that the defendant county was vicariously liable for the sheriff's personally-motivated wiretapping of his secretary's telephone.

The issue has been raised in the context of an employee recording a conversation with his employer. See Campbell v. Mississippi Employment Security Comm'n, 782 So. 2d 751 (Miss. Ct. App. 2000). In Campbell, the court held that an employee did not engage in misconduct, by secretly recording a conference with his employer for the employee's own protection, which would preclude the employee's receipt of unemployment compensation. Id. at 754. The dissent, written by Judge Southwick, found both that "[s]ecretly taping a meeting with a supervisor is something that could be found to be a willful denial of an employer's legitimate interests," and that such secret recording of a private meeting "shows a deceitfulness that an employer is entitled to prohibit in relations with employees." Id. at 756, 758. The dissent, however, also acknowledged that Miss. Code Ann. § 41-29-531(e) does not prohibit such secret recording if one person gives consent or is a party to the conversation; thus, there "may not have been anything actionable" about what the employee did. Id. at 759.

1. ***Wiretapping.*** Miss. Code Ann. §§ 41-29-501 -537 presently sets forth the state's statutory scheme for interception of wire or oral communications in criminal controlled substances investigations upon application by an authorized prosecutor and issuance of a court order. Interception and monitoring of communications in violation of this statute supports a civil action, Miss. Code Ann. § 41-29-529. Civil liability exceptions set forth in Miss. Code Ann. § 41-29-531 include prior consent of a party to the conversation, unless for some purpose independently unlawful. Miss. Code Ann. § 41-29-701 also authorizes the use of pen registers by state Bureau of Narcotics agents to record outgoing numbers dialed. There are no other relevant statutes.

Miss. Code Ann. § 41-29-535 provides that Miss. Code Ann. §§ 41-29-501 et seq. does not apply to "a person who is a subscriber to a telephone . . . and who intercepts a communication on a telephone to which he subscribes . . . [or] to persons who are members of the household of the subscriber who intercept communications on a telephone in the home or subscriber." This exception has been litigated chiefly in domestic relations cases in Mississippi's Chancery courts. For example, relying on this exception, the Mississippi Supreme Court recently held erroneous a Chancellor's order that a wife cease to record her husband's telephone conversations with their child. Rogers v. Morin, 791 So.2d 815 (Miss. 2001).

The upshot of Mississippi's statutory scheme is that it specifically prohibits secret taping of conversations, whether the conversations are face-to-face or electronically transmitted. Nonetheless, the statute only makes "eavesdropping" actionable -- namely, recording when no one involved in the conversation is aware of the recording. See Miss. Code Ann. § 41-29-531(e).

2. ***Electronic Communications.*** This issue has not been addressed directly in the privacy context. However, the Mississippi Court of Appeals upheld the Mississippi Employment Security Commission's denial of benefits where a male employee sent e-mails to a female co-worker, in violation of management's order to refrain from doing so, even though the e-mail was sent from home. In the case, the employee who sent the e-mail knew that his e-mail contact with female employees had been restricted, and the restriction was reasonably related to job performance and environment. Captain v. Mississippi Employment Security Commission, 817 So. 2d 634 (Miss. Ct. App. 2002).

3. ***Other Electronic Monitoring.*** No cases.

B. Mail

No cases.

C. Surveillance/Photographing

The only Mississippi case discussing this issue arose in the criminal context. In Wells v. State, 604 So. 2d 271 (Miss. 1992), an employer suspected an employee, a casher, of embezzlement. After discussions with local police, the employer set up a surveillance tape to monitor the employee during her shift. The employer had no prior policy of monitoring employees with surveillance. After surveillance caught the employee in the act of stealing, she was charged and convicted. The Court gave no suggestion that what the employer had done was improper.

VI. ACTIVITIES OUTSIDE THE WORKPLACE

A. Statute or Common Law

In Baker Donelson Bearman Caldwell & Berkowitz v. Seay, 42 So. 3d 474 (Miss. 2010), the defendant law firm was sued for negligent supervision after one of its attorneys was alleged to have had an affair with a client's wife. On appeal, the Mississippi Supreme Court reversed the trial court's denial of the law firm's motion for summary judgment on the negligent supervision claim. In so doing, the Court noted that "[u]nder Mississippi law, 'employers do not have a duty to supervise their employees when the employees are off-duty or not working . . . .Moreover, an employer's duty to supervise does not include a duty to uncover his employees' *concealed, clandestine, personal activities.*'"

B. Employees' Personal Relationships

1. ***Romantic Relationships Between Employees.*** In the two cases which raised the propriety of common law privacy claims, the employer was held to have a legitimate concern justifying its intrusion into sexual relationships between co-workers. See Glasgow v. Sherwin-Williams Co., 901 F. Supp. 1185, 1192 (N. D. Miss. 1995), summarily aff'd, 146 F.3d 867 (5th Cir. 1998) (discharge of alleged sex harasser, and Watkins v. United Parcel Service, Inc., 797 F. Supp. 1349, 1359 (S.D. Miss. 1992), aff'd, 979 F.2d 1535 (5th Cir. 1992) (violation of anti-fraternization policy).

2. ***Sexual Orientation.*** No cases in Mississippi. However, the United States Court of Appeals for the Fifth Circuit, in Woodland v. City of Houston, 918 F. Supp. 1047 (S.D. Tex. 1996), vacated, 1996 WL 752803 (5th Cir. 1996), recognized the possibility that a claim of invasion of privacy could be brought based on inquiries about homosexual conduct and other sexual behavior. The plaintiffs in that case had been required to submit to polygraph examinations as a condition of employment; during those examinations, questions were asked about homosexual behavior, sexual activity with animals, and marital and extramarital sexual activity. Although the Fifth Circuit reversed a jury verdict for the plaintiffs and remanded the case, the district court, on remand, found that the questions asked were unreasonably intrusive and therefore violated the right to privacy. Id. This decision was subsequently vacated upon the request of the parties. Woodland v. City of Houston, 1996 WL 752803 (5th Cir. 1996).

3. ***Marital Status.*** No cases.

C. Smoking

Miss. Code Ann. § 71-7-33 states that an employer may not require an employee to abstain from smoking or using tobacco products during non-working hours as a condition of employment. In MS Employment Security Comm'n v. Barnes, 853 So.2d 153, 157 (Miss. Ct. App. 2003), the Court held an employee was disqualified from receiving unemployment benefits where the employee was found smoking outside employer's designated smoking area, in violation of the employer's safety guidelines.

D. Blogging

No cases.

VII. RECORDS

Mississippi's general common law of privacy has not been applied to claims of wrongful disclosure or procurement of personnel records or criminal records in an employment context. There is no constitutional or statutory restriction on point. However, Miss. Code Ann. § 71-7-15 provides that any information or test results obtained by an employer through its drug and alcohol testing program are confidential communications, and may not be used without the employee's permission. There is one case in which a privacy objection was deemed inadequate to bar public records disclosure, one rejecting liability premised on a medical records subpoena, and one affirming liability based on litigation misuse of fraudulently obtained medical records.

The Mississippi Employment Protection Act, 2008 Miss. Laws ch. 312 (S.B. No. 2988), requires every employer in Mississippi to register and utilize the United States Department of Homeland Security's E-Verify system. The system, which allows employers to submit the social security numbers of new hires to verify their employment eligibility, requires employers to enter into a memorandum of understanding with the U.S. Department of Homeland Security, by which the employer agrees to safeguard the information on employees it receives via E-Verify, and to make employment records available to DHS and the Social Security Administration.

A. Personnel Records

In Mississippi Department of Wildlife, Fisheries and Parks v. Mississippi Wildlife Enforcement Officers' Association, 740 So.2d 925 (Miss. 1999), an employee association complaining about the agency's comp. time practices made a public records request for related personnel records. The agency released the names and accrued comp. time of several hundred employees during the relevant period. The association then made a broader request. Going against an Attorney General Opinion that such records are to be disclosed under the relevant statute, the agency then asserted a privacy objection and contended that its subsequent release during litigation of comp. time data without corresponding employee names should be regarded an appropriate balancing of the statute's disclosure requirement with the affected employees' privacy interests. The court held that public employees have no such privacy interest which might justify anything less than full disclosure of their public employer's records.

B. Medical Records.

See Miss. Code Ann. § 71-7-15, regarding prohibition on release of employee's drug and alcohol test results by employer.

In Williamson v. Keith, 786 So.2d 390 (Miss. 2001), our Supreme Court affirmed a grant of summary judgment for the defendant attorney who had subpoenaed a special education student's medical records in connection with her due process hearing. The student sought to compel the school district to replace the magnet, coil and cord of her cochlear implant device after she lost them. The district scheduled a hearing on her claim. The student's counsel designated a medical expert. The district's attorney served a medical records subpoena upon that expert's records custodian, but failed to assure that the student's lawyer was sent a copy, as required. The records were produced and the parties settled the case before the hearing. Following the settlement, the student sued the district's attorney for publishing private facts. Affirming summary judgment, the Court distinguished the "publication" element of defamation from the "publicity" which supports privacy invasion liability. The Court quoted Restatement (Second) of Torts § 652D, comment a (1977) in its holding that privacy invasion occurs only when private information is disseminated among the public at large, "or to so many persons that the matter must be regarded as substantially certain to become one of public knowledge." The district's attorney, in contrast, had conveyed the student's medical records only to his staff and to the district's Special Education Director. In addition, the Court held that the student had failed to show that her medical records were private. The record in this case showed that the student had disclosed them in the course of a prior, public hearing. That disclosure, said the Court, was fatal to her privacy claim.

McKorkle v. McKorkle, 2001 WL 19727 (Miss. Ct. App. Jan. 9, 2001) affirmed a $175,000 compensatory damages verdict and remanded for punitive damages trial in the case of a son who, angry with a timber company's advantageous purchase of logging rights from his father, obtained his father's Veterans Administration medical records, and used them in several, well-publicized, unsuccessful attempts to have his father adjudged mentally incompetent. The evidence was sufficient to sustain the verdict that the father had not consented to the records' disclosure, and to suggest that the son had obtained them on false pretenses. The Court deemed this a textbook case of tortious publicity of private facts, rejected the argument that the father had previously publicized the same information, and approved a jury instruction that the son could not have lawful possession of the records unless the father consented, because the medical file in question was made confidential by state and federal statutes.

In Ekugwum v. City of Jackson, 2010 WL 149027 (S.D. Miss.), plaintiff sued her employer for allegedly divulging confidential medical information she had submitted for FMLA leave to others in the office. The court granted summary judgment in favor of the City holding that the plaintiff had not produced evidence that the medical information had been shared with a large enough group of persons to be actionable.

C. Criminal Records

See "Fingerprints" section of outline, II E, above.

D. Subpoenas / Search Warrants

Ayles v. ex rel. Allen v. Allen,907 So. 2d 300 (Miss. 2005), a former wife and her daughter from a previous marriage brought suit against the former husband and his attorney for abuse of process and invasion of privacy, after the former husband, through his attorney who represented him in a custody dispute over the parties' child, attained production of the daughter's school records. The former husband, through his counsel, served a subpoena duces tecum on his former step-daughter's school, demanding production of her school records to use against his former wife in a custody dispute. The subpoena directed the school to produce the records within ten (10) days of receipt of the subpoena. However, the school produced the records to the process server (the attorney's secretary) immediately upon receipt of the subpoena. The attorney, upon receipt of the records, placed the records in a file and no other person, including his client, viewed the documents. Because the attorney did not "publicize" the documents, the attorney nor his client could be liable for invasion of privacy just because they served a subpoena seeking the documents and actually received the documents.

VIII. ACTIONS SUBSEQUENT TO EMPLOYMENT

A. References

No cases.

B. Non-Compete Agreements

Mississippi law does not favor covenants not to compete and will only enforce such covenants if the party seeking enforcement proves that they are reasonable. Herring Gas Co. v. Magee, 813 F. Supp. 1239 (S.D. Miss. 1993); Thames v. Davis & Goulet Ins., Inc., 420 So.2d 1041, 1043 (Miss. 1982) (quoting Texas Rd. Boring Co. of Louisiana-Mississippi v. Parker, 194 So.2d 885, 889 (Miss. 1967). In determining reasonableness, the Court looks at three major aspects of the covenant not to compete: the rights of the employer, the rights of the employee, and the rights of the public. Herring Gas Co. v. Magee, 813 F. Supp. 1239 (S.D. Miss. 1993). Reasonableness as to time and space limitations are also considerations. Texas Rd. Boring Co. of Louisiana-Mississippi v. Parker, 194 So.2d 885, 889 (Miss. 1967). If a court finds that the limitations contained in a covenant not to compete are unreasonable, then the court will modify the limitations so that they are reasonable. Redd Pest Control Co. v. Heatherly, 248 Miss. 34, 157 So.2d 133, 135-36 (1963). Covenants not to compete which restrict a party from competitive activities within fifty miles of the drafter's business or businesses comport with the requirements of reasonableness under Mississippi law. Herring Gas Co. v. Magee, 813 F. Supp. 1239 (S.D. Miss. 1993).

The Mississippi Court of Appeals, in Timber Lake Foods, Inc. v. Estess, 72 So. 3d 521 (Miss. Ct. App. 2011), held that a covenant not to compete between plaintiff and its former employee (a meat and poultry broker) protected a legitimate business interest of the employer. The court so held, even though the potential customers were nonexclusive and the price of brokered poultry was listed in a national market report. In reaching its conclusion, the court observed that the plaintiff provided extensive training and opportunities to the defendant (who had no prior sales experience), and referred to testimony supporting the effect of the broker-customer relationship on price, and evidence establishing that the overwhelming majority of the defendant's sales during her employment with the new employer were to former costumers of the plaintiff.

The Mississippi Court of Appeals also held in a breach of contract action between a rehabilitative therapy services contractor and a nursing home that the parties' covenant not to hire operated as an unreasonable restraint on trade and was unenforceable. *Cain v. Cain,* 2007 WL 1816047 (Miss. Ct. App. 2011). The restrictive covenant provided that the nursing home would not directly or indirectly hire "personnel employed by" the contractor for a period of two years following termination of the contract, however, the provision lacked specificity as to which individuals were limited by the covenant not to hire. For example, the covenant was ambiguous as to whether the nursing home was restricted from hiring employees who were dismissed by the contractor following the nursing home's termination of the contract. The court's consideration of a "covenant not to hire" was a matter of first impression.

IX. OTHER ISSUES

A. Statutes of Limitations

Claims of invasion of privacy are subject to the one-year bar which governs defamation claims, Miss. Code Ann. § 15-1-35. Lane v. Strang Communications Company, 297 F.Supp.2d 897, 899 (N.D. MS 2003); Malloy v. Sears, Roebuck & Company, 1997 WL 170313 (N.D. Miss. Mar. 4, 1997); Campbell v. Jackson Business Forms Co., 841 F. Supp. 772, 774 (S.D. Miss. 1994); Watkins v. United Parcel Service, Inc., 797 F. Supp. 1349, 1360 (S.D. Miss. 1992); Young v. Jackson, 572 So.2d 378,382 (Miss. 1990); McCorkle v. McCorkle, 2001 WL 19727 (Miss. App. Jan. 9, 2001). As explained in Hervey v. Metlife General Insurance Corporation System Agency of Mississippi, Inc., 154 F. Supp. 2d 909 (S.D. Miss. 2001), this formerly clear rule has recently been confused by decisions favoring or applying the three-year catch-all statute, Miss. Code Ann. § 15-1-49. A recent attempt was made to clarify the confusion. The Mississippi Court of Appeals applied the one year statute of limitations to an intentional tort claim. Slaydon v. Handford, 830 So.2d 686 (Miss. App. 2002).

B. Jurisdiction

The Mississippi Constitution grants circuit courts original jurisdiction in all civil and criminal matters which are not vested in some other court. Miss. Code Ann. § 9-7-81. Circuit courts have original jurisdiction in actions where the principal of the amount in controversy is in excess of $200 and are given the power to hear all civil matters meeting this threshold except those which are exclusively cognizable before another court. *Id.* Thus, the circuit court would have jurisdiction over employee privacy claims. The application of this statute to employment claims has not been discussed in any published opinion.

C. Worker's Compensation Exclusivity

Mississippi Code Section 71-3-9 provides, in part, that "[t]he liability of an employer to pay compensation shall be exclusive and in place of all other liability of such employer to the employee...." Miss. Code Ann. § 71-3-9 (Rev.2000) (emphasis added). However, based upon the statutory requirement that the "injury" be "accidental" to be compensable under the Act, see Mississippi Code Sections 71-3-3(b), 71-3-7, the Mississippi Supreme Court has found that some intentional torts are outside the scope of the exclusivity provision in Mississippi Code Section 71-3-9. Miss. Code Ann. §§ 71-3-3(b), 71-3-7 (Rev.2000). See Royal Oil Co. v. Wells, 500 So.2d 439, 442 (Miss. 1986) ("the [Act] does not bar an employee from pursuing a common law remedy against his employer for an injury caused by his employer's willful and malicious act"); Miller v. McRae's, Inc., 444 So.2d 368 at 371 (Miss. 1984) ("where an injury is caused by the willful act of an employee acting in the course and scope of his employment and in the furtherance of his employer's business, the [Act] is not the exclusive remedy available to the injured party"); **Oliver v. Food Giant Supermarkets, Inc., 2012 WL 3580683 (N.D. Miss. Aug. 17, 2012) ("Unlike negligence claims, the intentional tort of fraudulent misrepresentation would most likely not be barred by the Mississippi Workers' Compensation Act.").**

While there are no cases specifically discussing worker's compensation exclusivity as it applies to privacy torts, for the worker's compensation exclusivity provision to apply, the complained of tort must be unintentional.

D. Pleading Requirements

Mississippi law imposes no heightened pleading requirement upon common law privacy claimants. The Mississippi Supreme Court has often stated that, because Mississippi's Rules of Civil Procedure have been patterned after the federal rules, it looks to authoritative constructions by federal courts of the comparable federal rule for guidance. *E.g.,* Penn Nat'l Gaming, Inc. v. Ratliff, 954 So. 2d 427, 432 (Miss. 2007). However, the Mississippi Supreme Court has not yet passed judgment on whether it will adopt the plausibility standard for Rule 12(b)(6) motions set forth in Bell Atl. Corp. v. Twombly, **550 U.S. 544, 570** (2007), which retired the former "no set of facts" standard. **The defendant in Thompson v. True Temper Sports, Inc., 74 So. 3d 936, 938-39 (Miss. Ct. App. 2011) urged the Mississippi Court of Appeals to follow "the new and more stringent federal pleading standards established in Twombly," but the appellate court never reached the issue, as the appeal was dismissed for lack of jurisdiction. Id.**

SURVEY OF MISSOURI EMPLOYMENT LIBEL LAW

John J. Moellering
Joseph E. Martineau
Lewis, Rice, & Fingersh, L.C.
500 North Broadway, Suite 2000
St. Louis, Missouri 63102
Phone: (314) 444-7600; Fax: (314) 241-6056
jmoellering@lewisrice.com
jmartineau@lewisrice.com

(With Developments Reported Through **November 1, 2012**)*

GENERAL COMMENTS

None.

SIGNIFICANT DEVELOPMENTS SINCE THE 2012 *SURVEY*

None.

I. GENERAL LAW

A. General Employment Law

1. ***At Will Employment.*** Under Missouri's employment-at-will doctrine, an employer can discharge an at-will employee at any time for any reason, with or without cause. Fleshner v. Pepose Vision Inst., P.C., 304 S.W.3d 81, 91 (Mo. 2010) (citing Johnson v. McDonnell Douglas Corp., 745 S.W.2d 661, 663 (Mo. 1988) (en banc)). An at-will employee generally has no cause of action for wrongful discharge. Id. In Fleshner v. Pepose Vision Institute, P.C., however, the Supreme Court of Missouri expressly recognized a public-policy exception to the employment-at-will doctrine. Fleshner, 304 S.W.3d at 92. Under this exception, "[a]n at-will employee may not be terminated (1) for refusing to violate the law or any well-established and clear mandate of public policy as expressed in the constitution, statutes, regulations promulgated pursuant to statute, or rules created by a governmental body or (2) for reporting wrongdoing or violations of law to superiors or public authorities." Id. at 92. Any employee terminated for either reason has a cause of action in tort for wrongful discharge. Fleshner, 304 S.W.3d at 92. (The defendant must be a former employer before a cause of action can be brought. See Taylor v. St. Louis Co. Bd. of Elec. Comm., 625 F.3d 1025 (E.D. Mo. 2010).) To properly state a claim, an employee must plead with particularity the public policy that the employer's action allegedly violated. Grimes v. City of Tarkio, 246 S.W.3d 533, 536 (Mo. Ct. App. W.D. 2008), overruled in part on other grounds, by Fleshner, 304 S.W.3d 81; Adolphsen v. Hallmark Cards, Inc., 907 S.W.2d 333, 338 (Mo. Ct. App. W.D. 1995). Under the second theory of wrongful discharge, "a legal duty will not be forced upon parties who have agreed to an at-will relationship . . . absent a sufficiently definite statute, regulation based on statute, constitutional provision, or rule promulgated by a government body that clearly gives notice to the parties of its requirements." Margiotta v. Christian Hosp., 315 S.W.3d 342, 348 (Mo. 2010) (en banc); see Frevert v. Ford Motor Co., 614 F.3d 466 (8th Cir. 2010) (court held there is no Missouri public policy "encouraging the uncovering and disciplinary violations of company policy.") The Missouri Supreme Court has approved the "contributing factor" standard as the standard for causation in wrongful discharge cases. Fleshner, 304 S.W.2d at 94-95. See also MAI 38.03 [2012 Revision]. Under the contributing factor standard, the test is whether an illegitimate purpose was a "contributing factor" in the employment decision. See Fleshner, 304 S.W.2d at 94 (citing Daugherty v. City of Maryland Heights, 231 S.W.3d 814, 820 (Mo. 2007) (en banc)); MAI 38.03 [2012 Revision].

An employer also cannot discharge an employee for exercising his or her rights under Missouri Workers' Compensation Act. See Crabtree v. Bugby, 967 S.W.2d 66, 70 (Mo. 1998) (en banc). In contrast to the contributing factor standard under Fleshner, an employee must be fired exclusively for filing a worker's compensation claim in order to state a claim under the Act. See Northcutt v. City of Wildwood, No. 4:05CV00851, 2007 U.S. Dist. LEXIS 23420 at *11-12 (E.D. Mo. Mar. 30, 2007).

Employers are well served to have policies in place that reinforce Missouri's employment-at-will doctrine. Employee handbook language should clearly articulate the at-will rule and disclaim any contractual relationship, and receipt of the handbook should be acknowledged by employees in writing. See Johnson, 745 S.W.2d at 662 (court found that "given

---

* This work is a revision of work originally prepared by Carol K. DeWald, of Shank & Hamilton, P.C. in Kansas City, Missouri, to whom considerable credit is due.

the general language of the handbook and the employer's reservation of power to alter the handbook, a reasonable at will employee could not interpret its distribution as an offer to modify his at will status"). Where, however, an employment contract expressly incorporates the terms of the handbook, at-will status can be modified. Verni v. Cleveland Chiropractic College, WD62808, 2005 Mo. App. LEXIS 1544 at *23 (Mo. Ct. App. W.D. October 25, 2005), rev'd on other grounds, 212 S.W.3d 150 (Mo. 2007); see also Dunn v. Industrial Group, Inc. v. City of Sugar Creek, 112 S.W.3d 421, 435 n.5 (Mo. 2003) (en banc) (court found that "matters incorporated into a contract by reference are as much a part of the contract as if they had been set out in the contract in haec verba"). When drafting offer letters to prospective employees, employers should be mindful of referencing the at-will nature of the employment relationship.

B. Elements of Defamation Claim

1. ***Basic Elements.*** Under Missouri law, the "generic" or "unified" tort of defamation has largely subsumed the previously independent torts of slander and libel. See State ex rel. BP Products North America Inc. v. Ross, 163 S.W.3d 922, 927, n.5 (Mo. 2005); Overcast v. Billings Mutual Ins. Co., 11 S.W.3d 62, 70 (Mo. 2000); Nazeri v. Missouri Valley College, 860 S.W.2d 303, 313 (Mo. 1993); see also Boyd v. Schwan's Sales Enterprises, Inc., 23 S.W.3d 261, 265, n.3 (Mo. Ct. App. 2000) ("Modern law combines libel and slander as the generic tort of defamation."). The unification of these two torts and the abolition of the per se/per quod damages distinction have caused confusion regarding the requisite elements of the tort of defamation.

In Nazeri, the first case to merge slander and libel into the tort of defamation, the Supreme Court of Missouri held that "in defamation cases the old rules of per se and per quod do not apply and plaintiff need only to plead and prove the unified defamation elements set out in [the] MAI." Nazeri, 860 S.W.2d at 313. The newly-numbered versions of these Missouri Approved Instructions, MAI 23.06(1) and 23.10(1), set out the elements for a libel and slander action, respectively. See MAI 23.06(1) [1980 New]; MAI 23.10(1) [1980 New]. These two sets of instructions are essentially the same, except for minor differences accounting for the traditional distinction between libel and slander. Compare MAI 23.06 (1) with MAI 23.10(1). Combined, the elements of these two instructions are as follows: (1) the defendant published the defamatory statement; (2) the defendant was at fault for publishing the statement; (3) the statement tended to expose the plaintiff to hatred, contempt, and ridicule or deprive the plaintiff of the benefit of public confidence and social associations; (4) such statement was read or heard by other persons or by the public; and (5) plaintiff's reputation was thereby damaged. MAI 23.06(1); MAI 23.10(1). Notably, neither set of instructions requires the plaintiff to prove the falsity of the statement as an element of its prima facie case.

In subsequent cases, however, the Supreme Court of Missouri developed a new, independent doctrinal structure for the tort of defamation. In Overcast v. Billings Mutual Ins. Co., the Court held that "[t]he elements of defamation in Missouri are: 1) publication, 2) of a defamatory statement, 3) that identifies the plaintiff, 4) that is false, 5) that is published with the requisite degree of fault, and 6) damages the plaintiff's reputation." 11 S.W.3d at 70 (citing Nazeri, 860 S.W.2d at 303). In contrast to Nazeri, the Court in Overcast thus included falsity as an element of plaintiff's prima facie defamation case. Overcast, 11 S.W.3d at 70. In Kenney v. Wal-Mart Stores, Inc., 100 S.W.3d 809 (Mo. 2003), the Court recognized the tension between Nazeri and Overcast, but refused to dispose of the issue, instead classifying it as a potentially constitutional question unnecessary to the disposition of the case. See Kenney, 100 S.W.3d at 814, n. 2. Since Kenney, however, both the Supreme Court of Missouri and several Missouri appellate courts have included falsity in the plaintiff's prima facie case. See e.g., Ross, 163 S.W.3d at 929; Topper v. Midwest Div., Inc., 306 S.W.3d 117, 127 (Mo. Ct. App. W.D. 2010) (citation omitted); Johnson v. Allstate Indem. Co., 278 S.W.3d 228, 235 (Mo. 2009); Hayes v. Lange, No. 08-0042-CV-W-HFS, 2010 U.S. Dist. LEXIS 26871 at *13 (Mo. Ct. App. W.D. March 22, 2010) (citing Gray v. AT&T Corp., 357 F.3d 763 (8th Cir. 2004); see also Sifagus v. St. Louis Post-Dispatch L.L.C., 109 S.W.3d 174,176 (Mo. Ct. App. E.D. 2003) (filed on April 1, 2003, the same day as Kenney). Thus, under current Missouri precedent, it is likely that the plaintiff, in order to establish a prima facie case of defamation, must prove (1) publication, (2) of a defamatory statement, (3) that identifies the plaintiff, (4) that is false, (5) that is published with the requisite degree of fault, and (6) damages the plaintiff's reputation. Ross, 163 S.W.3d at 929; Overcast, 11 S.W.3d at 70; Johnson, 278 S.W.3d at 235; Topper, 306 S.W.3d at 127; Sifagus, 109 S.W.3d at 176; but see Kenney, 100 S.W.3d at 814, n. 2 (whether falsity is an element of plaintiff's prima facie case or truthfulness is an affirmative defense remains an unresolved issue); Mo. Rev. Stat. § 509.210 (2000 & Supp. 2009) ("The defendant may, in his answer, allege both the truth of the matter charged as defamatory and any mitigating circumstances admissible in evidence to reduce the amount of damages . . ."). If a qualified privilege applies, a private-figure plaintiff must assume the pleading and proof burden of a public-figure plaintiff. See McDowell v. Credit Bureaus of Southeast Missouri, Inc., 747 S.W.2d 630, 632 (Mo. 1988) (en banc); Cash v. Empire Gas Corp., 547 S.W.2d 830, 834 (Mo. Ct. App. E.D. 1976).

A public-figure plaintiff must plead and prove the elements set forth in MAI 23.06(2) for a libel action and in MAI 23.10(2) for a slander action. Combined, the elements of these two instructions are as follows: (1) defendant published the defamatory statement; (2) the statement was false; (3) defendant published it with knowledge it was false or with reckless disregard for its falsity or veracity; (4) the statement tended to expose plaintiff to hatred, contempt, and ridicule (or deprive plaintiff of the benefit of public confidence and social associations); (5) the statement was read or heard by other persons or by the public; and (6) plaintiff's reputation was thereby damaged. MAI 23.06(2) [1980 New] (stating the elements for libel); MAI 23.10(2) [1980 New] (stating the elements for slander).

A public-figure plaintiff must plead and prove that the publication was made "with knowledge that it was false, or with reckless disregard for whether it was true or false at a time when defendant had serious doubt as to whether it was true." See MAI 23.06(2); MAI 23.10(2). A public-figure plaintiff must also prove the statement was false. Id. See also Balderree v. Beeman, 837 S.W.2d 309, 326 (Mo. Ct. App. S.D. 1992) (quoting Philadelphia Newspapers, Inc. v. Hepps, 475 U.S. 767, 768-69, 776-77 (1986)), overruled on other grounds by, Amick v. Pattonville-Bridgeton Terrace Fire Prot. Dist., 91 S.W.3d 603 (Mo. 2002) (en banc). As discussed at I.B.1, supra, some uncertainty exists whether a private-figure plaintiff must plead and prove falsity.

2. ***Fault.*** Every defamation plaintiff must prove fault. Henry v. Halliburton, 690 S.W.2d 775, 782 (Mo. 1985) (en banc); Hoeflicker v. Higinsville Advance, Inc., 818 S.W.2d 650, 651 (Mo. Ct. App. W.D. 1991). The level of fault depends upon the plaintiff's status as a private or public figure. It is unclear whether the distinction between matters of private and public concern also affects the level of fault to be proved.

a. ***Private* Figure Plaintiff/Matter of *Public* Concern**. Negligence is likely the level of fault necessary for a claim filed by a private-figure plaintiff involving a matter of public concern. Deckard v. O'Reilly Automotive, Inc., 31 S.W.3d 6, 21 (Mo. Ct. App. W.D. 2000), overruled on other grounds by, Hampton v. Big Boy Steel Erection, 121 S.W.3d 220 (Mo. 2003) (en banc); Hyde v. City of Columbia, 637 S.W.2d 251, 266 (Mo. Ct. App. W.D. 1982); see Englezos v. Newspress & Gazette Co., 980 S.W.2d 25, 31 (Mo. Ct. App. W.D. 1998); see also Govan v. Missouri Dep't of Corrections, No. 2:02CV72 JCH, 2005 U.S. Dist. LEXIS 32011, at *27, n. 12. (E.D. Mo. Dec. 9, 2005) ("The requisite degree of fault for a private figure is negligence, or, to recover punitive damages, malice.") (quoting Overcast, 11 S.W.3d at 70), aff'd by Govan v. Gammon, 218 Fed.Appx. 559 (8th Cir. Mar 13, 2007) (No. 06-1472). But see Committee Comment MAI 23.06(1) (jury should determine applicable level of fault); Committee Comment (MAI 23.10(1) (same). See Englezos, 980 S.W.2d at 30-31 ("[N]o Missouri authority for application of a standard other than fault even where the articles concern a matter of public concern.").

b. ***Private* Figure Plaintiff/Matter of *Private* Concern.** Negligence is likely the level of fault in the context of a claim filed by a private-figure plaintiff involving a matter of private concern. Deckard, 31 S.W.3d at 21; Hyde, 637 S.W.2d at 266; see Englezos, 980 S.W.2d at 27, 31; see also Govan, 2005 U.S. Dist. LEXIS 32011 at *27 n. 12 ("The requisite degree of fault for a private figure is negligence, or, to recover punitive damages, malice.") (quoting Overcast, 11 S.W.3d at 70).

c. ***Public* Figure Plaintiff/Matter of *Public* Concern.** Where the plaintiff is a public figure, Missouri courts apply the actual malice standard set forth in New York Times Co. v. Sullivan, 376 U.S. at 280. Englezos, 980 S.W.2d at 30-31; Glover v. Herald Co., 549 S.W.2d 858, 860-61 (Mo. 1977) (en banc); see Bauer v. Ribaudo, 926 S.W.2d 38, 42 (Mo. Ct. App. E.D. 1996) (actual malice standard applied to defamation action brought by candidate for public office). To succeed in a defamation claim, a public-figure plaintiff must show that the defendant published the statement either "with knowledge of its falsity or with reckless disregard for whether it was true or false." Goven, 2005 U.S. Dist. Lexis, at *27, n. 12 (quoting Reliance Insurance Co. v. Shenandoah South, Inc., 81 F.3d 789, 792 (8th Cir. 1996)). Actual malice is discussed at II.A.2.d.(1), infra. A plaintiff may be classified as a public figure either because "(a) he achieves such pervasive fame or notoriety that he becomes a public figure for all purposes and in all contexts, or (b) he voluntarily injects himself or is drawn into a particular public controversy and thereby becomes a public figure for a limited range of issues." Gertz v. Robert Welch, 418 U.S. 323, 351 (1971).

3. ***Falsity.*** Private-figure and public-figure plaintiffs must prove the falsity of the published statement. Anton v. St. Louis Suburban Newspapers, Inc., 598 S.W.2d 493, 498 (Mo. Ct. App. E.D. 1980) (citing Cox Broadcasting Corp. v. Cohn, 420 U.S. 469, 490 (1975); Gertz v. Robert Welch, Inc., 418 U.S. 323, 347 (1974)). The necessity of a plaintiff proving falsity is the counterpart to truth being a complete affirmative defense. See Kenney, 100 S.W.3d at 814 n. 2. See I.B.1, supra. Recent case law suggests that a plaintiff must prove falsity as part of its prima facie case. See Ross, 163 S.W.3d at 929; Overcast, 11 S.W.3d at 70; Johnson, 278 S.W.3d at 235; Sifagus, 109 S.W.3d at 176. The issue remains somewhat uncertain as the Supreme Court of Missouri expressly left it "unresolved." See Kenney, 100 S.W.3d at 814 n. 2.

4. ***Defamatory Statement of Fact.*** A statement of fact is defamatory if it "tends to so harm the reputation of another as to lower him in the estimation of the community or to deter third persons from associating or dealing with him." Kennedy v. Jasper, 928 S.W.2d 395, 399-400 (Mo. Ct. App. E.D. 1996). To defame an individual's professional

standing, the language used must "impute a lack of knowledge, skill, capacity, or fitness to perform one's duties; or fraud, want of integrity, or misconduct in the line of one's calling." Nazeri, 860 S.W.2d at 311; see Brown v. Kitterman, 443 S.W.2d 146, 154 (Mo. 1969); Capobianco v. Pulitzer Publishing Co., 812 S.W.2d 852, 856 (Mo. Ct. App. E.D. 1991). General disparagement, equally discrediting to all, is not sufficient unless the characteristic disparaged is peculiarly important to the plaintiff's profession or business. Swafford v. Miller, 711 S.W.2d 211, 215 (Mo. Ct. App. S.D. 1986) (quoting Jacobs v. Transcontinental & Western Air, 216 S.W.2d 523, 525 (Mo. 1948)). "The mere statement that someone has been terminated from employment is not in and of itself defamatory." Klein v. Victor, 903 F. Supp. 1327, 1336, 24 Media L. Rep. 1417 (E.D. Mo. 1995); see also BPSS, Inc. v. Wilhold, No. 4:08CV1063, 2009 U.S. Dist. LEXIS 21630 (E.D. Mo. Mar. 18, 2009). A corporation may state a claim for defamation for damage to its business reputation. Jenkins, 925 S.W.2d at 944.

The defamatory nature of a statement is a question of law. Jordan v. City of Kansas City, 972 S.W.2d 319, 323 (Mo. Ct. App. W.D. 1998); see also Kitterman, 443 S.W.2d at 150. To determine whether a statement is defamatory, the court divests the statement of any pleaded innuendo and construes the statement in its most innocent sense. Nazeri, 860 S.W.2d at 311 (citing Walker v. Kansas City Star Co., 406 S.W.2d 44, 51 (Mo. 1966); Langworthy v. Pulitzer Publishing Co., 368 S.W.2d 385, 388 (Mo. 1963)). The court also considers the context of the statement, giving it its plain and ordinary meaning. See Nazeri, 860 S.W.2d at 311. Finally, the statement is "to be taken in the sense which is most obvious and natural and according to the ideas [it is] calculated to convey to those to whom [it] was addressed." Id. (citing Kirk v. Ebenhoch, 191 S.W.2d 643, 645 (Mo. 1945); see Chastain v. Kansas City Star, 50 S.W.3d 286, 288 (Mo. Ct. App. W.D. 2001). If the court determines a statement is capable of having a defamatory meaning, a jury decides whether it is actually defamatory. Pape v. Reither, 918 S.W.2d 376, 379 (Mo. Ct. App. E.D. 1996) (citing Henry, 690 S.W.2d at 779).

5. ***Of and Concerning Plaintiff.*** The defamatory statement must refer to the plaintiff in some way. Duggan v. Pulitzer Publishing Co., 913 S.W.2d 807, 811 (Mo. Ct. App. E.D. 1995) (citing Capobianco, 812 S.W.2d at 858). It is sufficient to generally allege that words were published concerning the plaintiff. Mo. Rev. Stat. § 509.210; Duggan, 913 S.W.2d at 811 (citation omitted). If the defamatory statement does not refer specifically to the plaintiff, the focus is on whether the statement's recipient reasonably understood the defamatory statement to refer to the plaintiff, not on the intent of the alleged defamer. May v. Greater Kansas City Dental Society, 863 S.W.2d 941, 945 (Mo. Ct. App. W.D. 1993). If the defamatory statement is unambiguous, the issue is for the court. Id. at 944-45. If, however, a question exists whether the defamatory statement concerns the plaintiff, the issue is for the jury. Id. at 944. If a defamatory statement is directed at a small group whose individual members are readily identifiable as those to whom the statement is referred, each individual member will have a cause of action. Smith v. UAW-CIO Federal Credit Union, 728 S.W.2d 679, 682 n.1 (Mo. Ct. App. W.D. 1987).

6. ***Publication.*** Publication is the communication of defamatory matter to a third person. Rice v. Hodapp, 919 S.W.2d 240, 243 (Mo. 1996) (en banc) (quoting Nazeri, 860 S.W.2d at 313). A publication may occur when one intentionally or unreasonably fails to remove defamatory matter known to be exhibited on land or chattels in one's possession or control. See Kenney v. Wal-Mart, WD 59936, 2002 Mo. App. LEXIS 1801, at *37 (Mo. Ct. App. W.D. Aug. 30, 2002), rev'd on other grounds, 100 S.W.3d 809 (Mo. 2003) (citing Restatement (Second) of Torts § 577(2)).

In Bogan v. General Motors Corp., the court granted summary judgment to plaintiff's employer ("GM") on plaintiff's libel claim. 437 F. Supp.2d 1040, 1050 (E.D. Mo. 2006), rev'd and remanded on other grounds, 500 F.3d 828 (8th Cir. 2007). Defendant GM terminated plaintiff's employment after she had been accused of selling drugs at work. Id. at 1043-44. Plaintiff was arrested on three counts of drug trafficking, although the charges later were dismissed. Id. Plaintiff sued GM, alleging libel based on a newspaper article that she had been charged with selling drugs at work. Id. at 1044. Plaintiff offered no evidence that GM was involved in the publication of the article, other than the article quoted a GM spokesperson stating that "GM has 'an absolute zero tolerance of this type of behavior." Id. at 1050. The court found this insufficient to establish publication.

a. **Intracorporate Communication.** "[C]ommunications between officers of the same corporation in the due and regular course of the corporate business, or between different offices of the same corporation, are not publications to third persons." Rice, 919 S.W.2d at 243 (quoting Hellesen v. Knaus Truck Lines, Inc., 370 S.W.2d 341, 344 (Mo. 1963)). In either case, the communication is deemed to be a communication by the corporation to itself. Lovelace v. Long John Silver's, Inc., 841 S.W.2d 682, 685 (Mo. Ct. App. W.D. 1992) (citing Hellesen, 370 S.W.2d at 344). Resolution of personnel problems is part of the "due and regular course of the corporate business." Lovelace, 841 S.W.2d at 685. Intracorporate communications concerning the reason for terminating an employee include statements to managers, to the corporate team investigating the employee's conduct, to the supervisor of the employee's supervisor, to the human resources manager, and to the human resources clerk processing the termination paperwork. See Gray v. AT&T Corp., 357 F.3d 763, 766 (8th Cir. 2004); see also Hayes v. Lange, 08-0042-CV-W-HFS, 2010 U.S. Dist. LEXIS 26871, at *15 (W.D. Mo. March 22, 2010) (statements made to corporate officers regarding fellow employee fell within the intracorporate communication exception); Lovelace, 841 S.W.2d at 685 (statements made by fellow employees to supervisor regarding another employee's conduct fell within protection of the rule). Corporate officers' or supervisors' communications to non-supervisory personnel may constitute publication, but may also be qualifiedly privileged. See Rice, 919 S.W.2d at 243-44 (court applied qualified privilege analysis but referred to the privileged statements as intracorporate communications). Excessive dissemination exceeding the exigencies of the situation may be construed as abusive and, therefore, an exception to the privilege. Id. at 244-45.

Missouri previously declined to extend the intracorporate immunity rule to inter-corporate communications. Lovelace, 841 S.W.2d at 685. The Eighth Circuit Court of Appeals, however, has recognized a "need to know" component, thereby extending the intracorporate doctrine to include communications between separate corporations. See Gray, 357 F.3d at 767. In Lovelace and prior decisions (see Washington v. Thomas, 778 S.W.2d 792, 797 (Mo. Ct. App. E.D. 1989)), Missouri appellate courts found no "compelling reason" to extend the rule beyond communications within the same corporation. Lovelace, 841 S.W.2d at 685. In Gray, however, the plaintiff claimed her former employer had defamed her by publishing defamatory statements about her termination, including to an outside company that the employer regularly used to handle unemployment claims. Gray, 357 F.2d at 766. The Eighth Circuit ruled there was no actionable publication under the facts of the case. See Id. The court observed that "[f]or many years, the law of libel and slander has recognized a general exemption to the publication rule for corporate communications to necessary third parties authorized to act on behalf of the corporation." Id. at 766-67 (citing Oklahoma, Tennessee, and Washington cases). The court further reasoned that, "[c] orporations, particularly small businesses, often rely on outside companies to perform many of their complicated regulatory compliance duties, imposed by a host of laws and regulations." Id. at 767. The court therefore concluded that, "Missouri would apply a similar 'need to know' concept for communications between the separate corporations under the facts of [the plaintiff's] claim." Id.; see also Hayes, 2010 U.S. Dist. LEXIS 26871, at *13-15 (intracorporate immunity rule has be "sufficiently expanded" to apply to statements made by corporate employees to the INS and the corporation's immigration attorney regarding another employee) (citing Gray, 357 F.3d at 766; Blake v. May Dep't Stores Co., 882 S.W.2d 688, 689 (Mo. Ct. App. E.D. 1994)).

Communications within a noncorporate context satisfy the publication requirement, at least to the extent of submitting the issue to the jury. See Dvorak v. O'Flynn, 808 S.W.2d 912, 917 (Mo. Ct. App. E.D. 1991) (communications within police academy); Ramacciotti v. Zinn, 550 S.W.2d 217, 223 (Mo. Ct. App. E.D. 1977) (communications between chief of police and city manager). The intracorporate immunity rule has been applied to "quasi-public corporations," such as state universities that carry out their "duties and functions much as a private corporate entity would." Dean v. Wissmann, 996 S.W.2d 631, 634-35 (Mo. Ct. App. W.D. 1999) (faculty member reported student cheating to superiors; no publication because faculty member's communication protected by intracorporate immunity rule).

When an employer is communicating the reasons for an employee's discharge within its own organization, the best way for the employer to avoid liability is to limit such communications to key personnel who have a "need to know." To the extent such information is communicated beyond such individuals, the content of the information conveyed should be considered carefully.

b. **Compelled Self-Publication.** Missouri recognizes an exception to the publication requirement if "the utterer of the defamatory matter intends, or has reason to suppose, that in the ordinary course of events the matter will come to the knowledge of some third person." Neighbors v. Kirksville College of Osteopathic Medicine, 694 S.W.2d 822, 824 (Mo. Ct. App. W.D. 1985) (quoting Herberholt v. DePaul Community Health Center, 625 S.W.2d 617, 624 (Mo. 1981) (per curiam), superseded by statute on other grounds as stated in Gloria v. University of Health Sciences, 713 S.W.2d 32, 33 (Mo. Ct. App. W.D. 1986); see Mauzy v. Mexico School District No. 59, 878 F. Supp. 153, 157 (E.D. Mo. 1995); see also Arthaud v. Mutual of Omaha Insurance Co., 170 F.3d 860, 862 (8th Cir. 1999) (applying Missouri law) (citations omitted) (elements of compelled self-publication defamation claim reviewed). In Neighbors, the plaintiff based her libel claim upon the service letter she received from her former employer. Neighbors, 694 S.W.2d at 824. Despite the third-party-publication requirement, the plaintiff survived a motion to dismiss by alleging that the service letter was given to her to use as a reference to find another job and that prospective employers actually read the letter. Id. at 824-25.

Compelled self-publication has not been recognized when the former employee's communication to the prospective employer embellishes upon the former employer's stated reason for discharge. See Deckard, 31 S.W.3d at 19 (plaintiff did not republish former employer's communication to a prospective employer where plaintiff communicated his own interpretation of his former employer's communication).

"In the compelled self-defamation context, an employee must demonstrate a causal connection between the employer's false statement and a lost job opportunity to show actual professional damages." Arthaud, 170 F.3d at 862 (citations omitted). Mere communication of the alleged defamatory statement to the prospective employer is insufficient. Id. To demonstrate a causal connection, a plaintiff must prove the prospective employer actually relied on the alleged defamatory statement in denying employment to the plaintiff. Id. (citations omitted).

c. **Republication.** The communication of defamatory matter to a third person constitutes publication, even if the individual communicating such information learned of the defamatory matter from another. See Moritz v. Kansas City Star Co., 258 S.W.2d 583, 585-86 (Mo. 1953) (en banc) ("The fact that someone else previously has communicated false facts does not justify knowingly repeating false facts."). However, the original publisher of the alleged defamatory communication has no liability for the subsequent republication, if the republication resulted from the unauthorized or independent conduct of others and if the original publication was privileged. Pulliam v. Bond, 406 S.W.2d 635, 643 (Mo. 1966); Willman v. Donner, 770 S.W.2d 275, 282 (Mo. Ct. App. W.D. 1989). In the context of an intracorporate communication, discussed at I.B.6.a, supra, repetition or republication of the defamatory statement does not satisfy the publication requirement. Blake v. May Dep't Stores Co., 882 S.W.2d 688, 690 (Mo. Ct. App. E.D. 1994) (citation omitted). If the original publication was opinion, discussed at II.B.2, infra, and a matter of public importance, the republication is absolutely privileged under the First Amendment. Henry, 690 S.W.2d at 786-87.

7. ***Statements versus Conduct.*** Although Missouri has no cases on point, case law suggests that nonverbal communication, such as gestures or sign language, may provide the basis for a defamation claim. See Bogan, 437 F. Supp. 2d at 1050 (quoting Roberson, 790 S.W.2d at 950); Boomshaft v. Klauber, 190 S.W. 616, 618 (Mo. Ct. App. E.D. 1916).

8. ***Damages.*** Missouri has abandoned the per se/per quod distinction regarding damages; the plaintiff must prove actual damages in all cases. See Nazeri, 860 S.W.2d at 313; Kennedy, 928 S.W.2d at 400; see also Hoyt v. GE Capital Mortgage Services, Inc., 193 S.W.3d 315, 324-25 (Mo. Ct. App. E.D. 2006) "Actual damages resulting from defamatory falsehood are not limited to monetary loss, but customarily include 'impairment of reputation and standing in the community, personal humiliation, and mental anguish and suffering.'" O'Brien v. Dekalb-Clinton Counties Ambulance District, No. 94-6121-CV-SJ-6, 1996 U.S. Dist. LEXIS, at *7, (W.D. Mo. June 24, 1996) (quoting Gertz v. Robert Welch, Inc., 418 U.S. 323, 349-50 (1974)) (citing Carter v. Willert Home Prod., 714 S.W.2d 506, 510 (Mo. 1986) (en banc)).

To recover for a claim of defamation, however, damages to a plaintiff's reputation are indispensable and must be proved in the first instance. Kenney, 100 S.W.3d at 813-14, 817 (citations omitted); see MAI 23.06(1). Only upon proof of reputational harm may a plaintiff recover for other related injuries, such as emotional distress. Kenney, 100 S.W.3d at 813-14 (citations omitted); see Scott v. LeClereq, 136 S.W.3d 183, 193-94 (Mo. Ct. App. W.D. 2004). There must be concrete proof that plaintiff's reputation has been injured. Weidner v. Anderson, 174 S.W.3d 672, 683 (Mo. Ct. App. S.D. 2005) (citation omitted). A plaintiff cannot recover based on only the plaintiff's testimony, conclusory statements, or inferred damages. See Scott, 136 S.W.3d at 194; Weidner, 174 S.W.3d at, 683-84. For example, in Kenney v. Wal-Mart, the plaintiff offered insufficient evidence to prove that she suffered actual damages. Kenney, 100 S.W.3d at 817. The plaintiff "made only a conclusory statement that her reputation was injured and that she felt 'embarrassed, shocked, mad.'" Id. Plaintiff "did not name a single person who held her in lower regard" after seeing the alleged defamatory poster, and the plaintiff did not "resent anyone who respected her less or thought of her reputation as being lowered by the poster." Id. Finally, the plaintiff failed to adduce testimony or other evidence of "stress or sleeplessness over the incident," and had "apparently suffered no symptoms associated with mental distress." Id. at 817-18. The court thus concluded that "[t]here was little, if any, evidence of 'quantifiable professional or personal injury, such as interference with job performance, psychological or emotional distress, or depression'." Id. at 818 (citation omitted). In contrast, in Scott, the plaintiff offered the testimony of a third party who testified that the plaintiff's reputation had been damaged professionally. Scott, 136 S.W.3d at 195-96. The plaintiff was a high school principal, and the third party was his supervisor, the superintendent. Id. The court found that such testimony was sufficient to establish proof of damage to plaintiff's reputation. Id.

To establish actual damages, a plaintiff must demonstrate that "defamatory statements caused a quantifiable professional or personal injury, such as interference with job performance, psychological or emotional distress, or depression." Arthaud, 170 F.3d at 862 (citations omitted). "In the compelled self-defamation context, an employee must demonstrate a causal connection between the employer's false statement and a lost job opportunity to show actual professional damages." Arthaud, 170 F.3d at 862 (citations omitted).

If unable to collect the judgment, a plaintiff may be eligible to recover from the Tort Victims' Compensation Fund if the plaintiff is unable to collect a monetary judgment. See Mo. Rev. Stat. § 537.675 (2000 & Supp. 2009).

a. **Presumed Damages and Defamation Per Se.** With the abolition of per se and per quod rules, Missouri has abolished presumed damages and the need to prove special damages. Kennedy, 928 S.W.2d at 400; see Nazeri, 860 S.W.2d at 313. Special damages refer to "a loss of money or of some advantage capable of being assessed in monetary value, such as loss of a marriage, employment, income, profits, or even gratuitous hospitality." Nazeri. 860 S.W.2d at 308 (citation omitted).

(1) **Employment-Related Criticism.** There are no Missouri cases on point. If such cases exist, however, it appears they no longer would be applicable, because Missouri abolished presumed damages and defamation per se.

(2) **Single Instance Rule.** There are no Missouri cases on point. If such cases exist, however, it appears they no longer would be applicable, because Missouri abolished presumed damages and defamation per se.

b. **Punitive Damages.** To recover punitive damages, a private-figure or public-figure plaintiff must establish actual malice by clear and convincing evidence. Englezos, 980 S.W.2d at 30 (citing Gertz, 418 U.S. at 347-48; Williams v. Pulitzer Broadcasting Co., 706 S.W.2d 508, 512 (Mo. Ct. App. E.D. 1986); Kennedy, 928 S.W.2d at 400)). Actual malice is defined as "publication of the defamatory matter with either knowledge of, or reckless disregard of, the falsity of the information published." Williams, 706 S.W.2d at 512; see Wright, 945 S.W.2d at 485 (quoting Smith, 728 S.W.2d at 683). The test for actual malice is subjective. "The test not being whether a reasonably prudent person would have had serious doubts as to the truth of the publication, but whether the defendant in fact entertained such doubts." In re Westfall, 808 S.W.2d 829, 836-37 (Mo. 1991) (en banc) (citing St. Amant v. Thompson, 390 U.S. 727, 730 (1968)). There must be "sufficient evidence to permit the conclusion that the defendant in fact entertained serious doubts as to the truth of his publication." Englezos, 980 S.W.2d at 33 (quoting St. Amant, 390 U.S. at 731). Proof of falsity is not proof of malice. Williams, 706 S.W.2d at 512 (citation omitted). Failure to investigate, without more, also does not establish malice. Malice may be found, however, if "there are obvious reasons to doubt the veracity of the informant or the accuracy of his reports." Wright, 945 S.W.2d at 497 (internal quotations and citations omitted); see Rice, 919 S.W.2d at 244 (recklessness standard is satisfied if statement made without any basis in fact).

The Supreme Court has long made clear that "[p]unitive damages may properly be imposed to further a State's legitimate interests in punishing unlawful conduct and deterring its repetition." Philip Morris USA v. Williams, 549 U.S. 346, 352 (U.S. 2007) (citation omitted). The Missouri Approved Jury Instructions include punitive damages instructions for defamation cases. See MAI 4.15 [1980 New] (private-figure plaintiff; used in conjunction with MAI 23.06(1) or 23.10(1)); MAI 4.16 [1980 New] (public-figure plaintiff) (used in conjunction with MAI 23.06(2) or 23.10 (2)). In assessing punitive damages, juries may consider aggravating and mitigating circumstances. See Maugh v. Chrysler Corp., 818 S.W.2d 658, 662 & n.2 (Mo. Ct. App. W.D. 1991). Mitigating circumstances include "provocation, the absence of malice, the presence of good faith, and that the defendant acted under the advice of counsel." Id. at 662. Juries consider many factors when assessing punitive damages, including (1) the degree of malice, positive wrongdoing or criminality characterizing the act; (2) the age, sex, health, financial worth, and injury suffered by the injured party; (3) the intelligence, standing or affluence, financial worth, and character of the defendant; and (4) all circumstances surrounding the bad act. Id. at 662, n. 2. As part of the 2005 tort reform initiative, the Missouri legislature has limited an award of punitive damages to the greater of: (a) five hundred thousand dollars ($500,000.00) or (b) five times the net amount of the judgment awarded to the plaintiff against the defendant. Mo. Rev. Stat. § 510.265 (Supp. 2009).

II. PRIVILEGES AND DEFENSES

A. Scope of Privileges

1. ***Absolute Privilege.*** Absolute immunity is limited to situations in which "there is an obvious policy in favor of permitting complete freedom of expression, without any inquiry as to the defendant's motives," such as executive, legislative, and judicial proceedings or otherwise required by or provided for by law. Wright, 945 S.W.2d at 485 (citations omitted); see also Barge v. Ransom, 30 S.W.3d 889, 890 (Mo. Ct. App. S.D. 2000) (citations omitted). It is the occasion, not the place or time, that decides whether publication of a defamatory communication is privileged and whether that privilege is absolute or qualified. Hester v. Barnett, 723 S.W.2d 544, 557 (Mo. Ct. App. W.D. 1987) (internal citation omitted). If a defendant asserts a privilege, the defendant has the burden of showing its applicability. Williams, 706 S.W.2d at 511 (citation omitted). Whether a privilege attaches is a question of law for the court. See *id.* An absolute privilege is not destroyed by malice. Id.

One absolute privilege is the "judicial privilege," which includes "defamatory statements made by judges, lawyers, witnesses or parties in the course of a judicial proceeding if the defamatory statements are relevant to the proceeding." Pape, 918 S.W.2d at 381 (citing Wright v. Truman Road Enterprises, Inc., 443 S.W.2d 13, 15 (Mo. Ct. App. W.D. 1969)). The immunity with respect to participation in judicial proceedings has been extended statutorily to "[a]ny person, official, or institution complying with the [statutory provisions] in the making of a report . . . or in cooperating with the division, or any other law enforcement agency, juvenile office, court, or child-protective service agency", unless that "person, official or institution intentionally [files] a false report, [acts] in bad faith, or with ill intent." Mo. Rev. Stat. §210.135 (2000 & Supp. 2009); see Clark v. Mickes, No. 05-CV-0100-ERW, 2006 U.S. Dist. LEXIS 46116, at *17-18 (E.D.

Mo. Jul. 6, 2006) (plaintiff, who taught students with behavioral problems, brought a defamation claim against his employer based on co-worker's statement to DFS that plaintiff "gets a little rough with students"; court dismissed claim because employer was immune from liability based on § 210.135), aff'd, 258 Fed. Appx. 916 (8th Cir. 2007). Statements made in the context of a quasi-judicial proceeding generally are held to be absolutely privileged if relevant to the proceedings. Entwistle v. Mo. Youth Soccer Ass'n, 259 S.W.3d 558, 567-68 (Mo. Ct. App. E.D. 2008) (citing Li v. Metropolitan Life Insurance Co., Inc., 955 S.W.2d 799, 803 (Mo. Ct. App. E.D. 1997)); Wright, 945 S.W.2d at 492; Bakhtiari v. Beyer, No. 4:06-CV-1489, 2009 U.S. Dist. LEXIS 27286, at *13-14 (E.D. Mo. Mar. 30, 2009) (letter sent to Immigration and Naturalization Service in connection with a deportation proceeding was absolutely privileged). A statement is relevant if it is made during the course of a proceeding and has some relation to the proceeding. Li, 955 S.W.2d at 804. A proceeding is quasi-judicial if the agency possesses traditional powers, such as being able to conduct hearings at which witnesses may be summoned and examined, subpoena documents, and hand down judgments." Id. at 803.

In Rockwood Bank v. Gaia, a bank president's alleged defamatory statements about a bank employee made to bank examiners during a routine bank examination were not entitled to absolute immunity. See 170 F.3d 833 (8th Cir. 1999) (applying Missouri law), cert. denied, 120 S. Ct. 407 (1999). Although the bank examiners (the FDIC and the Missouri Division of Finance) possess quasi-judicial powers, such powers and corresponding safeguards are not utilized in a routine bank examination. Id. at 839-40. An individual's statements made to police department internal affairs investigators through the department's official complaint procedure were not entitled to absolute immunity. See Barge v. Ransom, 30 S.W.3d 889 (Mo. Ct. App. S.D. 2000). The court held that such a grievance procedure did not qualify as a "quasi-judicial" proceeding and was otherwise not entitled to the application of an absolute privilege. Id. at 891-92. The Health Care Quality Improvement Act may provide limited immunity for statements made in the context of peer review and medical privilege revocation. Lee v. Trinity Lutheran Hospital, No. 00-0716-CV-W-HFS, 2004 U.S. Dist. LEXIS 1800, at *15-17 (W.D. Mo. Jan. 29, 2004), aff'd, 408 F.3d 1064 (8th Cir. 2005), reh'g denied, 2005 U.S. App. LEXIS 14781 (8th Cir. July 20, 2005).

2. ***Qualified Privileges.*** Missouri courts recognize two common-law qualified privileges. Id. at 780. First, the "fair comment" doctrine conditionally privileges fair and honest expressions of opinion or comments upon matters of public concern that are based upon the truth. See Henry, 690 S.W.2d at 780 (citing McClung v. Pulitzer Publishing Co., 214 S.W. 193 (Mo. 1919)(en banc); Cook v. Pulitzer Publishing Co., 145 S.W. 480, 488 (Mo. 1912)). Conditional privilege attaches where "[t]he publication of defamatory matter concerning another in a report of an official action or proceeding or of a meeting open to the public that deals with a matter of public concern. . . if the report is accurate and complete or a fair abridgement of the occurrence reported." Shafer v. Lamar Pub. Co., 621 S.W.2d 709, 711 (Mo. Ct. App. W.D. 1981) (quoting Restatement Second (Torts) § 611); see also Spradlin's Market, Inc. v. Springfield Newspapers, Inc. 398 S.W.2d 859, 864 (Mo. 1966); Erickson v. Pulitzer Pub. Co., 797 S.W.2d 853, 857 (Mo. Ct. App. E.D. 1990). Second, comments made under certain defined circumstances may also be qualifiedly privileged. Henry, 690 S.W.2d at 780. This second privilege conditionally privileges: "all statements made bona fide in performance of a duty, or with a fair and reasonable purpose of protecting the interest of the person making them, or the interest of the person to whom they are made." Id. at 780 (citation omitted). "A communication made bona fide upon any subject matter in which the party communicating has an interest, or in reference to which he has a duty, is privileged, if made to a person having a corresponding interest or duty." Id.

A qualified privilege is conditioned upon good motives, reasonable behavior, and is forfeited if abused. Hester, 723 S.W.2d at 558 (internal quotations and citation omitted). The existence of a qualified privilege precludes an inference of malice from the publication of defamatory material, and a plaintiff must prove actual malice by clear and convincing evidence. Herberholt, 625 S.W.2d at 625; Deckard, 31 S.W.3d at 21. The existence of a qualified privilege is a question of law, and may be appropriately resolved on a motion for summary judgment. Erickson, 797 S.W.2d at 857 (citation omitted).

Generally, statements in the context of union activity are qualifiedly privileged. See Wright, 945 S.W.2d at 493. See e.g., Manning v. McAllister, 454 S.W.2d 597, 600 (Mo. Ct. App. E.D. 1970) (reviewing numerous cases, many in the employment context, in which the communication was deemed qualifiedly privileged). A qualified privilege generally attaches to communications regarding the character or qualifications of an employee or former employee, if made in good faith by a person having a duty, whether legal, moral or social in nature, to one who has a definite interest in the communication. Fleischaker v. Headlee, 99 S.W.3d 540, 545 (Mo. Ct. App. S.D. 2003) (citation omitted). Additionally, a qualified privilege attaches to statements made to law enforcement for the purpose of apprehending a criminal. See Brown v. P.N. Hirsch & Co. Stores, Inc., 661 S.W.2d 587, 591 (Mo. Ct. App. W.D. 1983) (store manager's statements to police that plaintiff had shoplifted were qualifiedly privileged); see Smith v. IT Newberry Co., 395 S.W.2d 472, 475-76, 479 (Mo. Ct. App. E.D. 1965) (manager's statement to employee that there was proof enough for him of employee's stealing was qualifiedly privileged); see also Gardner v. 4 U Technology, Inc., 88 F. Supp. 2d 1005, 1009 (E.D. Mo. 2000) (corporate officer or director may be individually liable for alleged defamatory statement to the police if corporate officer or director does not indicate in signed statement that he or she is signing in official capacity as officer or director of corporation).

a. **Common Interest.** "A communication is qualifiedly privileged if made between persons having an interest in or duty concerning the subject matter." Dvorak, 808 S.W.2d at 918 (citation omitted). This interest or duty includes those of a "personal, private, moral, and social nature." Id.; see also McDowell, 747 S.W.2d at 632 (citation omitted); Henry, 690 S.W.2d at 781; Lee, 23 S.W.2d at 60. "A qualified privilege has been applied to credit reporting agencies, or mercantile agencies, if the agency communication is made to a subscriber having an interest in the financial position of that business or individual." McDowell, 747 S.W.2d at 632. A business/customer relationship may create the requisite common interest. See Deckard, 31 S.W.3d 6, 17 (Mo. Ct. App. W.D. 2000) (qualified privilege exists in company's communication to defrauded customer concerning employee's misuse of customer's account and actions taken to remedy situation). A common interest also may exist as to communications between supervisory and non-supervisory personnel. See, e.g., Rice, 919 S.W.2d at 244 (communications from supervisors to non-supervisory personnel concerning sexual harassment investigation were qualifiedly privileged because "[e]mployees have a legitimate interest in their employer's guidelines for appropriate behavior"); Deckard, 31 S.W.3d at 17 (manager's statements to non-managerial employees that assistant manager was no longer with the company due to theft were qualifiedly privileged because management reasonably needed to inform employees that assistant manager no longer worked for company and management had an interest in preparing employees to deal with questions from customers regarding assistant manager's absence).

b. **Duty.** "A communication is qualifiedly privileged if made between persons having an interest in or duty concerning the subject matter." Dvorak, 808 S.W.2d at 918. "This interest or duty includes those of a personal, private, moral, and social nature." Id.; see also McDowell, 747 S.W.2d at 632; Henry, 690 S.W.2d at 781; Lee, 23 S.W.2d at 60; Fisher v. Wal-Mart Stores, Inc., No. 08-0512-CV-W-DGK, 2009 U.S. Dist. LEXIS 62278, at *12-18 (W.D. Mo. July 6, 2009) (incorrect statement by store security officer to police dispatcher that customer was trying to pass fake money orders was protected by qualified privilege because security officer had duty to protect store assets).

c. **Criticism of Public Employee.** "Criticism of official conduct is protected by the requirement to plead and prove actual malice." Nazeri, 860 S.W. 2d at 315; see Ramacciotti, 550 S.W.2d at 224. At a minimum, public officials are "those among the hierarchy of government employees who have, or appear to the public to have substantial responsibility for or control over the conduct of governmental affairs." Id. at 225 (quoting Rosenblatt v. Baer, 383 U.S. 75, 85 (1966)). "Law enforcement personnel are also considered to be public officials. Westhouse v. Biondo, 990 S.W.2d 68, 70 (Mo. Ct. App. E.D. 1999) (citations omitted). Application of the actual malice standard is not restricted to comments on public conduct because private conduct may touch upon the public employee's fitness for office. Id. at 71 (citations omitted).

d. **Limitation on Qualified Privileges.**

(1) **Actual Malice.** Actual malice in the publication of a statement destroys the immunity of a qualified privilege. Wright, 945 S.W.2d at 490 (citation omitted). The existence of malice is a jury question, "unless there is no substantial evidence of express or actual malice, in which case the court should direct a verdict." Id. (citation omitted). The plaintiff has the burden of proving actual malice. Id. at 494. For purposes of defamation claims, "acting with 'actual malice' in the publication of a statement means that the defendant acted with knowledge that the statement was false or with reckless disregard for whether it was true or false at a time when defendant had serious doubts as to whether it was true." Id. (citations omitted). Actual malice "does not mean . . . that defendant was actuated by spite, ill will and a purpose to injure the plaintiff." Id. (citations omitted); see New York Times Co., 376 U.S. at 280; Rockwood Bank, 170 F.3d at 841 (8th Cir. 1999). Failure to investigate is alone insufficient to establish reckless disregard for the truth. Wright, 945 S.W.2d at 497 (internal quotations and citations omitted). "Rather, the publishers must act with a high degree of awareness of . . . probable falsity." Id. [S]ubjective awareness of probable falsity may be found if "there are obvious reasons to doubt the veracity of the informant or the accuracy of his reports." Id.; see also Rice, 919 S.W.2d at 244; McClanahan v. Global Security Service, Co., Inc., 26 S.W.3d 291, 293 (Mo. Ct. App. E.D. 2000).

The Eighth Circuit Court of Appeals has held that federal labor law partially preempts Missouri defamation law when a defamation claim arises in the context of a labor dispute. See Ruzicka Electric & Sons, Inc. v. Int'l Brotherhood of Electrical Workers, Local 1, AFL-CIO, 427 F.3d 511, 523 (8th Cir. 2005). If the context implicates federal labor law, the defamation plaintiff must show actual malice. Id. Consequently, "[s]tate libel and slander actions may be maintained within the context of a labor dispute but only if the defamatory publication is shown by clear and convincing evidence to have been made with knowledge that it was false or with reckless disregard of whether it was false or not." Id. (internal citations and quotations omitted). In Ruzicka Electrical & Sons, Inc., a school district hired the plaintiff, a non-union electrical company, to perform work. Id. at 513-14. The union picketed the job site. Id. at 514. In addition, a business representative of the union made a statement to the school board that he "felt" the non-union electrical company's work was not up to code, improper, and dangerous. Id. at 517. The Eighth Circuit concluded that the statement was opinion and commented there was "little evidence" the plaintiff "met the heightened actual malice standard." Id. at 523, 523 n.4. It seems the outcome would be similar applying Missouri defamation law, which recognizes a qualified privilege in the context of union activity, discussed at II.A.2, supra.

(2) **Common Law Malice.** Common-law malice, unlike actual malice, requires establishing ill-will. Englezos, 980 S.W.2d at 33. Missouri courts have recognized that the existence of common law malice can defeat a qualified privilege. Henry, 690 S.W.2d at 781; Willman v. Dooner, 770 S.W.2d 275, 281 (Mo. Ct. App. W.D. 1989).

e. **Question of Fact or Law.** The existence of a qualified privilege is a question of law. Dvorak, 808 S.W.2d at 918.

f. **Burden of Proof.** The plaintiff has the burden of overcoming the qualified privilege defense. Snodgrass v. Headco Industries, Inc., 640 S.W.2d 147, 153 (Mo. Ct. App. W.D. 1982). The plaintiff may discharge this burden and recover if plaintiff shows "that the statement was made with *malice* by producing substantial evidence that defendant made the statements knowing they were false or without knowledge of whether they were true or false in reckless disregard for the plaintiff's rights. Id. at 153-54 (emphasis original) (citing Ramacciotti, 550 S.W.2d at 225). Whether malice exists is a question to be determined by the jury. Id. (citation omitted).

B. Standard Libel Defenses

1. ***Truth.*** Truth is an absolute or complete defense to a defamation claim. Mo. Const. Art. 1, § 8; Capobianco, 812 S.W.2d at 859; Briggs, 569 S.W.2d at 762. If the communication alleged to be defamatory is true, no privilege defense is necessary. Pulliam v. Bond, 406 S.W.2d 635, 642 (Mo. 1966); see also Moore v. Credit Info. Corp. of America, 673 F.2d 208, 210 (8th Cir. 1982) (applying Missouri law). Substantial truth is also a defense. See Thurston v. Ballinger, 884 S.W.2d 22, 26 (Mo. Ct. App. W.D. 1994) ("A person is not bound to exact accuracy in his statements about another, if the statements are essentially true"); Turnbull v. Herald Co., 459 S.W.2d 516, 518-19 (Mo. Ct. App. E.D. 1970) (statement substantially true if it does "not alter the complexion of the essential facts"). The defendant must plead truth as an affirmative defense. See V.C., infra. For examples of truth serving as a complete defense to defamation in the employment context, see Bogan, discussed at I.B.6, supra; Boone v. Wal-Mart Stores, Inc., No. 4:08CV9 HEA, 2009 U.S. Dist. LEXIS 32123, at *12-16 (E.D. Mo. Apr. 16, 2009) (supervisor's statement that employee had been terminated for "integrity issues" was protected by absolute truth defense because plaintiff had indeed been terminated for using a deodorant stick in violation of store policy).

Whether a private-figure plaintiff must prove falsity as an element of its prima facie case is unclear. See I.B.1, supra. Under the current Missouri Approved Instructions, a public-figure plaintiff must prove falsity, while a private-figure plaintiff need only show the defendant was at fault in publishing the statement. Compare MAI 23.06(2) , and MAI 23.10(2), with MAI 23.06(1), and MAI 23.10(1); see also Balderree, 837 S.W.2d at 326. If, however, a qualified privilege applies in the case of a private-figure plaintiff, then the public-figure plaintiff jury instructions are used. Notes on Use, (1980 New) MAI 23.06(1); Notes on Use, (1980 New) MAI 23.10.(1).

2. ***Opinion.*** Statements of opinion are protected by an absolute privilege rooted in the First Amendment to the United States Constitution. Nazeri 860 S.W.2d at 314; Henry, 690 S.W.2d at 784; Pape, 918 S.W.2d at 380. Such statements cannot give rise to a cause of action even if made maliciously or insincerely." Pape, 918 S.W.2d at 380 (citing Diez v. Pearson, 834 S.W.2d 250, 253 Mo. Ct. App. E.D. 1992). Statements of opinion that necessarily imply the existence of a defamatory fact are the only exception under Missouri law. Id. (citing Henry, 690 S.W.2d at 787). The First Amendment protects opinion not only on matters of public importance, but also on political, economic, and social matters. Henry, 690 S.W.2d at 786; see Connick, 461 U.S. at 147 ("[A]n employee's false criticism of his employer on grounds not of public concern may be cause for his discharge but would be entitled to the same protection in a libel action accorded an identical statement made by a man on the street") (quoted in Henry, 690 S.W.2d at 785).

The Supreme Court's seminal decision in Milkovich v. Loraine Journal Co. limited the absolute privilege to "those statement[s] of opinion relating to matters of public concern that [do] not contain a provably false factual connotation." Milkovich, 497 U.S. 1 (1990). After Milkovich, the Supreme Court of Missouri stated that "[t]he test to be applied to an ostensible 'opinion' is whether a reasonable factfinder could conclude that the statement implies an assertion of objective fact." Nazeri, 860 S.W.2d at 314 (citing Milkovich, 497 U.S. at 21). The gravamen of the test is whether the facts implied by the statement are "demonstrably false." Id. "Imaginative expression" and "rhetorical hyperbole" are not actionable as defamation. Id. (citing Milkovich, 497 U.S. at 20). Thus, an expression of opinion that does not contain an implied assertion of objective fact is absolutely privileged under Missouri law. See Id.; see also Henry, 690 S.W.2d at 784; Pape, 918 S.W.2d at 380.

Whether a defamatory statement is opinion or fact is a question of law. Nazeri, 860 S.W.2d at 314; Henry, 690 S.W.2d at 789. In analyzing whether a statement is opinion or fact, Missouri courts have traditionally examined the totality of the circumstances, including the common usage or meaning of the allegedly defamatory statement, the verifiability of the statement, and the statement's full context. Henry, 690 S.W.2d at 788. After Milkovich and Nazeri, however, verifiability has emerged as the guiding consideration. Nazeri, 860 S.W.2d at 314 (court examines whether defamatory statement is demonstrably false); Pape, 918 S.W.2d at 381, 382, n.4 ("Since *Henry*, 'verifiability' has broken loose from the pack to emerge as the guiding consideration in this analysis, and our opinion reflects and approves this development.").

3. ***Consent.*** Consent may render an otherwise potentially defamatory statement absolutely privileged. Johnson v. Baptist Medical Center, 97 F.3d 1070, 1074 (8th Cir. 1996) (applying Missouri law). Williams v. School District of Springfield R-12, 447 S.W.2d 256, 268 (Mo. 1969) (quoting Restatement (Second) of Torts § 583). The extent of the privilege is determined by the terms of the consent. Johnson v. City of Buckner, 610 S.W.2d. 406, 411 (Mo. Ct. App. W.D. 1980) (quoting Restatement (Second) of Torts § 583, comment d). In Johnson, for example, the court held that a discharged employee who asks the employer to give grounds for termination in front of other people has consented to the publication. Id. at 411-12; see also School District of Springfield R-12, 447 S.W.2d at 267-69 (Mo. 1969).

4. ***Mitigation.*** A defendant may raise mitigating circumstances to reduce the amount of damages, even if the defendant asserts no justification for the alleged defamatory conduct. Mo. Rev. Stat. § 509.210 (2000 & Supp. 2009); Mo. Sup. Ct. Rule 55.20; see Hall v. Brookshire, 285 S.W.2d 60, 66 (Mo. Ct. App. E.D. 1955) (mitigating circumstances are not a defense to defamation claim). Missouri case law restricts consideration of mitigating circumstances to punitive damages. See, e.g., Anderson v. Shockley, 140 S.W. 755, 756 (Mo. Ct. App. W.D. 1911).

III. RECURRING FACT PATTERNS

A. Statements in Personnel File

Placing an alleged defamatory statement in an employee's personnel file, without more, does not constitute actionable publication. Hellesen, 370 S.W.2d at 344-45; Washington, 778 S.W.2d at 796; Ellis v. Jewish Hosp., 581 S.W.2d 850, 851 (Mo. Ct. App. E.D. 1979). A corporation "does not publish writings which are prepared in the ordinary course of business, placed in the corporate files, but not distributed outside the corporate structure." Washington, 778 S.W.2d at 797. Consequently, statements or notes placed in corporate files or on the corporate computer system are generally not actionable publication. Gray, 357 F.3d at 766 n.5.

B. Performance Evaluations

Alleged defamatory statements in an employee's performance evaluation that are placed in the employee's personnel file and read by the employee's supervisors are not published, and are therefore, not actionable. Ellis, 581 S.W.2d at 851.

C. References

Simply stating that an employee was discharged, if true, is not defamatory. See Cash, 547 S.W.2d at 834-35. If the employer's communication relates to a current or former employee's qualifications or character, the communication is qualifiedly privileged if the following conditions are satisfied: (1) the statement is made by one with a legal, moral, or social duty to do so; (2) the recipient has a legitimate interest regarding the subject matter (e.g., a prospective employer); and (3) the statement was made in good faith. Fleischaker, 99 S.W.3d at 545; Cash, 547 S.W.2d at 833; see also Stelzer v. Carmelite Sisters of Divine Heart of Jesus of Mo., 619 S.W.2d 766, 767-68 (Mo. Ct. App. E.D. 1981).

Defamation claims regarding a discharged employee frequently occur when an employee requests a service letter stating the true cause for discharge. See Mo. Rev. Stat. § 290.140.1 (2000 & Supp. 2009). As an employer is under a legal duty to issue a service letter, a qualified privilege attaches to statements therein. Herberholt, 625 S.W.2d at 625; see also Cash, 547 S.W.2d at 834-35 (employer's response to background check by former employee's prospective employer was qualifiedly privileged). To overcome this privilege, the employee plaintiff must prove that "the contents of the letter were false and that the falsity was actuated by express malice." Neighbors, 694 S.W.2d at 824 (citing Herberholt, 624 S.W.2d at 625)). Further, an employer may not argue that the statement was not published to a third party, because publication occurs where "the utterer of the defamatory matter intends, or has reason to suppose, that in the ordinary course of events the matter will come to the knowledge of some third person." Id. at 824 (citing Herberholt, 824 S.W.2d at 624); see, e.g., id. at 824-25 (employee survived motion to dismiss by alleging exception to third-party publication requirement; employee pled that she received service letter to use as a reference to find other employment and that prospective employers read service letter). The standard defenses to defamation also apply in this context. See e.g. Irwin v. Wal-Mart Stores, Inc., 813 S.W.2d 99, 102 (Mo. Ct. App. W.D. 1991) (truth is complete defense to service letter that reported "cold facts," namely, that employee's "drug test showed an unacceptable level of controlled substance").

Missouri law also provides statutory immunity to employers who respond to a request for information when certain conditions are satisfied. See Mo. Rev. Stat. § 290.152.4 (2000 & Supp. 2009). Under Section 290.152.2, an employer may be entitled to immunity if it responds in writing to a written request concerning a current or former employee from an entity or person which the employer reasonably believes to be a prospective employer of such employee. Id. The employer may disclose the nature and character of service rendered by the employee and the duration of the employee's employment. The employer may also state for what cause, if any, such employee was discharged or voluntarily quit such service. Mo. Rev. Stat. § 290.152.2 (2000 & Supp. 2009). The information provided must be "consistent with the content of any service letter provided pursuant to section 290.140 for the same employee." Id. An employer who responds to a written reference request in accordance with Section 290.152 is " immune from civil liability for any response made . . . or for any consequences of such response, unless such response was false and made with knowledge that it was false or with reckless disregard for whether such response was true or false." Mo. Rev. Stat. § 290.152.4 (2000 & Supp. 2009). In Missouri, there is no statute requiring employers to respond to requests for references or to employment verification requests. If an employer feels compelled to respond to such requests, however, following the requirements of § 290.152 will protect against defamation claims brought by a current or former employee. As truth is a complete defense, providing truthful information will also allow an employer to defend against a defamation claims arising out of the content of any job reference. See e.g., Irwin, 813 S.W.2d at 102.

D. Intracorporate Communication

The intracorporate communication doctrine, discussed at I.B.6.a., supra, applies when a corporation communicates with itself through communications between its officers or different offices in the due and regular course of the corporate business. Rice, 919 S.W.2d at 243 (quoting Hellesen, 370 S.W.2d at 344)). If the doctrine applies, there is no actionable defamation claim because the defamatory statement has not been published. Lovelace., 841 S.W.2d at 684 (citing Hellesen, 370 S.W.2d at 344); Gray, 357 F.3d at 767-68. Generally, employee statements made to supervisory personnel regarding the conduct of other employees constitute intracorporate communications. See e.g., Blake v. May Dep't Stores Co., 882 S.W.2d 688, 691 (Mo. Ct. App. E.D. 1994); Lovelace, 841 S.W.2d at 684. Corporate officers or supervisors' communications to non -supervisory personnel, however, may not fall within the traditional intracorporate communication rule. Such communications may, however, be privileged. See Rice, 919 S.W.2d at 244 (court applied qualified privilege analysis but referred to the privileged statements as intracorporate communications). Under certain circumstances, the intracorporate communication doctrine has been extended to include communications between separate corporations and communications to third parties. See e.g., Gray, 357 F.3d at 767 (no actionable publication in employer's statements about reason for employee's discharge to outside company that employer regularly used to handle unemployment claims); Hayes, 2010 U.S. Dist. LEXIS 25871 at *14-15 (statements made by officers of corporation to the INS and the corporation's attorney fell within the ambit of the intra corporate communications privilege).

Solving personnel problems constitutes activity in the regular course of business. In Lovelace, for example, an employee's sexual harassment complaint to management was protected by the intracorporate communication doctrine. 841 S.W.2d at 583. In contrast, cautioning non-supervisory personnel about dating co-workers is not in the regular course of business. See Snodgrass, 640 S.W.2d at 151, 160 (statements by supervisor to new receptionist regarding conduct of third-party employee were not intracorporate communications because new receptionist was not an officer and statements were not made within the due and regular course of company business). An Eighth Circuit decision has suggested that a Title VII plaintiff may be subject to defamation liability for filing false charges, lying to investigators, and defaming co-employees. See Gilooly v. Missouri Dep't of Health & Senior Services, 421 F.3d 734, 740 (8th Cir. 2005).

E. Statements to Government Regulators

Statements made to the Missouri Division of Employment Security protesting or pertaining to a claim for unemployment benefits are absolutely privileged. Mo. Rev. Stat. § 288.250 (2000 & Supp. 2009); Remington v. Wal-Mart Stores, Inc., 817 S.W.2d 571, 574-75 (Mo. Ct. App. S.D. 1991); Washington v. Thomas, 778 S.W.2d 792, 796 (Mo. Ct. App. E.D. 1989); Tucker v. Delmar Cleaners, Inc., 637 S.W.2d 222, 224 (Mo. Ct. App. E.D. 1982).

F. Reports to Auditors and Insurers

Pursuant to the Missouri Fraudulent Insurance Act, a qualified privilege exists for the National Association of Insurance Commissioners regarding the collection, review, analysis, and dissemination of data collected from statutorily required filings. Mo. Rev. Stat. § 375.041.3 (2000 & Supp. 2009). A qualified privilege also exists for an insurer regarding the filing of reports or furnishing of information required by statute or by the Department of Insurance. Mo. Rev. Stat. § 375.993.2 (2000 & Supp. 2009).

G. Vicarious Liability of Employers for Statements Made by Employees

1. ***Scope of Employment***. An employer is vicariously liable for the defamatory conduct of an employee if the employee is acting within the course and scope of employment at the time of publication. Wright, 945

S.W.2d at 490; see Carter v. Willert Home Prods. Inc., 714 S.W.2d 506, 511-12 (Mo. 1986) (en banc) (employer's liability for employee's alleged defamatory conduct premised on respondeat superior doctrine; scope of employment discussed at length), abrogated on other grounds by Nazeri, 860 S.W.2d at 308. Whether an employee acted within the scope of employment is determined on a case-by-case basis. Davenport v. Armstead, 255 S.W.2d 132, 0136-37 (Mo. Ct. App. W.D. 1952); see also Brown, 661 S.W.2d at 592 (defendant cannot argue on appeal that employee was acting outside her scope of employment in uttering slanderous remarks when defendant never took that position at trial). Although the question of whether an employee was acting within the scope of employment is one of fact, it may be decided as a matter of law if the alleged defamatory conduct served no business purpose and was not related to performance of the employee's tasks. See Herberholt, 625 S.W.2d at 626; Davenport, 255 S.W.2d at 137.

Employers should be mindful of potential liability for electronic correspondence (such as e-mail) sent by employees. Employers should implement written employment policies articulating what is expected of employees when they engage in such correspondence. Also, such policies should advise employees (in the private sector, at least) that employees have no expectation of privacy on company-owned computers/systems and that all activity may be monitored without the employee's consent.

2. ***Damages***. Case law pertaining to damages, discussed at I.B.8, supra, applies to defamation claims based upon vicarious liability. See, e.g., Carter, 714 S.W.2d at 512.

H. Privacy Issues

Employers are increasing security through the use of searches, surveillance, and other means, to prevent and/or avoid theft by employees. In a private-sector workplace, employers are not bound by federal constitutional constraints. However, the privacy concerns of private-sector employees are often protected by state laws and the common law. In Missouri, an individual's right of privacy is legally protected. Biederman's of Springfield, Inc. v. Wright, 322 S.W.2d 892, 895 (Mo. 1959) (citations omitted). Missouri courts protect this general right through a common law action for "invasion of privacy," a general term used to describe four different torts: (1) tortious intrusion upon seclusion, (2) appropriation of someone's name or likeness; (3) public disclosure of private facts; and (4) publicity that unreasonably places another in a false light before the public. Corcoran v. Southwestern Bell Telephone Co., 572 S.W.2d 212, 214 (Mo. App. W.D. 1978) (quoting Restatement (Second) of Torts § 652A); Meyerkord v. Zipatoni Co., 276 S.W.3d 319, 322 (Mo. Ct. App. E.D. 2008). Tortious intrusion upon seclusion is the most relevant in the employment context.

1. ***Tortious Intrusion upon Seclusion.*** To establish a claim for intrusion upon seclusion, a plaintiff must show the following: (1) the existence of a secret and private subject matter; (2) a right to keep the subject matter private; and (3) the defendant's obtaining of information about that subject matter through unreasonable means. Corcoran, 572 S.W.2d at 215. The plaintiff must prove that the defendant engaged in unreasonable or highly offensive conduct. Sofka v. Thal, 662 S.W.2d 502, 511 (Mo. 1983). The defendant must have obtained the information through deception, illegal activity, or other unreasonable methods. St. Anthony's Medical Center v. H.S.H., 974 S.W.2d 606, 610 (Mo. App. E.D. 1998). An employer who obtains information in the ordinary course of business or in response to a discovery request during litigation does not engage in unreasonable or offensive conduct." Thomas v. Corwin, 483 F.3d 516, 531 (8th Cir. 2007) (citing St. Anthony's Medical Center, 974 S.W.2d at 610) (employer did not employ unreasonable means to obtain information by requiring employee to undergo a FFD evaluation under threat of termination to determine employee's ability to return to work, or by acquiring medical records when voluntarily produced by employee's attorney in discovery). An employer can protect against tort liability by obtaining the employee's consent prior to engaging in the activity in question. For example, if the employer is going to conduct surveillance, they should consider requiring employees to sign a policy stating that employees may be surveilled.

2. ***Public Disclosure of Private Facts.*** To establish a claim for public disclosure of private facts, a plaintiff must show publication of private matters in which the public has no legitimate concern, so as to bring shame or humiliation to a person of ordinary sensibilities. Corcoran, 572 S.W.2d at 214-15. "Publication" is communication to the public in general or to a large number of persons, as distinguished from one individual or a few." Biederman's of Springfield, Inc., 322 S.W.2d at 898; Corcoran, 572 S.W.2d at 215. In Brown v. Mullarkey, for example, an employee's manager allowed attorneys requesting discovery in an auto negligence action to review the employee's entire personnel file, even though the file concededly contained documents revealing more information than the attorneys had requested. 632 S.W.2d 507 (Mo. Ct. App. E.D. 1982). The court found that the publication was insufficient to constitute communication to a large number of persons. Id. at 509-10; but see Rowe v. Roadway Express, Inc., No. 4:04CV1272, 2006 U.S. Dist. LEXIS 25132 at *17-20 (E.D. Mo. May 1, 2006) (genuine issue of material fact existed where employer distributed plaintiff's psychiatric evaluation to fellow employees with an allegedly legitimate interest in its content).

3. ***Publicity that Unreasonably Places Another in a False Public Light.*** An action for false light invasion of privacy is available when an individual is subject to unreasonable and highly objectionable publicity that

attributes to him characteristics, conduct, or beliefs that are false, and thereby is placed before the public in a false position. Meyerkord v. Zipatoni Co., 276 S.W.3d 319, 323 (Mo. Ct. App. E.D. 2008) (citing Restatement (Second) of Torts § 652E, cmt. b (1977)). The plaintiff must show that defendant's conduct was "highly offensive to a reasonable person," and that the actor "had knowledge of or acted in reckless disregard as to the falsity of the publicized matter." Id. (citing Restatement (Second) of Torts § 652E). Further, there must be "such a misrepresentation of one's character, history, activities, or beliefs that serious offense may reasonably be expected to be taken by a reasonable person in his or her position." Id. (citation omitted). Whether a misrepresentation is seriously offensive is a question of fact to be determined by the jury. Id. at 326 (citation omitted). The tort of false light invasion of privacy has been recognized in the employment context. In Meyerkord v. Zipatoni Co., a Missouri appellate court held that plaintiff, a former employee of defendant, adequately stated a cause of action for false light invasion of privacy. The plaintiff in Meyerkord filed a false light tort claim against his former employer because the employer listed plaintiff as the registrant on a website plaintiff had no involvement with and after plaintiff no longer worked for the employer. Id. at 321-22. The website and those associated with it were subject to public criticism for the website's content. Id. Ruling on a motion to dismiss, the court held that, because plaintiff alleged that the content of the website was publicly and wrongfully attributed to him and that he suffered harm thereby, his complaint sufficiently stated a false light claim. Id. at 326.

4. ***Surveillance.*** Section 565.253 prohibits the knowing, nonconsensual viewing, photographing or filming of another while the person is in a state of undress in a place where one would have a reasonable expectation of privacy. Mo. Rev. Stat. § 565.253 (2000 & Supp. 2009). A place where a person "would have a reasonable expectation of privacy" is "any place where a reasonable person would believe that a person could disrobe in privacy, without being concerned that the person's undressing was being viewed, photographed, or filmed by another." Mo. Rev. Stat. § 565.250(3) (2000 & Supp. 2009); See e.g. Turner v. General Motors Corp., 750 S.W.2d 76 (Mo. Ct. App. E.D. 1988) (there is no reasonable expectation of privacy in an employer's parking lot). Employers who wish to engage in surveillance in the workplace can avoid application of this statute by refraining from videotaping areas where employees might be expected to disrobe at work.

IV. OTHER ACTIONS BASED ON STATEMENTS

A. Negligent Hiring, Retention, and Supervision

A claim of negligent hiring or retention requires proof that "(1) the employer knew or should have known of the employee's dangerous proclivities, and (2) the employer's negligence was the proximate cause of the plaintiff's injuries." Gibson v Brewer, 952 S.W.2d 239, 246 (Mo. 1997) (en banc); see Gaines v. Monsanto Co., 655 S.W.2d 568, 570 (Mo. Ct. App. E.D. 1983) ("Negligent hiring or retention liability is independent of respondeat superior liability for negligent acts of an employee acting within the scope of his employment."). A claim of negligent supervision relates to the employer's duty to control the employee's conduct. Gibson, 952 S.W.2d at 247 (citing Restatement (Second) of Torts § 317). There are no Missouri cases on point concerning whether plaintiffs may use these causes of action to circumvent defamation requirements.

B. Intentional Infliction of Emotional Distress

To state a claim for the intentional infliction of emotional distress, a plaintiff must allege "extreme and outrageous conduct by a defendant who intentionally or recklessly causes severe emotional distress that results in bodily harm." Nazeri, 860 S.W.2d at 316 (citation omitted). Without distinct wanton and outrageous behavior, a mere defamatory statement will not support a claim for the intentional infliction of emotional distress. Id. To allow mere employment decisions to be actionable "would effectively subvert the law of this state to allow a claim for termination by an at will employee to be brought under the guise of an action for emotional distress." Rice, 919 S.W.2d at 245 (quoting Neighbors, 694 S.W.2d at 824); see also Bailey v. Bayer Cropscience, LP, No. 06-287-CV-W-DW, 2007 U.S. Dist. LEXIS 79033, at *4 (W.D. Mo. Oct. 23, 2007) (plaintiff employees may not "state an action under Missouri law for emotional distress resulting from termination," as "to do so would allow plaintiffs to undermine Missouri's doctrine of at-will employment.").

C. Interference with Economic Advantage

A plaintiff may base a tortious interference with economic advantage claim on a successful showing of defamation. "Tortious interference with a contract or business expectancy requires proof of: (1) a contract or valid business expectancy; (2) defendant's knowledge of the contract or relationship; (3) a breach induced or caused by defendant's intentional interference; (4) absence of justification; and (5) damages." Nazeri, 860 S.W.2d at 316 (citations omitted). The plaintiff must affirmatively show a lack of justification. Stehno v. Sprint Spectrum, L.P., 186 S.W.3d 247, 252 (Mo. 2006) (en banc). If the defendant has a legitimate interest in the expectancy plaintiff seeks to protect, then the plaintiff "must show that the defendant employed improper means in seeking to further only his own interests." Id.; see also Topper v. Midwest Division, Inc. 306 S.W.3d 117, 126 (Mo. Ct. App. W.D. 2010). Improper means are "those that are independently wrongful, such as threats, violence, trespass, *defamation*, misrepresentation of fact, restraint of trade, or any other wrongful act recognized by statute or the common law." Stehno, 186 S.W.3d at 252 (emphasis added). See Stehno, 186 S.W.3d at 252-53 (defendants may not use improper means - such as defamation - to protect their economic interests, but under facts of case court found that plaintiff failed to prove a reasonable business expectancy and an absence of justification for defendants' actions); Topper, 306 S.W.3d at 126-30 (while reversing and remanding the overall jury verdict in favor of plaintiff doctor, court held that, on one count, jury could have found tortious interference with a contract predicated on defamation where defendant hospital and its supervisors used defamatory means to terminate plaintiff's employment). Missouri courts will not, however, permit suits based upon absolutely privileged defamatory statements to be brought under the disguise of interference with business expectancy. See, e.g., Remington, 817 S.W.2d at 575.

D. Prima Facie Tort

A plaintiff may not use a prima facie tort theory to circumvent the requirements of a defamation claim. Under Missouri law, the elements of a prima facie tort are: "(1) an intentional lawful act by defendant; (2) defendant's intent to injure the plaintiff; (3) injury to the plaintiff, and (4) an absence of or insufficient justification for defendant's act." Nazeri, 860 S.W.2d at 315. Courts will dismiss prima facie tort claims "when it is clear that the theory is being asserted merely to circumvent an established body of law, or when it is not supported by the pleading of the factual elements giving rise to the claim." Id. at 316, n.9 (citations omitted). See Id. at 315-16 ("Recovery for untrue statements should be in defamation . . . [w]hile it may be possible for a plaintiff to plead facts that could establish a count in prima facie tort as an alternative to a separate recognized claim, appellant has not done so here.").

In addition, such a claim cannot be used as a mechanism to circumvent the employment-at-will doctrine. Dake v. Tuell, 687 S.W.2d 191, 192-3 (Mo. 1985) (en banc); see also Hanrahan v. Nashua Corp., 752 S.W.2d 878, 883-4 (Mo. Ct. App. E.D. 1988) ("[I]t is of no matter what particular legal theory an employee asserts against an employer for a claim of wrongful discharge, whether it be for prima facie tort . . . or any other legal theory which may seek to allege such a claim . . . there is no claim for wrongful discharge absent a valid contract, constitutional provision, statute, or regulation based on statute.") (citations omitted).

E. Injurious Falsehood

The tort of injurious falsehood protects a different interest than the tort of defamation. Ross, 163 S.W.3d at 929 (citing Restatement (Second) of Torts § 623A, cmt. g). The tort of defamation protects the injured party's personal reputation, while the tort of injurious falsehood protects "the economic interests of the injured party against pecuniary loss." Id. Under a claim for injurious falsehood, "[o]ne who publishes a false statement harmful to the interests of another is subject to liability for pecuniary loss resulting to the other if (1) he intends for publication of the statement to result in harm to interests of the other having a pecuniary value, or either recognizes or should recognize that it is likely to do so, and (2) he knows that the statement is false or acts in reckless disregard of its truth or falsity." Ross, 163 S.W.3d at 928. Proof of pecuniary loss is required. Id. In Ross, the plaintiffs, a company and its president, brought an injurious falsehood claim against several former employees and other parties. Id. at 923-24. Plaintiffs sought damages for "humiliation, embarrassment, disgrace, fright, injury to feeling, injury to reputation, emotional trauma and mental anguish based on defendants' statements that plaintiffs had stolen certain machinery." Id. at 929. Defendants argued the injurious falsehood claims were actually defamation claims, and thus barred by the shorter statute of limitations for defamation. Id. The court agreed, finding that plaintiffs' damages were not pecuniary, and thus not recoverable under injurious falsehood. Id.

IV. OTHER ISSUES

A. Procedural Issues

1. ***Statutes of Limitation.*** The statute of limitations for a defamation action is two years. Mo. Rev. Stat. § 516.140 (2000 & Supp. 2009); Ross, 163 S.W.3d at 924. The two-year statute of limitations applicable to defamation claims bars recovery of damages for reputational injury in a claim for injurious falsehood, although recovery for pecuniary damages falls within the five-year limitation period. Id. Under Missouri law, statutes of limitations are procedural rather than substantive. Consolidated Financial Investments, Inc. v. Manion, 948 S.W.2d 222, 224 (Mo. Ct. App. E.D. 1997). Under conflict of laws analysis, procedural questions are determined by the law of the forum state. Id. (citation omitted). Accordingly, Missouri's statute of limitations applies to defamation actions brought in Missouri, unless Missouri's borrowing statute mandates application of a shorter limitation period. See id.; Sangamon Associates, Ltd., 2004 Mo. App. Lexis 1519, at *9 (citing Mo. Rev. Stat. § 516.190).

Under Missouri law, the statute of limitations for defamation begins to run when damages were sustained and capable of ascertainment. Thurston, 884 S.W.2d at 26 (citing Mo. Rev. Stat. § 516.100); Jones v. Pinkerton's Inc., 100 S.W.2d 4569, 458-60 (Mo. Ct. App. W.D. 1985). Damages are ascertained "when the fact of damage appears, not when the extent or the amount of the damage is determined." Thurston, 884 S.W.2d at 26. Damages may be sustained and ascertainable upon publication. See, e.g., Ashby v. Haney, 2000 WL 33374419, at *3, (W.D. Mo. 2000) (cause of action accrued at time of publication where plaintiffs failed to adduce any evidence that damages were not immediately ascertainable). Missouri courts will likely follow the single publication rule, which dictates the number of causes of action a plaintiff might have and when the statute of limitations begins to run. Givens v. Quinn, 877 F. Supp. 485, 488-90 (W.D. Mo. 1994).

2. ***Conflicts of Law.*** Missouri has adopted the "most significant relationship" test of Restatement (Second) of Conflict of Laws to resolve conflict of laws issues in tort cases. Kennedy v. Dixon, 439 S.W.2d 173, 184 (Mo. 1969) (en banc). Under a conflicts analysis, the plaintiff's domicile is key, because defamation "produces a special kind of injury that has its principal effect among one's friends, acquaintances, neighbors and business associates in the place of one's residence." Elmore v. Owens-Illinois, Inc., 673 S.W.2d 434, 437 (Mo. 1984) (en banc) [citing Restatement (Second) of Conflicts § 150(2) (1971)). See also Fuqua Homes, Inc. v. Beattie, 388 F.3d 618, 622 (8th Cir. 2004)].

B. Jurisdiction, Venue, & Applicable Law

1. ***Personal Jurisdiction.*** In order for a Missouri court to exercise personal jurisdiction over a non-resident defendant, the defendant must have sufficient minimum contacts with the state to satisfy the requirements of due process and Missouri's long-arm statute. Norman v. Fischer Chevrolet-Oldsmobile, 50 S.W.3d 313, 316-17 (Mo. Ct. App. E.D. 2001). Missouri courts generally exercise personal jurisdiction over non-resident defendants who commit a tortious act within the state. Mo. Rev. Stat. § 506.500.1(3) (2000 & Supp. 2009); see Stevens v. Redwing, 146 F.3d 538, 543 (8th Cir. 1998) (applying Missouri law). Sending a defamatory communication into the state may be sufficient to subject the defendant to personal jurisdiction. Norman, 50 S.W.3d at 317. In Norman, the court refused to exercise personal jurisdiction over non-resident defendant whose only contact with Missouri was an alleged defamatory communication. Recognizing that a single defamatory contact could establish personal jurisdiction, the court nonetheless declined jurisdiction because both parties were non-residents and the defendant had no other contacts with Missouri. See Id. at 317-18.

2. ***Applicable Law.*** State defamation claims may be preempted by applicable federal law under certain circumstances. In Gore v. TWA, for example, the Eighth Circuit ruled that the Railway Labor Act preempted plaintiff's defamation claims based on communications made during the investigation of employee misconduct. The court found that the statements were inextricably intertwined with interpreting the rights and duties under the collective bargaining agreement. 210 F.3d 944, 951-52 (8th Cir. 2000). Another Eighth Circuit decision, however, declined to find that the Labor Management Relations Act preempted plaintiff's defamation claims. See Graham v. Contract Transportation, Inc., 220 F.3d 910, 913-14 (8th Cir. 2000). The Graham court noted the conflicting precedent in the Eighth Circuit and emphasized that a narrower approach to preemption is more faithful to Supreme Court precedent. Id. at 914.

3. ***Venue.*** Venue in Missouri is determined solely by statute. State ex rel. Rothermich v. Gallagher, 816 S.W.2d 194, 196 (Mo. 1991) (en banc).

Where the plaintiff was first injured in the state of Missouri, venue must be in the county where the plaintiff was first injured. Mo. Rev. Stat. § 510.010.4 (2009). Where the plaintiff was first injured outside the state of Missouri, venue is either a) in the county of the defendant's principle place of residence in the state of Missouri, or, if the defendant is a corporation, where its registered agent is located or b) in the county of the plaintiff's principal place of residence on the date plaintiff was first injured, if such place of residence was in the state of Missouri on the date plaintiff was first injured. Mo. Rev. Stat. § 508.010.5(1)-(2) (Supp. 2009). If the defamatory statement was first published in the state of Missouri, then venue is proper in the county in which it was first published. See Mo. Rev. Stat. § 508.010.4 & .8 (Supp. 2009). If, however, the defamatory statement was first published outside the state of Missouri, then venue depends upon the status of the defendant and whether the plaintiff resided in the state of Missouri at the time of the injury. See Mo. Rev. Stat. § 508.010.5 (1)-(2) & .8 (Supp. 2009).

In a defamation action, the plaintiff is considered first injured in the county where the defamation or invasion was first published. Mo. Rev. Stat. § 508.010.8 (Supp. 2009). "In deciding where a defamation or invasion of privacy was first published for venue purposes, Missouri courts have looked to the location where the defamation or invasion was originally issued." State ex rel. Drake Publishers, Inc. v. Baker, 859 S.W.2d 201, 204 (Mo. Ct. App. E.D. 1993) (citing State ex rel. Allen v. Barker, 581 S.W.2d 818, 826 (Mo. 1979) (en banc)); Litzinger v. Pulitzer Publishing Co., 356 S.W.2d 81, 84-85 (Mo. 1962), cert. denied, 374 U.S. 831 (1963)); see also Mo. Rev. Stat. § 508.010.9 & .8 (Supp. 2009).

C. Worker's Compensation Exclusivity

The Missouri Workers' Compensation Act likely does not bar an employee's defamation claim, because damages arising there from are not covered by the Act. Deckard, 31 S.W.3d at 15; Gambrell v. Kansas City Chiefs Football Club, Inc., 562 S.W.2d 163, 165 (Mo. Ct. App. 1978); see also Giandinoto v. Chemir Analytical Servs., 545 F. Supp. 2d 952, 960 (E.D.

Mo. 2007); see also Mo. Rev. Stat. § 287.120.2 (2000 & Supp. 2009). The Workers' Compensation Act covers "personal injury or death of the employee by accident arising out of and in the course of the employee's employment." Mo. Rev. Stat § 287.120.1 (2000 & Supp. 2009). The term "injury" is defined as "violence to the physical structure of the body and to the personal property which is used to make up the physical structure of the body" of an employee. Mo. Rev. Stat § 287.020.3(5) (2000 & Supp. 2009). The Workers' Compensation Act does not likely cover the type of damages resulting from defamation and therefore does not bar an employee's defamation claim. See Deckard, 31 S.W.3d at 15; Gambrell, 562 S.W.2d at 165; Giandinoto., 545 F. Supp. 2d at 960; Mo. Rev. Stat. § 287.120.2 (2000 & Supp. 2009). While the Workers' Compensation Act likely does not bar employee defamation claims, the forum in which this determination is made is still unsettled. Compare Lovelace, 841 S.W.2d at 685-86 (whether an employee plaintiff's injury, allegedly sustained due to defamatory statements made by management personnel, was within the Workers' Compensation Act . Plaintiff is determined by the Labor and Industrial Relations Commission under the doctrine of primary jurisdiction) Deckard, 31 S.W.3d at 15 (stating that employee's defamation claim "did not fall within the exclusive jurisdiction of the Workers' Compensation Law," because it "contains no provision for compensation for damage sustained by an employee from defamation by his employer."); Giandinoto, 545 F. Supp. 2d at 960 (holding that the Workers' Compensation Act does not bar employee plaintiff's libel claim).

D. Pleading Requirements

The pleading requirements for a defamation claim are currently unclear. In Nazeri, the Supreme Court of Missouri held that, "in defamation cases the old rules of per se and per quod do not apply and plaintiff need only to plead and prove the unified defamation elements set out in MAI 23.06(1) and 23.10(1)]." Nazeri, 860 S.W.2d at 313. Combined, these two instructions require pleading and proof of the following elements: (1) the defendant published the defamatory statement; (2) the defendant was at fault for publishing the statement; (3) the statement tended to expose the plaintiff to hatred, contempt, and ridicule or deprive the plaintiff of the benefit of public confidence and social associations; (4) such statement was read or heard by other persons or by the public; and (5) plaintiff's reputation was thereby damaged. MAI 23.06(1) [1980 New]; MAI 23.10(1) [1980 New]. Notably, neither set of instructions requires the plaintiff to plead the falsity of the statement as an element of its case. Recent precedent suggest, however, that "the plaintiff, who is not a public figure, must plead and prove the following elements: (1) publication, (2) of a defamatory statement, (3) that identifies the plaintiff, (4) that is false, (5) that is published with the requisite degree of fault, and (6) that damages the plaintiff's reputation." Deckard, 31 S.W.2d at 18; Topper, 306 S.W.3d at 127; see also Ross, 163 S.W.3d at 929; Overcast, 11 S.W.3d at 70; Johnson, 278 S.W.3d at 235; Sifagus, 109 S.W.3d at 176. These cases require plaintiff to plead falsity as an element of its case. It is therefore unclear whether the plaintiff in a defamation claim must plead falsity as an element of its claim, or if truth is an affirmative defense.

Plaintiff need not plead extrinsic facts to show application of the alleged defamatory statement to the plaintiff. Mo. Rev. Stat. § 509.210 (2000 & Supp. 2009). Stating that the alleged defamatory statement was "published or spoken concerning the plaintiff" is sufficient. Mo. Rev. Stat. § 509.210 (2000 & Supp. 2009); Mo. Sup. Ct. R. 55.20. For libel claims, the alleged defamatory statement must be pled "in haec verba, or in the exact words alleged to be defamatory." Nazeri, 860 S.W.2d at 313 (citation omitted). A slander claim, however, only requires "that there 'be certainty as to what is charged' as the slander." Id. (citation omitted).

Truth is an affirmative defense that must be pled, and the answer shall include a short factual statement showing the defendant is entitled to assert the defense. Mo. Rev. Stat. §§ 509.090, 509.210 (2000 & Supp. 2009); Mo. Sup. Ct. R. 55.08, 55.20. The defendant may also assert in the answer mitigating circumstances admissible in evidence to reduce the amount of damages. Mo. Rev. Stat. § 509.210 (2000 & Supp. 2009).

E. Defamation and the Internet

In at least one 2004 Missouri appellate case, the Internet provided the backdrop for an employment-related defamation claim. In Scott v. LeClercq, discussed at I.B.8, infra, plaintiff, a high school principal, brought a defamation claim against his wife's paramour, claiming that defendant published defamatory statements to a school student in an online chat room. 136 S.W.3d 183, 194-96 (Mo. Ct. App. W.D. 2004). The court held that, based on third-party testimony, the defamatory statements caused harm to plaintiff's reputation. Id. at 195-96.

SURVEY OF MISSOURI EMPLOYMENT PRIVACY LAW

Mark Sableman, Paul R. Klein, and R. Nelson Williams
Thompson Coburn LLP
One U.S. Bank Plaza, Suite 3500
St. Louis, Missouri 63101-1693
Telephone: (314) 552-6000; Facsimile: (314) 552-7000
E-mail: msableman@thompsoncoburn.com

(With Developments Reported Through **November 1, 2012**)

GENERAL COMMENTS

Missouri has uniform trial court rules that generally follow the Federal Rules of Civil Procedure. There are, however, some significant differences, and in addition some Missouri statutes provide some additional -- and at times overlapping -- rules. Many jurisdictions have additional local rules that can be obtained from the appropriate court clerk's office.

SIGNIFICANT DEVELOPMENTS SINCE THE 2012 *SURVEY*

The narrowness of false light claims was recently emphasized in Farrow v. St. Francis Medical Ctr., No. ED 96532, 2012 WL 2395156 (Mo. App. E.D. June 26, 2012) (emphasis in original). In Farrow, a nurse asserted a variety of claims against her former employer, including defamation and false light. Id. In support of her false light claim, the plaintiff alleged that a doctor made a series of defamatory statements about her, "to-wit: that she was not writing up the activity of the day on the board, was not following orders, and had altered doctor's orders and ignored instructions." Id. at *12. In finding that her claims did not meet the threshold for legitimate false light violations, the court stressed that false light claims only apply, "when the defendant knows the plaintiff, as a reasonable person, would be justified in the eyes of the *community* in feeling *seriously offended* and *aggrieved* by the publicity." Id. at *12. (emphasis in original). Moreover, "[i]t is only when there is such a *major misrepresentation* of one's *character, history, activities, or beliefs* that *serious offense*" is likely to result, thereby causing an invasion of privacy. Id. The court then distinguished the privacy-damaging viral marketing website in Meyerkord v. The Zipatoni Co., 276 S.W.3d 319, 323, 37 Media L. Rep. 1161 (Mo. App. 2008), from Farrow's allegations, holding her situation was, "one of a supervisor making critical assessments of [the plaintiff's] job performance, based upon his personal knowledge and opinion, to other employees in the workplace." Id. As such, the court affirmed the grant of summary judgment to the defendant. Id. at *13. Surprisingly, the court did not explicitly base its ruling on the inapplicability of the false light tort to alleged defamatory content, under Missouri's landmark ruling in Sullivan v. Pulitzer Broadcasting Co., 709 S.W.2d 475, 12 Media L. Rep. (BNA) 2187 (Mo. 1986).

The Eighth Circuit Court of Appeals recently affirmed the dismissal of the employee's false light claim. Cockram v. Genesco, Inc., 689 F.3d 1046, 1057 (8th Cir. 2012).

I. GENERAL LAW OF PRIVACY

A. Legal Basis of Privacy Claims

The Missouri Constitution contains no explicit right of privacy. Although the Missouri Supreme Court's landmark decision in Barber v. Time Inc., 348 Mo. 1199, 1206, 159 S.W.2d 291, 294, 1 Media L. Rep. (BNA) 1779, 1782 (Mo. 1942), held that the right of privacy "is, or at least grows out of, a constitutional right," Missouri courts since Barber have been reluctant to develop any special state constitutional right of privacy. See State v. Walsh, 713 S.W.2d 508, 513 (Mo. banc 1986) ("the application of Missouri's right of privacy to date has not paralleled the right of privacy said to inhere in the Federal Constitution...[W]hatever justification there may be for a nonoriginalist interpretation of the older United States Constitution, we believe that our Constitution of 1945 must be interpreted according to its plain language and original intent"); Cruzan by Cruzan v. Harmon, 760 S.W.2d 408, 417, n.13 (Mo. banc 1988) ("Missouri's constitution must be interpreted according to its plain language and in a manner consistent with the understanding of the people who adopted it;" suggestion in Barber of state constitutional right of privacy held "inapplicable in cases involving decisions of personal autonomy").

No Missouri statutes codify the common law torts arising under invasion of privacy. Missouri was one of the first states to recognize the tort of invasion of privacy in Munden v. Harris, 153 Mo. App. 652, 134 S.W. 1076 (Mo. App. 1911), a misappropriation case. Additionally, the Missouri Supreme Court decided Barber in 1942, one of the earliest and most frequently cited private facts cases in the nation. Missouri courts have also expressly recognized the invasion of privacy tort of intrusion. Although Missouri courts do not recognize a cause of action for false light in situations of classic defamation, a decision by the Missouri Court of Appeals found the false light claim potentially appropriate for situations where a false but non-defamatory statement is sufficiently serious "that serious offense may reasonably be expected to be taken by a reasonable person in his or her position." Meyerkord v. The Zipatoni Co., 276 S.W.3d 319, 323, 37 Media L. Rep. 1161 (Mo. App. 2008).

B. Causes of Action

Missouri Courts have now recognized all four invasion of privacy torts set forth in the Restatement (Second) of Torts § 652 (1977): publication of private facts, intrusion, misappropriation, and false light. In Missouri, invasion of privacy is a cause of action that is only available to individuals or groups. Corporations, however, cannot claim a right to privacy. W.C.H. of Waverly v. Meredith Corp., 1986 U.S. Dist. LEXIS 18125, 13 Media L. Rep. (BNA) 1648 (W.D. Mo. 1986).

1. ***Misappropriation/Right of Publicity.*** This state early recognized the tort action for invasion of privacy in Munden v. Harris, 153 Mo. App. 652, 134 S.W. 1076 (Mo. App. 1911). The Munden court held that a published picture of a five-year-old plaintiff used for advertising their merchandise business without the plaintiff's consent had misappropriated the plaintiff's rights of publicity. Id., 153 Mo. App. at 660, 134 S.W. at 1079. In defining this novel cause of action, the court reasoned that:

> ... one has an exclusive right to his picture, on the score of its being a property right of material profit. We also consider it to be a property right of value, in that it is one of the modes of securing to a person the enjoyment of life and the exercise of liberty, and that novelty of the claim is no objection to relief. If this right is, in either respect, invaded, he may have his remedy, either by restraint in equity or damages in an action at law. If there are special damages, they may be stated and recovered; but such character of damage is not necessary to the action, since general damages may be recovered without a showing of specific loss; and if the element of malice appears, as that term is known to the law, exemplary damages may be recovered." Id. at 1079.

In Haith v. Model Cities Health Corporation of Kansas City, the court held that the unauthorized use of plaintiffs' names as doctors participating in a specific health program in order to secure a federal grant for defendant's health care operation presented genuine issues of fact as to whether defendant wrongfully appropriated plaintiffs' names to its advantage. 704 S.W.2d 684, 688 (Mo. App. 1986). The court followed Munden, stating explicitly that private, ordinary citizens have a cause of action in privacy for the appropriation of their names or likenesses. Id. at 687-88. In rejecting defendants' argument, the court stated that the, "'Right of Publicity' in the sense used by a celebrity has nothing to do with this case." Id. at 688. In Nemani v. St. Louis University, the Missouri Supreme Court refused to extend Haith and held that in the circumstances where the name of a research professor was used on a grant application while the professor was working for the University and had expressed an interest in working on the project, the professor had impliedly consented to the University's use of his name on grant applications. 33 S.W.3d 184 (Mo. banc 2000). The Court distinguished Haith because the doctors in Haith had been terminated before their names were listed on the grant application, and thus they did not consent to the use of their names by the applicant/employer. Id. at 189.

Doe v. TCI Cablevision, 110 S.W.3d 363, 31 Media L. Rep. (BNA) 2025 (Mo. 2003), cert. denied, McFarlane v. Twist, 540 U.S. 1106 (2004), involved a former hockey player's suit against a comic book writer and others, alleging misappropriation based upon use of the plaintiff's name for a villain character in a comic book series and related video. The Missouri Supreme Court characterized plaintiff's claims as right-of-publicity action, because the plaintiff was seeking recovery for damage to the commercial value of his name. Id. at 368. In a right of publicity case, a plaintiff must prove that the defendant intended to use the plaintiff's name without consent to obtain a commercial advantage. Id. at 369-70. The court held that the plaintiff had presented sufficient evidence to establish that defendants used his name for commercial advantage. Rejecting the defendants' First Amendment defense, the court applied a "predominant use" balancing test:

> If a product is being sold that predominantly exploits the commercial value of an individual's identity, that product should be held to violate the right of publicity and not be protected by the First Amendment, even if there is some "expressive" content in it that might qualify as "speech" in other circumstances. If, on the other hand, the predominant purpose of the product is to make an expressive comment on or about a celebrity, the expressive values could be given greater weight. Id. at 374 (citing Mark S. Lee, Agents of Chaos: Judicial Confusion in Defining the Right of Publicity-Free Speech Interface, 23 Loy. L.A. Ent. L. Rev. 471, 500 (2003)).

Here, the court found that the use and identity of the plaintiff's name was "predominantly a ploy to sell comic books and related products rather than an artistic or literary expression." 110 S.W.3d 363, 374. Although the court reversed the judgment notwithstanding the verdict on legal grounds, it affirmed the order of a new trial because the verdict director allowed the jury to render a verdict for plaintiff without a finding that defendants intended to obtain a commercial advantage. Id. at 375-76.

In the second trial, the jury rendered a verdict for the plaintiff and the Court of Appeals affirmed. Doe v. McFarlane, 207 S.W.3d 52, 79 U.S.P.Q.2d 1727, 34 Media L. Rep. 2057 (Mo. App. E.D. 2006). The court approved the trial judge's decision to use a modified version of the Missouri Approved Instructions. The court also permitted expert testimony on the subject of what the plaintiff could have expected in endorsement revenue even though the plaintiff had no prior endorsement revenues.

2. ***False Light.*** The Missouri Supreme Court has expressly refused to recognize a cause of action for false light invasion of privacy in situations of classic libel. See Sullivan v. Pulitzer Broadcasting Co., 709 S.W.2d 475, 12 Media L. Rep. (BNA) 2187 (Mo. 1986); Nazeri v. Missouri Valley Coll., 860 S.W.2d 303 (1993) (holding that allegedly false statements were not actionable as prima facie tort or "false light" invasion of privacy). In Sullivan, the Missouri Supreme Court scrutinized the basis and validity of false light theory where it overlaps with defamation and concluded that there was no justification for such a broad theory. Sullivan, 709 S.W.2d at 479, 12 Media L. Rep. at 2190. The Court stated that the tort might be a non-substantive and unnecessary duplication of the tort of defamation. Id. The Court, however, left the door open for the recognition of false light as a cause of action in the future, but under more limited circumstances. The Court indicated that it might recognize a false light cause of action where "one publicly attributes to the plaintiff some opinion or utterance, whether harmful or not, that is false, such as claiming that the plaintiff wrote a poem, article or book which the plaintiff did not in fact write." Id. at 480, 12 Media L. Rep. at 2192.

In Meyerkord v. The Zipatoni Co., 276 S.W.3d 319, 37 Media L. Rep. 1161 (Mo. App. 2008) the Missouri Court of Appeals for the first time recognized the false light tort. In Meyerkord, the Missouri Court of Appeals vacated and remanded the trial court's dismissal of a plaintiff's claim alleging that the plaintiff's former employer, Zipatoni, had cast the plaintiff in a false light by failing to remove him as the registrant of a certain website. Id. Meyerkord received criticism in online forums when "concern, suspicion, and accusations" arose about the website. Although Meyerkord did not in fact create or control the website, he claimed that it was "publicly attributed" to him, resulting in the invasion of the plaintiff's privacy and causing him to suffer "shame, embarrassment, humiliation, harassment, and mental anguish." Id. at 321-322. The Court of Appeals held that the facts of Meyerkord fit the opening left by Sullivan for a "classic case" of false light, and found the tort of false light potentially appropriate for situations where a false but non-defamatory statement is sufficiently serious "that serious offense may reasonably be expected to be taken by a reasonable person in his or her position." Id. at 323.

The combination of Meyerkord and Sullivan leaves Missouri with what one may call "classical" false light – not recognized in classic defamation situations, but recognized in classic false light situations. This conclusion was reinforced by the Western District of Missouri's dismissal of a false light claim based solely on defamatory comments. Cockram v. Genesco, Inc., No. 09-1007-cv-W-JTM, 2010 WL 2349064, *2 (Mo. App. June 8, 2010). In Cockram, a former employee sued her former employer claiming that a press release stating that an employee had used highly inappropriate language was terminated constituted a false light invasion of privacy. Id. at *1. In dismissing the plaintiff's claim, the court held that even after Meyerkord, "there is no cause of action for false light invasion of privacy when recovery is sought for alleged defamatory statements." Id. **The Eighth Circuit Court of Appeals recently affirmed the dismissal of the employee's false light claim. Cockram v. Genesco, Inc., 689 F.3d 1046, 1057 (8th Cir. 2012).**

The narrowness of false light claims in Missouri was recently emphasized in Farrow v. St. Francis Medical Ctr., No. ED 96532, 2012 WL 2395156 (Mo. App. E.D. June 26, 2012) (emphasis in original). In Farrow, a nurse asserted a variety of claims against her former employer, including defamation and false light. Id. In support of her false light claim, the plaintiff alleged that a doctor made a series of defamatory statements about her, "to-wit: that she was not writing up the activity of the day on the board, was not following orders, and had altered doctor's orders and ignored instructions." Id. at *12. In finding that her claims did not meet the threshold for legitimate false light violations, the court stressed that false light claims only apply, "when the defendant knows the plaintiff, as a reasonable person, would be justified in the eyes of the *community* in feeling *seriously offended* and *aggrieved* by the publicity." Id. at *12. (emphasis in original). Moreover, "[i]t is only when there is such a *major misrepresentation* of one's *character, history, activities, or beliefs* that *serious offense*" is likely to result, thereby causing an invasion of privacy. Id. The court then distinguished the privacy-damaging viral marketing website in Meyerkord, from Farrow's allegations, holding her situation was, "one of a supervisor making critical assessments of [the plaintiff's] job performance, based upon his personal knowledge and opinion, to other employees in the workplace." Id. As such, the court affirmed the grant of summary judgment to the defendant. Id. at *13. Surprisingly, the court did not explicitly base its ruling on the inapplicability of the false light tort to alleged defamatory content, under Missouri's landmark ruling in Sullivan v. Pulitzer Broadcasting Co., 709 S.W.2d 475, 12 Media L. Rep. (BNA) 2187 (Mo. 1986).

3. ***Publication of Private Facts.*** The Barber court set out the tort of public disclosure of private facts in textbook fashion. See I.A, supra. The plaintiff, a Kansas City woman, entered a hospital for treatment of chronic over-eating. Barber, 348 Mo. at 1202, 159 S.W.2d at 293, 1 Media L. Rep. (BNA) at 1780. A wire service reporter came to interview her with a photographer who took her picture without consent. Id. Time magazine picked up the story and published it, treating the condition humorously and headlining it "Starving Glutton." Id. at 1202, 159 S.W.2d at 293, 1 Media L. Rep. (BNA) at 1780. A jury returned a verdict for Barber, and the Missouri Supreme Court upheld the verdict establishing that medical conditions and hospital stays are private facts, and that a person's medical condition and treatment lay at the core of his or her right to privacy. Id. at 1207-08, 159 S.W.2d at 295-96, 1 Media L. Rep. at 1782.

The four elements needed for a cause of action in tort for public disclosure of private facts are: (1) publication or publicity, (2) absent of any waiver or privilege, (3) of private matters in which the public has no legitimate concern, (4) so as to bring shame or humiliation to a person of ordinary sensibilities. Childs v. Williams, 825 S.W.2d 4, 7 (Mo. App. 1992) (quoting Y.G. v. Jewish Hosp. of St. Louis, 795 S.W.2d 488, 498-499 (Mo. App. 1990)). More than minimal publication may be needed to support a claim for public disclosure of private facts. Corcoran v. Southwestern Bell Tel. Co., 572 S.W.2d 212, 215 (Mo. App. 1978) (stating that "[t]he publication requirement means publicity in the sense of communication to the public in general or to a large number of persons, as distinguished from one individual or a few"). In Childs, the plaintiff failed to prove her claim of invasion of privacy where a psychiatrist, to whom she had been referred to by her employer, wrote a letter to her supervisor describing her emotional disorders and urging that she be transferred to a less stressful position. Id., 825 S.W.2d at 7. The court held that the review of the letter by her supervisors and others with a legitimate interest in the employee did not constitute publication. Id. Similarly, in Balke v. Ream, 33 S.W.3d 589 (Mo. App. 2000) the court held that one person's recording of a telephone conversation to which he was a party did not constitute a private facts violation because of the lack of communication to the public in general or to a large number of persons.

In Cooksey v. Boyer, 289 F.3d 513 (8th Cir. 2002), a mayor disclosed to the board of alderman that the chief of police was being treated for stress and also disclosed information relating to his treatment. The chief brought a § 1983 claim against the mayor and the board for releasing private medical information. The court held that because the job of a police chief is a stressful one, releasing information regarding those matters did not rise to the level of "shocking degradation" or "egregious humiliation" required for § 1983 claim.

In Buller v. Pulitzer Pub. Co., the court found that a plaintiff failed to state a cause of action for public disclosure of private facts because the petition did not sufficiently allege the absence of waiver or privilege. 684 S.W.2d 473, 482, 11 Media L. Rep. (BNA) 1289, 1295 (Mo. App. 1984). Although the plaintiff alleged that prior to publication she lived a secluded life, the court said that "this alone does not indicate to us a refusal to have anything to do with the press." Id. at 483, 11 Media L. Rep. at 1296.

A union's publication of notice in a trade union publication advising readers that certain supervisory employees were members of the city fire department, but not members of the local union, did not amount to a tortious invasion of privacy entitling the supervisory employees to injunctive relief where there was nothing in the notice which would bring shame or humiliation to a person of ordinary sensibilities. Claspill v. Craig, 586 S.W.2d 458 (Mo. App. 1979).

Where an employee subject to a collective-bargaining agreement raises claims of false light or private facts, those claims are preempted by the Labor and Management Relations Act ("LRMA") if interpretation of the collective bargaining agreement is necessary. 29 U.S.C.S. § 185; Gore v. TWA, 210 F.3d 944, 949 (8th Cir. 2000); Cf. Meyer v. Schnucks Markets, Inc., 163 F.3d 1048, 1052 (8th Cir. 1998) (holding that plaintiff's claim for intentional infliction of emotional distress based on publication of private facts was not preempted by LRMA because it is "not based on rights created by, or substantially dependent on an analysis of" the collective-bargaining agreement).

4. ***Intrusion.*** The three elements necessary to make a submissible case of intrusion are: (1) the existence of a secret and private subject matter; (2) a right possessed by plaintiff to keep that subject matter private; and (3) the obtaining of information about that subject matter by defendant through some method objectionable to the reasonable man. Corcoran, 572 S.W.2d at 214-15. Publicity is not required to establish a tort on the theory of intrusion. Id.

There is no liability unless the interference with the plaintiff's seclusion is a substantial one, and in Sofka v. Thal, the Court found that six to eight polite telephone calls made to plaintiff over a period of several months does not amount to the type of intrusion that could be found highly offensive to the ordinary person or to constitute "hounding." 662 S.W.2d 502, 511 (Mo. banc 1984).

In Duckworth v. Sayad, a police officer was discharged for allegedly engaging in sexual misconduct with an unnamed female contrary to the good order and discipline of the police department and its rules. 670 S.W.2d 88, 92 (Mo. App. 1984). The Court of Appeals held that a police officer's alleged sexual conduct in his dormitory room, which was visible only by standing in a particular spot on a balcony outside his room, was within an area where the police officer had a constitutional right to expect privacy, and that the evidence did not establish that police officer's alleged sexual conduct in his dormitory room was publicly visible or likely to become publicly known and thereby subject to regulation by rules of the Board of Police Commissioners. Id. Thus, the charge was not supported by substantial and competent evidence. Id.

In Crow v. Crawford & Co., an employee and his wife were videotaped outside of the workplace by his employer for purposes of demonstrating workers' compensation fraud. 259 S.W.3d 104, 111 (Mo. App. 2008). Part of the videotape revealed the employee's wife urinating in a public place near a boat ramp at a public park. The wife claimed intrusion upon seclusion because the area where she was videotaped was wooded and secluded. The Court of Appeals entered judgment for the employer and found that while "the elimination of bodily wastes would ordinarily be considered a private matter…there is no genuine dispute that the alleged urination occurred in a public place, on or near a boat ramp at a public park." Id. at 120. If the location was truly secluded, it would not have been so easy to videotape the alleged incident in the first place. Id.

An employee may release his or her employer from liability for invasion of privacy. In Schmalz v. Hardy Salt Co., the court held that the plaintiff had released his employer from privacy and other claims in a severance agreement. Id., 739 S.W.2d 765, 767 (Mo. App. 1987). The court rejected the employee's claims that the severance release lacked consideration, that it was waived by plaintiff's continued employment, and that it was executed under duress. Id. The court reasoned that because plaintiff was an at-will employee, who could be terminated at any time with or without cause, the employer's agreement to continue plaintiff on the payroll for at least another six weeks and to pay him one month severance pay constituted sufficient consideration by the employer for the release. Id.

C. Other Privacy-related Actions

One Missouri Supreme Court decision provides some authority for the proposition that plaintiffs cannot use general tort theories to circumvent the constitutional and common law defenses applicable to privacy claims. Sullivan v. Pulitzer Broadcasting Co., 709 S.W.2d 475, 481, 12 Media L. Rep. (BNA) 2187, 2192 (Mo. banc 1986). In Sullivan, the Court ruled that the "false light" privacy theory could not be used to circumvent traditional defenses available in libel cases. Id., 709 S.W.2d at 481, 12 Media L. Rep. at 2192. By analogy, general tort theories should not be used to circumvent traditional defenses to privacy claims. Id.

1. ***Intentional Infliction of Emotional Distress.*** A former employee stated an intentional infliction of emotional distress claim against the employer, where the alleged motive behind the employer's conduct was retaliation for the employee's exposing misrepresentations by her immediate supervisor which falsely enhanced the performance of the employer's operation and all acts attributed to employer. These actions, taken together, were so outrageous as to be utterly intolerable in civilized community. Polk v. INROADS/St. Louis, Inc., 951 S.W.2d 646, 648 (Mo. App. 1997). To state a claim for intentional infliction of emotional distress, a plaintiff must plead extreme and outrageous conduct by a defendant who intentionally or recklessly causes severe emotional distress that results in bodily harm. K.G. v. R.T.R., 918 S.W.2d 795, 799 (Mo. banc 1996). The conduct must have been "so outrageous in character, and so extreme in degree, as to go beyond all possible bounds of decency, and to be regarded as atrocious, and utterly intolerable in a civilized community." Warrem v. Parrish, 436 S.W.2d 670, 673 (Mo. 1969). The conduct must be "intended only to cause extreme emotional distress to the victim." K.G., 918 S.W.2d at 799; see Crow v. Crawford & Co., 259 S.W.3d 104, 119 (Mo. App. 2008) (finding that videotape of employee and his wife used to show workers' compensation fraud was not extreme or outrageous because the motivating factor was not to distress employee).

In Tatum v. City of Berkeley, 408 F.3d 543 (8th Cir. 2005), former African-American employees filed a complaint of intentional infliction of emotional distress against their former employer, based on alleged racially-motivated adverse treatment by a supervisor. Affirming the district court's award of judgment as a matter of law in favor of the city, the Eighth Circuit held that the majority of the plaintiffs did not present legally sufficient evidence to establish an issue of fact as to whether the City's conduct was illegal, much less "extreme and outrageous." Id. at 555 (noting that even illegal harassment may not rise to the level of "extreme and outrageous" conduct). Even if the plaintiffs had shown the City's conduct was extreme and outrageous, they failed to present legally sufficient evidence that they suffered severe emotional distress. Id. at 556.

2. *Interference With Prospective Economic Advantage*

a. **Private Employers.** To establish a claim for tortious interference with a contract or business relationship, a plaintiff must prove: (1) the existence of a contract or a valid business relationship; (2) defendant's knowledge of the contract or relationship; (3) defendant's intentional interference inducing or causing a breach of the contract or relationship; (4) absence of justification; and (5) damages. Baldwin Props., Inc. v. Sharp, 949 S.W.2d 952, 956 (W.D. Mo. 1997); K.G. v. R.T.R., 918 S.W.2d at 799; Sloan v. Bankers Life and Cas. Co., 1 S.W.3d 555 (Mo. App. 1999); Tri-Continental Leasing Co. v. Neidherdt, 540 S.W.2d 210, 212 (Mo. App. 1976); Harber v. Ohio Nat'l Life Ins. Co., 390 F.

Supp. 678, 683 (E.D. Mo. 1974). With regard to the justification issue, an absence of justification is the absence of any legal right on the part of the defendant to take the action about which the plaintiff complains. Taylor v. Zoltek Cos., Inc., 18 S.W.3d 541, 547 (E.D. Mo. 2000). A valid contract that allows for consultants to be hired away, with or without a fee, provides sufficient justification and does not constitute tortious interference with a contract or business relationship. Comp & Soft, Inc. v. AT&T Corp., 252 S.W.3d 189, 195 (Mo. App. 2008). A defendant does not necessarily need to have an economic interest at stake to be justified in interfering with a contract or business expectancy. Sharp, 949 S.W.2d 952, 957. In Chandler v. Allen, 108 S.W.3d 756 (W.D. Mo. 2003), a federal court held that Missouri state officials were justified in procuring the termination of a registered violent sex offender who was employed in a government office building. Id. at 760. The record showed that the plaintiff employee had an extensive criminal background that included sex offenses involving the use of weapons and coercive force against women who were strangers to him, and that his position as clerk in a deli gave him access to the building and its employees and access to various culinary tools in the cafeteria that could be used as weapons. Id. at 761. Finding that government officials were justified in requesting plaintiff's dismissal, the court upheld summary judgment for the employer on plaintiff's claim of tortious interference with an employment relationship. Id. at 763.

In Hensen v. Truman Medical Center, Inc., 62 S.W.3d 549 (Mo. App. 2001), a specially trained nurse left his position at a hospital to work for an outsourcing company, expecting to be assigned to fulfill the same functions at the same hospital, which had signed a contract with the outsourcing company. The nurse returned to work in the same hospital under the new company. That company then received complaints about inappropriate comments made by the nurse to co-workers. He was ordered to training and was told he could return to work after a probationary period. However, the hospital refused to allow him to return, causing the nurse to be reassigned to another specialty and in another facility—where his work product suffered and his employment terminated. Due to the circumstances of his employment—that the nurse left his job specifically so that he could do the same work at the same hospital—the court found that tortious interference was a jury submissible issue. Id. at 558. Defenses found in Rice v. Hodapp, 919 S.W.2d 240 (Mo. banc 1996) (termination legally justified under employer's duty to investigate offensive conduct and proceed accordingly) or Fleisher v. Hellmuth, Obata & Kassabaum, Inc., 870 S.W.2d 832 (Mo App. 1993) (qualified privilege to protect business interests) did not apply in this instance. Id. at 557-58. The court upheld the jury finding of tortious interference.

A federal court in Missouri has implicitly ruled that Missouri would recognize a cause of action for tortious interference with credit expectancy. Bruce v. First U.S.A. Bank, 103 F.Supp.2d 1135 (E.D. Mo. 2000), citing Bell v. May Dept. Stores, 6 S.W.3d 871 (Mo. 1999) (holding that a credit expectancy cannot be too remote at the time derogatory information was reported to a potential creditor); see also Taylor v. Zoltek Companies, 18 S.W.3d 541 (Mo. App. 2000) (implicitly recognizing claim for tortious interference with employee's long-term incentive plan).

b. **Public Employers.** Official immunity does not bar Missouri state law claims for tortious interference with contractual relations where the official's discretionary act was undertaken in bad faith or with malice. Hawkins v. Holloway, 316 F.3d 777, 789 (8th Cir. 2003). In Hawkins, the court held that sheriff's department employees who alleged they were terminated after reporting that sheriff had groped them, made lewd sexual comments, and threatened them with death or physical harm had provided ample evidence of bad-faith conduct. Id. Consequently, official immunity did not bar plaintiffs' state law claims of tortious interference with contractual relations. Id.

3. ***Prima Facie Tort.*** The elements of prima facie tort under Missouri law are: (1) intentional lawful act by the defendant, (2) intent to cause injury to the plaintiff, (3) injury to the plaintiff, and (4) an absence of any justification or an insufficient justification for the defendant's act. Porter v. Crawford & Co., 611 S.W.2d 265, 268-69 (Mo. App. 1980). However, "the doctrine is applicable only when the factual basis of the complaint does not fall within the parameters of an established tort." Kwon v. Southeast Missouri Prof'l Standards Review Org., 622 F. Supp. 520, 531 (E.D. Mo. 1985). This rule should prevent effective use of the prima facie tort theory where more traditional common law or statutory privacy claims cover the conduct in question.

A public school principal whose contract was not renewed prior to a school board hearing on charges of sexual harassment did not state a cause of action for prima facie tort. In Reed v. Rolla 31 Public School Dist., 374 F. Supp. 2d 787 (E.D. Mo. 2005), Plaintiff alleged that the school board committed prima facie tort, because its decision not to hold a scheduled hearing on charges against her was motivated by an improper purpose. Id. at 812. The court observed, "'[t]he Supreme Court of Missouri has noted that it is difficult to find any reported cases in which a recovery for prima facie tort has been established,'" and found no evidence that the Board had any intent to injure Plaintiff. Id. (quoting Kelly v. Golden, 352 F.3d 344, 351 (8th Cir. 2003)).

II. EMPLOYER TESTING OF EMPLOYEES

A. Psychological or Personality Testing

1. ***Common Law and Statutes.*** No state statutes.

2. ***Private Employers.*** Childs v. Williams, 825 S.W.2d 4 (Mo. App. 1992) (which does not technically involve employer testing) involved an employee who was demoted after her treating psychologist, relying on psychological testing, sent a letter to her supervisor urging that she be transferred to a less stressful position. See I.B.3, supra; Childs at 7. The employee filed suit against the psychologist for intentional infliction of emotional distress and invasion of privacy. Id. at 10. In the court's discussion, it stated that to prove a claim for intentional infliction of emotional distress, where there has been no physical injury, medical expert testimony is required to prove the "emotional distress or mental injury." Id.

3. ***Public Employers.*** The Missouri Court of Appeals held that the a police department inspector's office may require an accused police department member to submit to reasonable physical or psychological tests for purposes of determining fitness to perform duties or whether there has been a violation of departmental rules. Macchi v. Whaley, 586 S.W.2d 70, 75 (Mo. App. 1979). The accused department member may also request such tests. Id.

B. Drug Testing

1. ***Common Law and Statutes.*** In State Board of Nursing v. Berry, 32 S.W.3d 638 (Mo. App. 2000), the court held that the Missouri State Board of Nursing could discipline a licensed practical nurse based on an adverse drug test and the nurse's failure to respond to the Board's request for admissions. The court held that in an administrative proceeding for discipline for a licensed nurse under Mo. Rev. Stat. §335.066.2(14), the Board could satisfy its burden of proving possession of a controlled substance with evidence from a private employer's drug test and the nurse's failure to respond timely to a request for admission, because that evidence satisfied the preponderance of the evidence standard applicable to such administrative proceedings.

Missouri courts strictly interpreted a state statute disqualifying people for unemployment compensation in instances of misconduct connected with work. To disqualify the employee under Mo. Rev. Stat. § 288.045, the employer must include in its alcohol and drug policy the word "misconduct" to put employees on notice that they jeopardize their unemployment benefits by violating the policy. Christensen v. American Food & Vending Servs., Inc., 191 S.W.3d 88 (Mo. App. E.D. 2006). See also Div. of Emp't Sec. v. Comer, 199 S.W.3d 915 (Mo. App. SD 2006); Gaylord v. Wal-Mart Assocs., Inc., 193 S.W.3d 807, Unempl. Ins. Rep. (CCH) P 8633 (Mo. App. WD 2006).

However, in 2005, the Missouri legislature overruled a court's 2001 holding that an employer must show that using drugs actually affected the employee's on-the-job responsibilities rather than just violating a company policy prohibiting drug use. See Baldor Elec. Co. v. Reasoner, 66 S.W.3d 130 (Mo. App. 2001) (superseded by Mo. Rev. Stat. § 288.045(1)). The legislature amended the statute, indicating a specific intent to overrule Baldor's requirement that job impairment be shown.

In Winco Mfg., Inc. v. Capone, the court found that the Labor and Industrial Relations Commission erred in awarding unemployment compensation benefits to an employee who voluntarily quit his job after being asked to submit to a drug test. 133 S.W.3d 555 (Mo. App. 2004). The employee was asked to submit to a drug and alcohol test pursuant to company policy after he was presented with a reprimand for failing to report an absence. Id. The employee testified that he was told that, if he refused to take drug and alcohol test, he would be terminated, yet he voluntarily chose not to submit to the test, left work, and did not return. Id.

In Ward v. Durham Co., the court found that an employer who terminated an employee who refused to take a drug test committed misconduct by refusing to follow the employer's rules. 304 S.W.3d 736, 738 (Mo. App. 2010). The employee did not challenge the existence, content, or reasonableness of the employer's policy giving it the right to require its employees to submit to drug tests or that the employee violated that policy when he refused to submit to a drug test. Id. Instead, the employee argued that the policy's discretionary language regarding testing and discipline meant that failing to comply with the policy should not be ipso facto misconduct. Id. The court rejected the employee's argument and found that the employee's refusal to take a drug test pursuant to the employer's policy could constitute misconduct. Id.

2. ***Private Employers.*** In Rothweil v. Wetterau, Inc., the court held that the discharge of an at-will employee for failing to comply with drug policy did not constitute a wrongful discharge, even where the policy was changed after the employment relationship began. 820 S.W.2d 557, 559 (Mo. App. 1991). The Court first noted that the federal Equal Opportunity for Individuals with Disabilities Act of 1990, which is similar to the Missouri human rights law, explicitly excludes from protection, an employee "who is currently engaging in the illegal use of drugs." Id. Although Missouri's human rights law does not explicitly exclude current illegal drug users from its protection, the court concluded, "based on public policy and as a matter of law, that the term 'handicap' [under the Missouri Act] does not include self-inflicted addiction to illegal drugs." Id.

A plaintiff failed to state a claim for libel or slander when an employer included information in an employee's service letter concerning the results of his drug test. Irwin v. Wal-Mart Stores, 813 S.W.2d 99 (Mo. App. 1991). A third-party drug screening company, SmithKline, performed the drug test and reported to Wal-Mart only that the plaintiff's urinalysis showed that his urine contained cocaine. Id. at 101. Wal-Mart, in turn, reported in the plaintiff's service letter only that his drug test showed an unacceptable level of a controlled substance in his system. Id. The court found that, contrary to the plaintiff's allegations, neither defendant accused him of illegally obtaining a drug or illegally using a drug. Id. at 101-02. They each reported cold facts, which coincidentally may have led others to infer illegal drug use. Id. at 102.

3. ***Public Employers.*** After the city terminated a correctional officer for failing a random drug test, the officer sued under 42 U.S.C. § 1983, alleging that the city had violated his Fourth Amendment and due process rights because the test was not random and the search was unreasonable. Booker v. City of St. Louis, 309 F.3d 464 (8th Cir. 2002), *cert. denied*, 124 S.Ct. 52, (Oct 06, 2003) (NO. 02-1511). The Eighth Circuit held that even if a female drug-test monitor stood a foot behind the male correctional officer as he provided a urine sample in a bathroom stall while other employees came in and out of the room, the manner of collection was not so intrusive as to constitute an unreasonable search in violation of the Fourth Amendment. Id. at 467. The court relied on Vernonia Sch. District 47J v. Acton, 515 U.S. 646 (1995), in which the U.S. Supreme Court upheld a school district's random drug testing of student athletes using methods similar to that employed by the city correctional institution. 309F.3d 464, 468. The court also noted that the Fourth Amendment does not require same-sex monitoring of production of urine samples for drug testing. Id. Although plaintiff stated he "believed" that he was singled out for drug testing, this belief alone did not raise a reasonable inference that he was not randomly selected by the city for testing. Id. at 467.

C. Medical Testing

1. ***Common Law and Statutes.*** Employers are not permitted to use genetic information in making employment decisions. Mo. Rev. Stat. § 375.1306. A railroad's requirement that employees provide medical documentation or submit to testing to determine an employee's ability to work was not covered by Missouri law. State ex rel. Union Pacific R. Co. v. Dierker, 961 S.W.2d 816, 818 (Mo. banc 1998). That requirement constituted a "minor dispute" requiring interpretation of the meaning of a collective-bargaining agreement between a union and the railroad and was preempted by the Railway Labor Act. Id. at 819-20.

2. ***Private Employers.*** A section of the Missouri public health code, Mo. Rev. Stat. § 191.665, brings individuals with HIV infection, AIDS, and ARC under the anti-discrimination protections of chapter 213 of Missouri Statutes, the Missouri Fair Employment Practices Act. This protection does not, however, apply to an individual who has a contagious disease or infection and who, because of it, "would constitute a direct threat to the health or safety of other individuals or who, by reason of the currently contagious disease or infection, is unable to perform the duties of their employment." Id., at § 191.665(1).

Since January 1, 1999, it is illegal for employers in Missouri to use genetic information, or genetic test results, for employment decisions, unless the information relates directly to ability to perform assigned job responsibilities. Mo. Rev. Stat. § 375.1306. Health insurers are also restricted from using genetic information. Mo. Rev. Stat. § 375.1303.

3. ***Public Employers.*** A Missouri statute prohibits disclosure of any information or records held or maintained by any state agency concerning an individual's HIV infection status or the results of any HIV testing. Mo. Rev. Stat. § 191.656.

D. Polygraph Tests

Law enforcement officers may be dismissed for refusing polygraph testing. See Gardner v. Missouri State Highway Patrol Superintendent, 901 S.W.2d 107 (Mo. App. 1995). In Marciano v. Civil Service Com'n of City of St. Louis, 747 S.W.2d 758 (Mo. App. 1988), the court held that the Civil Service Commission properly used a polygraph examination to provide job applicant with opportunity to substantiate his denial of drug use, and thus remain on the fire fighter eligibility list because use of polygraph examination was related to business of city in fairly evaluating fire fighter applicants.

In a case decided prior to the Federal Employee Polygraph Protection Act of 1988, 29 U.S.C. 2001-2009, the Court of Appeals reversed an intentional infliction of emotional distress judgment in favor of an employee who was required to undergo a polygraph examination. See Gibson v. Hummel, 688 S.W.2d 4 (Mo. App. 1985). The employee, who was suspected of theft, claimed to have been distressed by the polygraph examination and the questions she was asked. Id. at 6. Among other things, she claimed that the questions were highly offensive, the polygraph room made her feel claustrophobic, and the polygraph itself looked like an "octopus" that would shock or electrocute her. Id. The court ruled, however, that plaintiff had failed to show that the defendant's conduct in making her take the polygraph examination was "extreme and outrageous" as required under the emotional distress tort. Id. The court noted that the employer had evidence that reasonably led it to suspect the plaintiff of employee theft, and "[i]t was not unreasonable for employer to take steps to halt the shortages." Id. at 8. The court further noted that the plaintiff was an at-will employee who "could be fired for no reason at all, and could be required to submit to a polygraph examination as a condition of continued employment." Id.

In another pre-1988 case, the use of polygraphic examinations in the course of a lawful investigation related to the business of a City was allowed. See Campbell v. Personnel Bd. of Kansas City, 666 S.W.2d 806 (Mo. App. 1984). Employees unsuccessfully challenged the use of polygraphic examination in the course of a lawful investigation of a loss of property and the refusal of two employees to submit to such an examination followed by the decision of the City that such refusal was a refusal or failure to cooperate in that investigation. Id. at 808. While the test results of polygraphic examinations are inadmissible in criminal trial proceedings, the requirement to submit to such examinations and the use of such techniques in lawful investigations is not prohibited. Id. at 811.

E. Fingerprinting

The following administrative codes require certain professionals to submit fingerprints as a prerequisite for licensure:

> 4 Mo. Code Regs. 15-2.010 (acupuncturists); 4 Mo. Code Regs. 70-2.040 (chiropractors); 4 Mo. Code Regs. 197-2.010 (massage therapists); 4 Mo. Code Regs. 200-4.020 (nurses); 4 Mo. Code Regs. 220-2.450 (pharmacists); 4 Mo. Code Regs. 255-2.010 (respiratory care practitioners); 4 Mo. Code Regs. 80-800.200 (teachers); 4 Mo. Code Regs. 75-13.020 (peace officers); 4 Mo. Code Regs. 10-2.020 (private security); 4 Mo. Code Regs. 30-40.342 (emergency medical technicians); 4 Mo. Code Regs. 30-61.045 (home daycare providers); 4 Mo. Code Regs. 30-62.042 (group daycare providers); 4 Mo. Code Regs. 95-2.020 (eff. June 30, 2005) (Professional Counselors).

III. SEARCHES

A. Employee's Person

No cases.

B. Employee's Work Area

In U.S. v. Thorn, 375 F.3d 679, 684 (8th Cir. 2004), vacated by 125 S.Ct. 1065 (Jan 24, 2005), reinstated by 413 F.3d 820, 824 (8th Cir. 2005), the Eighth Circuit found that a government employee may have had a legitimate expectation of privacy in his office, desk, and filing cabinet; however, any such expectation was limited because other agency employees had keys that allowed them to access the office and the contents of the desk and cabinets, and because the office, desk, and filing cabinet were all state-issued property and not the employee's personal belongings. Assuming without deciding that the employee had some minimal expectation of privacy in his office, desk, and filing cabinet, the court held that the employer's search of those areas did not violate the Fourth Amendment's prohibition against unreasonable searches. Id. The employee had authorized a search of his desk, where child pornography was discovered. Id. The discovery of pornography during a search of the desk allowed expansion of the scope of the investigation to include places and items where computer-generated pornographic materials could be stored. Id.

C. Employee's Property

In United States v. Chandler, 197 F.3d 1198, 1199 (8th Cir. 1999), a former St. Louis police officer was convicted of several controlled substance offenses after officers conducted a warrantless search of defendant officer's duty bag. Id. The defendant challenged the search under the Fourth Amendment protection against infringing "an expectation of privacy that society is prepared to consider reasonable." Id. at 1200 (quoting United States v. Jacobsen, 466 U.S. 109 (1984)). The court adopted the standard of O'Connor v. Ortega, 480 U.S. 709, 717 (1987), for warrantless searches by public employers by balancing an employee's reasonable expectation of privacy at work against the employer's legitimate interest in a justifiable warrantless search of the workplace. Id. Thus, the search was not unconstitutional because the defendant abandoned his duty bag at police station after his initial suspension, forfeiting any expectation of privacy in the duty bag. Id. In addition, the court stated that the controlled substances would inevitably have been discovered through an inventory process upon the officer's suspension. Id. at 1200-01.

In U.S. v. Thorn, see Section III.B supra., the Eighth Circuit applied the test articulated in O'Connor v. Ortega and affirmed the denial of a motion to suppress evidence of child pornography obtained during the search of a government employee's office. 375 F.3d at 683-84. The court found that, based on the government agency's computer use policy, the employee had no legitimate expectation of privacy as to the use and contents of his office computer, and therefore evidence found during a warrantless search of the computer was admissible in his prosecution. Id. at 683. The computer use policy specifically barred certain unauthorized use of the agency's computers, provided that employees had no personal right of privacy with respect to their use, and further provided that the agency had a right to access the computers to audit their use. Id.

In State v. Faruqi, the Missouri Supreme Court found evidence from an employee's work computer admissible when the employee consented to the search. 344 S.W.3d 193, 204 (Mo. banc 2011). The court further held that the employee could not assert vicariously the privacy rights of his employer in the computer. Id. at 205.

IV. MONITORING OF EMPLOYEES

A. Telephones and Electronic Communications

It is legal under Missouri law for a person to record or intercept a wire communication if the person is a party to the communication or if one of the parties to the communication has given prior consent to the interception, unless the communication is being intercepted for the purpose of committing a criminal or tortious act. Mo. Rev. Stat. § 542.402.2(2). Interceptions using wireless devices do not appear to be allowable even if one party consents. Mo. Rev. Stat. § 542.402.2(3).

Privacy considerations do not mandate a broad right to free line blocking of telephone numbers from the "caller identification" system. See State ex rel. Office of Public Counsel v. Missouri Public Service Com'n, 884 S.W.2d 311 (Mo. App. 1994). The Missouri Court of Appeals rejected the arguments made by the Office of Public Counsel that free line blocking is necessary to enable various persons, such as doctors, lawyers, or other professionals and service providers, to communicate confidentially. Id. at 315. The Public Counsel argued that failure to permit these groups of persons to have free line blocking would risk that their return calls would reveal their activities to others in the home or workplace, and that abuse victims, lawyers, doctors, other professionals, and citizens will be harassed or traced by those who intend to harm them as the result of accidental transmission of their telephone numbers. Id. The court deferred to the Public Service Commission's determination that per call blocking was sufficient to serve those needs, especially since phones are available which will automatically dial the blocking code when each call is made. Id. at 316-17.

1. ***Wiretapping.*** Missouri Revised Statutes § 542.400 et seq. is the Missouri Wiretap Act. The purpose of the Wiretap Act is to protect the privacy of individuals by limiting the use of information obtained in court authorized wiretapping in a criminal proceeding. It is a one-party consent statute; that is, it permits one party to a communication to record the communication. § 542.402.2. In Phillips v. American Motorist Ins. Co., the Missouri Court of Appeals construed a key provision of the Act, and held that that provision "does not mean what it says." 996 S.W.2d 584, 591 (Mo. App. 1999). Section 542.418.1 provides that "the contents of any wire communication or evidence derived therefrom shall not be received in evidence or otherwise disclosed in any civil or administrative proceeding except in civil actions brought pursuant to this section." Id. Read literally, this section would bar any use of a recorded communication, even one lawfully made by one party to that communication. "Literal application of the statute would mean that no Missouri court could ever allow any testimony concerning any telephone call, e-mail communication or telegram in any civil case except for a case brought under § 542.418.2for violation of the Wiretap Act itself .... Nor would any evidence of the contents, or any evidence derived therefrom, be admissible." Id. Because such a literal interpretation of the section would "wreck havoc with some business litigation claims," and "unreasonably deny access to justice in many instances," the court refused to follow that interpretation. Id. Rather, the court interpreted the section narrowly as prohibiting evidence derived from authorized law enforcement wiretaps in criminal cases to be used in collateral or unrelated civil or administrative proceedings. Id. at 592.

A civil claim may be brought under the Act, even in the case of a one-party consent recording, where it is alleged that the consenting party acted for the purpose of committing a criminal or tortious act. Mo. Rev. Stat. § 542.402.2 (3); Balke v. Ream, 983 S.W.2d 579 (Mo. App. 1998). The wiretapping claim of the plaintiff was later dismissed based on the plaintiff's failure to specify the alleged tortious purpose of the recordings. See, Balke v. Ream, 33 S.W.3d 589 (Mo. App. 2000). Moreover, the Court of Appeals rejected the plaintiff's innovative public disclosure of private facts theory in which the plaintiff claimed that the recording of his conversation by the other party to the conversation constituted a private facts violation. Id. at 594. The court found that in the situation where a conversation is taped by a party to that conversation, the publication element was missing. Id.

2. ***Electronic Communications.*** In Phillips, the court stated that portions of the Missouri Wiretap Act may be read to cover not only wiretapping but also "any telephone communications, fax communications, internet transactions, or e-mail communications." Id., 996 S.W.2d at 591.

3. ***Other Electronic Monitoring.*** No relevant statutes or cases.

B. Mail

No relevant statutes or cases.

C. Surveillance/Photographing

In Turner v. General Motors Corp., the court held that neither the plaintiff, employee, or plaintiff's son, had a cause of action for invasion of privacy after plaintiff's son was videotaped by surveillance cameras while masturbating in defendant's parking lot. 750 S.W.2d 76, 78 (Mo. App. 1988). The court held that plaintiff had no reasonable expectation of privacy for the acts he committed on another's property. Id. at 79. However, if a person is in a place where there is a "reasonable expectation of privacy," Missouri law prohibits viewing or filming a person nude or partially nude without knowledge or consent. Mo. Rev. Stat. § 565.253.

In Doe by Doe v. BPS Guard Services, Inc., the court affirmed a jury's award of $1,000 in compensatory damages to each of 12 female models at a fashion show at the St. Louis Convention Center against security guards who used surveillance cameras to watch and videotape the models as they changed their clothes in a makeshift dressing area. 945 F.2d 1422, 1424 (8th Cir. 1991), appeal after remand, 5 F.3d 347 (8th Cir. 1993). "So long as there was an objectionable intrusion into the plaintiffs' enjoyment of an area in which the plaintiffs had a right and expectation of privacy, it is not necessary to the plaintiffs' cause of action that they be viewed in a state of undress." 945 F.2d at 1427.

V. ACTIVITIES OUTSIDE THE WORKPLACE

A. Statute or Common Law

Chapter 130 of Missouri Revised Statutes prohibits employers and labor unions from taking action against employees based on their political activity or non-activity. Mo. Rev. Stat. § 130.028. In Int'l Bhd. of Elec. Workers v. St. Louis County, 117 F. Supp. 2d 922 (E.D. Mo. 2000), the court upheld a Civil Service Commission Rule on Political Activity prohibiting county employees from displaying political insignias on their personal vehicles if used for work, or while parked on county property. Employer policy prohibiting off-duty drug use is relevant to determining if behavior is in fact misconduct, and if such misconduct is connected with work, for the purposes of determining whether denial of unemployment compensation benefits is justified. Baldor Elec. Co. v. Reasoner, 66 S.W.3d 130 (Mo. App. 2001).

B. Employees' Personal Relationships

1. ***Romantic Relationships Between Employees.*** No state statutes explicitly cover this area. On a related issue, a police officer commanded to terminate an off-duty relationship with an individual on probation sought declaratory relief alleging that the city employer's regulation prohibiting the relationship was unconstitutional and violated his right to privacy. Wieland v. City of Arnold, 100 F. Supp. 2d 984 (E.D. Mo. 2000). The court adopted the balancing test of Pickering v. Board of Educ., 391 U.S. 563, 568, 88 S.Ct. 1731, 1735 (1968), and found that the city's interest in maintaining "strict order and efficiency" among its police department outweighed the officer's interest in his intimate association with the felon probationer. Wieland, 100 F. Supp. 2d at 988-89. The Eighth Circuit adopted the Pickering balancing test in Sexton v. Martin, 210 F.3d 905, 910 (8th Cir. 2000)). The Court also stated in dictum that a city may strictly regulate the behavior of its police officers although the city "certainly could not enforce [the] regulation . . . .against the general public, and probably could not enforce it against other civic employees." Wieland, at 990.

2. ***Sexual Orientation.*** Ordinances in the City of St. Louis, the City of St. Joseph, and Kansas City prohibit discrimination based on sexual orientation. The Missouri Human Rights Act does not explicitly cover this area. Mo. Rev. Stat. § 213.055. In an unusual case, a state social service worker who objected to foster parents who followed "alternative lifestyles" prevailed on a discrimination claim in which he alleged that action was taken against him because of his religious beliefs. Phillips v. Collings, 256 F.3d 843 (8th Cir. 2001).

A claim of intentional infliction of emotional distress in the workplace will avoid preemption under the Labor Management Relations Act if the employer's outrageous conduct violates its duty to every member of society, not just to the employees covered by the collective bargaining agreement. Plaintiff's allegations of discrimination based upon sexual orientation did not meet this threshold in Oberkramer v. IBEW-NECA Service Center, Inc., 151 F.3d 752 (8th Cir. 1998).

Evidence of an employee's sexual orientation may be offered if it is used to provide an alternative explanation for the employee voluntarily leaving his or her employment. Ratcliff v. Spring Mo., Inc., 261 S.W.3d 534, 544 (Mo. App. April 1, 2008). In Ratcliff, an employee left his job after complaining about injuries sustained at the workplace. Id. at 540. The employer responded by offering "evidence to rebut [employee's] reason for leaving his employment," including evidence from his diary that he felt discriminated against because of his homosexuality. Id. at 544. Despite the fact that the employee found evidence of his sexual orientation "irrelevant, inflammatory, and embarrassing," the Court of Appeals upheld the trial court in admitting evidence of the employee's sexual orientation. Id.

3. ***Marital Status.*** The Missouri Human Rights Act does not explicitly prohibit discrimination based on marital status. Mo. Rev. Stat. § 213.055.

C. Smoking

A state statute makes it an "improper employment practice" for an employer to take action against an employee "because the individual uses lawful alcohol or tobacco products off the premises of the employer during hours such individual is not working for the employer, unless such use interferes with the duties and performance of the employee, the employee's coworkers, or the overall operation of the employer's business." Mo. Rev. Stat. § 290.145. However, this section "shall not be deemed to create a cause of action for injunctive relief, damages or other relief." Id. The Missouri Indoor Clean Air Act, Mo. Rev. Stat. § 191.765 et seq., regulates smoking in public places in Missouri.

D. Blogging

No relevant statutes or cases.

VI. RECORDS

Chapter 610 of Missouri Revised Statutes, the Missouri Sunshine Law, provides that it is the public policy of the State of Missouri that public meetings and the deliberations of public bodies shall be open to the public, with some exceptions.

A. Personnel Records

The Fair Employment Practices Act prohibits employers from using any form of application for employment or from making any inquiry in connection with prospective employment which directly or indirectly limits employment according to race, color, religion, national origin, sex, ancestry, handicap (including HIV, AIDS or ARC), or age unless based upon a bona fide occupational qualification.

Discovery of personnel records even in employment litigation should be tailored to the issues and structured to avoid collateral embarrassment or harm. In State ex rel. Madlock v. O'Malley, the Missouri Supreme Court strongly disapproved of broad discovery tactics used to elicit "unlimited" access to a plaintiff's employment records, including "*any and all information of any nature whatsoever and concerning any time whatsoever*, which you may possess concerning the ... employment, personnel records, wage records, workers compensation records, disability claim records and *any other information....*" 8 S.W.3d 890, 891 (Mo. banc 1999) (emphasis in original). The Court stated that "[t]he discovery process was not designed to be a scorched earth battlefield upon which the rights of the litigants and the efficiency of the justice system should be sacrificed to mindless overzealous representation of plaintiffs and defendants." Id. The Court held that the trial court's protective order that simply limited the recipients of plaintiff's employment records did not go far enough, and plaintiff should have been protected as well from any disclosure to her adversaries of "information that may be irrelevant but embarrassing, or even harmful." Id. at 892. Additionally, the Court stated that where the parties could not agree on the scope of records authorization forms, it may be appropriate for either the court or a special master paid by the parties to conduct an in-camera inspection of the records. Id. at 891.

Discovery of an employee's entire personnel records for the collateral purpose of impeaching a witness is prohibited under Missouri law. In State ex rel. Delmar Gardens North Operating, LLC v. Gaertner, 239 S.W.3d 608, 609 (Mo. banc 2007), an employer objected to a request for production of the entire personnel record of an employee who witnessed alleged misconduct by the defendant. Id. at 610. After the trial court ordered the personnel records produced, the Supreme Court entered a writ of prohibition, holding that allowing discovery of an employee's entire personnel record "solely for a collateral matter such as impeachment would eviscerate the right of privacy that employees enjoy as to those records." Id. at 612. Allowing discovery of private personnel information would likely have the effect of discouraging witnesses from reporting incidents of misconduct in the workplace. Id. Accordingly, discovery that is permitted of confidential personnel records must be limited to information that relates to matters put at issue in the pleadings, especially in relation to sensitive personal information. Id.

Individuals need not provide to their opposing parties in private litigation authorizations for access to all of their past employment records. In State ex rel. Pierson v. Griffin, the court noted that personal information contained in a party's personnel records are subject to a fundamental right of privacy. 838 S.W.2d 490, 492 (Mo. App. 1992); see also State ex rel. Crowden v. Dandurand, 970 S.W.2d 340, 343 (Mo. banc 1998) (recognizing litigant's right of privacy in his employment records, but finding waiver of right because he asserted lost earnings claim in the litigation). Therefore, a blank authorization "directed to the world" permitting unlimited access to the individual's past employment records was overbroad; "The authorization should be tailored to seek only that information which is relevant to issues in these lawsuits upon which employment records would be relevant." Griffin, 970 S.W.2d at 493.

Tax and financial records of bank employees who are co-defendants in a tort case against the bank were held to be discoverable in State ex rel. Helt v. O'Malley, 53 S.W.3d 623 (Mo. App. 2001), because, despite the legitimate privacy interest of the bank employees implicated by disclosure of the records, the records were relevant and could be adequately protected through a protective order.

The terms of a settlement agreement between the city and an employee were not exempt from disclosure. In rejecting that contention, the court emphasized that the terms of the agreement were neither atypical nor unusual, and thus were unlikely to reveal the Board's thought processes or unduly infringe upon the employee's legitimate privacy interests. See Tuft v. City of St. Louis, 936 S.W.2d 113, 24 Media L. Rep. (BNA) 2260 (Mo. App. 1996). To protect a plaintiff's privacy interests in his employment records, attorneys for defendants may not be present at an in camera inspection of the records by the court. State ex rel. Stecher v. Dowd, 912 S.W.2d 462 (Mo. banc 1995). Under Missouri's Open Records and Meetings Law, a person affected by discussions held in a closed meeting is not allowed to open that meeting. Brown v. Weir, 675 S.W.2d 135 (Mo. App. 1984). The court held that the decision whether to close the meeting and vote belongs to the Board. A public employer may invite one or more members of the public into a closed session in which it deliberates on employment matters. Smith v. Sheriff, 982 S.W.2d 775, 27 Media L. Rep. (BNA) 1314 (Mo. App. 1998). Not only is protection of the employee's privacy and reputation involved, but there also exists a proper concern for promoting free and open discussion among members of the Board. In Hudson v. School District, the court said, "The opinion of the Attorney General of Missouri implicitly recognizes that the personnel exemption of the statute is based upon protection of the privacy of the employee." 578 S.W.2d 301, 308 (Mo. App. 1979). However, in Hawkins v. City of Fayette, this quotation was held to relate to general employees, and not to one such as the mayor, who was the elected presiding executive officer of the city. See id., 604 S.W.2d 716 (Mo. App. 1980). The court found that the question of whether his compensation as mayor should be increased in consideration of his assumption of additional duties, which could be performed by another employee such as a city manager, was one of sufficient public importance to require a public notice of any special meeting where those matters would be discussed and voted upon by the board of aldermen. Id. at 723.

In Pulitzer Pub. Co. v. Missouri State Employees' Retirement System, the court found that public governmental bodies are authorized to close the individually identifiable personnel records of current and past state officers and employees. See id., 927 S.W.2d 477 (Mo. App. 1996). However, recognizing the public's overriding interest in knowing how its tax money is spent, the court found that such protected personnel records did not include the names, positions, salaries and lengths of service of officers and employees of public agencies. Id. at 479. While public employees and contractors may not wish their employment contracts known, such contracts must be available upon request because "[e]ntering into a contract with a public governmental entity is simply not a personal matter." North Kansas City Hosp. Bd. of Trustees v. St. Luke's Northland Hosp., 984 S.W.2d 113, 121 (Mo. App. 1998).

In a liquidation proceeding the State Supreme Court required disclosure of compensation records for key employees of the receivership. Transit Cas. Co. ex rel. Pulitzer Publishing Co. v. Transit Cas. Co. ex rel. Intervening Employees, 43 S.W.3d 293 (Mo. banc 2001). The Court held, based on a limited record, that insurance liquidation proceedings were covered by the open records statute. Id. at 301-02. The Court reversed the lower court's decision that privacy interests of the Receivership's key employees outweighed the public interest in disclosure and held that there is a strong presumption for access to court records which can be overcome only by compelling justification for closure. The trial court's conclusory finding of need for confidentiality of compensation records was held insufficient, where the only supporting evidence was speculative and the liquidation did not allege in its pleadings specific factual circumstances to justify closure. Id. at 303-04.

In Grinnell Fire Protection Sys. Comp. v. NLRB, 272 F.3d 1028 (8th Cir. 2001), an employer submitted an appeal from a decision of the NLRB that the company must disclose the names and home addresses of employee's in the Union's bargaining unit. The court held that the while the names of those on the bargaining unit were presumptively important, the same could not be said of the addresses. The court noted that the ready availability of the home addresses weakened the union's need for the material.

Where a hospital injected quality assurance issues into litigation and selectively disclosed peer review records that would otherwise be covered by the statutory peer review privilege of Mo. Rev. Stat. §537.035, the hospital had waived its right to protect physician personnel files from discovery. In Re State of Missouri ex rel. St. John's Reg. Medial Center v. Dally, 90 S.W.3d 209 (Mo. App. 2002).

B. Medical Records

In workers' compensation proceedings, individuals need not provide to the opposing parties access to all of their past medical records. Although workers' compensation proceedings waive the physician-patient privilege, the scope of this waiver is limited to testimony and medical records regarding the condition for which compensation is being sought. State ex rel. Maloney v. Allen, 26 S.W.3d 244, 248 (Mo. App. 2000). A broader reading of Chapter 287 et seq. (see, e.g., §§ 287.140.6 and 287.140.7, Mo. Rev. Stat. (1994) and Mo. Rev. Stat. (Cum. Supp. 1998)) would be "inconsistent with the purpose of the privilege to invite confidence between physician and patient." Allen, 26 S.W.3d at 248.

C. Criminal Records

No relevant statutes or case law.

D. Subpoenas / Search Warrants

No relevant statutes or case law.

VII. ACTIONS SUBSEQUENT TO EMPLOYMENT

A. References

No relevant statutes or case law.

B. Non-Compete Agreements

Every contract, combination or conspiracy in restraint of trade or commerce in this state is unlawful. Mo. Rev. Stat. § 416.031. Restrictive covenants limiting individuals in the exercise or pursuit of their occupations are in restraint of trade. Sturgis Equip. Co., Inc. v. Falcon Indus. Sales Co., 930 S.W.2d 14, 16 (Mo. App. 1996). Post-employment restrictions are generally considered restraints of trade. House of Tools & Engineering, Inc. v. Price, 504 S.W.2d 157, 159 (Mo. App. 1973).

In Schmersahl v. McHugh, 28 S.W.3d 345, 349 (Mo. App. 2000), the court stated that a restrictive covenant in an employment agreement is only valid and enforceable if it is necessary to protect one of two well-defined interests, trade secrets and customer contacts, and if it is reasonable as to time and place. An employer can only "fairly require" the protection of these narrowly defined and well recognized interests against possible appropriation by a former employee. Id. Additionally, covenants not to compete are enforceable even if they are contained in employment contracts that do not provide a definite period of employment. Wilson Mfg. Co. v. Fusco, 258 S.W.3d 841, 844 (Mo. App. May 20, 2008).

VIII. OTHER ISSUES

A. Statutes of Limitations

No Missouri limitations statute specifically covers privacy actions. The two-year libel statute may apply to privacy claims that are similar to libel claims, such as false light. Mo. Rev. Stat. § 516.140; White v. Fawcett Publications, 324 F. Supp. 403 (W.D. Mo. 1971). However, where no specific limitations period is prescribed for a cause of action, the five-year general statute will apply. Mo. Rev. Stat. § 516.120. In Turen v. Equifax, Inc., 571 F.2d 411, 414 (8th Cir. 1978), the court dismissed a libel claim as being time-barred by the two-year statute of limitations but let the case proceed to trial on a claim for invasion of privacy. However, the court did not discuss which statute of limitations provision applies to invasion of privacy actions.

Though not an employment case, the Missouri Supreme Court has held claims requesting non-pecuniary damages are governed by the two-year statute of limitations for defamation, whereas claims requesting pecuniary damages are governed by the five-year statute of limitations for injurious falsehood. State ex rel. BP Prods. North America Inc. v. Ross, 163 S.W.3d 922 (Mo. banc 2005).

Missouri cases have rejected a "discovery" rule for libel actions. White v. Fawcett Publications, 324 F. Supp. 403, 404 (W.D. Mo. 1970) ("a libel action accrues at the time of publication of the allegedly libelous statements.... It does not matter that plaintiff may not have seen the issue until later."); Brown v. Chicago, Rock Island & Pacific Railroad Co., 212 F. Supp. 832 (W.D. Mo. 1963), aff'd, 323 F.2d 420 (8th Cir. 1963). Particularly for private torts similar to libel, like false light, these authorities should also bar a "discovery" rule in privacy actions. However, the "capability of ascertainment" exception of Mo. Rev. Stat. § 516.100 applies to most limitations periods, and hence the limitations period does not begin to run until the damages are "capable of ascertainment." Jones v. Pinkerton's Inc., 700 S.W.2d 456 (Mo. App. 1985) (an allegedly libelous publication is incapable of ascertainment by the plaintiff at the time of publication, for purposes of Mo. Rev. Stat. § 516.100, only when plaintiff was *actively prevented* from becoming aware of the publication (emphasis added); "mere ignorance of the plaintiff will not prevent the running of the statute of limitations." Id.).

B. Jurisdiction

1. ***Subject Matter.*** Where an employee subject to a collective-bargaining agreement raises claims of false light or private facts, those claims are preempted by the Labor and Management Relations Act ("LMRA") if interpretation of the collective bargaining agreement is necessary. 29 U.S.C.S. § 185; Gore v. TWA, 210 F.3d 944, 949 (8th Cir. 2000); Cf. Meyer v. Schnucks Markets, 163 F.3d 1048 (8th Cir. 1998) (holding that plaintiff's claim for intentional

infliction of emotional distress based on publication of private facts was not preempted by LMRA because it is "not based on rights created by, or substantially dependent on an analysis of" the collective-bargaining agreement).

C. Workers' Compensation Exclusivity

The Missouri Workers' Compensation Act requires employers to provide compensation for personal injuries of the employee that occur "by accident arising out of and in the course of the employee's employment." Mo. Rev. Stat. § 287.120.1; Miller v. Wackenhut Servs., Inc., 808 F. Supp. 697, 701 (W.D. Mo. 1992). Under the statute, the Missouri Workers' Compensation Act provides the exclusive remedy for all such claims:

> The rights and remedies herein granted to an employee shall exclude all other rights and remedies of the employee, his wife, her husband, parents, personal representatives, dependents, heirs or next kin, at common law or otherwise, on account of such injury or death, except such rights and remedies as are not provided for by this chapter.

Mo. Rev. Stat. § 287.120.2. The statute creates the Labor and Industrial Relations Commission ("LIRC") to adjudicate all workers' compensation claims.

In addition to exclusive jurisdiction over the claims themselves, the LIRC has exclusive jurisdiction to determine whether an employee's injury is the result of an accident or the intentional act of an employee, Goodrum v. Asplundh Tree Expert Co., 824 S.W.2d 6, 8 (Mo. banc 1992); Killian v. J & J Installer, Inc., 802 S.W.2d 158, 160-61 (Mo. banc 1991), and whether an employee's injury arose out of and in the course of employment. Yount v. Davis, 846 S.W.2d 780, 782 (Mo. Ct. App. 1993).

In Massey v. Victor L. Phillips, Co., 827 F. Supp. 597, 597 (W.D. Mo. 1993), an employee brought an invasion of privacy claim against her former employer, alleging that supervisors utilized a peephole to spy on her in the women's restroom. The employer moved to dismiss the invasion of privacy claim contending that the claim was preempted by Missouri's workers' compensation exclusivity. Massey, 827 F. Supp. at 597. The court held that Missouri's Labor and Industrial Relations Commission had exclusive jurisdiction to determine whether the conduct alleged was an accident covered by workers' compensation. Id. The court concluded that:

> [r]ecent Missouri Supreme court cases . . . suggest that . . . in all instances where an injured person seeks to hold his or her employer liable under any common law tort theory, including intentional torts, for injuries resulting from the work experience, the LIRC has first crack at determining whether the injuries are the result of an accident covered by workers' compensation. If they are, workers' compensation provides the exclusive remedy. If not, the injured person can proceed in court. This rule of law governs cases such as the instant one where the acts complained of are in no way accidental.

Id. at 599 (emphasis added) (citations omitted). Accordingly, an employee's invasion of privacy claim against an employer may be preempted by Missouri's workers' compensation exclusivity.

D. Pleading Requirements

Missouri courts require fact pleading. Therefore, each element of a cause of action must be plead and supported with facts that, if proven, would support a verdict in favor of the pleader. Under Missouri's fact pleading requirements, a pleader must state the ultimate facts, or allegations which infer those facts, which support every element of the cause of action pleaded to survive a motion to dismiss. Rule 55.05(1); Sofka v. Thal, 662 S.W.2d 502, 508 (Mo. banc 1983); Kennedy v. Microsurgery and Brain Research Inst., 18 S.W.3d 39, 44 (Mo. App. 2000).

SURVEY OF MONTANA EMPLOYMENT LIBEL LAW

Peter Michael Meloy
Meloy Law Firm
P.O. Box 1241
Helena MT 59624
Telephone: (406) 442-8670

(With Developments Reported Through **November 1, 2012**)

GENERAL COMMENTS

State trial courts in Montana are organized into twenty-two judicial districts, with one to five judges in each district. Appeal of right is directly to the Montana Supreme Court; there is no intermediate court of appeals. The State of Montana is a single federal district, with appeal to the Ninth Circuit.

While this outline uses standard citation format, the Montana Supreme Court adopted a vendor-neutral citation system for briefs submitted to the court after Jan. 1, 1998. This citation includes the calendar year in which the opinion or substantive order is issued, followed by the Montana U.S. Postal Code (MT), followed by a consecutive number beginning each year with "1" (for example, 1998 MT 1). For opinions which are not to be cited as precedent and for all substantive orders, the consecutive number is followed by the letter "N." This citation should be followed by regular, vendor-based citations (e.g., Doe v. Roe, 1998 MT 12,286 Mont. 175,989 P.2d 1312). See In Re: the Matter of Opinion Forms and Citation Standards of the Supreme Court of Montana; and the Adoption of a Form of Public Domain and Neutral-format Citation (Mont. Dec. 17, 1997).

SIGNIFICANT DEVELOPMENTS SINCE THE 2012 *SURVEY*

In Albert v. City of Billings, 2012 MT 159, 365 Mont. 454, 282 P.3d 704 (July 24, 2012), the Montana Supreme Court held that a news story reporting that Plaintiff slept with goggles and a mask as protection against cockroaches was not actionable slander.

I. GENERAL LAW

A. General Employment Law

1. ***At Will Employment.*** Montana continues to provide for "employment at will." Mont. Code Ann. § 39-2-503. Nevertheless, Montana requires an employer to have cause to terminate an employee who has completed any probationary period and allows for a wrongful discharge cause of action pursuant to Montana's Wrongful Discharge From Employment Act, Mont. Code Ann. §§ 39-2-901 et seq. A discharge under Montana's statutory scheme is wrongful only if: 1) it was in retaliation for the employee's refusal to violate public policy or for reporting a violation of public policy; 2) the discharge was not for good cause and the employee had completed the employer's probationary period of employment; or 3) the employer violated the express provisions of its own written personnel policy. Mont. Code Ann. § 39-2-904. Mont. Code Ann. § 39-2-905(2) limits the recovery of punitive damages in a wrongful discharge action to those situations in which the discharge is in violation of public policy.

B. Elements of a Libel Claim

1. ***Basic Elements.*** Defamation involves the publication of information about an individual that is false and injurious to his or her reputation. There are two types of defamation claims. The first is libel, in which the plaintiff must show a false and unprivileged publication by writing, printing, picture effigy, or other fixed representation to the eye which exposes any person to hatred, contempt, ridicule, or obloquy or which causes him or her to be shunned or avoided or which has a tendency to injure the person in his or her occupation. Mont. Code Ann. § 27-1-802. The other is slander, which involves a false and unprivileged publication other than libel which: 1) charges any person with crime or with having been indicted, convicted, or punished for crime; 2) imputes in him or her the present existence of an infectious, contagious, or loathsome disease; 3) tends directly to injure the person in respect to his or her office, profession, trade, or business, either by imputing general disqualification in those respects which the office or other occupation peculiarly requires or by imputing something with reference to his office, profession, trade, or business that has a natural tendency to lessen its profit; 4) imputes to him or her impotence or want of chastity; or 5) by natural consequence causes actual damage. Mont. Code Ann. § 27-1-803. See Hale v. City of Billings, 295 Mont. 495, 986 P.2d 413, 28 Media L. Rep. 1321 (1999), for recent discussion of defamation standards. **In Albert v. City of Billings, 2012 MT 159, 365 Mont. 454, 282 P.3d 704 (July 24, 2012), the Montana Supreme Court held that a news story reporting that Plaintiff slept with goggles and a mask as protection**

against cockroaches was not actionable slander. Defamation claims which are so totally devoid of merit as to constitute bad faith justifies an award of attorney fees incurred in defense of the claims. Dick Anderson Constr. Inc. v. Monroe Construction, 2009 MT 416, 353 Mont. 534, 221 P.3d 675 (2009).

2. ***Fault.*** The level of fault that must be shown depends on the plaintiff's private or public status. A public figure must prove that the defamatory statement was made with actual malice in order to recover damages. "A private figure must show some degree of fault to recover ... but does not have to prove actual malice except to recover presumed or punitive damages." Kurth v. Great Falls Tribune Co., 246 Mont. 407, 410, 804 P.2d 393, 395, 18 Media L. Rep. 1971 (1991) (citing Gertz v. Robert Welch, Inc., 418 U.S. 323, 1 Media L. Rep. 1633 (1974)). On remand, the district court found that defendant was guilty of libel but also that the libelous article had a minimal effect on plaintiff's reputation. The court awarded $2,000 in damages. On appeal, the Montana Supreme Court upheld the district court's damage award. Kurth v. Great Falls Tribune Co., 290 Mont. 530, 977 P.2d 342 (1998).

The Montana Supreme Court stated in Madison v. Yunker, 180 Mont. 54, 66-67, 589 P.2d 126, 132-33 (1978), that whether the plaintiff is a public or private figure is a question for the jury. In Roots v. Montana Human Rights Network, 275 Mont. 408, 913 P.2d 638 (1996), and Kurth v. Great Falls Tribune Co., 246 Mont. 407, 804 P.2d 393 (1991), the court reversed orders granting summary judgment because there were factual issues in dispute regarding the plaintiff's status. Nonetheless, in Williams v. Pasma, 202 Mont. 66, 73-74, 656 P.2d 212, 215-16 (1982), the court held that a political activist and former candidate for the U.S. Senate was a public figure as a matter of law.

a. **Private Figure Plaintiff/Matter of Public Concern.** A private figure plaintiff must prove 1) that the published material was false; 2) that defendant is chargeable with fault in the publication; and 3) that actual injury to plaintiff ensued, for which he or she may recover actual damages; 4) if plaintiff proves the publication was made with knowledge of its falsity or in reckless disregard for the truth or falsity thereof, he or she may recover punitive damages for such malice, but such malice does not include hatred, personal spite, ill-will, or a desire to injure. Madison v. Yunker, 180 Mont. 54, 67, 589 P.2d 126, 133, 4 Media L. Rep. 1337 (1978) (citing New York Times v. Sullivan, 376 U.S. 254, 1 Media L. Rep. 1527 (1964)). Montana follows the rule established in Gertz v. Robert Welch, Inc., 418 U.S. 323, 1 Media L. Rep. 1633 (1974), to determine the standard of balancing a private figure plaintiff's right to privacy against the interests of the public's right to know. The public's interest in accurate information about attorney discipline outweighs the state's interest in preserving the confidentiality of Commission on Practice investigation when information is obtained lawfully. Lence v. Hagadone Inc. Co., 258 Mont. 433, 853 P.2d 1230, 21 Media L. Rep. 1641 (1993) (overruled on other grounds in Sacco v. High Country Independent Press, Inc., 271 Mont. 209, 230, 896 P.2d 411, 423 (1995).

b. **Private Figure Plaintiff/Matter of Private Concern.** There are no reported decisions in Montana regarding a private figure plaintiff in a matter of private concern.

c. **Public Figure Plaintiff/Matter of Public Concern.** If the plaintiff was a public figure at the time of the alleged libel, then he or she cannot recover without showing the statement was made with actual malice. Public figures are subdivided into two subcategories: public figures for all purposes and public figures for a limited purpose. Either category of public figure must show the statement was made with actual malice. Kurth v. Great Falls Tribune Co., 246 Mont. 407, 409-10, 804 P.2d 393, 394, 18 Media L. Rep. 1971 (1991) (quoting New York Times v. Sullivan, 376 U.S. 254, 280, 1 Media L. Rep. 1527 (1964), and citing Gertz v. Robert Welch, Inc., 418 U.S. 323, 1 Media L. Rep. 1633 (1974)). In Williams v. Pasma, 202 Mont. 66, 656 P.2d 212, 9 Media L. Rep. 1004 (1982), the court adopted the distinction between public figures and public officials as given in Gertz. The court then went on to distinguish that "general fame or notoriety in the community" does not require national fame or notoriety; fame or notoriety within the local community is enough to determine public figure status. Williams, 202 Mont. at 73-74, 656 P.2d at 215-16.

3. ***Falsity.*** Falsity is an element of the plaintiff's case for both libel and slander. Mont. Code Ann. §§ 27-2-802, 803. In State v. Helfrich, 277 Mont. 452, 922 P.2d 1159 (1996), the court found that Montana's criminal defamation statute, Mont. Code Ann. § 45-8-212, was unconstitutional, citing Garrison v. Louisiana, 379 U.S. 64, 1 Media L. Rep. 1548 (1964). The court determined that truth is a defense even when the offending publication is not made with good motives and for justifiable ends. (The statute has since been amended.) A plaintiff who is a public official or public figure may recover only if he or she proves the threshold fact that the publication was made with knowledge of its falsity or reckless disregard for its truth or falsity. Madison v. Yunker, 180 Mont. 54, 589 P.2d 126, 4 Media L. Rep. 1337 (1978).

4. ***Defamatory Statement of Fact.*** In Hale v. City of Billings, 255 Mont. 495, 986 P.2d 413, 28 Media L. Rep. 1321 (1999), the court held that if an opinion creates a reasonable inference that it is based on undisclosed defamatory facts, it can give rise to liability for defamation. Such a statement of opinion can cause damages and is actionable only if it contains a probably false connotation or can reasonably be interpreted as stating facts about an individual. The Hale court relied in part on the Montana Constitution's mandate that the jury "shall determine the law and the facts" in defamation

cases, Mont. Const. art. II §7, to reverse summary judgment on the question of falsity in that case. However, a court may dispose of defamation claims where there are no issues of fact warranting a jury trial. See Knievel v. ESPN, 393 F.3d 1068 (9th Cir. 2005), (Ninth Circuit held that a cause of action for defamation under Montana law was not established because although the term "pimp" was capable of defamatory meaning, a reasonable person would not construe a photo caption on ESPN's website as implying the celebrity was a pimp or implying that his wife was a prostitute).

In Anderson v. City of Troy, 316 Mont. 39, 68 P.3d 805 (2003), the Montana Supreme Court held that reference by a city's police chief to a resident as a "gang banger" was not slanderous *per se* because the reference did not accuse the resident of any specific criminal activity or impute to him any particular opprobrious characteristic, and term in its modern usage seemed to denote either a bona fide member of a street gang or a "wannabe," which added up to nothing more than innuendo.

In McKonkey v. Flathead Electric Cooperative, 330 Mont. 48, 61, 125 P.3d 1121, 1130 (2005), the Court held that "claims of defamatory libel may not be based on innuendo or inference."

5. ***Of and Concerning Plaintiff***. Montana allows for a defamation action where a plaintiff is not actually named in the defamatory statement if the plaintiff can prove that the statement was made of and concerning the plaintiff. In order to establish defamation, plaintiff must prove that the community perceived the statement as relating to the plaintiff. A plaintiff who is not listed in the alleged libelous statement may present "evidence of the surrounding circumstances and facts" to meet the burden of proving that plaintiff was the person to whom the statement referred. Granger v. Time, Inc., 174 Mont. 42, 47, 568 P.2d 535, 539, 3 Media L. Rep. 1021 (citing Nolan v. Standard Pub. Co., 67 Mont. 212, 216 P. 571 (1923)). This burden is met if the statement was understood by readers to specifically refer only to plaintiff or to refer to plaintiff as a member of a group small enough that the defamation may reasonably be understood to apply to each group member. "Libel and damage consist in the apprehension of the hearers, not in the mind of the author of the statement. ... In order that there be actionable libel ... a plaintiff must show that people in the community other than the plaintiff perceived the statement to refer to the plaintiff." Granger, 174 Mont. at 49-50, 568 P.2d at 540 (1977).

In McKonkey, 330 Mont. at 61, 125 P.3d at 1130, the Court held that "allegedly libelous statements must be aimed specifically at the person claiming injury."

6. ***Publication.*** When a defamatory statement is published in a magazine or periodical, Montana has adopted the Multi-publication rule. The Multi-publication rule is that each time a libelous article is brought to the attention of a third person a new publication has occurred; each publication is a separate actionable tort; and each time a magazine containing libelous material is sold or distributed, a new publication has occurred and a fresh tort has been committed, which is actionable. Lewis v. Reader's Digest, 162 Mont. 401, 512 P.2d 702 (1973).

a. **Intracorporate Communication.** No reported decisions in Montana.

b. **Compelled Self-Publication.** No reported decisions in Montana.

c. **Republication.** No reported decisions in Montana.

7. ***Statements versus Conduct.*** No reported decisions in Montana.

8. ***Damages.*** Defamation plaintiffs who do not prove knowledge of falsity or reckless disregard for the truth are restricted to compensation for actual injury. The more customary types of actual harm inflicted by defamatory falsehood include impairment of reputation and standing in the community, personal humiliation, and mental anguish and suffering. A plaintiff who is a public official or public figure may recover only if he or she proves the threshold fact that the publication was made with knowledge of its falsity or reckless disregard for its truth or falsity. The plaintiff could then recover actual and punitive damages. Madison v. Yunker, 180 Mont. 54, 589 P.2d 126, 4 Media L. Rep. 1337 (1978). In an action involving a private figure, the plaintiff proved defamation but was awarded nominal damages in a bench trial. On appeal, the Montana Supreme Court affirmed the district court's finding that the libelous article had only minimal effect on plaintiff's reputation. Kurth v. Great Falls Tribune Co., 290 Mont. 530, 977 P.2d 342 (1998).

a. **Presumed Damages and Libel Per Se.** Montana defines libel per se as follows: "for words to be actionable per se their injurious character must be a fact of such common notoriety as to be established by the general consent of men so that the court takes judicial notice of it. ... 'Where the language complained of is clear and unambiguous, it is the duty of the court to determine whether it is actionable.'" Griffin v. Opinion Pub. Co., 114 Mont. 502, 138 P.2d 580, 584 (1943) (quoting 33 Am.Jur. § 294, p. 277) (overruled on other grounds by State v. Helfrich, 277 Mont. 452, 922 P.2d 1159, 1161 n. 1 (1996)).

(1) **Employment-Related Criticism.** Montana statutorily bars certain employment related criticism. "If any person, after having discharged an employee from his service, prevents or attempts to prevent by word or writing of any kind such discharged employee from obtaining employment with any other person, such person is punishable as provided in § 39-2-804 and is liable in punitive damages to such discharged person, to be recovered by civil action. No person is prohibited from informing by word or writing any person to whom such discharged person or employee has applied for employment a truthful statement of the reason for such discharge." Mont. Code Ann. § 39-2-802. Upon demand from the discharged employee, the employer must provide a written statement of the reason for discharge. Mont. Code Ann. § 39-2-801(1). However, the statement may be modified at any time and does not limit the employer's defense in any action by the discharged employee. Mont. Code Ann. § 39-2-801(3). The latter provision was enacted in 1999 and overrules prior court decisions holding that only reasons set forth in the discharge letter were relevant in a wrongful discharge action. A supervisor's statements expressing dissatisfaction with employee's job performance, made in the context of evaluating employee's performance, are not actionable. Frigon v. Morrison-Maierle, Inc., 233 Mont. 113, 760 P.2d 57 (1988) (overruled on other grounds in Sacco v. High Country Independent Press, Inc., 271 Mont. 209, 235, 896 P.2d 411, 426-27 (1995).

(2) **Single Instance Rule.** Montana has no reported decisions.

b. **Punitive Damages.** A plaintiff who proves that a publication was made with knowledge of its falsity or in reckless disregard for the truth may recover punitive damages. Madison v. Yunker, 180 Mont. 54, 589 P.2d 126, 4 Media L. Rep. 1337 (1978).

II. PRIVILEGES AND DEFENSES

A. Scope of Privileges

1. ***Absolute Privilege.*** An absolute privilege protects any statement made "in any legislative or judicial proceeding or in any other official proceeding authorized by law." Mont. Code Ann. § 27-1-804(2). See, e.g., Montana Bank of Circle, N.A. v. Ralph Myers & Son, Inc., 236 Mont. 236, 245, 769 P.2d 1208, 1213 (1989) (judicial complaint); Burgess v. Silverglat, 217 Mont. 186, 188, 703 P.2d 854, 855-56 (1985) (report submitted by court-appointed psychiatrist for indigent criminal defendant); Skinner v. Pistoria, 194 Mont. 257, 262-63, 633 P.2d 672, 675-76 (1982) (citizen's comments at city commission meeting).

Montana law also confers a privilege on statements made in the "proper discharge of an official duty." Mont. Code Ann. § 27-1-804(1). The Supreme Court has previously held that this privilege is absolute. See, e.g., Storch v. Board of Directors, 169 Mont. 176, 181-82, 545 P.2d 644, 647-48 (1976). However, in Hale v. City of Billings, 295 Mont. 495, 986 P.2d 413, 28 Media L. Rep. 1321 (1999), the court clarified that this privilege is absolute only when the defendant was required by law to publish the defamatory matter. Hale, 986 P.2d at 422. Otherwise, the word "proper" in the statute implies the privilege is qualified. For additional pre-Hale cases on privilege, see Marcy v. Delta Airlines, 18 Mont. Fed. Rep. 401 (D. Mont. 1994) (employer's statements to Department of Labor and Industry in connection with plaintiff's application for unemployment benefits), and Wall v. Corral West Ranchwear, Inc., 17 Mont. Fed. Rep. 489 (D. Mont. 1994) (employer's request to another to prepare document detailing allegations of theft against plaintiffs). In McLeod v. State ex rel. Dept. of Transp., 2009 MT 130, 350 Mont. 285, 206 P.3d 956, the Montana Supreme Court held that a report to a state licensing board criticizing a real estate appraiser's work was absolutely privileged and affirmed the lower court's dismissal of a defamation claim.

In Cooper v. Glaser, 2010 MT 55, 355 Mont. 342, 228 P.3d 443 (2010), the Court recognized an absolute privilege from liability for defamation claims brought by a constituent for comments made by a legislator on the House floor during a legislative session, citing Article 5, Section 8 of the Montana Constitution.

2. ***Qualified Privileges.***

a. **Common Interest.** A communication without malice to an interested person by one who is also interested, or by one who stands in such relation to the person interested as to afford a reasonable ground for supposing the motive for the communication innocent, or who is requested by the person interested to give the information is privileged. Mont. Code Ann. § 27-1-804(3); see Rasmussen v. Bennett, 228 Mont. 106, 110, 741 P.2d 755, 758 (1987) (applying qualified privilege to statements by church officials in course of disciplinary proceeding against members). Rasmussen also held that incidental communication to other parties does not automatically destroy the privilege.

b. **Duty.** A statement made "in the proper discharge of an official duty" is privileged. Mont. Code Ann. § 27-1-804(1). The Supreme Court has previously held that this privilege is absolute. See, e.g., Storch v. Board of Directors, 169 Mont. 176, 181-82, 545 P.2d 644, 647-48 (1976). However, in Hale v. City of Billings, 295 Mont. 495, 986 P.2d 413, 28 Media L. Rep. 1321 (1999), the court clarified that this privilege is absolute only when the defendant was required by law to publish the defamatory matter. See Hale, 986 P.2d at 422. Otherwise, the word "proper" in the statute implies the privilege is qualified.

For purposes of this now-qualified privilege, the court has generally construed the definition of "official duty" broadly. See, e.g., Wolf v. Williamson, 269 Mont. 397, 889 P.2d 1177 (1995) (police chief's response to request for information about plaintiff's employment history); Denny Driscoll Boys Home v. State of Montana, 227 Mont. 177, 737 P.2d 1150 (1987) (official statements to press regarding criminal investigation); Nye v. Department of Livestock, 196 Mont. 222, 639 P.2d 498 (1982) (statements made in course of firing public employee); see also Hale, 986 P.2d at 421-22 (suggesting that "official duty" could include duties associated with private employment); but see Shors v. Branch, 221 Mont. 390, 720 P.2d 239 (1986) (holding that unsolicited complaint to police is civic, not official, duty and not privileged).

c. **Criticism of Public Employee.** Montana has adopted the language of the Restatement of the Law of Torts §§ 606 & 607: "privilege of criticism ... includes a privilege to criticize the public conduct of all [public] officers ... in so far as the conduct of such officer ... is a matter of public concern to those to whom the criticism is published." Griffin v. Opinion Pub. Co., 114 Mont. 502, 138 P.2d 580, 588 (1943) (quoting Restatement of the Law of Torts, c. 25 § 607) (overruled on other grounds by State v. Helfrich, 277 Mont. 452, 922 P.2d 1159, 1161 n. 1 (1996)). "Every person has a right to comment on matters of public interest and general concern, provided he does so fairly and with an honest purpose." Griffin, 138 P.2d at 589.

A fair and true report without malice of a judicial, legislative, or other public official proceeding or of anything said in the course thereof is privileged. Mont. Code Ann. §27-1-804(4); Hale v. City of Billings, 295 Mont. 495, 986 P.2d 413, 423, 28 Media L. Rep. 1321 (1999); Cox v. Lee Ent., Inc., 222 Mont. 527, 723 P.2d 238, 13 Media L. Rep. 1230 (1986). Cox held that a "judicial proceeding" includes pleadings filed but not yet acted upon so that a newspaper report of the contents of a complaint was covered by the privilege. A preliminary investigation by the State Bar's Commission on Practice is also part of a judicial proceeding. Lence v. Hagadone, Inc., 258 Mont. 433, 443, 853 P.2d 1230, 1237, 21 Media L. Rep. 1641 (1993) (overruled on other grounds in Sacco v. High Country Independent Press, Inc., 271 Mont. 209, 230, 896 P.2d 411, 423 (1995).

d. **Limitation on Qualified Privileges.**

(1) **Constitutional or Actual Malice.** The Montana Supreme Court has rarely addressed the standard for overcoming a qualified privilege. In Rasmussen v. Bennett, 228 Mont. 106, 741 P.2d 755 (1987), the court indicated that constitutional malice -- "knowledge that [the statement] was false [or] reckless disregard of whether it was false or not" -- would overcome the "common interest" privilege. Rasmussen 228 Mont. at 111, 741 P.2d at 758 (citing Williams v. Pasma, 202 Mont. 66, 656 P.2d 212, 9 Media L. Rep. 1004 (1982), and New York Times v. Sullivan, 376 U.S. 254, 1 Media L. Rep. 1527 (1964)). However, that standard does not appear to be the exclusive means for overcoming a qualified privilege. See II.A.2.d(2), infra.

(2) **Common Law Malice.** The Montana Supreme Court has rarely addressed the standard for overcoming a qualified privilege. In addition to constitutional malice, see II.A.2.d(1), supra, a privilege may be overcome based on statutory or common law standards. In Hale v. City of Billings, 295 Mont. 495, 986 P.2d 413, 28 Media L. Rep. 1321 (1999), the court indicated that the limits of the "official duty" privilege are determined by the language of Mont. Code Ann. § 27-1-804(1). Thus, the question is whether the exercise of official duty was "proper." In Rasmussen v. Bennett, 228 Mont. 106, 741 P.2d 755 (1987), the court faced the "common interest" privilege, which § 27-1-804(3) states is available only for statements made "without malice." Although the court focused on the constitutional malice standard, it also listed the following ways in which a privilege can be lost through abuse: excessive publication, use of the occasion for an improper purpose, and lack of belief or grounds for belief in the truth of the statement. Rasmussen, 228 Mont. at 111, 741 P.2d at 758 (citing Prosser, Law of Torts, 4th ed. § 115, p. 796).

e. **Question of Fact or Law.** Whether a statement is privileged is a question of law for the court to decide, but whether a qualified privilege has been abused and thus lost is a question for the jury. Hale v. City of Billings, 295 Mont. 495, ¶ 35, 986 P.2d 413, 421, 28 Media L. Rep. 1321 (1999).

f. **Burden of Proof.** The plaintiff bears the burden of showing that a qualified privilege has been abused. Rasmussen v. Bennett, 228 Mont. 106, 111, 741 P.2d 755, 758 (1987).

B. Standard Libel Defenses

1. ***Truth.*** Truth is an absolute defense to a defamation claim; a publication which is truthful cannot constitute slander or libel. Mont. Code Ann. §§ 27-1-802, 803. See also Griffin v. Opinion Pub. Co., 114 Mont. 502,138 P.2d 580 (1943); Citizens First Nat'l Bank v. Moe Motor Co., 248 Mont. 495, 813 P.2d 400 (1991). Montana's criminal defamation statute, Mont. Code Ann. § 45-8-212(3)(a), formerly provided that truth was a defense to defamation only if the statement was "communicated with good motives and for justifiable ends." In State v. Helfrich, 277 Mont. 457, 922 P.2d

1159 (1996), the court held that this provision was unconstitutional, determining that truth is a defense even when the offending publication is not made "with good motives and for justifiable ends." The statute has since been amended to conform to this decision.

2. ***Opinion.*** Opinions cannot generally be considered defamation. A supervisor's opinion of an employee is not actionable when expressed in the context of the evaluating the employee's job performance. Frigon v. Morrison-Maierle, Inc., 233 Mont. 113, 760 P.2d 57 (1988). But in Hale v. City of Billings, 295 Mont. 495, 986 P.2d 413, 28 Media L. Rep. 1321 (1999), the court held that if an opinion creates a reasonable inference that it is based on undisclosed defamatory facts, it can give rise to liability for defamation. Such a statement of opinion can cause damages and is actionable only if it contains a provably false connotation or can reasonably be interpreted as stating facts about an individual.

3. ***Consent.*** Consent of the person defamed is an absolute defense. Griffin v. Opinion Pub. Co., 114 Mont. 502, 138 P.2d 580 (1943) (overruled on other grounds by State v. Helfrich, 277 Mont. 452, 922 P.2d 1159, 1161 n. 1 (1996)).

4. ***Mitigation.*** Montana Code Annotated 27-1-818 requires a defamed person to give those alleged to be responsible for publication or broadcast a reasonable opportunity to correct the defamatory matter.

III. RECURRING FACT PATTERNS

A. Statements in Personnel File

Montana has no reported decisions on the actionability of defamatory statements contained in personnel files. However, in Montana Human Rights Division v. City of Billings, 199 Mont. 434, 649 P.2d 1283 (1982), the court held that an employer has standing to challenge a subpoena for such information where disclosure could result in the employer's liability for invading employees' privacy.

B. Performance Evaluations

Supervisors' opinions expressed in the context of evaluating performance are generally not actionable. Frigon v. Morrison-Maierle, Inc., 233 Mont. 113, 760 P.2d 57 (1988), overruled on other grounds, Sacco v. High Country Indep. Press, Inc., 271 Mont. 209, 896 P.2d 411 (1995). An employee may, however, have a right of privacy in this information. Missoulian v. Bd. of Regents, 207 Mont. 513, 675 P.2d 962 (1984) (holding that public university president had protected privacy interest in performance evaluation).

C. References

Montana has two statutes that deal with providing information about a discharged employee. Mont. Code Ann. § 39 -2-802 protects discharged employees from prior employers making statements by word or in writing that would prevent employee from obtaining future employment. The statute does not prohibit employers "from informing by word or writing any person to whom such discharged person or employee has applied for employment a truthful statement of the reason for such discharge." Mont. Code Ann. § 39-2-803 prohibits blacklisting of discharged employees.

D. Intracorporate Communication

No reported decisions in Montana.

E. Statements to Government Regulators

No reported decisions in Montana

F. Reports to Auditors and Insurers

No reported decisions in Montana.

G. Vicarious Liability of Employers for Statements Made by Employees

An employer is liable for actions of its employee, if the employee was acting within the scope of employment at the instance of injury. Keller v. Safeway Stores, Inc., 111 Mont 28, 108 P.2d 605 (1940). "Respondent superior imposes liability on an employer for the wrongful acts of an employee which are committed within the scope of his employment. ... The servant or agent must have been acting in the course of his employment, in furtherance of his employer's interest, or for the benefit of his master; in the scope of his employment, etc. But a servant who acts entirely for his own benefit is generally held to be outside the scope of his employment and the master is relieved of liability." Maguire v. Montana, 254 Mont. 178, 182, 835 P.2d 755, 758 (1992) (internal quotation marks omitted). An employer is not liable for an employee's defamatory statements if the statements were not made in the course and scope of employment. Wall v. Corral West Ranchwear, Inc., 17 Mont. Fed. Rep. 489 (1994).

1. ***Scope of Employment.*** Montana determines if the injury was caused during the scope of the employee's employment. "The tort of an agent is within the course of his employment where the agent, in performing it, is endeavoring to promote the principal's business." Keller v. Safeway Stores, Inc., 111 Mont 28, 108 P.2d 605, 611 (1940). The determination of whether an employee is acting within the scope of his employment is a factual inquiry. MacPheat v. Schauf, 308 Mont. 215, 41 P.3d 895 (2002). In Denke v. Shoemaker, 2008 MT 418, 347 Mont. 322, 194 P.3d 284 the Montana Supreme Court held that a city commissioner was acting within the course and scope of his employment rendering the city liable for his retaliatory conduct in writing letters containing false information designed to harm the city clerk. The Court rejected the City's argument that illegal activity cannot fall within the course and scope of employment and when acting as a legislator he was immune from liability.

a. **Blogging**. There are no cases addressing employers' liability for comments on employee's authorized or unauthorized blogs.

2. ***Damages.*** Montana cases have not distinguished the damages that may be recovered from a vicariously liable employer from those that may be recovered from any other defendant.

H. Internal Investigations

There are no cases addressing application of libel law to an employer's internal investigations. But see generally, Section III (c) on References.

IV. OTHER ACTIONS BASED ON STATEMENTS

A. Negligent Hiring, Retention, and Supervision

Montana recognizes claims for negligent hiring, retention, and supervision. Maguire v. Montana, 254 Mont. 178, 835 P.2d 755 (1992); see also Bruner v. Yellowstone County, 272 Mont. 261, 900 P.2d 901 (1995) (affirming summary judgment on negligent retention claim where conduct complained of was subject to discrimination law). However, there are no reported decisions involving such claims based solely on statements.

B. Intentional Infliction of Emotional Distress

Montana allows an independent cause of action for intentional infliction of emotional distress. Sacco v. High Country Indep. Press, 271 Mont. 209, 896 P.2d 411 (1995). The court in Sacco adopted the Restatement (Second) of Torts § 46 in defining "serious" emotional distress. That standard requires "extreme and outrageous conduct" which goes so far "beyond all possible bounds of decency" that is "regarded as atrocious, and utterly intolerable in a civilized community." Sacco, 271 Mont. at 235-36, 896 P.2d at 427 (quoting Restatement (Second) of Torts § 46). In Bleek v. Supervalu, Inc., 25 Mont. Fed. Rep. 5, 11-12 (D. Mont. 1999), the Montana Federal District Court found that material issues of fact precluded summary judgment where the employee was diagnosed with post-traumatic stress disorder prior to termination, employer knew about the PTSD diagnosis, and the terminated employee claimed severe emotional distress because of his peculiar susceptibility to stress. In Jacobsen v. Allstate Ins. Co., 2009 MT 248, 351 Mont. 464, 206 P.3d, 351, WL 2217529, the Supreme Court held that the requirement to show serious or severe emotional distress applies only to independent claims of negligent or intentional infliction of emotional distress, but a plaintiff need not make a threshold showing of serious or severe emotional distress before a claim for emotional distress damages parasitic to an underlying tort is allowed to go to the jury; overruling First Bank (N.A.)-Billings v. Clark, 236 Mont. 195, 771 P.2d 84; see also Amondson v. North West Corp., 2009 MT 331, 353 Mont. 28, 220 P.3d 1 (2009); Johnson v. Supersave Markets, Inc., 211 Mont. 465, 686 P.2d 209; Noonan v. First Bank Butte, 227 Mont. 329, 740 P.2d 631.

C. Interference with Economic Advantage

Montana allows an action for tortious interference with contractual or business relations. To establish a prima facie case of interference with contractual, employment, or business relations, it must be shown that the acts 1) were intentional and willful; 2) were calculated to cause damage to the plaintiff in his or her business; 3) were done with the unlawful purpose of causing damage or loss, without right or justifiable cause on the part of the actor; and 4) resulted in actual damages and loss. Hardy v. Vision Service Plan, 328 Mont. 385, 390, 120 P.3d 402, 406 (2005); Bolz v. Myers, 200 Mont. 286, 295, 651 P.2d 606, 611 (1982). In an unpublished Montana Supreme Court decision in Jacobsen v. Montana, 294 Mont. 554, 996 P.2d 884 (1999), plaintiff, an elected official, was suspended for actions relating to his employment as city-county coroner, unsuccessfully prosecuted, and then reinstated to his former position. After losing his bid for reelection following his acquittal, plaintiff claimed interference with economic or business advantage. The Supreme Court found that plaintiff was paid retroactively after he was acquitted, the prosecution was done with a lawful purpose, and that any claim that he lost the election due to bad publicity was speculative, in affirming summary judgment for respondents. In Nelson v. Livingston Rebuild Center, Inc., 294 Mont. 408, 410, 981 P.2d 1185, 1186 (1999), plaintiff's claim for wrongful discharge included an allegation that defendants intentionally and maliciously interfered with his right to receive unemployment benefits. The arbitrator concluded that plaintiff had not proven his claim for interference with unemployment benefits and awarded no damages on that count.

D. Prima Facie Tort

The Montana Supreme Court has addressed the prima facie tort doctrine only in the context of insurance bad faith. Lipinski v. Title Ins. Co., 202 Mont. 1, 655 P.2d 970 (1982).

V. OTHER ISSUES

A. Statute of Limitations

The statute of limitations for a defamation claim -- whether for libel or slander -- is two (2) years. Mont. Code Ann. § 27-2-204(1). Montana follows the multi-publication rule, so that a new tort occurs each time a magazine containing defamatory material is sold or distributed. Lewis v. Reader's Digest, 162 Mont. 401, 512 P.2d 702 (1973).

In Edwards v. Cascade County Sheriff, 2009 MT 451, 354 Mont. 307, 223 P.3d 187 (2009), the Court ruled that a tort claim for discharge based on political beliefs was barred by the exclusive remedy provisions of the Human Rights Act, when the plaintiff failed to file an administrative claim under the Act within the 180 day statute of limitations.

B. Jurisdiction

Montana has no reported decisions.

C. Worker's Compensation Exclusivity

Mont. Code Ann. § 39-71-411, provides, the right to recover compensation for occupational diseases and injuries sustained by an employee and arising out of and in the course of employment, whether resulting in death or not, is the exclusive remedy against an employer who is properly insured under the Workers' Compensation Act and the Occupational Disease Act of Montana. This provision does not apply to willful, intentional or malicious acts of the employer or co-employees, Mont. Code Ann. § 39-71-413. To show malice and avoid exclusivity, a tort claimant must establish that the employer acted intentionally or had "knowledge of facts or intentionally disregarded facts that created a high probability of injury and: (a) deliberately proceeded to act in conscious or intentional disregard of the high probability of injury; or (b) deliberately proceeded to act with indifference to the high probability of injury. Mont. Code Ann. § 27-1-221(2). Sherner v. Conoco, Inc., 2000 MT 50, 298 Mont. 401, 995 P.2d 990. An injured worker also retains rights against a third party whose negligence was the cause of the injury. Mont. Code Ann § 39-71-412.

D. Pleading Requirements

To recover damages for a defamation claim, plaintiff must plead defamation in the complaint as a separate and independent claim from any claim for wrongful discharge. Ruzicka v. First Healthcare Corp., 45 F.Supp.2d 809 (D. Mont. 1997). In a recent case, the Montana Supreme Court held that the doctrine of *res judicata* precluded litigation of a defamation claim raised in a second action that could have been raised in the first suit. See Xu v. McLaughlin Research Institute for Biomedical Science, Inc., 328 Mont. 232, 119 P.3d 100 (2005).

SURVEY OF MONTANA EMPLOYMENT PRIVACY LAW

Peter Michael Meloy
Meloy Law Firm
P.O. Box 1241, 80 So. Warren
Helena, MT 59601
Tel: 406-442-8670; Fax: 406-442-4953

(With Developments Reported Through **November 1, 2012**)

GENERAL COMMENTS

The Montana Supreme Court has adopted a vendor-neutral citation system for briefs submitted to the court after Jan. 1, 1998. This citation includes the calendar year in which the opinion or substantive order is issued, followed by the Montana U.S. Postal Code (MT), followed by a consecutive number beginning each year with "1" (for example, 1998 MT 1). For opinions which are not to be cited as precedent and for all substantive orders, the consecutive number is followed by the letter "N." This citation should be followed by regular, vendor-based citations (e.g, Doe v. Roe, 1998 MT 12,286 Mont. 175,989 P.2d 1312). See In Re: the Matter of Opinion Forms and Citation Standards of the Supreme Court of Montana; and the Adoption of a Form of Public Domain and Neutral-format Citation (Mont. Dec. 17, 1997).

While the Montana Supreme Court requires use of its vendor neutral system, the reporters contain a mix of the Montana preferred cite and the standard citation format. This outline intermixes them, to permit easy access to the cases. An attorney preparing a brief for the Montana Supreme Court would need find the MT cite for cases decided after 1998. (But even the Supreme Court does not always use the MT cite in its opinions.)

SIGNIFICANT DEVELOPMENTS SINCE THE 2012 *SURVEY*

In Billings Gazette v. City of Billings, 2011 MT 293, 362 Mont. 522, 267 P.3d 11 (Nov. 23, 2011), the Montana Supreme Court ruled that a former city employee did not have a reasonable expectation of privacy with respect to a letter from a police captain contained in her personnel file detailing the employee's alleged misuse of a city credit card.

I. GENERAL LAW OF PRIVACY

A. Legal Basis of Privacy Claim

Montana citizens are guaranteed an individual right of privacy under the Montana Constitution. Montana Constitution, Article II, Section 10. "Montana has a strong tradition of respect for the right of individual privacy." State v. Bullock, 272 Mont. 361, 383, 901 P.2d 61, 75 (1995). The constitutional right of privacy extends only to individual human persons and not to "non-human entities" such as corporations. The Great Falls Tribune v. The Montana Public Service Commission, 2003 MT 359, 319 Mont. 38, 82 P.3d 876. This right provides "significantly broader protection than does the federal constitution." Armstrong v. State, 1999 MT 261, ¶ 41, 296 Mont. 361, 989 P.2d 364. In a recent criminal case, the Montana Supreme Court provided a comprehensive summary of cases decided under the privacy provisions of the Montana Constitution, concluding that electronic monitoring of a suspect without his knowledge or consent violated his privacy rights. State v. Goetz, 2008 MT 296, 345 Mont. 421, 191 P.3d 489.

Montana courts have developed a two-part test to determine if a privacy interest is protected under the Montana Constitution. The test is 1) whether the person involved had a subjective or actual expectation of privacy; 2) whether society is willing to recognize that expectation as reasonable. State ex rel Great Falls Tribune Company v. Eighth Judicial District Court, 238 Mont. 310, 777 P.2d 345 (1989); Montana Human Rights Division v. City of Billings, 199 Mont. 434, 440-41, 649 P.2d 1283, 1287 (1982).

There is no expectation of privacy in the last four digits of a Social Security number for use on conservation licenses. Montana Shooting Sports Assn. v State, 2010 MT 8, 355 Mont. 49, 224 P.3d 1240 (2010).

B. Causes of Action

The Montana Constitution protects individuals from "unlawful governmental intrusion into one's privacy." Deserly v. Dept. of Corrections, 298 Mont. 328, ¶ 16, 995 P.2d 972 (2000). Thus, when privacy is invaded by a public entity, the victim can look to the Montana Constitution as the source of a claim for relief. In this regard, the court will look to the following factors: "(1) whether the person has an actual expectation of privacy; (2) whether society is willing to recognize that expectation as objectively reasonable; and (3) the nature of the state's intrusion." Id. at ¶ 16. Money damages are available for violation of rights protected by the Montana Constitution. Dorwart v. Caraway, 312 Mont. 1, 16, 58 P.3d 128, 137 (2002). Furthermore, qualified immunity is not applicable to such claims. Id. at 21, 58 P.3d at 140.

In an unpublished opinion, the Court held that individuals do not have a cause of action against a private citizen alleged to have violated right of privacy because the citizen is not acting under color of state law. Quam v. Halverson, 2010 MT 158N, WL 2842736.

1. ***Misappropriation/Right of Publicity.*** No reported cases in Montana.

2. ***False Light.*** The elements of a false light invasion of privacy claim are "(1) the publicizing of a matter concerning another that (2) places the other before the public in a false light, when (3) the false light in which the other is placed would be highly offensive to a reasonable person, and (4) the actor knew of or acted in reckless disregard as to the falsity of the publicized matter." Lence v. Hagadone Inv. Co., 258 Mont. 433, 444, 853 P.2d 1230, 1237 (1993) overruled on other grounds by Sacco v. High County Ind. Press, 258 Mont. 433, 853 P.2d 1230 (1993). Plaintiff must establish the falsity of the publication to prove a false light invasion of privacy claim. Id. In a situation where an individual requests that a meeting discussing a complaint filed against him be open to public, he waives his privacy claim of false light and releasing private facts to public. Board of Dentistry v. Kandarian, 268 Mont. 408, 886 P.2d 954 (1994).

3. ***Publication of Private Facts.*** In discussing the tort, the Montana court referenced the Restatement (Second) of Torts, § 652(d) which sets out the elements of public disclosure of private facts as follows: "One who gives publicity to a matter concerning the private life of another is subject to liability to the other for invasion of his privacy, if the matter publicized is of a kind that (a) would be highly offensive to a reasonable person, and (b) is not of legitimate concern to the public." Kandarian, 268 Mont. at 414, 886 P.2d at 957 (1994).

4. ***Intrusion.*** Montana recognizes an invasion of privacy tort theory. Invasion of privacy is defined as "a wrongful intrusion into one's private activities in such a manner as to outrage or cause mental suffering, shame, or humiliation to a person of ordinary sensibilities." Rucinsky v. Hentchel, 266 Mont. 502, 505, 881 P.2d 616, 618 (1994). The Court found no authority to support an employee's invasion of privacy tort claim when the employer asked the sheriff to attend a meeting "to keep the peace." Koepplin v. Zortman Mining, Inc., 267 Mont. 53, 881 P.2d 1306 (1994). If discovery of information is made by a person with a right to access that information, there is no violation. Thus, a justice of the peace had no privacy right in sexually explicit material accessed on a county-owned computer located in his county office where the material was discovered by an employee shutting down the office network. Harris v. Smartt, 2002 MT 239, 311 Mont. 507, 57 P.3d 58.

C. Other Privacy-related Actions

1. ***Intentional Infliction of Emotional Distress.*** Montana allows an independent cause of action for "infliction of emotional distress" "under circumstances where serious or severe emotional distress to the plaintiff was the reasonably foreseeable consequence of the defendant's negligent or intentional act or omission." Sacco v. High Country Independent Press, 271 Mont. 209, 237, 896 P.2d 411, 418 (1995). In Sacco, the court adopted the Restatement (Second) of Torts § 46 in defining "serious or severe" emotional distress. It should be noted that the tort itself is not subject to the analysis found in the Restatement as the actor's conduct does not have to be "outrageous." Judd v. The Burlington Northern and Santa Fe Railway Co., 2008 MT 181, ¶31, 343 Mont.416, ¶31, 186 P.3d 214, ¶31. But, "a privileged action cannot become the basis for such a claim." Id. In Judd, the court reiterated that an actor cannot be liable for infliction of emotional distress when he or she merely insists upon his or her legal rights. Id. at ¶30. In Jacobsen v. Allstate Ins. Co, 2009 MT 248, 206 P.3d 351, 351 Mont. 464, the Supreme Court held that the requirement to show serious or severe emotional distress applies only to independent claims of negligent or intentional infliction of emotional distress, but a plaintiff need not make a threshold showing of serious or severe emotional distress before a claim for emotional distress damages parasitic to an underlying tort is allowed to go to the jury; overruling First Bank (N.A.)-Billings v. Clark, 236 Mont. 195, 771 P.2d 84 Johnson v. Supersave Markets, Inc., 211 Mont. 465, 686 P.2d 209; Noonan v. First Bank Butte, 227 Mont. 329, 740 P.2d 631.

In Klein v. State, 2008 MT 189, 343 Mont. 520, 185 P.3d 986, the Montana Supreme Court held that a union employee of the state was not bound under her collective bargaining agreement to grieve or arbitrate tort claims for deceit and negligent infliction of emotional distress. The decision rested on the court's determination that the arbitration clause in the collective bargaining agreement was narrow and did not encompass the emotional distress claim. To decide that claim, the court was not required to interpret the collective bargaining agreement

2. ***Interference With Prospective Economic Advantage.*** Montana allows an action for tortious interference with contractual or business relations. To establish a prima facie case of interference with contractual, employment, or business relations, it must be shown that "the acts 1) were intentional and willful; 2) were calculated to cause damage to the pleader in his or her business; 3) were done with the unlawful purpose of causing damage or loss, without right

or justifiable cause on the part of the actor; and 4) that actual damages and loss resulted." Bolz v. Myers, 200 Mont. 286, 295, 651 P.2d 606, 611 (1982). See also Farrington v. Buttrey Food and Drug Stores, 272 Mont. 140, 900 P.2d 277 (1995) (question of fact as to whether grocery store's complete ban of delivery man from its premises, resulting in loss of delivery job, was justified under the circumstances).

3. ***Prima Facie Tort.*** Montana has not recognized this cause of action. Pospisil v. First Nat. Bank of Lewistown, 2001 MT 286, ¶27, 307 Mont. 392, 37 P.3d 704.

II. EMPLOYER TESTING OF EMPLOYEES

A. Psychological or Personality Testing

No reported cases in Montana.

B. Drug Testing

1. ***Common Law and Statutes.*** Mont. Code Ann. §§ 39-2-205 through -211 allows drug testing only in certain situations, under a qualified testing program, and allows for an employee's right of rebuttal should the test prove positive. The statute provides a limitation on adverse actions by employers if the employee presents a reasonable explanation or medical opinion regarding the test results, as well as providing conditions of confidentiality of test results. Montana has not established a difference between public employers and private employers in this regard.

2. ***Private Employers.*** In an unpublished opinion in Johnson v. Columbia Falls Aluminum Co., 350 Mont. 562, Slip Copy, 2009 WL 865308 (Table) (Mont., 2009), the Montana Supreme Court held that a drug testing policy in a collective bargaining agreement between a union and private employer did not violate the right of privacy because it was not state action.

3. ***Public Employers.*** See II.B.1, supra.

C. Medical Testing

Medical testing is allowed in Montana, however Mont. Code Ann. § 39-2-301 makes it unlawful for an employer to require an employee to pay the cost of a medical examination or the cost of furnishing any records of such an examination as a condition of employment. Montana has not established a difference between public employers and private employers in this regard.

While the withdrawal of blood by a government entity is considered a search, "consent constitutes a waiver of any reasonable expectation of privacy." State v. Notti, 2003 MT 170, ¶ 19, 316 Mont. 345, 71 P.3d 1233. Thus, in Notti, the court rejected the defendant's claim that creation of a DNA profile from a blood sample violated his right of privacy. The taking of blood might be implicated in connection with employer drug testing, but no cases have yet been decided in Montana on that issue.

D. Polygraph Tests

Montana does not allow employers to conduct polygraph or lie detector tests as a condition of employment or continuation of employment. Mont. Code Ann. § 39-2-304.

E. Fingerprinting

Montana does not have a statute or case law addressing fingerprinting in the workplace. Some professions, however, require fingerprinting as a condition of licensing, i.e., gaming employees and agents, Mont. Code Ann. § 23-7-306; applicants for admission to the state bar, Rules for Admission to the Bar, 247 Mont. 1; public safety communications officers, Mont. Code Ann. § 7-31-202; peace officers, Mont Code Ann. § 7-32-303; reserve officers, Mont. Code Ann. § 7-32-213; applicants for a license to operate a youth care facility, Mont. Code Ann. § 52-2-622.

III. SEARCHES

An individual's right to be free from unreasonable searches is provided for in the Fourth Amendment to the United States Constitution and Article II, Section 10 of the Montana Constitution. Harris v. Smartt, 2002 MT 239, ¶ 65, 311 Mont. 507, 57 P.3d 58. This right is "augmented" by Article II, Section 10 of the Montana Constitution, which provides for an individual right of privacy. State v. Smith, 2004 MT 234, ¶ 9, 322 Mont. 466, 97 P.3d 567. The two sections must be read together. Id.

The Montana court has held that, "[T]he threshold question in analyzing search and seizure issues is whether the person asserting invasion of these constitutional rights has a legitimate expectation of privacy in the area invaded." Dorwart v. Caraway, 1998 MT 191, ¶ 25, 290 Mont. 196, 966 P.2d 1121, overruled on other grounds in Trustees of Indiana Univ. v. Buxbaum, 315 Mont. 210, 69 P.3d 663 (2003). In State v. Smith, *supra*, the Montana Supreme Court held that a party guest had no legitimate expectation of privacy in the common areas of an apartment belonging to her host. She did, however, have a legitimate expectation of privacy in the apartment bathroom. Thus, the court held that a law enforcement officer's entry into the bathroom while occupied by Smith was not justified by "the community caretaker doctrine." NOTE: The community caretaker doctrine holds that law enforcement officers "have a duty not only to fight crime, but to investigate uncertain situations in order to ensure public safety." Id.

In determining whether an individual's expectation of privacy is "reasonable" the court will look at the facts of each case. State v. Dunn, 2007 MT 296, 340 Mont. 31, 172 P.3d 110. In Dunn, the court found that the defendant could not reasonably expect his fenced back yard was private where he was disturbing the peace by playing loud music and was smoking marijuana in the yard. Similarly, an individual has no expectation of privacy in the license plate on her automobile as the plate is public information. State v. Thomas, 2008 MT 206, 344 Mont. 150, 186 P.3d 864.

The United States Court of Appeals for the Ninth Circuit, on rehearing, held that a Montana employee could have a reasonable expectation of privacy in his office and in his workplace computer based upon the fact that his office was not shared with co-workers and was kept locked. The court, nonetheless held that a search of the worker's computer was reasonable because his employer retained control over the computer and gave consent to the search. The employer owned and regularly monitored workplace computers, informed employees that employee usage would be audited, and had a policy prohibiting employees from using work computers for anything other than official business. United States v. Ziegler, 474 F.3d 1184, 1192 (9th Cir. 2007). Ziegler was a criminal case where the defendant argued that evidence of child pornography found on the hard drive of his workplace computer should be suppressed because law enforcement had no warrant to search the computer.

A. Employee's Person

An employee frisked by a sheriff during a termination meeting does not have a claim for invasion of privacy when the employer did not participate in the decision to frisk the employee. Koepplin v. Zortman Mining, Inc., 267 Mont. 53, 881 P.2d 1306 (1994). The employer asked the county sheriff to be present at termination meeting to keep the peace. The sheriff made an independent decision to frisk the employee as he entered the meeting. No agency relationship was established and the employer did not proximately cause an invasion of privacy. Id. at 62, 881 P.2d at 1312.

The standard to be applied to personal searches was set out in Deserly v. Department of Corrections, 2002 MT 42, 298 Mont. 328, 995 P.2d 972. There, the court applied a balancing test to determine whether the wife of a prisoner could bring a claim based upon a warrantless strip search of her person. The court found that such searches were a permissible intrusion into the individual's right of privacy only if the search was supported by particularized "reasonable suspicion." Id. at ¶ 29. The court balanced the government's interest in security against the individual's right of privacy, noting that "requiring a person to take off his or her clothing in front of another person or persons, no matter how professionally and courteously conducted, is a degrading, embarrassing and humiliating experience, and an invasion of personal privacy." Id. at ¶ 28.

B. Employee's Work Area

Entry into county justice of the peace office to shut down a county-owned computer was not a search and, thus, sexually explicit material found by other employees was not excluded in disciplinary proceeding. Harris, 311 Mont. at 522, 57 P.3d at 68. An employer can protect itself by informing employees that computers and work areas belong to the employer, will be monitored regularly, and prohibiting use of computers for anything other than official business. United States v. Ziegler, 474 F.3d 1184, 1192 (9th Cir. 2007).

C. Employee's Property

See IIIB. supra. With regard to objects, the court has held that "an actual or subjective expectation of privacy" can be demonstrated when one places "an object beyond the purview of the public in a place from which the person has the right to exclude others." State v. Hill, 2004 MT 184, ¶ 25, 322 Mont. 165, 94 P.3d 752. The defendant in Hill was found to have no right to exclude officers from a rental car that he was driving unlawfully and without permission. Id. If an individual fails to take steps to protect his property from the public, then he may lose any protection the property has. Thus, an individual has no expectation of privacy in the license plate on her automobile as the plate is public information. State v. Thomas, 2008 MT 206, 344 Mont. 150, 186 P.3d 864. The court has also upheld a warrantless search of garbage cans on an open wooden rack in the alley behind a suspect's home. State of Montana v. a Blue in Color, 1993 Chevrolet Pickup, et al., 2005 MT 180, 328 Mont. 10, 116 P.3d 800. In the criminal context, however, the court will require "individual suspicion that a crime is being committed" before law enforcement officers can rummage through someone's trash. Id. at ¶ 19.

IV. MONITORING OF EMPLOYEES

A. Telephones and Electronic Communications

With some exceptions, private communications are protected from intrusion by both public and private entities in Montana. Under the Privacy in Communications statute, Mont. Code Ann. § 45-8-213, "electronic communications" cannot be recorded without the knowledge of all parties to the conversation. Similarly, it is a crime if a person "purposely intercepts an electronic communication." This particular subsection "does not apply to elected or appointed public officials or employees when the interception is done in the performance of official duty or to persons given warning of the interception." Id. The privacy in communications statute was amended by the 2005 Legislature to exclude emergency telephone communications made to healthcare facilities or government agencies. See Section VI.B. *infra.* See also State v. DuBray, 2003 MT 255, 317 Mont. 377, 77 P.3d 247 (prisoner had no expectation of privacy in telephone communications where he had been adequately notified that calls would be monitored and recorded).

1. ***Wiretapping.*** See IV.A., supra. Phone tapping of private, confidential conversations constitutes a wrongful intrusion into one's private activities in a manner likely to cause outrage, mental suffering, shame, or humiliation to an ordinary person. Rucinsky v. Hentchel, 266 Mont. 502, 881 P.2d 616 (1994).

2. ***Electronic Communications.*** See IV.A., supra. The federal district court in Montana has found taping voicemail messages is not an invasion of privacy because the person leaving the message has consented to the recording of their message by the fact that they left the message. Payne v. Norwest Corporation, et. al., 911 F. Supp. 1299, 20 Montana Federal Reports 398 (D. Mont. 1995), *rev'd on other grounds*, 113 F.3d 1079 (9th Cir. 1999). The Payne court was interpreting a federal statute and not state law. Without reference to the Privacy in Communications statute, the Montana Supreme Court has held that electronic monitoring of a suspect without his knowledge or consent violated his privacy rights. State v. Goetz, 2008 MT 296, 345 Mont. 421, 191 P.3d 489. There, the court was persuaded that a person being surreptitiously monitored and recorded while speaking with another person in his own home or vehicle had a reasonable expectation of privacy in the one-on-one conversation. Id. at ¶37.

3. ***Other Electronic Monitoring.*** See section III.B. above.

B. Mail

See IV.A. above. Previous prohibition repealed.

C. Surveillance/Photographing

Use of thermal imaging to search for heat generated by cultivation of marijuana is an illegal search. State v. Siegal, 281 Mont. 250, 279, 934 P.2d 176, 193 (1997), overruled on other grounds in State v. Kuneff, 1998 MT 287, 91 Mont. 474, 970 P.2d 556. In Siegal the court relied on the Montana constitutional right of privacy and noted that delegates to the 1972 Montana constitutional convention had specifically expressed concern about governmental intrusion by means of electronic or photographic surveillance equipment. Id. at 264, 276, 934 P.2d at 184, 191.

V. ACTIVITIES OUTSIDE THE WORKPLACE

A. Statute or Common Law

With a few exceptions, an employer cannot refuse to employ or license, and may not discriminate against an individual with respect to compensation, promotion, or the terms, conditions, or privileges of employment because the individual uses a lawful product off the employer's premises during nonworking hours. Mont. Code Ann. § 39-2-313 (2).

B. Employees' Personal Relationships

1. ***Romantic Relationships Between Employees.*** Employees cohabitating outside of the marital relationship would be construed as protected under Mont. Code Ann. § 49-2-303 and Mont. Code Ann. § 49-3-201. Chaplin v. RJR Nabisco, Inc. et al., 6 Mont. Federal Reports 196 (1990).

2. ***Sexual Orientation.*** Although there are no reported employment cases in Montana, the Montana Supreme Court has held that the right of privacy set out in the Montana Constitution "includes the right to engage in consensual, non-commercial, private, same-gender sexual conduct with other adults free of governmental interference or regulation." Gryczan v. State, 283 Mont. 433, 451, 942 P.2d 112, 123 (1997). In

The court has also held that Montana's public university system's health insurance plan violated the equal protection clause of the State Constitution because it allowed opposite sex couples who weren't married in the traditional way to gain coverage by signing an affidavit called a Declaration of Common-Law Spouse. Because the plan did not allow same-sex couples this opportunity, it was unconstitutional. In reaching its decision, the court said "We do make clear, however, that any organization that adopts an administrative procedure in order to provide employment benefits to opposite-sex partners who may not be in a legal marriage relationship, must do the same for same-sex couples. To not do so violates equal protection." Snetsinger, et al. v. Montana University System, et al., 2004 MT 390, ¶ 35, 325 Mont. 148, 104 P.3d 445.

3. ***Marital Status.*** Employees cannot be discriminated against because of marital status. Mont. Code Ann. § 49-2-303 and Mont. Code Ann. § 49-3-201. Vortex Fishing Systems, Inc. 303 Mont. 8, 38 P.3d 836 (2001) (employee denied continued employment after he announced intent to marry co-worker was a victim of marital status discrimination).

C. Smoking

The 2005 Montana Legislature made significant changes to the rules governing smoking in the workplace. Effective October 1, 2005, most workplaces must be completely nonsmoking. There is no smoking in public school buildings or on public school property. Similarly, any "indoor area, room, or vehicle" that is open to the general public or is a place of work must be smoke-free. Mont. Code Ann. § 50-40-104. Conversely, Montana protects the rights of smokers by prohibiting discrimination against employees who use tobacco products on their own time. Mont. Code Ann. § 39-2-313(1); McGillen v. Plum Creek Timber Co., 290 Mont. 264, 964 P.2d 18 (1998).

D. Blogging

No case law.

VI. RECORDS

A. Personnel Records

Employees have a privacy interest in their personnel files, applications and performance evaluations. Montana Human Rights Division v. City of Billings, 199 Mont. 434, 649 P.2d 1283 (1982); Missoulian v. Board of Regents of Higher Education, 207 Mont. 513, 675 P.2d 962 (1984). Similarly, social security numbers and driver's license numbers are protected. Jefferson County v. Montana Standard, 2003 MT 304, ¶ 20, 318 Mont. 173, ¶ 20, 79 P.3d 805, ¶ 20.

The privacy rights in a public employee's personnel records must be weighed against the public's right to know. Personnel records may be discoverable given the correct set of circumstance and after appropriate balancing tests are considered. State v. Burns, 253 Mont. 37, 830 P.2d 1318 (1992). An employer can refuse to disclose personal information of employees and applicants for employment if it would place the employer in jeopardy of being sued. The employer's potential economic injury is sufficient to establish standing to challenge a third party's attempts to obtain personnel records. Montana Human Rights Div. v. City Of Billings, 199 Mont. 434, 649 P.2d 1283 (1982).

The law favors the public's right to examine public records and will generally allow disclosure with only private information deleted or redacted. Yellowstone County v. Billings Gazette, 2006 MT 218, 333 Mont. 390, 143 P.3d 135, ¶ 27; City of Billings Police Department v. Owen, 2006 MT 16, ¶ 30, 331 Mont. 10, ¶ 30, 127 P.3d 1044, ¶ 30. The right to know can be waived. In Lee v. City of Missoula, 2008 MT 186, 343 MT 487, 187 P.3d 609, an applicant who was rejected by the police department because of a background investigation, demanded to see the contents of the investigative file. The department refused based upon the privacy interests of those who gave information. The Montana Supreme Court affirmed, declining to address the privacy rights of the informants, but finding that the plaintiff had executed a document that said he understood that the information would not be released "to any person, including myself." Id. at ¶2.

The Montana Supreme Court let stand a decision of a state district court that public school teachers had no expectation of privacy in disciplinary documents in their personnel files, or "in their conduct as public employees." Billings High School Dist. No. 2 v. The Billings Gazette, 2006 MT 329, ¶2, 335 Mont. 94, ¶2, 149 P.3d 565, ¶2. The teachers had been disciplined for inappropriate sexual conduct on the school premises and the local newspaper sought details of the incident and the punishment given the teachers. The district court released certain records and the school district sought a declaratory ruling on the issue. The Montana Supreme Court declined to address the merits of the case because the documents had already been released. **In Billings Gazette v. City of Billings, 2011 MT 293, 362 Mont. 522, 267 P.3d 11 (2011), the Montana Supreme Court ruled that a former city employee did not have a reasonable expectation of privacy with respect to a letter from a police captain contained in her personnel file detailing the employee's alleged misuse of a city credit card.**

B. Medical Records

Individuals have a subjective or actual expectation of privacy in their medical records and society is willing to recognize that expectation as reasonable. The Montana Constitution "guarantee of privacy encompasses confidential 'informational privacy.'" St. James Community Hospital v. District Court, 2003 MT 261, ¶ 8, 317 Mont. 419, 77 P.3d 534. Medical records are quintessentially "private" and deserve the utmost constitutional protection. State v. Nelson, 283 Mont. 231, 941 P.2d 441 (1997). The Montana Uniform Health Care Information Act, Mont. Code Ann. § 50-16-501, et. seq., also protects records from disclosure by health care providers without certain safeguards. The 2005 Montana Legislature amended the Montana privacy in communications statute, Mont. Code Ann. § 45-8-213, to specifically provide that a healthcare facility or government agency that deals with healthcare does not commit the crime of violating privacy in communications if it records a healthcare emergency telephone communication made to the facility or agency.

An employer challenging the cause of an injury may not use unauthenticated medical records to impeach an employee about the cause, in fact, of his injury. Cheff v. BNSF Ry. Co., 2010 MT 235, 358 Mont. 144, 243 P.3d 1115.

C. Criminal Records

The Criminal Justice Information Act, Mont. Code Ann. § 44-5-101, et seq. provides for the confidentiality of criminal justice information, however, the court in In Re Lacy, 239 Mont. 321, 780 P.2d 186 (1989), held that it is the court's duty to balance the competing rights of individual privacy and the public's right to know and in order to determine what, if any information should be given to a party requesting criminal information. It is incumbent upon a party to make a proper showing in order to be eligible to receive such specific confidential information. When the records in question evidence criminal violations by an elected official, the Montana Supreme Court has held that the public's right to know overcomes the individual's right of privacy. Jefferson County v. Montana Standard, 2003 MT 304, 318 Mont. 173, 79 P.3d 805.

An employee has no expectation of privacy in his or her arrest record because arrest records are not considered to be confidential. They are public information. Barr v. Great Falls International Airport Authority, et al., 2005 MT 36, 326 Mont. 93, 107 P.3d 471. Barr was brought by an airport security officer whose employment was terminated based upon the results of a criminal background check. Although the plaintiff claimed that criminal justice information had to be kept confidential, the court found that the arrest information was public information that anyone could obtain. Similarly, information regarding allegations of misconduct by persons holding positions of public trust, here a teacher, need not be withheld from public scrutiny. Svaldi v. Anaconda-Deer Lodge County, 2005 MT 17, 325 Mont. 365, 106 P.3d 548. See also, Billings High School Dist. No. 2 v. The Billings Gazette, 2006 MT 329, ¶2, 335 Mont. 94, ¶2, 149 P.3d 565, ¶2.

Notwithstanding the provisions of the Criminal Justice Information Act, applicants for certain positions are required to submit to criminal background checks. These include public communications safety officers, Mont. Code Ann. § 7-31-202; peace officers, Mont. Code Ann. § 7-32-303; reserve officers, Mont. Code Ann. § 7-32-213; and persons operating youth care facilities, Mont. Code Ann. § 52-2-622.

D. Subpoenas / Search Warrants

The Montana Uniform Health Care Information Act requires consent or an appropriate subpoena for obtaining health care records. Mont. Code Ann. § 50-16-536 (2005).

VII. ACTIONS SUBSEQUENT TO EMPLOYMENT

A. References

Montana does not have a specific law governing references. It does have a "blacklisting" statute which prohibits employers who have discharged an employee from preventing or attempting to prevent "by word or writing of any kind such discharged employee from obtaining employment with any other person." Mont. Code Ann. § 39-2-802. The statute does not prohibit an employer from providing "a truthful statement of the reason for such discharge" to a prospective employer. Id. Violation of the statute is a misdemeanor and can subject the violator to a civil action for punitive damages as well. Mont. Code Ann. § 39-2-802.

B. Non-Compete Agreements.

In Montana, covenants not to compete are invalid unless they are both reasonable and limited. The court has said that three elements must be satisfied for a covenant to be valid: "(1) [I]t must be partial or restricted in its operation in respect either to time or place; (2) it must be on some good consideration; and (3) it must be reasonable, that is, it should afford only a fair protection to the interests of the party in whose favor it is made, and must not be so large in its operation as to interfere with the interests of the public." Access Organics, Inc. v. Hernandez, 2008 MT 4, ¶6, 341 Mont. 73, ¶6, 175 P.3d 899, ¶6. There, the court found that a covenant not to compete and a nondisclosure agreement executed by a former employee of the plaintiff was invalid because it was not supported by good consideration. The employee had not signed the agreement prior to hire, but some four months after he began employment and he was not given a raise or guaranteed a certain period of employment in exchange for the agreement. Thus, he received no benefit and the employer incurred no detriment that would serve as consideration for the agreement. The court has upheld a covenant not to compete where three employees of an accounting partnership agreed, if they left the business within 12 months and did work for firm clients, that they would pay to their former employer 100% of what their former firm had billed any clients in the 12 months preceding termination of employment. Dobbins DeGuire & Tucker, P.C. v. Rutherford MacDonald & Olson, 218 Mont. 392, 708 P.2d 577 (1985). An agreement which prevents an employee from engaging in her profession is not reasonable and is therefore an unlawful restraint on trade. Montana Mountain Products v. Curl, 2005 MT 102, 327 Mont. 7, 112 P.3d 979.

VIII. OTHER ISSUES

A. Statutes of Limitations

The applicable statute of limitations period for an action on a liability not founded upon an instrument in writing is three years. Mont. Code Ann. § 27-2-204(1). A wrongful discharge claim must be filed within one year from the date of discharge. Exhaustion of an internal grievance procedure may extend the statute for no more than one hundred twenty days. Mont. Code Ann. § 39-2-911.

B. Jurisdiction

Article VII, § 4(1) of the Montana Constitution grants broad jurisdiction to district courts in Montana. Mont. Const. art. V!I, § 4(1) (providing that "The district court has original jurisdiction in all criminal cases amounting to a felony and all civil matters and cases at law and in equity."). The Montana Supreme Court has appellate jurisdiction over final judgments from district courts and general supervisory control over all other courts. Mont. Const., Art. VII, Section 2.

In order to attain jurisdiction over employment privacy claims, courts must have proper personal and subject matter jurisdiction. Subject matter jurisdiction regarding non-discharge employment privacy claims is a non-issue because of the broad jurisdictional grant to district courts. For employment privacy claims arising out a discharge from employment must fall within the Wrongful Discharge from Employment Act. for the courts to exercise subject-matter jurisdiction. However, employers based outside of Montana may contest personal jurisdiction. The analysis for personal jurisdiction over a nonresident involves a two-part test: (1) determine whether the nonresident defendant has "minimum contacts" with the forum state under Rule 4B M.R.Civ.P., that justify an appearance in court there; and (2) determine whether the exercise of personal jurisdiction does not offend due process. Spectrum Pool Products v. MW Golden Inc., 291 Mont. 439, 968 P.2d 728 (1998). In determining whether exercise would offend due process, a three part test is required: (1) the non-resident actor must do something to avail himself of the privilege of conducting activities in Montana, (2) the claim must arise out of forum related activities and (3) exercise of jurisdiction must be reasonable. Id.

C. Worker's Compensation Exclusivity

Mont. Code Ann. § 39-71-411,provides, the right to recover compensation for occupational diseases and injuries sustained by an employee and arising out of and in the course of employment, whether resulting in death or not, is the exclusive remedy against an employer who is properly insured under the Workers' Compensation Act and the Occupational Disease Act of Montana. This provision does not apply to willful, intentional or malicious acts of the employer or co-employees, Mont. Code Ann. § 39-71-413. To show malice and avoid exclusivity, a tort claimant must establish that the employer acted intentionally or had "knowledge of facts or intentionally disregarded facts that created a high probability of injury and: (a) deliberately proceeded to act in conscious or intentional disregard of the high probability of injury; or (b) deliberately proceeded to act with indifference to the high probability of injury. Mont. Code Ann. § 27-1-221(2. Sherner v. Conoco, Inc., 2000 MT 50, 298 Mont. 401, 995 P.2d 99. An injured worker also retains rights against a third party whose negligence was the cause of the injury. Mont. Code Ann § 39-71-412.

D. Pleading Requirements

See elements set out under causes of action above.

SURVEY OF NEBRASKA EMPLOYMENT LIBEL LAW

Michael C. Cox and Daniel J. Fischer
Koley Jessen P.C., L.L.O.
One Pacific Place, Suite 800
1125 South 103rd Street
Omaha, Nebraska 68124
Telephone: (402) 390-9500; Facsimile: (402) 390-9005

(With Developments Reported Through **November 1, 2012**)

GENERAL COMMENTS

Nebraska's County Court provides a six-person jury trial with an amount in controversy maximum limit of $51,000.00. Nebraska's District Court system provides a twelve-person jury system for both equity and legal actions in any amount.

Nebraska has a two-tiered appellate court system. The Nebraska Court of Appeals hears most appeals, although there is also a "bypass" procedure for direct review by the Supreme Court, and a "petition for further review" which offers a chance to take cases up to the Supreme Court after the Court of Appeals decision. Additionally, the Nebraska Supreme Court on its own motion will take cases originally slated for the Court of Appeals to fill its docket.

SIGNIFICANT DEVELOPMENTS SINCE THE 2012 *SURVEY*

In McKinney v. Okoye, 282 Neb. 880, 806 N.W.2d 571 (2011), the Nebraska Supreme Court held that an action for malicious prosecution is not barred by the absolute privilege afforded to judges, attorneys, parties, witnesses, and jurors against claims for defamation founded upon statements made in relation to judicial proceedings. Id. at 889, 806 N.W.2d 579 (overturning contrary ruling in Central Ice Machine Co. v. Cole, 2 Neb. App. 282, 509 N.W.2d 229 (1993)).

In James v. Nebraska, 2011 WL 4062517 (D. Neb. 2011), the plaintiff, after completing her fellowship at the University of Nebraska Medical Center, applied to the Nebraska Department of Health and Human Services (DHHS) for a full license to practice medicine. Id. at *1. The plaintiff had previously received a probationary temporary education permit. Id. After receiving a full license on a disciplinary probationary basis from the DHHS, the plaintiff requested a hearing with DHHS concerning its licensing decision. Id. Minutes from the Board's meetings regarding the plaintiff's applications were posted on DHHS website and were temporarily available to the public. Id. The plaintiff filed a complaint alleging defamation and several other causes of action. Id. The court held that absolute immunity applied to actions of the Chief Medical Officer because her "actions were 'functionally comparable' to that of a judge." Id. at *2. The court also found that absolute immunity was not available to the eight individual board members because they served no judicial function. Id. at *4. However, qualified immunity was appropriate for the eight board members under the Nebraska Uniform Licensing Law (Neb. Rev. Stat. § 71-161.19 (2003). Id. at *6. The statute provided immunity to any member "of a professional board for any profession or occupation credentialed by the department" when the board member "acts without malice and in the reasonable belief that such action ... is warranted by the facts known to him or her after a reasonable effort is made to obtain the facts on which such action is taken." Id. This provision has been replaced by a similar provision in the Uniform Credentialing Act (Neb. Rev. Stat. § 38-173). Id. at *8.

In American Home Assurance Co. v. Greater Omaha Packing Co., Inc., 2012 WL 2061941 (D. Neb. 2012), the defendant sold the plaintiffs raw beef allegedly contaminated with *E. Coli.* Id. The defendant filed a counterclaim for tortious interference with business relationships caused by an article published in the the *New York Times* that "allegedly contained false information supplied by [plaintiffs'] representatives." Id. Plaintiffs moved to dismiss the counterclaim arguing that the applicable statute of limitations was one-year, not four years, because the counterclaim was based upon "defamatory statements" and not tortious interference. Id. The plaintiffs' motion to dismiss was denied because "in Nebraska a tortious interference claim may be based upon defamatory statements and considered a separate and distinct claim from a claim of defamation." Id. at *2. The court also rejected the plaintiffs' claim that, because the newspaper article addressed a matter of national public import, the defendant was required to show actual malice. Id. The court held that it was unnecessary to show actual malice because this was not a required element of a tortious interference claim. Id.

I. GENERAL LAW

A. General Employment Law

1. ***At-Will Employment.*** If the employee has been hired on an at-will basis, the employer can fire the employee for any reason or no reason at all. Barks v. Cosgriff Co., 247 Neb. 660, 529 N.W.2d 749 (1995). While this is the general rule in Nebraska, the courts do allow a claim for wrongful termination of at-will employees if the employee was fired in violation of a constitutionally protected interest or if a statute or contract prohibits the employer from firing an employee without good cause or for a specific reason. White v. Ardan, Inc., 230 Neb. 11, 430 N.W.2d 27 (1988). See also, Riesen v. Irwin Industrial Tool Co., 272 Neb. 41, 46, 717 N.W.2d 907, 913 (2006) (stating general rule in Nebraska that unless constitutionally, statutorily, or contractually prohibited, employer may, without incurring liability, terminate at-will employee at any time with or without reason; noting public policy exception, however, that employee can claim damages for wrongful discharge when motivation for firing contravenes public policy); Simonsen v. Hendricks Sodding & Landscaping, Inc., 5 Neb. App. 263, 558 N.W.2d 825 (Neb. Ct. App. 1997) (against public policy to discharge an at-will employee for refusing to violate criminal law or public policy of the state); Ambroz v. Cornhusker Square Ltd., 226 Neb. 899, 416 N.W.2d 510 (1987) (against statutorily mandated public policy to discharge at-will employee who refused to take lie detector test); Wendeln v. The Beatrice Manor, Inc., 271 Neb. 373, 391, 712 N.W.2d 226, 242 (2006) (holding that, as matter of law, plaintiff may recover mental suffering in retaliatory discharge action brought by former at-will employee alleging discharge violated clear mandate of public policy). While the general rule of at-will employment was recently upheld in Goff-Hamel v. Obstetricians & Gynecologists, P.C., 256 Neb. 19, 588 N.W.2d 798 (1999), the court did allow a promissory estoppel claim to be brought where the plaintiff had quit her previous employment in reliance upon an offer of at-will employment and was not allowed to begin the promised employment Id. at 28, 558 N.W.2d at 204. The Nebraska Supreme Court has recently reaffirmed the principle that Nebraska is an at-will employment state. Dossett v. First State Bank, 261 Neb. 959, 627 N.W.2d 131, 137 (Neb. 2001). Unless prohibited by contract, statute, or the Constitution, an employer may terminate an at-will employee at any time with or without reason and will not incur liability. Id. However, oral representations may, even standing alone, constitute a promise sufficient to create contractual terms which could modify the at-will status of an employee. Gilmore v. Woodmen Acc. & Life Company, 357 F.Supp. 2d 1189, 1193 (D. Neb. 2005). But see, Blinn v. Beatrice Comm. Hosp. and Health Ctr., Inc., 270 Neb. 809, 820-22, 708 N.W.2d 235, 246-47 (2006) (statement that "we've got at least five more years of work to do" not sufficiently definite in form to constitute offer of definite employment and did not manifest intent to create unilateral contract modifying at-will employment; employee's subjective understanding of job security is insufficient to establish implied contract); Miller v. Steele, 2006 WL 1888636, *3 (D. Neb. 2006) (holding that where at-will employee retains employment with knowledge of new or changed conditions, new or changed conditions may become contractual obligation).

In Teetor v. Dawson Public Power District, 19 Neb. App. 474, 808 N.W.2d 86 (Neb. Ct. App. 2012), the Nebraska Court of Appeals held that the termination of an at-will employee was not a breach of the implied covenants of good faith and fair dealing allegedly created by the employee manual. 19 Neb. App. at 483, 808 N.W.2d at 94. Further, covenants of good faith and fair dealing will not be implied in relation to the termination of at-will employees absent evidence that the employee manual created such covenants. Id.

In Trosper v. Bag 'N Save, the Nebraska Supreme Court held that the public policy exception to the employment at-will doctrine applies when an employer wrongfully demotes an employee in retaliation for filing a workers' compensation claim and that the employee who alleged that employer demoted her in retaliation for reporting a work-related injury, stated a cause of action. Trosper v. Bag 'N Save, 273 Neb. 855, 865-66, 734 N.W.2d 704, 711-12 (2007).

The Nebraska Supreme Court has held that an at-will employment relationship is a "business relationship or expectancy" that may be the object of a tortious interference. Huff v. Swartz, 258 Neb. 820, 826, 606 N.W.2d 461, 467 (2000). In order for interference made by a co-employee or supervisor to be actionable, the actions of the co-employee or supervisor must be shown to have been committed in furtherance of some purpose other than the lawful purposes of the employer. Id. at 828, 606 N.W.2d at 468. Further, in order to prevail, the plaintiff must also establish that the interference was unjustified. Id.

In Blinn v. Beatrice Community Hosp. and Health Center, Inc., 13 Neb. App. 459, 696 N.W.2d 149 (Neb. Ct. App. 2005), the Nebraska Court of Appeals held that an alleged oral agreement to extend an at-will employee's employment until the employee chose to retire or for at least five years did not violate Nebraska's Statute of Frauds, Neb. Rev. Stat. § 36-202 (Reissue 2004), because in theory the employee could choose to retire within one year, making the agreement capable of being performed within one year. Blinn, 13 Neb. App. at 68-69, 696 N.W.2d at 157.

Private employers, while not normally liable for suits upon constitutional rights, can be held liable for violation of an employee's free speech rights if the private employer willfully participates in joint action with state officials to retaliate for the exercise of constitutional rights. Dossett v. First State Bank, 399 F.3d 940, 954 (8th Cir. 2005).

With respect to public employment, Nebraska recognizes the well-established principle that public employees have some legally cognizable property interest in continued employment that is guaranteed a certain amount of constitutional procedural protection before the employee is permanently deprived of that interest. Ginter v. City of Ashland, 2005 WL 2347234, *3 (D. Neb. 2005). This property interest is sufficient to trigger application of procedural due process guaranties. Id. Under Nebraska law, an employee is generally terminable at will in the absence of an employment contract, but the Nebraska Supreme Court has recognized that persons may have constitutionally protected property interests in continued public employment stemming from sources such as municipal ordinances, implied contracts, and the regulations of administrative agencies. Id. (citing Ritchie v. Walker Mfg. Co., 963 F.2d 1119, 1123 (8th Cir. 1992)). In Ginter, however, the plaintiff failed to allege any facts showing he had a legitimate claim of entitlement to working as a police officer for the City of Ashland and therefore no protected property interest was shown to exist. Id. at *3. Similarly, in Kozisek v. County of Seward, 2007 WL 3124632 (D. Neb. 2007), the court also concluded that the plaintiff had no protected property interest in his job with the county. Id at *2. The court found that because (1) there was no written employment contract, (2) the plaintiff's employee handbook stated he was terminable at-will, and (3) the plaintiff testified that he felt free to resign at any time, the plaintiff's procedural due process claim failed as a matter of law. Id.

B. Elements of Libel Claim

1. ***Basic Elements.*** A claim for libel requires: (1) a false and defamatory statement concerning the plaintiff; (2) an unprivileged publication to a third party; (3) fault amounting to at least negligence on the part of the publisher; and (4) either actionability of the statement irrespective of special harm or the existence of special harm caused by the publication. Norris v. Hathaway, 5 Neb. App. 544, 561 N.W.2d 583 (Neb. Ct. App. 1997).

2. ***Fault.***

a. Private Figure Plaintiff/Matter of Public Concern. There are no reported decisions directly addressing this issue. In Silence v. Journal-Star Printing Co., 201 Neb. 159, 266 N.W.2d 533, 536, 3 Media L. Rep. 2550 (1978), four members of the court, concurring in judgment, would have held plaintiff to be a private figure, and therefore, "the libel rules enunciated in Gertz should control." In P.W. Eagle, Inc. v. Schnase, 376 F.Supp. 2d 945 (D. Neb. 2005), the court noted that determining whether the First Amendment protects utterances requires a review of the context in which the statements were made, including whether the statement concerned public or private figures. P.W. Eagle, Inc., 376 F.Supp. 2d at 948 (citing Janklow v. Newsweek, Inc., 788 F.2d 1300, 1302-03 (8th Cir. 1986) (en banc), cert. denied, 479 U.S. 883, 107 S.Ct. 272, 93 L.Ed.2d 249 (1986)).

b. Private Figure Plaintiff/Matter of Private Concern. No reported cases. But see P.W. Eagle, Inc., supra.

c. Public Figure Plaintiff/Matter of Public Concern. Prior to Gertz, the Nebraska Supreme Court upheld liability without fault in cases of libel per se. See Rimmer v. Chadron Printing Co., 156 Neb. 533, 535 ,56 N.W.2d 806, 808 (1953). This rule is clearly contrary to Gertz and will not be followed. To make a prima facie case, the public figure plaintiff must establish actual malice by clear and convincing evidence in accordance with Gertz and must also establish falsity by clear and convincing evidence. Hoch v. Prokop, 244 Neb. 443, 507 N.W.2d 626 (1993). In Nolan v. Campbell, 13 Neb. App. 212, 690 N.W.2d 638 (Neb. Ct. App. 2004), the Nebraska Court of Appeals reiterated the rule in Hoch and determined that a city administrator was a public figure as defined by the parameters of Gertz. Nolan, 13 Neb. App. at 218, 690 N.W.2d at 647.

3. ***Falsity.*** Truth with "good motives" is a defense guaranteed by the Nebraska Constitution. Neb. Const., Art. I, Sec. 5. Truth is a complete defense unless the plaintiff proves actual malice (common law malice, e.g., spite, hate, ill will). Bartels v. Retail Credit Co., 185 Neb. 304. 308-09, 175 N.W.2d 292, 297 (1990). The Nebraska Court of Appeals has now recognized falsity as an essential element for both libel and false light privacy actions. Wadman v. State, 1 Neb. App. 839, 510 N.W.2d 426 (Neb. Ct. App. 1993). See also, Nolan v. Campbell, 13 Neb. App. 212, 690 N.W.2d 638 (Neb. Ct. App. 2004)(falsity is an element of both libel and false light invasion of privacy claims); Prokop v. McClurg, 2011 WL 2724222, *4 (Neb. Ct. App. 2011) (unpublished decision)(summary judgment for defendant appropriate when there is no evidence in record that any statements were false, "let alone both false and made maliciously with knowledge of falsity").

4. ***Defamatory Statement of Fact.*** No reported decisions in the employment libel context. In Nolan v. Campbell, 13 Neb. App. 212, 690 N.W.2d 638 (Neb. Ct. App. 2004), the Nebraska Court of Appeals found statements of fact published by the defendant libelous per se for defendant's failure to deny those portions of plaintiff's complaint. The Court of Appeals affirmed the District Court's finding. Nolan, 13 Neb. App. at 218-19, 690 N.W.2d at 647.

5. ***Of and Concerning Plaintiff.*** In the public official context, the plaintiff must prove that defamatory statements were made "of and concerning" him by clear and convincing evidence. Deaver v. Hinel, 223 Neb.

529, 391 N.W.2d 128, 13 Media L. Rep. 1219 (1986). Reference to "law enforcement" is not of and concerning sheriff. Id. Testimony that plaintiff understood statements to refer to him is insufficient. Id. In DeCamp v. Omaha World-Herald Co., 1993 WL 100131 (Neb. Ct. App. 1993), the court held that a candidate is not libeled by defamatory publication concerning his campaign staff.

6. ***Publication***.

a. Intracorporate Communication. In distinguishing between an employee's statements to co-workers about a customer's sexual harassment and statements to the employee's parents and law enforcement regarding the same, the Nebraska federal district court explained that the statements to the employee's parents and law enforcement were not within the scope of her employment and therefore, the employer could not be held liable under *respondeat superior*. McPherson v. Red Robin Int'l, Inc., 2005 WL 2671033, *6-7 (D. Neb. 2005) (McPherson I); McPherson v. Red Robin Int'l, Inc., 2006 WL 2707450 (D. Neb. 2006) (McPherson II). "Conditional or qualified privilege comprehends communications made in good faith, without actual malice, with reasonable or probable grounds for believing them to be true, on a subject matter in which the author of the communication has an interest, or in respect to which the author has a duty, public, personal, or private, either legal, judicial, political, moral, or social, made to a person having a corresponding interest or duty. A communication between those sharing a common interest is conditionally privileged." McPherson II, 2006 WL 2707450 at *5 (citing Turner v. Welliver, 411 N.W.2d 298, 307 (Neb. 1987); Helmstadter v. North Am. Biological, Inc., 559 N.W.2d 794, 800 (Neb. Ct. App. 1997)). Pursuant to the defendant's harassment policy, the harassed employee was required to report all incidents and accidents to management, and therefore were part of a common interest or duty entitled to the qualified privilege, which plaintiff failed to show was made with any malice. McPherson II, 2006 WL 2707450 at *5-6.

b. Compelled Self-Publication. In Molt v. Lindsay Mfg. Co., 248 Neb. 81, 532 N.W.2d 11 (1995), the wife of the plaintiff requested that the reason for her husband's termination be placed in writing. The defendant complied with that request by typing a letter, placing it in a sealed envelope, and delivering it only to the defendant's wife. There is no publication when the words are only communicated to the person who is defamed. Id.

c. Republication. Republication is not a defense to a libel action in Nebraska. "[I]t is no defense to show that a defamatory publication was first made by another person or newspaper and was simply copied with proper credit." McCune v. Neitzel, 235 Neb. 754, 457 N.W.2d 803 (1990); Sheibley v. Huse , 75 Neb. 811, 820, 106 N.W. 1028, 1032 (1906). However, republication can be pleaded to mitigate damages. Sheibley, at 820-21, 106 N.W. at 1032. Furthermore, a Nebraska Court of Appeals decision held truthful and not actionable a news story which correctly related that a former Omaha police chief (plaintiff) had been "accused" by private persons of committing child abuse, even though the accusations were alleged by plaintiff to be false. Wadman v. State, 1 Neb. App. 839 (1993). That is true particularly where a republication is made by the original publisher of the accusations. Such a republication would create a second cause of action, although the trial courts would take care not to permit a damages verdict where damages to reputation would be multiplied by the number of publications. A publisher also would likely be liable for foreseeable republication by others. The republisher, in general, would also be liable in a separate suit, though double recoveries are avoided as to the same injury.

In Nolan v. Campbell, 13 Neb. App. 212, 690 N.W.2d 638 (Neb. Ct. App. 2004), the Nebraska Court of Appeals narrowed the injunction ordered by the trial court but affirmed prohibiting republication of defendant's publications against the plaintiff. Nolan, 13 Neb. App. at 224, 690 N.W.2d at 650-51. Specifically, the court in Nolan held that the scope of the permanent injunction could only forbid republication of the statements and flyers specifically found to be libelous after trial, and it further held that the portion of the injunction against new publications of material containing similar words such as scam, con artist, and thief, had to be stricken as an overly broad prior restraint of free speech. Id.

7. ***Statements versus Conduct***. No reported cases.

8. ***Damages***.

a. Presumed Damages and Libel Per Se. Written words are libelous per se only if they falsely impute the commission of a crime involving moral turpitude, an infectious disease, or unfitness to perform the duties of an office or employment, or if they prejudice one in his or her profession or trade or tend to disinherit one. Nolan v. Campbell, 13 Neb. App. 212, 218, 690 N.W.2d 638, 647 (Neb. Ct. App. 2004)(citing Matheson v. Stork, 239 Neb. 547, 477 N.W.2d 156 (1991)). One who is liable for libel or for slander per se is liable for at least nominal damages. Hennis v. O'Connor, 223 Neb. 112, 388 N.W.2d 470 (1986). Plaintiff need not plead special damages in a case alleging slander per se. Hruby v. Kalina, 228 Neb. 713, 424 N.W.2d 130, 15 Media L. Rep. 1559 (1988). Whether Gertz may prohibit or limit any such nominal damages has not been discussed by the Nebraska Supreme Court.

(1) Employment-Related Criticism. In Bowley v. W.S.A., Inc., 264 Neb. 6, 645 N.W.2d 512 (2002), a former employee brought a libel suit against his former employer alleging that a letter that the former

employer sent to the plaintiff's current employer resulted in his termination. The jury awarded damages, but the trial court found them excessive and granted the defendant's motion for new trial. In reversing the lower court's grant of a new trial for the defendant, the Nebraska Supreme Court noted that evidence of the plaintiff's earnings before and after the termination of his employment was relevant in determining the amount of damages which resulted from the allegedly libelous letter. Id. at 14, 645 N.W.2d at 518.

(2) Single Instance Rule. No reported cases.

b. Punitive Damages. Nebraska does not allow punitive, vindictive, or exemplary damages. "The measure of recovery in all civil cases is compensation for the injury sustained." Miller v. Kingsley, 194 Neb. 123, 124, 230 N.W.2d 472, 474 (1975).

c. Injunctive Relief. An injunction may be granted in a libel action. Nolan v. Campbell, 13 Neb. App. 212, 224, 690 N.W.2d 638, 650-51 (Neb. Ct. App. 2004)(citing Sid Dillon Chevrolet v. Sullivan, 251 Neb. 722, 559 N.W.2d 740 (1997)). According to the court in Sid Dillon and as reiterated in Nolan, "absent a prior adversarial determination that the complaint of publication is false or a misleading representation of fact, equity will not issue to enjoin libel or slander, unless such libel or slander is published (1) in violation of a trust or contract or (2) in a aid of another tort or unlawful act, or injunctive relief is essential for the preservation of a property right." Id. Only those publications which are found to be libelous after an adversarial proceeding are exempted from the general prohibition against unconstitutional prior restraints on speech. Nolan, 13 Neb. App. at 225-26, 690 N.W.2d at 651-52. Accordingly, the court in Nolan enjoined the defendant from permanently republishing in any fashion or otherwise publicly displaying the publications found libelous by the trial court and further permanently enjoined the defendant specific phrases which the trial court found libelous and published with actual malice. Nolan, 13 Neb. App. at 227-28, 690 N.W.2d at 653. The court stated, however, that other individual words in the publication could not be enjoined because they are words that could be used by the defendant legitimately to talk about the plaintiff in the future in the plaintiff's capacity as a city administrator. Id.

9. ***Due Process Claims.*** "[I]n order to state a claim under 42 U.S.C. § 1983 for violation of the Due Process Clause, a plaintiff who complains of defamation must claim (1) the existence of a public false statement (or a statement that could be proved false) about him [or her] by a state actor, which is sufficiently derogatory to injury his [or her] reputation, and (2) some tangible and material state-imposed burden or alteration of his [or her] status or of a right in addition to the stigmatizing statement. These requirements are known as the "stigma plus" test. To meet the first prong, the "stigma," the plaintiff must show that a state actor made concrete false assertions about him that could injure his [or her] reputation. To meet the second prong, the "plus," the plaintiff must demonstrate an alteration or impairment of a right or status previously recognized by state law. Buser v. Reed, 2006 WL 298813 (D. Neb. 2006) (citations omitted) (citing Paul v. Davis, 424 U.S. 693, 96 S. Ct. 1155, 47 L.Ed.2d 405 (1976)). Because the defendant's statements were related to matters of public record, plaintiff could not prove the second prong of the test and therefore, the court granted summary judgment for the defendant. Id. at *4-6. See also, Walker v. Thomas, 2006 WL 1586559 (D. Neb. 2006) (holding that allegations of defamation based on injury to reputation do not state claim for deprivation of liberty or property protected by Due Process Clause of United States Constitution); **State v. Norman, 282 Neb. 990, 1007, 808 N.W.2d 48, 62 (2012) ("stigma" portion of the test may be similar to private defamation, but "plus" factor can only be satisfied by state action that could not have been initiated by private person).**

II. PRIVILEGES AND DEFENSES

A. Scope of Privileges

1. ***Absolute Privilege.*** Participants in judicial or quasi-judicial proceedings have an absolute privilege for statements made incident to and in the course of the proceedings, as long as defamatory statement has some relation to the proceedings. Cummings v. Kirby, 216 Neb. 314, 343 N.W.2d 747 (1983); Beckenhauser v. Predoehl, 215 Neb. 347, 338 N.W.2d 618 (1983); Sinnett v. Albert, 188 Neb. 176, 195 N.W.2d 506 (1972); Reller v. Ankeny, 160 Neb. 47, 68 N.W.2d 686 (1955). **However, "the powers and duties of coroners are not judicial" and the privilege afforded to witnesses does not immunize the witness when the claim is for malicious prosecution. McKinney v. Okoye, 282 Neb. 880, 889, 806 N.W.2d 571, 579 (2011).** Information provided to the Department of Labor in connection with the Employment Security Law is absolutely privileged and cannot be the basis for a libel action unless the information provided is false and malicious. Neb. Rev. Stat. § 48-612 (Cum. Supp. 2004). In State ex rel. Upper Republican Natural Resources Dist. v. District Judges of Dist. Court for Chase County, 273 Neb. 148, 152, 728 N.W.2d 275, 279 (2007), the court held that the Legislature did not intend to create an absolute privilege for all communications occurring while a public body is in closed session under the Open Meetings Act because, unlike other Nebraska statutes, this Act is notably silent in providing a discovery privilege. See also Neb. Rev. Stat. § 84-1410(1). The court also explained that while there is no absolute privilege in the Open Meetings Act for communications in closed sessions convened under the Act, to the extent the communications

implicate other evidentiary privileges, such as attorney-client privilege, the communications could still be protected. State ex re. Upper Republican Natural Resources Dist., 273 Neb. at 153-54, 728 N.W.2d at 280-81. In Payne v. Peter Kiewit Sons' Inc., 2007 WL 4320673 (D. Neb. 2007), the court held that any statements made by representatives of the employer to the Nebraska Equal Opportunity Commission regarding the employee's work performance were privileged and cannot form the basis of a claim for defamation. The court explained that under Nebraska law, there is an absolute privilege granted to parties in judicial and quasi-judicial proceedings. Payne, 2007 WL 4320673 at *7. **In James v. Nebraska, 2011 WL 4062517 (D. Neb. 2011), the court held that the actions of the chief medical officer, when conducting a hearing for the Nebraska Department of Health and Human Services, are entitled to absolute immunity because they are "'functionally comparable' to that of a judge." Id. at *2. However, absolute immunity was not available to the eight board members who participated in the hearing because they performed no such function. Id. at *4 (though they were entitled to other immunity).**

2. ***Qualified Privileges.***

a. Common Interest. A communication honestly made between interested parties where it is reasonable or proper to give the information (e.g., employer/employee) is protected by a qualified privilege. Dangberg v. Sears, Roebuck & Co., 198 Neb. 234, 252 N.W.2d 168 (1977); Aetna Life Insurance Co. v. Mutual Benefit Health & Accident Association, 82 F.2d 115 (8th Cir. 1936); Turner v. Welliver, 226 Neb. 275, 411 N.W.2d 298 (1987) (communications between an insurer and insured about an agent of the insured were privileged); White v. Ardan. Inc., 230 Neb. 11, 430 N.W.2d 27 (1988) (statement by security executive to management about employees); Young v. First United Bank of Bellevue, 246 Neb. 43, 516 N.W.2d 256 (1994) (a letter by a chairman of a corporation to the shareholders of the corporation criticizing a former president's performance); McPherson v. Red Robin Int'l, Inc, 2005 WL 2671033 (D. Neb. 2005) and McPherson v. Red Robin Int'l, Inc., 2006 WL 2707450 (D. Neb. 2006) (applying qualified privilege between co-employees when one employee reported customer's harassment to co-workers and management).

b. Public Employees. In Omaha Police Union Local 101 v. City of Omaha, 274 Neb. 70, 78 -82, 736 N.W.2d 375, 383-85 (2000), the Nebraska Supreme Court held that because the National Industrial Relations Act ("Act") is similar to the Nebraska Labor Relations Act ("NLRA"), the "deliberate or reckless untruth" standard for protected speech did not apply to public employees. The Court further held that the balancing test espoused by the United States Supreme Court in Pickering v. Board of Education, 391 U.S. 563, 88 S. Ct. 1731, 20 L.Ed. 2d 811 (1968), was likewise inapplicable to work-related speech for public employees. 274 Neb. at 82-83, 736 N.W.2d at 385-86. Instead, the Court was guided by federal authority under the Federal Labor Relations Authority ("FLRA") and held that "public employees [in Nebraska] belonging to a labor organization have the protected right to engage in conduct and make remarks, including publishing statements through the media, concerning wages, hours, or terms and conditions of employment. However, employees lose the statutory protection of the Act if the conduct or speech constitutes 'flagrant misconduct.' Flagrant misconduct includes, but is not limited to, statements or actions that (1) are of an outrageous or insubordinate nature, (2) compromise the public employer's ability to accomplish its mission, or (3) disrupt discipline. It would also include conduct that is clearly outside the bounds of any protection, including, for example, assault and battery or racial discrimination." Omaha Police Union Local 101, 274 Neb. at 86, 736 N.W.2d at 387-88.

c. Duty. Duty may be either public, personal, or private and either legal, judicial, political, moral, or social. Turner v. Welliver, 411 N.W.2d 298 (Neb. 1987); Helmstadter v. North Am. Biological, Inc., 559 N.W.2d 794 (Neb. Ct. App. 1997); McPherson, 2006 WL 2707540 at *5.

d. Criticism of Public Employee. No reported cases. But see Nolan v. Campbell, 13 Neb. App. 212, 690 N.W.2d 638 (Neb. Ct. App. 2004)(while not discussing privileges to libel and false-light invasion of privacy, court affirmed jury's verdict in favor of city administrator for libelous publications against city administrator).

e. Limitation on Qualified Privileges.

(1) Constitutional or Actual Malice. Proof of constitutional malice is not required to defeat a qualified privilege.

(2) Common Law Malice. Where a qualified privilege exists, recovery can only be had by the plaintiff where there is proof of malice. In order to establish malice the plaintiff must demonstrate that the publication was made with hate, spite, or ill will. Molt v. Lindsay Mfg. Co., 248 Neb. 81, 532 N.W.2d 11(1995).

(3) Neb. Rev. Stat. § 25-840 (Reissue 1995) provides that truth alone shall be a complete defense unless the plaintiff proves that publication was made with actual malice, though actual malice shall not be inferred or presumed from the publication.

f. Question of Fact or Law. Whether a publication was privileged is a question of law unless facts are in dispute, in which case it is a question for the jury. Turner v. Welliver, 226 Neb. 275, 411 N.W.2d 298 (1987)

g. Burden of Proof. The Nebraska Supreme Court has not expressly placed the burden of proof on either party. The court treats privilege as a defense, which suggests that the burden is on the defendant. A plaintiff can overcome a qualified privilege by proving that the defendant acted with malice. White v. Chicago, Burlington and Quincy Railroad, 417 F.2d 941, 946 (8th Cir. 1969). The question of malice is one of fact for the jury. Id. at 946.

h. Medical Peer Review. The Healthcare Quality Improvement Act of 1986 ("HCQIA") provides immunity to hospitals and the participants of professional reviews from damages, but the Act does not provide immunity for equitable relief. McLeay v. Bergan Mercy Health Systems Corp., 271 Neb. 602, 609-10, 615, 714 N.W.2d 7, 14-15, 18 (2006) (evaluating whether physician rebutted presumption by preponderance of evidence that professional review action met standards of Act and was entitled to immunity). McLeay held that the defendant's actions were immune from liability for damages on all causes of action under the HCQIA, but it remanded for further proceedings on plaintiff's claims for equitable relief because no immunity existed. McLeay, 271 Neb. at 615, 714 N.W.2d at 18-19.

B. Standard Libel Defenses

1. ***Truth.*** Truth with "good motives" is a defense guaranteed by the Nebraska Constitution. Neb. Const., Art. I, Sec. 5. Truth is a complete defense unless the plaintiff proves malice (common law malice, e.g., spite, hate, ill will). Neb. Rev. Stat. § 25-840 (Reissue 1995); Bartels v. Retail Credit Co., 185 Neb. 304, 308-09, 175 N.W.2d 292, 297 (1970). Helmstadter v. North American Biological, Inc., 5 Neb. App. 440, 559 N.W.2d 794 (Neb. Ct. App. 1997). Malice shall not be inferred or presumed from the publication and must be proved by the plaintiff. Neb. Rev. Stat. § 25-840; Whitcomb v. Nebraska State Education Association, 184 Neb. 31, 165 N.W.2d 99 (1965). Truth is not an essential element of a privileged communication. Bartels v. Retail Credit Co., 185 Neb. 304, 311, 175 N.W.2d 292, 297 (1970). Proof of malice is at issue only when truth or conditional privilege has been asserted as a defense. Chudy v. Murdza, 1992 WL 76311 (Neb. Ct. App. 1992).

In Recio v. Evers, 278 Neb. 405, 771 N.W.2d 121, 2009 WL 2634052 (2009), the Nebraska Supreme Court discussed malice as a defense to defamation but in the context of whether statements were justified or not as an element of meaning an intentional interference with business relations claim. Id. at *12-13. While noting that malicious motive is a factor to determine whether interference is unjustified, the Court held that "it is generally insufficient standing alone to establish that fact under § 767 of the Restatement. In general, § 772(a) does not permit *any* liability to be imposed for the communication of truthful information. Id. at *13 (emphasis in original). The Court also reiterated that actual malice may not be presumed from a communication and that, in this context, was defined as "hate, spite, or ill will," requiring that defendant have acted with a desire to harm the plaintiff unrelated to a desire to protect the defendant's rights and which was not reasonably related to the defense of a recognized property or social interest. Id. at *13. (Noting that there was insufficient evidence to support finding that the defendant's sexual harassment complaint was entirely motivated by malice).

The Nebraska Court of Appeals has now recognized falsity as an essential element for both libel and false light privacy actions. Nolan v. Campbell, 13 Neb. App. 212, 690 N.W.2d 638 (Neb. Ct. App. 2004); Wadman v. State, 1 Neb. App. 839, 510 N.W.2d 426 (Neb. Ct. App. 1993). Nebraska cases prior to Gertz suggest that the defendant has the burden of pleading and then proving truth as an affirmative defense. See Bartels v. Retail Credit Co., 185 Neb. 304, 175 N.W.2d 292 (1970). Deaver v. Hinel, 223 Neb. 529, 391 N.W.2d 128, 13 Media L. Rep. 1219 (1986) (places burden of proving falsity on a public official plaintiff). In 1988, the Legislature rejected a bill which would have put burden of proving falsity on plaintiffs in all cases. When the plaintiff is a public figure and the speech is a matter of public concern, the plaintiff must establish falsity by clear and convincing evidence. Hoch v. Prokop, 244 Neb. 443, 507 N.W.2d 626 (1993). Lastly, Neb. Rev. Stat. § 25-840 states that "the defendant may allege the truth of the matter charged as defamatory, prove the same and any mitigating circumstances to reduce the amount of damages, or prove either."

2. ***Opinion.*** Pure opinion is not actionable in a defamation case, even when non-media defendants are involved. Turner v. Welliver, 226 Neb. 275, 411 N.W.2d 298 (1987) (citing Gertz v. Robert Welch. Inc., 418 U.S. 323, 94 S. Ct. 2997, 41 L.Ed.2d 789 (1974)). The court in Turner acknowledged a constitutional basis for distinguishing opinion from fact, citing Gertz. However, the court adopted the test in Restatement (Second) of Torts § 566 at 170 (1977). Statements by a bank employee to plaintiff's relatives that plaintiffs farm was in trouble and that plaintiff would lose everything were expressions of pure opinion protected by First Amendment and not actionable under Neb. Rev. Stat. § 20-204. Schoenweis v. Dando, 231 Neb. 180, 435 N.W.2d 666 (1989). The Nebraska Supreme Court in Wheeler v. Nebraska State Bar Ass'n rejected the Milkovich test, 244 Neb. 786, 508 N.W.2d 917 (1994). Instead, Nebraska adopted the California "totality of the circumstances" test. See Baker v. Los Angeles Herald Examiner , 42 Cal. 3d 254, 260, 721 P.2d 87, 90, 228

Cal. Rptr. 206, 209 (1986), cert. denied, 479 U.S. 1032, 107 5. Ct. 880, 93 L.Ed.2d 531. To determine the objectivity and verifiability of a statement, the language of the statement and the context in which the statement was made are examined.

3. ***Consent.*** Consent to the publication of material is an absolute defense to an action for libel. Miller v. American Sports Co., 237 Neb. 676, 467 N.W.2d 653 (1991) (model who agreed to unrestricted use of her photographs to sell products consented to publication of photograph, and her consent provided a complete defense to action for libel).

4. ***Mitigation.*** No reported cases. However, Neb. Rev. Stat. § 25-840 (Reissue 1995) states that the defendant may as a defense prove any mitigating circumstance to reduce the amount of damages.

5. ***Claims Against State and Political Subdivisions.*** Claims against the state and any political subdivision thereof for libel and slander are not permitted. Neb. Rev. Stat. § 13-910(7) (Supp. 2005); Neb. Rev. Stat. § 81-8219(4) (Reissue 2003). See also Doe v. Omaha Public School Dist., 273 Neb. 79, 86, 727 N.W.2d 447, 455 (2000) (citing Neb. Rev. Stat. § 13-910(7) as excluding intentional torts from political subdivision Tort Claims Act, including libel and slander).

III. RECURRING FACT PATTERNS

A. Statements in Personnel File

No reported cases.

B. Performance Evaluations

The report of a department chairperson to a hospital quality review committee was protected by the federal Health Care Quality Improvement Act. In order to overcome immunity provided by statute to medical peer reviewers, plaintiff would have to show that information in the report was false and the person providing the information knew it was false. Shilling v. Moore, 249 Neb. 704, 545 N.W.2d 442 (1996).

C. References

No reported cases.

D. Intracorporate Communication

"A communication is privileged if made bona fide by one who has an interest in the subject matter to one who also has an interest in it or stands in such relation that it is a reasonable duty, or is proper, for the writer to give the information." White v. Ardan, Inc., 230 Neb. 11, 19, 430 N.W.2d 27, 32-33 (1988). In Molt v. Lindsay Mfg. Co., 248 Neb. 81, 532 N.W.2d 11 (1995), the court determined that notifying a shift manager of the reason for an employee's termination was appropriate where the manager was on duty at the time of the firing and escorted the employee from the building following the termination. In McPherson v. Red Robin Int'l, Inc., 2006 WL 2707450 (D. Neb. 2006), the court dismissed plaintiff's complaint for libel against an employer for statements made by an employee to other employees about alleged incident of harassment by plaintiff, finding that a qualified privilege existed as a matter of law and that the record failed to provide any evidence to rebut privilege. Id. at *5-7. Where a qualified privilege exists, the plaintiff cannot recover for libel unless there is a showing of malice. Kloch v. Rateliffe, 221 Neb. 241, 375 N.W.2d 916 (1985). In order to establish that a statement was communicated with malice, the plaintiff would have to show the publication was made with hate, spite, or ill will. Turner v. Welliver, 226 Neb. 275, 411 N.W.2d 298 (1987); McPherson, 2006 WL 2707450 at *6.

Also, the intracorporate conspiracy doctrine states that co-employees are shielded from claims of conspiracy when they act within the scope of their employment. Meyers v. Starke, 420 F.3d 738 (8th Cir. 2005)(ruling on claim under 42 U.S.C. § 1985(2) prohibiting conspiracies to deter by force intimidation or threat any party or witness in case where plaintiff alleges co-employees and supervisor pressured her to change testimony regarding placement of children in treatment by Department of Health and Human Services).

E. Statements to Government Regulators

Information provided to the Department of Labor in connection with the administration and requirements of the Employment Security Law is absolutely privileged and shall not be the basis of a suit for libel unless the statement is false and made with a malicious intent. Molt v. Lindsay Mfg. Co., 248 Neb. 81, 89, 532 N.W.2d 11, 17 (1995).

In Kocontes v. McQuaid, 279 Neb. 335, 778 N.W.2d 410 (2010), the plaintiff sought damages for alleged libelous statements made in a letter the defendants submitted to the Nebraska Board of Pardons urging the Board to reject the plaintiff's application for pardon of felony drug convictions in Nebraska, which were holding up the plaintiff's admission to practice law in Florida. The letter stated the plaintiff's pro hac vice status in Florida was withdrawn for misrepresentations to the court, the plaintiff lied about his convictions when registering to vote, the plaintiff was illegally practicing law in Florida and charging exorbitant fees, and the Board should investigate specific rumors of illegal behavior for which the plaintiff had not been charged or convicted. The Supreme Court of Nebraska concluded the Nebraska Board of Pardons is a quasi-judicial body. Id. at 346, 420. Therefore, because the Nebraska Board of Pardons should consider any statements or correspondence received when evaluating a case, the statements made in the letter were protected by an absolute privilege, and the plaintiff's case was dismissed. Id. at 353, 424.

F. Reports to Auditors and Insurers

No reported cases.

G. Vicarious Liability of Employers for Statements Made by Employees

1. *Scope of Employment*. In McPherson v. Red Robin Int'l, Inc., 2005 WL 2671033 (D. Neb. 2005), the court held that statements by an employee to her parents and to law enforcement regarding sexual harassment by plaintiff were not made within scope of employment and therefore employer could not be liable for defamation as a matter of law. Id. at *5-7.

a. Blogging. No reported cases.

2. *Damages*. No reported cases.

H. Internal Investigations

Statements by an employer made during a judicial or quasi-judicial proceeding, such as an NEOC or EEOC proceeding, are privileged and cannot form the basis of a defamation claim. Payne v. Peter Kiewit Sons', Inc., 2007 WL 4320673, * 7 (D. Neb. 2007). However, an internal investigation can support a viable claim for defamation against an employer. White v. Chicago, Burlington and Quency R.R., 417 F.2d 941 (8th Cir. 1969) (refusing to apply privilege to statements made to prosecutor from internal investigation which failed to interview employee and which appeared to "steer" complaining witness to file criminal charges against employee). But see Wheeler v. Nebraska State Bar Ass'n, 244 Neb. 786, 508 N.W.2d 917 (1993) (holding that subjective ratings of non-judicial members of bar association by state and federal judges did not constitute "statements of fact" susceptible of being proved true or false in order to meet necessary element of defamation claim by state court judge; also adopting use of "totality of the circumstances analysis" in determining whether statement at issue implies provably false factual assertion).

IV. OTHER ACTIONS BASED ON STATEMENTS

A. Negligent Hiring, Retention, and Supervision

There are no reported cases that deal with employee statements and cases of negligent hiring. The general rule is that in selecting an employee, the employer must exercise a degree of care commensurate with the nature of the business in which he is engaged and the nature of service for which the employee is intended, but the employer is only required to hire employees with the skill that is ordinarily and reasonably commensurate with the work to be performed by them. Strong v. K & K Investments, Inc., 216 Neb. 370, 376, 343 N.W.2d 912, 916 (1984).

In Johnson v. State of Nebraska, 270 Neb. 316, 700 N.W.2d 620 (2005), the Nebraska Supreme Court held that where a plaintiff's tort claim "is based on the mere fact of government employment (such as a respondeat superior claim) or only the employment relationship between the intentional tortfeasor and the government (such as a negligent supervision or negligent hiring claim), the exception in § 81-8, 219(4) applies and the State is immune from suit. Johnson, 270 Neb. at 323, 700 N.W.2d at 625 (interpreting Nebraska's intentional tort exception to the State Tort Claims Act).

B. Intentional Infliction of Emotional Distress

In Vergara v. Lopez-Vasquez, 1 Neb. App. 1141, 510 N.W.2d 550 (Neb. Ct. App. 1993), the Court of Appeals stated that there was not sufficient distress to base a claim for intentional infliction of emotional distress when an employee was asked to leave his job due to alleged incompetence. Id. at 1150, 510 N.W.2d at 555. The distress associated with being asked to leave a position is not so severe as no reasonable person could be expected to endure. In Wendeln v. The Beatrice Manor, Inc., 271 Neb. 373, 712 N.W.2d 226 (2006), the Nebraska Supreme Court distinguished mental suffering damages that are recoverable in a retaliatory discharge action from a separate claim of intentional infliction of emotional distress. Wendeln, 271 Neb. at 393, 712 N.W.2d at 243. Specifically, Wendeln found that mental suffering was simply an aspect to providing full recovery further along, where present, and that there was no rational reason to confine such full recovery to former employees whose mental suffering had been severe. Id. Wendeln noted that severe emotional distress is not an element of the tort of retaliatory discharge in contravention of public policy, noting a distinction between the proof requirements in an action for negligent or intentional infliction of emotional distress and damages from mental suffering sought where other interests had been invaded and tort liability has arisen apart from the emotional distress. Id. (affirming damages awarded by jury for mental suffering).

In Langford v. City of Omaha, 2006 WL 680886 (D. Neb. 2006), the court granted summary judgment for the defendant on plaintiff's claim for intentional infliction of emotional distress because the plaintiff could not meet the high standard of proof required to establish conduct so outrageous in character and so extreme in degree as to go beyond all possible bounds of decency on the undisputed facts. Langford, 2006 WL 680886 at *5.

C. Interference with Economic Advantage

Nebraska recognizes a cause of action for tortious interference with a business relationship or expectancy. The elements of a cause of action for tortious interference with a business relationship or expectancy are: (1) the existence of a valid business relationship or expectancy, (2) knowledge by the interferer of the relationship or expectancy, (3) an unjustified intentional act of interference on the part of the interferer, (4) proof that the interference caused the harm sustained, and (5) damage to the party whose relationship or expectancy was disrupted. Matheson v. Stork, 239 Neb. 547, 551, 477 N.W.2d 156, 160 (1991). In Matheson, the plaintiff claimed that two co-employees interfered with his business relationship with the employer by evaluating his performance as being poor and by making the evaluation intentionally, in bad faith, and with malice. Id. at 549, 477 N.W.2d at 158. The court ruled that the plaintiff failed to state a cause of action for tortious interference with a business relationship because he failed to plead facts supporting the conclusion that the evaluation caused harm to the plaintiff and that he suffered damages as a result. Id at 552, 477 N.W.2d at 160. **In American Home Assurance Co. v. Greater Omaha Packing Co., Inc., 2012 WL 2061941 (D. Neb. 2012), the court held that "a tortious interference claim may be based upon defamatory statements and considered a separate and distinct claim from that of defamation." Id. at *2.** The Nebraska Supreme Court has recently held that even an at-will employment relationship is a "business relationship or expectancy" that may be the object of a tortious interference. Huff v. Swartz, 258 Neb. 820, 826, 606 N.W.2d 461, 467 (2000). In order for interference made by a co-employee or supervisor to be actionable, the actions of the co-employee or supervisor must be shown to have been committed in furtherance of some purpose other than the lawful purposes of the employer. Id. at 828, 606 N.W.2d at 468. Further, in order to prevail, the plaintiff must also establish that the interference was unjustified. Id. In Meccatech v. Kiser, 2006 WL 680894 (D. Neb. 2006), the court found, for the purposes of a motion for preliminary injunction, that there was a likelihood the plaintiff would succeed on an intentional interference with business relationship claim because computer forensic evidence showed defendants were actively working and plotting against the plaintiff while the defendants were employed with plaintiff, doing so for the benefit of defendants' new business. Meccatech, 2006 WL 680894 at *5-6 (ultimately denying preliminary injunction because plaintiff failed to prove money damages were insufficient to compensate for any harm and because of likelihood school district interests would be prejudiced or impeded).

The factors to be used to determine whether interference is "unjustified" under Nebraska law are: (a) the nature of the actor's conduct; (b) the actor's motive; (c) the interests of the other with which the actor's conduct interferes; (d) the interest sought to be advanced by the actor; (e) the social interests in protecting the freedom of action of the actor and the contractual interests of the other; (f) the proximity or remoteness of the actor's conduct to the interference; and (g) the relations between the parties. Huff v. Swartz, 258 Neb. 820, 828, 606 N.W.2d 461, 468 (2000) (holding further that a co-employee's acts in furtherance of interests other than those of employer provides proof of interference but does not necessarily establish "unjustified" interference and while malicious motive is factor which may be considered in determining whether interference was unjustified, it may indeed weigh heavily toward such finding, it is generally insufficient standing alone to establish that element under seven-factor test). "[W]hether a particular action is unjustified depends upon a 'choice of values' and determination as to whether 'the conduct should be permitted without liability, despite its affect of harm to another.'" Macke v. Peirce, 266 Neb. 9, 15, 661 N.W.2d 313, 318 (2003) (quoting Huff, *supra*).

In Recio v. Evers, 278 Neb. 405, 771 N.W.2d 121, 2009 WL 2634052 (2009), the Nebraska Supreme Court rejected a tortious interference claim between two co-workers – university professors – because the defendant's conduct was not "unjustified." Id. at*10-11. In Recio, a university placed the plaintiff on probation and ordered her to attend counseling because it found merit in a sexual harassment complaint brought by defendant based on a number of emails the plaintiff sent to the defendant. The plaintiff's claim of tortious interference in her business relationship with the university failed because, after analyzing the seven-factor balancing test adopted from the Restatement of Torts (Second) § 767 for use in determining whether conduct is justified, the Nebraska Supreme Court held that "a person does not incur liability for interfering with a business relationship by giving truthful information to another. Such interference is not improper, even if the facts are marshaled in such a way that they speak for themselves and the person to whom the information is given immediately recognizes them as a reason for breaking a contract or refusing to deal with another." Id. at *11. (also citing Restatement of Torts (Second) § 772). The Nebraska Supreme Court also noted that while malice is one of the seven factors to consider in determining whether interference is unjustified, "it is generally insufficient standing alone to establish that fact under § 767 of the Restatement. In general, § 772(a) does not permit *any* liability to be imposed for the communication of truthful information." Id. at *13 (emphasis in original).

D. Prima Facie Tort

No reported cases.

V. OTHER ISSUES

A. Statute of Limitations

An action for libel or slander must be brought within one year of the date of publication. Neb. Rev. Stat. § 25-208 (Cum. Supp. 2004). The statute of limitations begins to run upon publication of the defamatory matter which is the basis of the action. Prokop v. Hoch, 258 Neb. 1009, 607 N.W.2d 535 (2000); Patterson v. Renstrom, 188 Neb. 78, 79, 195 N.W.2d 193, 194 (1972). Publication of an allegedly libelous statement occurs when it is communicated to someone other than the person defamed. Vergara v. Lopez-Vasquez, 1 Neb. App. 1141, 510 N.W.2d 550 (Neb. Ct. App. 1995). If the petition or complaint shows on its face that it is time barred, then in absence of fraudulent concealment, demurrer will be sustained. Carlson v. Chain, 490 N.W.2d 469 (1992) (opinion withdrawn by court). The one-year statute of limitations is tolled when a person bringing the cause of action had a mental disorder at the time the libel occurred. Vergara v. Lopez-Vasquez, 1 Neb. App. 1141, 510 N.W.2d 550 (1995); Neb. Rev. Stat. § 25-213 (Reissue 1995). An action for libel abates by the death of the defendant. Neb. Rev. Stat. § 25-1402 (Reissue 2008). **American Home Assurance Co. v. Greater Omaha Packing Co., Inc., 2012 WL 2061941 (D. Neb. 2012) (tortious interference claim based on defamatory statement is separate and distinct claim and therefore subject to four-year statute of limitations).**

Nebraska adopted the "single publication" rule in the process of creating a statutory civil privacy act. It is in essence the uniform rule and applies to privacy and libel. Neb. Rev. Stat. § 20-209 (Reissue 1997). It was enforced in Lewis v. Craig, 236 Neb. 602, 463 N.W.2d 318 (1990).

B. Jurisdiction

The district courts have original jurisdiction in all civil actions unless some statute otherwise provides. Neb. Rev. Stat. § 24-302 (Reissue 1995).

C. Worker's Compensation Exclusivity

The Nebraska Worker's Compensation Act, Neb. Rev. Stat. § 48-101 et seq., applies to cases in which an employee suffers a "personal injury" by an "accident or occupational disease, arising out of and in the course of his or her employment." Neb. Rev. Stat. § 48-101. Any disputed claim for worker's compensation must be submitted to the Nebraska Workers' Compensation Court. Neb. Rev. Stat. § 48-161; Peak v. Small Business Admin., 666 F.2d 1121, 1122 (8th Cir. 1981) (the Nebraska Workmen's Compensation Court has "exclusive jurisdiction" over claims brought under the Nebraska Worker's Compensation Act). In addition, the Compensation Court "shall have jurisdiction to decide any issue ancillary to the resolution of an employee's right to workers' compensation benefits." §48-161 (exempting matters involving income withholding for child support, garnishment, and administrative attachment and bank matching).

D. Pleading Requirements

Effective January 1, 2003, pursuant to a legislative directive, the Nebraska Supreme Court promulgated the Nebraska Rules of Pleading in Civil Actions. See Neb. Rev. Stat. § 25-801.01 (Cum.Supp. 2002). The new pleading rules replace Nebraska's prior "code pleading" system with rules patterned after the Federal Rules of Civil Procedure. There have been no appellate opinions addressing the effect of these changes on pleading libel or invasion of privacy cases. Presumably, a complaint need not now make as detailed factual allegations as under the prior rules. Section 6-1108 of the Nebraska Rules of Pleading in Civil Actions (renumbered as of July 1, 2008, formerly Rule 8) requires only that a pleading "contain (1) a caption, (2) a short and plain statement of the claim showing that the pleader is entitled to relief, and (3) a demand for judgment for the relief the pleader seeks."

"In an action for a libel or slander it shall be sufficient to state, generally, that the defamatory matter was published or spoken of the plaintiff, and if the allegation be denied, the plaintiff must prove on the trial the facts, showing that the defamatory matter was published or spoken of him." Neb. Rev. Stat. § 25-839 (Reissue 1995).

SURVEY OF NEBRASKA EMPLOYMENT PRIVACY LAW

Michael C. Cox and Daniel J. Fischer[1]
Koley Jessen P.C., L.L.O.
One Pacific Place, Suite 800
1125 South 103rd Street
Omaha, Nebraska 68124
Telephone: (402) 390-9500; Facsimile: (402) 390-9005

(With Developments Reported Through **November 1, 2012**)

GENERAL COMMENTS

Nebraska's County Court provides a six-person jury trial with an amount in controversy maximum limit of $51,000.00. Nebraska's District Court system provides a twelve-person jury system for both equity and legal actions in any amount.

Nebraska has a two-tiered appellate court system. The Nebraska Court of Appeals hears most appeals, although there is a "bypass" procedure for direct review by the Supreme Court, and a "petition for further review" which offers a chance to take cases up to the Supreme Court after the Court of Appeals decision. Additionally, the Nebraska Supreme Court on its own motion will take cases originally slated for the Court of Appeals to fill its docket.

SIGNIFICANT DEVELOPMENTS SINCE THE 2012 *SURVEY*

In American Home Assurance Co. v. Greater Omaha Packing Co., Inc., 2012 WL 2061941 (D. Neb. 2012), the defendant sold the plaintiffs raw beef allegedly contaminated with *E. Coli*. Id. The defendant filed a counterclaim for tortious interference with business relationships caused by an article published in the the New York Times that "allegedly contained false information supplied by [plaintiffs'] representatives." Id. Plaintiffs moved to dismiss the counterclaim arguing that the applicable statute of limitations was one-year, not four years, because the counterclaim was based upon "defamatory statements" and not tortious interference. Id. The plaintiffs' motion to dismiss was denied because "in Nebraska a tortious interference claim may be based upon defamatory statements and considered a separate and distinct claim from a claim of defamation." Id. at *2. The court also rejected the plaintiffs' claim that the defendant was required to show actual malice because the newspaper article addressed a matter of national public import. Id. The court held that it was unnecessary to show actual malice because this was not a required element of tortious interference. Id.

I. GENERAL LAW OF PRIVACY

A. Legal Basis of Privacy Claims

In Nebraska, there is no common law right of action for an invasion of privacy. Schoneweis v. Dando, 231 Neb. 180, 184-85, 435 N.W.2d 666, 669-70 (1989). The cause of action for an invasion of privacy is based upon statute.

B. Causes of Action

1. ***Misappropriation/Right of Publicity***. Nebraska has recognized a tort of misappropriation by statutory enactment. See Neb. Rev. Stat. § 20-202 (Reissue 1997). Section 20-202 provides that any person that exploits a natural person, name, picture, portrait, or personality for advertising or commercial purposes shall be liable for an invasion of privacy. In Miller v. American Sports Co. Inc., 237 Neb. 676, 467 N.W.2d 653 (1991), the court determined that no cause of action for an invasion of privacy existed where a model had agreed to the unrestricted use of her photographs to sell products. Id. at 680, N.W.2d at 656. An action for misappropriation must be brought within one year from the date the cause of action arose. Neb. Rev. Stat. § 20-211 (Reissue 1997).

2. ***False Light***. Nebraska has recognized the tort of false light invasion of privacy by statutory enactment. See Neb. Rev. Stat. § 20-204 (Reissue 1997). It is essential to a false light invasion of privacy claim that the matter publicized be false. Schoneweis v. Dando, 231 Neb. 180, 185-86, 435 N.W.2d 666, 670 (1993). It is also essential to a false light invasion of privacy claim that the matter either be communicated to the public at large, or to so many persons that it be regarded as substantially certain to become public knowledge. Id. at 185, 435 N.W.2d at 670. A statement of pure opinion is protected under the First Amendment. Id. at 188, 435 N.W.2d at 671. The elements of a claim for false light

---

1. We thank one of our law clerks, Clark R. Youngman, for his assistance in the research and update of this year's outline.

invasion of privacy are: "(1) placing another in a false light (2) which would be highly offensive to a reasonable person and (3) that the actor had knowledge or acted in reckless disregard as to the falsity of the publicized matter." Wadman v. State, 1 Neb. App. 839, 848, 510 N.W.2d 426, 432 (Neb. Ct. App. 1993). To survive as a separate cause of action, a false light claim must allege a nondefamatory statement. Moats v. Republican Party of Nebraska, 281 Neb. 411 (2011). "[I]t has been widely held that a false light invasion of privacy claim 'sufficiently duplicative of libel' is subsumed within the defamation claim. We agree with these authorities and conclude that a statement alleged to be both defamatory and a false light invasion of privacy is 'subsumed within the defamation claim and not separately actionable.'" Moats, 281 Neb. at 598. An action for a false light invasion of privacy must be brought within one year from the date the cause of action arose. Neb. Rev. Stat. § 20-211 (Reissue 1997).

In Nolan v. Campbell, 13 Neb. App. 212, 690 N.W.2d 638 (Neb. Ct. App. 2004), the Nebraska Court of Appeals granted summary judgment in favor of plaintiff on false light invasion of privacy based upon the undenied allegations that defendant distributed three publications alleging that the plaintiff, a city administrator, conducted scams involving deceit and collusion; that he stole, extorted, and embezzled; and that he was a con artist and thief. One of the publications also stated that the plaintiff retained political office "by oppression, deception, dilatory actions (which harm others), intimidation, and dishonoring City records." Nolan, 13 Neb. App. at 214-15, 220, 690 N.W.2d at 644-45, 648. The plaintiff sued after serving a retraction request pursuant to Neb. Rev. Stat. § 25-840.01 (Reissue 1995) and the defendant refused.

3. ***Publication of Private Facts***. When the Nebraska Legislature considered creating causes of action for invasion of privacy, it declined to create a cause of action for publication of private facts. Therefore, no such cause of action exists under Nebraska law.

4. ***Intrusion***. Nebraska recognizes the tort of intrusion. See Neb. Rev. Stat. § 20-203 (Reissue 1997). Trespassing upon a person in his or her place of solitude or seclusion is actionable if the intrusion would be highly offensive to a reasonable person. Photographing a woman in the privacy of a tanning salon without her consent constitutes an invasion of privacy. Sabrina W. v. Willman, 4 Neb. App. 149, 155, 540 N.W.2d 364, 369 (Neb. Ct. App. 1995). In order to recover for an intrusion, the plaintiff need not show that he or she suffered severe mental distress from the intrusion. Id. at 154, 540 N.W.2d at 369. An action for intrusion must be brought within one year from the date the cause of action arose. Neb. Rev. Stat. § 20-211 (Reissue 1997). In Biby v. Board of Regents of the University of Nebraska-Lincoln, 419 F.3d 845 (8th Cir. 2005), a university's search of an employee's office and computer was justified "when there are reasonable grounds for suspecting that the search is necessary for a non-investigatory work-related purpose." Id. at 850-51. In Biby, the search was pursuant to a pending arbitration and litigation between the university and a third party.

C. Other Privacy-Related Actions

1. ***Intentional Infliction of Emotional Distress.*** In Vergara v. Lopez-Vasquez, 1 Neb. App. 1141, 510 N.W.2d 550 (Neb. Ct. App. 1993), the Nebraska Court of Appeals stated that there was not sufficient distress to base a claim for intentional infliction of emotional distress when an employee was asked to leave his job due to alleged incompetency. Id. at 1150, 510 N.W.2d at 555. The distress associated with being asked to leave a position is not so severe as no reasonable person could be expected to endure.

In Dossett v. First State Bank, 399 F.3d 940 (8th Cir. 2005), the trial court found a seven-figure jury award for non-economic damages in the plaintiff's First Amendment retaliation case against a private employer excessive. In reviewing the district court's finding of excessiveness and subsequent reduction of the award, the Eighth Circuit compared amounts of damages in other First Amendment retaliation cases, and in doing so, cited several cases which awarded damages for emotional distress. Id. at 946.

The plaintiff in Walker v. Lowes Home Centers, Inc., 2005 WL 2044920 (D. Neb. 2005), failed to recover for emotional distress or for any other damages because the court found on summary judgment that the plaintiff failed to prove any of her three claims as a matter of law. Id. at *6.

2. ***Interference With Prospective Economic Advantage.*** Nebraska recognizes a cause of action for tortious interference with a business relationship or expectancy. The elements of a cause of action for tortious interference with a business relationship or expectancy are: (1) the existence of a valid business relationship or expectancy, (2) knowledge by the interferer of the relationship or expectancy, (3) an unjustified intentional act of interference on the part of the interferer, (4) proof that the interference caused the harm sustained, and (5) damage to the party whose relationship or expectancy was disrupted. Matheson v. Stork, 239 Neb. 547, 551, 477 N.W.2d 156, 160 (1991). **In American Home Assurance Co. v. Greater Omaha Packing Co., Inc., 2012 WL 2061941 (D. Neb. 2012), the court held that a "tortious**

interference claim may be based upon defamatory statements and considered a separate and distinct claim from that of defamation." Id. at *2. The district court properly granted defendant's motion to dismiss when the State had not waived its sovereign immunity with respect to claims against its officers and employees who, while acting in the scope of their duties, are alleged to have interfered with contractual rights. See Bojanski v. Foley, 18 Neb.App. 929, 940 (Neb. Ct. App. 2011). In Hoschler v. Kozlik, 3 Neb. App. 677, 529 N.W.2d 822 (Neb. Ct. App. 1995), the Nebraska Court of Appeals found that the plaintiff's petition stated a cause of action for tortious interference with a business relationship, even though the employee was operating under an at-will employment contract. The Nebraska Supreme Court has recently agreed with and adopted the Court of Appeals reasoning on this point. See Huff v. Swartz, 258 Neb. 820, 826, 606 N.W.2d 461, 467 (2000). In order for the interference made by a co-employee or supervisor to be actionable, the actions of the co-employee or supervisor must be shown to have been committed in furtherance of some purpose other than the lawful purposes of the employer. Huff, 258 Neb. at 828, 606 N.W.2d at 468. See also, Brian v. Westside Community School Dist., 2006 WL 2375482, *9 (D. Neb. 2006). Further, in order to prevail, the plaintiff must also establish that the interference was unjustified. Huff, 258 Neb. at 828, 606 N.W.2d at 468.

In an unreported case, the Nebraska Court of Appeals specifically noted Huff's holding that at-will employment status, in and of itself, does not preclude a claim for tortious interference with the employment relationship. Rastede v. Bright Horizons Resources for Survivors of Domestic Violence and Sexual Assault, Inc., 2005 WL 2206037 (Neb. App. 2005)(citing Huff v. Swartz, 258 Neb. 820, 606 N.W.2d 461 (2000)). The court in Rastede held that the plaintiff made only unsupported allegations that her employer acted in retaliation for filing a grievance and that there was no evidence that she was terminated for any reason other than perceived deficiencies in her ability to work effectively with others and her violation of co-workers' privacy. Id. 2005 WL 2206037, at *8. The plaintiff's suit against the supervisor who directly terminated her was also dismissed as a matter of law because there were justified reasons for the firing. Id. 2005 WL 2206037, at *9.

In Gilmore v. Woodmen Accident & Life Co, 357 F.Supp. 2d 1189 (2005), the plaintiff employees sued their former employer for tortious interference with business contracts by arguing that their relationships with other co-employees, who worked for or with the plaintiffs under separate contract, were damaged as a result of the termination. The district court disagreed, noting that the plaintiffs must prove that the defendant's actions were unjustified. Id. at 1197. Because the defendant was clearly entitled to terminate plaintiffs' employment-at-will contracts, no unjustified conduct occurred, and plaintiffs therefore failed to show that termination was for some purpose other than a lawful purposes. Id.

In MeccaTech Inc. v. Kiser, 2008 WL 1774992 (D. Neb. 2008), when faced with a request for a preliminary injunction, the court held that it was likely that the plaintiff would be able to show that the defendant had tortiously interfered with its business. Id. at *7. The plaintiff sued a number of its former employees, along with others, for participating in a scheme to divert the plaintiff's Nebraska business to a different company. Id. at *1. In regard to the first two elements of the tort, the court found that (1) that plaintiff had valid business relationships with approximately 180 school districts; and (2) the defendants knew of those business relationships. Id. at *7. Furthermore, the court found that plaintiff produced "compelling evidence," based on e-mail correspondence between the former employees, that the defendants were working to further the interest of one of the plaintiff's competitors. Id. Based on the evidence produced, the court concluded that "but for Defendants' allegedly unfair tactics," the plaintiff would have retained the school districts' business. Id.

In Recio v. Evers, 278 Neb. 405, 771 N.W.2d 121, 2009 WL 2634052 (2009), the Nebraska Supreme Court rejected a tortious interference claim between two co-workers – university professors – because the defendant's conduct was not "unjustified." Id. at*10-11. In Recio, a university placed the plaintiff on probation and ordered her to attend counseling because it found merit in a sexual harassment complaint brought by defendant based on a number of emails the plaintiff sent to the defendant. The plaintiff's claim of tortious interference in her business relationship with the university failed because, after analyzing the seven-factor balancing test adopted from the Restatement of Torts (Second) § 767 for use in determining whether conduct is justified, the Nebraska Supreme Court held that "a person does not incur liability for interfering with a business relationship by giving truthful information to another. Such interference is not improper, even if the facts are marshaled in such a way that they speak for themselves and the person to whom the information is given immediately recognizes them as a reason for breaking a contract or refusing to deal with another." Id. at *11. (also citing Restatement of Torts (Second) § 772). The Nebraska Supreme Court also noted that while malice is one of the seven factors to consider in determining whether interference is unjustified, "it is generally insufficient standing alone to establish that fact under § 767 of the Restatement. In general, § 772(a) does not permit *any* liability to be imposed for the communication of truthful information." Id. at *13 (emphasis in original).

3. ***Prima Facie Tort.*** No reported cases.

II. EMPLOYER TESTING OF EMPLOYEES

A. Psychological or Personality Testing

1. ***Common Law and Statutes***. Psychological testing of applicants for civil service positions is permissible under Neb. Rev. Stat. § 19-1830 (Reissue 1997 and L.B. 54 2005). However, the testing must be practical and must fairly determine the capacity of the person to perform the duties of the position. Id.

2. ***Private Employers***. No reported cases.

3. ***Public Employers***. No reported cases.

B. Drug Testing

1. ***Common Law and Statutes***. Drug tests can be used to deny continued employment or to discipline employees if statutory requirements for the testing are met. Preliminary indications of positive findings of either alcohol or drugs must be confirmed by subsequent tests. Neb. Rev. Stat. § 48-1903 (Reissue 2004). Employees who refuse lawful directives of an employer to provide a body fluid or breathe sample as provided in this section may be subject to disciplinary or administrative action by the employer, including denial of continued employment. Neb. Rev. Stat. § 48-1910 (Reissue 2004).

2. ***Private Employers***. In Ritchie v. Walker Mfg. Co., 963 F.2d 1119 (8th Cir. 1992), the court stated that the statutory right of privacy would extend to the employee's place of employment. Id. at 1123. However, in order to recover for an intrusion on the right of privacy, the employee must be subjected to an intrusion that is highly offensive to a reasonable person. Id. In Ritchie, the employer specifically limited the drug testing of employees to those who were suspected of being under the influence of a drug. By incorporating a probable cause element and by following the Nebraska statutes governing drug testing, the plaintiff could not show that there was an invasion of privacy. Id. at 1124. It is not a test within the meaning of Neb. Rev. Stat. § 48-1903 (Cum.Supp. 2000) to smell alcohol on the breath of an employee. Poole v. Burlington Northern R.R. Co., 987 F. Supp. 753, 770-71 (D. Neb. 1997). Because no test is involved, there is no need to use subsequent tests to confirm that the employee is under the influence of alcohol. Id. at 771. The Nebraska Supreme Court recently held that an employer's release of an employee's drug test results to the Airport Authority was not a violation of Neb. Rev. Stat. § 48-1906 (Reissue 1998) which prohibits the release of drug test results to the public. Polinski v. Sky Harbor Air Service, Inc., 263 Neb. 406, 640 N.W.2d 391 (2002). The court further noted that the taking of a specimen for a drug test does not violate Neb. Rev. Stat. § 20-203 (Reissue 1997). Id. at 412, 640 N.W.2d 391 at 396. In Ngrime v. Huntington Park Care Center, 2006 WL 1041815, *5 (D. Neb. 2006), the court held that the plaintiff failed to state a Title VII discrimination claim by the employer initiating a drug test because the employer had a written drug policy stating that it would administer a drug test upon reasonable suspicion, which the court found when the employer observed the plaintiff-employee pulled over in employer's parking lot by law enforcement for erratic driving. In Jackson v. Brotherhood's Relief & Comp. Fund, 279 Neb. 593, 779 N.W.2d 589 (2010), the plaintiff was a railroad worker who sued the compensation fund for wages while he was "held out of service" for refusing to provide a urine sample. The Nebraska Supreme Court held that an employee's refusal to provide a urine sample for a random drug test required by federal regulation (citing 49 C.F.R. §§ 40.191(a), 219.107 (2009)) was a willful or intentional violation that excepted the employee from compensation while suspended pursuant to the compensation fund's constitution. Jackson, 279 Neb. at 596-98, 779 N.W.2d at 592-93.

3. ***Public Employers***. In Rushton v. Nebraska Public Power Dist., 844 F.2d 562 (8th Cir. 1988), the drug testing policy of the Nebraska Public Power District was upheld. The court ruled that the policy did not constitute an unreasonable search and seizure and it was not a violation of the right to privacy. Id. at 566. The expectation of privacy of employees at a heavily regulated nuclear facility is significantly diminished and the safety concern for the potential release of radiation by employees operating under the influence of drugs justified the urinalysis testing. Id. The Eighth Circuit used similar reasoning in Louis v. Department of Correctional Services of Nebraska, 437 F.3d 697, 699-701 (8th Cir. 2006) when it held that due process does not require the state to fund confirmatory testing after initial drug testing yields a positive result and an inmate continues denying using illicit drugs. **In Petersen v. Nebraska Department of Health and Human Services, 19 Neb. App. 314, 805 N.W.2d 667 (Neb. Ct. App. 2011), the court upheld the termination of an employee working as mental health security for violating the drug testing policy of the Department of Health and Human Services, the Nebraska Association of Public Employees labor contract, and the facility's work rules. The court held that the employee's termination was for just cause and that progressive discipline was not required due to the type of infraction, type of work, and the violent past history at the facility. Id. at 325-26, 805 N.W.2d 674-75.**

C. Medical Testing

1. ***Common Law and Statutes***. No statutes.

2. ***Private Employers***. No reported cases.

3. ***Public Employers***. In Glover v. Eastern Neb. Coin. Office of Retardation, 867 F.2d 461 (8th Cir. 1989), the court prohibited the defendant from testing employees for hepatitis B or acquired immune deficiency syndrome. Id. at 462. Testing employees could not be justified under the Fourth Amendment as the risk to the patients of contracting the diseases from the staff was so minuscule as to be insufficient to justify the infringement on the employee's constitutional rights. Id. at 464.

D. Polygraph Tests

Polygraph tests cannot be administered as a condition of employment unless the employee is a public law enforcement officer. Neb. Rev. Stat. § 81-1932 (Reissue 1999). An employer may ask an employee to voluntarily submit to a polygraph examination, however, the employer must limit the questions that are asked during the examination and must inform the employee that he or she may discontinue the examination at any time. A corrections unit caseworker at the State Penitentiary Medium Security Unit was not involved in public law enforcement and not required by statute to submit to a polygraph examination. White v. State, 248 Neb. 977, 984, 540 N.W.2d 354, 359 (1995). Firing a private security guard who refused to submit to a polygraph examination was a violation of statutorily mandated public policy. Ambroz v. Cornhusker Square Ltd., 226 Neb. 899, 905, 416 N.W.2d 510, 515 (1987). In Trosper v. Bag 'N Save, 273 Neb. 855, 734 N.W.2d 704 (2007), the Nebraska Supreme Court expanded an employee's right to sue an employer when discharged for making a workers compensation claim to cases involving demotion. Trosper, 273 Neb. at 865, 734 N.W.2d at 712. In doing so, however, Trosper distinguished the polygraph statute because the express language of the statute prohibited only termination. Id. (distinguishing application of § 81-1932 in Collins v. Bakers' Supermarket, 223 Neb. 365, 389 N.W.2d 774 (1986), thereby implicitly suggesting § 81-1932 applies only to termination and not demotions).

E. Fingerprinting

Various Nebraska statutes require applicants for certain positions to submit a set of fingerprints and provide authorization for a criminal history record check. See Neb. Rev. Stat. § 14-702 (Reissue 1997) (requiring firefighters to submit a full set of fingerprints and authorization for a criminal history record check); Neb. Rev. Stat. § 19-1831 (Reissue 1997) (requiring civil service applicants to submit fingerprints); Neb. Rev. Stat. § 83-1217.02 (Reissue 1999) (requiring employees of state facilities providing developmental disabilities services to submit a full set of fingerprints if the employees are not licensed or certified as members of their profession).

A statute requiring certain non-resident applicants for the first issuance of a teachers certificate to file a set of fingerprints with the Commissioner of Education was repealed in 2003. See 2003 Neb. Laws L.B. 685 (May 15, 2003) (repealing Neb. Rev. Stat. § 79-8,111 (Reissue 1996)).

F. Genetic Testing

Neb. Rev. Stat. § 48-236 (Reissue 2004) prohibits an employer from requiring an employee applicant to submit to a genetic test or provide genetic information as a condition of employment or promotion, though the statute does not prohibit an employee from voluntarily providing to an employer genetic information that is related to the employee's health or safety in the work place. Neb. Rev. Stat. § 48-236(2)(d) & (3).

III. SEARCHES

A. Employees Person

1. ***Private Employers***. No reported cases.

2. ***Public Employers***. No reported cases.

B. Employees Work Area

1. ***Private Employers***. No reported cases.

2. ***Public Employers.*** In Biby v. Board of Regents of the University of Nebraska-Lincoln, 419 F.3d 845 (8th Cir. 2005), the Eighth Circuit ruled that a university was not liable for a warrantless search of an employee's computer for work-related materials because (1) the university conducted the search primarily to provide documentation related to pending lawsuit and arbitration with third party, (2) the university's computer policy permitted search, and (3) the university believed the employee had disregarded his superior's orders and exceeded his authority with respect to contracts with the third party. Id. at 850-51.

C. Employees Property

1. ***Private Employers***. No reported cases.

2. ***Public Employers***. In Westbrook v. City of Omaha, 2006 WL 547956 (D. Neb. 2006), the Nebraska federal district court held that a police department's order requiring a police officer to turn over his bank records in an internal investigation of a citizen complaint did not violate the police officer's constitutional protections from unreasonable searches and seizures under the United States Supreme Court's standard of reasonableness under the circumstances, as opposed to a warrant requirement, for internal disciplinary investigations of governmental employees by the employer. Id. at *6 (citing O'Conner v. Ortega, 480 U.S. 709, 107 S.Ct. 1492, 94 L.Ed.2d 714 (1987)). In Westbrook, the results of the internal investigation were not shared with those conducting a criminal investigation of the police officer, nor were the results shared with the city or county prosecutors. Id. at *8. Further, the police department had a policy requiring that financial records be turned over to internal affairs investigators, and there was no showing that such records were used in criminal investigations against the officer. Id. (noting O'Conner found that "special needs" may justify public employer's search of employee's desk).

In True v. Nebraska, 2009 WL 562239 (D. Neb. 2009), the Nebraska federal district court held that periodic, random and unannounced searches of employee vehicles parked in a prison facility parking lot did not constitute unreasonable searches under the Fourth Amendment. Id. at *3. In True, the plaintiff was employed by the Lincoln Correctional Center, a prison facility operated by the Nebraska Department of Correctional Services. Id. at *1. The state had a policy of conducting random, unannounced searches of vehicles parked within prison parking lots, including employee vehicles, a policy for which employees had notice. Id. When the plaintiff's vehicle was selected at random for a search, the plaintiff refused to consent to the search and his employment was terminated on that basis. Id. at *1-2. The plaintiff sued the State, alleging violation of his constitutional rights under the First, Fourth and Fourteenth Amendments. Id. The Court dismissed all three of the plaintiff's claims. Id. at *3. With regard to the plaintiff's Fourth Amendment claim, the Court held that correction officers employed at a detention facility have a lower reasonable expectation of privacy at work, and the demand to search the plaintiff's personal vehicle did not violate his Fourth Amendment rights. Id. at *4.

IV. MONITORING OF EMPLOYEES

A. Telephones and Electronic Communications

1. ***Wiretapping***. It is not unlawful for a person to intercept a wire, electronic, or oral communication when the person is a party to the communication or when one of the parties consents to the interception. Neb. Rev. Stat. § 86-290(2) (Cum. Supp. 2004).

2. ***Electronic Communications***. It is not unlawful to intercept or access an electronic communication made through an electronic communications system that is readily accessible to the general public. Neb. Rev. Stat. § 86-290(2) (Cum. Supp. 2004).

3. ***Other Electronic Monitoring***.

B. Mail

No reported cases.

C. Surveillance/Photographing

No reported cases.

V. ACTIVITIES OUTSIDE THE WORKPLACE

A. Statute or Common Law

No statutes or reported cases.

B. Employees' Personal Relationships

1. ***Romantic Relationships Between Employees***. No reported cases.

2. ***Sexual Orientation***. No reported cases.

3. ***Marital Status***. It is an unlawful employment practice for the employer to discriminate against any individual with respect to compensation, terms, conditions, or privileges of employment because of the individual's

marital status. Neb. Rev. Stat. § 48-1104 (Reissue 2004). It is also an unlawful employment practice to limit, advertise, solicit, segregate, or classify employees in any way which deprives an individual of employment opportunities on the basis of marital status. Id.

In Adams v. Tenneco Automotive Operating Co., Inc., 359 F.Supp. 2d 834 (D. Neb. 2005), the plaintiff sued under the Nebraska Fair Employment Practice Act, Neb. Rev. Stat. § 48-1104, arguing that he was discriminated against based upon marital status, specifically the fact that he was separated and subsequently divorced. The district court found that based upon Nebraska's definition of marital status – "the status of a person whether married or single" – pursuant to Neb. Rev. Stat. § 48-1102(12), no discrimination could occur because this definition did not include separated or divorced individuals. Adams, 359 F.Supp. 2d at 835-36. The court listed four reasons why Nebraska law did not prohibit discrimination in private employment upon the status of being separated or divorced: First, the plain words of the statute did not create such classifications. Id. at 836. Marital status is defined in a limited fashion, that is, married or single. Id. Second, the legislative history of Nebraska's Fair Employment Practice Act does not support any protection for separated or divorced individuals. Id. Third, Nebraska's legislature has defined marital status to include being single, married, widowed, or divorced, in statutes pertaining to discrimination by educational institutions and therefore the legislature clearly knew how to define marital status to include individuals who are divorced or separated. Id. Fourth, no Nebraska case supported the expansion of marital status beyond the plain and limited words of the statute. Id.

C. Smoking

Nebraska's revised Clean Indoor Act became effective on June 1, 2009. See Neb. Rev. Stat. §§ 71-5716 – 71-5734 (2009). The Act makes it unlawful for any person to smoke in a place of employment or a public place, except as provided in § 71-5730, which exempts certain guest rooms and suites rented to guests and are designated as smoking rooms, indoor areas used in connection with research studying the health effects of smoking, tobacco retail outlets, and cigar bars as defined in § 53-103. An employer did not commit a prohibited practice in implementing a "Tobacco-Free Worksite" policy to an existing collective bargaining agreement when the employer bargained in good faith, and the parties reached an impasse prior to the policy's implementation. Int'l Bhd. of Elec. Workers Local 763 v. Omaha Pub. Power Dist., 280 Neb. 889, 791 N.W.2d 310 (2010).

D. Blogging

No reported cases.

VI. RECORDS

A. Personnel Records

"Personal information in records regarding personnel of public bodies other than salaries and routine directory information" may be withheld from the public. Neb. Rev. Stat. § 84-712.05 (Reissue 2004). The State of Nebraska's Personnel Rules and Regulations provide in part that "[a]t the request of the employee, records of disciplinary action shall be removed from the employee's personnel file after two years after the discipline was imposed." Chitwood v. Lawson, 2004 WL 2516206 (Neb. App. 2004)(citing Vinci v. Nebraska Dept. of Correctional Services, 253 Neb. 423, 571 N.W.2d 53 (1997) and 273 Neb. Admin. Code, ch.11, § 004.03 (1993)). Any fingerprints received by the Civil Service Commission or information resulting from an investigation of fingerprints, shall not be a public record. Neb. Rev. Stat. § 19-1831 (Reissue 1997).

B. Medical Records

Case-specific and patient-identifying data obtained from the medical records of individual patients is for the confidential use of the Department of Health and Human Services. The information obtained from medical records is confidential and shall not be made public so as to disclose the identity of an individual whose medical records have been used to compile reports for the Department of Health and Human Services. Neb. Rev. Stat. § 81-668 (Reissue 2003). In workers compensation cases, the medical and hospital information relevant to the particular injury of an employee shall be made available on demand to the employer. Neb. Rev. Stat. § 48-120(4) (Reissue 2004).

C. Criminal Records

Criminal history record information maintained by criminal justice agencies is a public record and is open to inspection and copying by any person during normal business hours. Neb. Rev. Stat. § 29-3520 (Reissue 2004). Criminal history record information includes notations of issuance of arrest warrants, arrests, detentions, indictments, formal criminal charges, and any disposition arising from arrests, charges, sentencing, correctional supervision, and release, however, criminal history record information does not include intelligence or investigative information. Neb. Rev. Stat. § 29-3506 (Reissue 2004).

D. Subpoenas / Search Warrants

Rule 34A of Nebraska's Court Rules for Discovery In Civil Cases allows parties to subpoena relevant records from third parties not party to the litigation. The procedural scheme requires the party issuing the subpoena to include a copy of the rule, and it leaves time for the third party to object. The party issuing the subpoena is also required to pay for reasonable copying costs.

There are no reported cases in Nebraska on search warrants in the employment context. But see O'Connor v. Ortega, 480 U.S. 709, 721-22 (1987).

VII. SUBSEQUENT TO EMPLOYMENT

A. References

No statutes or reported cases.

B. Non-Compete Agreements

"To determine whether a covenant not to compete is valid, a court must determine whether a restriction is reasonable in the sense that it is not injurious to the public, that it is not greater than is reasonably necessary to protect the employer in some legitimate interest, and that it is not unduly harsh and oppressive on the employee." C & L Industries, Inc. v. Kiviranta, 13 Neb. App. 604, 610, 698 N.W.2d 240, 247 (Neb. Ct. App. 2005) (citing Professional Bus. Servs. v. Rosno, 268 Neb. 99, 110, 680 N.W.2d 176, 184 (2004)). In Nebraska, a covenant not to compete may only prohibit a former employee from working for or soliciting customers for whom the former employee actually did business or with whom the employee had contact. Professional Business Servs., 268 Neb. at 105, 680 N.W.2d at 181. "An employer has a legitimate business interest in protection against a former employee's competition by improper and unfair means, but is not entitled to protection against ordinary competition from a former employee." DCS Sanitation Management, Inc. v. Castillo, 453 F.3d 892, 897 (8th Cir. 2006) (setting forth above requirements for valid covenant not to compete in Nebraska and limiting restrictions to clients or accounts with whom former employee actually did business and had personal contact). Controlled Rain, Inc. v. Sanders, 2006 WL 1222772 (Neb. Ct. App. 2006), distinguished "ordinary competition" from "unfair competition" by focusing on employee's opportunity to appropriate the employer's goodwill by initiating personal contacts with the employer's customers. Id. at *9 (citing Mertz v. Pharmacists Mut. Ins. Co., 261 Neb. 704, 625 N.W.2d 197 (2001)). "Where an employee has substantial personal contact with the employer's customers, develops goodwill with such customers, and siphons away the goodwill under circumstances where the goodwill properly belongs to the employer, the employee's result in the competition is unfair, and the employer has a legitimate need for protection against the employee's competition. Id. (also citing Professional Bus. Servs., *supra*, and Moore v. Eggers Consulting Co., 252 Neb. 396, 562 N.W.2d 534 (1997)). In Controlled Rain, the court found the covenant at issue to be valid because it did not prevent the former employee from soliciting business from the employer's customers with whom the employee did not have contact while employed. Controlled Rain, 2006 WL 1222772, at *10. See also Aon Consulting, Inc. v. Midlands Financial Benefits, Inc., 275 Neb. 642, 748 N.W.2d 626 (2008) (holding that defendant breached non-compete agreement when, almost immediately after leaving employment, he solicited business from plaintiff's customers whom he had personal dealings with in the last years of his employment with plaintiff); Softchoice Corp. v. MacKenzie, 636 F.Supp.2d 927, 2009 WL 2003226, at *10 (D. Neb. 2009) (noncompetition agreement was overly broad and unenforceable under Nebraska law because it was not limited to customers who whom former employee did business and had contact).

In ADT Sec. Servs., Inc. v. A/C Sec. Systems, Inc., 15 Neb. App. 666, 703, 736 N.W.2d 737, 769 (Neb. Ct. App. 2007), the Nebraska Court of Appeals noted that courts have generally been more willing to uphold promises to refrain from competition made in connection with sales of goodwill than those made in connection with contracts of employment. The court further explained that the rationale behind the differential treatment is that in a sale of a business, "it is almost intolerable that a person should be permitted to obtain money from another upon solemn agreement not to compete for a reasonable period within a restricted area, and then use the funds thus obtained to do the very thing the contract prohibits." Id. However, the court also explained that the restraint of trade permissible in connection with a sale of good will as a business asset is "no greater than is necessary to attain the desired purpose—the purpose of making good will a transferable asset. It is lawful for the seller to restrict his [or her] own freedom of trade only so far as it necessary to protect the buyer in the enjoyment of the good will for which he [or she] pays. The restraint on his [or her] own freedom must be reasonable in character and in extent of space and time." Id. at 704, 736 N.W.2d at 769-770 (noting that the elimination of a competitor from a restricted area for a limited time in the business field does not constitute such a restraint of trade or tendency toward monopoly incompatible with the public's interest as to warrant party avoiding solemn agreement). The court also noted that the "customer specific" rule is not applicable to non-competition agreements pursuant to the sale of good will, and is instead enforceable as long as it is reasonable in both time and scope. Id. at 704, 736 N.W.2d at 770.

Nebraska does not follow the "blue pencil" rule, and courts cannot strike or alter a covenant not to compete in order to enforce what would be considered reasonable in the circumstances. H & R Block Tax Servs., Inc. v. Circle A Enterprises, Inc., 269 Neb. 411, 416, 693 N.W.2d 548, 553 (2005). In Nebraska, a covenant not to compete is either wholly enforceable or unenforceable.

VIII. OTHER ISSUES

A. Statutes of Limitations

A cause of action for invasion of privacy must be brought within one year from the date the cause of action arose. Neb. Rev. Stat. § 20-211 (Reissue 1997); LaBenz Trucking, Inc. v. Snyder, 246 Neb. 468, 473, 519 N.W.2d 259, 262 (1994). Actions for intentional infliction of emotional distress or tortious interference with a business relationship or expectancy must be brought within four years of the date the cause of action arose. See Neb. Rev. Stat. § 25-212 (Reissue 1995). **An action for tortious interference based upon defamatory statements is a separate and distinct claim from a defamation claim; therefore, the statute of limitations for a tortious interference claim based upon defamatory statements is four years. American Home Assurance Co. v. Greater Omaha Packing Co., Inc., 2012 WL 2061941 (D. Neb. 2012).**

B. Jurisdiction

The district courts have original jurisdiction in all civil actions unless a statute otherwise provides. Neb. Rev. Stat. § 24-302 (Reissue 1995).

C. Worker's Compensation Exclusivity

The Nebraska Worker's Compensation Act, Neb. Rev. Stat. § 48-101 et seq., applies to cases in which an employee suffers a "personal injury" by an "accident or occupational disease, arising out of and in the course of his or her employment." Neb. Rev. Stat. § 48-101. Any disputed claim for worker's compensation must be submitted to the Nebraska Workers' Compensation Court. Neb. Rev. Stat. § 48-161; Peak v. Small Business Admin., 666 F.2d 1121, 1122 (8th Cir. 1981) (the Nebraska Workmen's Compensation Court has "exclusive jurisdiction" over claims brought under the Nebraska Worker's Compensation Act). In addition, the Compensation Court "shall have jurisdiction to decide any issue ancillary to the resolution of an employee's right to workers' compensation benefits." §48-161 (exempting matters involving income withholding for child support, garnishment, and administrative attachment and bank matching).

D. Pleading Requirements

Effective January 1, 2003, pursuant to a legislative directive, the Nebraska Supreme Court promulgated the Nebraska Rules of Pleading in Civil Actions. See Neb. Rev. Stat. §25-801.01 (Cum. Supp. 2002). The new pleading rules replace Nebraska's prior "code pleading" system with rules patterned after the Federal Rules of Civil Procedure. There have been no appellate opinions addressing the effect of these changes on pleading libel or invasion of privacy cases. Presumably, a complaint need not now make as detailed factual allegations as under the prior rules. Section 6-1108 of the Nebraska Rules of Pleading in Civil Actions (renumbered as of July 1, 2008, formerly Rule 8) requires only that a pleading "contain (1) a caption, (2) a short and plain statement of the claim showing that the pleader is entitled to relief, and (3) a demand for judgment for the relief the pleader seeks."

SURVEY OF NEVADA EMPLOYMENT LIBEL LAW

Wendy M. Krincek
R. Calder Huntington
Littler Mendelson
3960 Howard Hughes Parkway, Suite 300
Las Vegas, NV 89169

Mark Hinueber
Stephens Media
P.O. Box 70
Las Vegas, NV 89125

(With Developments Reported Through **November 1, 2012**)

GENERAL COMMENTS

With no intermediate court of appeals, Nevada generates relatively little published case law. Therefore, it is not uncommon for years to go by without a published decision by the Nevada Supreme Court regarding libel law.

There continues to be a marked increase of claims and causes of action brought in connection with wrongful discharge cases. The claims a Nevada employer can expect to see coupled with the claim for wrongful termination or discrimination include: defamation, invasion of privacy, intentional or negligent infliction of emotional distress, fraud, loss of consortium, interference with contract, interference with prospective economic advantage, false imprisonment, and assault and battery. These "tag along torts" are beneficial to plaintiffs because they enable a disgruntled former employee to recover large tort awards, including punitive damages, which are not normally available in a breach-of-contract case. It is important that Nevada employers understand the type of conduct that underlies such claims and recognize the liabilities that can result from them so that they may adopt preventative measures to minimize potential liability.

In addition, employers are coming under increasing attack for negligently hiring or permitting employees with problems, such as criminal records or histories of drug and alcohol abuse, to continue working. This is particularly true for workers whose performance can affect the health and safety of their coworkers or the public at large, such as employees operating motor vehicles or those providing services such as cleaning or repairing customers' homes. These relatively new causes of action are referred to as negligent hiring, negligent supervision, negligent retention, and negligent training. As is apparent from their titles, each claim is based on a theory of negligence, *i.e.*, that the employer failed to satisfy its duty to protect the plaintiff from the actions of the employer's employees, and that the plaintiff was damaged as a result.

SIGNIFICANT DEVELOPMENTS SINCE THE 2012 *SURVEY*

None.

I. GENERAL LAW

A. General Employment Law

1. ***At Will Employment***. Nevada has long recognized the doctrine of *at-will employment*, which generally holds that employment for an indefinite term may be terminated with or without notice, at any time, and without cause (*i.e.*, for any reason or no reason at all) so long as that reason is not otherwise illegal. Southwest Gas Corp. v. Ahmad, 99 Nev. 594, 668 P.2d 261 (1983).

But recently the at-will doctrine has been eroded by legislative action and judicial decision. The first limitation on at-will employment came in the form of legislative public policy exceptions. In response to the harsh results at-will terminations sometimes produced, legislatures identified and excluded special public policy areas of the employment relationship from the employer's power to terminate at will. These statutory exceptions have been expanded and supplemented by judicial interpretation to such an extent, some argue, that limitations on at-will employment are no longer the exception to the rule, but an exception that has nearly swallowed the rule. Despite this view, there is still room for the at-will employer in Nevada. As will be addressed later, such an employer generally has a carefully worded, signed agreement with its employees, expressly defining the employment relationship as one terminable with or without cause.

Statutory Exceptions. The Nevada legislature has enacted numerous exceptions to the at-will doctrine:

a. **Jury Service.** NRS § 6.190 makes the discharge of an employee for jury service a misdemeanor and provides a civil remedy to an employee discharged in violation of this section, including back pay, reinstatement, damages, and attorney's fees.

b. **Garnishment.** NRS § 31.298 prohibits discipline or discharge exclusively because the employer is required to withhold earnings pursuant to a writ of garnishment.

c. **Support**. NRS § 31A.290 provides that wage assignments and commissions for payments to collect support cannot be used to discipline or discharge an employee. The employer who violates this statute must fully reinstate the employee and pay a civil fine. In addition, the employer will be liable for any payments of support not paid and, if the employee prevails in an action, for an amount not less than $2,500 for payment of the employee's costs and attorney's fees incurred in the action.

d. **Witnesses.** NRS § 50.070 prohibits the employer from threatening to terminate or terminating an employee for serving as a witness or being a prospective witness in any judicial or administrative proceeding. Remedies for violation of this statute include restoration of lost wages and benefits, an order of reinstatement, damages equal to lost wages and benefits, and reasonable attorney's fees.

e. **Juvenile Proceedings.** Under Nevada law, it is a misdemeanor to terminate a parent, guardian, or custodian of a child for appearing in a juvenile proceeding if the employer is given notice. NRS § 62D.120; NRS § 62D.130. A discharged employee may recover civil damages and reasonable attorney's fees. NRS § 62D.130.

f. **Military Leave**. NRS §§ 281.145, 281.147 deal with public employees (not only state employees) who are active members of the military reserves, Nevada National Guard, or disaster technicians, as classified by the American Red Cross. If the employee requests leave and has written orders, the employer must grant military leave under Nevada Revised Statutes section 281.145 without loss of regular compensation for not more than fifteen working days in any calendar year. Similarly, a Red Cross-classified disaster technician must be granted leave, within certain geographical limitations, upon the Red Cross's request and employer approval.

g. **Disclosure Of Improper Governmental Action.** NRS §§ 281.611-281.671; NRS §§ 289.110-289.120 are Nevada's whistleblower statute. They apply to state employees and state officers. State employees and officers are prohibited from firing, demoting, transferring, disciplining, or otherwise interfering in any way with another state employee's or officer's disclosure of alleged improper governmental action. The employee may file an appeal alleging retaliation with the Department of Personnel. Criminal penalties are also possible.

h. **Local Government Employers.** Under Nevada's public sector collective bargaining statute, NRS § 288.270, a local government employer is prohibited from discriminating against an employee based on union involvement, "political or personal reasons or affiliations," or any other basis prohibited by law. The employee may pursue an unfair practice charge before the Employee Management Relations Board (EMRB) for violation of the statute.

i. **Voting.** NRS § 293.463 prohibits an employer from discharging, disciplining, or penalizing an employee who is absent from employment because he or she is voting in an election. Violation of this statute is a misdemeanor.

j. **Conferences and Other School-Related Activities.** Under NRS § 392.920, an employer may not terminate or threaten to terminate a parent, guardian, or custodian of a child based on attendance at a school conference requested by the school administrator or an emergency regarding the child at school. In addition, an employer may not terminate, demote, suspend or otherwise discriminate against a parent, guardian, or custodian of a child based on attendance at school-related activities, such as parent-teacher conferences, school-related activities during regular school hours, volunteering or involvement at school, and attendance at other school-related events. Violations of these provisions is a misdemeanor. The employee may recover civil damages and reasonable attorney's fees.

k. **Nevada National Guard Member.** Under NRS §§ 412.139-412.1395, an employer may not terminate a Nevada National Guard member because he/she is ordered to active duty or service. Violation of this statute is a misdemeanor. An employee discharged in violation of this statute may request a hearing before the labor commissioner and obtain full and immediate restoration of position.

l. **Search-And-Rescue Volunteers, Sheriff Reserves, and Civil Air Patrol Members.** NRS § 414.260 provides that no employer, including government employers, can recommend discharge or discharge an employee for any reason specifically relating to service as a volunteer search-and-rescue or reserve member in a sheriff's department, or a Civil Air Patrol unit, unless the employee fails to disclose membership to his/her employer, or the employer notifies the employee that the participant is prohibited during normal working hours. An employee discharged in violation of this statute is entitled to all wages and benefits lost as a result of the violation, full reinstatement and reasonable attorney's fees.

m. **Witness in Wage, Hour and Compensation Hearing.** Under NRS § 608.015, it is unlawful for anyone to threaten, discharge, or penalize in any manner, a person testifying in a wage, hour, and compensation hearing.

n. **Private Employment Agencies.** NRS § 611.265(2) provides that an employment agency may not cause or attempt to cause discharge of an employee. Violation of this statute is a misdemeanor.

o. **Candidates For Public Office.** NRS §§ 613.040, 613.070 prohibit an employer from making rules or regulations prohibiting or preventing an employee from engaging in politics or becoming a candidate for public office. Section 613.070 allows for a recovery of damages by an employee for injuries suffered as a result of a violation of section 613.040.

p. **Prohibition Against Spotters.** Nevada's "Spotter Statute," NRS § 613.160, prohibits employers from employing spotters for the purpose of investigating, obtaining, and reporting to the employer information concerning employees. Any disciplinary action or discharge based on such information is also prohibited where the employee's honesty, integrity, or breach of the employer's rules is at issue, unless the employer gives notice and an opportunity for a hearing to the accused employee. If the employee requests a hearing, the employee is entitled to confront the spotter and furnish testimony in his or her own defense. The exclusive remedy is a penalty of five thousand dollars per violation to be paid to the state. The state may also recover costs and attorney's fees.

q. **Covenants Not To Compete.** NRS § 613.200 prohibits an employer or any other person from willfully preventing a person who has left employment or who has been discharged for any cause from obtaining employment elsewhere in the state. The penalty for violation of this statute is a fine. The statute allows the employer and employee to enter into reasonable agreements regarding covenants not to compete and protection of trade secrets and other confidential information.

r. **Blacklisting.** NRS § 613.210 prohibits blacklisting an employee, but allows the employer to give a written statement to the employee at the time of discharge that includes the reasons for discharge. An employer may also give a statement regarding meritorious service at the time the employee leaves. Only an employee who has been employed for over sixty days may demand these letters. An individual who violates this law against blacklisting is guilty of a misdemeanor.

s. **Discrimination In Employment.** NRS §§ 613.330-613.430 are similar in structure to Title VII of the Civil Rights Act of 1974, 42 U.S.C. § 2000e, et seq., and the Age Discrimination in Employment Act, 29 U.S.C. § 621, et seq. State law protects a wider variety of classes than federal law, however. State law prohibits discrimination in employment based on race, color, religion, sex, sexual orientation, gender identity or expression, age, disability or national origin, including interference with aid or appliance for a disability and discrimination based on use of a hearing or seeing device or a guide dog. The prohibition of discrimination based on gender identity was added to the statute in 2011. The definition of "disability" includes "without limitation, the human immunodeficiency virus." NRS 613.310(1)(a). Presumably, AIDS may be included within this definition. Section 613.340 prohibits discrimination against an employee for opposing unlawful employment practices or for assisting in the investigation of unlawful employment practices. A person claiming discrimination under these sections files first with the Nevada Equal Rights Commission (NERC). NRS § 613.405. If the Commission does not conclude that a violation of the statute has occurred, the person may file his or her claim in state court within 180 days after the alleged act. NRS §§ 613.420 and 613.430.

t. **Polygraph Examinations.** NRS §§ 613.480-613.510 and NRS §§ 289.050, 289.070 prohibit employers from discharging, disciplining, or discriminating against an applicant or current employee based on the refusal to take a polygraph examination or the results of a polygraph examination, the filing of a claim alleging violation of this statute, and/or testifying about an alleged violation. Under the "peace officers' bill of rights," NRS 289, there are certain specific restrictions on polygraph examinations of peace officers.

u. **Smokers' Rights/Medical Use of Marijuana.** NRS § 613.333 is Nevada's "Smokers' Rights Act." It bars an employer from discharging or otherwise discriminating against any employee who engages in lawful use of any product outside the employer's premises during non-work hours if the use does not interfere with the ability to do the job or compromise the safety of coworkers. A violation of this statute can result in an order of reinstatement or an order directing that an offer of employment be made, damages equal to lost wages and benefits, and costs of suit and attorney's fees.

Section 613.333 of the NRS prohibits an employer from discriminating against its employees for the lawful use of any product outside its premises, as long as the use of the product does not adversely affect the employee's job performance or the safety of other employees. Although ostensibly drafted to protect smokers from discrimination in employment, the wording and application of this section are much broader.

Section 613.333 provides that an employer may not refuse to hire an applicant, or discharge, or otherwise discriminate against any employee concerning his compensation, terms, conditions, or privileges of employment because he engages in the lawful use of any product in Nevada outside the premises of the employer during nonworking hours, if that use does not adversely affect his ability to perform his job or the safety of other employees. However, this does not prevent the employer from implementing nonsmoking policies at its facilities.

The statute provides that an employee who is discriminated against in violation of this section may bring a civil action directly against the employer. Damages in these cases are limited to lost wages, benefits, and reinstatement without loss of position, seniority, or benefits. The prevailing party is also entitled to attorney's fees. Section 613.333 is the exclusive remedy for this violation; it would be difficult for an employee to credibly assert a public policy, tortious-discharge claim based on this statute.

v. **Genetic Testing.** Under Nevada's Fair Employment Practices Act, it is an unlawful employment practice for employers to require genetic testing of current employees. NRS 613.345(1). It is also unlawful for employers to require prospective employees to undergo genetic testing as a condition of employment, or to deny employment, alter the terms of employment, or terminate employment based upon genetic information. *Id.*

w. **Occupational Safety And Health.** NRS § 618.445 prohibits discharge or other retaliation for filing a claim under the state occupational safety and health statutes. If the employer violates this statute, the employee is entitled to reinstatement and reimbursement for lost wages and benefits.

x. **Retaliation.** Nevada also makes it an unlawful employment practice for an employer to retaliate against any of its employees or applicants for employment because an individual has opposed any practice made unlawful by sections 613.310 to 613.430 of the NRS. This prohibition of retaliation also extends to any employee who has made a charge, testified, assisted, or participated in any manner in an investigation, proceeding, or hearing under NRS sections 613.310 to 613.435.

To state a retaliation claim, an individual must show (1) he or she engaged in protected activity, (2) his employer subjected him to an adverse employment action, and (3) a "causal link" exists between the protected activity and the adverse action, i.e., the adverse action occurred because of a protected activity. Like the "burden shifting" analysis discussed above, the employer must present a legitimate reason for the adverse employment action. Once the employer presents a legitimate reason for the adverse employment action, the individual must demonstrate an important factual issue regarding whether the employer's reason was a "pretext," i.e., a mere excuse or a false reason.

Adverse employment action includes adverse treatment, such as a pay cut or the elimination of a flexible start time that is reasonably likely to deter employees from engaging in protected conduct, such as complaining about sexual harassment. Adverse employment actions also include transfers of job duties; undeserved performance ratings; distribution of an unfavorable job reference; exclusion from meetings, seminars, and positions that would have made the employee eligible for salary increases; denial of secretarial support; and a more burdensome work schedule. A single negative performance evaluation is not sufficient adverse action to support a retaliation claim. Mere "ostracism suffered at the hands of coworkers" is not adverse employment action, though more severe retaliatory harassment by coworkers may be sufficient to state a claim for retaliation.

y. **Case Law Exceptions.** While the Nevada Supreme Court has recognized that all employees in Nevada are presumptively at-will employees, American Bank Stationery v. Farmer, 106 Nev. 698, 703, 799 P.2d 1100, 1102 (1990), the Court has also recognized that employers and employees remain free to contractually modify an employee's at-will status, orally or in writing, Martin v. Sears, Roebuck & Co., 111 Nev. 923, 927, 899 P.2d 551, 554 (1995). The at-will presumption may be rebutted by proving, by a preponderance of the evidence, that there was an express or implied contract between the employer and the employee which indicates that the employer would only terminate the employee for cause. See id.; see also Vancheri v. GNLV Corp., 105 Nev. 417 (1989)(cited and applied by the Ninth Circuit Court of Appeals in Brooks v. Hilton Casinos, Inc., 959 F.2d 757, 759 (9th Cir.1992), cert. denied, 506 U.S. 906).

Moreover, just as the state legislature has imposed "public policy" limitations upon at-will employment, the Nevada Supreme Court has similarly limited the at-will doctrine. In this regard, the Nevada Supreme Court has created the following public policy exceptions to the at-will doctrine prohibiting conduct that encourages or requires the violation of law:

a. **Retaliatory/Tortious Discharge.** In MGM Grand Hotel-Reno v. Insley, 102 Nev. 513, 728 P.2d 821 (1986), an employee covered by a collective bargaining agreement required surgery because of an injury suffered while at work. The employer's insurance administrator denied industrial injury coverage. The employee appealed the decision, underwent surgery, and was discharged for an unexcused absence. He claimed that he was discharged in retaliation for appealing the denial of his industrial accident claim. The court held that the employee's claim was based on state public policy and was therefore a tort claim for retaliatory discharge and was not preempted by federal labor law. Presumably because the parties did not raise the issue, the court did not address whether the employee's claim would have been preempted by ERISA.

An often cited application of the judicial public policy exceptions to at-will employment is Hansen v. Harrah's, 100 Nev. 60, 675 P.2d 394 (1984). In Hansen, the Nevada Supreme Court considered for the first time whether Nevada should adopt a public policy exception to the at-will rule by recognizing a cause of action for retaliatory discharge for filing a workers' compensation claim. The court, affirming the established public policy of the state favoring economic security for employees injured on the job, upheld a narrow exception to the at-will employment doctrine, noting that a denial of such public policy claims would undermine the entire structure of the state workers' compensation law. The employees were allowed to maintain a tort cause of action.

Since deciding Hansen, the Supreme Court of Nevada has extended the public policy exception to cover varying circumstances. These circumstances include the termination of an employee for performing jury duty, see D'Angelo v. Gardner, 107 Nev. 704, 712, 819 P.2d 206, 212 (1991), refusing to engage in activities violative of the law or another public policy of the state, see Allum v. Valley Bank of Nevada, 114 Nev. 1313, 1323-24, 970 P.2d 1062, 1068 (1998), and for refusing to engage in unsafe conduct at his employer's request, D'Angelo v. Gardner, 107 Nev. at 719. See also K Mart Corp. v. Ponsock, 103 Nev. 39, 48, 732 P.2d 1364, 1369-80 (1987) (recognizing a similar tort of "bad faith discharge" for terminating an employee to prevent him from receiving retirement benefits), abrogated by Ingersoll-Rand Co. v. McClendon, 498 U.S. 133, 137 (1990) (holding that state law claims such as this are preempted by federal ERISA laws).

The Nevada Supreme Court has upheld its ruling in D'Angelo v. Gardner that it will not allow a claim for tortious discharge when an adequate statutory remedy already exists. Ozawa v. Vision Airlines, Inc., 216 P.3d 788, 791, 2009 Nev. LEXIS 45 (Oct. 1, 2009) citing D'Angelo v. Gardner, 107 Nev. at 720. In Ozawa, an employee who was terminated for organizing his coworkers to collectively seek increased compensation sought an exception to the at-will employment doctrine. Ozawa v. Vision Airlines, Inc., 216 P.3d at 791. The Nevada Supreme Court held that the employee could not bring a cause of action for tortious discharge when he had an alternative remedy under the federal Railway Labor Act, 45 U.S.C. §§ 151-188 (2006). Id. at 791-792.

To prevail on a tortious discharge claim "the employee must be able to establish that the dismissal was based upon the employee's refusing to engage in conduct that was violative of public policy or upon the employee's engaging in conduct which public policy favors." Bigelow v. Bullard, 111 Nev. 1178, 1181, 901 P.2d 630, 632 (1995). At base, a tortious discharge claim seeks to remedy the "wrongful, usually retaliatory, interruption of employment by means which are deemed to be contrary to the public policy of [the] state." D'Angelo v. Gardner, 107 Nev. 704, 718, 819 P.2d 206, 216 (1991). However, "[p]ublic policy tortious discharge actions are severely limited to those rare and exceptional cases where the employer's conduct violates strong and compelling public policy." Sands Regent v. Valgardson, 105 Nev. 436, 440, 777 P.2d 898, 900 (1989).

In Pope v. Motel 6, 121 Nev. 307, 114 P.3d 277 (2005), the Nevada Supreme Court held that retaliation actions are limited to those individuals that have actually opposed an unlawful employment practice or engaged in protected activity, not a third-party.

b. **Constructive Discharge.** In Dillard Dep't Stores, Inc. v. Beckwith, 115 Nev. 372, 989 P.2d 882, 885 (1999), rehearing denied by, (Feb. 22, 2000), cert. denied, 530 U.S. 1276 (2000), the Nevada Supreme Court affirmed a four-million-dollar jury verdict which found that Dillard's had constructively discharged an employee when she was demoted to an entry-level position with a forty percent pay cut after returning from workers' compensation leave. The Court's decision opened the door for even greater employer exposure in this area when it affirmed the use of a jury instruction which imposes a duty on the employer to "return the injured employee to the job he had before his injury," or risk liability.

c. **Bad Faith Discharge.** In K Mart Corp. v. Ponsock, 103 Nev. 39, 732 P.2d 1364 (1987), the Nevada Supreme Court determined that the discharged employee was a tenured employee rather than an at-will employee based upon a stipulation between the parties that the employee handbook was part of an employment contract, and that he had been terminated without good cause approximately six months before he was fully vested in his retirement benefits. The court, in discussing the development of the public policy exception to the at-will doctrine for retaliatory discharge, noted that an employer could not terminate an at-will employee for reasons that offended public policy, such as terminating an employee in order to avoid paying him or her retirement benefits. Noting that the case before it did not involve an at-will employee, the court chose to label the employee's discharge as a "bad faith discharge" giving rise to tort liability because plaintiff had been fired in violation of public policy. Presumably because the parties did not raise the issue, the court did not address whether the employee's claims were preempted by ERISA.

d. **Whistleblowing.** The Nevada Supreme Court has accepted reporting of illegal conduct of the employer as an exception to the "at-will" employment doctrine in one case, but has rejected it in two others. To establish a claim of retaliatory or tortious discharge based upon whistleblowing, the employee must demonstrate that retaliation for protected speech was the cause of his termination. Wiltsie v. Baby Grand Corp., 105 Nev. 291, 774 P.2d 432 (1989); see also

Blanck v. Hager, 360 F. Supp. 2d 1137, 1155 (D. Nev. 2005). An actual violation of the law by an employer is not essential. Biesler v. Prof'l Sys. Corp., 321 F. Supp. 2d 1165, 1169, n. 2 (D. Nev. 2004) (citing Allum v. Valley Bank of Nevada, 114 Nev. 1313, 970 P.2d 1062, 1067 (1998)), affirmed, 2006 U.S. App. Lexis 9902 (9thCir.). An employee's reasonable, good faith suspicion that the employer has engaged in illegal conduct is sufficient. Id.

In Wiltsie v. Baby Grand Corp., 105 Nev. 291, 774 P.2d 432 (1989), the Nevada Supreme Court reviewed the tortious-discharge claim of a casino employee who alleged he had been terminated for reporting the illegal conduct of his supervisor to his employer. The employer denied having been notified of the alleged illegal conduct. Stating that there is no more basic policy in Nevada than enforcement of gaming laws, the court went on to state that whistleblowing activity is protected only when the "employee's actions are not merely private or proprietary," but instead seek "to further the public good." Id. at 433. Because the employee in this case claimed he was discharged for reporting the illegal activity to his supervisor rather than the appropriate authorities, the court ruled that the employee was merely acting in a private or proprietary manner. The employee was denied an opportunity to pursue his tortious discharge claim.

In Biesler v. Prof'l Sys. Corp., 321 F. Supp. 2d 1165, 1169 (D. Nev. 2004), a Federal District Court in the District of Nevada similarly found that the employee's allegation that she "pointed out fraudulent and potentially illegal activities on the part of the company to management, including the CEO," was insufficient. "Such internal reporting or exposure is merely private or proprietary and is not sufficient to maintain a tortious discharge claim based upon whistleblowing." Id.; Schlang v. Key Airlines, Inc., 794 F. Supp. 1493 (D. Nev. 1992), vacated in part on other grounds by, 158 F.R.D. 666 (D. Nev. 1994) (employee's reporting of alleged violations of Federal Aviation Regulations to the National Mediation Board, Air Traffic Control, and in the aircraft log books insufficient because the employees did not report the alleged violations directly to the federal body charged with enforcing the FARs, the Federal Aviation Administration).

But when the Nevada Supreme court revisited whistleblowing as a basis for tortious discharge nine years later, it allowed the claim. In Allum v. Valley Bank, 114 Nev. 1313, 970 P.2d 1062 (1998), the court ruled that an employee who shows that he reasonably suspected in good faith that his employer had engaged in illegal conduct may maintain a tortious discharge claim. In this case, the employee claimed he had been fired for refusing to participate in suspected illegal activity relating to loan underwriting and whistleblowing. The court held that the employee did not have to prove that his employer actually participated in illegal activity. The Nevada Supreme Court also held that an employee who is fired for refusing to break the law can state a claim for tortious discharge in violation of public policy.

However, when whistleblowing is allowed as a basis for a tortious discharge claim, it may be limited by the particular facts of a case. In Shoen v. Amerco, Inc., 111 Nev. 735, 896 P.2d 469 (1995), rehearing denied by, (Oct. 19, 1995), the founder of a corporation alleged that he had been terminated because he testified against one of his children who was a major stockholder, an officer, and a director of Amerco, in an IRS tax trial. The father presented evidence that another of his sons, who also faced tax charges, assaulted and harassed him prior to and immediately after the trial. The court concluded, however, that a public policy tort would not be recognized in this case because the father had a comprehensive statutory remedy under Nevada Revised Statutes section 50.070, discussed supra, which prohibits employers from terminating an employee who was summoned to serve as a witness in any proceeding. The court noted that this statute provided an adequate tort-type remedy for the father.

e. **Refusal of Hazardous Assignment.** In D'Angelo v. Gardner, 107 Nev. 704, 819 P.2d 206 (1991), the Nevada Supreme Court clarified its earlier ruling in Valgardson, 105 Nev. 436, 777 P.2d 898 (1989), discussed infra, and held that an employee who had refused to work in a cyanide leach pit at the time he was suffering from a surgical wound had stated a cause of action for tortious discharge. Citing the Nevada Occupational Safety & Health Act (NOSHA), which expressly prohibits employers from requiring employees to go to or remain in unsafe or unhealthful places, the court held that "dismissal of an employee for seeking a safe and healthy working environment is contrary to the public policy of this state." D'Angelo, 819 P.2d at 216.

f. **Refusal to Violate the Law.** Nevada has recognized that a claim of tortious discharge may be supported by evidence that establishes outrageous condition that violates public policy, which includes the plaintiff's refusal to violate the law. State v. Eighth Judicial Dist. Court, 42 P.3d 233 (2002). In State v. Eighth Judicial Dist. Court, the employee's "impression" that he was asked to violate the law by unlawfully obtaining bank and telephone records was insufficient. The Nevada Supreme Court held that the employee's allegation must be supported by independent evidence.

No Exception Found. There are also several cases in which a public policy exception to the "at-will" doctrine has not been found:

a. **Age Discrimination.** In Sands Regent v. Valgardson, 105 Nev. 436, 777 P.2d 898 (1989), two card dealers, aged fifty-eight and fifty-two, were terminated by their employer, a casino. Consistent with the casino's desire to get rid of older people in the "pit" and give the pit a younger look, the employees were terminated because they were "too old." Later, the casino unsuccessfully attempted to rehire them. The employees eventually filed suit in state court alleging violation of Nevada's antidiscrimination law, NRS § 613.310 et seq.; the federal Age Discrimination in Employment Act (ADEA); and public policy wrongful discharge; among other state causes of action. The court concluded that "age discrimination does not fit into the public policy exception to the 'at-will' employment doctrine." Id. at 899. Acknowledging that Nevada has a public policy against age discrimination, the court said that "we do not perceive that our public policy against age discrimination is sufficiently strong and compelling to warrant another exception to the 'at-will' employment doctrine." Id. at 900. The court stated that age discrimination, however objectionable, did not rise to the same actionable tortious conduct level as in Hansen, supra, or K Mart Corp. v. Ponsock, supra. The court reemphasized that public policy tortious discharge actions are "severely limited to those rare and exceptional cases where the employer's conduct violates strong and compelling public policy." Id. at 900.

In D'Angelo v. Gardner, 107 Nev. 704, 819 P.2d 206 (1991), the court explained that it may have used some misleading language in its Valgardson opinion when the court stated that age discrimination was not a sufficient violation of public policy to warrant an exception to the at-will doctrine. The court explained that it had refused to allow recovery for age discrimination in Valgardson because the employee in that case had already recovered the equivalent of tort damages under the ADEA and the state antidiscrimination statute. The court explained that in Valgardson, the employee was unable to pursue his age-discrimination claim under the tortious-discharge theory because there was no need for an additional court-created remedy similar to the one the court fashioned in Hansen. The court further stated that the Nevada Occupational Safety and Health Act remedy was far less comprehensive than the remedy available to the employee in Valgardson. Because the employee in this case had no comprehensive statutory remedy to compensate him, he was entitled to pursue his action for tortious discharge against his employer.

In Marcoz v. Summa Corp., 106 Nev. 737, 801 P.2d 1346 (1990), the plaintiff, a casino employment representative, was terminated after he refused to accept voluntary early retirement. At the time of his termination, the employee was vested in the employer's retirement plan, but as a result of the termination he received less money than he would have received had he been able to remain on the job until age sixty-five. Among other claims, the employee alleged age discrimination in violation of the federal Age Discrimination in Employment Act and tortious discharge in violation of public policy. The court concluded the employee's claims of deliberate denial of ERISA benefits were preempted by federal law and could be heard only in a federal court. As for the employee's attempts to claim that some of his losses were not related to ERISA benefits, the court stated that under the K Mart case, the employee had not stated a cause of action for tortious discharge. The court further stated that K Mart did not apply to claims involving ERISA benefits.

In Martin v. Sears, Roebuck & Co., 111 Nev. 923, 899 P.2d 551 (1995), the discharged employee, a superintendent in a Sears store, was terminated because he improperly transferred funds and falsified company records. After an investigation, the employee resigned rather than accept a demotion. Among other claims, the employee alleged that he was constructively discharged in violation of public policy because of his age (forty-six) and because his employer desired to reduce costs. The court concluded that the employee lacked evidence to support his claim that the employer's actions were based on his age. Further, the court noted that under Valgardson, age discrimination cannot be the basis for tortious discharge in Nevada.

b. **Racial Discrimination.** In Bigelow v. Bullard, 111 Nev. 1178, 901 P.2d 630 (1995), rehearing denied by, (Feb. 28, 1996), employees alleged that they had been discharged because they objected to certain racial policies and activities on the part of their employer. In this case, there was little doubt that the employer had engaged in racially discriminatory practices and policies. After a detailed examination of the employees' failure to register their complaints directly with the employer, the court concluded that an employee's complaint to a fellow employee or some other third person about company policy could not sustain a claim for tortious discharge.

The court did suggest, however, that had either of the employees in this case presented evidence that they were terminated because they refused directives to engage in unlawful discriminatory policies, a tortious discharge claim might be sustained. The court provided several examples of tortious discharge already established by Nevada court decisions. The court cited a California case where an employee was terminated for refusing to commit perjury, suggesting that if presented with such a case, the Nevada Supreme Court might conclude that termination for refusal to commit perjury would be a sufficient basis for another exception to the at-will doctrine.

c. **Insubordination**. In another case, Smith v. Cladianos, 104 Nev. 67, 752 P.2d 233 (1988), the employer terminated the employment relationship after approximately four and one-half years because the employee paid funds to a company after being ordered not to do so. The employee claimed she had been given the order only after paying the funds and had been wrongfully terminated. The court, noting that no written contract of employment existed and that the employee admitted she was employed with no specific termination date, held that the employee was an at-will employee and could be terminated for any reason not in violation of public policy.

In Blankenship v. O'Sullivan Plastics Corp., 109 Nev. 1162, 866 P.2d 293 (1993), an employee was terminated from his position as an electrician because he refused to sign a substance abuse employee agreement that included a provision requiring each employee to waive his constitutional right against self-incrimination. The employer required all of its employees to sign this agreement in an attempt to comply with federal drug-free workplace legislation. The employee refused to sign because he was unwilling to waive his right against self-incrimination. Instead, the employee submitted an amended agreement to the employer. The employer then terminated him based solely on his refusal to sign the agreement.

The employee claimed that his refusal to waive such a fundamental right was guaranteed by the United States and Nevada Constitutions, and that his termination was a violation of both national and state public policy. The court analyzed the language of the agreement itself and concluded that neither a constitutional right nor a public policy was involved in the agreement. The court emphasized that federal and state constitutions prohibit a person from testifying against himself only in a *criminal case.* The language of the agreement did not in any way imply a criminal prosecution or a threat of prosecution. Rather, the agreement was the employer's misguided effort to prevent its employees from disrupting substance abuse testing in case of a plant accident or other suspicious behavior. The court noted that nothing in the agreement suggested that the employer was planning to turn over any evidence to the state for use in a criminal case. The court concluded that the employee's misinterpretation of the legal significance of the waiver could not form a basis for another public policy exception to the at-will doctrine. To allow such a claim to go forward, the court would be condoning public policy exceptions to the at-will doctrine based on "the brittle foundation of subjective assumptions, however erroneous." Blankenship v. O'Sullivan Plastics Corp., 109 Nev. 1162, 866 P.2d at 293 (1993).

In Wayment v. Holmes, 112 Nev. 232, 912 P.2d 816 (1996), the court addressed a tortious discharge claim raised by a public employee. The employee, a deputy district attorney, claimed that he had been discharged in violation of public policy because he repeatedly notified and then argued with his supervisor over alleged deficiencies in an indictment. The deputy claimed that he had an ethical duty under Nevada Supreme Court rules to inform his supervisor of the deficiencies and to try to convince his supervisor to remedy those deficiencies. He further claimed that he had a mandatory ethical duty to refrain from bringing a frivolous action and from prosecuting a charge that could not be supported by probable cause. By terminating him, he argued, the employer violated the strong public policy of having attorneys abide by Nevada Supreme Court rules.

The court noted that the deputy failed to produce any evidence that his termination was linked to his objections about the indictment. The employer had presented evidence that the deputy had been terminated because his work performance was unsatisfactory, and he was insubordinate. Further, the court noted that the deputy discharged his ethical duty when he notified his supervisor of the perceived deficiencies in the indictment. Noting that the Supreme Court Rules do not require an attorney to badger his supervisor about deficiencies, the court concluded that the deputy was terminated because he constantly argued with his supervisor and badgered him about the deficiencies. The court concluded that terminating an at-will public employee for insubordination does not violate Nevada public policy.

d. **Poor Performance.** In Beales v. Hillhaven, Inc., 108 Nev. 96, 825 P.2d 212 (1992), the court found that a nursing home administrator's termination, while wrongful, did not warrant tort damages. A discharge based on "poor performance," even if not one of the stated grounds for termination in an employee handbook, did not fall within the rare cases where tort liability is warranted.

e. **Position Elimination.** In another 1995 case, the court ruled that a twenty-one-year employee who had progressed through the ranks to become general manager of operations failed to state a claim for tortious discharge in violation of public policy when his position was eliminated during a corporate restructuring. The court concentrated its analysis on the employee's attempts to rebut the at-will presumption and merely concluded that the casino employer had done nothing that offended Nevada public policy. Yeager v. Harrah's Club, 111 Nev. 830, 897 P.2d 1093 (1995).

Implied Contract Found. At-will employment has also been eroded by the willingness of courts to find that the nature of the employment relationship has, by implication, given employees contractual protection against at-will terminations. There are two aspects to the implied contractual restrictions on at-will employment. The first is the implied-in-fact contract. The second is the implied-in-law covenant of good faith and fair dealing. These two limitations on the at-will doctrine are independent of the public policy exceptions discussed earlier in this chapter and exist without respect to public policy considerations.

Furthermore, employees who have no written contract of employment may nevertheless have the protections of an employment contract where the employer has made representations or has engaged in conduct that leads employees to believe that they are not terminable at will. The representations that establish an *implied-in-fact employment contract* vary greatly. They include statements made during the hiring process, statements contained in personnel or training manuals and employee handbooks, statements in memoranda or notices to employees, and statements made during employee evaluations. Conduct may take the form of performance-related pay increases, promotions, and the absence of any direct criticism of the employee's work, among other kinds of conduct. In the following cases, the evidence of an implied contract often is *both* oral and written. The cases have been divided to illustrate how the courts view oral evidence and written evidence.

a. **Stock-Purchase Agreement.** In Air Serv. Co. v. Sheehan, 95 Nev. 528, 594 P.2d 1155 (1979), the Nevada Supreme Court reviewed the evidence that the employee had presented to a jury. Noting that its review of the evidence was limited, the court found that there was sufficient evidence to conclude that the employee had reached a complete oral employment agreement. Evidence of the oral agreement included a stock purchase agreement and the employee's reliance upon this oral contract and the stock purchase agreement when he left his job and moved to Reno to undertake performance of the contract. There was enough evidence of the oral contract and performance under the contract that his breach-of-oral-contract claim could not be dismissed merely because it was not in written form.

b. **Verbal Assurances.** In 1985, the Court suggested that oral promises can form an employment contract if the parties intend such promises to constitute a term of employment. Tropicana Hotel Corp. v. Speer, 101 Nev. 40, 692 P.2d 499 (1985). Indefinite and vague statements regarding an employee's future with the company may be insufficient to form the basis of an enforceable contract, however. Bally's Grand Employees' Fed. Credit Union v. Wallen, 105 Nev. 553, 779 P.2d 956 (1989).

In American Bank Stationery v. Farmer, 106 Nev. 698, 799 P.2d 1100 (1990) the Nevada Supreme Court found that the employee sufficiently rebutted the presumption of at-will status by establishing that his employer orally promised to keep him as an employee so long as he performed adequately. The court held that such a specific offer would lead a reasonable person in the employee's position to believe that if the employee accepted the job, the employee could be fired only for good cause. Notably, however, the employer had a handbook stating that an employee could be discharged only for good cause. As in Western States, the court in Southwest Gas Corp. v. Vargas, 111 Nev. 1064, 901 P.2d 693 (1995), rehearing denied by, (Jan. 18, 1996), received comments and written evidence that had accumulated over the course of the employee's employment. While an employee's status might be clear at one point, the relationship can be modified to the point of confusion.

But the court in Brooks v. Hilton Casinos, 959 F.2d 757 (9th Cir. 1992), cert. denied, 506 U.S. 906, reached a different result. In Brooks, the employees argued that they could only be discharged for good cause, relying on evidence of their long-term employment, employment inducements, benefits, a progressive discipline system, past practices, and assurances that they would only be terminated if they failed to perform satisfactorily. The court found such factors insufficient to establish an implied contract to terminate only for just cause. And in Schlang v. Key Airlines, Inc., 794 F. Supp. 1493 (D. Nev. 1992), held that the employee failed to rebut his at-will employment status because there was no evidence showing that anyone in the personnel department had ever told him his job would be guaranteed if he performed reasonably.

c. **Employee Manual.** In Southwest Gas Corp. v. Ahmad, 99 Nev. 594, 668 P.2d 261 (1983), the court determined whether the parties were bound in contract by a termination clause that appeared in the employee information and benefits handbook provided to the employee. Based on testimony by the employee that she had knowledge of the termination section of the handbook throughout the length of her employment, the court found the handbook to be a part of the plaintiff's contract and that the employer was bound to follow the termination procedures contained in it.

In Hutton v. General Motors Corp., 775 F. Supp. 1373 (D. Nev. 1991), a federal court ruled that an employee who was discharged or who voluntarily resigned from his position should be allowed to go to trial to determine whether the employee had an express oral contract that prevented the employer from transferring him from his present location to an out-of-state location. Because the employee did not present any evidence by way of the employer's conduct or policies or manuals, however, the employee was not entitled to take his claim of an express written contract before a jury.

In Mannikko v. Harrah's Reno, 630 F. Supp. 191 (D. Nev. 1986), the employee received a booklet from her employer that included various pledges by the employer to treat employees fairly and give them an opportunity for promotion from within the company. Based on this booklet, the court determined that an implied employment contract existed between the employer and the employee that included all of the provisions contained in the handbook. The court determined that the employee could have relied on the assurances contained in the booklet. The court also stated that such an employer-issued booklet may be part of the employment contract, where the employee is given the booklet at the time of hiring and accepts a position in reliance upon the assurances set forth in the booklet.

In K Mart Corp. v. Ponsock, 103 Nev. 39, 732 P.2d 1364 (1987), an employee who had been employed for ten years was terminated ostensibly for applying spray paint to his forklift at work, thus "defacing" company property. The employer argued that its employment relationship with the employee was at will, but the Nevada Supreme Court determined that the employee was a tenured employee. The court based its determination on the employer's stipulation that the written provisions of its employee handbook were part of the contract between the parties. The court found that the employee had been hired "until retirement" and "for as long as economically possible." Id at 1366. In addition, the handbook provided for progressive discipline. Based upon these factors, the court determined that the employee was not an at-will employee and that the employer had breached its contract by terminating the employee without following the discipline provisions in the handbook. The court did not discuss the issue of ERISA preemption, presumably because the question was not raised by the parties.

In another case, Smith v. Cladianos, 104 Nev. 67, 752 P.2d 233 (1988), the employer terminated the employment relationship after approximately four and one-half years because the employee paid funds to a company after being ordered not to do so. The employee claimed that she had been given the order only after paying the funds and had been wrongfully terminated. The court reviewed the employee's claim that the probationary provision in the handbook created contractual rights. Because the employee was past her probationary period, this provision was not applicable. Nothing else in the handbook granted contractual rights. The court, further noting that no written contract of employment existed and that the employee admitted she was employed with no specific termination date, held that the employee was an at-will employee and could be terminated for any reason not in violation of public policy.

In Cordova v. Harrah's Reno Hotel-Casino, 707 F. Supp. 443 (D. Nev. 1988), the federal district court held that general statements in an employee handbook providing that an employee will have "maximum job security" are not specific enough to modify the employee's at-will status because they did not constitute specific statements regarding the employee's duration of employment.

Although the courts in Southwest Gas Corp. and K Mart Corp. v. Ponsock. limited an employer's ability to terminate an at-will employee based on a progressive discipline provision in the employer's handbook, the court in Vancheri v. GNLV Corp., 105 Nev. 417, 777 P.2d 366 (1989), held to the contrary. The Vancheri court recognized the positive aspects of standardized disciplinary procedures and held that if the disciplinary procedures were construed to convert an at-will employee into an employee who could be discharged only for cause, then employers would be reluctant to establish such procedures. The court stated that, as a matter of law, a disciplinary procedure was not sufficient to establish a *prima facie* case to rebut the at-will presumption.

Following its decision in Southwest Gas Corp. v. Ahmad, 99 Nev. 594, 668 P.2d 261 (1983), the Nevada Supreme Court concluded that the employer had issued a handbook containing statements that employees could be terminated for cause, and the employee in this case had received, read, and acknowledged its contents. The court also suggested that additional evidence of a contract was the employer's correspondence with the labor commissioner. The employer referred to the employee's violation of a specific work rule and stated that the employee had "acknowledged" his understanding of the handbook rules. D'Angelo v. Gardner, 107 Nev. 704, 819 P.2d 206 (1991).

In 1993, a federal court affirmed that under Nevada law there are some circumstances where provisions in an employee handbook may give rise to an inference of employment contract, thereby modifying at-will status. Alam v. Reno Hilton Corp., 819 F. Supp. 905 (D. Nev. 1993).

In Southwest Gas Corp. v. Vargas, 111 Nev. 1064, 901 P.2d 693 (1995), the court viewed a series of contradictory and confusing written statements in employee manuals and policies. This ambiguity created a triable issue of fact. The court was also impressed by the employee's reliance on the director of human resources, who told him that signing the later disclaimer would not affect his employment rights. While the court continues to state that such contradictions create questions of fact, the court indicated that disclaimers and language that appears to confer employment rights sometimes create questions of law. The court noted that contradictory language creates a question of law only when there is no doubt whether or not a contract exists. Barmettler v. Reno Air, Inc., 114 Nev. 441, 956 P.2d 1382 (1998).

d. **Real Estate Brokers.** There are a number of Nevada cases construing the employment relationships arising in the sale of real estate. In real estate employment cases, only moderate factual support is needed to sustain a claim of implied contract. For instance, an employment contract will be implied where the only evidence of the contract is the broker's receipt of price information from the seller and letters sent by the broker to the seller. Also significant is the seller's knowledge that the broker expects to be paid and the broker's continued belief that continued work on behalf of the seller will be compensated.

In Morrow v. Barger, 103 Nev. 247, 737 P.2d 1153 (1987), the plaintiff, a real estate broker, claimed she was entitled to a broker's commission pursuant to a written listing agreement, an oral listing agreement, or an implied listing agreement for the sale of a ranch. The Nevada Supreme Court stated that before a real estate agent is entitled to a commission, the agent must prove that an employment contract existed and that the agent was the procuring cause of the sale. The court concluded that plaintiff had presented sufficient evidence to go to trial.

In another real estate employment case, Matthews v. Collman, 110 Nev. 940, 878 P.2d 971 (1994), the dispute centered upon the relationship between a real estate company and its employee, a real estate broker. The employer believed that the broker's assistance in procuring and negotiating a sale of commercial real estate was on behalf of the buyer, and the employer therefore did not owe the broker a commission. The broker disagreed, claiming that she was owed a commission because she was acting on behalf of her employer, who had a partial interest in the property. The court stated that there was sufficient evidence to conclude that the employer's execution of documents listing the employee broker as the employer's agent supported an implied contract. The employee broker was entitled to the reasonable value of her services.

Existence of Implied Contract is Factual Question

a. **Employment Application.** In Stone v. Mission Bay Mortgage Co., 99 Nev. 802, 672 P.2d 629 (1983), the employee was terminated two weeks after she started working, during a thirty-day probationary period. She was terminated because the company's business declined. After beginning work and before being terminated, the plaintiff had completed and signed an "Application for Employment" that stated in small print above the signature that she could be terminated at any time without notice. The court, in reversing a summary judgment in favor of the employer, held that the phrase "probationary employee" did not necessarily mean that employees could be terminated without cause at any time during the probationary period and that the conditions of such a period could be set by agreement between the parties. The court further held that whether the employment application was intended to be a contract was an issue of fact for a jury.

Implied Contract Not Found

a. **Subjective Expectations.** In Vancheri v. GNLV Corp., 105 Nev. 417, 777 P.2d 366 (1989), the court ruled that contracts of employment cannot be created by an employee's subjective expectations. General expressions of long-term employment or job advancement do not convert an at-will employment relationship to one allowing termination only for cause. In Vancheri, the court found that the employer never orally told the employee he would be terminated only for cause, or that the employee would be employed for life, or that the employee had a specified period of employment duration.

In 1995, the Nevada Supreme Court reaffirmed the common law presumption that employees in Nevada are employed at will, absent some other specific agreement. Yeager v. Harrah's Club, 111 Nev. 830, 897 P.2d 1093 (1995). The court noted that the at-will presumption cannot be overcome by an employee's subjective expectations of continued employment or merely by uncorroborated self-serving allegations of verbal promises. The court stated that the at-will presumption could be overcome in some circumstances by the employer's handbook or correspondence, the employer's personnel practices, or witnesses to the specific employment contract. The decision whether evidence is sufficient to overcome the at-will presumption must be determined on a case-by-case basis. See also Hirschhorn v. Sizzler Restaurants Int'l, 913 F. Supp. 1393 (D. Nev. 1995) (where an employee's allegation that he "had a job as long as [he] wanted one" as long as his performance was satisfactory, was insufficient to rebut the at-will presumption).

b. **Change in Terms and Conditions of Employment.** Nevada law recognizes that employers may change the terms and conditions of employment for at-will employees because such employees are working without a consistent contract. Cotter v. Desert Palace, Inc., 880 F.2d 1142 (9th Cir. 1989). In Cotter, the Ninth Circuit Court of Appeals held that under Nevada law a casino was justified in changing the procedures by which its employees received tips, provided that the new procedure did not violate Nevada law or public policy.

B. Elements of Libel Claim

An exhaustive discussion of libel, defined as written defamation, can be found in People for the Ethical Treatment of Animals v. Bobby Berosini, Ltd., 111 Nev. 615, 895 P.2d 1269 (1995), rev'd on other grounds, City of Las Vegas Downtown Redevelopment Agency v. Hecht, 113 Nev. 644, 940 P.2d 134 (1997). In that case, an entertainer at a Las Vegas casino sued two nonprofit animal protection groups and several individuals for the taping of his last-minute preparations before going on stage. The tape showed the entertainer striking and poking his animals. One of the individually named defendants, an employee of the casino, videotaped the alleged physical abuse of the animals in his act. The court ultimately held that the publication of the videotape was not libelous.

1. ***Basic Elements.*** In order to establish a prima facie case of defamation, a plaintiff must prove: (1) a false and defamatory statement by defendant concerning the plaintiff; (2) an unprivileged publication to a third person; (3) fault, amounting to at least negligence, and (4) actual or presumed damages. Simpson v. Mars Inc., 113 Nev. 188, 929 P.2d 966 (1997), citing Chowdhry v. NLVH, Inc., 109 Nev. 478, 851 P.2d 459 (1993).

2. ***Fault.*** The only fault standards recognized under Nevada libel law are negligence and actual malice. Actual malice is the fault standard when the plaintiff is a public figure or public official. Negligence is the fault standard in all other cases.

a. **Private Figure Plaintiff/Matter of Public Concern.** Negligence is the fault standard for these cases. Nevada law does not make any distinction based upon whether the allegedly defamatory matter regards a matter of public or private concern. Simpson v. Mars Inc., 113 Nev. 188, 929 P.2d 966 (1997).

b. **Private Figure Plaintiff/Matter of Private Concern.** Negligence is the fault standard for these cases. Nevada law does not make any distinction based upon whether the allegedly defamatory matter regards a matter of public or private concern. Simpson v. Mars Inc., 113 Nev. 188, 929 P.2d 966 (1997).

c. **Public Figure Plaintiff/Matter of Public Concern.** Actual malice is the fault standard for cases involving a public figure plaintiff and a matter of public concern. Miller v. Jones, 114 Nev. 1291, 970 P.2d 571 (1998); Wynn v. Smith, 117 Nev. 6, 16 P.3d 424 (2001). Stephen A. Wynn, Chairman of Mirage Resorts, Inc., which owns, develops and operates many casino-based resorts, is an example of an individual whom Nevada has held is a public figure. The Nevada Supreme Court has also held that a Mexican restaurant was a "limited purpose" public figure for the purposes of a food review in a newspaper. Pegasus v. Reno Newspapers, Inc., 118 Nev. 706, 57 P.3d 82 (2002)("A limited-purpose public figure is a person who voluntarily injects himself or is thrust into a particular public controversy or public concern, and thereby becomes a public figure for a limited range of issues."), cert. denied, 540 U.S. 817 (2003). However, the Nevada Supreme Court concluded that a doctor is not a "limited-purpose" public figure unless that doctor voluntarily comes to the forefront of a national or local debate concerning medical issues or has "affirmatively step[ped] outside of [his] private realm [ ] of practice to attract public attention." Bongiovi v. Sullivan, 122 Nev. 556, 138 P.3d 433 (2006). In reaching the foregoing conclusion, the Court reasoned that in order for a defendant to prove the plaintiff is a "limited purpose" public figure the defendant must prove that: (1) the professional achievements of the plaintiff are sufficient to render him a "limited-purpose" public figure, (2) the plaintiff voluntarily thrust himself into a public controversy, and (3) the defamatory statements made against the plaintiff concerned a public controversy or issue and were made solely in the individual interest of the defendant and a third party.

The test for determining actual malice is subjective, with the focus on what the defendant believed and intended to convey, not what a reasonable person would have understood the message to be. Nevada Indep. Broadcasting Corp. v. Allen, 99 Nev. 404, 664 P.2d 337 (1983).

In an employment-related claim for defamation, a police officer relied upon as evidence a police chief's accusation in a press release that the police officer admitted he lied under oath. Posadas v. City of Reno, 109 Nev. 448, 851 P.2d 438, 441 (1993). The court concluded that the statement was capable of a defamatory construction as a matter of law because the chief's statement imputed dishonesty and unlawful conduct to the officer. The court went on to explain that because the employee-officer was a public officer, the chief's statement had to have been made with actual malice in order for the officer to recover for defamation. If the chief's statement was made with the knowledge of its falsity or if the chief recklessly disregarded whether the statement was true, the officer could recover for defamation. The officer had produced evidence surrounding the circumstances of these statements, and the court said there was sufficient evidence of actual malice for a jury to hear the case.

3. ***Falsity.*** The plaintiff must prove the falsity of the statements. People for the Ethical Treatment of Animals v. Bobby Berosini, Ltd., 111 Nev. 615, 895 P.2d 1269, 23 Media L. Rep. (BNA) 1961 (1995), overruled on other grounds, City of Las Vegas Downtown Redevelopment Agency v. Hecht, 113 Nev. 644, 940 P.2d 134 (1997); Nevada Indep. Broadcasting Corp. v. Allen, 99 Nev. 404, 664 P.2d 337 (1983). Determining the truth or falsity of an allegedly defamatory statement is an issue of fact left to the jury for resolution. Posadas v. City of Reno, 109 Nev. 448, 851 P.2d 438 (1993).

4. ***Defamatory Statement of Fact.*** The false statement must be a false statement of fact, as opposed to opinion. K-Mart Corp. v. Washington, 109 Nev. 1180, 866 P.2d 274 (1993). Furthermore, a statement is defamatory when under any reasonable definition such charges would tend to lower the subject in the estimation of the community and to excite derogatory opinions against him and to hold him up to contempt. Id.; People for the Ethical Treatment of Animals v. Bobby Berosini, Ltd., 111 Nev. 615, 895 P.2d 1269, 23 Media L. Rep. (BNA) 1961 (1995); Las Vegas Sun v. Franklin, 74 Nev. 282, 329 P.2d 867 (1958). It is a question of law and, therefore, within the province of the court, to determine if a statement is capable of a defamatory construction. If a statement can be interpreted as either defamatory or nondefamatory, resolution of the ambiguity is a question of fact for the jury. Branda v. Sanford, 97 Nev. 643, 637 P.2d 1223 (1981). The Nevada Supreme Court has implicitly recognized the incremental harm doctrine. People for the Ethical Treatment of Animals v. Bobby Berosini, Ltd., 111 Nev. 615, 895 P.2d 1269, 23 Media L. Rep. (BNA) 1961 (1995) (statement that Berosini beat his trained orangutans with steel rods was not defamatory even if the rods were actually made out of wood; The composition of the rods is of little moment; saying that they were steel does not defame Berosini).

5. ***Of and Concerning Plaintiff.*** The actionable words or assertions must refer to the party bringing the action, at least with reasonable certainty. Talbot v. Mack, 41 Nev. 245, 169 P. 25 (1917).

6. ***Publication.*** A plaintiff must prove publication to a third party. Publication is generally proven by direct evidence of the communication of the defamatory statement to a third person, that is, by the testimony of a third person that he heard the defamatory statement. Publication may also be proven, however, by circumstantial evidence of the communication of the defamatory statement to a third person, that is, by evidence that the defamatory statement was comprehensible to and uttered in the presence of a third person. M & R Inv. Co. v. Mandarino, 103 Nev. 711, 748 P.2d 488 (1987).

a. **Intracorporate Communication.** Publication of defamatory material to anyone other than the person defamed, even to agents or employees of a corporation, is publication for the purpose of making a prima facie case of defamation. Simpson v. Mars Inc., 113 Nev. 188, 929 P.2d 966 (1997), overruling Jones v. Golden Spike Corp., 97 Nev. 24, 623 P.2d 970 (1981). In Simpson v. Mars Inc., a divided Nevada Supreme Court, upsetting years of defamation law, concluded that a corporate employer's "publication" or communication of the reasons for an employee's termination to her coworkers stated a claim for defamation. Under previous Nevada case law, an employee claiming defamation had to show that the remarks were made to outside third parties in order to go to trial. In Simpson, the court reasoned that employees spend a great deal of time with friends and acquaintances at the workplace, and that the employer's communication of falsehoods about the employee is therefore especially damaging. Simpson, 929 P.2d at 967. However there are privileges that may apply to certain intracorporate communications, such as the common interest privilege. O'Connor v. Ortega, 480 U.S. 709 (1987). An intracorporate communication is only privileged if the communication occurs in the regular course of the corporation's business. Pope v. Motel 6, 121 Nev. 307, 114 P.3d 277 (2005).

Under Nevada Revised Statutes (NRS) section 41.755, an employer has immunity from civil liability for disclosures of information about an employee if the disclosure is made at the employee's request and the information is related to the employee's ability, diligence, skill, or reliability in performing the job, or an employee's illegal or wrongful act. There is no immunity for disclosures made with malice or ill will, disclosures made with information believed to be inaccurate, disclosures that the employer had no reasonable grounds for believing were accurate, disclosures made recklessly or intentionally of inaccurate information, and disclosures made in violation of state or federal law or an agreement with the employee. Because this statute is new and untested, employers are advised to consult with employment counsel before disclosing information about employees.

b. **Compelled Self-Publication.** No published decision specifically addresses the issue of compelled self-publication. Generally, a defendant cannot be held liable for willful publications made by the plaintiff. Potosi Zinc Co. v. Mahoney, 36 Nev. 390, 135 P. 1078 (1913).

c. **Republication.** A speaker can be held liable for his own republications, even when the republication is an attempted correction of the earlier defamatory statement. Nevada Indep. Broadcasting Corp. v. Allen, 99 Nev. 404, 664 P.2d 337 (1983). Generally, a republisher is liable to the same extent as if the republisher initially published the defamatory statement. Thompson v. Powning, 15 Nev. 195 (1880). In Wynn v. Smith, 117 Nev. 6, 16 P.3d 424 (2001), the Nevada Supreme Court declined to adopt the rule in other jurisdictions that the originator of the defamatory statement is liable for its foreseeable republication where there is a strong causal link between the actions of the originator and the damage caused by republication because, the Court found, the originator's statements were "much more qualified and couched in statements of investigative opinion than the ultimate phraseology" in the publication. A defendant who republishes a statement that is subject to multiple interpretations is entitled to choose the interpretation with which he agrees. Flowers v. Carville, 310 F. Supp. 2d 1157, 1164 (D. Nev. 2004), affirmed, 2006 U.S. App. Lexis 628 (9th Cir. 2006).

7. ***Statements versus Conduct.*** Words or conduct or the combination of words and conduct can communicate defamation. The Nevada Supreme Court has specifically held that the imputation of shoplifting, communicated through the act of handcuffing the plaintiff at a department store, constitutes slander per se. K-Mart Corp. v. Washington, 109 Nev. 1180, 866 P.2d 274 (1993).

8. ***Damages.*** Special damages are only those damages which a plaintiff alleges and proves that he has suffered in respect to his property, business, trade, profession or occupation, including such amounts of money as the plaintiff alleges and proves he has expended as a result of the alleged libel or slander. NRS 41.335. Special damages are those which flow directly from the injury to reputation caused by the defamation; not from the effects of the defamation. Branda v. Sanford, 97 Nev. 643, 637 P.2d 1223 (1981). Special damages must be specifically pleaded and proven in all cases that do not involve defamation per se. General damages are damages for loss of reputation, shame, mortification and hurt feelings. NRS 41.334.

a. **Presumed Damages and Libel Per Se.** The Nevada Supreme Court has recognized the four traditional types of defamation where the plaintiff need not prove damages: (1) the imputation of a crime; (2) the imputation of having a loathsome disease; (3) imputing lack of fitness for trade, business or profession; and (4) imputing serious sexual misconduct. K-Mart Corp. v. Washington, 109 Nev. 1180, 866 P.2d 274 (1993), citing, Las Vegas Sun v. Franklin, 329 P.2d 867 (1958). The fourth category includes imputing unchastity to a woman. Branda v. Sanford, 97 Nev. 643, 637 P.2d 1223 (1981). Statements made regarding a candidate for office are defamatory per se if they would tend to cause persons not to vote for the candidate. Nevada Indep. Broadcasting Corp. v. Allen, 99 Nev. 404, 664 P.2d 337 (1983).

(1) **Employment-Related Criticism.** Statements that criticize an employee's conduct will qualify as defamation per se if, taken as a whole, they clearly imply a want of qualities expected from that type of employee. Nevada Indep. Broadcasting Corp. v. Allen, 99 Nev. 404, 664 P.2d 337 (1983). This broad interpretation of defamation per se is tempered by a broad protection for evaluative opinions of an employee's conduct. Churchill v. Barach, 863 F. Supp. 1266 (D. Nev. 1994).

(2) **Single Instance Rule.** The Nevada Supreme Court has implicitly rejected the single instance rule. In Nevada Indep. Broadcasting Corp. v. Allen, 99 Nev. 404, 664 P.2d 337 (1983), the Court held that since three remarks were made relating to the delivery of one bad check by a candidate for governor, the remarks were defamatory per se.

b. **Punitive Damages.** Exemplary damages are damages which may, in the discretion of the court or jury, be recovered in addition to general and special damages for the sake of example and by way of punishing a defendant who has made a publication or broadcast with actual malice. NRS 41.333. For the purpose of determining whether exemplary damages may be awarded, actual malice means that state of mind arising from hatred or ill will toward the plaintiff and does not include that state of mind occasioned by a good faith belief in the truth of the publication or broadcast. NRS 41.332.

II. PRIVILEGES AND DEFENSES

A. Scope of Privileges

1. ***Absolute Privilege.*** This section describes types of publications that are absolutely immune from liability, and therefore nonactionable. Communications uttered or published in the course of judicial or quasi-judicial proceedings are absolutely privileged so long as they are in some way pertinent to the proceeding, whether or not they are false or malicious. Fink v. Oshins, 118 Nev. 428, 49 P.3d 640 (2002); Bank of America Nev. v. Bourdeau, 115 Nev. 263, 3, 982 P.2d 474 (1999); Sahara Gaming Corp. v. Culinary Workers Union Local 226, 115 Nev. 212, 216, 984 P.2d 164, 168 (1999), citing Circus Circus Hotels v. Witherspoon, 99 Nev. 56, 60, 657 P.2d 101 (1983); Knox v. Dick, 99 Nev. 514, 665 P.2d 267 (1983), distinguished on other grounds, Rust v. Clark County Sch. Dist., 103 Nev. 686, 689, 747 P.2d 1380 (1987). This privilege extends to communications made preliminary to a judicial proceeding. K-Mart Corp. v. Washington, 109 Nev. 1180, 866 P.2d 274 (1993).

Additionally, communications concerning another in a report of an official action or proceeding or of a meeting open to the public that deals with a matter of public concern is privileged ("fair report privilege") if the report is accurate and complete or a fair abridgment of the occurrence reported. Wynn v. Smith, 117 Nev. 6, 16 P.3d 424 (2001). Where the publication goes beyond the "fair, accurate, and impartial" reporting of judicial proceedings by presenting a one-sided viewed of the proceeding, the absolute "fair report" privilege may be inapplicable. Lubin v. Kunin, 117 Nev. 107, 17 P.3d 422 (2001). Unauthorized or confidential investigative reports do not qualify as an "official action or proceeding" under the fair report privilege. Wynn v. Smith, 117 Nev. 107, 16 P.3d 424 (2001).

By statute, Nevada law provides for an absolute privilege for all communications from an employer to the Employment Security Department, and from an applicant or licensee to the Gaming Control Board or Gaming Commission. NRS 612.265(12); NRS 463.3407; Hampe v. Foote, 118 Nev. 405, 47 P.3d 438 (2002).

The Nevada Supreme Court has held that the filing of a complaint against a police officer with an internal affairs bureau is absolutely privileged. Lewis v. Benson, 101 Nev. 300, 701 P.2d 751 (1985).

2. ***Qualified Privileges.*** A qualified privilege exists where a defamatory statement is made in good faith on any subject matter in which the person communicating has an interest, or in reference to which he has a right or duty, if it is made to a person with a corresponding interest or duty. Bank of America Nev. v. Bourdeau, 115 Nev. 263, 982 P.2d 474 (1999), citing Circus Circus Hotels v. Witherspoon, 99 Nev. 56, 657 P.2d 101 (1983). The Nevada Supreme Court held in Bank of America Nev. v. Bourdeau, that a background investigation of an employee is subject to a conditional privilege.

The Nevada Supreme Court recently held that communications made to police before the initiation of criminal proceedings are only subject to a qualified privilege. Pope v. Motel 6, 121 Nev. 307, 114 P.3d 277 (2005). In doing so, the court distinguished between statements made in court and statements made to the police. In court, "individuals must be free to risk impugning the reputations of others, in order to discharge public duties and protect individual rights," but citizens making informal complaints to police "should not enjoy blanket immunity from an action; instead, such statements should receive protection only if they were made in good faith, to discourage an abuse of the privilege."

Nevada's anti-SLAPP law, NRS 41.635 *et seq.*, provides a privilege for any: (1) communication that is aimed at procuring any governmental or electoral action, result or outcome; (2) communication of information or complaint to a legislator, officer or employee of federal, state or local government, regarding a matter reasonably of concern to the respective governmental entity; or (3) written or oral statement made in direct connection with an issue under consideration by a legislative, executive or judicial body, or any other official proceeding authorized by law. This privilege is lost if the speaker knows the communication or statement is false. NRS 41.637.

Nevada's anti-SLAPP statute states that when a plaintiff brings an action "against a person based upon a good faith communication in furtherance of the right to petition," the defendant may bring a special motion to dismiss within 60 days of service of the complaint. NRS 41.660(1)-(2). John v. Douglas County Sch. Dist., 219 P.3d 1276, 1281, 2009 Nev. LEXIS 68 (Nov. 25, 2009), cert. denied, 130 S. Ct. 3355 (2010). The Nevada Supreme Court has held that federal preemption does not prevent the application of Nevada's anti-SLAPP statute to a plaintiff's federal claims. Id. at 1283. The application of Nevada's anti-SLAPP statute applies to federal causes of action because it is a neutral and procedural statute that does not undermine any federal interests. Id. at 1287.

a. **Common Interest.** A qualified privilege exists where a defamatory statement is made in good faith on any subject matter in which the person communicating has an interest if it is made to a person with a corresponding interest. Circus Circus Hotels v. Witherspoon, 99 Nev. 56, 657 P.2d 101 (1983).

b. **Duty.** A qualified privilege exists where a defamatory statement is made in good faith on any subject matter in which the person communicating has a right or duty. Circus Circus Hotels v. Witherspoon, 99 Nev. 56, 657 P.2d 101 (1983). In Bank of America Nev. v. Bourdeau, the Nevada Supreme Court held that the Bank had an interest and a duty to cooperate with a Federal Deposit Insurance Corporation examiner to ensure that officers of a new bank are qualified and experienced.

c. **Criticism of Public Employee.** Criticism of a public employee would probably be covered by Nevada's anti-SLAPP law, NRS 41.635 et seq. The Nevada Supreme Court has held that the filing of a complaint against a police officer with an internal affairs bureau is absolutely privileged. Lewis v. Benson, 101 Nev. 300, 701 P.2d 751 (1985).

d. **Reply Privilege.** The Nevada Supreme Court adopted the conditional privilege of reply in State v. Eighth Judicial Dist. Court, 118 Nev. 140, 42 P.3d 233 (2002). This common law privilege grants those who are attacked with defamatory statements a limited right to reply. Where an individual is attacked in a newspaper, the individual may write to the paper to rebut the charges, and may retort upon the assailant, when such retort is a necessary part of the defense, or fairly arises out of the charges the assailant has made against the individual. This privilege may be lost, however, if the reply (1) includes substantial defamatory matter that is irrelevant or non-responsive to the initial statement; (2) includes substantial defamatory material that is disproportionate to the initial statement; (3) is excessively publicized; or (4) is made with malice in the sense of actual spite or ill will.

e. **Limitation on Qualified Privileges.** A qualified privilege is lost if the speaker abused the privilege by publishing the communication with bad faith, malice with spite, ill will, or some other wrongful motivation, and without belief in the statement's probable truth. Bank of America Nev. v. Bourdeau, 115 Nev. 263, 3, 982 P.2d 474 (1999); Circus Circus Hotels v. Witherspoon, 99 Nev. 56, 657 P.2d 101 (1983).

(1) **Constitutional or Actual Malice.** The test for determining actual malice is subjective, with the focus on what the defendant believed and intended to convey, not what a reasonable person would have understood the message to be. Nevada Indep. Broadcasting Corp. v. Allen, 99 Nev. 404, 664 P.2d 337 (1983). Constitutional or actual malice is not relevant in determining whether a qualified privilege has been abused.

In another employment-related claim for defamation, a police officer relied upon as evidence a police chief's accusation in a press release that the police officer admitted he lied under oath. Posadas v. City of Reno, 109 Nev. 448, 851 P.2d 438, 441 (1993) The court concluded that the statement was capable of a defamatory construction as a matter of law because the chief's statement imputed dishonesty and unlawful conduct to the officer. The court went on to explain that because the employee-officer was a public officer, the chief's statement had to have been made with actual malice in order for the officer to recover for defamation. If the chief's statement was made with the knowledge of its falsity or if the chief recklessly disregarded whether the statement was true, the officer could recover for defamation. The officer had produced evidence surrounding the circumstances of these statements, and the court said there was sufficient evidence of actual malice for a jury to hear the case.

(2) **Common Law Malice.** Malice in fact exists if the publication was in bad faith, with spite or ill will or some other wrongful motivation toward the plaintiff, and without a good faith belief in the statement's probable truth. Bank of America Nev. v. Bourdeau, 115 Nev. 263, 982 P.2d 474 (1999); Circus Circus Hotels v. Witherspoon, 99 Nev. 56, 657 P.2d 101 (1983). Malice can also be shown by proving that the publisher knew the communication was false or acted in reckless disregard for its veracity. Wynn v. Smith, 117 Nev. 6, 16 P.3d 424 (2001); Pope v. Motel 6, 121 Nev. 307, 114 P.3d 277 (2005). Reckless disregard for the truth or falsity of a publication may be found where the publisher entertained "serious doubt" as to the veracity of an informant or the accuracy of a report and the publisher failed to make reasonable efforts to investigate. Wynn v. Smith, 117 Nev. 6, 16 P.3d 424 (2001). Proof that a person would have investigated before publishing or refrained from publishing does not establish the requisite state of mind on the part of the defendant. Flowers v. Carville, 310 F. Supp. 2d 1157, 1163 (D. Nev. 2004), affirmed, 2006 U.S. App. Lexis 628 (9th Cir. 2006). A statement can be false without being malicious. Higgins v. Higgins, 103 Nev. 443, 445, 744 P.2d 530, 531 (1987). The mere fact that an individual informs police of possible criminal wrongdoing does not establish malice. Pope v. Motel 6, 114 P.3d 277 ("Suspicions of criminal wrongdoing are commonly expressed to police, and often the suspicion is misplaced").

f. **Question of Fact or Law.** Whether a particular communication is conditionally privileged by being published on a privileged occasion is a question of law for the court. Bank of America Nev. v. Bourdeau, 115 Nev. 263, 982 P.2d 474 (1999); Circus Circus Hotels v. Witherspoon, 99 Nev. 56, 657 P.2d 101 (1983).

g. **Burden of Proof.** The plaintiff bears the burden of proving that the defendant abused the privilege by publishing the communication with malice in fact. Bank of America Nev. v. Bourdeau, 115 Nev. 263, 982 P.2d 474 (1999), citing Circus Circus Hotels v. Witherspoon, 99 Nev. 56, 657 P.2d 101 (1983). The question goes to the jury only if there is sufficient evidence for the jury reasonably to infer that the publication was made with malice in fact. Id. The defendant corporation bears the burden of alleging and proving that a privilege is applicable to intracorporate communications. Pope v. Motel 6, 121 Nev. 307,114 P.3d 277(2005).

B. Standard Libel Defenses

1. ***Truth.*** Where the assertion is true, a claim of defamation cannot be maintained because liability can only be created based upon a false and defamatory statement. People for the Ethical Treatment of Animals v. Bobby Berosini, Ltd., 111 Nev. 615, 619, 895 P.2d 1269 (1995). Rhetorical hyperbole, exaggerations and overbroad generalizations are not actionable. Wellman v. Fox, 108 Nev. 83, 825 P.2d 208, 19 Media L. Rep. (BNA) 2028, cert. denied, 506 U.S. 820 (1992).

2. ***Opinion.*** Statements of opinion are not actionable. The Nevada Supreme Court has interpreted Milkovich v. Lorain Journal Co., 497 U.S. 1 (1990), as meaning that a statement can be libelous if it implies the existence of a false fact. Wellman v. Fox, 108 Nev. 83, 825 P.2d 208, 19 Media L. Rep. (BNA) 2028, cert. denied, 506 U.S. 820, 113 S. Ct. 68 (1992). Whether a statement is fact or opinion is a question of law. People for the Ethical Treatment of Animals v. Bobby Berosini, Ltd., 111 Nev. 615, 895 P.2d 1269, 23 Media L. Rep. (BNA) 1961 (1995); Wellman v. Fox, 108 Nev. 83, 825 P.2d 208, 19 Media L. Rep. (BNA) 2028, cert. denied, 506 U.S. 820 (1992).

3. ***Consent.*** No published Nevada decision specifically addresses the defense of consent. Generally, the Nevada Supreme Court follows the Restatement (Second) of Torts with regard to libel law. The Restatement (Second) of Torts, Section 583, provides that the consent to another to the publication of defamatory matter concerning him is a complete defense to a libel action.

4. ***Mitigation.*** A defendant may offer proof of mitigating circumstances, including the sources of information used in a publication. Las Vegas Sun v. Franklin, 74 Nev. 282, 329 P.2d 867 (1958).

III. RECURRING FACT PATTERNS

A. Statements in Personnel File

There are no reported cases in Nevada regarding this fact pattern, but a qualified privilege should apply to such communications. Circus Circus Hotels v. Witherspoon, 99 Nev. 56, 657 P.2d 101 (1983).

B. Performance Evaluations

There are no reported cases in Nevada regarding this fact pattern, but the Nevada Supreme Court has recognized that evaluative opinions are not actionable. People for the Ethical Treatment of Animals v. Bobby Berosini, Ltd., 111 Nev. 615, 895 P.2d 1269, 23 Media L. Rep. (BNA) 1961 (1995).

C. References

The release of inaccurate, misleading, or occasionally even truthful information about an employee or former employee may lead to an employer being sued for defamation. Under Nevada Revised Statutes (NRS) section 41.755, however, an employer has immunity from civil liability for disclosures of information about an employee if the disclosure is made at the employee's request and the information is related to the employee's ability, diligence, skill, or reliability in performing the job, or an employee's illegal or wrongful act. There is no immunity for disclosures made with malice or ill will, disclosures made with information believed to be inaccurate, disclosures that the employer had no reasonable grounds for believing were accurate, disclosures made recklessly or intentionally of inaccurate information, and disclosures made in violation of state or federal law or an agreement with the employee. Because this statute is relatively new and untested, employers are advised to consult with employment counsel before disclosing information about employees.

D. Intracorporate Communication

In 1997, the Nevada Supreme Court reversed an earlier decision and adopted the position set forth in the Restatement (Second) of Torts § 577(1) that publication to anyone other than the person defamed, even to agents, is publication for the purpose of making a prima facie case of defamation. Simpson v. Mars Inc., 113 Nev. 188, 929 P.2d 966 (1997), overruling Jones v. Golden Spike Corp., 97 Nev. 24, 623 P.2d 970 (1981). Certain intracorporate communications may be raised as defenses to a defamation action. Id. (citing Restatement (Second) of Torts §§ 593-596).

E. Statements to Government Regulators

In Bank of America Nev. v. Bourdeau, 115 Nev. 263, 982 P.2d 474 (1999), the Nevada Supreme Court held that because the Bank had an interest and a duty to cooperate with a Federal Deposit Insurance Corporation examiner to ensure that officers of a new bank are qualified and experienced, statements made to the FDIC were subject to a qualified privilege as a matter of law and could not be used to prove a claim unless the privilege was abused by bad faith, malice with spite, ill will, or some other wrongful motivation, and without belief in the statement's probable truth.

F. Reports to Auditors and Insurers

There are no reported cases in Nevada regarding this fact pattern, but a qualified privilege should apply to such communications. Circus Circus Hotels v. Witherspoon, 99 Nev. 56, 657 P.2d 101 (1983).

G. Vicarious Liability of Employers for Statements Made by Employees

1. ***Scope of Employment.*** *Respondeat superior* liability attaches only when the employee is under the control of the employer and when the act is within the scope of employment. Burnett v. C.B.A. Sec. Serv., 107 Nev. 787, 820 P.2d 750 (1991). The element of control requires that the employer have control and direction not only of the employment to which the contract relates but also of all of its details and the method of performing the work. Rockwell v. Sun Harbor Budget Suites, 112 Nev. 1217, 925 P.2d 1175 (1996).

a. **Blogging.** There are no reported cases in Nevada addressing this issue.

2. ***Damages.*** An employer who is held liable for an employee's acts is responsible for the compensatory damages awarded. An employer is liable for punitive damages if the employer, including a managing agent working on behalf of the employer, authorized or participated in the oppressive and malicious conduct that created the punitive damages liability. Cerminara v. California Hotel & Casino, 104 Nev. 372, 760 P.2d 108 (1988).

H. Internal Investigations

There are no reported cases in Nevada addressing this issue.

IV. OTHER ACTIONS BASED ON STATEMENTS

A. Negligent Hiring, Retention, and Supervision

These torts generally involve an examination of whether an employer was reasonably prudent when it hired, trained, or retained an employee. Accordingly, the traditional *respondeat superior* defense that an employee was not acting within the control and course and scope of the employer may be unavailing if the fact finder determines that the employee's misconduct was reasonably foreseeable by the employer.

As with many other tort claims in Nevada, it is becoming increasingly difficult to have these claims dismissed by way of summary judgment. The Nevada Supreme Court seems to be applying a totality-of-the-circumstances test in these claims and has implied that a jury or other fact finder should be reviewing whether an employer acts reasonably even when there is little evidence to support an inference that the employer knew, or should have known, the employee had a propensity for dishonesty or violent conduct.

Under the tort of negligent hiring, there is a general duty imposed on the employer to conduct reasonable background checks on potential employees to ensure that the employee is fit for the position. Burnett v. C.B.A. Sec. Serv., 107 Nev. 787, 820 P.2d 750 (1991). Thus, an employer may potentially be found negligent for not conducting a proper background check that might have revealed an employee's propensity toward dishonest or violent conduct. The plaintiff must show that the particular background check that the employer allegedly should have conducted would have uncovered conduct indicating that the employee hired was unfit for the position. Doe v. Green, 298 F. Supp. 2d 1025, 1040 (D. Nev. 2004).

At least some background investigation before hiring an applicant is highly advisable. At a minimum, the work history and references of any prospective employee should be confirmed to the greatest extent possible by contacting the appropriate parties. For some jobs a more extensive background investigation may be advisable. An employer need not perform exactly the same investigation on every applicant, provided that any differentiation is based upon legitimate and nondiscriminatory business interests and an investigation policy reasonably calculated to further those interests. An employer may also legitimately determine that applicants for managerial, supervisory, or policy-making positions will undergo a more rigorous background investigation due to their anticipated greater value to the employer and the greater potential for damage arising from wrongful conduct. However, a common land mine for employers conducting checks on current employees is violating the scope of an employee's consent or waiver to a background investigation. For example, employers often have concerns regarding promoting a person into management after conducting a credit check on the employee. The language and regulations of the Fair Credit Reporting Act make it crystal clear that an employer violates the employee's rights under the Act unless the employee's waiver and consent extends to performing checks during employment as well as in the initial hiring phase of employment. Accordingly, application materials (where such consent and waiver language is usually located) should be reviewed to determine whether they expressly authorize credit checks during any phase of employment.

Credit checks that have not been consented to by current employees could also arguably violate an employee's right to privacy, allowing the employee to recover for the tort of intrusion. This tort requires: (1) an intentional intrusion (2) on an employee's solitude or seclusion (3) that would be highly offensive to a reasonable person. People for the Ethical Treatment of Animals v. Bobby Berosini, Ltd., 111 Nev. 615, 895 P.2d 1269, 1278 (1995). Nonetheless, in light of the two decisions discussed below, it seems that employers should err on the side of obtaining broad releases and performing background checks whenever they reasonably believe it is appropriate.

In Rockwell v. Sun Harbor Budget Suites, 112 Nev. 1217, 925 P.2d 1175 (1996), the court reversed a granting of summary judgment entered by the district court on behalf of Sun Harbor on theories of negligent hiring, training, and supervision, among others. The plaintiff and his wife and son lived in an apartment at Sun Harbor Budget Suites. The plaintiff's wife was killed by a security guard working at Sun Harbor. Apparently, the plaintiff's wife and the security guard met at the apartment complex and allegedly began a sexual affair. When the plaintiff's wife attempted to end the affair, the security guard shot her eighteen times in his apartment, killing her. The security guard was hired by a property management service unrelated to Sun Harbor.

During the sexual affair, the plaintiff bitterly discussed his concerns with the security guard and the apartment manager. Afterward, the security guard repeatedly threatened to kill the plaintiff, while his wife moved back and forth between her family's apartment and the security guard's apartment. Finally, the plaintiff decided to move his family to another apartment complex. The wife decided to go with her family but wanted to say good-bye to the security guard in person. It was during this confrontation that he shot and killed her. The district court had dismissed the *respondeat superior*, negligent hiring, and negligent retention claims, apparently because the security guard was not an employee of Sun Harbor, and because the security guard was acting outside the course and scope of his employment. The Nevada Supreme Court found Sun Harbor to be a joint employer, specifying that Sun Harbor undertook a personal and non-delegable duty when it engaged security services. The court held that "it did not matter that the owners of Sun Harbor had an additional filter . . . [a management company], between themselves and the actual security guard." Id. at 1180. The court decided there was a genuine issue of material fact as to whether the security guard was acting within the scope of his employment even though he was off duty, in his apartment, and had allegedly been having a sexual affair with the woman he shot. The court pointed to the fact that off-duty security guards carried radios and responded to emergency situations as evidence of a genuine issue of material fact. The plaintiff also produced evidence that the security guard had been terminated from jobs for his violent behavior, was a convicted sex offender, had lied on his application about his criminal past, and had possibly lied about his military background in Morocco. The court concluded that all the evidence together created a genuine issue of material fact on the negligent hiring claim.

As to the causes of action for negligent supervision and training, the court examined evidence that Sun Harbor possessed authority to control the details and methods of performing the guard's work as well as to terminate the security guards. Additionally, the court examined evidence that Sun Harbor was aware that the plaintiff felt threatened by the security guard. The court held that Sun Harbor had enough information to conclude the security guard could be dangerous and that it acted negligently by not remedying the situation through adequate supervision or training.

Although it is unclear to what extent the court will be willing to extend this "nondelegable duty" in other employment contexts, it is clear that all contingent workers, including part-time employees, temporary employees, independent contractors, leased employees, and other employees with specific skills filling short-term or specialized needs of employers, are generally suspect. As a practical matter, most employers do not have the time or resources to check the backgrounds or résumés of these contingent workers. Indeed, this is precisely the reason many employers look to third parties to provide ready-to-go workers for the employer's workforce. A logical extension of this decision could be that employers utilizing very short-term workers provided by a temporary agency or some other source who injure or damage a third party or coworker will be liable for such injuries. A practical legal step may be to ensure that the company receives adequate written promises of indemnification and assurances that the agencies will conduct thorough background checks before workers are placed in the company's workforce. Nonetheless, it will not prevent the employer from being named in a lawsuit. The employer may be left holding the bag if the independent contractor or temporary agency has inadequate insurance or has gone out of business.

In Hall v. SSF, Inc., 112 Nev. 1384, 930 P.2d 94 (1996), a nightclub was sued because its bouncer significantly injured a patron when removing him from the club. There was, of course, some disagreement regarding the events that led up to the altercation. Although the district court found in favor of the plaintiff on claims for assault and battery (under *respondeat superior* theory), it dismissed claims for negligent hiring, training, supervision, and retention. Of particular concern was plaintiff's claim that the district court improperly disallowed certain evidence as to whether the bouncer had been discharged less than honorably from the military for striking a superior officer and had allegedly been in other altercations. There is no discussion in the opinion regarding whether the employer could have legitimately inquired into these topics before the bouncer was hired. The court held that the district court improperly excluded the evidence and remanded the case to trial on the issue of negligent hiring.

The Hall court went on to hold that employers also have a duty to use reasonable care in the training, supervision, and retention of its employees to make sure the employees are fit for their positions. The court remanded these claims to trial because the district court disallowed questioning regarding when and where the fights occurred, which "would have provided the district judge with information needed to determine whether [the employer] was aware of [the bouncer's] actions and whether [the employer] had acted negligently in training, supervising, and retaining [the bouncer]." Id. at 99. In overturning the district court's decision to exclude the evidence as improper character evidence, the court concluded that "such a ruling was manifestly wrong because while the evidence might have been improper character evidence regarding the issue of whether [the bouncer] tortiously hit [the plaintiff], it was certainly relevant on the issue of negligent training, supervision, and retention." Id.

The evidentiary effect of this decision remains somewhat unclear. However, it is possible that Nevada employers will find themselves defending this type of claim with the introduction of highly volatile and prejudicial evidence, without any initial showing that the employer knew or had a reason to know of the alleged conduct.

In Smith's Food & Drug Ctrs. v. Bellegarde, 114 Nev. 602, 958 P.2d 1208 (1998), abrogated, Countrywide Home Loans, Inc. v. Thitchener, 192 P.3d 243 (Nev. 2008), the Nevada Supreme Court upheld an award of punitive damages to a customer suspected of shoplifting who was wrongfully detained and searched when the acting store manager was not aware of, and had not been formally trained in, company procedures for detecting and handling shoplifters. This case illustrates that company policies and procedures are effective only insofar as they are adequately communicated to the company's employees. Courts and juries are increasingly willing to impose an affirmative duty on the employer to train its employees and make certain they understand the policies and procedures in effect.

Another illustrative case is Nittinger v. Holman, 119 Nev. 192, 69 P.3d 688 (2003), herein the court held that the employer could be held liable for compensatory damages where the employer is found to have ratified or approved the conduct by having the power and responsibility to stop tortious conduct, but failing to do so. Because the evidence did not establish that the supervisor had the authority to deviate from established policy or that he had any discretion or could exercise his independent judgment, he was not a managerial agent, and therefore, the employer could not be held liable for punitive damages. Mere supervisory status is not managerial agent status, and thus, is not enough to impose punitive damages upon the employer.

In the most recent published Nevada Supreme Court decision considering claims of negligent hiring, retention and supervision, the Nevada Supreme Court affirmed the District Court's grant of summary judgment in favor of a defendant employer based on dual grounds that (a) under NRS 41.745, an employer is not liable for harm caused by the intentional torts of an employee, and (b) an employee's intervening criminal act was a superseding cause that relieved Action Cleaning of liability. Wood v. Safeway, 121 Nev. 724, 121 P.3d 1026, 1031 (2005). The Court reiterated that the Nevada case law, as codified in NRS 41.745, provides that an employee's intentional conduct relieves an employer of liability when "the employee's tort is truly an independent venture of his own and not committed in the course of the very task assigned to him." Id. at 1035. The Court then noted that if "the willful tort is committed in the course of the very task assigned to the employee," then it is appropriate to extend liability to the employer. Id. Applying the foregoing standard, the Court concluded that a sexual assault committed by an employee of the employer was a "truly independent venture" and was not committed in the course of a "task assigned to the employee." Id. Moreover, the Court observed that NRS 41.745 requires the element of foreseeability to be proven (which, as noted by the court, has effectively raised the standard for establishing liability and, consequently, had made employers liable only when an employee's intentional conduct is reasonably foreseeable under the circumstances). Id.

Nonetheless, the plaintiff/appellant asserted that the employee's criminal actions were foreseeable because the employer's workforce was highly transient and not adequately trained or supervised, and because much of the employer's workforce were illegal aliens. Id. at 1036. In this regard, the plaintiff/appellant argued that the employee's criminal actions were foreseeable because a reasonable person would not have regarded it as "highly extraordinary" that, given the composition of the employer's workforce, its employees would sexually harass "vulnerable females" with whom they come into contact. Id.

In concluding the plaintiff/appellant's appeal was without merit, the Court found that there was no genuine issue of material fact as to the foreseeability of the employee's conduct. Id. at 1036-1037. Specifically, the Court explained the employee had no prior criminal history in the United States or Mexico, the employer required all applicants to show proof of identification, checked employment references, and completed the proper Immigration and Naturalization forms for every employee, the employer's district manager had not received complaints of sexual harassment regarding the employee or any other employee in the past ten years. Id. at 1037. Hence, the Court concluded that, under the facts of the case, it was not reasonably foreseeable that the defendant employer's employee would sexually assault another employee. Id.

B. Intentional Infliction of Emotional Distress

The tort of intentional infliction of emotional distress (also called the tort of outrage) is frequently asserted in wrongful discharge lawsuits.

In Nevada, in order to state a claim of intentional infliction of emotional distress, a plaintiff must establish that: (1) the defendant's conduct was extreme and outrageous, (2) the defendant intended to cause the plaintiff emotional distress or demonstrated reckless disregard for the probability of causing emotional distress, (3) the plaintiff actually suffered severe or extreme emotional distress, and (4) the defendant's conduct proximately caused the distress. Nelson v. Las Vegas, 99 Nev. 548, 665 P.2d 1141, 1145 (1983); Star v. Rabello, 97 Nev. 124, 625 P.2d 90 (1981). The elements of a claim for negligent infliction of emotional distress are identical, except that the element of intent or reckless disregard is replaced with simple negligence. The plaintiff, however, must plead and prove not only severe emotional distress, but also physical injury. Alam v. Reno Hilton Corp., 819 F. Supp. 905, 911 (D. Nev. 1993); Chowdhry v. NLVH, Inc., 109 Nev. 478, 851 P.2d 459, 462 (1993).

A recent development in the area of emotional distress damages is related to those claims where emotional distress damages are not secondary to physical injuries, but, rather precipitate physical symptoms. This scenario is typical in employment cases where there is a claim for emotional distress. In Olivero v. Lowe, 116 Nev. 395, 995 P.2d 1023 (Nev. 2000), a construction worker on a job site was confronted by the defendant. The defendant was apparently angered by the fact that construction was behind schedule. The defendant brandished a handgun, punched the worker in the face, and threatened to take the worker's life. The worker sued for assault, battery, and intentional infliction of emotional distress. This was obviously a case where physical injury was at issue.

The Nevada Supreme Court distinguished between cases in which emotional distress arises out of a physical injury and those cases where emotional distress damages are not secondary to physical injuries, but precipitate physical symptoms. The court held that "bare" claims for intentional or negligent infliction of emotional distress have a more stringent standard of proof than cases involving actual or imminent apprehension of physical injury (e.g., assault or battery). In "bare" claims for emotional distress "either a physical impact must have occurred or, in the absence of physical impact, proof of 'serious emotional distress' causing physical injury or illness must be presented." Id. at 1026. In physical injury cases, while the plaintiff must prove he or she suffered emotional distress, the plaintiff need not establish "serious emotional distress." Accordingly, it was not necessary for the worker to have sought medical or psychological treatment for the physical and emotional damages claimed. The court also concluded that the separate claim for intentional infliction of emotional distress was subsumed within the damages awarded in connection with the claims of assault and battery.

In the case of intentional infliction of emotional distress, the plaintiff's distress "must be so severe and of such intensity that no reasonable person could be expected to endure it." Alam, 819 F. Supp. at 911. In Alam, the court ruled that the plaintiff's feelings of inferiority, headaches, irritability, and loss of ten pounds did not constitute severe emotional distress. Id. The court decides whether the evidence of distress is sufficiently severe to allow the claim to go to a jury. Id.; Hirschhorn v. Sizzler Restaurants Int'l, 913 F. Supp. 1393, 1401 (D. Nev. 1995). Similarly, a plaintiff alleging negligent infliction of emotional distress must show that he/she suffered more than general physical or emotional discomfort. Chowdhry, 851 P.2d at 462.

In Nevada, it is well settled that the act of discharging an employee does not, by itself, rise to the level of extreme and outrageous conduct required for an emotional distress claim. Alam, 819 F. Supp. at 911. Liability is reserved for those rare cases where the defendant's conduct goes "beyond all possible bounds of decency, is atrocious and utterly intolerable." Id.; Hirschhorn, 913 F. Supp. at n.1 (citing Shoen v. Amerco, Inc. 111 Nev. 735, 896 P.2d 469 (1995)).

It is important for Nevada employers to recognize that the Nevada Supreme Court has held that the tort of intentional infliction of emotional distress can be maintained in an employment termination case. Shoen v. Amerco, Inc., 111 Nev. 735, 896 P.2d 469 (1995). In this case, the plaintiff was the founder of a successful corporation. His children, to whom he had essentially relinquished control and ownership of the corporation, attempted to terminate his contract of employment after a series of betrayals and misrepresentations. The court concluded that the employee-father had shown sufficient evidence to take his claim of intentional infliction of emotional distress to a jury.

As to negligent infliction of emotional distress brought by the direct victim, the Shoen court noted that Nevada cases have not expressly allowed recovery under this theory. The court recognized, however, that under Nevada case law bystanders can recover for negligent infliction of emotional distress under certain circumstances. Thus, the court reasoned that it was only logical that the direct victim, in this case the employee-father, should also be able to recover under this theory. Therefore, the court recognized that negligent infliction of emotional distress can be an element of damage in a negligence claim when the negligence was committed directly against the plaintiff-victim.

The Nevada Supreme Court again distinguished between compensable and noncompensable emotional distress in Maduike v. Agency Rent-A-Car, 114 Nev. 1, 953 P.2d 24 (1998). The court found that while a rental car company may be strictly liable for injuries resulting from renting a car with faulty brakes, it takes a lot more than inconsiderate or ignorant behavior to find intentional infliction of emotional distress or to warrant an award of punitive damages. The plaintiffs argued that the company's conduct in renting them a car that had readily apparent brake problems and failing to repair or replace the brakes constituted the "outrageous" conduct necessary to prevail on their claim for intentional infliction of emotional distress. Noting that "outrageous" conduct is "outside all possible bounds of decency" and must be "regarded as utterly intolerable in a civilized community," the court rejected this claim, finding that "persons must necessarily be expected and required to be hardened . . . to occasional acts that are definitely inconsiderate and unkind." Id. at 26.

The Maduike court also rejected that plaintiffs' claim that they were entitled to punitive damages. The Plaintiffs had argued that refusing to repair or replace an unsafe vehicle rented by a young couple with small children who are 400 miles from home should meet the definition of oppression necessary to recover on this claim. Citing the definition of oppression as "despicable conduct that subjects a person to cruel and unjust hardship with conscious disregard of the rights of the person," the court denied the claim. It found that "even unconscionable irresponsibility will not support a punitive damages award." Id.

In 1998, the Nevada Supreme Court adopted a new and seemingly much broader view of the claim of negligent infliction of emotional distress. In Crippens v. Sav On Drug Stores, 114 Nev. 760, 961 P.2d 761 (1998), the court adopted a general foreseeability test in a personal injury case involving a claim for negligent infliction of emotional distress. Thus, those who sue under this theory are now more likely to succeed. In the employment context, suing parties are certain to make the claim that negligent actions by the employer are actions that could foreseeably cause an individual to suffer emotional distress. Given the broad "foreseeability" language used by the Nevada Supreme Court, it will be difficult to get these claims dismissed before trial.

C. Intentional Interference with Economic Advantage

A former employer (and perhaps its managers and/or supervisors) may also be found liable for interference with a prospective economic advantage or another related interference claim. Such claims may arise when a company does not hire an applicant because of statements or acts by a former employer. This is not a contract claim, but a tort claim based on an interference with a potential agreement; that is, it does not depend on whether any underlying agreement is presently enforceable between the parties.

In Nevada, a plaintiff attempting to claim tortious interference with a present contract must show the following elements: (1) a valid and existing contract, (2) the defendant's knowledge of the contract, (3) intentional acts intended or designed to disrupt the contractual relationship, (4) actual disruption of the contract, and (5) resulting damage. Sutherland v. Gross, 105 Nev. 192, 772 P.2d 1287 (1989) (quiet title action). A person does not commit the necessary intentional-act inducement to commit breach of contract merely by entering into an agreement with knowledge that the other party cannot perform because there is an existing contract between the other party and a third person. J.J. Indus., LLC v. Bennett, 119 Nev. 269, 71 P.3d 1264 (2003), rehearing denied by, (Oct. 23, 2003).

A party cannot, as a matter of law, tortiously interfere with its own contract. Blanck v. Hager, 360 F. Supp. 2d 1137, 1154 (D. Nev. 2005). Agents, acting within the scope of their employment, i.e., the principal's interest, do not constitute intervening third parties, and therefore cannot tortiously interfere with a contract to which the principal is a party. Id.

The elements of a claim for tortious interference with prospective business relations are similar. Those elements are: (1) a prospective contractual relationship between the plaintiff and a third party, (2) knowledge by the defendant of the prospective relationship, (3) intent to harm the plaintiff by preventing the relationship, (4) the absence of privilege or justification by the defendant, and (5) actual harm to the plaintiff as a result of the defendant's conduct. Wichinsky v. Mosa, 109 Nev. 84, 847 P.2d 727, 729-30 (1993) (dispute arising from dissolution of partnership and submission of the dispute to arbitration).

D. Prima Facie Tort

In some states, an employer can be held liable for a newly recognized doctrine called a "*prima facie* tort" to a current or former employee if the employer intentionally and unjustifiably engages in conduct with the intent to injure the employee and the employee suffers injury as a result of the employer's action. However, some states have held that this doctrine is unavailable to remedy the termination of an at-will employee, even where he is terminated for bad cause. However, a claim for intentional infliction of emotional distress may be stated in the context of a public policy claim. No published Nevada decision addresses this doctrine.

V. OTHER ISSUES

A. Statute of Limitations

The statute of limitations for both libel and slander is two years. NRS 11.190(4)(c).

B. Jurisdiction

Nevada's long-arm statutes, NRS 14.065 and NRS 14.080, reach the limits of due process set by the United States Constitution. Judas Priest v. Second Judicial Dist. Court, 104 Nev. 424, 760 P.2d 137 (1988). Defamation and related tort claims are presumably not treated differently from any other causes of action.

C. Worker's Compensation Exclusivity

The law governing workers' compensation in Nevada, the Nevada Industrial Insurance Act (NIIA or the "Act"), is found in chapters 616A, 616B, 616C, 616D and 617 of the Nevada Revised Statutes. Section 616A.010 states that the provisions of the Nevada workers' compensation scheme are based on renunciation of the rights and defenses recognized at common law. Section 616A.020 expressly provides that chapters 616A to 616D are the exclusive remedy for the payment of compensation and the amount thereof for resulting injuries and death. Accordingly, Nevada courts have consistently held that the NIIA provides the exclusive remedy for workers on the job. Sims v. General Tel. & Elecs., 107 Nev. 516, 815 P.2d 151 (1991), overruled on other grounds, Tucker v. Action Equip. & Scaffold Co., 113 Nev. 1349, 951 P,2d 1027 (1997).

NRS 616A.265 defines "injury" and "personal injury" in pertinent part as "a sudden and tangible happening of a traumatic nature, producing an immediate or prompt result which is established by medical evidence, including injuries to prosthetic devices." Thus, once the court determines that a covered employee has sustained an "injury" or "personal injury" arising out of and in the course of employment, compensation is limited to that provided by the Act. Las Vegas-Tonopah-Reno Stage Line v. Nevada Indus. Comm'n, 81 Nev. 626, 408 P.2d 241 (1965). The *exclusive-remedy rule* means that no other common law statutory remedy may be sought against the employer in connection with an industrial injury. Nevada Indus. Comm'n v. Underwood, 79 Nev. 496, 387 P2d 663 (1963). An employee may only bring a common law tort action against his employer if the employee can establish that the injury or injuries are not industrial in nature; therefore, the employee must persuade the court that either the injury is not the result of an accident or that it did not arise out of and in the course of his employment.

Under Nevada law, negligent conduct, even gross negligence, is still considered "accidental" and subject to the *exclusive-remedy rule*. Kennecott Copper Corp. v. Reyes, 75 Nev. 212, 337 P.2d 624 (1959). In Kennecott Copper, the parents of a worker buried and killed in a mining pit brought a wrongful death action against the decedent's employer. The plaintiffs alleged that the employer had been grossly negligent in permitting the decedent to drive in an open pit because the employer had allegedly foreseen for some time that a slide would occur. In ruling that the suit was barred by Nevada's workers' compensation laws, the Nevada Supreme Court held that the fact that the injury might have been foreseeable did not mean it was not accidental. The court rejected the respondents' contention that the sudden and violent event resulting in the decedent's death was not an accident within the statutory definition because it was foreseen and expected by the appellant. The mere fact that the appellant had foreseen and expected that a slide would occur does not permit the conclusion that the event was not an accident even when coupled with negligence, albeit gross negligence, in permitting the operation to continue in view of lack of knowledge as to when the slide would occur, or even in view of its possible imminence. Id. at 215. In arriving at this conclusion, the court noted that while the Nevada legislature provided numerous express exceptions to the Act, it did not differentiate between degrees of negligence or even gross negligence. To hold otherwise, the court said, would provide an open bypass around the Act.

While Nevada has not specifically addressed the *exclusive-remedy rule* in the context of a libel claim, an employee could presumably pursue such a claim against his employer. See Barjesteh v. Faye's Pub. Inc., 106 Nev. 120, 787 P.2d 405 (1990) ("When an employer commits an intentional tort upon an employee, 'the employer will not be heard to say that his intentional act was an accidental injury and so under the exclusive provisions of the compensation act.'"). The Nevada Supreme Court recognizes that employers do not enjoy immunity from liability for their intentional torts under the exclusive remedy provision of the NIIA where an employer commits an intentional tort upon an employee. Conway v. Circus Circus, Inc., 116 Nev. 870, 8 P.3d 837, 840 (2000). "An employer who commits an intentional tort upon an employee cannot claim that the intentional act resulted in an accidental injury." Id. Thus, employees may avoid the exclusive remedy provision of the NIIA in regard to their injuries only if they can show that the employer deliberately and specifically intended to injure them. Id. at 875.

This rule regarding the exclusive coverage of the Act was reaffirmed in the Nevada Supreme Court's decision in Wood v. Safeway, 121 Nev. 724, 121 P.3d 1026 (2005). In that case, a mildly mentally handicapped employee of Safeway was sexually assaulted at work on three separate occasions by a night-time janitor who worked for Action Cleaning, a cleaning subcontractor hired to provide cleaning services at the Safeway where the employee worked. Citing ample evidence in the record, the court concluded that the sexual assaults occurred in the course of the injured employee's employment. Id. at 1033. The court then reviewed the evidence to determine if a causal link existed between the injured employee's work at Safeway and the sexual assaults.

To make this determination, the court approved the use of "an incidental or increased risk test that looks to whether the risk of harm is related to the conditions of employment or whether the employment increased the risk to the employee." Id. After reviewing the evidence under this test, the court held that the injured employee's "employment contributed to and increased the risk of assault beyond that of the general public" because the injured employee's "only contact with [the perpetrator] was through her employment." Id. Accordingly, the sexually assaulted employee's exclusive remedy against her employer was a claim arising under Nevada's workers' compensation laws.

The Federal District Court for Nevada has followed the exclusive remedy rule in interpreting the scope of exclusive coverage of the Act under Nevada law. In Prescott v. United States, 523 F. Supp. 918 (D. Nev. 1981), affirmed, 731 F.2d 1388 (9th Cir. 1984), the Federal District Court for Nevada held that a former employee at the Nevada test site, suffering from multiple myeloma, was barred from bringing a tort action alleging that his employer had intentionally sent him into areas of high radiation. The court in that case held that "willful intent" in sending workers into immediate areas of nuclear detonations in order to perform their jobs is not the same as intent to make the workers sick. Id. at 928.

In King v. Penrod Drilling Co., 652 F. Supp. 1331 (D. Nev. 1987), the plaintiff brought an action against his employer, alleging that he was injured by the acts of his employer which were "done intentionally or with reckless disregard." In granting a partial motion for summary judgment, the court held that no common law action could be brought against the employer unless the employer acted with specific intent to harm the plaintiff. In arriving at this conclusion, the court stated it believed that, if the Nevada Supreme Court were presented with the issue, it would not allow recovery by an employee for employer recklessness. The court reasoned that, in Nevada, a common law action may not be brought by an employee against an employer for personal injuries unless the employer acted with a deliberate intent to injure the employee.

The Nevada Supreme Court, however, upheld a limited exception to the exclusion of a common law action against an employer for personal injuries. In Nevada Power Co. v. Haggerty, 115 Nev. 353, 989 P.2d 870 (1999), the court found that in limited circumstances where there is an independent duty created by statute, there is an exception to the rule that provides employer immunity under workers' compensation laws.

In a separate case, the Nevada Supreme Court reiterated previous opinions holding that an employee who has pursued his or her remedies under the Nevada workers' compensation scheme may have waived any and all rights to file a civil action against the employer even where the injury is intentional. In Advanced Countertop Design, Inc. v. Second

Judicial District Court, 115 Nev. 268, 984 P.2d 756 (1999), the court held that an employee who files a workers' compensation claim and accepts a permanent partial disability award is barred from suing his employer even if he later alleges that the injury was the result of an intentional act by the employer. The court held that acceptance of the permanent partial disability award acts as an accord and satisfaction and extinguishes any common law right the employee might have had against the employer. The court also recognized that employers do not enjoy immunity under workers' compensation for intentional injuries. However, the court held that the employee having accepted benefits for an "accidental injury" could not now change his position and assert that the injury was not accidental. The court found that by accepting a permanent partial disability award the employee made an election of remedies.

Based on the foregoing caselaw, and to the extent an employee suffers an "injury" or "personal injury" as defined by the NIIA arising out of and in the course of employment, the employee may be able to avoid the exclusive remedy provision of the NIIA and pursue an intentional tort libel claim if he can show that the employer acted deliberately and with a specific intent to injure him.

D. Pleading Requirements

Nevada is a notice pleading jurisdiction. A court will construe a pleading liberally and draw every fair inference in favor of the pleading party. Special damages must be precisely pleaded. NRCP 9(g); Branda v. Sanford, 97 Nev. 643, 637 P.2d 1223 (1981).

In Simpson v. Mars Inc., 113 Nev. 188, 929 P.2d 966 (1997), the court reasoned that employees spend a great deal of time with friends and acquaintances at the workplace, and that the employer's communication of falsehoods about the employee is therefore especially damaging. Simpson, 929 P.2d at 967.

SURVEY OF NEVADA EMPLOYMENT PRIVACY LAW

Wendy M. Krincek
R. Calder Huntington
Littler Mendelson
3960 Howard Hughes Parkway, Suite 300
Las Vegas, NV 89169

Mark Hinueber
Stephens Media
P.O. Box 70
Las Vegas, NV 89125

(With Developments Reported Through **November 1, 2012**)

GENERAL COMMENTS

With no intermediate court of appeals, Nevada generates very little published case law. It is not uncommon for years to go by without a published decision of the Nevada Supreme Court regarding the law of privacy. Consequently, much of Nevada's law of privacy is based on only a few cases. In general, Nevada employment law is based almost entirely on federal statutes with a small number of relevant Nevada statutes.

SIGNIFICANT DEVELOPMENTS SINCE THE 2012 *SURVEY*

None.

I. GENERAL LAW OF PRIVACY

A. Legal Basis of Privacy Claims.

Nevada case law has long recognized the right to privacy. People for the Ethical Treatment of Animals v. Bobby Berosini, Ltd., 111 Nev. 615, 895 P.2d 1269, 23 Media L. Rep. (BNA) 1961 (1995), rev'd on other grounds, City of Las Vegas Downtown Redevelopment Agency v. Hecht, 113 Nev. 644, 940 P.2d 134 (1997). There are four kinds of privacy torts: (1) unreasonable intrusion upon the seclusion of another; (2) appropriation of the name or likeness of another; (3) unreasonable publicity given to private facts; and (4) publicity unreasonably placing another in a false light before the public. *Id.* In People, the Nevada Supreme Court adopted another tort, a cousin to the four just mentioned, the tort of invasion of the right of publicity.

In People, the court specifically addressed the tort of intrusion, the tort of appropriation, and the tort of invasion of the right of publicity. As for the claim of tort of intrusion, the court questioned whether the videotaping of his activities with his animals invaded the plaintiff's privacy. The court noted that this tort is basically an interference with an individual's right to be left alone. In order to recover for this tort, the following elements must be proved: (1) an intentional intrusion (physical or otherwise) (2) on the solitude or seclusion of another (3) that would be highly offensive to a reasonable person. People, 895 P.2d at 1279. The court determined that the plaintiff's main concern was that he be provided a space backstage where his animals would not be distracted. His concern was for the animals, not his personal privacy. The evidence showed that the plaintiff saw nothing wrong with his conduct. Moreover, he stated that he would have done the same thing if bystanders had been watching. Hence, the video camera was no more an intrusion than a bystander. The video camera had in no way disturbed the animals or interfered with the plaintiff's pre-act preparations. The court concluded that the plaintiff should not be able to proceed on his claim for a tort of intrusion. In reaching its conclusion, the court noted that there is a reduced expectation of privacy in the workplace.

The court further addressed whether the videotaping could be considered "highly offensive to a reasonable person" even if the plaintiff had been able to show that he had an expectation of privacy. Given the nonintrusive nature of the videotaping and the cameraman's good intentions in doing so, recovery would have been barred in any event.

The court then examined the plaintiff's claim that his privacy was invaded because his name and/or likeness had been appropriated. The court explained that appropriation requires the unwanted and unpermitted use of name or likeness of an ordinary citizen for commercial purposes. The court distinguished this tort from the right-of-publicity tort as recognized in Nevada statutes. NRS 597.770 – 597.810. The right-of-publicity tort involves a celebrity whose name or likeness is appropriated for commercial purposes. The court explained that the difference between these two torts is the interest to be protected. In the former tort, the plaintiff's interest is in personal privacy, whereas in the latter tort the plaintiff is concerned with the commercial loss associated with another's appropriation of celebrated status or identity.

Because the plaintiff-animal trainer's claim clearly fell into the tort of right of publicity, a claim he did not raise in his lawsuit, he could not recover under either theory.

B. Causes of Action.

1. ***Misappropriation/Right of Publicity.*** The Nevada Supreme Court has recognized the tort of misappropriation and the right of publicity tort as separate causes of action. The common law misappropriation tort ordinarily involves the unwanted and unpermitted use of the name or likeness of an ordinary, uncelebrated person for advertising or other such commercial purposes, although it is possible that the misappropriation tort might arise from the misuse of another's name for purposes not involving strictly monetary gain. The right of publicity, on the other hand, involves the appropriation of a celebrity's name or identity for commercial purposes. People for the Ethical Treatment of Animals v. Bobby Berosini, Ltd., 111 Nev. 615, 895 P.2d 1269, 23 Media L. Rep. (BNA) 1961 (1995). Nevada has codified the right of publicity tort. NRS 597.770 et. seq. The Nevada Supreme Court has recognized that a non-celebrity may assert a cause of action under the right of publicity statutes. Hetter v. District Court, 110 Nev. 513, 874 P.2d 762 (1994). The statute of limitations for a common law misappropriation claim is 2 years. NRS 11.190(4)(e). The statute of limitations for a statutory right of publicity claim is 3 years. NRS 11.190(3)(a).

2. ***False Light.*** While the Nevada Supreme Court has recognized the existence of the false light tort, the Court has never set forth the substantive elements of the tort. The Nevada Supreme Court has distinguished false light privacy actions from defamation actions by stating that the injury in privacy actions is mental distress from having been exposed to public view, while the injury in defamation actions is damage to reputation. People for the Ethical Treatment of Animals v. Bobby Berosini, Ltd., 111 Nev. 615, 622, 895 P.2d 1269, n.4, 23 Media. L. Rep. (BNA) 1961 (1995).

3. ***Publication of Private Facts.*** To maintain a cause of action for public disclosure of private facts one must prove that a public disclosure of private facts has occurred which would be offensive and objectionable to a reasonable person of ordinary sensibilities. There is no liability when the defendant merely gives further publicity to information about the plaintiff that is already public. Montesano v. Donrey Media Group, 99 Nev. 644, 668 P.2d 1081 (1983), cert. denied, 466 U.S. 959 (1983), citing Restatement (Second) of Torts § 652D.

4. ***Intrusion.*** To recover for the tort of intrusion, a plaintiff must prove the following elements: (1) an intentional intrusion (physical or otherwise); (2) on the solitude or seclusion of another; (3) that would be highly offensive to a reasonable person. People for the Ethical Treatment of Animals v. Bobby Berosini, Ltd., 111 Nev. 615, 895 P.2d 1269, 23 Media L. Rep. (BNA) 1961 (1995). To prevail, the plaintiff must show an action, subjective expectation of seclusion or solitude in the place, conversation or matter, and that the expectation was objectively reasonable. The Nevada Supreme Court has specifically stated, in the context of an intrusion claim, that there is, generally speaking, a reduced objective expectation of privacy in the workplace. *Id.*

C. Defenses.

Rules of conditional privilege that apply to a defamation claim are also applicable to invasion of privacy claims. State v. Eighth Judicial Dist. Court, 118 Nev. 140, 42 P.3d 233 (2002).

D. Other Privacy-Related Actions.

1. ***Intentional Infliction of Emotional Distress.*** The Nevada Supreme Court has held that the tort of intentional infliction of emotional distress can be asserted in an employment termination case. Shoen v. Amerco, Inc., 111 Nev. 735, 896 P.2d 469 (1995), reh'g denied by, (Oct. 19, 1995). The elements of a cause of action for intentional infliction of emotional distress are: (1) extreme and outrageous conduct with either the intention of, or reckless disregard for, causing emotional distress, (2) the plaintiff's having suffered severe or extreme emotional distress and (3) actual or proximate causation. Star v. Rabello, 97 Nev. 124, 625 P.2d 90 (1981). A former employee's speculation that he was asked to unlawfully obtain bank and telephone records does not provide a basis to establish outrageous conduct. State v. Eighth Judicial Dist. Court, 118 Nev. 140, 42 P.3d 233 (2002).

2. ***Interference With Prospective Economic Advantage.*** The Nevada Supreme Court has recognized a cause of action for interference with prospective economic advantage in contexts other than employment privacy law. Wichinsky v. Mosa, 109 Nev. 84, 847 P.2d 727 (1993). The elements of a cause of action for interference with economic advantage are: (1) a prospective contractual relationship between the plaintiff and a third party; (2) knowledge by the defendant of the prospective relationship; (3) intent to harm the plaintiff by preventing the relationship; (4) the absence of privilege or justification by the defendant; and (5) actual harm to the plaintiff as a result of the defendant's conduct. Leavitt v. Leisure Sports Inc., 103 Nev. 81, 734 P.2d 1221 (1987).

Privilege or justification can exist when the defendant acts to protect his own interests. Id. For example, free competition is a significant privilege or justification for interference with prospective economic advantage. Custom Teleconnect, Inc. v. Int'l Tele-Services, Inc., 254 F. Supp. 2d 1173 (D. Nev. 2003), citing Crockett v. Sahara Realty Corp., 95

Nev. 197, 591 P.2d 1135 (1979). However, courts have not given competitors carte blanche in their dealings with each other. A competitor is privileged to divert business to itself by all fair and reasonable means, so that a plaintiff in an interference with prospective economic advantage claim must show that the means used to divert the prospective advantage was unlawful, improper or was not fair and reasonable. Custom Teleconnect, Inc., 254 F. Supp. 2d at 1181. In Custom Teleconnect, Inc., because International Tele-Services breached a confidentiality agreement with Custom Teleconnect directly to the diversion of the economic advantage, the court held that the alleged breach would be conduct that was improper, unfair and unreasonable.

3. ***Prima Facie Tort.*** An employer can be held liable for a "prima facie tort" to a current or former employee if the employer intentionally and unjustifiably engages in conduct with the intent to injure the employee and the employee suffers injury as a result of the employer's action. However, other jurisdictions have held that this newly recognized doctrine "prima facie tort" is unavailable to remedy the termination of an at-will employee, even where he is terminated for bad cause. No published Nevada decision specifically addresses the cause of action known as "prima facie tort."

II. EMPLOYER TESTING OF EMPLOYEES

Pursuant to NRS 613.325, the Nevada Equal Rights Commission may adopt regulations, consistent with the provisions of 42 U.S.C. § 12101 *et seq.*, setting forth the types of examinations which an employer may require. To date, no such regulations have been promulgated. Pursuant to NRS 284.406 *et seq.*, public employees may be tested for drugs. Section 284.210 of the Nevada Revised Statutes sets forth the requirements for the competitive testing of applicants for public employment.

A. Psychological or Personality Testing.

Psychological testing in the employment arena has been attacked by employees as an unconstitutional invasion of their privacy.

When an employee is required as a condition of employment to submit to a medical examination, the employee has access to the results of the testing pursuant to NRS 629.061, unless disclosure of the results would compromise national security. Cleghorn v. Hess, 109 Nev. 544, 853 P.2d 1260, 1263-64 (1993). NRS 629.061 provides that health providers must make health care records available for inspection by the patient or their representative.

B. Drug Testing.

There are at least seven types of testing: (1) pre-employment screening; (2) routine or periodic testing, such as testing as part of a physical examination; (3) "reasonable suspicion" or other "cause" testing; (4) post-accident testing; (5) random testing; (6) return-to-duty testing; and (7) post-rehabilitation testing or "follow-up testing." In any testing program, the employer must take steps to assure the test's validity and maintain the confidentiality of any information obtained from the tests.

1. ***Common Law and Statutes.*** The Ninth Circuit has approved government-mandated drug testing as part of annual or periodic physical examinations. International Brotherhood of Teamsters, etc. v. DOT, 932 F.2d 1292 (9th Cir. 1991) (periodic testing did not violate the Fourth Amendment's prohibition against unreasonable searches and seizures). With respect to reasonable suspicion testing, one employee's association with another employee believed to be involved with drugs may not justify testing. Jackson v. Gates, 975 F.2d 648 (9th Cir. 1992), cert. denied sub nom, City of Los Angeles v. Jackson, 509 U.S. 905 (1993).

Furthermore, pursuant to NRS 613.333, it is unlawful for an employer to fail or refuse to hire a prospective employee or discharge or otherwise discriminate against any employee because he engages in the lawful use in this state of any product outside the premises of the employer during his nonworking hours, if that use does not adversely affect his ability to perform his job or the safety of other employers. Therefore, drug testing for alcohol and prescription medications may have limited use. The requirements for drug testing public employees are set forth in NRS 284.4065.

2. ***Private Employers.*** The Nevada Supreme Court has on several occasions examined employers' efforts to ensure that their employees are drug-free. In Blankenship v. O'Sullivan Plastics Corp., 109 Nev. 1162, 866 P.2d 293 (1993), an at-will employee was terminated for refusing to sign a substance abuse employment agreement. The Nevada Supreme Court upheld the dismissal and stated, "we are unaware of any prevailing public policy against employers seeking to provide safe and lawful working conditions through testing programs designed to identify and eliminate the use of illicit drugs and alcohol.

In Clevenger v. Nevada Employment Sec. Dep't, 105 Nev. 145, 770 P.2d 866 (1989), an employee who was involved in an industrial accident was ordered, per company policy, to submit to a drug screening. The results of the drug screening were positive for marijuana. The employee was allowed to return to work, subject to random drug tests. The results of a subsequent random drug test were positive, and the employee was terminated. The employee's request for unemployment benefits was denied because she was terminated for misconduct. The Nevada Supreme Court affirmed the denial of benefits and stated, "when off-the-job conduct violates an employer's rule or policy, such as prohibiting the use of marijuana, an analysis must be made to determine if the employer's rule or policy has a reasonable relationship to the work to be performed; and if so, whether there has been an intentional violation or willful disregard of that rule or policy."

In Fremont Hotel & Casino v. Esposito, 104 Nev. 394, 760 P.2d 122 (1988), an employer suspected an employee of being under the influence and ordered her to undergo an immediate drug test. When the employee refused to undergo the drug test, the employee was terminated. The employee's request for unemployment benefits was denied because she was terminated for misconduct. The Court affirmed the denial of benefits because "misconduct may be established by a 'deliberate violation or disregard on the part of the employee of standards of behavior which his employer has the right to expect.

In Nevada Empl. Sec. Dep't v. Holmes, 112 Nev. 275, 282, 914 P.2d 611 (1996), rehearing denied by, (Sept. 10, 1996), the Nevada Supreme Court held that a hair analysis drug test is an accepted and reliable scientific methodology for detecting illicit drug use. In Holmes, the employee was denied unemployment benefits as a result of her refusal to submit to drug testing. *Id.* at 283. The Court found that the drug-free policy had a reasonable relation to the work performed by Holmes because Holmes was entrusted with the employer's computer system and the employee's job duties included a substantial amount of personal interaction with guests. The Court held that the employer had a justifiable reason for demanding that Holmes refrain from using cocaine, and affirmed the denial of benefits.

NRS 612.385 provides that a former employee is not entitled to unemployment benefits if that individual was discharged for "misconduct." An employee's violation of the employer's drug and alcohol policy has been found to constitute "misconduct" under Nevada's unemployment compensation scheme such that the employee was not entitled to unemployment benefits. Nevada Employment Sec. Dep't v. Holmes, 112 Nev. 275, 914 P.2d 611 (1996).

3. ***Public Employers.*** Generally, a public employer may request an employee to submit to a drug test only if the public employer: (a) reasonably believes, based upon objective facts, that the employee is under the influence of alcohol or drugs which are impairing his ability to perform his duties safely and efficiently; (b) informs the employee of the specific facts supporting its belief and prepares a written record of these facts; and (c) informs the employee in writing: (1) of whether the test will be for alcohol or drugs, or both; (2) that the results of the test are not admissible in any criminal proceeding against him; and (3) that he may refuse the test, but that his refusal may result in his dismissal or in other disciplinary action being taken against him. NRS 284.4065(1). In addition, a public employer may request a law enforcement officer to submit to a drug test if the officer, during the performance of his duties: (1) discharges his firearm, other than by accident; or (2) drives a motor vehicle in such a manner as to cause bodily injury to himself or another person or substantial damage to property. NRS 284.4065(2). A public employer may place a public employee who submits to a drug test on administrative leave with pay until the employer receives the results of the test. NRS 284.4065(3). A public employer must provide a public employee who submits to a drug test with the results of the test within three working days after the public employer receives the results. NRS 284.4065(4)(c).

In the public sector, random drug testing has been upheld for employees in specific, narrowly defined job classifications or professions which may be categorized either as part of a pervasively regulated industry (when the employee has a diminished expectation of privacy given the nature of employment), or when their positions are critical to public safety or the protection of life, property, or national security. For example, the Ninth Circuit upheld random testing for certain pipeline workers in International Brotherhood of Electrical Workers, Local 1245 v. Skinner, 913 F.2d 1454 (9th Cir. 1990), for aviation personnel in Bluestein v. Skinner, 908 F.2d 451, 454 (9th Cir. 1990), cert. denied, 498 U.S. 1083 (1991), and for correctional officers who have contact with prisoners in American Fed'n of Gov't Employees v. Roberts, 9 F.3d 1464 (9th Cir. 1993).

C. Genetic Testing.

Under Nevada's Fair Employment Practices Act it is an unlawful employment practice for employers to require genetic testing of current employees. NRS 613.345(1). It is also unlawful for employers to require prospective employees to undergo genetic testing as a condition of employment, or to deny employment, alter the terms of employment, or terminate employment based upon genetic information. *Id.* "Genetic information" is information that is obtained from a genetic test. NRS 613.345(2)(a). A "genetic test" is a "test that uses deoxyribonucleic acid extracted from the cells of a person, or a diagnostic test that uses another substance extracted or otherwise obtained from the body of a person, which determines the presence of an abnormality or deficiency that: (1) is linked to a physical or mental disorder or impairment; or (2) indicates a susceptibility to an illness, a disease, an impairment or another physical or mental disorder." NRS 613.345(2)(b). However, a test to determine the presence of alcohol or a controlled substance in the system of the person tested is not a "genetic test."

D. Polygraph Tests.

NRS 613.480-613.510 and NRS 289.050 and 289.070 prohibit employers from discharging, disciplining, or discriminating against an applicant or current employee based on the refusal to take a polygraph examination or the results of a polygraph examination, the filing of a claim alleging violation of this statute, and testifying about an alleged violation. Employers who violate this statute may be required to hire, reinstate or promote the employee, and pay all lost wages and benefits. Under the Peace Officers' Bill of Rights, NRS chapter 289, there are also certain restrictions on polygraph examinations of peace officers.

Nevada law prohibits an employer from requiring an employee or prospective employee to take a polygraph test. NRS 613.480. However, NRS 613.510 sets forth significant exemptions to this general prohibition. An employer may request an employee to submit to a polygraph examination if the examination is administered in connection with an ongoing investigation involving economic loss or injury to the employer's business, including theft, embezzlement, misappropriation or an act of unlawful industrial espionage or sabotage. NRS 613.510(1)(a)(1). An employer may request a prospective employee to submit to a polygraph examination if the employer is in the primary business of providing armored car personnel, personnel engaged in the design, installation and maintenance of security alarm systems or other security personnel. NRS 613.510(1)(b).

The Employee Polygraph Protection Act (29 U.S.C. §§ 2001-2009) imposes severe restrictions on the use of lie-detector tests, effectively eliminating the use of polygraph testing as a pre-employment screening mechanism. The Act bars most private-sector employers from requiring, requesting, or suggesting that an employee or job applicant submit to a polygraph or lie detector test, and from using or accepting the results of such tests. The Act further prohibits employers from disciplining, discharging, or discriminating against any employee or applicant: (1) for refusing to take a lie-detector test, (2) based on the results of such a test, or (3) for taking any actions to preserve employee rights under the Act.

Initially, it is important to note that the Act only prohibits mechanical or electrical devices, not paper-and-pencil tests, chemical testing, or other nonmechanical or nonelectrical means that purport to measure an individual's honesty. Moreover, chemical testing is specifically excluded from the definition of lie detector, so as to affirmatively permit the use of medical tests to determine the presence of drugs or alcohol in an individual's bodily fluids.

The Act contains several limited exceptions to the general ban on polygraph testing, one of which permits the testing of prospective employees of security guard firms. To qualify for the security-firm exemption, however, the employer's primary business must consist of providing armored car personnel, persons who design, install, and maintain security alarm systems, or other uniformed or plainclothes security personnel. Thus, a security guard employed by an employer not in the business of supplying security services would not fall under this exemption. A second exemption is provided for employers who manufacture, distribute, or dispense controlled substances. The third, and only exception applicable to most private employers, permits any covered employer to test current employees who are reasonably suspected of involvement in a workplace incident that resulted in economic loss or injury to the employer's business.

Most employers may lawfully require an employee to submit to a polygraph test only under the following conditions: (1) the employer is engaged in an ongoing investigation involving economic loss or injury to the employer's business, (2) the employee to be tested had access to the property in question, and (3) the employer has a reasonable suspicion that the employee was involved in the incident. Moreover, employers should be aware that the only acceptable test is the polygraph test. Use of any other mechanical or electrical honesty testing device will be deemed a violation of the Act, even if the employer meets all of the other requirements of the exemption.

Additionally, the employer must provide the employee to be examined with a statement at least forty-eight hours prior to the test, in language understood by the examinee, which fully explains the specific incident or activity being investigated, and the basis for testing the particular employee. The notice must, at a minimum, identify the specific economic loss or injury to the business of the employer, describe with particularity the employee's access to the property that is the subject of the investigation, describe in detail the basis of the employer's reasonable suspicion that the employee was involved in the incident or activity under investigation, and include the signature of a person (other than the polygraph examiner) authorized to legally bind the employer. Furthermore, the employer must retain a copy of all such statements for at least three years.

E. Fingerprinting.

No statutes, regulations or case law limit the ability of an employer to request an employee to submit to fingerprinting. An employer may use the fingerprints of an employee who works with children to request information from the state regarding sexual offenses. NRS 179A.210. Fingerprinting is required for numerous privileged licenses, including gaming licenses. NRS 463.520.

III. SEARCHES

Although it is not specifically enumerated in the U.S. Constitution, the Supreme Court has held that there is a federal constitutional right to personal privacy. Griswold v. Connecticut, 381 U.S. 479 (1965). In Griswold, the Court found that the right to privacy is implicit in the Bill of Rights, which prohibits various types of unreasonable government intrusion upon personal freedom. In subsequent cases, the Court has expanded the scope of this right, particularly in areas in which an express guarantee exists, such as the Fourth Amendment's protection from unreasonable searches and seizures.

Although Article 1, Section 18 of the Nevada Constitution prohibits unreasonable searches and seizures, the Nevada Supreme Court has not found that the Nevada Constitution provides any greater protection against unreasonable searches and seizures than the Fourth Amendment to the United States Constitution. The constitutional prohibition on unreasonable searches applies only to persons acting under the color of state law. Golden v. State, 95 Nev. 481, 596 P.2d 495 (1979) (search of an air freight shipment by an airline employee did not implicate constitutional right to be free from unreasonable searches).

A. Employee's Person.

1. ***Private Employers***. Standard tort claims, including assault and battery, could presumably result from such searches.

Battery is generally defined as intentional and harmful or offensive contact by one person with another person. The intent required refers only to the intent to make physical contact; the defendant need not intend that the contact be offensive or harmful. Restatement (Second) of Torts § 16(1) (1965).

To successfully prove the tort of assault, a plaintiff must at least demonstrate: (1) intent to cause a harmful or offensive contact with the other person by the defendant, and (2) apprehension of such injury by the plaintiff. Restatement (Second) Of Torts § 21(1) (1965).

In Bigelow v. Bullard, 111 Nev. 1178, 901 P.2d 630 (1995), rehearing denied by, (Feb. 28, 1996), a former employee residing in her employer's rental project claimed assault and battery when the employer's agents attempted to force their way into the employee's apartment. The employee supplied evidence that she tried to push the employer's security guard to prevent him from entering, but he pulled a gun on her, pushed it into her stomach and said, "You push me again, bitch, and I'll bash your face in." There was sufficient evidence presented that a jury could have concluded that the security guard was acting within the course and scope of his duties and at the employer's request. The court concluded that the jury did not err in awarding punitive damages.

The court's discussion of compensatory and punitive damages in a footnote should give pause to Nevada employers. The jury found that the security guard committed an assault and a battery against the former employee and that he was acting within the course and scope of his employment. The jury assessed compensatory damages against the individual security guard for one thousand two hundred fifty dollars for the assault and one thousand two hundred fifty dollars for the battery. Punitive damages were assessed against the employer in the amount of ten thousand dollars for the assault and fifteen thousand dollars for the battery. The Nevada Supreme Court upheld this entire damage award.

2. ***Public Employers.*** By operation of law, federal constitutional prohibitions apply directly to public employers. Such employers must be especially careful, therefore, to avoid policies and practices that infringe upon the privacy rights of public employees. *See, e.g.*, O'Connor v. Ortega, 480 U.S. 709 (1987), on remand, Ortega v. O'Connor, 817 F.2d 1408 (9th Cir. 1987) (the Fourth Amendment's prohibition against unreasonable searches and seizures restricted a public employer's ability to search an employee's office).

In United States v. Gonzalez, 300 F.3d 1048 (9th Cir. 2002), a random search of a government employee's backpack by a store detective was held to be reasonable because the employee understood the established policy of the store requiring that employees allow such searches, which was known to the employee because he signed a form so indicating when he commenced employment, and because the scope of the search did not exceed the store's policy. The store was entitled to search his backpack for stolen merchandise only because the employee had clear notice before he ever came to work with his backpack that he would be subject to such a search. However, an employee on his first day who had not yet signed or learned of the store policy might be in a stronger position to have a reasonable expectation of privacy deserving protection from such searches.

In contrast, in Bernhard v. City of Ontario, 270 Fed.Appx. 518, 2008 U.S. App. LEXIS 6404 (9th Cir. 2008), the court found that a warrantless, covert video surveillance of a police department employee locker room in connection with a theft investigation was unreasonable because employees had an objective and subjective expectation of privacy. Two factors guided the court's decision: (1) people generally expect privacy in places where they engage in private activities, such as locker rooms, and (2) secret video surveillance is particularly intrusive to an employee's fourth amendment privacy rights.

B. Employee's Work Area.

A public employee may have a liberty interest in privacy, which is protected by the Fourth and Fourteenth Amendments to the Constitution. A deprivation of a liberty interest in *privacy* generally arises when a public employer improperly searches a public employee's office or desk or locker, then terminates that public employee based upon the results of the search. Drug testing also raises privacy right issues. A search is considered improper where the public employee has a reasonable expectation of privacy, and the public employer conducts the search without consent of the public employee or without a valid search warrant. O'Connor v. Ortega, 480 U.S. 709 (1987).

Schowengerdt v. General Dynamics Corp., 823 F.2d 1328 (9th Cir. 1987), cert. denied, 503 U.S. 951 (1992), illustrates this issue. Schowengerdt was a civil engineer working for the Navy. He was also in the Naval Reserve. The Navy and its private security entered Schowengerdt's locked office and searched his locked desk and credenza and seized personal correspondence and photographs. The Navy then discharged Schowengerdt from the Naval Reserve for homosexual activities. Schowengerdt ultimately resigned his civil engineering position. The Navy also made an adverse comment about Schowengerdt that held up the transfer of his security clearance for sixteen months. Under these facts, the Ninth Circuit Court of Appeals held that Schowengerdt could establish a deprivation of a liberty interest in privacy in violation of the Constitution.

A public employer can minimize the risk of depriving a public employee of a liberty interest in privacy. First, establish written policies for searches that reserve the right for employers to enter offices, desks, and lockers. Second, have all employees sign a receipt for these written policies. Third, retain copies of keys to all offices and desks and provide locks for all lockers. Fourth, obtain consent from the employee before conducting the search. Finally, if the employee does not consent or is unavailable to consent, obtain a valid search warrant.

IV. MONITORING OF EMPLOYEES

A. Telephones and Electronic Communications.

Title 18 of the Omnibus Control and Safe Streets Act (the Act) prohibits all private individuals and organizations, including employers, from intercepting the wire, oral, or electronic communications of others. 18 U.S.C. §§ 2510-2520. Generally, the Act provides for penalties and civil damages when a third person intercepts a telephone conversation without the consent of either of the conversing parties. 18 U.S.C. § 2511(1)(4)(a). In 1986, the Electronic Communications Privacy Act, more commonly known as the Federal Wiretap Act, amended the Omnibus Control and Safe Streets Act to cover interception of electronic communications.

The Act proscribes intentional interception of any "wire, oral, or electronic communication," and defines *intercept* as the "aural or other acquisition of the contents of any wire, electronic, or oral communication through the use of any electronic, mechanical, or other device." 18 U.S.C. § 2511(1)(a); § 2510(4). Thus, intercepting an electronic communication "essentially means acquiring the transfer of data." United States v. Reyes, 922 F. Supp. 818, 836 (S.D.N.Y. 1996).

Although the law is highly unsettled, the Ninth Circuit affirmed a district court ruling that stated that recording a voicemail message with a hand-held tape recorder, after the message was in voicemail, did not constitute an interception because the recording was not contemporaneous with the leaving of the message. Payne v. Norwest Corp., 911 F. Supp. 1299 (D. Mont. 1995), aff'd in part rev'd in part on other grounds, 113 F.3d 1079 (9th Cir. 1997). The court reasoned that the transmission over the system had ceased by the time the information was retrieved. Accordingly, under this line of reasoning, if the employer merely retrieves information, the employer has not engaged in an interception of information prohibited by Title 18. Although retrieval of electronically stored information is not considered a prohibited interception of communication, it may nonetheless be prohibited under Title II of the Federal Wiretap Act.

Title II of the Federal Wiretap Act "generally proscribes unauthorized access to stored wire or electronic communications." 18 U.S.C. §§ 2701-2711. Thus, while retrieval of electronic communications does not constitute interception, it is still prohibited as unlawful access under the Act, if the access is not authorized. Accordingly, the employer is well advised not to intercept or access electronically received or stored communications contained on an employee's private pager or electronic-mail or voicemail system.

Perhaps the most significant exception to the Federal Wiretap Act is found in 18 U.S.C. § 2511(2)(d), which provides that an employee may either expressly or impliedly consent to an otherwise impermissible monitoring of a communication. Accordingly, employers may avoid liability under the Act by procuring the consent of employees before monitoring communications.

The Federal Wiretap Act prohibits interception only through the use of any "electronic, mechanical, or other device." It expressly excludes telephone equipment or components furnished to the user by a provider of wire or electronic communications service in the ordinary course of business and being used by the subscriber in the ordinary course of business. 18 U.S.C. § 2510(5)(a). Thus, the monitoring of voicemail retrieval systems furnished by a communications service, such as Pacific Bell, may not constitute an interception for the purposes of this statute. Although it is unclear whether this exception would apply to a voicemail system, it appears less likely to apply to e-mail or other systems that do not rely on a "telephone or telegraph instrument, equipment or facility, or any component thereof."

1. ***Wiretapping.*** Pursuant to NRS 200.620, it is unlawful for any person to intercept a wire communication unless: (1) a court order is obtained; or (2) an emergency situation exists, one party consents and a court later ratifies the interception. In light of the Nevada Supreme Court's decision in Lane v. Allstate Ins. Co., 114 Nev. 1176, 969 P.2d 938 (1998), this statute must now be interpreted as requiring two-party consent for the recording of telephone conversations. In Lane, the Nevada Supreme Court held that telephone conversations recorded by the plaintiff without the consent of the other parties to the conversations could not be used in the plaintiff's wrongful discharge claim against his former employer.

2. ***Electronic Communications.*** The definition of wire communication set forth in NRS 200.610(2) is broad enough to include all transmissions via wire and cable. Therefore, most electronic communications, including computer E-mail are presumably subject to the two-party consent requirement set forth by the Nevada Supreme Court in Lane v. Allstate Ins. Co., 114 Nev. 1176, 969 P.2d 938 (1998). The definition of radio communication set forth in NRS 200.610(3) includes all transmissions via radio or other wireless methods. Therefore, cellular phone calls are presumably also subject to the two-party consent rule.

3. ***Other Electronic Monitoring.*** Nevada has not addressed other electronic monitoring. Existing federal law on this issue should be followed.

B. Mail.

Nevada law does not address this issue. Existing federal law regarding mail is the only law that needs to be followed.

C. Surveillance/Photographing.

No specific Nevada law addresses this issue. Presumably, an employer can, under certain circumstances, be sued for intrusion by an employee. However, the Nevada Supreme Court has specifically stated, in the context of an intrusion claim, that there is, generally speaking, a reduced objective expectation of privacy in the workplace. People for the Ethical Treatment of Animals v. Bobby Berosini, Ltd., 111 Nev. 615, 633, 895 P.2d 1269, 1281, n.20, 23 Media L. Rep. (BNA) 1961 (1995). NRS §§ 200.610(2); 200.620

V. ACTIVITIES OUTSIDE THE WORKPLACE

A. Statute or Common Law

The privacy rights of employees are protected by federal and state constitutional and statutory provisions. Accordingly, care should be taken to avoid unnecessary or unjustified attempts to regulate employee conduct outside of the workplace. For example, a blanket prohibition on *moonlighting*, or acceptance of outside employment, can be replaced with a requirement that employees must avoid actual or potential conflicts of interest, or the appearance of conflicts of interest, as well as outside activities that would interfere with the employee's loyalty to the employer and ability to fulfill all job responsibilities.

Pursuant to NRS 613.333, it is unlawful for an employer to fail or refuse to hire a prospective employee or discharge or otherwise discriminate against any employee because he engages in the lawful use in this state of any product outside the premises of the employer during his nonworking hours, if that use does not adversely affect his ability to perform his job or the safety of other employers.

NRS 613.330 makes it unlawful to discriminate based on sexual preference or sexual orientation. Therefore, prohibiting homosexual behavior outside the workplace would violate this law, and prohibiting a homosexual from discussing the issue or exhibiting homosexual tendencies in the workplace could violate the law.

NRS 613.330 also makes it unlawful to discriminate on the basis of gender expression or identity. Thus, prohibiting conduct based on employees' method of gender expression or professing their gender identity could violate the law. Also, prohibiting discussion of these issues or particular dress codes forcing gender stereotype conformance potentially could violate the law.

Care must also be taken by nonunion employers to avoid infringing on the rights of employees to organize. The National Labor Relations Act protects the rights of employees to engage in concerted activities for the purpose of collective bargaining or other mutual aid or protection. 29 U.S.C. § 157. Employer policies that interfere with, restrain, or coerce employees in the exercise of these rights constitute unfair labor practices. 29 U.S.C. § 158(a).

Notwithstanding these constraints, there remain many types of behavior which may be prohibited. It is generally recognized that the employee enters the workplace with the acceptance of the employer's authority and right to set reasonable rules of behavior. Nevertheless, the growing cultural expectation of unfettered individual freedom from traditional constraints is likely to foster claims and lawsuits attempting to establish violations when the employer attempts to constrain behavior outside the workplace or off the clock. Any written policy should be reviewed to verify that the particular standard does not run afoul of a specific law or infringe the rights of employees. The more business-related a policy is, the more likely it is to be enforceable. Additionally, any prohibition of conduct must be enforced in a nondiscriminatory manner to withstand a claim of discrimination.

B. Employees' Personal Relationships

1. ***Romantic Relationships Between Employees.*** Nevada law does not address the issue of romantic relationships between employees.

2. ***Sexual Orientation.*** NRS section 613.330 makes it an unlawful employment practice for an employer to discharge, fail to hire, or otherwise discriminate against its employees on the basis of race, color, religion, sex, sexual orientation, age, disability, or national origin. The Nevada Legislature amended section 613.330 effective October 1, 1999, to prohibit discrimination based upon sexual orientation. *Sexual orientation* is defined as "having or being perceived as having an orientation for heterosexuality, homosexuality, or bisexuality." NRS 613.310(6); NRS 610.010(5); NRS 338.125(4).

In addition to the amendment of section 613, the Nevada legislature also amended the Apprenticeship Law to prohibit discrimination in apprenticeship based upon sexual orientation, and the Public Works Discrimination Law to prohibit discrimination by state contractors based upon sexual orientation. NRS 610.020; NRS 338.125.

3. ***Marital Status.*** Nevada law does not prohibit discrimination by an employer on the basis of marital status. NRS 613.330.

C. Smoking.

NRS 613.333 is the Nevada Smokers' Rights Act. An employer may not discharge or otherwise discriminate against any employee who engages in lawful use of any product outside the employer's premises during nonwork hours if the use does not interfere with the ability to do the job or compromise the safety of coworkers. A violation of this statute may result in an order of reinstatement or an order directing that an offer of employment be made, damages equal to lost wages and benefits, and costs and attorney's fees.

D. Blogging.

Nevada has not specifically addressed blogging through statutory law or caselaw. Existing federal law on blogging must be followed. In addition, Nevada retaliatory discharge or whistleblowing caselaw may be extended to cover blogging.

VI. RECORDS

Public employers are frequently confronted with issues concerning the use and dissemination of employee records. Nevada's public record statute generally favors disclosure of records. Public employers seek guidance from the attorney general regarding application of this statute. The attorney general opinions regarding disclosure of medical records, personnel files, and the like, are particularly helpful. Careful review of the attorney general opinions is particularly important because the statute makes willful concealment, destruction, or alteration of public records and documents a category *C* felony.

NRS section 239.010 limits access to background information and personal history to state agencies and political subdivisions where the person who is the subject of the records and information has applied for a license, or is seeking employment or a contract for personal services. State agencies and political subdivisions may also obtain this information if there is a legitimate need to have such information for the protection of the agency or those within their jurisdictions.

A. Personnel Records.

NRS section 613.075 requires any employer, public or private, to allow its employees, or those under contracts of hire, to inspect any records that have information used by the employer to determine an employee's qualifications and any disciplinary actions, including termination, taken against the employee. This statute also applies to any labor organization referring a person to a prospective employer. The employee or person referred must be allowed access to information kept by a labor organization regarding positions on referral lists. The employee is also entitled to a copy of these records, and the employer may only charge the actual cost of providing access and the copies. Copies may be furnished only for employees or former employees who have or were employed more than sixty days. While the employer is prohibited from maintaining *secret* records, the employer is entitled to maintain a confidential *investigative* file. An employer who violates this statute may be assessed an administrative fine of not more than five hundred dollars for each violation.

Nevada law mandates encryption of sensitive human resources information. The recently passed NRS 603A.010-603A.920 applies to any organization doing business in Nevada that collects an individual's first name or initial and last name plus Social Security number, employee identification number, driver's license number, or credit or debit card number or financial account number with any required security code (collectively "Personal Information"). Every employer collects employees' SSNs in the ordinary course of business, and many employers assign employee identification numbers and collect driver's license numbers. Consequently, NRS 603A.010 et seq. applies to all employers.

NRS 603A.010 et seq. requires encryption in two circumstances. First, the electronic transmission of Personal Information must be encrypted unless the transmission (a) passes within a secure network, or (b) is sent by fax machine. 603A.215(2)(a). This means that intracorporate e-mail will not need to be encrypted as long as e-mails do not pass over the public Internet (which usually is the case). However, all e-mail to third parties, *i.e.*, e-mails that pass over the public Internet containing Personal Information, need to be encrypted.

Second, no "data storage device" which contains Personal Information may be taken off-site unless the Personal Information is encrypted. NRS 603A.215(2)(b). This new law's broad definition of "data storage device" includes laptops, iPhones, BlackBerrys, back-up tapes and disk drives, as well as virtually any other electronic device that can store Personal Information.

Employers who fail to comply with NRS 603A.010 et seq. will easily be discovered. Because Nevada's security breach notification law provides a safe harbor from notification for Personal Information that is encrypted, any notice of a security breach that discloses the loss of theft of a laptop, portable digital assistant, back-up tape or other electronic storage medium effectively would constitute an admission that the employer failed to comply with Nevada's encryption requirement. NRS 603A.220. Because that failure would violate a statutory standard, the absence of encryption most likely would be deemed negligent. For this reason, employers with operations in Nevada should develop plans for complying with the new Nevada encryption standard.

B. Medical Records.

Medical records are confidential under Nevada law. NRS 449.720 (1999). Information regarding prescriptions filled by a pharmacy is also confidential. NRS 639.238 (1995). Providers of health care must retain the health care records of patients for at least five years. NRS 629.051. Employers have no special right under the law to access employee's medical records. Medical records that are used in the state's industrial insurance system are also confidential. NRS 616B.012 (1999). Medical records and other medical information contained in files regarding public employees are probably not disclosable pursuant to Nevada's Open Records Act, NRS 239.010, due to the privacy interests of the public employees.

Federal law also addresses the issue of employee medical records. Specifically, the Americans with Disabilities Act (ADA) requires that any information relating to the medical condition or history of an applicant or employee be collected and maintained on separate forms, kept in separate medical files from the general personnel information, and treated as confidential. 42 U.S.C. § 12112(C)(3)(B)(1995). Disclosure of medical records or information is allowed only in three situations under the ADA: (1) when supervisors and managers need to be informed regarding necessary restrictions on work or duties of the employee and necessary accommodations; (2) when first-aid and safety personnel need to be informed about a disability that might require emergency treatment; and (3) when government officials investigating compliance with the ADA request access to such records or information. Thus, employers are wise to check the ADA Compliance Manual before using or disclosing medical information of any kind.

C. Criminal Records.

Under the Nevada statute regarding records of criminal history, employees and employers have certain rights and responsibilities. Some of those provisions are explained below.

Under NRS section 179A.100 (1999), employers or their authorized agents may request information regarding sexual offenses concerning an employee or a prospective employee, a volunteer or a prospective volunteer, if the employee gives the employer written consent to obtain this information. However, employers using a third party or outside vendor to gather such information must also comply with the federal Fair Credit Reporting Act.

NRS section 179A.150 (1987) allows any person who believes he/she may be the subject of information relating to sexual records or other records of criminal history to inspect such records maintained by the central repository, or the state, municipal, county, or metropolitan police agencies. This inspection must be done in person at the agency. However, investigative or intelligence files will not be disclosed.

Under NRS section 179A.190 (1987), an employer may consider information relating to sexual offenses in deciding to hire, retain, suspend, or discharge an employee, and the employee may not sue the employer for unlawful discrimination based on the employer's consideration of this information.

NRS section 179A.210 (1981) provides that the employer may only obtain notice of information relating to sexual offenses if there is an actual conviction or if there is an arrest or pending charge at the time the employer makes the request. Employers should be aware that an employee, a prospective employee, or a volunteer may recover actual damages in a civil action if the employer or the employer's agent disseminates the information regarding criminal history or sexual offenses to anyone else without express authority of law or a court order, and punitive damages if the disclosure was malicious. An employer may also be liable to a child *served by the employer* for damages if the child suffers a sexual offense by an employee for whom information about offenses relating to sexual conduct could have been discovered. The employer is not liable if the employee refused to give his written consent, as discussed earlier.

Under NRS section 179A.240(2) (1987), any person who unlawfully disseminates or attempts to disseminate information regarding sexual offenses is guilty of a misdemeanor.

D. Subpoenas / Search Warrants

NRS 50.165 imposes a duty upon a witness, who has been properly served with a subpoena, to appear at the trial at the date and time specified, to bring any specified papers which are under the witness' control, and to remain at trial until either the testimony is closed or the witness is discharged. A subpoena duces tecum commands a witness to bring to court documents or other tangible things under the witness' control. NRCP 45(b); see also NRS 50.165(1). The materials sought should be designated as specifically as possible.

A witness who is under subpoena is entitled to fees for each day of attendance and an allowance for mileage from the witness's residence. NRS 50.225; see Lamar v. Urban Renewal Agency, 84 Nev. 580, 445 P.2d 869 (1968), overruled on other grounds, Casey v. Williams, 87 Nev. 137, 482 P.2d 824 (1971). Unless at least one day's fees and mileage allowance have been paid, the witness is not required to appear. NRS 50.225. The amount for fees and mileage for lay witnesses is set forth in NRS 50.225.

NRCP 45 governs procedure related to witness subpoenas. Anyone who is eighteen years of age or older, but not a party to the action, may serve a subpoena. An attorney may not be permitted to serve a subpoena. Nevada Cornell Silver Mines, Inc. v. Hankins, 51 Nev. 420, 279 P. 27 (1929) (the attorney for the plaintiff was not permitted to serve a summons). A subpoena for trial may be served anywhere within the state. NRCP 45(e). Rule 45(c) requires that service be made personally, not through the mail or by delivering to an agent. It is accomplished by showing an original and giving a copy of the subpoena to the person.

Unless the subpoena is issued on behalf of the State of Nevada or its agency, the person under subpoena may require payment in advance of fees and allowable mileage for one day's attendance. NRCP 45(c). Fees and estimated mileage allowance should always be tendered with the subpoena since, under NRS 50.225(2)(a), a person is not obliged to testify unless one day's fees and mileage have been paid.

Failure to obey a subpoena without a legal excuse may be deemed a contempt of court. NRCP 45(f). If a witness fails to attend trial, a warrant may be issued to the county sheriff to arrest and bring the witness before the court. NRS 50.205. The witness must pay the aggrieved party $100 in addition to all damages sustained because of the failure to attend. NRS 50.195(2).

VII. ACTIONS SUBSEQUENT TO EMPLOYMENT

A. References

A job reference release signed by a former employee excusing the provider of information "from any liability," is unenforceable because it shields the wrongdoer from liability for intentional torts. McQuirk v. Donnelley, 189 F.3d 793 (9th Cir. 1999).

B. Non-Compete Agreements

Section 613.200 of the Nevada Revised Statutes generally prohibits employers from "blacklisting" employees in Nevada. Notwithstanding this general prohibition, the statute specifically allows employers and employees to enter into enforceable covenants not to compete. The statute, in pertinent part, reads as follows:

The provisions of this section do not prohibit a person, association, company, corporation, agent or officer from negotiating, executing and enforcing an agreement with an employee of the person, association, company or corporation which, upon termination of the employment, prohibits the employee from:

(A) Pursuing a similar vocation in competition with or becoming employed by a competitor of the person, association, company or corporation; or

(B) Disclosing any trade secrets, business methods, lists of customers, secret formulas or processes or confidential information learned or obtained during the course of his employment with the person, association, company or corporation; if the agreement is supported by valuable consideration and is otherwise reasonable in its scope and duration.

Historically, the Nevada Supreme Court forged a compromise by limiting enforcement of covenants not to compete to persons seeking employment with another company, as opposed to those entering self-employment. Hansen v. Edwards, 426 P.2d 792 (Nev. 1967). The court in Hansen focused its justification for refusing to extend enforceability on the basic tenet of commercial freedom, stating it was contrary to Nevada's public policy to put any restrictions on commerce or the right of an individual to pursue a livelihood in a chosen profession. In 1995, only after the adoption of the statutory language noted above did the Nevada Supreme Court change its position.

The Nevada Supreme Court has since announced that the legislative history of section 613.200(4) suggests that covenants not to compete are consistent with the public policy of Nevada. The Supreme Court also eliminated its distinction between employees who go on to work for other employers and those who go to work for themselves in its enforcement of covenants not to compete. Jones v. Deeter, 913 P.2d 1272 (Nev. 1996). This decision lifted a substantial restriction to many covenants not to compete, and many Nevada employers are now seeking the benefits of covenants not to compete. Now that covenants not to compete have been given a general blessing by the courts and the legislature, only noncompliance with the statute and general contractual principles should prevent their enforcement in Nevada in most circumstances.

Nevada law requires that covenants not to compete be supported by adequate consideration. NRS 613.200(2). Nevada courts address the question of what constitutes adequate consideration on a case-by-case basis. The Nevada Supreme Court has held that adding $0.50 an hour to an employee's hourly rate, satisfied the consideration requirement. Jones v. Deeter, 913 P.2d 1272 (Nev. 1996). The court has also held that "continued employment is valid consideration for an at-will employee's post-hire agreement not to compete." Camco, Inc. v. Baker, 936 P.2d 829 (Nev. 1997). The logical extension of this ruling would also require the court to consider an offer of initial employment to be adequate consideration to support a covenant not to compete entered into by a prospective at-will employee. However, the issue has not yet been ruled upon in Nevada.

Based on these rulings of the Nevada Supreme Court, failure of consideration is not a serious obstacle to the formation of an enforceable covenant not to compete. Despite these rulings regarding consideration, it is still recommended that employers reduce their covenants not to compete to writing. Not only does this help prove the existence of the covenant not to compete, it also allows the employer to take advantage of Nevada laws that presume adequate consideration exists for written contracts. NRS 47.250(18)(d).

Covenants not to compete consist of three principal elements: (1) what activity is restricted, (2) the geographic scope of the restriction, and (3) the duration of the restriction. The Nevada Supreme Court has succinctly set forth the basic rule for each element by refusing to enforce any restriction that is greater than necessary to protect the business and goodwill of the employer. Hansen v. Edwards, 426 P.2d 792 (Nev. 1967). In the Hansen case, the court declared that goodwill is a protectable interest and ruled to enforce a covenant not to compete in order to protect a medical group from losing patients to a recently departed doctor. Also in Hansen, the court elected to modify the geographic scope and the duration terms set forth in the agreement in order to make it reasonable. However, in a more recent decision, the Nevada Supreme Court refused without comment or explanation to modify the terms of an agreement it found to be overreaching, instead declaring that such an agreement is unenforceable. Jones v. Deeter,, 913 P.2d 1272. Accordingly, Jones supports the proposition that if employers try to be overly restrictive concerning any one of the three principal elements of the agreement, they risk the possibility of having the entire agreement struck down by the court rather than the court choosing to modify the agreement in order to make it reasonable.

The Nevada Supreme Court has looked to the specific activity of the employer and the contemplated activity of the employee in determining whether a covenant not to compete is needed to protect the employer from unfair competition. In

Ellis v. McDaniel, 596 P.2d 222 (Nev. 1974), the court held that an orthopedic surgeon leaving a general medical practice in Elko could not be restricted from practicing orthopedic medicine in Elko. The court reasoned that Elko needed the services of an orthopedic doctor (a public policy rationale against enforcement) and that because none of the remaining doctors practiced orthopedic medicine, the departing doctor would not be competing with them. However, the court upheld provisions of the covenant not to compete restricting the orthopedic doctor from practicing general medicine.

Many covenants not to compete restrict the employee from working anywhere within the State of Nevada. Such a restriction has never been upheld in Nevada. Usually, the farthest geographic boundary that will be found enforceable is a few miles beyond the limits of the city or perhaps the county in which the business operates. Hansen, 426 P.2d 792 (enforcing covenant to Reno's city limits); Ellis, 596 P.2d 222 (enforcing restriction on general practice to within five miles of Elko); Las Vegas Novelty, Inc. v. Fernandez, 787 P.2d 772 (Nev. 1990) (approving terms of covenant calling for restriction prohibiting employee from working within 20 miles of Las Vegas).

In the Hansen case, the court reserved the right to modify an injunction based upon a covenant not to compete that exceeded the geographic restrictions necessary to protect the legitimate interests of the employer. In that case, the injunction was modified from 100 miles around the city of Reno to the city's limits. However, the careful employer will not rely upon the court's power to modify a covenant to make it reasonable. As noted above, in the more recent case of Jones v. Deeter, 913 P.2d 1272 (Nev. 1996), the Nevada Supreme Court refused to use its power to modify the restrictions and instead held that the entire agreement, which restricted the employee from working within 100 miles of Reno for a period of five years, was unenforceable because it found that these terms were unreasonable.

In Camco, Inc. v. Baker, 936 P.2d 829 (Nev. 1997). the covenant prohibited former employees from starting a business, not only in the area where the employer was operating, but also in areas the employer had targeted for expansion of its business. The court held that covenants not to compete are only reasonable if they protect "existing" goodwill or customer contacts, and refused to modify or enforce the agreement.

The duration of a covenant not to compete must also be reasonably related to the protection of the employer's business. The longest period endorsed by the Nevada Supreme Court is four years. Las Vegas Novelty, 787 P.2d 772 (lower court modified agreement to one year, but the Supreme Court stated in its opinion that the original agreement of four years was reasonable). The court has also accepted terms of two years and modified an agreement without a time restriction to one year. Ellis, 596 P.2d 222; Hansen, 426 P.2d 792. The Nevada Supreme Court has refused, however, to enforce a five-year restriction. Jones, 913 P.2d 1272.

The Nevada Supreme Court has held that covenants not to compete may be enforced against third-party nonsignatories; such as a new employer, when the third party is in active concert with the principal in breaching the agreement. Las Vegas Novelty, 787 P.2d 772 (injunctive relief available against subsequent employers if they are in active concert with the principal in breaching the agreement). But the court has also held that the purchaser of a covenant not to compete assigned as part of an asset sale can not enjoin the employee subject to the covenant from working for a competitor, unless the covenant not to compete contains an assignability clause supported by separate and additional consideration. Traffic Control Servs., Inc. v. United Rentals Northwest, Inc., 87 P.3d 1054 (Nev. 2004) (holding that assignment of covenant not to compete as part of the sale of a business did not apply to employee because the employee agreed not to compete with his former company, not the purchasing company, and because covenant not to compete did not include an assignability clause supported by separate and additional consideration). The new employer may also be potentially liable for interference with contract and a variety of other tort-related claims. However, as set forth in the Trade Secret section below, if the competition involves the use of a trade secret, common law tort claims may not be available due to the preemptive effect of the Uniform Trade Secrets Act adopted by the Nevada Legislature.

Additionally, covenants not to compete arising in the sale of a business context are more readily enforced than similar covenants that arise only in the employment context. Economics Lab. v. Donnolo, 612 F.2d 405, 409 (9th Cir. 1979). The more strict enforcement in the sale of a business context is meant to protect the new owner of a business from a competing seller with established goodwill in the industry in the area. Id. Notwithstanding the pro-enforcement stance taken with sale-of-a-business covenants not to compete, Nevada courts still require any covenant not to compete to be reasonable as to territorial scope and duration. Hotel Riviera v. Torres, 632 P.2d 1155 (Nev. 1981).

The Nevada Supreme Court has not specifically ruled that restricting a particular profession with a covenant not to compete is against public policy, but it seemed to use the public policy of promoting the availability of medical services as a reason for only partially enforcing a covenant in Ellis v. McDaniel, 596 P.2d 222 (Nev. 1974).

Preliminary and permanent injunctive relief is specifically authorized by statute to uphold covenants not to compete. NRS 613.200(2). In addition, actual or threatened misappropriation [of a trade secret] may be enjoined. NRS 600A.040; see also Finkel v. Cashman Prof'l, Inc., 270 P.3d 1259 (Nev. 2012).

In one case the Nevada Supreme Court ruled that an accountant's testimony, based on analysis of prior yearly business trends that the amount of decline in his client's business was due to a former employee's competition was insufficient to prove the damages alleged. Gramanz v. T-Shirts and Souvenirs, 894 P.2d 342 (Nev. 1995).The court in Gramanz ruled that the former employer had not provided sufficient proof that the loss was caused by the former employee's breach of the covenant not to compete. The former employee argued, and the court agreed, that the losses could just as easily have been caused by an ailing economy. The court indicated that the former employer should have provided testimony from an expert economist to prove that the former employee's competition is what caused the loss in net profits.

VIII. OTHER ISSUES

A. Statutes of Limitations.

The statute of limitations for invasion of privacy and related tort claims based on the common law is two years. NRS 11.190(4)(e). The statute of limitations for claims based on a statute, such as right of publicity, is three years. NRS 11.190(3)(a).

B. Jurisdiction

Nevada's long-arm statutes, NRS 14.065 and NRS 14.080, reach the limits of due process set by the United States Constitution. Judas Priest v. Second Judicial Dist. Court, 104 Nev. 424, 760 P.2d 137 (1988). Privacy claims are presumably not treated any differently from any other causes of action.

C. Worker's Compensation Exclusivity

The law governing workers' compensation in Nevada, the Nevada Industrial Insurance Act (NIIA or the "Act"), is found in chapters 616A, 616B, 616C, 616D and 617 of the Nevada Revised Statutes. Section 616A.010 states that the provisions of the Nevada workers' compensation scheme are based on renunciation of the rights and defenses recognized at common law. Section 616A.020 expressly provides that chapters 616A to 616D are the exclusive remedy for the payment of compensation and the amount thereof for resulting injuries and death. Accordingly, Nevada courts have consistently held that the NIIA provides the exclusive remedy for workers on the job. Sims v. General Tel. & Elecs., 107 Nev. 516, 815 P.2d 151 (1991), overruled on other grounds, Tucker v. Action Equip. & Scaffold Co., 113 Nev. 1349, 951 P.2d 1027 (1997).

NRS 616A.265 defines "injury" and "personal injury" in pertinent part as "a sudden and tangible happening of a traumatic nature, producing an immediate or prompt result which is established by medical evidence, including injuries to prosthetic devices." Thus, once the court determines that a covered employee has sustained an "injury" or "personal injury" arising out of and in the course of employment, compensation is limited to that provided by the Act. Las Vegas-Tonopah-Reno Stage Line v. Nevada Indus. Comm'n, 81 Nev. 626, 408 P.2d 241 (1965). The *exclusive-remedy rule* means that no other common law statutory remedy may be sought against the employer in connection with an industrial injury. Nevada Indus. Comm'n v. Underwood, 79 Nev. 496, 387 P.2d 663 (1963). An employee may only bring a common law tort action against his employer if the employee can establish that the injury or injuries are not industrial in nature; therefore, the employee must persuade the court that either the injury is not the result of an accident or that it did not arise out of and in the course of his employment.

Under Nevada law, negligent conduct, even gross negligence, is still considered "accidental" and subject to the *exclusive-remedy rule*. Kennecott Copper Corp. v. Reyes, 75 Nev. 212, 337 P.2d 624 (1959). In Kennecott Copper, the parents of a worker buried and killed in a mining pit brought a wrongful death action against the decedent's employer. The plaintiffs alleged that the employer had been grossly negligent in permitting the decedent to drive in an open pit because the employer had allegedly foreseen for some time that a slide would occur. In ruling that the suit was barred by Nevada's workers' compensation laws, the Supreme Court held that the fact that the injury might have been foreseeable did not mean it was not accidental. The court rejected the parents' contention that the sudden and violent event resulting in the decedent's death was not an accident within the statutory definition because it was foreseen and expected by the employer. The mere fact that the employer had foreseen and expected that a slide would occur does not permit the conclusion that the event was not an accident even when coupled with negligence, albeit gross negligence, in permitting the operation to continue in view of lack of knowledge as to when the slide would occur, or even in view of its possible imminence. Id. at 215. In arriving at this conclusion, the court noted that while the Nevada legislature provided numerous express exceptions to the Act, it did not differentiate between degrees of negligence or even gross negligence. To hold otherwise, the court said, would provide an open bypass around the Act.

While Nevada has not specifically addressed the *exclusive-remedy rule* in the context of a privacy claim, an employee could presumably pursue a privacy claim against his employer. See Barjesteh v. Faye's Pub, Inc., 106 Nev. 120, 787 P2d 405 (1990) ("When an employer commits an intentional tort upon an employee, 'the employer will not be heard to say that his intentional act was an accidental injury and so under the exclusive provisions of the compensation act.'"). The Nevada Supreme Court recognizes that employers do not enjoy immunity from liability for their intentional torts under the exclusive remedy provision of the NIIA where an employer commits an intentional tort upon an employee. Conway v. Circus Circus, Inc., 116 Nev. 870, 8 P.3d 837, 840 (2000). "An employer who commits an intentional tort upon an employee cannot claim that the intentional act resulted in an accidental injury." Id. Thus, employees may avoid the exclusive remedy provision of the NIIA in regard to their injuries only if they can show that the employer deliberately and specifically intended to injure them. Id. at 875.

This rule regarding the exclusive coverage of the Act was reaffirmed by the Nevada Supreme Court decision in Wood v. Safeway, 121 Nev. 724, 121 P.3d 1026 (2005). In that case, a mildly mentally handicapped employee of Safeway was sexually assaulted at work on three separate occasions by a night-time janitor who worked for Action Cleaning, a cleaning subcontractor hired to provide cleaning services at the Safeway where the employee worked. Citing ample evidence in the record, the court concluded that the sexual assaults occurred in the course of the injured employee's employment. Id. at 1033. The court then reviewed the evidence to determine if a causal link existed between the injured employee's work at Safeway and the sexual assaults.

To make this determination, the court approved the use of "an incidental or increased risk test that looks to whether the risk of harm is related to the conditions of employment or whether the employment increased the risk to the employee." Id. After reviewing the evidence under this test, the court held that the injured employee's "employment contributed to and increased the risk of assault beyond that of the general public" because the injured employee's "only contact with [the perpetrator] was through her employment." Id. Accordingly, the sexually assaulted employee's exclusive remedy against her employer was a claim arising under Nevada's workers' compensation laws.

The Nevada Supreme Court further defined the "increased-risk test" by stating that an employee may recover in a workers' compensation action if that employee is subjected to a risk that is greater than what the general public is exposed to. Rio All Suite Hotel & Casino v. Phillips, 240 P.3d 2 (Nev. 2010). Thus, an act of employment which increases the frequency by which an employee is exposed to a potential risk of injury as compared to a member of the general public will be included in a workers' compensation action. Id. at 6-7.

The Federal District Court for Nevada has followed the exclusive remedy rule in interpreting the scope of exclusive coverage of the Act under Nevada law. In Prescott v. United States, 523 F. Supp. 918 (D. Nev. 1981), affirmed, 731 F.2d 1388 (9th Cir. 1984), the Federal District Court for Nevada held that a former employee at the Nevada test site, suffering from multiple myeloma, was barred from bringing a tort action alleging that his employer had intentionally sent him into areas of high radiation. The court in that case held that "willful intent" in sending workers into immediate areas of nuclear detonations in order to perform their jobs is not the same as intent to make the workers sick. Id. at 928.

In King v. Penrod Drilling Co., 652 F. Supp. 1331 (D. Nev. 1987), the plaintiff brought an action against his employer, alleging that he was injured by the acts of his employer which were "done intentionally or with reckless disregard." In granting a partial motion for summary judgment, the court held that no common law action could be brought against the employer unless the employer acted with specific intent to harm the plaintiff. In arriving at this conclusion, the court stated it believed that, if the Nevada Supreme Court were presented with the issue, it would not allow recovery by an employee for employer recklessness. The court reasoned that, in Nevada, a common law action may not be brought by an employee against an employer for personal injuries unless the employer acted with a deliberate intent to injure the employee.

The Nevada Supreme Court, however, upheld a limited exception to the exclusion of a common law action against an employer for personal injuries. In Nevada Power Co. v. Haggerty, 115 Nev. 353, 989 P.2d 870 (1999), the court found that in limited circumstances where there is an independent duty created by statute, there is an exception to the rule that provides employer immunity under workers' compensation laws.

In a separate case, the Nevada Supreme Court reiterated previous opinions holding that an employee who has pursued his or her remedies under the Nevada workers' compensation scheme may have waived any and all rights to file a civil action against the employer even where the injury is intentional. In Advanced Countertop Design, Inc. v. Second Judicial District Court, 115 Nev. 268, 984 P.2d 756 (1999), the court held that an employee who files a workers' compensation claim and accepts a permanent partial disability award is barred from suing his employer even if he later alleges that the injury was the result of an intentional act by the employer. The court held that acceptance of the permanent partial disability award acts as an accord and satisfaction and extinguishes any common law right the employee might have had against the employer. The court also recognized that employers do not enjoy immunity under workers' compensation for intentional injuries. However, the court held that the employee having accepted benefits for an "accidental injury" could not now change his position and assert that the injury was not accidental. The court found that by accepting a permanent partial disability award, the employee made an election of remedies.

Based on the foregoing caselaw, and to the extent an employee suffers an "injury" or "personal injury" as defined by the NIIA arising out of and in the course of employment, the employee may be able to avoid the exclusive remedy provision of the NIIA and pursue an intentional tort privacy claim if he can show that the employer acted deliberately and with a specific intent to injure him.

D. Pleading Requirements

Nevada is a notice pleading jurisdiction. A court will construe a pleading liberally and draw every fair inference in favor of the pleading party. Special damages must be precisely pleaded. NRCP 9(g); Branda v. Sanford, 97 Nev. 643, 637 P.2d 1223 (1981).

SURVEY OF NEW HAMPSHIRE EMPLOYMENT LIBEL LAW

Steven L. Winer
Jeremy D. Eggleton
Orr & Reno, P.A.
One Eagle Square
P.O. Box 3550
Concord, New Hampshire 03302-3550
Telephone: (603) 223-9152; Facsimile: (603) 224-2318

(With Developments Reported Through **November 1, 2012**)

GENERAL COMMENTS

New Hampshire does not have an abundance of defamation law arising specifically in the employment arena. There is, however, a fairly well-developed body of general defamation law in New Hampshire that does provide guidance applicable in the context of employer-employee relations.

SIGNIFICANT DEVELOPMENTS SINCE THE 2012 *SURVEY*

None.

I. GENERAL LAW

A. General Employment Law

1. ***At Will Employment.*** "In New Hampshire, absent a written employment contract, legislation, judicial exception, or a collective bargaining agreement, employment . . . is deemed to be . . . at will." Godfrey v. Perkin-Elmer Corp., 794 F. Supp. 1179, 1186 (D.N.H. 1992), rev'd on other grounds, 76 F.3d 413 (1st Cir. 1992); Panto v. Moore Business Forms, 130 N.H. 730, 547 A.2d 260 (1988); Cilley v. New Hampshire Ball Bearings, Inc., 128 N.H. 401, 514 A.2d 818 (1986); Monge v. Beebe Rubber Co., 114 N.H. 130, 316 A.2d 549 (1974). A wrongful discharge claim may be made, however, "if the employee proves the defendant was motivated by bad faith, malice, or retaliation, and the discharge resulted because the employee performed an act that public policy would encourage, or refused to do something that public policy would condemn." Godfrey, 794 F. Supp. 1179, 1186; Cloutier v. Great Atlantic & Pacific Tea Co., 121 N.H. 915, 436 A.2d 1140 (1981). In addition, RSA 354-A:6 disallows discrimination in employment based upon age, sex, race, creed, color, marital status, physical or mental disability, national origin, or sexual orientation. At-will employees may recover lost future earnings. Porter v. City of Manchester, 151 N.H. 30 (2004).

B. Elements of Libel Claim

1. ***Basic Elements.*** To prevail on a defamation claim, a plaintiff must prove that the defendant (1) failed to exercise reasonable care in publishing to a third party, (2) without a valid privilege, (3) a false and defamatory statement of fact (4) about the plaintiff. See Lilly Software Associates, Inc. v. Blue Ridge Designs, Inc., 2001 WL 531205, 2001 DNH 077 (D.N.H. Apr. 20, 2001) (citing Independent Mechanical Contractors, Inc. v. Gordon T. Burke & Sons, Inc., 138 N.H. 110, 118, 635 A.2d 487, 492 (1993)); O'Neil v. Valley Regional Health Care, Inc., 2001 WL 276968, 2001 DNH 054 (D.N.H. Mar. 21, 2001); Moss v. Camp Pemigewassett, Inc., 312 F.3d 503 (1st Cir. 2002). The statement in question must tend to lower a person in the esteem of "any substantial and respectable group, even though it might be quite a small minority." Douglas v. Pratt, 2000 WL 1513712, 2000 DNH 199 (D.N.H. Sept. 29, 2000) (citing Thomson v. Cash, 119 N.H. 371, 5 Media L. Rep. 1234 (1979)); accord Duschesnaye v. Munro Enterprises, Inc., 125 N.H. 244, 480 A.2d 123 (1984). The words alleged to be defamatory must be taken in context. Straughn v. Delta Airlines, Inc. and ESIS, Inc., 170 F. Supp. 2d 133 (D.N.H. 2000) (granting summary judgment in favor of defendant employer where employee's claim would require tortured construction of words used), aff'd, 250 F.3d 23 (1st Cir. 2001) (to establish defamation, there must be evidence that a defendant failed to exercise reasonable care in publishing, without a valid privilege, a false and defamatory statement of fact about the plaintiff to a third party). See Paster v. Glazier, 2005 WL 419688, 2005 DNH 028 (D.N.H. Feb. 17, 2005) (recognizing that pursuant to the Restatement (Second) of Torts § 559 "a statement is defamatory if it has a tendency to harm, regardless of whether it produces actual harm").

2. ***Fault.*** The level of fault that must be proven depends on the plaintiff's private or public status. No New Hampshire cases since Gertz v. Robert Welch, Inc., 418 U.S. 323 (1974), have examined the question of the applicable fault standard in a matter of private concern.

a. **Private Figure Plaintiff/Matter of Public Concern.** Although the standard of proof was neither briefed nor argued in McCusker v. Valley News, 121 N.H. 258, 428 A.2d 493, 7 Media L. Rep. 1343, cert. denied, 454 U.S. 1017 (1981), the court held that a private figure plaintiff need only prove negligence. Accord Duchesnaye v. Munro Enterprises, Inc., 125 N.H. 244, 480 A.2d 123 (1984). In Middleton v. Elizabeth Sutton, et al., 73 F.3d 355 (unpublished opinion), 24 Media L. Rep. 1639 (1st Cir. 1996), the First Circuit affirmed summary judgment in favor of the producer and distributor of the "Geraldo" show on the ground that the plaintiff could not prove they were negligent in broadcasting statements he claimed were false and defamatory. Those statements charged plaintiff, inter alia, with sexually abusing his children, using them in child pornography, engaging in satanic practices with them, and with being involved in an international child pornography and molestation ring.

The following plaintiffs have been determined to be private figures in cases decided under New Hampshire substantive law: a Veteran's Administration psychologist, see Kassel v. Gannett Co., 875 F.2d 935, 941 (1st Cir. 1989), and a manufacturing company, that was not publicly traded or involved in a controversial industry, Bruno & Stillman, Inc. v. Globe Newspaper Co., 633 F.2d 583, 591 (1st Cir. 1980).

b. **Private Figure Plaintiff/Matter of Private Concern.** In Lassonde v. Stanton, 157 N.H. 582, 956 A.2d 332 (2008), the court held that a dispute between a building contractor and property owners, in which the owners had made statements concerning allegedly defective workmanship by the contractor in building a home, was a purely private dispute, that the contractor could not be deemed a limited purpose public figure for purposes of analyzing the contractor's claim of defamation, and that the contractor therefore was entitled to damages on his defamation claim without a showing of actual malice. Similarly, in an action involving a private figure and a matter of private concern, the New Hampshire Supreme Court has noted that due to the reduced constitutional value of the speech, presumed damages are available absent a showing of constitutional actual malice. Touma v. St. Mary's Bank, 142 N.H. 762, 712 A.2d 619 (1998); see also Levinsky's, Inc. v. Wal-Mart Stores, Inc., 127 F. 3d 122 (1st Cir. 1999) (noting that Maine adheres to a minimum negligence standard for all defamation actions, and quoting Snead v. Redland Aggregates, Ltd., 998 F.2d 1325, 1334 (5th Cir.1993) ("the First Amendment imposes no minimum standard of fault in private/private libel cases")).

c. **Public Figure Plaintiff/Matter of Public Concern.** The status of the plaintiff as a public figure is ordinarily a jury issue under the "New Hampshire rule, which is unusual, that the determination of public official or public figure status is a jury question." Nash v. Keene Publishing Corp., 127 N.H. 214, 222, 498 A.2d 348, 353, 12 Media L. Rep. 1025 (1985); McCusker v. Valley News, 121 N.H. 258, 428 A.2d 493, 7 Media L. Rep. 1343 (1981); compare Kassel v. Gannett Co., 875 F.2d 935, 16 Media L. Rep. 1814 (1st Cir. 1989) (in a diversity action, federal law controls whether an issue goes to the jury, and under federal law the public official/figure issue is for the court to decide); Howard v. Antilla, 2000 WL 144387 (D.N.H. Nov. 17, 1999) (public figure issue one of law for the court) rev'd on other grounds, 294 F.3d 244, 30 Media L. Rep. 1936 (1st Cir. 2002).

A public figure plaintiff must prove actual malice in order to recover. Faigin v. Kelly, 184 F.3d 67, 76 (1st Cir. 1999); Simpkins v. Snow, 139 N.H. 735 (1995). Under this standard, "[e]ven if the plaintiff establishes that the defendants' statement is false, he can recover only on clear and convincing proof that the defendants acted 'with knowledge that it was false or with reckless disregard of whether it was false or not.'" Thomson v. Cash, 119 N.H. 371, 377, 402 A.2d 651, 655, 5 Media L. Rep. 1234 (1979), quoting New York Times v. Sullivan, 376 U.S. 254, 280 (1964); see also Faigin v. Kelly, 184 F. 3d 67 (1st Cir. 1999) ("as a condition precedent to recovery, such a plaintiff must prove by clear and convincing evidence that the defendant published the defamatory statement with actual malice, that is, that the defendant knew that the statement was false or, at least, recklessly disregarded its want of veracity").

In Snelling v. City of Claremont, 155 N.H. 674, 931 A.2d 1272 (2007), where the city fired the city tax assessor following the publication of an article in which the assessor criticized the city's tax system, the New Hampshire Supreme Court held, in an action for wrongful termination, that the assessor was not speaking pursuant to his official duties when he spoke with reporter who wrote the article and that the assessor spoke on a matter of public concern—namely, the fairness of the city's tax system and possible abuses of it. As such, the court upheld the jury's finding that the city had wrongfully terminated the assessor and its damages award. Id.; see Wentworth Douglass Hosp. v. Young & Novis Prof. Ass'n,, 2012 WL 1081172, Slip Op. at *7 (D.N.H. March 30, 2012) (merely providing quote to reporter concerning events in question was insufficient, in and of itself, to give rise to public figure status as a matter of law).

3. ***Falsity.*** Under New Hampshire law, the plaintiff bears the burden to prove that the statement at issue is false. Faigin v. Kelly, 184 F.3d 67, 75 (1st.Cir.1999) (citing Independent Mechanical Contractors, Inc. v. Gordon T. Burke & Sons, Inc., 138 N.H. 110 (1993)). "A statement is not actionable if it is substantially true." Simpkins v. Snow, 139 N.H. 735, 740, 661 A.2d 772, 776 (1995). On the other hand, since "a reasonable jury could plausibly find that [defendant's] statements substantially exaggerated the gravity of the complaints actually received, thereby giving the impression that [plaintiff] had been accused of serious sexual misconduct," summary judgment was denied. Moss v. Grabill, 2003 WL

22251159, 2003 DNH 163 (D.N.H. Sept. 30, 2003); see also Fecteau v. Foster & Co., 120 N.H. 406, 418 A.2d 1265, 6 Media L. Rep. 1688 (1980); Baer v. Rosenblatt, 106 N.H. 26, 203 A.2d 773 (1964), cert granted, 380 U.S. 941 (1965), rev'd, 383 U.S. 75 (1966), remanded, 108 N.H. 368 (1967); Chagnon v. Union Leader Corp., 103 N.H. 426, 174 A.2d 825 (1961) (superseded on other grounds by statute as stated in Hanchett v. Brezner Tanning Co., 107 N.H. 236, 221 A.2d 426 (1966)); Lilly Software Associates, Inc. v. Blue Ridge Designs, Inc., 2001 WL 531205, 2001 DNH 77 (D.N.H. Apr. 20, 2001) (citing Independent Contractors, Inc. v. Gordon T. Burke & Sons, Inc., 138 N.H. 110, 635 A.2d 487 (1993) (following the Restatement (Second) of Torts § 558 in laying out the elements of defamation, including a requirement of a "false and defamatory statement of fact")); Faigin v. Kelly, 184 F. 3d 67, 76 (1st Cir. 1999) ("Objective falsity is not only an element of a defamation action, but is also logically antecedent to questions bearing upon negligence or state of mind"); Straughn v. Delta Airlines, Inc., and ESIS, Inc., 170 F. Supp. 2d 133 (D.N.H. 2000) (employer not liable for statement about employee that was substantially true), aff'd, 250 F.3d 23 (1st Cir. 2001).

4. ***Defamatory Statement of Fact.*** In order to be defamatory, a statement "must tend to lower the plaintiff in the esteem of any substantial and respectable group even though it may be quite a small minority." Douglas v. Pratt, 2000 WL 1513712, 2000 DNH 199 (D.N.H. Sept. 29, 2000) (quoting Thomson v. Cash, 119 N.H. 371, 373 (1979)); see also Mills v. Merrimack Police Department, 2004 WL 1013380, 2004 DNH 79 (D.N.H. May 5, 2004) (police officer's statements in a local newspaper stating that plaintiff received more money in a post search and seizure refund than he was due, and would not likely return, were not considered defamatory where receipt of extra money did not lower him in the esteem of any group, and the statement that he would not likely return the money was pure opinion).

New Hampshire has not adopted any special test for distinguishing fact from opinion. In Pease v. Telegraph, 121 N.H. 62, 426 A.2d 463, 7 Media L. Rep. 1114 (1981), the court set aside a verdict for the plaintiff, ruling, as a matter of law, that a letter to the editor in which the plaintiff was referred to as the "'journalistic scum of the earth' could not reasonably be understood as assertions of fact" and was protected expression. Whether a statement is one of opinion or fact is initially a question of law for the court; if the trial court determines that the statement could be understood by the average reader in either sense, the issue is one for the jury. Id.; see also Catalfo v. Jensen, 657 F. Supp. 463, 13 Media L. Rep. 2356 (D.N.H. 1987) (newspaper article calling the plaintiff "sleazy" and likening him to "Ratso" in "Midnight Cowboy" is protected opinion); Powell v. Monitor Publishing Corp., 107 N.H. 83, 217 A.2d 193 (1966) (editorial about former governor suggesting that he was involved in "some kind of a deal" was capable of defamatory meaning).

The federal courts have further developed the law in this area. "While statements of fact may be defamatory, statements of opinion, as a general rule, are not. Baldi v. Amadon, 2003 WL 21355874, 2003 DNH 099 (D.N.H. June 29, 2003) (citing Nash v. Keene Publishing Corp., 127 N.H. 214, 498 A.2d 348, 12 Media L. Rep. 1025 (1985)). A statement of opinion is only actionable when "it may reasonably be understood to imply the existence of defamatory fact as the basis for the opinion." Id. (quoting Nash, 127 N.H. at 219, 498 A.2d at 351, 12 Media L. Rep. 1025). In Baldi, the court concluded that calling plaintiff a "bastard" could not reasonably be understood as implying he was engaged in illegal activities. Id; see also Gaylor v. McLaughlin, 2003 WL 22848929, 2003 DNH 206 (D.N.H. Nov. 19, 2003). In Gray v. St. Martin's Press, 221 F. 3d 243, 28 Media L. Rep. 2313 (1st Cir. 2000), cert. denied, 531 U.S. 1075 (2001), the First Circuit held that several statements could not be defamatory because they were not capable of being proved false; the statements involved matters of degree and speculation (statements included that plaintiff "had faked his closeness" with Reagan Administration officials; that plaintiff's business had "failed because it offered very little real substance; and that an official "might have asked [the plaintiff] to take on . . . controversial clients for the very purpose of spying on them."); see also Ben's Auto Body, Inc. v. Teitelbaum, 2008 WL 5244420 (D.N.H. Dec. 15, 2008) (unpublished opinion) (insurer's statement that auto repair shop was "overcharging" repair customer could not be considered as a matter of law a non-actionable opinion). Similarly, in Riley v. Harr, No. CA-98-712-M (D.N.H. Mar. 3, 2000), aff'd 292 F.3d 282, 30 Media L. Rep. 1961 (1st Cir. 2002), the court held that conditional "if/then" statements were not actionable because they did not imply underlying false facts. See also Douglas v. Pratt, 2000 WL 1513712, 2000 DNH 199 (D.N.H. Sept. 29, 2000) (an action in libel cannot be maintained on an artificial, unreasonable, or tortured construction imposed upon innocent words, nor when only supersensitive persons, with morbid imaginations, would consider the words defamatory); statements at issue related to the credibility of a valuation report provided in a divorce matter). However, in another case the federal district court held that a supervisor's statement that the plaintiff's "job isn't important and doesn't require brains" was a factual statement and thus actionable. Godfrey v. Perkin-Elmer Corp., 794 F. Supp. 1179 (D.N.H. 1992), rev'd on other grounds, 76 F.3d 413 (1st Cir. 1992). Similarly, statements to an employee in front of others including: "you have a lot of growing up to do;" "you have a bad attitude;" "who do you think you are working for;" and "you should learn what you're doing here" were found to be sufficiently factual to support a defamation claim. Id; see also Foster v. General Electric, No. 96-CV-151-SD (D.N.H. Sept. 2, 1998) (reference to former employee as a "liar" and "incompetent" implies underlying facts and is actionable). The mere statement of discharge from employment does not constitute defamation, unless the publication insinuates that the discharge was for some misconduct. Huard v. Town of Allenstown, 2011 WL 540766, 2011 DNH 022 (D.N.H. Feb. 8, 2011).

5. ***Of and Concerning Plaintiff.*** There is no case directly addressing the "of and concerning" requirement. See generally Morrissette v. Cowette, 122 N.H. 731, 449 A.2d 1221 (1982); Chagnon v. Union Leader Corp., 103 N.H. 426, 174 A.2d 825 (1961) cert. denied, 369 U.S. 830 (1961); see also Douglas v. Pratt, 2000 WL 1513712, 2000 DNH 199 (D.N.H. Sept. 29, 2000) ("it would be a stretch" to find statements to be "of and concerning" the plaintiff, where the statements were actually made about the plaintiff's expert in a divorce proceeding).

6. ***Publication.*** Under New Hampshire law, publication for the purpose of defamation occurs when the language complained of is actually communicated and understood in its defamatory sense. Waterfield v. Meredith Corp., 161 N.H. 707, 713, 20 A.3d 865 (2011); Chamberlain v. 101 Realty, Inc., 626 F. Supp. 865 (D.N.H. 1985). Publication to a single person is actionable. Duchesnaye v. Munro Enterprises, Inc., 125 N.H. 244, 480 A.2d 123 (1984). Intra-office publications concerning the reasons for an employee's discharge do not constitute defamation where statements are not publicized outside of the office. Marin v. Gonzales, 2005 WL 3464389, 2005 DNH 167 (D.N.H. Dec. 19, 2005) (denying former Assistant United States Attorney's defamation claim against her superior where allegedly false statements regarding her performance were disseminated amongst supervisory staff members. The court adopted the reasoning of Algarin v. Federal Express Corp., 56 F. Supp. 2d 172 (D.P.R. 1999) wherein privileged communications were deemed to include conversations from an employer to managers and supervisors of discharged employees). In the federal system, in order to survive summary judgment, the plaintiff must be able to allege who made the statement, to whom it was made, and where the statement was made, along with the general content (but not necessarily the exact words). Dube v. Hadco Corp., 1999 WL 1210885, 75 Empl. Prac. Dec. P 45,962 (D.N.H. Feb. 4, 1999).

a. **Intracorporate Communication.** It appears that intracorporate communication may constitute publication sufficient for defamation, depending upon the circumstances of the case. In two recent unpublished opinions, the federal district court sitting in New Hampshire twice addressed the issue of whether intra-corporate communications constitute publication for purposes of defamation law. See Foster v. Gen. Elec. Co., No. 96-151-SD (D.N.H. Sept. 2, 1998); Reale v. Riverbend Cmty Mental Health, Inc., No. 98-334-JD (D.N.H. Jan. 26, 1999). Although the New Hampshire Supreme Court has yet to specifically address this issue, the federal cases hold that intra-corporate communications meet the requirement of publication but are subject to a qualified privilege. In both cases, the federal court refused to grant summary judgment in favor of the defendant on the privilege issue, leaving the issue of the applicability of the privilege to the jury. In Chamberlain v. 101 Realty, Inc., 626 F. Supp. 865 (D.N.H. 1985), the former-employee plaintiff claimed that the company president defamed her by making statements to the company's comptroller which resulted in his writing a letter to the plaintiff demanding the return of some property claimed to be corporate property. The defendant argued that these statements were conditionally privileged under New Hampshire law which provides that a conditional privilege "is established if the facts, although untrue, were published on a lawful occasion, in good faith, for a justifiable purpose, and with a belief, founded on reasonable grounds of truth." Id. at 871 (citing Chagnon v. Union Leader Corp., 103 N.H. 426, 174 A.2d 825 (1961), cert. denied, 369 U.S. 830 (1962)). The Chamberlain court held that the question of whether these statements would be conditionally privileged was a jury question, given that there was a dispute of material facts regarding the president's good faith.

In Soto-Lebron v. Federal Express Corporation, 538 F.3d 45 (1st Cir. 2008), plaintiff was terminated from employment after investigation into the shipment of a package containing drugs. The package alleged to contain drugs was later proven not to contain any illicit drugs. Id. at 51. The court held that, under Puerto Rican law, the jury could fairly have concluded that the employer published defamatory material through intracorporate communication and that the qualified privilege of intracorporate communication was destroyed due to employer's reckless disregard for truth. The court observed that an employer's conditional privilege to communicate the reasons of an employee's discharge is "destroyed where an employer is on notice that the defamatory statements are of questionable validity and yet, with reckless disregard for the truth, fails to adequately investigate their veracity." Id. at 64. The court ruled that the jury was entitled to conclude that FedEx lost the benefit of the conditional privilege because it acted with reckless disregard for the truth, id., and therefore affirmed the trial court's denial of FedEx's motion for judgment as a matter of law on the libel claim.

b. **Compelled Self-Publication.** In Slater v. Verizon, the plaintiff alleged that he was a victim of compelled re-publication because the defendant employer "effectively forced him to republish to potential employers the false and defamatory statements defendant made regarding its reasons for terminating his employment." 2005 WL 488676, 2005 DNH 023 (D.N.H. Mar. 3, 2005). The district court predicted that, although the New Hampshire Supreme Court has not decided whether it will recognize a cause of action for defamation based upon forced republication, the supreme court would decline to adopt this theory because it reflects a minority view, and the trend is away from accepting the theory. Id.

c. **Republication.** New Hampshire follows the general rule of imposing liability on the ultimate publisher of defamatory material. For example, a newspaper may be held responsible for the publication of defamatory letters to the editor despite the fact that the newspaper was only "republishing" the defamatory statements of a third party. See Pease v. Telegraph Pub. Co., Inc., 121 N.H. 62, 426 A.2d 463, 7 Media L. Rep. 1114 (1981) (holding that the statements were non-actionable because they constituted protected opinion). New Hampshire does not have any published cases regarding the liability of the originator of the defamation for its republication by a third party.

7. ***Statements versus Conduct.*** While conduct, as opposed to words, may give rise to an action for slander, conduct that results in an impairment of reputation is not, in and of itself, sufficient. Rather, the plaintiff still bears the burden to prove all of the elements of defamation. Thus, where a general contractor fired a subcontractor and had it removed from the site, but no evidence was offered that any third party believed from the removal that the subcontractor had breached its contract, the defamation claim failed. Independent Mechanical Contractors, Inc. v. Gordon T. Burke & Sons, Inc., 138 N.H. 110, 635 A.2d 487 (1993); see also Panas v. Harakis, 129 N.H. 591, 529 A.2d 976 (1987) (jury found in favor of the plaintiff who had alleged that a false arrest was slanderous; the "arresting" security guard had said, loudly, that the plaintiff was under arrest and marched her into the K-Mart store where he detained her until a police officer arrived).

8. ***Damages.*** In Thomson v. Cash, the court held that "actual damages" in a defamation action include general damages for injury to reputation. 119 N.H. 371, 402 A.2d 651, 5 Media L. Rep. 1234 (1979) (citing Time Inc. v. Firestone, 424 U.S. 448 (1976) and Gertz v. Robert Welch, Inc., 418 U.S. 323, 349-50 (1974)). The court further stated that "the plaintiff does not need to allege special or specific monetary loss resulting from the publication where New York Times malice is shown." Id. at 376, 402 A.2d at 653 (citing Herbert v. Lando, 99 S. Ct. 1635 (1979); Gertz, 418 U.S. 323). It is up to the jury to decide whether the plaintiff has sustained actual damages and the extent thereof. These damages may be mitigated by a showing that the false and defamatory statement was based on general rumor in the community, Wetherbee v. Marsh, 20 N.H. 561 (1847), or the general bad character of the plaintiff, Lamos v. Snell, 6 N.H. 413 (1833). See RSA 515:6. However, once evidence of bad character is offered, the plaintiff may present evidence of good character. Dame v. Kenney, 25 N.H. 318 (1852).

a. **Presumed Damages and Libel Per Se.** In Touma v. St. Mary's Bank, 142 N.H. 762, 712 A.2d 619 (1998), the court held that in a private figure/matter of private concern case, presumed damages may be awarded absent a showing of constitutional actual malice. See also Lassonde v. Stanton, 157 N.H. 582, 956 A.2d 332 (2008) (plaintiff need not prove specific damages for libel *per se*). Other than these cases and Thomson v. Cash, 119 N.H. 371, 402 A.2d 651, 5 Media L. Rep. 1234 (1979), there is no case under this category decided since Gertz v. Robert Welch, Inc., 418 U.S. 323 (1974). Prior to Gertz, presumed damages were allowed in New Hampshire. See, e.g., Chagnon v. Union Leader Corp., 103 N.H 426, 174 A.2d 825 (1961).

In Jones v. Walsh, 107 N.H. 379, 222 A.2d 830 (1966), the court spoke to the slander per se issue in the employment context. There, a restaurant owner had, in effect, accused one of his waitresses of stealing, in front of the restaurant's patrons. The court stated that accusations of criminal activity constitute slander per se, and thus do not require proof of special damages. See also Chaulk Services, Inc. v. Fraser, 769 F.Supp. 37 (D.N.H. 1990) (proof of special damages not required in a defamation action by employer against former employee, where accusation of criminal activity constituted slander per se).

(1) **Employment-Related Criticism.** Employment-related criticism can result in liability if the criticism is published to persons without a legitimate interest in the information. Jones v. Walsh, 107 N.H. 379, 222 A.2d 830 (1966) (employer accused employee of stealing, in front of restaurant patrons; publication not privileged); see also Godfrey v. Perkin-Elmer Corp., 794 F. Supp. 1179 (D.N.H. 1992), rev'd on other grounds, 76 F.3d 413 (1st Cir. 1992) (supervisor yelled false criticism at employee in front of others). However, where a university faculty member had been arrested and banned from campus following a violent outburst towards a colleague, the university may notify a faculty member's colleagues of his arrest and campus ban and urge them to avoid contact with him and report to police if he is seen on campus. See Collins v. University of New Hampshire, 746 F.Supp.2d 358 (D.N.H. 2010) (noting that such statements are substantially true and privileged) (aff'd in Collins v. University of New Hampshire, 664 F.3d 8 (2011)). ..

In a recent unpublished federal district court decision, the court denied summary judgment to defendants in a situation in which comments were made by corporate employees regarding a former employee's conduct. Foster v. Gen. Elec. Co., No. CV-151-SD (D.N.H. Sept. 2, 1998). There, a former General Electric ("G.E.") employee who had been laid off created his own company through which he assisted G.E. customers with their audits and inspections of G.E. plants. G.E. began disallowing Foster access to its facilities, and made unflattering comments about him to several of the customers. The court found that, in context, G.E.'s comments could be found to be defamatory.

(2) **Single Instance Rule.** There is no New Hampshire case addressing the single instance rule.

b. **Punitive Damages.** New Hampshire does not allow punitive damages. RSA 507:16. However, a plaintiff may be entitled to "enhanced" measures of recovery upon a showing of common law malice, ill will, or the defendant's wanton disregard of the rights of the plaintiff. Baer v. Rosenblatt, 106 N.H. 26, 203 A.2d 773 (1964), rev'd on other grounds, 383 U.S. 75, 865 S. Ct. 669 (1966).

II. PRIVILEGES AND DEFENSES

A. Scope of Privileges

1. ***Absolute Privilege.*** "If a communication is absolutely privileged, the speaker is absolutely immune from suit regardless of his or her motive in making the communication." Pierson v. Hubbard, 147 N.H. 760, 764 (2002). The classification of absolutely privileged communications is narrow, and "must be reserved for those situations where the public interest is so vital and apparent that it mandates complete freedom of expression without inquiry into a defendant's motives." Id. The following communications are subject to absolute privilege: statements made by selectmen at town meetings as part of their legislative duties, Voelbel v. Town of Bridgewater, 144 N.H. 599, 747 A. 2d 252 (1999); pertinent statements made in the course of judicial proceedings, McGranahan v. Dahar, 119 N.H. 758, 408 A.2d 121(1979); statements made to one's attorney during the course of representation. Id.; statements made to law enforcement agencies and prosecuting authorities. Id.; Carey v. Eglody, 2006 WL 680867, 2006 DNH 32 (D.N.H. 2006) (recognizing that an absolute privilege exists both for formal and informal statements made to prosecuting authorities); attorney disciplinary proceedings, In re Grievance Procedure, 115 N.H. 310, 341 A.2d 272 (1975); statements made by employer to Department of Employment Security, RSA 282-A:122; pertinent pre-litigation communications between a witness and a litigant or attorney if the litigation was contemplated in good faith and under serious consideration by the witness, counsel, or possible party to the proceeding at the time of the communication. Provencher v. Buzzell-Plourde Assoc., 142 N.H. 848, 711 A.2d 251 (1998). In Pierson, however, the Supreme Court of New Hampshire declined to privilege the allegedly defamatory statements of a town clerk made at a meeting of the board of selectmen because she was acting in an administrative and not a legislative role when she made the statements. 147 N.H. at 764.

2. ***Qualified Privileges.*** In addition to those statements shielded by absolute privilege, other communications may be conditionally or qualifiedly privileged. In such a situation, the speaker's immunity from suit may be lost if the communication was not published on a lawful occasion, in good faith for a justifiable purpose, and with belief, founded on reasonable grounds, of truth. Pierson v. Hubbard, 147 N.H. 760, 764 (2002) (quotation omitted).

a. **Common Interest.** An employer's otherwise defamatory statement about an employee may be conditionally privileged if the circumstances lead the employer to reasonably believe that (a) facts exist which affect a sufficiently important interest of the employer, and (b) the recipient's knowledge of the matter will help to lawfully protect that interest. Jones v. Walsh, 107 N.H. 379, 222 A.2d 830 (1966); see also Collins v. University of New Hampshire, 746 F.Supp.2d 358 (D.N.H. 2010). This privilege can be lost through excessive publication. Id. In the sexual harassment context, the federal district court, relying on the Jones opinion, has ruled that, although the New Hampshire Supreme Court has not yet addressed the issue, employees' complaints of sexual harassment to management are protected by a qualified privilege. Caouette v. OfficeMax, Inc., 352 F. Supp. 134 (D.N.H. 2005). In the non-employment context, the New Hampshire Supreme Court has found the conditional common interest privilege not to apply when publication of a photograph of a restaurant property under foreclosure failed to note that the restaurant building, and not the plaintiff lessee, was for sale at auction. Touma v. St. Mary's Bank, 142 N.H. 762, 712 A.2d 769 (1998).

In Slocinsky v. Radwan., 83 N.H. 501, 144 A. 787 (1929), the court described the reasoning behind the common interest privilege in a way that seems particularly applicable to the employment context: "It is to the general interest of society that correct information shall be obtained as to the character of persons in whom others have a common interest, and hence the law grants to all the privilege of giving information concerning private individuals when given bona fide and to a person having a corresponding interest in the subject." Id. at 504, 144 A. at 789. See also discussion of the conditional privilege in the context of intracorporate communications contained in Soto-Lebron v. Federal Express Corporation, 538 F.3d 45 (1st Cir. Puerto Rico), applying Puerto Rican law, supra at I.B.6.(a).

b. **Duty.** In an old case, the New Hampshire Supreme Court held that an employer's statement to a minor employee's mother that the employee had stolen a sheet was privileged because it was within the employer's social duty to inform the mother of the problem. Moore v. Butler, 48 N.H. 161 (1868).

c. **Criticism of Public Employee.** If an allegedly defamatory statement is substantially true and concerns itself solely with the manner in which public officials and private individuals conduct the business affairs of a governmental entity, no liability can attach to the publisher. Fecteau v. George J. Foster & Co., Inc., 120 N.H. 406, 418 A.2d 1265 (1980). In addition, New York Times v. Sullivan malice rule applies to all government employees who have, or appear to have substantial responsibility for or control over conduct of governmental affairs. Nash v. Keene Pub. Corp., 498 A.2d 348 (1985), 127 N.H. 214; see also Kassel v. Gannet Co., Inc., 875 F. 2d 935 (1st Cir. 1989) (clinical psychologist at Veteran's Administration hospital not a public official); McCusker v. Valley News, 121 N.H. 258, 428 A.2d 493, cert. denied, 454 U.S. 1017 (deputy sheriff not necessarily a public official for purpose of actual malice rule); Catalfo v. Shenton, 102 N.H. 47, 149 A.2d 871 (1959) (political candidates); Palmer v. City of Concord, 48 N.H. 211 (1868) (criticism of administration of public affairs).

Further, a supervisor's criticism of a governmental employee may fall within the governmental immunity fair haven if the statement complained of was made within the "outer perimeter of the [speaker] official's line of duty." Kassel v. United States Veteran's Administration, 682 F. Supp 646, 654 (D.N.H. 1988) (finding individual defendant immune from defamation action because his comment was within the purview of his responsibilities); see also Rossi v. Town of Pelham, 35 F. Supp. 2d 58 (D.N.H. 1997) (same).

d. **Administration of Government**. In addition to those mentioned above, the federal district court has held that a town was privileged to order a police guard be stationed at the office of a town's clerk and tax collector to prevent her from removing records from the town hall under the "immunity that extends to government officials ensuring that 'the administration of government should not be hampered by the fear of lawsuits.'" Rossi v. Town of Pelham, 35 F. Supp. 2d 58 (D.N.H. 1997) (citing PROSSER & KEETON ON THE LAW OF TORTS § 11 at 774 (5th ed. 1984)). The court held, therefore, that even were the action otherwise slanderous, it was not actionable because the action was privileged. Id.

e. **Limitation on Qualified Privileges.**

(1) **Constitutional or Actual Malice.** Under New Hampshire law, actual or constitutional malice will not pierce certain conditional privileges. Thomas v. Telegraph Publishing Co., 155 N.H. 314, 929 A.2d 993 (2007).

(2) **Common Law Malice.** A qualified privilege may be defeated upon a showing of common law malice. Id.; see Moore v. Butler, 48 N.H. 161 (1868). Common law malice requires proof that the publication was made with "not only ill will, evil motive or intention to injure, but also a wanton disregard of the rights of others and the consequences likely to follow." Chagnon v. Union-Leader Corp., 103 N.H. 426, 438, 174 A.2d 825, 833 (1961).

f. **Question of Fact or Law.** Whether a defendant may claim a conditional privilege is traditionally held to be a question of fact for the jury. Pickering v. Frink, 123 N.H. 326, 461 A.2d 117 (1983); Supry v. Bolduc, 112 N.H. 274, 293 A.2d 767 (1972). However, the status of a public or private figure, upon which a defamation claim may turn, may constitute a threshold question of law for the trial court. See Nash v. Keene Publishing Corp., 127 N.H. 214, 498 A.2d 348, 12 Media L. Rep. 1025 (1985); see also Foster v. Gen. Elec. Co., No. 96-CV-151-SD (D.N.H. Sept. 2, 1998); Reale v. Riverbend Cmty Mental Health, Inc., No. 98-CV-334-JD (D.N.H. Jan. 26, 1999). Similarly, whether the situation is one in which a conditional privilege might apply can be a question of law. See Hayes v. Valley News, 141 N.H. 464, 685 A.2d 1237, 25 Media L. Rep. 1253 (1996) (Hayes case may be atypical because it dealt with the fair report privilege, which requires an objective review of whether the defamatory statement at issue was part of a fair and accurate report of an official proceeding or action, rather than the more subjective review demanded by other conditional privileges); Collins v. University of New Hampshire, 746 F.Supp.2d 358 (D.N.H. 2010) (noting that when no reasonable jury could find that employer acted in bad faith or that statements were not true, application of privilege was a question of law for the court to determine) .

g. **Burden of Proof.** The defendant bears the burden to prove the existence of a conditional privilege; however, once established, the plaintiff must prove malice in order to defeat the privilege. Duchesnaye v. Munro Enterprises, Inc., 125 N.H. 244, 480 A.2d 123 (1984).

B. Standard Libel Defenses

1. ***Truth.*** "A statement is not actionable if it is substantially true." Simpkins v. Snow, 139 N.H. 735, 740, 661 A.2d 772, 776 (1995) (private figure case); see also Straughn v. Delta Airlines, Inc., 170 F. Supp. 2d 133, (D.N.H. 2000) (employers' statements about employee doing something "very, very bad" were substantially true), aff'd, 250 F.3d 23 (1st Cir. 2001) (the record plainly demonstrated employee had, in fact, done something "very, very bad", as stated by two co-workers); Collins v. University of New Hampshire, 746 F.Supp.2d 358 (D.N.H. 2010) (statement by university that former employee had been arrested and was banned from campus not actionable because they were substantially true and offered in good faith); Fecteau v. Foster & Co., 120 N.H. 406, 418 A.2d 1265, 6 Media L. Rep. 1688 (1980) (public figure case); Baer v. Rosenblatt, 106 N.H. 26, 203 A.2d 773 (1964); Chagnon v. Union Leader Corp., 174 A.2d 825 (1961), 103 N.H. 426;

Faigin v. Kelly, 184 F. 3d 67 (1st Cir. 1999) (objective falsity an element of a defamation action); Noonan v. Staples, 556 F.3d 20, 37 Media L. Rep. 1321 (1st Cir. 2009) (where plaintiff was fired from his job as a salesman for allegedly padding expense reports, Staples executive's e-mail to employees informing them of the reason plaintiff was terminated held to be substantially true, and not published with actual malice; trial court correctly concluded there was no triable issue of fact on the question of truth, and that the employer did not act with actual malice so as to forfeit the defense of truth as provided under Massachusetts law).

2. ***Opinion.*** New Hampshire has not adopted any special test for distinguishing fact from opinion. In Pease v. Telegraph, 121 N.H. 62, 426 A.2d 463, 7 Media L. Rep. 1114 (1981), the court set aside a verdict for the plaintiff, ruling, as a matter of law, that a letter to the editor in which the plaintiff was referred to as the "'journalistic scum of the earth' could not reasonably be understood" as an assertion of fact and was protected expression. However, New Hampshire follows the general rule that a statement of opinion may be actionable if it reasonably implies the existence of defamatory facts as its basis. Thomas v. Telegraph Publishing Co., 155 N.H. 314, 929 A.2d 993 (2007). Whether a statement is one of opinion or fact is initially a question of law for the court; if the trial court determines that the statement could be understood by the average reader in either sense, the issue is one for the jury. Id.; see also Catalfo v. Jensen, 657 F. Supp. 463, 13 Media L. Rep. 2356 (D.N.H. 1987) (newspaper article calling the plaintiff "sleazy" and likening him to "Ratso" in "Midnight Cowboy" is protected opinion); Powell v. Monitor Publishing Corp., 107 N.H. 83, 217 A.2d 193 (1966) (editorial about former governor suggesting that he was involved in "some kind of a deal" was capable of defamatory meaning); see also Foster v. Gen. Elec., No. 96-CV-151-SD (D.N.H. Sept. 2, 1998) (reference to former employee as "liar" or "incompetent" implies underlying facts and is therefore actionable).

The federal courts have further developed law in this area. In Gray v. St. Martin's Press, 221 F.3d 243, 28 Media L. Rep. 2313 (1st Cir. 2000), cert. denied, 531 U.S. 1075 (2001), the First Circuit held that several statements complained of could not be defamatory because they were not capable of being proven false; the statements involved matters of degree and speculation. Similarly, in Riley v. Harr, No. CA-98-712-M (D.N.H. Mar. 3, 2000), aff'd 292 F.3d 282, 30 Media L. Rep. 1961 (1st Cir. 2002), the court held that conditional "if/then" statements were not actionable because they did not imply underlying false facts. See also Douglas v. Pratt, 2000 WL 1513712, 2000 DNH 199 (D.N.H. Sept. 29, 2000) (the first amendment unquestionably protects opinions from defamation liability; a protected opinion is one that involves expressions of personal judgment). If a statement of opinion either discloses the facts on which it is based or does not imply the existence of undisclosed facts, the opinion is not actionable. Id.; see also Ben's Auto Body, Inc. v. Teitelbaum, 2008 WL 5244420 (D.N.H. Dec. 15, 2008) (unpublished opinion) (insurer's statement that auto repair shop was "overcharging" repair customer could not be considered as a matter of law a non-actionable opinion).

3. ***Consent.*** No reported cases.

4. ***Mitigation.*** Pursuant to RSA 515:6, "[i]n actions for libel or slander, under the general issue, the defendant may prove, in mitigation of damages and to rebut evidence of actual malice, that the writing or words complained of were the repetition of common report, and that the conduct of the plaintiff was such as to create suspicion of the truth of the matters therein charged against him." See Wetherbee v. Marsh, 20 N.H. 561 (1847) (defendant may mitigate damages by showing that the false and defamatory statement was based upon general rumor in the community); Lamos v. Snell, 6 N.H. 413 (1833) (defendant may prove general bad character of the plaintiff). However, once evidence of his bad character is offered, the plaintiff may present evidence of good character. Dame v. Kenney, 25 N.H. 318 (1852).

In Thomas v. Telegraph Publishing Co., 155 N.H. 314, 929 A.2d 993 (2007), the Supreme Court of New Hampshire adopted the issue-specific libel-proof plaintiff doctrine. Under this doctrine a libel-proof plaintiff is one whose reputation is so diminished that, at the time of an otherwise libelous publication, it could not be further damaged. The issue-specific version of the doctrine applies to justify dismissal of defamation actions where the substantial criminal record of a libel plaintiff shows as a matter of law that he would be unable to recover anything other than nominal damages. In adopting the issue-specific libel proof plaintiff doctrine, the court held that a convicted criminal may have such a poor reputation that no further damage to it is possible at the time of an otherwise libelous publication and warned that the doctrine should be used with caution and sparingly.

To justify applying the doctrine, the record evidence must show that the plaintiff engaged in criminal or anti-social behavior in the past and that his activities were widely reported to the public. Id. at 325. "The evidence on the nature of the conduct, the number of offenses, and the degree and range of publicity received must make it clear, as a matter of law, that the plaintiff's reputation could not have suffered from the publication of the false or libelous statement." Id. Criminal convictions alone are not enough to justify application of the doctrine.

In Thomas, the court found that the issue-specific libel-proof plaintiff doctrine did not apply to the plaintiff, despite his robust criminal record, because he received little media attention. The Court held that publicity is part and parcel to the damage to a reputation necessary to trigger the issue-specific libel-proof plaintiff doctrine and noted that both the publicity surrounding the crimes and the attendant level of notoriety must be quite high to justify its application.

III. RECURRING FACT PATTERNS

A. Statements in Personnel File

There are no cases directly addressing this issue; however, on a closely related topic, the federal district court held that a school could not be held liable for defaming a student in his dismissal letter absent evidence that the letter was published to anyone other than the student. Gill v. Franklin Pierce Law Ctr., 899 F. Supp. 850 (D.N.H. 1995). In addition, the publication of a false statement regarding reasons for an employee's termination is actionable. O'Brien v. Papa Gino's of America, Inc., 780 F.2d 1067 (1st Cir. 1986) (decided under New Hampshire law; employer's half-truth regarding reasons for employee's termination may have properly been considered a lie by the jury).

B. Performance Evaluations

No cases under New Hampshire law. However, the First Circuit has ruled on this issue under Massachusetts law and held that there is a qualified privilege for an employer to evaluate and attempt to improve the performance of an employee. Anderson v. Boston Sch. Comm., 105 F.3d 762 (1st Cir. 1997).

C. References

A former employer's comments to a new or potential new employer may give rise to a cause of action in defamation or in intentional interference with contractual relations if the statements made are false and not privileged. See, e.g., Huskie v. Griffin, 75 N.H. 345, 74 A. 595 (1909) (former employee left on an honorable basis, but former employer implied to new employer that departure was dishonorable, resulting in employee's loss of new position); see also Foster v. Gen. Elec. Co., No. 97-CV-151-SD (D.N.H. Sept. 2, 1998) (statements of former employee to new business associates of employee). See Marin v. Gonzales, 2005 WL 3464389, 2005 DNH 167 (D.N.H. Dec. 19, 2005) (citing Algarin v. Federal Express Corp., 56 F. Supp. 2d 172 (D.P.R. 1999) (observing that "[a]mong the privileged communications so protected are those from an employer Y to prospective employers informing the reasons for the discharge of an employee; statements made in an employee's performance evaluation; and providing references of an employee to potential employers")).

D. Intracorporate Communication

See I.B.6.a, supra. In addition, while it is not absolutely clear, it appears that the communications complained about in O'Brien v. Papa Gino's of America, Inc., 780 F.2d 1067 (1st Cir. 1986), and Godfrey v. Perkin-Elmer Corp., 794 F. Supp 1179 (D.N.H. 1992), rev'd on other grounds, 76 F.3d 413 (1st Cir. 1992), were intracorporate in nature. See also the discussion of the conditional privilege in the context of intracorporate communications contained in Soto-Lebron v. Federal Express Corporation, 538 F.3d 45 (1st Cir. 2008) (applying Puerto Rican law, supra at I.B.6.(a)).

E. Statements to Government Regulators

Statements to the Department of Employment Security are absolutely privileged. RSA 282-A:122; Chamberlain v. 101 Realty, Inc., 626 F.Supp. 865 (D.N.H., 1985). In Chamberlain, an employee sued her former employer for defamation based on his contacts with the Department of Employment Security. Upon firing the plaintiff, the employer wrote a letter to the Department of Employment Security in which he stated that the employee was fired 'for reasons other than lack of work" and was therefore ineligible for unemployment benefits. When the employer was questioned by a Department of Employment Security representative regarding this allegation, the employer stated that the plaintiff did not spend enough time on her work, was frequently absent from the office, and failed to do her work in a proper manner. Pursuant to RSA 282-A:122, the court dismissed the plaintiff's defamation claim. RSA 282-A:122 provides that "[N]o action for slander or libel, either criminal or civil, shall be predicated upon information furnished by any employer or any employee to the commissioner [of the Department of Employment Security] in connection with the administration of any of the provisions of this chapter." Thus, where the defendant employer provided privileged information to the Department regarding plaintiff's discharge, such information failed to form the basis of an action for defamation.

F. Reports to Auditors and Insurers

No reported cases.

G. Vicarious Liability of Employers for Statements Made by Employees

1. ***Scope of Employment.*** The New Hampshire Supreme Court held that an employer can be held vicariously liable for an employee's statements made in the scope of employment. Pierson v. Hubbard, 147 N.H. 760, 802

A.2d 1162 (N.H. 2002). The First Circuit has also held that, under New Hampshire law, an employer will be vicariously liable for the defamatory statements of its employee if the statements were authorized by the employer or were incidental to duties that were authorized by the employer. Aversa v. United States, 99 F.3d 1200, 25 Media L. Rep. 1033 (1st Cir. 1996) (but for sovereign immunity, United States would have been liable for the intentional false statements about a criminal defendant made by an Assistant U.S. Attorney to the media). The federal district court has ruled that an employer is not liable for comments made that were not within the scope of employment, such as those made at a bar. Dube v. Hadco Corp., 1999 WL 1210885, 75 Empl. Prac. Dec. P 45, 962 (D.N.H. 1999).

a. **Blogging.** A recent New Hampshire Supreme Court case dealt with the need to balance a defamation plaintiff's right to protect its reputation with a defendant's right to exercise free speech anonymously. In Mortgage Specialists, Inc. v. Implode-Explode Heavy Industries, Inc., 160 N.H. 227, 38 Media L. Rep. 1641 (N.H. 2010), the court adopted the test announced in Dendrite International, Inc. v. Doe No. 3, 775 A.2 756 (N.J. Super. Ct. App. Div. 2001), which requires the proponent of disclosure of the author's identity to: (1) "'undertake effort[s] to notify the anonymous poster that they are the subject of ... [an] application for an order of disclosure;'" (2) "'set forth the exact statements purportedly made by each anonymous poster that plaintiff alleges constitutes actionable speech;'" and (3) produce "'sufficient evidence supporting each element of its cause of action, on a prima facie basis.'" If that burden of production is met, the trial court is to "'balance the defendant's First Amendment right of anonymous free speech against the strength of the prima facie case and the necessity for disclosure of the anonymous [poster].'"

2. ***Damages.*** No cases specifically address the damages issue in the context of vicarious liability.

H. Internal Investigations

In Caouette, the District Court of New Hampshire, applying New Hampshire law, found that complaints of sexual harassment by employees to management are protected by qualified privileged. Caouette v. OfficeMax, Inc., 352 F. Supp. 134 (D.N.H. 2005). As a matter of good practice, however, employers are advised to be circumspect while conducting investigations by qualifying the assertions of misconduct (*e.g.*, "purported allegations," " alleged misconduct," "the reported behavior," etc.) and limiting the dissemination of the allegations to the extent possible. In other words, allegations of misconduct are just that until substantiated. See Jones v. Walsh, 107 N.H. 379, 222 A.2d 830 (1966) (holding that employer's defamatory statements about an employee may not be conditionally privileged, if widely published).

IV. OTHER ACTIONS BASED ON STATEMENTS

New Hampshire has no cases specifically addressing the issue of whether a plaintiff can, in effect, circumvent the restrictions imposed on defamation actions through artful pleading of other causes of action. However, the First Circuit has addressed this issue, and has ruled in the context of a false light invasion of privacy claim that "it is not imaginable" that the claim could escape the constitutional constraints placed on defamation claims, and that the plaintiff must prove both falsity and fault in order to recover. Brown v. Hearst Corp., 54 F.3d 21, 23 Media L. Rep. 2204 (1st Cir. 1995). In addition, in Jimenez-Nieves v. United States, 682 F.2d 1 (1st Cir. 1982), the First Circuit stated that a claim that a communication resulted in damage to reputation sounds in defamation, regardless of the way it is pled, and is subject to the FTCA bar to defamation claims. These cases suggest that, at least in the federal courts, plaintiffs will not be allowed to avoid defamation restrictions through artful pleading.

A. Negligent Hiring, Retention, and Supervision

A third party successfully combined a slander and negligent hiring suit against K-Mart for the actions of the store's security guard in falsely accusing a woman of shoplifting. See Panas v. Harakis, 129 N.H. 591, 529 A.2d 976 (1987). However, an administrative agency acting in a quasi-judicial capacity cannot be held liable under a "negligent hiring" theory for the statements and conduct of its members in the course of proceedings, on account of sovereign immunity and quasi-judicial attaching to its actions. Shargal v. State Board of Examiners of Psychologists, 135 N.H. 242, 604 A.2d 559 (1992).

B. Intentional Infliction of Emotional Distress

New Hampshire does not allow an action for intentional infliction of emotional distress to be predicated merely upon a statement alleged to be defamatory. Provencher v. CVS Pharmacy, 145 F.3d 5 (1st Cir. 1998), rev'd on other grounds, 303 F.3d 387 (1st Cir. 2002), (Provencher fired by CVS; he claimed that another employee had sexually harassed him, and that his firing was in retaliation for reporting the harassment; accused harasser counter-claimed that she was wrongly removed from the store plaintiff managed by the police, and that this removal both constituted slander and intentional infliction of emotional distress; First Circuit upheld district court's ruling forcing plaintiff to elect between defamation and intentional infliction claim). If the facts pled go beyond a mere defamatory statement, a plaintiff may recover both for defamation and for intentional infliction. Young v. Conductron Corp., 899 F. Supp. 39 (D.N.H. 1995).

In addition, at least one case has held that the workers' compensation act in New Hampshire provides a complete defense to the employer for a claim of intentional infliction of emotional distress. RSA 281-A:8; see Rossi v. Town of Pelham, 35 F. Supp. 2d 58 (D.N.H. 1997) (statute immunizes employer from all liability and co-employees for liability for non-intentional torts); see also Reale v. Riverbend Cmty Mental Health, Inc., No. 98-CV-334-JD (D.N.H., order dated 1/26/99) (plaintiff conceded that his emotional distress claim was barred so long as there existed an employment relationship).

C. Interference with Economic Advantage

In an old case in New Hampshire, a former employee was allowed to proceed with an action against the employer for, in effect, intentional interference where the employee had left work under honorable circumstances, but the old employer implied to the new employer that the employee had left under dishonorable circumstances, and the employee then lost the new opportunity. Huskie v. Griffin, 75 N.H. 345, 74 A. 595 (1909); see also Foster v. Gen. Elec. Co., No. 97-JD-151-SD (D.N.H. Sept. 2, 1998) (summary judgment denied on claim that former employer's refusal to allow employee access to plant constituted intentional interference with contractual relations).

D. Prima Facie Tort

New Hampshire does not recognize the prima facie tort.

V. OTHER ISSUES

A. Statute of Limitations

Defamation actions of all types are subject to a three-year statute of limitations, with no discovery rule. RSA 508:4, II; see McNell v. Hugel, 1994 WL 264200 (D.N.H. May 16, 1994) (rejecting discovery rule and holding that cause of action accrued on date of first publication of the article), aff'd 77 F.3d 460 (1st Cir. 1996). New Hampshire follows the single publication rule. Keeton v. Hustler Magazine, Inc., 131 N.H. 6, 549 A.2d 1187, 16 Media L. Rep. 1077 (1988).

B. Jurisdiction

The New Hampshire long-arm statute has been held by the state supreme court to allow jurisdiction to the fullest extent permissible under the due process clause. Christian v. Barricade Books, Inc., 2003 WL 21146168, 31 Media L. Rep. 2303 (D.N.H., May 15, 2003) (corporation); Remsburg v. Docusearch, Inc., 2002 WL 130952, 2002 DNH 35 (D.N.H. Jan 31, 2002) (corporation); Phelps v. Kingston, 130 N.H. 166, 536 A.2d 740 (1987) (corporation); Estabrook v. Wetmore, 129 N.H. 520, 529 A.2d 956 (1987) (individual); Metcalf v. Lawson, 148 N.H. 35, 802 A.2d 1221(2002) (individual).

C. Worker's Compensation Exclusivity

As noted in section IV,B, supra, the federal court in New Hampshire has held that the workers' compensation act in New Hampshire provides a complete defense to the employer for a claim of intentional infliction of emotional distress. RSA 281-A:8; see also Rossi v. Town of Pelham, 35 F. Supp. 2d 58 (D.N.H. 1997) (statute immunizes employer from all liability and co-employees for liability for non-intentional torts); Reale v. Riverbend Cmty Mental Health, Inc., No. 98-CV-334-JD (D.N.H. Jan. 26, 1999) (plaintiff conceded that his emotional distress claim was barred so long as there existed an employment relationship). However, the federal district court in New Hampshire has held that the workers' compensation exclusivity bar does not preclude intentional tort claims against co-employees. E.g., Young v. Conductron Corp., 899 F.Supp. 39 (D.N.H. 1995).

D. Pleading Requirements

In the state system, the actual words used by the defendants must be alleged in slander actions. Gendron v. St. Pierre, 72 N.H. 400, 56 A.2d 915 (1903); Bassett v. Spofford, 11 N.H. 127 (1840). There is no case discussing this issue in the libel context. The federal district court dismissed a libel claim because the plaintiff, although alleging the document in question was defamatory, failed to plead the "actual content" of the document, thereby neglecting to adequately set forth a prima facie case. Baldi v. Amadon, 2003 WL 21355874, 2003 DNH 93 (D.N.H. June 9, 2003); Phantom Touring, Inc. v. Affiliated Publications, 953 F.2d 724, 728, n.6, 19 Media L. Rep. 1786 (1st Cir. 1992) (in libel action plaintiff restricted to statements that he claimed defamatory in his pleadings, because defendant entitled to notice of the words that plaintiff intended to complain about). At least in the federal courts, therefore, it appears that the specificity requirement will be applied to libel as well as slander actions. But see Dube v. Hadco Corp., 1999 WL 1210885, 75 Empl. Prac. Dec. P 45,962 (D.N.H. Feb. 4, 1999); Foster v. Gen. Elec. Corp., No. 96-CV-151-SD (D.N.H. Sept. 2, 1998) (suggesting plaintiff may not have to plead the exact words of defamatory statement, so long as he alleges the time and place of the statement, the speaker, and the listener). A defamation plaintiff need not identify specific persons to whom publication was made in his complaint. See Huard v. Town of Allenstown, 2011 WL 540766 (D.N.H. Feb. 8, 2011).

SURVEY OF NEW HAMPSHIRE EMPLOYMENT PRIVACY LAW

Steven L. Winer
Jeremy D. Eggleton
Orr & Reno, P.A.
One Eagle Square
P.O. Box 3550
Concord, New Hampshire 03302-3550
Telephone: (603) 223-9152; Facsimile: (603) 224-2318

(With Developments Reported Through **November 1, 2012**)

GENERAL COMMENTS

While New Hampshire historically has had only a modest body of case law relating to privacy matters in the employment context, the last several years have seen growth and development of the common law in this area.

SIGNIFICANT DEVELOPMENTS SINCE THE 2012 *SURVEY*

None.

I. GENERAL LAW OF PRIVACY

A. Legal Basis of Privacy Claims

The New Hampshire Constitution contains no specific provision guaranteeing the right to privacy. The New Hampshire Supreme Court has declared it unnecessary to determine the extent to which the right of privacy is protected as a constitutional matter without the benefit of statute, because the right exists as a matter of tort law in any event. Hamberger v. Eastman, 106 N.H. 107, 112, 206 A.2d 239, 242 (1964). Until 2003, Hamberger was the only case in which the state supreme court had ruled substantively on a claim for invasion of privacy, adopting the intrusion upon seclusion variant of the tort. In 2003, the New Hampshire Supreme Court recognized the tort of invasion of privacy by appropriation of an individual's name or likeness as set forth in the Restatement (Second) of Torts § 652C. Remsburg v. Docusearch, Inc., 149 N.H. 148, 816 A.2d 1001 (2003). No state statutes specifically provide a right of action for an invasion of privacy tort, although there may be invasion of privacy actions based upon statutory prohibitions.

In United States v. Burnette, 375 F.3d 10 (1st Cir. 2004), cert. granted, vacated, remanded, 543 U.S. 1181 (2005), aff'g original decision, 423 F.3d 22 (1st Cir. 2005), an individual defendant asserted that she had a "reasonable expectation of privacy" in the outside of mail that was sorted or stored in the open, common office area of a commercial mail receiving agency (CMRA). Comparing the CMRA to a shared office, the First Circuit held that while the analysis of reasonableness of the defendant's expectations is context specific, the record did not support the assertion that federal agents' search of the exterior of the defendant's mail violated her privacy or Fourth Amendment rights.

B. Causes of Action

In Hamberger v. Eastman, 106 N.H. 107, 206 A.2d 239 (1964), the New Hampshire Supreme Court discussed four variations of the tort of invasion of privacy: (1) intrusion upon the plaintiff's physical and mental solitude or seclusion; (2) public disclosure of private facts; (3) publicity which places the plaintiff in a false light; and (4) appropriation, for the defendant's benefit or advantage, of the plaintiff's name or likeness. The case involved a landlord's installation in the plaintiff tenants' bedroom of a concealed listening and recording device, capable of transmitting and recording sound. The court specifically adopted the first of the four variations of the privacy tort discussed above, and ruled that under the facts of the case, the plaintiffs could recover any damages they could prove. In Remsburg v. Docusearch, Inc., 149 N.H. 148, 816 A.2d 1001 (2003), the court expanded its recognition of torts based on invasion of privacy and adopted misappropriation of an individual's name or likeness as a cause of action.

New Hampshire's general three-year statute of limitations applies to this tort. RSA 508:4, I. There are no cases discussing specific procedural requirements.

1. ***Misappropriation/Right of Publicity.*** Unlike some states, New Hampshire has no statute relating to the right-of-publicity privacy tort and, although this tort was discussed in Hamberger v. Eastman, 106 N.H. 107, 206 A.2d 239 (1964), it was not adopted until 2003. In Remsburg v. Docusearch, Inc., 149 N.H. 148, 816 A.2d 1001 (2003), the New Hampshire Supreme Court for the first time recognized the tort of invasion of privacy by appropriation of an individual's name or likeness as set forth in the Restatement (Second) of Torts § 652C. Although recognizing the tort, the court held that

a plaintiff whose personal information is sold does not have a cause of action for appropriation against the investigator who sold the information because the investigator did not take advantage of the plaintiff's reputation, prestige or other value. Id.; see also Thompson v. C&C Research and Development, LLC, 153 N.H. 446, 898 A. 2d 495 (2006) (while individual has interest in controlling the use of his or her own name and likeness, when individual authorizes another and its licensee to use his or her image pursuant to a contract, such authorization precludes liability for misappropriation by either contracting party or its licensee); Rice v. Wal-Mart Stores, Inc., 2003 WL 22240349, 2003 DNH 166 (D.N.H. 2003) (employer's purchase of corporate-owned life insurance policies on lives of employees does not create viable commercial appropriation claim since employer did not exploit employees' reputations or prestige when it purchased policies); Doe v. Friendfinder Network, Inc., 540 F.Supp.2d 288 (D.N.H. 2008) (declining to dismiss Right of Publicity Claim for failure to state damages in pleading).

2. ***False Light.*** Although this tort was discussed in Hamberger v. Eastman, 106 N.H. 107, 206 A.2d 239 (1964), it has not been specifically adopted in New Hampshire. See Thomas v. Telegraph Publishing Co., 151 N.H. 435, 859 A.2d 1166 (2004) (noting that the New Hampshire Supreme Court has not yet determined whether claims for false light are recognized by state law). The federal district court, however, has held that New Hampshire would likely recognize the false light tort. See **Wentworth-Douglas Hospital v. Young & Novis Professional Ass'n, 2011 WL 446739 (D.N.H. Feb. 4, 2011);** Riley v. Harr, No. CA-98-712-M (D.N.H. Mar. 3, 2000), aff'd 292 F.3d 282, 30 Media L. Rep. 1961 (1st Cir. 2002). The court has not laid out the requirements of a *prima facia* case for this tort, but did indicate that it would be subject to the same constitutional strictures as defamation claims. See **Wentworth-Douglas;** Riley (New Hampshire likely would apply the Restatement (Second) of Torts §652 elements of the tort of false light invasion of privacy); O'Neill v. Valley Regional Health Care, Inc., 2001 WL 276968, 2001 DNH 054 (D.N.H. Mar. 21, 2001) (same); Young v. Plymouth State College, 1999 WL 813887 (D.N.H. Sept. 21, 1999) (observing that other jurisdictions recognizing false light invasion of privacy pursuant to the Restatement (Second) of Torts § 652 require a successful plaintiff to show that: (a) the false light representation would be highly offensive to a reasonable person, and (b) the actor had knowledge of or acted in reckless disregard as to the falsity of the publicized matter); Laramie and Hallem v. Cattell, N.H. Merr. Cty. Sup. Ct. Nos. 06-C-224 and 06-C-225 (8/27/07). (New Hampshire state superior court, in actions brought by two Department of Corrections employees alleging, inter alia, that co-employees had lied about their involvement in the assault of an inmate, which caused the plaintiffs to be fired, refused to grant summary judgment with respect to the plaintiffs' claim of false light invasion of privacy, adopting Restatement definition). As to the contours of the false light claim, the federal district court, relying upon federal case law, noted that the legitimacy of a false light claim may turn on whether the claimant was a public or a private figure. Wentworth Douglass Hosp. v. Young & Novis Prof. Ass'n,, 2012 WL 1081172, Slip Op. at *7 (D.N.H. March 30, 2012) (ruling, however, that merely providing quote to reporter concerning events in question was insufficient, in and of itself, to give rise to public figure status as a matter of law).

3. ***Publication of Private Facts.*** This tort, also identified in Hamberger v. Eastman, 106 N.H. 107, 206 A.2d 239 (1964), was first formally recognized in Karch v. Baybank FSB, 147 N.H. 525, 794 A.2d 763 (2002). There, the court stated that the claim requires "the invasion of something secret, secluded or private pertaining to the plaintiff; however, unlike intrusion, disclosure depends upon publicity." 147 N.H. at 535, 794 A.2d at 774 (internal quotations omitted). **To be actionable, the matter publicized must (1) be highly offensive to a reasonable person; and (2) not of legitimate public concern. Lovejoy v. Linehan, 161 N.H. 483, 20 A.3d 274 (2011).** Cf. State v. Mello, 162 N.H. 115 (2011) (declining to recognize, in criminal context, a privacy interest in subscriber information voluntarily provided to third party ISP); There are no New Hampshire statutes creating a cause of action for this variant of an invasion of privacy tort. However, there are statutes relevant to this tort in the employment context. For example, New Hampshire restricts AIDS testing and reporting. RSA 141-F. This statute also prohibits the disclosure of the identity of any individual tested for HIV, and requires that all research and information relating to HIV testing be maintained as confidential. Violations may result in criminal penalties and civil penalties of up to $5000.

In addition, New Hampshire's Fair Credit Reporting Act, RSA 359-B, limits an employer's use of "investigative consumer reports." These reports, sometimes used in connection with reference checks on job applicants, include information on an applicant's character, reputation, and personal characteristics, which can be obtained through personal interviews with the applicant's neighbors, friends, and associates. RSA 359-B:3, V. Employers requesting such reports must notify applicants that they have done so within three days, as well as notify applicants that they have a right to determine the scope of the requested investigation. RSA 359-B:6, I (a). If the applicant is ultimately denied a job based upon the report, the employer must notify the applicant of this fact and supply the applicant with the name and address of the reporting agency that supplied the report. RSA 359-B:15, I.

Other statutes protecting the privacy of information generated in the context of relationships deemed by law to be confidential include: RSA 329:26 (doctor and patient); RSA 330-A:19 (psychologists and other mental health providers and their patients); RSA 332-I:1 (medical records); RSA 359-C:1 et seq. (disclosure of information by financial institutions); RSA ch. 78-D (protecting private customer information in connection with retail purchase transactions); RSA 332-I (use and disclosure of protected health information and authorization and notice requirements for use of such information in connection with marketing and fundraising). See also Appeal of State Employees' Association of New Hampshire, Inc, 156 N.H. 426, 428 (2007) (State Employees' Association of New Hampshire ("SEA"), the decertified labor union of the New Hampshire Public Utilities Commission, appealed the denial by the New Hampshire Public Employee Labor Relations Board ("PELRB") of its request for the list of names and home addresses of employees in the bargaining unit, in connection with the decertification vote. The court held that the PELRB erred when it denied, based on an articulated concern for the privacy interests of the employees, the SEA's motion for the list, inasmuch as PELRB administrative rules entitled the union to such a list. The court presumed material prejudice to the union flowing from the denial of the motion and therefore remanded for a new decertification election.)

See VI, infra for discussion of public access to private facts through New Hampshire's Right-to-Know Law, RSA 91-A.

4. ***Intrusion.*** The tort of invasion of privacy through "intrusion upon the plaintiff's physical and mental solitude or seclusion" was specifically recognized in Hamberger v. Eastman, 106 N.H. 107, 110, 206 A.2d 239, 241 (1964). In that case, a landlord was held liable for placing a bug in his tenant's bedroom. New Hampshire adopted the Restatement (Second) definition of this tort, which provides that "'a person who unreasonably and seriously interferes with another's interest in not having his affairs known to others . . . is liable to the other . . . [but] only if the defendant's conduct was such that he should have realized that it would be offensive to persons of ordinary sensibilities. It is only where the intrusion has gone beyond the limits of decency that liability accrues.'" Id. at 111, 206 A.2d at 242 (quoting Restatement (Second) of Torts § 867, comment d); see also Remsburg v. Docusearch, Inc., 149 N.H. 148, 816 A.2d 1001 (2003) (person whose social security number ("SSN") is obtained by an investigator from a credit reporting agency without the person's knowledge or permission has a cause of action for intrusion upon seclusion for damages caused by the sale of the SSN, but must prove the intrusion was such it would be offensive to person of ordinary sensibilities; person whose work address was obtained by investigator's pretextual phone call does not have claim for intrusion upon seclusion since work address is not secret, secluded or private information); Rice v. Wal-Mart Stores, Inc., 2003 WL 22240349, 2003 DNH 166 (D.N.H. Sept. 30, 2003) (plaintiffs' claims that Wal-Mart obtained and used employees' confidential medical information without employees' knowledge or permission to purchase corporate-owned life insurance policies on employees' lives is sufficient to withstand summary judgment on intrusion upon seclusion claim); Karch v. Baybank, 147 N.H. 525, 794 A.2d 763 (2002) (passive party who received private information not liable for intrusion upon seclusion because the passive party did not engage in the actual intrusion); Fischer v. Hooper, 143 N.H. 585, 732 A.2d 396 (1999) (liability for intrusion upon seclusion claim only accrues when defendant's conduct has gone beyond limits of decency and he should know it would be offensive to ordinary person); Professional Firefighters of N.H. v. Local Government Ctr., 159 N.H. 699, 710 (2010) (declining to recognize publication of employee salaries as intrusion into privacy of employees' homes). However, when an intrusion is proven, the intrusion alone is sufficient to prove harm. Preferred Nat. Ins. Co. v. Docusource, Inc., 149 N.H. 759, 766-77 (2003) (citing Restatement (Second) of Torts s. 652H, comment a ("One who suffers an intrusion upon his solitude or seclusion… may recover damages for the deprivation of his seclusion.").

The First Circuit has affirmed a jury verdict in favor of a plaintiff's breach of privacy claim, apparently under this theory, in which the employer was found to have coerced the employee into taking a polygraph examination regarding drug use. O'Brien v. Papa Gino's of America, Inc., 780 F.2d 1067 (1st Cir. 1986).

See section VIII,C relating to the impact of the Workers' Compensation law exclusivity provision on intrusion claims.

C. Other Privacy-Related Actions

1. ***Intentional Infliction of Emotional Distress.*** New Hampshire recognizes the tort of intentional infliction of emotional distress as defined by the Restatement (Second) of Torts § 46: "One who by extreme and outrageous conduct intentionally or recklessly causes severe emotional distress to another is subject to liability for such emotional distress, and if bodily harm to the other results from it, for such bodily harm." Morancy v. Morancy, 134 N.H. 493, 593 A.2d 1158 (1991) (recognizing the tort for the first time in New Hampshire). This tort has become well established in New Hampshire. See, e.g., Moss v. Camp Pemigewassett, Inc., 312 F.3d 503 (1st Cir. 2002); Thompson v. Southwest Airlines Co., 2006 WL 287850, 2006 DNH 017 (D.N.H. Feb. 6, 2006); McNair v. McNair, 151 N.H. 343, 856 A.2d 5 (2004); Konefal v. Hollis/Brookline Co-op. School Dist., 143 N.H. 256, 723 A.2d 30 (1998); Asselin v. Waldrin, 2004 WL 57083, 2004 DNH 011 (D.N.H. Jan. 13, 2004) (noting that liability attaches only where conduct has been so outrageous in character, and so extreme in degree, as to go beyond all possible bounds of decency, and to be regarded as atrocious, and utterly intolerable in a civilized community. Generally, the case must be one wherein the recitation of facts to an average community member would arouse resentment against the actor, and lead one to exclaim, "Outrageous!").

Claims for intentional infliction of emotional distress may not be predicated merely upon a threat. Tessier v. Rockefeller, 162 N.H. 324, 33 A.3d 1118 (2011). Nor can a claim rest solely upon a statement claimed to be defamatory. Moss v. Camp Pemigewassett, Inc. 2001 WL 1326674, 2001 DNH 185 (D.N.H. Oct. 10, 2001), rev'd on other grounds, 312 F.3d 503; Provencher v. CVS Pharmacy, 145 F.3d 5 (1st Cir. 1998), rev'd on other grounds 303 F.3d 387; De Meo v. Goodall, 640 F. Supp. 1115 (D.N.H. 1986). The DeMeo court premised its ruling on this point on the fact that emotional distress is one of the elements of damages for a defamation action, and therefore no separate action for the distress could be brought. This reasoning likely could be applied to privacy torts as well.

See section VIII,C concerning effect of Workers' Compensation law exclusivity provision upon infliction of emotional distress claims.

2. ***Interference With Prospective Economic Advantage.*** New Hampshire recognizes the tort of intentional interference with prospective contractual relations. The plaintiff must prove that (1) the plaintiff had an economic relationship with a third party; (2) the defendant was aware of this relationship; (3) the defendant intentionally and improperly interfered with the relationship; and (4) the plaintiff was damaged by the interference. Tessier v. Rockefeller, 162 N.H. at 337 (citing Hughes v. N.H. Division of Aeronautics, 152 N.H. 30, 871 A.2d 18 (2005)); see Lilly Software Associates, Inc. v. Blue Ridge Designs, Inc., 2001 WL 531205, Slip Op. (D.N.H. Apr. 20, 2001) (holding defendants liable for interference where defendants made false statements of fact regarding plaintiff's software to potential customers with whom plaintiff's were engaged in sales discussions.); see generally Jet Wine & Spirits, Inc. v. Bacardi, Ltd., 158 F. Supp. 2d 162 (2001), rev'd on other grounds, 298 F. 3d 1 (1st Cir. 2002). No claim exists where the contractual obligations alleged to have been interfered with were in fact performed; and no claim exists where the party allegedly interfering was not a third party to the contract in question. Tessier v. Rockefeller, 162 N.H. at 337-38. The federal district court also has held that such claims require a plaintiff to "prove she had an already existing relationship that gives rise to a reasonable expectation of economic advantage." Sheppard v. River Valley Fitness One, 2003 WL 21688159, 2003 DNH 110 (D.N.H. July 16, 2003); Lilly Software Associates, Inc. v. Blue Ridge Designs, Inc., 2001 WL 531205, 2001 DNH 077 (D.N.H. Apr. 20, 2001); Preyer v. Dartmouth College, 968 F. Supp. 20 (D.N.H. 1997).

While in general a co-employee acting as an agent of the employer cannot be a third party for the purpose of intentional interference, this rule does not apply where the interfering co-employee is motivated by ill will, spite, hostility, bad faith, or a deliberate intent to injure the plaintiff. Id. But see Alexander v. Fujitsu Business Communication Systems, Inc., 818 F. Supp. 462 (D.N.H. 1993); Scarano v. Community Corrections Corp., 2001 WL 873059, 2001 DNH 133 (D.N.H. July 19, 2001); Hughes v. N.H. Division of Aeronautics, 152 NH 30, 871 A.2d 18 (2005) (granting State immunity on tortious interference with contractual relations claim where state actors reasonably believed their conduct to be legitimate in "refusing to exercise or waive the State's right of first refusal" regarding plaintiff's pending land purchase where State lacked sufficient funds to match plaintiff's offered price within requisite time period).

3. ***Prima Facie Tort.*** New Hampshire has not recognized this tort.

II. EMPLOYER TESTING OF EMPLOYEES

A. Psychological or Personality Testing

1. ***Common Law and Statutes.*** No reported state cases or statutes.

2. ***Private Employers.*** See II. A. 1, supra.

3. ***Public Employers.*** All uncertified police officers, state corrections officers and probation-parole officers are required to pass a psychological evaluation prior to assuming their duties. RSA 188-F:27, III-c.

B. Drug Testing

1. ***Common Law and Statutes.*** The labor statute and regulations forbid employers from requiring employees or job applicants to pay for the cost of drug or alcohol testing. See RSA 275:3; N.H. Admin. Rules, Lab. 803.03 (b). Further, after passage of the federal Drug-Free Workplace Act of 1988, New Hampshire adopted a regulation applicable to state employees providing, in part, that state employees convicted for use, possession, distribution, or manufacture of a controlled substance in the workplace must notify their employer within five days of the conviction. N.H. Admin. Rules, Per 1001.08(a).

2. ***Private Employers.*** See II. B. 1, supra.

3. ***Public Employers.*** All uncertified police officers, state corrections officers and probation-parole officers are required to pass a drug test prior to assuming their duties. RSA 188-F:27, III-a.

Refusal to reinstate transit employees in safety-sensitive positions following positive drug tests absent proof of successful treatment was justified by strong public policy, notwithstanding terms of collective bargaining agreement. In re Amalgamated Transit Union, Local 717, 144 N.H. 325, 328, 741 A.2d 66, 69 (1999).

C. Medical Testing

1. ***Common Law and Statutes.*** RSA 141-H:3 prohibits employers from requiring genetic testing as a condition of employment except "for the purpose of determining the employee's susceptibility or level of exposure to potentially toxic chemicals or potentially toxic substances in the workplace, if the employer does not terminate the employee, or take any other action that adversely affects any term, condition, or privilege of the employee's employment, as a result of genetic testing." RSA 141-H:3, IV(b). The exception is permitted only when the employee requests genetic testing and provides written, informed consent.

In addition, the New Hampshire regulations regarding hospitals, birthing centers, dialysis centers, ambulatory surgical centers, and adult day care centers specifically require that all employees have a physical examination and be tested for tuberculosis. See N.H. Admin. Rules, He-P 802.03, 810.03, 811.03, 812.03, and 818.03. Although these regulations have expired, they are still persuasive authority and, in some instances, may be the rules under which the executive agency operates.

The New Hampshire labor regulations also state that the employer may not require an employee or applicant to pay for the cost of a medical examination or drug or alcohol testing except to the extent the examination or testing is required by state or federal law. N.H. Admin. Rules, Lab. 803.03(b); RSA 141-F.

RSA Chapter 141-F restricts AIDS testing and reporting. RSA 141-F:9-a makes clear that it is not a statutory requirement for health care workers to be tested. RSA 141-F:9-b states that health care workers with known HIV may not participate in invasive procedures absent certification through a state procedure.

2. ***Private Employers.*** See II. C. 1, supra.

3. ***Public Employers.*** See II. C. 1, supra.

D. Polygraph Tests

In In re Waterman, 154 N.H. 437, 910 A.2d 1175 (2006), the New Hampshire Supreme Court held that an order made pursuant to the professional conduct and standards of the New Hampshire Department of Safety, Division of State Police, requiring a Division member take a polygraph test was lawful. As a matter of first impression in New Hampshire, the court found that a public employer can require a police officer to submit to a polygraph test as part of an investigation of his conduct. "Since a police officer must be above suspicion of violation of the laws that he is sworn to enforce and must perform his duty to investigate crime . . . and maintain the public trust, questions concerning the propriety of his conduct must be resolved promptly. In furtherance of this objective, polygraph tests can be administered, and an officer's refusal to submit to such an examination can result in his dismissal." Id. at 440.

In O'Brien v. Papa Gino's of America, Inc., 780 F.2d 1067 (1st Cir. 1986) (decided under New Hampshire law), the First Circuit affirmed a jury verdict in favor of the plaintiff for invasion of privacy based in part upon the employer's coercion of the employee to take a polygraph test relating to drug use, which the jury specifically found to be "highly offensive to a reasonable person and . . . invasive of plaintiff's privacy." Id. at 1071-1072.

E. Fingerprinting

Certain occupations in New Hampshire specifically require fingerprinting. These include all employees of a school district and independent contractors working for a school district in any capacity (including cafeteria workers, bus drivers, and custodians), RSA 189:13-a, police officers and private detectives, RSA 106-B and 106-F, certain vendors, RSA 31:102-b, II, licensed or registered child day care providers, RSA 170-E:7, certain town employees, RSA 41:9-b, nurses, RSA 326-B:15, physician assistants, RSA 328-D:3-a, physicians and surgeons, RSA 329:11-a, and alcohol and drug use professionals, RSA 330-C:20.

There are no cases on the rights of employers or employees as regards fingerprinting as a prerequisite for employment in other jobs.

III. SEARCHES

The New Hampshire Constitution provides in Part I, Article 19 that "[e]very subject hath a right to be secure from all unreasonable searches and seizures of his person, his houses, his papers, and all his possessions." This constitutional provision provides at least as much protection as does the federal constitution. State v. McBreairty, 142 N.H. 12, 697 A.2d 495 (1997); State v. McKinnon Andrews, 151 N.H. 19, 846 A.2d 1198 (2004) (analysis of constitutional framework); see also State v. McLellan, 144 N.H. 602, 744 A.2d 611, 614 (1999) (video surveillance of custodian in classroom did not violate privacy rights). Only criminal cases have been decided under this provision, and there is no other more generalized constitutional provision relating to privacy rights.

There is similarly no state statute directed at general privacy rights, or at searches and seizures in particular.

A. Employee's Person

1. ***Private Employers.*** No reported cases on point.

2. ***Public Employers.*** There are no reported cases decided under state law. However, in Rossi v. Town of Pelham, 35 F. Supp. 2d 58 (D.N.H. 1997), the federal district court found that while a police officer's prevention of a town clerk from removing records from town hall that were necessary for her to complete work due the next day could constitute a seizure of the person, in this case the intrusion on the plaintiff's rights was counter-balanced by the public interest in maintaining accurate financial records and by the somewhat voluntary nature of the town clerk's decision to remain at her office to complete her work. Thus, the court did not find a constitutionally impermissible seizure of the town clerk.

B. Employee's Work Area

In a criminal case decided in 1999, the state Supreme Court held that while an employee may have a reasonable expectation of privacy in an area given over to that employee's exclusive use, there is no such expectation of privacy in an area such as a classroom which is open to use by other employees and students. State v. McLellan, 144 N.H. 602, 744 A. 2d 611, 614 (1999) (custodian).

In Rossi v. Town of Pelham, 35 F. Supp. 2d 58 (D.N.H. 1997), the federal court ruled that a municipal town clerk and tax collector had a reasonable expectation of privacy in her office at the town hall, and that a police officer 's intrusion into that office infringed upon her reasonable expectation of privacy. The court also ruled that it was a constitutionally significant factor that the intrusion was by a police officer, rather than by the clerk's supervisor, because of the coercive authority with which the police officer is vested. As a result, the intrusion into the town clerk's office was a violation of her Fourth Amendment rights.

In Vega-Rodriquez v. Puerto Rico Telephone Co., 110 F. 3d 174 (1st Cir. 1997), the First Circuit ruled that there is no legitimate expectation of privacy in an open work area where there are no defined spaces assigned to particular employees. Therefore, the installation of video surveillance cameras, especially when this is announced ahead of time, does not create an invasion of privacy or constitute a Fourth Amendment violation.

C. Employee's Property

1. ***Private Employers.*** No reported cases on point.

2. ***Public Employers.*** There are no cases addressing this issue under state law. However, two federal cases discuss the federal constitutional privacy rights of public employees in their property. In Alinovi v. Worcester School Committee, 777 F.2d 776 (1st Cir. 1985), cert. denied, 479 U.S. 816 (1986), the First Circuit recognized that a teacher is entitled to protection against unreasonable searches and seizures by school officials. However, the reasonableness of the search or seizure will be viewed in light of the supervisor's legitimate oversight responsibilities, and the special duties of the complaining employee. Id. at 782. The court found in this instance that there was no legitimate expectation of privacy on the part of a teacher in a case-study she had done about a troubled student for submission in a graduate school course. Id. at 783.

In Rossi v. Town of Pelham, 35 F. Supp. 2d 58 (D.N.H. 1997), the federal court ruled that a municipal town clerk and tax collector had property rights in the town records she sought to bring to her home to continue her work on them there. However, the court also ruled that a police officer's prevention of her leaving town hall with the records (which required her to remain at the office to work on the papers) was of minimal intrusiveness and therefore did not on this ground violate her Fourth Amendment rights.

IV. MONITORING OF EMPLOYEES

A. Telephones and Electronic Communications

It is a criminal violation under New Hampshire law to "intercept" telecommunications or oral communications unless all parties to the communication consent. RSA 570-A:2. The New Hampshire Supreme Court has held that RSA 570-A applies to the use of cordless telephones in addition to wired telephones. Karch v. Baybank, 147 N.H. 525, 794 A.2d 763

(2002). The New Hampshire wiretapping and eavesdropping law generally is stricter, and more protective of an individual's right to privacy, than its federal counterpart. State v. Ayres, 118 N.H. 90, 383 A.2d 87 (1978), superseded on other grounds, State v. Kilgus, 128 N.H. 577, 519 A.2d 231 (1986). See also Desilets v. Wal-Mart Stores, Inc., 171 F. 3d 711 (1st Cir. 1999) (discussing damages for violations of federal wiretapping act).

1. ***Wiretapping.*** Wiretapping is prohibited except in accordance with the narrow exceptions listed in RSA 570-A:2. See State v. Locke, 144 N.H. 348, 761 A.2d 376 (1999) (informant must specifically consent to wiretap; consent to "monitoring" of conversation not sufficiently specific). New Hampshire's wiretapping statute, RSA 570-A, provides greater protection of individual rights than federal law because it requires authorization from the attorney general prior to conducting one-party intercepts. State v. Kepple, 151 N.H. 661 (2005). The New Hampshire Supreme Court held that RSA § 281-A does not bar an employee from bringing a claim of unlawful wiretapping and eavesdropping against an employer and a co-employee when the overheard conversation took place outside of the place and hours of employment. Karch v. Baybank, 147 N.H. 525, 794 A.2d 763 (2002); see also State of New Hampshire v. Windhurst, 2006 WL 2075119 (N.H. Super., July 13, 2006) (holding extraterritorial one-party intercepts permissible under New Hampshire law).

2. ***Electronic Communications.*** New Hampshire statute prohibits any person from intercepting any telecommunication or oral communication without the consent of all parties to the communication. RSA 570-A:2. Under RSA 570-A:1, "telecommunication means the transfer of any form of information in whole or in part through the facilities of a communications common carrier." Although there are no cases that expressly discuss how the aforementioned state statutes affect the interception of voicemail or electronic mail, the broadness of the definition of telecommunication arguably could give rise to a cause of action against employers who intercept voicemail or email. **See State v. Mello, 162 N.H. 115, 27 A.3d 771 (2011) (dicta recognizing privacy interest in content of electronic communications).** Transferring stored email files to another computer does not amount to the interception of electronic communications under 18 U.S.C. § 2511. Thompson v. Thompson, 2002 WL 1072342, 2002 DNH 108 (D.N.H. May 30, 2002). The district court, therefore, granted defendant's motion to dismiss because plaintiff failed to make a claim upon which relief could be granted. See New Hampshire v. Lott, 152 N.H. 436, 879 A.2d 1167 (2005) (holding that an undercover detective's acts of cutting and pasting text from an online instant messaging discourse he engaged in with a suspected child predator using Yahoo! did not qualify as an impermissible interception. The court noted that "unlike persons using a telephone persons using an instant messaging program are aware that their conversations are being recorded").

3. ***Other Electronic Monitoring.*** It is a misdemeanor under New Hampshire's Criminal Code for any person, without the consent of all parties, to install or use any device (a) for "observing, photographing, recording, amplifying or broadcasting or in any way transmitting images or sounds of the private body parts of a person including the genitalia, buttocks, or female breasts, or a person's body underneath that person's clothing; (b) in a private place, for the purpose of observing, photographing, recording, amplifying or broadcasting, or in any way transmitting images or sounds in such place; or (c) outside a private place, for the purpose of hearing, recording, amplifying, broadcasting, or in any way transmitting images or sounds originating in such place which would not ordinarily be audible or comprehensible outside such place." RSA 644:9, I(a)-(c). A private place, in turn, is defined as "a place where one may reasonably expect to be safe from surveillance including public restrooms, locker rooms, the interior of one's dwelling place, or any place where a person's private body parts including genitalia, buttocks, or female breasts may be exposed." RSA 644:9, II.

B. Mail

In United States v. Burnette, 375 F.3d 10 (1st Cir. 2004), cert. granted, judgment vacated, remanded, 543 U.S. 1181 (2005), aff'g original decision, 423 F.3d 22 (1st Cir. 2005), an individual defendant asserted that she had a "reasonable expectation of privacy" in the outside of mail that was sorted or stored in the open, common office area of a commercial mail receiving agency. The First Circuit held that while the analysis of reasonableness of the defendant's expectations is context specific, the record did not support the assertion that federal agents' search of the exterior of the defendant's mail violated her privacy or Fourth Amendment rights. Although the case did not involve an employment situation, the Court discussed the defendant's assertion that the facility is "the Fourth Amendment equivalent of a shared office," entitling one to a "reasonable expectation that the contents of the office will not be disturbed except by personal or business invitees." Id. at 16 (quoting Mancusi v. DeForte, 392 U.S. 364, 369, 88 S.Ct. 2120 (1968)).

C. Surveillance/Photographing

New Hampshire prohibits surveillance and photographing of individuals in any "private place" in which the employee has a reasonable expectation of safety from surveillance such as public restrooms, locker rooms or any place where a person's private body parts (genitalia, buttocks or female breasts) may be exposed. RSA 644:9. Under an earlier version of this criminal statute, the New Hampshire Supreme Court held that a defendant, who was a school custodian, could not challenge the video surveillance evidence against him in court under the previous version of RSA 644:9 because the classroom was not a place where the defendant could reasonably expect to be safe from surveillance and thus was not a "private place" under the aforementioned statute. State v. McLellan, 144 N.H. 602, 744 A.2d 611 (1999). See also Vega-Rodriquez v. Puerto Rico Telephone Co., 110 F. 3d 174 (1st Cir. 1997) (pre-announced video surveillance of open work area is not a privacy violation).

V. ACTIVITIES OUTSIDE THE WORKPLACE

A. Statute or Common Law

See V.B, infra. In addition, RSA 275:1 prohibits employers from coercing or compelling a person to enter into a written or verbal agreement not to join or become a member of any labor organization as a condition of employment. RSA 110-B:65 prohibits discrimination against employees and applicants for employment based upon National Guard membership, and prohibits attempts to dissuade enlistment in the National Guard through threatening adverse employment consequences. Further, the New Hampshire Human Rights Commission has ruled that anti-nepotism policies are unlawful except where they are based upon legitimate business needs. See Derry Cooperative Sch. Dist. v. Branley, ESMS 2606-84 (N.H. Human Rights Commission, Sept. 24, 1984).

B. Employees' Personal Relationships

1. ***Romantic Relationships Between Employees.*** No reported state cases or statutes.

2. ***Sexual Orientation.*** New Hampshire's equal employment opportunity statute prohibits employment-related discrimination based on sexual orientation. RSA 354-A:7, I. Sexual orientation is defined, effective January 1, 2007, at RSA 354-A:2, XIV-c.

Effective January 1, 2010, New Hampshire law permits same sex couples to marry; provides a means for converting previously established New Hampshire civil unions between same sex couples to marriages; and treats previously established civil unions between same sex couples from other states as marriages. See RSA 457-A.

3. ***Marital Status.*** New Hampshire's equal employment opportunity statute prohibits employment-related discrimination based on marital status. RSA 354-A:7, I. See also Derry Cooperative School District v. Branley, ESMS 2606-84 (N.H. Human Rights Commission, Sept. 24, 1984) (regarding anti-nepotism policies).

C. Smoking

RSA 275:37-a prohibits an employer from requiring as a condition of employment that any employee or applicant abstain from using tobacco products outside the course of employment, as long as the employee complies with workplace smoking policies required under the New Hampshire Indoor Smoking Act, RSA 155:64 et seq.

D. Blogging

No state statutes or reported cases.

VI. RECORDS

RSA 91-A, New Hampshire's Right-to-Know law, governs access to public records. The statute has been amended numerous times, generally to broaden and clarify its scope. The public's right to know is further safeguarded by a constitutional provision which states that "Government . . . should be open, accessible, accountable and responsive. To that end, the public's right of access to governmental proceedings shall not be unreasonably restricted." N.H. Const., Part I, Art. 8. The Right-to-Know law applies to the records of all public bodies, and to all public records not the subject of an exception enumerated by RSA 91-A:5 (which includes an exception for records whose disclosure might constitute an invasion of privacy).

A. Personnel Records

New Hampshire's Right-to-Know law specifically exempts personnel files, files relating to internal personnel practices, and "other files whose disclosure would constitute invasion of privacy" from disclosure pursuant to the provisions of the act. RSA 91-A:5; see generally Professional Firefighters of N.H. v. Local Government Center, 159 N.H. 699 (2010) and Union Leader Corp. v. New Hampshire Retirement System, 162 N.H. 673, 34 A.3d 725 (2011) (both holding this exemption inapplicable to certain employees' names and salary/retirement benefit information because public interest in government expenditures outweighs employees' privacy right in protecting individual salary or retirement benefit from disclosure); Lamy v. New Hampshire Public Utilities Commission, 152 N.H. 106, 872 A.2d 1006 (2005). The New Hampshire Supreme Court determined that this exemption did not apply to information regarding public school teachers' salaries, see Mans v. Lebanon Sch. Bd., 112 N.H. 160, 290 A.2d 866 (1972), or to information regarding names and addresses of substitute teachers employed by a school district while its regularly-employed teachers were on strike.

Timberlane Regional Educ. Ass'n v. Crompton, 114 N.H. 315, 319 A.2 d 632 (1974), exceptions overruled 115 N.H. 616, 347 A.2d 612 (1975); see, also, Montenegro v. City of Dover, 162 N.H. 641, 34 A.3d 717 (2011) (job titles of persons who monitor city surveillance equipment not subject to exemption for "internal personnel practice"). However, a report generated during the course of an investigation of claimed misconduct of a public employee was a record pertaining to "internal personnel practices" and therefore exempt from disclosure under New Hampshire's Right-to-Know law which includes an exception for records pertaining to internal personnel practices. Hounsell v. North Conway Water Precinct, 154 N.H. 1, 903 A.2d 987 (2006); see also Union Leader Corp. v. Fenniman, 136 N.H. 624, 620 A.2d 1039, 21 Media L. Rep. 1222 (1993) (documents compiled during an internal investigation of a police lieutenant accused of making harassing phone calls exempt from disclosure because they related to internal personnel practices).

All current and former employees in New Hampshire have the right to review and copy their personnel files. RSA 275:56; N.H. Admin. Rules, Lab. 803.04; see Rix v. Kinderworks, 136 N.H. 548, 618 A.2d 833 (1992). If, upon inspection of the file, the employee disagrees with information contained therein and the employer cannot agree upon removal or correction of this information, the employee may submit a written statement explaining his or her version of the information, which statement must be maintained in the personnel file. RSA 275:56, II. The New Hampshire statutes do not define "personnel file;" however, the state Labor Department's definition of this term can be found at N.H. Admin. Rules Lab. 802.09. The New Hampshire Supreme Court denied a police officer access to a document that at one time had been temporarily placed in his personnel file, as well as to an investigative file, holding that "until an internal investigation produces information that results in the initiation of disciplinary process, public policy requires that internal investigation files remain confidential." Pivero v. Largy, 143 N.H. 187, 191, 722 A. 2d 461, 463 (1998).

There are no state-law cases discussing whether disclosure of personnel records might constitute an invasion of privacy. However, in one old New Hampshire case, an employer was held liable for misrepresenting the terms of an employee's departure to a new employer, resulting in the employee' s losing the new opportunity. Huskie v. Griffin, 75 N.H. 345, 74 A.2d 595 (1909) (defamation-type claim); see also O'Brien v. Papa Gino's of America, Inc., 780 F.2d 1067 (1st Cir. 1986) (employer's half-truth about employee's termination may have properly been considered a lie by the jury on defamation claim); Gill v. Franklin Pierce Law Center, 899 F. Supp. 850 (D.N.H. 1995) (absent publication to a third party, dismissal letter could not result in defamation liability).

The federal district court has considered in several § 1983 actions the issue whether disclosure of an employee's personnel file by a state actor would violate a "clearly established" right of privacy, but has thus far determined that this right is not so clearly established as to prohibit qualified immunity for the state official. See Hansen v. Lamontagne, 808 F. Supp. 89 (D.N.H. 1992); Kassel v. United States Veterans Administration, 682 F. Supp. 646 (D.N.H. 1988). However, the same federal court in Kassel (II) determined that the "employees have a privacy interest in their employment history," and that disclosure of this information could constitute a violation of the Federal Privacy Act, 5 U.S.C.A. § 522a (West 1977 and Supp. 1992). See Kassel v. United States Veterans Administration, 709 F. Supp. 1194 (D.N.H. 1989). **However the federal court has compelled the limited disclosure of personnel records bearing on a party's credibility, despite the fact that "[P]ersonnel files contain perhaps the most private information about an employee within the possession of an employer." Moses v. Mele, 2011 WL 2174029, Civil No. 10-cv-253 (D.N.H. June 1, 2011).**

B. Medical Records

The New Hampshire Right-to-Know law specifically exempts medical records from disclosure. RSA 91-A:5. Further, the New Hampshire medical records law requires specific authorizations and notices prior to use and disclosure of protected health information. RSA 332-I, 1 et seq.

Several judicial opinions concerning disclosure or medical information also are informative. In May v. Dartmouth Hitchcock Medical Center, 2003 WL 21488697, 2003 DNH 111 (D.N.H. 2003), the federal district court held that it was "satisfied" the New Hampshire Supreme Court would recognize a tort based on the improper disclosure of privileged information. That court, however, concluded that the Medical Center employer of a physician employee who disclosed the plaintiff's confidential medical information was not vicariously liable since the physician employee disclosed the information on her own time, at a private function and entirely for her own purposes. Id. In another case involving medical records, the federal court determined that the plaintiff could not maintain a private cause of action under the Computer Fraud and Abuse Act ("CFAA"), 18 U.S.C. § 1030 (2000), against the employer on a theory of vicarious liability for the physician employee's intentional violation of the CFAA. Doe v. Dartmouth Hitchcock Medical Center, 2001 WL 873063, 2001 DNH 132 (D.N.H. July 19, 2001). In an earlier case, Borucki v. Ryan, 827 F.2d 836 (1st Cir. 1987), the First Circuit discussed the federal constitutional privacy rights implicated by the disclosure by a state actor of a prisoner's psychiatric records. The opinion also generally reviews the federal constitutional privacy interest in non-disclosure of personal matters, which also would be applicable to public employers.

C. Criminal Records

Employers may inquire regarding applicants' criminal convictions that have not been annulled, see RSA 651:5, X (c) (In any application for employment . . . a person may be questioned about a previous criminal record only in terms such as "Have you ever been arrested for or convicted of a crime that has not been annulled by a court?"), but not their arrest records unless the inquiry is justified by a bona fide business necessity. Even an annulled criminal conviction may be of sufficient public interest that its disclosure will not give rise to liability for invasion of privacy. Lovejoy v. Linehan, 161 N.H. 483 (2011) (no liability for disclosure of annulled criminal record of candidate for public office). Nevertheless, an employer is advised to be careful if the inquiry may have the effect of discouraging members of certain racial groups or other protected classes of applicants from applying for employment. If an employer desires to run a criminal background check, it may obtain a report regarding criminal convictions through the New Hampshire Department of Safety's State Police Central Repository of Criminal Records by submitting a written waiver on the Department's form containing the notarized signature of the subject along with a the appropriate fee. RSA 106-B:14.

In addition, certain occupations in New Hampshire require a criminal records check. These include all employees of a school district and independent contractors working for a school district in any capacity (including cafeteria workers, bus drivers, and custodians), RSA 189:13-a, police officers and private detectives, RSA 106-B and 106-F, certain vendors, RSA 31:102-b, II, licensed or registered child day care providers, RSA 170-E:7, certain town employees, RSA 41:9-b, nurses, RSA 326-B:15, physician assistants, RSA 328-D:3-a, physicians and surgeons, RSA 329:11-a, and alcohol and drug use professionals, RSA 330-C:20. Effective September 18, 2010, HB 1286 amended RSA 189:13-a to, among other things, permit private schools to require criminal history checks on certain employees and volunteers.

D. Subpoenas / Search Warrants

There are no statutes or reported cases on point. A cautious employer, however, typically resists a subpoena for the production of personnel records or other confidential records and instead will release such records only pursuant to a written authorization of the individual whose confidential records are being subpoenaed, or a court order.

VII. ACTIONS SUBSEQUENT TO EMPLOYMENT

A. References

There are no state statutes or reported decisions that address whether an employee has a privacy interest in the reference provided to a third party by his employer. Relying on other legal theories, however, a former employer's comments to a new or potential new employer may give rise to a cause of action for defamation or for intentional interference with contractual relations if the statements made are false and not privileged. See, e.g., Huskie v. Griffin, 75 N.H. 345, 74 A.595 (1909) (former employee left on an honorable basis, but former employer implied to new employer that departure was dishonorable, resulting in employee's loss of new position); see also Foster v. Gen. Elec. Co., No. 97-CV-151-SD (D.N.H. Sept. 2, 1998) (statements of former employee to new business associates of employee).

B. Non-Compete Agreements

New Hampshire "does not look with favor upon contracts in restraint of trade or competition." Merrimack Valley Wood Products, Inc. v. Near, 152 N.H. 192, 876 A.2d 757 (2005) (quoting Technical Aid Corp. v. Allen, 134 N.H. 1, 8 (1991)), cited in Maddog Software, Inc. v. Sklader, 382 F. Supp. 2d 268, 283 (D.N.H. 2005). Nonetheless, a restrictive covenant such as a non-competition agreement is valid and enforceable if the restraint is reasonable, given the particular circumstances. Merrimack Valley Wood Products, 152 N.H. at 197, 876 A.2d at 762;but see, Syncom Industries, Inc. v. Wood, 155 N.H. 73, 920 A.2d 1178 (2007) (restrictive employment covenant not enforceable where there has been a breach by employer of his own obligations under the contract) (applying Merrimack Valley test in detail). A restrictive covenant generally is reasonable provided it satisfies three criteria: (1) it must be no greater than necessary to protect the employer's legitimate interests; (2) it cannot impose an undue hardship on the employee; and (3) it cannot be injurious to the public interest. Id. Such contracts are to be narrowly construed. Id.

The New Hampshire Supreme Court has analyzed the first criterion in detail, noting that "[restrictive] covenants are enforceable only to the extent that they prevent employees from appropriating assets that are legitimately the employer's. Merrimack Valley Wood Products, 152 N.H. at 197, 876 A.2d at 762. In that case, involving an outside salesperson who, after leaving employer Merrimack Valley Wood Products, went to work for a competitor, the court stated that while "[a]n employee's special influence over an employer's customers, obtained during the course of employment, is one of the legitimate interests an employer may protect against competition," a non-competition covenant cannot extend "beyond the sphere of the employee's influence, either beyond the geographic area where the employee would have had actual client contact, or beyond the employee's own clients to the public at large." Merrimack Valley Woods Products, 152 N.H. at 198, 876 A.2d at 762-763. Accordingly, the court ruled that "it is unreasonable to prohibit the [employee] from soliciting customers with whom he previously had no contact." Merrimack Valley Wood Products, 152 N.H. at 199, 876 A.2d at 764.

In Merrimack Valley Wood Products, the supreme court, while recognizing a court's power to reform an overly broad restrictive covenant if the employer acted in good faith in the execution of the agreement, refused to reform the covenant at issue. Instead, the court ruled that the employer had acted in bad faith by failing to discuss the non-competition agreement with the employee prior to the start of his employment, by presenting the agreement to the employee six months after he started working, and by making his continued employment contingent on him signing the agreement. Merrimack Valley Wood Products, 152 N.H. at 200-201, 876 A.2d at 764-765.

In ACAS Acquisitions (Precitech) Inc. v. Hobert, 155 N.H. 381, 923 A.2d 1076, 1088 (2007), the defendant, as a condition of employment, signed a non-competition agreement with ACAS, agreeing that for a period of two years after termination he would not engage in any line of business that represented 5% of the gross revenues of ACAS or solicit any of ACAS' customers. The court held that ACAS had a legitimate business interest in protecting its trade secrets, confidential information, and customer goodwill and that the non-competition agreement was narrowly tailored to protect those interests. The court also found that the non-competition agreement did not work an undue hardship on the employee because the employee entered the employment relationship fully aware that the non-competition agreement would force him to relocate and, with this knowledge, the employee negotiated for a substantial severance package to lessen the impact of the covenant's enforcement. Finally, the non-competition agreement did not offend the public interest and therefore it was enforceable.

In ANSYS, Inc. v. Computational Dynamics North America, Ltd., Civ. No. 09-cv-284-SM, 2009 WL 4403745 (D.N.H. Nov. 25, 2009), aff'd 595 F.3d 75 (1st Cir. 2010), ANSYS, Inc. sought a preliminary injunction to enforce a former employee's one-year non-compete. Although the former employee had gone to work for a major competitor, Computational Dynamics North America, Ltd. ("CDNA"), ANSYS failed to demonstrate a "reasonable possibility" that he would disclose any confidential information to CDNA. Id. at *5. The decision rested in part on the differing software platforms between the two companies and on CDNA's strict policy prohibiting its employees from using confidential information obtained from prior employers. Id. at *6.

VIII. OTHER ISSUES

A. Statutes of Limitations

The statute of limitations for privacy claims is three years, and is governed by RSA 508:4, I, New Hampshire's general statute of limitations.

B. Jurisdiction

Claims based upon employment privacy are not subject to special jurisdictional requirements under New Hampshire law.

C. Workers' Compensation Exclusivity

The federal district court has held that the New Hampshire Workers' Compensation Law bars all emotional distress claims against an employer arising during the time of employment, and bars negligent infliction claims against co-employees. Rossi v. Town of Pelham, 35 F. Supp. 2d 58 (D.N.H. 1997); RSA 281-A:8; see Karch v. Baybank, 147 N.H. 525, 794 A.2d 763 (2002). The court also held in Rossi that, as a matter of law, the placement of a police guard on a town employee to prohibit her from taking town records home, to enable her to perform work while at home, was not "outrageous," and therefore could not give rise to an intentional infliction claim. Id. However, an employee may bring an intentional infliction of emotional distress claim against a co-employee if the conduct meets the outrageous conduct standard. See, e.g., Lemieux v. Freudenberg NOK General Partnership, 2000 WL 36958 (D.N.H. Nov.17, 1999); Fernandes v. TPD, Inc., 2000 WL 1466108 (D.N.H. Jan. 7, 2000); Karch v. Baybank, 147 N.H. 525 (2002). It should also be noted that, Rossi and Karch v. BayBank notwithstanding, several New Hampshire trial court judges do not believe that the Workers' Compensation Law bars such claims.

In Thompson v. Forest, 136 N.H. 215, 614 A.2d 1064 (1992), the supreme court held that tort claims alleging "willful, wanton and reckless" conduct by co-employees relating to the co-employees alleged failure to provide a safe and secure workplace did not constitute an allegation of an intentional tort, for purposes of applying the workers' compensation exclusivity provision. As a "non-intentional" tort the court held the claims were barred.

An employee is not barred by the Workers' Compensation Act, RSA 281-A, from bringing a claim of invasion of privacy based on intrusion against a co-employee when the co-employee eavesdropped on a private phone conversation. Karch v. Baybank, 147 N.H. 525, 794 A.2d 763 (2002).

D. Pleading Requirements

There are no special pleading requirements for an invasion of privacy claim.

SURVEY OF NEW JERSEY EMPLOYMENT LIBEL LAW

James P. Flynn
EpsteinBeckerGreen
One Gateway Center
Newark, NJ 07101
jflynn@ebglaw.com
Telephone (973) 642-1900; Telecopier (**973-642-0099**)

(With Developments Reported Through **November 1, 2012**)

GENERAL COMMENTS

(1) Practice rules for all courts in New Jersey are promulgated by the New Jersey Supreme Court and are set forth, with annotations, in Pressler, Current N.J. Court Rules. (2) In the absence of a substantial question arising under the federal or New Jersey Constitution or of a dissent in the Appellate Division, appeals to the New Jersey Supreme Court are discretionary. (3) Selected New Jersey Superior Court Law Division and Chancery Division decisions and New Jersey Superior Court Appellate Division decisions which are approved for publication are reported in New Jersey Superior Court Reports (N.J. Super.); all New Jersey Supreme Court decisions are reported in the New Jersey Reports (N.J.). Under N.J. Court Rule 1:36-3, an unpublished state court opinion may be cited in briefs and other court papers only if "all other parties are served with a copy of the opinion and of all other relevant unpublished opinions known to counsel including those adverse to the position of his client." There is no federal court rule restricting citation of unpublished cases.

Defamation suits and other intentional tort claims against public employees whose public employees are subject to the New Jersey Tort Claims Act, N.J.S.A. 59:3-1 et seq., require filing a written Notice of Claim with the entity pursuant to the Act, even if the employer is immune from liability and the employee can only be held liable on a showing of actual malice. Velez v. City of Jersey City, 180 N.J. 284, 850 A.2d 1238 (2004). The Velez case involved assault, but the ruling is broad enough to cover defamation claims. The Supreme Court made its ruling prospective only, since lower courts below had made conflicting rulings. In Donato v. Moldow, 374 N.J. Super. 475, 865 A.2d 711 (App. Div. 2005), the Federal Communications Decency Act was held to immunize the host of an online community bulletin board website from defamation claims. In Churchill v. State of New Jersey, 378 N.J. Super. 471, 876 A.2d 311 (App. Div. 2005) the Court held that the single publication rule applied to publication of an allegedly defamatory document on a governmental internet website. An allegedly defamatory press release posted on a company website discussing pending litigation was held to be non-actionable opinion, non-actionable rhetorical hyperbole and subject to a qualified privilege requiring a showing of actual malice to be actionable, Arista Records, Inc. v. Flea World, Inc., 356 F.Supp. 2d 411 (D. N.J. 2005). New Jersey now recognizes a cause of action against an employer for negligent misrepresentation of a former employee's work history if the following five (5) factors are proven: (1) the inquiring party clearly identifies the nature of the inquiry; (2) the employer voluntarily decides to respond to the inquiry, and thereafter unreasonably provides false or inaccurate information; (3) the person providing the inaccurate information is acting within the scope of his/her employment; (4) the recipient of the incorrect information relies on its accuracy to support an adverse employment action against the former employee; and (5) the former employee suffers quantifiable damages proximately caused by the negligent misrepresentation. Singer v. Beach Trading Co., Inc., 379 N.J. Super. 63, 69 (App. Div. 2005).

SIGNIFICANT DEVELOPMENTS SINCE THE 2012 *SURVEY*

As was the case during the previous reporting year, there were few reported or significant unreported employment libel cases.

I. GENERAL LAW

A. General Employment Law

1. ***At Will Employment.*** There is no cause of action for the mere discharge of an at will employee. Velantzas v. Colgate-Palmolive Co., 109 N.J. 189, 536 A.2d 237 (1988); El-Hewie v. Bergen County, et al., 348 Fed. Appx. 790 (September 17, 2009) (unpublished) (Board of Education had no obligation to renew one year contract of non-tenured public school teacher). An at-will employee has a cause of action against an employer for wrongful termination when the discharge violates state law or public policy. Id. The sources of public policy may come from legislation, administrative rules, regulations or decisions and in certain circumstances, professional codes of ethics. Pierce v. Ortho Pharmaceutical Corp., 84 N.J. 58, 417 A.2d 505 (1980). The New Jersey Supreme Court recently not only ratified the Pierce holdings, but essentially clarified and, to a certain extent, extended that decision by concluding that an employer's alleged violations of a Rule of Professional Conduct qualifies as a "source of public policy" permitting an at will employee to assert a cause of

action based upon wrongful discharge and that, while simple good faith disagreements about the meaning of a particular RPC will not alone support the relief requested, Pierce does not require proof of an external complaint as a prerequisite to recovery. Tartaglia v. UBS PaineWebber, Inc. 197 N.J. 81 (2008); Barnello, et al. v. AGC Chemicals Americas, Inc., et al., 2009 U.S. Dist. LEXIS 6410 (January 29, 2009). However, this ruling does not completely absolve a plaintiff from abiding by certain external reporting requirements, depending upon the types of claims asserted and against whom. For example, in Thomasian v. New Jersey Institute of Technology, 2009 U.S. Dist. LEXIS 7900 (Feb. 3 2009) (opinion and order), the District Court dismissed a plaintiff's libel, slander and defamation claims, in part due to his failure to file a notice of claim against NJIT, as required by the New Jersey Tort Claims Act for claims asserted against a public entity. Likewise, in Matthews v. The New Jersey Institute of Technology, 2010 U.S. Dist. LEXIS 27812 (March 23, 2010), the plaintiff's common law tort claims were dismissed for his failure to file a Notice of Claim against NJIT (a public entity), and its director (a public employee). That being said, it remains that a plaintiff's claim for common law wrongful discharge cannot be sustained absent the identification of a clear mandate of public policy about which an employee complained and that was the cause of the employee's discharge from employment, as required by Pierce. Leang v. Jersey City Board of Education, et al., 198 N.J. 557 (2009). Further, to establish a prima facie case of discriminatory retaliation, pursuant to N.J.S.A. 10:5-12(d), a plaintiff must demonstrate: (1) he or she engaged in a protected activity known by the employer; (2) thereafter the employer unlawfully retaliated against him or her; and (3) participation in the protected activity caused the retaliation. Stoecker v. North Hudson Regional Fire and Rescue, et al., 2009 N.J. Super Unpub. LEXIS 2783 (November 6, 2009), citing Tartaglia v. UBS PaineWebber, Inc. 197 N.J. 81 (2008).

While not actually raising issues relating to employment libel law, the United States District Court addressed interesting issues relating to the exercise of First Amendment free speech rights by an employee in Wiegand v. Motiva Enterprises, LLC, et al., 295 F. Supp.2d. 465 (D.N.J. 2003). In Wiegand, where the plaintiff ran a website offering for sale various racist and hate paraphernalia, the Court ruled that under New Jersey law, defendants did not violate a clear mandate of public policy when they determined that plaintiff's continued employment as supervisor of their convenience store, a job that required constant interaction with the consuming public, could not continue based on his dissemination of those racist items for commercial profit and that even if plaintiff could assert a First Amendment wrongful termination, he could not establish that defendants' decision to terminate was contrary to a clear mandate of public policy since it was not "clearly protected" by the First Amendment, due to its nature as commercial hate speech regulated by an employer. Continuing in that vein, in Brennan v. Township of Fairfield, 2008 U.S., Dist. Lexis 102805, the District Court recently reiterated that the First Amendment will not shield a police officer from disciplinary actions when he by-passed internal procedures and issued a memorandum on department letterhead explaining why he issued summonses to the township administrator. In so ruling, the District Court reasoned that since the police officer in question was making statements pursuant to his official duties and not as a private citizen, for First Amendment purpose, the Constitution did not insulate his communications from employer discipline. Likewise, in Stouch v. The Township of Irvington, 354 Fed. Appx. 660 (3d Cir. Court of Appeals, 11/24/2009), the Third Circuit Court of Appeals reiterated that in bringing a First Amendment wrongful termination claim, a public employee's statement is protected activity when (1) in making it, the employee spoke as a citizen, (2) the statement involved a matter of public concern, and (3) the government employer did not have an 'adequate justification for treating the employee differently from any other member of the general public' as a result of the statement he made. Id. at 665, citing Hill v. Borough of Kutztown, 455 F.3d 225, 241-42(3d. Cir. 2006).

B. Elements of Libel Claim

1. ***Basic Elements.*** In New Jersey, a defamatory statement has been defined as one that is false and injurious to the reputation of another or exposes another person to "hatred, contempt, or ridicule" or subjects another person to "a loss of the good will and confidence" in which he or she is held by others. Petersen, et al. v. Meggitt, et al., 407 N.J. Super. 63 (App. Div., 2009), quoting Romaine v. Kallinger, 109 N.J. 282, 289 (1988). Under New Jersey law, to prevail on a defamation claim, plaintiff must prove: (1) a false and defamatory statement concerning the plaintiff; (2) unprivileged publication to a third party; (3) fault amounting to at least negligence on the part of the publisher; and (4) damages. Ditzel v. University of Medicine and Dentistry of New Jersey, 962 F.Supp. 595 (D.N.J. 1997); Petersen, et al. v. Meggitt, et al., 407 N.J. Super. 63 (App. Div., 2009). Under the general fault standards for defamation, a plaintiff can prevail by showing either negligence, if the plaintiff is a private figure, or actual malice, if the defendant is a public figure. Costello v. Ocean County Observer, 136 N.J. 594, 643 A.2 1012 (1994). To state a defamation claim under New Jersey law, claimant must allege false and defamatory statement of fact about claimant, that defendant knew or should have known statement was false, and that statement was communicated to third parties causing damages. Arista Records, Inc. v. Flea World, Inc., 356 F.Supp. 2d 411 (D.N.J. 2005). Kiernan v. Williams, No. A-0531-04T1, A-0605-04T1 (Sup. Ct. N.J. B App. Div. August 23, 2006); Buying For the Home, LLC v. Humble Abode, LLC, 459 F.Supp. 2d 310 (D.N.J. 2006); Cataldo v. Moses, et al. No. A-4943-04T3 (Sup. Ct. N.J. – App. Div., May 26, 2006); Carlucci v. The Rugby School, 2007 WL 1827329 (App. Div. 2007); Bardinas, et al. v. Delaney, et al., BER-L-8291-06 (Sup. Ct. N.J. – Law Div., Feb. 8, 2007). Stevens Institute of Technology v. Hine, et al., 2007 WL 2188200 (N.J. Super. A.D.). D&D Associates, Inc. v. Board of Education of North Plainfield, 2007 WL 4554208 (D.N.J.).

2. ***Fault.*** The level of fault, if any, which must be shown depends on the plaintiff's private or public status and the private or public nature of the defendant's statement.

a. **Private Figure Plaintiff/Matter of Public Concern.** In Turf Lawnmower Repair v. Bergen Record Corp., 139 N.J. 392, 655 A.2d 417, 23 Media L. Rep. 1609 (1995), cert. denied, 516 U.S. 1066, 116 S. Ct. 752, 133 L. Ed. 2d 700 (1996), the Supreme Court extensively reviewed the standard of care applied by states in private figure defamation cases, noting that only three, Colorado, Indiana and New Jersey have adopted actual malice. New Jersey had previously held that the actual malice standard would be applied to articles about matters of public health, Dairy Stores, Inc., v. Sentinel Publishing Co., Inc., 104 N.J. 125, 516 A.2d 220, 13 Media L. Rep. 1594 (1986) (bottled water), and a highly regulated industry, Sisler v. Gannett Co., Inc., 104 N.J. 256, 516 A.2d 1083, 13 Media L. Rep. 1577 (1986) (banking). The lower court decision in Turf had ruled that the sale and repair of goods and services generally to the public was a matter of legitimate public interest, justifying the application of the actual malice standard, 269 N.J. Super. 370, 635 A.2d 575, 22 Media L. Rep. 1461 (App. Div. 1994). The Supreme Court retreated from this holding, but affirmed the dismissal on the basis that the article accused the plaintiffs of acts which violated the state's Consumer Fraud Act, and the public interest in deterring violations justified application of the actual malice rule. The Court stated that the activities of businesses generally, including advertising, did not make reporting on them a matter of public interest justifying a higher standard, and the negligence standard would apply. In Rocci v. Ecole Secondaire Macdonald-Cartier, et al., 165 N.J. 149, 755 A. 2D 583 (2000), the court determined there is a strong public interest in the behavior of teachers, especially concerning their conduct with and around their students. Therefore, although plaintiff herein is a private figure, the public concern involved requires a plaintiff to allege and prove pecuniary or reputational harm. The court, however, reserved for a future case the question whether the doctrine of presumed damages should apply to claims made by a private-figure plaintiff when no public interest is implicated. See I.B.8.a. infra. However, in Williams v. Associated Press, A-2840-00T1, 29 Media L. Rep. 2231 (App. Div., July 13, 2001), the Court found that Ms. Williams, a teacher, was a "limited purpose public figure" and therefore had the burden to prove by clear and convincing evidence that defendants published statements about her with actual malice. See I.B.4. infra. Under New Jersey law, there must be a showing of actual malice when nonpublic figure makes defamatory statement regarding matter of public concern. The actual malice standard will apply to statements concerning a business when business is charged with criminal fraud, substantial regulatory violation, or consumer fraud that raises legitimate public concern. Mayflower Transit, LLC v. Prince, 314 F.Supp. 2d 362 (D.N.J. 2004). In Salzano v. North Jersey Media Group, 403 N.J. Super. 403 (App. Div. 2008), the New Jersey Appellate Division held that, while plaintiff was clearly a private figure, because the alleged defamatory statements arose in the context of a bankruptcy matter involving his father's company, which was a business operating in a highly regulated industry and, further, there were potential criminal issues involved, he was deemed to have been embroiled in a public matter to which the actual malice standard applied. In Skoorka v. Kean University, et al., the Appellate Division considered claims filed by a tenured college professor against several defendants, including his employer, Kean University, the State of New Jersey, the Board of Trustees of Kean University, the Kean Federation of Teachers and other defendants alleging that because he is Jewish, objected to racial discrimination against a former colleague and disclosed or objected to other improper conduct, and because he filed a grievance and an Affirmative Action Complaint, he was denied promotion to Associate Professor and was subjected to a hostile work environment, contrary to the New Jersey Law Against Discrimination, the New Jersey Conscientious Employee's Protection Act and the New Jersey and Federal Constitutions. The Appellate Division, relied upon the United States Supreme Court Decision in Connick v. Myers, 461 U.S. 138 (1983) for the appropriate analysis in determining whether speech concerns a matter of public concern, i.e. "when a public employee speaks not as a citizen upon matters of public concern, but instead as an employee upon matters only of personal interest," the Court should not review the wisdom of a personnel decision allegedly taken in retaliation, but that speech is a matter of public concern if it relates to "any matter of political, social or other concern to the community," which must be determined by the content, form and context of a given statement, as revealed by the whole record. In Carlucci v. The Rugby School, Inc., et al., 2007 WL 1827329 (App. Div. 2007), cert. den. 193 N.J. 277 (2007) the Appellate Division considered claims by a former employee that she was fired for complaining about Rugby's procedure for preparing an individualized education program (IEP) for one of Rugby's students. Plaintiff alleged that her termination was discriminatory retaliation in violation of the Conscientious Employee Protection Act (CEPA), as well as asserting a common law claim for wrongful termination and claims for defamation. The Court held that the statements made by the individually named defendant who was the school principal (the statements relating to accusations, among other things, that plaintiff had failed to meet the school's standards, that plaintiff had undermined the principal's authority and had acted in an unethical manner) touched upon matters of public concern and that, as a result, plaintiff was required to show that such statements were made with actual malice.

b. **Private Figure Plaintiff/Matter of Private Concern.** A traditional negligence standard of fault is applicable, which is defined as communicating the false statement while acting negligently in failing to ascertain the truth or falsity of the statement before communicating it. Beck v. Tribert, 312 N.J. Super. 335, 349-350, 711 A.2d 951 (App. Div. 1998), certif. denied, 156 N.J. 424, 719 A.2d 1022 (1998). Fault may also be established by showing that the defendant knows the statement is false and that it defames plaintiff or the defendant acts with reckless disregard of its truth or falsity. Id. (citing Feggans v. Billington, 291 N.J. Super. 382, 390-91, 677 A.2d 771 (App. Div. 1996)(citations omitted)). An actual malice standard will not extend to all consumer investigative reporting and was held not to apply where plaintiff did not charge defendant with substantial fraud or regulatory violation, but rather claimed negligence in moving defendant's property. Plaintiff's moving business was deemed to be an everyday activity, and not an activity which "intrinsically involves a legitimate public interest," thus, negligence standard and not "actual malice" standard applied. Mayflower Transit, LLC v. Prince, 314 F.Supp. 2d 362 (D.N.J. 2004).

c. **Public Figure Plaintiff/Matter of Public Concern** A public figure (official) must prove with convincing clarity that the defamatory statements were published by the defendant with knowledge of their falsity or reckless disregard of whether they were true or false; reckless disregard in this context refers to the publishing of defamatory statements with a high degree of awareness of their probable falsity; reckless conduct is not measured by whether a reasonably prudent man would have published or would have investigated before publishing; defendant must have entertained serious doubts as to the truth of the publication. Lawrence v. Bauer Publishing & Printing Ltd., 89 N.J. 451, 466, 446 A.2d 469, 8 Media L. Rep. 1536 (1982), cert. denied, 459 U.S. 999, 8 Media L. Rep. 2454 (1982); Woods v. Township of Irvington, et a, 2009 N.J.Super. Unpub. LEXIS 2231 (App. Div. August 14, 2009) (Actual malice is standard of proof when public official is involved and requires the plaintiff to show by clear and convincing evidence that the defendants published the alleged defamatory statement with knowledge that it was false or with reckless disregard of whether it was false). The Appellate Division held that a candidate for the Board of Directors of a condominium association is a limited public figure and, therefore, must establish actual malice in order to maintain an action for defamation against a unit owner, who distributes an allegedly defamatory E-mail urging defeat of the candidate. Chandur Gulrajaney v. Stacey Petricha, et al., 381 N.J. Super. 241, 885 A.2d 496 (App. Div. 2005). See also, D&D Associates, Inc. v. Board of Education of North Plainfield, 2007 WL 4554208 (D.N.J.).

In Berkery v. Kinney, et al., 397 N.J. Super. 222, 936 A. 2d 1010 (App. Div. 2007), the Appellate Division considered the applicability of the actual malice standard, and the level of proof required to establish actual malice, in the context of a defamation action brought by a plaintiff who acknowledged having six criminal convictions. Plaintiff's claim arose out of two articles written by the defendant published in the Philadelphia Enquirer, which addressed the plaintiff's attempts to stop the publication of a book authored by another individual, entitled Confessions of a Second Story Man: Junior Kripplebauer and the K & A Gang, which focused on a criminal gang and which named the plaintiff as a member of the gang. The plaintiff alleged, inter alia, that plaintiff "has been a private individual with a right to privacy and not a public figure, limited-purpose public figure, or so-called 'involuntary' limited purpose public figure," that plaintiff had "shunned, rather than courted the press, and that the defendant had falsely accused the plaintiff of being 'a thug, thief, burglar, mob associate, lawbreaker, and murderer, statements that are libelous per se.'" The Appellate Division held that an individual who engages in criminal conduct does not automatically become a public figure for purposes of comment on a limited range of issues relating to his conviction; rather, certain criteria must be met for one to become a limited-purpose public figure: "The Court must consider (1) whether the alleged defamation involves a public controversy, and (2) the nature and extent of plaintiff's involvement in that controversy."

The Berkery Court continued, defining a "public controversy" as "a real dispute, the outcome of which affects the general public or some segment of it." The Court then concluded that an individual's involvement in publicized criminal activities and associations with organized criminal groups qualifies as a public controversy or issue that gives rise to limited-purpose public figure status. The Court also rejected plaintiff's argument that he is not a public figure because he now lives a private lifestyle, holding that once a person becomes a public figure in connection with a particular controversy, that person remains a public figure thereafter for purposes of later commentary or treatment of that controversy. The Court thus concluded that plaintiff clearly qualified as a limited-purpose public figure who must prove actual malice in order to recover in a defamation action and, further, even if he were not a limited-purpose public figure, he is still required to prove actual malice with respect to alleged defamatory statements relating to matters of legitimate public interest.

In Palamara v. Township of Irvington, et al., 2008 WL 516346 (N.J. Super. A.D.), the Appellate Division affirmed the trial court's grant of Summary Judgment on defamation claims asserted by the former Chief of Police who was demoted for insubordination, to Deputy Chief of Police, holding that the trial court, which had concluded that Palamara, admittedly a public figure, had failed to prove the elements of defamation and had further failed to prove evidence of actual malice. The Court also affirmed the rejection of Palamara's claim for intentional infliction of emotional distress because, among other things, he failed to prove physical injury resulting from the emotional stress he says he experienced.

Under New Jersey common law, the standard of liability turns on whether the publication at issue concerns a matter of public interest. Sisler v. Gannett Co., Inc., 104 N.J. 256, 270, 516 A.2d 1083, 13 Media L. Rep. 1577 (1986). In Turf Lawnmower Repair, Inc. v. Bergen Record Corp., 139 N.J. 392, 666 A. 2d 417, 23 Media L. Rep. 1609

(1995), cert. denied, 516 U.S. 1006, 116 S. Ct. 752, 133 L. Ed. 2d 700 (1996), the Supreme Court stated that a business serving the public was subject to the New York Times actual malice rule in an action against a newspaper for its consumer reporting article which alleged violations of the Consumer Fraud Act. In MacKay v. CSK Publishing Co., Inc., 300 N.J. Super. 599, 693 A.2d 546 (App. Div. 1997) the Appellate Division applied the test articulated in Turf for the application of actual malice standard and found that the actual malice standard applied because the allegations published by defendant, if true, would constitute a violation of the Consumer Fraud Act (stating that New Jersey case law has continued to recognize that the actual malice standard applies for private plaintiffs where the allegedly defamatory article relates to a legitimate public concern). In Lynch v. New Jersey Education Association, 161 N.J. 152, 735 A. 2d 1129, 1999 N.J. Lexis 846 (1999) the Court recognized plaintiff was a public figure (a state senator), however, it held that irresponsible political rhetoric is not actionable defamation rising to the level of actual malice. However, the court found the record to be quite different with respect to co-defendant Brendel & Associates and ordered a remand. In Lynch v. Brendel, A-4108-99 T5 (App. Div., April 16, 2001), the court determined that plaintiff provided sufficient evidence to show that a reasonable jury could find by clear and convincing evidence that Brendel caused the campaign material to be published with actual malice. An athletic director for a school district is a public official. Standridge v. Ramey, 323 N.J. Super. 538, 733 A. 2d 1197 (App. Div. 1999). The opinion of an expert on a television program regarding whether a search of an automobile by a police officer was constitutional was not based upon false or incomplete facts, and therefore defamatory, merely because he based his opinion on an edited tape of the search Hornberger v. American Broadcasting Companies, Inc., 351 N.J. Super. 577, 602, 799 A.2d 566, 580 (App. Div. 2002).

In Senna v. Florimont, 2007 WL 1542017 (App. Div. 2007) the appellate court had held that a libel plaintiff who operated boardwalk arcade games was subject to the actual malice standard, because such activities were subject to state licensing and a high degree of regulation. Upon certification to the Appellate Division, the New Jersey Supreme Court issued an opinion on September 22, 2008 reversing the Appellate Division, holding that, based on the content, form and context of the challenged speech, including the identity of the speaker and the intended audience, the speech involved did not touch on matters of public concern, and that the false and defamatory statements of defendants' employees, impugning the honesty of a business competitor, fall into the category of commercial speech not entitled to heightened protection under the actual-malice standard, but, rather, the negligence standard is the appropriate standard of care. In this case, the plaintiff and defendant operated competing Boardwalk arcade games, both regulated by the New Jersey Legalized Games of Chance Control Commission. The Court considered claims by the plaintiff that the defendant's employees had broadcast over a public address system that plaintiff was flimflamming the public, that plaintiff was "dishonest" and a "crook" who "ran away and screwed all of his customers in Seaside" (his former location) by not honoring their prize tickets and that he would cheat his Wildwood customers (his new location). In holding that the actual-malice standard did not apply, that plaintiff was not a public official or public figure and that the speech did not involve matters of public concern, the Court held that the invocation of the term "highly regulated industry" does not give every speaker immunity for his negligent, false and harmful speech and that many businesses are highly regulated. Rather, the critical inquiry in determining whether speech involves a matter of public interest is the content, form and context of the speech and that state law precedents did not support extending the actual-malice standard to the type of commercial speech which was before the Court.

3. ***Falsity.*** In a case decided before Philadelphia Newspapers, Inc. v. Hepps, 475 U.S. 767, 12 Media L. Rep. 1977 (1986), the New Jersey Supreme Court ruled that defendant bears the burden of proof on the defense of truth, which defense applies only if the truth is as broad as the defamatory imputation or sting of the statement. Lawrence v. Bauer Publishing & Printing Ltd., supra. Following Hepps, the New Jersey Supreme Court has held that a private figure plaintiff must prove that the statement made by a media defendant was false or was made with reckless disregard for the truth. Sisler v. Gannett Co., Inc., supra.; Dairy Stores, Inc. v. Sentinel Publishing Co., 104 N.J. 125, 131, 516 A.2d 220, 13 Media L. Rep. 1594 (1986); Durando, et al. v. The Nutley Sun, et al., 2010 N.J. Super Unpub. LEXIS 733 (April 8, 2010); Molin v. The Trentonian, 297 N.J. Super. 153, 687 A.2d 1022 (App. Div. 1997), certif. denied, 152 N.J. 190, 704 A.2d 20 (1997) (the trial judge, in granting summary judgment, concluded that the plaintiff was unable to prove the statements in the articles false). In deciding whether a statement is defamatory, a Court must examine three factors: content, verifiability and context. Dello Russo v. Nagel, 358 N.J. Super. 254, 817 A. 2d 826 (App. Div. 2003).

4. ***Defamatory Statement of Fact.*** A defamatory statement is one that is false and injurious to reputation of another or exposes another person to hatred, contempt, or ridicule or subjects another person to loss of good will and confidence in which he or she is held by others. Higgins v. Pascack Valley Hospital, 307 N.J. Super. 277, 704 A.2d 988, (App. Div. 1998), 158 N.J. 404, 730 A. 2d 327 (1999), affirmed dismissal of defamation claims. The threshold issue in any defamation case is whether the statement at issue is reasonably susceptible of a defamatory meaning. Ward v. Zelikovsky, 136 N.J. 516, 642 A.2d 972 (1994); Decker v. Princeton Packet, 116 N.J. 418, 424, 561 A.2d 1122, 16 Media L. Rep. 2194 (1989). In Williams v. Associated Press, A-2840-00 T1 (App. Div., July 13, 2001), the court noted that due to the racial overtones in the situation, the statements attributable to Williams containing ungrammatical syntax, could allow a reasonable reader to conclude Williams was uneducated or not as qualified a teacher as she claimed to be and therefore the statement

was capable of a defamatory meaning. See I.B.2.a. supra. In Hornberger v. American Broadcasting Companies, Inc., 351 N.J. Super. 577, 598-599, 799 A.2d 566, 578 (App. Div. 2002), although the Court recognized that whether a search of a motor vehicle is constitutional is a legal question, it treated same as a question of fact for the purpose of a defamation claim. A law firm's newspaper advertisement addressed to an eye surgeon's patients who had suffered a "bad result" was held non-defamatory. Dello Russo v. Nagel, 358 N.J. Super. 254, 817 A. 2d 426 (App. Div. 2003). One of an internet service provider's subscribers brought suit against provider for its alleged negligent failure to properly police its network in order to prevent two other subscribers from transmitting allegedly defamatory information about the first in internet chat room, or from transmitting a "punter" computer program to this first subscriber which shut down his computer. The United States District Court for the District of New Jersey granted provider's motion to dismiss. Subscriber appealed. The Court of Appeals held that internet service provider was statutorily immune from liability in tort, for its alleged negligent failure to properly police its network; provider, as a private, for-profit company, was not subject to constitutional free speech guarantees. Green v. America Online (AOL), 318 F. 3d 465 (3rd Cir. 2003). In Singer v. Beach Trading Co., Inc., 379 N.J. Super. 63, 81, 876 A.2d 885 (App. Div. 2005) the court held that incorrectly reporting employment history is not susceptible of any defamatory meaning as a matter of law, when there is no evidence that an employer intended to cast a former employee as a liar or as a person who would deliberately falsify information in a resume to defraud a potential employer. A tenant's defamatory statements about tenant's landlord, made to landlord's concierge, were made to landlord's agent, and not to a third party and therefore were not defamatory. The court further held that statements (about landlord hiring "goons" to harass her and to go through her mail) were not actionable because it was undisputed that the persons to whom the statements were made did not believe them. 30 River Court v. Capograsso, 383 N.J. Super. 470, 892 A.2d 711 (App. Div. 2006). City's disclosure of disciplinary notices to employee's union, even if improper, was not defamatory, under New Jersey law; notices which stated that employee had failed to perform his duties and was repeatedly late or absent were true and thus could not support a claim for defamation. McLaughlin v. City of Atlantic City. 2005 WL 1427498 (C.A.3 N.J. 2005). (Note: This case was not selected for publication in the Federal Reporter and is not precedential). School district did not defame tenured middle school teacher, under New Jersey law, by releasing to media notice that teacher was being suspended and listing charges; many charges were sustained by State Board of Education on appeal, there was no indication of malice, and information regarding dismissals of tenured teachers was public knowledge under New Jersey Right-to-Know Law. N.J.S.A. 47:1A-1 et seq. B Emri v. Evesham Tp. Bd. of Educ., 327 F.Supp. 2d 462 (D.N.J. 2004).

5. ***Of and Concerning Plaintiff.*** Although the statements at issue must be "of and concerning" the complaining party, Gnapinsky v. Goldyn, 23 N.J. 243, 253-254, 128 A.2d 697 (1957), the actual naming of plaintiff is not a necessary element as long as those who read or hear the libel reasonably understand plaintiff to be the person intended. Taj Mahal Travel, Inc. v. Delta Airlines, Inc., 164 F. 3d 186 (3rd Cir. 1998) (holding letter which informed passengers that their ticket had been reported stolen and that it was necessary for airline to retain ticket to assist in ongoing law enforcement investigation, linked plaintiff, travel agency to purported illegality, even though the agency was not named in the letter). Durski v. Chaneles, 175 N.J. Super. 418, 420, 419 A.2d 1134 (App. Div. 1980); Dijkstra v. Westerink, 168 N.J. Super 128, 133, 401 A.2d 1118 (App. Div. 1979), certif. denied, 81 N.J. 329 (1979); Mick v. American Dental Ass'n, 49 N.J. Super. 262, 286, 139 A.2d 570 (App. Div. 1958). Wilson v. Grant, 297 N.J. Super. 128, 687 A.2d 1009 (App. Div. 1996), certif. denied, 149 N.J. 34 (1997), cert. denied, 522 U.S. 139 L. Ed. 2d 76, 118 S. Ct. 591 (1997) (although not calling plaintiff by name, defendant sufficiently identified plaintiff as the person to whom comments were directed). Ditzel v. University of Medicine & Dentistry of NJ, 962 F. Supp. 595 (D.N.J. 1997) (holding that the absence of identifying language in the subject statement compelled the Court to reject plaintiff's claim that it defamed him). In applying this standard, the U.S. District Court for New Jersey held that a handful of individuals who wholly owned and controlled a close corporation could be libeled by a reference to the company name under which they do business. Shop Called East v. KYW Channel 3, 8 Media L. Rep. 1399 (D.N.J. Feb. 8, 1987). Further, the District Court has held that an individual plaintiff could be libeled by the libel of a corporation where the corporation was owned by a very few individuals, the person libeled was the principal of the corporation and was responsible for its major decisions and the corporation bore the name of the individual. Schiavone Constr. Co. v. Time, Inc., 619 F. Supp. 684, 697, 12 Media L. Rep. 1153 (D.N.J. 1985). In Graves v. Ryan, et al., (No. A-4203-93T5, App. Div., April 18, 1995), the Appellate Division held that comments critical of a professional's business activities were "of and concerning" her wholly owned business.

In Foxtons Inc. v. Cirri Germain Realty, et al., 2008 WL 465653 (N.J. Super. A.D.), the Appellate Division affirmed the trial court's dismissal of plaintiff's complaint, which arose from a single letter or flyer drafted and circulated by defendants, a licensed real estate agency and its principal, which was prepared on the agency's letterhead and signed by its principal. The Flyer was entitled "The Misleading 6% vs. 3% Commission Myth" and was addressed to homeowners urging them not to be fooled by advertised 3% commission rates. Plaintiff described itself in its complaint as a full service real estate brokerage that offered the public a "discounted commission rate of 3%," and alleged that defendant's flyer was defamatory and libelous per se. Plaintiff sought damages under the theories of tortious interference with a prospective economic advantage and product disparagement. Defendants argued that the flyer was not defamatory because the statements it contained were merely opinions expressed by a competitor and was privileged speech. Defendants also contended that because the real estate business was highly regulated, plaintiff must plead actual malice in the publication of the flyer and had failed to do so. Defendants further argued that the flyer never mentioned Foxtons by name and that the Complaint must fail as a matter of law because plaintiff could not demonstrate the allegedly defamatory statements were "of and concerning" plaintiff. Lastly, defendants contended that plaintiff failed to plead with the requisite specificity that it actually suffered damages as a result of the flyer's dissemination.

Addressing plaintiff's allegations and defendant's defenses, the Court noted that under New Jersey law, the actual naming of plaintiff is not a necessary element in an action for libel, and that it is enough that there is such reference to the plaintiff that those who read or hear the statement reasonably understand the plaintiff to be the person intended and, that if the defamatory comment fails to mention any specific name but is directed toward a group or class of individuals, a plaintiff may still establish a claim for libel by showing that he is a member of the defamed class and by establishing some reasonable application of the words to himself. The Court found that there were no facts asserted in the Complaint to support plaintiff's broad claims that "reasonable persons of ordinary intelligence who read defendants' libelous writing could only understand that plaintiff was the sole target." The Court affirmed that the test is whether reasonable third parties who read the flyer would surmise it referred to Foxtons. The Court also agreed with the motion judge that the contents of the flyer were not defamatory but, rather, were fair comment by a competitor extolling the virtues of its own services in comparison to those provided by other brokers, referring to the New Jersey Supreme Court holding that "boasts of a competitor concerning the prices of goods and services offered and their value are not defamatory." Printing Mart – Morristown v. Sharp Electronics Corp., et al., 116 N.J. 739 (1989). With respect to plaintiff's claim for tortious interference with prospective economic advantage, the Court noted that the fact that a party acted to advance its own interests and financial position does not establish the necessary malice or wrongful conduct, stating that when a business targets its competitor's customers, it exercises a valid business judgment and that alone does not constitute tortious interference with prospective economic advantage. Rather, a plaintiff must demonstrate that defendant's conduct was not sanctioned by the "rules of the game;" where a plaintiff's loss of business is merely the result of healthy competition, there is no compensable tort injury. Lastly, plaintiff argued that it sufficiently pled a *prima facie* claim for trade libel, but the Court found that even a most liberal reading of plaintiff's complaint demonstrated a complete failure to allege that defendants acted with the common law malice required for the tort.

6. ***Publication.*** Since the law of defamation seeks to secure reputation, there must be a communication to a third person, and without this essential element, neither libel nor slander is shown. Gnapinsky v. Goldyn, 23 N.J. 243, 128 A.2d 697 (1957). Communication is "published" to a third person for purposes of defamation under New Jersey law when it is communicated by way of writing, by way of spoken word or some other act. Bender v. Smith Barney, Harris Upham & Co., Inc., 901 F.Supp. 863 (D.N.J. 1994). While complaining about tenancy issues to the concierge of her apartment building, a tenant made slanderous statements about her landlord. The landlord sued her for defamation. Since the concierge was the landlord's agent and the tenants were invited to make complaints to the concierge, the statements made to the landlord's agent were not actionable in defamation because they were not published to a third party. As an agent, the concierge was a stand-in or conduit for the landlord, and was not a "third party" for purposes of the publication requirement. Appellate Division concluded that this analysis was particularly applicable to customer complaints and was consistent with State law protecting tenants. The Appellate Division also concluded that the statements were not actionable because the concierge did not believe them and, in that context, they had no potential to affect the landlord's reputation. 30 River Court East Urban Renewal Company, et al. v. Eleanor Capograsso, et al., 383 N.J. Super. 470, 892 A.2d 711 (App. Div. 2006).

a. **Intracorporate Communication.** Communications among employees of a corporation is sufficient for publication to have occurred. Lutz v. Royal Ins. Co. of America, 245 N.J. Super. 480, 586 A.2d 278 (App. Div. 1991). (Involved three separate publications among employees and supervisors).

b. **Compelled Self-Publication.** An allegation that a self-publication of the complained of statement to the employer's internal auditor served to toll the statute of limitations as a republication was rejected in Monroe v. Host Marriot Services Corp., 999 F.Supp. 599 (D.N.J. 1998).

c. **Republication.** Generally, the law of defamation in New Jersey provides redress against parties that reprint defamatory statements. Costello v. Ocean County Observer, 136 N.J. 594, 643 A.2d 1012 (1994). Under New Jersey law, one who republishes defamatory matter is generally subject to liability as if he or she had originally published it. Schiavone Const. Co. v. Time, Inc., 735 F.2d 94, on remand 619 F.Supp. 684 (3d. Cir. 1984). The fair report privilege is an exception to the general rule imposing liability for republication of defamatory matter. Fortenbaugh v. New Jersey Press, Inc., 317 N.J. Super. 439, 722 A. 2d 568 (App. Div. 1999). The New Jersey Supreme Court in Salzano v. North Jersey Media Group, 201 N.J. 500 (2010), reaffirmed that the purpose of the "fair report privilege" is to assure that people who report on official releases about public concerns will not be held responsible for the contents of the reports as long as the reporter has verified that the defamatory statement at issue was spoken, and that the substance of the statement is true before republication. However, the Salzano decision reversed the Appellate Court's conclusion that the fair reporting privilege did not apply to publications of preliminary pleadings such as Complaints before judicial action is taken. In so holding, the Court emphasized that it was crucial for the press to be able to report fairly and accurately on every aspect of the administration of justice, including the Complaint and Answer, without fear of having to defend a defamation case and without the inhibitory effect of such fear. Once the fair report privilege has been established the plaintiff must demonstrate by clear and convincing evidence that the defamatory statements were published with actual malice. Ricciardi v. Weber, 350 N.J. Super 453, 471, 795 A.2d 914, 924, 88 Fair Empl. Prac. Cas. (BNA) 1123 (App. Div. 2002). In Gallo v. Princeton University, 281 N.J. Super. 134, 656 A.2d 1267 (App. Div. 1995) certif. denied 42 N.J. 453, 663 A.2d 1159 (1995) statements in student and alumni publications repeating and reporting on university statements about plaintiff, a university employee terminated for misconduct, were held not to be republication attributable to defendant university. The standards and applicability of the "fair report" or "fair comment" privilege and the precedential cases giving rise to this privilege is well summarized in Salzano v. North Jersey Media Group, Inc., et al. 201 N.J. 500 (2010) and Petersen, et al. v. Meggitt, et al., 407 N.J. Super. 63 (App. Div. 2009).

7. ***Statements versus Conduct.*** In Schwartz v. Leasametric, Inc., 224 N.J. Super. 21, 539 A.2d 744 (App. Div. 1988), the court found that an employee's supervisor did not slander the employee by insisting upon searching through the employee's desk, personal belongings, and company car for an accident report kit in front of the employee's co-workers.

8. ***Damages.*** New Jersey courts have recognized the Gertz rule. Krumholz v. TRW, Inc., 142 N.J. Super 80, 83, 360 A.2d 413 (App. Div. 1976). The common law requirement that corporate libel plaintiffs plead and prove pecuniary business injury, Trenton Mut. Life & F. Ins. Co. v. Perrine, 23 N.J.L. 402 (Sup. Ct. 1852) was recognized in Canino v. New York News, Inc., 96 N.J. 189, 195, 475 A.2d 528, 10 Media L. Rep. 1852 (1984). General injury to reputation may be inferred from evidence proving special damages. Sisler v. Gannett Co., Inc., 104 N.J. 256, 516 A.2d 1083, 13 Media L. Rep. 1577 (1986). However, the per se-per quod distinction only applies to slander cases as far as the requirement for special damages is concerned. Arturi v. Tiebie, 73 N.J. Super. 217, 222-223, 179 A.2d 539 (App. Div. 1962). In order to prove damages stemming from slanderous remarks, the harm must result from the conduct of a third person and not from the defamer; emotional distress caused to person slandered by his knowledge that he has been defamed is not special harm even if the distress results in serious illness. Arturi, supra, at 223. Ward v. Zelikovsky, 136 N.J. 516, 541, 643 A.2d 972 (1994). An essential element of a defamation plaintiff's case is that plaintiff was harmed by the alleged defamation. Ricciardi v. Weber, 350 N.J. Super. 453, 795 A.2d 914 (App. Div. 2002). Tarus v. Borough of Pine Hill, 381 N.J. Super 412, 886 A.2d 1056 (App. Div. 2005) certif. granted 186 N.J. 255 (2006), aff'd in part, rev'd in part and remanded, 189 N.J. 498 (2007). Damages that a defamed plaintiff can recover are not damages for pain and suffering. Recovery for defamation exists solely to redress harm to reputation and are not deemed to be damages for pain and suffering. As such, the verbal threshold of the New Jersey Tort Claims Act, N.J.S.A. 59:9-2(d) is inapplicable to a defamation claim. O'Keefe v. State of New Jersey, Department of Labor, et al., 2007 WL 1975603 (N.J. Super. A.D. July 10, 2007). In Kurnik v. The Cooper Health Systems, 2008 WL 2829963 (N.J. Super. A.D.), involving a suit by a cardiologist against defendant hospital for breach of contract and breach of the implied covenant of good faith and fair dealings (plaintiff claiming that he was forced by defendants to step down as the head of its cardiology division in violation of the terms of his contract), the Appellate Division concluded that the trial court had erred in allowing plaintiff to pursue his claim for punitive damages. The Court held that the relationship between an employer and employee is not a fiduciary one, nor is it imbued with any special statutory or public duties, so as to fit with any of the exceptions to the rule that punitive damages are not awarded in contract cases. Indeed, while recognizing that some defamation actions still allow for presumed damages, the Appellate Division of the Superior Court of New Jersey recently commented that there is a general shift toward requiring plaintiffs in all defamation actions to prove actual damages through the production of concrete evidence of pecuniary losses or injury to their reputations. Vitanza v. James, 2010 N.J. Super Unpub. LEXIS 996 (May 6, 2010).

a. **Presumed Damages and Libel Per Se.** Traditionally, statements are defamatory per se when they: (1) charge commission of a crime, (2) impute certain loathsome diseases, (3) affect a person in his business, trade, profession or office or (4) impute unchastity to a woman. MacKay v. CSK Publishing Co., Inc., 300 N.J. Super. 599, 693 A.2d 546 (App. Div. 1997) (charging that a person in the Corvette restoration business had committed acts amounting to consumer fraud was defamatory per se). Arturi v. Tiebie, 73 N.J. Super. 217, 222, 179 A.2d 539 (App. Div. 1962). Geyer v. Faiella, 279 N.J. Super. 386, 652 A.2d 1245 (App. Div. 1995) (charging commission of a crime); Newman v. Delahunty, 293 N.J. Super. 469, 681 A.2d 659 (App. Div. 1996) affirming 293 N.J. Super. 491, 681 A. 2d 671 (Law Div. 1994) (charging a person with corruption and that person had someone "beaten up" is to charge criminal activity and was held to be libel per se). Stating a person has been terminated for cause is not defamatory per se, but it is not, as a matter of law, nondefamatory. Abella v. Barringer Resources, Inc., 60 N.J. Super. 92, 615 A.2d 288 (Ch. Div. 1992). Although statements may be defamatory per se, plaintiff bears a heavier burden in proving that the statements are also slanderous per se. Biondi v. Nassimos, 300 N.J. Super. 148, 692 A.2d 103 (App. Div. 1997) (refusing to expand the four slander per se categories to include statement which suggests that a person has "mob connections," implying that the person is capable of "committing a crime" or has an intention in such regard). The Court held that a genuine issue of fact existed as to whether statements made by an attorney related to a sexual harassment suit, not contained in his client's complaint, constituted slander per se. Ricciardi v. Weber, 350 N.J. Super 453, 478, 795 A.2d 914, 928, 88 Fair Empl. Prac. Case. (BNA) 1123 App. Div. 2002). In W.J.A. v. D.A., 4 A.3d 601 (App. Div. 2010), affirmed 210 N.J. 229, 43 A.3d 1148 (2012), the Appellate Division held that defamatory postings published on the Internet were properly considered libel, and not slander, and that the postings, in which a nephew accused his uncle of sexually molesting him as a child, were the type of defamatory statements for which damages may be presumed.

The jury charge was held erroneous as to presumed damages since "concrete proof" of injury is required by Sisler v. Gannett Co., Inc., 104 N.J. 256, 516 A.2d 1083, 13 Media L. Rep. 1577 (1986) and an impermissible burden on First Amendment rights would occur if otherwise allowed. Vassallo v. Bell, 221 N.J. Super. 347, 534 A.2d 724 (App. Div. 1987). There may be recovery for mitigated costs such as damages for loss of executive's time. Comdyne I, Inc. v. Corbin, 908 F.2d 1142, 1149-50 (3d Cir. 1990). A failure to demonstrate pecuniary or reputational harm, other than a minimal level of emotional distress, defeated the defamation claim. Rocci v. Ecole Secondaire MacDonald-Cartier, 323 N.J. Super. 18, 731 A. 2d 1205 (App. Div. 1999), aff'd on other grounds, 165 N.J. 149, 755 A. 2d 583, (2000). See I.B.2(a), supra.

The New Jersey Supreme Court seemingly confirmed the viability of the presumed damages doctrine but then sharply limited the doctrine, leaving private plaintiffs suing over a matter of non-public concern with only nominal damages (unless they can demonstrate concrete or actual damages). W.J.A. v. D.A., 210 N.J. 229, 43 A.3d 1148 (2012). If a plaintiff does not proffer evidence of actual damage to reputation, he may not recover for compensatory damages, but may survive summary judgment "to obtain nominal damages, thus vindicating his good name." Id. at 233. In so holding, the Court emphasized that private persons face "real risk of harm" given how easy it is to defame others on the Internet and that presumed damages therefore serve a legitimate interest that should remain part of the common law: "Presumed damages vindicate the dignitary and peace-of-mind interest in one's reputation that may be impaired through the misuse of the Internet." Id. at 249.

Prior to the W.J.A. decision, other New Jersey courts had followed a trend away from presumed damages. In Suarez v. Mecca, et al., 2008 WL 2547869 (N.J. Super. A.D.), the Appellate Division considered the claims of the plaintiff who, during the relevant time period, was the Mayor of the Borough of Ridgefield and who appealed from the grant of summary judgment to defendant Mecca who posted a statement on the Ridgefield forum on an Internet website claiming that police officers, a city councilman and the mayor came to his home at 6 a.m., saying that they were investigating an anonymous tip that he had an illegal apartment. In subsequent posts to the forum, defendant asserted that "the facts are correct," but during depositions defendant admitted that the alleged incident had been relayed to him by his attorney and friend, who was then the Ridgefield Municipal Prosecutor, and had not actually occurred either to him or his friend, but that he believed the story was true. Defendant denied that he was ever involved in any "raid" or "home inspection." In affirming the trial court's grant of summary judgment to the defendant, the Appellate Division reiterated that a public official such as plaintiff must show a defendant acted with "actual malice" in order to establish a prima facie case of defamation. The Court then continued to make clear that even were it to agree that defendant was acting in "reckless disregard," and was therefore acting with actual malice, plaintiff must nonetheless prove damages and, in so holding, rejected the applicability of the "doctrine of presumed damages." The Court then reviewed the history of the doctrine of presumed damages, noting that it has eroded over time and that such damages are now limited to claims of slander per se, but the Court concluded that the Internet posting at issue did not fit into any of the four slander per se categories. The Court then continued to note that presumed damages were previously generally available in libel cases, however, the availability of such damages was limited by Sisler v. Gannett Co., Inc., 104 N.J. 256, 281 (1986). In this context, the Court concluded that, regardless of whether the Internet postings are characterized as slander or libel, plaintiff could not avail himself of the "presumed damages" doctrine since the statement did not fit into any slander per se categories and, furthermore, where the allegedly defamatory remarks raise an issue of public concern, as it did in this case involving the public conduct of an elected official, a heightened standard of proof of damages is applied, requiring "substantial evidence" of reputational harm to satisfy the clear and convincing standard, and in order to survive a motion for summary judgment.

(1) **Employment-Related Criticism.** One who falsely and without privilege to do so publishes slander ascribing to another conduct, characteristics or condition incompatible with proper conduct of his lawful business, trade or profession is liable for slander per se. Sokolay v. Edlin, 65 N.J. Super 112, 167 A.2d 211 (App. Div. 1961). However, these statements must be of significance and importance to be actionable. Lutz v. Royal Ins. Co. of America, 245 N.J. Super. 480, 586 A.2d 278 (App. Div. 1991). A statement to parents that the band director falsified his resume and was improperly using a computer program purchased for defendants for his personal financial gain is slander per se as it states a claim for conduct incompatible with his business, trade or office. Kadetsky v. Egg Harbor Tp. Bd. of Educ., 82 F. Supp. 2d 327 (D.N.J. 2000).

(2) **Single Instance Rule.** There are no reported decisions where New Jersey courts have recognized the single instance rule.

b. **Punitive Damages.** The right of private and public figure plaintiffs to recover punitive damages is limited as a matter of New Jersey statutory law to those cases where plaintiff proves either "malice in fact" or defendant's failure to retract after a reasonable request for retraction has been communicated, N.J.S.A. 2A:43-2. Malice in fact under this statute has been equated with reckless disregard for the truth. Burke v. Deiner, 97 N.J. 465, 476-477, 479 A.2d 393 (1984).

II. PRIVILEGES AND DEFENSES

A. Scope of Privileges

1. ***Absolute Privilege.*** Defamatory statements made by participants in the course of and having some relation to judicial proceedings are absolutely privileged. Hawkins v. Harris, 141 N.J. 207, 661 A.2d 284 (1995). The case is a useful survey of the litigation privilege, and held, over a vigorous dissent, that an investigator for a litigant had an absolute privilege for defamatory statements so long as they bore some relation to the nature of the proceedings. See also Neuman v. Shebell, (No. A-3064-95T5) (App. Div. 1996) (a statement made in the course of a judicial proceeding is entitled to an absolute privilege whether or not it is defamatory); Rainier's Dairies v. Raritan Valley Farm, Inc., 19 N.J. 552, 117 A.2d 889 (1955); Lone v. Brown, 199 N.J. Super. 420, 489 A.2d 1192 (App. Div. 1985); Fleming v. UPS, 255 N.J. Super. 108, 604 A.2d 657 (Law Div. 1992). Defamatory statements, when made against a government entity, are absolutely protected under the First and Fourteenth Amendments to the U.S. Constitution, and thus are not actionable, even if admittedly false and malicious. College Savings Bank v. Florida Prepaid Postsecondary Educ. Expense Bd., 919 F. Supp. 756 (D.N.J. 1996). This "absolute litigation privilege" also applies in the context of administrative hearings. Zagami, LLC v. Cottrell, et al., 403 N.J. Super. 98 (App. Div. 2008) (Alleged defamatory statements made by parties in opposition to licensee's application to renew liquor license were protected under absolute litigation privilege as comprehensive regulatory scheme governing liquor license renewal hearings provided licensee sufficient safeguards by way of notice, hearing, neutrality, finality and review to protect licensee from allegedly false and malicious statements, statement were directly relevant to the core issue of the proceeding and the function performed by the issuing authority was quasi-judicial in nature, subject to higher review). See also, Phat Van Le v. Univ. of Med. & Dentistry, 2009 U.S. Dist. LEXIS 37672 (May 4, 2009) (Absolute privilege applied to statements made by students in connection with a student disciplinary hearing). However, while certain statements made in the course of quasi-judicial administrative proceedings are absolutely privileged, J.D. Constr. Corp. v. Isaacs, 51 N.J. 263, 239 A.2d 657 (1968), an appraisal proceeding under an insurance policy is not quasi-judicial for purposes of absolute privilege, Binkewitz v. Allstate Ins. Co., 222 N.J. Super. 501, 537 A.2d 723 (App. Div. 1988). Further, the New Jersey Appellate Division, in Nunez v. Pachman, et al., 2009 N.J. Super Unpub. LEXIS 3160 (November 29, 2009), recently cautioned that the applicability of this absolute privilege turns on a balance between the need for unfettered expression in a judicial, administrative or legislative proceeding and the individual's reputational interests. As such, whether the litigation privilege may attach outside a judicial setting will depend upon the nature of the administrative proceeding, the function performed, and the pertinency of the allegedly defamatory statement to the issues and contentions to be resolved. Statements made in a preliminary investigatory report submitted to the Township Administrator regarding plaintiff's fitness to become a police officer are part of a quasi-judicial proceeding and are absolutely privileged. Pollinger v. Loigman, 256 N.J. Super. 257, 606 A.2d 1113 (App. Div. 1992). The Appellate Division has adopted the Restatement (Second) of Torts, ' 590A (1976) formulation of absolute privilege and added that so long as the defamatory matter would not have been published except to inform the legislative body, and the material is relevant to the legislative proceeding, the privilege attaches regardless of whether the material is solicited or subpoenaed and regardless of whether it is given under oath, DeSantis v. Welfare Ass'n, 237 N.J. Super. 550, 554, 568 A.2d 565 (App. Div. 1990). Further, despite the truth or falsity of allegations in a criminal complaint, such a complaint does not constitute a defamatory statement due to the fact that criminal complaints are absolutely privileged. Pitts v. Newark Board of Education, 337 N.J. Super. 331, 766 A. 2d 1206, 151 Ed. Law Rep. 517 (App. Div. 2001). In, In re Quality Botanical Ingredients, Inc., 249 B.R. 619, 627 (Bankr. D.N.J., June 16, 2000) the Court held that a meeting convened by a U.S. Trustee to appoint an official committee of unsecured creditors in a bankruptcy case is part of a judicial proceeding and that statements made during the course of such a meeting are absolutely privileged. In Pitts v. Newark Board of Education, 337 N.J. Super. 331 (App. Div. 2001), the Court held that a school principal's filing of a criminal complaint against a custodian for criminal trespass based upon the custodian's alleged refusal to leave a school building was absolutely privileged as against custodian's ensuing defamation claim, even if allegations in criminal complaints were false. The court also held that even if the defendant's pronouncement to the police that the plaintiff had committed criminal trespass could be viewed as slander per se, Plaintiff was still required to prove actual damages since the matter involved a matter of public concern, namely, the safety and well-being of school children, and that in such a case, damages will not be presumed but, rather, plaintiff must prove actual damages. The Court also held the defendant principal was entitled to relief from the Judgment because the Judge failed to charge the jury on the qualified immunity under N.J.S.A. 59:3

-8 and that the Judge should have instructed the jury that, as a public employee, defendant could not be found "liable for injury caused by his instituting or prosecuting any judicial or administrative proceeding if he was acting within the scope of his employment," N.J.S.A. 59:3-8, unless he acted with "actual malice." N.J.S.A. 59:3-14. Statements made during settlement negotiations are absolutely privileged Dello Russo v. Nagel, 358 N.J. Super. 254, 817 A.2d 426 (App. Div. 2003). A United States Postal Service (USPS) employee sued his supervisor, the Postmaster General, and the United States, alleging, inter alia, defamation, and negligent hiring and retention. On motions by the Postmaster General and the United States to substitute the United States for the supervisor as defendant, and to dismiss complaint, the District Court, Cooper, J., held that: (1) Supervisor was absolutely immune from defamation claim; (2) Federal Tort Claims Act (FTCA) deprived District Court of subject matter jurisdiction over claims for invasion of privacy and intentional infliction of emotional distress; (3) Postmaster General was immune, under intentional-tort exception of Federal Tort Claims Act (FTCA), from claim of negligent hiring and retention; and (4) supervisor's alleged actions did not constitute retaliatory conduct under New Jersey Conscientious Employee Act (CEPA). Borawski v. Henderson, 265 F. Supp. 2d 475 (D.N.J. 2003). Letters from business rivals to federal regulators accusing party of violation of banking regulations were immune from defamation action on grounds of *Noerr B Pennington* doctrine. Caixa General de Depositor, A.A. CQD v. RodriguezCaixa General de Depositor, A.A. CQD v. Rodriguez, 2005 WL 1541055 (D.N.J. 2005). A pre-litigation demand letter by an attorney was protected by the absolute litigation privilege but extra-judicial statements by an attorney in anticipation of client's press conference were not protected by the absolute litigation privilege, in Williams v. Kenney, 379 N.J. Super. 118, 877 A.2d 277 (App. Div. 2005). In New Jersey, the litigation privilege protects attorneys not only from defamation actions, but also from a host of other tort-related claims. See, e.g., Rainier's Diaries v. Raritan Valley Farms, Inc., 19 N.J. 552, 564, 117 A.2d 889 (1955) ("If the policy, which is defamation actions affords an absolute privilege or immunity to statements made in judicial and quasi-judicial proceedings, is really to mean anything then we must not permit its circumvention by affording an almost equally unrestricted action under a different label."). Loigman v. Tp. Committee of Middletown, 185 N.J. 566, 889 A.2d 426 (2006). The Appellate Division recently reviewed in detail the New Jersey cases addressing the litigation privilege. In Kiernan v. Williams, No. A-0531-04T1, A-0605-04T1 (Sup. Ct. N.J. B App. Div. August 23, 2006), the Appellate Division stated, in part: "The litigation privilege provides complete immunity from liability and an absolute privilege to defamatory statements made in the course of a judicial proceeding, so long as the statement is relevant to the proceeding. *** The court must analyze whether the communication was " '(1) made in judicial or quasi-judicial proceedings; (2) by litigants or other participants authorized by law; (3) to achieve the objects of the litigation; and (5) that have some connection or logical relation to the action.'" Hawkins, supra, 141 N.J. at 216 (quoting Silberg v. Anderson, 786 P.2d 365, 369 (Cal. 1990)). In Hinkle v. United States, 2011 U.S. Dist. LEXIS 73662 (D.N.J. 2011), the United States District Court for the District of New Jersey dismissed a defamation action brought against a federal employee, holding that defamation "is not included in the list of actions for which the United States has waived immunity under the Federal Tort Claims Act." Similarly, in Montana v. Connor, 2011 U.S. Dist. LEXIS 107839 (D.N.J. 2011), the United States District Court for the District of New Jersey dismissed an action brought against a New Jersey Superior Court judge based on his criticism of an attorney's performance, holding that the defendant enjoyed absolute judicial immunity on such claims. A federal government contractor is absolutely immune from defamation liability to an employee because of reports made to the federal government pursuant to a governmentally-imposed duty. Mission1st Group v. Filak, 2010 U.S. Dist. LEXIS 127177 (D.N.J. 2010); Becker v. Philco Corp., 372 F.2d 771 (4th Circ. 1967).

The privilege encourages the search for the truth in the fact finding process by providing the participants with the "absolute freedom to express the truth" as they see it, without fear of recrimination. Id. at 217. The privilege extends beyond those statements made in a courtroom during a trial. Id. at 216. It includes statements made in settlement negotiations and attorney conferences, Dello Russo v. Nagel, 358 N.J. Super. 254, 266-67 (App. Div. 2003); communications by court-appointed psychologists to judges or others in the court system within the context of child custody proceedings, P.T. v. Richard Hall Cmty. Mental Health Care Ctr., 364 N.J. Super. 561, 583-84 (Law Div. 2002), aff'd o.b., 364 N.J. Super. 460 (App. Div. 2003), certif. denied, 180 N.J. 150 (2004); and attorney investigator's statements to third parties made during the course of pretrial discovery, Hawkins, supra, 141 N.J. at 219-21. The privilege extends to witnesses, litigants, their attorneys and representatives, and the attorney's employees. Id. at 214-20. However, the protection extends only "insofar as [the representative or employee] was engaged in a function which would be protected had it been undertaken by an attorney." Id. at 220 (quoting Leavitt v. Bickerton, 855 F. Supp. 455, 458 (D. Mass. 1994)).

The "extraordinary scope" of the privilege requires that it be "limited to situations in which authorities have the power both to discipline persons whose statements exceed the bounds of permissible conduct and to strike such statements from the records." Id. at 220 (quoting Moore v. Smith, 578 P.2d 26, 29 (Wash. 1978)). The privilege does not protect an attorney from professional discipline for unprofessional conduct; nor does it foreclose criminal penalties against the party or witness who commits perjury. Id. at 215. Nor does it insulate a litigant from civil liability for malicious prosecution or other tort-based claims arising from the improper initiation of administrative proceedings. Rainier's Diaries v. Raritan Valley Farms, Inc., 19 N.J. 552, 564-66 (1955).

The potential damage from a privilege that allows the declaration of harmful defamatory statements "is mitigated by the comprehensive control" afforded a trial judge over judicial proceedings and the conduct of the participants. Peterson, supra, 292 N.J. Super. at 588. For the reason, the privilege does not encompass "'statements made in situations for which there are no safeguards against abuse.'" Hawkins, supra, 141 N.J. at 221 (quoting Demopolis v. Peoples Nat'l Bank, 796 P. 2d 426, 430 (Wash. Ct. App. 1990). Distribution to the press of court-filed documents is not protected because it bears no relation to the purpose of the privilege, and only serves the interest of the distributor. Williams v. Kenney, 379 N.J. Super. 118, 135 (App. Div.), certif. denied, 185 N.J. 296 (2005). In Source Entertainment Group v. Baldonado & Associates, P.C., 2007 WL 1580157 (D.N.J. 2007), a federal court rejected a claimed litigation privilege for a letter sent to a third party, holding that the underlying case was inactive and the letter could not be said to be intended to achieve the purpose of the chancery litigation. In Kiernan v. Williams, 2006 WL 2418861, (App. Div. 2006), defendants made statements at a press conference and on a website related to a defendant in a homicide prosecution. A dismissal on the grounds of litigation privilege was reversed on appeal, the court holding that reasonable minds could differ as to whether defendant, through his attorney and his wife, caused republication of the allegedly defamatory statements outside of the courtroom.

In Mitan v. Neumann & Associates, 2010 US. Dist. LEXIS 121568 (D.N.J. 2010), the court held that the federal Communications Decency Act ("CDA") preempted a defamation claim. In this case, the plaintiff charged the defendant with libel, for the act of forwarding an email that the plaintiff claimed defamed him. The court said that because the defendant did not write the offending message, he was not the "information content provider" for the purposes of the CDA, and therefore could not be held liable on any state-law based claim.

2. ***Qualified Privileges.*** A person who makes a defamatory statement will not be subject to liability if a qualified, or conditional, privilege attaches. Coleman v. Newark Morning Ledger Co., 29 N.J. 357, 373, 149 A.2d 193 (1959). New Jersey recognizes several such privileges. As discussed infra, one such qualified privilege involves a "common interest" privilege, which is defined as "a communication made bona fide upon any subject matter in which the party communicating has an interest, or in reference to which he has a duty, is made to a person having a corresponding interest or duty, although it contains incriminatory matter which, without this privilege, would be slanderous and actionable." Professional Recovery Services, Inc. v. General Electric Capital Corporation, et al., 2009 U.S. Dist. LEXIS 50561 (June 16, 2009), quoting Williams v. Bell Tel. Lab., Inc., 132 N.J. 109 (1993). This common law privilege "arises out of a legitimate and reasonable need, in particular situations, for private people to be able freely to express private concerns to a limited and correlatively concerned audience, whether or not those concerns also touch upon the public interest in a broad sense." Id., quoting Bainhauer v. Manoukian, 215 N.J. Super. 9 (App. Div. 1987). The qualified privilege is abused where: (1) the publisher knows the statement is false or the publisher acts in reckless disregard of its truth or falsity; (2) the publication serves a purpose contrary to the interests of the qualified privilege; or (3) the statement is excessively published. Professional Recovery Services, Inc. v. General Electric Capital Corporation, et al., infra. Statements afforded qualified privilege further include statements made by nonconstitutional public officers arising from the exercise of administrative discretion, Hopkins v. City of Gloucester, 358 N.J. Super. 271, 817 A. 2d 436 (App. Div. 2003); statements by employees in report to supervisor reporting actual or suspected misconduct of co-employees Feggans v. Billington, 291 N.J. Super. 382, 677 A. 2d 771 (App. Div. 1996); persons who prepared company memorandum critical of employee, Monroe v. Host Marriot Services Corp., 999 F. Supp. 599 (D.N.J. 1998); performance evaluation of employee, Kennedy v. Chubb Group of Insurance Companies, 60 F. Supp. 2d 384 (D.N.J. 1999); statements by university officials to university community concerning investigation into misconduct in university department, Gallo v. Princeton University, 281 N.J. Super. 134, 656 A. 2d 1267 (App. Div. 1995), certif. denied, 142 N.J. 453, 663 A. 2d 1359 (1995); former employer's response to prospective employer of a discharged employee, Erickson v. Marsh & McLennan Co. Inc., 117 N.J. 539, 569 A. 2d 793 (1989); statements by hospital personnel to other hospital personnel concerning nurse's alleged substance abuse, Govito v. West Jersey Health System, Inc., 332 N.J. Super. 293, 753 A. 2d 716 (App. Div. 2000). Kass v. Great Coastal Express, Inc., 291 N.J. Super. 10, 676 A.2d 1099 (App. Div. 1996), aff'd in part, 152 N.J. 353, 706 A.2d 1293 (1998); report by an employee of abuse by another employee on a resident of a state facility for the developmentally disabled in any civil or criminal proceedings arising from the report, Fees v. Trow, 105 N.J. 330, 521 A.2d 824 (1987); statements by doctors and other medical personnel to hospital officials about another doctor's alleged incompetence if made to protect patients, Bainhauer v. Manoukian, 215 N.J. Super. 9, 520 A.2d 1154 (App. Div. 1987); statements by hospital personnel to other hospital personnel concerning nurse's alleged substance abuse, Govito v. West Jersey Health System, Inc. 332 N.J. Super. 293, 753 A.2d 716 (App. Div. 2000); communications by state officials with the media pertaining to matters within the scope of their responsibilities, Molnar v. Star Ledger, 193 N.J. Super. 12, 471 A.2d 1209, 10 Media L. Rep. 1823 (App. Div. 1984); statements by regional church officials regarding the management of a local church's finances, Augustave v. Cheatham, 2011 N.J. Super. Unpub. LEXIS 1304 (App. Div. 2011). In Sisler v. Gannett Co., Inc., 104 N.J. 256, 516 A.2d 1083, 13 Med. L.Rep. 1577 (1986), the court held that the common law fair comment privilege was applicable to the plaintiff's transactions with the bank he founded and formerly led in view of the bank's status in a highly regulated industry. The existence or absence of a qualified privilege in a defamation action is a question of law for the Court to decide. Tai v. Crown View Manor I Condominium Association, et al., 2008 WL 2696704 (N.J. Super. A.D.)

In Turf Lawnmower Repair v. Bergen Record Corp., 139 N.J. 392, 655 A. 2d. 417, 23 Med L.Rep. 1609 (1995), cert. denied, 516 U.S. 1066 (1996), the court rejected a lower court holding that criticism of activities of persons selling to the public were generally privileged, but held that the fair comment privilege applied to the articles because they accused plaintiffs of activities which would be violations of the state's Consumer Fraud Act. In Abdul Saquar v. Townley Sweeping Service, Inc., No. A-5014-03T1 (App. Div. May 16, 2005), the court found that the employer's communication of an employee's theft to The Division of Unemployment Insurance and to co-workers was protected by a qualified privilege, but ultimately held that the employee met his burden of proving the qualified privilege was overcome. Campaign statements made to prospective voters by a candidate for election to a condominium board are entitled to a conditional or qualified common law privilege, Gulrajaney v. Petricha, 381 N.J. Super. 241, 885 A.2d 496 (App. Div. 2005). Under New Jersey law, statements by attorney to press reporting on filing of allegedly defamatory complaint are protected by qualified privilege except on proof of malice. Arista Records, Inc. v. Flea World, Inc., 356 F.Supp. 2d 411 (D.N.J. 2005).

A qualified privilege may be abused if the defendant knows the statement is false or acts in reckless disregard of its truth or falsity, if publication serves a purpose contrary to the interest sought to be promoted by the privilege, or if the statement is excessively published. Reckless disregard as to truth or falsity exists when there is a high degree of awareness of probable falsity or serious doubt as to the truth of a statement. The question of abuse is for the fact-finder and must be proven by clear and convincing evidence. Cataldo v. Moses, et al. No. A-4943-04T3 (Sup. Ct. N.J. – App. Div. May 26, 2006). In Berrios v. PNC Bank, 2006 WL 2933899 (N.J. Super. A.D. 2006) the Appellate Division considered several claims, including tortious interference with prospective economic relations and defamation, asserted against defendant PNC Bank by a plaintiff who was employed as a security officer with a company which had contracted with PNC Bank to provide security services. Plaintiff's claims resulted from a report received by a PNC security analyst of unauthorized attempts to access a restricted computer location in the Bank, and resulted in PNC reporting the unauthorized computer access attempts to plaintiff's employer, with a request that the employer conduct an investigation. As a result of the investigation, plaintiff was removed from his assignment at PNC and transferred to new assignments with similar responsibilities and the same pay. Plaintiff rejected the new assignments, complaining that they were not "supervisory," and would be geographically inconvenient. In this context, the Court reviewed and reaffirmed the elements of a defamation claim and also considered whether PNC had abused its qualified privilege when it communicated to plaintiff's employer its suspicions about plaintiff's involvement in the alleged unauthorized computer access attempts, without carrying out a thorough investigation itself. The Court held that the plaintiff bears the burden of showing by clear and convincing evidence that defendant abused its discretion, and ruled that it could not conclude that PNC reported the incident to the plaintiff's employer with a reckless disregard for the truth since PNC was charged with the responsibility of safeguarding its client's sensitive and confidential information. The Court also held that there was nothing in the record to support a finding of excessive publication by PNC in reporting the incident. Summary judgment to defendant PNC was, therefore, affirmed.

In Gaglione v. New Community Corporation, 2007 WL 2141429 (N.J. Super. A.D. July 27, 2007), the Appellate Division considered an appeal filed by a former employee of defendant (a restaurant) whose employment had been terminated and which resulted in the assertion of several claims against defendant, including alleged violations of the Conscientious Employee Protection Act, N.J.S.A. 34:19-1 et seq.; of certain provisions of the New Jersey Worker's Compensation Act relating to the unlawful discharge of an employee claiming worker's compensation benefits; and defamation claims. The defamation claims were based upon an allegation that the plaintiff, who had applied for unemployment compensation benefits, had been defamed by virtue of a memorandum submitted by his former employer to another company which was acting as defendant's intermediary in preparing a defense to plaintiff's unemployment compensation claim. Plaintiff asserted that certain of the statements in the memo submitted by his former employer to that company, including statements that he drank alcohol on the job, that he had sexual relations at the restaurant after hours and that he took food and beverage from the restaurant for his personal use, were defamatory. The trial court dismissed all of plaintiff's claims on Motion for Summary Judgment and the dismissal was upheld by the Appellate Division, the Appellate Division holding that the trial Court had correctly determined that the statements, if false, were susceptible to defamatory meaning, but that defendant was entitled to a qualified special-interest privilege and that no reasonable fact-finder could find that plaintiff had demonstrated by clear and convincing evidence that defendant had abused the privilege. The Appellate Division held that the qualified privilege is based on the public policy that it is essential that true information be given whenever it is reasonably necessary for the protection of one's own interests, the interests of third persons, or certain interests of the public, and that a defendant abuses the privilege if he knows the statement is false or acts in reckless disregard of the truth or falsity, if publication serves a purpose contrary to the interest sought to be promoted by the privilege, or if the statement is excessively published. The Court held that an abuse of a qualified privilege must be proven by clear and convincing evidence and that such a determination is not exclusively reserved for a jury. The Court concluded that the plaintiff failed to demonstrate that the comments in the employer's memo were made in reckless disregard of their truth or falsity or under any other circumstances that would defeat the privilege and that, as a result, summary judgment was appropriate.

In Tai v. Crown View Manor I Condominium Ass'n, 2008 WL 2696704 (N.J. Super. A.D.), the Appellate Division affirmed the trial court's grant of Summary Judgment to the defendants with respect to plaintiff's claims of defamation arising out of a letter written to plaintiffs, long time owners and residents of a condominium development administered and managed by defendant Association. In the letter the Association's property manager notified plaintiff that he had been observed taking certain personal property from the lobby of the condominium building and demanded reimbursement. A copy of the property manager's letter was furnished to the Association's five board members, its attorney and to the managing agent of the property management company. Plaintiff filed suit asserting, among other claims, defamation and infliction of emotional distress. Plaintiff argued that the letter in question was not protected by a qualified privilege and that he was not a limited purpose public figure. The trial court, as well as the Appellate Division, concluded that the circumstances surrounding the publication of the letter rendered that letter qualifiedly privileged since it was written in connection with a common interest, namely, protecting the condominium's assets, and was sent only to those persons with a corresponding interest and duty to protect its property: board members, the Association's attorney, and one of the owners of the property management company. The Court also found that plaintiff had appeared at a regularly scheduled board meeting and distributed the letter to others. The Appellate Division thus concluded that the trial court did not err in dismissing plaintiffs' defamation claim and related claims of "legal malice," "failure to retract," "breach of duty to investigate," "outrage and/or infliction of emotional harm," also declining to address whether plaintiff was a limited purpose public figure because applicability of a qualified privilege is not dependent upon a finding that a plaintiff is a public figure.

a. **Common Interest.** A communication made bona fide upon any subject matter in which the party communicating has an interest is privileged if made to a person having a corresponding interest although it contains incriminating matter which, without such privilege, would be defamatory. Coleman v. Newark Morning Ledger Co., 29 N.J. 357, 375, 149 A.2d 193 (1959). New Jersey courts have extended this privilege to statements made by employees in furtherance of the common interests of the employer. Sokolay v. Edlin, 65 N.J. Super. 112, 125, 167 A.2d 211 (App. Div. 1961). For example, statements by employees in a petition to a supervisor reporting actual or suspected misconduct of a co-employee was found to be privileged. Feggans v. Billington, 291 N.J. Super 382, 677 A.2d 771 (App. Div. 1996). In Griffin v. Tops Appliance City, 337 N.J. Super. 15, 766 A. 2d 292, 2001 WL 62797 (App. Div. 2001), a qualified privilege was established when the employer told co-employees the reasons for plaintiff's termination. The defendants demonstrated a legitimate business purpose for the communications and there was no abuse of the privilege proven. See IV. B.2. infra.

b. **Duty.** A statement is not defamatory when the person who makes the communication has a moral duty to make it to a person who has an interest in hearing it, and both such conditions must exist in order that the statement may be privileged. Coleman v. Newark Morning Ledger Co., supra. A privilege exists with respect to an allegedly defamatory statement when legitimate public or private interests underlying the publication outweighs the interests of the individual. Abella v. Barringer Resources, Inc., 260 N.J. Super. 92, 615 A.2d 288 (Ch. Div. 1992).

c. **Criticism of Public Employee.** A police officer was held to be a public official subject to the actual malice standard in a suit by him against a critic of his official activities. DeAngelis v. Hill, 180 N.J. 1, 847 A.2d 1261 (2004). Nonelective government employees can be "public figures" for defamation purposes. Costello v. Ocean County Observer, 136 N.J. 594, 643 A.2d 1012 (1994). While not every public employee is a "public official" for defamation purposes, public officials are not limited to the upper echelons of government. Vassallo v. Bell, 221 N.J. Super. 347, 534 A.2d 724 (App. Div 1987). In Hogan v. Township of Haddon, et al., 2008 WL 647788 (C.A. 3 (N.J.)), the Third Circuit Court of Appeals considered a Complaint filed by a Township Commissioner which alleged violations of her constitutional rights, stemming from her attempts to publish articles in a Township Publication, and to post information on the Township's website or cable channel. The Court of Appeals affirmed the District Court, which had granted the Township's Motion for Summary Judgment, holding that the Commissioner did not have a First Amendment Right to publish articles in the Township Publication or to post on the Township's website and cable channel, and that there was no evidence that Township employees responded with retaliation to the Commissioner's public criticism of the employees.

d. **Limitation on Qualified Privileges.** The qualified privilege a statement enjoys from a possible defamation action is overcome on a showing of actual malice. Erickson v. Marsh & McLennan Co., 117 N.J. 539, 569 A.2d 793 (1990); Leang v. Jersey City Board of Ed., et al., 198 N.J. 557 (2009) (if Plaintiff can demonstrate existence of actual malice, immunity protection is inapplicable); Professional Recovery Services, Inc. v. General Electric Capital Corporation, et al., 2009 U.S. Dist. LEXIS 50561 (June 16, 2009). Abuse of a qualified privilege results in liability for defamation. Williams v. Bell Telephone Laboratories Inc., 132 N.J. 109, 623 A.2d 234 (1993). Qualified privilege is abused if the publisher knows the statement is false or if the publisher acts in reckless disregard of its truth or falsity, publication serves a purpose contrary to the interests of the qualified privilege, or a statement is excessively published. See id. In Kadetsky v. Egg Harbor Tp. Bd. of Educ., 82 F. Supp. 2d 327 (D.N.J. 2000), the court found there were sufficient allegations of abuse of the privilege where statements of the defendants were made maliciously and with knowledge of falsity or with serious doubt as to truth.

(1) **Constitutional or Actual Malice.** "Reckless disregard" for the truth, the constitutional standard for actual malice, means that the defendant "entertained serious doubts as to [the] truth of the

publication" or "had a high degree of awareness of [its] probable falsity." Harte-Hanks Communications v. Connaughton, 491 U.S. 657, 105 L. Ed 2d 562, 109 S. Ct. 2678 (1989). A conditional privilege is not abused by the mere existence in the mind of the publisher of the motive of unjustified indignation against the plaintiff. Trautwein v. Harbourt, 40 N.J. Super. 247, 123 A.2d 30, 59 A.L.R.2d 1274 (App. Div. 1956). Ricciardi v. Weber, 350 N.J. Super. 453, 795 A.2d 914 (App. Div. 2002) provides a useful survey of law of fair report, actual malice and slander. In the case, an attorney was sued for statements he made about a sexual harassment suit he had filed for a client. The court held that some statements were outside the fair report privilege and others raised triable issues of actual malice which would overcome the privilege. The Court also held the complained-of-statements stated a claim for slander per se. Public officers are cloaked with general discretionary immunity in the performance of their duties. Burke v. Deiner, 97 N.J. 465, 470, 479 A. 2d 393 (1984). "[I]n defamation actions against non-constitutional public officers arising from the exercise of administrative discretion, immunity will not be lost unless the defamation is made with actual malice in the New York Times v. Sullivan sense: 'with knowledge that it was false or with reckless disregard of whether it was fall or not.'" Id. at 475, 479 A. 2d 393 (quoting New York Times v. Sullivan, 376 U.S. 254, 279-80, 84 S. Ct. 710, 725-26, 11 L. Ed. 2d 686, 706 (1964)). Hopkins v. City of Gloucester, 358 N.J. Super. 271, 817 A. 2d 436 (App. Div. 2003).

(2) **Common Law Malice.** The New Jersey Supreme Court has rejected the common-law malice standard in favor of the New York Times malice standard. Burke v. Deiner, 97 N.J. 465, 623 A.2d 393 (1984).

e. **Question of Fact or Law.** Whether a privilege exists is a question for the judge. Lutz v. Royal Ins. Co. of America, 245 N.J. Super 480, 586 A.2d 278 (App. Div. 1991); Geyer v. Faiella, 279 N.J. Super. 386, 652 A.2d 1245 (App. Div. 1995). Whether allegedly defamatory statement is one of fact or opinion is question of law to be determined by court. Arista Records, Inc. v. Flea World, Inc., 356 F.Supp. 2d 411 (D.N.J. 2005). Kiernan v. Williams, No. A-0531-04T1, A-0605-04T1 (Sup. Ct. N.J. B App. Div. August 23, 2006)

f. **Burden of Proof.** The defendant has the burden of proof of showing entitlement to a privilege. Feggans v. Billington, 291 N.J. Super. 382, 677 A.2d 771 (App. Div. 1996); see also Bainhauer v. Manoukian, 215 N.J. Super. 9, 34, 520 A.2d 1154 (App. Div. 1987). Once a defendant proves his entitlement to a conditional or qualified privilege, the burden of proof shifts to plaintiff to establish defeasance by way of abuse, by clear and convincing evidence. Williams v. Bell Tel. Lab., Inc., 132 N.J. 109, 121, 623 A.2d 234 (1993); see also Feggans v. Billington, supra; Bainhauer v. Manoukian, 215 N.J. Super 9, 42, 520 A.2d 1154 (App. Div. 1987); Gomez v. Murdoch, 193 N.J. Super. 595, 475 A.2d 622 (App. Div. 1989); Mick v. American Dental Ass'n, 49 N.J. Super. 262, 139 A.2d 570 (App. Div. 1958). Gray v. Press Communications, L.L.C., 342 N.J. Super. 1, 775 A. 2d 678 (App. Div. 2001) certif. denied 170 N.J. 390, 788 A. 2d 774 (2001); Hopkins v. City of Gloucester, 358 N.J. Super. 271, 817 A. 2d 436 (App. Div. 2003), Dello Russo v. Nagel, 358 N.J. Super. 254, 817 A. 2d 426 (App. Div. 2003). In Abdul Saquar v. Townley Sweeping Service, Inc., No. A-5014-03T1 (Sup. Ct. N.J. B App. Div. May 16, 2005), the Appellate Division agreed that the employer's communication of an alleged theft by the employee to The Division of Unemployment Insurance and to co-workers was protected by a qualified privilege. However, the Appellate Division reversed the entry of Summary judgment in favor of the employer. The Appellate Division found that the employee should be given the benefit of all favorable inferences on summary judgment and had presented sufficient proofs to overcome the qualified privilege in two respects: (1) the employer acted with malice (an issue which does not lend itself to summary judgment); and (2) the employer sought to serve a purpose contrary to the interest of the qualified privilege, namely to deter employees from unionizing. The Appellate Division ordered a full trial on these issues.

In the context of a media defendant in a non-employment case, the N.J. Supreme Court has held that a plaintiffs' case may proceed past the summary judgment stage only where, in reviewing the record in the light most favorable to plaintiffs, the media defendant's "professions" of mistake "are unworthy of belief." Durando v. The Nutley Sun, 209 N.J. 235, 257, 37 A.3d 449, 462 (2012) (see also the dissenting opinion, which was critical of the majority's interpretation of the summary judgment standard and argued that credibility concerns existed such that the case should have been submitted to a jury).

B. Standard Libel Defenses

1. ***Truth***. Establishment of truth exonerates the publisher of a defamatory statement of fact. Lawrence v. Bauer Publishing & Printing Ltd., 89 N.J. 451, 460, 446 A.2d 469, 8 Media L. Rep. 1536 (1982), cert. denied, 459 U.S. 999, 8 Media L. Rep. 2454 (1982). Truth is always a defense in libel cases. MacKay v. CSK Publishing Co., Inc., 300 N.J. Super. 599, 693 A.2d 546 (App. Div. 1997); see also Van Englen v. Broadcast News Networks, Inc., 25 Media L. Rep. 1693 (D.N.J. 1997). Ditzel v. UMDNJ, 962 F. Supp. 595 (D.N.J. 1997) (liability for defamation cannot be imposed unless the defendant's statements of fact are false; thus, truth is an absolute defense to defamation); Protasiewicz v. Chemical Bank of N.J., (No. A-5436-95T1) (App. Div. 1996). Substantial truth is a well-established defense in New Jersey to a defamation action. Leers v. Greer, 24 N.J. 239, 257, 131 A.2d 781 (1957); Herrmann v. Newark Morning Ledger Co., 48 N.J. Super. 420, 431-32, 138 A.2d 61 (App. Div. 1958); **G.D. v. Bernard Kenny and The Hudson County Democratic**

Organization, Inc., 205 N.J. 275, 15 A.3d 300 (2011). Fortenbaugh v. New Jersey Press, 317 N.J. Super. 439, 722 A. 2d 568 (App. Div. 1999) is the first case in New Jersey holding that a defendant who publishes a defamatory statement made by a third party regarding the plaintiff, may not escape liability simply by demonstrating that it was true that the third party made the statement, but must show the underlying statement was true. This holding relies on dicta in Lawrence v. Bauer Pub. & Print, Ltd., 89 N.J. 451, 446 A. 2d 469, cert. den. 459 U.S. 99, 103 S. Ct. 357, 74 L. Ed. 2d 395 (1982). A professional athlete's claim of defamation by implication failed where the published statement comparing his criminal proceeding to another professional athlete's was truthful and did not imply that he was guilty of crimes of which he was acquitted. Montefusco v. ESPN, Inc., No. 01-3276, 2002 WL 31108927 (3rd Cir. Sept. 20, 2002). Truth is complete defense to a charge of defamation Arista Records, Inc. v. Flea World, Inc. 356 F.Supp. 2d 411 (D.N.J. 2005). In G.D. v. Bernard Kenny and The Hudson County Democratic Organization, Inc., 205 N.J. 275, 15 A.3d 300 (2011), the New Jersey Supreme Court held that expungement of a criminal conviction does not make the fact of the conviction any less true for the purpose of defending a defamation claim on grounds of truth, and that courts may give defendants in defamation cases access to expunged records for the purpose of establishing the truth of their assertions.

2. ***Opinion.*** The New Jersey Supreme Court held in Kotlikoff v. The Community News, 89 N.J. 62, 68, 444 A.2d 1086 Media L. Rep. 1549 (1982) that the common law "fair comment" privilege, as reflected in Section 566 of the Restatement (Second) of Torts (1977), has, after Gertz v. Welch, 418 U.S. 323, 94 S. Ct. 2997, 41 L. Ed. 2d 789 (1974), become obsolete insofar as its application is confined to mere expression of opinion. The New Jersey Supreme Court in Ward v. Zelikovsky, 136 N.J. 516, 643 A.2d 972 (1994) said that opinion statements which do not imply specific statements of fact are nondefamatory because they reflect the speaker's state of mind and are generally not capable of proof of truth or falsity. In Dairy Stores, Inc. v. Sentinel Pub. Co., 104 N.J. 125, 147, 516 A.2d 220, 13 Media L. Rep. 1594 (1986), the New Jersey Supreme Court held that "fair comment" should extend beyond opinion to statements of fact. Unlike false statements of fact, statements of opinion are not actionable unless they imply defamatory facts on which the declarent bases his statement. Karnell v. Campbell, 206 N.J. Super. 81, 89, 501 A.2d 1029, 12 Media L. Rep. 1703 (App. Div. 1985); Higgins v. Pascack Valley Hospital, 307 N.J. Super. 277, 704 A.2d 988 (App. Div. 1998); 158 N.J. 404, 730 A. 2d 327 (1999), affirmed dismissal of defamation claims. New Jersey decisions have reiterated the Kotlikoff standard, as a matter of state law, post Milkovich v. Lorain Journal Co., 497 U.S. 1, 110 S.Ct. 2695, 111 L.Ed.2d 1 (1990)(wherein the United States Supreme Court held that the First Amendment did not require a separate privilege for "opinion"). See Lutz v. Royal Ins. Co. Of Am., 245 N.J. Super. 480, 494-95, 586 A.2d 278 (1991); Cassidy v. Merin, 244 N.J. Super 466, 480-83, 582 A.2d 1039 (App. Div. 1990). Milkovich was discussed in Ward to the effect that opinion is defamatory only if it implies underlying facts which are in fact false or untrue. A statement by a Mayor about a borough resident at a public meeting, to the effect that "If he was a decent resident, we would have no problem", was held not to be defamatory, but rather clearly opinion, Tarus v. Borough of Pine Hill, 381 N.J. Super. 412, 886 A.2d 1056 (App. Div. 2005) certif.. granted 186 N.J. 255 (2006), aff'd in part, rev'd in part and remanded, 189 N.J. 497 (2007). An assessment of the adequacy of a person's (a physician's) skill level is necessarily a subjective opinion. Zheng v. Quest Diagnostics, 2006 WL 1993423 (D.N.J. 2006). Statements that are no more than rhetorical hyperbole or vigorous epithet are not defamatory. Arista Records, Inc. v. Flea World, Inc., 356 F.Supp. 2d 411 (D.N.J. 2005). However, a defamatory communication may consist of a statement in the form of an opinion, but a statement of this nature is actionable only if it implies the allegation of undisclosed defamatory facts as the basis for the opinion, and holding that characterizing a statement as an opinion does not trigger a "wholesale defamation exemption," citing Milkovich v. Lorain Journal Co., 497 U.S. 1, 18, 110 S.Ct. 2695, 2705, 111 L. Ed. 2d 1, 17 (1990). Levins v. Braccia, 2009 N.J. Super. Unpub. LEXIS 1473 (App. Div. March 24, 2009).

3. ***Consent.*** When publication of defamatory matter has been invited, instigated or procured by the one defamed, or by someone acting in his behalf, he generally cannot be heard to complain of the resulting injury, particularly when it was elicited for the purposes of predicating the action thereon. Mick v. American Dental Ass'n, 49 N.J. Super. 262, 139 A.2d 570 (App. Div. 1958). However, if the plaintiff, or someone at his request, made the inquiry which elicited the allegedly defamatory statement, action for libel in not barred provided the inquiry was made in good faith so as to ascertain whether the defamatory charges had been made against the plaintiff or perhaps to seek a clarification of an ambiguous remark. Id.

4. ***Mitigation.*** A defendant, in an action for libel, is entitled to plead in mitigation of damages his honest belief in the truth of the publication complained of. Schwartz Bros. Co. v. Evening News Pub. Co., 84 N.J.L. 486, 87 A. 148 (Sup. 1913).

III. RECURRING FACT PATTERNS

A. Statements in Personnel File

See the discussion under Performance Evaluations, infra.

B. Performance Evaluations

In Kennedy v. Chubb Group of Insurance Companies, 60 F. Supp. 2d 384 (D.N.J. 1999), it was not entirely clear if the statements contained in the performance evaluations were statements of fact or opinion, for only statements of fact are actionable in New Jersey. However, the Court went on to assume "arguendo" that they were statements of a factual nature and therefore shielded by a qualified privilege in this context. In Samodovitz v. Borough of New Providence, 2007 WL 1217359 (D. N.J. 2007) the United States District Court for the District of New Jersey considered plaintiff's claim that his employer, defendant Borough of New Providence, had defamed him through the denial of salary increases, false and biased evaluations and threats of firing and harassment. Plaintiff claimed that his professional reputation was damaged as a result. The court held that plaintiff could not meet his burden of establishing defamation through clear and convincing evidence and also held that defendant's actions, in denying plaintiff a salary increase and allegedly harassing and threatening to fire plaintiff, are not "statements." The Court also held that plaintiff had not provided the Court with any evidence that the statements in plaintiff's performance evaluation were false, but rather simply contained expressions of opinion. The Court also held that plaintiff did not demonstrate that any of his written evaluations were communicated to third parties. As a result, summary judgment on the defamation claims was granted to the defendant.

C. References

An employer's statements concerning an employee to another employer are protected by a qualified privilege. "[A] qualified privilege extends to an employer who responds in good faith to the specific inquiries of a third party regarding the qualifications of an employee." Erickson v. Marsh & McLennan Co., 117 N.J. 539, 562, 569 A.2d 793, 805 (1990).Even if such a statements is defamatory, it will not be actionable. Id. at 563,569 A.2d at 805. However, the privilege may be defeated by showing that the employer acted negligently in failing to ascertain the truth or falsity of reference information. Kass v. Great Coastal Express, Inc., 152 N.J. 353, 704 A. 2d 1293 (1998). New Jersey, along with many states, has not determined whether an employer has an affirmative duty to respond to a reference inquiry. See Kiren Dosanjh, Annotation, Former Employer's or Supervisor's Tort Liability to Prospective Employer or Third Person for Misrepresentation or Nondisclosure in Employment Reference, 68 A.L.R. 5th 1 (1994). However, employers who choose to respond to a reference inquiry may be held liable for negligent misrepresentation based on misleading or incomplete statements made in employment references. Id.

Health care entities are also afforded additional protections under the Health Care Professional Responsibility and Reporting Enhancement Act, N.J.S.A. 26:2H-12.2c, L. 2005, c. 83 (codified at N.J.S.A. 26:2H:12.2a to -12.2d, with amendments to other statutory provisions), which, among other things: (1) "prohibits health care entities from withholding certain information about current or former employees from other health care entities that request that information"; and (2) "provides immunity from civil liability if a health care entity or other person complies with its provisions." Senisch v. Carlino, 423 N.J. Super. 269, 279-80 (App. Div. 2011) (former employer's truthful reporting of the circumstances of plaintiff's termination protected under both qualified privilege and the Health Care Professional Responsibility and Reporting Enhancement Act).

D. Intracorporate Communication

The general theory of qualified privilege applies to intracorporate communications. In Bainhauer v. Manoukian, 215 N.J. Super. 9, 520 A.2d 1154 (App. Div. 1987), which considered whether a qualified privilege extended to a surgeon for statements made to various hospital executives concerning the responsibility of an anesthesiologist for the death of a patient, the court offered:

"[T]he critical test of the existence of the privilege is the circumstantial justification for the publication of the defamatory information. The critical elements of the test are the appropriateness of the occasion on which the defamatory information is published, the legitimacy of the interest thereby sought to be protected or promoted, and the pertinence of the receipt of that information by the recipient." Id. At 36-37, 520 A.2d at 1169-70; Taylor v. Amcor Flexibles, Inc., 669 F. Supp. 2d 501 (N.J.Dist., November 4, 2009) (communication is privileged where the defendant has a legitimate interest in the subject matter of the communication and it is made in good faith to a person with a corresponding interest or duty in the subject matter). In Govito v. West Jersey Health System, Inc., 332 N.J. Super. 293, 753 A.2d 716 (App. Div. 2000),the court determined that the Bainhauer privilege applied to a nurse who was defamed in the course of an "intervention" prompted by false allegations that the nurse was improperly diverting and using morphine, due to the strong public concern for the quality of nursing care.

In Lutz v. Royal Insurance Co. of America, 245 N.J. Super. 480, 586 A.2d 278 (App. Div. 1991), an insurance company employee's memo to a supervisor indicating that an agency vice president "constantly made sexist remarks," that he was "abusive, vulgar and offensive," and that he was disloyal to the company, was qualifiedly privileged, with regard to material that defamed the vice president. The court also found that subsequent memos, including one from the supervisor to the company's territorial vice president, were also qualifiedly privileged. Id. In a hostile environment workplace claim, the New Jersey Supreme Court found that if an employer had notice that co-employees were engaged, on a corporate electronic bulletin board, in a pattern of retaliatory harassment and defamation directed at a co-employee, the employer would have a duty to remedy such conduct. Blakey v. Cont'l Airlines, Inc., 164 N.J. 38, 751 A.2d 538 (2000).

In Feggans v. Billington, 291 N.J. Super. 382, 677 A.2d 771 (App. Div. 1996), plaintiff, a state employee sued fellow employees who had circulated a petition accusing her of being a disruptive employee. The court held the complained-of statements were subject to a qualified privilege.

In Fees v. Trow, 105 N.J. 330, 521 A.2d 824 (1987), a state employee's report to a superior accusing a fellow employee of misconduct was held entitled to the actual malice privilege.

In Gallo v. Princeton University, 281 N.J. Super. 134, 656 A.2d 1267 (App. Div. 1995) certif. denied 42 N.J. 453, 663 A.2d 1159 (1995), statements by the employer to the university community concerning the university's discharge of plaintiff for improper use of his employer's equipment were held subject to the actual malice standard.

In Rainsdell v. Pennsylvania R.R. Co., 79 N.J.L. 379, 75 Atl. 444 (Sup. Ct. 1910), a notice to railroad conductors re dismissal of a fellow conductor for failure to follow orders was held to be subject to a qualified privilege.

E. Statements to Government Regulators

Mandatory statements made by employers to the Unemployment Compensation Commission enjoy a qualified privilege. Rogozinski v. Airstream By Angell, 152 N.J. Super. 133, 377 A.2d 807 (Law Div. 1977). Letters from business rivals to federal regulators accusing party of violation of banking regulations were immune from defamation action on grounds of *Noerr B Pennington* doctrine. Caixa General de Depositor, A.A. CQD v. RodriguezCaixa General de Depositor, A.A. CQD v. Rodriguez, 2005 WL 1541055 (D.N.J. 2005). A pre-litigation demand letter by an attorney was protected by the absolute litigation privilege but extra-judicial statements by an attorney in anticipation of client's press conference were not protected by the absolute litigation privilege in Williams v. Kenney, 379 N.J. Super. 118, 877 A.2d 277 (App. Div. 2005). See also Abdul Saguar v. Townley Sweeping Service, Inc., No. A-5014-03T1 (Sup.Ct. N.J. B App. Div. May 16, 2005). Grievants in attorney ethics matters are absolutely immune from suit for filing an ethics complaint or making statements within the context of subsequent disciplinary proceedings, R. 1:20-9. Grievants are not immune for statements made outside the proceedings or to the media, R.M. v. Supreme Court, 185 N.J. 208, 883 A.2d 369 (2005). Health insurer that terminated physician from provider network and reported termination to State Board of Medical Examiners was immune from liability on claims of defamation, malicious prosecution and tortious interference with a prospective economic advantage; the insurer gave to physician several opportunities to respond to the perceived irregularities and to dispel its suspicions about physician's records and treatments, several departments at various times reviewed physician's case, the insurer thus made its report to the State Board of Medical Examiners in good faith and without malice. Feit v. Horizon Blue Cross and Blue Shield of New Jersey, 385 N.J. Super. 470, 897 A.2d 1075 (App. Div. 2006).

F. Reports to Auditors and Insurers

At least one New Jersey court has held that when sued for libel, auditors enjoy a qualified privilege. See Abella v. Barringer Resources Inc., 260 N.J. Super. 92, 99, 615 A.2d 288, 291 (Ch. Div. 1992). Noting that a qualified privilege exists when the legitimate public or private interest underlying the publication outweighs the interests of the individual, the Abella court, in dicta, held that it is "axiomatic" that an auditor's report serves a legitimate public and private interest. Id. ad 103, 615 A.2d at 294.

G. Vicarious Liability of Employers for Statements Made by Employees

1. ***Scope of Employment.*** Employer was held to be subject to liability under the principles of respondeat superior for defamatory statements by its employees. Printing Mart-Morristown v. Sharp Elecs. Corp., 116 N.J. 739, 563 A.2d 31 (1989). However, the statement in question must have been made within the employee's scope of employment. Id. Conduct is generally considered to be within the scope of employment if (1) it is of the kind that the employee is employed to perform; (2) it occurs substantially within the authorized time and space limits; and (3) it is actuated, at least in part, by a purpose to serve the master. DiCosala v. Kay, 91 N.J. 159, 169, quoted favorably in Singer v. Beach Trading Co., Inc., 379 N.J. Super. 63, 78 (App. Div. 2005). In Singer, the Court reversed the entry of summary judgment in favor of the employer because the record did not address the issue of whether the conduct was within the scope of employment. Singer, 379 N.J. at 78. While dismissing the underlying defamation claims as being improperly pled, the New Jersey District Court in Allia v. Target Corp., 2008 U.S. Dist. LEXIS 29591 (D.N.J. 2008), held that a Plaintiff does not need to plead *respondeat superior* as a separate cause of action when defamation claims have already been levied against the employees and the company. Doing so makes the *respondeat superior* claims redundant and subject to dismissal.

a. Blogging. In Goldhaber v. Kohlenberg, 359 N.J. Super. 380, 928 A.2d 948 (App. Div. 2007) the Court held that non-resident defendants in an internet libel case were subject to personal jurisdiction in New Jersey. The Court read their postings to a listserve, which were alleged to include disparaging or insulting references to a town, a police department and the New Jersey resident's neighbors on an unlicensed internet site for people to share travel experiences and to dispense advice, as targeting defendants in New Jersey, where they resided.

2. ***Damages.*** Exemplary damages may be assessed against a corporation in a libel action, if the wrongful act was committed by an employee so high in authority as to be fairly considered executive in character. Neigel v. Seaboard Fin. Co., 68 N.J. Super. 542, 173 A.2d 300 (App. Div. 1961).

H. Internal Investigations

In Berrios v. PNC Bank, 2006 WL 2933899 (N.J. Super. A.D. 2006) the Appellate Division considered several claims, including tortious interference with prospective economic relations and defamation, asserted against defendant PNC Bank by a plaintiff who was employed as a security officer with a company which had contracted with PNC Bank to provide security services. Plaintiff's claims resulted from a report received by a PNC security analyst of unauthorized attempts to access a restricted computer location in the Bank, and resulted in PNC reporting the unauthorized computer access attempts to plaintiff's employer, with a request that the employer conduct an investigation. As a result of the investigation, plaintiff was removed from his assignment at PNC and transferred to new assignments with similar responsibilities and the same pay. Plaintiff rejected the new assignments, complaining that they were not "supervisory," and would be geographically inconvenient. In this context, the Court reviewed and reaffirmed the elements of a defamation claim and also considered whether PNC had abused its qualified privilege when it communicated to plaintiff's employer its suspicions about plaintiff's involvement in the alleged unauthorized computer access attempts, without carrying out a thorough investigation itself. The Court held that the plaintiff bears the burden of showing by clear and convincing evidence that defendant abused its discretion, and ruled that it could not conclude that PNC reported the incident to the plaintiff's employer with a reckless disregard for the truth since PNC was charged with the responsibility of safeguarding its client's sensitive and confidential information. The Court also held that there was nothing in the record to support a finding of excessive publication by PNC in reporting the incident. Summary judgment to defendant PNC was, therefore, affirmed.

IV. OTHER ACTIONS BASED ON STATEMENTS

A. Negligent Hiring, Retention, and Supervision

An employer who negligently hires or retains in his employ an individual who is incompetent or unfit for the job "may be liable to a third party whose injury was proximately caused by the employer's" failure to exercise due care. Di Cosala v. Kay, 91 N.J. 159, 170, 450 A.2d 508 (1982). The existence of this tort is not confined to the narrow principles of respondeat superior. Negligent hiring focuses not on the application of principal-agent, but on the tort of negligently exposing members of the public to a potentially dangerous individual. Id. at 172. However, allegations that an employer violated the Immigration Reform and Control Act of 1986, were insufficient to establish a standard of conduct, of a reasonable employer, as required to state negligence in the hiring or retention of employees, even though the employee in question was had engaged in identity theft activities to the harm of other employees. Piscitelli v. Classic Residence By Hyatt, 408 N.J. Super. 83 (App. Div. 2009).

B. Intentional Infliction of Emotional Distress

1. ***Elements.*** To establish a claim for intentional infliction of emotional distress, a plaintiff must establish intentional and outrageous conduct by the defendant, proximate cause, and distress that is severe. Buckley v. Trenton Saving Fund Soc., 111 N.J. 355, 544 A.2d 857 (1988). Young v. Hobart West Group, 385 N.J. Super. 448, 897 A.2d 1063 (App. Div. 2005). For an intentional act to result in liability for the intentional infliction of emotional distress, the defendant must intend both to do the act and to produce emotional distress, and liability will also attach when the defendant acts recklessly and in deliberate disregard of a high degree of probability that emotional distress will follow. Id. See also BOHS v. The New York Times Co., 106 Fed. Appx. 109, 2004 (WL 1616354 (3d Cir. 2004), 32 Media L. Rep. 1993 (use of the name. "Larry BOHS" in a United Negro College Fund advertisement was not sufficiently outrageous and egregious to support a valid claim under New Jersey law). (Note: This case was not selected for publication in the Federal Reporter and is not precedential). The tort of intentional infliction of emotional distress requires emotional trauma that is severe. Young v. Hobart West Group, 385 N.J. Super. 448, 897 A.2d 1063 (App. Div. 2005). Proofs of alleged emotional distress should be considered by the finder of fact where an unlawful discrimination has occurred, even where there are no economic damages from a wrongful discharge. "Mixed motive" and retaliation are factors for the jury to consider in determining whether unlawful discrimination occurred, but a plaintiff is not entitled to special verdicts on these questions. The jury should, of course, be fully instructed in these respects. A jury should not be required to return special verdicts on the elements of the McDonnell Douglas burden-shifting principle. The jury should, of course, be fully instructed of this connection also. A

plaintiff who has prevailed on a claim of unlawful discrimination where there are no economic damages is entitled to an appropriate award of counsel fees in addition to whatever damages may be found for emotional distress. Cely Padilla v. Berkeley Educational Services of New Jersey, A-4559-03T5 (Sup. Ct. N.J. - App. Div. February 6, 2006).

In Kwiatkowski v. Merrill Lynch, et al., Docket No. A-2270-06T1 (Decided August 13, 2008), the Appellate Division considered plaintiff's appeal from Summary Judgment dismissing his claims of wrongful employment termination and harassment based on his sexual orientation, and for intentional infliction of emotional distress. In reversing the trial court's grant of Summary Judgment, one of the issues addressed by the Appellate Division was whether plaintiff's claim for intentional infliction of emotional distress was preempted by plaintiff's filing of a claim under the New Jersey Law Against Discrimination, N.J.S.A. 10:5-1 et seq. Defendants asserted that where an employee asserts a New Jersey Law Against Discrimination (LAD) claim, any common-law claims based upon the same allegations are preempted and should be dismissed. The Appellate Division held that the LAD does not "preempt" supplementary common-law causes of action, and that, by its very terms, the LAD does not exclude any independent right or action which may exist to provide relief from any unlawful discrimination. While noting that the United States Supreme Court has recognized that, in many cases, a common-law claim is merely duplicative of a law against discrimination claim, the Court held that where the common-law claim would "protect an interest in addition to or aside from those protected by the statutory action," it should not be deemed duplicative. The Appellate Division thus held that a claim for intentional infliction of emotional distress is not duplicative of a statutory claim for wrongful discharge based on unlawful discrimination, even though both claims may rely on the same set of facts. The Court then proceeded to outline the elements plaintiff must proof in order to prevail on a claim for intentional infliction of emotional distress, as follows: "Turning to the merits, to prevail on a claim for intentional infliction of emotional distress, a plaintiff must show that (1) the defendant acted intentionally or recklessly, both in doing the act and in producing emotional distress; (2) the conduct was so outrageous in character and extreme in degree as to go beyond all bounds of decency; (3) the defendant's actions were the proximate cause of the emotional distress; and (4) the distress was so severe that no reasonable person could be expected to endure it. Tarr v. Ciasulli, 181 N.J. 70, 77 (2004); Buckley v. Trenton Sav. Fund Soc'y, 111 N.J. 355, 366 (1988)."

2. ***Claims Based on Statements.*** It is difficult in New Jersey to establish the tort of intentional infliction of emotional distress based upon a statement. In Hart v. City of Jersey City, 308 N.J. Super. 487, 706 A.2d 256 (App. Div. 1998), a police officer's notice of suspension and an order to undergo outpatient alcohol treatment posted on a bulletin board were not found to rise to the level of misconduct to maintain an action. The court held that the plaintiff would have to show the defendants intended to cause distress or that they deliberately disregarded the risk that severe emotional distress would occur. Id. The New Jersey Supreme Court has held that even though many jurisdictions have stated that racial slurs uttered by a supervisor to an employee is not, as a matter of law, extreme and outrageous conduct that would give rise to an intentional infliction of emotional distress cause of action, it was a question best left for the jury. Taylor v. Metzger, 152 N.J. 490, 706 A.2d 685 (1998)(sheriff accused of calling black deputy a "jungle bunny"). While a racial slur between strangers on the street would not rise to the level of conduct required, a "jury could reasonably conclude that the power dynamics of the workplace contribute to the extremity and outrageousness of defendant's conduct." Id. at 511, 706 A.2d at 695 Accordingly, in Wigginton v. Servidio, 324 N.J. Super. 114, 734 A. 2d 798, 80 Fair Empl. Prac. Cas. (BNA) 1210 (App. Div. 1999), certif. denied, 163 N.J. 11,746 A.2d 457 (2000), the Court reversed the lower Court's dismissal of plaintiff's intentional infliction of emotional distress claim, finding that statements made during an incident involving plaintiff and three supervisory employees which only lasted seven to eight minutes, and, further where plaintiff's reaction was verified by two therapists, were sufficient to survive a motion to dismiss and should be determined by the factfinder. In Griffin v. Tops Appliance City, 337 N.J. Super. 15, 766 A. 2d 292 (App. Div. 2001), the court held that where an employer establishes a legitimate business purpose for the alleged defamatory statements made to other employees, the plaintiff cannot avoid the qualified privilege extended to such statements by relying upon them as the basis for an intentional infliction of emotional distress claim. See II.A.2.a. supra. In DeAngelis v. Hill, 180 N.J. 1, 847 A.2d 1265 (2004), the Supreme Court held that a public official plaintiff asserting a claim for intentional infliction of emotional distress must show actual malice similar to when asserting a defamation claim. In Vergopia v. Shaker, 383 N.J. Super. 256, 811 A.2d 644 (App. Div. 2006) aff'd with modifications, 191 N.J. 217 (2007) the New Jersey Supreme Court held that an attorney, who was also a corporate officer and outside counsel to a corporate client, who was named as a defendant in an action brought by former corporate officers against both the corporation and the attorney, asserting trade libel and emotional distress claims as a result of the attorney's role in preparing a press release for a corporation engaged in litigation, was entitled to indemnification under the broad indemnification provision in the corporation's Certificate of Incorporation. In so holding, the Court modified the decision of the Appellate Division which had found such an entitlement to indemnification on different grounds, i.e., as a corporate "agent" under the Delaware indemnification provision contained in Delaware's General Corporation Law.

C. Interference with Economic Advantage

1. ***Elements.*** To prove a claim for interference with an advantageous economic relationship. plaintiff must show: (1) the existence of a reasonable expectation of economic advantage; (2) intentional and malicious interference

with that expectation; (3) the interference caused plaintiff to lose the prospective economic advantage; and (4) damages. Printing Mart-Morristown v. Sharp Electronics Corp., 116 N.J. 739, 563 A.2d 31 (1989). See also, D&D Associates, Inc. v. Board of Education of North Plainfield, 2007 WL 4554208 (D.N.J.). Additionally, such a claim must be directed against a defendant who is not a party to the economic relationship. Id. See Patel v. Soriano, 369 N.J. Super. 192, 848 A.2d 803 (App. Div. 2004), cert. denied 182 N.J. 141 (2004) physician denied hospital privileges could recover from a competitor physician, who was the chief of vascular surgery at a hospital to which the plaintiff physician made application for privileges and who was alleged to have sabotaged plaintiff's application and communicated false statements about plaintiff to other members of the medical staff in order to continue his monopolistic control over the hospital's vascular surgery department. See also Vargo v. National Exchange Carriers Asso., Inc., 376 N.J. Super. 364, 380 (App. Div. 2005) (temporary employee, who was denied permanent position for failing a drug test, could not maintain a claim against the employer for tortious interference with prospective economic advantage since the employer was a party to the economic relationship in issue); see also Singer v. Beach Trading Co., Inc. 379 N.J. Super. 63, 81-82 (App. Div. 2005) (former employee failed to produce evidence that former employer intended to induce or cause current employer to terminate former employee by giving false information about former employee's job title). See also, Foxtons Inc. v. Cirri Germain Realty, et al., 2008 WL 465653 (N.J. Super. A.D.)

2. ***Claims Based on Statements.*** Claims of interference with economic advantage can be based on statements. Platinum Management, Inc., v. Dahms, 285 N.J. Super. 274, 666 A.2d 1028 (Law Div. 1995). The court in Dahms found that negative statements made by a former employee of a toy company to potential customers were tortuous interference with economic advantage. Id. See Patel v. Soriano, supra.

D. Prima Facie Tort.

1. ***Elements.*** Only one appellate level court has recognized the existence of a prima facie tort cause of action. See Trautwein v. Harbourt, 40 N.J. Super 247, 123 A.2d 30 (App. Div. 1956). While the New Jersey Supreme Court has not recognized the tort, it has stated that such a claim would probably be permitted only in limited situations where a plaintiff would have no other cause of action. Taylor v. Metzger, 152 N.J. 490, 706 A.2d 685 (1998) (cites omitted). In Stevens Institute of Technology v. Hine, et al., 2007 WL 2188200 (N.J. Super. A.D.) the Court considered defamation claims which were asserted by Stevens Institute of Technology against defendant Fund for a Better Waterfront, Inc., a not-for-profit corporation whose purpose was described in its Certificate of Incorporation as "educational and legal efforts to improve the environment and waterfront, the quality of life in Hoboken and neighboring communities," and certain individuals associated with the Fund in connection with the planning and construction by Stevens of a building on its campus in Hoboken which raised health hazard issues as the result of the presence of asbestos. The defendants expressed their concerns several ways, including in correspondence to the Mayor of Hoboken, in articles published in local newspapers and on its own website. Plaintiff Stevens Institute of Technology filed claims not only of defamation but also of prima facie tort, which tort has been recognized in New Jersey as "designed to redress unjustified intentional, willful or malicious harms where no adequate common law or statutory remedy exists." The Appellate Division affirmed the trial Court's grant of summary judgment to defendants on plaintiff's claim of prima facie tort, holding that plaintiff's claim of prima facie tort is essentially encompassed within its claim of defamation, and that the tort of defamation afforded plaintiff a legal avenue to seek to redress the wrongs allegedly caused by defendants' conduct and that there was thus no "gap" to fill through a prima facie tort claim.

2. ***Claims Based on Statements.*** There are no reported court decisions where statements served as the cause of action for a prima facie tort case.

E. Negligent Misrepresentation

New Jersey recognizes a cause of action against an employer for negligent misrepresentation of a former employee's work history. Singer v. Beach Trading Co., Inc., 279 N.J. Super. 63, 69 876 A.2d 885 (App. Div. 2005). The five (5) elements to be proven for this cause of action to proceed are: (1) the inquiring party clearly identifies the nature of the inquiry; (2) the employer voluntarily decides to respond to the inquiry, and thereafter unreasonably provides false or inaccurate information; (3) the person providing the inaccurate information is acting within the scope of his/her employment; (4) the recipient of the incorrect information relies on its accuracy to support an adverse employment action against the former employee; and (5) the former employee suffers quantifiable damages proximately caused by the negligent misrepresentation.

F. Violation of Due Process Rights Based on Injury To the Reputation of a Public Employee by the Government Employer

Both New Jersey state courts and federal courts in the Third Circuit have held that a public employee has no cognizable claim of a property right in his reputation entitled to substantive due process protection in connection with his termination or constructive discharge, but only, rather, a potential procedural due process right to refute the charges and clear one's name. Filgueiras v. Newark Pub. Sch., 426 N.J. Super. 449 (App. Div. 2012); Hill v. Borough of Kutztown, 455 F.3d 225 (3d Cir. 2006); **see also D&D Associates, Inc. v. Bd. of Educ. of North Plainfield, 2012 WL 1079583 (D.N.J. March 30, 2012).**

V. OTHER ISSUES

A. Statute of Limitations

The statute of limitations for a defamation action is one year. N.J.S.A. 2A:14-3. Cristelli v. Filomena II, Inc., 1999 WL 1081290, *3 (D.N.J. 1999). While the statute of limitations can be deemed waived as a defense if not raised prior to trial or even where it was raised in an Answer and then left to lie until a post trial brief, such a waiver does not occur when the defense is raised in either a summary judgment setting or other pre-trial motion. Plitsas v. Federal Express, Inc., 2010 U.S. Dist. LEXIS 39586 (April 22, 2010) (unpublished); Ramirez v. United Parcel Service, 2010 U.S. Dist. LEXIS 48351 (May 17, 2010) (unpublished). The one year statute of limitations also applies to claims of damages to a person's reputation and in "false light" claims. Guatam v. New Jersey Dept. of Banking and Insurance, 2008 N.J. Super. Unpub. LEXIS 1779 (App. Div. October 20, 2008) (plaintiff's claims that his reputation was harmed by being subjected to a psychiatric evaluation sounded in defamation to which a one year statute of limitations applied); Swan v. Boardwalk Regency Corp., 407 N.J. Super. 108 (App. Div. 2009) (Court applied one year statute of limitations to plaintiff's false light/invasion of privacy claims and rejected plaintiff's claim that the allegations should be treated as separate and distinct privacy torts sounding in an "injury to the person" subject to a two year statute of limitations). However, while reiterating that a one year statute of limitations applies to every action at law for libel or slander, the court in Thomasian v. New Jersey Institute of Technology, 2009 U.S. Dist LEXIS 7900, recognized that the statute does not begin to run in circumstances where an individual is subject to a continual, cumulative pattern of tortious conduct. Id. (While recognizing the existence of the equitable tolling of the statute of limitations, the court ultimately held that it did not apply to the facts of this case and dismissed the matter for failure to state a claim upon which relief could be granted.). Under New Jersey law, an action for slander per se also must be commenced within one year next after the publication of the alleged libel or slander. Campanello v. Port Auth., 590 F. Supp. 2d 694 (N.J.D. 2008). A suit by a physician for actions and statements causing plaintiff to be denied hospital privileges was held to be trade libel, subject to a six-year statute of limitations. Patel v. Soriano, 369 N.J. Super. 192, 848 A.2d 803 (App. Div. 2004), cert. denied 182 N.J. 141 (2004). New Jersey has adopted the "single publication" rule judicially. Barres v. Holt, Rinehart & Winston, Inc., 141 N.J. Super. 563, 359 A.2d 501 (App. Div. 1976), Aff'd 74 N.J. 461, 378 A.2d 1148 (1977). The Uniform Single Publication Act has not been adopted in New Jersey. Aggregator of telecommunications services sued the provider of long-distance services, alleging unjust enrichment and slander and libel under New Jersey law, and various claims under Communications Act. Long-distance provider counterclaimed for unpaid telephone use charges and shortfall charges. The United States District Court for the District of New Jersey, Nicholas H. Politan, J., granted summary judgment for long-distance provider, and entered judgment on counterclaim. Aggregator appealed. The Court of Appeals, Roth, Circuit Judge, held that provider's allegedly defamatory statements were subject to one-year statute of limitations for slander and libel under New Jersey law. 800 Services Inc v. AT&T Corp., 30 Fed. Appx. 21, 2002 WL 215625 (3rd Cir. (N.J.)). The single publication rule applies to publication on an internet website, Churchill v. State of New Jersey, 378 N.J. Super., 471, 876 A.2d 311, (App. Div. 2005).

In Cipriani Builders, Inc. v. Madden, 389 N.J.Super. 154, 912 A.2d 152 (App. Div. 2006) the Appellate Division held that the single publications rule did not apply to the facts in that case. The single publication rule is a limited exception to the general rule, namely, that any repetition of a defamatory statement gives rise to a new cause of action and that under the single publication rule a plaintiff asserting a defamation claim based upon a mass publication, such as a book or newspaper, has a single cause of action which arises at the first publication of an alleged libel, regardless of the number of copies of the publication distributed or sold, which prevents the constant tolling of the statute of limitations. The Court held that the single publication rule does not apply to the repetition of defamatory statements in any form other than multiple distributions of the same material by the mass media or a single communication heard at the same time by two or more persons. The Court thus held in Cipriani, supra, that any oral repetition by defendant of the alleged defamatory statements which had been contained in an earlier written memoranda did not constitute part of such a single publication and that, as a result, the single publication rule did not apply and the plaintiff's slander claims based on defendant's alleged defamatory oral statements were not barred by the statute of limitations.

In B.F. v. Accurate Dental Group, No. A-6369-08 (App. Div. 2011), the Appellate Division held that the discovery rule is inapplicable as a matter of law to defamation actions because the statute defines the limitation period in terms of the publication itself: "On this point, the Supreme Court has conclusively spoken. See Lawrence v. Bauer Publ'g & Printing Ltd., 78 N.J. 371, 375 (1979) (Pashman, J., concurring) (finding the discovery rule inapplicable as a matter of law to defamation actions). The statute does not define the limitation period in terms of the accrual of the cause of action, but the publication itself, thereby making the discovery rule inapplicable. Id. at 374-75." Therefore, the discovery rule cannot be used to provide an exception to the one-year statute of limitations, even if previous cases have hinted that re-examining Bauer may be appropriate. Id. See also Beljakovic v. Bishop Longin, 2011 N.J. Super. Unpub. LEXIS 2045 (App. Div. 2011).

B. Jurisdiction

Where some defendants and plaintiffs were residents of Israel, some were New Jersey residents, egregious misconduct was committed in New Jersey, elsewhere in the United States, and in Israel, by New Jersey residents, malicious defamation was published in and from this state, and where a fuller remedy was available to defendants under New Jersey law than in Israel, with regard to the scope of damages, then in light of the totality of the circumstances, New Jersey's interest in the controversy as a whole was paramount to Israel's interest, New Jersey defamation law would be applied and defendants' motion for dismissal on *forum non conveniens* grounds was denied. Almog v. ITAS, 298 N.J. Super. 145, 689 A.2d 158 (App. Div. 1997) appeal dismissed, 152 N.J. 361, 704 A.2d 1257 (1997). The federal district court has no jurisdiction to hear actions based on libel and slander when they are brought against the United States; the Federal Tort Claims Act ("FTCA") provides the exclusive remedy. Although the FTCA includes a specific waiver of sovereign immunity, it preserves sovereign immunity as a defense against certain claims, notably those based on libel and slander. Watts v. Internal Revenue Serv., 925 F. Supp. 271 (D.N.J. 1996).

Where both parties were New Jersey residents, the author and publisher were served in New Jersey and the book was distributed from a warehouse in the state and advertised in New Jersey newspapers, New Jersey law was found applicable. Barres v. Holt, Rinehart & Winston, Inc., 131 N.J. Super. 371, 377, 330 A.2d 38 (Law Div. 1974). Concerning the issue of personal jurisdiction, the Supreme Court found that defendants who published defamatory electronic messages, with knowledge that the messages would be published in New Jersey and could influence a claimant's efforts to seek a remedy under New Jersey's Law Against Discrimination, may properly be subject to the State's jurisdiction. Blakey v. Continental Airlines, Inc., 164 N.J. 38, 751 A.2d 538 (2000), reversing 322 N.J. Super. 187, 730 A. 2d 854 (App. Div. 1999). In Garfinkel v. Morristown Ob &Gyn., 333 N.J. Super. 291, 755 A. 2d 626 (App. Div. 2000), the court determined that claims of tortious interference and defamation were subject to arbitration pursuant to an employment contract where the arbitration clause contained broad language stating that it covered any claim or controversy arising out of and relating to the employment agreement, and both claims herein related to facts surrounding the employee's performance and termination. Non-resident buyers on ebay.com who purchased from a New Jersey seller and who complained of nondelivery and fraud and who were sued in New Jersey for conspiracy to defame and cause economic injury were held not subject to personal jurisdiction in New Jersey. Machulsky v. Hall, 210 F. Supp. 2d 531 (D.N.J. 2002). Operator of Internet coin auction business brought action under Racketeer Influenced and Corrupt Organizations (RICO) alleging that customers conspired with other Internet auction site users to defame her and cause her economic injury by ruining her business. On customers' motions to dismiss, the District Court, Brotman, J., held that customers were not subject to personal jurisdiction in New Jersey. Machulsky v. Hall, et al., 210 F. Supp. 2d 53 (D.N.J. 2002). In Team First Consulting, LLC v. Hangliter, 2007 WL 1302440 (D.N.J. 2007) the court held that personal jurisdiction did not lie in a suit by a New Jersey plaintiff against a non-resident defendant for statements made in the course of a project outside New Jersey even though the brunt of plaintiff's harm was suffered in New Jersey, because the defendant did not expressly aim his statements at New Jersey such that New Jersey can be said to be the focal point of the tortuous activity. In Goldhaber v. Kohlenberg, 395 N.J.Super. 380, 928 A.2d 948 (App. Div. August 2, 2007) the Court held that non-resident defendants in an internet libel case were subject to personal jurisdiction in New Jersey. The Court read their postings to a listserve as targeting defendants in New Jersey, where they resided. A libel claim which arose out of a contract containing an arbitration clause was held to be subject to arbitration. Philip Lehman Company, Ltd. v. William P. Smart Associates, 2006 WL 1971866 (App. Div. 2006). An employment agreement that contained an arbitration clause was held to be valid and enforceable in a defamation suit by a former employee. Blumert v. Wells Fargo and Co., 2011 N.J. Super. Unpub LEXIS 2199 (App. Div. 2011). A libel claim by a stockbroker against complaining customers was held subject to NASD arbitration. Welch v. Kotch, 2006 WL 1506957 (App. Div. 2006). In Deniscia v. International Association of Firefighters, et al., 2007 WL 1159967 (N.J. Super. A.D. 2007) the Superior Court of New Jersey, Appellate Division held that plaintiffs' claims of defamatory and libelous statements, alleged to have been made about them in a letter written by the President of plaintiffs' union, were subject to the internal union remedies provided in the Union Constitution and By-Laws, and that where an agreement provides grievance procedures for the settlement of controversies, a union member must exhaust those procedures before resorting to the Courts. The Court noted that there are certain exceptions to the general rule of exhaustion of remedies, none of which it found applicable to plaintiffs' defamation claims. In Stallworth v. Reheis Co., 2007 WL 1876495 (D.N.J. 2007) the plaintiff alleged various discrimination, tort and contract claims against his former employer and his former supervisor, including a number of claims arising under federal law, namely, Equal Protection, Title VII and ADEA claims. Summary judgment was granted to the defendants on all of the claims arising under federal law, resulting in the dismissal of plaintiff's pendent state law claims, which included a defamation claim, which pendent state claims were dismissed without prejudice but would not be deemed to be time-barred under 28 U.S.C. §1367(d). The United States District Court of the District of New Jersey, in 3 Lab, Inc. v.

Kim, 2007 WL 2177513 (D.N.J. 2007) granted defendants' motions to dismiss for lack of personal jurisdiction plaintiff's claims, which included claims for trade defamation, defamation, tortious interference and breach of the covenant of fair dealing, based upon an application of the "effects" test set forth in Calder v. Jones, 465 U.S. 783 (1984). Under the Calder effects test a plaintiff must demonstrate: (1) the defendant committed an intentional tort; (2) the forum was the focal point of the harm suffered by the plaintiff as a result of that tort; and (3) the defendant "expressly aimed" the tortious activity at the forum state, rather than simply asserting that the defendant knew that the plaintiff's principal place of business was located in the forum, which is insufficient to establish jurisdiction. The Court concluded that plaintiffs did not set forth any basis to indicate that defendants manifested any "behavior intentionally targeted at and focused" at New Jersey, as a result of which defendant's motions to dismiss for lack of personal jurisdiction were granted.

C. Worker's Compensation Exclusivity

The Workers' Compensation System in New Jersey was established by the legislature in order to provide a remedy to employees against their employer outside of the tort system. With certain exceptions, the Workers' Compensation System supersedes common law actions in tort, in order to provide an economical and efficient remedy for redress against the employer. N.J.S.A. 34:15-8 enumerates the "exclusivity rule" and its limited exceptions, i.e., the employee's remedy for a job-related injury is limited exclusively to the Workers' Compensation System "except for intentional wrong." Vetri v. Utica National Insurance, 2009 N.J. Super. Unpub. LEXIS 771 (April 28, 2009) (The Division of Workers' Compensation is deemed to have primary jurisdiction to decide compensability issues). In Kristiansen v. Morgan, et al., 153 N.J. 298, 708 A.2d 1173 (1998), the Court held that while the employee's right to recover against the employer exists exclusively under the Worker's Compensation System, an employee does have a remedy against negligent third-party tortfeasors, which remedy is not barred by the exclusivity remedy against the employer in Worker's Compensation. See also, Dettman v. Goldsmith, 11 N.J. Super 571, 78 A.2d 626 (Cty. Ct. 1951). As an exception to the exclusivity rule, if an employer has committed an intentional wrong, the employee may bring an action for damages outside the Worker's Compensation System. Laidlow v. Hariton Machinery Company, Inc., 170 N.J. 602 (2002); Millison v. E.I. DuPont deNemours & Co., 101 N.J. 61 (1985). The term "intentional wrong" is narrowly defined and requires a showing of deliberate intention to injure. Since the standard that defines an intention to injure is a subjective one, the Courts have adopted the "substantial certainty test," under which the conduct of the actor as well as the context in which the injury occurred are factors to be examined in determining the "deliberate intention." In Subbe-Hirt v. Baccigalupi, 94 F.3d 111 (3d Cir. 1996), an employee was permitted to sue her former employer for intentional infliction of emotional distress where the employer made derogatory comments to the plaintiff with an intention to verbally attack her until she quit. In Khair v. Campbell Soup Company, 893 F. Supp. 316 (D.N.J. 1995), in which an employee brought claims based upon age, race and nationality discrimination, the District Court held that the Worker's Compensation Act is not a bar to claims under the New Jersey Law Against Discrimination. Either subjective intent and/or substantial certainty of harm are sufficient to satisfy the requirement of an intentional wrong in order to escape the exclusivity provisions of the Worker's Compensation Action. New Jersey Manufacturers Insurance Company v. Joseph Oat Corporation, et al., 287 N.J. Super. 190, 670 A.2d 1071 (App. Div. 1995). By extension, the same requirements and results, as to the proofs necessary to satisfy the intentional wrong standard in order to escape the Workers' Compensation exclusivity rule, would appear likely to apply in the event of a libel claim by an employee against his or her employer.

D. Pleading Requirements

Although a verbatim transcription of the language complained of is not required, plaintiff must specify the defamatory words and the meaning he attaches to them. Miele v. Rosenblum, 254 N.J. Super. 8, 12-14, 603 A.2d 43, 20 Media L. Rep. 1667 (App. Div. 1991); Voorhees v. Preferred Mut. Ins., 246 N.J. Super, 564, 570, 588 A.2d 417 (App. Div. 1991); Zoneraich v. Overlook Hospital, 212 N.J. Super. 83, 101, 514 A.2d 53 (App. Div. 1986) cert. denied, 107 N.J. 32, 526 A. 2d 126 (1986); Kotok Building v. Charvine Co., 183 N.J. Super. 101, 443 A.2d 260 (Law Div. 1981); **Tyson v. Asbury Park Pub. Sch. Dist., No. A-0720-09T3, slip. op. (N.J. Super. App. Div. Aug. 1, 2011).** In order to state a claim for libel or slander, under New Jersey law, a complaint must allege the defamatory words, the person who uttered them, and when, where, and to whom they were published. Doug Grant, Inc. v. Great Bay Casino Corp., 3 F. Supp. 2d 518 (D.N.J. 1998). In Mangan v. Corporate Synergies Group, Inc., 2011 U.S. Dist. LEXIS 84661 (D.N.J. 2011), the court held that, in a federal court action, the pleading standards under Federal Rule of Civil Procedure 8, rather than New Jersey's heightened pleading standards, are to govern defamation cases in federal court. Under Rule 8, pleadings are to be "liberally construed", and so the plaintiff is not required to plead the specific words used. In Hopkins v. City of Gloucester, 358 N.J. Super 271, 817 A. 2d 436 (App. Div. 2003) the Court discussed the kind of evidence of actual malice which would defeat a motion for summary judgment by a privileged defendant. A state cause of action for defamation during a labor dispute is not preempted by federal labor law if the plaintiff can prove "that the statement was made with malice and injured him." Linn v. United Plant Guard Workers of America, Local 114, 383 U.S. 53, 55, 86 S.Ct. 657, 659, 15 L. Ed. 2d 582 (1966), quoted in Abdul Saquar v. Townley Sweeping Service, Inc., No. A-5014-03T1 (S.Ct. N.J. B App. Div. May 16, 2005). In Darakjian v. Hanna, 366 N.J.

Super. 238 (App. Div. 2004) the court dismissed count two of the Complaint since it failed to set forth particular factual allegation of actual malice. The court found a mere averment that the words printed were malicious is not sufficient. Id. To survive a motion for summary judgment, plaintiff must adduce "concrete proof" that third parties lowered their estimation of the plaintiff and that he or she suffered emotional or pecuniary harm as a result, Tarus v. Borough of Pine Hill, 381 N.J. Super. 412 886 A.2d 1056 (App. Div. 2005), certif. granted, 186 N.J. 225 (2006), *aff'd in part, rev'd in part and remanded*, 189 N.J. 497 (2007).

To prove trade libel, a plaintiff must show: (1) publication, (2) with malice, (3) of false allegations concerning [the plaintiff's] property, product or business, and (4) special damages." Bocobo v. Radiology Consultants of South Jersey, 2012 WL 1302576 (3d Cir. April 17, 2012) (quoting Arista Records, Inc. v. Flea World, Inc., 356 F. Supp. 2d 411, 424 (D.N.J. 2005)). In Bocobo, the court found that plaintiff pleaded only general damages, which fell short of the special damages required to establish a trade libel claim. Bocobo, at *8. Specifically, the court found that plaintiff, a radiologist who alleged he had been the victim of false accusations by his former employer in connection with his termination: (1) had failed to allege any loss of patients; and (2) failed to demonstrate that "the difference between his prior salary . . . and his current salary[,] . . . even if construed as specific damages, was a *direct* result of Defendants' purportedly libelous statements." Id. (emphasis in original).

SURVEY OF NEW JERSEY EMPLOYMENT PRIVACY LAW

Bruce S. Rosen and Kathleen A. Hirce
McCusker, Anselmi, Rosen & Carvelli
A Professional Corporation
210 Park Avenue, Suite 301
Florham Park, New Jersey 07932
Telephone: 973-635-6300; Facsimile: 973-635-6363
Email:brosen@marc-law.com
Website: www.marc-law.com

(With Developments Reported Through **November 1, 2012**)

GENERAL COMMENTS

New Jersey's Constitution embraces two separate privacy rights. Article I, paragraph 7 contains a search and seizure provision similar to the Fourth Amendment to the Federal Constitution. New Jersey also recognizes a constitutional right to privacy based upon that provision in varying contexts. Hennessey v. Coastal Eagle Point Oil Company, 129 N.J. 81, 95, 609 A.2d 11, 18 (1992). That provision provides "All persons are by their nature free and independent, and have certain inalienable rights, among which are those of enjoying and defending life and liberty, of acquiring, possessing, and protecting property, and of pursuing and obtaining safety and happiness."

Constitution-based privacy has been recognized in many contexts: marriage and familial association, Greenberg v. Kimmelman, 99 N.J. 552, 572, 494 A. 2d 294 (1985) (subject to "reasonable" regulation by the State); refusal of medical treatment, In re Conroy, 98 N.J. 321, 345, 486 A.2d 1209 (1985), In re Quinlan, 70 N.J. 10, 40, 355 A. 2d 647 (1976) (patient in persistent vegetative state), cert. denied, 429 U.S. 922, 97 S. Ct. 319, 50 L. Ed. 2d 289 (1976); consensual adult sexual relations, State v. Saunders, 75 N.J. 200, 213-14, 381 A.2d 333 (1977); disclosure of confidential personal information, In re Martin, 90 N.J. 295, 318, 324-35, 447 A.2d 1290 (1982) (balanced against government's need for information; Courts also require promulgation of regulations to prevent public dissemination of information provided by applicants for casino employment); and procreative rights, Right to Choose v. Byrne, 91 N.J. 287, 303-04, 450 A.2d 925 (1982) (elective abortion) (citing Schroeder v. Perkel, 87 N.J. 53, 66, 432 A.2d 834 (1981)); Berman v. Allan, 80 N.J. 421, 432, 404 A. 2d 8 (1979); Doe v. Bridgeton Hosp. Ass'n, 71 N.J. 478, 366 A.2d 641 (1976), cert. denied, 433 U.S. 914, 97 S. Ct. 2987, 53 L. Ed. 2d 1100 (1977); Comras v. Lewin, 183 N.J. Super. 42, 443 A.2d 229 (N.J. App. Div. 1982); In re Grady, 85 N.J. 235, 247-50, 426 A.2d 467 (1981) (voluntary sterilization).

SIGNIFICANT DEVELOPMENTS SINCE THE 2012 *SURVEY*

The Appellate Division reviewed the State Supreme Court's decision in State v. Reid, 194 N.J. 386 (2008), regarding searches of an employee's personal email account, as well as prior privacy decisions, in State v. DeFranco, 426 N.J. Super. 240, 43 A.3d 1253 (App. Div. 2012), where it declined to suppress evidence of a cell phone conversation between a teacher who allegedly sexually molested a student, and the complaining student. Police obtained the teacher's cell phone number from the school; the teacher had listed the number in the Staff Directory and provided it to parents and students, all without indicating the number was confidential. For these and other reasons, the Appellate Division reasoned that the teacher's "professed subjective expectation of privacy [was not] one that society would be willing to recognize as reasonable." Id. at 249-50.

In Capers v. FedEx Ground, No. 2:02-CV-5352, 2012 U.S. Dist. LEXIS 78818, at * 15 (D. N.J. June 6, 2012), Plaintiffs stated a claim for public disclosure of private facts in part because their allegations regarding disclosure of information from their paychecks by their employer were supported by the Restatment (Second) of Torts § 652(b) cmt. b (1977), in that "generally speaking, the law recognizes that information regarding a private employee's income is a private matter."

In granting summary judgment in favor of an employer on an employee's intentional infliction of emotional distress claim, the court in Polonsky v. Verizon Communications, Corp., No. 09-4756, 2011 U.S. Dist. LEXIS 134482, at * (D. N.J. Nov. 22, 2011) noted that "courts have consistently recognized that it is particularly difficult to establish intentional infliction of emotional distress in the employment context."

In Sahoury v. Meredith Corporation, No. 11-5180, 2012 U.S. Dist. LEXIS 108122 (D. N.J. Aug. 2, 2012) the District of New Jersey held that plaintiff's complaint failed to state a claim for invasion of privacy or right of publicity since she did not allege that defendant publishing company specifically sought to capitalize on her image when it posted a video featuring her to YouTube .

I. GENERAL LAW OF PRIVACY

A. Legal Basis of Privacy Claims

New Jersey recognizes the four classic privacy torts, Devlin v. Greiner, 147 N.J. Super. 446, 462, 371 A.2d 380 (Law Div. 1977), and relies heavily on the Restatement (Second) of Torts. See Bisbee v. John C. Conover Agency, 186 N.J. Super. 335, 339, 452 A.2d 689, 9 Media L. Rep. 1298 (App. Div. 1982); Rumbauskas v. Cantor, 138 N.J. 173, 179-182, 649 A. 2d 853 (1994); Tellado v. Time-Life Books, Inc., 643 F. Supp. 904 (D.N.J. 1986). The law of plaintiff's domicile will apply in libel and privacy actions if publication occurred there. Cibenko v. Worth Publishers, Inc., 510 F. Supp. 761, 766, 7 Media L. Rep. 1298 (D.N.J.1981); Barres v. Holt, Rinehart & Winston, Inc., 131 N.J. Super. 371 (Law Div. 1974), aff'd, 141 N.J. Super. 563, 330 A.2d 38 (App. Div. 1976), aff'd on opinion of trial court, 74 N.J. 461, 378 A.2d 1148 (1977). The tort of invasion of privacy focuses on the humiliation and intimate personal distress suffered by an individual as a result of intrusive behavior. While a corporation may have its reputation or business damages as a result of intrusive activity, it is not capable of emotional suffering. N.O.C., Inc. v. Schaefer, 197 N.J. Super. 249, 484 A.2d 729, 730-1 (Law Div. 1984). Privacy actions against state officials are subject to the state Tort Claims Act, N.J.S.A. 59:8-3. Rolax v. Whitman, 175 F. Supp.2d 720, 730 (D.N.J. 2001). The Appellate Division rejected the notion, raised by a trial judge, that invasion of privacy claims have "constitutional roots" and thereby trump statutory privileges or common law privileges such as a newsman's shield. Kinsella v. Welch, 362 N.J. Super. 143, 827 A.2d 325 (App. Div. 2003).

B. Causes of Action

1. ***Misappropriation/Right of Publicity.*** New Jersey has adopted the elements identified in the Restatement (Second) of Torts § 652C: one who appropriates to his own use or benefit the name or likeness of another is subject to liability to the other. Tellado v. Time-Life Books, Inc., 643 F. Supp. 904, 908, 13 Media L. Rep. 1401 (D.N.J. 1986). Misappropriation is the use of an individual's name or likeness for advertising or trade purposes without the individual's consent. Faber v. Condecor, Inc., 195 N.J. Super. 81, 86, 477 A.2d 1289, 1292 (App. Div. 1984), certif. denied, 99 N.J. 178, 481 A.2d 684 (1984). New Jersey courts may recognize a relational tort for misappropriation. Lamonaco v. CBS, Inc., No. 93-1975, 1993 WL 556536, at *4-6, 21 Media L. Rep. 2193 (D.N.J. July 29, 1993), aff'd, 27 F.3d 557, 22 Media L. Rep. 1831 (3d Cir. 1994). The defendant's use of plaintiff's likeness or name must be primarily with a commercial purpose. Faber, supra, 195 N.J. Super. 81; Tellado, supra, 643 F. Supp. 904 (use will be deemed commercial where it is "mainly for the purposes of trade, without a redeeming public interest, news or historical value"); Palmer v. Schoenhorn Enters., Inc., 96 N.J. Super. 72, 77-8, 232 A.2d 458, 461 (1967); Canessa v. J.I. Kislak, Inc., 97 N.J. Super. 327, 351, 235 A.2d 62, 75 (1967); Dorsey v. Black Pearl Books, Inc., No. 06-2940, 2006 WL 3327874, at *11; 2006 U.S. Dist. LEXIS 83093 (D. N.J. Nov. 14, 2006) (in analysis of motion for preliminary injunction, plaintiff had shown he was likely to prove that defendant book publisher used plaintiff's photograph for commercial purposes by placing it on the front and back covers of a book, in advertisement materials, and on the publisher's website) ; Zarrilli v. John Hancock Life Ins. Co., 231 Fed. Appx. 122, 125 (3d Cir. 2007) (failure to remove plaintiff's name from company correspondence and his voicemail message from the company phone system did not qualify as misappropriation because plaintiff "presented no evidence that [the company employer] acted with a commercial purpose or sought some other benefit from what it claimed had been a mistake."); G.D. v. Kenny, 205 N.J. 275, 311 (2011) (a misappropriation claim cannot stand where plaintiff's name and image was used in campaign flyers, and did not have a commercial purpose); Castro v. NYT Television, 370 N.J. Super. 282, 851 A.2d 88 (App. Div. 2004) (The broadcasting of videotape footage on a television show—in this case of emergency room patients—does not give a person who has been videotaped the right to maintain an action for misappropriation unless it has been used for "trade purpose"). It is irrelevant whether a videotape is broadcast in connection with a television story about important public events or a subject that provides only entertainment and amusement. Id.; see also Leibholz v. Hariri, No. 05-5148, 2006 WL 2023186, at *4, 2006 U.S. Dist. LEXIS 52993 (D. N.J. July 13, 2006) (differentiating Castro in the context of a business's website and noting that "[u]se of names and likenesses by non-media parties are different[ ]" from uses by a magazine); **Sahoury v. Meredith Corporation, No. 11-5180, 2012 U.S. Dist. LEXIS 108122 (D. N.J. Aug. 2, 2012) (plaintiff's complaint failed to state a claim for invasion of privacy or right of publicity since she did not allege that defendant publishing company specifically sought to capitalize on her image when it posted a video featuring her to YouTube)**

Having allowed the Plaintiff, a former college football player, to re-plead his misappropriation allegation against a video game developer to better "evoke the notion that Defendant has utilized Plaintiff's image in order to increase sales of its video game," Hart v. Elec. Arts, Inc., 740 F. Supp. 2d 658, 668 (D.N.J. 2010) (also elaborating upon the Castro standard and noting that "courts interpreting Castro have limited its holding to media defendants"), the District of New Jersey ultimately granted summary judgment to the Defendant, holding that Defendant was entitled to First Amendment protections against Plaintiff's misappropriation claim under both the "Transformative" test and the Rogers v. Grimaldi, 875 F.2d 994 (2d Cir. 1989) test. Hart v. Elec. Arts. Inc., No. 09-cv-5990, 2011 U.S. Dist. LEXIS 101254, at *103 (D.N.J. Sept. 9, 2011).

2. ***False Light.*** False light invasion of privacy is recognized as an independent cause of action consistent with the Restatement (Second) of Torts, subject to many of the privileges available in defamation actions. Devlin

v. Greiner, 147 N.J. Super. 446, 465, 371 A.2d 380, 390-91 (Law Div. 1977). It is designed to protect the individual's peace of mind about not having to appear before the public "in an objectionable light or false position," and to protect the individual's reputation. Salek v. Passaic Collegiate School, 255 N.J. Super. 355, 360, 605 A.2d 276, 20 Media L. Rep. 1196 (App. Div. 1992). New Jersey has adopted the elements identified in the Restatement (Second) of Torts § 652E: Liability for this form of privacy invasion is found when one gives publicity to a matter concerning another that places the other before the public in a false light [and] (a) the false light in which the other was placed would be highly offensive to a reasonable person, and (b) the actor had knowledge of an actor in reckless disregard as to the falsity of the published matter and the false light in which the other would be placed. Romaine v. Kallinger, 109 N.J. 282, 294, 537 A.2d 264, 290 (1988). Savely v. MTV Music Television, No. 11-1021, 2011 U.S. Dist. LEXIS 77621, at *13 (D.N.J. July 18, 2011) (noting that "[w]hile there is overlap between the torts of defamation and false light, it is not 'necessary to the action for invasion of privacy that the plaintiff be defamed.'").

Falsity. A fundamental requirement of the false light tort is that the disputed publicity be in fact false, or else "at least have the capacity to give rise to a false public impression as to plaintiff." Romaine, supra, 109 N.J. at 294; Salek v. Passaic Collegiate School, 255 N.J. Super. 355, 360-361; Bisbee v. John C. Conover Agency, 186 N.J. Super. 335, 340, 452 A.2d 689, 692, 9 Media L. Rep. 1298 (App. Div. 1982); Sherman v. Bordentown Reg'l Sch. Dist., 23 Media L. Rep. 1168 (Law Div. 1994); G.D. v. Kenny, 205 N.J. 275, 307-08 (2011) (affirming the dismissal of a false light and related privacy claims because the complained-of publication stating that plaintiff was convicted of a crime was true, regardless of the fact that plaintiff's conviction had been expunged).

Identification of Plaintiff. The publicized material in a false-light claim must constitute a major misrepresentation of plaintiff's character, history, activities or beliefs. Romaine v. Kallinger, 109 N.J. 282, 295, 537 A.2d 264 (1988).

Offensiveness. The tort does not extend to protection of the hypersensitive person; the material publicized "must be something that would be objectionable to the ordinary person under the circumstances." It is for the court to determine whether the communication in question is capable of the meaning assigned to it by plaintiff, and whether that meaning is highly offensive to a reasonable person. The court should not consider words or elements in isolation, but in the context of the whole article. Romaine, supra, 109 N.J. at 295; Salek, supra, 255 N.J. Super. at 361 (photograph in a high school yearbook implying sexual interest between two faculty members found not to be false light invasion); Cibenko v. Worth Publishers, Inc., 510 F. Supp. 761, 766, 7 Media L. Rep. 1298 (D. N.J.1981) (caption in textbook implying racial prejudice of police officer found not to be false light invasion); Sherman v. Bordentown Reg'l Sch. Dist. 23 Media L. Rep. 1168 (Law Div. 1994) (publicity must be highly offensive to reasonable person).

3. ***Publication of Private Facts.*** This tort occurs when it is shown that the matters revealed were actually private, that dissemination of such facts would be offensive to a reasonable person, and that there is no legitimate interest of the public in being apprised of the facts publicized. Bisbee v. John C. Conover Agency, 186 N.J. Super. 335, 340 (App. Div. 1982).

Public Disclosure. The court must first determine whether the published facts were in the public domain. Romaine v. Kallinger, 109 N.J. 282, 298 (1988); Sherman v. Bordentown Reg'l Sch. Dist. 23 Media L. Rep. 1168 (Law Div. 1994).

In the context of public access to an employment-related case for fraud where so-called confidential settlement documents touching on issues of public concern were discussed in the pleadings and attached, there is a presumption of public access to the materials and the proceeding. Lederman v. Prudential Life Ins. Co. of Am., 385 N.J. Super. 307 (App. Div.), certif. denied, 188 N.J. 353 (2006).

In G.D. v. Kenny, 205 N.J. 275, 309 (2011), the New Jersey Supreme Court dismissed a publication of private facts count where plaintiff could not establish he had a reasonable expectation of privacy in his expunged criminal conviction record.

Private Facts. If critical facts are private, publication of these facts would not constitute an actionable invasion of privacy if they are "newsworthy," and thus a matter of legitimate public concern. Romaine, supra, 109 N.J. at 300. Plaintiff must show that the matters revealed were actually private. Bisbee, supra, 186 N.J. Super. at 340. **In Capers v. FedEx Ground, No. 2:02-CV-5352, 2012 U.S. Dist. LEXIS 78818, at *15 (D. N.J. June 6, 2012), Plaintiffs stated a claim for public disclosure of private facts in part because their allegations regarding mistreatment of their paychecks by their employer were supported by the Restatement (Second) of Torts § 652(b) cmt. b (1977), in that "generally speaking, the law recognizes that information regarding a private employee's income is a private matter."**

Identification of Plaintiff. The reported cases do not specifically comment on identification of plaintiff; however, they assume that such an identification has occurred. Romaine, supra, 109 N.J. at 300; Bisbee, supra, 186 N.J. Super. at 340.

Offensiveness. Plaintiff must show that dissemination of private facts would be offensive to a reasonable person. Bisbee v. John C. Conover Agency, 186 N.J. Super. 335, 340, 452 A.2d 689, 691, 9 Media L. Rep 1298 (1982); Sherman v. Bordentown Reg'l Sch. Dist., 23 Media L. Rep. 1168 (Law Div. 1994).

Absence of Legitimate Concern to the Public. Plaintiff must show that the public has no legitimate interest in being apprised of the facts publicized. Bisbee, supra, 186 N.J. Super. at 340. University student newspaper's coverage of school investigation did not involve a purely private matter, and community had legitimate interest in being informed of results of investigation. Gallo v. Princeton Univ., 281 N.J. Super. 134, 148-49, 656 A.2d 1267 (App. Div.), certif. denied, 142 N.J. 453, 663 A.2d 1359 (1995). Claims for invasion of privacy by giving unreasonable publicity to the private life of another may not be predicated on the fact that a small group of people who filmed and edited a television show may have learned information concerning plaintiff's private lives. Castro v. NYT Television, 384 N.J. Super. 601 (App. Div. 2006).

4. ***Intrusion.*** New Jersey has adopted the elements identified in the Restatement (Second) of Torts § 652B: One who intentionally intrudes, physically or otherwise, upon the seclusion of another or his private affairs or concerns, is subject to liability to the other for invasion of his privacy, if the intrusion would be highly offensive to a reasonable person. Figured v. Paralegal Technical Servs., Inc., 231 N.J. Super. 251, 256, 555 A.2d 663 (App. Div. 1977). Bisbee, supra, 186 N.J. Super. at 339. Acts complained of must be established as unreasonably and offensively intrusive to the average person. Lingar v. Line-In Companions, Inc., 300 N.J. Super. 22, 692 A.2d 61 (App. Div. 1997). Hart v. City of Jersey City, 308 N.J. Super. 487, 493, 706 A.2d 256 (App. Div. 1998).

Unauthorized Intentional Intrusion or Prying into Plaintiff's Seclusion. Defendant is subject to liability only when he intrudes into a private place, or has invaded a private seclusion that plaintiff has thrown about his person or affairs. N.O.C., Inc. v. Schaefer, 197 N.J. Super. 249, 254, 484 A.2d 729, 731 (Law Div. 1984) (Court dismissed claim of purported polluter against adjoining property owner who built observation deck to monitor plaintiff's activities).

Offensiveness. Plaintiff must demonstrate that the intrusion would be "highly offensive" to a reasonable person. Figured, supra, 231 N.J. Super. at 256-257, 555 A.2d at 666, (citing Restatement (Second) of Torts § 652B).

As to Private Matter. There is no wrong where defendant did not actually delve into plaintiff's concerns, or where plaintiff's activities are already public or already known. Bisbee, supra, 186 N.J. Super. 335 (photograph of home could have been taken by any bystander and detailed information concerning home purchase and purchaser are matters of public record). Whatever the public may see from a public place cannot be private. Id.; N.O.C., Inc., supra, 197 N.J. Super. at 255; Figured, supra, 231 N.J. Super. at 258, 555 A.2d at 667.

Burden of Proof. Unreasonable intrusion upon seclusion, like defamation per se, is actionable in absence of proof of resulting special harm. Rumbauskas v. Cantor, 266 N.J. Super. 399, 629 A.2d 1359, 1362 (App. Div. 1993), rev'd on other grounds, 138 N.J. 173, 649 A. 2d 853 (1994).

C. Other Privacy-Related Actions

1. *Intentional Infliction of Emotional Distress.* In General. New Jersey recognizes the tort of intentional infliction of emotional distress, and has adopted the Restatement (Second) of Torts definition of the cause of action. Buckley v. Trenton Sav. Fund Soc'y, 111 N.J. 355, 544 A.2d 857 (1988). The cause of action for intentional infliction of emotional distress requires intentional and outrageous conduct by a tortfeasor causing another's severe emotional distress. The defendant must act intentionally or recklessly and intend to produce emotional distress in the plaintiff, or act recklessly in deliberate disregard of a high degree of probability that emotional distress will follow. Buckley, supra, 111 N.J. 355, 544 A.2d 857; Taylor v. Metzger, 152 N.J. 490, 706 A.2d 685 (1990); Voorhees v. Preferred Mut. Ins. Co., 128 N.J. 165, 607 A.2d 1255 (1992).

The Appellate Division affirmed dismissal of an intentional infliction of emotional distress claim brought by an employee who was in deep mourning regarding the death of her teenage daughter. Ingraham v. Ortho-McNeil Pharm., 422 N.J. Super. 12, 25 A.3d 1191 (App. Div. 2011). The employee was allegedly directed by her supervisor to remove the photographs and ballet slippers of her deceased daughter from her work cubicle, and not to talk about her daughter's death with co-workers. The Court held that the behavior did not rise to the extreme and outrageous standard, and that "the workplace has too many personal conflicts and too much behavior that might be perceived as uncivil for the courts to be used as the umpire for all but the most extreme workplace disputes." Id. at 13. Also, workplace conduct "will rarely be so egregious as to give rise to a claim of intentional infliction of emotional distress." Id.; **see also Polonsky v. Verizon**

Communications, Corp., No. 09-4756, 2011 U.S. Dist. LEXIS 134482 (D. N.J. Nov. 22, 2011) (noting that "courts have consistently recognized that it is particularly difficult to establish intentional infliction of emotional distress in the employment context.").

Statute of Limitations. In keeping with the applicability of defamation defenses to claims for intentional infliction of emotional distress, the libel and slander one-year limitations period is also applied to claims for intentional infliction of emotional distress based on allegedly defamatory statements. MacDonald v. Time, Inc., 7 Media L. Rep. 1981 (D. N.J. August 25, 1981). Although there is a two-year statute of limitations for personal injuries, the six-year statute of limitations can apply where personal rights, and not injuries, predominate. McGrogan v. Till, 167 N.J. 414, 423 (2001).

Other Procedural Matters. The court determines whether severe emotional stress can be found, and the jury decides if it is proven. Buckley, supra, 111 N.J. 355; DeAngelis v. Hill, 180 N.J. 1, 847 A.2d 1261 (2004); Lascurain v. City of Newark, 349 N.J. Super. 251, 793 A.2d 731 (App. Div. 2002). Where intentional infliction claim fails, accompanying claim for loss of consortium also must fail. Behrens v. Rutgers, No. 94-CV-358, 1996 WL 570989, at *1, 1996 U.S. Dist. LEXIS 22311 (D. N.J. 1996). A plaintiff may not pursue a claim for intentional infliction to circumvent the required elements of or defenses applicable to another cause of action that directly governs a particular form of conduct. Griffin v. Tops Appliance City, Inc., 337 N.J. Super. 15, 23-24, 766 A. 2d 292, 297 (App. Div. 2001). Except for the kind of aggravated discriminatory conduct involved in Taylor v. Metzger, 152 N.J. 490, 706 A.2d 685 (1998) (when an employer referred to an African American employee as a "jungle bunny"), "it is extremely rare to find conduct in the employment context that will rise to a level of outrageousness necessary to provide a basis of recovery for the tort of intentional infliction of emotional distress." Cox v. Keystone Carbon Co., 861 F.2d 390, 395 (3d Cir. 1988), cited in Griffin, supra, 337 N.J. Super at 25, 766 A. 2d at 297 (police officer brought action against resident for defamation, false light, intentional infliction of emotional distress, negligent infliction of emotional distress, harassment and actual malice after resident published a newsletter accusing the officer of perjury). "In order for plaintiff to prevail on an intentional infliction of emotional distress claim, he must show: 1) intentional conduct; 2) the conduct was extreme and outrageous; 3) the conduct proximately caused plaintiff's emotional distress; and 4) the emotional distress was severe." DeAngelis v. Hill, 180 N.J. 1, 847 A.2d 1261 (2004) (quoting Buckley v. Trenton Sav. Fund Soc'y. 111 N.J. at 366). "Expressions of anger, without more, are not extreme or outrageous" and while a complete expert report would not be necessary early in the litigation, a plaintiff should submit "some objective documentation of his claims" of suffering in order to make out a prima facie case. Juzwiak v. Doe, 415 N.J. Super. 442, 2 A.3d 428 (App. Div. 2010).

2. ***Negligent Infliction of Emotional Distress.*** In Govito v. West Jersey Health System, Inc., 332 N.J. Super. 293, 753 A.2d 716 (App. Div. 2000), the Court rejected defamation claims brought by a nurse against her employer alleging that she diverted narcotics for her addiction because a special-interest privilege applied and that nurses, like physicians, are "public figures," and the allegations did not rise to reckless disregard of the truth. The trial court had dismissed a claim for intentional infliction of emotional distress and this Court rejected her claims of negligent infliction because it was not wholly independent of the defamation alleged and the plaintiff could not meet the level of intent necessary to recover. In Decker v. Princeton Packet Inc., 116 N.J. 418, 432, 561 A. 2d 1122, 1130 (1989), the N.J. Supreme Court ruled that the first amendment requires the plaintiff establish at least the same level of intent to recover for infliction of emotional harm as is necessary to find defamation. While the Decker Court applied this ruling to media defendants, the Govito Court extended that application to "public interest" figures such as the plaintiff nurse. The relevant inquiry respecting a plaintiff's claim of negligent infliction of emotional distress is whether the defendant had a duty to plaintiff and breached it, proximately causing plaintiff's distress. Lascurain v. City of Newark, 349 N.J. Super 251, 279, 793 A.2d 731, 747 (App. Div. 2002).

3. ***Interference With Prospective Economic Advantage.*** Tortious interference with contractual relations is a distinct cause of action from tortious interference with prospective economic advantage. Thus, actionable interference can exist even in the absence of a contract. Printing-Mart Morristown v. Sharp Elecs., 116 N.J. 739, 750, 563 A.2d 31, 36 (1989); Harris v. Perl, 41 N.J. 455, 462, 197 A. 2d 359, 363 (1964). However, these claims are treated in the same general way by the New Jersey courts. Sys. Operations, Inc. v. Scientific Games Dev. Corp., 425 F. Supp. 130, 134 (D.N.J. 1977).

Existence of a Valid Contract Between Plaintiff and Third Party. One who unjustifiably interferes with the contract of another is guilty of a wrong and should not be heard to complain that the contract with which he interfered was unenforceable. Harris v. Perl, 41 N.J. 455, 197 A. 2d 359 (1964); accord Michael Halebian N.J., Inc. v. Roppe Rubber Corp., 718 F. Supp. 348 (D.N.J. 1989). Thus, contracts which are voidable by reason of the statute of frauds, formal defects, lack of consideration, lack of mutuality or uncertainty of terms still afford a basis for a tort action when the defendant interferes with their performance. Harris, supra, 41 N.J. 455, 197 A. 2d 359.

Knowledge By Defendant of Contract. Although the seminal case of Printing-Mart Morristown v. Sharp Electronics, 116 N.J. 739, 563 A. 2d 31 (1989) does not specifically require knowledge on the part of the defendant, federal cases interpreting New Jersey law and relying on Printing-Mart have identified this element as required for this cause of action. See Lightning Lube, Inc. v. Witko Corp., 4 F. 3d 1153, 1166 (3d Cir. 1993); Automated Salvage Transport, Inc. v. NV Koninklijke KNP BT, No. Civ.A.96-369, 1997 WL 576402, at *19, 1997 U.S. Dist. LEXIS 14062 (D. N.J. Sept. 12, 1997) (Wolin, J.).

Intentional and Improper Interference to Induce Nonperformance. Malice is an essential element of a claim for tortious interference with a contractual relationship, which requires proof not only that the interference was intentional, but also that it was without justification or excuse. E. Penn Sanitation, Inc. v. Grinnell Haulers, Inc., 294 N.J. Super. 158, 179-80, 682 A. 2d 1207, 1218 (App. Div. 1996), certif. denied, 148 N.J. 458, 690 A.2d 606 (1997). See O'Connor v. Harms, 111 N.J. Super. 22, 266 A. 2d 605 (App. Div.), certif. denied, 57 N.J. 137, 270 A.2d 40 (1970). In order to prove tortious interference with contract, plaintiff must prove that defendant's conduct was unconscionable and transgressed the generally accepted standards of morality. R.A. Intile Realty Co., Inc. v. Raho, 259 N.J. Super. 438, 477, 614 A.2d 167, 187 (Law Div. 1992). A non-party to a contractual relationship can recover for tortious interference with a contract only upon a showing that the defendant specifically intended to harm the non-party by interfering with the contract. Fineman v. Armstrong World Indus., 980 F. 2d 171 (3d Cir. 1992), cert. denied, 113 S. Ct. 1285 (1993).

Nonperformance of Contract Damaging to Plaintiff. Although the bare elements of the tort of tortious interference with contractual relations are actual interference with the contract and proof of malicious nature of the interference, the element of damage is nonetheless required. Norwood Easthill Assoc. v. Norwood Easthill Watch, 222 N.J. Super. 378, 384, 536 A. 2d 1317, 1320 (App. Div. 1988).

Reasonable Expectation of Entering into Valid Business Relationship. "An action for tortious interference with a prospective business relation protects the right to pursue one's business, calling or occupation free from undue influence or molestation." Printing-Mart Morristown v. Sharp Electronics, 116 N.J. 739, 750, 563 A.2d 31, 36 (1989) (quoting Louis Kamm, Inc. v. Flink, 113 N.J.L. 582, 586 (E & A 1934)). In such an action, a plaintiff must allege a protectable right that gives rise to some reasonable expectation of economic advantage. The complaint must demonstrate that the plaintiff was in pursuit of business. Printing-Mart Morristown, supra, 116 N.J. at 751, 563 A.2d at 36; Harris v. Perl, 41 N.J. 455, 197 A. 2d 359 (1964). It is fundamental to a cause of action for tortious interference with prospective economic advantage that the claim be directed to defendants who are not parties to the relationship. Jenkins v. Region Nine Housing Corp., 306 N.J. Super. 258, 265, 703 A.2d 664, 667 (App. Div. 1997), certif. denied, 153 N.J. 405, 709 A.2d 798 (1998) (citing Printing-Mart Morristown, supra, 116 N.J. at 752).

Intentional and Improper Interference. A complaint for tortious interference with prospective economic advantage must allege facts claiming that the interference was done intentional and with malice. Malice is defined to mean that the harm was inflicted intentionally and without justification or excuse. Printing-Mart Morristown, supra, 116 N.J. at 751, 563 A.2d at 37. The standard of malice must be flexible and must focus on the defendant's actions in the context of the case presented. Id. The factors most pertinent to the malice standard in an intentional interference with prospective economic relations claim are (1) the nature of the actor's conduct, (2) the actor's motive, (3) the interest sought to be advanced by the actor, (4) the societal interest in protecting the freedom of action of the actor, and (5) the contractual interests of the other. MacDougall v. Weichert, 144 N.J. 380, 404-05, 677 A.2d 162, 174 (1996).

Loss of Prospective Advantage. A complaint for tortious interference with prospective economic advantage must allege facts leading to the conclusion that the interference caused the loss of prospective advantage. Printing-Mart Morristown, supra, 116 N.J. at 751, 563 A.2d at 37. Thus, the facts alleged must lead to the conclusion that a reasonable probability existed that, absent the interference, the plaintiff would have received the anticipated economic benefit. Leslie Blau Co. v. Alfieri, 157 N.J. Super. 173, 185-86, 384 A. 2d 859, 865 (App. Div.), certif. denied sub nom., Leslie Blau Co. v. Reitman, 77 N.J. 510 (1978). The complaint must further allege that the injury caused damage. Printing-Mart Morristown, supra, 116 N.J. at 752; 563 A.2d at 37.

Common Law Defenses. That the underlying contract may be unenforceable is no defense to a claim of tortious interference with contractual relations. Harris v. Perl, 41 N.J. 455, 197 A.2d 359 (1964); accord, Michael Halebian N.J., Inc. v. Roppe Rubber Corp., 718 F. Supp. 348 (D. N.J. 1989). The fact that a contract is illegal or void as against public policy is a defense to a claim of tortious interference with prospective contractual relations. Fineman v. Armstrong World Indus., 980 F.2d 171 (3d Cr. 1992). Similarly, no cause of action for tortious interference with prospective economic advantage exists where the plaintiff had no property or business interest, present or future, deserving of legal protection. JEM Marketing, LLC v. Cellular Telecomm. Indus. Ass'n., 308 N.J. Super. 160, 704 A. 2d 798 (App. Div. 1998). A party to an existing or prospective contractual relationship cannot be held directly liable for tortious interference with that relationship. Printing-Mart Morristown, supra, 116 N.J. at 750, 563 A.2d at 36; accord Kopp, Inc. v. United Techs., Inc., 223 N.J. Super. 548, 539 A.2d 309 (App. Div. 1988). Justification or privilege negates malice and is an affirmative defense to an action for tortious interference with contractual rights or business relations. Middlesex Concrete Prods. & Excavating Corp. v. Carteret

Indus. Ass'n, 37 N.J. 507, 519, 181 A. 2d 774, 781 (1962). Protection of the public interest affords a privilege to acts of interference with contractual or economic relations. Id. To determine the availability of a defense of privilege in an action for tortious interference, the court must take into account the relationship of the parties within the social and factual context presented, and weigh the relative merits of rights and advantages affected by the alleged tortious conduct. Id.

Burden of Proof. It is the plaintiff's burden to prove that the defendant acted intentionally and wrongfully without justification. Printing-Mart Morristown, supra, 116 N.J. at 751, 563 A.2d at 37 (citing Levin v. Kuhn Loeb & Co., 174 N.J. Super. 560, 573, 417 A. 2d 79 (App. Div. 1980)). The actual malice standard will apply where the nature of plaintiff's business intrinsically involves a matter of legitimate public interest; other businesses must satisfy only a negligence standard. Turf Lawnmower Repair, Inc. v. Bergen Record Corp., 139 N.J. 392, 655 A. 2d 417, 23 Media L. Rep. 1609 (1995), cert. denied, 516 U.S. 1066, 116 S. Ct. 752, 133 L. Ed. 2d 700 (1996). However, the New Jersey Supreme Court recently qualified the Turf holding in Senna v. Florimont, 196 N.J. 469, 958 A.2d 427 (2008), a case where the plaintiff—an operator of a boardwalk game—brought a defamation and tortuous interference claim against a direct competitor whose employees broadcast over a public loud speaker that plaintiff was "dishonest" and a "crook," among other detailed statements. In reversing the lower court's decision that actual malice should apply because games of chance involve a highly regulated industry, the Court examined the identity of the speaker and held: "When published by a media or media-related defendant, a news story concerning public health and safety, a highly regulated industry, or allegations of criminal or consumer fraud or a substantial regulatory violation will, by definition, involve a matter of public interest or concern." Id. at 496. For all other media and non-media cases, the Court held, the content, form, and context of the speech should be examined to determine whether the speech involves a matter of public concern or interest. Id. at 497. The Court noted: "when a business owner maligns his competitor in the marketplace for apparent economic gain, it is difficult to reach the conclusion that such commercially disparaging expressions are at the heart of free speech values or implicate any of the concerns that animated the New York Times [v. Sullivan] decision." Id. at 495. In Salzano v. N. Jersey Media Group Inc., 201 N.J. 500 (2010), the Supreme Court reaffirmed that in deciding whether speech involves a matter of public concern it applies the "content, form and context" standard from Dun & Bradstreet, Inc. v. Greenmoss Builders Inc., 472 U.S. 749, 761, 105 S. Ct. 2939, 2946, 86 L. Ed. 2d 593, 604 (1985) and looks at the "identity of the speaker and targeted audience" as referenced in Senna. 21 N.J. at 533.

Statute of Limitations. In Rex v. Hutner, 26 N.J. 489, 140 A. 2d 753 (1958), the New Jersey Supreme Court held that the six-year statute of limitations applies only to actions for tortious injury not encompassed by the provisions of the two-year statute of limitations on actions for injuries to the person.

4. ***Prima Facie Tort.*** In an ambiguous decision in Taylor v. Metzger, 152 N.J. 490, 706 A.2d 685 (1998), the New Jersey Supreme Court acknowledged that a New Jersey cause of action for prima facie tort had been recognized by various law review articles and one Appellate Division case—Trautwein v. Harbourt, 40 N.J. Super. 247, 266, 123 A.2d 30 (App. Div.), ("[w]e have no difficulty with the theoretical concept . . . that intentional, willful or malicious harms of any kind are actionable unless justified"), certif. denied, 22 N.J. 220, 125 A.2d 233 (1956). Id. at *17. The court considered the formulations of prima facie tort set forth in the Restatement (Second) of Torts § 870, and recognized that some jurisdictions limit applicability of prima facie tort to "instances in which a plaintiff would have no other cause of action." Id. Nevertheless, the court declared that prima facie tort "should not be invoked when the essential elements of an established and relevant cause of action are missing," and quoted with the approval the declaration of a New York court that "[p]rima facie tort should not become a 'catch-all' alternative for every cause of action which cannot stand on its legs." Id. (quoting Belsky v. Lowenthal, 405 N.Y.S. 2d 62, 65 (1978), aff'd, 47 N.Y. 2d 820, 418 N.Y.S. 2d 573, 392 N.E. 2d 560 (1979)). Holding that the trial court had properly dismissed the prima facie tort claim in the case at bar, the Taylor v. Metzger court declined to resolve whether the tort exists in New Jersey: "this case presents no opportunity for this Court to determine the applicability of a cause of action for prima facie tort." Id. at *18. See also Stevens Inst. of Tech. v. Hine, 2007 WL 2188200, at *9-10, 2007 N.J. Super. Unpub. LEXIS 1268 (App. Div. July 31, 2007) (applying Taylor analysis and affirming summary judgment grant against plaintiff on prima facie tort claim because "the same conduct of defendants underlies plaintiff's claim of prima facie tort as underlies its claim of defamation").

II. EMPLOYER TESTING OF EMPLOYEES

A. Psychological or Personality Testing

1. ***Common Law and Statutes.*** New Jersey recognizes that "[T]he use of psychological tests to predict or evaluate employee performance is a recognized part of the American workplace." In re Vey, 124 N.J. 534, 540, 591 A.2d 1333, 1336 (1991). An employer's right to conduct such testing, however, is not unlimited, and must be directed specifically to job performance. Id.; McKenna v. Fargo, 451 F. Supp. 1355 (D. N.J. 1978), aff'd (3d Cir. 1979) (In action brought by individual challenging constitutionality of City's requirement that applicant undergo psychological testing to determine ability to withstand psychological pressures in firefighting, the District Court held that the interest of the City in

screening out applicants who could not handle psychological pressures of job was sufficient to justify intrusion into privacy of applicant). In Griswold v. Oliva, No. 08-01839, 2009 U.S. Dist. LEXIS 84129 (D. N.J. 2009), the court denied a motion to dismiss the claims of applicants to the Port Authority of New York and New Jersey who alleged that questions on a personality test violated their privacy rights. The court held that instead of relying solely upon the analysis of McKenna, the defendant Port Authority ought to address balancing factors established by the Third Circuit in Fraternal Order of Police, Lodge No. 5 v. City of Philadelphia, 812 F.2d 105, 110 (3d Cir. 1987) and U.S. v. Westinghouse Elec. Corp, 638 F.2d 570, 577 (3d Cir. 1980).

Relying largely upon U.S. Supreme Court and Ninth Circuit precedent, in 1991 the New Jersey Supreme Court in Vey set forth a "validation" process involving three steps that must be satisfied in order for an employer to establish the required correlation between its psychological testing and job performance:

> First, the employer must specify the trait or characteristic that the selection device is being used to identify or measure. Next, the employer must establish that the particular trait or characteristic is an important element of work behavior. Finally, the employer must "demonstrate by 'professionally acceptable methods' that the selection device is 'predictive of or significantly correlated' with the element of work behavior identified in the second step."

In re Vey, 124 N.J. 534, 541, 591 A.2d 1333, 1336 (1991). In Vey, the Supreme Court remanded the case to the Merit System Board of the NJ Department of Personnel because the record described "a variety of seemingly unremarkable personality traits," such as "boldness" and "suspiciousness" which the Court at first glance could not deem significant of unfitness to be a police officer. The second time it heard Vey, the Supreme Court upheld the Board's determination after clarification. In re Vey, 135 N.J. 306, 639 A.2d 718 (1994).

Statutes. New Jersey statutes on the issue appear to arise only in the contexts of board of education employees and special law enforcement officers. N.J.S.A. 18A:16-2 which empowers School Boards to require the psychiatric or physical testing of any employee who shows deviation from normal physical or mental health. The compelling state interest to protect school children justifies the constitutionality of the statute. Kochman v. Keansburg Bd. of Educ., 124 N.J. Super. 203, 305 A.2d 807 (Ch. Div 1973). Gish v. Bd. of Educ. of Paramus, Bergen County, 145 N.J. Super. 96, 366 A.2d 1337(App. Div. 1976), certif. den. 74 N.J. 251, cert. denied. 98 S. Ct. 233, 434 U.S. 879, 54 L. Ed. 2d 160 (1977) (Appellate Division held that predicated on school board's determination, with the corroboration of two psychiatrists, that a teacher's actions in support of gay rights displayed evidence of deviation from normal mental health which might affect his ability to teach, discipline and associate with students, the board's directive that the teacher submit to a psychiatric evaluation was fair and reasonable and did not constitute a violation of his First or Fourteenth Amendment rights, nor was the failure of the board to produce the two psychiatrists for cross examination at the board hearing a denial of due process.) Psychological testing for special law enforcement officers is governed by N.J.S.A. 40A:14-146.10.

2. ***Private Employers.*** Although In re Vey, 135 N.J. 306, 639 A.2d 718 (1994), involved psychological testing for a civil service position, the reasoning of the New Jersey Supreme Court suggests that its "validation" process for such tests may also be required of private employees.

3. ***Public Employers.*** See II.A.1, supra.

B. Drug Testing

1. ***Common Law and Statutes.*** No New Jersey statute addresses the validity of drug testing of employees.

2. ***Private Employers.*** In Hennessey v. Coastal Eagle Point Oil Co., 129 N.J. 81, 609 A.2d 11 (1992), the New Jersey Supreme Court set forth guidelines for the testing of employees by private employers. In the case, an at-will employee of a private oil company who was terminated following a positive drug test brought suit for wrongful discharge. The question presented to the Court was whether the firing of an at-will employee for failing or refusing to take random urine tests was a violation of a "clear mandate of public policy," which under the Court's landmark decision of Pierce v. Ortho Pharm. Corp., 84 N.J. 58, 417 A.2d 505 (1980) had become an exception to the common law rule that an at-will employee could be fired "for good cause, no cause, or even for cause morally wrong . . . ." Without addressing whether random drug testing violates either common law or Constitutional privacy rights, the Court nonetheless looked to Article I Paragraph 1 of the New Jersey Constitution, as well as common law privacy, to see if they gave rise to a clear mandate of public policy that allows a fired employee to state a Pierce cause of action when drug testing is involved. Id. at 92-97. Based on the Hennessey Court's assessment, to constitute a "clear mandate of public policy" supporting a wrongful discharge suit, a balancing test must be applied to find that the employee's individual right of privacy outweighs the competing public interest in public safety. Pierce, supra, 84 N.J. at 100. The determinative factor in the balancing test is the nature of the employee's

work. If his/her position is "safety sensitive," the scale tips toward public safety, but the right to individual privacy prevails where there is a non-safety sensitive job. Id., Fredric Knapp & Laura Lences McLester, *The Dwindling Employment-at-Will Doctrine*, 151 N.J.Law. 11 (1993). ("whether or not a private employer will be permitted to conduct a random drug test will depend exclusively on the safety-sensitive nature of the positions involved therein"). The only clear instruction from the courts on the issue of "safety sensitive" positions is that it is fact specific. The Hennessey Court recognized this when it stated that the complex issue is "better addressed in the context of legislation action or labor relation agreements." Id. at 107. There has since been no widening of the definition set forth in Hennessey and it should be assumed that random testing is not permitted for employees with jobs not explicitly "fraught with hazard." See Robert Bernstein & Michael Bissinger, Employee Drug Testing: Is it Permissible? N.J. Supreme Court Leaves Many Unanswered Questions ("Unfortunately, absent firm guidelines, public employers are left to guess whether their interests meet [the guidelines] necessary to overcome the employees constitutional privacy rights").

In the meantime, if a private employer is justified in implementing a drug testing program, it should heed the Hennessey Court's strong recommendation to "implement measures designed to minimize intrusiveness of testing process," including the use of a procedure "which allows as much privacy and dignity as possible; and notice, close in time to the beginning of a testing program but sufficient to provide adequate advance warning that announces the program, details the method for selecting employees to be tested, warns employees of lingering effect of certain drugs in the system, explains how the sample will be analyzed, and notifies employees of consequences of testing positive or refusing to take test." Hennessey v. Coastal Eagle Point Co., 129 N.J. 81, 107, 609 A.2d 11, 23 (1992). "Furthermore, employers may conduct only those tests necessary to determine the presence of drugs in urine, and are under obligation not to disclose information obtained as result of testing." Id.

3. ***Public Employers.*** Any government compelled drug or alcohol test is a "search" and a "seizure" within the meaning of the Fourth Amendment of the United States Constitution and Article I, paragraph 7 of the New Jersey Constitution and must meet the "reasonableness requirement" under both provisions. N.J. Transit PBA Local 304 v. N.J. Transit Corp., 151 N.J. 531, 543, 701 A.2d 1243, 1251 (1997); see also Skinner v. Railway Labor Executives Ass'n, 489 U.S. 602, 617, 109 S. Ct. 1402, 1413 (1989); National Treasury Employees Union v. Von Raab, 489 U.S. 656, 665, 109 S. Ct. 1384, 1390 (1989); Rawlings v. Police Dep't of Jersey City, 133 N.J. 182, 188, 627 A.2d 602 (1993); O'Keefe v. Passaic Valley Water Comm'n, 132 N.J. 234, 242, 624 A.2d 578 (1993); Int'l Fed'n of Prof'l & Technical Eng'rs, Local 194A v. Burlington County Bridge Comm'n, 240 N.J. Super. 9, 14, 572 A.2d 204, 207 (App. Div. 1990), certif. denied, 122 N.J. 183, 584 A.2d 244 (1990). Generally, New Jersey has borrowed from traditional search and seizure law to find that state compelled drug tests are unreasonable searches in the absence of probable cause or individualized suspicion. N.J. Transit PBA Local 304, supra, 151 N.J. at 544-545, 701 A.2d at 1243, 1249. However, depending on the type of job, individual suspicion is not necessary. The New Jersey Supreme Court in N.J. Transit PBA Local 304 held that the random testing of transit police officers in safety sensitive positions who carry firearms was constitutional. Shoemaker v. Handel, 795 F.2d 1136, 1142 (3d Cir. 1986) (Warrantless drug and alcohol testing of persons engaged in heavily regulated horseracing industry are constitutionally reasonable). A judicial determination of whether a government employer may require suspicionless drug testing of its employees will consider whether the government has satisfied the "special needs" test, under which search by drug or alcohol test will be upheld if there is a "special need" beyond normal law enforcement and public interests outweigh private ones. State v. O'Hagen, 189 N.J. 140, 157-58, 914 A.2d 267, 277 (2007) (affirming that drug and alcohol testing programs will be analyzed under the New Jersey Constitution by using the "special needs" test, despite the United States Supreme Court's decision—Samson v. California, 547 U.S. 843, 126 S. Ct. 2193, 165 L. Ed. 2d 250 (2006)—seemingly in favor of the balancing test.) A drug test performed by a police department pursuant to its regulations and the Attorney General's Guidelines is a search subject to the requirements of the Fourth Amendment, however while probable cause is the general standard for permitting a search, a balance is struck because of the "special governmental need" and a diminished expectation of privacy on the part of the police officer and a test can be required in the case of "reasonable suspicion without probable cause." Tamburelli v. Hudson County Police Dep't, 326 N.J. Super. 551, 555, 742 A.2d 560, 562 (App. Div. 1999) (a previously reliable confidential informant's tip that an officer was using drugs presented sufficient particularized reasonable suspicion to require a test). The Court will also assess whether the government's procedures minimize the intrusiveness of drug testing and diminish the employee's reasonable expectation of privacy and the amount of notice given regarding the drug testing requirement. N.J.S.A. Const. Art. 1, ¶ 1; U.S.C.A. Const. Amend. 4; N.J. Transit PBA Local 304, supra, 151 N.J. at 548. Insofar as it was inconsistent with the special needs test, the N.J. Transit PBA Local 304 Court overruled the Appellate Division's previous rejection of a city's contention in Fraternal Order of Police, Newark Lodge No. 12 v. City of Newark, 216 N.J. Super. 461, 524 A.2d 430 (App. Div. 1987) that police officers are members of a highly regulated industry subject to random drug testing. See also O'Keefe v. Passaic Valley Water Comm'n, 132 N.J. 234, 242, 624 A.2d 578, 582 (1993) (reviewing the special needs test in dicta); State v. Hempele, 120 N.J. 182, 576 A.2d 793 (1990) (finding special needs not applicable to government search of garbage because no special needs were identified); Int'l Fed'n of Prof'l & Technical Eng'rs, Local 194A, supra, 240 N.J. Super. at 24-25, 572 A.2d 204, 213 (App. Div. 1990), certif.

denied, 122 N.J. 183, 584 A.2d 244 (1990) (applying special needs test in upholding urine testing of bridge workers at annual physical examinations). Reaffirming that New Jersey follows the U.S. Supreme Court on searches for drugs within public schools, and differentiating privacy interests protected under Article I, paragraph I, of the New Jersey Constitution (i.e. reproductive freedom) from those of persons in the public school context. Joye v. Hunterdon Cent. Reg'l High Sch., 176 N.J. 568, 826 A.2d 624 (2003).

C. Medical Testing

1. ***Common Law and Statutes.*** New Jersey law expressly provides that Boards of Education may require any of its employees to undergo physical examinations. N.J.S.A. 18A:16-2. State child labor law requires minors under 18 to undergo a complete medical physical. N.J.S.A. 34:2-21.8. No state statute otherwise requires or prohibits physical examinations or medical testing, except that employers are prohibited from deducting from wages to defray the costs of medical examinations of employees and prospective employees. N.J.S.A. 34:11-24.1.

2. ***Private Employers.*** The New Jersey Law Against Discrimination ("LAD"), N.J.S.A. 10:5-1, prohibits discrimination in hiring on the basis of disability. A physical examination for the purpose of determining whether the employee is capable of performing the job does not violate the LAD. Kube v. New Penn Motor Exp., Inc., 865 F. Supp. 221 (D. N.J. 1994).

3. ***Public Employers.*** New Jersey courts have recognized a right to privacy in medical information. See Shoemaker v. Handel, 795 F.2d 1136, 1144 (3d Cir. 1986), cert. denied, 479 U.S. 986, 107 S. Ct. 577 (1986). Nonetheless, this privacy interest is not absolute and must be balanced against the legitimate interests of the state in securing the information. The state must use the "narrowest means consistent with maintenance of its legitimate interests" when requesting the disclosure of personal medical information. Shoemaker v. Handel, 608 F. Supp. 1151 (D. N.J.1985), aff'd on other grounds, 795 F.2d 1136 (3d Cir. 1986).

D. Polygraph Tests

Law related to lie detector tests in New Jersey is set forth in N.J.S.A. 2C:40A-1. The statute makes it a disorderly person's offense for an employer to "influence, request or require an employee or prospective employee to take or submit to a lie detector test as a condition of employment or continued employment." The provisions of the Act do not apply if the employer manufactures, distributes or dispenses controlled dangerous substances or if the employee's duties are to handle such substances. Id. The interpretation of the statute has been strict with respect to its requirement that the test not be a condition of employment or continued employment. See State v. Cmty. Distribs., Inc., 64 N.J. 479, 317 A.2d 697 (1974). ("Despite employer's contention that its request of employees that they take polygraph test was not condition of employment or continued employment, request was to be considered as having been made such condition in view of employment relationship and psychological compulsion which accompanied it"). It is not necessary that an employee actually submit to a polygraph for an employer to be convicted as a disorderly person. State v. Vornado, Inc., 155 N.J. Super. 354, 357, 382 A.2d 945, 946 (App. Div. 1978). Even if the police suggest the use of the test to solve a theft, the employer may not involve himself in such a way that the test becomes a condition of employment. State v. Berkley Photo Inc., 150 N.J. Super. 56, 60, 374 A.2d 1226, 1228 (App. Div. 1977). Federal law, the Employee Polygraph Protection Act, 29 U.S.C. §§ 2001-2009, exempts federal employees from coverage under the New Jersey statute. Stehney v. Perry, 101 F.3d 925, 938 (3d Cir. 1996).

E. Fingerprinting

New Jersey law sets forth a number of occupations that are amenable to pre-employment fingerprint tests. They include employees of the Boxing Wrestling and Combative Sports Commission (N.J.S.A. 5:2A-5), casino workers (N.J.S.A. 5:12-70), certain educationally related jobs including bus drivers (N.J.S.A. 18A:6-4.14; N.J.S.A. 18A:6-7.2; N.J.S.A. 18A:39-17; N.J.S.A. 18A:39-19.1), Parking Authority Employees (N.J.S.A. 40:11A-22), health care employees (N.J.S.A. 30:4-3.6; N.J.S.A. 45:11-24.4), locksmiths (N.J.S.A. 45:5A-35); employees of licensed detectives (N.J.S.A. 45:19-16), all candidates for admission as attorneys to the New Jersey bar (R. 1:24-1), and check-cashing licensees, (N.J.S.A. 17:15A-36). Additionally New Jersey municipalities have the power to license and subsequently fingerprint particular workers such as Real Estate Brokers N.J.S.A. 40:52-1. Such an ordinance does not give the power to deny a license based on the results of fingerprinting. A statutory requirement to provide fingerprints is not a search. Doe v. Poritz, 142 N.J. 1, 662 A.2d 367 (1995).

III. SEARCHES

A. Employee's Person

1. ***Private Employers.*** The search and seizure clause of Article I, paragraph 7 of the New Jersey Constitution does not apply to searches by private parties, including private employers. Hennessey v. Coastal Eagle Point Oil Co., 129 N.J. 81, 95, 609 A.2d 11, 17 (1992); State v. Calcagno, 120 N.J. Super. 536, 295 A.2d 366 (App. Div. 1972).

However, a search by a private employer in concert with law enforcement is unlawful. State v. Ferrari, 141 N.J. Super. 67, 72, 357 A.2d 286, 289 (App. Div. 1976). Where a private employer suspected his employee of breaking into the business's computer system police detectives became involved and obtained a subpoena to compel information on the employee from the Internet Service Provider ("ISP") for her personal email account. State v. Reid, 389 N.J. Super. 563, 566, 914 A.2d 310, 311 (App. Div. 2007). The Appellate Division held that the subpoena violated the employee's right to be free from unwarranted searches and seizures . The Police Detectives had obtained the subpoena from a Municipal Court without jurisdiction and the employee "had a reasonable expectation of privacy in her ISP account information[.]" Id. at 574, 914 A.2d at 317. The New Jersey Supreme Court modified and affirmed the Appellate Division's decision in State v. Reid, 194 N.J. 386 (2008), and remanded the case for further proceedings. The Court agreed with the Appellate Division that the Trial Court had properly suppressed evidence regarding an employee's personal e-mail account, which had been obtained by a procedurally-defective subpoena. It also held that under the New Jersey State Constitution, citizens have a reasonable expectation of privacy in the subscriber information they give to their ISPs. Id. at 389. Further, this interest is similar to the one that New Jersey citizens have in their bank records and telephone billing records, and law enforcement officials can satisfy that interest and obtain internet subscriber information by serving an ISP with a grand jury subpoena, without notice to the subscriber. Id.

Soon after Reid was decided, the Appellate Division distinguished it in a case where an employee who had stolen approximately $8000.00 from his employer objected to a police search of his personal information, which was located on a computer the Appellate Division determined was owned by the employer. State v. M.A., 954 A.2d 503 (2008). The Appellate Division held: "that neither the law nor society recognize as legitimate defendant's subjective expectation of privacy in a workplace computer he used to commit a crime." Id. at 513. **For a review of Reid and prior state Supreme Court privacy decisions, see State v. DeFranco, 426 N.J. Super. 240, 249-50, 43 A.3d 1253 (App. Div. 2012) (Court declining to suppress evidence of a cell phone conversation between a teacher who allegedly sexually molested a minor and the complaining student because the teacher's "professed subjective expectation of privacy [was not] one that society would be willing to recognize as reasonable.")**

An employee had a reasonable expectation of privacy in her email correspondence with her attorney, sent and received through her company-issued laptop, but using her personal, password protected Yahoo! email account. Stengart v. Loving Care Agency, Inc., 201 N.J. 300 (2010). Plaintiff Stengart left her position at Loving Care Agency and later sued for employment discrimination. Prior to resigning, Stengart had used her company laptop to communicate with her attorney. The emails—clearly regarding confidential legal matters and bearing a "personal and confidential" legend when sent from Stengart's attorney—were located by Loving Care's forensic computer experts during discovery and then used by its attorneys. The court rejected Loving Care's arguments that the attorney-client privilege either did not attach to the emails or was waived by Stengart because she had taken reasonable steps to insure that her communications with her attorney were confidential and Loving Care's policy on internet use did not warn users that their personal email accounts might be forensically divulged by the company. The court further emphasized the importance of preserving attorney-client privilege and noted that while companies may lawfully adopt policies on computer use to protect their businesses, "employers have no need or basis to read the specific *contents* of personal, privileged, attorney-client communications in order to enforce corporate policy." The case was remanded to the trial court for a hearing regarding whether Loving Care's attorneys violated the professional responsibility rules with respect to the review of the emails.

2. ***Public Employers.*** In general, the search of a person, work area or property requires a warrant for it to be considered reasonable under the Fourth Amendment. Lovgren v. Byrne, 787 F.2d 857, 865 (3d Cir. 1986); State v. Bonaccurso, 227 N.J. Super. 159, 45 A.2d 853 (Law Div. 1988). Nonetheless, in closely regulated industries an exception to the warrant requirement exists for searches of premises pursuant to an administrative inspection scheme. Shoemaker v. Handel, 795 F.2d 1136, 1142, cert. denied 107 S. Ct. 577 (3rd Cir. 1986); see also Camara v. Mun. Court, 387 U.S. 523, 528-29, 87 S. Ct. 1727, 1730-31 (1967). Whether a warrantless search is nevertheless a reasonable one, depends on the expectation of privacy in the area searched, the importance of the governmental interest occasioning the search, and the degree to which alleged authority for the search is tailored to that interest and minimizes the intrusion. Lovgren v. Byrne, 787 F.2d 857, 865 (3d Cir. 1986); N.J.S.A. Const. Art. 1, par. 7. Essentially the bright line rule is that an administrative search may be made without a warrant if the industry is highly regulated. See Middlesex County Health Dep't v. Roehsler, 235 N.J. Super. 262, 267, 561 A.2d 1212, 1214-15 (Law Div. 1989). The Casino Control Act, N.J.S.A. 5:12-79(a)(6), is one example of an exception to the warrant requirement. The court has upheld the constitutionality of the statute, which allows the Division of Gaming Enforcement to conduct warrantless searches of licensees and their personal effects in a casino facility. In re Martin, 90 N.J. 295, 447 A.2d 1290 (1982). The Casino Control statute permits warrantless searches only of "premises wherein casino gaming is conducted; or gaming devices or equipment are manufactured, sold, distributed, or serviced; or wherein any records of such activities are prepared or maintained . . . ." N.J.S.A. 5:12-79(a)(1). The court has expressly held that warrantless searches on any other premises were not authorized and that employees' homes could not be searched pursuant to the statute. Martin, supra, 90 N.J. at 295.

B. Employee's Work Area

New Jersey follows the federal scheme that constitutional protection against unreasonable search and seizure in an individual's home is not as strong in commercial premises. State v. Bonaccurso, 227 N.J. Super. 159, 164, 545 A.2d 853, 855-6, (Law Div. 1988); see Donovan v. Dewey, 452 U.S. 594, 101 S. Ct. 2534 (1981). A search by a private employer or its agents does not implicate the Fourth Amendment. State v. Calcagno, 120 N.J. Super. 536, 537, 295 A.2d 366, 367 (App. Div. 1972). There is a diminished expectation of privacy in industries pervasively regulated by the government or historically subject to close supervision, such that the government may conduct searches of work areas of such industries without a search warrant. Lovgren v. Byrne, 787 F.2d 857, 865 (3d Cir. 1986); State v. Bonaccurso, supra, 227 N.J. Super. at 167. An employer may search those areas of the place of employment that are dedicated to the private personal use of his employees, and if employer finds evidence of illegal activity such evidence may be turned over to the police and used in a criminal prosecution. See State v. Ferrari, 136 N.J. Super. 61, 344 A.2d 332, (App. Div 1976); see also Calcagno, supra, 120 N.J. Super. at 536. Where there is collusive activity by officers of the government and private citizens however, the Fourth Amendment precludes the use of evidence that is the product of such activity. Ferrari, supra, 136 N.J. Super. at 61. Where a private employer owns the property being used by an employee, the employer maintains the right to search that property. State v. Robinson, 86 N.J. Super. 308, 315, 206 A.2d 779, 783 (Law Div. 1965) (where silver taken from the locker of an employee in employer's silver plant and employer had the right to enter the locker because it was the employer's property, and in contract between employer and union, of which employee was a member, it was provided that employer retained a master key to the locker). An employee does retain a reasonable expectation of privacy against intrusion into his locked desk by law enforcement officers. State v. Ferrari, 141 N.J. Super. 67, 72, 357 A.2d 286, 189 (App. Div. 1976).

C. Employee's Property

1. ***Private Employers.*** See III.A.1, B, supra.

2. ***Public Employers.*** See III.B, supra.

IV. MONITORING OF EMPLOYEES

A. Telephones and Electronic Communications

1. ***Wiretapping.*** The New Jersey Wiretapping and Electronic Surveillance Control Act ("Wiretapping Act"), N.J.S.A. 2A:156A-1 et seq., creates civil and criminal liability for anyone who "intentionally intercepts, endeavors to intercept, or procures any other person to intercept or endeavor to intercept, any wire, oral or electronic communication." It is lawful, however, to intercept a wire, electronic or oral communication where one person to the communication consents to the interception. N.J.S.A. 2A:156A-4(d). See State v. Lane, 279 N.J. Super. 209, 218-19, 652 A.2d 724, 729 (App. Div. 1995), certif. denied, 141 N.J. 94 (1995) (Although the taping of one's own telephone conversations with another is not an intercept within the meaning of the statute, it is unlawful and a violation of New Jersey's Wiretapping Act to tape the telephone conversations of others, including one's spouse without consent when the spouse or person taping the conversation is not a party to the conversation); see also State v. Gora, 148 N.J. Super. 582, 590-91, 372 A.2d 1335, 1339 (App. Div. 1977), certif. denied, 74 N.J. 275, 377 A.2d 679 (1977). Wire communications are protected under the statute regardless of whether the person making or receiving such communications has an expectation of privacy. PBA Local No. 38 v. Woodbridge Police Dept., 832 F. Supp. 808, 819 (D.N.J. 1993). There is an exception to the Wiretapping Act called the "telephone extension exception" or "business extension exception" which creates a viable defense if the defendant can establish two facts: 1) that either the phone company or the subscriber furnished the intercepting telephone or telegraph instrument, equipment, facility, or component; and 2) that the equipment was used in the ordinary course of business. Pascale v. Carolina Freight Carriers Corp., 898 F. Supp. 276, 279 (D. N.J. 1995). (former employees, whose personal telephone conversations were recorded by employer, sued employer under Federal and State Wiretapping and Electronic Surveillance Acts and the employer could not use the "business extension exception" because the intercepting device was tape recording equipment installed by the employer as opposed to a busboard installed by the telephone company, and the recorders were not "telephone instruments or equipment," for purposes of the exemption). It is also not a crime under the state or federal statutes for a law enforcement officer to intercept a wire, electronic or oral communication, where the officer is a "party to the communication or where another officer who is a party to the communication requests or requires him to make such interception." N.J.S.A. 2A:156A-4. Additionally it is not a crime for "any person acting at the direction of an investigative or law enforcement officer to intercept a wire, electronic or oral communication, where such person is a party to the communication or one of the parties to the communication has given prior consent to such interception; provided, however, that no such interception shall be made unless the Attorney General . . . or a county prosecutor . . . determines that there exists a reasonable suspicion that evidence of criminal conduct will be derived from such interception." Id. Lastly, it is not a crime for a person not acting under color of law to intercept a communication, where the person is a party to the communication or one of the parties to the communication has given prior consent to an interception. Essentially, anyone not

acting under the color of law may lawfully record any phone conversation to which they are a party, provided that the recording is not done for an unlawful purpose.

2. ***Electronic Communications.*** In Blakey v. Cont'l Airlines, 164 N.J. 38, 60, 751 A.2d 538, 551 (2000), the New Jersey Supreme Court pondered, but did not decide when it is appropriate for a corporation to monitor posting to an electronic bulletin board, said that although employers should have sexual harassment policies concerning postings, "That does not mean that employers have a duty to monitor employees' mail. Grave privacy concerns are implicated. . . . It may mean that employers may not disregard the posting of offensive messages on company or state agency e-mail systems when the employer is made aware of those messages." However, the recent decision in Doe v. XYZ Corporation, 382 N.J. Super. 122, 887 A.2d 1156 (App. Div. 2005), has established that when an employer has actual or implied knowledge that an employee is using his workplace computer to access pornography, possibly child pornography, and no privacy interest of the employee stands in the way, the employer is under a duty to investigate and effectively stop the employee's unauthorized activities, lest they result in harm to innocent third parties. In State v. Reid, 389 N.J. Super. 563, 574, 914 A.2d 310, 317 (App. Div. 2007), the Appellate Division held that an employee, who was under suspicion by her employer for computer data theft and who later became a criminal defendant in the case, could suppress information retrieved by police from the Internet Service Provider hosting her personal, home e-mail account. The Appellate Court noted that New Jersey Constitutional case law is "highly protective" of the right to privacy, "even when the information sought is, of necessity, in the hands of a third-party." Id. at 575, 914 A.2d 310, 317. That the employee and defendant used an anonymous screen name "manifested an intention to keep her identity publicly anonymous." Id.

The Supreme Court held that an employee had a reasonable expectation of privacy in her email correspondence with her attorney, sent and received through her company-issued laptop, but using her personal, password protected Yahoo! email account. Stengart v. Loving Care Agency, Inc., 201 N.J. 300 (2010). Plaintiff Stengart left her position at Loving Care Agency and later sued for employment discrimination. Prior to resigning, Stengart had used her company laptop to communicate with her attorney. The emails—clearly regarding confidential legal matters and bearing a "personal and confidential" legend when sent from Stengart's attorney—were located by Loving Care's forensic computer experts during discovery and then used by its attorneys. The court rejected Loving Care's arguments that the attorney-client privilege either did not attach to the emails or was waived by Stengart because she had taken reasonable steps to insure that her communications with her attorney were confidential and Loving Care's policy on internet use did not warn users that their personal email accounts might be forensically divulged by the company. The court further emphasized the importance of preserving attorney-client privilege and noted that while companies may lawfully adopt policies on computer use to protect their businesses, "employers have no need or basis to read the specific *contents* of personal, privileged, attorney-client communications in order to enforce corporate policy." The case was remanded to the trial court for a hearing regarding whether Loving Care's attorneys violated the professional responsibility rules with respect to the review of the emails.

3. ***Other Electronic Monitoring.*** There are no published New Jersey cases regarding an employee's right to privacy with respect to other forms of electronic monitoring in the workplace.

B. Mail

See III.A.1, and IV,A.2, supra

C. Surveillance/Photographing

While no New Jersey court has expressly ruled on this issue, the Appellate Division reversed a grant of summary judgment and allowed the plaintiff to pursue a claim that a company policy that entails extended inquiry by the employer or any surveillance by the employer of the extramarital sexual activities of married employees may violate an employee's right to privacy and/or the public policy of the state. Slohoda v. United Parcel Serv., Inc., 193 N.J. Super. 586, 475 A.2d 618 (App. Div. 1984).

V. ACTIVITIES OUTSIDE THE WORKPLACE

A. Statute or Common Law

No statutes.

B. Employees' Personal Relationships

1. ***Romantic Relationships Between Employees.*** No reported decision addresses the question of whether a private or public employer may regulate relationships between employees.

2. ***Sexual Orientation.*** The New Jersey Law Against Discrimination ("LAD") prohibits discrimination in employment on account of sexual orientation or sexual preference. N.J.S.A. 10:5-12. The LAD's prohibitions "applies to sexual harassment of woman by men, men by women, men by men, and women by women. The LAD protects both men and women and bars both heterosexual and homosexual harassment. Lehmann v. Toys 'R Us, Inc., 132 N.J. 587, 604, 626 A.2d 445, 454 (1993); see also Caldwell v. KFC Corp., 958 F. Supp. 962, 970 (D.N.J. 1997); Zalewski v. Overlook Hosp., 300 N.J. Super. 202, 204-5, 692 A.2d 131, 132 (Law Div. 1996).

3. ***Marital Status.*** The New Jersey Law Against Discrimination ("LAD") prohibits discrimination in employment on account of marital status. N.J.S.A. 10:5-12(a). For example, a company policy that an employee may be fired for "adultery" which does not extend to single people having sexual relations violates the LAD. Slohoda v. United Parcel Serv., Inc., 193 N.J. Super. 586, 475 A.2d 618 (App. Div. 1984). However, an anti-nepotism policy, which prohibits employment in management or supervisory positions of persons married to another employee, has been upheld as not violative of the LAD. Thomson v. Sanborn's Motor Express, Inc., 154 N.J. Super. 555, 382 A.2d 53 (App. Div. 1977); see Slohoda, supra, 193 N.J. Super. at 592.

C. Smoking

State statute prohibits employment discrimination on account of a worker's use or non-use of tobacco products. N.J.S.A. 34:6B-1. The law prohibits employers from refusing to hire, discharging, or taking other adverse action against an employee "because that person does or does not smoke or use other tobacco products, unless the employer has a rational basis for doing so which is reasonably related to the employment . . . ." Id.

D. Blogging

In both Dendrite Int'l, Inc. v. Does 1-114, 342 N.J. Super. 134, 775 A.2d 756 (App. Div. 2001) and Immunomedics, Inc. v. Does 1-10, 342 N.J. Super. 160, 775 A.2d 773 (App. Div. 2001), the Appellate Division established a balancing test to be used when plaintiffs seek to discover the identities of anonymous Internet bloggers. In writing for the court in both cases, the appellate panel adopted a case-by-case approach to issues of Internet anonymity, weighing the right of anonymous free speech against the right of a company to protect its own commercial interests. (The court denied Dendrite access to the poster's identities, noting that the company had failed to show it had been damaged by the allegedly defamatory statements posted about it online. In Immunomedics, however, the court ruled that the information posted could have only come from an employee violating their confidentiality agreements. In turn, the court allowed Immunomedics to subpoena the identities of the posters from Yahoo.com.); see also Juzwiak v. Doe, 415 N.J. Super. 442, 2 A.3d 428 (App. Div. 2010) (applying Dendrite and quashing a subpoena).

In Too Much Media v. Hale, 413 N.J. Super. 135, 163 (App. Div. 2010), involving a blogger who was not anonymous and sought to invoke the shield law, the court distinguished Dendrite, noting that the "protections of Dendrite have never been extended beyond ISPs." In its treatment of the case, the Supreme Court of New Jersey noted that the Defendant's reliance upon Dendrite was misplaced, as the case involved a question of reporter's privilege, not anonymous speech. 206 N.J. 209, 239 n.5, 20 A.3d 364 (2011).

VI. RECORDS

A. Personnel Records

N.J.S.A. 18A:6-7a requires removal from the personnel files of school employees any reference to a complaint of child abuse or neglect determined to be unfounded. Employer's records regarding employees' health must be made available to the Commissioner of Health. N.J.S.A. 34:6A-40.

B. Medical Records

The Bill of Rights for Hospital Patients, N.J.S.A. 26:2H-12.8(g) provides for privacy and confidentiality of all records "except as otherwise provided by law or third-party payment contract." The act does not allow a private right of action. Castro v. NYT Television, 370 N.J. Super. 282, 851 A.2d 88 (App. Div. 2004) (Alleging violation of the Act by a hospital for allowing videotaping of emergency room patients).

C. Criminal Records

There are numerous statutes that permit a criminal record inquiry for job applicants, particularly jobs involving children or public safety, but some require the consent of the applicant. These statutes typically provide that such information is to remain confidential. Certain public education employees can only be subject to a criminal history check with their written consent. N.J.S.A. 18A: 6-7.1, 2, 18A:39-19.1. The state's "Megan's Law" N.J.S.A. 2C: 7-1, et seq.

Provides for release of criminal history of sex offenders under certain situations. Motor vehicle record release is governed by N.J.S.A. 39:2-3.4.

D. Subpoenas / Search Warrants

The Third Circuit set forth the privacy balancing test that should be used where an administrative agency seeks to subpoena an employer for employee records. U.S. v. Westinghouse Elec. Corp., 638 F.2d 570, 578 (3d Cir. 1980). In Westinghouse, the National Institute for Occupational Safety and Health sought to subpoena employee health records. When weighing the privacy interests of employees against the government's interest in the requested files, the Third Circuit counseled courts to consider "the type of record requested, the information it does or might contain, the potential for harm in any subsequent nonconsensual disclosure, the injury from disclosure to the relationship in which the record was generated, the adequacy of safeguards to prevent unauthorized disclosure, the degree of need for access, and whether there is an express statutory mandate, articulated public policy, or other recognizable public interest militating towards access." Id. See Trade Waste Mgmt. Ass'n, Inc. v. Hughey, 780 F.2d 221, 234 (3d Cir. 1985) (applying the Westinghouse reasoning to a complaint by a waste management trade association regarding the requirement that businesses to file disclosure statements and noting that "New Jersey's strong interest in the qualifications of persons engaged in the hazardous and solid waste industries, coupled with the regulations of the Department of Environmental Protection safeguarding unauthorized disclosure, would require the conclusion that [a] privacy interest relied upon must yield."). See E.E.O.C. v. Bessemer Group, Inc., 105 Fed. Appx. 411, 414 (3d Cir. 2004) (affirming order to enforce a subpoena—in the context of an age discrimination case—for personnel files of former employees and their severance packages; noting "[t]raditionally, administrative agencies are granted broad investigatory powers to enforce the laws within their purview."); E.E.O.C. v. Twp. of Howell, Nos. 91-2731, 91-2732, 1991 WL 160350, at *2, 1991 U.S. Dist. LEXIS 11650 (D. N.J. Aug. 12, 1991) ("The subpoena of an administrative agency may be enforced where the investigation is within the authority of the agency, the subpoena is not too indefinite, and the information sought is reasonably relevant to the charge under investigation with the EEOC" (citing Univ. of Penn. v. EEOC, 110 S. Ct. 577, 583 (1990)).

Pursuant to N.J.S.A. 10:5-8(i), the New Jersey Law against Discrimination ("LAD") permits the Director of the Division on Civil Rights to administer oaths and subpoena witnesses to appear and give testimony under oath in connection with any investigation or hearing conducted pursuant to the LAD. In connection with this power, the Director may require for the production and examination of any books or papers relating to any subject matter under investigation or in question by the division. Vornado, Inc. v. Potter, 159 N.J. Super. 32, 386 A.2d 1342 (App. Div. 1978), certif. denied, 77 N.J. 489, 391 A.2d 503 (1978). The privilege against self-incrimination does not excuse a witness subpoenaed by the Attorney General, the Director or an ALJ from testifying or producing evidence in such cases. N.J.S.A. 10:5-11.

VII. ACTIONS SUBSEQUENT TO EMPLOYMENT

A. References

The Appellate Division's decision in Singer v. Beach Trading Co., 379 N.J. Super. 63, 876 A.2d 885 (App. Div. 2005), established that an employer can be held liable for negligent misrepresentation of a former employee's work history under certain defined circumstances: (1) the inquiring party clearly identifies the nature of the inquiry; (2) the employer voluntarily decides to respond to the inquiry and thereafter unreasonably provides false or inaccurate information; (3) the person providing the inaccurate information is acting within the scope of his/her employment; (4) the recipient of the incorrect information relies on its accuracy to support an adverse employment action against the plaintiff; and (5) the plaintiff suffers quantifiable damages proximately caused by the negligent misrepresentation. New Jersey, like many other states, has not determined whether an employer has an affirmative duty to respond to a reference inquiry.

B. Non-Compete Agreements

Non-compete provisions in employment agreements are not illegal per se. Maw v. Advanced Clinical Commc'ns, Inc., 179 N.J. 439, 447, 846 A.2d 604 (2004). As established in both the cases of Solari Indus., Inc., v. Malady, 55 N.J. 571, 264 A.2d 53 (1970) and Whitmyer Bros., Inc. v. Doyle, 58 N.J. 25, 274 A.2d 577 (1971), New Jersey now follows what is known as the Solari/Whitmyer test to determine whether a non-compete agreement is unreasonable and therefore unenforceable. Under the Solari/Whitmyer test, a non-compete agreement is enforceable when it protects the legitimate interests of the employer, imposes no undue hardship on the employee, and is not injurious to the public. The first two prongs of the test require a balancing of the employer's interests in protecting proprietary and confidential information and the asserted hardship on the employee. Ingersoll-Rand Co. v. Ciavatta, 110 N.J. 609, 634, 542 A.2d 879, 892 (1988). The third prong requires the reviewing court to analyze the public's broad concern in fostering competition, creativity and ingenuity. Ingersoll-Rand, supra, 110 N.J. at 639, 542 A.2d at 894.

VIII. OTHER ISSUES

A. Statutes of Limitations

The statute of limitations for a misappropriation claim is six years. Canessa v. J.I. Kislak, Inc., 97 N.J. Super. 327, 235 A.2d 62 (Law Div. 1967). As to false light and publication of private facts, the state Supreme Court looked favorably upon case law from other jurisdictions, which generally holds that such actions are subject to the statute of limitations applicable to defamation claims, which is one year under N.J.S.A. 2A: 14-3. Rumbauskas v. Cantor, 138 N.J. 173, 183 (1992). The cause of action for unreasonable intrusion upon seclusion is not governed by the two-year statute of limitations, as it did not relate to any personal or emotional injury, and was not one for "an injury to the person." Rumbauskas v. Cantor, 266 N.J. Super. 399, 629 A.2d 1359, 1362 (App. Div. 1993) (citing N.J.S.A. 2A: 14-2). While injuries to a person are covered by a two-year statute of limitations (N.J.S.A. 2A: 14-2), those torts not covered by the two-year limitation or the one-year defamation limitation (N.J.S.A. 2A:14-3) are subject to the general six year limitation (N.J.S.A. 14A:14-1).

B. Jurisdiction

In Blakey v. Cont'l Airlines, 164, N.J. 38, 751 A.2d 538 (2000), the New Jersey Supreme Court held that jurisdiction over claims of violation of the Law Against Discrimination, defamation and intentional infliction of emotional distress may lie in New Jersey, even if it originated from statements made on electronic bulletin boards physically existing outside of the state, if that bulletin board was closely related to the workplace environment and benefited the employer, and, if harassment on the bulletin board could be considered part of the workplace and the employer had a duty to remedy that harassment.

C. Worker's Compensation Exclusivity

Where the parties agree to be governed by it, New Jersey's Workers Compensation statute provides that an employee be compensated for personal injury or death caused on the job, with various exceptions relating to self-inflicted injury, intoxication and willful failures on the part of the employee. N.J.S.A. 34:15-7. Such compensation is to be provided regardless of the employer's fault, and, in turn, the employee surrenders virtually all potential civil remedies against the employer. N.J.S.A. 34:15-8; Millison v. E.I. DuPont DeNemours & Co., 101 N.J. 161 (1985) ("when, by express or implied agreement, the parties have accepted the provisions of the Compensation Act and the employee qualifies for benefits under the conditions of the Act, the employee shall ordinarily be barred from the pursuit of other remedies"). However, the statute specifically states that employees do not surrender claims where harm is intentionally caused, N.J.S.A. 34:15-8, and it has been held that intentional infliction of emotional distress claims are not barred by a Workers Compensation settlement. Sagaral v. Mountainside Hosp., No. 99-2785, 2001 U.S. Dist. LEXIS 6838, at *63-64 (D. N.J. Feb. 22, 2001). Certain employment discrimination claims under New Jersey's Law Against Discrimination and federal statutes have also been found to be exceptions to the exclusivity provision. Khair v. Campbell Soup Co., 893 F. Supp. 316, 330-31 (noting the lack of case law on point but stating: "we refuse to believe that the New Jersey Supreme Court or state legislature would find race or national origin discrimination to be an unfortunate but expected consequence of employment."), vacated in part by, 893 F. Supp. 316 (D. N.J. 1995).

D. Pleading Requirements

New Jersey recognizes notice pleading. A complaint suffices when it serves fairly to notify defendants of the facts and the alleged deprivation. Presbytery of N.J. of Orthodox Presbyterian Church v. Florio, 40 F.3d 1454 (3d Cir. 1994).

SURVEY OF NEW MEXICO EMPLOYMENT LIBEL LAW

Gregory P. Williams
Peifer, Hanson & Mullins, P.A.
P.O. Box 25245
Albuquerque, NM 87125
Telephone: 505-247-4800; Facsimile: 505-243-6458
gwilliams@peiferlaw.com

(With Developments Reported Through **November 1, 2012**)

GENERAL COMMENTS

New Mexico employees enjoy statutory immunity from liability for job references as long as the information was provided in good faith. However, if an employer chooses to provide a reference on an employee who poses a foreseeable risk of physical harm, New Mexico recognizes a duty of full disclosure to prospective employers and third parties. (See IV.A., infra.)

SIGNIFICANT DEVELOPMENTS SINCE THE 2012 *SURVEY*

The New Mexico Supreme Court has made clear that New Mexico requires a showing of injury to one's reputation to establish liability for defamation. Evidence of humiliation and mental anguish, without evidence of actual injury to reputation, is insufficient to establish a cause of action for defamation. Smith v. Durden, 2012-NMSC-010, ¶ 1, 276 P.3d 943. In addition, the New Mexico Supreme Court has newly addressed the absolute privilege that grants immunity to litigants and their attorneys from being sued for defamation based on public statements they make about a judicial proceeding either before or after the judicial proceeding is filed. Helena Chemical Co. v. Uribe, 2012-NMSC-21, 281 P.3d 237.

I. GENERAL LAW

A. General Employment Law

1. ***At Will Employment.*** New Mexico employers and employees are governed by the "employment-at-will rule," under which employment relationships for an indefinite term can be terminated at any time or no reason, without liability. Hartbarger v. Frank Paxton Co., 115 N.M. 665, 857 P.2d 776 (1993). However, New Mexico courts have recognized an exception to the "at will" rule when circumstances surrounding an employment relationship create an "implied contract" between an employer and an employee. Forrester v. Parker, 93 N.M. 781, 606 P.2d 191 (1980). An implied contract may arise when the conduct of the parties, through either oral or written expressions, indicates that the parties intend to limit the employer's right to discharge an employee either substantively (such as imposing a "good cause" standard for discharge), or procedurally (such as requiring progressive discipline steps). Hartbarger, supra. Whether an implied contract exists is a question of fact to be determined on a case by case basis, taking into account the totality of the circumstances. Kestenbaum v. Pennzoil Co., 108 N.M. 20, 766 P.2d 280 (1988). See also Newberry v. Allied Stores, Inc., 108 N.M. 424, 773 P.2d 1231 (1989); Shull v. N.M. Potash Corp., 111 N.M. 132, 802 P.2d 641 (1990); Zarr v. Washington Tru Solutions, L.L.C., 2009-NMCA-050, ¶ 22, 146 N.M. 274, 208 P.3d 919.

New Mexico also recognizes an exception to the at-will employment rule for wrongful termination under facts disclosing unlawful retaliatory discharge. Lopez v. Kline, 1998-NMCA-016, ¶ 11, 124 N.M. 539, 541, 953 P.2d 304, 306. A claim for retaliatory discharge is only available to at-will employees because if "an employee is already protected from wrongful discharge by a contract," any retaliatory discharge claim would essentially "duplicate rights already adhering to the employee under contract," Weise v. Washington Tru Solutions, L.L.C., 2008-NMCA-121, ¶ 26, 144 N.M. 867, 192 P.3d 1244 (quoting Barreras v. State of N.M. Corr. Dep't, 2003 NMCA-027, ¶ 22, 133 N.M. 313, 62 P.3d 770). In making a claim for wrongful termination, a plaintiff may allege constructive discharge. Constructive discharge is not an independent cause of action, such as a tort or a breach of contract. Instead, constructive discharge is a doctrine that permits an employee to recast a resignation as a de facto firing, depending on the circumstances surrounding the employment relationship and the employee's departure. An employee must allege facts sufficient to find that the employer made working conditions so intolerable, when viewed objectively, that a reasonable person would be compelled to resign. Gormley v. Coca-Cola Enterprises, 2005-NMSC-003, ¶¶ 9-10, 137 N.M. 192, 194-95, 109 P.3d 280, 282-83.

B. Elements of Libel Claim

1. ***Basic Elements.*** The elements of a defamation action are as follows: (1) a false and defamatory communication; (2) published by the defendant; (3) to a third person; (4) of an asserted fact; (5) of and concerning the

plaintiff; and, (6) proximately causing actual injury to the plaintiff. Newberry v. Allied Stores, Inc., 108 N.M. 424, 429, 773 P.2d 1231, 1236 (1989); see also NM UJI 13-1002 (New Mexico has a section of uniform jury instructions dedicated to claims for defamation (NM UJI 13-1001 et seq.)).

2. ***Fault.*** The level of fault, if any, that must be shown depends upon a plaintiff's private or public status and the private or public nature of the defendant's statement.

a. **Private Figure Plaintiff/Matter of Public Concern.** The plaintiff has the burden of proving the falsity of the statement when the plaintiff is a public figure, or when the statements are matters of public concern published by the defendant. Andrews v. Stallings, 119 N.M. 478, 486, 892 P.2d 611, 619 (Ct. App. 1995). Truth is a defense when a private plaintiff alleges the defamatory statement was not of public concern. See also Comments to NM UJI 13-1002.

b. **Private Figure Plaintiff/Matter of Private Concern.** New Mexico has adopted the ordinary common law negligence standard of proof with respect to private defamation plaintiffs when dealing with matters of private concern. Marchiondo v. Brown, 98 N.M. 394, 649 P.2d 462, 470 8 Media L. Rep. 2233 (1982).

c. **Public Figure Plaintiff/Matter of Public Concern.** Plaintiff must prove falsity when he is a public figure when he makes statements of public concern. Andrews v. Stallings, 119 N.M. 478, 486, 892 P.2d 611, 619 (Ct. App. 1995).

3. ***Falsity.*** One or more statements of fact in the communication must be false in a material way. Insignificant inaccuracies of expression are not sufficient. NM UJI 13-1006. The plaintiff has the burden of proving the falsity of the statement when the Plaintiff is a public figure, or when the statements are matters of public concern. Andrews v. Stallings, 119 N.M. 478, 486, 892 P.2d 611, 619 (Ct. App. 1995); see also Committee Comment to NM UJI 13-1006. If a defamatory statement is made to a person who knows that the statement is untrue, then a publication has not occurred. Silverman v. Progressive Broadcasting, Inc., 1998-NMCA-107, 125 N.M. 500, 964 P.2d 61.

4. ***Defamatory Statement of Fact.*** Under New Mexico law, a statement is considered defamatory if it has a tendency to render the party about whom it is published contemptible or ridiculous in public estimation, or expose him to public hatred or contempt, or hinder "virtuous men" from associating with him. Bookout v. Griffith, 97 N.M. 336, 639 P.2d 1190 (1982). A statement is deemed to be defamatory per se, if, without reference to extrinsic evidence and viewed in its plain and obvious meaning, the statement imputes to plaintiff . . . unfitness to perform duties of office or employment for profit, or the want of integrity in discharge of duties of such office or employment; [or] some falsity which prejudices plaintiff in his or her profession or trade; or unchastity of a woman Marchiondo v. New Mexico State Tribune Co., 98 N.M. 282, 287-88, 648 P.2d 321, 8 Media L. Rep. 1915 (1981), cert. quashed, 98 N.M. 336, 648 P.2d 794 (1982). The appropriate test for defamation is whether the plain and obvious meaning of the communication was defamatory. Moore v. Sun Pub. Corp., 118 N.M. 375, 881 P.2d 735, 23 Media L. Rep. 1072 (Ct. App. 1994). Stating that an anthropologist was unqualified to work on a project is not defamatory where there is evidence that the statements were not taken literally by the recipients, because similar statements usually are not taken literally in the academic context in which they were made, and such statements do not convey, or at least in this case did not convey, a defamatory meaning, and were understood by the recipients to be opinions and not actual facts. Fikes v. Furst, 2003-NMSC-033, 134 N.M. 602, 81 P.3d 545; see also NM UJI 13-1004.

5. ***Of and Concerning Plaintiff.*** To support a claim for defamation, the communication must be concerning the plaintiff. The communication is concerning the plaintiff if the person to whom it was communicated reasonably understood that it was intended to refer to the plaintiff. NM UJI 13-1005. A statement which was alleged to have defamed an individual, but which referred to the individual's company rather than to him individually, was actionable. Poorbaugh v. Millen, 99 N.M. 11, 653 P.2d 511 (Ct. App. 1982). New Mexico does recognize liability for defamation by implication. Moore v. Sun Pub. Corp., 118 N.M. 375, 881 P.2d 735 (Ct. App. 1994); see also NM UJI 13-1005.

6. ***Publication.*** Publication is an intentional or negligent communication to one other than the person defamed. Poorbaugh v. Millen, 99 N.M. 11, 21, 653 P.2d 511, 521 (Ct. App. 1982). Publication does not occur where the writing is sent only to the person defamed and a third person intercepts and reads it before it reaches the person defamed. Chico v. Frazier, 106 N.M. 773, 750 P.2d 473 (Ct. App. 1988). If a defamatory statement is made to a person who knows the statement is untrue, then a publication has not occurred. Silverman v. Progressive Broadcasting, Inc., 1998-NMCA-18, ¶ 23, 125 N.M. 500, 964 P.2d 61; see also NM UJI 13-1003.

a. **Intracorporate Communication**. In Hagebak v. Stone, 2003-NMCA-007, 133 N.M. 75, 61 P.3d 201, the court rejected a lower court's adoption, in a case of first impression, of an absolute privilege for intracorporate communications. The court instead adopted a qualified-privilege approach, which it said "affords substantial protection to the corporation, while at the same time preserving defamation remedies for the worst kind of abuse that causes unprivileged injury to reputation." Hagebak, at ¶ 23.

b. **Compelled Self-Publication.** No cases reported in New Mexico.

c. **Republication.** There is no New Mexico Uniform Jury Instruction on the issue of "republication." Former NM UJI 10.26 stated no instruction exists because there is no New Mexico case law in point on the matter and the rulings from other states are in conflict. Under NM UJI 13-1003 "Directions for Use," it states, "This observation is still true and no instruction has been promulgated."

In Woodhull v. Meinel, 2009-NMCA-015, ¶ 12, 145 N.M. 533, 202 P.3d 126, the New Mexico Court of Appeals stated that a republication occurs upon "a separate aggregate publication from the original, on a different occasion, which is not merely a delayed circulation of the original edition" (quoting Firth v. State, 98 N.Y.2d 365, 747 N.Y.S.2d 69, 775 N.E.2d 463 (2002). The court analyzed the rule in the context of Internet publications and stated that mere technical modifications or the act of updating a website with information that is unrelated to the original defamatory statement are not sufficient to constitute a republication. Id. at ¶ 13. The question of whether a republication has occurred is highly factual and is determined by how the content of the second publication relates to the first publication. Id. at ¶ 16.

7. ***Statements versus Conduct.*** No cases reported in New Mexico.

8. ***Damages.*** Damages recoverable in a defamation action are limited to actual and special damages; punitive damages are recoverable only if there is proof by clear and convincing evidence that the publication was made with knowledge of its falsity or with a reckless disregard for whether it was false or not. NM UJI 13-1011; see also Poorbaugh v. Millen, 99 N.M. 11, 653 P.2d 511 (Ct. App. 1982). **New Mexico requires a showing of injury to one's reputation to establish liability for defamation. Evidence of humiliation and mental anguish, without evidence of actual injury to reputation, is insufficient to establish a cause of action for defamation. Smith v. Durden, 2012-NMSC-010, ¶ 1, 276 P.3d 943. A jury, after deciding in favor of a plaintiff on the question of liability for defamation, may award damages for injuries including personal humiliation and mental anguish and suffering if the plaintiff proves that the defamatory communication caused one or more of these injuries. Id. at ¶ 28; see also NM UJI 13-1010 (listing types of injuries which a plaintiff may recover). The process to be followed is first establishing the cause of action, which includes proving actual injury to reputation, and then moving to the apportionment of damages necessary to compensate for that injury to reputation. Id. at ¶¶ 30-31.** Under New Mexico law, actual injury is not limited to out-of-pocket loss; more customary types of actual harm include impairment of reputation and standing in the community, personal humiliation and mental anguish and suffering. Brown v. Presbyterian Healthcare Services, 101 F.3d 1324 (10th Cir. 1996); see also NM UJI 13-1010.

a. **Presumed Damages and Libel Per Se.** Under New Mexico law, plaintiff must prove actual injury to state a claim for defamation. Damages cannot be presumed. Brown v. Presbyterian Healthcare Services, 101 F.3d 1324 (10th Cir. 1996). The libel per se/per quod distinction "has probably been overtaken by rulings of the New Mexico Supreme Court." Newberry v. Allied Stores, Inc., 108 N.M. 424, 429, 773 P.2d 1231, 1236 (1989). While the New Mexico Supreme Court has not abolished the distinction outright, the latest version of the New Mexico Uniform Jury Instructions does not contain any such distinction. Schuler v. McGraw-Hill Companies, Inc. 989 F. Supp. 1377, 25 Media L. Rep. 2409 (D.N.M. 1997), aff'd, 145 F.3d 1346, 26 Media L. Rep. 1604 (10th Cir. 1998).

(1) **Employment-Related Criticism.** No cases reported.

(2) **Single Instance Rule.** No cases reported.

b. **Punitive Damages.** In defamation actions, punitive damages are recoverable if there is proof of actual malice. Newberry v. Allied Stores, Inc., 108 N.M. 424, 773 P.2d 1231 (1989). In Aken v. Plains Elec. Generation & Transmission Co-op., Inc., 2002-NMSC-021, 132 N.M. 401, 49 P.3d 662 (2002), a non-media defamation case, the New Mexico Supreme Court held that an award of punitive damages is to be reviewed de novo as a matter of federal constitutional law. Id. citing Cooper Industries v. Leatherman Tool Group, Inc., 532 U.S. 424 (2001).

II. PRIVILEGES AND DEFENSES

A. Scope of Privileges

1. ***Absolute Privilege.*** An absolute or unqualified privilege means absolute immunity from liability for defamation. Gregory Rockhouse Ranch, L.L.C. v. Glenn's Water Well Service, Inc., 2008-NMCA-101, ¶18, 144 N.M. 690, 696, 191 P.3d 548, 554, citing Neece v. Kantu, 84 N.M. 700, 705, 507 P.2d 447, 452 (Ct. App. 1973). The application of an absolute privilege is confined to very few situations in which there is an obvious policy in favor of complete freedom of expression regardless of the defendant's motives. Baker v. Bhajan, 117 N.M. 278, 281, 871 P.2d 374, 377 (1994).

Examples: (1) Generally, statements made in the course of judicial proceedings enjoy an absolute privilege from later charges of defamation. Gregory Rockhouse Ranch, at ¶ 18, 84 N.M. at 696, 507 P.2d at 554, citing Superior Constr., Inc. v. Linnerooth, 103 N.M. 716, 719, 712 P.2d 1378, 1381 (1986); and see generally Restatement (Second) of Torts § 635 (1977). **"The absolute privilege doctrine applies to pre-litigation statements made by attorneys in the presence of the press, if (1) the speaker is seriously and in good faith contemplating class action or mass-tort litigation at the time the statement is made, (2) the statement is reasonably related to the proposed litigation, (3) the attorney has a client or identifiable prospective client at the time the statement is made, and (4) the statement is made while the attorney is acting in the capacity of counsel or prospective counsel." Helena Chemical Co. v. Uribe, 2012-NMSC-21, ¶ 2, 281 P.3d 237.** New Mexico has recognized that an attorney-at-law is absolutely privileged to publish false and defamatory matter of another in communications preliminary to a proposed judicial proceeding, or in the institution of, or during the course and as a part of, a judicial proceeding. This has been applied to protect statements made by an attorney in a letter regarding a proposed lawsuit. Romero v. Prince, 85 N.M. 474, 513 P.2d 717, 720 (Ct. App. 1973). In cases involving application of the privilege to statements made by attorneys related to judicial proceedings, all doubt should be resolved in favor of recognizing the privilege. Only in extreme cases will a publication made in connection with a judicial proceeding serve as the basis for a defamation action. Penny v. Sherman, 101 N.M. 517, 684 P.2d 1182 (Ct. App. 1984). The recipient of the communication need not have a direct interest in the proceedings for the privilege to apply. Id. Under appropriate circumstances, this privilege applies even to statements made outside the proceedings themselves. "It is not absolutely essential, in order to obtain the benefits of absolute privilege, that the language claimed to be defamatory be spoken in open court or contained in a pleading, brief, or affidavit.... If the alleged defamatory statement is made to achieve the objects of the litigation, the absolute privilege applies even though the statement is made outside the courtroom and no function of the court or its officers is invoked." Romero v. Prince, 85 N.M. 474, 477, 513 P.2d 717, 720 (Ct. App. 1973). Statements made in close proximity to the initiation of judicial proceedings may be absolutely privileged, but statements made more than seven months before the commencement of litigation, when litigation was not seriously contemplated at the time the communications were made, were not absolutely privileged. Gregory Rockhouse Ranch, LLC v. Glenn's Water Well Service, Inc., 2008-NMCA-101, ¶ 219, 144 N.M. 690, 668, 191 P.3d 548, 555. (2) New Mexico also has recognized that publications made with the consent of a person defamed are absolutely privileged. This has been applied to protect statements made by a former employer regarding a former employee's capabilities, where the employee consented to the communication. Gengler v. Phelps, 92 N.M. 465, 589 P.2d 1056 (Ct. App.1978), cert. denied, 92 N.M. 353, 588 P.2d 554 (1979). (3) Fair and accurate reports of judicial proceedings and other official or public proceedings are absolutely privileged. Henderson v. Dreyfus, 26 N.M. 541, 191 P. 442 (1919); Stover v. Journal Publishing Co., 105 N.M. 291, 731 P.2d 1335 (Ct. App. 1985). This includes fair reports of criminal proceedings. Rockafellow v. New Mexico Broadcasting, 74 N.M. 652, 397 P.2d 303 (1964). The privilege under Restatement (Second) of Torts § 611 is applicable even when a media defendant reports on its own libel litigation. Stover v. Journal Publishing Co., 105 N.M. 291, 731 P.2d 1335 (Ct. App.1985) (discussing the application of comment C). (4) Statements by executive officers are absolutely privileged if they are made in the exercise of executive function and are in some way related to an official proceeding. Adams v. Tatsch, 68 N.M. 446, 362 P.2d 984, 989-990 (1961). Statements made by a Highway Commissioner during a public commission meeting were so privileged. Id. at 990. Only statements made *by* executive officers are so privileged (statements made by parties in the course of an administrative water rights adjudication were not absolutely privileged). Gregory Rockhouse Ranch, 2008-NMCA-101, ¶23, 144 N.M. 690, 698, 191 P.3d 548, 555. (5) Statements made during the course of a quasi-judicial labor grievance arbitration proceeding are privileged. Neece v. Kantu, 84 N.M. 700, 507 P.2d 447, 453 (Ct. App. 1975). (5) There is an absolute immunity from liability for defamatory statements made in court proceedings or at administrative hearings, e.g., testimony offered at unemployment security hearings. Zuniga v. Sears, Roebuck & Co., 100 N.M. 414, 671 P.2d 662 (Ct. App. 1983). (6) Statements made in pleadings are privileged if they are reasonably related to the subject matter of the action. Allegations of fraud in a complaint were so privileged. Barber Supermarkets, Inc. v. Stryker, 84 N.M. 181, 500 P.2d 1304 (Ct. App. 1972), cert. denied, 84 N.M. 180, 500 P.2d 1303 (1972). (7) Statements made in a letter to professional associations seeking "peer review" and the convening of a grievance committee to investigate the competency of a physician were so privileged. Franklin v. Blank, 86 N.M. 585, 525 P.2d 945 (Ct. App. 1974)) (superceded by statute as stated in Gregory Rockhouse Ranch, LLC v. Glenn's Water Well Service, Inc., 2008-NMCA-101, 144 N.M. 690, 191 P.3d 548 cert. denied, 2008). (8) A person who submits to an investigation of his conduct when he knows that the results of the investigation will be published consents to the publication of any findings which may be defamatory. Rodriguez v. Conant, 105 N.M. 746, 737 P.2d 527 (1987). (Polygraph examination results case) (Adopting Restatement (Second) of Torts § 583, comments and illustrations 2 and 3). (9) Where a defendant claimed an absolute privilege based on his exercise of the constitutional right to petition the government and pursuant to a statutory right to protest, and further claimed that the privilege would thus protect statements directed to governmental authorities and nominally designated petitions or protests, the Court of Appeals declined to find such a privilege. Gregory Rockhouse Ranch, L.L.C. v. Glenn's Water Well Service, Inc., 2008-NMCA-101, ¶24, 144 N.M. 690, 698, 191 P.3d 548, 556.

2. ***Qualified Privileges.***

a. **Common Interest.** Defamatory matters may be qualifiedly privileged between parties who have common business or personal interest in subject matter of the publication if they are made in good faith in order to protect one's interest or in the discharge of public or private duty. Poorbaugh v. Millen, 99 N.M. 11, 653 P.2d 511 (Ct. App. 1982). New Mexico has adopted the qualified privilege approach because it precludes lawsuits (1) if the defamatory statements are made in good faith and (2) protects corporations with regard to internal communications. Hagebak v. Stone, 2003-NMCA-007, 133 N.M. 75, 61 P.3d 201. In Hagebak, the Court of Appeals determined that "damage to one's reputation within a corporate community may be just as devastating as that effected by defamation spread to the outside." The Court of Appeals then rejected the intracorporate communication exception. Id. at 80, 61 P.3d at 206

b. **Duty.** A qualified privilege exists as a defense to a claim of defamation where there is a good faith publication in discharge of a public or private duty, but the privilege is abused if a person said to be privileged lacks the belief, or reasonable grounds to believe, the truth of the alleged defamation. Bookout v. Griffith, 97 N.M. 336, 639 P.2d 1190 (1982). The qualified privilege [against a defamation claim] to make statements about a former employee must be for a proper purpose and to one having a legitimate interest in the statements. Baker v. Bhajan, 117 N.M. 278, 282, 871 P.2d 374, 378 (1994); see also NM UJI 13-1012.

c. **Criticism of Public Employee.** There are no specific cases reported in New Mexico. However, a common law privilege of fair comment in context of a libel action is available to one who comments and communicates regarding a matter of public interest. Mauck, Stastny & Rassam, P.A. v. Bicknell, 95 N.M. 702, 625 P.2d 1219 (Ct. App. 1980). The common law privilege against defamation claims provides an employer qualified immunity for good-faith disclosures about employee performance, thereby encouraging such disclosure for the benefit of prospective employers and third parties who may be placed in harm's way without it. Davis v. Board of County Com'rs, 1999-NMCA-110, 127 N.M. 785, 987 P.2d 1172.

d. **Limitation on Qualified Privileges**. A qualified privilege applies to communications that are made by individuals or entities with legitimate interests at stake. An occasion makes a publication conditionally privileged if the circumstances induce a correct or reasonable belief that (a) there is information that affects a sufficiently important interest of the publisher, and (b) the recipient's knowledge of the defamatory matter will be of service in the lawful protection of the interest. Gregory Rockhouse Ranch, L.L.C. v. Glenn's Water Well Service, Inc., 2008-NMCA-101, ¶ 27, 2008 WL 3397453, 6, citing Restatement (Second) of Torts § 594 (1977). A qualified privilege applies to communications that are made to individuals or entities who may act in the public interest. An occasion makes a publication conditionally privileged if the circumstances induce a correct or reasonable belief that (a) there is information that affects a sufficiently important public interest, and (b) the public interest requires the communication of the defamatory matter to a public officer or a private citizen who is authorized or privileged to take action if the defamatory matter is true. Id. at ¶ 28, citing Restatement (Second) of Torts § 598 (1977).

Abuse of privilege arises out of publisher's lack of belief, or reasonable grounds for belief, in the truth of the alleged defamation or by the publication of material for improper use, by the publication to a person not reasonable necessary for the accomplishment of the purpose. Mahona-Jojanto, Inc. N.S.L. v. Bank of New Mexico, 79 N.M. 293, 442 P.2d 783 (1968). Once an employer makes a prima facie case of conditional privilege, the employee then has the burden to prove that the employer did not act in good faith. DiMarco v. Presbyterian Healthcare Services, Inc., 2007-NMCA-053, ¶ 8, 141 N.M. 735, 738, 160 P.3d 916, 919. A conditional or qualified privilege will be lost if it is abused. Id. at ¶ 10, citing Baker v. Bhajan, 117 N.M. 278, 283, 871 P.2d 374, 379 (1994). An employer abuses its privilege if it lacks belief or reasonable grounds for belief in the truth of the information disclosed; if it provides information for an improper use; if it provides information to a person unnecessary for the accomplishment of the purpose; or if it provides information beyond the scope reasonably necessary to accomplish the purpose. Id. at ¶ 11.

(1) **Constitutional or Actual Malice.** When there is a qualified privilege, it can be defeated by a showing of actual malice. Leyba v. Renger, 874 F.Supp. 1218 (D.N.M. 1994). To show malice under New Mexico law, the plaintiff must show that the statements were made with knowledge that they were false, or with reckless disregard for whether they were false. It is not enough for a plaintiff to show ill will on an employer's part. Id.

(2) **Common Law Malice.** The former common law definition of malice in New Mexico was ill will or personal hatred of the plaintiff by the defendant. Colbert v. Journal Publishing Co., 19 N.M. 156, 142 P. 146 (1914).

e. **Question of Fact or Law.** The question of whether an occasion gives rise to a qualified privilege is one for the court as an issue of law. Stewart v. Ging, 64 N.M. 270, 274, 327 P.2d 333, 336 (1958). If the Judge decides that a qualified privilege exists, "the question whether it was abused . . . is ordinarily for the jury." However, "where but one conclusion can be drawn from the evidence, the court may determine as a matter of law that the privilege has been abused or that it constitutes a defense to the action." Id. at 275, 327 P.2d at 337.

f. **Burden of Proof.** New Mexico recognizes that a qualified privilege is an affirmative defense which must be pleaded by the defendant. NM UJI 13-1012 informs the jury of the existence of the qualified privilege and assigns the burden of proof to the plaintiff to demonstrate the privilege has been abused and thus is inapplicable. See Zuniga v. Sears, Roebuck & Co., 100 N.M. 414, 418, 671 P.2d 662, 666 (Ct. App. 1983).

B. Standard Libel Defenses

1. ***Truth.*** An employer may assert truth as an affirmative defense to a defamation action. The truth must go to the underlying implication of the statement, not simply whether the statement published is accurate. In Schwartz v. American College of Emergency Physicians, 215 F.3d 1140, 28 Media L. Rep. 1929 (10th Cir. 2000), the Tenth Circuit Court of Appeals reaffirmed New Mexico's adherence to the substantial truth doctrine by holding that while a statement that a doctor was "being sued for stock fraud" was technically inaccurate, the gist of the comment was substantially true and could not serve as the basis for a defamation action.

2. ***Opinion.*** Relying on Gertz v. Robert Welch, Inc., 418 U.S. 1030, 111 S.Ct. 2720, 115 L.Ed.2d 789 (1974), New Mexico has held that ideas and opinions are constitutionally protected. Material as a whole, however, must contain full disclosure of the facts upon which the publisher's opinion is based and allow the reader to reach his own conclusion. Coronado Credit Union v. KOAT Television, Inc., 99 N.M. 233, 237, 656 P.2d 896, 900, 9 Media L. Rep. 1031 (Ct. App. 1982). Where a statement is unambiguously fact or opinion, the court must determine as a matter of law that the statement is fact or opinion. An opinion can be actionable "if it implies the allegation of undisclosed defamatory facts as the basis for the opinion." Andrews v. Stallings, 119 N.M. 478, 482, 892 P.2d 611, 615 (Ct. App. 1995). Where the alleged defamatory remarks could be determined either as fact or opinion, and the court cannot say as a matter of law that the statements were not understood as fact, there is a triable issue of fact for the jury. Marchiondo v. Brown, 98 N.M. 394, 649 P.2d 462, 8 Media L. Rep. 2233 (N.M. 1982)

3. ***Consent.*** Under New Mexico law, consent of Plaintiff giving rise to an absolute privilege will be implied where circumstances show that plaintiff gave his implied consent to publication, statement is relevant to purpose for which that consent was given, and publication is limited to those with a legitimate interest in its publication. Hill v. Cray Research, Inc., 864 F. Supp. 1070 (D.N.M 1991)

4. ***Mitigation.*** No cases reported.

III. RECURRING FACT PATTERNS

A. Statements in Personnel File.

No cases reported in New Mexico.

B. Performance Evaluations

A section of the New Mexico Review Organization Immunity Act (NMROIA), NMSA 1978, § 41-9-3 (Repl.Pamp.1989), creates a qualified privilege for persons providing information to a health care review organization. See Leyba v. Renger, 114 N.M. 686, 845 P.2d 780 (1992).

C. References

An employer is qualifiedly or conditionally privileged to make statements about an employee if for a proper purpose and to one having a legitimate interest in the subject matter of the statements. The employer's privilege arises from both common law (see, e.g., Gengler v. Phelps, 92 N.M. 465, 468, 589 P.2d 1056, 1059 (Ct. App. 1978) and statute (NMSA § 50-12-1) (stating that "when requested to provide a reference on a former or current employee, an employer acting in good faith is immune from liability for comments about the former employee's job performance."). Once an employer makes a prima facie case of conditional privilege, the employee then has the burden to prove that the employer did not act in good faith. DiMarco v. Presbyterian Healthcare Services, Inc., 2007-NMCA-053, ¶ 8, 141 N.M. 735, 738, 160 P.3d 916, 919. A conditional or qualified privilege will be lost if it is abused. Id. at ¶ 10, citing Baker v. Bhajan, 117 N.M. 278, 283, 871 P.2d 374, 379 (1994). An employer abuses its privilege if it lacks belief or reasonable grounds for belief in the truth of the information disclosed; if it provides information for an improper use; if it provides information to a person unnecessary for the accomplishment of the purpose; or if it provides information beyond the scope reasonably necessary to accomplish the purpose. Id. at ¶ 11. Public policy supports full and accurate disclosure of non-confidential information to an employee's prospective employers by the employee's current or former employers. Davis v. Board of County Com'rs, 1999-NMCA-110, 127 N.M. 785, 987 P.2d 1172.

New Mexico has adopted the qualified privilege approach because it precludes lawsuits 1) if the defamatory statements are made in good faith; and 2) protects corporations with regard to internal communications. Hagebak v. Stone, 2003-NMCA-007, 133 N.M. 75, 79, 61 P.3d 201, 205. In Hagebak, the Court of Appeals determined that "damage to one's reputation within a corporate community may be just as devastating as that effected by defamation spread to the outside."

D. Intracorporate Communication

In Hagebak v. Stone, 2003-NMCA-007, 133 N.M. 75, 61 P.3d 201, the court rejected a lower court's adoption, in a case of first impression, of an absolute privilege for intracorporate communications. The court instead adopted a qualified-privilege approach, which it said "affords substantial protection to the corporation, while at the same time preserving defamation remedies for the worst kind of abuse that causes unprivileged injury to reputation." Hagebak, at ¶ 23.

Where statements were made concerning an alleged attempted theft of a television set belonging to a store by discharged employee were made in initial report by security employee who had a duty to protect store's property, those statements were subject to a qualified privilege absent a showing of abuse of privilege. Zuniga v. Sears Roebuck & Co., 100 N.M. 414, 671 P.2d 662 (Ct. App. 1983).

E. Statements to Government Regulators

No cases reported, but would probably be covered under good faith discharge of public duty.

F. Reports to Auditors and Insurers

No cases reported, but would probably be covered under good faith discharge of a private duty.

G. Vicarious Liability of Employers for Statements Made by Employees

1. ***Scope of Employment.*** An employer may be held liable for compensatory damages which result from defamatory statements of employees acting within the scope of employment, regardless of the culpability of the employer. Newberry v. Allied Stores, Inc., 108 N.M. 424, 431, 773 P.2d 1231, 1238 (1989).

a. ***Blogging.*** No reported cases.

2. ***Damages.*** An employer is liable for punitive damages for defamatory statements of an employee acting within the scope of his employment and where the employer in some way participated in, authorized or ratified the tortious conduct of the employee. Newberry v. Allied Stores, Inc., 108 N.M. 424, 431, 773 P.2d 1231, 1238 (1989).

H. Internal Investigations. No reported cases.

IV. OTHER ACTIONS BASED ON STATEMENTS

A. Negligent Hiring, Retention, and Supervision

In order to support a claim on negligent hiring and retention, there must be evidence that employee was unfit, considering nature of employment and risk he posed to those with whom he would foreseeably associate, and that employer knew or should have known that employee was unfit; liability flows from direct duty running from employer to those members of public whom employer might reasonably anticipate would be placed in position of risk or injury as a result of hiring. Valdez v. Warner, 106 N.M. 305, 742 P.2d 517 (Ct. App. 1987). Although New Mexico law recognizes a statutory privilege allowing employers to make good faith statements regarding former employees, the Court of Appeals has held that an employer owes prospective employees and foreseeable third persons a duty of reasonable care not to misrepresent material facts in the course of making an employment recommendation about a present or former employee, when a substantial risk of physical harm is foreseeable. Davis v. Board of County Comm'rs, 1999-NMCA-110, 127 N.M. 785, 987 P.2d 1172. In this case, the alleged misrepresentation by an employer occurred prior to the adoption of New Mexico's statutory privilege adopted in 1995. However, the Court of Appeals refused to address the issue of whether such a cause of action could still exist under this statute because the issue was not directly before the court. For the basic elements of negligent hiring, supervision, or retention, see New Mexico Uniform Jury Instruction 13-1647.

B. Intentional Infliction of Emotional Distress

The tort of intentional infliction of emotional distress "provides recovery to victims of socially reprehensible conduct, and leaves it to the judicial process to determine, on a case-by-case basis, what conduct should be so characterized."

Baldonado v. El Paso Natural Gas Company, 2008-NMSC-005, ¶24, 143 N.M. 288, 293, 176 P.3d 277, 282, citing Daniel Givelber, The Right to Minimum Social Decency and the Limits of Evenhandedness: Intentional Infliction of Emotional Distress by Outrageous Conduct, 82 Colum. L.Rev. 42, 42 (1982). "Perhaps because of its indeterminacy, its main purpose seems to be to 'provide the basis for achieving situational justice.'" Id. at 74-75, 638 P.2d 423.

To recover for the intentional infliction of emotional distress a plaintiff must show that the defendant's conduct was extreme and outrageous, and was done recklessly or with the intent to cause severe emotional distress. Mantz v. Follingstad, 84 N.M. 473, 480, 505 P.2d 68, 75 (Ct. App. 1972), overruled on other grounds by Peralta v. Martinez , 90 N.M. 391, 392, 564 P.2d 194, 195 (Ct. App. 1977). Extreme and outrageous conduct is 'beyond all possible bounds of decency, and to be regarded as atrocious, and utterly intolerable in a civilized community." Id. As a general proposition, accurate publication of newsworthy events does not give rise to a cause of action for intentional infliction of emotional distress. Andrews v. Stallings, 119 N.M. 478, 492, 892 P.2d 611, 625 (Ct. App. 1995). Only in extreme circumstances can the act of firing an employee support a claim of intentional infliction of emotional distress. Stock v. Grantham, 1998-NMCA-081, ¶ 35, 125 N.M. 564, 964 P.2d 125. "Being fired is a common occurrence that rarely rises to the level of being 'beyond all possible bounds of decency' and 'utterly intolerable in a civilized community.'" Trujillo v. Northern Rio Arriba Elec. Co-op, Inc., 2002-NMSC-004, ¶ 27, 131 N.M. 607, 617, 41 P.3d 333, 343.

C. Interference with Economic Advantage

To recover for intentional interference with a contract, a plaintiff must prove: (1) defendant had knowledge of the contract; (2) plaintiff was unable to fulfill his or her contract obligations; (3) defendant played an active and substantial part in causing plaintiff to lose the benefits of the contract; (4) plaintiff suffered damages resulting from the breach; and (5) defendant induced the breach without justification or privilege to do so. Deflon v. Sawyers, 2006-NMSC-025, 139 N.M. 637, 646, 137 P.3d 577, 586, citing Ettenson v. Burke, 2001-NMCA-003, 130 N.M. 67, 17 P.2d 440.

When an employment relationship is at-will, a claim for interference with contractual relations is treated as an interference with a prospective employment relationship. Zarr v. Washington Tru Solutions, L.L.C., 2009-NMCA-050, ¶ 17, 146 N.M. 274, 208 P.3d 919. In a cause of action for interference with prospective contractual relations, improper motive must be the *sole* motive for interfering with a prospective or at-will contract. Fikes v. Furst, 2003-NMSC-033, ¶ 21, 134 N.M. 602, 81 P.3d 545. Interference with a prospective contract is therefore distinguishable from the cause of action for interference with an existing contract, which does not have this sole motive requirement. Id. As an alternative to showing improper motive, a plaintiff may also show that the defendant used improper means to interfere with the plaintiff's prospective contractual relations. If the plaintiff claims that the defendant used improper means, it is not necessary to show that the defendant's sole motive was to harm the plaintiff. Zarr v. Washington Tru Solutions, L.L.C., 2009-NMCA-050, ¶ 11, 146 N.M. 274, 208 P.3d 919. What may qualify as "improper means" may include, but is not limited to, "predatory behavior, violence, threats or intimidation, deceit or misrepresentation, bribery, economic pressure, unfounded litigation, defamation, unlawful conduct, and perhaps violation of business ethics and customs." Id. Where there is at least in part a legitimate business reason for the act, then a claim based on improper means fails. Los Alamos National Bank v. Martinez Surveying Services, LLC, 2006-NMCA-081, 140 N.M. 41, 46, 139 P.3d 201, 206.

Parties to a contract cannot bring an action for tortious interference with an existing contract against each other. Deflon v. Sawyers, 2006-NMSC-025, 139 N.M. 637, 646, 137 P.3d 577, 586. Conduct sufficient to establish intentional infliction of emotional distress might also be sufficient to establish intentional interference with a contract, but unlike a claim for IIED, a plaintiff making a claim for intentional interference with a contract need not establish "extreme and outrageous" conduct in order to prove that defendant, without justification or privilege, played an active and substantial part in causing plaintiff to lose the benefits of his or her employment. Id.

D. Prima Facie Tort

Under New Mexico law, elements of prima facie tort are an intentional, lawful act by defendant, with the intent to injure the plaintiff, injury to the plaintiff, and absence of justification or insufficient justification for defendant's acts. Yeitrakis v. Schering-Plough Corp., 804 F.Supp. 238 (D.N.M. 1992). To state a claim for prima facie tort, a plaintiff cannot merely reallege the facts in support of the other causes of action, adding only a bare recital of the elements of prima facie tort relating to intent and justification. A prima facie tort claim may not be used as a means of avoiding the more stringent requirements of other torts. The value and validity of prima facie tort as a separate cause of action depends upon its ability to offer relief for the intentional infliction of harm where the actor's otherwise lawful conduct cannot be brought within other more traditional categories of liability. Healthsource, Inc. v. X-Ray Associates of N.M., 2005-NMCA-097, ¶¶ 34-36, 138 N.M. 70, 80-81, 116 P.3d 861, 871-72. Village council member could not rely on prima facie tort theory against newspaper to circumvent established defenses to defamation in context in matters involving issues of public concern. Andrews v. Stallings, 119 N.M. 478, 892 P.2d 611 (Ct. App. 1995).

Prima facie tort demands a high degree of judicial inquiry because the trial court must engage in a balancing test that weighs (1) the injury; (2) the culpable character of the conduct; and (3) whether the conduct is unjustifiable under the circumstances. Celnik v. Congregation B'Nai Israel, 2006-NMCA-039, 139 N.M. 252, 257, 131 P.3d 102, 107, citing Beavers v. Johnson Controls World Servs., Inc., 120 N.M. 343, 348-49, 901 P.2d 761, 766-67 (Ct. App. 1995). In a case where a rabbi alleged that his congregation and its members intentionally disseminated one-sided and negative information about him with the intent to sway other members against him and to compel him to lose his employment with the congregation, the New Mexico Court of Appeals upheld a dismissal of his claims for prima facie tort, stating that "[t]o act as a judicial referee to this particular dispute, applying the intrusive balancing test called for under prima facie tort analysis would require us to ignore the core principles of the church autonomy doctrine." Id.

V. OTHER ISSUES

A. Statute of Limitations.

The statute of limitations for defamation claims in New Mexico is three years. NMSA Sec. 37-1-8 (1990 Repl. Pamp.)

B. Jurisdiction.

No cases reported in New Mexico.

C. Worker's Compensation Exclusivity

The New Mexico Workers' Compensation Act is codified in NMSA 1978, §§52-1-1 – 52-10-1. The compensation scheme of the Act is the exclusive remedy for a worker's injuries when at the time of the accident (1) the employer has complied with the insurance provisions of the act, (2) the employee was performing services arising out of and in the course of his employment, and (3) the injury or death is proximately caused by an accident arising out of and in the course of the employee's employment and is not intentionally self-inflicted. In 2001, the New Mexico Supreme Court broadened the scope of what would be considered an intentional act on the part of an employer, allowing an independent tort action, to include intentional or willful acts by the employer that cause a worker to suffer an injury that would otherwise be exclusively compensable under the Act. Delgado v. Phelps Dodge Chino, Inc., 2001-NMSC-034, ¶ 24, 131 N.M. 272, 34 P.3d 1148. In so holding, the Court stated that it was required by the Act not to construe the Act in favor of the employee or the employer, and the "actual intent" test that had been previously applied (requiring actual intent on the part of the employer to injure the employee) favored the employer. Id. at ¶ 17.

The Delgado Court set out a 3-prong test for when willfulness renders an employee's injury non-accidental and, therefore, outside the scope of the Act: (1) the worker or employer engages in an intentional act or omission, without just cause or excuse, that is reasonably expected to result in the injury suffered by the worker; (2) the worker or employer expects the intentional act or omission to result in the injury, or has utterly disregarded the consequences; and (3) the intentional act or omission proximately causes the injury. Id. at ¶ 26. When analyzing tort actions brought by an employee after Delgado, the New Mexico Court of Appeals has used the facts of Delgado; which involved a combination of deadly conditions, profit-motivated disregard for easily implemented safety measures, complete lack of worker training, and an outright denial of assistance to a worker in a terrifying situation; as a guide in determining the level of egregious conduct required on the part of the employer. Morales v. Reynolds, 2004-NMCA-098, ¶ 10, 136 N.M. 280, 97 P.3d 612.

Neither the Act nor any cases reported in New Mexico directly address the issue of liability or immunity under the for a defamation claim by an employee against an employer.

D. Pleading Requirements.

Defendants do not bear the burden to discern how an article has defamed plaintiffs. Rather, the latter "must plead precisely the statements" about which they complain. Andrews v. Stallings, 119 N.M. 478, 892 P.2d 611 (Ct. App. 1995); see also Weise v. Washington Tru Solutions, 2008-NMCA-121, ¶¶ 21-22, 144 NM 867, 875-76, 192 P.2d 1244, 1252-53 (defamation complaint must specifically state which statements defamed Plaintiff).

SURVEY OF NEW MEXICO EMPLOYMENT PRIVACY LAW

Thomas L. Stahl
Jennifer L. Duprez
Rodey, Dickason, Sloan, Akin & Robb, P.A.
201 Third Street NW, Suite 2200
Post Office Box 1888
Albuquerque, New Mexico 87103
Telephone: (505) 765-5900; Facsimile: (505) 768-7395

(With Developments Reported Through **November 1, 2012**)

GENERAL COMMENTS

Citations to NMSC or NMCA, e.g., "1996-NMSC-024, ¶ 11" are in the vendor neutral form required by New Mexico state courts for decisions filed after January 1, 1996. This form indicates the year of decision, the court (either Supreme Court or Court of Appeals), the case number, and a paragraph number as a pinpoint citation. For statutes, the form includes the enactment date of the section cited. For details, see In re Adoption of Vendor Neutral Citations for Appellate Opinions, 1998-NMSC-8500, 1998 N.M. LEXIS 1.

SIGNIFICANT DEVELOPMENTS SINCE THE 2012 *SURVEY*

None.

I. GENERAL LAW OF PRIVACY

A. Legal Basis of Privacy Claims

No New Mexico statutory or constitutional provision creates a general right to privacy. The New Mexico State Constitution prohibits unreasonable searches and seizures. N.M. Const. art. II, § 10. This provision, however, does not apply to intrusions by private persons. State v. Johnston, 108 N.M. 778, 780, 779 P.2d 556, 558 (Ct. App. 1989).

New Mexico common law explicitly recognizes the tort of invasion of the right to privacy, or "the right to be let alone." See Blount v. T D Publ'g Corp., 77 N.M. 384, 388, 423 P.2d 421, 424 (1966); Andrews v. Stallings, 119 N.M. 478, 492, 892 P.2d 611, 625 (Ct. App. 1995); Smith v. City of Artesia, 108 N.M. 339, 340, 772 P.2d 373, 374 (Ct. App. 1989); McNutt v. New Mexico State Tribune Co., 88 N.M. 162, 165, 538 P.2d 804, 807 (Ct. App. 1975). This tort encompasses four distinct theories of recovery: misappropriation, false light, publication of private facts, and intrusion. See Andrews, 119 N.M. at 492, 892 P.2d at 625. Several general limitations on recovery for invasion of privacy have been noted. First, liability attaches "only if the defendant's conduct was such that he should have realized it would be offensive to persons of ordinary sensibilities." Bitsie v. Walston, 85 N.M. 655, 657, 515 P.2d 659, 661 (Ct. App. 1973) (internal quotation marks omitted). Second, the individual's right to privacy is generally subordinate to the public interest in the dissemination of newsworthy material. McNutt, 88 N.M. at 166, 538 P.2d at 808. Third, except for the tort of misappropriation, a claim for invasion of privacy can be maintained only by a living person whose privacy has been invaded. Smith, 108 N.M. at 341, 772 P.2d at 375.

B. Causes of Action

1. ***Misappropriation/Right of Publicity.*** "The tort of misappropriation of likeness occurs when someone appropriates to his own use or benefit the name or likeness of another.'" Benally v. Hundred Arrows Press, Inc., 614 F. Supp. 969, 978 (D.N.M. 1985), rev'd on other grounds sub nom. Benally v. Amon Carter Museum of W. Art, 858 F.2d 618 (10th Cir. 1988) (quoting Restatement (Second) of Torts § 652C (1977)). The appropriation is not tortious unless the defendant deliberately uses the plaintiff's name or likeness to exploit its value for advertising or trade purposes. Id. at 979.

2. ***False Light.*** False light is a close relative of defamation, but here a plaintiff must show only that "'he is given unreasonable and highly objectionable publicity that attributes to him characteristics, conduct or beliefs that are false, and so is placed before the public in a false position.'" Moore v. Sun Publ'g Corp., 118 N.M. 375, 383, 881 P.2d 735, 743 (Ct. App. 1994) (quoting Restatement (Second) of Torts § 652E cmt. b (1977)). Most importantly, false light requires proof of a false statement of fact. Andrews, 119 N.M. at 492-93, 892 P.2d at 625-26.

3. ***Publication of Private Facts.*** "'This tort involves the publication of true but intimate or private facts about the plaintiff, such as matters concerning the plaintiff's sexual life or health.'" Moore v. Sun Publ'g Corp., 118 N.M. 375, 383, 881 P.2d 735, 743 (Ct. App. 1994) (quoting R. Smolla, Law of Defamation § 10.01[2], at 10-3 (1994)). In Fernandez-Wells v. Beauvais, 1999-NMCA-071, 127 N.M. 487, 983 P.2d 1006, the first state case actually addressing such a

claim, the New Mexico Court of Appeals enumerated the elements of this tort as "public disclosure of private facts, disclosure which would be objectionable to a reasonable person, and a lack of legitimate public interest in the information." Id. ¶ 8; see also Benally v. Hundred Arrows Press, Inc., 614 F. Supp. 969, 983 (D.N.M. 1985), rev'd on other grounds sub nom. Benally v. Amon Carter Museum of W. Art, 858 F.2d 618 (10th Cir. 1988) (tort committed if matter publicized would be highly offensive to a reasonable person and is not of legitimate concern to the public). "Public disclosure" in this context means that the matter is communicated "'to the public at large, or to so many persons that the matter must be regarded as substantially certain to become one of public knowledge.'" Fernandez-Wells, 1999-NMCA-071, ¶ 9, (quoting Restatement (Second) of Torts § 652D cmt. a (1977)). Even limited dissemination of the private information may be actionable if the plaintiff enjoys a "special relationship" with the recipients. Id. A claim for publication of private facts fails if the facts disclosed are already public. McNutt v. New Mexico State Tribune Co., 88 N.M. 162, 166, 538 P.2d 804, 808 (Ct. App. 1975).

4. ***Intrusion.*** A defendant is liable for intrusion if he invades the defendant's private space or solitude, for example, by eavesdropping on private conversations or peeking through a bedroom window. Moore v. Sun Publ'g Corp., 118 N.M. 375, 383, 881 P.2d 735, 743 (Ct. App. 1994). The intrusion need not be physical, but it must be upon the plaintiff's "'private affairs or concerns.'" Schuler v. McGraw-Hill Companies, 989 F. Supp. 1377, 1390, 24 Media L. Rep. 2409, 2417 (D.N.M. 1997) (quoting Restatement (Second) of Torts § 652B (1977)), aff'd, 145 F.3d 1346 (10th Cir.1998). The tort of intrusion is concerned with the manner in which a defendant obtains information, not with what he does with the information later; the latter is addressed by a claim for public disclosure of private facts. Fernandez-Wells, 1999-NMCA-071, ¶ 9.

C. Other Privacy-Related Actions

1. ***Intentional Infliction of Emotional Distress.*** A plaintiff may prevail on a claim of intentional infliction of emotional distress if he shows emotional distress caused by the defendant's "extreme and outrageous" conduct, "done recklessly or with the intent to cause severe emotional distress." Andrews v. Stallings, 119 N.M. 478, 491, 892 P.2d 611, 624 (Ct. App. 1995). Extreme and outrageous conduct goes "'beyond all possible bounds of decency, and [is] to be regarded as atrocious, and utterly intolerable in a civilized community.'" Id. (quoting Restatement (Second) of Torts § 46 (1965)). The defendant's conduct must have inflicted emotional distress so severe that no reasonable person could be expected to endure it. Dominguez v. Stone, 97 N.M. 211, 215, 638 P.2d 423, 427 (Ct. App. 1981). The New Mexico Court of Appeals has noted with apparent disapproval the tendency to use intentional infliction of emotional distress as an "end run" around the requirements of a defamation claim. Andrews, 119 N.M. at 491, 892 P.2d at 624. The actions of a defendant employer's employees or managers will be viewed in the aggregate to determine whether the employer acted with the culpable mental state necessary to support intentional infliction of emotional distress. Coates v. Wal-Mart Stores, Inc., 1999-NMSC-013, ¶ 48, 127 N.M. 47, 976 P.2d 999. An employee's claim for intentional infliction of emotional distress against a labor union must involve acts or omissions of agents or officials of the union. Akins v. United Steel Workers of America, 2009-NMCA-051, ¶30, 146 N.M. 237, 208 P.3d 457.

2. ***Interference With Prospective Economic Advantage.*** To recover on a claim for tortious interference with existing or prospective contractual relations, a plaintiff must show that the defendant "interfered [with contractual relations] with an improper motive or by improper means, or acted without justification or privilege." Quintana v. First Interstate Bank, 105 N.M. 784, 786, 737 P.2d 896, 898 (Ct. App. 1987) (internal citations omitted). An "improper motive" exists when the defendant acts solely to harm the plaintiff. M & M Rental Tools, Inc. v. Milchem, Inc., 94 N.M. 449, 454, 612 P.2d 241, 246 (Ct. App. 1980). "Improper means" include "violence, threats or other intimidation, deceit or misrepresentation, bribery, unfounded litigation, defamation, or disparaging falsehood." Id. (internal quotation marks omitted); see also Diversey Corp. v. Chem-Source Corp., 1998-NMCA-112, ¶ 21, 125 N.M. 748, 965 P.2d 332, cause dismissed, 129 N.M. 386, 9 P.3d 69 (N.M. Nov. 6, 1998) (No. 25,293) (improper means defined as predatory behavior, or behavior that is wrongful under statute, regulation, common law rule, or established standard of trade or profession). Regarding common-law privileges, see, for example, Ettenson v. Burke, 2001-NMCA-003, ¶ 17, 17 P.3d 440, 446-47 (Dec. 7, 2000) ("[A] corporate officer is privileged to interfere with his corporation's contracts only when he acts in good faith and in the best interests of the corporation, as opposed to his own private interests."), cert. denied 20 P.3d 810 (N.M. Jan. 19, 2001). The improper means necessary for contractual interference need not satisfy the elements of another, independent tort. Diversey Corp., 1998-NMCA-112, ¶ 20. The plaintiff bears the burden of proving improper interference, and that burden is heavier where prospective advantage is at issue: "'a strong showing must be made that the defendant acted not from a profit motive but from some other motive, such as personal vengeance or spite.'" Anderson v. Dairyland Ins. Co., 97 N.M. 155, 158 -59, 637 P.2d 837, 840-41 (1981) (quoting J. Henderson & R. Pearson, The Torts Process 1166 (2d ed. 1981)). A party alleging interference with contractual relations based upon improper means was not required to establish that defendants used improper means with the sole intention of harming plaintiff; the improper means test was governed by the nature of the conduct required to be shown. Zarr v. Washington Tru Solutions, LLC, 2009-NMCA-050, ¶¶ 10-11, 146 N.M. 274, 208 P.3d 919, overruling Los Alamos National Bank v. Martinez Surveying Services, LLC, 2006-NMCA-081, 140 N.M. 41, 139 P.3d 201.

3. ***Prima Facie Tort.*** In New Mexico, recovery for prima facie tort requires (1) a lawful but intentional act; (2) intent to injure the plaintiff; (3) injury to the plaintiff; and (4) no justification for the defendant's acts. Schmitz v. Smentowski, 109 N.M. 386, 394, 785 P.2d 726, 734 (1990). The cause of action is intended "to provide remedy for intentionally committed acts that do not fit within the contours of accepted torts." Id. at 396, 785 P.2d at 736. Thus, it "should not be used to evade stringent requirements of other established doctrines of law." Id. at 398, 785 P.2d at 738. At least three courts have rejected prima facie tort "end runs" around the requirements of defamation or invasion of privacy. See Schuler v. McGraw-Hill Cos., 989 F. Supp. 1377, 1391, 24 Media L. Rep. 2409, 2418 (D.N.M. 1997), aff'd, 145 F.3d 1346 (10th Cir. 1998); Fernandez-Wells v. Beauvais, 1999-NMCA-071, ¶ 23, 127 N.M. 487, 983 P.2d 1006; Andrews v. Stallings, 119 N.M. 478, 494, 892 P.2d 611, 627 (Ct. App. 1995); see also Padwa v. Hadley, 1999-NMCA-067, ¶ 27, 127 N.M. 416, 981 P.2d 1234 (rejecting attempt to claim prima facie tort as alternative to meeting requirements of intentional infliction of emotional distress). While a plaintiff can plead prima facie tort in the alternative, New Mexico courts have held that where a plaintiff does not assert any separate factual basis to support its prima facie claim, and the plaintiff's proof is susceptible to submission under another tort, the action should be submitted to the jury on the other cause of action and not as a prima facie tort claim. Guest v. Allstate Insurance Co., 2009-NMCA-037, ¶ 33, 145 N.M. 797, 205 P.3d 844.

II. EMPLOYER TESTING OF EMPLOYEES

A. Psychological or Personality Testing

No New Mexico law on point.

B. Drug Testing

1. ***Common Law and Statutes.*** There is no New Mexico statute or common law rule specifically governing drug testing in the workplace, but the New Mexico Constitution prohibits unreasonable searches and seizures by state actors. N.M. Const. art. II, § 10. See also Lara v. City of Albuquerque, 1999-NMCA-012, 126 N.M. 455, 971 P.2d 846 (city did not violate plaintiff's interest in privacy through its discovery of his drug testing agreement because there were no specific promises of confidentiality concerning the plaintiff's agreement to submit to drug testing and the legal consequences of failing to appear for the testing).

2. ***Private Employers.*** No New Mexico law on point.

3. ***Public Employers.*** As state actors, public employers are subject to the search and seizure provisions of the state and federal constitutions. Although warrantless searches are generally unreasonable, a public employer may subject an employee to a suspicionless search "'where the privacy interests implicated by the search are minimal, and where an important governmental interest furthered by the intrusion would be placed in jeopardy by a requirement of individualized suspicion.'" Barreras v. New Mexico Corrections Dept., 114 N.M. 366, 369, 838 P.2d 983, 986 (1992) (quoting Skinner v. Railway Labor Executives Ass'n, 489 U.S. 602, 624 (1989)) (suspicionless drug testing of corrections officers not unreasonable search). But there must be more than mere speculation that the need for government intrusion will materialize; the asserted governmental interests must be tied to the "operational realities of the workplace." Jaramillo v. City of Albuquerque, 1998-NMCA-062, ¶ 17, 125 N.M. 194, 958 P.2d 1244 (drug test of city employee unjustified where no showing that he would actually perform hazardous work) (internal quotation marks omitted).

C. Medical Testing

1. ***Common Law and Statutes.*** A New Mexico statute provides that "[n]o person may require an individual to disclose the results of a human immunodeficiency virus related test as a condition of hiring, promotion or continued employment, unless the absence of human immunodeficiency virus infection is a bona fide occupational qualification of the job in question." NMSA 1978, § 28-10A-1(A) (1989). This statute has not been applied in any reported case. No other New Mexico statute or common law rule restricts or specifically addresses the medical testing of employees, except in connection with the continued receipt of workmen's compensation benefits. NMSA 1978, § 52-1-51(H) (2003) ("If a worker fails or refuses to submit to [a medical] examination in accordance with this section, he shall forfeit all workers' compensation benefits that would accrue or become due to him except for such failure or refusal to submit to examination during the period that he persists in such failure and refusal unless he is by reason of disability unable to appear for examination"). Although it appears that a public or private employer is free to subject his employees to mandatory physical examinations, he may run afoul of the New Mexico Human Rights Act if he discriminates against an employee based on a disability revealed by such an examination. See NMSA 1978, § 28-1-7 (E & J) (2003); Martinez v. Yellow Freight Sys., Inc., 113 N.M. 366, 369-71, 826 P.2d 962, 965-67 (1992). Furthermore, an employer may be held vicariously liable for the medical malpractice of a physician who is negligent in connection with the examination of an employee. Baer v. Regents of Univ. of Cal., 118 N.M. 685, 690, 884 P.2d 841, 846 (Ct. App. 1994).

2. *Private Employers.* No New Mexico law on point.

3. *Public Employers.* No New Mexico law on point.

D. Polygraph Tests

New Mexico has imposed no restrictions on the administration of polygraph tests by employers. The Peace Officer's Employer-Employee Relations Act expressly authorizes mandatory polygraphs, under certain circumstances, for police officers who are under investigation by their superiors. NMSA 1978, § 29-14-5 (1991). The Tenth Circuit has held that mandatory polygraph examinations for employees do not violate New Mexico public policy for purposes of a common law retaliatory discharge claim and do not constitute an invasion of privacy under New Mexico law. Zaccardi v. Zale Corp., 856 F.2d 1473, 1475-76 (10th Cir. 1988).

E. Fingerprinting

There is no New Mexico statute or common law generally authorizing or restricting the fingerprinting of employees or prospective employees. Applicants for the position of fireman in large municipalities are required to provide their fingerprints for screening by the FBI. NMSA 1978, § 3-18-11.1 (1985). The same is true of applicants for employment with the public school system, NMSA 1978, § 22-10A-5(A) (2003), as well as volunteers and staff at juvenile justice facilities, NMSA 1978, § 9-2A-23 (2007). All New Mexico lottery board members and prospective lottery employees must be fingerprinted. NMSA 1978, § 6-24-12 (1999).

III. SEARCHES

"The people shall be secure in their persons, papers, homes and effects, from unreasonable searches and seizures, and no warrant to search any place, or seize any person or thing, shall issue without describing the place to be searched, or the persons or things to be seized, nor without a written showing of probable cause, supported by oath or affirmation." N.M. Const. art. II, § 10.

A. Employee's Person

1. *Private Employers.* The constitutional right to be free from unreasonable searches and seizures does not protect against intrusions by private persons. State v. Johnston, 108 N.M. 778, 780, 779 P.2d 556, 558 (Ct. App. 1989).

2. *Public Employers.* The only New Mexico cases on point are those addressing drug testing of public employees. See II.B.3, supra.

B. Employee's Work Area

No New Mexico law on point.

C. Employee's Property

1. *Private Employers.* The constitutional right to be free from unreasonable searches and seizures does not protect against intrusions by private persons. Johnston, 108 N.M. at 780, 779 P.2d at 558. If an individual's expectation of privacy is breached by a private actor, then subsequent investigation by the state is not an unreasonable search or seizure under the Fourth Amendment, so long as the subsequent investigation does not expand upon the scope of the original breach. State v. Rivera, 2009-NMCA-049, ¶ 13, 146 N.M. 194, 207 P.3d 1171. **Additionally, an individual will lose his expectation of privacy if he voluntarily relinquishes possession of his property to a third party. State v. Ballard, 2012-NMCA-043, ¶ 14, 276 P.3d 976. Under such circumstances, seizure of the property by a government official is considered reasonable and lawful under the Fourth Amendment and under Article II, Section 10 of the New Mexico Constitution. Id.**

2. *Public Employers.* There are no reported cases on point, but the rules applicable to drug testing of public employees would presumably apply here as well. See II.B.3, supra.

IV. MONITORING OF EMPLOYEES

A. Telephones and Electronic Communications

1. *Wiretapping.* The Abuse of Privacy Act prohibits interference with communications, which includes knowingly and without lawful authority "cutting, breaking, tapping or making any connection with any telegraph or telephone line, wire, cable or instrument belonging to or in the lawful possession or control of another, without the consent of such person owning, possessing or controlling such property." NMSA 1978, § 30-12-1(B) (1979). Interference with

communications also includes knowingly and without lawful authority "reading, interrupting, taking or copying any message, communication or report intended for another by telegraph or telephone without the consent of a sender or intended recipient thereof." Id. § 30-12-1(C) (1979). The violation of this statute constitutes a misdemeanor and subjects the perpetrator to civil liability. Id. §§ 30-12-1 (1979), 30-12-11 (1973). There is no case law addressing whether the Abuse of Privacy Act restricts an employer's right to monitor its employees' communications. There is no illegal intrusion if one party to the communication consents to the eavesdropping or recording. State v. Arnold, 94 N.M. 385, 387, 610 P.2d 1214, 1216 (Ct. App. 1979), rev'd on other grounds, 94 N.M. 381, 610 P.2d 1210 (1980).

2. ***Electronic Communications.*** It is unclear whether the Abuse of Privacy Act applies only to communications by telephone or telegraph, or whether its protections extend to other communications such as e-mail.

3. ***Other Electronic Monitoring.*** No New Mexico law on point.

B. Mail

No New Mexico law on point.

C. Surveillance/Photographing

No New Mexico law on point.

V. ACTIVITIES OUTSIDE THE WORKPLACE

A. Statute or Common Law

The New Mexico Human Rights Act generally addresses the unlawfulness of an employer discriminating against an employee based on "race, age, religion, color, national origin, ancestry, sex, sexual orientation, gender identity, physical or mental handicap or serious medical condition, or, if the employer has fifty or more employees, spousal affiliation." NMSA 1978, § 28-1-7(A) (2003).

B. Employees' Personal Relationships

1. ***Romantic Relationships Between Employees.*** No New Mexico law on point.

2. ***Sexual Orientation.*** The New Mexico Human Rights Act prohibits discrimination in the employment context on the basis of sexual orientation by employers with more than fifteen employees. NMSA 1978, § 28-1-7(A) (2004). According to NMSA 1978, § 28-1-2(P) (2003), sexual orientation means heterosexuality, homosexuality or bisexuality, whether actual or perceived.

3. ***Marital Status.*** The New Mexico Human Rights Act prohibits discrimination in the employment context on the basis of spousal affiliation, but only if the employer has fifty or more employees. NMSA 1978, § 28-1-7(A) (2004).

C. Smoking

The Employee Privacy Act makes it unlawful for an employer to discriminate against an employee or applicant because he is a smoker or nonsmoker or prohibit an employee from smoking during nonworking hours, unless a bona fide occupational requirement is involved. NMSA 1978, § 50-11-3 (1991). An employee aggrieved by a violation of the Employee Privacy Act may bring a civil suit for damages. Id. § 50-11-4 (1991).

Additionally, the Dee Johnson Clean Indoor Air Act, NMSA 1978, §§ 24-16-1 -20 (2007), prohibits an employer from discharging, refusing to hire or retaliating against an employee or applicant for employment because that employee or applicant exercised rights afforded by the Act, such as smoking in a designated smoking area, or reported a violation of the Act. NMSA 1978, § 24-16-19(A) (2007). This Act applies to any indoor workplace, indoor public place, buses, taxicabs, or other means of public transit not specifically exempted under the Act. NMSA 1978, § 24-16-4 (2007).

D. Blogging

No New Mexico law on point.

VI. RECORDS

Every employer shall keep a true and accurate record of hours worked and wages paid to each employee for at least one year after the entry of the record. NMSA 1978 § 50-4-9 (2000). The Inspection of Public Records Act gives every citizen the right to inspect any public records of the state except, among other things, records pertaining to physical or mental examinations, letters of reference concerning employment or licensing, letters or memoranda in personnel files that are matters of opinion, and except as otherwise provided by law. NMSA 1978, § 14-2-1 (2011).

A. Personnel Records

The exception in the Inspection of Public Records Act for "matters of opinion" has been held to protect from public inspection the personnel files of former state employees who were terminated for disciplinary reasons. State ex rel. Barber v. McCotter, 106 N.M. 1, 1-2, 738 P.2d 119, 119-20 (1987). The Act's catch-all exception has been applied to protect records of a public employee's personal position regarding union representation. City of Las Cruces v. Public Employee Labor Relations Bd., 1996-NMSC-024, ¶ 11, 121 N.M. 688, 917 P.2d 451. Applications for public employment have repeatedly been held to constitute public records. See City of Farmington v. Daily Times, 2009-NMCA-057, ¶¶ 19-22, 146 N.M. 349, 210 P.3d 246, overruled in part on other grounds by Republican Party of N.M. v. N.M. Taxation & Revenue Dep't, 2012-NMSC-026, ¶ 16, 283 P.3d 288; State ex rel. Blanchard v. City Comm'rs, 106 N.M. 769, 750 P.2d 469 (Ct. App. 1988). The Act generally protects letters of reference, documents concerning infractions and disciplinary action, and personnel evaluations. State ex rel. Newsome v. Alarid, 90 N.M. 790, 794, 568 P.2d 1236, 1240 (1977). A separate statute requires credit bureaus that furnish personnel-reporting services to keep such information confidential except in connection with personnel investigations. NMSA 1978, § 56-3-5 (1969).

B. Medical Records

The Inspection of Public Records Act protects public employees' personnel records pertaining to illness, injury, disability, inability to perform a job task, and sick leave. State ex. rel. Newsome v. Alarid, 90 N.M. 790, 794, 568 P.2d 1236, 1240 (1977).

C. Criminal Records

The Criminal Offender Employment Act allows state agencies regulating trades, businesses or professions to take criminal convictions into consideration in determining eligibility for licenses, permits or certificates, but a conviction cannot "operate as an automatic bar to obtaining authority to practice a trade, business or profession." NMSA 1978, § 28-2-3 (1974). Records of arrest without conviction and misdemeanors not involving moral turpitude may not be used, distributed or disseminated in connection with an application for public employment, license or other authority. Id.

The Caregivers Criminal History Screening Act, NMSA 1978, §§ 29-17-2 to -5 (1998), requires criminal history screening for anyone working as a "caregiver" in settings such as skilled nursing facilities, psychiatric facilities, rehabilitation facilities and other facilities that provide similar types of care. *See* §§ 29-17-4(A) to (C) (defining "caregiver" and the types of employment that require criminal history screening). Section 29-17-5(I) requires strict confidentiality with regard to the records and information obtained during the criminal history screening process. *See* § 29-17-4(I). Although the screening process is actually completed by the New Mexico Department of Health, it is possible that the employer/prospective employer for which the screening was undertaken will receive at least some information relating to the results of the screening process that is considered confidential under § 29-17-4(I). That possibility raises concerns both with regard to personnel record keeping and references provided to subsequent employers. An employer in such a situation should be especially careful to comply with the confidentiality provisions of the Act in order to avoid the imposition of penalties pursuant to § 29-17-4(I).

D. Subpoenas / Search Warrants

An employer must comply with a lawfully issued administrative subpoena issued in connection with a claim for failure to pay wages. NMSA 1978, § 50-4-9(E) (1953). Further, an employer, even if not a party to a pending lawsuit, must comply with a lawfully issued subpoena issued in connection with ongoing litigation. Rule 1-045, NMRA. An employer may move to quash an otherwise lawfully issued subpoena on grounds that the subpoena "requires disclosure of privileged or other protected matter and no exception or waiver applies." Rule 1-045(C)(3)(a)(iii). "[A]bsent a court order," a party responding to a subpoena "shall not respond to the subpoena prior to the expiration of fourteen (14) days after the date of service of the subpoena." Rule 1-045(C)(2)(a)(ii).

Although there is no New Mexico law that directly addresses an employer's liabilities, rights and obligations in responding to a search warrant involving the workplace, an employer in New Mexico may provide valid consent to such searches in the absence of a warrant under very specific circumstances. In the absence of probable cause or a search warrant, a search will generally be deemed lawful if voluntary consent is obtained from an authorized person. See State v. Duffy, 1998-NMSC-014, ¶ 72, 126 N.M. 132, 967 P.2d 807. In order to validly consent to a warrantless search in the workplace, one must have "common authority over the specific areas that were searched" or "other sufficient relationship to the premises.'" See State v. Madrid, 91 N.M. 375, 378, 574 P.2d 594, 597 (Ct. App. 1978).

VII. ACTIONS SUBSEQUENT TO EMPLOYMENT

A. References

"When requested to provide a reference on a former or current employee, an employer acting in good faith is immune from liability for comments about the former employee's job performance." NMSA 1978, § 50-12-1 (1995). "The immunity shall not apply when the reference information supplied was knowingly false or deliberately misleading, was rendered with malicious purpose or violated any civil rights of the former employee." Id. Section 50-12-1 "would appear to track much of the common-law privilege relating to defamation and good-faith comments in the employment context." Davis v. Bd. of County Comm'rs, 1999-NMCA-110, ¶ 30, 127 N.M. 785, 794, 987 P.2d 1172, 1182 (employers providing an employee reference may remain silent, but once they speak they may be held liable to third parties for negligently misrepresenting or omitting information concerning an employee's dangerous and violent propensities); see also id. at ¶ 28 ("public policy supports full and accurate disclosure of non-confidential information by employers, and we seek to encourage employers in that direction"). Section 50-12-1 provides only a qualified privilege against liability to an employer providing post-employment reference information. Id. at ¶ 29.

New Mexico courts have also recognized an absolute privilege from liability for provision of a post-employment reference where the employee has consented, in writing or otherwise, to release of employment information. Baker v. Bhajan, 117 N.M. 278, 281-82, 871 P.2d 374, 377-788 (1994) (former employee waived "any right of action, cause of action, or other means of redress . . . against any person or entity . . . which might arise from supplying information concerning [his] background to [the prospective employer]," and thus gave rise to absolute privilege (internal quotation marks omitted)); Gengler v. Phelps, 92 N.M. 465, 589 P.2d 1056 (Ct. App. 1978) (consent inferred and absolute privilege granted, when former employee knew, upon filling out application, that prospective employer would seek information from former employer).

B. Non-Compete Agreements

A New Mexico court will enforce a non-competition covenant as long as the court deems the covenant reasonable. Insure New Mexico, LLC v. McGonigle, 2000-NMCA-018, ¶ 24, 128 N.M. 611, 995 P.2d 1053 (citing Bowen v. Carlsbad Ins. & Real Estate, Inc., 104 N.M. 514, 516, 724 P.2d 233, 225 (1986) (noting that "Courts are more reluctant to disturb restrictive covenants in buy-sell agreements than those in employment contracts")). Restrictive covenants must be reasonable as to both term and geographic scope. Bowen, 104 N.M. at 516-17, 724 P.2d at 225-26. "Whether there is a reasonable restraint depends on the facts of a particular case, and is a matter of law for the courts to decide." Id. at 516, 724 P.2d at 225.

VIII. OTHER ISSUES

A. Statutes of Limitations

The New Mexico federal district court has held that a state court would apply an independent statute of limitations to each of the four privacy causes of action. Benally v. Hundred Arrows Press, Inc., 614 F. Supp. 969, 978 (D.N.M. 1985), rev'd on other grounds sub nom, Benally v Amon Carter Museum of W. Art, 858 F.2d 618 (10th Cir. 1988). Because the interest violated by misappropriation of likeness is in the nature of a property interest, the four-year limitations period for actions for injuries to property governs misappropriation. NMSA 1978, § 37-1-4 (1880); Benally, 614 F. Supp. at 978-79. An action for injury to property accrues when the aggrieved party discovers the injury. NMSA 1978, § 37-1-7 (1880). Public disclosure of private facts is more in the nature of a personal injury, so the three-year personal injury statute of limitations applies to that claim. Id. § 37-1-8 (1976); Benally, 614 F. Supp. at 980-81. This limitations period begins to run from the date of injury, or publication. Benally, 614 F. Supp. at 981 (citing New Mexico Elec. Serv. v. Montanez, 89 N.M. 278, 551 P.2d 634 (1976)). Although no case has decided which limitations period is applicable to false light or intrusion, both are basically personal injury actions and should be subject to the same three-year statute of limitations.

If an action for intentional infliction of emotional distress, prima facie tort, or negligent hiring, retention or supervision involves recovery for personal injury or analogous damages, the three-year limitations period generally governing personal injury claims will apply, and it will run from the time of injury. NMSA 1978, § 37-1-8 (1976). If the claim seeks recovery for property damage, the statute of limitations will be four years and will accrue upon discovery of the injury. Id. § 37-1-4 (1880).

B. Jurisdiction

No New Mexico law on point.

C. Worker's Compensation Exclusivity

No New Mexico law on point.

D. Pleading Requirements

Aside from the necessary elements of the various causes of action described above, there is no law in New Mexico addressing the procedural requirements of pleading with specific regard to privacy claims. Generally, a pleading must be sufficient to give fair notice of the claim asserted, so as to enable the adverse party to answer and prepare for trial. See Las Luminarias of N.M. Council of Blind v. Isengard, 92 N.M. 297, 304, 587 P.2d 444, 451 (Ct. App. 1978) (Sutin, J., concurring). **New Mexico has specifically declined to follow the federal pleading standard as outlined in Ashcroft v. Iqbal, 556 U.S. 662 (2009), thereby confirming that New Mexico is a notice-pleading state. Madrid v. Village of Chama, 2012-NMCA-071, ¶ 17.**

SURVEY OF NEW YORK EMPLOYMENT LIBEL LAW

Charles S. Sims
Proskauer Rose LLP
Eleven Times Square
New York, New York 10036
Telephone: (212) 969-3950; Fax: (212) 969-2900

(With Developments Reported Through **November 1, 2012**)

GENERAL COMMENTS

None.

SIGNIFICANT DEVELOPMENTS SINCE THE 2012 *SURVEY*

A New York appellate court overruled the court's policy of recognizing imputing homosexuality as defamation *per se* in light of modern public policy and legislative intent. Yonaty v. Mincolla, 945 N.Y.S.2d 774, 779 (3d Dep't 2012).

I. GENERAL LAW

A. General Employment Law

1. ***At Will Employment.*** There is no cause of action for the mere discharge of an at will employee. **Sullivan v. Harnisch, 19 N.Y.3d 259 (2012);** Horn v. New York Times, 100 N.Y.2d, 85, 790 N.E.2d 753, 760 N.Y.S.2d 378 (2003); Murphy v. Am. Home Prods. Corp., 58 N.Y.2d 293, 461 N.Y.S.2d 232, 448 N.E.2d 86 (1983). But see Wieder v. Skala, 80 N.Y.2d 628, 593 N.Y.S.2d 752, 609 N.E.2d 105 (1992) (acknowledging a narrow exception for certain self-regulated professions, such as lawyers). "[A]n employee may not circumvent this rule by using other causes of action to substitute for such a claim," including defamation. La Duke v. Lyons, 250 A.D.2d 969, 973, 673 N.Y.S.2d 240, 244 (3d Dep't 1998). A terminated at will employee may bring a defamation action, however, where the alleged defamation consists of statements by the defendants that are distinct from the termination. See Kelleher v. Corinthian Media, Inc., 208 A.D.2d 477, 617 N.Y.S.2d 726 (1st Dep't 1994). While there are no general public policy-based exceptions to the "At-Will Doctrine," there are several statutory exceptions, such as N.Y. Labor Law § 740, "the whistleblower's statute," which prohibits employers from retaliating against any employee who reports or threatens to report illegal employer activity that threatens public health or safety. See e.g., Carter v. New York City Dep't of Corrections, 7 Fed. Appx. 99 (2d Cir. 2001).

B. Elements of Defamation Claim

1. ***Basic Elements.*** Defamation, which includes libel and slander, is the invasion of a person's interest in his reputation and good name. Albert v. Loksen, 239 F.3d 256, 265 (2d Cir. 2001). Defamation arises from making a false statement that tends to expose the plaintiff to public contempt, hatred, ridicule, aversion or disgrace. **Thomas H. v. Paul B., 18 N.Y.3d 580, 965 N.E.2d 939, 942 N.Y.S.2d 437 (2012);** see also Town of Massena v. Healthcare Underwriters Mutual Insurance Company, 98 N.Y.2d 435, 779 N.E.2d 167, 749 N.Y.S.2d 456 (2002); Foster v. Churchill, 87 N.Y.2d 744, 751 (1996) (quoting Rinaldi v Holt, Rinehart & Winston, 42 N.Y.2d 369, 379 (1977)). To make out a defamation claim in New York, plaintiffs must establish: (1) a false and defamatory statement of fact; (2) concerning the plaintiff; (3) published without privilege or authorization to a third party; (4) constituting fault rising at least to the level of negligence; and (5) causing special harm or constituting defamation *per se*. See Fordham v. Islip Union Free School District, 662 F. Supp. 2d 261 (E.D.N.Y. 2009); Moccio v. Cornell Univ., No. 09 Civ. 3601, 2009 U.S. Dist. LEXIS 62052 (S.D.N.Y. July 20, 2009); Dillon v. City of New York, 261 A.D.2d 34, 38, 704 N.Y.S.2d 1 (1st Dept. 1999). A defamatory statement that is expressed in writing or print is subject to the common law cause of action of libel. **E.g., Parrino v. SunGard Avail. Servs., L.P., No. CV-11-3315, 2012 WL 826946 at *3 (citing Church of Scientology v. Behar, 238 F.3d 168, 173 (2d Cir. 2001)).** Libel claims differ from slander claims in libel claims require a statements to be in writing. See, e.g., Rizzo v. Edison, Inc., 172 Fed. Appx. 391, 395 (2d Cir. 2006); Dibella v. Hopkins, 403 F.3d 102, 110 (2d Cir. 2005).

For claims pleaded in state court, plaintiffs must allege in the pleadings "the particular words complained of . . . but their application to the plaintiff may be stated generally." N.Y. C.P.L.R. § 3016(a) (Consol. 2012); see Sokol v. Leader, 74 A.D.3d 1180, 1183, 904 N.Y.S.2d 153, 156-57 (2d Dep't 2010) (holding plaintiff had adequately pled defamation because plaintiff had stated with specificity the "particular words complained of" despite defendant's argument to the contrary); Pappalardo v. Westchester Rockland Newspapers, Inc., 101 A.D.2d 830, 830, 475 N.Y.S.2d 487, 488 (2d Dep't 1984) (holding plaintiff had adequately pled defamation because plaintiff attached copy of allegedly defamatory newspaper article as exhibit to complaint). See V.D. infra. Federal courts applying New York law do not require as great an amount of specificity at the pleading stage. Mahmud v. Bon Secours Charity Health Sys., 289 F. Supp. 2d 466, 476 (S.D.N.Y. 2003) (holding plaintiff must plead who made allegedly defamatory statements, to whom statements were made, and at what time they were made). Federal courts apply Fed. R. Civ. P. 8(a)(2) which merely requires a short plain statement of the claim alleged. Geisler v. Petrocelli, 616 F.2d 636, 640, 6 Media L. Rep. 1023 (2d Cir. 1980). See also Pasqualini v. MortgageIT, Inc., 498 F. Supp. 2d 659, 671-72 (S.D.N.Y. 2007) (noting that under Federal law, defamation is not one of the delineated claims in F.R.C.P. 9(b), thus the requirements in F.R.C.P. 8(a)(2) apply). The plaintiff has the burden of pleading and proving the alleged defamatory statement is false. Freeman v. Johnston, 84 N.Y.2d 52, 56, 637 N.E.2d 268, N.Y.S.2d 377 (1994); Guerrero v. Carva, 10 A.D.3d 105, 779 N.Y.S.2d 12 (1st Dep't 2004). New York states courts are "hesitant to find defamation based on the omission of facts." Biro v. Conde Nast, No. 11-CV-4442, 2012 WL 3264059 at *17 (S.D.N.Y. Aug. 9, 2012). One Southern District judge has allowed for the possibility of defamatory implication where the implication can be "derive from unchallenged facts" and on an "especially rigorous showing that (1) the language may be reasonably read to impart the false innuendo and (2) the author intends or endorses the inference." Id. (citing Chapin v. Knight-Ridder, Inc., 993 F.2d 1087, 1093 (4th Cir. 1993)). State court cases have not gone that far.

2. ***Fault.*** Some degree of fault is constitutionally required for every defamation claim. Gertz v. Robert Welch, Inc., 418 U.S. 323, 346-347, 94 S. Ct. 2997, 1 Media L. Rep. 1633 (1974).The level of fault that a plaintiff must demonstrate depends on the plaintiff's private or public status and the private or public nature of the defendant's statement.

a. **Private Figure Plaintiff/Matter of Public Concern.** Where a defendant speaks on a matter of public concern, a private figure plaintiff must plead and demonstrate that false statement was published in a grossly irresponsible manner "without due consideration for the standards of information gathering and dissemination ordinarily followed by responsible parties." Huggins v. Moore, 94 N.Y.2d 296, 302, 726 N.E.2d 456, 460, 704 N.Y.S.2d 904, 908 (1999) (quoting Chapadeau v. Utica Observer-Dispatch, 38 N.Y.2d 196, 199, 341 N.E.2d 569, 379 N.Y.S.2d 61, 1 Media L. Rep. 1693 (1975)); see also McGill v. Parker, 179 A.D.2d 98, 582 N.Y.S.2d 91, 19 Media L. Rep. 2170 (1st Dep't 1992) (applying Chapadeau standard to cases involving non-media defendants). "With respect to whether speech is on a matter of public concern, a court must 'tak[e] into account the content, form, and context of a given statement as revealed by the record as a whole.'" Licopoli v. Mineola Union Free Sch. Dist., No. 09-3974, 2010 U.S. Dist. LEXIS 127090, *16 (E.D.N.Y. Dec. 1, 2010) (citing Ruotolo v. New York, 514 F.3d 184, 189 (2d Cir. 2008) (internal citation and quotation marks omitted)). However, "a speaker's motive is not dispositive in determining whether his or her speech addresses a matter of public concern." Sousa v. Roque, 578 F.3d 164, 173 (2d Cir. 2009). An employee who speaks on a matter and is motivated by her own personal grievances may nevertheless be speaking on a matter of public concern. Id. (citing Connick v. Myers, 461 U.S. 138, 148-49 (1983)).

b. **Private Figure Plaintiff/Matter of Private Concern.** The Court of Appeals has not decided what level of fault, if any, must be shown in the context of a private figure in a matter of private concern. While traditional common law rules do not require fault, the at least some level of fault is required under the United States Constitution. Gertz, 418 U.S. at 346-347. Accordingly, New York's lower courts have required that plaintiffs demonstrate defendants acted at least negligently. Hogan v. Herald Co., 84 A.D.2d 470, 475 n. 3, 446 N.Y.S.2d 836, 8 Media L. Rep. 1137 (4th Dep't 1982), aff'd, 58 N.Y.2d 630, 444 N.E.2d 1002, 458 N.Y.S.2d 538, 8 Media L. Rep. 2567 (1982); Lee v. City of Rochester, 663 N.Y.S.2d 738, 174 Misc. 2d 723 (Sup. Ct. 1997), aff'd 254 A.D.2d 790, 677 N.Y.S.2d 848 (4th Dep't 1998). But see Albert v. Loksen, 239 F.3d 256, 270 (2d Cir. 2001) (criticizing some lower New York courts for concluding "without discussion or authority" that negligence principles should be applied).

c. **Public Figure Plaintiff/Matter of Public Concern.** When a public figure is the subject of an allegedly defamatory statement in a matter of public concern, the federal constitutional standard from New York Times v. Sullivan, 376 U.S. 254, 380 (1964) — actual malice — applies. See, e.g., Kipper v. NYP Holdings Co., 12 N.Y.3d 348, 912 N.E. 26, 884 N.Y.S.2d 194, 37 Media L. Rep. 1673 (2009) (requiring a defendant to show on summary judgment there were deficiencies in the record to prevent plaintiff from proving actual malice by clear and convincing evidence); Porcari v. Gannett Satellite Information Network, Inc., 50 A.D.3d 993, 856 N.Y.S.2d 217 (2d Dep't 2008) (finding plaintiff was not required to plead or prove that the defamatory statements were published with actual malice because plaintiff did not qualify as a public official). See II.A.2.d.(1), infra. Questions of actual malice are often difficult to resolve on pre-discovery summary judgment. See Fehlhaber v. Bd. of Educ. of the Utica City Sch. Dist., No. 6:09-CV-1380, 2010 U.S. Dist. LEXIS 115408, *16 (N.D.N.Y. Oct. 29, 2010) (denying motion to dismiss because "the 'resolution of the falsity and actual malice inquiries typically requires discovery'" (quoting Church of Scientology Int'l v. Behar, 238 F.3d 168, 173 (2d Cir. 2001)). Whether a plaintiff is a public figure is a question of law for the court. See, e.g., Celle v. Filipino Reporter Enters., 209 F.3d 163, 176-77 (2d Cir. 2000).

A plaintiff may be a public figure generally, or for a limited purpose. The Second Circuit has set forth a four part test for determining whether someone is a limited purpose public figure. A defendant must show the plaintiff has: (1) successfully invited public attention to his views in an effort to influence others prior to the incident that is the subject of litigation; (2) voluntarily injected himself into a public controversy related to the subject of the litigation; (3) assumed a position of prominence in the public controversy; and (4) maintained regular and continuing access to the media. Lerman v. Flynt Distributing Co., Inc., 745 F.2d 123, 136-37 (2d Cir. 1984). A plaintiff's prominence must be substantively related to the "particular controversy giving rise to the defamation." Pisani v. Staten Island Univ. Hosp., No. 06-CV-1016, 2008 WL 1771922, at *16 (E.D.N.Y. Apr. 15, 2008) (quoting Contemporary Mission, Inc. v. N.Y. Times Co., 842 F.2d 612, 617 (2d Cir. 1988)). A plaintiff found to be a limited issue public figure must demonstrate the additional elements of: "1) falsity with convincing clarity, 2) actual malice with convincing clarity, and, beyond a preponderance of the evidence, 3) some degree of fault." Chandok v. Klessig, 648 F.Supp.2d 449, 459 (N.D.N.Y. 2009), aff'd 632 F.3d 803 (2d Cir. 2011).

3. ***Falsity.*** When the defamatory statement involves a public figure or a private figure and a matter of public concern, the plaintiff has an additional burden to plead and prove falsity. Stern v. News Corp., No. 08 Civ. 7624, 2010 U.S. Dist. LEXIS 133119, *14–15 (S.D.N.Y. Oct. 4, 2010) (citing Philadelphia Newspapers v. Hepps, 475 U.S. 767 (1986)). Whether the common law rule continues to apply in cases involving matters of private concern remains unsettled, but at least one lower court has held that it does. See King v. Tanner, 142 Misc. 2d 1004, 539 N.Y.S.2d 617 (Sup. Ct. 1989) (placing burden of proving statement's truth on the defendant). See also II.A.f, infra (burdens of proof where privilege applies).

4. ***Defamatory Statement of Fact.*** A defamatory statement is a "false statement which tends to 'expose the plaintiff to public contempt, ridicule, aversion or disgrace, or induce an evil opinion of him in the minds of right-thinking persons, and to deprive him of their friendly intercourse in society.'" Foster v. Churchill, 87 N.Y.2d 744, 751, 665 N.E.2d 153, 157, 642 N.Y.S.2d 583, 587 (1996) (quoting Rinaldi v. Holt, Rinehart & Winston, 42 N.Y.2d 369, 366 N.E.2d 1299, 397 N.Y.S.2d 943, 2 Media L. Rep. 2169 (1977)). Although statements of "pure opinion" are not necessarily protected from defamation under the U.S. Constitution, they are protected under the New York State Constitution. Joyce v. Thompson Wigdor & Gilly LLP, No. 06 Civ. 15315, 2008 WL 2329227, at *5 (S.D.N.Y. June 3, 2008). Whether a particular statement could be found to be defamatory is a question of law for the court. Baraliu v. Vinya Capital, L.P., No. 07 Civ. 4626, 2009 U.S. Dist. LEXIS 35712 (S.D.N.Y. Mar. 30, 2009) (citing Golub v. Enquirer/Star Group, 89 N.Y.2d 1074, 681 N.E.2d 1282, 659 N.Y.S.2d 836 (1997)); Aronson v. Wiersma, 65 N.Y.2d 592, 483 N.E.2d 1138, 493 N.Y.S.2d 1006, 12 Media L. Rep. 1150 (1985); see, e.g., Karedes v. Ackerley Group, Inc., 423 F.3d 107 (2d Cir. 2005) (explaining how New York courts interpret disputed language of an allegedly defamatory statement or publication).

5. ***Of and Concerning Plaintiff.*** A defamation plaintiff must prove that the contested statement was "of and concerning" him or her. Excellus Health Plan, Inc. v. Tran, 287 F. Supp. 2d 167, 173 (W.D.N.Y. 2003); see Chicherchia v. Cleary, 207 A.D.2d 855, 855, 616 N.Y.S.2d 647, 647 (2d Dep't 1994); Allen v. Gordon, 86 A.D.2d 514, 446 N.Y.S.2d 48, 8 Media L. Rep. 1124 (1st Dep't 1982), aff'd, 56 N.Y.2d 780, 437 N.E.2d 284, 452 N.Y.S.2d 25 (1982). A statement is "of and concerning" the plaintiff if it is "reasonable to conclude that the publication refers to him." Chicherchia v. Cleary, 207 A.D.2d 855, 856, 616 N.Y.S.2d 647, 648 (2d Dep't 1994). Whether a statement is of and concerning the plaintiff is a question for the jury, but a court may grant summary judgment if no reasonable jury could find the statement was of and concerning the plaintiff. Excellus, 287 F. Supp. 2d at 174 (citing Cardone v. Empire Blue Cross & Blue Shield, 884 F. Supp. 838, 847 (S.D.N.Y. 1995)).

6. ***Publication.*** A defamation plaintiff must allege and prove that the purportedly defamatory statement was published to a third party. See Van-Go Transp. Co. v. New York City Bd. of Educ., 971 F. Supp. 90 (E.D.N.Y. 1997); Murphy v. Cadillac Rubber & Plastics, Inc., 946 F. Supp. 1108 (W.D.N.Y. 1996); Weintraub v. Phillips, Nizer, Benjamin, Krim, & Ballon, 172 A.D.2d 254, 568 N.Y.S.2d 84 (1st Dep't 1991). "Publication occurs when the [defamatory] words are read 'by someone other than the person libeled and the person making the charges.'" Van-Go Transp. Co., 971 F. Supp. at 102 (citing Fedrizzi v. Washingtonville Cent. Sch. Dist., 2004 A.D.2d 267, 268, 611 N.Y.S.2d 584 (2d Dep't 1994)).

a. **Intracorporate Communication.** Communications among employees of a corporation are considered to be published, see, e.g., Levine v. Bd of Educ. of City of N.Y., 186 A.D.2d 743, 589 N.Y.S.2d 181 (2d Dep't 1992), but are often protected by a qualified privilege. See III.D, infra.

b. **Compelled Self-Publication.** The courts are split as to whether New York recognizes defamation claims arising from "compelled self-publication." See Ascione v. Pfizer, 312 F. Supp. 2d 572, 579 (S.D.N.Y. 2004) ("The status of the tort of defamation by 'compelled self-publication' is, at best, unclear under New York law"); Van-Go Transp. Co. v. New York City Bd. of Educ., 971 F. Supp. 90, 104 (E.D.N.Y. 1997) (analyzing New York and 2d Circuit law and determining "[i]t seems reasonable to assume the New York Court of Appeals would adopt the doctrine [of self-publication] in a form that allowed for liability where . . . there was a high degree of compulsion that required the reporting of the defamatory matter."). However, a plaintiff who voluntarily republishes the alleged defamatory words cannot maintain a defamation claim. See Wellington Funding & Bus. Consultants, Inc. v. Cont'l Grain Co., 259 A.D.2d 323, 686 N.Y.S.2d 425 (1st Dep't 1999) (affirming libel verdict based on foreseeable consequences of initial publication); Weintraub v. Phillips, Nizer, Benjamin, Krim, & Ballon, 172 A.D.2d 254, 568 N.Y.S.2d 84 (1st Dep't 1991) (where plaintiff did not allege publication to a third party by defendant, plaintiff could not state a claim based on his own republication);.

c. **Republication.** The originator of a defamatory statement is not liable for its repetition if the originator had no control over the republication. Van-Go Transp. Co. v. New York City Bd. of Educ., 971 F. Supp. 90 (E.D.N.Y. 1997). The originator may be held liable for the defamatory statement's republication if this repetition was reasonably foreseeable, but the foreseeability standard for republication is interpreted narrowly. Geraci v. Probst, 15 N.Y.3d 336, 938 N.E.2d 917, 912 N.Y.S.2d 484 (2010). When an author has "no knowledge of and played no role in" the republication of a statement, no liability will attach. Id. at 344, 922, 489. Publishers may be found liable if they are grossly irresponsible in republishing defamatory statements. Karaduman v. Newsday, Inc., 51 N.Y.2d 531, 416 N.E.2d 557, 435 N.Y.S.2d 556, 6 Media L. Rep. 2345 (1980) (finding editor not liable for republication because he was not grossly irresponsible). Such liability is contrary to the single instance rule, I.B.8.A.2 infra, but the exception is justified if "the subsequent publication is intended to and actually reaches a new audience.'" Liverpool v. Con-Way, Inc., No. 08-CV-4076, 2010 U.S. Dist. LEXIS 122419, *14 (E.D.N.Y. Nov. 18, 2010) (quoting Firth v. State, 98 N.Y.2d 365, 371 (2002)), **aff'd No. 11-1528-cv, 2012 U.S. App. LEXIS 13528 (2d Cir. July 3, 2012).**

7. ***Statements versus Conduct.*** A defamatory statement must ordinarily be either oral or written. See Hayes v. Sweeney, 961 F. Supp. 2d 467, 481 (W.D.N.Y. 1997) (holding that unspoken conduct cannot, in and of itself, be defamatory under New York law); see also Contes v. City of New York, No. 99 Civ. 1597, 1999 WL 500140 at *9 (S.D.N.Y. July 14, 1999) (holding mere conduct without statements made to others cannot be defamatory); Borquin v. Brink's Inc., No. 97 CIV 7522, 1999 WL 108766, at *3 (S.D.N.Y. Mar. 3, 1999) (same).

8. ***Damages.*** A plaintiff must plead special damages in a defamation action unless the claim falls into one of the categories of defamation *per se*, see I.B.8.a, infra, in which case damages are presumed. **Robertson v. Dowbenko, 443 Fed. Appx. 659 (2d Cir. 2011)**; Liberman v. Gelstein, 80 N.Y.2d 429, 605 N.E.2d 344, 590 N.Y.S.2d 857, 21 Media L. Rep. 1079 (1992); Rufeh v. Schwartz, 50 A.D.3d 1002, 858 N.Y.S.2d 194 (2d Dep't 2008). Special damages contemplate "the loss of something having economic or pecuniary value" flowing directly from reputational injury caused by the defamation. **See Lan v. AOL Time Warner, Inc., No. 11 Civ. 2870, 2012 U.S. Dist. LEXIS 65307 (S.D.N.Y. May 9, 2012) (citing DiFolco v. MSNBC Cable, LLC, No. 06 Civ. 4278, 2011 U.S. Dist. LEXIS 131506, at *34 (S.D.N.Y. Nov. 9, 2011));** Liberman, 80 N.Y.2d at 434, 605 N.E.2d at 347, 590 N.Y.S. 2d at 860; Hassig v. Fitzrandolph, 8 A.D.3d 930, 779 N.Y.S.2d 613 (3d Dep't 2004). Presumed damages are not permitted in statements of public concern cases unless the plaintiff establishes that the defendant acted with actual malice. See Yesner v. Spinner, 765 F. Supp. 48 (E.D.N.Y. 1991); Friends of Animals, Inc. v. Associated Fur Mfrs., 46 N.Y.2d 1065, 390 N.E.2d 298, 416 N.Y.S.2d 790 (1979); 60 Minute Man Ltd. v. Kossman, 161 A.D.2d 574, 555 N.Y.S.2d 152 (2d Dep't 1990). A failure to itemize special damages is deemed a representation of general damages. Larsan v. Albany Med. Ctr., 252 A.D.2d 936, 676 N.Y.S.2d 293 (3d Dep't 1998); see also Boehner v. Heise, No. 03 Civ. 05453, 2009 U.S. Dist. LEXIS 41471 (S.D.N.Y. May 14, 2009); Drug Research Corp. v. Curtis Publ'g Co., 7 N.Y.2d 435, 166 N.E.2d 319, 199 N.Y.S.2d 33 (1960). Mere allegations of lost income will not suffice. Aronson v. Wiersma, 65 N.Y.2d 592, 595, 483 N.E.2d 1138, 493 N.Y.S.2d 1006 (1985).

a. **Presumed Damages and Defamation *Per Se*.** A defamatory statement is one that causes an individual to be vulnerable to "public hatred, shame, obloquy, contumely, odium, contempt, ridicule, aversion, ostracism, degradation, or disgrace". Treppel v. Biovail Corporation, No. 03 Civ. 3002, 2004 U.S. Dist. LEXIS 20714, at *30 (S.D.N.Y. Oct. 15, 2004) (quoting Celle v. Filipino Reporter Enters., 209 F.3d 163, 177 (2d Cir. 2000)); **Thomas H. v. Paul B., 18 N.Y.3d 580, 965 N.E.2d 939, 942 N.Y.S.2d 437 (2012).** Defamation *per se* "requires statements (i) charging plaintiff with a serious crime; (ii) that tend to injure another in his or her trade, business or profession; (iii) that plaintiff has a loathsome disease, or (iv) imputing unchastity to a woman." Torain v. Clear Channel Broadcasting, Inc., 651 F. Supp. 2d 125, 152 (S.D.N.Y. 2009).

A statement that inaccurately accuses someone of serious criminal conduct constitutes defamation *per se*. **Thomas H. v. Paul B., 18 N.Y.3d 580, 965 N.E.2d 939, 942 N.Y.S.2d 437 (2012);** see D'Lima v. Cuba Mem. Hosp., Inc., 833 F. Supp. 2d 383, 390 (W.D.N.Y. 2011) (finding allegations that defendant told a third party the plaintiff used illegal drugs was slander *per se*); Kasada, Inc. v. Access Capital, Inc., No. 01 Civ. 8893, 2004 U.S. Dist. LEXIS 25257 at *58 (S.D.N.Y. Dec. 10, 2004) (finding allegations of fraud, theft, and fraudulent conveyance" were slander *per se*); Sharrat v. Hickey, 20 A.D.3d 734, 799 N.Y.S.2d 299 (3d Dep't 2005) (holding defamation *per se* statements must allege serious crimes, not unlawful behaviors amounting to minor offenses).

A statement that would "tend to cause injury" to a person in her trade or profession constitutes defamation *per se*. Geraci v. Probst, 15 N.Y.3d 336, 344, 938 N.E.2d 317, 922, 912 N.Y.S.2d 484, 491 (2010) (citing Liberman v. Gelstein, 80 N.Y.2d 429, 435, 605 N.E.2d 344, 590 N.Y.S.2d 857 (1992)). See Henneberry v. Sumitomo Corporation of America, No. 04 Civ. 2128, 2005 U.S. Dist. LEXIS 7475, at *59 (S.D.N.Y. April 27, 2005) (finding statements that "disgraced plaintiff's business aptitude" constitute slander *per se*); cf. Bell v. Alden Owners, 299 A.D.2d 207, 209, 750 N.Y.S.2d 27, 29 (1st Dep't 2002) (finding allegedly defamatory remarks did not constitute slander *per se* because they were unrelated to plaintiff's business).

Suggestions that a person has contracted a "loathsome" disease are defamation *per se*, **but loathsome diseases are generally limited to venereal disease or diseases which are "loathsome and communicable." See Marino v. Jonke, No. 11 CV 430 & 4425, 2012 U.S. Dist. LEXIS 78661 at *34 (S.D.N.Y. Mar. 30, 2012). Mental illness does not qualify as such a loathsome disease, id.,** nor does cancer. Sam v. Enquirer/Star Group, Inc., 223 A.D.2d 360, 636 N.Y.S.2d 49 (1st Dep't 1996) (holding that cancer is not among the diseases that expose a person to public scorn or contempt), aff'd sub nom. Golub v. Enquirer/Star Group, Inc., 89 N.Y.2d 1074, 681 N.E.2d 1282, 659 N.Y.S.2d 836, 25 Media L. Rep. 1863 (1997).

Imputations of unchastity or serious sexual misconduct constitute slander *per se*. Walia v. Vivek Purmasir & Assocs., 160 F. Supp. 2d 380 (E.D.N.Y. 2000) (holding that telling multiple people, including a television reporter, in plaintiff's community that plaintiff was a "whore" and a "slut" constituted slander *per se*); Rejent v. Liberation Publications, Inc., 197 A.D.2d 240, 611 N.Y.S.2d 866, 22 Media L. Rep. 1826 (1st Dep't 1994) (holding the unauthorized publication of photograph of plaintiff in advertisement for sexually suggestive materials imputed sexual promiscuity); but see Ava v. NYP Holdings, Inc., 64 A.D.3d 407, 885 N.Y.S.2d 247 (1st Dep't 2009) (holding, in context, a newspaper's publication of sexual fantasies allegedly attributed to plaintiff did not constitute an imputation of unchastity or promiscuity).

New York courts had generally recognized imputations of homosexuality as an unofficial "fifth per se category," but at least one department has explicitly overruled those decisions on the basis of modern public policy and legislative intent. Yonaty v. Mincolla, 945 N.Y.S.2d 774, 779 (3d Dep't 2012). See also Stern v. Cosby, 645 F. Supp. 2d 258, 37 Media L. Rep. 2288 (S.D.N.Y. 2009) (indicating that defamatory nature of a statement depends on social mores, and that imputations of homosexuality are not *per se* defamation in 2009).

(1) **Employment-Related Criticism.** A defamation action cannot be based merely on the fact that an employee was terminated. Nichols v. Item Publishers, Inc., 309 N.Y. 596, 601, 132 N.E.2d 860, 862 (1956) ("The mere fact of one's removal from office carries no imputation of dishonesty or lack of professional capacity."); Weintraub v. Phillips, Nizer, Benjamin, Krim, & Ballon, 172 A.D.2d 254, 254, 568 NY.S.2d 84, 85 (1st Dep't 1991). A statement that merely reflects an unfavorable opinion of work performance does not constitute slander *per se*. See DG&A Mgmt. Servs, LLC v. Secs. Indus. Ass'n, 52 A.D.3d 992, 859 N.Y.S.3d 305 (3d Dep't 2008). Statements that criticize an employee's conduct are not defamation *per se* unless they impute fraud, dishonesty, incompetence, incapacity, or unfitness in the performance of the employee's trade. See **Lan v. AOL Time Warner, Inc., No. 11 Civ. 2870, 2012 U.S. Dist. LEXIS 65307 at *7 (S.D.N.Y. May 9, 2012) (statement that plaintiff was fired for being "lazy" alleged the employee lacks "an essential character . . . necessary to the performance of any and all professions or callings.");** Nicholls v. The Brookdale University Hospital Medical Center, No. 03-CV-6233 (Weinstein, J.), 2004 U.S. Dist. LEXIS 12816 *32 (E.D.N.Y. 2004) (holding accusations of fraud and forgery could "affect plaintiff's ability to carry on her trade or occupation"); Ives v. Guilford Mills, Inc., 3 F. Supp. 2d 191, 200 (N.D.N.Y. 1998) (reference to plaintiff's practice of letting things "go out the back door" could constitute slander per se); Zysk v. Fid. Title Ins. Co., 14 A.D.3d 609, 790 N.Y.S.2d 135 (2d Dep't 2005) (holding statements such as "you ought to be ashamed of yourself," "you are disgraceful," and "you are disgusting" . . . "did not imply behavior that was incompatible with the proper conduct of [a lawyer]"). A supervisor's charge that a train crew dispatcher abused drugs was held not to relate specifically to plaintiff's employment status, but was rather "more [a] general reflection upon the plaintiff's character," and therefore did not fall into the "trade, business or profession" exception. Harris v. Hirsh, 228 A.D.2d 206, 208, 643 N.Y.S.2d 556, 559 (1st Dep't 1996), appeal denied, 89 N.Y. 2d 805, 676 N.E.2d 499 (1996). However, a memorandum from a school president to the faculty was libel *per se* when it stated that the school had no responsible alternative but to replace the plaintiff as the chair of a department because the memorandum implied the existence of undisclosed facts. Kovacs v. Briarcliff School, Inc., 208 A.D.2d 686, 617 N.Y.S.2d 804 (2d Dep't 1994).

(2) **Single Instance Rule.** The "single instance rule" limits the defamation *per se* doctrine. Under the rule, when a statement relates to only one instance of professional or business malfeasance, presumed damages are not available, and the plaintiff must plead and prove special damages. Armstrong v. Simon & Schuster, 85 N.Y.2d 373, 379 n.5, 649 N.E.2d 825, 828 n.5 625 N.Y.S.2d 477, 480 n.5 (1995); November v. Time Inc., 13 N.Y.2d 175, 194 N.E.2d 126, 244 N.Y.S.2d 309 (1963); see also Cook v. Relin, 280 A.D.2d 897, 721 N.Y.S.2d 885 (4th Dep't 2001) (holding that statement implying that plaintiff was intoxicated at a social outing was subject to the single instance rule); but cf. Allen v. CH Energy Group, Inc., 58 A.D.3d 1102 (3d Dep't 2009) (defendant who allegedly accused customer service employee of defecating in public was beyond the scope of the single instance rule because employee would be unfit to continue work). **Online publication is considered a single instance of publication, even if the posting is continuously available. FTA Market Inc., v. Vevi, Inc., No. 11 CV 4789, 2012 WL 383945 at *7 (S.D.N.Y. Feb. 1, 2012) (collecting cases).**

b. **Punitive Damages.** Punitive damages are not available in defamation cases unless the plaintiff proves that the defendant acted with common law malice. Prozeralik v. Capital Cities Communications, Inc., 82 N.Y.2d 466, 626 N.E.2d 34, 605 N.Y.S.2d 218, 2 Media L. Rep. 2169 (1993). In Prozeralik, the Second Circuit held that actual malice — i.e., reckless disregard for the truth — was insufficient and a plaintiff seeking punitive damages must instead show that the defendant acted with "hatred, ill will, spite [or] criminal mental state." Id. See also **Weiss v. Lowenberg, 95 A.D.3d 405, 407, 944 N.Y.S.2d 27, 29-30 (1st Dep't 2012) (holding mere allegations that plaintiff was committing perjury and fraud by signing a probate petition did not rise to the level of "criminal indifference to civil obligations" required for punitive damages);** Dobies v. Brefka, 45 A.D.3d 999, 1001, 846 N.Y.S.2d 669, 671 (3d Dep't 2007) (finding punitive damages appropriate when defendant raised unfounded allegations of child sexual abuse against plaintiff). Punitive damages may be awarded on a showing of common law malice because they punish the defendant for intending to harm the plaintiff and are not related to the truth or falsity of any statement. Morsette v. "The Final Call", 309 A.D.2d 249, 255 (1st Dep't 2003).

II. PRIVILEGES AND DEFENSES

A. Scope of Privileges

1. ***Absolute Privilege.*** A statement made in the course of legal proceedings is absolutely privileged if it is "material and pertinent to the questions involved." **Sash v. Rosahn, 450 Fed. Appx. 42, 44 (2d Cir. 2011);** Ingber v. Mallilo, 52 A.D.3d 569, 860 N.Y.S.2d 180 (2d Dep't 2008) ("Statements made . . . in the course of a judicial or quasi-judicial proceeding are absolutely privileged, notwithstanding the motive with which they are made, as long as they are material and pertinent to the issue to be resolved in the proceeding."); see also Missick v. Big V Supermarkets, Inc., 115 A.D.2d 808, 495 N.Y.S.2d 994 (3d Dep't 1985), appeal dismissed 67 N.Y.2d 938, 493 N.E.2d 944, 502 N.Y.S.2d 1028 (1986) (statements made during proceeding before state agency could not be basis for defamation claim). Absolute privilege also attaches to statements made on the subject of pending litigation, Sexter & Warmflash, P.C. v. Margrabe, 38 A.D.3d 163, 828 N.Y.S.2d 315 (1st Dep't 2007), and statements submitted to judicial or quasi-judicial bodies that later become public records. See Bernstein v. Seeman, 593 F. Supp. 2d 630, 636 (S.D.N.Y. 2009) (collecting cases). See also Chimarev v. TD Waterhouse Investor Servs., 99 Fed. Appx. 259, 262-63 (2d Cir. 2004) (noting statements made in the course of litigation are absolutely privileged); Able Energy v. Marcum and Kliegman LLP, 69 A.D.3d 443, 893 N.Y.S.2d 36 (1st Dep't 2010) (holding statements in a letter to Securities Exchange Commission are absolutely privileged, regardless of whether agency commences proceedings in matter discussed); Herzfeld & Stern, Inc. v. Beck, 175 A.D.2d 689, 572 N.Y.S.2d 683 (1st Dep't 1991) (holding report submitted to New York Stock Exchange and Securities Exchange Commission concerning reasons for employee's termination is absolutely privileged). The privilege arises as a matter of common law and statute in New York. N.Y. Civ. Rights Law § 74 (Consol. 2012); Willson v. Association of Graduates of U.S. Military Academy, 946 F. Supp. 294 (S.D.N.Y. 1996). Absolute privilege protects public officials from liability for libel if the otherwise libelous act takes place within the sphere of their public duties. See Rosenberg v. Metlife, Inc., 8 N.Y.3d 359, 365, 866 N.E.2d 439, 442, 834 N.Y.S.2d 494, 497 (2007) (noting absolute privilege protects public officials so they can discharge their public function without fear of liability in a subsequent civil action). Additional statutory rights protect against defamation liability when the publication is "a fair and true report of any judicial proceeding." N.Y. Civ. Rights Law § 74 (McKinney 2012). *See D'Annunzio v. Ayken, Inc.*, No. 11-CV-3303, 2012 WL 2906248 at *4-5 (E.D.N.Y. July 17, 2012).

a. **Limitation on Absolute Privilege**. Absolute privilege applies to any person participating in the official processes of government. See, e.g., Park Knoll Assocs. v. Schmidt, 59 N.Y.2d 205, 209, 451 N.E.2d 182, 184, 464 N.Y.S.2d 424, 426 (1983). If absolute privilege is abused during a judicial proceeding, the privilege may be lost. Youmans v. Smith, 153 N.Y. 214, 220, 47 N.E. 265, 267 (1897) (holding privilege may be lost if a lawsuit is "needlessly defamatory" or "so obviously impertinent as not to admit of discussion"). The sole criterion for determining whether absolute privilege is abused is the pertinence of the statement in question to the proceedings. Seltzer v. Fields, 20 A.D.2d 60, 62, 244 N.Y.S.2d 792, 795 (1st Dep't 1963) affirmed 14 N.Y.2d 624, 198 N.E.2d 368, 249 N.Y.S.2d 174 (1964). Pertinence is a question of law for courts to determine. Sexter & Warmflash, P.C. v. Margrabe, 38 A.D.3d 163, 828 N.Y.S.2d 315 (1st Dep't 2007). The test for pertinence is "extremely liberal" and "any doubts are to be resolved in favor of pertinence." Casa de Meadows (Cayman Islands), 76 A.D.3d 917, 920, 908 N.Y.S.2d 628, 631 (1st Dep't 2010) (internal citations omitted). If the statement meets the bare minimum for pertinence, the statement is protected by the privilege. *Id.*

2. ***Qualified Privileges.*** A person who makes a defamatory statement without actual malice or common law malice will not be subject to liability if a qualified, or conditional, privilege attaches. New York recognizes several such privileges.

a. **Common Interest.** The common interest privilege is a qualified privilege insulating from liability communications made between parties with common legal interests in furtherance of those interests. **Chao v. Mount Sinai Hospital, No. 11-1328-cv, 2012 U.S. App. LEXIS 7617, at *3 (2d Cir. Apr. 17, 2012) (quoting Libeman v. Gelstein, 80 N.Y.2d 429, 437, 605 N.E.2d 344, 590 N.Y.S.2d 857 (1992)); Bulow v. Women in Need, Inc., 89 A.D.3d 525, 526, 933 N.Y.S.2d 222, 223 (1st Dep't 2011) (holding statements made between supervisory employees and, allegedly, between supervisor and employee about reasons for former employee's termination were protected by common**

interest privilege); Mancuso v. Allergy Associates of Rochester, 70 A.D.3d 1499, 895 N.Y.S.2d 756 (4th Dep't 2010) (statements by employer to employees about co-employee subject to qualified privilege); El-Hennawy v. Davita, Inc., 50 A.D.3d 625, 853 N.Y.S.2d 925 (2d Dep't 2008). The qualified privilege is most clearly applicable where statements are made in a confidential setting to a small group of individuals vitally interested in the subject matter of a meeting and the plaintiff is present. See Kasachkoff v. City of N.Y., 107 A.D.2d 130, 485 N.Y.S.2d 992 (1st Dep't 1985), aff'd, 68 N.Y.2d 654, 496 N.E.2d 226, 505 N.Y.S.2d 67 (1986). A qualified privilege also attaches to statements between employees, provided the statement is in furtherance of the employer's common interest. Loughry v. Lincoln First Bank, N.A., 67 N.Y.2d 369, 494 N.E.2d 70, 502 N.Y.S.2d 965 (1986). **Statements about an employee's work performance are normally protected by the common interest privilege, even if made to other employers. See Geltzer v. J.B. Hunt Transport, Inc., No. 09-CV-3865, 2012 U.S. Dist. LEXIS 48500 (E.D.N.Y. Mar. 30, 2012).** See also III.A infra.

b. **Duty.** The common interest privilege cases sometimes refer to a duty, which is sufficient but not necessary for the privilege to apply. Statements made pursuant to a duty or common interest and communicated to someone with a corresponding interest or duty are protected by the qualified privilege. Morgenstern v. County of Nassau, No. 04-CV-0058, 2008 U.S. Dist. LEXIS 91746 (E.D.N.Y. Sept. 29, 2008) (holding public official had "duty" to make statements to the media about ongoing scandal to advise the public); Hagemann v. Molinari, 14 F. Supp. 2d 277, 287-88 (E.D.N.Y 1998) (same). See Wyllie v. Dist. Att'y, 2 A.D.3d 714, 770 N.Y.S.2d 110 (2d Dep't 2003) (statement made by spokesperson for District Attorney's office covered by qualified privilege); Abeles v. Mellon Bank Corp., 298 A.D.2d 106, 106, 747 N.Y.S.2d 372, 373 (1st Dep't 2002) ("defendants' statements, even if construed as defamatory, were all made in the course of the investigation and consequent termination of plaintiff, and, as such, were qualifiedly privileged"); Kasachkoff v. City of N.Y., 107 A.D.2d 130, 134, 485 N.Y.S.2d 992, 995 (1st Dep't 1985) ("A communication made bona fide upon any subject matter in which the party communicating has an interest, or in reference to which he has a duty, is privileged if made to a person having a corresponding interest or duty") (quoting Byam v. Collins, 111 N.Y. 143, 19 N.E. 75 (1888)), aff'd, 68 N.Y.2d 654, 496 N.E.2d 226, 505 N.Y.S.2d 67 (1986).

c. **Criticism of Public Employee.** The common interest qualified privilege protects criticism of a public employee or official. Diaz v. Espada, 8 A.D.3d 49, 50, 778 N.Y.S. 2d 38, 40 (1st Dep't 2004) (holding statements made in the course of an election campaign could receive qualified privilege); Patane v. Griffin, 164 A.D.2d 192, 195, 562 N.Y.S.2d 1005, 1008 (3d Dep't 1990) (holding criticism of town supervisor protected by qualified privilege), appeal denied, 77 N.Y.2d 810, 575 N.E.2d 399, 571 N.Y.S.2d 913 (1991). In most instances, the plaintiff is a public figure and the statements pertain to a matter of public concern; the plaintiff will therefore bear the burden of demonstrating actual malice. See I.B.2.c, supra.

d. **Limitation on Qualified Privileges.** Qualified privilege is defeated by showing defendants acted with constitutional malice (actual malice) or solely with common law malice. **Thomas H. v. Paul B., 18 N.Y.3d 580, 965 N.E.2d 939, 942 N.Y.S.2d 437 (2012);** Shaw v. Club Mgrs. Ass'n. of Am., 84 A.D. 3d 928, 930, 923 N.Y.S.2d 127, 131 (2d Dep't 2011) ("[T]he shield provided by a qualified privilege may be dissolved if a plaintiff can demonstrate that a defendant spoke with spite or ill will (common-law malice) or with a high degree of awareness of the statements' probable falsity (constitutional malice)"); see Whitney Information Network, Inc. v. Weiss, No. 06-CV-6569, 2008 WL 731024 (E.D.N.Y. Mar. 18, 2008); Brown v. Albany Citizens Council on Alcoholism Inc., 199 A.D.2d 904, 605 N.Y.S.2d 577 (3d Dep't 1993) (malice adequately pled by allegation that defendant brought "slanted documents" suggesting plaintiff was guilty of misconduct before employer council at a time when plaintiff was not present to defend herself). The qualified privilege will also be defeated if defendants have engaged in "excessive publication" by spreading the statement to those with no legitimate interest in the matter. Stukuls v. State, 42 N.Y.2d 272, 281, 366 N.E.2d 829, 835, 397 N.Y.S.2d 740, 746 (1977); see also Anas v. Brown, 269 A.D.2d 761, 702 N.Y.S.2d 732 (4th Dep't 2000) (noting excessive publication must involve publication to those without a common interest in the information); McNaughton v. City of N.Y., 234 A.D.2d 83, 650 N.Y.S.2d 688 (1st Dep't 1996), appeal denied, 90 N.Y.2d 806, 686 N.E.2d 223, 663 N.Y.S.2d 511 (1997).

(1) **Constitutional or Actual Malice.** "Reckless disregard" for the truth, the constitutional standard for actual malice, means the defendant "entertained serious doubts as to the truth of his publication" or "had a high degree of awareness of [its] probable falsity." Harte-Hanks Communications v. Connaughton, 491 U.S. 657, 667, 16 Media L. Rep. 1881 (1989). Mere failure to investigate the truth of a statement, without more, is insufficient to prove "reckless disregard" for the truth even if a prudent person would have investigated. Carone v. Venator Group, Inc., 11 A.D.3d 399, 783 N.Y.S.2d 565 (1st Dep't 2004); see Croy v. A.O. Fox Mem'l Hosp., 68 F. Supp. 2d 136, 145 (N.D.N.Y. 1999).

(2) **Common Law Malice.** Common law malice involves "hatred, ill will, spite [or] criminal mental state, not just reckless disregard for the truth. Prozeralik v. Capital Cities Communications, Inc., 82 N.Y.2d 466, 479, 626 N.E.2d 34, 42, 605 N.Y.S.2d 218, 226, 2 Media L. Rep. 269 (1993). To establish common law malice, plaintiff must show defendant's sole motive for making a statement was malice. See, e.g., Morsette v. "The Final Call", 309 A.D.2d

249, 255, 764 N.Y.S.2d 416, 421 (1st Dep't 2003) (newspaper alteration and publication of a picture suggesting plaintiff had spent time in jail was not common law malice because there was no evidence actions was motivated by ill will toward the plaintiff); Present v. Avon Products, Inc., 253 A.D.2d 183, 189, 687 N.Y.S.2d 330, 334 (1st Dep't 1999) ("[T]he fact that defendants may have harbored ill will towards plaintiff is insufficient, without some evidence that this animus was the one and only cause for the publication" (internal citation omitted)). Malice cannot be implied from the mere falsity of a defamatory statement. See Kasachkoff v. City of N.Y., 107 A.D.2d 130, 134, 485 N.Y.S.2d 992 (1st Dep't 1985), aff'd, 68 N.Y.2d 654, 496 N.E.2d 226, 505 N.Y.S.2d 67 (1986).

e. **Question of Fact or Law.** The application of qualified privilege is a matter of law for the court to decide, based on either undisputed facts or, if the facts are disputed, the facts found by a jury. John W. Lovell Co. v. Houghton, 116 N.Y. 520, 525, 22 N.E. 1066, 1066 (1889); see also Phelan v. Huntington Tri-Vil. Little League, Inc., 57 A.D.3d 503, 505, 868 N.Y.S.2d 737, 738-39 (2d Dep't 2008) (holding plaintiff must raise triable issue of fact to prevent summary judgment if defendant presents facts that alleged defamatory statement was motivated by something other than malice); Harris v. Hirsh, 228 A.D.2d 206, 207, 643 N.Y.S.2d 556, 557 (1st Dep't 1996) appeal denied, 89 N.Y.2d 805, 676 N.E.2d 499, 653 N.Y.S.2d 917 (1996) (finding once facts were established the question of whether the privilege applied was one for the court).

f. **Burden of Proof.** A qualified privilege is an affirmative defense that must be pled by the defendant. See Clark v. McGee, 49 N.Y.2d 613, 616, 404 N.E.2d 1283, 1285, 427 N.Y.S.2d 740, 742 (1980) (noting qualified immunity among affirmative defenses); **Fletcher v. Dakota, 2012 NY Slip Op 5338, 2012 N.Y. App. Div. LEXIS 5245 at *20 (1st Dep't July 3, 2012) (declining to act on qualified privilege defense before it had been affirmatively pled by defendant).** Once the defendant proves a statement was made upon a privileged occasion, good faith is presumed, and the burden shifts to the plaintiff to show malice or other grounds for setting the privilege aside. Hemmens v. Nelson, 138 N.Y. 517, 34 N.E. 342 (1893); see also Foster v. Churchill, 87 N.Y.2d 744, 751-52, 665 N.E.2d 153, 157, 642 N.Y.S.2d 583, 587 (1996) (explaining instances where qualified privilege may be defeated or is otherwise inapplicable); Wilcox v. Newark Valley Central School District, 74 A.D.3d 1558, 904 N.Y.S.2d 523 (3d Dep't 2010); Bogoni v. Simpson, 306 A.D.2d 125, 760 N.Y.S.2d 497 (1st Dep't 2003).

B. Standard Defamation Defenses

1. ***Truth***. At common law, truth is an affirmative defense to a defamation action. This rule continues to apply in New York law in cases involving matters of private concern. **See Rosenfeld v. City of New York, No. 06-cv-1979, 2012 U.S. Dist. LEXIS 39548 at *20-22 (E.D.N.Y. Mar. 22, 2012) (dismissing defamation claim based on statements about the number of negative evaluations a teacher received because plaintiff failed to prove the number was false);** Nicholls v. The Brookdale University Hospital and Medical Center, No. 03-CV-6233, 2005 U.S. Dist. LEXIS 12582 at *104 (E.D.N.Y. 2005); Guarneri v. Korea News, 214 A.D.2d 649, 650, 625 N.Y.S.2d 291, 292, 23 Media L. Rep. 2215 (2d Dep't 1995) (dismissing claim against newspaper because information in articles was true). See also I.B.3, supra. In cases involving matters of public concern, however, the burden of proving falsity rests with the plaintiff. See I.B.3, supra. Where a defendant has the burden of proving truth, proof that a statement later turns out to be true will defeat a defamation action. See Kraus v. Brandstetter, 167 A.D.2d 445, 562 N.Y.S.2d 127 (2d Dep't 1990) (statement by defendant that plaintiff employee would be fired in the future was not actionable because plaintiff was in fact fired).

2. ***Opinion***. A properly plead defamation claim must be based on statements verifiable as true or false, not on opinion. Mann v. Abel, 10 N.Y.3d 271, 885 N.E.2d 884, 856 N.Y.S.2d 31 (2008) Only statements alleging fact are properly the basis for an action sounding in defamation. Id.; see Jewell v. NYP Holdings, Inc., 23 F. Supp 2d 348, 374 (S.D.N.Y. 1998); Gross v. New York Times Co., 82 N.Y.2d 146, 623 N.E.2d 1163, 603 N.Y.S.2d 813, 21 Media L. Rep. 2142 (1993); Ginther v. Ginther, 52 A.D.3d 1250, 858 N.Y.S.2d 637 (4th Dep't 2008). Statements must be evaluated in context to determine if a statement may be categorized as fact or opinion. **Thomas H. v. Paul B., 18 N.Y.3d 580, 965 N.E.2d 939, 942 N.Y.S.2d 437 (2012).** Expressions of opinion, including statements of evaluative judgments, are deemed privileged and, no matter how offensive, cannot be the subject of an action for defamation. Mann, 10 N.Y.3d at 276. **See also Doe v. French, 458 Fed. Appx. 21, 2012 U.S. App. LEXIS 1005 (2d Cir. 2012).** New York's constitution provides absolute immunity for opinion, provided those opinions are based on fully disclosed facts. N.Y. Const. art. I, § 8 ("Every citizen may freely speak, write and publish his or her sentiments on all subjects"). See Celle v. Filipino Reporter Enters., 209 F.3d 163, 178 (2d Cir. 2000) (noting the New York Constitution provides an absolute privilege for opinion); Compare Milkovich v. Lorain Journal Co., 497 U.S. 1, 17, Media L. Rep. 2009 (1990) (stating federal standard for opinion in defamation context) with Immuno AG v. Moor-Jankowski, 77 N.Y.2d 235, 249-50, 567 N.E.2d 1270, 1278, 566 N.Y.S.2d 906, 914 (1991) (holding the New York Constitution offers broader protection for freedom of speech than the United States Constitution). Whether a statement is an expression of fact or opinion is a question of law for the court. Mann, 10 N.Y.3d at 276; Aguinaga v. 342 E. 72nd St. Corp., 14 A.D.3d 304, 305, 787 N.Y.S.2d 283, 284 (1st Dep't 2005).

The following factors are used to distinguish between opinion and fact: (1) whether the specific language at issue has a precise meaning which is readily understood; (2) whether the statements are capable of being proven true or false; and (3) whether either the full context of the communication in which the statement appears or the broader social context and surrounding circumstances are such as to signal … readers or listeners that what is being read or heard is likely to be opinion, not fact. **Thomas H. v. Paul B., 18 N.Y.3d 580, 584, 965 N.E.2d 939, 942, 942 N.Y.S.2d 437, 441 (2012) (internal citations omitted).** Courts have also found subjective characterizations that cannot be objectively verified to be nonactionable opinion. Joyce v. Thompson Wigdor & Gilly, LLP, No. 06-Civ.-15315, 2008 U.S. Dist. LEXIS 43210, 36 Media L. Rep. 2030 (S.D.N.Y. June 3, 2008); Farrow v. O'Connor, Redd, Gollihue & Sklarin, LLP, 51 A.D.3d 626, 627, 857 N.Y.S.2d 235, 236 (2d Dep't 2008). Courts place the most importance on whether a reasonable reader or listener could conclude that the statement, in context, conveyed facts about the plaintiff. Flamm v. Am. Ass'n of Univ. Women, 201 F.3d 144, 153, 28 Media L. Rep. 1329 (2d Cir. 2000); Gross v. New York Times Co., 82 N.Y.2d 146, 152, 623 N.E.2d 1163, 1167, 603 N.Y.S.2d 813, 817 (1993). Courts examine what the reasonable interpretation of the statement would be when viewed in the context in which it was written or spoken to make this determination. See, e.g., **Couloute v. Ryncarz, No. 11-CV-5986, 2012 U.S. Dist. LEXIS 20534 at *17-18 (S.D.N.Y. Feb. 15, 2012) (holding statements regarding plaintiff's character were hyperbole when taken in context);** Brian v. Richardson, 87 N.Y.2d 46, 51, 660 N.E.2d 1126, 1129-30, 637 N.Y.S.2d 347, 350-51 (1995) (holding article published in newspaper's op-ed section by an interested party in the subject of the article would be viewed as opinion); **Gisel v. Clear Channel Communications, 94 A.D.3d 1525, 1526, 942 N.Y.S.2d 751, 752-53 (4th Dep't 2012) (holding comments made on a radio talk show would not be taken by the listener to be facts when heard in context).**

a. Pure Opinion. "Pure opinion" is a statement of opinion that is accompanied by the facts upon which it is based or, if unaccompanied by a factual recitation, one that does not imply that it is based upon undisclosed facts. Steinhilber v. Alphonse, 68 N.Y.2d 283, 289, 501 N.E.2d 550, 552-53, 508 N.Y.S.2d 901, 903-04, 13 Media L. Rep. 1562 (1986); Brown v. Albany Citizens Council on Alcoholism Inc., 199 A.D.2d 904, 605 N.Y.S.2d 577 (3d Dep't 1993). Pure opinion is not actionable, no matter how unreasonable it may be. Steinhilber, 68 N.Y.2d at 288, 501 N.E.2d at 552, 508 N.Y.S.2d at 903 (message that plaintiff union member was a who refused to participate in strike was a "scab" and lacked "talent, ambition, and initiative" in recorded telephone message was "pure opinion"); see, e.g., Torain v. Liu, 279 Fed. Appx. 46, 37 Media L. Rep. 1028 (2d Cir. 2008) (holding statement that plaintiff was a "racist pedophile" and "sick" was non-actionable as opinion); **Pecile v. Titan Capital Group, LLC, 947 N.Y.S.2d 66 (1st Dep't 2012) (holding "loose, hyperbolic" language such as characterizing a lawsuit as "without merit" and describing it as a "shakedown" was pure opinion and therefore non-actionable);** Shchegol v. Rabinovich, 30 A.D.3d 311, 311-12, 819 N.Y.S.2d 224, 225 (1st Dep't 2006) (holding publication of "polemic" in newspaper which disclosed all facts on which opinion was based was non-actionable).

b. Mixed Opinion. A statement of "mixed opinion" is one that expresses an opinion but implies undisclosed facts. Unlike pure opinion, mixed opinion may give rise to a defamation claim. **See Fehlhaber v. Bd. of Educ. of the Utica City Sch. Dist., 6:09-CV-1380, 2012 U.S. Dist. LEXIS 92072 at *43-44 (N.D.N.Y. July 3, 2012) (holding negative statements about a public employee's job performance made to newspaper could support defamation claim because statements implied undisclosed facts);** Arts4All, Ltd. v. Hancock, 5A.D. 106, 109, 773 N.Y.S.2d 348, 352 (1st Dep't 2004) (holding defendant's opinions were actionable as mixed opinion because they "impl[ied] that defendant … knows undisclosed, detrimental facts about" how plaintiff's business was run); Guerrero v. Carva, 10 A.D.3d 105, 779 N.Y.S.2d 12 (1st Dep't 2004) (holding statement by tenant in multiple flyers and newspaper interview that plaintiff was racist, unfit to manage buildings, and evicting tenants illegally is an example of mixed-opinion and is therefore actionable); Kraus v. Brandstetter, 167 A.D.2d, 445, 446, 562 N.Y.S.2d 127, 128 (2d Dep't 1990) (finding board's report that it had voted "no confidence" in nursing supervisor could imply knowledge of undisclosed facts).

3. ***Consent.*** Consent represents a complete defense to a defamation action. LeBreton v. Weiss, 256 A.D.2d 47, 47, 680 N.Y.S.2d 532, 532 (1st Dep't 1998). Consent need not be explicitly stated. See Dickson v. Slezak, 73 A.D.3d 1249, 902 N.Y.S.2d 206 (3d Dep't 2010) (holding that by hiring a private investigator to elicit statements reasonably anticipated to be defamatory, plaintiff implicitly consented to those statements being made) Hirschfeld v. Inst'l Investor, Inc., 260 A.D.2d 171, 172, 688 N.Y.S.2d 31, 32 (1st Dep't 1999) (holding plaintiff consented to defamation when she requested a written statement of the reason for termination). Consent must be "specific consent" that "clearly indicates the plaintiff was aware of and agreed to the possibility that the defamatory statements might be published." McNamee v. Clemens, 726 F. Supp. 2d 584, 604-05 (E.D.N.Y. 2011).

4. ***Mitigation.*** A defendant may offer proof to mitigate the circumstances surrounding an otherwise defamatory statement, "including the sources of his information and the grounds for his belief," whether or not the defendant has pleaded any defense. N.Y. Civ. Rights Law § 78 (Consol. 2012).

III. RECURRING FACT PATTERNS

A. Statements in Personnel File

Employers generally have a qualified privilege, based on common interest, to make statements in a personnel file. See **Campanella v. Cty. Of Monroe, No. 10-CV-6236L, 2012 WL 537495 at *4-5 (W.D.N.Y. Feb. 17, 2012) (holding critical memorandum in personnel file was qualifiedly privileged);** McNaughton v. City of New York, 234 A.D.2d 83, 650 N.Y.S.2d 688 (1st Dep't 1996) (holding privilege covers statements in disciplinary memoranda evaluating plaintiff's performance); Williams v. Varig Brazilian Airlines, 169 A.D.2d 434, 438, 564 N.Y.S.2d 328, 331 (1st Dep't 1991), appeal denied, 78 N.Y.2d 854, 577 N.E.2d 1059, 573 N.Y.S.2d 467 (1991) (holding memoranda criticizing work performance covered by qualified privilege). See II.A.2, supra.

Such statements may also be protected as opinion. See II.B.2, supra.

B. Performance Evaluations

Evaluations of an employee's work performance are generally not actionable because courts typically find that these statements constitute opinion. See Reilly v. Natwest Markets Group Inc., 181 F.3d 253, 271 (2d Cir. 1999) (holding that statement by one of employee's superiors to another that employee's performance was unsatisfactory constituted opinion), cert. denied, 528 U.S. 1119 (2000); Protic v. Dengler, 46 F. Supp. 2d 277, 281 (S.D.N.Y. 1999) (holding that supervisor's assessment of employee constituted opinion), aff'd, 205 F.3d 1324 (2d Cir. 1999); Farrow v. O'Connor, Redd, Gollihue & Sklarin, LLP, 51 A.D.3d 626, 857 N.Y.S.2d 235 (2d Dep't 2008). See II.B.2, supra.

Qualified privilege may also protect an employer's evaluation of an employee's work performance. Stillman v. Ford, 22 N.Y.2d 48, 238 N.E.2d 304, 290 N.Y.S.2d 893 (1968) (holding privilege applies to statements made by board members concerning president of board); McDowell v. Dart, 201 A.D.2d 895, 607 N.Y.S.2d 735 (4th Dep't 1994) (statements by employer evaluating employee's work performance are within common interest privilege); see also Colantino v. Mercy Med. Ctr., 73 A.D.3d 966, 968, 901 N.Y.S.2d 370, 374 (2d Dep't 2010) (holding discussion of allegedly false statements by hospital board was protected by qualified privilege provided defendants could prove absence of malice). See II.A.2, supra.

C. References

An employer's statement concerning an employee to another employer is generally protected by a qualified privilege based on common interest. Ott v. Automatic Connector, Inc., 193 A.D.2d 657, 658, 598 N.Y.S.2d 10, 11 (2d Dep't 1993); see also Qureshi v. St. Barnabas Hosp. Ctr., 430 F. Supp. 2d 279, 291-92 (S.D.N.Y. 2006) (holding reference to medical residency program could constitute actionable statement of mixed opinion and fact but medical programs share common interest); Serratore v. Am. Port Serv., Inc., 293 A.D.2d 464, 465, 739 N.Y.S.2d 452, 454 (2d Dep't 2002) ("[t]he responses of the plaintiff's former employer to a questionnaire from the plaintiff's prospective employer cannot support a cause of action to recover damages for defamation"). The privilege attaches even if the prospective employer did not request a reference. See Buckley v. Litman, 57 N.Y.2d 516, 443 N.E.2d 469, 457 N.Y.S.2d 221 (1982). See II.A.2, supra.

However, as with any qualified privilege, evidence of actual or common law malice will defeat the qualified privilege for references. **Apionishev v. Columbia Univ., No. 09-Civ-6471, 2012 U.S. Dist. LEXIS 8160 at *41 (S.D.N.Y. Jan. 23, 2012);** Qureshi, 430 F. Supp. 2d at 292.

References may also be protected as opinion. See II.B.2, supra.

D. Intracorporate Communication

A qualified privilege will generally attach to statements disseminated within a corporation in furtherance of the corporation's operations and interests. See Hutchinson v. Zurich Scudder Invs., Inc., 7 A.D.3d 329, 776 N.Y.S.2d 270 (1st Dep't 2004) (holding statement by supervisor to investment professionals employed by the firm explaining why plaintiff was fired was protected); Levine v. Board of Educ. of City of N.Y., 186 A.D.2d 743, 589 N.Y.S.2d 181 (2d Dep't 1992). Qualified privilege also attaches to statements made by an employee to his employer regarding a matter in the employer's interest. See Vaughn v. Am. Multi. Cinema, No. 09-Civ-8911, 2010 U.S. Dist. LEXIS 96609 at *9-10 (S.D.N.Y. Sept. 11, 2010). See II.A.2, supra.

E. Statements to Government Regulators

An absolute privilege shields written statements submitted to quasi-judicial bodies, even if the statement is part of a preliminary investigation and no charges are filed. Rosenberg v. Metlife, Inc., 8 N.Y.3d 359, 365 866 N.E.2d 439, 443 834 N.Y.S.2d 494, 498 (2007) (holding statements made by an employer on a U-5 form as part of a securities investigation is subject to an absolute privilege); Herzfeld & Stern v. Beck, 175 A.D.2d 689, 572 N.Y.S.2d 683 (1st Dep't 1991) (holding report submitted to New York Stock Exchange and Securities Exchange Commission concerning reasons for employee's termination is absolutely privileged), appeal dismissed, 79 N.Y.2d 914, 590 N.E.2d 251, 581 N.Y.S.2d 666 (1992); see also Cicconi v. McGinn, Smith & Co., Inc., 27 A.D.3d 59, 808 N.Y.S.2d 604 (2d Cir. 2005) (upholding the absolute privilege adopted in Herzfeld & Stern). Statements made to law enforcement officials, however, are subject to qualified immunity. Black v. Green Harbour Homeowners' Ass'n, Inc., 19 A.D.3d 962, 963-64, 798 N.Y.S.2d 753, 755 (3d Dep't 2005) (statements made to Attorney General's office enjoy qualified privilege); Dolan v. Buffalo News, 188 A.D.2d 1039, 592 N.Y.S.2d 197 (4th Dep't 1992) (same). The privilege arises as a matter of both common law and statute in New York. Willson v. Assn. of Graduates of U.S. Military Academy, 946 F. Supp. 294 (S.D.N.Y. 1996); see N.Y. Civ. Rights Law § 74 (McKinney 2005).

F. Reports to Auditors and Insurers

Reports to auditors or insurers are generally subject to qualified privilege. See Shapiro v. Health Ins. Plan of Greater New York, 7 N.Y.2d 56, 62-63, 163 N.E.2d 333, 337, 194 N.Y.S.2d 509, 514 (1959) (holding statements made to and by medical insurer regarding plaintiff's loss of malpractice insurance were protected by qualified immunity); East Point Collision Works, Inc. v. Liberty Mutual Ins. Co., 271 A.D.2d 471, 706 N.Y.S.2d 700 (2d Dep't 2000) (holding statements made by insured to insurance investigator were protected by qualified privilege); Neufeld v. Schachner, 61 A.D.2d 952, 952, 403 N.Y.S.2d 41, 42-43 (1st Dep't 1978) (holding qualified privilege could protect report from appraiser to insurer if report is made without malice); see also II.A.2, supra..

G. Vicarious Liability of Employers for Statements Made by Employees

1. ***Scope of Employment.*** An employer may be held vicariously liable for defamatory statements made by an employee if the employee was acting within the scope of employment at the time that the statement was made. D'Lima v. Cuba Mem'l Hosp., 833 F. Supp. 2d 383, 391 (W.D.N.Y. 2011) (quoting Perks v. Town of Huntington, 251 F. Supp. 2d 1143, 1166 (E.D.N.Y. 2003)) (holding if employee was instructed to make statements by hospital CEO such statements are part of employee's scope of employment and hospital could be vicariously liable); Loughry v. Lincoln First Bank, N.A., 67 N.Y.2d 369, 494 N.E.2d 70, 502 N.Y.S.2d 965 (1986) (holding employer liable for slander by agents in course of employment). There is no vicarious liability in cases where the alleged defamatory statement was made for personal motives unrelated to the furtherance of the employer's business. See Perks, 251 F. Supp. 2d at 1167, 1171 (E.D.N.Y. 2003) (dismissing vicarious liability claim where town council member acted out of purely personal motives); Seymour v. New York State Elec. & Gas Corp., 215 A.D.2d 971, 627 N.Y.S.2d 466 (3d Dep't 1995) (findingno vicarious liability where the employee whose duties did not include travel or car maintenance allegedly defamed auto body shop worker).

a. **Blogging.** In general, an employer cannot be held liable for defamatory third party postings on a company blog unless the employer had some involvement as an author. Shiamili v. Real Estate Group of New York, Inc., 17 N.Y.3d 281, 293, 952 N.E.2d 19, 1020, 929 N.Y.S.2d 19, 28, 39 Media L. Rep. 1922 (2011) (recognizing broad immunity for internet service providers under the federal Communications Decency Act). No cases have been reported in New York discussing whether or under what circumstances an employer may be held liable for defamatory statements made by its employees on blogs or other internet sites. However, the analysis would likely be the same as in III.G.1.

2. ***Damages.*** An employer who is held vicariously liable for an employee's defamation is responsible for the compensatory damages awarded. See Loughry v. Lincoln First Bank, N.A., 67 N.Y.2d 369, 494 N.E.2d 70, 502 N.Y.S.2d 965 (1986); Murray v. Watervliet City School Dist., 130 A.D.2d 830, 515 N.Y.S.2d 150 (3d Dep't 1987). However, the employer is not liable for punitive damages unless management has ordered, participated in, or ratified the conduct. Loughry, 67 N.Y.2d at 377-78, 494 N.E.2d at 74-75, 502 N.Y.S.2d at 969-70; see generally, Dean v. City of Buffalo, 579 F. Supp. 2d 391, 412-13 (W.D.N.Y. 2008) (finding no ratification for alleged assault by security guard defeats claim for punitive damages).

H. Internal Investigations

1. ***Elements.*** An employer may be liable for making defamatory statements about an employee in the course of an internal investigation. Albin v. Cosmetics Plus, Ltd., No. 97 Civ. 2670, 1997 U.S. Dist. LEXIS 15217 (S.D.N.Y. Oct. 3, 1997). Such liability is subject to qualified privilege. See, e.g., Salvatore v. Kumar, 45 A.D.3d 560, 563, 845 N.Y.S.2d 384, 388 (2d Dep't 2007) (publication of statements made during and as a result of internal investigation were qualifiedly privileged); Harris v. Hirsh, 228 A.D.2d 206, 207 (1st Dep't 1996) (defendant employer accusation that employee was drug user was qualifiedly privileged). An employer may also be liable for reporting an internal investigation to third parties, subject to privilege. See Salvatore, 45 A.D.3d at 563, 845 N.Y.S.2d at 388; Present v. Avon Prods., 253 A.D.2d 183, 187-188, 687 N.Y.S.2d 330, 333-34 (1st Dep't 1999).

2. ***Pre-emption***. State defamation claims are pre-empted by federal law where pursuing such claims would require the interpretation of the terms of labor agreements or contracts. Panczykowski v. Laborers Int'l Union, No. 97-CV-0036A, 1998 U.S. Dist. LEXIS 23269 at *24 (W.D.N.Y. 1998); See generally Semper v. New York Methodist Hosp., 786 F. Supp. 2d 566, 583-84 (E.D.N.Y. 2011) (holding any state law claims that would require interpretation of collective bargaining agreement are preempted by § 301 of the Labor Management Relations Act (LMRA)); c.f. Harris v. Hirsh, 86 N.Y.2d 207, 213, 654 N.E.2d 975, 979, 630 N.Y.S.2d 701, 705 (1995) (allegedly defamatory accusation by defendant employer did not require interpretation of collective bargaining agreement and therefore was not preempted by federal law).

IV. OTHER ACTIONS BASED ON STATEMENTS

A. Negligent Hiring, Retention, and Supervision

1. ***Elements.*** An employer may be liable for hiring or retaining an employee the employer knew (or had reason to know) had a propensity for conduct that caused plaintiff harm. Estevez-Yalcin v. Children's Village, 331 F. Supp. 2d 170, 174-75 (S.D.N.Y. 2004); Hassan v. Marriott Corp., 243 A.D.2d 406, 663 N.Y.S.2d 558 (1st Dep't 1997).

2. ***Claims Based on Statements.*** New York courts are not hospitable to attempts to evade the requirements of defamation law by alleging other torts based on statements rather than conduct. See, e.g., Cantor Fitzgerald, L.P. v. Peaslee, 88 F.3d 152, 157 (2d Cir. 1996) (noting plaintiff cannot avoid limitation on personal jurisdiction for defamation cases by recasting claims as other torts). Courts will generally not allow a negligent hiring action to go forward if the complaint more properly sounds in defamation. See St. John v. Town of Marlborough, 163 A.D.2d 761, 763, 558 N.Y.S.2d 332, 334 (3d Dep't 1990) (rejecting negligent supervision claim based on comments made by police officer because "any remedies available to plaintiff would lie with the traditional intentional torts such as slander"). However, courts may allow a negligent hiring and retention claim to move forward if it is pled alongside a colorable defamation claim. See Baez v. JetBlue Airways, 745 F. Supp. 2d 214, 225-26 (E.D.N.Y. 2010)

B. Intentional Infliction of Emotional Distress

1. ***Elements.*** New York follows the Restatement (Second) of Torts § 46 definition of intentional infliction of emotional distress ("IIED"). Howell v. New York Post Co., 81 N.Y.2d 115, 121, 612 N.E.2d 699, 702, 596 N.Y.S.2d 350, 353 (1993). There are four IIED elements: (1) extreme and outrageous conduct; (2) intent to cause, or reckless disregard of a substantial probability of causing, severe emotional distress; (3) a causal connection between the conduct and injury; and (4) severe emotional distress. **Marino v. Jonke, Nos. 11-CV-430, 4425, 2012 WL 1871623 at *10-11 (S.D.N.Y. Mar. 30, 2012);** Howell, 81 N.Y.2d at 121, 612 N.E.2d at 702, 596 N.Y.S.2d at 355. New York courts permit recovery for IIED only where "the conduct has been so outrageous in character, and so extreme in degree, as to go beyond all possible bounds of decency, and to be regarded as atrocious, and utterly intolerable in a civilized community." **Cusimano v. United Serv. Hosps., Inc., 91 A.D.3d 1149, 1152, 937 N.Y.S.2d 413, 418 (3d Dep't 2012) (quoting Murphy v. Am. Home Prods. Corp., 58 N.Y.2d 293, 303, 448 N.E.2d 86, 461 N.Y.S.2d 232 (1983)).** IIED causes of action are dismissed when the "conduct complained of falls well within the ambit of other traditional tort liability." Demas v. Levitsky 291 A.D.2d 653, 660, 738 N.Y.S.2d 402, 409 (3d Dep't 2002). An IIED claim may survive if all other traditional tort claims stemming from the same conduct are dismissed. 164 Mulberry St. Corp v. Columbia Univ., 4 A.D.3d 49, 58, 771 N.Y.S.2d 16, 23 (1st Dep't 2004).

2. ***Claims Based on Statements.*** **IIED claims in New York are almost never successful. See Marino, 2012 WL 1871623 at *10 (citing Howell and noting the Court of Appeals had rejected every IIED claim to come before it).** It is possible for statements that are not defamatory to nevertheless meet the standard for IIED, but it is extremely rare. See Esposito-Hilder v. SFX Broad. Inc., 236 A.D.2d 186, 188-90, 665 N.Y.S.2d 697, 700-01 (3d Dep't 1997) (holding a radio station's disparagement of a woman as an ugly bride, while not defamatory, could support a claim for IIED). Where a plaintiff is a private figure, the remarks are not about a matter of public concern, and intent to injure can be inferred, it is possible mere statements may support an IIED claim. Id. 236 A.D.2d at 190-91, 665 N.Y.S.2d at 700-01. **Cf. Reilly v. Garden City Free Union Sch. Dist., 89 A.D.3d 1075, 1077, 934 N.Y.S.2d 204, 206 (2d Dep't 2011) leave to appeal denied, 18 N.Y.3d 809, 967 N.E.2d 704, 944 N.Y.S.2d 479 (2012) (holding multiple false statements by school district that plaintiffs' deceased children were driving drunk when they were killed were not sufficiently outrageous to support IIED claim).**

C. Interference with Contract or Economic Advantage

1. ***Elements.*** A claim for tortious or intentional interference with an existing contract must allege: (1) a valid contract; (2) defendant's knowledge of the contract; (3) defendant's intentional procurement of the breach; and (4) resulting damages. Don King Prod. v. Smith, 47 Fed. Appx. 12, 15 (2d Cir. 2002); see TVT Records v. The Island Def Jam Music Group, 412 F.3d 82, 87 (2d Cir. 2005). At will employment agreements cannot support a claim of tortious interference with an existing contract because such agreements are merely "prospective contractual relations." Watts v. Jackson Hewitt

Tax Serv., Inc., 675 F. Supp. 2d 274, 281-82 (E.D.N.Y. 2009) (internal quotation marks and citations omitted). Id. A defendant may defend against a tortious interference claim by asserting its actions were in its own economic interests. White Plains Coat & Apron Co. v. Cintas Corp., 8 N.Y.3d 422, 426, 867 N.E.2d 381, 383, 835 N.Y.S.2d 530, 532 (2007). An economic interest defense can be defeated by a showing of malice or fraudulent or illegal means on the part of the defendant. Foster v. Churchill, 87 N.Y.2d 744, 751, 665 N.E.2d 153, 157, 642 N.Y.S.2d 583, 587 (1996).

For claims of interference with prospective economic advantage, a plaintiff must allege that the defendant acted with the sole purpose of harming plaintiff or employed dishonest, unfair or improper means. **Posner v. Lewis, 18 N.Y.3d 566, 570 n.3, 965 N.E.2d 949, 952 n.3, 942 N.Y.S.2d 447, 450 n.2 (2012).** The plaintiff must plead that he or she "would have consummated a contract but for defendant's interference." Maas v. Cornell Univ., 245 A.D.2d 728, 731, 666 N.Y.S.2d 743, 746 (3d Dep't 1997).

2. ***Claims Based on Statements.*** New York courts will not allow plaintiffs "to bring a defamation action . . . in the guise of an economic tort." Entertainment Partners Group, Inc. v. Davis, 198 A.D.2d 63, 64, 603 N.Y.S.2d 439, 440 (1st Dep't 1993). Plaintiffs cannot avoid the one-year defamation statute of limitations "by denominating the action as one for intentional interference with economic relations, prima facie tort, or injurious falsehood if, in fact, the claim seeks redress for injury to reputation." Id. Dissemination of defamatory materials can constitute interference with contract and prospective advantage provided "defendant's motives were solely to injure [Plaintiff's] reputation and to harm his business" and prospective business. Butler v. Delaware Otsego Corp., 218 A.D.2d 357, 360-61, 638 N.Y.S.2d 805, 807 (3d Dep't 1996).

D. Prima Facie Tort

1. ***Elements.*** The elements of prima facie tort are: "(1) intentional infliction of harm, (2) causing special damages, (3) without excuse or justification, (4) by an act or series of acts that would otherwise be lawful." **Posner v. Lewis, 18 N.Y.3d 566, 570 n.1, 965 N.E.2d 949, 951 n.1, 942 N.Y.S.2d 447, 449 n.1 (2012);** Curiano v. Suozzi, 63 N.Y.2d 113, 117, 469 N.E.2d 1324, 1327, 480 N.Y.S.2d 466, 469 (1984). Prima facie tort plaintiffs must prove the defendant was motivated solely by "disinterested malevolence." Curiano, 63 N.Y.2d at 117, 469 N.E.2d at 1327, 480 N.Y.S.2d at 469; Simaee v. Levi, 22 A.D.3d 559, 563, 802 N.Y.S.2d 493, 497 (2d Dep't 2005). Prima facie torts are designed to provide alternative remedies for intentional actions that cause harm but are not addressed by traditional torts and are not a "catch all alternative." Etzion v. Etzion, 62 A.D.3d 646, 651-52, 880 N.Y.S.2d 79, 84-85 (2d Dep't 2009).

2. ***Claims Based on Statements.*** **Prima facie tort may not be used as an alternative where a plaintiff could not prove other torts, including defamation, but may be plead in addition to causes of action sounding in defamation. See Diorio v. Ossining Union Free Sch. Dist., 96 A.D.3d 710, 946 N.Y.S.2d 195, 198-99 (2d Dep't 2012) (finding plaintiff had properly pled libel, libel per se, and prima facie tort by pleading special damages and a plausible case for malice and disinterested malevolence); see also Posner, 18 N.Y.3d at 572, 965 N.E.2d at 953, 942 N.Y.S.2d at 451 (holding blackmail in addition to repeated statements about plaintiff's private life to employer school to affect plaintiff's tenure evaluation was sufficient to support a prima facie tort claim).**

V. OTHER ISSUES

A. Statute of Limitations

The statute of limitations for a defamation action is one year. N.Y. C.P.L.R. § 215(3) (Consol. 2012). **However, if the real party in interest as defendant is a government official or municipal body, the statute of limitations is one year and ninety (90) days. N.Y. Gen. Mun. Law § 50-i; Coe v. Town of Conklin, 94 A.D.3d 1197, 1198, 942 N.Y.S.2d 255, 256 (3d Dep't 2012).**

B. Jurisdiction

Jurisdiction over a non-domiciliary is specifically excluded in defamation cases under N.Y. C.P.L.R. § 302(a)(2) and (3) (McKinney 2008). Plaintiffs cannot evade this exclusion by "recasting their cause of action as something other than defamation." Cantor Fitzgerald, L.P. v. Peaslee, 88 F.3d 152, 157 (2d Cir. 1996). Long-arm jurisdiction is available under N.Y. C.P.L.R. § 302(a) (1) (McKinney 2008) if the alleged defamation stems from the defendant's purposeful transaction of business in New York. World Wrestling Fed'n Entm't v. Bozell, 142 F. Supp. 2d 514, 533, 29 Media L. Rep. 1929 (S.D.N.Y. 2001) (collecting cases). **However, New York courts must take "particular care . . . to make certain that nondomiciliaries are not haled into court in a manner that potentially chills free speech without an appropriate showing that they purposefully transacted business [in New York] and that the proper nexus exists between the transaction and the defamatory statements at issue." SPCA of Upstate New York, Inc. v. American Working Collie Assoc., 18 N.Y.3d 400, 405-06, 963 N.E.2d 1226, 1230, 940 N.Y.S.2d 525, 529 (2012). See Penachio v. Benedict, 461 Fed. Appx. 4 (2d Cir. 2012). A website accessible from New York but not created in New York on which allegedly**

defamatory statements are posted does not, without more, constitute a sufficient nexus to New York to trigger jurisdiction. SPCA of Upstate New York, Inc., 18 N.Y.3d at 405, 963 N.E.2d at 1230, 940 N.Y.S.2d at 529.

C. Workers' Compensation Exclusivity

New York's workers' compensation law bars suits by employees against their own employers. See N.Y. Workers' Comp. Law § 29(6) (Consol. 2012); Torres v. Pisano, 116 F.3d 625, 640 (2d Cir. 1997); Pasqualini v. MortgageIT, Inc., 498 F. Supp. 2d 659, 666 (S.D.N.Y. 2007); Burlew v. American Mut. Ins. Co., 63 N.Y.2d 412, 416, 472 N.E.2d 682, 684, 482 N.Y.S.2d 720, 722 ("[A]ll employer conduct that is regulated by the Workers' Compensation Law is subject to the protection of that law's exclusivity."). The law does not cover intentional acts by the employer or co-employees, including defamation. See Merritt v. Shuttle, Inc., 13 F. Supp. 2d 371, 387 (E.D.N.Y. 1998).

D. Pleading Requirements

A defamation complaint must set forth the particular statements alleged to be defamatory "in haec verba," but may describe the circumstances of the communication in general terms. N.Y. C.P.L.R. 3016(a) (McKinney 2012); see also Lore v. City of Syracuse, 583 F. Supp. 2d 345, 383 (S.D.N.Y. 2008) (noting a defamation plaintiff must plead with particularity the words giving rise to her claim, the time, place, and manner of their delivery, and the persons to whom the statements were made); Massa Constr., Inc. v. George M. Bunk, P.E., P.C., 68 A.D.3d 1725, 1725 891 N.Y.S.2d 836, 836-37 (4th Dep't 2009) (same). **The complaint must not be based principally on conclusory statements and must put the defendant on notice as to the specific statements alleged to be defamatory. Davison v. Goodwill Industries of Greater New York and N. New Jersey, No. 10-CV-2180, 2012 U.S. Dist. LEXIS 43283 (E.D.N.Y. Mar. 28, 2012);** see Reilly v. Natwest Markets Group Inc., 181 F.3d 253, 271 (2d Cir. 1999) (holding complaint alleging a supervisor said "something bad" about employee is insufficiently pled). See I.B.1 supra.

SURVEY OF NEW YORK EMPLOYMENT PRIVACY LAW

Peter M. Panken, Esq.
Epstein Becker & Green, P.C.
250 Park Avenue
New York, New York 10177
Telephone: (212) 351-4500; Facsimile: (212) 661-0989

(With Developments Reported Through **November 1, 2012**)

GENERAL COMMENTS

None.

SIGNIFICANT DEVELOPMENTS SINCE THE 2012 *SURVEY*

None.

I. GENERAL LAW OF PRIVACY

A. Legal Basis of Privacy Claims

1. ***Constitutional Law.*** The New York State Constitution contains a search and seizure provision similar to the Fourth Amendment to the federal Constitution. See N.Y. Const. art. I, § 12. While it has been construed to provide greater protection against governmental searches and seizures than its federal counterpart, see People v. Scott, 79 N.Y.2d 474, 593 N.E.2d 1328, 583 N.Y.S.2d 920 (1992), there is no general constitutional protection for privacy in New York outside the search and seizure context.

2. ***Statutory Law.***

a. **Civil Rights Law §§ 50-51.** The only private right of action for invasion of privacy recognized as a matter of New York law is codified in Sections 50 and 51 of the Civil Rights Law, which protect living individuals from the use of their names or images in advertising and similar material without their written consent. See Freihofer v. Hearst Corp., 65 N.Y.2d 135, 480 N.E.2d 349 1056, 490 N.Y.S.2d 735, 12 Media L. Rep. 1056 (1985); Groden v. Random House, Inc., 61 F.3d 1045, 1049 (2d Cir. 1995); N.Y. Civ. Rights Law §§ 50-51 (McKinney 2005); Alfano v. NGHT, Inc., 623 F. Supp. 2d 355, 359 (E.D.N.Y. 2009).

Under Section 50 of the Civil Rights Law, to state a claim a living person must show that defendant: (i) used plaintiff's name, portrait, picture; (ii) for advertising or trade purposes; and (iii) without first having obtained the written consent of such person. Polimeni v. Asbestos Lead & Hazardous Wast Laborers' Local 78, 89 A.D.3d 826, 932 N.Y.S.2d 350 (2d Dep't 2011); Otero v. Houston Street Owners Corp., No. 104819/10, 2012 WL 692037 (N.Y. Sup. Ct. N.Y. Cty. Feb. 28, 2012). Although Civil Rights Law § 51 permits "equitable action" and a suit to recover "damages for injuries sustained", as well as "exemplary damages" for "knowingly" using the image in violation of Civil Rights Law § 50 there are certain exceptions including:

(1) Photographers who exhibit their work at their establishment, but not after they have received written notice from the person portrayed objecting to the use of their picture. (N.Y. Civ. Rights Law § 51).

(2) Publishers using the name, portrait or picture of any composer or artist in connection with the sale of their work. (N.Y. Civ. Rights Law § 51). Helm v. BBDO Worldwide, Inc., 93 A.D.3d 428, 938 N.Y.S.2d 892 (1st Dep't 2012); Scroggins v. Scroggins, No. 09 CV 5735, 2012 WL 3229282 (E.D.N.Y. Aug. 6, 2012).

But use of the portrait of any unrelated individual on a CD cover was still actionable under N.Y. Civ. Rights Law §§ 50and 51. Sang Lan v. AOL Time Warner, Inc., No. 11 Civ. 2870, 2011 WL 7807290 (S.D.N.Y. Nov. 21, 2011).

(3) Use in connection with newsworthy events or events of public interest. Child v. Renda, No. 603075/05, 2012 WL 3767166 (N.Y. Sup. Ct. N.Y. Cty. Aug. 20, 2012) (eccentric fashion model); Pisano v. English, No. 25146/09, 2012 WL 2842282 (N.Y. Sup. Ct. Nassau Cty. Mar. 22, 2012); Scott v. WorldStarHipHop, Inc., No. 10 Civ. 9538, 2012 WL 1592229 (S.D.N.Y. May 3, 2012).

(4) Satiric use. Sondik v. Kimmel, 33 Misc. 3d 1237(A), 941 N.Y.S.2d 541, 2011 WL 6381452 (N.Y. Sup. Ct. Kings Cty. 2011).

The New York State Senate proposed new legislation in February 2010 to amend Civil Rights Law §§ 50-51 by providing a postmortem right of publicity, which prohibits any person, firm or corporation from using the "persona" of any "deceased personality" for purposes of advertising or trade without having obtained the written consent of the registered rights holder. The bill would extend New York's narrowly-defined "right of publicity" to a personality's estate for 70 years following his/her death and would apply retroactively. The bill has been referred to the Codes Committee. (New York State Senate Bill 6790). Additionally, a similar bill was introduced in 2009 which would amend Civil Rights Law § 50 to prohibit the use, name, portrait and/or picture of a deceased personality, thereby creating a right of privacy and publicity for deceased persons. (New York State Senate Bill 5066).

(1) **Misdemeanor**. A person, firm, or corporation that uses for advertisement purposes, or for the purposes of trade, the name, portrait, or picture of any living person, without having first obtained the written consent of such person, is guilty of a misdemeanor. N.Y. Civ. Rights Law § 50.

(2) **Private Right of Action**. Any person whose name, portrait, or picture is used in violation of § 50 may sue for injunctive relief and money damages. N.Y. Civ. Rights Law § 51. See Caesar v. Chem. Bank, 66 N.Y.2d 698, 487 N.E.2d 275, 496 N.Y.S.2d 418 (1985) (statute applies to use of employees' likeness in employer's advertisement). See also Waldman v. NYNEX Corp., No. 102117/97, 1999 WL 292634, at *7 (N.Y. Sup. Ct. N.Y. Cty. Jan. 8, 1999), aff'd, 265 A.D.2d 164, 696 N.Y.S.2d 39 (1st Dep't 1999) (employee whose letterhead and signature were used by his former employer after his dismissal stated a cause of action under Section 51). See Yasin v. Q-Boro Holdings, 27 Misc. 3d 1214(A), 910 N.Y.S.2d 766, 2010 WL 1704889 (N.Y.Sup. Ct. Kings Cty. 2010). (defendant violated plaintiff's statutory right to privacy under Civil Rights Law § 51 when defendant used a photograph of plaintiff without her consent on its book cover).

(3) **Mitigation**. Neither oral nor implied consent is a complete defense to a privacy action under Civil Rights Law § 51. However, § 51 does authorize juries to exercise discretion on the issue of exemplary damages and, in that regard, oral and implied consent are available as partial defenses in mitigation of damages. Caesar, 66 N.Y.2d at 700-01, 487 N.E.2d at 275, 496 N.Y.S.2d at 419; see, e.g., Morse v. Studin, 283 A.D.2d 622, 725 N.Y.S.2d 93 (2d Dep't 2001) (plastic surgeon's contention that a patient orally modified her consent, so as to allow the use of her photographs in the surgeon's advertisements, was insufficient to avoid liability under the Civil Rights Law).

B. Causes of Action

1. *Misappropriation/Right of Publicity*

No Common Law Right to Privacy. New York courts have refused to create a private right of action for invasion of privacy as a matter of common law to supplement the rights established by Sections 50 and 51 of the Civil Rights Law. See Messenger v. Gruner + Jahr Printing and Publ'g, 94 N.Y.2d 436, 727 N.E.2d 549, 706 N.Y.S.2d 52, 28 Media L. Rep. 1491 (2000) (New York does not recognize a common-law right of privacy); Howell v. New York Post Co., 81 N.Y.2d 115, 596 N.Y.S.2d 350, 612 N.E.2d 699, 596 N.Y.S.2d 350, aff'd in part, 82 N.Y.2d 690, 619 N.E.2d 650, 601 N.Y.S.2d 572 (1993); Clark v. Elam Sand and Gravel, Inc., 4 Misc. 3d 294, 777 N.Y.S.2d 624 (N.Y. Sup. Ct. N.Y. Cty. 2004) ("[i]n this State the right to privacy is governed exclusively by sections 50 and 51 of the Civil Rights Law; we have no common law of privacy") (citing Howell); Adams v. Rizzo, 13 Misc. 3d 1235(A), 831 N.Y.S.2d 351, 2006 WL 3298383 (N.Y. Sup. Ct. Onondaga Cty. 2006) (Sections 50 and 51 of the Civil Rights Law "were drafted narrowly to encompass only the commercial use of an individual's name, portrait or picture and no more") (citing Arrington v. N.Y. Times Co., 55 N.Y.2d 433, 439 N.E.2d 1313, 449 N.Y.S.2d 941 (1982)). For details on Sections 50 and 51, see sec. A.2.a., supra.

2. ***False Light***. New York does not recognize false light claims, which allege that the defendant cast the plaintiff in a highly offensive light. Howell, 81 N.Y.2d at 123, 612 N.E.2d at 703, 596 N.Y.S.2d at 354; Alfano, 623 F. Supp. 2d at 360 (quoting Messenger). Sections 50 and 51 of the Civil Rights Law are read narrowly to exclude false light claims. Finger v. Omni Publ'g Int'l, Ltd., 77 N.Y.2d 138, 141, 566 N.E.2d 141, 143, 564 N.Y.S.2d 1014, 1016 (1990); see also Costanza v. Seinfeld, 181 Misc. 2d 562, 564, 693 N.Y.S.2d 897, 899 (N.Y. Sup. Ct. N.Y. Cty. 1999) (dismissing false light and invasion of privacy for failure to state a claim), aff'd, 279 A.D.2d 255, 719 N.Y.S.2d 29 (1st Dep't 2001); School of Visual Arts v. Kuprewicz, 3 Misc. 3d 278, 288, 771 N.Y.S.2d 804, 812-13 (N.Y. Sup. Ct. N.Y. Cty. 2003) (alleged use of plaintiff's name on false job listings on internet website and in connection with subscribing to pornographic websites and catalogs was not for advertising purposes or for the purposes of trade, as required to support claim under § 51).

3. ***Publication of Private Facts.*** New York does not permit causes of action for publication of true but private facts. Howell, 81 N.Y.2d at 123, 612 N.E.2d at 703, 596 N.Y.S.2d at 354.

4. ***Intrusion.*** In New York, there is no cause of action sounding in invasion of privacy for intrusion upon seclusion or solitude of a person in his private concerns. Howell, 81 N.Y.2d at 123, 612 N.E.2d at 703; 596 N.Y.S.2d at 354,; see also Hurwitz v. United States, 884 F.2d 684 (2d Cir. 1989).

C. Other Privacy-Related Actions

1. ***Intentional Infliction of Emotional Distress.***

a. **Elements**. New York has adopted the Restatement definition of intentional infliction of emotional distress: Extreme and outrageous conduct intentionally or recklessly caus[ing] severe emotional distress to another. Restatement (Second) of Torts § 46 (1999). See Freihofer, 65 N.Y.2d at 143, 480 N.E.2d at 355, 490 N.Y.S.2d at 741; Howell, 81 N.Y.2d at 121, 612 N.E.2d at 702, 596 N.Y.S.2d at 353. The elements of intentional infliction of emotional distress are: (i) extreme and outrageous conduct; (ii) intent to cause, or disregard of a substantial probability of causing, severe emotional distress; (iii) a causal connection between the conduct and injury; and (iv) severe emotional distress. Howell, 81 N.Y.2d at 121, 612 N.E.2d at 702, 596 N.Y.S.2d at 353; Sylvester v. City of New York, 23 Misc. 3d 1139(A), 889 N.Y.S.2d 508, 2009 WL 1651494, at *4 (N.Y. Sup. Ct. N.Y. Cty. June 4, 2009); see also Smigo v. NYP Holdings, Inc., No. 108756/2008, 2010 WL 1047679 (N.Y. Sup. Ct. N.Y. Cty. Mar. 16, 2010). New York courts have permitted recovery for intentional infliction of emotional distress only where the conduct has been so outrageous in character, and so extreme in degree, as to go beyond all possible bounds of decency, and to be regarded as atrocious, and utterly intolerable in a civilized community. Id. (quoting Restatement (Second) of Torts § 46, comment d); see, e.g., Cavanaugh v. Doherty, 243 A.D.2d 92, 102, 675 N.Y.S.2d 143, 150 (3d Dep't 1998) (termination of a government employee who has expressed political views contrary to those of the incumbent administration and, in the context of an off-duty argument arising out of those political differences, has admittedly referred to a higher-ranking government official in a vulgar and disparaging manner, can hardly be said to be so outrageous in character, and so extreme in degree, as to go beyond all possible bounds of decency); see also Beck v. Cornell Univ., 42 A.D.3d 609, 839 N.Y.S.2d 575 (3d Dep't 2007) (alleged abusive language toward employee in workplace was not so outrageous in character and so extreme in degree to state a cause of action to recover damages for intentional infliction of emotional distress).

b. **Relationship to Employment Law**. Some New York courts have expressed concern about the danger of allowing plaintiffs to circumvent the state's bar on wrongful termination suits by alleging intentional infliction of emotional distress. See Cerick v. MTB Bank, 240 A.D.2d 274, 274, 658 N.Y.S.2d 311, 312 (1st Dep't 1997) (it appears that plaintiff is attempting to circumvent the employee at will discharge rule by pleading intentional infliction); DeFilippo v. Xerox Corp., 223 A.D.2d 846, 848, 636 N.Y.S.2d 463, 465 (3d Dep't 1996) ("we find the gravamen of such allegations more closely resembling a claim alleging the wrongful discharge of an at-will employee, a cause of action not recognized in New York"). Although there are no reported cases addressing this point, New York courts presumably would be similarly reluctant to allow a plaintiff who does not meet the standards of Sections 50 and 51 of the Civil Rights Law to pursue a privacy claim masked as a claim of intentional infliction of emotional distress. In any event, decisions reaching the substance of plaintiffs' allegations have noted that it is exceptionally difficult to prove intentional infliction. See, e.g., Howell, 81 N.Y.2d at 122, 612 N.E.2d at 702, 596 N.Y.S.2d at 353 (because the tort could be broad enough to create liability for otherwise lawful behavior, requirements are rigorous).

2. ***Interference with Prospective Economic Advantage.***

a. **Elements.** A claim for tortious or intentional interference with an existing contract must allege: (1) a valid contract; (2) defendant's knowledge of the contract; (3) defendant's intentional interference with the contract without justification; (4) a breach; and (5) resulting damages. Snyder v. Sony Music Entm't, Inc., 252 A.D.2d 294, 299, 684 N.Y.S.2d 235, 238 (1st Dep't 1999); Anesthesia Assoc. of Mount Kisco, LLP v. Northern Westchester Hosp. Ctr., 59 A.D.3d 473, 873 N.Y.S.2d 679 (2d Dep't 2009). At-will employment agreements, which are classified as only prospective contractual relations, cannot support a claim for tortious interference with an existing contract. Id. See also Thawley v. Turtell, 289 A.D.2d 169, 736 N.Y.S.2d 2 (1st Dep't 2001). Where a defendant's acts were motivated by its own economic interests, no cause of action lies in the absence of malice, fraud or illegal means. WMW Mach. Co. v. Koerber AG, 240 A.D.2d 400, 401, 658 N.Y.S.2d 385, 386 (2d Dep't 1997).

For claims of interference with prospective economic advantage, a plaintiff must allege that the defendant acted with the sole purpose of harming plaintiff or employed dishonest, unfair or improper means. Protic v. Dengler, 46 F. Supp. 2d 277, 279 (S.D.N.Y.), aff'd, 205 F.3d 1324 (2d Cir. 1999); Snyder, 252 A.D.2d at 299-300, 684 N.Y.S.2d at 239. The plaintiff must plead that he or she would have entered into an economic relationship but for the defendant's wrongful conduct. Vigoda v. DCA Prods. Plus Inc., 293 A.D.2d 265, 266-67, 741 N.Y.S.2d 20, 23 (1st Dep't 2002); Maas v. Cornell Univ., 245 A.D.2d 728, 731, 666 N.Y.S.2d 743, 746 (3d Dep't 1997), aff'd, 94 N.Y.2d 87, 721 N.E.2d 966, 699 N.Y.S.2d 716 (1999); see also 30 CPS, LLC v. Board of Mgrs. of Cent. Park S. Med. Condo., 23 Misc. 3d

1024, 874 N.Y.S.2d 879 (N.Y. Sup. Ct. N.Y. Cty. 2009) (distinguishing between an interference with an existing contract and an interference with a prospective economic advantage).

b. **Relationship to Employment Law.** There are no reported cases involving claims of invasion of privacy cast as allegations of tortious interference.

3. ***Prima Facie Tort.***

a. **Elements.** In New York, the elements of prima facie tort are: (1) intentional infliction of harm, (2) causing special damages, (3) without excuse or justification, (4) by an act or series of acts that would otherwise be lawful. Curiano v. Suozzi, 63 N.Y.2d 113, 117, 469 N.E.2d 1324, 1326, 480 N.Y.S.2d 466, 468 (1984); see also Gray v. Grove Mfg. Co., 971 F. Supp. 78 (E.D.N.Y. 1997) (applying Curiano standard); Klinge v. Ithaca Coll., 167 Misc. 2d 458, 464, 634 N.Y.S.2d 1000, 1004 (N.Y. Sup. Ct. Tompkins Cty. 1995) (requirements are the presence of malice, the absence of any lawful excuse or justification, and the lack of any traditional remedy at law or equity), aff'd as modified, 235 A.D.2d 724, 652 N.Y.S.2d 377 (3d Dep't 1997). Prima facie tort plaintiffs must plead special damages and that the defendants were motivated solely by disinterested malevolence. Curiano, 63 N.Y.2d at 117, 469 N.E.2d at 1327 480 N.Y.S.2d at 469; see Gorgone v. Capozzi, 238 A.D.2d 308, 656 N.Y.S.2d 49 (2d Dep't 1997) (affirming dismissal because the plaintiff did not plead special damages and the record suggested none existed); Rosario-Suarz v. Wormuth Bros. Foundry, Inc., 233 A.D.2d 575, 649 N.Y.S.2d 225 (3d Dep't 1996) (granting summary judgment where the plaintiff offered insufficient proof of disinterested malevolence); Starishevsky v. Parker, 225 A.D.2d 480, 639 N.Y.S.2d 377 (1st Dep't 1996) (finding sufficient cause of action where plaintiff set forth special damages in the form of lost wages and benefits and established that defendant, motivated by a personal vendetta to see plaintiff fired, acted solely with disinterested malevolence in advising third party to file false claim against plaintiff and leaking information about confidential proceeding); Beck (noting that plaintiff failed to plead special damages, a necessary element of a prima facie tort claim). Also see McKenzie v. Dow Jones & Co., 355 F. App'x 533 (2d Cir. 2009) (affirming dismissal of prima facie tort as thinly-veiled defamation claim finding defendant's actions were not solely motivated by malevolence).

b. **Relationship to Employment Law.** New York will not permit a cause of action for prima facie tort in circumvention of the unavailability of a tort claim for wrongful discharge or the contract rule against liability for discharge of an at will employee. Murphy v. Am. Home Prods. Corp., 58 N.Y.2d 293, 304, , 448 N.E.2d 86, 91, 461 N.Y.S.2d 232, 237 (1983); see also U.S. Reinsurance Corp. v. Humphreys, 240 A.D.2d 264, 667 N.Y.S.2d 2, 3 (1st Dep't 1997) (an allegation of prima facie tort may not be invoked as a basis to sustain a pleading that otherwise fails to state a cause of action in traditional tort); Beck (granting motion to dismiss where claim was merely an improper effort to circumvent at will employment rule). This reasoning may make courts reluctant to entertain prima facie tort claims that appear to attempt to avoid the strict limits of New York privacy law.

II. EMPLOYER TESTING OF EMPLOYEES

A. Psychological or Personality Testing

1. ***Common Law and Statutes.*** New York law bars the use of psychological stress evaluators on employees. Employers may neither administer such tests, which purport to discern truthfulness from vocal fluctuations, nor utilize the results of such testing. N.Y. Lab. Law § 735 (McKinney 1999). Courts have distinguished between these stress evaluators and polygraphs, which employers may use in limited circumstances. See II.D, infra. By a law passed in 1983, applicants for employment as corrections officers must submit to psychological testing. N.Y. Correct. Law § 8 (McKinney 2002). **This statute expired on September 1, 2011.**

2. ***Private Employers.*** New York does not explicitly regulate the use of personality tests such as MMPI, but employers must be wary of problems that may arise from these tests. For instance, the New York Human Rights Law and the federal Title VII bar employers from using tests with discriminatory purpose or impact. If confronted with a discrimination claim, the employer will have to demonstrate the job-relatedness of the test. See Michael Delikat and Rene Kathawala, Personality and Aptitude Tests: A Good Idea for Employers?, N.Y.L. J., Dec. 29, 1997, at 1; Kimberli R. Black, Personality Screening in Employment, 32 Am. Bus. L. J. 69 (1994).

3. ***Public Employers.*** A public employee's employment or medical history is not subject to disclosure under the Freedom of Information Law. See N.Y. Pub. Off. Law § 89 (2)(b) (McKinney 2002).

B. Drug Testing

1. ***Common Law and Statutes.*** There are no New York statutes specifically regulating drug testing. Santiago v. Greyhound Lines, Inc., 956 F. Supp. 144, 151 (N.D.N.Y. 1997). However, under New York law, drug addiction

can be considered a protected disability. Doe v. Roe, Inc., 143 Misc. 2d 156, 539 N.Y.S.2d 876 (N.Y. Sup. Ct. N.Y. Cty. 1989), aff'd, 160 A.D.2d 255, 553 N.Y.S.2d 364 (1st Dep't 1990). Though recently, courts have held otherwise. See Kirk v. City of New York, 47 A.D.3d 406, 848 N.Y.S.2d 169 (1st Dep't 2008) (clarifying that although alcohol dependency qualifies as a disability under the Human Rights Law, drug abuse does not); see also In re Shugg, 62 A.D.3d 1199, 882 N.Y.S.2d 317 (3d Dep't 2009); and see Weinstock v. Columbia Univ., 224 F.3d 33, 42 n.1 (2d Cir. 2000).

Employers who administer drug tests must be careful not to violate statutory law barring discrimination against an employee or applicant on the basis of a protected disability. See N.Y. Exec. Law §§ 296, 292.21 (McKinney 2002); see also Kevin G. Chapman, Drug Testing of Employees and Applicants: Legal and Practical Considerations for Private Employers in New York, 66 N.Y. St. B.J. 14 (1994). One court has found that a public employee may bring a negligence action arising out the manner in which a laboratory conducted a random drug test on the job. Coleman v. Town of Hempstead, 30 F. Supp. 2d 356 (E.D.N.Y. 1999). Courts may also have limited authority in sharing the results of drug tests with an individual's employer. See In re Janyce B., 37 A.D.3d 459, 831 N.Y.S.2d 189 (2d Dep't 2007) (family court order directing the Department of Social Services to reveal the results of a mother's drug test in the course of a child protective proceeding exceeded the court's authority).

2. ***Private Employers.*** New York courts will not entertain suits asserting that private employer-mandated drug screening violates employees' privacy rights or state or federal constitutional rights concerning searches and seizures. See Santiago; Claim of Atkinson, 185 A.D.2d 415, 586 N.Y.S.2d 319 (3d Dep't 1992) (test by a private person or a nongovernmental entity does not violate constitutional rights); Doe, 143 Misc. 2d at 158, 539 N.Y.S.2d at 877 (while Supreme Court rulings recognizing the Government's interest in creating a drug-free workplace do not directly affect private employment, the decisions likely will be construed as supporting private workplace testing).

3. ***Public Employers.*** While public employers are subject to constitutional search and seizure provisions, New York courts have approved drug testing where the employer has a reasonable suspicion or where there is a strong state interest in monitoring the job that the employees perform. Delaraba v. Nassau County Police Dep't, 83 N.Y.2d 367, 632 N.E.2d 1251, 610 N.Y.S.2d 928 (2d Dep't 1994); see also United States v. Abbadessa, 848 F. Supp. 369, 378 (E.D.N.Y. 1994), vacated sub nom, United States v. DeRiggi, 45 F.3d 713 (2d Cir. 1995). Random testing of certain public employees is permissible based on the state's crucial interest in the integrity of law enforcement. See Seelig v. Koehler, 76 N.Y.2d 87, 556 N.E.2d 125, 128-29, 556 N.Y.S.2d 832, 835-36 (1990) (corrections officers); Caruso v. Ward, 72 N.Y.2d 432, 530 N.E.2d 850, 853, 439, 534 N.Y.S.2d 142, 145 (1988) (elite police unit). Blanket drug testing of probationary public school teachers, however, was held not permissible absent reasonable suspicion based on supportable objective facts and established administrative standards. Patchogue-Medford Congress of Teachers v. Board of Educ. Patchogue-Medford Union Free Sch. Dist., 70 N.Y.2d 57, 510 N.E.2d 325, 517 N.Y.S.2d 456 (1987). While public employees may be entitled to due process when they are dismissed on the basis of drug testing, the availability of an Article 78 proceeding to challenge the dismissal satisfies the constitutional requirement for post-termination due process. Fleming v. Kerlikowske, No. 97-CV-0999E(H), 1999 WL 307696, at *4 (W.D.N.Y. May 7, 1999), aff'd, 201 F.3d 431 (2d Cir. 1999); see also Stenson v. Kerlikowske, No. 98-CV-0316E(H), 1999 WL 409496, at *3 (W.D.N.Y. June 10, 1999), aff'd, 205 F.3d 1324 (2d Cir. 2000) (pre-termination due process satisfied where employee was made aware of drug testing results two weeks prior to termination).

C. Medical Testing

1. ***Permissible Examinations.*** New York generally recognizes the right of employers to require physical examinations. See Patchogue-Medford Congress of Teachers, 70 N.Y.2d at 70, 510 N.E.2d at 331, 517 N.Y.S.2d at 462. For instance, a court has held that mandatory annual physical examinations of doctors working in hospitals does not violate the doctors' right to privacy. Ritterband v. Axelrod, 149 Misc. 2d 135, 562 N.Y.S.2d 605 (N.Y. Sup. Ct. Albany Cty. 1990). The Legislature has approved mandatory medical testing for employees of local boards of education. N.Y. Educ. Law § 913 (McKinney 2002). However, because persons with certain medical conditions are protected against discrimination, employers who require medical examinations must use caution not to violate anti-discrimination statutes. See N.Y. Exec. Law § 296(1)(a) (McKinney 2002).

2. ***Testing Procedures.*** However, under Federal law employer may not conduct a medical examination until after an offer of employment is made and may not condition the offer on the results of the medical examination. 42 U.S.C. §§ 12112(d)(3)-(4); see also Hirschmann v. Hassapoyannes, 16 Misc. 3d 1014, 1018, 843 N.Y.S.2d 778 (N.Y. Sup. Ct. N.Y. Cty. 2007), aff'd, 52 A.D.3d 221, 859 N.Y.S.2d 150 (1st Dep't 2008). It is unlawful for any employer to require any applicant for employment to pay the cost of a medical examination required by the employer as a condition of original employment. N.Y. Lab. Law § 201-b(1) (McKinney 2002). Whenever an employer requires a physical examination of a woman by a physician, she is entitled to have the examination made by a woman or to have another woman present if a male physician performs the examination. N.Y. Lab. Law § 206-a (McKinney 2002). The employer requiring the examination must post a notice informing the party to be examined of her rights under this section. Id. An employer who

requires an employee to undergo a physical examination may have a duty to inform the employee of any dangerous, or potentially dangerous, disease or condition disclosed by that examination. See McKinney v. Bellevue Hosp., 183 A.D.2d 563, 565, 584 N.Y.S.2d 538, 540 (1st Dep't 1992); but see Petrosky v. Brasner, 181 Misc. 2d 897, 902, 695 N.Y.S.2d 281, 285 (N.Y. Sup. Ct. N.Y. Cty. 1999), aff'd, 279 A.D.2d 75, 718 N.Y.S.2d 340 (1st Dep't 2001) (holding that defendant insurance company could not be held liable in negligence to a plaintiff for failure to disclose the insured's medical condition where defendant insurance company had not assumed a professional and expert position with respect to the insured's physical condition).

3. ***HIV/AIDS***. New York law requires that anyone performing an HIV-related test first receive the written, informed consent of the person being tested. N.Y. Pub. Health Law § 2781(1), (4). A person authorized pursuant to law to order the performance of an HIV-related test must provide to the person seeking the test an opportunity to remain anonymous and provide written, informed consent through use of a coded system with no linking of individual identity to the test request or results. N.Y. Pub. Health Law § 2781(4). Violation of the confidentiality provisions relating to HIV/AIDS testing creates a private right of action for the patient, who may be able to recover punitive damages. See Doe v. Roe, 190 A.D.2d 463, 599 N.Y.S.2d 350 (4th Dep't 1993).

D. Polygraph Tests

Although New York, by statute, regulates the use of psychological tests, it has not done the same for polygraphs. See II.A, supra. Courts have interpreted this as a statement of New York public policy and have refused to create common law regulation of polygraph testing. See Hall v. United Parcel Serv. of Am., Inc., 76 N.Y.2d 27, 555 N.E.2d 273, 556 N.Y.S.2d 21 (1990). The absence of regulation of polygraphs per se does not insulate employers from all potential liability arising from the use of such tests. See People by Abrams v. Hamilton, 125 A.D.2d 1000, 511 N.Y.S.2d 190 (4th Dep't 1986) (finding against employer on basis of incidents of sexual harassment during pre-employment lie detector tests). Indeed, under the Federal Employee Polygraph Protection Act, 29 U.S.C. § 2001 et seq., most uses of polygraphs in private employment are prohibited

E. Fingerprinting

Public employers may require fingerprinting of prospective or current employees. Private employers may not do so. N.Y. Lab. Law § 201-a (McKinney 2003); see also Utility Workers Union of Am. AFL-CIO v. Nuclear Regulatory Comm'n, 664 F. Supp. 136, 138-39 (S.D.N.Y. 1987) (collecting cases); Friedman v. Valentine, 177 Misc. 437, 30 N.Y.S.2d 891 (N.Y. Sup. Ct. N.Y. Cty. 1941), aff'd, 266 A.D. 561, 42 N.Y.S.2d 593 (1st Dep't 1943).

III. SEARCHES

A. Employee's Person

1. ***Private Employers***. A private employer's search of an employee does not give rise to a cause of action based on privacy. Santiago v. Greyhound Lines, Inc., 956 F. Supp. 144 (N.D.N.Y. 1997); see also Claim of Atkinson, 185 A.D.2d 415, 586 N.Y.S.2d 319 (3d Dep't 1992).

2. ***Public Employers.*** A search by a public employer of an employee's person is allowed when it is necessary for a work-related purpose unrelated to a criminal investigation or based on reasonable grounds to suspect that the search will produce evidence of work-related misconduct. Caruso, 72 N.Y.2d at 437, 530 N.E.2d at 852, 534 N.Y.S.2d at 144 (citing O'Connor v. Ortega, 480 U.S. 709 (1987)); Morris v. Port Auth. of N.Y. & N.J., 290 A.D.2d 22, 27, 736 N.Y.S.2d 324, 328 (1st Dep't 2002).

B. Employee's Work Area

1. ***Private Employers***. Although there are no reported cases, courts have found in the public employer context that reasonable searches of an employee's work area for work-related purposes, as well as for investigations of work-related misconduct, are permissible. See O'Connor, 480 U.S. at 719-726; Sheppard v. Beerman, 18 F.3d 147, 152 (2d Cir. 1994) (dismissing claims based on search of a judge's clerk because clerk, as an employee, had no reasonable expectation of privacy in his office furniture or file cabinet); see also Gudema v. Nassau County, 163 F.3d 717, 722-723 (2d Cir. 1998) (permitting searches of work area regarded as reasonable and normal under all the circumstances) (citing O'Connor, 480 U.S. 709). The same standard should apply to private employers as well.

2. ***Public Employers***. As noted above, courts will uphold reasonable searches by public employers of an employee's work area – without the need for a search warrant – when done in the public entity's role as employer for work -related purposes or to investigate work-related misconduct. The standard for such a search is one of reasonableness under all the circumstances. See O'Connor, 480 U.S. at 725-26; see also City of Ontario, Ca. v. Quon, 130 S. Ct. 2619 (2010);

Gudema, 163 F.3d at 722-723; Sheppard, 18 F.3d at 152. Established office practices, procedures or regulations can factor into the reasonableness of an employee's expectation of privacy. See O'Connor, 480 U.S. at 716-18; see also United States v. Reilly, No. 01-CR-1114(RPP), 2002 WL 1163572, at *3 (S.D.N.Y. June 3, 2002).

C. Employee's Property

1. ***Private Employers.*** There are no reported cases, but no cause of action based on invasion of privacy is recognized in New York. See I.B.4, supra.

2. ***Public Employers.*** A public employer's search of an employee's property must be reasonably related to the circumstances giving rise to the suspicion concerning the employee; the conduct of the search should not be excessively intrusive in light of the nature of the suspected misconduct. People v. Postall, 153 Misc. 2d 167, 170-72, 580 N.Y.S.2d 975, 977-78 (N.Y. Sup. Ct. Kings Cty. 1992). See also Chenkin v. Bellevue Hosp. Ctr., 479 F. Supp. 207, 214-15 (S.D.N.Y. 1979) (holding that a public hospital's policy of conducting random spot inspections of employees' packages to prevent pilfering was not unreasonable and did not violate the Fourth Amendment where the hospital had announced the inspection policy and provided employees with an alternative procedure to check their packages and avoid searches altogether); People v. Desnoyers, 183 Misc. 2d 871, 878, 705 N.Y.S.2d 851, 857 (N.Y. Sup. Ct. N.Y. Cty. 2000) (although not reaching the issue, indicating that a hospital's search policy would be unconstitutional because it lacked an underlying public policy goal and was implemented in an unreasonable and non-random manner).

A public employee's locker is the employee's property for the purposes of determining the legality of the employer's search of the locker. Postall, 153 Misc. 2d at 170, 580 N.Y.S.2d at 977.

IV. MONITORING OF EMPLOYEES

A. Telephones and Electronic Communications

1. ***Wiretapping.*** Public employers in New York are subject to a provision of the New York State Constitution relating to searches and seizures that explicitly preserves that right of the people to be secure against unreasonable interception of telephone and telegraph communications. N.Y. Const. art. I, § 12. Further, a statute that applies to both public and private employers criminalizes the monitoring or recording of phone conversations without a court order or the permission of one party. N.Y. Penal Law §§ 250.00, 250.05 (McKinney 2002). However, a third party may monitor and record such a conversation if one participant consents, whether or not the other participants know of or consent to the monitoring. See N.Y. Penal Law §§ 250.05 cmt (McKinney 2002); People v. Lasher, 58 N.Y.2d 962, 447 N.E.2d 70, 460 N.Y.S.2d 522 (1983). Notably, telephone subscribers, including employers, may not intercept communications on their own telephone lines when the subscriber is not a party to the conversation and none of the parties has consented. In such situations, employers may not intercept communications even to determine whether an employee is disloyal or dishonest. N.Y. Penal Law § 250.05 cmt.

2. ***Electronic Communications (E-mail).*** Intentional collection or recording of an electronic communication without the consent of the sender or intended recipient is a felony. N.Y. Penal Law § 250.05. The definition of electronic communication encompasses e-mail, faxes, and display pagers (but not pagers that only emit tones). See N.Y. Penal Law §§ 250.05 cmt, 250.00(5)(b).

While the rule for telephone lines described above may be applied by analogy, recent cases indicate that an employee may not have a reasonable expectation of privacy for e-mail sent over an employer's computer system. See In re Asia Global Crossing, Ltd., 322 B.R. 247, 257-59 (Bankr. S.D.N.Y. 2005) (surveying case law); Chimarev v. TD Waterhouse Investor Serv., Inc., 280 F. Supp. 2d 208, 216 (S.D.N.Y. 2003), aff'd, 99 F. App'x 259 (2d Cir. 2004) (stating that New York's limited right of privacy does not prohibit an employer from accessing employee email and other documents produced on the employer's system); see also Jeffrey S. Klein & Nicholas J. Pappas, Monitoring Internet Use in the Workplace, N.Y.L.J., Feb. 7, 2000, at 3 (collecting cases). Employers should also be sure to comply with the federal Electronic Communications Privacy Act, 18 U.S.C. § 2510 et seq., which is similar to the New York law but appears to permit some employer monitoring of communications. See Peter M. Panken & Jeffery D. Williams, Employers Need to Observe Limits on Monitoring the Workplace and Reduce Privacy Expectations, 71(7) N.Y. State B.J. 26 (1999); Ellen M. Martin & Tracy E. Diamond, Workplace Claims: Wrongful Termination, Collateral Torts, Privacy, Restrictions on Right to Compete, and Investigations, 571 PLI/Lit 649, 679-685 (1997).

3. ***Other Electronic Monitoring.***

B. Mail

Under New York law, it is a misdemeanor to open or read a sealed letter or other sealed private communication without the consent of the sender or intended recipient. N.Y. Penal Law § 250.25(1). This proscription may not apply to private communications sent to public employees at work. See People v. Freedman, 87 Misc. 2d 585, 586, 386 N.Y.S.2d 306, 307 (N.Y. City Ct. Rochester 1976) (holding that mail received by city employees is public). New York courts have not addressed the application of this law to mail sent to a private workplace.

C. Surveillance/Photographing

Employer and its president did not have common-law or statutory duty to protect privacy of former employee in the workplace and therefore their installation and maintenance of telephone and video surveillance equipment in workplace without employee's knowledge did not support claim for negligent infliction of emotional distress. Clark v. Elam Sand and Gravel, Inc., 4 Misc. 3d 294, 777 N.Y.S.2d 624 (N.Y. Sup. Ct. Ontario Cty. 2004).

Sanitation employees' rights to privacy were not invaded where pictures of them were taken without their permission to be shown to witnesses who claimed that sanitation employees were collecting waste from commercial enterprises for their own remuneration. DeLury v. Kretchmer, 66 Misc. 2d 897, 322 N.Y.S.2d 517 (N.Y. Sup. Ct. N.Y. Cty. 1971).

V. ACTIVITIES OUTSIDE THE WORKPLACE

A. Statute or Common Law

1. ***Discrimination Prohibited.*** Under the Legal Activities Law, it is unlawful for an employer to fire, refuse to hire, or discriminate against an employee or applicant because of the individual's political activities during non-working hours, legal use of consumable products during non-work hours when not on the employer's premises, or legal recreational activities outside working hours off the employer's property. N.Y. Lab. Law § 201-d (McKinney 2005). A defendant who claimed that she was fired as a result of statements that she made in a political argument at a restaurant stated a claim under Labor Law § 201-d. Cavanaugh v. Doherty, 243 A.D.2d 92, 99, 675 N.Y.S.2d 143, 148 (3d Dep't 1998); see also Baker v. City of Elmira, 271 A.D.2d 906, 707 N.Y.S.2d 513 (3d Dep't 2000) (denying city's motion for summary judgment in action alleging discrimination due to political activities where affidavits raised a genuine issue of material fact concerning city manager's political bias in making firefighter promotions); McCue v. County of Westchester, 18 A.D.3d 830, 796 N.Y.S.2d 384 (2d Dep't 2005) (holding that alleged violation of Labor Law § 201-d should not have been dismissed absent a factual finding that county employee had engaged in political activities during work hours, or on county premises, or with county equipment); but see Wehlage v. Quinlan, 55 A.D.3d 1344, 864 N.Y.S.2d 630 (4th Dep't 2008) (City did not discharge animal control officer for political activities outside the workplace, in violation of Labor Law, where officer did not run for public office, campaign for a candidate for public office, or participate in fund-raising activities for the benefit of a candidate, political party or political advocacy group).

B. Employees' Personal Relationship

1. ***Romantic Relationships Between Employees.*** Two state courts have held that enforcement of an employer's policy against employees dating each other does not violate the recreational activities statute. See Hudson v. Goldman Sachs & Co., 283 A.D.2d 246, 725 N.Y.S.2d 318 (1st Dep't 2001); State v. Wal-Mart Stores, Inc., 207 A.D.2d 150, 621 N.Y.S.2d 158 (3d Dep't 1995). However, another court ruled that cohabitation was protected under the statute, finding that the law covered social activities in general as long the activities occurred after work and off the employer's property. Pasch v. Katz Media Corp., No. 94 Civ. 8554 (RPP), 1995 WL 469710, at *3 (S.D.N.Y. Aug. 8, 1995); see also Aquilone v. Republic Nat'l Bank of N.Y., No. 98 Civ. 5451 (SAS), 1998 WL 872425, at *6 (S.D.N.Y. Dec. 15, 1998) ("'friendship' that occurs off the employer's premises, without use of the employer's equipment and not on the employer's time, should be considered a protected activity under § 201-d unless there is a material conflict of interest). Pasch and Aquilane were distinguished by McCavitt v. Swiss Reinsurance Am. Corp., 89 F. Supp. 2d 495, 499 (S.D.N.Y. 2000), aff'd, 237 F.3d 166 (2d Cir. 2001), which held that a dating relationship between employees does not fall within the protection of § 201-d of the New York Labor Law. One court has refused to characterize cohabitation with a man married to a different woman as a recreational activity within the meaning of Labor Law § 201-d(2)(c). Bilquin v. Roman Catholic Church, 286 A.D.2d 409, 729 N.Y.S.2d 519 (2d Dep't 2001).

2. ***Sexual Orientation.*** As of January 16, 2003, the New York Human Rights Law made sexual orientation a protected trait. N.Y. Exec. Law § 296(1)(a) (McKinney 2005); see also Logan v. Salvation Army, 10 Misc. 3d 756, 759, 809 N.Y.S.2d 846, 849 (N.Y. Sup. Ct. N.Y. Cty. 2005) (applying state sexual orientation provision prospectively only). Moreover, the New York City Human Rights Law also explicitly prohibits discrimination by employers on the basis of sexual orientation and therefore may provide an additional cause of action. N.Y.C. Admin. Code § 8-107(1)(a) (McKinney 2005); see also Priore v. New York Yankees, 307 A.D.2d 67, 72-73, 761 N.Y.S.2d 608, 613 (1st Dep't 2003) (contrasting state and city statutes); Martinez v. County of Monroe, 50 A.D.3d 189, 850 N.Y.S.2d 740 (4th Dep't 2008) (holding employer unlawfully discriminated against employee, in violation of Executive Law, by refusing to recognize employee's valid Canadian same-sex marriage when she applied for spousal health care benefits, as the sole reason for employer's rejection of the marital status of employee was her sexual orientation).

3. ***Marital Status.*** Under the New York Human Rights Law, employers may not, on the basis of marital status, fire, refuse to hire or discriminate against a person with regard to terms or conditions of employment. N.Y. Exec. Law § 296. Courts have interpreted this law to mean that employers may no longer decide whether to hire, fire, or promote someone because he or she is single, married, divorced, separated or the like. Manhattan Pizza Hut, Inc. v. New York State Human Rights Appeal Bd., 51 N.Y.2d 506, 512, 415 N.E.2d 950, 953, 434 N.Y.S.2d 961, 964 (1980); cf. Kipper v. Doron Precision Sys., Inc., 194 A.D.2d 855, 598 N.Y.S.2d 399 (3d Dep't 1993) (reversing summary judgment for defendant where plaintiff presented evidence that supervisor stated that one reason plaintiff was being laid off was that he was single). However, employers may maintain antinepotism policies governing the employment of spouses. See Manhattan Pizza Hut, 51 N.Y.2d at 513, 415 N.E.2d at 954, 434 N.Y.S.2d at 964-65 (upholding policy barring relatives, including spouses, from working in supervisory relationship); Campbell Plastics, Inc. v. New York State Human Rights Appeal Bd., 81 A.D.2d 991, 440 N.Y.S.2d 73 (3d Dep't 1981) (holding that employer's refusal to hire woman whose husband already worked for employer did not constitute discrimination based on marital status). It may also be permissible for employers to limit or deny insurance benefits based on facts apart from marital status itself. See, e.g., Police Ass'n of City of Mount Vernon v. New York State Pub. Employment Relations Bd., 126 A.D.2d 824, 510 N.Y.S.2d 742 (3d Dep't 1987) (city's proposal to deny health insurance benefits to employees eligible for similar coverage under spouse's insurance did not discriminate on basis of marital status); Funderburke v. Uniondale Union Free Sch. Dist. No. 15, 251 A.D.2d 622, 676 N.Y.S.2d 199 (2d Dep't 1998) (school district's decision not to extend health insurance benefits to same-sex partners of employees did not discriminate on the basis of marital status).

C. Smoking

One appellate court has held that smoking outside the workplace, without more, is not a disability under N.Y. State law. Fortunoff Fine Jewelry & Silverware, Inc. v. New York State Div. of Human Rights, 227 A.D.2d 557, 642 N.Y.S.2d 710 (2d Dep't 1996) (annulling determination that defendant discriminated against plaintiff by refusing to accept her application for employment because she was a smoker). However, it appears that smoking cigarettes would be protected by the Legal Activities Law as legal use of consumable products. See N.Y. Lab. Law § 201-d(2)(b) (McKinney 2005). Even if that protection applies, employers may still pass on to employees who smoke the added incremental cost of their health, disability, or life insurance. N.Y. Lab. Law § 201-d(6). Smoking is now banned in the workplace under the N.Y. Health Laws, § 1399-n, et seq.

D. Blogging

There are no reported New York cases on point.

E. Domestic Violence Victim Status

As of July 7, 2009, employers are prohibited from discriminating against victims of domestic violence or stalking based upon status as a domestic violence victim. 2009 Sess. Law News of N.Y. Ch. 80 (A. 755-A) (McKinney's).

VI. RECORDS

A. Personnel Records

1. ***Basic Information.*** Every employer must keep a record of each employee's name, social security number, and salary. N.Y. Lab. Law. § 575 (McKinney 2005). This record is open to inspection by the Department of Labor. Id. However, the information acquired by the Department from employers is not open to the public and cannot be used in court unless the Commissioner of the Department of Labor is a party to the lawsuit. N.Y. Lab. Law § 537 (McKinney 2005). Employees in the private sector have no recognized right to inspect records pertaining to them.

2. ***Invasion of Privacy.*** No reported case in New York has held that disclosure of personnel records gives rise to a cause of action for invasion of privacy.

3. ***No Right of Access to Records of Certain Public Employees.*** Public employers' records are generally open to the public, including to the public employees who are subjects of the records. See N.Y. Pub. Off. Law § 84 et seq. (McKinney 2001). However, disclosure of employment, medical or credit histories, as well as the personal references of applicants for employment, is barred by statute. N.Y. Pub. Off. Law § 89(2)(b) (McKinney 2002). These records may be disclosed, however, with identifying details deleted or upon the request or consent of the subject of the records. Id. § 89(2)(c). In addition, the New York Civil Rights Law protects personnel records of police officers, firefighters, paramedics, and corrections officers from disclosure under the Freedom of Information Law. N.Y. Civ. Rights § 50-a (McKinney 2002); see generally Daily Gazette Co. v. City of Schenectady, 93 N.Y.2d 145, 710 N.E.2d 1072 , 688 N.Y.S.2d 472 (1999); see also New York City Police Officers v. City of New York, 34 A.D.3d 392, 826 N.Y.S.2d 22 (1st Dep't 2006) (§ 50-a does not

require the release of personnel records to third parties); Brewster v. State, 13 Misc. 3d 1246(A), 831 N.Y.S.2d 358, 2006 WL 3545428 (Ct. Cl. 2006) (the protections of § 50-a are limited to those categories of employees set forth in the statute); Crowe v. Kelly, 38A.D.3d 435, 437, 835 N.Y.S.2d 4 (1st Dep't 2007) (there is a two-step process for overcoming the confidentiality requirements applicable to personnel records of police, firemen and certain other civil servants involving first a hearing as to whether the facts warrant a request of the records for in camera review, and a determination as to whether they are relevant and material to the underlying action).

a. Grievance Records. Grievances filed against corrections officers are personnel records exempt from disclosure under the Freedom of Information Law. See Daily Gazette Co., 93 N.Y.2d at 156-57, 710 N.E.2d at 1076-77; 688 N.Y.S.2d at 476-77; Prisoners' Legal Serv. of N.Y. v. New York State Dep't of Corr. Serv., 73 N.Y.2d 26, 31, 535 N.E.2d 243, 245, 538 N.Y.S.2d 190, 192 (1988).

b. No Private Right of Action. The law making personnel records confidential does not create a private right of action. See Carpenter v. City of Plattsburgh, 105 A.D.2d 295, 299, 484 N.Y.S.2d 284, 286 (3d Dep't), aff'd, 66 N.Y.2d 791, 488 N.E.2d 839, 497 N.Y.S.2d 909 (1985); New York City Police Officers, 34 A.D.3d 392, 826 N.Y.S.2d 22.

B. Medical Records

1. ***Certain Records Protected.*** The confidentiality of certain medical records is protected by statute. See II.C.3, supra (confidentiality of HIV/AIDS testing). Absent specific statutory protection, employees' medical records may be open to disclosure by employers because New York does not allow common-law invasion of privacy claims. See Waldron v. Ball Corp., 210 A.D.2d 611, 619 N.Y.S.2d 841 (3d Dep't 1994) (rejecting privacy claim where defendant falsely represented that plaintiff's decedent had consented to release of medical records). For purposes of litigation, unless a patient waives confidentiality or if certain exceptions apply, a medical professional may not disclose any information acquired in his or her professional capacity. N.Y. C.P.L.R. § 4504 (McKinney 2004); see also Gunn v. Sound Shore Med. Ctr. of Westchester, 5 A.D.3d 435, 436, 772 N.Y.S.2d 714, 715 (2d Dep't 2004) (The physician-patient privilege [§ 4504] shields the patient's medical information (diagnosis, prognosis and propensities) from disclosure.) (citation omitted). However, in Keshecki v. St. Vincent's Med. Ctr., 5 Misc. 3d 539, 543, 785 N.Y.S.2d 300, 303 (N.Y. Sup. Ct. Richmond Cty. 2004), one trial court recently held that § 4504 was preempted by the Health Insurance Portability and Accountability Act of 1996 (HIPAA) to the extent that the New York statute would provide less protection than HIPAA. But see Ottinger v. Mausner, 11 Misc. 3d 1070(A), 816 N.Y.S.2d 698, 2006 WL 777066 (N.Y. Sup. Ct. Nassau Cty. 2006) (agreeing with those other trial courts that have found that HIPAA did not preempt existing New York State law regarding waiver of the physician-patient privilege.). Currently, state and federal courts remain divided over the issue of whether and/or to what extent post-note of issue interviews with treating physicians may take place. Compare Bayne v. Provost, 359 F. Supp. 2d 234 (N.D.N.Y. 2005) (finding that New York does not have a more stringent standard as it may relate to the disclosure of health information and therefore HIPAA appears to preempt or trump New York law regarding *ex parte* communications with health care providers) with Valli v. Viviani, 7 Misc. 3d 1002(A), 801 N.Y.S. 2d 243, 2005 WL 735872 (N.Y. Sup. Ct. Suffolk Cty. 2005) (declining to follow Kreshecki and holding that HIPAA does not preempt state law which clearly permits post note of issue interviews with treating physicians.).

Under the Federal Health Insurance Portability and Accountability Act of 1996, 42 U.S.C. §§ 1320d-2 and 1320d-4, sec. 264 of Pub. L. 104-191, most medical information is protected.

2. ***Waiver of Confidentiality.*** Public employers may require a waiver of confidentiality for records concerning work-related illness or injury, but any waiver of confidentiality for medical records in their entirety must be the subject of collective bargaining. See Schenectady Police Benevolent Ass'n v. New York State Pub. Employment Relations Bd., 85 N.Y.2d 480, 487, 650 N.E.2d 373, 376, 626 N.Y.S.2d 715, 718 (1995).

C. Criminal Records

1. ***Unproven Accusations.*** By statute, it is unlawful for any public or private employer to inquire about any arrest or criminal accusation that was followed by a termination of that criminal action or proceeding in favor of the individual or to take an adverse action against an applicant or employee based on such an arrest or accusation. N.Y. Exec. Law § 296(16) (McKinney 2005). The statute was amended to expressly strike any requirement for a person to disclose any criminal accusation to an employer that is not pending and was resolved favorably for that person. N.Y. Exec. Law § 296(16) (McKinney 2009). Courts appear to require an aggrieved individual to show that the arrest was the but-for cause of the employer's action. See Gonzalez v. Dynair Serv. Co., 728 F. Supp. 100, 103 (E.D.N.Y. 1990) (plaintiff would have to show that he was discharged because of his arrest and that the employer had no bona fide business reasons for the discharge); Salanger v. U.S. Air, 611 F. Supp. 427, 432 (N.D.N.Y. 1985) (same); but see Giles v. Lockport Sav. Bank, 142 A.D.2d 943,

530 N.Y.S.2d 367 (4th Dep't 1988) (holding that statute does not protect employee discharged after arrest but before dismissal of charges). An employer may consider independent evidence of conduct leading to criminal charges. New York State Dep't of Mental Hygiene v. State Div. of Human Rights, 103 A.D.2d 546, 549, 481 N.Y.S.2d 371, 374 (2d Dep't 1984), aff'd, 66 N.Y.2d 752, 488 N.E.2d 107, 497 N.Y.S.2d 361 (1985).

2. ***Convictions.*** New York statutory law generally makes it unlawful for any public or private employer to deny any license or employment to any individual by reason of his having been convicted of one or more criminal offenses, or by reason of a finding of a lack of good moral character that is based upon the individual's having been convicted of one or more criminal offenses. N.Y. Exec. Law § 296(15) (McKinney 2005). See State Div. of Human Rights on Complaint of Maymi v. Sorrento Cheese Co., 115 A.D.2d 323, 324, 495 N.Y.S.2d 865, 866 (4th Dep't 1985). However, an exception permits the consideration of criminal offenses if there is a direct relationship between one or more of the previous criminal offenses and the specific license or employment sought. N.Y. Correction Law § 752(1) (McKinney 2003); see also Al Turi Landfill, Inc. v. New York State Dep't of Envtl. Conservation, 289 A.D.2d 231, 232, 735 N.Y.S.2d 61, 63 (2d Dep't 2001), aff'd, 98 N.Y.2d 758, 781 N.E.2d 892, 751 N.Y.S.2d 827 (2002) (holding that corporate landfill operator's criminal convictions for filing false tax returns, coupled with convictions of its principals on extortion and fraud charges, had a direct relationship to operator's application and denial of an expansion permit); Stewart v. Civil Serv. Comm'n of City of N.Y., 84 A.D.2d 491, 492-93, 446 N.Y.S.2d 948, 949-50 (1st Dep't 1982) (holding that candidate for traffic enforcement agent was properly denied position because he lied on his application about previous criminal convictions). In addition, Correction Law § 752 prohibits discrimination against persons previously convicted of one or more criminal offenses unless the issuance of the license or the granting of the employment would involve an unreasonable risk to property or to the safety or welfare of specific individuals or the general public. N.Y. Correct. Law § 752(2) (McKinney 2003); see also Grafer v. New York City Civil Serv. Comm'n, 181 A.D.2d 614, 581 N.Y.S.2d 337 (1st Dep't 1992) (rejecting complaint of would-be firefighter because criminal offenses involving drunk driving posed unreasonable risk to property and welfare of the general public); Marra v. City of White Plains, 96 A.D.2d 17, 25, 467 N.Y.S.2d 865, 871 (2d Dep't 1983) (reversing denial of license where past crimes were only somewhat related to license, and commissioner and lower court failed to consider evidence of rehabilitation).

D. Subpoenas / Search Warrants

There are no reported New York cases on point.

VII. ACTIONS SUBSEQUENT TO EMPLOYMENT

A. References

Communication between a former and prospective employer for the purpose of eliciting a reference for an employee is subject to a qualified privilege as to the character of a former employee even though some of the information communicated may ultimately be proven inaccurate. See Nicholls v. Brookdale Univ. Hosp. and Med. Ctr., No. 03-CV-6233, 2005 WL 1521239, at *26 (E.D.N.Y. June 22, 2005), aff'd, 205 F. App'x 858 (2d Cir. 2006) (citing Cellamare v. Millbank, Tweed, Hadley & McCloy LLP, No. 03-CV-0039(FB)(LB), 2003 WL 22937683, at *9 (E.D.N.Y. Dec. 2, 2003); see also Serratore v. Am. Port Servs., Inc., 293 A.D.2d 464, 465-66, 739 N.Y.S.2d 452, 454 (2d Dep't 2002). The qualified privilege can only be overcome by showing that the remarks were made with actual malice. See Nicholls, 2005 WL 1521239, at *26. To show actual malice under the common law, a plaintiff must prove spite, ill will, or such culpable recklessness or gross negligence as constitutes a wanton disregard of the rights of others. Id. (citation omitted).

B. Non-Compete Agreements

New York courts tend to disfavor restrictive covenants and will enforce them only to the extent they are reasonable and necessary to protect valid business interests. Lucente v. International Bus. Mach. Corp., 310 F.3d 243, 254 (2d Cir. 2002). As set forth in BDO Seidman v. Hirshberg, 93 N.Y.2d 382, 389, 712 N.E.2d 1220, 1223, 690 N.Y.S.2d 854, 857 (1999) a restrictive covenant will only be subject to specific enforcement to the extent that it is reasonable in time and area, necessary to protect the employer's legitimate interests, not harmful to the general public and not unreasonably burdensome to the employee. (citation omitted). In general, New York courts limit broad restraints on competition but will recognize an employer's legitimate interests in seeking protection against misappropriation of the employer's trade secrets or confidential customer lists, or protection from competition by a former employee who may possess unique or extraordinary services. Id. at 389, 712 N.E.2d at 1223, 690 N.Y.S.2d at 857. The employer may also have a protectable interest in preventing former employees from exploiting or appropriating the goodwill of a client or customer, which has been created and maintained at the employer's expense, to the employer's detriment. Id. at 392, 712 N.E.2d at 1225, 690 N.Y.S.2d at 859.

VIII. OTHER ISSUES

A. Statutes of Limitations

1. ***§ 51 of the Civil Rights Law.*** A plaintiff claiming a violation of her right of privacy under Section 51 of the Civil Rights Law must commence suit within one year. N.Y. C.P.L.R. § 215(3) (McKinney 2003); see also Nussenzweig v. diCorcia, 9 N.Y.3d 184, 187, 878 N.E.2d 589, 848 N.Y.S.2d 7 (N.Y. Sup. Ct. N.Y. Cty. 2007), aff'd, 50 A.D.3d 586, 855 N.Y.S.2d 366 (1st Dep't 2008) (holding that under the single publication rule, the statute of limitations on a claim for unauthorized use of likeness began to run when photograph was first exhibited); see also Shatriya v. Gilden, 16 Misc. 3d 1137(A), 851 N.Y.S.2d 61, 2007 WL 2609792 (N.Y. Sup. Ct. N.Y. Cty. 2007) (dismissing privacy claim under the single publication rule).

2. ***Intentional Infliction of Emotional Distress.*** The statute of limitations for intentional infliction claims is one year. N.Y. C.P.L.R. § 215(3) (McKinney 2003); see also Lamb v. Citibank, N.A., No. 93 Civ. 2358 (MBM), 1994 WL 497275, at *6 (S.D.N.Y. Sept. 12, 1997) (It is well established under New York law that a claim of intentional infliction of emotional distress has a one-year statute of limitations.), aff'd, 122 F.3d 1056 (2d Cir. 1995). However, it may be that where a defendant's pattern of conduct extends back in time more than one year, the plaintiff may maintain a claim only as to those tortious actions within the past year. See Weisman v. Weisman, 108 A.D.2d 853, 485 N.Y.S.2d 570 (2d Dep't 1985); but see Neufeld v. Neufeld, 910 F. Supp. 977 (S.D.N.Y. 1996) (holding that pattern and practice of outrageous conduct tolls statute of limitations). See also Mariani v. Consolidated Edison Co. of N.Y., Inc., 982 F. Supp. 267, 273-74 (S.D.N.Y. 1997) (citing cases supporting both views), aff'd, 172 F.3d 38 (2d Cir. 1998).

3. ***Interference with Contract or Economic Advantage.*** The statute of limitations for actions predicated on damage to property interests is three years and is not a continuing tort. N.Y. C.P.L.R. § 214(4) (McKinney 2005); Monex Fin. Serv. Ltd. v. Dynamic Currency Conversion, Inc., 19 Misc. 3d 1113(A), 859 N.Y.S.2d 904, 2008 WL 880209. at *2 (N.Y. Sup. Ct. Nassau Cty. 2008), aff'd as modified, 62 A.D.3d 675, 878 N.Y.S.2d 432 (2d Dep't 2009). This limitations period applies to claims of interference with contracts and prospective business relationships. Classic Appraisals Corp. v. DeSantis, 159 A.D.2d 537, 552 N.Y.S.2d 402 (2d Dep't 1990).

4. ***Prima Facie Tort.*** The limitations period for claims of prima facie tort appears to vary according to the underlying conduct. For instance, where the claim arises from negligence, the plaintiff must file suit within three years. See Marine Midland Bank, N.A. v. Renck, 208 A.D.2d 688, 617 N.Y.S.2d 507 (2d Dep't 1994). In contrast, where the plaintiff alleges intentional wrongdoing by the defendants, courts will apply the one-year statute of limitations. See Della Villa v. Constantino, 246 A.D.2d 867, 668 N.Y.S.2d 724 (3d Dep't 1998). However, courts will not permit a plaintiff to avoid the one-year statute of limitations for intentional torts by creatively labeling the action as a prima facie tort. Yong Wen Mo v. Gee Ming Chan, 17 A.D.3d 356, 358-59,792 N.Y.S.2d 589, 591 (2d Dep't 2005).

B. Jurisdiction and Venue

General jurisdiction exists when a defendant is "present" in New York. N.Y. C.P.L.R. 301. In addition to actual physical presence, a defendant may engage in purposeful activity within the state that is so systematic and continuous that the party will be considered to be "present" in New York. See, e.g., Landoil Resources Corp. v. Alexander & Alexander Servs., Inc., 77 N.Y. 2d 28, 33, 565 N.E.2d 488, 490 563 N.Y.S.2d 739 (1990). Under New York law, a defendant is present when it is "doing business" in New York. N.Y. C.P.L.R. 301. If general jurisdiction is lacking, a defendant may still be subject to jurisdiction in New York based on specific acts directed at the state, provided the action arises out of those acts. In contrast to the "doing business" test, a single, isolated act may serve as a basis for asserting specific jurisdiction if it is substantially related to the claims asserted. See Alan Lupton Assoc., Inc. v. Northeast Plastics, Inc., 105 A.D. 2d 3, 5, 482 N.Y.S.2d 647, 649-50 (4th Dep't 1984).

Article 5 of the N.Y. C.P.L.R. sets forth New York's rules of venue, i.e, the place of trial of state Supreme Court actions. The geographic subdivisions (counties) of the state Supreme Court extend throughout the state. Lower courts, such as the Civil Court of the City of New York, are divided into five counties and, as a result, require venue rules. *See* Article 3, New York City Civil Court Act § 301 to 307. The same is true of the District Courts located in Nassau and Suffolk Counties on Long Island. Article 3, Uniform District Court Act § 301 to 307. All other cities throughout the state (other than New York City) consist of a single subdivision and do not require venue rules. Where venue is concerned, convenience, not competence, is the guiding principle. An action will not be dismissed if the venue rules are violated, but the court will either transfer the matter to the appropriate county or render a binding judgment. N.Y. C.P.L.R. 509. New York venue rules separates actions into several categories. These are: local actions, such as those affecting title or possession of real property (N.Y. C.P.L.R. 50), transitory actions, which include all other actions (N.Y. C.P.L.R. 50), replevin actions which the plaintiff may treat as either local or transitory (N.Y. C.P.L.R. 50), and actions where a contractual choice of venue is made by the parties, regardless of whether the action is transitory or local (N.Y. C.P.L.R. 50).

C. Worker's Compensation Exclusivity

If an employee is injured or killed on the job, that worker (or surviving dependent) surrenders the right to maintain a civil action against the employer and coemployers in exchange for limited, virtually no-fault recovery. N.Y. Work. Comp. Law § 11, 29(6). The employer avoids the costs of litigation and the exposure to larger judgments in exchange for paying the premiums under the statute. Gonzales v. Armac Indus., Ltd., 81 N.Y.2d 1, 7, 611 N.E. 2d 261, 264, 595 N.Y.S.2d 360, 363 (1993). A worker's "employer" for purposes of the exclusivity rule is defined broadly, with a focus on determining who controls and directs the manner, details, and ultimate result of the employee's work. Fung v. Japan Airlines Co., 9 N.Y.3d 351, 880 N.E.2d 845, 850 N.Y.S.2d 359 (2007). There are a number of exceptions to the exclusivity rule allowing a worker to maintain a civil action against the employer, including situations where the employer fails to provide coverage for the worker at the time of the accident (N.Y. Work. Comp. Law § 11, 26-1); intentional torts against the employee (Burlew v. American Mut. Ins. Co., 63 N.Y. 2d 412, 417, 472 N.E. 2d 682, 687, 482 N.Y.S.2d 720, 723 (1984)); federal civil rights actions (McClary v. O'Hare, 786 F.2d 83, 85 (2d Cir. 1986)), and third party injuries (Coley v. Arnot Ogden Mem. Hosp., 107 A.D.2d 67, 485 N.Y.S.2d 867, 878 (3d Dep't 1985). Because third party injuries were being used as a work-around to seek damages from employers, in 1996, the State Legislature passed the Omnibus Workers' Compensation Reform Act, which prohibits a third party sued by an employee from impleading an employer for contribution, unless it is shown that the employee suffered a "grave injury." N.Y. Work. Comp. Law § 11.

D. Pleading Requirements

Statements in a pleading must be sufficiently particular to give the court and parties notice of the transactions, occurrences, or series of transactions or occurrences, intended to be proved and the material elements of each cause of action or defense. N.Y. C.P.L.R. § 3013 (McKinney 2007). In an action for libel or slander, the particular words complained of must be set forth in the complaint, but their application to the plaintiff may be stated generally. Id. § 3016. Where a cause of action or defense is based upon misrepresentation, fraud, mistake, willful default, breach of trust or undue influence, the circumstances constituting the wrong must be stated in detail. Id. In an action involving the sale and delivery of goods, or the performing of labor or services, the plaintiff should set forth and number in a verified complaint the items of the claim and the reasonable value or agreed price of each. The defendant by verified answer should indicate specifically those items in dispute and whether in respect of delivery or performance, reasonable value or agreed price. Id. In an action for personal injuries arising out of negligence in the use or operation of a motor vehicle, the complaint must state that the plaintiff has sustained a serious injury or economic loss greater than basic economic loss. Id. In an action or proceeding based upon the conduct of a director, officer or trustee, the complaint must be verified and must state whether or not the complaint is based upon gross negligence or intentional infliction of harm. Id.

SURVEY OF NORTH CAROLINA EMPLOYMENT LIBEL LAW

Brian D. Barger and Jonathan E. Buchan
McGuireWoods LLP
201 North Tryon Street, Suite 3000
P.O. Box 31247 (Zip 28231)
Charlotte, North Carolina 28202
Telephone: (704) 343-2000; Facsimile: (704) 343-2300
E-mail: bbarger@mcguirewoods.com; jbuchan@mcguirewoods.com

(With Developments Reported Through **November 1, 2012**)

GENERAL COMMENTS

North Carolina has developed an unusual and somewhat confusing three-tiered classification of defamatory statements. A careful review of the principal cases is essential before venturing into the cross-currents created by these classifications.

SIGNIFICANT DEVELOPMENTS SINCE THE 2012 *SURVEY*

Although not directly addressed by North Carolina courts, communications between employees of a company implicitly have been treated as published. See, e.g., Moore v. Cox, 341 F. Supp.2d 570 (M.D. N.C. 2004); Arnold v. Sharpe, 296 N.C. 533, 251 S.E.2d 452, 456 (1979); Pressley v. Continental Can Co., 39 N.C. App. 467, 250 S.E.2d 276, rev. denied, 297 N.C. 177, 254 S.E.2d 37 (1979); Alpar v. Weyerhaeuser Co., 20 N.C. App. 340, 201 S.E.2d 503, rev. denied, 285 N.C. 85, 203 S.E.2d 57 (1974). However, in a case of first impression, the North Carolina Court of Appeals addressed the issue of whether circulation of an annual performance evaluation by the reviewing supervisor to the supervisor's superior and in-house counsel constituted "publication". In holding that publication had occurred, the court noted that "intra-office communications can be published in terms of defamation if the individual who reads the communication is independent of the process by which the communications were produced." Because the Dean of Engineering and in-house counsel were not involved in preparing the review in question, the court held that publication had occurred. Implicit in the ruling, however, was the finding that circulation of intra-office communications between employees of an entity who are *collectively involved in the preparation of the communication itself* (e.g., an evaluation, disciplinary warning) does not, on its own, constitute publication. See White v. Trew, __ N.C. App. __, 720 S.E.2d 713 (2011); rev. allowed, __ N.C. __, 722 S.E.2d 59 (2012).

I. GENERAL LAW

A. General Employment Law

1. ***At Will Employment.*** As a general rule, with the exception of employment contracts for a specific duration, employees may be terminated "at will" by an employer at any time, for any or no reason, with or without cause. Still v. Lance, 279 N.C. 254, 182 S.E.2d 403 (1971); Salt v. Applied Analytical, Inc., 104 N.C. App. 652, 655, 412 S.E.2d 97, 99 (1991), rev. denied, 331 N.C. 119, 415 S.E.2d 200 (1992). North Carolina courts have, however, adopted a public policy exception to the employment "at-will" rule, such that employees may bring an action for wrongful discharge if terminated by an employer "for an unlawful reason or purpose that contravenes [North Carolina] public policy." Sides v. Duke Univ., 74 N.C. App. 331, 342, 328 S.E.2d 818, 826, rev. denied, 314 N.C. 331, 333 S.E.2d 490 (1985), overruled on other grounds, 347 N.C. 329, 493 S.E.2d 420 (1997). The fact that a plaintiff could potentially avail himself of federal or state statutory remedies does not "automatically preclude a claim for wrongful discharge based on the public policy exception . . . ." Amos v. Oakdale Knitting Co., 331 N.C. 348, 356, 416 S.E.2d 166, 171 (1992). North Carolina courts have further held that although the definition of public policy "does not include a laundry list of what is or is not 'injurious to the public or against the public good,' at the very least public policy is violated when an employee is fired in contravention of express policy declarations contained in the North Carolina General Statutes." Amos v. Oakdale Knitting Co., supra (discharge for refusing to work for less than the minimum wage). See also Lenzer v. Flaherty, 106 N.C. App. 496, 418 S.E.2d 276 (1992) (discharge for reporting allegations of patient abuse); Coman v. Thomas Manuf. Co., 325 N.C. 172, 381 S.E.2d 445 (1989) (termination for refusing to violate U.S.D.O.T. safety regulations). In addition, the North Carolina Court of Appeals has held that any exception to the at-will employment doctrine should be adopted only with substantial justification grounded in compelling considerations of public policy as expressed in the state's statutes or constitution. Considine v. Compass Group USA, Inc., 145 N.C. App. 314, 321, 551 S.E.2d 179, 184, aff'd, 354 N.C. 568, 557 S.E.2d 528 (2001). See also Schult v. Int'l Bus. Mach. Corp., 123 Fed.Appx. 540 (4th Cir. 2004) (holding that a public policy exception to the state's employment at-will doctrine did not extend to an employer's conduct in allegedly asking an employee to lie during the course of a private, internal harassment investigation).

North Carolina law also provides numerous statutory causes of action for retaliatory/wrongful discharge, including claims where an employee is discharged because he or she: (1) has filed a workers' compensation claim or participated in such a proceeding (N.C. Gen. Stat. § 97-6.1 (2012)); (2) has served on a jury (N.C. Gen. Stat. § 9-32 (2012)); (3) has filed a state Occupational Safety and Health Act complaint or testified in such a proceeding (N.C. Gen. Stat. § 95-130 (8) (2012)); (4) has testified at an Employment Security Commission proceeding (N.C. Gen. Stat. § 96-15.1 (2012)); (5) has filed a complaint under the State Wage and Hour Act (N.C. Gen. Stat. § 95-25.20 (2012)); (6) is not a union member or has refused to participate in labor union activity (N.C. Gen. Stat. § 95-81 (2012)); (7) is "handicapped" (15 or more employees) (N.C. Gen. Stat. § 168A-11C (2012)); (8) has the AIDS virus or HIV infection (N.C. Gen. Stat. § 130A-148(i) (2012)); (9) has sickle cell or hemoglobin C traits (N.C. Gen. Stat. § 95-28.1 (2012)); (10) is of a particular race, religion, color, national origin, age or sex or is disabled (N.C. Gen. Stat. § 143-422.2 (2012)); (11) has participated in National Guard service (N.C. Gen. Stat. § 127A-201(2012)); or (12) has participated in military service (N.C. Gen. Stat. § 127B-10 (2012)).

B. Elements of Libel Claim

1. ***Basic Elements.*** Libel is the publication of false and defamatory statements about another in written or broadcast form. Slander is the oral utterance of false and defamatory statements to another. See Donovan v. Fiumara, 114 N.C. App. 524, 532, 442 S.E.2d 572, 577, 22 Media L. Rep. 2173 (1994). When defamatory words are spoken with the intent that the words be reduced to writing, and the words are, in fact, reduced to writing, the publication is both slander and libel. Phillips v. Winston-Salem/Forsyth County Bd. of Educ., 117 N.C. App. 274, 450 S.E.2d 753 (1994), rev. denied, 340 N.C. 115, 456 S.E.2d 318 (1995). Defamation consists of (1) a false and defamatory statement of fact; (2) of and concerning the plaintiff; (3) communicated to a third person; and (4) causing injury to plaintiff's reputation. Arnold v. Sharpe, 296 N.C. 533, 251 S.E.2d 452 (1979); Renwick v. News & Observer, 310 N.C. 312, 312 S.E.2d 405, 10 Media L. Rep. 1443, cert. denied, 469 U.S. 858 (1984).

North Carolina recognizes three common-law classifications of libel. These three classes are: "(1) publications obviously defamatory which are called libelous per se; (2) publications susceptible of two interpretations, one of which is defamatory and the other not; and (3) publications not obviously defamatory but when considered with innuendo, colloquium, and explanatory circumstances become libelous, which are termed libels per quod." Renwick v. News & Observer, supra. For a publication to be libelous per se, the words must be susceptible of but one meaning and "of such nature that the court can presume as a matter of law that they tend to disgrace and degrade the party or hold him up to public hatred, contempt or ridicule, or cause him to be shunned and avoided." Renwick v. News & Observer, supra, 310 N.C. at 317 -18, 312 S.E.2d at 409. To be libelous per se, the statement must be defamatory on its face, stripped of all insinuation, innuendo, colloquium, and explanatory circumstances. Tyson v. L'Eggs Prods., Inc., 84 N.C. App. 1, 351 S.E.2d 834 (1987). Accord Cummings v. Lumbee Tribe of N.C., 590 F. Supp.2d 769 (E.D. N.C. 2008) (dismissing employee's libel per se claim where information in a published memo "requires an explanation of the circumstances," but allowing plaintiff's libel per quod claims to proceed); Jackson v. Mecklenburg County, NC, 2008 WL 2982468 (W.D. N.C. July 30, 2008) (dismissing former employee's defamation and slander per claims, where the statement was an insinuation and did not mention the plaintiff by name); Jolly v. Acad. Collection Serv., Inc., 400 F. Supp.2d 851, 2005 WL 3082260 (M.D. N.C. 2005) (granting motion to dismiss where plaintiff's allegations against a defendant collection agency and one of its employees was "completely conclusory" and did not "give either the wording of any defamatory statements or even describe their nature); Broughton v. McClatchy Newspapers, Inc., 161 N.C. App. 20, 588 S.E.2d 20, 32 Media L.Rep. 1313 (2003) (affirming summary judgment for defendants where plaintiff "complain[ed] only of insinuations and innuendos by alleging what defendants intended to mean"). It is for the court to determine whether a publication is capable of only one interpretation and whether that interpretation is defamatory. Renwick v. News & Observer, supra. Accord Broughton v. McClatchy Newspapers, Inc., supra. To determine whether statements are libelous per se, the court must read them in the context of the entire article and as the "mythical ordinary man" would read them. EEE ZZZ Drain Co. v. Lakeland Ledger Publishing Corp., 28 Media L. Rep. 1954, 1956-58, 2000 WL 33422618 (W.D. N.C. February 8, 2000). When a publication is susceptible of two interpretations, one of which is defamatory, the jury determines whether the publication is defamatory. Renwick v. News & Observer, supra. If the case is one of libel per quod, the court determines whether the publication is reasonably susceptible of a defamatory meaning so as to warrant a consideration of the issue by the jury. Bell v. Simmons, 247 N.C. 488, 101 S.E.2d 383 (1958). In an action for libel per quod, the plaintiff must allege and prove the innuendo and special damages. Renwick v. News & Observer, supra. **See also Pierce v. Atlantic Group, Inc., __ N.C. App. __, 724 S.E.2d 568; rev. denied, __ N.C. __, 731 S.E.2d 413 (2012) (upholding the dismissal of a former employee's libel per quod claim for failure to plead special damages, where plaintiff merely alleged that the defamation "damaged [Plaintiff's] economic circumstances").**

North Carolina recognizes both libel per se and libel per quod. Libel per se is defined as a publication which, when considered alone without explanatory circumstances: (1) charges that a person has committed an infamous crime; (2) charges a person with having an infectious disease; (3) tends to impeach a person in that person's trade or profession; or (4) otherwise tends to subject one to disgrace, ridicule or contempt. Phillips v. Winston-Salem/Forsyth County Bd. of Educ., supra.

North Carolina also recognizes both slander per se and slander per quod. Only three types of defamatory statements will support an action for slander per se: (1) those charging plaintiff with a crime or offense involving moral turpitude; (2) those impeaching plaintiff in his/her trade or profession; and (3) those imputing to plaintiff a loathsome disease. The plaintiff may recover for slander per se without specifically pleading or proving special damages. Although a statement that "holds one up to disgrace, ridicule or contempt" may be libelous per se, it is not slanderous per se unless it falls within one of these three categories. Donovan v. Fiumara, 114 N.C. App. 524, 532, 442 S.E.2d 572, 577, 22 Media L. Rep. 2173 (1994). Moreover, to fall within the class of slander per se with respect to a person's trade or profession, a defamatory statement must do more than merely harm a person in his or her business – it must: (1) touch the person in his or her special trade or occupation, and (2) contain an imputation necessarily hurtful in its effect on his or her business. Market America, Inc. v. Christman-Orth, 135 N.C. App. 143, 520 S.E.2d 570 (1999), rev. denied, 351 N.C. 358, 542 S.E.2d 213 (2000). See also Farmer v. Lowe's Companies, 188 F. Supp.2d 612, 616 (W.D. N.C. 2001) (applying the Market America test regarding a person's trade or profession to claims of libel per se). A federal court applying North Carolina law has further held that a plaintiff cannot state a claim of slander per se merely by putting a defendant's thoughts or the hearer's impression of them at issue, but must point to actual statements that amount to a false accusation. Dobson v. Central Carolina Bank & Trust, 240 F. Supp.2d 516 (M.D. N.C. 2003) (granting motion for judgment on the pleadings and dismissing a claim of slander per se brought by a bank customer who alleged that the bank's manager defamed him by telling a police dispatcher that he was acting suspiciously and that the manager had instructed tellers not to remove their cash drawers, implying that she suspected he was planning to rob the bank).

2. ***Fault.*** The degree of fault, if any, that a defamation plaintiff must plead and prove depends in part upon the plaintiff's private or public figure status.

a. **Private Figure Plaintiff/Matter of Public Concern.** Without addressing whether the publication at issue was a matter of public concern, the North Carolina Court of Appeals held in McKinney v. Avery Journal, Inc., 99 N.C. App. 529, 393 S.E.2d 295, 18 Media L. Rep. 1204, rev. denied, 327 N.C. 636, 399 S.E.2d 123 (1990), that a private figure libel plaintiff must prove fault or negligence. Moreover, in Neill Grading & Constr. Co. v. Lingafelt, 168 N.C. App. 36, 606 S.E.2d 734, rev. granted, 359 N.C. 635, 616 S.E.2d 541, rev. improvidently allowed, 360 N.C. 172, 622 S.E.2d 490 (2005), the North Carolina Court of Appeals expressly held that negligence is the standard of fault for defamatory speech regarding a matter of public concern where the plaintiff is a private figure. See also Mathis v. Daly, 695 S.E.2d 807, 38 Media L. Rep. 2161 (2010) (dismissing plaintiff's defamation claim, where bare allegation that speech involves "matters that are still actively before the public eye, in the public dialogue and in the public courts" is insufficient to show such comments relate to matters of public concern").

b. **Private Figure Plaintiff/Matter of Private Concern.** In Sleem v. Yale Univ., 843 F. Supp. 57, 21 Media L. Rep. 1897 (M.D. N.C. 1993), a federal district court applying North Carolina law refused to dismiss plaintiff's claims for presumed damages and punitive damages after the court held that the case involved a private figure plaintiff and did not involve a matter of public concern. The court held that "presumed damages and presumed malice (strict liability) are the rule" when the publication is defamatory per se or capable of two reasonable interpretations, and the issue is not one of public concern.

c. **Public Figure Plaintiff/Matter of Public Concern.** The federal constitutional standard of New York Times v. Sullivan, 376 U.S. 254, 1 Media L. Rep. 1527 (1964), applies in cases involving public figure and public official plaintiffs. See Branch v. Guida, 2011 U.S. Dist. LEXIS 49912 (W.D. N.C. May 9, 2011) (public official); Griffin v. Holden, 180 N.C. App. 129, 636 S.E.2d 298 (2006) (public official); Varner v. Bryan, 113 N.C. App. 697, 440 S.E.2d 295 (1994) (public official); Taylor v. Greensboro Daily News, 57 N.C. App. 426, 291 S.E.2d 852, 8 Media L. Rep. 2023 (1982), app. dismissed, 307 N.C. 459, 298 S.E.2d 385 (1983) (public figure); Hall v. Piedmont Publishing Co., 46 N.C. App. 760, 266 S.E.2d 397, 6 Media L. Rep. 1333 (1980) (public official). See also Phifer v. City of Rock Mount, 2010 WL 3834565 (E.D. N.C. Aug. 12, 2010) (extending public official status to a former police officer after his resignation, where the alleged defamatory statements related to his past public service). That constitutional malice standard has been applied to non-media defendants. Varner v. Bryan, supra. **See also Mayfield v. Nat'l Assoc. for Stock Car Auto Racing, Inc., 674 F.3d 369 (4th Cir. 2012) (upholding the dismissal of a driver's defamation claim involving a NASCAR press conference where his positive drug tests were reported, noting that conclusory allegations of malice that are "a mere recitation of the legal standard" are insufficient);** Branch v. Guida, 2011 U.S. Dist. LEXIS 49912 (W.D. N.C. May 9, 2011) (dismissing a slander claim against a mayor who stated that a former police officer was a "pervert" and a "child stalker", noting that even if such statements were assumed unsupported, the officer conceded he had no evidence that the mayor made the statements with malice). In addition, under North Carolina law, an individual may in some circumstances become a "limited purpose public figure" by injecting himself or being drawn into an important public controversy that gives rise to the alleged defamation. Gaunt v. Pittaway, 135 N.C. App. 442, 520 S.E.2d 603 (1999), aff'd on reh'g, 139 N.C. App. 778, 534 S.E.2d 660 (2000), rev. denied, 353 N.C. 371, 547 S.E.2d 810 (2001), cert. denied, 534 U.S. 950 (2001) (affirming the trial court's determination that a plaintiff infertility specialist's clinic was a limited-purpose public figure for purposes of statements made by other doctors about the specialist's training and testing practices as quoted in a newspaper story on *in vitro* fertilization). See also Mathis v. Daly, 695 S.E.2d 807, 38 Media L. Rep. 2161 (2010) (holding that limited purpose public official status did not apply where the public controversy – a flood – did not in any way relate or give rise to the alleged defamatory statement); Boyce & Isley, PLLC v. Cooper, 153 N.C. App. 25, 568 S.E.2d 893 (2002) (holding that limited purpose public official status occurs where an individual engages in purposeful activity amounting to "thrusting his personality into the vortex of an important public controversy").

3. ***Falsity.*** Without addressing whether the defamatory statement involved a matter of public concern, the North Carolina Court of Appeals has held that plaintiff bears the burden of proving falsity. Cochran v. Piedmont Publishing, 62 N.C. App. 548, 302 S.E.2d 903, 9 Media L. Rep. 1918, rev. denied, 309 N.C. 819, 310 S.E.2d 348 (1983), cert. denied, 469 U.S. 816 (1984). That is a reversal of the traditional common-law rule, which held that truth is an affirmative defense, and Rule 8(c) of the N.C. Rules of Civil Procedure lists truth in an action for defamation as an affirmative defense which must be pled. See also Alvis Coatings, Inc. v. John Does One Through Ten, 2004 WL 2904405 (W.D. N.C. Dec. 2, 2004) (holding that although the right to speak anonymously is protected under the First Amendment, in the context of commercial speech on the Internet, a plaintiff who makes a prima facie showing that the speaker's statements are false and damaging to its business is entitled to compel the production of the speaker's identity).

4. ***Defamatory Statement of Fact.*** North Carolina's broad definition of libel per se includes any statements that tend to hold one up to disgrace, contempt, hatred or ridicule or which cause one to be shunned or avoided. Renwick v. News & Observer, 310 N.C. 312, 312 S.E.2d 405, 10 Media L. Rep. 1443, cert. denied, 469 U.S. 858 (1984). Slander per se is limited to statements charging plaintiff with a crime or an offense involving moral turpitude, impeaching plaintiff in his/her trade or profession, or imputing to plaintiff a loathsome disease. Gibby v. Murphy, 73 N.C. App. 128, 325 S.E.2d 673 (1985). Thus, the critical issue in North Carolina defamation cases is usually whether a statement is, when considered within the four corners thereof, as ordinary persons would understand it, capable of only one meaning, which is defamatory. If it does not meet that standard, the debate becomes whether the statement is reasonably susceptible of any defamatory meaning and whether special damages have been properly pled. The following statements have been held to be defamatory: (1) alleged false report by a company manager to other managers and third parties that plaintiff had used profanity and made derogatory comments against management held sufficient to state a claim for defamation per quod. Moore v. Cox, 341 F. Supp.2d 570 (M.D. N.C. 2004); (2) manager's statement that plaintiffs over billed, double dipped and were untrustworthy held potentially slanderous per se. Guider v. Hertz Corp., Rent-A-Car Div., 2004 WL 1497611 (M.D. N.C. June 28, 2004); (3) alleged false statements about a former police chief's insubordination, refusal to follow orders and unwillingness to communicate with his supervisors were held sufficient to state a libel per se claim. Bradley v. Ramsey, 329 F. Supp.2d 617 (W.D. N.C. 2004); (4) employees' alleged oral statements to customers at a trade show, editors, and others that plaintiff was mismanaging its company, engaged in unethical and morally repugnant dealings with employees/customers, performed shoddy work, and was going bankrupt held "sufficient to reach the level of slander per se." Eli Research, Inc. v. United Communications Group, LLC, 312 F. Supp.2d 748 (M.D. N.C. 2004); (5) statements that a private club manager practiced "character assassination", propagated misinformation, executed documents without consultation in violation of club by-laws, and engaged in conduct that caused the declarant to "question his integrity" and be "sick inside" were held potentially libelous per se. Martin v. Boyce, 2000 WL 1264148 (M.D. N.C. July 20, 2000); (6) statement that textile worker had been arrested as a strike ringleader held actionable as tending to prevent him from obtaining employment. Lay v. Gazette Publishing Co., 209 N.C. 134, 183 S.E. 416 (1936); (7) statement by a store employee about a customer's alleged criminal abuse of a child was held to constitute a statement charging plaintiff with a crime "involving moral turpitude". Dobson v. Harris, 352 N.C. 77, 530 S.E.2d 829 (2000); (8) statements that plaintiff misappropriated funds. Richardson v. Mancil, 2010 N.C. App. LEXIS 2323 (Dec. 21, 2010); (9) defendant's statements to industry association members and other third-parties describing plaintiff as a "lease jumper," "bitch," and "billboard whore," and describing plaintiff's actions as unprofessional, despicable and unethical found to support defamation claim. Beroth Oil Co. v. Whiteheart, 173 N.C. App. 89, 618 S.Ed.2d 739 (2005); (10) alleged false statements that plaintiff sexually harassed defendant held potentially defamatory. Smith-Price v. Charter Behavioral Health Sys., 164 N.C. App. 349, 595 S.E.2d 778 (2004); (11) statements to a former employee's mortgage lender that the employer suspected the employee had taken client files, that the employer had called the police, and implying that the employee had committed loan fraud were held actionable given their capacity to harm the employee in his trade or profession. Ausley v. Bishop, 133 N.C. App. 210, 515 S.E.2d 72 (1999) (Ausley I), vacated in part and rev'd in part on other grounds after remand, 150 N.C. App. 56, 564 S.E.2d 252 (Ausley II), rev'd, 356 N.C. 422, 572 S.E.2d 153 (2002), reh'g denied, 356 N.C. 696, 577 S.E.2d 109 (2003); (12) statements by a district attorney that plaintiff was fired because of incompetence held to constitute libel and slander per se. Clark v. Brown, 99 N.C. App. 255, 393 S.E.2d 134, rev. denied, 327 N.C. 426, 395 S.E.2d 675 (1990); (13) statement to plaintiff's colleague, that plaintiff was "a liar, deceitful, absolutely useless, and does not have a Ph.D. and was a fraud" was actionable. Raymond U v. Duke Univ., 91 N.C. App. 171, 182, 371 S.E.2d 701, 709, rev. denied, 323 N.C. 629, 374 S.E.2d 590 (1988); and (14) statements by insurance agents to customers that plaintiff's company "cheats people", is unreliable and unprofessional, overcharges and does poor work were held actionable.

Pack Bros. Body Shop, Inc. v. Nationwide Mut. Ins. Co., 2003 NCBC 1, 2003 WL 21017395 (N.C. Super. January 10, 2003). The following statements have been held to be nondefamatory: **(1) statement that an employee is "violent, angry, emotional and frustrated." Bess v. County of Cumberland, 2011 WL 4809879 (E.D. N.C. Oct. 11, 2011);** (2) conclusive allegations that certain employees are dishonest, possess a poor attitude and make "racist, inflammatory and hateful personal remarks." Jackson v. Mecklenburg County, NC, 2008 WL 2982468 (W.D. N.C. July 30, 2008); (3) general statement that identified plaintiff business owner and his employees as persons who do not pay debts. Jolly v. Acad. Collection Serv., Inc., 400 F. Supp.2d 851, 2005 WL 3082260 (M.D. N.C. 2005); (4) statements in advertisements making alleged false comparisons between a company's products/experience and those of plaintiff were held as "better understood" as the factual basis for a Lanham Act claim. Eli Research, Inc. v. United Communications Group, LLC, 312 F. Supp.2d 748 (M.D. N.C. 2004); (5) co-worker remarks that plaintiff was faking her illness, made excuses to miss work, and was having sexual relations with her supervisors did not "as a matter of law rise to the level of slander per se." Arbia v. Owens-Illinois, Inc., 2004 WL 1345091 (M.D. N.C. June 4, 2004), aff'd, 124 Fed.Appx 202 (4th Cir. 2005); (6) bank manager's statements to a police dispatcher that a customer was acting suspiciously and that the manager had instructed tellers not to take their cash drawers to the vault held not slanderous per se. Dobson v. Central Carolina Bank & Trust, 240 F. Supp.2d 516 (M.D. N.C. 2003); (7) statement that a director of a corporate board had "retired" held not libelous per se or per quod. Farmer v. Lowe's Companies, 188 F. Supp.2d 612, 616 (W.D. N.C. 2001); **(8) email from a contractor to plaintiff's employer that plaintiff "falsified his time sheet" held not libelous per se. Pierce v. Atlantic Group, Inc., __ N.C. App. __, 724 S.E.2d 568; rev. denied, __ N.C. __, 731 S.E.2d 413 (2012);** (9) statement that plaintiff's attorney "can get you off a drug test" held not slanderous per se. Losing v. Food Lion, L.L.C., 185 N.C. App. 278, 648 S.E.2d 261 (2007), rev. denied, 362 N.C. 236, 659 S.E.2d 735 (2008); (10) statements that plaintiff committed a simple assault held not slanderous per se. Richardson v. Mancil, supra; (11) statements that county employees "were doing things and moving money around for various and sundry motives" and that there was some level of impropriety in the transfer of county funds held not libelous per se. Griffin v. Holden, 180 N.C. App. 129, 636 S.E.2d 298 (2006); (12) statements regarding a female plaintiff's alleged flirting with and expressing affections toward male co-workers held not slanderous per se. Coremin v. Sherrill Furniture Co., 170 N.C. App. 697, 614 S.E.2d 607, 2005 WL 1330966, rev. denied, 360 N.C. 62, 621 S.E.2d 178 (2005); (13) statement that a candidate was not a resident of the town in which he was running held not libelous per se where, although a Class I felony, such act did not rise to the level of an infamous crime or sufficiently affect his alleged lost "opportunity for employment." Aycock v. Padgett, 134 N.C. App. 164, 516 S.E.2d 907 (1999); (14) statement that plaintiff was "gay" or "bisexual" held not slanderous per se or libelous per se. Donovan v. Fiumara, 114 N.C. App. 524, 442 S.E.2d 572, 22 Media L. Rep. 2173 (1994); (15) statement that plaintiff had been discharged for misconduct and a dishonest act held not actionable per se. Stutts v. Duke Power Co., 47 N.C. App. 76, 266 S.E.2d 861 (1980); and **(16) statement that an employee was "untrustworthy," "set traps" for people in the business and was "holding the company back" held not libelous per se. Yates v. Brown, 2012 WL 1287715 (N.C. Super. April 13, 2012).**

5. ***Of and Concerning Plaintiff.*** A defamation plaintiff must prove that the contested statement was "of and concerning" him or her. Arnold v. Sharpe, 296 N.C. 533, 251 S.E.2d 452 (1979). A defendant's statement that "someone" who worked at a restaurant had contracted the AIDS virus could not support a defamation claim by the restaurant's nine employees because the statements were not "of and concerning" the nine, but instead concerned a single unidentified member of the group. Chapman v. Byrd, 124 N.C. App. 13, 475 S.E.2d 734 (1996), rev. denied, 345 N.C. 751, 485 S.E.2d 50 (1997).

6. ***Publication.*** A defamation plaintiff must prove that the defamatory statement was published to a third party. Arnold v. Sharpe, 296 N.C. 533, 251 S.E.2d 452 (1979). See also RDLG, LLC v. RPM Group, LLC, 2010 U.S. Dist. LEXIS 142881 (W.D. N.C. Dec. 21, 2010) (holding that specific allegations of publication to a third party and of the content of the alleged defamatory statements are necessary to support a defamation claim); Esancy v. Quinn, 2006 WL 322607 (W.D. N.C. February 10, 2006) (dismissing plaintiff's state law defamation claim for lack of publication where "Plaintiff admits that Defendant never made any of the alleged defamatory statements"); Taylor v. Jones Bros. Bakery, 234 N.C. 660, 68 S.E. 313 (1951) (holding that statements made by an employer to an employee regarding the reasons for the employee's termination do not constitute publication sufficient to support an action for slander).

a. **Intracorporate Communication.** Although not directly addressed by North Carolina courts, communications between employees of a company implicitly have been treated as published. See, e.g., Moore v. Cox, 341 F. Supp.2d 570 (M.D. N.C. 2004); Arnold v. Sharpe, 296 N.C. 533, 251 S.E.2d 452, 456 (1979); Bloch v. Paul Revere Life Ins. Co., 143 N.C. App. 228, 547 S.E.2d 51 (2001), rev. denied, 354 N.C. 67, 553 S.E.2d 35 (2001); Barker v. Kimberly-Clark Corp., 136 N.C. App. 455, 524 S.E.2d 821 (2000); Long v. Vertical Technologies, Inc., 113 N.C. App. 598, 439 S.E.2d 797 (1994); Shreve v. Duke Power Co., 97 N.C. App. 648, 389 S.E.2d 444, rev. denied, 326 N.C. 598, 393 S.E.2d 883 (1990); Pressley v. Continental Can Co., 39 N.C. App. 467, 250 S.E.2d 276, rev. denied, 297 N.C. 177, 254 S.E.2d 37 (1979); Alpar v. Weyerhaeuser Co., 20 N.C. App. 340, 201 S.E.2d 503, rev. denied, 285 N.C. 85, 203 S.E.2d 57 (1974). See also **White v. Trew, __ N.C. App. __, 720 S.E.2d 713 (2011); rev. allowed, __ N.C. __, 722 S.E.2d 59 (2012) (holding that**

"intra-office communications can be published in terms of defamation if the individual who reads the communication is independent of the process by which the communications were produced"); Cranford v. Frick, 2007 WL 676687 (M.D. N.C. Feb. 28, 2007) (holding that statements by a Sheriff to officers that their fellow officer was mentally ill and "should be committed" were sufficient to prove communication to a third person). The same is true with respect to communications between a company and its shareholders. Farmer v. Lowe's Companies, 188 F. Supp.2d 612, 616 (W.D. N.C. 2001). Communications between employees of a company are protected by a qualified privilege. See III.D, infra. However, merely storing statements in an employee's personnel file does not amount to publication, even if the materials contained in such files are potentially available for others to read. Pressley v. Continental Can Co., supra. See also Harrell v. City of Gastonia, 2008 WL 2139619 (W.D. N.C. May 20, 2008), aff'd, 2010 WL 3314567 (4th Cir. Aug. 24, 2010) (dismissing libel per se claim regarding termination memo contained in plaintiff's personnel file, where there was no evidence of publication to potential employers or other third parties). **Likewise mere direct communications with an employee plaintiff do not constitute publication. See Bess v. County of Cumberland, 2011 WL 4809879 (E.D. N.C. Oct. 11, 2011) (holding that an employer's written letter communicated to an employee in response to the employee's internal complaint of discrimination cannot be used to support a claim for defamation given the lack of publication).** Further, because individual defendants cannot be held liable for defamatory comments under respondeat superior, plaintiffs cannot pursue a slander claim against them where "they did not themselves communicate such statements." Arbia v. Owens-Illinois, Inc., 2004 WL 1345091 (M.D. N.C. June 4, 2004), aff'd, 124 Fed.Appx 202 (4th Cir. 2005).

b. **Compelled Self-Publication.** As a general rule, disclosure of a libel procured or invited by the employee himself is not sufficient to constitute publication. See Harrell v. City of Gastonia, 2010 WL 3314567 (4th Cir. Aug. 24, 2010) (holding that no publication existed where an employee requested and consented to the release of his personnel file); Johnson v. Wal-Mart Stores East, L.P., 2011 WL 2183155 (W.D. N.C. June 6, 2011) (applying North Carolina law to dismiss an employee's self-defamation claim regarding the reason for her termination, noting that "recognition of such a tort would effectively end the doctrine of at-will employment. . .inasmuch as an employee aggrieved by termination could create a lawsuit against a former employer by simply telling prospective employers the reason the former employer gave for termination"); Pressley v. Continental Can Co., 39 N.C. App. 467, 468, 250 S.E.2d 676, 678, rev. denied, 297 N.C. 177, 254 S.E.2d 37 (1979) (showing of an alleged libelous employee evaluation to others by the plaintiff); Ryan v. Univ. of North Carolina Hosp., 168 N.C. App. 729, 609 S.E.2d 498, 2005 WL 465554 (2005) (holding that an alleged libelous letter submitted as part of a medical peer review of plaintiff's performance as a resident physician was "invited. . .by [plaintiff's] participation in the residency program and subjecting himself to defendants' evaluation of his work"). Cf. Arbia v. Owens-Illinois, Inc., 2004 WL 1345091 (M.D. N.C. June 4, 2004), aff'd, 124 Fed.Appx 202 (4th Cir. 2005) (holding that "[p]laintiff's own reiteration of slanderous comments" does not extend the statute of limitations). Otherwise, North Carolina has not expressly addressed the issue of compelled self-publication. But see Ryan v. Univ. of North Carolina Hosp., supra, and Ryan v. Univ. of North Carolina Hosp., 128 N.C. App. 300, 494 S.E.2d 789, rev. granted, 348 N.C. 501, 510 S.E.2d 655, rev. improvidently allowed, 349 N.C. 349, 507 S.E.2d 39 (1998) (both noting that plaintiff had originally initiated an action alleging, among other things, "self-defamation against the defendants").

c. **Republication.** A person who republishes a defamatory statement that originated with another may be liable for it. Cf. McKinney v. Avery Journal, Inc., 99 N.C. App. 529, 393 S.E.2d 295, 18 Media L. Rep. 1294, rev. denied, 327 N.C. 636, 399 S.E.2d 123 (1990) (finding newspaper not liable for republication because it relied upon reputable news services and was, therefore, not negligent). But see Morgan v. Moug, 2008 WL 2115158 (W.D. N.C. May 16, 2008) (holding that reporting on defamatory accusations for the specific purpose of debunking the claims does not support a claim for republication liability); Arbia v. Owens-Illinois, Inc., supra, (holding that "[p]laintiff's own reiteration of slanderous comments" does not extend the statute of limitations").

7. ***Statements versus Conduct.*** Defamation ordinarily must be either oral or written. Non-verbal conduct is generally immune from claims of defamation. See Shillington v. K-Mart Corp., 102 N.C. App. 187, 402 S.E.2d 155 (1991). See also Curry v. Philip Morris USA, Inc., 2010 WL 431692 (W.D. N.C. Feb. 4, 2010) (holding that a search of an employee's vehicle by security personnel did not give rise to a claim for defamation).

8. ***Damages.***

a. **Presumed Damages and Libel Per Se.** The North Carolina Supreme Court in Renwick v. News & Observer, 310 N.C. 312, 312 S.E.2d 405, 10 Media L. Rep. 1443, cert. denied, 469 U.S. 858 (1984), without addressing the First Amendment issues raised in Gertz v. Robert Welch, Inc., 418 U.S. 323, 1 Media L. Rep. 1633 (1974), stated that when an unauthorized publication is libelous per se, actual damages are presumed from the fact of publication and no proof is required of any resulting injury. See Sleem v. Yale Univ., 843 F. Supp. 57 (M.D. N.C. 1993) (holding presumed damages in libel cases do not violate the First Amendment, the Due Process Clause of the United States Constitution or the Law of the Land Clause of the North Carolina Constitution). But see Ellis v. Northern Star Co., 326 N.C. 219, 388 S.E.2d 127 (1990) (questioning whether malice and damages may constitutionally be presumed after Gertz). See also Hugger v.

Rutherford Inst., 94 Fed.Appx. 162, 2004 WL 765067 (4th Cir. 2004) (applying North Carolina law to hold that if the subject matter of the allegedly defamatory statement involves a matter of public concern, presumed damages are recoverable only if the defamer acts with actual malice). Likewise, when a statement is slanderous per se, a prima facie presumption of malice and a conclusive presumption of legal injury and damage arise, such that allegation and proof of special damages is not required. Donovan v. Fiumara, 114 N.C. App. 524, 532, 442 S.E.2d 572, 577, 22 Media L. Rep. 2173 (1994).

Actual damages include pecuniary losses, damages for physical pain and inconvenience, damages for mental suffering, and damages for injury to reputation. Osborn v. Leach, 133 N.C. 427, 45 S.E. 783 (1903). See also First Union Sec., Inc. v. Lorelli, 168 N.C. App. 398, 607 S.E.2d 674 (2005) (holding that although North Carolina ordinarily does not allow a prevailing party to recover attorneys' fees on a defamation claim, an arbitration panel acting under NYSE Rules may award attorneys' fees in addition to general damages). If the publication is defamatory only per quod, special damages must be alleged and proved. Renwick v. News & Observer, supra; Williams v. Rutherford Freight Lines, 10 N.C. App. 384, 179 S.E.2d 319 (1971). However, mere "conclusory allegations" of humiliation and reputational harm do not suffice to show actual damages, because permitting recovery on such basis would be no different than permitting recovery of presumed damages. Hugger v. Rutherford Inst., supra. See also Arbia v. Owens-Illinois, Inc., 2004 WL 1345091 (M.D. N.C. June 4, 2004), aff'd, 124 Fed.Appx 202 (4th Cir. 2005) (holding that alleged humiliation and embarrassment alone does not demonstrate special damages). Special damages, as used in the law of defamation, means pecuniary loss as distinguished from humiliation, emotional distress or mental suffering. Stutts v. Duke Power Co., 47 N.C. App. 76, 266 S.E.2d 861 (1980). Potential pecuniary damages, including harm to professional reputation and career prospects, and emotional distress, are insufficient to support a claim actionable per quod. Salgado v. Joyner Management Services, Inc., 127 N.C. App. 209, 490 S.E.2d 253, 26 Media L. Rep. 1595, rev. denied, 347 N.C. 403, 494 S.E.2d 419 (1997). A candidate's loss of an election, allegedly resulting from the publication of libelous statements about him, does not constitute special damages for which a court may grant relief. Aycock v. Padgett, 134 N.C. App. 164, 516 S.E.2d 907 (1999). But see Cranford v. Frick, 2007 WL 676687 (M.D. N.C. Feb. 28, 2007) (claims that defamatory statements resulted in plaintiff's inability to find further employment as a law enforcement officer and caused her "emotional distress" were sufficient allegations of special damages to prevent Rule 12(b)(6) dismissal of slander per quod claim). In order to be permitted to offer evidence of mitigating circumstances which would reduce the amount of compensatory damages, defendant must plead mitigating circumstances in its answer. Littlejohn v. Piedmont Publishing, 7 N.C. App. 1, 171 S.E.2d 227 (1969).

(1) **Employment-Related Criticism.** Statements that criticize an employee's conduct will not qualify as slander per se unless they impeach the employee's trade or profession. To fall within this category, statements must do more than merely injure a person in his or her business. Rather, the statement in question must (a) be false, (b) touch plaintiff in his or her special trade or occupation, and (c) contain an imputation which is necessarily hurtful in its effect on plaintiff's business. Long v. Vertical Technologies, Inc., 113 N.C. App. 598, 439 S.E.2d 797, 801 (1994) (holding that a statement by a president of the company that plaintiffs did not handle business correctly and engaged in "shady" transactions did not injure plaintiffs in their trade, business or profession, and thus did not constitute slander per se). See also Jackson v. Mecklenburg County, NC, 2008 WL 2982468 (W.D. N.C. July 30, 2008) (accusations that an employee is dishonest and possess a poor attitude toward team-building are insufficient to state a claim for slander or defamation per se); Mbadiwe v. Union Mem'l Reg'l Med. Ctr, Inc., 2005 WL 3186949 (W.D. N.C. Nov. 28, 2005) (applying North Carolina law to hold that statements to a medical executive committee and others that plaintiff's "patients do not understand that another physician is actually providing the care" and "my staff and I feel that this is dishonest" are insufficient to support a claim for defamation); Moore v. Cox, 341 F. Supp.2d 570 (M.D. N.C. 2004) (holding that alleged false report by a company manager to other managers and third parties that plaintiff had used profanity and made derogatory comments against management held sufficient to state a claim for defamation per quod); Bradley v. Ramsey, 329 F. Supp.2d 617 (W.D. N.C. 2004) (holding that alleged false statements about a former police chief's insubordination, refusal to follow orders and unwillingness to communicate with his supervisors were sufficient to state a claim for libel per se); Stewart v. Nation-Wide Check, 279 N.C. 278, 287, 182 S.E.2d 410, 416 (1971) (holding that some of the employer's statements to plaintiff's relatives concerning alleged misappropriation of funds were slanderous per se in the absence of any common interest or duty by such individuals); Penner v. Elliott, 225 N.C. 33, 33 S.E.2d 124, 125 (1945) (false statement that plaintiff was a man who could not pay his debts, would not work and who respectable people would best have nothing to do with was not slanderous per se); **Pierce v. Atlantic Group, Inc., __ N.C. App. __, 724 S.E.2d 568; rev. denied, __ N.C. __, 731 S.E.2d 413 (2012) (email from a contractor to plaintiff's employer that plaintiff "falsified his time sheet" held not libelous per se);** Bloch v. Paul Revere Life Ins. Co., 143 N.C. App. 228, 547 S.E.2d 51 (2001), rev. denied, 354 N.C. 67, 553 S.E.2d 35 (2001) (holding that alleged statements that an employee was a poor manager, could not be trusted and should not be confided in, along with other evidence, were sufficient to create a question of fact as to whether such actions constituted tortious interference with plaintiff's employment contract); Barker v. Kimberly-Clark Corp., 136 N.C. App. 455, 524 S.E.2d 821 (2000) (alleged false statements by plaintiff's manager to other management and non-management personnel regarding an employee's illegal drug use on company premises and accessing of pornography on the Internet presented a question of fact as to whether such accusations constituted slander per se and tortious interference or were qualifiedly privileged); Ausley v. Bishop, 133 N.C.

App. 210, 515 S.E.2d 72 (1999) (Ausley I), vacated in part and rev'd in part on other grounds after remand, 150 N.C. App. 56, 564 S.E.2d 252 (Ausley II), rev'd, 356 N.C. 422, 572 S.E.2d 153 (2002), reh'g denied, 356 N.C. 696, 577 S.E.2d 109 (2003) (statements to former employee's mortgage lender that the employer suspected the employee had taken client files, that the employer had called the police, and implying that the employee had committed loan fraud were held actionable as slander given their capacity to harm the employee in his trade or profession); Gibson v. Mut. Life Ins. Co. of New York, 121 N.C. App. 284, 289, 465 S.E.2d 56, 60 (1996) (holding that a regional vice president's statement to a former employee over the telephone that plaintiff was a liar and could not be trusted did not constitute slander per se, as North Carolina courts have "consistently held that alleged false statements . . . calling plaintiff 'dishonest' or charging that plaintiff was untruthful and an unreliable employee, are not actionable per se"); Talbert v. Mauney, 80 N.C. App. 477, 343 S.E.2d 5 (1986) (statement by the president of a bank that plaintiff was a drug dealer was slander per se); Morris v. Bruney, 78 N.C. App. 668, 338 S.E.2d 561 (1986) (a neighbor's statements that plaintiff was immature, unintelligent and unfit as a mother were not slanderous per se because these statements did not reflect on her fitness to serve as nursery school employee); Tallent v. Blake, 57 N.C. App. 249, 291 S.E.2d 336, 339 (1982) (holding that a superintendent's statement that plaintiff lied about why she left her job was not slanderous per se because it did not impeach the plaintiff's occupation); Angel v. Ward, 43 N.C. App. 288, 258 S.E.2d 788 (1979) (holding that a letter to an IRS supervisor from an outside accountant criticizing an agent's work was libelous per se); Williams v. Rutherford Freight Lines, Inc., 10 N.C. App. 384, 179 S.E.2d 319 (1979) (statement by employee that plaintiff's union representatives were "a bunch of gangsters" was not slanderous per se because it did not charge them with specific, indictable crimes); **Yates v. Brown, 2012 WL 1287715 (N.C. Super. April 13, 2012) (statement that an employee was "untrustworthy," "set traps" for people in the business and was "holding the company back" held not libelous per se).** Such statements, however, will be subject to a qualified privilege. Long v. Vertical Technologies, Inc., supra. See also II.A.2, infra. Cf. Schult v. Int'l Bus. Mach. Corp., 123 Fed.Appx. 540 (4th Cir. 2004) (holding that a public policy exception to the state's employment at-will doctrine did not extend to an employer's conduct in allegedly asking an employee to lie during the course of a private, internal harassment investigation); Deerman v. Beverly California Corp., 135 N.C. App. 1, 518 S.E.2d 804 (1999), rev. denied, 351 N.C. 353, 542 S.E.2d 208 (2000) (holding that the termination of a registered nurse following her advice to a patient's family that they should reconsider their current choice of physicians constituted wrongful discharge in violation of North Carolina public policy).

(2) **Single Instance Rule.** North Carolina has not addressed the issue of whether a plaintiff must plead and prove special damages where a statement relates only to "a single instance" of professional or trade misfeasance.

b. **Punitive Damages.** To recover punitive damages for a false and defamatory statement, a plaintiff must prove actual malice as defined by the federal constitutional standard of New York Times v. Sullivan, 376 U.S. 254, 1 Media L. Rep. 1527 (1964), by showing that the defendant published the defamatory material with a high degree of awareness of its probable falsity. Cochran v. Piedmont Publishing, 62 N.C. App. 548, 302 S.E.2d 903, 9 Media L. Rep. 1918, rev. denied, 309 N.C. 819, 310 S.E.2d 348 (1983), cert. denied, 469 U.S. 816 (1984). North Carolina cases have not determined whether a private figure plaintiff in a case involving an issue of non-public concern must prove constitutional malice to recover punitive damages. But see Sleem v. Yale Univ., 843 F. Supp. 57, 21 Media L. Rep. 1897 (M.D. N.C. 1993) (acknowledging but declining to decide that issue). However, if the subject matter of the allegedly defamatory statements involves a matter of public concern, punitive damages are recoverable only if the defamer acted with constitutional malice. Hugger v. Rutherford Inst., 94 Fed.Appx. 162, 2004 WL 765067 (4th Cir. 2004) (applying North Carolina law).

In addition, North Carolina's punitive damages statute, N.C.G.S. § 1D-1-50 (2012), limits punitive damages to three times the amount of compensatory damages or $250,000, whichever is greater, and requires clear and convincing proof of fraud, common law malice, or willful or wanton conduct for the award of punitive damages.

II. PRIVILEGES AND DEFENSES

A. Scope of Privileges

1. ***Absolute Privilege.*** There is an absolute privilege against liability for defamatory statements made during a judicial proceeding. Jarman v. Offutt, 239 N.C. 468, 80 S.E.2d 248 (1954); Harman v. Belk, 165 N.C. App. 819, 600 S.E.2d 43 (2004). The privilege is not restricted to trials but includes every proceeding of a judicial nature before a competent court or before a tribunal or an officer clothed with judicial or quasi-judicial powers. The absolute privilege has been held to extend to written statements submitted in connection with statements made in court filings in child custody cases, an adoption proceeding and proceedings to terminate parental rights (McManaway v. LDS Family Servs., 2010 N.C. App. LEXIS 2224 (N.C. Ct. App. Dec. 21, 2010)); statements made as part of a state Employment Security Commission claim (Howard v. Food Lion, Inc., 232 F. Supp.2d 585 (M.D. N.C. 2002) (citing N.C. Gen. Stat. § 96-4(t)(5); Griffin v. South Piedmont Community College, 2011 WL 3841562 (W.D. N.C. Aug. 30, 2011)); statements made in affidavits filed in mental commitment proceedings (Fowle v. Fowle, 255 N.C. 720, 122 S.E.2d 722 (1961)), an arrest warrant (LaComb v. Jacksonville

Daily News, 142 N.C. App. 511, 543 S.E.2d 219, 29 Media L. Rep. 1595, rev. denied, 353 N.C. 727, 550 S.E.2d 779 (2001); Jones v. City of Greensboro, 51 N.C. App. 571, 277 S.E.2d 562 (1981), overruled on other grounds, 334 N.C. 345, 435 S.E.2d 530 (1993)), a letter written in the course of an investigation by the Board of Medical Examiners (Mazzucco v. Bd. of Medical Examiners, 31 N.C. App. 47, 228 S.E.2d 529, app. dismissed, 291 N.C. 323, 230 S.E.2d 676 (1976)), statements made in a deposition (Harman v. Belk, supra), statements made during a break in a deposition in connection with questions asked during the deposition (Gibson v. Mutual Life Insurance Co. of New York, 121 N.C. App. 284, 290-91, 465 S.E.2d 56, 60-61 (1996)), statements made by a witness to another in communications preliminary to a judicial proceeding (Rickenbacker v. Coffey, 103 N.C. App. 352, 405 S.E.2d 585 (1991)), and out-of-court statements between parties to a judicial proceeding or their attorneys made in correspondence (Burton v. NCNB Nat'l Bank of North Carolina, 85 N.C. App. 702, 355 S.E.2d 800 (1987)). The North Carolina Court of Appeals reinforced the breadth of the absolute privilege by holding that an attorney's statement to a potential witness in a case in which the attorney represents a party is absolutely privileged, provided the statement is "not so palpably irrelevant to the subject matter of the controversy that no reasonable man can doubt its irrelevancy or impropriety" and "so related to the subject matter of the controversy that it may [have] become the subject of inquiry in the court of the trial." See Jones v. Coward, 193 N.C. App. 231, 666 S.E.2d 877, 880 (2008) (dismissing as privileged a statement by attorney to potential witness that the plaintiff in a lawsuit "got run out of town for drugs"). It is a question of law for the court to determine whether the statement is sufficiently relevant to the proceeding at issue to be privileged. Scott v. Statesville Plywood & Veneer Co., 240 N.C. 73, 81 S.E.2d 146 (1954). Testimony given during a grand jury hearing on issues material to the inquiry is absolutely privileged, even if the testimony is given with express malice and knowledge of its falsity. Houpe v. The City of Statesville, 128 N.C. App. 334, 497 S.E.2d 82, rev. denied, 348 N.C. 72, 505 S.E.2d 871 (1998). Cf. Jacobs v. Mallard Creek Presbyterian Church, Inc., 214 F. Supp.2d 552 (W.D. N.C. 2002) (holding that civil court claims for, among other things, state slander, defamation and invasion of privacy related to a church's investigation and discipline of the pastor's conduct and the Permanent Judicial Committee of the Presbytery's ruling with respect thereto are barred by the Free Exercise and Establishment Clauses of the United States Constitution); Angel v. Ward, 43 N.C. App. 288, 258 S.E.2d 788 (1979) (holding that a defamatory statement written in response to a request by an I.R.S. agent's supervisor is absolutely privileged as a part of a quasi-judicial proceeding). Moreover, the Fourth Circuit Court of Appeals, applying North Carolina law, has held that the absolute privilege for quasi-judicial proceedings applies to statements in letters written to the President regarding qualifications of candidates for U.S. Attorney position. Smith v. McDonald, 895 F.2d 147, 17 Media L. Rep. 1499 (4th Cir. 1990). North Carolina courts have also indicated, without so holding, that statements made in legislative proceedings and reports made by military personnel to superiors are absolutely privileged. Ramsey v. Cheek, 109 N.C. 270, 13 S.E. 775 (1891). Although the North Carolina Court of Appeals did not address the issue as one of absolute privilege, it has further held that publication of a libelous statement "procured or invited by the plaintiff" will not support a claim for defamation. Pressley v. Continental Can Co., 39 N.C. App. 467, 250 S.E.2d 676, rev. denied, 297 N.C. 177, 254 S.E.2d 37 (1979); Ryan v. Univ. of North Carolina Hospitals, 168 N.C. App. 729, 609 S.E.2d 498, 2005 WL 465554 (2005). However, in CNC/Access, Inc. v. Scrugg, 2006 NCBC 20, 2006 WL 3350854 (N.C. Super. Nov. 15, 2006), a North Carolina Business Court judge held that mere complaints by an employer to government agencies about a former employee are not entitled to an absolute privilege, where none of the entities in question were actively investigating the employee at the time the complaints were filed.

2. ***Qualified Privilege.*** A person who makes a defamatory statement will not be subject to liability if the statement is protected by a qualified privilege.

a. **Common Interest**. A communication subject to a qualified or conditional privilege is one made in good faith on any subject matter in which the person communicating has an interest, or in reference to which he has a right or duty, to a person having a corresponding interest or duty, on a privileged occasion and in a manner and under circumstances fairly warranted by the occasion and duty, right or interest. The privilege arises from the necessity of full and unrestricted communication concerning a matter in which the parties have an interest or duty. Stewart v. Nation-Wide Check, 279 N.C. 278, 182 S.E.2d 410 (1971).

b. **Duty**. The duty need not be legal. It is sufficient if it is a moral or social duty. Stewart v. Nation-Wide Check, 279 N.C. 278, 182 S.E.2d 410 (1971); Ramsey v. Cheek, 109 N.C. 270, 13 S.E. 775 (1891).

c. **Criticism of Public Employee**. A citizen has the right to criticize a public official if that criticism is in good faith and the speaker has probable cause to believe its truth. Ramsey v. Cheek, 109 N.C. 270, 13 S.E. 775 (1891). A citizen also has the right to criticize candidates for public office, and such criticism is protected by qualified privilege. Bird v. Hudson, 113 N.C. 203, 18 S.E. 209 (1893). A statement by a school board's communications officer to a school superintendent may be subject to a qualified privilege. Phillips v. Winston-Salem/Forsyth County Bd. of Educ., 117 N.C. App. 274, 450 S.E.2d 753 (1994), rev. denied, 340 N.C. 115, 456 S.E.2d 318 (1995). A memorandum from a university department head to department employees providing a synopsis of events leading to plaintiff employee's dismissal was protected by qualified privilege. Hanton v. Gilbert, 126 N.C. App. 561, 486 S.E.2d 432, rev. denied, 347 N.C. 266, 493 S.E.2d 454 (1997).

d. **Limitation on Qualified Privileges.** When a qualified privilege exists, there is a presumption that the defendant acted in good faith and without malice. However, an action involving a qualified privilege may be maintained if the plaintiff can prove the falsity of the charge and common-law actual malice. Stewart v. Nation-Wide Check, supra; Smith-Price v. Charter Behavioral Health Sys., 164 N.C. App. 349, 595 S.E.2d 778 (2004); Phillips v. Winston-Salem/Forsyth County Bd. of Educ., 117 N.C. App. 274, 450 S.E.2d 753, 756 (1994), rev. denied, 340 N.C. 115, 456 S.E.2d 318 (1995); Clark v. Brown, 99 N.C. App. 255, 393 S.E.2d 134, rev. denied, 327 N.C. 426, 395 S.E.2d 675 (1990); Boston v. Webb, 73 N.C. App. 457, 326 S.E.2d 104, rev. denied, 314 N.C. 114, 332 S.E.2d 479 (1985). See also CNC/Access, Inc. v. Scrugg, 2006 NCBC 20, 2006 WL 3350854 (N.C. Super. Nov. 15, 2006) (holding that "there is no qualified privilege for complaints knowingly filed with an agency that has no jurisdiction to hear the claims asserted"). Cf. Bradley v. Ramsey, 329 F. Supp.2d 617 (W.D. N.C. 2004) (holding that public official immunity will not protect town officials if their alleged actions are corrupt, malicious, outside and beyond the scope of their duties, or if they involve intentional torts such as libel per se and/or intrusion). But see Dempsey v. Halford, 183 N.C. App. 637, 645 S.E.2d 201 (2007) (holding that mere disputing the factual accuracy of allegations made by defendants concerning plaintiff does not amount to actual malice).

(1) **Constitutional or Actual Malice.** A plaintiff may overcome a qualified privilege by demonstrating that the defendant published the defamatory statement with knowledge that it was false, with reckless disregard for its truth or with a high degree of awareness of its probable falsity. Clark v. Brown, supra.

(2) **Common Law Malice.** North Carolina courts continue to permit the qualified privilege to be overcome by proof of common law actual malice defined as "evidence of ill-will or personal hostility on the part of the declarant." Clark v. Brown, supra. See also Phifer v. City of Rock Mount, 2010 WL 3834565 (E.D. N.C. Aug. 12, 2010) (dismissing defendant's motion for summary judgment, where a question of fact remained whether a Chief of Police's statements in a F5-B Report of Separation of Law Enforcement Officer was made in good faith or in retaliation for plaintiff's prior complaint regarding the Chief's affair with another officer). That standard is questionable because it appears, in effect, to deny the qualified privilege to a speaker who has both a reasonable, good faith belief in the truth of his/her statement as well as personal hostility toward the subject of the statement.

e. **Question of Fact or Law.** Whether the occasion is privileged is a question of law to be decided by the court. Stewart v. Nation-Wide Check, supra; Hartsfield v. Harvey C. Hines Co., 200 N.C. 356, 157 S.E. 16 (1931); Market America, Inc. v. Christman-Orth, 135 N.C. App. 143, 520 S.E.2d 570 (1999), rev. denied, 351 N.C. 358, 542 S.E.2d 213 (2000).

f. **Burden of Proof.** A qualified privilege is an affirmative defense, and the facts upon which it is predicated must be specifically pled. Presnell v. Pell, 298 N.C. 715, 260 S.E.2d 611, aff'd in part and rev'd in part on other grounds, 298 N.C. 715, 260 S.E.2d 611 (1979). The burden of proof generally is on the defendant who asserts a qualified privilege to establish its existence. The burden then shifts to the plaintiff to overcome the privilege by showing that the defendant acted with actual malice. Dobson v. Harris, 134 N.C. App. 573, 521 S.E.2d 710 (1999), rev'd on other grounds, 352 N.C. 77, 530 S.E.2d 829 (2000); Clark v. Brown, supra. However, if a declarant acts pursuant to a statutory reporting obligation that provides not merely conditional immunity upon proof of good faith but a mandatory "good faith" immunity presumption, the defendant is relieved of the initial burden of putting forward evidence of his or her good faith. Dobson v. Harris, 352 N.C. 77, 530 S.E.2d 829 (2000). Actual malice may be proved by evidence of ill-will or personal hostility on the part of the declarant or by a showing that the declarant published the statement with knowledge that it was false, with reckless disregard for the truth, or with a high degree of awareness of its probable falsity. Dobson v. Harris, 134 N.C. App. 573, 521 S.E.2d 710 (1999), rev'd on other grounds, 352 N.C. 77, 530 S.E.2d 829 (2000); Clark v. Brown, supra. A plaintiff who must negate a conditional or mandatory presumption of good faith with proof of actual malice cannot rely on "bare allegation and suspicion" of a defendant's retaliatory motives. Dobson v. Harris, 352 N.C. 77, 530 S.E.2d 829, 873 (2000) (affirming summary judgment in favor of defendant on plaintiff's slander per se claim). A plaintiff may, however, be able to rebut the presumption of a qualified privilege by alleging specific facts that a jury could find demonstrate actual malice. See, e.g., Bloch v. Paul Revere Life Ins. Co., 143 N.C. App. 228, 547 S.E.2d 51 (2001), rev. denied, 354 N.C. 67, 553 S.E.2d 35 (2001) (holding that defendants' alleged false statements to senior management about plaintiff's performance, their desire to have plaintiff terminated, and their attempts to channel crucial business information away from plaintiff constituted sufficient evidence to rebut the presumption of a qualified privilege with respect to plaintiff's tortious interference claims); Barker v. Kimberly-Clark Corp., 136 N.C. App. 455, 524 S.E.2d 821 (2000) (holding that the defendant's alleged exhibition of anger, personal hostility and ill-will towards the plaintiff, the inclusion of plaintiff on an alleged "hit list" of employees to "get rid of", and defendant's admitted desire to end plaintiff's employment and failure appropriately to investigate allegations against her constituted sufficient evidence to rebut the presumption of a qualified privilege raised in defense to plaintiff's slander per se claim).

B. Standard Libel Defenses

1. ***Truth***. North Carolina recognizes and applies the doctrine of "substantial truth" as a defense to defamation actions. White v. Town of Chapel Hill, 899 F. Supp. 1428 (M.D. N.C.), aff'd, 70 F.3d 1264 (4th Cir. 1995) (statement that plaintiff was a "gunman" held to be "a fair representation of the full truth"); Brewer v. Dungan, 1993 WL 441306, 21 Media L. Rep. 1926 (N.C. 1993). See also I.B.3, supra; Branch v. Guida, 2011 U.S. Dist. LEXIS 49912 (W.D. N.C. May 9, 2011) (dismissing a slander claim against a mayor, holding that the statement at issue was not proven to be false given that evidence in the record provided support for such comments); Losing v. Food Lion, L.L.C., 185 N.C. App. 278, 648 S.E.2d 261 (2007), rev. denied, 362 N.C. 236, 659 S.E.2d 735 (2008) (denying defamation claim where statements that plaintiff failed a drug test, failed to follow store policy and was fired for such were true, albeit later tests ultimately showed the results were a false positive and plaintiff was reinstated); Ryan v. Univ. of North Carolina Hosp., 168 N.C. App. 729, 609 S.E.2d 498, 2005 WL 465554 (2005) (denying plaintiff's defamation claims where defendants described plaintiff as a "problem resident" and his work as "unacceptable", holding that "[p]laintiff's argument is unpersuasive because there is no showing that these statements are untrue"); Wingard v. Hall, 34 Media L. Rptr. 1537 (N.C. Super. 2006) (statements in a book that "[b]y the time [plaintiff] graduated [from high school] she was pregnant with her first child," held substantially true, where plaintiff had become pregnant within three months of graduation).

2. ***Opinion***. In addition to the broad defenses of absolute and qualified privilege, North Carolina cases have recognized the defense of "opinion" but have noted that "[p]urported statements of 'opinion' concerning the personal honesty, integrity and conduct of individuals have been sufficiently capable of being proven false to support a libel action." Renwick v. News & Observer, 63 N.C. App. 200, 304 S.E.2d 593 (1983), rev'd on other grounds, 310 N.C. 312, 312 S.E.2d 405, 10 Media L. Rep. 1443, cert. denied, 469 U.S. 858 (1984). Furthermore, the North Carolina Court of Appeals relied on Milkovich v. Lorain Journal Co., 497 U.S. 1, 17 Media L. Rep. 2009 (1990), to hold that statements of opinion related to matters of public concern that do not contain provably false connotations are constitutionally protected. Gaunt v. Pittaway, 135 N.C. App. 442, 520 S.E.2d 603 (1999), aff'd on reh'g, 139 N.C. App. 778, 534 S.E.2d 660 (2000), rev. denied, 353 N.C. 371, 547 S.E.2d 810 (2001), cert. denied, 534 U.S. 950 (2001) (affirming summary judgment in favor of defendant doctors whose statements about another doctor's training and testing practices were published in a newspaper story about *in vitro* fertilization, finding that such statements were opinions protected under Milkovich, or alternatively, that actual malice was not proven). See also Branch v. Guida, 2011 U.S. Dist. LEXIS 49912 (W.D. N.C. May 9, 2011) (dismissing a slander claim against a mayor for statements that a former police officer was a "pervert" and "child stalker", in part, because "rhetorical hyperbole and expressions of opinion not asserting provable facts are protected speech"); Mbadiwe v. Union Mem'l Reg'l Med. Ctr. Inc., 2005 WL 3186949 (W.D. N.C. Nov. 28, 2005) (applying North Carolina law to hold that statements to a medical executive committee and others that plaintiff's "patients do not understand that another physician is actually providing the care" and "my staff and I feel that this is dishonest" are not actionable because they are statements "of opinion" and not provable as false); **Lewis v. Rapp, __ N.C. App. __, 725 S.E.2d 597, 40 Media L. Rep. 1805 (2012) (holding that defendant blogger's statement claiming a judge had violated the Code of Judicial Conduct contained "provable false connotations and was not defendant's subjective opinion");** Nucor Corp. v. Prudential Equity Group, LLC, 189 N.C. App. 731, 659 S.E.2d 483 (2008) (holding that statements by a financial service analyst regarding a steel manufacturer in an investor update used rhetorical language and constituted opinion statements without alleging libelous facts); Daniels v. Metro Magazine Holding Co., 179 N.C. App. 533, 634 S.E.2d 586, 34 Media L. Rep. 2363 (2006), rev. denied, 361 N.C. 6921, 654 S.E.2d 251 (2007) (holding that "[a]lthough someone cannot preface an otherwise defamatory statement with 'in my opinion' and claim immunity from liability, a pure expression of opinion is protected because it fails to assert actual fact"). **In addition, the Federal District Court for the Eastern District of North Carolina applied North Carolina law in dismissing an employee's claim regarding a negative employment evaluation, noting that "[c]ourts have held that an employer's evaluations of an employee's abilities or performance constitute opinions and are not actionable under a defamation claim." Whitaker v. Nash County, 2012 WL 3840375 (E.D. N.C. Sept. 5, 2012).** Although North Carolina courts recognize many forms of qualified privilege, they are not usually discussed in terms of "fair comment."

3. ***Consent.*** There are no North Carolina cases addressing this issue.

4. ***Mitigation.*** In order to offer evidence of mitigating circumstances which would reduce the amount of compensatory damages, defendant must plead mitigating circumstances in its answer. Littlejohn v. Piedmont Publishing, 7 N.C. App. 1, 171 S.E.2d 227 (1969).

III. RECURRING FACT PATTERNS

A. Statements in Personnel File

A qualified privilege generally protects statements by private and public employers in an employee's personnel file where the person communicating the information made the statement in good faith on a subject matter in which he or she has an interest or duty to a person having a corresponding interest or duty. Arnold v. Sharpe, 296 N.C. 533, 251 S.E.2d 452, 456 (1979) (holding that a qualified privilege covers a supervisor's evaluation in an employee's personnel records); Davis v. Durham City Sch., 91 N.C. App. 520, 372 S.E.2d 318, 320 (1988) (granting summary judgment on plaintiff's defamation claim because the principal's report regarding plaintiff's alleged physical abuse of students was an accurate representation of the students' complaints, such that there could be no showing of actual malice). Cf. Angel v. Ward, 43 N.C. App. 288, 258 S.E.2d 788 (1979) (holding that a letter to an IRS supervisor from an outside accountant contained in the agency's evidentiary file in support of its decision to terminate plaintiff was absolutely privileged in light of the quasi-judicial nature of the administrative proceeding). Merely storing statements in an employee's personnel file does not amount to publication, even if the materials contained in such files are potentially available for others to read. Pressley v. Continental Can Co., 39 N.C. App. 467, 250 S.E.2d 676, rev. denied, 297 N.C. 177, 254 S.E.2d 37 (1979). See also Harrell v. City of Gastonia, 2009 WL 234064 (W.D. N.C. 2009) (holding that without any other showing, disclosure of personnel file contents to a third-party at plaintiff's request does not constitute publication, given that the mere placement of information in the file itself is insufficient), aff'd, 2010 WL 3314567 (4th Cir. Aug. 24, 2010) (holding that no publication existed where an employee requested and consented to the release of his personnel file); Griffin v. South Piedmont Community College, 2011 WL 3841562 (W.D. N.C. Aug. 30, 2011) (holding that "plaintiff cannot base her defamation claim on the placing of a statement regarding the cause for termination in her personnel file").

B. Performance Evaluations

Intracorporate publication of employee evaluations is protected by a qualified privilege. See Hanton v. Gilbert, 126 N.C. App. 561, 568, 486 S.E.2d 432, 436 (1997), rev. denied, 347 N.C. 266, 493 S.E.2d 454 (1997) (memorandum from a biology department chairman stating that plaintiff was discharged because she was insubordinate and received several "unsatisfactory" performance evaluations was qualifiedly privileged because the chairman "had an interest in the smooth running and morale of his department"); Pressley v. Continental Can Co., 39 N.C. App. 467, 250 S.E.2d 676, rev. denied, 297 N.C. 177, 254 S.E.2d 37 (1979) (report from one manager to another referring to the plaintiff as a "racist, socialist, anti-world, sneak, conniving, lazy" was subject to a qualified privilege); Ryan v. Univ. of North Carolina Hosp., 168 N.C. App. 729, 609 S.E.2d 498, 2005 WL 465554 (2005) (denying plaintiff's defamation claims where an alleged libelous letter submitted as part of a medical peer review of plaintiff's performance was "invited. . .by [plaintiff's] participation in the residency program and subjecting himself to defendants' evaluation of his work" and, therefore, not "published"); Alpar v. Weyerhaeuser Co., Inc., 20 N.C. App. 340, 201 S.E.2d 503, 507-08 (1974), rev. denied, 285 N.C. 85, 203 S.E.2d 57 (1974) (interoffice memo in which plaintiff's supervisor stated that plaintiff is clinically paranoid was subject to a qualified privilege because it was made in the corporation's interest). Cf. Collins v. TIAA-CREF, 2009 WL 3077555 (W.D. N.C. Sept. 23, 2009), aff'd, 2010 WL 2640416 (4th Cir. July 29, 2010) (dismissing plaintiff's libel claims, in part, where there was no allegation that the performance appraisal in question was shared with anyone else or otherwise published); Dempsey v. Halford, 183 N.C. App. 637, 645 S.E.2d 201 (2007) (dismissing slander claims concerning statements made to a Medical Review Committee regarding plaintiff's performance, holding that merely disputing the factual accuracy of allegations does not amount to actual malice). But see Braswell v. Haywood Reg'l Med. Ctr., 352 F. Supp.2d 639 (W.D. N.C. 2005) (holding that plaintiff's state law defamation and other claims against a hospital and members of its disciplinary and peer review boards were not barred under the federal peer review privilege). **Further, in Whitaker v. Nash County, 2012 WL 3840375 (E.D. N.C. Sept. 5, 2012), the United States District Court for the Eastern District of North Carolina recently applied North Carolina law in dismissing an employee's claim regarding a negative employment evaluation, noting that "an employer's evaluation of his employee's performance contains an inherent degree of subjectivity," such that "[c]ourts have held that an employer's evaluations of an employee's abilities or performance constitute opinions and are not actionable under a defamation claim."**

C. References

N.C. Gen. Stat. § 14-355 (2012) provides that it shall be unlawful for any person, agent, company or corporation to prevent or attempt to prevent, by word or writing, any of its discharged employees from obtaining employment, except that such provision "shall not be construed as prohibiting any person or agent of any company or corporation from furnishing in writing upon request . . . a truthful statement of the reason for such discharge." This "blacklisting" statute authorizes a cause of action for punitive damages only. Houpe v. The City of Statesville, 128 N.C. App. 334, 497 S.E.2d 82, rev. denied, 348 N.C. 72, 505 S.E.2d 871 (1998). In addition, to constitute a violation of the statute, statements to a prospective employer must be unsolicited. Cortes v. McDonald's Corp., 955 F. Supp. 531 (E.D. N.C. 1996); Friel v. Angell Care, Inc., 113 N.C. App. 505, 440 S.E.2d 111 (1994). Truthful statements made about a former employee in response to a request from a prospective employer are privileged under this section. Friel, supra. Cf. Webb v. K.R. Drenth Trucking, Inc., 780 F. Supp.2d 409 (W.D. N.C. 2011) (dismissing employer's motion for summary judgment, holding that statements to a prospective employer that the employee was terminated because he caused a preventable accident were sufficient to support a defamation claim); Joiner v. Revco Discount Drug Ctr., Inc., 467 F. Supp.2d 508 (W.D. N.C. 2006) (holding that employee's state law claim for blacklisting was preempted by the federal Fair Credit Reporting Act); Webb v. Harris, 378 F. Supp.2d 608 (M.D. N.C. 2005) (holding that a claim for post-employment defamation relating to an alleged statement made to a prospective employer "arose out of employment" for purposes of determining whether the claim was subject to mandatory arbitration); Baqir v. Principi, 288 F. Supp.2d 706 (W.D. N.C. 2003) (holding that a former federal employee's state law blacklisting and defamation claims were preempted by Title VII, given that such causes of action relied on the same alleged conduct that formed the basis for plaintiff's Title VII retaliation claims); Ihekwu v. City of Durham, 129 F. Supp.2d 870 (M.D. N.C. 2000) (denying former employee's federal ADA/blacklisting claim related to the alleged placement of medical information in his personnel file); Couch v. Bradley, 179 N.C. App. 852, 635 S.E.2d 492 (2006)(enforcing a consent and forbearance agreement against a former coworker/defendant resolving a libel action, where defendant later provided a copy of the agreement to a neighbor, who forwarded the agreement and a letter concerning the earlier suit to plaintiff's prospective employers); Wuchte v. McNeil, 130 N.C. App. 738, 505 S.E.2d 142 (1998) (holding that merely withholding a recommendation for employment regarding a former public employee is insufficient to invoke due process protection); Gibby v. Murphy, 73 N.C. App. 128, 325 S.E.2d 673 (1985) (holding that evidence of an oral reference falsely accusing an employee of being charged with embezzlement is sufficient to uphold a jury finding of slander per se).

In response to ongoing concerns about the potential liability of employers responding to requests for reference checks, effective October 1, 1997, North Carolina adopted a new statute providing qualified immunity from civil liability to employers who disclose information about past or current employees. See N.C. Gen. Stat. § 1-539.12 (2012). This statute provides that an employer who discloses information about a current or former employee's job history or job performance to a prospective employer "upon request" of the prospective employer or the employee is "immune from civil liability and is not liable in civil damages for the disclosure or any consequences of the disclosure." N.C. Gen. Stat. § 1-539.12(a) (2012). For purposes of this statute, "job performance" is defined to include statements concerning the suitability of the employee for reemployment, the reason for the employee's separation and the employer's opinion concerning the employee's "skills, abilities, and traits as they may relate to suitability for future employment." N.C. Gen. Stat. § 1-539.12(a) and (b) (2012). Such qualified immunity, however, may be overcome where the plaintiff can demonstrate both that the information disclosed was false and that the employer providing the information "knew or reasonably should have known that the information was false." N.C. Gen. Stat. § 1-539.12(a)(1) and (2) (2012).

D. Intracorporate Communication

A qualified privilege exists for statements made within a corporation. See Schult v. Int'l Bus. Mach. Corp., 123 Fed.Appx. 540 (4th Cir. 2004) (statements by company personnel concerning a private, internal investigation of alleged harassment and related dismissals held subject to a qualified privilege); Cupples v. Amsan, LLC, 2007 WL 1075178 (W.D. N.C. March 30, 2007), aff'd, 282 Fed.Appx. 205 (4th Cir. 2008) (holding that "the social interest in ensuring free and open channels of communication between an employer and its employees for the purpose of reporting and redressing suspected sexual harassment" gives rise to a qualified privilege); Arnold v. Sharpe, 296 N.C. 533, 251 S.E.2d 452, 456 (1979) (bank vice president who reported to the president that plaintiff "gossiped" and was a "troublemaker" acted under a qualified privilege); Jones v. Hester, 260 N.C. 264, 132 S.E.2d 586 (1963) (corporate president's statements made during the course of investigation of an employee held to be subject to a qualified privilege); Hartsfield v. Harvey C. Hines Co., 200 N.C. 356, 157 S.E. 16 (1931) (corporate president's statement that plaintiff had misappropriated money was qualifiedly privileged, as it was made to the vice president, bookkeeper and night clerk, all of whom had an interest in the subject matter in question); Hearn v. Ostrander, 194 N.C. 753, 140 S.E. 724, 725 (1927) (superintendent's statement that plaintiff had stolen company property was subject to a qualified privilege because the superintendent made the statement while conducting a company investigation); Elmore v. Atlantic Coast Line R. Co., 189 N.C. 658, 127 S.E. 710, 714 (1925) (statements by railroad superintendent to a co-conspirator employee accusing plaintiff of theft were subject to a qualified privilege); Radcliff v. Orders Distr. Co., Inc., 2008 WL 2415976 (N.C. App. June 17, 2008) (holding that statements reporting alleged employee conflicts with a contractor to supervisors, who in turn reported concerns to the contractor's management, were subject to a qualified privilege); Kinesis Adver., Inc. v. Hill, 652 S.E.2d 284 (2007), rev. denied, 362 N.C. 177, 658 S.E.2d 485 (2008) (holding that statements alleging plaintiff stole millions of dollars from his employer were subject to a qualified privilege, given that they were made in the course of an internal investigation/inventory of assets); Coremin v. Sherrill Furniture Co., 170 N.C. App. 697, 614 S.E.2d 607, rev. denied, 360 N.C. 62, 621 S.E.2d 178 (2005) (corporate vice president's statements made during the course of an investigation into sexual harassment allegations held subject to a qualified privilege); Smith-Price v. Charter Behavioral Health Sys., 164 N.C. App. 349, 595 S.E.2d 778 (2004) (holding that employee had "a legitimate interest in reporting any incidents of improper sexual advances or conduct to plaintiff's supervisor" that provides a qualified privilege if exercised in good faith); Bloch v. Paul Revere Life Ins. Co., 143 N.C. App. 228, 547 S.E.2d 51 (2001), rev. denied, 354 N.C. 67, 553 S.E.2d 35 (2001) (holding that alleged statements that an employee was a poor manager, could not be trusted and should not be confided in, along with other evidence, were sufficient to create a question of fact as to whether such actions constituted tortious interference or were qualifiedly privileged); Barker v. Kimberly-Clark Corp., 136 N.C. App. 455, 524 S.E.2d 821 (2000) (alleged false statements by plaintiff's manager to other management and non-management personnel regarding an employee's illegal drug use on company premises and accessing of pornography on the Internet presented a question of fact as to whether such accusations constituted slander per se and tortious interference or were qualifiedly privileged); Market America, Inc. v. Christman-Orth, 135 N.C. App. 143, 520 S.E.2d 570 (1999), rev. denied, 351 N.C. 358, 542 S.E.2d 213 (2000) (a bulletin circulated to managing distributors by the President of an employee's former company that likened the employee to "termites," "parasites" and "vermin" because of her attempts to recruit distributors into a competitive organization was protected by a qualified privilege); Long v. Vertical Technologies, Inc., 113 N.C. App. 598, 439 S.E.2d 797, 800 (1994) (statements made by a company president to employees that the plaintiffs did not handle business correctly and engaged in "shady" transactions were subject to a qualified privilege, despite the fact that comments were made in a staff meeting called to discuss plaintiffs' terminations); Harris v. Proctor & Gamble Mfg. Co., 102 N.C. App. 329, 401 S.E.2d 849, rev. denied, 329 N.C. 269, 407 S.E.2d 836 (1991) (statements identifying individuals suspected of drug use to managers and announcing individuals discharged for drug use to all employees were protected by a qualified privilege); Shreve v. Duke Power Co., 97 N.C. App. 648, 389 S.E.2d 444, rev. denied, 326 N.C. 598, 393 S.E.2d 883 (1990) (after a supervisor had reported that plaintiff threatened him, management's internal discussions regarding such accusations were subject to a qualified privilege); Pressley v. Continental Can Co., 39 N.C. App. 467, 250 S.E.2d 676, rev. denied, 297 N.C. 177, 254 S.E.2d 37 (1979) (report from one manager to another referring to plaintiff as a "racist, socialist, anti-world, sneak, conniving, lazy" was subject to a qualified privilege); Alpar v. Weyerhaeuser Co., Inc., 20 N.C. App. 340, 201 S.E.2d 503, 507-08, rev. denied, 285 N.C. 85, 203 S.E.2d 57 (1974) (interoffice memo in which plaintiff's supervisor stated that the plaintiff is clinically paranoid was subject to a qualified privilege because it was made in the corporation's interest). Cf. Priest v. Sobeck, 160 N.C. App. 230, 584 S.E.2d 867 (2003) (statements by a labor union in its newsletter mailed to membership regarding the actions of certain members in allowing non-union employees to work were protected by a qualified privilege), rev. denied, 358 N.C. 155, 592 S.E.2d 694 (2004).

E. Statements to Government Regulators

An absolute privilege attaches to statements made to government regulators in judicial or quasi-judicial proceedings. Holmes v. Eddy, 341 F.2d 477 (4th Cir.), cert. denied, 382 U.S. 892 (1965) (applying North Carolina law to hold that a stockbroker's sending of a letter received from a corporation to the Securities Exchange Commission and executing an affidavit to that effect at the request of the Commission was protected by an absolute privilege); Larrowe v. Bank of the Carolinas, 2011 WL 3793411 (M.D. N.C. Aug. 25, 2011) (applying North Carolina law to hold that employee statements to a bank examiner are protected by a qualified privilege); Horton v. Alltel Communications, Inc., 2009 WL 1940059 (W.D. N.C. July 2, 2009) (applying North Carolina law to hold that statements made during the course of an unemployment hearing "falls within the absolute privilege as judicial testimony"); Howard v. Food Lion, Inc., 232 F. Supp.2d 585 (M.D. N.C. 2002) (applying North Carolina law to hold that statements and information submitted in connection with a state Employment Security Commission claim are absolutely privileged in light of the quasi-judicial nature of such proceeding); (Angel v. Ward, 43 N.C. App. 288, 258 S.E.2d 788 (1979) (holding that statements in a letter to an IRS supervisor criticizing an agent's performance were absolutely privileged given that the letter was part of a quasi-judicial IRS administrative proceeding regarding the agent's termination); Mazzucco v. North Carolina Bd. of Medical Examiners, 31 N.C. App. 47, 228 S.E.2d 529, rev. denied, 291 N.C. 323, 230 S.E.2d 676 (1976) (holding that an absolute privilege applies to communications made in a Board of Medical Examiners' investigation of a physician given the quasi-judicial nature of such proceedings). Statements made pursuant to a public duty are also given qualified privilege protection. See, e.g., Goforth v. Avemco Life Ins. Co. of Silver Springs, Md., 368 F.2d 25 (4th Cir. 1966) (applying North Carolina law to hold that an insurance company's letter to the department of insurance was prima facie qualifiedly privileged); Dobson v. Harris, 352 N.C. 77, 530 S.E.2d 829 (2000) (store employee's statements to the local Department of Social Services regarding a customer's suspected child abuse are protected by a statutory privilege under N.C. Gen. Stat. § 7B-309 such that good faith of the person making the report is not merely conditional but is mandatorily presumed, thereby relieving the defendant of the initial burden of putting forward evidence of his or her good faith); Hartsfield v. Harvey C. Hines Co., 200 N.C. 356, 157 S.E. 16 (1931) (holding that statements made by a company's president to a deputy sheriff imputing theft by the company's treasurer were subject to a qualified privilege); Troxler v. Charter Mandala Ctr., Inc., 89 N.C. App. 268, 365 S.E.2d 665, rev. denied, 322 N.C. 838, 371 S.E.2d 284 (1988) (statements by the employer to protective services and the police concerning plaintiff's alleged sexual relations with a minor patient were protected by a qualified privilege). See also N.C. Gen. Stat. § 7A-377 (2012), which provides that testimony and other evidence presented to the Judicial Standards Commission (which hears complaints of judicial misconduct) is privileged in any action for defamation, but that no other publication of such testimony or evidence is privileged except the record filed with the Supreme Court. But see Logan v. Hodges, 146 N.C. 38, 59 S.E. 349 (1907) (holding that a letter imputing theft to a county treasurer sent to an official with no power to hear or redress the issue was not subject to a qualified privilege). Cf. Van Pelt v. UBS Fin. Servs., 2006 WL 1698861 (W.D. N.C. June 14, 2006) (upholding a NASD arbitration panel's decision that statements explaining an employee's termination in a Form U-5 were defamatory and should be amended); Farmer v. Lowe's Companies, 188 F. Supp.2d 612, 616 (W.D. N.C. 2001) (libel action regarding reference to the "retirement" of a corporate director contained in a company's Definitive Proxy Statement filed with the Securities and Exchange Commission, which was in turn sent to all company shareholders).

F. Reports to Auditors and Insurers

There are no reported cases in North Carolina, although reports to auditors and insurers by employers should be subject to a qualified privilege. The North Carolina Supreme Court has, however, held that there was a genuine issue of material fact concerning whether statements to a chairman of a company's internal audit committee were made with actual malice, where there was some evidence of potential ill-will and hostility toward plaintiff by the president of the employer. See Lee v. Lyerly, 343 N.C. 115, 468 S.E.2d 60 (1996). See also Griffin v. Holden, 180 N.C. App. 129, 636 S.E.2d 298 (2006) (upholding the dismissal of plaintiff's libel claims regarding the publication of an investigatory audit report and other statements concerning the handling of county money, citing, among other things, insufficient evidence of actual malice); N.C. Gen. Stat. § 58-39-110 (2012), which provides that no cause of action in the nature of defamation, invasion of privacy or negligence may arise from the furnishing of personal or privileged information to an insurance institution, agent or insurance support organization unless the information is false and provided with "malice or willful intent to injure." Cf. N.C. Gen. Stat. § 58-63-15 (2012), which provides that defamation, in the context of false statements calculated to injure an insurer, constitutes an unfair trade practice.

G. Vicarious Liability of Employers for Statements Made by Employees

1. ***Scope of Employment.*** An employer may be held vicariously liable for defamatory statements by its employees when done in accordance with such employer's express or implied authority or when such actions are within the course and scope of the employee's employment. Gillis v. Great Atlantic & Pacific Tea Co., 223 N.C. 470, 27 S.E.2d 283 (1943). Cf. Stutts v. Duke Power Co., 47 N.C. App. 76, 266 S.E.2d 861, 865 (1980) (holding that defamatory statements made by an employee months after plaintiff's discharge were not made within the employee's scope of employment and were not attributable to the defendant). See also Lee v. Cannon Mills Co., 107 F.2d 109, 111 (4th Cir. 1939) (holding that despite the fact that a co-worker's complaint regarding plaintiff was subsequently found to be false, there was no showing of actual malice when the company discharged plaintiff for theft as a result of such allegations, where the company believed such statements to be true and governed its actions accordingly); Guider v. Hertz Corp., Rent-A-Car Div., 2004 WL 1497611 (M.D. N.C. June 28, 2004) (holding that manager's statement that plaintiffs over billed, double dipped and were untrustworthy held potentially slanderous per se); Arbia v. Owens-Illinois, Inc., 2003 WL 21297330 (M.D. N.C. June 4, 2003) (holding that co-worker remarks that plaintiff was faking her illness and having sexual relations with her supervisors were insufficient to state a slander claim against the employer based on vicarious liability, absent allegations that the statements were made in furtherance of the employer's interests or its employee's obligations to the company); Spencer v. Byrd, 917 F. Supp. 368, 374 (M.D. N.C. 1995) (deputy's report to sheriff stating that plaintiff was terminated for false statements was protected by a qualified privilege, where the deputy acted within the scope of his employment in performing his duty to report the facts surrounding such event); Merritt, Flebotte, Wilson, Webb & Caruso, PLLC v. Hemmings, 196 N.C. App. 600, 676 S.E.2d 79 (2009) (dismissing plaintiff's slander claims, in part on the grounds that statements by a law firm's office administrator after work in a social setting about former associates were not authorized or made acting as the law firm's agent); Barker v. Kimberly-Clark Corp., 136 N.C. App. 455, 524 S.E.2d 821 (2000) (holding that a genuine issue of fact existed as to whether an employer ratified its managers' conduct in allegedly making false statements to other management and non-management personnel about an employee's illegal drug use on company premises and accessing of pornography on the Internet, precluding summary judgment for employer on plaintiff's tortious interference claim); Dobson v. Harris, 134 N.C. App. 573, 521 S.E.2d 710 (1999), rev'd on other grounds, 352 N.C. 77, 530 S.E.2d 829 (2000) (holding that a store employee's statements to the local Department of Social Services regarding a customer's suspected child abuse did not subject the employer to respondeat superior liability, where there was no showing of authorization or ratification by the employer and, because of an existing privilege for such reports, the employee could only be held liable if the statements were made with actual malice, which action would be outside of the course and scope of her employment); Shillington v. K-Mart Corp., 102 N.C. App. 187, 402 S.E.2d 155 (1991) (security guard's statement to police that plaintiff had trespassed on store property to loot merchandise was protected by a qualified privilege because the statements were made in the scope of the guard's duties); Kwan-Sa You v. Roe, 97 N.C. App. 1, 387 S.E.2d 188, 194 (1990) (holding that if statements by a co-worker concerning alleged threats of violence by plaintiff "are found to be in furtherance of a malicious purpose of his own, they are outside the scope of his employment and Duke University cannot be held liable"); Troxler v. Charter Mandala Ctr., Inc., 89 N.C. App. 268, 365 S.E.2d 665, rev. denied, 322 N.C. 838, 371 S.E.2d 284 (1988) (holding that an employee's statement to his supervisors that plaintiff had engaged in sexual relations with a minor patient did not constitute defamatory statements that could be imputed to the employer, because if the employee was motivated by actual malice towards plaintiff, such conduct was outside the scope of the employee's employment). Cf. Hoffman v. United States, 182 F.3d 907 (4th Cir. 1999) (affirming the dismissal of a federal employee's North Carolina slander and libel claims against two co-workers, holding that the employees' statements about the plaintiff were made within the scope of their employment and out of a desire for self-preservation, such that the United States' concurrent motions to substitute itself for the defendant employees in the action and to dismiss plaintiff's claims on the basis of sovereign immunity should be granted); Market America, Inc. v. Christman-Orth, 135 N.C. App. 143, 520 S.E.2d 570 (1999), rev. denied, 351 N.C. 358, 542 S.E.2d 213 (2000) (affirming the

dismissal of a former employee's slander per se claims against her previous employer for negative voicemail messages left about her by two of the employer's independent distributors, on the grounds that under North Carolina law, an employer is not vicariously liable for the torts of its independent contractors).

a. **Blogging.** There are no statutes under North Carolina law regarding blogging by employees or other individuals. However, in Alvis Coatings, Inc. v. John Does One Through Ten, 2004 WL 2904405 (W.D. N.C. Dec. 2, 2004), a federal district court applying federal and North Carolina law denied defendants' motion to quash a subpoena in connection with state law claims for, among other things, defamation and tortious interference with business relations where anonymous individuals posted negative comments on Internet home improvement message boards operated by bobvila.com and oldhouse.com concerning plaintiff's business, products and employees. Ruling on an issue of first impression, the court in Alvis Coatings held that although the right to speak anonymously is protected under the First Amendment, in the context of commercial speech on the Internet, a plaintiff who makes a prima facie showing that the speaker's statements are false and damaging to its business is entitled to compel the production of the speaker's identity. See also Burleson v. Toback, 391 F. Supp.2d 401 (M.D. N.C. 2005) (holding that a non-resident entity's semi-interactive website, individual defendants' Internet postings/blogging on a web forum, and a single e-mail exchange between defendant and plaintiff were insufficient, standing alone, to confer specific personal jurisdiction); Accu-Sport Int'l, Inc. v. Swing Dynamics, Inc., 367 F. Supp.2d 923 (M.D. N.C. 2005) (holding that a passive, informational website maintained by a non-resident company was insufficient contact with the forum to subject the defendant to personal jurisdiction of the court for slander and other claims, where the website's interactivity was limited to links that allowed the user to e-mail defendant's employees and to access the website of an unrelated company); Dailey v. Pompa and Beaver, 191 N.C. App. 64, 662 S.E.2d 12 (2008) (holding that mere posting of defamatory statements about plaintiff on an Internet bulletin board are insufficient to support personal jurisdiction, even where the effect of the defamation occurred in North Carolina).

2. ***Damages***. Employers who are held vicariously liable for an employee's defamatory statements are potentially liable for compensatory damages flowing from such conduct. See Gillis v. Great Atlantic & Pacific Tea Co., supra. To recover punitive damages for false and defamatory statement on an issue of public concern, a plaintiff must prove constitutional malice as defined by New York Times v. Sullivan, 376 U.S. 254, 1 Media L. Rep. 1527 (1964), by showing that the defendant published the defamatory material with knowledge of its falsity or with reckless disregard for its truth. Cochran v. Piedmont Publishing, 62 N.C. App. 548, 302 S.E.2d 903, 9 Media L. Rep. 1918, rev. denied, 309 N.C. 819, 310 S.E.2d 348 (1983), cert. denied, 469 U.S. 816, (1984). North Carolina cases have not determined whether a private figure plaintiff in a case involving an issue of non-public concern must prove actual malice to recover punitive damages. But see Sleem v. Yale Univ., 843 F. Supp. 57, 21 Media L. Rep. 1897 (M.D. N.C. 1993) (acknowledging but declining to decide that issue).

North Carolina has not addressed whether plaintiff must also show common law malice to recover punitive damages. See Roth v. Greensboro News, 217 N.C. 13, 6 S.E.2d 882 (1940). See Sam J. Ervin, Jr., *Punitive Damages in North Carolina*, 59 N.C. L. Rev. 1225 (1981). Punitive damages are not recoverable as a matter of right, but only in the discretion of the jury, Hinson v. Dawson, 244 N.C. 23, 92 S.E.2d 393 (1956). Punitive damages in a libel case may be recovered only in an amount not excessively disproportionate to the circumstances demonstrated by the evidence. Bouligny, Inc. v. United Steelworkers, 270 N.C. 160, 154 S.E.2d 344 (1967).

H. Internal Investigations

Depending on the nature of the investigation, there may be an absolute privilege against liability for defamatory statements made during the course of a quasi-governmental, internal employee review. See, e.g., Mazzucco v. Bd. of Medical Examiners, 31 N.C. App. 47, 228 S.E.2d 529, app. dismissed, 291 N.C. 323, 230 S.E.2d 676 (1976) (conferring an absolute privilege against liability for defamatory statements made during the course of an investigation by the Board of Medical Examiners). In addition, as a general rule, a qualified privilege exists for statements made during the course of internal investigations conducted in good faith. See, e.g., Schult v. Int'l Bus. Mach. Corp., 123 Fed.Appx. 540 (4th Cir. 2004) (statements by company personnel concerning a private, internal investigation of alleged harassment and related dismissals held subject to a qualified privilege); Horton v. Alltel Communications, Inc., 2009 WL 1940059 (W.D. N.C. July 2, 2009) (e-mails between employees during the investigation of plaintiff's fraud held subject to a qualified privilege); Cupples v. Amsan, LLC, 2007 WL 1075178 (W.D. N.C. March 30, 2007), aff'd, 282 Fed.Appx. 205 (4th Cir. 2008) (holding that "the social interest in ensuring free and open channels of communication between an employer and its employees for the purpose of reporting and redressing suspected sexual harassment" gives rise to a qualified privilege); Jones v. Hester, 260 N.C. 264, 132 S.E.2d 586 (1963) (corporate president's statements made during the course of investigation of an employee held to be subject to a qualified privilege); Hartsfield v. Harvey C. Hines Co., 200 N.C. 356, 157 S.E. 16 (1931) (corporate president's statement that plaintiff had misappropriated money was qualifiedly privileged, as it was made to the vice president, bookkeeper and night clerk, all of whom had an interest in the subject matter in question); Hearn v. Ostrander, 194 N.C. 753, 140 S.E. 724, 725 (1927) (superintendent's statement that plaintiff had stolen company property was subject to a qualified privilege because the superintendent made the statement while conducting a company investigation); Elmore v. Atlantic Coast Line R. Co., 189 N.C. 658, 127 S.E. 710, 714 (1925) (statements by railroad superintendent to a co-conspirator employee accusing plaintiff of theft were subject to a qualified privilege); Kinesis Adver., Inc. v. Hill, 187 N.C. App. 1, 652 S.E.2d 284 (2007), rev. denied, 362 N.C. 177, 658 S.E.2d 485 (2008) (holding that statements alleging plaintiff stole millions of dollars from his employer were subject to a qualified privilege, given that they were made in the course of an internal investigation/ inventory of assets); Coremin v. Sherrill Furniture Co., 170 N.C. App. 697, 614 S.E.2d 607, rev. denied, 360 N.C. 62, 621 S.E.2d 178 (2005) (corporate vice president's statements made during the course of an investigation into sexual harassment allegations held subject to a qualified privilege); Smith-Price v. Charter Behavioral Health Sys., 164 N.C. App. 349, 595 S.E.2d 778 (2004) (holding that employee had "a legitimate interest in reporting any incidents of improper sexual advances or conduct to plaintiff's supervisor" that provides a qualified privilege if exercised in good faith); Shreve v. Duke Power Co., 97 N.C. App. 648, 389 S.E.2d 444, rev. denied, 326 N.C. 598, 393 S.E.2d 883 (1990) (after a supervisor had reported that plaintiff threatened him, management's internal discussions regarding such accusations were subject to a qualified privilege). Cf. Jacobs v. Mallard Creek Presbyterian Church, Inc., 214 F. Supp.2d 552 (W.D. N.C. 2002) (holding that civil court claims for, among other things, state slander, defamation and invasion of privacy related to a church's investigation and discipline of the pastor's conduct and the Permanent Judicial Committee of the Presbytery's ruling with respect thereto are barred by the Free Exercise and Establishment Clauses of the United States Constitution). But see Schult v. Int'l Bus. Mach. Corp., 123 Fed.Appx. 540 (4th Cir. 2004) (holding that a public policy exception to the state's employment at-will doctrine did not extend to an employer's conduct in allegedly asking an employee to lie during the course of a private, internal harassment investigation).

IV. OTHER ACTIONS BASED ON STATEMENTS

A. Negligent Hiring, Retention, and Supervision

North Carolina recognizes a tort claim for an employer's negligent hiring of employees where the plaintiff can prove: (1) the specific negligent act on which the action is founded; (2) incompetence by inherent unfitness or previous specified acts of negligence, from which incompetence can be inferred; (3) either actual notice to the employer of such unfitness or constructive notice, by showing that the employer could have known the relevant facts had it used ordinary care in oversight and supervision; and (4) that the injury to the plaintiff resulted from such incompetence. See Medlin v. Bass, 327 N.C. 587, 398 S.E.2d 460 (1990); Stanley v. Brooks, 112 N.C. App. 609, 436 S.E.2d 272 (1993), rev. denied, 335 N.C. 772, 442 S.E.2d 521 (1994). Actions for negligent retention/supervision have likewise been recognized in North Carolina where a plaintiff can prove the general elements of a claim for negligent hiring, except that the focus of inquiry will be on information obtained by the employer after an employee is hired, not before. See, e.g., Braswell v. Braswell, 330 N.C. 363, 410 S.E.2d 897 (1991); Smith v. Privette, 128 N.C. App. 490, 495 S.E.2d 395, app. dismissed, 348 N.C. 284, 501 S.E.2d 913 (1998); B.B. Walker Co. v. Burns Int'l Sec. Services, Inc., 108 N.C. App. 562, 424 S.E.2d 172, rev. denied, 333 N.C. 536, 429 S.E.2d 552 (1993). North Carolina courts have also allowed plaintiffs to assert negligent retention/supervision claims along with separate claims for defamation. See, e.g., Carter v. Rockingham County Bd. of Educ., 158 N.C. App. 687, 582 S.E.2d 69 (2003); Barker v. Kimberly-Clark Corp., 136 N.C. App. 455, 524 S.E.2d 821 (2000); Houpe v. The City of Statesville, 128 N.C. App. 334, 497 S.E.2d 82, rev. denied, 348 N.C. 72, 505 S.E.2d 871 (1998); Shillington v. K-Mart Corp., 102 N.C. App. 187, 402 S.E.2d 155 (1991).

B. Intentional Infliction of Emotional Distress

Individuals may assert an action under North Carolina law for intentional infliction of emotional distress where a plaintiff can demonstrate: (1) extreme and outrageous conduct, (2) that is intended to cause and does cause, (3) severe emotional distress or reckless indifference to the likelihood that the conduct will cause such distress. See Dickens v. Puryear, 302 N.C. 437, 276 S.E.2d 325 (1981). The conduct in question, however, must be "so outrageous in character, and so extreme in degree, as to go beyond all possible bounds of decency, and to be regarded as atrocious, and utterly intolerable in a civilized community." Hardin v. Champion Int'l. Corp., 685 F. Supp. 527, 531 (W.D. N.C. 1987). In addition, liability for intentional infliction claims generally "does not extend to mere insults, indignities [or] threats . . . . [t]here is no occasion for the law to intervene in every case where someone's feelings are hurt." Hogan v. Forsyth Country Club, 79 N.C. App. 483, 340 S.E.2d 116, rev. denied, 317 N.C. 334, 346 S.E.2d 140 and 346 S.E.2d 141 (1986). See also Mbadiwe v. Union Mem'l Reg'l Med. Ctr, Inc., 2005 WL 3186949 (W.D. N.C. Nov. 28, 2005) (holding that defendants' consultation and/or decision regarding the restriction of plaintiff's medical privileges and statements that plaintiff's "patients do not understand that another physician is actually providing the care" and "my staff and I feel that this is dishonest" are insufficiently extreme or outrageous to support a claim for intentional infliction of emotional distress); Swaim v. Westchester Academy, Inc., 208 F. Supp.2d 579 (M.D. N.C. 2002) , aff'd, 60 Fed. Appx. 944, 2003 WL 1908821 (4th Cir. 2003) (alleged unjustified work-related criticism of an employee by her supervisor was not sufficiently extreme and outrageous to support a claim for intentional infliction of emotional distress); Binkley v. Loughran, 714 F. Supp. 768 (M.D. N.C. 1988), cert. denied, 714 F.

Supp. 774 (1989), aff'd, 940 F.2d 651 (4th Cir. 1991) (plaintiff's intentional infliction of emotional distress claim based on her employer's publication to co-workers of true but embarrassing facts about her treatment by a psychiatrist was preempted by the federal Labor Management Relations Act); Dobson v. Harris, 134 N.C. App. 573, 521 S.E.2d 710 (1999), rev'd on other grounds, 352 N.C. 77, 530 S.E.2d 829 (2000) (store employee's statements to the local Department of Social Services regarding a customer's suspected child abuse, even if exaggerated or fabricated, do not constitute "extreme and outrageous conduct which is utterly intolerable in a civilized community"); Ausley v. Bishop, 133 N.C. App. 210, 515 S.E.2d 72 (1999) (Ausley I), vacated in part and rev'd in part on other grounds after remand, 150 N.C. App. 56, 564 S.E.2d 252 (Ausley II), rev'd, 356 N.C. 422, 572 S.E.2d 153 (2002), reh'g denied, 356 N.C. 696, 577 S.E.2d 109 (2003) (statements to former employee's mortgage lender that the employer suspected the employee had taken client files, that the employer had called the police, and implying that the employee had committed loan fraud were insufficient to support an intentional infliction of emotional distress claim); Shillington v. K-Mart Corp., 102 N.C. App. 187, 402 S.E.2d 155 (1991) (a security guard's statement to police that plaintiff had trespassed on store property to loot merchandise did not reach the level of "being extreme and outrageous" given, among other things, the fact that the event occurred during a state of emergency following a tornado); Troxler v. Charter Mandala Ctr., Inc., 89 N.C. App. 268, 365 S.E.2d 665, 668, rev. denied, 322 N.C. 838, 371 S.E.2d 284 (1988) (holding that an employee's statement that plaintiff had engaged in sexual relations with a minor patient was made for malicious purposes outside the scope of his employment, thereby precluding plaintiff from recovering for intentional infliction of emotional distress).

C. Interference with Economic Advantage

A plaintiff may assert a claim for tortious interference with contract under North Carolina law where an individual, without legal justification, knowingly and intentionally causes or induces one party to a contract to breach that contract and thereby causes damage to the other contracting party. See, e.g., Carolina Overall Corp. v. East Carolina Linen Supply, Inc., 8 N.C. App. 528, 174 S.E.2d 659 (1970). A plaintiff must show that: (1) a valid contract existed between plaintiff and a third-party, (2) the defendant outsider to the contract had knowledge of the contract, (3) the defendant intentionally induced the third-party not to perform the contract, (4) the defendant acted without justification, and (5) the plaintiff suffered actual damages as a result. Rhodes, Inc. v. Morrow, 937 F. Supp. 1202 (M.D. N.C. 1996); Sides v. Duke Univ., 74 N.C. App. 331, 346, 328 S.E.2d 818, 828, rev. denied, 314 N.C. 331, 333 S.E.2d 490 (1985), overruled on other grounds, 347 N.C. 329, 493 S.E.2d 420 (1997). Employers are covered by a qualified privilege to interfere with employment contracts so long as the motives for doing so are related to a business interest in the contract. See Riley v. Dowd Corning Corp., 767 F. Supp. 735, 738 (M.D. N.C. 1991), recon. denied, 876 F. Supp 728 (M.D. N.C. 1992), aff'd, 986 F.2d 1414 (4th Cir. 1993); Lenzer v. Flaherty, 106 N.C. App. 496, 513, 418 S.E.2d 276, 286, rev. denied, 332 N.C. 345, 421 S.E.2d 348 (1992). North Carolina courts have, however, held that tortious interference with contractual rights is a common law wrong and may constitute a claim for relief in addition to an action for libel or slander where defamatory statements are the alleged means of interference. See, e.g., Coremin v. Sherrill Furniture Co., 170 N.C. App. 697, 614 S.E.2d 607, 2005 WL 1330966, rev. denied, 360 N.C. 62, 621 S.E.2d 178 (2005); Bloch v. Paul Revere Life Ins. Co., 143 N.C. App. 228, 547 S.E.2d 51 (2001), rev. denied, 354 N.C. 67, 553 S.E.2d 35 (2001); Barker v. Kimberly-Clark Corp., 136 N.C. App. 455, 524 S.E.2d 821 (2000); Varner v. Bryan, 113 N.C. App. 697, 440 S.E.2d 295 (1994); Friel v. Angell Care, Inc., 113 N.C. App. 505, 440 S.E.2d 111 (1994); Kwan-Sa You v. Roe, 97 N.C. App. 1, 9-10, 387 S.E.2d 188, 192 (1990); Angel v. Ward, 43 N.C. App. 288, 258 S.E.2d 788, 792 (1979); Presnell v. Pell, 39 N.C. App. 538, 251 S.E.2d 692, 695, aff'd in part and rev'd in part on other grounds, 298 N.C. 715, 260 S.E.2d 611 (1979). But see Joiner v. Revco Discount Drug Ctr., Inc., 467 F. Supp.2d 508 (W.D. N.C. 2006) (holding that employer's report to consumer reporting agency and potential employers did not constitute tortious interference with employee's prospective economic advantage, where employer gained no advantage by filing the report, had not intent to injure employee and had a legitimate justification in reporting employee information to the agency); Braswell v. Haywood Reg'l Med. Ctr., 352 F. Supp.2d 639 (W.D. N.C. 2005) (holding that a defendant hospital's failure to send a physician's records to another hospital as part of recredentialing did not give rise to a claim for tortious interference with contract where the plaintiff refused to sign a release of claims related to the records transmission and the defendant had no affirmative duty to forward the materials).

North Carolina common law also recognizes a claim for tortious interference with a prospective advantage. See, e.g., Johnson v. Gray, 263 N.C. 507, 509, 139 S.E.2d 551, 552-53 (1965) (holding that "[w]e think the general rule prevails that unlawful interference with the freedom of contract is actionable, whether it consists in maliciously procuring breach of a contract, or in preventing the making of a contract when this is done, not in the legitimate exercise of the defendant's own rights, but with design to injure the plaintiff, or gaining some advantage at his expense. . . . Maliciously inducing a person not to enter into a contract with another, which he would otherwise have entered into, is actionable if damage results"). See also Owens v. Pepsi Cola Bottling Co., 330 N.C. 666, 412 S.E.2d 636 (1992); Bohannon v. Wachovia Bank & Trust Co., 210 N.C. 679, 188 S.E. 390 (1936); Spartan Equip. Co. v. Air Placement Equip. Co., 263 N.C. 549, 559, 140 S.E.2d 3, 11 (1965).

D. Prima Facie Tort

North Carolina has not recognized a cause of action for "prima facie tort" claims. See Beasley v. Nat'l Savings Life Ins. Co., 75 N.C. App. 104, 330 S.E.2d 207 (1985), rev. dismissed, 316 N.C. 372, 341 S.E.2d 338 (1986); Von Hagel v. Blue Cross and Blue Shield, 91 N.C. App. 58, 370 S.E.2d 695 (1988).

V. OTHER ISSUES

A. Statute of Limitations

N.C. Gen. Stat. § 1-54(3) (2012) imposes a one-year statute of limitations for libel and slander. The statute begins to run at the date of publication, regardless of when damage results or the identity of the author is discovered, Williams v. Rutherford Freight Lines, 10 N.C. App. 384, 179 S.E.2d 319 (1971); Price v. J.C. Penney Co., 26 N.C. App. 249, 216 S.E.2d 154, rev. denied, 288 N.C. 243, 217 S.E.2d 666 (1975), and regardless of when plaintiff discovers that the defamatory statement was made, Gibson v. Mut. Life Ins. Co. of New York, 121 N.C. App. 284, 465 S.E.2d 56 (1996). Each act of defamation is a separate tort that, in most instances, a plaintiff must specifically allege. English Boiler & Tube, Inc. v. W. C. Rouse & Son, Inc., 172 F.3d 862 (4th Cir. 1999) (holding that because plaintiff failed to mention a second letter in its original complaint or even allege a separate defamatory publication, the second letter did not arise out of the same "conduct, transaction or occurrence described in the original complaint" and, therefore, did not relate back to the original complaint for statute of limitations purposes). Moreover, a "[p]laintiff's own reiteration of slanderous comments" does not extend the statute of limitations. Arbia v. Owens-Illinois, Inc., 2004 WL 1345091 (M.D. N.C. June 4, 2004), aff'd, 124 Fed.Appx 202 (4th Cir. 2005). There are no North Carolina cases addressing the "single instance" publication rule.

B. Jurisdiction

A statement about a North Carolina resident made by an out-of-state defendant who was not otherwise subject to jurisdiction in North Carolina does not confer jurisdiction over defendant. Bullard v. USAir, Inc., 114 N.C. App. 791, 443 S.E.2d 80 (1994).

C. Worker's Compensation Exclusivity

The North Carolina Workers' Compensation Act generally provides the exclusive remedy for claims arising out of workplace injuries. See N.C. Gen. Stat. § 97-10.1 (2012). See also Regan v. Amerimark Bldg. Prods., Inc., 118 N.C. App. 328, 454 S.E.2d 849, rev. denied, 340 N.C. 59, 458 S.E.2d 189 (1995), cert. denied, 342 N.C. 659, 467 S.E.2d 72 (1996); Andrews v. Peters, 55 N.C. App. 124, 284 S.E.2d 748 (1981), rev. denied, 305 N.C. 395, 290 S.E.2d 364 (1982). However, North Carolina courts have held that the Act does not bar a common law action by an employee against his employer "for the intentional conduct of the employer." Hogan v. Forsyth Country Club Co., 79 N.C. App. 483, 40 S.E.2d 116, rev. denied, 317 N.C. 334, 346 S.E.2d 140 (1986) (denying defendant's assertion that N.C. Gen. Stat. § 97-10.1 barred plaintiff's claim for intentional infliction of emotional distress). North Carolina courts have also carved out two additional exceptions. In Pleasant, the court held that an injured employee may pursue a civil action against a *co-employee* on the basis of willful, wanton and reckless negligence. Pleasant v. Johnson, 312 N.C. 710, 325 S.E.2d 244 (1985). In Woodson, the court held that an injured employee may sue an *employer* for damages when the employer "intentionally engages in misconduct knowing it is substantially certain to cause serious injury or death to employees." Woodson v. Rowland, 329 N.C. 330, 407 S.E.2d 222 (1991). This last exception has been held to apply "only in the most egregious cases of employer misconduct." Whitaker v. Town of Scotland Neck, 357 N.C. 552, 597 S.E.2d 665 (2003). However, the federal District Court for the Middle District of North Carolina has applied and extended the ruling in Hogan to hold that N.C. Gen. Stat. § 97-10.1 does not bar claims against an employer for negligent infliction of emotional distress. See Strickland v. Jewell, 562 F. Supp.2d 661 (M.D. N.C. 2007); Ridenhour v. Concord Screen Printers, Inc., 40 F. Supp.2d 744 (M.D. N.C. 1999).

No known North Carolina ruling exists regarding the application of the Workers' Compensation exclusivity rule with respect to state claims of libel or slander.

D. Pleading Requirements

The defamatory words attributed to the defendant must be alleged substantially in haec verba, or with sufficient particularity to enable the court to determine whether the statement was defamatory. They need not be pled verbatim. Stutts v. Duke Power Co., 47 N.C. App. 76, 266 S.E.2d 861 (1980). See also N.C. Gen. Stat. § 1A-1, Rule 9(i) (2012), which provides that libel and slander must be specially pled. Recent decisions, however, have held that this heightened pleading standard does not apply in federal court, where defamation cases fall under the liberal pleading requirement of Fed. R. Civ. P. 8(a) and require only a short and plain statement showing that the pleader is entitled to relief. Moore v. Cox, 341 F. Supp.2d 570 (M.D. N.C. 2004); Eli Research, Inc. v. United Communications Group, LLC, 312 F. Supp.2d 748 (M.D. N.C. 2004);

North Carolina Motorcoach Ass'n v. North Carolina State Bd. of Educ., 2003 WL 23713733 *6 (E.D. N.C. April 17, 2003), aff'd, 103 Fed.Appx 481 (4th Cir. 2004); Martin v. Boyce, 2000 WL 1264148 *8-9 (M.D. N.C. July 20, 2000). But see **Mayfield v. Nat'l Assoc. for Stock Car Auto Racing, Inc., 674 F.3d 369 (4th Cir. 2012) (upholding the dismissal of a NASCAR driver's defamation claim, noting that conclusory allegations of malice that are "a mere recitation of the legal standard" are insufficient to state a defamation claim); Russell v. Merrill Lynch, Inc., 2011 WL 6742506 (M.D. N.C. Dec. 22, 2011) (granting the employer's motion to dismiss plaintiff's defamation claims regarding a statement that plaintiff was fired for failing to meet performance standards, "because there is no plausible allegation of falsity");** Esancy v. Quinn, 2006 WL 322607 (W.D. N.C. February 10, 2006) (dismissing plaintiff's defamation claim for, among other things, plaintiff's failure sufficiently to plead "the time and place of the alleged defamatory communication"); Mbadiwe v. Union Mem'l Reg'l Med. Ctr. Inc., 2005 WL 3186949 (W.D. N.C. Nov. 28, 2005) (general allegations regarding statements made to a medical executive committee and other individuals "that plaintiff was engaged in dishonesty tantamount to defrauding patients" held inadequate to state a claim for defamation given the lack of particularity); Carter v. Duke Medical Ctr., 1995 U.S. Dist. LEXIS 16145 (M.D. N.C. 1995) (holding that while allegedly defamatory words need not be pleaded verbatim, they must be alleged "'substantially' in haec verba"). Moreover, a former employee's "bare bones assertion that he is suing for slander" which contains "no factual allegations at all – no indication of the date of the. . .slander. . .or what the alleged slanderous statements were" is insufficient to state a claim. Franklin v. Wiggins, 179 N.C. App. 434, 634 S.E.2d 273, 2006 WL 2528010 (2006). See also Sturdivant v. Kone, Inc., 2010 WL 2723729 (W.D. N.C. July 8, 2010) (dismissing plaintiff's claim regarding alleged defamatory statements made about his violation of company policy, where plaintiff failed to provide evidence other than his own pleadings and deposition testimony); Iannucci v. Mission Hosp., 2008 WL 5220641 (W.D. N.C. Dec. 11, 2008) (holding that an allegation that an employer created an environment that included "libel + slander" does not satisfy even the requirements of notice pleading); Reid Pointe, LLC v. Stevens, 2008 NCBC 15, 2008 WL 3846174 (N.C. Super. Aug. 18, 2008) (holding that the plaintiff must plead the time and place of an alleged defamatory statement, such that assertions that a party "communicated unfavorably" with regulators and "undermined the confidence of service providers" fail to state a claim).

SURVEY OF NORTH CAROLINA EMPLOYMENT PRIVACY LAW

Brian D. Barger and Jonathan E. Buchan
McGuireWoods LLP
201 North Tryon Street, Suite 3000
P.O. Box 31247 (Zip 28231)
Charlotte, North Carolina 28202
Telephone: (704) 343-2000; Facsimile: (704) 343-2300
E-mail: bbarger@mcguirewoods.com; jbuchan@mcguirewoods.com

(With Developments Reported Through **November 1, 2012**)

GENERAL COMMENTS

North Carolina courts have limited common law actions for "invasion of privacy" to two categories of claims: (1) commercial misappropriation of another's likeness, and (2) intrusion into the seclusion of another. However, as outlined below, North Carolina does provide a number of statutory and other common law protections to employees that govern the extent to which employers may monitor, collect and utilize information about employees.

SIGNIFICANT DEVELOPMENTS SINCE THE 2012 *SURVEY*

None.

I. GENERAL LAW OF PRIVACY

A. Legal Basis of Privacy Claims

Although North Carolina has long recognized a common law cause of action for commercial misappropriation of another's likeness, it has expressly rejected the expansion of its invasion of privacy jurisprudence by declining to recognize common law claims of false light or invasion of privacy by the publication of true but embarrassing facts. It was not until 1996 that North Carolina expressly recognized the common law tort of invasion of privacy by intrusion into the seclusion of another. North Carolina courts have, however, held that the North Carolina Constitution does provide protection against invasions of privacy. See ACT-UP Triangle v. Comm'n for Health Services, 345 N.C. 699, 483 S.E.2d 388 (1997); Treants Enter., Inc. v. Onslow County, 83 N.C. App. 345, 350 S.E.2d 365 (1986), aff'd, 320 N.C. 776, 360 S.E.2d 783 (1987).

B. Causes of Action

1. ***Misappropriation/Right of Publicity.*** North Carolina recognizes a common law cause of action for the unauthorized use of one's likeness or photograph in an advertisement or for other commercial purpose. Flake v. Greensboro News, 212 N.C. 780, 195 S.E. 55 (1937). The North Carolina Supreme Court in Flake held that a plaintiff may establish a prima facie cause of action for invasion of privacy/misappropriation by presenting evidence of the use in an advertisement of plaintiff's likeness without consent, thereby entitling plaintiff to nominal damages and injunctive relief without the necessity of proving special damages. In Barr v. Southern Bell Telephone & Telegraph Co., 13 N.C. App. 388, 185 S.E.2d 714 (1972), the North Carolina Court of Appeals recognized a cause of action where defendant had mistakenly published the photograph of a stranger identified as plaintiff. But see Merritt, Flebotte, Wilson, Webb & Caruso, PLLC v. Hemmings, 196 N.C. App. 600, 676 S.E.2d 79 (2009) (holding that the continued existence of an html code on a third-party server that could be used to retrieve former employees' biographies and images through general search engines did not constitute misappropriation, where the employer otherwise removed links to the defendants from its website and deleted other web references under its control).

2. ***False Light.*** North Carolina has expressly declined to recognize a common law cause of action for false light invasion of privacy. Renwick v. News & Observer, 310 N.C. 312, 312 S.E.2d 405, 10 Media L. Rep. 1443, cert. denied, 469 U.S. 858, 105 S. Ct. 187, 83 L. Ed. 2d 121 (1984). The Supreme Court reasoned that a cause of action for "false light" invasion of privacy duplicated other common law actions recognized in North Carolina such as libel and intentional infliction of emotional distress. See also Curry v. Philip Morris USA, Inc., 2010 WL 431692 (W.D. N.C. Feb. 4, 2010) (dismissing invasion of privacy claim focused on the "negative message" that allegedly arose out of a search of the employee's car, holding that any such connotation is "irrelevant. . .as North Carolina does not recognize a tort for invasion of privacy through portrayal in a false light); Sabrowski v. Albani-Bayeux, Inc., 2003 WL 23018827 (M.D. N.C. Dec. 19, 2003).

3. ***Publication of Private Facts.*** North Carolina has expressly declined to recognize a cause of action for invasion of privacy by publication of truthful but embarrassing information. Bradley v. Ramsey, 329 F. Supp.2d 617 (W.D. N.C. 2004); Sabrowski v. Albani-Bayeux, Inc., supra; French v. U.S. Dept. of Human Health and Human Service, 55

F. Supp.2d 379 (W.D. N.C. 1999); Hall v. Salisbury Post, 323 N.C. 259, 372 S.E.2d 711, 15 Media L. Rep. 2329 (1988). See also **Benzing v. Tharrington Smith, 2012 WL 169946 (E.D. N.C. Jan. 19, 2012) (holding that publication of information inappropriately obtained through a consumer credit report cannot support a claim for "distribution of non-public information," slander and defamation, as "North Carolina does not recognize a claim for invasion of privacy by publication of true but private facts");** Alexander v. City of Greensboro, 762 F.Supp.2d 764 (M.D. N.C. 2011) (holding that disclosure of settlement information regarding plaintiffs, even if derived in part from plaintiffs' personnel files, did not constitute intrusion, where defendant properly received the information and there was no allegation that defendant "improperly ascertained the amount of the City's settlement offer" or other details); McFadyen v. Duke Univ., 786 F.Supp.2d 887, 2011 WL 1260207 (M.D. N.C. 2011) (holding that a university employee's disclosure of student financial and educational records and violation of FERPA "does not create a state tort claim for invasion of privacy"); Fisher v. Communication Workers of Am., 2008 WL 4754850 (N.C. Super. Oct. 30, 2008) (dismissing plaintiffs' claims involving the publication of employee Social Security numbers, in part, on the grounds that North Carolina courts "have not recognized a cause of action for invasion of privacy by public disclosure of private facts"). Cf. Fisher v. Communication Workers of America, __ N.C. App. __, 716 S.E.2d 396, 2011 WL 3569964 (2011); rev. denied, __ N.C. __, 721 S.E.2d 231 (2012) (dismissing non-union employee's invasion of privacy action again union for posting of the employees' social security numbers on a workplace bulletin board as preempted by the NLRA).

4. ***Intrusion.*** North Carolina has expressly recognized the common law cause of action of intrusion upon the seclusion or solitude of another. Miller v. Brooks, 123 N.C. App. 20, 472 S.E.2d 350 (1996), rev. denied, 345 N.C. 344, 483 S.E.2d 172 (1997). The court held that such intrusion upon the seclusion of another would be actionable if the intrusion would be highly offensive to a reasonable person. In Miller, plaintiff presented evidence that his estranged wife, or her agents, had placed a hidden video camera in his home that recorded him undressing and showering. Plaintiff also presented evidence that defendants had intercepted and opened some of his mail. See also Jennings v. Univ. of North Carolina, 444 F.3d 255 (4th Cir. 2006), cert. denied, 552 U.S. 887, 128 S. Ct. 247, 169 L. Ed. 2d 147 (2007) (applying North Carolina law to hold that a coach's two isolated inquiries into an athlete's dating relationships did not rise to the level of egregious conduct sufficient to support a claim for intrusion); Bradley v. Ramsey, 329 F. Supp.2d 617 (W.D. N.C. 2004) (applying North Carolina law to hold that a former police chief stated a claim for unlawful intrusion where his supervisor sought and obtained a confidential letter that revealed the chief's alternative sexual lifestyle and used it to blackmail the chief and cover up the supervisor's own corrupt practices); French v. U.S. Dept. of Human Health and Human Service, 55 F. Supp.2d 379 (W.D. N.C. 1999) (applying North Carolina law to hold that a former employer's unauthorized disclosure of confidential medical records to a tribal officer in order to prevent the employee's reinstatement is sufficient to state a claim for intrusion); Toomer v. Garrett, 155 N.C. App. 462, 574 S.E.2d 76 (2002), rev. denied, 357 N.C. 66, 579 S.E.2d 576 (2003) (holding that the alleged unauthorized disclosure of medical, financial and other private information from a former State employee's personnel file to the news media and the public is sufficient to state a claim for intrusion into seclusion); Smith v. Jack Eckerd Corp., 101 N.C. App. 566, 400 S.E.2d 99 (1991) (detention of plaintiff by a security guard who suspected her of shoplifting and searched her person with an electronic scanner held not sufficiently offensive to constitute invasion of privacy by intrusion). Cf. Sabrowski v. Albani-Bayeux, Inc., 124 Fed.Appx. 159 (4th Cir. 2005) (holding that although the disclosure of an individual's private personnel files and medical records would amount to a per se intrusion if the records contained sensitive materials, there was no such disclosure); Sherman v. Univ. of North Carolina at Wilmington, 2008 WL 4461911 (E.D. N.C. Aug. 13, 2008) (magistrate recommending dismissal of plaintiff's intrusion claim, where alleged unauthorized disclosure of false and misleading statements concerning tenured employment, suspension and termination did not rise to level of conduct that would be highly offensive to a reasonable person), aff'd in relevant part, 2008 WL 4461935 (E.D.N.C. Sept. 30, 2008); Burgess v. Eforce Media, Inc., 2007 WL 3355369 (W.D. N.C. Nov. 9, 2007) (dismissing plaintiff's intrusion claims involving placement of viruses on a computer that redirected internet searches, holding that "frustration of purpose is not an invasion of privacy); Fisher v. Communication Workers of Am., 2008 WL 4754850 (N.C. Super. Oct. 30, 2008) (distinguishing Toomer v. Garrett to hold that the public disclosure of Social Security numbers may violate the North Carolina Identity Theft Protection Act but "is not the type of 'intentional intrusion, physically or otherwise' necessary to state a claim for invasion of privacy by intrusion into seclusion"); Broughton v. McClatchy Newspapers, Inc., 161 N.C. App. 20, 588 S.E.2d 20, 32 Med.L.Rep. 1313 (2003) (holding that "[g]enerally, there must be a physical or sensory intrusion or an unauthorized prying into confidential personal records to support a claim for invasion of privacy by intrusion").

C. Other Privacy-Related Actions

1. ***Intentional Infliction of Emotional Distress.*** Individuals may assert an action under North Carolina law for intentional infliction of emotional distress where a plaintiff can demonstrate: (1) extreme and outrageous conduct, (2) that is intended to cause and does cause, (3) severe emotional distress or reckless indifference to the likelihood that the conduct will cause such distress. See Dickens v. Puryear, 302 N.C. 437, 276 S.E.2d 325 (1981). The conduct in question must be "so outrageous in character, and so extreme in degree, as to go beyond all possible bounds of decency, and to be regarded as atrocious, and utterly intolerable in a civilized community." Hardin v. Champion Int'l. Corp., 685 F. Supp.

527, 531 (W.D. N.C. 1987). In addition, liability for intentional infliction claims generally "does not extend to mere insults, indignities, threats . . . There is no occasion for the law to intervene in every case where some one's feelings are hurt." Hogan v. Forsyth Country Club, 79 N.C. App. 483, 493, 340 S.E.2d 116, 123, rev. denied, 317 N.C. 334, 346 S.E.2d 140 and 346 S.E.2d 141 (1986).

See also Hooper v. North Carolina, 379 F. Supp.2d 804 (M.D. N.C. 2005) (holding that defendants' alleged actions in, among other things, unlawfully wiretapping and surveilling a state employee was sufficient to state a claim for intentional infliction of emotional distress); Sabrowski v. Albani-Bayeux, Inc., 2003 WL 23018827 (M.D. N.C. Dec. 19, 2003) (holding that employer's alleged calls to plaintiff's sister and "probing and intrusive questions" concerning plaintiff's mental health and alleged use of illegal drugs does not rise to the level of extreme and outrageous conduct sufficient to support an intentional infliction of emotional distress claim); Haburjak v. Prudential Bache Securities, 759 F. Supp. 293 (M.D. N.C. 1991) (holding that even an unlawful discharge does not in and of itself amount to "outrageous conduct"); Binkley v. Loughran, 714 F. Supp. 768 (M.D. N.C. 1988), cert. denied, 714 F. Supp. 774 (1989), aff'd, 940 F.2d 651 (4th Cir. 1991) (holding that plaintiff's intentional infliction of emotional distress claim based on her employer's publication of true but embarrassing facts about her treatment by a psychiatrist to co-workers was preempted by the federal Labor Management Relations Act); Arledge v. Peoples Services, Inc., 2002 WL 1591690 (N.C. Gen. Ct. April 18, 2002) (holding that the termination of an employee because of his status as a transsexuals does not rise to the level of "extreme and outrageous" conduct necessary to support an intentional infliction of emotional distress claim); Troxler v. Charter Mandala Ctr., Inc., 89 N.C. App. 268, 365 S.E.2d 665, 668, rev. denied, 322 N.C. 838, 371 S.E.2d 284 (1988) (holding that an employee's statement that plaintiff had engaged in sexual relations with a minor patient was made for malicious purposes outside the scope of his employment, thereby precluding plaintiff from recovering for intentional infliction of emotional distress). Cf. French v. U.S. Dept. of Human Health and Human Service, 55 F. Supp.2d 379 (W.D. N.C. 1999) (applying North Carolina law to hold that a former employer's unauthorized disclosure of confidential medical records to a tribal officer in order to prevent the employee's reinstatement is sufficient to state a claim for intentional infliction of emotional distress); Miller v. Brooks, 123 N.C. App. 20, 472 S.E.2d 350 (1996), rev. denied, 345 N.C. 344, 483 S.E.2d 172 (1997) (holding that a husband could pursue an intrusion, trespass and intentional infliction of emotional distress claim against his estranged wife based on the videotaping of plaintiff in his bedroom and opening/sorting through his personal mail); Woodruff v. Miller, 64 N.C. App. 364, 307 S.E.2d 176 (1983) (reversing the trial court's judgment notwithstanding the verdict where plaintiff was awarded $20,000 in damages for circulation of plaintiff's criminal record from the Clerk of Court among plaintiff's acquaintances).

2. ***Interference With Prospective Economic Advantage.*** A plaintiff may assert a claim for tortious interference with contract under North Carolina law where an individual, without legal justification, knowingly and intentionally causes or induces one party to a contract to breach that contract and thereby causes damage to the other contracting party. See, e.g., Carolina Overall Corp. v. East Carolina Linen Supply, Inc., 8 N.C. App. 528, 174 S.E.2d 659 (1970). A plaintiff must show that: (1) a valid contract existed between plaintiff and a third-party, (2) the defendant outsider to the contract had knowledge of the contract, (3) the defendant intentionally induced the third-party not to perform the contract, (4) the defendant acted without justification, and (5) the plaintiff suffered actual damages as a result. Rhodes, Inc. v. Morrow, 937 F. Supp. 1202 (M.D. N.C. 1996); Sides v. Duke Univ., 74 N.C. App. 331, 346, 328 S.E.2d 818, 828, rev. denied, 314 N.C. 331, 333 S.E.2d 490 (1985), overruled on other grounds, 347 N.C. 329, 493 S.E.2d 420 (1997). Employers are protected by a qualified privilege to interfere with employment contracts so long as the motives for such action are related to a business interest in the contract. See Riley v. Dow Corning Corp., 767 F. Supp. 735, 738 (M.D. N.C. 1991), aff'd, 986 F.2d 1414 (4th Cir 1993); Lenzer v. Flaherty, 106 N.C. App. 496, 513, 418 S.E.2d 276, 286, rev. denied, 332 N.C. 345, 421 S.E.2d 348 (1992). North Carolina courts have, however, allowed plaintiffs to assert claims for tortious interference with contractual rights in addition to claims for intrusion/violation of state confidentiality requirements. See, e.g., Houpe v. City of Statesville, 128 N.C. App. 334, 497 S.E.2d 82, rev. denied, 348 N.C. 72, 505 S.E.2d 871 (1998); Cameron v. New Hanover Mem. Hosp., 58 N.C. App. 414, 293 S.E.2d 901 (1982). Cf. Combs & Assocs., Inc. v. Kennedy, 147 N.C. App. 362, 555 S.E.2d 634 (2001). But see Braswell v. Haywood Reg'l Med. Ctr., 352 F. Supp.2d 639 (W.D. N.C. 2005) (holding that a defendant hospital's failure to send a physician's records to another hospital as part of recredentialing did not give rise to a claim for tortious interference with contract where the plaintiff refused to sign a release of claims related to the records transmission and the defendant had no affirmative duty to forward the materials).

North Carolina common law also recognizes a claim for tortious interference with prospective advantage. See, e.g., Johnson v. Gray, 263 N.C. 507, 509, 139 S.E.2d 551, 552-53 (1965) (holding that "[w]e think the general rule prevails that unlawful interference with the freedom of contract is actionable, whether it consists in maliciously procuring breach of a contract, or in preventing the making of a contract when this is done, not in the legitimate exercise of the defendant's own rights, but with design to injure the plaintiff, or gaining some advantage at his expense . . . . Maliciously inducing a person not to enter into a contract with another, which he would otherwise have entered into, is actionable if damage results"). See also Owens v. Pepsi Cola Bottling Co., 330 N.C. 666, 412 S.E.2d 636 (1992); Bohannon v. Wachovia Bank & Trust Co., 210 N.C. 679, 188 S.E. 390 (1936); Spartan Equip. Co. v. Air Placement Equip. Co., 263 N.C. 549, 559, 140 S.E.2d 3, 11 (1965).

3. ***Prima Facie Tort.*** North Carolina has not recognized a cause of action for "prima facie tort" claims. See Beasley v. Nat'l Savings Life Ins. Co., 75 N.C. App. 104, 330 S.E.2d 207 (1985), rev. dismissed, 316 N.C. 372, 341 S.E.2d 338 (1986); Von Hagel v. Blue Cross and Blue Shield, 91 N.C. App. 58, 370 S.E.2d 695 (1988).

II. EMPLOYER TESTING OF EMPLOYEES

A. Psychological or Personality Testing

1. ***Common Law and Statutes.*** There are no North Carolina statutes or cases that specifically limit the use of psychological or personality testing in the employment context. The North Carolina Handicapped Persons Protection Act, however, provides that it is a discriminatory practice for employers with 15 or more employees "to fail to hire or consider for employment or promotion, to discharge, or otherwise to discriminate against a qualified handicapped person on the basis of a handicapping condition with respect to compensation or the terms, conditions, or privileges of employment." N.C. Gen. Stat. § 168A-5 (2012). That statute further prohibits an employer from requiring "an applicant to identify himself as handicapped prior to a conditional offer of employment; however, any employer may invite an applicant to identify himself as handicapped in order to act affirmatively on his behalf." N.C. Gen. Stat. § 168A-5(a)(4) (2012). The statute does allow employers to "make an employment decision on the basis of State and federal laws or regulations imposing physical, health, mental or psychological job requirements." N.C. Gen. Stat. § 168A-5(b)(1) (2012). The statute also allows employers to administer pre-employment tests, provided that the tests: (1) measure only job-related abilities, (2) are required of all applicants for the same position (unless limited to determining the extent of an applicant's ability to perform the duties of a job in question or potential accommodations), and (3) "accurately measure the applicant's aptitude, achievement level, or whatever factors they purport to measure rather than reflecting the handicapped person's impaired sensory, manual or speaking skills" (unless those skills are requirements for the position in question). N.C. Gen. Stat. § 168A-5(b)(8) (2012). But see Anderson v. Farr Assoc., Inc., 1997 WL 896407, p. 4 (M.D. N.C. 1997) (applying North Carolina law in denying the employer's motion to dismiss plaintiff's claim for intrusion, where plaintiff asserted that the employer "forced him to participate in group sessions and evaluations which resulted in his disclosure of deeply personal information").

The North Carolina Handicapped Persons Protection Act allows individuals to assert a private right of action for relief in the Superior Court of the county in which the unlawful act occurred or where the plaintiff or defendant resides. See N.C. Gen. Stat. § 168A-11(a) (2012). Such action must be brought within 180 days after plaintiff became aware of, or with reasonable diligence should have become aware of, the unlawful practice. N.C. Gen. Stat. § 168A-12 (2012).

2. ***Private Employers.*** See II.A.1, supra.

3. ***Public Employers.*** See II.A.1, supra.

B. Drug Testing

1. ***Common Law and Statutes.*** Under North Carolina law, public and private employers may request applicants for employment and/or employees to be tested for illegal drugs at a laboratory approved in accordance with state guidelines. See N.C. Gen. Stat. §§ 95-230 to 95-235 (2012); N.C. Admin. Code Title 13 §§ 20.0101 to 20.0602 (2012). Although the statute does not impose limitations on the use of drug tests or the circumstances when such tests may be administered, the statute does specify the procedures that must be followed both during and after testing. N.C. Gen. Stat. § 95 -232 (2012). The statute further provides that a confirmation test must be conducted if initial test results are positive (at the cost of the employer). N.C. Gen. Stat. § 95-232(c1) (2012). See also N.C. Gen. Stat. § 14-357.1 (2012). Applicants for employment and employees may also request a retest of a confirmed, positive sample at the same or another approved laboratory (at the employee's expense). See N.C. Gen. Stat. § 95-232(f) (2012).

Employers who violate the requirements of the state drug testing statute are subject to civil penalties of up to $250 per affected examinee with a maximum not to exceed $1,000 per investigation by the North Carolina Commissioner of Labor or his or her authorized representative. N.C. Gen. Stat. § 95-234 (2012). These amounts, when finally determined, may be recovered in a civil action brought by the Commissioner in state court. N.C. Gen. Stat. § 95-234(b) (2012). However, the statute does not directly authorize a private action by employees for violations of its terms. But see Garner v. Rentenbach Constructors, Inc., 350 N.C. 567, 515 S.E.2d 438 (1999) (holding that an employee's termination as a consequence of a positive drug test performed at a laboratory that was not certified as required by the state's drug testing statute did not give rise to a wrongful discharge claim where the employee failed to forecast any evidence that the employer knew or even suspected that the laboratory did not qualify as an approved lab or that his discharge "was for an unlawful reason or for a purpose that contravenes public policy").

In addition to the above, the North Carolina Handicapped Persons Protection Act, N.C. Gen. Stat. § 168A-1, et seq. (2012), prohibits discrimination by employers with 15 or more employees "against a qualified handicapped person on the basis of a handicapping condition with respect to compensation or the terms, conditions or privileges of employment." N.C. Gen. Stat. § 168A-5 (2012). The statute, however, provides that the definition of "handicapped" does not include "active alcoholism or drug addiction or abuse." N.C. Gen. Stat. § 168A-3 (2012). The statute also allows employers "to fail to hire, transfer or promote, or to discharge a handicapped person who has a history of drug abuse or who is unlawfully using drugs where the job in question is in an establishment that manufactures, distributes, dispenses, conducts research, stores, sells or otherwise handles controlled substances regulated by the North Carolina Controlled Substances Act." N.C. Gen. Stat. § 168A-5 (2012). Both of these exceptions run directly counter to federal protections provided by the Americans with Disabilities Act of 1990 (ADA) to current alcoholics or individuals with a history of alcoholism or drug abuse. See also Meyer v. Qualex, Inc., 426 F. Supp.2d 344 (E.D. N.C. 2006) (where an applicant who had been extended a conditional offer of employment that was withdrawn after a positive drug test sued the employer, alleging that the test result was caused by the applicant's taking prescription medication for a psychological condition, and asserting a claim of discrimination under the ADA).

2. ***Private Employers.*** See II.B.1, supra. In addition, in Harris v. Proctor & Gamble Mfg. Co., 102 N.C. App. 329, 401 S.E.2d 849, rev. denied, 329 N.C. 269, 407 S.E.2d 836 (1991), an employee sued Proctor & Gamble for defamation, negligence and intentional infliction of emotional distress arising from plaintiff's discharge for asserted drug use. The primary dispute in Harris began when the company interviewed several employees, including plaintiff, concerning alleged drug use at the facility, after which a meeting was held where management was told of individuals who were suspected of using drugs. The company later terminated eight individuals for drug use and advised all employees of the names of the individuals discharged and the reasons for such action. The employer argued that its communication was protected by a qualified privilege, and plaintiff countered that the company exceeded the scope of the privilege by communicating the details of his discharge to all employees. The Court of Appeals rejected plaintiff's argument, holding that plaintiff did not demonstrate actual malice or excessive publication merely by presenting evidence that the employer told all facility employees about his dismissal. See Harris v. Proctor & Gamble Mfg. Co., supra. See also Regan v. Westpoint Stevens, Inc., 139 F.3d 892, 1998 WL 112725 (4th Cir. 1998) (applying North Carolina law to hold that plaintiff's termination for failure to cooperate in the employer's request for drug testing did not constitute "wrongful discharge" in violation of North Carolina public policy); Meyer v. Qualex, Inc., 388 F. Supp.2d 630 (E.D. N.C. 2005) (holding that an employer's pre-employment illegal drug test was not a "medical examination" under the ADA and that withdrawal of a conditional offer of employment following a positive drug screen did not support an ADA or other claim, where the applicant failed to inform the employer or testing service that he was taking alleged prescription medication that could affect the test); Smith v. R.J. Reynolds Tobacco Co., 2003 WL 355646 (M.D. N.C. February 11, 2003) (holding that a drug test in and of itself does not constitute "adverse employment action" by an employer); Garner v. Rentenbach Constructors, Inc., 350 N.C. 567, 515 S.E.2d 438 (1999) (holding that an employee's termination as a consequence of a positive drug test performed at a laboratory that was not certified as required by the state's drug testing statute did not give rise to a wrongful discharge claim where the employee failed to forecast any evidence that the employer knew or even suspected that the laboratory did not qualify as an approved lab or that his discharge "was for an unlawful reason or for a purpose that contravenes public policy"); Losing v. Food Lion, L.L.C., 185 N.C. App. 278, 648 S.E.2d 261 (2007), rev. denied, 362 N.C. 236, 659 S.E.2d 735 (2008) (denying defamation claim where statements that plaintiff failed a drug test, failed to follow store policy and was fired for such were true, albeit later tests ultimately showed the results were a false positive and plaintiff was reinstated); Couch v. Bradley, 179 N.C. App. 852, 635 S.E.2d 492 (2006)(enforcing a consent and forbearance agreement against a former coworker/defendant resolving a libel action, where a defendant coworker circulated memoranda throughout campus accusing plaintiff of, among other things, using cocaine); Barker v. Kimberly-Clark Corp., 136 N.C. App. 455, 524 S.E.2d 821 (2000) (holding that alleged false statements by plaintiff's manager to other management and non-management personnel regarding, among other things, an employee's illegal drug use on company premises presented a question of fact as to whether such accusations constituted slander per se and tortious interference or were qualifiedly privileged).

3. ***Public Employers.*** See II.B.l, supra. See also Best v. Department of Health and Human Services, 149 N.C. App. 882, 563 S.E.2d 573, aff'd, 356 N.C. 430, 571 S.E.2d 586 (2002) (holding that hospital officials did not have reasonable cause to require state employees to submit to drug testing, such that the Department had no basis for terminating such employees for refusing to comply with requested testing); Hawkins v. State, 117 N.C. App. 615, 453 S.E.2d 233 (1995) (action by a state employee under §§ 1981 and 1983, the North Carolina Constitution and for intentional infliction of emotional distress arising from his discharge for refusal to submit to a urine test for drugs); Boesche v. Raleigh-Durham Airport Auth., 111 N.C. App. 149, 432 S.E.2d 137, rev. granted, 334 N.C. 687, 436 S.E.2d 370, rev. denied on reconsideration, 334 N.C. 687, 437 S.E.2d 370 (1993) (holding that the drug testing policy applied by the local airport authority did not violate Fourth Amendment search and seizure protections, as plaintiff's maintenance mechanic position was one with an overriding public safety concern); Jones v. Graham Co. Bd. Of Educ., 197 N.C. App. 279, 677 S.E.2d 171 (2009) (distinguishing Boesche and holding that employees do not have "a reduced expectation of privacy by virtue of their employment in a public school system," such that a policy requiring random, suspicionless drug and alcohol testing of *all* board of education employees violated the North Carolina Constitution's guarantee against unreasonable searches). Cf. Vanwijk v. Professional Nursing Services, Inc., __ N.C. App. __, 713 S.E.2d 766 (2011) (dismissing former police officer's

negligence action against a private party drug testing service for failure to exhaust administrative remedies, where plaintiff never filed a notice for administrative hearing regarding the underlying test and employment termination).

C. Medical Testing

1. ***Common Law and Statutes***. N.C. Gen. Stat. § 14-357.1 (2012) provides that it is unlawful for an employer with 25 or more employees to require an applicant to pay the cost of a medical examination or the cost of furnishing any records required by the employer as a condition of hiring. A recent North Carolina statute effective August 1, 1997 also provides that no person or entity may deny or refuse employment to any person or discharge any employee from employment on account of such individual's "having requested genetic testing or counseling services, or on the basis of genetic information obtained concerning the person or a member of the person's family." N.C. Gen. Stat. § 95-28.1A (2012).

The North Carolina Communicable Disease Act provides that no HIV/AIDS test may be given to employees to determine their suitability for continued employment. N.C. Gen. Stat. § 130A-148 (2012). That statute further provides that it is unlawful to discriminate against a person with the AIDS virus or HIV infection because of his or her condition in determining suitability for continued employment (unless an exception applies). N.C. Gen. Stat. § 130A-148 (2012). North Carolina law also prohibits employers and other entities from engaging in discrimination in employment because a person has a sickle cell or hemoglobin C trait. See N.C. Gen. Stat. § 95-28.1 (2012). However, although AIDS testing for job applicants is prohibited by the general provisions of the Americans with Disabilities Act of 1990 (ADA), North Carolina law expressly allows such testing. See N.C. Gen. Stat. § 130A-148(i)(1) (2012). North Carolina also does not prohibit discrimination against individuals with confirmed positive AIDS test results in hiring for employment. See N.C. Gen. Stat. § 130A-148(i)(2) (2012). See also Weston v. Carolina Medicorp, Inc., 102 N.C. App. 370, 402 S.E.2d 653, rev. denied, 330 N.C. 123, 409 S.E.2d 611 (1991) (upholding the suspension of a physician's staff privileges for failure to notify other medical personnel about the known HIV positive status of one of his patients, noting that although N.C. Gen. Stat. § 130A-143 does not "require" the release of HIV information to medical personnel, the physician violated the hospital's internal blood and body fluid isolation policy).

The North Carolina Communicable Disease Act allows individuals to assert a private right of action for relief in the Superior Court of the county in which the unlawful act occurred or where plaintiff or defendant resides. See N.C. Gen. Stat. § 130A-148(i) (2012). Such action must be brought within 180 days after plaintiff became aware of, or with reasonable diligence should have become aware of, the unlawful practice. Id.

In addition to the above, N.C. Gen. Stat. § 168A-5 (2012) provides that it is a discriminatory practice for a public or private employer with 15 or more employees to, among other things, "fail to hire or consider for employment or promotion, to discharge, or otherwise to discriminate against a qualified handicapped person on the basis of a handicapping condition with respect to compensation or the terms, conditions, or privileges of employment." That statute further prohibits an employer from requiring "an applicant to identify himself as handicapped prior to a conditional offer of employment." N.C. Gen. Stat. § 168A-5(a)(4) (2012). This statute does, however, affirmatively allow employers to: (1) "invite an applicant to identify himself as handicapped in order to act affirmatively on his behalf," (2) inquire whether a person has the ability to perform the duties of a job in question, and (3) "obtain medical information or to require or request a medical examination where such information or examination is for the purpose of establishing an employee health record." N.C. Gen. Stat. §§ 168A-5(a)(4), 168A-5(b)(5) and 168A-5(b)(7) (2012). Accord Sabrowski v. Albani-Bayeux, Inc., 2003 WL 23018827 (M.D. N.C. Dec. 19, 2003) (holding that "merely asking someone who is returning from medical leave to disclose[medical] information potentially relevant to her fitness to return to duty" does not constitute prohibited intrusion, and declining to hold, in the absence of North Carolina precedent, that the medical examination and inquiry provisions of N.C. Gen. Stat. § 168A-5 or the American's With Disabilities Act rise to the level of North Carolina public policy sufficient to support a state wrongful discharge claim).

N.C. Gen. Stat. § 168A-5 further allows employers to require or request a person to undergo a medical examination, which may include a medical history, for the purposes of determining the person's ability to perform the duties of available jobs or to aid in possible reasonable accommodations. N.C. Gen. Stat. § 168A-5(b)(6) (2012). Such medical examinations may only be required where an offer of employment has been made: (1) on the condition that the person meets the physical and mental requirements of the job, with or without a reasonable accommodation; and (2) the examination is required of all persons conditionally offered employment for the same position regardless of handicapping condition (unless limited to determining potential accommodations or the extent to which a person's condition would interfere with his ability to perform the job). N.C. Gen. Stat. § 168A-5(b)(6) (2012).

2. ***Private Employers.*** See II.C.1., supra.

3. ***Public Employers.*** See II.C.1, supra. North Carolina personnel law provides that it is the State's policy not to discriminate in employment against any applicant for public employment or public employee who has or is

suspected of having the AIDS virus or HIV infection, provided that the individual is capable of performing the duties of the job satisfactorily and there is no medical indication that the employee's condition is a health threat to co-workers or the public. See N.C. Admin. Code Title 25 § 1L.0204 (2012). State public employee law also prohibits medical tests and examinations for the presence of HIV or associated conditions, except as authorized by State and federal law or required by the rules of the Commission for Health Services. See N.C. Admin. Code Title 25 § 1L.0205 (2012). The regulation further requires applicable agencies to maintain confidentiality regarding a public employee's status with respect to such conditions. N.C. Admin. Code Title 25 § 1L.0206 (2012). However, State employees may be required to meet physical fitness standards based on pre-employment physical examinations, provided that the requirements are reasonably necessary for the specific work to be performed and are uniformly and equally applied to all applicants, regardless of age or sex. See N.C. Admin. Code Title 25 § 1C.0202(c)(2) (2012). But see N.C. Executive Order 18-85 (prohibiting discrimination in the administration of performance appraisals because of any protected characteristic, e.g. handicap status).

In addition to the above, the North Carolina Supreme Court has held that the elimination of anonymous HIV testing by local health departments and its replacement with a program of confidential testing did not amount to a violation of state constitutional rights, where N.C. Gen. Stat. § 130A-143 was deemed to provide adequate protection against unlawful disclosure. See ACT-UP Triangle v. Comm'n for Health Services, 345 N.C. 699, 483 S.E.2d 388 (1997).

D. Polygraph Tests

Although North Carolina statutes require "detection of deception examiners" to be licensed and monitored by the State in order to provide some level of examiner competency, North Carolina does not have a separate state statute similar to the federal Employee Polygraph Protection Act which governs the administration and use of polygraph tests. See N.C. Gen. Stat. §§ 74C-2 and 74C-3(5) (2012). However, the North Carolina Court of Appeals held in Warren v. City of Asheville, 74 N.C. App. 402, 328 S.E.2d 859, rev. denied, 314 N.C. 336, 333 S.E.2d 496 (1985), that a police officer could not be required to submit to a polygraph examination to answer questions about whether he was a homosexual unless the city informed the officer that: (1) the questions will relate specifically and narrowly to the performance of official duties; (2) the answer cannot be used against the officer in any subsequent criminal prosecution; and (3) the penalty for refusal is dismissal. But see also Truesdale v. Univ. of North Carolina, 91 N.C. App. 186, 371 S.E.2d 503 (1988), rev. denied, 323 N.C. 706, 377 S.E.2d 229 (1989), cert. denied, 493 U.S. 808, 110 S. Ct. 50, 107 L. Ed. 2d 19 (1989), overruled on other grounds, 330 N.C. 761, 413 S.E.2d 276 (1992) (holding that there is no fundamental right to engage in homosexual activity, such that there is no invasion of privacy in asking control questions in a polygraph test related to such actions).

E. Fingerprinting

North Carolina has not addressed the issue of whether fingerprinting of current or prospective employees unreasonably invades such individuals' privacy. Moreover, North Carolina statutes specifically require and allow for fingerprinting of employees in certain specified occupations. See, e.g., N.C. Gen. Stat. §§ 110-90.2, 114-19.5 and 131D-10.3A (2012) (child care providers); N.C. Gen. Stat. §§ 114-19.2, 115C-238.29(k) and 115C-332 (2012) (public school system employees); N.C. Gen. Stat. § 114-19.4 (2012) (foster care workers); N.C. Gen. Stat. § 84-24 (2012) (applicants for the North Carolina State Bar); N.C. Gen. Stat. § 74D-8 (2012) (alarm system employees); N.C. Gen. Stat. § 58-71-50 (2012) (bail bondsmen or runners); and N.C. Gen. Stat. § 53-243.05 (2012) (licensed mortgage brokers, mortgage bankers and loan officers).

III. SEARCHES

A. Employee's Person

1. ***Private Employers.*** There is no North Carolina statute that governs or regulates public or private employer searches of an employee's person, work area or property. N.C. Gen. Stat. § 14-72.1 (2012), however, provides that any merchant, his agent or employee or a peace officer who detains or causes the arrest of any person for suspected shoplifting may not be held civilly liable for detention, malicious prosecution, false imprisonment or false arrest if the detention "upon the premises of the store or in a reasonable proximity thereto, is in a reasonable manner for a reasonable length of time." Such statute further provides that in order to shield the acting party from potential liability, the individual or entity involved in the detention or arrest must have "probable cause to believe" that the individual committed a shoplifting crime. N.C. Gen. Stat. § 14-72.1 (2012).

In Hall v. Post, 85 N.C. App. 610, 615, 355 S.E.2d 819, 823, 14 Media L. Rep. 1129 (1987), rev'd on other grounds, 323 N.C. 259, 372 S.E.2d 711, 15 Media L. Rep. 2329 (1988), the North Carolina Court of Appeals noted in dicta that the tort of intrusion could potentially be based on such acts as "physically invading a person's home or other private place, eavesdropping by wiretapping or microphones, peering through windows, persistent telephoning, unauthorized prying into a bank account, and opening personal mail of another." Id. In addition, although there are apparently no North Carolina cases concerning searches of an employee's person in the context of an intrusion claim, other general tort and property claims such as conversion, trespass and false imprisonment have been found to provide limitations on employer action. See, e.g., Parrish v. Boysell Mfg. Co., 211 N.C. 7, 188 S.E. 817 (1936) (holding that an employee's physical search of a co-worker in connection with an attempt to find wages lost by other employees was outside the course and scope of the employee's employment, thereby precluding plaintiff's recovery against the employer for false arrest and imprisonment); Williams v. Boylan-Pearce, Inc., 69 N.C. App. 315, 317 S.E.2d 17, rev. denied, 312 N.C. 625, 323 S.E.2d 927 (1984), aff'd, 313 N.C. 321, 327 S.E.2d 870 (1985) (upholding judgment against employer for malicious prosecution where its employee, among other things, examined the contents of plaintiff's purse without her consent and subjected plaintiff to a body search). Cf. Smith v. Jack Eckerd Corp., 101 N.C. App. 566, 400 S.E.2d 99 (1991) (holding that an employer's search of a customer and the customer's children using a hand-held scanner after the customer triggered the store's merchandise alarm was not "highly offensive to a reasonable person").

2. ***Public Employers.*** See III.A.1, supra. There are no reported cases concerning searches of an employee's person in the public employment context.

B. Employee's Work Area

There are no reported cases where employees have framed an action based on an employer's search of their work area in the context of an intrusion claim. Employees have, however, asserted actions for trespass, conversion, false imprisonment and intentional infliction of emotional distress for searches of their offices and other work areas. See, e.g., Binkley v. Loughran, 714 F. Supp. 768 (M.D. N.C. 1988), cert. denied, 714 F. Supp. 774 (M.D. N.C. 1989), aff'd, 940 F.2d 651 (4th Cir. 1991) (holding that plaintiff's claims for intentional infliction of emotional distress, trespass and conversion arising out of the employer's search through her personal belongings in her desk at the company fell under the terms of a collective bargaining agreement and were, therefore, preempted by the federal Labor Management Relations Act); Daniel v. Carolina Sunrock Corp., 110 N.C. App. 376, 430 S.E.2d 306, 310 (1993) (holding that the employer's actions in, among other things, counting and screening plaintiff's personal calls and inspecting the contents of her desk while she attended a funeral were not sufficiently "extreme and outrageous" to constitute intentional infliction of emotional distress); Raymond U. v. Duke Univ., 91 N.C. App. 171, 371 S.E.2d 701, rev. denied, 323 N.C. 629, 374 S.E.2d 590 (1988) (employee action for malicious prosecution, conversion, libel and slander arising from the employer's search of his office and alleged conversion of property in the course of the same).

C. Employee's Property

1. ***Private Employers.*** See III.A.1 and B, supra.

2. ***Public Employers.*** See III.A.1 and B, supra. See also **Brookshire v. Bumcombe County, 2012 WL 136899 (W.D. N.C. Jan. 18, 2012) (holding that use of a GPS device attached to a truck did not give rise to Fourth Amendment unreasonable search / invasion of privacy claim, since there is no reasonable expectation of privacy by persons traveling in an automobile on public streets);** Caldwell v. Linker, 901 F. Supp. 1010 (M.D. N.C. 1995) (applying North Carolina law to hold that the defendant community college did not convert an instructor manual previously in the possession of plaintiff, where the college retained ownership of the manual as purchaser and licensee of the teaching program).

IV. MONITORING OF EMPLOYEES

A. Telephones and Electronic Communications

1. ***Wiretapping.*** N.C. Gen. Stat. § 15A-287 (2012) makes it a Class H felony for any person to willfully intercept, disclose, use, endeavor to intercept, or procure any other person to intercept, the contents of any wire, oral or electronic communication, unless at least one party to the communication consents. The statute further prohibits the use or attempted use of any electronic, mechanical or other device to intercept any oral communication when: (1) the device is affixed to or otherwise transmits a signal through a wire, cable or other like connection, or (2) the device transmits communications by video or interferes with the transmission of such communications. N.C. Gen. Stat. § 15A-287(a)(2) (2012). By amendment to the statute effective August 28, 1997, the definition of "wire communication" has been expanded to include the radio portion of a cordless telephone communication that is transmitted between the "telephone handset and the base unit." N.C. Gen. Stat. § 15A-286(21) (2012). It is not unlawful, however, to intercept or access an electronic communication system that is configured so the electronic communication is readily accessible to the public. N.C. Gen. Stat. § 15A-287(b)(1) (2012). The statute also allows switchboard operators and officers, employees and agents of a provider of electronic communication services to intercept, disclose or use electronic communications "in the normal course of employment while engaged in any activity that is a necessary incident to the rendition of his or her service or to the protection of the rights or property of the provider of that service." N.C. Gen. Stat. § 15A-287(c) (2012). Even then, a provider of wire

or electronic communication service "may not utilize service observing or random monitoring except for mechanical or service quality control checks." N.C. Gen. Stat. § 15A-287(c) (2012).

N.C. Gen. Stat. § 15A-296 (2012) allows for the institution of a civil action by any individual whose wire, oral or electronic communication has been intercepted in violation of N.C. Gen. Stat. § 15A-287. Potential damages for such violations include actual damages (not less than liquidated damages, computed at the rate of $100 a day for each day of violation or $1,000, whichever is higher), punitive damages and attorneys' fees/other litigation costs. N.C. Gen. Stat. § 15A-296 (2012).

In addition to the above, N.C. Gen. Stat. § 14-155 (2012) provides that it is unlawful for any person to tap or make any connection with any wire or apparatus of any telephone or telegraph company operating in the state, except as authorized by the person or entity engaged in such operations. See also Weeks v. Union Camp Corp., 215 F.3d 1323, 2000 WL 727771 (4th Cir. June 7, 2000) (affirming the dismissal of federal wiretapping claims against plaintiffs' former employer, finding that there was no triable issue of fact as to whether the employer knew or had reason to know at the time the employer used a recording that another employee had intentionally tape recorded the plaintiffs' conversation); Food Lion, Inc. v. Capital Cities/ABC, Inc., 194 F.3d 505 (4th Cir. 1999) (applying North Carolina and South Carolina law to hold that news reporters for ABC who were hired as Food Lion grocery store employees breached their duty of loyalty to Food Lion and improperly trespassed on Food Lion property by secretly videotaping activities in areas to which non-employees would not have had access); Hooper v. North Carolina, 379 F. Supp.2d 804 (M.D. N.C. 2005) (dismissing a public employee's North Carolina wiretapping claim against the State, his state university employer and other defendants sued in their official capacities because of sovereign immunity, but allowing plaintiff's wiretapping and intentional infliction of emotional distress claims to proceed against certain defendants in their individual capacities); Bryant v. Wagoner, 1998 WL 1037922 (M.D. N.C. Dec. 14, 1998) (dismissing defendant's motion for partial summary judgment on plaintiff's federal wiretapping claims where a question of fact existed as to the degree to which defendant's husband consented to the taping of personal telephone calls placed from or coming into his residence); Food Lion, Inc. v. Capital Cities/ABC, Inc., 887 F. Supp. 811, 23 Media L. Rep. 1673 (M.D. N.C. 1995), aff'd, 116 F.3d 472 (4th Cir. 1997) (dismissing plaintiff's claim alleging violation of the federal wiretapping statute in an action arising out of the undercover video surveillance of a Food Lion grocery store by a Prime Time Live reporter); Binkley v. Loughran, 714 F. Supp. 768 (M.D. N.C. 1988), cert. denied, 714 F. Supp. 774 (M.D. N.C. 1989), aff'd, 940 F.2d 651 (4th Cir. 1991) (holding that despite the fact that the issue of whether an employee's telephone was monitored fell under the terms of a collective bargaining agreement, the employee could pursue an invasion of privacy claim under state law based on the monitoring of her telephone at home and at work, as her right to be free of unauthorized wiretapping was non-negotiable); Kinesis Adver., Inc. v. Hill, 652 S.E.2d 284 (2007), rev. denied, 362 N.C. 177, 658 S.E.2d 485 (2008) (holding that employer's retrieval of employees' stored voicemail and e-mail messages did not violate North Carolina's state wiretapping law, given that the employer had a right to retrieve business-related correspondence and retrieval of such stored data did not constitute "interception" within the meaning of the Act); Huber v. North Carolina State Univ., 163 N.C. App. 638, 594 S.E.2d 402 (2004), rev. denied, 358 N.C. 731, 601 S.E.2d 531 (2004) (holding that state university employer's alleged unauthorized recording of plaintiff's personal calls "for illicit and personal purposes" outside of the ordinary course of business and unconnected to any investigative or law enforcement purpose are sufficient to demonstrate a potential claim for violation of state and federal wiretapping law); Barker v. Kimberly-Clark Corp., 136 N.C. App. 455, 524 S.E.2d 821 (2000) (holding that alleged false statements by plaintiff's manager to other management and non-management personnel regarding, among other things, an employee's accessing of pornography on the Internet presented a question of fact as to whether such accusations constituted slander per se and tortious interference or were qualifiedly privileged); Daniel v. Carolina Sunrock Corp., 110 N.C. App. 376, 430 S.E.2d 306 (1993) (holding that the employer's actions in, among other things, counting and screening plaintiff's personal calls at work were not sufficiently "extreme and outrageous" to constitute intentional infliction of emotional distress); Hall v. Post, 85 N.C. App. 610, 355 S.E.2d 819, 823, 14 Media L. Rep. 1129 (1987), rev'd on other grounds, 323 N.C. 259, 372 S.E.2d 711, 15 Media L. Rep. 2329 (1988) (noting that examples of activity that may rise to the level of a tort for intrusion include "physically invading a person's home or other private place, eavesdropping by wiretapping or microphones, peering through windows, persistent telephoning, unauthorized prying into a bank account, and opening personal mail of another"). Cf. Miller v. Brooks, 123 N.C. App. 20, 472 S.E.2d 350 (1996), rev. denied, 345 N.C. 344, 483 S.E.2d 172 (1997) (holding that a husband could pursue an intrusion, trespass and intentional infliction of emotional distress claim against his estranged wife based on the videotaping of plaintiff in his bedroom and opening/sorting through his personal mail).

2. ***Electronic Communications.*** See IV.A.1, supra. See also Mason v. ILS Technologies, LLC, 2008 WL 731557 (W.D. N.C. Feb. 29, 2008) (affirming that the attorney-client privilege applied and a reasonable expectation of privacy existed as to e-mail sent by an employee to his attorney from the employee's work computer, where the employer could not show that the employee had knowledge of the employer's electronic communication policy that expressly disclaimed any privacy expectation); Burgess v. Eforce Media, Inc., 2007 WL 3355369 (W.D. N.C. Nov. 9, 2007) (holding that placing of spyware on plaintiff's computer was not so egregious as to give rise to a claim for invasion of privacy through

"intrusion," but would support a claim for trespass to chattels); Culbreth v. Ingram, 389 F. Supp.2d 668 (E.D. N.C. 2005) (holding that the sender of an e-mail loses his legitimate expectation of privacy for Fourth Amendment purposes once it reaches the recipient's account); Alvis Coatings, Inc. v. John Does One Through Ten, 2004 WL 2904405 (W.D. N.C. Dec. 2, 2004) (holding that although the right to speak anonymously is protected under the First Amendment, in the context of commercial speech on the Internet, a plaintiff who makes a prima facie showing that the speaker's statements are false and damaging to its business is entitled to compel the production of the speaker's identity).

3. ***Other Electronic Monitoring.*** See IV.A.1 and IV.A.2, supra.

B. Mail

With the exception of adult care/nursing home residents and patients and State mental health facility clients, there is no North Carolina statute that directly addresses the opening of private communications and/or mail addressed to individuals. See N.C. Gen. Stat. §§ 122C-62(a)(1), 131D-21(10) and 131E-117(8) (2012). However, in Hall v. Post, 85 N.C. App. 610, 355 S.E.2d 819, 823, 14 Media L. Rep. 1129 (1987), rev'd on other grounds, 323 N.C. 259, 372 S.E.2d 711, 15 Media L. Rep. 2329 (1988), the North Carolina Court of Appeals noted in dicta that examples of activity that may rise to the level of a tort for intrusion include "physically invading a person's home or other private place, eavesdropping by wiretapping or microphones, peering through windows, persistent telephoning, unauthorized prying into a bank account, and opening personal mail of another." Cf. Miller v. Brooks, 123 N.C. App. 20, 472 S.E.2d 350 (1996), rev. denied, 345 N.C. 344, 483 S.E.2d 172 (1997) (holding that a husband could pursue an intrusion, trespass and intentional infliction of emotional distress claim against his estranged wife based on the videotaping of plaintiff in his bedroom and opening/sorting through his personal mail).

C. Surveillance/Photographing

There are no North Carolina statutes that directly address the surveillance and/or photographing of employees or other individuals. N.C. Gen. Stat. §§ 74C-1 to 74C-33 (2012) does, however, require "private protective services professionals" to be licensed, which include "any person, firm, association, or corporation which discovers, locates, or disengages by electronic, electrical, or mechanical means any listening or other monitoring equipment surreptitiously placed to gather information concerning any individual, firm, association, or corporation for a fee or other valuable consideration." N.C. Gen. Stat. § 74C-3(a)(3) (2012). Nonetheless, N.C. Gen. Stat. §§ 74C-3(b)(13) and 74C-3(b)(14) (2012) expressly exempt any "person who works regularly and exclusively as an employee of an employer in connection with the business affairs of that employer" and any "employee of a security department of a private business that conducts investigations exclusively on matters internal to the business affairs of the business."

In addition, the North Carolina Electronic Surveillance Act, N.C. Gen. Stat. § 15A-287 (2012), prohibits the attempted use of electronic, mechanical or other devices to intercept any oral communication when the device transmits communications by video or interferes with the transmission of such communications. North Carolina law also prohibits "stalking" of a person where an individual willfully on more than one occasion "follows or is in the presence of another person without legal purpose and with the intent to cause death or bodily injury or with the intent to cause emotional distress by placing that person in reasonable fear of death or bodily injury." See N.C. Gen. Stat. § 14-277.3 (2012).

See also Food Lion, Inc. v. Capital Cities/ABC, Inc., 194 F.3d 505 (4th Cir. 1999) (applying North Carolina and South Carolina law to hold that news reporters for ABC who were hired as Food Lion grocery store employees breached their duty of loyalty to Food Lion and improperly trespassed on Food Lion property by secretly videotaping activities in areas to which non-employees would not have had access); Geller v. Provident Life & Accident Ins. Co., 2011 WL 1239835 (W.D. N.C. March 30, 2011) (granting motion to remand intrusion claim where plaintiff was subjected to surveillance in her backyard by a investigation firm engaged by plaintiff's disability insurance carrier); Hooper v. North Carolina, 379 F. Supp.2d 804 (M.D. N.C. 2005) (holding that defendants' alleged actions in, among other things, unlawfully wiretapping and surveilling a state employee was sufficient to state a claim for intentional infliction of emotional distress); Food Lion, Inc. v. Capital Cities/ABC, Inc., 887 F. Supp. 811, 23 Media L. Rep. 1673 (M.D. N.C. 1995), aff'd, 116 F.3d 472 (4th Cir. 1997) (dismissing plaintiff's claim alleging violation of the federal wiretapping statute in an action arising from undercover video surveillance of a grocery store by a reporter); Barksdale v. Int'l Business Machines Corp., 620 F. Supp. 1380, 1383 (1985), aff'd, 1 IER Cases 560 (4th Cir. 1986) (holding that plaintiffs were unable to establish a claim for fraud, intentional infliction of emotional distress and intrusion where the employer's observation and recording of the number of errors that plaintiffs made in tasks that they were expected to perform at work "can hardly be considered an intrusion upon the Plaintiffs' 'solitude or seclusion . . . or [their] private affairs or concerns'"); Wright v. Town of Zebulon, 202 N.C. App. 540, 688 S.E.2d 786 (2010), rev. denied, 364 N.C. 334, 701 S.E.2d 682 (2010) (holding that surveillance of a town police officer's verbal communications in his police car did not violate the N.C. Electronic Surveillance Act, where the integrity check conducted was not for bad purpose or without justifiable excuse and, therefore, was not "willful"); Hall v. Post, 85 N.C. App. 610, 355

S.E.2d 819, 823, 14 Media L. Rep. 1129 (1987), rev'd on other grounds, 323 N.C. 259, 372 S.E.2d 711, 15 Media L. Rep. 2329 (1988) (noting that examples of activity that may rise to the level of a tort for intrusion include "physically invading a person's home or other private place, eavesdropping by wiretapping or microphones, peering through windows, persistent telephoning, unauthorized prying into a bank account, and opening personal mail of another"). Cf. Terry v. PPG Indus., Inc., 156 N.C. App. 512, 577 S.E.2d 326 (2003), rev. denied, 357 N.C. 256, 583 S.E.2d 290 (2003) (upholding the Industrial Commission's failure to consider video tape surveillance of a claimant, where the employer improperly showed a portion of the video to claimant's physician without her knowledge or consent): Groves v. Travelers Ins. Co., 139 N.C. App. 795, 535 S.E.2d 105, rev'd on other grounds, 354 N.C. 206, 552 S.E.2d 141 (2001) (holding that the exclusivity provision of the North Carolina Workers' Compensation Act did not bar an employee's claims against her employer and the employer's workers' compensation carrier for intentional infliction of emotional distress allegedly resulting from the employer's forwarding of a videotape to plaintiff's evaluating physician that failed to show all aspects of the plaintiff's job); Miller v. Brooks, 123 N.C. App. 20, 472 S.E.2d 350 (1996), rev. denied, 345 N.C. 344, 483 S.E.2d 172 (1997) (holding that a husband could pursue an intrusion, trespass and intentional infliction of emotional distress claim against his estranged wife based on the videotaping of plaintiff in his bedroom and opening/sorting through his personal mail). But see **Brookshire v. Bumcombe County, 2012 WL 136899 (W.D. N.C. Jan. 18, 2012) (holding that use of a GPS device attached to a truck did not give rise to Fourth Amendment unreasonable search / invasion of privacy claim, since there is no reasonable expectation of privacy by persons traveling in an automobile on public streets);** Keyzer v. Amerilink, Ltd., 173 N.C. App. 284, 618 S.E.2d 768 (2005), aff'd, 360 N.C. 397, 627 S.E.2d 462 (2006) (holding that defendants' hiring of private investigators who posed as potential clients, interviewed plaintiff without disclosing their connection to defendants, and tape-recorded conversations without plaintiffs' knowledge in order to determine whether plaintiff and his attorney were abiding by the confidentiality terms of a prior settlement agreement did not support a claim for intrusion).

V. ACTIVITIES OUTSIDE THE WORKPLACE

A. Statute or Common Law

N.C. Gen. Stat. § 95-28.2 (2012) provides that it is an unlawful employment practice for an employer to fail or refuse to hire an applicant or to discharge or otherwise discriminate against an employee where such individual "engages in or has engaged in the lawful use of lawful products if the activity occurs off the premises of the employer during nonworking hours and does not adversely affect the employee's job performance or the person's ability to properly fulfill the responsibilities of the position in question or the safety of other employees." The statute allows an employee to bring a civil action against the employer within one year of the date of the alleged violation, the damages for which may include any wages or benefits lost as a result of the violation, an order of reinstatement without loss of position, seniority or benefits; or an order directing the employer to offer employment to the prospective employee, as applicable. N.C. Gen. Stat. § 95-28.2(e) (2012). The statute further provides that a court may order reasonable expenses, including court costs and attorneys' fees, to the prevailing party in such an action. N.C. Gen. Stat. § 95-28.2(f) (2012). The statute does, however, allow employers to discharge, discipline or take other action against employees because of their failure to comply with the requirements of the employer's substance abuse policies or the recommendations of a substance abuse prevention counselor employed or retained by the employer. N.C. Gen. Stat. § 95-28.2 (c) (3) (2012). The statute further allows employers to restrict the lawful use of lawful products during nonworking hours if the restrictions relate to: (1) a bona fide occupational requirement that is reasonably restricted to the employment activities, or (2) the fundamental objectives of the organization. N.C. Gen. Stat. § 95 -28.2(c)(1) and (2) (2012).

In addition to the above, state personnel law prohibits public employers from discriminating on the basis of the political affiliation or political opinions of employees. See N.C. Admin. Code Title 25 §§ 1C.0202(e) and 1C.0203(a)(2) (2012). These prohibitions, however, do not protect employees in various pay grades depending on the specific length of their service with the public employer. See N.C. Admin. Code Title 25 § 1C.0202(e) (2012).

B. Employees' Personal Relationships

1. ***Romantic Relationships Between Employees.*** There are no statutes under North Carolina law regarding romantic relationships between employees in the privacy context. However, the Fourth Circuit Court of Appeals has held that a county's anti-nepotism policy barring spouses from working in the same department did not significantly interfere with the fundamental right to marry or violate plaintiffs' Fourteenth Amendment rights. See Waters v. Gaston County, 57 F.3d 422 (4th Cir. 1995). See also Arbia v. Owens-Illinois, Inc., 2004 WL 1345091 (M.D. N.C. June 4, 2004), aff'd, 124 Fed.Appx 202 (4th Cir. 2005) (holding that a co-worker's remarks that plaintiff was faking her illness, made excuses to miss work, and was having sexual relations with her supervisors did not "as a matter of law rise to the level of slander per se"); Jacobs v. Mallard Creek Presbyterian Church, Inc., 214 F. Supp.2d 552 (W.D. N.C. 2002) (dismissing claims for, among other things, state slander, defamation and invasion of privacy related to a church's investigation and discipline of a pastor for engaging in a sexual relationship with a church member, on the grounds that such civil court claims

were barred by the Free Exercise and Establishment Clauses of the United States Constitution); Couch v. Bradley, 179 N.C. App. 852, 635 S.E.2d 492 (2006)(enforcing a consent and forbearance agreement against a former coworker/defendant resolving a libel action, where a defendant coworker circulated memoranda throughout campus accusing plaintiff of, among other things, an affair with a former employee); Johnson v. York, 134 N.C. App. 332, 517 S.E.2d 670 (1999) (dismissing plaintiff employee's claims for invasion of privacy and intentional infliction of emotional distress on governmental immunity grounds in an action arising from a defendant manager's involvement in a confrontation at plaintiff's home with her then husband regarding her affair with another man, all of the parties of which were employees of the same public employer). Cf. Jennings v. Univ. of North Carolina, 444 F.3d 255 (4th Cir. 2006), cert. denied, 552 U.S. 887, 128 S. Ct. 247, 169 L. Ed. 2d 147 (2007) (applying North Carolina law to hold that a coach's two isolated inquiries into an athlete's dating relationships did not rise to the level of egregious conduct sufficient to support a claim for intrusion).

2. ***Sexual Orientation.*** North Carolina law does not bar discrimination against individuals on the basis of sexual orientation. Nevertheless, N.C. Gen. Stat. § 130A-148(i) (2012) provides that it is unlawful to discriminate against any person with AIDS or HIV infection because of their condition in determining such individual's suitability for continued employment. See also Bradley v. Ramsey, 329 F. Supp.2d 617 (W.D. N.C. 2004) (applying North Carolina law to hold that a former police chief stated a claim for unlawful intrusion where his supervisor sought and obtained a confidential letter that revealed the chief's alternative sexual lifestyle and used it to blackmail the chief and cover up the supervisor's own corrupt practices); Chapman v. Byrd, 124 N.C. App. 13, 475 S.E.2d 734 (1996), rev. denied, 345 N.C. 751, 485 S.E.2d 50 (1997) (holding that the plaintiff had stated a claim for intentional infliction of emotional distress when the director of a county EMS service repeated a rumor that a certain restaurant had an employee suffering from AIDS or HIV); Warren v. City of Asheville, 74 N.C. App. 402, 328 S.E.2d 859, rev. denied, 314 N.C. 336, 333 S.E.2d 496 (1985) (holding that the city could not demand that an officer answer questions about whether he was a homosexual absent some other behavior). Cf. Bradley v. N.C. Dept. of Transp., Div. of Motor Vehicles, 286 F. Supp.2d 697 (W.D. N.C. 2003) (dismissing plaintiff's state law intrusion and negligent infliction of emotion distress claims involving the release of a confidential letter regarding plaintiff's alternative lifestyle for lack of supplemental federal jurisdiction). But see Bradley v. Ramsey, supra, (holding that disclosure of a former police chief's alternative sexual lifestyle in and of itself was not actionable under North Carolina law); Arledge v. Peoples Services, Inc., 2002 WL 1591690 (N.C. Gen. Ct. April 18, 2002) (holding that the termination of an employee because of his status as a transsexuals does not violate North Carolina public policy, nor does transsexualism rise to the level of a disability protected by N.C. Gen. Stat. § 143-422.2); Truesdale v. Univ. of North Carolina, 91 N.C. App. 186, 371 S.E.2d 503 (1988), rev. denied, 323 N.C. 706, 377 S.E.2d 229 (1989), cert. denied, 493 U.S. 808, 110 S. Ct. 50, 107 L. Ed. 2d 19 (1989), overruled on other grounds, 330 N.C. 761, 413 S.E.2d 276 (1992) (holding that there is no fundamental right to engage in homosexual activity, such that there is no privacy invasion in asking control questions in a polygraph test related to such actions).

3. ***Marital Status.*** North Carolina law does not expressly bar discrimination or employment action against individuals on the basis of their marital status. Cf. Broughton v. McClatchy Newspapers, Inc., 161 N.C. App. 20, 588 S.E.2d 20, 32 Med.L.Rep. 1313 (2003) (holding that there can be no intrusion claim for disclosure of plaintiff's divorce based on the use of public records as to which plaintiff had no expectation of privacy). N.C. Gen. Stat. § 143-422.2 (2012) does, however, provide that for employers that regularly employ 15 or more employees, it is the public policy of the state to prohibit discrimination on account of, among other things, an individual's sex.

C. Smoking

See V.A, supra. In addition to the North Carolina statute concerning the lawful use of lawful products (N.C. Gen. Stat. § 95-28.2 (2012)), North Carolina has also enacted statutory provisions that prohibit the enactment or modification of local ordinances regulating smoking after October 15, 1993 that exceed or are more stringent than the State's anti-smoking provisions. See N.C. Gen. Stat. §§ 143-595 to 143-601 (2012). See also GASP v. Mecklenburg County, 42 N.C. App. 225, 256 S.E.2d 477 (1979) (holding that the state Handicapped Persons Protection Act was not intended to cover minor pulmonary problems or all individuals who are harmed or irritated by tobacco smoke); State v. Futrell, 39 N.C. App. 674, 251 S.E.2d 715 (1979) (holding that the North Carolina Toxic Vapors Act, N.C. Gen. Stat. § 90-113.8A *et seq.*, does not prohibit the smoking of tobacco products).

D. Blogging

There are no statutes under North Carolina law regarding blogging by employees or other individuals. However, in Alvis Coatings, Inc. v. John Does One Through Ten, 2004 WL 2904405 (W.D. N.C. Dec. 2, 2004), a federal district court applying federal and North Carolina law denied defendants' motion to quash a subpoena in connection with state law claims for, among other things, defamation and tortious interference with business relations where anonymous individuals posted negative comments on Internet home improvement message boards operated by bobvila.com and oldhouse.com concerning plaintiff's business, products and employees. Ruling on an issue of first impression, the court in Alvis Coatings held that although the right to speak anonymously is protected under the First Amendment, in the context of commercial speech on the Internet, a plaintiff who makes a prima facie showing that the speaker's statements are false and damaging to its business is entitled to compel the production of the speaker's identity. See also Burleson v. Toback, 391 F. Supp.2d 401 (M.D. N.C. 2005) (holding that a non-resident entity's semi-interactive website, individual defendants' Internet postings/blogging on a web forum, and a single e-mail exchange between defendant and plaintiff were insufficient, standing alone, to confer specific personal jurisdiction); Accu-Sport Int'l, Inc. v. Swing Dynamics, Inc., 367 F. Supp.2d 923 (M.D. N.C. 2005) (holding that a passive, informational website maintained by a non-resident company was insufficient contact with the forum to subject the defendant to personal jurisdiction of the court for slander and other claims, where the website's interactivity was limited to links that allowed the user to e-mail defendant's employees and to access the website of an unrelated company). Cf. Merritt, Flebotte, Wilson, Webb & Caruso, PLLC v. Hemmings, 196 N.C. App. 600, 676 S.E.2d 79 (2009) (holding that the continued existence of an html code on a third-party server that could be used to retrieve former employees' biographies and images through general search engines did not constitute a misappropriation of likeness, where the employer otherwise removed all links and references to the defendants from its website).

VI. RECORDS

A. Personnel Records

North Carolina law does not provide any statutory or common law protection to employees of private employers for information contained their personnel files. N.C. Gen. Stat. § 126-22 (2012), however, provides that personnel files of State employees, former State employees or applicants for State employment "shall not be subject to inspection and examination." Information protected under this statute is limited to that: (1) gathered by the employing state agency or considered in an individual's application for employment, and (2) which relates to the individual's "application, selection or non-selection, promotions, demotions, transfers, leave, salary, suspension, performance evaluation forms, disciplinary actions, and termination of employment"). News & Observer Publishing Co. v. Poole, 330 N.C. 465, 412 S.E.2d 7, 19 Media L. Rep. 1873 (1992). N.C. Gen. Stat. §§ 126-23 and 126-24 (2012) further provide that with the exception of general background information and other specifically enumerated exceptions, all "other information contained in a [State employee's] personnel file is confidential and shall not be open for inspection and examination."

N.C. Gen. Stat. § 131E-257.2 (2012) similarly provides that notwithstanding the provisions of the North Carolina Public Records Act, "personnel files of employees and applicants for employment maintained by a public hospital are subject to inspection and may be disclosed *only* as provided" by such statute. (Emphasis added). N.C. Gen. Stat. § 131E-257.2 (2012) does, however, further provide that the following general data regarding each public hospital employee is non-confidential in nature and a matter of public record: name, age, date of original employment, current position title, current salary, date and amount of the most recent salary increase or decrease, date of the most recent promotion, demotion, transfer, suspension, separation or other change in position classification, and the office to which the employee is currently assigned. See also Knight Publ'g Co. v. Charlotte-Mecklenburg Hosp. Auth., 172 N.C. App. 486, 616 S.E.2d 602, rev. denied, 360 N.C. 176, 626 S.E.2d 299 (2005) (holding that under the North Carolina Public Hospital Personnel Act, other than as expressly provided in such statute, any information satisfying the Act's definition of "personnel file" is confidential and exempt from disclosure under the state Public Records Act, including information regarding employment contracts, severance agreements, non-salary compensation/benefits, and expense reimbursements paid to current or former employees).

See also Washington v. City of Charlotte, 219 Fed.Appx. 273 (4th Cir. 2007) (holding that although city employee personnel files are protected from disclosure, N.C. Gen. Stat. § 160A-168 specifically allows for release of such information under court order); Sabrowski v. Albani-Bayeux, Inc., 124 Fed.Appx. 159 (4th Cir. 2005) (noting that the disclosure of an individual's private personnel files and medical records would amount to a per se intrusion if the records contain sensitive materials); Foxx v. Town of Fletcher, 2008 WL 4000626 (W.D. N.C. Aug. 26, 2008) (holding that plaintiff's general assertion that personnel files may contain information relevant to his claims was insufficient to compel production); Brown v. SLS Int'l, Inc., 2006 WL 3694535 (W.D. N.C. Dec. 13, 2006) (holding that the need for production of employee personnel files during discovery must be balanced against the privacy interests of such individuals); James v. Peter Pan Transit Management, Inc., 1999 WL 735173 (E.D. N.C. Jan. 20, 1999) (holding that "personal privacy and the confidentiality of personnel files are important public policy concerns"); News Reporter Co., v. Columbus County, 184 N.C. App. 512, 646 S.E.2d 390 (2007) (holding that portions of a county employee's letter sent to the Board of Commissioners addressing the employee's experience with a co-worker are protected from disclosure under N.C. Gen. Stat. § 153A-98 as confidential personnel file information, but portions of the letter concerning recommendation of such employee for the position of county medical director are not); Toomer v. Garrett, 155 N.C. App. 462, 574 S.E.2d 76 (2002), rev. denied, 357 N.C. 66, 579 S.E.2d 576 (2003) (holding that the alleged unauthorized disclosure of medical, financial and other private information from a former State employee's personnel file to the news media and the public is sufficient to state a claim for intrusion into seclusion, among other claims); N.C. Gen. Stat. §§ 115C-319, 115C-320, 115C-321 and 115C-325(b) (2012) (confidentiality of personnel files for applicants for employment and current and former employees of local boards of education); N.C. Gen.

Stat. §§ 115D-27 to 115D-30 (2012) (confidentiality of personnel files for applicants for employment and current and former employees of community colleges); N.C. Gen. Stat. § 153A-98 (2012) (confidentiality of personnel records for applicants for employment and current and former county employees); N.C. Gen. Stat. § 160A-168 (2012) (confidentiality of personnel files for applicants for employment and current and former city employees). But see Pressley v. Continental Can Co., 39 N.C. App. 467, 468, 250 S.E.2d 676, 678, rev. denied, 297 N.C. 177, 254 S.E.2d 37 (1979) (merely storing statements in an employee's personnel file does not amount to publication, even if the materials contained in such files are potentially available for others to read); N.C. Gen. Stat § 126-30 (2012) (any applicant for state employment who "knowingly and willfully discloses false or misleading information, or conceals dishonorable military service; or conceals prior employment history or other requested information. . . ." may be disciplined or dismissed). Cf. McDougal-Wilson v. Goodyear Tire & Rubber Co., 232 F.R.D. 246 (E.D. N.C. 2005) (upholding the redaction of medical, insurance and social security number information from personnel file records requested in discovery out of concern for employee privacy); Hinton v. Conner, 225 F.R.D. 513 (M.D. N.C. 2005) (holding that "in all instances where employment records of non-parties are sought [in discovery], particularly disciplinary records, there is a privacy interest involved for which some protection may be considered even sua sponte"); Cason v. Builders Firstsource-Southeast Group, Inc., 159 F. Supp.2d 242 (W.D. N.C. 2001) (noting that although employee personnel records are not covered by a per se privilege as confidential, "there is a strong public policy against the public disclosure of personnel files").

B. Medical Records

Information and records, whether publicly or privately maintained, that identify a person who has the AIDS virus or has or may have a "reportable communicable disease" are protected from disclosure. N.C. Gen. Stat. §§ 130A-133 and 130A-143 (2012). Communications between physician and patient, including confidential information contained in medical documents, are privileged and "shall not be considered public records under G.S. 132-1." N.C. Gen. Stat. § 8-53 (2012). Confidential information acquired in attending or treating a mental patient in a State-licensed facility is also protected from disclosure. N.C. Gen. Stat. § 122C-52 (2012). In addition, in French v. U.S. Dept. of Human Health and Human Service, 55 F. Supp.2d 379 (W.D. N.C. 1999), a federal district court applying North Carolina law held that a former employer's unauthorized disclosure of confidential medical records to a tribal officer in order to prevent the employee's reinstatement is sufficient to state a claim for intrusion into the employee's private affairs. See also II.C, supra; Sabrowski v. Albani-Bayeux, Inc., 124 Fed.Appx. 159 (4th Cir. 2005) (noting that the disclosure of an individual's private personnel files and medical records would amount to a per se intrusion if the records contain sensitive materials); Toomer v. Garrett, 155 N.C. App. 462, 574 S.E.2d 76 (2002), rev. denied, 357 N.C. 66, 579 S.E.2d 576 (2003) (holding that the alleged unauthorized disclosure of, among other things, medical information from a former State employee's personnel file to the news media and the public is sufficient to state a claim for intrusion). But see Sabrowski v. Albani-Bayeux, Inc., supra, (dismissing plaintiff's wrongful discharge claims, holding that there is no North Carolina authority establishing a public policy that shield's an employee's medical records from his or her employer). Cf. Iannucci v. Mission Hosp., 2008 WL 5220641 (W.D. N.C. Dec. 11, 2008) (upholding the dismissal of an employee's privacy claim under HIPAA where a manager allegedly "pulled up" plaintiff's medical records in front of other employees, on the grounds that "[t]here is no private cause of action under HIPAA"); Ihekwu v. City of Durham, 129 F. Supp.2d 870 (M.D. N.C. 2000) (denying former employee's federal ADA/blacklisting claim related to the alleged placement of medical information in his personnel file); Burgess v. Busby, 142 N.C. App. 393, 544 S.E.2d 4, rev. improvidently allowed, 354 N.C. 351, 553 S.E.2d 679, reh'g denied, 355 N.C. 224, 559 S.E.2d 554 (2001) holding that letters sent by a physician to local colleagues naming jurors in his former civil suit as having "found a doctor guilty" may give rise to an intentional infliction of emotional distress claim); Crist v. Moffatt, 326 N.C. 326, 389 S.E.2d 41 (1990) (holding that considerations of patient privacy and the confidential relationship between doctor and patient preclude ex parte verbal contacts between a worker's compensation plaintiff's non-party treating physician and defense counsel absent plaintiff's express consent); Salaam v. N.C. Dep't of Transp., 122 N.C. App. 83, 468 S.E.2d 536 (1996), rev. improvidently allowed, 345 N.C. 494, 480 S.E.2d 51 (1997) (prohibiting ex parte verbal contacts between a plaintiff's non-party treating physician and defense counsel in the medical malpractice context); Mayfield v. Hannifin, 174 N.C. App. 386, 621 S.E.2d 243 (2005), rev. denied, 360 N.C. 364, 629 S.E.2d 855 (2006) (applying Salaam and Crist to prohibit employer's counsel from posing interrogatory-like questions to plaintiff's non-party treating physician by facsimile).

But see Tillet v. Onslow Memorial Hosp., Inc., 715 S.E.2d. 538, 2011 WL 3904615 (W.D. N.C. Sept. 6, 2011) (holding that hospital employee's accessing, viewing and publishing of autopsy x-ray photographs did not constitute intrusion upon seclusion since the originals may be inspected and examined by the public, subject to certain time and place restrictions); EEOC v. Sheffield Fin., LLC, 2007 WL 1726560 (M.D. N.C. June 13, 2007) (holding that the EEOC's general assertion that plaintiff's medical and pharmaceutical records are private does not preclude their production, where plaintiff seeks compensatory damages for past and future emotional distress, humiliation, anxiety, inconvenience, and loss of enjoyment of life); Sabrowski v. Albani-Bayeux, Inc., 2003 WL 23018827 (M.D. N.C. Dec. 19, 2003) (holding that "merely asking someone who is returning from medical leave to disclose [medical] information potentially relevant to her fitness to return to duty" does not constitute prohibited intrusion, and declining to hold, in the absence of North Carolina precedent, that the medical examination and inquiry provisions of N.C. Gen. Stat. § 168A-5 or the American's With Disabilities Act rise to the level of North Carolina public policy sufficient to support a state wrongful discharge claim); Watts v. Cumberland County Hosp. System, 75 N.C. App. 1, 330 S.E.2d 242, rev. denied, 314 N.C. 548, 335 S.E.2d 27 (1985), rev'd on other grounds, 317 N.C. 321, 345 S.E.2d 201 (1986) (holding that in the context of a health care provider's unauthorized disclosure of a patient's confidences, claims of invasion of privacy and breach of fiduciary duty/confidentiality should be treated as a claims for medical malpractice); Smith v. State of North Carolina, 298 N.C. 115, 131, 257 S.E.2d 399, 408 (1979) (holding that privacy of patient medical records "does not extend to hospital administrators or employees who need the information in order to facilitate the patient's treatment or properly administer the hospital"); N.C. Gen. Stat. § 58-39-110 (2012) (which provides that no cause of action in the nature of defamation, invasion of privacy or negligence may arise from the furnishing of personal or privileged information to an insurance institution, agent or insurance support organization unless the information is false and provided with "malice or willful intent to injure"). In addition, newly adopted N.C. Gen. Stat. § 97-25.6 (2012) provides that "[n]otwithstanding the provisions of G.S. 8-53, any law relating to the privacy of medical records or information, and the prohibition against ex parte communications at common law," an employer or insurer paying medical compensation to a provider rendering treatment under the Workers' Compensation Act may obtain records of that treatment without the express authorization of the employee and, upon written notice to the employee, may obtain directly from the medical provider medical records relating to evaluation or treatment of the current injury or condition for which the employee is claiming compensation. N.C. Gen. Stat. § 97-25.6 further provides that an employer or insurer paying compensation for an admitted claim or paying without prejudice pursuant to N.C. Gen. Stat. § 97-18(d) may communicate with an employee's medical provider in writing, limited to specific questions promulgated by the North Carolina Industrial Commission, to determine, among other information, the diagnosis for the employee's condition, the reasonable and necessary treatment, the anticipated time that the employee will be out of work, the relationship, if any, of the employee's condition to the employment, the restrictions from the condition, the kind of work for which the employee may be eligible, the anticipated time the employee will be restricted, and the permanent impairment, if any, as a result of the condition. When these questions are used, a copy of the written communication must be provided to the employee at the same time and by the same means as the communication is made to the health care provider. But see Silvers v. Mastercraft Fabrics, LLC, 630 S.E.2d 255, 2006 WL 1528974 (N.C. App. June 6, 2006) (holding that a human resources manger's non-consensual attendance at an employee's medical appointments made in connection with the employee's ongoing workers' compensation claim violated the physician-patient privilege of N.C. Gen. Stat. § 8-53).

C. Criminal Records

North Carolina does not prohibit the use of criminal records and information in the employment setting. In addition, North Carolina statutes specifically require and allow for criminal background searches on applicants for employment and employees in certain specified occupations. See, e.g., N.C. Gen. Stat. § 62-333 (2012) (utility or utility contractor employees with access to nuclear power facilities or control over nuclear material); N.C. Gen. Stat. §§ 110-90.2, 114-19.5 and 131D-10.3A (2012) (child care providers); N.C. Gen. Stat. §§ 114-19.4 and 131D-10.3A (2012) (foster care workers); N.C. Gen. Stat. §§ 114-19.2, 115C-238.29(k) and 115C-332 (2012) (public school system employees); N.C. Gen. Stat. § 114-19.3 (2012) (hospital, nursing home, adult care home, home care agency, child placement agency, residential child care facility and other employees/providers of treatment or services to children, the elderly, mental health patients, the sick and disabled); N.C. Gen. Stat. § 114-19.6 (2012) (Department of Health and Human Services applicants and employees); N.C. Gen. Stat. §§ 114-9.3 and 131D-40 (2012) (adult care provider employees); N.C. Gen. Stat. §§ 114-19.3 and 131E-265 (2012) (nursing home/ home care agency employees); N.C. Gen. Stat. § 74C-11 (2012) (employees of licensed protective service providers); N.C. Gen. Stat. § 74D-8 (2012) (alarm system employees); N.C. Gen. Stat. § 95-47.2 (2012) (owners, officers, directors and managers of private personnel services); N.C. Gen. Stat. § 58-71-50 (2012) (licensed bail bondsmen or runners). But see Woodruff v. Miller, 64 N.C. App. 364, 307 S.E.2d 176 (1983) (reversing the trial court's judgment notwithstanding the verdict where plaintiff was awarded $20,000 in damages for the circulation of plaintiff's criminal record from the Clerk of Court among plaintiff's acquaintances); Scroggs v. N.C. Criminal Justice Educ. & Training Standards Comm'n, 101 N.C. App. 699, 400 S.E.2d 742 (1991) (holding that the Commission's decision to terminate a law enforcement officer was arbitrary and capricious, where the employee had written on his application that he had used marijuana and other non-prescription drugs on a "teenage experimental basis" and the Commission had knowledge of such information for more than 5 years prior to taking action).

D. Subpoenas / Search Warrants

General requirements regarding the form, substance and issuance of subpoenas are set forth in N.C. Gen. Stat. § 1A-1, Rule 45 (2012). N.C. Gen. Stat. § 1A-1, Rule 45(c)(2) (2012) further specifically provides for special procedures for the production of public records or hospital medical records. For example, where a custodian of hospital medical records is ordered to produce certain records in the custodian's custody, the custodian may tender to the court certified copies of the record requested. N.C. Gen. Stat. § 1A-1, Rule 45(c)(2) (2012). In addition, "[a]ny original or certified copy of records or an affidavit delivered according to the provisions of [such rule], unless otherwise objectionable, shall be admissible in any action or proceeding without further certification or authentication." Id. Cf. N.C. Gen. Stat. § 122C-54(a) (2012) (requiring disclosure of confidential information acquired in attending or treating a mental patient in a State-licensed facility upon issuance of an order by a court of competent jurisdiction compelling disclosure).

Likewise, when a subpoena requires disclosure of a trade secret or other "confidential research, development, or commercial information, a court may, to protect a person subject to or affected by the subpoena, quash or modify the subpoena", absent a showing of substantial need by the requesting party that cannot otherwise be met without undue hardship. N.C. Gen. Stat. § 1A-1, Rule 45(c)(7) (2012). Cf. Bennett v. CSX Transp., Inc., 2011 WL 4527430 (E.D. N.C. Sept. 26, 2011) (denying motion to compel employee social security numbers absent a showing that the moving party made every reasonable attempt to contact the employees without such numbers); McDougal-Wilson v. Goodyear Tire & Rubber Co., 232 F.R.D. 246 (E.D. N.C. 2005) (upholding the redaction of medical, insurance and social security number information from personnel file records requested in discovery out of concern for employee privacy); Hinton v. Conner, 225 F.R.D. 513 (M.D. N.C. 2005) (holding that "in all instances where employment records of non-parties are sought [in discovery], particularly disciplinary records, there is a privacy interest involved for which some protection may be considered even sua sponte"); Cason v. Builders Firstsource-Southeast Group, Inc., 159 F. Supp.2d 242 (W.D. N.C. 2001) (noting that although employee personnel records are not covered by a per se privilege as confidential, "there is a strong public policy against the public disclosure of personnel files"). But see **Wood v. Town of Warsaw, 2011 WL 6748797 (E.D. N.C. Dec. 22, 2011) (compelling a non-party supervisor of plaintiff to produce non-privileged electronic records contained on the hard drive of the supervisor's personal home computer using key word searches related to claims and defenses asserted by the parties, since "in this age of smart phones and telecommuting, it is increasingly common for work to be conducted outside of the office and through the use of personal electronic devices");** Bulter v. Burroughs Wellcome, Inc., 920 F. Supp. 90 (E.D. N.C. 1996) (compelling plaintiff to comply with defendant's subpoena and discovery requests, holding that employees who bring ADA actions, like plaintiffs in medical malpractice actions, waive all privileges and privacy interests related to their claim by virtue of filing a complaint); Media Network, Inc. v. Mullen Advertising, Inc., 2006 NCBC 6, 2006 WL 1066640 (N.C. Super. April 21, 2006) (holding that the defendant in a contract action could obtain discovery of a former co-defendant's settlement with the plaintiff to establish the possibility of witness bias or prejudice, even though the terms of the settlement were confidential per agreement of the settling parties).

Besides the general records subpoena statute, N.C. Gen. Stat. § 97-25.6 (2012) provides that "[n]otwithstanding the provisions of G.S. 8-53, any law relating to the privacy of medical records or information, and the prohibition against ex parte communications at common law," an employer or insurer paying medical compensation to a provider rendering treatment under the Workers' Compensation Act may obtain records of that treatment without the express authorization of the employee and, upon written notice to the employee, may obtain directly from the medical provider medical records relating to evaluation or treatment of the current injury or condition for which the employee is claiming compensation. N.C. Gen. Stat. § 97-25.6 further provides that an employer or insurer paying compensation for an admitted claim or paying without prejudice pursuant to N.C. Gen. Stat. § 97-18(d) may communicate with an employee's medical provider in writing, limited to specific questions promulgated by the North Carolina Industrial Commission, to determine, among other information, the diagnosis for the employee's condition, the reasonable and necessary treatment, the anticipated time that the employee will be out of work, the relationship, if any, of the employee's condition to the employment, the restrictions from the condition, the kind of work for which the employee may be eligible, the anticipated time the employee will be restricted, and the permanent impairment, if any, as a result of the condition. When these questions are used, a copy of the written communication must be provided to the employee at the same time and by the same means as the communication is made to the health care provider.

In addition, in Alvis Coatings, Inc. v. John Does One Through Ten, 2004 WL 2904405 (W.D. N.C. Dec. 2, 2004), a federal district court applying federal and North Carolina law denied defendants' motion to quash a subpoena in connection with state law claims for, among other things, defamation and tortious interference with business relations where anonymous individuals posted negative comments on Internet home improvement message boards operated by bobvila.com and oldhouse.com concerning plaintiff's business, products and employees. Ruling on an issue of first impression, the court in Alvis Coatings held that although the right to speak anonymously is protected under the First Amendment, in the context of commercial speech on the Internet, a plaintiff who makes a prima facie showing that the speaker's statements are false and damaging to its business is entitled to compel the production of the speaker's identity.

VII. ACTIONS SUBSEQUENT TO EMPLOYMENT

A. References

N.C. Gen. Stat. § 14-355 (2012) provides that it shall be unlawful for any person, agent, company or corporation to prevent or attempt to prevent, by word or writing, any of its discharged employees from obtaining employment, except that such provision "shall not be construed as prohibiting any person or agent of any company or corporation from furnishing in writing upon request . . . a truthful statement of the reason for such discharge." This "blacklisting" statute authorizes a cause of action for punitive damages only. Houpe v. The City of Statesville, 128 N.C. App. 334, 497 S.E.2d 82, rev. denied, 348 N.C. 72, 505 S.E.2d 871 (1998). In addition, to constitute a violation of the statute, statements to a prospective employer must be unsolicited. Cortes v. McDonald's Corp., 955 F. Supp. 531 (E.D. N.C. 1996); Friel v. Angell Care, Inc., 113 N.C. App. 505, 440 S.E.2d 111 (1994). See also Harrell v. City of Gastonia, 2008 WL 2139619 (W.D. N.C. May 20, 2008) (holding that employer statements to media outlets repeatedly challenging plaintiff to waive his right of privacy regarding his employment records did not constitute an "unsolicited statement" to prospective employers). Truthful statements made about a former employee in response to a request from a prospective employer are privileged under this section. Friel, supra. Cf. **Smith v. Waverly Partners, LLC, 2012 WL 3645324 (W.D. N.C. Aug. 23, 2012) (holding that a corporate recruiter's disclosure to plaintiff's current employer of the fact that plaintiff was considering other employment in contradiction of plaintiff's instructions presented a triable issue of fact as to plaintiff's breach of contract claim);** Smith v. Waverly Partners, LLC, 2011 WL 1655592 (W.D. N.C. April 29, 2011) (holding that a corporate recruiter's disclosure to plaintiff's current employer of the fact that plaintiff was considering other employment did not rise to the level of intrusion, where plaintiff did not allege that defendant "made a physical or other sensory intrusion, or pried without authorization into her confidential records"); Webb v. Harris, 378 F. Supp.2d 608 (M.D. N.C. 2005) (holding that a claim for post-employment defamation relating to an alleged statement made to a prospective employer "arose out of employment" for purposes of determining whether the claim was subject to mandatory arbitration); Baqir v. Principi, 288 F. Supp.2d 706 (W.D. N.C. 2003) (holding that a former federal employee's state law blacklisting and defamation claims were preempted by Title VII, given that such causes of action relied on the same alleged conduct that formed the basis for plaintiff's Title VII retaliation claims); Ihekwu v. City of Durham, 129 F. Supp.2d 870 (M.D. N.C. 2000) (denying former employee's federal ADA/blacklisting claim related to the alleged placement of medical information in his personnel file); News Reporter Co., v. Columbus County, 184 N.C. App. 512, 646 S.E.2d 390 (2007) (holding that portions of a county employee's letter sent to the Board of Commissioners recommending a co-worker for the position of county medical director are not protected from disclosure under N.C. Gen. Stat. § 153A-98 as confidential personnel file information); Couch v. Bradley, 179 N.C. App. 852, 635 S.E.2d 492 (2006)(enforcing a consent and forbearance agreement against a former coworker/defendant resolving a libel action, where defendant later provided a copy of the agreement to a neighbor, who forwarded the agreement and a letter concerning the earlier suit to plaintiff's prospective employers); Wuchte v. McNeil, 130 N.C. App. 738, 505 S.E.2d 142 (1998) (holding that merely withholding a recommendation for employment regarding a former public employee is insufficient to invoke due process protection); Gibby v. Murphy, 73 N.C. App. 128, 325 S.E.2d 673 (1985) (holding that evidence of an oral reference falsely accusing an employee of being charged with embezzlement is sufficient to uphold a jury finding of slander per se).

In response to ongoing concerns about the potential liability of employers responding to requests for reference checks, effective October 1, 1997, North Carolina adopted a new statute providing qualified immunity from civil liability to employers who disclose information about past or current employees. See N.C. Gen. Stat. § 1-539.12 (2012). This statute provides that an employer who discloses information about a current or former employee's job history or job performance to a prospective employer "upon request" of the prospective employer or the employee is "immune from civil liability and is not liable in civil damages for the disclosure or any consequences of the disclosure." N.C. Gen. Stat. § 1-539.12(a) (2012). For purposes of this statute, "job performance" is defined to include statements concerning the suitability of the employee for reemployment, the reason for the employee's separation and the employer's opinion concerning the employee's "skills, abilities, and traits as they may relate to suitability for future employment." N.C. Gen. Stat. § 1-539.12(a) and (b) (2012). Such qualified immunity, however, may be overcome where the plaintiff can demonstrate both that the information disclosed was false and that the employer providing the information "knew or reasonably should have known that the information was false." N.C. Gen. Stat. § 1-539.12(a)(1) and (2) (2012).

B. Non-Compete Agreements

As a general rule, covenants not to compete must meet six criteria to be considered valid and enforceable under North Carolina law. A covenant must be (1) in writing; (2) made a part of the contract of employment; (3) based on valuable consideration; (4) reasonable as to time and territory; (5) designed to protect a legitimate business interest of the employer; and (6) otherwise not against North Carolina public policy. United Laboratories, Inc. v. Kuykendall, 322 N.C. 643, 370 S.E.2d 375 (1988); Precision Walls, Inc. v. Servie, 152 N.C. App. 630, 568 S.E.2d 267 (2002); Farr Assoc., Inc. v. Baskin, 138 N.C. App. 276, 530 S.E.2d 878 (2000).

With respect to the requirement regarding writing, N.C. Gen. Stat. § 75-4 (2012) provides that "[n]o contract or agreement hereafter made, limiting the right of any person to do business anywhere in the State of North Carolina, shall be enforceable unless such agreement is in writing duly signed by the party who agrees not to enter into any such business within such territory . . . ." North Carolina, however, follows the minority rule that outside verbal or "parol" evidence may be used to establish the consideration provided for a non-compete (e.g., a pay raise/promotion). See Brooks Distribution Co. v. Pugh, 324 N.C. 326, 378 S.E.2d 31 (1989). Moreover, the terms of a verbal non-compete may be enforceable in some circumstances if later reduced to writing and signed by the employee. See, e.g., Robin & Weill v. Mason, 70 N.C. App. 537, 320 S.E.2d 693 (1984).

With respect to the second requirement, it is clear that a covenant not to compete is made part of "the employment contract" if it is entered into: (1) at the beginning of employment; or (2) later during employment when supported by adequate, new consideration. Some North Carolina cases, however, have implied that a non-compete must not only be attendant to an established employment relationship, but "entered into at the time and as part of *the contract*" of employment. (Emphasis added). See, e.g., Statesville Medical Group, P.A. v. Dickey, 106 N.C. App. 669, 418 S.E.2d 256 (1992).

Under North Carolina law, the signing of a covenant not to compete prior to or at the beginning of the employment relationship (i.e., upon hire) provides sufficient "consideration" to the employee to support the non-compete. Farr Assoc., supra. Similarly, a significant, beneficial change in the terms and conditions of an individual's employment may provide sufficient consideration to support a covenant not to compete entered into after an employment relationship has already begun (e.g., a promotion, raise or new incentive plan that the employee would not have been otherwise entitled to receive). Whittaker Gen. Med. Corp. v. Daniel, 324 N.C. 523, 379 S.E.2d 824 (1989); Cox v. Dine-A-Mate, Inc., 129 N.C. App. 773, 501 S.E.2d 353, rev. denied, 349 N.C. 355, 525 S.E.2d 449 (1998).

Continued employment or the promise of continued employment in and of itself will not provide sufficient consideration to support a non-compete entered into after an employment relationship has already begun. Greene Co. v. Kelley, 261 N.C. 166, 134 S.E.2d 16 (1964); Forrest Paschal Mach. Co. v. Millholen, 27 N.C. App. 678, 220 S.E.2d 190 (1975). Consideration provided by an employer in exchange for a non-compete also cannot be "illusory" (e.g., a promise of potential, future wholly discretionary bonuses). See, e.g., Milner Airco, Inc. of Charlotte v. Morris, 10 N.C. App. 323, 433 S.E.2d 811 (1993).

To be valid, a non-compete must also be reasonable as to both time and territory/scope. Farr Assoc., supra. See also Kennedy v. Kennedy, 160 N.C. App. 1, 584 S.E. 2d 328 (2003). With respect to the issue of time, limitations of six months to two years generally have been held to be reasonable, depending upon the position at issue. See, e.g., Market America, Inc. v. Christman-Orth, 135 N.C. App. 143, 520 S.E.2d 570 (1999), rev. denied, 351 N.C. 358, 542 S.E.2d 213 (2000) (six months); Amdar, Inc. v. Satterwhite, 37 N.C. App. 410, 246 S.E.2d 165 (1978) (one year); Forrest Paschal Machine Co., supra (two years); Wilmar, Inc. v. Corsillo, 24 N.C. App. 271, 210 S.E.2d 427 (1974) (one year). Cf. Eng'r Assoc., Inc., v. Pankow, 268 N.C. 137, 150 S.E.2d 56 (1966) (striking down a 5-year non-compete as over broad); Hartman v. Odell & Assoc., Inc., 117 N.C. App. 307, 450 S.E.2d 912 (1994) (striking down a ten-year, eight-county non-compete). Longer restrictions have been held to be valid in the case of covenants tied to dual shareholders/employees as part of the sale of a business. See, e.g., Bicycle Transit Auth., Inc. v. Bell, 314 N.C. 219, 333 S.E.2d 299 (1985) (citing Jewel Box Stores v. Morrow, 272 N.C. 659, 662-63, 158 S.E.2d 840, 843 (1968)).

With respect to the issue of territory, North Carolina courts have held that the restrictions contained in a non-compete must be no broader in scope than is necessary to protect the legitimate business interests of the employer. See, e.g., Southeastern Outdoor Prods., Inc. v. Lawson, 172 N.C. App. 592, 616 S.E.2d 693 (N.C. App. 2005); Hartman, supra. A major factor in such consideration is the reasonableness of the territorial restriction when related to the type of position occupied by the employee, and the skills and/or knowledge obtained by the employee while in his or her prior position(s). Thus, when determining the reasonableness of a territorial restriction, if the primary concern is the employee's knowledge of customers and/or accounts, courts have held that the territory should be limited only to areas in which the employee made contacts during the period of his or her employment. See, e.g., Farr Assoc., supra. Other factors relevant in determining the reasonableness of a geographic restriction include the area/scope of the restriction, area assigned to the employee, the area where the employee actually worked or was subject to work, the area in which the employer operated, nature of the business involved; and the nature of the employee's duty and his/her knowledge of the employer's business operation. See VisionAir, Inc. v. James, 167 N.C. App. 504, 606 S.E.2d 359 (2004); Hartman, supra. In addition, North Carolina courts will generally enforce a customer non-solicitation provision (as opposed to a broader non-compete) without reference to geographical limits. Farr Assoc., supra. But see Prof'l Liab. Consultants, Inc. v. Todd, 345 N.C. 176, 478 S.E.2d 201 (1996) (per curia) (overruling a North Carolina Court of Appeals' decision and approving the reasoning of the lower court's dissent, without comment, which struck down a customer non-solicitation provision with no geographical limit as unreasonable).

As to the last required factor for enforcing North Carolina non-competes, North Carolina courts have held that there are generally two separate and distinct bases for enforcing restrictive covenants: (1) intimate knowledge of a company's business operations and/or confidential information; and (2) personal contact and association with customers or intimate knowledge of customer needs and habits. Reynolds & Reynolds Co. v. Tart, 955 F. Supp. 547 (W.D. N.C. 1997); United Laboratories, supra; Hartman, supra. Customer relationships and goodwill are legitimate business interests protectable by non -competes in North Carolina. Id. An employer does not, however, have a legitimate protectable interest in merely preventing ordinary competition by a former employee. Cox, supra. In addition, even if an employee has no customer contacts or information, a non-compete may be enforceable against an employee if he/she acquired intimate knowledge of the nature and character of the business that was not otherwise generally known and available to the public. See Chemimetals Processing, Inc. v. McEneny, 124 N.C. App. 194, 476 S.E.2d 374 1996). But see Masterclean v. Guy, 82 N.C. App. 45, 345 S.E.2d 692 (1986) (refusing to issue an injunction when the only information the employer sought to protect was "unique" but not confidential or patented procedures).

Lastly, as a general rule, North Carolina courts will not rewrite or revise (blue pencil) portions of covenants not to compete found to be overly broad or unreasonable. Whittaker, supra; Southeastern Outdoor Prods., supra; Beasley v. Banks, 90 N.C. App. 458, 368 S.E.2d 885 (1988). As such, if a non-compete agreement is deemed to be over broad, courts will not rewrite the agreement but will simply strike and not enforce the entire provision. Id. If the contract terms are, however, separable and the remaining provisions are deemed to be reasonable, a court may choose to blue pencil/strike unreasonable, separable terms such that the other provisions remain. Id.

VIII. OTHER ISSUES

A. Statutes of Limitations

Although North Carolina law has no specific statute providing for a limitations period for invasion of privacy actions, N.C. Gen. Stat. § 1-52(2) (2012) provides for a three-year statute of limitations where no other limitations period is established by statute. See also Losing v. Food Lion, L.L.C., 185 N.C. App. 278, 648 S.E.2d 261 (2007), rev. denied, 362 N.C. 236, 659 S.E.2d 735 (2008) (affirming that "[t]he applicable statute of limitations for the tort of invasion of privacy is three years").

B. Jurisdiction

The status of an Alabama resident psychiatrist as the owner of a medical practice whose activities were carried out in North Carolina was sufficient to confer jurisdiction over defendant for an action alleging invasion of privacy and intentional infliction of emotional distress. Acosta v. Byrum, 180 N.C. App. 562, 638 S.E.2d 246 (2006).

C. Worker's Compensation Exclusivity

The North Carolina Workers' Compensation Act generally provides the exclusive remedy for claims arising out of workplace injuries. See N.C. Gen. Stat. § 97-10.1 (2012). See also Regan v. Amerimark Bldg. Prods., Inc., 118 N.C. App. 328, 454 S.E.2d 849, rev. denied, 340 N.C. 59, 458 S.E.2d 189 (1995), cert. denied, 342 N.C. 659, 467 S.E.2d 72 (1996); Andrews v. Peters, 55 N.C. App. 124, 284 S.E.2d 748 (1981), rev. denied, 305 N.C. 395, 290 S.E.2d 364 (1982). However, North Carolina courts have held that the Act does not bar a common law action by an employee against his employer "for the intentional conduct of the employer." Hogan v. Forsyth Country Club Co., 79 N.C. App. 483, 40 S.E.2d 116, rev. denied, 317 N.C. 334, 346 S.E.2d 140 (1986) (denying defendant's assertion that N.C. Gen. Stat. § 97-10.1 barred plaintiff's claim for intentional infliction of emotional distress). North Carolina courts have also carved out two additional exceptions. In Pleasant, the court held that an injured employee may pursue a civil action against a *co-employee* on the basis of willful, wanton and reckless negligence. Pleasant v. Johnson, 312 N.C. 710, 325 S.E.2d 244 (1985). In Woodson, the court held that an injured employee may sue an *employer* for damages when the employer "intentionally engages in misconduct knowing it is substantially certain to cause serious injury or death to employees." Woodson v. Rowland, 329 N.C. 330, 407 S.E.2d 222 (1991). This last exception has been held to apply "only in the most egregious cases of employer misconduct." Whitaker v. Town of Scotland Neck, 357 N.C. 552, 597 S.E.2d 665 (2003). However, the federal District Court for the Middle District of North Carolina has applied and extended the ruling in Hogan to hold that N.C. Gen. Stat. § 97-10.1 does not bar claims against an employer for negligent infliction of emotional distress. See Strickland v. Jewell, 562 F. Supp.2d 661 (M.D. N.C. 2007); Ridenhour v. Concord Screen Printers, Inc., 40 F. Supp.2d 744 (M.D. N.C. 1999).

No known North Carolina ruling exists regarding the application of the Workers' Compensation exclusivity rule with respect to state claims of intrusion / invasion of privacy.

D. Pleading Requirements

There are no heightened pleading requirements for invasion of privacy claims.

SURVEY OF NORTH DAKOTA EMPLOYMENT LIBEL LAW

Steven R. Anderson, Kathlyn E. Noecker, John P. Borger[1],
Daniel G. Prokott, Leita Walker and David Merritt
Faegre & Benson, L.L.P.
2200 Wells Fargo Center
90 South Seventh Street
Minneapolis, Minnesota 55402
Telephone: (612) 766-7000; Facsimile: (612) 766-1600
http://www.faegre.com/

(With Developments Reported Through **November 1, 2012**)

GENERAL COMMENTS

None.

SIGNIFICANT DEVELOPMENTS SINCE THE 2012 *SURVEY*

None.

I. GENERAL LAW

A. General Employment Law

1. ***At-Will Employment.*** In North Dakota, the traditional common law rule of employment at-will has been adopted by statute. N.D.C.C. § 34-03-01 provides:

An employment having no specified term may be terminated at the will of either party on notice to the other, except when otherwise provided by this title.

2. ***Statutory Exceptions to the "At-Will" Doctrine.*** North Dakota does not allow an employer to discharge an employee because of race, color, religion, sex, national origin, age, physical or mental disability, marital status, public assistance status, participation in lawful activity off the employer's premises during non-working hours which does not directly conflict with the essential business-related interests of the employer. N.D. Cent. Code § 14-02.4-03 (1997); see also Koehler v. County of Grand Forks, 658 N.W.2d 741, 745–46 (N.D. 2003).

Under N.D.C.C. § 34-01-20, an employer may not discharge an employee because the employee or person acting on behalf of employee reports a violation of law or rule to an employer, government body or law enforcement officer. In addition, an employee may not be discharged if requested to participate in an investigation, hearing or inquiry or if employee refuses an employer's order to perform an action the employee believes violates state or federal law or rule or regulation.

3. ***Case Law Exceptions to the "At-Will" Doctrine.*** The presumption of at-will employment can be overcome by the existence of a contract that takes the employment out of the at-will rule. Bykonen v. United Hosp., 479 N.W.2d 140, 141 (N.D. 1992). An employer and employee can define their contractual rights regarding termination. Thompson v. Associated Potato Growers, Inc., 610 N.W.2d 53, 56 (N.D. 2000). An employee can be terminated for good cause even if the contract does not specifically mention good cause but provides for other termination reasons. Id. at 57. Good cause is an objective standard under which an employer may terminate for "fair and honest reasons, regulated by good faith on the part of the employer, that are not trivial, arbitrary or capricious, unrelated to business needs or goals, or pretextual." Id. at 59. An employee's "impression" from his job interview that he has been hired for "permanent type" and "career type position" does not establish a contract of employment outside the at-will rule. Hillesland v. Federal Land Bank Ass'n, 407 N.W.2d 206, 211 (N.D. 1987). Describing a job as "permanent employment" during a job interview and stating that "as long as you want the job, it's yours," also does not overcome the presumption. Phillips v. Dickinson Mgmt., 580 N.W.2d 148, 150 (N.D. 1998). The use of terms such as "permanent employment," "life employment," and "as long as the employee chooses" are presumed to mean "steady employment," and do not overcome the presumption. Aaland v. Lake Region Grain Coop., 511 N.W.2d 244, 246 (N.D. 1994). Although a promise by an employer to allow an employee to remain at his position "until he found another job" does not overcome the at-will presumption and create an employment contract, the employer must continue employment for a "reasonable time" to allow the employee to look for a job. Id.

1. Licensed in North Dakota.

Employee handbooks that contain promises of specific treatment in specific situations can overcome the at-will presumption if they create an expectation that its provisions will be followed. See Eldridge v. Evangelical Lutheran Good Samaritan Soc'y, 417 N.W.2d 797, 799 (N.D. 1987); Bailey v. Perkins Restaurants, 398 N.W.2d 120, 122 (N.D. 1986). The entire manual must be examined to determine if its language creates an intent to overcome the at-will presumption and create an employment contract. Hunt v. Banner Health Sys., 720 N.W.2d 49 (N.D. 2006); Schmidt v. Ramsey County, 488 N.W.2d 411, 413 (N.D. Ct. App. 1992). A clear disclaimer, stating that the manual's policies are not intended to create contractual rights, is an important factor in determining whether the presumption has been overcome. See, e.g., Humann v. KEM Elec. Coop., Inc., 497 F.3d 810, 813 (8th Cir. 2007) (concluding employment remained at-will where defendant's policy bulletin stated that employment "has no specified term and may be terminated at the will of either the employee or the [employer] on notice to the other"); Good Bird v. Twin Buttes Sch. Dist., 733 N.W.2d 601, 605 (N.D. 2007) (concluding the handbook was not an express contract where it stated its "primary purpose ... is to serve as a resource guide to provide school staff with information and guidance regarding conditions of employment, work expectations, resources, procedures, professional ethics...."); Schmidt, 488 N.W.2d 411. Even when a handbook encourages employees to rely on its provisions as a "source of information you can look to with authority and completeness," the at-will presumption is not overcome if it contains a disclaimer that specifically and clearly states that the handbook's provisions do not create contractual rights. Olson v. Souris River Telcoms. Coop., 558 N.W.2d 333, 337 (N.D. 1997). In Dahlberg v. Lutheran Soc. Servs., 625 N.W.2d 241 (N.D. 2001), the North Dakota Supreme Court held that a progressive discipline policy promulgated after the employee handbook does not "override the at-will presumption preserved in the unambiguous language" of the handbook. See id. at 247–48. The court found that both the handbook and signed acknowledgement receipt contained specific and clear disclaimers stating that the handbook was not a contract and that the employer could terminate an employee for any reason or no reason. See id. It concluded that the handbook and the policy had to be construed together as a whole. See id. Similarly, where a policy states that employment is at-will and where an employee signs a receipt acknowledging the at-will employment status, the employee may not rely on equitable estoppel theories regarding termination claims. Humann, 497 F.3d at 813. Additionally, if the policy states that employment will depend on the employee's satisfactory performance but does not state that employment will depend *only* on satisfactory service, the employee is similarly barred from equitable estoppel theories. Id. If the intention of the parties can be ascertained from the terms of the personnel manual alone, its interpretation is a question of law. Bykonen, 479 N.W.2d at 142.

North Dakota follows the majority of states in declining to recognize an implied covenant of good faith and fair dealing in employment at-will situations. Jose v. Norwest Bank ND, N.S., 599 N.W.2d 293, 296 (N.D. 1999); see also Dalan v. Paracelsus Healthcare Corp. of N.D., Inc., 640 N.W.2d 726, 731 (N.D. 2002) (decided on other grounds but laying out the North Dakota cases in which the doctrine of implied covenant of good faith and fair dealing has been rejected). The court has stated that, "[w]e refuse to recognize a cause of action for breach of an implied covenant of good faith and fair dealing where, as in this case, the claimant relies upon an employment contract which contains no express term specifying the duration of employment." Hillesland v. Federal Land Bank Ass'n, 407 N.W.2d 206, 215 (N.D. 1987).

North Dakota recognizes claims for wrongful discharge in limited circumstances. See Wadeson v. American Family Mut. Ins. Co., 343 N.W.2d 367 (N.D. 1984); see also Peterson v. N.D. Univ. Sys. , 678 N.W.2d 163, 174 (N.D. 2004); Long v. Samson, 568 N.W.2d 602 (N.D. 1997); Soentgen v. Quain & Ramstad Clinic, P.C., 467 N.W.2d 73 (N.D. 1991). The court in Soentgen affirmed the dismissal of a wrongful discharge claim because Soentgen did not exhaust her administrative remedies. Soentgen, 467 N.W.2d at 73. An employer's decision to terminate an employee for cause must be assessed by the trier of fact under an objective standard of reasonableness. Thompson v. Associated Potato Growers, Inc., 610 N.W.2d 53, 59 (N.D. 2000).

The North Dakota Supreme Court has also recognized that even where an employee is at-will employee, and therefore may be terminated with or without cause, if the employee is a shareholder then the termination may trigger a claim that the employer acted in a manner that was unfairly prejudicial toward the employee in violation of the employee-shareholder's rights under the North Dakota Business Corporation Act (N.D.C.C. ch. 10-19.1). Kortum v. Johnson, 755 N.W.2d 432 (N.D. 2008).

The North Dakota Century Code prohibits employer retaliation against so-called "whistle blowers." Under N.D.C.C. § 34-01-20, it is unlawful for an employer to discharge, discipline or penalize an employee who reports a suspected violation of law in good faith, participates in an investigation of wrongdoing by public bodies, or refuses an employer's order to perform an action that the employee believes to be unlawful. See Vandall v. Trinity Hosps., 676 N.W.2d 88, 90–93 (N.D. 2004). To establish a prima facie case of retaliatory discharge under the North Dakota statute, the employee must show: (1) the employee engaged in a protected activity; (2) the employer took an adverse action against the employee; and (3) the existence of a causal connection between the employee's protected activity and the employer's adverse action. Heng v. Rotech Med. Corp., 720 N.W.2d 54 (N.D. 2006); Jacob v. Nodak Mut. Ins. Co., 693 N.W.2d 604, 611 (N.D. 2005); Vandall, 676 N.W.2d at 92; Dahlberg, 625 N.W.2d at 253; see also Anderson v. Meyer Broad. Co., 630 N.W.2d 46, 55 (N.D. 2001) (concluding that any evidence of a causal connection was missing and that the court would not draw "an inference of causation from the mere fact [that the plaintiff] reported violations and was subsequently fired" as that would be based on "pure speculation"). To receive protection, the employee must make a report "for the purpose of blowing the whistle to expose an illegality, and the reporter's purpose must be assessed at the time the report is made." Dahlberg, 625 N.W.2d at 255–56; see also Vukelic v. Bartz, 245 F. Supp. 2d 1068 (D.N.D. 2003) (analysis of defamation, First Amendment protection and unlawful retaliation in a public employment context under federal law); Heng, 720 N.W.2d at 60–63 (holding the evidence was sufficient to support the court's findings that plaintiff's reports were made in good faith and that her termination from employment was causally related to a good-faith report of a violation of law where plaintiff told her regional manager and director that the defendant employer was not complying with North Dakota respiratory care regulations and repeatedly sought clarification from them on how to effectuate compliance with the regulation); Jacob, 693 N.W.2d at 606 (concluding that letter from plaintiffs' counsel to North Dakota Insurance Investigator advising of plaintiffs' participation in company's internal investigation, requesting inspection of documents, and stating that "[w]hen we have this information, we will be in a better position to assess pursuit of our claims and complaints under the North Dakota Uniform Fair Trade Practices Act" was not protected activity because letter failed to specify any law alleged to have been violated); Vandall, 676 N.W.2d at 90–93 (finding that when both a common law and statutory action for retaliatory discharge coexist but with different statute of limitations periods, the statute of limitations provided by the statutory law governs a claim for retaliatory discharge).

The North Dakota Supreme Court has recognized public policy exceptions to the at-will presumption. Peterson v. N.D. Univ. Sys. , 678 N.W. 2d 163, 174 (N.D. 2004); Vandall, 676 N.W.2d at 91; Jose v. Norwest Bank ND, N.A., 599 N.W.2d 293, 298 (N.D. 1999). In Ressler v. Humane Soc'y, 480 N.W.2d 429, 432 (N.D. 1992), the court held that public policy prohibits an employer from discharging an employee for honoring a subpoena and for testifying truthfully. In Krein v. Marian Manor Nursing Home, 415 N.W.2d 793, 794 (N.D. 1987), the court held that public policy prohibits retaliatory discharge of an employee for seeking workers compensation benefits. However, to qualify as an at-will exception, the public policy relied on must be evidenced by a constitutional or statutory provision. Jose, 599 N.W.2d at 298, 299. In Jose, the court dismissed the retaliatory discharge claims of two employees because there was no constitutional or statutory provision that indicated that it was against public policy to fire employees for their participation in an internal investigation of their supervisor's job performance. Id.

The at-will employment doctrine is limited when employers engage in discriminatory practices. Koehler v. County of Grand Forks, 658 N.W.2d 741, 745–46 (N.D. 2003); see also Fatland v. Quaker State Corp., 62 F.3d 1070 (8th Cir. 1995). Under N.D.C.C. § 14-02.4-03 it is a discriminatory practice for an employer to discharge an employee "because of race, color, religion, sex, national origin, age, physical or mental disability, status with respect to marriage or public assistance, or participation in lawful activity off the employer's premises during nonworking hours which is not in direct conflict with the essential business-related interests of the employer." See also Koehler, 658 N.W.2d at 745 ("The Act's purpose is to prevent and eliminate discrimination in employment relations, and it prohibits an employer from taking certain adverse employment actions on the basis of, among other things, physical disability.").

A "letter of call" issued by a religious organization to a chaplain that reserves its right to terminate his employment does not affect the at-will presumption when the employer of the chaplain did not issue or sign the letter. Hougum v. Valley Mem'l Homes, 574 N.W.2d 812, 820 (N.D. 1998).

B. Elements of Defamation Claim

1. ***Basic Elements***. Under North Dakota law, defamation is classified as either libel or slander. N.D.C.C. § 14-02-02 (2005). The North Dakota Supreme Court has held that every person has the right to be protected from defamation (libel or slander). Fish v. Dockter, 671 N.W.2d 819, 822–23 (N.D. 2003); Bertsch v. Duemeland, 639 N.W.2d 455, 459–60 (N.D. 2002); Moritz v. Medical Arts Clinic, P. C., 315 N.W.2d 458, 460 (N.D. 1982). North Dakota's libel statute, N.D.C.C. § 14-02-03, provides that:

> Libel is a false and unprivileged publication by writing, printing, picture, effigy, or other fixed representation to the eye, which exposes any person to hatred, contempt, ridicule, or obloquy, or which causes him to be shunned or avoided, or which has a tendency to injure him in his occupation.

See also Mr. G's Turtle Mt. Lodge, Inc. v. Roland Twp., 651 N.W.2d 625, 633 (N.D. 2002). Therefore, the essential elements of a workplace libel claim include the publication by the employer of unprivileged, false information that is believed to be defamatory by the person or persons to whom it is published. See Forster v. W. Dakota Veterinary Clinic, Inc., 689 N.W.2d 366, 379 (N.D. 2004). Section 14-02-05 of the North Dakota Century Code recognizes communications that are deemed to be privileged and provides as follows:

> *Privileged communications.* A privileged communication is one made:
>
> In the proper discharge of an official duty;
>
> In any legislative or judicial proceeding or in any other proceeding authorized by law;
>
> In a communication, without malice, to a person interested therein by one who also interested, or by one who stands in such relation to the person interested as to afford a reasonable ground for supposing the motive for the communication innocent, or who is requested by the person interested to give the information; and
>
> By a fair and true report, without malice, of a judicial, legislative, or other public official proceeding, or of anything said in the course thereof
>
> In the cases provided for in subsections 3 and 4, malice is not inferred from the communication or publication. See Humann v. KEM Elec. Coop., Inc., 450 F. Supp. 2d 1006, 1016 (D.N.D. 2006), aff'd 497 F.3d 810 (8th Cir. 2007).
>
> Under N.D.C.C. § 14-02-04 civil slander is defined as follows:
>
> False and unprivileged publication, other than libel, which: 1. Charges any person with crime, or with having been indicted, convicted, or punished for crime; 2. Imputes to him the present existence of an infectious, contagious, or loathsome disease; 3. Tends directly to injure him in respect to his office, profession, trade, or business, either by imputing to him general disqualifications in those respects which the office or other occupation peculiarly requires, or by imputing something with reference to his office, profession, trade, or business that has a natural tendency to lessen its profits; 4. Imputes to him impotence or want of chastity; or 5. By natural consequence causes actual damage.

See also Fish, 671 N.W.2d at 822.

2. ***Fault.*** North Dakota has had no libel cases involving the issue of public/private figures, nor has North Dakota had any cases defining actual malice since New York Times Co. v. Sullivan, 376 U.S. 254 (1964). Some early cases, however, discussed various forms of malice (malice in law, legal malice, actual malice, presumed malice). See Wrege v. Jones, 100 N.W. 705 (N.D. 1904); Lauder v. Jones, 101 N.W. 907 (N.D. 1904).

3. ***Falsity.*** For a statement to be libelous or slanderous, and therefore defamatory, it must first be false. See Witzke v. City of Bismarck, 718 N.W.2d 586 (N.D. 2006) (holding that failure to show that statements made by city prosecutor to city officials were false precluded individual from prevailing on defamation claim); Mr. G's, 651 N.W.2d at 634–35 ("This Court had indicated defamation will not lie where only a forced construction will place a defamatory connotation on the communication. . . . We conclude that the truthful and innocuous language of the letters is not fairly susceptible of a defamatory meaning."); Bertsch, 639 N.W.2d at 461–62 ("Duemeland's communication about Bertsch's business capabilities could be construed as injuring Bertsch in his occupation by imputing to him general disqualifications in his occupation. . . . We conclude Duemeland's communication is susceptible to a meaning that is defamatory, and it is ordinarily a question for the trier of fact to determine whether the recipient . . . understood it in that light."). North Dakota's Constitution allows truth as a defense if the communication is "published with good motives and for justifiable ends." N.D. Const. Art. I, § 4. In dealing with political speech, a false statement made in good faith is deemed protected by the First Amendment. See District One Republican Comm. v. District One Democratic Comm., 466 N.W.2d 820 (N.D. 1991). If the language of an alleged libel is fairly susceptible of a construction rendering it defamatory and therefore actionable, though also susceptible to contrary construction, it is for the jury to determine whether the words were used in an innocent or defamatory sense. See Rickbeil v. Grafton Deaconess Hosp., 23 N.W.2d 247 (N.D. 1946); Meyerle v. Pioneer Publishing Co., 178 N.W. 792 (N.D. 1920); McCue v. Equity Coop. Publishing Co., 167 N.W. 225 (N.D. 1918); Lauder v. Jones, 101 N.W. 907 (N.D. 1904). In addition, there can be no defamation unless the recipient of the communication believes it to be defamatory, i.e., the plaintiff is defamed in the recipient's eyes. Little v. Spaeth, 394 N.W.2d 700 (N.D. 1986). In Jose v. Norwest Bank ND, N.A., 599 N.W.2d 293, 299 (N.D. 1999), the North Dakota Supreme Court held that a "Staff Changes" memorandum that correctly noted that two employees had been terminated was not defamatory even though third parties may have drawn inferences about the employees as a result of the memorandum.

4. ***Defamatory Statement of Fact.*** In Myers v. Richland County, 2004 U.S. Dist. LEXIS 19944, *42 (D.N.D. Sept. 30, 2004), the District Court of North Dakota held that a statement of fact will not be considered defamatory simply because the speaker "places a defamatory connotation on the statement." The court will construe the statement of fact according to the general meaning of the words, and will not consider the statement to be defamatory unless it is "fairly

susceptible of a defamatory meaning." Id. at 42 (citing Moritz v. Medical Arts Clinic P.C., 315 N.W.2d 458, 460 (N.D. 1982), for the rule that words must be construed as people generally understand them and according to their ordinary meaning). In the employment context, a statement of fact may be considered defamatory if the statement imputes general disqualifications to the plaintiff that are peculiarly required by the plaintiff's occupation. Id. at *41; see also Fjelsta v. Zogg Dermatology, PLC, 488 F.3d 804, 811 (8th Cir. 2007) (vague statement regarding reasons for termination not reasonably interpreted as implying a damaging, provable false statement of fact).

5. ***Of and Concerning Plaintiff.*** No reported cases.

6. ***Publication.*** North Dakota courts have been relatively liberal with the concept of publication. In Rickbeil v. Grafton Deaconess Hosp., 23 N.W.2d 247, 255 (N.D. 1946), the North Dakota Supreme Court concluded that a letter defaming its recipient met the requirement of publication, because it was "published" when the author dictated it to his secretary. Id. Similarly, in Emo v. Milbank Mut. Ins. Co., 183 N.W.2d 508 (N.D. 1971), the court concluded that publication to one's spouse of defamatory matter is sufficient to give rise to a cause of action for defamation, as allegedly defamatory matter communicated to a third party is publication. See also Farmers Ins. Exch. v. Schirado, 717 N.W.2d 576 (N.D. 2006) (accepting circumstantial evidence of publication that after communicating with former employer, prospective employers no longer had available positions for plaintiff); Forster v. W. Dakota Veterinary Clinic, Inc., 689 N.W.2d 366, 377 (N.D. 2004) (accepting circumstantial evidence that some recipients of communication had changed their behavior after communicating with defendant as sufficient to find that publication had occurred, and that statements were understood as defamatory).

North Dakota has enacted the Uniform Single Publication Act at N.D.C.C. § 14-02-10, which provides:

> No person may have more than one claim for relief for damages for libel or slander or invasion of privacy or any other tort founded upon any single publication or exhibition or utterance, such as any one edition of a newspaper or book or magazine or any one presentation to an audience or any one broadcast over radio or television or any one exhibition of a motion picture. Recovery in any action must include all damages for any such tort suffered by the plaintiff in all jurisdictions.
>
> A judgment in any jurisdiction for or against the plaintiff upon the substantive merits of any action for damages founded upon a single publication or exhibition or utterance as described in this section bars any other action for damages by the same plaintiff against the same defendant founded upon the same publication or utterance.

a. **Intracorporate Communication.** While no cases have specifically addressed intracorporate communication, in light of North Dakota's liberal treatment of publication it appears likely that a North Dakota court would hold that intracorporate communication constitutes publication. See Rickbeil v. Grafton Deaconess Hosp., 23 N.W.2d 247 (N.D. 1946) (holding that a letter was published when its author dictated it to his secretary). However, in Jose, 599 N.W.2d at 299, the North Dakota Supreme Court held that a "Staff Changes" memorandum that correctly noted that two employees had been terminated was not defamatory even though third parties may have drawn inferences about the employees as a result of the memorandum.

b. **Compelled Self-Publication.** In Jose, 599 N.W.2d at 300, the North Dakota Supreme Court declined to decide "whether the element of publication in a defamation case is satisfied when an employee is compelled to disclose to a prospective employer the reason given for termination by a former employer," because the plaintiffs in that case failed to present evidence to support the elements necessary to apply the doctrine. The court noted that other jurisdictions have held that an employee may "assert a claim for compelled self-publication defamation in the employment context when: (1) the defendant employer makes a defamatory statement to the plaintiff employee; (2) it was reasonably foreseeable to the defendant that the plaintiff would be under a strong compulsion to disclose the content of that statement to prospective employers; (3) the plaintiff, under compulsion, communicates the defamatory statement to a prospective employer; and (4) because of that communication, the plaintiff was damaged." Id. at 299-300.

c. **Republication.** The author of a defamation is not liable for an unauthorized republication that he reasonably could not have anticipated. Waite v. Stockgrowers' Credit Corp., 249 N.W. 910 (N.D. 1933).

7. ***Statements versus Conduct.*** There are no published cases in North Dakota on the issue of whether conduct alone could constitute defamation. However, the North Dakota Supreme Court has hinted that defamation by conduct may be an actionable claim under the proper set of circumstances: "Ordinarily, publication in a slander case is accomplished by the communication of the allegedly defamatory matter to a third party by spoken words, by transitory gestures, or by any form of communication other than such form as would make it a libel." Gowin v. Hazen Mem'l Hosp. Ass'n, 311 N.W.2d 554, 558 (N.D. 1981).

8. **Damages.** Both general and special damages are recoverable in North Dakota for harm arising from libel or slander. Vanover v. Kansas City Life Ins. Co., 553 N.W.2d 192 (N.D. 1996). A jury may also award exemplary damages in addition to compensatory damages, if there was oppression, fraud, or malice by the defendant. N.D.C.C. § 32-03.2-11. The original complaint may not seek exemplary damages, rather the party must move to amend the pleadings to claim exemplary damages. Vanover, 553 N.W.2d at 194. The motion must be accompanied by one or more affidavits alluding to the factual basis for the exemplary damages. Id.

a. **Presumed Damages and Libel Per Se.** After Vanover v. Kansas City Life Ins. Co., 553 N.W.2d 192 (N.D. 1996), North Dakota no longer recognizes a distinction between libel per quod and libel per se and therefore proof of special damages is no longer necessary in an action for libel per quod. See also Forster, 689 N.W.2d 366, 377–78 (N.D. 2004).

(1) **Employment-Related Criticism.** The North Dakota Supreme Court has stated that "generally communications by an employer concerning the conduct of an employee are, when necessary to protect interests of the employer, qualifiedly privileged." Soentgen v. Quain & Ramstad Clinic, P.C., 467 N.W.2d 73, 78–79 (N.D. 1991). This privilege is "based upon the sound public policy that some communications are so socially important that the full and unrestricted exchange of information requires some latitude for mistake." Id. The privilege may be defeated by proof of actual malice. See also Vukelic v. Bartz, 245 F. Supp. 2d 1068 (D.N.D. 2003) (analysis of defamation, First Amendment protection and unlawful retaliation in a public employment context under federal law).

(2) **Single Instance Rule.** No reported cases.

b. **Punitive Damages.** North Dakota allows punitive damages for defamation claims if there is evidence of oppression, fraud, or actual malice. N.D.C.C.§ 32-03.2-11. Proof of any compensatory or actual damages will support an award of exemplary damages. Vanover v. Kansas City Life Ins. Co., 553 N.W.2d 192 (N.D. 1996).

II. PRIVILEGES AND DEFENSES

A. Scope of Privileges

Under North Dakota law a privileged communication is defined by statute. N.D.C.C. § 14-02-05 states that a privileged communication is one made:

1. In the proper discharge of an official duty;

2. In any legislative or judicial proceeding, or in any other proceeding authorized by law;

3. In a communication, without malice, to a person interested therein by one who also is interested, or by one who stands in such relation to the person interested as to afford a reasonable ground for supposing the motive for the communication innocent, or who is requested by the person interested to give the information; and

4. By a fair and true report, without malice, of a judicial, legislative, or other public official proceeding, or of anything said in the course thereof.

See also Fish v. Dockter, 671 N.W.2d 819, 822–23 (N.D. 2003).

In Jose v. Norwest Bank ND, N.A., 599 N.W.2d 293, 299, the North Dakota Supreme Court held that a "Staff Changes" memorandum that correctly noted that two employees had been terminated was a privileged communication because it was a "communication between persons of common interest."

In Humann v. KEM Elec. Co-op., Inc., , 1010 (D.N.D. 2006), aff'd 497 F.3d 810 (8th Cir. 2007), the court held that a letter from KEM's attorney to Humann's attorney was privileged because it referenced a likely judicial proceeding and because the corresponding response concerned possible defenses.

1. ***Absolute Privilege.*** The North Dakota Supreme Court has held that the absolute privilege created by subsections (1) and (2) of N.D.C.C. § 14-02-05 is warranted because under those circumstances "the free exchange of information is so important that even defamatory statements made with actual malice are privileged." Soentgen v. Quain & Ramstad Clinic, P.C., 467 N.W.2d 73, 78 (N.D. 1991); Witzke v. City of Bismarck, 718 N.W.2d 586, 591 (N.D. 2006) (concluding that any defamatory statements made by the city prosecutor were privileged communication because the statements were made while the city prosecutor was discharging his official duty during a judicial proceeding). In Rykowsky v. Dickinson Pub. Sch. Dist. #1, 508 N.W.2d 348 (N.D. 1993), an employee was accused at a school board meeting of costing the school district money because he irresponsibly managed the district's bus system. The North Dakota Supreme Court held

that the statements fell under § 14-02-05(1) and therefore were not actionable. Id. at 351; see also Riemers v. State, 738 N.W.2d 906 (N.D. Ct. App. 2007) (child support reports were privileged official communications under defamation statute). The court stated that school board meetings had been recognized as "official proceedings authorized by law" within the meaning of similar statutes. 508 N.W.2d at 351. However, the court noted that the communication, even if covered by the absolute privilege, must still be pertinent to be free of liability. Id. In this case, the communication was pertinent because it concerned a matter over which the school board had responsibility. Id.; see also Humann v. KEM Elec. Co-Op., Inc., 497 F.3d 810 (8th Cir. 2007) (statements made in letter response to letter threatening judicial proceeding privileged); Zutz v. Kamrowski, 787 N.W.2d 286 (N.D. 2010) (interpreting Minnesota law, which the district court held was consistent with North Dakota law, and affirming decision that report of private investigator commissioned by county attorney was absolutely privileged); Voigt v. State, 759 N.W.2d 530, 533 (N.D. 2008) (statements made during a legislative proceeding were absolutely privileged); Fish, 671 N.W.2d at 823–24 (co-worker's statements about another worker's maintenance of his work vehicle that were made during a federal administrative hearing were entitled to an absolute privilege); In re Dvorak, 611 N.W.2d 147 (N.D. 2000) (answers given in response to guardian ad litem's questionnaire are absolutely privileged). In Wagner v. Miskin, 660 N.W.2d 593 (N.D. 2003), the state supreme court determined that while the absolute privilege protected defamatory, privileged statements, "[a] privileged statement, such as one made in a judicial proceeding, is not privileged for all subsequent publications by virtue of initially being spoken in a privileged proceeding. . . . Even an 'absolute' privilege does not permit an individual to categorically republish possibly defamatory statements without consequence." Id. at 596–97.

2. ***Qualified Privileges.*** The North Dakota Supreme Court has held that subsections (3) and (4) of N.D.C.C. § 14-02-05 provide a qualified privilege, rather than an absolute one, because the danger of abuse is greater. Soentgen v. Quain & Ramstad Clinic, P.C., 467 N.W.2d 73, 78 (N.D. 1991). An analysis of qualified privilege requires a two -step process to determine (1) if the attending circumstances of a communication occasion a qualified privilege, and (2) if so, whether the privilege was abused. Id. at 73; see also Forster v. W. Dakota Veterinary Clinic, Inc., 689 N.W.2d 366, 379 (N.D. 2004). In Soentgen, the court found that statements made at a meeting regarding the conduct and alleged drug and alcohol dependency of an employee-physician were covered by qualified privilege, and privilege was not abused. The court explained its ruling by stating that, "generally communications by an employer concerning the conduct of an employee are, when necessary to protect interests of the employer, qualifiedly privileged." Soentgen, 467 N.W.2d at 79. Moreover, the court stated that public policy supported the privilege in this case because of the employer's duty to protect the public from incompetent or impaired physicians. Id.; see also Fish, 671 N.W.2d at 823 (when a co-worker is required, by job duty and/or company policy, to report to his employer about the conditions of another worker's truck, those statements are entitled to a qualified privilege).

a. **Common Interest.** In Soentgen, 467 N.W.2d at 79, the court found that statements made at a meeting regarding the conduct and alleged drug and alcohol dependency of an employee-physician were qualifiedly privileged and that this privilege was not abused. The court explained its ruling by stating that "generally communications by an employer concerning the conduct of an employee are, when necessary to protect interests of the employer, qualifiedly privileged." Id.; see also Khokha v. Shahin, 767 N.W.2d 159, 169 (N.D. 2009) (holding that statements doctor made to patient's family regarding the cause of her death were protected by qualified privilege because they were made to interested persons; further holding that doctor's alleged failure to comply with hospital policy involved whether he abused the privilege, which was an issue of fact for the jury).

b. **Duty.** In Soentgen, 467 N.W.2d at 79, the court also based its finding of qualified privilege on the fact that public policy supports the privilege in cases when an employer's duty to protect the public from incompetent or impaired physicians exists.

c. **Criticism of Public Employee.** There is no statute expressly providing for immunity for criticism of public employees generally, but such statements may be qualifiedly privileged under N.D.C.C. § 14-02-05. See II.A, supra. In addition, the North Dakota legislature has provided specific grants of absolute immunity for statements made regarding public employees in certain limited circumstances. An example is found in N.D.C.C. § 15-47-38, which provides that "[n]o cause of action for libel or slander may be brought for any statement expressed either orally or in writing at any executive session of [a] school board" for the purpose of determining whether to discharge a teacher.

In Riemers v. Mahar, 748 N.W.2d 714, 721-22 (N.D. 2008), the North Dakota Supreme Court held that individuals who assist in drafting state ballot initiatives qualify as limited purpose public figures for defamation purposes. The limited purpose public figure status is appropriate, the court said, because initiative drafters voluntarily assume a role of special prominence in a social controversy to influence its outcome. Id. at 721. As a result, the plaintiff, who had drafted the Family Law Reform Initiative and was one of its main proponents, was required to present clear and convincing evidence that the defendant's statements were false and made with actual malice. Id.

d. <u>**Limitation on Qualified Privileges**</u>. Under North Dakota law, a "qualified privilege is abused if statements are made with actual malice, without reasonable grounds for believing them to be true, and on a subject matter irrelevant to the common interest or duty. . . . If the occasion is one of qualified privilege, actual malice is not inferred from the communication or publication even if statements are slander per se." <u>Soentgen</u>, 467 N.W.2d at 79.

(1) **Constitutional or Actual Malice**. Evidence of constitutional malice would defeat a qualified privilege, but a plaintiff does not have to meet this high standard. <u>Id.</u> A qualified privilege is abused if statements are made with common law malice (defined as malice in fact, ill-will or wrongful motive), without reasonable grounds for believing them to be true, and on a subject matter irrelevant to the basis for the privilege. <u>Id.</u>

(2) **Common Law Malice.** A qualified privilege is abused if statements are made with common law malice (defined as malice in fact, ill-will or wrongful motive), without reasonable grounds for believing them to be true, and on a subject matter irrelevant to the basis for the privilege. <u>Id.</u>

e. <u>**Question of Fact or Law**</u>. The court in <u>Soentgen</u> further delineated the province of the court and the jury. When the circumstances surrounding the communication are not in dispute, the determination of whether there is a qualified privilege is a question of law for the court, but whether that qualified privilege is abused is generally a question of fact. <u>Id.</u>

Moreover, actual malice and abuse of a qualified privilege generally are questions of fact. <u>Id.</u> The court however went on to state that, "where the facts and inferences are such that reasonable minds could not differ, factual issues are questions of law." <u>Id.</u>

f. <u>**Burden of Proof**</u>. The <u>Soentgen</u> court ruled that once a defendant establishes that a statement is entitled to a qualified privilege, the burden shifts to the plaintiff to prove abuse of the privilege. <u>Id.</u>

B. Standard Libel Defenses

1. ***Truth.*** In view of the fact that the essence of a defamation claim is the falsity of the communication, truth is clearly the best defense to a libel claim. North Dakota's Constitution allows truth as a defense if the communication is published with good motives and for justifiable ends. N.D. Const. Art. I, § 4. A trial court has held that material is not false if it is substantially true. <u>Klem v. Dickinson Press</u>, Civ. No. 90C-162, slip op. (SW Judicial Dist. Ct. July 28, 1992).

In <u>Eli v. Griggs County Hosp. & Nursing Home</u>, 385 N.W.2d 99 (N.D. 1986), an employee was fired for breach of confidentiality when she made inappropriate remarks about her supervisor and employer in general. A summary of the remarks, documenting her misconduct, was placed in her personnel file. <u>Id.</u> at 100. Although the plaintiff alleged that this constituted defamation, the court found otherwise based on its conclusion that the summary was a truthful synopsis of the plaintiff's actions. <u>Id.</u> at 101.

2. ***Opinion.*** North Dakota courts have not considered this issue in the post-<u>Gertz</u> or post-<u>Milkovich</u> era, thus case law reflects common law doctrines of fair comment, etc. There is no "test" to distinguish opinion from fact. <u>See</u> <u>Langer v. Courier News</u>, 179 N.W. 909 (1920); <u>McCue v. Equity Coop. Publ'g Co.</u>, 167 N.W. 225 (1918).

3. ***Consent.*** No reported cases.

4. ***Mitigation.*** <u>See</u> <u>Forster v. W. Dakota Veterinary Clinic, Inc.</u>, 689 N.W.2d 366, 380–82 (N.D. 2004) (following Restatement (Second) of Torts § 918(2) (1977), which takes a restrictive view of the victim's obligation to mitigate damages in cases involving intentional torts).

III. RECURRING FACT PATTERNS

There have been relatively few cases related to libel in an employment setting in North Dakota, and therefore there are no identifiable recurring fact patterns that would lead to a predictable pool of case law. Typically, communications to an employee regarding the employee's performance are considered "qualifiedly privileged" under North Dakota law. <u>Soentgen v. Quain & Ramstad Clinic, P.C.</u>, 467 N.W.2d 73, 79 (N.D. 1991).

A. Statements in Personnel File

In <u>Eli v. Griggs County Hosp. & Nursing Home</u>, 385 N.W.2d 99 (N.D. 1986), an employee was fired for breach of confidentiality when she made inappropriate remarks about her supervisor and employer in general. <u>Id.</u> at 100. A summary of the remarks documenting her misconduct was placed in her personnel file. <u>Id.</u> Although the plaintiff alleged that this constituted defamation, the court found otherwise based on its conclusion that the summary was a truthful synopsis of the plaintiff's actions. <u>Id.</u> at 101.

B. Performance Evaluations

Typically, communications to an employee regarding the employee's performance are considered "qualifiedly privileged" under North Dakota law. Soentgen, 467 N.W.2d at 79.

C. References

Employers have been given qualified immunity under North Dakota statutory law when they give references. N.D.C.C. § 34-02-18 provides that:

> 1. An employer, or an employer's agent, who truthfully discloses date of employment, pay level, job description and duties, and wage history about a current or former employee to a prospective employer of the employee is immune from civil liability for the disclosure and the consequences of the disclosure of that information.
>
> 2. An employer, or an employer's agent, who discloses information about a current or former employee's job performance to a prospective employer of the employee is presumed to be acting in good faith. Unless lack of good faith is shown, the employer or employer's agent is immune from civil liability for the disclosure and the consequences of providing that information. The presumption of good faith may be rebutted by a preponderance of the evidence that the information disclosed was:
>
> (1) Knowingly false;
>
> (2) Disclosed with reckless disregard for the truth;
>
> (3) Deliberately misleading; or
>
> (4) Rendered with malicious purpose.
>
> 3. The immunity provided by subsection 2 does not apply if the information provided is in violation of a nondisclosure agreement, or was otherwise confidential according to applicable law.

In a case decided before the August 1, 1997, enactment of N.D.C.C. § 34-02-18, an employee recovered substantial damages for an employer's post-termination statements about the employee. Vanover v. Kansas City Life Ins. Co., 553 N.W.2d 192 (N.D. 1996). In Vanover, the general counsel of Vanover's former employer, Kansas City Life Ins. Co., sent a letter to Vanover's current employer and others stating that Vanover had been terminated "for cause." Id. at 194. Vanover was terminated shortly thereafter and Vanover subsequently sued Kansas City for defamation, alleging that Kansas City had made "unprivileged and false statements by letter and telephone that he had been terminated 'for cause.'" Id. at 194. Vanover was awarded $1,400,250 in damages. Id. at 199.

D. Intracorporate Communications

No reported cases. But see Rickbeil v. Grafton Deaconess Hosp., 23 N.W.2d 247 (N.D. 1946) (the court held that a letter was "published" when the author dictated it to his secretary).

E. Statements to Government Regulators

There are no specific cases addressing this issue. The absolute privilege for statements made "in any legislative or judicial proceeding" or the qualified privilege for "a communication, without malice, to a person interested therein by one who also is interested" provided for in N.D.C.C. § 14-02-05 may apply. See Voigt, 759 N.W.2d at 533 (holding that statements made by a Special Assistant Attorney General for Workforce Safety and Insurance to an interim workers' compensation review committee were absolutely privileged).

F. Reports to Auditors and Insurers

No reported cases. But see III.E, supra.

G. Vicarious Liability of Employers for Statements Made by Employees

1. **Blogging.** No reported cases.

H. Internal Investigations

No reported cases.

IV. OTHER ACTIONS BASED ON STATEMENTS

A. Negligent Hiring, Retention, and Supervision

North Dakota has recognized the torts of negligent hiring, negligent retention and negligent supervision. See, e.g., Mentz v. United States, 359 F. Supp. 2d 856, 859 (D.N.D. 2005); Koehler v. County of Grand Forks, 658 N.W.2d 741, 749 (N.D. 2003). In McLean v. Kirby Co., 490 N.W.2d 229, 232 (N.D. 1992), the North Dakota Supreme Court ruled that when an employer's placement of an employee poses a "peculiar unreasonable risk of physical harm to others," an employer must take precautions and exercise reasonable care in the selection of employees. Similarly, in Nelson v. Gillette, 571 N.W.2d 332, 340 (N.D. 1997), the North Dakota Supreme Court ruled that an employer may be liable for negligent supervision when the "foreseeable misconduct of an employee" causes harm to other employees or third parties, but only if the harm occurs when the employee is on the premises of the employer or using the employer's chattel (e.g. company vehicles). "Because the claim is based on negligence principles, the plaintiff has the burden of demonstrating a duty, breach of that duty, causation, and damages." Koehler, 658 N.W.2d at 749 (affirming summary judgment for employer due to plaintiff's failure to demonstrate any pecuniary loss). An employer cannot be liable for independent claims of negligent supervision brought by employees suffering loss of employment, absent physical injury. Kongelf v. Sears Holding Corp., 2010 WL 1977955, No. 4:09-cv-038 (D.N.D. April 12, 2010). Such a claim of negligent supervision is foreclosed by the employment at-will doctrine codified at N.D.C.C. §34-03-01. Id.

Generally, one who employs an independent contractor is not liable for the independent contractor's negligence. See Pechtl v. Conoco, Inc., 567 N.W.2d 813, 816 (N.D. 1997). However, when an employer, retains control over the independent contractor's work in terms of the "method, manner, and operative detail of the work," the employer is "subject to liability for physical harm to others for whose safety the employer owes a duty to exercise reasonable care." Fleck v. ANG Coal Gasification Co., 522 N.W.2d 445, 447 (N.D. 1994); Restatement (Second) of Torts § 414 (1965); Gasal v. CHS Inc., 2011 U.S. Dist. LEXIS 81833 (D. N.D. July 22, 2011) (finding that an employer did not owe plaintiff a duty to protect him from injuries caused by a subcontractor's acts or omissions because the employer did not retain any degree of control over the work performed by the subcontractor). In Rogstad v. Dakota Gasification Co., 623 N.W.2d 382 (N.D. 2001), the court determined that the contract between the employer and the independent contractor provided that the independent contractor retained "'complete control over its employees and all of its Subcontractors' and was 'solely responsible for all means, methods, techniques, sequences, and portions of the Work in complying with the Agreement.'" Id. at 387. It concluded that the employer's safety manual and orientation video were not included as part of the contract between the employer and independent contractor. See id. at 386–87. Because the independent contractor retained complete control over its employees and the employer never retained actual control over these employees, the court affirmed the summary judgment motion dismissing the negligence action brought by the independent contractor's employee against the employer. See id. at 389. **Further, North Dakota does not allow independent contractors to sue employers under premise liability for a hazardous or dangerous worksite. Armes v. Petro-Hunt, LLC, 2012 U.S. Dist. LEXIS 59002 (D.N.D. Apr. 27, 2012) (holding that premise liability is not a viable cause of action in North Dakota).**

B. Intentional Infliction of Emotional Distress

The North Dakota Supreme Court has recognized the tort of intentional infliction of emotional distress. See Vandall v. Trinity Hosps., 676 N.W.2d 88, 96–97 (N.D. 2004); Weiss v. Collection Ctr., 667 N.W.2d 567, 573–74 (N.D. 2003); Muchow v. Lindblad, 435 N.W.2d 918, 923–25 (N.D. 1989); see also RDO Foods Co. v. United Brands Int'l, Inc., 194 F. Supp. 2d 962, 974 (D.N.D. 2002) ("If . . . RDO engaged in a personal vendetta to ruin James Osgood and his business, the Court finds that this could cause an ordinary citizen, upon hearing the facts, to exclaim 'Outrageous!', the benchmark for this tort."). To prove intentional infliction of emotional distress, a claimant must show (1) extreme and outrageous conduct that is (2) intentional or reckless and causes (3) severe emotional distress. Muchow, 435 N.W.2d at 923–25. The "extreme and outrageous" threshold is narrowly limited to conduct that exceeds "all possible bounds of decency" and which would arouse resentment against the actor and lead to an exclamation of 'outrageous' by an average member of the community. Id. at 924; see also G.K.T. v. T.L.T, 798 N.W.2d 872 (N.D. 2011) (holding that mother's attempts to foster a relationship between her child and the child's biological father and mother's threat to adoptive father to tell the child that he was not the child's father were insufficient as a matter of law to support a claim by the adoptive father for intentional infliction of emotional distress because such actions did not satisfy the "beyond all possible bounds of decency" standard). Moreover, "liability clearly does not extend to mere insults, indignities, threats, annoyances, petty oppressions, or other trivialities." Id.; see also Geraci v. Women's Alliance, Inc., 436 F. Supp. 2d 1022 (D. N.D. 2006) (holding that county's conduct in creating and carrying out a visitation plan at a rape crisis center for two children was not extreme and outrageous). In Dahlberg v. Lutheran Soc. Servs., 625 N.W.2d 241 (N.D. 2001), the state supreme court affirmed summary judgment for the employer based upon lack of extreme and outrageous conduct in the termination context. See id. at 249–50. The court concluded that any termination may produce stress and mental anguish but "the test is not whether or not the termination was traumatic, but whether or not the termination was outrageous." Id. at 248. Actionable conduct would have to be "regarded as atrocious and utterly intolerable in a civilized community." Id. at 250; see also Weiss, 667 N.W.2d at 573–74. The court held in Swenson v. Northern Crop Ins., Inc., 498 N.W.2d 174, 185 (N.D. 1993), when an employer was accused of gender discrimination, that the "position of the parties is relevant when examining the facts for instances of extreme and outrageous conduct." The Swenson court also held that although a defendant's knowledge of a plaintiff's susceptibility to stress is not conclusive of extreme and outrageous conduct, it is relevant when determining whether conduct was extreme and outrageous.

C. Interference with Economic Advantage

Although no reported cases in the state have addressed interference with economic advantage, North Dakota courts recognize the tort of interference with contractual relations. See Tracy v. Central Cass Pub. Sch. Dist., 574 N.W.2d 781 (N.D. 1998); Fronteer Directory Co. v. Maley, 567 N.W.2d 826, 829 (N.D. 1997); Bismarck Realty Co. v. Folden, 354 N.W.2d 636, 642 (N.D. 1984). To prevail on this tort, plaintiffs must plead and prove the existence of a valid contract between themselves and a third party, and the defendant's intentional and improper interference to induce nonperformance. Bismarck Realty, 354 N.W.2d at 642; see also Minto Grain, LLC v. Tibert, 776 N.W.2d 549 (N.D. 2009).

In Bismarck Realty, the court stated that intentional and improper interference to induce nonperformance must be proven as two separate elements: (1) "the defendant instigated the breach," and (2) "the defendant did so without justification." Id.. The latter element is explained: "Where interference with contractual rights is done for the indirect purpose of injuring the plaintiff or benefiting the defendant at the plaintiff's expense, it is unjustifiable." Id. The trial court did not award compensatory damages on the tortious interference claim, but it did award punitive damages. Id. The North Dakota Supreme Court affirmed the judgment on the claim, but reversed on the punitive damages award because the requisite "oppression, fraud, or malice, actual or presumed," was not shown. Id. at 643.

In 2001, the North Dakota Supreme Court recognized the existence of the common law tort claim for unlawful interference with business. Trade 'N Post, L.L.C. v. World Duty Free Ams., Inc., 628 N.W.2d 707 (N.D. 2001); see also Smith Enters. v. In-Touch Phone Cards, Inc., 685 N.W.2d 741, 747–48 (N.D. 2004). To prevail on such a claim, the plaintiff must prove five elements: (1) the existence of a valid business relationship or expectancy; (2) knowledge by the interferer of the relationship or expectancy; (3) an independently tortious or otherwise unlawful act of interference by the interferer: (4) proof that the interference caused the harm sustained; and (5) actual damages to the party whose relationship or expectancy was disrupted. Trade 'N Post, 628 N.W.2d at 717. The court discussed the third element, supra, and determined the type of wrongful conduct that must be shown: "By independently tortious we do not mean that the plaintiff must be able to prove an independent tort. Rather, we mean only that the plaintiff must prove that the defendant's conduct would be actionable under a recognized tort." Id. at 720 (citation omitted); see also RDO Foods Co. v. United Brands Int'l, Inc., 194 F. Supp. 2d 962, 973 –74 (D.N.D. 2002) (holding that this tort requires that the "interference be with an identifiable *third* party"); Lochthowe v. Peterson Estate, 692 N.W.2d 120, 127 (N.D. 2005) (finding unlawful interference where legally invalid lien is imposed); Mr. G's Turtle Mt. Lodge, Inc. v. Roland Twp., 651 N.W.2d 625, 633 (N.D. 2002) (in concluding that no causal link had been established, the court stated, "When the only witnesses who might have been influenced by the alleged interference testify that it had no effect upon their decision whether to enter into a business relationship with the plaintiff, there has been no showing of unlawful interference.").

D. Prima Facie Tort

Only two reported cases in North Dakota mention a claim for prima facie tort. See Thiele v. Lindquist &Vennum, 404 N.W.2d 52 (N.D. 1987); Hurt v. Freeland, 589 N.W.2d 551 (N.D. 1999). In neither case does the court base its decision or elaborate on the claim or its requirements in this state.

V. OTHER ISSUES

A. Statute of Limitations

N.D.C.C.§ 28-01-18 provides a two-year statute of limitation for actions for libel or slander. North Dakota has also enacted the single publication rule, as N.D.C.C. § 14-02-10, which provides:

> No person may have more than one claim for relief for damages for libel or slander or invasion of privacy or any other tort founded upon any single publication or exhibition or utterance, such as any one edition of a newspaper or book or magazine or any one presentation to an audience or any one broadcast over radio or television or any one exhibition of a motion picture. Recovery in any action must include all damages for any such tort suffered by the plaintiff in all jurisdictions.
>
> A judgment in any jurisdiction for or against the plaintiff upon the substantive merits of any action for damages founded upon a single publication or exhibition or utterance as

described in this section bars any other action for damages by the same plaintiff against the same defendant founded upon the same publication or utterance.

B. Jurisdiction

In Wilkie v. Dept. of Health and Human Services, 2008 WL 818892 (D.N.D. 2008), the court held in abeyance claims relating to libel, slander, defamation, and whistle-blowing where plaintiff had not yet exhausted her administrative remedies for her Title VII claim.

C. Worker's Compensation Exclusivity

Under the North Dakota workers' compensation act, an employee generally gives up the right to sue the employer in exchange for sure and certain benefits for all workplace injuries, regardless of fault. Trinity Hosps. v. Mattson, 723 N.W.2d 684, 688 (N.D. 2006); N.D.C.C. § 65-01-0. An "employee" is "a person who performs hazardous employment for another for remuneration," and an "employer" is "a person who engages or received the services of another for remuneration." N.D.C.C. § 65-01-0(16) and (17). Under N.D.C.C. § 65-01-0, injured employees do not have a claim for relief against a "contributing employer or against any agent, servant, or other employee of the employer for damages for personal injuries, but shall look solely to the fund for compensation." "Employers who comply with the provisions of [N.D.C.C. ch. 65-04] shall not be liable to respond in damages at common law or by statute for injury to or death of any employee." N.D.C.. § 65-04-28. There are no reported cases addressing workers' compensation exclusivity in the context of libel or defamation claims.

D. Pleading Requirements

The only special pleading requirement that applies to defamation claims is that exemplary damages may not be pleaded in the original complaint, but may only be added afterwards with a motion to amend. N.D.C.C. § 32-03.2-11.

SURVEY OF NORTH DAKOTA EMPLOYMENT PRIVACY LAW

Steven R. Anderson, Kathlyn E. Noecker, John P. Borger[1],
Daniel G. Prokott, Leita Walker and David Merritt
Faegre & Benson, L.L.P.
2200 Wells Fargo Center
90 South Seventh Street
Minneapolis, Minnesota 55402
Telephone: (612) 766-7000; Facsimile:(612) 766-1600
http://www.faegre.com/

(With Developments Reported Through **November 1, 2012**)

GENERAL COMMENTS

None.

SIGNIFICANT DEVELOPMENTS SINCE THE 2012 *SURVEY*

None.

I. GENERAL LAW OF PRIVACY

A. Legal Basis of Privacy Claims

The North Dakota Supreme Court has never expressly recognized a tort claim for invasion of privacy. See Hougum v. Valley Mem'l Homes, 574 N.W.2d 812, 816 (N.D. 1998); Am. Mut. Life Ins. Co. v. Jordan, 315 N.W.2d 290, 295–96 (N.D. 1982). In Hougum, the court noted that such claims are recognized in "virtually all jurisdictions." 574 N.W.2d at 816. The court, assuming without deciding that such a claim exists in North Dakota, held that the plaintiff failed to raise disputed issues of material fact sufficient to support such a claim. Id. Therefore, it seems likely that on the right facts, the court will recognize such a claim in the future.

B. Causes of Action

1. ***Misappropriation/Right of Publicity.*** No reported cases.

2. ***False Light.*** No reported cases.

3. ***Publication of Private Facts.*** No reported cases.

4. ***Intrusion.*** No reported cases.

C. Other Privacy-Related Actions

1. ***Intentional Infliction of Emotional Distress.*** The North Dakota Supreme Court has recognized the tort of intentional infliction of emotional distress. See Weiss v. Collection Ctr., 667 N.W.2d 567, 573–74 (N.D. 2003); Muchow v. Lindblad, 435 N.W.2d 918, 923–25 (N.D. 1989); Hougum, 574 N.W.2d 812; see also Myers v. Richland County, 2004 U.S. Dist. LEXIS 19944, *32 (D.N.D. Sept. 30, 2004) aff'd in part, vacated in part, remanded, 429 F.3d 740 (8th Cir. 2005) (not finding intentional infliction of emotional distress where plaintiff failed to show extreme and outrageous conduct by the individual defendants); RDO Foods Co. v. United Brands Int'l, Inc., 194 F. Supp. 2d 962, 974 (D.N.D. 2002) ("If . . . RDO engaged in a personal vendetta to ruin James Osgood and his business, the Court finds that this could cause an ordinary citizen, upon hearing the facts, to exclaim, 'Outrageous!', the benchmark for this tort."). To prove intentional infliction of emotional distress, a claimant must show (1) extreme and outrageous conduct that is (2) intentional or reckless and causes (3) severe emotional distress. Muchow, 435 N.W.2d at 923–25. The "extreme and outrageous" threshold is narrowly limited to conduct that exceeds "all possible bounds of decency" and that would arouse resentment against the actor and lead to an exclamation of "outrageous" by an average member of the community. Id. at 924; see also G.K.T. v. T.L.T, 798 N.W.2d 872 (N.D. 2011) (holding that mother's attempts to foster a relationship between her child and the child's biological father and mother's threat to adoptive father to tell the child that he was not the child's father were insufficient as a matter of law to support a claim by the adoptive father for intentional infliction of emotional distress because such actions did not satisfy the "beyond all possible bounds of decency" standard); Geraci v. Women's Alliance, Inc., 436 F. Supp. 2d 1022 (D. N.D. 2006)

---

1. Licensed in North Dakota.

(holding that county's conduct in creating and carrying out a visitation plan at a rape crisis center for two children was not extreme and outrageous). Moreover, "liability clearly does not extend to mere insults, indignities, threats, annoyances, petty oppressions, or other trivialities." Muchow, 435 N.W.2d at 924. In Dahlberg v. Lutheran Social Services, 625 N.W.2d 241 (N.D. 2001), the state supreme court affirmed summary judgment for the employer based upon lack of extreme and outrageous conduct in the termination context. See id. at 249–50. The court concluded that any termination may produce stress and mental anguish but "the test is not whether or not the termination was traumatic, but whether or not the termination was outrageous." Id. at 248; see also Eklind v. Cargill Inc., 2009 U.S. Dist. LEXIS 72444, *22 (D.N.D. Aug. 14, 2009) (finding that "the circumstances surrounding Eklind's termination from employment with Cargill likely caused her to experience anxiety and stress; however, Cargill's conduct simply does not rise to the level of outrageousness required to support a cause of action for intentional infliction of emotional distress.") Actionable conduct would have to be "regarded as atrocious and utterly intolerable in a civilized community." Dahlberg, 625 N.W.2d at 248; Weiss, 667 N.W.2d at 573–74. The court held in Swenson v. Northern Crop Insurance, Inc., 498 N.W.2d 174, 185 (N.D. 1993), when an employer was accused of gender discrimination, that the "position of the parties is relevant when examining the facts for instances of extreme and outrageous conduct." The Swenson court also held that although a defendant's knowledge of a plaintiff's susceptibility to stress is not conclusive of extreme and outrageous conduct, it is relevant when determining whether conduct was extreme and outrageous. Id. at 186.

2. ***Interference with Economic Advantage.*** In 2001, the North Dakota Supreme Court recognized the existence of the common law tort claim for unlawful interference with business. See Lochthowe v. Peterson Estate, 692 N.W.2d 120, 126 (N.D. 2005); see also Smith Enters., Inc. v. In-Touch Phone Cards, Inc., 685 N.W.2d 741, 747-48 (N.D. 2004); Trade 'N Post, L.L.C. v. World Duty Free Ams., Inc., 628 N.W.2d 707 (N.D. 2001). The tort is only recognized in situations involving a contractual or business relationship. See Carlson v. Roetzel & Andress, 2008 U.S. Dist. LEXIS 27084 (finding that the tort of unlawful interference with business does not apply to a claim for interference with workers compensation benefits). To prevail on such a claim, the plaintiff must prove five elements: (1) the existence of a valid business relationship or expectancy; (2) knowledge by the interferer of the relationship or expectancy; (3) an independently tortious or otherwise unlawful act of interference by the interferer: (4) proof that the interference caused the harm sustained; and (5) actual damages to the party whose relationship or expectancy was disrupted. Trade 'N Post, 628 N.W.2d at 717. The court discussed the third element, supra, and determined the type of wrongful conduct that must be shown: "By independently tortious we do not mean that the plaintiff must be able to prove an independent tort. Rather, we mean only that the plaintiff must prove that the defendant's conduct would be actionable under a recognized tort." Id. at 720 (citation omitted); see also Mr. G's Turtle Mt. Lodge, Inc. v. Roland Twp., 651 N.W.2d 625, 633 (N.D. 2002) (in concluding that no causal link had been established, the court stated, "When the only witnesses who might have been influenced by the alleged interference testify that it had no effect upon their decision whether to enter into a business relationship with the plaintiff, there has been no showing of unlawful interference."); Bertsche v. Duemeland, 639 N.W.2d 455, 462–63 (N.D. 2002) (reiterating that actual damages are an essential element of tortious interference with a business relationship, stating that "plaintiffs are held to a stringent standard, and they must show they would have obtained the economic benefit in the absence of the interference."); see also RDO Foods Co. v. United Brands Int'l, Inc., 194 F. Supp. 2d 962, 973–74 (D.N.D. 2002) (holding that this tort requires that the "interference be with an identifiable *third* party").

North Dakota courts also recognize the tort of interference with contractual relations. See Tracy v. Central Cass Pub. Sch. Dist., 574 N.W.2d 781 (N.D. 1998); Fronteer Directory Co. v. Maley, 567 N.W.2d 826, 829 (N.D. 1997); Bismarck Realty Co. v. Folden, 354 N.W.2d 636, 642 (N.D. 1984). To prevail on this tort, plaintiffs must plead and prove the existence of a valid contract between themselves and a third party, and the defendant's intentional and improper interference to induce nonperformance. Lochthowe, 692 N.W.2d at 126; Bismarck Realty, 354 N.W.2d at 642; see also Minto Grain, LLC v. Tibert, 776 N.W.2d 549 (N.D. 2009).

In Bismarck Realty, the court stated that intentional and improper interference to induce nonperformance must be proven as two separate elements: (1) "the defendant instigated the breach," and (2) "the defendant did so without justification." Id. The latter element is explained: "Where interference with contractual rights is done for the indirect purpose of injuring the plaintiff or benefiting the defendant at the plaintiff's expense, it is unjustifiable." Id. The trial court did not award compensatory damages on the tortious interference claim, but it did award punitive damages. Id. The North Dakota Supreme Court affirmed the judgment on the claim, but reversed on the punitive damages award because the requisite "oppression, fraud, or malice, actual or presumed," was not shown. Id. at 643.

3. ***Prima Facie Tort.*** Only two reported cases in North Dakota mention a claim for prima facie tort. See Hurt v. Freeland, 589 N.W.2d 551 (N.D. 1999); Thiele v. Lindquist & Vennum, 404 N.W.2d 52 (N.D. 1987). In neither of these cases does the court base its decision or elaborate on the claim or its requirements in this state.

II. EMPLOYER TESTING OF EMPLOYEES

A. Psychological or Personality Testing

There are no relevant decisions or statutes specifically addressing psychological or personality testing under North Dakota law, however, any such testing probably would be limited under the North Dakota Human Rights Act by the limitations on both pre-employment and post-employment testing already defined under the Americans with Disabilities Act. Because of the sparse case law interpreting the North Dakota Human Rights Act, North Dakota courts have looked to the Americans with Disabilities Act for guidance. See McClean v. Case Corp., 314 F. Supp. 2d 911 (D.N.D. 2004); Engel v. Montana Dakota Utils., 595 N.W.2d 319, 321 (N.D. 1999); Eklind v. Cargill Inc., 2009 U.S. Dist. LEXIS 72444 (D.N.D. Aug. 14, 2009). Consequently, North Dakota courts would likely impose parallel limitations established under the ADA in determining the scope of acceptable testing pursuant to the NDHRA.

B. Drug Testing

N.D.C.C. § 34-01-15 requires an employer to pay for a drug or alcohol test when the employer requires an applicant or employee to take a drug or alcohol test as a condition of obtaining or retaining employment. Any employer violating this provision is guilty of an infraction.

C. Medical Testing

N.D.C.C. § 14-02.4-10 expressly states it is not discriminatory practice for an employer to require the following after a conditional offer of employment: (a) Require a person to undergo physical examination for the purpose of determining the person's capability to perform the essential functions of the job with or without reasonable accommodations if every entering employee in the same job category is subjected to the examination; or (b) Conduct an investigation as to the person's medical history for the purpose of determining the person's capability to perform available employment if every entering employee in the same job category is subjected to the investigation. Any medical history obtained under this section must be kept confidential and maintained separate from non-medical information. Id. N.D.C.C. § 34-01-15 states that whenever an employer requires an employee, or prospective employee, to take a medical examination, as condition of retaining or obtaining employment, the employer shall bear the cost of the examination.

D. Polygraph Tests

No relevant statutes or case law.

E. Fingerprinting

No relevant statutes or case law.

III. SEARCHES

A. Employees Person

No relevant statutes or case law.

B. Employees Work Area

No relevant statutes or case law.

C. Employees Property

No relevant statutes or case law.

IV. MONITORING OF EMPLOYEES

A. Telephones and Electronic Communications

1. ***Wiretapping.*** Section 12.1-15-02, N.D.C.C., makes it a Class C felony to intentionally intercept, use or disclose wire or oral communications, and a Class A misdemeanor to eavesdrop. Section 12.1-15-03, N.D.C.C., deals with the sale of the interception devices, while Section 12.1-15-04, N.D.C.C., defines various forms of communications and communication devices. Section 12.1-15-05, N.D.C.C., makes it a Class A misdemeanor to intercept written communications. Sections 29-29.2-01 through 29-29.2-05, N.D.C.C., deal with drug-related wiretapping. There is a one-party consent exception under both sections. N.D.C.C. §§ 12.1-15-02, 29-29.02-05.

2. ***Electronic Communications.*** See IV.A.1, supra.

3. ***Other Electronic Monitoring.*** See IV.A.1, supra.

B. Mail

No reported cases.

C. Surveillance/Photographing

No reported cases.

V. ACTIVITIES OUTSIDE THE WORKPLACE

A. Statute or Common Law

N.D.C.C. § 14-02.4-03 expressly prohibits discrimination in hiring or employment based on an employee's "participation in lawful activity off the employer's premises during nonworking hours which is not in direct conflict with the essential business-related interests of the employer." The North Dakota Supreme Court has held that the statute was enacted to preclude employers from inquiring into employees' on-work conduct including employees' weight, smoking, marital and sexual habits. Hougum v. Valley Mem'l Homes, 574 N.W.2d 812, 820 (N.D. 1998). **For an employee to establish that an employer has violated N.D.C.C. § 14-02.4-03, the employee must show that the lawful activity the employee engaged in "did not conflict with an indispensable or necessary business-related interest of [the employer]." Clausnitzer v. Tesoro Refining and Marketing Co., 820 N.W.2d 665, 670-672 (N.D. 2012) (concluding that an employee's actions in driving a company vehicle with a blood alcohol level above the .04 limit imposed by employer's policies conflicted with employer's essential business-related interests, and, thus, employee failed to show that he was a member of a protected class under North Dakota's Human Rights Act).**

B. Employees' Personal Relationships

N.D.C.C. § 14-02.4-03 expressly prohibits discrimination in hiring or employment based on an employee's "participation in lawful activity off the employer's premises during nonworking hours which is not in direct conflict with the essential business-related interests of the employer." The North Dakota Supreme Court has held that the statute was enacted to preclude employers from inquiring into employees' non-work conduct including employees' weight, smoking, marital and sexual habits. Hougum, 574 N.W.2d at 820.

1. ***Romantic Relationships Between Employees.*** No reported cases.

2. ***Sexual Orientation.*** Sexual orientation is not a protected characteristic under the North Dakota Human Rights Act.

3. ***Marital Status.*** It is unlawful to discriminate against an employee or applicant based on marital status. N.D.C.C. § 14-02.4-03.

C. Smoking

N.D.C.C. § 14-02.4-03 expressly prohibits discrimination in hiring or employment based on an employee's "participation in lawful activity off the employer's premises during nonworking hours which is not in direct conflict with the essential business-related interests of the employer." The North Dakota Supreme Court has held that the statute was enacted to preclude employers from inquiring into employees' non-work conduct including employees' weight, smoking, marital and sexual habits. Hougum, 574 N.W.2d at 820.

D. Blogging

No reported cases.

VI. RECORDS

A. Personnel Records

Public Employee File Contents. Under N.D.C.C. § 54-06-21, there are limits on the types of documents that may be placed in public employee personnel files. No documents addressing an employee's character or performance may be put in the file unless the employee has the opportunity to read and answer the material. Id. The employee's answer must be attached to the file copy of any such material. In addition, no anonymous letter may be placed in a file. Id.

Public Employee Access to Files. Under N.D.C.C. § 54-06-21, an employee or the employee's representative must be allowed to examine and copy personnel file materials during regular business hours at the employee's expense. Id.

Access by Third Persons to Public Employee Files. The North Dakota Supreme Court has consistently held that under N.D.C.C. § 44-04-18 and N.D. Const. Art. XI § 6, personnel files of state and municipal employees are "public records" open to inspection during business hours by any member of the public. See Grand Forks v. Grand Forks Herald, 307 N.W.2d 572 (N.D. 1981). In Grand Forks Herald, a newspaper sought access to the personnel file of the city's former chief of police to determine why he had resigned and the terms of the negotiated settlement of resignation between the police chief and the city. Id. at 573. The court rejected the former police chief's argument that the records of former employees are not public records subject to inspection. Id. at 576. In addition, the court rejected the chief's argument that such access would be an impermissible intrusion on his privacy. Id. at 579. An exception to the open-records law may not be implied, rather the Legislature must directly address the status of the record in question. Hovet v. Hebron Pub. Sch. Dist., 419 N.W.2d 189 (N.D. 1988).

Confidential Information in Public Employee Files. Under N.D.C.C. § 44-04-18.1, personal information such as home address; home telephone number; photographs; birth dates; social security numbers and financial information is not to become part of an employee's personnel file and is confidential. N.D.C.C. § 44-04-18.1. In addition, medical information and records of employee assistance program treatment are confidential and may not be released without the written consent of the employee. Id.

B. Medical Records

Under state workers' compensation laws, the claimant's name; date of birth; injury date; employer name; type of injury; whether the claim is accepted, denied, or pending; and whether the claim is in active or inactive pay status will be available to the public. N.D.C.C. § 65-05-32. Other "information contained in the claim files and records of injured employees is confidential and is not open to public inspection." Id. Access to such files is limited to representatives of the claimant; employers when reviewing files of their own injured workers; physicians treating claimants or giving advice to the Workers Compensation Bureau; and other persons rendering assistance to the Bureau. Id.

C. Criminal Records

The North Dakota Supreme Court has held that the public has a right to inspect the records of criminal proceedings after such proceedings are completed and entered in the docket of the court. State ex rel. Williston Herald, Inc. v. O'Connell, 151 N.W.2d 758, 763 (N.D. 1967). This right is not an unlimited one, and a court may in its discretion deny inspection of files in a given case when justice so requires. Id. In addition, the right of inspection of criminal records is subject to reasonable rules and regulations as to who may inspect the records and where and how such inspection may be made. Id.

D. Subpoenas / Search Warrants

No relevant cases.

VII. ACTIONS SUBSEQUENT TO EMPLOYMENT

A. References

N.D.C.C. § 34-02-18(1) provides that an employer or an employer's agent who truthfully discloses date of employment, pay level, job description and duties, and wage history about a current or former employee to a prospective employer of the employee is immune from civil liability for the disclosure and the consequences of the disclosure of that information. The statute also provides that an employer or employer's agent who provides such information is presumed to be acting in good faith and is immune from civil liability for such disclosure unless lack of good faith is shown. N.D.C.C. § 34-02-18(2). The presumption of good faith may be rebutted by a preponderance of the evidence that the information disclosed was (a) knowingly false; (b) disclosed with reckless disregard for the truth; (c) deliberately misleading; or (d) rendered with malicious purpose. Id.; see also Forster v. W. Dakota Veterinary Clinic, Inc., 689 N.W.2d 366, 380 (N.D. 2004) (implying that immunity under N.D.C.C. § 34-02-18 would not exist where information was volunteered to rather than requested by the prospective employer). The immunity provided by N.D.C.C. § 34-02-18(2) does not apply if the information is disclosed in violation of a nondisclosure agreement or was otherwise confidential according to applicable law. N.D.C.C. § 34-02-18(3).

B. Non-Compete Agreements

Covenants not to compete are void, with exceptions for situations involving the sale of a business and covenants made in anticipation of a partnership dissolution. N.D.C.C. § 9-08-06. This statute invalidates provisions in employment contracts prohibiting an employee from working for a competitor after completion of employment or imposing a penalty for doing so. Werlinger v. Mutual Serv. Casualty Ins. Co., 496 N.W.2d 26, 30 (N.D. 1993). However, the general proscription of N.D.C.C. § 9-08-06 does not apply to covenants not to solicit the employer's employees. Warner & Co. v. Solberg, 634 N.W.2d 65, 71–73 (N.D. 2001) (holding that a noncompetition agreement which prohibited an insurance agent from post-employment solicitations of former clients/insureds was an illegal restraint on trade but that a provision which prohibited the agent from soliciting or seeking to influence former employees to leave the agency and join the agent at his new place of employment was not void and was enforceable); see also CDI Energy Servs., Inc. v. West River Pumps, Inc., 2007 WL 4395703 (D.N.D. Dec. 13, 2007) (recognizing that "for more than seventy years the North Dakota Supreme Court has consistently held that employment contracts cannot lawfully contain a restraint of trade").

VIII. OTHER ISSUES

A. Statutes of Limitations

N.D.C.C. § 28-01-22 provides that the statute of limitations for an action for relief not otherwise provided for must be commenced within ten years after the claim for relief has accrued. Under North Dakota law, the statute of limitations period is not tolled by the absence of a party from the state if the state has jurisdiction over the absent party. Atkinson v. McLaughlin, 462 F. Supp. 2d 1038 (D.N.D. 2006).

B. Jurisdiction

No relevant statutes or case law.

C. Worker's Compensation Exclusivity

Under the North Dakota workers' compensation act, an employee generally gives up the right to sue the employer in exchange for sure and certain benefits for all workplace injuries, regardless of fault. Trinity Hosps. V. Mattson, 723 N.W.2d 684, 688 (N.D. 2006); N.D.C.C. § 65-01-02(16) and (17). Under N.D.C.C. § 65-01-08, injured employees do not have a claim for relief against a "contributing employer or against any agent, servant, or other employee of the employer for damages for personal injuries, but shall look solely to the fund for compensation." "Employers who comply with the provisions of [N.D.C.C. ch. 65-04] shall not be liable to respond in damages at common law or by statute for injury to or death of any employee." N.D.C.C. § 65-04-28. There are no reported cases addressing workers' compensation exclusivity in the context of employment privacy claims.

D. Pleading Requirements

No relevant statutes or case law.

SURVEY OF OHIO EMPLOYMENT LIBEL LAW

Kevin T. Shook
Frost Brown Todd LLC
One Columbus, Suite 2300
Columbus, Ohio 43215-3484
Telephone: (614) 559-7214; Facsimile: (614) 464-1737
E-mail: kshook@fbtlaw.com

(With Developments Reported Through **November 1, 2012**)

GENERAL COMMENTS

In Ohio Supreme Court cases, unlike those of other states, where there is an inconsistency between the language of the Court's syllabus and the text of its opinion, the syllabus controls.

SIGNIFICANT DEVELOPMENTS SINCE THE 2012 *SURVEY*

On an issue of first impression, the Ohio Supreme Court ruled that a client could not be vicariously liable for its attorney's allegedly defamatory statements, absent a showing that the client had authorized or ratified the statements. Am. Chem. Soc. v. Leadscope, Inc., 2012 WL 4201288, 2012-Ohio-4193 (September 18, 2012).

I. GENERAL LAW

A. General Employment Law

1. ***At Will Employment.*** It is a fundamental tenet of Ohio employment law that, in the absence of an agreement for a specified term, the employment relationship is at will. Gill v. Monetary Management Corp., 1996 Ohio App. LEXIS 4088 (Cuyahoga). Under Ohio law, unless otherwise agreed to, either party may terminate an at will employment relationship for any reason that is not illegal. Mers v. Dispatch Printing Co., 19 Ohio St. 3d 100, 483 N.E.2d 150 (1985). The presumption in favor of at will employment can be rebutted by showing the existence of a contract evidencing something other than an at will arrangement, or an implied employment contract based upon a promise made by the employer. Id. at 104 -105. Although the presumption of at will employment may be rebutted by an implied employment contract based upon such a promise, an employee's *subjective* view that a contract exists is not sufficient to establish the same. Rolsen v. Lazarus, Inc., 2000 Ohio App. LEXIS 4466 (Hamilton). The presumption can also be rebutted by asserting the theory of promissory estoppel, or by showing termination of at will employment in violation of a statute. Id. The presumption may also be countered by establishing a termination of at will employment in violation of public policy of as serious an import as the violation of a statute. Painter v. Graley, 70 Ohio St. 3d 377, 384, 639 N.E.2d 51 (1994), reconsideration denied, 70 Ohio St. 3d 1477, 640 N.E.2d 849.

Under Ohio law, there is generally no claim for wrongful discharge as applied to the at will employment context. Mers v. Dispatch Printing Co., 19 Ohio St. 3d 100, 483 N.E.2d 150 (1985). An at will employee may sue for wrongful discharge, however, if the employer fires her for a reason that contravenes public policy. Powers v. Springfield City Schools, 1998 Ohio App. LEXIS 2827, *13 (Clark), cert. denied, 84 Ohio St. 3d 1411 (1998). Put another way, the Ohio Supreme Court has recognized that public policy warrants an exception to the at will doctrine when an employee is discharged for a reason that is prohibited by statute or violates a clearly defined public policy. Greeley v. Miami Valley Maintenance Contractors, Inc., 49 Ohio St. 3d 228, 234-235 (1990).

B. Elements of Libel Claim

1. ***Basic Elements.*** "In Ohio, defamation occurs when a publication contains a false statement made with some degree of fault, reflecting injuriously on a person's reputation, or exposing a person to public hatred, contempt, ridicule, shame or disgrace, or affecting a person adversely in his or her trade, business or profession." Jackson v. City of Columbus, 117 Ohio St. 3d 328, 883 N.E.2d 1060 (2008). The elements of the tort of libel are (a) there must be a statement of fact; (b) the statement must be false; (c) the statement must have a defamatory meaning toward the plaintiff; (d) the statement must be published by the defendant; (e) the publication must be the proximate cause of injury to the plaintiff; and (f) the defendant must have acted with the requisite degree of fault in failing to publish the truth about the plaintiff. Celebreeze v. Dayton Newspapers, Inc., 41 Ohio App. 3d 343, 346-47, 535 N.E. 2d 755, 15 Media L. Rep. 1589 (Cuyahoga 1988); Dennis v. Coventry Local School Dist. Board of Education, 2006 Ohio 2847, 30, 2006 Ohio App. LEXIS 2674 (Ohio Ct. App. 2006); Molnar v. Klammer, 2005 Ohio 6905, 114, 2005 Ohio App. LEXIS 6227 (Ohio Ct. App. 2005); Rich v. Thompson Newspapers, Inc., 164 Ohio App. 3d 477, 484, 842 N.E.2d 1081 (Ashtabula 2005). Although generally, the term "libel" refers to defamation in a written form, defamatory statements made within the context of a television/radio broadcast

constitute libel, pursuant to the Restatement of Torts and the Supreme Court of Ohio. Holley v. WBNS 10TV, Inc., 2002 Ohio App. LEXIS 4346 (Franklin), citing 3 Restatement of the Law 2d Torts (1977) and Perez v. Scripps-Howard Broadcasting Co., 35 Ohio St. 3d 215, 520 N.E.2d 198, 15 Media L. Rep. 1318 (1988), cert. denied, 488 U.S. 870 (1988); see also Sethi v. WFMJ Television, Inc., 134 Ohio App. 3d 796, 732 N.E.2d 451 (1999) (applying libel standard to television broadcast), appeal denied, 88 Ohio St. 3d 1411, 723 N.E.2d 118 (2000).

2. ***Fault.***

a. **Private Figure Plaintiff/Matter of Public Concern.** In Lansdowne v. Beacon Journal Publishing Co., 32 Ohio St. 3d 176, 512 N.E.2d 979, 14 Media L. Rep. 1801 (1987), the Ohio Supreme Court held that in all private figure defamation actions, where a prima facie showing of defamation is made by a plaintiff, the plaintiff must prove by clear and convincing evidence that the defendant failed to act reasonably in attempting to discover the truth or falsity or defamatory character of the publication. The Supreme Court of Ohio had earlier adopted this negligence standard for defamation cases by private plaintiffs against the media in Embers Supper Club, Inc. v. Scripps-Howard Broadcasting Co., 9 Ohio St. 3d 22, 457 N.E.2d 1164, 10 Media L. Rep. 1729 (1984), cert. denied 467 U.S. 1226 (1984). In Lansdowne, the Court did not develop a distinction between matters of public and private concern for private figure defamation actions. Lansdowne, 32 Ohio St. 3d at 187 (Brown, J., dissenting).

b. **Private Figure Plaintiff/Matter of Private Concern.** In Lansdowne, the Ohio Supreme Court held that in private figure defamation actions, where a prima facie showing of defamation is made by a plaintiff, the plaintiff must prove by clear and convincing evidence that the defendant failed to act reasonably in attempting to discover the truth or falsity or defamatory character of the publication. No distinction is made between matters of public or private concern. See Lansdowne, 32 Ohio St. 3d at187 (Brown, J., dissenting).

c. **Public Figure Plaintiff/Matter of Public Concern.** The Ohio Supreme Court has applied the standard of Rosenblatt v. Baer, 383 U.S. 75, 86, 1 Media L. Rep. 1558 (1966) in determining whether an individual is a public official. Scott v. News-Herald, 25 Ohio St. 3d 243, 245, 496 N.E.2d 699, 702, 13 Media L. Rep. 1241 (1986). Quoting from Rosenblatt, the Court stated: "Where a position in government has such apparent importance that the public has an interest in the qualification and performance of the person who holds it, beyond the general public interest in the qualifications and performance of all government employees . . . the New York Times malice standard applies. Id. Thus in public official libel actions, the plaintiff must prove that the defendant published a false statement "with knowledge that it is false or with reckless disregard of whether it was false or not." Perez v. Scripps Howard Broadcasting Co., 35 Ohio St. 3d 215, 520 N.E.2d 198, 15 Media L. Rep. 1318 (1988), cert. denied, 488 U.S. 870 (1988). The plaintiff must prove actual malice with convincing clarity. Robb v. Lincoln Publishing (Ohio) Inc., 114 Ohio App. 3d 595, 683 N.E.2d 823 (Hamilton 1996), appeal not allowed, 78 Ohio St. 3d 1410, 675 N.E.2d 1249 (1997); Conese v. Nichols, 1998 Ohio App. LEXIS 965, 26 Media L. Rep. 1907 (Hamilton), overruled in part on other grds. by Riston v. Butler, 2002 Ohio App. Lexis 2316 (Hamilton). Examples of public officials are: a superintendent of a school system, Scott, 25 Ohio St. 3d at 245; a deputy sheriff, Perez, 35 Ohio St. 3d at 215; a county treasurer, Varanese v. Gall, 35 Ohio St. 3d 78, 79, 518 N.E.2d 1177, 1179, 14 Media L. Rep. 2361 (1988); a municipal law director, Grau v. Kleinschmidt, 31 Ohio St. 3d 84, 509 N.E. 2d 399, 14 Media L. Rep. 1353 (1987); a mayoral candidate, Dupler v. Mansfield Journal Co., 64 Ohio St. 2d 116, 413 N.E.2d 1187, 6 Media L. Rep. 2362 (1980), cert. denied, 452 U.S. 962 (1981); a city council member, id.; a sheriff, Peck v. The Dispatch Printing Co., Fairfield App. No. 47-CA-86, unreported (1987); a university police officer, Waterson v. Cleveland State University, 93 Ohio App. 3d 792, 639 N.E.2d 1236 (1994); and a police officer, Carpenter v. Gebhart, 1999 Ohio App. LEXIS 1624 (Butler App. 1999). A public school principal is not, however, a public official under Ohio law. East Canton Educational Ass'n v. McIntosh, 85 Ohio St. 3d 465, 709 N.E.2d 468 (1999), reconsid. denied, 86 Ohio St. 3d 1421, 711 N.E.2d 1014 (1999), cert. denied, Slick v. McIntosh, 528 U.S. 1061 (1999).

Ohio follows the Gertz definition of a public figure: a person who achieves pervasive fame is a public figure for all purposes, and a person who voluntarily injects him or herself or is drawn into a particular public controversy is a public figure for limited purposes. See, e.g., Scott v. The News-Herald, 25 Ohio St. 3d 243, 257, 496 N.E. 2d 699, 711, 13 Media L. Rep. 1241 (1986) (Douglas J., concurring). Thus in public figure defamation actions, the plaintiff must prove that the defendant acted with actual malice. Curtis Publishing Co. v. Butts, 388 U.S. 130, 1 Media L. Rep. 1568 (1964), reh'g denied, 389 U.S. 889 (1967). The Scott court disapproved generally of the decision in Milkovich v. News-Herald, 15 Ohio St. 3d 292, 473 N.E.2d 1191, 11 Media L. Rep. 1598 (1984), cert. denied, 474 U.S. 953, where the court decided that a well-known high school wrestling coach was not a public figure despite his involvement in a local controversy."

"The determination of whether a party is a private or public figure is a matter of law." Great Lakes Capital, Ltd. v. Plain Dealer Publ'g. Co., 2008-Ohio-6495, 2008 Ohio App. LEXIS 5414 (Cuyahoga App. 2008) (citing Milkovich v. News-Herald, 15 Ohio St. 3d at 294). Examples of public figures are: a front office executive of a professional football organization, Nussbaumer v. Time, Inc., 1986 Ohio App. LEXIS 8956, 13 Media L. Rep. 1753 (Cuyahoga); a restaurant and its owner for purposes of commenting about the food, service, and décor of the restaurant, Greer v. Columbus Monthly, 4 Ohio App. 3d 235, 448 N.E.2d 157, 8 Media L. Rep. 2129 (Franklin 1982); the owner of a private arts school for the purpose of commenting about the operation of the school, Cooper School of Art, Inc. v. Plain Dealer Pub. Co., 1986 Ohio App. LEXIS 6698, 12 Media L. Rep. 2283 (Cuyahoga); and an attorney who injected himself into the abortion debate, Condit v. Clermont County Review, 93 Ohio App. 3d 166, 635 N.E.2d 44 (1994). A high school principal is not, however, a public figure or official for defamation purposes. East Canton Educational Ass'n. v. McIntosh, 1997 Ohio App. LEXIS 3957 (Stark), aff'd on reh'g., 85 Ohio St. 3d 465, 709 N.E.2d 468 (1999). A retired schoolteacher who had worked for the public school system and regularly spoke at school board meetings was a limited public figure for purposes of analyzing statements made about his behavior at a school board meeting. Featherstone v. CM Media, Inc., 2002-Ohio-6747, 2002 Ohio App. LEXIS 6509 (Franklin App. 2002). A local high school football coach who was vocal about his religious views both on the field and in the classroom was considered a limited purpose public figure after his tenure became a public controversy. Daubenmire v. Sommers, 156 Ohio App. 3d 322, 2004-Ohio-914, 805 N.E. 2d 571 (Madison App. 2004).

3. ***Falsity.*** Truth is always a defense in any action for libel. Shifflet v. Thomson Newspapers, Inc., 69 Ohio St. 2d 179, 431 N.E. 2d 1014, 8 Media L. Rep. 1199 (1982). Ohio Rev. Code Ann. § 2739.02 provides that truth, when pleaded and proven by the defendant, is a complete defense to an action for libel and slander. When the allegedly defamatory publication is about a matter of legitimate public concern, the plaintiff has the burden of proving falsity. Philadelphia Newspapers, Inc. v. Hepps, 475 U.S. 767, 12 Media L. Rep. 1977 (1986); accord, Wilson v. Scripps Howard Broadcasting Co., 642 F.2d 371, 7 Media L. Rep. 1169 (6th Cir. 1981), cert. dismissed, 454 U.S. 1130 (1981). It is sufficient for the defendant to show that the imputation is substantially true, or as is often put, to justify the "gist, or " the "sting." A plaintiff cannot establish a prima facie case of falsity where the record reveals that the published report was substantially true. National Medic Serv. Corp. v. E.W.Scripps Co., 61 Ohio App. 3d 752, 573 N.E. 2d 1148 (Hamilton 1989); accord, Cooper School of Art, Inc. v. Plain Dealer Pub. Co., 1986 Ohio App. LEXIS 6698, 12 Media L. Rep. 2283 (Cuyahoga); Nussbaumer v. Time, Inc., 1986 Ohio App. LEXIS 8956, 13 Media L. Rep. 1753 (Cuyahoga).

4. ***Defamatory Statement of Fact.*** In order to constitute a defamatory statement of fact, it is enough that the statement is reasonably capable of being understood as something defamatory. East Canton Education Association v. McIntosh, 1997 Ohio App. LEXIS 3957 (Stark), aff'd on reh'g, 85 Ohio St. 3d 465, 709 N.E.2d 468 (1999). While the court determines as a matter of law whether a statement is capable of bearing a defamatory meaning, the jury determines whether such a statement was understood by its reader to be defamatory. Id. at *19. "Ohio has seemingly adopted the "innocent-construction rule." Mann v. Cincinnati Enquirer, 2010 WL 3328631, 2010 -Ohio- 3963, ¶13 (Hamilton Aug. 25, 2010). A plaintiff must allege defamatory statements of fact with requisite specificity. Bansal v. Mt. Carmel Health Sys., 2011 WL 3359992, 2011 -Ohio- 3827, ¶43 (Ohio App. 10 Dist. 2011) (allegations that hospital and/or doctors made statements that internal medicine physician whom hospital had removed from its emergency room on-call list "suffered from emotional disturbances," that physician was "unreachable when needed," that physician "has caused substantial risk management activity," together with statements regarding physician's "prowess as a physician" were insufficient to state claim for defamation, where physician's allegations lacked sufficient specificity about substance of claim). Under the innocent-construction rule, "if allegedly defamatory words are susceptible to two meanings, one defamatory and one innocent, the defamatory meaning should be rejected and the innocent meaning adopted. Id. However, Ohio does now recognize a false light invasion of privacy claim. Welling v. Weinfeld. 113 Ohio St. 3d 464, 2007-Ohio-2451, 866 N.E.2d 1051. The Ohio Supreme Court decided that, since Ohio already recognizes invasion of privacy based on publicizing true, but embarrassing facts, the right to privacy "naturally extends" to publicizing false embarrassing statements of fact, even if they are not defamatory. Id. Thus, plaintiffs who are unable to allege a defamatory statement of fact, may resort to bringing a false light claim. To prevail upon such a claim, the plaintiff must prove actual malice, discussed below.

5. ***Of and Concerning Plaintiff.*** A publication that is libelous per se must not only refer to some person, but the plaintiff must show that he or she is the person about whom the statement was made. Smith v. Huntington Publishing Co., 410 F. Supp. 1270 (S.D. Ohio 1975), aff'd, 535 F.2d 1255 (6th Cir); Lambert v. Garlo, 19 Ohio App. 3d 295, 484 N.E.2d 260 (1985). Statements made in a letter that were interpreted by the recipient to mean that the plaintiff fraudulently obtained title to a vehicle were not actionable because they did not reference the Plaintiff anywhere and were not "of and concerning" the Plaintiff. Christopher v. Auto. Fin. Corp., 2008 Ohio 2972, 2008 Ohio App. LEXIS 2494 (Mahoning App. June 13, 2008). Statements made generally about a tax department and not the tax administrator himself are not actionable. Stow v. Coville, 96 Ohio App. 3d 70, 644 N.E. 2d 673 (1994). Statements made generally about a business and the operation of that business's on-line service are not of and concerning the operator of that business because the statements did not mention the operator by name. Worldnet Software Co. v. Gannett Satellite Information Network, Inc., 122 Ohio App. 3d 499. 702 N.E.2d 149, 25 Media L. Rep. 2331 (Hamilton 1997).

6. ***Publication.*** Under Ohio law, publication of defamatory matter is its communication intentionally or by negligent acts to one other than the person being defamed. Any act by which defamatory matter is communicated to a third party is publication, even if the matter is communicated to one person only, and even if that person has been sworn to

secrecy. Hecht v. Levin, 66 Ohio St. 3d 458, 613 N.E.2d 585 (1993). An allegedly defamatory letter from employer to a former employee's attorney discussing reasons for the employee's termination and stating, "I understand [employee] is working for cash while he rides out his unemployment benefits," pertained to employee's claim under the Age Discrimination in Employment Act and was therefore held not to be publication to a third party. Snyder v. Ag Trucking, Inc., 57 F.3d 484 (6th Cir. 1995). A confidential letter to plaintiff's attorney from the plaintiff's former employer listing reasons for the plaintiff's discharge was not "published" just because the letter was stamped "copy sent." Wood v. Dorcas, 126 Ohio App. 3d 730, 711 N.E.2d 291 (Lucas, 1998), appeal not allowed, 82 Ohio St. 3d 1473, 696 N.E.2d 602 (1998). Publication occurred when oil refinery's director of security gave an oral report regarding an alleged drug transaction to the plant manager and when he directed preparation of a memorandum which contained allegedly defamatory statements and presented it to the plant manager for his signature. Ball v. British Petroleum Oil, 108 Ohio App. 3d 129, 670 N.E.2d 289 (Lucas 1995). Summary judgment in favor of defendants on the issue of publication was improper where security guards for the Department of Human Services posted a photo of the plaintiff with defamatory comments written below the photo. Jones v. White, 1997 Ohio App. LEXIS 4636 (Summit). Statements made regarding the discharge of a governmental employee were not defamatory because those statements were not made public. Fields v. Ariss, 2000 Ohio App. LEXIS 3866 (Warren). Statements that an employer put in an employee's file were not actionable because they were never published to a third party. Potter v. RETS Tech Ctr. Co., 2008 Ohio 993, 2008 WL 615423, 2008 Ohio App. LEXIS 858 (Montgomery App. March 7, 2008) (finding that employee's concern that prospective employers would find out about the statements in the future was not sufficient to create a cause of action). A notice suspending a member of a club was not actionable because it was not published to anyone but the club member. McPeek v. Leetonia Italian-American Club, 174 Ohio App. 3d 380, 882 N.E.2d 450 (Columbiana App. December 19, 2007). However, where an allegedly defamatory report was released only pursuant to a public records request, a publication was found to take place and the defendant could not claim immunity. Mehta v. Ohio Univ., 2011-Ohio-3484 ¶63, 2011 WL 2739639 (Ohio App. 10 Dist. 2011).

a. **Intracorporate Communication.** Publication occurred when oil refinery's director of security gave an oral report regarding an alleged drug transaction to the plant manager and when he directed preparation of a memorandum which contained allegedly defamatory statements and presented it to the plant manager for his signature. Ball v. British Petroleum Oil, 108 Ohio App. 3d 129, 670 N.E.2d 289 (Lucas 1995).

b. **Compelled Self-Publication.** Ohio courts have not recognized the doctrine of compelled self-publication. Atkinson v. Stop-N-Go Foods, Inc., 83 Ohio App. 3d 132, 614 N.E.2d 784 (Cuyahoga 1992); Schact v. Ameritrust Co. N.A., 1994 Ohio App. LEXIS 1125, *8 n.3 (Cuyahoga). As a general principle, compelled self-publication, or forced republication, provides for proof of publication where a defamed person is forced to republish defamatory statements to a third party. Schacht, 1994 Ohio App. LEXIS at *20.

c. **Republication.** Parties may not avoid the consequences of publishing a libelous statement merely by saying that they are repeating the words of another, even when that person is identified. The general rule is that one who repeats a libelous remark is liable for his or her republication. Theiss v. Scherer, 396 F.2d 646, 46 Ohio Ops. 2d 55 (6th Cir. 1968). In some cases, however, Ohio courts have reached a contrary result, without discussing the issue. See, e.g., Joplin v. WEWS, 1980 Ohio App. LEXIS 12131, 6 Media L. Rep. 1331 (Cuyahoga) (television station report repeated statement that plaintiff was rape suspect). The plaintiff's participation in eliciting the defamation in an honest investigation to ascertain its existence, source, content or meaning is not a defense to an action for republication, but the result might be otherwise if the plaintiff invited or procured the defamation with the intent to bring suit or trick the defendant. Rainey v. Shaffer, 8 Ohio App. 3d 262, 263-64, 456 N.E.2d 1328, 1331 (Lake 1983). Letters written by a fellow doctor to the hospital's chairman charging that the plaintiff was incompetent to perform a surgical procedure were not "republished" simply because they were incorporated into the plaintiff's employee file and were therein read by several others. Frank v. Gindi, 1980 Ohio App. LEXIS 13714 (Cuyahoga). In a suit brought by a former employee against a former employer's biggest client, it was not republication when the former supervisor merely referred to a memorandum in a meeting with that employee where the memorandum was written a month prior, and where the supervisor was not employed by the client. Sawyer v. Devore, 1994 Ohio App. LEXIS 4954 (Cuyahoga). The republication of a defamatory statement 10 years after the original publication did not restart the statute of limitations. Friedler v. The Equitable Life Assurance Society of the United States, 86 Fed. Appx. 50 (6th Cir. 2003).

7. ***Statements versus Conduct.*** Under Ohio law, conduct, standing alone, does not constitute defamation. Lawson v. AK Steel Corporation, 121 Ohio App. 3d 251, 699 N.E.2d 951 (Butler 1997). "An adverse employment action is not a "statement," for purposes of a defamation claim; it is an action." Wissler v. Ohio Dep't of Job & Family Servs., 2009-Ohio-2826, 2009 Ohio Misc. LEXIS 75 (Ohio Ct. of Claims 2009). The act of demoting an employee, standing alone without any other supporting evidence of actual publication, is not sufficient to establish publication. Id. at *11. Merely escorting a suspected shoplifter to the store office in front of other customers does not, without more, amount to defamation. Hodges v. Meijer, Inc., 129 Ohio App., 3d 318, 717 N.E.2d 806 (Butler 1998). Merely using security guards to escort a terminated employee from the building is similarly not actionable as defamation. Paolucci v. Robinson, 1995 Ohio

App. LEXIS 886 (Portage) (unreported), appeal not allowed, 73 Ohio St. 3d 1414, 65 N.E.2d 1311. It may, however, create a claim under other legal theories unless the employer had a legitimate reason for use of the security guards at termination. *Cf.* Aker v. N.Y. and Co., 364 F. Supp. 2d 661, 668-69, 2005 U.S. Dist. LEXIS 5449 (N.D. Ohio 2005) (defamatory conduct included employee being searched and escorted from workplace while in the presence of co-workers and others).

8. ***Damages.*** Except in cases involving actual malice, plaintiffs must prove actual injury to recover in a libel action. Thomas Maloney & Sons, Inc. v. E.W. Scripps Co., 43 Ohio App. 2d 105, 334 N.E.2d 494 (1974), cert. denied, 423 U.S. 883 (1975). Actual injury includes not only out-of-pocket expenses, but also impairment of reputation, personal humiliation, mental anguish and suffering. Id.; Kanjuka v. Metrohealth Medical Center, 151 Ohio App. 3d 183, 2002 Ohio 6803, 783 N.E.2d 920 (Cuyahoga App. 2002). To recover damages for emotional distress, expert evidence proving serious emotional injury "is necessary in all but the most extraordinary cases." Shariff v. Rahman, 152 Ohio App.3d 210, 2003-Ohio-1336, 787 N.E. 2d 72 (Cuyahoga App. 2003). The plaintiff may also recover for lost income and loss of earning capacity where the evidence establishes a nexus between the damages and the defamation. The jury has wide discretion to determine defamation damages. Kluss v. Aluminum Corp., 106 Ohio App. 3d 528, 666 N.E.2d 603 (Cuyahoga 1995). **With regard to defamation per quod, a Plaintiff cannot simply allege "special harm" in conclusory fashion, but must tie the alleged harm to the separate allegations in other sections of the complaint and comply with Civ.R. 9(G), which states that "[w]hen items of special damage are claimed, they shall be specifically stated." McWreath v. Cortland Bank, 2012 WL 2522933, 2012-Ohio-3013 (Trumbull App. June 29, 2012).** Mere proof of a drop in income is insufficient evidence of damages inasmuch as Ohio requires that "the particular contracts, sales, customers, patients, or clients lost be alleged as a prerequisite to recovery of special damages. Moore v. P.W. Publishing Co., Inc., 3 Ohio St. 2d 183, 190, 209 N.E.2d 412, 416 (1965), cert. denied, 382 U.S. 978 (1966). Damages for "great pain and anguish" suffered as a result of a per quod defamatory statement are "of such a nature that they do not necessarily follow from a defamatory remark" and are therefore special damages. King v. Bogner, 88 Ohio App. 3d 564, 624 N.E.2d 364 (Montg. 1993). However, under modern practice, it may be sufficient to aver generally the special damages, although they must still be proved with particularity. J.V.Peters & Co. v. Knight Rider Co., 1984 Ohio App. LEXIS 9064, 10 Media L. Rep. 1576 (Summit). Special damages may include a percentage of the "total amount of overall happiness" a plaintiff lost due to the defamatory remark, quantified as a dollar figure by assigning a daily value to the plaintiff's state of mind. Kanjuka v. Metrohealth Med. Ctr., 151 Ohio App.3d 183, 2002-Ohio-6803, 783 N.E.2d 920 (Cuyahoga App. 2002). Ohio follows the "incremental harm" doctrine where a measure is made between the incremental reputational harm inflicted by the challenged statements beyond the harm imposed by the non-actionable remainder of the publication. Frigo v. UAW Local 549, 2005 Ohio 3981, 2005 Ohio App. LEXIS 3641 (Ohio Ct. App. 2005).

a. **Presumed Damages and Libel Per Se.** Libel per se occurs when material is defamatory on its face. Becker v. Toulmin, 165 Ohio St. 549, 556, 138 N.E.2d 391 (1956); Gosden v. Louis, 116 Ohio App. 3d 195, 687 N.E.2d 481 (Summit 1996), appeal not allowed, 78 Ohio St. 3d 1456, 677 N.E.2d 816 (1997). To constitute defamation *per se*, the words must be of such a nature that courts can presume as a matter of law that they tend to degrade or disgrace the person of whom they are written or spoken or hold him up to public hatred, contempt or scorn. A statement will be considered defamation *per se* if the statement tends to injure a person and is in his or her trade, profession or occupation. When a statement is found to be defamation *per se*, both damages and actual malice are presumed to exist. Whether a statement is defamation *per se* is a question of law that an appellate court properly may determine. Knowles v. The Ohio State University, 2002 Ohio 6962, 2002 Ohio App. LEXIS 6779 (Franklin App. 2002). Written matter is libelous per se if, on its face, it reflects upon a person's character in such a manner that will cause him to be ridiculed, hated, or held in contempt, or injures him in his trade or profession. Becker, 165 Ohio St. at 533. Written words that accuse a person of a crime are libelous per se. Gosden, 116 Ohio App. 3d at 207. Referring to another as a racist may constitute defamation per se. Lennon v. Cuyahoga County Juvenile Court, 2006 Ohio 2587, 28, 2006 Ohio App. LEXIS 2443 (Ohio Ct. App. 2006). Statement that the sole owner of a business was dying was defamatory per se because it impacted his relationships with his customers and his employees. *Murray v. Knight-Ridder, Inc.*, 2004-Ohio-821, 2004 Ohio App. LEXIS 763 (Belmont App. 2004). In an employee's defamation suit based on his former employer's allegations of sexual harassment, the communications about the allegations were defamation per se because the employee presented evidence that the communications were injurious to his employment, and thus the employee had no need to plead or prove special damages. Shoemaker v. Community Action Organization of Scioto County, Inc., 2007 Ohio 3708 (Ct. App. Scioto County 2007). When a publication is libelous per se, the plaintiff is entitled to recover presumed damages if he can prove that the statements were about him, that the statement were false, that the defendant published the statements, and that the defendant was negligent in doing so. Moore v. P.W. Publishing Co., 3 Ohio St.2d 183, 188, 209 N.E.2d 412 (1965), cert. denied, 382 U.S. 978 (1966); Gosden, 116 Ohio App. 3d at 211. A letter from an electrical contractor to a construction contractor alleging that another electrical contractor gave kickbacks in order to secure jobs constituted libel per se. Douglas Electric Corp. v. Grace, 70 Ohio App. 3d 7, 590 N.E.2d 363 (1990). A cablegram sent from an attorney to his clients notifying them that "we have found it desirable to terminate employment of our employee" was not libel per se. Becker v. Toulmin, 165 Ohio St. 549, 138 N.E.2d 391 (1956). Simply stating that a person is not a loyal employee is not libel per se. Johnson v. Campbell, 91 Ohio App. 483, 108 N.E.2d 749

(Franklin 1952). A supervisor's comments about an employee's alleged depression, difficulty getting to work on time, and difficulty in getting up to go to work bear directly on the ability to successfully fulfill professional responsibilities and may constitute defamation per se. Kanjuka v. Metrohealth Med. Ctr., 151 Ohio App.3d 183, 2002-Ohio-6803, 783 N.E.2d 920 (Cuyahoga App. 2002). A union member's statements in a union newsletter criticizing a supervisor's procedures for recording and granting equalization records qualified as libel per se, because they reflected upon her character as a supervisor. Jacobs v. Budak, 156 Ohio App. 3d 160, 2004 Ohio 522, 805 N.E. 2d 111 (Trumbull App. 2004). A statement that a police officer's child is a criminal reflects poorly on the police officer's reputation and professional ability and is defamatory *per se*. Williams v. Gannett Satellite Info. Network, Inc., 2005 Ohio 4141, 2005 Ohio App. LEXIS 3769 (Ohio Ct. App. 2005).

(1) **Employment-Related Criticism.** A former employer's letter to Virginia State Board of Medicine in the peer review context about professional character of former resident podiatrist was protected by qualified privilege because employer had duty to inform. Jacobs v. Frank, 60 Ohio St. 3d 111, 573 N.E.2d 609 (1991). In a suit brought by non-union mail carriers against a union for publication of materials criticizing plaintiffs for crossing picket lines, the term "scab" was a federally protected term. Old Dominion Branch No 496 v. Austin, 418 U.S. 264 (1974); Local Lodge 1297 v. Allen, 22 Ohio St. 3d 228, 490 N.E.2d 865 (1986). A disparaging email sent by a supervisor to 35 of plaintiff's co-workers does not constitute defamation because immunity protections are afforded when 1) the place of employment is defined as a governmental agency and 2) the email is written within the scope of supervisor's employment. Jackson v. McDonald, 144 Ohio App. 3d 301, 760 N.E.2d 23 (Stark 2001), appeal not allowed, 93 Ohio St. 3d 1458, 756 N.E.2d 1235 (2001). An employee was required to prove actual malice even though the statements on their face constituted libel per se because this controversy concerned a labor dispute, which requires a higher standard of proof in that the plaintiff must prove actual malice by clear and convincing evidence. Jacobs v. Budak, 2008 Ohio 2756, 2008 WL 2332543, 2008 Ohio App. LEXIS 2308 (Turmbull App. June 6, 2008).

(2) **Single Instance Rule.** Ohio has not adopted the single instance rule for defamatory statements.

b. **Punitive Damages.** In order to recover punitive damages in a defamation action involving a private plaintiff on a matter of private concern, a plaintiff must show that the defendant acted with common law express malice: that is, the defendant must have acted with ill-will, vengefulness, hatred, or reckless disregard of the plaintiff's rights. Gosden v. Louis, 116 Ohio App. 3d 195, 687 N.E.2d 481 (Ohio App. 9 Dist. 1996), appeal not allowed, 78 Ohio St. 3d 1456, 677 N.E.2d 816 (1997). The private plaintiff need not, however, show that the defendant acted with actual malice: knowledge of falsity or reckless disregard for the truth of a statement need only be proved by public figure/official plaintiffs, or private plaintiffs involved in a public matter in order to collect punitive damages. Id. at 213. See also Robb v. Lincoln Publishing Co., 114 Ohio App. 3d 595, 621, 683 N.E.2d 823 (Brown 1996), appeal not allowed, 78 Ohio St. 3d 1410, 675 N.E.2d 1249 (1997) (evidence was sufficient to demonstrate actual malice on the part of a newspaper in publishing an advertisement containing false statements about the county clerk of courts, and thus to warrant instruction as to punitive damages in action by clerk).

II. PRIVILEGES AND DEFENSES

A. Scope of Privileges

1. ***Absolute Privilege.*** Ohio Rev. Code § 2744, et seq., provides governmental immunity to political subdivisions and their employees. Specifically, Ohio Rev. Code § 2744.02(A)(1) provides that "a political subdivision is not liable in damages in a civil action for injury, death, or loss to person or property allegedly caused by any act or omission of the political subdivision *or* an employee of the political subdivision in connection with a governmental or proprietary function." "An intentional tort claim such as a defamation claim does not fit under any of the enumerated exceptions [in Ohio Rev. Code 2744.02]." Vaughn v. Lake Metropolitan Housing Auth., 2010 WL 3081473 (Ohio App. 11 Dist.), 2010-Ohio-3686, ¶46. Therefore, "[a] political subdivision performing governmental functions is immune from liability for an intentional tort such as defamation." Id. However, one court of appeals has found that political subdivision immunity does not apply to defamation actions filed "by an employee . . . against his political subdivision relative to any matter that arises out of the employment relationship between the employee and the political subdivision[.]" Buck v. Reminderville, 2010 WL 5551003, 2010-Ohio-6497 ¶10 (Ohio App. 9 Dist.); **see also Steinbrink v. Greenon Local School Dist., 2012 WL 1080735 2012-Ohio-1438 (Clark App. March 30, 2012).**

An "employee" is defined by Ohio Rev. Code § 2744.01(B), in part, as "an officer, agent, employee, or servant, *** who is authorized to act and is acting within the scope of the officer's, agent's, employee's, or servant's employment for a political subdivision." Ohio Rev. Code § 2744.03(A)(6) "provides absolute immunity to employees whether [the plaintiff's] claims are based in negligence or are an intentional tort, such as defamation." Stoll v. Gardner, 2009-Ohio-1865, 2009 Ohio App. LEXIS 1571 (Summit App.2009). An employee's immunity remains intact as a defense to any civil claims unless a plaintiff can prove under Ohio Rev. Code § 2744.03(A)(6), that: "(a) the employee's acts or omissions were manifestly outside the scope of the employee's employment or official responsibilities; "(b) the employee's acts or omissions were [committed] with malicious purpose, in bad faith, or in a wanton or reckless manner; [or] (c) [c]ivil liability is expressly imposed upon the employee by a section of the Revised Code."

Where an employer is required to supply information to the Ohio Bureau of Unemployment Compensation about an employee's discharge, an absolute privilege exists which precludes recovery for defamation. Jackson v. City of Columbus, 117 Ohio St. 3d 328, 883 N.E.2d 1060 (2008); Wolf v. First National Bank, 20 Ohio Op. 3d 262 (C.P. 1980). Statements made in connection with an employee's unemployment compensation hearing are made in the course of quasi-judicial hearings and are therefore absolutely privileged when they are relevant to the issues at hand. Horsley v. Wal-Mart, Inc., 1997 Ohio App. LEXIS 5988 (Lawrence). Defamatory statements made during a deposition that were at least remotely related to the case at bar are privileged and cannot form the basis of a defamation complaint. Fiore v. Plating Tech., 2004 Ohio 6611, 2004 Ohio App. LEXIS 6010 (Ohio Ct. App. 2004). Statements allegedly made by union, employee, and union steward during meetings and investigations of grievance are protected by absolute privilege under § 1 of the National Labor Relations Act. Stiles v. Chrysler Motor Corp., 89 Ohio App. 3d 256, 624 N.E.2d 238 (Ohio App. 6 Dist. 1993), dismissed, jurisdictional motion overruled, 67 Ohio St. 3d 1502, 622 N.E.2d 651, interpreting 29 U.S.C.A. § 151. Statements made in a mayor's investigative report concerning wrongdoing of public employees are not subject to an absolute privilege; that privilege applies only to statements made in judicial and legislative proceedings, and has not been extended to statements made in the discharge of local executive authority. Marcum v. Rice, 1999 Ohio App. LEXIS 3365 (Franklin 1999), appeal not allowed, 87 Ohio St. 3d 1449, 719 N.E.2d 966 (1999). Under R.C. § 2305.25, no member of a peer review or professional standards review committee of a state or local society composed of doctors or pharmacists, and no member or employee of a utilization review committee, or a tissue committee of a hospital or community mental health center, or of a utilization committee composed of doctors may be held liable for any action taken or recommendation made within the scope of the functions of that committee. A federal court has held, however, that the state hospital peer review privilege described in the statute does not prevent discovery by a physician of peer review proceedings needed to prove a sexual discrimination case. LeMasters v. The Christ Hospital, 791 F. Supp. 188 (S.D. Ohio 1991).

2. ***Qualified Privileges.*** Under Ohio law, statements made in good faith about a matter of common interest between an employer and an employee regarding a third party employee, or between two employees regarding a third employee, are subject to a qualified privilege. Jacobs v. Frank, 60 Ohio St. 3d 111, 573 N.E.2d 609 (1991); Worrell v. Multipress, Inc., 45 Ohio St. 3d 241, 543 N.E.2d 1277 (1989); Taylor v. National Group of Companies, Inc., 729 F. Supp. 575 (N.D. Ohio 1989), reconsideration denied, 765 F. Supp. 411 (N.D. Ohio 1990); Horsley v. Walmart Inc., 1997 Ohio App. LEXIS 5988 (Lawrence); Holloman v. Rutman Wine Company, 11 Ohio App. 3d 257 (1983). The application of this privilege means that the plaintiff, in order to prevail, must prove not only that the statements were untrue, but that they were made with actual malice. Contadino v. Tilow, 68 Ohio App. 3d 463, 589 N.E.2d 48 (Hamilton 1990). An employee can defeat an employer's qualified privilege if the employee shows by clear and convincing evidence that the employer made the defamatory communication with actual malice. Coleman v. Barnovsky, 2005 Ohio 5867, 19, 2005 Ohio App. LEXIS 5287 (Ohio Ct. App. 2005). Statements made in a union grievance proceeding were qualifiedly privileged. Gray v. Allison Division, General Motors Corp., 52 Ohio App. 2d 348, 370 N.E.2d 747 (Cuyahoga 1977). An employee's statement to police and to his employer regarding a second employee threatening physical harm at work is protected by the qualified privilege. Franklin v. Miami Univ., 2008 Ohio 7044, 2008 Ohio Misc. LEXIS 297 (Ohio Ct. of Claims 2008). A company president's statement to his brother, also an officer in the company, regarding an employee's alleged leak of confidential information to a customer was protected by qualified privilege. Olson v. Holland Computers, 2007 Ohio 4727 (Ct. App. Lorain County 2007). Statements regarding reason for employee's termination made in good faith and solely within employer's management team were held to be protected by qualified privilege. Daff v. Associated Bldg. Suppliers, Inc., 2007 Ohio 3238 (Ct. App. Summit County 2007). Qualified privilege protected employer's documents relating to employee's reprimand and subsequent termination, where the documents were created in the scope of their author's employment, were distributed only to those managerial employees who had a need to know the information contained within, and were a matter of common interest. Hatton v. Interim Health Care of Columbus, Inc., 2007 Ohio 1418, P17 (Ct. App. Franklin County 2007). A letter from a company official to a discharged building engineer and statements made by company president in presence of another official to building engineer, both about reasons for engineer's discharge, were protected by qualified privilege because they concerned the activities of the engineer arising out of his employment with the company. Rinehart v. Maiorano, 76 Ohio App. 3d 413, 602 N.E.2d 340 (Lucas 1984). An employer's statements to police that a convenience store employee had stolen money were not made with reckless disregard for the truth and thus were qualifiedly privileged. Atkinson v. Stop-N-Go Foods, Inc., 83 Ohio App. 3d 132, 614 N.E.2d 784 (Montgomery 1992). A threat made by an employee in the presence of a co-worker was qualifiedly privileged when that threat was relayed to a supervisor and the incident was later repeated to a potential future employer. Temethy v. Huntington Bancshares, Inc., 2004-Ohio-1253, 2004 Ohio App. LEXIS 1111 (Cuyahoga App. 2004). Communications from an insurance company to some of its policyholders informing them that it had terminated an agent who had previously dealt with them were qualifiedly privileged. Hahn v. Kotten, 43 Ohio St.2d 237, 331

N.E.2d 713 (1975). Language used by employer in an employee's termination letter protected by qualified privilege. Smith v. Westlake PVC Corp., 1997 U.S. App. LEXIS 34536 (6th Cir. 1997). Statements made in a letter from an employer to the Ohio Bureau of Employment Services are protected by qualified privilege. Matthias v. Wendy's of Pearl, Inc., 1997 Ohio App. LEXIS 4227 (Cuyahoga). Good faith statements made by an employer to the Ohio Bureau of Workers' Compensation's fraud division are protected by qualified privilege; that privilege applies only to statements that are communicated to the appropriate parties and that are necessary to make a proper inquiry. Stephenson v. Yellow Freight Systems, 1999 Ohio App. LEXIS 4994 (Franklin), appeal not allowed, 88 Ohio St. 3d 1432, 724 N.E.2d 809 (Franklin 1999). Statements made by a physician's employer to the physician's patients are protected by a qualified privilege. Johnson v. Lakewood Hospital, 1997 Ohio App. LEXIS 4016 (Cuyahoga). Good faith statement by employer that conviction of the crime of marijuana possession is a crime of dishonesty is qualifiedly privileged. Schacht v. Ameritrust Co., 1994 Ohio App. LEXIS 1125 (Ct. App. Mar. 17, 1994) (unreported). When defamatory statements are related to information about criminal charges against the plaintiff, they are privileged, even if the statements are only regarding work performance. Frigo v. UAW Local 549, 2005 Ohio 3981, 2005 Ohio App. LEXIS 3641 (Ohio Ct. App. 2005). Communications made between a supervisor and a secretary, both employees of the same company, are qualifiedly privileged. Byvank v. Fidelity Orthopedic, Inc., 1999 Ohio App. LEXIS 2396 (Montgomery App. 1999). R.C. § 4113.71 provides a qualified privilege under certain circumstances for employee references. However, see Robinson v. Shell Oil, 519 U.S. 337 (1997), re: former employees' Title VII discrimination or retaliation causes of action based on references.

Ohio courts have also recognized a "public interest" qualified privilege. "The 'public interest' privilege 'involves communications made to those who may be expected to take official action of some kind for the protection of some interest of the public.'" Watley v. Ohio Dep't of Rehab. & Corr., 2008 Ohio 3691, 2008 WL 2854535, 2008 Ohio App. LEXIS 3260 (Franklin App. July 24, 2008) (finding "persons employed within the prison system, especially correction officers who are directly involved with the inmate population, be afforded a qualified privilege in reporting violations of prison rules in order to maintain the safety and security of the institution, its prisoners, and its employees."); Miller v. Cent. Ohio Crime Stoppers, Inc., 2008 Ohio 1280 (Ohio March 20, 2008) (finding that Crime Stoppers was entitled to the qualified privilege when it released its "Most Wanted" list to assist the police in reducing crime). The Supreme Court of Ohio recognized such a privilege in Jacobs v. Frank, 60 Ohio St.3d 111, 573 N.E.2d 609 (1991). There, the court held that "[p]ublic policy concerns dictate that those who provide information to licensing boards . . . be given a qualified privilege in order to aid in the dissemination of information to those boards, thereby improving the quality of health care administered to the general public." Id.

Some Ohio court's have applied a qualified privilege specifically for statements made in labor disputes. For example, an employee was required to prove actual malice even though the court found that the statements on their face constituted libel per se because the statements were made in a controversy concerning a labor dispute. Jacobs v. Budak, 2008 Ohio 2756, 2008 WL 2332543, 2008 Ohio App. LEXIS 2308 (Turmbull App. June 6, 2008).

a. **Common Interest.** A communication, when made in good faith on a matter of common interest between an employer and an employee, or between two employees concerning a third employee, is protected by a qualified privilege. Stearns v. Ohio Savings Ass'n, 15 Ohio App. 3d 18, 472 N.E.2d 372 (Cuyahoga 1984); Shugars v. Allied Machine & Engineering Corporation, 2003 Ohio 4672, 2003 Ohio App. LEXIS 4202 (Tuscarawas App. 2003); Kalbfell v. Marc Glassman, Inc., 2003 Ohio 3489, 2003 Ohio App. LEXIS 3183 (Columbiana App. 2003); Lennon v. Cuyahoga County Juvenile Court, 2006 Ohio 2587, 28, 2006 Ohio App. LEXIS 2443 (Ohio Ct. App. 2006). It is also worth noting that "[c] ourts in Ohio have found a 'common business interest' privilege exists where two entities share a mutual business interest, even if (1) the entities are not 'related' other than having a common business interest, or (2) the person making the statement and the recipient of the statement do not have the same employer." Georgalis v. Ohio Turnpike Comm, 2010 WL 3934589, 2010 -Ohio- 4898 (Cuyahoga October 7, 2010).

The communication must be limited in scope to the common purpose and made to proper parties only. Vitale v. Modern Tool & Die Co., 2000 Ohio App. LEXIS 2743 (Cuyahoga), appeal not allowed, 90 Ohio St. 3d 1472, 738 N.E.2d 383 (2000). Where statements made by officers of a business are made concerning activities of an employee arising out of his employment status with company, such statements are afforded a qualified privilege because they concern matters of common business interest between the parties. Evely v. Carlon Co., Div. of Indian Head, Inc., 4 Ohio St. 3d 163, 447 N.E.2d 1290 (1983). Any statements made by the Better Business Bureau are privileged for libel purposes, so long as they are made in good faith on a subject matter in which the Bureau has an interest, right, or duty, and so long as they are made to a person having a corresponding interest, right, or duty. Smith v. Ameriflora, 96 Ohio App. 3d 179, 644 N.E.2d 1038, dismissed, appeal not allowed, 642 N.E.2d 635m 71 Ohio St. 3d 1427 (Franklin 1994). A hospital's statements about an employee suspended due to alleged sexual harassment are protected by qualified privilege because they are communicated in an employment setting concerning matters of hospital interest. Hanly v. Riverside Methodist Hospital, 603 N.E.2d 1126, 78 Ohio App. 3d 73 (Franklin 1991). Statements made by company employees to management regarding plaintiff's sex-related gossiping during the normal course of a sexual harassment investigation and pursuant to the company's established sexual harassment policy are privileged. Bisbee v. Cuyahoga Board of Elections, 2001 Ohio App. LEXIS 759 (Cuyahoga). Statements made in the minutes of a hospital board meeting about the performance of a doctor-employee and distributed to other hospital personnel are protected by qualified privilege when such statements are only distributed to those who had in interest in such information. Michael v. Memorial Hospital, 1996 Ohio App. LEXIS 4846 (Sandusky), appeal not allowed, 78 Ohio St. 3d 1441, 676 N.E.2d 1187 (1997). A hospital employee's identification of a contract physician as having used a stolen credit card is protected by a qualified privilege. Doe v. Lodi Community Hospital, 2000 Ohio App. LEXIS 5802 (Medina). A statement made by a vendee to its vendor trucking company that one of the vendor's truck drivers intended to terminate his employment was privileged, since the two companies had a contractual relationship, and the future employment of a truck driver was important to both businesses. Jurczak v. J&R Schugel Trucking Company, 2003-Ohio-7039, 2003 Ohio App. LEXIS 6362 (Franklin App. 2003).

b. **Duty.** A communication made in good faith on any subject matter in which the person communicating has an interest, or in reference to which he has a duty, is privileged if made to a person having a corresponding interest or duty, even though it contains matter which, without the privilege, would be actionable, and even though the duty is not a legal one, but a moral or societal one. Hahn v. Kotten, 43 Ohio St.2d 237, 331 N.E.2d 713 (1975). Even if defamation claim was timely and communications by state commission administrator and directors regarding an employee were defamatory, the communications were protected by a qualified privilege because the communicators of the information were under a duty to inform of the employee's misconduct. Miller v. Ohio Rehab. Service Commission, 685 N.E.2d 616, 86 Ohio Misc.2d 97 (Ohio Ct. Cl., 1997). Former employer's letter to Virginia State Board of Medicine about professional character of former resident podiatrist was protected by qualified privilege because employer had a duty to inform in the peer review context. Jacobs v. Frank, 60 Ohio St. 3d 111, 573 N.E.2d 609 (1991). A child care center cannot be held liable for defamation in connection with its executive director's statutory duty to report teacher's suspected child abuse. Lail v. Madisonville Child Care Project, Inc., 55 Ohio App. 3d 37, 561 N.E.2d 1063 (Hamilton 1989). An employer cannot be found liable for defamation where a collective bargaining agreement imposed a duty on the employer to distribute employee termination letters to the union representative. Snell v. Drew, 1985 Ohio App. LEXIS 9187 (Lucas). There is no duty on the part of a former employer to inform plaintiff's current employer that plaintiff was never at work when she should have been; such duties are limited to occasions when a former employer is informing a *prospective* employer of an applicant's qualifications. Dodley v. Budget Car Sales, Inc., 1999 Ohio App. LEXIS 1790 (Franklin 1999).

c. **Criticism of Public Employee.** There is some authority for the proposition that criticism of the government short of sedition is absolutely privileged. Grafton v. American Broadcasting Co., 70 Ohio App. 2d 205, 435 N.E.2d 1131, 7 Media L. Rep. 1134 (1980). However, courts will typically apply the qualified privilege to an employer's criticism of a public employee. Jackson v. City of Columbus, 117 Ohio St. 3d 328, 883 N.E.2d 1060 (2008). Police officers are public officials and thus in defamation actions must prove that false statements were made with actual malice. Id.; Deoma v. Shaker Heights, 68 Ohio App. 3d 72, 587 N.E.2d 425 (Cuyahoga 1990).

d. **Limitation on Qualified Privileges.** The essential elements of the qualified privilege are a) good faith; b) interest to be upheld; c) statement limited in scope to the proper purpose; d) statement limited in scope to the proper occasion; and e) publication in proper manner and to proper parties. Kremer v. Cox, 682 N.E.2d 1006, 114 Ohio App. 3d 41 (Summit 1996), dismissed, appeal not allowed, 674 N.E.2d 372, 77 Ohio St. 3d 1519, reconsideration denied, 675 N.E.2d 1253, 78 Ohio St. 3d 1416. The qualified privilege may be overcome by the plaintiff upon a showing of actual malice. In this context, actual malice means that the defendant acted with knowledge that the statements were false, or with reckless disregard as to their truth or falsity. Kremer, 682 N.E.2d 1006. In determining whether the plaintiff has overcome the defendant's qualified privilege, actual malice may not be inferred. Rather, there must be adequate evidence to allow a conclusion that the defendant seriously doubted the truth of the publication. Id. Union members' publication and distribution to the local union of a form accusing plaintiffs of stealing money from employees' paychecks and demanding compensation did not constitute privileged statements in the course of a bargaining session between representatives of management and representatives of employees. Bailey v. Sams, 24 Ohio App. 3d 137, 493 N.E.2d 966 (Hardin 1985). Sheriff's allegedly defamatory statements about a former employee, made after a legislative session adjourned and reported by a local newspaper, were not subject to an absolute or qualified privilege. April v. Reflector-Herald, Inc., 46 Ohio App. 3d 95, 546 N.E.2d 466, 15 Media L. Rep. 2455 (Huron 1988). A former employer's statements to plaintiff's current employer that the plaintiff was never at work when she should have been exceeds the scope of the qualified privilege and constitutes defamation. Dodley v. Budget Car Sales, 1999 Ohio App. LEXIS 1790 (Franklin 1999). Defamatory statements made by Clerk of Court's employees are protected under Ohio Rev. Code § 2744.02(A)(1), as long as the employees did not act negligently and statements were made within the scope of their employment. Macklin v. Turner, 2005 U.S. Dist. LEXIS 19616 (N.D. Ohio 2005). A qualified privilege does not apply to statements made by a union official at a union meeting accusing an employee of theft with the knowledge that the accusations were false. Simpson v. Bakers/Local No. 57, 1998 Ohio App. LEXIS 1855 (Hamilton App. 1998). While a political subdivision and its employees engaged in a judicial or prosecutorial function normally receive immunity for making allegedly defamatory remarks, employee immunity may be defeated with a showing of malicious or reckless acts. However, employee liability does not alter the immunity of the political subdivision. Aronson, et al. v. City of Akron, 2001 Ohio App. LEXIS 1583 (Summit).

(1) **Constitutional or Actual Malice.** The qualified privilege may be overcome by the plaintiff upon a showing of actual malice. In this context, actual malice means that the defendant acted with knowledge that the statements were false, or with reckless disregard as to their truth or falsity. Kremer, 682 N.E.2d 1006. In determining whether the plaintiff has overcome the defendant's qualified privilege, actual malice may not be inferred. Rather, there must be adequate evidence to allow a conclusion that the defendant seriously doubted the truth of the publication. Id.

The Ohio Supreme Court has adopted the definition of actual malice appearing in New York Times v. Sullivan, 376 U.S. 254, 279-80 (1964): publishing a false and defamatory statement "'with knowledge that it is false or with reckless disregard of whether it was false or not.'" Perez v. Scripps Howard Broadcasting Co., 35 Ohio St. 3d 215, 218, 520 N.E.2d 198, 202, 15 Media L. Rep. 1318 (1988), cert. denied, 488 U.S. 870 (1988). To show reckless disregard for the truth, plaintiff must show with convincing clarity that (1) false statements were made with a high degree of awareness of their probable falsity, or (2) the defendant entertained serious doubts as to the truth of the publication. Id. Under New York Times v. Sullivan, plaintiffs must make a showing of actual malice when attempting to recover from a public official or public figure.

Actual malice may exist where the contents of a publication are so inherently improbable on their face that the defendant must have realized the material was probably false. Varanese v. Gall, 35 Ohio St. 3d 78, 84, 518 N.E.2d 1177, 1184, 14 Media L. Rep. 2361 (1988), cert. denied, 487 U.S.1206 (1988); Robb v. Lincoln Publishing (Ohio) Inc., 114 Ohio App. 2d 595, 683 N.E.2d 823 (Brown 1996), appeal not allowed, 78 Ohio St. 3d 1410, 675 N.E.2d 1249 (1997). Actual malice must be determined at the time of publication, id., and must be determined by the "totality of the circumstances which led to the publication of the statements." Grau v. Kleinschmidt, 31 Ohio St. 3d 84, 89, 509 N.E.2d 399, 402, 14 Media L. Rep. 1353 (1987). Unfair, one-sided attacks do not constitute actual malice. Perez, 35 Ohio St. 3d at 219, 520 N.E.2d at 203. The omission of information does not demonstrate a disregard for the truth. Id. at 220, 520 N.E.2d at 204. Entertaining doubts about the possible falsity of a publication is immaterial; the issue is whether the defendant had a high degree of awareness of the probable falsity of the publication. Varanese, 35 Ohio St. 3d at 82, 518 N.E.2d at 1182. The mere presence of conflicting stories in the defendant's own files does not constitute actual malice. Id., 35 Ohio St. 3d at 81, 518 N.E.2d at 1181. Failure to investigate does not establish actual malice. Id., 35 Ohio St. 3d at 81, 84, 518 N.E.2d at 1181, 1183; Becker v. Internatl. Assn. of Firefighters Local 4207, 2010 WL 2892766 (Ohio App. 12 Dist.), 2010 -Ohio- 3467 ¶24 (Warren July 26, 2010) ("since reckless disregard is not measured by lack of reasonable belief or of ordinary care, even evidence of negligence in failing to investigate the facts is insufficient to establish actual malice; investigatory failure alone, without a high degree of awareness of probable falsity, may raise the issue of negligence but not the issue of actual malice"). Actual malice on the part of the defendants is not demonstrated by the plaintiff's allegation or belief that the statements are false where the plaintiff failed to establish that the defendants had doubts about the truth of the statements and acted with reckless disregard of the truth. *Featherstone v. CM Media*, 2002 Ohio 6747, 2002 Ohio App. LEXIS 6509 (Franklin App. 2002). Instigating an investigation of an employee's background does not constitute malice, provided that the employer relies upon competent and credible information. Marinucci v. Ohio Dep't of Transportation, 2000 Ohio App. LEXIS 93 (Franklin). An employee's admitted dislike for his co-worker was not sufficient to show actual malice when that employee reported to a supervisor that his co-worker had threatened to bring a gun to work. Temethy v. Huntington Bancshares, Inc., 2004-Ohio-1253, 2004 Ohio App. LEXIS 1111 (Cuyahoga App. 2004). Mere negligence does not constitute actual malice. Id., 35 Ohio St. 3d at 83, 518 N.E.2d at 1183. Publishing information following a warning that it is libelous does not constitute actual malice. Id., 35 Ohio St. 3d at 83, 518 N.E.2d at 1183. A defamation plaintiff that submits a self-serving affidavit, which is not corroborated by any evidence, has not established a material issue of fact on the issue of actual malice. Watley v. Ohio Dep't of Rehab. & Corr., 2008 Ohio 3691, 2008 WL 2854535, 2008 Ohio App. LEXIS 3260 (Franklin App. July 24, 2008); Lansky v. Ciaravino, 2008 Ohio 2666, 2008 WL 2257753, 2008 Ohio App. LEXIS 2238 (Cuyahoga App. June 2, 2008); **Lucas v. Perciak, 2012 WL112983, 2012-Ohio-88 (Cuyahoga App. 2012).** However, evidence of statements or acts made subsequent to the defamatory statement which shows its ill-will, spite, or malice is admissible as evidence of actual malice. Katz v. Enzer, 29 Ohio App. 3d 118, 504 N.E.2d 427 (1987). Also, an employer who publishes a critical report about an employee and specifically qualifies that the information contained in the report is based on an unreliable source, may still be found to have published a statement with actual malice. Jackson v. City of Columbus, 117 Ohio St. 3d 328, 883 N.E.2d 1060 (2008). Malice can be inferred when the defendant's own testimony establishes that the information he has does not support his statements. Condit v. Clermont County Review, 93 Ohio App. 3d 166, 638 N.E.2d 96 (1994). "If the [deliberate] alteration [of a statement] changes the meaning of the subject's statement thus bearing upon its defamatory character, the alteration will be probative of a finding of actual malice." Murray v. Knight-Ridder, Inc., 2004-Ohio-821, 2004 Ohio App. LEXIS 763 (Belmont App. 2004).

If there is a basis for a finding of malice by a corporate employee at any position in the chain of communication, there is a jury issue of corporate malice. Ball v. British Petroleum Oil, 108 Ohio App. 3d 129, 670

N.E.2d 289 (Lucas 1995). In defamation claims based on statements made by and about participants in a public-sector labor dispute, the actual malice standard applies. Dale v. Ohio Civil Service Employees Ass'n., 57 Ohio St. 3d 112, 567 N.E.2d 253 (1991), cert. denied, 501 U.S. 1231 (1991). A "labor dispute" is any controversy over the terms and conditions of employment or the representation of employees for collective bargaining purposes, regardless of whether the disputants stand in the relation of employer and employee, and regardless of whether the dispute is subject to the jurisdiction of the National Labor Relations Board, the State Employment Relations Board, or some other administrative agency. Dale, 57 Ohio St. 3d at 116. Statements in a union newsletter that an employee who was responsible for payroll had trouble adding which resulted in the suspension of the union member, were made in the broad context of a labor dispute and therefore the plaintiff needed to establish actual malice in order to recover. Bertsch v. Communications Workers of America, 101 Ohio App. 3d 186, 655 N.E.2d 243 (Summit 1995), appeal not allowed, 72 Ohio St. 3d 1436, 625 N.E.2d 624. A union employee's article in a union newsletter criticizing a supervisor's procedures for recording and granting equalization records qualified as a labor dispute, thus the actual malice standard applied. Jacobs v. Budak, 156 Ohio App. 3d 160, 2004 Ohio 522, 805 N.E. 2d 111 (Trumbull App. 2004).

(2) **Common Law Malice.** Common law malice connotes ill will, hatred, spite, vengeance, or a conscious disregard for the rights and safety of other persons that has a great probability of causing substantial harm. Jacobs v. Frank, 60 Ohio St. 3d 111, 573 N.E.2d 609, quoting Preston v. Murry, 32 Ohio St. 3d 334, 512 N.E.2d 1174 (1987). While plaintiffs must make a showing of actual malice in the public official defamation context, in purely private defamation cases the plaintiff need only establish common law malice. Malone v. Courtyard by Marriot L.P., 74 Ohio St. 3d 440, 445-46, 659 N.E.2d 1242 (1996); Gosden v. Louis, 116 Ohio App. 3d 195, 687 N.E.2d 481 (1996), appeal not allowed, 78 Ohio St. 3d 1456, 677 N.E.2d 816 (1997). Once an employer establishes a qualified privilege, however, an employee must make a showing of actual malice in order to overcome that privilege. Jacobs v. Frank, 60 Ohio St. 3d 111, 573 N.E.2d 609 (1991).

e. **Question of Fact or Law.** Where the circumstances of the occasion for alleged defamatory statements are not in dispute, the determination of whether a qualified privilege exists is a question of law for the court. Horsley v. Wal-Mart, Inc., 1997 Ohio App. LEXIS 5988 (Lawrence); A & B-Abell Elevator Co. v. Columbus/Cent. Ohio Bldg. & Constr.Trades Council, 73 Ohio St. 3d 1, 651 N.E.2d 1283 (1995); Kremer v. Cox, 114 Ohio App. 3d 41, 682 N.E.2d 1006 (Summit 1996), dismissed, appeal denied, 674 N.E.2d 372, 77 Ohio St. 3d 1519, reconsideration denied, 675 N.E.2d 1253, 78 Ohio St. 3d 1416.

f. **Burden of Proof.** Once a privilege is found to exist, the burden is on the plaintiff to establish that the defendant acted with actual malice in order to overcome the privilege. Kremer v. Cox, 114 Ohio App. 3d 41, 682 N.E.2d 1006 (Summit 1996), dismissed, appeal denied, 674 N.E.2d 372, 77 Ohio St. 3d 1519, reconsideration denied, 675 N.E.2d 1253, 78 Ohio St. 3d 1416. For purposes of overcoming a qualified privilege, actual malice is acting with knowledge that statements were false or acting with reckless disregard as to their truth or falsity. Kremer v. Cox, 114 Ohio App. 3d 41, 682 N.E.2d 1006 (Summit 1996).

B. Standard Libel Defenses

1. ***Truth.*** Truth is always a defense in any action for libel. Shifflet v. Thomson Newspapers, Inc., 69 Ohio St. 2d 179, 431 N.E. 2d 1014, 8 Media L. Rep. 1199 (1982). Ohio Rev. Code Ann. § 2739.02 provides that truth, when pleaded and proven by the defendant, is a complete defense to an action for libel and slander. When the allegedly defamatory publication is about a matter of legitimate public concern, the plaintiff has the burden of proving falsity. Philadelphia Newspapers, Inc. v. Hepps, 475 U.S. 767, 12 Media L. Rep. 1977 (1986); accord, Wilson v. Scripps Howard Broadcasting Co., 642 F.2d 371, 7 Media L. Rep. 1169 (6th Cir. 1981), cert. dismissed, 454 U.S. 1130 (1981). It is sufficient to show that the imputation is substantially true, or as is often put, to justify the "gist, or the sting." A plaintiff cannot establish a prima facie case of falsity where the record reveals that the published report was substantially true. National Medic Serv. Corp. v. E.W. Scripps Co., 61 Ohio App. 3d 752, 573 N.E. 2d 1148 (Hamilton 1989); accord, Cooper School of Art, Inc. v. Plain Dealer Pub. Co., 1986 Ohio App. LEXIS 6698, 12 Media L. Rep. 2283 (Cuyahoga); Nussbaumer v. Time, Inc., 1986 Ohio App. LEXIS 8956, 13 Media L. Rep. 1753 (Cuyahoga). Even if three statements are individually substantially true, if such statements are taken out of context, the meaning is substantially altered, thus they may be defamatory. Murray v. Knight-Ridder, Inc., 2004-Ohio-821, 2004 Ohio App. LEXIS 763 (Belmont App. 2004). In a libel action against a former employer for statements made about the reasons for the former employee's termination, the former employer's statements were not actionable because the statements were true and there was no showing of actual malice. Davis v. Customized Transporation Inc., 854 F. Supp. 513 (N.D. Ohio 1994). Mayor's and police chief's reasons for discharging police officer were true and thus they were protected from officer's defamation claim, based on the fact that the officer admitted to eight allegations which served as grounds for the discharge. Hadad v. Croucher, 970 F. Supp. 1227 (N.D.Ohio 1997). Reports that employee was encouraging a third party to file suit and that employee was late on annual reports was not defamatory because the employee failed to prove that the reports were untrue. Miller v. Ohio Rehab. Services Commission, 86 Ohio Misc.2d 97, 685 N.E.2d

616 (Ohio Ct. Cl. 1997). Statements made by co-workers to an employer that one of the employees was carrying a handgun to work were not defamatory. Dryden v. Cincinnati Bell Telephone, 135 Ohio App. 3d 394, 734 N.E.2d 409 (Hamilton 1999). The employee never denied carrying a handgun to work, and thus the employer was not liable for legitimate safety concerns made by other employees. See id. at *15. Statements that a dentistry practice was more concerned about quantity of work rather than quality, made by a dentist who was formerly employed by the plaintiff, were not actionable because they were substantially true. Dental Care Clinic v. McDonough, 1986 Ohio App. LEXIS 5742, 12 Media L. Rep. 2323 (Cuyahoga).

2. ***Opinion.*** Statements of opinion cannot be defamatory. Van Deusen v. Baldwin, 99 Ohio App. 3d 416, 650 N.E.2d 963 (1994). Whether an alleged defamatory statement constitutes fact or opinion is a question of law. Rich v. Thompson Newspapers, Inc., 164 Ohio App. 3d 477, 484 842 N.E.2d 1081 (Ashtabula 2005) (citing Scott v. News Herald, 25 Ohio St. 3d 243, 250 496 699 (1986); Lennon v. Cuyahoga County Juvenile Court, 2006 Ohio 2587, 29, 2006 Ohio App. LEXIS 2443 (Ohio Ct. App. 2006). When determining whether speech is protected opinion, Ohio courts must consider the totality of circumstances surrounding the speech at issue. Specifically, courts must consider the specific language used, whether the statement is verifiable, the general context of the statement, and the broader context in which the statement appeared. Vail v. The Plain Dealer Publishing Co., 72 Ohio St. 3d 279, 649 N.E.2d 182, 23 Media L. Rep. 1881 (1995), cert. denied, 516 U.S. 1043 (1995). The Ohio Constitution does not afford greater protection to opinion than the federal Constitution. Milkovich v. News-Herald, 70 Ohio App. 3d 480, 591 N.E.2d 394 (Ohio App. 11 Dist. 1990), cause dismissed, 59 Ohio St. 3d 702, 571 N.E.2d 137. Words such as "thought" and "believed" automatically show that a speaker is stating his/her opinion and, as such, the statement does not constitute a factual statement for purposes of a defamation claim. Molnar v. Klammer, 2005 Ohio 6905, 114, 2005 Ohio App. LEXIS 6227 (Ohio Ct. App. 2005). Merely using the phrase "in my opinion," however, does not invoke protection from a defamation claim. Davis v. Black, 70 Ohio App. 3d 359, 591 N.E.2d 11 (Franklin 1991). A statement recommending that an employee not be rehired cannot be defamatory because it is impossible to verify whether the person should be rehired and the decision fully depends on the supervisor's opinion. Byrne v. Univ. Hosps., 2011 WL 3630483, 2011-Ohio-4110, ¶15 (Ohio App. 8 Dist. 2011).

Referring to a plant manager as "Little Hitler" and accusing him of running a "concentration camp" were expressions of opinion and thus were protected in the context of a labor dispute. Yeager v. Local Union 20, 453 N.E.2d 666, 6 Ohio St. 3d 369 (1983). The use of factual references does not automatically transform an opinion into a factual report for purposes of a defamation claim. Rich v. Thompson Newspapers, Inc., 164 Ohio App. 3d 477, 484 842 N.E.2d 1081 (Ashtabula 2005). A newspaper article that quoted a labor negotiator as saying that the county prosecutor gave "very incompetent legal advice" and that also stated the underlying nondefamatory facts on which the opinion was based was nonactionable opinion. Plough v. Schneider, 8 Media L. Rep. 1620 (Ohio Ct. App. Portage 1982). The opinion privilege applies not only to the media, but extends to nonmedia defendants as well. Wampler v. Higgins, 93 Ohio St. 3d 111, 752 N.E.2d 962, 29 Media L. Rep. 2377 (2001). The status of a defendant does not affect a plaintiff's burden of proving falsity. Because an opinion cannot be false, an opinion cannot be defamatory regardless of the status of the parties. See id. Union member's flier regarding plaintiff's qualifications for union office were not protected opinion because flier did not expressly note that statements contained therein were union member's own opinions; rather, reasonable reader would understand the information to be factual. Smith v. Papp, 114 Ohio App. 3d 442, 683 N.E.2d 384 (Cuyahoga 1996), appeal not allowed, 77 Ohio St. 3d 1548, 674 N.E.2d 1186. Vulgar letters that appeared on police department bulletin boards and in mailboxes of certain personnel fell within realm of protected speech because letters were so couched in exaggeration and were so subjective in tone that a reasonable person could only believe author was expressing his or her opinion. Bross v. Smith, 80 Ohio App. 3d 246, 608 N.E.2d 1175 (Butler 1992), rehearing denied, 65 Ohio St. 3d 1467, 60 N.E.2d 1175, cert. denied, 508 U.S. 909 (1993). Homeowners' association trustee's statements to homeowners in a letter regarding one homeowner's "intimidation of children," "allow[ing] no person, pet or plaything to touch his property," and initiation of legal action against his neighbors for "petty violations" constituted protected opinion because it was language that was loosely definable and had various interpretable meanings. Heidel v. Amburgy, 2003-Ohio-3073, 2003 Ohio App. LEXIS 2752 (Warren App. 2003). Where the published statements were contained in the Letters to the Editor section of a newspaper; were modified by the words "supposedly" and "apparently"; and it was clear from the tone of the letter that the author is not attempting to be impartial, the statements are opinions, and therefore not defamatory. Rich v. Thompson Newspapers, Inc., 2004-Ohio-1431, 2004 Ohio App. LEXIS 1269 (Ashtabula App. 2004). "Merely because an editorial article contains factual references does not transform an opinion into a factual article." Rich v. Thompson Newspapers, Inc., 2004-Ohio-1431, 2004 Ohio App. LEXIS 1269 (Ashtabula App. 2004) (citing Sikora v. Plain Dealer Publishing Co., 2003-Ohio-3218, 2003 Ohio App. LEXIS 2880 (Cuyahoga App. 2003)). Statements that the employee was "unhinged" and a "hazard" were not defamatory because they were based on an opinion and not a professional diagnosis. Frigo v. UAW Local 549, 2005 Ohio 3981, 2005 Ohio App. LEXIS 3641 (Ohio Ct. App. 2005).

3. ***Consent.*** An employee who becomes a member of a union whose collective bargaining agreement requires written notice of dismissal of any employee cannot sue for defamation based on the contents of that letter, because the employee has consented to such a writing. Holloman v. Rutman Wine Co., 11 Ohio App. 3d 257, 464 N.E.2d 180 (Cuyahoga 1983).

4. ***Mitigation.*** Under § 2730.02 of the Ohio Revised Code, defendants in a libel action may prove mitigating circumstances in order to reduce damages. Under the common law, one who is injured by a defamatory publication may demand an apology or retraction from the defendant. But unless the plaintiff accepts such an apology or retraction as a satisfaction, it cannot be a complete defense to a libel claim; rather, it would only be considered in mitigation of damages. Byers v. Meridian Printing Co., 84 Ohio St. 408, 422, 95 N.E. 917, 919 (1911). Furthermore, just because the defendant asserts a belief in the truth of his publication does not mean he has established a defense. Such a belief is not a defense, but will go only to the existence of malice and the mitigation of damages. Alpin v. Morton, 21 Ohio St. 536 (1871); Waterman v. Martin, 1981 Ohio App. LEXIS 12137; Gray v. General Motors Corp., 52 Ohio App. 2d 348, 350, 370 N.E.2d 747, 750 (1977). If, in response to a defamation charge, the defendant responds only with a general denial, the truth of the alleged libel cannot be considered a defense, but can only be considered in mitigation of damages. Spencer v. News Publishing Co., 79 Ohio App. 519, 74 N.E.2d 282 (1947).

III. RECURRING FACT PATTERNS

A. Statements in Personnel File

A written report by an employee's department supervisor evaluating the employee on his work duties and filed with company superiors was conducted in the scope of supervisor's employment and is therefore protected by a qualified privilege. Senften v. Massillon Community Hospital, 1983 Ohio App. LEXIS 13137 (Stark). Statements that an employer put in an employee's file were not actionable because they were never published to a third party. Potter v. RETS Tech Ctr. Co., 2008 Ohio 993, 2008 WL 615423, 2008 Ohio App. LEXIS 858 (Montgomery App. March 7, 2008)

B. Performance Evaluations

A written warning issued to a hospital employee to cease his harassment of fellow employees does not provide a basis for defamation claim. Bartlett v. Daniel Drake Memorial Hospital, 75 Ohio App. 3d 334, 599 N.E.2d 403 (Hamilton 1991). A written report by employee's department supervisor evaluating employee on his work duties and filed with company superiors was conducted in the scope of supervisor's employment and is therefore protected by a qualified privilege. Senften v. Massillon Community Hospital, 1983 Ohio App. LEXIS 13137 (Stark). Merely recommending that action be taken to investigate or evaluate an employee's performance does not provide a basis for a libel claim. Boutsicaris v. Akron General Medical Center, 1997 Ohio App. LEXIS 2041 (Summit).

C. References

A qualified privilege exists in the employment reference setting, and thus an employer may communicate to a prospective employer facts, opinions, or suspicions without fear of a defamation action, so long as such statements are not made maliciously. Rainey v. Shaffer, 8 Ohio App. 3d 262, 456 N.E.2d 1328 (Lake 1983). A company official's statements to a prospective employer concerning reasons for a building engineer's discharge are protected by a qualified privilege. Rinehart v. Maiorano, 76 Ohio App. 3d 448, 602 N.E.2d 340 (Lucas 1991). However, see Robinson v. Shell Oil, 519 U.S. 337 (1997) re: former employees' Title VII discrimination or retaliation causes of action based on references.

D. Intracorporate Communication

A statement which appears in a company's financial statement and reports a lawsuit pending against a former employee does not provide a basis for a libel action. Seredich v. Joseph Industries, Inc., 1991 Ohio App. LEXIS 4240 (Cuyahoga).

E. Statements to Government Regulators

Statements made to government officials who may be expected to take action with regard to the qualifications of bidders for public-works contracts are protected by a qualified privilege. A&B Abell Elevator Co., Inc. v. Columbus/Central Ohio Building & Construction Trades Council, 73 Ohio St. 3d 1, 651 N.E.2d 1283 (1995).

F. Reports to Auditors and Insurers

Under R.C. § 3904.22, those who, in good faith, furnish truthful, personal or privileged information to an insurance institution, agent, or insurance support organization are immune from liability for defamation. Those who furnish such information to the division of insurance fraud of the department of insurance are likewise protected from liability. Mann v. American Packaging Corp., 1993 U.S. App. LEXIS 29939 (6th Cir.) (Ohio law).

G. Vicarious Liability of Employers for Statements Made by Employees

Managing editors of newspapers can be held individually liable for libel printed in their newspapers, even though they do not have actual knowledge of the libel contained therein. Goudy v. Dayton Newspapers, Inc., 14 Ohio App. 2d 207,

237 N.E.2d 909 (Montgomery 1967). A corporation can be held liable for the defamatory statements of its employees and/or agents. Ball v. British Petroleum Oil, 108 Ohio App. 3d 129, 670 N.E.2d 289 (Lucas 1995). Building owners cannot be held liable for the libelous graffiti that is written on the walls of their building, even though the plaintiff may have given notice of the graffiti and the building owner took no action. Scott v. Hull, 22 Ohio App. 2d 141, 259 N.E.2d 160 (3 Dist. 1970). An employer is not liable for independent acts of employees which in no way facilitate or promote the employer's business. Schulman v. Cleveland, 30 Ohio St. 2d 196, 283 N.E.2d 175 (1972). **A client may be vicariously liable for its attorney's defamatory statements only if the client authorized or ratified the conduct. Am. Chem. Soc. v. Leadscope, Inc., 2012 WL 4201288, 2012-Ohio-4193 (September 18, 2012).**

1. ***Scope of Employment.*** Absent facts that comments were within scope of employment, employers cannot be held liable for allegedly defamatory statements made by employees about co-workers. Trader v. People Working Cooperatively, Inc., 104 Ohio App. 3d 690, 663 N.E.2d 335 (Hamilton 1994), appeal allowed, 72 Ohio St. 3d 1544, 674 N.E.2d 1389, appeal dismissed as improvidently allowed, 74 Ohio St. 3d 1286, 660 N.E.2d 737. An employer will not be held responsible, under the doctrine of respondeat superior, when an unidentified employee posts a sign denouncing a fellow employee as an "experienced drinking companion," without showing that the tort was committed within the scope of employment and without a showing of specific and personalized liability. Shanahan v. B.F. Goodrich Aerospace Co., 993 F. Supp. 1107 (N.D. Ohio 1998), aff'd, 181 F.3d 103 (6th Cir. 1999). An employer has no respondeat superior liability when an employee types a defamatory letter outside the scope of employment about another employee; further, because defamation is an intentional tort, it is necessary to establish that the letter is calculated to facilitate or promote the business. Baeppler v. McMahan, 2000 Ohio App. LEXIS 1653 (Cuyahoga). Employees who make allegedly defamatory statements in the course of an employee's unemployment compensation hearing are acting within scope of employment and therefore may be protected by either an absolute or qualified privilege. Horsley v. Wal-Mart, Inc., 1997 Ohio App. LEXIS 5988 (Lawrence App.). Employers cannot be held liable for defamatory statements made by outside investigators absent evidence that investigator was working as employer's agent. Gaumont v. Emery Air Freight Corp., 61 Ohio App. 3d 277, 572 N.E.2d 747 (Montgomery 1989). Hotel desk clerk was not acting within the scope of her employment when she wrote a letter to plaintiff's employer complaining about plaintiff's behavior and intoxication at an employment seminar held at the hotel. Anderson v. Toeppe, 116 Ohio App. 3d 429, 688 N.E.2d 538 (Lucas 1996). A dispatcher, who identified himself as such, does not have apparent authority to make statements regarding a former employee's work ethic. Because the dispatcher was not acting under the authority of the employer, the employer is not liable to the plaintiff for the defamatory statements. Young v. Oh. Bulk Transfer, Inc., 2005 Ohio 4426, 17-18, 2005 Ohio App. LEXIS 4013 (Ohio Ct. App. 2005).

a. **Blogging.** No cases reported.

2. ***Damages.*** No cases reported.

H. Internal Investigations

Statements regarding reason for employee's termination made in good faith and solely within employer's management team during an internal investigation are protected by qualified privilege. Daff v. Associated Bldg. Suppliers, Inc., 2007 Ohio 3238, 2007 WL 1827626 (Ct. App. Summit County 2007):

A supervisor's statements regarding an employees threats of violence in the workplace, that were made at the request of her superior while in an employer's supervisory meeting, were protected by a qualified privilege. Temethy v. Huntington Bancshers, Inc., 2004 Ohio 1253, 2004 WL 528820 (Ct. App. Cuyahoga County 2004).

IV. OTHER ACTIONS BASED ON STATEMENTS

A. Negligent Hiring, Retention, and Supervision

To recover under a claim based on negligent hiring a plaintiff must prove: 1) the existence of an employment relationship; 2) the employee's incompetence; 3) the employer's actual or constructive knowledge of such incompetence; 4) the employee's act or omission causing the plaintiff's injuries; 5) the employer's negligence in hiring or retaining the employee as the proximate cause of plaintiff's injuries. Ruta v. Breckenridge-Remy Co., 1980 Ohio App. LEXIS 12410 (Erie Co., 1980), aff'd, 69 Ohio St. 2d 66 (1982); Anderson v. Toeppe, 116 Ohio App. 3d 429, 688 N.E.2d 538 (Lucas 1996). The courts of Ohio also have applied these elements to claims of negligent supervision. Harmon v. GZK, Inc., 2002 Ohio App. LEXIS 480 (Montgomery). The Ohio cases involve claims of third-parties against employers, and it is argued in Ohio that such claims by employees are barred by the workers' compensation system. In an action for negligent hiring and supervision of a hotel employee based on statements in a letter written by the employee to plaintiff's employer, complaining about plaintiff's behavior at an employment seminar, defendant hotel had no actual or constructive knowledge of incompetence on the part of the employee and thus plaintiffs were barred from recovery. Anderson, 116 Ohio App. 2d at 438; 688 N.E.2d at 543. This cause of action is most commonly applied in cases involving criminal behavior of an employee or negligent acts of an employee. See, e.g., Kropf v. Vermillion Board of Education, 1986 Ohio App. LEXIS 7795 (Erie); Reichardt v. Designed Metal Products Co., 1995 Ohio App. LEXIS 3627 (Richland), appeal not allowed, 73 Ohio St. 3d 1453, 654 N.E.2d 989 (1996); Evans v. Ohio State University, 112 Ohio App. 3d 724, 680 N.E.2d 161 (Franklin 1996), appeal not allowed, 77 Ohio St. 3d 1494, 673 N.E.2d 149 (1996); Kuhn v. Youlten, 118 Ohio App. 3d 168, 692 N.E.2d 226 (Cuyahoga 1997); Venger v. Davis, 1994 Ohio App. LEXIS 2940 (Summit). As such, it is premised primarily on conduct, not statements, of employees. The Ohio Supreme Court has, however, held that an action against an employer for negligently hiring and retaining employees may be predicated upon allegations of workplace sexual harassment by an employee. Kerans v. Porter Paint Co., 61 Ohio St. 3d 486, 575 N.E.2d 428 (1991). The case is viewed not as a negligent hire/supervision case so much as a workplace safety and sexual harassment case. Interestingly, with regard to the second element of negligent supervision/retention (i.e., employee's incompetence), "sexually harassing behavior is per se incompetent behavior." Harmon, 2002 Ohio App. LEXIS at *43-*44.

B. Intentional Infliction of Emotional Distress.

The Ohio Supreme Court recognized a cause of action for intentional or reckless infliction of emotional distress in Yeager v. Local Union 20, 6 Ohio St. 3d 369, 453 N.E.2d 666 (1983). In order to prevail on a claim for intentional infliction of emotional distress, a plaintiff must establish: 1) that the defendant either intended to cause emotional distress or knew or should have known that actions taken would result in serious emotional distress to the plaintiff; 2) that the defendant's conduct was so extreme and outrageous as to go beyond all possible bounds of decency and was such that it can be considered as utterly intolerable in a civilized community; 3) that the defendant's actions were the proximate cause of plaintiff's injury; and 4) that the mental anguish suffered by plaintiff is serious and of a nature that no reasonable man could be expected to endure it. Tschantz v. Ferguson, 97 Ohio App. 3d 693, 647 N.E.2d 507 (1994), citing Pyle v. Pyle, 11 Ohio App. 3d 31, 34, 463 N.E.2d 98 (1983). See also Yeager v. Local Union 20, 6 Ohio St. 3d 369, 375, 453 N.E.2d 666. Intent, in and of itself, without extreme and outrageous conduct, is insufficient to constitute a cause of action for intentional infliction of emotional distress. Hale v. City of Dayton, 2002 Ohio App. LEXIS 474, appeal denied, 95 Ohio St. 3d 1474, 768 N.E.2d 1182 (Montgomery). In fact, in Yeager, the Ohio Supreme Court stated: Liability "clearly does not extend to mere insults, indignities, threats, annoyances, petty oppressions, or other trivialities. The rough edges of our society are still in need of a good deal of filing down, and in the meantime plaintiffs must necessarily be expected and required to be hardened to a certain amount of rough language, and to occasional acts that are definitely inconsiderate and unkind. There is no occasion for the law to intervene in every case where some one's (sic) feelings are hurt. There must still be freedom to express an unflattering opinion, and some safety valve must be left through which irascible tempers may blow off relatively harmless steam." Yeager, 6 Ohio St. 3d at 374. Ohio also recognizes an actionable form of emotional distress in cases where the business relationship of the plaintiff and defendant creates a situation where the plaintiff is entitled to protection by the defendant. Meyers v. Hot Bagels Factory, Inc., 131 Ohio App. 3d 82, 721 N.E.2d 1068 (Hamilton 1999), appeal not allowed, 85 Ohio St. 3d 1487, 709 N.E.2d 1214 (1999). Examples of such situations include where a streetcar operator removes a ten-year-old boy from a streetcar at night because the only coin he had for fare was mutilated, Cincinnati Northern Traction Co. v. Rosnagle, 84 Ohio St. 310, 95 N.E. 884 (1911); and a hotel's refusal to provide a guest access to his room because he had HIV, Phillips v. Mufleh, 95 Ohio App. 3d 289, 642 N.E.2d 411 (1994). In these situations, liability is premised on the special relationship between the plaintiff and defendant and requires the defendant to extend respectful and decent treatment to his guests. Meyers, 1999 Ohio App. LEXIS at *18. A plaintiff cannot prevail on a claim of intentional infliction of emotional distress where his employer calls a team meeting in which the employer dispels rumors that the plaintiff was sexually harassing another employee. Wilson v. Proctor & Gamble, 1998 Ohio App. LEXIS 5290 (Hamilton 1999), appeal not allowed, 85 Ohio St. 3d 1427, 707 N.E.2d 517 (1999).

The Ohio Supreme Court has further recognized that, under some circumstances, at will employees can maintain a cause of action against their former employers for intentional infliction of emotional distress arising out of their employment. Russ v. TRW, Inc., 59 Ohio St. 3d 42, 570 N.E.2d 1076 (1991), reh'g denied, 60 Ohio St. 3d 720, 574 N.E. 2d 1084 (1991). To support a claim of intentional infliction of emotional distress, a plaintiff must prove that the emotional distress is serious: liability does not extend to mere insults, threats, indignities, or annoyances. Volkert v. Talbott, 1998 Ohio App. LEXIS 1121 (Franklin). Most commonly, however, such a claim is applied in circumstances in which an employee has been discharged in response to whistle blowing, see, e.g., Anders v. Specialty Chemical Resources, Inc., 121 Ohio App. 3d 348, 700 N.E.2d 39 (Cuyahoga 1997), or in circumstances in which an employer is accused of discriminating against an employee on the basis of race or handicap. See, e.g., Takach v. Americal Medical Technology Inc., 128 Ohio App. 3d 457, 715 N.E.2d 577 (Cuyahoga 1998), appeal allowed, 82 Ohio St. 3d 1482, 696 N.E.2d 1088 (1998), dismissed, 85 Ohio St. 3d 1213, 709 N.E.2d 169 (1999); Morgan v. Taft Place Medical Center, 1998 Ohio App. LEXIS 2541 (Butler); Dunn v. Rossborough Manufacturing Co., 1998 Ohio App. LEXIS 1806 (Lorain), appeal not allowed, 83 Ohio St. 3d 1429, 699 N.E.2d 945 (1998). As such, these claims are premised on the defendant's conduct, and not the defendant's statements. Note, however, that a large number of discrimination and harassment cases are filed based upon words uttered in the workplace, and nothing more. Court affirmed dismissal of defamation and intentional infliction claims arising from employee's termination due to his allegedly having made a sexually harassing comment which violated the employer's work environment policy, holding employee did not state a defamation claim and that "it is not extreme or outrageous to report conduct which may violate company policy, even when the alleged infraction involved no ill will or animus." Adkins v. DuPont Vespel Parts & Shapes, Inc., 2007 Ohio 2770, 2007 WL 1643208 (Ct. App. Cuyahoga County 2007).

Ohio had an employment intentional tort statute, which provided that an employer was liable if a plaintiff, who was either an employee or the dependent survivor(s) of a deceased employee, proved by clear and convincing evidence that the employer deliberately committed all of the elements of an employment intentional tort. O.R.C. § 2745.01(B). "Employment intentional tort" meant an act committed by an employer in which the employer deliberately and intentionally injured, caused an occupational disease of, or caused the death of an employee. O.R.C. § 2745.01(D)(1). However, the Ohio Supreme Court has recently found this statute to be unconstitutional. Johnson v. BP Chemical, Inc., 85 Ohio St. 3d 298, 707 N.E.2d 1107 (1999).

C. Interference with Economic Advantage

Ohio recognizes the tort of "business interference," which occurs when a person, without privilege, induces or otherwise purposely causes a third party not to enter into, or continue, a business relationship, or perform a contract with another. Juhasz v. Quik Shops Inc., 55 Ohio App.2d 51, 379 N.E.2d 235 (Summit Cty. 1977); Smith v. Ameriflora 1992, Inc., 96 Ohio App.3d 179, 644 N.E.2d 1038 (Franklin Cty. 1994). The interference must be intentional, rather than negligent. Ohio does not acknowledge interference with a business relationship that is merely negligent. Diamond Wine & Spirits, Inc. v. Dayton Heidelberg Dist. Co., Inc., 2002 Ohio App. LEXIS 4066 (Allen). Whether there is a privilege depends on (1) the nature of the actor's conduct, (2) the nature of the expectancy with which his conduct interferes, (3) the relations between the parties, (4) the interest sought to be advanced by the actor and (5) the social interests in protecting the expectancy on the one hand and the actors's freedom of action on the other hand. Juhasz, 55 Ohio App.2d at 57. The Ohio Supreme Court has cited Juhasz for the proposition that the law recognizes the tort of interference with business relationships. Haller v. Borror Corp., 50 Ohio St.3d 10, 552 N.E.2d 207 (1990), reh'g denied, 51 Ohio St. 3d 704, 555 N.E.2d 322 (1990). Actual malice is not a necessary element of a tortious interference claim. However, once a qualified privilege has been asserted, actual malice must be demonstrated in order to defeat the qualified privilege defense. Smith v. Ameriflora, supra.

Ohio also recognizes the tort of intentional interference with a contract. The elements of this tort are: (1) the existence of a contract; (2) the wrongdoer's knowledge of the contract; (3) the wrongdoer's intentional procurement of the contract's breach; (4) the lack of justification; and (5) resulting damages. Kenty v. Transamerica Premium Ins. Co., 72 Ohio St.3d 415, 650 N.E.2d 863 (1995).

In a claim alleging, among other things, intentional interference with a contractual relationship, the Hamilton County Court of Appeals found that the plaintiff entered into a valid written agreement relieving a defendant from all liability arising from its administration of the psychological tests. Pinger v. Behavioral Science Center, 52 Ohio App.3d 17, 556 N.E.2d 209 (Hamilton Cty. 1988).

Former employer did not tortiously interfere with plaintiff's economic advantage by informing plaintiff's patients that plaintiff was no longer an employee at the hospital or by informing plaintiff's prospective employer that plaintiff and employer had a "disagreement." Johnson v. Lakewood Hospital, 1997 Ohio App. LEXIS 4016 (Cuyahoga).

D. Prima Facie Tort

No cause of action exists in Ohio for a prima facie tort. Costell v. Toledo Hospital, 38 Ohio St. 3d 221, 527 N.E.2d 858 (1988); Huffman v. Lemmon, 1982 Ohio App. LEXIS 12910; Bajpayee v. Rothermich, 53 Ohio App. 2d 117, 372 N.E.2d 817 (Franklin 1977).

V. OTHER ISSUES

A. Statute of Limitations

An action for libel must be brought within one year after the cause accrues. Ohio Rev. Code Ann. § 2305.11. Where a party's negligent and intentional infliction of emotional distress claims "sound in" defamation, meaning that the emotional distress claims arise from the defamatory communication, the one-year statute of limitations for the defamation claim applies to the emotional distress claims as well. Breno v. City of Mentor, 2003-Ohio-4051, 2003 Ohio App. LEXIS 3610 (Cuyahoga App. 2003). A recently bankrupted business owner's claim against a news company that filmed him moving out of his home, which depicted him as attempting to escape his creditors, was a defamation claim, not invasion of privacy, and was therefore subject to the one-year statute of limitations for defamation claims. Salupo v. Fox, 2004-Ohio-149, 2004 Ohio App. LEXIS 136 (Cuyahoga App. 2004). An action for libel accrues upon the first publication of the matter complained of. Guccione v. Hustler Magazine, 17 Ohio St. 3d 88, 477 N.E.2d 630 (1985). It is well settled under Ohio law that the statute of limitations begins to run when the defamatory statement is first published, not when the defamed person discovers the injury associated with the act. Cramer v. Fairfield Med. Ctr., 2009-Ohio-3338, 2009 Ohio App. LEXIS 2877 (Fairfield App. 2009). Simply mailing a complaint to the court to be filed within one year after the cause accrues does not satisfy the statute; it must actually be received by the court and filed within that time. Rice v. Hawkins, Lake County Common Pleas, Case No. 97 CV 001083 (May 23, 1997). However, the statute is not a bar when an indigent defendant does everything in his power to file the complaint on time and when the timely filing is prevented through the fault of the clerk of courts. Pollock v. Rashid, 117 Ohio App. 3d 361, 690 N.E.2d 903 (Hamilton 1996). The burden of proving the statute of limitations defense is on the defendant. Rainey v. Shaffer, 8 Ohio App. 3d 262, 263, 456 N.E.2d 1328, 1330-31 (1983); Karlen v. Carfangia, 2001 WL 58931, *6 (Ohio Ct. App. 2001). In a defamation case against an employer for distributing copies of a reprimand letter in the employee lunchroom, publication for purposes of determining the statute of limitations occurred on the date the letter was received by the employee and his union representative, not on the (later) date that it was distributed in the lunchroom. Snell v. Drew, 1985 Ohio App. LEXIS 9187 (Lucas). The republication of a defamatory statement 10 years after the original publication did not restart the statute of limitations. Friedler v. The Equitable Life Assurance Society of the United States, 86 Fed. Appx. 50 (6th Cir. 2003). Even though plaintiff's original complaint for defamation was barred by the statute of limitations, because plaintiff, in his response to defendant's motion to dismiss, alleged defendant made other defamatory statements within the statutory period, plaintiff should be granted leave to amend his complaint. Ziegler v. Findlay Indus., 2005 U.S. Dist. LEXIS 15936 (N.D. Ohio 2005). **The one-year statute of limitations applicable to defamation claims applies, rather than statute of limitations for actions against the State, where a complaint plainly presents allegations of defamation against a state entity and likewise plainly sets forth the date when plaintiff contends the wrongful action took place. Shampine v. Ohio Dept. of Job & Family Servs., 2011 WL 5878158, 2011-Ohio-6057 (Franklin App. 2012).**

B. Jurisdiction

The Ohio Supreme Court has found that Ohio's long-arm statute confers jurisdiction on a non-resident who posted statements on the Internet from outside the state because the statements were technically published in Ohio when read by five Ohio residents. Kauffman Racing Equip. v. Roberts, 126 Ohio St.3d 81 (Ohio June 10, 2010). Kauffman is the first decision to recognize personal jurisdiction over a non-resident based on Internet postings, and may well open the door to more cross-state libel suits testing the limits of jurisdiction.

C. Worker's Compensation Exclusivity

Section 35, Article II of the Ohio Constitution and Ohio Rev. Code § 4123.74 provide an employer under Ohio's Workers' Compensation system is immune from suit by its employees for occupational injuries except for injuries resulting from intentional torts. See Jones v. VIP Development Company (1984), 15 Ohio St.3d 90. Ohio has statutorily created an employer intentional tort, but that statute expressly does not apply to defamation claims. Ohio Rev. Code § 2745.01. Liability may be imposed against employers who commit intentional torts that do not implicate the hazards of the workplace, including defamation. McGee v. Goodyear Atomic Corp. (1995), 103 Ohio App. 3d 236, 249.

D. Pleading Requirements

To state a cause of action for defamation, allegedly defamatory statements must be set forth in the complaint substantially in the language used. Sorin v. Board of Education, 464 F. Supp. 50 (N.D. Ohio 1978); but see Baxter Travenol Lab. Inc. v. LeMay, 93 F.R.D. 379, 381 (D.C. Ohio 1981) (holding that it was "not necessary to adhere to the strict pleading requirements for libel and slander that existed at common law."). The publication element of defamation can be properly pled through "any act that communicates information" even when it may be difficult to prove that those who observed the conduct drew a negative inference regarding the plaintiff's character. Siebert v. Dana Corp., 2005 U.S. Dist. LEXIS 5450 (N.D. Ohio 2005) (*citing* Hecht v. Levin, 66 Ohio St. 3d 458, 460, 613 N.E. 2d 585 (1993).

SURVEY OF OHIO EMPLOYMENT PRIVACY LAW

John C. Greiner
Graydon Head & Ritchey LLP
1900 Fifth Third Center
511 Walnut Street
Cincinnati, Ohio 45202-3157
Telephone: (513) 621-6464; Facsimile: (513) 651-3836
E-mail: jgreiner@graydon.com

(With Developments Reported Through **November 1, 2012**)

GENERAL COMMENTS

In Ohio Supreme Court cases, unlike those of other states, where there is an inconsistency between the language of the state court's syllabus and the text of its opinion, the syllabus controls.

Cases by and for Ohio courts should be cited in the following format: Housh v. Peth (1956), 165 Ohio St. 35, 133 N.E.2d 340. Citations in this outline follow this format.

SIGNIFICANT DEVELOPMENTS SINCE THE 2012 *SURVEY*

None.

I. GENERAL LAW OF PRIVACY

A. Legal Basis of Privacy Claims

In Ohio, the right to privacy was first recognized by the Ohio Supreme Court in Housh v. Peth (1956), 165 Ohio St. 35, 133 N.E.2d 340. In Ohio, the right of privacy is the right to be free from unwarranted publicity, and to live without unwarranted interference by the public in matters with which the public is not necessarily concerned. Ohio recognizes actions for invasion of privacy based upon: (1) the unwarranted appropriation or exploitation of one's personality; (2) the publicizing of information that places a person in a false light in the public eye; (3) the publicizing of a person's private affairs with which the public has no legitimate concern; and (4) the wrongful intrusion into one's private activities in such a manner as to outrage or cause mental suffering, shame or humiliation to a person of ordinary sensibilities. Welling v. Weinfeld, 113 Ohio St.3d 464, 2007-Ohio-2451, 866 N.E.2d 1051.

The Ohio Privacy Act, Ohio Revised Code (O.R.C.) Chapter 1347, regulates the copying and use of personal information by state and local governments.

B. Causes of Action

1. ***Misappropriation/Right of Publicity***. An actionable invasion of the right to privacy includes the unwarranted appropriation or exploitation of one's personality. Housh v. Peth, supra. The fundamental wrong of this tort is the appropriation of the plaintiff's identity or persona for the use or benefit of defendant. Brooks v. Am. Broad. Co. (N.D.Ohio 1990), 737 F. Supp. 431, aff'd, (C.A.6, 1993), 999 F.2d 167, cert. denied, (1993) 114 S.Ct. 609. Mere incidental use of a person's name or likeness is not actionable under "right of publicity." Vinci v. Am. Can Co. (1990), 69 Ohio App.3d 727, citing Zacchini v. Scripps Howard Broad. Co. (1977), 47 Ohio St.2d 224, 351 N.E.2d 454, paragraph one of the syllabus, rev'd on other grounds, 433 U.S. 562, 97 S.Ct. 2849, 53 L.Ed.2d 965. There is no misappropriation when the person's name or likeness is used in the context of general news reporting. Brooks v. Am. Broad. Co., supra.

In general, there is a four-year statute of limitation for invasion of privacy claims. O.R.C. 2305.09(D). In order to determine the applicable statute of limitations for a particular claim, it is necessary to determine the true nature or subject matter of the acts giving rise to the complaint. Hidey v. Ohio State Highway Patrol (1996), 116 Ohio App.3d 744; 689 N.E.2d 89; Doe v. First United Methodist Church (1992), 68 Ohio St.3d 531, 629 N.E.2d 402.

An action for invasion of privacy did not merge with an action for libel so as to be barred by the one-year statute of limitations applicable to libel claims. Guccione v. Hustler (1978), 64 Ohio Misc. 59, 413 N.E.2d 860.

2. ***False Light***. The Ohio Supreme Court has stated that Ohio recognizes a false light invasion of privacy action. Welling v. Weinfeld, 113 Ohio St.3d 464, 2007-Ohio-2451, 866 N.E.2d 1051. In Ohio, an individual can be liable to another if that individual spreads negative publicity about the other in an attempt to place the other in a false light before the public. In order for a plaintiff to prevail on a false light invasion of privacy theory, that plaintiff must show that

"(a) the false light in which the other was placed would be highly offensive to a reasonable person, and (b) the actor had knowledge of or acted in reckless disregard as to the falsity of the publicized matter and the false light in which the other would be placed." Welling, 113 Ohio St.3d at 473. "The liability clearly does not extend to mere insults, indignities, threats, annoyances, petty oppressions, or other trivialities." Riehl v. City of Rossford, 6th Dist. No. WD-06-050, 2007-Ohio-3824.

Ohio's "false light" theory of the tort of invasion of privacy does not address that issue within the federal law context of U.S.C. 1983 actions. Thornton v. Summit Cty. Children Servs. Bd., 9th Dist. No. 2005-07-3935, 2007-Ohio-4657.

3. ***Publication of Private Facts***. Ohio recognizes a cause of action for publication of a person's private affairs of which the public has no legitimate concern. Housh v. Peth, (1956), 165 Ohio St. 35, 133 N.E.2d 340; Sustin v. Fee (1982), 69 Ohio St.2d 143, 431 N.E.2d 992. The elements of this tort are: (1) publicity, i.e., the disclosure must be of a public nature; (2) the facts disclosed must concern the private life of the individual; (3) the matter publicized must be one which would be highly offensive and objectionable to a reasonable person of ordinary sensibilities; (4) the publication must have been made intentionally, not negligently; and (5) the matter publicized must not be of legitimate concern to the public. Killilea v. Sears, Roebuck & Co. (1985), 27 Ohio App.3d 163, 499 N.E.2d 1291; Hobbs v. Lopez (1994), 96 Ohio App.3d 670, 645 N.E.2d 1261. Ohio courts are not unanimous in approving all of the above elements. For example, the First District Court of Appeals has rejected the requirement that a disclosure must be intentional, rather than negligent. Greenwood v. Taft, Stettinius & Hollister (1995), 105 Ohio App.3d 295, 303, 663 N.E.2d 1030. However, all Ohio courts require the element of "publicity." Scroggins v. Bill Furst Florist And Greenhouse, Inc., 2d Dist. No. 19519, 2004-Ohio-79.

"Publicity" means communicating the matter to the public at large, or to so many persons that the matter must be regarded as substantially certain to become one of public knowledge as opposed to "publication" as that term of art is used in connection with liability for defamation as meaning any communication by the defendant to a third person. Scroggins v. Bill Furst Florist And Greenhouse, Inc., supra, citing Killilea v. Sears, Roebuck & Co., supra. Thus, disclosure to one single person does not fit the definition of publicity. Seta v. Reading Rock, Inc. (1995), 100 Ohio App.3d 731, 654 N.E.2d 1061. Not even disclosure to a group of four people constitutes "publicity." Davis v. City of Cleveland, 8th Dist. No. 83665, 2004-Ohio-6621.

Originally, it was held that intent or recklessness was the necessary standard of fault for establishing invasion of privacy. McCormick v. Haley (1973), 37 Ohio App.2d 73, 307 N.E.2d 34. More recent cases indicate that recovery can be allowed upon a showing of negligence as well as intent. Prince v. St. Francis - St. George Hosp., Inc. (1985), 20 Ohio App.3d 4, 484 N.E.2d 265; Sowards v. Norbar Inc. (1992), 78 Ohio App.3d 545, 605 N.E.2d 468. The actual malice standard of New York Times Co. v. Sullivan (1964), 376 U.S. 254, 845 S.Ct. 710, 11 L.Ed.2d 686, applies to invasion of privacy claims by public officials and public figures. E. Canton Edn. Assn. v. McIntosh (1999), 85 Ohio St.3d 465, 709 N.E.2d 468 (holding that a public school principal was not a public figure). However, case by case analysis is necessary to make that determination. Sovchik v. Roberts (May 9, 2001), 9th Dist. No. 3090-M, unreported.

Ohio has a four-year statute of limitations for most tort actions. O.R.C. 2305.09(D). However, claims based on publication, such as libel and slander, have a one-year statute of limitations. O.R.C. 2305.11(A). Invasion of privacy generally is subject to the four-year statute of limitations of 2305.09(D). However, a court will determine the true nature or subject matter of the acts giving rise to a complaint in order to determine the statute of limitations for an invasion of privacy claim. Hidey v. Ohio State Highway Patrol (1996), 116 Ohio App.3d 744, 689 N.E.2d 89.

A plaintiff cannot make a claim for wrongful publication of private facts based upon publication of the act of moving out of a home; "the act of moving is not the type of private fact the law protects." Salupo v. Fox, Inc., 8th Dist. No. 82761, 2004-Ohio-149. Likewise, there is no claim for publication of private facts arising against one who turns what he believes to be evidence of a crime over to police. Graham v. Byerly, 3d Dist. No. 5-04-09, 2004-Ohio-4530.

4. ***Intrusion***. Ohio recognizes a cause of action for intrusion based upon the intentional intrusion, physical or otherwise, upon the solitude or seclusion of another or his private affairs or concerns. Sustin v. Fee (1982), 69 Ohio St.2d 143, 431 N.E.2d 992; Jackson v. Playboy Enter. (S.D.Ohio 1983), 574 F. Supp. 10; Housh v. Peth (1956) 165 Ohio St. 35, 133 N.E.2d 340; Haller v. Phillips (1990), 69 Ohio App.3d 574, 591 N.E.2d 305. Actionable intrusion is the wrongful intrusion into one's private activities in such a manner as to outrage or cause mental suffering, shame, or humiliation to a person of ordinary sensibilities. "Wrongful" may relate to the manner of the intrusion. Housh v. Peth, supra.; Strutner v. Dispatch Printing Co. (1982), 2 Ohio App.3d 377, 442 N.E.2d 129, 8 Media L. Rep. 2344. The existence of this cause of action for invasion of privacy has been recognized by Ohio courts. Sowards v. Norbar, Inc. (1992), 78 Ohio App.3d 545, 605 N.E.2d 468. Invasion of privacy need not be committed intentionally or maliciously in order to be actionable; simple negligence suffices. Sowards v. Norbar, Inc., supra.

Taking on certain public roles or consenting to certain procedures affects the ability to bring an invasion of privacy claim. A public official who acts within the scope of his or her official duties in conducting an investigation or surveillance is immune from liability for invasion of privacy unless he or she acts in bad faith. Sustin v. Fee (1982), 69 Ohio St.2d 143, 431 N.E.2d 992. A person consenting to procedures in a teaching hospital necessarily gives up certain elemental rights of privacy. Adams v. St. Elizabeth Hosp. Medical Center (Mar. 16, 1989), 7th Dist. No. 87-CA-180, unreported. A private investigator hired by an employer to conduct surveillance on an employee to determine whether that employee was misusing FMLA leave would not cause outrage, mental suffering, shame, or humiliation in a person of ordinary sensibilities. Stonum v. U.S. Airways, Inc. (S.D.Ohio 1999), 83 F. Supp. 2d 894. The employer was therefore entitled to summary judgment on the employee's "wrongful intrusion" invasion of privacy claim. Id. See also York v. Gen. Elec. Co. (2001), 144 Ohio App.3d 191, 759 N.E.2d 865. ("It is not unreasonable for an employer to conduct an investigation into a person's injury while the person is receiving workers' compensation benefits" as long as the activities were open to the public -- i.e. not within their home).

Ohio has a statute requiring disclosure of a political campaign contributor's current employer where the amount of the contribution exceeds $100. O.R.C. 3517.10(E)(2). A city charter amendment requiring the identification and disclosure of the primary employer of every person who contributed $50 or more to any campaign for municipal office does not violate the First Amendment. Frank v. City of Akron (N.D.Ohio 1999), 95 F. Supp. 2d 706. The alleged intrusions upon the privacy rights of contributors as a result of this disclosure are minimal, at best. Id.

Originally, it was held that intent or recklessness was the necessary standard of fault for establishing invasion of privacy. McCormick v. Haley (1973), 37 Ohio App.2d 73, 307 N.E.2d 34. More recent cases indicate that recovery can be allowed upon a showing of negligence as well as intent. Prince v. St. Francis - St. George Hosp., Inc. (1985), 20 Ohio App.3d 4, 484 N.E.2d 265; Lynn v. Allied Corp. (1987), 41 Ohio App.3d 392, 536 N.E.2d 25; Sowards v. Norbar Inc., supra.

The test is whether a disclosure is substantially certain to become public knowledge. Rowe v. Guardian Automotive Products, Inc. (N.D.Ohio 2005), 2005 WL 3299766, at *3. Disclosures of private information via email messages are not substantially certain to become public knowledge, therefore the likelihood that they would become public knowledge has more persuasive power than the number of persons to whom the email was sent. Roe v. Heap, 10th Dist. No. 03AP-586, 2004-Ohio-2504.

Use of a professional copying company to reproduce a case file for use in preparation of a related legal malpractice case does not constitute a "wrongful intrusion into one's private activities in such a manner as to outrage or cause mental suffering, shame or humiliation to a person of ordinary sensibilities." Hahn v. Satullo (2004), 156 Ohio App.3d 412, 428, 806 N.E.2d 567, 580.

The four-year statute of limitations found at O.R.C. 2305.09(D) is applied in non-media invasion of privacy claims not based on publication. Hidey v. Ohio State Highway Patrol (1996), 116 Ohio App.3d 744, 689 N.E.2d 89.

C. Other Privacy-Related Actions

1. ***Intentional Infliction of Emotional Distress.*** The same legal standard for wrongful intrusion claims is applied to intentional infliction of emotional distress claims. Wharton v. Gorman-Rupp Co. (N.D.Ohio 2008), 2008 WL 1696942, at *16. One who by extreme and outrageous conduct intentionally or recklessly causes serious emotional distress to another is subject to liability for such emotional distress, and if bodily harm to the other results from it, for such bodily harm. Yeager v. Local Union 20 (1983), 6 Ohio St.3d 369, 453 N.E.2d 666, overruling Bartow v. Smith, 149 Ohio St. 301, 78 N.E.2d 735. In order to recover on an action for intentional infliction of emotional distress, the plaintiff must establish four elements: (1) that the actor either intended to cause emotional distress or knew or should have known that actions taken would result in serious emotional distress to the plaintiff; (2) that the actor's conduct was so extreme and outrageous as to go beyond all possible bounds of decency and was such that it can be considered as utterly intolerable in a civilized community; (3) that the actor's actions were the proximate cause of plaintiff's psychological injury; and (4) that the injury suffered by plaintiff is serious and of a nature that no reasonable person could be expected to endure. Pyle v. Pyle (1983), 11 Ohio App.3d 31, 463 N.E.2d 98; Yeager v. Local Union 20, supra; Reese v. K-Mart Corp. (N.D.Ohio 1994), No. 1:93CV0797, 10 IER Cases 202, 1994 U.S. Dist. LEXIS 19637; 1994 WL 757564; Weir v. Krystie's Dance Academy, 11th Dist. No. 2007-T-0050, 2007-Ohio-5910. Severe emotional distress may be found where a reasonable person, normally constituted, would be unable to cope adequately with mental distress engendered by the circumstances of the case. Paugh v. Hanks, (1993), 6 Ohio St.3d 72, 451 N.E.2d 759; Smith v. Ameriflora (1994), 96 Ohio App.3d 179, 644 N.E.2d 1038.

The original version of Ohio's employment intentional tort statute provided that an employer was liable if a plaintiff, who was either an employee or the dependent survivor(s) of a deceased employee, proved by clear and convincing evidence that the employer deliberately committed all of the elements of an employment intentional tort. O.R.C. 2745.01(B). "Employment intentional tort" meant an act committed by an employer in which the employer deliberately and intentionally injured, caused an occupational disease of, or caused the death of an employee. O.R.C. 2745.01(D)(1). However, the Ohio

Supreme Court found that statute to be unconstitutional. Johnson v. BP Chem., Inc. (1999), 85 Ohio St.3d 298, 707 N.E.2d 1107; Funk v. Rent-All Mart, Inc. (2001), 91 Ohio St.3d 78, 742 N.E.2d 127.

As a result of Johnson, the determination of an employer intentional tort claim was made under the common -law test explained in Fyffe v. Jeno's Inc. (1991), 59 Ohio St.3d 115, 570 N.E.2d 1108. Jurasek v. Gould Electronics, Inc., 11th Dist. No. 2001-L-007, 2002-Ohio-6260. In Fyffe, the Supreme Court of Ohio set forth the common law standard for "proving an employer intentional tort." Jurasek, 2002 WL3154351 at *2. "In order to establish 'intent' for the purpose of proving the existence of an intentional tort committed by an employer against his employee, the following must be demonstrated: (1) knowledge by the employer of the existence of a dangerous process, procedure, instrumentality or condition within its business operation; (2) knowledge by the employer that if the employee is subjected by his employment to such dangerous process, procedure, instrumentality or condition, then harm to the employee will be a substantial certainty; and (3) that the employer, under such circumstances, and with such knowledge, did act to require the employee to continue to perform the dangerous task." Id. "The mere knowledge and appreciation of a risk – something short of substantial certainty – is not intent." Id. Under the common law standard, "an employer is not liable for a plaintiff's emotional distress if the employer does no more than insist upon his legal rights in a permissible way, even though he is well aware that such insistence is certain to cause emotional distress." Ekstrom v. Cuyahoga Cty. Community College (2002), 150 Ohio App.3d 169, 183, 779 N.E.2d 1067, 1077; citing Foster v. McDevitt (1986), 31 Ohio App.3d 237, 239, 511 N.E.2d 403. Absent something more, there is no claim for intentional infliction of emotional distress. Mendlovic v. Life Line Screening of Am., Ltd., 173 Ohio App.3d 46, 2007-Ohio-4674, 877 N.E.2d 377.

Next, the Ohio General Assembly enacted a revised version of the statute, which provided that an employer must be "substantially certain" that an employee will be injured by the employer's acts. O.R.C. 2745.01(A). In light of the new statutory standard, the common law standard under Fyffe no longer applies. Harding v. Transforce, Inc., No. 2:11-cv-244, 2012 WL 628747, at *3 (S.D.Ohio Feb. 27, 2012).

Thus, merely terminating an employee's employment – absent extreme, outrageous, or intolerable conduct on the part of the employer – does not create a cause of action for intentional infliction of emotional distress. Craddock v. Flood Co., 9th Dist. No. 23882, 2008-Ohio-112, citing Mendlovic v. Life Line Screening of Am., Ltd., 173 Ohio App.3d 46, 2007-Ohio-4674, 877 N.E.2d 377, at ¶ 49. Likewise, an employer is not liable for a plaintiff's emotional distress when the employer has a legal obligation to reprimand and/or warn plaintiff regarding plaintiff's offensive conduct in the workplace. Courie v. ALCOA, 162 Ohio App.3d 133, 2005-Ohio-3483, 832 N.E.2d 1230

An independent tort claim of intentional infliction of emotional distress, absent any physical injury, may be recognized in an employment setting. Antalis v. Ohio Dep't of Commerce (1990), 68 Ohio App.3d 650, 589 N.E.2d 429; Yeager, supra. Ohio courts have only recognized sexual harassment claims in this context. Browning v. Ohio State Hwy. Patrol, 151 Ohio App.3d 798, 2003-Ohio-1108, 786 N.E.2d 94.

A qualified privilege defense is applicable to actions for intentional infliction of emotional distress. Foster v. McDevitt, supra.

Where intentional infliction of emotional distress is claimed and the employee is unusually sensitive because of an existing mental health problem, the employee must present evidence that the employer was aware of the condition. Scroggins v. Furst, 2d Dist. No. 19519, 2004-Ohio-79. Compare Garrison v. Bobbitt (1999), 134 Ohio App.3d 373, 382, 731 N.E. 2d 216, 223 (emphasizing that the defendant was aware of plaintiff's mental state).

Employees who have binding arbitration agreements with their employers will have to submit their claims for intentional infliction of emotional distress to arbitration, when the arbitration agreement reasonably contemplated the situation giving rise to the claim. Robbins v. Country Club Retirement Center IV, Inc., 7th Dist. No. 04 BE 43, 2005-Ohio-1338 (claims for intentional infliction of emotional distress arising out of wrongful discharge must be submitted to arbitration when the arbitration agreement stated that matters are arbitrable if they arise out of or relate to employment or termination of employment).

Ohio also recognizes the tort of negligent infliction of emotional distress. Schultz v. Barberton Glass Co. (1983), 4 Ohio St.3d 131, 447 N.E.2d 109. Ohio does not, however, recognize the tort of negligent infliction of emotional distress in the employment context. See McCrone v. Bank One Corp. (2005), 107 Ohio St.3d 272, 279; Crihfield v. Monsanto Co. (S.D.Ohio 1994), 844 F. Supp. 371; Tschantz v. Ferguson (1994), 97 Ohio App.3d 693, 647 N.E.2d 507 ("Ohio courts do not recognize a separate tort for negligent infliction of emotional distress in the employment context."). Moreover, the tort of negligent infliction of emotional distress assumes that a bystander or witness to a sudden, negligently caused event is traumatized by its emotionally distressing occurrence. Bartlett v. Daniel Drake Mem'l Hosp. (1991), 75 Ohio App.3d 334, 599 N.E.2d 403. The tort has been limited mostly to situations involving automobile accidents. Tschantz, 97 Ohio App.3d at 714. In order for an uninjured bystander to recover for negligent infliction of emotional distress, the emotional distress must be both serious and reasonably foreseeable. Paugh v. Hanks (1983), 6 Ohio St.3d 72, 451 N.E.2d 759. Both intentional and negligent causes of action require that the emotional distress be severe unless it is accompanied by a contemporaneous physical injury. Audia v. Rossi Bros. Funeral Home, Inc. (2000), 140 Ohio App.3d 589, 592, 748 N.E.2d 587, 596, citing Binns v. Fredendall (1987), 32 Ohio St.3d 244, 513 N.E.2d 278. Severe emotional distress, which is both severe and debilitating, may be found where a reasonable person, normally constituted, would be unable to cope adequately with the mental distress engendered by the circumstances of the case. Lynn v. Allied Corp. (1987), 41 Ohio App.3d 392, 536 N.E.2d 25.

2. ***Interference with Prospective Economic Advantage.*** Ohio recognizes the tort of "business interference," which occurs when a person, without privilege, induces or otherwise purposely causes a third party not to enter into, or continue, a business relationship, or perform a contract with another. Juhasz v. Quik Shops Inc. (1977), 55 Ohio App.2d 51, 379 N.E.2d 235; Smith v. Ameriflora 1992, Inc. (1994), 96 Ohio App.3d 179, 644 N.E.2d 1038. Whether there is a privilege depends on (1) the nature of the actor's conduct, (2) the nature of the expectancy with which his conduct interferes, (3) the relations between the parties, (4) the interest sought to be advanced by the actor and (5) the social interests in protecting the expectancy on the one hand and the actor's freedom of action on the other hand. Juhasz, 55 Ohio App.2d at 57. The Ohio Supreme Court has cited Juhasz for the proposition that the law recognizes the tort of interference with business relationships. Haller v. Borror Corp. (1990), 50 Ohio St.3d 10, 552 N.E.2d 207. Actual malice is not a necessary element of a tortious interference claim. However, once a qualified privilege has been asserted, actual malice must be demonstrated in order to defeat the qualified privilege defense. Smith v. Ameriflora, supra.

Ohio also recognizes the tort of intentional interference with a contract. The elements of this tort are: (1) the existence of a contract; (2) the wrongdoer's knowledge of the contract; (3) the wrongdoer's intentional procurement of the contract's breach; (4) the lack of justification; and (5) resulting damages. **Belvino LLC v. Empson (USA) Inc., No. 97305 July 5, 2012, 2012-Ohio-3074, at ¶ 39**, citing Kenty v. Transamerica Premium Ins. Co. (1995), 72 Ohio St.3d 415, 650 N.E.2d 863.

In a claim alleging, among other things, intentional interference with a contractual relationship, the Hamilton County Court of Appeals found that the plaintiff entered into a valid written agreement relieving a defendant from all liability arising from its administration of the psychological tests. Pinger v. Behavioral Sci. Ctr. (1988), 52 Ohio App.3d 17, 556 N.E.2d 209.

3. ***Prima Facie Tort.*** Ohio does not recognize a cause of action for prima facie tort. Wolf v. Lakewood Hosp. (1991) 73 Ohio App.3d 709, 715, citing Costell v. Toledo Hosp. (1988), 38 Ohio St.3d 221, 527 N.E.2d 858.

II. EMPLOYER TESTING OF EMPLOYEES

A. Psychological or Personality Testing

1. ***Common Law and Statutes.*** Ohio has no law prohibiting psychological testing, and at least one court has found for the employer in a claim alleging negligence, defamation and intentional interference with a contractual relationship. The claim arose based on the results of psychological testing – the Minnesota Multiphasic Personality Inventory – required by the employer. However, the plaintiff had entered into a valid written agreement relieving the defendant from all liability arising from its administration of the psychological tests. Pinger v. Behavioral Sci. Ctr. (1988), 52 Ohio App.3d 17, 556 N.E.2d 209.

The Equal Employment Opportunity Commission's Enforcement Guidance on Pre-employment Disability-Related Questions and Medical Examinations explains that the Americans with Disabilities Act prohibits employers from conducting medical examinations that seek information about physical or mental impairments or health. (EEOC Notice 915.002, Oct. 10, 1995, reprinted in EEOC Compl. Man. (CCH) ¶ 6903). However, employers are permitted to make inquiries or require medical examinations when there is a need to determine whether an employee is still able to perform the essential functions of the job. EEOC Interpretive Guidance on ADA, 29 C.F.R. pt. 1630 Appx 1630.14(c). Psychological examinations are medical if they provide evidence that would lead to identifying a mental disorder or impairment listed in the American Psychiatric Association's most recent Diagnostic and Statistical Manual of Mental Disorders. Tests designed to measure traits such as honesty, tastes and habits are not medical. Post-offer medical examinations are allowed if all entering employees in the same job category are subjected to the examination, regardless of disability, and if the medical information is kept confidential. 42 U.S.C.A. 12112(d)(3); 29 C.F.R. 1630.14(c)(1)-(2).

2. ***Private Employers.*** If an employee enters into a valid written agreement with the employer who conducts a personality or psychological test, the employer is relieved of liability arising from its administration of the test. Pinger v. Behavioral Sci. Ctr., supra.

3. ***Public Employers***. No cases reported, but the EEOC Enforcement Guidance would apply to public employers under the standards of the Rehabilitation Act of 1973. 29 U.S.C.A. 793(d); 794(d) (which relies on the standards of the 1990 Americans with Disabilities Act, 42 U.S.C.A. 12111). See EEOC Notice 915.002, Oct. 10, 1995, reprinted in EEOC Compl. Man. (CCH) ¶ 6903.

B. Drug Testing

1. ***Common Law and Statutes***. O.R.C. 4112.02(Q)(2)(a) allows an employer to adopt or administer reasonable policies or procedures, including, but not limited to, testing for the illegal use of any controlled substance, that are designed to ensure that the employee, applicant, or other person who has successfully completed a supervised drug rehabilitation program and no longer is engaging in the illegal use of any controlled substance, or the employee, applicant, or other person who otherwise successfully has been rehabilitated and no longer is engaging in that illegal use, in fact is no longer engaging in the illegal use of any controlled substance.

The Federal Omnibus Transportation Employee Testing Act of 1991 ("FOTETA") (P.L. 102-143; 105 Stat. 952, codified at 49 U.S.C. 31306(b); 49 C.F.R. 382.305) mandates random drug testing on an annual basis for a certain percentage of an employer's employees holding a commercial driver's license. The preamble to the Act noted Congress's recognition of the significant dangers to the nation from alcohol abuse and illegal drug use in the transportation industry. Cleveland Bd. of Educ. v. Int'l Bhd. of Firemen & Oilers, Local 701 (1997), 120 Ohio App.3d 63, 696 N.E.2d 658.

Under O.R.C. 4123.54 ("Rebuttable Presumption" Law), employers may seek the denial of an injured employee's workers' compensation claim if the employee tests positive for alcohol or specified controlled substances (drugs), or refuses a test following a work-related accident. If an employee tests positive or refuses a test, the burden of proof shifts to the employee to prove the presence of the alcohol or drugs was not the proximate cause of the work-related injury.

A drug test performed to determine the illegal use of drugs is not considered a medical exam. 42 U.S.C.A. 12114(d)(1), 29 C.F.R. 1630.16(c).

2. ***Private Employers***. Drug testing does not constitute an invasion of an employees' common law right to privacy. Groves v. Goodyear Tire & Rubber Co. (1991), 70 Ohio App.3d 656, 591 N.E.2d 875; Reese v. K-Mart Corp. (N.D.Ohio 1994), No. 1:93CV0797, 10 IER Cases 202, 1994 U.S. Dist. LEXIS 19637, 1994 WL 757564; Seta v. Reading Rock, Inc. (1995), 100 Ohio App.3d 731, 654 N.E.2d 1061.

Individual agents of private employers that engage in "federal action" may be sued for violations of an employee's constitutional rights ("Bivens" actions). Hammons v. Norfolk S. Corp. (C.A.6, 1998), 156 F.3d 701. Therefore, if a corporate policy at issue, e.g., drug testing, has violated an employee's constitutional rights, and the policy is attributable to the federal government, the employee would be entitled to relief. Id. However, the U.S. Supreme Court has declined to extend Bivens claims against private employers. Arar v. Ashcroft (C.A.2, 2008), 532 F.3d 157, citing Correctional Service Corp. v. Malesko (2001), 534 U.S. 61, 122 S.Ct. 515, 151 L.Ed.2d 456.

3. ***Public Employers***. Public employees have a heightened expectation of privacy in their employment. The conduct of public employers is covered by the Fourth Amendment to the United States Constitution, as applied to the states through the Fourteenth Amendment. O'Connor v. Ortega (1987), 480 U.S. 709, 107 S.Ct. 1492, 94 L.Ed.2d 714; Feliciano v. City of Cleveland (C.A.6, 1993), 988 F.2d 649. Drug testing implicates the Fourth Amendment, as drug testing through urinalysis is a search. In order to succeed on a due process claim, a plaintiff must show that the drug test does not bear a reasonable relation to a legitimate government interest, that the test procedures were so unreliable that they were irrational or led to irrational results, or that the procedures to collect the urine shock the conscience. Feliciano, 988 F.2d at 657. Drug tests of police officers charged with the job of drug interdiction bear a reasonable relation to the legitimate government interest of preventing those officers from abusing illegal drugs. Feliciano, 988 F.2d at 657; Nat'l Treasury Employees Union v. Von Raab (1989), 489 U.S. 656, 668-69, 109 S.Ct. 1384, 103 L.Ed.2d 685.

C. Medical Testing

1. ***Common Law and Statutes***. The Americans with Disabilities Act applies to employers and prevents medical examinations or inquiries as to whether an applicant is an individual with a disability or the nature and severity of the disability. 42 U.S.C.A. 12112(d)(2)(A). The ADA allows post-offer medical examinations with safeguards. 42 U.S.C.A. 12112(d)(3). Section 504 of the Rehabilitation Act prohibits Federal Fund recipients from conducting pre-employment medical examinations or making pre-employment inquiries regarding handicaps. Post-offer medical examinations are permitted. Ohio Law permits pre-employment medical examinations, if they are designed to (1) determine whether an applicant can perform the job without significantly increasing the occupational hazards to himself or herself, to others, to the general public, or to the work facilities; (2) determine whether the job requires the handicapped person to

routinely undertake any task, the performance of which is substantially and inherently impaired by his or her handicap; and (3) determine whether the person has a handicap that requires accommodation. OAC 4112-5-08(C)(1). Information obtained by a medical examination must be collected only through the use of separate forms which are accorded confidentiality as medical records. OAC 4112-5-08(C)(2). Medical examinations may not be used to exclude an applicant, unless the handicap creates a significant occupational hazard or prevents substantial job performance. OAC 4112-5-08(C)(1)(c). Employers shall not require any prospective employee or applicant for employment to pay the cost of a medical examination required by the employer as a condition of employment. O.R.C. 4113.21.

HIV and AIDS testing is governed by O.R.C. 3701.242. That section requires informed consent before an HIV test is performed. Consent may be given orally or in writing, and the person to be tested must be given an oral or written explanation of the test and testing procedures; an oral or written explanation that the test is voluntary, that consent to be tested may be withdrawn (for outpatients, any time before the individual leaves the premises where the blood is taken; for in-patients, within one hour after the blood is taken for the test), and that the individual may elect to have an anonymous test; and an oral or written explanation about behaviors known to pose risks for transmission of HIV. O.R.C. 3701.242(A) limits the persons to whom disclosure of a positive HIV test may be made.

2. ***Private Employers***. The Sixth Circuit Court of Appeals has held that the ADA permits medical examinations in limited circumstances; the focus is on job-relatedness and business necessity. EEOC v. Prevo's Family Market, Inc. (C.A.6, 1998), 135 F.3d 1089. In Prevo's, the legitimate business purpose and business necessity for requiring an HIV-positive employee to submit to a medical examination was to protect the health of its employees, other employees, and the general public from HIV infection. EEOC v. Prevo's Family Market, Inc., 135 F.3d at 1094. The employee was a produce clerk in a grocery store, who used knives in his job and was prone to cuts and scrapes. Id.

3. ***Public Employers***. The ADA or Rehabilitation Act applies to public employers and medical examinations must be job-related and consistent with business necessity. EEOC v. Prevo's Family Market, Inc., supra; Sullivan v. River Valley Sch. Dist. (W.D.Mich. 1998), 20 F. Supp. 2d 1120; Denman v. Davey Tree Expert Co. (C.A.6, 2007), 266 Fed. Appx. 377, 379

D. Polygraph Tests

The federal Employee Polygraph Protection Act of 1988 prohibits most private employers from requiring employees or applicants to take a lie detector examination or to make any employment decision based on the results of a lie detector examination or the refusal to take an exam. 29 U.S.C.A. 2001 et seq; 29 CFR 801.1 et seq. However, Ohio has no law prohibiting written "honesty tests."

A court determined that no invasion of privacy occurred when a security company launched an investigation into several employees, ordered background checks of the employees and conducted voluntary polygraph examinations after the employees' ATM machines "showed a shortage." The court determined that the investigation was appropriate, reasonable and necessary, especially in light of the fact that the employees signed an Employee Acknowledgment form agreeing to cooperate with any investigation. Powers v. Pinkerton, Inc., 8th Dist. No. 76333, 2001-Ohio-4119.

The situation is different, though, for public employers, who can require their employees to take a polygraph test and discharge them if they refuse. Warrensville Heights v. Jennings (1991), 58 Ohio St.3d. 206, 569 N.E.2d 489 (holding that a police department had just cause to terminate an officer for when he refused to take a polygraph test). Similarly, when a public employee is accused of inappropriate behavior towards a co-worker, and subsequently gives "evasive answers" to a polygraph test, his public employer is justified in terminating his employment, even when he has an otherwise spotless record. Perez v. Cuyahoga County Auditor, 8th Dist. No. 84804, 2005-Ohio-1187.

E. Fingerprinting

Several sections of the Ohio Revised Code provide for fingerprinting of applicants for certain types of employment and licenses. This includes an applicant for a license as a masseur or masseuse (O.R.C. 503.45(D)); applicants for pre-school employment in positions requiring the care, custody or control of a child (O.R.C. 3301.541); Head Start employees (O.R.C. 3301.32); applicants for positions as teachers, educational aides and assistants, school district treasurers and business managers (O.R.C. 3319.291; this section was amended effective June 12, 2008 by the 2008 Law File 111, Sub. H.B. 428, to render professional or permanent teaching certificates inactive for failure to submit fingerprints within the requisite period); applicants for employment with home health agencies in positions providing direct care to older adults or children (O.R.C. 3701.881(B)); applicants for licenses issued by the state racing commission (O.R.C. 3769.03); applicants for private investigator and security guard licenses (O.R.C. 4749.03(C)(1), 4749.06(B)(2) (This section amended effective July 1, 2005 by the General Assembly, 2005 H.B. 68. The amendments did not change the relevancy to this issue); applicants for employment in positions responsible for child care (O.R.C. 5104.011, 5104.012(A), 5104.013(A); however, the June 12, 2008 amendment allows permission for certain additional private companies and certain employers to make requests for the superintendant to investigate applicants under 5104.012, 5104.013, and 5126.28) and applicants for employment or appointment with a County Board of Mental Retardation and Developmental Disabilities (O.R.C. 5126.28(C)). In addition, candidates for the position of County Sheriff are required to be fingerprinted, (O.R.C. 311.01(B)(6)), as are applicants for admission to the Bar of the State of Ohio (Gov. Bar R. I(2)(B)(3)). A Board of Education of a city school district may require that prospective employees be fingerprinted. 1961 OAG 2703.

There are no cases reported addressing the fingerprinting issue among private sector employers.

III. SEARCHES

A. Employee's Person

1. ***Private Employers***. Private employers are generally not subject to the strictures of the Fourth Amendment. Lovvorn v. City of Chattanooga (C.A.6, 1988), 846 F.2d 1539, 1560, (Guy, J. dissenting), vacated, reh'g. en banc, granted, 861 F.2d 1388 (C.A.6, 1988). One who intrudes, physically or otherwise, upon the solitude or seclusion of another person is subject to liability for invasion of privacy, if the intrusion would be highly offensive to a reasonable person. Haller v. Phillips (1990), 69 Ohio App.3d 574, 591 N.E.2d 305 Quoting Restatement (Second) Torts 652B, at 378-79 (1977); Proffitt v. Int'l Paper Co. (S.D.Ohio 1996), 953 F. Supp. 207. "A person's expectations of privacy in the workplace is informed by the rules and regulations under which he or she works." Proffitt, 953 F. Supp. at 211. The rules under which an employee works may come from a collective bargaining agreement, in which case state law invasion of privacy claims would be preempted by § 301 of the Labor Management Relations Act. Id.

2. ***Public Employers***. Searches and seizures by government employers or supervisors of the private property of their employees are subject to Fourth Amendment restraints. O'Connor v. Ortega (1987), 480 U.S. 709. "[G] overnment employees' Fourth Amendment rights are implicated only when the conduct of government employers or supervisors infringes upon an expectation of privacy in the workplace that society is prepared to consider reasonable." Brannen v. Kings Local School Dist. Bd. of Educ. (2001), 144 Ohio App.3d 620, 629, 761 N.E.2d 84, 91. The workplace includes those areas and items that are related to work and are generally within the employer's control, including hallways, offices, locker rooms, break rooms, cafeterias, desks, and file cabinets. Id. A public employee's expectation of privacy in the workplace may be reduced by virtue of actual office practices, work procedures, or regulation. Id. at 630.

B. Employee's Work Area

Generally, invasion of an area where an employee has a legitimate expectation of privacy, such as a locker for which the employer does not have a master key or the combination, can constitute an actionable invasion of privacy. Sowards v. Norbar, Inc. (1992), 78 Ohio App.3d 545, 605 N.E.2d 468. Employees, however, have no legitimate expectation of privacy where they have been given advance notification that their lockers and personal belongings may be subject to unannounced searches. Although the search itself may not be actionable, the manner of the search may be actionable if particularly intrusive or objectionable. Am. Postal Workers Union v. United States Postal Serv. (S.D.Ohio 1987), 671 F. Supp. 497, aff'd, (C.A.6, 1989), 871 F.2d 556; O'Connor v. Ortega (1987), 480 U.S. 709.

C. Employee's Property

1. ***Private Employers***. A truck driver had a legitimate right of privacy in a hotel room in which he was staying during a layover, even though the room was paid for by the employer. Sowards v. Norbar, supra.

2. ***Public Employers***. Generally, employees, including those who work in the public sector, have been considered to possess a reasonable expectation of privacy in their possessions and work stations. However, public employees' expectations of privacy in their offices, desks and file cabinets, like similar expectations of employees in the private sector, may be reduced by virtue of actual office practices or procedures, or by legitimate regulation. O'Connor v. Ortega, supra; Am. Postal Workers Union v. United States Postal Serv., supra.

IV. MONITORING OF EMPLOYEES

A. Telephones and Electronic Communications

1. ***Wiretapping***. O.R.C. 2933.52 is similar to the Federal Electronic Communications Privacy Act (ECPA). It prohibits any person from intercepting, attempting to intercept or procuring another person to intercept a wire, oral, or electronic communication. "Wire communication" is defined in O.R.C. 2933.51(A) to mean "an aural transfer that is made in whole or in part through the use of facilities for the transmission of communications by the aid of wires or similar methods of connecting the point of origin of the communication and the point of reception of the communication in a

switching station, if the facilities are furnished or operated by a person engaged in providing or operating the facilities for the transmission of communications." "Wire communication" includes an electronic storage of wire communication. The interception and recording of cordless telephone conversations constitutes a violation of O.R.C. 2933.52. State ex rel. Master v. City of Cleveland (1996), 76 Ohio St.3d 340, 667 N.E.2d 974. Cordless telephone communications received over a neighbor's electronic baby monitor were "oral communications" within meaning of statute prohibiting person from purposely intercepting wire or oral communications. O.R.C. 2933.51(B). State v. Bidinost (1994), 71 Ohio St.3d 449, 644 N.E.2d 318.

Both the federal and Ohio wiretap statutes require only that one party to a communication consent to its interception. 18 U.S.C.A. 2511(2)(c) (amended July 10, 2008 concerning foreign interception), O.R.C. 2933.521(B)(2)(b); Ohio Domestic Violence Network v. Pub. Util. Comm. (1994), 70 Ohio St.3d 311, 638 N.E.2d 1012. Therefore, one party to a telephone conversation may record that conversation.

A county agency director who secretly recorded four employees' conversations was personally liable under the federal wiretapping statute. Dorris v. Absher (C.A.6, 1999), 179 F.3d 420. The director tape recorded conversations, played the conversations for his wife and friends, and used the conversations in drafting termination notices for two of the employees. The employees had a reasonable expectation of privacy in those conversations. Id. The director's wife did not violate the wiretapping statute by listening to the conversations, because simply listening is not considered an illegal "use" of the communication. Id.

2. ***Electronic Communications***. "Electronic communication" is defined as "a transfer of a sign, signal, writing, image, sound, datum, or intelligence of any nature that is transmitted in whole or in part by a wire, radio, electromagnetic, photo-electronic, or photo-optical system." O.R.C. 2933.51(N).

O.R.C. 2933.52 is similar to the Federal Electronic Communications Privacy Act (ECPA). It prohibits any person from intercepting, attempting to intercept or procuring another person to intercept a wire, oral, or electronic communication. However, the statute does not prevent an operator of a switchboard, or an officer, employee, or agent of a provider of wire or electronic communication service, whose facilities are used in the transmission of a wire or electronic communication to intercept, disclose, or use that communication in the normal course of employment while engaged in an activity that is necessary to the rendition of service or to the protection of the rights or property of the provider of that service. 18 U.S.C.A. 2511 (2)(a)(i); O.R.C. 2933.52(2).

Employer does not invade employee's privacy when employee who knew that employer had access to her email and should not have a reasonable expectation of privacy in either her emails or her telephone calls made at work. Olson v. Holland Computers, Inc., 9th Dist. No. 06CA008941, 2007-Ohio-4727. Knowledge of the employer's access to her email served as implied consent necessary for lawful interception of wire, oral, or electronic communication. 18 U.S.C. 2511(2)(d)(2007).

3. ***Other Electronic Monitoring***. No cases reported.

B. Mail

No cases reported.

C. Surveillance/Photographing

While reasonable surveillance of employees in an institutional setting is a reasonable investigative tool, an employee's consent to searches by her employer did not authorize surveillance of the employee from the bathroom ceiling. Speer v. Ohio Dep't of Rehab. & Corr. (1993), 89 Ohio App.3d 276, 624 N.E.2d 251, judgment entered, on remand, 68 Ohio Misc. 2d 13, 646 N.E.2d 273 (Ct. Cl. 1994).

At least one Ohio court has recognized an employer's right to videotape an employee who is receiving workers' compensation benefits so long as the activities videotaped were open to the public -- i.e. not within their home. York v. Gen. Elec. Co. (2001), 144 Ohio App.3d 191, 759 N.E.2d 865.

The Twelfth Ohio District Court of Appeals recognized a public school district's right to conduct video surveillance in a custodians' break room. The court noted that there was no Fourth Amendment violation because the custodial employees did not have a reasonable expectation of privacy in the break room. Brannen Bd. of Educ. of Kings Local Sch. Dist. (2001), 144 Ohio App.3d 620, 761 N.E.2d 84.

V. ACTIVITIES OUTSIDE THE WORKPLACE

A. Statute or Common Law

See V.B, infra.

B. Employees' Personal Relationships

1. ***Romantic Relationships Between Employees.*** Policies prohibiting or restricting romantic relationships between employees have not been found invalid, but such a policy cannot be applied differently to men and women. Russell v. United Parcel Serv., 110 Ohio App.3d 95, 2004-Ohio-2668, 673 N.E.2d 659. However, the punishment for violating the policy may be more severe for employees in a supervisory role. Koski v. Willowwood Care Ctr. of Brunswick, Inc., 158 Ohio App.3d 248, 2004-Ohio-2668, 814 N.E.2d 1235 (noting that an employer might distinguish between a supervisor and a non-supervisor who have embarked on a romantic relationship and punish the supervisor more harshly because his conduct places the organization in danger of lawsuits and threatens company morale).

2. ***Sexual Orientation.*** The question of whether a defendant tortuously invaded plaintiff's privacy by spreading information about his sexual orientation was for a jury. Sexual orientation may be a private fact for which disclosure may be offensive to a reasonable person. Greenwood v. Taft, Stettinius & Hollister (1995), 105 Ohio App.3d 295, 663 N.E.2d 1030. **Ohio does not have a general law prohibiting discrimination based on sexual orientation. However, Ohio has prohibited discrimination based on sexual orientation in state employment through Executive Orders. Former Governor Strickland signed Executive Order 2007-10S on May 30, 2007, and Governor Kasich signed Executive Order 2011-05K on January 21, 2011.**

Twenty-nine Ohio cities and counties now have anti-discrimination ordinances that include sexual orientation. The following Ohio cities and counties have ordinances that protect all individuals from discrimination based on sexual orientation: Akron, Athens, Bowling Green, Canton, Cincinnati, Cleveland, Cleveland Heights, Columbus, Dayton, East Cleveland, Lakewood, North Olmstead, Oberlin, Oxford, Shaker Heights, Toledo, and Yellow Springs. These Ohio cities and counties only protect city or county employees from discrimination based on sexual orientation: Cuyahoga County, Cuyahoga Falls, Franklin County, Gahanna, Hamilton, Hamilton County, Laura, Lima, Lucas County, Montgomery County, Summit County, and Wood County.

The Sixth Circuit Court of Appeals has held that homosexuals are not part of a suspect class against whom alleged employment discrimination would trigger strict constitutional scrutiny. Likewise, those who associate with homosexuals do not constitute a suspect class. However, a public employer must show a rational basis for refusing to hire or promote an individual who associates with homosexual rights groups. General animus towards homosexuals is not a rational governmental purpose. Scarborough v. Morgan County Board of Education (C.A.6, 2006), 470 F.3d 250.

The Supreme Court has held that a Texas law prohibiting consensual homosexual sexual activity was unconstitutional because there was no "state interest which can justify [the] intrusion into the personal and private life of the individual." Lawrence v. Texas (2003), 539 U.S. 558, 123 S. Ct. 2472, 156 L.Ed.2d. 508.

The majority's opinion concerning the privacy of homosexuals may have a lasting impression on future state decisions. The Court stated, "These matters, involving the most intimate and personal choices a person may make in a lifetime, choices central to personal dignity and autonomy, are central to the liberty protected by the Fourteenth Amendment. At the heart of liberty is the right to define one's own concept of existence, of meaning, of the universe, and of the mystery of human life....Persons in a homosexual relationship may seek autonomy for these purposes, just as heterosexual persons do." Id. at 2481-2482.

Lawrence does not stand for the proposition that all consensual sexual activity between adults must be constitutionally protected. State laws prohibiting adult relatives from engaging in sexual activity, including relatives through marriage, are subject only to a rational basis test. State v. Lowe, 112 Ohio St.3d 507, 2007-Ohio-606, 861 N.E.2d 512.

3. ***Marital Status.*** An anti-nepotism policy that prevents married couples from working together is subject to rational basis scrutiny, unless the burden on the right to marry is "direct and substantial." Montgomery v. Carr (C.A.6, 1996), 101 F.3d 1117. In Montgomery, a school district prevented married couples from working in the same building. The court upheld the policy, finding that the reasons proffered by the school district were rational and noting that marital status discrimination is subject to rational basis scrutiny. Montgomery, 101 F.3d at 1128.

C. Smoking

Ohio has no law protecting the right to smoke or use tobacco products outside of the workplace.

The Smoke Free Workplace Act, effective December 7, 2006, prohibits all forms of tobacco smoke in all public places of employment and areas that in close proximity to the entrance and exit of the public place. O.R.C. Ch. 3794. In accordance with the Act, Executive Order 99-03T prohibits smoking in most state facilities. This Executive Order superseded Executive Order 93-01V, which contained the same prohibition. As a result of Executive Order 93-01V, an unfair labor practice charge challenging the unilateral implementation of a no-smoking policy was rendered moot. Ohio Civil Serv.

Employees Ass'n, AFSCME, Local 11, AFL-CIO v. Ohio Dep't of Transp. (1995), 104 Ohio App.3d 340, 662 N.E.2d 44. The choice to smoke in public or semi-public places is not a "privacy right" that deserves special constitutional protection. Operation Badlaw, Inc. v. Licking County Gen. Health Dist. Bd. of Health (S.D.Ohio 1992), 866 F. Supp. 1059. Federal and state courts in Ohio have yet to address whether individuals have the right to smoke in their own homes or whether employees have the right to smoke away from work.

D. Blogging

Sharing emotions on a blog about a trial while contemporaneously serving jury duty did not create the need for a new trial because the blog had no effect in the rendering of the verdict. State v. Goehring, 6th Dist. No. OT-06-023, 2007-Ohio-5886.

VI. RECORDS

Public records are defined at O.R.C. 149.43(A) to mean any record that is kept by any public office, including, but not limited to, state, county, city, village, township, and school district units, and records pertaining to the delivery of educational services by an alternative school in Ohio kept by a nonprofit or for profit entity operating such alternative school pursuant to O.R.C. 3313.533. (This section amended to include students who have been released from the custody of the department of youth services under O.R.C. 5139.51 by 2004 Ohio Laws File 102 (Am. Sub. H.B. 106).) Several exceptions to this definition are listed. O.R.C. 149.43(A). Certain privileged communications to or from an Ohio governor are exempted from disclosure under the Public Records Act. State ex rel. Dann v. Taft, 109 Ohio St.3d 364, 2006-Ohio-1825, 848 N.E.2d 472. Public records document the organization, functions, policies, decisions, procedures, operations or other activities of the public office. State ex rel. Wilson-Simmons v. Lake County Sheriff's Dep't (1998), 82 Ohio St.3d 37, 693 N.E.2d 789.

In order to determine whether an entity is a "public office," Ohio uses a "functional-equivalency test." Among the factors a court will consider are "(1) whether the entity performs a government function, (2) the level of government funding, (3) the extent of government involvement or regulation, and (4) whether the entity was created by the government or to avoid the requirements of the Public Records Act." State ex rel. Oriana House, Inc. v. Montgomery, 110 Ohio St.3d 456, 462, 2006 -Ohio-4854, 854 N.E.2d 193; State ex rel. Repository v. Nova Behavioral, 112 Ohio St.3d 338, 2006-Ohio-6713, 859 N.E.2d 936.

All public records must be promptly prepared and made available for inspection to any person at all reasonable times during regular business hours. Upon request, the person responsible for public records shall make copies available at cost, within a reasonable period of time. O.R.C. 149.43(B). The constitutional right to privacy, however, outweighs the statutory right to a prompt disclosure, so the disclosure of public records may be delayed until Social Security numbers have been redacted. State ex rel. Siroki, 108 Ohio St.3d 207, 2006-Ohio-662, 842 N.E.2d 508; 2005 OAG 47.

When a request for a copy of a public record has been denied, the proper remedy is to file a writ of mandamus with either the trial court or the appellate court in the county where the request was made. State ex rel. Cincinnati Enquirer v. Winkler, 101 Ohio St.3d 382, 2004-Ohio-1581, 805 N.E.2d 1094. The entity refusing to release the records then has the burden of proving that the requested records were excepted from disclosure under the Public Records Act. Gilbert v. Summit County, 104 Ohio St.3d 660, 2004-Ohio-7108, 821 N.E.2d 564. If the entity's refusal to release records is based on a rational stance on an unsettled legal issue, the court will not award attorney's fees against it. State ex rel. Cincinnati Enquirer v. Daniels, 108 Ohio St.3d 518, 525, 2006-Ohio-1215, 844 N.E.2d 1181, 1187.

The Ohio Supreme Court interprets O.R.C. 149.43 "liberally in favor of broad access, with any doubt resolved in favor of disclosure of public records." State ex rel. Morgan v. New Lexington, 112 Ohio St.3d 33, 40, 2006-Ohio-6365, 857 N.E.2d 1208 (noting that "we do not require perfection in public-records requests").

To obtain a writ of mandamus to access public records from a public official, not otherwise permitted under the Public Records Act of O.R.C. 149.43, employees must establish a clear legal right to the records, a corresponding clear legal duty on behalf of the public official to provide these records, and the lack of an adequate remedy in the ordinary course of the law. State ex rel. Dreamer v. Mason, 115 Ohio St.3d 190, 2007-Ohio-4789, 874 N.E.2d 510, citing State ex rel. Boccuzzi v. Cuyahoga Cty. Bd. of Comm'rs, 112 Ohio St.3d 438, 2007-Ohio-323, 860 N.E.2d 749.

Ohio Civ. R. 26 was amended to clarify that discovery of electronically stored information is permitted (amendment effective July 1, 2008 as Ohio Order 08-25). However, the trial judge regulates whether the cost of production is too burdensome compared to the value of discovery and regulates the allocation of costs in producing electronically stored information. Ohio Civ. R. 26.

A. Personnel Records

Public records are defined at O.R.C. 149.43(A) to mean any record that is kept by any public office, including, but not limited to, state, county, city, village, township, and school district units. Several exceptions to this definition are listed.

O.R.C. 149.43(A). Personnel records reflecting the discipline of police officers are required to be disclosed pursuant to O.R.C. 149.43. State ex rel. Dispatch Printing Co. v. Wells (1985), 18 Ohio St.3d 382, 481 N.E.2d 632; Superseded by statute as stated in State ex rel. Beacon Publ'g Co. v. Akron Metro. Hous. Auth., (Apr. 13, 1988), 9th Dist. No. 13575, unreported; State ex rel. National Broad. Co. v. Cleveland (1988), 38 Ohio St.3d 79, 526 N.E.2d 786, 15 Media L. Rep. 1853; Reversing in part, (1991), 57 Ohio St.3d 77, 566 N.E.2d 146. See also State ex rel. Ohio Patrolmen's Benevolent Assoc. v. City of Mentor (2000), 89 Ohio St.3d 440, 732 N.E.2d 969, (noting that "public employee personnel records, including personnel records of police officers reflecting discipline, are generally regarded as public records, absent proof of an exception"), citing State ex rel. Multimedia, Inc. v. Snowden (1995), 72 Ohio St.3d 141, 647 N.E.2d 1374.

In order to access records related to a public employment termination, the terminated employee need not specify the date and author of the requested records. State ex rel. Morgan, 112 Ohio St.3d at 40.

"Any provision in a collective bargaining agreement that establishes a schedule for the destruction of public records is unenforceable if it conflicts with or fails to comport with all of the dictates of the Public Records Act." Keller v. City of Columbus, 100 Ohio St.3d 192, at syllabus, 2003-Ohio-5599, 797 N.E. 2d 964.

Not everything within a personnel file may be subject to disclosure as a public record. Documents within personnel files that are neither required to be maintained by law nor are necessary to respondents' execution of their duties and responsibilities fall outside the scope of O.R.C. 149.43 and are not subject to public disclosure. Habe v. South Euclid Civil Serv. Comm'n (Feb. 4, 1993), 8th Dist. No. 61786, unreported. To the extent an item in a state employee's personnel file is not a public record and is "personal information," under O.R.C. 1347.01(E), a public office has an affirmative duty to prevent its disclosure. State ex rel. Fant v. Enright (1993), 66 Ohio St.3d 186, 610 N.E.2d 997; O.R.C. 1347.05(G). (2005 HB 104 3, effective Feb. 17, 2006, amended O.R.C. 1347.01, noting the General Assembly's intent that this section supersede all county or municipal ordinances pertaining to government databases of personal information.). For example, state employees' home addresses are not "public records" subject to disclosure under the Public Records Act. State ex rel. Dispatch Printing Co. v. Johnson, 106 Ohio St.3d 160, 2005-Ohio-4384, 833 N.E.2d 274. Documents relating to a community fire company's investigation of alleged sexual harassment and its decision to terminate two volunteers' association with the company were not exempt from disclosure under the Public Records Act's exemption for confidential law enforcement investigatory records. State ex rel. Freedom Communications, Inc. v. Elida Comty. Fire Co. (1998), 82 Ohio St.3d 578, 697 N.E.2d 210. However, a record sealed under O.R.C. 2953.52 after a finding of not guilty of a criminal offense or having an indictment dismissed "does not violate the public's constitutional right of access to public records." State ex rel. Cincinnati Enquirer v. Winkler, 101 Ohio St.3d 382, at syllabus, 805 N.E.2d 1094. Once a case is sealed, because "the public had a right of access to any court record before, during, and for a period of time after the criminal trial," the basis for access to the records no longer exists. Id. at 385.

Likewise, police officers have a constitutionally protected privacy interest under the substantive component of the Fourteenth Amendment Due Process Clause. This protection prevented the City of Columbus from disclosing certain personal information contained in personnel files absent a showing that the disclosure narrowly serves a compelling state interest. Kallstrom v. City of Columbus (C.A.6, 1998), 136 F.3d 1055. The Ohio Supreme Court adopted Kallstrom in State ex rel. Keller v. Cox, 85 Ohio St.3d 279, 1999-Ohio-264, 707 N.E.2d 931. The First District, Court of Appeals, applied Kallstrom when it upheld withholding the identities of wounded police officers in State ex rel. The Cincinnati Enquirer v. Streicher, 1st Dist. No. C-100820, 2011-Ohio-4498. Not all police officer personnel information is protected, just the "information of the sort likely to facilitate intrusion on the liberty/security interest of officers." Smith v. City of Dayton (S.D.Ohio 1999), 68 F. Supp. 2d 911. The release of Information in a police officer's personnel file relating to a diagnosis of post-traumatic stress disorder did not violate his constitutional right to privacy, because it did not make it more likely that persons would intrude upon his liberty/security interests. In addition, peace officers have no expectation of privacy in otherwise public records held by another public office which "does not disclose the fact that the information relates to a peace officer" (e.g. documents held by the county recorder.) Ohio Attorney General Opinion No. 2000-021 (April 18, 2000). Peace officers are also protected by O.R.C. 2921.24, which prohibits employees or officers of law enforcement agencies or courts from disclosing, during the pendency of any criminal case, the home address of any peace officer who is a witness or arresting officer. Photographs of police officers constitute familial and residential information and are exempt from disclosure under O.R.C. 149.43(A)(7)(b). State ex rel Plain Dealer Publishing Co. v. Cleveland, 106 Ohio St.3d 70, 2005-Ohio-3807, 831 N.E.2d 987.

A public employer may not claim statutory immunity under O.R.C. 2744.03 (2002) in an invasion of privacy claim when that claim arises out of the plaintiff's employment with the public employer. Ross v. Trumbull County Child Support Enforcement Agency (Feb. 8, 2001), 11th Dist. No. 2000-T-0025, unreported.

A public or private employer in Ohio who is requested by an employee or a prospective employer of an employee to disclose to a prospective employer of an employee information relating to that employee's job performance and who discloses the information to the prospective employer is not liable in damages in a civil action to that employee, the prospective employer, or any other person for any harm sustained as a proximate result of making the disclosure or of any information disclosed, unless the employer knows the information is false, deliberately intends to mislead the prospective employer or another person, or provides the information in bad faith or with malicious purpose, or if the disclosure of the information constitutes a discriminatory practice. O.R.C. 4113.71(B).

The Equal Employment Opportunity Commission has authority to serve subpoenas to gain access to any evidence relevant to the charge under investigation. 42 U.S.C. 2000e-5(b). EEOC v. Roadway Express (N.D.Ohio 1999), 75 F. Supp. 2d 767. This includes information concerning an employer's hiring practices with regard to minorities or women, as long as the requested information is relevant, does not put an undue burden on the employer, and the Charge set forth the necessary information. Id.

In the United States' action against abortion protesters and their organization alleging violations of the Freedom of Access to Clinic Entrances Act, protesters were entitled to discover the identity of the targeted clinics' employees with whom they allegedly interfered. United States v. Operation Rescue (S.D.Ohio 1999), 112 F. Supp. 2d 696. Since the plaintiff's complaint alleged interference with the clinics' employees, the Defendants were entitled to discovery on the identity of those employees. Id.

During discovery for a federal lawsuit an attorney is not bound by the limits of Ohio Civ. R. 26, and may therefore seek public records for purposes of the litigation pursuant to the Ohio Public Records Act. Gilbert v. County of Summit, 9th Dist. No. 21521, 2003-Ohio-6012.

B. Medical Records

Employers may be found liable for disclosing an employee's confidential medical history. Levias v. United Airlines (1985), 27 Ohio App.3d 222, 500 N.E.2d 370. An invasion of privacy action may be brought by a patient who alleges that a physician invaded her privacy by sending a bill with a medical diagnosis of alcoholism to her husband's employer's office. Such conduct raised a genuine issue of material fact whether there was a publication by a physician of private information about patient's alcoholism. Prince v. St. Francis-St. George Hosp., Inc. (1985), 20 Ohio App.3d 4, 484 N.E.2d 265. A healthcare provider can be liable under federal law for mistakenly sending an individual's medical records to that individual's employer. Herman v. Kratche, 8th Dist. No. 86697, 2006-Ohio-5938. No invasion of privacy action exists where plaintiff cannot establish that his former employer disclosed plaintiff's drug addiction to prospective employers and when plaintiff voluntarily disclosed his drug addiction to prospective employers. Such an admission was an indication that the plaintiff did not expect to be able to conceal that aspect of his professional career. Hall v. The Jewish Hosp. of Cincinnati (June 2, 2000), 1st Dist. No. C-990571, unreported. In Ohio, an independent tort exists for the unauthorized, unprivileged disclosure to a third party of nonpublic medical information that a physician or hospital has learned within a physician-patient relationship. Biddle v. Warren Gen. Hosp. (1999), 86 Ohio St.3d 395, 715 N.E.2d 518. Following Biddle, a court upheld withholding non-party patient records from a terminated nurse, who sought them to determine whether the hospital treated similarly situated nurses in a like manner in Kapp v. Jewish Hospital, Inc. (July 7, 2011), S.D. Ohio No. 1:09-CV-949, unreported. This limitation extends to putative representative plaintiffs for purposes of determining class membership in bringing a class action. A hospital need not disclose names of potential class members without first securing consent of those potential class members. Walker v. Firelands Community Hospital, 6th Dist. No. E-03-009, 2004-Ohio-681. Even if the requested reports contain "protected health information" as defined by the Health Insurance Portability and Accountability Act ("HIPAA"), and even if the entity operates as a "covered entity" pursuant to HIPAA, the reports would still be subject to disclosure under the "required by law" exception to the HIPAA privacy rule because the Ohio Public Records Law requires disclosure of these reports, and HIPAA does not supersede state disclosure requirements. State ex rel. Cincinnati Enquirer v. Daniels, 108 Ohio St.3d 518, 2006-Ohio-1215, 844 N.E.2d 1181. Waiver of medical confidentiality for litigation purposes is limited to the specific case for which the records are sought. Hageman v. Southwest Gen. Health Ctr., 119 Ohio St.3d 185, 2008-Ohio-3343, 893 N.E.2d 153. An attorney who violates this limited waiver by disclosing the records to a third party unconnected to the litigation may be held liable for these actions under the Ohio's independent tort outlined in Biddle. Id. at 5.

C. Criminal Records

There is no statutory provision that allows a court to partially seal official records relating to a criminal case. State v. Lynch (2008), 145 Ohio Misc. 2d 84, 87, 883 N.E.2d 485, 487. The definition of "official records" as "all records that are possessed by any public office or agency that relate to a criminal case" is all-inclusive and without limitation, except for the specific exceptions in O.R.C. 2953.53 (statute covering application to have records sealed) and except for records or reports maintained by a public children services agency or department of job and family services maintained pursuant to O.R.C. 2151.421. State v. Lynch, supra.

O.R.C. 2953.33(B) provides that in any application for employment, license, or other right or privilege, any appearance as a witness, or any other inquiry, a person may be questioned only with respect to convictions not sealed, unless the question bears a direct and substantial relationship to the position for which the person is being considered (amended by 2008 Ohio Laws File 111 (Sub. H.B. 428) to include section 3319.232, adding the Braille competency standards for certain teaching licenses). The 2008 Amended version of O.R.C. 2953.33 provides that the state board of education and the state department of education may question an applicant "for issuance or renewal of any license with respect to any criminal offense committed or alleged to have been committed by the applicant." However, if the allegations or convictions have been sealed or expunged, the applicant may not be questioned unless the offense bears a direct and substantial relationship to the issuance or renewal of the license or to the position for which the applicant is applying. O.R.C. 2953.33. Questions regarding criminal convictions or allegations that are sealed or expunged are not part of the public record under O.R.C. 149.43. A trial court abused its discretion in denying a motion to seal a record of conviction, since the decision was based on the court's belief that expungement would prevent the Supreme Court from obtaining a complete picture of a law student's fitness to practice law. State v. Greene (1991), 61 Ohio St.3d 137, 573 N.E.2d 110. Applicants who intend to take the Ohio bar examination must file an application that includes a form that authorizes the release of sealed criminal records to the authorities investigating the applicant's fitness for admission to the bar. Gov. Bar. R. I(2)(B)(6). Anyone may gain access to the sealed records if specifically authorized by the person whose records were sealed. O.R.C. 2953.32(D)(3), (amended in 2008 by Ohio Laws File 128, effective July 1, 2008 to have the procedure request comply with O.R.C. 109.572 (Sub. H.B. 195)). O.R.C. 2953.33(B) encompasses any inquiry that bears a direct and substantial relationship to other rights and privileges associated with a professional license. In re Niehaus (1989), 62 Ohio App.3d 89, 574 N.E.2d 1104.

Ohio has a sexual predator registration law, and the General Assembly has determined that a person who is found to be a sexual predator or a habitual sex offender has a reduced expectation of privacy because of the public's interest in public safety and in the effective operation of government. O.R.C. 2950.02(A)(5) (2002). This law was found not to constitute an invasion of a sex offender's right to privacy. State v. Williams, 88 Ohio St.3d 513, 2000-Ohio-428, 728 N.E.2d 342. For more than a decade, both the Supreme Court of Ohio and the United States Supreme Court have repeatedly upheld sex offender registration schemes against claims of unconstitutionality. State v. Wade, 10th Dist, No. 10AP-159, 2010-Ohio-6395. The information that would be disseminated to the public is a public record, and the right to privacy encompasses only personal information and not information readily available to the public. Id. There is also nothing in the registration law that violates an individual's right to pursue a lawful occupation. Id.

D. Subpoenas / Search Warrants

Legitimate needs of the government in maintaining the records of prosecutions for operating a vehicle while under the influence of alcohol (OVI), including the public's right of access to these records, outweighs any interests of an individual in having the records of such a case sealed. O.R.C. 2953.52. Official records include all subpoenas issued in the criminal case. State v. Lynch, 145 Ohio Misc. 2d 84, 2008-Ohio-307, 87, 883 N.E.2d 485, 487, citing O.R.C. 2953.51(D).

Search warrants can authorize persons present at the location. State v. Mullins, 12th Dist. No. CA2007-08-194, 2008-Ohio-3516. Illegal drugs found by un-uniformed police officer constitutes evidence lawfully obtained because police officer, though not a named party to the warrant, was on location during the execution of the warrant and aided spontaneously out of concern the suspect might be reaching for a weapon, establishing his credibility. Id. at *3.

VII. ACTIONS SUBSEQUENT TO EMPLOYMENT

A. References

Ohio law recognizes a qualified privilege for an employer to "pass on to a prospective employer facts, opinions, or suspicions regarding a former employee and not be subject to an action for slander." Rainey v. Shaffer (1983), 8 Ohio App.3d 262, 264-65, 456 N.E.2d 1328. This protection was codified in 1996 at O.R.C. 4113.71, which provides: "An employer who is requested by an employee or a prospective employer of an employee to disclose to a prospective employer of that employee information pertaining to the job performance of that employee for the employer and who discloses the requested information to the prospective employer is not liable in damages in a civil action to that employee, the prospective employer, or any other person for any harm sustained as a proximate result of making the disclosure or of any information disclosed, unless the plaintiff in a civil action establishes, either or both of the following: (1) By a preponderance of the evidence that the employer disclosed particular information with the knowledge that it was false, with the deliberate intent to mislead the prospective employer or another person, in bad faith, or with malicious purpose; (2) By a preponderance of the evidence that the disclosure of particular information by the employer constitutes an unlawful discriminatory practice . . ." O.R.C. 4113.71(B).

B. Non-Compete Agreements

The Ohio Supreme Court has stated that "reasonable" covenants not to compete will be enforced, and courts may modify unreasonable ones to make them enforceable. Rogers v. Runfola & Associates, Inc. (1991), 57 Ohio St.3d 5, 565 N.E.2d 540. Generally, covenants are deemed reasonable when they are necessary to protect the employer's business interests, and they are not unnecessarily burdensome to the employee or harmful to the public. Raimonde v. Van Vlerah (1975), 42 Ohio St.2d 21, 325 N.E.2d 544. Courts are understandably reluctant to enforce covenants that are so broad, either in geography or duration that they impede upon a terminated employee's ability to earn a living. Rogers v. Runfola & Associates, Inc., supra. However, in instances where the employee was left with viable, though less than ideal, options for employment, the covenant was enforced. Columbus Medical Equipment Co. v. Watters (1983), 13 Ohio App.3d 149, 468 N.E.2d 343 (holding that a covenant which prevented a sales agent from selling competitive products for two years within his former employer's territory was enforceable because the sales agent could work outside the former employer's territory or sell non-competitive items).

VIII. OTHER ISSUES

A. Statutes of Limitations

Ohio has a four-year statute of limitations for most tort actions. O.R.C. 2305.09(D). Claims based on publication, such as libel and slander, have a one-year statute of limitations. O.R.C. 2305.11. However, a two-year statute of limitations applies where an employee alleges bodily injury as the result of an employer's intentional tort. Funk v. Rent-All Mart, Inc., 91 Ohio St.3d 78, 2001-Ohio-270, 742 N.E.2d 127. Invasion of privacy is generally subject to the four-year statute of limitations of 2305.09(D). However, a court will determine the true nature or subject matter of the acts giving rise to a complaint in order to determine the statute of limitations for an invasion of privacy claim. Hidey v. Ohio State Highway Patrol (1996), 116 Ohio App.3d 744, 689 N.E.2d 89.

B. Jurisdiction

"Where an employee undergoes a return-to-work physical examination following a strike at his employer's plant, a test of his urine reveals the presence of cannabinoids, and he is not hired back because of his failure of the drug-screening test, a court of common pleas has no jurisdiction to hear his complaint for 'negligent performance,' invasion of privacy and wrongful discharge, since the complained-of conduct of the employer is arguably prohibited by the National Labor Relations Act and, therefore, within the exclusive jurisdiction of the National Labor Relations Board." Anderson v. U.S. Gypsum Co. (1987), 42 Ohio App.3d 112, 536 N.E.2d 1180, syllabus.

C. Worker's Compensation Exclusivity

The general rule in Ohio is that an employee injured during the course of employment is to limited redress through the Ohio Workers' Compensation Act. O.R.C. 4123.90. Although generally comprehensive, there are limited exceptions to the exclusivity of the Ohio Workers' Compensation Act.

Surveillance of injured workers is a common practice. In York v. General Electric Co. (2001), 144 Ohio App.3d 191, 759 N.E.2d 865, the court held that the videotaping of an employee who was receiving workers' compensation benefits did not constitute invasion of privacy. The worker told a claims representative about his motorcycle hobby despite his work-related back injury. Therefore, the employer conducted surveillance of the worker and contested his claim based on the surveillance video. The appellate court upheld summary judgment for the employer because it is not unreasonable for an employer to conduct surveillance of an employee who is receiving workers' compensation benefits, so long as the surveillance does not invade the worker's privacy (e.g., outside in public view).

D. Pleading Requirements

Ohio Civil Rule 8 requires that any pleading contain a short and plain statement of the claim showing that the party is entitled to relief and a demand for judgment for the relief to which the party claims to be entitled. If the party seeks more than twenty-five thousand dollars, the party shall so state in the pleading but shall not specify in the demand the amount of recovery sought. Defenses and denials shall also be stated in short and plain terms. Civil R. 8(B). Affirmative defenses must be pleaded, and averments to which a responsive pleading is required, if not denied are admitted. Civ. R. 8(C)-(D). Pleadings shall be simple, concise and direct.

Under Civil Rule 8 all that is required to establish a claim is "a short and plain statement of the claim showing that the party is entitled to relief, and ... a demand for judgment for the relief to which the party claims to be entitled." Civil R. 8 (A). It is clear that under the liberal requirements of the civil rules few complaints are properly subject to dismissal for failure to state a claim. Where the complaint states any facts which if proven would entitle the pleader to relief as a matter of law the motion to dismiss should be denied. Laster v. Bowman (1977), 52 Ohio App.2d 379, 370 N.E.2d 767.

Civil Rule 11 requires an attorney of record to sign every pleading, motion or other paper, with the attorney's name, address and registration number.

SURVEY OF OKLAHOMA EMPLOYMENT LIBEL LAW

J. Patrick Cremin and Stephanie T. Gentry
Hall, Estill, Hardwick, Gable, Golden & Nelson, P.C.
320 South Boston, Suite 200
Tulsa, Oklahoma 74103
Telephone (918) 594-0400; Telecopier (918) 594-0505

(With Developments Reported Through **November 1, 2012)**

GENERAL COMMENTS

The Oklahoma state court system is comprised of the Supreme Court, the Court of Criminal Appeals, the Court of Civil Appeals, and seventy seven District Courts, one for each county in the state. The District Courts are the primary state trial courts; they have general jurisdiction and handle most civil and criminal cases. Decisions of the District Courts are generally unreported and unpublished. Unlike many states, Oklahoma has two courts of last resort: civil appeals are heard by the Oklahoma Supreme Court, and criminal appeals are heard by the Oklahoma Court of Criminal Appeals. All appeals from civil cases are first filed with the Oklahoma Supreme Court, which usually assigns the case to one of the four divisions of the Oklahoma Court of Civil Appeals. Opinions of the Oklahoma Court of Civil Appeals do not have precedential value unless the Oklahoma Supreme Court releases them for publication. Occasionally, if a case involves issues of first impression, important questions of law, or great public interest, the Oklahoma Supreme Court will retain cases appealed from the trial courts, rather than assign them to the Oklahoma Court of Civil Appeals.

The citation format used in this outline follows Okla. Sup. Ct. R. 1.200(e), which requires that published opinions of the Oklahoma Supreme Court and Oklahoma Court of Civil Appeals promulgated after May 1, 1997 be cited using the paragraph citation form contained in the rule. Parallel citation to Pacific Reporter is required; parallel citation to Oklahoma Reports is proscribed. Parallel citation to the official paragraph citation form is strongly encouraged for opinions promulgated prior to May 1, 1997.

SIGNIFICANT DEVELOPMENTS SINCE THE 2012 *SURVEY*

None.

I. GENERAL LAW

A. General Employment Law

1. ***At Will Employment.*** Oklahoma courts have long recognized the basic principle that an employment contract of unspecified duration may be terminated by either party without notice or cause at anytime without incurring liability for breach of contract. Hinson v. Cameron, 1987 OK 49, 742 P.2d 549, 552 n.6; Foster v. Atlas Life Ins., 1931 OK 617, 6 P.2d 805, 154 Okla. 30. Such indefinite employment contracts are deemed terminable-at-will. The classic statement of the at-will rule is that an employer may discharge an employee for good cause, for no cause, or even for cause morally wrong, without being thereby guilty of legal wrong. Burk v. K-Mart Corporation, 1989 OK 22, 770 P.2d 24. Principles of freedom of contract and the importance of economic growth are attributed to the development of the terminable-at-will doctrine. Id. at 26 (citing Parnar v. American Hotels, Inc., 65 Haw. 370, 652 P.2d 625, 628 (1982)).

The at-will doctrine has been judicially limited by two exceptions that restrict the grounds on which an at-will employee may be discharged. First, the Oklahoma Supreme Court has recognized that implied contractual provisions may restrict an employer's freedom to discharge an employee at will, and that such restrictions may arise from employee manuals, oral assurances, and the like. See Hinson, 1987 OK 49, 742 P.2d 549; see also Johnson v. Nasca, 1990 OK CIV APP 87, 802 P.2d 1294. However, employers may disclaim or deny any intent to make the provisions of a personnel manual a binding part of the employment relationship, as long as the disclaimer is clear and the company has not engaged in conduct negating the disclaimer's effect. Russell v. Bd. of County Comm'rs, 1997 OK 80, ¶ 24, 952 P.2d 492, 502.

Second, in Burk, the Oklahoma Supreme Court recognized a public policy exception to the at–will doctrine. Known in Oklahoma as a "Burk" tort, such a claim must allege (1) an actual or constructive discharge (2) of an at-will employee (3) in significant part for a reason that violates an Oklahoma public policy goal (4) that is found in Oklahoma's constitutional, statutory, or decisional law or in a federal constitutional provision that prescribes a norm of conduct for Oklahoma and (5) no statutory remedy exists that is adequate to protect the Oklahoma policy goal." Kruchowski v. Weyerhaeuser Co., 2008 OK 105, ¶24, 202 P.3d 144, 152.

Oklahoma does not recognize an implied covenant of good faith and fair dealing in at–will employment contracts. Burk, 1989 OK 22, 770 P.2d 24.

B. Elements of Libel Claim

1. ***Basic Elements.*** Oklahoma law provides two causes of action for defamation: libel and slander. Slander is defined as a false and unprivileged communication which: (a) charges a person with a crime, or having been indicted, convicted, or punished for a crime; (b) imputes to a person an infectious, contagious, or loathsome disease; (c) tends directly to injure an individual in respect to his office, profession, trade or business, either by imputing to him general disqualification in those respects in which his office or other occupation peculiarly requires, or by imputing something with reference to the individual's office, profession, trade or business that has a natural tendency to lessen its profit; (d) imputes to a person impotence or lack of chastity; or (e) which by natural consequences, causes actual damage. Okla. Stat. tit. 12, § 1442.

Libel is defined as a false or malicious unprivileged publication by writing, printing, picture, or effigy or other fixed representation to the eye, which exposes a person to public hatred, contempt, ridicule or obloquy, or which tends to deprive him of public confidence, or to injure him in his occupation, or any malicious publication as aforesaid, designed to blacken or vilify the memory of one who is dead, and tending to scandalize his surviving relatives or friends. Okla. Stat. tit. 12, § 1441 (emphasis added).

Elements of a libel or slander action involve (1) identifying the defamatory matter; (2) showing that it was broadcast, published, or spoken of the plaintiff; (3) that the broadcaster failed to exercise ordinary care; and (4) that damage flowed from the defamatory broadcast. Peterson v. Grisham, 2008 WL 4363653 (E.D.Okla) (not reported in F.Supp.); Cardtoons, L.C., v. Major League Baseball Players' Ass'n, 335 F.3d 1161 (10th Cir. 2000); Hetherington v. Griffin Television, Inc., 430 F. Supp. 493 (W.D. Okla. 1977). See also Springer v. Richardson Law Firm, 2010 OK CIV APP 72, ¶ 7, 239 P.3d 473, 475 (quoting Trice v. Burress, 2006 OK CIV APP 79, ¶ 10, 137 P.3d 1253, 1257) ("In order to recover for defamation, a private figure must prove (1) a false and defamatory statement,)3) an *unprivileged* publication to a third party, (3) fault amounting at least to negligence on the part of the publisher; and (4) either the actionability of the statement irrespective of special damage, or the existence of special damage caused by the publication."). The pivotal issue in a defamation case is whether the plaintiff's reputation has been harmed. Zeran v. Diamond Broadcasting, Inc., 203 F.3d 714, 719 (10th Cir. 2000) (applying Oklahoma law). It is the injury to reputation *and not to the feelings of the individual* that is the subject of redress. Id. The language in the alleged defamatory communication must tend to lower the plaintiff in the estimation of men whose standard of opinion the court can recognize. Wiley v. Oklahoma Press Publishing Co., 1924 OK 350, 233 P. 224, 106 Okla. 52. Further, a communication is defamatory if it tends to so harm the reputation of another so as to lower him in the estimation of the community or to deter third persons from associating or dealing with him. Herbert v. Okla.Christian Coalition, 1999 OK 90, 992 P.2d 322, 327 n.4. Being teased or ridiculed because of the statement does not rise to the level of defamation, but rather, the issue is whether another person believed the statement and thereby lowered his opinion of the plaintiff. Colbert v. World Publishing Co., 1987 OK 116, 747 P.2d 286, 14 Media L. Rep. 2188; Mitchell v. Griffin Television, L.L.C., 2002 OK CIV APP 115, 60 P.3d 1058. Further, an action for defamation may lie where the recipient of the communication mistakenly but reasonably believes that the communication referred to the plaintiff. Gonzales v. Sessom, 2006 OK CIV APP 61, ¶¶ 12–13, 137 P.3d 1245.

2. ***Fault.*** The Supreme Court of Oklahoma has aligned libel and slander law with the constitutional perceptions of the United States Supreme Court. Martin v. Griffin Television, Inc., 1976 OK 13, 549 P.2d 85. The liability imposed on one publishing a defamatory falsehood about another is that one is liable for making such a publication willfully, as well as for doing so without utilizing the ordinary care a prudent person would use to ascertain whether the statement is true or false. Hence, the constitutionally required fault elements underlying liability for defamation in Oklahoma are willfulness or gross negligence. It is important to note, however, that Oklahoma distinguishes between the issues of public and private concern, and different standards of proof are applied to each. Public concern matters involving a plaintiff who is a private figure are analyzed under the negligence standard, whereas private concern matters invoke a recklessness standard. Additionally, if the public concern involves a public figure, actual malice must be established.

a. **Private Figure Plaintiff/Matter of Public Concern.** In order to recover on a libel or slander claim under Oklahoma law, a private figure plaintiff with regard to a matter of public concern, must show that the defendant failed to exercise ordinary care, i.e., was negligent. Metcalf v. KFOR-TV, Inc., 828 F. Supp. 1515, 21 Media L. Rep. 1481, (W.D. Okla. 1992); Malson v. Palmer Broadcasting Group, 1998 OK CIV APP 68, 963 P.2d 13, 14; Gaylord Entertainment Co. v. Thompson, 1998 OK 30, 958 P.2d 128; Magnusson v. New York Times Co. d/b/a KFOR, 2004 OK 53, 98 P.3d 1070.

b. **Private Figure Plaintiff/Matter of Private Concern.** Liability attaches to anyone who publishes a defamatory falsehood concerning a private person or a public official or figure regarding a purely private matter not affecting his official conduct, fitness or capacity if (1) the utterer knows the statement is false, or (2) the publisher acts in reckless disregard of whether such statement is false or not, or (3) the speaker acts negligently in failing to ascertain that the statement is false. Anson v. Erlanger Minerals & Metals, Inc., 1985 OK CIV APP 24, 702 P.2d 393; Gaylord, 1998 OK 30, 958 P.2d 128; Magnusson, 2004 OK 53, 98 P.3d 1070; Jenkins v. Gonzalez, 2006 WL 2773231, * 4 (W.D. Okla. Sep. 25, 2006);

c. **Public Figure Plaintiff/Matter of Public Concern.** The federal constitutional standard from New York Times v. Sullivan, 376 U.S. 254 (1964), actual malice, also applies to these cases in Oklahoma. See, e.g., Grogan v. KOKH, L.L.C., 2011 OK CIV APP 34, ¶ 9, 256 P.3d 1021, 1027; Peterson v. Grisham, 2008 WL 4363653 (E.D.Okla) (not reported in F.Supp.); Herbert v. Oklahoma Christian Coalition 1999 OK 90, 992 P.2d 322; Mitchell v. Griffin Television, L.L.C., 2002 OK CIV APP 115, 60 P.3d 1058; Revell v. Hoffman, 309 F.3d 1228 (10th Cir. 2002) (applying Oklahoma law); Miskovsky v. Oklahoma Publishing Co., 1982 OK 8, 654 P.2d 587, 7 Media L. Rep. 2607, cert. denied, 459 U.S. 923; Luper v. Black Dispatch Publishing Co., 1983 OK CIV APP 54, 675 P.2d 1028. A plaintiff who is a public figure or public official is required to demonstrate that the defamatory publication was made with actual malice in order to recover. Strong v. Oklahoma Publishing Co., 1995 OK CIV APP 89, 899 P.2d 1185, 24 Media L. Rep. 1315; Jordan v. World Pub. Co., 1994 OK CIV APP 30, 872 P.2d 946, 948, 22 Media L. Rep. 1796. Additionally, actual malice must be established by clear and convincing evidence. Herbert, 992 P.2d at 327. Absent some false allegation of criminal behavior, criticism of public officials on matters of public concern is absolutely protected. Okla. Stat. tit. 12, § 1443.1 See also Peterson.

It is essential to recovery in such cases that a plaintiff show evidence of deliberate falsification or reckless publication despite the publisher's awareness of provable falsity. Washington v. World Pub. Co., 1972 OK 166, 506 P.2d 913. Failure to conduct a thorough investigation is not a sufficient basis to establish actual malice. Herbert, 992 P.2d at 328; Jurkowski v. Crawley, 1981 OK 110, 637 P.2d 56, 61, 7 Media L. Rep. 2113. Further, a showing of negligence is not enough to meet to the level of actual malice, and malice may not be inferred simply from the plaintiff's showing that a publication was untrue. Herbert, 992 P.2d at 328. Even a showing that a statement was published out of ill will, spite, hatred, or a desire to injure the public figure is not, standing alone, enough to meet the New York Times actual malice standard adopted by Oklahoma courts. Id. at 329, 331. The focus of the inquiry must be on the defendant's subjective attitude toward the truth or falsity of the alleged defamatory statement, not on the defendant's attitude toward the plaintiff. Id. at 331. Reckless disregard may be established by clear and convincing proof that the defendant proceeded to publish the statement despite a high degree of awareness of probable falsity, or that the defendant did, in fact, entertain serious doubts as to the truth of the statement. Id. at 332. The question of whether the evidence in the record is sufficient to support a finding of actual malice is a question of law. Herbert, 992 P.2d at 328, 332; Johnson v. The Black Chronicle, Inc., 1998 OK CIV APP 77, 964 P.2d 924, 928. Oklahoma law will not allow a plaintiff to couch a defamation claim in negligence terms in order to overcome the plaintiff's burden of proving actual malice. Jordan v. World Pub. Co., 1994 OK CIV APP 30, 872 P.2d 946, 948, 22 Media L. Rep. 1796.

3. ***Falsity.*** To recover for defamation, a public figure plaintiff must show evidence of deliberate falsification or reckless publication despite the publisher's awareness of probable falsity. Jordan v. World Pub. Co., 1994 OK CIV APP 30, 872 P.2 946, 947-48, 22 Media L. Rep. 1796; Washington v. World Publishing Co., 1972 OK 166, 506 P.2d 913. It is not clear under Oklahoma defamation law, to the extent it remains unmodified by constitutional requirements, whether falsity is an element of a private plaintiff's prima facie case or truth is an affirmative defense. Metcalf v. KFOR-TV, Inc., 828 F.Supp. 1515, 21 Media L. Rep. 1481 (W.D. Okla. 1992). Under Oklahoma defamation law, statements by media defendants on matters of public concern must be provable as false before liability attaches. Id.

4. ***Defamatory Statement of Fact.*** In Oklahoma, statements which are a matter of opinion and not factual in nature and which cannot be verified as true or false are not actionable as slander or libel. Metcalf v. KFOR-TV, Inc., 828 F. Supp. 1515, 21 Media L. Rep. 1481 (W.D. Okla. 1992); Bird Construction Co., Inc. v. Oklahoma City Housing Authority, 2005 OK CIV APP 12, ¶ 10, 110 P.3d 560. Whether a statement is one of fact or opinion, for purposes of determining defamation liability, is a question of law. Id. When a statement is determined to be one of fact, the public figure plaintiff must establish deliberate falsification or recklessness as an element of the offense. Washington v. World Publishing Co., 1972 OK 166, 506 P.2d 913. However, Oklahoma courts have not determined if private figure plaintiffs must also establish the untruthfulness of a factual statement in order to establish a prima facie case. Metcalf v. KFOR-TV, Inc., 828 F.Supp. 1515, 21 Media L. Rep. 1481 (W.D. Okla. 1992).

5. ***Of and Concerning Plaintiff.*** The "of and concerning" element in defamation actions requires that the alleged defamatory comment refer to the plaintiff. McCullough v. Cities Service Co., 1984 OK 1, 676 P.2d 833, 10 Media L. Rep. 1411; Gentry v. Wagoner County Publishing Co., 1960 OK 84, 351 P.2d 718. However, general references to the undesirability of physicians with inadequate training performing surgery in their own offices were held to be of and concerning physician plaintiff, sufficient to maintain his claim, although he was not specifically named in those statements. Metcalf v. KFOR-TV, Inc., 828 F.Supp. 1515, 21 Media L. Rep. 1481 (W.D. Okla. 1992). In addition, an action for defamation may lie where the recipient of the communication mistakenly but reasonably believes that the communication referred to the plaintiff. Gonzales v. Sessom, 2006 OK CIV APP 61, ¶¶ 12–13, 137 P.3d 1245.

6. ***Publication.*** Publication of a defamatory statement is the communication of the matter to some third person. An alleged defamatory statement must be published to predicate liability of an employer for libel. Patrick v. Thomas, 1962 OK 190, 376 P.2d 250. See also Exhibition of alleged libelous matter to others by plaintiff's agent at

plaintiff's request is not actionable publication. Taylor v. McDaniels,, 1929 OK 378, 281 P. 967, 189 Okla. 262. Where alleged defamatory words regarding a discharged employee were spoken by supervisory employees in the presence and hearing of a fellow employee only, there was no publication and hence the words were not actionable. Since publication requires the communication of defamatory matter to a third person, there is no action for defamation for statements made among a corporate employer's managers, since neither agents nor employees of a corporation are third persons in relation to the corporation. Magnolia Petroleum Co. v. Davidson, 1944 OK 182, 148 P.2d 468.

a. **Intracorporate Communications.** Intracorporate communications do not constitute publications that will give rise to defamation actions, and therefore, liability cannot turn on the content of, or intent behind, the intracorporate communication. Magnolia Petroleum Co. v. Davidson, 1944 OK 182, 148 P.2d 468. Under Oklahoma law, communications between employees of a corporation which concerned the basis for firing of a store manager and which were alleged to be defamatory were protected by the intracorporate communications privilege and could not be considered a publication for purposes of a defamation action. Starr v. Pearle Vision, Inc., 54 F.3d 1548 (10th Cir. 1995); Tatum v. Philip Morris Inc., 809 F. Supp. 1452 (W.D. Okla. 1992). All that is required for a statement to be protected under the intracorporate communication privilege is that the speaker and the listener are employees of the common employer at the time of the discourse. Starr, 54 F.3d 1548; Angove v. Williams Sonoma, Inc., 70 Fed.Appx. 500, 2003 WL 21529409 (10th Cir. (Okla.)) (unpublished opinion). Even communications between employees and agents of the employer may qualify for the intracorporate communications privilege. Ishmael v. Andrew, 2006 OK CIV APP 82, ¶¶ 12–18, 137 P.3d 1271.

b. **Compelled Self-Publication.** No Oklahoma court has considered whether to adopt or reject the compelled self-publication theory. However, the U.S. Court of Appeals for the Tenth Circuit has declined to assume that Oklahoma would recognize a claim for compelled self-publication. Starr v. Pearle Vision, Inc., 54 F.3d 1548 (10th Cir. 1995).

c. **Republication.** Republication of a defamatory "letter to the editor" regarding a public figure could be the subject of an action in libel. Weaver v. Pryor Jeffersonian, 1977 OK 163, 569 P.2d 967, 3 Media L. Rep. 1425. However, the fair report privilege provided a newspaper with a complete defense to a libel claim brought by a plaintiff who was named in connection with a drug investigation when it republished information from the district attorney's press conference. Wright v. Grove Sun Newspaper Company, Inc., 1994 OK 37, 873 P.2d 983, 22 Media L. Rep. 1801. The fair report privilege affords a qualified or conditional privilege to the media when they republish defamatory material in an account of a public or official proceeding. Id. The republication of allegedly defamatory statements concerning a former employee, at an unemployment compensation proceeding, did not give rise to a claim for slander; to be slanderous, a statement must be nonprivileged, while communications made during unemployment hearings are absolutely privileged. Hensley v. Armstrong World Industries, Inc., 798 F. Supp. 653 (W.D. Okla. 1992).

Not only is an original speaker who republishes his or her own publications held liable for slander, a third person who republishes the publication is also held liable. Additionally, if it was foreseeable to the original speaker that the republication was likely, the original speaker can be held liable for the republication by a third person. Weaver v. Pryor Jeffersonian, 1977 OK 163, 569 P.2d 967, 3 Media L. Rep. 1425.

7. ***Statements versus Conduct.*** Oklahoma recognizes the continuing vitality of the legal distinction between statements which are defamatory per se and those which are defamatory per quod. The term per se is applied to words which are actionable because they, of themselves, without anything more, are opprobrious. A publication is actionable per se when the language used therein is susceptible of but one opprobrious meaning and the publication on its face shows that the derogatory statements, taken as a whole, refer to the plaintiff, and not to some other person. Strong v. Oklahoma Publishing Co., 1995 OK CIV APP 89, 899 P.2d 1185, 24 Media L. Rep. 1315; Trice v. Burress, 2006 OK CIV APP 79, ¶ 10, 137 P.3d 1253. A false statement is deemed defamatory per quod if the words are reasonably susceptible of both a defamatory and an innocent meaning. Brock v. Thompson, 1997 OK 127, 948 P.2d 279, 292; Trice at ¶ 10. In determining whether a publication amounts to libel per se or libel per quod, the court considers the publication in its entirety and ascribes to words used in their ordinary, natural, and obvious meanings. Id. There is no fixed rule by which the court can determine whether or not a statement is defamatory per se. Fite v. Oklahoma Publishing Co., 1930 OK 554, 293 P. 1073. Under the Oklahoma statute governing slander, false statements that charge a person with a crime, impute the presence of an existence of infectious, contagious, or loathsome disease, tend to injure the subject directly in his or her business or profession, or impute to the subject impotence or want of chastity, constitute slander per se. In comparison, the statute provides that false statements, which by natural consequences cause actual damage, constitute slander per quod. Starr v. Pearle Vision, Inc., 54 F.3d 1548 (10th Cir. 1995). A statement that an employee was terminated due to accusations that she had stolen money from a store constituted a statement that charged the employee with the commission of a crime and could be considered slander per se. Id. Whether a statement is defamatory per se is always a question of law for the court; defamation per quod requires proof of extrinsic facts to show a defamatory meaning, and thus presents a fact issue for determination by a jury. Brock v. Thompson, 1997 OK 127, 948 P.2d at 292. In Turner v. Boy Scouts of America, Inc., 2009 WL 2567962 (W.D.Okla. 2009),

a written statement by the plaintiff's former supervisor that the plaintiff's employment had been terminated for a major infraction that rendered him ineligible for benefits, when the plaintiff claimed he had resigned, did not meet the definition for slander under Oklahoma law.

In Berman v. Laboratory Corp. of America, 2011 OK 106, ¶¶ 7-9268 P.3d 68, 71, the Oklahoma Supreme Court made clear that the distinction between statements and conduct is relevant for purposes of determining whether the privilege set forth in Okla. Stat. tit. 12, § 1443.1 applies. See Section II(A)(1) below.

8. ***Damages.*** In a defamation action by a private figure plaintiff against a media defendant, where the published matter is of public concern, the plaintiff must show actual malice in order to recover presumed and punitive damages. However, a private figure plaintiff is not constitutionally required to prove that same degree of culpability to recover presumed and punitive damages in a defamation action against a non-media defendant involving a publication of purely private concern. Metcalf v. KFOR-TV, Inc., 828 F. Supp. 1515, 21 Media L. Rep. 1481 (W.D. Okla. 1992); Martin v. Griffin Television, Inc., 1976 OK 13, 549 P.2d 85. Actual malice is defined as having knowledge that it was false or with reckless disregard of whether it was false or not. Washington v. World Publishing Co., 1972 OK 166, 506 P.2d 913. If there is evidence of heedless conduct to show wanton indifference to consequences so as to permit the conclusion that media defendants entertained serious doubts as to the truth of a publication regarding a public figure or public official and thus there is a finding of actual malice, the news item is libelous per se and the plaintiff can recover both general and special damages. Akins v. Altus Newspapers, Inc., 1977 OK 179, 609 P.2d 1263, 3 Media L. Rep. 1449, cert. denied 449 U.S. 1010 (1980). The more customary types of actual harm inflicted by defamatory falsehood include impairment of reputation and standing in the community, personal humiliation, and mental anguish and suffering. A plaintiff who is a public figure or public official is required to demonstrate that publication was made with actual malice in order to recover damages in a defamation action. Herbert v. Okla. Christian Coalition, 1994 OK 90, 992 P.2d 322, 327; Strong v. Oklahoma Publishing Co., 1995 OK CIV APP 89, 899 P.2d 1185, 24 Media L. Rep. 1315. In the case of slander per quod, the plaintiff must establish evidence of special damages. Zeran v. Diamond Broadcasting, Inc., 203 F.3d 714, 718, 26 Med. L. Rep. 1401(10th Cir. 2000); Trice, 2006 OK CIV APP 79, ¶ 10; Springer v. Richardson Law Firm, 2010 OK CIV APP 72, ¶ 7, 239 P.3d 473, 475.

a. **Presumed Damages and Defamation Per Se.** Slander per se does not require proof of actual damages. Accordingly, one who is found to have made a statement that constituted defamation per se is liable for both general and special damages. M.F. Patterson Dental Supply Co. v. Wadley, 401 F.2d 167 (10th Cir. 1968). On the issue of libel per quod, only special damages are recoverable on requisite pleading and proof. Id. The more customary types of actual harm inflicted by defamatory falsehood include impairment of reputation and standing in the community, personal humiliation, and mental anguish and suffering. Akins v. Altus Newspapers, Inc., 1977 OK 179, 609 P.2d 1263, 3 Media L. Rep. 1449. In a libel action against a public official or public figure, it is constitutionally impermissible to presume actual malice, even though statements involved are libelous per se. Morgan v. Winters, 1979 OK 68, 594 P.2d 1220, 5 Media L. Rep. 1653.

(1) **Employment Related Criticism.** No reported cases.

(2) **Single Instance Rule.** No reported cases.

b. **Punitive Damages.** A private figure plaintiff is not required to establish actual malice in order to recover presumed and punitive damages in a defamation action against a non-media defendant involving publication of a purely private concern. Metcalf v. KFOR-TV, Inc., 828 F. Supp. 1515, 21 Media L. Rep. 1481 (W.D. Okla. 1992). Punitive damages are recoverable for defamation per quod based on a specific finding of malice and special damages. M.F. Patterson Dental Supply Co. v. Wadley, 401 F.2d 167 (10th Cir. 1968).

II. PRIVILEGES AND DEFENSES

A. Scope of Privileges

1. ***Absolute Privilege.*** Statements made in judicial pleadings or proceedings are absolutely privileged. Okla. Stat. tit. 12, §1443.1; Jones v. England, 402 Fed.Appx. 326, 328, 2010 WL 4487115 (10th Cir. (Okla.)); Lindsey v. Brinker Int'l., 2011 WL 2493047 (W.D.Okla. June 22, 2011) (allegedly slanderous statements made by employer during unemployment compensation proceedings were privileged); Bennett v. McKibben, 1966 OK CIV APP 22, 915 P.2d 400; Pryor v. Findley, 1997 OK CIV APP 74, 949 P.2d 1218. Moreover, the absolute privilege attaches to a communication which is a preliminary step to a quasi-judicial proceeding. Hatcher v. Sumpter, 1992 OK CIV APP 3, 825 P.2d 638. For example, information sent to regulatory agencies designed to prompt enforcement are considered part of the official proceeding and enjoy the protection of absolute immunity to defamation actions. Presson v. Bill Beckman Co., Inc., 1995 OK CIV APP 44, 898 P.2d 179. The privilege provided by Okla. Stat. tit. 12 § 1443.1 provides the media with a complete defense to libel on matters pertaining to official proceedings. McGhee v. Newspaper Holdings, Inc., 2005 OK CIV APP 41, ¶

6, 115 P.3d 896. Additionally, attorneys are immune under litigation privileges from defamation liability, even absent an attorney-client relationship, while soliciting clients. Samson Investment Co. v. Chevaillier, 1999 OK 19, 988 P.2d 327. The litigation privilege does not give free reign to attorneys to defame; rather the litigation privilege applies only when the communication is (1) relevant or has some relation to the proposed proceeding and (2) circumstances surrounding the communication have some relation to the proposed proceeding. Id. The litigation privilege applies regardless of whether the communications are true or false. Id.; Cardtoons, L.C., v. Major League Baseball Players' Ass'n, 335 F.3d 1161 (10th Cir. 2000); Burkett v. Tal, 2004 OK CIV APP 57, 94 P.3d 114. See also Springer v. Richardson Law Firm, 2010 OK CIV APP 72, ¶ 7, 239 P.3d 473, 475 (holding that litigation privilege applied to exempt defendants from defamation action based on alleged defamatory statements contained in a petition filed to initiate judicial proceedings).

In Kirschstein v. Haynes, 1990 OK 8, 799 P.2d 941, the Oklahoma Supreme Court extended the "litigation privilege" to communications made prior to judicial or quasi-judicial proceedings if the statement had some relation to the proposed proceedings. The privilege bars not only defamation claims but also claims for intentional infliction of emotional distress and negligence as well, if such claims are based on the same *communication* at issue in the defamation claim. Id. at ¶ 30, 788 P.2d at 954. However, the privilege does not bar a negligence claim (or presumably an intentional infliction of emotional distress claim) that arises out of the same set of circumstances where the negligence claim is based on the defendant's conduct, as opposed to its communications. See, e.g., Berman v. Laboratory Corp. of America, 2011 OK 106, ¶¶ 7-9268 P.3d 68, 71.

In addition, under Oklahoma law, public officials are immune from tort liability for actions taken within the scope of their employment. Montgomery v. City of Ardmore, 365 F.3d 926 (10th Cir. 2004).

2. ***Qualified Privileges.***

a. **Common Interest.** A privileged communication is one made in good faith, upon any subject matter in which the party communicating has an *interest*, or in reference to which he has, or honestly believes he has, a duty, and which contains matter which, without the occasion upon which it is made, would be defamatory and actionable. Magnolia Petroleum Co. v. Davidson, 1944 OK 182, 148 P.2d 468. Thus, Oklahoma courts have held that statements made by one company employee to another company employee are privileged communications as there is a common interest between the communicators. Tatum v. Philip Morris Inc., 809 F. Supp. 1452 (W.D. Okla. 1992). See also Sections (I)(B)(6)(a) above and (II)(D) below.

b. **Duty.** Oklahoma's statutory privilege of fair report and fair comment, Okla. Stat. tit. 12, §1443.1, protects from civil liability the publication of (a) an accurate account of judicial, legislative or other proceedings authorized by law, as well as (b) opinions and criticisms upon the official proceedings. The statutory privilege's fair-report component was established in order to provide the public the information they need in order to be informed of public or official proceedings. The privilege protects the republication of accurate accounts of official actions or proceedings, even though the reports may contain defamatory statements. To fall within the privilege, a report need not be exact in every detail. It is enough that it is substantially accurate, or if its "gist" or "sting" is true. Crittendon v. Combined Communications Corp., 1985 OK 111, 714 P.2d 1026, 12 Media L. Rep. 1649; McGhee v. Newspaper Holdings, Inc., 115 P.3d 896, 898 (Okla.Civ.App.2005).

The statutory comment-and-criticism privilege, on the other hand, affords legal immunity for the expression of opinion on matters relating to official proceedings. The defense of fair comment is predicated upon the principle that the interests of society are furthered through a free discussion of public affairs and matters of public interest. The §1443.1 shield from state-law liability imposes upon the defendant the duty of interposing the statutory privilege as an affirmative defense and proving its elements. Gaylord Entertainment Co. v. Thompson, 1998 OK 30, 958 P.2d 128.

c. **Criticism of Public Employees.** Similarly, the criticism of public employees is protected by Okla. Stat. tit. 12 §1443.1. Cases applying the statutory fair-report privilege are: (a) Cooper v. Parker-Hughey, 1995 OK 35, 894 P.2d 1096 (a prosecution witness in a criminal trial is immune from civil liability for damages caused by his testimony); (b) Kirschstein v. Haynes, 1990 OK 8, 788 P.2d 941 (attorneys, parties and witnesses are immune from defamation suits where those suits are based upon communications made during or preliminarily to judicial proceedings, as long as the communications are in some way relevant to the proceeding); (c) Wright v. Grove Sun Newspaper Co., Inc., 1994 OK 37, 873 P.2d 983, 22 Media L. Rep. 1801 (the republication of statements made at a district attorney's press conference was privileged); (d) Crittendon v. Combined Communications Corp., 1985 OK 111, 714 P.2d 1026, 12 Media L. Rep. 1649 (the statements made in a television broadcast concerning a medical malpractice action brought against a physician were a fair and true report of a default hearing and hence privileged under §1443.1); Johnson v. KFOR-TV, 2000 OK CIV APP 64, 6 P.3d 1067 (statements made in a television broadcast relating to a dentist and disciplinary proceedings against the dentist were covered by the statutory privilege found in §1443.1).

d. **Communications Between Church Members.** In Trice v. Burress, 2006 OK CIV APP 79, 137 P.3d 1253, the court held that, in addition to absolute protection from tort liability under the First Amendment of the United States Constitution, statements by a church pastor to a member of the congregation indicating that the reason for the former youth director's discharge was "because he was questioning his sexuality" were protected by a conditional or qualified privilege. The court stated, "where the alleged defamatory statements are exchanged by or between members of the congregation during or as a result of either a church's decision to employ, retain or terminate a clergyman or lay employee, or a church's review of the performance of a clergyman or lay employee, the conditional privilege shields the church from liability for defamation." Trice at ¶ 10.

e. **Limitation on Qualified Privileges.**

(1) **Constitutional or Actual Malice.** A qualified privilege is a privilege which may be lost by abuse. For example, that type abuse occurs when a defendant publishes the statement knowing it to be false or acting in reckless disregard as to its truth or falsity. Therefore, in order to lose the qualified privilege defense, a plaintiff must show that the defendant acted with actual malice. Wright v. Haas, 1978 OK 109, 586 P.2d 1093.

(2) **Common Law Malice.** It has been suggested that common law imposes strict liability for the publishing of a false and defamatory statement about another, but also allows a conditional privilege to protect certain defined interest, if that privilege is not abused. However, following the dictates of the U.S. Supreme Court in Robert Welch, Inc. v. Gertz, 459 U.S. 1226 (1983), Oklahoma courts found, as unconstitutional, statutes affording a presumption of malice when a publication was false or injurious. Martin v. Griffin Television, Inc., 1976 OK 13, 549 P.2d 85. The publication of matters of public interest is privileged if communicated in good faith without malice to those who have an interest in the subject-matter of the publication, and when such publication is made in an honest belief that the communication is true, when the belief is based upon reasonable and probable grounds. Holway v. World Pub. Co., 1935 OK 356, 44 P.2d 881, 171 Okla. 306.

(3) **Other Limitations on Qualified Privileges.** In a libel action, in order for the alleged defamatory publication to be shielded on the ground that the statement was qualifiedly privileged, the communication must be a privileged one, uttered on a privileged occasion, by a privileged person, to one within the privilege. In other words, for a qualified privilege to be applicable, there must be a showing that some special private relationship was involved, such as fraternal, fiduciary, business, or professional. Fawcett Pub., Inc. v. Morris, 1962 OK 183, 377 P.2d 42. However, in Oklahoma, there is no longer a conditional privilege available, either by statute or common law, as a defense to a public figure plaintiff in a defamation action. Wright v. Haas, 1978 OK 109, 586 P.2d 1093.

f. **Question of Fact or Law.** Where the circumstances of a publication are not in dispute and the publication's language is plain and unambiguous, the issue of whether a publication is privileged under §1443.1 is a question of law. Price v. Walters, 1996 OK 63, 918 P.2d 1370, 1375.

g. **Burden of Proof.** Oklahoma law determined that a previously existing statute which allowed a plaintiff to recover in a defamation action simply by proving that the alleged defamatory statement was published or spoken and that it concerned the plaintiff was unconstitutional. Martin v. Griffin Television, Inc., 1976 OK 13, 549 P.2d 85. With the required proof of actual malice, then the abuse, and resulting loss, of any common law qualified privilege is also proven; however, proof of mere negligence is not treated as sufficient to amount to abuse of a qualified privilege. Wright v. Haas, 1978 OK 109, 586 P.2d 1093. While ordinarily the burden of proving actual malice is upon the party who complains of defamation, on a motion for summary judgment in a libel action, the defendant has the burden of showing there is no issue of actual malice. Id.

B. Standard Libel Defenses

1. ***Truth.*** Truth is an affirmative defense and the burden of proving truth rests upon the defendant. Hetherington v. Griffin Television, Inc., 430 F. Supp. 493 (W.D. Okla. 1977). Literal truth of a report is a complete bar to a defamation action since true statements cannot be defamatory as a matter of law. Melton v. City of Oklahoma City, 928 F.2d 920 (10th Cir. 1991); Tatum v. Philip Morris Inc., 809 F. Supp. 1452 (W.D. Okla. 1992).). See also Grogan v. KOKH, L.L.C., 2011 OK CIV APP 34, ¶ 11, 256 P.3d 1021, 1027-28

2. ***Opinion.*** As a general rule statements which are a matter of opinion and not factual in nature, which cannot be verified as true or false, are not actionable as slander or libel under Oklahoma law. Metcalf v. KFOR-TV, Inc., 828 F. Supp. 1515, 21 Media L. Rep. 1481 (W.D. Okla. 1992); Magnusson, 2004 OK 53, 98 P.3d 1070; Bird Construction Co., Inc. v. Oklahoma City Housing Authority, 2005 OK CIV APP 12, ¶ 10, 110 P.3d 560. Whether a statement is one of fact or opinion, for purposes of determining defamation liability, is a question of law for the court. Id. Oklahoma law follows the U.S. Supreme Court's holding in Milkovich v. Lorain Journal Co., 479 U.S. 1 (1990), and finds that if a

statement of opinion on a matter of public concern reasonably implies false and defamatory facts regarding public figures or officials, those individuals must show that such statement were made with knowledge of their false implications or with reckless disregard for their truth. Herbert v. Okla. Christian Coalition, 1999 OK 90, 992 P.2d 322, 327. In Herbert, a lobbyist's conclusions and comments concerning a state representative, which were published in a Voters Guide, were in the form of non-actionable judgmental statements and were opinionative, not factual. Id.

3. ***Consent.*** No reported cases.

4. ***Mitigation.*** No reported cases.

III. RECURRING FACT PATTERNS

A. Statements in Personnel File

Defamatory statements made between employees of a corporation regarding the basis for firing of a store manager were protected by the intracorporate communications privilege and could not be considered published for purposes of a libel action. Tatum v. Philip Morris Inc., 809 F. Supp. 1452 (W.D. Okla. 1992). Thus, an employer has the right to discharge an employee and to notify customers and prospective customers of the discharge, and to tell customers the reason for the employee's discharge, even though that reason may be injurious or damaging to the discharged employee, provided it was done without malice or evil intent to injure or damage the former employee and for the purpose of protecting or promoting the employer's business. Id. However, a statement that an employee was discharged due to accusations that she had stolen money from a store could be considered slander per se since the employee was charged with the commission of a crime. Starr v. Pearle Vision, Inc., 54 F.3d 1548 (10th Cir. 1995). Conversely, where a representative of a collective bargaining agent of a discharged employee read an allegedly defamatory letter written by the employer's manager to the representative to state the purported reason for discharge of the employee, there was no publication on which to predicate liability of the employer and manager for libel. Patrick v. Thomas, 1962 OK 190, 376 P.2d 250.

B. Performance Evaluations

Defamatory statements made between a supervisor and an employee during a performance evaluation, and then repeated to a third party within the organization, were protected by the intra-corporate communications privilege and could not be considered actionable under a libel claim. Patrick v. Thomas, 1962 OK 190, 376 P.2d 250; Tatum v. Philip Morris Inc., 809 F. Supp. 1452 (W.D. Okla. 1992).

C. References

In 1995, the Oklahoma legislature passed a bill creating a statute limiting an employer's liability for disclosing information about a current or prospective employee, codifying the common law. Although the statute does not provide absolute protection for the employer, it is extremely helpful in defending defamation actions. Okla. Stat. tit. 40, §61 (West Supp. 1998) provides in pertinent part:

> An employer may disclose information about a current or former employee's job performance to a prospective employer of the current or former employee upon request of the prospective employer and with consent of the current or former employee, or upon request of the current or former employee. . . . The employer is presumed to be acting in good faith, unless lack of good faith is shown by a preponderance of the evidence. The current or former employer shall be immune from civil liability for the disclosure or any consequences of such disclosure unless the presumption of good faith is rebutted upon a showing that the information is disclosed by the current or former employer was false and the employer providing the information had knowledge of its falsity or acted with malice or reckless disregard for the truth.

D. Intracorporate Communication

Discussions between employees of a corporation, concerning the reasons a store manager was fired, were protected by the intracorporate communications privilege and could not be considered published for purposes of a libel action even though the statements appeared to be libelous. Tatum v. Philip Morris Inc., 809 F. Supp. 1452 (W.D. Okla. 1992). An employer may terminate an employee and then inform both existing and prospective customers of the reasons for termination. This communication is protected even if the stated reasons may be damaging or detrimental to the discharged employee's reputation. However, it must lack malice or evil intent to injure or damage the former employee and be done for the purpose of protecting or promoting the employer's business. Id. Additionally, a representative of a collective bargaining agent of a terminated employee had the occasion to read an allegedly defamatory letter that suggested the reason for discharge. While the letter was written by the employer's manager to the representative, the Court held there was no publication to establish liability of the employer and manager for libel. Patrick v. Thomas, 1962 OK 190, 376 P.2d 250. Conversely, an employee who was discharged because of allegations that she had appropriated money from a store, and that reason was stated to others, could establish slander per se since the statement concerned the commission of a crime. Starr v. Pearle Vision, Inc., 54 F.3d 1548 (10th Cir. 1995); Angove v. Williams Sonoma, Inc., 70 Fed.Appx. 500, 2003 WL 21529409 (10th Cir. (Okla.)) (unpublished opinion). Richardson v. Watco Companies, Inc., 2011 WL 1500504, * 3 (W.D.Okla. April 19, 2011).

E. Statements to Government Agencies

Communications by a company which processed an employee's unemployment claims to the Oklahoma Employment Security Commission (OESC) were privileged and could not form the basis for libel or slander. Allen v. T.G.& Y. Stores Co., 699 F. Supp. 867 (W.D. Okla. 1987). Thus, a former employer's statements to the OESC that an employee was discharged for stealing property and for insubordination were privileged communications where the statements were made in response to the OESC's request for information. Tatum v. Philip Morris Inc., 809 F. Supp. 1452 (W.D. Okla. 1992). Accordingly, information sent to regulatory agencies designed to insure prompt enforcement of claims are considered part of the official proceeding and enjoy the protection of absolute immunity to defamation actions. Presson v. Bill Beckman Co. Inc., 1995 OK CIV APP 44, 898 P.2d 179.

F. Reports to Auditors and Insurers.

No reported cases.

G. Vicarious Liability of Employers for Statements Made by Employees

1. ***Scope of Employment.*** An employer could not be held liable for a co-worker's allegedly slanderous statement concerning a former employee where the coworker who published the statement was away from her workplace, and conversation was neither attendant to the employer's business nor was intended to further the interest of the employer. Hensley v. Armstrong World Industries, Inc., 798 F. Supp. 653 (W.D. Okla. 1992); Montgomery v. City of Ardmore, 365 F.3d 926 (10th Cir. 2004); Wilson v. City of Tulsa, 2004 OK CIV APP 44, 91 P.3d 673.

a. **Blogging**. No reported cases.

H. Internal Investigations

In Ishmael v. Andrew, 2006 OK CIV APP 82, ¶¶ 12–18, 137 P.3d 1271, the Oklahoma Court of Civil Appeals held that false statements made by an attorney during an internal investigation were not slander and were protected by the intracorporate privilege. In Ishmael, the attorney had been hired by the employer to investigate the attempted poisonous contamination of an employee's beverage. During the course of conducting the investigation, the attorney interviewed the plaintiff and accused him of being the person who had contaminated the employee's drink. The court held that such conduct could not sustain either a slander claim or a claim for intentional infliction of emotional distress.

IV. OTHER ACTIONS BASED ON STATEMENTS

A. Negligent Hiring, Retention and Supervision

It is well settled that Oklahoma recognizes a cause of action for negligent hiring and retention. Schovanec v. Archdiocese, 2008 OK 70, 188 P.3d 158; N.H. v. Presbyterian Church (U.S.A.), 1999 OK 88, 998 P.2d 592; Jordan v. Cates, 1997 OK 9, 935 P.2d 289; and Mistletoe Express Service, Inc. v. Culp, 1959 OK 250, 353 P.2d 9. Liability results when the employer had reason to believe that the person hired would cause an undue risk of harm to others, and under the circumstances, the employer did not take the care which a prudent person would have taken in selecting the person for the business at hand. Escue v. Northern OK College, 450 F.3d 1146, 1156 (10th Cir. Okla. 2006); Blazier v. St. John Medical Ctr., Inc., 2006 WL 2599199, * 8 (N.D.Okla.2006). This theory of recovery may be available when vicarious liability cannot be established, but the critical element for a plaintiff's recovery is the employer's prior knowledge of the employee's propensity to create the specific danger from which harm was suffered. N.H. v. Presbyterian Church, 1999 OK 88, 998 P.2d at 600. What precautions must be taken by an employer depend upon the situation. An employer can normally assume that an employee who offers to perform simple work is competent. If, however, the work is likely to subject third persons to serious risk of great harm, there is a special duty of investigation. Jackson v. Remington Park, Inc., 1994 OK CIV APP 30, 874 P.2d 814. Without evidence of wrongful conduct by the individual hired, a plaintiff does not have a valid claim for negligent hiring, retention or supervision. Mitchell v. City of Moore, 218 F.3d 1190, 1201 (10th Cir. 2000) (upholding summary judgment granted by the Western District of Oklahoma on state claims in favor of defendant employer). However, "the hirer of an independent contractor is not liable to employees of the independent contractor for negligent hiring." Young v. Bob Howard Automotive, Inc., 2002 OK CIV APP ¶ 21, 52 P.3d 1045.

B. Intentional Infliction of Emotional Distress

Oklahoma recognizes as an independent tort, intentional infliction of emotional distress. Also known as a tort of outrage, it is governed by the narrow standards of the Restatement (Second) of Torts §46. An action for intentional infliction of emotional distress will lie only where there is extreme and outrageous conduct coupled with severe emotional distress. Liability has been found only where the conduct has been so outrageous in character, and so extreme in degree, as to go beyond all possible bounds of decency, and to be regarded as atrocious and utterly intolerable in a civilized community. Gaylord Entertainment Co. v. Thompson, 1998 OK 30, 958 P.2d 128. In order to recover for intentional infliction of emotional distress, a plaintiff must prove that "(1) the defendant acted intentionally or recklessly; (2) the defendant's conduct was extreme and outrageous; (3) the defendant's conduct caused the plaintiff emotional distress; and (4) the resulting emotional distress was severe." Computer Publications, Inc. v. Welton, 2002 OK 50, ¶ 7, 49 P.3d 732; Miner v. Mid-America Door Company, 2003 OK CIV APP 32, 68 P.3d 212; EEOC v. Voss Elec. Co. d/b/a Voss Lighting, 257 F.Supp.2d 1354, 1363 (W.D.Okla. 2003); Campbell v. Wal-Mart Stores, Inc., 272 F.Supp.2d 1276, 1302 (N.D.Okla. 2003); Trentadue v. U.S., 386 F.3d 1322, 1336 (10th Cir. 2004); Bolin v. Oklahoma Conference of the United Methodist Church, 397 F.Supp.2d 1293, 1298 (N.D.Okla. 2005); Escue v. Northern OK College, 450 F.3d 1146, 1158 (10th Cir. 2006); Charlton v. Ardent Health Services, L.L.C., 2006 WL 1836048, * 3 (N.D.Okla. June 30, 2006); Freeman v. Sikorsky Aircraft Corp., 2006 WL 2385311, * 4 (N.D. Okla. Aug. 17, 2006). A viable claim for intentional infliction of emotional distress must cause physical suffering or injury. Hussein v. Duncan Regional Hosp., Inc., 2009 WL 1212278 (W.D.Okla. 2009) (citing Gaylord at 49, n. 93).

In Ishmael v. Andrew, 2006 OK CIV APP 82, 137 P.3d 1271, the Oklahoma Court of Civil Appeals held that statements made by a corporate employer's attorney during an investigation falsely accusing the plaintiff of having poisonously contaminated a co–worker's beverage could not sustain a cause of action for intentional infliction of emotional distress because the statements were not sufficiently outrageous, atrocious or beyond all possible bounds of decency in that context. Id. at ¶¶ 19–20. In Peterson v. Grisham, 2008 WL 4363653 (E.D.Okla) (not reported in F.Supp.), the court held that criticisms of public officials contained in three published books documenting two murder cases in the town of Ada, Oklahoma, were not sufficiently extreme and outrageous to support a claim for intentional infliction of emotional distress.

A claim for intentional infliction of emotional distress cannot be based on privileged communications that would otherwise be defamatory. Kirschstein v. Haynes, 1990 OK 8, 788 P.2d 941. However, such a claim (or one for negligence) may be grounded on conduct that is related to such privileged statement. Berman v. Laboratory Corp. of America, 2011 OK 106, 268 P.3d 68.

C. Interference with Economic Advantage

Under Oklahoma law, the elements of a cause of action for tortious interference with a contract, or wrongful interference with an existing advantageous relation, are (1) the existence of a business or contractual right with which there was interference; (2) that the interference was malicious and wrongful; (3) that the interference was neither justified, privileged, nor excusable; and (4) that damage was proximately sustained as a result of the complained interference. Gonzalez v. Sessom, 2006 OK CIV APP 61, 137 P.3d 1245; Morrow Dev. Corp. v. American Bank & Trust Co., 1994 OK 26, 875 P.2d 411, 416; Cardtoons, L.C., v. Major League Baseball Players' Ass'n, 335 F.3d 1161 (10th Cir. 2003); Angove v. Williams Sonoma, Inc., 70 Fed.Appx. 500, 2003 WL 21529409 (10th Cir. (Okla.)) (unpublished opinion). The right to recover for unlawful interference with the performance of a contract presupposes the existence of a valid enforceable contract. While every interference is not necessarily tortious, in the context of defamation and libel, most causes of action arise under the tortious theory. First American Kickapoo Operations v. Multimedia Games, Inc., 412 F.3d 1166 (10th Cir. 2005); Ellison v. An-Son Corp., 1987 OK CIV APP 71, 751 P.2d 1102; Tatum v. Philip Morris Inc., 809 F. Supp. 1452 (W.D. Okla. 1992); Green Bay Packaging, Inc. v. Preferred Packaging, Inc., 1996 OK 121, 932 P.2d 1091; Vice v. Conoco, Inc., 150 F.3d 1286 (10th Cir. 1998). An employer may not be liable for interfering with an employee's employment, because the business relationship allegedly interfered with must be with a third party. Gabler v. Holder & Smith, Inc., 2000 OK CIV APP 107, 11 P.3d 1269.

Plaintiff can establish malicious and wrongful conduct by showing reckless disregard or conscious indifference to the consequences. Graham v. Keudel, 1993 OK 6, 847 P.2d 342, 362. Further, Oklahoma courts hold that the interference is not actionable if the action was taken fairly and honestly and was done to better the actor's business, not to expressly harm another. Morrow Dev. Corp., 875 P.2d at 416 (quoting Del State Bank v. Salmon, 1976 OK 42, 548 P.2d 1024, 1027).

D. Prima Facie Tort

Oklahoma The Oklahoma Supreme Court has not expressly adopted a prima facie tort theory of recovery. Tarrant v. Guthrie First Capital Bank, 2010 OK CIV APP 82, ¶ 15, 241 P.3d 280, 284; Grossman v. Fannie Mae, 431 Fed.Appx. 699,

2011 WL 2871101 (10th Cir. (Okla.)) (Oklahoma does not recognize prima facie tort). See also Cardtoons v. Major League Baseball Players Association, 335 F.3d 1161, 1167 (10th Cir. 2003), citing Patel v. OMH Med. Ctr., Inc., 1999 OK 33, 987

V. OTHER ISSUES

A. Statute of Limitations

The statute of limitations for a defamation action is one year. Okla. Stat. tit. 12, §95(A)(4). However, [t]he discovery rule applies to libel actions when the publication is likely to be concealed or published in a secretive manner which would make it unlikely to come to the attention of the injured party. Digital Design Group, Inc. v. Information Builders, 2001 OK 21, ¶18, 24 P.3d 834; Bolin v. Oklahoma Conference of the United Methodist Church, 397 F.Supp.2d 1293, 1298 (N.D.Okla. 2005); Martin v. Cornell Companies, Inc., 2009 WL 1856200 (W.D.Okla).

B. Jurisdiction

Jurisdiction for claims made pursuant to the Oklahoma statutory provisions for slander and libel lies in the state district courts. However, as often is the case, when defamation or other state tort claims are asserted in conjunction with claims made under federal employment laws, such as Title VII or the Americans with Disabilities Act, the preferred jurisdiction is in the federal district courts, which assume supplemental jurisdiction over the state tort claims pursuant to 28 U.S.C. §1367.

C. Worker's Compensation Exclusivity

The Oklahoma Worker's Compensation Act provides the exclusive rights and remedies of injured workers. Section 11 of the Worker's Compensation Act prescribes employer liability "for the disability or death of an employee resulting from an accidental injury sustained by the employee arising out of and in the course of employment, without regard to fault." Okla. Stat. tit. 85, § 11. Section 12 makes that liability "exclusive and in place of all other liability of the employer."

There are no reported cases applying Oklahoma's worker's compensation exclusivity provision to defamation claims brought against employers, but Oklahoma courts have routinely dismissed actions based upon the provision wherein an employee who sustains an injury through the alleged negligence of the employer, that arises out of and in the course of employment, brings a claim for such negligence. This exclusive remedy provision may not apply if an employee was willfully injured by his employer. In Parret v. UNICCO Serv. Co., 2005 OK 54, 127 P.3d 572, the Oklahoma Supreme Court answered a certified question about the standard of intent necessary for an employee's tort claim against an employer to fall outside the protection of the Worker's Compensation Act. The Supreme Court adopted a "substantial certainty" standard, which requires that the employer desired to bring about the worker's injury or intended the act that caused the injury with knowledge that the injury was substantially certain to follow.

D. Pleading Requirements

In all civil actions to recover damages for libel or slander, it shall be sufficient to state generally what the defamatory matter was, that it was published or spoken of the plaintiff, and to allege any general or special damage caused thereby. Okla. Stat. tit. 12, §1444.1. Oklahoma's adoption of notice pleading has not eliminated the need to allege special damages when libel or slander per quod is claimed. See Niemeyer v. U.S. Fidelity & Guar. Co., 1990 OK 32, 789 P.2d 1318, 1321; Sturgeon v. Retherford Pub., 1999 OK CIV APP 78, 987 P.2d 1218, 1224; Finnell v. Jebco Seismic, 2003 OK 35, 67 P.3d 339. See also Hester v. Express Metal Fabricators, LLC, 2011 WL 5837086 (N.D.Okla.) (Plaintiff stated a plausible claim for slanderous defamation under federal Rule 12(b)(6) standard, even where only facts plead in the complaint were that the defendant had made an allegedly false allegations of felony vandalism against the plaintiff to the local sheriff and police department. However, the plaintiff did not state sufficient facts to indicate that his claim for libel *per se* was plausible where the plaintiff had made only bald assertions of harm and, therefore, the libel *per se* claim was subject to dismissal).

SURVEY OF OKLAHOMA EMPLOYMENT PRIVACY LAW

J. Patrick Cremin and Molly Aspan
Hall, Estill, Hardwick, Gable, Golden & Nelson
320 South Boston – Suite 200
Tulsa, Oklahoma 74103-3706
Telephone: 918-594-0595; Fax: 918-594-0505

(With Developments Reported Through **November 1, 2012**)

GENERAL COMMENTS

The Oklahoma Anti-Discrimination Act ("OADA") generally prohibits discrimination in the workplace by both private and public employers on the basis of race, color, national origin, sex, religion, creed, age, disability, or genetic information. The OADA also applies to compensation and terms and conditions of employment and to decisions about hiring and discharge. See Okla. Stat. tit. 25, §§ 1301, et seq. **On July 1, 2012, the Oklahoma Human Rights Commission, the agency tasked with investigating claims under the OADA, merged into the Oklahoma Attorney General's Office, Office of Civil Rights Enforcement.** While most employment related grievances are brought before the Equal Employment Opportunity Commission and federal district court, with that court assuming supplemental jurisdiction over state law claims, it is worth noting the Oklahoma authority for preventing discrimination in the workplace.

The citation format used in this outline follows Okla. Sup. Ct Rule 1.200(e), which requires that published opinions of the Oklahoma Supreme Court and Oklahoma Court of Civil Appeals promulgated after May 1, 1997 be cited using the paragraph citation form contained in the rule. Parallel citation to Pacific Reporter is required; parallel citation to Oklahoma Reports is proscribed. Parallel citation to the official paragraph citation form is strongly encouraged for opinions promulgated prior to May 1, 1997.

SIGNIFICANT DEVELOPMENTS SINCE THE 2012 *SURVEY*

The Oklahoma legislature abolished the Oklahoma Human Rights Commission ("OHRC") effective July 1, 2012. Responsibilities and duties of the OHRC are now with the Office of Civil Rights Enforcement, part of the Oklahoma Attorney General's Office ("OCRE"). The OCRE is now responsible for investigating claims of employment discrimination made under state law.

The Oklahoma Standards for Workplace Drug and Alcohol Testing Act, Okla. Stat. tit. 41, § 551, et seq., which regulates employer-mandated testing programs, significantly changed effective November 1, 2011. Some additional changes were made this past year and became effective May 8, 2012. The additional changes relate primarily to alcohol tests using breath, types of testing, confidentiality, and unemployment proceedings.

The Oklahoma Firearms Act and Oklahoma Self-Defense Act prohibit employers from establishing any policy or rule that has the effect of prohibiting any person, except a convicted felon, from transporting and storing firearms locked in or locked to a motor vehicle on any property set aside for any motor vehicle. The 2012 legislature amended this to encompass not only firearms, but also ammunition. Okla. Stat. tit. 21, § 1290.22.

The Oklahoma Supreme Court recently decided two cases related to non-compete agreements. In Howard v. Nitro-Lift Technologies, L.L.C., 2011 OK 98, ___ P.3d ___, the Court found a non-compete covenant void and unenforceable, and refused to judicially modify the covenant where it would have to be substantially excised leaving only a shell of the original agreement and would require the addition of at least one material term. In Smoot v. B&J Restoration Services, 2012 OK CIV APP 58, 279 P.3d 805, the Court analyzed personal liability for breach of a non-compete agreement in connection with the sale of a business.

I. GENERAL LAW OF PRIVACY

A. Legal Basis of Privacy Claims

Oklahoma has both statutory and common law bases for privacy causes of action. Oklahoma statutes provide a cause of action for unauthorized use of another person's rights of publicity. Okla. Stat. tit. 12, § 1449. Additionally, there is statutory language that provides criminal liability for such unauthorized use of another's likeness. Okla. Stat. tit. 21, § 839.1. Furthermore, on November 1, 2006, an Oklahoma statute became effective that provides criminal liability for the unauthorized use of the likeness of any service member of the United States Armed Forces, including both active duty members as well as former members of the Armed Forces of the United States. Okla. Stat. tit. 21, § 839.1A.

The Oklahoma Supreme Court has adopted a limited invasion of privacy cause of action "to afford some redress to plaintiffs who have suffered from certain previously non-actionable forms of anti-social behavior," however, with the restriction that "[t]here is simply no room in the framework of our society for permitting one party to sue on the event of every intrusion into the psychic tranquility of an individual." Munley v. ISC Fin. House, Inc., 1978 OK 123, 584 P.2d 1336, 1339. Oklahoma has adopted the standard set forth in the Restatement of Torts (Second) § 652 for invasion of privacy causes of action which is predicated upon activity which is "highly offensive to a reasonable person." Id. Oklahoma recognizes four scenarios upon which an invasion of privacy claim may be based: (1) unreasonable intrusion upon seclusion of another; (2) appropriation of another's name or likeness; (3) unreasonable publicity given to another's private life; or (4) publicity that places another in false light before the public. See, e.g., McCormack v. Okla. Publ'g Co., 1980 OK 98, 613 P.2d 737, 739.

In Gens v. Casady School, 2008 OK 5, 177 P.3d 565, the court denied defendant's motion to dismiss and permitted a mother to assert a constitutional claim of invasion of privacy on behalf of her son. Oklahoma's statutory law provides that minors may protect their rights by suing through their "next friend," and the mother is stepping into her son's shoes as opposed to asserting a claim on her behalf for the violation of her son's constitutional right of privacy. See id. (citing Okla. Stat. tit. 12, § 2017).

B. Causes of Action

Oklahoma has recognized a cause of action for each of the four above categories of invasion of privacy, either statutorily or judicially. See Okla. Stat. tit. 12, § 1449 (setting forth the requirements for a claim based upon misappropriation of another's likeness); McCormack v. Okla. Publ'g Co., 1980 OK 98, 613 P.2d 737, 739 (recognizing the tort of invasion of privacy in all four categories as set out in the Restatement of Torts (Second) § 652); Munley v. ISC Fin. House, Inc., 1978 OK 123, 584 P.2d 1336 (recognizing intrusion upon seclusion as an invasion of privacy claim).

In Woods v. Prestwick House, Inc., 2011 OK 9, 247 P.3d 1183, the Oklahoma Supreme Court examined the statute of limitations and the discovery rule for misappropriation/right of publicity claims under Okla. Stat. tit. 12, § 1449. The Court held that because the concept of misappropriation of another's name or likeness as the tort of invasion of privacy arose before the legislature's enactment of Okla. Stat. tit. 12, §1449, the causes of action arising under the statute are governed by Okla. Stat. tit. 12, § 95(3) providing for a two year statute of limitations period for an action for injury to the rights of another. The Court then held that, where applicable, the discovery rule tolls the limitations period until a plaintiff learns of an injury and, through prudent investigation, can obtain sufficient facts to state a cause of action. See also VIII.A., infra.

1. ***Misappropriation/Right of Publicity***. Oklahoma statutes provide that any person who knowingly uses another's name, voice, signature, photograph, or likeness, in any manner, on or in products, merchandise, or goods, or for purposes of advertising or selling, or soliciting purchases of products, merchandise, goods, or services, without such person's consent shall be liable for any damages sustained by the person injured as a result of such use. Further, any profits attributable to the unauthorized use shall be taken into account in computing the actual damages. Okla. Stat. tit. 12, § 1449 (A). In establishing the profits attributable to unauthorized use, the plaintiff must show the gross revenue from such use, and the defendant bears the burden of showing any deductible expenses. Okla. Stat. tit. 12, § 1449(A). Under the provisions of the statute, punitive damages may be awarded to the plaintiff and attorney fees may be awarded to the prevailing party. Okla. Stat. tit. 12, § 1449(A). The statute exempts from liability the use of a name, voice, signature, photograph, or likeness in connection with any news, public affairs, or sports broadcast or account, or any political campaign. Okla. Stat. tit. 12, § 1449 (D). Additionally, misappropriation of another's likeness is deemed a misdemeanor under Oklahoma law. Okla. Stat. tit 21, § 839.1. Furthermore, on November 1, 2006, an Oklahoma statute became effective that provides criminal liability for the unauthorized use of the likeness of any service member of the United States Armed Forces, including both active duty members as well as former members of the Armed Forces of the United States. Okla. Stat. tit. 21, § 839.1A.

In Brill v. The Walt Disney Co., 2010 OK CIV APP 132, 246 P.3d 1099, the Oklahoma Court of Civil Appeals issued the first Oklahoma state court decision addressing this right of publicity claim under Okla. Stat. tit. 12, § 1449 (A). In Brill, the Plaintiff argued that the fictional animated race car character "Lightning McQueen" in the movie *Cars* constitutes a misappropriation of his likeness and violates his right of publicity pursuant to common law and Okla. Stat. tit. 12, § 1449. Plaintiff argued that the common law right of publicity is broader than the statutory right in that the use of one's "identity" is actionable even if one's "likeness" or name is not used. The Court disagreed and held that the common law right of publicity is limited to the appropriation of "the name or likeness of another." In order to establish a *prima facie* case of statutory violation of the right of publicity, a plaintiff must plead facts establishing three elements of the claim: (1) that defendant knowingly used plaintiff's name or likeness, (2) on products, merchandise, or goods, (3) without plaintiff's prior consent. The Court in Brill held that any similarities of Plaintiff's car to Lightning McQueen do not equate to a knowing use of Plaintiff's personal likeness.

2. ***False Light.*** To present an adequate claim for false light invasion of privacy, a plaintiff must prove that (1) the defendant gave publicity to the matter placing the plaintiff before the public in a false light; (2) the false

light would be highly offensive to reasonable persons under the circumstances; and (3) defendant had knowledge of or acted in reckless disregard as to the falsity of the publicized matter and the false light. Grogan v. KOKH, LLC, 2011 OK CIV APP 34, 256 P.3d 1021, 1030; Warren v. U.S. Specialty Sports Ass'n, 2006 OK CIV APP 78, 138 P.3d 580, 586; Tanique, Inc. v. Okla. Bureau of Narcotics & Dangerous Drugs, 2004 OK CIV APP 73, 99 P.3d 1209; Grimes v. CBS Broad. Int'l of Canada, Ltd., 905 F.Supp. 964 (N.D. Okla. 1995). Although the Oklahoma Supreme Court has not articulated what constitutes a "highly offensive" depiction or statement in a claim for false light invasion of privacy, it adopted the view of the Restatement of Torts (Second) § 652(E). Grimes, 905 F. Supp. at 969. The rule set forth by the Restatement states that to be "highly offensive" requires that serious offense could reasonably be expected to be taken by a reasonable person in the same situation. Id.

Based upon the Oklahoma Supreme Court's view that the question of whether a publication is defamatory in a libel or slander action is a matter of law, and upon the Court's adoption of the Restatement in false light cases, an Oklahoma federal district court concluded that it is the role of the court to make the threshold determination of whether a matter in a false light claim is highly offensive. Id. at 968. Additionally, a claim for false light invasion of privacy cannot be premised on mere harm to one's feelings, but rather requires conduct which is intentional and would reasonably be regarded as extreme or outrageous. Colbert v. World Publ'g Co., 1987 OK 116, 747 P.2d 286, 289-90.

Oklahoma courts hold that whether a statement is capable of the meaning alleged is a question of law. Grogan, 256 P.3d at 1029.. Then, upon determining whether the first two elements of a false light invasion of privacy claim are met, the court should view the facts in the light most favorable to plaintiff. Id. at 1030. Upon examining the third element, whether the defendant had knowledge of or acted in reckless disregard as to the falsity of the publicized matter and the false light, Oklahoma courts have adopted the actual malice test. Id.; Colbert, 747 P.2d at 290-91. In other words, actual malice must be proven with convincing clarity by showing that the defendant had a high degree of awareness of probable falsity or, in fact, entertained serious doubts as to the truth of the publication. Colbert, 747 P.2d at 291. The actual malice element of the false light tort contains two components stated in the alternative - either (1) the defendant knows the publication is false and would portray the plaintiff in a false light, or (2) the defendant acts with reckless disregard as to whether the statement is false and would portray the plaintiff in a false light. Grogan, 256 P.3d at 1031.

Oklahoma courts recognize that there is sometimes an overlapping between false light invasion of privacy and defamation claims, and that a cause of action may lie in both in some cases. McCormack, 613 P.2d at 741. However, Oklahoma courts have recognized three basic differences between a false light invasion of privacy claim and a defamation claim: (1) a false light claim is not limited to matters actually defamatory, either on their face or in context, but may be brought for any false portrayal that is highly offensive to a reasonable person; (2) although any publication gives rise to a defamation action, the false light claim requires publication to a substantial portion of the general public; and (3) the essence of a defamation action is injury to reputation, but a false light plaintiff may recover for subjective suffering, embarrassment, and outrage in the absence of damage to reputation. Grogan, 256 P.3d at 1036 (citing 62A Am. Jur. 2d *Privacy* § 128 (2005)).

Oklahoma courts also recognize that, unlike a claim for libel per se, a claim for false light invasion of privacy can properly rest on a defendant stating a falsehood by implication - such as through the use of innuendo. Peterson v. Grisham, 594 F.3d 723, 730-31 (10th Cir. 2010). However, there must be a clear connection between a defendant's statement and the falsehood that the statement purportedly implies. Id. In Peterson, the Tenth Circuit affirmed the District Court's granting of Defendants' Motion to Dismiss on Plaintiffs' false light claims as Plaintiffs failed to allege the necessary nexus between the Defendants' statements and the proposition that Plaintiffs were involved in a crime. Id. Peterson involved claims brought by an Oklahoma District Attorney, a former police officer, and a former state criminologist against author John Grisham, and others, based on Mr. Grisham's book *The Innocent Man* and another book *Journey Toward Justice*. Ronald Williamson and Dennis Fritz were wrongfully convicted of a rape and murder and were later exonerated after spending over a decade in jail. Mr. Grisham wrote the book *The Innocent Man*, and Mr. Fritz wrote the book *Journey Toward Justice*, telling the story of Mr. Williamson and Mr. Fritz. The books did not paint the Plaintiffs in a positive light. Plaintiffs brought these claims against Defendants after the release of these books.

3. ***Publication of Private Facts.*** The prima facie elements required for a claim of invasion of privacy due to public disclosure of private facts are (1) that there was a public disclosure; (2) that the facts disclosed were private and not of legitimate public concern; and (3) the disclosure was one which would be offensive to a reasonable person. McCormack, 613 P.2d at 740-41. Disclosure to the general public is the extent of publicity required to give rise to an action for public disclosure of private facts. Eddy v. Brown, 1986 OK 3, 715 P.2d 74, 78. It is not necessary that the statements be untrue. McCormack, 613 P.2d at 737. However, if the facts are a matter of public record, plaintiff does not have a valid claim under this category of invasion of privacy. Id. at 741-42 (adopting Restatement of Torts (Second) § 252(D)).

4. ***Intrusion.*** The case by which Oklahoma adopted the tort of invasion of privacy involved claims of intrusion upon seclusion. See Munley v. ISC Fin. House, Inc., 1978 OK 123, 584 P.2d 1336. See also Williams v. City of Tulsa, 393 F. Supp. 2d 1124, 1131 (N.D. Okla. 2005). In Munley, the plaintiff claimed that defendant, a collection agency,

employed collection practices which unlawfully intruded upon plaintiff's privacy; however, in upholding summary judgment in favor of defendant, the Oklahoma Supreme Court held that defendant's action were not so extreme and outrageous as to constitute an invasion of plaintiff's privacy. The requirements established by the Restatement of Torts (Second) § 652(B) were adopted by the Oklahoma Supreme Court as the elements necessary for an intrusion of privacy claim, and are as follows: "[o]ne who intentionally intrudes, physically or otherwise, upon the solitude or seclusion of another, or his private affairs or concerns, is subject to liability to the other for invasion of his privacy, if the intrusion would be highly offensive to a reasonable person." Munley, 584 P.2d at 1339. In Munley, the court held that the defendant's actions in attempting to collect a debt owned by plaintiff, conduct which consisted of numerous phone calls to plaintiff's home and current and past employers, as well as personal visits to plaintiff's home, apartment manager and neighbors, did not constitute "highly offensive" behavior to a reasonable person. Id. at 1339-40. Even in a public place, there may be some matters so private that the invasion of which can create liability under this invasion of privacy claim. See Williams, 393 F. Supp. 2d at 1131. For additional discussion of Oklahoma law concerning "highly offensive" conduct, see I.B(2), supra.

C. Other Privacy-related Actions

1. **Intentional Infliction of Emotional Distress.** Oklahoma recognizes intentional infliction of emotional distress as an independent tort. See e.g., Chenoweth v. City of Miami, 2010 OK CIV APP 91, 240 P.3d 1080; Schovanec v. Archdiocese of Oklahoma City, 2008 OK 70, 188 P.3d 158; Warren v. U.S. Specialty Sports Ass'n, 2006 OK CIV APP 78, 138 P.3d 580, 585; Ishmael v. Andrew, 2006 OK CIV APP 82, 137 P.3d 1271, 1276; Estate of Trentadue ex rel. Aguilar v. United States, 397 F.3d 840, 855-56 (10th Cir. 2005), remanded to 560 F. Supp. 2d 1124 (W.D. Okla. 2008); Worsham v. Nix, 2004 OK CIV APP 2, 83 P.3d 879, 888 n.4; Breeden v. League Servs. Corp., 1978 OK 27, 575 P.2d 1374. In Breeden, the Oklahoma Supreme Court adopted the test set forth in the Restatement of Torts (Second) § 46 that for a defendant's conduct to be actionable as intentional infliction of emotional distress, the conduct must be of such a character as would reasonably be regarded as extreme and outrageous. Breeden, 575 P.2d at 1376. Additionally, it is for the trial court to make the initial determination of whether the defendant's conduct may reasonably be regarded as extreme and outrageous so as to allow recovery by the plaintiff, and where it is such that reasonable minds could differ, it is a decision for the jury. Id. at 1377. More specifically stated, the test is whether the defendant's conduct is "so outrageous in character and extreme in degree as to go beyond all possible bounds of decency, and to be regarded as atrocious, and utterly intolerable in a civilized community." Eddy v. Brown, 1986 OK 3, 715 P.2d 74, 75. It is a very high standard. The plaintiff must prove that "(1) the defendant acted intentionally or recklessly; (2) the defendant's conduct was extreme and outrageous; (3) the defendant's conduct caused the plaintiff emotional distress; and (4) the resulting emotional distress was severe." Durham v. McDonald's Restaurants of Oklahoma, Inc., 2011 OK 45, 256 P.3d 64, 66; Computer Publ'n, Inc. v. Welton, 2002 OK 50, 49 P.3d 732, 735. The plaintiff's emotional distress must be "so severe that no reasonable person could be expected to endure it." See Chellen v. John Pickle Co., 446 F. Supp. 2d 1247, 1292 (N.D. Okla. 2006) (citing Computer Publ'g, Inc., 49 P.3d at 735). While emotional distress includes all highly unpleasant mental reactions, it is only where the emotional distress is so extreme that liability arises. See id. There is not a cause of action for intentional infliction of emotional distress against the State. Tanique, Inc. v. Okla. Bureau of Narcotics & Dangerous Drugs, 2004 OK CIV APP 73, 99 P.3d 1209.

Oklahoma law requires that the offending behavior be intentional or reckless in order to be actionable, and the determination of "outrageous and extreme" should not be considered in a "sterile setting," but rather within "the milieu in which [the conduct] took place." Eddy, 715 P.2d at 76-77. The test is whether the conduct "has so totally and completely exceeded the bounds of acceptable social interaction that the law must provide redress," or whether "the recitation of the facts to an average member of the community would arouse his resentment against the actor, and lead him to exclaim 'Outrageous.'" Worsham, 83 P.3d at 888 n.4 (citing Miller v. Miller, 1998 OK 24, 956 P.2d 887, 901). Liability for this tort does not extend to "mere insults, indignities, threats, annoyances, petty oppressions, or other trivialities." Chellen, 446 F. Supp. 2d at 1292 (quoting Eddy, 715 P.2d at 77). In Eddy, the plaintiff sought recovery from his employer, supervisor, and foreman for harassment and ridicule he received in the workplace because of his union support, speech impediment, and psychiatric counseling. Id. The court found that although the defendants' conduct might have been unreasonable and hurtful, it was not so extreme and outrageous as to be actionable. Id. In Durham, the plaintiff sought recovery from his employer for a statement allegedly made to him by his manager. Durham, 256 P.3d at 66. The court reversed summary judgment for defendant and found that plaintiff's alleged "highly unpleasant mental reactions" were reasonable and justified under the circumstances and "go beyond mere hurt feelings, insult, indignity, and annoyance and could be reasonable regarded to constitute emotional distress so severe that no reasonable person could be expected to endure it." Id. at 68-69.

2. **Interference With Prospective Economic Advantage.** Oklahoma recognizes the tort of interference with prospective economic advantage, and in doing so declines to accept that tort as synonymous with the tort of interference with contractual or business relationships. See Fulton v. People Lease Corp., 2010 OK CIV APP 84, 241 P.3d 255; Champagne Metals v. Ken-Mac Metals, Inc., 458 F.3d 1073, 1094 (10th Cir. 2006); McNickle v. Phillips Petro. Co., 2001 OK CIV APP 54, 23 P.3d 949, 953; Gaylord Entm't Co. v. Thompson, 1998 OK 30, 958 P.2d 128, 149-50 n.96; Overbeck v. Quaker Life Ins. Co., 1984 OK CIV APP 44, 757 P.2d 846, 848. Interference with a prospective economic

advantage usually involves interference with some type of reasonable expectation of profit; however, defining the scope of liability and allowable damages are unsettled issues. See Overbeck, 757 P.2d at 847. In most instances, this claim is not actionable unless some intentional or improper conduct exists on the part of the defendant. Id. Recognizing that legitimate and fair competition is essential to our free enterprise system, Oklahoma law holds that persuading another to change his employment status or business practices is not alone deemed unlawful. Id. See also Boyle Servs., Inc. v. Dewberry Design Group, Inc., 2001 OK CIV APP 63, 24 P.3d 878, 880. The essential elements of a claim for intentional interference with prospective economic advantage are the existence of a valid business relation or expectancy, knowledge of the relationship or expectancy on the part of the interferer, an intentional interference inducing or causing a breach or termination of the relationship or expectancy, and resultant damage to the party whose relationship has been disrupted. See Gonzalez v. Sessom, 2006 OK CIV APP 61, 137 P.3d 1245, 1249.

3. **Prima Facie Tort.** Oklahoma does not currently recognize a prima facie tort theory of liability. Tarrant v. Guthrie First Capital Bank, 2010 OK CIV APP 82, 241 P.3d 280. In 1990, the Tenth Circuit recognized that Oklahoma was among a handful of states to adopt a prima facie tort theory of liability. Merrick v. Northern Natural Gas Co., 911 F.2d 426, 433 (10th Cir. 1990). The prima facie tort doctrine permits the recovery of damages for conduct that does not fall within the traditional category of tort liability. Id. The Merrick case cited Restatement (Second) of Torts § 870, which states that the plaintiff only needs to establish that the defendant's "conduct is generally culpable and not justified under the circumstances." Id. The elements of prima facie tort include: (1) intentional infliction of harm; (2) by otherwise lawful activity; (3) without excuse or justification; and (4) causing damage or unjustified detriment. Id.

There are no Oklahoma cases addressing prima facie tort specifically concerning a privacy issue, and there have been few Oklahoma cases addressing prima facie tort at all. In Cardtoons v. Major League Baseball Players, 335 F.3d 1161, 1167 (10th Cir. 2003), the Tenth Circuit found that it was questionable whether this tort was ever recognized in Oklahoma. Id. (citing Patel v. OMH Med. Ctr., Inc., 1999 OK 33, 987 P.2d 1185, 1189-90 n.2). Then, in the 2010 Tarrant case, the Oklahoma Court of Civil Appeals clarified the position that there is no prima facie tort by holding that "[t]he Oklahoma Supreme Court has not previously recognized a theory of recovery based on prima facie tort, and we decline to do so in this case." Tarrant, 241 P.3d at 285.

II. EMPLOYER TESTING OF EMPLOYEES

A. Psychological or Personality Testing

No reported cases. No generally applicable statutory law.

1. ***Common Law and Statutes.*** The Oklahoma statutes require and set forth the procedure for psychological testing of applicants for armed security guard licensing, police or peace officers, and municipal police officers. See Okla. Stat. tit. 11, § 34-101.1; Okla. Stat. tit. 59, § 1750.3A; Okla. Stat. tit. 70, § 3311(E).

2. ***Private Employers.*** No reported cases.

3. ***Public Employers.*** No reported cases.

B. Drug Testing

1. ***Common Law and Statutes.*** The Oklahoma legislature enacted the Standards for Workplace Drug and Alcohol Testing Act, which became effective in June 1993 and regulates employer-mandated testing programs. See Okla. Stat. tit. 40, §§ 551, et seq. This Act was significantly changed effective November 1, 2011. **Additional changes became effective May 8, 2012.**

The statutory provisions comprising the Standards for Workplace Drug and Alcohol Testing Act are lengthy and detailed. A brief summary is provided here. See Okla. Stat. tit. 40, §§ 551, et seq. for specific issues. The employer must have a written policy setting forth the specifics of its drug or alcohol testing program. Okla. Stat. tit. 40, § 555. For an applicant to be required to submit to a drug test, the applicant must have received a conditional offer of employment. Okla. Stat. tit. 40, § 552(2); Okla. Stat. tit. 40, § 554(1).

For-cause testing of employees is allowed if at any time the employer reasonably believes that the employee may be under the influence of drugs or alcohol. Okla. Stat. tit. 40, § 554(2). If provided for in the employer's policy, random testing by private employers is allowed. Okla. Stat. tit. 40, § 554(4). However, public employers may perform random drug testing on only limited employee groups. Okla. Stat. tit. 40, § 554(4). Oklahoma courts have rejected the claim that an employer's requirement of participation in random drug testing violates Oklahoma's general statutory right to privacy which states that "[e]very person is bound, without contract, to abstain from injuring the person or property of another, or infringing upon any of his rights." See Gilmore v. Enogex, Inc., 1994 OK 76, 878 P.2d 360, 365 (citing Okla. Stat. tit. 76, § 1).

Testing must be deemed work time for purposes of compensation and benefits of current employees. Okla. Stat. tit. 40, § 556. An employer may take disciplinary action against an employee who refuses to undergo drug or alcohol testing in accordance with the Act or who tests positive for the presence of drugs or alcohol. Okla. Stat. tit. 40, § 562.

As of this date, there have been only two judicial interpretations of these provisions, McClure v. ConocoPhillips Company, 2006 OK 42, 142 P.3d 390, and Estes v. ConocoPhillips Company, 2008 OK 21, 184 P.3d 518. Both these cases relate to the use of evidential breath testing ("EBT") devices to test for alcohol.

In McClure, the Oklahoma Supreme Court, in response to certified questions, held that EBT devices are appropriate for both initial and confirmation testing and that employers are not required to utilize different machines for the first or second tests or to preserve a breath sample from the initial test to be analyzed the second time.

In Estes, the Oklahoma Supreme Court, in response to certified questions, held that (1) evidential breath tests to determine an employee's blood alcohol level are laboratory services which must be confirmed by a licensed testing facility before an employer may take disciplinary action in reliance on those test results, and (2) the term "willful violation" means conscious, purposeful violations or deliberate disregard of the Act by those who know or should have known of its provisions.

In addition to these two cases based upon claims brought under the Oklahoma Standards for Workplace Drug and Alcohol Testing Act, Oklahoma courts have found that in order for issues concerning an employer's drug testing policy to be actionable, an employee must show either that the policy is discriminatory or that a violation of the drug policy which results in termination is contrary to a clear mandate of public policy, or in other words, is an exception to Oklahoma's modified at-will employment doctrine. See Gilmore v. Enogex, Inc., 1994 OK 76, 878 P.2d 360. If the employer can show that it has a legitimate interest in requiring drug testing and that the testing procedures are administered fairly, there are no public policy violations nor violations of the employees' constitutional rights. Id. In Gilmore, the plaintiff's refusal to submit to random drug testing and his termination resulting from that refusal were found not to fall within any of the public policy exceptions to Oklahoma's at-will employment doctrine. Id. at 364.

Further, the public policy exception to at-will employment is a narrow one which requires showing (1) the employee was fired for refusing to do something that public policy would condemn and (2) the employer was motivated by bad faith, malice, or retaliation when it discharged the employee. Id. at 364. An employee's refusal to submit to a random drug test can constitute a violation of public policy only where such refusal is articulated by clear constitutional, statutory, or decisional law. Id.

Oklahoma law holds that an employer has a legitimate interest in maintaining a work force that is free from the adverse effects of illegal drug and alcohol abuse. Safety issues and other concerns such as efficiency are legitimate reasons for an employer to take steps to ensure that its employees are neither intoxicated on the job nor performing under par because of off-duty drug and alcohol abuse, even if the drug testing is somewhat intrusive. Id. In Gilmore, the random drug testing was announced several weeks before the actual testing which gave employees an opportunity to cease any illegal drug activity prior to being tested. Id. The fact that a drug policy does not require dismissal of employees who test positive, but rather requires that they undergo counseling, is evidence that the employer's intent is to maintain a drug-free workplace, not simply to replace drug dependent employees. Id.

Additionally, for purposes of workers' compensation, no employee who tests positive for the presence of certain substances or who refuses to take a drug or alcohol test required by the employer shall be eligible for such compensation. Okla. Stat. tit. 40, § 554(3). See also Newquist v. Hall Building Products, Inc. 2004 OK CIV APP 92, 100 P.3d 1060, 1061-63 (discussing burden of proof for intoxication/impairment defense); Bayard Drilling v. Martin, 1999 OK CIV APP 67, 986 P.2d 530, 531.

2. ***Private Employers.*** Oklahoma law holds that private employers have a legitimate interest in ensuring drug and alcohol-free work environments and that where the employer's drug testing program is reasonably designed to achieve that end, at-will employees have no cognizable claim for wrongful discharge. Gilmore, 878 P.2d at 364. The constitutional right of privacy affords protection against governmental intrusions and is not enforceable against private individuals or corporations. Id. at 365. See II.B(1), supra, for discussion of the applicability of Oklahoma's statutory Standards for Workplace Drug and Alcohol Testing Act to private employers.

3. ***Public Employers.*** The Oklahoma Supreme Court recognizes the U.S. Supreme Court's directive that, under defined circumstances, mandatory drug testing of employees by public employers will be upheld. See id. at 367 (citing Skinner v. Railway Labor Executives Ass'n, 489 U.S. 602, 109 S. Ct. 1402, 103 L.Ed.2d 639 (1989)). The drug-testing procedures of public employers are evaluated under the Fourth Amendment using these criteria: (1) the presence of state action by either a governmental entity or a private party acting as an instrument or agent of the government; (2) a

mandatory drug test; (3) the absence of particularized suspicion; and (4) a compelling state interest in ensuring that employees do not use drugs. Id. See II.B(1), supra, for discussion of the applicability of Oklahoma's statutory Standards for Workplace Drug and Alcohol Testing Act to public employers.

C. Medical Testing

1. ***Common law and statutes.*** An employer may condition an offer of employment on the results of a pre-employment medical examination that is given to all applicants regardless of disability and for the sole purpose of measuring an applicant's ability to perform job-related functions. Okla. Admin. Code § 335:15-9-4(a). Information obtained from these tests must be collected on separate forms and kept confidential except from supervisors and managers, safety and first aid personnel, and government officials who need the information, under the same conditions as they would have access to information that applicants voluntarily provide about their disability as part of a permissible pre-employment inquiry. Okla. Admin. Code § 335:15-9-4(d). This has not changed due to the Privacy Rule, because the Privacy Rule only preempts state law if it is contrary, meaning that it is impossible to comply with both requirements. 45 C.F.R. § 160.202-03. Further, the Privacy Rule itself provides exceptions to the general rule of federal preemption for contrary state laws, including state laws that relate to the privacy of individually identifiable health information and provide greater privacy protections or privacy rights with respect to such information. Id.

The Privacy Rule, published in final form on August 14, 2002, was adopted pursuant to the Health Insurance Portability and Accountability Act of 1996 ("HIPAA"), Pub. Law 104-191. The Privacy Rule attempts to assure that individuals' health information is properly protected while allowing the flow of health information needed to provide and promote high quality health care and to protect the public's health and well being.

The Privacy Rule standards address the use and disclosure of individuals' health information (called "protected health information") by organizations subject to the Privacy Rule (called "covered entities"), as well as standards for individuals' privacy rights to understand and control how their health information is used. "Covered entities" include health plans, health care clearinghouses, and health care providers who transmit any health information in electronic form in connection with a covered transaction. 45 C.F.R. § 160.103.

A covered entity may not use or disclose protected health information, except either (1) as the Privacy Rule permits or requires; or (2) as the individual who is the subject of the information (or the individual's personal representative) authorizes in writing. 45 C.F.R. § 164.502(a). "Protected health information" is individually identifiable health information held or transmitted by a covered entity or its business associate, in any form or medium, whether electronic, paper, or oral. 45 C.F.R. § 160.103. However, this definition does not include various records, including employment records held by a covered entity in its role as employer. Id.

A covered entity, except in certain exceptions, must make reasonable efforts to use, disclose, and request only the minimum amount of protected health information needed to accomplish the intended purpose of the use, disclosure, or request. 45 C.F.R. §§ 164.502(b), 164.514(d).

2. ***Private Employers.*** No reported cases.

3. ***Public Employers.*** No reported cases.

D. Polygraph Tests

Oklahoma has not enacted legislation regarding the use of polygraph testing as a condition of employment. However, the Oklahoma Supreme Court noted that the Employee Polygraph Protection Act, enacted by Congress in 1988, makes it unlawful, except in limited situations, for an employer to "directly or indirectly, require, request, suggest, or cause any employee or prospective employee to take or submit to any lie detector test." See Pearson v. Hope Lumber & Supply Co., 1991 OK 112, 820 P.2d 443, 445.

Oklahoma has not expressly authorized the use of polygraph testing by employers. However, in Vernon v. Seven-Eleven Stores, 1976 OK 34, 547 P.2d 1300, compensation was denied for an accidental injury sustained during employment when the employee had a mental illness induced by his submission to a polygraph test required by his employer.

E. Fingerprinting

There are no reported cases or statutory provisions concerning fingerprinting in the context of employment. However, in a matter of criminal concern, an Oklahoma court has noted that fingerprinting is not punishment and is useful in many circumstances, only some of which relate to law enforcement. See Lester v. State of Okla., 1966 OK CR 85, 416 P.2d 52, 57. In Lester, the court held that unless the burdens fingerprinting places on the individual are unreasonable, it will be upheld as one of those annoyances that must be suffered for the common good. Id.

III. SEARCHES

A. Employee's Person

No reported cases relating to an employment matter.

1. ***Private Employers.*** No reported cases.

2. ***Public Employers.*** No reported cases.

B. Employee's Work Area

The Court of Criminal Appeals of Oklahoma, relying on New York v. Burger, 482 U.S. 691, 107 S. Ct. 2626, 96 L.Ed.2d 601 (1987), stated that there is a different and lesser expectation of privacy on commercial property than there is in one's home, particularly in closely regulated industries. State v. Howerton, 2002 OK CR 17, 46 P.3d 154, 156-57. See also U.S. v. Johnson, 408 F.3d 1313, 1320-22 (10th Cir. 2005), cert. denied, 546 U.S. 951 (2005). The court used the three part test established in the Burger case to determine whether a warrantless inspection of a closely regulated industry was reasonable. There must be (1) "a 'substantial' government interest that informs the regulatory scheme pursuant to which the inspection is made…"; (2) the inspection must be necessary to further that scheme; and (3) the inspection program "must provide a constitutionally adequate substitute for a warrant." Id. at 157 (quoting New York, 482 U.S. at 702-03 (1987)). See also U.S. v. Gwathney, 465 F.3d 1133 (10th Cir. 2006) (permitting warrantless search of a commercial truck). Courts distinguish cases of an employee's expectation of privacy in his own office from an employee's expectation of privacy in other areas of the workplace. See Williams v. City of Tulsa, 393 F. Supp. 2d 1124, 1129-30 (N.D. Okla. 2005). Whether an employee has an objectively reasonable expectation of privacy is an easier question where an area is not enclosed, where activities can be easily observed, and where other personnel have easy access to the area. See id.

In Lewis v. Tripp, 604 F.3d 1221 (10th Cir. 2010), the Tenth Circuit reversed the District Court's denial of summary judgment in favor of Defendant and remanded the case with instructions that the District Court enter summary judgment in favor of Defendant, Ronald Tripp. Oklahoma state authorities had revoked the Plaintiff's license to practice chiropractic medicine, but they suspected him of continuing his practice unlawfully. Thus, they sent out an administrative subpoena and searched his office. Specifically, they handed the subpoena to an employee while Dr. Lewis was out of the office and the receptionist handed over patient treatment cards she had at the front desk. It was also disputed whether records were taken from inside his personal desk. Dr. Lewis sued claiming that the search was carried out in violation of his Fourth Amendment rights and naming, among others, Dr. Tripp, the president of the Oklahoma Board of Chiropractic Examiners. However, the Tenth Circuit's Opinion did not focus on the search itself (although it found that Dr. Lewis did not demonstrate a constitutional violation), but rather found that summary judgment should be entered in favor of Dr. Tripp because Dr. Lewis did not present any evidence that Dr. Tripp, as the president of the Board, somehow knew or should have known that an unlawful investigation would follow from his decision to report Dr. Lewis's unauthorized practice of medicine, and was thus protected by qualified immunity.

C. Employee's Property

In U.S. v. Angevine, the Tenth Circuit held that a college professor did not have a reasonable expectation of privacy in his university issued computer. U.S. v. Angevine, 281 F.3d 1130, 1134 (10th Cir. 2002), cert. denied 537 U.S. 845 (2002). The court said that the privacy expectations of a public employee may be decreased by "actual office practices and procedures, or by legitimate regulation." Id. (quoting O'Connor v. Ortega, 480 U.S. 709, 717, 107 S. Ct. 1492, 94 L.Ed.2d 714 (1987)). The court listed additional factors taken into consideration, including, "(1) the employee's relationship to the item seized; (2) whether the item was in the immediate control of the employee when it was seized; and (3) whether the employee took actions to maintain his privacy in the item." Id. (quoting United States v. Anderson, 154 F.3d 1225, 1229 (10th Cir. 1998)).

Similar to U.S. v. Angevine, the Tenth Circuit held in U.S. v. Barrows that an employee did not have a reasonable expectation of privacy in his personal computer that he brought to work for business purposes. U.S. v. Barrows, 481 F.3d 1246 (10th Cir. 2007). Even though it was his own personal computer, the Court examined the factors set forth in Angevine and held that the employee did not have a legitimate expectation of privacy because the computer was being used for business purposes, the employee voluntarily moved his personal computer to a public place for work-related use, and the employee failed to password protect his computer, turn it off, or take any other steps to prevent third-party use. Id. at 1248-49.

The 2004 Oklahoma legislature enacted a bill that amended the Oklahoma Firearms Act and the Oklahoma Self-Defense Act and prohibited employers from establishing any policy or rule that had the effect of prohibiting any person, except a convicted felon, from transporting and storing firearms in a locked vehicle on any property set aside for the vehicle. See H.B. 2122, 49th Leg., 2d Reg. Sess. (Okla. 2004) (amending Okla. Stat. tit. 21, §§ 1289.7a, 1290.22). These statutes were initially introduced as a reaction to rulings in a lawsuit filed in 2002, Bastible, et al v. Weyerhauser Co., 437 F.3d 999 (10th Cir. 2006). In Bastible, six contractors were discharged for having weapons in their vehicle in violation of Weyerhauser policy. Id. They brought public policy wrongful discharge claims against Weyerhauser, and the Court, in that case, found for Weyerhauser. Id. The Tenth Circuit affirmed the District Court's opinion. Id.

This new law was initially to become effective on November 1, 2004, but the Court entered an Order permanently enjoining the State of Oklahoma from enforcing the statute, finding that it was a violation of the property owners' 5th and 14th Amendment rights as an impermissible taking, is unconstitutionally vague, deprives property owners of due process, and is pre-empted by federal law. See Whirlpool Corp. v. Henry, No. 04-CV-820 (N.D. Okla. temp. restraining order granted Oct. 29, 2004). In response to this ruling, the 2005 Oklahoma legislature enacted a bill amending the OFA. See H.B. 1243, 50th Leg., 1st Reg. Sess. (Okla. 2005) (amending Okla. Stat. tit. 21, § 1289.7a). Thus, the Court in Whirlpool (now known as ConocoPhillips Company v. Henry) addressed both the 2004 and 2005 bills in determining whether to issue a permanent injunction. ConocoPhillips Company v. Henry, 520 F. Supp. 2d 1282 (N.D. Okla. 2007). The Court found that the bills impermissibly conflicted with and were preempted by federal law, specifically the Occupational Safety and Health Act ("OSHA"). See id. Thus, the Court enjoined the enforcement of the 2004 and 2005 amendments to the OFA and OSDA against any entity that is an "employer" as defined by OSHA. See id. However, in 2009, the Tenth Circuit reversed the District Court's grant of a permanent injunction and upheld the amendments to the OFA and OSDA permitting employees the right to keep firearms in their locked vehicles. Ramsey Winch, Inc. v. Henry, 555 F.3d 1199 (10th Cir. 2009). **The 2012 legislature amended the statute to prohibit employers from establishing any policy or rule that has the effect of prohibiting any person, except a convicted felon, from transporting and storing firearms or ammunition in a locked motor vehicle, or from transporting and storing firearms or ammunition locked in or locked to a motor vehicle on any property set aside for any motor vehicle. Okla. Stat. tit. 21, § 1290.22.**

1. ***Private Employers.*** No reported cases. See III.C, supra.

2. ***Public Employers.*** No reported cases.

IV. MONITORING OF EMPLOYEES

A. Telephones and Electronic Communications

Under the Security of Communications Act, Okla. Stat. tit. 13, §§ 176.1, et seq., it is unlawful, in Oklahoma, to willfully intercept, use, or disclose any contents of a wire, oral or electronic communication. Okla. Stat. tit. 13 § 176.3. This includes both telephone and electronic communications. Okla. Stat. tit. 13 § 176.2. A violation of this Act is a felony punishable by a fine of not less than five thousand dollars ($5,000) and/or imprisonment of not more than five (5) years. Okla. Stat. tit. 13 § 176.3. Oklahoma allows an exception if one of the interceptors is a party to the conversation or if consent was given by one of the parties to the conversation. Okla. Stat. tit. 13 § 176.4. Although it is not an employment case, State v. Serrato, 2007 OK CR 44, 176 P.3d 356, provides guidance on the application of the Oklahoma Security of Communications Act.

1. ***Wiretapping.*** No reported cases. See IV.A, supra.

2. ***Electronic Communications.*** No reported cases. See IV.A, supra.

3. ***Other Electronic Monitoring.*** No reported cases. See IV.A, supra.

B. Mail

No reported cases.

C. Surveillance/Photographing

In Williams v. City of Tulsa, 393 F. Supp. 1124 (N.D. Okla. 2005), the Court examined whether various surveillance and recording allegations violated the Electronic Communications Privacy Act, 18 U.S.C. § 2510, et seq. However, the Court determined that the Plaintiffs were unable to show an interception of their communications and therefore establish a claim under the Act. Id.

V. ACTIVITIES OUTSIDE THE WORKPLACE

A. Statute or Common Law

See V.C, infra, for discussion of Oklahoma's statutory provisions relating to employees' tobacco use. See II.B, supra, for discussion of Oklahoma's statutory provisions relating to drug and alcohol testing of employees.

B. Employees' Personal Relationships

No case specifically speaks about monitoring employees relationships, but in N.H. v. Presbyterian Church (U.S.A.), 1999 OK 88, 998 P.2d 592, the court noted that an employer's query to an employee about sexual behavior may be subject to constitutional claims for invasion of privacy and sexual harassment.

1. ***Romantic Relationships Between Employees.*** No reported cases.

2. ***Sexual Orientation.*** No reported cases.

3. ***Marital Status.*** No reported cases.

C. Smoking

Under Oklahoma law, it is unlawful for an employer to discharge or otherwise discriminate against employees or applicants for employment on the basis that they smoke or do not smoke or because they use tobacco products during nonworking hours. Okla. Stat. tit. 40, § 500(1). Additionally, an employer may not require as a condition of employment that an employee or applicant abstain from smoking or using tobacco products during nonworking hours. Okla. Stat. tit. 40, § 500(2). However, employers may impose conditions for smoking on the job or in the workplace, or restrict smoking based upon a bona fide occupational qualification or an applicable collective bargaining agreement that prohibits or allows off-duty tobacco use. Okla. Stat. tit. 40, §§ 501-02. Damages available to employees for violation of this statute are wages and benefits the employee was denied because of the employer's violation, plus reasonable attorney's fees and court costs. Okla. Stat. tit. 40, § 503.

D. Blogging

No reported cases.

VI. RECORDS

A. Personnel Records

Personnel records of public employees which relate to employment decisions may be kept confidential, as well as, any personnel records the disclosure of which would "constitute a clearly unwarranted invasion of personal privacy." Okla. Stat. tit. 51, § 24A.7(A). Additionally, public bodies shall keep confidential the home address, telephone numbers, and social security numbers of public employees. Okla. Stat. tit. 51, § 24A.7(D). However, personnel records of public employees consisting of employment applications, dates of employment and final disciplinary actions shall be made available to the public. Okla. Stat. tit. 51, § 24A.7(B). State employers may disclose a current or former employee's job performance information to prospective employers only if the disclosure is made at the request of or with the consent of the employee. 1997 OK AG 48. There is no similar requirement for private employers. See Nichols v. Pray, Walker, Jackman, Williamson & Marler, 2006 OK CIV APP 115, 144 P.3d 907, n.7.

In December 2009, the Oklahoma Attorney General, in response to a request, submitted an opinion responding to various questions about the confidentiality of public records. 2009 OK AG 33. The opinion provides that (1) a public body has discretion to determine that disclosing a personnel record indicated the date of birth of a public employee is un unwarranted invasion of the employee's personal privacy under Okla. Stat. tit. 51, § 24A.7(A)(2), (2) in making the determination, the public body may weigh the employee's interest in non-disclosure against the public's interest in having access to the record, and (3) where the employee's interest in non-disclosure is dominant, birth dates should be kept confidential while releasing the balance of the requested personnel record. Id. The opinion also addresses the circumstances in which a public body must disclose the name of an employee who is on administrative leave with pay and facing potential disciplinary action. Id. If under the public body's personnel policies placing an employee on administrative leave with pay is the usual procedure during an internal personnel investigation, the public body may keep any record related to that action confidential under Okla. Stat. tit. 51, § 24A.7(A). Id. Once an investigation is complete and a final disciplinary action that qualifies under Okla. Stat. tit. 51, § 24A.7(B) occurs, the records indicating that action must be available for public inspection and copying. Id.

In Okla. Public Employees Ass'n v. State ex rel. Okla. Office of Personnel Management, 2011 OK 68, 267 P.3d 838, the Oklahoma Supreme Court issued an opinion in response to two requests to obtain information about the disclosure of the names, birth dates, and employee identification numbers of all state employees. The Court held that the legislative language utilized in Okla. Stat. tit. 51, § 24A.7(A)(2) indicates the legislature intended to provide a non-exclusive list of examples of information, release of which may amount to a clearly unwarranted invasion of State employees' personal privacy; and, that where a claim is made that disclosure would constitute a clearly unwarranted invasion of personal privacy within the meaning of the statute, application of a case-by-case balancing test is utilized to determine whether personal information is subject to release. Id. The Court applied a balancing test, determined that significant privacy interests are at stake while the public's interest either in employee birth dates or employee information numbers is minimal, and held that the release of birth dates and employee identification numbers of State employees "would constitute a clearly unwarranted invasion of personal privacy" under Okla. Stat. tit. 51, § 24A.7(A)(2). Id.

B. Medical Records

Under Oklahoma law, where the content of an employee's medical records is shown to be of legitimate concern to others in the workplace, for example an employee's supervisor, there is no liability for disclosing the content of those records to the other person. See Eddy v. Brown, 1986 OK 3, 715 P.2d 74, 77.

Records pertaining to all drug or alcohol testing are the property of the employer and, upon request of the applicant or employee tested, shall be made available for inspection and copying to the applicant or employee. Okla. Stat. tit. 40, § 560. **The employer may not release such records to any person other than the applicant, employee, or the review officer, except for the following purposes: (1) as admissible evidence by an employer or the individual tested in a case or proceeding before a court of record or administrative agency if either the employer or the individual tested are named parties in the case or proceeding; (2) in order to comply with a valid judicial or administrative order; or (3) to an employer's employees, agents, or representatives who need access to such records for certain purposes. Id.** Additionally the testing facility may not disclose to the employer any information relating to the general health, pregnancy, or other physical or mental condition of the applicant or employee. Id.

A covered entity, except in certain exceptions, must make reasonable efforts to use, disclose, and request only the minimum amount of protected health information needed to accomplish the intended purpose of the use, disclosure, or request. 45 C.F.R. §§ 164.502(b), 164.514(d).

A covered entity must develop and implement written privacy policies and procedures that are consistent with the Privacy Rule. 45 C.F.R. § 164.530(i). These policies and procedures, as well as privacy practices notices, disposition of complaints, and other actions, activities, and designations required by the Privacy Rules must be maintained until six years after the later of the date of their creation or last effective date. 45 C.F.R. § 164.530(j).

See II.C, supra, for more information regarding the Privacy Rule and HIPAA.

C. Criminal Records

Oklahoma has enacted the Open Records Act which entitles individuals to certain records maintained by a "public body," including most criminal records. See Okla. Stat. tit. 51, § 24A.8. See also Lawson v. Curnutt, 2010 OK CIV APP 78, 239 P.3d 192; Okla. State Bd. of Med. Licensure & Supervision v. Migliaccio, 1996 OK CIV APP 37, 917 P.2d 483. An employer, however, may not require an employee or applicant to disclose any information contained in sealed criminal records. Okla. Stat. tit. 22, § 19(F). Oklahoma law specifically authorizes an employer to obtain criminal records for some types of employment. See, e.g., Okla. Stat. tit. 63, § 1-1950.1(B)(1) (authorizing an employer to obtain criminal records for certain medical professionals employed in particular industries). However, those records generally are to remain confidential, and shall be destroyed after one year from the end of employment. See, e.g., Okla. Stat. tit. 63, § 1-1950.1(E).

D. Subpoenas/Search Warrants

No reported cases.

VII. ACTIONS SUBSEQUENT TO EMPLOYMENT

A. References

Under Oklahoma law, an employer may provide an employment reference to a prospective employer of a current or former employee with the consent of or at the request of the current or former employee. The employer is presumed to be acting in good faith, unless lack of good faith is shown by a preponderance of the evidence. The current or former employer shall be immune from civil liability for the disclosure or any consequences of such disclosure unless the presumption of good faith is rebutted upon a showing that the information disclosed by the current or former employer was false and the employer providing the information had knowledge of its falsity or acted with malice or reckless disregard for the truth. See Okla. Stat. tit. 40, § 61. Under this qualified immunity statute, an employer is not required to provide job performance information. That is, an employer could issue a "no comment" or remain silent. See Nichols v. Pray, Walker, Jackman, Williamson & Marler, 2006 OK CIV APP 115, 144 P.3d 907. Oklahoma declined, in this opinion, to impose a duty on employers to even verify employment. See id.

B. Non-Compete Agreements

Oklahoma statutes specifically provide that non-compete agreements are void and unenforceable, although the former employee may not directly solicit established customers of the employer if there is a non-solicitation agreement. See Okla. Stat. tit. 15, §§ 217, 219A. Although past Oklahoma cases allow non-compete agreements under a reasonable standard, these cases no longer offer precedential value.

The first case decided based upon this statute was Cardiovascular Surgical Specialists v. Mammana, 2002 OK 27, 61 P.3d 210. In Mammana, the Court reversed an arbitration panel and a District Court decision finding a non-compete provision enforceable. The Court found that part of the non-compete provision was void and unenforceable, as it was a "provision[] by which an employer sought to go beyond a prohibition on active solicitation and thus prevent fair competition." See id. The next case based upon this statute was Vanguard Environmental, Inc. v. Curler, 2008 OK CIV APP 57, 190 P.3d 1158. In Vanguard, the Court found that the non-complete provision was void and unenforceable and held that the provision could not be judicially reformed to make it enforceable because that would require extensive judicial alteration and the addition of material terms and provisions essential to the parties' contract. Id. The opinion in Vanguard provides a history of Oklahoma law on restraint of trade. The courts have recently decided a few cases providing more guidance on non-compete agreements in Oklahoma. First, in 2009, the Court affirmed the granting of a temporary injunction requiring a former employee (and former seller of the business) to comply with the terms of a non-compete agreement. Inergy Propane, LLC v. Lundy, 2009 OK CIV APP 8, 219 P.3d 547. This agreement fell into the exception to Oklahoma's restraint of trade provision with respect to the sale of a business. Id. (citing to Okla. Stat. tit. 15, § 218). **In 2011, the Court found that the non-compete covenant at issue was void and enforceable as against Oklahoma's public policy expressed in § 219A, and refused to judicially modify the covenant where it would have to be substantially excised leaving only a shell of the original agreement and would require the addition of at least one material term. Howard v. Nitro-Lift Technologies, L.L.C., 2011 OK 98, __ P.3d __. In 2012, the Court also analyzed personal liability for breach of a non-compete agreement in connection with the sale of a business. Smoot v. B&J Restoration Services, 2012 OK CIV APP 58, 279 P.3d 805.**

VIII. OTHER ISSUES

A. Statutes of Limitations

Oklahoma law provides a two year statute of limitations for an action for injury to the rights of another, not arising on contract, and not specifically enumerated as otherwise in the statute. Okla. Stat. tit. 12, § 95(3). In an action brought by an employee claiming mental anguish and emotional distress suffered on the job, the Oklahoma Supreme Court held that an injury to the rights of another not arising on contract must be brought within two years, unless it falls among those specifically enumerated tort claims which must be brought within one year. Williams v. Lee Way Motor Freight, 1984 OK 64, 688 P.2d 1294, 1297.

The Oklahoma Supreme Court also applied this two year statute of limitations to a false light invasion of privacy claim. Colbert v. World Publ'g Co., 1987 OK 116, 747 P.2d 286, 288-89. The Court's rationale in Colbert indicates the same limitations period is applicable for all privacy torts, negligent hiring, and intentional infliction of emotional distress claims. In addressing the "new tort theory" of false light invasion of privacy the court stated:

> This Court held that the Legislature's failure to include this new tort theory with the other more traditional theories, which had to be initiated within one year, was indicative of the Legislature's intent that action of this type be governed by the more general, two-year statute of limitation provided by 12 O.S. 1981 § 95(3). This reasoning is applicable here because the tort theory of false light invasion of privacy is not listed with those specific theories which must be sued upon within one year.

Id. at 289.

The Oklahoma Supreme Court recently examined the statute of limitations and the discovery rule for invasion of privacy claims in Woods v. Prestwick House, Inc., 2011 OK 9, 247 P.3d 1183. The Court held that because the concept of misappropriation of another's name or likeness as the tort of invasion of privacy arose before the legislature's enactment of Okla. Stat. tit. 12, §1449, the causes of action arising under the statute are governed by Okla. Stat. tit. 12, § 95(3) providing for a two year statute of limitations period for an action for injury to the rights of another. The Court then held that, where applicable, the discovery rule tolls the limitations period until a plaintiff learns of an injury and, through prudent investigation, can obtain sufficient facts to state a cause of action.

B. Worker's Compensation Exclusivity

The Oklahoma Worker's Compensation Act was substantially revised by the legislature in 2011. The Act still provides the exclusive rights and remedies of injured workers. The liability prescribed in the Act is exclusive and in place of all other liability of the employer and any of his or her employees, at common law or otherwise, for such injury, loss of services, or death to the employee, or the spouse, personal representative, parents, or dependents of the employee, or any other person, exception in the case of intentional tort, or where the employer has failed to secure the compensation of payment for the injured employee. Okla. Stat. tit. 85, § 302(A). An intentional tort exists only when the employee is injured as a result of willful, deliberate, specific intent of the employer to cause such injury, and allegations or proof that the employer had knowledge that such injury was substantially certain to result from the employer's conduct does not constitute an intentional tort. Okla. Stat. tit. 85, § 302(B).

There are no reported cases applying Oklahoma's worker's compensation exclusivity provision to privacy claims brought against employers, but Oklahoma courts have routinely dismissed actions based upon the provision wherein an employee who sustains an injury through the alleged negligence of the employer, that arises out of and in the course of employment, brings a claim for such negligence. This exclusive remedy provision may not apply if an employee was willfully injured by his employer. In Parret v. UNICCO Serv. Co., 2005 OK 54, 127 P.3d 572, the Oklahoma Supreme Court answered a certified question about the standard of intent necessary for an employee's tort claim against an employer to fall outside the protection of the Worker's Compensation Act. The Supreme Court adopted a "substantial certainty" standard, which requires that the employer desired to bring about the worker's injury or intended the act that caused the injury with knowledge that the injury was substantially certain to follow. See also Price v. Howard, 2010 OK 26, 236 P.3d 82; CompSource Oklahoma v. L&L Constr., Inc., 2009 OK CIV APP 28, 207 P.3d 415.

C. Pleading Requirements

In order to adequately plead an invasion of privacy cause of action based upon unreasonable publicity given to a person's private life, a plaintiff must allege that the published facts are private and not of public record and must also set forth facts sufficient to show the plaintiff's action were not of legitimate public concern. McCormack v. Okla. Publ'g Co., 1980 OK 98, 613 P.2d 737, 741; Sturgeon v. Retherford Publ'n, 1999 OK CIV APP 78, 987 P.2d 1218, 1224.

SURVEY OF OREGON EMPLOYMENT LIBEL LAW

Paula A. Barran
Barran Liebman LLP
601 SW 2nd Avenue, Suite 2300
Portland, Oregon 97204
Telephone: (503) 228-0500; Facsimile (503) 274-1212

(With Developments Reported Through **November 1, 2012**)

GENERAL COMMENTS

Oregon has a unified system of state trial and appellate courts. Oregon maintains a Supreme Court (the highest judicial tribunal), and a single level Court of Appeals (the intermediate level appellate court). Trial courts are the circuit courts and Oregon Tax Court. Formerly the state recognized limited jurisdiction district courts, but those merged into circuit courts in 1998. Trial court decisions are not reported. There is a reporter system for decisions of the Oregon Court of Appeals and a separate reporter system for decisions of the Oregon Supreme Court.

SIGNIFICANT DEVELOPMENTS SINCE THE 2012 *SURVEY*

None.

I. GENERAL LAW

A. General Employment Law

1. ***At Will Employment***. Employment is at will, but Oregon recognizes exceptions for contract, statute, and public policy. Patton v. J.C. Penney Co., 301 Or. 117, 719 P.2d 854 (1986). The public policy tort extends protection to conduct in support of an important public function or policy such as jury duty (Nees v. Hocks, 272 Or. 210, 536 P.2d 512 (1975)), or refusing to defame an employee (Delaney v. Taco Time, Int'l, 297 Or. 10, 681 P.2d 114 (1984)) as well as to employees who pursue important statutory rights related to their status as an employee (Brown v. Transcon Lines, 284 Or. 597, 588 P.2d 1087 (1978)).

Personnel policy statements, however, can create contractual obligations between an employee and an employer. Yartzoff v. Democrat-Herald Publishing Co., 281 Or. 651, 576 P.2d 356 (1978), though an employer may reserve the unilateral power to make a final decision if properly stated in the manual. Lund v. Arbonne Intern., Inc., 132 Or. App. 87, 887 P.2d 817 (1994). Express at will language in an employment contract may be modified by statements or conduct inconsistent with at will status including progressive discipline. Bennett v. Farmers Insurance Co., 332 Or. 138, 26 P.3d 785 (2001).

B. Elements of Libel Claim

1. ***Basic Elements***. While Oregon generally distinguishes between libel and slander, both are generally called defamation. An oral statement is slander; a statement in written form is a libel. An oral slanderous statement which is then published in written form is a libel. Newton v. Family Federal Sav. and Loan Ass'n, 48 Or. App. 373, 616 P.2d 1213 (1980).

State law requires a defamatory statement, defined to be one which subjects a person to hatred, contempt or ridicule or tends to diminish the esteem, respect, goodwill or confidence in which the subject is held, or which excites adverse, derogatory or unpleasant feelings or opinions against the subject. Worley v. Oregon Physicians Service, 69 Or. App. 241, 686 P.2d 404 (1984), rev. denied, 298 Or. 334, 691 P.2d 483 (1984). The communication must be both false and defamatory. Reesman v. Highfill, 327 Or. 597, 965 P.2d 1030 (1998), must concern the plaintiff, Id., and must be published to a third person. Downs v. Waremart, Inc., 324 Or. 307, 926 P.2d 314 (1966).

2. ***Fault***.

a. **Private Figure Plaintiff/Matter of Public Concern**. A public figure is one who enters a public controversy to influence its resolution. Wheeler v. Green, 286 Or. 99, 593 P.2d 777 (1979). With media defendants, and speech on an issue of public concern, private plaintiffs must show that the defendants acted negligently. Bank of Oregon v. Independent News, Inc., 298 Or. 434, 693 P.2d 35, 11 Media L. Rep. 1313 (1985), cert. den. 474 U.S. 826, 106 S.Ct. 84, 88 L.Ed.2d 69 (1985). The Oregon Supreme Court has held, however, that the Gertz standard only applies to media defendants. Harley-Davidson v. Markley, 279 Or. 361, 568 P.2d 1359 (1977). Public figures and public officials must still prove actual malice, regardless of the defendant's status. Wheeler v. Green, 286 Or. 99, 593 P.2d 777 (1979).

b. Private Figure Plaintiff/Matter of Private Concern. Oregon courts have not addressed the applicable fault standard in cases involving private figure plaintiffs and speech that is not of public concern.

c. Public Figure Plaintiff/Matter of Public Concern. A public figure must prove that the allegedly defamatory statement was made with actual malice, that is, knowledge of its falsity or with reckless disregard of whether it was false or not. Reesman v. Highfill, 149 Or. App. 374, 942 P.2d 891 (1997), rev'd in part, 327 Or. 597, 965 P.2d 1030 (1998). Proof must be by clear and convincing evidence, for actual malice is not presumed and may not be inferred from the fact of a defamatory publication alone. Lonsdale v. Swart, 143 Or. App. 331, 922 P.2d 1263 (1996), rev. denied, 325 Or. 247, 936 P.2d 363; Victoria v. LeBlanc, 168 Or. App. 586, 7 P.3d 668 (2000). A recently terminated city administrator is still a public official for purposes of defamation where the statements in question criticized work done while a public official.

3. ***Falsity***. There is no liability if the statement is substantially true or if defendant is able to justify the gist or sting of the statement. Shirley v. Freunscht, 81 Or. App. 221, 724 P.2d 907 (1986), rev'd on other grounds, 303 Or. 234, 735 P.2d 600 (1987), citing Prosser and Keeton Torts 842, § 116 (5th ed 1984). A plaintiff must prove falsity in cases that involve public figures or public concerns. Hickey v. Settlemeier, 141 Or. App. 103, 917 P.2d 44 (1996), rev.den. 323 Or. 690, 920 P.2d 549 (1996). Falsity must be shown. Greenwood v. Tillamook County, 2006 WL 2400075 (D. Or. 2006) (plaintiff failed to prove falsity of statements that he behaved inappropriately by relying on general non-specific statements of others that he was generally well-behaved).

4. ***Defamatory Statement of Fact***. It is a question of law whether an assertion is capable of a defamatory meaning, Reesman v. Highfell, 327 Or. 597, 965 P.2d 1030 (1998), and whether it constitutes a fact or an opinion. Bock v. Zittenfield, 66 Or. App. 97, 672 P.2d 1237 (1983), rev. den. 296 Or. 486, 677 P.2d 702 (1984). Simpson v. Burrows, 90 F. Supp. 2d 1108 (D. Or. 2000). Buckner v. Home Depot U.S.A., Inc., 188 Or. App. 307, 71 P.3d 150 (2003), rev. den. 336 Or. 92, 79 P.3d 313 (2003) (also holding that a statement in the form of an opinion may be treated as a representation of fact if the parties are on an unequal footing and do not have equal knowledge or means of knowledge so that what on the surface appears as an opinion actually implies the existence of facts that are undisclosed to the listener). Whether statements are defamatory is a question of fact for the jury to decide. Bendl v. Parks, 164 Or. App. 699, 994 P.2d 802 (2000). Oregon adopts Restatement (Second) of Torts § 566 (1981), noting two kinds of expressions of opinion including an opinion in form or context apparently based on facts regarding the plaintiff or his conduct that have not been stated by the defendant or assumed to exist by the parties to the communication, and citing Adler v. American Standard Corp., 538 F. Supp. 572 (D. Md.1982) (statement that plaintiff was terminated for "unsatisfactory performance" capable of defamatory meaning because based on undisclosed defamatory facts with a reasonable implication that the plaintiff was guilty of some misconduct, negligence or incompetence in the performance of duties); Slover v. Oregon State Bd. of Clinical Social Workers, 144 Or. App. 565, 927 P.2d 1098 (1996) (statement that social worker engaged in dubious therapeutic technique with boys could have been understood to be based on undisclosed facts and therefore not protected as opinion). Statement in respect to drug testing that "nothing less than 100% accuracy is acceptable" not capable of defamatory meaning. Ishikawa v. Delta Air Lines, 149 F.Supp.2d 1246 (D. Or. 2001). Statement by supervisor that plaintiff was terminated for altering a urine specimen but that other reasons were reflected in her personnel file is too vague to be capable of defamatory meaning. Id. There can be defamation by implication if a defamatory inference can be drawn from a facially non-defamatory communication. In such a case the length between the communication and the defamatory inference must not be "too tenuous," that is, that the inference must be reasonable. See Brown v. Gatti, 341 Or 452, 145 P.3d 130 (2006).

5. ***Of and Concerning Plaintiff.*** Even if a statement does not directly refer to a person by name, a jury may infer that the publication relates to him or her, including through the direct testimony of the recipient of the publication. Direct testimony of the recipients' understanding of the defamatory nature is not required if other evidence is sufficient to permit an inference of such an understanding. Wheeler v. Green, 286 Or. 99, 593 P.2d 777 (1979). Direct testimony of the recipients' understanding of the defamatory nature of a libel is not required if other evidence is sufficient to permit an inference of such an understanding. Wheeler v. Green, 286 Or. 99, 593 P.2d 777 (1979) (published letter referring to a "supertrainer" known in the industry), citing Beecher v. Montgomery Ward & Co., Inc., 267 Or. 496, 517 P.2d 667 (1973) and Glenn v. Esco Corp., 268 Or. 278, 520 P.2d 443 (1974).

6. ***Publication***.

a. Intracorporate Communication. Publication is an essential element of an action for defamation; that is proved when a statement is communicated to a third party. Because the interest protected by the law of defamation is an individual's interest in his or her reputation, both in the community at large and in that individual's professional community, Oregon has refused to adopt the intracorporate, nonpublication rule. Instead, a defamatory communication from one corporate employee to another corporate employee concerning the job performance of a third employee is published for purpose of a defamation claim. Wallulis v. Dymowski, 323 Or. 337, 918 P.2d 755 (1996) (statement by employee who was also union official made to supervisor); Lansford v. Georgetown Manor Inc., 192 Or. App. 261, 84 P.3d 1105 (2004), mod., 193 Or. App. 59, 88 P.3d 305 (2004), rev. denied, 337 Or. 182, 94 P.3d 877 (2004) (statement that plaintiff had misappropriated company property by taking home merchandise she planned to purchase was published for purposes of defamation claim when it was communicated to other managers). However an inadvertent publication is insufficient to satisfy this element. Morrow v. II Morrow Inc., 139 Or. App. 212, 911 P.2d 964 (1996), rev. denied, 323 Or. 153, 916 P.2d 312 (1996) (publication to a third person must be intentional or negligent; employer did not libel employee by inadvertent or accidental publication through inadequately erasing memo from drive of computer network).

b. **Compelled Self-Publication**. The Oregon Court of Appeals initially recognized the tort of compelled self-publication defamation in Downs v. Waremart, 137 Or. App. 119, 903 P.2d 888 (1995); on appeal, the Oregon Supreme Court did not specifically reach the issue despite an appeal on that precise issue. Downs v. Waremart, 324 Or. 307, 926 P.2d 314 (1996). The matter was settled by the Oregon legislature with ORS 30.178(2) holding that an action for defamation may not be maintained by an employee against an employer based on a claim that in seeking subsequent employment the former employee will be forced to reveal the reasons given by the employer for the termination. In Koanui v. Cenveo, 2004 WL 2632785 (D. Or. 2004) (dismissing defamation claim) and 2005 WL 2465813 (D. Or. 2005) (granting employer motion for summary judgment on remaining claims), the federal court for the District of Oregon refused to accept such a claim, but without citing the statute.

c. **Republication**. An oral statement made to a newspaper reporter which is then published is a libel. Newton v. Family Federal Sav. and Loan Ass'n, 48 Or. App. 373, 616 P.2d 1213 (1980). Liability flows if the republication is authorized or intended, or that the original speaker could reasonably have expected such republication. Wheeler v. Green, 286 Or. 99, 593 P.2d 777 (1979). Statements posted on a union website do not result in liability because the provider of a website (an interactive computer service) is not a publisher of the content posted by another. Roskowski v. Corvallis Police Officers' Association, 2005 WL 555398 (findings and recommendation granting summary judgment on defamation) and 2005 WL 1429917 (D. Or. 2005) (adopting magistrate findings and recommendation), aff'd 250 Fed. Appx. 816 (9th Cir. 2007), citing the Communications Decency Act of 1996.

7. ***Statements versus Conduct***. Conduct is actionable as defamation as long as the inference from the conduct is not "too tenuous" to support the claim. Bickford v. Tektronix, Inc., 116 Or. App. 547, 842 P.2d 432 (1992) (posting guard who did nothing more than stand and observe from some distance too tenuous to render act possibly defamatory).

8. ***Damages***. Compensatory damages are measured by the injury to plaintiff's reputation and the resulting humiliation and mental anguish. Wheeler v. Green, 286 Or. 99, 593 P.2d 777 (1979).

Damages may be reduced by proof that plaintiff had a poor reputation (but not character) before the allegedly defamatory statements were made. Reputation is an essential element of the plaintiff's claim and of the defense. Shirley v. Freunscht, 81 Or. App. 221, 724 P.2d 907 (1986), rev'd on other grounds 303 Or. 234, 735 P.2d 600 (1987). A defendant may also offer evidence of any mitigating circumstances. Shirley v. Freunscht, 81 Or. App. 221, 724 P.2d 907 (1986) rev'd on other grounds 303 Or. 234, 735 P.2d 600 (1987) citing ORCP 20E(2). Pleading mitigation in the answer is permissive, not mandatory, and evidence may be offered notwithstanding a failure to plead. Shirley v. Freunscht, 81 Or. App. 221, 724 P.2d 907 (1986) rev'd on other grounds 303 Or. 234, 735 P.2d 600 (1987).

a. **Presumed Damages and Libel Per Se**. A libel (written form) is defamatory per se. A slander imputing unfitness to perform the duties of one's employment is actionable per se. Newton v. Family Federal Sav. and Loan Ass'n, 48 Or. App. 373, 616 P.2d 1213 (1980).

A statement that a construction worker had been drinking before coming to work and was intoxicated on the job site is capable of a per se defamatory meaning. Affolter v. Baugh Construction Oregon, Inc., 183 Or. App. 198, 51 P.3d 642 (2002).

A statement that a worker had threatened to torture a company official to get information as a result of being turned away from a job is not defamatory *per se* because it does not attack competence to perform job duties as an electrician. Kofoed v. Rosendin Electric, Inc., 157 F. Supp. 2d 1152 (D. Or. 2001).

A statement that an employee has committed theft is defamatory as a matter of law, even if it does not specifically relate to work performance. Worley v. Oregon Physicians Service, 69 Or. App. 241, 686 P.2d 404 (1984), rev. denied, 298 Or. 334, 691 P.2d 483 (1984).

Statements accusing someone of conduct that would be criminal are defamatory per se even if the speaker has not explicitly given the conduct the name of a particular crime. Muresan v. Philadelphia Romanian Pentecostal Church, 154 Or. App. 465, 962 P.2d 711 (1998), rev. denied, 327 Or. 621, 971 P.2d 413 (1998).

Where the defamation is actionable per se, the plaintiff need not allege or prove any special damages. General damages are presumed and may be recovered without evidence of the harm incurred. Benassi v. Georgia Pacific, 62 Or. App. 698, 662 P.2d 760 (1983), mod., 63 Or. App. 672, 667 P.2d 532, rev. denied, 295 Or. 730, 670 P.2d 1035 (1983). Loss of earning capacity is part of the damage to business reputation, and evidence of inability to secure employment caused by the defamation is admissible to show that loss. Cook v. Safeway Stores Inc., 266 Or. 77, 511 P.2d 375 (1973).

Oregon limits the rule in Gertz v. Robert Welch, Inc., 418 U.S. 323, 94 S. Ct. 2997, 41 L.Ed.2d 789 (1974) to media defendants so long as the plaintiff is neither a public official nor a public figure. All defendants, however, not just media defendants, are protected by the rule in New York Times Company v. Sullivan, 376 US 254, 84 S. Ct. 710, 11 L.Ed.2d 686 (1964), in cases involving comment upon public officials and public figures. Wheeler v. Green, 286 Or. 99, 593 P.2d 777 (1979).

(1) **Employment-Related Criticism**. In the professional context a statement is defamatory if false and relates conduct characteristics or a condition incompatible with the proper conduct of a lawful business trade or profession. See Brown v. Gatti, 341 Or 452, 145 P.3d 130 (2006). A slander imputing unfitness to perform the duties of one's employment is actionable per se. Newton v. Family Federal Sav. and Loan Ass'n, 48 Or. App. 373, 616 P.2d 1213 (1980). A statement falsely ascribing to a person characteristics or conduct that would adversely affect his fitness for his occupation or profession is capable of having a defamatory meaning. Bock v. Zittenfield, 66 Or. App. 97, 672 P.2d 1237 (1983), rev. denied, 296 Or. 486, 677 P.2d 702 (1984) (statement that news reporter was discharged because of unsatisfactory coverage on two occasions, and second statement that he "simply didn't perform his job" both actionable because a jury could find in each an implication that plaintiff lacked the qualities or skill and competence normally expected of a reporter). See also Walsh v. Consolidated Freightways, 278 Or. 347, 563 P.2d 1205 (1977) (statement that "I wouldn't hire him as a supervisor" could have been understood to be defamatory as impugning plaintiff's work record); Newton v. Family Federal Savings & Loan, 48 Or. App. 373, 616 P.2d 1213 (1980) (statement that plaintiff was "administratively incapable" capable of defamatory meaning). However, a racially derogatory statement that certain jobs were suitable only for members of a particular race is not defamatory per se without additionally stating that plaintiff is unable to do his work. L&D of Oregon, Inc. v. American States Insurance Company, 171 Or. App. 17, 14 P.3d 617 (2000).

A statement that an employee has committed theft is defamatory as a matter of law, even if it does not specifically relate to work performance. Worley v. Oregon Physicians Service, 69 Or. App. 241, 686 P.2d 404 (1984), rev. denied, 298 Or. 334, 691 P.2d 483 (1984). However, a statement that an employee was terminated because of an inability to return to work was not defamatory. Walleri v. Federal Home Loan Bank, 83 F.3d 1575 (9th Cir 1996). A statement that plaintiff had purchased an appliance without paying for it was not defamatory as a matter of law where plaintiff had failed to follow procedures for prior approval of employee purchases and had not paid for the item until 5 months after she received it. Hardie v. Legacy Health System, 167 Or. App. 425, 6 P.3d 531 (2000) rev. denied, 332 Or. 656, 36 P.3d 973 (2001). A statement that plaintiff was fired for misappropriation of company property is capable of defamatory meaning because "misappropriate" can suggest a dishonest or unlawful taking. Lansford v. Georgetown Manor Inc., 192 Or. App. 261, 84 P.3d 1105 (2004), mod., 193 Or. App. 59, 88 P.3d 305 (2004), rev. denied, 337 Or. 182, 94 P.3d 877 (2004).

A statement that a construction worker had been drinking before coming to work and was intoxicated on the job site is capable of a per se defamatory meaning. Affolter v. Baugh Construction Oregon, Inc., 183 Or. App. 198, 51 P.3d 642 (2002).

Tubra v. Cooke, 233 Or. App. 339, 225 P.3d 862 (2010), rev. denied 348 Or. 621, 237 P.3d 221 (2010), presented the unusual circumstance of a defamation claim brought by a former pastor against his church and certain church officials. Defendants raised the free exercise clause as a defense. The court concluded that the free exercise clause bars a defamation claim by a pastor against his or her church if the organization is of religious character, if the alleged statements relate to its religious beliefs and practices and are of a kind that can only be classified as religious, but that if the statements are not exclusively religious in character the free exercise clause does not necessarily prevent adjudication although the statements may be qualifiedly privileged.

(2) **Single Instance Rule**. Statement of a single act of conduct that would adversely affect fitness for an occupation or profession is actionable if the act fairly implies an habitual course of similar conduct, or the want of the qualities or skill that the public is reasonably entitled to expect of persons engaged in such a calling. Bock v. Zittenfield, 66 Or. App. 97, 672 P.2d 1237 (1983), rev. denied, 296 Or. 486, 677 P.2d 702 (1984), citing Restatement (Second) of Torts § 573, comment d.

b. **Punitive Damages**. The Oregon Constitution does not permit recovery of punitive damages for speech, even though punitive damages are generally available in the state for non-speech related conduct. Wheeler v. Green, 286 Or. 99, 593 P.2d 777 (1979). This is so even if the tort is different. Hall v. May Dept. Stores Co., 292 Or. 131, 637 P.2d 126 (1981).

II. PRIVILEGES AND DEFENSES

A. Scope of Privileges

1. ***Absolute Privilege***. Oregon has recognized only a handful of situations in which defamatory statements are absolutely privileged, practically limited to legislative and judicial proceedings and other acts of state. Grubb v. Johnson et al, 205 Or. 624, 289 P.2d 1067 (1955); Wallulis v. Dymowski, 323 Or. 337, 918 P.2d 755 (1996); Janal v. Aramark, 2000 WL 1297708 (D. Or. 2000) (public officers acting under official duty or authority). Statements made to carry out a statutory requirement are also absolutely privileged. Christensen v. Marvin, 273 Or. 97, 539 P.2d 1082 (1975); Wallulis v. Dymowski, 323 Or. 337, 918 P.2d 755 (1996). DeLong v. Yu Enterprises Inc., 170 Or. App. 609, 13 P.3d 1012 (2000), which had held that an employer's report to police that money was missing during plaintiff's tenure was subject to an absolute privilege, was reversed. DeLong v. Yu Enterprises Inc., 334 Or. 166, 47 P.3d 8 (2002) with the court holding that a citizen making an informal statement to police should not enjoy blanket immunity from an action but rather that statements should receive protection only if they were made in good faith so as to discourage an abuse of the privilege. The court acknowledged that an earlier opinion in Ducosin v. Mott, 292 Or. 764, 642 P.2d 1168 (1982) might be read to say otherwise; to the extent that the dictum in that case could be read to suggest that informal statements to police are absolutely privileged, it is disavowed. Chamberlain v. City of Portland, 184 Or. App. 487, 56 P.3d 497 (2002), stated the rule that executive officers of public entities have an absolute privilege that in some circumstances acts as a complete bar to a claim for defamation. The Court of Appeals stated the rule adopted by the Supreme Court in Shearer v. Lambert, 274 Or 449, 547 P.2d 98 (1976), extending the privilege to inferior state officers in order to protect the right of public officers to discharge their duties free from intimidation, and applied this rule to the sworn police sergeant. A public official is protected even if statements are not made in connection with judicial or quasi-judicial proceedings. Instead, statements made as a result of an executive's status as a public official engaged in the performance of official duties are absolutely privileged. Johnson v. Brown and Deschutes County, 193 Or. App. 375, 91 P.3d 741 (2004) clarified 194 Or. App. 486, 95 P.3d 235 (2004) (statements by employee during investigation into possible official misconduct and work related wrongdoing by plaintiff absolutely privileged). But see Clifford v. City of Clatskanie, 204 Or. App. 566, 131 P.3d 783 (2006), rev. denied, 341 Or. 216, 140 P.3d 1133 (2006) (no absolute privilege for statements made by police officer to persons to whom he has no official duty to impart the information). The court concluded the privilege was not shown where a police officer told students that a fellow student had reported their drinking. Cross v. Safeway, Inc., 2004 WL 1969407 (findings and recommendation on summary judgment) and 2004 WL 2203257 (adopting findings and recommendation) (D. Or. 2004) (letter responding to union letter about effecting arbitration award absolutely privileged because labor arbitration is quasi-judicial). The absolute privilege which belongs to an executive officer also belongs to lower level executive officials such as a state LEDS education manager who reports having received complaints that the plaintiff employee had cheated on a certification test. Lucas v. Lake County, 2007 WL 1413001 (D. Or. 2007). But see Sizemore v. City of Madras, 2004 WL 1502891 (D. Or. 2005), rejecting mayor's motion for summary judgment due to lack of evidence that publication of allegedly defamatory letter was a statement he was required or authorized to make. Prosecutors are absolutely immune for statements made as prosecutor-advocates, but that protection does not extend to statements made to press despite argument that it is important to keep public informed. Christy v. Schrunk, 2006 WL 1515549 (D. Or. 2006). Statement made to a law school honor code committee for the purpose of initiating a claim and in furtherance of that process are absolutely privileged because such a committee acts as a quasi-judicial body in evaluating conduct and credentialing students. See Singh v. Tong, 2006 WL 3063495 (D. Or. 2006). Statements made to the Employment Department in connection with employee applications for benefits are absolutely privileged. Martinez- Delacruz v. Stuart Olson Farms, Inc., 2007 WL 3046489 (D. Or. 2007). Where the alleged defamatory statements are made by city police officers in the course and scope of their duties such as preparation of a police report, the conduct is not absolutely privileged but more properly the employees are protected by principles of absolute immunity. Nash v. Lewis, 365 Fed.Appx. 48 (9th Cir. 2010).

2. ***Qualified Privileges***.

a. **Common Interest**. A conditional privilege to make a defamatory statement can arise when it is made to protect the interests of an employer or when it is on a subject of mutual concern to the publisher and those to whom it is made. Wattenburg v. United Medical, 269 Or. 377, 525 P.2d 113 (1974); Worley v. Oregon Physicians Service, 69 Or. App. 241, 686 P.2d 404 (1984), rev. denied, 298 Or. 334, 691 P.2d 483 (1984). This includes statements made by an employer to employees other than the subject of the statement where there is a mutual interest such as internal security. Worley v. Oregon Physicians Service, 69 Or. App. 241, 686 P.2d 404 (1984), rev. denied, 298 Or. 334, 691 P.2d 483 (1984). Oregon law provides examples of many such situations including statements made to protect employee morale in the context of the termination of another, Bickford v. Tektronix, 116 Or. App. 547, 842 P.2d 432 (1992); statements made to a consultant or to persons who share a business interest in or with the speaker, Lund v. Arbonne Intern., Inc., 132 Or. App. 87, 887 P.2d 817 (1994); statements made by an insurance agent to protect insurer's reputation with former clients and retain them as customers and explain why plaintiff's proposals were not right for their situations, Shirley v. Freunscht, 81 Or. App. 221, 724 P.2d 907 (1986), rev'd on other grounds, 303 Or. 234, 735 P.2d 600 (1987). Statements that drug testing laboratory was

100% accurate, that plaintiff had altered her urine specimen and statements about plaintiff's termination for failing drug test were conditionally privileged and plaintiff failed to present evidence that the speaker lacked good faith belief in the truth of the matter. Ishikawa v. Delta Air Lines, 149 F.Supp.2d 1246 (D. Or. 2001).

Statements accusing someone within an employer's organization are necessarily on a subject of mutual concern to an employer and to its top management. Vanderselt v. Pope, 155 Or. App. 334, 963 P.2d 130 (1998), rev. denied, 328 Or. 194, 977 P.2d 1172 (1998). Cross v. Safeway, Inc., 2004 WL 1969407 and 2004 WL 2203257 (D. Or. 2004) (sending copies of letter responding to union letter about effecting arbitration award subject to qualified privilege where sent to union representative, store manager, division president, operations manager, human resources director, district manager and company arbitration attorney; all parties were appropriate recipients). Thompson v. Mentor Graphics Corporation, 2004 WL 2584022 (D. Or. 2004) (discussions with managers and reorganization consultants conditionally privileged). **The same principles governing qualified privilege apply to statements made not about a fellow employee but about a vendor or supplier of labor. Mannex Corp. v. Bruns, 250 Or. App. 50, 60, 279 P.3d 278, 285 (2012).** See also Blocker v. Wells Fargo Bank, 2010 WL 6403721 (D. Or. 2010) (bank had qualified privilege to communicate with its employees on the subject of a hold placed on depositor's bank account pending investigation into possible fraud).

Harrell v. Costco, 2010 WL 331773 (D. Or. 2010) aff'd 422 Fed. Appx. 635 (9th Cir. 2011) (employees who provided written statements of possible theft to police were conditionally privileged; good faith report of possible crime is conditionally privileged and there was no evidence that defendants abused the privilege).

However, motivation to act on behalf of an employer is not the only factual prerequisite for the qualified privilege which may be lost if the speaker does not believe the statement is true or lacks reasonable grounds for believing the truth of the statement. Affolter v. Baugh Construction Oregon, Inc., 183 Or. App. 198, 51 P.3d 642 (2002); Wilson v. Dollar Tree Stores, Inc., 161 Fed.Appx. 695 (9th Cir 2006) (employee needed to offer evidence of state of mind to show employer exceeded scope of privilege but failed to do so; employer could reasonably infer from undisputed facts that employee had permitted subordinate to work off the clock).

b. **Duty**. A qualified privilege exists generally, unless there is sufficient connection to a judicial or quasi-judicial forum for an absolute privilege to attach in which case the greater protection applies. Adamson v. Bonesteele, 295 Or. 815, 671 P.2d 693 (1983); Mount v. Welsh, 118 Or. 568, 247 P. 815 (1926).

c. **Criticism of Public Employee**. See Fender v. City of Oregon City, 811 F. Supp. 554, aff'd 37 F.3d 1505 (9th Cir. 1994), Roskowski v. Corvallis Police Officers' Association, 2005 WL 555398 (magistrate findings and recommendation) and 2005 WL 1429917 (D. Or. 2005) (adopting magistrate findings and recommendation). See also 250 Fed.Appx. 816 (9th Cir. 2007) (appeal on claim against union). **In Brocato v. City of Baker, 2012 WL 1085493 (D. Or. 2012), 2012 WL 1079805 (D. Or. 2012), defamation claims against city councilors related to city manager's discharge were rejected where statements were made during city council meeting or in response to inquiries by citizens, or in the course of recall campaign and therefore shielded by state Tort Claims Act.**

d. **Limitation on Qualified Privileges**. Oregon has adopted the portion of the Restatement (Second) of Torts § 599 on how a privilege can be abused, including the publisher's lack of belief or reasonable grounds for belief in the truth of the defamatory matter, because the defamatory matter is published for some purpose other than that for which the privilege is given, because the publication is made to some person not reasonably believed to be necessary for the accomplishment of the purpose of the privilege, or because the publication includes defamatory matter not reasonably believed to be necessary to accomplish the purpose for which the occasion is privileged. Schafroth v. Baker, 276 Or. 39, 553 P.2d 1046 (1976); Wilson v. Dollar Tree Stores, Inc., 161 Fed.Appx. 695 (9th Cir 2006) (employee needed to offer evidence of state of mind to show employer exceeded scope of privilege but failed to do so; employer could reasonably infer from undisputed facts that employee had permitted subordinate to work off the clock). And see U.S. Ex Rel Chartraw v. Cascade Healthcare Community, Inc., 2009 WL 588, 664 (D. Or. 2009). There the federal court held that in order to challenge a qualified privilege, the complaining party must show that the privilege was abused. A privilege can be abused if the speaker does not believe in good faith that the statement is true. To survive a motion for summary judgment on this issue a plaintiff must offer some evidence creating an issue of fact about the mental state of the speaker at the time the statement was made. **A privilege may also be abused if the speaker is motivated to discredit the target solely because the speaker wants the target's job. Javansalehi v. BF & Associates, Inc., 2011 WL 5239752 (D. Or. 2011), related opinion on wage claims 2012 WL 1566184 (D. Or. 2012).**

Where the privileged occasion is dissemination to other employees, that is limited. An employer is privileged to disseminate to its employees a certain amount of information regarding the discharge of another employee, but the amount of defamatory material that it is privileged to publish may depend on the position of the employees to whom the information is given. Benassi v. Georgia Pacific, 62 Or. App. 698, 662 P.2d 760 (1983), mod. 63 Or. App. 672, 667 P.2d

532, rev. denied, 295 Or. 730, 670 P.2d 1035 (1983). An employer may disclose allegedly defamatory matter about employee's termination to small group of employees involved in termination process or who worked directly with plaintiff. Lewis v. Carson Oil Company, 204 Or. App. 99, 127 P.3d 1207 (2006), rev. denied, 341 Or. 245, 142 P.3d 73 (Table) (2006). A statement in a temporary employee staffing employer's national database about plaintiff's criminal convictions was conditionally privileged where accessible only to managers and supervisors involved in placement. Olson v. ASI Staffing, Inc., 2005 WL 1839015 (D. Or. 2005).

A privilege is not abused by including truthful extraneous matter in the publication. IC Marketing Inc. v. Outdoor Empire Publishing, Inc., 2005 WL 525635 (D. Or. 2005). An individual retains the protection of the qualified privilege by taking reasonable steps to ascertain the truth of information. Sweet v. Tigard-Tualatin School District, 124 Fed.Appx. 482 (9th Cir. 2005) (school principal e-mails alerting staff to threats privileged where he spoke to administrative team and verified facts with two sources of information).

Plaintiff must provide some evidence of the mental state of the declarant at the time of the statement to demonstrate that the statements were made without a reasonable belief as to their truthfulness. Bickford v. Tektronix, Inc., 116 Or. App. 547, 842 P.2d 432 (1992), Bendl v. Parks, 164 Or. App. 699, 994 P.2d 802 (2000); Wilson v. Dollar Tree Stores, Inc., 161 Fed.Appx. 695 (9th Cir 2006) (employee needed to offer evidence of state of mind to show employer exceeded scope of privilege but failed to do so; employer could reasonably infer from undisputed facts that employee had permitted subordinate to work off the clock).

An executive's discussion with several top management employees of an accusation that plaintiff "ran the Consumer Products division for his own personal gain" in the course of determining how to respond to the accusation was held not to be an abuse of the conditional privilege even though the executive had no opinion whether the allegation was true because the discussion presented the charges as an allegation, not as a fact. Vanderselt v. Pope, 155 Or. App. 334, 963 P.2d 130 (1998), rev. denied, 328 Or. 194, 977 P.2d 1172 (1998).

Where the only evidence the defendant had about plaintiff's alleged misconduct as a public official came from attending city council meetings, there was evidence from which a jury could conclude the defendant either did not believe the accusations or made no attempt to determine whether they were true. Victoria v. LeBlanc, 168 Or. App. 586, 7 P.3d 668 (2000).

Summary judgment is not appropriate and a jury may conclude that the speaker lacked a reasonable basis to believe that plaintiff had engaged in a dishonest act where there was evidence that she had taken merchandise home consistent with company policy and while waiting to be quoted the employee price, and that therefore defendant employer did not believe she was actually trying to steal the merchandise but nevertheless characterized her conduct as misappropriation. Lansford v. Georgetown Manor Inc., 192 Or. App. 261, 84 P.3d 1105 (2004), mod., 193 Or. App. 59, 88 P.3d 305 (2004), rev. denied, 337 Or. 182, 94 P.3d 877 (2004).

There can be circumstances in which whether statements are privileged requires an interpretation of the labor agreement; if that is so, the claims are converted into claims under § 301 of the National Labor Relations Act. Kofoed v. Rosendin Electric, Inc., 157 F. Supp. 2d 1152 (D. Or. 2001) and if the agreement must be construed, the defamation claim is preempted. Kofoed v. Shiprack, 2004 WL 2473304 (D. Or. 2004), affd 2006 WL 2494864 (9th Cir. 2006).

Hakanson v. Boise, Inc., 435 Fed. Appx. 648 (9th Cir. 2011) (employee's defamation claim alleging union encouraged other union members to file false police report was not preempted and police report intended to give advantage in grievance procedures was not protected because it was not made in a grievance procedure).

(1) **Constitutional or Actual Malice**. Proof of constitutional malice is not required to defeat a qualified privilege.

(2) **Common Law Malice**. Proof of a malicious motive is not required before a jury may find that the speaker abused a conditional privilege. Worley v. Oregon Physicians Service, 69 Or. App. 241, 686 P.2d 404 (1984), rev. denied, 298 Or. 334, 691 P.2d 483 (1984). Repetition of a defamatory utterance outside a privileged circumstance is evidence of malice. Phelan v. Beswick, 213 Or. 612, 326 P.2d 1034 (1958).

e. **Question of Fact or Law.** The court determines whether a statement is capable of a defamatory meaning and whether the occasion can be privileged, though it is a question of fact whether the privilege is lost. Worley v. Oregon Physicians Service, 69 Or. App. 241, 686 P.2d 404 (1984), rev. denied, 298 Or. 334, 691 P.2d 483 (1984). It is also a question of law whether an assertion constitutes a fact or an opinion. Bock v. Zittenfield, 66 Or. App. 97, 672 P.2d 1237 (1983), rev. denied, 296 Or. 486, 677 P.2d 702 (1984).

f. **Burden of Proof.** Once a privilege is properly raised as a defense by the employer, it is the plaintiff's burden to prove that the privilege was abused. Walsh v. Consolidated Freightways, 278 Or. 347, 563 P.2d 1205 (1977).

To prove that defendant lacked a reasonable belief in the truth of the statement, plaintiff must offer evidence creating a question of fact as to the mental state of the defendant at the time the statement was made. Lund v. Arbonne Intern., Inc., 132 Or. App. 87, 887 P.2d 817 (1994), citing Bickford v. Tektronix, Inc., 116 Or. App. 547, 842 P.2d 432 (1992); Wilson v. Dollar Tree Stores, Inc., 161 Fed.Appx. 695 (9th Cir 2006) (employee needed to offer evidence of state of mind to show employer exceeded scope of privilege but failed to do so; employer could reasonably infer from undisputed facts that employee had permitted subordinate to work off the clock).

B. Standard Libel Defenses

1. ***Truth***. There is no liability if the statement is substantially true or if defendant is able to justify the gist or sting of the statement. Shirley v. Freunscht, 81 Or. App. 221, 724 P.2d 907 (1986), rev'd on other grounds, 303 Or. 234, 735 P.2d 600 (1987), citing Prosser and Keeton on Torts 842, §116 (5th ed. 1984). Even though falsity is an element of the claim, a defendant bears the burden of proof of truth. Fowler v. Donnelly, 225 Or. 287, 358 P.2d 485 (1960). A statement that plaintiff had falsified her employment application was true because the application contained affirmative misrepresentations and there was a material omission. Olson v. ASI Staffing, Inc., 2005 WL 1839015 (D. Or. 2005).

2. ***Opinion***. Expressions of opinion are not actionable as libel or slander. King v. Menolascino, 276 Or. 501, 555 P.2d 442 (1976). It is a question of law whether an assertion constitutes a fact or an opinion. Bock v. Zittenfield, 66 Or. App. 97, 672 P.2d 1237 (1983), rev. denied, 296 Or. 486, 677 P.2d 702 (1984). Oregon adopts Restatement (Second) of Torts § 566 (1981), noting two kinds of expressions of opinion including an opinion in form or context apparently based on facts regarding the plaintiff or his conduct that have not been stated by the defendant or assumed to exist by the parties to the communication, and citing Adler v. American Standard Corp., 538 F. Supp. 572 (D. Md 1982) (statement that plaintiff was terminated for "unsatisfactory performance" capable of defamatory meaning because based on undisclosed defamatory facts with a reasonable implication that the plaintiff was guilty of some misconduct, negligence or incompetence in the performance of duties); Slover v. Oregon State Bd. of Clinical Social Workers, 144 Or. App. 565, 927 P.2d 1098 (1996) (statement that social worker engaged in dubious therapeutic technique with boys could have been understood to be based on undisclosed facts and therefore not protected as opinion).

However, a statement that was expressed as opinion to the effect that plaintiff had had too much to drink may still be actionable because it implied the unstated underlying facts that plaintiff had been drinking before coming to work in the construction industry in violation of an industry-wide zero tolerance policy. Affolter v. Baugh Construction Oregon, Inc., 183 Or. App. 198, 51 P.3d 642 (2002).

Statements to the effect that plaintiff was "a disgraced academic with a shady past" are not actionable; statements cannot be shown to be anything more than "rhetorical hyperbole" "parody" or "lose or figurative speech." DuBoff v. Playboy Enterprises International Inc., 2007 WL 1876513 (D. Or. 2007).

3. ***Consent***. There is an absolute privilege for publications that are consented to, even when the allegedly defamed person did not consent to the exact words that are published as long as the person had reason to believe the consented to publication would be defamatory. Christensen v. Marvin, 273 Or. 97, 539 P.2d 1082 (1975); Lee v. Paulsen, 273 Or. 103, 539 P.2d 1079 (1975) (request at board meeting that reasons for termination be discussed constituted consent where plaintiff knew reasons were defamatory when the discussion was requested). Consent, however must be proved. Dell v. K.E. McKay's Market, Inc., 273 Or. 752, 543 P.2d 678 (1975) (no evidence distraught wife was agent of her husband in inquiring of reasons for husband's termination, in response to which defamatory statement was made).

4. ***Mitigation***. Mitigation applies, but most case law is sparse and old. In general, mitigation may be proved by evidence of events that provoked the statement, or by evidence of related acts of business misconduct. See, e.g., Upton v. Hume, 24 Or. 420, 33 P.2d 810 (1893) (holding limited; see Harley-Davidson Motorsports, Inc. v. Markley, 279 Or. 361, 568 P.2d 1359 (1977); Peck v. Coos Bay Times Pub. Co., 122 Or. 408, 259 P. 307 (1927); Shirley v. Freunscht, 303 Or. 234, 735 P.2d 600 (1987).

III. RECURRING FACT PATTERNS

A. Statements in Personnel File

So long as statement in personnel files are not published they are unlikely to be sufficient to support a defamation claim; inadvertent publication is insufficient to satisfy this element. Morrow v. II Morrow Inc., 139 Or. App. 212, 911 P.2d

964 (1996), rev. denied, 323 Or. 153, 916 P.2d 312 (1996) (publication to a third person must be intentional or negligent; employer did not libel employee by inadvertent or accidental publication through inadequately erasing memo from drive of computer network). Statements in evaluations are conditionally privileged, employers need to ensure vitality and productivity of employees, and management deliberations during evaluations are necessary part of due process. A manager may rely on information provided by others. Hutchinson v. Menlo Logistics, 2006 WL 44196 (D. Or. 2006).

B. Performance Evaluations

Since inadvertent publication is insufficient to satisfy this element, Morrow v. II Morrow Inc., 139 Or. App. 212, 911 P.2d 964 (1996), rev. denied, 323 Or. 153, 916 P.2d 312 (1996) (publication to a third person must be intentional or negligent; employer did not libel employee by inadvertent or accidental publication through inadequately erasing memo from drive of computer network), performance evaluations retained in files are unlikely to support a defamation claim.

C. References

The common law rule recognizes a qualified privilege to make a defamatory communication about the character or conduct of an employee to present or prospective employers, or for an employee to make a communication to that employee's supervisor concerning another employee's work performance to protect the interests of the employer or on a subject of mutual concern. Wallulis v. Dymowski, 323 Or. 337, 918 P.2d 755 (1996). ORS 30.178(1) extends the common law protection to employers providing references in good faith. Statements made to mortgage company inaccurately reporting plaintiff had resigned caused no harm, since an accurate report would have led to same result. Bellairs v. Beaverton School District, 2005 WL 2077934 (D. Or. 2005). **The qualified privilege is a shield that protects employers only from good faith communications; statement that employee was terminated "for cause" could be defamatory. Gordon v. Kleinfelder West, Inc., 2012 WL 844200 (D. Or. 2012).**

D. Intracorporate Communication

Publication is an essential element of an action for defamation; that is proved when a statement is communicated to a third party. Because the interest protected by the law of defamation is an individual's interest in his or her reputation, both in the community at large and in that individual's professional community, Oregon has refused to adopt the intracorporate nonpublication rule. Instead, a defamatory communication from one corporate employee to another corporate employee concerning the job performance of a third employee is published for the purpose of a defamation claim. Wallulis v. Dymowski, 323 Or. 337, 918 P.2d 755 (1996); Lansford v. Georgetown Manor Inc., 192 Or. App. 261, 84 P.3d 1105 (2004), mod., 193 Or. App. 59, 88 P.3d 305 (2004). However, such publications may be conditionally privileged. Olson v. ASI Staffing, 2005 WL 1839015 (D. Or. 2005), rev. denied, 337 Or. 182, 94 P.3d 877 (2004) (statement in database about prior conviction).

E. Statements to Government Regulators

Whether statements to government regulators are absolutely privileged depends upon the function of the regulator. Communications to a medical examiner as the initial step in a judicial proceeding are absolutely privileged. Ducosin v. Mott, 292 Or. 764, 642 P.2d 1168 (1982).

F. Reports to Auditors and Insurers

A statement to an insurer writing a fidelity bond on which an employer sought to make a claim was conditionally privileged and the employee was required to prove actual malice. Phelan v. Beswick, 213 Or. 612, 326 P.2d 1034 (1958).

G. Vicarious Liability of Employers for Statements Made by Employees

1. ***Scope of Employment.*** The principal or corporate employer is liable for defamatory statements made in furtherance of the corporations' business or within the scope of his authority or when he, himself, made the statement. Wheeler v. Green, 286 Or. 99, 593 P.2d 777 (1979); Bradbury v. Teacher Standards and Practices Com'n, 151 Or. App. 176, 947 P.2d 1145 (1997), rev'd on other grounds, 328 Or. 391, 977 P.2d 1153 (1999). An employee acts within the scope of employment when acting substantially within the time and space limits authorized by the employer, when the employee is motivated at least in part by a purpose of serving the employer, and when the act is of the kind the employee was hired to perform. Downs v. Waremart, Inc., 137 Or. App. 119, 903 P.2d 888 (1995), aff'd in part, rev'd in part, 324 Or. 307, 926 P.2d 314 (1995), Araujo v. General Electric Information Services, 82 F. Supp. 2d 1161 (D. Or. 2000), aff'd and rem., 25 Fed. Appx. 615, 2002 WL 24553 (9th Cir 2002). Preparation of a report about a fellow officer's conduct during an event that was part of their official duty was within the scope of a sworn officer's official duties for application of the absolute privilege enjoyed by a sworn police officer. Chamberlain v. City of Portland, 184 Or. App. 487, 56 P.3d 497 (2002). There was sufficient evidence to avoid summary judgment on the question of vicarious liability where an administrator told plaintiff's

employer plaintiff had used cocaine where the statement was said to be made during the work day and where the administrator's job description gave her full responsibility for management and control and charges her with promoting and maintaining good community relationships. Coney v. Fagan and Landa S Inc., 195 Or.App. 282, 97 P.3d 1252 (2004).

a. Blogging. Although not strictly a blogging case, Barnes v. Yahoo! Inc., 565 F.3d 560 (9th Cir. 2009), amended 2009 WL 1740755 (9th Cir. 2009), addresses defamation claims in the context of postings to provider websites. The defendant internet service provider successfully argued that the Communications Decency Act provided it immunity from plaintiff's negligence claim arising out of a refusal to remove a harmful profile of plaintiff posted by her former boyfriend. The statute precludes liability if the duty the plaintiff alleges derives from the defendant's status or conduct as a "publisher or speaker." **In Obsidian Finance Group LLC v. Cox, 2011 WL 5999334 (D. Or. 2011), the Oregon federal court held that a self-described "investigative blogger" was not a "media" defendant or journalist.**

2. ***Damages***. Defamation per se is actionable without pleading or proof of special damages. General damages (including damage to business reputation) are presumed in such a case and may be recovered without evidence of the harm incurred. Loss of earning capacity is a part of the damage to business reputation and evidence of the inability to secure employment caused by the defamation is admissible to show that loss. Cook v. Safeway Stores Inc., 266 Or. 77, 511 P.2d 375 (1973). The inability to obtain employment that the plaintiff would have obtained but for the currency of the slander is a special harm and may be recovered if there is poof of causation, that is if the statement was a substantial factor in causing the harm. Benassi v. Georgia Pacific, 62 Or. App. 698, 662 P.2d 760 (1983), mod. 63 Or. App. 672, 667 P.2d 532, rev. denied, 295 Or. 730, 670 P.2d 1035 (1983). Nominal damages are available. Quigley v. McGee, 12 Or. 22, 5 P. 347 (1885).

H. Internal Investigations

An employer may be vicariously responsible for defamatory statements of employees operating within the course and scope of employment. *See* Tenold v. Weyerhaeuser Company, et al., 127 Or.App.511, 873 P.2d 413 (1994) (employer liable for defamatory statements of county sheriff deputy accusing employee of theft, where deputy carried out county obligations to provide forestry patrol and field investigation; agreement between county and employer was ambiguous and whether employer had right to control deputy was a question of fact for the jury to decide). *See also* Wallulis v. Dymowski 323 Or. 337, 918 P.2d 755 (1996) (union steward who reported manager's substance abuse problem could simultaneously be agent of employer and union for purposes of employer vicarious liability for defamation).

IV. OTHER ACTIONS BASED ON STATEMENTS

A. Negligent Hiring, Retention, and Supervision

A negligent supervision claim will lie for the release of confidential information; in such cases the proper statute of limitations is the two year statute for torts, rather than the one year statute for defamation, unless the claim is fairly characterized as defamation. Bradbury v. Teacher Standards and Practices Com'n, 151 Or. App. 176, 947 P.2d 1145 (1997), rev'd on other grounds, 328 Or. 391, 977 P.2d 1153 (1999).

B. Intentional Infliction of Emotional Distress

Oregon recognizes the tort, which requires proof of an extraordinary transgression of the bounds of socially tolerable conduct. Hall v. May Dept. Stores Co., 292 Or. 131, 637 P.2d 126 (1981). Plaintiff must also prove severe emotional distress resulting from the act, and intent or reckless disregard. McGanty v. Staudenrauss, 321 Or. 532, 901 P.2d 841 (1995). The tort does not provide recovery for the kind of temporary annoyance or injured feelings that can result from friction and rudeness among people in day-to-day life even when the intentional conduct causing distress otherwise qualifies for liabilities. Accusing a school employee of being a sex abuser, which could result in permanent public stigmatization, meets the requirement of the tort (conduct exceeding all bounds of social toleration). Kraemer v. Harding, 159 Or. App. 90, 976 P.2d 1160 (1999), rev. denied, 329 Or. 357, 994 P.2d 124 (1999). Publication of allegedly defamatory letter does not rise to level of abusiveness required to prove claim for intentional infliction of severe emotional distress. Sizemore v. City of Madras, 2004 WL 1502891 (D. Or. 2005). Police association's press releases and website seeking resignation of Chief not extreme or outrageous. Roskowski v. Corvallis Police Officers' Association, 2005 WL 555398 (findings and recommendation granting summary judgment on defamation) and 2005 WL 1429917 (D. Or. 2005) (adopting magistrate findings and recommendation), aff'd 250 Fed. Appx. 816 (9th Cir. 2007). However, "a defendant's publication of a defamatory or otherwise significantly stigmatizing statement, knowing the statement to be false, unfounded, or unsubstantiated, is conduct that, if found to be true by a factfinder, constitutes an extraordinary transgression of what is socially tolerable." If the defamation serves an ulterior purpose or takes advantage of an unusually vulnerable individual, those factors can be evaluated in considering the "socially outrageous quality." Checkley v. Boyd, 198 Or.App. 110, 107 P.3d 651 (2005), rev. denied, 338 Or. 583, 114 P.3d 505 (2005). Accord, Gunter v. The Guardian Press Foundation, Inc., 2006 WL 1030182 (D. Or. 2006). But see House v. Hicks, et al, 218 Or.App. 348, 179 P.3d 730 (2008) (university employee's complaint about plaintiff's unwanted contact, even though arguably not entirely true, was not sufficiently stigmatizing to qualify as outrageous since there was no reference to plaintiff's character, or the substance or context; the employee had no relationship with plaintiff so as to impose a duty on her, and the statements were made privately); **Boon v. Union Pacific R. Co., 2011 WL 7452732 (D. Or. 2011) (findings and recommendations) and 2012 WL 707172 (D. Or. 2012) (adopting findings and recommendation) (employer statement that employee suspended for violating policy not an extraordinary transgression of bounds of socially tolerable conduct).**

C. Interference with Economic Advantage

Oregon recognizes the tort of interference with prospective economic advantage which requires proof of a relationship, improper motivation or improper means, and damage beyond the fact of the interference. To be actionable, the interference must be by a stranger to the relationship, not by one acting "as" the entity or within the course and scope of employment. McGanty v. Staudenrauss, 321 Or. 532, 901 P.2d 841 (1995). Defamation can be an improper means, Kraemer v. Harding, 159 Or. App. 90, 976 P.2d 1160 (1999), rev. denied, 329 Or. 357, 994 P.2d 124 (1999), but if the challenged statements are privileged, they are not an improper means. Lund v. Arbonne Intern., Inc., 132 Or. App. 87, 887 P.2d 817 (1994) (no improper means based on allegedly defamatory statements made in the context of a business relationship where statements were qualifiedly privileged and no evidence the privilege was abused); Walsh v. Consolidated Freightways, Inc., 278 Or. 347, 563 P.2d 1205 (1977). However, where parents believed a school bus driver behaved improperly towards their children and sought his removal from employment, while they had a right to protest and seek his removal, they did not have the right to do so by publishing false accusations without believing reasonably that they were true. Kraemer v. Harding, 159 Or. App. 90, 976 P.2d 1160 (1999), rev. denied, 329 Or. 357, 994 P.2d 124 (1999).

D. Prima Facie Tort

Oregon does not recognize prima facie tort. Nees v. Hocks, 272 Or. 210, 536 P.2d 512 (1975).

V. OTHER ISSUES

A. Statute of Limitations

The statute of limitations for both libel and slander is one year. ORS 12.120(2). Where publication is of a confidential nature, the "discovery rule" applies and the statute commences when the employee could have discovered the event with the exercise of reasonable diligence. White v. Gurnsey, 48 Or. App. 931, 618 P.2d 975 (1980). The discovery rule does not extend to defamation expressed in open or public forums or media. Workman v. Rajneesh Foundation Intern., 84 Or. App. 226, 733 P.2d 908, rev. denied, 303 Or. 700, 740 P.2d 1213 (1987). Where the discovery rule applies, a plaintiff need not know the "exact content" of the statement; knowledge of "substantially all" was sufficient to trigger the statute of limitations. Holdner v. Oregon Trout Inc., 173 Or. App. 344, 22 P.3d 244 (2001). The Oregon Supreme Court reversed a lower court opinion in Bradbury v. Teacher Standards and Practices Com'n, 151 Or. App. 176, 947 P.2d 1145 (1997), rev'd on other grounds, 328 Or. 391, 977 P.2d 1153 (1999) (which cited Magenis v. Fisher Broadcasting, Inc., 103 Or. App. 555, 798 P.2d 1106 (1990) to hold that a negligence claim alleging improper release of a damaging but arguably false confidential report was not actionable outside the one year statute). Bradbury v. Teacher Standards and Practices Commission, 328 Or. 391, 977 P.2d 1153 (1999), rev'd on other grounds, 328 Or. 391, 977 P.2d 1153 (1999), held that the mere allegation that the information was false was not enough to transform an action for negligent supervision into one for defamation. The tort is identified by the nature of the conduct complained of – the predominant characteristic of the tort.

Each publication of a defamatory statement is a discrete tort for which the publisher may be liable, and the statute of limitations on each statement begins to run on the date the statement is made. Kraemer v. Harding, 159 Or. App. 90, 976 P.2d 1160 (1999), rev. denied, 329 Or. 357, 994 P.2d 124 (1999).

Where a defamation claim is preempted on the grounds that a bargaining agreement will need to be construed to determine whether there was a qualified privilege to make certain statements, the claims are converted into claims under § 301 of the National Labor Relations Act and the limitation period is six months. Kofoed v. Rosendin Electric, Inc., 157 F. Supp. 2d 1152 (D. Or. 2001).

B. Jurisdiction

Oregon state courts have jurisdiction, including under the state's long arm statute. Rosenlund v. Transnational Ins., Co., 237 F. Supp. 599 (D. Or. 1964).

A plaintiff must plead the defamatory matter with sufficient particularity to permit employers to identify constitutional or other privileges in responding. Rice v. Comtek Mfg. of Oregon, Inc., 766 F. Supp. 1539 (D.Or. 1990). Falsity must be alleged. Fowler v. Donnelly, 225 Or. 287, 358 P.2d 485 (1960).

Special damages must be alleged. Cook v. Safeway, 266 Or. 77, 511 P.2d 375 (1973). And see Marleau v. Truck Ins. Exch., 333 Or. 82, 37 P.3d 148 (2001), (dismissing complaint where no special damages claimed and no per se cause of action; distinguishing Cook v. Safeway).

Claim of absolute privilege must be asserted affirmatively; labeling defense broadly "absolute privilege," together with express incorporation of earlier allegations is sufficiently broad to meet pleading standard. Johnson v. Brown and Deschutes County, 193 Or. App. 375, 91 P.3d 741 (2004), clarified 194 Or. App. 486, 95 P.3d 235 (2004).

Oregon has enacted Anti-SLAPP legislation. ORS 31.150 et seq.

C. Worker's Compensation Exclusivity

In Stone v. Finnerty, 182 Or. App. 452, 50 P.3d 1179 (2002), mod. recon. 184 Or.App. 111, 55 P.3d 531 (2002), the court cited to Michigan case law to the effect that the exclusive remedy provision of the workers' compensation legislation does not bar claims for invasions of a worker's interest such as might occur in the case of defamation.

D. Pleading Requirements

Or. Rules Civ. Proc.20 sets out pleading requirements, specifically that a plaintiff need not plead extrinsic facts for the purpose of showing the application to the plaintiff of the defamatory matter, but rather may state generally that it was published or spoken concerning the plaintiff. A defendant may allege both the truth of the matter charged as defamatory, and any mitigating circumstances, to reduce the amount of damages. Falsity must be alleged. Fowler v. Donnelly 225 Or. 287, 291-292, 358 P.2d 485, 488 (1960). A pleading that remarks "reflected on plaintiff individually" is insufficient under this standard set out by the Rules. Patzer v. Liberty Communications, Inc. 58 Or.App. 679, 683, 650 P.2d 141, 143 (1982). **And see Ziya v. Global Linguistic Solution, 2012 WL 1357678 (D. Or. 2012) (claim must include facts that show a defendant made an untrue statement to a third party that subjects the plaintiff to hatred, contempt or ridicule and detrimentally affects good reputation in the community).** Where the complaint is of false light privacy, a plaintiff must allege that the defendant had knowledge of or acted in reckless disregard of the falsity of the published matter and the false light in which it would place him. Dean v. Guard Pub. Co., Inc. 73 Or.App. 656, 660, 699 P.2d 1158, 1160 - 1161 (1985). It is unnecessary to plead or prove special damage if defamation is *per se*, although a plaintiff must allege any special harm. Benassi v. Georgia Pacific, 62 Or. App. 698, 662 P.2d 760 (1983), mod., 63 Or. App. 672, 667 P.2d 532, rev. denied, 295 Or. 730, 670 P.2d 1035 (1983).

SURVEY OF OREGON EMPLOYMENT PRIVACY LAW

Jenna L. Mooney
Carol A. Noonan
Davis Wright Tremaine LLP
1300 SW 5th Avenue, Suite 2300
Portland, Oregon 97201
Telephone: (503) 241-2300; Facsimile: (503) 778-5299

(With Developments Reported Through **November 1, 2012**)

SIGNIFICANT DEVELOPMENTS SINCE THE 2012 *SURVEY*

None.

I. GENERAL LAW OF PRIVACY

A. Legal Basis of Privacy Claims

1. ***Constitutional Law.*** The Oregon Constitution contains a search and seizure provision similar to the Fourth Amendment to the federal Constitution; however, it has generally been construed to provide greater protection against governmental searches and seizures than its federal counterpart. Or. Const., Art. I, Sec. 9., State v. Caraher, 293 Or. 741, 653 P.2d 942 (1982).

2. ***Statutory Law.*** Oregon's Criminal Code provides that a person commits the crime of invasion of privacy if the person knowingly observes, or photocopies, or makes a visual recording of another person, without consent, in a state of nudity where the other person has a reasonable expectation of privacy. ORS 163.700.

In 2005, the Oregon legislature created a new cause of action for invasion of personal privacy that allows recovery of compensatory damages and attorney fees, but not punitive damages. ORS 30.865; 2005 Or. Laws Ch. 544 (July 15, 2005). See I.B.5. below.

3. ***Common Law.*** Oregon law regarding tortious invasion of privacy is comparatively sparse. The Oregon Supreme Court has, however, recognized a legal right of privacy. Hinish v. Meier and Frank Co., 166 Or. 482, 113 P.2d 438 (1941); Anderson v. Fisher Broadcasting Cos., 300 Or. 452, 712 P.2d 803 (1986). In Anderson, the court commented that the invasion of privacy torts as they are classified in the Restatement (Second) of Torts, while not necessarily authoritative statements of Oregon law, could be accepted for convenience. Id. at 460. The Oregon appellate courts have adopted the four causes of action that make up the tort of invasion of privacy in one form or another.

B. Causes of Action

1. ***Misappropriation of Name or Likeness.*** Oregon courts have recognized a cause of action for misappropriation of name or likeness. Hinish v. Meier and Frank Co., 166 Or. 482, 113 P.2d 438 (1941). The Oregon appellate courts have analyzed such claims in terms of the Restatement (Second) of Torts § 652C (1977). Under Oregon law, plaintiffs may recover damages when their names, pictures or other likenesses have been used without their consent to advertise a defendant's product, to accompany an article sold, to add luster to the name of a corporation, or for some other business purpose. Martinez v. Democrat-Herald Pub. Co., 64 Or. App. 690, 669 P.2d 818 (1983). Generally, it is held that plaintiffs have no cause to action when a person's picture is use to illustrate a noncommercial, newsworthy article. Id. Likewise, incidental use of a name or likeness does not constitute the tort Restatement (Second) of Torts § 652C, comments C and D. Under Oregon law, a plaintiff may state a claim for appropriation of name or likeness in the absence of commercial benefit to the defendant. Anderson v. Fisher Broadcasting Cos., 300 Or. 452, 712 P.2d 803 (1986). Such a claim will not give rise to damages for mental or emotional distress, however, unless "the manner or purpose of defendant's conduct is wrongful in some respect apart from causing the plaintiff's hurt feelings." 300 Or. at 469.

2. ***False Light.*** A person who places another before the public in a false light may be liable for resulting damages. Dean v. Guard Publishing Co., 73 Or. App. 656, 659, 699 P.2d 1158 (1985). The focus of the tort is not on the truth or falsity of a particular statement, but instead it is whether what has been said leads others to believe something about the plaintiff that is false. Phillips v. Lincoln County Sch. Dist., 161 Or. App. 429, 984 P.2d 947 (1999). Like defamation, a false light claim involves publication. The publication requirement is different, however, in that for a false light claim there must be publication to the public generally or a large number of persons. Morrow v. II Morrow, Inc., 139 Or. App. 212, 911 P.2d 964 (1996). To recover under a false light claim, a plaintiff must plead and prove the defendant "had knowledge of or acted in reckless disregard as to the falsity of a publicized matter and the false light in which the other would

be placed." Flowers v. Bank of America, 67 Or. App. 791, 797, 679 P.2d 1385 (1984). False light invasions of privacy and defamation causes of actions are very similar; however, they are theoretically distinct. Defamation focuses on damage to reputation, while a false light claim focuses on the mental distress or anguish that a person suffers because the "false light" that is cast by a communication is highly offensive. Reesman v. Highfill, et al., 327 Or. 597, 602, 965 P.2d 1030 (1998). See also Magenis v. Fisher Broadcasting, Inc., 103 Or. App. 555, 798 P.2d 1106 (1990) (false light claim focuses on plaintiff's interest in being left alone).

3. ***Publication of Private Facts.*** To maintain a claim for publication of private facts in Oregon, plaintiffs must plead and prove: (1) the facts disclosed are private facts; (2) the defendant disclosed them to the public generally or to a large number of persons as distinguished from one or a few; and (3) the disclosure was in a form of publicity of the highly objectionable kind. Tollefson v. Price, 247 Or. 398, 430 P.2d 990 (1967); L & D of Oregon, Inc. v. American States Ins. Co., 171 Or. App. 17, 14 P.3d 617 (2000). Disclosure of facts that are a matter of public record does not constitute an invasion of privacy. Ayers v. Lee Enterprises, Inc., 277 Or. 527, 561 P.2d 998 (1977). The right of privacy is not so broad as to create a right of action for every unauthorized disclosure of personal information. Hamilton v. Crown Life Ins., 246 Or. 1, 423 P.2d 771 (1967).

4. ***Intrusion.*** To prevail on a claim for intrusion upon seclusion in Oregon a plaintiff must establish: (1) an intentional intrusion, physical or otherwise; (2) upon plaintiff's private affairs or concerns; and (3) that the intrusion would be offensive to a reasonable person. Leggett v. First Interstate Bank of Oregon, 86 Or. App. 523, 739 P.2d 1083 (1987). Even where an intrusion has occurred, the intruder's legitimate interest in making the intrusion "must be balanced against the nature and extent of the intrusion in deciding if an invasion of privacy has occurred." Leggett v. First Interstate Bank of Oregon, 86 Or. App. at 527.

5. ***Invasion of Personal Privacy.*** In 2005, the Oregon legislature created a new cause of action for invasion of personal privacy that allows recovery of compensatory damages and attorney fees, but not punitive damages. To prove the cause of action, the plaintiff must establish any one of the following: (1) the defendant knowingly made or recorded a photograph, motion picture or other visual recording of plaintiff in a state of nudity without the consent of the plaintiff where there was a reasonable expectation of privacy; (2) the defendant was in a location to observe the plaintiff in a state of nudity without consent for the purpose of arousing or gratifying the defendant's sexual desire; (3) the defendant made a photograph, motion picture of other visual recording of an intimate area of the plaintiff without the plaintiff's consent or viewed an intimate area of the plaintiff without consent for the purpose of arousing or gratifying sexual desire of any person; or (4) the defendant disseminated a photograph, motion picture, videotape or other visual recording of the plaintiff in a state of nudity when the plaintiff had an expectation of privacy and without the consent of the plaintiff. ORS 30.865.

C. Defenses

1. ***Absolute Privilege.*** The absolute privileges that exist for defamation apply to the publication of any matter that is an invasion of privacy. Wollam v. Brandt, 154 Or. App. 156, 961 P.2d 219 (1998); Lee v. Nash, 65 Or. App. 538, 671 P.2d 703 (1983). Thus, publications in the context of legislative, judicial proceedings or other acts of state or publications made to carry out statutory requirements are absolutely privileged. Wallulis v. Dymowski, 323 Or. 337, 918 P.2d 755 (1996); Shearer v. Lambert, 274 Or. 449, 547 P.2d 98 (1976). However, a lawyer may not invoke the absolute privilege defense merely because he or she is an attorney. The protected statements are only those made to further the judicial proceedings; statements to the press (for instance) will generally be viewed under the same standards as if made by a non-lawyer. Brown v. Gatti, 195 Or. App. 695, 99 P.3d 299 (2004); rev'd, in part on other grounds, 145 P.3d 130 (2006).

2. ***Qualified Privilege.*** The qualified privileges that exist for defamation apply to the publication of any matter that is an invasion of privacy, except where the invasion of privacy action does not involve publicity. Leggett v. First Interstate Bank of Oregon, 86 Or. App. 523, 739 P.2d 1083 (1987). A conditional privilege can arise when a publication is made to protect the interests of an employer or when it is on a subject of mutual concern to the publisher and those to whom it is made. Worley v. Oregon Physicians Service, 69 Or. App. 241, 686 P.2d 404 (1984).

3. ***Consent.*** Consent to any publication of matter that invades privacy creates an absolute privilege so long as the publication does not exceed the scope of the consent. Castagna v. Western Graphics, 38 Or. App. 403, 590 P.2d 291 (1979).

D. Other Privacy-Related Actions

1. ***Negligent Hiring, Retention, and Supervision.*** A negligent supervision claim can arise from the release of confidential information. In such cases the proper statute of limitations is the two-year statute for torts, rather than the one-year statute for defamation. See Bradbury v. Teacher Standards and Practices Comm'n, 328 Or. 391, 977 P.2d 1153 (1999).

2. ***Intentional Infliction of Emotional Distress.*** Oregon recognizes the tort which requires proof of an extraordinary transgression of the bounds of socially tolerable conduct. Hall v. May Dep't. Stores Co., 292 Or. 131, 637 P.2d 126 (1981). A plaintiff must also prove severe emotional distress resulting from the act, and intent or reckless disregard. McGanty v. Staudenraus, 321 Or. 532, 901 P.2d 841 (1995). The tort does not provide recovery for the kind of temporary annoyance or injured feelings that can result from friction and rudeness among people in day-to-day life, even when the intentional conduct causing distress otherwise qualifies for liabilities. Accusing a school employee of being a sex abuser, which could result in a permanent public stigmatization, meets the requirement of the tort (conduct exceeding all bounds of social toleration). Kraemer v. Harding, 159 Or. App. 90, 976 P.2d 1160 (1999).

3. ***Interference with Economic Advantage.*** Oregon recognizes the tort of interference with prospective economic advantage which requires proof of a relationship, improper motivation or improper means, and damages beyond the fact of the interference. To be actionable, the interference must be by a stranger to the relationship, not by one acting "as" the entity or within the course and scope of employment. McGanty v. Staudenraus, 321 Or. 532, 901 P.2d 841 (1995). Defamation can be an improper means, but if the challenged statements are privileged, they are not an improper means. Lund v. Arbonne Int'l., Inc., 132 Or. App. 87, 887 P.2d 817 (1994) (no improper means based on allegedly defamatory statements made in the context of a business relationship where statements qualified privileged and no evidence the privilege was abused); Walsh v. Consolidated Freightways, Inc., 278 Or. 347, 563 P.2d 1205 (1977).

4. ***Prima Facie Tort.*** Oregon does not recognize prima facie tort. Nees v. Hocks, 272 Or. 210, 563 P.2d 512 (1975).

II. EMPLOYER TESTING OF EMPLOYEES

A. Psychological or Personality Testing

It is an unlawful employment practice under Oregon law to subject a public or private employee, directly or indirectly, to a psychological stress test or brain wave test to detect deception through use of instrumentation or mechanical devices. ORS 659A.300.

At least one reported decision upholds an employer's order for an employee to submit to a psychological exam where the employee's ability to perform his job was at issue. Langer v. Employment Div., 111 Or. App. 154, 826 P.2d 6 (1992).

B. Drug Testing

The Oregon Legislature has, at least implicitly approved drug testing of employees by providing that an individual who has been terminated for failing a reasonable drug-testing program, including random testing, is disqualified from receiving unemployment benefits. ORS 657.176(9)(a). Generally, Oregon statutes do not restrict an employer's right to engage in drug and alcohol testing. Oregon law makes it a crime to use or possess to use any substance or device designed to falsify results of a drug test. An employer may not administer a Breathalyzer test unless (1) the employee or prospective employee consents, or (2) the employer has reasonable grounds to believe that the individual is intoxicated. ORS 659.840, ORS 659A.300. Although there is no Oregon case as yet on point, it is likely that a drug or alcohol test of a public employee would be deemed a seizure within the meaning of Article I, Section 9 of the Oregon Constitution. It is also likely that testing based upon individualized suspicion will pass constitutional muster. See AFSCME Local 2623 v. Dep't. of Corr., 315 Or. 74, 843 P.2d 409 (1992).

In April 2010, the Oregon Supreme Court issued its decision in Emerald Steel Fabrications, Inc. v. Bureau of Labor and Industries, 348 Or. 159, 230 P.3d 518 (2010), which decided that employers are not required to accommodate for medical marijuana use outside of the work place under Oregon's disability discrimination laws. The Court concluded that ORS 475.306(1)—Oregon's statute allowing medical use of marijuana—is not enforceable because it is preempted by the federal Controlled Substances Act. Therefore, because the employee was engaged in the illegal use of drugs and the employer discharged him for that reason, Oregon's disability discrimination laws did not apply. This case makes clear that as long as marijuana is considered a "Schedule I" drug under the Controlled Substances Act, federal law preempts the Oregon Medical Marijuana Act and employers will not be required to accommodate an employee's use of the drug.

C. Medical Testing

Oregon Civil Rights of Disabled Persons Act, ORS 659A.122 et seq., like the federal Americans with Disabilities Act, 42 USC § 1112 (d), restricts an employer's ability to conduct medical examinations. Examinations are limited to post offer of employment exams or situations where the employee's ability to safely perform his or her job duties is at issue. The employer is required to keep all medical information resulting from such tests in a separate, confidential file. ORS 659A.133 (applicants); ORS 659A.136 (employees). The employer may not require the employee to pay the cost of any such medical examination, except where the examination is required pursuant to a collective bargaining agreement, state or federal statute, or city or county ordinance. ORS 659A.306.

In 2009, the Oregon Legislature amended the Oregon Civil Rights of Disabled Persons Act, ORS 659A.122 et seq., regarding the criteria that an individual must meet to establish a disability under the statute. The amendment increases the scope of activities and functions that are considered major life activities for the purpose of determining if an individual has a disability. These include but are not limited to: caring for oneself, performing manual tasks, seeing, hearing, eating, sleeping, walking, standing, lifting, bending, speaking, breathing, learning, reading, concentrating, thinking, communicating, working, socializing, sitting, reaching, interacting with others, employment, ambulation, transportation and operation of a major bodily function. This change affects 659A.136 because an employer may not subject an employee to a medical examination or make inquiries regarding whether an employee has such a disability or to the nature or severity of such a disability, unless the examination or inquiry is shown to be job-related and consistent with business activity. However, an employer may conduct voluntary medical examinations and employees may voluntarily give information regarding their medical histories. The information obtained by employers must be collected and maintained on separate forms and in separate medical files and must be treated as confidential medical records.

The Oregon Court of Appeals, in Heiple v. Henderson, 229 Or. App. 693 (2009), reviewed and affirmed a lower court's order, holding that the Oregon Employment Department was entitled to request an employee submit to a medical examination based on job relatedness and business necessity. The employee asserted that she was discriminated against based on her disability when she refused to submit to an independent medical examination (IME) and was later terminated. The court held that the request for examination was job related and based on business necessity because the request flowed directly from complaints regarding the employee's interactions with coworkers and clients and their concerns that she posed a safety risk at work.

It is an unlawful employment practice in Oregon to subject a public or private employee or prospective employee to genetic testing absent informed consent of the individual and only so long as the test assists in determining a bona fide occupational requirement. ORS 659A.303; ORS 659A.300. It is also a crime to unlawfully obtain, retain or disclose genetic information. ORS 192.539.

D. Polygraph Testing

It is an unlawful employment practice to subject any employee or prospective employee to a polygraph examination, even if the employee consents. ORS 659.840.

E. Fingerprinting

Oregon law does not restrict or limit an employer's ability to fingerprint an employee or prospective employee.

III. SEARCHES

A. Employee's Person

1. ***Private Employers.*** No statute or judicial decision *per se* limits or restricts a private employer's right to search the person or property of a private employee. It is clear, however, that employers may be held liable if the manner of the search is unreasonable, degrading and humiliating. Bodewig v. K-Mart, Inc., 54 Or. App. 480, 635 P.2d 657 (1981). See VII.B, infra.

2. ***Public Employers.***

a. **Federal Law** The Fourth Amendment of the U.S. Constitution protects individuals from unreasonable searches and seizures at the hands of any state actor. This protection extends into the workplace of all federal and, through the Fourteenth Amendment, state employers. See O'Connor v. Ortega, 480 U.S. 709 (1987). However, the protections provided by the Fourth Amendment are limited. Only "unreasonable searches" performed where the employee has a "reasonable expectation of privacy" are unconstitutional. Also, to be lawful a search by a public employer of an employee's person must either be necessary for a non-investigatory, work-related purpose or be based on reasonable grounds to suspect that the search will produce evidence of work-related misconduct.

Employees whose Fourth Amendment rights have been violated may recover for the emotional shock or physical harm of the unlawful search, but may not recover for any resulting injury to their employment status or position. See Bivens v. Six Unknown Agents of the Fed. Bureau of Narcotics, 456 F.2d 1339 (2d Cir. 1972).

b. **State Law** In AFSCME Local 2623 v. Dep't. of Corr., 315 Or. 74, 843 P.2d 409 (1992), the Oregon Supreme Court upheld, against a facial invalidation challenge, Administrative Rule OAR 291-41-005(3), which authorized the search of an employee's person, vehicle or possessions. The court held that the rule's requirement of individualized suspicion satisfied the requirements of the search and seizure provision of the Oregon Constitution, Article I, Section 9.

B. Employee's Work Area

1. ***Federal Law*** The same standards apply to searches of a public employee's person and work area. See United States v. Horowitz, 806 F.2d 1222, 1224 (4th Cir. 1986) (whether employee's privacy interest will be recognized depends upon "whether the individual had a reasonable expectation of privacy in the area searched, not merely in the items found"); see, e.g. United States v. Simons, 206 F.3d 392 (4th Cir. 2000) (employee had legitimate expectation of privacy in his office because he did not share it, and there was no evidence of any workplace practices, procedures, or regulations that had the effect of lowering such expectation); cf. Schowengerdt v. United States, 944 F.2d 483, 485, 488-89 (9th Cir. 1991) (holding that civilian employee of Navy weapons plant lacked legitimate expectation of privacy in private office when office was regularly searched in employee's absence, employee was aware that such searches occurred, and employee had participated in searches of co-workers' offices); United States v. Taketa, 923 F.2d 665, 672-73 (9th Cir. 1991) (rejecting argument that government employee lacked a legitimate expectation of privacy in his office because regulation requiring clean desks implied that office was subject to inspection, in part on ground that the regulation had not been enforced by a practice of inspections).

2. ***State Law*** See III.A, supra.

C. Employee's Property

1. ***Federal Law*** Whether or not a governmental employer's search of an employee's property is improper will be tested by a standard of reasonableness under all the circumstances, which requires a balancing of the employee's privacy expectations against the governmental employer's need for supervision, control and an efficient workplace. O'Connor v. Ortega, 480 U.S. 709 (1987) (employee doctor had an expectation of privacy in his desk and file cabinets because they were used only by the doctor and he had kept personal items there for a long time); Faulkner v. State of Maryland, 317 Md. 441, 564 A.2d 785 (Md. 1989) (search of locker for drugs or alcohol not unreasonable where the employer periodically cut padlocks off to clean lockers on a regular schedule); McDonell v. Hunter, 809 F2d 1302 (8th Cir. 1987) (search of correctional officers' vehicles within prison confines found reasonable); Shields v. Burge, 874 F.2d 1201 (7th Cir. 1989) (police officer's search of another officer's closed, personal briefcase found inside automobile being lawfully searched as part of internal misconduct investigation was reasonable); but see Leventhal v. State of New York, 2001 WL 1159812 (2d Cir., Sept. 26, 2001) (state agency employee had reasonable expectation of privacy in contents of his office computer where employee occupied private office with door and had exclusive use of computer, and agency did not routinely conduct searches of office computers, nor had it adopted policy against mere storage of personal files, as opposed to use of agency time for personal business; however, agency possessed individualized suspicion justifying search).

2. ***State Law*** See III.A, supra.

IV. MONITORING OF EMPLOYEES

A. Telephones and Electronic Communications

It is unlawful under Oregon law for any person "to obtain or attempt to obtain the whole or any part of a telecommunication" unless at least one party has consented. ORS 165.540(1)(a). It is unlawful under Oregon law for any person "to obtain or attempt to obtain the whole or any part of a conversation by means of any device . . . if all participants in the conversation are not specifically informed that the conversation is being obtained." ORS 165.540(1)(c).

1. ***Wiretapping.*** See IV.A, supra.

2. ***Electronic Communications.*** See IV.A, supra.

3. ***Other Electronic Monitoring.*** See IV.A, supra.

B. Mail

A "person commits the crime of mail theft or receipt of stolen mail if the person intentionally:...(e) conceals or possesses mail...knowing that the mail...has been unlawfully taken or obtained." ORS 164.162.

C. Surveillance/Photographing

In the only case to consider the issue, the Oregon Supreme Court in McLain v. Boise Cascade Corp., 271 Or. 549, 533 P.2d 343 (1975), held that the videotaped surveillance of an individual who had filed a workers' compensation claim did not violate the individual's right of privacy. The court decided that a person who seeks to recover damages for alleged injuries waives the right of privacy to the extent of a reasonable investigation. The court went on to hold that surveillance is not necessarily unreasonable, particularly when the individual is unaware of it and when the activities being watched and filmed are open to neighbors and passersby. 271 Or. at 556.

V. ACTIVITIES OUTSIDE THE WORKPLACE

A. Statute or Common Law

See V.B, infra. In 2010, the Oregon Legislature enacted legislation prohibiting employers from using credit histories in making employment-related decisions. Or. Admin. R. 839-005-0070. Effective July 1, 2010, the legislation makes it "an unlawful employment practice for an employer to obtain or use for employment purposes information contained in the credit history of an applicant for employment or an employee, or to refuse to hire, discharge, demote, suspend, retaliate or otherwise discriminate against an applicant or an employee with regard to promotion, compensation or the terms, conditions or privileges of employment based on information in the credit history."

B. Employee's Personal Relationships

1. ***Romantic Relationships between Employees.*** The Oregon Supreme Court has held that an employer's restrictions on romantic relationships between employees do not implicate any constitutional or societal right. Patton v. J.C. Penney Co., 301 Or. 117, 719 P.2d 854 (1986), abrogated on other grounds by McGanty v. Staudenraus, 321 Or. 532, 901 P.2d 841 (1995).

2. ***Sexual Orientation.*** In a controversial decision, the Oregon Court of Appeals for the first time interpreted Oregon's anti-discrimination status, ORS 659.030(1)(b), as implicitly including sexual orientation as a protected class. Tanner v. OHSU, 157 Or. App. 502, 516, 971 P.2d 435 (1998). The state Bureau of Labor & Industries views the Tanner decision as creating a new protected class. The Cities of Portland, Eugene, Corvallis and Ashland by ordinance explicitly prohibit discrimination by employers on the basis of sexual orientation.

The Oregon Legislature has passed a statute codifying the decision in Tanner v. OHSU, 157 Or. App. 502, 516. Sexual orientation is now a protected class similar to race, national origin, religion, gender, marital status, and disability, and "sexual orientation" includes an individual's actual or perceived homosexuality, bisexuality or gender identity. ORS 659A.003; ORS 174.100(6).

3. ***Marital Status.*** It is an unlawful employment practice for an employer to discriminate against any employee or prospective employee because of that individual's marital status. ORS 659A.030.

4. ***Domestic Partnership.*** Same-sex couples may now choose to register as "domestic partners" in their respective counties of residence. "Domestic partnership" means a civil contract entered into in person between two individuals of the same sex who are at least 18 years of age, who are otherwise capable and at least one of whom is a resident of Oregon. Any privilege, immunity, right or benefit granted by statute, administrative or court rule, policy, common law or any other law to a person because of marriage is granted to a person in a domestic partnership. 2007 Or. Laws Ch. 106, §§ 1 to 9.

Under Oregon's domestic partnership law enacted in 2007, any privilege, immunity, right or benefit granted by statute, administrative or court rule, policy, common law or any other law to a person because of marriage is granted to a person in a domestic partnership. The Oregon Insurance Division issued a bulletin interpreting the law to require all group health insurance policies issued or renewed in Oregon on or after April 1, 2008 to provide the same rights to domestic partners as provided to spouses. Thus, an employer with a health insurance policy issued in Oregon must offer the same policy coverage for both spouses and domestic partners. The domestic partnership legislation does not mandate employers extend any benefit under an employee benefit plan that is subject to federal regulation under the Employee Retirement Income Security Act (ERISA) (e.g., retirement plans and self-insured health plans), but insured plans are subject to indirect regulation through the Oregon Insurance Code. However, employers may voluntarily extend such benefits to domestic partners as long as they note the different federal tax treatment of benefits provided to spouses (usually tax exempt) as opposed to domestic partners (often a taxable benefit).

C. Smoking

It is an unlawful employment practice for an employer to require, as a condition of employment, any employee or prospective employee to refrain from using lawful tobacco products during non-working hours except when the restriction relates to a bona fide occupational requirement or when an applicable collective bargaining agreement prohibits off duty use of tobacco products. ORS 659A.315.

D. Blogging

No Oregon statute or case specifically addresses blogging. Employers should consider adopting and disseminating a blogging policy that clearly lays out the expectations and restrictions.

E. Expression of Breast Milk

For employers who have 25 or more employees, employees may be allowed to express breast milk during unpaid break periods. An employer must make a reasonable effort to provide a location, other than a public restroom or toilet stall, in close proximity to the employee's work area for the employee to express milk in private. An employer is not required to provide rest periods for the expression of breast milk only if to do so would impose an undue hardship on the operation of the employer's business. ORS 653.077(2); see also 29 U.S.C. §207(r)(1) (setting forth same requirements for employers with 50 or more employees).

F. Employee Leave for Certain Crime Victims

In 2007, the Oregon Legislature enacted legislation requiring employers with six or more employees to allow employees affected by sexual assault, domestic violence or stalking crimes to take time off to address their circumstances including leave to attend proceedings, obtain healthcare, and to relocate or secure their homes. In 2011, the law was extended to also cover victims of criminal harassment. 2011 Or. Laws Ch. 210, § 3. To be eligible, an employee must be a victim of, or the parent or guardian of a victim of, sexual assault, domestic violence, and stalking crimes. The employee must have worked at least an average of 25 hours per week during the 180 days prior to the leave. Employers must allow a reasonable amount of leave, unless it causes an undue hardship, which is defined as "significant difficulty and expense" in consideration of the size of the employer and the need for the employee's services. The leave is unpaid except that employers must allow employees to use any available vacation or other paid time off. Employees must provide reasonable advance notice of the need for leave, unless giving notice is not feasible. The employer can require the employee to provide certification justifying the need for leave. Certification can include a copy of a police report, protective order, or other evidence from a court or attorney or member of law enforcement, health care provider, member of the clergy or victim services provider. All records must be kept confidential. ORS 659A.190-659A.198; 2007 Or. Laws Ch. 180, §§ 2 to 7.

VI. RECORDS

A. Personnel Records

No Oregon statute requires an employer to maintain personnel records *per se*. If such records are maintained, public and private employers must, upon request, *provide the employee the records within 45 days of receipt of the request*, and allow the employee to inspect those personnel records which are used or have been used to determine the employee's qualification for employment, promotion, additional compensation or employment termination or other disciplinary action. Upon termination of employment, the employer shall keep the terminated employee's personnel records for not less than 60 days. At the request of the employee, within the 60-day period or at any time if the employer has retained the records at the time of the request, the employer shall furnish all certified copies of such records within 45 days of receipt of the request. ORS 652.750(2)-(3).

Personnel records regarding crime victims and their immediate family members who take state-mandated leaves of absence to attend a criminal proceeding are to be kept confidential. See ORS 659A.196(2).

Public employee personnel records are public records within the meaning of Oregon's Public Records Act. Personnel disciplinary actions and documents related thereto, ORS 192.501(12) (2001), are exempt from disclosure. Also, information "of a personal nature" kept in a "personal (sic) medical or similar file" is exempt absent clear and convincing evidence of the public interest if "disclosure would constitute an unreasonable invasion of privacy" ORS 192.502(2) (2001).

B. Medical Records

Under Oregon's Civil Rights of Disabled Persons Act, ORS 659A.122 et seq., employers are required to maintain employee medical records in separate, confidential files.

C. Criminal Records

In the public sector, under ORS 181.534, authorized agencies including the Oregon State Lottery and any criminal justice agencies defined in ORS 181.010, may request that the Department of State Police conduct a criminal records check on an individual for non-criminal justice purposes. When a state criminal records check is completed, the Department of

State Police shall destroy the fingerprint cards and results of the criminal records check provided to the authorized agency and shall retain no facsimiles or other material from which a fingerprint can be reproduced.

Authorized agencies can use criminal record checks for agency employment purposes including: 1) to determine when and under what conditions a subject individual may be hired on a preliminary basis pending a criminal records check or 2) to define the conditions under which a subject individual may participate in training, orientation and work activities pending completion of a criminal records check. Any criminal offender information is confidential. Authorized agencies and the Department of State Police have rules to restrict the dissemination of information received under this section to persons with a demonstrated and legitimate need to know the information. Lastly, if an authorized agency requires a criminal records check of employees or prospective employees the application forms of the authorized agency must contain a notice that the person is subject to fingerprinting and a criminal records check.

D. Subpoenas / Search Warrants

The Commissioner of the Bureau of Labor and Industries may conduct investigations, issue subpoena, and subpoenas duces tecum when the information sought is relevant to a lawful investigative purpose and is reasonable in scope. A party subject to the subpoena may object to providing information. After being served with a subpoena, if a person refuses, without reasonable cause, to be examined, to answer any question or to produce any document or other thing as required by the subpoena, the commissioner may petition the circuit court in the county in which the investigation is pending for an order directing the person to show cause why the person has not complied with the subpoena and should not be held in contempt. ORS 651.060.

Under Oregon's Constitution and the Fourth Amendment of the United States Constitution, a subpoena duces tecum seeking an employer's records and documents, which may include employee files, is not an unreasonable search and seizure. State v. Van Drimmelen, 240 Or. 347, 349, 401 P.2d 298 (1965); Pope & Talbot, Inc. v. St. Tax Comm., 216 Or. 605, 614-616, 340 P.2d 960 (1959).

Oregon Rules of Civil Procedure provide procedural requirements attorneys must follow when issuing a subpoena for individually identifiable health information. ORCP 55 H. The individual (or his or her attorney) must receive 14 days prior notice before issuing the subpoena. The health care provider must be told that such notice has been given and that he or she did not object within the 14 days.

E. Court Filings

Oregon's rules of Civil Procedure and Uniform Trial Court Rules prohibit the filing of documents that contain a social security number. The social security number must be redacted.

VII. ACTIONS SUBSEQUENT TO EMPLOYMENT

A. References

Employers have a qualified privilege when responding to references from prospective employers. Providing the information is provided at the request of the prospective employer and discloses information about the former employee's job performance, the privilege applies. ORS 30.178(1).

B. Non-Compete Agreements

Non-compete agreements are enforceable only if the employer informs the employee in a written employment offer received by the employee at least two weeks before the first day of the employee's employment that a non-competition agreement is required as a condition of employment; or the non-competition agreement is entered into upon a subsequent bona fide advancement of the employee by the employer. ORS 653.295.

In order to be enforceable an employee must have access to the employer's protectable interest such as trade secrets, competitively sensitive confidential business, or professional information that include product development plans, product launch plans, marketing strategy or sales plans. ORS 653.295.

These non-compete agreements may only be entered into with an employee who meets the "white collar exemption." The employee must also be paid more than the median gross income for a family of four at the time of termination (approximately $62,000). These requirements will only affect agreements effective January 1, 2008 or later, and will not affect non-solicitation agreements. If an employer fails to meet these requirements, an employer may buy an enforceable non -compete by paying at least 50% of the employee's annual gross salary for up to two years or 50% of the median family income for a 4 person family, whichever amount is greater. ORS 653.295.

VIII. OTHER ISSUES

A. Statute of Limitations

In general, the two-year statute of limitations for torts provided in ORS 12.110 applies to actions for invasion of privacy. However, actions for placing the plaintiff in a false light must be commenced within one year. Magenis v. Fisher Broadcasting Inc., 103 Or. App. 555, 798 P.2d 1106 (1990).

B. Jurisdiction

Oregon state courts have jurisdiction, including under the state's long arm statute. Rosenlund v. Transnational Ins., Co., 237 F. Supp. 599 (D. Or. 1964).

C. Workers' Compensation Exclusivity

The Oregon Workers' Compensation Act ("Act"), ORS Chapter 656, provides the exclusive remedy for employees' injuries arising out of and in the course of employment. ORS 656.018. The Act requires that employers either obtain insurance or show proof of self-insurance to cover work related injuries. The system operates as a "no fault" system by granting employees sure and certain relief for both medical and wage loss benefits while generally freeing employers from the threat of common law remedies such as emotional distress, pain and suffering and outrageous conduct. The Workers' Compensation Division of the Department of Consumer and Business Services administers the Act. However, employers may still be liable directly to an employee under the Oregon Employers' Liability Act. The Employers' Liability Act provides that an employer who is either an owner, contractor, or subcontractor and who violates health and safety laws may be held liable for damages that result from the consequent injury or death of an employee. The negligence of a fellow employee is not a defense, nor is the contributory negligence of the injured employee, although it may be taken into account by the jury in determining the amount of damages. Moreover, in 2002, the Oregon Supreme Court issued a decision holding that the exclusive remedy provision of the workers compensation system did not apply when a person applied for benefits and was denied benefits. In other words, if the insurer found that the injury was due, for instance, to a preexisting injury rather than a work place accident or condition, and the employee was therefore not eligible for benefits, the employee could then bring a negligence action directly against the employer. *Smothers v. Gresham Transfer Inc.,* 332 Or. 83, 23 P.3d. 333 (2001).

D. Pleading Requirements

Where the complaint is of false light privacy, a plaintiff must allege that the defendant had knowledge of or acted in reckless disregard of the falsity of the published matter and the false light in which it would place him. Dean v. Guard Pub. Co., Inc., 73 Or.App. 656, 660, 699 P.2d 1158, 1160 - 1161 (1985).

E. Damages

1. ***Mental Distress Damages.*** In Oregon, damages for mental distress and suffering are recoverable if they are directly related to the invasion of privacy. Dean v. Guard Publ'g Co., 73 Or. App. 656, 699 P.2d 1158 (1985). To be recoverable, the claimed emotional stress must be a direct result of the invasion of privacy. Leggett v. First Interstate Bank of Oregon, 86 Or. App. 523, 739 P.2d 1083 (1987).

2. ***Punitive Damages.*** Punitive damages are generally recoverable in invasion of privacy claims. Leggett v. First Interstate Bank of Oregon, 86 Or. App. 523, 739 P.2d 1083 (1987). However, in accordance with Article 1, Section 8 of the Oregon Constitution, punitive damages are barred when the harm results solely from abusive speech. Wheeler v. Green, 286 Or. 99, 593 P.2d 777 (1979).

SURVEY OF PENNSYLVANIA EMPLOYMENT LIBEL LAW

Stacy Alison Fols
Kristen E. Polovoy
Montgomery, McCracken, Walker & Rhoads, LLP
123 South Broad Street
Philadelphia, PA 19103
Telephone: (215) 772-1500; Facsimile: (215) 772-7620

(With Developments Reported Through **November 1, 2012**)

GENERAL COMMENTS

Pennsylvania's judicial system has four levels. The highest level is the Supreme Court, which administers all the courts within the state. It hears discretionary appeals from the Superior and Commonwealth courts by allowance, direct appeals from the courts of Common Pleas in cases specified by statute, and direct appeals from the Commonwealth Court in its original jurisdiction. The next level includes two appellate courts: the Superior Court and the Commonwealth Court. The Superior Court hears civil and criminal appeals from the Court of Common Pleas. The Commonwealth Court hears original civil cases commenced by and against the Commonwealth of Pennsylvania, appeals from decisions by state agencies and from the Courts of Common Pleas involving the Commonwealth and local agencies. The third level is the Court of Common Pleas, which hears major civil and criminal cases, and appeals from the Special Courts. The final level is the Special Courts, which hear minor non-jury civil and criminal matters.

The opinions of the Pennsylvania Supreme Court, which are cited to as "Pa.," are published in the Pennsylvania Reports and/or the Atlantic Reporter. Citations to "Pa. Super." reference the Pennsylvania Superior Court, whose opinions are published in the Pennsylvania Superior Court Reports and/or the Atlantic Reporter. Pennsylvania Superior Court cases after January 1999 are published in public domain format, as indicated by citations to "Pa. Super." Citations to "Pa. Commw." reference the Pennsylvania Commonwealth Court, whose opinions are published in the Pennsylvania Commonwealth Court Reports and/or the Atlantic Reporter. The opinions of the Pennsylvania Court of Common Pleas, which are cited to as "Pa. D. & C.," are reported in the Pennsylvania District and County Reports.

SIGNIFICANT DEVELOPMENTS SINCE THE 2012 *SURVEY*

This year, in Krajewski v. Gusoff, ___ A.3d ___, 2012 WL 3292225, *7 (Pa. Super. Aug. 14, 2012), the court stressed that, in determining whether a statement is capable of a defamatory meaning, courts must look to the full context when "consider[ing] what effect the statement would have on the minds of the average persons among whom the statement would circulate." The court looked at many factors, including the placement of items on a page and the timing of the statements in holding that statements and a cartoon critical of plaintiff council member's acceptance of payments from Philadelphia's Deferred Retirement Option Plan "might suggest to the average reader that [plaintiff] acted to the detriment of her constituents in accepting a large payout of public funds that might otherwise have sustained a branch of the Philadelphia Free Library."

Over the past year, federal courts in Pennsylvania have applied the "truth defense" to a RESTATEMENT (SECOND) OF TORTS § 772(a) claim for tortious interference with contractual relations -- as adopted by the Pennsylvania Supreme Court in 2011 -- with the federal courts finding that applicability of the defense turns on the facts of each case. However, a defendant's improper intent is irrelevant, "so long as [the statement] is truthfully and honestly given." Manning v. Flannery, No. 2:10-cv-178, 2012 WL 1111188, at *1, 25-26 (W.D. Pa. Mar. 31, 2012).

I. GENERAL LAW

A. General Employment Law

1. ***At Will Employment.*** Pennsylvania is an at-will employment state. Pipkin v. Pa. State Police, 548 Pa. 1, 4, 693 A.2d 190, 191 (1997). The presumption is that all employment is at-will, and that the employer or employee can terminate the employment relationship for any reason or no reason at all. Luteran v. Loral Fairchild Corp., 455 Pa. Super. 364, 371, 688 A.2d 211, 214 (1997) (language in handbook stating that the employer would "discharge for just cause" did not establish contract that employee could only be fired for just cause); Nelson v. DeVry, Inc., No. 07-4436, 2008 U.S. Dist. LEXIS 55696 (E.D. Pa. July 22, 2008) (refusing to recognize a cause of action for "negligent termination of employment" and noting that such a claim is at "odds with Pennsylvania's presumption of at-will employment."). Thus, Pennsylvania recognizes no common law cause of action against an employer for termination of an at-will employment relationship. Rapagnani v. Judas Co., 1999 Pa. Super. 203, 206, 736 A.2d 666, 669 (1999); Guerra v. Redevelopment Authority of City of

Philadelphia, 2011 Pa. Super. 181, 27 A.3d 1284 (Pa. Super. 2011) (noting that exceptions to this rule have been recognized in only the most limited of circumstances, where discharges of at-will employees would threaten the clear mandates of public policy).

The at-will presumption can be rebutted if the employee establishes one of the following exceptions: "(1) an agreement for a definite duration; (2) an agreement specifying that the employee will be discharged for just cause only; (3) sufficient additional consideration; or (4) an applicable recognized public policy exception." Luteran, 455 Pa. Super. at 371, 688 A.2d at 214. To establish the first exception, an employee must show clear and precise evidence that the parties intended to enter an employment contract for a definite term, and "comments wheich merely evince an employers *hope* that the employee will remain" are inadequate to provie a contract for a definite term. Marsh v. Boyle, 530 A.2d 491, 493 (Pa. Super. 1987). **See also Edwards v. Geisinger Clinic, 459 Fed. Appx. 125, 2012 WL 171967 (3d Cir. 2012) (noting that "aspirational statement of employer and employee expectations" that the employment would last a number of years does not establish an express contract under Pennsylvania law)**; Ruzicki v. Catholic Cemeteries Ass'n of Diocese of Pittsburgh, 416 Pa. Super. 37, 41, 610 A.2d 495, 497 (1992). In order to "contract-away" the presumption, however, the contract must be sufficiently definite and of a specific duration. Veno v. Meredith, 357 Pa. Super. 85, 96, 515 A.2d 571, 577 (1986), appeal denied, 532 Pa. 665, 616 A.2d 986 (1992); Schecter v. Watkins, 395 Pa. Super. 363, 372-73, 577 A.2d 585, 589-90 (1990), appeal denied, 526 Pa. 638, 584 A.2d 320 (1990). See Rapagnani, 1999 Pa. Super. 203, ¶ 8, 736 A.2d at 670 ("Generally, an employment contract for a broad, unspecified duration does not overcome the presumption of at-will employment . . . Definiteness is required. . . ."); see, e.g., Marsh v. Boyle, 366 Pa. Super. 1, 7, 530 A.2d 491, 494 (1987) (an employer's assurance that the employee would be working as a publisher for at two least years was not sufficiently definite); Darlington v. Gen. Elec., 350 Pa. Super. 183, 194, 504 A.2d 306, 312 (1986), overruled on other grounds by Clay v. Advanced Computer Applications, Inc., 522 Pa. 86, 559 A.2d 917 (1989) (a contract for "permanent employment" or to work on a long-term project is insufficient) (internal citations omitted). However, while the Eastern District has noted that "Pennsylvania law does not permit a claim based on promissory estoppel by an employee; a claim based on promissory estoppel by an independent contractor does not appear to be precluded." Inoff v. Craftex Mills, Inc., No. 06-3675, 2007 U.S. Dist. LEXIS 91552 at *35, 38 (E.D. Pa. Dec. 11, 2007) (holding that if the plaintiff "was not an employee, but was an independent contractor as defendants allege, a theory of promissory estoppel is a permissible alternative argument to the presence of a term contract."). "[A]n employee handbook does not overcome the 'at-will' presumption unless the handbook's language clearly expresses the employer's intent to do so." In re Grose, 2005 Pa. Super. 8. ¶10, 886 A.2d 437, 441 (2005), appeal denied, 889 A.2d 89 (Pa. 2005). If such a contract is proven, then the employee cannot be terminated during that period unless the employer has "just cause." Greene v. Oliver Realty, Inc., 363 Pa. Super. 534, 543, 526 A.2d 1192, 1196 (1987), appeal denied, 517 Pa. 607, 536 A.2d 1331 (1987).

Like the first exception, the second exception applies where an agreement exists, either express or implied, that the employee will be discharged for just cause only. Luteran v. Loral Fairchild Corp., 455 Pa. Super. 364, 371, 688 A.2d 211, 214 (1997), appeal denied, 549 Pa. 717, 701 A.2d 578. Such a contract must clearly establish that the parties intend the employee to be terminated only for just cause, and this intention will not be unheedingly inferred. Veno v. Meredith, 357 Pa. Super. 85, 99, 515 A.2d 571, 577 (1992), appeal denied, 532 Pa. 655, 616 A.2d 986. The Pennsylvania Superior Court declined to find such an intention in Luteran v. Loral Fairchild Corp., 455 Pa. Super. 364, 688 A.2d 211, despite language in an employee handbook advising employees that they "may only be discharged for just cause," where the handbook also stated that it was to be used merely as an informational guideline regarding the employer's business, policies, and procedures, and the employer retained the right to amend the handbook unilaterally at any time. Id. at 369-71, 688 A.2d at 213-15. However, a collective bargaining agreement containing specific language guaranteeing termination for just cause only is sufficient to overcome the "at will" presumption. Dee v. Borough of Dunmore, 549 F.3d 225, 231 (3d Cir. 2008) (holding that a collective bargaining agreement containing such language created a property interest in continued employment). Note that persons who hold a property interest in their positions are not necessarily due a pre-suspension hearing or notice, depending on the circumstances. Smith v. Borough of Dunmore, 633 F.3d 176, 182 (3d Cir. 2011) (recognizing that "the strong government interest in public safety" could justify suspension without a prior hearing in some cases). Also, an employee has no property interest in a job where his contract specifies that he can be terminated immediately for cause but with ninety days notice without cause. Greene v. Street, 2011 WL 208382 (E.D. Pa., Jan. 20, 2011). Although there is no express definition of the term "just cause," the Pennsylvania courts have explained that "the promise to discharge only for cause provides an objective measure by which to evaluate the dismissal: What was the reason for the dismissal, and in the circumstances did the reason amount to just cause?" Martin v. Capital Cities Media, Inc., 354 Pa. Super. 199, 210, 511 A.2d 830, 836 (1986), appeal denied, 514 Pa. 643, 523 A.2d 1123. The Pennsylvania Superior Court, in an early decision, explained that an employer is "not compelled to keep an employee, hired for a given term, in his [or her] service until the master's business has suffered pecuniary loss, where the employee is disobedient and quarrelsome with co-employees." O'Neil v. Schneller, 63 Pa. Super. 196, 200 (1916). Rather, "[w]hen the [employer] is justified in believing that the employee's conduct is such that an injury or loss to the business or disorganization of affairs is likely to flow from such conduct if it is permitted to continue, the [employer] would be warranted in discharging the employee." Id.

The third exception permits even a contract of indefinite duration to rebut the presumption of at-will employment, if the employee proves that he or she gave the employer additional consideration. Luteran, 455 Pa. Super. at 374, 688 A.2d at 216. "Additional consideration" may be found when the employee bestows upon the employer a substantial benefit other than the services for which the employee was hired to perform, or when the employee undergoes a substantial hardship other than the services for which the employee was hired to perform. Rapagnani v. Judas Co., 1999 Pa. Super. 203, ¶ 11, 736 A.2d 666, 671. If the employee successfully establishes sufficient additional consideration, the employee cannot be discharged absent just cause. Luteran, 455 Pa. Super. at 375, 688 A.2d at 216. Pennsylvania case law differs on what acts constitute sufficient additional consideration. See Rapagnani, 1999 Pa. Super. 203, ¶ 12, 736 A.2d 666, 671 (where there is an expectation in the profession that the employee accepting the subject employment position must leave his or her residence, there is no support for a finding of additional consideration); Veno, 357 Pa. Super. 85, 101, 515 A.2d 571, 580 (an employee's relocation from Newark, New Jersey to Pennsylvania to accept a position with the employer was not sufficient additional consideration but rather a detriment incurred by all manner of salaried professionals); But see Lucacher v. Kerson, 158 Pa. Super. 437, 443, 45 A.2d 245, 248 (1946), aff'd, 355 Pa. 79, 48 A.2d 857 (1946) (an individual's act of leaving a current job to relocate his family from New York to Philadelphia to take a new position with the employer constituted sufficient additional consideration); **Ciari v. Laurel Media Inc., 2012 WL 70656, *4 (W.D. Pa. Jan. 9, 2012) (noting that additional consideration cannot be the "detriments commensurate with those incurred by all manner of salaried professionals," but finding that plaintiff stated a claim based on the additional consideration exception with allegations that she had relocated from Florida to Pennsylvania and her employer paid to move her belongings but terminated her after only 16 days).** "It is a question of fact whether, in a given case, the additional consideration furnished by the employee is sufficient to rebut the at-will presumption." Cashdollar v. Mercy Hosp. of Pittsburgh, 406 Pa. Super. 606, 612, 595 A.2d 70, 73 (1991). Note that where an employee receives compensation for the alleged additional consideration provided, the employee does not provide more than the services the employee is hired to perform and the presumption will not be overcome. Clinkscales v. CHOP, 2009 U.S. Dist. LEXIS 38939, at *22-24 (E.D. Pa. May 6, 2009) (citing Veno v. Meredith, 515 A.2d 580 (Pa. Super. Ct. 1986) (holding that an employee who renders additional consideration creates an implied contract and is due a reasonable duration of employment prior to dismissal)). Also, even where additional consideration is furnished, the implied contract protects the employee against dismissal only for a "reasonable" period of time. Id. See Chalfont v. U.S. Electrodes, 2010 WL 5341846 (E.D.Pa., Dec. 28, 2010) (noting that, typically, such implied contracts are found where the employees in question were terminated after extremely brief periods of employment between four days and three months, and rejecting the argument that an implied contract lasting seventeen years could have been created by additional consideration).

The final exception permits the employee to rebut the at-will presumption if termination of the employment relationship by the employer violated some recognized public policy. Brozovich v. Dugo, 651 A.2d 641, 643-44 (Pa. Commw. Ct. 1994), appeal denied, 541 Pa. 643, 663 A.2d 694 (1995). Under the public policy exception, the employer cannot: (1) require the employee to commit a crime, (2) prevent the employee from complying with a statutorily imposed duty, or (3) discharge the employee when specially prohibited from doing so by statute. Donahue v. Fed. Express Corp., 2000 Pa. Super. 146, ¶ 19, 753 A.2d 238, 244 (2000). The public policy exception to the at-will employment doctrine is a narrow one: an employee "must show a violation of a clearly mandated public policy which 'strikes at the heart of a citizen's social rights, duties and responsibilities.'" Turner v. Letterkenny Fed. Credit Union, 351 Pa. Super. 51, 505 A.2d 259, 261 (1985). Courts have found public policy exceptions where employees have been discharged for refusing to submit to a polygraph test, for filing an unemployment compensation claim, and for submitting a worker's compensation claim. See Rothrock v. Rothrock Motor Sales, Inc., 584 Pa. 297, 883 A.2d 511, 515 (2005). The public policy exception has also been applied when discharge results from conduct by the employee that is required by law, or when an employee refuses to engage in conduct prohibited by law. Clark v. Modern Group Ltd., 9 F.3d 321, 328 (3d Cir. 1993). The court has found public policy violated where an employee was terminated for serving on a jury, Reuther v. Fowler & Williams, Inc., 255 Pa. Super. 28, 32, 386 A.2d 119, 121 (1978); for reporting a violation of federal nuclear regulations, Field v. Philadelphia Elec. Co., 388 Pa. Super. 400, 418-25, 565 A.2d 1170, 1179-82 (1989); and for filing a Worker's Compensation Claim, Shick v. Shirey, 552 Pa. 590, 604, 716 A.2d 1231, 1238 (1998). The courts, however, have rejected claims that a private employer violated a public policy by firing an employee for whistleblowing when the employee was under no legal duty to report the acts at issue. Donahue v. Fed. Express Corp., 2000 Pa. Super. 146, ¶ 20, 753 A.2d 238, 244. Additionally, the Third Circuit has stated that under Pennsylvania law an employee's mere "speculation" as to the lawfulness of required acts is "insufficient for [the court] to conclude" that the conduct allegedly required would have violated a law or legal requirement. Martinez v. Rapidigm, Inc., 290 Fed. Appx. 521, 527 (3d Cir. 2008). The Third Circuit has further held that Pennsylvania courts would not use the First Amendment as a source of a public policy exception where no state action exists. Fraser, 352 F. 3d at 112-13; accord Brennan v. Cephalon, Inc., No. 04-3241 2005 U.S. Dist. LEXIS 25170, *55-56 (D. N.J. Oct. 25, 2005) (applying Pennsylvania Law); but see Novosel v. Nationwide Ins. Co., 721 F.2d 894 (3d Cir. 1983) (holding that firing an employee based on their refusal to participate in compelled political speech violated public policy). The Eastern District court has noted that under Pennsylvania law, "a plaintiff may only bring a claim for wrongful termination if his or her termination violated the public policy of *Pennsylvania*." Conklin v. Moran Industries, Inc., 2011 WL 2135647 (E.D.Pa., May 31, 2011) (noting "the possibility that an individual's termination violated federal law is itself insufficient to establish that his or her termination violated Pennsylvania public policy"). The Third Circuit has indicated that the public policy exception to at-will employment would apply to independent contractors as well as employees. Fraser v. Nationwide Mut. Ins. Co., 352 F. 3d 107, 111 (3d Cir. 2003).

B. Elements of Libel Claim

1. ***Basic Elements.*** In Pennsylvania, the elements for a claim of defamation are defined by statute. Pursuant to this statute, the plaintiff carries the burden of proving the following: (1) the defamatory character of the communication; (2) its publication by the defendant; (3) its application to the plaintiff; (4) the understanding by the recipient of its defamatory meaning; (5) the understanding by the recipient of it as intended to be applied to the plaintiff; (6) special harm resulting to the plaintiff from its publication; and (7) abuse of a conditionally privileged occasion. 42 PA. CONS. STAT. ANN. § 8343(a) (West 1998).

Once the above is established, the defendant must then prove by affirmative defense the following: (1) the truth of the defamatory communication; (2) the privileged character of the occasion on which it was published; and (3) the character of the subject matter of defamatory comment as of public concern. Id. § 8343(b).

In order to ensure freedom of speech and the press, particularly in cases involving public issues or figures, courts are tasked with the job of carefully scrutinizing defamation claims, and summary judgment is encouraged where the minimum legal requirements have not been met. First Lehigh Bank v. Cowen, 700 A.2d 498, 502 (Pa. Super. 1997) (emphasizing the "important function" of summary judgment in the context of First Amendment limits on defamation claims, noting: "For the stake here, if harassment succeeds, is free debate") (internal citations omitted).

2. ***Fault.*** The questions of the level of fault that plaintiff must establish and which party bears the burden of proving truth or falsity depends upon whether the plaintiff is a public or private figure and whether the allegedly defamatory statement was on a matter of public concern.

It is the function of the trial court to ascertain in the first instance whether the plaintiff is a public or private figure. Iafrate v. Hadesty, 423 Pa. Super. 619, 622, 621 A.2d 1005, 1007, 21 Media L. Rep. 1378 (1993). In Pennsylvania, there are two classes of public figures. The first class concerns an individual who achieves such pervasive fame or notoriety that he or she becomes a public figure for all purposes and in all contexts. Id. at 623. The second class concerns a "limited purpose public figure," which is an individual who voluntarily injects himself or herself or is drawn into a particular public controversy and thereby becomes a public figure for a limited range of issues. Id. Such a person uses "purposeful activity" to thrust "his personality" into a "public controversy." Id. A private individual, however, is not automatically transformed into a public figure just by becoming involved in or associated with a matter that attracts public attention. Id. See Heimbecker v. Drudge, 2011 WL 828418, *1 (Pa. Com. Pl., January 31, 2011) (noting that plaintiff "became a public figure by creating a controversy" concerning the nomination of Justice Alito to the Supreme Court "and by publicizing the fact that he filed a judicial misconduct complaint against Justice Alito").

A communication is of public concern if it is "a real dispute, the outcome of which affects the general public or some segment of it in an appreciable way." Iafrate. at 624, 621 A.2d at 1009. See, e.g., Matus v. Triangle Publications, 445 Pa. 384, 286 A.2d 357 (1971), *overruled on other grounds,* 506 Pa. 304, 485 A.2d 374 (1984) (talk show host's allegation that a snow remover had overcharged and should not be in business what a matter of private concern); Dougherty v. Boyertown Times, 377 Pa. Super. 462, 474-75, 547 A.2d 778, 784, 15 Media L. Rep. 2433 (1988) (holding that letter concerning qualifications of chiropractor was of public concern because of regulation by statute of the medical profession).

a. **Private Figure Plaintiff/Matter of Public Concern.** Private figure libel plaintiffs must prove "that the defamatory matter was published with 'want of reasonable care and diligence to ascertain the truth' or, in the vernacular, with negligence." Rutt v. Bethlehems' Globe Publ'g Co., 335 Pa. Super. 163, 186, 484 A.2d 72, 83 (1984). Private figure plaintiffs need only prove negligence on the part of defendant, regardless of whether the defamatory statement was a matter of public or private concern. Am. Future Sys., Inc. v. Better Bus. Bureau of E. Pa., 592 Pa. 66, 84, 923 A.2d 389, 400 (Pa. 2007) (holding that the plaintiff at issue was a public rather than private figure, but noting that negligence is "the appropriate standard relative to a private-figure plaintiff " in all contexts because of the "Pennsylvania Constitution's protections in the area of reputational interests"). Negligence in this context is the publication of information with a want of reasonable care to ascertain the truth. Joeseph v. Scranton Times L.P., 959 A.2d 322, 342 (Pa. Super. 2008). See also 42 PA. CONS. STAT. ANN. § 8343. Some case law, exists, however, that incorrectly suggests that a higher standard than negligence applies. See, e.g., Moore v. Vislosky, 240 Fed. Appx. 457, 2007 WL 1182021 (3d Cir. 2007) (in which the Court of Appeals for the Third Circuit, based on the trial court opinion in American Future Systems and a month prior to the Pennsylvania Supreme Court's decision and statement to the contrary, predicted "that the Pennsylvania Supreme Court would now require a private-figure plaintiff suing on matters of public concern to show that the statements were made with actual malice to defeat a conditional privilege under Pennsylvania law").

b. **Private Figure Plaintiff/Matter of Private Concern**. Private figure plaintiffs who commence a defamation action against a defendant for a defamatory communication of private concern need only demonstrate negligence in order to recover compensatory damages. Am. Future Sys., 592 Pa. at 84, 923 A.2d at 400; Rutt, 335 Pa. Super. at 186, 484 A.2d at 83. See also 42 PA. CONS. STAT. ANN. § 8343.

c. **Public Figure Plaintiff/Matter of Public Concern.** If the plaintiff is a public official or public figure and the statement relates to a matter of public concern, then to satisfy First Amendment strictures the plaintiff must establish that the defendant made a false and defamatory statement with actual malice. **Krajewski v. Gusoff, ___ A.3d ___, 2012 WL 3292225, *7 (Pa. Super. Aug. 14, 2012) ("When raised by a public official concerning statements bearing on a matter of public concern, claims for defamation are subject to an onerous standard of proof, owing to considerations of free speech that inhere to any claim that implicates the First Amendment");** Am. Future Systems, 592 Pa. at 85, 923 A.2d at 400. In other words, the plaintiff must prove "that the defamatory statements were made with knowledge of their falsity or with reckless disregard for the truth." Iafrate v. Hadesty, 423 Pa. Super. 619, 622, 621 A.2d 1005, 1007, 21 Media L. Rep. 1378 (1993). Although the term "reckless disregard for the truth" is incapable of precise definition, "the defendant must have made the false publication with a high degree of awareness of . . . probable falsity, . . . or must have entertained serious doubts as to the truth of his [or her] publication." Sprague v. Walter, 441 Pa. Super. 1, 25, 656 A.2d 890, 904 (1995), appeal denied, 543 Pa. 695, 670 A.2d 142 (1996). Moreover, "actual malice is proven by applying a subjective standard by evidence that the defendants in fact entertained serious doubts as to the truth of its publication by clear and convincing evidence." Weaver v. Lancaster Newspapers, Inc., 2005 Pa. Super. 165, ¶ 22, 875 A.2d 1093, 1103, 33 Media L. Rep. 1609 (2005), rev'd and remanded on other grounds, 926 A.2d 899, 35 Med. L. Rep. 2170 (Pa. 2007) (holding that subsequent republication of the statement, after the defendant is notified that it is allegedly defamatory, is relevant in determining whether actual malice exists). However, pure negligence arising from a failure to investigate alternative sources is not sufficient to show that actual malice existed. See Blackwell v. Eskin, WCAU-TV, 2007 Pa. Super. 20, 916 A.2d 1123, 1126, 35 Media L. Rep. 1720 (Pa. Super. Ct. 2007) (holding that defendant's failure to confirm the truth behind source's statements would not show that actual malice existed even if it were deemed negligent); Skiff RE Business, Inc. v. Buckingham Ridgeview, LP, 991 A.2d 956, 965 (Pa.Super. 2010) (noting that failing to investigate the truth of an honestly or reasonably believed statement, without more, will not support a finding of malice).

3. ***Falsity.*** Both plaintiffs who are public figures and plaintiffs suing over statements that are a matter of public concern have the burden of affirmatively establishing that the statement is false. Pennsylvania requires the public figure plaintiff to prove falsity. Ertel v. Patriot-News Co., 544 Pa. 93, 99, 674 A.2d 1038, 1041, 24 Media L. Rep. 2233 (1996), cert. denied, 519 U.S. 1008 (1996). Also, the private figure plaintiff who commences a defamation action against a defendant for a defamatory communication of a public concern must prove falsity. ToDay's Housing v. Times Shamrock Communications, Inc., 2011 Pa. Super. 91, 21 A.3d 1209 (Pa. Super. Ct. 2011) (noting that the "activities of highly regulated industries are generally deemed matters of public concern"). See also Dougherty v. Boyertown Times, 377 Pa. Super. 462, 475-76, 547 A.2d 778, 784-85, 15 Media L. Rep. 2433 (1988); Philadelphia Newspapers, Inc. v. Hepps, 475 U.S. 767, 12 Media L. Rep. 1977 (1986). In all other defamation matters, namely those concerning a private figure plaintiff and a communication of private concern, the plaintiff need not prove falsity, but the defendant has the burden of proving the truth of the statement. Simms v. Exeter Architectural Prods., 916 F. Supp. 432, 437 (M.D. Pa. 1996).

4. ***Defamatory Statement of Fact.*** The threshold determination to be made in a defamation case is whether the communication at issue is capable of defamatory meaning. Kurowski v. Burroughs, 994 A.2d 611, 616 (Pa. Super. 2010; Weinstein v. Bullick, 827 F. Supp. 1193, 1196, 22 Media L. Rep. 1481 (E.D. Pa. 1993), aff'd, 77 F.3d 465 (3d Cir. 1996). The initial determination of whether a communication is defamatory presents a question of law. MacElree v. Philadelphia Newspapers, Inc., 544 Pa. 117, 124, 674 A.2d 1050, 1053 (1996). The court must consider the impression the communication would engender in the minds of the average persons among whom it is intended to circulate and in the context in which it was made. Baker v. Lafayette Coll., 516 Pa. 291, 296, 532 A.2d 399, 402 (1987); **Krajewski v. Gusoff, ___ A.3d ___, 2012 WL 3292225, *7 (noting that "the court will consider what effect the statement would have on the minds of the average persons among whom the statement would circulate," and holding that statements and a cartoon critical of plaintiff council member's acceptance of payments from Philadelphia's Deferred Retirement Option Plan "might suggest to the average reader that [plaintiff] acted to the detriment of her constituents in accepting a large payout of public funds that might otherwise have sustained a branch of the Philadelphia Free Library");** Maier v. Maretti, 448 Pa. Super. 276, 671 A.2d 701 (1995) ("The words must be given by judges and juries the same significance that other people are likely to attribute to them).. If the court finds as a matter of law that the communication is capable of defamatory meaning, the jury can then consider whether the communication was understood as such by the recipient. Parano v. O'Connor, 433 Pa. Super. 570, 574, 641 A.2d 607, 609 (1994). However, if a court determines that a communication has multiple plausible

interpretations, including both a defamatory and innocent one, a jury must be permitted to decide the issue. **Reed v. Pray, ___ A.3d ___, 2012 WL 3590690, at *5 (Pa. Cmwlth. Aug. 22, 2012) (reversing grant of summary judgment in part because, although statement at issue was capable of an innocuous meaning, it was also capable of a defamatory meaning).** See also Tucker v. Merck & Co., No. 02-2421, 2003 U.S. Dist. LEXIS, at *31-32 (E.D. Pa. May 2, 2003), aff'd, 102 Fed. Appx. 247 (3d Cir. 2004); Maier v. Maretti, 448 Pa. Super. 276, 671 A.2d 701, 704 (1995) ("if there is an innocent interpretation and an alternate defamatory interpretation, the issue must proceed to the jury"). In making such a determination, the court should consider the context of the communication, judging the effect the alleged communication would produce in the minds of the audience among whom it was intended to circulate." See Baker v. Lafayette Coll., 516 Pa. 291, 532 A.2d 399, 402 (1987). See also Bochetto v. Gibson, No. 3722, 2002 WL 434551, at *7 (Pa. Com. Pl. March 13, 2002), rev'd on other grounds by 580 Pa. 245, 860 A.2d 67, 32 Media L. Rep. 2474 (2004) (holding that a court, when determining whether a communication is defamatory, "may not look at the statement in a vacuum").

Pennsylvania uses two distinct standards to measure whether the particular written or spoken communication is defamatory. The first standard, or "traditional standard," provides that a communication is defamatory if it blackens the plaintiff's reputation; holds the plaintiff up to ridicule, contempt or public hatred; or injures the plaintiff in his or her business or profession. Baker, 516 Pa. at 296, 532 A.2d at 402; Schnabel v. Meredith, 378 Pa. 609, 612, 107 A.2d 860, 862 (1954); Collins v. Dispatch Publ'g Co., 152 Pa. 187, 190, 25 A. 546, 547 (1893); Tucker v. Merck, 2000 Pa. Super. 183, ¶ 6, 757 A.2d at 943.

The second standard, or "alternative standard," provides that a communication is defamatory if it tends to harm the reputation of another as to lower him or her in the estimation of the community or deter others from associating or dealing with him or her. Davis v. Resources for Human Dev., Inc., 2001 Pa. Super. 73, ¶ 5, 770 A.2d 353, 357; Tucker v. Merck, 2000 Pa. Super. 183, ¶ 6, 757 A.2d at 943; Constantino v. Univ. of Pittsburgh, 2001 Pa. Super. 4, ¶ 15, 766 A.2d 1265, 1270; Parano, 433 Pa. Super. at 574, 641 A.2d at 609; Synygy, Inc. v. Scott-Levin, Inc., 51 F. Supp. 2d 570, 580 (1999), aff'd, 229 F.3d 1139 (2000); Weinstein v. Bullick, 827 F. Supp. 1193, 1197, 22 Media L. Rep. 1481 (E.D. Pa. 1993), aff'd, 77 F.3d 465 (3d Cir. 1996). The "community" may include the plaintiff's business, trade or profession. Barclay v. Keystone Shipping Co., 128 F. Supp. 2d 237, 247 (E.D. Pa. 2001) (citing Maier v. Maretti, 448 Pa. Super. 276, 671 A.2d 701 (1995)). For example, in Barclay v. Keystone Shipping Co., 128 F. Supp. 2d 237, the United States District Court for the Eastern District of Pennsylvania held that a letter from a defendant vessel operator to the United States Coast Guard that the plaintiff seaman was a deserter was capable of defamatory meaning given the serious consequences of such a designation in the maritime world. Id. at 247.

The Pennsylvania courts have consistently ruled that certain communications, although offensive to the plaintiff, are not defamatory. Kryeski v. Schott Glass Techs., Inc., 426 Pa. Super. 105, 116, 626 A.2d 595, 601 (1993) (1994) (employee's statement to another that a fellow employee was "crazy" was not defamatory). For instance, the courts have held that words that are merely annoying, offensive or embarrassing have no defamatory meaning. Id.; Maier v. Moretti, 448 Pa. Super. 276, 671 A.2d 701, 704 (1995). Moreover, statements of fact, and not expressions of opinions, are defamatory. Constantino v. Univ. of Pittsburgh, 2001 Pa. Super. 4, ¶ 16, 766 A.2d 1265, 1270 (2001). This is because statements of opinion without more are not defamatory unless the plaintiff can "demonstrate that the communicated opinion may reasonably be understood to imply the existence of undisclosed defamatory facts justifying the opinion." Weinstein, 827 F. Supp. at 1197, 22 Media L. Rep. 1481. In determining whether a particular statement is merely annoying, embarrassing, hyperbolic or a vigorous epithet, as opposed to implying genuine defamatory facts, the court will consider the context, the relationship between the parties and the events surrounding the statement. Mathias v. Carpenter, 402 Pa. Super. 358, 587 A.2d 1, 2 (Pa. Super.Ct. 1991); Mitchell v. Plasmacare, Inc., 2011 WL 2181414 (W.D.Pa., June 2, 2011) (noting that, in particular, the use of statements implying sexual misconduct can be either capable of defamatory meaning or not, depending on the attendant circumstances); **Krajewski v. Gusoff, ___ A.3d ___, 2012 WL 3292225, *7 (noting that defendants' "resurrecting the controversy that surrounded the payment of [plaintiff's Deferred Retirement Option Plan] account" nearly a year after it had first been raised, together with also linking the issue with the unrelated public library closing were "circumstances equally probative of defamatory meaning"); Balletta v. Spadoni, 47 A.3d 183, 197-200 (Pa. Cmwlth. Ct. 2012) (holding that statements following sheriff's sale that unsuccessful bidders were "anarchists," "paper terrorists" or "fellow travelers" of certain anti-government groups or that they "could be after a quick buck" and "they may simply be opportunists" were not capable of a defamatory meaning because "the article fully discloses the facts upon which" the statements were made and did not imply the existence of undisclosed facts. The court also noted, "Pennsylvania courts hold that to call a person a name descriptive of his political, economic or sociological philosophies does not give rise to an action for libel").**

5. ***Of and Concerning Plaintiff.*** The defamatory statement must be about the plaintiff, not persons in general. Garvey v. Dickinson Coll., 761 F. Supp. 1175, 1188 (M.D. Pa. 1991). For example, a statement alleging that criminal activity occurred at the plaintiff's place of business, without alleging that the plaintiff was involved in the activity, is not defamatory as to the plaintiff. Richwine v. Pittsburgh Courier Publ'g Co., 186 Pa. Super. 644, 649, 142 A.2d 416, 418

(1958). The defamatory communication must be reasonably understood as referring to the plaintiff. Garvey, 761 F. Supp. at 1188. As such, the plaintiff need not be named in the statement or communication, as long as he or she is reasonably identifiable as its subject. Cosgrove Studio & Camera Shop, Inc. v. Pane, 408 Pa. 314, 319, 182 A.2d 751, 753 (1962). "Reasonably identifiable" means that a reasonable reader (not the plaintiff), in the context of the publication, would have known the statement to be about the plaintiff. Garvey, 761 F. Supp. at 1188; see also Harris by Harris v. Easton Publ'g Co., 335 Pa. Super. 141, 157, 483 A.2d 1377, 1385-86, 11 Media L. Rep. 1209 (1984).

Pennsylvania courts recognize that defamation by innuendo is actionable. "To establish defamation by innuendo, the innuendo must be warranted, justified and supported by the publication." Livingston v. Murray, 417 Pa. Super. 202, 612 A.2d 443, 449 (1992), appeal denied, 533 Pa. 601, 617 A.2d 1275 (1992). See also Thomas Merton Center v. Rockwell Int'l Corp., 497 Pa. 460, 442 A.2d 213, 217 (1981); Sarkees v. Warner-West Corp., 349 Pa. 365, 368-69, 37 A.2d 544, 546 (1944) (question of whether innuendo is actionable as defamatory is a question of law; the legal test to be applied is whether the challenged language could "fairly and reasonably be construed" to imply the alleged defamatory meaning); Franklin Prescriptions, Inc. v. New York Times, Co., 267 F. Supp. 2d 425, 435 (E.D. Pa. 2003), aff'd, 424 F.3d 336 (3d Cir. 2005) (holding that article, although not naming plaintiff specifically, could be defamatory because "if the defendant juxtaposes a series of facts so as to imply a defamatory connection between them, or otherwise creates a defamatory implication . . . he may be held responsible for [that] implication. . . ." Id. at *20 (citation omitted); ToDay's Housing v. Times Shamrock Communications, Inc., 2011 Pa. Super 91, 21 A.2d 1209, 1214 (2010) (rejecting argument that five articles, taken as a whole, falsely implied that plaintiff manufactured the modular homes it sold).

6. ***Publication.*** "Publication" is defined as the "communication intentionally or by a negligent act to one other than the person defamed" of the defamatory matter. Agriss v. Roadway Express, Inc., 334 Pa. Super. 295, 309, 483 A.2d 456, 465 (1984). No matter what or how serious the defamatory language, there cannot be a defamation absent a publication or dissemination of the information by the defendant to a third person (i.e., someone other than the plaintiff). Ertel v. Patriot-News Co., 544 Pa. 93, 102, 674 A.2d 1038, 1043 (1994), cert. denied, 519 U.S. 1008 (1996); Elia v. Erie Exch., 430 Pa. Super. 384, 391, 634 A.2d 657, 660 (1993). See Davis v. Resources for Human Dev., Inc., 2001 Pa. Super. 73, ¶ 6, 770 A.2d 353, 358 (there is no publication where there was a communication between four authors of a defamatory letter because, while four people signed the letter, none of those was a third party). The occasion of the publication and identity of the recipients must be pled. Raneri v. De Polo, 65 Pa. Commw. 183, 186, 441 A.2d 1373, 1375 (1982). "[S] ubstantial circumstantial evidence may be sufficient to prove publication in the context of defamation." Porter v. Joy Realty, Inc., 2005 Pa. Super. 129, ¶ 7, 872 A.2d 846, 849 (2005). **Cf. Rentzell v. Dollar Tree Store, 2012 WL 707005 (E.D. Pa. March 5, 2012) (holding that there was insufficient circumstantial evidence to support the element of publication at the relevant time where proofs showed that (1) a representative of defendant had made negative comments about plaintiff three years following his termination, and (2) plaintiff had been unable to get another job after he was terminated despite a number of prospects and "positive interviews").** Note that, in Pennsylvania, the specificity with which the publication element must be set forth in the complaint varies as between state court and federal court, as noted below.

a. **Intracorporate Communication.** The fact that the defamatory statement is made in the corporate setting does not alter the publication requirement. An absolute or a conditional privilege, however, may protect a publication made in this context. See Agriss, 334 Pa. Super. 295, 309-10, 483 A.2d 456, 463-64 (the publication of warning letters to parties who were proper recipients under collective bargaining agreements between the employer and the union was absolutely privileged); DeLuca v. Reader, 227 Pa. Super. 392, 399, 323 A.2d 309, 313 (1974) (employers have an absolute privilege to publish defamatory matter in notices of employee termination) (internal citations omitted). See III.D., infra. Furthermore, the publication requirement is not met when the intra-company recipient already knows the defamatory statement from another source. Beyda v. USAir, Inc., 697 F. Supp. 1394, 1397 (W.D. Pa. 1988).

b. **Compelled Self-Publication.** "Compelled self-publication" occurs "when a defendant makes a defamatory statement to the plaintiff who later is compelled to communicate the defamatory matter to a third party, and it was foreseeable to the defendant that the plaintiff would be compelled to publish the matter." Strange v. Nationwide Mut. Ins. Co., 867 F. Supp. 1209, 1221 (E.D. Pa. 1994). Pennsylvania has not recognized a claim for compelled self-publication. Yetter v. Ward Trucking Corp., 401 Pa. Super. 467, 472, 585 A.2d 1022, 1025 (1991), appeal denied, 529 Pa. 623, 600 A.2d 539 (1991); Strange, 867 F. Supp. at 1221; Ritter v. Pepsi Cola Operating Co. of Chesapeake & Indianapolis, 785 F. Supp. 61, 64 (M.D. Pa. 1992). In Yetter v. Ward Trucking Corp., 401 Pa. Super. 467, 585 A.2d 1022, the Superior Court held "that where the defamation action rests on the publication of an employee termination letter by the employer to the employee only, the requirement that the defamatory matter be published by the defendant is not met through proof of compelled self-publication." Id. at 472, 585 A.2d at 1025. The court left open, however, the question "as to whether under a different set of circumstances, compelled self-publication of the defamatory material by the defamed person, rather than by the defendant, to a third party will suffice." Id. These "different set of circumstances" have not been addressed by the Pennsylvania courts.

c. **Republication.** Pennsylvania has not abandoned the common law rule that the republisher of a defamatory statement is subject to liability similar to that of the original defamer. First Lehigh Bank v. Cowen, 700 A.2d 498, 502, 26 Media L. Rep. 1075 (Pa. Super. Ct. 1997); Wilson v. Slatalla, 970 F. Supp. 405, 417, 25 Media L. Rep. 2281 (E.D. Pa. 1997). However, the Eastern District of Pennsylvania has held that the Communications Decency Act preempts Pennsylvania law and bars claims for defamation against providers and users of interactive computer service providers that publish defamatory statements authored by others. Dimeo v. Max, 433 F. Supp. 2d 523, 531, 34 Media L. Rep. 1921 (E.D. Pa. 2006) (citing 47 U.S.C. § 230(c)(1), (e)(3)), aff'd 248 Fed. Appx. 280 (3d Cir. 2007); Parker v. Google, Inc., 422 F. Supp. 2d 492, 501 (E.D. Pa. 2006) (granting motion to dismiss defamation claim based on the Communications Decency Act). However, republication of a statement by the original defamer, after notification that the statement may be defamatory, should also be considered in determining whether actual malice existed in the original publication. Weaver v. Lancaster Newspapers, Inc., 35 Med. L. Rep. 2170, 926 A.2d 899 (Pa. 2007).

7. ***Statements versus Conduct.*** Pennsylvania permits a defamation action based on nonverbal communication or conduct. D'Errico v. DeFazio, 2000 Pa. Super. 354, ¶ 18 n.4, 763 A.2d 424, 432 n.4 (2000); appeal denied, 566 Pa. 663, 782 A.2d 546 (2001); Berg v. Consol. Freightways Inc., 280 Pa. Super. 495, 501 n.1, 421 A.2d 831, 501 n.1 (1980); Doe v. Kohn Nast. & Graf. 862 F. Supp. 1310, 1327 (E.D. Pa. 1994). At least one federal court has noted that all Pennsylvania cases "in which a plaintiff was permitted to proceed with a defamation claim based on conduct[,] [the case] involved acts imputing criminal behavior." Jones v. Johnson & Johnson, McNeil - PPC, Inc., No. 94-7473, 1997 WL 549995, *9 (E.D. Pa. Aug. 22, 1997), aff'd, 166 F.3d 1205 (3d Cir. 1998). See Bennett v. Norban, 396 Pa. 94, 151 A.2d 476 (1959) (defamation found where the plaintiff was followed out of the store by the manager, who ordered the plaintiff to remove her coat and empty the contents of her purse, suggesting the plaintiff was a thief).

8. ***Damages.*** By statute, damages cannot be recovered for defamation unless the publication was made maliciously or negligently. 42 PA. CONS. STAT. ANN. § 8344. When the plaintiff is a public figure or a private figure complaining of statements that are a matter of public concern, the plaintiff must allege and prove that the publisher acted maliciously, that is, with knowledge of falsity or reckless disregard of the truth. Johnson v. Resources for Human Dev., Inc., 860 F. Supp. 218, 221 (E.D. Pa. 1994). In cases which do not involve matters of public concern and the plaintiff is a private figure, the plaintiff need only prove that the publisher acted negligently. Rutt v. Bethlehems' Globe Publ'g Co., 335 Pa. Super. 163, 185, 484 A.2d 72, 83 (1984). Additionally, a plaintiff must prove special harm, which has been defined as "monetary or out-of-pocket loss borne by the defamation." Bochetto v. Gibson, 2002 WL 434551, at *9 (Pa. Com. Pl. March 13, 2002), rev'd on other grounds by 580 Pa. 245, 860 A.2d 67, 32 Media L. Rep. 2474 (2004) (also noting the contrast between special damages and general damages, which is "proof that one's reputation was actually affected by the slander, or that she suffered personal humiliation, or both") (quoting Walker v. Grand Central Sanitation, Inc., 430 Pa. Super. 236, 245-46, 634 A.2d 237, 241-42 (1993)); Davitt v. Wood Co., 58 Pa. D. & C.4th 279, 291 (Lehigh Cty 2002) (holding that "[s]pecial harm means harm of an economic or pecuniary nature"). Mere loss of reputation is not enough to prove special harm. Id. At least one court has suggested that the libel-proof plaintiff doctrine should apply in Pennsylvania. Griffin v. Griffin, Nos. 1477 and 032793, 2008 Phila. Ct. Comm. Pl. LEXIS 300 at *2 (Nov. 21, 2008). The doctrine states that libel actions cannot stand where (1) the plaintiff's reputation is already too low, or (2) the true portions of the libelous statement have a significantly damaging effect. Id.

a. **Presumed Damages and Libel Per Se.** Libel per se, slander per se and libel per quod are ancient common law doctrines that have apparently been abolished in Pennsylvania. Agriss v. Roadway Express, Inc., 334 Pa. Super. 295, 318, 483 A.2d 456, 468 (1984) (plaintiffs need not prove special damages; proof of harm to reputation is sufficient, and it is irrelevant whether the damage was done by words defamatory on their face). But see Bochetto, 2002 WL 434551, at *9 (noting that when alleging defamation per se, a plaintiff does not have to prove special damages, i.e., economic or pecuniary loss but must still must make some showing of general damages); Davitt, 58 Pa. D. & C.4th at 291 (observing that when alleging slander per se, a plaintiff is not required to prove special harm). Accordingly, Pennsylvania courts have not addressed employment related criticism or the single instance rule which flow from the defamation per se doctrine. But see Tucker v. Fischbein, No. 97-6150, 2005 U.S. Dist. LEXIS 410, at *7, 33 Media L. Rep. 1193 (E.D. Pa. Jan. 11, 2005) ("Plaintiff is required to plead special harm resulting from the publication of the alleged defamatory statement" in slander per quod action); Synygy, Inc. v. Scott-Levin, Inc., 51 F. Supp. 2d 570 (E.D. Pa. 1999), aff'd, 229 F.3d 1139 (2000) (summary judgment granted to defendant on basis that plaintiff failed to prove special damages).

(1) **Employment-Related Criticism.** No reported cases.

(2) **Single Instance Rule.** No reported cases.

b. **Punitive Damages.** Punitive damages are available to a defamation plaintiff as in any other tort action, except that public figures must prove both actual malice and common law malice. Sprague v. Walter, 441 Pa. Super. 1, 35-41, 656 A.2d 890, 906-08 (1995), appeal denied, 543 Pa. 695, 670 A.2d 142 (1996). Common law malice involves outrageous conduct that is the result of bad motive or reckless indifference to the rights of others. DiSalle v. P.G. Publ'g Co., 375 Pa. Super. 510, 520, 544 A.2d 1345, 1350, 15 Media L. Rep. 1873 (1988), appeal denied, 521 Pa. 620, 557 A.2d 724 (1989), cert. denied, 492 U.S. 906 (1989). Pennsylvania Courts have been inconsistent in requiring a private figure plaintiff to prove actual malice. See Geyer v. Steinbronn, 351 Pa. Super. 536, 566 & n.12, 506 A.2d 901, 917 & n.12 (1986) (holding that although the two standards overlap significantly, actual malice is the appropriate standard for awarding punitive damages); Paul v. Hearst Corp., 261 F. Supp. 2d 303, 306-07 (M.D. Pa. 2002) (holding that "[u]nder Pennsylvania law, a finding of actual malice is sufficient to trigger consideration of punitive damages" but noting the overlap between the two malice standards and the uncertainty regarding whether a private figure plaintiff in a public concern matter is also required to show common law malice); Sprague v. Walter, 357 Pa. Super. 570, 516 A.2d 706, 13 Media L. Rep. 1177 (1986), aff'd, 518 Pa. 425, 543 A.2d 1078 (1988) (both actual malice and common law malice must be proven for a private figure to receive punitive damages if the publication is of public concern); PPG Industries, Inc. v. Zurawin, 52 Fed. Appx. 570, 2002 WL 31289285 (3d Cir. Oct. 11, 2002) (3d Cir. Oct. 11, 2002) (holding that defendant "incorrectly collapse[d] the distinction between actual and common law malice" and therefore, common law malice not shown by mere submission of sufficient evidence to conclude actual malice). It is worthwhile to note that punitive damages are not available for claims brought pursuant to the Pennsylvania Human Relations Act. Hoy v. Angelone, 554 Pa. 134, 142, 720 A.2d 745, 749 (1998).

II. PRIVILEGES & DEFENSES

A. Scope of Privileges

1. ***Absolute Privilege.*** In general, a defendant who publishes defamatory matter within the scope of an absolute privilege is immune from liability regardless of occasion or motive. Agriss v. Roadway Exp., Inc., 334 Pa. Super. 295, 309, 483 A.2d 456, 463 (1984). This privilege may be lost, however, if the scope of the privilege is exceeded by publishing the defamation to unauthorized parties. Id. Pursuant to Pennsylvania's policy favoring private resolution of disputes between employers and employees, Pennsylvania law recognizes an absolute privilege of employers to publish a false, defamatory statement, regardless of motive, when an employer notifies the employee of the basis for the dismissal. Yetter v. Ward Trucking Corp., 401 Pa. Super. 467, 471, 585 A.2d 1022, 1024 (1991), appeal denied, 529 Pa. 623, 600 A.2d 539 (1991). The purpose of the absolute privilege is to encourage the employer's communication to the employee of the reasons for discharge by eliminating the risk that the employer will possibly be subject to liability for defamation. Valjet v. Wal-Mart, No. 06-01842. 2007 U.S. Dist. LEXIS 90845 at *27 n.6, 2007 WL 4323377 (E.D. Pa. Dec. 11, 2007). This absolute privilege applies with equal force to warning or notice of termination letters. Davis v. Resources for Human Dev., Inc., 2001 Pa. Super. 73, ¶ 6, 770 A.2d 353, 358; Agriss, 334 Pa. Super. at 309, 483 A.2d at 463-64. **Recently, the Court of Common Pleas has held this privilege applicable to statements made by a third-party to an employer and the police where "the communications alleged to be defamatory concerned Plaintiffs' work performance" and the reasons for their termination. Woodward v. Viropharma Inc., 2012 WL 2365313 (Pa. Com. Pl., May 25, 2012) (in case involving defendants' communications to its contract commercial cleaning and maintenance company that they believed employees of that company had stolen a laptop from the premises).**

There is also an absolute privilege to publish defamatory material in judicial, legislative and regulatory proceedings about employment disputes, as well as in public records. Milliner v. Enck, 709 A.2d 417, 420 (1998) (holding that an employer's letter to unemployment compensation office stating the reasons for termination to be absolutely privileged as long as the communication is sufficiently related to the proceeding). The judicial privilege only applies to publications within the proceedings themselves; it does not extend to "extrajudicial act[s] that occur[] outside of the regular course of the judicial proceedings." Bochetto v. Gibson, 580 Pa. 245, 253, 860 A.2d 67, 73, 32 Media L. Rep. 2474 (2004) (no absolute privilege for lawyer who faxed copy of filed complaint to reporter at legal publication). However, the privilege does apply to documents that are issued "as a regular part of legal proceedings, and pertinent and material to those proceedings," such as an expert report. Reece v. Nestarick, 2011 WL 1097081 (Pa. Com. Pl. 2011) (real estate appraiser's report prepared for use in administrative license proceedings fell within the scope of immunity). The privilege extends to "quasi-judicial" proceedings, but only where there is "government involvement." Overall v. Univ. of Pa., 412 F.3d 492, 496-97 (3d Cir. 2005) (noting that an "entirely private proceeding" conducted by an employer did not qualify as quasi-judicial). However, even if the fair reporting privilege applied to a workers' compensation hearing where the account of the official proceeding was fair, accurate and complete, and not published solely for the purpose of causing harm to the person defamed, the privilege does not apply to preclude liability on the part of a newspaper for publishing allegedly defamatory statements purportedly made by a citizen while a township board meeting was in recess. DeMary v. Latrobe Printing & Publ'g Co., 2000 Pa. Super. 339, ¶ 14, 762 A.2d 758, 765.

Pennsylvania law also extends the doctrine of absolute privilege to "high public officials" when the statements at issue are made within the scope of their authority. Linder v. Mollan, 544 Pa. 487, 490, 677 A.2d 1194, 1194 (Pa. 1996); see also Hall v. Kiger, 795 A.2d 497, 502 (Pa. Commw. Ct. 2002), appeal denied, 544 Pa. 487, 677 A.2d 1194 (2002) (holding that a borough councilman was "high public official" and entitled to raise absolute privilege defense for allegedly defamatory remarks made about a citizen during a public meeting; councilman's comments did not exceed the scope of his authority); McKibben v. Schmotzer, 700 A.2d 484, 491 (Pa. Super. 1997) (holding that a mayor's statements to the press as to why she fired a borough police chief, although "harsh" and untrue, were within her duties, but a latter statement in which she accused the chief of lying was outside her duties because there, the mayor "was no more than a private citizen seeking to enforce her private criminal complaint")(emphasis removed); Smith v. Borough of Dunmore, 633 F.3d 176, 182 (3d Cir. 2011) (disclosure to the press of a letter prepared in the scope of a council member's official duties did not remove it from the absolute privilege). Pennsylvania courts have recognized that school superintendents and presidents of school boards qualify as high public officials under this doctrine. Ruder v. Pequea Valley School District, ___ F.Supp.2d ___, 2011 WL 1832794 (E.D. Pa. 2011) (holding that these officials were entitled to immunity but other members of the school board were not); **Reed v. Pray, ___ A.3d ___, 2012 WL 3590690 (Pa. Cmwlth. Ct. 2012) (where council member "reasonably and appropriately expressed her concerns about the propriety of Borough action to law enforcement officials," statements were privileged).**

The absolute privilege applies even when the high public official obtains information concerning the defamatory statement by violating a policy of his office. Heller v. Fulare, 454 F.3d 174, 180 (3d Cir. 2006) ("It follows that because Pennsylvania courts have repeatedly applied immunity to false statements as well as malicious ones, the fact that Fulare may have obtained his information in violation of a Board policy, does not remove the shield of immunity.").

The Pennsylvania Supreme Court has expressly stated that it will not recognize the neutral reportage privilege as a matter of state or federal constitutional law. Norton v. Glenn, 860 A.2d 48, 58-59 (Pa. 2004), cert. denied 125 S. Ct. 1700 (2005). This privilege would have immunized media defendants from liability for defamation, even if actual malice could be shown, where they repeated "newsworthy comments regarding a public official" made outside of the course of any official proceedings. Id. at 53.

Additionally, sovereign immunity bars suit for defamation against the United States as an employer because it is not specifically waived under the Federal Tort Claims Act. Izzo v. U.S. Gov't, 138 Fed.Appx. 387, 2005 U.S. App. LEXIS 8955, at *4 (3d Cir. May 18, 2005). **Sovereign immunity also bars suits for defamation against Pennsylvania governmental entities. Balletta v. Spadoni, 47 A.3d 183, 195 (Pa. Cmwlth. Ct. 2012) (noting that a plaintiff suing a governmental entity in Pennsylvania must show that the tortious act falls within one of the exceptions to governmental immunity set forth in 42 Pa.C.S. § 8542(b), and that defamation claims do not fall within an exception).**

2. ***Qualified Privileges.***

a. **Common Interest.** A publication that might otherwise be defamatory is subject to a conditional privilege " 'if the publisher reasonably believes that the recipient shares a common interest in the subject matter and is entitled to know." ' *Miketic v. Baron,* 675 A.2d 324, 330 (Pa.Super. 1996) (quoting *Daywalt v. Montgomery Hosp.,* 573 A.2d 1116, 1118 (Pa.Super.1990)). The communication must be made on a proper occasion, from proper motive and in a proper manner. See Maier v. Maretti, 448 Pa. Super. 276, 286, 671 A.2d 701, 706 (1995), appeal denied, 548 Pa. 637, 694 A.2d 622 (1997) (supervisor's communication to branch manager and personnel director of statement made by employee was privileged because the supervisor, branch manager and personnel director had a common interest in an employee who had been suspended). See also Tucker v. Merck & Co. Inc., No. 02-2421, 2003 U.S. Dist. LEXIS 7672, at *28 (E.D. Pa. May 2, 2003), aff'd, 102 Fed. Appx. 247 (3d Cir. 2004) (holding that conditional privilege will apply to statements made during an employer's investigation of employee "so long as it is conducted in a proper manner") (citation omitted). The "occasion is conditionally privileged when the circumstances are such as to lead any one of several persons having a common interest in a particular subject matter correctly or reasonably to believe that facts exist which another sharing such common interest is entitled to know." Davis v. Res. for Human Dev., Inc., 2001 Pa. Super. 73, ¶ 6, 770 A.2d at 358 (council members had a legitimate interest in a letter accusing another council member of stealing items from her hotel room and displaying inappropriate behavior, and each were entitled to know the contents therein as it concerned a council matter) (citing Miketic v. Baron, 450 Pa. Super. 91, 675 A.2d 324, 329 (1996)). See also Donaldson v. Informatica Corp., No. 10-1229, 2011 WL 1108200, at *2-3, 420 Fed. Appx. 204, 207-08 (3d Cir. 2011) (affirming district court's grant of summary judgment to defendant where claim arose out of an e-mail sent to several Informatica executives and the parties agreed that the e-mail was "conditionally privileged" under the law, meaning that "the speaker and recipient share a common interest in the subject matter and both are entitled to know about the information" and thereby requiring plaintiff, in order to set forth a per se defamation claim, to show that the privilege was abused because the statement was: "(1) actuated by malice or negligence; (2) made for a purpose other than that for which the privilege is given; (3) made to a person not reasonably believed to be necessary for the accomplishment of the purpose of the privilege; or (4) includes defamatory matter not reasonably believed to be necessary for the accomplishment of the purpose").

b. **Duty.** A conditional privilege exists where an employer's statement is made pursuant to a duty. See Goralski v. Pizzimenti, 115 Pa. Commw. 210, 219, 540 A.2d 595, 599-600 (1988) (a school district manager's discharge letter fell within the scope of his duties). See also Baker v. Lafayette Coll., 350 Pa. Super. 68, 73, 504 A.2d 247, 249 (1986), aff'd, 516 Pa. 291, 532 A.2d 399 (1987) (employer contractually compelled to communicate).

c. **Criticism of Public Employee.** Although there are no reported cases in Pennsylvania regarding defamation of a public employee in the employment realm, a conditional privilege exists where a recognized interest of the public will be involved. Generally, Pennsylvania recognizes a conditional privilege, for defamation purposes, where some interest of the publisher of the defamatory material is involved, where some interest of the recipient of the matter or third party is involved, or where a recognized interest of the public is involved. See Elia v. Erie Ins. Exch., 430 Pa. Super. 384, 634 A.2d 657 (1993), appeal denied, 537 Pa. 662, 644 A.2d 1200 (1994). See also Cimino v. DiPaolo, 786 A.2d 309, 311 (Pa. Commw. Ct. 2001) (holding that because he was acting within the scope of his duties, District Justice was protected by sovereign immunity when reporting Constable's alleged improprieties).

In addition to proving abuse of the privilege, the plaintiff, if a public official, has the burden of proving actual malice. See I.B.8., supra.

d. **Limitations on Qualified Privileges.** A privilege will be lost upon a showing by the plaintiff that a conditional privilege has been abused. Abuse of a conditional privilege occurs when the publication is: (1) actuated by malice or negligence; (2) is made for a purpose other than that for which the privilege is given; (3) is made to a person not reasonably believed to be necessary for the accomplishment of the purpose of the privilege; or (4) includes defamatory matter not reasonably believed to be necessary for the accomplishment of the purpose. Elia, 430 Pa. Super. at 393, 634 A.2d at 661; Maier v. Maretti, 448 Pa. Super. 276, 286-87, 671 A.2d 701, 706-07 (1995), appeal denied, 548 Pa. 637, 694 A.2d 622 (1997).

(1) **Constitutional or Actual Malice.** Proof of constitutional malice is not required to defeat a qualified privilege. See II.A.2.d., supra.

(2) **Common Law Malice.** A privilege will be lost upon a showing by the plaintiff that a conditional privilege has been abused. Abuse of a conditional privilege occurs when the publication is: (1) actuated by malice or negligence; (2) is made for a purpose other than that for which the privilege is given; (3) is made to a person not reasonably believed to be necessary for the accomplishment of the purpose of the privilege; or (4) includes defamatory matter not reasonably believed to be necessary for the accomplishment of the purpose. Elia, 430 Pa. Super at 393, 634 A.2d at 661; Maier, 448 Pa. Super. at 286-87, 671 A.2d at 706-07. See Howard v. Deklinski, No. 01-4171, 2002 U.S. App. LEXIS 25269, at *9-12, 2002 WL 31501850 (3d Cir. Nov. 12, 2002) (holding that subjective malice inferred from employer's "supposed antipathy" towards employee as a result of an alleged disagreement alone was not sufficient to overcome conditional privilege); Smith v. Borough of Dunmore, No. 3:05-CV-1343, 2007 U.S. Dist. LEXIS 21396 (M.D. Pa. March 7, 2007) (holding that the conditional privilege held by the Borough of Dunmore was abused by "their failure to exercise reasonable care and diligence to ascertain the truth before giving currency to what amounted to an untrue communication.").

(3) **Other Limitations on Qualified Privileges.** No reported cases.

e. **Question of Fact or Law.** When the question involved is whether a conditional privilege exists, it is to be decided by the court. Bargerstock v. Washington Greene Cmty. Action Corp., 397 Pa. Super. 403, 411, 580 A.2d 361, 364 (1990), appeal denied, 529 Pa. 655, 604 A.2d 247 (1992). When the issue to be decided is whether the privilege has been abused or vitiated, it is a question of fact for the jury to decide. Id.

f. **Burden of Proof.** Once the defendant establishes a prima facie privilege, the plaintiff has the burden of proving the abuse of that privilege. Baird v. Dun & Bradstreet, Inc., 446 Pa. 266, 273, 285 A.2d 166, 170 (1971); Geyer v. Steinbronn, 351 Pa. Super. 536, 550, 506 A.2d 901, 908 (1986); Barclay v. Keystone Shipping Co., 128 F. Supp. 2d 237, 248 (E.D. Pa. 2001).

B. Standard Libel Defenses

1. ***Truth.*** Truth is always an absolute defense to a defamation claim. American Future Systems, Inc. v. Better Business Bureau of Eastern Pennsylvania, 592 Pa. 66, 77-78, 923 A.2d 389, 396 (2007); Bobb v. Kraybill, 354 Pa. Super. 361, 364, 511 A.2d 1379, 1380 (1986), appeal denied, 513 Pa. 633, 520 A.2d 1384 (1987).

Substantial Truth. Substantial truth is sufficient to constitute truth as a defense. Chicarella v. Passant, 343 Pa. Super. 330, 337-38, 494 A.2d 1109, 113-14 (1985). "Although there is no specific formula for substantial truth, 'Pennsylvania has determined proof of a substantial truth must go to the 'gist' or 'sting' of the alleged defamatory matter." Tucker v. Merck & Co., Inc., No. 02-2421, 2003 U.S. Dist. LEXIS 7672, at *18 (E.D. Pa. May 2, 2003), aff'd, 102 Fed. Appx. 247 (3d Cir. 2004); Keeshan v. Home Depot, U.S.A. Inc., 11 AD Casts 1509, 2001 U.S. Dist. LEXIS 3607, 2001 WL

310601 (E.D. Pa. 2001), aff'd 35 Fed. Appx. 51, 2002 U.S. App. LEXIS 10160 (3d Cir. 2002). For example, in Marier v. Lance, Inc., No. 07-4284, 2009 U.S. App. LEXIS 2713, 2009 WL 297713 (3d Cir. Feb. 9, 2009), the Third Circuit held that the statement that the plaintiff had been escorted by the police off of another's property was substantially true where the party voluntarily left after police had been called to the scene. 2009 U.S. App. LEXIS at *6.

Summary Judgment Determination of Truth. Because the truth or falsity of a statement is generally a factual determination, the defense will, at best, be available only at the summary judgment phase of the proceeding, and may likely end up being a jury question. See, e.g., Geyer v. Steinbronn, 351 Pa. Super. 536, 551-52, 506 A.2d 901, 909 (1986) (holding that the defendants failed to overcome their burden of proving the truth of the defamatory communication for purposes of summary judgment because the jury was free to resolve the factual issues in favor of the plaintiff).

Burden of Proving Falsity. The burden of proving falsity also may be affected by the nature of the statement because, regardless of the Pennsylvania statute, the burden is constitutionally shifted to the plaintiff if the statement is of public concern. Philadelphia Newspapers, Inc. v. Hepps, 475 U.S. 767, 775-76, 12 Media L. Rep 1977 (U.S. 1986); see also Bobb v. Kraybill, 354 Pa. Super. 361, 366, 511 A.2d 1379, 1381 (1986), appeal denied, 513 Pa. 633, 520 A.2d 1384 (1987) (where publication is of public concern, summary judgment will be granted unless the plaintiff comes forward with evidence of falsity).

2. ***Opinion.*** A statement of opinion cannot be the basis of a defamation action. Kryeski v. Schott Glass Techs., 426 Pa. Super. 105, 116, 626 A.2d 595, 601 (1993), appeal denied, 536 Pa. 643, 639 A.2d 29 (1994); 42 PA. CONS. STAT. ANN. § 8343(a). An opinion may be held defamatory, however, if "the plaintiff can demonstrate that the communicated opinion may be reasonably understood to imply the existence of undisclosed defamatory facts justifying the opinion.'" Tucker v. Merck & Co., No. 02-2421, 2003 U.S. Dist. LEXIS 7672, at *32 (E.D. Pa. May 2, 2003), aff'd, 102 Fed. Appx. 247 (3d Cir. 2004) (quoting Baker v. Lafayette Coll., 516 Pa. 291, 532 A.2d 399, 402 (1987) (quoting Beckman v. Dunn, 276 Pa. Super. 527, 419 A.2d 583, 587 (1980)).

Pure Opinion. The statement must be "pure" opinion and, therefore, not actionable because it cannot be subjected to a test as to its truth or falsity. Because a statement must be false to be defamatory, if it is of a type that cannot be measured for its falsity, it cannot be defamatory. Also, a statement that clearly sets forth both an opinion and the facts on which that opinion is based cannot be defamatory. For example, in Burns v. Supermarkets General Corp., 615 F. Supp. 154 (E.D. Pa. 1985), the employer's statement that the employee's "reducing the price of good produce improperly is like stealing" was held to be mere opinion and not an allegation of theft. Id. at 159. Presumably, the reader can judge for himself or herself whether the conclusion is correct or not because he or she has the speaker's facts. Id. at 158. Similarly, in Alston v. Keel Commc'ns., 980 A.2d 215 (Phila. Ct. Com. Pl. 2009), the court held that a statement in a newspaper article that plaintiff was "no more than a land speculator who cloaks himself in the guise of a community activist" was mere opinion because it was based upon facts disclosed in the article and did not imply the existence of undisclosed facts. In Baker v. Lafayette College, 516 Pa. 291, 532 A.2d 399 (1987), the court held that because it was not reasonable for a person to imply from the defendant's statement of opinion the existence of undisclosed defamatory facts justifying the opinion, the statement could not be defamatory. 516 Pa. at 297, 532 A.2d at 402; but see Donaldson v. Informatica Corp., No. 08-605, 2009 U.S. Dist. LEXIS 15528 at *10 – 13 (W.D.Pa. Feb. 25, 2009) (holding as sufficient to imply the existence of undisclosed defamatory facts the statement to an e-mail recipient that "[i]f [plaintiff] wants to talk about integrity, I would encourage [plaintiff] to be honest enough to tell you the full true story"). **A statement in which a person "expresses concern" about or "feels" that possible illegal activity has occurred is expressing opinion and not making a factual allegation of criminal conduct. Reed v. Pray, ___ A.3d ___, 2012 WL 3590690, at *5 (Pa. Cmwlth. Ct. Aug. 22, 2012) (noting that "concerns" and "beliefs" were mere expressions of opinion at most, but that a plain statement that plaintiff "took $100,000" from the Borough was capable of a defamatory meaning).**

Mixed Fact and Opinion. If a statement is a declaration of mixed fact and opinion or implies the speaker has an undisclosed knowledge of facts to support it, it can be the basis for a defamation action. Mixed statements of fact and opinion, where the facts are inaccurate, are not protected as opinion. Pino v. Prudential Ins. Co. of Am., 689 F. Supp. 1358, 1365-68 (E.D. Pa. 1988).

Province of Court and Jury. Because the determination of whether a statement is pure opinion or a mixed fact and opinion is part of the analysis of whether a statement is defamatory, the trial court makes a determination of the issue, not the jury. See Burns v. Supermarkets Gen. Corp., 615 F. Supp. 154 (E.D. Pa. 1985). Therefore, a demurrer is the proper vehicle for raising the question. Mathias v. Carpenter, 402 Pa. Super. 358, 364, 587 A.2d 1, 9-10, 18 Media L. Rep. 1818 (1991), appeal denied, 529 Pa. 650, 602 A.2d 860 (1992).

No Constitutional Protection for Opinion. Pennsylvania courts had assumed that even mixed statements of fact and opinion were constitutionally protected in some instances. See, e.g., Fram v. Yellow Cab Co. of Pittsburgh, 380 F.

Supp. 1314 (W.D. Pa. 1974). These decisions, however, predate the United States Supreme Court's decision that constitutional protection for opinion does not exist. Milkovich v. Lorain Journal, 497 U.S. 1, 17 Media L. Rep. 2009 (1990). Nevertheless, Pennsylvania continues to hold that common law protection for opinion exists. See Mathias v. Carpenter, 402 Pa. Super. 358, 362, 587 A.2d 1, 3, 18 Media L. Rep. 1818 (1991), appeal denied, 529 Pa. 650, 602 A.2d 860 (1992).

3. ***Consent.*** No action will lie where the communications were expressly or by implication consented to by the plaintiff. See Baker v. Lafayette Coll., 516 Pa. 291, 296, 532 A.2d 399, 402 (1987) (affirming that employee evaluations were consensual because they were required by the faculty handbook and, therefore, non-actionable). See also Sobel v. Wingard, 366 Pa. Super 482, 487, 531 A.2d 520, 522 (1987) (employee evaluations are deemed to be consented to, and therefore, an absolute privilege attaches) (internal citations omitted). See also PPG Indus., Inc. v. Zurawin, 52 Fed. Appx. 570, 2002 WL 31289285 (3d Cir. Oct. 11, 2002) ("Under Pennsylvania law, consent is an absolute defense to a defamation claim.").

4. ***Mitigation.*** In Pennsylvania, mitigating circumstances are not recognized as a defense to a defamation claim. Defenses are limited to proving truth of the statement, proving that the subject matter of the statement was of public concern, or that the occasion on which the statement was made or published was of a privileged character. U.S. Healthcare, Inc., v. Blue Cross of Greater Phila., 898 F.2d 914, 923, 17 Media L. Rep. 1681 (3d Cir. 1990), cert. denied, 498 U.S. 816 (1990).

III. RECURRING FACT PATTERNS

A. Statements in Personnel File

A statement in a personnel file memorializing an investigation of alleged employee misconduct is not defamatory. Tucker v. Merck & Co., Inc., No. 02-2421, 2003 U.S. Dist. LEXIS 7672, at *32-35 (E.D. Pa. May 2, 2003), aff'd, 102 Fed. Appx. 247 (3d Cir. 2004) (contention that file letter memorializing a meeting regarding the employee's alleged misconduct was "frivolous" where the letter stated that the claim was unsubstantiated and absolved the employee of liability; the file letter "was an appropriate action on the part of [the employer]" and "serves the proper management purpose of memorializing the unsubstantiated allegation against the employee and absolving him of liability"). Furthermore, "compan[ies] must be allowed to investigate allegations made against its employees, and to record their findings." Id. at *34. See also Merkam v. Wachovia Corp., No. 2397, 2008 WL 2214649, at * (Pa. Com. Pl. 2008) (statements made by supervisor in corrective action and counseling report, which notified employee that he was being terminated for violating employer's code of conduct, were incapable of defamatory meaning; the statements constituted supervisor's opinion that plaintiff engaged in misconduct warranting the termination of his employment as an "at will" employee).

B. Performance Evaluations

In Pennsylvania, employee consent to evaluation by an employer creates an absolute privilege. Sobel, 366 Pa. Super. at 487, 531 A.2d at 522. See also Bloch v. Temple Univ., 939 F. Supp. 387, 397 (E.D. Pa. 1996) (absolute privilege extended to statements made during professor's tenure evaluation) (internal citations omitted); Keddie v. Pa. State Univ., 412 F. Supp. 1264, 1276-77 (M.D. Pa. 1976) (employer's evaluative statements of an employee that were critical of the employee's job performance were not defamatory). But see Frymire v. Painewebber, Inc., 87 B.R. 856, 859 (Bankr. E.D. Pa. 1988) (declining to follow Sobel's statement that an employer is absolutely privileged to publish defamatory statements in employee evaluations distributed to third parties; finding that such privilege is only conditional, at least in the absence of consent). Performance evaluations are also often considered opinion, and therefore, not capable of defamatory meaning. Baker v. Lafayette Coll., 516 Pa. 291, 297, 532 A.2d 399, 402 (1987) (holding that although the evaluations of an art professor's performance by department chairman did not portray the professor in glowing terms, the substance of the report was "frank opinion void of innuendo" and therefore pure opinion). Compare Forrest v. Owen J. Roberts Sch. Dist., No. 09-3014, 2011 WL 1549492, at *18 (E.D. Pa. Apr. 1, 2011) (school district superintendent stated colorable defamation claim to survive school board's motion to dismiss where plaintiff alleged the "deliberate and malicious dissemination of [job performance] appraisals that profoundly differ[ed] from her prior appraisals and specific accomplishments as to go beyond mere opinion and impl[ied] the existence of undisclosed defamatory facts").

C. References

A qualified privilege protects an employer's statements to a prospective employer of a former employee. Frymire v. PaineWebber, Inc., 107 B.R. 506, 512 (Bankr. E.D. Pa. 1989) (statement that employee was terminated for poor attitude and less than satisfactory performance was conditionally privileged where there was no evidence that the privilege was abused, in other words, that: (1) the former employer acted with malice or ill will, (2) did not have reasonable grounds for the statements, or (3) there was publication outside the scope of the privilege). See also Walker v. Grand Cent. Sanitation, Inc., 430 Pa. Super. 236, 634 A.2d 237 (1993), appeal denied, 539 Pa. 652, 651 A.2d 539 (1994); Geyer v. Steinbronn, 351 Pa.

Super 536, 506 A.2d 901 (1986); Momah v. Albert Einstein Med. Ctr., 978 F. Supp. 621 (E.D. Pa 1997), aff'd, 229 F.2d 1138 (3d Cir. 2000); Garvey v. Dickinson Coll., 763 F. Supp. 796, 798 (M.D. Pa. 1991) (communication to prospective employer, providing fair account of employment performance, including "account of circumstances which caused [plaintiff] some difficulty and perhaps detracted from his job performance," were "clearly conditionally privileged"; the conditional privilege may be "forfeited if the author of the defamatory communication is motivated solely by spite or ill-will against the plaintiff and not by a desire to benefit a common legitimate objective through full disclosure"). Moreover, a statement from a former employer to a prospective employer that the employee was terminated from employment or terminated for cause, without more, does not constitute defamation. Livingston v. Murray, 417 Pa. Super. 202, 212, 612 A.2d 443, 448, 20 Media L. Rep. 1824 (1992), appeal denied, 533 Pa. 601, 617 A.2d 1275 (1992). But see Varrato v. Unilife Corp., No. 1:11–CV–398, 2011 WL 1522170, at *4 (M.D. Pa. Apr. 20, 2011) (noting that while a statement that a plaintiff was terminated from her employment is not alone capable of defamatory meaning, a statement that could reasonably be construed as claiming that plaintiff was fired for accepting bribes might be capable of a defamatory meaning). Likewise, the fact that an employee may foreseeably be required to relate to a prospective employer or others a defamatory statement made to him or her by his or her employer in communicating the reasons for the employee's termination is not defamation. Pilkington v. CGU Ins. Co., Inc., 2001 U.S. Dist. LEXIS 3668, *16, 2000 WL 33159253, at *5 (E.D. Pa. Feb. 9, 2001).

D. Intracorporate Communication

Statements made in furtherance of a corporation's business interests are conditionally privileged. In Simms v. Exeter Architectural Products, Inc., 916 F. Supp. 432 (M.D. Pa. 1996), the court held that a director of a corporation was conditionally privileged to communicate to shareholders allegations of wrongdoing by other directors as the information would affect the shareholders' interest in the corporation. Id. at 436. See also Fort Washington Res. v. Tannen, 846 F. Supp. 354 (E.D. Pa. 1994); Jackson v. J.C. Penney Co., Inc., 616 F. Supp. 233, 235 (E.D. Pa. 1985) (accusations by employer of employee theft while in the presence of corporate security personnel were conditionally privileged); Foster v. UPMC South Side Hosp., 2 A.3d 655, 663 (Pa. Super. 2010) (co-worker physician's apparently false statement that plaintiff physician had caused paralysis in a patient was subject to the conditional privilege applied to communications made by employees concerning matters of discipline and termination with respect to another employee, and thus was not defamation); Kia v. Imaging Sciences Int'l, Inc., 735 F. Supp. 2d 256, 275 (E.D. Pa. 2010) (allegedly defamatory e-mail sent by co-owner of dental imaging corporation to the vice president of the company and to its human resources consultant, concerning the work of employee, was protected by conditional privilege, as necessary for the operation of the business); Truong v. Dart Container Corp., No. 09-3348, 2010 WL 4611980, at *2 (E.D. Pa. Nov. 12, 2010) (a qualified privilege applies to communications between an employer and physicians with whom it contracts to examine employees who sustain on-the-job injuries).

E. Statements to Government Regulators

An alleged defamatory communication is absolutely privileged when it is published by an employer prior to or during a regulatory or judicial proceeding, as long as the communication has some reference to the subject matter of the inquiry. See Pino v. Prudential Ins. Co. of Am., 689 F. Supp. 1358, 1367 (E.D. Pa. 1988) (life insurer's allegedly defamatory letter about insurance broker sent to the Pennsylvania Insurance Commission was absolutely privileged; however, the defendant-insurance agent's allegedly defamatory letter about plaintiff-broker to professional organizations of insurance agents enjoyed only a conditional privilege (as the organization served the public interest by promoting high standards of professionalism in insurance industry)). See also Milliner v. Enck, 709 A.2d 417, 420-21 (Pa. Super. Ct. 1998) (employer's sending of a termination letter and cover letter explaining the allegations of the termination letter to the Pennsylvania Department of Labor and Industry Job Center for the purposes of an unemployment compensation benefits claim was privileged). But see Preiser v. Rosenzweig, 418 Pa. Super. 341, 347-49, 614 A.2d 303, 305-07 (1992), aff'd, 538 Pa. 139, 646 A.2d 1166 (1994) (absolute privilege did not extend to statements made to the Allegheny County Fee Dispute Committee -- voluntary association of lawyers seeking to mediate a county fee dispute -- because the statements at issue were not made to either a judge or an officer appointed by a court during judicial proceedings). See also Reliant Healthcare Mgmt., Inc. v. Ashton Hall, No. 3083, 2011 WL 1097024 (Pa. Com. Pl. Feb. 22, 2011) (letter terminating management agreement between nursing home owner and nursing home management company that incorrectly set forth the bases of the termination and that was copied to the Pennsylvania Department of Health and the U.S. Offices of the Attorney General and the Department of Health and Human Services was not defamatory).

The doctrine of collateral estoppel may not apply, in a later civil defamation proceeding, to the prior findings of fact by Unemployment Compensation Board. Rue v. K-Mart Corp., 552 Pa. 13, 17-21, 713 A.2d 82, 84-87 (1998). However, in Spyridakis v. Riesling Group, 2009 U.S. Dist. LEXIS 93507, at *17 (E.D. Pa. Oct. 6, 2009), the court found that it is possible for collateral estoppel to apply to unemployment compensation proceedings if the elements of collateral estoppel are met. The court explained that Rue does not definitively hold that collateral estoppel does not apply to unemployment compensation proceedings; rather, Rue denied a preclusive effect where the elements of collateral estoppel were not met, and Rue is silent as to whether a decision in an unemployment compensation proceeding per se can ever meet those elements. Id.

Subsequently, the Third Circuit in Spyridakis v. The Riesling Group, Inc., No. 09-4315, 398 Fed. Appx. 793, 2010 WL 3818055, at *3 (3d Cir. Oct. 3, 2010), distinguished Rue because, inter alia, Spyridakis concerned the preclusive effect of a decision by a Pennsylvania court on a question of law, not a decision by an unemployment compensation referee on a question of fact). See also Bakery, Confectionery, Tobacco Workers & Grain Millers Int'l Union, AFL-CIO, CLC Local 6 v. Morabito Baking Co., No. 10-CV-5141, 2011 WL 1883298, at *4 (E.D. Pa. May 18, 2011) ("As for its preclusion argument, Respondent not only cited no case holding that an unemployment compensation decision has preclusive effect, but ignored cases holding that such a decision does *not* have preclusive effect").

F. Reports to Auditors and Insurers

Although no cases have been reported specifically alleging defamatory material in reports to auditors or insurers, Pennsylvania courts recognize a conditional privilege where inquiries or reports are made by auditors and insurers under a common interest theory. For example, in Krochalis v. Insurance Co. of North America, 629 F. Supp. 1360 (E.D. Pa. 1985), the Court held that inquiries by an auditor to a former employee were conditionally privileged for purposes of a defamation action by the worker against his employer and supervisor, even if implication of the inquiries and the discharge were to reaffirm accusations against worker's wife relating to impropriety of wife's employment by the worker, as the parties had a common business interest in the communications in ensuring propriety in the conduct of the employer's business affairs. Id. at 1369-70. See also Elia v. Erie Exchange, 430 Pa. Super. 384, 634 A.2d 657 (1993), appeal denied, 537 Pa. 662, 644 A.2d 1200 (1994); Chicarella v. Passant, 343 Pa. Super. 330, 494 A.2d 1109 (1985). Accordingly, it would appear that the same privilege would apply in the reverse situation.

G. Vicarious Liability of Employers for Statements made by Employees

1. ***Scope of Employment.*** Where an employee publishes a defamatory statement, the employer will not be vicariously liable unless the employee was acting with the authority or on behalf of the employer. See Michelson v. Exxon Research & Eng'g Co., 629 F. Supp. 418, 422 (W.D. Pa. 1986), aff'd, 808 F.2d 1005 (3d Cir. 1987) (principal was liable for defamation so long as agent was apparently authorized to make defamatory statement). See also Momah v. Albert Einstein Med. Ctr., 978 F. Supp. 621 (E.D. Pa. 1997), aff'd, 229 F.2d 1138 (3d Cir. 2000); Deklinski v. Marchetti, 30 Pa. D. & C. 4th 435 (C.C.P., Dauphin County 1996); Morgenstern v. Fox Television Stations of Philadelphia, No. 08-0562, 2008 WL 4792503, at *7-8 (E.D. Pa. Oct. 31, 2008) (allowing discovery to proceed as to whether the union employee made the alleged defamatory statements within the authorized time and space limits of employment and whether the statement was of a kind and nature he was employed to perform); Savonikas v. Borough of Avoca, No. 3:07-CV-2311, 2008 WL 2622904, at *7-8 (M.D. Pa. June 27, 2008) (explaining the four elements of vicarious liability: "The conduct of an employee is within the scope of employment if it is of a kind and nature that the employee is employed to perform, it occurs substantially within the authorized time and space limits, it is actuated, at least in part, by a purpose to serve the employer, and if force is intentionally used by the employee against another, the use of force is not unexpected by the employer"); Flamm v. Sarner & Associates, P.C., No. 02-4302, 2002 WL 31618443, at *7 (E.D. Pa. Nov. 6, 2002) (denying motion to dismiss defamation claim against defendants who hired a process server and debt collector to pressure plaintiff to pay her debts, where the debt collector went to plaintiff's place of employment and made statements such as "I don't know what kind of sneaky little thieves you hire, but Mara Flamm stole thousands of dollars from a doctor and hasn't paid").

a. **Blogging** No reported cases.

2. ***Damages.*** No reported cases.

H. Internal Investigations

In Berg v. Consolidated Freightways, Inc., the Superior Court found that the plaintiff's claim for defamation against defendant, plaintiff's former employer, properly went to the jury where the facts established that the plaintiff "was forced to resign amidst an investigation for theft, along with the actual thieves, and there was also evidence adduced which showed communications from appellants reflecting on [plaintiff's] character and reputation, which proved to be untrue, and which were shown to be communicated to third persons." Berg, 280 Pa. Super. 495, 500, 421 A.2d 831, 833 (Pa. Super. Ct. 1980). The Court also affirmed the lower court's finding that the defendant employer's actions were entitled to a conditional privilege and instructing the jury that such privilege would not be a valid defense if the jury found the defendant acted with malice, including a finding that the defendant acted with a reckless disregard as to whether the statements about plaintiff were false. Berg, 280 Pa. Super at 501-02, 421 A.2d 831, 834.

In Paul v. Lankenau Hospital, the Superior Court, attempting to expand the holding in Berg, held that the dismissal of an employee after an internal investigation for theft could form the basis of a claim for defamation and granted the plaintiff a new trial. Paul, 375 Pa. Super. 1, 20, 543 A.2d 1148, 1158 (Pa. Super. 1988), aff'd in part, denied in part 524 Pa. 90 (1990). The Court stated "regardless of whether [the defendant] did or did not communicate verbally with any unprivileged employee regarding [the plaintiff's] discharge, his termination could have served as an injury to reputation and could have been subject to a defamatory construction." Id. The Court noted that a privilege may protect statements made in this context but that the question of abuse of privilege should have been before the jury. Id. The Court stated that "[u]nder Pennsylvania law, the dismissal of an innocent employee for theft could constitute communication that that employee was a thief, and support a cause of action for defamation." Id; but see Paul, 375 Pa. at 33, 543 A.2d at 1164 (Cavanaugh J. dissenting) (finding that the plaintiff had not stated a cause of action for defamation where there was "no evidence that any publication of allegedly defamatory communication took place" and that even "if [the Court] were to accept [plaintiff's] resignation under pressure as a defamatory act, it is nothing more than an opinion – that [defendant] believed in good faith . . . that the refrigerators were taken by [plaintiff] without permission."). The Supreme Court reversed the Superior Court's grant of a new trial finding that the issue had been waived. Paul v. Lankenau Hospital, 524 Pa. 90, 95, 569 A.2d 346, 349 (Pa. 1990); but see Paul 524 Pa. at 97, 569 A.2d at 349 (Zappalam J. concurring) (finding that the issue was not waived but concurring on the Court's reversal finding that there was no "evidence to establish any communication of defamatory material.").

In accord with these prior decisions, in Bowman v. Burroughs, the District Court for the Western District of Pennsylvania refused to grant the defendant's motion to dismiss where the plaintiff claimed that certain defendants "defamed him during the course of the [internal] investigation by providing false statements regarding Plaintiff's conduct to" another defendant. Bowman, No. 2:07-00185, 2007 U.S. Dist. LEXIS 36538 at *1-2, 2007 WL 1468528, at *1-2 (May 18, 2007). The Court held that it could not conclude "at this early state of the proceedings, that Plaintiff will be able to state no set of facts in support of his defamation claim that would defeat [Defendants'] defenses of absolute and/or conditional privilege." 2007 U.S. Dist. LEXIS at *4; 2007 WL 1468528, at *2. See also Beyda v. USAir, Inc., 697 F. Supp. 1394 (W.D. Pa. 1988) (internal communications between discharged pilot's superiors in course of investigating incident of alleged misconduct were privileged and did not give rise to any actionable defamation).

IV. OTHER ACTIONS BASED ON STATEMENTS

As a general rule, Pennsylvania Courts do not permit plaintiffs to "mislabel" a defamation cause of action where the alleged injury arises from the act of publication. See Evans v. Philadelphia Newspapers, Inc., 411 Pa. Super. 244, 249, 601 A.2d 330, 333, 19 Media L. Rep. 1868 (1991) (contractual interference claim in a complaint arose out of the publication of a libelous report and, therefore, was merely a defamation claim misnomered to circumvent the one-year statute of limitations); Atiyeh Publishing, LLC v. Times Mirror Magazines, Inc., No. 00-CV-1962, 2000 WL 18886574, at *4 (E.D. Pa. Dec. 7, 2000) (noting that the court will "look to the gravamen of the action . . . and not to the label applied" by plaintiff). **Cf. Manning v. Flannery, No. 2:10-cv-178, 2012 WL 1111188, at *1, 17-18 (W.D. Pa. Mar. 31, 2012) (acknowledging Evans v. Philadelphia Newspapers but agreeing with plaintiff that the one year statute of limitations for defamation claims did not apply to his intentional interference with contractual relations claims (having a two year statute of limitations), which were based on "derogatory opinions communicated by Defendants [and] allegedly interfered with Plaintiff's rights under his Executive Agreement, thus resulting in economic harm to Plaintiff"; distinguishing Evans on the facts because Manning's intentional interference claims were based on opinions and statements other than those offered in support of his defamation claims).**

In addition, Pennsylvania has very broadly interpreted the exclusivity provision of its Workers' Compensation law so as to bar many claims such as: intentional infliction of emotional distress, invasion of privacy, fraud, misrepresentation, bad faith and loss of consortium. See, e.g., Santiago v. Pa. Nat'l Mut. Cas. Ins. Co., 418 Pa. Super. 178, 613 A.2d 1235 (1992); Kline v. Arden H. Verner Co., 503 Pa. 251, 469 A.2d 158 (1983). As stated earlier, however, defamation claims are not subject to the exclusivity provision. See V. C., infra. Accord Fox v. The Devereux Foundation, No. 90-0830, 1990 WL 97796, at *6 (E.D. Pa. July 10, 1990) ("Devereux's alleged defamatory conduct was its termination of Fox. Devereux's conduct did not arise during the course of Fox's employment, but at its end. Accordingly, I find that the Pennsylvania courts do not hold the Workers' Compensation Act as a bar to a claim of defamation"); Pilkington v. CGU Insurance Co., Inc., No. 00-2495, 2000 WL 33159253, at *4 E.D. Pa. Feb 9, 2001) (defamation claim against employer not barred by exclusivity provision of the Pennsylvania Workers' Compensation Act since the Act was not intended to redress injury to reputation); Urban v. Dollar Bank, 725 A.2d 815 (Pa. Super. 1999) (employee's defamation claim was not barred by the exclusivity provisions of the Workers' Compensation Act).

A. Negligent Hiring, Retention, and Supervision

Pennsylvania recognizes causes of action for negligent hiring, retention, and supervision. See, e.g., Fuhrman v. Quill, No. 1:09-CV-00841, 2010 WL 411698, at *9 (M.D. Pa. Jan. 27, 2010) ("Employers in Pennsylvania have a duty to exercise reasonable care in selecting, supervising, and controlling employees. To fasten liability upon an employer under RESTATEMENT (SECOND) OF TORTS § 317, it must be shown that the employer knew, or in the exercise of ordinary care, should have known of the necessity for exercising control of his employee"); Hutchison by Hutchison v. Luddy, 560 Pa. 51, 742 A.2d 1052 (1999); Dempsey v. Walso Bureau, Inc., 431 Pa. 562, 246 A.2d 148 (1968). An employer has a "duty not to hire or retain employees that it knows or should know have a propensity for [tortious conduct]." Hutchison by Hutchison, 560 Pa. at 64, 742 A.2d at 1059. Therefore, "[w]here the plaintiff can establish that [the employer] knew or reasonably should have known of such a propensity, the [employer] will generally be liable for the foreseeable [tortious conduct] . . . by that employee." Id. Further, "[l]iability based on negligent hiring or retention is not limited to [tortious conduct] that occurs" while the employee is working. Id. An employer may be liable for tortious acts committed by its employees outside of work "where there is a causal connection between the particular injury and the fact of employment." Id. An employer "can be held liable for injuries suffered after it knew or should have known of the employee's propensity." Id. There is no Pennsylvania case law holding employers liable for their employees' defamatory statements under a negligent hiring, retention, or supervision theory.

B. Intentional Infliction of Emotional Distress

"While the Pennsylvania Supreme Court has yet to formally recognize a cause of action for intentional infliction of emotional distress, see Taylor v. Albert Einstein Med. Ctr., 562 Pa. 176, 754 A.2d 650, 652 (2000), the Pennsylvania Superior Court has recognized the cause of action and has held that, 'in order for a plaintiff to prevail on such a claim, he or she must, at the least, demonstrate intentional outrageous or extreme conduct by the defendant, which causes severe emotional distress to the plaintiff.'" Reedy v. Evanson, 615 F.3d 197, 231 (3d Cir. 2010). Accord Sullivan v. Warminster Township, 765 F. Supp. 2d 687, 708 (E.D. Pa. Mar. 15, 2011) ("The Pennsylvania Supreme Court has never explicitly recognized the tort of IIED under Pennsylvania law. The Third Circuit, however, has predicted that the Supreme Court of Pennsylvania would adopt the IIED tort as set forth in Section 46 of the Restatement (Second) of Torts"); Monroe v. Mullooley, No. 10-1208, 2011 WL 337333, at *3 (W.D. Pa. Feb. 3, 2011) ("Although it is unsettled whether Pennsylvania recognizes the tort of intentional infliction of emotional distress, it is generally assumed that the tort requires proof of conduct that is so outrageous in character, and so extreme in degree, as to go beyond all possible bounds of decency, and to be regarded as atrocious, and utterly intolerable in a civilized society") (citing RESTATEMENT (SECOND) OF TORTS § 46 cmt. d (1965)); Pope v. Rostraver Shop & Save, No. 06-01009, 2008 WL 1776507, at *14 (W.D. Pa. Apr. 16, 2008); Pacheco v. Golden Living Ctr. Summit, No. 3:10cv1641, 2011 WL 744656, at *6, 7 (M.D. Pa. Feb. 23, 2011) ("The Pennsylvania Superior Court has adopted . . . section 46 of the RESTATEMENT (SECOND) OF TORTS" but "[t]he Pennsylvania Supreme Court has found that only the most serious conduct justifies recovery"). See also Strickland v. Univ. of Scranton, 700 A.2d 979, 987 (Pa. Super. Ct. 1997); NTP Marble, Inc. v. AAA Hellenic Marble, Inc., No. 09-cv-5783, 2011 WL 2582135, at *5-6 (E.D. Pa. June 30, 2011) (alleged conduct by defendant in publishing a press release containing allegedly defamatory statements about competitor's employee, and then refusing to retract the press release in light of competitor's agent admitting sole responsibility for posting the fake negative reviews of defendant, was not sufficiently outrageous to sustain a cause of action for IIED, although it was "boorish and unprofessional").

In order to recover for IIED, the plaintiff must establish the existence of the following four criteria: (1) the defendant's conduct was intentional or reckless; (2) the defendant's conduct was extreme and outrageous; (3) the defendant's conduct caused emotional distress; and (4) the emotional distress is severe. **Vives v. Rodriguez, No. 09-2728, 2012 WL 298760, at *1, 13 (E.D. Pa. Jan. 31, 2012) (failure to return nearly $40,000 pursuant to a contractual arrangement "falls far short of the outrageousness that Hunger v. Grand Cent. Sanitation, 447 Pa. Super. 575, 670 A.2d 173, 177 (1996) requires");** Mascarini v. Quality Employment Serv. & Training, No. 1:10–CV–1546, 2011 WL 332425, at *9 n.3 (M.D. Pa. Jan. 31, 2011); Wilson v. Am. Gen. Fin., Inc., No. 10–412, 2011 WL 344168, at *1 (W.D. Pa. Aug. 8, 2011) (although a publication imputing unworthiness of credit is libelous under Pennsylvania law, the defendant-mortgagee's statement that plaintiff-mortgagors' accounts were past due as a result of delinquent payments was not sufficiently outrageous in character to support mortgagor's intentional infliction of emotional distress claim under Pennsylvania law); Hanczyc v. Valley Distrib. and Storage Co., Inc., No. 3:10-CV-2397, 2011 WL 1790093, at *3 (M.D. Pa. May 9, 2011) ("Generally, the case is one in which the recitation of the facts to an average member of the community would arouse his resentment against the actor, and lead him to exclaim, 'outrageous!'"); Halterman v. Tullytown Borough, No. 10–7166, 2011 WL 2411020, at *7 (E.D. Pa. June 14, 2011) (no actionable IIED claim where defendant told others that plaintiff "used vulgarity in public, repeatedly declined to follow a police officer's instructions, and was consequently arrested, detained, and charged with minor offenses"); Ruder v. Pequea Valley Sch. Dist., No. 10-442, 2011 WL 1832794, at *11 (E.D. Pa. May 12, 2011) ("The Third Circuit Court of Appeals has held that it is 'extremely rare' in the employment context for conduct to rise to the level of outrageousness necessary to support recovery for IIED . . . Pennsylvania courts have permitted claims of IIED to proceed in the employment context in situations such as where an employer engages in both sexual harassment and other retaliatory behavior"). Accord Brooks v. Systems Mfg. Corp., No. 03-1523, 2003 WL 23023826, at *3 (E.D. Pa. Dec. 18, 2003); Benn v. Universal Health Sys., Inc., No. 99-CV-6526, 2001 WL 1251207, at *10 (E.D. Pa. July 24, 2001); Frankel v. Warwick Hotel, 881 F. Supp. 183, 187 (E.D. Pa. 1995) (citing RESTATEMENT (SECOND) OF TORTS § 46(1) (1992)).

A plaintiff must substantiate the emotional harm with proof of physical bodily injury. Hanczyc, 2011 WL 1790093, at *3 (plaintiff must allege physical injury); Stewart v. Xrimz, LLC, No. 3:10-CV-2147, 2011 WL 1002207, at *6 (M.D. Pa.

Mar. 18, 2011) (plaintiffs must allege physical injury); Marchese v. Umstead, 110 F. Supp. 2d 361, 368-69 (E.D. Pa. 2000) (discussing the physical injury requirement for an IIED claim and "the narrow circumstances under which this tort has evolved and been recognized"); Goodson v. Kardashian, 413 Fed. Appx. 417, 418, 2011 WL 167272, at *1 (3d Cir. Jan. 20, 2011) (liability for infliction of emotional distress "clearly does not extend to mere insults, indignities, threats, annoyances, petty oppressions, or other trivialities"); Mort v. Lawrence County Children and Youth Serv., No. 2:10-cv-1438, 2011 3862641, at *18 (W.D. Pa. Aug. 31, 2011) ("Pennsylvania courts routinely require an averment of physical injury to sustain a cause of action for negligent infliction of emotional distress"); Whiting v. Bonazza, No. 09-1113, 2011 WL 500797, at *14 (W.D. Pa. Feb. 10, 2011) (allegations of harassment, unlawful arrest, and excessive force do not go beyond all possible bounds of decency as required by Pennsylvania courts); Gagliardi v. Equifax, No. 09–1612, 2011 WL 337331, at *1 (W.D. Pa. Feb. 3, 2011) ("no reasonable trier of fact could conclude that [plaintiff's] 'emotional distress' was proximately caused" by alleged conduct by Equifax in providing plaintiff's credit score to a gas company that concluded plaintiff failed to meet its credit guidelines for service); Hunger v. Grand Cent. Sanitation, 447 Pa. Super. 575, 583, 670 A.2d 173, 177 (1996) (same), appeal denied, 545 Pa. 664, 681 A.2d 178 (1996). Accord Moeller v. Twp. of N. Strabane, No. 05-0135, 2008 U.S. Dist. LEXIS 60469, at *19-20, 2008 WL 3072975, at *5 (W.D. Pa. Aug. 1, 2008); Bonson v. Diocese of Altoona-Johnstown, 67 Pa. D. & C. 4th 419, 439-40 (Pa. Com. Pl. 2004); Paith v. County of Washington, 394 Fed. Appx. 858, 861, 2010 WL 3622670, at *3 (3d Cir. 2010); Patton v. Pasqualini, No. 09–4893, 2011 WL 3803505, at *12 (E.D. Pa. Aug. 25, 2011) ("a plaintiff must support the claim of emotional distress with competent medical evidence, in the form of expert medical evidence"); Barnett v. York County, No. 1:CV–11–0906, 2011 WL 2790467, at *26 n.20 (M.D. Pa. June 24, 2011).

To state a cognizable claim for IIED, a plaintiff must also have been present when the allegedly tortious conduct that caused the serious mental distress occurred. Weiley v. Albert Einstein Med. Ctr., No. 339-EDA-2011, 2012 WL 2478185, at *1, 10, n. 14 (Pa. Super. 2012) (citing Taylor v. Albert Einstein Med. Ctr., 754 A.2d 650, 654 (Pa. 2000))

Additionally, although "Pennsylvania's Workers' Compensation Act is the exclusive remedy for . . . intentional or negligent infliction of emotional distress arising out of an employment relationship," the Act does not bar suit for "conduct that occurred after the termination of employment and that did not arise out of the course of employment or relate thereto." Equal Employment Opportunity Commission v. Creative Playthings, Ltd., 375 F. Supp. 2d 427, 438 (E.D. Pa. 2005). See also Minto v. J.B. Hunt Transport Serv., Inc., 971 A.2d 1280, 1283 (Pa. Super. 2009) ("The Act bars actions in tort by an employee against his or her employer, with certain limited exceptions. One such exception is where the courts determine that the injury did not arise in the course of employment").

C. Interference with Advantageous Economic Relations / Interference with Prospective Contractual Relations

"Pennsylvania recognizes two interference based claims. First, Pennsylvania has adopted the RESTATEMENT (SECOND) approach to interference with advantageous economic relations or with performance of a contract. Second, Pennsylvania recognizes a cause of action for interference with prospective contractual relations. The names of these two bases of liability vary across jurisdiction, but ultimately represent a tort based on interference with existing relations and a tort based on interference with prospective relations." Flannery v. Mid Penn Bank, No. 1:CV–08–0685, 2008 WL 5113437, at *8 -9 (M.D. Pa. Dec. 3, 2008) (plaintiff alleged three separate interference based torts: (1) interference with business advantage, (2) interference with prospective advantage, and (3) intentional interference with contractual relations). See also Ruffing v. 84 Lumber Co., 410 Pa. Super. 459, 467, 600 A.2d 545, 549 (1991), appeal denied, 530 Pa. 666, 610 A.2d 46 (1992) (Pennsylvania recognizes a cause of action for intentional interference with prospective contractual relations). "Pennsylvania does not recognize a tort for 'intentional interference with prospective economic advantage,' but does apply its 'intentional interference with contractual relations' tort to prospective contracts." ClubCom, Inc. v. Captive Media, Inc., No. 02:07–cv–1462, 2009 WL 249446, at *7 (W.D. Pa. Jan. 31, 2009). **"To plead a tortious interference with contract claim, the party must demonstrate that: [1] either a contract or prospective contractual relationship exists between the complainant and a third party; [2] there must be purposeful action by the defendant to harm the relationship or prevent the relationship from occurring; [3] the absence of privilege or justification on the part of the defendant for their actions must be shown; [and] [4] plaintiff must prove that defendant's conduct resulted in actual legal damage to the plaintiff." Pierre v. Post Commercial Real Estate Corp., No. 0384, 2012 WL 2872015, at *1 (Pa. Com. Pl. July 2, 2012) (citing Strickland v. Univ. of Scranton, 700 A.2d 979, 985 (Pa. Super. 1997) and finding defendants were entitled to judgment as a matter of law because plaintiff failed to meet the first prong).**

To state a claim for intentional interference with prospective contractual relations, a plaintiff must establish four elements: (1) a prospective contractual relation; (2) the purpose or intent to harm the plaintiff by preventing the relation from occurring; (3) the absence of privilege or justification on the part of the defendant; and (4) actual damage resulting from the defendant's conduct. Thompson Coal Co. v. Pike Coal Co., 488 Pa. 198, 208, 412 A.2d 466, 471 (1979); **Rantnetwork, Inc. v. Underwood, No. 4:11-CV-1283, 2012 WL 1021326, at *1, 14-15 (M.D. Pa. Mar. 26, 2012) (confirming that**

Thompson Coal is binding authority regarding the elements of a claim for intentional interference with prospective contractual relations); Flannery, 2008 WL 5113437, at *8-9 (as for a claim for intentional interference with contractual relations, "Pennsylvania permits tort claims against one who, without privilege to do so, induces or otherwise purposely causes a third person not to (a) perform a contract with another or (b) enter into or continue a business relation with another"); Brotech Corp. v. White Eagle Int'l Tech. Group, Inc., No. Civ.A. 03–232, 2003 WL 22797730, at *8 n.1 (E.D. Pa. Jan. 16, 2003) ("The elements of claims for tortious interference with existing and prospective business relations under Pennsylvania law are identical to the elements of claims for tortious interference with existing and prospective contractual relations, and are based on Sections 766 and 766B of the RESTATEMENT (SECOND) OF TORTS"); Perrano v. Arbaugh, No. 10–cv–01623, 2011 WL 1103885, at *18-19 (E.D. Pa. Mar. 25, 2011) ("As recognized by the Third Circuit, the elements of intentional interference with a contractual relation under Pennsylvania law, whether existing or prospective, are as follows…").

A prospective contractual relation is "'something less than a contractual right, something more than a mere hope.'" Id. at 209, 412 A.2d 471; American Food & Vending Corp. v. Full Serv. Vending Co., No. 3:10cv2576, 2011 WL 2632798, at *5 (M.D. Pa. July 5, 2011) ("Courts have concluded that defining a 'prospective contractual relationship' can be difficult. The term has an evasive quality, eluding precise definition. It is something less than a contractual right, something more than a mere hope. Still, a plaintiff must demonstrate a reasonable likelihood or probability of the parties agreeing to a contract. Courts apply an objective standard for determining whether a reasonable likelihood or possibility exists") (internal citations omitted). "Specific intent to harm" is not required under this test. Ruffing, 410 Pa. Super. at 469. **"In determining the 'reasonable likelihood or probability' of a prospective contractual relationship, courts must apply an objective standard." RX Home Care, Inc. v. Dubin, No. 2010-C-2694, 2012 WL 2603382, at *1 (Pa. Com. Pl. June 2012) ("Pennsylvania courts have consistently required more evidence than the existence of a current business or contractual relationship"). Plaintiff must show an "objectively reasonable probability that a contract will come into existence. This 'reasonable probability may result from an unenforceable express agreement, an offer, or the parties' current dealings, but not merely from prior dealings or an existing business relationship between the parties.") Manning v. Flannery, No. 2:10-cv-178, 2012 WL 1111188, at *1, 29-30 (W.D. Pa. Mar. 31, 2012) (plaintiff's evidence was insufficient to establish the existence of a prospective business relationship to support a claim for intentional interference with prospective contractual relationship where plaintiff offered no evidence that he obtained an offer, oral agreement or had actual current dealings for employment beyond preliminary discussions and interviews for positions).**

In addition, absence of privilege or justification is "closely related to the element of intent [and] . . . is not susceptible of precise definition." Silver v. Mendel, 894 F.2d 598, 603 n.7 (3d Cir. 1990), cert. denied, 496 U.S. 926 (1990). One who is "an actor is privileged to interfere with another's performance of a contract when: (1) the actor has a legally protected interest; (2) he or she acts or threatens to act to protect the interest; and (3) the threat is to protect by proper means." Ruffing, 447 Pa. Super. at 582, 600 A.2d at 548.

When addressing an intentional interference with prospective contractual relations claim, Pennsylvania courts consider the totality of the factual circumstances, focusing on the propriety of the defendant's conduct. Id. at 582, 600 A.2d at 549 (citation omitted). The courts have used the following factors to determine the propriety of a defendant's conduct: (1) the nature of the actor's conduct; (2) the actor's motive; (3) the interests of the other with which the actor's conduct interferes; (4) the interests sought to be advanced by the actor; (5) the social interests in protecting the freedom of action of the actor and the contractual interests of the other; (6) the proximity or remoteness of the actor's conduct to the interference; and (7) the relations between the parties. Ruffing, 410 Pa. Super. at 582, 600 A.2d at 600 (citing RESTATEMENT (SECOND) OF TORTS § 767 (1992)).

Recently, the Pennsylvania Supreme Court expressly adopted RESTATEMENT (SECOND) OF TORTS § 772(a) and held that the act of providing truthful information cannot support a claim for tortious interference with contractual relations. Walnut Street Assoc's, Inc. v. Brokerage Concepts, Inc., 20 A.3d 468 (Pa. 2011). In Walnut Sreet, a customer of insurance services cancelled its long-standing contract with its broker after it was informed in a letter from its insurance plan administrator the exact amount of commissions earned by its broker on its account. The Court reasoned that Section 772(a) was consistent with existing Pennsylvania law, and it explained that providing truthful information cannot be "improper," as is required to establish a claim for tortious interference. Id. at 479. Distinguishing Walnut Street on the facts, the court in Feldman & Pinto, P.C. v. Seithel, LLC, No. 11-5400, 2011 WL 6758460, at *1, 9 n.2 (E.D. Pa. Dec. 22, 2011), found that the "defense of truth" did not apply because the letters an attorney sent in an attempt to solicit clients from her former law firm were not truthful. **The court in Rantnetwork, Inc. v. Underwood, No. 4:11-cv-1283, at *1, 2, 3, 16 (M.D. Pa. Mar. 26, 2012) -- where plaintiff software-developer allegedly suffered over $5 million in damages as a result of a "fateful e-mail" that defendants sent to plaintiff's CEO and several of its investors "scaring off potential investors" (e.g., ". . . not one single promise made by Rant has ever been kept . . . you have not been proactive in keeping investors updated . . .") -- dismissed plaintiff's intentional interference with prospective contractual relations claim based on the truth defense adopted by Walnut Street: "[A] defendant's raising a truthfulness defense per RESTATEMENT (SECOND) OF**

TORTS § 772(a) against a claim of tortious interference obviates the need for an analysis of the relative weights of the seven otherwise-applicable considerations in § 767 of the RESTATEMENT." Id. at *16. Similarly, analogizing the case before it to Walnut Street, the court in Manning v. Flannery, No. 2:10-cv-178, 2012 WL 1111188, at *1, 25-26 (W.D. Pa. Mar. 31, 2012) -- involving communications made during a search for a new corporate vice president -- granted summary judgment to defendant on plaintiff's claims of intentional interference with existing contractual/business relationships: "The Defendant's improper intent is not relevant to determining whether Section 772 applies. Even though the advice given may have been self-serving, so long as it is truthfully and honestly given, the interference [with business relationship] will be deemed proper." Id. at *26.

"Pennsylvania recognizes the tort of contractual interference as separate and distinct from the torts of slander and libel." Fennell v. Van Cleef, No. 2754, 2000 WL 33711042, at *3 (Pa. Com. Pl. Sept. 25, 2000).

D. Prima Facie Tort

Pennsylvania remains resistant to recognition of a cause of action for prima facie tort. D'Errico v. DeFazio, 2000 Pa. Super. 354, ¶ 22, 763 A.2d 424, 433 (2000), appeal denied, 566 Pa. 663, 782 A.2d 546 (2001) ("Pennsylvania has not adopted intentional or *prima facie* tort as set forth in § 870 of the Restatement because only our supreme court and the legislature can adopt new causes of action in Pennsylvania").

Although some courts have dismissed such a claim, predicting that the Pennsylvania Supreme Court would not recognize it, others have allowed the claim to proceed. The court in Charles Shaid of Pa., Inc. v. George Hyman Constr. Co., 947 F. Supp. 844, 855-56 (E.D. Pa. 1996), predicted that "if presented with a claim for prima facie tort, the Pennsylvania Supreme Court would not recognize such a cause of action under Pennsylvania law." 947 F. Supp. at 856. However, "a few federal district courts" have permitted the claims for prima facie tort under Pennsylvania law, and "[s]ome of these courts have allowed prima facie tort claims without any analysis or citation." Utz v. Johnson, No. 94-cv-0437, 2004 WL 1368824, at *1, 2 (E.D. Pa. June 16, 2004) (citations omitted); L&M Beverage Co. v. Guinness Imp. Co., No. 94-CV-4492, 1995 WL 771113, at *5 (E.D. Pa. Dec. 29, 1995). But see Cotner v. Yoxheimer, No. 1:07-cv-1566, 2008 U.S. Dist. LEXIS 51388 at *19-21, 2008 WL 2680872, at *7 (M.D. Pa. July 2, 2008) (internal citation and quotation omitted) (dismissing claim for prima facie tort and noting that "it is not a cognizable legal theory in Pennsylvania" and that "the great majority of federal district courts, several of which engaged in a lengthy examination of the issue not to be repeated here, have uniformly concluded that the Pennsylvania Supreme Court would not recognize such a cause of action under Pennsylvania law").

The Third Circuit has not yet made a prediction on whether a claim for prima facie tort will be approved by the Supreme Court of Pennsylvania. Devon IT, Inc. v. IBM Corp., No. 10–2899, 2011 WL 1331888, at *16 (E.D. Pa. Mar. 31, 2011) ("Plaintiffs acknowledge that Pennsylvania has not recognized a claim for a prima facie tort, but submit that it has not been rejected either, and that they should be allowed to pursue the claim"). ;

V. OTHER ISSUES

A. Statute of Limitations

The statute of limitations for defamation is one year. 42 PA. CONS. STAT. ANN. § 5523. The cause of action for defamation accrues on the date of the publication of the defamatory statement. Morris v. Hoffa, No. 01-3420, 2002 U.S. Dist. LEXIS 5975, at *7 (E.D. Pa. Apr. 18, 2002). In Pennsylvania, the discovery rule does not apply to defamation actions, at least with respect to mass media defamation. Barrett v. Catacombs Press, 64 F. Supp. 2d 440, 444, 27 Media L. Rep. 2493 (E.D. Pa. 1999). Pennsylvania does recognize the single publication rule; however, it has a slightly different variation on the rule. Bradford v. Am. Media Operations, 882 F. Supp. 1508, 1517, 23 Media L. Rep. 1941 (E.D. Pa. 1995). Essentially, Pennsylvania protects against more than one action for the same publication only if it is by the same publisher. Graham v. Today's Spirit, 503 Pa. 52, 57-58, 468 A.2d 454, 457-58, 10 Media L. Rep. 1337 (1983). At least one court has declined to apply the single publication rule to a report from a subscription service providing background information on potential employees. Pendergrass v. ChoicePoint, Inc., No. 08-188, 2008 U.S. Dist. LEXIS 99767 at *17 – 18, 2008 WL 5188782 (E.D. Pa. Dec. 10, 2008). In Pendergrass, the plaintiff was terminated by his former employment under suspicion of theft. Id. at *2. The former employer then reported the theft to the subscription service, to which multiple prospective new employers subscribed. Id. at *3. The plaintiff was repeatedly denied new employment based on the report. Id. at *3 – 4. The court held that, because the subscription service was not a mass publication, the rationale for the single publication rule was not present, and therefore allowed the plaintiff to maintain defamation causes of action for each time the report was accessed within the one year limitations period. Id. at *17 – 18.

B. Jurisdiction

Although the reported cases addressing jurisdiction are outside of the employment arena, it is important to note that a defendant may be subject to jurisdiction in Pennsylvania where the plaintiff is a Pennsylvania resident, despite de minimus publication within the state. See Friedman v. Israel Labour Party, 957 F. Supp. 701, 708, 25 Media L. Rep. 2153 (E.D. Pa. 1997) (an article about a Pennsylvania resident in Boston Globe, which has daily circulation of fewer than 25 copies in the entire state of Pennsylvania, subjects the Globe to Pennsylvania jurisdiction in a libel suit challenging the article). But see Barrett, 64 F. Supp. 2d 440 (a web site in Oregon without more contacts is insufficient to establish jurisdiction in Pennsylvania).

C. Worker's Compensation Exclusivity

The Workmen's Compensation Act ("WCA") provides the exclusive remedy for injuries arising during the course of employment. 77 PA. CONS. STAT. ANN. § 481(b) (2002). The statute reflects a compromise whereby employees give up their common law cause of action for work-related injury in favor of an exclusive statutory right to compensation. Jackson v. Rohm & Haas Co., 56 Pa. D. & C.4th 449, 453 (2002) (citing Socha v. Metz, 385 Pa. 632, 637, 123 A.2d 837, 839 (1956)). Pennsylvania courts have held that the exclusivity provision of the WCA applies not only in cases involving negligence, but also when the employer commits an intentional tort. Poyser v. Newman & Co., Inc., 514 Pa. 32, 36, 522 A.2d 548, 550 (1987).

The WCA's limits recovery to those situations in which damages arise from injury or death occurring within the scope of employment. 77 PA. CONS. STAT. ANN. § 481(a) (2002). Damages arising from conduct outside the scope of employment and damages not arising due to personal injury fall outside the Act's scope. See Urban v. Dollar Bank, 1999 Pa. Super. 33, 725 A.2d 815, 818 (1999); Krasevic v. Goodwill Indus. Of Cent. Pa., Inc., 2000 Pa. Super. 348, 764 A.2d 561, 567 (2000). Courts in Pennsylvania have held that injury to reputation does not qualify as personal injury for purposes of the WCA's exclusivity provision. Urban, 725 A.2d at 819; Care v. Reading Hosp. and Med. Ctr., No. 2003-CV-04121, 2005 U.S. Dist. LEXIS 5469 at 12, 2005 WL 746772 (E.D. Pa. March 31, 2005). Therefore, actions for libel are not barred by the WCA. Urban, 725 A.2d at 821.

D. Pleading Requirements

The Pennsylvania Rules of Civil Procedure require that a pleading contain the material facts upon which a cause of action is based. 42 PA. CONS. STAT. ANN. 1019(a).

Defamation is subject to a more stringent pleading standard. Zugarek v. Southern Tioga Sch. Dist., 214 F. Supp. 2d 468, 481 (M.D. Pa. 2002) (quoting Smith v. Sch. Dist. of Philadelphia, 112 F. Supp. 2d 417, 429 (E.D. Pa. 2000). Generally, the plaintiff must identify and plead the precise words that he or she claims to be defamatory. Moses v. McWilliams, 379 Pa. Super. 150, 157, 549 A.2d 950, 953 (1988), appeal denied, 521 Pa. 630, 558 A.2d 532 (1989). **See also Lilac Meadows, Inc. v. Rivello, 2012 WL 1230494 (Pa.Com.Pl., April 5, 2012) (striking phrase "as well as diverse others" in complaint following specific alleged statements and noting that "[t]he inclusion of an averment regarding 'other' unidentified instances of slander clearly does not satisfy Moses and its progeny . . ..").**

The occasion of the publication and identity of the recipients must be pled. Raneri v. De Polo, 65 Pa. Commw. 183, 186, 441 A.2d 1373, 1375 (1982). But see Beascoechea v. Sverdrup & Parcel & Assocs., Inc., 486 F. Supp. 169 (E.D. Pa. 1980) (holding that a summary of the defamatory words was sufficient); Linker v. Custom-Bilt Mach., Inc., 594 F. Supp. 894 (E.D. Pa. 1984) (the difference between federal and state decisions on pleading may lie in the more liberal "notice pleading" federal rules). Under Pennsylvania pleading standards, a complaint for defamation should specifically identify what allegedly defamatory statements were made by whom and to whom. Gross v. United Eng'rs and Constructors, Inc., 224 Pa. Super. 233, 302 A.2d 370, 371 (Pa. Super. Ct. 1973; Raneri v. Depolo, 65 Pa. Cmwlth. 183, 441 A.2d 1373, 1375 (Pa. Commw. Ct. 1982). However, cases in federal court, even on removal, apply the more liberal federal pleading standards and do not require such specificity. Willy v. Coastal Corp., 503 U.S. 131, 134-35, 112 S.Ct. 1076, 117 L.Ed.2d 280 (1992); Varrato v. Unilife Corp., 2011 WL 1522170 (M.D. Pa., April 20, 2011).

A plaintiff must also allege with particularity the persons making the defamatory statements. Sylk v. Bernstein, 2003 WL 1848565, at *8 (Pa. Com. Pl. Feb. 4, 2003) (citing Itri v. Lewis, 281 Pa. Super. 521, 524, 422 A.2d 591, 592 (1980)). Recently, in Pilchesky v. Gatelli, 2011 Pa. Super. 3, 12 A.2d 430 (Pa. Super. Ct. 2011), the Pennsylvania Superior Court addressed, as an issue of first impression in Pennsylvania, the appropriate standard to be applied to a request for the disclosure of the identity of a John Doe defendant in a defamation claim. Appellee Judy Gatelli brought defamation claims against, inter alia, forty-six John Doe defendants who had posted statements on an internet message board using pseudonyms. The trial court had ordered the disclosure of the true identity of six individuals. Addressing the issue as an appeal of a collateral order, the Superior Court adopted a "modified version" of the tests adopted by the New Jersey Appellate Division in Dendrite Int'l, Inc. v. Doe, No. 3, 342 N.J. Super 134, 775 A.2d 756 (App. Div. 2001), and by the Delaware Supreme Court in Doe No. 1 v. Cahill, 884 A.2d 451 (De. 2005). Id. at 439-42. The court noted that four requirements "are necessary to ensure the proper balance between a speaker's right to remain anonymous and a defamation plaintiff's right to seek redress." Id. at 442. Specifically: (1) the John Doe defendant must receive proper notification of a petition to disclose his identity and a reasonable opportunity to contest the petition; (2) the plaintiff must "present sufficient evidence to establish a prima facie case for all elements of a defamation claim, within the plaintiff's control, such as would survive a motion for summary judgment;" (3) the plaintiff must submit an affidavit asserting that the requested information is sought in good faith, is unavailable by other means, is directly related to the claim and is fundamentally necessary to secure relief; and (4) the reviewing court "must expressly balance the defendant's First Amendment rights against the strength of the plaintiff's prima facie case," considering such factors as the nature of the comments, the quantity and quality of the evidence presented, and the context in which the comments were made. Id. at 442-46. The Superior Court noted that the trial court had not undertaken a balancing test, so it vacated the order and remanded for further proceedings.

SURVEY OF PENNSYLVANIA EMPLOYMENT PRIVACY LAW

Jaime S. Tuite, Emilie R. Hammerstein and Ashley L. Yeager
Buchanan Ingersoll & Rooney PC
One Oxford Centre, 20th Floor
301 Grant Street
Pittsburgh, PA 15219
Telephone: (412) 562-8800; Facsimile: (412) 562-1041

(With Developments Reported Through **November 1, 2012**)

GENERAL COMMENTS

The federal courts in Pennsylvania make use of an Electronic Case Filing ("ECF") system. Any subscriber to WebPACER may read, download, store, and print the full content of electronically filed documents. Therefore, by way of both Local Rules of Civil Procedure and also Standing Rules of Court, the Pennsylvania federal courts prohibit the inclusion of certain personal information in court filings, absent certain limited exceptions. Such personal information generally includes Social Security numbers (only last four digits permitted), names of minor children, dates of birth (only year permitted), financial account numbers, and in some situations home addresses (only city and state permitted). See Local Rule 5.1.1 (W.D. Pa.); Local Rule 5.2 (M.D. Pa.); and Local Rule 5.1.3 (E.D. Pa.).

SIGNIFICANT DEVELOPMENTS SINCE THE 2012 *SURVEY*

In *Trail v. Lesko*, No. GD-10-017249 (C.P. Alleg. Co. July 3, 2012 Wettick, J), Judge Stanton Wettick provided a detailed analysis of the discoverability of private Facebook content, ultimately denying both parties' respective motions to discover the information.

I. GENERAL LAW OF PRIVACY

A. Legal Basis of Privacy Claims

1. ***Constitutional Protection.*** Article 1, Section 8 of the Pennsylvania Constitution bars unreasonable governmental searches and seizures. See PA. CONST. Art. I, § 8. Although the language of the state provision is essentially identical to that of the Fourth Amendment of the United States Constitution, greater protection is offered under the state constitution than under the federal. See, e.g., Commonwealth v. Beaman, 880 A.2d 578, 584 (Pa. 2005) (holding that suspicionless sobriety checkpoints pass muster under Article I, Section 8 of the state constitution, which affords "greater individual privacy protections" than the United States Constitution); Commonwealth v. Gillispie, 821 A.2d 1221, 1226 (Pa. 2003) ("Article I, § 8, . . . 'may be employed to guard individual privacy rights against unreasonable searches and seizures more zealously than the federal government does under the Constitution of the United States.'") (quoting Commonwealth v. Melilli, 555 A.2d 1254, 1258 (Pa. 1989)); Commonwealth v. Matos, 672 A.2d 769, 776 (Pa. 1996) (holding that police pursuit of an individual constitutes a "seizure" under Article I, Section 8 of the state constitution, notwithstanding that such a pursuit would not constitute a "seizure" for Fourth Amendment purposes); Commonwealth v. Edmunds, 586 A.2d 887, 905-06 (Pa. 1991) (holding that Article I, Section 8 of the state constitution does not incorporate "good faith" exception to exclusionary rule unlike Fourth Amendment jurisprudence); Commonwealth v. Sell, 470 A.2d 457, 468 (Pa. 1983) (holding that person charged with a possessory offense has "automatic standing" to assert protection against unreasonable searches and seizures under Article I, Section 8 of the state constitution, although such "automatic standing" is not available when asserting Fourth Amendment protection); Commonwealth v. J.B., 719 A.2d 1058, 1064 (Pa. Super. Ct. 1998) (noting strength of implicit right to privacy under Article 1, Section 8).

Privacy is also protected by the Pennsylvania Constitution's general declaration of rights, which includes the right to protect one's "reputation." See PA. CONST. Art. I, § 1 ("All men are born equally free and independent, and have certain inherent and indefeasible rights, among which are those of enjoying and defending life and liberty, of acquiring, possessing and protecting property and reputation, and of pursuing their own happiness."); In re T.R., 731 A.2d 1276, 1279-80 (Pa. 1999) (citing In re June 1979 Allegheny Cty. Inv. Gr. Jury, 415 A.2d 73, 77 (Pa. 1980) (plurality opinion) and In re B., 394 A.2d 419, 425 (Pa. 1978) (plurality opinion)) (noting that individuals' privacy interest in their personal matters, including their psychiatric records, finds explicit protection in Article I, Section 1 of the state constitution). Like the other provisions of the Pennsylvania Constitution's "Bill of Rights," Article 1, Section 1 has been read to directly bar only state action. See Western Pa. Socialist Workers 1982 Campaign v. Connecticut, 515 A.2d 1331, 1335 (Pa. 1986) (noting that the Declaration of Rights in the state constitution does not reach the acts of purely private actors); Borse v. Piece Goods Shop, Inc., 963 F.2d 611, 620 (3d Cir. 1992) (predicting that, if squarely faced with the issue, the Pennsylvania Supreme Court would hold that the right to privacy protected by the state constitution does not encompass invasions of privacy committed by private actors); but cf. Moses v. McWilliams, 549 A.2d 950, 954 (Pa. Super. Ct. 1988) (discussing constitutional right to privacy in the context of a physician's disclosures in a civil suit) superseded by statute as stated in White v. Behlke, 65 Pa. D.&C.4th 479, 486 (Comm. Pleas Ct. Lackawanna Co. 2004). Within this context, however, Section 1 has been invoked to protect public employees, (see Denoncourt v. Com., State Ethics Comm'n, 470 A.2d 945, 950 (Pa. 1983) (plurality opinion) (school directors)), and in regard to the receipt of post-employment government benefits (see McCusker v. Workmen's Comp. Appeal Bd., 639 A.2d 776, 778-82 (Pa. 1994) (workmen's compensation benefits)).

The Section 1 privacy right excludes certain "public records" from disclosure under the state "Right to Know Act," 65 P.S. §§ 66.1-66.9, repealed effective January 1, 2009 by 65 P.S. § 3102(2)(ii), but does not serve to prohibit disclosure of salary information for public employees. Pennsylvania State Univ. v. State Employees' Retirement Bd., 935 A.2d 530, 539, 36 Media L. Rep. 1017 (Pa. 2007). The Pennsylvania Supreme Court resolved a long-standing dispute when holding that the phone records for city-issued mobile phones used by city council members are not protected from disclosure under the Right to Know Act's personal security and privacy exceptions, but telephone numbers had to be redacted before disclosure of the records. Tribune-Review Publishing Co. v. Bodack, et al., 961 A.2d 110, 117-18, 37 Media L. Rep. 1195 (Pa. 2008). Although this dispute arose under Pennsylvania's predecessor Right to Know Act, which was replaced effective January 1, 2009, the Bodack opinion may have some precedential value as to the new Right to Know Act because the personal security and privacy exceptions in the predecessor law continue to have effect under the new law. Compare 65 P.S. §§ 66.1, repealed effective January 1, 2009 by 65 P.S. § 3102(2)(ii), with 65 P.S. § 67.708(b). Just as in phone records cases, the Commonwealth Court ruled that while the definition of a public record under the predecessor Right to Know Law does not expressly exclude home addresses, the independent constitutional right of privacy prohibits disclosure of home addresses when public records are disclosed. Pennsylvania State Educ. Ass'n v. Commonwealth, 981 A.2d 383, 386, 38 Media L. Rep. 1350 (Pa. Commw. Ct. Aug. 6, 2009).

A recent Commonwealth Court decision held that the Right to Know Act does not authorize the charging of labor costs in producing the documents requested, and agencies may only charge the proscribed $0.25 per page. State Employees' Retirement Sys. v. Office of Open Records, 10 A.3d 358, 363 (Pa. Commw. Ct. 2010); Indiana Univ. of Pa. v. Loomis, 23 A.3d 1126, 1128 (Pa. Commw. Ct. 2011) (holding an agency may generally withhold access to the documents requested until the requester pays the applicable fees).

Entities contracting with the government should also be aware that the Pennsylvania courts have interpreted §506(d)(1) of the Right to Know Act as "providing that a record in the possession of a party with whom an agency has contracted to perform a governmental function on behalf of the agency shall be deemed a 'public record,' and, as a consequences, shall be accessible under the [Right to Know Act]." Allegheny Cnty. Dep't. of Admin. Serv. v. A Second Chance, Inc., 13 A.3d 1025, 1039 (Pa. Commw. Ct. 2011).

Neither the federal constitution, nor the state constitution, provides a right to privacy in one's Social Security number. See McCauley v. Computer Aid Inc., 447 F. Supp. 2d 469, 472-73 (E.D. Pa. 2006) (granting employer's motion to dismiss employee's claim of violation of constitutional right to privacy based on employer's request for employee's Social Security number).

2. ***Statutory Protection.*** The Pennsylvania Wiretap Act, 18 PA. CONS. STAT. ANN. § 5701 (West 1983), et seq., prohibits the interception, use, and disclosure of any wire, electronic, or oral communication. Id. § 5703. See IV, infra.

3. ***Common Law Protection.*** Pennsylvania common law provides a cause of action for all four varieties of "invasion of privacy" claims:

(a) misappropriation of likeness;

(b) false light;

(c) publicity given to private facts; and

(d) intrusion upon seclusion.

See, e.g., Santillo v. Reedel, 634 A.2d 264, 266, 22 Media L. Rep. 1381 (Pa. Super. Ct. 1993) (citing Culver by Culver v. Port Allegheny Reporter Argus, 598 A.2d 54, 56, 19 Media L. Rep. 1638 (Pa. Super. Ct. 1991)); Harris by Harris v. Easton Publ'g Co., 483 A.2d 1377, 1383, 11 Media L. Rep. 1209 (Pa. Super. Ct. 1984). Pennsylvania appellate courts have adopted the interpretations of these torts provided by the Restatement (Second) of Torts, see Harris, 483 A.2d at 1383, following the lead shown by the Pennsylvania Supreme Court in Vogel v. G.T. Grant Co., 327 A.2d 133, 136 (Pa. 1974) (commenting with approval on the Restatement's tentative draft). The four types of claims are treated as analytically distinct torts and are typically pled separately. See Santillo, 634 A.2d at 266-67; Neish v. Beaver Newspapers, Inc., 581 A.2d 619, 624, 18 Media

L. Rep. 1251 (Pa. Super. Ct. 1990); and Larsen v. Phila. Newspapers, Inc., 543 A.2d 1181, 1188, 16 Media L. Rep. 1705 (Pa. Super. Ct. 1988).

Common law invasion of privacy claims are subject to a one-year statute of limitations. See 42 PA. CONS. STAT. ANN. § 5523(1) (West 1981) (actions for "libel, slander or invasion of privacy" must be commenced within one year).

In addition to the common law causes of action themselves, the common law "right to privacy" may, under certain circumstances, create a public policy exception to Pennsylvania's at-will employment doctrine. See Borse v. Piece Goods Shop, Inc., 963 F.2d 611, 626 (3d Cir. 1992) (terminating employee for refusing drug test that tortiously invades her right to privacy may amount to wrongful discharge); but cf. Hershberger v. Jersey Shore Steel Co., 575 A.2d 944, 949 (Pa. Super. Ct. 1990) (permitting the discharge of an employee who failed a drug test without requiring administration of a second, confirming test).

B. Causes of Action

1. ***Misappropriation/Right of Publicity.*** A cause of action based on the "right of publicity" (i.e., misappropriation of likeness) has been recognized in Pennsylvania. See, e.g., Marks v. Bell Telephone Co., 331 A.2d 424, 430 (Pa. 1975); Vogel v. G.T. Grant Co., 327 A.2d 133, 136 (Pa. 1974); Fanelle v. LoJack Corp., 79 F. Supp. 2d 558, 563-64 (E.D. Pa. 2000) (granting in pt. and denying in pt. defendant's motion to dismiss). Although not yet formally adopted by the Pennsylvania Supreme Court, the form of the appropriation of likeness analysis in the Restatement (Second) of Torts has, to this date, been utilized and followed by the courts in defining the contours of the misappropriation of likeness cause of action in Pennsylvania. See Marks, 331 A.2d at 430, Vogel, 327 A.2d at 136, Fanelle, 79 F. Supp. 2d at 563-64. The right of publicity involves the right to "control the commercial exploitation of [one's] inherent distinctive name and likeness;" the right thus protects against a defendant's "appropriating [plaintiff's] valuable name or likeness, without authorization, to defendant's commercial advantage." Phila. Orchestra Ass'n v. Walt Disney Co., 821 F. Supp. 341, 349 (E.D. Pa. 1993) (citing Zacchini v. Scripps-Howard Broad. Co., 433 U.S. 562, 2 Media L. Rep. 2089 (1977)). One need not be a celebrity to assert the right. Fanelle v. LoJack Corp., 79 F. Supp. 2d 558, 563-64 (E.D. Pa. 2000) (denying defendant's motion to dismiss remaining claims). For the appropriation of a name to be actionable, the name must have "secondary meaning." Id.

The right of publicity inures to individuals and groups, id., but does not inhere in a corporate trademark. See Eagle's Eye v. Ambler Fashion Shop Inc., 627 F. Supp. 856, 862 (E.D. Pa. 1985).

2. ***False Light.*** The cause of action for false light invasion of privacy requires:

(a) publicity, given to a

(b) false statement, that

(c) would be highly offensive to a reasonable person, where

(d) the defendant has knowledge of or acted in reckless disregard as to the falsity of the publicized matter and the false light in which the other would be placed.

See Wecht v. PG Publ'g Co., 725 A.2d 788, 790, 27 Media L. Rep. 2210 (Pa. Super. Ct. 1999) (citing the RESTATEMENT (SECOND) OF TORTS § 652E 1977); Neish v. Beaver Newspapers, Inc., 581 A.2d 619, 624, 18 Media L. Rep. 1251 (Pa. Super. Ct. 1990).

a. **Publicity**. "Publicity" exists where information is "made public, by communicating it to the public at large, or to so many persons that the matter must be regarded as substantially certain to become one of public knowledge." Harris by Harris v. Easton Publ'g Co., 483 A.2d 1377, 1384, 11 Media L. Rep. 1209 (Pa. Super. Ct. 1984). "Wide spread dissemination" of the statement is required. Marion v. City of Philadelphia, No. 00-3553, 2002 U.S. Dist. LEXIS 23716, at *17, 18 (E.D. Pa. Dec. 9, 2002). It will be necessary, of course, for the information at issue to be identified, or at least identifiable, with the plaintiff. Harris, 483 A.2d at 1385.

In finding a lack of publicity, courts have emphasized three factors: the number of people; the "contained" nature of the audience; and the audience's "need to know."

There is insufficient publicity where a statement is made only to a small number of people. See Kryeski v. Schott Glass Techs., Inc., 626 A.2d 595, 601-02 (Pa. Super. Ct. 1993) (one or two); Harris, 483 A.2d at 1384 (one); Vogel v. G.T. Grant Co., 327 A.2d 133, 137-38 (Pa. 1974), (two or four). There is also insufficient publicity where a statement is communicated only within a discrete group. See Curran v. Children's Serv. Ctr., 578 A.2d 8, 13 (Pa. Super. Ct. 1990) (managerial staff involved in employee's termination); Chicarella v. Passant, 494 A.2d 1109, 1114 (Pa. Super. Ct.

1985) (insurance company investigating a claim); Faison v. Parker, 823 F. Supp. 1198, 1206 (E.D. Pa. 1993) (files of court and prison system); Wells v. Thomas, 569 F. Supp. 426, 437 (E.D. Pa. 1983) (among employees at staff meetings); Rogers v. I.B.M. Corp., 500 F. Supp. 867, 870 (W.D. Pa. 1980) (employees in a managerial capacity); Marion, 2002 U.S. Dist. LEXIS 23716, at *17, 18 (employee's written psychiatric evaluation forwarded to employer's medical evaluation unit). There is also likely to be insufficient publicity where the statement is made only to people with an "interest" in the information. See, e.g., Rush v. Phila. Newspapers, Inc., 732 A.2d 648, 654 (Pa. Super. Ct., 1999) (finding newspaper articles in the School District of Philadelphia discussing award of school district vending contract to plaintiff school board member's husband not actionable, as public has "an interest in and a right to know about their public school system"); Strickland v. Univ. of Scranton, 700 A.2d 979, 987 (Pa. Super. Ct. 1997) (holding that disclosure of pending settlement to judgment creditor and ex-spouse of appellant not actionable, as both had an interest in settlement monies); Curran, 578 A.2d at 13 (only communication made was "that necessary to enable the defendant employer to make a decision regarding the termination of appellant's employment"); Avins v. Moll, 610 F. Supp. 308, 325 (E.D. Pa. 1984) (disclosure insufficient where communication from certifying entity only went to law school administration); Wells, 569 F. Supp. at 437 (disclosure of terms of employee's separation agreement to other employees at staff meetings in response to questions by individual employees does not constitute "publicity"); Rogers, 500 F. Supp. at 870 (disclosure not actionable, as there was a "need for such information" to properly address the concerns of subordinate employees).

By contrast, there will probably be sufficient publicity when the statement is heard by a moderately large group. See Harris by Harris v. Easton Publ'g Co., 483 A.2d 1377, 1385-86, 11 Media L. Rep. 1209 (Pa. Super. Ct. 1984) (under the circumstances, receipt of information by 17 people is publicity as a matter of law). There will be sufficient publicity where the statement is communicated to the public at large. See Harris, 483 A.2d at 1383-84. There also may be sufficient publicity where a statement somehow spreads throughout an entire industry, despite having been originally issued only to those with a "need to know." See Krochalis v. Ins. Co. of Am., 629 F. Supp. 1360, 1371 (E.D. Pa. 1985) (refusing to grant summary judgment based on lack of publicity, although communication was only made to employees at staff meeting, where there was evidence that substance of communication became public knowledge, and there was a genuine issue of material fact as to whether the individual making the communication knew it would become public knowledge). However, the mere possibility that a communication to a limited audience might spread is insufficient to prove publicity. See Kryeski, 626 A.2d at 602 (publication to a popular and talkative individual held insufficient, in itself, to prove publicity).

b. **Falsity**. In cases where the facts reported are "simply . . . not false," there is no claim for false-light invasion of privacy. See Santillo v. Reedel, 634 A.2d 264, 266, 22 Media L. Rep. 1381 (Pa. Super. Ct. 1993) (statements by police officers that complaint was filed against judicial candidate were true and, therefore, were not actionable); McCabe v. Village Voice, Inc., 550 F. Supp. 525, 529, 8 Media L. Rep. 2580 (E.D. Pa. 1982) (nude photo of woman taking a bath would not be actionable under a false-light theory unless, at minimum, woman does not actually take baths). Moreover, minor inaccuracies will not amount to falsity. See Seale v. Gramercy Pictures, 964 F. Supp. 918, 925 (E.D. Pa. 1997) (scene in movie showed plaintiff purchasing guns in a dark room from an Asian gun dealer; although plaintiff testified that he was given guns by an Asian man and purchased guns only at hardware stores during normal business hours, court held that such "minor factual inaccuracies" do not amount to falsity).

However, the selective publication of true facts can create an actionably false "impression." A false impression may thus be created by the omission of important background information. See Seale, 964 F. Supp. at 927-28 (omission of plaintiff's leadership at a particular rally depicted him in a false light); but see Santillo, 634 A.2d at 267 (when publishing complaint filed against police officer, failure to provide commendations of police officer does not create false impression). The mere failure to include unrelated exculpatory information in a true report does not amount to the creation of a tortiously false impression. Id. 267.

As is the case in defamation, expressions of opinion that suggest the existence of underlying false facts are probably actionable. See Santillo, 634 A.2d at 266.

c. **Highly Offensive**. Publicity given to false facts is actionable if "a reasonable person of ordinary sensibilities would find such publicity highly offensive"; i.e., if the invasion of privacy is "committed in such a manner as to outrage or cause mental suffering, shame, or humiliation to a person of ordinary sensibilities." Harris, 483 A.2d at 1384-85 (publication in newspaper of application information given by recipients of public assistance may be highly offensive); Dice v. Johnson, No. 1:CV-08-0956, 2010 WL 1791138, at *14 (M.D. Pa. May 3, 2010) (reasonable person would not be seriously offended by being misrepresented as a puppy supplier or seller).

Courts typically find charges of criminal or ethical impropriety and revelation of intimate details "highly offensive"; by contrast, temperate evaluations of performance on the job or in the public sphere, even if critical, are generally not found "highly offensive."

Publicity can be "highly offensive" when given to accusations of criminal behavior, see Santillo, 634 A.2d at 266, ("sexual abuse of a minor"); Jenkins v. Bolla, 600 A.2d 1293, 1296, 19 Media L. Rep. 2059 (Pa. Super. Ct. 1992) (sexual offenses); professionally unethical conduct, Larsen v. Phila. Newspapers, Inc., 543 A.2d 1181, 1189-90, 16 Media L. Rep. 1705 (Pa. Super. Ct. 1988) (judge's perjury and failure to recuse himself where warranted); and "immoral" activity, Weinstein v. Bullick, 827 F. Supp. 1193, 1202-03 (E.D. Pa. 1993) (fraudulent claim of rape); Martin v. Mun. Publ'ns, 510 F. Supp. 255, 259 (E.D. Pa. 1981) ("closet transvestite" who likes to "get stinking drunk"). In addition, publicity can be highly offensive when given to the intimate personal details of a private life. See Harris, 483 A.2d at 1387-88 (personal and confidential family information including daughter's pregnancy from letter of application for public assistance); Tucker v. Fischbein, 237 F.3d 275 (3d Cir. 2001) (summary judgment in favor of defendant attorney reversed because reasonable jury could conclude that defendant attorney had actual knowledge that plaintiffs were not seeking in underlying case to recover damage to sexual relationship when defendant attorney made allegedly defamatory comments) , cert. denied, 534 U.S. 815 (2001); McCabe, 550 F. Supp. at 529 (nude photo).

By contrast, the examination and evaluation of an employee or public figure's job performance, even if critical, will generally not be considered "highly offensive." See, e.g., Parano v. O'Connor, 641 A.2d 607, 609 (Pa. Super. Ct. 1994) (description as "adversarial," "uncooperative," and "less than helpful"); Wells v. Thomas, 569 F. Supp. 426, 437 (E.D. Pa. 1983) (details of a separation agreement). Opinions about public figures will not be actionable unless they are "far out of proportion with the facts." Neish v. Beaver, 581 A.2d 619, 623-24, 18 Media L. Rep. 1251 (Pa. Super. Ct. 1990) (criticism of town solicitor's absence from town meetings); see also Curran v. Children's Serv. Ctr., 578 A.2d 8, 13 (Pa. Super. Ct. 1990) ("An employee must expect and cannot complain when his or her performance on the job is examined and evaluated by a superior."); Giampolo v. Somerset Hosp. Ctr. for Health, Inc., No. 95-133J, 1998 U.S. Dist. LEXIS 14388, at *50 n.19 (W.D. Pa. May 29, 1998) (qualifying remarks as non-defamatory professional differences of opinion regarding patient treatment and hospital policy), aff'd, 189 F.3d 464 (3d Cir. 1999).

d. **Knowledge or reckless disregard of the truth**. Pennsylvania case law does not contain a substantial discussion of the "actual malice" requirement in the false-light context. There is no reason to believe, however, that the standard would differ from that applied in the defamation context.

e. **Public figures**. Even outside constitutional considerations, public figures will be less able to sustain a claim for false-light invasion of privacy, as they should expect to have their behavior "scrutinized and evaluated." See Parano, 641 A.2d at 610 (false-light claim dismissed in part because of plaintiff's status as administrator of hospital); Neish, 581 A.2d at 624-25 ("Appellant's stature in the community as a public figure resulted in a relinquishment of insulation from scrutiny of his public affairs."); Seale v. Gramercy Pictures, 964 F. Supp. 918, 924 (E.D. Pa. 1997) (noting that those who choose to be in the public eye, such as celebrities and politicians, clearly have less privacy, at least concerning their public affairs).

f. **Privileges**. Communications issued in the regular course of judicial proceedings have absolute immunity from charges of false-light invasion of privacy. See Buschel v. Metrocorp, 957 F. Supp. 595, 598-99 (E.D. Pa. 1996). There is no exemption from a public official's immunity for defamation if the statement made by the public official is untrue. See Smith v. Borough of Dunmore, 633 F.3d 176, 180 (3d Cir. 2011).

Under Pennsylvania law, "reports of potential threats to public safety are privileged and cannot be subject to any kind of invasion of privacy claim." Primus v. Burnosky, No. 02-713, 2003 U.S. Dist. LEXIS 6713, at *41-43 (E.D. Pa. Apr. 16, 2003) (holding that where nursing home reported to pertinent authorities that plaintiff had sexually abused his daughter, a nursing home patient, nursing home was not subject to a claim for false-light invasion of privacy because its actions were appropriate and required by law) (citing RESTATEMENT (SECOND) OF TORTS § 595 1977).

g. **Comparison with defamation**. A claim of false-light invasion of privacy is treated similarly, in many ways, to a claim of defamation. See Weinstein v. Bullick, 827 F. Supp. 1193, 1202, 22 Media L. Rep. 1481 (E.D. Pa. 1993).

However, an action for false-light invasion of privacy can sometimes be sustained where an action for defamation cannot, in that a statement can be "highly offensive" without rising to the level of defamatory meaning. See id.; Primus v. Burnosky, No. 02-713, 2003 U.S. Dist. LEXIS 6713, at *41-43 (E.D. Pa. Apr. 16, 2003) (noting that in a false-light claim, "the false statement need not be defamatory") (citing Weinstein, 827 F. Supp. at 1202).

Conversely, while a "publication" may be actionable defamation if made only to one person, an action for false-light invasion of privacy requires a statement to actually be made "public," or disseminated widely. Weinstein, 827 F. Supp. at 1202 (television broadcast); Harris by Harris v. Easton Publ'g Co. , 483 A.2d 1377, 1384-85, 11 Media L. Rep. 1209 (Pa. Super. Ct. 1984) (communication to 17 individuals); Marion v. City of Philadelphia, No. 00-3553, 2002 U.S. Dist. LEXIS 23716, at *17, 18 (E.D. Pa. Dec. 9, 2002).

3. ***Publication of Private Facts.*** A cause of action for the tort of "publicity given to private life" requires:

(a) publicity; given to

(b) private facts,

(c) which would be highly offensive to a reasonable person, and that

(d) are not of legitimate concern to the public.

See Jenkins v. Bolla, 600 A.2d 1293, 1296, 19 Media L. Rep. 2059 (Pa. Super. Ct. 1992) (citing Harris, 483 A.2d at 1384).

a. **Publicity**. Pennsylvania courts do not draw any substantive distinctions between the standard of "publicity" applied in false-light cases and that applied in claims of publication-of-private-facts. See Kelleher v. City of Reading, No. 01-3386, 2002 U.S. Dist. LEXIS 9408, at *28 (E.D. Pa. May 29, 2002) (recognizing in a publicity of private life claim that "[t]he publicity element requires that the matter be communicated 'to the public at large, or to so many persons that the matter must be regarded as substantially certain to become one of public knowledge'") (quoting Harris, 483 A.2d at 1384); Rapid Circuits, Inc. v. Sun Nat'l Bank, No. CV-10-6401, 2011 WL 1666919, *15 (E.D. Pa. May 3, 2011) (it is insufficient to send the communication to a "discrete list of customers").

b. **Private facts**. Private facts are those "that [have] not already been made public." See Harris, 483 A.2d at 1384. Going further, one court has suggested (in dicta) that where a company reveals a fact that would have been revealed anyway, the "inevitable" publication is not of a private fact, and thus not actionable. See Wells v. Thomas, 569 F. Supp. 426, 437-38 (E.D. Pa. 1983). A determination of whether facts are private hinges on whether the publication of the information would "offend standards of common decency." Kelleher v. City of Reading, No. 01-3386, 2002 U.S. Dist. LEXIS 9408, at *29 (E.D. Pa. May 29, 2002) (holding that publication of suspension of city council clerk did not offend the standards of decency) (citing RESTATEMENT (SECOND) OF TORTS § 652D cmt. h).

A communicated fact will not be "private" where the recipient had "prior knowledge of that fact"; so there can be no recovery of damages for the publication of facts that "were already known to the recipients of the publication prior to publication." See Harris, 483 A.2d at 1386; Morgan by and through Chambon v. Celender, 780 F. Supp. 307, 310, 19 Media L. Rep. 1862 (W.D. Pa. 1992).

In addition, facts in the public record are not private. See Jenkins v. Bolla, 600 A.2d 1293, 1296, 19 Media L. Rep. 2059 (Pa. Super Ct. 1992); Morgan, 780 F. Supp. at 380. However, the passage of time may make private a fact that was once public, if over time that fact loses its "nexus" to the public interest. See Jenkins, 600 A.2d at 1297 (past sex offenses of operator of publicly funded boarding house for mentally ill held to be of public interest).

c. **Highly Offensive**. Pennsylvania case law does not draw a substantive distinction between the standard of "highly offensive" applied in false-light claims and that applied in publicity-to-private-life claims. See e.g., Boring v. Google, 362 F. App'x 273, 280 (3d Cir. 2010) (photograph taken by internet search engine of plaintiffs' house, garage and pool would not be highly offensive to person of ordinary sensibilities).

d. **Public Concern**. The public's legitimate concerns encompass "the community-at-large's pecuniary well-being [and] its legal rights and liabilities." See Jenkins, 600 A.2d at 1297. The scope of the public's concern has been described as "[including] matters of the kind customarily regarded as 'news.'" See Culver v. Port Allegany Reporter Argus, 598 A.2d 54, 56, 19 Media L. Rep. 1638 (Pa. Super. Ct.. 1991) (fact of parents' request that school board pay for privately retained psychologist held to be of public concern).

In part, then, the public has a legitimate concern in the character or history of those in whom it puts its trust. See Jenkins, 600 A.2d at 1297 (operator of publicly funded boarding house for mentally ill). Accordingly, the public will have a legitimate concern in the character of those who occupy (or seek to occupy) public positions (see Santillo, 634 A.2d at 266 (individual running for office of District Justice)); the conduct of public figures (see Morgan, 780 F. Supp. at 310 (former police chief); Coughlin v. Westinghouse Broad. and Cable, 603 F. Supp. 377, 390, 11 Media L. Rep. 1681 (E.D. Pa. 1985) (police officer); and the history of those whose activities will have a significant effect on the public (see Jenkins, 600 A.2d at 1297; Harris, 483 A.2d at 1387).

The public also has a legitimate interest in knowing how its money is spent (see Jenkins, 600 A.2d at 1297; Culver, 598 A.2d at 56) and in the provision of useful information to the public, (see Harris, 483 A.2d at 1387). Along similar lines, the public has an interest in private investigations regarding the possibility of fraud. See Forster v. Manchester, 189 A.2d 147, 150 (Pa. 1963).

The public does not have a legitimate interest in the intimate personal details of a private figure's life where publication would serve no interest more important than the satisfaction of "mere curiosity." See Harris, 483 A.2d at 1387 (no legitimate public concern in personal and confidential family information given in application for public assistance); McCabe v. Village Voice, Inc., 550 F. Supp. 525, 529 (E.D. Pa. 1982) ("I am not persuaded that a woman taking a bath is newsworthy. Many people engage in that practice daily and the media does not consider it worth reporting publicly."). However, personal details that relate to an issue of legitimate public concern may themselves be of public interest. See Jenkins, 600 A.2d at 1297 (past sex offenses of operator of publicly funded boarding house for mentally ill held to be of public interest); Morgan, 780 F. Supp. at 310 (name and age of victim of sexual abuse).

A claim of publication of private facts will not be made actionable simply by the manner in which the facts were obtained, even if "illegally, unethically, and deceptively." See Morgan, 780 F. Supp. at 310 (newspaper published statements that reporter assured were "off the record").

4. ***Intrusion upon seclusion.*** A cause of action for an intrusion upon seclusion claim requires:

(a) intentional and

(b) substantial

(c) intrusion, into another's seclusion, solitude, or private affairs, that is done in a

(d) highly offensive manner.

See Doe v. Kohn, Nast & Graf, P.C., 862 F. Supp. 1310, 1326 (E.D. Pa. 1994).

a. **Intentional**. For an intrusion to be intentional, it is necessary that the defendant believe, or be substantially certain, that he or she "lacks the necessary legal or personal permission to commit the intrusive act." See O'Donnell v. U.S., 891 F.2d 1079, 1083 (3d Cir. 1989); Kohn, Nast & Graf, P.C., 862 F. Supp. at 1326. Where the intrusion is not intentional, there is no liability for the tort. See Harris by Harris v. Easton Publ'g Co., 483 A.2d 1377, 1384 (Pa. Super. Ct. 1984) (facts voluntarily exposed to one defendant; facts received unsolicited by another defendant); O'Donnell, 891 F.2d at 1083 (reasonable belief that release of hospital records had been authorized by the plaintiff); Rudas v. Nationwide Mut. Ins. Co., No. 96-5987, 1997 U.S. Dist. LEXIS 169, at *15 (E.D. Pa. Dec. 13, 1997) (voluntary exposure); Rogers v. I.B.M. Corp., 500 F. Supp. 867, 870 (W.D. Pa. 1980) (voluntary exposure). See also Primus v. Burnosky, No. 02-713, 2003 U.S. Dist. LEXIS 6713, at *41-43 (E.D. Pa. Apr. 16, 2003) (holding that plaintiff failed to state a claim for intrusion as a matter of law because defendant nursing home had a duty to protect patient under their care from potential abuse by plaintiff).

Even where an otherwise authorized intrusion intentionally or recklessly treads on a protected sphere of privacy, it may be actionable. See Borse v. Piece Goods Shop, Inc., 963 F.2d 611, 621 (3d Cir. 1992) (manner in which observation of urine collection, or search of employee's personal property, is done may be actionable); Wolfson v. Lewis, 924 F. Supp. 1413, 1435, 24 Media L. Rep. 1609 (E.D. Pa. 1996) (persistent videotaping done not for the purposes of newsgathering, but to coerce a reluctant third-party into agreeing to an interview, is actionable); Doe v. Kohn, Nast & Graf, P.C., 866 F. Supp. 190, 195-96 (E.D. Pa. 1994) (opening employee's mail, marked personal but received at the business, may be actionable).

b. **Substantial**. The requirement that an actionable intrusion be "substantial" probably parallels the requirement that it be "highly offensive." Compare DeAngelo v. Fortney, 515 A.2d 594, 595 (Pa. Super. Ct. 1986) ("Business solicitations are generally inoffensive inquiries accepted as part of daily living," and thus typically do not constitute a substantial intrusion) with Kohn, Nast & Graf, P.C., 862 F. Supp. at 1326 (search of a plaintiff's office, resulting in the discovery of a personal letter, may be substantial intrusion).

c. **Intrusion into seclusion**. An actionable intrusion may take one of three forms:

(1) physical intrusion into a place in which the plaintiff has secluded him or herself;

(2) use of the defendant's senses to oversee or overhear the plaintiff's private affairs; or

(3) some other form of investigation or examination into the plaintiff's private concerns.

See Kelleher v. City of Reading, No. 01-3386, 2002 U.S. Dist. LEXIS 9408, *23 (E.D. Pa. May 29, 2002); Harris by Harris v. Easton Publ'g Co., 483 A.2d 1377, 1383 (Pa. Super. Ct. 1984).

Actionable *intrusions* typically require the defendant's movement into, or observation of, the plaintiff's private life; requests or demands that the plaintiff do even very private things are typically not actionable.

Absent any action, a mere request to obtain certain information will not constitute an intrusion. See Spencer v. General Tel. Co. of Pa., 551 F. Supp. 896, 899 (M.D. Pa. 1982) (request that employee allow security investigations is not an intrusion).

It is also typical for a claim to involve a defendant who "does not believe that he has the legal authority to do the intrusive act." See Rapid Circuits, Inc. v. Sun Nat'l Bank, No. CV-10-6401, 2011 WL 1666919, *14-15 (E.D. Pa. May 3, 2011) (finding that because the defendants "*believed* their actions were legally permissible," plaintiff did not have a claim for intrusion into seclusion).

Similarly, the demand that a party take certain action of their own accord, even in the private sphere, will not necessarily constitute an intrusion. See Frankel v. Warwick Hotel, 881 F. Supp. 183, 188 (E.D. Pa. 1995) (a father dismissing his employee son for refusing to divorce his wife is not an intrusion).

Actionable intrusions into *seclusion* typically do not occur in the public and semi-public spheres. For example, a plaintiff whose employer took pictures of him praying in a mosque could not prevail in his intrusion into seclusion claim because he was praying in a public place in plain view; therefore, he could not establish that he had an expectation of privacy. Tagouma v. Investigative Consultant Services, Inc., No. 987 MDA 2009, 2010 WL 3123173, at *5 (Pa. Super. Ct. Aug. 10, 2010). However, even in the public sphere, particularly egregious actions may intrude upon a person's seclusion.

Typically, photographs taken in "a place open to the public" will not constitute an intrusion into seclusion. See Fogel v. Forbes, Inc., 500 F. Supp. 1081, 1087, 6 Media L. Rep. 1941 (E.D. Pa. 1980) (photo taken in airport lounge not an intrusion as a matter of law). However, an action may lie where the plaintiff is "hounded" by investigators, even if only in a public or semi-public space. See Wolfson v. Lewis, 924 F. Supp. 1413, 1420, 24 Media L. Rep. 1609 (E.D. Pa. 1996) (constant harassment by television crew may constitute intrusion upon seclusion).

The scope of a plaintiff's personal affairs does not extend to material contained within company records. See Rogers v. I.B.M. Corp., 500 F. Supp. 867, 870 (W.D. Pa. 1980). However, opening a plaintiff's personal mail, received at a business, may be actionable. See Vernars v. Young, 539 F.2d 966, 969 (3d Cir. 1976); Kohn, Nast & Graf, P.C., 862 F. Supp. at 1326.

d. **Highly offensive**. The "highly offensive" requirement apparently parallels that of the false-light and publicity-given-to-private-life torts. See Chicarella v. Passant, 494 A.2d 1109, 1114 (Pa. Super. Ct. 1985) ("highly offensive" causes "mental suffering, shame or humiliation to a person of ordinary sensibilities") (citation omitted). "The requirement that the intrusion be highly offensive is a difficult standard to satisfy. . . ." Tucker v. Merck & Co., No. 02-2421, 2003 U.S. Dist. LEXIS 7672, at *38-39 (E.D. Pa. May 2, 2003), aff'd, 102 Fed. Appx. 247, 2004 U.S. App. LEXIS 13347 (3d Cir. 2004) (holding that threshold showing of "highly offensive" conduct was not met where employer questioned employee's husband about employee's violation of company's conflict of interest policy even though questions may have made the husband "uncomfortable" or were "impolite").

e. **Lack of publication requirement**. There is no publication requirement in actions for intrusion upon seclusion. See Vernars, 539 F.2d at 969.

C. Other Privacy-Related Actions

1. ***Intentional Infliction of Emotional Distress.*** Pennsylvania recognizes a cause of action for intentional infliction of emotional distress ("IIED"). Strickland v. Univ. of Scranton, 700 A.2d 979, 987 (Pa. Commw. Ct. 1997). Nevertheless, "[l]iability has been found only where the conduct has been *so outrageous in character, and so extreme in degree, as to go beyond all possible bounds of decency, and to be regarded as atrocious, and utterly intolerable in a civilized society.*" Id. (additional quotations omitted) (italics in original). To recover, a plaintiff must establish the existence of four criteria:

(1) defendant's conduct must be intentional or reckless;

(2) it must be extreme and outrageous;

(3) it must cause emotional distress; and

(4) the emotional distress must be severe.

Frankel v. Warwick Hotel, 881 F. Supp. 183, 187 (E.D. Pa. 1995) (citing RESTATEMENT (SECOND) OF TORTS § 46(1) (1992)). Moreover, a plaintiff must substantiate the emotional harm with proof of physical bodily injury. Hunger v. Grand Cent. Sanitation, 670 A.2d 173, 177 (Pa. Super. Ct. 1996).

Pennsylvania courts have been cautious in awarding recovery for this cause of action in the employment context. See Snyder v. Specialty Glass Products, Inc., 658 A.2d 366, 375 (Pa. 1995) (denying IIED claim when employee suffered verbal abuse and demotion for coming in late after providing emergency medical treatment to an accident victim); Strickland v. Univ. of Scranton, 700 A.2d 979, 987 (Pa. Super. Ct. 1997) (holding that University's termination of administrator after civil and criminal action commenced against him is not outrageous conduct); Hunger, 670 A.2d at 178 (refusing recovery because plaintiff could not prove resultant bodily injury); Kryeski v. Schott Glass Techs., Inc., 626 A.2d 595, 600 (Pa. Super. Ct. 1993) (rejecting claim that superior's sexual advances are extreme and outrageous conduct); see also Andrews v. City of Philadelphia, 895 F.2d 1469, 1487 (3d Cir. 1990) ("[I]t is extremely rare to find conduct in the employment context that will give rise to the level of outrageousness necessary to provide a basis for recovery for the tort of intentional infliction of emotional distress.") (quotations omitted); Warmkessel v. East Penn Mfg. Co., Inc., No. Civ.A.03-CV -02941, 2005 WL 1869458, *5 (E.D. Pa. July 28, 2005) (dismissing by summary judgment an IIED claim intended to hold the employer vicariously liable when the plaintiff's supervisor "would touch, grab or pinch plaintiff's groin, nipples, buttocks and genitals; look under bathroom stalls when plaintiff was using the bathroom; and often creep up behind plaintiff and thrust his hips against plaintiff's buttocks, simulating a sexual act"); United States ex rel. Magin v. Wilderman, No. Civ.A.96-CV-4346, 2005 WL 469590, *5 (E.D. Pa. Feb. 28, 2005) ("Mere allegations of criminal conduct are insufficient to establish that a person acted in an extreme or outrageous manner."); Imboden v. Chowns Communications, 182 F. Supp. 2d 453, 457 (E.D. Pa. 2002) (stating that in order to make out a cause of action for IIED that will rise to the requisite level of outrageousness, a plaintiff must "allege retaliation based on a rejection of sexual advances or propositions") (citations omitted); Steffenino v. G.G.D. Jr., Inc., No. 94-5333, 1995 U.S. Dist. LEXIS 5083, at *5 (E.D. Pa. Apr. 17, 1995) (dismissing IIED claim); Frankel, 881 F. Supp. at 188 (holding that employer's discharge of employee (his son) for refusing to divorce his wife was not extreme and outrageous conduct); but see Denton v. Silver Stream Nursing and Rehab. Ctr., 739 A.2d 571, 577 (Pa. Super. Ct. 1999) (holding that allegation of employer-condoned death threats in response to employee's "whistleblower" activities, if proven, would qualify as extreme and outrageous conduct and therefore reversing dismissal of IIED claim); Chuy v. Phila. Eagles Football Club, 595 F.2d 1265, 1275, 4 Media L. Rep. 2537 (3d Cir. 1979) (holding that team doctor's knowingly false statements that player had fatal disease are sufficient to support jury verdict in favor of player for IIED); Fitzpatrick v. QVC, Inc., No. 98-CV-3815, 1999 U.S. Dist. LEXIS 3155, at *10, 11 (E.D. Pa. Mar. 15, 1999) (allowing intentional infliction of emotional distress claim in sexual harassment suit where employee experienced retaliation as a result of rejecting employer's sexual advances). But Hoy v. Angelone, 720 A.2d 745, 754 (Pa. 1998) (holding that retaliation should be one of a number of factors used in weighing intentional infliction of emotional distress claims in sexual harassment cases because "[b]y regarding retaliation as a weighty factor, but not a mandated factor, we allow for the rare case in which a victim of sexual harassment is subjected to blatantly abhorrent conduct, but in which no retaliatory action is taken"). Employers may be vicariously liable for punitive damages in addition to compensatory damages for the extreme and outrageous acts of their employees. See Chuy, 595 F.2d at 1279.

2. ***Negligent Infliction of Emotional Distress***

a. **Common Law**. Pennsylvania recognizes a cause of action for negligent infliction of emotional distress. See, e.g., Sinn v. Burd, 404 A.2d 672, 686 (Pa. 1979). To state a claim for negligent infliction of emotional distress, the Superior Court of Pennsylvania has explained that a plaintiff must establish:

(1) that he or she experienced a contemporaneous sensory observance of physical injuries being inflicted on another family member; or

(2) that he or she nearly experiences a physical impact by virtue of being in the zone of danger created by the defendant's tortious conduct.

See Hunger v. Grand Cent. Sanitation, 670 A.2d 173, 178 (Pa. Super. Ct. 1996) (citations omitted).

b. **Application to the Employment Context**. The Superior Court of Pennsylvania has arguably recognized an additional basis on which a claim for negligent infliction of emotional distress may lie. This expansion of the law of negligent infliction of emotional distress in the Commonwealth of Pennsylvania finds its genesis in Judge Beck's concurring opinion in Hunger, where he observed that recovery may be based on a claim of negligent infliction of emotional distress where the defendant breaches a preexisting duty to the plaintiff which causes the plaintiff emotional distress. Id. at 183. Thereafter, in Denton v. Silver Stream Nursing and Rehab. Ctr., 739 A.2d 571 (Pa. Super. Ct. 1999), the Superior Court applied the expanded approach advocated by Judge Beck to a negligent infliction of emotional distress claim flowing from the harassment of the plaintiff by a co-worker. 739 A.2d at 578. However, in affirming the grant of a demurrer to the negligent infliction of emotional distress claim, the Denton Court found no duty on the part of the employer to protect its employees from emotional distress. Id.; see also McKeeman v. Corestates Bank, N.A., 751 A.2d 655, 661 (Pa. Super. Ct. 2000) (apparently recognizing the validity of Judge Beck's expanded "duty-based" approach to the law of negligent infliction of emotional distress). Similarly, in Pirolli v. World Flavors, Inc., No. 98-3596, 1999 U.S. Dist. LEXIS 18092 (E.D. Pa. Nov.

24, 1999), the District Court for the Eastern District of Pennsylvania discussed the expanded approach to negligent infliction of emotional distress claims advocated in Denton, then applied the expanded approach in ruling on the plaintiff's claim that the harassment that he suffered from his co-workers caused him emotional distress. Id. at *33-35. Upon review, the Pirolli Court concluded that the plaintiff's failure to even allege a duty on the part of his employer to protect him from the harassment was fatal to his claim of negligent infliction of emotional distress. Id. at *35. However, the Third Circuit reversed and remanded Pirolli, without opinion, 262 F.3d 159 (3d Cir. 2001).

3. ***Interference With Prospective Economic Advantage***

a. **Common Law.** Pennsylvania recognizes a cause of action for intentional interference with contractual relations. Ruffing v. 84 Lumber Co., 600 A.2d 545, 549 (Pa. Super. Ct. 1991) (citation omitted). To state a claim for intentional interference with contractual relations, a plaintiff must establish four elements:

(1) a prospective contractual relation;

(2) the purpose or intent to harm the plaintiff by preventing the relation from occurring;

(3) the absence of privilege or justification on the part of the defendant; and

(4) actual damage resulting from the defendant's conduct.

Thompson Coal Co. v. Pike Coal Co., 412 A.2d 466, 471 (Pa. 1979). "Specific intent to harm" is not required under this test. Yaindl v. Ingersoll-Rand Co., 422 A.2d 611, 622 n.11 (Pa. Super. Ct. 1980) (abrogated on other grounds). In addition, absence of privilege or justification is "closely related to the element of intent [and] . . . is not susceptible of precise definition." Silver v. Mendel, 894 F.2d 598, 603 n.7 (3d Cir. 1990). "[A]n actor is privileged to interfere with another's performance of a contract when: (1) the actor has a legally protected interest; (2) he acts or threatens to act to protect the interest; and (3) the threat is to protect by proper means." Ruffing, 600 A.2d at 548 (citations omitted).

In analyzing claims for intentional interference with prospective contractual relations, Pennsylvania courts consider the totality of the factual circumstances, focusing on the propriety of the defendant's conduct. Id. at 549 (citing Adler, Barish, Daniels, Levin and Creskoff v. Epstein, 393 A.2d 1175, 1183-84 (Pa. 1987)). Courts have applied the following factors to determine more specifically the propriety of a defendant's conduct:

(1) the nature of the actor's conduct;

(2) the actor's motive;

(3) the interests of the other with which the actor's conduct interferes;

(4) the interests sought to be advanced by the actor;

(5) the social interests in protecting the freedom of action of the actor and the contractual interests of the other;

(6) the proximity or remoteness of the actor's conduct to the interference; and

(7) the parties' relationship.

Id. at 468-69; 600 A.2d at 549 (citing RESTATEMENT (SECOND) OF TORTS § 767 (1979)).

b. **Application to the Employment Context.** It is well settled under Pennsylvania law that a corporation cannot tortiously interfere with a contract to which it is a party. Nix v. Temple Univ., 596 A.2d 1132, 1137 (Pa. Super. Ct. 1991). Thus, to the extent that an employee or former employee claims injury for interference with their employment relationship with the defendant/employer, such claims must fail as a matter of Pennsylvania law. An employee states a claim for intentional interference with contractual relations against his former employer when the employer, absent possession of a valid non-compete clause, threatens to sue a prospective employer if the employee is hired. See Ruffing, 600 A.2d at 553 (allowing jury award in favor of plaintiff whose former employer threatened competitor with injunction if it hired plaintiff); Kachmar v. Sungard Data Sys., Inc., 109 F.3d 173, 186 (3d Cir. 1997) (denying employer's motion for summary judgment when employer threatened to sue prospective employer if it hired plaintiff). More often, however, courts have rejected employee claims, ruling that plaintiffs failed to meet the elements of the cause of action. See Pyle v. Meritor Sav. Bank, Nos. 92-7361, 92-7362, 1996 U.S. Dist. LEXIS 3042, at *15-16 (E.D. Pa. Mar. 11, 1996); Steffenino v. G.G.D., Jr., Inc., No. 94-5333, 1995 U.S. Dist. LEXIS 5083, at *8-9 (E.D. Pa. Apr. 17, 1995); Milione v. Hahnemann Univ., No. 89-6761, 1992 U.S. Dist. LEXIS 3339, at *11 (E.D. Pa. Mar. 17, 1992); McMorris v. Williamsport Hosp., 597 F. Supp. 899, 917 (M.D. Pa. 1984).

4. ***Prima Facie Tort.*** Pennsylvania has not recognized an independent cause of action for *prima facie* tort. See West Coast Franchising Co. v. WCV Corp., 30 F. Supp. 2d 498, 500 (E.D. Pa. 1998); Charles Shaid of Pa., Inc. v. George Hyman Constr. Co., 947 F. Supp. 844, 855-56 (E.D. Pa. 1996) (predicting that Pennsylvania Supreme Court would not recognize *prima facie* tort as a cause of action under Pennsylvania law); L & M Beverage Co. v. Guinness Imp. Co., No. 94-CV-4492, 1995 WL 771113, at *5 (E.D. Pa. Dec. 29, 1995).

II. EMPLOYER TESTING OF EMPLOYEES

A. Psychological or Personality Testing

There is no Pennsylvania statute or regulation prohibiting psychological or personality testing by employers. Medical psychological information, however, is entitled to some protection against disclosure under the common law of privacy. See Fraternal Order of Police, Lodge 5 v. City of Philadelphia (F.O.P., Lodge 5), 812 F.2d 105, 113 (3d Cir. 1987) (mental health information sought by questions asked of police applicants are entitled to privacy protection); see also Paul P. v. Verniero, 170 F.3d 396, 406 (3d Cir. 1999) (remanding for determination of whether adequate procedural safeguards exist to ensure that notification provisions of Megan's Law do not violate plaintiffs' constitutional right to privacy). This principle has been applied in the public employment context by balancing the individual's privacy expectations against the government's interests. F.O.P., Lodge 5, 812 F.2d at 112-14; Murray v. Pittsburgh Bd. of Educ., 759 F. Supp. 1178, 1181-83 (W.D. Pa. 1991) (privacy interest in psychiatric information overridden by state's legitimate interest in obtaining psychiatric information of teachers). Application questions asked of potential police officers regarding their mental health were found to be constitutional because of the need for mentally capable officers and the corresponding reduced expectation that information regarding mental health would not be requested. F.O.P., Lodge 5, 812 F.2d at 114. Although not deciding the constitutionality issue, a district court denied a teacher's motion for preliminary injunction to enjoin a psychological examination resulting from the teacher's prolonged absences and an incident with another employee. Murray, 759 F. Supp. at 1183.

B. Drug Testing

1. ***Common Law and Statutes.*** There are no Pennsylvania statutes specifically regulating drug testing. Under Pennsylvania common law, if a private sector employee is discharged as a result of a drug test, and the manner of testing is a substantial and highly offensive invasion of the employee's privacy, the employee may have a common law claim for wrongful discharge in violation of public policy. Borse v. Piece Goods Shop, Inc., 963 F.2d 611, 621-22 (3d Cir. 1992). The manner of the test may be an invasion of privacy if the test was directly observed or was done in such a way as to reveal personal matters unrelated to the workplace. 963 F.2d at 621. However, in determining whether there is just cause for an employee to disobey an employer's request for drug testing, the employer's interests must be balanced against the burden imposed on the employee's privacy rights. See, e.g., Rowles v. Automated Prod. Sys., Inc., No. 1:CV-98-0707, 1999 U.S. Dist. LEXIS 21605, at *40 (M.D. Pa. March 26, 1999) (citations omitted) (noting that an individual's privacy interests trumps his employer's efficiency concerns where the invasion of privacy occasioned by the test is highly offensive to the reasonable person), mot. for recons. denied in part, 92 F. Supp. 2d 424 (M.D. Pa. 2000). As the Pennsylvania Supreme Court has stated:

> [I]f an employer's request [for drug testing] can be deemed circumstantially reasonable, after considering the burden to the employee, then the employee has an implied obligation to cooperate. Although there might be practical reasons that can justify an employee's refusal to cooperate, such noncompliance cannot be predicated upon asserted common law and property rights. As to employer requests that are reasonable in the above sense, the employee has waived those rights as a basis for noncompliance; he waived them when he voluntarily assumed the legal relationship with his employer.

Rebel v. Unemployment Compensation Board of Review, 723 A.2d 156 (Pa. 1998) (quoting Simpson v. Unemployment Comp. Bd. of Review, 450 A.2d 305, 311 (Pa. Commw. Ct. 1982)). The Rebel court held that the employee's refusal to submit to an employer's drug testing program constituted willful misconduct, thereby disqualifying the employee for unemployment compensation benefits. Simpson, 450 A.2d at 311.

2. ***Private Employers.*** Discharge of a private sector at-will employee may constitute a claim for wrongful discharge in violation of public policy if the drug testing related to that discharge was directly observed or was done in such a way as to reveal personal matters unrelated to the workplace. Borse, 963 F.2d at 621-22. However, there is no clear mandate of public policy prohibiting a private employer from discharging an employee on the basis of a positive drug test without confirming the results of the initial drug test by another scientifically distinct test. Hershberger v. Jersey Shore Steel Co., 575 A.2d 944, 948-49 (Pa. Super. Ct. 1990). Nor does a third party who is hired by a private employer to conduct a pre-employment drug screening of a prospective employee owe him or her a duty of care to properly conduct the screening. Ney v. Axelrod, 723 A.2d 719, 722-23 (Pa. Super. Ct. 1999) But cf. Sharpe v. St. Luke's Hosp., 821 A.2d 1215 (Pa. 2003) (a third party hired by an employer to perform a drug test on a *current* employee does owe a duty of reasonable care to that

employee). See also Hammond v. City of Philadelphia, 164 F. Supp. 2d 481, 483 (E.D. Pa. 2001) (private laboratory owed no duty of care to police officer terminated by police department for positive drug test).

3. ***Public Employers.*** A government agency may conduct warrantless and suspicionless drug testing in a random testing program of those employees in the following areas: law enforcement, the heavily regulated horse-racing industry, and safety-sensitive positions, such as operators or maintenance personnel of railway, airline or shipping equipment. See Transp. Workers Local 234 v. SEPTA, 884 F.2d 709, 713 (3d Cir. 1988) (affirming constitutionality of random testing of transportation workers in safety-sensitive positions); Policemen's Benevolent Ass'n, Local 318 v. Washington Township, 850 F.2d 133, 135 (3d Cir. 1988) (random testing of police officers held to be constitutional); Shoemaker v. Handel, 795 F.2d 1136, 1142 (3d Cir. 1986) (upholding law requiring jockeys to submit to breathalyzer and random urinalysis testing); see also Wilcher v. City of Wilmington, 139 F.3d 366, 380 (3d Cir. 1998) (method of observing urine collection does not violate firefighters' Fourth Amendment rights); **Mollo v. Passaic Valley Sewerage Com'rs, 406 Fed. Appx. 664, 669-70 (3d Cir. 2011) (subjecting a landscaper at publicly-owned wastewater treatment plant to suspicionless, random drug testing pursuant to policy applicable to all facility employees engaged in 'safety sensitive' work did not violate landscaper's rights to be free from unreasonable searches and seizures).**

On the other hand, compulsory, suspicionless testing of an employee in a non-safety-sensitive position, such as the maintenance custodian of a transportation system, is not permitted. Bolden v. SEPTA, 953 F.2d 807, 823-24 (3d Cir. 1991). Therefore, the voluntary consent of the employee is required; however, consent is not voluntary where the employer is faced with job loss, even if the employee voices no objection. Id. at 824.

C. Medical Testing

Medical information is entitled to privacy protection against disclosure. Fraternal Order of Police, Lodge 5 (F.O.P., Lodge 5) v. City of Philadelphia, 812 F.2d 105, 113 (3d Cir. 1987).

This principle has been applied in the public employer context by balancing the individual's privacy expectations against the Government's interests. Id. at 112; see Murray v. Pittsburgh Bd. of Educ., 759 F. Supp. 1178, 1181 (W.D. Pa. 1991). Application questions about potential police officers' physical health were found constitutional because of the need for physically capable officers and the corresponding reduced expectation of privacy. F.O.P., Lodge 5, 812 F.2d at 114.

In Grimminger v. Maitra, M.D., 887 A.2d 276 (Pa. Super. Ct. 2005), the Pennsylvania Superior Court reviewed a case in which the U.S. Postal Service directly questioned an employee's physician regarding a lifting restriction the physician placed on the employee. Specifically, postal inspectors came to the physician's office, showed a surveillance film of the employee, and obtained an opinion from the physician that it appeared the employee had "recovered." Id. at 278, 280-81. The employee pursued a civil action against the physician for breach of the physician-patient privilege. The Superior Court held that the manner in which the employer obtained the medical information did not breach the physician-patient privilege. Id. at 280-81.

D. Polygraph Tests

A Pennsylvania statute makes it a second-degree misdemeanor for an employer to require a polygraph test as a condition for employment. 18 PA. CONS. STAT. ANN. § 7321 (West 1985). This statute does not apply to employees "in the field of public law enforcement or who dispense or have access to dangerous narcotics or drugs." Id.

This statute supports a claim under Pennsylvania law for wrongful discharge in violation of public policy by a discharged at-will employee alleging that he was discharged for refusing to take a polygraph test. Kroen v. Bedway Sec. Agency, Inc., 633 A.2d 628, 633 (Pa. Super. Ct. 1993) (reversing entry of summary judgment on wrongful discharge claim); Perks v. Firestone Tire & Rubber Co., 611 F.2d 1363, 1366 (3d Cir. 1979) (same). On the other hand, because of the law-enforcement exception to the statute, a polygraph test administered to applicants for jobs in the city police and corrections department does not violate applicants' rights to due process and equal protection of the laws. Anderson v. City of Philadelphia, 845 F.2d 1216, 1222-24 (3d Cir. 1988). At least one court has denied a cause of action for wrongful discharge based on violation of this statute when an employee suspected of theft voluntarily agreed to a polygraph examination. King v. United Parcel Service, Inc., 15 Pa. D.&C.4th 538, 541-42 (Comm. Pleas Ct. Delaware Co. 1992).

E. Fingerprinting

Under some circumstances, Pennsylvania law requires employers to obtain fingerprints from applicants, for submission to the Federal Bureau of Investigation for the purpose of obtaining federal criminal history record information. For example:

Applicants applying for employment (including independent contractors) with any public or private school, when such applicant has not been a resident of Pennsylvania for at least two years preceding the date of application. 24 P.S. § 1-111. This does not apply for employees or independent contractors who have no direct contact with children. Id.

· Applicants applying for employment with a licensed security guard agency or private detective agency. 22 P.S. § 23.

· Applicants applying for the training program required for employment as a weapons-carrying officer in a county probation or parole department. 61 P.S. § 332.7.

III. SEARCHES

Following the U.S. Supreme Court's decision in O'Connor v. Ortega, 480 U.S. 709, 715 (1987), public employees may invoke the Fourth Amendment to the United States Constitution to bring a cause of action for an illegal employer search. Pennsylvania's State Constitution similarly provides in part that "[t]he people shall be secure in their persons, houses, papers, and possessions from unreasonable searches and seizures . . . ." PA. CONST. Art. I, § 8. The Pennsylvania Supreme Court has emphasized that "the notion of privacy implicit in Article I, Section 8 is particularly strong . . . ." Commonwealth v. Cass, 709 A.2d 350, 359 (Pa. 1998). Nonetheless, this provision, like its federal counterpart, "applies only to the actions of governmental authorities, and is inapplicable to the conduct of private parties." Simpson v. Unemployment Comp. Bd. of Review, 450 A.2d 350, 309 & n.2 (Pa. Commw. Ct. 1982) (citations omitted).

There are no Pennsylvania statutes specifically regulating employer searches of an employee's person, work area, or property, regardless of whether the employer is public or private. Claims alleging illegal private employer searches "arise, for the most part, from common law property rights." Id. at 310. While Pennsylvania recognizes "intrusion upon seclusion" as a common law tort protecting an individual's private affairs and property, see § I.B.4., supra, the Pennsylvania Supreme Court has been silent on the issue of whether employer searches can be intrusions upon seclusion. Several decisions applying Pennsylvania law discussed below suggest that the issue should be analyzed in a manner consistent with that cause of action.

A. Employee's Person

1. ***Private Employers***. There are no reported cases in Pennsylvania applying privacy principles to private employer searches of an employee's person.

2. ***Public Employers***. Because of the extreme intrusiveness of a full body cavity search, a public employer must justify the search by showing "a clear indication that the suspect is carrying contraband in a body cavity." McKenna v. City of Philadelphia, 771 F. Supp. 124, 126 (E.D. Pa. 1991) (holding that police department may have violated police officer's Fourth Amendment rights by forcing him to submit to body cavity search upon his return to active duty). However, correctional officers have a diminished expectation of privacy and may be subject to random pat downs upon entering a prison facility. Allegheny County Prison Employees Indep. Union v. County of Allegheny, 315 F. Supp. 2d 728, 738-40 (W.D. Pa. 2004).

B. Employee's Work Area

1. ***Private Employers***. It may be unreasonable for a supervisor to search an employee's office, read a personal letter, and disseminate the information. Doe v. Kohn Nast & Graf, P.C., 862 F. Supp. 1310, 1326 (E.D. Pa. 1994) ("A search of an employee's workplace which is done in such a way as to reveal matters unrelated to the workplace, may constitute a tortious invasion of the employee's privacy" if it is "substantial, and highly offensive to the reasonable person.").

2. ***Public Employers***. A Fourth Amendment claim cannot stand when a supervisor, acting within the scope of her responsibilities, retrieves work-related materials from an employee's desk during his leave of absence, despite the fact that the supervisor may be exposed to some of the employee's personal items. Williams v. Philadelphia Hous. Auth., 826 F. Supp. 952, 954 (E.D. Pa. 1993) (searching computer disk containing both work and personal files).

C. Employee's Property

1. ***Private Employers***. An employer's search of an employee's lunch bucket was "circumstantially reasonable" because the employer's on-site security concerns outweighed its employee's right to privacy attendant to the lunch bucket. Simpson v. Unemployment Comp. Bd. of Review, 450 A.2d 305, 311 (Pa. Commw. Ct. 1982). On the other hand, the Third Circuit predicted that a personal property search as part of a drug prevention program could violate Pennsylvania public policy if it "tortiously invaded the employee's privacy." Borse v. Piece Goods Shop, Inc., 963 F.2d 611, 626 (3d Cir. 1992). The Third Circuit predicted, however, that the Pennsylvania Supreme Court would not "require private employers to

limit . . . personal property searches to employees suspected of drug use or to those performing safety-sensitive jobs." Id. at 625 (italics in original). In an earlier case, the Third Circuit also predicted that an invasion of privacy claim would lie when a corporate board member opened and read a corporate officer's personal mail without the officer's permission. Vernars v. Young, 539 F.2d 966, 968-69 (3d Cir. 1976) (employees have a reasonable expectation that their personal mail will not be opened and read by persons lacking their consent).

2. ***Public Employers***. A city police department's search of employee lockers did not result in a Fourth Amendment violation because the department had in place a directive both authorizing the searches and requiring officers to provide their superiors with duplicate keys to their lockers. Brambrinck v. City of Philadelphia, No. 94-1673, 1994 U.S. Dist. LEXIS 16538, at *46 (E.D. Pa. Nov. 14, 1994). The directive eliminated any reasonable expectation of privacy officers had in their assigned lockers. Id. at *28. Nonetheless, the directive's language did not eliminate the officers' reasonable expectation of privacy in the *contents* of their lockers. Id. Rather, a search of the contents must be preceded by suspicion that is reasonable at its inception and limited in its scope. Id. at *37-46.

IV. MONITORING OF EMPLOYEES

A. Telephones and Electronic Communications

1. ***Wiretapping***. The Pennsylvania Wiretap Act, 18 PA. CONS. STAT. ANN. § 5701 (West 1983), et seq., prohibits the interception, use and disclosure of any wire, electronic or oral communication. Id. § 5703. Telephone conversations fall under the definition of "oral communication." Id. § 5702. Text messages, on the other hand, fall under the definition of "electronic communication." Id.; Commonwealth v. Cruttenden, 976 A.2d 1176, 1181 (Pa. Super. Ct. 2009) ("text messages constitute electronic communications as statutorily defined"). The Pennsylvania Superior Court has distinguished "oral communications" (i.e., telephone calls) from "electronic communications" (i.e., text messages) in holding that the statute prohibits interception, disclosure, or use of text messages regardless of whether an expectation of privacy exists. Cruttenden, 976 A.2d at 1182. In other words, interception of a text message violates the Pennsylvania statute regardless of whether the sender or receiver had a reasonable expectation of privacy. A text message is "intercepted" under the Act if the recipient poses as someone else when using their cellular phone to send or receive a text message. Cruttenden, 976 A.2d at 1181. But see Commonwealth v. Frattaroli, No. CP-14-CR-1758-2009, 2010 WL 925170 (Pa. Com. Pl. Jan. 15, 2010) (a police officer does not violate the Wiretap Act if a confidential informant receives text messages and shows them to the police officer). A recording of a person's voice over a speakerphone, where the speaker knows they have been placed on speakerphone but does not know (and thus does not consent) to recording, is prohibited by the Wiretap Act and is inadmissible in court. Commonwealth v. Deck, 954 A.2d 603, 605, 609 (Pa. Super. Ct. 2008). A communication is not an "oral communication" as defined in the Act unless the victim has a reasonable expectation of non-interception. Commonwealth v. McIvor, 670 A.2d 697, 703 (Pa. Super. Ct. 1996). Courts consider whether an individual had an expectation of privacy in the communication in analyzing whether an expectation of non-interception existed. Id. at 703. For example, when an employee hides a tape recording device under a coworker's desk for the purpose of recording personal conversations unbeknownst to the coworker, the analysis of whether the Pennsylvania Wiretap Act was violated will depend on whether the coworker had a reasonable expectation of privacy in workplace conversations recorded by the device. See Commonwealth v. Ward, 3 Pa. D.&C.5th 268, 277 (Comm. Pleas Ct. Lawrence Co. December 12, 2007) (finding a violation under these facts).

Any unlawful interception can potentially result in both criminal (third degree felony) and civil (actual and punitive damages) liability. 18 PA. CONS. STAT. ANN. §§ 5703, 5725. Furthermore, any intentional, unauthorized access to a stored wire communication (voice mail) is an offense subject to a fine under the Act. Id. § 5741(a).

"Interception" is defined so as to exclude interceptions made by a telephone extension furnished for use in the ordinary course of business. Id. § 5702. Thus, the acquisition of communications by use of a telephone extension or other equipment in the ordinary course of business is likely not a violation. Id. Compare with Commonwealth v. Rosa, 21 A.3d 1264, 1270 (Pa. Super. Ct. 2011) (concluding that even though the callers spoke directly with each other, the communications were still intercepted because the detective spoke to the defendants under false pretenses and posed as the owner of the phone).

Under the Pennsylvania Wiretap Act, the consent defense requires the consent of all parties to a communication. Id. § 5704. Because of this, customers should be advised by a recording that calls may be monitored.

2. ***Electronic (e-mail) Communications***. The Pennsylvania Wiretap Act specifically provides that the interception, use and disclosure of electronic communications, including e-mail, are prohibited. Id. §§ 5702, 5703. Any unlawful interception can potentially result in both criminal (third degree felony) and civil (actual and punitive damages) liability. Id. §§ 5703, 5725. Furthermore, any intentional, unauthorized access to a stored electronic communication is an offense subject to a fine under the Act. Id. § 5741(a).

The consent defense under the Act requires the consent of all parties to the communication. Id. § 5704. Thus, interception of e-mail sent outside the employer is prohibited.

Any right of privacy in intercompany e-mail was held to be limited in Smyth v. Pillsbury Co., 914 F. Supp. 97, 101 (E.D. Pa. 1996). In Smyth, an employee was terminated for making unprofessional comments over company e-mail. Id. at 98-99. Although the employee had been assured that e-mail messages were confidential and would not be intercepted by management, there was no "reasonable expectation of privacy in e-mail communications voluntarily made by an employee to his supervisor over the company e-mail system" used by all employees. Id. at 101. Furthermore, the court held that even if there was a reasonable expectation of privacy, the employer's interception of e-mail messages did not constitute a substantial and highly offensive invasion. Id. at 101. Because there was no invasion of privacy asserted, the employee did not state a claim for wrongful discharge in violation of public policy. Id. But see Kelleher v. City of Reading, No. 01-3386, 2002 U.S. Dist. LEXIS 9408, at *24-25 (E.D. Pa. May 29, 2002) (recognizing that the holding in Smyth does "not necessarily foreclose the possibility that an employee might have a reasonable expectation of privacy in certain e-mail communications, depending upon the circumstances of the communication and the configuration of the email systems"). The court in Kelleher, however, did not elaborate on these reasons, and held only that where an employer's guidelines regarding the expectation of privacy in e -mail are uncontroverted and explicit, there is no reasonable expectation of privacy. Id. at *25.

3. ***Other Electronic Monitoring.*** The Pennsylvania Wiretap Act is the only statute in Pennsylvania governing electronic monitoring of employees.

B. Mail

The Third Circuit has predicted that a cause of action for invasion of privacy exists under Pennsylvania law for the unauthorized opening and reading by a corporate board member of a corporate officer's mail which was delivered to the corporation's office but addressed to the corporate officer and marked personal. Vernars v. Young, 539 F.2d 966, 968-69 (3d Cir. 1976).

Where an employee asserted an invasion of privacy claim against his employer (a law firm) for allegedly opening multiple items of mail, some marked personal and confidential, the district court denied the employer's motion for summary judgment, holding that "[a]n employer is not authorized to open mail addressed to a person at his workplace that appears to be personal." Doe v. Kohn, Nast & Graf, P.C., 866 F. Supp. 190, 195-96 (E.D. Pa. 1994). The court stated that even if the employer were authorized to open mail related to firm business, the opening of the mail might constitute intrusion upon the employee's seclusion if that method failed to give due regard to the employee's privacy or revealed personal matters unrelated to the workplace. Id. at 196.

C. Surveillance/Photographing

The Pennsylvania Wiretap Act does not apply to recording without sound, and thus video surveillance is not regulated by the Act. 18 Pa. C.S. § 5702. Video evidence obtained from a camera directed at the work area of an employee who was suspected of wrongdoing was not suppressed under the Fourth Amendment when the employee knew that there was video surveillance in the area. United States v. O'Reilly, No. 91-678, 1992 U.S. Dist. LEXIS 8187, at *2 (E.D. Pa. Mar. 13, 1992). Because of his knowledge of the general video surveillance, the employee did not have a legitimate expectation of privacy with respect to the camera. Id.

D. Consumer Reports

Under the federal Fair Credit Reporting Act ("FCRA"), an employer may obtain consumer reports on employees "for the purpose of evaluating a consumer for employment, promotion, reassignment or retention as an employee." 15 U.S.C. §1681a(h).

In Kelchner v. Sycamore Manor Health Ctr., 305 F. Supp. 2d 429, 436 (M.D. Pa. 2004), the court held that an employee has no wrongful termination cause of action when her employer conditions continued employment on the employee signing a release giving the employer access to the employee's consumer reports. The court noted, however, that the reports are only "to be used for legitimate, narrowly defined, employment purposes," and "once an employer decides to use these reports and takes adverse action against their employees, they must follow procedures to ensure that they are being used fairly and accurately. Id.

In ATM Corp. of America v. Unemployment Compensation Board of Review, 892 A.2d 859, 860 (Pa. Commw. Ct. 2006), the Pennsylvania Commonwealth Court reviewed a case in which an employer sought to avoid unemployment compensation benefits on the basis that the employee was terminated for refusing to execute an authorization permitting the employer to obtain consumer reports and investigative consumer reports as background checks. The employer established that there was a known workplace rule prohibiting insubordination, but the employee was not given advance notice that refusing to cooperate with a background check would result in termination. Id. at 861-62. The Commonwealth Court held that requiring a background check was not unreasonably intrusive into the employee's privacy, and that the employee's refusal to authorize the background check without explanation constituted willful misconduct, rendering the employee ineligible for unemployment compensation benefits. Id. at 867-68.

V. ACTIVITIES OUTSIDE THE WORKPLACE

A. Statutory Law

The Pennsylvania legislature has not specifically addressed the subject of a private or public employee's personal conduct outside the workplace as it affects the employer/employee relationship.

It is worth noting, however, that municipalities have enacted ordinances regulating off-duty conduct of police officers. See, e.g., Fabio v. Civil Serv. Comm'n, 414 A.2d 82, 84 & n.1 (Pa. 1980) (citing Art. I, § 1.75 of the Philadelphia Police Department Duty Manual (providing for dismissal for "conduct unbecoming a police officer -- repeated violations of departmental rules and regulations, or any other course of conduct indicating that a member has little or no regard for his responsibility as a member of the Police Department")); Feliciano v. Borough of Norristown, 758 A.2d 295, 295 (Pa. Commw. Ct. 2000) (citing Article IX, Section 4-64(f)(2) and (4) of The Borough Administrative Code and Section 1190(2) and (4) of The Borough Code, Act of Feb. 1, 1966, P.L. 1656 (1965), as amended, 53 P.S. § 46190(2) and (4)); Faust v. Police Civil Serv. Comm'n, 347 A.2d 765, 767 & n.2 (Pa. Commw. Ct. 1975) (citing Section 1191 of The Borough Code, Act of Feb. 1, 1966, P.L. 1656 (1965), as amended, 53 P.S. § 46191). Both the Supreme and Commonwealth Courts ruled that disciplining officers under these statutes for their adulterous behavior did not violate the officer's privacy rights because of the higher standard to which police officers are subject, the fact that the behavior affected the workplace, and the state's interest in maintaining an effective police force. Fabio, 414 A.2d at 89-90; Faust, 347 A.2d at 768-69.

B. Employees' Personal Relationships

1. ***Romantic Relationships Between Employees***. A public employee discharged for engaging in an intimate relationship with another employee may have an invasion of privacy claim under the United States Constitution if the relationship is of the character to which constitutional intimate association protection attaches. See Angelilli v. Borough of Conshohocken, No. 96-3391, 1996 U.S. Dist. LEXIS 16994, at *11-12 (E.D. Pa. Nov. 15, 1996) (remanding for further factual findings).

2. ***Sexual Activity Outside the Workplace***. Police officers discharged for failing to answer questions pertaining to their personal intimate behavior pursuant to an official investigation may have an invasion of privacy claim under the United States Constitution. See Shuman v. City of Philadelphia, 470 F. Supp. 449, 459-60 (E.D. Pa. 1979) ("In the absence of a showing that a policeman's private, off-duty personal activities have an impact upon his on-the-job performance, . . . inquiry into those activities violates the constitutionally protected right of privacy."). The broad questioning in Shuman which had little or no attachment to the workplace, can be contrasted with the ordinances upheld by the courts in Fabio and Faust, which were focused on adultery affecting the workplace (see Statutory Law, above). See Shuman, 470 F. Supp. at 461; Fabio, 414 A.2d at 90; Faust, 347 A.2d at 769.

The Commonwealth Court determined that Pennsylvania's Unemployment Compensation Board of Review could not deny benefits to a former vice president of a private company who was discharged for engaging in an intimate relationship with the owner's wife, Jones v. Unemployment Comp. Bd. of Review, 562 A.2d 935, 936-37 (Pa. Commw. Ct. 1989), but could deny benefits to a former hospital employee dismissed for failing to terminate an intimate relationship with a patient, Turner v. Unemployment Comp. Bd. of Review, 381 A.2d 223, 224 (Pa. Commw. Ct. 1978). In both cases, the court's decision hinged on a determination of whether the behavior in question amounted to work-related willful misconduct. Jones, 562 A.2d at 937; Turner, 381 A.2d at 224.

3. ***Sexual Orientation***. An employer's discriminatory treatment on the basis of sexual orientation is not actionable under Pennsylvania's constitution, any state statute, or public policy. DeMuth v. Miller, 652 A.2d 891, 900 (Pa. Super. Ct. 1995). In contrast, at least three Pennsylvania cities have enacted ordinances prohibiting employment discrimination on the basis of sexual orientation. See City of Pittsburgh Code of Ordinances §§ 651.04(n) and 659.02 (defining "sexual orientation" as "[m]ale or female homosexuality, heterosexuality and bisexuality or perceived homosexuality, heterosexuality and bisexuality"); City of Harrisburg Code of Ordinances §§ 4-101.2 and 4-101.6(dd) (defining "sexual preference/orientation" as "male or female homosexuality, heterosexuality and bisexuality, by preference, practices or as perceived by others"); City of Philadelphia Code of Ordinances §§ 9-1102(y) and 9-1103 (defining "sexual orientation" as "[m]ale or female homosexuality, heterosexuality and bisexuality, by preference, practice or as perceived by others"). See also Wortman v. Philadelphia Comm'n on Human Relations, 591 A.2d 331, 332-33 (Pa. Commw. Ct. 1991)

(considering appeal from adjudication applying ordinance); See Pa. Transp. Auth. v. City of Phila., 20 A.3d 558, 568 (Pa. Commw. Ct. 2011) (jurisdiction of the Philadelphia Commission on Human Relations (PCHR) is more expansive than the Pennsylvania Human Relations Commission in that it covers discrimination based on sexual orientation).

Additionally, Pennsylvania does not consider employer discrimination on the basis of transsexualism to be actionable. See Holt v. Northwest Pa. Training P'ship Consortium, Inc., 694 A.2d 1134, 1139 (Pa. Commw. Ct.1997) (holding that transsexualism does not qualify as disability under Pennsylvania Human Relations Act (PHRA)); Dobre v. Nat'l R.R. Passenger Corp., 850 F. Supp. 284, 287-90 (E.D. Pa. 1993) (holding that transsexualism does not qualify as sex discrimination, handicap, or mental or physical disability under PHRA); see also Ashlie v. Chester-Upland Sch. Dist., No. 78-4037, 1979 U.S. Dist. LEXIS 12516, at *15-16 (E.D. Pa. May 9, 1979) (holding that employer discrimination based on transsexualism does not support invasion of privacy claim).

4. ***Marital Status***. "Neither Title VII nor the PHRA prohibits discrimination based solely on marital status." Myers v. Chestnut Hill Coll., No. 95-6244, 1996 U.S. Dist. LEXIS 1655, at *21 (E.D. Pa. Feb. 13, 1996). Marital status discrimination under these statutes is only actionable if a plaintiff can show that an employer is applying a different standard to a sub-class, e.g., treating unmarried men differently than unmarried women. Id. at 21-22; see also Kovich v. Mansfield State Coll., 478 A.2d 950, 953 (Pa. Commw. Ct. 1984) (holding that plaintiff failed to state marital discrimination claim under PHRA because she failed to establish that men married to faculty members were treated differently than women married to faculty members).

In addition, discharging an employee for refusing to divorce his spouse is not actionable under Pennsylvania common law. Frankel v. Warwick Hotel, 881 F. Supp. 183, 188 (E.D. Pa. 1995).

Again, local ordinances enacted by Pennsylvania cities may provide protection that the state statutes do not -- in this case, against employment discrimination based on marital status. See, e.g., City of Philadelphia Code of Ordinances §§ 9-1102(r) and 9-1103 (prohibiting employment discrimination based on "marital status" and defining that term to mean "[t] he status of being single, married, separated, divorced, widowed or a life partner"); City of Harrisburg Code of Ordinances §§ 4-101.2 and 4-101.6(u) (prohibiting employment discrimination based on "marital status" and defining that term to include "(1) the presence or absence of a religiously or civilly recognized marital union; (2) single, divorced or separated status; or (3) any association of two or more adults unless otherwise illegal under established and reasonable occupancy requirements").

5. ***General Familial Privacy***. The public policy exception to Pennsylvania's "at-will" doctrine favoring privacy rights does not prohibit an employer from discharging an employee for being a victim of domestic violence and rape. See Green v. Bryant, 887 F. Supp. 798, 801 (E.D. Pa. 1995). Nor does it prohibit an employer from discharging employees for violating company policy by failing to report that subordinates had disclosed to them, in confidence, they had been subjected to improper sexual behavior by fellow male employees. See McDaniel v. Am. Red Cross, 58 F. Supp. 2d 628, 631-35 (W.D. Pa. 1999).

C. Smoking

No Pennsylvania statutes or reported cases specifically address the right of employers to prohibit employees from smoking outside the workplace. By statute, however, employers are required to implement a policy to regulate smoking in the workplace. 35 PA. CONS. STAT. ANN. § 1230.1(a) (West 1993).

D. Blogging/Social Media

As of the time of this update, there are no reported Pennsylvania statutory or regulatory provisions regarding blogging. regarding termination of employment for blogging content or activities. **In *Trail v. Lesko*, No. GD-10-017249 (C.P. Alleg. Co. July 3, 2012 Wettick, J), Judge Stanton Wettick provided a detailed analysis of the discoverability of private Facebook content, ultimately denying both parties' respective motions to discover the information. The denial of the Facebook information was based upon Pennsylvania Rule of Civil Procedure 4011(b), which prohibits discovery that would cause "unreasonable annoyance, embarrassment [or] oppression . . . to any person or party." Judge Wettick stated that granting a party access to an individual's Facebook account is intrusion because the party given access will likely come across information that is irrelevant to the litigation and which may be embarrassing. However, on a scale of one to ten with one being the lowest, Judge Wettick stated the intrusion caused by most Facebook discovery is likely at the level of a two. To determine if the intrusion is unreasonable, Judge Wettick stated the court should balance the level of intrusion with the "potential value of the discovery" to the requesting party. In the case at issue, the potential value was insufficient to justify the intrusion.**

In Zimmerman v. Weis Markets, No. CV-09-1535, 2011 WL 2065410, *5 (Comm. Pleas Ct. Northumberland Co. May 19, 2011), the Northumberland County Pennsylvania trial court ordered a former forklift operator to make available to his former employer his social media information from his MySpace and Facebook accounts. Despite claiming serious and permanent health problems and diminution in enjoying life's pleasures, his employer found public postings about Zimmerman enjoying motorcycle riding and bike stunts. Id. at *1. The Zimmerman court concluded the employer's right to discover relevant information about Zimmerman on the non-public portions of his Facebook and MySpace pages outweighed any of Zimmerman's alleged privacy interests. Id. at *2. It stated: "Zimmerman placed his physical condition in issue, and Weis Markets is entitled to discovery thereon." Id. at *4.

The 2010 McMillen decision, the seminal Pennsylvania case, addressed three key principals. McMillen v. Hummingbird Speedway, Inc., No. 113-2010 CD, 2010 WL 4403285, *1 (Comm. Pleas Ct. Jefferson Co. Sept. 9, 2010) (requiring plaintiff to provide login and password information because plaintiff's public profile indicated relevant information may be in the private portion). First, under Pennsylvania law, there is no privilege for information posted in the non-public sections of social websites. Id. at *2. Second, the postings on social media sites, such as Facebook and MySpace, cannot be considered confidential because: (a) their purpose is to disseminate information in an open, public way that is easily shared with and by others and (b) their use terms make clear that information shared on the sites is not private and may be disclosed. Id. at *3. Third, liberal discovery is generally allowable, and the pursuit of the truth related to the alleged claims is paramount to discovery. Based on its analysis of those factors, the McMillen court ordered McMillen to provide the name of his social network computer site(s), his user name(s), his login name(s), and his password(s). Id. at *5-6.

See also Largent v. Reed, No. 09-1823, 2011 WL 5632688 (Comm. Pleas Ct. Franklin Co. Nov. 8, 2011) (holding plaintiff must produce login and password information because information on plaintiff's public profile were relevant and discoverable); Arcq v. Fields, No. 08-2430 (Comm. Pleas Ct. Franklin Co. Dec. 2011) (denying defendant's discovery request for plaintiff's login and password information because defendant failed to provide a factual showing that the public portions of plaintiff's profile contained relevant information); Martin v. Allstate Fire & Casualty Ins. Co., No. 1104022438 (Comm. Pleas Ct. Phila. Co. Dec. 13, 2011) (denying defendant's request for plaintiff's Facebook account information because defendant failed to show the profile may contain relevant information); Kennedy v. Norfolk Southern Corp., No. 100201473 (Comm. Pleas Ct. Phila. Co. Jan. 4, 2011) (denying defendant's motion for plaintiff's account information); Kalinowski v. Kirschenheiter, No. 10-6779 (Comm. Pleas Ct. Luzerne Co. 2011) (denying defendant's motion for plaintiff's account information); Piccolo v. Paterson, No. 09-04979 (Comm. Pleas Ct. Bucks Co. Mar . 2011) (denying defendant's request for access to plaintiff's photographs on Facebook because plaintiff already provided photographs and defendant failed to show need for the information); **Gallagher v. Urbanovich, No. 10-33418 (Comm. Pleas Ct. Montgomery Co. Feb. 27, 2012) (ordering defendant to provide plaintiff with his Facebook account information for a period of seven days).**

VI. RECORDS

A. Personnel Records

Public employers have a duty to maintain "complete and accurate records of [an employee's] employment history." Quinones v. United States, 492 F.2d 1269, 1280 (3d Cir. 1974). Public employees can enforce this duty on a general negligence theory. Id. Additionally, all employers must allow employees to inspect their personnel files at reasonable times upon request. 23 PA. CONS. STAT. ANN. § 1322 (West 1993). However, the Third Circuit has held that public employees do not have a reasonable expectation of privacy in their personnel files such that an employer does not violate the Fourth Amendment by searching and using them. Roberts v. Mentzer, No. 09-3251, 2010 WL 2113405, at *4 (3d Cir. April 20, 2010).

The Pennsylvania Legislature has been silent with respect to the confidentiality of personnel files. Notwithstanding, the public has the right to access attendance records and payroll registers of public employees. See Kanzelmeyer v. Eger, 329 A.2d 307, 310 (Pa. Commw. Ct. 1974); Commonwealth v. Brister, 16 A.3d 530, 536 (Pa. Super. Ct. 2011) (holding that a police officer did not have statutory right to privacy in his personnel files).

On December 20, 2005, Pennsylvania enacted the Breach of Personal Information Notification Act. See 73 P.S. §§ 2301-2308. The Act, which became effective June 20, 2006, requires notification to Pennsylvania residents whose personal information was or may have been disclosed due to a security system breach. Id. § 2303. "Personal information" means an individual's first name or first initial, with last name, linked to their Social Security number, driver's license number, financial account numbers, or credit card numbers (the latter two in combination with a password or security code). The Act applies broadly to business entities, including Pennsylvania governmental agencies and financial institutions. Id. § 2302. The Act requires notification, "without unreasonable delay," when any breach of security occurs and personal information about a Pennsylvania resident was, or is reasonably believed to have been, accessed and acquired by another person. Id. § 2303. If the notice is provided to more than 1,000 persons at one time, then notice must also be provided, without unreasonable delay, to all consumer reporting agencies. Id. § 2305. There are certain limited exemptions and exceptions to the notice requirement. Id. §§ 2304, 2307. In addition to the notice requirements, a violation of the Act is deemed to be an unfair or deceptive trade practice under the Pennsylvania Unfair Trade Practices and Consumer Protection Law. Id. § 2308.

B. Medical Records

To determine whether employee medical records are discoverable, a court must balance the employee's privacy interests with the public's need to know the information. See United States v. Westinghouse Elec. Corp., 638 F.2d 570, 580 (3d Cir. 1980); P.F. v. Mendres, 21 F. Supp. 2d 476, 482 (D.N.J. 1998) ("The Third Circuit has held that an individual has a constitutionally recognized right to privacy in medical records, records of prescription medication, and other personal medical information."). Courts applying Pennsylvania law have applied this balancing test to determine the propriety of an employer's disclosure and use of employee medical records. See Doe v. Southeastern Pa. Transp. Auth., 72 F.3d 1133, 1143 (3d Cir. 1995) ("[A] self-insured employer's need for access to employee prescription records under its health insurance plan, when the information disclosed is only for the purpose of monitoring the plans by those with a need to know, outweighs an employee's interest in keeping his prescription drug purchases confidential."); F.O.P., Lodge 5 v. City of Phila., 812 F.2d 105, 117 (3d Cir. 1987) ("Although most of the [medical, financial, and behavioral] information requested [in police application questionnaire] is entitled to privacy protection, the questions are specific, relevant, and permissible because the City's need for the information overrides the applicants' rights not to disclose it."); Schofield v. Trustees of the Univ. of Pa., 161 F.R.D. 302, 304, No. 94-CV-5887, 1995 U.S. Dist. LEXIS 6423, at *4 (E.D. Pa. May 8, 1995) ("Since the situation warrants issuance of some sort of confidentiality order, we strongly encourage the parties to negotiate an agreement that properly balances [plaintiff's] concerns for privacy with defendant's need for flexibility in defending its case.").

The confidentiality provision of Pennsylvania's Mental Health Procedures Act, 50 P.S. § 7111, which provides a "statutory privilege of confidentiality on the patient's records," may protect information regarding past sexual conduct between an institution's employees and the institution's employees or patients from discovery in civil litigation. T.M. v. Elwyn, Inc., 950 A.2d 1050, 1061 (Pa. Super. Ct. 2008). In some circumstances, disclosure of mental health treatment records is prohibited by the Psychologist-Patient Privilege Act, 42 Pa. C.S.A. § 5944. "[T]he right of privacy of mental health treatment and the records created pursuant to that treatment is of utmost importance, as evidenced by the statutory privileges accorded to such records." Commonwealth v. Makara, 980 A. 2d 138, 141 (Pa. Super. Ct. 2009).

C. Criminal Records

In Pennsylvania, arrest records are not afforded any privacy protection. See Fraternal Order of Police, Lodge 5 v. City of Philadelphia, 812 F.2d 105, 117 (3d Cir. 1987).

Under the Pennsylvania Criminal History Record Information Act, 18 P.S. §§ 9101-9183, court dockets, police blotters, and press releases (and information contained therein) are considered public records. When deciding whether to hire or reject an applicant for employment, the statute limits an employer use of criminal history record information to felony and misdemeanor convictions and only to the extent that such convictions "relate to the applicant's suitability for employment in the position for which he has applied." 18 P.S. § 9125. The employer must notify the applicant in writing if the employer's decision to reject an applicant is based in whole or in part on criminal history record information. Id. The statute provides a private right of action against agencies, employers, and individuals, and provides for recovery of actual damages, costs of litigation/attorney's fees, and punitive damages. Schmidt v. Deutsch Larrimore Farnish & Anderson, LLP, 876 A.2d 1044, 1047 (Pa. Super. Ct. 2005); 18 P.S. § 9183.

The Pennsylvania Superior Court has held that even assuming the Criminal Record History Act is a clear statement of Pennsylvania public policy regarding hiring decisions based in whole or in part on convictions, the statute does not support a wrongful termination claim based on a decision to terminate a current employee (not an applicant) for conduct believed to be criminal, even if it turns out that the conduct at issue does not result in a criminal conviction. See Cisco v. United Parcel Services, Inc., 476 A.2d 1340, 1343-44 (Pa. Super. Ct. 1984) (implicitly overruled as authority for an unrelated principle by Krajsa v. Keypunch, Inc., 622 A.2d 355, 358-59 (Pa. Super. Ct. 1993).

D. Subpoenas / Search Warrants

The Third Circuit mandates consideration of seven factors when determining whether a subpoena calling for production of employment records should be quashed due to privacy concerns. United States v. Westinghouse Electric Corp., 638 F.2d 570, 578 (3d Cir. 1980). Those are: the type of record requested; the information contained; the potential harm caused by nonconsensual disclosure; the injury (if any) to the relationship that generated the record; the adequacy of any safeguards that could be utilized to prevent unauthorized disclosure; the degree of need for access to the record; and whether there is an express public policy or interest favoring access. Id.

Utilizing the above seven factors, the Third Circuit has held that "a self-insured employer's need for access to employee prescription records under its health insurance plan, when the information disclosed is only for the purpose of monitoring the plans by those with a need to know, outweighs an employee's interest in keeping his prescription drug purchases confidential." Doe v. SEPTA, 72 F.3d 1133, 1143 (3d Cir. 1995).

Certain information regarding employees of Pennsylvania agencies, including salary and years of service information, are available to Pennsylvania citizens without the use of a subpoena, through use of the state "Right to Know Act." The Right to Know Act, 65 P.S. §§ 66.1-66.9, repealed effective January 1, 2009 by 65 P.S. § 3102(2)(ii), gives Pennsylvania citizens access to "public records," a defined term with few exceptions, and the requester need not provide any reason for the request. Privacy interests in employment information, including salary data, will not prevent disclosure unless such interests are so strong that disclosure "would operate to the prejudice or impairment of a person's reputation or personal security." Pennsylvania State Univ. v. State Employees' Retirement Bd., 935 A.2d 530, 533, 36 Media L. Rep. 1017 (Pa. 2007). Social Security numbers would ordinarily not be obtainable under the statute. Id.; Pa. State Troopers Ass'n v. Scolforo, 18 A.3d 435, 440 (Pa. Commw. Ct. 2011) (finding troopers did not establish that they would be put at substantial risk if forced to disclose supplementary employment forms and supported documents if "appropriately redacted"). Effective January 1, 2009, a new Pennsylvania "Right to Know" law took effect. 65 P.S. §§ 67.301-305, 1310. The new law, which changed its predecessor in both substantive and procedural ways, was intended to fundamentally change Pennsylvania law in favor of public access to public records. As with the predecessor law, certain types of records raising privacy concerns, such as medical records, certain personnel records, and records containing certain personal information (such as Social Security numbers), will be exempt from disclosure. 65 P.S. § 67.708.

VII. ACTIONS SUBSEQUENT TO EMPLOYMENT

A. References

Under a Pennsylvania statute that became effective August 15, 2005, Pennsylvania employers enjoy an immunity from civil liability for disclosing job performance information about a current or former employee to a prospective new employer, unless a lack of good faith is shown by clear and convincing evidence. 42 Pa. C.S. § 8340.1.

B. Non-Compete Agreements

Restrictive post-employment covenants are not favored in Pennsylvania, because they are viewed as a restraint on trade. Non-compete agreements will be enforced, however, where they are reasonably necessary for the protection of legitimate business interests of the former employer, and where the scope, geographic, and temporal limitations are reasonable. See generally, Omicron Sys., Inc. v. Weiner, 860 A.2d 554, 559-560 (Pa. Super. Ct. 2004).

VIII. OTHER ISSUES

A. Statutes of Limitations

Under Pennsylvania law, the statutory limitations period for claims of defamation and invasion of privacy is one year. 42 PA. CONS. STAT. ANN. § 5523 (West 1981). The statute of limitations for negligent hiring, retention and supervision is two years. Id. § 5524(7). The statute of limitations for intentional infliction of emotional distress is two years. Id. § 5524 (7). If a claim is based on breach of physician-patient confidentiality, however, such as when an employee files suit against a healthcare provider for making an unauthorized disclosure of drug abuse treatment to the employer in response to a request for records relevant to a workers' compensation claim, the statutory limitations period is two years. Burger v. Blair Medical Assoc., Inc., 964 A.2d 374, 381 (Pa. 2009).

Under the discovery rule, the statute of limitations does not begin to run "until the plaintiff has discovered the injury, or, in the exercise of reasonable diligence, should have discovered his injury." Pocono Int'l Raceway v. Pocono Produce, 468 A.2d 468, 471 (Pa. 1983);

B. Jurisdiction

The Pennsylvania legislature establishes the jurisdiction of the various courts in the Commonwealth. 42 Pa. C.S.A. § 701 et seq. The highest appellate court is the Pennsylvania Supreme Court, which has minimal original jurisdiction. Id. § 721. Most final orders from the intermediate appellate courts are not appealable as of right, and may be reviewed by the Pennsylvania Supreme Court upon allowance of appeal (grant of allocatur). Id. § 724. There are two intermediate appellate courts -- the Commonwealth Court and the Superior Court. The Superior Court has exclusive appellate jurisdiction of all appeals from final orders of the trial courts without regard to the nature or amount of the controversy, unless the Supreme or Commonwealth Court has exclusive appellate jurisdiction. Id. § 742. In addition to serving as an intermediate appellate court, the Commonwealth Court has considerable original jurisdiction, dealing principally with governmental and criminal affairs. Id. § 761. Pennsylvania trial courts, known as the Courts of Common Pleas, are the point of origin for most civil and criminal cases. Except when another court in the Commonwealth system has exclusive original jurisdiction, the Courts of Common Pleas have, as a general rule, unlimited original jurisdiction of all actions and proceedings. Id. § 931.

C. Workers' Compensation Exclusivity

The Pennsylvania Workers' Compensation Law provides the exclusive remedy for workplace injuries and deaths:

> The liability of an employer under this act shall be exclusive and in place of any and all other liability to such employer, his legal representative, husband or wife, parents, dependents, next of kin or anyone otherwise entitled to damages in any action at law or otherwise on account of any injury or death as defined in section 301(c)(1) and (2) or occupational disease as defined in section 108.

77 P.S. § 481(a).

The purpose of this exclusivity is to immunize an employer from civil suits brought by their employees for work-related injuries. Kline v. Arden H. Verner Co., 469 A.2d 158 (Pa. 1983). The Pennsylvania Supreme Court has held that injuries to employees are exclusively within the Pennsylvania Workers' Compensation Law even when there was intentional misconduct by the employer, and even when the claim asserted is an intentional tort. Barber v. Pittsburgh Corning Corp., 555 A.2d 766, 770 (Pa. 1989); Poyser v. Newman & Co. Inc., 522 A.2d 548, 550 (Pa. 1987). Under the "personal animus exception," an employee may bring any available common law claim against the employer if the injury, although occurring in the workplace, was caused by an act of a third person intending to injure the employee for reasons personal to the employee, not related to status as an employee or because of employment. 77 P.S. § 411(1). Workers' compensation exclusivity does not apply to a claim against an employer for violating the Pennsylvania Wiretap Act, 18 PA. CONS. STAT. ANN. § 5725 (West 1983), by recording employee's private phone calls without their knowledge or consent. Provenzo v. Conard, 24 Pa. D.&C.4th 515, 518 (Comm. Pleas Ct. Westmoreland Co. 1995).

Trial courts often rely on workers' compensation exclusivity grounds when dismissing invasion-of-privacy claims brought by employees based on employer conduct. See, e.g., King v. United Parcel Service, Inc., 15 Pa. D.&C.4th 538, 541-42 (Comm. Pleas Ct. Delaware Co. 1992) (dismissing claims of invasion of privacy, intentional infliction of emotional distress, defamation, and malicious prosecution on workers' compensation exclusivity grounds); Jackson v. Rohm and Haas Co., 56 Pa. D.&C.4th 449, 459-61 (Comm. Pleas Ct. Phil. Co. 2002).

D. Pleading Requirements

There are no reported cases relevant to this issue in the context of privacy and employment. Generally, however, under the fact pleading requirements of the Pennsylvania Rules of Civil Procedure, as opposed to the notice pleading requirements under the Federal Rules of Civil Procedure, a pleading must contain the material facts upon which a cause of action is based. Pa.R.C.P. 1019(a); see RegScan, Inc. v. Conway Transp. Serv., Inc., 875 A.2d 332, 341 (Pa. Super. Ct. 2005) (failure to plead essential facts of a claim means that such claim is waived); Therefore, under Pennsylvania law, "the pleadings must define the issues, and thus every act or performance essential to that end must be set forth in the complaint." Swift, 690 A.2d at 723 (citing Santiago v. Pa. Nat'l Mut. Cas. Ins. Co., 613 A.2d 1235, 1238 (Pa. Super. Ct. 1992)).

SURVEY OF PUERTO RICO EMPLOYMENT LIBEL LAW

Juan R. Marchand, Esq.
P.O. Box 9024227
San Juan, P.R. 00902-4227
Telephone: (787) 721-2495; Facsimile: (787) 725-3066
E-mail: juanmarchand@microjuris.com

(With Developments Reported Through **November 1, 2012**)

GENERAL COMMENTS

Local court decisions are reported in "Decisiones de Puerto Rico" (D.P.R.), available in English as Puerto Rico Reports (PRR) up to volume 100; from that volume onward, decisions in English start with vol. 1 of the Official Translations; advance copies are available through Westlaw, sometimes in English translations when available. While this chapter cites some rulings of the Puerto Rico Circuit Court of Appeals (Tribunal de Apelaciones (T.A.)), decisions of this court are not binding precedent, and are also available through Westlaw. The U.S. District Court sits in San Juan and reports to the First Circuit.

Commonwealth court proceedings are conducted in Spanish, and civil cases are held before judges without juries. Motions for summary judgment are resolved by the ultimate trier of fact. For First Amendment purposes, the Commonwealth is treated like any State. See El Vocero v. Puerto Rico, 508 U.S. 147 (1993); Rivera-Puig v. Garcia-Rosario, 983 F.2d 311 (1st Cir. 1992); Posadas v. Commonwealth Tourism Co., 478 U.S. 328, 330 (1986).

SIGNIFICANT DEVELOPMENTS SINCE THE 2012 *SURVEY*

None.

I. GENERAL LAW

A. General Employment Law

1. ***At Will Employment.*** Law No. 80 of 1976, 29 LPRA §§ 185 et seq. is the exclusive remedy for employees contracted without a fixed time and discharged without just cause, providing for severance pay equal to one month of salary, plus one week's wages for each complete year of employment. Acevedo v. Western Digital Caribe, Inc., 96 JTS 42; Porto v. Bentley Puerto Rico, Inc., 132 D.P.R. 331 (1992; Arroyo v. Rattan Specialties Inc., 117 D.P.R. 35 (1986); Rivera v. Security National Life Ins., 106 D.P.R. 517, 527 (1977). In Baralt v. Nationwide Mut. Ins. Co., 86 F. Supp. 2d 31 (D.P.R. 2000), the court reiterated the doctrine, citing cases. However, the statutory remedy does not shield an employer from civil liability if it intentionally or negligently commits any tortious or libelous act concomitantly with the termination. Roig v. Iberia Lineas, 688 F. Supp. 810 (D.P.R. 1988); Aponte v. Puerto Rico Marine Management, Inc., 794 F. Supp. 55 (D.P.R. 1992). See also Secretario del Trabajo v. ITT, 108 D.P.R. 536 (1979); Schneider v. Tropical Gas, 95 D.P.R. 626 (1958); Cassasus v. Escambron, 86 D.P.R. 375 (1962); Wolf v. Neckware, 80 D.P.R. 537 (1958); Long v. Tribunal, 72 D.P.R. 788 (1951).

The fact that employees are unionized does not prevent them from receiving information from another labor association. In Asociación de Maestros v. Secretario de Educación, 2002 TSPR 058, the P.R. Supreme Court held constitutionally invalid a regulation that prevented teacher's association from meeting in public schools and speaking to union employees, on the topic of their labor contract and employment matters. The lower courts had confirmed the validity of the regulation, arguing that only the labor union that had won recent elections could communicate with employees on these subjects in school property. The court reversed, finding that the association has a constitutional right to expression under the First Amendment, citing Tinker v. Des Moines Indep. School District, 393 U.S. 503, 507-510 (1969), and that such right may not be impeded on the basis of content, absent evidence that meetings were disruptive of schools' operations

B. Elements of Defamation Claim

1. ***Basic Elements.*** Defamation consists of the publication of a false statement of fact, regarding the plaintiff, which causes injury to plaintiff's reputation. The Libel and Slander Statute of 1902, 32 LPRA §§ 3141 et seq., only survives insofar as it is compatible with the Commonwealth Constitution. Ojeda v. El Vocero, 94 J.T.S. 131 (1994); Méndez Arocho v. El Vocero de P.R., 92 J.T.S. 94 (1992); González Martínez v. López, 118 D.P.R. 190 (1987); Clavell v. El Vocero de P.R., 115 D.P.R. 685, 690 (1984); Oliveras v. Paniagua, 115 D.P.R. 257 (1984); Torres Silva v. El Mundo, 106 D.P.R. 415 (1977); Cortés Portalatín v. Hau, 103 D.P.R. 734 (1975). Traditional distinctions between libel and slander are practically nonexistent in these cases. The modern development of Puerto Rico law on libel and slander has been under Art. 1802 of the Civil Code (31 LPRA §5141), regarding general negligence, and this type of action in negligence covers damages for mental

suffering experienced by the person of whom the defamatory remarks were made, as well as those of family members collaterally affected, who had no remedy under the Libel and Slander Statute of 1902. Sociedad v. El Vocero, 94 J.T.S. 13 (1994); Pages v. Manuel Feingold, 928 F. Supp. 148, (D.P.R. 1996). However, a defendant may claim the traditional defense of privilege as it might under the Libel and Slander Statute of 1902.

In Torrado v. Centro de Diagnóstico, 2003 WL 23280235 (TCA Aug. 29, 2003) the court found that the basic elements of defamation had not been pleaded, in a case where the employee was fired pursuant to a hand delivered letter. The court held that there was no publication of a falsity before third persons, applying media and non-media precedents without distinction. Thus, it held that even in the labor context, publication, falsity, negligence and damages are the essential elements of a cause of action for defamation.

2. ***Fault.*** The level of fault that a plaintiff must allege and prove depends on her status as a public or a private figure. In the cited cases, the P.R. Supreme Court has developed a "functional" or "dynamic" analysis, in which the individual's rank and official responsibility, prior notoriety, as well as the nature of her involvement in reported matter, are taken into consideration.

a. **Private Figure Plaintiff/Matter of Public Concern.** In Villanueva v. Hernández, 128 D.P.R. 618 (1991) the court held that the plaintiff, a public school teacher, was a private figure plaintiff who must establish negligence at the summary judgment stage, which is "critical," and that the plaintiff must make a showing of sufficient evidence to prevail at trial on all issues. The court reversed a denial of summary judgment and dismissed the claim for lack of evidence on the issue of negligence. In Torres Silva v. El Mundo, 106 D.P.R. 415 (1977), a well known retired bandleader was held to be a private figure in relation to an article about the arrest of individual who claimed to be his son, because plaintiff had never participated in public debate on issues other than music and recordings. Here, the court upheld the grant of summary judgment, but on grounds of absence of negligence.

b. **Private Figure Plaintiff/Matter of Private Concern.** In Porto v. Bentley Puerto Rico Inc., 92 J.T.S. 175 (1992), a private figure involved in an issue of limited concern (alleged corporate indiscipline) had to prove that defendant abused the conditional privilege for intracorporate communications. See also Chico v. Editorial Ponce, 101 D.P.R. 753 (1973), in which the court stated that an alleged family dispute was of limited concern, as compared to information on organized crime, drug trafficking, and other such incidents which have a more pervasive impact on society.

c. **Public Figure Plaintiff/Matter of Public Concern.** In Zequeira v. El Mundo, 106 D.P.R. 432 (1977) and García Cruz v. El Mundo, 108 D.P.R. 174 (1978), the court held that actual malice must be established by the plaintiff. The plaintiff in Zequeira was a recently retired judge, but the publication dealt with alleged official conduct. In García Cruz the plaintiff was a recently defeated political candidate, and the published information dealt with his fitness for office; not enough time had passed for him to be deemed a private figure at the time of publication. In Garib v. Clavell, 94 JTS 36 (1994) the plaintiff was a physician specialized in the care of AIDS patients and author of a book on the subject; the court held him to be a public figure in relation to a publication criticizing his positions on treatment of the illness and related subjects. The case was dismissed, based on findings that the publications constituted opinion and rhetoric hyperbole.

3. ***Falsity.*** The plaintiff bears the burden of proving falsity. Torres Silva v. El Mundo, 106 D.P.R. 415 (1977); accord Garib v. Clavell, 135 D.P.R. 475 (1994).

4. ***Defamatory Statement of Fact.*** For liability to exist regarding a written or verbal expression, it must be objectively provable as true or false. Exaggerated language used in voicing an opinion will not qualify as such a statement. Garib v. Clavell, 135 D.P.R. 475 (1994).

5. ***Of and Concerning Plaintiff.*** Plaintiff, a former employee, could not recover from employer on a defamation claim based on a former supervisor's alleged statement to another employee that plaintiff was having an affair, where concrete evidence was not offered to establish that the former supervisor was referring to the plaintiff. Flamand v. American Intern. Group, Inc., 876 F. Supp. 356 (D.P.R. 1994). In Rosado v. Fluor International, S.A., 81 D.P.R. 608 (1959) a sign placed by an employer, stating generally that it had lost valuable materials because of employee theft, was held not to identify any of its 156 employees, and thus was not actionable. However, in Parrilla v. Airport Catering Services, 93 J.T.S. 71 (1993) the arrest of three employees in the presence of others provided the requisite identification even though a notice posted in the corporate bulletin board, the day following the arrest, did not identify the arrested employees by name.

6. ***Publication.*** In general, publication is defined as actually showing the statement to a third party with intent to have its contents be known by such third parties. In Pardo Hernandez v. Citibank, N.A., 141 F.Supp.2d 241 (D.P.R. 2001), summary judgment was granted to defendant when plaintiff could not produce admissible evidence of publication of alleged slanderous expression. Gossip and general comments by co-employees were inadmissible to identify the defendant as stating that plaintiff had been terminated for falsifying certain documents. Publication is an essential element

of the cause of action for slander under 32 LPRA sec. 3143, and absence of evidence justifies summary disposition as matter of law.

a. **Intracorporate Communication.** In Porto v. Bentley Puerto Rico, Inc., 92 J.T.S. 175 (1992), the Court held that within the corporation there was publication among executives involved in firing an employee. However, it went on to find that there had been no abuse of privilege because the executives consulted or informed were key supervisors whose duties included taking action in the matter. See also Acevedo Santiago v. Western Digital, 96 J.T.S. 42 (1996); Vargas v. Royal Bank of Canada, 604 F. Supp. 1036 (D.P.R. 1985). In Ramirez de Arellano v. American Airlines, Inc., 957 F. Supp. 359 (D.P.R. 1997), the court held that the conditional privilege was not abused when the plaintiff's termination was discussed in the presence of another employee, since the employee was legitimately present as an invitee of the plaintiff as provided by the employer's regulations.

In Torrado v. Centro de Diagnóstico, 2003 WL 23280235 (TCA Aug. 29, 2003) the intermediate court of appeals affirmed a dismissal of libel claim by employee who was fired on grounds expressed hand delivered letter. The court held that there was no abuse of privilege because only those executives essentially involved in the firing of the plaintiff were made aware of the dismissal and grounds therefor. Citing Porto, supra, the court virtually accepts that intramural discussion or investigation is privileged, and that cause of action for defamation will not proceed if there is no publication outside corporate channels. A similar result was obtained in Suero v. Eli Lilly, Inc., 2003 WL 23280166 (TCA Oct. 17, 2003), where the intermediate court of appeals affirmed the dismissal of a cause of action for libel and illegal detention filed by suspended employee. The court noted that employee voluntarily stayed at meeting with superiors, and that there is technically no publication of defamatory utterance before third persons, so there was no abuse of conditional privilege under statute.

In Martinez v. Sam's Club 2004 WL 3237321 (TCA), the court rejected the employer's defense that no publication had been made before a third party, holding that the fact that the employee would soon marry his fiancee (who was present when defamatory statements were proffered), did not make her his wife in relation to whether the expressions were made before a third party. No blood or family relationship was found, and therefore the employer was denied a motion for summary judgment

b. **Compelled Self-Publication.** In Acevedo v. Western Digital Caribe, Inc. 96 J.T.S. 42 (1996) the court rejected as speculative a fired employee's allegations that he would have to divulge the details of his termination when seeking future employment. Moreover, the court reasoned that even if the prospective employer were informed of the letter of termination, such a publication would also be covered by the conditional privilege. See also Algarin v. Federal Express Corp., 56 F. Supp. 2d 172 (D.P.R. 1999).

c. **Republication.** In Roman v. Timberland, 2003 WL 23268891 (TCA Jan. 21, 2003), the intermediate court of appeals affirmed the dismissal of a libel action by a former employee of defendant, based on negative recommendation to prospective employer. Defendant had conditional privilege, under the Puerto Rico statute, to reply and inform the prospective employer of the reasons for previously firing the plaintiff ("aggressive behavior," among other things). The court reasoned that such communications should be fostered and protected, because entities with a common business purpose can share such information regarding past and potential employees. The court does not discuss whether defendant's expression to the prospective employer is a publication, but clearly accepts the publication as a premise, in its comments that such expression is privileged.

7. ***Statements versus Conduct.*** In Parrilla v. Airport Catering Services, 93 J.T.S. 71 (1993), the court held that the employee's arrest, in plain view of fellow employees, was sufficient to identify them as the culprits in a bulletin board memorandum, posted days afterwards, stating that certain unnamed employees had been suspended for pilferage. No abuse of privilege was found by the court in Tejada Batista v. Fuentes Agostini, 87 F. Supp. 2d 72 (D.P.R. 2000), where plaintiff's sec. 1983 action against the Department of Justice was based on wrongful termination for criticizing agency matters before the media. The court noted that the speech involved was of public concern, protected by the First Amendment, and that prior to "going public" the plaintiff had exhausted administrative remedies.

8. ***Damages.***

a. **Presumed Damages and Libel Per Se.** Puerto Rico does not allow presumed or punitive damages. Aponte v. Puerto Rico Marine Management, Inc., 830 F. Supp. 95 (D.P.R. 1993). Under Art. 1802 of the Civil Code, 31 LPRA § 5141, there must be causal connection between the defamatory expression and special damages alleged.

(1) **Employment-Related Criticism.** In Mendez v. Kraidman, 63 D.P.R. 281 (1944), a store supervisor called her employee a "thief." No privilege was recognized to the employer for said statement. See also Casanova v. González Padín, 47 D.P.R. 488 (1934).

(2) **Single Instance Rule.** No reported cases.

b. **Punitive Damages.** There are no punitive damages in Puerto Rico. See Aponte v. Puerto Rico Marine Management, Inc., 830 F. Supp. 95 (D.P.R. 1993) and cases cited therein.

II. PRIVILEGES AND DEFENSES

A. Scope of Privileges. In general, common law malice is presumed in regards to defamatory remarks or statements, written or verbal, as long as their effect is to injure reputation, or dishonor a victim. The effect of claiming privilege is to shift the burden of proof to the plaintiff so that malice is established by admissible evidence.

1. ***Absolute Privilege.*** No reported cases on this point.

2. ***Qualified Privileges.***

a. **Common Interest.** The Libel and Slander Statute specifically provides that common law malice shall not be presumed in communications "between persons having business in partnerships, or other similar associations." 32 L.P.R.A. § 3145. This provision embodies conditional or qualified privileges for communications made under specific circumstances. Chico v. Editorial Ponce, Inc., 101 D.P.R. 759, 768 (1973); Diaz v. Puerto Rico Railway, Light and Power Co., 63 D.P.R. 808 (1944). In Porto v. Bentley Puerto Rico, Inc., 92 J.T.S. 175 (1992) the court held that intracorporate communications made in good faith to persons with a right to be so informed are not libelous, since they have a legitimate interest in knowing the reasons for an employee's dismissal. See also Aponte v. Puerto Rico Marine Management, 830 F. Supp. 95, 98 (D.P.R. 1993); Acevedo Santiago v. Western Digital, 96 J.T.S. 42.

In Roman v. Timberland, 2003 WL 23268891 (TCA Jan. 21, 2003), the court affirmed the dismissal of a libel action by a former employee of defendant, where the defendant had given adverse information requested by prospective employer of the plaintiff. Although defendant was not compelled to give such information, its expression was held to be privileged because the communication is between entities with "common business interests" under P.R. statute.

b. **Duty.** An employer is immune from a suit for defamation when it files informative tax returns of former employees with the appropriate authorities, or when it files a proof of claim in bankruptcy court. Gierbolini Rosa v. Banco Popular, 930 F. Supp. 712 (D.P.R. 1996). Compliance with applicable laws establishes a duty and such filings are not actionable by the former employee. In early 1992, the bank conducted an investigation into complaints of unauthorized withdrawals from the accounts of bank customers. As a result of this investigation, and despite her claim of innocence, the bank fired Mrs. Gierbolini, along with several bank cashiers. Due to pressing economic obligations arising from the loss of her job, Mrs. Gierbolini and her husband filed for bankruptcy under Chapter 13 of the Bankruptcy Code.

c. **Criticism of Public Employee.** No reported cases on point.

d. **Limitation on Qualified Privileges.**

(1) **Constitutional or Actual Malice.** No reported cases on point.

(2) **Common Law Malice.** If statements regarding an employee are made in good faith and the situation is not used to launch an attack against an employee, such statements will be privileged and no cause of action for defamation will be recognized. Porto v. Bentley Puerto Rico, 92 J.T.S. 175 (1992).

e. **Question of Fact or Law.** Since there are no juries in civil cases in Puerto Rico, the same judge would sit at trial to resolve factual controversies.

f. **Burden of Proof.** Once the privilege attaches, it is incumbent upon plaintiff to establish by extrinsic evidence the elements of a defamation claim. Quinones v. J.T. Silva Banking and Commercial Co., 16 D.P.R. 696 (1910); Jimenez v. Diaz Caneja, 14 D.P.R. 9 (1908). Once a colorable claim of privilege has been raised, the burden shifts to the plaintiff to show that the defendant has abused the privilege. Gierbolini Rosa v. Banco Popular, 930 F. Supp. 712 (D.P.R. 1996); Franco v. Martinez, 29 D.P.R. 237 (1921).

B. Standard Libel Defenses

1. ***Truth.*** There are no reported cases on point. However, it is fair to conclude that substantial truth would be available as a defense to an employer, as established for media defendants in Mendez Arocho v. El Vocero, 92 J.T.S. 94 (1992). The defense of truth will be available to a defendant if imprecisions in the statement do not cause an impression which is substantially different from the subjacent truth.

2. ***Opinion.*** There are no reported cases on point.

3. ***Consent.*** There are no reported cases on point.

4. ***Mitigation.*** There are no reported cases on point. However, in Torres Silva v. El Mundo, 106 D.P.R. 415 (1977) great weight was given to a prompt and candid retraction on the part of defendant newspaper.

III. RECURRING FACT PATTERNS

A. Statements in Personnel File

There are no reported cases on point.

B. Performance Evaluations

There are no reported cases on point.

C. References

There are no reported cases on point.

D. Intracorporate Communication

A conditional privilege applies to statements within the corporate structure in furtherance of the corporation's legitimate interests. Ramirez de Arellano v. American Airlines, Inc., 957 F. Supp. 359 (D.P.R. 1997); Acevedo Santiago v. Western Digital, 96 J.T.S. 42 (1996); Porto v. Bentley Puerto Rico, Inc., 92 J.T.S. 175 (1992); Vargas v. Royal Bank of Canada, 604 F. Supp. 1036 (D.P.R. 1985).

In Martinez v. Sam's Club 2004 WL 3237321 (TCA), the Intermediate Court of Appeals rejected a claim of privilege on the part of employer's security guard, for expressions made to ex-employee who had been terminated months before a visit to the store. The court held that no privilege applies to expressions made at that time, because they were not tied to the act of firing the employee, nor in furtherance of the corporation's business.

E. Statements to Government Regulators

An employer who complies with the legal obligation of filing of an ex-employee's informative tax returns with the appropriate authorities is immune from a claim for defamation. Gierbolini Rosa v. Banco Popular, 930 F. Supp. 712 (D.P.R. 1996).

F. Reports to Auditors and Insurers

No reported cases on point.

G. Vicarious Liability of Employers for Statements Made by Employees

1. ***Scope of Employment.*** No cases.

   a. **Blogging.** No cases.

2. ***Damages.*** No cases.

H. Internal Investigations

No cases.

IV. OTHER ACTIONS BASED ON STATEMENTS

A. Negligent Hiring, Retention, and Supervision

No reported cases on point.

B. Intentional Infliction of Emotional Distress

No reported cases on point.

C. Interference with Economic Advantage

No reported cases on point.

D. Prima Facie Tort

No reported cases on point.

V. OTHER ISSUES

A. Statute of Limitations

The limitations period is one (1) year from the date of publication, and in mass media publications, the starting point is presumably the date of publication. Ojeda v. El Vocero, 94 J.T.S. 131 (1994). In Colón Pratts v. Municipality of San Sebastián, 194 F.Supp.2d 67 (D.P.R. 2002), a journalist and radio station owner filed within the one-year limitations period against municipality for violation of 42 U.S.C. sec. 1983, because such period runs from the date of knowledge of allegedly discriminatory actions.

B. Jurisdiction

In Colón Pratts v. Municipality of San Sebastián, 194 F.Supp.2d 67 (D.P.R. 2002), the court conceded that "using government funds to punish political speech by members of the press and to attempt to coerce commentary favorable to the government would run afoul of the First Amendment," citing El Día, Inc. V. Rosselló, 165 F.3d 106, 109 (1st Cir. 1999), 27 Med. L. Rptr. 1185. However, it held that allegations by the plaintiff journalist, at best, would tend to establish a cause of action belonging to the corporation, who was not a party. The case was dismissed for lack of justiciability, since even if plaintiff's expressions triggered retaliation by the municipality against the station, it is the latter which could bring a cause of action for its own damages.

C. Worker's Compensation Exclusivity

The exclusivity provisions of the Workers Accident Compensation Act. P.R.Laws Ann., tit. 11, § 2, exclude defamation claims by an employee against an employer under worker's compensation scheme.

D. Pleading Requirements

No reported cases on point.

SURVEY OF PUERTO RICO EMPLOYMENT PRIVACY LAW

Juan R. Marchand, Esq.
P.O. Box 9024227
San Juan, P.R. 00902-4227
Telephone: (787) 721-2495; Facsimile: (787) 725-3066
E-mail: juanmarchand@microjuris.com

(With Developments Reported Through **November 1, 2012**)

GENERAL COMMENTS

Local court decisions are reported in "Decisiones de Puerto Rico" (D.P.R.), available in English as Puerto Rico Reports (PRR) up to volume 100; from that volume onward, decisions in English start with vol. 1 of the Official Translations; advance copies are available through Westlaw, sometimes in English translations when available. While this chapter cites some rulings of the Puerto Rico Circuit Court of Appeals (Tribunal de Apelaciones (T.A.)), decisions of this court are not binding precedent. See R. 11(D), Reglamento del Tribunal de Apelaciones. The U.S. District Court sits in San Juan and reports to the First Circuit.

Commonwealth court proceedings are conducted in Spanish, and civil cases are held before judges without juries. Motions for summary judgment are resolved by the ultimate trier of fact. For First Amendment purposes, the Commonwealth is treated like any State.. See El Vocero v. Puerto Rico, 508 U.S. 147 (1993); Rivera-Puig v. Garcia-Rosario, 983 F.2d 311 (1st Cir. 1992); Posadas v. Commonwealth Tourism Co., 478 U.S. 328, 330 (1986).

SIGNIFICANT DEVELOPMENTS SINCE THE 2012 *SURVEY*

None.

I. GENERAL LAW OF PRIVACY

A. Legal Basis of Privacy Claims

Privacy of the individual and family life is constitutionally guaranteed under Art. II, Sec. 8 of the Commonwealth Constitution adopted in 1952, which protects the individual from "abusive attacks to his honor, reputation, and private or family life." Its provisions operate ex proprio vigore, and no statute has been adopted. The Puerto Rico Supreme Court has fleshed out its application in diverse contexts. The right to privacy has been established as a right of the highest rank. Colón v. Romero Barceló, 112 D.P.R. 573 (1982); Figueroa Ferrer v. ELA, 107 D.P.R. 250 (1978); ELA v. Hermandad de Empleados, 104 D.P.R. 436, 439-440 (1975); García Santiago v. Acosta, 104 D.P.R. 321 (1975); Sucesión de Victoria v. Iglesia Pentecostal, 102 D.P.R. 20 (1974); Alberio Quiñones v. ELA, 90 D.P.R. 812 (1964); González v. Ramírez Cuerda, 88 D.P.R. 125 (1963). State action is not required, for a cause of action lies against any private individual who violates a plaintiff's right to privacy. Colón, supra. See also Rivera Sanchez v. MARS, 30 F. Supp. 2d 187 (D.P.R. 1998), citing Arroyo v. Rattan Specialties, 117 D.P.R. 35 (1986), where plaintiff alleged that his fundamental privacy rights under the Commonwealth and federal constitutions were violated, because his love affair with the employee of a business client was allegedly a private matter, and that constitutional privacy requires no specific enabling legislation, and it applies to claims of violations of privacy. The case was dismissed for lack of diversity among the parties, without an adjudication on the merits.

B. Causes of Action

None of the cases listed in the preceding paragraph follow the Prosser classifications itemized in this section, infra. In fact, those classifications are not even mentioned in said cases.

1. ***Misappropriation/Right of Publicity.*** No reported cases deal with the employment context. However, in Colón v. Romero Barceló, 112 D.P.R. 573 (1982) the court recognized a cause of action to the widow and family of a person who was killed during an armed robbery. A photograph of the deceased's corpse was used by defendant as part of a campaign for a constitutional referendum related to the right to pretrial bond in criminal cases, without abiding by the widow's refusal to grant permission for such use. The court also held that the use of the photograph was not the only nor the most effective way of illustrating the defendant's position regarding the public debate on the matter. Also worthy of note is the fact that the same photograph had already been published months before, as part of news articles reporting the details of the murder of plaintiff's husband.

2. ***False Light.*** No reported cases on point.

3. ***Publication of Private Facts.*** No reported cases on point.

4. ***Intrusion.*** In Vega v. P.R. Telephone, 110 F.3d 174 (1st Cir. 1997) the court held that (1) the employees lacked an objectively reasonable expectation of privacy against the disclosure of soundless video surveillance footage taken while they were working in an open and undifferentiated work area; (2) the employees lacked a fundamental right to be free from surveillance; and (3) the surveillance did not violate the employees' substantive due process rights. In Vega v. Puerto Rico Telephone, 2002 TSPR 50, the P.R. Supreme Court basically decided the issues in the same manner as the First Circuit at 110F.3d 174 (1st Cir. 1997), recognizing the existence of a compelling need for electronic surveillance on the part of the defendant for the protection of company property. However, it added that since employees do not have an opportunity to controvert the contents of tapes, they cannot be used for any other purposes. Additionally, the telephone company cannot take action against employees based on conduct observed or taped, if said conduct is unrelated to the security and property interests advanced to justify surveillance of the workplace.

In U.S. v. Suarez Rodriguez, 200 F.Supp.2d 68 (D.P.R. 2002), the court dismissed employees' lawsuit for violation of right to privacy, where FedEx had policies in place allowing their security to search anyone on the premises. The court held that plaintiffs failed to prove that employer had made prearrangement with police, and thus ongoing investigation did not constitute "state action" for purposes of jurisdiction under 42 U.S.C. sec. 1983. The sole fact that FedEx had dealt with police officers as to ongoing investigations "is not proof of a prearrangement or of a conspiracy. It is unsupported speculation which can be safely ignored by the court." Id., p. 72.

In Lugo v. Caribbean Cinemas, 2003 WL 23221214 TCA, the court held that cause of action for infliction of emotional distress and invasion of privacy by intrusion and oppression does not require publication before third parties; therefore, it is not decisive that the utterances were not made outside the corporation. This type of action is better suited for plenary hearing, and hence summary judgment should not be favored in these circumstances.

C. Other Privacy-related Actions

1. ***Intentional Infliction of Emotional Distress.*** In Lugo v. Caribbean Cinemas, 2003 WL 23221214 TCA, the intermediate appellate court reversed a grant of summary judgment in favor of the employer, reasoning that the cause of action by fired employee was for invasion of privacy and individual oppression, and not defamation. Publication was not necessary for the cause of action to be recognized; hence, keeping matter from the eyes of third parties does not make employer immune from privacy tort action. The court added that this type of action, unlike defamation (where the actionable expression is easily established) is better suited for plenary hearing, and hence summary judgment should not be favored in these circumstances.

2. ***Interference With Prospective Economic Advantage.*** No reported cases on point.

3. ***Prima Facie Tort.*** No reported cases on point.

II. EMPLOYER TESTING OF EMPLOYEES

A. Psychological or Personality Testing

1. ***Common Law and Statutes.*** No statutes or reported cases on point.

2. ***Private Employers.*** No statutes or reported cases on point.

3. ***Public Employers.*** No statutes or reported cases on point.

B. Drug Testing

1. ***Common Law and Statutes.*** No reported cases on point. See 29 LPRA sec 161a-e, which establishes standards that employers must follow in order to require drug testing,, and providing for liability for violating such requirements.

2. ***Private Employers.*** In Congreso de Uniones Industriales de P.R. v. Bacardi Corp., 961 F. Supp. 338, 343 (D.P.R. 1997), the court approved defendant's "Policy on Controlled Substances" in light of its legitimate business interest, and in light of the specific circumstances in which such testing could be performed: 1) when the security and health of Bacardi's employees may be affected, and 2) when a reasonable basis exists to believe an employee is using or under the influence of controlled substances.

3. ***Public Employers.*** No reported cases on point; statute referred in par. 1 of this section is applicable to all employers.

C. Medical Testing

1. ***Common Law and Statutes.*** No statutes or reported cases on point.

2. ***Private Employers.*** No statutes or reported cases on point.

3. ***Public Employers.*** No statutes or reported cases on point.

D. Polygraph Tests

In Arroyo v. Rattan Specialties, Inc., 117 D.P.R. 35 (1986) the court held unconstitutional the employer's regulations regarding polygraph tests as a condition for continued employment, with a detailed analysis of the various levels of intrusion into the employee's thoughts and private opinions. The employee had been working for defendant, a furniture factory, for many years and the testing was instituted against all employees of the firm.

E. Fingerprinting.

No statutes or reported cases on point.

III. SEARCHES

A. Employee's Person

1. ***Private Employers.*** No reported cases on point.

2. ***Public Employers.*** No reported cases on point.

B. Employee's Work Area. No reported cases on point.

C. Employee's Property

1. ***Private Employers.*** In U.S. v. Suarez Rodriguez, 200 F.Supp.2d 68 (D.P.R. 2002), the court dismissed employees' lawsuit for violation of right to privacy, where FedEx had policies in place allowing their security to search anyone on the premises. The court held that plaintiffs failed to prove that employer had made prearrangement with police, and thus ongoing investigation did not constitute "state action" for purposes of jurisdiction under 42 U.S.C. sec. 1983. The sole fact that FedEx had dealt with police officers as to ongoing investigations "is not proof of a prearrangement or of a conspiracy. It is unsupported speculation which can be safely ignored by the court." Id., p. 72.

2. ***Public Employers.*** No reported cases on point.

IV. MONITORING OF EMPLOYEES

A. Telephones and Electronic Communications

1. ***Wiretapping.*** No reported cases on point.

2. ***Electronic Communications.*** No reported cases on point.

B. Mail.

No reported cases on point.

C. Surveillance/Photographing

In Vega v. P.R. Telephone, 110 F.3d 174 (1st Cir.1997) the First Circuit allowed video surveillance (without audio) of the work area of employees (see I.B.4, supra). The court stressed that the camera was fixed and visible to all employees in the area.

V. ACTIVITIES OUTSIDE THE WORKPLACE

A. Statute or Common Law

In ELA v. Hermandad de Empleados, 104 D.P.R. 436, 439-440 (1975), picketing of the Labor Secretary at his home, after office hours, was held to be a violation of his privacy. The court held that even a public employee had the right to be let alone at home, and that the defendants had ample opportunity to demonstrate against him during office hours in the vicinity of his workplace.

B. Employees' Personal Relationships

1. ***Romantic Relationships Between Employees.*** In Cruz v. Wal-Mart, 2006 WL 2171492 (TCA), plaintiff's cause of action for unjust termination was based on a claim of privacy regarding his consensual relationship with another employee. The court dismissed the claim because only prejudice or bias against married employees is protected by law; the court rejected "reading into" the statute the situation of coemployees who are not legally married. Therefore, consensual relation was not protected from employer's regulations and dismissal of the plaintiff was upheld

2. ***Sexual Orientation.*** No reported cases on point.

3. ***Marital Status.*** In Cruz v. Wal-Mart, 2006 WL 2171492 (TCA), employer's regulation regarding marriage between employees was held not to apply when the relationship was merely consensual.

C. Smoking.

No reported cases on point.

D. Blogging.

No reported cases on point.

VI. RECORDS

A. Personnel Records.

No reported cases on point.

B. Medical Records.

No reported cases on point.

C. Criminal Records.

In U.S. v. Millan Ferrer, 129 F.Supp.2d 112 (D.P.R. 2001), it was held that the prohibition under 28 CFR sec. 20.32 (1979), regarding the maintenance and dissemination of personal information in data bases, was not violated when videotapes and photographs were taken of individuals arrested for trespassing on U.S. Navy territory in the island of Vieques. The court held that taking such photographs for use in trial court on trespassing charges is justified, because such use is "to ensure that the multitude of defendants associated with the ongoing Vieques saga are not misidentified." Id., p. 113.

D. Subpoenas / Search Warrants

No reported cases on point.

VII. ACTIONS SUBSEQUENT TO EMPLOYMENT

A. References.

No case law.

B. Non-compete Agreements

For a non-competition agreement to be valid: (1) The employer must have a legitimate interest in the agreement; (2) the scope of the prohibition must fit the employer's interest but not exceed twelve months; (3) the employer shall offer a consideration in exchange for the employee signing the non-competition covenant other than mere job tenure; (4) the non-competition agreement must be valid a contract; and, (5) the non-competition covenants must be in writing. Arthur Young & Co. v. Vega III, 136 D.P.R. 157, 175-76, 1994 WL 909262 (P.R. May 24, 1994) (P.R. Offic.Trans. at 16-17 (1994)).

VIII. OTHER ISSUES

A. Statutes of Limitations

Since privacy is established under Art. II, sec. 8 of the Puerto Rico constitution, enabling statutes are unnecessary and causes of action may be brought *ex proprio vigore.* Therefore, damage cases based on invasion of privacy are brought under the general negligence (tort) articles of the Civil Code (31 LPRA §§ 5141 et seq.), and the applicable period is one year.

B. Jurisdiction

In Colón Pratts v. Municipality of San Sebastián, 194 F.Supp.2d 67 (D.P.R. 2002), 30 Med. L. Rptr. 2113, the court conceded that "using government funds to punish political speech by members of the press and to attempt to coerce commentary favorable to the government would run afoul of the First Amendment," citing El Día, Inc. v. Rosselló, 165 F.3d 106, 109 (1st Cir. 1999), 27 Med. L. Rptr. 1185. However, it held that allegations by the plaintiff journalist, at best, would tend to establish a cause of action belonging to the corporation, who was not a party to the case. The case was dismissed for lack of justiciability, since even if plaintiff's expressions triggered retaliation by the municipality against the station, it is the latter which could bring a cause of action for its own damages.

C. Worker's Compensation Exclusivity

The exclusivity provisions of the Workers Accident Compensation Act. P.R.Laws Ann., tit. 11, § 2, exclude defamation claims by an employee against an employer under worker's compensation scheme.

D. Pleading Requirements.

No reported cases on point.

SURVEY OF RHODE ISLAND EMPLOYMENT LIBEL LAW

Stephen J. MacGillivray and Raymond M. Ripple
Edwards Wildman Palmer LLP
2800 Financial Plaza
Providence, Rhode Island 02903-2499
Telephone: (401) 274-9200; Facsimile: (401) 276-6611

(With Developments Reported Through **November 1, 2012**)

GENERAL COMMENTS

The Rhode Island courts are comprised of four Superior Courts: Providence County Superior Court; Kent County Superior Court; Newport County Superior Court; and Washington County Superior Court. Rhode Island does not have an "intermediate" appellate court. Consequently, any appeal from a final judgment or order entered in one of the foregoing Superior Courts is made directly to the Rhode Island Supreme Court.

SIGNIFICANT DEVELOPMENTS SINCE THE 2012 *SURVEY*

None.

I. GENERAL LAW

A. General Employment Law

1. ***At Will Employment.*** Rhode Island is, with one limited (and debatable) exception, an employment -at-will jurisdiction. Roy v. Woonsocket Inst. for Savings, 525 A.2d 915 (R.I. 1987). See DelSignore v. Providence Journal Co., 691 A.2d 1050, 1051 n.5 (R.I. 1997) ("[I]n Rhode Island the general rule is that employees . . . who are hired for an indefinite period with no contractual right to continued employment are at-will employees subject to discharge at any time for any permissible reason or for no reason at all"). See also Galloway v. Roger Williams University, 777 A.2d 148, 150 (R.I. 2001); Payne v. K-D Mfg. Co., 520 A.2d 569 (R.I. 1987).

The narrow exception to this rule is the product of a holding by the United States District Court for the District of Rhode Island that an at-will employee "possesses a cause of action in tort against an employer who discharges the employee for reporting employer conduct that violates an express statutory standard." Cummins v. EG&G Sealol, Inc., 690 F. Supp. 134, 139 (D.R.I. 1988) (interpreting Volino v. General Dynamics, 539 A.2d 531 (R.I. 1988)). See also Dunfey v. Roger Williams University, 824 F. Supp. 18, 23 (D. Mass. 1993) (discussing Rhode Island employment law and the holding in Cummins).

In a 1993 per curiam decision, the Supreme Court observed that its 1988 decision in Volino v. General Dynamics, might have misleadingly suggested the existence of a non-statutory wrongful discharge cause of action; the Supreme Court then explicitly stated: "[W]e now unequivocally state that in Rhode Island there is no cause of action for wrongful discharge." Pacheco v. Raytheon Co., 623 A.2d 464, 465 (R.I. 1993). See Andrade v. Jamestown Housing Authority, 82 F.3d 1179, 1188 (1st Cir. 1996) (noting the unequivocal nature of the holding in Pacheco). Accordingly, the continued viability of the Federal Court holding in Cummins, can be questioned in view of the Supreme Court's unequivocal subsequent statement in Pacheco.

In addition, the General Assembly's adoption of the Whistleblowers' Act should be noted; that Act indicates with some degree of specificity when an employee may seek to recover for reporting suspected misconduct by the employer. See Marques v. Fitzgerald, 99 F.3d 1 (1st Cir. 1996) (applying the Rhode Island statute). See also III. E, infra.

The Rhode Island Supreme Court has expressly declined to rule on the question of whether employment manuals or employment policies can be a basis for rights which would not otherwise be available to "at will" employees. Roy, 525 A.2d at 918. See Andrade v. Jamestown Housing Authority, 82 F.3d at 1186 (declining to extend Rhode Island law in this regard).

B. Elements of Libel Claim

1. ***Basic Elements.*** The Rhode Island Supreme Court has expressly held that an action in defamation "requires proof of '(a) a false and defamatory statement concerning another; (b) an unprivileged publication to a third party; (c) fault amounting at least to negligence on the part of the publisher'; and (d) damages, unless the statement is actionable irrespective of special harm." Lyons v. R.I. Public Employees Council 94, 516 A.2d 1339, 1341 (R.I. 1986) (quoting

Restatement (Second of Torts § 558 (1977)). See Swerdlick v. Koch, 721 A.2d 849, 859-860 (R.I. 1998) (summarizing the elements of a defamation claim). **See also Burke v. Gregg, 2012 WL 2587852 (R.I. July 5, 2012) (reiterating the elements of a defamation claim)**; Nassa v. Hook SupeRx, Inc., 790 A.2d 368, 373 (R.I. 2002). The plaintiff must prove that the statement at issue was published and also that it was defamatory. Elias v. Youngken, 493 A.2d 158, 161 (R.I. 1985); Gaudette v. Carter, 214 A.2d 197, 199 (R.I. 1965).

Defamation claims in the context of a labor dispute are discussed in the First Circuit's decision in Intercity Maint. Co. v. Local 254, Service Employees Int'l Union, 241 F.3d 82, 89-90 (1st Cir. 2001).

The Rhode Island Supreme Court has frequently held that whether the meaning of a communication is defamatory is a question of law for the court. See e.g., **Burke, 2012 WL 2587852 *4 ("It is well settled that whether a particular communication is defamatory or not is a question of law for the court to decide, and not an issue of fact for a jury.")**; DiBattista v. State, 808 A.2d 1081, 1088 (R.I. 2002) ("Courts are responsible for deciding as a matter of law whether the particular statement or conduct alleged to be defamatory is capable of containing a defamatory construction, taking into account the context of the statement in which the publication occurs and the plain and ordinary meaning of the words in the community in which the publication occurred."); Kevorkian v. Glass, 774 A.2d 22, 25 (R.I. 2001) (citing Beattie v. Fleet Nat'l Bank, 746 A.2d 717, 721 (R.I. 2000) and Gordon v. St. Joseph's Hospital, 496 A.2d 132, 136 (R.I. 1985)). See also Budget Termite & Pest Control, Inc. v. Bousquet, 811 A.2d 1169, 1172 (R.I. 2002).

A statement is defamatory if it (1) "imputes conduct that injuriously affects a person's reputation;" (2) "tends to degrade him or her in society;" or (3) "[tends to] bring him or her into public hatred and contempt." McCann v. Shell Oil Co, 551 A.2d at 698 (citing cases). See also Swerdlick v. Koch, 721 A.2d 849, 860 (R.I. 1998).

2. ***Fault.*** Regardless of the status of the plaintiff or defendant, the degree of fault can never be less than negligence in a defamation action under Rhode Island law. Lyons, 516 A.2d 1339.

a. **Private Figure Plaintiff/Matter of Public Concern.** The private figure defamation plaintiff "is only held to the ordinary standard of negligence." Capuano v. Outlet Co., 579 A.2d 469, 472 (R.I. 1990). See also Beattie, 746 A.2d at 723 n.2; DeCarvalho v. DaSilva, 414 A.2d 806, 812-813 (R.I. 1980). In DeCarvalho, the Rhode Island Supreme Court expressly held that, with respect to the applicability of the actual malice standard outlined in New York Times Co. v. Sullivan, 376 U.S. 254 (1964), there should be no distinction between media defendants and nonmedia defendants. 414 A.2d at 813. While both types of defendants would have to establish that the plaintiff was a public official or public figure in order to benefit from the actual malice standard, there should be no differentiation among defendants. Id. (noting that a distinction between media and nonmedia defendants "raises many types of equal protection problems.") In the seminal DeCarvalho decision, the Rhode Island Supreme Court also stated that, even with regard to private figures, liability may not be established without fault and the defamation plaintiff must show "at least ordinary negligence." Id. at 812-813.

b. **Private Figure Plaintiff/Matter of Private Concern.** Although no Rhode Island decision is squarely on point, the DeCarvalho decision indicates that a showing of negligence is a minimum requirement in *all* defamation actions. See also Marcil v. Kells, 936 A.2d 208, 212 (R.I. 2007) (stating that to prevail on a defamation action plaintiff must show "fault amounting at least to negligence").

c. **Public Figure Plaintiff/Matter of Public Concern.** The public figure plaintiff must prove actual malice by clear and convincing evidence. Capuano, 579 A.2d at 472; Kempen v. Town of Middletown, 2010 R.I. Super. LEXIS 14, 16-17 (R.I. Super. Ct. 2010). See also Major v. Drapeau, 507 A.2d 938 (R.I. 1986) (explaining the concept of "actual malice").

Rhode Island's definition of "public official" is very broad. Hall v. Rogers, 490 A.2d 502 (1985) (holding that a police sergeant and a special police officer are public officials).

By contrast, the approach of the Rhode Island courts to the question of who is a "public figure" has been more nuanced. It is true that several decisions have interpreted this category in a broad and liberal manner. See, e.g., Harris Nursing Home, Inc. v. Narragansett Television, Inc., 24 Media L. Rep. 1671, 1995 WL 865486 (R.I. 1995) (nursing home corporation held to be a public figure); Capuano, 579 A.2d 469 (holding that the plaintiffs, who were operators of a waste disposal business, were limited purpose public figures); Martin v. Wilson Publ'g Co., 497 A.2d 322 (R.I. 1985) (commercial property developer held to be a public figure in the region in which the newspaper at issue was circulated); DeCarvalho, 414 A.2d 806 (holding that a man who had been very prominent and active in Portuguese-American affairs for 25 years was a pervasive public figure in the Portuguese-American community).

It should be noted, however, that the record of the Rhode Island courts with respect to the public figure issue cannot be said to have been uniformly broad and liberal. See, e.g., Leddy v. Narragansett Television, L.P., 843

A.2d 481, 486-487 (R.I. 2004) (holding that a fire investigator was not a public official); Healey v. New England Newspapers, Inc., 555 A.2d 321 (R.I. 1989) (holding that a medical doctor was not a public figure with respect to what he allegedly failed to do in his medical capacity, even though the nature of the doctor's reaction to the medical emergency which provoked media comment occurred while the doctor was presiding at a YMCA board meeting, in which latter capacity he was held to be a limited purpose public figure), cert. denied, 493 U.S. 814 (1989).

The public figure analysis of Chief Judge Lagueux in the case of Quantum Electronics Corp. v. Consumers Union of United States, Inc., 881 F. Supp. 753 (D.R.I. 1995) is meticulous and should be consulted. The court in that case concluded that the plaintiff (a manufacturer and seller of ozone generating air purifiers) was a limited purpose public figure.

Although it is dictum, the Rhode Island Supreme Court's discussion in Beattie of what constitutes an issue of public concern would seem to indicate that the Court will approach that issue in a broad and liberal manner. 746 A.2d at 724-725 & n.3. The reader should also consult the First Circuit's discussion of what constitutes a matter of public concern in Levinsky's Inc. v. Wal-Mart Stores, Inc., 127 F.3d 122, 132-133 (1st Cir. 1997).

3. ***Falsity.*** In Lyons, 516 A.2d 1339, the Supreme Court explicitly stated that "Rhode Island law incorporates the concept of falsity into its definition of a defamatory statement." Id. at 1342 (footnote omitted).

4. ***Defamatory Statement of Fact.*** It is for the court to decide whether a particular statement is capable of bearing a defamatory meaning. Mills v. C.H.I.L.D., Inc., 837 A.2d 714, 720 (R.I. 2003) (quoting Wilkinson v. State Crime Lab. Comm'n, 788 A.2d 1129, 1142 (R.I. 2002)). See Fudge v. Penthouse Int'l, Ltd., 840 F.2d 1012, 1018 (1st Cir.), cert. denied, 488 U.S. 821 (1988); Socha v. Nat'l Ass'n of Letter Carriers, 883 F. Supp. 790, 806 (D.R.I. 1995).

5. ***Of and Concerning Plaintiff.*** A defamation plaintiff must establish that the allegedly defamatory statement was "of and concerning" the plaintiff. The "of and concerning" requirement is discussed in Budget Termite & Pest Control v. Bousquet, 811 A.2d 1169, 1172-1173 (R.I. 2002). See Connery v. Kalian, 205 A.2d 587, 589 (R.I. 1964). See also Lyons, 516 A.2d at 1342.

6. ***Publication.***

a. **Intracorporate Communication.** No reported Rhode Island cases.

b. **Compelled Self-Publication.** No reported Rhode Island decision has dealt with the issue of compelled self-publication in the employment context or otherwise.

c. **Republication.** Rhode Island adheres to the traditional rule that the republication of a defamatory statement renders the republisher liable. Trainor v. Std. Times, 924 A.2d 766, 770 (R.I. 2007) ("[I]t is well settled that one who republishes libelous or slanderous material is subject to liability just as if he had published it originally.") (quoting Martin v. Wilson Publ'g Co., 497 A.2d 322, 327 (R.I. 1985)). At the same time it should be noted that the Supreme Court has held that no liability will attach if the sources of a statement appear reliable. Lyons v. Rhode Island Public Employees Council 94, 559 A.2d 130, 136 (R.I. 1989).

7. ***Statements versus Conduct.*** No reported cases.

8. ***Damages.***

a. **Presumed Damages and Libel Per Se.** "In Rhode Island, a common law action for defamation requires proof of 'damages, unless the statement is actionable irrespective of special harm.'. . . Under the common law rule damages are presumed, and the need to offer evidence obviated, if the defamatory statement is libelous per se." Intercity Maint. Co. v. Local 254, Service Employees Int'l Union, 241 F.3d 82, 90 n.7 (1st Cir. 2001) (quoting from Swerdlick v. Koch, 721 A.2d 849, 859-861 (R.I. 1998)). See also Nassa v. Hook-SupeRx, Inc., 790 A.2d 368, 374-375 (R.I. 2002).

b. **Punitive Damages.** Whether the facts suffice to support a punitive damages award is a question of law for the court. Kingstown Mobile Home Park v. Strashnick, 774 A.2d 847, 859 (R.I. 2001); Mark v. Congregation Mishkon Tefiloh, 745 A.2d 777, 779-780 (R.I. 2000); Sherman v. McDermott, 329 A.2d 195, 196 (R.I. 1974). See also Gordon v. St. Joseph's Hospital, 496 A.2d 132, 137 (R.I. 1985). The finder of fact then determines whether punitive damages should be awarded and in what amount. Scully v. Matarese, 422 A.2d 740, 741 (R.I. 1980).

Rhode Island courts generally consider an award of punitive damages to be "[d]isfavored in the law" and to be "an extraordinary sanction permitted only with great caution and within narrow limits." Picard v. Barry Pontiac-Buick, Inc., 654 A.2d 690, 696 (R.I. 1995). See also Fenwick v. Oberman, 847 A.2d 852, 856 (R.I. 2004); Palmisano

v. Toth, 624 A.2d 314, 318 (R.I. 1993). With respect to common law actions, the Rhode Island Supreme Court has also emphasized that "[c]ourts in this jurisdiction only allow punitive damages when the evidence indicates that the defendant acted maliciously or in bad faith." Sarkasian v. Newspaper, Inc., 512 A.2d 831, 836 (R.I. 1986). See generally Wilson Auto Enter., Inc. v. Mobil Oil Corp., 778 F. Supp. 101, 107 (D.R.I. 1991) ("In Rhode Island, punitive damages must be based upon *intentional* and *malicious* conduct toward the plaintiff") (emphasis in original).

The case of Johnson v. Johnson, is also of interest with respect to the subject of punitive damages. 654 A.2d 1212 (R.I. 1995). In that non-media slander case, the Supreme Court, even though it upheld a finding that the defendant had "acted out of spite and ill will," ruled that since the defendant's statement was uttered "under enormous provocation" the utterance of the slanderous statement did not meet Rhode Island's rigorous standard for punitive damages. Id. at 1216. The Court in Johnson reiterated the rule that punitive damages are not to be awarded without "evidence of such willfulness, recklessness or wickedness, on the part of the party at fault as amounts to criminality, which for the good of society and warning to the individual, ought to be punished."

The Court in Johnson also discussed the decision of the United States Supreme Court in Dun & Bradstreet, Inc. v. Greenmoss Builders, Inc., 472 U.S. 749 (1985). The Rhode Island court expressly stated that, pursuant to the plurality opinion of the United States Supreme Court "buttressed by" two concurring opinions, the present rule is that where "defamatory statements do not involve matters of public concern, the First Amendment . . . does not require a showing of 'actual malice' for either compensatory or punitive damages . . . ." 654 A.2d at 1216. (It should be noted that the plaintiff in Johnson was a private figure. In addition, the Rhode Island Supreme Court specifically held that "the defamatory statements made by the defendant in that case were not matters of public concern." Id. (footnote omitted)).

(1) **Employment-Related Criticism.** No reported cases.

(2) **Single Instance Rule.** No reported cases.

II. PRIVILEGES AND DEFENSES

A. Scope of Privileges

1. ***Absolute Privilege.*** Rhode Island follows the generally prevailing American rule according an absolute privilege to "libelous matter in pleadings filed in judicial proceedings . . . where the statements are material, pertinent or relevant to the issues therein . . . ." Vieira v. Meredith, 123 A.2d 743, 744 (R.I. 1956). See also Pawtucket Credit Union v. LaScola, 693 A.2d 1031 (R.I. 1997). In addition, in O'Coin v. Woonsocket Institution Trust Co., 535 A.2d 1263, 1267 (R.I. 1988), the Supreme Court recognized a privilege (apparently absolute) with respect to a witness who is required to testify in response to a question at trial.

In Western Mass. Blasting Corp. v. Metropolitan Property and Casualty Ins. Co., 783 A.2d 398 (R.I. 2001), the Supreme Court held that assertions made in an arbitration proceeding are privileged. The court did not explicitly state that the privilege would be absolute, but that would seem to be a fair inference.

Additionally, in Bartlett v. Am. Power Conversion Corp., C.A. No. 05-084-ML, 2006 WL 2709404, at *8 (D.R.I. Sept. 20, 2006), the court granted the employer's motion for summary judgment on the employee-plaintiff's defamation claims. The plaintiff had alleged that her employer defamed her in statements filed with the Equal Employment Opportunity Commission. The court dismissed these claims holding that "[c]ommunications made in judicial proceedings are absolutely privileged." Id. (citing to Vieira v. Meredith, 123 A.2d at 744).

2. ***Qualified Privileges.***

a. **Common Interest**. An employer's communication to his or her employees about the misconduct of a fellow employee is often qualifiedly privileged under the "common interest" heading. Ponticelli v. Mine Safety Appliance Co., 247 A.2d 303, 307 (R.I. 1968). See Nelson v. City of Cranston, 116 F. Supp.2d 260, 268 (D.R.I. 2000); Hayden v. Hasbrouck, 84 A. 1087 (R.I. 1912). It is for the court (and not the jury) to determine whether the privilege applies to a particular factual situation. See Swanson v. Speidel Corp., 293 A.2d 307 (R.I. 1972); Di Biasio v. Brown & Sharpe Mfg. Co., 525 A.2d 489, 491 (R.I. 1987). See generally Ventetuolo v. Burke, 596 F.2d 476, 485 (1st Cir. 1979) (discussing and applying Rhode Island law).

If the court so determines, then the case may be submitted to a jury for factual findings as to possible forfeiture of the qualified privilege -- unless the Court rules that there is insufficient evidence upon which to base such a finding. See Swanson, 293 A.2d 307; Di Biasio, 525 A.2d at 491. See generally Ventetuolo, 596 F.2d at 485 (1st Cir. 1979).

In Froess v. Bulman, 610 F. Supp. 332 (D.R.I. 1984), The United States District Court for the District of Rhode Island applied the Vieira holding to litigation-related statements by an attorney. (The First Circuit affirmed without published opinion. 767 F.2d 905 (1985).)

It should also be noted that a Rhode Island statute provides qualified immunity for the one giving an employment reference. R.I. Gen. Laws §28-6.4-1. In addition, case law recognizes the existence of such a privilege as a matter of common law.

The case of Martin v. Wilson Publ'g Co., 497 A.2d 322 (R.I. 1985) is significant even though it did not arise out of the employment context. Martin involved the republication of a defamatory rumor; the repetition of rumors can be actionable in the context of employment references. See e.g., Sigal Construction Corp. v. Stanbury, 586 A.2d 1204, 1215-1216 (D.C. 1991).

Under Rhode Island law, a jury (provided that there is enough evidence for the case to go to a jury) can find that the qualified privilege has been forfeited by virtue of common law malice (as distinguished from constitutional "actual malice") on the defendant's part. Ponticelli, 247 A.2d at 308. The plaintiff has the burden of showing that "*the primary motivating force* for the communication was the publisher's ill will or spite toward him." Id. (emphasis added). The court in Ponticelli added the following clarification: "Where. . . the causative factor was the common interest, a publisher's resentment toward the person defamed is immaterial and any incidental gratification is without legal significance." Id. (citations omitted). See also Boston Mutual Life Ins. Co. v. Varone, 303 F.2d 155, 159 (1st Cir. 1962). ("Incidental gratification of personal feelings is irrelevant."); Nelson v. City of Cranston, 116 F. Supp. 2d 260, 269 (D.R.I. 2000).

b. **Duty.** In Bartlett v. Am. Power Conversion Corp., 2006 WL 2709404 (D.R.I. Sept. 20, 2006), the court granted summary judgment to an employer on an employee's defamation claim based on the qualified privilege of duty. The employee had alleged that her employer's reporting to the Rhode Island Department of Labor and Training regarding her termination for poor work performance constituted defamation under Rhode Island law. Judge Lisi held that an employer can avoid liability "if the occasion for the publication is such that the publisher acting in good faith correctly or reasonably believes that he has a legal, moral, or social duty to speak out, or that to speak out is necessary to protect either his own interests, or those of third persons, or certain interests of the public." Id. at *8 (citing Ponticelli v. Mine Safety Appliance Co., 247 A.2d 303, 305-06 (R.I. 1968)). See generally Sylvester v. D'Ambra, 54 A.2d 418 (R.I. 1947) (recognizing the existence of a qualified privilege for a communication to a law enforcement officer). See also Curtis v. State Dept. for Children & Their Families, 522 A.2d 203 (R.I. 1987) (discussing the statutory duty to report suspected child abuse).

c. **Criticism of Public Employee.** Rhode Island has a very broad definition of public official. Hall v. Rogers, 490 A.2d 502 (1985) (holding that a police sergeant and a special police officer are public officials). Because of the respect accorded to the First Circuit by the Rhode Island courts, the reader should note the recent statement by Judge Selya of the First Circuit that "criticism of the workings of government is at the core of conduct protected by the First Amendment." Levinsky's Inc. v. Wal-Mart Stores, Inc., 127 F.3d 122, 132 (1997) (citing New York Times Co. v. Sullivan, 376 U.S. 254, 282-283 (1964)).

d. **Limitation on Qualified Privileges.**

(1) **Constitutional or Actual Malice.** Proof of constitutional "actual malice" is not required to defeat a qualified privilege.

(2) **Common Law Malice.** The qualified common interest privilege can only be overcome with proof of common law malice. Nelson v. City of Cranston, 116 F. Supp. 2d 260, 269 (D.R.I. 2000); Gordon v. St. Joseph's Hosp., 496 A.2d 132, 137 (R.I. 1985); Swanson v. Speidel Corp., 293 A.2d 307, 311 (R.I. 1972). See also Di Biasio, 525 A.2d at 492; Belliveau v. Rerick, 504 A.2d 1360, 1363 (R.I. 1986); Ponticelli, 247 A.2d at 308.

e. **Question of Fact or Law.** It is for the court (and not the jury) to determine whether the privilege applies to a particular factual situation. Ponticelli, 247 A.2d at 307. See also Swanson v. Speidel Corp., 293 A.2d 307 (R.I. 1972); Di Biasio, 525 A.2d at 491. See generally Ventetuolo v. Burke, 596 F.2d 476, 485 (1st Cir. 1979) (discussing and applying Rhode Island law). When the evidence provides a basis for such a finding, a jury may find that the qualified privilege has been forfeited. Gordon, 496 A.2d at 137.

f. **Burden of Proof.** The plaintiff has the burden of proving that a defendant who relies on the defense of qualified privilege acted with common law malice. Nelson v. City of Cranston, 116 F. Supp. 2d 260, 269 (D.R.I. 2000).

B. Standard Libel Defenses

1. ***Truth.*** The Rhode Island Supreme Court has held that "truth is an absolute defense to a charge of libel." Lyons v. Rhode Island Public Employees Council 94, 516 A.2d 1339, 1343 (R.I. 1986). See also Lundgren v. Pawtucket Firefighters Ass'n, 595 A.2d 808, 815 (R.I. 1991) (same). In addition, a Rhode Island statute provides that truth is a "sufficient" defense unless the statement in question was "published or uttered from malicious motives . . . ." R.I. Gen. Laws § 9-6-9. See Johnson v. Johnson, 654 A.2d 1212 (R.I. 1995).

One pre-Sullivan case held that the failure to substantiate truth may provide a basis for an award of punitive damages. Marley v. Providence Journal Co., 134 A.2d 180 (R.I. 1957). It should be emphasized, however, that there is no similar published Rhode Island decision subsequent to the U.S. Supreme Court's decision in Phila. Newspapers, Inc. v. Hepps, 475 U.S. 767 (1986).

The Rhode Island Supreme Court's decision in Johnson v. Johnson, 654 A.2d 1212, upheld an award of compensatory damages for defamatory statements that were not matters of public concern. The defamatory statement consisted of the defendant's having called the plaintiff (his ex-wife) a "whore" in the presence of between fifty and seventy-five people. The trial justice's finding that the plaintiff in fact "fit the definition of the defamatory term [whore]" was not disturbed by the Supreme Court. Nevertheless, the Supreme Court looked to the provisions of the above-cited state statute (R.I. Gen. Laws § 9-6-9) to the effect that "the truth, unless published or uttered from malicious motives, shall be a sufficient defense to the person charged." In light of that statutory language (which is entirely consistent with article 1, section 20, of the Rhode Island Constitution) and the trial justice's finding that the defendant had acted out of spite and ill will, the Supreme Court upheld the jury's award of compensatory damages. The Court held that defendant's federal constitutional defenses had not been preserved, since they were not raised at trial. If the Court had reached those defenses, it seems likely that the slander claim would have been dismissed even though the defendant was not a media defendant and the statement at issue did not involve a matter of public concern. See, e.g., Diane Leenheer Zimmerman, *False Light Invasion of Privacy*, 64 N.Y.U. L. REV. 364, 423 n.316 (1989) ("Although it has not explicitly ruled on the question, an examination of the Supreme Court's defamation cases leaves little doubt that a defense of truth is constitutionally required without regard to the defendant's motives").

2. ***Opinion.*** In Froess v. Bulman, 610 F. Supp. 332 (D.R.I. 1984), the United States District Court indicated that the opinion privilege can be invoked regardless of whether or not the plaintiff is a public figure and regardless of whether or not the issue is one of public interest. Id. at 339 n.3, aff'd mem., 767 F.2d 905 (1st Cir. 1985). See also Socha v. Nat'l Ass'n of Letter Carriers, 883 F. Supp. 790, 806 (D.R.I. 1995).

In Beattie v. Fleet Nat'l Bank, the Rhode Island Supreme Court discussed the principle that an opinion which is based upon disclosed, non-defamatory facts does not "constitute an actionable-defamatory communication." 746 A.2d 717, 719 (2000). Although Beattie did not involve the employment context (but rather an alleged libel of an independent real estate appraiser by a bank's own chief appraiser), it is of general usefulness with respect to the subject of "opinion" in defamation law. The case is also noteworthy for its discussion of the United States Supreme Court's decision in Milkovich v. Lorain Journal Co., 497 U.S. 1 (1990) (declining to create an unlimited exemption from defamation claims for statements disguised in the form of "opinions" because the existing jurisprudence on the subject provided the requisite "breathing space" which "freedoms of expression require in order to survive.") With respect to the post-Milkovich opinion doctrine in general, one should also consult the First Circuit's important opinion in Phantom Touring, Inc. v. Affiliated Publications, 953 F.2d 724, cert. denied, 504 U.S. 94 (1992). See also Abner J. Mikva, *"In My Opinion, Those Are Not Facts,"* 11 GEORGIA ST. U. L. REV. 291 (1995).

In Burke v. Gregg, a recent Rhode Island Supreme Court decision, the court acknowledged that "opinions are afforded greater protections under the law" in the context of a defamation case. 2012 WL 2587852 *11 (R.I. July 5, 2012). The defamation at issue consisted of an on-the-air rant by a well known radio talk show host, sparked by an "openly critical" article published in the Providence Journal. Id. at *1-2. The court relied upon Gertz v. Robert Welch, Inc., 418 U.S. 323 (1974), in reiterating that a "statement in the form of an opinion is actionable only if it implies the allegation of undisclosed defamatory facts for the basis of the opinion." The court reasoned that an opinion based on disclosed, non-defamatory facts is not actionable as a defamation because "readers will understand that they are getting the author's interpretation of the facts presented" and accordingly, are "unlikely to construe the statement as insinuating the existence of additional, undisclosed [defamatory] facts." Burke, 2012 WL 2587852 *12; Beattie, 746 A.2d at 721 (quoting Standing Comm. on Discipline v. Yagman, 55 F.3d 1430, 1439 (9th Cir. 1995)). The court embarked upon a 2 part analysis: (1) whether the basis for the speaker's opinion was disclosed to his audience, and (2) whether the speaker's opinion was itself defamatory. Burke, 2012 WL 2587852 *12. While the radio host embarked on a "rambling diatribe" which would "ruffle the sensibilities of any listener," he disclosed that his opinions sprang from the newspaper article and openly referred to it throughout the broadcast. Id. at *13. The court reasoned

that even if the newspaper's allegations were false or inaccurate, they were not defamatory as a matter of law. Id. Accordingly, the judgment of the Superior Court dismissing plaintiff's claim was affirmed. Id.

The opinion defense is also discussed in Budget Termite & Pest Control, Inc. v. Bousquet, 811 A.2d 1169 (R.I. 2002) and Cullen v. Auclair, 809 A.2d 1107 (R.I. 2002). The Budget Termite case is unusual in that the plaintiff corporation based its defamation claim on a cartoon that appeared in the comics section of a Sunday newspaper.

The First Circuit has held that the word "trashy" as applied to a retail store is not actionable because it "admits of numerous interpretations" and because it is "quintessentially subjective." Levinsky's Inc. v. Wal-Mart Stores, Inc., 127 F.3d 122, 130 (1997). Although the Levinsky's case arose in Maine, the First Circuit cited cases from numerous jurisdictions in support of its conclusion that the "trashy" comment constituted "loose language that cannot be objectively verified" and so falls in the category of protected opinion. Id.

3. ***Consent.*** No reported cases.

4. ***Mitigation.*** No reported cases.

III. RECURRING FACT PATTERNS

A. Statements in Personnel File

See III.C, infra.

B. Performance Evaluations

See III.C, infra.

C. References

Pursuant to R.I. Gen. Laws §28-6.4-1, a qualified privilege is accorded to an employer making a reference.

It should also be noted that alleged breaches of contractual agreements specifying the contents of references that will be given with respect to a former employee can be actionable. See Wells v. Uvex Winter Optical, Inc., 635 A.2d 1188, **1194** (R.I. 1994).

D. Intracorporate Communication

No reported cases.

E. Statements to Government Regulators

In Global Waste Recycling, Inc. v. Mallette, 762 A.2d 1208 (R.I. 2000), the Supreme Court upheld the Superior Court's grant of summary judgment under the Rhode Island anti-SLAPP statute in favor of two individuals whose critical and allegedly defamatory statements about a controversial recycling facility were published in a local newspaper. The Court rejected the appellant's argument that, in order to benefit from the protection of the anti-SLAPP statute, the allegedly defamatory statements had to have been made before a legislative, judicial or administrative body. In rejecting that argument, the Court emphasized the language of the anti-SLAPP statute which seeks to protect "robust discussion of issues of public concern before the legislative, judicial, and administrative bodies, and in other public fora." Id. (quoting from the anti-SLAPP statute and from Hometown Properties, Inc. v. Fleming, 680 A.2d 56, 61 (R.I. 1996)).

In all likelihood Rhode Island would consider most statements to government regulators to be qualifiedly privileged, even when the statements do not qualify for protection under the anti-SLAPP statute. See Kissell v. Dunn, 793 F. Supp. 389, 393 (D.R.I. 1992) (holding that "statements made to a police agency in support of a request for an arrest warrant are entitled only to a qualified privilege").

In addition, the Rhode Island Whistleblowers' Protection Act should be noted. R.I. Gen. Laws § 28-50-1, et seq. The statute provides rights to an employee who reasonably suspects violations of law by the employer and reports those suspicions to a public body. See Zinno v. Patenaude, 770 A.2d 849, 851 (R.I. 2001) ("For conduct to fall within the purview of the act, a plaintiff must report or threaten to report misconduct to a public body. . . ."). See generally Marques v. Fitzgerald, 99 F.3d 4 (1st Cir. 1996) (discussing the Rhode Island statute). The Rhode Island Supreme Court has held that this statute does not apply when such reports are made by an employee to a newspaper reporter. Picard v. State, 694 A.2d 754, **755** (R.I. 1997).

F. Reports to Auditors and Insurers

No reported cases.

G. Vicarious Liability of Employers for Statements Made by Employees

1. ***Scope of Employment.*** The Rhode Island courts have consistently held that the principal is not liable in *punitive* damages under a respondeat superior theory for the tortious conduct of the agent unless the principal has "participated in, authorized, or ratified" the actions of the agent or employee. Reccko v. Criss Cadillac Co., Inc., 610 A.2d 542, 545 (R.I. 1992). See AAA Pool Service & Supply, Inc. v. Aetna Casualty & Surety Co., 479 A.2d 112, 116 (R.I. 1984) (holding that the trial court erred in finding principal liable in punitive damages when the principal did not participate in, authorize, or ratify the actions of the agent). See also Wills v. Brown University, 184 F.3d 20, 30-31 (1st Cir. 1999) (discussing the circumstances under which Rhode Island law imposes liability on the employer for an assault and battery by an employee). By contrast, the principal is liable in compensatory damages for the tortious conduct of the agent which is committed while the agent is acting within the scope of his/her authority. Piscitelli v. DeFelice Real Estate, Inc., 512 A.2d 117, 119-120 (R.I. 1986).

The Rhode Island Supreme Court's decision in George v. Fadiani, 772 A.2d 1065 (R.I. 2001) deals with some of the issues that arise when a plaintiff alleges, on the basis of apparent authority principles, that a particular defendant was an employee or agent of a corporate entity and not an independent contractor.

Although it is not an employment law case, the federal court decision in Butler v. McDonald's Corp., 110 F. Supp.2d 62 (D.R.I. 2000) contains a particularly useful summary of Rhode Island agency law principles.

a. **Blogging.** No reported cases or statutes on this subject.

2. ***Damages.*** The Rhode Island Supreme Court has stated in dictum that "a principal's liability for the libel of its agent generally extends only to compensatory damages, not to punitive damages." Gordon v. St. Joseph's Hosp., 496 A.2d 132, 137 n.2 (R.I. 1985). See also Reccko v. Criss Cadillac Co., Inc., 610 A.2d at 544-545; AAA Pool Service & Supply, Inc., 479 A.2d at 116; Manocchia v. Narragansett Television, L.P., 25 Media L. Rep. 1619, 1628, 1996 WL 937020 (R.I. Super. 1996) ("A principal is liable for punitive damages only where it ratifies, authorizes or participates in the wrongful conduct of its agent").

H. Internal Investigations

No reports cases or statutes on this subject.

IV. OTHER ACTIONS BASED ON STATEMENTS

A. Negligent Hiring, Retention, and Supervision

The issue of negligent hiring is extensively considered in Welsh Mfg. Div. of Textron, Inc. v. Pinkerton's, Inc., 474 A.2d 436 (R.I. 1984), 44 ALR 4th 603. The Rhode Island Supreme Court in that case upheld a finding of liability arising from the defendant security company's negligent hiring of a guard who served as a security officer at a manufacturing plant which incurred thefts of gold, which thefts were facilitated by the security officer. See also Wills v. Brown University, 184 F.3d 20, 28 (1st Cir. 1999) (noting that Rhode Island law requires that "an employer exercise reasonable care in selecting its employees"); Fraioli v. Lemcke, 328 F. Supp. 2d 250, 264 (D.R.I. 2004) ("An employer's liability for negligent hiring is based on a failure to exercise reasonable care, by selecting a person who the employer knew or should have known was unfit or incompetent for the work assigned . . . ."). In Liu v. Striuli, 36 F. Supp. 2d 452 (D.R.I. 1999), the federal district court granted summary judgment to the defendant college with respect to the plaintiff's claim that the college had been negligent in hiring an individual who several years later allegedly sexually harassed the plaintiff. The court emphasized the lack of allegations as to "facts in existence about [the alleged harasser] at the time of his hiring which would have given the College a reason to believe that [the alleged harasser] was a sexual harassment risk." Id. at 467. The Liu decision also discusses the Rhode Island law regarding negligent supervision, but held that the plaintiff in that case had not pointed to enough evidence supportive of such a claim to survive the defendant college's motion for summary judgment. Id. at 468.

The Rhode Island Supreme Court does not seem to be anxious to expand the number or scope of duties in tort law. See generally Ferreira v. Strack, 636 A.2d 682, 685 (R.I. 1994) (discussing the concept of "duty" in the law of torts in general --albeit in the context of a physical injury to the plaintiff). See also Butler v. McDonald's Corp., 110 F. Supp.2d 62 (D.R.I. 2000).

The Rhode Island Supreme Court's decision in Rivers v. Poisson, 761 A.2d 232 (R.I. 2000) is also noteworthy for its application, in the context of criminally harassing telephone calls made by a janitor to a third party without the employer's knowledge, Rhode Island law concerning negligent supervision, and negligent retention. The court held that the employer had no duty as a matter of tort law "to control the use of the telephone by the janitor in the absence of any knowledge that the janitor would use such telephone to make harassing calls to the plaintiff." Id. at 236.

B. Intentional Infliction of Emotional Distress

In Champlin v. Washington Trust Co., 478 A.2d 985 (R.I. 1984), the court addressed this tort and expressly adopted the criteria set forth in Restatement (Second) of Torts § 46. Id. at 989.

In addition, the court in Champlin held that a physical manifestation of the severe emotional distress was required. Id. at 990. The courts have continued to insist upon the physical symptomatology requirement. See Hoffman v. Davenport-Metcalf, 851 A.2d 1083, 1089-90 (R.I. 2004). See also Wills v. Brown University, 184 F.3d 20, 28 (1st Cir. 1999); Marques v. Fitzgerald, 99 F.3d 1, 7 (1st Cir. 1996).

In Elias v. Youngken, 493 A.2d 158 (R.I. 1985), the Supreme Court expressly stated that the "extreme and outrageous" requirement applies to intentional infliction claims brought by an employee against a supervisor.

C. Interference with Economic Advantage

Rhode Island recognizes the tort of interference with a contractual relationship. See Jolicoeur Furniture Co., Inc. v. Baldelli, 653 A.2d 740, 752 (R.I.), cert. denied, 516 U.S. 964 (1995). The following are the four elements of a claim based on this tort: "(1) the existence of a contract; (2) the alleged wrongdoer's knowledge of the contract; (3) his intentional interference; and (4) damages resulting therefrom." Smith Dev. Corp. v. Bilow Enter., Inc., 308 A.2d 477, 482 (R.I. 1973). See also Ed Peters Jewelry Co., Inc. v C&J Jewelry Co., Inc., 51 F. Supp. 2d 81, 101 (D.R.I. 1999), aff'd, 215 F.3d 182 (1st Cir. 2000); UST Corp. v. General Rd. Trucking Corp., 783 A.2d 931, 937 (R.I. 2001).

Although good motives do not negate the existence of the tort (intent to interfere being sufficient), some interferences are legally justified and thus not actionable. See Jolicoeur Furniture Co., Inc. v. Baldelli, 653 A.2d at 753. The plaintiff bears "the initial burden of showing that the interference was not legally privileged or justified." Stop & Shop Supermarket Co. v. Blue Cross & Blue Shield, 239 F. Supp.2d 180, 194 (D.R.I. 2003).

If the plaintiff successfully makes such a showing, then the burden shifts to the defendant to prove that a particular interference was justified. Id.; see also URI Cogeneration Partners, L.P. v. Board of Governors, 915 F. Supp. 1267, 1289 (D.R.I. 1996); Mesolella v. City of Providence, 508 A.2d 661, 670 (R.I. 1986).

The statute of limitations applicable to claims of interference with contract is the ten-year statute set forth in R.I. Gen. Laws § 9-1-13(a). See McBurney v. Roszkowski, 687 A.2d 447 (R.I. 1997).

In addition, Rhode Island recognizes the closely related cause of action for interference with *prospective* contractual relations (sometimes called tortious interference with advantageous business relations). Wooler v. Hancock, 988 F. Supp. 47, 49 (D.R.I. 1997), vacated w/o pub. op., 187 F.3d 624 (1st Cir. 1998); Pride Hyundai, Inc. v. Chrysler Fin. Co., LLC, 263 F. Supp. 2d 374, 398 (D.R.I. 2003); New England Multi-Unit Housing Laundry Ass'n v. RIHMFC, 893 F. Supp. 1180, 1193 (D.R.I. 1995). See also Intercity Maint. Co. v. Local 254 Service Employees Int'l Union, 62 F. Supp.2d 483, 500 n.4 (D.R.I. 1999) (noting the similarities between this tort and the tort of interference with contract).

The causation which a plaintiff must establish in order to prevail with respect to either interference tort is discussed (and pertinent cases are cited) in Ed Peters Jewelry Co., 51 F. Supp.2d 81, 102, aff'd, 215 F.3d 182 (1st Cir. 2000). The plaintiff bears the burden of proof as to the causation issue. Wooler v. Hancock, 27 Med.L.Rptr. 2141, 1998 U.S. App. LEXIS 28408 (1st Cir. 1998).

A federal court decision, applying Rhode Island law, has held that on occasion even the dissemination of *truthful* information (e.g., the truthful fact that a lawsuit was pending in another jurisdiction) can constitute tortious interference with contractual relations in some circumstances. C.N.C. Chemical Corp. v. Pennwalt Corp., 690 F. Supp. 139, 142-143 (D.R.I. 1988). The court in that case stated as follows: "The general rule that communicating truthful information does not constitute 'improper' interference should not be viewed as absolute. Its applicability depends upon the circumstances." Id. at 143. (A scholarly article in the Hastings Constitutional Law Quarterly concluded that the Pennwalt court acted "erroneously" in holding that truth is not an absolute defense to an interference with contractual relations claim. Robert L. Tucker, *"And the Truth Shall Make You Free": Truth as a First Amendment Defense in Tortious Interference with Contract Cases*, 24 HASTINGS CONST. L.Q. 709, 721 (1997).)

D. Prima Facie Tort

No reported cases.

V. OTHER ISSUES

A. Statute of Limitations

The statute of limitations for slander (or "words spoken") is one year, whereas libel is governed by the general three-year tort statute of limitations. R.I. Gen. Laws § 9-1-14. See Mikaelian v. Drug Abuse Unit, 501 A.2d 721 (R.I. 1985). See generally Lyons v. Town of Scituate, 554 A.2d 1034, 1036 (R.I. 1989); Arnold v. R. J. Reynolds Tobacco Co., 956 F. Supp. 110, 113 (D.R.I. 1997).

The statute of limitations for a defamation claim begins to run on the date when the statements at issue were spoken or published. Sola v. Leighton, 45 A.3d 502, 502 (R.I. 2012) ("the rule that obtains in this jurisdiction, is that the statute of limitations for a defamation claim begins to run on the date when the statements at issue were spoken or published.").

The Supreme Court in Mills v. Toselli, 819 A.2d 202 (R.I. 2003) discusses the circumstances under which the discovery rule is applicable in the context of an action for "words spoken."

Although defamation actions do not ordinarily survive the death of the plaintiff, a special statute permits an action for damages to be brought for defamation "in an obituary or similar account" within three months of the date of death. R.I. Gen. Laws § 10-7.1-1, et seq.

B. Jurisdiction

Rhode Island has a very expansive minimum contacts statute. R.I. Gen. Laws § 9-5-33. Pursuant to that statute, Rhode Island will exercise jurisdiction to the extent that such exercise is "not contrary to the provisions of the constitution of or laws of the United States." Id. See Riverhouse Publ'g Co. v. Porter, 287 F. Supp. 1 (D.R.I. 1968) (discussing the Rhode Island statute and applying it in the context of a libel action.). See also Geary v. Goldstein, 782 F. Supp. 725 (D.R.I. 1992).

C. Workers' Compensation Exclusivity

The Rhode Island Supreme Court has held that statutory invasion of privacy claims asserted by an employee against his/her employer are barred by the exclusive-remedy provision of the Workers' Compensation Act. Manzi v. State, 687 A.2d 461, 461 (R.I. 1997). See also **Lafreniere v. Dutton, 44 A.3d 1241, 1243 (R.I. 2012) (reiterating the Manzi holding)**. See generally Iacampo v. Hasbro, Inc., 929 F. Supp. 562, 581-582 (D.R.I. 1996) (observing that "[t]he scope and breadth of [the Workers' Compensation Act] is not to be underestimated"); Cianci v. Nationwide Ins. Co., 659 A.2d 662, 670 (R.I. 1995) (stating that there is "no intentional tort exception to the exclusivity provisions" of the Rhode Island Workers' Compensation Act).

Nonetheless, the Supreme Court reversed a ruling by the Superior Court on a motion for summary judgment and held that the exclusive-remedy provision of the Workers' Compensation Act does not bar work-related *defamation* claims filed in court by an employee against his or her employer or coworker. Nassa v. Hook SupeRx, Inc., 790 A.2d 368 (R.I. 2002). In so holding, the Supreme Court was required to distinguish a number of its own previous decisions which had held that numerous intentional torts were preempted by the exclusive-remedy provision of the Rhode Island statute. The Supreme Court did not overrule those previous decisions, but rather based its decision on the ground that the nature of the tort of defamation differs from the nature of those other intentional torts.

D. Pleading Requirements

A slander claim must "set forth the words substantially as used." Kenyon v. Cameron, 17 R.I. 122, 124 (R.I. 1890).

A more recent and broader rule as to pleading requirements was articulated by the First Circuit in Phantom Touring Inc. v. Affiliated Publications, 953 F.2d 724, 728 n.6 ("a defendant is entitled to knowledge of the precise language challenged as defamatory"), cert. denied, 504 U.S. 94 (1992). Although Phantom Touring was not decided under Rhode Island law, it seems probable that the Rhode Island courts would adhere to the same rule.

The Rhode Island Supreme Court's decision in Kevorkian v. Glass, 774 A.2d 22 (R.I. 2001), emphasized the importance of the moving party's adhering to the notice requirements of Rule 56 of the Rules of Civil Procedure. (The case involved allegations of defamation in the employment context.)

SURVEY OF RHODE ISLAND EMPLOYMENT PRIVACY LAW

Stephen J. MacGillivray and Raymond M. Ripple
Edwards Wildman Palmer LLP
2800 Financial Plaza
Providence, Rhode Island 02903-2499
Telephone: (401) 274-9200; Facsimile: (401) 276-6611

(With Developments Reported Through **November 1, 2012**)

GENERAL COMMENTS

The Rhode Island courts are comprised of four Superior Courts: Providence County Superior Court; Kent County Superior Court; Newport County Superior Court; and Washington County Superior Court. Rhode Island does not have an "intermediate" appellate court. Consequently, any appeal from a final judgment or order entered in one of the foregoing Superior Courts is made directly to the Rhode Island Supreme Court.

SIGNIFICANT DEVELOPMENTS SINCE THE 2012 *SURVEY*

None.

I. GENERAL LAW OF PRIVACY

A. Legal Basis of Privacy Claims

In Rhode Island, an action for invasion of privacy cannot be maintained at common law. Washburn v. Rite Aid Corp., 695 A.2d 495, 501 n.10 (R.I. 1997); Clift v. Narragansett Television, L.P., 688 A.2d 805, 814, 25 Media L. Rep. 1417, 1425 (R.I. 1996); Henry v. Cherry & Webb, 30 R.I. 13, 73 A. 97 (1909). See also Pontbriand v. Sundlun, 699 A.2d 856, 863 (R.I. 1997); Gravina v. Brunswick Corp., 338 F. Supp. 1, 2-3 (D.R.I. 1972).

In 1972, shortly after the decision in Gravina (declining to grant relief to a plaintiff whose photograph had allegedly been used for commercial promotional purposes without her consent), the General Assembly provided a statutory cause of action for the unauthorized commercial use of one's name, portrait or picture. R.I. Gen. Laws § 9-1-28. See generally Mendonsa v. Time, Inc., 678 F. Supp. 967, 970 (D.R.I. 1988). That particular Rhode Island statute did *not*, however, adopt the other three aspects of the privacy right which are recognized by the Restatement (Second) of Torts § 652A-E. See Kalian v. People Acting Through Cmty. Effort, Inc., 408 A.2d 608, 609 (R.I. 1979).

Thereafter, in 1980, the General Assembly enacted another privacy statute, which includes the four aspects of the right to privacy recognized by the Restatement (Second) of Torts. R.I. Gen. Laws § 9-1-28.1 (the "Privacy Act"). See generally Mendonsa, 678 F. Supp. at 970.

The courts in Rhode Island often look to the Restatement (Second) of Torts for guidance with respect to privacy torts. Intercity Maint. Co. v. Local 254 Serv. Employees Int'l Union, 62 F. Supp. 2d 483, 506 (D.R.I. 1999).

The Privacy Act provides a private right of action for violation of the several enumerated statutory privacy rights. R.I. Gen. Laws § 9-1-28.1(b). If the plaintiff successfully establishes the elements of the cause of action which are explicitly set forth in the statute, the defendant shall be liable "in an action at law, suit in equity or any other appropriate proceedings . . . ." Id. Although the Act does authorize the court to award attorneys' fees and court costs to the prevailing party, it makes no provision for punitive damages. Likewise, the statute is silent as to a right to trial by jury; and, absent such statutory authorization, neither the federal nor state constitution would appear to make a jury trial available under this statute.

An invasion of privacy claim may not be maintained on behalf of a deceased person, since "the right to privacy dies with the person." Clift, 688 A.2d at 814, 25 Media L. Rep. at 1425.

Similarly, Rhode Island courts have adopted the position of the Restatement (Second) of Torts to the effect that corporations do not enjoy privacy rights and have no cause of action for invasion of the four privacy torts recognized in §§652B-E of the Restatement. Intercity Maint. Co., 62 F. Supp. 2d at 506.

In Manocchia v. Narragansett Television, L.P., 1996 WL 937020, 25 Media L. Rep. 1619 (R.I. Super. 1996), the Superior Court for Providence County ruled that punitive damages are not available under Rhode Island's Privacy Act. Id. at 1624 ("If the General Assembly had intended to permit the Court to award punitive damages, . . . it would have said so").

In Doe v. Prudential Ins. Co. of Am., 744 F. Supp. 40 (D. R.I. 1990), the court denied a petition by the parents of an AIDS victim who had sought to proceed under fictitious names in their action against their son's insurance carrier. Although

Rhode Island's statutory right to privacy was not involved, the court nonetheless indicated that it "is very solicitous of individual rights to privacy and is sympathetic to efforts to protect those rights." Id. at 41. While the court concluded that it could not grant the requested relief under the circumstances of the case, it also stated (in dictum) that the decision whether or not to publicize the identities of parties in a case of this nature "is not a determination for the Court to make," but rather "depends upon the editorial judgment and sensitivity of those in a position to disseminate such information." Id. at 42.

B. Causes of Action

1. ***Misappropriation/Right of Publicity.*** Two separate statutes deal with the wrongful use of one's name or likeness. R.I. Gen. Laws § 9-1-28 and § 9-1-28.1 (a)(2). The first statute prohibits the nonconsensual use of a person's "name, portrait or picture . . . for advertising purposes or for the purposes of trade." The second cited statute grants the "right to be secure from an appropriation of one's name or likeness," but it further requires that any such appropriation be without the permission of the claimant and be of benefit to someone other than the claimant.

The relationship between these two statutes was judicially analyzed in Mendonsa. 678 F. Supp. at 967. See also Leddy v. Narragansett Television, L.P., 843 A.2d 481, 490 (R.I. 2004). The Court in Mendonsa held that § 9-1-28.1 (a)(2) applies only to misappropriations for non-commercial purposes, while § 9-1-28 deals with the nonconsensual use of one's name, portrait or picture in a commercial context. 678 F. Supp. at 973.

It should also be noted that the commercial misappropriation statute, § 9-1-28, authorizes the court, in its discretion, to award treble damages to the successful plaintiff; but, unlike the non-commercial misappropriation statute, § 9-1-28.1 (a)(2), it does not expressly authorize the award of attorneys' fees or court costs. Both statutes are completely silent with respect to any jury trial right.

2. ***False Light.*** The false light cause of action in Rhode Island is purely statutory. R.I. Gen. Laws § 9-1-28.1 (a)(4). See Fudge v. Penthouse Int'l, Ltd., 840 F.2d 1012, 1018 n.3, 14 Media L. Rep. 1238, 1243 (1st Cir. 1988), cert. denied, 488 U.S. 821 (1988). The First Circuit in Fudge indicated that it is proper to look to the state law of defamation for analogies to guide analysis of the false light statute. Id. at 1018 ("[I]t is widely recognized that claims for defamation and false light have much in common"). The Rhode Island Supreme Court took the same approach in Swerdlick v. Koch, 721 A.2d 849, 859 (R.I. 1998) ("We next address plaintiffs' defamation and false-light claims together because the applicable law is similar.")

To establish a violation of the false light aspect of the right to privacy, the plaintiff must show that there has been a "publication of a false or fictitious fact which implies an association which does not exist" and that the implied association "would be objectionable to the ordinary reasonable man under the circumstances." R.I. Gen. Laws § 9-1-28.1 (a)(4)(A). See Swerdlick, 721 A.2d at 861. See also Alves v. Hometown Newspapers, Inc., 857 A.2d 743, 751 (R.I. 2004) (discussing the elements of a cause of action for portraying an individual in a false light); Cullen v. Auclair, 809 A.2d 1107, 1112 (R.I. 2002) (same). The statute (§ 9-1-28.1 (a)(4)(B)) further states that the fact which is disclosed "need not be of any benefit to the discloser." The United States District Court in its decision in the above-referenced Fudge case stated that the "gravamen" of Rhode Island's statutory false light tort "is that the objectionable material be false." 1987 U.S. Dist. LEXIS 5468, 14 Media L. Rep. 1238, 1243 (D.R.I. June 4, 1987).

The plaintiffs in Fudge were four schoolgirls, aged eight to twelve, and their parents. 840 F.2d at 1014. At issue was the publication by Penthouse magazine of a syndicated picture and story concerning fights between boy and girl students during recess periods at a public elementary school. Id. With respect to their false light claim, plaintiffs alleged that there was an implication that they had consented to the use of the photograph and story by Penthouse. Judge Coffin, writing for the Court of Appeals, held that there could be no objectionable "association" based on an implication that the plaintiffs had consented to publication in Penthouse, since the magazine had expressly stated that the photograph and story in question were from among a number of items which had been "culled from the nation's press." Id. at 1019 (quoting from the magazine itself). The First Circuit held that, when faced with a false light claim, "the court should make the threshold determination of whether a statement is capable of implying the objectionable association of which the plaintiff complains." Id. at 1018. The court unanimously upheld the District Court's grant of a Rule 12(b)(6) motion to dismiss with respect to all of plaintiffs' claims, including the false light claim.

In Cullen v. Auclair, 809 A.2d 1107, 1112 (R.I. 2002), the Rhode Island Supreme Court explicitly held that "the same protections afforded opinions in a defamation claim also apply in the context of a false-light claim."

The decision of the First Circuit in the case of Brown v. Hearst Corp., 54 F.3d 21, 23 Media L. Rep. (1995), should also be mentioned. Although that decision applied the substantive law of Massachusetts, the First Circuit forthrightly stated that "it is not imaginable that [a false light claim] could escape the same constitutional constraint as [a] defamation claim." Id. at 27 (citing Time v. Hill, 385 U.S. 374 (1976)). The First Circuit then went on to hold that the plaintiff in that case, who was a private figure, would have to show both falsity and negligence in order to raise a jury question with respect to his false light claim. Id.

3. ***Publication of Private Facts.*** The Rhode Island Privacy Act grants a right "to be secure from unreasonable publicity given to one's private life." R.I. Gen. Laws § 9-1-28.1 (a)(3). In order to recover for a violation of this right, the plaintiff must establish that there has been a publication of a private fact and the fact which has been made public is "one which would be offensive or objectionable to a reasonable man of ordinary sensibilities." Id.; **Lamarque v. Centreville Sav. Bank, 22 A.3d 1136, 1140 (R.I. 2011).** It is not required that the disclosed fact be of any benefit to the discloser. R.I. Gen. Laws § 9-1-28.1 (a)(4)(ii). Washburn v. Rite Aid Corp., 695 A.2d 495 (R.I. 1997) and Pontbriand v. Sundlun, 699 A.2d 856 (R.I. 1997), both analyze this prong of the statute in detail and are discussed infra. See also Hatch v. Town of Middletown, 311 F.3d 83, 86 (1st Cir. 2002) (discussing the meaning of the term "private fact" in the Rhode Island statute).

This statutory provision differs from the Restatement in that it requires only that the information be *published*, not necessarily that "publicity" be given to it. Pontbriand, 699 A.2d at 856 (citing Gaudette v. Carter, 214 A.2d 197, 199 (1965)).

The entire Privacy Act is subject to the express provision that nothing in the Act "shall be construed to limit or abridge any existing right of access" with respect to "records kept by any agency of state or municipal government." R.I. Gen. Laws § 9-1-28.1 (c). This latter provision was relied upon by the Rhode Island Supreme Court in rejecting a claim that the Privacy Act should be read so as to prohibit newspaper publication of Family Court records concerning divorce. Doe v. Edward A. Sherman Publ'g Co., 593 A.2d 457 (R.I. 1991). Since Family Court records concerning divorce are public records pursuant to a separate statute (R.I. Gen. Laws § 8-10-21), the Court held that the Privacy Act did not authorize an injunction against the newspaper's publishing that information. Id. at 459. In dictum the Rhode Island Supreme Court in Doe stated that, even if the extent of the Privacy Act were not limited as a matter of statutory construction, plaintiffs would not have a constitutional right to privacy in this situation because the United States Supreme Court's ruling in Cox Broad. Corp. v. Cohn, 420 U.S. 469 (1975) would bar such an action. (In Cox, the Court held that "the First and Fourteenth Amendments will not allow exposing the press to liability for truthfully publishing information released to the public in official court records." Id. at 496). See also Veilleux v. Nat'l Broad. Co., 206 F.3d 92, 132 (1st Cir. 2000) (stating in dictum that "[t]he constitutional validity of the unreasonable publication tort is unclear.")

4. ***Intrusion.*** The Rhode Island Privacy Act establishes the "right to be secure from unreasonable intrusion upon one's physical solitude or seclusion." R.I. Gen. Laws § 9-1-28.1 (a)(1). In a case construing this statutory language, the United States Court of Appeals for the First Circuit gave special emphasis to the Rhode Island statute's use of the adjective "physical." Russell v. Salve Regina College, 890 F.2d 484, 488 (1989), rev'd on other grounds, 499 U.S. 225 (1991).

In order to recover for a violation of this right, the plaintiff must establish that there has been an invasion of something that is entitled to be or would be expected to be private and that the invasion was offensive or objectionable under a reasonable person test. **Koolen v. Town of Warren, No. C.A. 12–121M, 2012 WL 2576325 (D.R.I. July 3, 2012) (granting defendant's motion to dismiss when plaintiff provided no facts in his complaint that could plausibly establish that the defendant intruded on anything of plaintiff's "that was entitled to be private or expected to be private.").**

There is no requirement that the person who disclosed the information in question benefit from that disclosure.

In Swerdlick v. Koch, 721 A.2d 849 (R.I. 1998), the Rhode Island Supreme Court found no violation of the intrusion prong of the Privacy Act in a situation stemming from a neighbor's non-trespassory photographic and personal scrutiny of the comings-and-goings at another house on the street in the context of a dispute over alleged violations of the zoning ordinance. Even though the Swerdlick case did not involve the employment milieu, the court's analysis of the Privacy Act is instructive.

The Rhode Island Supreme Court also dealt with the intrusion branch of the privacy statute in the case of Washburn v. Rite Aid Corp., 695 A.2d 495 (1997), a decision which has numerous practical ramifications. Washburn is noteworthy for the fact that it found a violation of both the intrusion prong of the privacy statute and the provision which recognizes the right of the individual to be secure from unreasonable publicity of his or her private life. R.I. Gen. Laws §§ 9-1-28.1(a)(1) and (3). (The court did not clearly explain how there could be an actionable intrusion where the defendant pharmacy rightfully possessed the information at issue.) The defendant in Washburn was a pharmacy which, upon receipt of a subpoena issued by plaintiff's divorce attorney, mailed the plaintiff's prescription drug records directly to the attorney rather than complying with the strict letter of the law by bringing the health-care records to the Family Court. It should be added, however, that the Washburn court reiterated the rule that exemplary damages are available only if the plaintiff shows that there has been "malice-amounting-to-criminality" in the circumstances surrounding the tort or statutory violation. Id. at 499.

Another significant privacy case is Pontbriand, 699 A.2d 856. The principal defendant in the Pontbriand case was Bruce Sundlun, who at all pertinent times was Governor of Rhode Island. In the context of a major controversy as to which citizens would greatly benefit from legislation designed to deal with a banking crisis, the Governor released to the media the names of 900 individuals who had deposits in excess of $100,000 at certain closed banks. Id. at 859. Interestingly, the release to the media was accompanied by a memo which stated: "We strongly urge you to respect the private nature of the enclosed information." Id. at 861. The Supreme Court held that no cause of action was stated under the "intrusion" prong of the Rhode Island privacy statute, R.I. Gen. Laws § 9-1-28.1(a)(1). That holding was premised upon the fact that there were "no allegations in the complaint that the information possessed by the Governor was acquired through any wrongful or improper means." Id. at 863. By contrast, however, the Supreme Court held that a cause of action was stated with respect to the "private facts" claim brought under R.I. Gen. Laws § 9-1-28.1(a)(3).

Also significant is the federal district court's decision in Liu v. Striuli, 36 F. Supp. 2d 452 (D.R.I. 1999). The court in that case, denying the named defendant's motion for summary judgment, held that the Privacy Act's intrusion prong would be satisfied if (as was alleged) the defendant had in fact burst into the plaintiff's apartment and raped her. Id. at 479. The court also suggested that the same statutory provision would have been violated if (as was alleged), the defendant had without consent "disclosed to a third party . . . . details about [the] sexual relationship" between plaintiff and defendant Striuli. Id. at 479-480.

In DaPonte v. Ocean State Job Lot, Inc., 21 A.3d 248, 253 (R.I. 2011), the plaintiff unsuccessfully attempted to rely upon Liu's interpretation of Rhode Island's privacy statute as extending to an "invasion of the body". The Supreme Court affirmed the Superior Court's dismissal of the action, stating that Liu was "easily distinguished in its facts." Id. Whereas Liu dealt with rape and serial harassment, the contact at issue in DaPonte was nonsexual in nature (the only touching alleged involved putting a sticker on an outer garmet), and took place in a public place of business. Id. The court noted that "to transform the defendant's public, boorish touching of the outer garment of the plaintiff's shoulder . . . into a right-to-privacy action would transform every non-permitted touching into a parallel right-to-privacy action under § 9-1-28.1(a)(1)." Id.

The Rhode Island Supreme Court has recognized that not every isolated intrusive act is enough to constitute actionable intrusion under the statute. See Clift v. Narragansett Television, L.P., 688 A.2d 805, 814, 25 Media L. Rep. 1417 (R.I. 1996) (holding that the family of a man who committed suicide after barricading himself in his house had no cause of action for intrusion with respect to a news reporter's single call to the man while he was barricaded). See also Brousseau v. Town of Westerly, 11 F. Supp. 2d 177, 183 (D.R.I. 1998) (rejecting a claim that a pat-down search of a student conducted in a public school in an attempt to find a missing knife was an *unreasonable* invasion of privacy and also stating that "it is difficult to believe that the Rhode Island General Assembly intended to confer liability [under the privacy statute] for constitutionally permissible searches by government officials.")

A Rhode Island criminal statute imposes penal sanctions upon a person who makes harassing telephone calls. R.I. Gen. Laws §11-35-17. See Rivers v. Poisson, 761 A.2d 232 (R.I. 2000) (discussing the employer's responsibilities when such calls are made from the workplace by means of the employer's telephones).

C. Other Privacy-Related Actions

1. ***Intentional Infliction of Emotional Distress.*** Rhode Island recognizes the tort of intentional infliction of emotional distress. Champlin v. Washington Trust Co., 478 A.2d 985, 988 (R.I. 1984). See also Elias v. Youngken, 493 A.2d 158 (R.I. 1985). See generally **Jalowy v. Friendly Home, 818 A.2d 698, 709-710 (R.I. 2003);** Clift, 688 A.2d at 813-814, 25 Media L. Rep. 1423; Russell v. Salve Regina College, 649 F. Supp. 391, 400-403 (D.R.I. 1986), aff'd, 890 F.2d 484 (1st Cir. 1989), rev'd on other grounds, 499 U.S. 225 (1991).

The intentional infliction cause of action in Rhode Island is consistent with the description contained in Restatement (Second) of Torts § 46. See Champlin, 478 A.2d at 988. See also Borden v. Paul Revere Life Ins. Co., 935 F.2d 370, 380 (1st Cir. 1991). In the case of Fudge v. Penthouse Int'l, Ltd., the First Circuit opined that the Rhode Island Supreme Court would follow the Restatement (Second) of Torts in requiring that, as a threshold inquiry, courts would be required to determine that the conduct had been sufficiently extreme and outrageous to permit recovery. 840 F.2d 1012, 1021, 14 Media L. Rep. 1238 (1st Cir. 1988), cert. denied, 488 U.S. 821 (1988). The Court defined extreme and outrageous conduct as being conduct which is "atrocious and utterly intolerable in a civilized community." Id. The First Circuit in Fudge also noted that "the 'extreme and outrageous' standard is a difficult one to meet;" and further commented that this tort "is not well-established in Rhode Island." Id. at 1020-1021. The court asserted that "conduct that is intentional or reckless and causes severe emotional distress does not ipso facto constitute extreme and outrageous conduct." Id. (citing Champlin, 478 A.2d at 989). See also Forbes v. R.I. Brotherhood of Corr. Officers, 923 F. Supp. 315, 329 (D.R.I. 1996).

The following four elements must exist for there to be liability under this theory as a matter of Rhode Island law: "(1) the conduct must be intentional or in reckless disregard of the probability of causing emotional distress, (2) the conduct must be extreme and outrageous, (3) there must be a causal connection between the wrongful conduct and the emotional distress, and (4) the emotional distress in question must be severe." Champlin, 478 A.2d at 989. See also Norton v. McOsker, 407 F.3d 501, 510 (1st Cir. 2005) (reciting the four factors); Marques v. Fitzgerald, 99 F.3d 1, 7 & n.12 (1st Cir. 1996) (same); Russell v. Salve Regina College, 649 F. Supp. at 400-403 (describing the parameters of this tort under Rhode Island law and opining that it applies in a variety of relationships).

One of the requisite elements of the tort is that the plaintiff exhibit physical symptoms of the alleged emotional distress. Norton, 407 F.3d at 510; Hoffman v. Davenport-Metcalf, 851 A.2d 1083, 1089 (R.I. 2004); DiBattista v. State, 808 A.2d 1081, 1088-1089 (R.I. 2002); Reilly v. United States, 547 A.2d 894, 898-899 (R.I. 1988). Also, in order to survive a motion to dismiss, a plaintiff claiming intentional infliction of emotional distress may not simply allege "pain and suffering" without being more specific. Socha v. Nat'l Ass'n of Letter Carriers, 883 F. Supp. 790, 805 (D.R.I. 1995).

A decision of the First Circuit arising under Rhode Island law held that at least in some circumstances expert testimony would be necessary to prove that the plaintiff's emotional distress was *caused* by the defendant's conduct. Andrade v. Jamestown Housing Authority, 82 F.3d 1179, 1185 (1st Cir. 1996). A per curiam decision of the Rhode Island Supreme Court appears to be to the same effect. Pawtucket Credit Union v. La Scola, 693 A.2d 1031, 1032 (R.I. 1997).

It should also be noted that, under Rhode Island law (as construed by the First Circuit), once "liability for intentional infliction has been satisfactorily established, a plaintiff must carry no additional burden to establish his eligibility for exemplary [punitive] damages." Borden, 935 F.2d at 382.

Rhode Island also recognizes a cause of action for negligent infliction of emotional distress. See Iacampo v. Hasbro, Inc., 929 F. Supp. 562, 581 (D.R.I. 1996).

2. ***Interference With Prospective Economic Advantage.*** Rhode Island recognizes the tort of interference with a contractual relationship. See W. Mass. Blasting Corp. v. Metro. Prop. & Cas. Ins. Co., 783 A.2d 398, 401 (R.I. 2001); Jolicoeur Furniture Co., Inc. v. Baldelli, 653 A.2d 740, 752 (R.I. 1995). The following are the four elements of a claim based on this tort: "(1) the existence of a contract; (2) the alleged wrongdoer's knowledge of the contract; (3) his intentional interference; and (4) damages resulting therefrom." Smith Dev. Corp. v. Bilow Enter., Inc., 308 A.2d 477, 482 (R.I. 1973). Although good motives do not negate the existence of the tort (intent to interfere being sufficient), some interferences are legally justified and thus not actionable. See Jolicoeur Furniture Co., 653 A.2d at 753.

This cause of action is not available to an at-will employee in an action against his/her employer. Roy v. Woonsocket Inst. for Sav., 525 A.2d 915, 917-919 (R.I. 1987). It may, however, be asserted against a third party. Nationwide Life Ins. Co. v. Steiner, 722 F. Supp. 2d 179, 188 (D.R.I. 2010) ("[T]ortious interference with contract applies only to parties outside the agreement.") (quoting URI Cogeneration Partners, L.P. v. Bd. of Governors for Higher Educ., 915 F. Supp. 1267, 1289 (D.R.I. 1996)); D'Andrea v. Calcagni, 723 A.2d 276, 278 (R.I. 1999);

A Federal Court decision, applying Rhode Island law, has held that the dissemination of truthful information (viz., that a lawsuit was pending in another jurisdiction) can constitute tortious interference with contractual relations in some circumstances. C.N.C. Chem. Corp. v. Pennwalt Corp., 690 F. Supp. 139, 142-143 (D.R.I. 1988). The Court stated as follows: "The general rule that communicating truthful information does not constitute 'improper' interference should not be viewed as absolute. Its applicability depends upon the circumstances." Id. at 143. See Robert L. Tucker, *"And the Truth Shall Make You Free: Truth as a First Amendment Defense in Tortious Interference with Contract Cases,"* 24 HASTINGS CONST. L.Q. 709, 721 (1997) (stating that the Pennwalt court had "erroneously" held that truth is not an absolute defense to an action for tortious interference with contractual relations).

3. ***Prima Facie Tort.*** No reported cases.

II. EMPLOYER TESTING OF EMPLOYEES

A. Psychological or Personality Testing

No cases or statutes.

B. Drug Testing

1. ***Common Law and Statutes.*** Employers and their agents are prohibited by statute from requesting employees to submit a sample of "urine, blood, or other bodily fluid or tissue for testing as a condition of continued employment . . . ." R.I. Gen. Laws § 28-6.5-1. The statute then goes on to authorize an employer to require the testing of a specific employee with respect to the use of controlled substances if certain specified conditions are met.

2. ***Private Employers.*** The just-mentioned statute applies to all private employers and their agents.

3. ***Public Employers.*** The pre-employment drug testing authorized by § 28-6.5-2 does not apply.

C. Medical Testing

1. ***Common Law and Statutes.*** Genetic testing is statutorily prohibited as a condition of employment. An employer may not request or require genetic testing as a condition of employment, nor may the results of genetic testing be used to affect the terms, conditions or continuation of employment. R.I. Gen. Laws § 28-6.7-1, et seq.

2. ***Private Employers.*** By statute, information obtained through an employee's participation in an employee assistance program is confidential. Even the names of employees participating in such programs are to be kept confidential. R.I. Gen. Laws § 28-6.8-1, et seq.

3. ***Public Employers.*** No reported cases.

D. Polygraph Tests

See R.I. Gen. Laws § 28-6.1-1, et seq., which prohibits polygraph tests as a condition of employment or continued employment. Carr v. Mulhearn, 601 A.2d 946, 951 (R.I. 1992).

E. Fingerprinting

Fingerprinting is required by Rhode Island law with respect to employment background checks in the educational field (including pre-school programs). R.I. Gen. Laws § 16-48.1-1, et seq. Fingerprints obtained for that purpose are to be destroyed at the conclusion of the background check. R.I. Gen. Laws § 16-48.1-8. The fingerprinting requirement in this context has been held to be constitutional. Henry v. Earhart, 553 A.2d 124 (R.I. 1989). The Supreme Court in Henry also specifically held that the fingerprinting requirement did not invade the plaintiffs' right to privacy. Id. at 128.

III. SEARCHES

A. Employee's Person

1. ***Private Employers.*** No reported cases. There is, however, a statute (R.I. Gen. Laws § 11-41-26) prohibiting the use of two-way mirrors or video cameras in the dressing rooms of retail establishments.

2. ***Public Employers.*** There are no reported cases that are directly on point. See generally Brousseau v. Town of Westerly, 11 F. Supp. 2d 177 (D.R.I. 1998).

B. Employee's Work Area

No Rhode Island statute or reported judicial decision directly addresses this issue, but the Privacy Act should be consulted. See also Washburn v. Rite Aid Corp., 695 A.2d 495 (R.I. 1997) (discussing the intrusion prong of the Privacy Act). It should also be noted that the Rhode Island Supreme Court has upheld the constitutionality of a warrantless search of a "pervasively regulated business." Keeney v. Vinagro, 656 A.2d 973, 975 (R.I. 1995). The Court held that such a search violates neither the Fourth Amendment to the United States Constitution nor art. 1, sec. 6 of the Rhode Island Constitution. Id. at 975.

C. Employee's Property

1. ***Private Employers.*** No Rhode Island statute or reported judicial decision directly addresses this issue, but the Privacy Act should be consulted. See also Washburn, 695 A.2d 495 (discussing the intrusion prong of the Privacy Act).

It should be noted that a statute, R.I. Gen. Laws § 5-3.1-23 prohibits the disclosure of the confidential information to which accountants are privy by virtue of their profession. See McFarland v. Brier, 769 A.2d 605, 613 n.9 (R.I. 2001).

2. ***Public Employers.*** No Rhode Island statute or reported judicial decision directly addresses this issue, but the Privacy Act should be consulted. See also Washburn, 695 A.2d 495 (discussing the intrusion prong of the Privacy Act).

IV. MONITORING OF EMPLOYEES

A. Telephones and Electronic Communications

1. ***Wiretapping.*** Rhode Island has a separate statute dealing with the unauthorized interception of "any wire or oral communication." R.I. Gen. Laws § 11-35-21. The Rhode Island statute is fairly benign, however, since it

declares that interception is not unlawful if accomplished by a party to the communication or if authorized by the prior consent of one of the parties. R.I. Gen. Laws § 11-35-21 (c)(3). Nonetheless, even those interceptions may not be carried out for the purpose of committing any criminal or tortious or "other injurious" act. Id.

The one-party-consent feature of the Rhode Island statute has been noted by the courts. Pulawski v. Blais, 506 A.2d 76, 77 (R.I. 1986); State v. Ahmadjian, 438 A.2d 1070, 1080 (R.I. 1981).

The Rhode Island Supreme Court has upheld a criminal conviction for the surreptitious videotaping and simultaneous audio recording of sexual activity between two college students. State v. O'Brien, 774 A.2d 89 (R.I. 2001). The decision in O'Brien discusses the Rhode Island wiretapping statutes at considerable length.

2. ***Electronic Communications.*** No specific Rhode Island statute addresses the issue of an employer's interception of or intrusion into an employee's computer-based communications or files. It would seem that, in appropriate circumstances, one or more provisions of the Rhode Island Privacy Act could be successfully invoked -- unless the courts were to rule that an employer's ownership interest in the computer system effectively prevents the successful assertion of a privacy claim. Although it cannot be so stated with certainty, it would seem likely that some degree of protection would be accorded to the contents of an employee's genuinely personal computer-based correspondence that was read or disseminated by the employer without business necessity. See generally Washburn, 695 A.2d 495; Manocchia v. Narragansett Television L.P., 25 Media L. Rptr. 1619, 1996 WL 937020 (R.I. Super. 1996).

3. **Other Electronic Monitoring.** No Rhode Island statute or reported judicial decision has addressed this issue.

B. Mail

See R.I. Gen. Laws § 9-1-28.1(a)(1) (recognizing the "right to be secure from unreasonable intrusion upon one's physical solitude or seclusion."). See Washburn, 695 A.2d 495. See also Pontbriand v. Sundlun, 699 A.2d 856, 863-864 (R.I. 1997).

C. Surveillance/Photographing

See R.I. Gen. Laws § 9-1-28.1(a)(1) (recognizing the "right to be secure from unreasonable intrusion upon one's physical solitude or seclusion."); Washburn, 695 A.2d 495. See also Pontbriand, 699 A2d at 863-864; Manocchia, 25 Media L. Rep. 1619, 1996 WL 937020.

V. ACTIVITIES OUTSIDE THE WORKPLACE

A. Statute or Common Law

By statute, no employer or agent of the employer may request or require any applicant for employment to provide copies of federal or state income tax returns or related tax documents. R.I. Gen. Laws § 28-6.9-1, et seq.

B. Employees' Personal Relationships

1. ***Romantic Relationships Between Employees.*** No statute or reported case has addressed this issue.

2. ***Sexual Orientation.*** Discrimination in employment on the basis of an individual's sexual orientation is prohibited. R.I. Gen. Laws § 28-5-7.

3. ***Marital Status.*** Although no Rhode Island case specifically states, it is generally believed that the state statutory prohibition against discrimination on the basis of sex would include discrimination on the basis of marital status.

C. Smoking

No Rhode Island statute or reported judicial decision has addressed this issue.

D. Blogging

No Rhode Island statute or reported judicial decision has addressed this issue.

VI. RECORDS

A. Personnel Records

No relevant statutes or case law.

B. Medical Records

Rhode Island has a comprehensive statute dealing with the confidentiality of medical information. R.I. Gen. Laws § 5-37.3-1 et seq. (the "Confidentiality of Health Care Information Act"). See generally In re John Doe Grand Jury Proceedings, 717 A.2d 1129, 1133 (R.I. 1998) (discussing the history of the present statute and concluding that "[a] presumption in favor of privacy exists . . . ."). In pertinent part, this statute prohibits the non-consensual release or transfer of a patient's confidential health care information except in one of the several statutorily permitted situations. R.I. Gen. Laws § 5-37.3-4. Criminal penalties are contained in the statute for those who "intentionally and knowingly" violate its provisions. R.I. Gen. Laws § 5-37.3-9(b). In addition, the statute declares that "[a]ny one who violates the provisions of [the confidentiality statute] may be held liable for actual and exemplary damages." The penalty provisions of the confidentiality statute have not yet been authoritatively construed, and it is not certain if the courts will hold that republication by the media of confidential health care information which the media obtained without the commission of a crime would be considered to be violative of the statute and, if so, whether such a provision would be constitutional. In this regard, the provisions of § 5-37.3-9(c) would seem to provide the media with a statutory argument that republication under such circumstances would not be violative of the confidentiality statute: "The civil and criminal penalties above shall also be applicable to anyone who obtains confidential health care information through the commission of a crime." Some of these issues are addressed in Manocchia, 25 Media L. Rep. 1619, 1996 WL 937020.

The Confidentiality of Health Care Communications and Information Act (then known as the Confidentiality of Health Care Information Act) is also extensively analyzed in Washburn v. Rite Aid Corp., 695 A.2d 495 (R.I. 1997). That case is particularly noteworthy for its exigent standards with regard to the obligations of the custodian of health care records even when the custodian has been served with a subpoena. (The defendant in that case was a pharmacy which had been served with a subpoena issued by the attorney for one of the parties in a divorce proceeding).

C. Criminal Records

No relevant statutes or case law.

D. Subpoenas / Search Warrants

No relevant statutes or case law; however, attorneys seeking to serve subpoenas on corporations should be cognizant of the strictures of the Rhode Island Confidentiality of Health Care Communications and Information Act, see R.I. Gen. Laws § 5-37.3-1 et seq.

VII. ACTIONS SUBSEQUENT TO EMPLOYMENT

A. References

No relevant statutes or case law.

B. Non-Compete Agreements

Rhode Island permits the use of non-competition agreements by employers to restrict an employee's ability to compete with the employer post-employment, subject to a reasonableness analysis. "Because non-competition agreements are not favored, they are subject to judicial scrutiny and will be enforced as written only if the contract is reasonable and does not extend beyond what is apparently necessary for the protection of those in whose favor it runs." Durapin, Inc. v. Amer. Prods., Inc., 559 A.2d 1051, 1053 (R.I. 1989). When considering the validity of a non-competition agreement, the crucial issue is reasonableness, and that test is dependent upon the particular circumstances surrounding the agreement." Id. Reasonableness of non-competition agreements turns on: "(1) whether the provision is narrowly tailored to protect the legitimate interests; (2) whether it is reasonably limited in activity, geographic area, and time; (3) whether the promisee's interests are not outweighed by the hardship to the promisor; and (4) whether the restriction is likely to injure the public." **R.J. Carbone Co. v. Regan, 582 F. Supp. 2d 220, 225 (D.R.I. 2008) (citing Nestle Food Co. v. Miller, 836 F. Supp. 69, 73 (D.R.I. 1993)); F. Saia Rests., LLC v. Pat's Italian Food to Go, Inc., 2012 R.I. Super. LEXIS 86 (R.I. Super. Ct. 2012). While covenants not to compete that lack both temporal and geographic limitations "are not unenforceable per se, courts should uphold them only to the extent they are necessary to protect the promisee's legitimate interests." Cranston Print Works Co. v. Pothier, 848 A.2d 213, 219 (R.I. 2004).**

VIII. OTHER ISSUES

A. Statutes of Limitations

In general, there is a three-year statute of limitations applicable to personal injury actions. R.I. Gen. Laws § 9-1-14 (b). Actions for "words spoken" must be brought within one year. R.I. Gen. Laws § 9-1-14 (a).

B. Jurisdiction

Original jurisdiction over claims involving the privacy issues discussed in this chapter would reside with the Rhode Island Superior Courts.

C. Workers' Compensation Exclusivity

In Folan v. State, 723 A.2d 287, 291-292 (R.I. 1999), the Rhode Island Supreme Court reiterated its 1997 holding in Manzi v. State, 687 A.2d 461, to the effect that the exclusivity provision of the Workers' Compensation Act bars a statutory invasion of privacy claim by the employee against his or her employer. See also Iacampo v. Hasbro, Inc., 929 F. Supp. 562, 581-582 (D.R.I. 1996) ("The scope and breadth of the [Workers' Compensation Act] is not to be underestimated . . . ."); Cianci v. Nationwide Insur. Co., 659 A.2d 662, 670 (R.I. 1995) (stating that there is "no intentional tort exception to the exclusivity provisions" of the Workers' Compensation Act). It should be noted, however, that in its decision in the case of Nassa v. Hook-SupeRx, Inc., 790 A.2d 368 (2002), the Rhode Island Supreme Court held that the exclusive-remedy provision of the Rhode Island Workers' Compensation does not bar work related *defamation* claims filed in court by an employee against his or her employer or coworker.

D. Pleading Requirements

Although no Rhode Island case addresses this issue in the privacy law context, one can reasonably anticipate that the Rhode Island courts would apply a rule analogous to that formulated by the First Circuit in a defamation case: "[A] defendant is entitled to knowledge of the precise language challenged . . . ." Phantom Touring Inc. v. Affiliated Publications, 935 F.2d 724, 728 n.6, cert. denied, 504 U.S. 94 (1992).

SURVEY OF SOUTH CAROLINA EMPLOYMENT LIBEL LAW

Amos A. Workman, Wallace K. Lightsey and J. Theodore Gentry
Wyche, P.A.
44 East Camperdown Way
Greenville, South Carolina 29601
Telephone: (864) 242-8200; Facsimile: (864) 235-8900

(With Developments Reported Through **November 1, 2012**

GENERAL COMMENTS

The South Carolina law of defamation largely comprises common law principles, with no substantial statutory modifications. South Carolina appellate courts first addressed First Amendment standards in 1978 and have decided several cases on such issues since then. All Federal Court cites refer to cases interpreting South Carolina law. South Carolina state appellate decisions are located in West's Southeastern Reporter.

SIGNIFICANT DEVELOPMENTS SINCE THE 2012 S*URVEY*

See Fountain v. First Reliance Bank, 398 S.C. 434, 730 S.E. 2d 305 (S.C. 2012), for a recent discussion of current defamation law in South Carolina. It is not an employer-employee case, but quite helpful.

I. GENERAL LAW

A. General Employment Law

1. ***At-Will Employment.*** South Carolina is an employment-at-will state, which means that an employee without a contract for a definite term may be discharged at any time for any reason that does not violate a statute. Culler v. Blue Ridge Electric Co-op, Inc., 309 S.C. 243, 422 S.E.2d 91 (1992), Williams v. Grimes Aerospace Co., 988 F.Supp. 925 (D.S.C. 1997). However, there has developed a trend toward judicially created exceptions to the policy. One exception courts recognize is a discharge for a reason that violates public policy. Garner v. Morrison Knudsen Corporation, 318 S.C. 223, 456 S.E.2d 907 (1995). Under the "public policy exception" to the at will employment doctrine, an at-will employee has a cause of action in tort for wrongful termination where there is a retaliatory termination of the at-will employee in violation of a clear mandate of public policy. Barron v. Labor Finders of South Carolina, 393 S.C. 609, 713 S.C. 2d 634 (S.C. 2011). The public policy exception clearly applies to cases where either: (1) the employer requires the employee to violate the law, Ludwick v. This Minute of Carolina, Inc. 287 S.C 219, 337 S.E.2d 213 (1985), or (2) the reason for the employee's termination itself is a violation of criminal law, Culler v. Blue Ridge Elct. Co-op., Inc., 309 S.C. 243, 422 S.E. 2d 91 (1992) (employee was terminated after he refused to contribute to political action fund, and his termination violated S. C. Code Ann. §16-17-560). Barron, supra. While the public policy exception applies to situations where an employer requires an employee to violate the law or the reason for the termination itself is a violation of criminal law, the public policy exception is not limited to these situations. See Garner v. Morrison Knudsen Corp., 318 S.C. 223, 456 S.E.2d 907 (1995); Kieger v. Citgo, Coastal Petroleum, Inc., 326 S.C. 369, 482 S.E.2d 792 (Ct. App. 1997). In both of these cases, the courts declined to address whether the public policy exception applied because, in their procedural posture, it was not appropriate to decide the novel issue without further developing the facts of the case. Barron v. Labor Finders of South Carolina, 393 S.C. 609, 713 S.C. 2d 634 (S.C. 2011). In Stiles v. American General Life Insurance Co., 335 S.C. 222, 516 S.E.2d 449 (1999), the employer contended that the employee could not raise a public policy exception to the at-will doctrine because of an employment agreement providing for 30-day notices to either party before termination. The Supreme Court disagreed, allowing the employee to proceed with his claim for wrongful termination, finding that a notice provision does not eliminate an individual's ability to sue for wrongful discharge based on a public policy exception.

And in Evans v. Taylor Made Sandwich Co., 337 S.C. 95, 522 S.E.2d 350 (Ct. App. 1999), the Court affirmed a jury verdict in favor of employees who successfully prosecuted claims for unpaid wages under the Wage Payment Act and for wrongful discharge in violation of public policy. Evans also acknowledges that where a statutory remedy for wrongful discharge is available to an employee, the public policy exception is unavailable, citing Stiles v. American Gen. Life Ins. Co., 335 S.C. 222, 516 S.E.2d 449 (1999) (Toal, J., concurring) (citing Dockins v. Ingles Markets, Inc., 306 S.C. 496, 413 S.E.2d 18 (1992) and Epps v. Clarendon County, 304 S.C. 424, 405 S.E.2d 386 (1991)). However, the Evans opinion has very recently been revisited by the state Supreme Court. Barron, supra. The Supreme Court overruled Evans to the extent the Evans court held that a jury may determine whether discharging an employee on certain grounds is a violation of public policy. The determination of what constitutes public policy is a question of law for the courts to decide, not the jury. Barron, supra.

The public policy exception was recently limited by the South Carolina Supreme Court to cases where either an employer requires an employee to violate a law, or the reason for the employee's termination was itself a violation of criminal law, Lawson v. S.C. Department of Corrections, 340 S.C. 346, 532 S.E.2d 259 (2000), and the Court of Appeals refused to extend this exception to cases where an employee is terminated for refusing to comply with a directive which she simply believes would require her to violate the law. Antley v. Shepherd, 340 S.C. 541, 532 S.E.2d 294 (Ct. App. 2000). See also the recent unpublished case of Keeshon v. Eu Clare Coop. Health Centre, Inc.,, 394 Fed Appx. 987 C.A. 4 (S.C.) 2010, where the Court granted employer summary judgment on an employee's wrongful discharge claim. In advancing her claim, the employee argued the public policy exception to the employment at will doctrine. However, the Court determined she was not an at will employee but an employee under a continuing contract, and therefore the public policy exception did not apply.

Another exception to at-will employment can arise when an employee handbook is deemed to give rise to contractual obligations. A comprehensive discussion of this law is contained in Jones v. General Electric Co., 503 S.E.2d 173 (Ct. App. 1998). See also Nolte v. Gibbs Inter., Inc., 335 S.C. 72, 515 S.E.2d 101 (Ct. App. 1999), cert. denied, No. 2887 (filed Sept. 24, 1999) and Williams v. Riedman, 339 S.C. 251, 529 S.E.2d 28 (Ct. App. 2000). Hessenthaler v. Tri-County Sister Help, 365 S.C. 101, 616 S.E. 2d 694 (2005); **Tompkins v. Eckerd d/b/a Rite Aid, 2011 WL 4549173 (D.S.C.).**

A decade of South Carolina jurisprudence saw South Carolina courts steadily broaden the circumstances under which an employee handbook will be treated as an employment contract. This judicial trend presented employers with a dilemma: while handbooks can be an effective communication tool in the workplace – and indeed may be critical in limiting liability under the federal discrimination statutes – their benefits could be lost if they can be construed as contracts. Disgruntled employees have increasingly succeeded in finding some otherwise innocent element of a handbook that they say was "violated," and then suing for a "breach" of that provision. The South Carolina Legislature addressed this problem by promulgating S.C. Code § 41-1-110 (the "Act"), signed by Governor Sanford on March 16, 2004. The Act affirms the at-will nature of employment relationships in South Carolina and provides a specific safe harbor for ensuring that a handbook is not an employment contract:

> It is the public policy of this State that a handbook, personnel manual, policy, procedure, or other document issued by an employer or its agent after June 30, 2004, shall not create an express or implied contract of employment if it is conspicuously disclaimed. For purposes of this section, a disclaimer in a handbook or personnel manual must be in underlined capital letters on the first page of the document and signed by the employee. For all other documents referenced in this section, the disclaimer must be in underlined capital letters on the first page of the document. Whether or not a disclaimer is conspicuous is a question of law.

Compliance with the Act should significantly reduce the risk that written communications inadvertently become binding contracts.

In Angus v. Burroughs & Chapin, 358 S.C. 498, 596 S.E. 2d 67, (S.C. Ct. App. May 12, 2004), the S.C. Court of Appeals did rule that an at-will employee can sue for conspiracy against a third party if that person causes a firing, even if the employee has no claim against his or her former employer. Also, in Katherine Burns v. Universal Health Services, Inc., 603 S.E.2d 605, 361 S.C. 221, (Ct. App. 2004) the South Carolina Court of Appeals reinstated a jury verdict finding an employment contract and a subsequent breach of implied covenant of good faith and fair dealing by the employer. And in Cape v. Greenville County School District, 365 S.C. 316, 618 S.E.2d 881 (S.C. 2005), the South Carolina Supreme Court ruled that, under certain circumstances, a contract for a specific term can also be an at-will contract.

More recently, the Court of Appeals has also held that an employee's status as an at-will employee is not altered by the employer's election to give warnings to other salaried employees. Grant v. Mount Vernon Mills, 370 S.C. 138, 634 S.E. 2d 15 (Ct. App. 2006). And, in Greene v. Quest Diagnostics Clinical Laboratories, Inc., 455 F. Supp. 2d 483 (2006), the South Carolina District Court discussed the public policy exception to the at-will doctrine, and found no violation of public policy because the employee was not being asked to violate a criminal law, nor was the employee being terminated a violation of criminal law. Additionally, the Court found that there was sufficient disclaimer in the employee handbook such that no employment contract existed. Also, see Jaggers v. Odyssey Healthcare, 276 Fed. Appx. 310, C.A.4 (S.C.) 2008, and Barron v. Labor Finders of South Carolina, 393 S.C. 609, 713 S.C. 2d 634 (S.C. 2011), where the South Carolina Supreme Court did not find employee's claims for wrongful termination within the public policy exception to the at-will doctrine because the employee did not pursue any claims under the Payment of Wages Act but stated: "We do not foreclose the possibility that a claim for wrongful termination in violation of public policy may exist when an employee is terminated in retaliation for instituting a claim under the Act." Barron, supra.

B. Elements of Libel Claim

1. ***Basic Elements***. Under South Carolina law, the elements of defamation include: "(1) a false and defamatory statement concerning another; (2) an unprivileged publication to a third party; (3) fault on the part of the publisher; and (4) either actionability of the statement irrespective of special harm or the existence of special harm caused by the publication." Holtzscheiter v. Thomson Newspapers, Inc., 332 S.C. 502, 506 S.E.2d 497, 26 Media L. Rep. 2537, (S.C. 1998) ("Holtzscheiter II"); West v. Todd Morehead, Columbia City Paper, LLC and Paul Blake, 396 S.C. 1, 720 S.E. 2d 495 (Ct. App. 2011), and **Fountain v. First Reliance Bank, 398 S.C. 434, 730 S.E. 2d 305 (S.C. 2012)**. See also Murray v. Holnam, Inc., 344 S.C. 129, 542 S.E.2d 743 (Ct. App. 2001) and Goodwin v. Kennedy, 347 S.C. 30, 552 S.E.2d 319 (S.C. Ct. App., 2001). Holtzscheiter II is an attempt by the South Carolina Supreme Court to clarify the law of defamation and address the confusion created by Holtzscheiter v. Thomson Newspapers, Inc., 306 S.C. 297, 411 S.E.2d 664 (1991) ("Holtzscheiter I"). The court referred to "the need to reconsider many of our defamation cases in light of changing constitutional principles." The court further cautioned the bench and bar that "this area of the law is constantly evolving, and consequently all prior decisions must be read in the context of the current status of the law." Holtzscheiter II must be carefully consulted in any libel or slander action in this jurisdiction, as it not only interprets and clarifies Holtzscheiter I but it also discusses at length the elements of libel and slander under South Carolina law. The volatility of the law is even more pronounced because of Justice Toal's concurring opinion in Holtzscheiter II. See also Fleming v. Rose, 526 S.E.2d 732, 338 S.C. 524 (Ct. App., 2000), rev'd, 350 S.C 488, 567 S.E.2d (S.C. 2002).

2. ***Fault.*** The level of fault that must be shown depends on the plaintiff's private or public status.

a. **Private Figure Plaintiff/Matter of Public Concern.** The Constitution forbids imposing liability for defamation without some showing of fault on the part of the defendant. Normally, this is done by proving the negligence of the defendant in publishing the defamatory statement. Jones v. Sun Pub. Co., 278 S.C. 12, 292 S.E.2d 23 (1982). Fleming v. Rose, 526 S.E.2d 732, 338 S.C. 524 (Ct. App. 2000), rev'd, 350 S.C 488, 567 S.E.2d (S.C. 2002). It was previously thought that South Carolina had adopted a negligence standard. Jones v. Sun Publishing Co., 278 S.C. 12, 292 S.E.2d 23 (1982), cert. denied, 459 U.S. 944 (1983). In Floyd v. WBTW, 2007 WL 4458924 (D.S.C. Dec. 17, 2007), the federal district court questioned whether South Carolina continued to apply the negligence standard for private-figure plaintiffs. The Floyd court suggested that the South Carolina Supreme Court had created confusion on this issue through its statement in Erickson v. Jones Street Publishers, LLC, 368 S.C. 444, 629 S.E.2d 653 (2006), that in cases involving matters of public concern, a private-figure plaintiff is required "to plead and prove common law malice," 629 S.E.2d at 670, since common law malice consists of ill will or reckless indifference toward the rights of the plaintiff. Floyd, supra, at *3 n.3.

b. **Private Figure Plaintiff/Matter of Private Concern.** In Erickson v. Jones Street Publishers, LLC, 368 S.C. 444, 475-76, 629 S.E.2d 653, 670, 34 Media L. Rep. 1610 (2006), the South Carolina Supreme Court held that, in suits by a private-figure plaintiff against a media defendant where the publication involves a matter of public controversy or concern, the common law presumptions of falsity, malice, and damages do not apply, and the plaintiff in such a suit must prove constitutional actual malice by clear and convincing evidence in order to recover punitive damages against a media defendant. It has not been decided whether a plaintiff may recover without proof of fault when the subject of the defamatory statement is not a public figure and the statement concerns a purely private matter. Dun & Bradstreet, Inc. v. Greenmoss Builders, Inc., 472 U.S. 749 (1985). Fleming v. Rose, 338 S.C. 524, 526 S.E.2d 732 (Ct. App. 2000), reversed on other grounds by the State Supreme Court in Fleming v. Rose, 350 S.C. 488, 567 S.E.2d 857 (S.C. 2002).

c. **Public Figure Plaintiff/Matter of Public Concern.** The federal constitutional standard from New York Times v. Sullivan, 376 U.S. 254 (1964) — actual malice — applies in South Carolina. South Carolina courts have issued a number of opinions applying the New York Times standard of liability. See e.g., Peeler v. Spartan Radiocasting, Inc., 478 S.E.2d 282, 25 Media L.Rep. 1310 (S.C. 1996); Miller v. City of West Columbia, 322 S.C. 224, 471 S.E.2d 683 (S.C. 1996); Doe v. Berkeley Publishers, 322 S.C. 307, 471 S.E.2d 731 (S.C. App. 1996); Gause v. Doe, 317 S.C. 39, 451 S.E.2d 408 (Ct. App. 1994);. The first case was Stevens v. Sun Publishing Co., 270 S.C. 65, 240 S.E.2d 812 (1978), cert. denied, 436 U.S. 945, (1979), in which the Court accorded public official status to a former State senator. A public figure plaintiff suing for defamation must prove, by clear and convincing evidence, the defamatory falsehood was made with knowledge of its falsity or reckless disregard for its truth. Miller v. City of West Columbia, 322 S.C. 224, 471 S.E.2d 683 (S.C. 1996); Botchie v. O'Dowd, 315 S.C. 126, 432 S.E.2d 485 (1993) (Botchie II); Holtzscheiter v. Thomson Newspapers, 306 S.C. 297, 411 S.E.2d 664 (1991) (Toal, J., dissenting). In George v. Fabri, 345 S.C. 440, 548 S.E.2d 868 (S.C. 2001), the South Carolina Supreme Court adopted as a matter of state law the holding of Anderson v. Liberty Lobby, Inc., 477 U.S. 242, 106 S. Ct. 2505 (1986), that a standard of "clear and convincing evidence" of actual malice applies to summary judgment motions in defamation actions brought by public officials and public figures. The Court also found that a corporation closely connected with the plaintiff, a candidate for public office, was a public figure in connection with the allegedly defamatory statements.

3. ***Falsity.*** Under the common law, truth is an absolute defense in an action for defamation. Ross v. Columbia Newspapers, Inc., 266 S.C. 75, 80, 221 S.E.2d 770, 772 (1976); Haulbrooks v. Overton, 295 S.C. 380, 383, 368 S.E.2d 676, 678 (Ct. App. 1988); see Reinhardt v. State-Record Co., 235 S.C. 480, 488, 112 S.E.2d 500, 504 (1960). The traditional common-law rule was that, because truth is a defense, the defendant bore the burden of proving the truth of the statement. Smith v. Smith, 194 S.C. 247, 263, 99 S.E.2d 584, 591 (1940). However, the traditional common law rule is no longer good law. It is well established now that the party asserting libel has the obligation to prove falsity, Parker v. Evening Post Publishing Co., 317 S.C. 236, 452 S.E.2d 640 (Ct. App. 1994), at least where the publication concerns a matter of public concern and was published by a media defendant. Erickson v. Jones Street Publishers, LLC, 368 S.C. 444, 466, 629 S.E.2d 653, 665, 34 Media L. Rep. 16109 (2006) (citing Philadelphia Newspapers, Inc. v. Hepps, 475 U.S. 767 (1986)); Boone v. Sunbelt Newspapers, Inc., 347 S.C. 571, 556 S.E.2d 732, 30 Media L. Rep. 1010 (Ct. App. 2001) (citing Hepps, 475 U.S. 767 (1986)).

The standard for judging whether a statement is true, and hence immune from liability, is that of substantial truth. Ross v. Columbia Newspaper, Inc., 266 S.C. 75, 80, 221 S.E.2d 770, 772-73 (1976); Dauterman v. State-Record Co., 249 S.C. 512, 514, 154 S.E.2d 919 (1967) (per curiam); Haulbrooks v. Overton, 295 S.C. 380, 383, 368 S.E.2d 676, 678 (Ct. App. 1988); see Jackson v. Record Pub. Co., 175 S.C. 211, 222, 178 S.E. 833, 837 (1935). Under the standard of substantial truth, "[i]t is not necessary to establish the literal truth of the precise statement made. Slight inaccuracies . . . are immaterial provided that the defamatory charge is true in substance." Restatement (Second) of Torts § 581A, comment f (1977); accord, Anderson v. Stanco Sports Library, Inc., 542 F. 2d 638, 641 (4th Cir. 1976) (applying South Carolina law). See 20 S.C. Juris. Libel & Slander §§ 33-34.

4. ***Defamatory Statement of Fact.*** To be defamatory, the words complained of, on their face or by reason of extrinsic facts, must tend to impeach or injure the reputation of the plaintiff. Capps v. Watts, 271 S.C. 276, 246 S.E.2d 606 (1978). Thus, a statement that injures the reputation of the plaintiff's spouse is not defamatory. Johnson v. Life Ins. Co., 227 S.C. 351, 88 S.E.2d 260 (1955). Likewise, because the essential element is injury to reputation, words that are "undoubtedly impolite, coarse and vulgar" Stokes v. Great Atlantic & Pacific Tea Co., 202 S.C. 24, 28, 23 S.E.2d 823, 825 (1943) or which are abusive and scurrilous, Capps v. Watts, 271 S.C. 276, 246 S.E.2d 606 (1978), but which do not tend to injure reputation, are not defamatory. Mere "vulgar name calling" is not defamatory if it is clearly understood in this sense. Smith v. Phoenix Furniture Co., 339 F. Supp. 969, 971-72 (D.S.C. 1972) (plaintiff called a "bastard" and "son of a bitch"). Nor is it defamatory to charge someone in a hypothetical manner if the charge is conditioned on future events that may never occur. Warner v. Rudnick, 280 S.C. 595, 313 S.E.2d 359 (Ct. App. 1984). Conversely, however, it is defamatory to charge someone with the commission of a crime even if that person could not have committed the crime, because it is the charge which makes the statement actionable, not the possibility of its being true. Flowers v. Zayre Corp., 286 F. Supp. 119, 121 (D.S.C. 1968). See 20 S.C. Juris. Libel & Slander § 15; McBride v. School District of Greenville County, 389 S.C. 546, 698 S.C. 2d 845 (S.C. App. 2010).

In Elder v. Gaffney Ledger, Inc., 333 S.C. 651, 511 S.E. 2d 383 (1999), rev'd on other grounds, Elder v. The Gaffney Ledger, 341 S.C. 108, 533 S.E.2d 899, 28 Media L. Rep. 2295 (S.C. 2000), a newspaper column headline that asked whether drug dealers were bribing the police chief, followed by publication of an alleged anonymous caller's statement that the caller often wondered if the drug dealers were paying the police chief, were defamatory in that they went beyond a mere inquiry and could reasonably be construed to imply that the former police chief was guilty of bribery; the headline question implied an affirmative answer when read in conjunction with the text of the column.

In Goodwin v. Kennedy, 347 S.C. 30, 552 S.E.2d 319 (S.C. Ct. App. 2001), the Court of Appeals rejected the defense that the defendant's characterization of the plaintiff, an African-American assistant principal of a high school, as the "house nigger" of the Caucasian principal, was merely opinion and epithet and therefore not actionable. The Court held that, under the circumstances in which the defamatory statement was uttered, it could be construed as a charge that the plaintiff was unfit in his profession as an assistant principal. The Court also held that an assistant school principal does not qualify as a public official. See also Kwarteng v. Morgan State University, 128 Fed. Appx. 301 (4th Circuit, March 31, 2005).

Any living person may be defamed. A cause of action for defamation is personal, however, and dies with the person defamed. Belcher v. South Carolina Bd. of Corrections, 406 F. Supp. 805, 808 (D.S.C. 1978) (dictum); Carver v. Morrow, 213 S.C. 199, 48 S.E.2d 814 (1948) (per curiam). In Hospital Care Corp. v. Commercial Cas. Ins. Co., 194 S.C. 370, 9 S.E.2d 796 (1940), it was held that a corporation may be defamed if the statement relates to the business of the corporation.

South Carolina recognizes the distinction between defamation per se and per quod. The decision in Holtzscheiter v. Thomson Newspapers, Inc., 332 S.C. 502, 506 S.E.2d 497, 26 Media L. Rep. 2537, (S.C. 1998), endeavors to clarify the law in South Carolina regarding the meaning of the terms per se, per quod, and "actionable per se." The Court stated: "Much confusion arises from defamation law's use of the term "per se" in two different senses. There is the question whether the statement is defamatory per se or per quod. A separate issue is whether the statement is "actionable per se" or not. This issue is one of pleading and proof, and is always a question of law for the court. If a defamation is actionable per se, then under common law principles the law presumes the defendant acted with common law malice and the plaintiff suffered *general* damages. If a defamation is not actionable per se, then at common law the plaintiff must plead and prove common law actual malice and *special* damages. The Court strongly discouraged use of the term "actionable per quod" and suggested the issue be posed as "actionable per se" and "not actionable per se".

The Holtzscheiter II Court also distinguished between defamation in the form of libel, and that in the form of slander when assessing the issue of actionable per se. The court stated "essentially all libel is actionable per se. In contrast to libel, slander is actionable per se only if it charges the plaintiff with one of five types of acts or characteristics: (1) commission of a crime of moral turpitude; (2) contraction of a loathsome disease; (3) adultery; (4) unchastity; or (5) unfitness in one's business or profession. While some states limit actionable per se libel to the same categories of slander which are actionable per se, this is not the law in South Carolina. See, e.g., Hubbard and Felix The South Carolina Law of Torts 402 (1990). To the extent Holtzscheiter I may be read to impose this limitation on actionable per se libel, it is overruled." Holtzscheiter II, 332 S.C. 502, 511, 506 S.E.2d 497, 502.

5. ***Of and Concerning Plaintiff.*** It is well settled that the plaintiff complaining of defamation must prove that he is the person with reference to whom the defamation was made. Neeley v. Winn-Dixie Greenville, Inc., 255 S.C. 301, 308, 178 S.E.2d 662, 666 (1971);Smith v. Phoenix Furniture Co., 339 F. Supp. 969, 972 (D.S.C., 1972); Kendrick v. Citizens and Southern National Bank, 266 S.C. 540, 223 S.E.2d 866 (1976). In Smith, the court held that words spoken to the plaintiff under the mistaken belief that he was the plaintiff's brother, and which were so understood by those who overheard the remarks, did not refer to the plaintiff and therefore were not defamatory as to him. Smith v. Phoenix Furniture Co., 339 F. Supp. 969, 972 (D.S.C., 1972).

The plaintiff's name need not be mentioned. In Nash v. Sharper, 229 S.C. 451, 456, 93 S.E.2d 457, 460 (1956), the Court held "It is sufficient that there is a description of, or reference to, him, by which he may be known." Where the plaintiff was shown in a photograph but never named in an article about organized crime, the court held that was a question of fact as to whether the article referred to the plaintiff. Holmes v. Curtis Pub. Co., 303 F. Supp. 522, 527 (D.S.C. 1969). If it is uncertain whether a statement refers to the plaintiff, the factfinder must decide this issue. Wilhoit v. WCSC, Inc., 293 S.C. 34, 358 S.E.2d 397 (Ct. App. 1987). See 7 S.C. Juris. Libel & Slander § 22.

In Holtzscheiter II the statement in issue was "there simply was no family support to encourage [Shannon] to continue her education". The court held that there was evidence from which a jury could have found that the statement about family support was "of and about" the young woman's mother. 332 S.C. 502, 509, 506 S.E.2d 497, 501.

6. ***Publication.*** Defamation is not actionable without publication. Kendrick v. Citizens & Southern Nat'l Bank, 266 S.C. 450, 223 S.E.2d 866 (1976); Duckworth v. First Nat'l Bank, 254 S.C. 563, 176 S.E.2d 297 (1970); Burris v. Electro Motive Mfg. Co., 247 S.C. 579, 148 S.E.2d 687 (1966); Tucker v. Pure Oil Co., 191 S.C. 60, 3 S.E.2d 4547 (1939). Publication is the communication of a statement and the statement need not be in oral form. Lily v. Belk's Dept. Store, 178 S.C. 278, 182 S.E. 889 (1935). There must be a communication to someone other than the person defamed. Kendrick v. Citizens & Southern Nat'l Bank, 266 S.C. 450, 223 S.E.2d 866 (1976); Duckworth v. First Nat'l Bank, 254 S.C. 563, 176 S.E.2d 297 (1970). The plaintiff may prove publication by establishing the presence of a third person when the defamatory statement was made and close enough to hear it. Duckworth v. First Nat'l Bank, 254 S.C. 563, 176 S.E.2d 297 (1970); Tucker v. Pure Oil Co., 191 S.C. 60, 3 S.E.2d 547 (1939). In Hampton v. Conso Products, Inc., 808 F. Supp. 1227 (D.S.C., 1992) the court held that an employer's actions in forcing an employee to take a medical leave did not constitute a publication. See, more recently, Williams v. Lancaster County School District, 369 S.C.293, 631 S.E.2d 286 (2006).

Johnson v. Dillard's, Inc., 2007 WL 2792232 (D.S.C. 2007) held that an employee's action in having the plaintiff escorted from work by a police officer was "undefamatory" as a matter of law, whereas in Lynch v. Toys 'R' Us-Delaware, Inc., 375 S.C. 604, 654 S.E.2d 541 (Ct. App. 2007), the court held that it was for the jury to decide whether the defendant defamed the plaintiff by having a shopper arrested for suspected shoplifting.

a. **Intracorporate Communication.** Certain communications may not be actionable if they occur between persons with a common interest like a corporate business. For example, an officer of a business entity generally has a qualified privilege as to communications made to other officers in the same entity. Bell v. Bank of Abbeville, 208 S.C. 490, 38 S.E.2d 641 (1946).

In Wright v. Sparrow, 298 S.C. 469, 381 S.E.2d 503 (S.C. Ct. App. 1989), the plaintiff claimed that her former supervisor had defamed her by placing documents critical of her job performance in her personnel file, and then revealing those documents to other employees. The Court of Appeals held that these communications related to plaintiff's job performance were qualifiedly privileged, and affirmed the trial court's grant of summary judgment in favor of the defendant since the defendant failed to establish a genuine issue of fact as to "actual malice" on the part of the supervisor.

As the Fourth Circuit explained in Austin v. Torrington Co., 810 F.2d 416, 423-25 (4th Cir. 1987), cert denied, 108 S. Ct. 489 (1987), under South Carolina law, there is a qualified privilege for communications between persons with a serious common interest; employment performance constitutes such an interest. And where that qualified privilege exists (as it does here), the burden falls on the plaintiff to prove "actual malice." This showing of actual malice requires both "ill will and consciousness of wrongdoing," and a mere inference of malice is insufficient. 810 F.2d at 425.

Other South Carolina cases have reached the same result by concluding that communications made between various company employees in the ordinary course of their business are not publications for defamation purposes. See Anderson v. Southern R. Co., 224 S.C. 65, 77 S.E.2d 350 (1953) (holding as a matter of law that no publication of alleged defamatory statements occurred when various company managers discussed in private meeting their suspicions of embezzlement by an employee); Watson v. Wannamaker, 216 S.C. 295, 57 S.E.2d 477 (1950) (holding as a matter of law that dictation of defamatory comments to secretary is not a publication of the comments to a third party); Rodgers v. Wise, 193 S.C. 5, 7 S.E.2d 517 (1940) (same).

b. **Compelled Self-Publication.** No South Carolina cases directly discuss this point. See, however, Murray v. Holnam, Inc., 344 S.C. 129, 542 S.E.2d 743 (Ct. App. 2000), wherein no self-publication was found when Plaintiff employee merely reported to his superiors about events and accusations surrounding the alleged defamatory statement.

c. **Republication.** In Taub v. McClatchy Newspapers, Inc., 504 F. Supp. 2d 74, (D.S.C. 2007), the federal District Court held that a newspaper could be liable for posting on its website, via an automatic feed, a defamatory article circulated by the Associated Press wire service. The court recognized the wire service defense, but held that it did not apply in this case because the article originated from the defendant newspaper itself: "[T]his case does not present the typical scenario whereby a newspaper publishes an article from a reputable wire service or news agency that the wire service or news agency picked up from a different source. Instead, the article at issue here originated from a *Gazette* article, and the *Gazette* then republished on its website the AP's altered version of its original article. Therefore, the *Gazette* at least had some reason to be aware of the article's inaccuracies." Id. at *5; see also Jennings v. Southern Railway Co., 156 S.C. 92, 152 S.E. 821 (1930) (each separate publication of libel constitutes a separate cause of action); Johnson v. Great Atlantic and Pacific Tea Co., 25 F. Supp. 449 (E.D.S.C., 1939)(same). In Smith v. Dunlap Tire & Rubber Co., 186 S.C. 456, 196 S.E. 174 (1938), the court held that the repetition of a slanderous statement by the original publisher, in response to a question made in good faith by the person slandered, was actionable.

7. ***Statements versus Conduct.*** Conduct alone can give rise to defamation. See I.B.6, supra. In Tyler v. Macks Stores of South Carolina, Inc., 275 S.C. 456, 272 S.E.2d 633 (1980), the plaintiff was fired immediately after taking a polygraph test. He filed suit alleging that the defendant's conduct gave others the impression that he had been terminated for wrongful conduct. The defendant demurred to the plaintiff's complaint, alleging that the facts set out in the complaint did not support a publication. The trial court denied the defendant's demurrer. The supreme court affirmed the trial court's decision based on the general rule that "a defamatory insinuation may be made by actions or conduct as well as by word."

In Lynch v. Toys 'R' Us-Delaware, Inc., 375 S.C. 604, 654 S.E.2d 541 (Ct. App. 2007), the court held that it was for the jury to decide whether the defendant defamed the plaintiff by having a shopper arrested for suspected shoplifting. Johnson v. Dillard's, Inc., 2007 WL 2792232 (D.S.C. Sept. 24, 2007), however, held that an employee's action in having the plaintiff escorted from work by a police officer was "undefamatory" as a matter of law.

8. ***Damages.*** Recovery is allowed for both actual and punitive damages as in other civil actions. Rogers v. Florence Printing Co., 233 S.C. 567, 106 S.E.2d 258 (1968). For a recovery of actual damages in a libel action by a private individual the degree of proof is by a preponderance of the evidence. DeLoach v. Beaufort Gazette, 281 S.C. 484, 316 S.E.2d 139 (1984), cert. denied, 469 U.S. 981 (1984). Actual damages may be requested in a particular amount. See Rules 8 (a), S.C.R.C.P. and F.R.C.P. In an action per se, special damages need not be pled or proved to recover; Holtzscheiter v. Thomson Newspapers, 306 S.C. 297, 411 S.E.2d 664 (1991); but in a per quod situation, special damages must be alleged and proved. Capps v. Watts, 271 S.C. 276, 246 S.E.2d 606 (1978); Drakeford v. Dixie Home Stores, 233 S.C. 519, 105 S.E.2d 711 (1959). Hurt feelings do not suffice as proof of special damage; special damage must consist of some provable material loss to the plaintiff as a result of the injury to his reputation, Wardlaw v. Peck, 282 S.C. 199, 318 S.E.2d 270 (Ct. App. 1984); however, humiliation and wounded feelings are recoverable damages. Smith v. Smith, 194 S.C. 247, 9 S.E.2d 584 (1940). The award of actual damages rests in the discretion of the trial judge. Miller v. City of West Columbia, 322 S.C. 224, 471 S.E.2d 683 (S.C. 1996).

a. **Presumed Damages and Libel Per Se.** Under the common law, in a slander per se action the plaintiff is not required to prove general damages as they are presumed as a matter of law. Constant v. Spartanburg Steel Products, Inc., 339 F. Supp. 969 (D.S.C., 1972). However, in Erickson v. Jones Street Publishers, LLC, 368 S.C. 444,

475-76, 629 S.E.2d 653, 670, 34 Media L. Rep. 1610 (2006), the South Carolina Supreme Court held that, in suits by a private-figure plaintiff against a media defendant where the publication involves a matter of public controversy or concern, the common law presumptions of falsity, malice, and damages do not apply.

(1) **Employment-Related Criticism.** No South Carolina cases discuss this issue.

(2) **Single Instance Rule.** Although its opinion is not clear, the South Carolina Court of Appeals may have obliquely rejected the rule in Moosally v. W.W. Norton & Co, 358 S.C. 320, 594 S.E.2d 878 (Ct. App. 2004). Reversing the dismissal of a book publisher under the South Carolina "Door-Closing Statute," S.C. Code 15-5-150 (1977), the Court of Appeals held that "[t]he dissemination of the book in South Carolina is a continuing libel in each and every instance [of publication]. The tort of libel occurs wherever the offending material is circulated." Id. at 339, 594 S.E.2d at 888. Quoting these statements from Moosally, the federal District Court concluded in Taub v. McClatchy Newspapers, Inc., 504 F. Supp. 2d 74 (D.S.C. 2007), that South Carolina state law does not follow the single publication rule. The District Court criticized the reasoning of the Moosally opinion, see Taub, 504 F. Supp. 2d at 79, but felt bound to follow it under the Erie doctrine as a matter of state law in the diversity case before the District Court. As a result, the District Court held that an article posted on a newspaper's website continued to be published until it was removed from the website. Id. at 80.

b. **Punitive Damages.** For a private individual to recover punitive damages in a libel action, actual malice must be proved by clear and convincing evidence. Erickson v. Jones Street Publishers, LLC, 368 S.C. 444, 475 -76, 629 S.E.2d 653, 670, 34 Media L. Rep. 1610 (2006); Peeler v. Spartan Radiocasting, Inc., 324 S.C. 261, 478 S.E.2d 282, 25 Media L. Rep. 1310 (S.C. 1996); DeLoach v. Beaufort Gazette, 281 S.C. 484, 316 S.E.2d 139 (1984), cert. denied, 469 U.S. 981 (1984). This is a judicial recognition of the Gertz punitive damages doctrine. See also S.C. Code Ann., § 15-33-135 (Law. Co-op. Supp. 1996), which requires punitive damages to generally be proved by clear and convincing evidence for causes of action arising or accruing on or after April 5, 1988. Punitive damages must be requested in general terms only and not for a stated sum. See Rule 8(a), S.C.R.C.P. Punitive damages may be requested for a sum certain in Federal Court. See Rule 8(a), F.R.C.P. The trial judge must conduct a post-trial review of an award of punitive damages, pursuant to Gamble v. Stevenson, 305 S.C. 104, 306 S.E.2d 350 (1991), to determine if the award withstands constitutional challenge. Weir v. Citicorp National Services, Inc., 312 S.C. 511, 435 S.E.2d 864 (1963). An award of punitive damages does not violate public policy even though the award relates to activities undertaken in furtherance of investigating allegations of sexual harassment. Miller v. City of West Columbia, 322 S.C. 224, 471 S.E.2d 683 (S.C. 1996).

II. PRIVILEGES AND DEFENSES

A. Scope of Privileges

1. ***Absolute Privilege.*** There is an absolute privilege against liability for defamatory statements in all executive, legislative and judicial proceedings. Johnston v. Independent Life & Acci. Ins. Co., 94 F. Supp. 959, 961-62 (E.D.S.C. 1951); Fulton v. Atlantic C.L.R. Co., 220 S.C. 287, 67 S.E.2d 425 (1951); Restatement (Second) of Torts § 591 (1977). In Wright v. Sparrow, 298 S.C. 469, 381 S.E.2d 503 (Ct. App. 1989), the court held there was no absolute privilege applicable to a discussion by an executive official concerning a government employee with the employee's agency. The opinion implies that only legislative and judicial officers enjoy an absolute privilege. See id. at 474, 381 S.E.2d at 505. In Eubanks v. Smith, 292 S.C. 57, 354 S.E.2d 898 (1987), the court held that there was no absolute privilege for remarks made by an executive official in press releases concerning a criminal investigation by his department.

2. ***Qualified Privileges.*** A qualified privilege exists if the defendant correctly or reasonably believes some important interest of his own or of a third party is threatened. **Fountain v. First Reliance Bank, 398 S.C. 434, 730 S.E. 2d 305 (S.C. 2012);** Callum v. Dun & Bradstreet, Inc., 228 S.C. 384, 90 S.E.2d 370 (1955). The privilege only exists when the publication has occurred in a proper manner and to proper parties only. Swinton Creek Nursery v. Edisto Farm Credit, 326 S.C. 426, 483 S.E.2d 789 (S.C. App. 1997); Abofreka v. Alston Tobacco Co., 288 S.C. 122, 341 S.E.2d 622 (1986). Essential elements are good faith, an interest to be upheld, a statement relative in its scope to this purpose, a proper occasion, and publication in a proper manner and to proper parties only. Swinton Creek Nursery v. Edisto Farm Credit, 326 S.C. 426, 483 S.E.2d 789 (S.C. Ann. 1997); Manley v. Manley, 291 S.C. 325, 353 S.E.2d 312 (Ct. App. 1987). This privilege does not prevent liability for statements made with actual malice. Swinton Creek Nursery v. Edisto Farm Credit, 326 S.C. 426, 483 S.E.2d 789 (S.C. App. 1997); Eubanks v. Smith, 292 S.C. 57, 354 S.E.2d 898 (1987). An inference of malice is insufficient, however, where statements are found to be qualifiedly privileged. Austin v. Torrington Co., 810 F.2d 416 (4th Cir. 1987). In Wright v. Sparrow, 298 S.C. 469, 381 S.E.2d 503 (S.C. Ct. App. 1989), the plaintiff claimed that her former supervisor had defamed her by placing documents critical of her job performance in her personnel file, and then revealing those documents to other employees. The Court of Appeals held that these communications related to plaintiff's job performance were qualifiedly privileged, and affirmed the trial court's grant of summary judgment in favor of the defendant since the defendant failed to establish a genuine issue of act as to "actual malice" on the part of the supervisor. As the Fourth Circuit explained in Austin v. Torrington Co., 810 F.2d 416, 423-25 (4th Cir. 1987), cert. denied, 108 S. Ct. 489, under South Carolina law, there

is a qualified privilege for communications between persons with a serious common interest; employment performance constitutes such an interest. And where that qualified privilege exists (as it does here), the burden falls on the plaintiff to prove "actual malice." This showing of actual malice requires both "ill will and consciousness of wrongdoing," and a mere inference of malice is insufficient. 810 F.2d at 425.

For particularly good discussions of qualified privilege, see True v. Southern Railway Co., 159 S.C., 454, 157 S.E. 618, (S.C. 1931); Conwell v. Spur Oil Co., 240 S.C. 170, 125 S.E.2d 270 (1962), and Lesesne v. Willingham, 83 F. Supp. 918 (E.D.S.C. 1949). See also 7 S.C. Juris Libel & Slander § 54-58; Swinton Creek Nursery v. Edisto Farm Credit, 326 S.C. 426, 483 S.E.2d 789 (S.C. App. 1997); 334 S.C. 469, 514 S.E.2d 126 (S.C. 1999), and Murray v. Holnam, Inc., 344 S.C. 129, 542 S.E.2d 743 (Ct. App. 2000). "Factual inquiries, such as whether the defendants acted in good faith in making the statement, whether the scope of the statement was properly limited in its scope, and whether the statement was sent only to the proper parties, are generally left in the hands of the jury to determine whether the privilege was bused." Murray, 542 S.E.2d at 749. See also Bell v. Evening Post Publishing Co., 318 S.C. 558, 459 S.E.2d 315 (S.C. App., 1995).

The fair report qualified privilege was also extensively discussed in West v. Todd Morehead, Columbia City Paper, LLC and Paul Blake, 396 S.C. 1, 720 S.E. 2d 495 (Ct. App. 2011), which discussed reporting on contents of public files and judicial proceedings. Conflicting evidence was presented, and the Court concluded that the jury was to determine whether or not the privilege was available.

a. **Common Interest.** A qualified privilege attaches to statements made by one person to another on a subject of common interest. Bell v. Bank of Abbeville, 208 S.C. 490, 38 S.E.2d 641 (1946); Manley v. Manley, 291 S.C. 325, 353 S.E.2d 312 (Ct. App. 1987).

b. **Duty.** When a communication is published in the discharge of a legal, social or moral duty, it is qualifiedly privileged. Montgomery Ward & Co. v. Watson, 55 F.2d 184 (4th Cir., 1932).

c. **Criticism of Public Employee.** No South Carolina cases discuss this point.

d. **Limitation on Qualified Privileges.** A qualified privilege is defeated by a showing that defendants acted with actual malice. Eubanks v. Smith, 292 S.C. 57, 354 S.E.2d 898 (1987). A defendant may also lose the protections of qualified privilege through excessive publication or abuse, Abofreka v. Alston Tobacco Co., 288 S.C. 122, 341 S.E.2d 622 (1986); by publishing the statement to persons other than those within the privilege, Bell v. Bank of Abbeville, 208 S.C. 490, 38 S.E.2d 641 (1946); or by exceeding the requirement of the occasion involved, Prentiss v. Nationwide Mutual Insurance Co., 256 S.C. 141, 181 S.E.2d 325 (1971).

(1) **Constitutional or Actual Malice.** Constitutional malice means knowledge of falsity or reckless disregard of the truth. Scott v. McCain, 272 S.C. 198, 201, 250 S.E.2d 118, 120 (1978). Fleming v. Rose, 338 S.C. 524, 526 S.E.2d 732 (Ct. App., 2000), rev'd, 350 S.C 488, 567 S.E.2d (S.C. 2002). When required by the First Amendment to prove actual malice, one must "demonstrate with clear and convincing evidence that the defendant realized that the statement was false or that he subjectively entertained serious doubt about the truth of his statement." Bose Corp. v. Consumers Union of United States, Inc., 466 U.S. 485, 511 n.30 (1984). Peeler v. Spartanburg Herald-Journal Div. of New York Times Co., 681 F. Supp. 1144, 1147 (D.S.C. 1988). A good faith belief in the truth of the statement precludes malice in the constitutional sense. New York Times Co. v. Sullivan, 376 U.S. 254, 286 (1964).

Recklessness under the constitutional malice standard is measured by evidence that the defendant actually knew of falsity or had serious doubts as to the truth of the publication. St. Amant v. Thompson, 390 U.S. 727, 731 (1968). Plaintiff must proffer clear and convincing evidence that defendant published the defamatory statement with a "high degree of awareness of probable falsity." Beckley Newspapers Corp. v. Hanks, 389 U.S. 81, 84 (1967) (per curiam). For constitutional actual malice, a plaintiff may prove the defendant's state of mind through circumstantial evidence, including such factors as departure from professional standards or motive; while courts should not place too much reliance on such factors, it cannot be said that evidence concerning motive or care never bears any relation to the actual malice inquiry. Elder v. Gaffney Ledger, Inc., 333 S.C. 651, 511 S.E.2d 383 (Ct. App. 1999). However, the South Carolina Supreme Court reversed the Court of Appeals, finding that there was evidence of malice and held that: (1) the editor's failure to investigate or verify information left by anonymous caller did not establish that newspaper acted with actual malice in publishing editorial column; (2) the editor's failure to introduce into evidence tape of anonymous phone call that was basis for editorial column did not create an inference of malice; (3) the fact that the editor had been rude to police chief's wife was not relevant to question of whether editorial was published with actual malice; and (4) the editor's alleged ill will toward police chief did not demonstrate that editor deliberately published editorial column with a high degree of awareness of its probable falsity. Elder v. The Gaffney Ledger, 341 S.C. 108, 533 S.E.2d 899, 28 Media L. Rep. 2295 (S.C. 2000).

In Fleming v. Rose, the South Carolina Supreme Court rendered a decision recently that is significant, not for making new law in South Carolina, but for reversing a highly suspect decision by the South Carolina Court of Appeals. Fleming v. Rose, 350 S.C 488, 567 S.E.2d 857 (S.C. 2002). The case arose from a press release concerning an internal investigation by the South Carolina Department of Public Safety into allegations of a cover-up of facts concerning an automobile accident in which several highway patrol troopers were involved. There was evidence that the vehicle in which the troopers were riding was traveling at a high rate of speed and that there were open containers of alcohol in that vehicle. After accusations were made that this evidence had been covered up by the state agency, investigators for the Department of Public Safety looked into the matter and concluded that the plaintiff, a trooper who was not in the accident, had learned of the evidence of speeding but failed to report it to his supervisor. In the press release at issue in the case, the defendant (the director of the Department of Public Safety) stated that the plaintiff "learned key details about the accident [but] did not report this information to his superiors." The trial court granted summary judgment, ruling the plaintiff was a public figure and that the publication was not made with actual malice. The Court of Appeals, relying on the usual standards for summary judgment motions and not even mentioning Anderson v Liberty Lobby, Inc., 417 U.S. 242 (1986), held that defendant's approval of the press release without any knowledge of whether it was true or false constituted sufficient evidence of "actual malice" to withstand summary judgment. Fleming v. Rose, 338 S.C. 524, 526 S.E.2d 732 (Ct. App. 2000). The Supreme Court reversed, holding that a public-figure plaintiff must demonstrate actual malice with "clear and convincing proof" to defeat a motion for summary judgment. The Supreme Court reviewed the record in detail and found no proof of knowledge of falsity or reckless disregard of the truth, but to the contrary showed that the defendant "relied on the results and conclusions of an investigation conducted by two highly respect investigators." Because there was no reason for the defendant to doubt the results of the investigation, actual malice could not be predicted on the defendant's failure to conduct his own investigation. Fleming, 350 S.C. at 497, 567 S.E.2d at 861.

In George v. Fabri, 345 S.C. 440, 548 S.E.2d 868 (S.C. 2001), the South Carolina Supreme Court adopted as a matter of state law the holding of Anderson v. Liberty Lobby, Inc., 477 U.S. 242, 106 S. Ct. 2505 (1986), that a standard of "clear and convincing evidence" of actual malice applies to summary judgment motions in defamation actions brought by public officials and public figures. Likewise, the State Supreme Court reaffirmed that "actual malice is governed by a subjective standard which tests the defendant's good faith belief in the truth of her statements. There must be sufficient evidence to conclude either that the defendant made the statements with a 'high degree of awareness of ¼ probable falsity,' or that the defendant 'in fact entertained serious doubts as to the truth of his publication.'" George, 345 S.C. at 456, 548 S.E.2d at 876. However, failure to investigate before publishing a defamatory statement does not constitute malice, unless "there are obvious reasons to doubt the veracity of the statement or informant." George, 345 S.C. at 459, 548 S.E.2d at 878. For this reason, the Supreme Court rejected the argument that there was sufficient proof of malice in defendant's admission that she did not "know" that what she had said was true.

More recently, in Metts v. Mims, 370 S.C. 529, 635 S.E.2d 640 (Ct. App. 2006), the Court of Appeals held that "simply because the reporter was aware that [the source of the defamatory statement] and [the plaintiff's] supervisor were political adversaries does not mean the reporter had obvious reasons to doubt [the source's] credibility as a source of information." Id. at 537, 635 S.E.2d at 644. Accordingly, the plaintiff failed to prove actual malice. The Supreme Court reversed, however, on the ground that information known to the reporter that contradicted the source's statements created a jury issue as to whether there was clear and convincing evidence of malice. Metts v. Mims, 384 S.C. 491, 501-02, 682 S.E.2d 813, 819, 37 Media L. Rep. 2275 (2009). See also West v. Todd Morehead, Columbia City Paper, LLC and Paul Blake, 396 S.C. 1, 720 S.E. 2d 495 (Ct. App. 2011).

(2) **Common Law Malice.** Under common law, malice is an element of defamation. Scott v. McCain, 272 S.C. 198, 201, 250 S.E.2d 118, 120 (1978). Malice, in the common law sense, means ill will, a design or purpose by defendant to carelessly and wantonly injure plaintiff, perhaps such recklessness as to represent conscious indifference toward plaintiff's rights. Jones v. Garner, 250 S.C. 479, 488, 158 S.E.2d 909, 914 (1968); Middlebrooks v. Curtis Pub. Co., 281 F. Supp. 1, 7 (D.S.C., 1968), aff'd, 413 F.2d 141 (4th Cir. 1969); Eubanks v. Smith, 292 S.C. 57, 63, 354 S.E.2d 898, 902 (1987); Duncan v. Record Pub. Co., 145 S.C. 196, 276, 143 S.E. 31, 56 (1927). Constant v. Spartanburg Steel Products, Inc., 316 S.C. 86, 447 S.E.2d 194 (S.C. 1994). See, recently, West v. Todd Morehead, Columbia City Paper, LLC and Paul Blake, 396 S.C. 1, 720 S.E. 2d 495 (Ct. App. 2011).

(3) **Other Limitations on Qualified Privileges.** None.

e. **Question of Fact or Law.** If the facts supporting a claim of privilege are in dispute, the question whether a statement is privileged would be for the jury. Swinton Creek Nursery v. Edisto Farm Credit, ACA, 334 S.C. 469, 514 S.E.2d 126 (S.C. 1999); Murray v. Holnam, Inc., 344 S.C. 129, 542 S.E.2d 743 (Ct. App. 2000); Goodwin v. Kennedy, 347 S.C. 30, 552 S.E.2d 319 (S.C. Ct. App. 2001); Anderson v. The Augusta Chronicle, 365 S.C. 589, 619 S.E.2d 428 (S.C. 2005); West v. Todd Morehead, Columbia City Paper, LLC and Paul Blake, 396 S.C. 1, 720 S.E. 2d 495 (Ct. App. 2011).

f. **Burden of Proof.** A qualified privilege is an affirmative defense that must be pleaded by the defendant. Sierra v. Skelton, 307 S.C. 217, 414 S.E.2d 169 (Ct. App. 1991); S.C.R.C.P. Rule 8(c); Rivers v. Florence Printing Co., 141 S.C. 364, 139 S.E. 781 (1927).

B. Standard Libel Defenses

1. ***Truth.*** Substantial truth of the matters published is a valid and complete defense to a defamation action. Weir v. Citicorp National Services, Inc., 312 S.C. 511, 435, S.E.2d 864 (1993); Ross v. Columbia Newspapers, Inc., 266 S.C. 75, 221 S.E.2d 770 (1976); Anderson v. Stanco Sports Library, Inc., 542 F.2d 638 (4th Cir. 1976). See also Parker v. Evening Post Publishing Co., 317 S.C. 236, 452 S.E.2d 640 (Ct. App. 1994); Wesay Financial Corp. v. Lingefelt, 316 S.C. 442, 450 S.E.2d 580 (Ct. App. 1994); Holtzscheiter v. Thomson Newspapers, 306 S.C. 297, 411 S.E.2d 664 (1991) (Toal, J. dissenting); Dauterman v. State Record Co., 249 S.C. 512, 154 S.E.2d 919 (1967). Fleming v. Rose, 338 S.C. 524, 526 S.E.2d 732 (Ct. App., 2000), rev'd, 350 S.C 488, 567 S.E.2d 857 (S.C. 2002). **Fountain v. First Reliance Bank, 398 S.C. 434, 730 S.E. 2d 305 (S.C. 2012).**

In Parrish v. Allison, 376 S.C. 308, 656 S.E.2d 382 (Ct. App. 2007), the court reaffirmed the common-law rule that truth is an affirmative defense, and held that the defendant had waived the defense by failing to plead it in his Answer. This holding is questionable in light of the well established rule that the plaintiff bears the burden of proving falsity.

2. ***Opinion.*** The Supreme Court of South Carolina has long recognized a constitutional basis for the privilege of fair comment. As early as 1921, anticipating the United States Supreme Court by forty years, the South Carolina Supreme Court held that "[f]air and just criticism of a juror's work in the discharge of his duty is in the interest of the administrator of justice and a sound public policy and when such criticism is fair and just, there is no defamation." Oliveros v. Henderson, 116 S.C. 77, 83, 106 S.E. 855, 858 (1921). The court's holding was based in part on the proposition that "freedom of speech is the necessary attribute of every free government." Id. at 84, 106 S.E. at 858.

In Goodwin v. Kennedy, 347 S.C. 30, 552 S.E.2d 319 (Ct. App. 2001), the Court of Appeals rejected the defense that the defendant's characterization of the plaintiff, an African-American assistant principal of a high school, as the "house nigger" of the white principal, was merely opinion and epithet and therefore not actionable. The Court held that, under the circumstances in which the defamatory statement was uttered, it could be construed as a charge that the plaintiff was unfit in his profession as an assistant principal. The Court ruled that it was not error for the trial court to reject the defendant's requested jury instruction that "'the mere expression of opinion is not slander' ... because [defendant's] request to charge appears to exempt all opinion as non-defamatory comment without qualification, we find no error in the [trial] court's decision to deny [defendant's] proposed jury charge." Id., 347 S.C. at 41, 552 S.E.2d at 325. Similarly, in Anderson v. Augusta Chronicle, 355 S.C. 461, 585 S.E.2d 506, 31 Media L. Rep. 1393 (S.C. App. 2003), aff'd on other grounds, 365 S.C. 589, 619 S.E.2d 428, 34 Media L. Rep. 1022 (2006), the Court of Appeals found that statements that the plaintiff had been "exposed as a liar" and was a "proven prevaricator" were not protected expressions of opinion, notwithstanding the fact that they were made in an editorial. One doctor's opinions concerning another doctor's treatment of several accident victims was held to be protected since the opinions could not reasonably be interpreted as stating actual facts. Woodward v. Weiss, 932 F. Supp. 723 (D.S.C. 1996). See Faltas v. State Newspaper, 928 F. Supp. 637 (D.S.C. 1996), aff'd, 155 F.3d 557 (4th Cir. 1998) (Table) (author of an opinion piece in newspaper's editorial section was a "limited purpose public figure" when addressing the author's defamation claim against the newspaper for subsequently printing various "letters to the editor" which were in response to opinion piece. The author had alleged the "letter to the editor" had defamed her and the newspaper had promoted the defamation by publishing the letters).

The current standard in South Carolina for distinguishing between statements of fact and statements of opinion is a multi-factor analysis comprising the following considerations: (a) whether the statement can be characterized as true or false; (b) whether the choice of words indicate that the statement is fact or opinion; (c) whether the context of the statement indicates that it is opinion (for example, the editorial page of a newspaper); and (d) the broader social context in which the statement fits. Sunshine Sportswear & Electronics, Inc. v. WSOC Television, Inc., 738 F. Supp. 1499, 1506 (D.S.C. 1989). See 7 S.C. Juris. Libel & Slander § 38.

3. ***Consent.*** A person may not sue for a defamatory statement that he has authorized, consented to, solicited or induced. Smith v. Dunlap Tire and Rubber Co., 186 S.C. 456, 196 S.E. 174 (1938); Gathers v. Harris Teeter Supermarket, Inc., 282 S.C. 220, 317 S.E.2d 748 (Ct. App. 1984).

4. ***Mitigation.*** Several South Carolina cases speak to the availability of mitigation of damages. For example,

> "Matters may be considered in mitigation of damages which do not amount to justification," Johnston v. Life & Casualty Ins. Co., 192 S.C. 518, 525, 7 S.E.2d 463, 465 (1940).

"Retraction of a libel is matter to be considered in mitigation." Rogers v. Florence Printing Co., 233 S.C. 567, 579, 106 S.E.2d 258, 263 (1958).

By way of mitigation, a defendant may introduce evidence that his actions were provoked by the plaintiff, if "not only the connection between the publications be manifest, but also that the provocation is so recent as to induce a fair presumption that the injury complained of was inflicted during the continuance of feelings and passions excited by the provocation. A distinct and independent libel published by the defendant is not mitigation." McLeod v. American Pub. Co., 126 S.C. 363, 120 S.E. 70 (1923).

Evidence of the character of a person claiming defamation may be tendered in mitigation. McLeod v. American Pub. Co., 126 S.C. 363, 120 S.E. 70 (1923).

III. RECURRING FACT PATTERNS

A. Statements in Personnel File

Employers have a qualified privilege, based on common interest, to make statements in a personnel file. Wright v. Sparrow, 298 S.C. 469, 381 S.E.2d 503 (Ct. App. 1989).

B. Performance Evaluations

See III.A, supra.

C. References

An employer's statements concerning an employee to another employer are protected by a qualified privilege. Austin v. Torrington Company, 810 F.2d 416 (4th Circuit, 1987). S.C. Code Ann. § 41-1-65 grants employers immunity from civil liability for the disclosure of an employee's or former employee's dates of employment, pay level, and wage history to a prospective employer. An employer who responds in writing to a written request concerning a current employee or former employee from a prospective employer of that employee shall be immune from civil liability for disclosure of the following information to which an employee or former employee may have access: (1) written employee evaluations; (2) official personnel notices that formally record the reasons for separation; (3) whether the employee was voluntarily or involuntarily released from service and the reason for the separation; and (4) information about job performance. This protection and immunity shall not apply where an employer knowingly or recklessly releases or discloses false information.

D. Intracorporate Communication

See I.B.6.a, supra. Generally, intracorporate communications are protected by a qualified privilege. Bell v. Bank of Abbeville, 211 S.C. 167, 44 S.E.2d 328 (1947).

E. Statements to Government Regulators

No South Carolina cases discuss this point.

F. Reports to Auditors and Insurers

No South Carolina cases discuss this point.

G. Vicarious Liability of Employers for Statements Made by Employees

No South Carolina cases discuss this point.

1. ***Scope of Employment.*** No cases.

    a. ***Blogging.*** No cases.

2. ***Damages.*** No cases.

H. Internal Investigations

No South Carolina cases discuss this point.

IV. OTHER ACTIONS BASED ON STATEMENTS

A. Negligent Hiring, Retention, and Supervision

In Doe by Doe v. Greenville Hospital System, 323 S.C. 33, 448 S.E.2d 564 (Ct. App. 1994), the jury returned a verdict in a negligent hiring claim, where a male employee whom the employer had hired despite a prior record of sexual incident, sexually assaulted plaintiff at work. See also Doe by Roe v. Orangeburg County School Dist. No. 2, 329 S.C. 221, 495 S.E.2d 230, 123 Ed. Law Rep. 368 (Ct. App. 1998). In Sabb v. South Carolina State University, 350 S.C. 416, 567 S.E.2d 231 (S. Ct., 2002) the South Carolina Supreme Court noted that the exclusivity provision of the Workers' Compensation Act may provide a defense for injuries sustained by an employee asserting a negligent hiring or supervision claim, but that such a defense can be waived. Sabb also discusses an employer's responsibilities and duties to the employee on receiving grievances from an employee. See also Longshore v. Saber Security Services and Marc A. Shafer, 365 S.C. 554, 619 S.E.2d 5 (S.C. Ct. Appeals 2005) and Doe v. ATC, Inc., 367 S.C. 199, 624 S.E. 2d 447 (Ct. App. 2005). In Doe the Court of Appeals held that a single incident of an inappropriate sexual advance to a fellow employee did not necessarily trigger liability, although it appears the employee's theory of liability was flawed. The Court also explored distinctions between claims for negligent retention and negligent supervision. Doe, *supra*. See, also, Kirk v. Mumford, Inc., Unpublished Opinion No. 2006 UP 179 (S.C. Ct. Appeals, April 4, 2006).

In James v. Kelly Trucking, 377 S.C. 628, 661 S.E.2d 329 (2008), the Supreme Court concluded that South Carolina law does not prohibit a plaintiff from pursuing a negligent hiring, training, supervision or entrustment claim once *respondeat superior* liability has been admitted.

B. Intentional Infliction of Emotional Distress

1. ***Elements.*** South Carolina recognized the tort of intentional infliction of emotional distress or "outrage" in the case of Ford v. Hutson, 276 S.C. 157, 276 S.E.2d 776 (1981), by upholding a verdict in favor of a real estate agent who, after years of harassment by a disappointed purchaser, suffered serious emotional and physical injuries. In order to recover for the intentional infliction of emotional distress, a plaintiff must establish that "(1) the defendant intentionally or recklessly inflicted severe emotional digress, or was certain or substantially certain that such distress would result from his conduct; (2) the conduct was so extreme and outrageous as to exceed all possible bounds of decency and must be regarded as atrocious and utterly intolerable in a civilized community; (3) the actions of the defendant caused the plaintiff's emotional distress; and (4) the emotional distress suffered by the plaintiff was so severe that no reasonable person could be expected to endure it." Upchurch v. New York Times, 314 S.C. 531, 431 S.E.2d 558 (1993). Fleming v. Rose, 338 S.C. 524, 526 S.E.2d 732, (Ct. App., 2000), rev'd, 350 S.C 488, 567 S.E.2d 857 (S.C. 2002).

See Shipman v. Glenn, 314 S.C. 327, 443 S.E.2d 921 (S.C. Ct. App. 1994) (employer who verbally abused and ridiculed speech impediment of employee with cerebral palsy, while "callous and offensive," was not guilty of outrage); Barber v. Whirlpool Corp., 34 F.3d 1268, 1276 (4th Cir. 1994) (verbal abuse of employee by former marine officer, while "despicable," did not constitute outrage); Gattison v. South Carolina State College, 318 S.C. 148, 151-156, 456 S.E.2d 414, 416-19 (Ct. App. 1995) (employee who was deprived of secretarial support, given inferior office, humiliated at meetings, and taunted about being fired did not make out a claim of outrage); Corder v. Champion Road Mach. Int'l Corp., 283 S.C. 520, 523, 324 S.E.2d 79, 81 (Ct. App. 1984) (retaliatory discharge, which may be reprehensible conduct, insufficient to state a claim for outrage), cert. denied, 286 S.C. 126, 332 S.E.2d 533 (1985) superceded by statute in Hines v. United Parcel Service, Inc., 736 F. Supp. 675 (1990); Satterfield v. Lockheed Missiles & Space Co., 617 F. Supp. 1359, 1365-69 (D.S.C. 1985) (plaintiff terminated over faulty urinalysis test, whose status was kept in doubt for two weeks, did not make out an outrage claim); Frazier v. Badger, Unpublished Opinion #2002-UP-513, (Ct. App. Aug. 2002) (constant harassment and reprisals by assistant school principal visited upon teacher did make outrage claim.)

Outrage is not available where an existing tort remedy is already available. This was the express holding of Todd v. South Carolina Farm Bureau Mutual Insurance Co., 283 S.C. 155, 173, 321 S.E.2d 602, 613 (Ct. App. 1984), quashed on other grounds, 287 S.C. 190, 336 S.E.2d 472 (1985). Noting that the "tort of outrage was designed not as a replacement of existing tort actions," the Court of Appeals held that outrage was not available where the wrong alleged fell under the heading of defamation. However, in Frazier v. Badger, 361 S.C. 94, 603 S.E. 2d 587 (S.C. 2004) the S.C. Supreme Court allowed a school teacher to pursue a claim based on outrage, even though she had a statutory claim of sexual harassment. Further, the Court held that tort immunity for government employees does not obtain under the facts of this case, as the unwanted sexual advances were not within the "scope of the employee's employment or part of his official duties." In Singleton v. Department of Corrections, 115 Fed. App. 119 (unpublished case, November 17, 2004), the 4th Circuit did not find sexual harassment, though a prison librarian was the subject of repeated off-color comments from an assistant warden. Would a tort of outrage been recognized? See, also, more recently, Williams v. Lancaster County School District, 369 S.C. 293, 631 S.E. 2d 286, 210 Ed. Law Rep. 479 (Ct. Appeals, 2006).

In Hansson v. Scalise Builders of South Carolina, 374 S.C. 352, 650 S.E. 2d 68 (S.C. 2007), the Supreme Court ruled that to make a prima facie case for intentional infliction of emotional distress, an employee must show a genuine issue of material fact to each essential element of the plaintiff's claim, not just one element. Otherwise, summary judgment is appropriate.

2. ***Claims Based on Statements.*** In the view of the Court of Appeals of South Carolina, the tort of outrage is not available where there is a remedy available under a traditional tort such as defamation. Accordingly, the Court of Appeals of South Carolina has excluded from the scope of the tort of outrage those wrongs that could be brought under traditional tort actions. Folkens v. Hunt, 290 S.C. 194, 348 S.E.2d 839 (Ct. App. 1986); Todd v. South Carolina Farm Bureau Mut. Ins. Co., 283 S.C. 155, 321 S.E.2d 602 (Ct. App. 1984), rev'd on other grounds, 287 S.C. 190, 336 S.E.2d 472 (1985). Indeed, in Folkens v. Hunt, the Court of Appeals held that "[a]t most, [defendant] defamed [plaintiff] by making false accusations of criminal conduct," which was insufficient to establish a cause of action for outrage. 290 S.C. at 204, 348 S.E.2d at 845. However, this view seems to have been questioned by the South Carolina Supreme Court in dictum, in Upchurch v. New York Times Co., 314 S.C. 531, 431 S.E.2d 558 (1993), where the court seemed to suggest that an intentional infliction of emotional distress action might be available where a publisher made a deliberate decision to print mere rumors and suspicions, even if they proved to be true.

C. Interference with Economic Advantage

1. ***Elements.*** South Carolina recognizes both interference with contractual relations and interference with prospective contractual relations. In order to recover for interference with contractual relations, a plaintiff must establish "(1) the contract; (2) the wrongdoer's knowledge thereof; (3) his intentional procurement of its breach; (4) the absence of justification; and (5) damages resulting therefrom." DeBerry v. McCain, 275 S.C. 569, 274 S.E.2d 293 (1981). See also F.P. Hubbard & R.L. Felix, South Carolina Law of Torts (1990).

Overruling two prior decisions declining to recognize intentional interference of prospective contractual relations, the Supreme Court of South Carolina recognized the cause of action in Crandall Corp. v. Navistar Intern, 302 S.C. 265, 395 S.E.2d 179 (1990). In Crandall, the Supreme Court held that a plaintiff must prove "(1) the defendant intentionally interfered with the plaintiff's potential contractual relations; (2) for an improper purpose or by improper methods; (3) causing injury to plaintiff." Id. at 266. The court continued to state that, "[i]f a defendant acts for more than one purpose, his improper purpose must predominate in order to create liability," that "[a]s an alternative to establishing an improper purpose, the plaintiff may prove the defendant's method of interference was improper under the circumstances." Id. Improper methods of interference are those that are illegal or independently tortious. Improper methods may include violence, threats, bribery and the like. Love v. Gamble, 316 S.C. 203, 448 S.E.2d 876 (Ct. App. 1994).

And in Greenlee v. Godlan, 78 Fed. Appx. 299, another 4th Circuit case involving a South Carolina employer, the Court upheld a sizeable jury verdict against an employer that tried to enforce an invalid non-compete agreement. The employee's new employer had terminated the employee because she failed to disclose the non-compete agreement. The employee then sued her former employer and won. Greenlee v. Godlan.

2. ***Claims Based on Statements.*** To establish the claim for breach of contract accompanied by a fraudulent act one must prove (1) a breach of contract; (2) fraudulent intent related to the breach; and (3) a fraudulent act directly connected to the breach. Hendrix v. Eastern Distribution, Inc., 316 S.C. 34, 446 S.E.2d 440 (S.C. App. 1994) affirmed in part, vacated in part (on other grounds) by Hendrix v. Eastern Distribution, Inc., 320 S.C. 218, 464 S.E.2d 112 (S.C. 1995). In Hendrix the court found sufficient evidence to support a determination that an employer was guilty of breach of contract accompanied by fraudulent act when it hired a saleswoman with assurances she would not be terminated once she began to generate commissions, yet the employer terminated her once she did begin to generate commissions, allegedly because of economic conditions and a need to eliminate sales force, yet hired an alleged Vice President who performed in a sales capacity.

In Prescott v. Farmers Telephone Co-op, 328 S.C. 379, 491 S.E.2d 698 (S.C. App. 1997), the court apparently recognized intentional interference with contract as a cause of action in an employment setting, although finding no factual basis for this claim in this case. It is noted that an action for willful interference with contract requires interference by a third party. U.S. for the Use & Benefit of Williams Elec. Co., Inc., v. Metric Constructors, Inc., 325 S.C. 129, 480 S.E.2d 447 (S.C. 1997).

D. Prima Facie Tort

No South Carolina case has recognized, accepted, rejected or discussed prima facie tort.

V. OTHER ISSUES

A. Statute of Limitations

The limitation of action for libel or slander is two (2) years. S.C. Code Ann. § 15-3-550 (Law Co-op Supp. 2001). In Jones v. City of Folly Beach, 326 S.C. 360, 483 S.E.2d 770 (S.C. App. 1997), the court declined to adopt a "discovery" rule for defamation and/or libel/slander claims holding such causes of action accrue when the plaintiff has a legal right to sue. See Scott v. McCain, 272 S.C. 198, 250 S.E.2d 118 (1978) (amendment to complaint allowed in libel action after expiration of statute of limitations where amendment only amplified and made more definite and certain the original allegations of malice). The courts have not addressed the single publication rule, nor is there any statutory provision affecting it. See I.B.6.c supra.

B. Jurisdiction

General jurisdictional and venue authorities apply to defamation actions. South Carolina has broad "long-arm" statutes, S.C. Code Ann., §§ 36-2-802, 803 (2001).

However, employment contracts containing mediation and arbitration clauses may require mediation and arbitration of even tort claims related to employment and privacy. Stokes v. Metropolitan Life, 351 S.C. 606, 571 S.E. 2d 711 (S.C. Ct. Appeals, 2002).

C. Workers' Compensation Exclusivity

Actions for slander are not barred by the exclusivity provision of the Workers' Compensation Act. *Dockins v. Ingles Markets, Inc.*, 306, S.C. 287, 288, 411 S.E.2d 437, 438 (S.C. 1991)(overruled on other grounds by *Sabb v. S.C. State Univ.*, 350 S.C. 416, 422, 567 S.E.2d 231, 234 (S.C. 2002). S.C. Code Ann. § 42-1-540 provides that the rights and remedies granted by the Act are exclusive and bar all other claims against the employer on account of personal injury or death by accident. Although actions for intentional torts committed by the employer are not excluded by this provision, a claim against an employer for negligent supervision of a co-employee who committed an intentional tort would be excluded if it is in the nature of a personal injury. *Dickert v. Metro. Live Ins. Co.*, 311 S.C. 218, 219, 428 S.E.2d 700, 701 (S.C. 1993). However, in *Dockins*, the Supreme Court held that slander does not constitute a "personal injury," but rather is an injury to the plaintiff's proprietary interest in his reputation and does not come within the scope of the Act. 306 S.C. 287 at 288, 411 S.E.2d 437 at 438. *See also Loges v. Mack Trucks, Inc.*, 308 S.C. 134, 136, 417 S.E.2d 538, 540 (holding that an action for slander was not barred by the Act); *Cason v. Duke Energy Corp.*, 348 S.C. 544, 547, 560 S.E.2d 891, 893 (S.C. 2002) (exception to exclusivity exists where the tort is slander and injury is to reputation).

D. Pleading Requirements

The pleading of a cause of action for libel or slander is governed generally by the South Carolina Rules of Civil Procedure and specifically by Rule 9(h), which provides that "it is not necessary to state in the pleading any extrinsic facts for the purpose of showing the application to the pleader of the defamatory matter out of which the action arose; but it is sufficient to state generally that the same was published or spoken concerning the pleader." Rule 9(h), S.C.R.C.P. In a case of defamation that is actionable per se, "it is not necessary to plead malice . . . or special damages." H. Lightsey and J. Flanagan, South Carolina Civil Procedure 142 (1985) (citing Matthews v. U.S. Rubber Co., 219 F. Supp. 831 (D.S.C. 1963), aff'd, 352 F.2d 597 (4th Cir. 1964); Brown v. National Home Ins. Co., 239 S.C. 488, 123 S.E.2d 850 (1962).

Libel or slander is not actionable unless it causes or has a natural and direct tendency to cause damage to the plaintiff's reputation. Capps v. Watts, 271 S.C. 276, 246 S.E.2d 606 (1978). In an action for defamation that is action per se, it is not necessary to allege special damages for the defamation to be actionable. Renew v. Serby, 237 S.C. 116, 115 S.E.2d 664 (1960); Stokes v. Great Atlantic & Pacific Tea Co., 202 S.C. 24, 23 S.E.2d 823 (1943); Buffkin v. Pridgen, 154 S.C. 53, 151 S.E. 105 (1930). If the defamatory statement is not actional per se, a plaintiff "must show that he was actually damaged by pleading and proving special damage." Capps v. Watts, 271 S.C. 276, 289, 246 S.E.2d 606, 611 (1978); see also Wilhoit v. WCSC, Inc., 293 S.C. 34, 358 S.E.2d 397 (Ct. App. 1987). Even if the defamation is actionable per se, any special damages the plaintiff seeks to recover "must be pled and proved." Capps v. Watts, 271 S.C. 276, 246 S.E.2d 606 (1978).

Rule 9(h) of the South Carolina Rules of Civil Procedure provides that the defendant may in his answer "allege both the truth of the matter charged as defamatory, and any mitigating circumstances reducing the amount of damages and, whether he prove the justification or not, he may give in evidence the mitigating circumstances." Rule 9(h), S.C.R.C.P. The language of the rule is somewhat obsolete since, in most cases now, the plaintiff is constitutionally required to bear the burden of proving the falsity of the defamatory statement. Privilege is an affirmative defense. Rutledge v. Junior Order of United American Mechanics, 185 S.C. 142, 193 S.E. 434 (1937); Moore v. New South Express Lines, 184 S.C. 266, 192 S.E. 261 (1937).

SURVEY OF SOUTH CAROLINA EMPLOYMENT PRIVACY LAW

Wallace K. Lightsey, Amos A. Workman, J. Theodore Gentry and Mark W. Bakker
Wyche, P.A.
44 East Camperdown Way
Greenville, South Carolina 29601
Telephone: (864) 242-8200 Facsimile: (864) 235-8900

(With Developments Reported Through **November 1, 2012**

GENERAL COMMENTS

None.

SIGNIFICANT DEVELOPMENTS SINCE THE 2012 *SURVEY*

South Carolina, like several other states, has legislation pending that will ban employers from asking employees and prospective employees for passwords to their social media sites. (H.B. 5105, introduced in the General Assembly on March 29, 2012). Currently the bill is pending in the House Judiciary Committee.

In Milliken & Company v. Brian Morin, Opinion #27154 (S.C. August 1, 2012), the state Supreme Court considered certain employee confidentiality and invention assignment clauses and held them to not be in restraint of trade, and further, should not be strictly construed in favor of an employee. Under a reasonableness standard of enforceability, the employer's agreements were reasonable and served a legitimate business interest.

I. GENERAL LAW OF PRIVACY

A. Legal Basis of Privacy Claims

The Supreme Court of South Carolina first recognized a right of privacy in Holloman v. Life Insurance Co. of Virginia, 192 S.C. 454, 7 S.E.2d 169, 127 A.L.R. 110 (1940). Invasion of privacy was defined by the Supreme Court in Meetze v. The Associated Press, 230 S.C. 330, 335, 95 S.E.2d 606, 608 (1956) as: "The unwarranted appropriation or exploitation of one's personality, the publicizing of one's private affairs with which the public has no legitimate concern, or the wrongful intrusion into one's private activities, in such manner as to outrage or cause mental suffering, shame or humiliation to a person of ordinary sensibilities." The Court of Appeals of South Carolina has interpreted the definition to mean that three separate and distinct causes of action, each significantly different from the other, arise under the heading of invasion of privacy: (1) wrongful appropriation of personality; (2) wrongful publicizing of private affairs; (3) wrongful intrusion into private affairs. Meetze v. Associated Press, 230 S.C. 330, 335, 95 S.E.2d 606, 608 (1956); Rycroft v. Gaddy, 281 S.C. 119, 314 S.E.2d 39 (Ct. App. 1984); Snakenberg v. The Hartford Casualty Ins. Co., 299 S.C. 164, 383 S.E.2d 2 (Ct. App. 1989); Wright v. Sparrow, 298 S.C. 469, 381 S.E.2d 503 (Ct. App. 1989); O'Shea v. Lesser, 308 S.C. 10, 416 S.E.2d 629 (S.C. 1992); Swinton Creek Nursery v. Edisto Farm Credit, 334 S.C. 469, 476, 514 S.E.2d 126, 130 (1999); Sloan v. S.C. Dept. of Public Safety, 355 S.C. 321, 586 S.E.2d 108, 110 (2003); Frasier v. Verizon Wireless, 2008 WL 724037 (D.S.C. March 17, 2008). See, more recently, Gignilliat v. Gignilliat, Savitz & Bettis, L.L.P., 385 S.C. 452, 684 S.E.2d 756 (S.C. 2009).

B. Causes of Action

1. ***Misappropriation/Right of Publicity***. The Court of Appeals of South Carolina has interpreted the Supreme Court of South Carolina's broad definition of right of privacy to include wrongful appropriation of personality, which it defined in Snakenberg v. The Hartford Cas. Ins. Co., 299 S.C. 164, 383 S.E.2d 2 (Ct. App. 1989): "Wrongful appropriation of personality involves the intentional, unconsented use of the plaintiff's name, likeness, or identity by the defendant for his own benefit. The gist of the action is the violation of the plaintiff's exclusive right at common law to publicize and profit from his name, likeness and other aspects of personal identity."

The plaintiff would be obligated to prove the elements of the cause of action by the preponderance of the evidence. While lack of consent is identified as an element of the cause of action, proof of consent by the defendant would be an affirmative defense which must be established by a preponderance of the evidence. A three-year statute of limitations governs this action. S.C. Code Ann. § 15-3-530(5) (1976).

2. ***False Light.*** For many years, South Carolina appellate decisions listed the three forms of invasion of privacy listed above; see, IA, supra, without stating whether or not the tort of "false light" was a viable claim in this state. In Brown v. Pearson, 326 S.C. 409, 483 S.E.2d 477 (Ct. App. 1997) (per curiam), the Court of Appeals explicitly held that South Carolina does not recognize false light invasion of privacy. Id., 326 S.C. at 420; accord Bidzirk, LLC v. Smith, 2007

WL 3119445, at *4, 35 Media L. Rep. 2478 (D.S.C. Oct. 22, 2007) ("[T]his cause of action does not exist under South Carolina law.").

3. ***Publication of Private Facts.*** South Carolina recognized the publication of private facts as a tort in Rycroft v. Gaddy, 281 S.C. 119, 314 S.E.2d 39 (1984). In order to establish a cause of action for publication of private facts the plaintiff must plead and prove the publicizing of his/her private affairs with which the public has no legitimate concern.

South Carolina courts have repeatedly stated that "the gravamen of [publication of private facts] is publicity as opposed to mere publication." Snakenberg v. Hartford Casualty Insurance Company, Inc., 299 S.C. 164, 170, 383 S.E.2d 2, 6 (S.C. Ct. App. 1989). In Wright v. Sparrow, 298 S.C. 469, 381 S.E.2d 503 (Ct. App. 1989), an employee's personnel file was reviewed by her immediate supervisor, then two superiors. The court concluded that the plaintiff's private facts claim should be dismissed because there was no public disclosure of the employee's file. "Liability for invasion of privacy does not arise from communication to a single individual or a small group of people absent a breach of contract, trust or other confidential relationship." Id. at 505. See also Rycroft v. Gaddy, 281 S.C. 119, 314 S.E.2d 39 (Ct. App. 1984) (exhibiting the plaintiff's bank records, which were subpoenaed in a pending litigation, to another person did not qualify as "publicity or as a public disclosure"); Swinton Creek Nursery v. Edisto Farm Credit, 326 S.C. 426, 435, 483 S.E.2d 789, 794 (Ct. App. 1997) ("the disclosure of private facts must be a public disclosure, and not a private one; there must be, in other words, publicity"). See also McCormick v. England, 328 S.C. 627, 640, 494 S.E.2d 431, 437 (Ct. App. 1997) ("the gravamen of the tort is publicity as opposed to mere publication"); Brown v. Pearson, 326 S.C. 409, 421, 483 S.E.2d 477, 484 (Ct. App. 1997) (per curiam) (private facts action does not lie where only publicizing of private facts was done by plaintiffs).

There is no bright line test for what constitutes a private fact under the South Carolina decisions. See, e.g., Doe v. Berkeley Publishers, 329 S.C. 412, 496 S.E.2d 636 (1998) (identity of a person who was the victim of a homosexual rape while incarcerated in county jail was, as a matter of law, a matter of public interest rather than a private fact); Meetze v. The Associated Press, 230 S.C. 330, 95 S.E.2d 606 (1956) (no recovery for publication of private facts for publishing the identity of a married 12-year-old who gave birth to a child); but see Hawkins v. Multimedia, Inc., 288 S.C. 569, 344 S.E.2d 145 (1986) (a jury award of actual and punitive damages upheld in a case identifying a teenager alleged to be the father of an illegitimate child).

South Carolina follows the rule that the right of privacy protects only the "ordinary sensibilities of an individual," and in order to constitute a claim for an invasion of privacy, the act "must be of such a nature as a reasonable man can see might and probably would cause mental distress and injury to anyone possessed of ordinary feelings and intelligence." Meetze v. The Associated Press, 230 S.C. 330, 338, 95 S.E.2d 606, 610 (1956). In McCormick v. England, 328 S.C. 627, 494 S.E.2d 431 (Ct. App. 1997), the court reiterated that "an invasion of privacy claim narrowly proscribes the conduct to that which is 'highly offensive' and 'likely to cause serious mental injury.'" Id. 328 S.C. at 640.

Finally, with respect to the requirement that the private affairs disclosed be of no legitimate concern to the public, the leading South Carolina commentators have noted, "the concept of legitimate public interest affects and limits the concept of private matter, and some cases suggest that the two are mutually exclusive." F.P. Hubbard & R.L. Felix, South Carolina Law of Torts (1990), 3rd edition, at 536. See, e.g., Meetze v. The Associated Press, 230 S.C. 330, 338, 95 S.E.2d 606, 610 (1956). In Meetze, the court noted that the unusual fact of a 12-year-old girl giving birth to a child was a "biological occurrence which would naturally excite public interest." The court did caution that "newsworthiness" is not necessarily the test of whether a matter is of legitimate public interest. In Hawkins, the court upheld a damage award in favor of a minor identified as the putative father of an illegitimate child, and even though the article was a sidebar to a story concerning the problem of teenage pregnancies, the court held that whether a fact is a matter of public interest is a question of fact for the jury. The court softened this stance somewhat in Doe v. Berkeley Publishers, 329 S.C. 412, 496 S.E.2d 636 (1998). There the court explained that "[t]he issue in an invasion of privacy claim is whether the occurrence is a matter of legitimate public or general interest. While ordinarily the issue whether an occurrence meets this test is a question of fact for the jury, under some circumstances it may be a question of law for the court." Id. 312 S.C. at 413. The court went on to hold that the occurrence at issue – a newspaper's publication of the identity of a person who was the victim of a homosexual rape while incarcerated in county jail – involved a matter of public interest as a matter of law. The court also rejected the argument that it was for the jury to decide whether publishing Doe's name as the victim of sexual assault was a matter of public significance. "Under state law, if a person, whether willingly or not, becomes an actor in an event of public or general interest, 'then the publication of his connection with such an occurrence is not an invasion of his right to privacy.'" Id. 329 S.C. at 414 (quoting Meetze). Similarly, in Parker v. Evening Post Pub. Co., 317 S.C. 236, 244, 452 S.E.2d 640, 645 (Ct. App. 1994), the court upheld a directed verdict on a private facts claim, stating "If the public has a legitimate interest in knowing that a 12-year-old girl gave birth to a child as a matter of law, it likewise has a legitimate interest in knowing that the purchaser of a car dealership may be liable for the debts of the former owner as a matter of law. Accordingly, we find the entire article, including the limited references to Parker, involve matters of public concern." In Brown v. Pearson, 326 S.C.

409, 483 S.E.2d 477 (Ct. App. 1997) (per curiam), the Court of Appeals held as a matter of law that a report of sexual harassment and abuse by the pastor of a church was "of some legitimate public interest, albeit to a limited group." Id., 326 S.C. at 421-22.

In Burton v. York County Sheriff's Department, 358 S.C. 339, 594 S.E.2d 888 (Ct. App. 2004), a case involving the "privacy" exemption to disclosure in the South Carolina Freedom of Information Act, S.C. Code §§ 30-4-10 to -165, the Court of Appeals opined that information contained in the personnel records of law enforcement officers relating to allegations of misconduct and disciplinary action against them, even though embarrassing and of a personal nature, did not come within the exemption, because of the strong public interest in such information.

In a footnote in an intentional infliction of emotional distress case, the Supreme Court commented that, "a newspaper is generally shielded from liability when it prints truthful information of public significance which it has lawfully obtained." Upchurch v. New York Times, 314 S.C. 531, 431 S.E.2d 558 (1993).

The constitutional dimension of the right of privacy tort was considered by the Supreme Court in Meetze v. The Associated Press, 230 S.C. 330, 95 S.E.2d 606, 609 (1956). The court stated "[t]he right of privacy is not an absolute right. Some limitations are essential for the protection of the right of freedom of speech and of the press and the interest of the public in having a free dissemination of news and information. None of these rights are without qualification. Courts have encountered considerable difficulty in seeking to balance these conflicting interests. In almost every case involving assertion of a right of privacy, the court if called upon to resolve a conflict between the rights of the individual on the one hand and the interests of society on the other." Generally, however, South Carolina courts have required plaintiffs to prove the absence of legitimate public interest as an element of their claim, rather than requiring the defendant to prove the existence of public interest as a privilege or defense. See Doe v. Berkeley Publishers, 329 S.C. 412, 496 S.E.2d 636 (1998); Brown v. Pearson, 326 S.C. 409, 483 S.E.2d 477 (Ct. App. 1997) (per curiam).

Consent is an affirmative defense, and requires a showing that the injured party consented to the publication of private facts. Hawkins v. Multimedia, Inc., 288 S.C. 569, 344 S.E.2d 145 (1986).

Truth is not a defense to an invasion of privacy claim. Meetze v. The Associated Press, 230 S.C. 330, 95 S.E.2d 606 (1956). Malice is not an element of the tort, and is relevant only when the plaintiff seeks punitive damages. Hawkins v. Multimedia, Inc., 288 S.C. 569, 344 S.E.2d 145 (1986).

No South Carolina decision explicitly addresses the issue of what damages are recoverable for an invasion of privacy, but general damages for injury to the privacy interest and for the mental suffering resulting from the invasion are elements of general damages recognized in Restatement (Second) of Torts § 652H. Punitive damages are recoverable upon a showing of malice. Hawkins v. Multimedia, Inc., 288 S.C. 569, 344 S.E.2d 145 (1986).

South Carolina's rape victim shield statute provides for criminal penalties for the publication of the identity of the victim of criminal sexual conduct. The Supreme Court of South Carolina has held that the statute does not provide a private right of action. Dorman v. Aiken Communications, Inc., 303 S.C. 63, 398 S.E.2d 687 (1990). No other confidentiality statute has been asserted as the basis of a private cause of action. The statute barring publication of the name or picture of a child under the jurisdiction of the family court was declared unconstitutional to the extent that it seems to limit truthful publication by the media of information lawfully obtained concerning a juvenile charged with a crime. State ex rel. The Times & Democrat 276 S.C. 26, 274 S.E.2d 910 (1981). South Carolina's Freedom of Information Act provides that certain information is exempt from disclosure, including "[i]nformation of a personal nature where the public disclosure thereof would constitute unreasonable invasion of personal privacy," S.C. Code Ann § 30-4-40(a)(2), and that public bodies may hold meetings closed to the public to discuss certain matters, id. § 30-4-70. The Supreme Court has rejected the claim, however, that the Act's exemptions to the requirement of disclosure and exceptions to the requirement of open meetings create an expectation of confidentiality. Bellamy v. Brown, 304 S.C. 291, 408 S.E.2d 219 (1991).

South Carolina law would require the plaintiff to prove by a preponderance of the evidence each element of the private facts invasion of privacy. The defendant would have the burden of proof on affirmative defenses such as consent. Hawkins v. Multimedia, Inc., 288 S.C. 569, 344 S.E.2d 145 (1986). The statute of limitations for invasion of privacy claims arising on or after April 5, 1988, is three years. S.C. Code Ann. § 15-3-530(5) (1976). The statute of limitations for libel and slander actions is two years. S.C. Code Ann. § 15-3-550 (1976).

4. ***Intrusion.*** Intrusion was discussed in Meetze v. The Associated Press, 230 S.C. 330, 95 S.E.2d 606 (1956), but no case has been decided where intrusion was the basis of an invasion of privacy claim against a media defendant. In Meetze, the court held that there was no cause of action for reporting that a 12-year-old girl had given birth to a child. On a less forgiving note, though, the court ended its opinion by stating: "In conclusion, we desire to say that there is some justification for the complaint made by plaintiffs as to the conduct of this newspaper reporter. He visited the mother's

room on the day following the birth of the child. It would seem he could have waited a reasonable time before seeking to interview her. He was obviously an unwelcome visitor and a source of great annoyance. We regret that we cannot give legal recognition to Mrs. Meetze's desire to avoid publicity, but the courts do not sit as censors of the manners of the Press." 95 S.E.2d 606 at 610. South Carolina requires that the defendant's act or course of conduct be intentional. Snakenberg v. The Hartford Casualty Ins. Co., 299 S.C. 164, 383 S.E.2d (Ct. App. 1989).

The South Carolina Court of Appeals has stated that what constitutes an intrusion is a factual matter to be decided on a case-by-case basis, and it may consist of "watching, spying, prying, besetting, overhearing, or other similar conduct." Snakenberg v. The Hartford Casualty Ins. Co., 299 S.C. 164, 171, 383 S.E.2d 2, 6 (Ct. App. 1989). The intrusion must be substantial and unreasonable as the law does not provide a remedy for every annoyance occurring in everyday life. Id. The intrusion must concern those elements of a person's home, family, personal relationships and communications which one normally expects will be free from exposure. Id.

Where the invasion of privacy claim is based on "intrusion" alone without evidence of public disclosure, the plaintiff must show "a blatant and shocking disregard of his rights and serious mental or physical injury or humiliation to himself resulting therefrom." Rycroft v. Gaddy, 281 S.C. 119, 124, 314 S.E.2d 39, 43 (Ct. App. 1984). The conduct must be of a nature that would cause mental injury to a person of ordinary feelings and intelligence. The law protects normal sensitivities, not heightened sensitivity. Snakenberg v. The Hartford Casualty Ins. Co., 299 S.C. 164, 383 S.E.2d 2 (Ct. App. 1989).

No South Carolina decision specifically discusses the relationship of intrusion to trespass or other privacy torts, but the Court of Appeals has held that where a claim is made based on intrusion without publication, the plaintiff must show a blatant and shocking disregard of his rights and serious mental or physical injury or humiliation resulting from the intrusion. Rycroft v. Gaddy, 281 S.C. 119, 314 S.E.2d 39 (Ct. App. 1984). See Moore v. Rural Health Servs. Inc., 2007 WL 666796 (D.S.C., Feb. 27, 2007) ("Considering the evidence in the light most favorable to the Plaintiff, Hamrick's motives and conduct in providing this admittedly confidential material to a newspaper reporter could constitute a blatant and shocking disregard of Plaintiff's rights, at least sufficient to survive summary judgment.").

No South Carolina case has discussed damages in an intrusion claim, but general damages are likely to be allowed. Since the plaintiff must prove that the defendant's intrusion was intentional, punitive damages could be recoverable.

C. Other Privacy-Related Actions

1. Intentional Infliction of Emotional Distress

a. ***Elements.*** South Carolina recognized the tort of intentional infliction of emotional distress or "outrage" in the case of Ford v. Hutson, 276 S.C. 157, 276 S.E.2d 776 (1981), by upholding a verdict in favor of a real estate agent who, after years of harassment by a disappointed purchaser, suffered serious emotional and physical injuries. In order to recover for the intentional infliction of emotional distress, a plaintiff must establish that "(1) the defendant intentionally or recklessly inflicted severe emotional distress, or was certain or substantially certain that such distress would result from his conduct; (2) the conduct was so extreme and outrageous as to exceed all possible bounds of decency and must be regarded as atrocious and utterly intolerable in a civilized community; (3) the actions of the defendant caused the plaintiff's emotional distress; and (4) the emotional distress suffered by the plaintiff was so severe that no reasonable person could be expected to endure it." Upchurch v. New York Times, 314 S.C. 531, 431 S.E.2d 558 (1993). Williams v. Lancaster County School District, 396 S.C. 293, 631 S.E. 2d 286, 210 Ed. Law Rep. 479 (S.C. Ct. Appeals, May, 2006).

b. ***Relationship to Employment Law.*** A claim of outrage will lie only under extreme circumstances. A plaintiff must show (1) conduct by the defendant which is atrocious, utterly intolerable in a civilized community, and so extreme and outrageous as to exceed all possible bounds of decency; (2) the defendant acted with intent to inflict emotional distress or acted recklessly when it was certain or substantially certain such distress would result from his conduct; (3) the actions of the defendant caused the plaintiff to suffer emotional distress; and (4) the emotional distress suffered by the plaintiff was so severe that no reasonable man could be expected to endure it. Wright v. Sparrow, 298 S.C. 469, 471, 381 S.E.2d 503, 505 (Ct. App. 1989); Frazier v. Badger, Unpublished Opinion #2002-UP-513 (Ct. App. Aug. 2002). **Frazier v. Badger, 361 S.C. 94, 603 S.E.2d 587 (S.C. 2004)**

See Shipman v. Glenn, 314 S.C. 327, 443 S.E.2d 921 (Ct. App. 1994) (employer who verbally abused and ridiculed speech impediment of employee with cerebral palsy, while "callous and offensive," was not guilty of outrage); Barber v. Whirlpool Corp., 34 F.3d 1268, 1276 (4th Cir. 1994) (verbal abuse of employee by former marine officer, while "despicable," did not constitute outrage); Gattison v. South Carolina State College, 318 S.C. 148, 152-157, 456 S.E.2d 414, 416-19 (Ct. App. 1995) (employee who was deprived of secretarial support, given inferior office, humiliated at meetings, and taunted about being fired did not make out a claim of outrage); Corder v. Champion Road Mach. Int'l Corp., 283 S.C. 520, 523, 324 S.E.2d 79, 81 (Ct. App. 1984) (retaliatory discharge, which may be reprehensible conduct, insufficient to state a claim for outrage), cert. denied, 286 S.C. 126, 332 S.E.2d 533 (1985); Satterfield v. Lockheed Missiles & Space Co., 617 F. Supp. 1359, 1365-69 (D.S.C. 1985) (plaintiff terminated over faulty urinalysis test, whose status was kept in doubt for two weeks, did not make out an outrage claim). Fleming v. Rose, 350 S.C. 488, 567 S.E. 2d 857 (2002) (press release which stated that a state policeman had set a "deplorable example" in the handling of an internal investigation not so extreme and outrageous as to support a claim for intentional infliction of emotional distress.); Frazier v. Badger, Unpublished Opinion #2002-UP-513, (Ct. App. August, 2002) (Constant harassment and reprisals by assistant school principal visited upon teacher did make outrage claim.). **Frazier v. Badger, 361 S.C. 94, 603 S.E.2d 587 (S.C. 2004)**

To prevent claims for intentional infliction of emotional distress from becoming a "panacea for wounded feelings" rather than reprehensible conduct, the South Carolina Supreme Court recently emphasized the significant gatekeeping role a court should play in analyzing a defendant's motion for summary judgment when claims of intentional infliction of emotional distress are asserted. See Hansson v. Scalise Builders of South Carolina, 374 S.C. 352, 650 S.E.2d 68 (S.C. 2007). Emotional distress allegedly sustained by the plaintiff-employee, as result of being constantly derided by supervisor with callous and vulgar remarks and gestures related to homosexuality, which caused lost sleep and teeth grinding, was not sufficiently severe to establish a prima facie claim of intentional infliction of emotional distress against his employer and supervisor. Id. In Hansson, the plaintiff admitted that he neither visited nor received treatment or medication from any other physician or counselor, and he stated that his coworkers' conduct did not cause him to lose any time from work, affect his relationship with his wife, or affect his ability to perform his job. Consequently, the Court granted summary judgment. Id.; see also Westmoreland v. AB Beverage Co., Inc.. 2007 WL 2749450 (D.S.C., Sept. 20, 2007) (even assuming that physical attack in the employment setting, on an employee with a known pre-existing heart condition, constitutes extreme and outrageous conduct, claim for intentional infliction of emotional distress failed because plaintiff did not present sufficient evidence of resulting severe emotional distress).

It has been contended that outrage is not available where an existing tort remedy is already available. This was the holding of Todd v. South Carolina Farm Bureau Mutual Insurance Co., 283 S.C. 155, 173, 321 S.E.2d 602, 613 (Ct. App. 1984), quashed on other grounds, 287 S.C. 190, 336 S.E.2d 472 (1985). Noting that the "tort of outrage was designed not as a replacement of existing tort actions," the Court of Appeals held that outrage was not available where the wrong alleged fell under the heading of defamation. However, in Frazier v. Badger, 361 S.C. 94, 603 S.E.2d 587 (S.C. 2004) the S.C. Supreme Court allowed a school teacher to pursue a claim based on outrage, even though she had a statutory claim of sexual harassment. Further, the Court held that tort immunity for government employees does not obtain under the facts of this case, as the unwanted sexual advances were not within the "scope of the employee's employment or part of his official duties."

2. Interference With Prospective Economic Advantage

a. ***Elements.*** South Carolina recognizes both interference with contractual relations and interference with prospective contractual relations. In order to recover for interference with contractual relations, a plaintiff must establish "(1) the contract; (2) the wrongdoer's knowledge thereof; (3) his intentional procurement of its breach; (4) the absence of justification; and (5) damages resulting therefrom." DeBerry v. McCain, 275 S.C. 569, 274 S.E.2d 293 (1981); Kinard v. Crosby, 315 S.C. 237, 240, 433 S.E.2d 835, 837 (1993); Camp v. Springs Mortgage Corp., 310 S.C. 514, 426 S.E.2d 304 (1993); Collins Entertainment Corp. v. Coats & Coats Rental Amusement, 355 S.C. 125, 584 S.E.2d 120 (2003). See generally F.P. Hubbard & R.L. Felix, South Carolina Law of Torts, 3rd Edition.

Overruling two prior decisions declining to recognize intentional interference with prospective contractual relations, the Supreme Court of South Carolina recognized the cause of action in Crandall Corp. v. Navistar Int'l Transp. Corp., 302 S.C. 265, 395 S.E.2d 179 (1990). In Crandall, the Supreme Court held that a plaintiff must prove "(1) the defendant intentionally interfered with the plaintiff's potential contractual relations; (2) for an improper purpose or by improper methods; (3) causing injury to plaintiff." Id. at 265. The court stated that, "[i]f a defendant acts for more than one purpose, his improper purpose must predominate in order to create liability," that "[a]s an alternative to establishing an improper purpose, the plaintiff may prove the defendant's method of interference was improper under the circumstances." Id. Improper methods of interference are those that are illegal or independently tortious. Improper methods may include violence, threats, bribery, and the like. Love v. Gamble, 316 S.C. 203, 448 S.E.2d 876 (Ct. App. 1994)l; United Educ. Distribs., LLC v. Educ. Testing Servs., 350 S.C. 7, 564 S.E.2d 324 (Ct. App. 2002).

b. ***Relationship to Employment Law.*** South Carolina courts have indicated support for a cause of action for tortious interference with contract in the context of enforcing restrictive covenants. In Oxman v. Sherman, 239 S.C. 218, 122 S.E. 2d 559 (S.C. 1961), the employer sued to enforce by injunction an insurance agent's non-compete/non-solicitation agreement wherein the agent agreed not to "directly or indirectly induce or attempt to induce any ... employees . . . to terminate their association" with the employer. While the main holding of Oxman was the court's declaration that the provision at issue was reasonable and violated no public policy, the court also held: "It is merely a recognition of the right of respondents to be immune from malicious interference by a third person with any contractual relations they have with their employees. This is a right which exists independently of contract, for it is well settled that it is unlawful for a third person to maliciously cause or induce another to breach his contract." 239 S.C. at 226,122 S.E.2d at 562; see also Wolf v. Colonial Life & Accident Ins. Co., 309 S.C. 100, 420 S.E.2d 217 (Ct. App. 1992) (discussing elements of enforcing a restrictive covenant but not finding sufficient evidence to establish interference with contractual relations).

An analogous case decided by the Fourth Circuit is informative. In Barnes Group, Inc. v. C & C Prods., Inc., 716 F.2d 1023 (4th Cir. 1983), the court addressed the interplay of restrictive covenants and tortious interference with contract after six salesmen from the Bowman division of Barnes Group signed contracts with C & C, a Bowman competitor, and commenced selling to former Bowman customers in violation of their contractual covenants not to compete. One of the Bowman salesmen was a South Carolina resident. The Fourth Circuit determined that although the district court misapplied the choice-of-law provision (in favor of Ohio), the error was harmless as applied to the South Carolina salesman because, like Ohio, "South Carolina...recognize(s) a classic common law cause of action for tortious interference with contract." 716 F.2d at 1033. The district court found that C & C interfered with the contractual relationship between Bowman and its salesmen by: (1) soliciting and enticing Bowman salesman to leave by stating that the restrictive covenant was not enforceable and by promising that C & C would pay any legal expenses if Bowman sued them; (2) by encouraging the Bowman salesmen hired by C & C to breach their restrictive covenants and to use confidential information to divert their customer accounts; (3) by encouraging Bowman salesmen to work for and transfer their Bowman accounts to C & C before resigning from Bowman; and (4) by encouraging the salesmen to bring other Bowman salesmen with them. 716 F.2d at 1027 n.5 (noting that "these factual findings are not clearly erroneous, and provide ample support for the district court's ultimate finding of liability on the tortious interference claim to the extent the covenants are enforceable ones under governing law").

In an unpublished case, Greenlee v. Godlan, Inc., 78 Fed. Appx. 299, C.A. 4 (S.C.) 2003, the Fourth Circuit addressed a suit by an employee against a former employer for tortiously interfering with her relationship with her new employer.

> Greenlee [the Plaintiff-employee] introduced evidence in this case demonstrating that Godlan [her former employer] asserted to Greenlee and to Saint-Gobain [her new employer] that Greenlee had a valid non-compete agreement that Godlan intended to enforce, and thereafter faxed to Saint-Gobain an acknowledgment page signed by Greenlee to a non-compete agreement from a superseded manual knowing it had been superseded and was invalid. Greenlee also introduced evidence that the same afternoon Saint-Gobain received the fax, it suspended Greenlee and then terminated her because she failed to disclose the no longer valid non-compete agreement. We find Greenlee introduced sufficient evidence to prove the essential elements of her claim of tortious interference with contract under South Carolina law.

The court further upheld the jury award to Plaintiff of $200,000 even though the Plaintiff's employment with her new employer was at-will, noting that future damages were supported by sufficient evidence and that such an award was not speculative. **See Uhlig v. Shirley, 2012 WL 2923242 (D.S.C.), wherein the District Court let stand a jury verdict for damages on this type of claim.**

South Carolina has declined to recognize a cause of action for the recovery of pure pecuniary harm, however, resulting from a tortfeasor's negligent interference with a plaintiff's contractual relationships. Self v. Norfolk Southern Corp. 2007 WL 540373 (D.S.C., Feb. 15, 2007) (citing Edens & Avant Investment Properties, Inc. v. Amerada Hess Corp., 318 S.C. 134, 456 S.E.2d 406, 407 (Ct. App.1995)).

3. **Prima Facie Tort.** No South Carolina case has recognized, accepted, rejected or discussed prima facie tort.

II. EMPLOYER TESTING OF EMPLOYEES

A. Psychological or Personality Testing

No South Carolina decisions or statutes on this point.

B. Drug Testing

1. ***Common Law and Statutes.*** South Carolina has enacted a statute to govern drug testing in the workplace, balancing the need for a drug-free workplace with the need for employee privacy. S.C. Code Ann. § 41-1-15 allows an employer, public or private, to establish a substance abuse policy in the workplace that includes random testing. It must cover all employees. All information, interviews/reports, statements, memoranda, and test results, written or otherwise,

received by the employer through a substance abuse testing program are confidential communications but may be used or received in evidence obtained in discovery or disclosed in any civil or administrative proceeding. Information on test results shall not be released for or used or admissible in any criminal proceeding against the employee.

2. ***Private Employers.*** See II.B.1, supra

3. ***Public Employers.*** See II.B.1, supra

C. Medical Testing

No South Carolina statutes or cases discuss this issue.

D. Polygraph Tests

No South Carolina statutes or cases discuss this issue directly. In Todd v. South Carolina Farm Bureau Mut. Ins. Co., 283 S.C. 155, 321 S.E.2d 602 (Ct. App. 1984), quashed in part on other grounds, 287 S.C. 190, 336 S.E.2d 472 (S.C. 1985), the court held in the absence of a state statute barring polygraph tests as a condition for hiring or continuation of employment, an employee who is terminated for refusing to take a polygraph test may not bring a wrongful discharge in violation of public policy. But see 29 U.S.C. § 2002 (prohibiting employers from taking certain action against employees solely on the basis of polygraph results).

E. Fingerprinting

No South Carolina statutes or cases discuss this issue.

III. SEARCHES

A. Employee's Person

No South Carolina statutes or cases discuss this issue.

1. ***Private Employers.*** No South Carolina statutes or cases discuss this issue.

2. ***Public Employers.*** No South Carolina statutes or cases discuss this issue. However, the South Carolina Constitution, Article I, Section 10, provides: "The right of the people to be secure in their persons, houses, papers and effects against unreasonable searches and seizures and unreasonable invasions of privacy shall not be violated . . ." S. C. Constitution, Article 1, § 10.

B. Employee's Work Area

No South Carolina statutes or cases discuss this issue.

C. Employee's Property

No South Carolina statutes or cases discuss this issue.

1. ***Private Employers.*** No South Carolina statutes or cases discuss this issue.

2. ***Public Employers.*** No South Carolina statutes or cases discuss this issue. See III.A.2, supra.

IV. MONITORING OF EMPLOYEES

A. Telephones and Electronic Communications

S.C. Code Ann. § 16-17-470 (Supp. 1993) prohibits Peeping Tom eavesdropping upon another's property. 18 U.S.C. § 2510 et seq. generally defines and prescribes methods and circumstances during which it is proper to intercept wire, electronic and oral communications, and recovery of damages for illegal interception. S.C. Code Ann. § 16-17-470 (Supp. 1993) establishes a misdemeanor offense for eavesdropping, with a fine of up to $500 and/or up to 3 years imprisonment. The South Carolina courts have not yet addressed whether this statute creates a private cause of action. The South Carolina Court of Appeals has determined that this statute does not apply to reporters attempting to overhear proceedings of a city council conducted in an executive session. Herald Publishing Co. v. Barnwell, 291 S.C. 4, 351 S.E.2d 878 (Ct. App. 1986).

1. ***Wiretapping (Telephone).*** A corporation's use of a "voice logger" continuously recording all telephone conversations undertaken on some of the telephone lines with extensions in its security office unlawfully "intercepted" wire or oral communications of a security officer in violation of the Federal Wiretapping Act; the logger did not

qualify for the business use exception in that it was not a "telephone or telegraph instrument, equipment or facility" or component thereof and was not sold by a telephone company in the ordinary course of business, nor was it used in the ordinary course of the corporation's business, despite claimed fear of bomb threats, where evidence of bomb threats was scant, no threats were received during the period recordings were made, and the corporation never notified security guards, other than a supervisor, that recordings were being made. Sanders v. Robert Bosch Corp., 38 F.3d 736 (4th Cir. 1994).

However, there was no unlawful interception of a security officer's conversations during the period after a corporation which retained the security firm turned off the voice logger on telephone lines with extensions in the security office, even though, due to a design defect, a handset microphone remained able to pick up ambient noise in guards' office and transmitted it to corporation's security control room; corporation never acquired the "contents" of any conversations taking place in the guards' office where corporation was not aware of the situation and there was no evidence that any of its employees ever listened to or recorded any conversations and corporation did not act intentionally. Sanders v. Robert Bosch Corp., 38 F.3d 736 (4th Cir. 1994).

The U.S. Court of Appeals for the Fourth Circuit determined that civil liability for an alleged unlawful wiretapping required proof of criminal willfulness (i.e., intentional or reckless disregard of legal obligations) by a party engaged in the purported illegal interception. Malouche v. JH Management Co., Inc., 839 F.2d 1024 (4th Cir. 1988). In Weeks v. Union Camp Corp., 215 F.3d 1323 (Table), C.A. 4 (S.C.) 2000, (unpublished), the Fourth Circuit Court of Appeals considered the use of a tape of employees' conversations as taped by another employee. The taping employee had received a negative peer review and claimed racial motivation. Employer listened to the tape and fired the employees for their racial harassment. The fired employees claimed a violation of the Federal Wiretapping Act. The Court ruled that the employer acted reasonably in listening to and relying on the tape, and thus was not liable.

Under the South Carolina Homeland Security Act, §17-30-10 to §17-30-145, employers are allowed to monitor the communication of employees under certain circumstances. Employers may intercept a wire, oral, or electronic communication when a party to the communication or one of the parties has given previous consent to the interception. Employers may monitor and/or review the contents of an employee's e-mail, telephone conversation, and/or voice mail with (1) prior consent or (2) disclosure by a party to the communication. But the law prohibits an employer from:

1. directing a party to the communication to disclose information; and/or

2. using a device to monitor the contents of its electronic and/or oral communication applications without prior consent.

Violation of either provision is a felony. S.C. Code §§ 17-30-10 et seq. Prior consent is not defined in the new law.

2. ***Electronic Communications (E-mail).*** No South Carolina cases discuss this point. See IV.A, supra.

3. ***Other Electronic Monitoring.*** No South Carolina cases discuss this point. See IV.A., supra. **However, South Carolina, like several other states, has legislation pending that will ban employers from asking employees and prospective employees of passwords to their social media cites. (H.B. 5105, introduced in the General Assembly on March 29, 2012.). The bill is currently in the House Judiciary Committee.**

B. Mail.

No South Carolina statutes or cases discuss this issue.

C. Surveillance/Photographing.

See IV.A, supra.

V. ACTIVITIES OUTSIDE THE WORKPLACE

A. Statute or Common Law

Under South Carolina law, a person's use of tobacco products outside the workplace may not be the basis of adverse personnel action. S.C. Code Ann. § 41-1-85. In Connelly v. Wometco, 314 S.C. 188, 442 S.E.2d 204 (Ct. App. 1994) the South Carolina Court of Appeals affirmed a verdict on an employee's wrongful discharge claim. The employee claimed that the employer violated S.C. Code Ann. §41-1-70 which imposes liability on an employer who dismisses or demotes an employee for compliance with a subpoena or service on a jury.

In Dixon v. Coburg Dairy, 330 F.2d 250 (4th Cir. 2003), new decision after rehearing en banc, 369 F.3d 811 (4th Cir. 2004), the Fourth Circuit considered a case in which a long-term employee of the Coburg Dairy was an active member of the Sons of the Confederate Veterans. He attached Confederate battle flag stickers to his toolbox used at work as a show of support for South Carolina flying the Confederate flag at the state capitol. An African-American co-worker objected to the toolbox display as being racially motivated and in violation of the dairy's harassment policy. In an effort to compromise, the dairy offered to buy the employee a new "unflagged" toolbox. The employee rejected the compromise and was terminated.

The employee then sued the dairy, claiming his termination violated his constitutional right of free speech and was also a violation of South Carolina Code Ann. §16-17-560, which reads as follows:

> Assault Or Intimidation On Account Of Political Opinions Or Exercise Of Civil Rights. It is unlawful for a person to assault or intimidate a citizen, discharge a citizen from employment or occupation, or reject a citizen from a rented house, land, or other property because of political opinions or the exercise of political rights and privileges guaranteed to every citizen by the Constitution of laws of the United States or by the Constitution and laws of this State.
>
> A person who violates the provisions of this section is guilty of a misdemeanor and, upon conviction, must be fined not more than one thousand dollars or imprisoned not more than two years, or both.

In its initial decision, the court dismissed the constitutional claim on the basis that constitutional protection applies only as a shield from government interference. The Court also dismissed employee's claim under the statute, reasoning that the law protected his political support of the Confederate flag, but that protection is not extended to activity in the private sector workplace. The court concluded that there has to be a balance between free speech and an employer's right to preserve a harmonious and efficient work environment. The court did state that the South Carolina statute would have protected an employee who was attending a political rally at the capitol, flying a Confederate flag at home, or participating in a march. Dixon v. Coburg Dairy, 330 F.2d 250 (4th Cir. 2003).

This ruling aroused substantial interest in 2003 and could have profoundly affected employment privacy law in South Carolina. But after rehearing, en banc, the 4th Circuit Court of Appeals concluded that the case did not raise a substantial enough federal question to warrant federal court jurisdiction. Matthew Dixon v. Coburg Dairy, 369 F.3d 811 (4th Circuit 2004).

Another Fourth Circuit case bears brief mention, though it originates in Maryland. Booth v. State of Maryland, 327 F.3d 377 (4th Cir. 2003). In that case the court considered the right of an individual to exercise his religious beliefs by maintaining a Rastafarian dread locks hair style at work, despite employer policies limiting permissible hairstyles. The employer prevailed in the case as the Court rejected employee's claims under § 1981 and § 1983, but in a very limited holding.

B. Employees' Personal Relationships

1. ***Romantic Relationships Between Employees.*** No South Carolina statutes or cases discuss this point.

However, one case may be of interest. In Stone v. Traylor, 360 S.C. 271, 600 S.E. 2d 551 (Ct. App. 2004) the Court of Appeals affirmed a decision of The Industrial Commission rejecting a worker's compensation claim by an employee who was injured in a fight with another man over a former girlfriend. The Commission concluded that the injury originated out of personal relationships, not "out of" and "in the course of employment."

2. ***Sexual Orientation.*** S.C. Code Ann. § 20-1-15 prohibits same sex marriages and declares that such marriages are void ab initio. No South Carolina cases discuss the effect of this statute in the workplace and/or with employee benefits.

3. ***Marital Status.*** No South Carolina statutes or cases discuss this issue. See also V.B.2, supra.

C. Smoking

See V.A, supra. South Carolina has adopted the Clean Indoor Air Act, S.C. Code Ann, § 44-95-20, which prohibits smoking in many public facilities and requires smoking/non-smoking designated areas when smoking is permitted.

D. Blogging

No South Carolina statutes or cases discuss this issue.

VI. RECORDS

A. Personnel Records

In Wright v. Sparrow, 298 S.C. 469, 381 S.E.2d 503 (Ct. App. 1989), an employee's personnel file was reviewed by her immediate supervisor, then two superiors. The court concluded there was no public disclosure of the employee's file. Liability for invasion of privacy does not arise from communication to a single individual or a small group of people absent a breach of contract, trust or other confidential relationship.

S.C. Code Ann. §41-1-65 (1996) gives immunity from civil liability for employers who give written responses to written requests concerning an employee or former employee when the employer discloses: (1) written employee evaluations; (2) official personnel notices that formally record the reasons for separation; (3) whether the employee was voluntarily or involuntarily released from service and the reason for the separation; and (4) information about job performance.

This immunity is waived if the employer knowingly or recklessly releases or discloses false information.

B. Medical Records

No South Carolina cases discuss this issue. S.C. Code Ann. § 1-13-85 (1996) requires separate forms and files for employee medical records, and they must be treated as a confidential medical record.

C. Criminal Records.

No South Carolina statutes or cases discuss this issue.

D. Subpoenas / Search Warrants

No South Carolina statutes or cases discuss this issue.

VII. ACTIONS SUBSEQUENT TO EMPLOYMENT

A. References.

See VI, A, supra.

B. Non-Compete Agreements.

South Carolina courts will review restrictive covenants very carefully and construe them narrowly. The restrictive covenant must meet each of the requirements set forth in Rental Uniform Serv. Of Florence, Inc. v. Dudley, 278 S.C. 674, 675-76, 301 S.E.2d 142, 143 (1983): (1) it is necessary for the protection of the employer's legitimate interests, (2) it is reasonably limited in its operation with respect to time and place, (3) it is not unduly harsh and oppressive in curtailing the legitimate efforts of the employee to earn a livelihood, (4) it is reasonable from the standpoint of sound public policy, and (5) it is supported by a valuable consideration. See also Stringer v. Herron, 309 S.C. 529, 531, 424 S.E.2d 547, 548 (Ct. App. 1992) (citing the elements in Dudley); Milliken v. Morin, 386 S.C. 1, 685 S.E.2d 828 (Ct. App. 2009).

South Carolina courts have held that a restrictive covenant that safeguards against the loss of customers may legitimately protect an employer's interest. See Caine & Estes Ins. Agency, Inc. v. Watts, 278 S.C. 207, 293 S.E.2d 859 (1982); Standard Register Co. v. Kerrigan, 238 S.C. 54, 119 S.E.2d 533 (1961); Wolf v. Colonial Life & Accident Ins. Co., 309 S.C. 100, 420 S.E.2d 217 (Ct. App. 1992); Dickerson v. People's Life Ins. Co., 284 S.C. 356, 326 S.E.2d 423 (Ct. App. 1984). However, restrictions cannot be overbroad or vague in time, place, or application. See Lapman v. Dewolff Boberg & Associates, Inc., 319 Fed. Appx. 293, C.A. 4 (S.C.) 2009, for a recent discussion of the law of South Carolina as to non-compete agreements. Generally, courts will find that at-will employment is sufficient consideration for restrictive covenants signed and executed at the commencement of employment. But see Poole v. Incentives, Inc., 345 S.C. 378, 548 S.E.2d 207 (2001) (holding that a non-competition agreement formed after years of employment was void for lack of consideration).

See also Stonhard, Inc. v. Carolina Flooring Specialists, Inc., Daniel Parham and Manuel T. Parham, 366 S.C. 156, 621 S.E.2d 352 (2005). Stonhard affirms a principal of South Carolina law whereby South Carolina courts will construe the terms in a non-compete agreement according to the law of other states, but will not enforce those terms if it would make the agreement invalid under South Carolina law or violates public policy. See also Nucor Corp. v. Bell, 482 F. Supp. 2d 714 (D.S.C. 2007).

Dove Data Products, Inc. v. Deveaux, Unpublished Opinion No. 2008-UP-202 (S. C. Ct. Appeals, March 24, 2008), provides a good primer on the additional consideration requirements for non-compete agreements arrived at with existing employees. Also, Dove Data holds that non-solicitation agreements are governed by the same consideration rules as non-compete agreements when it comes to enforcement. Additional consideration is needed when a current employee is asked to sign either a non-compete or a non-solicitation agreement.

South Carolina courts will not modify a territorial restriction in a non-compete to make it more reasonable and, therefore, enforceable. Poynter Investments, Inc. v. Century Builders of Piedmont, Inc., 387 S.C. 583, 694 S.E.2d 15 (S.C. 2010). **Team 1A, Inc. v. Lucas, 395 S.C. 237, 717 S.E.2d 103 (Ct. App. 2011). However, the court in Team 1A also suggested that alternative territorial restrictions in the original agreement could save the agreement.**

In Milliken & Company v. Brian Morin, Opinion #27154 (S.C. August 1, 2012), the state Supreme Court considered certain employee confidentiality and invention assignment clauses and held them to not be in restraint of trade, and further, should not be strictly construed in favor of the employee. Under a reasonableness standard of enforceability, the employer's agreements were reasonable and served a legitimate business interest.

A recent South Carolina District Court decision also let stand a jury verdict for actual and punitive damages awarded to an employer when a former employee misappropriated confidential customer lists. Uhlig v. Shirley, 2012 WL 2923242 (D.S.C.)

Non-compete agreements are extensively discussed by Phillip Kilgore and Jeff Dunlaevy, *Battle-Worthy Non-Competes*, THE SOUTH CAROLINA LAWYER, May, 2008, at 24.

VIII. OTHER ISSUES

A. Statutes of Limitations

No South Carolina cases have directly discussed the statute of limitations for these causes of action, but it seems clear that a three-year statute of limitations will apply, S.C. Code Ann. § 15-3-530 (2001). The discovery rule, generally applicable to statutes of limitations, applies to outrage claims alleging past sexual abuse, regardless of whether at the time of "discovery" it was possible to realize the extent of injuries. Doe v. R.D. & E.D., 308 S.C. 139, 417 S.E.2d 541 (1992). In cases of "repressed memory" the statute has been held to run when plaintiff has enough evidence to think abuse could have occurred, even though she did not experience something perceived as a memory of an actual event until later. Roe v. Doe, 28 F.3d 404 (4th Cir. 1994).

B. Jurisdiction

General jurisdictional and venue authorities apply to privacy actions. South Carolina has broad "long-arm" statutes, S.C. Code Ann., §§ 36-2-802, 803 (2001).

However, employment contracts containing mediation and arbitration clauses may require mediation and arbitration of even tort claims related to employment and privacy. Stokes v. Metropolitan Life, 351 S.C. 606, 571 S.E. 2d 711, (S.C. Ct. Appeals, 2002).

C. Workers' Compensation Exclusivity

There is authority that at least some types of privacy claims are not barred by the exclusivity provision of the Worker's Compensation Act. S.C. Code Ann. § 42-1-540 provides that the rights and remedies granted by the Act are exclusive and bar all other claims against the employer on account of personal injury or death by accident. Actions for intentional torts, including intentional infliction of emotional distress, committed by the employer are not excluded by this provision. Dickert v. Metro. Life Ins. Co., 311 S.C. 218, 219, 428 S.E.2d 700, 701 (S.C. 1993). However, when the intentional tort is committed by another employee, a claim against an employer for negligent supervision of the co-employee would be excluded if the tort is in the nature of a personal injury. *Id.* Therefore, to the extent that a privacy action is founded on emotional distress to the plaintiff caused by the actions of a co-employee, the S.C. Supreme Court has held that such a claim is in the nature of a personal injury and is precluded by the Act. *Id.* at 702. The court in *Dickert* recognized, however, that some privacy claims might be founded on harm done to the employee's proprietary interests rather than to his person, and stated that these claims would not be barred. *Id.* More recently, the U.S. District Court for South Carolina held that a claim for invasion of privacy was not precluded by the Act under S.C. law. Frasier v. Verizon Wireless, C.A. No. 8:08-356-HMH, 2008 WL 724037 at *3 (D.S.C. 2008).

D. Pleading Requirements

Todd v. South Carolina Farm Bureau Mut. Ins. Co., 276 S.C. 284, 278 S.E.2d 607 (1981), appeal after remand, 283 S.C. 155, 321 S.E.2d 602 (Ct. App. 1984), quashed in part on other grounds, 287 S.C. 190, 336 S.E.2d 472 (1985) held that allegations by a former employee, in a suit against his former employers and third parties, that defendants wrongfully accused the former employee of leaking information from an investigation of fire loss claims to an arsonist, and that defendants published these accusations to the public, supported the former employee's cause of action against defendants for invasion of his right of privacy, and therefore the trial court did not err in overruling defendants' demurrer to the cause of action based on that right.

In order to state a cause of action for invasion of privacy, plaintiff must allege the unwarranted appropriation or exploitation of his personality, the publicizing of his private affairs with which the public has no legitimate concern, or the wrongful intrusion into one's private activities in such a manner as to outrage or cause mental suffering, shame or humiliation to a person of ordinary sensibilities. Corder v. Champion Road Machinery Intern. Corp., 283 S.C. 520, 324 S.E.2d 79 (Ct. App. 1984), cert. denied, 286 S.C. 126, 332 S.E.2d 533 (1985).

SURVEY OF SOUTH DAKOTA EMPLOYMENT LIBEL LAW

Heather C. Knox
Lynn, Jackson, Shultz & Lebrun, P.C.
P.O. Box 8250, Rapid City, SD 57709
Telephone: 605-342-2592; Facsimile: 605-342-5185
www.lynnjackson.com

(With Developments Reported Through **November 1, 2012**)

GENERAL COMMENTS

None.

SIGNIFICANT DEVELOPMENTS SINCE THE 2012 *SURVEY*

None.

I. GENERAL LAW

A. General Employment Law

1. ***At Will Employment***. South Dakota recognizes no cause of action for the discharge of an at will employee, absent certain court-created exceptions. Reynolds v. Ethicon Endo-Surgery, Inc., 454 F.3d 868, (S.D. 2006), see also Zavadil v. Alcoa Extrusions, Inc., 363 F.Supp.2d 1187 (S.D. 2005) (list of exceptions provided by court). South Dakota courts have recognized that a discharged employee may have a valid defamation claim. Nelson v. WEB Water Dev. Assn. Inc., 507 N.W.2d 691 (S.D. 1993). The defamation claims may arise from comments made concerning the discharged employee's job performance. Nelson, supra.

An employer creates a protected property right in continued employment for its employees when it surrenders its statutory at-will power and adopts a discharge policy that provides termination will occur only for cause. Aberle v. City of Aberdeen, 2006 S.D. 60, 718 N.W.2d 615 (2006).

B. Elements of Libel Claim

1. ***Basic Elements***. Libel is considered a false and unprivileged publication, in writing, printing, picture or effigy, which exposes the person to hatred, contempt, ridicule, or obloquy, or which has a tendency to injure him in his occupation. S.D.C.L. § 20-11-3. Slander is defined as a false and unprivileged communication, other than libel, which charges anyone with a crime, imputes to him an infectious or loathsome disease, tends directly to injure him in respect to his office or occupation, either by imputing general disqualification to perform, or to lessen profit, imputes impotence or lack of chastity, or by natural consequence, causes actual damage. S.D.C.L. § 20-11-4.

2. ***Fault***. The level of fault is dependent upon the plaintiff's public or private status. Nelson v. WEB Water Dev. Assn. Inc., 507 N.W.2d 691 (S.D. 1993). If the employee/plaintiff has thrust himself into the public arena through his employment activities, he is considered a limited purpose public figure for fault analysis in any employment defamation claim. Id.

A public employee who offers his or her personal opinions or beliefs, especially in the work setting, does not implicate matters of "public concern," as element for First Amendment protection of public employee speech. Gilbert v. Flandreau Santee Sioux Tribe, 2006 S.D. 109, 725 N.W.2d 249 (2006).

a. **Private Figure Plaintiff/Matter of Public Concern**. See Nelson v. WEB Water Dev. Assn. Inc., 507 N.W.2d 691 (S.D. 1993), discussed supra.

b. **Private Figure Plaintiff/Matter of Private Concern**. No cases.

c. **Public Figure Plaintiff/Matter of Public Concern**. See Gilbert v. Flandreau Santee Sioux Tribe, 2006 S.D. 109, 725 N.W.2d 249 (2006), discussed supra.

3. ***Falsity***. Public figure plaintiffs bear the burden of proving the falsity of any statement. Janklow v. Viking Press, 459 N.W.2d 415, 17 Media L. Rep. 2220 (S.D. 1990) (overruled on other grounds).

In order to recover under clear and convincing evidentiary standard in libel action, public-figure plaintiff must show that defendant knew defamatory statements were false or acted with reckless disregard of truth in publishing statements, and to establish actual malice must show that false publication was made with high degree of awareness of its probable falsity. Krueger v. Austad, 1996 S.D. 26, 545 N.W.2d 205 (1996); Saathoff v. Kuhlman, 2009 SD 17, 763 N.W.2d 800 (2009) (trial court obligated to use clear and convincing standard to assess actual malice at summary judgment stage). Absent plaintiff's proof of the viability of his claim, the court will not reach other defenses raised. Saathoff, supra.

Under South Dakota law, neither libel nor slander requires a showing that the publisher of the false publication has knowledge of the falsity of the publication. Cincinnati Ins. Co. v. Pro Enters., Inc., 394 F.Supp.2d 1127 (S.D. 2005).

4. ***Defamatory Statement of Fact.*** In all trials for libel, both civil and criminal, the truth, when published with good motives and for justifiable ends, shall be a sufficient defense. Gilbert v. Flandreau Santee Sioux Tribe, 2006 S.D. 109, 725 N.W.2d 249 (2006). See Section B.1 supra.

5. ***Of and Concerning Plaintiff.*** In a libel suit, it must appear that alleged defamatory language refers to some ascertained or ascertainable person and that person must be plaintiff, although action may be maintained where defamed person is not named but is sufficiently identified by reference in article to facts and circumstances from which others may understand that such person is referred to. Brodsky v. Journal Pub. Co., 73 S.D. 343, 42 N.W.2d 855 (1950).

6. ***Publication.***

a. **Intracorporate Communication**. South Dakota has recognized a defamation claim concerning statements made by the employer to the discharged employee's co-workers. Petersen v. Dacy, 1996 S.D. 72, 550 N.W.2d 91 (1996). The statements, however, were deemed privileged.

b. **Compelled Self-Publication**. Mentioned in dicta, but not yet recognized by the South Dakota Supreme Court. Schwaiger v. Avera Queen of Peace Health Servs., 2006 S.D. 44, 714 N.W.2d 874 (S.D. 2006).

c. **Republication**. General rule is anyone who takes part in any publication of the material may be liable for defamation. Janklow v. Viking Press, 378 N.W.2d 875, 17 Media L. Rep. 2220 (S.D. 1985) (overruled on other grounds).

7. ***Statements versus Conduct.*** No reported cases in South Dakota.

8. ***Damages.*** Plaintiff must plead special damages unless complaint can allege libel per se. Brodsky v. Journal Publishing Co., 73 S.D. 343, 42 N.W.2d 855 (S.D. 1950) (citing Niblo v. Ede, 35 S.D. 359, 152 N.W. 284 (1915) and Adams v. Scott, 33 S.D. 194, 145 N.W. 446 (1914).

a. **Presumed Damages and Libel Per Se.** Defamation per se is generally defined by statute. See Section B.1 supra.

(1) **Employment-Related Criticism**. No reported cases in South Dakota.

(2) **Single Instance Rule**. No reported cases in South Dakota.

b. **Punitive Damages**. Punitive damages are available in defamation claims in South Dakota when the defendant acted with malice. S.D.C.L. § 21-3-2.

II. PRIVILEGES AND DEFENSES

A. Scope of Privileges

1. ***Absolute Privilege.*** See S.D.C.L. § 20-11-5 (1) and (2). South Dakota recognizes an absolute privilege for statements made in a judicial or legislative proceeding. Flugge v. Wagner, 532 N.W.2d 419 (S.D. 1995). The absolute privilege extends to statements made to peer review boards. Id. (communications to State Board of Accountancy accorded absolute privilege). An absolute privilege is also afforded to public officials in the discharge of their duties. Hackworth v. Larson, 83 S.D. 674, 165 N.W.2d 705 (1969) (press release by Secretary of State concerning termination of two deputies considered to be within her official duties and subject to absolute privilege). The absolute privilege does not extend to an employer's internal investigation of employee misconduct, and statements made during the investigation, as the employer's investigation cannot be considered an official proceeding" under the statute. Pawlovich v. Linke, 2004 S.D. 109, 688 N.W.2d 218. However, a qualified "common interest" privilege will apply. S.D.C.L. § 20-11-5(3).

2. ***Qualified Privileges***

a. **Common Interest**. Statements between "interested persons" are afforded a qualified privilege. Petersen v. Dacy, 1996 S.D. 72, 550 N.W.2d 91 (1996) (Statements made to co-workers about dismissal of another employee considered to be between "interested persons," and subject to qualified privilege). See S.D.C.L. § 20-11-5 (3).

b. **Duty**. The privilege for discharge of an official duty is absolute. S.D.C.L. § 20-11-5(1). Ruple v. Weinaug, 328 N.W.2d 857 (S.D. 1983) (city manager's communication to mayor concerning finance officer, made without malice and in proper discharge of city manager's official duty, was absolutely privileged). Hackworth v. Larson, 83 S.D. 674, 165 N.W.2d 705 (1969).

c. **Criticism of Public Employee**. A person whose position grants them responsibility or control over conduct of governmental affairs or who holds a position of apparent importance which fosters the independent interest of the public may be considered a "public figure" or "public official" under First Amendment for libel purposes. Sparagon v. Native American Publishers Inc., 1996 S.D. 3, 542 N.W.2d 125 (S.D. 1996).

d. **Limitation on Qualified Privileges**.

(1) **Constitutional or Actual Malice.** Reckless disregard requires the plaintiff to show the defendant entertained serious doubts as to the truth of his publications. Uken v. Sloat, 296 N.W.2d 540 (S.D. 1980). The evidence must show that the defendant actually had a high degree of awareness of the probable falsity of the statements. Janklow v. Viking Press, 459 N.W.2d 415 (S.D. 1990) (overruled on other grounds); Krueger v. Austad, 1996 S.D. 26, 545 N.W.2d 205 (1996)

(2) **Common Law Malice.** Malice is not presumed from the falsity of any statement. Uken v. Sloat, 296 N.W.2d 540 (S.D. 1980).

Malice, which would defeat qualified privilege, cannot be assumed from a defamatory communication alone. Plaintiff must show either the presence of malice or reckless disregard of the truth. S.D.C.L. § 20-11-5; Schwaiger v. Avera Queen of Peace Health Servs., 714 N.W.2d 874 (S.D. 2006).

(3) **Other Limitations on Qualified Privileges**

e. **Question of Fact or Law**. Existence of privilege in defamation action is question for the court. Schwaiger v. Avera Queen of Peace Health Servs., 2006 S.D. 44, 714 N.W.2d 874 (S.D. 2006); Sparagon v. Native American Publishers Inc., 1996 S.D. 3, 542 N.W.2d 125 (1996)

f. **Burden of Proof**. The plaintiff has the burden to allege both the falsity of the statements, and the fact that no privilege would apply. Tibke v. McDougall, 479 N.W.2d 898 (S.D. 1992). Plaintiff also has the burden to prove that if conditionally privileged, there was a reckless disregard for the truth on the part of the defendant. Id.

Public figure or public official bringing libel action faces higher burden of proof than ordinary civil litigant as result of "New York Times rule," which prohibits public figure or official from recovering damages for defamatory falsehood relating to his official conduct unless he proves that statement was made with "actual malice," or with knowledge that it was false or with reckless disregard of whether it was false or not, and further requires that actual malice be shown with "convincing clarity," or "clear and convincing proof." Sparagon v. Native American Publishers Inc., 542 N.W.2d 125, 1996 S.D. 3 (S.D. 1996).

B. Standard Libel Defenses

1. ***Truth***. Truth is a defense to all defamation claims, regardless of the existence of a privilege. S.D. Const. Art. VI, § 5.

2. ***Opinion***. There is no constitutional privilege for a broad category of speech labeled "opinion"; expressions of opinion may often imply assertions of objective fact, and those statements are actionable. Paint Brush Corp. v. Neu, 1999 S.D. 120, 599 N.W.2d 384 (1999), overruling Janklow v. Viking Press, 459 N.W.2d 415, 17 Media L. Rep. 2220 (S.D. 1990).

3. ***Consent***. No reported cases in South Dakota.

4. ***Mitigation***. A party to an action for libel charging the plaintiff with the commission of a crime which he fails to justify, is subject to actual damages, circumstances may be shown in mitigation may constitute a partial defense by exempting a defendant from a verdict for exemplary damages in addition to actual damages. Williams v. Black, 24 S.D. 501, 124 N.W. 728 (S.D.1910).

III. RECURRING FACT PATTERNS

A. Statements in Personnel File

Statements in a personnel file appear to be subject to the qualified privilege based upon common interest. Petersen v. Dacy, 1996 S.D. 72, 550 N.W.2d 91 (1996). No specific case addressing this issue is reported.

B. Performance Evaluations

See Section III, A. above.

C. References

South Dakota has one reported case in which a former employee filed a defamation action based upon statements communicated to a prospective employer. Guilford v. Northwestern Public Serv., 1998 S.D. 71, 581 N.W.2d 178 (1998). The action was dismissed because the employee failed to prove the falsity of the statements. The Court did not address the question of whether a common interest qualified privilege might apply.

D. Intracorporate Communication

Intracorporate communications should be subject to a qualified privilege of common interest. Petersen v. Dacy, 1996 S.D. 72, 550 N.W.2d 91 (1996).

E. Statements to Government Regulators

An absolute privilege exists for statements made to judicial or legislative bodies. These include administrative agencies and peer review boards. Flugge v. Wagner, 532 N.W.2d 419 (S.D. 1995).

F. Reports to Auditors and Insurers

No reported cases.

G. Vicarious Liability of Employers for Statements Made by Employees

1. ***Scope of Employment***. No reported cases, although the Court has discussed an employer's defamation liability in the context of statements made by an employee in the course of his employment. Guilford v. Northwestern Public Serv., 1998 S.D. 71, 581 N.W.2d 178 (1998).

a. **Blogging.** No reported cases.

2. ***Damages***. No reported cases.

H. Internal Investigations

No Reported Cases.

IV. OTHER ACTIONS BASED ON STATEMENTS

A. Negligent Hiring, Retention, and Supervision

South Dakota recognizes a tort based upon negligent hiring and/or supervision. Rehm v. Lenz, 1996 S.D. 51, 547 N.W.2d 560 (1996).

B. Intentional Infliction of Emotional Distress

This tort is recognized in South Dakota. Kjerstad v. Ravellette Publications, Inc., 517 N.W.2d 419 (S.D. 1994). The tort may be proved either by intentional or reckless conduct causing severe emotional distress. Id. In Speck v. Federal Land Bank of Omaha, 494 N.W.2d 628 (S.D. 1993), the allegations of intentional infliction of emotional distress were based upon allegedly defamatory statements. The Court dismissed the action upon other grounds, and did not specifically address the issue of whether the claim can be supported if based upon statements.

C. Interference with Economic Advantage

South Dakota recognizes this action. Tibke v. McDougall, 479 N.W.2d 898 (S.D. 1992). The essential elements of tortious interference with business relations or expectancy include: (1) the existence of a valid business relationship or expectancy; (2) knowledge by the interferer of the relationship or expectancy; (3) an intentional and unjustified act of interference on the part of the interferer; (4) proof that the interference caused the harm sustained; and (5) damage to the party whose relationship or expectancy was disrupted. Mueller v. Cedar Shore Resort, Inc., 2002 SD 38, ¶ 35, 643 N.W.2d 56, 68 (citing Tibke v. McDougall, 479 N.W.2d 898, 908 (S.D.1992)). In Guilford v. Northwestern Public Serv., 1998 S.D. 71, 581 N.W.2d 178 (1998), Plaintiff raised the issue based upon statements made to a prospective employer, but the Court rejected the action upon other grounds.

D. Prima Facie Tort

South Dakota has no reported decisions explicitly accepting or rejecting a prima facie tort theory. The Court dismissed a wrongful termination case brought, in part, under this theory since the employee was terminable at will. Blote v. First Federal Sav. and Loan Assn., 422 N.W.2d 834 (S.D. 1988).

V. OTHER ISSUES

A. Statute of Limitations

The statute of limitations is two (2) years. S.D.C.L. § 15-2-15.

B. Jurisdiction

Defamation claims are excluded from the jurisdiction of the small claims courts.

C. Worker's Compensation Exclusivity

Worker's compensation is the exclusive remedy for all personal injury or death claims arising out of one's employment, excepting those arising from an intentional tort. S.D.C.L. §62-3-2. No specific cases have addressed whether the statute applies to defamation claims, although the exclusive remedy provision has been broadly interpreted by the South Dakota Courts to prevent such common law claims against the employer.

D. Pleading Requirements

It is sufficient to generally plead the facts concerning the allegedly defamatory statements, and that the same were published about the plaintiff. S.D.C.L. § 15-6-9(i).

SURVEY OF SOUTH DAKOTA EMPLOYMENT PRIVACY LAW

Heather C. Knox
Lynn, Jackson, Shultz & Lebrun, P.C.
P.O. Box 8250
Rapid City, SD 57709
Telephone 605-342-2592; Facsimile 605-342-5185
www.lynnjackson.com

(With Developments Reported Through **November 1, 2012**)

GENERAL COMMENTS

None.

SIGNIFICANT DEVELOPMENTS SINCE THE 2012 *SURVEY*

None.

I. GENERAL LAW OF PRIVACY

A. Legal Basis of Privacy Claims

South Dakota by common law recognizes a general, all encompassing cause of action sounding in the invasion of the right of privacy. Truxes v. Kenco Enters. Inc., 80 S.D.104, 119 N.W.2d 914 (1963). An actionable violation of the right of privacy has been acknowledged by this court to be: The unwarranted appropriation or exploitation of one's personality, the publicizing of one's private affairs with which the public has no legitimate concern, or the wrongful intrusion into one's private activities, in such manner as to outrage or cause mental suffering, shame, or humiliation to a person of ordinary sensibilities. Hart v. Miller, 2000 S.D. 53, 609 N.W.2d 138 (S.D., 2000) (quoting Truxes v. Kenco Enters. Inc., 80 S.D. 104, 119 N.W.2d 914, 916 (1963).

B. Causes of Action

1. ***Misappropriation/Right of Publicity***. South Dakota has not explicitly accepted or rejected a misappropriation tort. In Montgomery Ward v. Shope, 286 N.W.2d 806 (S.D. 1979), the Court cited with approval, as a recognized invasion of the right of privacy classification, the Restatement (Second) of Torts section stating that the right of privacy is invaded by appropriation of the other's name or likeness.

2. ***False Light***. South Dakota has not expressly adopted the false light tort, but the South Dakota Supreme Court has implied that a false light claim may be cognizable. Truxes v. Kenco Enters. Inc., 80 S.D. 104, 119 N.W.2d 914 (1963).

3. ***Publication of Private Facts***. South Dakota has not expressly accepted or rejected a publication of private facts tort. The Supreme Court has noted, however, that the right of privacy may be invaded by unreasonable publicity given one's private life. Montgomery Ward v. Shope, 286 N.W.2d 806 (S.D. 1979).

4. ***Intrusion***. While South Dakota has not expressly accepted an intrusion tort, the Court has indicated that the tort of invasion of the right of privacy includes an intrusion element. Kjerstad v. Ravellette Publications Inc., 517 N.W.2d 419 (S.D. 1994); see also Roth v. Farner-Bocken Co., 667 N.W.2d 651(S.D. 2003) (Court recognized intrusion-type claim for employer's interception and opening of employee's private mail).

C. Other Privacy-Related Actions

1. ***Intentional Infliction of Emotional Distress.*** South Dakota does recognize a tort cause of action for the intentional infliction of emotional distress. Kjerstad v. Ravellette Publications Inc., 517 N.W.2d 419 (S.D. 1994). To establish intentional infliction of emotional distress one must demonstrate: an act by the defendant that amounts to extreme and outrageous conduct; that the defendant intended to cause extreme emotional distress on the plaintiff; causation; and that the plaintiff "suffered an extreme disabling emotional response to defendant's conduct." Murphy v. Kmart Corp., 2011 WL 887908 (D.S.D. Mar. 14, 2011).

2. ***Interference with Prospective Economic Advantage.*** The tort of interference with prospective advantage was adopted by the Court in Tibke v. McDougall, 479 N.W.2d 898 (S.D. 1992). Plaintiff must prove (1) the existence of a business expectancy; (2) knowledge by the interferer of the expectancy; (3) an intentional and unjustified act of interference; (4) proof that the interference caused harm; and (5) damage to the party whose expectancy was disrupted.

3. ***Prima Facie Tort.*** South Dakota has not expressly accepted or rejected this theory.

II. EMPLOYER TESTING OF EMPLOYEES

A. Psychological or Personality Testing

1. ***Common Law and Statutes.*** No reported cases.

2. ***Private Employers.*** No reported cases.

3. ***Public Employers.*** No reported cases.

B. Drug Testing

1. ***Common Law and Statutes.*** No reported cases, although the Court has affirmed a case where an employer used a drug test to raise a statutory defense to a worker's compensation action. Goebel v. Warren Transp., 2000 S.D. 79, 612 N.W.2d 18 (2000).

2. ***Private Employers.*** No reported cases.

3. ***Public Employers.*** No reported cases.

C. Medical Testing

1. ***Common law and statutes.*** No reported cases.

2. ***Private Employers.*** No reported cases.

3. ***Public Employers.*** No reported cases.

D. Polygraph Tests

No reported cases.

E. Fingerprinting

No reported cases.

III. SEARCHES

A. Employee's Person

No reported cases.

1. ***Private Employers.*** No reported cases.

2. ***Public Employers.*** No reported cases.

B. Employee's Work Area

No reported cases. The Court has noted, in another context, that an employer has an expected right of privacy in the employee's work area. Gateway 2000 Inc. v. Limoges, 1996 S.D. 81, 552 N.W.2d 591 (1996) (company may disallow service of civil summons in employee work areas).

C. Employee's Property. No reported cases.

1. ***Private Employers.*** No reported cases.

2. ***Public Employers.*** No reported cases.

IV. MONITORING OF EMPLOYEES

A. Telephones and Electronic Communications.

While there are no reported cases regarding an employer monitoring an employee's telephonic and electronic communications, the District Court for the District of South Dakota recently suggested people have no expectation of privacy in addressing information on their phones, such as the numbers dialed, because they have voluntarily conveyed this information to their phone carrier. This does not necessarily extend to the content of the phone call. U.S. v. Yazzie, 2011 WL 590112 (D.S.D. Jan. 25, 2011).

1. ***Wiretapping***. S.D.C.L. § 22-21-1 criminalizes a trespass on property with the intent to subject anyone to eavesdropping or surveillance in a private place, or the installation in any private place, without the consent of the person entitled to privacy therein, of any device for observing, photographing, recording, amplifying, or broadcasting sounds or events in such place.

2. ***Electronic Communications***. No reported cases.

3. ***Other Electronic Monitoring.*** No reported cases.

B. Mail

No reported cases.

C. Surveillance/Photographing

See Section IV, A.1 above.

V. ACTIVITIES OUTSIDE THE WORKPLACE

A. Statute or Common Law

South Dakota has one reported case in which an employee was terminated due to outside the workplace activities. Butterfield v. Citibank of S.D. N.A., 437 N.W.2d 857 (S.D. 1989) (The employee was terminated for an outside stock analysis business). The Court refused to grant the employee a cause of action since he was terminable at will.

B. Employees' Personal Relationships

The Court declined to find misconduct in an unemployment insurance case for an employee of the State who attempted to solicit a personal relationship with a client of his agency. Wernke v. State, 1999 S.D. 32, 590 N.W.2d 260 (1999).

1. ***Romantic Relationships Between Employees.*** No reported cases.

2. ***Sexual Orientation.*** No reported cases.

3. ***Marital Status.*** No reported cases.

C. Smoking

South Dakota by statute prohibits the discrimination against any employee for his off duty use of tobacco, unless the restriction relates to a bona fide occupational requirement and is reasonably related to the employee's employment activities. Wood v. S.D. Cement Plant, 1999 S.D. 8, 588 N.W.2d 227 (1999). S.D.C.L. § 60-4-11.

D. Blogging

No reported cases.

VI. RECORDS

A. Personnel Records

No reported cases.

B. Medical Records

No reported cases.

C. Criminal Records

No reported cases.

D. Subpoenas / Search Warrants

Employers may be compelled to allow the search of an employee's desk, etc., when presented with a search warrant. State v. Helland, 2005 S.D. 121, 707 N.W.2d 262, (S.D. 2005).

VII. ACTIONS SUBSEQUENT TO EMPLOYMENT

A. References

S.D.C.L. § 60-4-12 provides a presumption of good faith in any action arising out of claimed defamation for a post-employment reference if the employer responds in writing to a written request by a prospective employer for an evaluation of the former employee's job performance.

B. Non-Compete Agreements

Generally considered a contract in restraint of trade and disfavored. However, non-compete agreements are upheld if the agreement comports with the territorial and temporal limitations set by statute. S.D.C.L. § 53-9-11. Ward v. Midcom Inc., 1998 S.D. 10, 575 N.W.2d 233. The prevailing party in an action to enforce the non-compete agreement may be awarded attorney's fees in the event the parties' agreement so provided. Midcom Inc. v. Oehlerking, 2006 S.D. 67, 722 N.W.2d 722 (S.D. 2006).

VIII. OTHER ISSUES

A. Statutes of Limitations

Privacy claim must be brought within the general statute for tort claims of three years. S.D.C.L. § 15-2-14. An action for "wages" must be brought within two years. S.D.C.L. § 15-2-15. The statute of limitations on a privacy claim is tolled when employer fraudulently conceals an invasion of employee's privacy and employee acts with due diligence in discovering the invasion. Roth v. Farner-Bocken Co., 2003 S.D. 80, 667 N.W.2d 651 (S.D. 2003).

B. Jurisdiction

No cases.

C. Worker's Compensation Exclusivity

Worker's compensation is the exclusive remedy for all personal injury or death claims arising out of one's employment, excepting those arising from an intentional tort. S.D.C.L. § 62-3-2. No specific cases have addressed whether the statute applies to defamation claims, although the exclusive remedy provision has been broadly interpreted by the South Dakota Courts to prevent such common law claims against the employer.

D. Pleading Requirements

Pleading shall set forth a plain statement of the claim showing the pleader is entitled to relief; and a demand for judgment. S.D.C.L. § 15-6-8(a).

SURVEY OF TENNESSEE EMPLOYMENT LIBEL LAW

Lucian T. Pera, Esq.
Adams and Reese LLP
Brinkley Plaza
80 Monroe Ave., Suite 700
Memphis, Tennessee 38103
Telephone: (901) 524-5278
Facsimile: (901) 524-5378
Email: Lucian.Pera@arlaw.com
Website: www.arlaw.com

Margaret R. T. Myers, Esq.
Adams and Reese LLP
Fifth Third Center
424 Church Street, Suite 2800
Nashville, Tennessee 37219
Telephone: (615) 259-1009
Facsimile: (615) 259-1470
Email: Margaret.Myers@arlaw.com
Website: www.arlaw.com

(With Developments Reported Through **November 1, 2012**)

GENERAL COMMENTS

The Tennessee appellate court system is two-tiered, consisting of the Tennessee Supreme Court and the Court of Appeals in civil cases. Opinions of the Supreme Court are generally published in the West reporter. Tennessee Court of Appeals opinions are generally not published unless an application for permission to appeal to the Tennessee Supreme Court is denied. Most Tennessee unpublished decisions may be ordered from the Tennessee Attorneys Memo by telephone at (615) 248-5900. Most Tennessee appellate decisions issued since about 1995 are also available without charge at a web site maintained by the Tennessee Supreme Court at www.tsc.state.tn.us and available by subscription at the Tennessee Bar Association's site, TBALink, at www.tba.org.

SIGNIFICANT DEVELOPMENTS SINCE THE 2012 *SURVEY*

None.

I. GENERAL LAW

A. General Employment Law

1. ***At Will Employment.*** A presumption arises in Tennessee that an employee is an employee at-will. Davis v. Connecticut General Life Ins. Co., 743 F. Supp. 1273, 1280 (M.D. Tenn. 1990). Without a clear contract under which rights may vest, employees possess no contractual right under the employment at-will doctrine. Bennett v. Steiner-Liff Iron & Metal Co., 58 Fair Empl. Prac. Cas. (BNA) 733, 826 S.W.2d 119 (Tenn. 1992). When employment is terminable at will, there is no property interest in future employment. Sudberry v. Royal & Sun Alliance, No. M2008-00751-COA-R3-CV, 2008 Tenn. App. LEXIS 607 (Tenn. Ct. App., Western Section, Oct. 3, 2008). The doctrine of employment at-will has long been recognized in this state with the concomitant right of either party to terminate such a relationship at any time for good cause, bad cause, or no cause. Whittaker v. Care-More, Inc., 621 S.W.2d 395 (Tenn. Ct. App.), appeal denied (Tenn. 1981); Chism v. Mid-South Milling Co., Inc., 762 S.W.2d 552, 555 (Tenn. 1988); Bennett, supra; Forrester v. Stockstill, 869 S.W.2d 328 (Tenn. 1994); **Thompson v. Memphis Light, Gas & Water, No. W2009-02447-COA-R3-CV, 2011 Tenn. App. LEXIS 206 (Tenn. Ct. App. Apr. 29, 2011), appeal denied (Tenn. Oct. 18, 2011).** A contract of employment for a definite term may not be terminated before the end of the term, except for good cause or by mutual agreement, unless the right to do so is reserved in the contract. Nelson Trabue, Inc. v. Professional Management-Automotive, Inc., 589 S.W.2d 661 (Tenn. 1979); Bennett, supra; **Hutchings v. Jobe, Hastings & Assocs., No. M2010-01583-COA-R3-CV, 2011 Tenn. App. LEXIS 442 (Tenn. Ct. App. Aug. 12, 2011) (no appeal sought).** An employee handbook can become part of an employment contract if the language in the handbook specifically shows the employer's intent to be bound by the handbook's provisions. Smith v. Morris, 778 S.W.2d 857, 858 (Tenn. Ct. App. 1988), appeal denied (Tenn. 1989); Claiborne v. Frito-Lay, Inc., 718 F. Supp. 1319 (E.D. Tenn. 1989); Brown v. City of Niota, 214 F.3d 718 (6th Cir. 2000).

Tennessee common law and statutes recognize that employers are prevented from terminating employees for reasons that offend well-defined public policy. By statute, an employer cannot terminate an employee because of his/her race, creed, color, religion, sex, age, or national origin, Tenn. Code Ann. § 4-21-401(a)(1) (1998); on the basis of any physical, mental, or visual handicap, unless the handicap prevents the individual from performing the duties required by the employment sough or impairs the performance of the work involved, Tenn. Code Ann. § 8-50-103(a) (2002); because the employee reports or participates in an investigation or prosecution of workplace safety violations, Tenn. Code Ann. § 50-3-106(7) (1999); because the employee, after providing the required advanced notice, misses work to serve on a jury, Tenn. Code Ann. § 22-4-108(f) (Supp. 1992); because the employee asserts a worker's compensation claim, Tenn. Code Ann. § 50-6-114 (1999); Clanton v. Cain-Sloan Co., 677 S.W.2d 441 (Tenn. 1984); Anderson v. Standard Register Co., 857 S.W.2d 555 (Tenn. 1993); **Johnson v. Total Renal Care, Inc., No. 1:11-cv-01047-JDB-egb2012, U.S. Dist. LEXIS 35172 (W.D. Tenn.**

Mar. 15, 2012); Caraway v. Goodman Mfg. Co., L.P., No. 1:10-cv-2472011, U.S. Dist. LEXIS 139897 (E.D. Tenn. Dec. 5, 2011); because the employee uses a legal tobacco product, i.e. smokes so long as it is done in a manner compliant with all applicable employer policies regarding such use, such use during work time, Tenn. Code Ann. § 50-1-304(e); or because the employee refuses to participate in or be silent about illegal activity in the workplace, Tenn. Code Ann. § 50-1-304(a)-(d) (Supp. 2002) (popularly known as the "whistle-blower" statute); **Sykes v. Chattanooga Hous. Auth., 343 S.W.3d 18 (Tenn. 2011).**

The common law tort of retaliatory discharge is also recognized. Chism v. Mid-South Milling Co., Inc., 762 S.W.2d 552 (Tenn. 1988); Robins v. Flagship Airlines, Inc., 956 S.W.2d 4 (Tenn. Ct. App.), appeal denied (Tenn. 1997); Baines v. Wilson County, 86 S.W.3d 575 (Tenn. Ct. App. 2002) (plaintiff firefighter failed to state a claim for retaliatory discharge against his supervisor in his individual capacity, because he was not the firefighter's employer, a required element of a retaliatory discharge claim); Mountjoy v. City of Chattanooga, slip op., No. E2001-02017-COA-R3-CV, 2002 Tenn. App. LEXIS 277 (Tenn. Ct. App., Eastern Section, April 23, 2002) (court found city employer retaliated against employee for filing sexual harassment claim by demoting her); See also Sloan v. Tri-County Elec. Mbrshp. Corp., slip op., No. M2000-01794-COA-R3-CV, 2002 Tenn. App. LEXIS 109 (Tenn. Ct. App., Middle Section, February 7, 2002) (defendant asked that plaintiff or her husband resign because of company's anti-nepotism policy. Plaintiff failed to maintain an action for wrongful discharge since an employment practice that prohibits concurrent employment of spouses violates no clear public policy mandate). Note that establishing the common law tort of retaliatory discharge requires proof that the employee's protected activity played a "substantial role" in the employee's termination, but establishing a claim under the "whistle-blower" statute, Tenn. Code Ann. § 50-1-304 (Supp. 2002), requires that the plaintiff prove that the "sole reason" for termination was that the employee was engaged in protected activity. The Tennessee Supreme Court has recently recognized that in-house counsel could bring a common-law action of retaliatory discharge resulting from counsel's compliance with an ethical duty that represented a clear and definitive statement of public policy. Crews v. Buckman Labs. Int'l, 78 S.W. 3d 852 (Tenn. 2002). The court found that the elements of a common-law retaliatory discharge claim were satisfied since: (1) there was an at-will employment relationship; (2) a clear public policy evidenced by the ethical duty not to aid in the unauthorized practice of law existed; (3) plaintiff did not voluntarily leave her employment; and (4) the sole motivation for the constructive discharge was plaintiff's adherence to her ethical duties to report the unauthorized practice of law. Id. See, II.A.1, infra.

At common law, Tennessee recognizes the employment at will rule which provides that employment for an indefinite term is a contract at will and can be terminated by either party, at any time, without cause. This principle is still viable in Tennessee, except where modified by statute. Tenn. Code Ann. § 50-1-304 (Supp. 2002) is a narrowly crafted statutory exception to the common law rule. Tenn. Code Ann. § 50-1-304 (Supp. 2002) provides, in pertinent part, that no employee shall be discharged or terminated solely for refusing to participate in or for refusing to remain silent about illegal activities. "Illegal activities" means activities which are in violation of the criminal or civil code of this state or of the United States or any regulation intended to protect the public health, safety, or welfare. An employee terminated in violation of this code section has a cause of action against the employer for retaliatory discharge and any other damages to which the employee may be entitled. Tenn. Code Ann. § 50-1-304 (Supp. 2002); see Darnall v. A+ Homecare, Inc., slip op., No. 01A01 -9807-CV-00347, 1999 Tenn. App. LEXIS 339, 15 IER CAS 353 (Tenn. Ct. App., Middle Section, June 2, 1999). Allowing an employment contract to expire on its own terms does not constitute a "termination" for purposes of the whistleblower statute. Howard v. Life Care Ctrs., slip op., No. E2004-00212-COA-R3-CV, 2004 Tenn. App. LEXIS 534 (Tenn. Ct. App., Eastern Section, Aug. 20, 2004). The Tennessee Supreme Court recently clarified that a common-law whistleblower cause of action survived the enactment of Tenn. Code Ann. § 50-1-304 (Supp. 2002). Thus, an employee in Tennessee may sue under either the statute or the common law. The primary benefit for the employee proceeding under common law is the ability to avoid the statutory requirement that the termination be "solely" as a result of the protected activity. Guy v. Mut. of Omaha Ins. Co., 79 S.W.3d 528 (Tenn. 2002).

B. Elements of Libel Claim

1. ***Basic Elements.*** Defamation consists of a false and defamatory statement of fact regarding the plaintiff which is communicated to a third party causing injury to the plaintiff's reputation. Sullivan v. Young, 678 S.W.2d 906 (Tenn. Ct. App.), appeal denied (Tenn. 1984); Stones River Motors, Inc. v. Mid-South Publ'g Co., 651 S.W.2d 713 (Tenn. Ct. App.), appeal denied (Tenn. 1983). Defamation also protects an individual's business reputation in his professional community along with his general standing in the greater community. Forsman v. Rouse, No. 3:07-0327, 2008 U.S. Dist. LEXIS 47266 (M.D. Tenn. June 16, 2008) (a false accusation that an individual used profanity in his business or trade may be defamatory if it causes ridicule or disgrace within his professional community). To be defamatory, a statement must hold the plaintiff up to a level of public hatred, contempt, ridicule, or disgrace. Naylor Med. Sales & Rentals, Inc. v. Invacare Continuing Care, Inc., No. 09-2344-STA-cgc, 2011 U.S. Dist. LEXIS 263, at *42 (W.D. Tenn. Jan. 3, 2011). There is no valid claim for defamation when an individual defendant does not personally publish the allegedly defamatory statement. Jackson v. Dempsey, No. 1:09-CV-240, 2010 U.S. Dist. LEXIS 32823 (E.D. Tenn. Apr. 2, 2010) (defamation claim failed because alleged defamatory statement was issued by an organization, not the individual defendant). Plaintiffs are required to

prove actual damages in all defamation cases regardless of whether the defamatory meaning was obvious or not. Pate v. Service Merchandise Co., 959 S.W.2d 569 (Tenn. Ct. App. 1996), appeal denied (Tenn. 1997), cert. denied, 118 S. Ct. 76 (U.S. Oct. 6, 1997).

Tennessee has historically categorized a claim for defamation as either libel or slander. Libel is defined as a publication expressed in printing or writing, or by pictures or signs, tending to injure the character of an individual, or diminish his reputation. Dunn v. Winters, 21 Tenn. (2 Humph.) 512 (1841). The speaking of base and defamatory words that tend to prejudice the reputation, office, trade, business or means of getting a living of another is slander. J.M. James Co. v. Continental Nat'l Bank, 105 Tenn. 1, 58 S.W. 261 (Tenn. 1900). Tennessee no longer distinguishes between libel per se and libel per quod. Pate, supra.

It is a question of law for the court to decide whether a communication is defamatory. If it is, the jury then decides whether it was understood as defamatory by those to whom it was published. Myers v. Pickering Firm, Inc., 959 S.W.2d 152 (Tenn. Ct. App.), appeal denied (Tenn. 1997); Grubb v. Prince, slip op., 1986 Tenn. App. LEXIS 2918 (Tenn. Ct. App., Western Section, April 14, 1986) (trial court correctly granted summary judgment for defendant where statements were non-defamatory as a matter of law); Memphis Publ'g Co. v. Nichols, 569 S.W.2d 412, 419 (Tenn. 1978); Biltcliffe v. Hailey's Harbor, Inc., slip op., No. M2003-02408-COA-R3-CV, 2005 Tenn. App. LEXIS 676 (Tenn. Ct. App., Middle Section, Oct. 27, 2005) (no appeal sought); **Jimenez v. Vanderbilt Landscaping, LLC, No. 3-11-02762011, U.S. Dist. LEXIS 81726 (M.D. Tenn. July 25, 2011) (denying plaintiff's motion to dismiss defendant's defamation counterclaim because it is the fact-finder's role to determine whether the statements made against the defendant were true or false).**

2. ***Fault.*** The level of fault that must be shown depends on the plaintiff's private or public status and the private or public nature of the defendant's statements. There is no relevant case law that provides a bright-line test for distinguishing between matters of private and public concern. Determination of whether an individual attains "public figure" or "public official" status is a question of law for the court to determine. Ferguson v. Union City Daily Messenger, Inc., 845 S.W.2d 162 (Tenn. 1992).

a. **Private Figure Plaintiff/Matter of Public Concern.** The Tennessee Court of Appeals applied negligence as the relevant level of fault in a case involving the spreading of a rumor that a private physician was HIV+, but did not engage in any specific discussion or analysis as to whether any higher standard than negligence would be appropriate because the rumors involved a matter of public concern. Whitehurst v. Martin Med. Ctr., P.C., slip op., No. W2001-03034-COA-R3-CV, 2003 Tenn. App. LEXIS 619 (Tenn. Ct. App., Western Section, Aug. 28, 2003) (no appeal sought). Negligence standard applied by Tennessee Court of Appeals to private figure who was the brother-in-law of a high-ranking public official. Lewis v. Newschannel 5 Network, L.P., slip op., Nos. 00C-2704, 01C-1873 (Tenn. Cir. Ct., Davidson County, Jan. 10, 2005).

b. **Private Figure Plaintiff/Matter of Private Concern.** Negligence is the requisite level of fault that must be established by a private figure plaintiff bringing a defamation action regarding a matter of private concern. Press, Inc. v. Verran, 569 S.W.2d 435, 442 (Tenn. 1978) (adopting standards set forth in Restatement (Second) of Torts " 580A & 580B (1977)). The court must decide whether by a preponderance of the evidence the defendant exercised reasonable care and caution in checking the truth or falsity and the defamatory character of the communication before publishing it. Memphis Publ'g Co. v. Nichols, 569 S.W.2d 412, 418 (Tenn. 1978). This standard also applies to public figures involving matters of a purely private nature not affecting the public figure's conduct, fitness or role in their public capacity. Trigg v. Lakeway Publishers, Inc., 720 S.W.2d 69 (Tenn. Ct. App.), appeal denied (Tenn. 1986); Stones River Motors, Inc. v. Mid-South Publ'g Co., 651 S.W.2d 713 (Tenn. Ct. App.), appeal denied (Tenn. 1983); Press, Inc. v. Verran, supra. The Tennessee Supreme Court excluded from the Gertz heightened standard suits by private plaintiffs for matters of private concern. Safro v. Kennedy, slip op., No. E2006-01638-COA-RS-CV, 2007 Tenn. App. LEXIS 248 (Tenn. Ct. App., Eastern Section, Apr. 25, 2007) (no appeal sought).

c. **Public Figure Plaintiff/Matter of Public Concern.** "The occupant of any position in any branch of government who exercises any public function is subject to the New York Times rule as to all conduct in his official capacity or as to any conduct that might adversely affect his fitness for public office, if he has, or appear[s] to the public to have, substantial responsibilities for or control over the conduct of governmental affairs." Id. at 441 (citation omitted). However, the mere appointment to a government board does not demonstrate substantial responsibility over governmental affairs in order to be classified as a public official. Mason v. Chattanooga News Weekly, slip op., No. 03A01-9408-CV-00310, 1995 Tenn. App. LEXIS 423 (Tenn. Ct. App., Eastern Section, June 23, 1995), appeal denied (Tenn. Nov. 6, 1995). A government or public employee who is not in a position to make decisions or in upper management is generally not considered a public official for purposes of the defamation analysis. Brasfield v. Dyer, slip op., No. E2008-01774-COA-R3-CV, 2010 Tenn. App. LEXIS 9 (Tenn. Ct. App., Eastern Section, Jan. 12, 2010), appeal denied (Tenn. Sept. 2, 2010). However, if the alleged defamation relates to a public employee's job performance, performance of their duties required by public service, or matters of "public interest," the public employee is a public figure. Id. Rosenblatt means that states cannot be more restrictive than the United States Constitution in determining who is a public official, but they can be less restrictive and reach "lower in to the governmental hierarchy than that which is required by the United States Constitution and lesser officers or employees can be designated 'public officials.'" Campbell v. Robinson, 955 S.W.2d 609 (Tenn. Ct. App.), appeal denied (Tenn. 1997).

Public figures are those who have thrust themselves into the vortex of an important public controversy, those who achieve such pervasive fame or notoriety that they become public figures for all purposes and in all contexts, those who voluntarily inject themselves, or are drawn into public controversies, and become public figures for a limited range of issues, and those who assume special prominence in the resolution of public questions. Press, Inc. v. Verran, 569 S.W.2d 435 (Tenn. 1978); see also Hibdon v. Grabowski, 195 S.W.3d 48 (Tenn. Ct. App.), appeal denied (Tenn. Sept. 27, 2006) (owner of jet ski customizing business who injected himself into public controversy); Trigg v. Lakeway Publishers, Inc., 720 S.W.2d 69 (Tenn. Ct. App.), appeal denied (Tenn. 1986) (spokesman for citizen tax reform group who injected self into public controversy); Cloyd v. Press, Inc., 629 S.W.2d 24 (Tenn. Ct. App. 1981), appeal denied, (Tenn. 1982) (citizen who voluntarily injects himself into public controversy regarding municipal referendum); Taylor v. Nashville Banner Publ'g Co., 573 S.W.2d 476 (Tenn. Ct. App. 1976), cert. denied, (Tenn. 1978), cert. denied, 441 U.S. 923 (1979) (candidate for the Tennessee Supreme Court); Tomlinson v. Kelly, 969 S.W. 2d 402 (Tenn. Ct. App. 1997), appeal denied, (Tenn. May 4, 1998) (municipal mayor and city manager); Street v. National Broad. Co., 645 F.2d 1227 (6th Cir.), cert. dismissed per stipulation, 454 U.S. 1095 (1981) (prosecutrix in Scottsboro case held to be public figure during Scottsboro trials and public figure for purposes of later televised dramatization of Scottsboro trial); Lane v. New York Times, 8 Media L. Rep. 1623 (W.D. Tenn. 1982) (attorney who had published books on subjects of broad public interest and former business manager for the Peoples' Temple in Jonestown, Guyana); Ray v. Time, Inc., 452 F. Supp. 618 (W.D. Tenn. 1976), aff'd, 582 F.2d 1280 (6th Cir. 1978) (convicted murderer of national civil rights leader). In Wilson v. Scripps-Howard, 642 F.2d 371 (6th Cir.), cert. dismissed per stipulation, 454 U.S. 1130 (1981), plaintiff, a cattleman who had received media attention seven years prior to controversy forming basis of defamation action, was held not to be a public figure where prior media attention was unconnected to present controversy, plaintiff did not knowingly inject himself into present controversy and did not have regular and continuing access to media. Further, a businessman's participation in civic and charitable activities does not make him a public figure where the published controversy is only associated with his business dealings. Mason v. Chattanooga News Weekly, slip op., No. 03A01-9408-CV-00310, 1995 Tenn. App. LEXIS 423 (Tenn. Ct. App., Eastern Section, June 23, 1995), appeal denied, 1995 Tenn. LEXIS 679 (Tenn. Nov. 6, 1995); See also Woodruff v. Ohman., slip op., No. 99-6037, 99-6128, 2002 U.S. App. LEXIS 2087 (6th Cir. Feb. 6, 2002) (post-doctoral research assistant is not a public figure). A mayor's wife who traveled out of the state and country as the "spouse of the Mayor" and was a guest writer and commentator for a local newspaper is a public figure. Piper v. Mize, slip op., No. M2002-00626-COA-R3-CV, 2003 Tenn. App. LEXIS 429, at *28-29 (Tenn. Ct. App., Middle Section, June 10, 2003). An incumbent grants writer for the City of Clarksville who was also a former candidate for mayor, the subject of numerous articles in local city newspapers, a featured speaker for civic groups, and the host of a local radio talk show, is a public figure. Id.

A person may also be deemed to be an "involuntary" public figure when, through no purposeful action of his own, the person is drawn into a particular public controversy, or when the person's conduct is related in an integral and meaningful way to the conduct of a public official. Lewis v. NewsChannel 5 Network, L.P., 238 S.W.3d 270 (Tenn. Ct. App. 2007) (citing Gertz v. Robert Welch, Inc., 418 U.S. 323 (1974) and Rosenbloom v. Metromedia, Inc., 403 U.S. 29 (1971)); appeal denied (Tenn. 2007). Elaborating on Justice White's concurrence in Rosenbloom v. Metromedia, Inc. discussing the manner in which a private person might become an involuntary public figure, the Tennessee Court of Appeals added that the private person's "appearance in the story must be an integral and meaningful part of addressing the conduct of the public official with regard to a matter of public concern." Lewis v. NewsChannel 5 Network, L.P., (appellant brother-in-law of a police official was an involuntary public figure because the story in question involved a matter of public concern regarding the discipline of said high-ranking public official due to his alleged interference with the plaintiff's arrest); **see also Milligan v. United States, 670 F.3d 686 (6th Cir. 2012) (holding that a broadcast of plaintiff being falsely arrested by police was an official action; finding the report that plaintiff was arrested with a "warrant in hand" was a fair and accurate report of what police had done, despite police arresting the wrong individual due to a clerical error; and that plaintiff failed to show that defendant televised the report with actual malice)**.

Tennessee courts follow the "actual malice" rule as the standard of liability for public officials or figures. Press, Inc. v. Verran, 569 S.W.2d 435 (Tenn. 1978). Restatement (Second) of Torts ' 580A (1977). Actual malice is the making of a statement with the knowledge that it is false, or the reckless disregard for its truth or falsity. Since employee had presented her research to the professor as an abstract, professor must have known that his statements regarding the employee's production were false. The court held that the professor acted with sufficient recklessness by placing the employee's professional and immigration status at great risk for questionable motives. Woodruff v. Ohman, 166 Fed. Appx. 212 (6th Cir.), rehearing en banc denied (May 22, 2006). The Tennessee Court of Appeals has held that, even if the plaintiff's claim was true, the defendants could have conducted a better investigation before airing a report about him, nevertheless, his defamation claim could not satisfy the actual malice standard requiring the plaintiff to present evidence of the defendants' purposeful or reckless avoidance of the truth. Lewis v. NewsChannel 5 Network, L.P., 238 S.W.3d 270 (Tenn. Ct. App. 2007), appeal denied (Tenn. 2007). Whether there is "actual malice" is a proper question for summary judgment. Trigg v. Lakeway Publishers, Inc., 720 S.W.2d 69 (Tenn. Ct. App.), appeal denied (Tenn. 1986); Piper v. Mize, slip op., No. M2002-00626-COA-R3-CV, 2003 Tenn. App. LEXIS 429, at *13-14 (Tenn. Ct. App., Middle Section, June 10, 2003) (stating that "the appropriate summary judgment question" is "whether the evidence in the record could support a reasonable jury finding either that plaintiff has shown actual malice by clear and convincing evidence or that the plaintiff has not"). When a defendant negates the element of actual malice by means of affidavits and other materials filed in support of a motion for summary judgment, the burden is shifted to the plaintiff to produce evidence of specific facts that establish a genuine issue of material fact on that issue. Shamblin v. Martinez, No. M2010-00974-COA-R3-CV, 2011 Tenn. App. LEXIS 182, at *15 (Tenn. Ct. App., Middle Section, April 13, 2011) (citing Martin v. Norfolk Southern Railway Co., 271 S.W.3d 76, 84 (Tenn. 2008)). Public figures must show with "convincing clarity" the facts which make up the actual malice. Ramsey v. Cleveland Daily Banner, (Tenn. Ct. App., Eastern Section, Nov. 24, 1982), cert. denied, concurring in results only, 1983 Tenn. App. LEXIS 747 (Tenn. Dec. 5, 1983) (sheriff conceded to be public official). The Tennessee Court of Appeals has required a public figure to demonstrate actual malice in a defamation claim against a non-media defendant. Trigg, supra. The Court of Appeals has yet to outline the standard for "convincing clarity." Selby v. Ilabaca, slip op., No. 02A01-9503-CV-00058, 1996 Tenn. App. LEXIS 254 (Tenn. Ct. App., Western Section, April 29, 1996) (no appeal sought). However, the Tennessee Supreme Court, in Hodges v. S.C. Toof & Co., 833 S.W.2d 896, 901 n.3 (Tenn. 1992), held that punitive damages may be awarded only when the egregious conduct could be proven by clear and convincing evidence, being "evidence in which there is no serious or substantial doubt about the correctness of the conclusions drawn from the evidence."

Testimony showing that the defendant did not care whether the statements he published were true or false amounted to reckless disregard of whether the article was true or false. Moore v. Bailey, 628 S.W.2d 431, 433-34 (Tenn. Ct. App.), appeal denied (Tenn. 1981); Moman v. M.M. Corp., slip op., No. 02A01-9608-CV00182, 1997 Tenn. App. LEXIS 233 (Tenn. Ct. App., Western Section, April 10, 1997) (no appeal sought). "Actual malice" is a term of art with its meaning differing from the manner in which it is commonly understood. Holbrook v. Harman Automotive, Inc., 58 F.3d 222 (6th Cir. 1995). Actual malice is not synonymous with malice, a term that connotes ill will, spite, or animosity. Id. In Moore v. Bailey, 628 S.W.2d 431 (Tenn. Ct. App.), appeal denied (Tenn. 1981), the court held that "past history of bad blood" is relevant to the determination of knowledge of falsity or reckless disregard for the truth and affirmed a jury verdict against a non-media defendant in public official's action. But see Windsor v. The Tennessean Corp., 654 S.W.2d 680 (Tenn. Ct. App.), appeal denied (Tenn. 1983), cert. denied, 465 U.S. 1030 (1983) (liability not predicated upon "hatred, spite, ill will, and desire to injure" but on "knowledge of falsity or reckless disregard of the truth").

3. ***Falsity.*** The damaging words must be factually false. If they are true, or essentially true, they are not actionable, even though the published statement contains other inaccuracies that are not damaging. Thus, the defense of truth applies so long as the "sting" (or injurious part) of the statement is true. Ali v. Moore, 984 S.W. 2d 224 (Tenn. Ct. App. 1998); Shamblin v. Martinez, No. M2010-00974-COA-R3-CV, 2011 Tenn. App. LEXIS 182, at *15 (Tenn. Ct. App., Middle Section, April 13, 2011) (statement at issue was held to not be defamatory though it contained portions that were factually false); Wagner v. Fleming, slip op., No. E2002-02304-COA-R3-CV, 2004 Tenn. LEXIS 579 (Tenn., Jan. 6, 2004) (statements on signs were not false; therefore, no material evidence to support jury's finding of any false statements); Coker v. Sundquist, slip op., No. 01A01-9806-BC-00318, 1998 Tenn. App. LEXIS 708 (Tenn. Ct. App., Middle Section, Oct. 23, 1998), appeal denied (Tenn. May 10, 1999); Moman v. M.M. Corp., slip op., No. 02A01-9608-CV00182, 1997 Tenn. App. LEXIS 233 (Tenn. Ct. App., Western Section, April 10, 1997) (no appeal sought); Stones River Motors, Inc. v. Mid-South Publ'g Co., 651 S.W.2d 713, 721-722 (Tenn. Ct. App.), appeal denied (Tenn. 1983). The proper question is whether the meaning reasonably conveyed is defamatory, that is, "whether the libel as published would have a different effect on the mind of the reader from that which the pleaded truth would have produced." Nichols, 569 S.W.2d 412, 420 (Tenn. 1978) (quoting Fleckenstein v. Friedman, 266 N.Y. 19, 193 N.E. 537, 538 (N.Y. 1938)). Comments upon, or characterizations of published facts are not in themselves actionable if the published facts commented upon are true. Stones River Motors, 651 S.W.2d at 721-722. An opinion is not actionable as libel unless it implies the existence of unstated defamatory facts. Id. As long as the true facts on which the opinion is based are published, the opinion itself is not actionable. Id. **Questions can be libelous under certain circumstances where the question can reasonably be read as an assertion of a false fact. Eisenstein v. WTVF-TV, News Channel 5 Network, LLC, No. M2011-02208-COA-RS-CV, 2012 Tenn. App. LEXIS 515, *14-15 (Tenn. Ct. App., Middle Section, July 30, 2012) (no appeal sought; dismissing a judge's libel claim based on a news broadcast that began with the question, "Is the presiding judge of Davidson County's general sessions court facing an ethics investigation?", because, even though there was no pending investigation, the court found the question was not answered in the affirmative during the broadcast).**

4. ***Defamatory Statement of Fact.*** The U.S. Court of Appeals for the Sixth Circuit has held, as a matter of federal constitutional law, that a private figure plaintiff must prove that a statement on a matter of public concern is false and negligently published. Wilson v. Scripps-Howard, 642 F.2d 371 (6th Cir.), cert. dismissed per stipulation, 454 U.S. 1130 (1981). Where a plaintiff did not even know what statements had been made to the government as part of a mandatory investigation, plaintiff cannot prove that any statements made were false. Newsom v. Textron Aerostructures, 924 S.W.2d 87 (Tenn. Ct. App. 1995), appeal denied (Tenn. 1996). Defamation may also exist where incomplete statements of true fact create a false and defamatory impression through innuendo, or where words not defamatory on their face are shown to be so in light of extrinsic evidence. Anderson v. Watchtower Bible & Tract Soc'y of N.Y., Inc., slip op., No. M2004-01066-COA-R9-CV, 2007 Tenn. App. LEXIS 29, *102-*103 (Tenn. Ct. App., Middle Section, Jan. 19, 2007), appeal denied (Tenn. 2007), cert. denied, 128 S. Ct. 323 (U.S. 2007).

Prior to Gertz, statements of opinion were protected under the common law fair comment privilege. Venn v. Tennessean Newspapers, Inc., 201 F. Supp. 47 (M.D. Tenn. 1962), aff'd, 313 F.2d 639 (6th Cir.), cert. denied, 374 U.S. 839 (1963). Following Gertz v. Robert Welch, Inc., 418 US 323 (1974), expressions of opinion are constitutionally protected. Stones River Motors, Inc. v. Mid-South Publ'g Co., 651 S.W.2d 713 (Tenn. Ct. App.), appeal denied (Tenn. 1983). But see Zius v. Shelton, slip op., No. E1999-01157-COA-R9-CV, 2000 Tenn. App. LEXIS 360 (Tenn. Ct. App., Eastern Section, June 6, 2000) (providing that "The United States Supreme Court has since held that there is no wholesale defamation exception for anything that might be labeled 'opinion,'" citing Milkovich v. Lorain Journal Co.); Kersey v. Wilson, slip op., No. M2005-02106-COA-R3-CV, 2006 Tenn. App. LEXIS 826, *10-*11 (Tenn. Ct. App., Middle Section, Dec. 29, 2006) (citing Zius v. Shelton), appeal denied (Tenn. 2007), cert. denied, 128 S. Ct. 285 (U.S. 2007). A statement of opinion that implies the allegation of undisclosed defamatory facts as the basis for opinion is actionable. Id.; Hicks v. Metropolitan Govt., slip op., No 86-49-II, 1986 Tenn. App. LEXIS 3599 (Tenn. Ct. App., Middle Section, Oct. 3, 1986). An expression of opinion based on disclosed or assumed nondefamatory facts is not actionable, even though the opinion may be unjustified and unreasonable. Binkley v. Tennessee Farmers Mut. Ins. Co., slip op., 1985 Tenn. App. LEXIS 3436 (Tenn. Ct. App., Middle Section, Nov. 8, 1995). See also Satterfield v. Bluhm, slip op., No. E2003-01609-COA-R3-CV, 2004 Tenn. App. LEXIS 244 (Tenn. Ct. App., Eastern Section, April 16, 2004) (rejecting argument that Zius abrogated distinction between fact and opinion; no appeal sought). Tennessee has not adopted a special constitutionally-based test for distinguishing opinion from fact. The determination of whether a statement is protected opinion or fact is a question of law for resolution by the court. Klein v. People Weekly Magazine, slip op., No. 82-2626-M (W.D. Tenn. June 6, 1983) (order on pending motions). Statements must be factually false in order to be actionable; thus comments upon or characterizations of published facts are not in themselves actionable. Moman v. M.M. Corp., supra (citing Gertz, 418 U.S. 264). Statements interpreting the meaning of literary work are considered matters of opinion and readers of the work enjoy "considerable latitude" in their interpretations. Kersey v. Wilson, slip op., No. M2005-02106-COA-R3-CV, 2006 Tenn. App. LEXIS 826 (Tenn. Ct. App., Middle Section, Dec. 29, 2006), appeal denied (Tenn. 2007), cert. denied, 128 S. Ct. 285 (U.S. 2007) (church member's comment to a police officer that another member's written poem "threatened the life of" a church member was not actionable defamation because interpretation of the poem was not a statement of fact).

For a communication to be libelous, it must constitute a serious threat to the plaintiff's reputation. A libel does not occur just because the publication is annoying, offensive, or embarrassing. The actions taken must reasonably be construed as holding the plaintiff up to public hatred, contempt or ridicule. They must carry with them an element of disgrace. Stones River Motors, Inc. v. Mid-South Publ'g Co., 651 S.W.2d 713, 719 (Tenn. Ct. App.), appeal denied (Tenn. 1983); Butler v. Diversified Energy, Inc., slip op., No. 03A01-9804-CV-00146, 1999 Tenn. App. LEXIS 55 (Tenn. Ct. App., Eastern Section, Jan. 28, 1999) (letter to employer complaining of "disruptive problems" from two employees and requesting that they not come onto complainant's property deemed not actionable; no appeal sought); Naylor Med. Sales & Rentals, Inc. v. Invacare Continuing Care, Inc., No. 09-2344-STA-cgc, 2011 U.S. Dist. LEXIS 263, at *42 (W.D. Tenn. Jan. 3, 2011). The gravamen of an action for defamation is injury to the reputation of the plaintiff, not injury to his self-esteem, emotions or mental state. The basis of an action for defamation, whether it be for slander or libel, is that defamation results in injury to the person's character and reputation. The words "character" and "reputation" were intended to mean reputation in respect to character, for character may be shown only by reputation. Coker v. Sundquist, slip op., No. 01A01-9806-BC-00318, 1998 Tenn. App. LEXIS 708 (Tenn. Ct. App., Middle Section, Oct. 23, 1998), appeal denied (Tenn. May 10, 1999). **Statements that plaintiff was "dangerous" and dealt with "machine guns" held not defamatory. Krasner v. Arnold, No. W2011-00580-COA-R3-CV, 2011 Tenn. App. LEXIS 688 (Tenn. Ct. App., Western Section, Dec. 28, 2011) (no appeal sought).**

Even though statements in news articles were "literally true," the publication of an article was held actionable where "the meaning reasonably conveyed by the published is defamatory." Memphis Publ'g Co. v. Nichols, 569 S.W.2d 412 (Tenn. 1978) (implication of adultery); see also Stones River Motors, Inc., supra (distinguishing Nichols as inapplicable to constitutionally-protected opinion or characterization of fact). While store clerks' identifications of plaintiff in a photo line-up as a woman who used a credit card to purchase VCR's were not defamatory on their face, they conveyed a defamatory meaning because of the existence of an investigation of credit card theft. Pate v. Service Merchandise Co., 959

S.W.2d 569 (Tenn. Ct. App. 1996), appeal denied (Tenn. 1997), cert. denied, 118 S. Ct. 76 (Oct. 6, 1997). A sarcastic tone of voice does not render non-defamatory verbal communication actionable. Hunt v. Tangel, slip op., No. 01A01-9705-CV-00199, 1997 Tenn. App. LEXIS 914 (Tenn. Ct. App., Western Section, Dec. 19, 1997) (no appeal sought). Statements that plaintiff had spent two and one-half years on a project and had not been able to accumulate enough data for a single paper was false and libelous because it clearly related to her professional reputation. Woodruff v. Ohman, 166 Fed. Appx. 212 (6th Cir.), rehearing en banc denied (May 22, 2006). Merely requesting an investigation by the U.S. Attorney and the FBI of an apparent forged check does not amount to slander. Henegar v. Agilysys, Inc., slip op., No. 3:06-cv-21, 2006 U.S. Dist. LEXIS 56773 (E.D. Tenn. Aug. 11, 2006). Statement that one "wrote a poem that threatened the life of one of our members," held to be nondefamatory. Kersey v. Wilson, slip op., No. M2005-02106-COA-R3-CV, 2006 Tenn. App. LEXIS 826, *10-*11 (Tenn. Ct. App., Middle Section, Dec. 29, 2006), appeal denied (Tenn. 2007), cert. denied, 128 S. Ct. 285 (U.S. 2007). Court ruled defendant's allegedly defamatory statement that Plaintiff attempted to "steal" was an obvious exaggeration, much like the words "swindling, ripping-off, or pirating", and not a defamatory statement. Farmer v. Hersh, slip op., No. W2006-01937-COA-R3-CV, 2007 Tenn. App. LEXIS 513 (Tenn. Ct. App. Aug. 9, 2007). The court found no prima facie case of defamation existed because the statement was made between business associates regarding normal employment behavior; where information shared to different offices of the defendant benefited its work, the court found that this was type of communication the workplace privilege was intended to protect, and there was no publication. Hood v. Tenn. Bd. of Regents, slip op., No. 3:04-0473, 2006 U.S. Dist. LEXIS 65881 (M.D. Tenn. Sept. 14, 2006) (application for permission to appeal filed October 6, 2006). Courts cannot determine whether a statement is defamatory when it will be required to examine the correctness of the decision of a religious body to determine the falsity of the statements. Anderson v. Watchtower Bible & Tract Soc'y of N.Y., Inc., slip op., No. M2004-01066-COA-R9-CV, 2007 Tenn. App. LEXIS 29 (Tenn. Ct. App., Middle Section, Jan. 19, 2007), appeal denied (Tenn. 2007), cert. denied, 128 S. Ct. 323 (U.S. 2007).

Defamatory statements can also be "couched in the form of a question." Secured Financial Solutions, LLC v. Winer, slip op., No. M2009-00885-COA-R3-CV, 2010 Tenn. App. LEXIS 70, *8 (Tenn. Ct. App., Middle Section, Nov. 5, 2009), appeal denied (Tenn. Aug. 25, 2010); **see also Eisenstein v. WTVF-TV, News Channel 5 Network, LLC, No. M2011-02208-COA-RS-CV, 2012 Tenn. App. LEXIS 515, *14-15 (Tenn. Ct. App., Middle Section, July 30, 2012) (no appeal sought; dismissing a judge's libel claim based on a news broadcast that began with the question, "Is the presiding judge of Davidson County's general sessions court facing an ethics investigation?", because, even though there was no pending investigation, the court found the question was not answered in the affirmative during the broadcast).** To be defamatory, however, the question "must be reasonably read as an assertion of false fact." Id. A mere inquiry in a "genuine effort to obtain information," regardless of whether it is "embarrassing or unpleasant to its subject," is not an accusation. Id. For example, an email asking whether someone has heard that the president of another company is in trouble and might get "shut down" and adding, "[s]ure hope it's true," was not defamatory where it was deemed a legitimate inquiry into something the person heard and was a legitimate effort to determine the truth of the information. Id. at *3-9. Publication of advertisements in the newspaper by a challenger in county sheriff's election insinuating that the incumbent sheriff allowed a local automotive repair business to repeatedly overcharge the county was found libelous notwithstanding defendant's arguments that his ads were directed at the incumbent sheriff, rather than the local automotive repair company. Repair company subsequently lost their contract with the county, and at trial, evidence was offered of the damage to the reputation of the company, as well as defendant's admission that he made errors in the calculations in his ads, and had no actual support for some of his assertions of overcharging. Clemons v. Cowan, slip op., No. M2008-02600-COA-R3-CV, 2010 Tenn. App. LEXIS 88 (Tenn. Ct. App., Western Section, Feb. 4, 2010), appeal denied (Tenn. Aug. 25, 2010). Letter from physician stating plaintiff should stop taking narcotics was not defamatory where plaintiff had consented to disclosure of her protected health information in consent forms, and where such disclosure was copied to plaintiff's prior treating physician and worker's compensation claim handler. Gard v. Harris, slip op., No. 2008-01939-COA-R3-CV, 2010 Tenn. App. LEXIS 187, 2010 WL 844810 (Tenn. Ct. App., Eastern Section, Mar. 11, 2010) (no appeal sought). Simply alleging that defamatory information would "spread like wildfire" because of the size of an organization is not sufficient to meet the public requirement for defamation. Lamdin v. Aerotek Commer. Staffing, No.: 3:10-CV-280, 2010 U.S. Dist. LEXIS 105306 (E.D. Tenn. Sept. 30, 2010).

5. ***Of and Concerning Plaintiff.*** Plaintiff must establish that the statement is in fact understood by a third person as referring to the plaintiff. Insurance Research Servs, Inc. v. Associates Fin. Corp., 134 F. Supp. 54 (M.D. Tenn. 1955); Stones River Motors, Inc., supra; see also Tompkins v. Wisener, 33 Tenn. (1 Sneed) 458 (Tenn. 1853) (affirming summary judgment in favor of defendant newspaper which had edited out specific reference to plaintiffs in letter to editor); Lyons v. State, slip op., No 01A01-9304-BC-00160, 1993 Tenn. App. LEXIS 668 (Tenn. Ct. App., Middle Section, Oct. 20, 1993) (plaintiff was never identified in 44 seconds of air time); see also Henderson v. Clear Channel Broad., Inc., 34 Media L. Rep. 1125, 2005 Tenn. App. LEXIS 592 (Tenn. Ct. App., Western Section, Sept. 21, 2005) (no appeal sought) (affirming judgment in favor of defendants since defamatory statements were made about plaintiff's daughter and not the plaintiff or plaintiff's business). The appropriate test is whether the third party recipient of the communication reasonably

understood the publication as referring to the plaintiff and not whether the plaintiff subjectively understands that he is the subject of the communication. Stones River Motors, Inc., supra.

Adult cabaret and three female employees failed to state a defamation claim against a county commissioner based on the commissioner's general statement that the adult entertainment businesses tended to employ women who were sexually abused and were addicted to drugs and alcohol, because neither the plaintiff cabaret nor its three employees were named in a statement the court deemed non-actionable opinion. Steele v. Ritz, slip op., No. W2008-02125-COA-R3-CV, 2009 Tenn. App. LEXIS 843 (Tenn. Ct. App., Western Section, Dec. 16, 2009) (no appeal sought).

6. ***Minors and Libel.*** A minor cannot be held liable for torts, including defamation committed by a minor's agent or servant, such as a minor's parents. L.W. v. Knox Co. Board of Ed., slip op., No 3:05-CV-274, 2006 U.S. Dist. LEXIS 64138 (E.D. Tenn. Sept. 6, 2006); Messer v. Reid, 208 S.W.2d 528, 530 (Tenn. 1948) (same).

7. ***Publication.*** "Publication" is a term of art meaning the communication of defamatory matter to a third person. Quality Auto Parts Co. v. Bluff City Buick Co., 876 S.W.2d 818, 821 (Tenn. Ct. App.), reh'g denied (Tenn. 1994); Little Stores v. Isenberg, 26 Tenn. App. 357, 172 S.W.2d 13 (Tenn. Ct. App.), cert. denied (Tenn. 1943). It is an elementary rule that publication is an essential element of a libel action without which a libel action must be dismissed. Ward v. Wal-Mart Stores, Inc., slip op., No. 3:05-0777, 2006 U.S. Dist. LEXIS 79220 (M.D. Tenn. Oct. 30, 2006); Woods v. Helmi, 758 S.W.2d 219 (Tenn. Ct. App.), appeal denied (Tenn. 1988); Applewhite v. Memphis State Univ., 495 S.W.2d 190 (Tenn. 1973); Mason v. USEC, Inc., No. 3:07-cv-10, 2008 U.S. Dist. LEXIS 75714 (E.D. Tenn. Aug. 26, 2008). Plaintiff cannot base a cause of action for defamation based upon plaintiff's own republication. Railroad v. Delaney, 102 Tenn. (18 Pickle) 289, 52 S.W. 151 (Tenn. 1899); Sylvis v. Miller, 96 Tenn. (12 Pickle) 94, 33 S.W. 921 (Tenn. 1896); Cawood v. Booth, No. E2007-02537-COA-R3-CV, 2008 Tenn. App. LEXIS 715 (Tenn. Ct. App., Eastern Section, Nov. 25, 2008), appeal granted, 2009 Tenn. LEXIS 370 (Tenn., June 15, 2009); see also Multari v. Bennett, slip op., No. 1:05-CV-355, 2006 U.S. Dist. LEXIS 64135 (E.D. Tenn. Sept. 6, 2006) (finding summary judgment is appropriate where motion to amend to add libel claim would be futile because the plaintiff could not show the required element of publication to a third party); A plaintiff is limited to a single cause of action based upon the circulation of copies of an edition of a book, newspaper, or periodical. Applewhite v. Memphis State Univ., 495 S.W.2d 190, 194 (Tenn. 1973); **see also Milligan v. United States, 670 F.3d 686, 698 (6th Cir. 2012) (commenting that a plaintiff's cause of action accrues only once, at the time of publication, and subsequent publications do not give rise to additional causes of action for defamation; where a news report originally aired on a television station's news broadcast related to the arrest of plaintiff; any additional publications, including on the television station's website, are not separately actionable under Tennessee's single publication rule).** In an action for defamation based upon defendants' communication of defamatory information to the National Practitioner Data Bank which information was subsequently transmitted to third parties, the single publication rule was not applicable to multiple instances where the information was transmitted by the Data Bank to third parties. Swafford v. Memphis Individual Practice Ass'n, slip op., No. 02A01-9612-CV-00311, 1998 Tenn. App. LEXIS 361 (Tenn. Ct. App., Western Section, June 2, 1998), appeal denied (Tenn. Jan. 25, 1999). Where the evidence raises reasonable inferences that nearby third parties heard and understood alleged defamatory statements, a genuine issue of material fact as to publication to third parties is raised warranting submission of the case to a jury. Safro v. Kennedy, slip op., No. E2006-01638-COA-R3-CV, 2007 Tenn. App. LEXIS 248 (Tenn. Ct. App., Middle Section, Apr. 25, 2007) (vacating trial court's dismissal of a defamation claim based on store surveillance video clips showing patrons in the immediate area while the alleged defamatory statements were made); Grubman v. Morgan Stanley DW, Inc., No. 3:06-0705, 2008 U.S. Dist. LEXIS 86628 (M.D. Tenn. Sept. 16, 2008) (granting summary judgment for defendants because of a failure to communicate the form to third parties). **Communications among agents of the same corporation made within the course and scope of their employment relative to duties performed for that corporation are not to be considered statements communicated or publicized to third persons. Washington v. Vogel, No. M2010-02461-COA-R3-CV, 2011 Tenn. App. LEXIS 393 (Ten. Ct. App., Middle Section, July 20, 2011) (no appeal sought), citing Woods v. Helmi, 758 S.W.2d 219 (Tenn. Ct. App. 1988).**

a. **Intracorporate Communication** Communication among agents of the same corporation made with the scope and course of their employment relative to duties performed for that corporation are not to be considered statements communicated or publicized to third persons. Ward v. Wal-Mart Stores, Inc., slip op., No. 3:05-0777, 2006 U.S. Dist. LEXIS 79220 (M.D. Tenn. Oct. 30, 2006) (statement made by plaintiff's supervisor/manager in front of three other managers is not published); Bernard v. Sumner Regional Health Sys., slip. op., No. M2000-01478-COA-R3-CV, 2002 Tenn. App. LEXIS 213 (Tenn. Ct. App., Middle Section, March 26, 2002) (comments about plaintiff doctor are privileged when communicated for the sole purpose of a sexual harassment investigation); Reinshagen v. PHP Cos., slip op., No. E2001-00025-COA-R3-CV, 2001 Tenn. App. LEXIS 845 (Tenn. Ct. App., Eastern Section, Nov. 14, 2001) (employee's supervisor's dissemination of his job performance reviews was not publication); Tate v. Baptist Memorial Hospital No. W1999-00553-COA-R3-CV, 2000 Tenn. App. LEXIS 505 (Tenn. Ct. App., Western Section, July 28, 2000); Woods v. Helmi, 758 S.W.2d 219 (Tenn. Ct. App.), appeal denied (Tenn. 1988) (comments concerning nurse anesthetist's performance qualifiedly privileged when communicated to those responsible for overseeing nurse's performance, even though persons receiving communication were employed by different corporate entities since made "within scope and course of employment relative to duties performed for corporation" and made to those "in the 'need to know' channel"); Hood v. Tenn. Bd. of Regents, slip op., No. 3:04-0473, 2006 U.S. Dist. LEXIS 65881 (M.D. Tenn. Sept. 14, 2006) (summary judgment granted to defendant for plaintiff's failure to satisfy publication requirement because the alleged defamatory letter is the type of intracorporate communication that the workplace privilege was intended to protect, thereby precluding application of "need to know exception"); Clark v. Hoops, 709 F. Supp. 2d 657, 672 (W.D. Tenn. 2010) (email sent to 150 recipients sufficient to create fact question regarding "need to know" status of recipients); Freeman v. Dayton Scale Co., 159 Tenn. 413, 19 S.W.2d 255, 256 (Tenn. 1929); Southern Ice Co. v. Black, 136 Tenn. 391, 189 S.W. 861 (Tenn. 1916); Bradfield v. Dotson, slip op., No. 02A01-9902-CV-00060, 1999 Tenn. App. LEXIS 552 (Tenn. Ct. App., Western Section, Aug. 16, 1999) (all communications between employees occurred during course and scope of employment; no appeal sought); Evans v. Amcash Mortg. Co., Inc., slip op., No. 01A01-9608-CV-00386, 1997 Tenn. App. LEXIS 535 (Tenn. Ct. App., Middle Section, Aug. 1, 1997) (communication to employee by manager that past manager was terminated for touching blouse of an employee not actionable even though minimal investigation of incident occurred); Perry v. Fox, slip op., No. 01A01-9407-CV-00337, 1994 Tenn. App. LEXIS 763 (Tenn. Ct. App., Middle Section, Dec. 21, 1994) (publication did not occur when an allegedly defamatory memorandum was disseminated to plaintiff's fellow employees); Revis v. McClean, 31 S.W. 3d 250 (Tenn. Ct. App.), appeal denied (Tenn. 2000) (statement made by CEO that "there was no room in plant for [plaintiff's] attitude, as well as letter posted by CEO describing plaintiff's facial expression during meeting as "menacing, denigrating, threatening . . . " did not amount to defamation because both were opinion of CEO); McLeay v. Huddleston, slip op., No. M2005-02118-COA-R3-CV, 2006 Tenn. App. LEXIS 655 (Tenn. Ct. App., Western Section, Oct. 6, 2006), appeal denied (Tenn. 2007) (communication of the circumstances surrounding one employee's termination to other employees in the hospital through the use of correspondence and notations in employee's employment file does not satisfy the publication requirement for a defamation claim). The legal conclusion that an intracorporate communication does not amount to a publication for defamation purposes applies equally to for-profit and not-for-profit corporations alike. Siegfried v. Grand Krewe, slip op., No. W2002-02246-COA-R3-CV, 2003 Tenn. App. LEXIS 845 (Tenn. Ct. App., Western Section, Oct. 14, 2003) (no appeal sought).

b. **Compelled Self-Publication.** The Tennessee Supreme Court reversed the holding of the Tennessee Court of Appeals, in a case by a discharged employee against her former employer, that compelled self-publication does not satisfy the publication element essential to a prima facie case of defamation. Sullivan v. Baptist Mem'l Hosp., 995 S.W. 2d 569 (Tenn. 1999). Publication element not satisfied where defendant allowed copies of a newsletter "to be placed on the counter of his place of business" for customers to take freely, but had "no part in the writing, publishing, editing or actively disseminating" the newsletters, and where there was no evidence any third party took or read a copy of the newsletter. Piper v. Mize, slip op., No. M2002-00626-COA-R3-CV, 2003 Tenn. App. LEXIS 429, at *20-25 (Tenn. Ct. App., Middle Section, June 10, 2003). McLeay v. Huddleston, slip op., No. M2005-02118-COA-R3-CV, 2006 Tenn. App. LEXIS 655 (Tenn. Ct. App., Western Section, Oct. 6, 2006) (finding any defamatory information that was made public was done so by plaintiff's own action), appeal denied (Tenn. 2007); see also Cawood v. Booth, No. E2007-02537-COA-R3-CV, 2008 Tenn. App. LEXIS 715 (Tenn. Ct. App., Eastern Section, Nov. 25, 2008), appeal granted, 2009 Tenn. LEXIS 370 (Tenn., June 15, 2009); Boynton v. Southeastern Tenn. State Reg'l Corr. Facility, slip op., No. 1:06-cv-30 Lee, 2007 U.S. Dist. LEXIS 44888 (E.D. Tenn. June 20, 2007) (citing Tennessee Supreme Court's refusal to recognize self-publication as constituting publication for defamation purposes even when the employee is compelled to self-publish plaintiff's former employer's allegedly defamatory reasons for plaintiff's termination by prospective employers). Recent Tennessee case law suggests that self-publication of drug test results by employees can vitiate their *prima facie* defamation/false light case. Yancy v. Barr-Nunn Transportation Inc., slip op., No. 2:09-cv-02207-JPM-egb, 2010 U.S. Dist. LEXIS 42707, 2010 WL 1780229 (W.D. Tenn. April 30, 2010) (granting summary judgment to employer on defamation and false light claims in suit of terminated employee who admitted he had informed every prospective employer about his termination from employer due to a positive drug test; finding employer had not released terminated employee's drug test results to prospective employers and thus, employee had failed to establish the first element of his *prima facie* case, that the employer had "published" statements, i.e. the drug test results).

c. **Republication.** Every separate and distinct publication of a libel gives rise to a separate action. Underwood v. Smith, 93 Tenn. 687, 27 S.W. 1008 (Tenn. 1894) (author of same article published in two newspapers held liable in separate actions); but see Multari v. Bennett, slip op., No. 1:05-CV-355, 2006 U.S. Dist. LEXIS 64135 (E.D. Tenn. Sept. 6, 2006) (no republication to a third party when allegedly defamatory alert distributed only to members of the Chamber of Commerce, a corporation). An authorized repetition or successive publication of libelous matters affords in itself a right of action. Riley v. Dun & Bradstreet, 172 F.2d 303 (6th Cir. 1949).

8. ***Statements versus Conduct.*** Tennessee cases only deal with written or spoken actions. An action for defamation is based on either libel or slander. Libel is written defamation, while slander is spoken. Ryerson v. American Surety Co. of New York, 213 Tenn. 182, 373 S.W.2d 436 (Tenn. 1963); Shipley v. Tennessee Farmers Mut. Ins. Co., slip op., No. 01-A01-9011-CV-00408, 1991 Tenn. App. LEXIS 346 (Tenn. Ct. App., Western Section, May 15, 1991).

9. ***Damages.***

a. **Presumed Damages and Libel Per Se.** Following Gertz, plaintiff must plead and prove actual injury resulting from a defamatory communication. Pate v. Service Merchandise Co., Inc., 959 S.W.2d 569 (Tenn. Ct. App. 1996), appeal denied (Tenn. 1997), cert. denied, 118 S. Ct. 76 (U.S. Oct. 6, 1997); Memphis Publ'g Co. v. Nichols, 569 S.W.2d 412 (Tenn. 1978); Chera v. Penn, No. 3:07-0165, 2008 U.S. Dist. LEXIS 102364 (M.D. Tenn. Dec. 16, 2008) (no showing of evidence that statements caused any injury). Damages are not presumed in defamation cases. Emerson v. Garner, 732 S.W.2d 613 (Tenn. Ct. App.), appeal denied (Tenn. 1987); see Dolan v. Poston, slip op., No. M2003-2573-COA-R3-CV, 2005 Tenn. App. LEXIS 631 (Tenn. Ct. App., Middle Section, Sept. 29, 2005) (no appeal sought) (loss of employment is sufficient to prove actual damages). Although a court can draw reasonable inferences from plaintiff's proof, plaintiff in a defamation action must still prove damages; a court will not infer them. Glennon v. Dean Witter Reynolds, 83 F.3d 132 (6th Cir.), reh'g en banc denied, 1996 U.S. App. LEXIS 18395 (6th Cir. July 15, 1996) (applying Tennessee law); see also Reyes v. Seaton Enters., LLC, slip op., No. 1:07-cv-196, 2008 U.S. Dist. WL 2066447 (E.D. Tenn. May 13, 2008) (noting that there is no substantive element of special damages in the tort of defamation under Tennessee law, and therefore there is no requirement that a defamation plaintiff specifically plead to any "item of special damage."). Damages must directly result from the defamatory impact of the published statement. Expenses that the plaintiff incurs in attempting to mitigate the effect of the defamation are not recoverable. Electric Furnace Corp. v. Deering Miliken Research Corp., 325 F.2d 761 (6th Cir. 1963). Where the lone recipient of the publication stated that his estimation of the plaintiff was undiminished, there were no actual damages. Sullivan v. Young, 678 S.W.2d 906 (Tenn. Ct. App.), appeal denied (Tenn. 1984). Plaintiff's testimony that being accused of shoplifting made him look "bad" created sufficient evidence to go to the jury on the question of damages. Miller v. Piggly Wiggly Supermarket, slip op., No. 02A01-9403-CV-00048, 1995 Tenn. App. LEXIS 121 (Tenn. Ct. App., Eastern Section, Feb. 24, 1995). It is reasonable to infer compensatory damages where plaintiff had not been able to find a job at the level at which he had been previously employed. Lineberry v. State Farm Fire & Cas. Co., 885 F. Supp. 1095 (M.D. Tenn. 1995). The jury was permitted to award damages for emotional distress resulting from the communication of defamatory statements when plaintiff testified about the devastation, humiliation, and distress that a defamatory engineering report caused them after having spent 40 years building their reputation in the architecture business despite lack of evidence of injury to reputation. Myers v. Pickering Firm, Inc., 959 S.W.2d 152 (Tenn. Ct. App.), appeal denied (Tenn. 1997). There was no material evidence to support an award of $250,000 in pecuniary damages when the evidence failed to show that losses resulted from an unprivileged rather than a privileged report. Id. There was no material evidence to support an award of $200,000 for injuries to plaintiff's reputation when the evidence indicated that injuries to reputation resulted from privileged communications of a report rather than unprivileged communications. Id. Plaintiff police officer did not suffer actual damages where no disciplinary action was taken toward him, no internal investigation resulted, he had nightmares and difficulty sleeping but missed no work, and where his superior officer did not change his opinion of plaintiff. Dowlen v. Mathews, slip op., No. M2001-03160-COA-R3-CV, 2003 Tenn. App. LEXIS 215, at *13-14 (Tenn. Ct. App., Middle Section, Mar. 14, 2003). Trial court's award of $1,000,000 in compensatory damages to police officer who had established actual malice in the making of false statements about him that "effectively destroyed [his] fourteen year career" affirmed. Spicer, 2004 Tenn. App. LEXIS 436; see also McWhorter v. Barre, 132 S.W.3d 354, 367 (Tenn. Ct. App. 2003), appeal denied (Tenn. 2004) (affirming award of $25,000 in compensatory damages to pilot who suffered personal humiliation, mental anguish and suffering, and decreased marketability as a result of defamatory letter sent to the FAA). Judge noted that plaintiff father's personal humiliation and mental anguish was a normal reaction to hearing a public radio broadcast that his daughter was having an affair with a married man; however, plaintiff offered no proof as to the exact cause of his emotional distress and there was no evidence that clearly showed his business suffered any injury as a result of the broadcast. Henderson v. Clear Channel Broad., Inc., 34 Media L. Rep. 1125, 2005 Tenn. App. LEXIS 592 (Tenn. Ct. App., Western Section, Sept. 21, 2005) (no appeal sought). It is for the jury to decide whether there is injury and the extent of damages for suffering of "anguish, severe emotional distress, anxiety and loss of sleep," as well as general injury to one's reputation and standing as a professional; court stated it had no trouble concluding that calling a lawyer an "ambulance chaser" was a defamatory remark. Safro v. Kennedy, slip op., No. E2006-01638-COA-R3-CV, 2007 Tenn. App. LEXIS 248, *14-*16 (Tenn. Ct. App., Eastern Section, Apr. 25, 2007) (no appeal sought). Court found that plaintiff nurse was not injured by alleged defamatory statements in her employment file because was granted a position in an emergency room (even though she was not placed on the schedule due to the lack of open positions) as well as the fact that she chose not to fully pursue applications with other facilities. McLeay v. Huddleston, slip op., No. M2005-02118-COA-R3-CV, 2006 Tenn. App. LEXIS 655 (Tenn. Ct. App., Middle Section, Oct. 6, 2006), appeal denied (Tenn. 2007); see also Riccardi v. Vanderbilt Univ. Med. Ctr., Nos. 3:06cv0065, 3:06cv0615, 2008 U.S. Dist. LEXIS 438 (M.D. Tenn. Jan. 2, 2008) (recommending a remitter of the damages award to $250,000 because the original award of $1,500,000 was so clearly excessive as to shock the conscience). Courts cannot enforce a remedy for economic damages that inevitably occur from shunning within a religious organization, because it would place an impermissible burden upon a protected activity. Anderson v. Watchtower Bible & Tract Soc'y of N.Y., Inc., slip op., No. M2004-01066-COA-R9-CV, 2007 Tenn. App. LEXIS 29 (Tenn. Ct. App., Middle Section, Jan. 19, 2007), appeal denied (Tenn. 2007), cert. denied, 128 S. Ct. 323 (U.S. 2007).

(1) Employment-Related Criticism. See II.A.2, infra.

(2) Single Instance Rule. No cases.

b. **Punitive Damages.** Unless "actual malice" is shown, punitive damages are not permitted. Emerson v. Gardner, 732 S.W.2d 613 (Tenn. Ct. App.), appeal denied (Tenn. 1987); Woodruff v. Ohman, 166 Fed. Appx. 212 (6th Cir.), rehearing en banc denied (May 22, 2006). An award of punitive damages in a public official slander action was upheld on appeal, but Court of Appeals opinion does not discuss the precise standard of liability. Moore v. Bailey, 628 S.W.2d 431 (Tenn. Ct. App.), appeal denied (Tenn. 1981). An appellate court reduced an award of punitive damages where the words that formed the basis of the libel action did not evidence oppression or continuing malicious acts. Edmondson v. Church of God, slip op., No. 85-151-II, 1988 Tenn. Ct. App. LEXIS 743 (Tenn. Ct. App., Middle Section, Nov. 23, 1988); see also Riccardi v. Vanderbilt Univ. Med. Ctr., Nos. 3:06cv0065, 3:06cv0615, 2008 U.S. Dist. LEXIS 438 (M.D. Tenn. Jan. 2, 2008) (reducing the award of punitive damages to a maximum of $250,000 because the injuries were not particularly debilitating). There was sufficient evidence of actual malice to support an award of $100,000 in punitive damages when record indicated that the plaintiff had requested that the defendant correct errors and retract defamatory statements but defendant failed to do so. Myers v. Pickering Firm, Inc., 959 S.W.2d 152 (Tenn. Ct. App.), appeal denied (Tenn. 1997); McWhorter, 132 S.W.3d at 367 (affirming punitive damages award of $42,500 where actual malice found and compensatory damages award of $25,000 made); see also Hodges v. S.C. Toof & Co., 833 S.W.2d 896 (Tenn. 1992) (general standard for awards of punitive damages).

II. PRIVILEGES AND DEFENSES

A. Scope of Privileges

1. ***Absolute Privilege.*** Relevant and responsive testimony of witnesses before legislative committees is absolutely privileged. Logan Supermarkets, Inc. v. McCalla, 208 Tenn. 68, 343 S.W.2d 892 (Tenn. 1961). The privilege extends to those testifying before subordinate legislative bodies such as city councils. Boody v. Garrison, 636 S.W.2d 715 (Tenn. Ct. App. 1981), appeal denied (Tenn. 1982). Members of subordinate legislative bodies are absolutely privileged from defamation actions regarding comments relating to matters within the scope of the legislative bodies' authority. Cornett v. Fetzer, 604 S.W.2d 62 (Tenn. Ct. App.), cert. denied (Tenn. 1980); Evans v. Nashville Banner Publ'g Co., 15 Media L. Rep. 2216, 1988 Tenn. App. LEXIS 638 (Tenn. Ct. App., Middle Section, Oct. 12, 1988) (relevant statements made at local zoning board hearing). Relevant statements made in course of judicial proceedings or quasi-judicial administrative proceedings are absolutely privileged. Lambdin Funeral Servs., Inc. v. Griffith, 559 S.W.2d 791 (Tenn. 1978) (administrative proceedings); Cashion v. State, No. 01A01-9903-BC-00174, 1999 Tenn. App. LEXIS 623 (Tenn. Ct. App., Middle Section Sept. 17, 1999), appeal denied (Tenn. Feb. 28, 2000); Tabor v. Eakin, slip op., No. 03A01-9902-CV-00043, 1999 Tenn. App. LEXIS 328 (Tenn. Ct. App., Eastern Section, May 26, 1999) (Tennessee Board of Licensing Contractors; no appeal sought); Jones v. Trice, 210 Tenn. 535, 360 S.W.2d 48 (Tenn. 1962) (judicial proceedings). Allegations in an arrest warrant broadcast after its issuance are absolutely privileged as part of a judicial proceeding. Sullivan v. Young, 678 S.W.2d 906 (Tenn. Ct. App.), appeal denied (Tenn. 1984). The issuance of an arrest warrant by a county clerk is absolutely privileged because it is a judicial function. Jackson v. Thomas, No. M2010-01242-COA-R3-CV, 2011 Tenn. App. LEXIS 141 (Tenn. Ct. App. Dec. 7, 2010) (county clerk was immune from defamation claim in professional role because the issuance of an arrest warrant is a judicial function; no claim for defamation even when arrest warrant was negligently issued). "[C]ommunications preliminary to a proposed judicial proceeding," are absolutely privileged and, thus, a report produced by an engineering company hired to determine the cause of construction defects, design problems, and the entities responsible for the problems for use in the defense of a lawsuit was privileged, but the publication of that report to a third-party contractor hired to complete the project and to a third-party company hired to market the project was not privileged. Myers v. Pickering Firm, Inc., 959 S.W.2d 152 (Tenn. Ct. App. 1997), appeal denied (Tenn. 1997); Snedeker v. Fed. Mogul Friction, slip op., No. 2:06-00022, 2006 U.S. Dist. LEXIS 40791 (M.D. Tenn. June 14, 2006) (statements in the course of judicial proceedings that are relevant and pertinent to the issues in the proceeding are absolutely privileged and cannot be the basis for a state law defamation action; no appeal sought). An attorney is absolutely privileged to publish defamatory matter concerning another in communications preliminary to a proposed judicial proceeding, or in the institution of, or during the course and as part of, a judicial proceeding in which he participates as counsel, if it has some relation to the proceeding. Simpson Strong-Tie Co. v. Stewart, Estes & Donnell, 232 S.W.3d 18 (Tenn. 2007); **Sony/ATV Music Publishing, LLC v D.J. Miller Music Distributors, Inc., No. 3:09-cv-01098, 2011 US. Dist. LEXIS 116158 (M.D. Tenn. Oct. 7, 2011) (defendants' assertion that defamatory statements were made by plaintiffs, "directly or through their agents, representatives, and/or attorneys," was insufficient on its own to give rise to litigation privilege)**; see also Carry v. Gonzalez, slip op., No. 3:06-0157, 2006 U.S. Dist. LEXIS 75952 (M.D. Tenn. Oct. 18, 2006) (statements relevant and pertinent to criminal proceedings made during the course of "settlement discussions" are absolutely privileged);. The absolute privilege that protects statements made in connection with legal proceedings does not extend to preliminary or investigatory matters of an administrative proceeding. Glennon v. Dean Witter Reynolds, 83 F.3d 132 (6th Cir.), reh'g en banc denied, 1996 U.S. App. LEXIS 18395 (6th Cir. July

15, 1996) (applying Tennessee law); Delk v. Home Quality Management, Inc., slip op., No. 2:06-00021, 2006 U.S. Dist. LEXIS 61248 (M.D. Tenn. Aug. 28, 2006) (administrative proceedings, including employer's communications to State unemployment agency about employee's claim for unemployment benefits pursuant to Tenn. Code Ann. § 50-7-701(c)). The use of information in an out-of state administrative hearing also is absolutely privileged. Environmental Capital Holdings v. Recycling Advocates of Middle Tennessee, Memorandum and Order, No. 97-336-III (Tenn. Chancery Ct., Davidson County, Sept. 19, 1997). An employer's records concerning an employee that were required to be submitted to the department of employment security were absolutely privileged. Tenn. Code Ann. § 50-7-701 (Supp. 1997); see also Hite v. Glazer Steel Corp., slip op., No. 03A01-9808-CV-00256, 1999 Tenn. App. LEXIS 220 (Tenn. Ct. App., Eastern Section, April 1, 1999) (no appeal sought); Roy v. City of Harriman, 279 S.W.3d 296 (Tenn. Ct. App. 2008); appeal denied (Tenn. 2009) (statements made in a peer review process are protected by privilege). Trau-Med of Am., Inc. v. Allstate Ins. Co., 71 S.W.3d 691 (Tenn. 2002) (where the action is not based upon defamation, absolute privilege will not be extended to claims for intentional interference with business relationships). Anderson v. Watchtower Bible & Tract Soc'y of N.Y., Inc., slip op., No. M2004-01066-COA-R9-CV, 2007 Tenn. App. LEXIS 29 (Tenn. Ct. App., Middle Section, Jan. 19, 2007), appeal denied (Tenn. 2007), cert. denied, 128 S. Ct. 323 (U.S. 2007) (in a church membership expulsion situation, statements made within a congregation and based on ecclesiastical doctrine enjoy an absolute privilege from scrutiny by the secular authority, including claims of defamation during or arising from those disciplinary proceedings).

Tennessee now explicitly recognizes the "larger conspiracy" exception to the testimonial privilege. Brown v. Birman Managed Care, Inc., 42 S.W.3d 62 (Tenn. 2001). Tennessee generally recognizes an absolute testimonial privilege that protects relevant statements made by witnesses in the course of judicial proceedings or quasi-judicial administrative proceedings. However, Tennessee now recognizes an exception to that absolute testimonial privilege in cases where the testimony is false and was given as part of a "larger conspiracy" to defraud or otherwise damage another.

Consent is also an absolute privilege to defamation, and will defeat a plaintiff's defamation claim where, for example, a plaintiff has consented to treatment by defendant physician and to the disclosure of protected health information. Gard v. Harris, slip op., No. 2008-01939-COA-R3-CV, 2010 Tenn. App. LEXIS 187, 2010 WL 844810 (Tenn. Ct. App., Eastern Section, Mar. 11, 2010) (no appeal sought).

2. ***Qualified Privileges.*** A conditional interest is recognized when the interest in which the defendant is seeking to vindicate or further is regarded as sufficiently important to justify some latitude for making mistakes. Pate v. Service Merchandise Co., 959 S.W.2d 569 (Tenn. Ct. App. 1996), appeal denied (Tenn. 1997), cert. denied, 118 S. Ct. 76 (U.S. Oct. 6, 1997). Fair and accurate reporting of judicial proceedings is qualifiedly privileged, Langford v. Vanderbilt Univ., 199 Tenn. 389, 287 S.W.2d 32 (Tenn. 1956), as is fair and accurate reporting of a public meeting, Evans v. Nashville Banner Publ'g. Co., 15 Media L. Rep. 2216, 1988 Tenn. App. LEXIS 638 (Tenn. Ct. App., Middle Section, Oct. 12, 1988) (report of statements made at local zoning board meeting), as is fair and accurate reporting by the media "of police arrests or stops of public interest," Lewis v. Newschannel 5 Network, L.P., slip op., Nos. 00C-2704, 01C-1873 (Tenn. Cir. Ct., Davidson County, Jan. 10, 2005). However, official actions and proceedings are the core of the privilege, which does not extend to provide protection from liability for fair and accurate reports of statements made by any governmental employee in *any* circumstance, rather, it is limited to reports of statements made in "circumstances involving public proceedings or official actions of government that have been made public." Lewis v. NewsChannel 5 Network, L.P., 238 S.W.3d 270 (Tenn. Ct. App. 2007); appeal denied (Tenn. 2007). (holding that the fair and accurate report privilege does not extend to protect broadcaster's entire story from a defamation claim since the story was not limited to the contents of the Chief of Police's press release, and instead, the report did more than broadcast to members of the public what they would have read or heard had they only received a copy of the press release). Comment upon facts, expression of views, or opinions are qualifiedly privileged. Venn v. Tennessean Newspapers, Inc., 201 F. Supp. 47 (M.D. Tenn. 1962), aff'd, 313 F.2d 639 (6th Cir.), cert. denied, 374 U.S. 30 (1963). **Milligan v. United States, 670 F.3d 686 (6th Cir. 2012) (holding that a broadcast of plaintiff being falsely arrested by police was an official action and finding report that plaintiff was arrested with a "warrant in hand" was a fair and accurate report of what police had done).**

Any communication made in good faith upon any subject matter in which the communicating party has an interest, or in reference to which he has a duty to a person having a corresponding interest or duty, is qualifiedly privileged and the privilege is defeated only upon plaintiff's demonstration that the words spoken were used with express malice towards him. Southern Ice Co. v. Black, 136 Tenn. 391, 189 S.W. 861 (Tenn. 1916); Dickson v. Nissan, slip op., No. 87-289-II, 1988 Tenn. App. LEXIS 80 (Tenn. Ct. App., Middle Section, Feb. 10, 1988); See also Bernard v. Sumner Regional Health Sys., slip. op., No. M2000-01478-COA-R3-CV, 2002 Tenn. App. LEXIS 213 (Tenn. Ct. App., Middle Section, March 26, 2002). "Malice" sufficient to defeat a qualified privilege is knowledge of falsity or reckless disregard for truth or falsity. Ivy v. Damon Clinical Lab., slip op., No. 41, 1984 Tenn. App. LEXIS 3083 (Tenn. Ct. App., Western Section, Aug. 20, 1985); accord Turner v. Garrow, 12 Media L. Rep. 2314 (W.D. Tenn. 1986); McWhorter, 132 S.W.3d 354; contra Lewis v. Pinkerton's, Inc., slip op., 1985 Tenn. App. LEXIS 2805 (Tenn. Ct. App., Middle Section, April 12, 1985) (malice defined as ill will).

Tennessee's "anti-SLAPP" statute, Tenn. Code Ann. § 4-21-1003 (1998), provides that, when persons in connection with a public or governmental issue communicate information regarding another person or entity to any agency of the federal, state, or local government regarding a matter of concern to that agency they shall be immune from civil liability on claims based upon the communication to the agency. The statute provides attorney's fees and the recovery of costs if the defendant prevails upon the defense of immunity as provided in this section. Immunity is not conferred if the person communicating the information knew the information to be false, communicated the information in reckless disregard for its falsity, or when the information pertains to a person other than a public figure and the communication was made negligently in failing to ascertain the falsity of the information. The Governmental Tort Liability Act prohibits claims against governmental entities for libel and slander. Tenn. Code Ann. § 29-20-205(2). See Bly v. Keesling, No. E2002-01115-COA-R3-CV, 2002 Tenn. App. LEXIS 909 (Tenn. Ct. App., Eastern Section, Dec. 6, 2002) (no appeal sought); Shorter v. Tenn. Dep't Children Serv., Inc., No. M2003-02713-COA-R3-CV, 2005 Tenn. App. LEXIS 119 (Tenn. Ct. App., Middle Section, Feb. 9, 2005) (no appeal sought); Jackson v. Dempsey, No. 1:09-CV-240, 2010 U.S. Dist. LEXIS 32823 (E.D. Tenn. Apr. 2, 2010); Jackson v. Thomas, No. M2010-01242-COA-R3-CV, 2011 Tenn. App. LEXIS 141 (Tenn. Ct. App., Middle Section, Dec. 7, 2010).

The question of whether a publication is privileged is a question of law which the court determines, and the appellate court reviews de novo, with no presumption of correctness for the trial court's findings. Smith v. Reed, 944 S.W.2d 623 (Tenn. Ct. App. 1996), appeal denied (Tenn. 1997); see also Trotter v. Grand Lodge F. & A.M., slip op., 2006 Tenn. App. LEXIS 155 (Tenn. Ct. App., Eastern Section, Mar. 6, 2006) (no appeal sought) (the determination of whether a publication is privileged cannot be determined until the specific group of persons to whom the statements were made is established as a matter of fact). The report of a mercantile credit reporting agency is qualifiedly privileged. Riley v. Dun & Bradstreet, 172 F.2d 303 (6th Cir. 1949). An employer is qualifiedly privileged to comment upon an employee's job performance. Varner v. Hillcrest Medical Nursing Inst., Inc., slip op., 1984 Tenn. App. LEXIS 2612 (Tenn. Ct. App., Eastern Section, June 20, 1984); Russell v. Cleveland Country Club, slip op. (Tenn. Ct. App., Eastern Section, June 29, 1982). Also, the written contents of an employee file accessible only by management are qualifiedly privileged. Andrews v. Hagood, slip op., 1985 Tenn. App. LEXIS 2739 (Tenn. Ct. App., Eastern Section, Mar. 14, 1985). When a communication is qualifiedly privileged, it is actionable only if there is proof of actual malice. Smith v. Reed, 944 S.W.2d 623 (Tenn. Ct. App. 1996), appeal denied, (Tenn. 1997) (defendant's article covered under "fair reporting privilege" because more inflammatory word "forced" reflected the basic allegation of involuntariness and removal of double negative was not a material or misleading change); Woods v. Helmi, 758 S.W.2d 219 (Tenn. Ct. App. 1988), appeal denied, (Tenn. 1988) (comments concerning nurse anesthetist's performance qualifiedly privileged when communicated to those responsible for overseeing nurse's performance, even though persons receiving communication were employed by different corporate entities); see also Lineberry v. State Farm Fire & Cas. Co., 885 F. Supp. 1095 (M.D. Tenn. 1995) (arbitration panel could have properly found under Tennessee law that filing of termination report was not protected by any privilege; arbitration panel's finding of actual malice was a fact determination and not subject to review); Stem v. Gannett Satellite Info. Network, Inc., 866 F. Supp. 355 (W.D. Tenn. 1994) (defendant's article, which was based on allegations made in an affidavit in a proceeding to which the plaintiff was not a party, was within the fair report privilege); Evans v. Amcash Mortgage Co., Inc., slip op., No. 01A01-9608 -CV-00386, 1997 Tenn. App. LEXIS 535 (Tenn. Ct. App., Western Section, Aug. 1, 1997) (no appeal sought; in action by terminated employee, held that there was no publication of statement from corporate defendant's attorney to one of defendant's employees and that statement was subject to qualified privilege); Raiteri v. RKO Gen., Inc., slip op., No. 56, 1989 Tenn. App. LEXIS 791 (Tenn. Ct. App., Western Section, Dec. 6, 1989) (communications regarding defendant's performance made to employees in "need to know" positions of within proper chain of command deemed not published; statements by defendant that "it would be all right to fire plaintiff" may show malice sufficient to defeat privilege); Rose v. United Parcel Serv., slip op., No. 85-269-II, 1986 Tenn. App. LEXIS 2989 (Tenn. Ct. App., Middle Section, May 9, 1986) (where collective bargaining agreement required employer to send union a copy of any discharge letter, employer's discharge letter constituted a statement made pursuant to the collective bargaining agreement, and so was unqualifiedly privileged). The Tennessee Court of Appeals has adopted the Restatement (Second) of Torts ' 598 (1977) as law with respect to the public interest privilege as it applies to communications with private citizens. Pate v. Service Merchandise Co., 959 S.W.2d 569 (Tenn. Ct. App. 1996), appeal denied (Tenn. 1997), cert. denied, 118 S. Ct. 76 (U.S. Oct. 6, 1997).

A guardian ad litem is entitled to quasi-judicial immunity from liability for defamation that might occur while acting in the scope of his or her duty as guardian. Winchester v. Little, 996 S.W. 2d 818 (Tenn. Ct. App. 1998).

a. **Common Interest.** There is no case law in Tennessee dealing with this issue.

b. **Duty.** See II.A.1.- 2., supra.

c. **Criticism of Public Employee.** See I.B.2., supra.

d. Limitation on Qualified Privileges.

(1) **Constitutional or Actual Malice.** "Malice" sufficient to defeat a qualified privilege is knowledge of falsity or reckless disregard for truth or falsity. Ivy v. Damon Clinical Lab., slip op., No. 41, 1984 Tenn. App. LEXIS 3083 (Tenn. Ct. App., Western Section, Aug. 20, 1985); accord Turner v. Garrow, 12 Media L. Rep. 2314 (W.D. Tenn. 1986); contra Lewis v. Pinkerton's, Inc., slip op., 1985 Tenn. App. LEXIS 2805 (Tenn. Ct. App., Middle Section, April 12, 1985) (malice defined as ill will). **The Sixth Circuit affirmed the the grant of summary judgment in favor of a television station in an action by a plaintiff who appeared in a news report while being arrested, based in part on no finding of actual malice. Milligan v. United States, 670 F.3d 686, 698 (6th Cir. 2012). The plaintiff's arrest was due to a clerical error, as plaintiff was not the person listed on the original arrest warrant; however, the television station was unaware of this fact when it participated in a "ride along" with law enforcement during the arrest. Id. at 690-91. The criminal charges against plaintiff were dropped; however, the following day, the television broadcast the news report and also ran a story on the station's website. Id. at 691. Upon being contacted by plaintiff's attorney regarding the incorrect report, the television station stopped broadcasting the report and removed all direct links to the report from its web site. Id. at 692. Due to technical difficulties, the report was accessible on the website through a keyword search for an additional 10 days. Id. The court found no actual malice because there was no argument that the station knew the arrest was erroneous, and no evidence demonstrated that the reporter entertained serious doubts as to the truth of plaintiff's arrest. Id. at 698.**

(2) **Common Law Malice.** In Lewis v. Pinkerton's, Inc., slip op., 1985 Tenn. App. LEXIS 2805 (Tenn. Ct. App., Middle Section, April 12, 1985), a Tennessee appellate court defined the malice sufficient to defeat a qualified privilege as ill will.

(3) **Other Limitations on Qualified Privileges.** No cases.

e. **Question of Fact or Law.** The question of whether a publication is privileged is a question of law which the court determines, and the appellate court reviews de novo, with no presumption of correctness for the trial court's findings. Smith v. Reed, 944 S.W.2d 623 (Tenn. Ct. App. 1996), appeal denied (Tenn. 1997). The determination concerning whether a plaintiff is a public figure is a question of law, as is the determination of whether a public figure has come forward with clear and convincing evidence that the defendant was acting with actual malice. Lewis v. NewsChannel 5 Network, L.P., 238 S.W.3d 270 (Tenn. Ct. App. 2007); appeal denied (Tenn. 2007).

f. **Burden of Proof.** If the defendant is able to show grounds of privilege, the plaintiff has the burden of showing actual or express malice to overcome the privilege. Once privileged, the statement is presumed to be made without malice. Langford v. Vanderbilt Univ., 318 S.W.2d 568 (Tenn. Ct. App. 1958); Evans v. Nashville Banner Publ'g Co.,15 Media L. Rep. 2216, 1988 Tenn. App. LEXIS 638 (Tenn. Ct. App., Middle Section, Oct. 12, 1988); Dickson v. Nissan, slip op., No. 87-289-II, 1988 Tenn. App. LEXIS 80 (Tenn. Ct. App., Middle Section, Feb. 10, 1988); see also Evans v. Amcash Mortg. Co., Inc., slip op. No. 01A01-9608-CV-00386, 1997 Tenn. App. LEXIS 535 (Tenn. Ct. App., Middle Section, Aug. 1, 1997) (communication to employee by manager that past manager was terminated for touching blouse of an employee held not actionable even though minimal investigation of incident occurred). When reviewing a grant of summary judgment to a defendant in such a case, an appellate court must determine, not whether there is material evidence in the record supporting the plaintiff, but whether or not the record discloses clear and convincing evidence upon which a trier of fact could find actual malice. Lewis v. NewsChannel 5 Network, L.P., 238 S.W.3d 270 (Tenn. Ct. App. 2007); appeal denied (Tenn. 2007).

B. Standard Libel Defenses

1. ***Truth.*** Truth is available as an absolute defense to libel only when the defamatory meaning conveyed by the words is true. The literal truth of each portion of a communication does not constitute a defense when the communication, taken as a whole, conveys a false and defamatory impression due to failure to state complete facts. Memphis Publ'g Co. v. Nichols, 569 S.W.2d 412 (Tenn. 1978); Woodruff v. Ohman, 166 Fed. Appx. 212 (6th Cir.), rehearing en banc denied (May 22, 2006). Defendant must only demonstrate the substantial truth of an alleged defamatory communication. Stones River Motors, Inc. v. Mid-South Pub. Co., 651 S.W.2d 713 (Tenn. Ct. App. 1983), appeal denied (Tenn. 1983); Carroll v. Times Printing Co., 14 Media L. Rep. 1210, 1987 Tenn. App. LEXIS 3186 (Tenn. Ct. App., Eastern Section, May 5, 1987); Spence v. Keenan, slip op., No. 89-284-II, 1990 Tenn. App. LEXIS 130 (Tenn. Ct. App., Middle Section, Feb. 28, 1990); Hicks v. Metropolitan Gov't, slip op., No. 86-49-II, 1986 Tenn. App. LEXIS 3599 (Tenn. Ct. App., Middle Section, Oct. 3, 1986); Robbins v. Ferguson, slip op., No. 86-20-II, 1986 Tenn. App. LEXIS 3089 (Tenn. Ct. App., Middle Section, June 18, 1986); Kallenberg v. Knox County Bd. of Educ., No. 3:06-CV-371, 2008 U.S. Dist. LEXIS 89645 (E.D. Tenn. Aug. 12, 2008) (raising a genuine issue of fact as to whether the defendant acted with negligence or reckless disregard as to the truth of a statement). Truth is available as an absolute defense only when the defamatory meaning conveyed by the words is true. Moman v. M.M. Corp., slip op., No. 02A01-9608-CV00182, 1997 Tenn. App. LEXIS 233 (Tenn. Ct. App., Western

Section, April 10, 1997) (no appeal sought); see also Robertson v. The Leaf Chronicle, No. M2007-01025-COA-R3-CV, 2007 Tenn. App. LEXIS 789 (Tenn. Ct. App. December 20, 2007) (court of appeals affirming trial court ruling that the defendant newspaper was entitled to defense of truth because the newspaper article accurately covered a public criminal judicial proceeding); Gallagher v. The E.W. Scripps Co., No. 08-2153-STA, 2009 U.S. Dist. LEXIS 45709 (W.D. Tenn. May 29, 2009) (failure to state a claim when all statements are either true or substantially true); Moore v. John Deere Health Plan, Inc., No.: 3:07-CV-484, 2010 U.S. Dis. LEXIS 22741, at *49 (E.D. Tenn. March 11, 2010) (summary judgment appropriate where defendant's allegedly defamatory statements were entirely true); **Spivey v. King, No. E2011-01114-COA-R3-CV, 2012 Tenn. App. LEXIS 67 (Tenn. Ct. App., Eastern Section, Feb. 2, 2012) (no appeal sought; holding that a party cannot shift the burden of production for summary judgment purposes by an affidavit that merely asserts, in blanket form, that every derogatory statement they made was true; no appeal sought).**

2. ***Opinion.*** Prior to Gertz, statements of opinion were protected under the common law fair comment privilege. Venn v. Tennessean Newspapers, Inc., 201 F. Supp. 47 (M.D. Tenn. 1962), aff'd, 313 F.2d 639 (6th Cir.), cert. denied, 374 U.S. 830 (1963). Following Gertz, expressions of opinion formerly protected by the fair comment privilege are constitutionally protected. Street v. National Broad. Co., 645 F.2d 1227 (6th Cir.), cert. dismissed per stipulation, 454 U.S. 1095 (1981); Stones River Motors, Inc., supra. The determination of whether a statement is protected opinion or fact is a question of law for resolution by the court. Klein v. People Weekly Magazine, No. 82-2626-M (W.D. Tenn. June 6, 1983) (order on pending motions). A statement of opinion that implies the allegation of undisclosed defamatory facts as the basis for the opinion is actionable. Stones River Motors, Inc., supra; Hicks, supra; Binkley v. Tennessee Farmers Mut. Ins. Co., slip op., 1985 Tenn. App. LEXIS 3436 (Tenn. Ct. App., Middle Section, Nov. 8, 1985) (expression of opinion based on disclosed or assumed nondefamatory facts is not actionable, even though the opinion may be unjustified and unreasonable). But see Zius v. Shelton, No. E1999-1157-COA-RA-CV, 2000 Tenn. App. LEXIS 360 (Tenn. Ct. App., Eastern Section, June 6, 2000) (opining that there is no wholesale defamation exemption for anything that might be labeled "opinion" and reasoning that such an exemption would ignore that fact that expressions of "opinion" often imply an assertion of objective fact; citing Milkovich v. Lorain Journal Co., 497 U.S. 1, 111 L. Ed. 2d 1, 110 S. Ct. 2695 (1990)). Tennessee has not adopted a special constitutionally-based test for distinguishing opinion from fact. See also Reinshagen v. PHP Cos., slip op., No. E2001-00025-COA-R3-CV, 2001 Tenn. App. LEXIS 845 (Tenn. Ct. App., Eastern Section, November 14, 2001) (supervisor's mere statement of opinion is not slander). Statements interpreting the meaning of literary work are considered matters of opinion and readers of the work enjoy "considerable latitude" in their interpretations. Kersey v. Wilson, slip op., No. M2005-02106-COA-R3-CV, 2006 Tenn. App. LEXIS 826 (Tenn. Ct. App., Middle Section, Dec. 29, 2006), appeal denied (Tenn. 2007), cert. denied, 128 S. Ct. 285 (U.S. 2007) (church member's comment to a police officer that another member's written poem "threatened the life of" a church member was not actionable defamation because interpretation of the poem not a statement of fact).

The statement that plaintiffs had not "heard a word about business and let's face it they weren't the brightest guys who ever lived" held to be statements of rhetorical hyperbole or epithet and, therefore, constitutionally protected. Further, a statement that plaintiff "misrepresents the facts" held to be mere epithetical characterization in light of plaintiff's statement the defendant was "an idiot" and plaintiff's characterization of defendant's previous statements as "bull." Klein v. People Weekly Magazine, No. 82-2626-M (W.D. Tenn. June 6, 1983) (order on pending motions). A statement that plaintiff's news reporting was "biased and unbalanced" was opinion and not actionable. Raiteri v. RKO General, slip op., No. 56, 1989 Tenn. App. LEXIS 791 (Tenn. Ct. App., Western Section, Dec. 6, 1989). An editorial using the terms "harangue," "bleating and breast beating," "braggadocio," "swagger and bluster," and "blather," and analogizing a county attorney's conduct to that of the "Nixon White House" were permissible hyperbole and not actionable. McCluen v. Roane County Times, Inc., 936 S.W.2d 936, 941 (Tenn. Ct. App. 1996), appeal denied (Tenn. 1996). A caricature, in conjunction with its title and an article contained in the same newspaper, could be interpreted as stating actual facts about the plaintiff because the article clearly implied that the plaintiff took public money and left town, and the caricature could be reasonably understood to imply that the plaintiff took public money and moved to another city. Moman v. M.M. Corp., slip op., No. 02A01-9608-CV 00182, 1997 Tenn. App. LEXIS 233 (Tenn. Ct. App., Western Section, April 10, 1997) (no appeal sought). A letter to property owners containing statements about plaintiff's management capabilities was not actionable because the statements at issue merely voiced the opinion of the defendant. Thompson v. Hayes, 748 F. Supp. 2d 824 (E.D. Tenn. 2010).

Effects of Milkovich. A pre-Milkovich state case was cited for the proposition that opinion is constitutionally protected in a post-Milkovich non-media case. Shaw v. Wood, slip op., No. 03A01-9105-CV-165, 1991 Tenn. App. LEXIS 789 (Tenn. Ct. App., Eastern Section, Oct. 1, 1991). In another Tennessee appellate court case, the Milkovich analysis was arguably applied. In Zius v. Shelton, No. E1999-1157-COA-RA-CV, 2000 Tenn. App. LEXIS 360 (Tenn. Ct. App., Eastern Section, June 6, 2000), the Tennessee Court of Appeals explicitly adopted Milkovich; see also Revis v. McClean, No. 1999-00658-COA-R3-CV, 2000 Tenn. App. LEXIS 149 (Tenn. Ct. App., Middle Section, Mar. 13, 2000); but see Satterfield v. Bluhm, slip op., No. E2003-01609-COA-R3-CV, 2004 Tenn. App. LEXIS 244 (Tenn. Ct. App., Eastern Section, April 16, 2004) (rejecting argument that Zius abrogated distinction between fact and opinion; no appeal sought). It is not true that a statement couched in the form of an opinion can never be found to be defamatory; however, a statement of opinion is only actionable if it implies the allegation of undisclosed defamatory facts as the basis for the opinion. Kersey v. Wilson, slip op., No. M2005-02106-COA-R3-CV, 2006 Tenn. App. LEXIS 826 (Tenn. Ct. App., Middle Section, Dec. 29, 2006), appeal denied (Tenn. 2007), cert. denied, 128 S. Ct. 285 (U.S. 2007). Religious belief, opinion, and interpretation are subject to an additional constitutional protection. Anderson v. Watchtower Bible & Tract Soc'y of N.Y., Inc., slip op., No. M2004-01066-COA-R9-CV, 2007 Tenn. App. LEXIS 29 (Tenn. Ct. App. Jan. 19, 2007), appeal denied (Tenn. 2007), cert. denied, 128 S. Ct. 323 (U.S. 2007).

3. ***Consent.*** There are no cases in Tennessee that refer to this topic.

4. ***Mitigation.*** If the article sued on was published in good faith, and there were reasonable grounds for believing that the published statements were true, and if, within ten days of being notified of the plaintiff's intent to sue, the defendant newspaper or periodical publishes a full and fair correction, apology or retraction, giving it the statutorily required prominence, the plaintiff is not entitled to recover punitive damages. Tenn. Code Ann. § 29-24-103 (1980). Notice to the defendant of intent to sue under this statute is not a precondition for maintenance of a defamation action. Langford v. Vanderbilt Univ., 287 S.W.2d 32 (Tenn. 1956); Ramsey v. Cleveland Daily Banner (Tenn. Ct. App., Eastern Section, Nov. 24, 1982), cert. denied, concurring in results only, 1983 Tenn. LEXIS 747 (Tenn. Dec. 5, 1983) (sheriff conceded to be public official). To be considered in mitigation of damages, a retraction must unambiguously admit the defamation, admit that it was without proper foundation, and offer the regrets and apology of the publisher. Knoxville Publ'g Co. v. Taylor, 31 Tenn. App. 368, 215 S.W.2d 27 (Tenn. Ct. App. 1996), cert. denied (Tenn. 1948) (not decided under retraction statute).

III. RECURRING FACT PATTERNS

A. Statements in Personnel File

An employer is qualifiedly privileged to comment upon an employee's job performance. Varner v. Hillcrest Med. Nursing Inst., Inc., slip op., 1984 Tenn. App. LEXIS 2612 (Tenn. Ct. App., Eastern Section, June 20, 1984); Russell v. Cleveland Country Club, slip op. (Tenn. Ct. App., Eastern Section, June 29, 1982). Also, the written contents of an employee file accessible only by management are qualifiedly privileged. Andrews v. Hagood, slip op., 1985 Tenn. App. LEXIS 2739 (Tenn. Ct. App., Eastern Section, Mar. 14, 1985).

B. Performance Evaluations

Federal employees enjoy qualified immunity in defamation actions based upon the contents of personnel evaluations of federal employees. Rowe v. Pierce, 467 F. Supp. 14 (E.D. Tenn. 1979); Woods v. Helmi, 758 S.W.2d 219 (Tenn. Ct. App.), appeal denied (Tenn. 1988) (comments concerning nurse anesthetist's performance qualifiedly privileged when communicated to those responsible for overseeing nurse's performance, even though persons receiving communication were employed by different corporate entities); see also Ironside v. Simi Valley Hosp., 188 F.3d 350 (6th Cir. 1999) (affirming summary judgment for defendant hospital under Tennessee's Peer Review Act, Tenn. Code Ann. § 63-6-219(d), where information published was not false); Crabtree v. Dodd, No. 01A01-9807-CH-00370, 1999 Tenn. App. LEXIS 556 (Tenn. Ct. App., Middle Section, Aug. 17, 1999) (holding that a medical malpractice insurer's notification of a medical peer review board of the plaintiff-doctor's withdraw from an alcohol treatment center was entitled to qualified immunity under the Tennessee Peer Review Act); Raiteri v. RKO Gen., Inc., slip op., No. 56, 1989 Tenn. App. LEXIS 791 (Tenn. Ct. App., Western Section, Dec. 6, 1989) (communications regarding defendant's performance made to employees in "need to know" positions within proper chain of command deemed not published; statements by defendant that "it would be all right to fire plaintiff" may show malice to defeat privilege); Rose v. United Parcel Serv., slip op., No. 85-269-II, 1986 Tenn. App. LEXIS 2989 (Tenn. Ct. App., Middle Section, May 9, 1986) (where collective bargaining agreement required employer to send union a copy of any discharge letter, employer's discharge letter constituted a statement made pursuant to the collective bargaining agreement, and so was unqualifiedly privileged); See also Reinshagen v. PHP Cos., slip op., No. E2001-00025-COA-R3-CV, 2001 Tenn. App. LEXIS 845 (Tenn. Ct. App., Eastern Section, Nov. 14, 2001) (supervisor's performance review of employee was not defamatory because it had not been published); Roy v. City of Harriman, 279 S.W.3d 296 (Tenn. Ct. App. 2008); appeal denied, (Tenn. 2009) (statements made in a peer review process are protected by privilege).

C. References

"A qualified immunity" has been statutorily created in Tennessee that protects a former employer when an employer is requested to provide information within the context of a job reference concerning a former employee. Tenn. Code Ann. § 50-1-105 (1999); see also I.B.6(b), supra. Any employer who, upon request by a perspective employer or a current or former employee, provides truthful, fair and unbiased information about the job performance of the current or former employee is presumed to be acting in good faith and is granted a qualified immunity for the disclosure of the information and the consequences of the disclosure of that information. Tenn. Code. Ann. § 50-1-105 (1999). The statutorily created presumption of good faith is, however, rebuttable. Good faith may be rebutted upon a showing by a preponderance of the evidence that the disclosed information was (a) knowingly false; (b) deliberately misleading; (c) disclosed for malicious purpose; (d) disclosed in reckless disregard for its falsity or defamatory nature; or (e) Violative of the current or former employee's civil rights pursuant to current employment discrimination laws. Id.

D. Intracorporate Communication

See I.B.6., supra.

E. Statements to Government Regulators

See II.A.2., supra.

F. Reports to Auditors and Insurers

There is no case law in Tennessee in this area.

G. Vicarious Liability of Employers for Statements Made by Employees

1. ***Scope of Employment*** Corporations may be held liable for libelous words they ratify. Southern Ice Co. v. Black, 136 Tenn. 391, 189 S.W. 861 (Tenn. 1916). Corporations can be held liable for slanderous statements made by agents when uttered within the agent's scope of employment and in performance of duties in the course of transacting the business of the corporation. Tate v. Baptist Memorial Hospital, No. W1999-00553-COA-R3-CV, 2000 Tenn. App. LEXIS 505 (Tenn. Ct. App., Western Section, July 28, 2000); Buckeye Cotton Oil v. Sloan, 250 F. 712 (6th Cir. 1918); see also Bullion v. Ford Motor Co., 60 F. Supp. 2d 765 (M.D. Tenn. 1999). There is no liability when there is a material variance between the statement authorized by the principal and the statement published by the agent, unless the principal subsequently ratifies the latter. Dawson & Campbell v. Holt, 79 Tenn. 583 (1883). Generally, an employer is not liable for the torts of an independent contractor. Carr v. Carr, 726 S.W.2d 932 (Tenn. Ct. App. 1986), appeal denied (Tenn. 1987). An independent contractor is one who contracts to do a piece of work according to his own methods, and without being subject to the control of his employer, except as a result of his work. Masiers v. Arrow Transfer & Storage Co., 639 S.W.2d 654, 656 (Tenn. 1982); Shipley v. Tennessee Farmers Mut. Ins., slip op., No. 01-A-01-9011-CV-00408, 1991 Tenn. App. LEXIS 346 (Tenn. Ct. App., Western Section, May 15, 1991). The principal factor in determining whether an existing relationship is one of master and servant or one of employer and independent contractor is the right to control or direct the manner in which the work is done. Parker v. Vanderbilt Univ., 767 S.W.2d 412 (Tenn. Ct. App. 1988), appeal denied (Tenn. 1989); Knight v. Hawkins, 173 S.W.2d 163 (Tenn. 1941); Shipley, supra. The doctrine of respondeat superior applies only when the relationship is that of master and servant. W.N.C. Motor Transp. Co. v. Brooks, 121 S.W.2d 559 (Tenn. 1938); see also Huber v. Marlow, No. E2007-01879-COA-R9-CV, 2008 Tenn. App. LEXIS 319 (Tenn. Ct. App. Feb. 12, 2008) (holding that when statute of repose extinguished plaintiff's cause of action against the non-party employee, the employer cannot then be held vicariously liable solely on the actions of the non-party employee). The burden is on the employer to prove that the alleged employee is an independent contractor. National Life & Accident Insurance Co. v. Morrison, 162 S.W.2d 501 (Tenn. 1942); Shipley, supra.

There is a factual presumption that an editor is aware of what is published and authorizes it, but this presumption is rebuttable. Knoxville Publ'g Co. v. Taylor, supra; Southern College of Optometry v. Tennessee Academy of Ophthalmology, 13 Media L. Rep. 1205, slip op., No. 40, 1986 Tenn. App. LEXIS 3157 (Tenn. Ct. App. 1986) (issue of fact required reversal of summary judgment for individual defendants on question of personal liability for alleged defamatory communications); Stevenson v. J.C. Bradford Futures, Inc. (In re Cannon), 230 B.R. 546 (W.D. Tenn. 1999).

a. **Blogging.** There is no case law in Tennessee in the area of employers' liability for comments on employees' (authorized and unauthorized) blogs.

b. **Social Networking.** There is no case law in Tennessee in the area of employers' liability for comments on employees' (authorized and unauthorized) social networking sites, e.g. Facebook, MySpace, Twitter, LinkedIn.com, Flickr.com, Bebo.com, Tagged.com, BlackPlanet.com, Goodreads.com, Friendster.com, Plaxo.com, and Classmates.com.

2. ***Damages.*** See I.B.8., supra.

H. Internal Investigations

A Tennessee court recently determined that the dissemination of an email to 150 employees detailing the results of an internal investigation and corresponding termination of employees raised an issue of fact to whether all recipients were in the "need to know pipeline." Thompson v. Hayes, 748 F. Supp. 2d 824 (E.D. Tenn. 2010).

IV. OTHER ACTIONS BASED ON STATEMENTS

A. Negligent Hiring, Retention, and Supervision

Tennessee recognizes the tort of negligent hiring. The tort of negligent hiring stems from the principle that a person conducting an activity through employees is liable for harm resulting from negligent conduct in the employment of improper persons or instrumentalities in work involving risk of harm to others. Phipps v. Walker, slip op., No. 03A01-9508-CV-00294, 1996 Tenn. App. LEXIS 210 (Tenn. Ct. App., Western Section, April 4, 1996) (no appeal sought). Three elements necessary for recovery under such theory are: (1) the applicant is unfit for the particular job; (2) the applicant for employment, if hired, would pose an unreasonable risk to others; (3) the prospective employer knew or should have known that the historic criminality of the applicant would likely be repetitive. Id. (citing Gates v. McQuiddy Office Products, slip op., No. 02A01-9410-CV-000240, 1995 Tenn. App. LEXIS 715 (Tenn. Ct. App., Eastern Section, Nov. 2, 1995)); **see also Maynard v. CitiFinancial Auto Credit, Inc., No. 3:09-CV-334, 2011 U.S. Dist. LEXIS 85029 (E.D. Tenn. Aug. 1, 2011)**. Gates concluded that negligent hiring arises only when a particular unfitness of a job applicant creates a danger of harm to others which the employer should have known. Id. In order to establish negligence, the plaintiff must establish proximate cause, which cannot be done if the actionable behavior by the employee was committed outside the scope of employment. Phipps, supra; Corder v. Metropolitan Gov't, 852 S.W.2d 910 (Tenn. Ct. App. 1992), appeal denied (Tenn. 1993); Doe v. Rogers, slip op., No. 03A01-9606-CV-00212, 1997 Tenn. App. LEXIS 68 (Tenn. Ct. App., Eastern Section, Jan. 31, 1997) (no appeal sought); **Holt v. Macy's Retail Holdings, Inc., 719 F. Supp. 2d 903 (W.D. Tenn. 2010) (granting company's motion for summary judgment finding plaintiff's contention that repetitive unprofessional outbursts posed an unreasonable risk to clientele was insufficient to establish negligent hiring, in part, because plaintiff failed to present proof that employer knew or should have known about the employee's alleged unprofessionalism).** Once a duty to plaintiff is established and negligence of defendant is established, the ultimate question is whether the negligence of defendant was the proximate or legal cause of plaintiff's injuries. Long v. Brookside Manor, 885 S.W.2d 70 (Tenn. Ct. App. 1994), appeal denied (Tenn. 1994); Lancaster v. Montesi, 390 S.W.2d 217, 220 (Tenn. 1965). Tennessee recognizes the tort of negligent supervision. This cause of action is brought mainly against employers or principals for the damages caused by their employees or agents. Negligent supervision is not, however, founded solely on the respondeat superior theory, rather, it is an additional tort allowing for independent recovery. There are four elements of negligent supervision which are: (1) a duty owed by the defendant to the plaintiff; (2) a breach of duty; (3) injury or damage to the plaintiff; and (4) a proximate causal relationship between the breach of duty and the injury. In re Cannon 230 B.R. 546 (W.D. Tenn. 1999); see also Jones v. Bedford County, M2006-02710-COA-R3-CV, 2007 Tenn. App. LEXIS 669 (Tenn. Ct. App. Oct. 31, 2007) (noting that under proximate cause element of a negligent supervision claim, the plaintiff must establish that the employer should have reasonably foreseen or anticipated that the plaintiff would be at risk of injury).

B. Intentional Infliction of Emotional Distress

Intentional infliction of emotional distress and outrageous conduct are simply different names for the same cause of action. Bain v. Wells, 936 S.W.2d 618 (Tenn. 1997) (hospital and physician not liable for outrageous conduct when they placed patient in same hospital room with fellow patient infected with HIV without giving warning or obtaining consent). There are three essential elements to a cause of action for outrageous conduct: (1) the conduct complained of must be intentional or reckless; (2) the conduct must be so outrageous that it is not tolerated by civilized society; and (3) the conduct must result in serious mental injury. Id.; Macdermid v. Discover Financial Services, 488 F.3d 721 (6th Cir. 2007) (reversing dismissal of outrageous conduct claim based on defendant's threats of criminal prosecution for failure to pay a purely civil debt where the court disagreed with defendant's contention that the plaintiff was necessarily criminally liable for credit card fraud); Attea v. Eristoff, slip. op., No. M2005-02834-COA-R3-CV, 2007 Tenn. App. LEXIS 316 (Tenn. Ct. App., Middle Section, May 18, 2007) (dismissing the intentional infliction of emotional distress claim because plaintiff failed to prove that the alleged conduct of two New York taxing authorities was "so outrageous" when the authorities merely challenged the plaintiff's change of state residency and threatened to assess taxes, fines, interest, and penalties against the plaintiff); Chera v. Penn, No. 3:07-0165, 2008 U.S. Dist. LEXIS 102364 (Tenn. Ct. App., Middle Section, Dec. 16, 2008) (conduct that is simply "hasty and rash" is not punished by the tort of intentional infliction of emotional distress); Nairon v. Holland, slip op., No. M2006-00321-COA-R3-CV, 2007 Tenn. App. LEXIS 118 (Tenn. Ct. App., Middle Section, Mar. 1, 2007) (reversing grant of summary judgment to defendant medical equipment company because a jury *could* reasonably find that the "hundreds" of alleged calls made by defendant to plaintiff's home for retrieval of a rented wheelchair rose to the level of outrageous conduct); White v. Fort Sanders-Park West Med. Ctr., slip op., No. E2006-00330-COA-R3-CV, 2007 Tenn. App. LEXIS 53 (Tenn. Ct. App., Eastern Section, Jan. 29, 2007) (affirming dismissal of a claim for intentional infliction of emotional distress where plaintiff avers she was discriminated against based on her age, and yet fails to offer material evidence proving that she was replaced at all, much less by a younger person); Grubman v. Morgan Stanley DW, Inc., No. 3:06-cv-0705, 2008 U.S. Dist. LEXIS 86628 (Tenn. Ct. App., Middle Section, Sept. 16, 2008) (granting summary judgment to dismiss because a mere showing of retaliatory conduct and discrimination does not amount to a claim for intentional infliction of emotional distress); Massi v. Walgreen, No. 3:05-CV-425, 2006 U.S. Dist. LEXIS 82306 (E.D. Tenn. Nov. 9, 2006) (dismissing claim for outrageous conduct where neither the defendant's refusal to pay for the plaintiff's medical treatment nor the defendant's alleged negligent filing of a prescription constituted conduct "so outrageous"); See, V.B., infra, Anderson v. Watchtower Bible and Tract Soc'y of N.Y., Inc., slip op., No. M2004-01066-COA-R9-CV, 2007 Tenn. App. LEXIS 29 (Tenn. Ct. App., Middle Section, Apr. 14, 2005), appeal denied (Tenn. 2007), cert. denied, 128 S. Ct. 323 (2007) (doctrine of ecclesiastical abstention mandates dismissal of the *intentional infliction of emotional distress claim* for lack of subject matter jurisdiction because such an inquiry would require the court to adjudicate the correctness of the church's membership expulsion decision); Dodson v. St. Thomas Hosp., slip op., No. M2004-01102-COA-R3-CV, 2005 Tenn. App. LEXIS 205 (Tenn. Ct. App., Middle Section, Apr. 7, 2005) (facts of the case did not arouse the level of resentment necessary to state a claim for intentional infliction of emotional distress); Graham v. Liberty Mut. Ins. Co., No. 1:08-CV-299, 2009 U.S. Dist. LEXIS 32919 (E.D. Tenn. Apr. 17, 2009) (must allege bad faith to state a claim for intentional infliction of emotional distress); Leach v. Taylor, 124 S.W.3d 87 (Tenn. 2004), rev'g 2002 Tenn. App. LEXIS 925 (Tenn. Ct. App., Western Section, Dec. 30, 2002), (allegations that funeral home employees falsely stated that decedent's body had been mutilated by unauthorized harvesting of organs sufficient to state claim for outrageous conduct); Parks v. Nelson, slip. op. No. E2000-02943-COA-R3-CV, 2002 Tenn. App. LEXIS 230 (Tenn. Ct. App., Eastern Section, April 9, 2002) (conduct about which plaintiff complains must be based on plaintiff's own knowledge and not on information learned from a third party); Johnson v. Woman's Hosp., 527 S.W.2d 133, 134 (Tenn. Ct. App. 1975), cert. denied (Tenn. 1975); Medlin v. Allied Inv. Co., 217 Tenn. 469, 479, 398 S.W.2d 270, 274 (Tenn. 1966). In a recent claim of reckless infliction of emotional distress, the Tennessee Supreme Court stated that it expressed no opinion concerning whether claims of *intentional* infliction of emotional distress must be based on conduct that was directed at a specific individual. Doe 1 ex rel. Doe 1 v. Roman Catholic Diocese of Nashville, 154 S.W.3d 22 (Tenn. 2005) (holding, however, that a "claim of reckless infliction of emotional distress need not be based upon conduct that was directed at a specific person or that occurred in the presence of the plaintiff") rev'g slip op., No. M2001-01780-COA -R3-CV, 2003 Tenn. App. LEXIS 685 (Tenn. Ct. App. Sept. 22, 2003); see also Lourcey v. Estate, 146 S.W. 3d 48 (Tenn. 2004) (opting not to address argument that conduct must be "directed at" the plaintiff). **An employer may be liable for its employees' infliction of emotional distress "if its corporate supervisors and officials engage in conduct that rises to the level of reckless disregard of outrageous conduct." Theus v. Glaxosmithkline, 452 Fed. Appx. 596, 603 (6th Cir. Tenn. 2011) (quoting Pollard v. E.I. Dupont De Nemours, Inc., 412 F.3d 657, 665 (6th Cir. 2005)).** Liability for mental distress damages clearly does not extend to mere insults, indignities, annoyances, petty oppression or other trivialities. Medlin, 398 S.W.2d at 274 (adopting Restatement (Second) of Torts ' 46, comment d (1965)); **West v. Genuine Parts Co., No. 3:11-CV-252, 2011 U.S. Dist. LEXIS 105595 (E.D. Tenn. Sept. 16, 2011) (dismissing plaintiff's IIED claim, stating that simply being terminated by employer does not rise to the level of outrageous conduct without further proof of circumstances that are in the extreme);** Johnson v. Cantrell, slip op., No. 01A01-9712-CV-00690, 1999 Tenn. App. LEXIS 7 (Tenn. Ct. App., Middle Section, Jan. 20, 1999) (use of profane, abusive language not enough to constitute outrageous conduct; no appeal sought); Barbee v. Wal-Mart Stores, Inc., 2004 Tenn. App. LEXIS 88 (complaints of emotional injury such as embarrassment and humiliation without further proof will not satisfy requirement of serious mental injury); Lester v. Cracker Barrel Old Country Store, Inc., slip op., No. M2003-02409-COA-R3-CV, 2004 Tenn. App. LEXIS 348 (Tenn. Ct. App., Middle Section, June 2, 2004) (applying Restatement (Second) of Agency § 229 in determining whether restaurant was liable for intentional conduct of its employee). **To determine what rises to the level of severe mental injury, courts should analyze a claim using the following nonexclusive factors: (1) evidence of physiological manifestations of emotional distress, including but not limited to nausea, vomiting, headaches, severe weight loss or gain, and the like; (2) evidence of psychological manifestations of emotional distress, including but not limited to sleeplessness, depression, anxiety, crying spells or emotional outbursts, nightmares, drug and/or alcohol abuse, and unpleasant mental reactions such as fright, horror, grief, shame, humiliation, embarrassment, anger, chagrin, disappointment, and worry; (3) evidence that the plaintiff sought medical treatment, was diagnosed with a medical or psychiatric disorder such as post-traumatic stress disorder, clinical depression, traumatically induced neurosis or psychosis, or phobia, and/or was prescribed medication; (4) evidence regarding the duration and intensity of the claimant's physiological symptoms, psychological symptoms, and medical treatment; (5) other evidence that the defendant's conduct caused the plaintiff to suffer significant impairment in his or her daily functioning; and (6) in certain instances, the extreme and outrageous character of the defendant's conduct is itself important evidence of serious mental injury. Rogers v. Louisville Land Co., 367 S.W.3d 196 (Tenn. 2012).**

Tennessee courts have not considered whether speech not actionable as defamation may nonetheless support a claim for intentional infliction of emotional distress. Henderson v. Mullady, 1999 U.S. App. LEXIS 18316 (6th Cir. Aug. 2, 1999)) (order), also reported at 187 F.3d 635 (6th Cir. 1999) (table). Acting with an intent which is tortious, criminal, or which has been characterized as 'malice' or with a degree of aggravation which would entitle the plaintiff to punitive damages for another tort, however, does not create liability for the tort of outrageous conduct. Newsom v. Textron Aerostructures, 924 S.W.2d 87 (Tenn. Ct. App. 1995), appeal denied (Tenn. 1996) (quoting Blair v. Allied Maintenance Corp., 756 S.W.2d 267, 273 (Tenn. Ct. App. 1988) (no appeal sought), and Restatement (Second) of Torts ' 46, comment d (1965)).

In considering whether a standard has been met for intentional infliction of emotion distress, it is the court's burden in the first instance to decide whether the conduct alleged is sufficiently outrageous as to allow a reasonable jury to find in favor of the plaintiff. Henderson v. Mullady, 1999 U.S. App. LEXIS 18316 (6th Cir. Aug. 2, 1999)) (order), also reported at 187 F.3d 635 (6th Cir. 1999) (table); See Menuskin v. Williams, 145 F.3d 755, 768 (6th Cir. 1998). The cumulative effect of multiple acts by a defendant can rise to a level sufficient to constitute outrageous conduct. Levy v. Franks, 159 S.W.3d 66 (Tenn. Ct. App. 2004).

C. Interference with Economic Advantage

Until recently, Tennessee explicitly refused to recognize the tort of interference with prospective economic advantage/expectancy (also known as tortious interference with business relations.) See Nelson v. Martin, 958 S.W.2d 643, 646 (Tenn. 1997). However, in Trau-Med of Am., Inc. v. Allstate Ins. Co., 71 S.W.3d 691 (Tenn. 2002), the Tennessee Supreme Court overruled, in part, its prior decision in Nelson and held that Tennessee now recognizes the tort of interference with business relations. The Court held that the elements of the tort are: (1) an existing business relationship with specific third parties or a prospective relationship with an identifiable class of third parties; (2) the defendant's knowledge of that with the defendant's intent to relationship and not a mere awareness of the plaintiff's business dealings with others in general, (3) the defendant's intent to cause the breach or termination of the business relationship, (4) the defendant's improper motive or improper means, and (5) damages resulting from the tortious interference. Id. at 701. The relations protected against intentional interference include all prospective contractual relations except those leading to contracts to marry. Id. The Court specifically noted that employment relationships would be protected by this tort. Id. With regard to the requirement that the defendant must have acted with improper motive, the Court held that an all encompassing definition would be impossible and will vary with the facts of each case. Id. at n.5; see also Rennell v. Through the Green, Inc., No. M2006-01429-COA-R3-CV, 2008 Tenn. App. LEXIS at *21–22 (Tenn. Ct. App. March 14, 2008) (such facts include "whether the corporate officer was acting outside the general scope of his authority and for his own interests instead of the interests of the corporation"). However, the Court held that with regard to improper motive, the plaintiff must demonstrate that the defendant's predominant purpose was to injure the plaintiff. Id. Allegations that there was interference with general categories of persons, such as employees, are insufficient as specific third parties must be identified. Overnite Transp. Co. v. Teamsters Local Union No. 480, 149 Lab. Cas. (CCH) P59,857, 2004 Tenn. App. LEXIS 139 (Tenn. Ct. App., Middle Section, Feb. 27, 2004), reh'g denied, 2004 Tenn. App. LEXIS 212 (Tenn. Ct. App., April 15, 2004) (no appeal sought). See, V.B., infra, Anderson v. Watchtower Bible and Tract Soc'y of N.Y., Inc., slip op., No. M2004-01066-COA-R9-CV, 2007 Tenn. App. LEXIS 29 (Tenn. Ct. App., Middle Section, Apr. 14, 2005), appeal denied (Tenn. 2007), cert. denied, 128 S. Ct. 323 (2007) (doctrine of ecclesiastical abstention mandates dismissal of the *tortious interference claim* for lack of subject matter jurisdiction because such an inquiry would require the court to adjudicate the correctness of the church's membership expulsion decision).

Recognized by the Tennessee Supreme Court in Waste Conversion Sys., Inc. v. Greenstone Indus., Inc., 33 S.W.3d 779 (Tenn. 2000), the "qualified privilege" of a parent company to interfere in the contractual relations of a wholly-owned subsidiary does not apply where the parent company owns less than 100% of its subsidiary. Cambio Health Solutions, LLC v. Reardon, 213 S.W.3d 785 (Tenn. 2006) (finding that a parent company is not immune from a claim of tortuous interference with contractual relations where the former CEO of the parent company's subsidiary alleged that the parent company interfered with his executive consulting agreement with the subsidiary that is not wholly-owned).

There is a statutory and common law tort of inducement or procurement of breach of contract. Tenn. Code Ann. § 47-50-109; Holloway v. Collier, 969 S.W.2d 407 (Tenn. Ct. App. 1997), appeal denied (Tenn. 1998). The elements of this cause of action are: (1) knowledge of the wrongdoer of a legal contract for a designated term; (2) malicious intent of the wrongdoer to induce the breach of the contract; (3) a resultant breach of the contract proximately caused by the wrongdoer's acts; and (4) the plaintiff was damaged as a result of the breach of the contract. Lee v. Strickland, slip op., No. 03A01-9801-CH-00195, 1999 Tenn. App. LEXIS 251 (Tenn. App., Eastern Section, April 11, 1999) (no appeal sought); Myers v. Pickering Firm, Inc., 959 S.W.2d 152, 158 (Tenn. Ct. App.), appeal denied (Tenn. 1997); New Life Corp. of Am. v. Thomas Nelson, Inc., 932 S.W.2d 921 (Tenn. Ct. App.), appeal denied (Tenn. 1996); Forrester v. Stockstill, 869 S.W.2d 328 (Tenn. 1994) (holding that a corporate director, officer, or employee is generally not liable for interference with the corporation's contracts); Campbell v. Matlock, 749 S.W.2d 748 (Tenn. Ct. App. 1987), appeal denied (Tenn. 1988); TSC Indus. Inc. v. Tomlin, 743 S.W.2d 169 (Tenn. Ct. App.), appeal denied (Tenn. 1987); Dynamic Motel Management, Inc. v. Erwin, 528 S.W.2d 819, 822 (Tenn. Ct. App.), appeal denied (Tenn. 1975). Tennessee also recognizes the tort of interference with an employment relationship. Forrester, supra. At least one other court has recognized that the breach of the employment contract recognized in Forrester relied upon an authority that did not limit the type of contract that could be breached. Judds v. Pritchard, slip op., No. 01A01-9701-CV-00030, 1997 Tenn. App. LEXIS 647 (Tenn. Ct. App., Western Section, Sept. 24, 1997) (no appeal sought); see also Owens v. University Club of Memphis, slip op., No. 02A01-9705-CV-00103, 1998 Tenn. App. LEXIS 688 (Tenn. Ct. App., Western Section, Oct. 15, 1998) (recognizing tort of interference with employment contract where subsequent employer learned from previous employer that "there had been problems with employee at work" when employee had actually been terminated for refusal to break the law), appeal denied (Tenn. Dec. 30, 1998); Isbell v. Travis

Electric Co., slip op., No. M1999-00052-COA-R3-CV, 2000 Tenn. App. LEXIS 809 (Tenn. Ct. App., Middle Section, Dec. 13, 2000) (noting plaintiff's claim of tortious interference of contract failed "due to the lack of evidence of an express or implied contract;" no appeal sought). Federated Rural Elec. Ins. Exch. v. Hill, slip op., No. M2005-02461-COA-R3-CV, 2007 Tenn. App. LEXIS 152 (Tenn. Ct. App., Middle Section, Mar. 26, 2007), appeal denied (Tenn. 2007) (affirming dismissal of plaintiff's suit against his former employer for intentional tortuous interference with an employment contract where plaintiff's termination resulted after he was caught on videotape building a barn while he was out from work and collecting total disability benefits for his on-the-job knee injuries); Wyatt v. TVA, slip op., No. 3:05-0834, 2007 U.S. Dist. LEXIS 1763 (M.D. Tenn. Jan. 8, 2007) (granting defendant's motion for summary judgment because plaintiff failed to state a claim of intentional interference with business relationships since plaintiff's termination of employment with the defendant's subcontractor was neither for an improper purpose nor for the intentional purpose of injuring plaintiff, but rather, due to the defendant's legitimate purpose of banning employees who test positive on drug tests); Forsman v. Rouse, No. 3:07-0327, 2008 U.S. Dist. LEXIS 47266 (M.D. Tenn. June 16, 2008) (stating that the elements that must be proved to bring a claim for intentional interference with a business relationship applies equally to a claim for intentional interference with employment).

D. Prima Facie Tort

There are no cases in Tennessee that specifically consider this cause of action.

V. OTHER ISSUES

A. Statute of Limitations

An action for slander must be commenced within six months of the defamatory utterance. Tenn. Code Ann. § 28-3-103 (2000); Quality Auto Parts Co. v. Bluff City Buick Co., 876 S.W.2d 818, 820 (Tenn. 1994) (declining to adopt a discovery rule"); see also Rose v. Cookeville Regional Medical Center, No. M2007-02368-COA-R3-CV, 2008 Tenn. App. LEXIS 286 (Tenn. Ct. App. May 14, 2008) (rejecting a "continuous defamation" exception to the six month slander statute of limitations).

An action for libel must be commenced within one year after cause of action accrues. Tenn. Code Ann. § 28-3-104 (a)(1) (Supp. 2000); Thompson v. Wilson, slip op., No. E2003-00885-COA-R3-CV, 2004 Tenn. App. LEXIS 50 (Tenn. Ct. App., Eastern Section, Jan. 26, 2004) (no appeal sought) (erroneous filing of defamation claim in federal court instead of state court does not toll the one-year statute of limitations); Wyatt v. Carey, slip op., No 03A01-9809-CV-00307, 1999 Tenn. App. LEXIS 579 (Tenn. Ct. App., Eastern Section, Aug. 25, 1999), appeal sought (Tenn. Oct. 4, 1999). The period of ion runs text of the single publication rule, a libel claim accrues on the date of first distribution in the county where the action was brought. Gibbons v. Schwartz-Nobel, 928 S.W.2d 922 (Tenn. Ct. App.), appeal denied (Tenn. 1996); see also Shell v. State, 893 S.W.2d 416 (Tenn. 1995) (in an action for negligent deprivation of constitutional rights based on prosecutors' dissemination of false information, claim accrues when information disseminated); Applewhite v. Memphis State Univ., 495 S.W.2d 190, 194 (Tenn. 1973). Where libel is disseminated by communication not accessible to the general public, the claim accrues when the plaintiff knew or should have known of the existence of the libelous communication. Leedom v. Bell, slip op., No. 03A01-9704-CV-00136, 1997 Tenn. App. LEXIS 742 (Tenn. Ct. App., Eastern Section, Oct. 29, 1997) (no appeal sought). But see Ali v. Moore, slip op., No. 03A01-9708-CV-00347, 1998 Tenn. App. LEXIS 398 (Tenn. Ct. App., Eastern Section, June 16, 1998) (limiting Leedom to its facts and applying date of publication as date claim accrues in broadcast libel action), appeal denied, 1998 Tenn. App. LEXIS 754 (Tenn. 1998). In an action for defamation based upon the defendants' communication of defamatory information to the National Practitioner Data Bank, which subsequently transmitted the information to third parties, the claim accrued on each date third parties received information from Data Bank, not the date the defendants transmitted the information to the Data Bank. Swafford v. Memphis Individual Practice Ass'n, slip op., No. 02A01-9612-CV-00311, 1998 Tenn. App. LEXIS 361 (Tenn. Ct. App., Western Section, June 2, 1998), appeal denied (Tenn. Jan. 25, 1999).

Despite libel claims' one-year statute of limitation period in Tennessee, in the context of a motion to amend a complaint, claims arising out of the same conduct, transaction, or occurrence set forth in the original pleading will be allowed and are not time barred under the relation back provision of Fed. R. Civ. P. 15(c). Multari v. Bennett, slip op., No. 1:05-CV-355, 2006 U.S. Dist. LEXIS 64135 (E.D. Tenn. Sept. 6, 2006) (allowing plaintiff to amend complaint to add claims occurring seventeen months after libel cause of action arose though relation back provision).

Unlike a slander action in which the period begins to run as soon as the defamatory words are uttered, the "discovery rule" applies to the limitations period for libel based on an alleged libel made in documents not available to the general public. Watson v. Fogolin, slip op., No. M2009-00327-COA-R3-CV, 2010 Tenn. App. LEXIS 250 (Tenn. Ct. App., Eastern Section, Apr. 1, 2010) (no appeal sought). Accordingly, the statute of limitations will not begin to run until the plaintiff knows, or with reasonable diligence should know, of the publication where the libel claim is based on documents not available to the general public. Id. (noting, however, that the discovery rule does not apply to libel actions based on a public broadcast); **Kinser v. Bechtel Power Corp., No. 1:10-CV-312, 2012 U.S. Dist. LEXIS 76096 (E.D. Tenn. May 31, 2012) (finding that statute of limitations began to run once employee became aware of statements made by his employer in employee's security file).**

B. Jurisdiction

A plaintiff may bring a libel action in any county in which publication occurs, but is restricted to a single action for each edition of the offending publication. Applewhite v. Memphis State Univ., 495 S.W.2d 190 (Tenn. 1973). A nonresident author was held subject to in personam jurisdiction in a libel action arising out of the publication of a book and an interview related to that book where research and interviews for the book were conducted in Tennessee. Klein v. People Weekly Magazine, slip op., No. 82-2626-M (W.D. Tenn. June 6, 1983) (order on pending motions). A nonresident defendant whose agent faxed an allegedly libelous letter from office in Connecticut to Indiana was held subject to in personam jurisdiction on the basis that defendant committed tortious act outside Tennessee which proximately caused damage within Tennessee. See also Overton v. Raffone, slip op., No. 03A01-9305-CV-00192, 1994 Tenn. App. LEXIS 37 (Tenn. Ct. App., Eastern Section, Feb. 3, 1994); Nat'l Publ'g Auction House Co. v. Anderson Motor Sports, LLC, No. 3:10-00509, 2011 U.S. Dist. LEXIS 10914 (M.D. Tenn. Jan. 31, 2011) (specific jurisdiction proper under Tennessee long arm statute where libelous statements knowingly targeted Tennessee businesses and citizens). Multistate defamation may have occurred where an untrue termination report was filed in New York, recorded in Maryland, and later used in Tennessee by a different corporation to deny plaintiff a job. Tennessee substantive law applied because Tennessee had the most significant relationship to the defamation. Lineberry v. State Farm Fire & Cas. Co., 885 F. Supp. 1095 (M.D. Tenn. 1995). Nonresident authors of a Sports Illustrated article suggesting that the plaintiff, a nationally-known boxer residing in Tennessee, uses cocaine and fixed a fight in which he participated were held not to be subject to personal jurisdiction in Tennessee where the preparation of the article, including interviews, was accomplished entirely outside of Tennessee. Cobb v. Time Inc., 23 Media L. Rep. 2021, 1995 U.S. Dist. LEXIS 13682 (M.D. Tenn. 1995). The defendant's use of computer transfer with a Tennessee library was not sufficient to establish minimum contacts with a forum state for purposes of obtaining personal jurisdiction. Gibbons v. Schwartz-Nobel, 928 S.W.2d 922 (Tenn. Ct. App.), appeal denied (Tenn. 1996); Cullen v. Ybarrolaza, slip op., No. 04C197 (Tenn. Cir. Ct., Davidson County, Feb. 14, 2005) (general posting on the Internet insufficient to indicate purposeful direction of activities to forum state and did not support personal jurisdiction for defamation action). A federal district court may decline to exercise supplemental jurisdiction for a defamation action when all federal claims have been dismissed. Thorpe v. Alber's, Inc., 922 F. Supp. 84 (E.D. Tenn. 1996); Smith v. White, slip op., No. 95-6104, 1996 U.S. App. LEXIS 22378 (6th Cir. Aug. 1, 1996) (order), also reported at 92 F.3d 1186 (6th Cir. 1996) (table), cert. denied, 117 S. Ct. 1261 (1997). Federal courts may also decline to exercise supplemental jurisdiction to permissive counterclaim when state defamation claim does not have logical relationship to underlying constitutional claims. L.W. v. Knox Co. Board of Ed., slip op., No 3:05-CV-274, 2006 U.S. Dist. LEXIS 64138 (E.D. Tenn. Sept. 6, 2006). The Tennessee Claims Commission has exclusive jurisdiction over claims of libel or slander against state employees acting within the scope of their employment, but when the complaint makes no allegation that the defendants were acting as state employees when they allegedly slandered or defamed the plaintiff, the circuit court has subject matter jurisdiction to try the case. Bradfield v. Dotson, slip op., No. 02A01-9902-CV-00060, 1999 Tenn. App. LEXIS 552 (Tenn. Ct. App., Western Section, Aug. 16, 1999) (no appeal sought); Walz v. Mitchell, No. E2008-00349-COA-R3-CV, 2009 Tenn. App. LEXIS 153 (Tenn. Ct. App. Apr. 21, 2009) (when cause of action is for unliquidated damages related to defamation of character, circuit court is the proper place to file). Trial court erred in failing to treat termination of Pastor's employment as a civil wrong where defendant's alleged slanderous statements were made outside the confines of the church after Pastor had been terminated and were made in the presence of Church members, local law enforcement, and members of the surrounding community. Ausley v. Shaw, 193 S.W.3d 892 (Tenn. Ct. App. 2005), appeal denied (Tenn. 2006). In an action alleging defamation stemming from the act of informing church members of disciplinary or expulsion actions taken against specific members, the doctrine of ecclesiastical abstention mandates dismissal of the defamation claim for lack of subject matter jurisdiction because such an inquiry would require the court to adjudicate the correctness of the church's membership expulsion decision and thereby become excessively entangled in religious doctrine. Anderson v. Watchtower Bible and Tract Soc'y of N.Y., Inc., slip op., No. M2004-01066-COA-R9-CV, 2007 Tenn. App. LEXIS 29, (Tenn. Ct. App., Middle Section, Apr. 14, 2005), appeal denied (Tenn. 2007), cert. denied, 128 S. Ct. 323 (2007). Even though the fact of expulsion carries negative implications, such as sinful behavior or spiritual violations, the mere statement that a person has been expelled from church membership is not actionable if the fact of expulsion is true. Id.

Under the Federal Tort Claims Act (FTCA), the United States must be substituted as the defendant in place of its federal employees where the employees are sued for their commission of torts while acting within the scope of employment. Although the FTCA waives the government's sovereign immunity for many torts, suits for libel and slander are excluded from the waiver. As a result, upon substitution of the United States as defendant, a motion to dismiss a libel or slander claim must be granted for lack of subject matter jurisdiction based on the government's sovereign immunity. Jones v. Pittman, slip op., No. 3:06-0228, 2007 U.S. Dist. LEXIS 25663 (M.D. Tenn. Apr. 5, 2007).

C. Workers' Compensation Exclusivity

Tennessee's Workers' Compensation law provides the exclusive remedy for employees (as well as the employee's personal representative, dependents or next of kin) who are injured during the course and scope of their employment. Tenn. Code Ann. § 50-6-108; Clawson v. Burrow, 250 S.W.3d 59 (Tenn. Ct. App. 2007), appeal denied (Tenn. 2008). Under Tennessee's Workers' Compensation exclusivity provision, employees are precluded from seeking tort damages for the injury. Valencia v. Freeland & Lemm Const. Co., 108 S.W.3d 239 (Tenn. 2003); see also Lang v. Nissan North America, Inc., 170 S.W.3d 564 (Tenn. 2005) (finding hedonic damages, or damages for the loss of enjoyment of life, were not a basis for recovery of workers' compensation benefits as the workers' compensation statute did not provide for such common-law tort recovery; recognizing hedonic damages as a basis for recovering benefits would run counter to the exclusive remedy provisions of the workers' compensation law); **see also Poole-Henry v. Johnson & Johnson Health Care Sys., No. 11-2695 -STA, 2011 U.S. Dist. LEXIS 143683 (W.D. Tenn. Dec. 12, 2011)**. Tennessee's Workers' Compensation exclusivity provision does not violate due process clauses of Federal and Tennessee Constitutions. Nichols v. Benco Plastics, Inc. 469 S.W.2d 135 (Tenn. 1971). Tennessee's Workers' Compensation exclusivity provision protects the immediate employer, general contractors and fellow employees. Scott v. AMEC Kamtech, Inc., 583 F. Supp. 2d 912 (E.D. Tenn. 2008).

It is not contrary to Tennessee's Constitution that, under Tennessee's Workers' Compensation law, injured employees may choose to file a claim for compensation from his employer under Tennessee's Workers' Compensation laws or proceed against a third person liable for the injuries, or proceed against both, but they cannot recover against both. Mitchell v. Usilton, 242 S.W. 648 (Tenn. 1922).

To avoid Tennessee's exclusive remedy provisions of the Workers' Compensation Act, Tennessee courts require proof of an *actual* intent by the employer to injure the employee. Gonzales v. Alman Const. Co., 857 S.W.2d 42 (Tenn. Ct. App. 1993); Scarborough v. Brown Group, Inc., 935 F. Supp. 954 (W.D. Tenn. 1996); Blair v. Allied Maintenance Corp., 756 S.W.2d 267 (Tenn. Ct. App. 1988). An employer's alleged willful, wanton, deliberate and grossly negligent conduct did not fall within the intentional tort exception to the exclusivity provisions of Tennessee's workers' compensation law. Scarborough v. Brown Group, Inc., 935 F. Supp. 954 (W.D. Tenn. 1996). The intent necessary to qualify for an exception "must be equivalent to a deliberate determination on the part of the employer to cause injury combined with the undertaking of some means appropriate to that purpose." Burke v. Bradley Cnty. Gov't, No. 1:11-CV-19,2011 U.S. Dist. LEXIS 36070, at *8 (E.D. Tenn. Apr. 1, 2011).

An employer was deemed to have waived its argument that the exclusivity provision of Tennessee's workers' compensation law barred the former employee's claim for intentional infliction of emotional distress after the employer failed to plead the same in its answer or at any time prior to submitting a reply brief as part of a second appeal. Pollard v. E.I. DuPont De Nemours, Inc., 412 F.3d 657 (6th Cir. 2005).

Employee was receiving workers' compensation benefits from the employer but, also, sued employer under products liability theory because employer manufactured the equipment that caused the workplace injury. The court rejected employee's "dual capacity" theory. Morris v. Johns Manville International, Inc., slip op., No. 1:09-cv-232, 2010 U.S. Dist. LEXIS 101030, 2010 WL 3825867 (E.D. Tenn. Sept. 24, 2010).

Workers' Compensation exclusive remedy rule does not bar further employee action under Title VII and the Tennessee Human Rights Act. Reagan v. City of Knoxville, 692 F.Supp. 2d 891 (E.D. Tenn. 2010).

D. Pleading Requirements

The common law rule requiring pleading of slanderous words in haec verba is no longer applicable in light of the Tennessee Rules of Civil Procedure. Handley v. May, 588 S.W.2d 772 (Tenn. Ct. App.), appeal denied (Tenn. 1979); Evans v. Nashville Banner Publ'g Co., slip op., No. 87-164-II, 1988 Tenn. App. LEXIS 638, 15 Media L. Rep. 2216 (Tenn. Ct. App., Middle Section, Oct. 12, 1988). But a complaint still must allege both the time and place of the slanderous utterance. Millsaps v. Millsaps, 1989 Tenn. App. LEXIS 317 (Tenn. App., Western Section, May 3, 1989), appeal denied (Tenn. Sept. 5, 1989); Hayes v. Tyson, slip op., No. W2004-00750-COA-R3-CV, 2005 Tenn. App. LEXIS 227 (Tenn. Ct. App., Western Section, Apr. 19, 2005) (no appeal sought) (defamation action dismissed for failure to specifically plead defamatory remarks); TIG Ins. Co. and Fairmont Specialty Group v. Titan Underwriting Managers, LLC, No. M2007-01977-COA-R3-CV, 2008 Tenn. App. LEXIS 777 (Tenn. Ct. App. Nov. 7, 2008), appeal denied, 2009 Tenn. LEXIS 247 (Tenn. May, 11, 2009) (claim dismissed by trial court because of failure to plead the substance of a slanderous statement). Accordingly, Tennessee does not recognize a "continuing defamation" exception to the "time and place" pleading requirement. Rose v. Cookeville Regional Medical Center, No. M2007-02368-COA-R3-CV, 2008 Tenn. App. Lexis 286 (Tenn. Ct. App. May 14, 2008). The Tennessee Supreme Court recently held that an insurer can be held vicariously liable for the acts or omissions of an attorney hired to represent an insured when those acts or omissions were directed, commanded, or knowingly authorized by the insurer. Specifically, the liability will arise when the insurer undertakes to exercise actual control over the actions of the insured's attorney, then it may be held vicariously liable for any harm to a plaintiff proximately caused thereby. Givens v. Mullikin, slip op., No. W1999-01783-SC-R11-CV, 2002 Tenn. LEXIS 153 (Tenn. March 25, 2002). A defendant cannot be held liable for the acts of its attorney, however, based solely upon the mere existence of the attorney-client relationship. Laurent v. Suntrust Bank, slip op., No. E2003-014808-COA-R3-CV, 2003 Tenn. App. LEXIS 856 (Tenn. Ct. App., Eastern Section, Oct. 17, 2003) (no appeal sought). **An employee may be precluded from bringing a cause of action for defamation after a determination is made by an administrative law judge. Sullivan v. Wilson County, No. M2011-00217-COA-R3-CV, 2012 Tenn. App. LEXIS 332 (Tenn. Ct. App. May 22, 2012) (no appeal sought). In Sullivan, an employee was terminated by a local power board after a detective sent his employer a letter stating the employee sold narcotic drugs from the truck the employee used during his shift and that the employee admitted selling the drugs. Id. The employee denied selling illegal drugs or making such an admission to the detective, but the administrative law judge in charge of the evidentiary hearing determined that the statements in the detective's letter were true. Id. The employee later filed suit against the detective who authored the letter, his supervisors, and the county employing the individual defendants. The former employee asserted causes of action for defamation, negligence, false light invasion of privacy, and intentional infliction of emotional distress. Id. The trial court concluded that the former employee was collaterally estopped from re-litigating the veracity of the statements in the detective's letter leading to the plaintiff's termination.**

E. Due Process

A person's good name, reputation, honor, and integrity are among the liberty interests protected by the due process clause of the Fourteenth Amendment." Chilingirian v. Boris, 882 F.2d 200, 205 (6th Cir. 1989). Defamation alone, however, is insufficient to invoke due process concerns. See Paul v. Davis, 424 U.S. 693, 711, 96 S. Ct. 1155, 47 L. Ed. 2d 405 (1976). "Some alteration of a right or status 'previously recognized by state law,' such as employment, must accompany damage to reputation." Quinn v. Shirey, 293 F.3d 315, 319 (6th Cir. 2002) (quoting Paul, 424 U.S. at 711-12). A non-tenured public employee is entitled to a name-clearing hearing when he shows that he has been stigmatized by the public dissemination of false information during the decision to terminate his employment. Paul, 424 U.S. at 709-10.

Five elements must be satisfied to implicate a liberty interest in one's reputation: (1) the stigmatizing comments must be made in conjunction with the plaintiff's termination; (2) plaintiff's employer must do more than allege merely improper or inadequate performance, incompetence, neglect of duty or malfeasance; (3) the stigmatizing statements must be made public; (4) the plaintiff must claim that the statements made against her were false; and (5) the public dissemination must have been voluntary. See Ludwig v. Bd. of Trs. of Ferris State Univ., 123 F.3d 404, 410 (6th Cir. 1997). "Once a plaintiff has established the existence of all five elements, [she] is entitled to a name-clearing hearing if [she] requests one." Quinn, 293 F.3d at 320.

F. Standing

A Defamation action accrues at the time of the publication of an allegedly defamatory statement and provides for the right to recover for alleged injury to a person's reputation. See Applewhite v. Memphis State Univ. , 495 S.W.2d 190 (Tenn. 1973); Gibbons v. Schwartz, 928 S.W.2d 922 (Tenn. Ct. App. 1996); Stones River Motors, Inc. v. Mid-South Publ'g Co., 651 S.W.2d 713 (Tenn. Ct. App. 1983). Moreover, tort actions involving personal injuries and wrongs done to a person, reputation, or feelings of the injured party are unassignable. Can Do, Inc. Pension and Profit Sharing Plan and Successor Plans v. Manier Herod, Hollabaugh & Smith, 922 S.W.2d 865, 867 (Tenn. 1996). The person or entity with a justiciable interest in a defamation action can not assign that interest to another. Garland v. Bellsouth Adver. & Publ. Corp., slip op., No. 3:06-CV-14, 2006 U.S. Dist. LEXIS 72261 (D. Tenn. 2006).

SURVEY OF TENNESSEE EMPLOYMENT PRIVACY LAW

Lucian T. Pera, Esq.
Adams and Reese LLP
Brinkley Plaza
80 Monroe Ave., Suite 700
Memphis, Tennessee 38103
Telephone: (901) 524-5278
Facsimile: (901) 524-5378
Email: Lucian.Pera@arlaw.com
Website: www.arlaw.com

Margaret R. T. Myers, Esq.
Adams and Reese LLP
Fifth Third Center
424 Church Street, Suite 2800
Nashville, Tennessee 37219
Telephone: (615) 259-1009
Facsimile: (615) 259-1470
Email: Margaret.Myers@arlaw.com
Website: www.arlaw.com

(With Developments Reported Through **November 1, 2012**)

GENERAL COMMENTS

The Tennessee appellate court system is two-tiered, consisting of the Tennessee Supreme Court and the Court of Appeals in civil cases. Opinions of the Supreme Court are generally published in the West reporter. Tennessee Court of Appeals opinions are generally not published unless an application for permission to appeal to the Tennessee Supreme Court is denied. Most Tennessee unpublished decisions may be ordered from the Tennessee Attorneys Memo by telephone at (615) 248-5900. Most Tennessee appellate decisions issued since about 1995 are also available without charge at a web site maintained by the Tennessee Supreme Court at www.tsc.state.tn.us and available by subscription at the Tennessee Bar Association's site, TBALink, at www.tba.org.

SIGNIFICANT DEVELOPMENTS SINCE THE 2012 *SURVEY*

None.

I. GENERAL LAW OF PRIVACY

A. Legal Basis of Privacy Claims

Although there is no specific direct mention of a right to privacy in the United States Constitution, a law governing privacy and invasions of that privacy has arisen as a result of judicial interpretations of the common law as well as developments in statutory law addressing specific concerns of narrowly defined privacy interests. One of the earliest judicial recognitions of the law of privacy involved the unauthorized use of a photograph of the plaintiff and a bogus testimonial attributed to him which appeared in a newspaper advertisement for a life insurance company. The litigation which followed this conduct resulted in the Georgia Supreme Court's recognition that there is a law of privacy that prevents unauthorized use of an individual's likeness for advertising purposes. Pavesich v. New England Life Ins. Co., 122 Ga. 190, 50 S.E. 68 (1905). Generally, actions for invasion of privacy fall into four categories: (1) appropriation of the name or likeness of another; (2) unreasonable intrusion upon the seclusion of another; (3) unreasonable publicity given to the private life of another; and (4) publicity that unreasonably places another in a false light. Restatement (Second) of Torts § 652A (1977). Tennessee has adopted the Restatement (Second) of Torts § 652A as the basis for an action in Major v. Charter Lakeside Hosp., slip op., No. 42, 1990 Tenn. Ct. App. LEXIS 621 (Tenn. App., Western Section, Aug. 31, 1990) (no appeal sought).

It is generally conceded that Tennessee judicially recognized a common law right of privacy in 1956. A plaintiff brought a lawsuit against Vanderbilt University alleging that a publication of Vanderbilt University invaded the privacy of the plaintiff by publishing information which it had obtained from the plaintiff's pleadings in previously filed litigation not involving the University. The court held that the University's newspaper was privileged to publish a fair and accurate report of matters of public record, including pleadings in litigation. Langford v. Vanderbilt Univ., 287 S.W.2d 32 (Tenn. 1956). Subsequently, judicial recognition of rights to privacy in Tennessee by Tennessee courts has included denial of an invasion of privacy claim by an individual who consensually posed for a photograph to be used in a publication for a private club, Martin v. Senators, Inc., 418 S.W.2d 660 (Tenn. 1967); as well as a case involving allegations of invasion of privacy and outrageous conduct following a six-month surveillance by the defendant of the plaintiff, Swallows v. Western Elec. Co., 543 S.W.2d 581 (Tenn. 1976); however, the unauthorized copying and distribution of a photograph of the plaintiff depicting a personal part of her anatomy was sufficient to give rise to a cause of action for invasion of privacy, Dunn v. Moto Photo, Inc., 828 S.W.2d 747 (Tenn. Ct. App. 1991); Fann v. Fairview, 905 S.W.2d 167 (Tenn. Ct. App. 1994), appeal denied (Tenn. 1995). The Tennessee Supreme Court found that private employers are not prohibited from requiring employees to submit to random drug tests and that such a requirement did not violate any state constitutional guarantee of privacy. Stein v. Davidson Hotel Co., 945 S.W.2d 714 (Tenn. 1997); see also Tidman v. The Salvation Army, slip op., No. 01-A-01-9708-CV-00380, 1998 Tenn. App. LEXIS 475, 136 Lab. Cas. (CCH) & 58,441 (Tenn. Ct. App., Middle Section, July 15, 1998) (denying invasion of privacy claim when employer attempted to discover whether employee was having an affair on grounds that information sought related to employee's ability to effectively serve as officer in the Salvation Army; no appeal sought).

Federal courts in Tennessee have expanded upon our appellate court decisions by looking at the law and assuming further that our courts would recognize the four areas of invasion of privacy contained in the Restatement. Cordell v. Detective Publications, Inc., 307 F. Supp. 1212 (E.D. Tenn. 1968), aff'd, 419 F.2d 989 (6th Cir. 1969); Beard v. Akzona, Inc., 517 F. Supp. 128 (E.D. Tenn. 1981); International Union v. Garner, 601 F. Supp. 187 (M.D. Tenn. 1985); Scarbrough v. Brown Group, Inc., 935 F. Supp. 954 (W.D. Tenn. 1995); Doe v. Hendersonville Hosp. Corp., 1999 U.S. App. LEXIS 848 (6th Cir. Jan. 13, 1999) (order), also reported at 172 F.3d 872 (6th Cir. 1999) (table).

B. Causes of Action

1. ***Misappropriation/Right of Publicity.*** In Martin v. Senators, Inc., 418 S.W.2d 660 (Tenn. 1967), the plaintiff was employed as a "hat check girl" for a private club in Knox County. She consented for her photographic likeness to be used on a bulletin board within the club. When the club used the photographic likeness in an advertisement published in a newspaper in Knox County, she sued for invasion of privacy. The court, citing Langford v. Vanderbilt Univ., supra, held that, because she had consented to the public use of her photograph by the club and because the conduct of the club in publishing her photograph in conjunction with the newspaper advertisement did not offend persons of ordinary sensibility nor go beyond the limits of decency, there was no cause of action for invasion of privacy. In Major v. Charter Lakeside Hosp., slip op., No. 42, 1990 Tenn. App. LEXIS 621 (Tenn. Ct. App., Western Section, Aug. 31, 1990), the Tennessee Court of Appeals adopted the Restatement (Second) of Torts § 652A as the basis for a cause of action for invasion of privacy. Employer's use of a fictional character portrayed by the plaintiff in an advertising campaign did not involve the use or appropriation of plaintiff's personal traits, but rather the use of copyrightable advertisements. Stanford v. Caesars Entm't, Inc., 430 F. Supp. 2d 749 (W.D. Tenn. 2006).

Every individual has, by Tennessee statute, a property right in the use of their name, photograph, or likeness in any medium in any manner. These individual rights constitute property rights which are freely assignable and licensable and do not expire upon the death of the individual, whether or not the rights were commercially exploited by the individual during their lifetime, but are descendible to the heirs, executors, and devisees of the individual. Tenn. Code Ann. § 47-25-1103 (2001); but cf. Stanford v. Caesars Entertainment, Inc., 430 F. Supp. 2d 749 (W.D.Tenn. 2006) (ruling that a former employee's state statutory claim alleging unauthorized use of his image and voice in an advertising campaign was preempted by federal copyright law where the works of authorship at issue depicted the entertainer playing a role, rather than his persona or likeness, and thus did not involve exploitation or misappropriation of his identity); McKee v. Meltech, Inc., slip op., No. 10 -2730, 2011 U.S. Dist. LEXIS 49612 (W.D. Tenn. May 9, 2011) (noting authority for proposition that appropriation of one's name or likeness *may* form the basis of a claim for invasion of privacy under Tennessee law, but also noting lack of any authority for proposition that a person of ordinary sensibilities would be offended by a defendant's using an image or video of that person's likeness where he voluntarily provided the defendant with the image or video; finding that, because wife submitted photos/materials of herself, sometimes with her husband, to company through a website pursuant to a contract, nothing in the allegations by husband suggested that the company should have realized that using the images and videos of the husband would be offensive and, for that reason, husband failed to state a plausible claim for invasion of privacy). The individual property rights, which are descendible, are exclusive to the individual and subject to assignment and licensing during that individual's lifetime and to the executors, heirs, assigns or devisees for a period of 10 years after the death of the individual. See Polygram Records, Inc. v. Legacy Entertainment Group, slip op., 2006 Tenn. App. LEXIS 41, 77 U.S.P.Q. (BNA) 1680 (Tenn. Ct. App., Middle Section, Jan. 20, 2006), appeal denied (Tenn. Sept. 25, 2006) (holding that original recordings of Hank Williams came under the description of personal property or individual rights and because those rights were never assigned by Williams they pass to his heirs). The executor, assignee, heir or devisee has the right to use the name, photograph or likeness of the individual for any commercially appropriate purpose so long as that use is commenced within 10 years after death, and the exclusive right for commercial exploitation continues until the exploitation terminates or is unused for a period of two years following the expiration of the tenth anniversary of the death of the individual. Tenn. Code Ann. § 47-25-1104 (2001). Unauthorized use of the name or likeness of an individual, even after death, is prohibited and, depending upon the nature of the violation of this statutory prohibition, may be punishable as a Class A misdemeanor as well as actionable civilly. Tenn. Code Ann. § 47-25-1105 (2005) (as amended by 2005 Tenn. Acts, ch. 395, §§ 4, 5, eff. July 1, 2005) (violations occurring prior to July 1, 2005 are punishable only as a "Class C" misdemeanor). Among the remedies available to redress violations of this Act are actions in the circuit or chancery courts to enjoin unauthorized use, the impoundment of materials violating the rights, and their destruction. As part of the injunction, the court may authorize the confiscation of all unauthorized items and seize all instrumentalities used in connection with the violation of the individual's rights. Tenn. Code Ann. § 47-25-1106 (Supp. 2005) (as amended by 2005 Tenn. Acts, ch. 395, § 6, eff. July 1, 2005). Among the damages recoverable for violation of the Act are the actual damages suffered as a result of the knowing use or infringement of the individual's rights together with any profits attributable to the use or infringement. Id. These remedies are considered cumulative and in addition to any others provided for by law. Id.

2. ***False Light***. The Tennessee Supreme Court recently recognized "false light" as a distinct, valid cause of action in Tennessee. West v. Media General Convergence, Inc., 53 S.W.3d 640 (Tenn. 2001); see Creal v. City of Cleveland, No.: 1:07-CV-61, 2008 U.S.Dist. LEXIS 41521 (E.D. Tenn. May 22, 2008) (federal district court noting that because the plaintiff's claim raised an issue of state law based the tort of "false light" that had just been recognized in Tennessee within the past decade, that the claim would be better left for the state courts to handle); McKee v. Meltech, Inc., slip op., No. 10-2730, 2011 U.S. Dist. LEXIS 49612 (W.D. Tenn. May 9, 2011). The Court adopted Section 652E of the Restatement (Second) of Torts as a true statement of the elements of the false light cause of action in Tennessee. Id. at *15-20. Thus, in Tennessee, one who gives publicity to a matter concerning another that places the other before the public in a false light is subject to liability to the other for invasion of his privacy, if (a) the false light in which the other was placed would be highly offensive to a reasonable person, and (b) the actor had knowledge of or acted in reckless disregard as to the falsity of the publicized matter and the false light in which the other would be placed. Id. Actual malice is the appropriate standard in cases where the plaintiff is a public official or public figure or when the claim is asserted by a private individual about a matter of public concern. Id. at *22-23; Lewis v. NewsChannel 5 Network, L.P., 238 S.W.3d 270 (Tenn. Ct. App. 2007), appeal denied (Tenn. 2007) (holding that the plaintiff, a private citizen, is an "involuntary" public figure that failed to satisfy the actual malice standard for his false light invasion of privacy claim against NewsChannel 5 for its report about the plaintiff's brother-in-law, a high-ranking public official, who was disempowered because of his alleged interference with the plaintiff's arrest). See also Shamblin v. Martinez, slip op., No. M2010-00974-COA-R3-CV, 2011 Tenn. App. 182 (Tenn. Ct. App., Middle Section, Apr. 13, 2011); Flatt v. Tenn. Secondary Schs. Athl. Ass'n, slip op., No. M2001-01817-COA-R3-CV, 2003 Tenn. App. LEXIS 7 (Tenn. Ct. App., Middle Section, Jan. 9, 2003); Gunter v. Emerton, slip op., No. M2001-00364-COA-R3-CV, 2002 Tenn. App. LEXIS 360 (Tenn. Ct. App., Middle Section, May 21, 2002). Roberts v. Dover, 525 F. Supp. 987 (M.D. Tenn. 1981); Coker v. Redick, slip op., No. 01A01-9806-BC-00318, 1995 Tenn. App. LEXIS 137 (Tenn. Ct. App., Middle Section, March 3, 1995); Overton v. Raffone, slip op., No. 03A01-9305-CV-00192, 1994 Tenn. App. LEXIS 37 (Tenn. Ct. App., Eastern Section, Feb. 3, 1994); Brooks v. Collinwood Church of God, slip op., No. 846, 1989 Tenn. App. LEXIS 474 (Tenn. Ct. App., Western Section, July 6, 1989). **The Sixth Circuit affirmed the grant of summary judgment in favor of a television station in an action by a plaintiff who appeared in a news report while being arrested, based in part on no finding of actual malice. Milligan v. United States, 670 F.3d 686, 698 (6th Cir. 2012). The plaintiff's arrest was due to a clerical error, as plaintiff was not the person listed on the original arrest warrant; however, the television station was unaware of this fact when it participated in a "ride along" with law enforcement during the arrest. Id. at 690-91. The criminal charges against plaintiff were dropped; however, the following day, the television broadcast the news report and also ran a story on the station's website. Id. at 691. Upon being contacted by plaintiff's attorney regarding the incorrect report, the television station stopped broadcasting the report and removed all direct links to the report from its web site. Id. at 692. Due to technical difficulties, the report was accessible on the website through a keyword search for an additional 10 days. Id. The court found no actual malice because there was no argument that the station knew the arrest was erroneous, and no evidence demonstrated that the reporter entertained serious doubts as to the truth of plaintiff's arrest. Id. at 698.** In cases involving a private individual and a private matter, negligence is the appropriate standard. West, 53 S.W.3d at 648. Other parameters of the false light cause of action are defined by Sections 652F - 652I of the Restatement (Second) of Torts. Id. While the Tennessee Supreme Court has recognized the tort of false light invasion of privacy as a separate and distinct tort from defamation in *West v. Media General Convergence Inc.*, the publication of information must go outside the employer for the claim to succeed. White v. Fort Sanders-Park W. Med. Ctr., slip op., No. E2006-00330-COA-R3-CV, 2007 Tenn. App. LEXIS 53 (Tenn. Ct. App., Eastern Section, Jan. 29, 2007); **West v. Genuine Parts Co., No. 3:11-CV-252, 2011 U.S Dist. LEXIS 105595 (E.D. Tenn. Sept. 16, 2011) (holding that a letter sent to a state official to review a workers compensation award did not arise to the "publicity" required for a claim of false light); Secured Fin. Solutions, LLC v. Winer, slip op., No. M2009-00885-COA -R3-CV, 2010 WL 3346444 (Tenn. Ct. App. Middle Section, Jan 28, 2010), appeal denied (Tenn. Aug. 25, 2010) (sending an email to one person and making oral comments to another person does not satisfy the publicity requirement for false light invasion of privacy)**. There is no claim for false light when the statements at issue are true or substantially true or are privileged (as accurate reports of judicial proceedings and court records) and the plaintiff failed to show how such true and privileged statements would be highly offensive to a reasonable person. Gallagher v. The E.W. Scripps Co., No. 08-2153-STA, 2009 U.S. Dist. LEXIS 45709 (W.D. Tenn. May 29, 2009).

The cause of action for false light lies only for individuals. Id. Corporations, organizations and business entities may not maintain a cause of action for false light. Id.

Plaintiffs seeking to recover on false light claims must specifically plead and prove damages allegedly suffered from the invasion of their privacy. Id. As with defamation there must be proof of actual damages. Id. If there is proof of actual damages, a false light plaintiff may recover damages for: (a) the harm to the individual's interest in privacy, (b) the individual's mental distress provided that the mental distress was actually suffered and is the kind that normally results from such an invasion of privacy, and (c) special damage of which the invasion is a legal cause. Id.; See also Shamblin v. Martinez, slip op., No. M2010-00974-COA-R3-CV, 2011 Tenn. App. 182 (Tenn. Ct. App., Middle Section, Apr. 13, 2011).

The statute of limitations for a false light claim is the same six month statute that applies to claims of slander or the one year state of limitation that applies to libel, which are codified at Tenn. Code. Ann. §§ 28-3-103 and 28-3-104(a)(1), depending on whether the publicity is spoken or printed. Id.; see Barbee v. Wal-Mart Stores, Inc., slip op., No. W2003-00017-COA-R3-CV, 2004 Tenn. App. LEXIS 88 (Tenn. Ct. App., Western Section, Feb. 9, 2004), appeal denied, 2004 Tenn. App. LEXIS 762 (Tenn. Sept. 6, 2004); Daniel v. Taylor, No. E2008-01248-COA-R3-CV, 2009 Tenn. App. LEXIS 110 (Tenn. Ct. App. Mar. 25, 2009). **Absent any showing of injurious statements made to a third party within six months of the filing of plaintiff's complaint barred recovery under a false light theory. Caruana v. Marcum, No. 3:01-1567, 2011 U.S. Dist. LEXIS 79890 (M.D. Tenn. July 21, 2011).**

Recent Tennessee case law suggests that self-publication of drug test results by employees can vitiate their *prima facie* defamation/false light case. Yancy v. Barr-Nunn Transportation Inc., slip op., No. 2:09-cv-02207-JPM-egb, 2010 U.S. Dist. LEXIS 42707, 2010 WL 1780229 (W.D. Tenn. April 30, 2010) (granting summary judgment to employer on defamation and false light claims in suit of terminated employee who admitted he had informed every prospective employer about his termination from employer due to a positive drug test; finding employer had not released terminated employee's drug test results to prospective employers and thus, employee had failed to establish the first element of his *prima facie* case, that the employer had "published" statements, i.e. the drug test results).

3. ***Publication of Private Facts.*** Publicity of a matter concerning the private life of an individual may create an action for invasion of privacy if the matter publicized is of a kind that: (a) would be highly offensive to a reasonable person, and (b) is not of legitimate concern to the public. Restatement (Second) of Torts § 652D (1977). The decision to inform fellow employees of plaintiff's involuntary hospitalization for psychiatric problems was held not actionable when all of the employees had work-related reasons to know of plaintiff's condition. Doe v. Hendersonville Hosp. Corp., 1999 U.S. App. LEXIS 848 (6th Cir. Jan. 13, 1999) (order), also reported at 172 F.3d 872 (6th Cir. 1999) (table); Beard v. Akzona, Inc., 517 F. Supp. 128 (E.D. Tenn. 1981); Robinson v. Omer, slip op., No. 01A01-9510-CV-00434, 1996 Tenn. App. LEXIS 317 (Tenn. Ct. App., Western Section, May 24, 1996), rev'd on other grounds, 952 S.W.2d 423 (Tenn. 1997); see also Cawood v. Booth, No. E2007-02537-COA-R3-CV, 2008 Tenn. App. LEXIS 715 (Tenn. Ct. App., Eastern Section, Nov. 25, 2008) (when there is only limited exposure to a small group of people, it is not sufficient to make out a cause for invasion of privacy), appeal granted, 2009 Tenn. LEXIS 370 (Tenn., June 15, 2009); Harris v. Horton, 341 S.W.3d 264, (Tenn. Ct. App. 2009) (a person involved in a fatal car accident is considered an involuntary public figure and the use of private facts related to that event will bar any recovery for publication of private facts).

Where the license tags on private vehicles were recorded during a surveillance activity conducted by police officers involving individuals attending union organization meetings, such conduct did not create an action for public disclosure of private facts. International Union v. Garner, 601 F. Supp. 187 (M.D. Tenn. 1985). The Garner decision follows and cites with approval the 1981 decision of Beard v. Akzona, Inc., 517 F. Supp. 128 (E.D. Tenn. 1981), where the Restatement (Second) of Torts § 652D was cited as the rationale for establishing the elements of a cause of action based upon publication of private information.

Drug experience reports containing the names of physicians who submit the reports which are submitted pursuant to affirmative provisions of federal law, and which contain headings under categories such as the identification of patients and submitting physicians indicating that they are "confidential" create an expectation of privacy so that physicians filing the reports have a good reason to believe that they are made in confidence and will not be disclosed. Newsom v. Breon Lab., Inc., 709 S.W.2d 559 (Tenn. 1986); see also Tidman v. The Salvation Army, slip op., No. 01-A-01-9708-CV-00380, 1998 Tenn. App. LEXIS 475, 136 Lab. Cas. (CCH) & 58,441 (Tenn. Ct. App., Middle Section, July 15, 1998) (denying a cause of action for public disclosure of private information on grounds that complaint did not allege that private information was disclosed to anyone outside of Salvation Army corporate structure; no appeal sought).

4. ***Intrusion.*** The tort of intrusion occurs when one intentionally intrudes, physically or otherwise, on the solitude or seclusion of another or their private affairs or concerns if the intrusion would be highly offensive to a reasonable person. Swallows v. Western Elec. Co., 543 S.W.2d 581 (Tenn. 1976); Coker v. Redick, slip op., No. 01-A-01-9410-CH-00500, 1995 Tenn. App. LEXIS 127 (Tenn. Ct. App., Middle Section, March 3, 1995); Stein v. Davidson Hotel Co., slip op, No. 01A01-9509-CV-00407, 1996 Tenn. App. LEXIS 280 (Tenn. Ct. App., Middle Section, May 8, 1996), aff'd, 945 S.W. 2d 714 (Tenn. 1997); Vanrooyen v. Wipro Gallagher Solutions, Inc., slip. op., No. 1:09-0005, 2010 U.S. Dist. LEXIS 77967 (M.D. Tenn. July 30, 2010) (male co-worker yelling at employee on one occasion, raising his fist, and saying to female co-worker that she should be hit, even if true, did not rise to this level or constitute such extreme, outrageous conduct; granting summary judgment in favor of employer); see also Restatement (Second) of Torts § 652B (1977); Harris v. Horton, 341 S.W.3d 264, (Tenn. Ct. App. 2009) (the taking of photographs of a car accident by paramedic and using those photos as illustrative aides for safety class does not rise to the level of intrusion of private affairs). Federal courts applying and interpreting Tennessee law have assumed this intrusion to be an element of the Tennessee law of privacy. An employee who was allegedly discriminated against by a supervisor of their employer stated a valid cause of action when they alleged

that the supervisor had followed the employee home on more than one occasion and had even attempted to gain entrance to the home through a window. Scarbrough v. Brown Group, Inc., 935 F. Supp. 954 (W.D. Tenn. 1995). Participation in a union meeting has been held to be not a matter of individual solitude or seclusion and surveillance of the meeting place together with a recording of the license tag numbers on vehicles driven by individuals attending meetings does not give rise to an invasion of privacy. International Union v. Garner, 601 F. Supp. 187 (M.D. Tenn. 1985); see also Tidman v. The Salvation Army, slip op., No. 01-A-01-9708-CV-00380, 1998 Tenn. App. LEXIS 475, 1369 Lab. Cas. (CCH) & 58,441 (Tenn. Ct. App., Middle Section, July 15, 1998) (no claim for unreasonable intrusion when information sought by employers regarding whether employee had had an affair related directly to whether employee could serve as an officer in the Salvation Army and all alleged inquiries took place at work, within an official circle that had to make that determination; no appeal sought). An employee may waive a cause of action for intrusion upon seclusion. Martin v. Senators, Inc., 418 S.W.2d 660 (Tenn. 1967).

C. OTHER PRIVACY-RELATED ACTIONS

1. ***Intentional Infliction of Emotional Distress***. Intentional infliction of emotional distress and outrageous conduct are simply different names for the same cause of action. Bain v. Wells, 936 S.W.2d 618 (Tenn. 1997) (hospital and physician not liable for outrageous conduct when patient was placed in same hospital room with patient infected with HIV without giving warning or obtaining consent). There are three essential elements to a cause of action for outrageous conduct: (1) the conduct complained of must be intentional or reckless; (2) the conduct must be so outrageous that it is not tolerated by civilized society; and (3) the conduct must result in serious mental injury. Id.; Harvey v,. America's Collectibles Network, Inc., slip op., No. 3:09-CV-523, 2011 U.S. Dist. LEXIS 5662 (E.D. Tenn. Jan. 20. 2011) (an employer throwing employee's doctors letters across a table "may not be polite or professional behavior, it is hardly conduct that is 'atrocious and utterly intolerable in a civilized community' . . . [sufficient to meet] the 'high threshold standard' necessary to maintain a claim for outrageous conduct under Tennessee law;" finding employer had every right to request current medical information from employee's doctor's for a pending ADA reasonable accommodation request); Kiger v. Jennings Funeral Homes, Inc., slip op., No. 2-10-0084, 2011 U.S. Dist. LEXIS 704 (M.D. Tenn. Jan 4, 2011) (employee's termination and manager's conduct in being agitated at employee during termination was not so outrageous to rise to the level of intentional infliction of emotional distress); **Johnson v. BellSouth Telecomms. Inc., No. 3:09-CV-323, 2012 U.S. Dist. LEXIS 34220 (E.D.Tenn. Mar. 14, 2012) (conduct in allegedly discharging employee because of his complaints regarding unethical sales practices does not rise to the level of "atrocious" or "utterly intolerable" conduct);** MacDermid v. Discover Financial Services, 488 F.3d 721 (6th Cir. 2007) (reversing dismissal of outrageous conduct claim based on defendant's threats of criminal prosecution for failure to pay a purely civil debt where the court disagreed with defendant's contention that the plaintiff was necessarily criminally liable for credit card fraud); Massi v. Walgreen, slip op., No. 3:05-CV-425, 2006 U.S. Dist. LEXIS 82306 (E.D. Tenn. Nov. 9, 2006) (dismissing claim for outrageous conduct where neither the defendant's refusal to pay for the plaintiff's medical treatment nor the defendant's alleged negligent filing of a prescription constituted conduct "so outrageous"); Attea v. Eristoff, slip. op., No. M2005-02834-COA-R3-CV, 2007 Tenn. App. LEXIS 316 (Tenn. Ct. App., Middle Section, May 18, 2007) (dismissing the intentional infliction of emotional distress claim because plaintiff failed to prove that the alleged conduct of two New York taxing authorities was "so outrageous" when the authorities merely challenged the plaintiff's change of state residency and threatened to assess taxes, fines, interest, and penalties against the plaintiff); Nairon v. Holland, slip op., No. M2006-00321-COA-R3-CV, 2007 Tenn. App. LEXIS 118 (Tenn. Ct. App., Middle Section, Mar. 1, 2007) (reversing grant of summary judgment to defendant medical equipment company because a jury *could* reasonably find that the "hundreds" of alleged calls made by defendant to plaintiff's home for retrieval of a rented wheelchair rose to the level of outrageous conduct); White v. Fort Sanders-Park West Med. Ctr., slip op., No. E2006-00330-COA-R3-CV, 2007 Tenn. App. LEXIS 53 (Tenn. Ct. App., Eastern Section, Jan. 29, 2007) (affirming dismissal of a claim for intentional infliction of emotional distress where plaintiff avers she was discriminated against based on her age, and yet fails to offer material evidence proving that she was replaced at all, much less by a younger person); Grubman v. Morgan Stanley DW, Inc., No. 3:06-cv-0705, 2008 U.S. Dist. LEXIS 86628 (Tenn. Ct. App., Middle Section, Sept. 16, 2008) (granting summary judgment to dismiss because a mere showing of retaliatory conduct and discrimination does not amount to a claim for intentional infliction of emotional distress); See, V.B., infra, Anderson v. Watchtower Bible and Tract Soc'y of N.Y., Inc., slip op., No. M2004-01066-COA-R9-CV, 2007 Tenn. App. LEXIS 29 (Tenn. Ct. App., Middle Section, Apr. 14, 2005), appeal denied (Tenn. 2007), cert. denied, 128 S. Ct. 323 (U.S. 2007) (doctrine of ecclesiastical abstention mandates dismissal of the *intentional infliction of emotional distress claim* for lack of subject matter jurisdiction because such an inquiry would require the court to adjudicate the correctness of the church's membership expulsion decision); Leach v. Taylor, 124 S.W.3d 87 (Tenn. 2004), rev'g 2002 Tenn. App. LEXIS 925 (Tenn. Ct. App., Western Section, Dec. 30, 2002) (allegations that funeral home employees falsely stated that decedent's body had been mutilated by unauthorized harvesting of organs sufficient to state claim for outrageous conduct); Parks v. Nelson, slip. op. No. E2000-02943-COA-R3-CV, 2002 Tenn. App. LEXIS 230 (Tenn. Ct. App., Eastern Section, April 9, 2002) (conduct about which plaintiff complains must be based on plaintiff's own knowledge and not on information learned from a third party); Johnson v. Woman's Hosp., 527 S.W.2d 133, 134 (Tenn. Ct. App.), cert. denied (Tenn. 1975); Medlin v. Allied Inv. Co., 398 S.W.2d 270, 274 (Tenn. 1966). The

actionable conduct under a theory of intentional infliction of emotional distress must be set out in the pleadings. Federated Rural Elec. Ins. Exch. v. Hill, slip op., No. M2005-02461-COA-R3-CV, 2007 Tenn. App. LEXIS 152 (Tenn. Ct. App., Middle Section, Mar. 26, 2007); Graham v. Liberty Mut. Ins. Co., No. 1:08-CV-299, 2009 U.S. Dist. LEXIS 32919 (E.D. Tenn. Apr. 17, 2009) (must allege bad faith to state a claim for intentional infliction of emotional distress). In a recent claim for reckless infliction of emotional distress, the Tennessee Supreme Court stated that it expressed no opinion concerning whether claims of *intentional* infliction of emotional distress must be based on conduct that was directed at a specific individual. Doe 1 ex rel. Doe 1 v. Roman Catholic Diocese of Nashville, 154 S.W.3d 22, n.29 (Tenn. 2005) (holding, however, that a "claim of reckless infliction of emotional distress need not be based upon conduct that was directed at a specific person or that occurred in the presence of the plaintiff") rev'g slip op., No. M2001-01780-COA-R3-CV, 2003 Tenn. App. LEXIS 685 (Tenn. Ct. App. Sept. 22, 2003). Liability for mental distress damages clearly does not extend to mere insults, indignities, annoyances, petty oppression or other trivialities. Medlin, 398 S.W.2d at 274 (adopting Restatement (Second) of Torts § 46, comment d (1965)); Barbee v. Wal-Mart Stores, Inc., 2004 Tenn. App. LEXIS 88 (complaints of emotional injury such as embarrassment and humiliation without further proof will not satisfy requirement of serious mental injury); Rogers v. Louisville Land Co., slip op., No. E2010-00991-COA-R3-CV, 2011 Tenn. App. LEXIS 273 (Tenn. Ct. App., Eastern Section, May 25, 2011) (plaintiff failed to prove serious mental injury despite being "very, very emotional, very tearful" about the way Defendant had maintained her sons' gravesite, given the record was "devoid of any evidence that Plaintiff suffered from any other physical manifestations of emotional distress . . . [such as] nightmares, insomnia, depression, loss of weight, or inability to work, socialize, or lead her day-to-day life . . . [or] that Plaintiff sought or obtained any psychiatric, psychological, or medical treatment for her alleged mental distress."); Leu v. Embraer Aircraft Maint. Servs., slip op., No. 3:10-0322, 2011 U.S. Dist. LEXIS 38336 (M.D. Tenn. Apr. 7, 2011) (finding employee's unsubstantiated deposition testimony that he has headaches and stomach pain, is afraid of co-worker, and had a few anxiety attacks shortly before his deposition, but conceded he had not sought medical assistance and has been able to continue to perform his job, "are simply insufficient evidence of the 'serious mental injury' necessary to demonstrate IIED."). **To determine what rises to the level of severe mental injury, courts should analyze a claim using the following nonexclusive factors: (1) evidence of physiological manifestations of emotional distress, including but not limited to nausea, vomiting, headaches, severe weight loss or gain, and the like; (2) evidence of psychological manifestations of emotional distress, including but not limited to sleeplessness, depression, anxiety, crying spells or emotional outbursts, nightmares, drug and/or alcohol abuse, and unpleasant mental reactions such as fright, horror, grief, shame, humiliation, embarrassment, anger, chagrin, disappointment, and worry; (3) evidence that the plaintiff sought medical treatment, was diagnosed with a medical or psychiatric disorder such as post-traumatic stress disorder, clinical depression, traumatically induced neurosis or psychosis, or phobia, and/or was prescribed medication; (4) evidence regarding the duration and intensity of the claimant's physiological symptoms, psychological symptoms, and medical treatment; (5) other evidence that the defendant's conduct caused the plaintiff to suffer significant impairment in his or her daily functioning; and (6) in certain instances, the extreme and outrageous character of the defendant's conduct is itself important evidence of serious mental injury. Rogers v. Louisville Land Co., 367 S.W.3d 196 (Tenn. 2012).**

Under the Tennessee Governmental Tort Liability Act ("GLTA"), government agencies are immune from claims of outrageous conduct by government employees acting in their official capacity. Tenn. Code Ann. § 29-20-201(a); Houchins v. Jefferson County Bd. of Educ., No.: 3:10-CV-14, 2011 U.S. Dist. LEXIS 120717 (E.D. Tenn. Oct. 18, 2011).

Tennessee courts have not considered whether speech not actionable as defamation may nonetheless support a claim for intentional infliction of emotional distress. In Henderson v. Mullady, 1999 U.S. App. LEXIS 18316 (6th Cir. Aug. 2, 1999)) (order), also reported at 187 F.3d 635 (6th Cir. 1999) (table), the Sixth Circuit found that one remark to an AIDS-infected patient by his physician did not constitute outrageous conduct when not accompanied by other objectionable conduct. Acting with an intent which is tortious, criminal, or which has been characterized as "malice" or with a degree of aggravation which would entitle the plaintiff to punitive damages for another tort, however, does not create liability for the tort of outrageous conduct. Newsom v. Textron Aerostructures, 924 S.W.2d 87 (Tenn. Ct. App. 1995), appeal denied (Tenn. 1996) (citing Blair v. Allied Maintenance Corp., 756 S.W.2d 267, 273 (Tenn. Ct. App. 1988) (no appeal sought), and Restatement (Second) of Torts § 46, comment d (1965).

The "discovery" rule has been determined to apply to claims for intentional infliction of emotional distress. Leach v. Taylor, 124 S.W.3d at 91.

2. ***Interference with Economic Advantage.*** Until recently, Tennessee explicitly refused to recognize the tort of interference with prospective economic advantage/expectancy (also known as tortious interference with business relations.) See Nelson v. Martin, 958 S.W.2d 643, 646 (Tenn. 1997). However, in Trau-Med of Am., Inc. v. Allstate Ins. Co., 71 S.W.3d 691 (Tenn. 2002), the Tennessee Supreme Court overruled, in part, its prior decision in Nelson and held that Tennessee now recognizes the tort of interference with business relations. The Court held that the elements of the tort are: (1) an existing business relationship with specific third parties or a prospective relationship with an identifiable class of third parties; (2) the defendant's knowledge of that relationship and a not a mere awareness of the plaintiff's business

dealings with others in general; (3) the defendant's intent to cause the breach or termination of the business relationship; (4) the defendant's improper motive or improper means; and (5) damages resulting from the tortious interference. Id. at 701; see also Thompson v. Hayes, 748 F. Supp. 2d 824 (E.D. Tenn. 2010). The relations protected against intentional interference include all prospective contractual relations except those leading to contracts to marry. Id. The Court specifically noted that employment relationships would be protected by this tort. Id. With regard to the requirement that the defendant must have acted with improper motive, the Court held that an all encompassing definition would be impossible and will vary with the facts of each case. Id.; see also Rennell v. Through the Green, Inc., No. M2006-01429-COA-R3-CV, 2008 Tenn. App. LEXIS at *21–22 (Tenn. Ct. App. March 14, 2008) (such facts include "whether the corporate officer was acting outside the general scope of his authority and for his own interests instead of the interests of the corporation"). However, the Court held that with regard to improper motive, the plaintiff must demonstrate that the defendant's predominant purpose was to injure the plaintiff. Id. Allegations that there was interference with general categories of persons, such as employees, are insufficient as specific third parties must be identified. Overnite Transp. Co. v. Teamsters Local Union No. 480, 149 Lab. Cas. (CCH) P59,857, 2004 Tenn. App. LEXIS 139 (Tenn. Ct. App., Middle Section, Feb. 27, 2004), reh'g denied, 2004 Tenn. App. LEXIS 212 (Tenn. Ct. App., April 5, 2004) (no appeal sought). See, V.B., infra, Anderson v. Watchtower Bible and Tract Soc'y of N.Y., Inc., slip op., No. M2004-01066-COA-R9-CV, 2007 Tenn. App. LEXIS 29 (Tenn. Ct. App., Middle Section, Apr. 14, 2005), appeal denied (Tenn. 2007), cert. denied, 128 S. Ct. 323 (2007) (doctrine of ecclesiastical abstention mandates dismissal of the *tortious interference claim* for lack of subject matter jurisdiction because such an inquiry would require the court to adjudicate the correctness of the church's membership expulsion decision). A refusal to deal was not improper motive but was, instead, privileged. Watson's Carpet & Floor Covering, Inc. v. McCormick, 247 S.W.3d 169 (Tenn. Ct. App. 2007), appeal denied (Tenn. 2007).

Recognized by the Tennessee Supreme Court in Waste Conversion Sys., Inc. v. Greenstone Indus., Inc., 33 S.W.3d 779 (Tenn. 2000), the "qualified privilege" of a parent company to interfere in the contractual relations of a wholly-owned subsidiary does not apply where the parent company owns less than 100% of its subsidiary. Cambio Health Solutions, LLC v. Reardon, 213 S.W.3d 785 (Tenn. 2006) (finding that a parent company is not immune from a claim of tortious interference with contractual relations where the former CEO of the parent company's subsidiary alleged that the parent company interfered with his executive consulting agreement with the subsidiary that is not wholly-owned).

There is a statutory tort of inducement or procurement of breach of contract. Tenn. Code Ann. § 47-50-109 (2001); Holloway v. Collier, 969 S.W.2d 407 (Tenn. Ct. App. 1997), appeal denied (Tenn. 1998). The elements of this cause of action are: (1) knowledge of the wrongdoer of a legal contract for a designated term; (2) malicious intent of the wrongdoer to induce the breach of the contract; (3) a resultant breach of the contract proximately caused by the wrongdoer's acts; and (4) the plaintiff was damaged as a result of the breach of the contract. B&L Corp. v. Thomas and Thorngren, Inc., slip op., No. M2002-02355-COA-R3-CV, 2004 Tenn. App. LEXIS 94 (Tenn. Ct. App., Middle Section, Feb. 4, 2004), appeal denied (Tenn. 2005); Lamdin v. Aerotek Commer. Staffing, No.: 3:10-CV-280, 2010 U.S. Dist. LEXIS 105306 (E.D. Tenn. Sept. 30, 2010); Lee v. Strickland, slip op., No. 03A01-9801-CH-00195, 1999 Tenn. App. LEXIS 251 (Tenn. Ct. App., Eastern Section, April 11, 1999) (no appeal sought); Myers v. Pickering Firm, Inc., 959 S.W.2d 152, 158 (Tenn. Ct. App.), appeal denied (Tenn. 1997); New Life Corp. of Am. v. Thomas Nelson, Inc., 932 S.W.2d 921 (Tenn. Ct. App.), appeal denied (Tenn. 1996); Forrester v. Stockstill, 869 S.W.2d 328 (Tenn. 1994) (holding that a corporate director, officer, or employee is generally not liable for interference with the corporation's contracts); Thompson v. Memphis Light, Gas & Water, slip op., No. W2009-02447-COA-R3-CV, 2011 Tenn. App. LEXIS 206 (Tenn. Ct. App., Western Section, Apr. 29, 2011); Campbell v. Matlock, 749 S.W.2d 748 (Tenn. Ct. App. 1987), appeal denied (Tenn. 1988); TSC Indus. Inc. v. Tomlin, 743 S.W.2d 169 (Tenn. Ct. App.), appeal denied (Tenn. 1987); Dynamic Motel Management, Inc. v. Erwin, 528 S.W.2d 819, 822 (Tenn. Ct. App.), appeal denied (Tenn. 1975); Tennessee also recognizes the tort of interference with an employment relationship. Forrester, supra; Thompson, supra. At least one other Court has recognized that the breach of the employment contract recognized in Forrester relied upon an authority that did not limit the type of contract that could be breached. See Judds v. Pritchard, slip op., No. 01A01-9701-CV-00030, 1997 Tenn. App. LEXIS 647 (Tenn. Ct. App., Western Section, Sept. 24, 1997) (no appeal sought); Owens v. University Club, slip op., No. 02A01-9705-CV-00103, 1998 Tenn. App. LEXIS 688 (Tenn. Ct. App., Western Section, Oct. 15, 1998), appeal denied (Tenn. Dec. 30, 1998). It is, however, important to note that, although both the tort of intentional interference with employment relations and the tort of inducement or procurement of a breach of contract may be applicable to a single set of facts, they are distinct causes of actions. Leemis v. Russell, No. W1999-00352-COA-R3-CV, 2000 Tenn. App. LEXIS 348, at *10 n.3 (Tenn. Ct. App., Western Section, May 24, 2000); Rennell v. Through the Green, Inc., No. M2006-01429-COA-R3-CV, 2008 Tenn. App. LEXIS at *n.3 (Tenn. Ct. App. March 14, 2008); see also Wyatt v. TVA, slip op., No. 3:05-0834, 2007 U.S. Dist. LEXIS 1763 (M.D. Tenn. Jan. 8, 2007) (granting defendant's motion for summary judgment because plaintiff failed to state a claim of intentional interference with business relationships since plaintiff's termination of employment with the defendant's subcontractor was neither for an improper purpose nor for the intentional purpose of injuring plaintiff, but rather, due to the defendant's legitimate purpose of banning employees who test positive on drug tests); Federated Rural Elec. Ins. Exch. v. Hill, slip op., No. M2005-02461-COA-R3-CV, 2007 Tenn. App. LEXIS 152 (Tenn. Ct. App., Middle Section, Mar. 26, 2007) (affirming dismissal of plaintiff's suit against his former employer for intentional tortious interference with an employment contract where plaintiff's termination resulted after he was caught on videotape building a barn while he was out from work and collecting total disability benefits for his on-the-job knee injuries); Forsman v. Rouse, No. 3:07-0327, 2008 U.S. Dist. LEXIS 47266 (M.D. Tenn. June 16, 2008) (stating that the elements that must be proved to bring a claim for intentional interference with a business relationship applies equally to a claim for intentional interference with employment).

3. **Prima Facie Tort**. There are no cases in Tennessee that specifically consider this cause of action.

II. EMPLOYER TESTING OF EMPLOYEES

A. Psychological or Personality Testing

1. ***Common Law and Statutes.*** There are no Tennessee statutes or case law in this area. Employers should beware of questions asked during any psychological testing as they could be construed as a subtle attempt by the employer to discern whether the employee suffers from any mental illness or psychological problems, such as depression, which could be protected under the American with Disabilities Act.

2. ***Private Employers.*** No cases.

3. ***Public Employers.*** No cases.

B. Drug Testing

1. ***Common Law and Statutes.*** "The Tennessee Drug-Free Workplace Act," Tenn. Code Ann. §§ 50 -9-101-112 (1999) was drafted to allow employers to promote drug-free workplaces and to further the theme "that drug and alcohol abuse be discouraged" and that employees who choose to engage in drug or alcohol abuse "face the risk of unemployment and the forfeiture of worker's compensation benefits." Id. Employers adopting the act's provisions receive discounts on their worker's compensation premiums. If an employer adopts a drug-free workplace program in accordance with the provisions of the act, including notice, education, and procedural requirements for testing, then the employee may be required to submit to a drug or alcohol test and, if such a drug or alcohol level is found to be present, then the employee may be terminated and the employee forfeits eligibility for worker's compensation medical and indemnity benefits.

The program adopted by the employer must warn all employees that it is a condition of employment for all employees to refrain from reporting to work or working with the presence of drugs or alcohol in their body. If the employee refuses to submit to a test for drugs or alcohol, the employee forfeits eligibility for worker's compensation medical and indemnity benefits. The program differentiates between employees in safety-sensitive positions and those who are not. Safety -sensitive position employees may be tested for drug or alcohol use at any occasion. Tenn. Code Ann. § 50-9-106 (a)(2) - (5) (1999). Employees not in safety-sensitive positions may only be tested based upon reasonable suspicion as defined in Tenn. Code Ann. § 50-9-103(15) (1999). The act requires that employers give all employees written policy statements containing complete information on all requirements and consequences of an employee's failure to comply with the requirements of the act. Tenn. Code Ann. § 50-9-105 (Supp. 2002). Tennessee recently amended the act to clarify that testing may be conducted on employees who are minors and that the results of the drug testing may be reported to the parents or guardians of minors without liability provided that the minor is informed that the results of any such testing will be disclosed to their parents or guardians. Tenn. Code Ann. §§ 50-9-109(e) & 50-9-105(f) (Supp. 2002).

2. ***Private Employers.*** The Tennessee Supreme Court has found that private employers are not prohibited from requiring employees to submit to random drug tests, that such a requirement does not violate any state constitutional guarantee of privacy, and that no clear mandate of public policy is violated by such a requirement. Stein v. Davidson Hotel Co., 945 S.W.2d 714 (Tenn. 1997). Private sector employees who left their most recent job either to "avoid taking a drug or alcohol screening test, or after receiving a positive result to a drug or alcohol screening test" are not entitled to unemployment compensation. Tenn. Code Ann. §§ 50-7-303 (Supp. 2002). However, an employees' admitted illegal drug use outside of work – that did not result in a positive drug test – does not amount to work-related misconduct disqualifying employee from receiving unemployment benefits. Dura Automotive Systems, Inc. v. Neeley, No. M2009-00908-COA-R3-CV, 2010 Tenn. App. LEXIS 44, 2010 WL 204090 (Tenn. Ct. App., Western Section, Jan. 21, 2010) (finding employee's admitted marijuana use had not affected his work performance and thus, did not constitute work-related misconduct such that he was ineligible for unemployment benefits, irrespective of the fact such conduct violated Company policies and that termination of employment under pursuant to such policies was justified); But cf., Hale v. Neeley, 335 S.W.3d 599 (Tenn. Ct. App. 2010) (rejecting employee's argument that "it was error for him to be found guilty of work-related misconduct so as to deny him unemployment benefits, since the drug possession arrest was made while he was on vacation and not on [employer's] premises, and had no connection whatsoever to his work; ruling employee violated the employer's drug policy by being charged and convicted of possession of cocaine and failing to report his conviction under a criminal drug statute to

his employer within the requisite three day window, noting it was undisputed the employee violated the policy, he knew about the policy, as his signature on the written acknowledgment shows, and violated a duty owed to his employer as opposed to society in general, and thus employee's conduct constituted work-related misconduct, disqualifying him from unemployment benefits).

3. ***Public Employers.*** The Tennessee Legislature, pursuant to Tenn. Code Ann. § 49-6-4213 (2002), has legalized and endorsed the testing of public school students where there are "reasonable indications to the principal that [the] student may have used or [is] under the influence of drugs." The legislature has also specifically mandated that security personnel employed by the department of corrections and youth development be tested as a condition of employment. Tenn. Code. Ann. § 41-1-122 (1997). The legislature also commented that workers who engage in drug abuse face "the risk of loss of employment and the forfeiture of worker's compensation benefits." Tenn. Code Ann. § 50-9-101(a) (1999). All employees of the narcotics investigation division are required to submit to mandatory drug tests. Tenn. Code Ann. § 38-6-205 (Supp. 2002).

In Knox County Educ. Assoc. v. Knox County Board of Educ., 158 F. 3d 361 (6th Cir. 1998), cert. denied, 120 S. Ct. 46, 145 L. Ed. 2d 41 (U.S. 1999), the Sixth Circuit upheld a law requiring that all teachers in the Knox County public school system submit to two separate levels of drug testing: (1) suspicionless drug testing, and (2) "reasonable suspicion" drug and/or alcohol testing of all school employees. The Sixth Circuit found that the drug policies did not violate the Fourth Amendment due to the unique role of teachers who "stand in the place of student's natural parents and are responsible for their safekeeping." Id.; see also Smith County Educ. Ass'n v. Smith County Bd. of Educ., slip op., No. 2:08-0076, 2011 U.S. Dist. LEXIS 14681 (M.D. Tenn. Feb. 14, 2011) (finding the absence of any evidence that Smith County teachers perform roles which are different in any significant way from those of the Knox County teachers, the court was bound by the Sixth Circuit conclusion in Knox County Educ. Assoc. v. Knox County Board of Educ. that teachers in Tennessee, including the teachers in this case, stand *in loco parentis* to their students, and occupy "safety sensitive" positions). Evaluating whether the need for ongoing, *random* drug testing outweighed the privacy interests, including being protected against unreasonable searches and seizures, of its teachers in violation of teachers' Fourth Amendment rights, a Tennessee federal court found that, "the School Board ha[d] demonstrated a need for a drug policy and the need for random drug testing, but that the policy [was] constitutionally flawed by its lack of notice of what drugs [were] the subject of testing and how the policy [was] to be implemented." Id. at *46. Thus, while the federal court ruled that "random suspicionless drug testing of Smith County teachers under the 2007 drug policy in its current form and implementation is unreasonably intrusive and violates the Fourth Amendment," the court thereafter made it clear that "[i]n so holding, the [c]ourt is not finding that the random drug testing of Smith County teachers is unconstitutional *per se*. If the unconstitutional aspects of the 2007 Policy and its implementation are cured, the Court is of the opinion that the random drug testing will comply with the Fourth Amendment." Id. Mandatory drug testing of employees by a government contractor was also allowed when the employees serviced a government nuclear weapons plant and the risk to national security and safety were high. Ensor v. Rust Eng'g Co., 704 F. Supp. 808 (E.D. Tenn. 1989), aff'd, 935 F.2d 269 (6th Cir. 1991).

C. Medical Testing

1. ***Common Law and Statutes.*** See Barnes v. Goodyear Tire and Rubber Co., 48 S.W.3d 698 (Tenn. 2000) (reversing judgment of Court of Appeals and reinstating jury verdict for plaintiff under the Tennessee Handicap Act, Tenn. Code Ann. § 8-50-103 (2002), for discharge on account of a "perceived disability").

2. ***Private Employers.*** No cases.

3. ***Public Employers.*** See Satterfield v. Bluhm, 15 Am. Disabilities Cas. (BNA) 860, 2004 Tenn. App. LEXIS 244 (Tenn. Ct. App., Eastern Section, April 16, 2004) (state commercial motor vehicle inspector discharged after being required to submit to, and failing, a physical examination; no appeal sought).

D. Polygraph Tests

The Tennessee Polygraph Examiners Act, Tenn. Code Ann.§ 62-27-101(d) (1997) prevents an examiner from inquiring into any of the following areas during the examination: religious beliefs or affiliations; beliefs or opinions regarding racial matters; political beliefs or affiliations; beliefs or affiliations regarding unions or labor organizations; sexual preferences or activities; any disability covered by the Americans with Disabilities Act; or actions or activities more than five years preceding the date of the examination, except for felony convictions and violations of the Tennessee Drug Control Act. Exceptions arise when the examination is administered as a result of an investigation of illegal activity in such area and the inability to pose such questions would be detrimental to the investigation. Tenn. Code Ann. § 62-27-125(1)(a) - (d) (1997) states that the examinee must consent to the examination, has the right to refuse to take a polygraph exam, has the right to refuse to answer any question and may terminate the exam at any time. Tenn. Code Ann. § 62-27-128 (1997) requires that an employer may not take any personnel action based solely upon the results of a polygraph examination. See Vick & Dickerson

v. Krystal Co., slip op, 1991 Tenn. App. LEXIS 753, 122 Lab. Cas. (CCH) & 57,026 (Tenn. Ct. App., Western Section, Sept. 18, 1991) (finding that Tennessee Polygraph Examiners Act does not specifically govern the employer-employee relationship and does not prohibit employers from discharging employees who refuse to submit to polygraph examinations), aff'd 1992 Tenn. LEXIS 707 (Tenn. Dec. 21, 1992)). But see Tisdale v. Kayo Oil Co., slip op., No. 88-244-II, 1989 Tenn. App. LEXIS 59, 116 Lab. Cas. (CCH) & 56,318 (Tenn. Ct. App. Middle Section, Jan. 25, 1989) (finding that employee may present a cause of action for wrongful discharge when the employee refused to sign a consent to a polygraph examination which contained a full release of liability as to the employer and polygraph examiner). The Krystal court found that no evidence existed that plaintiff was discharged for refusing to waive rights granted to him in the statute and distinguished Tisdale based on the fact that Tisdale was rendered prior to several Tennessee Supreme Court opinions, including Chism v. Mid-South Milling, 762 S.W.2d 552 (Tenn. 1988), which required "a clear violation of some well-defined and established public policy" as evidenced by an "unambiguous constitutional, statutory or regulatory provision."

E. Fingerprinting

There is no statute regarding whether private employers are allowed to fingerprint employees. The following statutes govern situations in which a public employer is required or allowed to obtain fingerprinting from prospective employees. Tenn. Code Ann. §§ 33-2-1201 (2010) (Tennessee department of mental health employees or volunteers with direct contact or direct responsibility for persons with mental illness, serious emotional disturbance, or developmental disabilities); 37-5-511 (2001) (registration to screen child care providers); 37-1-414 (persons working with children in connection with the child welfare agency); 37-5-117 (2001) (youth service officers); 39-17-1351 (Supp. 2002) (application for handgun carry permit); 41-1-116 (1997) (corrections officers); 41-21-107 (1997) (inmate information); 49-5-413 (2002) (public school teachers); 62-32-301 and -312 (1997) (alarm systems contractors registration of employees); 62-35-105 (1997) (contract security company licenses and applications); 68-11-233 (2001) (home health care workers or volunteers); 71-3-507 (Supp. 2002) (child care agency workers).

III. SEARCHES

A. Employee's Person

1. ***Private Employers.*** Newsom v. Thalheimer Bros., Inc., 901 S.W.2d 365 (Tenn. Ct. App. 1994) (no tort for false imprisonment where employee felt "mentally restrained," as evidence must establish a restraint against the plaintiff's will such as "where [employee] yields to force, to the threat of force or to assertion of authority"). See also Roberts v. Essex Microtel Associates, 46 S.W.3d 205 (Tenn. Ct. App. Nov. 27, 2000), appeal denied (Tenn. 2001) (no tort for invasion of privacy or false imprisonment against hotel owner or desk clerk when after desk clerk provided police with statistical information obtained from plaintiff's driver license plaintiff was detained and arrested for two hours until police determined plaintiff was not suspect wanted on outstanding warrant.) There is no case law on the issue of when an employer is allowed to search an employee and how invasive the search may be. See also II.B., E, supra.

2. ***Public Employers.*** In Holmes v. Owens, slip op., No. 02A01-9706-CV-00115, 1998 Tenn. App. LEXIS 132, 14 I.E.R. Cas. (BNA) 345 (Tenn. Ct. App., Western Section, Feb. 23, 1998), appeal denied (Tenn. 1998), the court adopted the test first developed in United States v. Janis, 428 U.S. 433 (1976), and later refined in National Treasury Employees Union v. Von Raab, 489 U.S. 656 (1989), in which the public interest in perfecting the search must be balanced against the employee's privacy concerns. Holmes found that the reasonableness of the search was the paramount consideration in determining the validity of that search and declared that the privacy expectations of deputies in the narcotics department involved with the interdiction of drugs and the need to carry a firearm are outweighed by the compelling interest in safeguarding society and providing for the public safety.

In Butler v. Board of Commissioners, slip op., No. 625, 1988 Tenn. App. LEXIS 369 (Tenn. Ct. App., Eastern Section, June 2, 1988), the court adopted language from O'Connor v. Ortega, 480 U.S. 709 (1987), in which the U.S. Supreme Court drew a distinction between job-related search and seizures and those in criminal cases: "The employee's expectation of privacy must be assessed in the context of the employment relation. Given the great variety of work environments in the public sector, the question of whether an employee has a reasonable expectation of privacy must be addressed on a case-by-case basis. There is a plethora of contexts in which the employers will have occasion to intrude to some extent upon employee's expectation of privacy." The Butler court concluded that an employee's job as a fireman and the fact that the urine analysis was given only in conjunction with a required physical at least once every 36 months did not violate the employee's expectation of privacy and a "close nexus existed between the testing and the government's public safety concern." In State v. Stoddard, 909 S.W. 2d 454 (Tenn. Crim. App. 1994), the court adopted the language from Ortega and held that the search of a police officer's personal suitcase found in the trunk of his patrol car did not violate his reasonable expectation of privacy because officers had been verbally notified that their patrol cars were liable to be searched. See also II.B., E, supra.

B. Employee's Work Area

See Swallows v. Western Elec. Co., 543 S.W.2d 581 (Tenn. 1976) (court does not comment on what actions by employer could constitute invasion of privacy but does state that liability could attach if the employer's behavior was offensive and the intrusion exceeds the limits of decency); Vanrooyen v. Wipro Gallagher Solutions, Inc., 2010 U.S. Dist. LEXIS 77967 (M.D. Tenn. July 30, 2010) (male co-worker yelling at employee on one occasion, raising his fist, and saying to female co-worker that she should be hit, even if true, did not rise to this level or constitute such extreme, outrageous conduct which would be beyond the pale of decency; granting summary judgment in favor of employer).

C. Employee's Property

In State v. Harris, slip op., No. 85, 1990 Tenn. Crim. App. LEXIS 748 (Tenn. Crim. App., Eastern Section, Nov. 8, 1990), appeal denied (Tenn. 1991), the court determined that a car salesman employed by a local car dealer and furnished with a "demo" model to drive had a protected right to privacy while he maintained control over the vehicle. Once the "demo" was returned to the dealership however, the employee did not have a recognized privacy interest and the true owner of the vehicle the dealership had the right to allow authorities to search the vehicle.

1. ***Private Employers.*** See III.A.1., supra.

2. ***Public Employers.*** See III.A.2., supra.

IV. MONITORING OF EMPLOYEES

A. Telephones and Electronic Communications

1. ***Wiretapping.*** Tenn. Code Ann. §§ 39-13-601 to - 606 (1997 and Supp. 2002) governs the recording and interception of wire, oral, and electronic communication. Tenn. Code Ann. § 39-13-601(b)(5) provides that it is lawful for a party to intercept a wire, oral, or electronic communication where the person is a party to the conversation or where one of the parties has given prior consent. See State v. Bacon, slip op., No. 03C01-9608-CR-00308, 1998 Tenn. Crim. App. LEXIS 31 (Tenn. Crim. App., Eastern Section, Jan. 8, 1998), aff'd after remand, 1998 Tenn. Crim App. LEXIS 869 (Tenn. Crim. App., Eastern Section, Aug. 17, 1998). If there is consent to the use of a videotape and audiotape to record, there can be no violation of the statute. Cawood v. Booth, No. E2007-02537-COA-R3-CV, 2008 Tenn. App. LEXIS 715 (Tenn. Ct. App., Eastern Section, Nov. 25, 2008), appeal granted, 2009 Tenn. LEXIS 370 (Tenn., June 15, 2009). The statute does not state whether an employer may monitor electronic transmissions. However, the wording of the statute appears to imply that employers need to obtain prior written consent in order to listen in on employee conversations at work. Tenn. Code Ann. § 39-13-603 (1997) sets forth applicable damages if a violation of § 39-13-601 (1997) occurs including attorney's fees, punitive damages, actual damages, and statutory damages of $100 per day or $10,000, whichever is greater. The court has no discretion to award nominal damages for a violation and must award the greater of actual damages or the statutory penalty. See Robinson v. Fulliton, slip op., No. W2001-01753-COA-R3-CV, 2003 Tenn. App. LEXIS 122 (Tenn. Ct. App., Western Section, Feb. 14, 2003), appeal denied, 2003 Tenn. LEXIS 790 (Tenn., Sept. 2, 2003). Violators are deemed to have committed a Class D felony. Tenn. Code Ann. § 39-13-602 (1997). Tenn. Code Ann. § 39-13-606 (1997) governs the use of electronic tracking devices in motor vehicles. All owners of the vehicle must be informed of any electronic devices placed in the vehicle. Compare Tenn. Code Ann. § 39-13-606(a)(1) with § 39-16-606(b)(2) (1997). Cellular and cordless phones are governed by Tenn. Code Ann. §§ 40-6-301 to 40-6-311 (1997).

2. ***Electronic Communications.*** Tenn. Code Ann. §§ 40-6-301 to -311 (1997) is known as the "Wiretapping and Electronic Surveillance Act of 1994" and should be interpreted in conjunction with Tenn. Code Ann. §§ 39 -13-601 to -606 (1997 and Supp. 2002). Tenn. Code Ann. § 40-6-301 concerns cellular and cordless transmissions. No specific guidance is given regarding whether employers are allowed to monitor and record such telephone conversations. However, in State v. Pendergrass, slip op., No. 01C01-9306-CR-00189, 1995 Tenn. Crim. App. LEXIS 188 (Tenn. Crim. App., Middle Section, Mar. 9, 1995), rev'd on other grounds, 937 S.W.2d 834 (Tenn. 1996), the court held that one does not have a reasonable expectation of privacy in cordless transmissions and that eavesdropping on cordless telephone conversations is lawful. See also State v. Munn, slip op., No. 01C01-9801-CC-00007, 1999 Tenn. Crim. App. LEXIS 304 (Tenn. Crim. App., Middle Section, April 1, 1999), aff'd in part, rev'd in part, 56 S.W.3d 486 (Tenn. 2001).

Under Tenn. Code Ann. § 10-7-512 (1999) any state, agency, institution or political subdivision that maintains an electronic mail communications system is required to adopt a written policy on the monitoring of the mail communications. This policy must also include a statement to the effect that correspondence of the employee in the form of electronic mail may be a public record and may be subject to public inspection.

3. ***Electronic Monitoring.*** No cases.

B. Mail

There is no Tennessee statute concerning this matter.

C. Surveillance/Photographing

Tenn. Code Ann. § 39-13-605 (Supp. 2002) provides that it is unlawful to knowingly photograph an individual if that person would have a reasonable expectation of privacy and a reasonable person would be offended and the purpose of the photograph was for the purpose of arousal or sexual gratification. See Swallows v. Western Elec. Co., 543 S.W.2d 581 (Tenn. 1976) (court does not comment on what actions by employer could constitute invasion of privacy but does state that liability could attach if the employer's behavior was "offensive and the intrusion exceeds the limits of decency").

Although not directly on point, the issue of when an employer has gone too far in seeking information about the employee's private life was indirectly addressed in Tidman v. The Salvation Army, slip op. 01-A-01-9708-CV-00380, 1998 Tenn. App. LEXIS 475, 136 Lab. Cas. (CCH) & 58,441 (Tenn. Ct. App., Middle Section, July 15, 1998) (denying claim of unreasonable intrusion when information sought by employers regarding whether employee had had an affair related directly to whether employee could serve as an officer in the Salvation Army and all alleged inquiries took place at work, within an official circle that had to make that determination; no appeal sought); See also Kidd v. Cigna Corp., slip op., No. 3:10-0020, 2010 U.S. Dist. LEXIS 120801 (M.D. Tenn. Nov. 12, 2010) (invasion of privacy claim by employee who was secretly videotaped by a third party working for the employer's long term disability insurance carrier, when the employee was undergoing a Functional Capacity Evaluation related to her receipt of long term disability benefits, was a question of reasonableness and a question for a jury to decide whether the employee's "privacy was invaded by considering the degree, context, circumstances, motives and setting surrounding the intrusion.")

V. ACTIVITIES OUTSIDE THE WORKPLACE

A. Statute or Common Law

No cases.

B. Employees' Personal Relationships

1. ***Romantic Relationships Between Employees.*** The Tennessee Court of Appeals held in Tidman v. The Salvation Army, slip op., No. 01-A-01-9708-CV-00380, 1998 Tenn. App. LEXIS 475, 136 Lab. Cas. (CCH) & 58,441 (Tenn. Ct. App., Middle Section, July 15, 1998) (no appeal sought), that an employer was justified in attempting to discover information relating to an alleged affair the employee had when such behavior would directly affect the employee's ability to effectively serve as an officer in the Salvation Army and when all inquiries took place only at work within "the official circle that had to make that determination." Termination of employment of plaintiff county employee who had an intimate relationship with a married co-worker, whose wife also worked in the same county courthouse as plaintiff was not wrongful because it was rationally based and for a plausible policy reason. Beecham v. Henderson County, 422 F.3d 372 (6th Cir. 2005). See Letner v. Wal-Mart Discount Department Store, 172 F.3d 873, 1999 WL 68766 (6th Cir. 1999), for a discussion of anti-fraternization policies.

2. ***Sexual Orientation.*** There is no statutory or case law dealing with whether an employer may inquire into an employee's sexual orientation. In Hall v. Baptist Memorial Health Care Corp., 215 F.3d 618 (6th Cir. 2000), the Sixth Circuit held that the termination of an employee with a Baptist-affiliated college after being ordained as a lay minister in a church with a large gay and lesbian membership was not wrongful nor did it amount to discrimination based on religion as alleged by the complainant.

3. ***Marital Status.*** There is no statutory or case law that prohibits an employer from inquiring about the employee's marital status. An employer should be cautious in doing so, however, as this could be construed as a subtle means of gender discrimination. In Vaughn v. Lawrenceburg Power System, 269 F.3d 703 (6th Cir. 2001), the Sixth Circuit upheld the termination of former municipal employees who were terminated after they married in violation of their employer's anti-nepotism policy. The Court reasoned that the policy was rationally related to the employer's legitimate goals and did not violate the employee's First Amendment association rights. See also Roberts-Deckard v. City of Sevierville, No. E2008-01580-COA-R3-CV, 2009 WL 1409981 (Tenn. Ct. App. Middle Section May, 20, 2009); Sloan v. Tri-County Electric Membership Corp., slip op., No. M2000-01794-COA-R3-CV, 2002 Tenn. App. LEXIS 109 (Tenn. Ct. App., Middle Section, Feb. 7, 2002).

C. Smoking

Tenn. Code Ann. § 50-1-304(e)(1) and (2) (Supp. 2002) provides that no employee may be terminated for using "agricultural products not regulated by the Alcoholic Beverage Commission" if the employee complies with all applicable employer policies regarding such use during times when the employee is working. Tenn. Code Ann. § 50-1-304(e)(2) (Supp. 2002) does not allow an employee to be terminated if the employee smokes when not on the job.

D. Blogging

No cases.

E. Social Networking

No cases.

VI. RECORDS

A. Personnel Records

An employer is qualifiedly privileged to comment upon an employee's job performance. Varner v. Hillcrest Med. Nursing Inst., Inc., slip op., 1984 Tenn. App. LEXIS 2612 (Tenn. Ct. App., Eastern Section, June 20, 1984); Russell v. Cleveland Country Club, slip. op. (Tenn. Ct. App., Eastern Section, June 29, 1982). Also, written contents of employee files accessible only by management are qualifiedly privileged. Andrews v. Hagood, slip. op., 1985 Tenn. Ct. App. LEXIS 2739 (Tenn. Ct. App., Eastern Section, Mar. 14, 1985). Tenn. Code Ann. §§ 10-7-503 and 504 (2000) govern the availability and confidentiality of certain public records, including those relating to public employees. Medical records, criminal investigative files, documents related to national, military security, records regarding public school students, records of the state attorney general's office, and contingency plans of law enforcement agencies in response to violent incidents such as bombings are several examples of records that are not available for public dissemination.

B. Medical Records

Tenn. Code Ann. §§ 10-7-503 and -504 (Supp. 2002) govern the availability and confidentiality of certain public records, including those relating to public employees. Medical records, criminal investigative files, documents related to national, military security, records regarding public school students, records of the state attorney general's office, and contingency plans of law enforcement agencies in response to violent incidents such as bombings are several examples of records that are not available for public dissemination. An employer may be liable for an employee's disclosure of an employee's confidential medical record when the employee was also a customer of the employer. Doe v Walgreens Co., No. W2009-02235-COA-R3-CV, 2010 Tenn. App. LEXIS 734 (Tenn. Ct. App. Nov. 24, 2010) (reversing a trial courts dismissal of the case because an employee, without authorization, disseminated an employee's HIV status to her fiancé by checking which prescriptions she was having filled at the store).

C. Criminal Records

Tenn. Code Ann. §§ 10-7-503 and -504 (Supp. 2002) govern the availability and confidentiality of certain public records, including those relating to public employees. Medical records, criminal investigative files, documents related to national, military security, records regarding public school students, and records of the state attorney general's office are several examples of records that are not available for public dissemination.

D. Subpoenas / Search Warrants

Corporations and other collective agencies may not assert a Fifth Amendment privilege to resist a subpoena to produce company records. See Toyota of Morristown, Inc. v. Third Nat'l Bank in Knoxville, 120 B.R. 925, 927 (Bankr. E.D. Tenn. 1990) (citing Braswell v. United States, 487 U.S. 99 (1988)). A custodian of corporate records is not entitled to resist a subpoena for such records on the ground that production will incriminate him in violation of the Fifth Amendment. United States v. Ellwest Stereo Theatres of Memphis, Inc., 927 F.2d 244, 246B47 (6th Cir. 1991) (citing Braswell, 487 U.S. 99 (1988)). When a corporate officer or custodian possesses corporate records in an individual capacity, i.e., when the individual leaves the company's employ, the Fifth Amendment may then be asserted to resist producing such records. See Toyota, 120 B.R. at 928 (quoting In re Grand Jury Subpoenas Duces Tecum, 722 F.2d 981, 986B87 (2d Cir. 1983)). Whether or not subpoenaed records were prepared by a corporation is not directly relevant. Id. See also Tenn. R. Civ. P. 45.02.

There are no Tennessee cases discussing search warrants served on employers seeking to search an employee's files or an employee's workspace.

VII. ACTIONS SUBSEQUENT TO EMPLOYMENT

A. References

Section 50-1-105 of the Tennessee Code imposes a good faith obligation on employers when providing employee information to prospective employers. If the information disclosed is truthful, fair, and unbiased, the employer is presumed to have acted in good faith and will be immune from the consequences of disclosure. Id. The presumption of good faith is rebuttable if it is shown by a preponderance of the evidence that the disclosure was: "(1) knowingly false; (2) deliberately misleading; (3) disclosed for a malicious purpose; (4) disclosed in reckless disregard for its falsity or defamatory nature; or (5) violative of the current or former employee's civil rights pursuant to current employment discrimination laws." Id. Under this statute, mere negligence will not be enough to rebut the presumption that the employer acted in good faith. Sullivan v. Baptist Mem'l Hosp., 995 S.W.2d 569, 575 (Tenn. 1999); Gard v. Harris, slip op., No. 2008-01939-COA-R3-CV, 2010 Tenn. App. LEXIS 187 , at *3 (Tenn. Ct. App. Mar. 11, 2010) (noting "[a] written statement is not libel simply because the person who is the subject of the publication found it to be annoying, offensive, or embarrassing, but the words must be reasonably construed to hold the plaintiff up to public hatred, contempt or ridicule, and they must carry with them an element 'of disgrace.'")

A former employee's compelled self-publication of defamatory statements on an employment application, referencing former employment and the reasons such employment was terminated, is not sufficient to hold a former employer liable for defamation. Sullivan, 995 S.W.2d 569. Compelled self-publication conflicts with Tennessee's employment-at-will doctrine. Id. at 574.

Governmental employees may not claim a liberty interest deprivation when employment references are made that result in the employee appearing less attractive to other employers but leaving open a definite range of opportunity. See Rowe v. Chattanooga Bd. of Educ., 938 S.W.2d 351, 356 (Tenn. 1996) (citing Board of Regents of State Colleges v. Roth, 408 U.S. 564, 569B70 (1972)). To implicate liberty interests, the defamatory reference must "stigmatize or otherwise burden the plaintiff so that he is not able to take advantage of other employment." See Rowe, 938 S.W.2d at 356 (citing Joelson v. United States, 86 F.3d 1413, 1420B21 (6th Cir. 1996)).

B. Non-Compete Agreements

Rhetorically, covenants not to compete are disfavored in Tennessee because they are viewed as a restraint of trade. As such, they are to be construed strictly in favor of the employee. Hasty v. Rent-A-Driver, Inc., 671 S.W.2d 471, 472 (Tenn. 1984). Nevertheless, most of the Tennessee cases on the topic have resulted in enforcement, to a greater or lesser extent, of the covenant not to compete.

The Tennessee Supreme Court has stated that the enforceability of a covenant not to compete is dependent upon the following factors: (1) the consideration supporting the covenant; (2) the threatened danger to the employer in the absence of the covenant; (3) the economic hardship imposed on the employee by the covenant; and (4) whether the covenant is inimical to the public interest. Hasty, 671 S.W.2d at 472-473; Allright Auto Parks, Inc. v. Berry, 409 S.W.2d 361, 363 (Tenn. 1966).

The first factor enumerated above, requiring adequate consideration supporting the covenant, has been liberally interpreted. In 1984, the Tennessee Supreme Court concluded that a covenant not to compete signed prior to, contemporaneously with, or shortly after employment begins is part of the original agreement, and is therefore supported by adequate consideration. Central Adjustment Bureau, Inc. v. Ingram, 678 S.W.2d 28, 33 (Tenn. 1984). The Ingram court also observed that adequate consideration for a non-compete agreement could exist even where the agreement was executed well after employment had commenced. Id. at 33-35 (noting that the court will look to the length of the continued employment after execution of the non-compete and how the employment ultimately ended).

The second factor, whether the employer has a sufficient interest at stake to require the employee to adhere to the restrictive covenant, is at issue in most reported Tennessee decisions. In Tennessee, an employer does not have a protectable interest in restraining ordinary competition from a former employee and must demonstrate that the former employee would gain an unfair advantage in future competition with the employer. Vantage Technologies, LLC v. Cross, 17 S.W.3d 637, 644 (Tenn. Ct. App. 1999); See also Intermodal Cartage Co. v. Cherry, 227 S.W.3d 580 (Tenn. Ct. App. 2007) (disputed issues of fact with regard to the element of unfair advantage alone merit the reversal of summary judgment). Tennessee courts have found a legitimate protectable interest where (1) the employer has provided the employee with specialized training; (2) the employee is given access to trade or business secrets or confidential information; and (3) where the employer's customers tend to associate the employer's business with the employee due to the employee's repeated contacts with the customers on behalf of the employer. Id. These considerations may operate individually or in tandem to give rise to a properly protectable business interest. An employer, however, will not be considered to have provided an employee with specialized training that would give him/her an unfair advantage in future competition if: (a) the training sessions were not taught by the employer, but rather a third party; (b) the employer did not provide materials to be presented by the third party at the training sessions; (c) the training seminars did not provide specialized techniques or practices of the employer, and instead imparted general knowledge of a particular industry; (d) the training programs were not solely for the employer's employees, but were open to any participants who wanted to apply, pay and attend, including those from other professionals from competing businesses. Girtman & Associates, Inc. v. St. Amour, slip op., No. M2005-00936-COA-R3-CV, 2007 Tenn. App. LEXIS 271, at *18-23 (Tenn. Ct. App., Middle Section, Apr. 27, 2007) (finding no colorable proof that: (1) the former employee gained specialized or unique knowledge through expensive third-party training; (2) employer had a protectable business interest because it had not given the employee access to customer lists that could not be ascertained through public sources or to trade secrets, such as up-to-date pricing schedules and discounts available to customers, that were current and unique to the employer; or (3) employer's customers associated its business with the employee to the extent that they identified him with it); see also Columbus Med. Servs., LLC v. David Thomas & Liberty Healthcare Corp., 308 S.W.3d 368, at 389 (Tenn. Ct. App. 2009) (the nature of an employment agency's business is unique in that its main service is to provide the "costly and valuable commodity" of time, effort, and expense in finding and putting together prospective employees and employers and negotiating contracts related to their employment. Non-compete provisions may be included in the employees' contracts to protect the agency's investment by preventing unfair disintermediation, i.e., usurpation of the agency's role by the client hiring the employees directly or through another employment agency. Thus, to the extent that an employment agency has invested resources with respect to a particular employee, the agency may have a legitimate business interest in protecting itself against unfair disintermediation). Furthermore, Tennessee courts have upheld employment agreements restricting employees from using private security business services to solicit employment for themselves, any other employee or any of the employer's customers. Int'l Sec. Mgmt. Group, Inc. v. Sawyer, No.: 3:06cv04562006, U.S. Dist. LEXIS 37059 (M.D. Tenn. June 6, 2006); see also International Mktg. Group, Inc. v. Speegle, No.: M1999-00468-COA-R3-CV, 2000 Tenn. App. LEXIS 229 (Tenn. Ct. App. Mar. 30, 2000) (affirming the trial court's decision to enforce a restrictive covenant prohibiting solicitation of current employees, and affirming damages judgment against former employees for injuries resulting from their "stripping" of more than one half of the former employer's sale force and almost half of its customers).

Tennessee law requires that something more than a breach of contract be alleged to warrant an injunction giving effect to a non-compete agreement; specifically, a plaintiff must also prove a competitive injury. Chromalox, Inc. v. Ga. Oven, slip op., No. 3:060546, 2007 U.S. Dist. LEXIS 5520 (M.D. Tenn. Jan. 25, 2007) (despite the former employee's breach of his employment contract that clearly precluded his employment with any firm in the heating industry for a period of one year, the court denied the former employer's motion for an injunction because it failed to establish "the likelihood of competitive injury" that might result from the former's employee's potential disclosure of confidential trade secrets).

Where an employer has a legitimate business interest to support the non-compete agreement, the agreement must be drafted such that the temporal and territorial restrictions are no greater than necessary to protect the employer's legitimate business interests. Allright Auto Parks, Inc. v. Berry, 409 S.W.2d 361, 363 (Tenn. 1966). When a Tennessee court is confronted with a non-compete agreement which is broader than reasonably necessary to protect the employer's legitimate interests, the court is authorized to void the non-compete obligations (where the employer is found to have acted in bad faith by insisting upon deliberately unreasonable and oppressive restrictions) or it may judicially modify the agreement such that it conforms to the employer's legitimate interests. Central Adjustment Bureau, Inc. v. Ingram, 678 S.W.2d 28, 36-37 (Tenn. 1984); see also BFS Retail and Commercial Operations, LLC v. Smith, 232 S.W.3d 756 (Tenn. Ct. App. 2007) (finding that reasonable construction of a non-compete clause referencing "those areas where you worked or had responsibilities at the time of your separation" could lead to the conclusion that application of the non-compete agreement is not limited by a geographic component, therefore, rejecting the former employee's argument that he had not violated the non-compete agreement since he was located outside the geographic location in which he was previously employed). "Absence of [an] explicit geographic limitation does not render [a] non-compete agreement unmodifiable" or overly broad so as to be unenforceable. Carrigan v. Arthur J. Gallagher Risk Mgmt. Servs., slip op., No. 3:10-cv-1089, 2011 U.S. Dist. LEXIS 13373 (M.D. Tenn. Feb. 10, 2011).

Few cases have turned exclusively on the third factor -- the hardship imposed on the employee -- as the decisions generally turn on the finding that the employer's business interest in enforcing a non-compete is insufficient and does not outweigh the employee's hardship. Selox, Inc. v. Ford, 675 S.W.2d 474 (Tenn. 1984).

Tennessee law does permit the invalidation of a non-compete agreement on public policy grounds. Murfreesboro Medical Clinic, P.A. v. Udom, 166 S.W.3d 674 (Tenn. 2005) (enforcement of covenants not to compete against physicians, except for certain agreements specifically covered by statute, is contrary to Tennessee public policy); **Columbus Med. Servs., LLC v. David Thomas & Liberty Healthcare Corp., 308 S.W.3d 368 (Tenn. Ct. App. 2009), appeal denied (Tenn. 2010) (holding that public policy concerns of a physician's continuity of care for at-risk patients outweighs the enforcement of restrictive covenants)**. The Udom decision may signal a willingness in Tennessee, where important public policy considerations are involved, to invalidate other types of post-employment restrictions believed to have anti-competitive effects. Id. at 679; see also Spiegel v. Thomas, Mann & Smith, P.C., 811 S.W.2d 528, 529-30 (Tenn. 1991) (voiding a law firm's "deferred compensation agreement" as effectively constituting a non-compete agreement in violation of lawyer ethics rules).

When an employer threatens to terminate an at-will employee if the employee refuses to sign a non-compete agreement, the non-compete agreement will not be held unenforceable due to duress because the employer was asserting a legal right, i.e. the legal right to terminate an at-will employee without cause. Cummings Inc. v. Dorgan, slip op., No. M2008 -00593-COA-R3-CV, 2009 Tenn. App. LEXIS 639, 2009 WL 3046979, at *13-14 (Tenn. Ct. App., Western Section at Nashville, Sept. 23, 2009), *appeal denied* (Tenn. June 17, 2010).

VIII. OTHER ISSUES

A. Statutes of Limitations

Slander is governed by a six-month statute of limitations. Tenn. Code Ann. § 28-3-103 (2000); see also Rose v. Cookeville Regional Medical Center, No. M2007-02368-COA-R3-CV, 2008 Tenn. App. LEXIS 286 (Tenn. Ct. App. May 14, 2008) (rejecting a "continuous defamation" exception to the six month slander statute of limitations). Libel is governed by a one-year statute of limitations. Tenn. Code Ann. § 28-3-104(a)(1) (1980), Quality Auto Parts v. Bluff City Buick Co., 876 S.W.2d 818, 820 (Tenn. 1994) (declining to adopt "discovery rule"); Wyatt v. Carey, slip op., No 03A01-9809-CV-00307, 1999 Tenn. App. LEXIS 579 (Tenn. Ct. App., Eastern Section, Aug. 25, 1999), appeal denied (Tenn. Jan. 31, 2000); **Kinser v. Bechtel Power Corp., No. 1:10-CV-312, 2012 U.S. Dist. LEXIS 76096 (E.D. Tenn. May 31, 2012) (finding that the statute of limitations began to run once employee became aware of statements made by his employer in the employee's security file).**

B. Jurisdiction

No cases.

C. Worker's Compensation Exclusivity

Tennessee's Workers' Compensation law provides the exclusive remedy for employees (as well as the employee's personal representative, dependents or next of kin) who are injured during the course and scope of their employment. Tenn. Code Ann. § 50-6-108; Clawson v. Burrow, 250 S.W.3d 59 (Tenn. Ct. App. 2007), appeal denied (Tenn. 2008). Under Tennessee's Workers' Compensation exclusivity provision, employees are precluded from seeking tort damages for the injury. Valencia v. Freeland & Lemm Const. Co., 108 S.W.3d 239 (Tenn. 2003); see also Lang v. Nissan North America, Inc., 170 S.W.3d 564 (Tenn. 2005) (finding hedonic damages, or damages for the loss of enjoyment of life, were not a basis for recovery of workers' compensation benefits as the workers' compensation statute did not provide for such common-law tort recovery; recognizing hedonic damages as a basis for recovering benefits would run counter to the exclusive remedy provisions of the workers' compensation law); **see also Poole-Henry v. Johnson & Johnson Health Care Sys., No. 11-2695 -STA, 2011 U.S. Dist. LEXIS 143683 (W.D. Tenn. Dec. 12, 2011)**. Tennessee's Workers' Compensation exclusivity provision does not violate due process clauses of Federal and Tennessee Constitutions. Nichols v. Benco Plastics, Inc. 469 S.W.2d 135 (Tenn. 1971). Tennessee's Workers' Compensation exclusivity provision protects the immediate employer, general contractors and fellow employees. Scott v. AMEC Kamtech, Inc., 583 F. Supp. 2d 912 (E.D. Tenn. 2008).

It is not contrary to Tennessee's Constitution that, under Tennessee's Workers' Compensation law, injured employees may choose to file a claim for compensation from his employer under Tennessee's Workers' Compensation laws or proceed against a third person liable for the injuries, or proceed against both, but they cannot recover against both. Mitchell v. Usilton, 242 S.W. 648 (Tenn. 1922).

To avoid Tennessee's exclusive remedy provisions of the Workers' Compensation Act, Tennessee courts require proof of an *actual* intent by the employer to injure the employee. Gonzales v. Alman Const. Co., 857 S.W.2d 42 (Tenn. Ct. App. 1993); Scarborough v. Brown Group, Inc., 935 F. Supp. 954 (W.D. Tenn. 1996); Blair v. Allied Maintenance Corp., 756 S.W.2d 267 (Tenn. Ct. App. 1988); see also Burke v. Bradley County, slip op., No. 1:11-CV-19, 2011 U.S. Dist. LEXIS 36070 (E.D. Tenn. Apr. 1, 2011). An employer's alleged willful, wanton, deliberate and grossly negligent conduct did not fall within the intentional tort exception to the exclusivity provisions of Tennessee's workers' compensation law. Scarborough v. Brown Group, Inc., 935 F. Supp. 954 (W.D. Tenn. 1996).

An employer was deemed to have waived its argument that the exclusivity provision of Tennessee's workers' compensation law barred the former employee's claim for intentional infliction of emotional distress after the employer failed to plead the same in its answer or at any time prior to submitting a reply brief as part of a second appeal. Pollard v. E.I. DuPont De Nemours, Inc., 412 F.3d 657 (6th Cir. 2005).

Employee was receiving workers' compensation from the employer but, also, sued employer under products liability theory because employer manufactured the equipment that caused the workplace injury. The court rejected employee's "dual capacity" theory. Morris v. Johns Manville International, Inc., slip op., No. 1:09-cv-232, 2010 U.S. Dist. LEXIS 101030, 2010 WL 3825867 (E.D. Tenn. Sept. 24, 2010).

Workers' Compensation exclusive remedy rule does not bar further employee action under Title VII and the Tennessee Human Rights Act. Reagan v. City of Knoxville, 692 F. Supp. 2d 891 (E.D. Tenn. 2010).

D. Pleading Requirements

The common law rule requiring pleading of slanderous words in haec verba is no longer applicable in light of Tenn. R. Civ. P. Handley v. May, 588 S.W.2d 772 (Tenn. Ct. App.), appeal denied (Tenn. July 6, 1979); Evans v. Nashville Banner Publ'g Co., slip op., No. 87-164-II, 1988 Tenn. App. LEXIS 638, 15 Media L. Rep. 2216 (Tenn. Ct. App., Middle Section, Oct. 12, 1988) (no appeal sought). But a complaint still must allege both the time and place of the slanderous utterance. TIG Ins. Co. and Fairmont Specialty Group v. Titan Underwriting Managers, LLC., No. M2007-01977-COA-R3-CV, 2008 Tenn. App. LEXIS 777 (Tenn. Ct. App. Nov. 7, 2008), appeal denied, 2009 Tenn. LEXIS 247 (Tenn. May, 11, 2009) (claim dismissed by trial court because of failure to plead the substance of a slanderous statement); Millsaps v. Millsaps, slip op., 1989 Tenn. App. LEXIS 317 (Tenn. Ct. App., Western Section, May 3, 1989), appeal denied (Tenn. Sept. 5, 1989). Accordingly, Tennessee does not recognize a "continuing defamation" exception to the "time and place" pleading requirement. Rose v. Cookeville Regional Medical Center, No. M2007-02368-COA-R3-CV, 2008 Tenn. App. Lexis 286 (Tenn. Ct. App. May 14, 2008). See also Tennessee Rule of Civil Procedure 8.01.

An employee may be precluded from bringing a cause of action for defamation after a determination is made by an administrative law judge. Sullivan v. Wilson County, No. M2011-00217-COA-R3-CV 2012 Tenn. App. LEXIS 332 (Tenn. Ct. App. May 22, 2012) (no appeal sought). In Sullivan, an employee was terminated by a local power board after a detective sent his employer a letter stating the employee sold narcotic drugs from the truck the employee used during his shift and that the employee admitted selling the drugs. Id. The employee denied selling illegal drugs or making such an admission to the detective, but the administrative law judge in charge of the evidentiary hearing determined that the statements in the detective's letter were true. Id. The employee later filed suit against the detective who authored the letter, his supervisors, and the county employing the individual defendants. The former employee asserted causes of action for defamation, negligence, false light invasion of privacy, and intentional infliction of emotional distress. Id. The trial court concluded that the former employee was collaterally estopped from re-litigating the veracity of the statements in the detective's letter leading to the plaintiff's termination.

SURVEY OF TEXAS EMPLOYMENT LIBEL LAW

John K. Edwards
Jackson Walker L.L.P.
1401 McKinney, Suite 1900
Houston, Texas 77010
Telephone: (713) 752-4200; Telecopier: (713) 752-4221

(With Developments Reported Through **November 1, 2012**)

GENERAL COMMENTS

None.

SIGNIFICANT DEVELOPMENTS SINCE THE 2012 *SURVEY*

There were no significant appellate court rulings this past year in employment libel cases in Texas, but a few decisions that built on prior precedent are worth mentioning. The Fort Worth Court of Appeals confirmed that allegedly false statements in a termination letter placed in a personnel file are not actionable without publication to a third party. Bell v. Express Energy Services Operating, LP, 2012 WL 2036437, *3-4 (Tex. App.—Fort Worth June 7, 2012, no pet.). The Waco Court of Appeals relied on substantial precedent in applying the common interest qualified privilege to communications by a former employer to prospective employers and headhunters. Gonzalez v. Methodist Charlton Medical Center, 2011 WL 6091255 (Tex. App.—Waco Dec. 7, 2011, no pet.). In Becker v. Clardy, 2011 WL 6756999 (Tex. App.—Austin Dec. 22, 2011, no pet.), the Austin Court of Appeals rejected a defamation claim made by a teacher at a parochial school against a co-worker, holding that the ecclesiastical abstention doctrine deprived the courts of jurisdiction to hear the claim.

I. GENERAL LAW

A. General Employment Law

1. **At Will Employment.** The long standing rule in Texas is that employment for an indefinite term may be terminated at will and without cause. Midland Jud. Dist. Cmty. Supervision & Corrs. Dep't v. Jones, 92 S.W.3d 486, 487 (Tex. 2002); Montgomery County Hosp. Dist. v. Brown, 965 S.W.2d 501, 502 (Tex. 1998); Federal Express Corp. v. Dutschmann, 846 S.W.2d 282, 283 (Tex. 1993); Winters v. Houston Chronicle Pub. Co., 795 S.W.2d 723 (Tex. 1990); East Line & R.R.R. Co., v. Scott, 72 Tex. 70, 10 S.W. 99, 102 (1888); Mayfield v. Lockheed Eng'g Servs. Co., 970 S.W.2d 185, 186 (Tex. App.–Houston [14th Dist.] 1998, pet. denied); Lumpkin v. H&C Communications, Inc., 755 S.W.2d 538 (Tex. App.–Houston [1st Dist.] 1988, writ denied); Benoit v. Polysar Gulf Coast, Inc., 728 S.W.2d 403 (Tex. App.—Beaumont 1987, writ ref'd n.r.e.). Given this statement of the law, Texas is generally recognized as an "at will" employment state. "Thus, the employer may, without liability, discharge an employee for good reason, bad reason, or no reason at all." Garcia v. Allen, 2000 WL 731781 (Tex. App.–Corpus Christi 2000, no pet.) (stating employer has no duty to investigate information about an at-will employee prior to termination); Currey v. Lone Star Steel Company, 676 S.W.2d 205 (Tex. App.–Fort Worth 1984, no writ); see also Welch v. Doss Aviation, Inc., 978 S.W.2d 215, 220 (Tex. App.–Amarillo 1998, no pet.). General comments that an employee will not be discharged as long as his work is satisfactory do not in themselves manifest an intent to modify an employee's at-will status. Brown, 965 S.W.2d at 502. However, there are many ways that an employer, either intentionally or unintentionally, may modify the employment terms of the at will status of its employees. See, e.g., County of Dallas v. Wiland, 216 S.W.3d 344, 348 (Tex. 2007) (modification by contract or rules and policies); In re Jebbia, 2000 WL 1405671 (Tex. App.–Houston [14th Dist.] 2000, no pet. h.) (stating to prove a modification of an at-will employment contract, the party asserting the modification must prove notice and acceptance of the change); Jones v. Fujitsu Network Communications, Inc., 81 F. Supp.2d 688 (N.D. Tex. 1999); City of Odessa v. Barton, 967 S.W.2d 834, 835 (Tex. 1998); see also Muncy v. City of Dallas, 335 F.3d 394, 398 (5th Cir. 2003) (stating that at-will status may be abrogated by "statute, rule, handbook, or policy which limits the condition under which the employment may be terminated").

To date, the Texas Supreme Court has created only two exceptions to the at will employment doctrine: (1) where an employee is discharged for the sole reason that the employee refused to perform an illegal act that carries criminal penalties; and (2) where an employee demonstrates that the principal reason for discharge was the employer's desire to avoid contributing or paying benefits under the employer's pension fund. See City of Midland v. O'Bryant, 18 S.W.3d 209, 215 (Tex. 2000) (stating that the Texas Supreme Court has only recognized an illegal act exception); Winters, 795 S.W.2d at 723 -724; Sabine Pilot Serv., Inc. v. Hauck, 687 S.W.2d 733 (Tex. 1985). However, the Texas Supreme Court has specifically declined to recognize a cause of action for private employees who are discharged for reporting illegal activities. Austin v. Healthtrust, Inc. - The Hospital Co., 967 S.W.2d 400 (Tex. 1998); Winters, 795 S.W.2d at 724-725; see also Mayfield, 970

S.W.2d at 187. The appellate court in Johnston v. Del Mar Distrib. Co., 776 S.W.2d 768 (Tex. App.–Corpus Christi 1989, writ denied) expanded the exception created in Sabine Pilot to include claims by employees who are merely attempting to determine whether actions they are required to perform are illegal. See also Garza v. Doctors on Wilcrest, P.A., 976 S.W.2d 899, 901 (Tex. App.–Houston [14th Dist.] 1998, pet. denied); Mayfield, 970 S.W.2d at 187. The court held that the plaintiff must only show that she had a good faith belief that the act might be illegal. Johnston, 776 S.W.2d 768.

Generally, in Texas, there is not a cause of action for wrongful discharge of an at will employee, without more. There is no duty of good faith and fair dealing in an employment relationship. City of Midland, 18 S.W.3d at 216. However, an employee who can prove that his employment at will is subject to an oral or written agreement that he will not be terminated except for good cause can recover for wrongful discharge, even if the employee has not agreed to remain in service for a definite length of time. See Mansell v. Texas & Pacific Ry. Co., 135 Tex. 31, 137 S.W.2d 997, 999-1000 (1940).

The Texas Legislature has also placed restrictions upon the at will employment doctrine and has enacted several statutes that protect specific classes of employees from various types of retaliation. See Austin, 967 S.W.2d at 401-402. For example, § 554.002 of the Government Code protects public employees from retaliation for reporting, in good faith, violations of law to an appropriate law enforcement agency. Tex. Gov't Code § 554.002. Similarly, a physician cannot be retaliated against for reporting to the State Board of Medical Examiners the acts of another physician that pose a continuing threat to the public welfare. Tex. Occ. Code § 160.012 (Vernon 2000). Additionally, a statute exists that prohibits retaliation against nursing home employees who report abuse or neglect of a nursing home resident. Tex. Health & Safety Code § 242.133. Also, employers who use hazardous chemicals may not retaliate against employees for reporting a violation of the Hazard Communication Act. Id. at § 502.017. Nor can employers retaliate against employees for opposing or reporting discriminatory practices in the workplace. Tex. Lab. Code § 21.055.

However, there is no statute protecting private sector "whistleblowers." The Texas Supreme Court has declined to recognize a cause of action for private sector whistleblowers. City of Midland, 18 S.W.3d at 215-16; Austin v. HealthTrust, Inc. – The Hosp. Co., 967 S.W.2d 400 (Tex. 1998); see also Melendez v. Exxon Corp., 998 S.W.2d 266, 273 (Tex. App.–Houston [14th Dist.] 1999, no pet. h.) (court of appeals declined to recognize cause of action for private sector whistleblowers).

There are numerous other restrictions and exceptions to the at will doctrine created by the Texas Legislature. See Winters, 795 S.W.2d at 724, n. 1.

B. Elements of Libel Claim

1. **Basic Elements.** The only cause of action in Texas for libel is under the statutory provision set forth in Section 73.001, et. seq. of the Texas Civil Practice and Remedies Code. The statutory definition of libel in Texas is: "a defamation, expressed in written or other graphic form that tends to blacken the memory of the dead or that tends to injure a living person's reputation and thereby expose the person to public hatred, contempt or ridicule, or financial injury or to impeach any person's honesty, integrity, virtue, or reputation or to publish the natural defects of anyone and thereby expose the person to public hatred, ridicule, or financial injury."

Tex. Civ. Prac. & Rem. Code § 73.001 (Vernon Supp. 1999); Dallas Independent School District v. Finlan, 27 S.W.2d 220 (Tex. App.–Dallas 2000, pet. denied), cert. denied, 122 S. Ct. 342 (Oct. 9, 2001); see also Turner v. KTRK Television, Inc., 38 S.W.3d 103, 29 Media L. Rep. 1673 (Tex. Dec. 31, 2000); \s "memo" \c 0Abbott v. Pollock, 946 S.W.2d 513, 519 (Tex. App.–Austin 1997, writ denied); M. N. Dannenbaum, Inc. v. Brummerhop, 840 S.W.2d 624, 633-34 (Tex. App.–Houston [14th Dist.] 1992, writ denied).

To prove defamation (libel or slander) in Texas, an employee must show that the employer said something untrue about the employee, that the employer knew that the statement was untrue or failed to reasonably investigate the truth or the falsity of the statement, that the statement was published (to a third party) either orally or in writing, and that the employee's reputation was damaged as a result. See Smith v. McMullen, 589 F. Supp. 642, 644, 10 Media L. Rep. 2250 (S.D. Tex. 1984); Huckabee v. Time Warner Entm't Co., 19 S.W.3d 413, 429 (Tex. 2000); Randall's Food Mkts., Inc. v. Johnson, 891 S.W.2d 640, 646 (Tex. 1995). Additionally, the employee must be able to overcome any assertion that the statement was privileged. Id. A corporation may be held liable for defamation by its agent if such defamation is referable to the duty owing by the agent to the corporation and was made in the discharge of that duty. Wal-Mart Stores, Inc. v. Lane, 31 S.W.3d 282 (Tex. App.–Corpus Christi 2000, pet. denied).

2. **Fault.** "A cause of action for libel accrues if the defendant publishes a false, defamatory statement of fact of and concerning the plaintiff and if the defendant was at fault." Hanssen v. Our Redeemer Lutheran Church, 938 S.W.2d 85, 92 (Tex. App.–Dallas 1996, writ denied); Holly v. Cannady, 669 S.W.2d 381, 383, 10 Media L. Rep. 2291 (Tex. App.–Dallas 1984, no writ). Fault is a constitutional prerequisite for defamation liability. WFAA-TV, Inc. v. McLemore,

978 S.W.2d 568, 571, 26 Media L. Rep. 2385 (Tex. 1998), cert. denied, 526 U.S. 1051 (1999) (citing Gertz v. Robert Welch, Inc., 418 U.S. 323, 347 (1974)). Depending on the status of the plaintiff, the standard of care required of a defendant will be either negligence or actual malice.

a. **Private Figure Plaintiff/Matter of Public Concern**. The Supreme Court of Texas applies the negligence standard of fault for defamation cases in which the plaintiff is a private figure. Dolcefino v. Randolph, 19 S.W.3d 906, 917 (Tex. App.–Houston [14th Dist.] 2000, pet. denied); Foster v. Laredo Newspapers, Inc., 541 S.W.2d 809, 819 (Tex. 1976), cert. denied, 429 U.S. 1123 (1977); McLemore, 978 S.W.2d at 571 (citing Foster, 541 S.W.2d at 819). In Foster v. Laredo Newspapers, Inc., 541 S.W.2d 809, 819 (Tex. 1976), cert. denied, 429 U.S. 1123 (1977), the Texas Supreme Court held that in cases involving private figure plaintiffs and matters of public concern, "a private individual may recover damages from a publisher or broadcaster of a defamatory falsehood as compensation for actual injury upon a showing that the publisher ... knew or should have known that the defamatory statement was false." See also Granada Biosciences, Inc. v. Barrett, 958 S.W.2d 215, 223 (Tex. App.–Amarillo 1997, pet. denied); Delta Air Lines, Inc. v. Norris, 949 S.W.2d 422, 426 (Tex. App.–Waco 1997, writ denied); Lomas Bank USA v. Flatow, 880 S.W.2d 52, 54 (Tex. App. – San Antonio 1994, writ denied); Dannenbaum, Inc. v. Brummerhop, 840 S.W.2d 624, 633 (Tex. App.–Houston [14th Dist.] 1992, writ denied).

b. **Private Figure Plaintiff/Matter of Private Concern**. In light of the Supreme Court's plurality opinion in Dun & Bradstreet, Inc. v. Greenmoss Builders, Inc., 472 U.S. 749, 760-61 (plurality), 763-64 (Burger, C.J., concurring), 773-74 (White, J., concurring), 11 Media L. Rep. 2417 (1985), the Fifth Circuit found that in cases involving private figure plaintiffs and matters of private concern, "the Constitution imposes no minimum standard of care." The Fifth Circuit further found that a plaintiff does not have to prove that the defamatory statement was made with actual malice in order to recover presumed or punitive damages. Snead v. Redland Aggregates, Ltd., 998 F.2d 1325, 1333, 21 Media L. Rep. 1865 (5th Cir. 1993)(applying Texas law). Rather, the plaintiff simply has to show common law malice, i.e, ill will. Peshak v. Greer, 13 S.W.3d 421 (Tex. App.–Corpus Christi 2000, no pet.) (holding exemplary damages in defamation case between private litigants can be supported if utterance is made with malice).

c. **Public Figure Plaintiff/Matter of Public Concern**. The question of public figure/public official status is one of constitutional law. Colson v. Grohman, 24 S.W.3d 414, 420 (Tex. App.–Houston [1st Dist.] 2000, pet. denied). The United States Supreme Court held in Rosenblatt v. Baer that "public officials" include "those among the hierarchy of government employees who have, or appear to the public to have, substantial responsibility for or control over the conduct of governmental affairs." Rosenblatt v. Baer, 383 U.S. 75, 85, 1 Media L. Rep. 1558 (1966); Rogers v. Cassidy, 946 S.W.2d 439, 444 (Tex. App.–Corpus Christi 1997, n.w.h.). In addition, the designation "public official" may include those who hold a position which "has such apparent importance that the public has an independent interest in the qualifications and performance of the person who holds it, beyond the general public interest in the qualifications and performance of all government employees". Rosenblatt, 383 U.S. at 86. There is no definite rule to determine "how far down into the lower ranks of government employees the 'public official' designation extend[s] ... or otherwise to specify categories of persons who would or would not be included." New York Times Co. v. Sullivan, 376 U.S. 254, 283 n.23 (1964); Rogers, 946 S.W.2d at 444. Significantly, though, the Texas Supreme Court has recognized that even a "lower echelon" municipal employee may be a public official for defamation purposes. See Dolcefino, 19 S.W.3d at 928 (holding city controller was public figure); see Foster v. Laredo Newspapers, Inc., 541 S.W.2d 809 (Tex. 1976), cert. denied, 429 U.S. 1123 (1977).

In Gertz v. Robert Welch, Inc., 418 U.S. 323, 1 Media L. Rep. 1633 (1974), the United States Supreme Court decided that "public figures" are those who fit into either of two categories: (1) those who achieve such pervasive fame or notoriety that they become public figures for all purposes and in all contexts; or (2) those who voluntarily inject themselves or are drawn into a particular public controversy, thereby becoming public figures for a limited range of issues. Swate v. Schiffers, 975 S.W.2d 70, 76, 26 Media L. Rep. 2258 (Tex. App.–San Antonio 1998, pet. denied) (citing Gertz, 418 U.S. at 351); San Antonio Exp. News v. Dracos, 922 S.W.2d 242, 251 (Tex. App.–San Antonio 1996, no writ); Simmons v. Ware, 920 S.W.2d 438, 449 (Tex. App.–Amarillo 1996, no writ); see also WFAA-TV, Inc. v. McLemore, 978 S.W.2d 568, 571, 26 Media L. Rep. 2385 (Tex. 1998), cert. denied, 526 U.S. 1051 (1999); TSM AM-FM TV v. Meca Homes, Inc., 969 S.W.2d 448, 452-53 (Tex. App.–El Paso 1998, pet. denied). These two categories are generally referred to as "general purpose public figures" and "limited purpose public figures," respectively. See Dracos, 922 S.W.2d at 251; Simmons, 920 S.W.2d at 449; Einhorn v. LaChance, 823 S.W.2d 405, 413 (Tex. App.–Houston [1st Dist.] 1992, writ dism'd w.o.j.), cert. denied, 517 U.S. 1135 (1996); see also McLemore, 978 S.W.2d at 571; TSM AM-FM TV, 969 S.W.2d at 452-53. The question of whether a person is a public figure is question of law for the court to decide. Rosenblatt, 383 U.S. at 88; Trotter v. Jack Anderson Enters., Inc., 818 F.2d 431, 433, 14 Media L. Rep. 1180 (5th Cir. 1987); McLemore, 978 S.W.2d at 571; Dracos, 922 S.W.2d at 251; Simmons, 920 S.W.2d at 449; Einhorn, 823 S.W.2d at 413. The Fifth Circuit has adopted the following three-prong test to determine whether a person is a limited purpose public figure:

1. the controversy at issue must be public both in the sense that people are discussing it and people other than the immediate participants in the controversy are likely to feel the impact of its resolution;

2. the plaintiff must have more than a trivial or tangential role in the controversy; and

3. the alleged defamation must be germane to the plaintiff's participation in the controversy.

Trotter v. Jack Anderson Enters., Inc., 818 F.2d 431, 433, 14 Media L. Rep. 1180 (5th Cir. 1987). In WFAA-TV, Inc. v. McLemore, 978 S.W.2d 568, 26 Media L. Rep. 2385 (Tex. 1998), cert. denied, 119 S. Ct. 1358 (1999), the Texas Supreme Court adopted the Trotter test (which had previously been adopted by two Texas courts of appeals (Einhorn, 823 S.W.2d at 413 and TSM- AM-FM TV v. Meca Homes, Inc., 969 S.W.2d 448, 453 (Tex. App.–El Paso 1998, pet. denied)).

The Texas courts have found that a "public controversy" is not just a matter of interest to the public, but rather "involves a real dispute, the outcome of which affects the general public or some segment of it in an appreciable way." TSM- AM-FM TV, 969 S.W.2d at 453; Einhorn, 823 S.W.2d at 411. Likewise, "a public controversy is a dispute that in fact has received public attention because its ramifications will be felt by persons who are not direct participants." TSM- AM-FM TV, 969 S.W.2d at 453; Einhorn, 823 S.W.2d at 412. Furthermore, "private concerns or disagreements do not become public controversies simply because they attract attention." Einhorn, 823 S.W.2d at 412 (citing Time, Inc. v. Firestone, 424 U.S. 448, 454-55 (1976)); see also TSM-AM-FM TV, 969 S.W.2d at 453.

For example, the court in Barbouti v. Hearst Corp. found that the alleged illegal export of chemicals and technology to Libya and Iraq by the plaintiff was a public controversy because the issue involved "prohibiting access to materials or technology that Iraq or Libya could use to wage war or inflict death or destruction," and "involve[d] the security of the United States and the international community." Barbouti, 927 S.W.2d 37, 48 (partial publication, pages 40-62 unpublished in official reporter) (pages 40-62 appear in Westlaw, cited as Barbouti v. Hearst Corp., 927 S.W.2d 37 (Tex. App.–Houston 1996, writ denied) (No. 01-94-00907-CV)). However, in the same case, the court found that a lawsuit between the plaintiff and a pipeline company and its owner, who sued the plaintiff for conspiring and attempting to steal the company's pipe-coating technology and export it to Libya and Iraq, was not a public controversy. Id. In Einhorn v. LaChance, the court decided that a dispute regarding overtime compensation and safety regulations for EMS pilots was a public issue, because the issue had received public exposure in various ways over the course of several years. Einhorn, 823 S.W.2d at 412-13; see also McLemore, 978 S.W.2d at 572 (ATF agents' failed assault on Branch Davidian compound at Mount Carmel was a public controversy); Swate v. Schiffers, 975 S.W.2d 70, 76, 26 Media L. Rep. 2258 (Tex. App. – San Antonio 1998, pet. denied) (physician's questionable medical practice is information that interests the public); Ross v. Labatt, 894 S.W.2d 393, 395 (Tex. App.–San Antonio 1994, writ dism'd, w.o.j.) (political debate over proposed reservoir, which had resulted in two local public referendums, was a public controversy).

In New York Times Co. v. Sullivan, 376 U.S. 254 (1964), the United States Supreme Court held that a public official cannot recover damages for a defamatory statement relating to the performance of official duties unless the public official proves that the defamatory statement was made with actual malice. Dolcefino, 19 S.W.3d at 917, 929; Colson, 24 S.W.3d at 421 (stating actual malice is a stringent culpability standard); See McLemore, 978 S.W.2d at 571 (citing New York Times, 376 U.S. 279-80 (1964)); Turner v. KTRK Television, Inc., 38 S.W.3d 103, 29 Media L. Rep. 1673 (Tex. Dec. 31, 2000); Carr v. Brasher, 776 S.W.2d 567, 569 (Tex. 1989) (citing New York Times, 376 U.S. at 279-80); Casso v. Brand, 776 S.W.2d 551, 554 (Tex. 1989); Beck v. Lone Star Broad. Co., 970 S.W.2d 610, 613 (Tex. App.–Tyler 1998, pet. denied); Rogers, 946 S.W.2d at 444; Morris v. Dallas Morning News, Inc., 934 S.W.2d 410, 415 (Tex. App.–Waco 1996, writ denied); Hailey v. KTBS, Inc., 935 S.W.2d 857 (Tex. App.–Texarkana 1996, no writ). The same rule also applies in cases involving public figures engaged in speech on matters of public concern. El Paso Times, Inc. v. Trexler, 447 S.W.2d 403, 405 (Tex. 1969); see Gertz, 418 U.S. at 342; McLemore, 978 S.W.2d at 571 (citing Curtis Publ'g Co. v. Butts, 388 U.S. 130 (1967). However, it should be noted that public official plaintiffs do not have to prove actual malice when defamatory statements made about them do not relate to their official capacity. Rogers, 946 S.W.2d at 444 (citing Monitor Patriot Co. v. Roy, 401 U.S. 265, 273-75, 1 Media L. Rep. 1619 (1971)); New York Times, 376 U.S. at 283 n.23; Foster, 541 S.W.2d at 814 -15; Villarreal v. Harte-Hanks Communications, Inc., 787 S.W.2d 131, 133 (Tex. App.–Corpus Christi 1990), cert. denied, 499 U.S. 923 (1991)); see also Guinn v. Tex. Newspapers, Inc., 738 S.W.2d 303, 305-306, 16 Media L. Rep. 1024 (Tex. App. –Houston [14th Dist.] 1987, writ denied), cert. denied, 488 U.S. 1041 (1989).

A public official or public figure plaintiff must establish actual malice by clear and convincing evidence. Gertz, 418 U.S. at 342; Casso, 776 S.W.2d at 554; Howell v. Hecht, 821 S.W.2d 627, 630 (Tex. App.–Dallas 1991, writ denied). "Actual malice, as used in defamation cases, ... does not include ill will, spite, or evil motive, but rather requires 'sufficient evidence to permit the conclusion that the defendant in fact entertained serious doubt as to the truth of his publication.'" Casso, 776 S.W.2d at 558 (quoting St. Amant v. Thompson, 390 U.S. 727, 731 (1968)); New Times, Inc. v.

Isaacks, 2004 WL 1966014, *14 (Tex. Sept. 3, 2004); Forbes Inc. v. Granada Biosciences, Inc., 124 S.W.3d 167, 171 (Tex. 2003); Knox v. Taylor, 992 S.W.2d 40, 54 (Tex. App.–Houston [14th Dist.] 1999, no pet.); Beck, 970 S.W.2d at 613 (quoting St. Amant, 390 U.S. at 731); see also Dolcefino v. Turner, 987 S.W.2d 100, 110-11 (Tex. App.–Houston [14th Dist.] 1998), aff'd sub. nom. Turner v. KTRK Television, Inc., 38 S.W.3d 103, 29 Media L. Rep. 1673 (Tex. Dec. 31, 2000); Morris, 934 S.W.2d at 445; Howell, 821 S.W.2d at 630. In order to prove that the defendant acted with actual malice, the plaintiff must show that the defendant either knew that the defamatory statement was false when it was made or made the statement with reckless disregard of whether the statement was false. New Times, Inc., 2004 WL 1966014, *14; Forbes Inc., 124 S.W.3d at 171; WFAA-TV, Inc. v. McLemore, 978 S.W.2d 568, 573-74, 26 Media L. Rep. 2385 (Tex. 1998), cert. denied, 526 U.S. 1051 (1999); Randall's Food Mkts., Inc., v. Johnson, 891 S.W.2d 640, 646 (Tex. 1995); Carr v. Brasher, 776 S.W.2d 567, 571, 16 Media L. Rep. 1942 (Tex. 1989); Knox, 992 S.W.2d at 54 (citing Randall's, 891 S.W.2d at 646); Beck, 970 S.W.2d at 613; Rogers, 946 S.W.2d at 449; Morris, 934 S.W.2d at 415. "'Reckless disregard' is defined as a high degree of awareness of probable falsity, for proof of which the plaintiff must present 'sufficient evidence to permit the conclusion that the defendant in fact entertained serious doubts as to the truth of his publication.'" Carr, 776 S.W.2d at 571 (citing St. Amant, 390 U.S. at 731; Casso, 776 S.W.2d at 558); Forbes Inc., 124 S.W.3d at 171; Dolcefino, 19 S.W.3d at 929; Turner, 987 S.W.2d at 110; Beck, 970 S.W.2d at 616; Rogers, 946 S.W.2d at 445; see also McLemore, 978 S.W.2d at 574.

The mere failure of a defendant to investigate the accuracy of a published statement does not constitute actual malice. See St. Amant v. Thompson, 390 U.S. 727, 733 (1968); New Times, Inc., 2004 WL 1966014, *20; El Paso Times v. Trexler, 447 S.W.2d 403, 406 (Tex. 1969); Turner, 987 S.W.2d at 110 (citing St. Amant, 390 U.S. at 733); Beck, 970 S.W.2d at 617. Furthermore, evidence of ill will or spite is not evidence of actual malice. See Turner, 987 S.W.2d at 110 (citing Masson v. New Yorker Magazine, Inc., 501 U.S. 496, 510 (1991)). In addition, falsity alone does not establish actual malice. Turner, 987 S.W.2d at 114. "Actual malice may be inferred from the relation of the parties, the circumstances attending the publication, the terms of the publication itself, and from the defendant's words or acts before, at or after the time of the communication." Turner, 987 S.W.2d at 111 (citing International & G.N.R. Co. v. Edmundson, 222 S.W.2d 181, 184 (Tex. Comm'n App. 1920, holding approved)); Frank B. Hall & Co. v. Buck, 678 S.W.2d 612, 621 (Tex. App.–Houston [14th Dist.] 1984, writ ref'd n.r.e.) cert. denied, 105 U.S. 2704 (1985). However, "[m]ere surmise or suspicion of malice [cannot] form the basis of a legal inference of malice, and circumstantial evidence must be sufficient to permit the conclusion that the defendant entertained serious doubts as to the truth of his publication." Turner, 987 S.W.2d at 112 (citing Proctor & Gamble Mfg. Co. v. Hagler, 880 S.W.2d 123, 127 (Tex. App.–Texarkana 1994), writ denied per curiam, 884 S.W.2d 771 (Tex. 1994)); St. Amant, 390 U.S. at 731). In Dolcefino v. Turner, 987 S.W.2d 100, 119 (Tex. App. – Houston [14th Dist.] 1998),aff'd sub. nom. Turner v. KTRK Television, Inc., 38 S.W.3d 103, 29 Media L. Rep. 1673 (Tex. Dec. 31, 2000), a court of appeals held that reliance upon a source motivated by a strong political bias does not amount to evidence of actual malice. The court stated that "[political motivation does not equate with knowing or reckless falsity." Id. at 119.

3. **Falsity.** A statement is defamatory only if it is a false statement of fact. A.H. Belo Corp. v. Rayzor, 644 S.W.2d 71, 79, 8 Media L. Rep. 2425 (Tex. App.–Fort Worth 1982, writ ref'd n.r.e.); see AccuBanc Mortg. Corp. v. Drummonds, 938 S.W.2d 135, 149 (Tex. App.–Fort Worth, 1996, writ denied).

In cases involving media defendants, the courts have held that the plaintiff has the burden of proving falsity. Dolcefino, 19 S.W.3d at 917; McIlvain v. Jacobs, 794 S.W.2d 14, 15, 17 Media L. Rep. 2207 (Tex. 1990); Rayzor, 644 S.W.2d at 79-80; see Gertz, 418 U.S. at 35; Swate v. Schiffers, 975 S.W.2d 70, 74, 26 Media L. Rep. 2258 (Tex. App.–San Antonio 1998, pet. denied) (plaintiff still bears burden of proving falsity when pleading libel per se); Rogers v. Dallas Morning News, Inc., 889 S.W.2d 467, 472 n.7 (Tex. App.–Dallas 1994, writ denied). For instance, in Rogers v. Dallas Morning News, Inc., a case involving a media defendant, the court of appeals stated that "[r]egardless of whether [the plaintiff] is considered a private person or a public figure, she would still be required to prove that [the defendant's] objectionable statements were false." Rogers, 889 S.W.2d at 472 n.7 (citing McIlvain, 794 S.W.2d at 15).

On the other hand, in a case involving a non-media defendant, the Texas Supreme Court stated that "[i]n suits brought by private individuals, truth is an affirmative defense to slander." Randall's Food Mkts., Inc. v. Johnson, 891 S.W.2d 640, 646 (Tex. 1995); see David L. Aldridge Co. v. Microsoft Corp., 995 F. Supp. 728, 741 (S.D. Tex. 1998); Knox v. Taylor, 992 S.W.2d 40, 54 (Tex. App.–Houston [14th Dist.] 1999, no pet.) (citing Randall's, 891 S.W.2d at 646); Frank B. Hall & Co. v. Buck, 678 S.W.2d 612, 623 (Tex. App.–Houston [14th Dist.] 1984, writ ref'd n.r.e.) cert. denied, 105 U.S. 2704 (1985); Campbell v. Salazar, 960 S.W.2d 719, 726 (Tex. App. El Paso 1997, pet. denied); Rios v. Texas Commerce Bancshares, Inc., 930 S.W.2d 809, 817 (Tex. App.–Corpus Christi 1996, writ denied); Duran v. Furr's Supermarkets, Inc., 921 S.W.2d 778, 793 (Tex. App.–El Paso 1996, writ denied). There, the burden falls on the defendant to prove the truth of the given statement. Knox, 992 S.W.2d at 54; Buck, 678 S.W.2d at 623; but compare Turner v. Church of Jesus Christ and Latter Day Saints, 18 S.W.3d 877, 902 (Tex. App.–Dallas 2000, pet. denied), cert. denied, 121 S. Ct. 2594 (2001) (stating that plaintiff missionary had burden to show church's statements were false).

The Texas libel statute also provides that truth is a defense to an action for libel. Tex. Civ. Prac. & Rem. Code § 73.005 (Vernon 1997); see also Evans v. Dolcefino, 986 S.W.2d 69, 76 (Tex. App.–Houston [1st Dist.] 1999, no pet.) ; TSM AM-FM TV v. Meca Homes, Inc., 969 S.W.2d 448, 452 (Tex App.–El Paso 1998, pet. denied); Granada Biosciences, Inc., v. Barrett, 958 S.W.2d 215, 224 (Tex. App.–Amarillo 1997, pet. denied) (citing Mitcham v. Bd. of Regents, Univ. of Tex. Sys., 670 S.W. 2d 371, 373 (Tex. App.–Texarkana 1984, no writ)); Randall's Food Mkts., Inc. v. Johnson, 891 S.W.2d 640, 646 (Tex. 1995).

Nevertheless, in Brown v. Petrolite Corp., 965 F.2d 38, 43 (5th Cir. 1992), the Fifth Circuit concluded that Texas law requires the plaintiff to prove falsity as an element of a cause of action for defamation, and this case did not involve a media defendant. Following the Fifth Circuit's interpretation of Texas law in Brown, other Texas cases have held that this burden rests on the plaintiff. David L. Aldridge Co. v. Microsoft Corp., 995 F. Supp. 728, 741 (S.D. Tex. 1998); see also Spectators' Communication Network, Inc. v. Anheuser-Busch Inc., No. 3:95-CV-2390-P, 1998 WL 874848, at *10 (N.D. Tex. Nov. 24, 1998) (mem.), aff'd in part & rev'd in part, 253 F.3d 215 (5th Cir. 2001) (citing Brown, 965 F.2d at 43).

In Randall's Food Mkts., Inc., the Texas Supreme Court stated that it need not decide whether truth is an affirmative defense in slander cases brought by public officials or public figures. Randall's, 891 S.W.2d at 646 n.6. Earlier, however, the Texas Supreme Court, in Carr v. Brasher, 776 S.W.2d 567, 569, 16 Media L. Rep. 1942 (Tex. 1989), held that to sustain a defamation claim, a public official or public figure must prove that the defendant published a statement that was defamatory of the plaintiff and that the false statement was made with actual malice.

In any event, it is clear under Texas law that the "substantial truth" test is used to determine the truth or falsity of complained of statements. Dolcefino, 19 S.W.3d at 918; Delta Air Lines, Inc. v. Norris, 949 S.W.2d 422, 426 (Tex. App.–Waco 1997, writ denied); KTRK Television v. Felder, 950 S.W.2d 100, 105, 25 Media L. Rep. 2418 (Tex. App. – Houston [14th Dist.] 1997, no writ); Simmons v. Ware, 920 S.W.2d 438, 447 (Tex. App.–Amarillo 1996, no writ); Rogers v. Dallas Morning News, Inc., 889 S.W.2d 467, 472 (Tex. App.–Dallas 1994, writ denied) (citing McIlvain v. Jacobs, 794 S.W.2d 14, 15 (Tex. 1990)); see also Knox, 992 S.W.2d at 54. Under this test, the court examines each statement in question, in its entirety, and decides whether the evidence shows that the "gist" of the statement is substantially true. Dolcefino, 19 S.W.3d at 921 (stating where facts are undisputed as to gist of libelous charge, court disregards any variance regarding items of secondary importance); McIlvain, 794 S.W.2d at 15-16; Evans v. Dolcefino, 986 S.W.2d 69, 76 (Tex. App.–Houston [1st Dist.] 1999, no pet. h.) (citing McIlvain, 794 S.W.2d at 16, and KTRK Television v. Felder, 950 S.W.2d 100, 105-106 (Tex. App.–Houston [1st Dist.] 1997, no writ)); Turner v. KTRK Television, Inc., 38 S.W.3d 103, 29 Media L. Rep. 1673 (Tex. Dec. 31, 2000); Swate v. Schiffers, 975 S.W.2d 70, 75, 26 Media L. Rep. 2258 (Tex. App.–San Antonio 1998, pet. denied); Norris, 949 S.W.2d at 426; Felder, 950 S.W.2d at 105; Simmons, 920 S.W.2d at 447; Rogers, 889 S.W.2d at 472. This test "involves consideration of whether the alleged defamatory statement was more damaging to [the plaintiff's] reputation in the mind of the average [person who heard or read the statement] than a truthful statement would have been." Dolcefino, 19 S.W.3d at 918; McIlvain, 794 S.W.2d at 15-16; Knox, 992 S.W.2d at 54; Evans, 986 S.W.2d at 76; Swate, 975 S.W.2d at 75; Norris, 949 S.W.2d at 426; Felder, 950 S.W.2d at 105; Simmons, 920 S.W.2d at 447; Rogers, 889 S.W.2d at 472. If the court decides that the statement is substantially true, then it may end its inquiry and determine substantial truth as a matter of law. McIlvain, 794 S.W.2d at 16; Evans, 986 S.W.2d at 76; Swate, 975 S.W.2d at 75; Norris, 949 S.W.2d at 426; Simmons, 920 S.W.2d at 447; Lewis v. A.H. Belo Corp., 818 S.W.2d 856, 857, 19 Media L. Rep. 1566 (Tex. App.–Fort Worth 1991, writ denied).

The Beaumont Court of Appeals held that the omission of a true statement from a report did not render defamatory an otherwise true statement actually contained in the report that represented the gist of the communication. In Louis v. Mobil Chemical Co., 254 S.W.3d 602 (Tex. App.—Beaumont 2008, pet. denied), a former employee sued Mobil Chemical Company and two supervisors for, among other things, defamation based on a report by an investigator on the audit staff for ExxonMobil Corporation. The investigation at issue was undertaken to determine whether Plaintiff Louis had falsified preventive maintenance records. Id. at 610. The resulting report concluded that Louis had falsified records and it was Louis's idea and decision to do so. Id. Although Louis admitted to falsifying the records, he contended that the investigation report made him appear to be more culpable by stating that was his idea, when in reality a supervisor had pressured Louis to complete the records the way that he did. Id. at 610-11. The Court of Appeals rejected this argument, holding that the facts left out of the report about being pressured related to the supervisor's culpability and did not diminish Louis's personal responsibility to accurately record the work he performed. Id. at 611. Thus, the allegedly false fact concerning whose idea it was did not render an otherwise true statement defamatory. Id.

4. **Defamatory Statement of Fact.** "A statement is defamatory if the words tend to injure a person's reputation, exposing the person to public hatred, contempt, ridicule, or financial injury." Campbell v. Salazar, 960 S.W.2d 719, 726 (Tex. App.–El Paso 1997, n.w.h.) (citing Tex. Civ. Prac. & Rem. Code Ann.§ 73.001 (Vernon 1997); Duran, 921 S.W.2d at 792; Einhorn v. LaChance, 823 S.W.2d 405, 410-11 (Tex. App.–Houston [1st Dist.] 1992, writ dism'd w.o.j.), cert. denied, 517 U.S. 1135 (1996); see also I.B.1., supra (statutory definition). Whether or not a statement is capable of a defamatory meaning is initially a question of law for the court to decide. Dolcefino, 19 S.W.3d at 917; Carr, 776 S.W.2d at

569; Musser v. Smith Protective Servs., Inc., 723 S.W.2d 653, 654-55 (Tex. 1987); Turner, 987 S.W.2d at 109 (citing Musser, 723 S.W.2d at 654-55); Garcia v. Burris, 961 S.W.2d 603, 605 (Tex. App.–San Antonio 1997, pet. denied) (citing Carr, 776 S.W.2d at 569); Campbell, 960 S.W.2d at 725; Duran, 921 S.W.2d at 792. However, this determination becomes a question of fact where the court determines that the language is ambiguous or of doubtful meaning. Raymer v. Doubleday & Co., 615 F.2d 241, 246, 6 Media L. Rep. 1245 (5th Cir. 1980); Smith v. McMullen, 589 F. Supp. 642, 644 (S.D. Tex. 1984); Norris, 949 S.W.2d at 426; Campbell, 960 S.W.2d at 725; Einhorn, 823 S.W.2d at 411. The question of whether or not a statement is defamatory "should not be submitted to the jury unless the court determines that the language is ambiguous or of doubtful import." Garcia, 961 S.W.2d at 605 (citing Musser, 723 S.W.2d at 655); Barrett, 958 S.W.2d at 222 (citing Musser, 723 S.W.2d at 655); see also Ortiz v. San Antonio City Employees Federal Credit Union, 974 S.W.2d 833, 836 (Tex. App.–San Antonio 1998, no pet.).

In making its determination as to whether a statement is defamatory, the court considers the statement "as a whole in light of surrounding circumstances based upon how a person of ordinary intelligence would perceive the entire statement." Dolcefino, 19 S.W.3d at 917; Cecil v. Frost, 14 S.W.3d 414, 417 (Tex. App.–Houston [14th Dist.] 2000, no pet.); Musser v. Smith Protective Servs., Inc., 723 S.W.2d 653, 655 (Tex. 1987); Turner, 987 S.W.2d at 109; Campbell v. Salazar, 960 S.W.2d 719, 725 (Tex. App.–El Paso 1997, n.w.h.); Garcia v. Burris, 961 S.W.2d 603, 605 (Tex. App.–San Antonio 1997, pet. denied); therefore, "[t]he opinion of the parties has no bearing on whether the complained of words are actually defamatory." Schauer v. Memorial Care Sys., 856 S.W.2d 437, 446 (Tex. App.–Houston [1st Dist.] 1993, no writ); Bradbury v. Scott, 788 S.W.2d 31, 37-38 (Tex. App.–Houston [1st Dist.] 1989, writ denied). "A statement may be false, abusive, unpleasant and objectionable to the plaintiff without being defamatory." Free v. American Home Assur. Co., 902 S.W.2d 51, 54 (Tex. App.–Houston [1st Dist.] 1995, no writ); Schauer, 856 S.W.2d at 446; Rawlins v. McKee, 327 S.W.2d 633, 635 (Tex. Civ. App.–Texarkana 1959, writ ref'd n.r.e.). For example, in Einhorn v. LaChance, 823 S.W.2d 405, 411 (Tex. App. – Houston [1st Dist.] 1992, writ dism'd w.o.j.), cert. denied, 517 U.S. 1135 (1996), the court found that accusing employees of attempting to form a union was not defamatory, even though there was a strong sentiment against union activity in the given industry, because forming a union is not a crime and is not unethical. Also, in Roberson v. Corporation for Economic Development of Harris County, Inc., 2004 WL 2366937 (Tex. App.–Houston [1st Dist.] 2004, n.p.h.), the Houston First Court of Appeals rejected a defamation claim by a former employee against her former employer because the claim was too vague. The former employee brought claims of wrongful termination, defamation, and intentional infliction of emotional distress. However, the employee could not identify any specific statements made by the employer that were defamatory, but thought that "something is probably out there." Id. at *4. Further, the employee could not prove that any future employers had refused to hire her because she had been terminated from employment. Thus, she failed to show any defamatory statements were made that injured her reputation. Id.

In deciding whether a statement is defamatory, the court will give words their ordinary meaning as read and construed by persons of ordinary intelligence. Columbia Valley Regional Med. Ctr. v. Bannert, 112 S.W.3d 193. 199 (Tex. App.–Corpus Christi 2003, no pet.); Taylor v. Houston Chronicle Pub. Co., 473 S.W.2d 550, 554 (Tex. Civ. App.–Houston [1st Dist.] 1971, writ ref'd n.r.e.); see also Musser, 723 S.W.2d at 655; Turner, 987 S.W.2d at 109; Campbell, 960 S.W.2d at 725; Garcia, 961 S.W.2d at 605. Furthermore, the court will look at the entire communication and not separate sentences or piecemeal portions. Musser, 723 S.W.2d at 655; Swate v. Schiffers, 975 S.W.2d 70, 75, 26 Media L. Rep. 2258 (Tex. App.–San Antonio, 1998, pet. denied); San Antonio Exp. News v. Dracos, 922 S.W.2d 242, 248 (Tex. App.–San Antonio 1996, no writ); Schauer, 856 S.W.2d at 446. Likewise, statements may not be made defamatory by taking them out of context. Raymer v. Doubleday & Co., 615 F.2d 241, 244-45, 6 Media L. Rep. 1245 (5th Cir. 1980); Schauer, 856 S.W.2d at 446; see Simmons v. Ware, 920 S.W.2d 438, 444 (Tex. App.–Amarillo 1996, no writ).

Texas courts continue to scrutinize complained of statements closely to determine if they are reasonably capable of defamatory meaning. The San Antonio Court of Appeals recently held that a former employer's statement that an employee quit their job is not defamatory. Cram Roofing Co., Inc. v. Parker, 131 S.W.3d 84 (Tex. App.–San Antonio, 2003 no pet.). In Parker, a former general manager for a roofing company brought a libel claim, among other claims, against his former employer, alleging that a statement in a letter by the employer's attorney to prospective customers indicating that the general manager "voluntarily terminated" his employment with the company was libelous. Id. at 87-88. The Court concluded that such a statement was not defamatory as a matter of law because, construed in light of the surrounding circumstances, stating that one has quit his employment does not injure a person's reputation. Id. at 90. In Durckel v. St. Joseph Hospital, 78 S.W.3d 576 (Tex. App.–Houston [14th Dist.] 2002, no pet.), a former employee sued its employer hospital and director of marketing for breach of contract and defamation based on alleged statements implying incompetency and theft by the dismissed employee. The Court held that the plaintiff was not identified by name with respect to the charge of incompetency, and in any event, the statements made were not reasonably capable of a defamatory meaning. Id. at 583-84. With respect to the theft charge, the Court held that the statement at issue only referenced a missing camera that the hospital wanted back, and no charge of theft was made; thus, the statement was not capable of defamatory meaning. In Columbia Valley Regional Med. Ctr. v. Bannert, 112 S.W.3d 193 (Tex. App.–Corpus Christi 2003, no pet.), the complained of statement in a memo by a supervisor contained the comment that "the apparent lack of discipline in her [plaintiff's] department is an affront to the professionalism I expect in any department under me." Id. at 199. The Court held that this statement was only an opinion, and in any event, an ordinary reader would not reasonably understand the statement to have a defamatory meaning. Id.

In Marx v. Electronic Data Systems Corp., 2009 WL 1875505 (Tex. App.—Amarillo, June 30, 2009, n.p.h.), a former employee sued EDS for wrongful termination and slander after his resignation based on the allegation that he was directed to engage in fraudulent overbilling and co-workers made false and defamatory statements about him before and after his resignation. The majority of defamatory statements included that the plaintiff was a "sneaky snake," a "hunt and peck" typist and "slow pecker," that he needed to go home and take medication "for your problems," and a statement to the plaintiff that he should wash out a co-worker's coffee mug "before you get laid off." Id. at *8. The appeals court affirmed summary judgment in favor of EDS, holding that the statements at issue were not defamatory as a matter of law. Id. at *9. The Court pointed out that the plaintiff conceded in his deposition that each comment could be considered jokes or "kidding." Id.

In Gumpert v. ABF Freight System, Inc., 2009 WL 1395906 (Tex. App.—Dallas, May 20, 2009, n.p.h.), two male employees sued their employer for alleged sex discrimination and libel, among other claims, based on offensive business cards and flyers posted throughout the workplace beginning in 1997. The cards and flyers included references to fictional occurrences, exaggerations of work-related events, and homosexual conduct by employees, including the plaintiffs, and were deemed by the court to be "rude and offensive" and "perverted and mean-spirited." Id. at *5. However, the appeals court noted that the comments were pervasive and directed at a broad range of employees over a number of years. Id. at 7-8. The appellate court affirmed summary judgment in favor of the employer, holding that while the postings at issue were "vulgar and puerile," they were not defamatory because none of the publications could be understood as conveying actual facts about the plaintiffs and, instead, were "clearly beyond reality" and described "ridiculous events" of an exaggerated nature and, thus, were "obviously satirical." Id.

The defamatory statement made about the plaintiff in a libel action must be a false statement of fact rather than a pure comment or opinion. Gertz v. Robert Welch, Inc., 418 U.S. 323 (1974); Associated Press v. Cook, 17 S.W.3d 447, 454 (Tex. App.–Houston [1st Dist.] 2000, no pet.); Howell v. Hecht, 821 S.W.2d 627, 631 (Tex. App.–Dallas 1991, writ denied); see also Evans v. Dolcefino, 986 S.W.2d 69, 78 (Tex. App.–Houston [1st Dist.] 1999, no pet. h.) (citing Howell, 821 S.W.2d at 631); Brewer v. Capital Cities/ABC, Inc., 986 S.W.2d 636, 643, 27 Media L. Rep. 1235 (Tex. App.–Ft. Worth 1998, no pet.); A.H. Belo Corp. v. Rayzor, 644 S.W.2d 71, 79, 8 Media L. Rep. 2425 (Tex. App.–Fort Worth 1982, writ ref'd n.r.e.). For example, hyperbole is a type of speech that can be protected because it does not impart a false statement of fact. In Yiamouyiannis v. Thompson, 764 S.W.2d 338 (Tex. App.–San Antonio 1988, writ denied), cert denied, 493 U.S. 1021 (1990), the court held that references to an opponent of drinking water fluoridation as a quack, hoke artist, fearmonger, and as lacking solid credentials and expressing incomprehensible mumbo jumbo were "vintage hyperbole" and therefore statements of opinion rather than fact. A claim of defamation based on references to a prospective employer must identify specific statements of fact and not generalized "negative information." Brown v. Swett & Crawford of Texas, Inc., 2005 WL 2234052, *8 (Tex. App.–Houston [1st Dist.] 2005, no pet. h.). Statements that amount to no more than name calling, and do not imply the existence of verifiable facts, are protected as opinion and are not actionable. Id. at *7. Whether a statement is an assertion of fact or opinion is a question of law. Carr v. Brasher, 776 S.W.2d 567, 570, 16 Media L. Rep. 1942 (Tex. 1989); Delta Air Lines, Inc. v. Norris, 949 S.W.2d 422, 426 (Tex. App.–Waco 1997, writ denied); Simmons, 920 S.W.2d at 451 (citing New York Times Co. v. Sullivan, 376 U.S. 254 (1964)); Casso v. Brand, 776 S.W.2d 551, 558, 16 Media L. Rep. 1929 (Tex. 1989)); Schauer, 856 S.W.2d at 447; El Paso Times v. Kerr, 706 S.W.2d 797, 798 (Tex. App.–El Paso 1986, writ ref'd n.r.e.), cert. denied, 480 U.S. 932 (1987).

Texas courts have traditionally rejected the theory of libel by implication, wherein liability can be founded on a statement not published but merely inferred from a published statement. For example, in KTRK Television, Inc. v. Fowkes, 981 S.W.2d 779, 789 (Tex. App.–Houston [1st Dist.] 1998, pet. denied), a court of appeals asserted that under Texas Supreme Court precedent, namely Randall's Food Mkts., Inc. v. Johnson, 891 S.W.2d 640, 646 (Tex. 1995), there is no cause of action for libel by implication, i.e., true or substantially true statements cannot give rise to liability regardless of the unpublished implications that may be inferred from published statements. Similarly, in Evans v. Dolcefino, 986 S.W.2d 69 (Tex. App.–Houston [1st Dist.] 1999, no pet. h.), the First Court of Appeals again held that "[t]he notion that a plaintiff can assert a cause of action for libel by implication, where the facts stated are substantially true, has been rejected by the Texas Supreme Court." Id. at 78.

However, this line of cases rejecting libel by implication claims was called into question by the Texas Supreme Court case of Turner v. KTRK Television, Inc., 38 S.W.3d 103, 29 Media L. Rep. 1673 (Tex. Dec. 31, 2000). The Turner case involved a libel action by 1991 Houston mayoral candidate Sylvester Turner, who lost his run-off election bid against candidate Bob Lanier, against KTRK Television and its investigative reporter, Wayne Dolcefino, based on a broadcast raising questions about Turner's involvement in a multi-million dollar insurance fraud. KTRK defended the broadcasts, in part, on the basis that the statements contained in the broadcast were true or substantially true. Indeed, in the majority opinion, the Texas Supreme Court twice acknowledged that an accurate broadcast would have raised "serious" and "troubling" questions about Turner's associations and yet still would not have been actionable. The Texas Supreme Court also concluded "that most of the broadcast's individual statements are literally true and that most of those not literally true are substantially true." The court held, however, that a publication "can convey a false and defamatory meaning by omitting or juxtaposing facts, even though all of the story's individual statements" are substantially true. The court reasoned that since the substantial truth doctrine allows for defendants to support the truth of a story based on the story's "gist" or "sting," the converse should also apply – that a plaintiff should be able to impose liability based on the story's "gist" or "sting." In this case, the court opined that the gist of the broadcast was that Turner was a knowing participant in a multi-million dollar insurance fraud. While the Court did not label such a cause of action "libel by implication," it nevertheless permitted a plaintiff to sue based on the impression created by the publication "as a whole."

5. **Of and Concerning Plaintiff.** The plaintiff in a libel action "must be the particular person about whom the allegedly defamatory statement [ ][is] made." Dolcefino v. Randolph, 19 S.W.3d 906, 931 (Tex. App.–Houston [14th Dist.] 2000, no pet. h.) (plaintiff not specifically mentioned, and no showing that alleged defamatory statement was "of and concerning" plaintiff); Cox Tex. Newspapers, L.P. v. Penick, 219 S.W.3d 425, 433 (Tex. App.—Austin 2007, pet. denied); Campbell v. Salazar, 960 S.W.2d 719, 726 (Tex. App.–El Paso 1997, n.w.h.); Rosenblatt v. Baer, 383 U.S. 75, 81, 1 Media L. Rep. 1558 (1966) (holding that jury could not find liability without evidence that published statement was "of and concerning" plaintiff); Newspapers, Inc. v. Matthews, 161 Tex. 284, 339 S.W.2d 890, 893 (1960); see also Texas Beef Group v. Winfrey, 11 F. Supp.2d 858, 864, 26 Media L. Rep. 1498 (N.D. Tex. 1998), aff'd, 201 F.3d 650 (5th Cir. 2000); Evans v. Dolcefino, 986 S.W.2d 69, 77 (Tex. App.–Houston [1st Dist.] 1999, no pet.); Galveston County Fair v. Glover, 880 S.W.2d 112, 119 (Tex. App.–Texarkana 1994, writ denied); Baubles & Beads v. Louis Vuitton, S.A., 766 S.W.2d 377, 381 (Tex. App.–Texarkana 1989, no writ). Likewise, at least one person must reasonably understand that the plaintiff is the object of the defamatory statement. Campbell, 960 S.W.2d at 725; Diaz v. Rankin, 777 S.W.2d 496, 499-500, 16 Media L. Rep. 2458 (Tex. App.–Corpus Christi 1989, no writ). However, the plaintiff does not have to be specifically referred to in the defamatory statement. It is enough that those who know and are acquainted with the plaintiff understand that the defamatory statement refers to the plaintiff. Matthews, 339 S.W.2d at 894; Evans, 986 S.W.2d at 78; Campbell, 960 S.W.2d at 725; Simmons, 920 S.W.2d at 451; Glover, 880 S.W.2d at 119; Davis v. Davis, 734 S.W.2d 707, 711 (Tex. App. – Houston [1st Dist.] 1987, writ ref'd n.r.e.).

Where a group is named in a defamatory statement, a readily identifiable member or leader of that group can be libeled if those who know and are acquainted with the plaintiff understand that the libelous statement refers to the plaintiff. Sellards v. Express News Corp., 702 S.W.2d 677 (Tex. App.–San Antonio 1985, writ ref'd n.r.e.); Eskew v. Plantation Foods, Inc., 905 S.W.2d 461, 462 (Tex. App.–Waco 1995, no writ) ("[A] member of a group has no cause of action for a defamatory statement directed to some or less than all of the group when there is nothing to single out the plaintiff."); see also Evans, 986 S.W.2d at 77 (citing Eskew, 905 S.W.2d at 462). Here, a cause of action for defamation exists only if the individual plaintiff is identifiable as an individual by the statement. See Webb v. Sessions, 531 S.W.2d 211, 213 (Tex. Civ. App.–Eastland 1975, no writ).

The First Court of Appeals remanded a libel case for trial, even though the "gist" of the allegedly libelous newspaper article as a whole was not of and concerning the Plaintiff. Klentzman v. Brady, 312 S.W.3d 886 (Tex. App.—Houston [1st Dist.] 2009, no pet).

6. **Publication.** Publication is a "negligent or intentional act that communicates a defamatory matter to a person other than the person defamed." Shearson Lehman Hutton, Inc. v. Tucker, 806 S.W.2d 914, 921-22 (Tex. App.–Corpus Christi 1991, writ dism'd w.o.j.); see KTRK Television v. Felder, 950 S.W.2d 100, 105, 25 Media L. Rep. 2418 (Tex. App.–Houston [14th Dist.] 1997, no writ). A defamatory statement is "published" if it is communicated orally or in writing to a third person who is capable of understanding its defamatory import and is communicated in such a way that the person understands its defamatory import. See Campbell v. Salazar, 960 S.W.2d 719, 726 (Tex. App.–El Paso 1997, n.w.h.); Abbott v. Pollock, 946 S.W.2d 513, 519 (Tex. App.–Austin 1997, writ denied); AccuBanc Mortg. Corp. v. Drummonds, 938 S.W.2d 135, 147 (Tex. App.–Fort Worth 1996, writ denied); Marshall Field Stores, Inc. v. Gardiner, 859 S.W.2d 391, 399 (Tex. App. –Houston [1st Dist.] 1993, writ dism'd w.o.j.); Ramos v. Henry C. Beck Co., 711 S.W.2d 331, 335 (Tex. App.–Dallas 1986, no writ). Usually the plaintiff must show that at least one person did, in fact, understand that the communication was defamatory. Diesel Injection Sales & Servs. v. Renfro, 656 S.W.2d 568, 573 (Tex. App.–Corpus Christi 1983, writ ref'd n.r.e.). There also must be sufficient proof that the defamatory communication came from the defendant, and not from some other source. Gardiner, 859 S.W.2d at 399-400.

Negligent publication occurs where a reasonable person would recognize that his actions create an unreasonable risk that the defamatory matter will be communicated to a third party. Campbell, 960 S.W.2d at 726; First State

Bank v. Ake, 606 S.W.2d 696, 701 (Tex. Civ. App.–Corpus Christi 1980, writ ref'd n.r.e.). The defendant's liability here is the same as it is for an intentional publication. Campbell, 960 S.W.2d at 726; Ake, 606 S.W.2d at 701.

Recent appellate opinions hold that an employee cannot satisfy the publication element of a defamation claim through conclusory affidavit testimony during a summary judgment proceeding. Specifically, in Zepeda v. Industrial Site Services, Inc., 2008 WL 4822205 (Tex. App.—Corpus Christi, Nov. 6, 2008, n.p.h.), the defendant employer ordered a background check on an employee from a third-party vendor that erroneously reflected that the employee had a prior felony drug conviction, which led to the employee's termination. The employee sued the former employer, and others, alleging libel and slander per se based on publication of the background check to other employees at Industrial Site Services. During the summary judgment proceeding, the plaintiff submitted an affidavit to the effect that everyone at the company knew of his supposed felony conviction, and that the only person with reason to know had published the information to others. Id. at *5. The appellate court affirmed the trial court's grant of summary judgment in favor of the employer, holding that the plaintiff's statements concerning publication were speculative and conclusory and, thus, did not constitute competent summary judgment evidence. Id.

Similarly, in Atchison v. Spawmaxwell Co., L.P., 2007 WL 1500328 (Tex. App.—Houston [1st Dist.] 2007, no pet), the Court examined whether the appellant's affidavit testimony to the effect that he had been told that a former employer was making disparaging remarks (accusations of theft) to prospective employers was sufficient to establish publication. The Court held that the statements were entirely conclusory and failed to identify the person with the former employer who made the statements, to whom the statements were made, and the specific statements made. Thus, the publication element had not been satisfied, requiring dismissal of the defamation claim.

a. **Intracorporate Communication**. Statements to a fellow employee are considered to be published. Ramos v. Henry C. Beck Co., 711 S.W.2d 331, 335 (Tex. App.–Dallas 1986, no writ). Communications occurring within a corporation fall within the qualified privilege if the communications relate to a common duty among the author to the recipient. See Willis v. Roche Biomedical Laboratories, Inc., 61 F.3d 313, 316-17 (5th Cir. 1995). See III.D., infra.

b. **Compelled Self-Publication**. The general rule in Texas is that a plaintiff cannot complain of a publication of which he "consented to, authorized, invited, or procured." Lyle v. Waddle, 144 Tex. 90, 188 S.W.2d 770, 772 (Tex. 1945); Saucedo v. Rheem Mfg. Co., 974 S.W.2d 117, 120 (Tex. App.–San Antonio 1998, pet. denied) (citing Smith v. Holley, 827 S.W.2d 433, 436 (Tex. App.–San Antonio 1992, writ denied)); Hooper v. Pitney Bowes, Inc., 895 S.W.2d 773, 778 (Tex. App.–Texarkana 1995, writ denied); Frank B. Hall & Co. v. Buck, 678 S.W.2d 612, 617 (Tex. App.–Houston [14th Dist.]1984, writ ref'd n.r.e.) cert. denied, 105 U.S. 2704 (1985). However, several courts of appeal have recognized a theory referred to as "self-publication" or "self-defamation," whereby an action lies despite the fact that the defamed party is the one who published the defamatory matter. Drummonds, 938 S.W.2d at 135; Dewald v. Home Depot, No. 05-98-00013-CV, 2000 WL 1207124, * 7-10 (Tex. App.–Dallas August 25, 2000, no pet. h.); Chasewood Constr. Co. v. Rico, 696 S.W.2d 439 (Tex. App.–San Antonio 1985, writ ref'd n.r.e.); First State Bank v. Ake, 606 S.W.2d 696, (Tex. Civ. App.–Corpus Christi 1980, writ ref'd n.r.e.); see Purcell v. Seguin State Bank & Trust Co., 999 F.2d 950, 959 (5th Cir. 1993) (noting that Texas courts recognize narrow exception of self-compelled defamation). Nevertheless, one Fifth Circuit case treated the issue of whether self-defamation constitutes a publication as an open question. Duffy v. Leading Edge Prods., Inc., 44 F.3d 308, 312 n.5, 23 Media L. Rep. 1455 (5th Cir. 1995). To date, the Texas Supreme Court has not recognized a cause of action based on self-publication. Patton v. United Parcel Serv., Inc., 910 F. Supp. 1250, 1275 (S.D. Tex. 1995).

The test for self-publication adopted by the Ake and Rico courts is a pure foreseeability test. Here, self publication occurs if the defamed person communicates the defamatory statements to a third party and the surrounding circumstances indicate that the communication was likely. Rico, 696 S.W.2d at 445; Ake, 606 S.W.2d at 701-02. As stated by the Ake court, "[o]ne who communicates defamatory matter directly to the defamed person, who himself communicates it to a third party, has not published the matter to the third person if there are no other circumstances. If the circumstances indicated that communication to a third party is likely, however, a publication may properly be held to have occurred." Ake, 606 S.W.2d at 701 (citing Restatement (Second) of Torts § 577, cmt. m (1977)). In addition to the foreseeability test used by the Ake and Rico courts, several courts have embraced a two part test for a self-defamation claim. This test requires the following: (1) the defamed person must be unaware of the defamatory nature of the matter; and (2) the circumstances must indicate that the communication to the third party would be likely. Estate of Martineau v. ARCO Chemical Co., 203 F.3d 904, 914 (5th Cir. 2000); Drummonds, 938 S.W.2d at 148; Doe v. SmithKline Beecham Corp., 855 S.W.2d 248, 259 (Tex. App.–Austin 1993), aff'd and modified on other grounds, 903 S.W.2d 347 (Tex. 1995). This test follows the language of the Restatement (Second) of Torts § 577, cmt. m (1977).

A Houston appellate court rejected the use of a private investigator by a plaintiff in an attempt to uncover alleged defamatory references made by a former employer to prospective employers In Oliphant v. Richards, 167 S.W.3d 513 (Tex. App.–Houston [14th Dist.] 2005, pet. denied), a former employee brought claims of defamation, negligence and intentional infliction of emotional distress against a former employer and supervisor based on a negative employment reference. After encountering difficulty in securing employment after a termination allegedly based on performance and other issues, "all of which are related to alcohol" according to a former supervisor, the plaintiff hired a private investigator to call the past employer to confirm whether negative references were being made. The investigator was told that Plaintiff had been terminated for "substance abuse problems." The appellate court began its analysis by examining prior consent cases holding that a plaintiff may not recover on a defamation claim based on a publication to which he has consented or which he has authorized, procured, or invited. Id. at 516 (citing Lyle v. Waddle, 188 S.W.2d 770, 772 (Tex. 1945)). "By hiring an investigator to check his references under these circumstances, [plaintiff] invited the defamation, and therefore his claim is barred." Id. Since the underlying defamation claim was barred, so too were the claims for negligence and intentional infliction of emotional distress. Id. at 517-18.

More recently, in a case involving the absolute privilege attaching to judicial or quasi-judicial proceedings, including proceedings before the Texas Workforce Commission ("TWC"), the Corpus Christi Court of Appeals recently held that self-publication to a prospective employer of a TWC determination that an employee had been terminated from previous employment due to "theft" did not waive the former employer's assertion of judicial privilege. Linan v. Strafco, Inc., 2006 WL 1766204 (Tex. App.–Corpus Christi 2006, no pet.). In Linan, the former employee alleged that he was required to publish a TWC record reflecting that he was terminated from his most recent employment due to theft to several prospective employers. Id. at *3. The former employee did so in an attempt to explain the circumstances of being fired, and thus argued that this was a foreseeable self-publication outside the scope of the privilege that should result in waiver of the former employer's privilege to report reasons for termination to the TWC. Id. The Court rejected this reasoning, holding that to extend waiver of the privilege to instances where the allegedly defamed person self-publishes the complained of material outside the judicial context would render the judicial privilege meaningless. Id.

The self-publication cases indicate that libel or slander may arise when a plaintiff feels compelled to explain the reasons for his or her termination to a prospective employer. For an action to lie under a self-publication theory, however, there must be actual publication to support a claim for self-compelled publication. Speculation about what a prospective employer may or may not do once the employee is self-compelled to publish the defamation is insufficient. Estate of Martineau, 203 F.3d at 914 (record that is unclear as to whether employee actually mentioned statements to potential employers will not support self-defamation claim); Reeves v. Western Co. of N. Am., 867 S.W.2d 385, 387 (Tex. App.–San Antonio 1993, writ denied), abrogated on other grounds, Cain v. Hearst Corp. 878 S.W.2d 577, 22 Media L. Rep. 2161 (Tex. 1994).

In a recent case applying the compelled self-publication doctrine, the Fort Worth Court of Appeals analyzed the appellant's claim that he was compelled to repeat his former employer's allegedly defamatory remarks – that he was terminated for falsifying his expense report – to third persons when seeking new employment. The Court rejected appellant's argument, holding that appellant was aware that the allegation that he falsified his expense report, if untrue, was defamatory, thus failing the requirement that the defamed person's communication be made without an awareness of its defamatory nature. Moon v. Star-Telegram Operating, Ltd., 2007 WL 2460256 (Tex. App.—Fort Worth 2007, no pet).

c. **Republication**. The Texas courts have held that "a person may be liable for repeating a slanderous statement that was already made by another; every repetition of a slander is a willful publication, making the person who repeats it subject to liability." Johnson v. Randall's Food Mkts., Inc., 869 S.W.2d 390, 396-97 (Tex. App.–Houston [1st Dist.] 1993), rev'd on other grounds, 891 S.W.2d 640 (Tex. 1995) (citing Patterson & Wallace v. Frazer, 93 S.W. 146, 150 (Tex. Civ. App. 1906), rev'd on other grounds, 100 Tex. 103, 94 S.W. 324 (1906)); McDonald v. Glitsch, Inc., 589 S.W.2d 554, 556 (Tex. Civ. App.–Eastland 1979, writ ref'd n.r.e.) (citing Houston Chronicle Publ'g Co. v. Wegner, 182 S.W. 45 (Tex. Civ. App.–Galveston 1915, writ ref'd)); see Renfro Drug Co. v. Lawson, 138 Tex. 434, 160 S.W.2d 246, 251 (1942). Furthermore, "a person who publishes a defamatory statement made by another becomes responsible for doing so." Johnson, 869 S.W.2d at 397 (citing Patterson, 93 S.W. at 150)).

In Holloway v. Butler, 662 S.W.2d 688, 690, 10 Media L. Rep. 1068 (Tex. App.–Houston [14th Dist.] 1983, writ ref'd n.r.e.), the court adopted the Uniform Single Publication Act. This act provides that a plaintiff cannot have "more than one cause of action for damages for libel or slander or invasion of privacy or any other tort founded upon any single publication ... Recovery in any action shall include all damages for any such tort suffered by the plaintiff in all jurisdictions." Holloway, 662 S.W.2d at 690. However, the court in this case found that the single publication rule does not limit a plaintiff "to a single cause of action in the event the same information appears in separate printings of the same publication or in different publications. The single publication rule applies strictly to multiple copies of a libelous article published as part of a single printing." Holloway, 662 S.W.2d at 692. It should be noted that Holloway involved a libel action brought for statements made in a magazine, and was not an employment law case. Cf. Stephan v. Baylor Medical Center at Garland, 20 S.W.3d 880, 888-90 (Tex. App.–Dallas 2000, no pet. h.) (holding that although the allegedly defamatory information provided by Baylor about Stephan was contained in a single report made available to a wide audience through the National Practitioner Data Bank ("NPDB"), the confidential nature of the dissemination did not create a "mass publication" as contemplated by the single publication rule – since a physician may suffer a new and distinct injury with each republication of an allegedly defamatory report by the NPDB, each transmission of the report is a new publication and a possible separate tort.)

In Stephan v. Baylor Medical Center at Garland, 20 S.W.3d 880, 888-90 (Tex. App.–Dallas 2000, no pet. h.), the Dallas appellate court more recently held that although the allegedly defamatory information provided by a hospital about the plaintiff was contained in a single report made available to a wide audience through the National Practitioner Data Bank ("NPDB"), the confidential nature of the dissemination did not create a "mass publication" as contemplated by the single publication rule – since a physician may suffer a new and distinct injury with each republication of an allegedly defamatory report by the NPDB, each transmission of the report is a new publication and a possible separate tort.

In Freedom Communications, Inc. v. Sotelo, 2006 WL 1644602 (Tex. App. Eastland, no pet. h.), an arrestee brought a libel suit against media companies after television news broadcasts and newspaper articles incorrectly labeled the arrestee as a sex offender. In determining whether the plaintiff had to prove falsity of the underlying assertion that the arrestee was a sex offender, the Court concluded that publications should be compared, not with actual fact, but with the governmental reports that defendants republished. Id. at *3. After comparing the newspaper article and the broadcasts to the news release issued by the police department, the Court found that both the newspaper article and the broadcasts were accurate and complete reports, or a fair abridgement, of the news release issued by the police department. Id.

7. **Statements versus Conduct.** A plaintiff might establish publication through conduct if a defamatory message is communicated to a third party and understood by that third party, even when there is no written or oral statement in words. See Restatement (Second) of Torts § 568, comment d; see also Reicheneder v. Skaggs Drug Center, 421 F.2d 307, 312 (5th Cir. 1970) (having the police take the plaintiff from the defendant's store in view of employees who had been told that a shoplifter had been taken into custody, constituted publication); but see Marshall Field Stores v. Gardiner, 859 S.W.2d 391, 399 (Tex. App.–Houston [1st Dist.] 1993, writ dism'd w.o.j.) (publication by conduct theory failed when store security officer escorted employee accused of stealing money through store). The court in Gardiner did not rule out the possibility that publication by conduct could be established with a broader definition given to the jury. Id. at 399.

8. **Damages.** Actual damages, or general damages, which are recoverable in a libel case include compensation for injuries to reputation or character, mental anguish, and other like wrongs incapable of money valuation. Wenco of El Paso/Las Cruces v. Nazaro, 783 S.W.2d 663, 666-67 (Tex. App.–El Paso 1989, no writ) (citing Ryder Truck Rentals, Inc. v. Latham, 593 S.W.2d 334 (Tex. Civ. App.–El Paso 1980, writ ref'd n.r.e.)); West Tex. Utils. Co. v. Wills, 164 S.W.2d 405, 412 (Tex. Civ. App.–Austin 1942, no writ); see Kelly v. Diocese of Corpus Christi, 832 S.W.2d 88, 94 (Tex. App.–Corpus Christi 1992, writ dism'd w.o.j.). Actual damages may be presumed in libel per se cases. See I.B.8(a) & 8(b), infra. Special damages such as lost income are also recoverable. See Shearson Lehman Hutton, Inc. v. Tucker, 806 S.W.2d 914, 922 (Tex. App.–Corpus Christi 1991, writ dism'd w.o.j.). For instance, where a plaintiff can show that his special damages were caused directly by the publication and circulation of defamatory statements, his special damages may include damages for loss of employment. Houston Belt & Terminal Ry. Co. v. Wherry, 548 S.W.2d 743, 753 (Tex. Civ. App.–Houston 1976, writ ref'd n.r.e.). In addition, special damages may include "loss of time," where that item is synonymous with loss of earnings and the jury is properly instructed as to its meaning. Vista Chevrolet, Inc. v. Baron, 698 S.W.2d 435, 441 (Tex. App.–Corpus Christi 1985, no writ). Furthermore, decreased earning capacity damages may be recoverable as an item of special damages where a jury instruction regarding these damages would not be duplicitous of a jury instruction on loss of earnings. Baron, 698 S.W.2d at 441-42. Exemplary damages are also available if certain requirements are met. See I.B.8(b), infra.

The Fourteenth Court of Appeals in Houston recently vacated a nearly half-million dollar jury verdict in favor of a former employee because there was no adequate segregation of damages among claims for wrongful termination and defamation. In Exxon Mobil Corp. v. Hines, 252 S.W.3d 496 (Tex. App.—Houston [14th Dist.] 2008, pet. denied), the trial court granted summary judgment to the former employer on an age discrimination claim, but allowed the defamation claim concerning internal company publication of alleged violation of a matching college gift program to proceed to trial. The jury found that Exxon had defamed the plaintiffs and awarded damages totaling $467,500. Id. at 498. The Court of Appeals reversed, holding first that the evidence failed to identify any damages apart from those caused by the alleged wrongful termination itself and, thus, was insufficient to sustain an award of economic damages for the alleged excessive internal publication of the reasons for termination. Id. at 503-504. The Court also held that evidence of mental anguish and reputational harm caused by the fact of termination, as opposed to the alleged internal defamatory communications, was insufficient to sustain an award of non-economic damages. Id. at 505-507. Thus, the jury verdict was reversed and judgment rendered that the plaintiffs take nothing.

In Kastner v. Gutter Management, Inc., 2010 WL 3010941 (Tex. App.—Houston [1st Dist.] no pet. h.), the Houston Fourteenth Court of Appeals affirmed summary judgment in favor of an employer, Gutter Management, sued by a former employee, Kastner, for, among other things, allegedly making defamatory statements about the employee in a criminal proceeding and to the Texas Board of Law Examiners while investigating Kastner's fitness for admission to the Texas Bar. The Court of Appeals quickly disposed of the defamation claim based on testimony in a criminal proceeding brought by Kastner for assault against a former principal of Gutter Management – the Court held that the statements were protected by the absolute privilege applicable to judicial proceedings. Id. at *7. With respect to statements allegedly made to the Board of Law Examiners by the principals at Gutter Management (including that Kastner had committed criminal trespass, assault, was terminated for insubordination, and possessed symptoms of bi-polar disorder), the Court concluded that Kastner had produced no evidence raising a genuine issue of fact that the Board had completed its investigation or made a determination as to Kastner's bar admission, or even that the Board considered the alleged defamatory statements during its investigation. Id. at *3. Thus, there was no evidence of causation and damages presented. Id.

a. **Presumed Damages and Libel Per Se**. Some statements are so damaging to the plaintiff's reputation that they are considered defamatory as a matter of law, or defamation "per se." Bayoud v. Sigler, 555 S.W.2d 913, 915 (Tex. Civ. App.–Beaumont 1977, writ dism'd). Where a defamatory statement constitutes defamation "per se," the statutory element of injury to the plaintiff's reputation is presumed. Knox v. Taylor, 992 S.W.2d 40, 50 (Tex. App. – Houston [14th Dist.] 1999, no pet.); Tucker, 806 S.W.2d at 921. Here, the plaintiff is not required to plead or prove special damages. Tucker, 806 S.W.2d at 921. Where a statement is considered libelous "per se," the plaintiff may recover general damages without proof of other injury. Leyendecker & Assocs., Inc. v. Wechter, 683 S.W.2d 369, 374 (Tex. 1984) (citing Guisti v. Galveston Tribune, 105 Tex. 497, 150 S.W. 874 (1912); Peshak v. Greer, 13 S.W.3d 421, 427 (Tex. App.–Corpus Christi 2000, no pet. h.). Under the old Texas common law rule, if a defamation rose to the level of libel per se, actual damages were presumed by law. See Wenco, 783 S.W.2d at 666; Bayoud, 555 S.W.2d at 915. General damages for injury to character, reputation, feelings, mental suffering or anguish, or other wrongs not susceptible to monetary valuation are presumed, although the damages awarded may be nominal. Texas Disposal Sys. Landfill, Inc. v. Waste Mgmt. Holdings, Inc., 219 S.W.3d 563, 584 (Tex. App.—Austin 2007, pet. denied).

However, in Gertz v. Robert Welch, Inc., 418 U.S. 323, 349, 1 Media L. Rep. 1633 (1974), the United States Supreme Court held that presumed and punitive damages are unconstitutional where liability is based on a standard of fault less than the "actual malice" standard. In addition, in Dun & Bradstreet, Inc. v. Greenmoss Builders, Inc., 472 U.S. 749, 760-61 (plurality), 763-64 (Burger, C.J., concurring), 773-74 (White, J., concurring), 11 Media L. Rep. 2417 (1985), a plurality of the United States Supreme Court agreed that proof of "actual malice" is not required to recover presumed or punitive damages under state defamation law in cases involving private plaintiffs and speech on matters of purely private concern. In light of the Supreme Court's decisions in Gertz and Dun & Bradstreet, the Fifth Circuit found that in cases involving private plaintiffs and statements of purely private concern, the plaintiff does not need to show actual malice in order to be entitled to presumed damages and punitive damages. Snead v. Redland Aggregates Ltd., 998 F.2d 1325, 1333, 21 Media L. Rep. 1865 (5th Cir. 1993). However, in cases involving either public figures (or public officials) or statements regarding matters of public concern, the plaintiff must show actual malice in order to be entitled to presumed and punitive damages. See Snead, 998 F.2d at 1333. Actual damages which the law presumes include injury to character or reputation, humiliation, mental anguish, and other wrongs and injuries incapable of money valuation. Wenco, 783 S.W.2d at 666-67; Wills, 164 S.W.2d at 412.

It is important to note that while pleading libel per se eliminates the requirement of pleading or proving special damages, it does not shift the burden for proving the falsity of the allegedly defamatory statements. Swate v. Schiffers, 975 S.W.2d 70, 74, 26 Media L. Rep. 2258 (Tex. App. – San Antonio 1998, pet. denied) (citing Leyendecker, 683 S.W.2d at 374).

The types of statements that constitute defamation "per se" under Texas law include the following:

(a) a false accusation which charges a person with the commission of a crime; Matta v. May, 118 F.3d 410, 414, 25 Media L. Rep. 2398 (5th Cir. 1997); Leyendeckfer, 683 S.W.2d at 374 (citing Christy v. Stauffer Publications, Inc., 437 S.W.2d 814 (Tex. 1969)); Smith v. McMullen, 589 F. Supp. 642, 644, 10 Media L. Rep. 2250 (S.D. Tex. 1984) (citing Raymer v. Doubleday & Co., 615 F.2d 241, 246, 6 Media L. Rep. 1245 (5th Cir. 1980)); GMC Enterprises, Inc. v. Sunwest Bank of El Paso, No. 08-99-00384, 2000 WL 730780, *2 (Tex. App. – El Paso, June 08, 2000, no pet. h.).

(b) a false accusation that a person has committed an act regarded by the public as involving moral turpitude; see Eidenoff v. Andress, 321 S.W.2d 368, 369-70 (Tex. Civ. App. – El Paso 1959, writ ref'd n.r.e.);

(c) a statement that injures a person in his office, business, profession or occupation, including statements attributing financial impropriety or bankruptcy to a person; Wenco, 783 S.W.2d at 665 (citing Tatum v. Liner, 749 S.W.2d 251 (Tex. App. – San Antonio 1988, no writ)); Gulf Constr. Co. v. Mott, 442 S.W.2d 778, 784 (Tex. Civ. App. – Houston [14th Dist.] 1969, no writ); see also Knox v. Taylor, 992 S.W.2d 40, 50 (Tex. App. – Houston [14th Dist.] 1999, no pet.); and

(d) a false statement that a person has a "loathsome disease"; see Scheidler v. Brochstein, 73 S.W.2d 907, 908 (Tex. Civ. App. – Galveston 1934, no writ).

Additionally, statements that accuse someone of sexual harassment are defamatory per se and injury to reputation is presumed. Fox v. Parker, 98 S.W.3d 713, 726 (Tex. App. B Waco 2003, pet. denied). In City of Brownsville v. Pena, 716 S.W.2d 677, 682 (Tex. App. – Corpus Christi 1986, no writ), the court found that false statements about a city employee alleging that he had racist attitudes towards legal Mexican residents working in Texas constituted libel per se.

(1) **Employment-Related Criticism**. Criticisms of an employee can rise to the level of actionable defamation but are generally protected by a qualified privilege when made to a person having an interest in or duty regarding the conduct of employees. See Leatherman v. Rangel, 986 S.W.2d 759, 762 (Tex. App.–Texarkana 1999, pet. denied). For example: comments made during performance review and evaluation of an employee, Schauer v. Memorial Care Systems, 856 S.W.2d 437, 449 (Tex. App. B Houston [1st Dist.] 1993, no writ); Boze v. Branstetter, 912 F.2d 801, 806 (5th Cir. 1990); accusations made during an investigation of employee wrongdoing, including statements made by one employee against another employee, Randall's Food Markets, Inc. v. Johnson, 891 S.W.2d 640, 646 (Tex. 1995); Wal-Mart Stores, Inc. v. Lane, No. 13-98-250-CV, 2000 WL 867594, *5 (Tex. App.–Corpus Christi, June 29, 2000, no pet. h.); Bergman v. Oshman's Sporting Goods, Inc., 594 S.W.2d 814, 816 (Tex. Civ. App.–Tyler 1980, no writ); statements to potential employer of a former employee, including references and reasons for termination, Patrick v. McGowan, 104 S.W.3d 219, 224 (Tex. App.–Texarkana 2003, no pet.); Hardwick v. Houston Lighting & Power Co., 881 S.W.2d 195 (Tex. App.–Corpus Christi 1994, writ dism'd w.o.j.); Hamamcy v. Wyckoff Heights Hosp., 786 S.W.2d 32 (Tex. App.–Fort Worth 1990, writ denied); Duncantell v. Universal Life Ins. Co., 446 S.W.2d 934 (Tex. Civ. App.–Houston [14th Dist.] 1969, writ ref'd n.r.e.). See III., infra.

(2) **Single Instance Rule**. There are no reported cases on this topic.

b. **Punitive Damages**. In order to recover punitive damages in a libel action, a plaintiff must show that the statement was made with malice. Tatum v. Liner, 749 S.W.2d 251, 253 (Tex. App.–San Antonio 1988, no writ). It is important to note that the malice required to support a punitive damage award is different from the "actual malice" fault standard imposed in cases involving public officials, public figures, or statements on matters of public concern. See I.B.2(a) & 2(c), supra. In the context of punitive damages, malice is defined as:

> (1) a specific intent by the defendant to cause substantial injury to the claimant; or
>
> (2) an act or omission: (a) which when viewed objectively from the standpoint of the actor at the time of its occurrence involves an extreme degree of risk, considering the probability and magnitude of the potential harm to others; and (b) of which the actor has actual, subjective awareness of the risk involved, but nevertheless proceeds with conscious indifference to the rights, safety, or welfare of others.

Tex. Civ. Prac. & Rem. Code § 41.001(7) (Vernon 1997). Malice may be inferred where a statement is published with reckless disregard and knowledge of its falsity. Leyendecker & Assocs., Inc. v. Wechter, 667 S.W.2d 822, 828 (Tex. App.–Houston [14th Dist.] 1983), aff'd in part, rev'd in part on other grounds, 683 S.W.2d 369 (Tex. 1984) ****(citing Houston Belt & Terminal Ry. Co. v. Wherry, 548 S.W.2d 743 (Tex. Civ. App.–Houston [1st Dist.] 1976, writ ref'd n.r.e.)). Although some courts have indicated that "actual malice" is the standard required to support a finding of punitive damages, that is a minority view which has been superceded by the exemplary damages statutes for cases accruing on or after September 1, 1995. See Tex. Civ. Prac. & Rem. Code § 41.001(7) & § 41.002(a) (Vernon Supp. 1999); Shearson Lehman Hutton, Inc. v. Tucker, 806 S.W.2d 914, 924 (Tex. App.–Corpus Christi 1991, writ dism'd w.o.j.). Furthermore, the Fifth Circuit has interpreted the Supreme Court's plurality opinion in Dun & Bradstreet, Inc. v. Greenmoss Builders, Inc., 472 U.S. 749,760-61 (plurality), 763-64 (Burger, C.J., concurring), 773-74 (White, J., concurring), 11 Media L. Rep. 2417 (1985), to mean that in cases involving private plaintiffs and statements of purely private concern, the plaintiff does not need to show "actual malice" in order to be entitled to punitive damages. Snead v. Redland Aggregates Ltd., 998 F.2d 1325, 1333, 21 Media L. Rep. 1865 (5th Cir.1993).

Punitive damages are generally not recoverable in a libel action without an award of actual damages. Snead, 998 F.2d at 1334; AccuBanc Mortg. Corp. v. Drummonds, 938 S.W.2d 135, 150 (Tex. App.–Fort Worth 1996, writ denied); Doubleday & Co., Inc. v. Rogers, 674 S.W.2d 751, 754-55, 10 Media L. Rep. 2173 (Tex. 1984). Nevertheless, for libel causes of action accruing on or after September 1, 1995, punitive damages may be awarded, even if only nominal actual damages have been awarded, if the plaintiff establishes by clear and convincing evidence that the harm to the plaintiff resulted from malice as defined in section 41.001(7)(A) of the Texas Civil Practice and Remedies Code. Tex. Civ. Prac. & Rem. Code § 41.004(b) (Vernon Supp. 1999).

II. PRIVILEGES AND DEFENSES

A. Scope of Privileges

1. **Absolute Privilege.** Texas recognizes a number of absolute privileges which protect defendants from defamation claims. A civil action for libel or slander will not lie against an absolutely privileged communication even though the language is false and uttered or published with express malice. South Padre Island v. Jacobs, 736 S.W.2d 134, 143 (Tex. App.–Corpus Christi 1986, writ denied). An absolute privilege applies to statements made between husband and wife and statements made in the context of executive, legislative or judicial proceedings. Zarate v. Cortinas, 553 S.W.2d 652 (Tex. App.–Corpus Christi 1977, no writ). The privilege extends to quasi-judicial proceedings such as those before the Texas Workforce Commission adjudicating claims of unemployment compensation. Wal-Mart Stores, Inc. v. Lane, 31 S.W.3d 282 (Tex. App.–Corpus Christi 2000, pet. denied); Hardwick v. Houston Lighting & Power Co., 881 S.W.2d 195, 198 (Tex. App.–Corpus Christi 1994, writ dism'd w.o.j.). It also extends to reports made to committees such as the Texas State Bar Unauthorized Practice of Law Committee, Crain v. Smith, 22 S.W.3d 58 (Tex. App.–Corpus Christi 2000, no writ), and to the Southwest Airlines Flight Attendants' Board of Adjustment. Soileau v. Southwest Airlines, 1999 WL 1140883 (N.D. Tex. Dec. 13, 1999), aff'd, 232 F.3d 210 (5th Cir. 2000). More broadly, in Dolenz v. Texas State Bd. of Med. Examiners, 981 S.W.2d 487 (Tex. App.–Austin 1998, no pet.), the appellate court held that dissemination of information pertaining to disciplinary information was subject to an absolute privilege because the reporting duty arose by statute.

Any communication made in the due course of a judicial proceeding is absolutely privileged. Id.; see also Schwager v. Telecheck Servs., Inc., 2002 WL 31995012 (Tex. App.–Houston [14th Dist.] 2002, no pet.); Knox v. Taylor, 992 S.W.2d 40, 54 (Tex. App.–Houston [14th Dist.] 1999, no pet.). If the statement bears some relation to proposed or existing litigation, no action will lie to recompense any injury which those statements may cause. See Hill v. Harold Post Pub. Co., 877 S.W.2d 774, 782 (Tex. App.–El Paso 1994), rev'd on other grounds, 891 S.W.2d 638 (Tex. 1994). The immunity is absolute even if the statement is false and uttered or published with express malice. Dallas Independent School District v. Finlan, 27 S.W.3d 220 (Tex. App.–Dallas 2000, pet. denied), cert. denied, 122 S. Ct. 342 (Oct. 9, 2001). This privilege extends to any statement made by the judge, jurors, counsel, parties, or witnesses, and attaches to all aspects of a judicial proceeding, including statements made in open court, pretrial hearings, depositions, affidavits, and in any of the pleadings or other papers filed in the case. See, e.g., Bird v. W.C.W., 868 S.W.2d 767, 771 (Tex. 1994) (affidavits filed in pretrial proceedings are absolutely privileged). Statements made during the course of settlement negotiations are also within the absolute privilege afforded to statements made in the course of judicial proceedings. Bennett v. Computer Associates, Inc., 932 S.W.2d 197, 201 (Tex. App.–Amarillo 1996, writ denied).

In a non-employment case but one of first impression involving the absolute privilege, the Fort Worth Court of Appeals held that statements made to the City Council of Forth Worth by a law firm competing for a legal services contract about a competing law firm were absolutely privileged and could not serve as the basis for a defamation claim. Perdue, Brackett, Flores, Utt & Burns, v. Linbarger, Goggan, Blair, Sampson & Meeks, L.L.P., 2009 WL 1270848 (Tex. App.—Fort Worth, May 7, 2009, n.p.h.). The Court held that the City Council possessed quasi-judicial powers, and since the statements at issue were made during the course of quasi-judicial decision making in awarding the contract, the absolute privilege applied. Id. at *4.

In Schwager v. Telecheck Servs., Inc., 2002 WL 31995012 (Tex. App.–Houston [14th Dist.] 2002, no pet.), the plaintiff alleged that her employer defamed her in a letter accusing plaintiff of theft, fraud, unlawful activity, extortion, and lying. The letter at issue was sent by an attorney for the defendant to the attorney for the plaintiff and stated that plaintiff was being terminated and noted the reasons for doing so. Id. at *6. The defendant asserted an absolute privilege afforded communications made in connection with a judicial proceeding. The Court noted that before the letter was sent, plaintiff had already filed a formal discrimination complaint, which is a prerequisite to a lawsuit for statutory discrimination. Id. The Court concluded: "In light of the increasingly adversarial relationship that had developed between them, their resort to legal counsel, the filing of a formal complaint and ultimately a lawsuit, there can be little doubt that a judicial proceeding was reasonably contemplated at the time the letter was sent, and any such doubt must be resolved in favor of the letter relating to the subsequent proceeding." Id.

In Henderson v. Wellman, 43 S.W.3d 591 (Tex. App.–Houston [1st Dist.] 2001, no pet.), the Houston First District Court of Appeals determined that statements made during an arbitration hearing were absolutely privilege. A former university employee sued a coworker for, among other things, libel and slander, based on alleged sexual harassment incidences that led to the plaintiff's termination. The matter was first handled through arbitration, and the plaintiff alleged that the complained of libel and slander were republished during the arbitration hearing sufficient to satisfy the statute of limitations. Id. at 198. However, the court determined that the arbitration was a quasi-judicial proceeding, and any statements at the hearing were absolutely privileged and could not serve as the basis for claims of libel or slander. Id. at 600.

This privilege also attaches to out-of-court communications if the communication bears some relationship to the proceeding and is in furtherance of the attorney's representation. Finlan, 27 S.W.3d 220. In Finlan, the Dallas Court of Appeals evaluated whether delivering pleadings to the news media and issuance of an out-of-court press release by attorneys were actionable. The Court concluded that mere delivery did not amount to publication, and that issuance of the press release was sufficiently related to the ongoing judicial proceeding to be absolutely privileged. Recently, the Houston Fourteenth Court of Appeals held that the pre-litigation verbal and written communications by an attorney on behalf of his clients (a television station and its reporter) to the opposing party (an elected official) challenging the opposing party's denial of media access to a public building were "statements made in contemplation of litigation" and thus were absolutely privileged. Randolph v. Jackson Walker L.L.P., 29 S.W.3d 271 (Tex. App.–Houston [14th Dist.] 2000, pet. denied).

Reaching a contrary result, the Houston First Court of Appeals rejected a claim of absolute privilege asserted by an attorney arising out of his communications to the supervisor of another attorney. Helfand v. Coane, 12 S.W.3d 152 (Tex. App.–Houston [1st Dist.] 2000, pet. denied). In the Helfand case, the allegation was that a communication by one attorney to his opposing attorney's in-house counsel contact was grounds for defamation. The lawyer sending the communication asserted that it was absolutely privileged because it was made in the course of judicial proceedings, and thus contended that the trial court was justified in freezing discovery. The Helfand court disagreed, holding discovery on this issue should not have been frozen, because the communicator had not established as a matter of law that his communication was absolutely privileged.

The absolute privilege attaches to proceedings before the Texas Workforce Commission ("TWC"), and is not lost or waived by an employer even if the employee publishes the contents of a TWC record to others. In Linan v. Strafco, Inc., 2006 WL 1766204 (Tex. App.–Corpus Christi 2006, no pet.), the Corpus Christi Court of Appeals held that self-publication to a prospective employer of a TWC determination that an employee had been terminated from previous employment due to "theft" did not waive the former employer's assertion of judicial privilege. The former employee alleged that he was required to publish a TWC record reflecting that he was terminated from his most recent employment due to theft to several prospective employers. Id. at *3. The former employee did so in an attempt to explain the circumstances of being fired, and thus argued that this was a foreseeable self-publication outside the scope of the privilege that should result in waiver of the former employer's privilege to report reasons for termination to the TWC. Id. The Court rejected this reasoning, holding that to extend waiver of the privilege to instances where the allegedly defamed person self-publishes the complained of material outside the judicial context would render the judicial privilege meaningless. Id.

Additionally, an absolute privilege attaches to statements made by government employers because the law seeks to "protect[] the public interest by shielding responsible government officials against harassment and inevitable hazards of vindictive or ill founded damage suits brought on account of actions taken in the exercise of their official responsibilities". Id. Absolute privilege may apply "even though at times, it may result in individual citizens suffering pecuniary loss as a result of repressive or malicious actions by government officials." South Padre, 736 S.W.2d at 143.

The Amarillo court of appeals held in 1998 that an absolute privilege applied in the context of a report by one colleague of another colleague's performing questionable medical procedures, and that the physician making the report was, therefore completely immune from defamation liability. See Attaya v. Shoukfeh, 962 S.W.2d 237 (Tex. App.–Amarillo, 1998, pet. denied). In 2000, however, the Dallas Court of Appeals ruled that a hospital was not entitled to absolute immunity from liability for defamation for statements in an adverse action report reported to the Texas Board of Medical Examiners or the National Practitioner Data Bank. Stephan v. Baylor Medical Center at Garland, 20 S.W.3d 880 (Tex.App.–Dallas 2000, no pet.). The Court held that an absolute privilege attaches to a proceeding, not to the parties involved in the communication, citing Gallegos v. Escalon, 993 S.W.2d 422, 424 (Tex. App.—Corpus Christi 1999, no pet.), and that because the communication in this case was not sent as part of a judicial or quasi- judicial proceeding, but rather merely to comply with administrative obligations under federal law, the communication was not immune from attack.

2. **Qualified Privileges.** A qualified privilege extends only to communications (1) made in good faith, (2) upon a subject in which the speaker or author has an interest or a duty, (3) to another having a corresponding interest or duty, and (4) made in a lawful manner for a lawful purpose. See also Schauer v. Memorial Care Sys., 856 S.W.2d 437, 449 (Tex. App.–Houston [1st Dist.] 1993, no writ) (accusations or comments concerning an employee made to persons conducting a performance review of the employee were subject to a qualified privilege). The law presumes good faith and lack of malice where the statement is qualifiedly privileged. Marathon Oil Co. v. Salazar, 682 S.W.2d 624, 630 (Tex. App. – Houston [1st Dist.] 1984, writ ref'd n.r.e.).

Communications about an employee by his employer are qualifiedly privileged so long as they are made only to others with a similar interest with the employee. Randall's Food Markets, 891 S.W.2d at 646; Childers, 2005 WL 774512, *3; Saudi v. Brieven, 2004 WL 2415659, *6 (Tex. App.–Houston [1st Dist.] 2004, n.p.h.); Leatherman v. Rangel, 986 S.W.2d 759, 762 (Tex. App.–Texarkana 1999, pet. denied); see also Reeves v. Western Co. of North Am., 867 S.W.2d

385 (Tex. App.–San Antonio 1993, no writ) (a statement by a prospective employer to the wife of a job applicant that the job applicant had failed a drug test was entitled to a qualified privilege as the wife was within the interest group), abrogated on other grounds, Cain v. Hearst Corp. 878 S.W.2d 577, 22 Media L. Rep. 2161 (Tex. 1994).

Additionally, communications among employees in certain circumstances may be subject to a qualified privilege. Martin v. Southwestern Elec. Power Co., 860 S.W.2d 197 (Tex. App.–Texarkana 1993, writ denied)(statements in a letter from the employer's president to supervisors reporting the poor work habits of an employee were held to be qualifiedly privileged because the comments, even if defamatory, were made to persons who had specific duties to supervise the employees in their work and safety practices); Wilson v. UT Health Center, 973 F.2d 1263 (5th Cir. 1992) (jury was entitled to find that allegedly libelous statement was fabricated, and therefore malicious); Schauer v. Memorial Care Sys., 856 S.W.2d 437, 449 (Tex. App.–Houston [1st Dist.] 1993, no writ); Knox, 992 S.W.2d at 55; see also Leatherman, 986 S.W.2d at 763 ("Where the facts are undisputed and the statements are not ambiguous, the question of privilege is one of law for the court."); Ramos v. Henry C. Beck Co., 711 S.W.2d 331, 335 (Tex. App.–Dallas 1986, no writ) (an accusation by the employer to the employee's foreman that the employee had allegedly taken the employer's equipment from the job site was qualifiedly privileged because the foreman and the employer had a common interest in the employee's discharge); Bergman v. Oshman's Sporting Goods, Inc., 594 S.W.2d 814, 816 (Tex. Civ. App.–Tyler 1980, no writ) (accusations or reports of wrongdoing made by an employee against another employee, if made to a person having an interest in or duty regarding the conduct of employees, is qualifiedly privileged).

In an important case involving publication of allegedly defamatory statements beyond the scope of the qualified privilege, the El Paso Court of Appeals held that evidence an officer of a company republished the complained of statement concerning a former employee to the employee's former supervisor several months after the termination supported loss of the privilege. In Richard Rosen, Inc. v. Mendivil, 2005 WL 3118005 (Tex. App.–El Paso 2005, pet. denied), a former employee brought suit against his former employee alleging defamation and intentional infliction of emotional distress based on conduct leading to and after the end of his employment. A jury found in favor of the employee, and the trial court awarded damages on the verdict, except for punitive damages. The Court of Appeals overturned the award on the infliction of distress claim, but sustained the award as to the defamation claim. Id. at *12-13. The Court determined that the former employer had not conclusively established its qualified privilege because the false statement that the employee had been fired was repeated by an officer of the company to the employer's former supervisor "several months" after employment had ended. Id. at *12. The Court found that that there was no business reason for the communication, and the former supervisor did not have an interest or duty with regard to the information at that point in time. Id.

Ramos v. Henry C. Beck Co., 711 S.W.2d 331, 335 (Tex. App.–Dallas 1986, no writ) (an accusation by the employer to the employee's foreman that the employee had allegedly taken the employer's equipment from the job site was qualifiedly privileged because the foreman and the employer had a common interest in the employee's discharge); Bergman v. Oshman's Sporting Goods, Inc., 594 S.W.2d 814, 816 (Tex. Civ. App.–Tyler 1980, no writ) (accusations or reports of wrongdoing made by an employee against another employee, if made to a person having an interest in or duty regarding the conduct of employees, is qualifiedly privileged).

In 2002, the Texas Supreme Court reversed an appellate court that upheld a jury verdict in a case involving the qualified privilege attached to communications occurring during company investigations. In Minyard Food Stores, Inc. v. Goodman, 80 S.W.3d 573 (Tex. 2002), the Texas Supreme Court reversed the Fort Worth Court of Appeals, which had upheld a jury verdict that a manager had acted within the course and scope of employment when making statements about an employee during a misconduct investigation. The statements at issue were not shown to have been made "in furtherance of the employer's business, and for the accomplishment of the objective for which the employee was employed." Id. at 578. The Court criticized the appellate court's analysis of the employee's "general authority" as a store manager, as opposed to an analysis of whether the defamatory remarks were in furtherance of the employer's business. While the evidence showed that employees must participate in workplace investigations, these policies did not demonstrate that the defamation at issue would further the employer's business. Id. at 578-79. The Court in Davila v. Pay & Save Corp., 2003 WL 22413632, *1 (Tex. App. –El Paso 2003, n.p.h.) recently held that to establish that an employee is acting within the scope of employment, the plaintiff must put forth evidence that "the employee's statements were made in furtherance of the employer's business, and for the accomplishment of the objective for which the employee was employed." Id.

The San Antonio Court of Appeals reiterated that reports and information obtained during an investigation of employee wrongdoing, and then published in connection with the investigation, are privileged. In Gonzales v. Levy Strauss & Co., 70 S.W.3d 278 (Tex. App.–San Antonio 2002, no pet.), former employees brought suit against their employer and supervisor for defamation due to statements made during an investigation leading to their termination for violating company rules by disclosing information concerning another employee. The evidence demonstrated that the supervisor relied on reports and information furnished by other employees in the line of duty, and as such, there was no evidence of actual malice to overcome the qualified privilege that attached. Id. at 382-83. Moreover, "minor inconsistencies" as to the reasons for their termination do not establish knowledge of any false statements. Id. at 383.

In Bozeman v. Watson Wyatt & Co., 2003 WL 22938953 (N.D. Tex. 2003), a federal district court held that statements between co-workers and supervisors of the plaintiff, which constituted an evaluation of plaintiff's performance on a project, were privileged. Id. at *4. The Court noted that these individuals had an interest in the plaintiff's performance, and to hold otherwise would undermine the central policy of the privilege, which "recognizes the need for free communication of information to protect business and personal interests." Id.

Texas courts recognize that the qualified privilege can protect statements by former employers to prospective employers in response to employment reference requests. See, e.g., Patrick v. McGowan, 104 S.W.3d 219, 224 (Tex. App.–Texarkana 2003, no pet.); Free v. American Home Assur. Co., 902 S.W.2d 51, 55-56 (Tex. App.–Houston [1st Dist.] 1995, no writ); Pioneer Concrete of Texas, Inc. v. Allen, 858 S.W.2d 47 (Tex. App.–Houston [14th Dist.] 1993, writ denied); Smith v. Holley, 827 S.W.2d 433, 436 (Tex. App.–San Antonio 1992, writ denied). An employer has a qualified privilege to investigate allegations concerning employee wrongdoing, and therefore, communications made during such an investigation are privileged. Wal-Mart Stores, Inc. v. Lane, 31 S.W.3d 282 (Tex. App.–Corpus Christi 2000, pet. denied).

The qualified privilege is not lost so long as the speaker believes in the truth of the communication. Id. Once the court finds that the communication is subject to a qualified privilege, the plaintiff can overcome the privilege only by showing that the statement was made with actual malice. Randall's Food Markets, Inc., 891 S.W.2d at 646; Saudi v. Brieven, 2004 WL 2415659, *7 (Tex. App.–Houston [1st Dist.] 2004, n.p.h.); Rodriguez v. Wal-Mart Stores, Inc., 52 S.W.3d 814, 822 (Tex. App.–San Antonio 2001, no pet. h.); Leatherman v. Rangel, 986 S.W.2d 759, 762 (Tex. App.–Texarkana 1999, pet. denied). (For a more detailed discussion of "actual malice" in defamation suits, see I.B.2.c., supra.) The plaintiff must show actual malice even if the communication is defamatory per se. Marathon Oil Co. v. Salazar, 682 S.W.2d 624, 630 (Tex. App.–Houston [1st Dist.] 1984, writ ref'd n.r.e.). Actual malice in the defamation context does not include ill will, spite, or evil motive, but rather requires "sufficient evidence to permit the conclusion that the defendant in fact entertained serious doubts as to the truth of his publication." Hagler v. Proctor & Gamble Mfg. Co., 884 S.W.2d 771, 771-72 (Tex. 1994); Leatherman, 986 S.W.2d at 762. (For a more detailed discussion of "actual malice" in defamation suits, see I.B.2.c., supra.) In Hagler, a forty year employee was terminated for allegedly stealing a telephone. After the defendant posted a notice of the reason for the termination, the employee sued. The Texas Supreme Court found that, even though the court of appeals misconstrued the test for actual malice, there was not sufficient evidence to conclude that the defendant posted the notice with serious doubts as to the truth of the statement. Id.; see also Wilson v. UT Health Center, 973 F.2d 1263 (5th Cir. 1992) (jury was entitled to find that allegedly libelous statement was fabricated, and therefore malicious); Ramos v. Henry C. Beck Co., 711 S.W.2d 331, 335 (Tex. App.–Dallas 1986, no writ) (defendant failed to show absence of malice in communicating allegations of theft).

In Crouch v. Trinque, 2008 WL 2764594 (Tex. App.—Eastland 2008, n.p.h.), a former university employee sued a university vice-president and former supervisor for, among other things, defamation. Plaintiff Crouch was terminated from her job as the annual giving officer at Tarleton State University ostensibly for failure to perform her job adequately, failure to follow appropriate guidelines and office policy, and insubordination. Id. at *2-3. The trial court granted summary judgment in favor of the defendants. On appeal, Crouch argued that several facts defeated summary judgment, including false accusations concerning job performance, alleged threats and intimidation of her supervisor that did not occur, verbal abuse by her supervisor, and repeated instances in which the defendants' summary judgment affidavits were rebutted. For example, the supervisor attempted to justify her fear of Crouch by alleging that Crouch had previously assaulted someone and had been arrested for the crime when, in fact, Crouch had not been arrested for the crime but was, instead, the victim. Id. at *3. The Court of Appeals reversed in part, holding that there were issues of fact that precluded summary judgment on the defamation claim because the supervisor failed to conclusively establish an absence of malice as part of her conditional privilege defense. In particular, there were disputed facts as to whether the supervisor made statements knowing of their falsity or with reckless disregard as to their truth. Id. at *5.

In Knox v. Taylor, 992 S.W.2d 40, 54 (Tex. App.–Houston [14th Dist.] 1999, no pet.), the court of appeals affirmed a jury verdict awarding damages to a managing general agent for an indemnity company's contract surety against a competing contract surety for libel and tortious interference with contract based on a memorandum written by the competitor concerning Plaintiff. The court noted that a conditional or qualified privilege applies to the giving of information to persons interested in the trade and commercial standing of another at the time the information is given. The Court concluded, however, that when the competitor wrote the memorandum about the agent, any qualified privilege that may have attached to the memorandum was defeated by evidence of actual malice, based on the "the damaging nature of the statements to [Plaintiff's] professional reputation, the context in which they were made, [Defendant's] lack of personal verification, and the statements falsity." Id. at 56. In Saucedo v. Rheem Mfg. Co., 974 S.W.2d 117, 120 (Tex. App.–San Antonio 1998, pet. denied), a former employee brought a defamation claim, among others, against his employer and supervisor based on his termination. The employee claimed that the employer told other employees that they could not give any information regarding Plaintiff if called by prospective employees, which Plaintiff contended lead the listener to believe there was adverse information concerning the Plaintiff.. The Court held that the Plaintiff had no claim for defamation because there was no publication. Id. at 120-21. In Grant v. Stop-N-Go Market of Texas, Inc., 994 S.W.2d 867, 874 (Tex. App.–Houston [1st Dist.] 1999, no pet.), the Court held that an employer lost any qualified privilege that may attach to a communication regarding possible shoplifting when the employer accused the person of shoplifting in front of members of the public Id. at 874 ("That [Plaintiff] was publicly accused (instead of privately questioned) is sufficient to prevent Stop-N-Go from invoking the qualified privilege.").

A recent case addressed the application of a qualified privilege to an employer's statements to law enforcement personnel concerning an employee's misconduct. In Rodriguez v. Wal-Mart Stores, Inc., 52 S.W.3d 814 (Tex. App.–San Antonio 2001, no pet. h.), a former Wal-Mart employee, who had been arrested after a check was written on an employer's account was returned for insufficient funds, sued the store that received the check for several claims, including libel. The court determined that Wal-Mart's statements to the district attorney regarding the NSF check were qualifiedly privileged. Id. at 822. The Wal-Mart employees that talked to the district attorney testified in their depositions that they did not know the plaintiff, and they turned the check over for collection in accordance with Wal-Mart's policy. Id. Although there was evidence that Wal-Mart was aware of a potential for misidentification, the plaintiff was unable to present evidence that a Wal-Mart employee knew that plaintiff did not sign the check, or that a Wal-Mart employee entertained serious doubts as to the information provided to the district attorney's office. Id.

Also, in Borninksi v. Williamson, 2003 WL 22952571 (N.D. Tex. 2003), a federal court held that in the absence of a showing of malice, "an employer's posting photos or other information necessary to keep a former employee from entering a secure facility would not constitute defamation." Id. at *6. The Court also addressed whether the employer's letter to the FBI noting Plaintiff's involvement in $25,000 in missing funds from a credit union and other matters related to the plaintiff's employment was protected by privilege. The Court noted that under our criminal justice system, an employer must have the ability to communicate to peace officers the alleged wrongful acts of others without fear of civil action for honest mistakes. Id. at *7.

In Spring v. Walthall, Sachse & Pipes, Inc., 2010 WL 2102988 (Tex. App.—San Antonio, no pet. h.), the San Antonio Court of Appeals reversed and remanded in part a summary judgment entered against a former employee, Spring, who had counterclaimed in a non-compete suit brought by a former employer, Walthall, Sachse & Pipes, that the company had, among other things, defamed her. The former employer lost at trial on affirmative claims related to breach of a non-compete agreement and theft of trade secrets, and Spring appealed the adverse summary judgment ruling that denied recovery for defamation. Id. at *2. The defamation claim related to another employee of Walthall, Sachse & Pipes who allegedly told Spring's new employer that Spring had stolen and destroyed documents and computer files. Id. The former employer argued on appeal that the statements at issue were made in the course of an internal investigation, but never presented evidence in support of this argument. Id. Nor did the former employer ever argue, at trial or on appeal, that the alleged statements were published without malice. Id. Thus, the trial court erred in granting summary judgment in favor of the former employer. Id. at *3.

a. **Common Interest**. Communications about an employee by his employer are qualifiedly privileged so long as they are made only to others with a similar interest with the employee. Randall's Food Mkts., 891 S.W.2d at 646; Knox v. Taylor, 992 S.W.2d 40, 54 (Tex. App.–Houston [14th Dist.] 1999, no pet.). In Randall's Food Mkts., during an investigation into an employee's alleged theft of store property, discussions among members of store management and with a coworker who had witnessed the incident concerning the allegations were privileged, because the management had an interest or duty in the matter. Id. at 647.

In Minyard Food Stores, Inc. v. Goodman, 80 S.W.3d 573 (Tex. 2002), the Texas Supreme Court reversed the Fort Worth Court of Appeals, which had upheld a jury verdict that a manager had acted within the course and scope of employment when making statements about an employee during a misconduct investigation. The statements at issue were not shown to have been made "in furtherance of the employer's business, and for the accomplishment of the objective for which the employee was employed." Id. at 578. The Court criticized the appellate court's analysis of the employee's "general authority" as a store manager, as opposed to an analysis of whether the defamatory remarks were in furtherance of the employer's business. While the evidence showed that employees must participate in workplace investigations, these policies did not demonstrate that the defamation at issue would further the employer's business. Id. at 578-79.

More broadly, a qualified privilege applies "to the giving of information to persons interested in the trade and commercial standing of another at the time the information is given . . . ." Knox, 999 S.W.2d at 55. "The privilege applies as long as the communication passes only to persons having an interest or duty in the matter to which the communications relate." Grant v. Stop-N-Go Market of Texas, Inc., 994 S.W.2d 867, 874 (Tex. App.–Houston [1st Dist.] 1999, no pet.). Therefore, an employer that accuses a person of shoplifting in front of members of the public loses the qualified privilege with respect to that communication. Id. at 874.

In an important case concerning complaints made against co-workers, the Court of Appeals in Roberts v. Davis, 160 S.W.3d 256 (Tex. App.–Texarkana 2005, pet. denied) focused on whether the complaints alleged violations of law. In Roberts, a CAT-scan technician brought a libel suit against two radiologists after complaints were made to their employer (a medical center) about the plaintiff's performance, work habits, and attitude in two letters to the director of radiology at the medical center. One letter presented a critique of the plaintiff's job performance, accusing her of deliberate obstruction and deteriorating behavior in her work and relationships with other employees. Id. at 261. The court held that this letter was not defamatory because it did not accuse the plaintiff of a crime or question her honesty, integrity, or virtue, and all of the criticism related to her work. Id. The second letter, however, was different. It accused the plaintiff of violations of state and federal law, repetitious and malicious illegal malpractice, manufacture of false reasons for violating orders, and illegally practicing medicine. Id. at 262. The court held that a fact issue existed as to whether the second letter was false and defamatory. With respect to the qualified privilege defense, the court held that the medical center conclusively established each element of the defense except one – lack of malice. Since the plaintiff controverted the employer's conclusory assertion of lack of malice, and the statements were such that malice could be inferred, the court held that a fact issue existed warranting a trial. Id. at 263.

In Austin v. Inet Technologies, Inc., 118 S.W.3d 491 (Tex. App.–Dallas 2003, n.p.h.), the Dallas Court of Appeals broadly construed the qualified privilege by holding that a statement made by a supervisor to a co-worker and friend of the plaintiff, who had already been fired, was protected by the privilege. The Court noted that the complained of statement was made to a friend of the plaintiff only after the friend asked the supervisor for the reason that the plaintiff had been fired. Id. at 498. The Court concluded that the plaintiff's friend had an interest or duty in the matter related to plaintiff's dismissal for insubordination. Id.

In Gonzalez v. Methodist Charlton Medical Center, 2011 WL 6091255 (Tex. App.—Waco Dec. 7, 2011, no pet.), the Waco Court of Appeals affirmed a district court summary judgment ruling that applied the common interest qualified privilege to employer communications to a headhunter and co-worker of the plaintiff. The plaintiff, a former hospital employee, contended that she was wrongfully discharged and the hospital libeled and slandered her by statements made on an internet database to a headhunter and, verbally, to a co-worker. Id. at *14. The Court of Appeals disagreed, holding in part that the employer and the head hunter, as well as the co-worker, all shared a common interest in information concerning the reasons for termination of an employee. Id. The interest was not lost by dissemination beyond an audience that shared the interest because the information was placed on a subscriber-only database used by health care providers and otherwise shared only with employees. Id. at *14. Nor was there evidence of actual malice. Id. at *15-16.

A trial court that refuses to submit a jury question on the "common interest" qualified privilege commits reversible error if the privilege was properly raised by the pleadings and evidence. In Thomas-Smith v. Mackin, 2007 WL 2790761 (Tex. App.—Houston [14 Dist.] 2007, no pet.).

b. **Duty**. Communications are also qualifiedly privileged if they are made by an employer or supervisor in the fulfillment of their employment duties, which often overlaps with the common interest privilege. In Baldwin v. University of Texas Medical Branch, 945 F. Supp. 1022 (S.D. Tex. 1996), aff'd, 122 F.3d 1066 (5th Cir. 1997), the plaintiff, a medical resident, sued for failure of the hospital to renew his residency contract based on poor performance evaluations, which he alleged were defamatory. The court concluded that the evaluations were protected by a qualified privilege because the physicians prepared the evaluations as part of their supervisory duties and were directed to the residency program director, who had a duty with regard to a resident's performance. Id. at 1035-36.

More generally, any communication made because it is required by law is subject to at least a qualified privilege. Moore & Associates v. Metropolitan Life Ins., 604 S.W.2d 487, 489-90 (Tex. Civ. App.—Dallas 1980, no writ) (concluding that a letter sent pursuant to the requirements of ERISA was privileged). The Restatement (Second) of Torts applies an absolute privilege to such communications. Restatement (Second) of Torts § 592A. The recent decision of Dolenz v. Texas State Bd. of Med. Examiners, 981 S.W.2d 487 (Tex. App.–Austin 1998, no pet.) suggests that an absolute privilege applies where a duty requiring disclosure of information is imposed by statute. Id. at 489 (Board of Medical Examiners protected by absolute privilege concerning dissemination of report and summary of disciplinary orders because the information was required to be disclosed by statute).

c. **Criticism of Public Employee**. Criticism regarding the official acts or conduct of public officials and candidates for public offices, or their qualifications for office, is privileged and not libelous. Casso v. Brand, 776 S.W.2d 551 (Tex. 1989)(Gonzalez, J. concurring and dissenting) (citing Rawlins v. McKee, 327 S.W.2d 633, 637 (Tex. Civ. App.–Texarkana 1959, writ ref'd n.r.e.)). The fair comment privilege has been codified in part with respect to the press in Section 73.002 of the Texas Civil Practices & Remedies Code. In most instances, because the plaintiff will be a public official, the plaintiff will also have the heavy burden of proving actual malice by clear and convincing evidence. See I.B.2.c., supra.

d. **Limitation on Qualified Privileges**.

(1) **Constitutional or Actual Malice**. Once the court finds that the communication is subject to a qualified privilege, the plaintiff can overcome the privilege only by showing that the statement was made with actual malice. Randall's Food Mkts., Inc. v. Johnson, 891 S.W.2d 640, 646 (Tex. 1995); Childers v. King Ranch, Inc., 2005 WL 774512, *3 (Tex. App. – Corpus Christi 2005, no pet. h.); Henriquez v. Cemex Management, Inc., 2005 WL 497663 (Tex. App. – Houston [1st Dist.] 2005, pet. denied); Saudi v. Brieven, 2004 WL 2415659, *7 (Tex. App.–Houston [1st Dist.] 2004, n.p.h.); Knox v. Taylor, 992 S.W.2d 40, 54 (Tex. App.—Houston [14th Dist.] 1999, no pet.); Leatherman v. Rangel, 986 S.W.2d 759, 762 (Tex. App.—Texarkana 1999, pet. denied). The plaintiff must show actual malice even where the communication is defamatory per se. Marathon Oil Co. v. Salazar, 682 S.W.2d 624, 630 (Tex. App.—Houston [1st Dist.] 1984, writ ref'd n.r.e.). Actual malice in the defamation context does not include ill will, spite, or evil motive, but rather requires "sufficient evidence to permit the conclusion that the defendant in fact entertained serious doubts as to the truth of his publication." Haglar v. Proctor & Gamble Mfg. Co., 884 S.W.2d 771, 771-72 (Tex. 1994). See I.B.2.c., supra. In Haglar, a forty year employee was terminated for allegedly stealing a telephone. After the defendant posted a notice of the reason for the termination, the employee sued. The Texas Supreme Court found that, even though the court of appeals misconstrued the test for actual malice, there was not sufficient evidence to conclude that the defendant posted the notice with serious doubts as to the truth of the statement. Id.

The Texas Supreme Court has noted that since the actual malice inquiry focuses on the defendant's state of mind at the time of publication, direct evidence that the defendant knew the statements to be false will rarely be available to the plaintiff. See Bentley v. Bunton, 94 S.W.3d 561, 597 (Tex. 2002) (noting that plaintiff need not produce "smoking gun" proving knowledge of falsity). Instead, a plaintiff may, and often must, use circumstantial evidence to show that the defendant acted with reckless disregard and "entertained serious doubts as to the truth of his publication." See id. at 591.

In addition, as noted earlier, selectively omitting facts in order to create a false impression may constitute evidence of actual malice. Huckabee, 19 S.W.3d at 425-26; Texas Disposal Sys. Landfill, Inc., 219 S.W.3d at 578.

In Gonzales v. Levy Strauss & Co., 70 S.W.3d 278 (Tex. App.–San Antonio 2002, no pet.), former employees brought suit against their employer and supervisor for defamation due to statements made during an investigation leading to their termination for violating company rules by disclosing information concerning another employee. The evidence demonstrated that the supervisor relied on reports and information furnished by other employees in the line of duty, and as such, there was no evidence of actual malice to overcome the qualified privilege that attached. Id. at 382-83. Moreover, "minor inconsistencies" as to the reasons for their termination do not establish knowledge of any false statements. Id. at 383.

In Crouch v. Trinque, 2008 WL 2764594 (Tex. App.—Eastland 2008, n.p.h.), a former university employee sued a university vice-president and former supervisor for, among other things, defamation. Plaintiff Crouch was terminated from her job as the annual giving officer at Tarleton State University ostensibly for failure to perform her job adequately, failure to follow appropriate guidelines and office policy, and insubordination. Id. at *2-3. The trial court granted summary judgment in favor of the defendants. On appeal, Crouch argued that several facts defeated summary judgment, including false accusations concerning job performance, alleged threats and intimidation of her supervisor that did not occur, verbal abuse by her supervisor, and repeated instances in which the defendants' summary judgment affidavits were rebutted. For example, the supervisor attempted to justify her fear of Crouch by alleging that Crouch had previously assaulted someone and had been arrested for the crime when, in fact, Crouch had not been arrested for the crime but was, instead, the victim. Id. at *3. The Court of Appeals reversed in part, holding that there were issues of fact that precluded summary judgment on the defamation claim because the supervisor failed to conclusively establish an absence of malice as part of her conditional privilege defense. In particular, there were disputed facts as to whether the supervisor made statements knowing of their falsity or with reckless disregard as to their truth. Id. at *5.

In Spring v. Walthall, Sachse & Pipes, Inc., 2010 WL 2102988 (Tex. App.—San Antonio, no pet. h.), the San Antonio Court of Appeals held that a former employer failed to meet its summary judgment burden to support a qualified privilege when there was no evidence presented in support of an internal investigation triggering the privilege. Moreover, the former employer never argued, at trial or on appeal, that the alleged statements were published without malice. Id. at *2. Thus, the trial court erred in granting summary judgment in favor of the former employer. Id. at *3.

(2) **Common Law Malice**. At common law, a qualified privilege could be overcome by a showing of malice, defined as "ill will, bad motive, or such gross indifference to the rights of others as will amount to a willful or wanton act." Buck v. Savage, 323 S.W.2d 363 (Tex. Civ. App.–Houston 1959, writ ref'd n.r.e.). However, Texas now follows the U.S. Supreme Court decisions applying the constitutional actual malice standard set forth in New York Times Co. v. Sullivan, 376 U.S. 254 (1964) to overcome a qualified privilege. Haglar v. Proctor & Gamble Mfg.

Co., 884 S.W.2d 771, 771-72 (Tex. 1994); Saudi v. Brieven, 2004 WL 2415659, *7 (Tex. App.–Houston [1st Dist.] 2004, n.p.h.); Leatherman v. Rangel, 986 S.W.2d 759, 762 (Tex. App.–Texarkana 1999, pet. denied); Hanssen v. Our Redeemer Lutheran Church, 938 S.W.2d 85, 92 (Tex. App.–Dallas 1996, writ denied). See I.B.2.c., supra.

(3) **Other Limitations on Qualified Privileges.**

e. **Question of Fact or Law**. Whether a communication is subject to a qualified privilege is a question of law. Schauer v. Memorial Care Sys., 856 S.W.2d 437, 449 (Tex. App.–Houston [1st Dist.] 1993, no writ); Knox, 992 S.W.2d at 55; see also Leatherman, 986 S.W.2d at 763 ("Where the facts are undisputed and the statements are not ambiguous, the question of privilege is one of law for the court.").

f. **Burden of Proof**. In a defamation case, the qualified privilege operates as an affirmative defense that must be plead and proven. Richard Rosen, Inc. v. Mendivil, 2005 WL 3118005 (Tex. App.–El Paso 2005, pet. denied); Schauer v. Memorial Care Sys., 856 S.W.2d 437, 449 (Tex. App.–Houston [1st Dist.] 1993, no writ).

In Bryant v. Lucent Technologies, Inc., 2005 WL 2155196 (Tex. App.–Waco 2005, no pet. h.), a former at-will employee who allegedly was told to provide sales leads at no cost to certain dealers filed suit against her employer for a variety of claims, including defamation and intentional infliction of emotional distress. The trial court granted the employer a summary judgment on the defamation claim, among others, and a jury rendered a take-nothing verdict on the emotional distress and a breach of contract claim. On appeal, the plaintiff challenged the trial court's summary judgment rulings, including dismissal of the defamation claim based on her employer incorrectly identifying plaintiff as a "Marketing Manager" rather than a "Marketing Director" to third parties. Id. at *4. The employer relied on the qualified privilege defense, thus bearing the burden of conclusively establishing each element of the privilege to prevail at summary judgment. Id. The court held that the employer offered no summary judgment evidence to prove its affirmative defense, but instead erroneously asserted that the plaintiff bore the burden of proving actual malice to defeat the privilege. Id. Thus, the lower court erred in granting summary judgment to the employer.

B. Standard Libel Defenses

1. **Truth.** The truth of the statement in the publication is an absolute defense to a libel action. Reeves v. Western Co. of N. Am., 867 S.W.2d 385, 393 (Tex. App.–San Antonio 1993, no writ), abrogated on other grounds, Cain v. Hearst Corp. 878 S.W.2d 577 (Tex. 1994). For example, a statement by a prospective employer to a job applicant that the job applicant had failed a drug screening test was true and therefore not defamatory. Id. at 388. The court held that so long as the statement was "substantially true," it was not actionable. Id. at 395 (holding that employer's statement that employee's urine test revealed a .4 % rather than the actual .04% alcohol content did not destroy truth defense). A statement by a supervisor or a co-worker that an employee was physically unable to perform all of the functions of his job because of a previous injury is not defamatory where the evidence indicates that such information was substantially true. Garcia v. Allen, 28 S.W.3d 587 (Tex. App.–Corpus Christi 2000, pet. denied).

In employment defamation actions, truth is an affirmative defense which shifts the burden of proof back to the plaintiff. Randall's, 891 S.W.2d at 646.

In Randall's Food Mkts., Inc., an employee was investigated for leaving the store without paying for merchandise. Id. at 640. Throughout the investigation the employer merely communicated that the employee had left the store without paying for a Christmas wreath - a fact which the employee did not dispute. Id. at 646. The employer did not speculate or make accusations regarding the employee's intent. Id. The employee claimed slander because the accusation might infer dishonesty. Id. The court held that truth is a complete defense to defamation. Id.

In determining the truth or falsity of an allegedly defamatory publication, Texas uses the "substantial truth" test. See McIlvain v. Jacobs, 794 S.W.2d 14, 15 (Tex. 1990); Dolcefino v. Randolph, 19 S.W.3d 906, 918 (Tex. App.–Houston [14th Dist.] 2000, pet. denied); Knox v. Taylor, 992 S.W.2d 40, 54 (Tex. App.–Houston [14th Dist.] 1999, no pet.); KTRK Television v. Felder, 950 S.W.2d 100, 105 (Tex. App.–Houston [14th Dist.] 1997, no writ). For a more detailed discussion of the "substantial truth" test, see I.B.3., supra.

In Louis v. Mobil Chemical Co., 254 S.W.3d 602 (Tex. App.—Beaumont 2008, pet. denied), a former employee sued Mobil Chemical Company and two supervisors for, among other things, defamation based on a report by an investigator on the audit staff for ExxonMobil Corporation. The investigation at issue was undertaken to determine whether Plaintiff Louis had falsified preventive maintenance records. Id. at 610. The resulting report concluded that Louis had falsified records and it was Louis's idea and decision to do so. Id. Although Louis admitted to falsifying the records, he contended that the investigation report made him appear to be more culpable by stating that was his idea, when in reality a supervisor had pressured Louis to complete the records the way that he did. Id. at 610-11. The Court of Appeals rejected this argument, holding that the facts left out of the report about being pressured related to the supervisor's culpability and did not diminish Louis's personal responsibility to accurately record the work he performed. Id. at 611. Thus, the allegedly false fact concerning whose idea it was did not render an otherwise true statement defamatory. Id.

2. **Opinion**. A pure expression of opinion is protected free speech and does not constitute defamation. Shearson Lehman Hutton, Inc. v. Tucker, 806 S.W.2d 914 (Tex. App.–Corpus Christi 1991, writ dism'd w.o.j.), the court found that an employer's statement that the plaintiff "was going to lose his stock broker's license, was in big trouble with the Securities & Exchange Commission and would never work again as a stock broker" to be actionable fact statements. Id. at 920. The employer had argued that the statements were predictions regarding future events that could not be proven false and were therefore protected opinion. The court disagreed, citing Milkovich v. Lorain Journal Co., 497 U.S. 1 (1990), as holding that there is no separate constitutional privilege for opinion, and that opinions or ideas may be actionable if they imply false statements of objective fact. The court reasoned that even though the remarks could be characterized as opinions, the statements clearly imputed the existence of undisclosed facts. Id. But see Simmons v. Ware, 920 S.W.2d 438, 449 (Tex. App.–Amarillo 1996, no writ) (whether reporter's stories were "biased" was in the eye of the beholder and incapable of definitive proof one way or the other). See also I.B.4.b., infra.

In Columbia Valley Regional Med. Ctr. v. Bannert, 112 S.W.3d 193 (Tex. App.–Corpus Christi 2003, no pet.), the complained of statement in a memo by a supervisor contained the comment that "the apparent lack of discipline in her [plaintiff's] department is an affront to the professionalism I expect in any department under me." Id. at 199. The Court held that this statement was only an opinion, and in any event, an ordinary reader would not reasonably understand the statement to have a defamatory meaning. Id. Moreover, a claim of defamation based on references to a prospective employer must identify specific statements of fact and not generalized "negative information" that amounts to opinion. Brown v. Swett & Crawford of Texas, Inc., 2005 WL 2234052, *8 (Tex. App.–Houston [1st Dist.] 2005, no pet. h.). For example, statements that amount to no more than name calling, and do not imply the existence of verifiable facts, are protected as opinion and are not actionable. Id. at *7.

The Dallas Court of Appeals has held that use of the word "crazy" to describe an employee was not actionable. In Shaw v. Palmer, 197 S.W.3d 854, 857-58 (Tex. App.–Dallas 2006, no pet. h.), the Dallas Court of Appeals held that use of the word "crazy" does not, in its common usage, convey a verifiable fact, but is by its nature is indefinite and ambiguous. Id. at 857. The statement did not imply an assertion of fact, but rather was used in its popular sense, and as such was an expression of opinion, and thus the trial court erred in concluding that it was actionable slander. Id. at 858.

3. **Consent**. If the plaintiff invites, requests or consents to a statement an action for defamation is barred. Reeves v. Western Co. of N. Am., 867 S.W.2d 385, 394 (Tex. App.–San Antonio 1993, no writ), abrogated on other grounds by Cain v. Hearst Corp. 878 S.W.2d 577, 22 Media L. Rep. 2161 (Tex. 1994); Smith v. Holley, 827 S.W.2d 433, 436 (Tex. App.–San Antonio 1992, writ denied); see also Sedona Contracting, Inc. v. Ford, Powell & Carson, Inc., 995 S.W.2d 192, 198 (Tex. App.–San Antonio 1999, pet. denied) (Plaintiff's participation in construction project bidding process effectively served as consent to the possibility of defamation during the bidding process). The plaintiff's consent to publication gives the employer an absolute privilege to publish the statement even if the statement proves to be defamatory. Smith, 827 S.W.2d at 436. A plaintiff does not consent, however, unless the plaintiff knew or had reason to anticipate that the statement could be defamatory. Ramos v. Henry C. Beck Co., 711 S.W.2d 331, 336 (Tex. App.–Dallas 1986, no writ). Where a consent or authorization form is involved, the terms of the consent must be carefully examined to determine whether the information disclosed is actually encompassed by the authorization. Smith, 827 S.W.2d at 439.

In Oliphant v. Richards, 167 S.W.3d 513 (Tex. App.–Houston [14th Dist.] 2005, pet. denied), a former employee brought a claim of defamation against a former employer based on a negative employment reference. However, the plaintiff had hired a private investigator to call the past employer to confirm whether negative references were being made. The investigator was told that Plaintiff had been terminated for "substance abuse problems." "By hiring an investigator to check his references under these circumstances, [plaintiff] invited the defamation, and therefore his claim is barred." Id.

The San Antonio Court of Appeals has stated clearly that an employee who initiates an investigation, as in cases of requested reinstatement, have consented to communications that occur in connection with the investigation. In Rouch v. Continental Airlines, Inc., 70 S.W.3d 170 (Tex. App.–San Antonio 2001, pet. denied), an employee sued her employer for wrongful termination and defamation. The defendant employer claimed that the employee consented to the alleged defamation by challenging her termination and submitted to an investigation and review. The Court, noting that a party who submits her conduct to investigation consents to certain publications, held that the plaintiff had consented to the results of the investigation being published at a reinstatement hearing. Id. at 173.

The First Court of Appeals in Houston recently held that a defamation claim against a former employer in the context of a termination based upon alleged theft was barred because the uncontroverted summary judgment evidence established that the plaintiff herself published the same statements to co-workers, stating essentially that "they took me back there and they fired me, they said I took $100." Rerich v. Lowe's Home Centers, Inc., 2007 WL 1412881 (Tex. App.—Houston [1st Dist.] 2007, no pet.).

4. **Mitigation**. A libel defendant may give evidence regarding the following matters to determine the extent and source of actual damages and to mitigate exemplary damages: (1) all material facts and circumstances surrounding the claim for damages and defenses to the claim; (2) all facts and circumstances under which the libelous publication was made; and (3) any public apology, correction, or retraction of the libelous matter made and published by the defendant. Tex. Civ. Prac. & Rem. Code § 73.003. Under the first prong, "libel proof" evidence, i.e., the plaintiff's reputation was already damaged prior to the publication, is admissible. McBride v. New Braunfels Herald-Zeitung, 894 S.W.2d 6, 9 (Tex. App.–Austin 1994, writ denied); Finklea v. Jacksonville Daily Progress, 742 S.W.2d 512, 517 (Tex. App.–Tyler 1987, writ dism'd w.o.j.). Under the second prong, a defendant may offer evidence that the source of the information was generally reliable, Shely v. Harney, 163 S.W.2d 839, 840 (Tex. Civ. App.–San Antonio 1942, writ ref'd w.o.m.), or that the plaintiff himself provoked or invited the allegedly defamatory statement, Buck v. Savage, 323 S.W.2d 363, 371-72 (Tex. Civ. App.–Houston 1956, writ ref'd n.r.e.). Finally, evidence that the defendant apologized or published a retraction can be offered to mitigate damages. Express Publ'g Co. v. Gonzalez, 350 S.W.2d 589, 592 (Tex. Civ. App.–Eastland 1961, writ ref'd n.r.e.).

III. RECURRING FACT PATTERNS

A. Statements in Personnel File

In Leatherman v. Rangel, 986 S.W.2d 759 (Tex. App.–Texarkana 1999, pet. denied), the appeals court addressed the plaintiff's claim that it was likely that a copy of her termination letter in her personnel file would be disclosed in the future, thus constituting publication of allegedly defamatory statements. Id. at 763. The Court rejected the notion that there was a cause of action for "anticipatory defamation" where the facts upon which relief was sought had not yet occurred. Id. at 764.

In another reported case involving a personnel file, Ellert v. Lutz, 930 S.W.2d 152 (Tex. App.–Dallas 1996, no writ), a secretary brought an action against her former supervisor based on statements in a memorandum that was placed in the secretary's personnel file. The narrow issue before the court was whether the discovery rule tolling the statute of limitations applied to a libel claim. The evidence indicated that the secretary had access to her personnel file all along, and thus the statements were not inherently undiscoverable. Id. at 156-57.

In Roberts v. Davis, 2007 WL 3194813 (Tex. App.—Texarkana 2007, pet. denied), the Texarkana Court of Appeals affirmed a jury finding that Plaintiff Roberts' libel claim, based on a letter from a doctor to the Roberts' immediate supervisor at a hospital, was barred by the applicable one-year statute of limitations. Roberts argued that the April 9, 2001 letter, which accused Roberts of violations of state and federal law, repetitious and malicious illegal malpractice, manufacture of false reasons for violating orders, and illegally practicing medicine, was concealed from her for over a year after it was communicated to her supervisor. Id. at *2. However, the evidence presented to the jury revealed that the letter was placed in Roberts' personnel file after a June 7, 2001 counseling session during which Roberts was given an opportunity to review the letter. Id. Since Roberts knew of the letter, and based on the statutory right of a public employee to have complete access to his or her personnel file under Texas law, the Court held that there was evidence that Roberts was both aware of the letter's existence and contents, and had continuing access to the letter. Id. Accordingly, since suit was not filed until almost two years after the initial publication, her libel claim was barred by limitations.

In Bell v. Express Energy Services Operating, LP, 2012 WL 2036437 (Tex. App.—Fort Worth June 7, 2012, no pet.), the Fort Worth Court of Appeals affirmed summary judgment in favor of an employer when sued on multiple claims, including defamation, by several employees. When evaluating the claim of a salesman terminated based upon customer complaints, the Court determined that allegedly false statements in a termination letter placed in a personnel file did not give rise to a claim of defamation because there was no publication to any third party. Id. at S*3-4.

B. Performance Evaluations

In Texas, a qualified privilege normally attaches to statements contained in performance evaluations. In Schauer v. Memorial Care Sys., 856 S.W.2d 437 (Tex. App.–Houston [1st Dist.] 1993, no writ), the court upheld summary judgment for the employer for a claim based upon a mediocre employment appraisal. The plaintiff admitted that most of the statements were true and most of the remaining comments were expressions of opinion or incapable of a defamatory meaning. Id. at 447 -48. Moreover, the appraisal was subject to a qualified privilege for accusations or comments about an employee by an employer that are made to a person having an interest or duty in the matter to which the communication relates. Id. at 449. Finally, there was no actual malice shown to overcome the qualified privilege. Id. at 449-50.

The Fifth Circuit also recognizes the qualified privilege rule under Texas law in reference to performance evaluations. In Boze v. Branstetter, 912 F.2d 801, 806 (5th Cir. 1990), the court held that a qualified privilege attaches to discussions regarding an employee's performance evaluation. In Boze, the plaintiff, Boze, was an in-house attorney for Chevron. He resigned after receiving a very critical performance evaluation prepared by Branstetter, his immediate supervisor and Chevron's regional counsel. Branstetter published the written performance evaluation to Chevron's general and associate general counsels. During a meeting to discuss the performance evaluation, Branstetter told Boze in the presence of Chevron's associate general counsel that Boze was "the worst rated lawyer throughout [Branstetter's] tenure with Gulf and . . . the worst rated lawyer in the Chevron USA law department. Boze sued Branstetter and Chevron claiming that he was defamed by the performance evaluation and by Branstetter's comment that he was the worst rated lawyer. The Court held that Branstetter and his bosses in the general counsel's office, had a shared interest in Boze's work performance and the evaluation of his performance. Therefore, all of Branstetter's comments were protected by qualified privilege. Id. at 806.

Recently, in Bozeman v. Watson Wyatt & Co., 2003 WL 22938953 (N.D. Tex. 2003), a federal district court held that statements between co-workers and supervisors of the plaintiff, which constituted an evaluation of plaintiff's performance on a project, were privileged. Id. at *4. The Court noted that these individuals had an interest in the plaintiff's performance, and to hold otherwise would undermine the central policy of the privilege, which "recognizes the need for free communication of information to protect business and personal interests." Id.

Comments regarding a person's job performance are often the subject of defamation claims. For example, in Associated Press v. Cook, 17 S.W.3d 447, 454 (Tex. App.–Houston [1st Dist.] 2000, no pet.), the defendant county sheriff stated that plaintiff, a member of the Texas Rangers, was a "blight on law enforcement." The court held that the statement was a non-actionable opinion, no matter how objectionable, comparing it to the statement at issue in Howell v. Hecht, 821 S.W.2d 627, 631 (Tex. App. B Dallas 1991, writ denied), where a political opponent was described to be "widely considered an embarrassment to the judiciary and Republican party"--a statement that was considered constitutionally protected opinion, not a statement of fact.

C. References

False statements in letters of reference can support a claim for defamation. However, references are usually subject to a qualified privilege that prevents the employee from recovering on a defamation claim unless the employee can show the employer made the statements with actual malice. Patrick v. McGowan, 104 S.W.3d 219, 224 (Tex. App.–Texarkana 2003, no pet.). In Duncantell v. Universal Life Ins. Co., 446 S.W.2d 934 (Tex. Civ. App.–Houston [14th Dist.] 1969, writ ref'd n.r.e.), a statement by a former supervisor to a prospective employer pursuant to a plaintiff-requested inquiry by the prospective employer "not to fool with" the plaintiff because the plaintiff had taken money from the former employer and could not be trusted, related to the work record of the plaintiff and was qualified privileged and therefore created no liability absent malice. Id. at 936-37.

Plaintiffs who complain of bad references to prospective employers must plead and prove specific defamatory statements. A claim of defamation in references to a prospective employer must identify specific statements of fact and not generalized "negative information." Brown v. Swett & Crawford of Texas, Inc., 2005 WL 2234052, *8 (Tex. App.–Houston [1st Dist.] 2005, no pet. h.).

In Oliphant v. Richards, 167 S.W.3d 513 (Tex. App.–Houston [14th Dist.] 2005, pet. denied), a former employee brought claims of defamation, negligence and intentional infliction of emotional distress against a former employer and supervisor based on a negative employment reference. After encountering difficulty in securing employment after a termination allegedly based on performance and other issues, "all of which are related to alcohol" according to a former supervisor, the plaintiff hired a private investigator to call the past employer to confirm whether negative references were being made. The investigator was told that Plaintiff had been terminated for "substance abuse problems." The appellate court began its analysis by examining prior consent cases holding that a plaintiff may not recover on a defamation claim based on a publication to which he has consented or which he has authorized, procured, or invited. Id. at 516 (citing Lyle v. Waddle, 188 S.W.2d 770, 772 (Tex. 1945)). "By hiring an investigator to check his references under these circumstances, [plaintiff] invited the defamation, and therefore his claim is barred." Id.

In Saucedo v. Rheem Mfg. Co., 974 S.W.2d 117, 120 (Tex. App.–San Antonio 1998, pet. denied), the appellate court reiterated that when a plaintiff requests that a prospective employer contact a prior employer for references, any adverse statements made by the former employer concerning plaintiff are subject to a qualified privilege. Id. at 121.

In a decision where references were not specifically requested or provided to a particular potential employer, the Waco Court of Appeals held that statements made by a former employer in a database accessible by potential employers were privileged. In Gonzalez v. Methodist Charlton Medical Center, 2011 WL 6091255 (Tex. App.—Waco Dec. 7, 2011, no pet.), the court affirmed a summary judgment ruling in favor of a hospital, based on the common interest qualified privilege, when statements about the termination of an employee were placed on a subscriber-only internet database accessible by potential employers of the plaintiff. Id. at *14-16.

D. Intracorporate Communication

An intracorporate communication is covered by the qualified privilege if the communication relates to a common duty among the author or speaker to the recipient of the communication. If the statement, albeit defamatory, relates to a shared interest, the application of the qualified privilege is present. See Willis v. Roche Biomedical Laboratories, Inc., 61 F.3d 313, 316-17 (5th Cir. 1995) (communicating the results of a drug screening was privileged).

E. Statements to Government Regulators

An absolute privilege shields any communication made in the due course of a "quasi-judicial" proceeding. See Village of Bayou Vista v. Glaskow, 899 S.W.2d 826, 829-830 (Tex. App.–Houston [14th Dist.] 1995, no writ). The privilege for communications in the course of quasi-judicial proceedings extends to complaints to licensing boards. See, e.g., Rose v. First American Title Ins. Co. of Texas, 907 S.W.2d 639, 642 (Tex. App.–Corpus Christi 1995, no writ) (letter initiating grievance with State Board of Public Accountancy was absolutely privileged); Reagan v. Guardian Life Ins. Co., 140 Tex. 105, 166 S.W.2d 909, 9913 (1942) (complaint to state Insurance Board was absolutely privileged).

Additionally, an oral or written statement made to the Texas Employment Commission or to an employee of the commission in connection with the discharge of the commission's or employees official statutory duties is absolutely privileged and may not serve as the basis for a defamation action. See Hardwick v. Houston Lighting & Power Co., 881 S.W.2d 195, 198 (Tex. App.–Corpus Christi 1994, writ dism'd w.o.j). Similarly, statements made to the Texas Workforce Commission ("TWC") are privileged. Linan v. Strafco, Inc., 2006 WL 1766204 (Tex. App.–Corpus Christi 2006, no pet.).

In Kastner v. Gutter Management, Inc., 2010 WL 3010941 (Tex. App.—Houston [1st Dist.] no pet. h.), the Houston Fourteenth Court of Appeals affirmed summary judgment in favor of an employer, Gutter Management, sued by a former employee, Kastner, for, among other things, allegedly making defamatory statements about the employee in a criminal proceeding and to the Texas Board of Law Examiners while investigating Kastner's fitness for admission to the Texas Bar. The Court of Appeals quickly disposed of the defamation claim based on testimony in a criminal proceeding brought by Kastner for assault against a former principal of Gutter Management – the Court held that the statements were protected by the absolute privilege applicable to judicial proceedings. Id. at *7. With respect to statements allegedly made to the Board of Law Examiners by the principals at Gutter Management (including that Kastner had committed criminal trespass, assault, was terminated for insubordination, and possessed symptoms of bi-polar disorder), the Court concluded that Kastner had produced no evidence raising a genuine issue of fact that the Board had completed its investigation or made a determination as to Kastner's bar admission, or even that the Board considered the alleged defamatory statements during its investigation. Id. at *3. Thus, there was no evidence of causation and damages presented. Id.

F. Reports to Auditors and Insurers

There are no reported cases on this topic.

G. Vicarious Liability of Employers for Statements Made by Employees

1. **Scope of Employment.** An employer is liable for its officer's or agent's defamatory remark if the officer or agent was acting within the course and scope of employment when the defamatory remark was made. Davila v. Pay & Save Corp., 2003 WL 22413632, *1 (Tex. App.–El Paso 2003, n.p.h.); Hooper v. Pitney Bowes, Inc., 895 S.W.2d 773, 777-78 (Tex. App.–Texarkana 1995, writ denied). Neither express authorization nor subsequent ratification by the employer is necessary to establish liability. Texam Oil Corp. v. Poynor, 436 S.W.2d 129, 130 (Tex. 1968); Hooper, 895 S.W.2d at 777-78. However, in Estate of Martineau v. ARCO Chemical Co., 203 F.3d 904, 913-14 (5th Cir. 2000), the court held that the defendant corporation was entitled to summary judgment on plaintiff's defamation claim against a supervisor because there was no evidence showing that the corporation ratified the statements made by the supervisor.

In Lyon v. Allsup's Convenience Stores, Inc., 997 S.W.2d 345, 347 (Tex. App.–Fort Worth 1999, no pet.), the Fort Worth appellate court recently held that an employer is not liable for an employee's defamation if it occurs beyond the course and scope of employment. In Lyon, a supervisor falsely accused the Plaintiff of theft and fired her. The evidence suggested that the supervisor accused the Plaintiff to conceal his own unauthorized activities. The court held that the employer could not be held liable for alleged defamation and intentional infliction of emotional distress occurring during the Plaintiff's termination because the supervisor's statements did not relate to a duty performed on behalf of the employer, but in fact related to accomplishing an object outside the scope of employment. Id. at 347.

The Waco Court of Appeals recently clarified the test for establishing vicarious liability of an employer for the defamations of an employee. In Mars, Inc. v. Gonzalez, 71 S.W.3d 434 (Tex. App.–Waco 2002, pet. denied), a supervisor sued his employer and two independent contractors for defamation. In addressing the issue of vicarious liability, the Court stated the test for holding a corporate entity for an employee's defamation: there must be evidence that (1) an agent of the company; (2) acting "on behalf of the corporation"; (3) communicated a false statement; (4) to a person a) other than an employee, or b) to an employee whose course and scope of duties did not require receipt of the false communication; (5) and that communication proximately caused; (6) damages. Id. at 437. On the facts presented, involving unauthorized use of an e-mail system, the investigation of wrongdoing involved only employees necessary to conclude the investigation. With respect to an e-mail sent to an employee's wife, the Court held that the distribution of the e-mail was not on behalf of the employer; thus, no corporate liability attached. Id. at 434.

In addition to agent liability, a corporation can be liable if a vice-principal of the corporation (defined as an officer or person with authority to employ, direct, and discharge employees) makes defamatory statements. Wal-Mart Stores, Inc. v. Lane, 31 S.W.3d 282 (Tex. App.–Corpus Christi 2000, pet. denied). The presence or absence of entity liability for defamatory conduct does not affect the liability of the individual who published the defamatory statement.

a. **Blogging.** There are no reported cases on this topic.

2. **Damages.** A corporation may be liable for punitive damages for defamation by one of its corporate officers, even if the employee's malicious conduct was neither authorized nor ratified by the corporation. Wal-Mart Stores, Inc. v. Odem, 929 S.W.2d 513, 530 (Tex. App.–San Antonio 1996, writ denied).

H. Internal Investigations

In 2002, the Texas Supreme Court reversed an appellate court that upheld a jury verdict in a case involving the qualified privilege attached to communications occurring during company investigations. In Minyard Food Stores, Inc. v. Goodman, 80 S.W.3d 573 (Tex. 2002), the Texas Supreme Court reversed the Fort Worth Court of Appeals, which had upheld a jury verdict that a manager had acted within the course and scope of employment when making statements about an employee during a misconduct investigation. The statements at issue were not shown to have been made "in furtherance of the employer's business, and for the accomplishment of the objective for which the employee was employed." Id. at 578. The Court criticized the appellate court's analysis of the employee's "general authority" as a store manager, as opposed to an analysis of whether the defamatory remarks were in furtherance of the employer's business. While the evidence showed that employees must participate in workplace investigations, these policies did not demonstrate that the defamation at issue would further the employer's business. Id. at 578-79. The Court in Davila v. Pay & Save Corp., 2003 WL 22413632, *1 (Tex. App. –El Paso 2003, n.p.h.) held that to establish that an employee is acting within the scope of employment, the plaintiff must put forth evidence that "the employee's statements were made in furtherance of the employer's business, and for the accomplishment of the objective for which the employee was employed." Id.

The San Antonio Court of Appeals reiterated that reports and information obtained during an investigation of employee wrongdoing, and then published in connection with the investigation, are privileged. In Gonzales v. Levy Strauss & Co., 70 S.W.3d 278 (Tex. App.–San Antonio 2002, no pet.), former employees brought suit against their employer and supervisor for defamation due to statements made during an investigation leading to their termination for violating company rules by disclosing information concerning another employee. The evidence demonstrated that the supervisor relied on reports and information furnished by other employees in the line of duty, and as such, there was no evidence of actual malice to overcome the qualified privilege that attached. Id. at 382-83. Moreover, "minor inconsistencies" as to the reasons for their termination do not establish knowledge of any false statements. Id. at 383.

In Spring v. Walthall, Sachse & Pipes, Inc., 2010 WL 2102988 (Tex. App.—San Antonio, no pet. h.), the San Antonio Court of Appeals reversed and remanded in part a summary judgment entered against a former employee, Spring, who had counterclaimed in a non-compete suit brought by a former employer, Walthall, Sachse & Pipes, that the company had, among other things, defamed her. The former employer argued on appeal that the statements at issue were made in the course of an internal investigation, but never presented evidence in support of this argument. Id. at *2. Nor did the former employer ever argue, at trial or on appeal, that the alleged statements were published without malice. Id. Thus, the trial court erred in granting summary judgment in favor of the former employer. Id. at *3.

In Dworschak v. Transocean Offshore Deepwater Drilling, Inc., 2011 WL 435717 (Tex. App.—Houston [14th Dist.] Sept. 20, 2011, n.p.h.), the Fourteenth Court of Appeals built upon previous case law in rejecting a libel/business disparagement claim brought by a senior project manager against his employer, on grounds that there was no evidence of malice when the employer relied upon witness reports during an internal investigation of misconduct where such reports were not shown to be untrue or made themselves with ill will. Accordingly, summary judgment for the employer was appropriate. Id. at *6.

IV. OTHER ACTIONS BASED ON STATEMENTS

A. Negligent Hiring, Retention, and Supervision

Texas courts recognize a cause of action for negligent hiring and supervision. See, e.g., LaBella v. Charlie Thomas, Inc., 942 S.W.2d 127, 137 (Tex. App.–Amarillo 1997, writ denied) (recognizing a duty for an employer to "make inquiry into the competence and qualifications of those he considers for employment"); Akins v. Estes, 888 S.W.2d 35, 42 (Tex. App.–Amarillo 1994) ("The courts of Texas have long recognized that a master has a duty to inquire as to the competence and qualifications of those he considers for employment."), aff'd in part & rev'd in part sub nom., 926 S.W.2d 287 (Tex. 1996). When an employer hires an incompetent or unfit employee, the employer is liable to a third party whose injury was proximately caused by the employer's negligence. Mackey v. U.P. Enterprises, Inc., 935 S.W.2d 446, 459 (Tex. App.–Tyler 1996, no writ) ("An employer has a duty to adequately hire, train, and supervise employees," and if these tasks are performed negligently, the employer may be liable to injuries resulting from the failure to take reasonable precautions to protect the person injured from the misconduct of the employee).

For a finding of liability for negligent hiring, there must be negligence on the part of the employer in hiring or retaining the employee when the employer knows or by the exercise of reasonable care should know that the employee was incompetent or unfit for employment. See, e.g., LaBella, 942 S.W.2d at 137 (stating that an employer is negligent in hiring an employee if the master knows or by the exercise of reasonable care should have known that the employee was incompetent or unfit, thereby creating an unreasonable risk of harm to others). There is no requirement that the conduct complained of arise from acts committed in the course and scope of employment. Mackey, 935 S.W.2d at 459.

While there are few reported Texas cases addressing whether a negligent hiring and supervision claim can be successfully asserted against an employer for the defamatory statement of an employee, a recent appellate decision indicates that such a claim will fail when the defamation claim fails. In Dolcefino v. Randolph, 19 S.W.3d 906 (Tex. App.–Houston [14th Dist.] 2000, pet. denied), where the plaintiff alleged numerous causes of action, including defamation and negligent supervision, the court held that a cause of action for negligent supervision depends entirely on the validity of the defamation claim. Id. at 932 (citing KTRK Television v. Felder, 950 S.W.2d 100, 108 (Tex. App.–Houston [14th Dist.] 1997, no writ) (holding that claims grounded entirely on defamation claim are precluded when defamation claim has no merit because the statements are substantially true). The court concluded: "Because we hold that appellants did not defame [Plaintiffs/ Appellees], we find their claims based on negligent supervision and conspiracy are without merit." Id.

B. Intentional Infliction of Emotional Distress

Under Texas law, the tort of intentional infliction of emotional distress consists of (1) intentional or reckless conduct; (2) that is extreme or outrageous; (3) that caused emotional distress; (4) that was severe in nature. Free v. American Home Assurance Co., 902 S.W.2d 51, 56 (Tex. App. – Houston [1st Dist.] 1995, no writ). Texas courts have held that a plaintiff may not evade the constitutional requirements of a defamation claim, including proof of falsity and actual malice where applicable, by asserting a non-libel claim grounded on the same speech. Evans v. Dolcefino, 986 S.W.2d 69 (Tex. App.–Houston [1st Dist.] 1999, no pet.); KTRK Television v. Felder, 950 S.W.2d 100, 108 (Tex. App.–Houston [1st Dist.] 1997, no writ). Thus, if the defamation claim fails, a claim of intentional infliction of emotional distress must normally fail as a matter of law. Oliphant v. Richards, 167 S.W.3d 513 (Tex. App.–Houston [14th Dist.] 2005, pet. denied) (since underlying defamation claim was barred, so too were the claims for negligence and intentional infliction of emotional distress); Evans, 986 S.W.2d at 79 (non-libel claims, including intentional infliction of emotional distress, must fail if defamation claim fails); Hailey v. KTBS, Inc., 935 S.W.2d 857, 861 (Tex. App.–Texarkana 1996, no writ) ("Since any [intentional infliction of emotional distress] recovery would necessarily be derived from the same defamatory utterances to which we have applied the New York Times rule, the same reasoning would preclude recovery for emotional distress."); Rose v. First Am. Title Ins. Co., 907 S.W.2d 639, 643 (Tex. App.–Corpus Christi 1995, no writ) (applying privilege to both defamation and intentional infliction of emotional distress because otherwise "a litigant could plead around the defamation privilege . . . by labeling his defamation case as one for intentional infliction of emotional distress").

However, in the employment context, courts generally allow claims for intentional infliction of emotional distress to proceed independently from a defamation claim. At least one court has allowed recovery for intentional infliction of emotional distress even though a defamation claim was unsuccessful as invited or procured by the plaintiff. See Hooper v. Pitney Bowes, Inc., 895 S.W.2d 773, 776-77 (Tex. App.–Texarkana 1995, writ denied). Other courts addressing defamation in the work place have allowed intentional infliction claims to proceed separately even though based on statements claimed to also be defamatory. See, e.g., Cote v. Rivera, 894 S.W.2d 536, 542 (Tex. App.–Austin 1995, no writ); Schauer v. Memorial Care Systems, 856 S.W.2d 437, 450-51 (Tex. App.–Houston [1st Dist.] 1993, no writ) (rejecting claim that performance appraisal was defamatory but considering, and ultimately rejecting, intentional infliction claim independently). In Kooken v. The Leather Center, Inc., 2000 WL 381926 (Tex. App.–Dallas, n.p.h.) (unpublished), the appellate court rejected an employee's claim of intentional infliction of emotional distress based on an accusation of wrongdoing and subsequent termination. The court held that an employer must be able to supervise, review, criticize, demote, transfer, and discipline employees, including termination of employment. Id. at *6-7. But see Oliphant v. Richards, 167 S.W.3d 513 (Tex. App—Houston [14th Dist.] 2005, pet. denied).

C. Interference with Economic Advantage

To recover for tortious interference with an employment contract, a plaintiff must prove: (1) the existence of a business relationship subject to interference; (2) the occurrence of an act of interference that was willful and intentional; (3) that the act was a proximate cause of plaintiff injury; and (d) actual damage or loss occurred. KTRK Television, Inc v. Fowkes, 981 S.W.2d 779, 790 (Tex. App.–Houston [1st Dist.] 1998, pet. denied); see also Holloway v. Skinner, 898 S.W.2d 793, 795-96 (Tex. 1995).

Texas law also protects against tortious interference with prospective business relations. Juliette Fowler Homes, 793 S.W.2d at 665. To recover for tortious interference with a prospective business relationship, a plaintiff must show that: (1) there was a reasonable probability that the plaintiff would have entered into a business relationship; (2) the defendant acted maliciously and intentionally preventing the relationship from occurring with the purpose of harming the plaintiff; (3) the defendant was not privileged or justified in his actions; and (4) actual harm or damage occurred to the plaintiff as a result of the interference. American Medical Int'l v. Giurintano, 821 S.W.2d 331 (Tex. App.–Houston [14th Dist.] 1991, no writ).

One is privileged to interfere with another's contractual relations if it is done as a bona fide exercise of one's own rights. Victoria Bank & Trust Co. v. Brady, 811 S.W.2d 931, 939 (Tex. 1991); Martinez v. Hardy, 864 S.W.2d 767, 776 (Tex. App.–Houston [14th Dist.] 1993, no writ). The Texas Supreme Court in Texas Beef Cattle Co. v. Green 921 S.W.2d 203, 212 (Tex. 1996), recently clarified the relevance of good faith to a defendant's assertion of the legal justification defense. The Court clarified that common law actual malice, such as ill-will, spite, evil motive, etc., does not vitiate the defense of justification and expressly:

> disavow[ed] good faith as relevant to the justification defense when the defendant establishes its legal right to act as it did. Only when mistaken, but colorable claims of legal rights are asserted is the good faith of the actor legally significant. Only then must the jury determine whether the defendant believed in good faith that it had a colorable legal right.

Id. In Thorpe v. Alsaeed, 2000 WL 567617 (Tex. App.–Houston [1st Dist.] pet. denied), cert. denied, 531 U.S. 1112 (2001) (unpublished), the court made clear that if a privilege attaches to a communication, the communication can not be the subject of a claim for tortious interference. However, if the lawful purpose of the communication is not established, the tort claim may proceed. Id. Actual malice is only relevant in the context of punitive damages. Id. at 210-212.

Texas recognizes a cause of action for tortious interference with an employment contract, even though the contract is terminable at will. See, e.g., Knox v. Taylor, 992 S.W.2d 40, 54 (Tex. App.–Houston [14th Dist.] 1999, no pet.); Goodrich v. Superior Oil Co., 640 S.W.2d 680, 681 (Tex. App.–Houston [14th Dist.] 1982, no writ). The Texas Supreme Court has held that an at will employment relationship may give rise to a tortious interference claim. Sterner v. Marathon Oil Co., 767 S.W.2d 686, 688-89 (Tex. 1989); c.f. Williams v. Wal-Mart Stores, 882 F.Supp 612 (S.D. Tex. 1995).

Texas courts adhere to the holding enunciated in Hustler Magazine, Inc. v. Falwell, 485 U.S. 46 (1988) that litigants may not attempt an end run around the constitutional defenses against the tort of defamation by pleading torts which do not require falsity, actual malice, etc. See Cain v. Hearst, 878 S.W.2d 577 (Tex. 1994); Evans v. Dolcefino, 986 S.W.2d 69 (Tex. App.–Houston [1st Dist.] 1999, no pet. h.).

Claims for tortious interference based upon the allegedly false and defamatory character of the statements complained of are indistinguishable from the claims for defamation themselves, and are, therefore, barred. See Evans, 986 S.W.2d at 79 (where allegedly defamatory statements are substantially true, non-libel tort claims must fail); Moore & Associates v. Metropolitan Life Ins., Co., 604 S.W.2d 487, 491 (Tex. Civ. App.–Dallas 1980, no writ); see also Rogers v. Dallas Morning News, 889 S.W.2d 467 (Tex. App.–Dallas 1994, writ denied) (court's finding that the defendants were entitled to summary judgment with respect to the libel claim automatically precluded the plaintiff from recovering on her non-libel claims, including tortious interference with contract, as a matter of law); Martinez v. Hardy, 864 S.W.2d 767, 775-76 (Tex. App.–Houston [14th Dist.] 1993, no writ) (court found the allegedly defamatory language to be privileged and ruled that privileged language could not support a claim for tortious interference with employment contract); Griffin v. Rowden, 702 S.W.2d 692, 695 (Tex. App.–Dallas 1985, writ ref'd n.r.e.) (language which is privileged against a claim of slander is likewise privileged in a tortious interference case).

D. Prima Facie Tort

Texas courts have not recognized a cause of action for prima facie tort. The tort has been considered by Texas courts, but rejected. See, e.g., Tatum v. Nationsbank of Texas, N.A., 1995 WL 437413, *5 (Tex. App.–Dallas 1995, writ denied) (unpublished); A.G. Services, Inc. v. Peat, Marwick, Mitchell & Co., 757 S.W.2d 503, 507 (Tex. App.–Houston [1st Dist.] 1988, writ denied). In Tatum, the appellate court recited the definition of "prima facie tort" in Texas as "the infliction of an intentional harm without excuse or justification by an act or series of acts which otherwise would be lawful and which results in special damage." Id. (citing Martin v. Trevino, 578 S.W.2d 763, 772 (Tex. Civ. App.–Corpus Christi 1978, writ ref'd n.r.e.). The court noted, however, that no Texas court has adopted a cause of action for prima facie tort, and the Tatum court declined to do so.

V. PROCEDURAL ISSUES

A. Statute of Limitations

The statute of limitations for defamation claims in Texas is one year. Tex. Civ. Prac. & Rem. Code §16.002 (Vernon 1986); Williamson v. New Times, Inc., 980 S.W.2d 706 (Tex. App.–Fort Worth 1998, no pet.); Marshall Field Stores, Inc. v. Gardiner, 859 S.W.2d 391, 394 (Tex. App.–Houston [1st Dist.] 1993, writ dism'd w.o.j.). The limitations period begins to run from the date the cause of action accrues. Roe v. Walls Regional Hosp., 21 S.W.3d 647, 651 (Tex. App. –Waco 2000, n.p.h); Gardiner, 859 S.W.2d at 394. Generally, a cause of action for libel accrues when the injury occurs and limitations runs against the action to recover damages for the consequences from the date of the communications ... and not from the date of consequences." Moore & Assoc. v. Metropolitan Life Ins. Co., 604 S.W.2d 487, 491 (Tex. Civ. App.–Dallas 1980, no writ); see also Roe, 21 S.W.2d at 651.

The discovery rule has been applied in cases of "credit libel" to toll the running of the limitations period until the time that the plaintiff learns of the defamation. Kelley v. Rinkle, 532 S.W.2d 947, 949 (Tex. 1976); but see Ellert v. Lutz, 930 S.W.2d 152 (Tex. App.–Dallas 1996, no writ) (discovery rule held inapplicable in a defamation suit based on a memorandum that was placed in the employee's personnel file because the employee had access to file and could have discovered memorandum).

In a case applying the one-year statute of limitations applicable to defamation actions, the Waco Court of Appeals held that a cause of action accrues, and should be discoverable, from the date of termination when an employee claims that a past employer provided false and defamatory information to the terminating employer. In Johnson v. Baylor Univ., 188 S.W.3d 296 (Tex. App.—Waco 2006, pet. denied), an aircraft pilot was fired from working for Baylor University based allegedly on chronic obesity and poor grammar and diction, which Baylor believed diminished the image of Baylor. While a discrimination suit was pending against Baylor (which ended unsuccessfully), the pilot accepted a position at Kitty Hawk Air Cargo, Inc. on a probationary basis. In his pre-employment interview, the pilot informed Kitty Hawk that he had been terminated from Baylor because of his obesity and not because of his performance as a pilot. Id. at 299. Kitty Hawk received a background information report revealing that the pilot had in fact been terminated from Baylor for misconduct and was ineligible for rehire. Id. Kitty Hawk terminated the pilot, informing him that information received from Baylor led to the decision. Id. Sixteen months after the termination, the pilot obtained the actual records provided to Kitty Hawk from Baylor and sued, alleging defamation and tortuous interference with contract. Id. The Court of Appeals affirmed summary judgment for Baylor on the defamation claim, holding that the pilot knew or should have known of his wrongfully caused injury when he was terminated by Kitty Hawk and told that it was because of information received from Baylor. Id. at 302.

In Roberts v. Davis, 2007 WL 3194813 (Tex. App.—Texarkana 2007, pet. denied), the Texarkana Court of Appeals affirmed a jury finding that Plaintiff Roberts' libel claim, based on a letter from a doctor to the Roberts' immediate supervisor at a hospital, was barred by the applicable one-year statute of limitations. Roberts argued that the April 9, 2001 letter, which accused Roberts of violations of state and federal law, repetitious and malicious illegal malpractice, manufacture of false reasons for violating orders, and illegally practicing medicine, was concealed from her for over a year after it was communicated to her supervisor. Id. at *2. However, the evidence presented to the jury revealed that the letter was placed in Roberts' personnel file after a June 7, 2001 counseling session during which Roberts was given an opportunity to review the letter. Id. Since Roberts knew of the letter, and based on the statutory right of a public employee to have complete access to his or her personnel file under Texas law, the Court held that there was evidence that Roberts was both aware of the letter's existence and contents, and had continuing access to the letter. Id. Accordingly, since suit was not filed until almost two years after the initial publication, her libel claim was barred by limitations.

Each distinct publication inflicts an independent injury from which a separate cause of action may arise. Carr v. Mobile Video Tapes, Inc., 893 S.W.2d 613, 619 (Tex. App.–Corpus Christi 1994, no writ); Gardiner, 859 S.W.2d at 394. However, Texas recognizes the "single publication rule" which establishes the publication date when a defamatory statement is published in a mass medium. See Stephan v. Baylor Medical Center at Garland, 20 S.W.3d 880, 889 (Tex. App.–Dallas

2000 n.p.h). Under the single publication rule, each copy of a newspaper or magazine is not a separate publication. Publication is complete upon the last day of the mass distribution of the printed matter. See Holloway v. Butler, 662 S.W.2d 688, 690 (Tex. App.–Houston [14th Dist.] 1983, writ ref'd n.r.e.); see also I.B.6.c., supra. However, the rule is limited in application in that it does not apply to separate printings of the same publication or to situations in which the same information appears in different publications (known as the "new audience" rationale). Stephan, 20 S.W.3d at 889. In Stephan, the Dallas Court of Appeals held that the single publication rule did not apply to adverse action reports made to the National Practitioner Data Bank (NPDB) concerning physician performance. Each dissemination of the report was held to reach a "separate and discrete audience with each dissemination by the NPDB." Id.

B. Jurisdiction

The constitutional district courts and statutory county courts at law have jurisdiction over defamation claims. Tex. Gov't Code § 25.003 et seq. Neither the constitutional county courts nor the Justice of the Peace or Small Claims Courts have jurisdiction over libel or slander claims. Tex. Gov't Code § 26.0043; Tex. Gov't Code § 27.031. The Texas Long-Arm Statute, Tex. Civ. Prac. & Rem. Code §§ 17.041-17.045, governs personal jurisdiction and the amenability of process for a nonresident.

Venue in a defamation case lies in any of the following: (1) the county of the plaintiff's residence at the time of the accrual of the cause of action; (2) the county in which the defendant resided at the time suit was filed, (3) the county of the residence of the defendant, or (4) any of the preceding, or the domicile of any corporate defendant. Tex. Civ. Prac. & Rem. Code § 15.017. This provision establishes mandatory venue.

Federal preemption can be an issue in employment defamation cases. In Frank v. Delta Airlines, Inc., 314 F.3d 195 (5th Cir. 2002), the Fifth Circuit held that state tort law claims, including a defamation claim, were preempted by federal law in a case where an employee sued an employer for based on termination for refusal to test when the plaintiff, an airline mechanic, submitted adulterated urine sample after being selected for random drug test. The Court held that the state law claims, which included negligence, intentional infliction of emotional distress, and defamation, were all preempted by the Omnibus Transportation Employee Testing Act (OTETA) and Federal Aviation Administration (FAA) regulations. With respect to the defamation claim, the Court held that federal law "substantially subsume" the subject matter of plaintiff's defamation claim. Id. at 203.

Under the common law, Texas courts lack jurisdiction over defamation claims made in church settings under the ecclesiastical abstention doctrine. In Becker v. Clardy, 2011 WL 6756999 (Tex. App.—Austin Dec. 22, 2011, no pet.), the Austin Court of Appeals addressed a defamation claim made by a teacher at a parochial school against a co-worker. The trial court sustained a plea to the jurisdiction based on the ecclesiastical abstention doctrine, and the appeals court affirmed, holding that the complained-of statements were all made to students, administrators, or faculty related to Plaintiff's actions as a teacher at the school and addressed subject matters related to teacher discipline and interaction with students and teachers. Id. at *3-4. Further, since the alleged damages were limited to the church community and implicated the school's code of ethics and moral standards of the Catholic faith and Canon law, a civil action resolving the claims would inappropriately encroach on the church's ability to manage its internal affairs. Id. at *5.

C. Workers' Compensation Exclusivity

The Texas Workers' Compensation Act creates a system that provides for the payment of compensation and other benefits to employees, or the employee's beneficiaries, for injuries or death arising out of the employee's course of employment. See Tex. Lab. Code § 401.001, et. seq. In Texas, "[r]ecovery of workers' compensation benefits is the exclusive remedy of an employee covered by workers' compensation insurance coverage or a legal beneficiary against the employer or an agent or employee of the employer for the death of or work-related injury sustained by the employee." Tex. Lab. Code § 408.001(a).

Texas courts have not applied the exclusivity provision to defamation claims brought by employees against their employers. However, Texas Courts support the proposition that "[a]lthough the Workers' Compensation Act bars an employee's common law action for negligence against his employer, the Act does not exempt employers from common law liability for intentional torts." Massey v. Armco Steel Co., 652 S.W.2d 932, 933 (Tex. 1983) (emphasis added). Thus, an injured employee covered by the workers' compensation system still retains the right to seek common law remedies for intentional torts committed by either the employer or an agent of the employer. See Rodriguez v. Naylor Indus., Inc., 763 S.W.2d 411, 412 (Tex. 1989). The intentional tort exception is "very limited" because "[i]n the workers' compensation setting, the Texas Supreme Court has defined intent to mean 'the actor desires to cause consequences of his act, or that he believes that the consequences are substantially certain to result from it.'" Prescott v. CSPH, Inc., 878 S.W.2d 692, 695 (Tex. App.–Amarillo 1994, writ denied) (citing Reed Tool Co. v. Copelin, 689 S.W.2d 404, 406 (Tex. 1985)).

It should also be noted that an allegedly defamatory statement made in connection with a worker's compensation claim may be deemed subject to privilege. See Pisharodi v. Barrash, 116 S.W.3d 858, 864 (Tex. App.–Corpus Christi 2003, pet. denied).

D. Pleading Requirements

Under Texas law, a pleading that sets forth a defamation claim must state with particularity the alleged defamatory statements. It is not clear whether the statements must be set forth in haec verba, Perkins v. Welch, 57 S.W.2d 914 (Tex. Civ. App.–San Antonio 1933, no writ), or whether it is sufficient to refer to the existence of statements whose substance and meaning are allegedly defamatory, Kahn v. Beicker Engineering, Inc., 1995 WL 612402 (Tex. App. – San Antonio 1995, writ denied) (unpublished), cert. denied, 519 U.S. 965 (1996). Recently, in Natkin Service Co. v. Winiarz, 2000 WL 852834 (Tex. App.–Austin, n.p.h.), a petition was found sufficient to support a default judgment on a defamation claim, even though the petition merely alleged that the defendant had falsely claimed that plaintiff was incompetent, dishonest, and had engaged in theft, fraud, and deception, without setting forth the specific statements at issue. In Fields v. Keith, 2000 WL 748152 (N.D. Tex.), aff'd, 273 F.3d 1099 (5th Cir. 2001), a federal court in Texas held that a complaint that merely stated that an employee had defamed Plaintiff by accusations of theft was insufficient to state a claim for defamation because not enough facts were pleaded concerning the specific conduct giving rise to the claim.

Special damages are only recoverable in a defamation action if they are plead. Shearson Lehman Hutton, Inc. v. Tucker, 806 S.W.2d 914 (Tex. App.–Corpus Christi 1991, writ dism'd w.o.j.). A claim of libel per se does not require further pleading of special damages. Swate v. Schiffers, 975 S.W.2d 70, 76, 26 Media L. Rep. 2258 (Tex. App.–San Antonio 1998, pet. denied).

SURVEY OF TEXAS EMPLOYMENT PRIVACY LAW

Christie M. Alcalá
Allysun E. Atwater
Vinson & Elkins L.L.P.
1001 Fannin Street, Suite 2500
Houston, TX 77002
Telephone: (713) 758-2787; Facsimile: (713) 615-5112

(With Developments Reported Through **November 1, 2012**)

GENERAL COMMENTS

Texas case authority should be cited in accordance with the citation rules contained within the *Texas Rules of Form*. See Texas Rules of Form (Texas Law Review Ass'n et al. eds., 11th ed. 2006).

SIGNIFICANT DEVELOPMENTS SINCE THE 2012 *SURVEY*

On September 1, 2012, House Bill 300 ("HB 300"), an expansion of the Texas medical record privacy law went into effect. The law applies to covered entities which it defines broadly as persons (or agents, employees or contractors of such persons) who assemble, collect, analyze, use, evaluate, store, transmit, obtain or come into possession of protected health information ("PHI"). Covered entities may include business associates, health care payers, governmental units, information or computer management entities, schools, health researchers, health care facilities, clinics, health care providers, or persons who maintain an internet site. Tex. Health & Safety Code Ann. § 181.001 (Vernon 2010). HB 300 prohibits the disclosure of PHI without authorization and requires that covered entities post notification if PHI is subject to electronic disclosure. Id. § 181.154. Additionally, HB 300 prohibits the sale of PHI by a covered entity. However, authorization is not required for disclosure to another covered entity for the purposes of treatment, payment, health care operations, or insurance or health maintenance organization functions. Id. §§ 181.153, 181.154. HB 300 requires covered entities to provide training for their employees regarding both state and federal laws concerning PHI. The training must be tailored to the scope of the employee's position and the covered entity's particular course of business. Covered entities must provide the training no more than 60 days after the date of hire and at least once every two years thereafter. Id. § 181.101. HB 300 carries steep penalties for the unlawful disclosure of patient PHI. These penalties range from fines of $5,000 per violation to $1.5 million per year for violations occurring with a frequency that constitutes a pattern or practice Id. § 181.201. Additionally, HB 300 requires any person who conducts business in Texas and owns or licenses computerized data that includes PHI or other sensitive information to notify individuals whose sensitive personal information has been or is believed to have been acquired by an unauthorized person. Tex. Bus. & Com. Code Ann. § 521.053 (Vernon 2009). The breach notification requirement carries heightened penalties for failure to notify individuals of a breach of PHI. Those penalties are $100 per individual, per day that the individual has not been informed of the breach, not to exceed $250,000 for all individuals for whom notification is due. Id. § 521.151.

I. GENERAL LAW OF PRIVACY

A. Legal Basis of Privacy Claims

1. ***Constitutional Law.*** The Texas Constitution provides that "The people shall be secure in their persons, houses, papers and possessions, from all unreasonable seizures or searches, and no warrant to search any place, or to seize any person or thing, shall issue without describing them as near as may be, nor without probable cause, supported by oath or affirmation." Tex. Const. Art, I, § 9. Although there is no explicit guarantee of the right to privacy in the Texas Constitution, as under the United States Constitution, several provisions of the Texas Bill of Rights have been held to create "zones of privacy" which together serve to "protect[] personal privacy from unreasonable intrusion." Tex. State Employees Union v. Tex. Dep't of Mental Health & Mental Retardation, 746 S.W.2d 203, 205 (Tex. 1987). Constitutional privacy rights, however, can only be invoked when there is government action. Kaminski v. Tex. Employment Comm'n, 848 S.W.2d 811, 812-13 (Tex. App.— Houston [14th Dist.] 1993, no writ) (holding that the denial of unemployment benefits by the Texas Employment Commission does not convert a private employer's actions to government action unless the Free Exercise Clause of the First Amendment is implicated, by requiring an individual to act contrary to the requirements of his religion). As such, in the private employment context, there is no right to privacy under the Texas Constitution.

Whether the government unlawfully invaded an employee's privacy rights under the Texas Constitution is assessed in light of a balancing test. Tex. State Employees Union, 746 S.W.2d at 205-06. The government must demonstrate a compelling objective which cannot be achieved through less intrusive, more reasonable means to overcome an individual's privacy right. Id. (holding Texas Department of Mental Health and Mental Retardation's requirement of polygraph testing an unconstitutional violation of privacy rights where testing was required during investigations involving suspected patient abuse, theft or other criminal activity on the Department's facilities, or an activity posing a threat to the health and safety of patients or employees). Greater deference is afforded to the government where the objectives at issue are directly involved in the state goal of protecting the safety of the public. Id. at 206 (citing Richardson v. City of Pasadena, 500 S.W.2d 175, 177 (Tex. Civ. App.—Houston [14th Dist.] 1973), rev'd on other grounds, 513 S.W.2d 1 (Tex. 1974)). See also Thompson v. City of Arlington, 838 F. Supp. 1137 (N.D. Tex. 1993) (holding no unconstitutional invasion of privacy to require, as a condition of police officer's reinstatement to active duty after suicide attempt and drug therapy, disclosure of her past and contemporaneous mental health records).

2. ***Statutory Law.*** There is no statutory recognition of a general right to privacy under Texas law. However, various statutes address disclosure of records and other issues that relate to privacy issues. For example, a person who owns a property right in the name, voice, signature, photograph or likeness of a deceased person has a statutory cause of action for another's unauthorized use of such property right. Tex. Prop. Code Ann. § 26.013 (Vernon Supp. 2000).

3. ***Common Law.*** Texas recognizes three of four "classic" invasion of privacy torts. Cain v. Hearst Corp., 878 S.W.2d 577, 578 (Tex. 1994); Billings v. Atkinson, 489 S.W.2d 858 (Tex. 1973). The classic four are: "1. Intrusion upon the plaintiff's seclusion or solitude, or into his private affairs; 2. Public disclosure of embarrassing private facts about the plaintiff; 3. Publicity which places the plaintiff in a false light in the public eye; [and] 4. Appropriation, for the defendant's advantage, of the plaintiff's name or likeness." Industrial Found. of the South v. Tex. Indus. Accident Bd., 540 S.W.2d 668, 682 (Tex. 1976) (quoting from William L. Prosser, Privacy, 48 Cal. L. Rev. 383, 389 (1960)). Texas does not recognize the tort of false light. Cain, 878 S.W.2d at 578. The statute of limitations for an invasion of privacy claim is two years. Tex. Civ. Prac. & Rem. Code Ann. § 16.003(a) (Vernon 1986 & Supp. 2000); see also Stevenson v. Koutzarov, 795 S.W.2d 313, 319 (Tex. App.—Houston [1st Dist.] 1990, writ denied).

Consent is an absolute defense to an invasion of privacy claim. Farrington v. Sysco Food Servs., 865 S.W.2d 247, 253-54 (Tex. App.—Houston [1st Dist.] 1993, writ denied); Jennings v. Minco Tech. Labs, Inc., 765 S.W.2d 497, 500 (Tex. App.—Austin 1989, writ denied). As in the context of defamation claims, the scope of the consent and whether the conduct complained of falls within it may be an issue of fact. See, e.g., Smith v. Holley, 827 S.W.2d 433 (Tex. App.—San Antonio 1992, writ denied). In addition, some invasion of privacy claims may be preempted by federal law when a collective bargaining agreement controls the relationship. Dancy v. Fina Oil & Chem. Co., 921 F. Supp. 1532 (E.D. Tex. 1996) (holding that an invasion of privacy claim for posting absentee employees' names was preempted by the Labor Management Relations Act since it required interpreting the breadth of the management rights clause addressing absenteeism policies). Further, in the public employment context, official immunity may bar privacy claims. See Moulton v. Vaughn, 982 S.W.2d 107 (Tex. App.—Houston [1st Dist.] 1998, pet. denied).

B. Causes of Action

1. ***Misappropriation/Right of Publicity.*** The use of a person's name or likeness in connection with a commercial undertaking or advertisement without permission is an invasion of privacy, even if the person is a public figure. See Benavidez v. Anheuser Busch, Inc., 873 F.2d 102, 104 (5th Cir. 1989); Kimbrough v. Coca-Cola/USA, 521 S.W.2d 719 (Tex. Civ. App.—Eastland 1975, writ ref'd n.r.e.) (former college football star stated valid claim for misappropriation when his picture was used to advertise soft drinks); Matthews v. Wozencraft, 15 F.3d 432, 437 (5th Cir. 1994); cf. Moore v. Big Picture Co., 828 F.2d 270 (5th Cir. 1987) (holding that a contractor was liable for misappropriation of name for representing in bidding that it had hired the plaintiff when it had not). There are three elements to a misappropriation claim under Texas law: (1) that the defendant appropriated the plaintiff's name or likeness for the value associated with it, and not in an incidental manner or for a newsworthy purpose; (2) that the plaintiff can be identified from the publication; and (3) that there was some advantage or benefit to the defendant. Brown v. Ames, 201 F.3d 654, 657-58 (5th Cir. 2000) (applying Texas law); Matthews, 15 F.3d at 437; Express One Int'l v. Stienbeck, 53 S.W.3d 895, 900 (Tex. App.—Dallas 2001, no pet.).

Texas law does not protect a name per se, but the value associated with it. Stienbeck, 53 S.W.3d at 900. Liability for invasion of privacy arises only when the defendant appropriates for his own benefit the commercial standing, reputation or other values associated with the plaintiff's name. Id. Generally, an appropriation becomes actionable when the name is used "to advertise the defendant's business or product, or for some similar commercial purpose." Id.

2. ***False Light.*** False light invasion of privacy is not a recognized tort under Texas law. Cain v. Hearst Corp., 878 S.W.2d 577 (Tex. 1994). The claim is seen as duplicative of defamation claims without any of the procedural protection. Id.

3. ***Publication of Private Facts.*** To prevail on a claim for wrongful publication of private facts, a plaintiff must establish the disclosure of "information containing highly intimate or embarrassing facts about a person's

private affairs," that the publication be "highly objectionable to a person of ordinary sensibilities," that the information be "communicat[ed] to more than a small group of persons," and that "the matter publicized is not of legitimate public concern." Industrial Found. of the South v. Tex. Indus. Accident Bd., 540 S.W.2d 668, 682-83 (Tex. 1976); see also Star-Telegram, Inc. v. Doe, 915 S.W.2d 471, 473-74 (Tex. 1995). The definition of "public disclosure" requires widespread publicity as opposed to publication to a single person, i.e. "the matter must be communicated to the public at large, such that the matter becomes one of public knowledge." Industrial Foundation, 540 S.W.2d at 683-84; see also Wilhite v. H.E. Butt Co., 812 S.W.2d 1, 6 (Tex. App.—Corpus Christi 1991, no writ) (holding that a discussion only among management was not public disclosure), abrogated on other grounds, Cain v. Hearst Corp., 878 S.W.2d 577, 578 (Tex. 1994); Ellenwood v. Exxon Shipping Co., 6 I.E.R. Cas. (BNA) 1623 (D. Me. 1991), aff'd in part, rev'd in part on other grounds, 984 F.2d 1270 (1st Cir. 1993) (holding under Texas law that employee failed to prove public disclosure of private facts invasion of privacy where his employer told only a small group of co-workers that he had undergone treatment for alcoholism). Furthermore, private *facts* about an individual must have been published; if the published information is false, no cause of action will arise. See Doe v. United States, 83 F. Supp. 2d 833, 841-42 (S.D. Tex. 2000).

Whether information is of legitimate public concern depends on the facts of each case, considering the nature of the information and the public's interest in its disclosure. Star-Telegram, 915 S.W.3d at 474. While there is a presumption that private facts are not of legitimate public concern, this presumption is rebuttable. Industrial Found. of the South v. Tex. Indus. Accident Bd., 540 S.W.2d 668, 682, 685 (Tex. 1976). Once a matter has become part of the public record, there is no liability for subsequent publication. Id. at 684; see also Anonsen v. Donahue, 857 S.W.2d 700, 704 (Tex. App.—Houston [1st Dist] 1993, writ denied) (crimes such as incest and rape are matters of legitimate public concern and cannot form the basis of an invasion of privacy action).

4. ***Intrusion.*** This form of invasion of privacy requires an "intentional intrusion upon the solitude. . . of another or her private affairs, which would be highly offensive to a reasonable person." Wilson v. Sysco Food Servs. of Dallas, Inc., 940 F. Supp. 1003, 1014 (N.D. Tex. 1996); Thompson v. City of Arlington, 838 F. Supp. 1137, 1154 (N.D. Tex. 1993); see also Valenzuela v. Aquino, 853 S.W.2d 512, 513 (Tex. 1993); Billings v. Atkinson, 489 S.W.2d 858, 859 (Tex. 1973) (defining invasion of privacy as, among other things, "humiliati[ng] to a person of ordinary sensibilities"). Either a physical intrusion upon a person's property or something similar to eavesdropping or wiretapping is required. Vaughn v. Drennon, 202 S.W.3d 308, 320 (Tex. App.—Tyler 2006, no pet.); Wilhite v. H.E. Butt Co., 812 S.W.2d 1, 6 (Tex. App.—Corpus Christi 1991, no writ), abrogated on other grounds, Cain v. Hearst Corp., 878 S.W.2d 577, 578 (Tex. 1994); Wilson, 940 F. Supp. at 1015.

In determining whether actions by an employer constitute an intrusion, courts consider whether the employee has a legitimate and reasonable expectation of privacy with respect to the area searched or investigated. For example, in K-Mart Corp. v. Trotti, 677 S.W.2d 632 (Tex. App.—Houston [1st Dist.] 1984), writ ref'd n.r.e., 686 S.W.2d 593 (Tex. 1985) (per curiam), the employee recovered a six-figure damage award for invasion of privacy where the employer, who suspected her of theft, broke into her company locker and examined its contents. The court reasoned that because the store allowed employees to provide their own personal locks for the lockers and because there was no company policy that provided for random searches, the employee had a legitimate expectation of privacy in the locker that had been violated by the employer.

C. Other Privacy-related Actions

1. ***Intentional Infliction of Emotional Distress.*** In Texas, the elements of intentional infliction of emotional distress are: (1) the defendant acted either intentionally or recklessly; (2) the conduct was extreme or outrageous; (3) the defendant's actions caused the plaintiff emotional distress; and (4) the emotional distress was severe. Wornick Co. v. Casas, 856 S.W.2d 732, 734 (Tex. 1993); Twyman v. Twyman, 855 S.W.2d 619, 621 (Tex. 1993).

The "outrageous conduct" required for a claim of intentional infliction of emotional distress is that which goes beyond all possible bounds of decency, and is regarded as atrocious, and utterly intolerable in a civilized society. See Wornick, 856 S.W.2d at 734; Stokes v. Puckett, 972 S.W.2d 921, 924 (Tex. App.—Beaumont 1998, pet. denied). "The threshold question of whether 'outrageous' conduct existed . . . is an issue of law to be determined by the courts." Farrington v. Sysco Food Servs., Inc., 865 S.W.2d 247, 254 (Tex. App.—Houston [1st Dist.] 1993, writ denied); see also Wornick, 856 S.W.2d at 734; DeWald v. Home Depot, No. 05-98-00013-CV, 2000 WL 1207124 (Tex. App.—Dallas Aug. 25, 2000, no pet.) (holding that falsely depicting a former employee in the community as a thief is not sufficiently outrageous to raise a fact issue to preclude summary judgment).

For employees at will, "the fact of discharge itself as a matter of law cannot constitute outrageous behavior." Wornick, 856 S.W.2d at 735 (citing Diamond Shamrock Ref. & Mktg. Co. v. Mendez, 844 S.W.2d 198, 202 (Tex. 1992)). In order to make out the claim of intentional infliction of emotional distress, a plaintiff must allege and prove conduct independent of a termination itself that is outrageous. Sebesta v. Kent Elecs. Corp., 886 S.W.2d 459, 464 (Tex. App.—

Houston [1st Dist.] 1994, writ denied) (holding "exit parade" at the busiest time of the day to escort plaintiff out after her termination, being yelled at for serving on a jury and not doing something to avoid jury duty, and the company's attitude about jury duty not outrageous as a matter of law).

Further, employment-related disputes that commonly occur, such as the discharge of an employee or conflicts between management and employees, cannot constitute extreme and outrageous acts forming the basis for a claim of intentional infliction of emotional distress. MacArthur v. Univ. of Tex. Health Ctr., 45 F.3d 890, 898 (5th Cir. 1995); Johnson v. Merrell Dow Pharms., Inc., 965 F.2d 31, 33-34 (5th Cir. 1992); Horton v. Montgomery Ward & Co., 827 S.W.2d 361, 367-70 (Tex. App. —San Antonio 1992, writ denied); McClendon v. Ingersoll-Rand Co., 757 S.W.2d 816 (Tex. App.—Houston [14th Dist.] 1988), rev'd on other grounds, 779 S.W.2d 69 (Tex. 1989), rev'd on other grounds, 498 U.S. 133 (1990). The wrongful termination of an employee does not, standing alone, constitute intentional infliction of emotional distress. Davila v. Pay & Save Corp., No. 08-02-00452-CV, 2003 WL 22413632 (Tex. App.—El Paso Oct. 23, 2003, no writ).

Liability under a claim of intentional infliction of emotional distress does not extend to mere insults, indignities, threats, annoyances or petty oppressions. See, e.g., Ugalde v. W.A. McKenzie Asphalt Co., 990 F.2d 239, 243 (5th Cir. 1993) (citing Wilson v. Monarch Paper Co., 939 F.2d 1138, 1143 (5th Cir. 1991)) (supervisor's reference to Title VII constructive discharge plaintiff as a "Mexican" and a "wetback" over period of time not extreme and outrageous); Horton, 827 S.W.2d at 367-70 (subjecting employee to derogatory name calling and ostracism, defacing her pictures, or refusing to discipline her tormentors does not constitute extreme and outrageous behavior).

"[H]arassing and retaliatory conduct, without more, is likewise insufficient to support a cause of action for intentional infliction of emotional distress." Amador v. Tan, 855 S.W.2d 131, 135 (Tex. App.—El Paso 1993, writ denied). While insensitive or rude behavior, requiring an employee to work under a supervisor she dislikes, or intentionally creating an onerous or unpleasant work environment does not ordinarily constitute outrageous conduct, the Fifth Circuit has held that a fact issue existed on whether it was outrageous for a manager to assign the plaintiff to report to a supervisor with whom she had previously been romantically involved but from whom she had broken up after finding out he had sexually abused her daughter. See Benningfield v. City of Houston, 157 F.3d 369 (5th Cir. 1998), cert. denied sub nom., Benningfield v. Nuchia, 526 U.S. 1065 (1999). Even conduct which may be illegal in an employment context may not be the sort of conduct constituting extreme and outrageous conduct. Thomas v. Clayton Williams Energy, Inc., 2 S.W.3d 734 (Tex. App.—Houston [14th Dist.] 1999, no pet.) (holding constant barrage of racial slurs, jokes, insults and harassment from supervisors and employees, although condemnable, does not rise to the level of extreme and outrageous conduct necessary to support a claim for intentional infliction of emotional distress). Likewise, conduct is not necessarily extreme and outrageous simply because it is tortuous or wrongful. Bradford v. Vento, 48 S.W.3d 749, 758 (Tex. 2001).

"'Severe emotional distress' means distress so severe that no reasonable person would be expected to endure it." See Stokes v. Puckett, 972 S.W.2d 921, 924-25 (Tex. App.—Beaumont 1998, pet. denied). Any party seeking to recover for mental anguish must prove more than mere worry, anxiety, vexation, embarrassment, or anger. See id.; see also GTE Sw., Inc. v. Bruce, 998 S.W.2d 605, 618-19 (Tex. 1999). Testimony regarding problems such as depression, anxiety, embarrassment, loss of self-esteem, humiliation, and various physical manifestations of mental anguish has been found to constitute sufficient evidence of severe emotional distress. See Stokes, 972 S.W.2d at 924-25. However, proof of a physical manifestation of the plaintiff's emotional distress is not required. See id.

An employee's claim for severe emotional distress is not a compensable injury under the Texas Workers' Compensation Act and thus is not barred by the Act. Bruce, 998 S.W.2d at 605 (finding that because injuries were caused by repetitive mental trauma rather than an ascertainable event, there can be no recovery under the Act). When an employee's complaint is for sexual harassment, the plaintiff must proceed solely under a statutory claim unless there are additional facts, unrelated to sexual harassment, to support an independent tort claim for intentional infliction of emotional distress. Hoffmann-La Roche Inc. v. Zeltwanger, 144 S.W.3d 438 (Tex. 2004).

Texas does not recognize the tort of negligent infliction of emotional distress. Twyman v. Twyman, 855 S.W.2d 619, 621 (Tex. 1993); Boyles v. Kerr, 855 S.W.2d 593, 594 (Tex. 1993).

2. ***Interference With Prospective Economic Advantage.*** A party to a contract has a cause of action for tortious interference against any third person who wrongly induces another contracting party to breach the contract. See Holloway v. Skinner, 898 S.W.2d 793, 794-95 (Tex. 1995). Under Texas law, the elements of the cause of action of tortious interference with an existing contract are: (i) a contract or relationship existed between the plaintiff and some third party, (ii) the defendant intentionally interfered with such contract or relationship, and (iii) this intentional interference was the proximate cause of actual damages sustained by the plaintiff. See, e.g., Exxon Corp. v. Allsup, 808 S.W.2d 648, 654 (Tex. App.—Corpus Christi 1991, writ denied). The Texas Supreme Court has held that "the terminable-at-will status of a contract is no defense to an action for tortious interference with its performance." Sterner v. Marathon Oil Co., 767 S.W.2d 686, 689 (Tex. 1989). See also Martin v. Kroger Co., 65 F. Supp. 2d 516, 561 (S.D. Tex. 1999).

In order to recover for tortious interference with a prospective business relation a plaintiff must prove that (1) a reasonable probability that the parties would have entered into a contractual relationship; (2) an independently tortious or unlawful act by the defendant that prevent the relationship from occurring; (3) the defendant did such an act with a conscious desire to prevent the relationship from occurring or knew that the interference was certain or substantially certain to occur as a result of his conduct; (4) the plaintiff suffered actual harm or damages as a result of the defendant's interference. Wal-Mart Stores, Inc. v. Sturges, 52 S.W.3d 711, 713, 726 (Tex. 2001); Allied Capital Corp. v. Cravens, 67 S.W.3d 486, 491 (Tex. App.—Corpus Christi 2002, no pet.); Baty v. Protech Ins. Agency, 63 S.W.3d 841, 860 (Tex. App.—Houston [14th Dist.] 2001, pet. denied). This does not mean that the plaintiff must be able to prove an independent tort. Id. It means that the plaintiff must be able to prove that the defendant's conduct would be actionable under a recognized tort. Id. For example, a plaintiff may recover for tortious interference from a defendant who makes fraudulent statements about the plaintiff to a third person without proving that the third person was actually defrauded. Id. Likewise, a plaintiff may recover for tortious interference from a defendant who threatens a person with physical harm if he does business with plaintiff. Id. The plaintiff need prove only that the defendant's conduct toward the prospective customer would constitute assault. Id.

By definition, the person who wrongfully induces the breach usually cannot be one of the contracting parties. See Holloway, 898 S.W.2d at 795. When the defendant serves the dual roles of a corporate agent and the third party who allegedly induced the corporation's breach, the question arises as to whether the actions of the corporate agent are to be deemed the actions of the corporation itself, or the acts of the agent as an individual. See id. To preserve the logically necessary rule that a party cannot tortiously interfere with its own contract, a prima facie case of tortious interference is established if the alleged act of interference is performed in order to further the defendant-agent's personal interests. See id. at 796. The plaintiff must show that the defendant acted in a manner so contrary to the corporation's best interests that his actions could only be motivated by personal interests. See id. The mere existence of a personal stake in the outcome, especially when any personal benefit is derivative of the improved financial condition of the corporation, will not alone constitute proof that the defendant-agent committed an act of intentional interference. See id. Furthermore, the burden of proving that an agent committed an act of interference for reasons personal to the agent is on the plaintiff. See id.

Interference with any contract may be legally justified under appropriate circumstances. Sterner v. Marathon Oil Co., 767 S.W.2d 686, 689 (Tex. 1989). Legal justification is an affirmative defense, and therefore, the burden of proof of legal justification or excuse lies with the party accused of interference. Id. at 690. Under the affirmative defense of legal justification or excuse, one is privileged to interfere with another's contract (1) if it is done in a bonafide exercise of one's own rights, or (2) if he has an equal or superior right in the subject matter to that of the other party. Id. at 691. Actual malice on the part of the allegedly interfering party (such as ill will toward the plaintiff) is *irrelevant* to determining whether his action is legally justified. Tex. Beef Cattle Co. v. Green, 921 S.W.2d 203, 211-212 (Tex. 1996). However, if the allegedly interfering party cannot establish as a matter of law the legal right to act as he did, he may nevertheless prevail on a justification defense if (1) the court determines that he interfered while exercising a colorable legal right, and (2) the jury determines that, although mistaken, the defendant exercised that colorable legal right in good faith. Id. at 211. Justification and privilege are defenses in a claim for tortious interference with prospective relations only to the extent that they are defenses to the independent tortiousness of the defendant's conduct. Wal-Mart Stores, Inc. v. Sturges, 52 S.W.3d 711, 713, 726 (Tex. 2001).

3. ***Prima Facie Tort.*** Texas courts have not recognized a cause of action for prima facie tort. See Martin v. Trevino, 578 S.W.2d 763, 772-73 (Tex. App.—Corpus Christi 1978, pet ref'd n.r.e.).

II. EMPLOYER TESTING OF EMPLOYEES

Unless otherwise agreed between employer and employee, employment in Texas is "at will," and as a result, the employer may modify the terms of employment at any time and require that the employee accept the modifications or quit. In re Halliburton Co., 80 S.W.3d 566, 568-69 (Tex. 2002); Hathaway v. Gen. Mills, Inc., 711 S.W.2d 227, 229 (Tex. 1986); Jennings v. Minco Tech. Labs, Inc., 765 S.W.2d 497, 499 (Tex. App.—Austin 1989, writ denied). An employee who continues in his or her employment after the employer modifies its terms is deemed to have accepted those terms and acquiesced to their application to him or her by the employer. In re Halliburton Co., 80 S.W.3d at 568-69.

Many employers require employees and applicants to undergo testing in connection with the application process or during employment. Such testing raises privacy considerations.

A. Psychological or Personality Testing

1. ***Common Law and Statutes.*** There are no Texas statutes in this area.

2. ***Private Employers.*** In the private sector, employers should analyze the viability of such testing in light of the general common law invasion of privacy principles discussed above and under the Americans with Disabilities

Act. While confidentiality concerns remain an important issue, the Fifth Circuit has concluded that it is not an "adverse employment action" when an employer requires an employee to undergo a psychological exam, if placed on paid leave at the time. Breaux v. City of Garland, 205 F.3d 150, 157-58 (5th Cir. 2000); Luckman v. United Parcel Serv., No. 3:00-CV-0739-G, 2001 WL 1029523, at * 5 (N.D. Tex. Aug. 30, 2001).

3. ***Public Employers.*** Testing can be justified based on public safety considerations. See Wuertz v. Wilson, 922 S.W.2d 268 (Tex. App.—Austin 1996, no writ) (holding that the EMS Director in public hospital was justified by the serious nature of a paramedic's job and the public safety concerns involved in ordering the paramedic to undergo psychological and physical tests, including drug tests, when supervisors reported erratic behavior). Presumably, a public employer wishing to conduct such testing could do so if the public objective can be met with no less intrusive, more reasonable means. See Tex. State Employees Union v. Tex. Dep't of Mental Health & Mental Retardation, 746 S.W.2d 203, 205-06 (Tex. 1987). Claims in connection with disclosure of psychological test results by public employees may, under appropriate circumstances, be subject to the defense of official immunity. See Moulton v. Vaughn, 982 S.W.2d 107 (Tex. App.—Houston [1st Dist.] 1998, pet. denied) (holding university police officer immune from liability from claim of improper disclosure of applicant's psychological test result to the police chief of another police department where applicant was currently employed, based on good faith disclosure and action within scope of authority).

A supervisor's referral of a police department employee for psychological testing was held not to be an "adverse employment action" in the context of a claim alleging retaliation for exercise of free speech rights under First Amendment. Benningfield v. City of Houston, 157 F.3d 369 (5th Cir. 1998), cert. denied sub. nom., Benningfield v. Nuchia, 526 U.S. 1065 (1999). The Fifth Circuit held that the referral was intended to assess fitness for duty and was appropriate for gathering facts to form the basis of an employment decision. Id.

B. Drug Testing

1. ***Common Law and Statutes.*** There are no Texas statutes specifically addressing drug testing by employers in Texas. However, employers should be aware that the Texas Commission on Human Rights Act contains a general provision that allows an employer to adopt a policy prohibiting the employment of an individual who currently uses or possesses a "controlled substance" (as defined under federal law) other than use or possession that is under the supervision of a licensed health care professional or any other use or possession authorized under the federal Controlled Substances Act or other federal or state law. See Tex. Lab. Code Ann. § 21.120(a) (Vernon 1996). However, a policy that is adopted or applied with the intent to discriminate on the basis of race, color, sex, national origin, religion, age, or disability is not permitted. Id. at § 21.120(b).

As of September 1, 2005, employers with 15 or more employees who have workers' compensation insurance coverage are no longer required to implement a drug abuse policy as previously required by Tex. Lab. Code Ann. § 411.091(a) (Vernon 1996). See Commissioner's Bulletin No. B-0038-05 (August 17, 2005) (available at http:// www.tdi.state.tx.us/ bulletins/2005/b-0038-05.html).

2. ***Private Employers.*** Under the common law, an employer may require an employee to consent to a drug testing program as a condition of continued employment. Jennings v. Minco Tech. Labs, Inc., 765 S.W.2d 497, 500-02 (Tex. App. –Austin 1989, writ denied) (upholding against privacy claim chip manufacturer's right to institute random drug testing); Tex. Employment Comm'n v. Hughes Drilling Fluids, 746 S.W.2d 796, 799-800 (Tex. App.—Tyler 1988, writ denied). There is no invasion of privacy where the employee signs a written consent to a drug screening because it is voluntary. Farrington v. Sysco Food Servs., Inc., 865 S.W.2d 247, 253 (Tex. App.—Houston [1st Dist.] 1993, writ denied). Consent is an "absolute defense" in any tort action based upon invasion of privacy. Jennings, 765 S.W.2d at 500. An employer must not only obtain the employee's consent to drug testing, but must also obtain the employee's consent to release the test results to the employer. Crocker v. Synpol, Inc., 732 S.W.2d 429 (Tex. App.—Beaumont 1987, no writ).

The validity of the consent cannot be attacked by merely arguing that it was signed under financial distress (such as economic circumstances requiring salary continuation). Jennings, 765 S.W.2d at 502. For the purposes of unemployment compensation, failure to provide consent for a drug test is misconduct justifying denial of unemployment compensation benefits because requiring such consent is not deemed to be an unreasonable condition of continued employment. Kaminski v. Tex. Employment Comm'n, 848 S.W.2d 811, 812 (Tex. App.—Houston [14th Dist.] 1993, no writ); Tex. Employment Comm'n, 746 S.W.2d at 800-01.

The Texas Supreme Court has ruled that negligent drug testing is *not* a recognized theory of liability for employers of at-will employees. Mission Petroleum Carriers, Inc. v. Solomon, 106 S.W.3d 705, 715-716 (Tex. 2003) (employers who collect in-house urine specimens under the Department of Transportation (DOT) regulations for random drug -testing of employees owe no duty of care to employees to conduct the drug test with reasonable care). Likewise, under Texas law, a laboratory owes no duty of reasonable care to an employee whose urine is tested for drugs at the request of his employer. Frank v. Delta Airlines, Inc., No. 3:00-CV-2772-R, 2001 WL 910386 at *2 (N.D. Tex. Aug. 3, 2001) (citing Willis v. Roche Biomedical Labs., Inc., 61 F.3d 313, 315 (5th Cir. 1995)).

3. ***Public Employers.*** The government has a compelling interest in assuring that employees who could injure the public safety are drug-free. Bailey v. City of Baytown, 781 F. Supp. 1210, 1218 (S.D. Tex. 1991). In Bailey, in the context of employees at a waste-water treatment plant, the court held that since urinalysis is accurate, routine, and not highly offensive, it is a reasonable means for achieving that governmental interest. Id.

C. Medical Testing

1. ***Common Law and Statutes.*** No employer in Texas may require an employee to take a test for AIDS or HIV unless "as a bona fide occupational qualification and there is not a less discriminatory means of satisfying the occupational qualification." Tex. Health & Safety Code Ann. § 81.102(a)(5)(A) (Vernon Supp. 2000). The employer bears the burden of proving that the test is necessary. Id. at § 81.102(b). Restrictions on disclosure of AIDS/HIV test results is discussed at VI.B, infra.

The employee may not have an expectation of privacy if a medical test or medical examination follows a work-related accident. Morrison v. Weyerhaeuser Co., 119 Fed. Appx. 581 (5th Cir. 2004) (rejecting employee's invasion of privacy claim where supervisor insisted on being present during a medical examination following a work-related accident, but nothing private was disclosed during the medical examination which consisted primarily of an x-ray).

An employer or labor organization commits an unlawful employment practice if it discriminates against an individual with respect to compensation or terms, conditions, or privileges of employment: (1) on the basis of genetic information or (2) because of the refusal of the individual to submit to a genetic test. Tex. Lab. Code § 21.402 (Vernon Supp. 2001). Employers should exercise caution in this area to the extent that test results may disclose disabilities and action based on such results could run afoul of the Americans with Disabilities Act or Texas Labor Code's prohibition against disability discrimination, Tex. Lab. Code § 21.051 (Vernon 1996). In addition, there are limitations on genetic testing under the Texas Insurance Code that apply to "group health benefit plan issuers." See VI.B, infra. Restrictions on the disclosure of genetic testing records are described at VI.B, infra.

2. ***Private Employers.*** No reported cases.

3. ***Public Employers.*** No reported cases.

D. Polygraph Tests

There is no state statute prohibiting the use of polygraph examinations by employers in Texas, except in certain specific public sector jobs. However, the federal Employee Polygraph Protection Act ("EPPA"), 29 U.S.C. § 2009 et. seq., makes it an unlawful employment practice to require employees or applicants to take or submit to any polygraph examination except under very limited circumstances. The Act does not apply to federal, state or local governments. The primary exceptions are for employers (a) whose primary business is providing security services for governmental purposes such as public transportation or currency, (b) authorized to manufacture or dispense a controlled substance, or (c) involved in an ongoing investigation of theft, embezzlement or espionage provided the employee is a reasonable suspect and the employer first provides the employee with specific statutory disclosures in writing. 29 U.S.C. § 2006.

The Texas Polygraph Examiners Act regulates polygraph examiners who practice in Texas. Tex. Occ. Code § 1703.002 (Vernon 2000). The examiner is permitted to disclose the results of a polygraph exam only to (i) the examinee, (ii) the person, business, or agency that requested the examination, and (iii) any licensing or regulatory agency. Id. at 1703.306 (Vernon 2000). If an employer requests a polygraph examination, information obtained from the examination may not be disclosed. Tex. Occ. Code § 1703.002 (Vernon 2000).

Determining whether a polygraph examiner is an "employer" under the EPPA requires a consideration of whether the examiner went beyond the role of an independent entity and exerted control, as a matter of "economic reality" over the employer's compliance with the EPPA. Calbillo v. Cavender Oldsmobile, Inc., 288 F.3d 721, 727 (5th Cir. 2002). If an examiner is hired for the sole purpose of administering an examination, then as a matter of economic reality, the examiner is generally not "acting in the interest of an employer in relation to an employee or prospective employee," and therefore, is not subject to suit under 29 U.S.C. § 2005 (c)(1). Id. The distinction is important, as an independent polygraph examiner hired by an employer to conduct polygraph examinations does not owe a duty of reasonable care to the employees tested. Id. at 729-30.

Public employers are government actors and thus must demonstrate both a compelling interest behind administering a polygraph examination and show that there is no less intrusive, more reasonable substitute. Tex. State Employees Union v. Tex. Dep't of Mental Health & Mental Retardation, 746 S.W.2d 203, 205 (Tex. 1987). The Texas Supreme Court has protected employee privacy rights when the government cannot show that an intrusion is reasonably warranted. See id. at 205 -06 (objectives of the Texas Department of Mental Health and Retardation in utilizing polygraph examinations of its employees were not adequately compelling to warrant invasion of the employees' privacy rights).

The state's interests in its role as an employer are different than those in its role as a governing body. As employees take on positions carrying more and more risk and authority, the state's interest in ensuring that such employees are honest and credible increases. The state's interest as an employer may be compelling with respect to matters relevant to the employee's job duties and performance. Firemen's & Policemen's Civil Serv. Comm'n v. Burnham, 715 S.W.2d 809, 811-12 (Tex. App.—Austin 1986, writ denied) (holding that allegations of criminal activity are relevant to a police officer's employment even if he was off-duty when the crimes occurred); but see Talent v. City of Abilene, 508 S.W.2d 592, 596 (Tex. 1974) (holding that allegations of off-duty criminal activity were not relevant to fireman's employment). However, consent is a defense to a privacy claim based on a polygraph examination. Town of S. Padre Island v. Jacobs, 736 S.W.2d 134, 139 (Tex. App.—Corpus Christi 1986, writ denied). In addition, even instances in which a polygraph examination is appropriate, the questions asked during the examination must be narrowly tailored to address the particular concerns of the state as an employer. Tex. State Employees Union, 746 S.W.2d at 205.

Firefighters and police officers in municipalities that have voted to adopt the Municipal Civil Service chapter of the Texas Local Government Code can only be required to take polygraph exams as part of internal investigations if they consent and pass or are ordered to under extraordinary circumstances that call the integrity of the officers or department into question. Tex. Loc. Gov't Code Ann. § 143.124 (Vernon 1999). Additionally, on request, the examination results must be provided 48 hours after testing and the relevant tests results cannot be used in any commission proceedings. Id. at §§ 143.124(c), (e). In addition, employees of the Texas Department of Justice cannot be suspended, discharged or subject to any other form of employment discrimination for refusal to take a polygraph test. Tex. Gov't Code Ann. § 493.022 (Vernon 1998).

E. Fingerprinting

Some categories of employers are specifically empowered by statute to require applicants to submit fingerprints as a condition of employment. See, e.g., Tex. Educ. Code Ann. § 51.215 (Vernon 1996) (permitting public colleges and similar educational institutions to require fingerprints for applicants to security-sensitive positions); Tex. Gov't. Code Ann. § 411.098 (Vernon 1998) (applying to Texas School for the Blind); Id. at § 411.113 (Texas School for the Deaf); Tex. Health & Safety Code Ann. § 533.007(d) (Vernon Supp. 2000) (applying to state and community mental health centers). There are no other Texas statutes or cases discussing fingerprinting in the employment context.

III. SEARCHES

A. Employee's Person

There are no reported cases about searches of an employee's person under Texas law. General case law regarding privacy rights in the context of investigations may be instructive. An employer may question an employee within a reasonable scope during business hours on business premises when the employer has reason to believe that the employee has stolen company property. Patton v. United Parcel Serv., Inc., 910 F. Supp. 1250, 1276 (S.D. Tex. 1995). See also Rackley v. Decker Food Co., No. 05-94-01052-CV, 1995 WL 447567 (Tex. App.—Dallas July 26, 1995, writ denied) (directed verdict on plaintiff's intrusion claim was not reversible error where employee consented to employer's investigation and to the content of other employees' interviews). However, an employee's reasonable expectation of privacy in his own person seems likely to overcome any employer need for search. See K-Mart Corp. v. Trotti, 677 S.W.2d 632, 637-38 (Tex. App.—Houston [1st Dist.] 1984), writ ref'd n.r.e., 686 S.W.2d 593 (Tex. 1985) (per curiam). As to an employee's alleged misconduct, the Texas Supreme Court has declined to recognize a cause of action against employers for negligent investigations of their at-will employee's alleged misconduct. Tex. Farm Bureau Mut. Ins. Cos. v. Sears, 84 S.W.3d 604 (Tex. 2002).

B. Employee's Work Area

The guidepost for the lawfulness of an employer's search of a work area is the employee's reasonable expectation of privacy in that area. K-Mart Corp. v. Trotti, 677 S.W.2d 632, 637-38 (Tex. App.—Houston [1st Dist.] 1984), writ ref'd n.r.e., 686 S.W.2d 593 (Tex. 1985) (per curiam). An employer may demonstrate "an interest both in maintaining control over . . . and in conducting legitimate, reasonable searches" of a locked locker or desk used by the employee when the employer retains a copy of the key with the employee's knowledge. Id. at 637. See also Dawson v. State, 868 S.W.2d 363, 370 (Tex. App. –Dallas 1993, pet. ref'd) (holding that the expectation of privacy is diminished when an employee knows "that others could search or have access to the locker or desk"). There is no reasonable expectation in common areas, such as a hallway outside of an employee's office. See Gillespie v. Dallas Hous. Auth., No. CA 3:01-CV-895-R, 2003 WL 102223 (N.D. Tex. Jan. 3, 2003).

However, when the employer does not retain a key to a desk or locker, and the employee locks his desk or locker, the employee's expectation of privacy is enhanced and the offensiveness of an intrusion increases. K-Mart, 677 S.W.2d at 637); Dawson, 868 S.W.2d at 370 (both contrasting searching an unlocked locker or entering an unlocked office door and holding that an employee had a reasonable expectation of privacy in her locker when she provided her own lock and had no notice of the possibility of searches by the employer). While employers can give police permission to conduct warrantless searches of employees' lockers, there must either be notice of such a policy or employer access to the lockers. Id.

Whether a public employee has a reasonable expectation of privacy in his or her workplace must be determined on a case by case basis. O'Connor v. Ortega, 480 U.S. 709, 718, 107 S. Ct. 1492, 94 L.Ed.2d 714 (1987). However, a public employer's intrusion upon the privacy interests of its employees for non-investigatory, work-related purposes, as well as for investigations of work-related misconduct, does not require a warrant and is judged by the standard of reasonableness. Id. Specifically, such workplace searches must be reasonable both at the inception and scope. Id. at 726.

C. Employee's Property

Chapter 52 of the Texas Labor Code was amended on June 17, 2011 to prohibit public and private employers from adopting and enforcing policies that deny employees the right to keep a lawfully possessed firearm or ammunition in a locked, private vehicle in parking lots or parking garages that employers provide for their employees. Tex. Lab. Code Ann. § 52.061 (Vernon Supp. 2011). In order to store a firearm in her vehicle, the employee must hold a concealed handgun license in accordance with Chapter 411 of the Texas Government Code or otherwise lawfully possess a firearm. § 52.061. The law excepts several employers from its coverage, including school districts, charter and private schools, chemical manufacturers, and oil and gas refineries. § 52.062(a)(2)(B)-(F).

1. ***Private Employers.*** Unlike a desk or locker provided by the employer, personal items such as a purse or briefcase are the property of the employee. As a result, the expectation of privacy is considerably higher for such personal items than for such areas as unlocked desk drawers. See, e.g., K-Mart Corp. v. Trotti, 677 S.W.2d 632, 638 (Tex. App.—Houston [1st Dist.] 1984, writ ref'd n.r.e., 686 S.W.2d 593 (Tex. 1985) (per curiam) (holding that "the single act of opening and inspecting the locker, and *certainly the purse*" support the jury's finding of an invasion of privacy) (emphasis added).

2. ***Public Employers.*** There are no cases in Texas distinguishing between employee property searches conducted by public versus private employers.

IV. MONITORING OF EMPLOYEES

A. Telephones and Electronic Communications

1. ***Wiretapping.*** It is a crime to intentionally intercept, endeavor to intercept, or procure another person to intercept or endeavor to intercept a wire, oral, or electronic communication. Tex. Pen. Code Ann. § 16.02 (Vernon 1994 and Supp. 2000). It is not an offense if the person making the interception is a party to the communication or if one of the parties to the communication has given prior consent. Id. at § 16.02(c)(4) (Vernon Supp. 2000). However, if the purpose of the interception is to commit a criminal or tortious act, the defense of consent does not apply. Id. In Burnett v. State, 789 S.W.2d 376 (Tex. App. – Houston [1st Dist.] 1990, pet. ref'd, the Court held that the interception by a security personnel employee of telephone conversation of store employee fell within statutory exception for ordinary course of business use to statute prohibiting persons from willingly intercepting communications.

2. ***Electronic Communications.*** It is an actionable invasion of privacy for a third party to listen to or record a phone call or other similar voice communication without consent of one of the parties to the communication. Tex. Civ. Prac. & Rem. Code Ann. §§ 123.001, 123.002 (Vernon 1997). However, consent of one party to the conversation, even if that person is the recorder, is sufficient for a lawful taping. Kotrla v. Kotrla, 718 S.W.2d 853 (Tex. App.—Corpus Christi 1986, writ ref'd n.r.e.) Any person who divulges information obtained through an illegal wiretap may be held liable. Tex. Civ. Prac. & Rem. Code Ann. § 123.002 (West 1997); Collins v. Collins, 904 S.W.2d 792 (Tex. App.—Houston [1st Dist.] 1995), writ denied, 923 S.W.2d 569 (Tex. 1996) (per curiam).

An employee does not have an expectation of privacy in e-mail messages sent over a company's e-mail system although the e-mail messages are stored in personal folders to which access is restricted by a personal password. McLaren v. Microsoft Corp., No. 05-97-00824-CV, 1999 WL 339015 (Tex. App.—Dallas May 28, 1999, no pet.).

It is a crime to intercept e-mail communications without prior consent or if the purpose is to commit a criminal or tortious act. Tex. Pen. Code Ann. § 16.02 (Vernon 1994 and Supp. 2000) (including "electronic communications" which is defined to cover e-mail communications in Tex. Code Crim. Proc. Ann. art. 18.20, § 1 (Vernon Supp. 2000)).

It is additionally a crime to intercept voice communications without prior consent or if the purpose is to commit a criminal or tortious act. Tex. Pen. Code Ann. § 16.02(c)(4) (Vernon Supp. 2000).

3. ***Other Electronic Monitoring.*** In 2009, Texas enacted a law criminalizing online harassment. Tex. Penal Code Ann. § 33.07. Specifically, the law prohibits online impersonation with the intent to cause harm. Id. at § 33.07(a). Under the statute, an individual may not use another person's name or persona to create a web page or to post one or more messages on a commercial social networking site, with the intent to defraud, harm, intimidate or threaten another person. Id. A violation of the law is classified as a third-degree felony, punishable by two to ten years imprisonment, and a fine not to exceed $10,000. Id. at § 33.07(c).

This law may prove helpful to employers that are attacked online by disgruntled, former employees using false personas to send emails to other employees or phony profiles on social networking sites to "spoof" a former supervisor. These impersonations are often defamatory, and this law should make it easier for prosecutors to uncover the identity of the perpetrator without any cost to the employer.

B. Mail

An employee does not have an expectation of privacy in e-mail messages sent over a company's e-mail system although the e-mail messages are stored in personal folders to which access is restricted by a personal password. McLaren v. Microsoft Corp., No. 05-97-00824-CV, 1999 WL 339015 (Tex. App.—Dallas May 28, 1999, no pet.).

It is a crime to intercept e-mail communications without prior consent or if the purpose is to commit a criminal or tortious act. Tex. Pen. Code Ann. § 16.02 (Vernon 1994 and Supp. 2000) (including "electronic communications" which is defined to cover e-mail communications in Tex. Code Crim. Proc. Ann. art. 18.20, § 1 (Vernon Supp. 2000)).

C. Surveillance/Photographing

An employee does not have an expectation of privacy "where one's movements are exposed to public views generally." Roberts v. Houston Indep. Sch. Dist., 788 S.W.2d 107, 111 (Tex. App.—Houston [1st Dist.] 1990, writ denied) (holding that a teacher had no expectation of privacy in her classroom). Where videotaping is done in public areas and does not record any private affairs, there is not invasion of privacy. Id. See also Price v. City of Terrell, No.3:99-CV-0269-D, 2000 WL 1872081 (N.D. Tex. Dec. 20, 2000).

A Texas statute permits electronic monitoring of a nursing home resident's room, upon request of the nursing home resident or his or her legal guardian. See Tex. Health & Safety Code Ann. §§ 242.841-852. (Vernon Supp. 2002) The law requires the institution to post a conspicuous notice at the entrance of the institution, and at the entrance of each monitored resident's room, warning employees and visitors that the room is being monitored by an electronic monitoring device. See id. at § 242.847(b) and 242.850. An institution may require the electronic monitoring device to be installed in a manner that is safe for residents, employees or visitors who may be moving about the room. Id. at § 242.847(g).

V. ACTIVITIES OUTSIDE THE WORKPLACE

A. Statute or Common Law

There are no Texas statutes specifically addressing employees' off-duty conduct. In Collingsworth General Hospital v. Hunnicutt, 988 S.W.2d 706 (Tex. 1998), the Texas Supreme Court held that unemployment compensation benefits were properly denied the plaintiff because she was terminated for "misconduct . . . 'connected with' her last work" under Section 207.044(a) of the Texas Labor Code, after pleading guilty to an aggravated assault for slashing another woman with a box cutter while off-duty. The Court held that while not all violations of personnel policies constitute "misconduct" within the meaning of the Texas Labor Code, the plaintiff's intentional violation of a law as well as engaging in conduct so fundamentally opposed to the hospital's policy against inflicting harm to persons that the conduct qualified. The Court noted that "[t]he adverse impact of an employee's misconduct on an employer will not always depend on whether the misconduct occurred while the employee was on-duty or off-duty or whether the misconduct occurred on or off the employer's premises." Id. at 708-09. Other case law in this area is set forth below.

B. Employees' Personal Relationships

1. ***Romantic Relationships Between Employees.*** In Helena Laboratories Corp. v. Snyder, 886 S.W.2d 767 (Tex. 1994), the Texas Supreme Court held that an employer could not be held liable to the spouses of two of its employees for failing to take action to prevent an extramarital affair between the two employees. The court held that the action was barred by former Texas Family Code § 4.06 (repealed 1997), which precludes claims for alienation of affection. In so holding, the Court refused to recognize a cause of action for negligent interference with the familial relationship.

Under Texas law, there is no constitutionally protected right to engage in adultery. According to the Supreme Court of Texas, unlike recognized privacy rights concerning child rearing, family relationships, procreation, marriage, contraception, and abortion, adulterous conduct involving an affair by one police officer with the wife of another officer is not a fundamental, constitutionally protected right. See City of Sherman v. Henry, 928 S.W.2d 464, 469 (Tex. 1996). According to the court, having sexual relations with the spouse of another is not a right that is "implicit in the concept of liberty" or "deeply rooted in this State's history and tradition." See id. at 473. As such, the plaintiff police officer's adulterous affair with the wife of another police officer could legitimately be the basis of a decision to deny the officer promotion. Id. at 474.

In Crosby v. Dallas County, 166 F. Supp. 2d 525 (N.D. Tex. 2001), the court refused to find that the two-level demotion of an employee based on his secret sexual relationship with a subordinate was race discrimination where other officers not belonging to employee's protected class had been similarly or more harshly disciplined in that a white officer had been terminated as consequence of consensual sexual relationship with a subordinate. Also, in Smith v. Wal-Mart Stores, 891 F.2d 1177 (5th Cir. 1990) the Court upheld the termination of an employee for violation of non-fraternization policy and found that such a termination was not grounds for gender-based discrimination claim.

2. ***Sexual Orientation.*** In Bailey v. City of Austin, 972 S.W.2d 180 (Tex. App.—Austin 1998, pet. denied), city employees and same sex partners sued after a city referendum was passed to eliminate insurance benefits to domestic partners. The court held that the referendum did not violate the equal protection clause of the Texas Constitution, reasoning that the change in insurance benefits was based on marital status and not on sexual orientation and was rationally related to the legitimate state purpose of recognizing and fostering marital relationships.

In City of Dallas v. England, 846 S.W.2d 957 (Tex. App.—Austin 1993, writ dism'd w.o.j.), the court affirmed the granting of an injunction against the City of Dallas' Police Department from relying on its hiring policy prohibiting the employment of homosexuals and the Texas Penal Code provision 21.06 on which it was based, which criminalizes private sexual relations between consenting adults of the same sex. Relying on its decision in State v. Morales, 826 S.W.2d 201 (Tex. App.—Austin 1992), rev'd on other grounds, 869 S.W.2d 941 (Tex. 1994), the court held that the employer could not consider this policy in rejecting the application of the plaintiff, a lesbian.

3. ***Marital Status.*** There are no Texas statutes or case law at present time regarding the consideration of marital status in employment relations.

C. Smoking

The City of Houston has an ordinance that prohibits smoking in all enclosed areas within places of employment and orders employers to communicate this prohibition to all prospective employees upon their application for employment. Houston Tex. Ordinance No. 2006-1054 (Oct. 18, 2006); Houston Code of Ordinances § 21-238. This ordinance became effective on September 1, 2007, repealing a previous section of the Houston Code which required an employer to adopt, implement and maintain a written employee smoking policy for places other than public areas. Houston Code of Ordinances § 2-239 (prior to September 1, 2007).

In Couey v. Arrow Coach Lines, Inc., 288 S.W.2d 192 (Tex. Civ. App.—Austin 1956, no writ), the Court discussed the validity of an arbitration award to an employee dismissed, for among other things, violation of employer's no-smoking while on duty policy.

D. Blogging

There are no Texas statutes at present time addressing employment-related blogging, but courts in Texas have granted an employer an injunction to prevent a former employee from causing financial harm to the employer by disclosing the employer's confidential information through blogging. Dynamic Sports Nutrition, Inc. v. Roberts, No. H-08-1929, 2009 WL 136023 (S.D. Tex. 2009) (granting employer's request for a permanent injunction against former employee who posted employer's confidential information and trade secrets on publicly accessible blogs and websites causing the employer to lose over $500,000 in profits).

VI. RECORDS

A. Personnel Records

1. ***Public Employers.*** The Texas Public Information Act requires all public employers to make all records available to the public except, among other things, "information in a personnel file, the disclosure of which would constitute a clearly unwarranted invasion of personal privacy." Tex. Gov't Code Ann. § 552.102. (Vernon 1994 & Supp. 2000). Also excepted are records deemed confidential, private personnel records, and the address and phone number of

members of law enforcement and those public employees who do not wish their address and telephone numbers to be disclosed. Id. §§ 552.101, 552.102, 552.117. Section 552.101 has been interpreted to protect all information the disclosure of which would be an invasion of privacy. The privacy analysis, however, applies to all records even if they are not personnel records. Industrial Found. of the South v. Tex. Indus. Accident Bd., 540 S.W.2d 668, 682 (Tex. 1976); Morales v. Ellen, 840 S.W.2d 519, 524 (Tex. App.—El Paso 1992, writ denied). Fire and police departments must maintain complete personnel files on all officers, which may not be disclosed except with consent or as mandated by law. Tex. Loc. Gov't Code Ann. § 143.089 (Vernon Supp. 1999). Teacher performance evaluations are confidential. Tex. Educ. Code Ann. § 21.355 (Vernon 1996). Charitable contributions made by state employees are confidential. Tex. Gov't Code Ann. § 659.135 (Vernon Supp. 2000).

2. ***Private Employers.*** Private employers are required to maintain those employment records specified by the Texas Workforce Commission and must provide them to the Commission on request. Tex. Lab. Code Ann. § 301.081(a) (Vernon 1996). The Commission must maintain the confidentiality of such records unless "necessary for the proper administration of this title." Id. at § 301.081(c). Employers are not required under any statute to make these records available to anyone else. However, employment records are discoverable through subpoena or discovery in litigation. A court's order that employment records of private sector employees be produced in discovery may be challenged as state action under a constitutional right to privacy theory. See Kessell v. Bridewell, 872 S.W.2d 837, 841 (Tex. App.—Waco 1994, orig. proceeding) (in mandamus proceeding, holding trial court's order that defendant insurance company produce performance evaluation records for employees involved in denial of claims in a bad faith action not abuse of discretion, based on employees' failure to establish privacy interest sufficiently; acknowledging, however, that "employment records might, under some circumstances, be included within the protected zone of privacy").

B. Medical Records

Effective September 1, 2012, House Bill 300 ("HB 300"), expands the Texas medical records privacy law and regulates the handling of protected health information ("PHI") by covered entities. A covered entity is defined broadly to include any person (or any employee, agent or contractor of such person) who assembles, collects, analyzes, uses, evaluates, stores, transmits, obtains or comes into possession of PHI. Tex. Health & Safety Code Ann. § 181.001 (Vernon 2010). Covered entities are required to train their employees with regard to the state and federal law concerning PHI within 60 days of the employee hire date and every two years thereafter. The training must be tailored to the employee's scope of employment and the covered entity's particular course of business with regard to PHI. Additionally, covered entities must document employee attendance at the training. Id. § 181.101. HB 300 prohibits the disclosure of PHI without authorization and requires that covered entities post notification if PHI is subject to electronic disclosure. Id. § 181.154. Additionally, HB 300 prohibits the sale of PHI by a covered entity. Id. § 181.153. However, authorization is not required and sale of PHI is not prohibited for disclosure to another covered entity for the purposes of treatment, payment, health care operations, or insurance or health maintenance organization functions. Id. §§ 181.153, 181.154. HB 300 levies penalties of $5,000 to $1.5 million for unauthorized disclosures of PHI. Id. § 181.201 Additionally, the law requires that anyone who conducts business in Texas and owns or licenses computerized data that includes PHI or other sensitive information must notify individuals of any breach that results in or is believed to have resulted in acquisition of PHI or sensitive information by an unauthorized person. Tex. Bus. & Com. Code Ann. § 521.053 (Vernon 2009). The penalties for failure to provide notification of such a breach are heightened under HB 300 and include fines of $100 per individual, per day that the individual has not been informed of the breach, not to exceed $250,000 for all individuals who should be notified. Id. § 521.151.

Several additional Texas statutes address privacy in medical records. To the extent that these statutes provide greater confidentiality for PHI than the new Texas privacy law, their validity is unaffected. Tex. Health & Safety Code Ann. § 181.002 (Vernon 2010). A professional treating a person for psychiatric or substance abuse problems may only disclose the communications with the patient's written consent or as otherwise permitted by law. Tex. Health & Safety Code Ann. § 611.004(a) (Vernon 2003). Cf. Thompson v. City of Arlington, 838 F. Supp. 1137 (N.D. Tex. 1993) (holding under federal law that the Arlington police force could require an officer who was being treated for depression and who attempted suicide to turn over all her psychiatric records in order to be considered for full reinstatement because the force's interest in evaluating the capacities of its officers outweighed her privacy interest).

Medical records may also be protected against disclosure under the U.S. and Texas Constitutions. Whether compelling the production of medical records in litigation is appropriate must be determined under the U.S. Constitution's guarantee of privacy. See Tarrant County Hosp. Dist. v. Hughes, 734 S.W.2d 675, 679 (Tex. App.—Fort Worth 1987, no writ) (ordering disclosure of identity of blood donors, holding that privacy interests of blood donors were outweighed by needs of accident victim who had contracted AIDS after receiving multiple transfusions).

An employer who obtains an HIV/AIDS test result regarding an employee must maintain such result in the strictest confidence. Tex. Health & Safety Code Ann. § 81.103 (Vernon 2001). Under the statute, "test result" includes any statement that an identifiable person has or has not been tested for AIDS or HIV infection, including a statement that the person is positive, negative, at risk, or has or does not have a specific level of antigen or antibody. Id. at § 81.101(5). Disclosure, except under very limited statutory exceptions, can result in criminal penalty. Id. at § 81.103 (j).

In addition, employers who qualify as "issuers" of "group health benefit plans," must maintain the confidentiality of any genetic testing information. Tex. Ins. Code Ann. art. 21.73 § 4(a) (Vernon Supp. 2000). Disclosure can be made only pursuant to a specific written consent form complying with the statute's requirements. Id. Although the term "issuer" is not defined, it appears that an employer would be covered by these provisions if it is a plan sponsor of a self-insured plan that provides for benefits for medical or surgical expenses incurred as a result of a health condition, accident or sickness. Whether an employer that merely sponsors an insured group health benefit plan is covered is less clear. Consequently, any employer that obtains genetic testing information regarding an employee should maintain it confidentially in accordance with Article 21.73 of the Texas Insurance Code.

C. Criminal Records

Employers may now obtain criminal records information through the Texas Department of Public Safety without individual consent. See Tex. Gov't Code Ann. §§ 411.088, 411.135 (Vernon 2000). Under the statute, a person who obtains this information may "use this information for any purpose" and may "release the information to any other person." Id. From a privacy claims standpoint, however, it would still be advisable to inform any applicant or employee that a criminal background check may be performed and to obtain written authorization. Similarly, it would be advisable to disclose the information only to those individuals who need to know it.

Other statutes provide that nursing homes and similar facilities are entitled to obtain a criminal history record for any applicant. Tex. Health & Safety Code Ann. § 250.002(a) (Vernon Supp. 2000). The records, however, may not be disclosed to anyone except under a court order or on written consent. Id. at § 250.007. It is not an invasion of privacy to inform a state trust company of any employee's involvement (known or suspected) in an unlawful activity. Tex. Fin. Code § 181.307 (Vernon Supp. 2000).

D. Subpoenas / Search Warrants

Employers have a legal duty to comply with a subpoena. However, employers may give the employee whose records are at issue advanced notice that they will be complying with the subpoena out of courtesy. If, for example, an employee's personnel file contains confidential, proprietary, or otherwise privileged company documents, the employer may follow the procedures set out in Texas Rule of Civil Procedure 176.6 and move for protection under Texas Rule of Civil Procedure 192.6(b) to resist compliance with the subpoena to the extent it is objectionable. Texas Rule of Civil Procedure 176.6 addresses subpoenas that command a person to produce documents or tangible things. 176.6(d) explains the process by which one can object to the subpoena: "A person commanded to produce and permit inspection or copying of designated documents and things may serve on the party requesting issuance of the subpoena—before the time specified for compliance written objections—to producing any or all of the designated materials. A person need not comply with the part of the subpoena to which objection is made as provided in this paragraph unless ordered to do so by the court. The party requesting the subpoena may move for such an order at any time after an objection is made." 176.6 (e) provides that "A person commanded to appear at a deposition, hearing, or trial , or to produce and permit inspection and copying of designated documents and things, and any other person affected by the subpoena, may move for a protective order under Rule 192.6(b)--before the time specified for compliance—either in court in which the action is pending or in a district court in the county where the subpoena was served."

Employment records are discoverable through subpoena or discovery in litigation. A court's order that employment records of private sector employees be produced in discovery may be challenged as state action under a constitutional right to privacy theory. See Kessell v. Bridewell, 872 S.W.2d 837, 841 (Tex. App.—Waco 1994, orig. proceeding) (in mandamus proceeding, holding trial court's order that defendant insurance company produce performance evaluation records for employees involved in denial of claims in a bad faith action not abuse of discretion, based on employees' failure to establish privacy interest sufficiently; acknowledging, however, that "employment records might, under some circumstances, be included within the protected zone of privacy").

VII. ACTIONS SUBSEQUENT TO EMPLOYMENT

A. References

False statements written in a letter of reference can give rise to a defamation claim. However, provided they meet enumerated requirements, most statements in connection with references will be covered by a qualified privilege. For instance, a Texas court ruled that a statement by an employee's former supervisor to a prospective employer "not to fool with" the plaintiff because the plaintiff had taken money from the former employer and could not be trusted, was held to be qualifiedly privileged because the statement concerned the former employee's work record as was not done with malice. Duncantell v. Universal Life Ins. Co., 446 S.W.2d 934 (Tex.Civ.App.—Houston [14th Dist.] 1969, writ ref'd n.r.e.). In defamation cases, the qualified privilege is an affirmative defense that must be pled. TRT Development Co. v. Meyers, 15 S.W.3d 281, 286 (Tex.App.—Corpus Christi 2000, no pet.). In order to be protected by the qualified privilege, the statement must be (1) made in good faith; (2) be upon a subject in which the speaker or author has an interest or a duty; (3) be made to another person having a corresponding interest or duty; and (4) be made in a lawful manner for a lawful purpose. Id. at 286; see also Bryant v. Lucent Technologies, 10-03-00330-CV, 2005 WL 2155196 at *15 (Tex.App.—Waco September 7, 2005); See also, Austin v. Inet Techs.,Inc., 118 S.W.3d 491, 496 (Tex.App.—Dallas 2003, no pet.); Diamond Shamrock Refining & Marketing v. Mendez, 844 S.W.2d 198, 210 (Tex. 1992).

In 1999, the Texas Legislature attempted to address the issue of defamation liability for employers in connection with employee references when it enacted Chapter 103 of the Texas Labor Code. In particular § 103.004 discusses immunity from civil liability and § 103.005 provides that Chapter 103 does not require that employment references be given. Following are the two statutory provisions:

Texas Labor Code 103.004. Immunity From Civil Liability; Employer Representatives.

> (a) An employer who discloses information about a current or former employee under Section 103.003 is immune from civil liability for that disclosure or any damages proximately caused by that disclosure unless it is proven by clear and convincing evidence that the information disclosed was known by that employer to be false at the time the disclosure was made or that the disclosure was made with malice or in reckless disregard for the truth or falsity of the information disclosed. For purposes of this subsection, "known" means actual knowledge based on information relating to the employee, including any information maintained in a file by the employer on that employee.
>
> (b) This chapter applies to a managerial employee or other representative of the employer who is authorized to provide and who provides information in accordance with this chapter in the same manner that it applies to an employer.

Texas Labor Code 103.005. Employment Reference.

This chapter does not require an employer to provide an employment reference to or about a current or former employee.

Section 103.004 creates immunity from civil liability provided disclosure of the covered information is not done with (1) knowledge that the information is false; (2) malice; or (3) reckless disregard as to its truth. The statute thus requires malice or actual malice to defeat immunity. See e.g., HBO v. Harrison, 983 S.W.2d 31, 40 (Tex.App.—Houston [14th Dist.] 1998, no pet.) ("Proof that a statement was motivated by actual malice, existing at the time of publication defeats the privilege."). "In the defamation context, a statement is made with actual malice when it is made with knowledge of its falsity or with reckless disregard as to its truth." Randall's Food Mkts., Inc., 891 S.W.2d 640, 646 (Tex. 1995); see also Forbes Inc. v. Granaga Biosciences, Inc., 124 S.W.3d 167 (Tex. 2003) ("Actual malice, in this context, 'is a term of art.' It is not ill will, spite, or evil motive."); Huckabee v. Time Warner, 19 S.W.3d 413, 420 ("actual malice" requires proof that the defendant made a statement "with knowledge that it was false or with reckless disregard of whether it was true or not.").

Section 103.005 had the effect of codifying the existing common law. "The law imposes no duty on anyone to talk about a former employee." Saucedo v. Rheem Mfg. Co., 974 S.W.2d 117, 122 (Tex.App.—San Antonio 1998, pet. denied) (quoting American Medical Int'l Inc. v. Giurintano, 821 S.W.2d 331, 337 (Tex-App.—Houston [14th District] 1991, no writ); see also Golden Spread Council, Inc. #562 v. Akins, 926 S.W.2d 287, 290-293 (Tex. 1996) (former employer has no duty to provide a reference to a prospective employer).

An important distinction between § 103.004 of the Texas Labor Code and the common law is that the statute explicitly states the sort of information which can be disclosed to a prospective employer. Tex. Lab. Code § 103.003 limits employers to disclosing information about a current or former employee's job performance to a prospective employer. "Job performance" is defined broadly as "the manner in which an employee performs a position of employment and includes an analysis of the employee's attendance at work, attitudes, effort, knowledge, behaviors, and skills." § 103.002. This definition should capture most subject matters discussed in an employee reference.

Three other defenses to defamation are (1) truth; (2) substantial truth; and (3) consent. See Tex. Civ. Prac. Rem. Code § 73.005 ("The truth of the statement in the publication on which an action for libel is based is a defense to the action."); Randall's Food Mkts. Inc., 891 S.W.2d at 646 (truth is complete defense to defamation); McIlvain v. Jacobs, 794 S.W.2d 14, 15-16 (Tex. 1990) (substantial truth is a complete defense to defamation and substantial truth means that it is no more damaging to the Plaintiff's reputation, in the mind of an average listener, than a truthful statement would have been); Reeves v. Western Co. of North America, 867 S.W.2d 385 (Tex.App.—San Antonio 1993, writ denied), abrogated on other grounds Cain v. Hearst Corp., 878 SW 2d. 577 (Tex. 1994) (job applicant who requested that his prospective employer tell his wife the reason the prospective employer was not going to hire him consented to the allegedly defamatory statements to his wife); Saucedo, 974 S.W.2d at 117 (court affirmed summary judgment on a former employee's defamation claim on consent grounds because the alleged defamatory statement was made only after employee requested a reference check when he suspected employer was giving a bad reference). However, although truth and substantial truth are defenses to defamation, the publication of the statement should not convey a false meaning. See Turner v. KTRK Television, Inc., 38 S.W.3d 103, 113-117 (Tex. 2000) (possible for publication to be defamatory even though all the individual statements in the publication are true if, by omission or juxtaposition of facts, the publication conveys a false meaning). The statement also must be true *when made*. See Gulf Constr. Co. v. Mott, 442 S.W.2d 778, 784 (Tex.Civ.App.—Houston [14th Dist.] 1969, no writ).

B. Non-Compete Agreements

Texas Business and Commerce Code §§ 15.50-15.52 provides the criteria for enforceability of covenants not to compete. The requirements listed in the statute are (1) it must be ancillary to or part of an otherwise enforceable agreement at the time the agreement is made and (2) it must be limited in the time, geographical area, and scope of activity to be restrained and (3) these limitations must be reasonable and not impose a greater restraint than is necessary to protect the goodwill or other business interest of the promisee. Section 15.51 also contains special criteria for persons licensed as a physician by the Texas State Board of Medical Examiners.

In Light v. Centel Cellular Co. of Texas, the Texas Supreme Court held that the following requirements must be met for a covenant-not-to-compete to be enforceable:

The employer must make a promise to the employee that is enforceable when made;

The promise must give rise to the employer's interest in restraining competition;

The employee must make a return promise; and

The covenant must be designed to enforce the employee's return promise.

883 S.W.2d 642, 674 (Tex. 1994). The Light Court's interpretation of the Covenant Not to Compete Act proved troublesome in practice, and three subsequent Texas Supreme Court decisions departed from its restrictive requirements, reflecting a growing trend toward the enforcement of non-competition agreements in Texas. See Marsh USA Inc. and Marsh & McLennan Companies, Inc v. Cook, 354 S.W.3d 764 (Tex. 2011); Mann Frankfort Stein & Lipp Advisors, Inc. v. Fielding, 289 S.W.3d 844 (Tex. 2009); Alex Sheshunoff Mgmt. Servs. L.P. v. Kenneth Johnson and Strunk & Assocs., 209 S.W.3d. 644 (Tex. 2006).

1. ***Ancillary to or part of Otherwise Enforceable Agreement.*** Much of the uncertainty regarding covenants not to compete has centered on the "otherwise enforceable agreement" requirement. See Curtis v. Ziff Energy Group, LTD, 12 S.W.3d 114 (Tex.App.—Houston [14th Dist.] 1999, no pet.) (holding that promise to provide confidential information and return promise to not disclose confidential information was an "otherwise enforceable agreement" and employer was not required to provide employee confidential information simultaneously with signing of covenant not to compete) cf. Trilogy Software v. Callidus Software, 143 S.W.3d 452, 461 n.6 (Tex. App.—Austin 2004, no pet. h.) (holding that there was no "otherwise enforceable agreement" because "there is no evidence that Trilogy provided [the employee] with confidential information *immediately upon or only momentarily after* he signed the agreement; instead, the event occurred *later that day*." (emphasis added)).

The Texas Supreme Court's decision in Sheshunoff alleviated much of the confusion surrounding this issue. In Sheshunoff, the employee signed an employment agreement containing a covenant not to compete. Sheshunoff, 209 S.W.3d. at 646-47. The employer promised to provide the employee special training and access to its confidential and proprietary information. Id. The employee promised to keep the information confidential. Id. Although the employer did eventually provide the employee training and confidential information, it did not do so at the time the employment agreement was executed. The appeals court held the agreement was unenforceable under Light. Id. at 647-48.

The Texas Supreme Court revisited and rejected the parts of the Light decision that precluded a unilateral contract from ever being enforceable because it was not enforceable at the time the agreement was made. Instead, the Court held that covenants not to compete can be made enforceable after an agreement is signed by performing the promises made in the agreement. Id. at 646. Therefore, a promise to give confidential information will support a covenant not compete even if the confidential information is not provided to the employee until some time after the covenant is signed. The Court also made an additional important statement as to the proper focus in determining enforceability. The Court explicitly commented that the "overly technical" disputes around whether a covenant was ancillary to an otherwise enforceable agreement that had been engendered by Light were inconsistent with the "core inquiry" required by the statute in determining enforceability—the covenant's reasonableness. Id. at 655-56.

A question that remained open after Sheshunoff was whether an enforceable non-compete agreement must contain an explicit promise by the employer to provide confidential information to the employee. In Mann, the Texas Supreme Court answered this question and held that the employer's promise to provide confidential information may be implied. Mann, 289 S.W.3d at 849.

In Mann, the Court held that even if the non-compete agreement does not contain an explicit promise by the employer to provide confidential information, if the nature of the employee's job will reasonably require the employer to do so, then an implied promise to provide confidential information exists and the non-compete agreement is enforceable as long as the other requirements of the Covenant Not To Compete Act are satisfied. Id. at 845-46. Brendan Fielding worked as a certified public account for Mann Frankfort, and neither party disputed that the job involved accessing confidential financial information. Id. at 846. The Court found that Fielding could not have acted on his promise to refrain from disclosing confidential information unless Mann Frankfort provided him with it, and Mann Frankfort's actual provision to Fielding of access to confidential information created an "otherwise enforceable agreement" under § 15.50 of the Act. Id. at 847.

In Marsh, the Texas Supreme Court further departed from Light and held that the consideration that an employer must give in order to support an enforceable covenant not to compete does *not* have to give rise to the employer's interest in restraining the employee from competing. Marsh, 354 S.W.3d 764, at 775. Marsh involved a managing director of an insurance firm, who was awarded stock options through a company incentive plan. Id. at 766. Approximately nine years after receiving the options, the employee exercised them, and in so doing, signed a three year non-solicitation agreement, as required by the incentive plan. Id. at 767. Shortly before the non-solicitation agreement expired, the employee went to work for a competitor, where he began to solicit Marsh's customers. Id. When Marsh challenged his right to do so, the employee argued that under the Light standard his non-solicitation obligations were unenforceable because the transfer of stock did not "give rise to" to Marsh's interest in restraining competition. Id. In issuing its opinion, the Marsh Court did not expressly overturn Light, but it rejected that case's approach and emphasized that nothing in the Covenant Not to Compete Act required the consideration for a non-competition agreement to give rise to the interest in restraining competition. Id. at 775. Instead, the Court emphasized that a covenant is "ancillary to or part of" an otherwise enforceable agreement—and thus enforceable—when the interest worthy of protection is "reasonably related" to the consideration given. Id. The options that Marsh granted were deemed to have met this test, as they "linked the interest of a key employee with the company's long-term business interests," and thus encouraged Cook to create goodwill on Marsh's behalf. Id. at 777. The Court also rejected the employee's argument that his non-solicitation agreement was invalid because he signed it years after being granted stock options and held that an employer's interest in restraining an employee can exist before the employer's consideration is given. Id. at 778.

Sheshunoff, Mann, and Marsh will likely mean that covenants not to compete for at-will employees in Texas will be less susceptible to technical challenges about the terms of the agreement and analyzed more for the reasonableness of the restrictions imposed on the employee.

2. ***Sufficient Business Interest.*** Texas courts recognize an employer's legitimate interest in protecting business good will, trade secrets, other confidential or proprietary information, and special training or knowledge acquired by an employee during the employment relationship. DeSantis v. Wackenhut Corp., 793 S.W.2d 670, 682 (Tex. 1990); Tom James Co. v. Mendrop, 819 S.W.2d 251, 253 (Tex. Ct. App.—Fort Worth 1991, no writ); Curtis v. Ziff Energy Group, LTD, 12 S.W.3d 114 (Tex.App.—Houston [14th Dist.] 1999, no pet.) (promise to provide confidential information and trade secrets gives rise to employer's interest in restricting employee from competing); but see Strickland v. Medtronic, 97 S.W.3d 835 (Tex.App.—Dallas 2003, pet. dism'd w.o.j.) (promise to give ninety days notice prior to terminating without cause and the promise to compensate employee in the event of economic hardship resulting from the non-compete agreement do not give rise to an interest worthy of protection by a covenant not to compete.).

3. ***Reasonableness.*** To be enforceable, a covenant not to compete must restrain no more activity than is necessary to protect the legitimate business interest of the employer. Most cases that address the scope of the activity to be restrained are found in the context of agreements prohibiting solicitation of customers or clients. Texas courts have insisted that such covenants be narrowly designed to negate the competitive advantage and knowledge the former employee might have gained about the clients *because of* his former employment. For instance, in Peat Marwick Main & Co. v. Haass, 818 S.W.2d 381 (Tex. 1991) and Juliette Fowler Homes v. Welch Associates, 793 S.W.2d 660, 663 (Tex. 1990), the Texas Supreme Court found unreasonable, and thus unenforceable, agreements potentially prohibiting a former employee from

soliciting customers or clients with whom the former employee had no contact and of whom the former employee had no confidential knowledge. See also John R. Ray & Sons, Inc. v. Stroman, 923 S.W.2d 80 (Tex. App.—Houston [14th Dist.] 1996, writ denied) (refusing to enforce covenants not to compete that include an industry-wide prohibition).

Texas courts have also refused to enforce agreements that vaguely prohibit all competitive activity or prohibit employment in any capacity for a competitive entity. E.g., McNeilus Companies, Inc. v. Sams, 971 S.W.2d 507 (Tex. App.—Dallas 1997, no writ); see also Posey v. Monier Resources, Inc., 768 S.W.2d 915, 918 (Tex. App.—San Antonio 1989, writ denied). Texas courts have also refused to enforce agreements that prohibit activity unrelated to the work the employee performed for the former employer. Bertotti v. C.E. Shepherd Co., Inc., 752 S.W.2d 648, 656 (Tex. App.—Houston [14th Dist.] 1988, no writ) (holding that language "selling or offering to sell goods or materials of any kind" was overbroad and reforming agreement to allow employee to sell non-competing products); Diversified Human Resources Group, Inc. v. Levinson-Polakoff, 752 S.W.2d 8, 11 (Tex. App.—Dallas 1988, no writ) (holding that agreement prohibiting recruiter from placing any type of employee was overbroad).

With regard to geographic limitations, Texas courts have determined that noncompetition agreements that contain no geographical limitations or fail to limit the scope of activity to be restrained are unreasonable and unenforceable. Juliette Fowler Homes, 793 S.W.2d at 663 (Tex. 1990) (determining that an agreement that contained no limitations on the geographical area or scope of activity was "an unreasonable restraint of trade and unenforceable on grounds of public policy"). However, covenants that contain no express geographic restriction, yet limit competition only to those clients with whom the employee personally worked, have been found reasonable. Totino v. Alexander & Associates, No. 01-97-01204-CV, 1998 WL 552818 at *16 (Tex. App.—Houston [1st Dist.] 1998) (No Publication). The client limitation was a substitute for the geographic restriction. *Id.* Courts may also allow a specific nonsolicitation clause that is connected to the employee's prior accounts or customers to substitute for a missing geographic restriction. See, e.g., American Express Financial Advisors, 955 F. Supp. 688, 692-93 (N.D. Tex. 1996).

The reasonableness of the area to be enforced will often depend on the particular circumstances of the situation. See Allan J. Richardson & Assocs. v. Andrews, 718 S.W.2d 833, 835 (Tex.Ct.App—Houston [14th Dist.] 1986, no writ) ("The breadth of enforcement of territorial restraints in noncompetition contracts depends upon the nature and extent of the employer's business and the degree of the employee's involvement... The covenant must bear some relationship to the activities of the employee..."). However, generally, a reasonable area of restraint consists only of the territory in which the employer worked while employed by the former employer. Zep Mfg. Co. v. Harthcock, 824 S.W.2d 654 (Tex.App.—Dallas 1992, no writ). Similarly, courts have also refused to enforce agreements with nationwide applicability when the employee did not truly have nationwide responsibilities for the former employer. Allan J. Richardson & Associates v. Andrews, 718 S.W.2d 833, 835-36 (Tex. App.—Houston [14th Dist.] 1986, no writ); see also Posey, 768 S.W.2d at 919 (reforming nationwide restriction to the area of work of the former employee). However, where it is necessary to protect trade secrets or confidential information, courts will enforce noncompetition agreements that have nationwide and even potential worldwide scope. Bertotti , v. C.E. Shepherd Co., Inc., 752 S.W.2d 648, 654 (Tex. App.—Houston [14th Dist.] 1988, no writ).

Generally courts have held that one and two year restrictions are reasonable. See, e.g., Guy Carperter & Co. v. Provenzale, 334 F.3d 459, 462 (5th Cir. 2003); Butler v. Arrow Mirror & Glass, Inc., 51 S.W.3d 787, 794 (Tex.Ct.App. —Houston [1st Dist.] 2001); Safeguard Bus. Sys. v. Schaffer, 822 S.W.2d 640, 644-45 (Tex.Civ.App.– Dallas 1991, no writ); Car Wash Sys. of Tex., Inc. v. Brigance, 856 S.W.2d 853, 859 (Tex.Ct.App.—Fort Worth 1993, no writ); American Express Fin. Advisors, Inc. v. Scott, 955 F.Supp. at 692-93. However, longer periods have been upheld. Evan's World Travel, Inc., 978 S.W.2d at 225 (three year restriction).

4. ***Reformation.*** Reformation is permitted by the statute. Tex. Bus. & Com. Code § 15.51(c); Evan's World Travel, Inc. v. Adams, 978 S.W.2d 225, 232-33 (Tex.Ct.App.—Texarkana 1998) (Court reformed geographic term to apply only to single county in which travel agent had actually worked and from which she had actually drawn customers). The employer must make a specific request for reformation at the trial court level. Daytona Group of Tex. v. Smith, 800 S.W.2d 285, 289 (Tex. Ct. App.—Corpus Christi 1990, writ denied). Note, however, that an employer cannot recover damages for the period of time that elapses before judicial reformation of an overbroad covenant. § 15.51(c). A non-disclosure agreement that is separable from but contained within the same contract as an unenforceable non-competition agreement is not rendered void by the non-competition agreement. Zep Mfg. Co. v. Harthcock, 824 S.W.2d 654, 659 (Tex. Ct. App.—Dallas 1992, no writ).

VII OTHER ISSUES

A. Statutes of Limitations

In Texas, a tort cause of action generally "accrues" for limitations purposes when the defendant's wrongful act causes an injury. Generally, accrual of a cause of action does not depend on when the plaintiff learns of injury, since the defendant's act is a legal injury in itself. See Moreno v. Sterling Drug, Inc., 787 S.W.2d 348, 351 (Tex. 1990). If the defendant's act is not wrongful in and of itself, the cause of action accrues at a later point when actual damages are sustained by the plaintiff. See Atkins v. Crosland, 417 S.W.2d 150, 153 (Tex. 1967). For example, a cause of action for negligence accrues on the date of the breach of duty, even though the injury is not immediately apparent. See Am. Centennial Ins. Co. v. Canal Ins. Co., 810 S.W.2d 246, 255 (Tex. App.—Houston [1st Dist.] 1991), aff'd in part, rev'd in part on other grounds, 843 S.W.2d 480 (Tex. 1992). An action for libel or slander accrues on the date defamatory material is published or spoken, not from the date the plaintiff experiences damaging consequences. See Langston v. Eagle Publ'g Co., 719 S.W.2d 612, 615 (Tex. App.—Waco 1986, writ ref'd n.r.e.).

Most tort causes of action are governed by a two-year statute of limitation found in the Texas Civil Practice and Remedies Code. See Tex. Civ. Prac. & Rem. Code Ann. § 16.003 (Vernon 1986 & Supp. 2000). The language of the statute expressly governs claims for all personal injuries and trespass violations. See id. Thus, except for defamation, virtually all tort litigation is governed by the two-year statute. Accordingly, the case law indicates that the following causes of action are governed by a two-year statute of limitations: (1) negligence actions, (2) invasion of privacy (including intrusion on seclusion; appropriation of name or likeness; public disclosure of private facts; placing a person in a false light); (3) intentional infliction of emotional distress; and (4) tortious interference with a business relationship. Defamation actions are governed by a separate one-year statute of limitations that is triggered upon the date of publication. See Tex. Civ. Prac. & Rem. Code Ann. § 16.002(a) (Vernon Supp. 2000).

B. Jurisdiction

Privacy torts are defined by state law, and therefore, state courts have jurisdiction over such claims. Many privacy claims are removed to federal court based on diversity or pendent jurisdiction.

A suit for damages for libel, slander, or invasion of privacy must be brought and can only be maintained in the county in which the plaintiff resided at the time of the accrual of the cause of action, or in the county in which the defendant resided at the time of filing suit, or in the county of the residence of the defendants, or any of them, or the domicile of any corporate defendant, at the election of the plaintiff. Tex. Civ. Prac. & Rem. Code Ann. § 15.017 (Vernon 1986). This statutory venue provision is mandatory. Acker v. Denton Publ'g Co., 937 S.W.2d 111, 114 (Tex. App.—Fort Worth 1996, no writ).

C. Worker's Compensation Exclusivity

The Texas Workers' Compensation Act is not the exclusive remedy for employer-employee disputes in the context of privacy claims against employers. The injuries alleged in privacy claims are not compensable injuries under the Texas Workers' Compensation Act, and thus are not barred by the Act. See, e.g, Wickel v. Knight Transp., Inc., No. EP-05-CA-0461-FM, 2006 WL 648047 at *3 (W.D. Tex. 2006) (holding that plaintiff's claim for defamation was not barred by the Texas Workers' Compensation Act because plaintiff had not alleged physical injuries or damage to the structure of his body caused by the employer's negligence).

D. Pleading Requirements

A petition in Texas must consist of a statement of the plaintiff's "cause of action" in plain language sufficient to give fair notice of the claim involved. See Tex. R. Civ. P. 45, 47. One court has stated that a plaintiff's petition must show on its face "that a primary legal right rests in the plaintiff, that there is a primary legal duty connected with this right resting on the defendant, and that there has been a breach of this duty by the defendant." Christy v. Hamilton, 384 S.W.2d 795, 796 (Tex. Civ. App.—Amarillo 1964, no writ). In addition to the requirement that the original petition allege a cause of action, the petition must help define the issues and provide information sufficient to enable the defendant to prepare a proper defense. See Tex. R. Civ. P. 45, 47. At least one court has defined the test for determining if a petition provides sufficient notice as whether an opposing attorney of reasonable competence could, with the pleading before her, determine the nature and basic issues of the dispute and the testimony which would probably be relevant. See Davis v. Quality Pest Control, 641 S.W.2d 324, 328 (Tex. App.—Houston [14th Dist.] 1982, writ ref'd n.r.e.).

A party may allege as many separate claims as he has against a single defendant regardless of whether the claims are based upon equitable or legal grounds or both and regardless of factual or legal consistency. See Tex. R. Civ. P. 48, 51(a). A party may also may set forth two or more statements of a claim alternatively or hypothetically, either in one count or in separate counts. See Tex. R. Civ. P. 48.

The plaintiff's original petition must articulate a demand for judgment (otherwise known as a prayer) for all the relief the plaintiff considers herself to be entitled. See Tex. R. Civ. P. 47. The omission of the prayer, like other defects in the pleadings, may be waived if the defendant proceeds to trial and judgment having failed to timely challenge the defect. See Am. Empire Life Ins. Co. v. Bryan, 357 S.W.2d 578, 580 (Tex. Civ. App.—Fort Worth 1962, no writ). A prayer for relief may be in the form of a general prayer, in which whatever relief plaintiff may be entitled to is generally asked for, a special prayer, in which a specific type of recovery is sought, or a combination of both. However, a prayer will not permit recovery when the petition fails to give fair and adequate notice of the cause of action pleaded or is inconsistent with the facts stated as a basis for recovery. See Kissman v. Bendix Home Sys., Inc., 587 S.W.2d 675, 677 (Tex. 1979).

On the defense side, an answer must contain all affirmative defenses to be relied upon. See Sci. Spectrum, Inc. v. Martinez, 941 S.W.2d 910, 911 (Tex. 1997); Gibbs v. Gen. Motors Corp., 450 S.W.2d 827, 828 (Tex. 1970); Tex. R. Civ. P. 94. However, affirmative defenses may be tried by consent. Tex. R. Civ. P. 67; Greenbelt Elec. Coop., Inc. v. Johnson, 608 S.W.2d 320, 323 n.5 (Tex. Civ. App. – Amarillo 1980, no writ).

SURVEY OF UTAH EMPLOYMENT LIBEL LAW

Scott S. Bell, Esq.
Parsons Behle & Latimer
One Utah Center
201 South Main Street, Suite 1800
Salt Lake City, Utah 84147-0898
Telephone: (801) 532-1234; Facsimile: (801) 536-6111

(With Developments Reported Through **November 1, 2012**)

GENERAL COMMENTS

Until 1974, Utah's official reporters were Utah and Utah 2d. When citing cases decided before 1974, the practitioner should include both the Utah reporter cite and the Pacific Reporter cite.

SIGNIFICANT DEVELOPMENTS SINCE THE 2012 *SURVEY*

The Utah federal district court, applying Utah law, held that in considering whether an article contains defamatory meaning, courts consider both the headline and the body of the article. Hogan v. Winder, 2012 WL 4356326, *9 (D. Utah Sept. 24, 2012). Reporting that a person was accused of extortion in an employment dispute was not defamatory because the article provided the context that the accusations were made in the heat of contentious civil litigation and did not imply that the person faced criminal extortion charges. Id. at *10. The court also held that the article's report on opinions of others were non-defamatory. Id., at *8. A report that an individual was terminated for poor performance and erratic behavior was held to be a non-actionable expression of opinion, at least partly because the allegations in the article were attributed to a former employer in the context of an employment dispute. Id.

The Utah Supreme Court held that the judicial proceedings privilege encompasses attorney conduct within the scope of a client's interests made in the course of judicial proceedings. Moss v. Parr Waddoups Brown Gee & Loveless, 712 Utah Adv. Rep. 41, 2012 WL 2629224, *6-8 (Utah July 6, 2012).

I. GENERAL LAW

A. General Employment Law

1. ***At Will Employment***. "The general rule is that an employment relationship for an indefinite time gives rise to a contractual arrangement that allows both the employer and the employee to terminate the employment for any reason and allows the employer to do so without extending any procedural safeguards to an employee, except as required by law." Rackley v. Fairview Care Centers, Inc., 23 P.3d 1022 (Utah 2001); Fox v. MCI Communications, Inc., 931 P.2d 857, 859 (Utah 1997). See also Uintah Basin Medical Center v. Hardy, 54 P.3d 1165, 1170 (Utah 2002); Brehany v. Nordstrom, Inc., 812 P.2d 49, 53 (Utah 1991); Berube v. Fashion Centre, Ltd., 771 P.2d 1033, 1044 (Utah 1989); Bihlmaier v. Carson, 603 P.2d 790, 792 (Utah 1979); Johnson v. Kimberly Clark Worldwide Inc., 86 F. Supp.2d 1119, 1120 (D. Utah 2000). The general rule can be overcome by demonstration that "(1) there is an implied or express agreement that the employment may be terminated only for cause or upon satisfaction of another agreed-upon condition; (2) a statute or regulation restricts the right of an employer to terminate an employee under certain conditions; or (3) the termination of employment constitutes a violation of a clear and substantial public policy." Rackley, 23 P.3d at 1026; Retherford v. AT&T Communications, 844 P.2d 949, 958-59 (Utah 1992); Heslop v. Bank of Utah, 839 P.2d 828, 836-38 (Utah 1992); Peterson v. Browning, 832 P.2d 1280, 1281-82 (Utah 1992); Hodges v. Gibson Prods. Co., 811 P.2d 151, 165 (Utah 1991). See generally Clark W. Sabey, Note, Scalpels and Meat Cleavers: Carving a Public Policy Limitation to the At-Will Employment Doctrine, 1993 Utah L. Rev. 597, 599-600 & n.28.

B. Elements of Libel Claim

1. ***Basic Elements.*** Utah follows the common law definitions of libel and slander per se. Allred v. Cook, 590 P.2d 318, 320-21 (Utah 1979) (slander). Words "are to be construed according to their usual, popular and common acceptation." Western States Title Ins. Co. v. Warnock, 415 P.2d 316, 318 (Utah 1966). See also DeBry v. Godbe, 992 P.2d 979, 982 (Utah 1999). The court will carefully examine the context in which the statement was made. West v. Thomson Newspapers, 872 P.2d 999, 1009 (Utah 1994). The guiding principle as to whether a statement may be considered defamatory is "the statement's tendency to injure a reputation in the eyes of its audience." Id. at 1008; see Utah Code Ann. § 45-2-2 (2003) (defining libel and slander); Utah Code Ann. § 76-9-501 (2004) (defining criminal libel).

2. ***Fault.***

a. **Private Figure Plaintiff/Matter of Public Concern.** The standard of conduct required in private figure plaintiff cases is that of due care. In order to establish libel, therefore, a "private individual" need show only that the defendant was negligent. In re I.M.L., 61 P.3d at 1045; Russell v. Thomson Newspapers, Inc., 842 P.2d 896, 903 n.20 (Utah 1992); Seegmiller v. KSL, Inc., 626 P.2d 968, 974 (Utah 1981); Cox v. Hatch, 761 P.2d 556, 560 (Utah 1988). No Utah case specifically addresses the issue of whether a higher standard would apply to matters of public concern. See Seegmiller, 626 P.2d at 978-79 n.10 (noting that constitutional standard of actual malice would probably apply to issues of public concern). Plaintiffs must prove malice and actual harm in defamation claims arising from labor disputes. Int'l Ass'n of United Mine Workers Union v. United Mine Workers of America, 2006 WL 1183245, *4 (D.Utah 2006).

b. **Private Figure Plaintiff/Matter of Private Concern.** The standard of conduct required in private figure plaintiff cases is that of due care. In order to establish libel, therefore, a "private individual" need show only that the defendant was negligent. Russell v. Thomson Newspapers, Inc., 842 P.2d 896, 903 n.20 (Utah 1992); Seegmiller v. KSL, Inc., 626 P.2d 968, 974 (Utah 1981); Cox v. Hatch, 761 P.2d 556, 560 (Utah 1988); Gascoigne v. Gascoigne, 2010 WL 1418881, *3 (D. Utah April 7, 2010) (citing Ferguson v. Williams & Hunt, 221 P.3d 205, 213 (Utah 2009)).

c. **Public Figure Plaintiff/Matter of Public Concern.** Utah follows the actual malice standard of New York Times Co. v. Sullivan in cases involving public officials and public figures. The Utah Supreme Court defines actual malice as "knowledge that statements were false, or made with reckless disregard of whether they were false or not." See In re I.M.L., 61 P.3d at 1045; Russell v. Thomson Newspapers Inc., 842 P.2d 896, 904 (Utah 1992); Seegmiller v. KSL, Inc., 626 P.2d 968, 972 (Utah 1981).

Utah also follows the New York Times Co. v. Sullivan and Rosenblatt v. Baer standards for defining "public official." Van Dyke v. KUTV, 663 P.2d 52, 54-55 (Utah 1983). Public officials are limited to those persons whose responsibilities are likely to influence matters of public policy in the civil, as distinguished from the cultural, educational, or sports realms. O'Connor v. Burningham, 2007 UT 58, ¶ 15, 165 P.3d 1214. Public officials are those who have the authority to make policy affecting life, liberty, or property. Id. A public high school athletic coach is not a public official. Id. Postal employees are not public officials by virtue of their status as "public employees." Cox v. Hatch, 761 P.2d 556, 560 (Utah 1988). A police officer who shoots a suspect while acting in his official capacity is a public figure. Madsen v. United Television Inc., 797 P.2d 1083, 1085 (Utah 1990). Utah law generally treats politicians or political candidates as public figures. West v. Thomson Newspapers, 872 P.2d 999, 1019-20 (Utah 1994); Utah State Farm Bureau Federation v. National Farmers Union Serv. Corp., 198 F.2d 20, 22 (10th Cir. 1952); Peterson v. New York Times Co., 106 F. Supp. 2d 1227 (D. Utah 2000) (holding politician who had resigned seat in state legislature was still public figure and thus had to prove actual malice for his claim to survive summary judgment).

It must not be lightly assumed that a person is an all-purposes public figure. Wayment v. Clear Channel Broad., Inc., 116 P.3d 271, 280 (Utah 2005). A television reporter who appeared on the local news five nights a week was held not to be an all-purposes public figure. Id. at 281. It may be that only a household name or a person who causes others to alter their conduct or ideas based on that person's actions is an all-purposes public figure. Id. at 280. Two steps are required to determine that someone is a limited-purpose public figure: first, a particular controversy related to the alleged defamation must be isolated; and second, the nature and extent of the person's participation in the alleged controversy must be such that she thrust herself to the forefront of the controversy in order to influence the resolution. Id. at 282-83; World Wide Ass'n of Specialty Programs v. Pure, Inc., 450 F.3d 1132, 1136-37 (10th Cir. 2006). A marketing company that actively promoted and defended its members' programs for treatment of at-risk teenagers was a limited-purpose public figure. Id. at 1137. A corporation that issued press releases, made other public statements, and actively sought media coverage to air its position about its embroilment in a high-profile copyright ownership dispute qualified as a limited-purpose public figure. SCO Group, Inc. v. Novell, Inc., 692 F.Supp.2d 1287, 1296 (D. Utah 2010).

3. ***Falsity.*** Falsity is an essential element of defamation. West v. Thompson Newspapers, 872 P.2d 999, 1007 (Utah 1994). Statements may be infected with some inaccuracy, innuendo, or falsity and still not be actionable so long as their "gist" is true. Jensen v. Sawyers, 2005 UT 81, ¶ 89, 130 P.3d 325; Magistro v. Day, 2010 UT App 397, 2010 WL 5550448, *2 (Utah Ct .App. Dec. 30, 2010). Although most cases place the burden of proof with respect to truth squarely on the defendant, one trade libel case stated that the plaintiff must prove the falsity of the statements made in order to prevail. Direct Import Buyers Ass'n v. KSL, Inc., 538 P.2d 1040, 1042 (Utah 1975). This assertion cannot be harmonized with any other Utah defamation case; consequently caution is warranted in relying upon it. At the very least, however, the plaintiff must in all cases aver that the defamatory material is false. Dowse v. Doris Trust Co., 208 P.2d 956, 958 (Utah 1949). There have been no post-Hepps or Milkovich decisions on the issue of burden of proof.

4. ***Defamatory Statement of Fact.*** To be defamatory, a statement must be a false representation of fact rather than an expression of opinion. Utah recognizes the "fair comment" privilege for opinions based upon true or

privileged assertions of fact. West v. Thomson, 872 P.2d 999, 1012 (Utah 1994). The Utah Constitution "provides an independent source of protection for expressions of opinion." Id. at 1013. However, that protection is abused "when the opinion states or implies facts that are false and defamatory." Id. at 1015. See also II.B.2, infra. To determine whether defamatory meaning exists, courts must consider whether a reasonable reader could reasonably infer defamation. Int'l Ass'n of United Mine Workers Union v. United Mine Workers of America, 2006 WL 1183245, *3 (D.Utah 2006). Whether a statement is capable of sustaining a defamatory meaning is a question of law to be decided by the Court. Jacob v. Bezzant, 2009 UT 37, 212 P.3d 535, 546 (Utah 2009); **Hogan v. Winder, 2012 WL 4356326, *7 (D. Utah Sept. 24, 2012). In considering whether an article contains defamatory meaning, courts consider the article's context, including both the headline and the body of the article. Id. at *9. Reporting that a person was accused of extortion in an employment dispute was not defamatory because the article provided the context that the accusations were made in the heat of contentious civil litigation and did not imply that the person faced criminal extortion charges. Id. at *10.** Stating that a person quit his or her job, absent additional commentary or detail, is not defamatory. Zoumadakis v. Uintah Basin Medical Ctr., 2009 UT App 135, 2009 WL 1423559, *1 (Utah Ct. App. May 21, 2009).

5. ***Of and Concerning Plaintiff.*** Before defamatory statements are actionable, they must refer to some ascertained or ascertainable person. Lynch v. Standard Pub. Co., 170 P. 770, 773 (Utah 1918). It must appear that third persons must have reasonably understood that the statements were of and concerning plaintiff, and that the libelous expressions referred to him. Simpson v. Steen, 127 F. Supp. 132, 137-38 (D. Utah 1954). The complaint does not have to allege intrinsic facts showing application of defamatory matter to plaintiff; it is sufficient to state generally that it was published/spoken concerning him. Utah R. Civ. P. 9(j) (1); People v. Ritchie, 42 P. 209, 210 (Utah 1895); Burton v. Mattson, 166 P. 979, 981 (Utah 1917); Fenstermaker v. Tribune Pub. Co., 45 P. 1097, 1098-99 (Utah 1896). Where the defamatory matter refers generally to a group and does not identify particular individuals, there is no cause of action for libel unless (i) the group is so small that the matter can reasonably be understood to refer to an individual, or (ii) the circumstances of publication give rise to the conclusion that there is particular reference to an individual. Pratt v. Nelson, 2007 UT 41, ¶ 49, 164 P.3d 366. However, when statements refer explicitly to an individual by name, regardless of whether the individual is part of a group or larger listing of names, the group defamation defense does not apply. Id. ¶ 57.

6. ***Publication.*** Publication is an essential element of defamation, West v. Thomson Newspapers, 872 P.2d 999, 1007 (Utah 1994), however, "excessive publication is only evidence of malice, not a substitute or equal thereof." DeBry v. Godbe, 992 P.3d 979, 985 (Utah 1992).

a. **Intracorporate Communication.** No Utah cases directly address this issue. However, the Utah Supreme Court has applied a conditional privilege to a communication between stockholders. See Brehany v. Nordstrom, Inc., 812 P.2d 49, 58 (Utah 1991); Lind v. Lynch, 665 P.2d 1276, 1279 (Utah 1983). One case held that a disciplinary report in an employee file was not published because the contents of the file were confidential and not disclosed to outside organizations. Zoumadakis v. Uintah Basin Medical Ctr., 2009 UT App 135, 2009 WL 1423559, *1 (Utah Ct. App. May 21, 2009).

b. **Compelled Self-Publication.** No Utah cases directly address this issue.

c. **Republication.** No Utah cases directly address this issue. However, in a case applying Utah law, the Tenth Circuit noted in dictum that "if the published statement is libelous as a matter of law, it is no defense that it was repeated from another source." Utah State Farm Bureau Federation v. National Farmers Union Serv. Corp., 198 F.2d 20, 23 (10th Cir. 1952). Utah follows common law rules of agency and respondeat superior to determine the liability of employers for defamatory statements of employees. Mounteer v. Utah Power & Light Co., 823 P.2d 1055, 1058 (Utah 1991).

7. ***Statements versus Conduct.*** No Utah cases directly address this issue.

8. ***Damages.*** If words are not held to be slanderous or libelous per se, special damages must be pleaded and proved. Auto West, Inc. v. Baggs, 678 P.2d 286, 290 (Utah 1984); Baum v. Gillman, 667 P.2d 41, 42-3 (Utah 1983); Prince v. Peterson, 538 P.2d 1325, 1328 (Utah 1975); Western States Title Ins. Co. v. Warnock, 415 P.2d 316, 317 (Utah 1966); Nichols v. Daily Reporter Co., 83 P. 573, 573 (Utah 1905). A plaintiff can only recover those damages that flow from the defendant's defamatory statements, not damages resulting from the plaintiff's or another person's activities. World Wide Ass'n of Specialty Programs v. Pure, Inc., 450 F.3d 1132, 1138 (10th Cir. 2006). The statement that an employee was discharged for "poor performance" does not constitute defamation per se even though it could impede acquisition of future employment. Larson v. SYSCO Corp., 767 P.2d 557, 560 (Utah 1989). In a suit for slander of title, the plaintiff "cannot prevail unless he alleges and proves pecuniary loss resulting from the act of the defendant." Dowse v. Doris Trust Co., 208 P.2d 956, 958 (Utah 1949). In the Dowse case, however, the court took a broad view of special damages, holding that attorneys' fees were a reasonable expense of litigation and thus constituted actual damage. Dowse, 208 P.2d at 958-59. In another slander of title case, attorney fees were held recoverable as special damages if incurred "to clear title or to undo any harm created by whatever slander of title occurred." Gillmor v. Cummings, 904 P.2d 703, 709 (Utah App. 1995),

quoting Bass v. Planned Management Servs., Inc., 761 P.2d 566, 568 (Utah 1988). The Utah Supreme Court recently expressed the concern, however, that although "[t]he intended meaning of the term 'per se' as used in Utah's statutes would seem to be 'actionable without proof of special damages,'" Gertz "make[s] it clear that, at least in the case of media defendants, there can be no liability absent actual damages." Seegmiller v. KSL, Inc., 626 P.2d 968, 977 n.7 (Utah 1981). The Seegmiller opinion may represent the first step in the abolition of the per se/per quod distinction. No Utah case explicitly deals with the issue of whether mental distress is compensable in a defamation case.

a. **Presumed Damages and Libel Per Se.** Words that "hold a person up to hatred, contempt or ridicule, or injure him in his business or vocations, [are] deemed actionable per se; and the law presumes that damages will be suffered there from." Prince v. Peterson, 538 P.2d 1325, 1328 (Utah 1975); see also Larson v. SYSCO Corp., 767 P.2d 567, 560 (Utah 1989). False or misleading charges of criminal conduct, loathsome disease, conduct incompatible with the exercise of a lawful business, trade, profession or office, and charges of the unchastity of a woman constitute "slander per se" under Utah law and give rise to presumed damages. Proctor & Gamble Co. v. Haugen, 222 F.3d 1262 (10th Cir. 2000) (headnotes 15, 16). "A statement is libelous per se if language is used concerning a person or that person's affairs that from its nature must, or presumably will as its natural and proximate consequence, cause pecuniary loss to the person about whom the statement is made. Farm Bureau Mut. Life Ins. Co. v. American Nat'l Ins. Co., 2007 WL 1343719 (D. Utah 2007). The presumption of damage inheres to the words of the writing itself." Computerized Thermal Imaging, Inc. v. Bloomberg, 312 F.3d 1292, 1297 (10th Cir. 2002) (applying Utah law). Absent special damages, a plaintiff must show defamation per se in order to recover. Larson, 767 P.2d at 560. Absent either a showing of defamation per se or special damages, a Plaintiff's claim will not survive a motion to dismiss. Computerized Thermal Imaging, Inc. v. Bloomberg, L.P., No. 1:00CV98K, 2001 WL 670927 (D. Utah Mar. 26. 2001). In a slander of title case, the Utah Supreme Court held that "'presumed or special damages' are insufficient in a slander of title action. 'A slander of title action requires proof of actual or special damages.'" Valley Colour v. Beuchert Builders, 944 P.2d 361, 364 (Utah 1997), citing First Security Bank of Utah, N.A. v. Banberry Crossing, 780 P.2d 1253, 1257 (Utah 1989). A newspaper's election notice rejecting charges against candidates for office made in an advertisement and apologizing to the candidates is not libelous per se. Jacob v. Bezzant, 2009 UT 37, 212 P.3d 535, 545-46 (Utah 2009).

(1) **Employment-Related Criticism.** A statement on a separation slip that plaintiff was fired for "poor performance" is insufficient. Larson, 767 P.2d at 560.

(2) **Single Instance Rule.** No Utah case specifically addresses this issue.

b. **Punitive Damages.** Punitive damages can be awarded only if the jury finds that the defendant exhibited actual malice, defined as "motivated by spite, hatred, or ill will against the subject." Fausett v. American Resources Management Corp., 542 F. Supp. 1234, 1242 (D. Utah 1982), citing Berry v. Moench, 331 P.2d 814, 820 (Utah 1958) (libel); accord, Prince v. Peterson, 538 P.2d 1325, 1329 (Utah 1975); Dowse, 208 P.2d at 958-9 (slander of title). There was no actual malice where, although a reporter was not fair and balanced in her reporting, she believed her reporting was accurate. Jensen v. Sawyers, 2005 UT 81, ¶¶ 121-25, 130 P.3d 325. The punitive damages awarded must bear a reasonable relationship to the actual damages found. Prince, 538 P.2d at 1329. In a slander of title action, punitive damages were awarded even though the defendant broker had acted in good faith and had reasonable grounds to believe that he was entitled to a lien. Olsen v. Kidman, 235 P.2d 510, 513 (Utah 1951). However, the jury awarded only $10, consequently, it appears that the award was merely exemplary and not punitive. There are no post-Dun & Bradstreet v. Greenmoss decisions.

II. PRIVILEGES AND DEFENSES

A. Scope of Privileges

1. ***Absolute Privilege.*** Utah recognizes an absolute privilege accorded in judicial proceedings, which requires proof of three elements. First, the statement must have been made during or in the course of a judicial proceeding. Second, the statement must have some reference to the subject matter of the proceeding. Third, the one claiming the privilege must have been acting in the capacity of a judge, juror, witness, litigant, or counsel. Allen v. Ortez, 802 P.2d 1307, 1312 (Utah 1990); Thompson v. Community Nursing Serv. & Hospice, 910 P.2d 1267, 1267-68 (Utah App. 1996) (finding statements by counsel and witnesses during administrative proceeding before EEOC absolutely privileged); Price v. Armour, 949 P.2d 1251, 1256-8 (Utah 1997) (finding statements about quality of counsel's ability by opposing party in pre-litigation communication absolutely privileged because made during judicial proceeding); DeBry v. Godbe, 992 P.2d 979, 983 (Utah 1999) (holding statements in a post-trial letter from attorney to judge raising possibility of ex-wife engaging in intimidation was privileged even though judge had taken the case under advisement at the time); Cline v. Utah, 2005 UT App 498, ¶ 37 (holding that testimony of child welfare worker in child custody proceeding was absolutely privileged); Pratt v. Nelson, 2007 UT 41, ¶ 32, 164 P.3d 366 (finding statements at a press conference to likely not qualify for the judicial proceeding privilege); Allen v. Dimeo, 2007 UT App 192 (holding that letters and affidavits written for Guardians Ad Litem to use in a custody case were privileged); O'Connor v. Burningham, 2007 UT 58, ¶ 32, 165 P.3d 1214 (holding that statements made

during community comment portion of school district meeting were not privileged); McNeil v. Kennecott Utah Copper Corp., 2009 WL 2554726 (D. Utah Aug. 18, 2009) (holding that the judicial proceeding privilege should be interpreted expansively and finding that employees' statements in interviews with their company counsel in anticipation of possible litigation were absolutely privileged). **The judicial proceedings privilege has also been extended to encompass attorney conduct within the scope of a client's interests made in the course of judicial proceedings. Moss v. Parr Waddoups Brown Gee & Loveless, 712 Utah Adv. Rep. 41, 2012 WL 2629224, *6-8 (Utah July 6, 2012).** Utah also recognizes an absolute privilege for filing of a lis pendens. Hansen v. Kohler, 550 P.2d 186, 190 (Utah 1976); but see Birch v. Fuller, 337 P.2d 964 (Utah 1959) (finding that only purpose of filing of lis pendens was to slander plaintiff's title). Utah law "generally holds that communications that are otherwise privileged lose their privilege if the statement is excessively published." DeBry v. Godbe, 992 P.2d 979, 985 (Utah 1999). In determining whether the judicial proceeding privilege has been lost due to excessively published, courts consider (1) whether the recipients of the publication have a sufficient connection to the judicial proceeding, and (2) whether the purpose of the judicial proceeding privilege would be furthered by protecting the publication. Pratt, 2007 UT 41, ¶ 36, 164 P.3d 366. Statements made about a case to the media at a press conference do not qualify for the judicial proceeding privilege. Id. ¶ 46.

When the privilege is found, it extends to "all claims arising from the same statements." Id. at 986 (extending judicial privilege to claim for intentional infliction of emotional distress). A pre-litigation demand fell within the scope of this privilege because it met the three criteria necessary for the judicial proceeding privilege. Krouse v. Bower, 20 P.3d 895 (Utah 2001). The Utah State Bar and its employees were immune from suit under the judicial proceeding privilege where they published the facts surrounding Plaintiff's professional misconduct in the Utah Bar Journal. Pendleton v. Utah State Bar, 16 P.3d 1230 (Utah 2000). The Supreme Court of Utah has also recognized an absolute legislative proceeding privilege. In Riddle v. Perry the court stated, "A witness is absolutely privileged to publish defamatory matter as part of a legislative proceeding in which he [or she] is testifying or in communications preliminary to the proceeding, if the matter has some relation to the proceeding." 40 P.3d 1128 (Utah 2002). Additionally, Utah specifically retains immunity for defamation under the Governmental Immunity Act. Utah Code Ann. § 63-30-10(2) (2005); Ostler v. Salt Lake City Corp., 2005 WL 2237631, *2 (D.Utah 2005); Cline, 2005 UT App 498, ¶ 33.

2. ***Qualified Privileges.*** "[E]xistence of a conditional privilege is a question for the court . . . [but] if there is any dispute about the facts, they are to be determined by the jury." Brehany v. Nordstrom, Inc., 812 P.2d 49. 58 (Utah 1991); Combes v. Montgomery Ward & Co., 228 P.2d 272, 274-75 (Utah 1951) (citing Hales v. Commercial Bank of Spanish Fork, 197 P.2d 910, 913 (Utah 1948)); Berry v. Moench, 331 P.2d 814, 818 (Utah 1958); Russell v. Thomson, Inc. Newspapers, 842 P.2d 896, 900 (Utah 1992); Wayment v. Clear Channel Broad., Inc., 116 P.3d 271, 288 (Utah 2005); and 4 Newell, Slander and Libel 395. When the public health and safety are involved, or when there is a legitimate issue with respect to the functioning of governmental bodies, officials, or public institutions, or with respect to matters involving the expenditure of public funds, defendants are protected by a conditional privilege which shields them from liability absent a showing of malice. See Russell, 842 P.2d at 902; Seegmiller v. KSL, Inc., 626 P.2d 968 (Utah 1981); see also Williams v. Standard-Examiner Publishing Co., 27 P.2d 1 (Utah 1933); Utah State Farm Bureau Federation v. National Farmers Union Serv. Corp., 198 F.2d 20, 22-3 (10th Cir. 1952). There is a qualified privileged for statements made in investigations leading to judicial proceedings. Cline v. Utah, 2005 UT App 498, ¶¶ 39-40. The Governmental Immunity Act shields public employees from defamation actions unless the public employees act with fraud or malice. Brown v. Wanlass, 18 P.3d 1137 (Utah Ct. App. 2001). In this context, malice means an improper motive such as a desire to do harm, or that the speaker did not honestly believe the statements were true. Becker v. Kroll, 494 F.3d 904, 927-28 (10th Cir. 2007) (holding that government statement about plaintiff's illegal acts after innocence had already been determined evidenced sufficient malice to overcome governmental immunity).

Although generally not applicable in employment cases, in 2008 the Utah Judicial Council adopted a rule of evidence that provides varying degrees of privilege to reporters to refuse to disclose (1) confidential source information, (2) confidential unpublished news information, and (3) other unpublished news information. Utah R. Evid. 509.

a. **Common Interest.** Utah recognizes a qualified privilege for communications between persons who share a common business interest. Lind v. Lynch, 665 P.2d 1276, 1278 (Utah 1983) (stockholder's proxy solicitation). This privilege protects an employer's communications to other interested parties concerning the reasons for an employee's discharge. Ferguson v. Williams & Hunt, Inc., 2009 UT 49, 221 P.3d 205, 214 (Utah 2009) (extending the privilege to statements made by a law firm to a client indicating that a former partner in the firm was discharged for overbilling). The common interest privilege protects a communication made necessary by the terms of a contract between an employer and the truck driver's union. Sowell v. IML Freight, Inc., 519 P.2d 884, 885 (Utah 1974). It also protects an employer's notations on dismissal slip. Richardson v. Grant Central Corp., 572 P.2d 395, 397 (Utah 1977). Communications between parties who share a common interest are qualifiedly privileged when disseminated for the purpose of a termination hearing which was demanded by the terminated party. Alford v. Utah League of Cities and Towns, 791 P.2d 201, 204-05 (Utah App. 1989). Statements made by an employer to its managers that employees' discharges had been drug-related are conditionally privileged where employer had legitimate interest in enforcing its drug policy. Brehany v. Nordstrom, Inc., 812 P.2d 49, 58-59 (Utah 1991) (expanding scope of Utah Code Ann. § 45-2-3(3)). Statements by a former employer to other interested parties concerning the reasons for the employee's discharge are conditionally protected. Watkins v. General Refractories Co., 805 F. Supp. 911, 918 (D. Utah 1992); Dubois v. Grand Central, 872 P.2d 1073, 1079 (Utah App. 1993) (affirming summary judgment and dismissal of employee's slander claim where employer's communications to co-workers did not allude to personal hostility or ill will toward employee). Statements between members of a limited liability company that shared a common interest. Mitchell v. Smith, 2010 WL 5172906, *6 (D.Utah Dec. 14, 2010). The qualified privilege also protects free and honest communication between opposing counsel on a case before the courts, Western States Title Ins. Co. v. Warnock, 415 P.2d 316 (Utah 1966), and a physician's disclosure of defamatory information about one of his patients in an effort to protect a third person, Berry, 331 P.2d at 817. The privilege protects the communications of parties seeking to enter into a business relationship. Thomas v. Pacificorp, 324 F.3d 1176, 1180 (10th Cir 2003) (applying Utah law). The privilege protects communications between a doctor, nurses, and a medical center discussing an employee's alleged drinking on the job and reasons for the employee's termination. Zoumadakis v. Uintah Basin Medical Ctr., 2009 UT App 135, 2009 WL 1423559, *1 (Utah Ct. App. May 21, 2009). Statements in a meeting between a human resources representative, an administrative assistant, and an employee were found to be privileged. Smith v. Nu Skin Enterprises, 2008 WL 4850526, *4 (D. Utah Nov. 6, 2008).

An individual's report of a matter of public interest to a legislator is protected by the public interest privilege if the matter affects the legislator's discharge of his or her duties. Tetra Financial Group, LLC v. Cell Tech Intern. Inc., 2011 WL 1749069, *3 (D. Utah May 6, 2011) (citing privilege found in Restatement (Second) of Torts § 598 in case where legislator was considering legislation on the topic which the communication addressed). The Utah Supreme Court has adopted a conditional privilege for communications that contain information relating to intra-family relationships. O'Connor v. Burningham, 2007 UT 58, ¶ 34, 165 P.3d 1214 (adopting standard from Restatement (Second) of Torts § 597).

b. **Duty.** A communication "between employer and employee is protected by the [qualified] privilege when it is made bona fide about a matter in which the writer had an interest or duty and the recipient had a corresponding interest or duty and the communication was made in the performance of that duty." Sowell v. IML Freight, Inc., 519 P.2d 884, 885 (Utah 1974).

c. **Criticism of Public Employee.** No Utah cases specifically address this issue.

d. **Limitation on Qualified Privileges.**

(1) **Constitutional or Actual Malice.** While constitutional malice would appear to qualify, "[t]he malice which plaintiff must show in order to overcome a conditional privilege is simply an improper motive such as a desire to do harm or that the defendant did not honestly believe his statements true or that the publication was excessive." Alford v. Utah League of Cities & Towns, 791 P.2d 201, 205 (Utah Ct. App. 1990). See also Lind v. Lynch, 665 P.2d 1276, 1279 (Utah 1983); Direct Import Buyers Ass'n v. KSL, Inc., 538 P.2d 1040, 1042 (Utah 1975). Cf. Combs v. Montgomery Ward, 228 P.2d 272, 276-77 (Utah 1951) (actual malice removes the conditional privilege). A plaintiff cannot overcome a conditional privilege by showing negligence or lack of reasonable grounds for believing the statement. Instead, in addition to other common law means, a plaintiff can show abuse of a conditional privilege where the defendant made the statement while knowing it to be false or acting in reckless disregard to its falsity. Ferguson v. Williams & Hunt, Inc., 2009 UT 49, 221 P.3d 205, 214-15 (Utah 2009).

(2) **Common Law Malice.** "The malice which plaintiff must show in order to overcome a conditional privilege is simply an improper motive such as a desire to do harm or that the defendant did not honestly believe his statements true or that the publication was excessive." Alford v. Utah League of Cities & Towns, 791 P.2d 201, 205/Utah App. (1990). See also Lind v. Lynch, 665 P.2d 1276, 1279 (Utah 1983); Direct Import Buyers Ass'n v. KSL, Inc., 538 P.2d 1040, 1042 (Utah 1975). Cf. Combs v. Montgomery Ward, 228 P.2d 272, 276-77 (Utah 1951) (actual malice removes the conditional privilege). Evidence of malice may include indications that the publisher made the statement with ill will, that statements were excessively published, or that the publisher did not reasonably believe the statements. Wayment, 116 P.3d at 288 (citing Russell, 842 P.2d at 905); see also Becker v. Kroll, 340 F.Supp.2d 1230, 1239 (D.Utah 2004).

Common law malice does not operate as a standard of fault; it is the degree of malice that must be proven to overcome the statutory privilege (Utah Code Ann. § 45-2-3). Russell v. Thomson Newspapers, Inc., 842 P.2d 896, 904 (Utah 1992). On the other hand, actual malice, the constitutional standard enunciated in New York Times v. Sullivan, refers to the "level of fault necessary in public figure cases." Id.

(3) **Other Limitations on Qualified Privileges.** A conditional privilege may be lost if defamatory statements are excessively published. Jacob v. Bezzant, 2009 UT 37, 212 P.3d 535, 544-45 (Utah 2009). A newspaper's posting an election notice on its web site and distributing the notice to city residents at the time of an election

was not considered excessive publication. Id.; see also Mitan v. BRCSLC, Inc., 2010 WL 5300898, *2 (D. Utah Dec. 20, 2010) (holding that simply posting something on the Internet does not ipso facto constitute excessive publication). In an unpublished decision, the Utah Court of Appeals suggested that a qualified privilege may be lost when "publication of the defamatory material extend[s] beyond those who had a legally justified reason for receiving it." Ellis v. Wal-Mart Stores, Inc., 2002 Utah App. 6 (Utah Ct. App. 2002). Publication to a realtor who had worked with the litigants and had an interest in the case, although not a litigant, did not constitute excessive publication. Campbell v. Castle Stone Homes, Inc., 2011 WL 902637, *13 (D. Utah March 15, 2011).

e. **Question of Fact or Law.** Whether qualifiedly privileged article was written with malicious motive is question for jury. Ogden Bus Lines v. KSL, 551 P.2d 222, 225 (Utah 1976); Demman v. Star Broadcasting Co., 497 P.2d 1378, 1380 (Utah 1972) (same) (Tuckett, J. concurring); Williams v. Standard-Examiner Pub. Co., 27 P.2d 1, 17 (Utah 1933) (in absence of proof of malice it is court's duty to say publication was without malice).

f. **Burden of Proof.** The burden of establishing the affirmative defense of privilege rests with the defendant. See, e.g., Williams v. Standard-Examiner Pub. Co., 27 P.2d 1, 17 (Utah 1933). Because the plaintiff does not have the initial burden of pleading the inapplicability of a qualified privilege, the plaintiff may not use that privilege as grounds for a motion dismiss for failure to state a claim. Zoumadakis v. Uintah Basin Med. Ctr., Inc., 2005 UT App 325, ¶¶ 6 -7, 122 P.3d 891. The plaintiff bears the burden to prove whether the defendant abused a qualified privilege. Brehany v. Nordstrom, Inc., 812 P.2d 49, 58 (Utah 1991). Abuse can be shown by proving malice. Id.; Seegmiller v. KSL, Inc., 626 P.2d 968, 976 (Utah 1981), citing Williams v. Standard-Examiner, 27 P.2d 1 (Utah 1933). The Utah Supreme Court has applied a standard of "preponderance of evidence" in non-media cases. Howarth v. Ostergaard, 515 P.2d 442, 444-45 (Utah 1973); Derounian v. Stokes, 168 F.2d 305, 306-07 (10th Cir. 1948).

B. Standard Libel Defenses

1. ***Truth.*** Truth is a complete and absolute defense to a charge of defamation. See In re I.M.L., 61 P.3d at 1043; Brehany v. Nordstrom, Inc., 812 P.2d 49, 57 (Utah 1991); Auto West, Inc. v. Baggs, 678 P.2d 286, 290 (Utah 1984); Direct Import Buyer's Ass'n v. KSL, Inc., 572 P.2d 692, 694 (Utah 1977) ("Direct Import Buyer's II"); Ogden Bus Lines v. KSL, Inc., 551 P.2d 222, 224 (Utah 1976); Derounian v. Stokes, 168 F.2d 305, 306 (10th Cir. 1948); Williams v. Standard-Examiner Pub., 27 P.2d 1, 13 (Utah 1933); see also Utah Const. art. I, Sec. 15. Furthermore, the Utah Supreme Court has held that when truth is pleaded in justification, "it is not necessary to prove the literal truth of the precise statement made. Insignificant inaccuracies of expression are immaterial, providing that the defamatory charge is true in substance." Auto West, Inc. v. Baggs, 678 P.2d at 290-91, citing Crellin v. Thomas, 247 P.2d 264, 266 (Utah 1952); Brehany v. Nordstrom, Inc., 812 P.2d at 57-58. For every rule, however, there is an exception. In the case of Berry v. Moench, which concerned the doctor-patient relationship, the Supreme Court concluded that if a doctor violates a patient's confidence and publishes derogatory matter concerning him, an action would lie for any injury suffered, without regard to the truth or falsity of the statements, assuming no statutory or common law privilege would otherwise protect the communication. 331 P.2d 814, 817 (Utah 1958).

2. ***Opinion.*** In general, Utah has followed the common law rule that the statement of a mere opinion does not give rise to a cause of action. Ogden Bus Lines v. KSL, Inc., 551 P.2d 222, 224-25 (Utah 1976) (discussing common law). The Utah Constitution, Article I, sections 1 and 15, protects expression of opinion. West v. Thomson Newspapers, 872 P.2d 999, 1015 (Utah 1994). Looking to pre-Milkovich case law, the Utah Supreme Court in West v. Thomson Newspapers held that the defamatory implication that mayor misled voters to get elected is protected opinion. The Court examined four factors in determining whether statements are protected opinions: "(i) the common usage or meaning of the words used; (ii) whether the statement is capable of being objectively verified as true or false [could a reasonable fact-finder conclude that the underlying statement conveys the alleged defamatory implication and if so, is that implication sufficiently factual to be susceptible of being proven true or false?]; (iii) the full context of the statement C for example, the entire article or column C in which the defamatory statement is made; and (iv) the broader setting in which the statement appears." West, 872 P.2d at 1018. **These factors remain the standard in determining whether a statement is an opinion or not. Hogan v. Winder, 2012 WL 4356326, *7 (D. Utah Sept. 24, 2012)** In West, the fact that the allegedly defamatory implication was not verifiable as true or false, and the context and broader setting it appeared in - criticism in an editorial column about an elected public official and his political position - meant it was protected opinion, not fact. The court will examine such statements with exacting constitutional scrutiny, and will be more likely to construe statements as opinions when made in the context of political campaigns. Id. at 1020. **News stories reporting on opinions of others are also protected. See Hogan, 2012 WL 4356326, *8. In Hogan, a newspaper report that an individual was terminated for poor performance and erratic behavior was held to be a non-actionable expression of opinion, at least partly because the allegations in the article were attributed to a former employer in the context of an employment dispute. Id. at *8.** Editorials relating to matters of public interest are subject to a qualified privilege and therefore are not actionable absent a showing of malice. Seegmiller v. KSL, Inc., 626 P.2d 968, 976-78 (Utah 1981); Williams v. Standard-Examiner Publishing

Co., 27 P.2d 1, 16-18 (Utah 1933). For effects of Milkovich, see West v. Thomson Newspapers, I.B.1, supra. In Russell v. Thomson Newspapers, Inc., the Utah Supreme Court held that allegations of misconduct against a local doctor and nurse, while matters of public concern, are not protected under the fair comment doctrine, where the statement concerning the nurse's alleged abortions purported to be a quote from a public official concerning the nurse's medical history. 842 P.2d 896, 902-3 (Utah 1992). The comment was a false assertion of fact and not an opinion. Id. In a footnote, the court made the following observation about the fair comment privilege: "Notwithstanding the fact that Milkovich subsumes a portion of the common law fair comment privilege, the common law privilege also protects an opinion that is based on privileged facts, a subject not discussed by the majority opinion in Milkovich. Consequently, the common law privilege remains viable independent of the Constitution, and we reaffirm our commitment to the privilege at this time." Russell, 842 P.2d at 903 n.19.

3. ***Consent.*** No Utah cases directly address this issue.

4. ***Mitigation.*** No Utah cases directly address this issue.

III. RECURRING FACT PATTERNS

A. Statements in Personnel File

The conditional privilege protects an employer's comments on an employee's discharge slip where there was no evidence of publication to anyone other than parties immediately concerned. Richardson v. Grand Central Corp., 572 P.2d 395, 397 (Utah 1977). Utah has adopted the Restatement (Second) of Torts § 594. Id.; Hales v. Commercial Bank of Spanish Fork, 197 P.2d 910, 913 (Utah 1948); Combes v. Montgomery Ward, 228 P.2d 272, 275 (Utah 1951).

B. Performance Evaluations

No Utah cases directly address this issue. However, the qualified privilege protects employer's communication to employee's union of reason for employee's dismissal where contract between employer and union required that communication. Sowell v. IML Freight, Inc. 519 P.2d 884 (Utah 1974).

C. References

No Utah cases directly address this issue. However, Utah's Employer Reference Immunity Statute, Utah Code Ann. Sec. 34-42-1, bars civil liability for an employer who provides in good faith an evaluation of a former or current employee to a prospective employer where that information is requested by the employee or the prospective employer. That statute creates a rebuttable presumption that the employer providing such information does so in good faith. Clear and convincing evidence of actual malice or an intent to mislead is required to overcome the presumption.

D. Intracorporate Communication

No Utah cases directly address this issue. However, a stockholder's letter to other stockholders is protected by a qualified privilege unless published with malice. Lind v. Lynch, 665 P.2d 1276, 1279 (Utah 1983). Statements between members of a limited liability company that share a common interest are protected by a qualified privilege. Mitchell v. Smith, 2010 WL 5172906 *6 (D.Utah Dec. 14, 2010).

E. Statements to Government Regulators

No Utah cases directly address this issue.

F. Reports to Auditors and Insurers

No Utah cases directly address this issue.

G. Vicarious Liability of Employers for Statements Made by Employees

No Utah cases directly address this issue. However, the Utah Workers' Compensation Act bars employers' vicarious liability for their employees' intentional acts. Mounteer v. Utah Power & Light, 773 P.2d 405, 407 (Utah App. 1989). Publishing of libelous statements by a person who works for an employer, but who is not an actual employee, likely fails to create liability in the employer. Proctor & Gamble Co. v. Haugen, 222 F.3d 1262 (10th Cir. 2000) (holding employer was not liable for distributor's statements because distributor was more akin to independent contractor rather than agent or employee). In Utah, the general test for whether a person is an independent contractor or employee is determined by the employer's "right to control" the manner and method of the worker's performance. See, Foster v. Steed, 432 P.2d 60, 62-63 (Utah 1967); see also, Glover v. Boy Scouts of Am., 923 P.2d 1383, 1385 (Utah 1996).

1. ***Scope of Employment.*** Even if an employer-employee relationship is established, an employer may only be vicariously liable under the doctrine of respondeat superior for the employee's harmful actions that are committed within the scope of its employment. Jackson v. Righter, 891 P.2d 1387, 1391 (Utah 1995). See also J.H. by D.H. v. West Valley City, 840 P.2d 115, 122 (Utah 1992); Clover v. Snowbird Ski Resort, 808 P.2d 1037, 1040 (Utah 1991); Birkner v. Salt Lake County, 771 P.2d 1053, 1056 (Utah 1989). To be considered within the scope of employment, an employee's conduct must (1) "be of the general kind the employee is employed to perform"; (2) "occur within the hours of the employee's work and the ordinary spatial boundaries of the employment"; and (3) "be motivated, at least in part, by the purpose of serving the employer's interest." Birkner, 771 P.2d at 1056-57. Whether an employee's conduct falls within the scope of employment is ordinarily a question of fact. Clover, 808 P.2d at 1040. However, where the employee's conduct is so clearly outside the scope of employment that reasonable minds cannot differ, the issue may properly be decided as a matter of law. Id.; Birkner, 771 P.2d at 1057.

a. **Blogging.** No Utah cases directly address this issue.

2. ***Damages.*** No Utah cases directly address this issue.

H. Internal Investigations

No Utah cases directly address this issue.

IV. OTHER ACTIONS BASED ON STATEMENTS

A. Negligent Hiring, Retention, and Supervision

Utah recognizes the general tort of negligent employment and characterizes negligent hiring, retention and supervision as subsets of that tort. Retherford v. AT&T Communications, 844 P.2d 949 (Utah 1992). The elements of the claim are: (1) the employer knew or should have known that its employee posed a foreseeable risk of engaging in the tortious conduct and causing the alleged harm; (2) the employee did indeed inflict such harm; and (3) the employer's negligence in hiring, supervising, or retaining the employee proximately caused the injury. Id. at 973. A claim by an employee for injury by the intentional torts of a co-worker is likely barred by the exclusive remedy of workers' compensation. Id. at 965 n.8.

B. Intentional Infliction of Emotional Distress

The cause of action for intentional infliction of emotional distress is not subsumed within defamation. Russell v. Thompson Newspapers, Inc., 842 P.2d 896, 905 (Utah 1992). To prevail on a claim of intentional infliction of emotional distress, a claimant must show that: (1) defendant's conduct was "outrageous and intolerable in that it offended against the generally accepted standards of decency and morality," Retherford, 844 P.2d at 970, (2) defendant "intended to cause, or acted in reckless disregard of the likelihood of causing, emotional distress," Id. at 970-71, (3) the claimant "suffered severe emotional distress," Id. at 971, and (4) defendant's actions proximately caused claimant's emotional distress. Id. See also White v. Blackburn, 787 P.2d 1315, 1317 (Utah Ct. App. 1990); Samms v. Eccles, 358 P.2d 344, 346-47 (Utah 1961); DeBry v. Godbe, 992 P.2d 979, 986 (Utah 1999); Skultin v. Bushnell, 82 F. Supp. 2d 1258, 1261 (D. Utah 2000); Matthews v. Kennecott Utah Copper Corp., 54 F. Supp. 2d 1067, 1075 (D. Utah 1999), aff'd, 208 F.3d 226 (10th Cir. 2000).

The nature and purposes of the two actions are distinct. Id. However, where an emotional distress claim is based on the same facts as a claim for defamation, the First Amendment rights of the parties must be considered. Id. at 906. A plaintiff may not recover for emotional distress by reason of defamation absent a showing of the requisite level of fault. Id. The Utah Supreme Court stated in dicta that the qualified privilege codified at Utah Code Ann. § 45-2-3(4) applies to other claims (including emotional distress) that are based on a defamatory publication. Id. at n.37. The absolute judicial privilege also applies to other claims (including emotional distress) where such a claim arises from the same statements that gave rise to the defamation claim. DeBry v. Godbe, 992 P.2d 979, 986 (Utah 1999). A claim for negligent infliction of emotional distress against an employer is barred by the exclusive remedy of the Utah Workers' Compensation Act. Mounteer v. Utah Power & Light Co., 823 P.2d 1055, 1058 (Utah 1991). A claim for intentional infliction of emotional distress against an employer based on actions of co-workers may also be barred thereunder, Retherford v. AT&T Communications, 844 P.2d 949, 965 n.8 (Utah 1992), unless it is shown that the employer "intended or directed the act which caused the emotional distress." Newsome v. McKesson Corp., 932 F.Supp. 1339, 1343 (D. Utah 1996).

C. Interference with Economic Advantage

No Utah cases specifically address this issue. However, Utah has recognized the tort of interference with prospective economic relations. See Leigh Furniture and Carpet Co. v. Isom, 657 P.2d 293, 304 (Utah 1982). To prove tortious interference under Leigh Furniture, a plaintiff must demonstrate that: "(1) the defendant intentionally interfered with the plaintiff's existing or potential economic relations, (2) for an improper purpose or by improper means, (3) causing injury to the plaintiff." See also, Proctor & Gamble Co. v. Haugen, 222 F.3d 1262 (10th Cir. 2000) (headnote 26).

D. Prima Facie Tort

Utah has not recognized a cause of action based on the doctrine of prima facie tort. Doit, Inc. v. Touche, Ross & Co., 926 P.2d 835, 841 n.11 (Utah 1996).

V. OTHER ISSUES

A. Statute of Limitations

Libel and slander actions are governed by a one-year statute of limitations. Utah Code Ann. Sec. 78-12-29(4) (1994). This one-year limitations period applies to all defamation actions and to false light invasion of privacy claims that flow from allegedly defamatory statements. Jensen v. Sawyers, 2005 UT 81, ¶¶ 33, 53, 130 P.3d 325. The Utah Supreme Court has applied the "discovery rule" to the one-year statute. Allen v. Ortez, 802 P.2d 1307, 1313-14 (Utah 1990) (alleged child abuse accusation); see also Watkins v. General Refractories Co., 805 F. Supp. 911, 917 (D. Utah 1992) (employee termination case). The Utah Court of Appeals recently applied the discovery rule to toll the running of the statute of limitations in a situation where the plaintiff knew of the publication of the alleged defamatory statements, but did not learn the identity of the speaker after a reasonable investigation. Robinson v. Morrow, 99 P.3d 341, 345 (Utah Ct. App. 2004). However, the Utah Supreme Court held in a media case "that an alleged defamation is reasonably discoverable, as a matter of law, at the time it is first published and disseminated in a newspaper which is widely available to the public." Russell v. Standard Corp, 898 P.2d 263, 264 (Utah 1995) (rejecting plaintiff's additional claim that amendment of complaint related back to date of original complaint). In a slander of title action, the Utah Supreme Court held that the two-year statute of limitations rule from Utah Code Ann. § 78-12-25.5(3) applies and that the running of the statute of limitations is triggered when one attempts to sell the property which is subject to the slander of title. Valley Colour v. Beuchert Builders, 944 P.2d 361, 364 (Utah 1997). There is a four-year statute of limitation for claims arising out of negligent employment. Retherford v. AT&T Communications, 844 P.2d 949 (Utah 1992).

B. Jurisdiction

A two-part test determines whether Utah courts can exercise personal jurisdiction over non-residents. Mori v. Mori, 896 P.2d 1237, 1239 (Utah App. 1995). First, the claim must arise from one of the activities enumerated in the Utah Long-Arm Statute, Utah Code Ann. Sec. 78-27-24. Id. Second, the defendant's contacts must be sufficient to satisfy the Due Process Clause of the Fourteenth Amendment. Id. A Tenth Circuit opinion interpreting the Utah Long-Arm Statute held that its enumeration of tortious injury applied to slander no differently than to any other tort. American Land Program v. Bonaventura, 710 F.2d 1449, 1453, 9 Media L. Rep. 1974 (10th Cir. 1983). In one case, a Utah court held that a series of allegedly defamatory calls made into Utah by a non-resident defendant amounted to tortious injury under the Utah Long-Arm Statute and subjected the defendant to personal jurisdiction in Utah. Berrett v. Life Ins. Co. of the Southwest, 623 F.Supp. 946 (D. Utah 1985). In another case, the court held that a California publisher of an online trade newsletter had sufficient minimum contacts with Utah to establish personal jurisdiction for a claim of defamation based on 60 Utah subscribers and harm done to Utah residents. Conlin Enter. Corp. v. SNEWS L.L.C., 2008 WL 803041, *7 (D. Utah March 24, 2008).

C. Worker's Compensation Exclusivity

An employee who incurs or suffers an accident, injury, or death in the course of the employee's employment is limited to the exclusive remedies established by the Workers' Compensation Act. Utah Code § 34A-2-105. The Workers' Compensation Act takes the place of any civil liability for employers and prevents any actions at law for injuries arising out of employment. Id. Employers must maintain adequate workers' compensation insurance for their employees. Id. § 34A-2-201.

The Utah Supreme Court has ruled that defamation claims by an employee against an employer are not subject to the exclusivity provisions of the Workers' Compensation Act (i.e., an employee may bring a lawsuit against an employer for defamation). Mounteer v. Utah Power & Light Co., 823 P.2d 1055, 1057 (Utah 1991). The Court reasoned that the Workers' Compensation Act provides the exclusive remedy for loss of earning power due to physical or mental injuries sustained in the workplace. Id. However, defamation causes damages to reputation, which is not covered by the Workers' Compensation Act. Id. at 1057-58.

D. Pleading Requirements

Utah is a notice pleading jurisdiction. Rule 8(a) of the Utah Rules of Civil Procedure "is to be liberally construed when determining the sufficiency of a plaintiff's complaint," Gill v. Timm, 720 P.2d 1352, 1353 (Utah 1986) and the text of Rule 8 itself declares that "all pleadings shall be so construed as to do substantial justice." Utah R. Civ. P. 8(f). "The days of strict adherence to draconian formalities at the pleading stage are over. Rather, the fundamental purpose of the liberalized pleading rules is to afford parties the privilege of presenting whatever legitimate contentions they have pertaining to their dispute, subject only to the requirement that their adversaries have fair notice of the nature and basis or grounds of the claim and a general indication of the type of litigation involved." Consolidated Realty Group v. Sizzling Platter, Inc., 930 P.2d 268, 275 (Utah App. 1996) (internal quotations omitted). Rule 9 states that a plaintiff need not set forth intrinsic facts showing the application to the plaintiff of the defamatory matter, but rather can state generally that the same concerned plaintiff. Utah R. Civ. P. 9(j)(1). However, a plaintiff's complaint must identify the defamatory statement either by its words or words to that effect; general conclusory statements are inadequate. McNeil v. Kennecott Utah Copper Corp., 2009 WL 2554726, *10 (D. Utah Aug. 18, 2009) (citing Zoumadakis v. Uintah Basin Med. Cntr., 122 P.3d 891, 892-93 (Utah Ct. App. 2005)). One decision upheld the dismissal of a complaint that failed to identify the specific statements that were defamatory and failed to demonstrate that the statements were false, not subject to privilege, or negligently published. Oman v. Davis School District, 2008 UT 70, 194 P.3d 956, 972 (Utah 2008). "A pleading does not contain the seeds for a claim of defamation or slander simply because an opposing party considers some of his adversary's accusations untrue." Novell, Inc. v. Vigilant Ins. Co., 2010 WL 1734771, *6 (D. Utah April 27, 2010). In pleading a defense, the defendant may allege both the truth of the matter charged as defamatory and any mitigating circumstances to reduce damages. Utah R. Civ. P. 9(j)(2).

SURVEY OF UTAH EMPLOYMENT PRIVACY LAW

Heidi E.C. Leithead, Jeffrey J. Hunt, and Michael S. Anderson
Parr Brown Gee & Loveless
185 South State, Suite 800
Salt Lake City, Utah 84111
Telephone: (801) 532-7840; Facsimile: (801) 532-7750
E-mail: hleithead@parrbrown.com
E-mail: jhunt@parrbrown.com
E-mail: manderson@parrbrown.com

(With Developments Reported Through **November 1, 2012**)

GENERAL COMMENTS

Until 1974, Utah's official reporters were the Utah and Utah 2d. When citing cases decided before 1974, the practitioner should include both the Utah reporter cite and the Pacific Reporter cite. Utah has adopted a public domain citation format for cases released on or after January 1, 1999. Thus, when citing Utah Supreme Court or Utah Court of Appeals cases after 1998, the practitioner should include both the public domain cite and the Pacific Reporter cite. See Utah Supreme Court Standing Order No. 4 (effective Jan. 18, 2000).

The Utah courts have had few opportunities to examine the subjects in this outline. With regard to many outline areas, there are simply no Utah cases or statutes on point.

SIGNIFICANT DEVELOPMENTS SINCE THE 2012 *SURVEY*

None.

I. GENERAL LAW OF PRIVACY

A. Legal Basis of Privacy Claims

The Utah Supreme Court has recognized the four invasion of privacy torts, as those torts are defined in the Restatement (Second) of Torts § 652 (1977), namely (1) Misappropriation, (2) False Light, (3) Publication of Private Facts, and (4) Intrusion. Cox v. Hatch, 761 P.2d 556, 562-66, 16 Media L. Rep. 1366 (Utah 1988). In Cox, three postal workers had posed for a photograph with Orrin Hatch, then a candidate for the United States Senate. When the photograph appeared in the candidate's campaign literature, the offended postal workers sued the candidate for defamation, abuse of personal identity (under Utah Code section 45-3-3) and "invasion of privacy." Cox, 761 P.2d at 557. In disposing of these claims, the Utah Supreme Court cited to § 652 of the Restatement (Second) of Torts and appeared to approve of its definitions of the privacy torts. Cox, 761 P.2d at 563; see also Donahue v. Warner Brothers Pictures, Inc., 194 F.2d 6, 10 (10th Cir. 1952) (defining the right of privacy protected by privacy torts "as the right of the ordinary person to enjoy life without his name or life being exploited for commercial purposes"). In addition to the common law invasion of privacy torts, the Utah Abuse of Personal Identity Act prohibits advertisers from using an individual's likeness "in a manner which expresses or implies" the individual's approval or endorsement of the subject matter of the advertisement. UTAH CODE ANN. § 45-3-3(1)(a). As discussed below, the Act "is similar to, although somewhat broader than, the action for appropriation of one's name or likeness under" the Restatement (Second) of Torts §§ 652A and 652C. Cox, 761 P.2d at 564 n.9.

B. Causes of Action

1. ***Misappropriation/Right of Publicity.*** As discussed supra, I.A, in Cox v. Hatch, the Utah Supreme Court recognized the tort of misappropriation of another's name or likeness ("misappropriation") and appeared to adopt the definition of the tort contained in § 652C of the Restatement (Second) of Torts. 761 P.2d 556, 564 n.9 (Utah 1988). Section 652C defines misappropriation as: "One who appropriates to his own use or benefit the name or likeness of another is subject to liability to the other for invasion of his privacy." Restatement (Second) of Torts § 652C (cited in Cox, 761 P.2d at 564 n.9). The Utah Court of Appeals formulated the elements for the tort of misappropriation as follows: "(1) appropriation, (2) of another's name or likeness that has some 'intrinsic value,' (3) for the use or benefit of another." Stien v. Marriott Ownership Resorts, Inc., 944 P.2d 374, 379 (Utah Ct. App. 1997) (citing Cox, 761 P.2d at 564)).

In addition to the common law tort, the Utah Abuse of Personal Identity Act prohibits the use of an individual's "personal identity" without that person's written consent. UTAH CODE ANN. § 45-3-1 *et seq.* Under the Act, the personal identity of an individual is abused if "(a) an advertisement is published in which the personal identity of that individual is used in a manner which expresses or implies that the individual approves, endorses, has endorsed, or will endorse the specific subject matter of the advertisement; and (b) consent has not been obtained for such use from the individual, or if the individual is a minor, then consent of one of the minor's parents or consent of the minor's legally appointed guardian." Id. § 45-3-3(1); see also Schwarz v. Salt Lake Tribune, 2005 UT App. 206, ¶ 3 (finding the plaintiff's abuse of personal identity claim failed because she had "consented to the use of her photograph in the article").

Under the Act, an advertisement is "a notice designed to attract public attention or patronage and includes a list of supporters for a particular cause." UTAH CODE ANN. § 45-3-2(1). Consent is "a person's voluntary agreement to the use of that person's name, title, picture, or portrait," and "may not be inferred by the failure of the person to request that the person's name, title, picture, or portrait not be used or that the person's name be removed from a mailing or supporter list." Id. § 45-3-2(3)(a), (b). The Act provides that "[a]n individual whose personal identity" is abused "may bring an action against a person who caused the publication of the advertisement, and is entitled to injunctive relief, damages alleged and proved, exemplary damages, and reasonable attorney's fees and costs." Id. § 45-3-4. The Act further provides, "(1) An individual whose personal identity has been abused under Section 45-3-3 of this act may bring an action against a person who published the advertisement: (a) if the advertisement, on its face is such that a reasonable person would conclude that it is unlikely that an individual would consent to such use; and (b) the publisher did not take reasonable steps to assure that consent was obtained. (2) In an action under this section, the plaintiff shall be entitled to injunctive relief, damages alleged and proved, exemplary damages, and reasonable attorney's fees and costs." Id. § 45-3-5. The Act does not, however, preclude or limit any causes of action otherwise available to the parties. Id. § 45-3-6; see Nature's Way Prods., Inc. v. Nature -Pharma, Inc., 736 F. Supp. 245, 251 (D. Utah 1990) (holding that plaintiff can bring action for misappropriation of common-law right of publicity and for violation of statutory right created under the Act).

The general limitations period applicable to most tort claims, presumably including a common-law misappropriation action, is four years. UTAH CODE ANN. § 78B-2-307(3). There are no Utah cases that consider whether the general limitations period applicable to torts also applies to misappropriation claims or whether the shorter limitations period of one year for defamation claims is appropriate. Based on the Court's holding in Jensen v. Sawyers, 2005 UT 81, 130 P.3d 325, 33 Media L. Rep. 2578, it is likely the general limitations period of four years would apply, except in cases where the operative facts of the misappropriation claim would support a defamation claim as well. See discussion of Jensen, 2005 UT 81, 130 P.3d 325, I.B.2, infra. The limitations period for the Act probably would be three years pursuant to Utah Code section 78B-2-305(4), which provides the limitations period for actions or claims created by statute.

In addition to providing potential tort liability for abuse of personal identity, Utah law also provides potential criminal penalties for a person who "knowingly or intentionally causes the publication of an advertisement in which the personal identity of an individual is used in a manner which expresses or implies that the individual approves, endorses, has endorsed, or will endorse the specific subject matter of the advertisement without the consent for such use by the individual." UTAH CODE ANN. § 76-9-407(2). A person who violates this criminal statute is guilty of a class B misdemeanor. Id. Under Utah law, a person convicted of a class B misdemeanor may be imprisoned for a term not exceeding six months. Id. § 76-3-204(2). In addition, a person convicted of a class B misdemeanor may be fined up to $1000. Id. § 76-3-301(1)(d). A corporation, association, or governmental entity convicted of the same may be fined up to $5000. Id. § 76-3-302(3).

2. ***False Light.*** The Utah Supreme Court recognized the tort of false light invasion of privacy in Cox v. Hatch, and adopted the definition of the tort contained in § 652E of the Restatement (Second) of Torts. 761 P.2d 556, 564 (Utah 1988) (see I.A, supra); see also Russell v. Thomson Newspapers, Inc., 842 P.2d 896, 907 (Utah 1992) (reversing grant of summary judgment in favor of defendants and remanding case to allow plaintiff-nurse opportunity to present evidence that defendant newspaper and public official had been negligent in publishing allegedly "false light" statements about her personal life); Stien v. Marriott Ownership Resorts, Inc., 944 P.2d 374, 380 (Utah Ct. App. 1997) (quoting Russell, 842 P.2d at 907). The definition of false light in Utah is: one who "gives publicity to a matter concerning another that places the other before the public in a false light is subject to liability to the other for invasion of his privacy, if (a) a false light in which the other person was placed would be highly offensive to a reasonable person, and (b) the actor had knowledge of or acted in a reckless disregard as to the falsity of the publicized matter and the false light in which the other would be placed." Restatement (Second) of Torts § 652E (cited in Cox, 761 P.2d at 563-64). A former employer's comments about an employee to a prospective employer could not be the basis for a false light claim because the statements were not "published" but rather were made during a private meeting. Watkins v. General Refractories, Co., 805 F. Supp. 911, 918 (D. Utah 1992).

In Int'l Ass'n of United Mine Workers Union v. United Mine Workers of America, a coal mining company brought a false light claim against a newspaper agency for statements the newspaper published concerning a dispute between the mining company and a miner's' labor union. No. 2:04cv00901, 2006 WL 1183245, at *3-6 (D. Utah April 30, 2006). The court dismissed the false light claim, reasoning that labor disputes are "highly publicized by nature," so the plaintiff was not able to "punish its opponents for the publicity that naturally arises from any labor dispute." Id. at *37. In support of its decision, the court also noted there was no evidence that the newspaper had acted in reckless disregard as to the information publicized. Id. In Jacob v. Bezzant, an individual brought a false light claim against the editor of a local weekly newspaper.

2009 UT 37, ¶¶ 6, 21, 212 P.3d 535. The individual paid to publish information in the paper about particular candidates for local office. Id. ¶ 3. The editor of the paper then published an apology to the candidates which identified the individual and expressed a view about a controversial issue involving the eligibility of the candidates to stand for election. Id. ¶ 4. The court found that the editor's statements were not actionable because they were an editorial opinion that "cannot be verified as either true or false." Id. ¶ 22.

The general limitations period applicable to most tort claims is four years. UTAH CODE ANN. § 78B-2-307 (3). However, in Jensen v. Sawyers, the Utah Supreme Court held that the statute of limitations for the tort of false light invasion of privacy is only one year. 2005 UT 81, 130 P.3d 325, 33 Media L. Rep. 2578. The court compared the tort of false light invasion of privacy with the tort of defamation. Finding that the two torts "have much in common," the court reasoned that false light claims should also be subject to the stricter limitation period of one year in order to accommodate freedom of speech. Id. ¶ 49. The plaintiff's defamation claim and false light claim were based on the same operative facts, and therefore, the court vacated the verdict related to the false light claim since the one-year period of limitations had run. Id. Nonetheless, the Court recognized that "a false light invasion of privacy claim may turn on operative facts that do not include defamation," and limited its holding to cases involving similar facts. Id. ¶ 53. Accordingly, it is possible that a plaintiff's false light claim may not be subject to the shorter one-year limitations period in instances where the facts would not support a defamation claim as well as a false light claim.

3. ***Publication of Private Facts.*** In Shattuck-Owen v. Snowbird Corp., 2000 UT 94, 16 P.3d 555, the Utah Supreme Court set forth the specific elements for the tort of public disclosure of private embarrassing facts ("private facts tort"). The court held that "(1) the disclosure of the private facts must be a public disclosure and not a private one; (2) the facts disclosed to the public must be private facts, and not public ones; (3) the matter made public must be one that would be highly offensive and objectionable to a reasonable person of ordinary sensibilities." Id. ¶ 11 (citing Stien v. Marriott Ownership Resorts, Inc., 944 P.2d 374, 380 (Utah Ct. App. 1997)). Previous to the Shattuck-Owen case, Utah courts had had few opportunities to address this tort. See Cox v. Hatch, discussed supra I; Jeppson v. United Television, Inc., 580 P.2d 1087, 1088-89, 3 Media L. Rep. 2513 (Utah 1978); see also Jones v. United States Child Support Recovery, 961 F. Supp. 1518, 1520-21 (D. Utah 1997). The Utah Supreme Court has not yet adopted the second prong of the test for unreasonable publicity given to another's private life as set forth in Restatement (Second) of Torts § 652D, which is that the matter publicized "is not of legitimate concern to the public." Restatement (Second) of Torts § 652D (cited in Cox, 761 P.2d at 563-64); see also Jones, 961 F. Supp. at 1520 (citing Restatement (Second) of Torts § 652D); Stien, 944 P.2d at 380 (same).

In Shattuck-Owen, a ski resort's employee was assaulted in a lounge area during a break, and surveillance cameras caught the assault on tape. In the course of investigating the incident to determine the identity of the assailant, the employer showed the surveillance video to eight management-level employees and five other people. Among those who viewed the videotape was a police officer from a nearby city investigating a rape, a rape victim from the same city, and "two or three other individuals who were walking in and out of the security office while the tape was showing." 2000 UT 94, ¶ 4, 16 P.3d 555. The Utah Supreme Court held that the display of the video to twelve or thirteen people during the course of the investigation did not constitute public disclosure, and thus the employee's claim for the private facts tort failed. Regarding the requirement in Restatement (Second) of Torts § 652D that the matter publicized not be of legitimate concern to the public, the court said, "[i]n light of our holding, we need not decide whether to adopt this requirement as an element of the invasion of privacy tort we address today." Id. ¶ 11 n.1.

In Barker v. Manti Telephone Co., an employee's wife who worked at the telephone company told him the amount of one of his co-workers phone bills and where the calls were made to. No. 2:06-CV-00812-TC-SA, 2009 WL 47110, at *1 (D. Utah Jan. 6, 2009). The employee then disclosed this information to three other co-workers. Id. The court found that disclosure to three people was "not sufficient to create a public disclosure" and that the disclosure was not "highly offensive and objectionable to a reasonable person of ordinary sensibilities." Id. at *5.

The general limitations period applicable to most tort claims, presumably including this one, is four years. UTAH CODE ANN. § 78B-2-307(3). There are no Utah cases that consider whether the general limitations period applies to private facts tort claims or whether the shorter limitations period for defamation is appropriate.

4. ***Intrusion.*** As discussed supra, I.A, in Cox v. Hatch, the Utah Supreme Court recognized the tort of unreasonable intrusion upon the seclusion of another ("intrusion upon seclusion") and appeared to adopt the definition of the tort contained in § 652B of the Restatement (Second) of Torts. 761 P.2d 556, 563-64 (Utah 1988); Stien v. Marriott Ownership Resorts, Inc., 944 P.2d 374, 378 (Utah Ct. App. 1997). The elements of the tort of intrusion in Utah are "(1) that there was 'an intentional substantial intrusion, physically or otherwise, upon the solitude or seclusion of the complaining party,' and (2) that the intrusion 'would be highly offensive to the reasonable person.'" Stien, 944 P.2d at 378 (quoting Turner v. General Adjustment Bureau, Inc., 832 P.2d 62, 67 (Utah Ct. App. 1992), overruled on other grounds by Campbell v. State Farm Mut. Auto Ins. Co., 2001 UT 89, 65 P.3d 1134); see also Cox, 761 P.2d at 563-64 (citing Restatement (Second)

of Torts § 652B). The first element, consisting of an invasion of an individual's solitude or seclusion, could potentially be satisfied by an invasion of an individual's "home or other quarters, or an illegal search of his shopping bag in a store." Stien, 944 P.2d at 378. Intrusion upon seclusion could also involve non-physical invasions such as eavesdropping, peeping into windows, and even persistent unwanted phone calls. Id. In Stien, the Court found that a video shown at a company party that jestingly described the plaintiffs' love life was clearly "intended to be a joke and nothing more"; thus, the second element requiring the intrusion to be highly offensive to a reasonable person was not satisfied. Id. at 379.

In Walston v. United Parcel Service, Inc., the court held that an employee was entitled to summary judgment on his intrusion claim where a tape recorder was secretly placed above an employee workspace. No. 2:07-CV-525 TS, 2008 WL 5191710, at *3 (D. Utah Dec. 10, 2008). The court found that the intrusion was highly offensive because the employees did not know they were being taped by the defendant and testified that their conversations would have been different had the defendant been present. Id. at *2-3. The court later held that "'one who suffers an intrusion upon his solitude or seclusion . . . may recover damages for the deprivation of his seclusion.'" Walston v. United Parcel Service, Inc., No. 2:07-CV-525 TS , 2009 WL 349837, at *3 (D. Utah Feb. 11, 2009) (quoting Restatement (Second) of Torts § 652H cmt. a.). In addition, one may also recover damages for emotional distress, personal humiliation. Id. Thus, the court granted damages for plaintiff's paranoia and distrust of co-workers and anxiety resulting in lack of sleep and loss of appetite. Id.

In Barker v. Manti Telephone Company, no intrusion was found where an employee disclosed to other employees the amount of a co-worker's telephone bill and to where the calls were placed. No. 2:06-CV-00812-TC-SA, 2009 WL 47110, at *3-4 (D. Utah Jan. 6, 2009). The disclosure to others did not factor into the intrusion analysis. Id. at *3. The court cited the Restatement (Second) of Torts §652B cmt. a (1977), explaining that "the tort of intrusion upon seclusion 'does not depend upon any publicity given to the person whose interest is invaded or to his affairs' . . . [but rather the] 'intentional interference with his interest in solitude or seclusion.'" Id. The court found no intrusion because the employee was not actively "involved in procuring" the information and "dissemination of what is learned in an intrusion by a passive recipient of the information is not itself an intrusion upon seclusion." Id. at *3-4.

The general limitations period applicable to most tort claims, presumably including this one, is four years. UTAH CODE ANN. § 78B-2-307(3). There are no Utah cases that consider whether the general limitations period applies to intrusion claims or whether the shorter limitations period for defamation is appropriate.

C. Other Privacy-Related Actions

1. ***Negligent Hiring, Retention, and Supervision.*** "The causes of action variously termed 'negligent hiring,' 'negligent supervision,' and 'negligent retention' are all basically subsets of the general tort of negligent employment . . . . These variants differ only in that they arise at different points in the employment relationship." Retherford v. AT&T Communications, 844 P.2d 949, 973 n.15 (Utah 1992). An employer can be liable for negligent employment only if its employee is liable for an independent tort. Id. at 970. To prevail in a claim of negligent employment, the claimant must prove that: (1) the employer knew or should have known that its employee posed a foreseeable risk of engaging in the tortious conduct and of causing the alleged harm, (2) "the employee[] did indeed inflict such harm," and (3) "the employer's negligence in hiring, supervising, or retaining the employee[] proximately caused the injury." Id. at 973.

Although the existence of a collective bargaining agreement does not necessarily cause federal preemption of this common law claim, if the existence of such an agreement were to become relevant, federal preemption questions might arise under the Labor Management Relations Act, 29 U.S.C. § 185(a). The federal law does preempt the state common law claim in cases where the resolution of the common law claim depends upon the interpretation of the collective bargaining agreement. For example, in making a determination of proximate cause, "a court might have to resort to the collective bargaining agreement to discover whether contractual limitations on the power of the employer to deal with the employee precluded it from taking steps to prevent the harm." Retherford, 844 P.2d at 974. In such a case, the federal law would preempt the common law claim.

The Utah Supreme Court has not yet directly addressed the issue of "whether a plaintiff who is mentally or physically injured by the intentional torts of a fellow employee can sue his or her employer for negligent employment, or whether workers' compensation provides the exclusive remedy for employer's negligence." Id. at 965 n.8. In Retherford, where plaintiff sought recovery under a theory of negligent employment for emotional distress inflicted by her fellow employees, the Supreme Court declined to address the workers' compensation issue because it had not been raised or briefed. Id. However, the court found in its prior decisions the suggestion "that workers' compensation would be an exclusive remedy" in such actions. Id. (discussing Mounteer v. Utah Power & Light Co., 823 P.2d 1055 (Utah 1991)).

The Utah Supreme Court has formally recognized "negligent credentialing" as a valid common law cause of action. See Archuleta v. St. Mark's Hospital, 2010 UT 36, ¶ 15, 238 P.3d 1044. In Archuleta, a woman underwent surgery at St. Mark's Hospital and was later admitted to a different hospital complaining of severe pain and complications from her recent surgery. Id. ¶ 2. The woman then brought suit against St. Mark's hospital, claiming the hospital was negligent for credentialing the doctor. Id. ¶ 3. While the suit was dismissed at the trial court, the Utah Supreme Court recognized that a "substantial majority of the other common law states recognize negligent credentialing as a valid claim." Id. ¶ 15 (internal citation omitted). The court allowed the claim, holding that negligent credentialing "is a natural extension of torts such as negligent hiring." Id.

2. ***Intentional Infliction of Emotional Distress.*** Utah recognizes intentional infliction of emotional distress as a valid cause of action. To prevail on a claim of intentional infliction of emotional distress, a claimant must show that: (1) defendant's conduct was "outrageous and intolerable in that it offended against the generally accepted standards of decency and morality," Retherford, 844 P.2d at 970, (2) defendant "intended to cause, or acted in reckless disregard of the likelihood of causing, emotional distress," Id. at 970-71, (3) the claimant "suffered severe emotional distress," Id. at 971, and (4) defendant's actions proximately caused claimant's emotional distress. Id.; see also Franciscomi v. Union Pacific RR, 2001 UT App. 350, 36 P.3d 999; White v. Blackburn, 787 P.2d 1315, 1317 (Utah Ct. App. 1990). Whether an actor's conduct meets the threshold requirement of outrageousness gets determined by an objective standard, whereas the existence of severe emotional distress is a subjective determination. "Consequently, a plaintiff claiming intentional infliction of emotional distress must show both that a reasonable person would consider the alleged conduct to be outrageous and that the plaintiff actually experienced subjective severe emotional anguish because of this objectively outrageous conduct." Retherford, 844 P.2d at 976 n.17.

In Retherford the court found sufficiently outrageous conduct to support a cause of action, where the plaintiff alleged months of persecution by her co-workers, including threatening looks and remarks, intimidation, and manipulation of circumstances to make her job more stressful. Id. at 978. On the other hand, in White v. Blackburn, the court found a clergyman's actions insufficient to support a claim of intentional infliction of emotional distress, where he had bought the plaintiff's child a plane ticket believing the forged permission slip given him by the child was authentic. White, 787 P.2d at 1317-18. Also, the court in Matthews v. Kennecott Utah Copper Corp., 54 F. Supp. 2d 1067 (D. Utah 1999), found ample support in Utah case law for the proposition that termination and demotion are not sufficiently outrageous actions to support an action for intentional infliction of emotional distress. Id. at 1075.

Recently, the Utah Supreme Court held an employer's failure to prevent a supervisor from inflicting emotional anguish on employees does not give rise to a valid claim of intentional infliction of emotional distress. See Cabaness v. Thomas, 2010 UT 23, ¶ 36, 232 P.3d 486. The case involved Cabaness, an employee, who was subjected to regular verbal abuse and intimidation from his immediate supervisor, Thomas, for twenty years. Id. ¶¶ 5-6. Although numerous employees complained to Thomas' supervisor, the supervisor warned the employees that any further complaints about Thomas could result in their termination. Id. ¶ 13. The court found that Thomas "frequently used gross profanity and consistently verbally harassed, intimidated, and ridiculed the employees he supervised." Id. ¶ 6. While the Court allowed a claim of intentional infliction of emotional distress against Thomas, it held that failure to prevent another from inflicting emotional distress did not constitute conduct directed toward Cabaness with the intent to inflict harm. Id. ¶ 37. While the Court opined that "there may be persuasive case law in other jurisdictions for extending the reach of intentional infliction of emotional distress to include situations where an individual appears to have some duty or obligation to prevent the outrageous conduct," it was not persuaded to "expand the rule at this time." Id.

A federal district court judge noted that normally, the Utah Workers' Compensation Act would provide the exclusive remedy for an employee's claim of negligent infliction of emotional distress where the employee claimed that she got pressured into telling her husband, also an employee at the same company, that he was fired because he had AIDS and other employees did not want to work with him. Richardson v. Valley Asphalt, 109 F. Supp. 2d 1332 (D. Utah 2000). The exclusive remedy provision is intended to shield employers from common law liability, "unless it is shown that the employer intended or directed the act which caused the emotional distress." Id. at 1340 (citing Newsome v. McKesson Corp., 932 F. Supp. 1339, 1343 (D. Utah 1996)). Therefore, in Richardson, the Utah Workers' Compensation Act exclusive remedy provision did not bar the plaintiff's claim for intentional infliction of emotional distress because the plaintiff properly alleged that the "employer intended or directed the act that caused the emotional distress." Id. at 1340. Finally, the court held that "disability discrimination," like sexual harassment, is outrageous and intolerable if performed with the requisite intent and thus the allegations of disability discrimination against the employee with AIDS satisfied the elements of the tort of intentional infliction of emotional distress. Id.

The Utah Court of Appeals held that a collective bargaining agreement preempted an employee's claim for intentional infliction of emotional distress. Peterson v. Delta Air Lines, 2002 UT App. 56, 42 P.3d 1253. In Peterson, the plaintiff, a retiring airline pilot, alleged that the employer committed intentional infliction of emotional distress by not allowing him to make a scheduled farewell flight. Id. ¶ 5. In determining whether the collective bargaining agreement preempted the pilot's claim, the court considered whether the employer had misused its authority or whether the tortious conduct was purely personal. Id. ¶ 14. The court held that the decision of whether or not to allow the pilot to fly was "an issue of managerial authority, which is governed by the [collective bargaining agreement]," and therefore the claim was preempted. Id. ¶ 15.

The general limitations period applicable to intentional infliction of emotional distress claims is four years. UTAH CODE ANN. § 78B-2-307(3); Retherford, 844 P.2d at 975. However, when the claim is alleged based on a pattern of continuous and ongoing tortious conduct, "the statute of limitations begins to run at the time the last injury occurred or the tortious conduct ceases." Cabaness, 2010 UT 23, ¶ 26, 232 P.3d 486 (modifying and clarifying the rule set forth in Hatch v. Davis, 2004 UT App. 378, 102 P.3d 774). The Court further held that when the claim is based on ongoing and continuous conduct, a plaintiff may support his claim with evidence of the defendant's entire course of conduct, even conduct that occurred outside the four-year statute of limitations. Id. ¶ 28 (allowing Cabaness to introduce evidence from over the course of twenty years to establish outrageous conduct). Similarly, a plaintiff may recover for injuries suffered during the entire course of defendant's conduct. Id. ¶ 27.

3. ***Interference with Prospective Economic Advantage.*** In Leigh Furniture and Carpet Co. v. Isom, 657 P.2d 293 (Utah 1982), the Utah Supreme Court expressly recognized interference with prospective economic advantage as an actionable tort, although the court referred to it as "interference with prospective economic relations." Id. at 302. The court discussed various definitions of the tort, finally accepting the definition adopted by Oregon. Id. at 304. Under the Oregon definition, to prevail under the theory of interference with prospective economic relations, the plaintiff must prove: "(1) that the defendant intentionally interfered with the plaintiff's existing or potential economic relations, (2) for an improper purpose or by improper means, (3) causing injury to the plaintiff." Id.; see also Ferguson v. Williams & Hunt, Inc., 2009 UT 49, ¶ 35, 221 P.3d 205 (citing Leigh, 657 P.2d at 307). A party may recover for injurious interference where the interference occurred through the use of "improper means" or, even if the means were proper, derived from some "improper purpose." The element of "improper means" is satisfied "where the means used to interfere with a party's economic relations are contrary to law, such as violations of statutes, regulations, or recognized common-law rules." Leigh, 657 P.2d at 308. In addition, although breach of contract standing alone does not constitute "improper means," "breach of contract (or lease), when done with a purpose to injure, satisf[ies] this element of the tort." Id. at 309. "The alternative of improper purpose . . . will support a cause of action for intentional interference with prospective economic relations even where the defendant's means were proper." Id. at 307. The element of improper purpose is satisfied "where it can be shown that the actor's predominant purpose was to injure the plaintiff." Id. (citing St. Louis-San Francisco Railway Co. v. Wade, 607 F.2d 126, 133 (5th Cir. 1979)).

In Pratt v. Prodata, Inc., 885 P.2d 786 (Utah 1994), where former employee sued former employer for contacting the Utah Department of Transportation, with whom the former employee had worked as an independent contractor, and informing UDOT that the former employee was in violation of a covenant not to compete, the Utah Supreme Court reaffirmed the principles set forth in Leigh. The court rejected defendant's assertion "that under Leigh a judgment for intentional interference with economic relations cannot be based on the transmission of truthful information." Id. at 790. Chief Justice Zimmerman, the author of the Pratt opinion, did express "grave doubts about the future vitality of Leigh's improper purpose prong, especially in the context of commercial dealings," Id. at 789 n.3, believing that "Leigh's improper-purpose test should be revisited and recast to minimize its potential for misuse." Id. However, the issue had not been raised, and Zimmerman relegated his concerns to the footnotes. Two of the three remaining justices expressed the contrary opinion in a concurrence, stating that the Pratt opinion "demonstrate[d] the soundness of the improper-purpose prong . . . ." Id. at 791; see also Watkins v. General Refractories, Co., 805 F. Supp. 911 (D. Utah 1992) (dismissing an employee's claim for interference with prospective economic advantage because an employer's statements about the employee to a prospective employer were not made solely for the improper purpose of preventing the employee from obtaining the job).

In Giusti v. Sterling Wentworth Corp., a recently hired executive claimed tortious interference with economic relations with his former company when he was terminated by defendants, his superiors. 2009 UT 2, ¶ 64, 201 P.3d 966. The court cited the Leigh elements and clarified that when defendants "are also employees . . . the plaintiff must establish that the defendants were acting outside the scope of their employment *for purely personal reasons*." Id. ¶ 65. An employee acts for "purely personal motives when their actions are *in no way connected with the employer's interest*." Id.; PrizeWise, Inc. v. Oppenheimer & Co., No. 2:07-CV-792 TS, 2010 WL 1417781, at *3-4 (D. Utah Apr. 5, 2010) (dismissing claim because employee's actions were done for personal reasons and were not of the kind the employer engaged him to perform). In Giusti, the court found that because the defendants were "high level executives with the responsibility for the operation of [the company], the right to terminate [was] clearly within the scope of [their] employment." 2009 UT 2 ¶ 68, 201 P.3d 966. Furthermore, the court acknowledged that even if defendants had mixed motives for terminating the plaintiff, as long as their actions were within the scope of employment, it did not prevent summary judgment in their favor. Id. ¶ 69.

In Iostar Corp. v. Stuart, the court granted summary judgment in favor of a company for interference with economic relations. No. 1:07-CV-133, 2009 WL 270037, at *16 (D. Utah 2009). The former president and member of the board of directors of a company claimed tortious interference when he felt forced to resign because of "unlawful and improper acts" by the CEO of the company, which the president "refused to ignore." Id. The court found that the predominant purpose of the CEO's actions was not to injure the plaintiff, but that he misappropriated money from the company for his own benefit. Id. at *17. Furthermore, the plaintiff could not demonstrate how the CEO's actions "were actually directed at his economic relations with [the company]." Id.

The Utah Supreme Court has held that for pecuniary losses, lost profits are the appropriate measure of damages for tortious interference with prospective economic relations. TruGreen Co. v. Mower Bros., Inc., 2008 UT 81, ¶ 21, 199 P.3d 929. The Court recognized, however, that lost profits may be difficult to ascertain in certain situations and so it may be appropriate to examine a defendant's gains. Id. ¶ 27.

4. ***Prima Facie Tort.*** In Doit, Inc. v. Touche, Ross & Co., 926 P.2d 835 (Utah 1996), plaintiffs brought a class action against various defendants related to failed thrift institutions, and asserted a cause of action against the accountant defendants titled prima facie tort. The Utah Supreme Court stated that "plaintiffs have not supplied, and we have been unable to find, any legal precedent which indicates that such a cause of action exists in Utah." Id. at 841 n.11. Furthermore, because the plaintiffs failed to plead the elements of a prima facie tort as established in other jurisdictions, the court declined to address the issue of whether such a cause of action does exist in Utah. Id.

II. EMPLOYER TESTING OF EMPLOYEES

A. Psychological or Personality Testing

1. ***Common Law and Statutes.*** No Utah cases or statutes discuss this issue.

2. ***Private Employers.*** No Utah cases or statutes discuss this issue.

3. ***Public Employers.*** Failure to perform a certain psychological test that purported to discover sexual deviancy did not give rise to a cause of action for negligent hiring, where a police officer had molested a juvenile. J.H. by D.H. v. West Valley City, 840 P.2d 115, 124-25 (Utah 1992).

B. Drug Testing

1. ***Common Law and Statutes.*** Utah Code sections 34-38-1 to -15 govern drug and alcohol testing by private employers. Utah Code sections 34-41-101 to -107 govern drug and alcohol testing of employees by local governmental entities or state institutions of higher education. Utah Code section 67-19-36 governs drug and alcohol testing of employees by Utah State Government or its administrative subdivisions.

2. ***Private Employers.*** The Utah Legislature has expressed a strong public policy supporting the maintenance of a drug free work environment. See UTAH CODE ANN. § 34-38-1. Utah statute defines an employer as any person, firm, or corporation that has "one or more workers or operators employed in the same business." UTAH CODE ANN. § 34-38-2(3). Another section of the code governs federal, state, and other local public employers. See II.B.1, supra.

Under Utah Code section 34-38-3(1), it is lawful to test employees and prospective employees for the presence of drugs or alcohol, but should the employer choose to implement such testing, the employer and management in general "shall submit to the testing themselves on a periodic basis." Employers involved in the storage or transportation of high-level nuclear waste must establish a mandatory drug and alcohol testing program for employees. Id. § 34-38-3(2). To perform the testing, an employer may require a sample and may even designate what that sample will be as between urine, blood, breath, saliva, or hair. See UTAH CODE ANN. § 34-38-4. In addition, the employer may require that the testee present reliable identification to the person collecting the samples. Id. Any drug testing must be performed during or immediately after the regular work period, and be deemed work time for purposes of compensation and benefits for current employees. UTAH CODE ANN. § 34-38-5(1). The employer is responsible for paying all costs associated with the testing, including transportation if the testing occurs away from the work site. Id. § 34-38-5(2).

The actual testing must conform to five requirements, the purpose of which is to ensure safety, reliability, and maximum privacy. First, the testing must be performed under "reasonable and sanitary conditions." UTAH CODE ANN. § 34-38-6(2). Second, the samples must be collected and tested "with due regard to the privacy of the individual being tested; and in a manner reasonably calculated to prevent substitutions or interference with the collection or testing of a reliable sample." UTAH CODE ANN. § 34-38-6(3). Third, the sample collection must be documented, and the documentation must include: (a) labeling of the samples to reasonably preclude the probability of erroneous identification; and (b) an opportunity for the testee to provide any information he or she considers relevant to the test, such as the use of prescription drugs. UTAH CODE ANN. § 34-38-6(4). Fourth, the collection, storage, and transportation must be "performed so as reasonably to preclude the probability of sample contamination or adulteration . . . ." UTAH CODE ANN. § 34-38-6(5). Finally, the testing must conform to "scientifically accepted analytical methods and procedures" and must include verification of positive test results by gas chromatography, gas chromatography-mass spectroscopy, or another comparably reliable method before an employer may use the test result as a basis for any action. UTAH CODE ANN. § 34-38-6(6).

The employer must perform any testing within the terms of a written policy, which has been distributed to the employees and is available for prospective employees to review. UTAH CODE ANN. § 34-38-7(1). An employer may use a verified positive drug or alcohol test, or a refusal to provide a sample for testing, as the basis for disciplinary or rehabilitative actions. UTAH CODE ANN. § 34-38-8(1). Such actions may include: (a) a requirement that the employee enroll in an employer-approved rehabilitation or counseling program, (b) suspension without pay, (c) termination, (d) refusal to hire, or (e) "other disciplinary measures in conformance with the employer's usual procedures, including a collective bargaining agreement." Id.

Utah law also provides the employer with various protections from liability related to drug or alcohol testing. No cause of action can arise against an employer who establishes a testing program pursuant to Chapter 38 for a failure to test for drugs or alcohol, or to test for a specific drug. UTAH CODE ANN. § 34-38-9(1). In addition, no cause of action can arise against an employer for failing to establish a testing program. UTAH CODE ANN. § 34-38-12. Under Utah Code section 34-38-10, no cause of action can arise against an employer who has taken disciplinary action under Utah Code section 34-38-8, unless the employer acted on the basis of a false test result. In a claim alleging that the employer acted based on a false test result, there is a rebuttable presumption that the result was valid if the testing conformed to the requirements of the statute. Id. § 34-38-10(2). If the test result was, in fact, false, the employer is not liable for monetary damages resulting from its action, so long as the employer's reliance on the result was reasonable and in good faith. Id. No cause of action for defamation, libel, slander, or damage to reputation arises against an employer who has established a testing program pursuant to Chapter 38, unless false results have been disclosed to an unauthorized person with malice, and all elements otherwise required by statute or common law to support such an action are present. UTAH CODE ANN. § 34-38-11.

All information, interviews, reports, statements, memoranda, or test results received through an employer testing program are the property of the employer, and are confidential communications, not to be disclosed, discovered, or received into evidence except in a proceeding related to an action taken by an employer regarding the results. UTAH CODE ANN. § 34-38-13(1). Furthermore, an employer may not undergo examination as a witness regarding the above information, except in a proceeding related to an action under Utah Code section 34-38-8, Utah Code section 34-38-11, or an action taken by the Division of Occupational and Professional Licensing under Utah Code section 58-1-401. UTAH CODE ANN. § 34-38-13(6). An employee or prospective employee whose positive test results are verified is not considered a person with a disability for purposes of the Utah Antidiscrimination Act, based on those test results alone. UTAH CODE ANN. § 34-38-14. Nor is a physician-patient relationship created between the testee and the employer or any person performing the test based on the establishment of a drug or alcohol testing program. UTAH CODE ANN. § 34-38-15.

An employer that discharges an employee for failing to pass a drug or alcohol test will not be liable for unemployment compensation benefits unless the employer fails to comply with the requirements of Chapter 38. See Johnson v. Dep't of Employment Sec., 782 P.2d 965 (Utah Ct. App. 1989) (finding that an employee that was discharged after testing positive for marijuana consumption on two occasions did not qualify for unemployment benefits where the employee had knowledge of the employer's drug testing policy). However, failure to conform to the requirements of Chapter 38 in the administration of a drug or alcohol testing program may leave the employer liable for unemployment compensation benefits if the employer bases termination of the employee on a positive result. For example, in Grace Drilling v. Board of Review, 776 P.2d 63 (Utah Ct. App. 1989), a Utah appellate court upheld the Industrial Commission's award of unemployment compensation benefits, where the employer "failed to demonstrate that its testing procedures met the enumerated criteria set forth in Section 34-38-6." Id. at 69. The court specifically pointed out that the employer violated Utah Code section 34-38-6 (3)(b), because the employee did not receive the opportunity to identify two prescription drugs he was taking before his termination. Id. In addition, the office manager's hearsay testimony was insufficient to demonstrate that the employer's procedures "conform[ed] to scientifically accepted analytical methods and procedures." Id. In a similar case, a Utah appellate court upheld unemployment insurance benefits for an employee who was terminated after testing positive on a drug test where the employer violated Utah Code section 34-38-6 by failing to give the employee an opportunity to explain the test results and by failing to show that scientific methods informed the administration of the test. See Autoliv ASP, Inc. v. Dep't. of Workforce Servs., 2001 UT App. 366, 38 P.3d 979.

Interpreting Utah law, the U.S. Court of Appeals for the Tenth Circuit held that "[w]hile UTAH CODE ANN. § 34-38-8 does permit an employer to terminate an employee for failing a drug test, it is permissive and not mandatory, and termination is only one of several discretionary and non-exclusive remedies." Kennecott Utah Copper Corp. v. Becker, 195 F.3d 1201, 1207 (10th Cir. 1999). Therefore, the Tenth Circuit was not "persuaded that these provisions constitute a clear public policy that prohibits reinstatement of an employee [after a positive drug test] . . . . The Utah provisions . . . simply do not suggest that every employee in a safety sensitive position that tests positive one time, with no other evidence of drug involvement, must be fired." Id. at 1206.

3. ***Public Employers.*** The Local Governmental Entity Drug-Free Workplace Policies statute governs drug testing by local governmental entities and state institutions of higher education. UTAH CODE ANN. §§ 34-41-101 to 107. This Statute is similar to the statute governing drug testing by private employers. Like private employers, a local governmental entity or state institution of higher education may only perform drug tests on employees and volunteers pursuant to a written policy that has been distributed to its employees and volunteers and made available for review by prospective employees and volunteers. Id. § 34-41-103(1)(a), (b). The Statute allows but does not require drug testing in connection with preemployment hiring or volunteer selection procedures, post-accident investigations, reasonable suspicion situations, preannounced periodic testing, rehabilitation programs, random testing in safety sensitive positions, or compliance with the federal Drug Free Workplace Act of 1988. Id. § 34-41-102(3). The standards for sample collection and testing are substantially the same as those for private employers; however, the Statute requires that entities independent of the local government or state institution of higher education perform all sample collection and testing for drugs, and that an independent laboratory prepare the instructions, chain of custody forms, and collection kits. Id. § 34-41-104(1).

The Utah State Government and its administrative subdivisions are more limited in their ability to perform drug and alcohol testing. Random drug testing may only be performed on employees in "highly sensitive positions, as identified in department class specifications . . . ," UTAH CODE ANN. § 67-19-36(2), and must be performed in accordance with rules set forth by the executive director pursuant to Utah Code section 67-19-34. UTAH CODE ANN. § 67-19-34(3)(b). Otherwise, a medically accepted drug test may only be performed when there is a "reasonable suspicion" that an employee is using a controlled substance or alcohol unlawfully "during work hours." UTAH CODE ANN. § 67-19-36(1). All testing must be conducted by a federally certified and licensed physician, medical clinic, or drug testing facility in accordance with the rules established by the executive director under Utah Code section 67-19-34, and must be kept confidential pursuant to the same rules. UTAH CODE ANN. § 67-19-36(3)(c). Utah law also protects any physician, medical facility, or testing facility from civil liability for acting or omitting to act in any way in good faith pursuant to this section. UTAH CODE ANN. § 67-19-36(4).

C. Medical Testing

1. ***Common Law and Statutes.*** There is no case law and little statutory law regarding medical testing in the employment context. Regulations addressing medical testing generally are directed at health facility licensure, where health itself is at issue. For example, skin testing of employees is mandatory to obtain and retain an ambulatory surgical center license. UTAH ADMIN. CODE r. 432-500-11(1)(d). Hepatitis testing, in addition to skin testing, is mandatory to obtain a license for end stage renal disease facilities. UTAH ADMIN. CODE r. 432-650-6(3). To prevent diseases transmissible through food, the Utah Department of Agriculture and Food may require "appropriate medical examinations, including collection of specimens for laboratory analysis, of a suspected employee and other employees." UTAH ADMIN. CODE r. 70-530-3.

Before it was withdrawn, the Pre-Employment Inquiry Guide, established pursuant to the Utah Antidiscrimination Act, *et seq*., stated that it is improper to require a potential employee to take a medical examination prior to an offer of employment. UTAH ADMIN. CODE r. 606-2-2(F)(2)(b) (repealed 2011). Along the same lines, Utah Code section 34-33-1 prohibits any "person, firm, corporation or partnership" from charging prospective employees and applicants a medical fee for physical examinations for employment with the employer. UTAH CODE ANN. § 34-33-1. Nor can any employer lawfully deduct the costs of physical examinations from an employee's earnings. Id. Finally, no employer shall, "as a condition of pre-employment, employment, or continued employment, require any employee or person applying for employment to submit to or obtain a physical examination, unless such employer shall pay all costs of such physical examination." Id. Violation of this statute results in a misdemeanor. UTAH CODE ANN. § 34-33-2.

The Genetic Testing Privacy Act, UTAH CODE ANN. § 26-45-101 *et seq*., and the Genetic Testing Restrictions on Employers Act, UTAH CODE ANN. § 34A-11-101 *et seq.*, protect employees from genetic testing. This legislation prohibits both public and private employers, in connection with a hiring, promotion or retention decision, from accessing or taking into consideration "private genetic information about an individual." UTAH CODE ANN. § 26-45-103(1)(a). In effect, the legislation prohibits employers from considering information resulting from a DNA test of a current or potential employee. In addition, employers may not "request or require an individual or his blood relative to submit to a genetic test." UTAH CODE ANN. § 26-45-103(1)(c). Under certain circumstances, however, an employer may obtain a court order requiring an employee to consent to release of DNA test results or to submit to a DNA test. UTAH CODE ANN. § 26-45-103(2). The legislation creates a private right of action for violation of the genetic testing prohibitions after June 30, 2003, UTAH CODE ANN. § 26-45-105, and the state attorney general may enforce the law through civil proceedings. UTAH CODE ANN. § 26-45-106. Primarily, the bill eliminates the potential for employers to use genetic testing as a means to determine which employees may have or may be susceptible to debilitating and expensive health problems, including cancer and other diseases.

2. ***Private Employers.*** No Utah cases or statutes discuss this issue.

3. ***Public Employers.*** No Utah cases or statutes discuss this issue.

D. Polygraph Tests

Utah has at least implicitly accepted the use of polygraph testing in the employment context by setting forth polygraph examiner licensure requirements that refer to employment situations. The Deception Detection Examiners Licensing Act, UTAH CODE ANN. §§ 58-64-101 *et seq.*, establishes a board to govern the use of deception detection tests, sets forth certain requirements for licensure, and mandates the use of equipment that meets certain minimum operating standards. The Act also makes it unlawful to perform certain types of deception detection tests in any context. For example, it is unlawful to conduct a deception detection examination performed: (a) outside the physical presence of the subject; (b) using any electronic means, including telephone; and (c) through any surreptitious means when the subject is not aware of the examination. UTAH CODE ANN. § 58-64-501(1). It is also unlawful for an examiner located outside the state to perform an examination by electronic means on a subject located inside the state. UTAH CODE ANN. § 58-64-501(2). Under the Act, unprofessional conduct includes using equipment that does not meet the standards established by the board, or using an instrument that does not make a permanent recording. UTAH CODE ANN. § 58-64-502. Engaging in unlawful or unprofessional conduct may result in various sanctions, including license denial, revocation, or suspension. UTAH CODE ANN. § 58-1-401.

More detailed regulations, found in the Utah Administrative Code R156-64-101 to -502, set forth specific requirements for licensure and describe additional unprofessional conduct. Under Utah Administrative Code R156-64-502 (7), it constitutes unprofessional conduct to use a polygraphy instrument that does not record at a minimum: (a) properly functioning respiration, (b) galvanic skin response, and (c) cardio vascular response. Utah Administrative Code R156-64-502 also sets forth exacting requirements for pre-employment interviews as well as periodic examinations. The duration of a pre-employment or periodic examination must be no less than 60 minutes. UTAH ADMIN. CODE r. 156-64-502(9)(b). If the examination is not pre-employment or periodic, it must be no less than a 90-minute duration. UTAH ADMIN. CODE r. 156-64-502(9)(c). During a pre-employment or periodic examination, decisions of truthfulness or deception must be based on no less than two repetitions of each question. UTAH ADMIN. CODE r. 156-64-502(4)(a). During a specific examination, such decision must be based on no less than three repetitions of each question. UTAH ADMIN. CODE r. 156-64-502(4)(b). It constitutes unprofessional conduct to ask any questions about the subject's sexual attitudes, political beliefs, union sympathies, or religious beliefs during a pre-employment examination unless there is some overriding reason to do so. UTAH ADMIN. CODE r. 156-64-502(12).

Polygraph testing in the employment context has been challenged only once in Berube v. Fashion Centre, Ltd., 771 P.2d 1033 (Utah 1989), where plaintiff asserted that the language in Utah Code section 58-64-501 (previously Utah Code section 34-37-16) that prohibited surreptitious examinations applied to all polygraph tests. The court "express[ed] no view approving or disapproving the use of polygraphs in employment situations," Berube, 771 P.2d at 1039 n.5, stating that it would "reserve judgment on this issue." Id. However, the court found plaintiff's interpretation too "far-reaching," Id. at 1038, in that it would bar the use of polygraphs to screen potential employees and examine current employees.

Although employers can subject their employees to polygraph tests, where an at-will employment situation has been modified by an implied covenant of good faith through a company policy, certain limitations apply. In Berube, despite the fact that the employer's policy specifically stated that an employee could get terminated for refusing to submit to a polygraph test, the court found that an employee who got terminated for refusing to submit to a polygraph test had not been terminated with just cause where she had already passed two previous polygraph tests regarding the same subject and had only requested postponement of the third test. Id. at 1047-49. The employer's termination of the employee for refusing to submit to the third test was not reasonable, and gave rise to an action for breach of an implied covenant of good faith. Id. at 1049.

A polygraph test, standing alone, might not be enough to constitute just cause for termination in the context of unemployment compensation. In Spartan AMC/Jeep v. Board of Review, 709 P.2d 395 (Utah 1985), the Utah Supreme Court upheld the Industrial Commission's Board of Review's decision to grant unemployment benefits, where Spartan relied heavily on a polygraph examination in terminating the employee, but failed to produce the test itself or the examiner for cross examination. Id. at 396. In the absence of other evidence, the polygraph test results were not enough to support a finding of just cause discharge. Id.

In addition to the Utah statutory law governing polygraph tests, Utah employers involved in, or affecting, interstate commerce are subject to the Employee Polygraph Protection Act of 1988. This Act prohibits employers from (1) directly or indirectly requiring, requesting, or causing any employee or prospective employee to submit to a lie detector test; (2) using, accepting, or inquiring into the results of a lie detector test taken by an employee or prospective employee; or (3) discharging, disciplining, discriminating against, denying employment or promotion, or threatening adverse action against any employee or prospective employee based on lie detector test results, or the employee's refusal to take a lie detector test. 29 U.S.C.A. § 2002. The Employee Polygraph Protection Act does not apply to federal or state governmental employers, security system companies, or certain manufacturers of controlled substances. 29 U.S.C.A. § 2006(a). Despite its varying prohibitions, the

Act does allow employers to conduct lie detector tests in connection with an "ongoing investigation involving economic loss or injury to the employer's business, such as theft, embezzlement, misappropriation," or similar losses. 29 U.S.C.A. § 2006(d)(1).

E. Fingerprinting

No Utah cases or statutes directly discuss this issue on a general level applicable to all Utah employers. However, Utah law requires specific classes of employees to submit to fingerprinting as a condition for employment or licensing in a particular field. See, e.g., UTAH CODE ANN. § 53A-6-401 (public education background checks); UTAH CODE ANN. § 61-2f-204 (real estate broker's licensing); and UTAH CODE ANN. § 58-47b-302 (massage therapy licensing). For example, in Sorenson's Ranch School v. Oram, the Utah Court of Appeals interpreted the meaning of a state law requiring public and private employers licensed to provide services and care to children and youth to submit to the Utah Department of Public Safety the "name and other identifying information, which may include fingerprints," of employees. 2001 UT App. 354, ¶ 7, 36 P.3d 528 (interpreting former version of Utah Code section 62A-2-120). The statute required the Department of Public Safety to conduct a background check on potential employees, owners and directors of licensed child and youth care providers. See id.

III. SEARCHES

A. Employee's Person

1. ***Private Employers.*** No Utah cases or statutes directly address this issue. Article I, Section 14 of the Utah Constitution does protect persons and their effects from unreasonable searches and seizures. However, the Utah Supreme Court has held that "unreasonable *private* searches are not subject to the protection of article I, section 14 of the Utah Constitution." State v. Watts, 750 P.2d 1219, 1221 (Utah 1988) (emphasis added); see also Atkinson v. Stateline Hotel Casino & Resort, 2001 UT App. 63, ¶ 30, 21 P.3d 667 (same). Therefore, the Utah Constitution offers no protection to employees from searches and seizures by private employers, even if performed unreasonably.

2. ***Public Employers.*** No Utah cases or statutes discuss this issue. However, it may be assumed that searches by public employers are subject to the protections of Article I, Section 14 of the Utah Constitution. See III.A.1, supra. Furthermore, the Fourth Amendment of the U.S. Constitution protects individuals from unreasonable searches and seizures. This protection extends to state employers through the Fourteenth Amendment. See O'Connor v. Ortega, 480 U.S. 709 (1987). Therefore, employees are protected from being subject to "unreasonable searches" where the employee has a "reasonable expectation of privacy." See O'Connor, 480 U.S. 709 (finding that the employee had a reasonable expectation of privacy in his office, and therefore, was entitled to a determination of whether an uninvited search of his office space violated his Fourth Amendment rights).

B. Employee's Work Area

No Utah cases or statutes discuss this issue. See III.A.1, supra.

C. Employee's Property

1. ***Private Employers.*** No Utah cases or statutes discuss this issue. See III.A.1, supra.

2. ***Public Employers.*** No Utah cases or statutes discuss this issue. See III.A.2, supra.

IV. MONITORING OF EMPLOYEES

A. Telephones and Electronic Communications

1. ***Wiretapping.*** Utah's broadly applicable Interception of Communications Act, UTAH CODE ANN. §§ 77-23a-1 *et seq.*, governs wiretapping in the employment context, as well as the interception of oral or electronic communications. In accordance with the Act, and "[t]o safeguard the privacy of innocent persons, the interception of wire or oral communications when none of the parties to the communication has consented to the interception should be allowed only when authorized by a court of competent jurisdiction and should remain under the control and supervision of the authorizing court." UTAH CODE ANN. § 77-23a-2(4). However, a person may intercept a wire, electronic, or oral communication "if that person is a party to the communication or one of the parties to the communication has given prior consent to the interception." UTAH CODE ANN. § 77-23a-4(7)(b). Also, in Hart v. Clearfield City, Davis County, 815 F. Supp. 1544 (D. Utah 1993), the Court held that a City dispatcher had no reasonable expectation of privacy with respect to personal telephone calls made during work hours given the nature of her employment and work environment and the routine review of telephone calls.

The Act authorizes a person whose communication has been intercepted to recover appropriate relief in a civil action against the violator. UTAH CODE ANN. § 77-23a-11. Appropriate relief may include: (1) preliminary and other equitable or declaratory relief, (2) damages and punitive damages, and (3) reasonable attorney's fee and litigation costs. UTAH CODE ANN. § 77-23-11(2). In such an action, the court may assess as damages whichever is the greater of the sum of the actual damages and any profits derived from violations, statutory damages of $100 for each day of violation, or $10,000. UTAH CODE ANN. § 77-23a-11(3)(a)(2), (b). It is a complete defense against any civil or criminal action that the violator relied in good faith upon a good faith determination that Utah Code section 77-23a-4 permitted the conduct complained of. UTAH CODE ANN. § 77-23a-11(4)(c). Under the Act, a civil action may not be commenced later than two years after the claimant discovered or had reasonable opportunity to discover the violation. UTAH CODE ANN. § 77-23a-11(5).

In order to introduce a wiretap recording into evidence at trial, a court must use sound discretion in determining "that the recording is accurate, authentic, and generally trustworthy." Chen v. Stewart, 2005 UT 68, ¶ 29, 123 P.3d 416. In addition, the recording must be obtained in accordance with the Act since the Act's exclusionary rule prohibits any wire, electronic, or oral communication that has been intercepted from being received into evidence in any trial or related adversarial proceeding where the information was obtained in violation of the Act. UTAH CODE ANN. § 77-23a-7. In Chen, the defendant argued that despite the exclusionary rule, an illegally procured wiretap recording should be admissible at trial for impeachment purposes, similar to the controlling federal evidence rule in criminal cases. 2005 UT 68, ¶ 31, 123 P.3d 416. The court rejected this argument, holding that "any impeachment exception to the Utah wiretap exclusionary rule does not extend to civil cases." Id. However, an aggrieved party still must carry the burden of proof in establishing the wiretap recording violates the Act and should therefore be excluded from being admitted into evidence. Id. ¶ 33.

In addition to the Utah cases and statutes governing wiretapping, a recent California Supreme Court decision may affect how Utah employers should approach issues relating to wiretapping, particularly employers that record telephone conversations. In Kearney v. Salomon Smith Barney, Inc., various California residents brought an invasion of privacy claim against a Georgia financial company for recording phone conversations without their consent. 39 Cal. 4th 95, 99, 137 P.3d 914, 917 (Cal. 2006). California is an "all-party" consent state, meaning every participant to a phone conversation must know and consent to recording, whereas Georgia is a "one-party" consent state like Utah. The phone calls originated from the residents in California, but were recorded by the company in Georgia. Id. The court ruled that the locus of the recording in Georgia was not as important as the privacy interests of the California residents; accordingly, the court found the Georgia company had violated the privacy rights of the California citizens. Id. at 128-30, 137 P.3d at 936-38. While the court refused to award damages since the decision centered on an issue of first impression, the court explicitly allowed for damages in future cases. Id. at 130-31, 137 P.3d at 938-39. As a result of the decision, any California resident who is recorded without consent in another state now has a claim in a California court. Therefore, Utah employers that record telephone conversations with out of state residents should notify callers and obtain their consent prior to recording.

2. ***Electronic Communications.*** The provisions of the Interception of Communications Act discussed above, see IV.A.1, supra, also apply to electronic communications. In addition, Utah Code sections 77-23b-1 to -9 provide further guidance regarding access to stored electronic communications. As might well be expected, it is a criminal offense to access a wire or electronic communication in electronic storage if the person accessing the communication intentionally accesses a facility through which electronic communications service is provided without authorization or while exceeding an authorization to access the facility. UTAH CODE ANN. § 77-23b-2. It is also unlawful for an electronic communication provider to divulge the contents of a stored electronic communication except under certain circumstances. UTAH CODE ANN. § 77-23b-3. For example, a provider may divulge the contents of an electronic communication "with the lawful consent of the originator or addressee or intended recipient of the communication . . . ." UTAH CODE ANN. § 77-23b-3(2)(c).

Similar to the Interception of Communications Act, Utah Code section 77-23b-8 authorizes any person aggrieved by a violation of Chapter 23b to recover relief in a civil action. The same forms of relief are available, see IV.A.2, supra, except that "in no case is a person entitled to recover less than $1,000." UTAH CODE ANN. § 77-23b-8(3). In addition, Chapter 23b allows recovery only for intentional violations. As under the "Interception of Communications Act," a civil action pursuant to this chapter may not be commenced later than two years after the claimant discovered or had a reasonable opportunity to discover the violation. UTAH CODE ANN. § 77-23b-8(5).

In Autoliv ASP, Inc. v. Dep't of Workforce Servs., 2001 UT App. 198, 29 P.3d 7, the Utah Court of Appeals found that two employees' use of their company e-mail system to send sexually explicit jokes, photographs and video clips flagrantly violated a universal standard of behavior, thus providing the employer with just cause for terminating the employees. The court reasoned that such material "exposes the employer to sexual harassment and sex discrimination lawsuits." Id. ¶ 26. The employees' termination came after an investigation by the employer turned up misuse of e-mail, prompting several company-wide warnings. Because the conduct constituted a flagrant violation of a universal standard of behavior, the Court of Appeals said that the employer did not have "an obligation to notify the claimant that his e-mail use differed significantly in content and extent from that of his co-workers . . . ." Id. ¶ 13.

3. ***Other Electronic Monitoring.*** No Utah cases or statutes discuss this issue.

B. Mail

No Utah cases or statutes discuss this issue.

C. Surveillance/Photographing

No Utah cases or statutes discuss this issue.

V. ACTIVITIES OUTSIDE THE WORKPLACE

A. Statute or Common Law

No Utah cases or statutes directly address this issue.

B. Employees' Personal Relationships

1. ***Romantic Relationships Between Employees.*** Although no Utah cases or statutes directly address this issue, the Utah Supreme Court has suggested that a cause of action may exist for an employee against an employer who meddles in his or her personal relationships. In Jackson v. Righter, 891 P.2d 1387 (Utah 1995), the court refused to hold the employer of plaintiff's wife liable for alienation of affection, where the employer had not prevented two of its employees from engaging in a romantic relationship with the plaintiff's wife. In so holding, the court relied partially on the fact that "absent some indication of harassment or intimidation, an employer who attempted merely upon the basis of its knowledge of a romantic relationship, to police the personal conduct of its employees may expose itself to liability for interfering with private relationships." Id. at 1393-94. On the other hand, in Oliverson v. West Valley City, 875 F. Supp. 1465 (D. Utah 1995), a Utah federal district court held that a married police officer's right to privacy under federal law had not been violated when he received a thirty-day suspension for engaging in sexual relations with at least one female member of the Police Explorer Post in violation of a Utah statute that prohibited adultery.

2. ***Sexual Orientation.*** Utah's Antidiscrimination Act, UTAH CODE ANN. §§ 34A-5-101 *et seq.*, is too narrow to encompass discrimination on the basis of sexual orientation. Before it was withdrawn, the Pre-Employment Inquiry Guide, promulgated pursuant to Utah's Antidiscrimination Act, stated that it would be improper to question a potential employee about his or her "sexual preferences." UTAH ADMIN. CODE r. 606-2-2(P)(2) (repealed 2011). It is doubtful that this guideline would have had any effect on an employer's ability to discriminate against an employee on the basis of sexual orientation. In Weaver v. Nebo School District, 29 F. Supp. 2d 1279 (D. Utah 1998), the Court discussed sexual orientation and employment law generally but ultimately held on a narrower issue that the employer violated the lesbian teacher's right to equal protection by prohibiting her from discussing her homosexual orientation while permitting other teachers to discuss their heterosexual orientations.

3. ***Marital Status.*** No Utah cases or statutes discuss this issue. Utah's Antidiscrimination Act, UTAH CODE ANN. §§ 34A-5-101 *et seq.*, is unusually narrow in that it does not protect employees or potential employees from discrimination on the basis of marital status. Although it is doubtful that it would have had any effect on an employer's ability to discriminate against an employee on the basis of marital status, the now-withdrawn Pre-Employment Inquiry Guide, see V.B.II, supra, formerly stated that it would be improper "to inquire into marital status unless based on legitimate bona fide occupational qualifications." UTAH ADMIN. CODE r. 606-2-2(A)(2) (repealed 2011). A "bona fide occupation qualification" in this context would have referred to "a characteristic applying to an employee: (i) that is necessary to the operation; or (ii) is the essence of the employee's employer's business." UTAH CODE ANN. § 34A-5-102(1)(b).

C. Smoking

No Utah cases or statutes directly address the relationship between an employer's actions and smoking outside the workplace. However, Utah has a comprehensive anti-smoking statute, the "Utah Indoor Clean Air Act," UTAH CODE ANN. §§ 26-38-1 *et seq.*, which requires employers to prohibit smoking in all "enclosed indoor places of public access and publicly owned buildings and offices," with very few exceptions. UTAH CODE ANN. § 26-38-3(1). Governmental employers, state institutions of higher education, and state institutions of public education may also be subject to local ordinances prohibiting smoking in "outdoor places of public access," in the event the local governing body enacts such legislation. UTAH CODE ANN. § 26-38-6(2). More detailed regulations promulgated pursuant to the Utah Indoor Clean Air Act appear in Utah Administrative Code rule 392-510.

D. Blogging

No Utah cases or statutes discuss this issue.

VI. RECORDS

A. Personnel Records

1. ***Private Employers.*** Every employer must keep "a true and accurate record of time worked and wages paid each pay period to each employee who is employed on an hourly or a daily basis . . . ." UTAH CODE ANN. § 34-28 -10(1)(a). These records must be kept on file for at least one year. UTAH CODE ANN. § 34-28-10(1)(b). Any employer who fails to comply with this requirement is guilty of a misdemeanor. UTAH CODE ANN. § 34-28-12. In addition, according to the rules established by the Utah Anti-Discrimination Division pursuant to Utah Code section 34A-5-104: "[a]ny personnel or employment record made or kept by an employer (including but not necessarily limited to application forms submitted by applicants and other records having to do with hiring, promotion, demotion, transfer, layoff or termination, rates of pay or other terms of compensation, and selection for training or apprenticeship) shall be preserved by the employer for a period of six months from the date of the making of the record and the personnel action involved, whichever occurs later." UTAH ADMIN. CODE r. 606-6-2C. If an employee has been involuntarily terminated, the personnel records of that employee must be kept for a period of six months after termination. Id. If a complaint of discrimination gets filed, the respondent employer must keep all personnel records relevant to the complaint until final disposition of the complaint. Id.

The Employment Selection Procedures Act, UTAH CODE ANN. § 34-46-101 *et seq.*, controls what information an employer may request from an applicant and how the employer can use the information it obtained through the selection process. Under the Act, employers are generally prohibited from asking for an applicant's date of birth, Social Security number or driver license number before offering the applicant a job. UTAH CODE ANN. § 34-46-201(1). An employer may not "use information about an applicant obtained through an initial selection process for a purpose other than to determine whether or not the employer will hire the applicant as an employee." Id. § 34-46-202(1)(a). Thus, an employer may not "provide information about an applicant through an initial process to a person other than the employer." Id. Employers cannot sell the information and are prohibited from using the information for marketing, profiling, or other similar purposes. Id. § 34-46-202(1)(b). In addition, employers are required to develop and "maintain a specific policy regarding the retention, disposition, access, and confidentiality of the information" obtained from an applicant. Id. § 34-46-203(1)(a). The employer must also provide an applicant the opportunity to review its retention policy if the applicant so requests. Id. § 34-46 -203(1)(b). Under the Act, if an employer does not hire the applicant within a two-year period, the employer is prohibited from retaining selection process information for more than two years after the applicant submitted the information. Id. § 34-46-203(2).

2. ***Public Employers.*** The Division of Human Resources Management (ADHRM) must maintain a computerized record of all state employees except those exempted under Utah Administrative Code rule 477-2-1. The computerized record must contain "performance ratings" and "[r]ecords of actions affecting employee salary history, classification history, title and salary range, employment status and other personal data." UTAH ADMIN. CODE r. 477-2-5(1) (b), (c). Individual state agencies must also maintain personnel records for each employee. UTAH ADMIN. CODE r. 477-2-5 (2). After a state employee's termination, the DHRM computerized records must be maintained for thirty years. UTAH ADMIN. CODE r. 477-2-5(6). Agency hard copy records must be maintained for at least two years, and then transferred to the State Record Center. Id. State counties are also required to keep certain personnel records. Specifically, county executives are required to create an office of personnel management, to be administered by a director of personnel management who has the duty of establishing and maintaining records of "all employees in the county service, setting forth as to each employee class, title, pay or status, and other relevant data." UTAH CODE ANN. § 17-33-5(2)(e).

The Government Records Access and Management Act, UTAH CODE ANN. §§ 63G-2-101 to 901, governs access to public employees' personnel files. The Act recognizes and attempts to balance two opposing constitutional rights. First, the "public's right of access to information concerning the conduct of the public's business . . . ." UTAH CODE ANN. § 63G-2-102(1)(a). Second, "the right of privacy in relation to personal data gathered by governmental entities." UTAH CODE ANN. § 63G-2-102(1)(b).

The following information in personnel records is considered public to the extent that it is not otherwise protected by a court rule, another state statute, federal statute, or federal regulation: names, gender, gross compensation, job titles, job descriptions, business addresses, business telephone numbers, number of hours worked per pay period, dates of employment, and relevant education, previous employment, and similar job qualifications of the governmental entity's former and present employees and officers. UTAH CODE ANN. § 63G-2-301(2)(b). This provision does not apply to the personnel records of undercover law enforcement personnel, or to those of investigative personnel where inappropriate. UTAH CODE ANN. § 63G-2-301(2)(b)(i), (ii).

Other personal information in public records gets divided into three categories: (1) private, (2) controlled, or (3) protected. Private information includes "medical data," UTAH CODE ANN. §63G-2-302(1)(b), and any record that would disclose an employee's, former employee's, or potential employee's "home address, home telephone number, Social

Security number, insurance coverage, marital status, or payroll deductions . . . ." Utah Code Ann § 63G-2-302(1)(f). In addition, information that is private if properly classified by a governmental entity includes: "performance evaluations and personal status information such as race, religion, or disabilities," UTAH CODE ANN. § 63G-2-302(2)(a), and "other records containing data on individuals the disclosure of which constitutes a clearly unwarranted invasion of personal privacy . . . ." UTAH CODE ANN. § 63G-2-302(2)(d). In Jones v. United States Child Support Recovery, 961 F. Supp. 1518 (D. Utah 1997), the court held that the defendant's public record defense to the plaintiff's claim of intrusion upon seclusion was without merit because state records regarding delinquent child support payments do not qualify as an open public record. Id. at 1522.

Effective July 1, 2003, "at-risk" current or former government employees may affirmatively request that the agency of a government entity holding a record or a part of a record that would disclose the employee's or the employee's family member's home address, home telephone number, social security number, insurance coverage, marital status, or payroll deductions classify those records as private. UTAH CODE ANN. § 63G-2-303(2). At-risk employees include peace officers, federal and state judges, U.S. Attorneys and assistant U.S. Attorneys, and certain prosecutors and law enforcement officials. UTAH CODE ANN. § 63G-2-303(1). The change adds little by way of privacy protection, however, since the previous law already protected such records.

Controlled information includes "medical, psychiatric, or psychological data about an individual," where releasing the information could harm the individual or violate normal professional practice and medical ethics. UTAH CODE ANN. § 63G-2-304. Protected information covers a wide variety of records, including "records, other than personnel evaluations, that contain a personal recommendation concerning an individual if disclosure would constitute a clearly unwarranted invasion of personal privacy, or disclosure is not in the public interest." UTAH CODE ANN. § 63-2-305(25). Access to private, controlled, and protected information is very limited. Details regarding access to information under each classification appear in Utah Code section 63G-2-202.

B. Medical Records

The Division of Occupational and Professional Licensing Act, UTAH CODE ANN. § 58-1-101 *et seq.*, mandates satisfaction of certain requirements to obtain and retain a license. The various sections governing licensure of medical professions include a provision discussing medical records, which provides as follows: "Medical records maintained by a licensee shall: (a) meet the standards and ethics of the profession; and (b) be maintained in accordance with division rules made in collaboration with the board." UTAH CODE ANN. § 58-67-803(1).

In State v. Ellingsworth, 966 P.2d 1220 (Utah Ct. App. 1998), the defendant argued that the obtainment of her medical records by Workers' Compensation Fund investigators constituted an unconstitutional seizure. Id. at 1222. The court held that the Workers' Compensation Fund employees did not engage in "state action" so as to implicate the Fourth Amendment, because they were investigating defendant's claim for the benefit of Workers' Compensation Fund and without the involvement of law enforcement. Id. at 1225. This was so despite the fact that local law enforcement benefited from the private investigation. Id. at 1224-25.

The Genetic Testing Privacy Act, UTAH CODE ANN. § 26-45-101 *et seq.*, and the Genetic Testing Restrictions on Employers Act, UTAH CODE ANN. § 34A-11-101 *et seq.*, protect employees from genetic testing. This legislation prohibits both public and private employers, in connection with a hiring, promotion or retention decision, from accessing or taking into consideration "private genetic information about an individual." UTAH CODE ANN. § 26-45-103(1)(a). In effect, the legislation prohibits employers from considering information resulting from a DNA test of a current or potential employee. Under certain circumstances, however, an employer may obtain a court order requiring an employee to consent to release of DNA test results or to submit to a DNA test. UTAH CODE ANN. § 26-45-103(2). Primarily, the legislation eliminates the potential for employers to use genetic testing as a means to determine which employees may have or may be susceptible to debilitating and expensive health problems, including cancer and other diseases.

C. Criminal Records

It is the duty of the Criminal Investigations and Technical Services Division, as created under Utah Code section 53-10-103(1), to maintain and provide access to criminal records. UTAH CODE ANN. § 53-10-104(2).

Generally, access to an individual's criminal record is limited to governmental agencies. However, a "qualifying entity" may gain access to criminal records to perform "employment background checks for their own employees and persons who have applied for employment with the qualifying entity . . . ." UTAH CODE ANN. § 53-10-108(1)(g). A qualifying entity in this context is "a business, organization, or a governmental entity that employs persons or utilizes volunteers who deal with: (a) national security interests; (b) care, custody, or control of children; (c) fiduciary trust over money; (d) health care to children or vulnerable adults; or (e) the provision of any of the following to a vulnerable adult: (i) care; (ii) protection; (iii) food, shelter, or clothing; (iv) assistance with the activities of daily living; or (v) assistance with financial resource management." UTAH CODE ANN. § 53-10-102(19). Before it was withdrawn, the Pre-Employment Inquiry Guide, promulgated pursuant to Utah's Antidiscrimination Act, stated that it would be proper for an employer to ask about felony convictions in a pre-employment interview. UTAH ADMIN. CODE r. 606-2-2(V) (repealed 2011). However, it would be considered improper to ask about arrest records. UTAH ADMIN. CODE r. 606-2-2(U) (repealed 2011).

The Utah Court of Appeals held that a convicted felon was not precluded from working as a plumber and maintenance worker at a licensed, private youth services facility despite a state statute that prohibited convicted felons from providing "child placing services, foster care, youth programs, substitute care, or institutionalized care." Sorenson's Ranch School v. Oram, 2001 UT App. 354, ¶ 7, 36 P.3d 528 (interpreting former version of Utah Code section 62A-2-120). The Utah Department of Public Safety had conducted a criminal background check on the maintenance worker and detected the convictions after the employee's name and other identifying information were submitted to the Department as required by law for licensed child and youth care facilities. Id.

D. Subpoenas / Search Warrants

No Utah employer may "deprive an employee of employment or threaten or otherwise coerce the employee regarding employment because the employee attends a deposition or hearing in response to a subpoena." UTAH CODE ANN. § 78B-1-132(1). Should the employer violate this mandate, the employer is guilty of criminal contempt and the employee may bring an action in court to recover lost wages, or to be reinstated, in addition to any other remedies available at law. UTAH CODE ANN. § 78B-1-132(2), (3). No Utah cases or statutes specifically discuss subpoenas that are served upon private employers for the purpose of obtaining information about employees. Notwithstanding, Utah Rule of Civil Procedure 45 governs subpoenas in general, and Utah Code section 63G-2-207 governs subpoenas for access to government records. Utah law provides special protection to "at-risk government employees," particularly, employees that have been involved in government legal occupations such as judges and prosecutors. UTAH CODE ANN. § 63G-2-303(1). "If the government agency holding the private record receives a subpoena for the records," the government agency must then attempt to notify the "at-risk government employee or former employee by mailing a copy of the subpoena to the employee's last-known mailing address." UTAH CODE ANN. § 63G-2-303(5). The at-risk employee may then authorize the release of the records being subpoenaed or "deliver to the government agency holding the private record a copy of a motion to quash filed with the court who issued the subpoena." UTAH CODE ANN. § 63G-2-303(5).

No Utah cases or statutes discuss the specific issue of search warrants served on employers for the purpose of searching employee files or workspace, nor does Utah law address an employer's attempt to resist such search warrants. Nonetheless, Utah law would likely allow an employer to consent to the search of an employee's files or workspace. State v. Duran, 2005 UT App 409, 131 P.3d 246, states that even a warrantless search "is reasonable if it is conducted with the consent of the defendant or some other person who 'possesse[s] common authority over or other sufficient relationship to the premises or effects sought to be inspected.'" Id. ¶ 11 (citing United States v. Matlock, 415 U.S. 164, 171 (1974)). Typically, common authority over the premises is found when "mutual use of the property by persons generally having joint access or control for most purposes," is present. Id. Accordingly, employers could likely consent to a search because most employers have joint access to, and generally control, employee workspace.

VII. ACTIONS SUBSEQUENT TO EMPLOYMENT

A. References

There is no direct regulation of references in Utah except for Utah Code section 34-42-1, which confers good faith immunity from liability for defamation on employers who write letters of reference in good faith. Id. § 34-42-1(1). Under this statute, there is a "presumption that an employer is acting in good faith when the employer provides information about the job performance, professional conduct, or evaluation of a former or current employee to a prospective employer of that employee, at the request of the prospective employer of that employee." Id. § 34-42-1(2). This presumption is "rebuttable only upon showing by clear and convincing evidence that the employer disclosed the information with actual malice or with intent to mislead." Id. § 34-42-1(3). An employer acts with "actual malice" in this context when the employer either knows about the falsity of the information or recklessly disregards the possibility that the information was false. Id. § 34-42-1(4).

Also, given the confidentiality restrictions on the disclosure of alcohol and drug test-related information under Utah Code section 34-38-13, see II.B.2, supra, employers should be cautious about providing such information in their references.

B. Non-Compete Agreements

Under Utah law, non-compete agreements "are enforceable if carefully drawn to protect only the legitimate interests of the employer." Robbins v. Finlay, 645 P.2d 623, 627 (Utah 1982). Specifically, such agreements are valid when (1) supported by consideration, (2) negotiated in good faith, (3) necessary to protect the employer's good will, and (4) reasonable in their restrictions as to geographic area and duration. System Concepts, Inc. v. Dixon, 669 P.2d 421, 425-26 (Utah 1983); see also Allen v. Rose Park Pharmacy, 120 Utah 608, 617-18, 237 P.2d 823, 828 (Utah 1951). In addition, to enforce such agreements employers must show that the employee's "services were special, unique, or extraordinary." Robbins, 645 P.2d at 628; see also Kasco Servs. Corp. v. Benson, 831 P.2d 86, 88 (Utah 1992).

In considering the reasonableness of the geographic restriction of a non-compete agreement, of primary importance "are the location and nature of the employer's clientele." System Concepts, Inc., 669 P.2d at 427. Accordingly, unlimited territorial restrictions are generally unreasonable when the potential scope of the employer's clientele is only local in nature. Id. Moreover, though Utah courts have not provided any guidance for discerning the reasonableness of the duration of a non-compete agreement, they have upheld such agreements with durations spanning anywhere from one year, Robbins, 645 P.2d at 624, to twenty-five years. Valley Mortuary v. Fairbanks, 119 Utah 204, 206-07, 225 P.2d 739, 741 (Utah 1950). Generally, however, the "reasonableness" of the restraints in non-compete agreements "is determined on a case-by-case basis, taking into account the particular facts and circumstances surrounding the case and the subject covenant." System Concepts, Inc., 669 P.2d at 427.

The Utah Supreme Court has held that lost profits is the appropriate measure of damages for breach of a contractual non-compete, non-disclosure, or non-solicitation provisions. TruGreen Co. v. Mower Bros., Inc., 2008 UT 81, ¶ 9, 199 P.3d 929. The Court reasoned the purpose of these damages is to compensate the nonbreaching party for any actual injury sustained and restore the party to the position it was in prior to the injury. Id. ¶ 10. However, an analysis of the profits of the breaching employee's new employer may be appropriate when damages are difficult to determine. Id. ¶¶ 13, 18.

VIII. OTHER ISSUES

A. Statutes of Limitations

The general limitations period applicable to most tort claims is four years. UTAH CODE ANN. § 78B-2-307. The same four-year limitation period applies to claims of negligent employment, Retherford v. AT&T Communications, 844 P.2d 949, 977 (Utah 1992), intentional infliction of emotional distress, Id. at 975, and presumably, interference with prospective economic advantage. In a situation where the claimant suffers an emotional injury as a result of ongoing or continuous tortious conduct, the Utah Supreme Court has held that "the statute of limitations begins to run at the time the last injury occurred or the tortious conduct ceases." Cabaness v. Thomas, 2010 UT 23, ¶ 26, 232 P.3d 486. Although the court in Retherford did not authoritatively address the issue, it did suggest that when an action for negligent employment is based on a situation where the claimant does not accrue a cause of action until the claimant experiences some subjective harm, "it may be contended that the employer's breach of duty has become evident long before that point . . . ." 844 P.2d at 977. Therefore, "one might argue that the statute of limitations against the employer for negligent employment should begin to run before the statute begins to run on the tort by the employee." Id.

The statute of limitation periods for misappropriation, false light, publication of private facts, and intrusion are discussed in I.B, supra under their respective headings. In the case of claims arising under the Interception of Communications Act, see IV.A.1, supra, or Utah Code section 77-23b-8, see IV.A.2, supra, a civil action cannot be commenced later than two years after the date the claimant first discovered or had a reasonable opportunity to discover the violation. UTAH CODE ANN. §§ 77-23a-11(5) and 77-23b-8(5). Unless otherwise specified by statute, the limitations period for any other claims created by statute is three years pursuant to Utah Code section 78B-2-305(4).

B. Jurisdiction

The district court is a trial court of general jurisdiction in Utah and has original jurisdiction of all matters, civil and criminal, not excepted by the Utah Constitution or by statute. See Utah Const., art. VIII, § 5; UTAH CODE ANN. § 78A-5-101, -102. The Utah Supreme Court is the highest appellate court in the state and has original appellate jurisdiction over cases as provided by statute, which generally includes civil employment privacy cases. UTAH CODE ANN. § 78A-3-102. The Supreme Court may, and sometimes does, however, transfer such cases to the Utah Court of Appeals for decision. Id.

In order to obtain jurisdiction over employment privacy claims, courts must have proper subject matter and personal jurisdiction. Because of Utah's broad constitutional and statutory grant of jurisdiction to the district court, subject matter jurisdiction of such claims generally will be proper in the district court. Employers based outside of Utah, however, may have grounds to contest personal jurisdiction. Whether a court has specific personal jurisdiction over a defendant hinges on a two-part test: "'First, do [the plaintiff's] claims arise from one of the activities listed in the [long-arm] statute,' and second, whether the 'defendant's contacts with this forum [are] sufficient to satisfy the due process clause of the fourteenth amendment.'" Pohl, Inc. v. Webelhuth, 2008 UT 89, ¶ 10, 201 P.3d 944 (quoting Anderson v. Am. Soc'y of Plastic & Reconstructive Surgeons, 807 P.2d 825, 226 (Utah 1990)).

C. Workers' Compensation Exclusivity

The Utah Workers' Compensation Act ("Act") compensates workers for mental and physical injuries that are sustained on the job. Shattuck-Owen v. Snowbird Corp., 2000 UT 94, ¶ 19, 16 P.3d 555. The exclusive remedy provision of the Act "bars common-law tort actions requiring proof of physical or mental injury." Id.; see also UTAH CODE ANN. § 34A-2 -105(1) ("The right to recover compensation pursuant to this chapter for injuries sustained by an employee, whether resulting in death or not, is the exclusive remedy against the employer and . . . the liabilities of the employer imposed by this chapter is in place of any and all other civil liability whatsoever[.]").

Although the Act's exclusive remedy provision does not bar intentional injuries, Helf v. Chevron U.S.A., Inc., 2009 UT 11, ¶ 43, 203 P.3d 962, or reputational damages, such as those arising from defamation claims, Mounteer v. Utah Power & Light Co., 823 P.2d 1055, 1056-57 (Utah 1991) (employee slander claim not barred), Utah courts have held that the Act bars invasion of privacy claims, Davis v. Utah Power & Light Co., Civil No. 87-C-0659G, 1990 WL 146097, at *2-4, 10-12 (D. Utah Feb. 2, 1990) (invasion of privacy claims barred); cf. Shattuck-Owen, 2000 UT 94, ¶¶ 10, 13, 16 P.3d 555 (affirming on other grounds district court's dismissal of invasion of privacy claim based on exclusive remedy provision of the Utah Workers' Compensation Act), intentional and negligent infliction of emotional distress claims, Mounteer, 823 P.2d at 1058-59 (intentional and negligent infliction claims barred); Hirase-Doi v. U.S. West Comms., Inc., 61 F.3d 777, 786-87 (10th Cir. 1995) (intentional infliction claim barred); Sauers v. Salt Lake County, 735 F. Supp. 381, 385 (D. Utah 1990) (intentional infliction claim barred), and employer negligence claims, Niles v. Jones, Case No. 2:03-CV-18, 2004 WL 724451, *5 (D. Utah Feb. 24, 2004) ("It is well-established that the Utah Workers' Compensation Act is the exclusive remedy for an employee's claims of negligence, including negligent supervision."); Retherford v. AT&T Comms., 844 P.2d 949, 965 n.8 (Utah 1992) (noting without deciding that workers' compensation would likely be an exclusive remedy for negligent employment claims).

The Utah Supreme Court recently examined when the exclusive remedy provision of Utah's Workers' Compensation Act precludes one employee from suing another in tort. See Stamper v. Johnson, 2010 UT 26, 232 P.3d 514. In Stamper, the Court clarified the language of the Act, stating workers' compensation was the exclusive remedy for employees injured by their employer, "officer, agent, or employee of the employer." Id. ¶ 12 (quoting UTAH CODE ANN. § 34A-2-105(1)). Thus, holding an employee may have a cognizable claim against any third party who cause the injury if that person is not "an employer, officer, agent, or employee of the employer." Id. (quoting UTAH CODE ANN. § 34A-2-106(1)).

D. Pleading Requirements

Utah has adopted liberal notice pleading requirements "to the end that the parties are afforded the privilege of presenting whatever legitimate contentions they have pertaining to their dispute." Cheney v. Rucker, 14 Utah 2d 205, 211, 381 P.2d 86, 91 (Utah 1963). Typically, the complaint need only "give the opposing party fair notice of the nature and basis or grounds of the claim and a general indication of the type of litigation involved." Blackham v. Snelgrove, 3 Utah 2d 157, 160, 280 P.2d 453, 455 (Utah 1955). No cases or statutes discuss specific pleading requirements with respect to claims discussed within this *Survey*.

SURVEY OF VERMONT EMPLOYMENT LIBEL LAW

Robert B. Hemley, Esq., and Matthew B. Byrne, Esq.
Gravel and Shea
76 St. Paul Street
P.O. Box 369
Burlington, VT 05402-0369
Telephone: (802) 658-0220; Facsimile: (802) 658-1456
E-mail: rhemley@gravelshea.com or mbyrne@gravelshea.com

(With Developments Reported Through **November 1, 2012**)

GENERAL COMMENTS

Civil cases in Vermont state court are generally brought in Superior Court. Appeals are taken directly to the Vermont Supreme Court and are heard as a matter of right; there are no intermediary appellate courts. Opinions of the Vermont Supreme Court are published in an official reporter, the Vermont Reporter, and are available online at www.vermontjudiciary.org. Opinions of the Superior Court are now available in a publication called Vermont Lawyer and Trial Court Reporter.

SIGNIFICANT DEVELOPMENTS SINCE THE 2012 *SURVEY*

None.

I. GENERAL LAW

A. General Employment Law

1. ***At Will Employment.*** The Vermont Supreme Court has implied that it will construe the at will employment doctrine narrowly. Dillon v. Champion Jogbra, Inc., 175 Vt. 1, 5, 819 A.2d 703, 706 (2002) ("we are mindful at the outset that at-will employment relationships have fallen into disfavor"). Nevertheless, employment for an indefinite period is still presumed to be employment at will, "terminable at any time, for any reason, or none at all." Sherman v. Rutland Hosp., Inc., 146 Vt. 204, 207, 500 A.2d 230, 232 (1985); see also Ross v. Times Mirror, Inc., 164 Vt. 13, 18, 665 A.2d 580, 583 (1995); Trombley v. Southwestern Vermont Med. Ctr., 169 Vt. 386, 392, 738 A.2d 103, 108 (1999); Dulude v. Fletcher Allen Health Care, Inc., 174 Vt. 74, 80, 807 A.2d 390, 395 (2002); Dillon, 175 Vt. at 5, 819 A.2d at 706-07 ("we have noted repeatedly that the presumption that employment for an indefinite term is an "at-will" agreement is simply a general rule of contract construction"). The at will nature of the employment relationship may, however, be modified by an employee handbook or company practice that is inconsistent with the at will status. Trombley, 169 Vt. at 392, 738 A.2d at 108; Farnum v. Brattleboro Retreat, Inc., 164 Vt. 488, 494-95, 671 A.2d 1249, 1254 (1995); Taylor v. National Life Ins. Co., 161 Vt. 457, 464, 652 A.2d 466, 470-71 (1993); see also Havill v. Woodstock Soapstone Co., Inc., 2004 VT 73 ¶¶ 11-13, 865 A.2d 335, 341 (2004) (finding that progressive discipline and just cause policy in employer's personnel manual modified at will relationship). In addition, former employees may use promissory estoppel affirmatively as an independent cause of action if the actions or communications of the employer reflect assurances of continued employment. Foote v. Simmonds Precision Prods. Co., 158 Vt. 566, 570-71, 613 A.2d 1277, 1280 (1992); Raymond v. Int'l Bus. Machines Corp., 954 F. Supp. 744, 748 (D. Vt. 1997), aff'd 148 F.3d 63 (2d Cir. 1998). Former at will employees may also maintain an independent claim in tort for wrongful discharge if the termination violates a "clear and compelling public policy." Murray v. St. Michaels College, 164 Vt. 205, 208-09, 667 A.2d 294, 298 (1995); see also LoPresti v. Rutland Reg'l Health Servs., Inc., 2004 VT 105, ¶ 23, 865 A.2d 1102, 1112 (2004). Vermont courts define public policy as "the community common sense and common conscience, extended and applied throughout the state to matters of public morals, public health, public safety, public welfare, and the like." Payne v. Rozendaal, 147 Vt. 488, 492, 520 A.2d 586, 588 (1986). Prior to the enactment of Vermont's Fair Employment Practices Act, the Vermont Supreme Court found a violation of public policy where an employer who was not covered by the Federal Age Discrimination in Employment Act terminated an employee's employment on the basis of age. Payne, 147 Vt. at 494, 520 A.2d at 589. Vermont does not recognize an implied covenant of good faith and fair dealing as to tenure in an unmodified at will employment relationship. Dicks v. Jensen, 172 Vt. 43, 52, 768 A.2d 1279, 1286 (2001); Madden, 165 Vt. at 313, 683 A.2d at 391; Ross, 164 Vt. at 23, 665 A.2d at 586. However, the Vermont Supreme Court has recently indicated the covenant may apply "in the employment termination context when a plaintiff's claim for damages is based on 'accrued benefits' and not solely on implied tenure, i.e., permanent employment until just cause for termination arises." LoPresti, 2004 VT 105 at ¶ 42, 865 A.2d at 1117 (noting that, for example, even "when the employment arrangement gives the employer absolute discretion to terminate the contract without cause, courts have held employers liable for breaching the covenant where the termination was based on the employer's desire to avoid paying the employee benefits earned under the contract").

B. Elements of Libel Claim

1. ***Basic Elements.*** The elements of defamation are (1) a false and defamatory statement concerning another, (2) some negligence, or greater fault, in publishing the statement, (3) publication to at least one third person, (4) lack of privilege in the publication, (5) special damages, unless actionable per se, and (6) some actual harm so as to warrant compensatory damages. Crump v. P&C Food Mkts., Inc., 154 Vt. 284, 291, 576 A.2d 441, 446 (1990); Lent v. Huntoon, 143 Vt. 539, 546-47, 470 A.2d 1162, 1168, 9 Media L. Rep. 2547 (1983); see Raymond v. Int'l Bus. Machines Corp., 954 F. Supp. 744, 754-55 (D. Vt. 1997). Any written defamation is actionable per se, with or without extrinsic evidence, and the plaintiff is not required to allege or prove special damages. Lent, 143 Vt. at 548, 470 A.2d at 1169. Oral defamation, on the other hand, must be established with allegations and proof of special damages to be actionable, unless the slander involves the traditional exceptions categorized as slander per se – imputation of a crime, statements injurious to ones business or trade, charges of having a loathsome disease, or impugning the chastity of a woman. Lent, 143 Vt. at 546, 470 A.2d at 1168; see Wood v. Wood, 166 Vt. 608, 609, 693 A.2d 673, 674 (1997). However, even if the defamation is actionable per se, the plaintiff must prove some actual harm, even if only nominal. Lent, 147 Vt. at 546-49, 470 A.2d at 1168-69; Ryan v. Herald Ass'n, Inc., 152 Vt. 275, 282, 285-86, 566 A.2d 1316, 1320, 1322, 16 Media L. Rep. 2472 (1989); Solomon v. Atlantis Dev., Inc., 147 Vt. 349, 359, 516 A.2d 132, 138 (1986).

2. ***Fault.*** A plaintiff must allege and prove "some negligence, or greater fault." Crump, 154 Vt. at 291, 576 A.2d at 446. If the plaintiff is a public figure, the action may be sustained only upon a showing of actual malice. Palmer v. Bennington Sch. Dist., 159 Vt. 31, 39, 615 A.2d 498, 503, 20 Media L. Rep. 1640 (1992). Currently, the Vermont Supreme Court does not appear to distinguish matters of public concern from matters of private concern in determining the appropriate standard of fault. Rather, the Court focuses on the public versus private status of the plaintiff. See Colombo v. Times-Argus Ass'n, 135 Vt. 454, 455, 380 A.2d 80, 82, 3 Media L. Rep. 1451 (1977) ("whatever the prior status . . . of a publication relating to an individual's involvement in 'a matter of public interest,' it must now be considered that it is the status of the individual, rather than the nature of the matter in which he is involved, that triggers the requirement for showing actual malice") (overruling Michlin v. Roberts, 132 Vt. 154 (1974)). It is uncertain whether a standard of fault other than negligence would be required in purely private defamation cases. While the Court has observed that the fault requirement of Gertz v. Robert Welch, Inc., 418 U.S. 323 (1974), may be limited to defamatory material of a public concern, see Ryan v. Herald Ass'n, Inc., 152 Vt. 275, 280 n.2, 566 A.2d 1316, 1319, 16 Media L. Rep. 2472 (1989), the Court has required "some negligence" in cases involving private plaintiffs and private employment-related matters. Lent v. Huntoon, 143 Vt. 539, 546, 470 A.2d 1162, 1168, 9 Media L. Rep. 2547 (1983); Crump v. P&C Food Markets, Inc., 154 Vt. 284, 291, 576 A.2d 441, 446 (1990) ("some negligence" is an element of defamation claim involving a private plaintiff and private employment matter).

a. **Private Figure Plaintiff/Matter of Public Concern.** Negligence is the standard of fault in cases brought by private plaintiffs concerning matters of public concern. Ryan, 152 Vt. at 280-81, 566 A.2d at 1319.

b. **Private Figure Plaintiff/Matter of Private Concern.** While the Vermont Supreme Court has acknowledged that Gertz may not require a showing of fault in such cases, it has twice held that "negligence, or some greater fault" is required in private employment defamation cases involving private plaintiffs. Crump, 154 Vt. at 291, 576 A.2d at 446; Lent, 143 Vt. at 546, 470 A.2d at 1168. Federal courts have similarly required a showing of negligence. See, e.g., Marcoux-Norton v. Kmart, 907 F. Supp. 766, 778-79 (D. Vt. 1993).

c. **Public Figure Plaintiff/Matter of Public Concern.** The federal constitutional "actual malice" standard applies to cases involving public figures and matters of public concern. Palmer, 159 Vt. at 39, 615 A.2d at 503 (1992); Furno v. Pignona, 147 Vt. 538, 544, 522 A.2d 746, 750 (1986); Colombo, 135 Vt. at 455, 380 A.2d at 82 (1977). To prove actual malice a plaintiff must show "that the defendant made a statement with knowledge of its falsity or with reckless disregard as to the statements truth or falsity." Palmer, 159 Vt. at 39, 615 A.2d at 503 (citing New York Times v. Sullivan, 376 U.S. 254, 285-86 (1964)).

3. ***Falsity.*** A plaintiff appears to bear the burden of proving falsity in all cases, even private cases concerning private matters. The Vermont Supreme Court has consistently listed a "false . . . statement concerning another" as an essential element to a defamation claim, including employment defamation claims involving private matters. Lent, 143 Vt. at 546, 470 A.2d at 1168; Crump, 154 Vt. at 291, 576 A.2d at 446; see also Marcoux-Norton, 907 F. Supp. at 778.

Truth is a complete defense to a defamation claim. Lent, 143 Vt. at 548. "Substantial truth," as opposed to literal truth, is adequate to support a complete defense. The Vermont Supreme Court has recently held that allegedly defamatory statements "should be judged using the common-sense 'substantial truth' standard," under which "it is not necessary to prove the literal truth of the accusation in every detail, [rather] it is sufficient to show that the imputation is substantially true"; in other words, that "the gist, the sting, of the matter is true." Russin v. Wesson, 2008 VT 22, ¶¶ 7-8, 949 A.2d 1019, 1021 (2008). "The inquiry is whether the alleged defamatory statement produces a different effect upon the reader than that which would be produced by the literal truth of the matter." Id. ¶ 8, 949 A.2d at 1021. See also Turgeon v.

Operating Engineers, Local No. 98, 2 Fed. Appx. 176, 180, 2001 WL 99578 at 3 (2d Cir. 2001) (concluding that, under Vermont law, statements that are either substantially true or "obvious exaggerations" cannot be defamatory); Russin, ¶ 12, 949 A.2d at 1022 (reversing finding of slander where defendant's statements that plaintiff was a thief and had stolen his property were substantially true, although plaintiff had been found liable only for conversion); Weisburgh v. Mahady, 147 Vt. 70, 73, 511 A.2d 304, 306, 12 Media L. Rep. 2293 (1986) (substantially accurate news story of criminal charge not actionable, so long as report does not assert guilt).

4. ***Defamatory Statement of Fact.*** A statement is defamatory when it "tends to so harm the reputation of another as to lower him in the estimation of the community or to deter third persons from associating or dealing with him." Weisburgh v. Mahady, 147 Vt. 70, 73 , 511 A.2d 304, 306, 12 Media L. Rep. 2293 (1986). The "community" may be a minority of the total community, but must be a substantial respectable group. Fin v. Middlebury College, 136 Vt. 543, 544, 394 A.2d 1152, 1153 (1978); see Marcoux-Norton v. Kmart Corp., 907 F. Supp. 766, 778 (D. Vt. 1993). While the court determines whether a statement is defamatory as a matter of law, an ambiguous statement must be submitted to the jury for determination. Lent, 143 Vt. at 547, 470 A.2d at 1168; see also Marcoux-Norton, 907 F. Supp. at 779. In order to prove defamation, the plaintiff's "evidence must show more than vague allegations of unspecified incompetence and more than the employment decision itself." Herrera v. Union No. 39 Sch. Dist., 2009 VT 35, ¶ 19, 975 A.2d 619, 626 (2009).

5. ***Of and Concerning Plaintiff.*** No cases on point.

6. ***Publication.*** A plaintiff must allege and prove publication of an allegedly defamatory statement to a third party as an element of the claim. Lent v. Huntoon, 143 Vt. 539, 546-47, 470 A.2d 1162, 1168, 9 Media L. Rep. (1983); Crump v. P&C Food Markets, Inc., 154 Vt. 284, 291, 576 A.2d 441, 446 (1990). Ordinarily, if the plaintiff is responsible for the publication, the element of publication is not satisfied. Raymond v. Int'l Bus. Machines Corp., 954 F. Supp. 744, 755 (D. Vt. 1997); but see I.B.6(b), infra. (addressing compelled self-publication).

a. **Intracorporate Communication.** An employer enjoys a conditional privilege to engage in limited intracorporate communications to protect its legitimate business interests. Crump, 154 Vt. at 292, 576 A.2d at 446; Lent, 143 Vt. at 548-49, 470 A.2d at 1169. This privilege is lost, however, if a defamation plaintiff shows either malice or abuse of the privilege. Id. One of two types of malice are sufficient to overcome this conditional privilege: (1) "knowledge of the statements falsity or with reckless disregard for its truth," (traditionally referred to as "actual malice") or (2) "conduct manifesting personal ill will, reckless or wanton disregard of plaintiffs rights, or carried out under circumstances evidencing insult or oppression" (traditionally referred to as "simple malice" or "common law malice"). Crump, 154 Vt. at 293, 576 A.2d at 447. Moreover, the plaintiff must prove malice by clear and convincing evidence. Id.

b. **Compelled Self-Publication.** The Vermont Supreme Court has not yet addressed whether it will recognize defamation claims arising from compelled self-publication. A federal decision concluded that Vermont would recognize the doctrine of compelled self-publication when an employer knows, or should know, that the former employee has no means of avoiding publication or is under a strong compulsion to publish the statement. Raymond v. Int'l Bus. Machines Corp., 954 F. Supp. 744, 755-56 (D. Vt. 1997), affd,148 F.3d 63 (2d Cir. 1998) (affirming on other grounds); but see Moss v. Mutual of Omaha Ins. Co., No. Civ. A 89-138, 1990 WL 485666 at *5 (D. Vt. Apr. 9, 1990) (Billings, J.) (concluding that Vermont would not recognize the doctrine of compelled self-publication); see also David J. Blyth, Workplace Defamation: Public Policy, Compelled Self-Publication, and the Vermont Constitution, 16 Vt. L. Rev. 341 (1991).

A recent federal decision noted the continuing uncertainty under Vermont law about the applicability of the doctrine of compelled self-publication. Knelman v. Middlebury College, No. 5:11-cv-213, 2012 WL 4481470 (D. Vt. Sept. 28, 2012).

c. **Republication.** A defendant who republishes the defamatory statement of another is liable as if he had originally published it. Lancour v. Herald & Globe Ass'n, 111 Vt. 371, 381, 17 A.2d 253, 257 (1941); see Stone v. Banner Publ'g Corp., 677 F. Supp. 242, 245 (D. Vt. 1988).

7. ***Statements versus Conduct.*** No cases on point.

8. ***Damages.*** To recover damages, a plaintiff must plead and prove some actual harm, which may include impairment of reputation in the community, personal humiliation, or mental anguish and suffering. Crump, 154 Vt. at 295, 576 A.2d at 448; Lent, 143 Vt. at 549, 470 A.2d at 1169; see Marcoux-Norton v. Kmart, 907 F. Supp. 766, 781 (D. Vt. 1993). Actual harm may be "slight," and nominal damages of $1.00 are sufficient to support liability. Ryan v. Herald Ass'n, Inc., 152 Vt. 275, 285-86, 566 A.2d 1316, 1322, 16 Media L. Rep. 2472 (1989). If the plaintiff shows constitutional malice, then actual damages may be presumed. Id. at 281, 566 A.2d at 1319.

a. **<u>Presumed Damages and Libel Per Se</u>.** Damages are presumed only if the plaintiff proves constitutional malice, even in private figure cases involving private concerns. Ryan, 152 Vt. at 281, 566 A.2d at 1390; Lent v. Huntoon, 143 Vt. 539, 549, 470 A.2d 1162, 1169-70, 9 Media L. Rep. 2547 (1983). While Vermont continues to recognize libel per se, in which case the plaintiff need not plead or prove special damages, see I.B.1., supra, a defamation plaintiff must nevertheless prove actual harm supporting compensatory damages, unless constitutional malice is shown. Ryan, 152 Vt. at 283, 566 A.2d at 1321.

(1) **Employment-Related Criticism.** Statements that criticize an employee's conduct may constitute defamation per se. See, e.g., Crump, 154 Vt. 284, 576 A.2d 441 (statements that employee stole property during work hours); Lent, 143 Vt. 539, 470 A.2d 1162 (statements that plaintiff had been discharged suggesting improper conduct, and statements that he had a "record a mile long"). However, general rumors surrounding the reasons for an employee's termination "are insufficient to establish a claim of defamation." Dulude v. Fletcher Allen Health Care, Inc., 174 Vt. 74, 86, 807 A.2d 390, 400 (2002).

(2) **Single Instance Rule.** Although the Vermont Supreme Court has not directly addressed the issue, Vermont does not appear to limit libel per se by the single instance rule (under which a statement concerning a single instance of professional malfeasance does not support libel per se and damages are thus not presumed). See, e.g., Crump, 154 Vt. 284, 576 A.2d 441 (libel per se action based upon single instance of alleged misconduct). Since Vermont does not permit presumed damages without a showing of constitutional malice in any event, the single instance rule would appear unnecessary.

b. **<u>Punitive Damages</u>.** Punitive damages are available only upon a showing of both constitutional malice and common-law malice. Ryan, 152 Vt. at 281, 566 A.2d at 1319; Lent, 143 Vt. at 550, 470 A.2d at 1170. While the Vermont Supreme Court has acknowledged that Dun & Bradstreet v. Greenmoss Builders, 472 U.S. 749 (1985) limited Gertz to cases involving matters of public concern, Ryan, 152 Vt. at 280 n.2, 566 A.2d at 1319 n.2, the Court has not yet held that punitive damages are available in private concern cases absent a showing of constitutional malice. Even if constitutional malice were not required in nonmedia cases not involving matters of public concern, Vermont law requires at least a showing of common law malice to support punitive damages. See Rubin v. Sterling Enters., Inc., 164 Vt. 582, 586-87, 674 A.2d 782, 78 (1996); Lent, 143 Vt. at 550, 470 A.2d at 1170; Crump, 154 Vt. at 297-98, 576 A.2d at 449.

II. PRIVILEGES AND DEFENSES

A. Scope of Privileges

1. ***Absolute Privilege.*** There is an absolute privilege for statements made by witnesses, judges, attorneys, and jurors during judicial proceedings. Politi v. Tyler, 170 Vt. 428, 431, 751 A.2d 788, 791 (2000); LaPlanca v. Laney, 134 Vt. 56, 58, 349 A.2d 235, 236 (1975); see Wilkinson v. Russell, 973 F. Supp. 437, 440 (D. Vt. 1997) (statements by child welfare official in response to a request made pursuant to a judicial order are absolutely privileged), aff'd, 182 F.3d 89 (2d Cir. 1999) (affirming result under qualified immunity standard after the Court concluded that the official was not acting pursuant to a court order). In addition, "[d]efamatory statements published by parties in the course of judicial proceedings . . . are absolutely privileged, so long as they bear some relation to the proceedings." Okemo Mountain, Inc. v. Sikorski, No. 1:93-CV-22, 2006 WL 335858, at *3 (D. Vt. Feb. 14, 2006). The privilege provides an absolute bar against any action arising from statements made within the judicial proceeding. LaPlanca, 134 Vt. at 48, 349 A.2d at 236. However, where statements made during judicial proceedings are "entirely foreign and irrelevant" to the judicial proceeding, the privilege will not apply. Letourneau v. Hickey, 174 Vt. 481, 484, 807 A.2d 437, 441 (2002) (to sustain an action for slander based on statements arising out of a judicial proceeding, a plaintiff "must show that the words spoken were not pertinent to the matter then in progress, and that they were spoken maliciously and with a view to defame"); Clemmons v. Danforth, 67 Vt. 617, 623, 32 A. 626, 628 (1895).

The Vermont Supreme Court recently extended absolute immunity to the county level state's attorneys. O'Connor v. Donovan, 2012 VT 27, ¶ 21. The Court also broadened the circumstances to which the immunity applied, although it is not clear what the limit of the immunity is.

By statute, statements made by an employer or an employee to the Commissioner of the Department of Employment and Training concerning an application for unemployment benefits "shall be absolutely privileged" and may not be the basis of a defamation suit "unless they are false in fact and malicious in intent." 21 V.S.A. § 1314(g); see Marcoux-Norton v. Kmart, 907 F. Supp. 766, 780 n.12 (D. Vt. 1993). While this privilege is labeled as "absolute," it is expressly qualified by the limitations of falsity and malice.

2. ***Qualified Privileges.*** A defamation defendant can defeat a claim if a conditional privilege applies. However, a plaintiff may overcome a conditional privilege by showing malice. See II.A.2(d), infra.

a. **Common Interest.** Vermont has not directly recognized a common interest privilege. Vermont does recognize a conditional privilege for intracorporate communications to protect legitimate business interests under which statements made among corporate supervisory employees with a legitimate common interest in a matter are conditionally privileged. See Crump v. P& C Food Mkts., Inc., 154 Vt. 284, 292, 576 A.2d 441, 446-47 (1990) (reports and statements accusing plaintiff of "theft" and being a "problem employee"); see also Moss v. Mutual of Omaha, Civ.A. 89-138, 1990 WL 485666 (D. Vt. Apr. 9, 1990) (internal discussions concerning plaintiffs discharge for sexual harassment).

b. **Duty.** Vermont recognizes a conditional privilege for statements made to protect the legitimate interests of third parties. Nott v. Stoddard, 38 Vt. 25, 32 (1865); Marcoux-Norton, 907 F. Supp. at 780. Under this privilege employers may, without malice, make statements concerning an employee to a party outside the corporation (such as other potential employers, or a financial institution from whom the employee has sought financing) upon the third party's request. Id.

c. **Criticism of Public Employee.** No cases specifically recognize a conditional privilege to criticize public employees. Cf. Lomberg v. Crowlet, 138 Vt. 420, 415 A.2d 1324 (1980) (public employees defamation claim against his supervisor remanded for findings related to supervisors potential immunity, including whether his criticism of plaintiff was "fair comment" made in an official capacity). However, because the plaintiff will in most cases be a public figure, the plaintiff will have to show actual malice. Palmer v. Bennington Sch. Dist., 159 Vt. 31, 615 A.2d 498, 20 Media L. Rep. 1640 (1992) (school principal); Colombo v. Times Argus Ass'n, 135 Vt. 454, 380 A.2d 80, 3 Media L. Rep. 1451 (1977) (police officer); see I.B.2, supra.

d. **Limitation on Qualified Privileges.** A conditional privilege may be defeated if the plaintiff shows malice by clear and convincing evidence, Lent v. Huntoon, 143 Vt. 539, 548-49, 470 A.2d 1162, 1169, 9 Media L. Rep. 2547 (1983), or abuse of privilege, Crump, 154 Vt. at 292, 576 A.2d at 446 (citing Restatement (Second) of Torts §§ 599-605A). One of two types of malice are sufficient to overcome this conditional privilege: (1) "knowledge of the statements falsity or with reckless disregard for its truth," (traditionally referred to as "actual malice") or (2) "conduct manifesting personal ill will, reckless or wanton disregard of plaintiffs rights, or carried out under circumstances evidencing insult or oppression" (traditionally referred to as "simple malice" or "common law malice"). Crump, 154 Vt. at 293, 576 A.2d at 447. Moreover, the plaintiff must prove malice by clear and convincing evidence. Id.

(1) **Constitutional or Actual Malice.** Constitutional malice is "knowledge of the statements falsity or with reckless disregard for its truth." Crump, 154 Vt. at 293, 576 A.2d at 447 (quoting Lent 143 Vt. at 549, 470 A.2d at 1169). To prove "reckless disregard," a plaintiff must produce "'sufficient evidence to permit the conclusion that the defendant in fact entertained serious doubts as to the truth of his publication,' . . . or that the defendant acted with a 'high degree of awareness of . . . probable falsity.'" Palmer, 159 Vt. at 39, 615 A.2d at 503 (citations omitted).

(2) **Common Law Malice.** Common law malice involves "conduct manifesting personal ill will, reckless or wanton disregard of plaintiff's rights, or carried out under circumstances evidencing insult or oppression." Crump, 154 Vt. at 293, 576 A.2d at 447 (quoting Lent, 143 Vt. at 550, 470 A.2d at 1170).

e. **Question of Fact or Law.** No cases directly address whether the existence of a conditional privilege is a question of fact or law. In one case, the court held that the defendant bore the burden of proving the privilege. Lent, 143 Vt. at 549, 470 A.2d at 1169. In another case, the court noted that the trial court found as a matter of law that the defendant enjoyed a privilege. Crump, 154 Vt. at 293, 576 A.2d at 446. The issue of whether a plaintiff has defeated a conditional privilege is a question of fact for the jury. Crump, 154 Vt. at 293, 576 A.2d at 447; Marcoux-Norton, 907 F. Supp. at 780.

f. **Burden of Proof.** The defendant bears the burden of proving that it enjoys a conditional privilege. Lent, 143 Vt. at 549, 470 A.2d at 1169. Once the defendant proves a privilege, the plaintiff can overcome the privilege by proving by clear and convincing evidence the requisite malice (see II.A.2(d), supra). Crump, 154 Vt. at 293, 576 A.2d at 447.

B. Standard Libel Defenses

1. ***Truth.*** Truth is a complete defense to a defamation claim. Lent, 143 Vt. at 548. "Substantial truth," as opposed to literal truth, may be adequate to support a complete defense. See Weisburgh v. Mahady, 147 Vt. 70, 73, 511 A.2d 304, 306, 12 Media L. Rep. 2293 (1986); Turgeon v. Operating Engineers, Local No. 98, AFL-CIO, 2 Fed. Appx. 176, 180, 2001 WL 99578 at 3 (2d Cir. 2001) (concluding that, under Vermont law, statements that are either substantially true or "obvious exaggerations" cannot be defamatory); Sweet v. Roy, 173 Vt. 418, 448, 801 A.2d 694, 716 (2002).

2. ***Opinion.*** No Vermont Supreme Court cases. One Superior Court held that "pure opinion" is protected by the Constitution and, therefore, not actionable. Killington, Ltd. v. Times Argus Ass'n, 14 Media L. Rep. 1314, 1316 (Vt. Super. Ct. 1987).

3. ***Consent.*** The Vermont Supreme Court has not addressed consent as a defense. A federal decision predicts that Vermont would allow the issue of consent to be submitted to the jury under a two-part inquiry: (1) whether the plaintiff reasonably should have been aware that defendants report would have been defamatory, and (2) whether plaintiff would have signed the consent form if he had been aware that the report might be defamatory. Marcoux-Norton, 907 F. Supp. at 781.

4. ***Mitigation.*** No recent case addresses mitigating circumstances. Nineteenth century cases hold that mitigating circumstances include evidence of rumor, belief, or suspicion that the plaintiff is guilty of the acts charged in the statement, Bridgman v. Hopkins, 34 Vt. 532 (1861), and evidence of the plaintiffs general bad character or reputation, Bowen v. Hall, 20 Vt. 232 (1848).

III. RECURRING FACT PATTERNS

A. Statements in Personnel File

No cases on point. However, the Vermont Supreme Court recently cited with approval a Second Circuit case which held that "extensively detailed lists of [an employee's] supposed professional failings" placed in "her personnel file, which was likely to be seen by potential future employers," were potentially defamatory. See Herrera v. Union No. 39 Sch. Dist., 2009 VT 35, ¶ 21, 975 A.2d 619, 627 (2009) (citing Donato v. Plainview-Old Bethpage Cent. Sch. Dist., 96 F.3d 623, 631-32 (2d Cir. 1996)).

B. Performance Evaluations

Vermont has not expressly recognized a conditional privilege for performance evaluations. The parties in one case presented the issue to the court in the context of a college tenure evaluation process, but the court declined to rule on the issue without a more complete factual record. Cockrell v. Middlebury College, 148 Vt. 557, 536 A.2d 547 (1987); see also Fin v. Middlebury College, 136 Vt. 543, 394 A.2d 1152 (1978) (declining to address privilege issue arising from letter written to college because the plaintiff failed to show injury to his reputation).

C. References

Vermont recognizes a conditional privilege for statements made to protect the legitimate interests of third parties, which appears to cover employment references. Nott v. Stoddard, 38 Vt. 25, 32, 1865 WL 2182 (1865); cf. Breslauer v. Fayston Sch. Dist., 163 Vt. 416 (1995) (arising from allegedly defamatory reference, but not addressing conditional privilege); see also Marcoux-Norton, 907 F. Supp. at 780 (conditional privilege recognized for a credit reference concerning employee). Further, in Agee v. Grunert, 349 F. Supp. 2d 838, 843 (D. Vt. 2004), Plaintiff claimed he was defamed when his colleagues informed the hospital where he had operating privileges that Plaintiff's ability to practice medicine was "impaired" and that he had been placed on "medical disability." The U.S. District Court for the District of Vermont concluded that the Vermont Supreme Court would recognize a conditional privilege for "[s]tatements concerning a physician's fitness to practice" made "in the interests of patients and other third parties." Id., at 843-44 (noting that "where the safety of patients is at stake, there is an even greater need for the conditional privilege" than in the case of "statements made for the protection of a lawful business interest").

The Vermont legislature has considered legislation that would have created a statutory qualified privilege for employment references. House Bill 166, "An Act Relating to Employment Reference Immunity" (1997). To date, no such legislation has been enacted.

D. Intracorporate Communication

An employer enjoys a conditional privilege to engage in limited intracorporate communications to protect its legitimate business interests. Crump v. P& C Food Mkts., Inc., 154 Vt. 284, 292, 576 A.2d 441, 446 (1990); Lent v. Huntoon, 143 Vt. 539, 548-49, 470 A.2d 1162, 1169, 9 Media L. Rep. 2547 (1983); see I.B.6(a), supra.

E. Statements to Government Regulators

No cases on point.

F. Reports to Auditors and Insurers

No cases on point.

G. Vicarious Liability of Employers for Statements Made by Employees

1. ***Scope of Employment.*** An employer may be held vicariously liable for "the tortious acts of an employee or servant committed during, or incidental to, the scope of employment." Brueckner v. Norwich Univ., 169 Vt. 118, 122-23, 730 A.2d 1086, 1090 (1999). Even if the conduct at issue is not actually authorized, the employer may be liable if the conduct is "of the same general nature as, or incidental to, the authorized conduct." Id. (citing Restatement (Second) of Agency § 229 (1) (1958)); see also McHugh v. Univ. of Vermont, 758 F. Supp. 945, 951 (D. Vt. 1991) (in determining the scope of employment, "the inquiry turns not on whether the act doing was authorized or was in violation of the employers policies, but rather whether the act can properly be seen as intending to advance the employers interests") (quoting Anderson v. Toombs, 119 Vt. 40, 45, 117 A.2d 250, 253 (1955)); Turgeon v. Operating Engineers, Local No. 98, AFL-CIO, 2 Fed. Appx. 176, 179, 2001 WL 99578 at 3 (2d Cir. 2001) (employer may be liable for defamatory statements made by an employee if the statements are made in furtherance of the employers business, or if the employer expressly or impliedly authorized the statements). There is no vicarious liability if an allegedly defamatory statement was made at a time when the speaker was no longer employed by the employer, even if the statement related to events that occurred during the employment. Breslauer v. Fayston Sch. Dist., 163 Vt. 416, 424, 659 A.2d 1129, 1134 (1995) (school district could not be vicariously liable for a negative reference given by a former principal at a time when the principal was no longer employed by the school district).

a. **Blogging.** No reported cases.

2. ***Damages.*** No cases directly address damages for vicarious liability arising from defamation. The Vermont Supreme Court has, however, recently addressed a corporation's liability for punitive damages based upon claims of vicarious liability and negligent supervision. In Brueckner v. Norwich University, 169 Vt. 118, 129, 730 A.2d 1086, 1095 (1999), the Court reaffirmed that punitive damages are available if a "plaintiff can demonstrate that a defendant acted with malice." The Court defined malice as "conduct manifesting personal ill will or carried out under circumstances evidencing insult or oppression or even by conduct showing a reckless or wanton disregard of ones rights." Id. The Court then reaffirmed that a corporation may be held liable for punitive damages if "the malicious or unlawful act relied upon [must be] that of the governing officers of the corporation or one lawfully exercising their authority, or, if the act relied upon is that of a servant or agent of the corporation, it must be clearly shown that the governing officers either directed the act, participated in it, or subsequently ratified it." Id. at 130, 730 A.2d at 1096 (citations omitted). However, inaction or inattention alone is inadequate to support an award of punitive damages. Id.

H. Internal Investigations

No reported cases. However, it is likely that a corporation's conditional privilege for intracorporate communications made to protect its legitimate business interests would apply in such situations. See I.B.6(a) and III.D, infra.

IV. OTHER ACTIONS BASED ON STATEMENTS

Vermont courts have not specifically addressed concerns about plaintiffs pleading alternative theories in an effort to circumvent limitations to a defamation claim. The courts have, however, addressed other tort claims that are commonly raised in the employment and employment libel context.

A. Negligent Hiring, Retention, and Supervision

Following the Restatement, Vermont recognizes that an employer may be liable if it is "negligent or reckless . . . in the employment of improper persons or instrumentalities in work involving risk of harm to others: in the supervision of the activity; or . . . in permitting, or failing to prevent, negligent or other tortious conduct by persons, whether or not [its] servants, upon premises or within instrumentalities under [its] control." Haverly v. Kaytec, Inc., 169 Vt. 350, 356-57, 738 A.2d 86, 91 (1999) (quoting Restatement (Second) of Agency § 213 (1958)); see also Brueckner, 169 Vt. at 126, 730 A.2d at 1093 ("A principal may, in addition to being found vicariously liable for tortious conduct of its agents, be found directly liable for damages resulting from negligent supervision of its agents activities"). The workers compensation statute, however, bars such claims by employees against their own employers. Dunham v. Chase, 165 Vt. 543, 674 A.2d 1279 (1996). Also, a former employee has no claim of negligent supervision for a negative reference given by a former supervisor if the reference was made at a time when the supervisor was no longer employed by the employer. Breslauer v. Fayston Sch. Dist., 163 Vt. 416, 659 A.2d 1129 (1995).

B. Intentional Infliction of Emotional Distress

Vermont recognizes a claim of intentional infliction of emotional distress for "outrageous conduct, done intentionally or with reckless disregard of the probability of causing emotional distress, resulting in the suffering of extreme emotional distress, actually or proximately caused by the outrageous conduct." Fromson v. Vermont, 2004 VT 29, ¶ 14, 176 Vt. 395, 399, 848 A.2d 344, 347 (2004); see also Morton v. Allstate Ins. Co., 58 F. Supp. 2d 325 (D. Vt. 1999); Crump v. P&C Food Mkts., Inc., 154 Vt. 284, 296, 576 A.2d 441, 448 (1990). A plaintiff's burden is a "heavy one." Fromson, 2004 VT at ¶ 14, 176 Vt. at 399, 848 A.2d at 347. An employer is not liable for the mere termination of employment, id., or for "mere insults, indignities, threats, annoyances, petty oppressions, or other trivialities." Denton v. Chittenden Bank, 163 Vt. 62, 66, 655 A.2d 703, 706 (1994). Outrageous conduct based solely on unlawful motives underlying the conduct is insufficient. Fromson, 2004 VT at ¶ 18, 176 Vt. at 401, 848 A.2d at 349. Vermont courts have not addressed whether the state will recognize claims for intentional infliction of emotional distress based only on statements alleged to be defamatory.

C. Interference with Economic Advantage

A plaintiff establishes a claim of tortious interference with a contract or business relationship with proof that the defendant "intentionally and improperly induced [a party] not to perform its contract." Gifford v. Sun Data, Inc., 165 Vt. 611, 612, 686 A.2d 472, 474 (1996) (mem.). The elements of the tort are: "(1) the existence of a valid business relationship or expectancy, (2) knowledge by the interferer of the relationship or expectancy, (3) an intentional act of interference on the part of the interferer, (4) damage to the party whose relationship or expectancy was disrupted, and (5) proof that the interference caused the harm sustained." Id., 165 Vt. at 613 n.2, 686 A.2d at 474 n.2; see also J.A. Morrissey, Inc. v. Smejkal, 2010 VT 66, ¶ 21 (Vermont Supreme Court affirmed jury verdict in which the jury awarded punitive damages for the intentional interference with prospective economic advantage); Von Turkovich v. APC Capital Partners, LLC, 259 F. Supp. 2d 314 (D. Vt. 2003) (refusing to grant summary judgment because there was sufficient evidence that lending company had intentionally interfered with the landlord/tenant relationship); Howard Opera House Assoc. v. Urban Outfitters, Inc., 166 F. Supp. 2d 917 (D. Vt. 2001) (no claim because legitimate noise complaints are not actionable interference).

Officers of a company may be liable for inducing the employer to break a contract with an employee if they acted outside the scope of their employment to further their own interests. Lyon v. Bennington College Corp., 137 Vt. 135, 139, 400 A.2d 1010, 1012 (1979); see also Murray v. St. Michaels College, 164 Vt. 205, 213, 667 A.2d 294, 300 (1995).

The State of Vermont is immune from suit based on intentional interference with contractual relations. See 12 V.S.A. § 5601(e)(6).

D. Prima Facie Tort

The Vermont Supreme Court has declined to recognize a claim for prima facie tort when the claim was used to overcome the deficiencies in a traditional tort. Fromson v. Vermont, 2004 VT 29, 176 Vt. 395, 848 A.2d 344 (2004).

V. OTHER ISSUES

A. Statute of Limitations.

The statute of limitation for libel cases is three years. 12 V.S.A. § 512. This period applies to actions for defamation and slander alike. "The statute of limitations runs from the time when a plaintiff can first sue and recover its demand." Rennie v. State, 171 Vt. 584, 586, 762 A.2d 1272, 1275 (2000) (employment defamation claim and related causes of action were time barred); see also Tindall v. Poultney High Sch. Dist., 414 F.3d 281, 284 (2d Cir. 2005) (noting that the statute of limitations runs from the date "the alleged defamatory statements were made"). Vermont courts apply a "discovery rule" in determining whether a defamation claim is barred by the statute of limitations. Dulude v. Fletcher Allen Health Care, Inc., 174 Vt. 74, 85, 807 A.2d 390, 399 (2002). Under this rule "the accrual of a cause of action in defamation may be deferred until the plaintiff discovers, or through the use of reasonable care and diligence, should have discovered the nature of the defamatory communication." Id. at 399 (citing Marshall Field Stores, Inc. v. Gardinder, 859 S.W.2d 391, 394 (Tex. App. 1993)); but see Lapinsky v. Copley Hosp., No. 1:05-cv-34, 2007 WL 3143331, at *5 (D. Vt. Oct. 25, 2007) (discovery rule did not extend the statute of limitations for plaintiff's defamation claim where plaintiff "knew the substance of the allegedly defamatory statements, who made the statements, and at least one person . . . to whom the statements were made").

B. Jurisdiction.

Vermont's long-arm statute extends the states jurisdiction to any case where personal jurisdiction is proper under the federal Due Process clause. See 12 V.S.A. § 913(b); Dall v. Kaylor, 163 Vt. 274, 658 A.2d 78 (1995).

C. Worker's Compensation Exclusivity

Vermont's worker's compensation statute provides the exclusive remedy for workplace injuries, subject to certain limited exceptions, including for intentional injuries committed by the employer. See Mead v. Western Slate, Inc., 2004 VT 11, ¶¶ 11-12, 176 Vt. 274, 278-79, 848 A.2d 257, 260 (2004). However, there do not appear to be any Vermont cases considering the issue of whether the statute bars defamation claims by employees against their employers. Moreover, the trend in recent cases seems to be that claims for intentional infliction of emotional distress by employees against their employers are not barred as a matter of law by the workers' compensation statute. See, e.g., Goodstein v. Bombardier Capital, Inc., 889 F. Supp. 760, 766-67 (D. Vt. 1995) (finding IIED claim by sexual harassment and discrimination in the workplace not barred); see also Buote v. Verizon New England, 190 F. Supp. 2d 693, 706 (D. Vt. 2002) ("Intentional actions aimed specifically at an employee with the intent the cause harm do not fall within the 'accidental' personal injuries compensable under section 618(a) of the VWCA."); Garger v. Desroches, 2009 VT 37, ¶ 8, 974 A.2d 597, 601-02 (2009) (in order for plaintiff to avoid WCA exclusivity provision, "defendant must have either had a specific intent to inure or have known with substantial certainty that injury would result").

D. Pleading Requirements.

Although a plaintiff is no longer required to plead the defamatory statements in haec verba, defamation must be alleged in sufficient detail to afford the defendant "sufficient notice of the nature of the communications complained of." Solomon v. Atlantis Dev., Inc., 147 Vt. 349, 358 (1986); see also Decker v. Vermont Educ. Television, Inc., 13 F. Supp. 2d 569, 573 (D. Vt. 1998). A complaint must plead "an adequate identification of the communication, and an identification of who made the communication, when it was made, and to whom it was communicated." Decker, 13 F. Supp. 2d at 573.

SURVEY OF VERMONT EMPLOYMENT PRIVACY LAW

Robert B. Hemley, Esq., and Matthew B. Byrne, Esq.
Gravel and Shea
76 St. Paul Street
P.O. Box 369
Burlington, VT 05402-0369
Telephone: (802) 658-0220; Facsimile (802) 658-1456
E-mail: rhemley@gravelshea.com or mbyrne@gravelshea.com

(With Developments Reported Through **November 1, 2012**)

GENERAL COMMENTS

Civil cases in Vermont state court are generally brought in Superior Court. Appeals are taken directly to the Vermont Supreme Court and are heard as a matter of right; there are no intermediary appellate courts. Opinions of the Vermont Supreme Court are published in an official reporter, the Vermont Reporter, and are available online at www.vermontjudiciary.org. Opinions of the Superior Court are now available in a publication called Vermont Lawyer and Trial Court Reporter.

SIGNIFICANT DEVELOPMENTS SINCE THE 2012 *SURVEY*

None.

I. GENERAL LAW OF PRIVACY

A. Legal Basis of Privacy Claims

The Vermont Supreme Court has rejected a claim for invasion of privacy based on the Due Process Clause of Vermont's Constitution. Levinski v. Diamond, 151 Vt. 178, 197, 559 A.2d 1073, 1085 (1989) (holding where plaintiff alleged defamation and invasion of privacy by public officials during the course of a medicaid fraud investigation, no substantive constitutional right stems from Article 4, therefore, it does not rise to the level of establishing a fundamental privacy right), overruled on other grounds, Muzzy v. State, 155 Vt. 279, 583 A.2d 82 (1990); McHugh v. University of Vermont, 758 F. Supp. 945, 952 (D. Vt. 1991) (holding University employee had no privacy claim under Vermont Constitution for alleged sexual harassment), aff'd, 966 F.2d 67 (1992); Vt. Const. Ch. 1 Art. 4.

Within the context of government searches of private property, Article 11 of the Vermont Constitution may afford greater protection to individual rights than does the Fourth Amendment to the Federal Constitution. State v. Birchard, 2010 VT 57, ¶ 12; State v. Rogers, 161 Vt. 236, 246, 638 A.2d 569, 575 (1993) ("As our paramount concern in search and seizure cases is to give effect to the core values of privacy underlying Article 11, we have not hesitated to depart from the parallel federal law when necessary to accomplish this goal"); State v. Kirchoff, 156 Vt. 1, 587 A.2d 988 (1991); State v. Welch, 160 Vt. 70, 76, 624 A.2d 1105, 1108 (1993); State v. Morris, 165 Vt. 111, 125, 680 A.2d 90, 100 (1996) Vt. Const. Ch. 1, Art. 11.

In the Article 11 area, the Vermont Supreme Court decided a case that may have implications for workplace privacy. See State v. Simmons, 2011 VT 69. In Simmons, the Court addressed the issue of whether a person had a reasonable expectation of privacy for information placed on social media sites. The Court stated that: "Given the necessary and willing exposure of an internet user's access point identification and frequency of use to third party internet service providers, such information cannot reasonably be considered confidential, especially when a provider such as MySpace openly declares a policy of disclosure." Id. at ¶ 15. While the case dealt with criminal investigations, the case could have broader implications for work place privacy.

Vermont has no statute providing a cause of action for invasion of privacy. Historically, the state tort liability statute exempted the state from liability for invasion of privacy. However, effective July 1, 1990, the legislature amended the state tort immunity statute, deleting the exception to the waiver of immunity for claims arising out of invasion of the right to privacy. 12 V.S.A. § 5601(e)(6). Thus, under current statutory law, there is no sovereign immunity for invasion of privacy claims.

The tort of invasion of privacy, however, has been recognized as a cause of action in the common law of the state. Staruski v. Continental Tel. Co., 154 Vt. 568, 581 A.2d 266 (1990); Denton v. Chittenden Bank, 163 Vt. 62, 655 A.2d 703 (1994); Hodgdon v. Mt. Mansfield Co., 160 Vt. 150, 624 A.2d 1122 (1992); Pion v. Bean, 2003 VT 79, 176 Vt. 1, 833 A.2d 1248 (2003).

B. Causes of Action

1. ***Misappropriation/Right of Publicity.*** Vermont recognizes a cause of action for invasion of privacy by the commercial appropriation of a person's identity. Staruski v. Continental Tel. Co., 154 Vt. 568, 581 A.2d 266 (1990). An advertisement for the commercial benefit of an employer which used an employee's name and photograph and falsely attributed a testimonial by the employee without the employee's consent entitled the employee to recover damages for injury for invasion of privacy. Id. The Supreme Court has not considered whether and to what degree the noncommercial appropriation of a person's name or likeness may be tortious in Vermont. Id. 154 Vt. at 572, n.4, 581 A.2d at 268.

2. ***False Light.*** Vermont recognizes a cause of action for invasion of privacy by publicity that unreasonably places a person in a false light. Staruski, 154 Vt. at 572, 581 A.2d at 268; Lemnah v. American Breeders Serv. Inc., 144 Vt. 568, 482 A.2d 700 (1984). The Lemnah Court applied the law on invasion of privacy as presented in the trial court's jury instructions, which recited the Restatement (Second) of Torts, without an independent analysis because there was no precedent in Vermont and the parties did not dispute the applicable law. Lemnah, 144 Vt. at 574, 482 A.2d at 704 (applying jury instruction that "invasion of privacy can be found in either of two ways: 1) the defendant gave unreasonable publicity to plaintiff's private life, or 2) the defendant gave publicity that unreasonably placed the plaintiff in a false light"). The court expressly stated that it would not address the general question of what elements comprise the tort of invasion of privacy in Vermont. Id. Without indicating which of the two forms of invasion of privacy applied to the facts in question, the court found defendant's tortious statement, that plaintiff was a drunk and sold refrozen bovine semen ineffective for insemination, made to only one other person was insufficient to constitute publicity for purposes of a cause of action for invasion of privacy. Lemnah, 144 Vt. at 575, 482 A.2d at 704. When publicity is an element of an invasion of privacy claim, the communication must be to a group larger than several people. Lemnah, 144 Vt. at 576, 482 A.2d at 705.

Preliminary to a discussion of invasion of privacy based on misappropriation, the Staruski Court acknowledged that the court, in Lemnah, had previously recognized two forms of invasion of privacy – a claim based on publicity which places a person in a false light, and a claim based on publicity regarding a person's private life. Staruski, 154 Vt. at 572, 581 A.2d at 268.

3. ***Publication of Private Facts.*** Vermont recognizes a cause of action for invasion of privacy by the unreasonable publicity of a person's private life. Staruski, 154 Vt. 568, 581 A.2d 266 (1990); Lemnah, 144 Vt. 568, 482 A.2d 700 (1984); see I.B.2, supra.

4. ***Intrusion.*** Vermont recognizes a cause of action for invasion of privacy based upon intrusion upon seclusion. Hodgdon v. Mt. Mansfield Co., 160 Vt. 150, 624 A.2d 1122 (1992); Denton v. Chittenden Bank, 163 Vt. 62, 655 A.2d 703 (1994); Pion v. Bean, 2002 VT 179, 833 A.2d 1248 (2003). Invasion of privacy is an intentional interference with a person's interest in solitude or seclusion, either as to the person or as to the person's private affairs or concerns, of a kind that would be highly offensive to a reasonable person. Hodgdon, 160 Vt. at 162, 624 A.2d at 1129 (single letter threatening termination if plaintiff failed to wear dentures at work was insufficient to constitute an invasion of privacy); Denton, 163 Vt. at 69, 655 A.2d at 707 (No invasion of privacy found where supervisor came to employee's house during employee's sick leave and questioned employee in front of guests about employee's illness and absence from work, because actions of supervisor were not substantial or an intrusion that would be highly offensive to a reasonable person); Pion v. Bean, 2002 VT 179, ¶ 34, 833 A.2d 1248, 1258 (2003) (affirming award of compensatory and punitive damages when landowner acted with malicious intent to drive out the other landowner by engaging "in a persistent pattern of intrusive conduct that amounted to 'hounding,'" including "filing false complaints with authorities and 'hurling insults and threats'").

The Vermont Supreme Court has held that sexual harassment allegations that a supervisor made inquiries of a personal nature and would lean close to employee at her work station is not the type of "substantial intrusion" upon private affairs that would be "highly offensive to a reasonable person" and, thus, no invasion of privacy tort had been committed. Vermont Ins. Mgmt. v. Lumbermens' Mut. Cas., 171 Vt. 601, 604, 764 A.2d 1213, 1216 (2000). However, in denying an employer's motion to dismiss, a Vermont federal district court held that a complaint alleging misconduct by an employee that included "making unwelcome and highly offensive sexual comments and insults to Plaintiff about her body and grabbing Plaintiff's buttocks" set forth "sufficient factual averments to support a claim of invasion of privacy" against the employer for the employee's actions. Crowley v. Erdmann, No. 1:07-CV-10, 2007 WL 1768708, at *1 (D. Vt. June 15, 2007).

In a Superior Court decision, it was held there was no basis for a claim for invasion of privacy based on allegations by a employee suffering from depression that her employer disclosed information about her clinical condition and remarked on her body odor. Boucher v. Northeast Kingdom Mental Health Serv., Docket No. 221-10-970scv, Orleans Superior Court, Sept. 21, 2000, 5 Vt. Tr. Ct. Rptr. 339 (May 31, 2001). The court held that there was no evidence that the employer misused knowledge of the plaintiff's condition and that body odor cannot be reasonably presumed to be safe from "invasion."

C. Other Privacy-Related Actions

1. ***Intentional Infliction of Emotional Distress.*** Vermont recognizes a claim of intentional infliction of emotional distress for "outrageous conduct, done intentionally or with reckless disregard of the probability of causing emotional distress, resulting in the suffering of extreme emotional distress, actually or proximately caused by the outrageous conduct." Fromson v. Vermont, 2004 VT 29, ¶ 14, 176 Vt. 395, 399, 848 A.2d 344, 347 (2004); see also Morton v. Allstate Ins. Co., 58 F. Supp.2d 325 (D. Vt. 1999); Crump v. P&C Food Mkts., Inc., 154 Vt. 284, 296, 576 A.2d 441, 448 (1990). A plaintiff's burden is a "heavy one." Fromson, 2004 VT at ¶ 14, 176 Vt. at 399, 848 A.2d at 347. An employer is not liable for the mere termination of employment, id., or for "mere insults, indignities, threats, annoyances, petty oppressions, or other trivialities." Denton v. Chittenden Bank, 163 Vt. 62, 66, 655 A.2d 703, 706 (1994). Outrageous conduct based solely on unlawful motives underlying the conduct is insufficient. Fromson, 2004 VT at ¶ 18, 848 A.2d at 349. Vermont courts have not addressed whether the state will recognize claims for intentional infliction of emotional distress based only on statements alleged to be defamatory or actions that constitute invasions of privacy.

2. ***Interference With Prospective Economic Advantage.*** A plaintiff establishes a claim of tortious interference with a contract or business relationship with proof that the defendant "intentionally and improperly induced [a party] not to perform its contract." Gifford v. Sun Data, Inc., 165 Vt. 611, 612, 686 A.2d 472, 474 (1996) (mem.). The elements of the tort are: "(1) the existence of a valid business relationship or expectancy, (2) knowledge by the interferer of the relationship or expectancy, (3) an intentional act of interference on the part of the interferer, (4) damage to the party whose relationship or expectancy was disrupted, and (5) proof that the interference caused the harm sustained." Id., 165 Vt. at 613 n.2, 686 A.2d at 474 n.2; see also J.A. Morrissey, Inc. v. Smejkal, 2010 VT 66, ¶ 21 (Vermont Supreme Court affirmed jury verdict in which the jury awarded punitive damages for the intentional interference with prospective economic advantage); Von Turkovich v. APC Capital Partners, LLC, 259 F. Supp. 2d 314 (D. Vt. 2003) (refusing to grant summary judgment because there was sufficient evidence that lending company had intentionally interfered with the landlord/tenant relationship); Howard Opera House Assoc. v. Urban Outfitters, Inc., 166 F. Supp. 2d 917 (D. Vt. 2001) (no claim because legitimate noise complaints are not actionable interference).

Officers of a company may be liable for inducing the employer to break a contract with an employee if they acted outside the scope of their employment to further their own interests. Lyon v. Bennington College Corp., 137 Vt. 135, 139, 400 A.2d 1010, 1012 (1979); see also Murray v. St. Michael's College, 164 Vt. 205, 213 (1995)

The State of Vermont is immune from suit based on intentional interference with contractual relations. See 12 V.S.A. 5601(e)(6).

3. ***Prima Facie Tort.*** The Vermont Supreme Court has declined to recognize a claim for prima facie tort when the claim was used to overcome the deficiencies in a traditional tort. Fromson v. Vermont, 2004 VT 29, 176 Vt. 395, 848 A.2d 344 (2004).

II. EMPLOYER TESTING OF EMPLOYEES

A. Psychological or Personality Testing

No cases or statutes.

B. Drug Testing

1. ***Common Law and Statutes.*** Vermont law regulates the use of drug testing for applicants and employees. 21 V.S.A. § 511 *et seq.*. An employer may not request or require that an applicant submit to a drug test, nor may an employer administer a drug test to an applicant for employment unless the applicant has been given an offer of employment conditioned on the applicant receiving a negative test result. 21 V.S.A. § 512. Likewise, an employer may not as a condition of employment, promotion or change of status, request or require that an employee submit to a drug test nor may an employer administer a drug test to an employee unless:

> 1) an employer has probable cause to believe that the employee is using or is under the influence of a drug on the job;
>
> 2) the employer has available for the tested employee a bona fide rehabilitation program for alcohol or drug abuse;
>
> 3) the employee may not be terminated if the test result is positive and the employee agrees to participate in and then successfully completes the employee assistance program. 21 V.S.A. § 513.

Employers may not conduct random tests or company-wide test unless such testing is required by federal law or regulations. 21 V.S.A. § 513(b).

The statute provides procedures for administration of drug tests. 21 V.S.A. § 514. Employers may not conduct their own drug tests; rather, they must contract with a medical review officer to review and evaluate all test results directly with the individual to be tested. Only confirmed drug test reports may be reported by the review officer to the employer. 21 V.S.A. § 514(11). Any information concerning the drug test results are confidential and must not be released to anyone except the employer, medical review officer, applicant or employee. 21 V.S.A. § 516. The enforcement provisions of the statute provides a private right of action by an applicant or an employee for injunctive relief, damages, costs and attorney's fees. 21 V.S.A. § 519.

2. ***Private Employers.*** No cases on point.

3. ***Public Employers.*** No cases on point.

C. Medical Testing

1. ***Common Law and Statutes***. It is unlawful for any employer to require any employee or applicant to pay the cost of a medical examination as a condition of employment. 21 V.S.A. § 301. It is also unlawful for any person to use genetic counseling or testing in any way relating to the terms, conditions or privileges of employment. 18 V.S.A. § 9333.

2. ***Private Employers***. In Vermont it is unlawful for any employer, employment agency, or labor organization to request or require an applicant, employee, or member to have an HIV-related blood test as a condition of employment or membership, classification, placement, or referral. 21 V.S.A § 495(a)(7). It is also unlawful for any employer to discriminate against, indicate a preference or limitation, refuse properly to classify or refer, or to limit or segregate membership, on the basis of a person's having a positive test result from an HIV-related blood test. 21 V.S.A. § 495(a)(6).

3. ***Public Employers.*** A similar provision prohibiting HIV testing or discrimination on the basis of HIV positive test results exists under the State Employees Labor Relations Act, where the employer is defined as the state of Vermont, including the state university and colleges. 3 V.S.A. § 961(7), (8).

D. Polygraph Tests

Vermont has a Polygraph Protection Act which prohibits polygraph testing as a condition of employment. 21 V.S.A. § 494a. Certain employers, such as police, the public safety department, or employers involved in the sale of precious metals or gems, or the manufacture or sale of regulated drugs, are permitted to require that an applicant for employment take a polygraph examination. 21 V.S.A. § 494b.

E. Fingerprinting

The Commissioner of Education, superintendents and headmasters of independent schools are required to request an FBI fingerprint check for any person applying for a job in a school. 16 V.S.A. § 255. Current school employees are grandfathered. Id.

III. SEARCHES

A. Employee's Person.

No cases on point.

B. Employee's Work Area

There are no reported cases on point. In an intrusion-upon-seclusion invasion of privacy case, however, a supervisor's search of an employee's files and desk drawers when the employee was on sick leave, a request by the supervisor asking the employee to empty his briefcase, and occasionally interrupting employee's business meetings without knocking, were facts alleged but not discussed or cited by the court as the reasons for declining to sustain the invasion of privacy claim. Denton v. Chittenden Bank, 163 Vt. 62, 655 A.2d 703 (1994) (no invasion of privacy found where supervisor came to employee's house during employee's sick leave and questioned employee in front of guests about employee's illness and absence from work, because actions of supervisor were not substantial or an intrusion that would be highly offensive to a reasonable person).

In a government search and seizure case which held that, under the Vermont Constitution, people have a privacy interest in their garbage bags left at curbside, the court cited with approval Justice Brennan's dissent in California v.

Greenwood, 486 U.S. 35 (1988), stating that rifling through desk drawers or intercepting phone calls, like the search of trash, "can divulge the target's financial and professional status, political affiliations, private thoughts, personal relationships, and romantic interests." State v. Morris, 165 Vt. 111, 116, 680 A.2d 90, 94 (1996). This may indicate the court's willingness, when state action is involved invoking constitutional privacy rights, to find that an employee has a privacy interest in his desk or work area.

C. Employee's Property

No cases on point.

IV. MONITORING OF EMPLOYEES

A. Telephones and Electronic Communications

1. ***Wiretapping.*** Vermont does not have a wiretapping statute. Further, there are no Supreme Court decisions in this area. A Superior court decision has recognized a claim against the State as employer for invasion of privacy by intrusion on seclusion based upon the wiretapping of private conversations of employees in the sheriff's office by the sheriff, although the claim was barred by the statute of limitations and the exception to waiver of state sovereign immunity statute (which has since been removed). Scribner v. Townsend, 2 Vt.Tr.Ct.Rptr. 56, Orange Superior Court Docket No. S119 -93, S125-93 and S144-93 (August 28, 1997).

Outside of the employment context, the Vermont Supreme Court has noted that warrantless electronic monitoring may offend the privacy values expressed in Article 11 of the Vermont Constitution when it is conducted in the home but not when conducted outside the home, such as in an automobile or parking lot or on unposted private property. State v. Costin, 168 Vt. 175, 180-81, 720 A.2d 866, 869-70 (1998); but see State v. Wetter, 2011 VT 111, ¶ 15 (finding no expectation of privacy in conversations with informant).

2. ***Electronic Communications.*** No reported decisions.

3. ***Other Electronic Monitoring.*** No reported decisions

B. Mail

No reported cases. Article 11 of the Vermont Constitution provides that, "the people have a right to hold themselves, their houses, their houses, papers and possessions free from search or seizure."

C. Surveillance/Photographing

No reported decisions. However, outside of the employment context, the Vermont Supreme court has, in dicta, noted that video surveillance of a protected area may trigger Constitutional privacy protections, citing other jurisdictions which prohibit warrantless video surveillance on private business premises. State v. Costin, 168 Vt. 175 (1998).

V. ACTIVITIES OUTSIDE THE WORKPLACE

A. Statute or Common Law

No cases directly on point. But, if the supervisor's actions are sufficiently egregious, there might be liability for the actions of a supervisor outside of the workplace. See Denton v. Chittenden Bank, 163 Vt. 62, 655 A.2d 703 (1994) (no invasion of privacy found where supervisor came to employee's house during employee's sick leave and questioned employee in front of guests about employee's illness and absence from work, because actions of supervisor were not substantial or an intrusion that would be highly offensive to a reasonable person).

B. Employees' Personal Relationships

1. ***Romantic Relationships Between Employees.*** No reported Vermont decisions on point. However, a federal district court case in Vermont held, under federal constitutional law, that social dating and the freedom to associate without interference from an employer, if constitutionally protected at all, derive that protection from the due process clause. Layfayette v. Frank, 688 F. Supp. 138 (D. Vt. 1988) (female postal worker who was reassigned because of her personal relationship with a postal contract carrier failed to show how interference with right of privacy constituted irreparable injury for purposes of preliminary injunctive relief).

In a hostile work environment sex discrimination claim brought by a female state police officer, the court relied on a number of incidents including comments by fellow employees regarding the plaintiff's relationships, including her relationship with a former state police officer and a supervisor's warning to plaintiff that her relationship with the former officer was antagonizing her colleagues and tarnishing the reputation of the force, which in the aggregate, among other factors, created a hostile work environment. In re Butler, 166 Vt. 423, 697 A.2d 659 (1997).

2. ***Sexual Orientation.*** The Vermont Fair Employment Practices Act prohibits employment discrimination based on sexual orientation. 21 V.S.A. § 495; 3 V.S.A. § 961 (public employers). The prohibition of discrimination based on sexual orientation does not prevent religious organizations from promoting their religious principles in any employment related matter. 21 V.S.A. § 495(e). Nor does this provision change the definition of family in an employee benefit plan. 21 V.S.A. § 495(f). It should be noted, however, that under 15 V.S.A. § 1204 parties to a civil union are granted the same benefits, protections and responsibilities as those granted to spouses in a marriage.

A constitutional invasion of privacy claim brought by a law clerk against her employers based on alleged reprimands by her employer for her gay rights activities outside of the workplace, was dismissed as premature because, among other reasons, she had not exhausted her administrative remedies. Aranoff v. Bryan, 153 Vt. 59, 569 A.2d 466 (1989).

3. ***Marital Status.*** No statute or reported cases on point. However, the marital relationship between a judge and a state police officer was determined to be insufficient to disqualify the judge to hear a case in which one of the witnesses was a co-worker of the judge's husband. State v. Putnam, 164 Vt. 558, 675 A.2d 422 (1996). It should be noted in passing that under 15 V.S.A. § 1204 parties to a civil union are granted the same benefits, protections and responsibilities as those granted to spouses in a marriage.

C. Smoking

No reported cases. Vermont law requires an employer to either prohibit smoking throughout the workplace or restrict smoking to a designated enclosed smoking area. 18 V.S.A. §§ 1421-1427.

D. Blogging

No reported decisions.

VI. RECORDS

It is a crime to knowingly, intentionally, and unlawfully access any computer, computer system, network, or data contained in such computers or systems. 13 V.S.A. § 4101 et seq. "'Access' means to instruct, communicate with, store data in, enter data in, retrieve data from or otherwise make use of any resources of a computer, computer system or computer network." In addition to criminal penalties, the law creates a private right of action for claimants to recover civil damages for unlawful access. The law applies to all businesses, employers, employees and all electronic records. Thus, this law provides, among other things, criminal and civil liability for unauthorized access by employees of an employer's records.

A. Personnel Records

Record keeping requirements of federal statutes are not discussed but would, of course, apply to Vermont employers covered by those statutes.

1. ***Public employees.*** Public employers' records are generally open to the public. See 1 V.S.A. § 316. However, personal documents contained in the personnel files of any employee of a public agency, or elsewhere, are exempt from public inspection and copying. 1 V.S.A § 317(c)(7). All information in personnel files of an individual employee of any public agency is available to that individual employee or his designated representative. Id. The Public Records Act has been construed liberally and favors the right of access to public documents. Trombley v. Bellows Falls Union High Sch. Dist. No. 27, 160 Vt. 101, 624 A.2d 857 (1992). Only "personal documents" that would constitute an invasion of privacy by revealing "intimate details of a person's life, including any information that might subject the person to embarrassment, harassment, disgrace, or loss of employment or friends" are protected from disclosure under the Act. Trombley, 160 Vt. at 110, 624 A.2d at 863 (holding that defendant school board failed to demonstrate that records regarding teacher's grievance were "personal" and thus exempted from the right to access public records act).

In a decision, the Vermont Supreme Court provided further guidance as to the test the court must employ to balance "an individual's privacy interest against the public interest in disclosure of records" sought pursuant to an access to public records request. Kade v. Smith, 2006 VT 44, ¶ 12, 180 Vt. 554, 559, 904 A.2d 1080, 1085-86 (2006). The court "must consider not only the relevance, if any, of the records to the public interest for which they are sought, but any other factors that may affect the balance, including: the significance of the public interest asserted; the nature, gravity, and potential consequences of the invasion of privacy occasioned by the disclosure; and the availability of alternative sources for the requested information." Id. ¶ 14, 180 Vt. at 560, 904 A.2d at 1086. Further, the Court instructed that should the lower court "determine that the balance favors nondisclosure, the court must also give careful consideration to redaction of the personal information and disclosure of the remainder." Id., 904 A.2d at 1087; see also Norman v. Vermont Office of Court Adm'r, 2004 VT 13, ¶¶ 8-10, 176 Vt. 593, 595, 844 A.2d 769, 772-73 (2004) (noting that the trial court should determine whether disclosure of personal information would reveal intimate details of person's life, including any information that might subject person to embarrassment, harassment, disgrace or loss of employment or friends and must consider the possibility of redacting the intimate information). The Kade Court also stated that a portion of the findings of fact may be issued under seal if necessary to maintain confidentiality. Kade, 2006 VT 44, ¶ 14, 180 Vt. at 560, 904 A.2d at 1087.

In the case of Rutland Herald v. City of Rutland, 2012 VT 26, ¶¶ 38-41, the Vermont Supreme Court held that where public employees used public computers to view pornography, disciplinary action resulting from the viewing should be available in a redacted form to the public.

2. ***Private employees.*** A Vermont statute requires litigants in most civil cases to follow certain procedures before they can obtain employee personnel records. 12 V.S.A § 1691a. The law requires that when personnel records are requested in civil litigation (except employment discrimination cases), the requesting party must inform the employee of the request and of the protections of the law. The employer is required to assist the litigant in providing notice to the employee by providing, upon request, the name and last-known address of the specific employee whose records are being sought. 12 V.S.A. § 1691a(c). The employee has twenty days after proper notice to state their intention to object, and the employee who objects has a right to a hearing before the court to state why the records should not be disclosed. Id. at § 1691a (f). In the definitions section of this statute, "civil action" is defined as an action commenced under the Vermont Rules of Civil Procedure, and thus, does not technically apply to actions brought in federal court. The law states that it is not intended to undermine other independent bases on which an employer could resist the production of records "as provided by law." Id. at § 1691a(j). Recently, a Vermont federal court considered an employee's privacy interests in ruling on a motion to compel personnel files in an employment discrimination case. The court denied plaintiff's motion which sought the files of a fellow employee, holding that the scope of the case was limited and "given the questionable relevance of the requested information, [the employee's] privacy interest outweighs [Plaintiff's] alleged need to review her files." Scanlan v. Potter, No. 1:05-CV-291, 2007 WL 602101, at *2 (D. Vt. Feb. 22, 2007).

Different versions of a bill providing employees and former employees with the right to review and copy their personnel files were passed by the senate and house, but the differences were not reconciled and the bill was not enacted into law. See House Bill 177 (1997), "An Act Relating to an Employee's Right to Review a Personnel File."

B. Medical Records

Access to pharmaceutical records is barred to all but authorized officials. 18 V.S.A. § 4211. Vermont recognizes the doctor/patient privilege. 12 V.S.A. § 1612. Patients' records are confidential; and physicians and other health professionals must not disclose any information acquired in attending a patient, without the patient's waiver. Id. A confidential public health record shall not be used to determine issues relating to employment or insurance for any individual. 18 V.S.A. § 1001(d)(2).

There are no reported cases directly on point. However, a warrantless inspection of pharmaceutical records of a nurse with a known drug history, employed by the state, was upheld under the regulated industry exception to warrantless searches, despite the nurse's legitimate expectation of privacy in pharmacy records. State v. Welch, 160 Vt. 70, 624 A.2d 1105 (1992). Also, the Vermont Supreme Court ordered the disclosure of State Board of Nursing files containing medical records of a nurse with a drug problem, despite a stipulation specifying that the investigation was to be confidential under the "investigative files" privilege. Douglas v. Windham Superior Court, 157 Vt. 34, 49 597 A.2d 774, 783 (1991) (dissent noting the peculiarly sensitive nature of medical records, triggering privacy interests of patients).

C. Criminal Records

An employer who is in the business of caring for the elderly or disabled adults may request the record of convictions of a person who is a current employee or contractor or a person to whom the employer has given a conditional offer of employment. 33 V.S.A. § 6914. Public and private schools are required to request a criminal record check, including an FBI fingerprint check, from the Vermont Criminal Information Center for any person applying for a job in a school. 16 V.S.A. § 255. The Vermont Criminal Information Center is authorized to release records of information requested under the above statutes. 20 V.S.A. § 2060.

The Vermont public safety statute regarding fingerprinting and criminal history records allows dissemination of criminal history records to employers that work with "vulnerable classes," such as children, the elderly and persons with disabilities, after the employer has made a conditional offer of employment to applicant and applicant has given a written authorization on a release form provided by the Vermont Crime Information Center. 20 V.S.A. § 2056c(b), (c). In addition, post-secondary school employers may obtain the criminal records for those applicants who will have access to student residential facilities. Id. § 2056c(d).

Records concerning the investigation of criminal conduct by public employees is categorically unavailable to the public. Rutland Herald v. City of Rutland, 2012 VT 26; Rutland Herald v. Vermont State Police, 2012 VT 24.

D. Subpoenas / Search Warrants

No reported decisions on the topics of subpoenas or search warrants. However, the statutes and case law discussed in Parts IV.A.1 & 2 above would apply to a subpoena to an employer calling for personnel records. Under Vermont Rule of Civil Procedure 45, a party served with a subpoena has 14 days in which to serve written objections, and may move to quash a subpoena that requires disclosure of "privileged or other protected matter" or of "a trade secret or other confidential research, development, or commercial information." See V.R.C.P. 45(c).

VII. ACTIONS SUBSEQUENT TO EMPLOYMENT

A. References

No reported decisions. However, Vermont recognizes a conditional privilege for statements made to protect the legitimate interests of third parties, which appears to cover employment references. Nott v. Stoddard, 38 Vt. 25, 32, 1865 WL 2182 (1865); cf. Breslauer v. Fayston Sch. Dist., 163 Vt. 416 (1995) (arising from allegedly defamatory reference, but not addressing conditional privilege); see also Marcoux-Norton, 907 F. Supp. at 780 (conditional privilege recognized for a credit reference concerning employee). Further, in Agee v. Grunert, 349 F. Supp. 2d 838, 843 (D. Vt. 2004), the U.S. District Court for the District of Vermont concluded that the Vermont Supreme Court would recognize a conditional privilege for "[s] tatements concerning a physician's fitness to practice" made "in the interests of patients and other third parties." Id., at 843-44 (noting that "where the safety of patients is at stake, there is an even greater need for the conditional privilege" than in the case of "statements made for the protection of a lawful business interest").

B. Non-Compete Agreements

The Vermont Supreme Court "will proceed with caution when asked to enforce covenants against competitive employment because such restraints run counter to public policy favoring the right of individuals to engage in the commercial activity of their choice." Systems & Software, Inc. v. Barnes, 2005 VT 95, ¶ 4, 178 Vt. 389, 391, 886 A.2d 762, 764 (2005); see also Roy's Orthopedic, Inc. v. Lavigne, 142 Vt. 347, 350, 454 A.2d 1242, 1244 (1982) ("[R]estrictions on doing business or on the exercise of an individual's trade or talent are subject to scrutiny for reasonableness and justification."). Nevertheless, the Court "will enforce such agreements 'unless the agreement is found to be contrary to public policy, unnecessary for protection of the employer, or unnecessarily restrictive of the rights of the employee, with due regard being given to the subject matter of the contract and the circumstances and conditions under which it is to be performed.'" Systems & Software, 2005 VT 95 at ¶ 4, 178 Vt. at 391, 886 A.2d at 764 (quoting Vt. Elec. Supply. Co. v. Andrus, 132 Vt. 195, 198, 315 A.2d 456, 458 (1974)). The scope of non-compete agreements in Vermont is not limited to trade secrets or confidential customer information, but may extend to protecting significantly broader "legitimate employer interests such as customer relationships and employee-specific goodwill." Id. at ¶ 5, 178 Vt. at 392, 886 A.2d at 764; see also Majestic Corp. of America v. Crepeau, Civ. No. 1:06CV35, 2007 WL 922267, at *6 (D. Vt. Mar. 23, 2007) (enforcing non-compete agreement with non-solicitation clause protecting employer's "customer relationships," which were "properly subject to protection" under Vermont law).

In Vermont, non-compete agreements will be enforced to the extent they are reasonable. This inquiry depends on several factors, including the type of prohibited activities, the length of time of the restriction, the geographic area of the restriction, and the consideration paid to the employee. The Vermont Supreme Court has observed that a restrictive agreement "is easier to justify if the restraint is limited to the taking of [the] former employer's customers as contrasted with competition in general." Id. at ¶ 9, 178 Vt. at 393, 886 A.2d at 765. However, the court will uphold a complete ban on competition that is "reasonably limited temporally and geographically" under the appropriate circumstances, including where "it would be difficult for an employer to determine when an employee is soliciting its customers," or for an employer "to monitor whether [a former employee] was using the good will and knowledge he acquired while working for [the employer] to gain a competitive advantage against [it]." Id. at ¶ 10. An agreement which prohibited an employee from selling to his active customers and "anyone within 50 miles of those customers" was found to be over-inclusive and unreasonable, where the employer provided "no justification for the 50 mile restriction," which was "unnecessarily restrictive of [employee's] rights," and failed to show that "such a broad restriction is necessary to protect its interests." Fisher v. Global Values, Inc., No 2:06-CV178, 2006 WL 3251488, at *5 (D. Vt. Nov. 2, 2006). Relying in part on a draft of the Restatement (Third) of Employment Law, the Vermont Supreme Court has held that "continued employment alone is sufficient consideration to support a covenant not to compete entered into during an at-will employment relationship." Summits 7, Inc. v. Kelly, 2005 VT 97, ¶¶ 18, 20, 178 Vt. 396, 404-05, 886 A.2d 365, 372-73 (2005) (stating that "[r]egardless of what point during the employment relationship the parties agree to a covenant not to compete, legitimate consideration for the covenant exists as long as the employer does not act in bad faith by terminating the employee shortly after the employee signs the covenant").

Finally, in Vermont, an employer's "trade secrets" may also be protected by the Vermont Trade Secrets Act. See 9 V.S.A. § 4601(3); see also Dicks v. Jensen, 172 Vt. 43, 46, 768 A.2d 1279, 1282 (2001) (noting that the Act, which is based on the Uniform Trade Secrets Act, "was enacted in 1996 to prevent the misuse of business information").

VIII. OTHER ISSUES

A. Statutes of Limitations

The statute of limitations for a privacy action is three years. 12 V.S.A. § 512.

B. Jurisdiction

Vermont's long-arm statute extends the states jurisdiction to any case where personal jurisdiction is proper under the federal Due Process clause. See 12 V.S.A. § 913(b); Dall v. Kaylor, 163 Vt. 274, 658 A.2d 78 (1995).

C. Worker's Compensation Exclusivity

Vermont's worker's compensation statute provides the exclusive remedy for workplace injuries, subject to certain limited exceptions, including for intentional injuries committed by the employer. See Mead v. Western Slate, Inc., 2004 VT 11, ¶¶ 11-12, 176 Vt. 274, 278-79, 848 A.2d 257, 260 (2004). However, there do not appear to be any Vermont cases considering the issue of whether the statute bars invasion of privacy tort claims by employees against their employers. Moreover, the trend in recent cases seems to be that claims for intentional infliction of emotional distress by employees against their employers are not barred as a matter of law by the workers' compensation statute. See, e.g., Goodstein v. Bombardier Capital, Inc., 889 F. Supp. 760, 766-67 (D. Vt. 1995) (finding IIED claim by sexual harassment and discrimination in the workplace not barred); see also Buote v. Verizon New England, 190 F. Supp. 2d 693, 706 (D. Vt. 2002) ("Intentional actions aimed specifically at an employee with the intent the cause harm do not fall within the 'accidental' personal injuries compensable under section 618(a) of the VWCA."); Garger v. Desroches, 2009 VT 37, ¶ 8, 974 A.2d 597, 601-02 (2009) (in order for plaintiff to avoid WCA exclusivity provision, "defendant must have either had a specific intent to inure or have known with substantial certainty that injury would result").

D. Pleading Requirements

A complaint alleging invasion of privacy must state that defendant's conduct was intentional, substantial, or highly offensive to a reasonable person. Harris v. Carbonneau, 165 Vt. 433, 439, 685 A.2d 296, 300 (1996) (a complaint alleging only that defendant "wrongfully invaded plaintiffs' privacy" by entering house "without permission and against plaintiff's wishes" failed to support anything more than alternatively pleaded theories of trespass and negligence).

SURVEY OF VIRGINIA EMPLOYMENT LIBEL LAW

Warren David Harless, Craig T. Merritt, David B. Lacy
Christian & Barton, L.L.P.
909 East Main Street, Suite 1200
Richmond, Virginia 23219
Telephone: (804) 697-4100; Facsimile: (804) 697-4112

(With Developments Reported Through **November 1, 2012**)

GENERAL COMMENTS

None.

SIGNIFICANT DEVELOPMENTS SINCE THE 2012 *SURVEY*

Although the Supreme Court of Virginia issued several opinions dealing with defamation law, none pertain to defamation in the employment context and none change the substantive law. A few Virginia Circuit courts issued noteworthy opinions. In particular, the Russell County Circuit Court held that the mere inclusion of a person's photograph in a negative article about another person is not defamatory as a matter of law. See Compton v. Foster, 82 Va. Cir. 279 (Russell Cir. Ct. 2011). Federal courts applying Virginia law have addressed such issues as: (1) substantial truth; (2) inferring defamatory meaning from context; and (3) qualified privilege for statements made in the context of workplace investigations. Although none of these cases altered the Commonwealth's substantive defamation law or addressed issues in a particularly novel way, they provide useful illustrations.

I. GENERAL LAW

A. General Employment Law

1. ***At Will Employment.*** Virginia strongly adheres to the at-will employment doctrine in the absence of a contract for a defined duration or a just cause requirement for termination. Norfolk S. Ry. v. Harris, 190 Va. 966, 59 S.E.2d 110 (1950); see also County of Giles v. Wines, 262 Va. 68, 546 S.E.2d 721 (2001) (holding that a statement in the personnel policy permitting dismissal for inefficiency, insubordination, misconduct, or other just cause was not sufficient to rebut the presumption that plaintiff was an at-will employee). Under the doctrine, either party to an employment relationship may end the association upon furnishing reasonable notice of termination. Lawrence Chrysler Plymouth Corp. v. Brooks, 251 Va. 94, 98, 465 S.E.2d 8906, 808 (1996). In Bowman v. State Bank of Keysville, 229 Va. 534, 331 S.E.2d 797 (1985), the Virginia Supreme Court carved out a "narrow exception to the employment-at-will rule" which prohibits discharge that violates a Virginia public policy. "Public policies" under the Bowman wrongful discharge doctrine are limited to those "polic [ies] underlying existing laws designed to protect the property rights, personal freedoms, health, safety, or welfare of the people in general." Miller v. SEVAMP, 234 Va. 462, 467-68, 362 S.E.2d 915, 918 (1987). The exception does not extend so far as to make actionable discharges of at-will employees that violate only private rights or interests. In Rowan v. Tractor Supply Co., 263 Va. 209, 559 S.E.2d 709 (2002), the Supreme Court of Virginia identified three circumstances where a cause of action for a wrongful discharge or a discharge in violation of public policy exists: (1) where an employer violates a policy enabling the exercise of an employee's statutorily created right; (2) where the public policy violated by the employer was explicitly expressed in the statute and the employee was clearly a member of that class of persons directly entitled to the protection enunciated by the public policy; and (3) where an employee is discharged based on the employee's refusal to engage in a criminal act. See Id. at 213, 559 S.E.2d at 710-711; see also McFarland v. Va. Ret. Servs. of Chesterfield, L.L.C., 477 F. Supp. 2d 727, 732-736 (E.D. Va. 2007) (plaintiff sufficiently pled claim for Bowman wrongful discharge under state statute mandating reporting of abuse at adult retirement facilities). A Bowman wrongful termination claim cannot be premised upon federal statutes. Stated differently, "a claim for wrongful discharge under Bowman cannot succeed unless the plaintiff identifies a *Virginia* statute establishing a public policy which was violated by the defendant in terminating the plaintiff." **Shomo v. Junior Corporation, 2012 U.S. Dist. LEXIS 76463, *19 (W.D. Va. June 1, 2012) (emphasis in original) (employee could not base Bowman claim on public policy embedded in the federal Constitution)**; Doss v. Jamco, Inc., 254 Va. 362, 367 n.3, 492 S.E.2d 441 (1997) (employee must be able to identify a Virginia statute establishing the public policy violated by the employer); Leverton v.Allied Signal, Inc., 991 F. Supp. 486, 490 (E.D. Va. 1998) (same). The statute upon which a plaintiff relies must expressly confer rights or duties upon the employee or other similarly situated employee of the employer. **Therefore, an employee terminated for her refusal to have an abortion could not state a Bowman claim based on Virginia's statutes restricting abortion because those statutes were intended to protect unborn children, not pregnant women. Shomo, 2012 U.S. Dist. LEXIS 76463, *17–18. Moreover, where an employee asserts a Bowman claim based on refusal to engage in a criminal act, the conduct must fit the precise definition and scope of the relevant criminal statute's prohibition. See id. at *15–17; Sewell v. Wells Fargo Bank, N.A., 2012 U.S.**

Dist. LEXIS 9376, *14–15 (W.D. Va. Jan. 27, 2012) (signing documents certifying that supervisees had falsified bank records did not fit within the scope of statutes prohibiting grand larceny, embezzlement, or falsifying bank records). Virginia does not recognize a generalized, common-law "whistleblower" retaliatory discharge claim as an exception to the employment at-will doctrine. Dray v. New Market Poultry Products, Inc., 258 Va. 187, 191, 518 S.E.2d 312, 313 (1999). The Virginia Human Rights Act ("VHRA"), Virginia Code Sections 2.2-3900 *et seq.*, prohibits various forms of discrimination that mirror, in large part, Title VII of the Civil Rights Act of 1964, 42 U.S.C. Sections 2000e, *et seq.*, and sets forth the public policy of Virginia regarding the discrimination prohibited therein. However, Section 2.2-2639(D) (formerly § 2.1-725(D)) of the VHRA prohibits any common law cause of action for wrongful discharge based on the policies reflected in the VHRA, regardless of whether that policy is articulated elsewhere. Conner v. National Pest Control Assoc., Inc., 257 Va. 286, 513 S.E.2d 398 (1999); Doss v. Jamco, Inc., 254 Va. 362, 492 S.E.2d 441 (1997); **see also Shomo, 2012 U.S. Dist. LEXIS 7643, *20–21 (employee could not state a Bowman claim based on the theory that her employer fired her on the basis of her religious convictions because freedom from religious discrimination is a policy reflected in the VHRA).** Section 2.2-2639(D) does not prohibit a common law cause of action for wrongful discharge based on public policies not reflected in the VHRA even though the underlying conduct might also violate a public policy that are reflected in the VHRA. Mitchem v. Counts, 259 Va. 179, 523 S.E.2d 246 (2000) (allowing a claim for wrongful discharge in violation of the public policy embodied in the Virginia statutes prohibiting fornication and lewd and lascivious behavior because those, public policies not reflected in the VHRA, when a woman alleged she was discharged for refusing to engage in a sexual affair with her supervisor). Unless otherwise required by statute, a plaintiff asserting a cause of action for wrongful termination under Bowman must only prove by a preponderance of the evidence that the discharge occurred because of factors that violate Virginia's public policy. A plaintiff is not required to prove that the employer's improper motive was the sole cause of the wrongful termination, or that "but for" the employee's protected activity, the employee would not have been terminated. Virginia has not presently adopted or considered application of the "mixed-motive" causation standard for wrongful discharge claims. Shaw v. Titan Corp., 255 Va. 535, 498 S.E.2d 696 (1998); Cooley v. Tyson Foods, Inc., 257 Va. 518, 514 S.E.2d 770 (1999) (statute required employee to prove that but for the employee's protected activity, the employee would not have been terminated).

Insulting Words Statute. Virginia Code Section 8.01-45 is known as the "insulting words" statute and provides an individual a cause of action when a person is addressed with insulting words "which from their usual construction and common acceptance are construed as insults and tend to violence and breach of the peace." "An action for insulting words ... is treated precisely as an action for slander or libel, for words actionable *per se*, with one exception, namely, no publication is necessary. The trial of an action for insulting words is completely assimilated to the common law action for libel or slander, and from the standpoint of the Virginia law it is an action for libel or slander." Carwile v. Richmond Newspapers, Inc., 196 Va. 1, 6-7, 82 S.E.2d 588, 591 (1954). In addition to the publication distinction, an action under the insulting words statute will not lie unless the insult tends to violence and breach of the peace. Allen & Rocks, Inc. v. Dowell, 252 Va. 439, 477 S.E.2d 741 (1996) (former employer's statements to prospective employers about plaintiff's job performance did not tend to violence or breach of the peace); Trail v. General Dynamics Armament & Tech. Prods., 697 F. Supp. 2d 654, 658 (W.D. Va. 2010) (denying Fed. R. Civ. P. 12(b)(6) motion to dismiss claim under § 8.01-45 because "a reasonable fact finder could infer that the mass distribution of the erroneous newspaper article and Green's termination letter constituted statements that could lead to violence."). **The plaintiff need not show that violence actually resulted; rather, the statement merely must objectively tend to provoke violence. Beaseley v. Consolidated Coal Co., 2012 U.S. Dist. LEXIS 81472, *15–16 (W.D. Va. June 13, 2012). For instance, false accusations of a crime, particularly a dangerous one, tend to provoke violence. Id. (accusing an underground coal miner of smoking in the mine, thereby endangering his co-workers' lives, fit within the statute).** The insulting words statute does not require that the words be uttered in a face -to-face confrontation. Trail, 697 F. Supp. 2d at 658-659. Defamation is a private cause of action. See Guide Publishing Co. v. Futrell, 175 Va. 77, 85, 7 S.E.2d 133, 137 (1940). Accordingly, the General Assembly did not promulgate in the "insulting words" statute any underlying Virginia public policy for Bowman purposes, but rather a policy for individual protection. See Pacquette v. Nestle USA, Inc., 2007 U.S. Dist. LEXIS 33448, *19 (W.D. Va. May 7, 2007) (dismissing Bowman wrongful termination claim premised on insulting words statute because the statute only concerns conduct between private individuals).

B. Elements of Libel Claim

1. ***Basic Elements.*** Unlike other states, Virginia makes no distinction between actions for libel and those for slander. Fleming v. Moore, 221 Va. 884, 889, 275 S.E.2d 632, 635 (1981); Jackson v. Hartig, 274 Va. 219, 228, 645 S.E.2d 303, 310 (Va. 2007) ("Virginia law allows a person who has been the subject of libel or slander to bring a cause of action for defamation.") (citation omitted). In general, under Virginia law the necessary elements of the tort of defamation are (1) publication about the plaintiff, (2) an actionable statement, and (3) the requisite intent. Jordan v. Kollman, 269 Va. 569, 575, 612 S.E.2d 203, 206 (2005); Chapin v. Greve, 787 F. Supp. 557, 562 (E.D. Va. 1992), aff'd, Chapin v. Knight-Ridder, Inc., 993 F.2d 1087, 1092 (4th Cir. 1993). An "actionable statement" is one that is both false and defamatory. Id. (citation omitted); Soo Choi v. Kyu Chul Lee, 312 Fed. Appx. 551, 553 (4th Cir. 2009) (citation omitted) (holding that trial

court abused its discretion by failing to instruct the jury that an actionable statement must be defamatory in addition to being false). A statement is defamatory if it "tends to so harm the reputation of another as to lower him in the estimation of the community or to deter third persons from associating or dealing with him," Soo Choi, 312 Fed. Appx. at 553, or if it renders him odious, contemptible, or ridiculous. Chaffin v. Lynch, 83 Va. 106, 1 S.E. 803 (1887). Merely offensive or unpleasant statements are not defamatory. Chapin v. Knight-Ridder, Inc., 993 F.2d 1087, 1092 (4th Cir. 1993); see also Marroquin v. Exxon Mobil Corp., 2009 U.S. Dist. LEXIS 44834, *23 (E.D. Va. May 27, 2009) (holding that statements that plaintiff had been terminated for doing "something very bad" and that plaintiff's dealings with a co-sponsor were "inappropriate" and "improper" were not defamatory because "[w]hile perhaps upsetting to Plaintiff, he is not able to show that these mild assessments of his termination diminished his reputation to anyone."). Whether a statement is capable of a defamatory construction is a question for the Court. Yeagle v. Collegiate Times, 255 Va. 293, 296, 497 S.E.2d 136, 138 (1998). In determining whether words are capable of a defamatory construction, they will be taken in their ordinary sense and plain import, and as they would be generally understood. Carwile v. Richmond Newspapers, Inc., 196 Va. 1, 7, 82 S.E.2d 588, 591 -592 (1954); see also Verrinder v. Rite Aid Corp., 2006 U.S. Dist. LEXIS 53385, *5-6 (W.D. Va. Aug. 2, 2006) (claim that employee-pharmacist "violated HIPPA" did not rise to the level of offensiveness needed to qualify as defamatory under Virginia law); Vaile v. Willick, 2008 U.S. Dist. LEXIS 5111, *7-8 (W.D. Va. Jan. 24, 2008) (plain and ordinary meaning of claim that plaintiff was found "guilty" of charges is that plaintiff was convicted of criminal charges, not that he was found liable in a civil lawsuit); **Nigro v. Virginia Commonwealth University/Medical College of Virginia, 2012 U.S. App. LEXIS 12862, *21–22 (4th Cir. June 21, 2012) (statements to the effect that a medical resident still had much to learn as a resident were not defamatory because the very purpose of residency is to provide training). Statements may be defamatory by inference, implication, insinuation, and context; moreover, surrounding circumstances can render otherwise harmless statements defamatory. Sewell v. Wells Fargo Bank, N.A., 2012 U.S. Dist. LEXIS 9376, *17–18 (W.D. Jan. 27, 2012) (employer bank's statements that employee was terminated for "not following procedure" and "because of money" were defamatory because listeners could have inferred that she was fired for dishonesty). Nevertheless, "[w]hile every fair inference in a pleading may be used to determine whether the words complained of are capable of a meaning ascribed by innuendo, inference cannot extend the statements, by innuendo, beyond what would be the ordinary and common acceptance of a statement." Yeagle, 255 Va. at 297, 497 S.E.2d at 138. Therefore, a plaintiff alleging that inclusion of her photograph with an identifying caption in a negative newspaper article about her son constituted defamation failed to state a claim. Compton v. Foster, 82 Va. Cir. 279 (Russell Cir. Ct. 2011). The plaintiff's construction of the statements extended well beyond ordinary and common acceptance and was unreasonable as a matter of law. Id.**

An action under the insulting words statute, Virginia Code Section 8.01-45, is treated as an action for defamation, except that the insulting words statute does not require publication of the defamatory statement to a third party. Carwile v. Richmond Newspapers, Inc., 196 Va. 1, 6-7, 82 S.E.2d 588, 591 (1954); Weist v. E-Fense, Inc., 356 F. Supp. 2d. 604, 608 (E.D. Va. 2005) (quoting Potomac Valve & Fitting v. Crawford Fitting Co., 829 F.2d 1280, 1284 (4th Cir. 1987)); Jarrett v. Goldman, 67 Va. Cir. 361, 379 (Portsmouth Cir. Ct. May 31, 2005). Additionally, proof of provocation is necessary to sustain a cause of action for insulting words, Allen & Rocks, Inc. v. Dowell, 252 Va. 439, 477 S.E.2d 741, 742-43 (1996) (holding that to recover under the insulting words statute, proponent must show that the words used tend to violence and a breach of the peace), but a face-to-face confrontation is not required. Trail v. General Dynamics Armament & Tech. Prods., 697 F. Supp. 2d 654, 658-59 (W.D. Va. 2010).

Virginia distinguishes words defamatory per se from words defamatory per quod. Although actual damages are presumed in an action for defamation per se, and the plaintiff need not present evidence of damages, the jury's verdict must still bear a rational relationship to the underlying facts of the case. Cretella v. Kuzminski, 640 F. Supp. 2d 741, 757 (E.D. Va. 2009) (evidence of actual damages becomes important for purposes of a remittitur analysis). For words defamatory per quod, special damages must be pleaded and proved. Fleming v. Moore, 221 Va. 884, 894, 275 S.E.2d 632, 639 (1981); Carwile v. Richmond Newspapers, Inc., 196 Va. 1, 6, 82 S.E.2d 588, 591 (1954). Words actionable per se fall into four categories: (1) words that impute to a person the commission of some criminal offense involving moral turpitude, by which the person, if the charge is true, may be indicted and punished; (2) words that impute to a person infection with a contagious disease, which, if true, would exclude the person from society; (3) words that impute to a person unfitness to perform the duties of an office or employment for profit, or want of integrity in the discharge of such duties; (4) words that prejudice a person in his or her profession or trade. Fleming v. Moore, 221 Va. at 889, 275 S.E.2d at 635. Category (1) is satisfied if the words impute commission of an offense punishable by confinement in a penal institution. Schnupp v. Smith, 249 Va. 353, 360, 457 S.E.2d 42, 46 (1995). Fleming v. Moore appears to have broadened substantially the types of loss that will constitute special damage.

Prior to the court's decision in Fleming, a long line of Virginia cases had recognized that in actions to recover for words not defamatory per se, special damages had to be both pleaded and proved. See, e.g., Shupe v. Rose's Stores, 213 Va. at 375-76, 192 S.E.2d at 767; Carwile v. Richmond Newspapers, Inc., 196 Va. at 7, 82 S.E.2d at 591; M.

Rosenberg and Sons v. Craft, 182 Va. 512, 518, 29 S.E.2d 375, 378 (1944). While in these cases there was little discussion of what actually constituted "special damage," it seemed clear that emotional upset and embarrassment did not. See, e.g., Shupe v. Rose's Stores, 213 Va. at 375-76, 192 S.E.2d at 767; Connelly v. Western Union Tel. Co., 100 Va. 51, 54, 40 S.E. 618, 619 (1902). In Fleming, the court stated that: "'Special damages' which under the common-law rule must be shown as a prerequisite to recovery where the defamatory words are not actionable per se, are not to be limited to pecuniary loss." 221 Va. at 894, 275 S.E.2d at 639. Since no reason is given for this expansion of the actionability of defamatory words, it arguably resulted from an inadvertent confusion of "actual damages" with "special damages". See R. Sack and S. Baron, Libel, Slander, and Related Problems 148 (2d ed. 1994). Whatever the cause for the radical change, three cases decided after Fleming have repeated this broad definition of special damages. See Sateren v. Montgomery Ward & Co., Inc., 234 Va. 303, 362 S.E.2d 324 (1987); The Gazette, Inc. v. Harris, 229 Va. 1, 13, 325 S.E.2d 713, 723, 11 Media L. Rep. 1609, 1613, cert. denied, 472 U.S. 1032 and 473 U.S. 905 (1985); Great Coastal Express, Inc. v. Ellington, 230 Va. 142, 334 S.E.2d 846, 12 Media L. Rep. 1100, 1103-04 (1985).

2. ***Fault.*** Although, depending on the facts of a particular case, the rules of defamation are sometimes discussed in terms of media and non-media defendants, see, e.g., Jackson v. Hartig, 274 Va. 219, 645 S.E.2d 303, 308 (2007), Union of Needletrades, Indus. & Textile Emples. v. Jones, 268 Va. 512, 519, 603 S.E.2d 920, 924 (2004) and WJLA-TV v. Levin, 264 Va. 140, 155, 564 S.E.2d 383, 391-392 (2002), the Supreme Court of Virginia has treated media and nonmedia defendants alike. See The Gazette, Inc. v. Harris, 229 Va. 1, 17, 325 S.E.2d 713, 726, 11 Media L. Rep. 1609, 1615, cert. denied, 472 U.S. 1032 and 473 U.S. 905 (1985); Great Coastal Express, Inc. v. Ellington, 230 Va. 142, 150, 334 S.E.2d 846, 852, 12 Media L. Rep. 1100, 1103 (1985). Instead of focusing on the status of the defendant, "[t]he requisite intent a plaintiff must prove in a defamation action depends upon the plaintiff's status as a public or private figure and the damages sought." Jordan v. Kollman, 269 Va. 569, 578, 612 S.E.2d 203, 207 (2005).

a. **Private Figure Plaintiff/Matter of Public Concern.** In defamation actions by private plaintiffs based on statements regarding matters of public concern, the plaintiff must prove "actual malice" to recover presumed or punitive damages. See, e.g., WJLA-TV v. Levin, 264 Va. 140, 155, 564 S.E.2d 383, 391-392 (2002) (holding that "where a private individual alleges defamation by a news-media defendant involving a matter of public concern, presumed damages cannot be awarded in the absence of actual malice."); Shenandoah Publishing House, Inc. v. Gunter, 245 Va. 320, 324, 427 S.E.2d 370, 372 (1993) (articles headlined "Lawyer's office searched for stolen items," and "Lawyer escapes having to produce confidential file" were held to report matters of public concern); Newspaper Publishing Corp. v. Burke, 216 Va. 800, 803, 224 S.E.2d 132, 135 (1976) (published statements suggesting that doctors were treating improperly "heavily sedated," i.e., brain damaged, babies involved a statement of public concern). However, where the defamatory statement makes substantial danger to reputation apparent, a private individual must only prove negligence to recover actual, compensatory damages for defamatory statements concerning matters of public concern. The Gazette, Inc. v. Harris, 229 Va. 1, 325 S.E.2d 713, 11 Media L. Rep. 1609, cert. denied, 472 U.S. 1032 and 473 U.S. 905 (1985).

b. **Private Figure Plaintiff/Matter of Private Concern.** In The Gazette, Inc. v. Harris, 229 Va. 1, 325 S.E.2d 713, 11 Media L. Rep. 1609, cert. denied, 472 U.S. 1032 and 473 U.S. 905 (1985), the Supreme Court of Virginia held that a negligence standard governs private figure defamation cases seeking an award of compensatory damages where the words uttered make substantial danger to reputation apparent. Where substantial danger to reputation is not apparent, a determination that is to be made by the trial court, actual malice must be proved by clear and convincing evidence. Id. at 15, 325 S.E.2d at 725, 11 Media L. Rep. at 1614. For cases in which a trial court, using an objective standard, evaluated whether substantial danger to reputation would have been apparent to a reasonable and prudent editor using ordinary care, see McCleary v. Keesling, 29 Va. Cir. 527, 527-28 (Fauquier Cir. Ct. December 1, 1992) (not apparent) and Rush v. Worrell Enterprises, 21 Va. Cir. 203, 209 (Charlottesville Cir. Ct. September 10, 1990) (apparent). In Harris, the court did not explain whether it was adopting a reasonable man or a reasonable editor standard. In Great Coastal Express, Inc. v. Ellington, 230 Va. 142, 151, 334 S.E.2d 846, 852, 12 Media L. Rep. 1100, 1103-04 (1985), the Virginia Supreme Court held that in a suit brought by a private individual it would "not, as a matter of state law, apply to speech actionable per se, involving no matters of public concern, the Gertz rule inhibiting presumed compensatory damages," but would continue to require "proof of New York Times malice for the recovery of punitive damages in all cases." (allegation of commercial bribery not a matter of public concern).

c. **Public Figure Plaintiff/Matter of Public Concern.** It appears that Virginia courts will apply the public figure/official doctrine conservatively, requiring a high threshold of public activity by the plaintiff. See, e.g., Fleming v. Moore, 221 Va. 884, 275 S.E.2d 632, 7 Media L. Rep. 1313 (1981); Chapin v. Knight-Ridder, Inc., 993 F.2d 1087, 1092 n.4, 21 Media L. Rep. 1449, 1450 n.4 (4th Cir. 1993); Reuber v. Food Chemical News, Inc., 925 F.2d 703, 18 Media L. Rep. 1689 (4th Cir.), cert. denied, 501 U.S. 1212 (1991); National Foundation for Cancer Research, Inc. v. Council of Better Business Bureaus, Inc., 705 F.2d 98, 9 Media L. Rep. 1915 (4th Cir.), cert. denied, 464 U.S. 830 (1983); Fitzgerald v. Penthouse, 691 F.2d 666, 8 Media L. Rep. 2340 (4th Cir. 1982), cert. denied, 460 U.S. 1024 (1983); Arctic Co. v. Loudoun Times-Mirror, 624 F.2d 518, 6 Media L. Rep. 1433 (4th Cir. 1980), cert. denied, 449 U.S. 1102 (1981); Freedlander v. Eden

Broadcasting, Inc., 734 F. Supp. 221, 17 Media L. Rep. 1659 (E.D. Va. 1990), aff'd, 923 F.2d 848 (1991); but see Massey Energy Co. v. UMWA, AFL-CIO, CLC, et al., 34 Media L. Rep. 2517, 2006 Va. Cir. LEXIS 129, *10 (Fairfax Cir. Ct. Aug. 4, 2006) (observing that "[a]lthough public-figure status requires that one has assumed a role of special prominence in the public controversy, prominence is not equivalent to general notoriety.") (citing Reuber v. Food Chemical News, Inc., 925 F.2d 703, 709 (4th Cir. 1991)). In Richmond Newspapers Inc. v. Lipscomb, 234 Va. 277, 362 S.E.2d 32, 14 Media L. Rep. 1953, 1955-57 (1987), cert. denied, 486 U.S. 1023 (1988), an English teacher and acting department head of a public high school was held not to be a public official. In Fleming v. Moore, supra, the Virginia Supreme Court, applying the standard under Gertz, found that a public college professor at the University of Virginia did not occupy a position of "such persuasive power and influence" that he could be deemed a public figure "for all purposes." 221 Va. at 891-92, 275 S.E.2d at 637, 7 Media L. Rep. 1313. The Virginia Supreme Court has not yet considered the public figure/official standards applicable to corporations, but the Fourth Circuit considers the same factors applicable to individuals in determining whether corporations were public or private figures. See, e.g., New Life Ctr., Inc. v. Fessio, 2000 U.S. App. LEXIS 20894, *24, 28 Media L. Rep. 2249 (4th Cir. August 16, 2000); National Foundation for Cancer Research, Inc., supra, 705 F.2d 98, 9 Media L. Rep. 915; Arctic Co., supra, 624 F.2d 518, 6 Media L. Rep. 1433. In Blue Ridge Bank v. Veribanc, Inc., 866 F.2d 681, 688-89 16 Media L. Rep. 1122 (4th Cir. 1989), the Fourth Circuit refused to classify a bank as a public figure, and, citing that case, has refused to so classify American Cyanamid, finding an absence of public controversy, Mylan Pharmaceuticals, Inc. v. American Cyanamid Co., 1995 U.S. App. LEXIS 4197, *9, 23 Media L. Rep. 1748 (4th Cir. March 3, 1995), cert. denied sub nom. McKnight v. American Cyanamid Co., 133 L. Ed. 2d 194 (1995). The Fourth Circuit also has held that persons publicly accused of serious sexual misconduct punishable by imprisonment cannot be deemed limited purpose public figures merely because they make reasonable public replies to the accusations, Foretich v. Capital Cities/ABC, Inc., 37 F.3d 1541, 1558, 22 Media L. Rep. 2353, 2367 (4th Cir. 1994), even where "some of their public statements were probably intended (at least in part) to influence the outcome . . . of the legislative debate in Congress," id. at 1563, 22 Media L. Rep. at 2371-72. But in Carr v. Forbes, Inc., 259 F.3d 273 (4th Cir. 2001), cert. denied, 535 U.S. 988 (2002), the Fourth Circuit found a developer of privately financed, public projects to be a limited purpose public figure because the public projects met the public controversy element and the plaintiff's substantial personal involvement in the public projects reflected an attempt to influence the outcome of the controversy, and, therefore, the plaintiff had voluntarily assumed a role of special prominence in a public controversy. Id. at 279-81. The determination of whether a party is a public figure or public official is a matter of law to be decided by the court, see, Fleming v. Moore, 221 Va. 884, 275 S.E.2d 632, 7 Media L. Rep. 138 (1981); Fitzgerald v. Penthouse, 639 F.2d 1076, 1080, 6 Media L. Rep. 2447, 2450 (4th Cir. 1981), cert. denied, 460 U.S. 1024 (1983); Ryan v. Brooks, 634 F.2d 726, 728 n.2, 6 Media L. Rep. 2155, 2156 n.2 (4th Cir. 1980), as is the determination of whether the words make substantial danger to reputation apparent, The Gazette, Inc. v. Harris, 229 Va. 1, 15, 325 S.E.2d 713, 725, 11 Media L. Rep. 1609, 1618, cert. denied, 472 U.S. 1032 and 473 U.S. 905 (1985).

3. ***Falsity.*** In every defamation action, the burden is on the plaintiff to prove that the alleged defamatory statement is false. Jordan v. Kollman, 269 Va. 569, 576, 612 S.E.2d 203, 207 (2005); Union of Needletrades, Indus. & Textile Emples. v. Jones, 268 Va. 512, 520, 603 S.E.2d 920, 924 (2004). Truth, however, is a complete defense to any defamation claim, including one under the insulting words statute. Alexandria Gazette Corp. v. West, 198 Va. 154, 159, 93 S.E.2d 274, 279 (1956); Spencer v. Am. Int'l Group, Inc., 2009 U.S. Dist. LEXIS 457, *16-17 (E.D. Va. Jan. 6, 2009) ("Because a defamatory statement must be false to be actionable and the facts alleged in the Complaint fail to support any plausible conclusion that the statement alleged in Paragraph 48(a) was false, the statement cannot form the basis of Plaintiff's defamation claim."); Cummings v. Moore, 2009 U.S. Dist. LEXIS 5093 (E.D. Va. Jan. 26, 2009), aff'd, 326 Fed. Appx. 162 (4th Cir. 2009), cert. denied, 130 S. Ct. 559, 560 (U.S. 2009), reh'g denied, 130 S. Ct. 1169 (U.S. 2010) (statement in letter to state court judge stating that the former employer had not lifted its ban on the plaintiff's entry onto the employer's campus was true and thus not actionable). Pleadings which do not allege the statements were false, only "without lawful justification," does not satisfy the pleadings standard needed to survive a 12(b)(6) motion to dismiss. Bates v. Strawbridge Studios, Inc., 2011 U.S. Dist. LEXIS 52442, *6-8 (W.D. Va. 2011). Slight inaccuracies of expression are immaterial provided the defamatory charge is true in substance, and it is sufficient to show that the imputation is "substantially true." Saleeby v. Free Press, Inc., 197 Va. 761, 763, 91 S.E. 2d 405, 407 (1956). "Substantially true" means that the statement is a fair and accurate description of the event in question. PBM Prods., LLC v. Mead Johnson Nutrition Co., 678 F. Supp. 2d 390, 400-01 (E.D. Va. 2009) (allegation that plaintiff had "lied" was substantially true because false advertising is "substantially synonymous" with lying). Absent an unequivocal admission by the plaintiff that the allegedly defamatory statement is true, whether the statement is false is a factual question to be resolved by the jury. Hyland v. Raytheon Tech. Servs. Co., 277 Va. 40, 48, 670 S.E.2d 746, 752 (Va. 2009); Soo Choi v. Kyu Chul Lee, 312 Fed. Appx. 551, 553 (4th Cir. 2009).

Where the defendant's state of mind is at issue and the plaintiff must prove some form of malice, the defendant may offer as evidence of good faith matter tending to prove the truth of the subject statements, even though truth has not been pleaded. See Rosenberg v. Mason, 157 Va. 215, 160 S.E. 190 (1931), overruled in part by The Gazette, Inc. v. Harris, 229 Va. 1, 8, 325 S.E.2d 713, 720, 11 Media L. Rep. 1609, cert. denied, 472 U.S. 1032 and 473 U.S. 905 (1985). If the defendant pleads and fails to prove the truth, such failure cannot be used as evidence of common-law malice unless the defendant had no basis for entering the plea. See Snyder v. Fatherly, 153 Va. 762, 765-7, 151 S.E. 149, 150 (1930). False statements made in reliance on the public record are privileged as long as the publication represents a "fair and substantially correct" restatement of the public record. Alexandria Gazette Corp. v. West, 198 Va. 154, 159-160, 93 S.E.2d 274, 279 (1956); Wiest v. E-Fense, Inc., 356 F. Supp. 2d 604, 609 (E.D. Va. 2005).

4. ***Defamatory Statement of Fact.*** While it is firmly established that "pure expressions of opinion" are protected, and therefore cannot form the basis for a defamation action, see II.B.2, infra, factual statements made to support or justify an opinion can form the basis for an action for defamation. Williams v. Garraghty, 249 Va. 224, 233, 455 S.E.2d 209, 215 (1995), cert. denied, 516 U.S. 814 (1995) (a charge of sexual harassment may be mere opinion, but statements supporting such a charge are factual in nature); Raytheon Tech. Servs. Co. v. Hyland, 273 Va. 292, 641 S.E.2d 84, 91 (2007) (expressions of opinion in employee review based on statements that can be proven true or false). The Virginia Supreme Court has held that a jury may determine whether statements of opinion "laden with factual content" are defamatory statements of fact about the plaintiff. Richmond Newspapers, Inc. v. Lipscomb, 234 Va. 277, 297-98, 362 S.E.2d 32, 43, 14 Media L. Rep. 1953, 1962 (1987), cert denied, 486 U.S. 1023 (1988). Under the circumstances of a labor dispute, the words "cocksucker" and "motherfucker" were held not to support liability under Virginia's insulting words statute because they could not be reasonably understood to convey a false representation of fact. Crawford v. United Steel Workers, AFL-CIO, 230 Va. 217, 234-35, 335 S.E.2d 828, 838-39 (1985); see also Jarrett v. Goldman, 67 Va. Cir. 361, 381-82 (Portsmouth Cir. Ct. May 31, 2005) (holding that calling someone "stupid" in conjunction with "motherfucker" cannot be understood to convey a false representation that the plaintiff lacked normal mental capacity). Calling the plaintiff a racist, on the other hand, has been viewed as defamatory. Fleming v. Moore, 221 Va. 884, 275 S.E.2d 632, 7 Media L. Rep. 1313 (1981). Milkovich v. Lorain Journal Co., 497 U.S. 1 (1990), has been cited by the Virginia Supreme Court in support of the principle that speech which does not contain a provably false factual connotation, or statements which cannot reasonably be interpreted as stating actual facts about a person, are statements of opinion that cannot form the basis of a common law defamation action. Yeagle v. Collegiate Times, 255 Va. 293, 497 S.E.2d 136 (1998) (words "Director of Butt Licking" cannot be understood to convey a false representation of fact). **Statements that an employee is "incompetent," has an "apathetic/ disinterested approach," has "poor time management," or has shown no improvement with respect to problems have been held to constitute nonactionable opinion. Nigro v. Virgnia Commonwealth University/Medical College of Virginia, 2012 U.S. App. LEXIS 12862, *19–20 (4th Cir. June 21, 2012); Kebaish v. Inova Health Case Services, 2012 Va. Cir. LEXIS 62, *6–7 (Fairfax Cir. Ct. June 25, 2012). Similarly, a statement that an employer was "very, very disappointed" in the quality of an employee's work was opinion because disappointment is inherently relative and solely contingent on the speaker's internal view point. Cook, Heyward, Hopper, & Feehan, P.C. v. Trump Virginia Acquisitions LLC, 2012 U.S. Dist. LEXIS 72065, *15 (E.D. Va. May 23, 2012). Courts have also held that where a party discloses detailed facts for the basis of his or her opinion, allowing the reader or listener to ascribe his or her own interpretation of the facts, the statement is more properly characterized as an opinion. Cummings v. Addison, No. CL11-510, slip op. at 5–6 (Norfolk Cir. Ct. Feb. 24, 2012).** Whether an alleged defamatory statement is one of fact or of opinion is a question of law to be resolved by the trial court. Raytheon Tech. Servs. Co. v. Hyland, 273 Va. 292, 641 S.E.2d at 91.

5. ***Of and Concerning Plaintiff.*** In Virginia, a defamation plaintiff must show that the alleged defamation was published "of or concerning" the plaintiff. This test is met if the plaintiff shows, absent his mention by name, that the publication, in its description or identification, was such as to lead those persons who know the plaintiff to believe that the publication was intended to refer to the plaintiff. The Gazette Inc. v. Harris, 229 Va. 1, 37, 325 S.E.2d 713, 738, cert. denied, 472 U.S. 1032 and 473 U.S. 905 (1985). An article about child abuse that used a fictitious name to identify an allegedly abused child but gave the child's age, the approximate date of the incident, the hospital where the child was treated and the general nature of the injuries was held to be of and concerning the child's parents. The Gazette Inc. v. Harris, 229 Va. at 35-37, 325 S.E.2d at 737-39. Similarly, the Fourth Circuit has found that a series of newspaper columns about the federal investigation of letters laced with anthrax provided sufficient information for a reasonable reader to identify the plaintiff, despite the fact that the columns never explicitly stated the plaintiff's name. See Hatfill v. New York Times Co., 416 F.3d 320 (4th Cir. 2005), cert. denied, 547 U.S. 1040 (2006). In WJLA-TV v. Levin, 264 Va. 140, 564 S.E.2d 383 (2002), the Supreme Court of Virginia held that "statements or publications by the same defendant regarding one specific subject or event and made over a relatively short period of time, some of which clearly identify the plaintiff and others which do not, may be considered together for the purpose of establishing that the plaintiff was the person 'of or concerning' whom the alleged defamatory statements were made. This is so even where the publication identifying the plaintiff is made subsequent to those that do not identify him." Id. at 153, 564 S.E.2d at 390. **Where a news program's allegedly defamatory statements concerned a particular tax preparation company, the company president failed to plead facts demonstrating that the statements could be imputed to him; rather, the news program's statements referred to tax preparers in general. Hanks v. WAVY Broadcasting, 2012 U.S. Dist. LEXIS 15729, *16–21 (E.D. Va. Feb. 8, 2012).**

6. ***Publication.*** To prove a statement actionable as defamation, the plaintiff must show that the communication was published to a third person. Montgomery Ward Co. v. Nance, 165 Va. 363, 378-79, 182 S.E. 264, 270 (1935). However, proof of publication is not necessary to properly plead an action for insulting words under Virginia Code Section 8.01-45, which provides that "[a]ll words shall be actionable which from their usual construction and common acceptance are construed as insults and tend to violence and breach of the peace." An action under the statute is treated "precisely as an action for slander or libel for words actionable per se, with one exception, namely, no publication is necessary." Carwile v. Richmond Newspapers, Inc., 196 Va. 1, 6, 82 S.E.2d 588, 591 (1954). Publication sufficient to sustain common-law defamation is uttering the slanderous words to some third person so as to be heard and understood by such person. Thalhimer Bros., Inc. v. Shaw, 156 Va. 863, 871, 159 S.E. 87, 90 (Va. 1931). In order to establish prima facie evidence of publication, a plaintiff is not required to present testimony from a third party regarding what that person heard and understood, or to identify the person to whom the defamatory words were published. Instead, a plaintiff may prove publication of defamatory remarks by either direct or circumstantial evidence that the remarks were heard by a third party who understood these remarks as referring to the plaintiff in a defamatory sense. Food Lion v. Melton, 250 Va. 144, 151, 458 S.E.2d 580, 585 (1995).

a. **Intracorporate Communication.** "Communication of [allegedly defamatory] statements to an employee required to transcribe or transmit the communication containing the defamatory statements is not a publication to a third party" that will support a cause of action for defamation. Larimore v. Blaylock, 259 Va. 568, 575, 528 S.E.2d 119, 122-23 (2000). This rule or privilege "applies broadly to all statements related to 'employment matters,' provided the parties to the communication have a duty or interest in the subject matter." Echten-Kamp v. Loudon Co. Public Schs., 263 F. Supp. 2d 1043, 1061 (E.D. Va. 2003). Notwithstanding, the privilege is qualified and may be lost if the defamatory words are spoken with common-law malice. Id. An allegation that the allegedly defamatory statements were made out of "hatred, ill will, or a desire to hurt the plaintiff" is sufficient to overcome a Fed. R. Civ. P. 12(b)(6) motion to dismiss based on the qualified privilege. Nigro v. Va. Commonwealth Univ. Med. College of Va., 2010 U.S. Dist. LEXIS 56229, 41-42 (W.D. Va. June 4, 2010). Furthermore, where a plaintiff makes a bare allegation of publication to other persons outside the corporation, "without specifying who 'others' were, the defendants have no ability to respond with a defense. The pleading is then fatally deficient." Loria v. Regelson, 38 Va. Cir. 283, 285 (Richmond Cir. Ct. December 26, 1995) (citing Hines v. Gravins, 136 Va. 313, 318, 112 S.E. 869, 870 (1922)). **Where a complaint fails to allege that an employer's allegedly defamatory statements were communicated to other employees who did not have a duty or authority to receive the communication, it fails to state a claim for defamation. Tomlin v. IBM, Corp., 2012 Va. Cir. LEXIS 26, *16 (Fairfax Cir. Ct. Feb. 13, 2012). Similarly, where a plaintiff fails to allege that his employer either read his termination letter out loud or circulated it to those outside the scope of the privilege, he fails to state a claim. Jafari v. The Old Dominion Transit Management Company, 462 Fed. Appx. 385, 390–91 (4th Cir. 2012).**

b. **Compelled Self-Publication.** It appears that a compelled publication by a plaintiff in an action for defamation is not a substitute for the requirement that a defendant publish the defamatory words to a third person. Cybermotion, Inc. v. Vedcorp, L.C., 41 Va. Cir. 348, 348-49 (Salem Cir. Ct. February 3, 1997) (citing Davis v. Heflin, 130 Va. 169, 172, 107 S.E. 673, 674 (1921)). The Fourth Circuit, in a case applying Maryland law, has determined that the theory of self-publication has not gained widespread acceptance, and refused to adopt this theory in the case before the court. DeLeon v. St. Joseph Hosp., Inc., 871 F.2d 1229 (4th Cir. 1989); see also Pacquette v. Nestle USA, Inc., 2007 U.S. Dist. LEXIS 33448, *26-27 (W.D. Va. May 7, 2007) ("The publication element of defamation cannot be met by compelled self-publication in Virginia."); **Ortiz v. Panera Bread Company, 2011 U.S. Dist. LEXIS 85463, *14 (E.D. Va. Aug. 2, 2011) ("Plaintiff's claim that he has been forced to defame himself is insufficient to support the publication requirement of a defamation claim.")**

c. **Republication.** "It is well settled that the author or originator of a defamation is liable for a republication or repetition thereof by third persons, provided it is the natural and probable consequence of his act, or he has presumptively or actually authorized or directed its republication." Weaver v. Beneficial Finance Co., 199 Va. 196, 199, 98 S.E.2d 687, 690 (1957). In addition, the party that repeats the defamatory comments will be liable for defamation as he has adopted the defamer's words as his own. Lee v. Dong-A Ilbo, 849 F.2d 876, 878 (4th Cir. 1988), cert. denied, 489 U.S. 1067 and 489 U.S. 1067 (1989). Liability for republication of the writings of others has been recognized by the Virginia Supreme Court, see Story v. Newspapers, Inc., 202 Va. 588, 118 S.E.2d 668 (1961); Ewell v. Boutwell, 138 Va. 402, 121 S.E. 912 (1924), and by the Fourth Circuit, see Blue Ridge Bank v. Veribanc, Inc., 866 F.2d 681, 16 Media L. Rep. 1122 (4th Cir. 1989). Actual damages are recoverable from employers for statements made by employees within the scope of their employment. See Slaughter v. Valleydale Packers, Inc., 198 Va. 339, 343-44, 94 S.E.2d 260, 263-64 (1956); Thalhimer Bros. v. Shaw, 156 Va. 863, 875-79, 159 S.E. 87, 92-93 (1931); Jordan v. Melville Shoe Corp., 150 Va. 101, 104-05, 142 S.E. 387, 387-88 (1928); W. T. Grant Co. v. Owens, 149 Va. 906, 913, 141 S.E. 860, 862-63 (1928). Punitive damages are recoverable only upon showing that the defamatory statements were authorized or ratified by the employer. See Id.

7. ***Statements versus Conduct.*** If conduct is actionable in Virginia, it is only when accompanied by statements that impute allegations of conduct or character that are defamatory. See, e.g., Zayre, Inc. v. Gowdy, 207 Va. 47, 147 S.E.2d 710 (1966).

8. ***Damages.*** The terms "actual damages" and "compensatory damages" are synonymous, and include all damages other than punitive damages. News Leader Co. v. Kocen, 173 Va. 95, 108, 3 S.E.2d 385, 391 (1939). Compensatory damages are allowed as recompense for the injury actually received, and include compensation for insult, pain, humiliation, mental suffering, injury to reputation and the like. Weatherford v. Birchett, 158 Va. 741, 746-47, 164 S.E. 535, 537 (1932). Special damages are a class of compensatory damages which, although a natural and probable consequence of the defamation, are not assumed to be necessary or inevitable, and must be shown by allegation and proof. Slaughter v. Valleydale Packers, Inc., 198 Va. 339, 346, 94 S.E.2d 260, 266 (1956). Compensatory damages, both general and special, are recoverable in all cases upon proof of actual injury. Fleming v. Moore, 221 Va. 884, 894, 275 S.E.2d 632, 638-39, 7 Media L. Rep. 1313, 1317-18 (1981). Where the defamation is per se actionable, compensatory damages are presumed. Great Coastal Express, Inc. v. Ellington, 230 Va. 142, 151, 334 S.E.2d 846, 852, 12 Media L. Rep. 1100, 1103-04 (1985). Although actual damages are presumed in an action for defamation per se, and the plaintiff need not present evidence of damages, the jury's verdict must still bear a rational relationship to the underlying facts of the case. Cretella v. Kuzminski, 640 F. Supp. 2d 741, 757 (E.D. Va. 2009) (evidence of actual damages becomes important for purposes of a remittitur analysis). An instruction on nominal damages apparently is permitted where there is no evidence of any particular amount of loss, News Leader Co. v. Kocen, 173 Va. 95, 107-08, 3 S.E.2d 385, 392 (1939), but is not required where there is no instruction inviting the jury to award "substantial" actual damages. The Gazette v. Harris, 229 Va. 1, 25, 32, 325 S.E.2d 713, 731, 735, 11 Media L. Rep. 1609, 1620, 1623, cert. denied, 472 U.S. 1032 and 473 U.S. 905 (1985). Generally speaking, "one with an unblemished reputation is entitled to more damages when subjected to defamatory statements than one whose reputation is 'little hurt' by the statements." Poulston v. Rock, 251 Va. 254, 262, 467 S.E.2d 479, 483 (1996).

a. **Presumed Damages and Libel Per Se.** In an action brought by a private individual for defamatory words involving no matters of public concern, if the published words are determined by the trial judge to be actionable per se, compensatory damages are presumed. Great Coastal Express, Inc. v. Ellington, 230 Va. 142, 151, 334 S.E.2d 846, 852, 12 Media L. Rep. 1100, 1103-04 (1985) (applying Dun & Bradstreet, Inc. v. Greenmoss Builders, Inc., 472 U.S. 749 (1985)). **Accordingly, where a former employee proves that an employer's statement falsely imputes to her unfitness to perform the duties of her employment, the employee need not prove that the statement proximately caused damage to her reputation. Askew v. Collins, 283 Va. 482, 485, 486, 722 S.E.2d 249, 251 (2012).**

(1) **Employment-Related Criticism.** Statements that criticize an employee's conduct, or assert terminable offenses, do not constitute defamation per se unless they constitute (1) words that impute to a person the commission of some criminal offense involving moral turpitude, by which the person, if the charge is true, may be indicted and punished; (2) words that impute to a person infection with a contagious disease, which, if true, would exclude the person from society; (3) words that impute to a person unfitness to perform the duties of an office or employment of profit, or want of integrity in the discharge of such duties; (4) words that prejudice a person in his or her profession or trade. Fleming v. Moore, 221 Va. 884, 889, 275 S.E.2d 632, 635 (1981). Hence, stating that an employee was fired for unsatisfactory job performance does not constitute defamation per se because "allegations of unsatisfactory job performance do not in and of themselves so harm [the employee's] reputation as to lower him in the estimation of the community or deter third persons from associating or dealing with him." McBride v. City of Roanoke Redev. & Housing Auth., 871 F. Supp. 885, 892 (W.D. Va. 1994), aff'd, 78 F.3d 579 (4th Cir. 1996); see also Marroquin v. Exxon Mobil Corp., 2009 U.S. Dist. LEXIS 44834, *23 (E.D. Va. May 27, 2009) (holding that statements that plaintiff had been terminated for doing "something very bad" and that plaintiff's dealings with a co-sponsor were "inappropriate" and "improper" were not defamatory because "[w]hile perhaps upsetting to Plaintiff, he is not able to show that these mild assessments of his termination diminished his reputation to anyone."). Furthermore, there must be a nexus between the content of the defamatory statement and the skills or character required to carry out the particular occupation of the plaintiff. Fleming v. Moore, supra, 221 Va. at 890, 275 S.E.2d at 636. Thus, because an attorney is required to adhere to the disciplinary rules, charging an attorney with unethical conduct is defamatory per se. Id.; see also Oberbroeckling v. Lyle, 234 Va. 373, 379, 362 S.E.2d 682 (1987) (holding that a memorandum accusing plaintiff of "mismanagement of funds" was defamatory because it implied that plaintiff was unfit to perform the duties of his employment or lacked integrity or was dishonest in performing them); but see Spencer v. Am. Int'l Group, Inc., 2009 U.S. Dist. LEXIS 457, *20-21 (E.D. Va. Jan. 6, 2009) ("Not every statement that reflects poorly on one's ability to practice law constitutes defamation per se."). Also, statements that a restaurant employee gave away liquor and food to friends may be defamatory *per se* because they imply embezzlement or larceny. Lemond v. Viamac, Inc., 57 Va. Cir. 25, 27-28 (Roanoke Cir. Ct. June 4, 2001).

(2) **Single Instance Rule.** No reported cases.

b. **Punitive Damages.** In all cases, the plaintiff must prove New York Times v. Sullivan malice to recover punitive damages. Great Coastal Express, Inc. v. Ellington, 230 Va. 142, 151, 334 S.E.2d 846, 852, 12 Media L. Rep. 1100, 1103-04 (1985); Fleming v. Moore, 221 Va. 884, 893, 275 S.E.2d 632, 638, 7 Media L. Rep. 1313, 1317 (1981). However, it is not necessary for a jury to intend an award to be punitive in order for it to be treated as such. A trial court recently held in a defamation case that a $10 million award was effectively punitive regardless of whether the jury so intended it to be, and accordingly, it reduced the award to $1 million. Sheckler v. Virginia Broadcasting Corp., 63 Va. Cir. 368, 379 (Charlottesville Cir. Ct. November 7, 2003). If the defamation is actionable per se, an award of compensatory damages is not necessary to support an award of punitive damages. Newspaper Publishing Corp. v. Burke, 216 Va. 800, 805, 224 S.E.2d 132, 136 (1976). The total amount awarded for punitive damages cannot exceed $350,000. Virginia Code § 8.01-38.1.

II. PRIVILEGES AND DEFENSES

A. Scope of Privileges

Privileges can be either absolute, meaning no suit can be brought for the statement at issue, or qualified, meaning suit can be maintained only upon a showing of common law malice.

1. ***Absolute Privilege.*** Virginia recognizes as absolutely privileged statements made in the course of judicial proceedings, so long as they are pertinent and relevant to the subject matter of the proceeding. Lindeman v. Lesnick, 268 Va. 532, 537, 604 S.E.2d 55, 58 (2004). The reason for the rule of absolute privilege in judicial proceedings is to encourage unrestricted speech in litigation, and because of the safeguards that exist in judicial proceedings, including liability for perjury and the applicability of the rules of evidence. Id. Judicial proceedings have been defined broadly, and are "not restricted to trials of civil actions or indictments, but . . . [include] every proceeding before a competent court or magistrate in the due course of law or the administration of justice which is to result in any determination or action of such court or officer." Darnell v. Davis, 190 Va. 701, 707, 58 S.E.2d 68, 71 (1950) (citing 53 C.J.S. Libel & Slander § 104 at 16). Watt v. McKelvie, 219 Va. 645, 248 S.E.2d 826, 4 Media L. Rep. 1781 (1978); Penick v. Ratcliffe, 149 Va. 618, 627-28, 140 S.E. 664, 667 (1927); Donohoe Construction Co., Inc. v. Mount Vernon Assocs., 235 Va. 531, 369 S.E.2d 857 (1988). **Accordingly, the absolute privilege extended to a draft complaint circulated among potential defendants for settlement purposes because the statement was made preliminary to a proposed proceeding, was related to a proceeding contemplated in good faith and under serious consideration, and was disclosed to interested parties. Mansfield v. Bernabei, 284 Va. 116, 121–26, 727 S.E.2d 69, 73–75 (2012); see also Cummings v. Addison, No. CL11-510, slip op. at 6 –15 (Norfolk Cir. Ct. Feb. 24, 2012).** The privilege also extends to quasi-judicial proceedings governed by safeguards that surround a judicial proceeding, an area that has recently seen increased litigation. See Elder v. Holland, 208 Va. 15, 155 S.E.2d 369 (1967) (administrative proceedings of state agencies exercising quasi-judicial functions may serve as the basis for a claim of absolute privilege); Lindeman v. Lesnick, 268 Va. 532, 537-38, 604 S.E.2d 55, 58 (2004) (Certain proceedings before the Virginia Workers' Compensation Commission "involve a quasi-judicial body contemplated by the privilege because the Commission, upon receipt of evidence submitted under penalty of perjury, resolves facts and legal disputes falling within its statutory authority between parties who seek to have their disputes over workers' compensation issues resolved by that body."); Moore v. PYA Monarch, LLC, 238 F.Supp.2d 724 (E.D. Va. 2002) (holding that statements made during Virginia Employment Commission hearing for unemployment compensation are privileged); Shabazz v. PYA Monarch, LLC, 271 F. Supp. 2d 797, 802-803 (E.D. Va. 2003) (statements made to Virginia Employment Commission in response to former employee's allegations of wrongful discharge and to EEOC in response to charge of discrimination are absolutely privileged); Katz v. Odin, Feldman & Pittleman, P.C., 332 F. Supp. 2d 909, 920 (E.D. Va. 2004) ("The attributes of fee arbitrations are sufficiently similar to judicial proceedings such that there is a firm basis for applying the absolute privilege in the arbitration context."); Shestul v. Moeser, 344 F. Supp. 2d 946, 951 (E.D. Va. 2004) ("[A]n absolute privilege should attach to any statements made to the Board of Bar Examiners in connection with an applicant to the Virginia bar. Although there seem to be no Virginia cases on point, the court agrees with other jurisdictions that have afforded such a privilege to these communications."); Martin v. Watkins, 2011 U.S. Dist. LEXIS 22463, *10 (W.D. Va. Mar. 3, 2011) ("Statements made in the course of, or in connection with grievance or arbitration procedures conducted pursuant to collective bargaining agreements are generally privileged under the law of defamation.") (citations omitted). But see Lockheed Information Management Systems Co. v. Maximus, Inc., 259 Va. 92, 524 S.E.2d 420 (2000) (holding that a bid protest proceeding does not have sufficient judicial safeguards to qualify as a basis for the absolute privilege defense). The absolute privilege applies to the proceedings of a legislative body, but only when the body is acting in its legislative capacity, not in its supervisory or administrative capacity. Isle of Wight County v. Nogiec, 281 Va. 140, 704 S.E. 2d 83 (2011). **At least one court has rejected the assertion that all reports to law enforcement are absolutely privileged under Virginia law. Beasley v. Consolidated Coal Co., 2012 U.S. Dist. LEXIS 81472, *9–10 (W.D. Va. June 13, 2012) (holding that statements made to the Virginia Department of Mines, Minerals, and Energy outside of quasi-judicial proceedings were not entitled to absolute privilege).**

2. ***Qualified Privileges.*** Stated broadly, Virginia courts will recognize a qualified privilege "where the author or publisher of the alleged slander acted in the bona fide discharge of a public or private duty, legal or moral, or in the prosecution of his own rights or interests" or in regard to "anything said or written by a master in giving the character of a servant who has been in his employment." Williams Printing Co. v. Sanders, 113 Va. 156, 176, 73 S.E. 472, 476 (1912); see Penick v. Ratcliffe, 149 Va. 618, 140 S.E. 664 (1927). However, the issue of privilege is not available on demurrer, especially when it is clear that the publication is not entitled to an absolute privilege. Cashion v. Smith, 2010 Va. Cir. LEXIS 240, *7 (Roanoke Cir. Ct. December 8, 2010). In The Gazette, Inc. v. Harris, 229 Va. 1, 18, 325 S.E.2d 713, 727, 11 Media L. Rep. 1609, 1616, cert. denied, 472 U.S. 1032 and 473 U.S. 905 (1985), the court held that the common-law privileges remain a defense in Virginia in addition to the defense provided by the requirement that the plaintiff prove fault. To defeat a qualified privilege, the plaintiff must prove either that the statements were made with common-law malice (which includes, but is not limited to, New York Times v. Sullivan malice) or that the privilege was otherwise exceeded. E.g., Smalls v. Wright, 241 Va. 52, 399 S.E.2d 805 (1991); Great Coastal Express, Inc. v. Ellington, 230 Va. 142, 334 S.E.2d 846, 12 Media L. Rep. 1100 (1985); Preston v. Land, 220 Va. 118, 120-21, 255 S.E.2d 509, 511 (1979); Crawford & Co. v. Graves, 199 Va. 495, 498-99, 100 S.E.2d 714, 716-17 (1957). This proof must be by clear and convincing evidence. Smalls v. Wright, 241 Va. at 55, 399 S.E.2d at 808; see Schnupp v. Smith, 249 Va. 353, 365, 457 S.E.2d 42, 48-49 (1995); Jarrett v. Goldman, 67 Va. Cir. 361 (Portsmouth Cir. Ct. May 31, 2005). Transmissions of defamatory statements between members of a corporate entity are presumed to be made without malice, and are entitled to qualified privilege. Larimore v. Blaylock, 259 Va. 568, 528 S.E.2d 119 (2000). "This privilege is lost if defamatory statements are communicated to third parties who have no duty or interest in the subject matter, even if those third parties are fellow employees." Id. at 575, 528 S.E.2d at 122. **Where a complaint fails to allege that an employer's allegedly defamatory statements were communicated to other employees who did not have a duty or authority to receive the communication, it fails to state a claim. Tomlin v. IBM, Corp., 2012 Va. Cir. LEXIS 26, *16 (Fairfax Cir. Ct. Feb. 13, 2012).** Additionally, a corporate employer may be liable for compensatory and punitive damages for a qualifiedly privileged defamatory communication by its agent if the agent's malicious conduct either was authorized by the principal or subsequently ratified by it. Oberbroeckling v. Lyle, 234 Va. 373, 382, 362 S.E.2d 682, 687 (1987). A qualified privilege applied to statements made in a report to a county Board of Supervisors acting in its non-legislative, supervisory capacity about museum repairs. Isle of Wight County v. Nogiec, 281 Va. 140, 704 S.E.2d 83 (2011).

The following sections of the Virginia Code create privileges under certain circumstances: 8.01-47 (school personnel reporting on alcohol or drug abuse); 8.01-49 (broadcast by radio or television station of statements made by another); 17.1-914 (filing papers and giving testimony before Judicial Inquiry and Review Commission); 38.2-618 (disclosure of personal or privileged information to an insurance institution, agent, or insurance-support organization); 38.2-2212(G) (statements made within context of cancellation or nonrenewal of insurance policy); 54.1-3908 (statements made by lawyer or law firm concerning the professional conduct of any member of the bar of Virginia before any bar association or committee thereof).

a. **Common Interest.** Where the existence of the privilege is based upon an interest or duty on the part of the speaker, the statement is qualifiedly privileged "if made to a person having a corresponding interest or duty." Taylor v. Grace, 166 Va. 138, 144, 184 S.E. 211, 213 (1936). "[C]ommunications between persons with corresponding interests or duties, whether legal, moral, or social, if made in good faith, are qualifiedly privileged." Dwyer v. Smith, 867 F.2d 184, 195 (4th Cir. 1989). Comments by an employer to his employees and other interested persons concerning the reason for the discharge of an employee are privileged. Kroger Company v. Young, 210 Va. 564, 172 S.E.2d 720 (1970); Peoples Life Ins. Co. v. Talley, 166 Va. 464, 168 S.E. 42 (1936); Chesapeake Ferry Co. v. Hudgins, 155 Va. 874, 156 S.E. 429 (1931). An employee does not have a common, corresponding duty or interest in the termination of an employee of a different company, even if the terminated employee's duties brought him in contact with the other company. Suarez v. Loomis Armored US, LLC, 2010 U.S. Dist. LEXIS 129335, *8-9 (E.D. Va. December 7, 2010). **Employees generally have an interest in ensuring that fellow employees follow the employer's rules; therefore, statements to management or other employees about misconduct are generally privileged in the absence of malice. See Nigro v. Virgnia Commonwealth University/Medical College of Virginia, 2012 U.S. App. LEXIS 12862, *22–24 (4th Cir. June 21, 2012).**

b. **Duty.** Where a defendant acts in performance of a duty, legal or social, or in defense of his own interests, the occasion is privileged. Chalkley v. Atlantic Coast Line R. Co., 150 Va. 301, 143 S.E. 631 (1928). Thus, for example, responses by bank employees to questions by investigating police officers are subject to a qualified privilege. Marsh v. Commercial and Savings Bank, 265 F. Supp. 614, 621 (W.D. Va. 1967). An employee does not have a common, corresponding duty or interest in the termination of an employee of a different company, even if the terminated employee's duties brought him in contact with the other company. Suarez v. Loomis Armored US, LLC, 2010 U.S. Dist. LEXIS 129335, *8-9 (E.D. Va. December 7, 2010). Therefore, the qualified privilege does not apply. Id.

c. **Criticism of Public Employee.** Virginia has not recognized any privilege peculiar to statements regarding public employees. Public employees are treated in all respects the same as private employees, subject to the same analysis of whether they are public or private figures, and determination of whether the comments were made in a context that gives rise to a qualified or absolute privilege. See, e.g., Richmond Newspapers, Inc. v. Lipscomb, 234 Va. 277,

362 S.E.2d 32, 14 Media L. Rep. 1953 (1987), cert. denied, 486 U.S. 1023 (1988); Elder v. Holland, 208 Va. 15, 55 S.E.2d 369 (1967).

d. **Limitation on Qualified Privileges.**

(1) **Constitutional or Actual Malice.** Virginia law treats New York Times malice as being subsumed by common law malice. Great Coastal Express, Inc. v. Ellington, 230 Va. 142, 149 n.3, 334 S.E.2d 846, 851 n.3 (1985). To defeat a qualified privilege, the plaintiff must prove by clear and convincing evidence that the statements were made with common-law malice (which includes, but is not limited to, New York Times v. Sullivan malice). See, e.g., Smalls v. Wright, 241 Va. 52, 399 S.E.2d 805 (1991); Great Coastal Express. Inc. v. Ellington, 230 Va. 142, 334 S.E.2d 846, 12 Media L. Rep. 1100 (1985); Taylor v. CNA Corp., 2010 U.S. Dist. LEXIS 89475, *51 (E.D. Va. August 27, 2010). Such a showing is sufficient to overcome a qualified privilege. Ellington, 230 Va. at 155, 334 S.E.2d at 854. Where a jury found actual malice, the court held that the "failure to instruct the jury on qualified privilege was harmless error because the privilege would have been lost upon the jury's finding of actual malice." Government Micro Resources, Inc. v. Jackson, 271 Va. 29, 44, 624 S.E.2d 63, 71 (2006).

(2) **Common Law Malice.** This malice in the context of defamation is "malice in fact, actual malice, existing at the time the words were spoken" and includes "wanton or willful disregard of the rights of the plaintiff." Preston v. Land, 220 Va. 118, 120, 255 S.E.2d 509, 511 (1979). It is "behavior actuated by motives of personal spite, or ill-will, independent of the occasion on which the communication was made." The Gazette, Inc. v. Harris, 229 Va. 1, 18, 325 S.E.2d 713, 727, cert. denied, 472 U.S. 1032 and 473 U.S. 905 (1985). Statements and conduct by the defendant after an allegedly defamatory utterance are probative to show malice. Oberbroeckling v. Lyle, 234 Va. 373, 380, 362 S.E.2d 682, 687 (1987). A showing of common law malice will defeat a qualified privilege. Preston v. Land, 220 Va. 118, 120-21, 255 S.E.2d 509, 511 (1979). However, the malice must be shown on the part of the speaker, not an individual who gives the speaker the information to make the allegedly defamatory statement. Nigro v. Virginia Commonwealth University Medical College of Va., 2010 U.S. Dist. LEXIS 123939, *49 (W.D. Va. November 23, 2010). An allegation that the allegedly defamatory statements were made out of "hatred, ill will, or a desire to hurt the plaintiff" is sufficient to overcome a Fed. R. Civ. P. 12(b)(6) motion to dismiss based on the qualified privilege. Nigro v. Va. Commonwealth Univ. Med. College of Va., 2010 U.S. Dist. LEXIS 56229, 41-42 (W.D. Va. June 4, 2010). **An employee cannot overcome the qualified privilege for statements made by her employer during the course of an investigation into the employee's misconduct when the employer's investigation was sufficiently thorough and had a logical basis. Shaheen v. The Wellpoint Companies, Inc., 2012 U.S. App. LEXIS 16236, *10–12 (4th Cir. Aug. 3, 2012). To survive a motion to dismiss on the grounds of qualified privilege, an employee cannot simply allege malice in a conclusory fashion but, rather, must specifically allege underlying facts showing that the defamatory statement was actuated by a corrupt motive. Tomlin v. International Business Machines Corporation, 2012 Va. Cir. LEXIS 26, *16–18 (Fairfax Cir. Ct. Feb. 13, 2012). Where, however, an employee shows that he had a history of conflict with an employer, that the employer waited six days to report the alleged misconduct, and that the details of his story changed over time, the employee has presented sufficient evidence to create a genuine issue of material fact as to malice and thereby survive summary judgment. Beasley v. Consolidated Coal Company, 2012 U.S. Dist. LEXIS 81472, *11–12 (W.D. Va. June 13, 2012).**

(3) **Other Limitations on Qualified Privileges.** None.

e. **Question of Fact or Law.** The determination of whether statements are privileged is a question of law for the court, whereas the determination of whether a privilege is abused is generally for the jury to decide. See, e.g., Bragg v. Elmore, 152 Va. 312, 147 S.E. 275 (1928); Fuste v. Riverside Healthcare Ass'n, 265 Va. 127, 135, 575 S.E.2d 858, 863 (2003).

f. **Burden of Proof.** The burden is on plaintiff to prove facts defeating a privilege, e.g., Preston v. Land, 220 Va. 118, 120-21, 255 S.E.2d 509, 511 (1979); Crawford and Co. v. Graves, 199 Va. 495, 498-99, 100 S.E.2d 714, 716-17 (1957), and such proof must be by clear and convincing evidence, Great Coastal Express, Inc. v. Ellington, 230 Va. 142, 334 S.E.2d 846, 12 Media L. Rep. 1100 (1985); see Schnupp v. Smith, 249 Va. 353, 365, 457 S.E.2d 42, 48-49 (1995). "Clear and convincing evidence is that degree of proof which produces in the mind of the trier of facts a firm belief or conviction upon the allegations sought to be established." Oberbroeckling v. Lyle, 234 Va. 373, 379, 362 S.E.2d 682, 685 (1987). This level of proof is required where New York Times malice must be shown, see Great Coastal Express, Inc. v. Ellington, 230 Va. at 152, 334 S.E.2d at 853, 12 Media L. Rep. at 1104 (punitive damages), and where one seeks to defeat a qualified privilege. In Ryan v. Brooks, 634 F.2d 726, 6 Media L. Rep. 2155 (4th Cir. 1980), the Fourth Circuit recognized that the burden of proof as applied to the question of whether actual malice exists is a difficult one for plaintiffs to satisfy. Nevertheless, resolution of a credibility issue in favor of the plaintiff's testimony has satisfied the burden in a state court. Schnupp v. Smith, 249 Va. 353, 457 S.E.2d 42 (1995).

B. Standard Libel Defenses

1. ***Truth.*** A defamatory statement must be false in order to be actionable, as truth is recognized as an absolute defense to a libel action. See Spencer v. Am. Int'l Group, Inc., 2009 U.S. Dist. LEXIS 457, *16-17 (E.D. Va. Jan. 6, 2009) ("Because a defamatory statement must be false to be actionable and the facts alleged in the Complaint fail to support any plausible conclusion that the statement alleged in Paragraph 48(a) was false, the statement cannot form the basis of Plaintiff's defamation claim."); Chaplin v. Greve, 787 F. Supp. 557 (E.D. Va. 1992); Freedlander v. Edens Broadcasting, Inc., 734 F. Supp. 221 (E.D. Va. 1990). In determining whether allegedly defamatory statements are true or false, "it is not necessary to prove the literal truth of statements made. Slight inaccuracies of expression are immaterial provided the defamatory charge is true in substance, and it is sufficient to show that the imputation is "substantially true." Saleeby v. Free Press, 197 Va. 761, 763, 91 S.E.2d 405, 407 (1956). **A former employer's statement that an employee was terminated "after allegations were made that accused [him] of . . . violating investment related statutes, regulations, rules, or industry standards of conduct" was true because the underlying accusations pertained to banking. Whitaker v. Wells Fargo Advisors, LLC, 2011 U.S. Dist. 111938, *8–10 (E.D. Va. Sept. 29, 2011). Moreover, the employer's alleged mischaracterization of the underlying accusations as "investment-related" was immaterial in any case because the "gist" of the statement was substantially true. Id. at * 10–11.** "Substantially true" means that the statement is a fair and accurate description of the event in question. PBM Prods., LLC v. Mead Johnson Nutrition Co., 678 F. Supp. 2d 390, 400-01 (E.D. Va. 2009) (allegation that plaintiff had "lied" was substantially true because false advertising is "substantially synonymous" with lying). A plaintiff cannot combine the damaging nature of certain true statements with the falsity of other, immaterial statements in order to provide the basis for a defamation claim. See Chapin v. Greve, 787 F. Supp. 557, 563 (E.D. Va. 1992) (citing AIDS Counseling & Testing Centers v. Group W Television, Inc., 903 F.2d 1000, 17 Media L. Rep. 1893 (4th Cir. 1990)). Similarly, "a defendant in a defamation action may not introduce into evidence every bad act of the plaintiff for the purpose of showing substantial truth." Massey Energy Co. v. UMWA, AFL-CIO, CLC, et al., 72 Va. Cir. 54, 60, 34 Media L. Rep. 2517 (Fairfax Cir. Ct. Aug. 4, 2006) (citing Restatement (Second) of Torts § 581A, cmt f; James v. Powell, 154 Va. 96, 106-107, 152 S.E. 539, 543 (1930)). If the defendant pleads and fails to prove the truth, such failure cannot be used as evidence of common-law malice unless the defendant had no basis for entering the plea. See Snyder v. Fatherly, 153 Va. 762, 765-7, 151 S.E. 149, 150 (1930). Truth is no longer an affirmative defense, instead a plaintiff must prove falsity. See Gazette Inc. v. Harris, 229 Va. 1, 15, 325 S.E.2d 713, 725 (1985), cert. denied, 472 U.S. 1032, 473 U.S. 905 (1985).

2. ***Opinion.*** In Chaves v. Johnson, 230 Va. 112, 335 S.E.2d 97 (1985), the Supreme Court of Virginia recognized that "[p]ure expressions of opinion, not amounting to fighting words, cannot form the basis of an action for defamation." 230 Va. at 119, 335 S.E.2d at 101-02. The court explained that "the First Amendment to the federal constitution and Article 1, Section 12 of the Constitution of Virginia protect the 'right of the people to teach, preach, write or speak any such opinion, however ill-founded'. . . ." Id. The court did not discuss in any detail what kinds of statements constitute pure opinion, but held that words charging that an architect lacked experience and charged excessive fees were protected. The question is one of law to be decided by the court. Id. The court reaffirmed these principles in Williams v. Garraghty, 249 Va. 224, 455 S.E.2d 209, cert. denied, 133 L. Ed. 2d 28 (1995), where the factual statements supporting an opinion or charges of sexual harassment were held to form the basis for a defamation action, and more recently in American Communications Network, Inc. v. Williams, 264 Va. 336, 341, 568 S.E.2d 683, 686 (2002), where statements relating to a former employee's job performance were held to be either true or opinions as a matter of law, and in Raytheon Tech. Servs. Co. v. Hyland, 273 Va. 292, 641 S.E.2d 84, 90-92 (2007), where some statements in an employee's performance evaluation were found capable of supporting plaintiff's defamation claim and others were held to be opinion as a matter of law. The Fourth Circuit has also recognized that statements of opinion cannot constitute actionable defamation. See Blue Ridge Bank v. Veribanc, Inc., 866 F.2d 681, 16 Media L. Rep. 1122 (4th Cir. 1989); Potomac Valve & Fitting, Inc. v. Crawford Fitting Co., 829 F.2d 1280 (4th Cir. 1988); National Foundation for Cancer Research, Inc. v. Council of Better Business Bureaus, Inc., 705 F.2d 98, 9 Med L. Rep. 1915 (4th Cir.), cert. denied, 464 U.S. 830 (1983). The words held to be protected opinion in National Foundation for Cancer Research were that plaintiff, a corporation, did not spend "a reasonable percentage" of its income on program services. In Lapkoff v. Wilks, 969 F.2d 78 (4th Cir. 1992), the remark "personally, I wouldn't trust him as far as I can throw him" was held to be opinion as a relative statement completely dependent on the speaker's obvious bias. See also Jafari v. Old Dominion Transit Mgmt. Co., 2008 U.S. Dist. LEXIS 97037 (E.D. Va. Nov. 26, 2008) (statement at meeting that plaintiff's skills as a supervisor had "diminished" to the point that he had to be terminated was not actionable as a statement of opinion). No precise test for distinguishing fact from opinion has been adopted by the Virginia Supreme Court. However, the court has defined "opinion" as "'speech which does not contain a provably false factual connotation, or statements which cannot reasonably be interpreted as stating actual facts about a person cannot form the basis of a common law defamation action. Statements that are relative in nature and depend largely upon the speaker's viewpoint are expressions of opinion. Jordan v. Kollman, 269 Va. 569, 576, 612 S.E.2d 203, 206 (2005) (quoting Fuste v. Riverside Healthcare Ass'n, Inc., 265 Va. 127, 132-33, 575 S.E.2d 858, 861 (2003)). The Portsmouth Circuit Court has held that statements that a former employee "had screwed up" and "would screw up" his employment responsibilities were best characterized as statements of opinion that were not actionable. Jarrett v. Goldman, 67 Va. Cir. 361 (Portsmouth Cir. Ct. May 31, 2005). A Virginia trial

court has held that medical critiques are opinions, but the statement "you just euthanized my patient" is actionable. Cashion v. Smith, 2010 Va. Cir. LEXIS 240, *6 (Roanoke Cir. Ct. December 8, 2010). The Fourth Circuit Court of Appeals, relying on the analysis in Milkovich v. Lorain Journal Co., 497 U.S. 1 (1990), has held that tenor, language, and content can demonstrate that statements constitute subjective views that are nonactionable opinion. Biospherics Inc. v. Forbes, Inc., 151 F.3d 180, 26 Media L. Rep. 2114 (4th Cir. 1998). Context is also relevant. See Arthur v. Offit, 38 Media L. Rep. 1508, 2010 U.S. Dist. LEXIS 21946, *13-14 (E.D. Va. Mar. 10, 2010) (quoting Snyder v. Phelps, 580 F.3d 206, 219 (4th Cir. 2009)). The caption "Director of Butt Licking" beneath the photograph of an assistant to a college Vice President of Student Affairs has been held to be nonactionable rhetorical hyperbole. Yeagle v. Collegiate Times, 255 Va. 293, 497 S.E.2d 136 (1998). In Motsinger v. Kelly, 9 Va. Cir 9 (Danville Cir. Ct. August 12, 1985), a trial court found an accusation that plaintiff was "the ugliest man in Danville" to be a statement of opinion. **Statements that an employee is "incompetent," has an "apathetic/disinterested approach," has "poor time management," or has shown no improvement with respect to problems have been held nonactionable opinion. Nigro v. Virgnia Commonwealth University/Medical College of Virginia, 2012 U.S. App. LEXIS 12862, *19–20 (4th Cir. June 21, 2012); Kebaish v. Inova Health Case Services, 2012 Va. Cir. LEXIS 62, *6–7 (Fairfax Cir. Ct. June 25, 2012). Similarly, a statement that an employer was "very, very disappointed" in the quality of an employee's work was opinion because disappointment is inherently relative and solely contingent on the speaker's internal view point. Cook, Heyward, Hopper, & Feehan, P.C. v. Trump Virginia Acquisitions LLC, 2012 U.S. Dist. LEXIS 72065, *15 (E.D. Va. May 23, 2012).** While pure expressions of opinion are not actionable, "factual statements made to support or justify an opinion can form the basis of an action for defamation." Raytheon Tech. Servs. Co. v. Hyland, 273 Va. 292, 303, 641 S.E.2d 84, 91 (2007) (internal quotations omitted); see also Richmond Newspapers, Inc. v. Lipscomb, 234 Va. 277, 297-98, 362 S.E.2d 32, 43, 14 Media L. Rep. 1953, 1962 (1987), cert denied, 486 U.S. 1023 (1988) (holding that jury may determine whether statements of opinion "laden with factual content" are defamatory statements of fact about the plaintiff). Milkovich v. Lorain Journal Co., 497 U.S. 1 (1990), has been cited by the court in support of the principle that speech which does not contain a provably false factual connotation, or statements which cannot reasonably be interpreted as stating actual facts about a person, cannot form the basis of a common law defamation action. Yeagle v. Collegiate Times, 255 Va. 293, 497 S.E.2d 136 (1988). Whether words are opinion is to be decided by the court. Yeagle, 255 Va. at 296, 497 S.E.2d at 138 (1998); Chaves v. Johnson, 230 Va. 112, 119, 335 S.E.2d 97, 102 (1985).

3. ***Consent.*** Although Virginia has not expressly adopted a consent defense, it has protected as privileged communications made by an employer to a union official acting on the plaintiff's behalf, Kroger Co. v. Young, 210 Va. 564, 172 S.E.2d 720 (1970), and publishing defamatory material at the plaintiff's request to family members or friends. Id.; Chesapeake Ferry Co. v. Hudgins, 155 Va. 874, 156 S.E. 429 (1931). See also Kay v. Collins, 39 Va. Cir. 150 (Richmond Cir. Ct. April 9, 1996) (discussing consent as a possible defense but distinguishing facts from case relied on by defendant).

4. ***Mitigation.*** Evidence of bad character is admissible to diminish damages, since the pain, the mortification, the insult are usually in proportion to a person's good or bad reputation, and the effect of a bad reputation is to reduce the damage inflicted. Stubbs v. Cowden, 179 Va. 190, 200, 18 S.E.2d 275, 280 (1942). However, the purpose of admitting evidence of bad reputation is to diminish the damage, not to bar the action. Weatherford v. Birchett, 158 Va. 741, 747, 164 S.E. 535, 537 (1932). Publications may offer proof of all the circumstances of publication in mitigation of all but "actual pecuniary damages," Va. Code Ann. § 8.01-48, and all defendants may offer in mitigation an apology before suit, or if there was no opportunity before suit, at the earliest opportunity after suit is filed, Va. Code Ann. § 8.01-46.

III. RECURRING FACT PATTERNS

A. Statements in Personnel File

Statements to the employee regarding the reasons for discharge, including a termination letter in the employee's personnel file documenting such reasons, are qualifiedly privileged in the absence of malice. Southeastern Tidewater Opportunity Project, Inc. v. Bade, 246 Va. 273, 435 S.E.2d 131 (1993); Thalhimer Bros. v. Shaw, 156 Va. 863, 159 S.E. 87 (1931). **Similarly, other employees' statements regarding the employee's termination are privileged provided they are not communicated to others outside the scope of the privilege. Ortiz v. Panera Bread Company, 2011 U.S. Dist. LEXIS 85463, *11–14 (E.D. Va. Aug. 2, 2011); Tomlin v. International Business Machines Corporation, 2012 Va. Cir. LEXIS 26, *16–18 (Fairfax Cir. Ct. Feb. 13, 2012). An employee cannot overcome the qualified privilege for statements made by her employer during the course of an investigation of the employee's misconduct where the evidence shows that the investigation was sufficiently thorough and had a logical basis. Shaheen v. The Wellpoint Companies, Inc., 2012 U.S. App. LEXIS 16236, *10–12 (4th Cir. Aug. 3, 2012).**

B. Performance Evaluations

Criticisms or reports of an employee's performance are also qualifiedly privileged in the absence of malice. Oberbroeckling v. Lyle, 234 Va. 373, 362 S.E.2d 682 (1987); Loria v. Regelson, 38 Va. Cir. 283,1995 WL 1056054 (1995).

The privilege is also lost if the criticisms or reports are communicated to third parties who have no duty or interest in the subject matter, even if those third parties are fellow employees. Larimore v. Blaylock, 259 Va. 568, 575, 528 S.E.2d 119, 122-23 (2000). While opinions expressed in a performance evaluation are not actionable, factual statements made to support or justify an opinion can form the basis of an action for defamation. Raytheon Tech. Servs. Co. v. Hyland, 273 Va. 292, 641 S.E.2d 84, 90-92 (2007) (determining which statements in the subject performance evaluation were capable of supporting plaintiff's defamation claim).

C. References

Job references are subject to a qualified privilege if the words used do not transcend the privilege, i.e., relate only to the employee's employment with the defendant, and the words are used in good faith without actual malice, i.e., a belief by the employer that the statements are true, and the existence of reasonable grounds for such belief. Rosenberg v. Mason, 157 Va. 215, 160 S.E. 190 (1931).

D. Intracorporate Communication

"Communication of [allegedly defamatory] statements to an employee required to transcribe or transmit the communication containing the defamatory statements is not a publication to a third party" that will support a cause of action for defamation. Larimore v. Blaylock, 259 Va. 568, 575, 528 S.E.2d 119, 122-23 (2000). Where a plaintiff makes a bare allegation of publication to other persons outside the corporation, "without specifying who 'others' were, the defendants have no ability to respond with a defense. The pleading is then fatally deficient." Loria, 38 Va. at 285 (citing Hines v. Gravins, 136 Va. 313, 318, 112 S.E. 869, 870 (1922)). **Similarly, where a complaint fails to allege that an employer communicated the allegedly defamatory statements to other employees outside the scope of the intracorporate privilege, it fails to state a claim. Tomlin v. IBM, Corp., 2012 Va. Cir. LEXIS 26, *16 (Fairfax Cir. Ct. Feb. 13, 2012).**

E. Statements to Government Regulators

Statements before governmental administrators and officials will be afforded an absolute privilege if the communication was made in proceedings that are judicial or quasi-judicial in nature. Otherwise, the communication is entitled only to a qualified privilege. See Elder v. Holland, 208 Va. 15, 155 S.E.2d 369 (1967) (where they are sufficiently similar to judicial proceedings, administrative proceedings of state agencies exercising quasi-judicial functions may serve as the basis for a claim of absolute privilege). **See also Beasley v. Consolidated Coal Co., 2012 U.S. Dist. LEXIS 81472, * 9–10 (W.D. Va. June 13, 2012) (holding that statements made to the Virginia Department of Mines, Minerals, and Energy outside of quasi-judicial proceedings were not entitled to absolute privilege).** In addition, the following sections of the Virginia Code create privileges under certain circumstances: 8.01-47 (school personnel reporting on alcohol or drug abuse); 2.1-37.14 (filing papers and giving testimony before Judicial Inquiry and Review Commission); 54.1-3908 (statements made by lawyer or law firm concerning the professional conduct of any member of the bar of Virginia before any bar association or committee thereof).

F. Reports to Auditors and Insurers

The following sections of the Virginia Code create privileges under certain circumstances: 38.2-618 (disclosure of personal or privileged information to an insurance institution, agent, or insurance-support organization) See, e.g., Goddard v. Protective Life Corp., 82 F. Supp. 2d 545 (E.D. Va. 2000) (holding that this statute barred a patient's defamation claim against the medical laboratory that administered his HIV test when the lab transmitted his indeterminate results to an insurance organization); 38.2-2212(G) (statements made within context of cancellation or nonrenewal of insurance policy).

G. Vicarious Liability of Employers for Statements Made by Employees

1. ***Scope of Employment.*** Actual damages are recoverable from employers for statements made by employees within the scope of their employment, and which grow out of an act connected with the employment. See Slaughter v. Valleydale Packers, Inc. of Bristoe, 198 Va. 339, 343-44, 94 S.E.2d 260, 263-64 (1956); Thalhimer v. Shaw, 156 Va. 863, 875-79, 159 S.E. 87, 92-93 (1931); Jordan v. Melville Shoe Corp., 150 Va. 101, 104-05, 142 S.E. 387, 387-88 (1928); W. T. Grant Co. v. Owens, 149 Va. 906, 913, 141 S.E. 860, 862-63 (1928). A plaintiff establishes a prima facie case of vicarious liability by proving the existence of an employer-employee relationship. The burden of proving that the employee acted outside the scope of his employment then shifts to the employer. Mann v. Heckler & Koch Def., Inc., 2008 U.S. Dist. LEXIS 79126, *21 (E.D. Va. Oct. 7, 2008); see also Gina Chin & Assocs., Inc. v. First Union Bank, 260 Va. 533, 537 S.E.2d 573 (2000); Majorana v. Crown Cent. Petroleum Corp., 260 Va. 521, 539 S.E.2d 426 (2000). **Employees' statements regarding another employee's termination do not fall outside the scope of employment simply because the employer warned its employees not to discuss the topic. Sewell v. Wells Fargo Bank, N.A., 2012 U.S. Dist. LEXIS 9376, *19–20 (W.D. Va. Jan. 27, 2012).**

a. Blogging. McGeorge Camping Ctr., Inc. v. Affinity Group, Inc., 2008 U.S. Dist. LEXIS 18611 (E.D. Va. Mar. 11, 2008) arose in part out of an allegedly defamatory comment posted on a blog. In refusing to find that the plaintiff had fraudulently joined a defendant to defeat diversity jurisdiction, the trial court suggested that blog postings can give rise to an actionable defamation claim. Id. at *5-6 (noting that statements in posting were likely too "innocuous" to survive a Fed. R. Civ. P. 12(b)(6) motion to dismiss). Similarly, in Woody v. Carter, 77 Va. Cir. 198 (Montgomery Cir. Ct. 2008), the court sustained a demurrer to a defamation/fighting words claim arising from a blog posting, but only on the grounds that the complaint failed to identify the underlying statements other than in conclusory legal terms. Id. at 199.

2. ***Damages.*** In connection with a qualifiedly privileged communication, corporations may be liable for compensatory and punitive damages only upon showing that the defamatory statements were authorized or ratified by the employer. Oberbroeckling v. Lyle, 234 Va. 373, 362 S.E.2d 682 (1987); Sun Life Assurance Co. v. Bailey, 101 Va. 443, 44 S.E. 692 (1903).

H. Internal Investigations

Applying North Carolina law, the Fourth Circuit affirmed a district court's awarding of summary judgment to an employer on the grounds that the allegedly defamatory statements made during an internal investigation concerning sexual harassment were privileged. See Schult v. IBM, 2003 U.S. Dist. LEXIS 27159, *12-16 (W.D.N.C. October 30, 2003), aff'd, 123 Fed. Appx. 540 (4th Cir. (N.C.) 2004). **Applying Virginia law, the Fourth Circuit recently held that an employee cannot overcome the qualified privilege for statements made by her employer during the course of an investigation into her alleged misconduct where the evidence shows that the investigation was sufficiently thorough and had a logical basis. Shaheen v. The Wellpoint Companies, Inc., 2012 U.S. App. LEXIS 16236, *10–12 (4th Cir. Aug. 3, 2012). The privilege, however, may be overcome by a showing that the investigation originated as a result of malice. See Beasley v. Consolidated Coal Company, 2012 U.S. Dist. LEXIS 81472, *11–12 (W.D. Va. June 13, 2012).**

IV. OTHER ACTIONS BASED ON STATEMENTS

A. Negligent Hiring, Retention, and Supervision

1. ***Negligent Hiring.*** Virginia has long recognized the tort of negligent hiring when the employer is alleged to have placed a person in an employment situation involving an unreasonable risk of harm to others, and when the employer knew or should have known that the person was unfit for the job. Hott v. VDO Yazaki Corp., 922 F. Supp. 1114, 1129 (W.D. Va. 1996); J. v. Victory Tabernacle Baptist Church, 236 Va. 206, 208, 372 S.E.2d 391, 393 (1988); Doe v. Bruton Parish Church, 42 Va. Cir. 467 (1997). Virginia allows both claims for negligent hiring and *respondeat superior* to be alleged in the same action. Fairshter v. American Nat'l Red Cross, 322 F. Supp. 2d 646, 653-54 (E.D. Va. 2004). To prove negligent hiring, a plaintiff must show that an employee's propensity to cause injury to others was either known or should have been discovered by reasonable investigation. Majorana v. Crown Cent. Petroleum Corp., 260 Va. 521, 531, 539 S.E.2d 426, 431-432 (2000).

2. ***Negligent Retention and Supervision.*** Virginia recognizes the independent tort of negligent retention. Southeast Apartments Management, Inc. v. Jackman, 257 Va. 256, 260-61, 513 S.E.2d 395, 397 (1999). The cause of action is based on the principle that an employer is subject to liability for harm resulting from the employer's negligence in retaining a dangerous employee who the employer knows or should have known was dangerous to fellow employees, customers, guests or other third persons to whom the employer owes a duty of care. Id. Because such claims appear to require that the hired or retained employee have a record or history of behavior that is dangerous, so as to place others at risk of harm, it does not appear that defamation alone will suffice to establish such claims. However, offensive or discriminatory behavior may also form the basis for a claim of negligent retention. In Thompson v. Town of Front Royal, 117 F.Supp.2d 522, 531 (W.D.Va. 2000), the court held that a plaintiff who had suffered harassment, discrimination, and racial slurs from co -workers had produced sufficient evidence to support his claim for negligent retention. Thus, it appears that an employer may be liable where the employer "knew or should have known of an employee's offending conduct." Id. at 531. Such claims, if available for defamation by a co-employee, are not barred by the Virginia's Workers Compensation Act, since it cannot be said that the personal damages flowing from such conduct constitute injury by accident. Williams v. Garraghty, 249 Va. 224, 455 S.E.2d 209 (1995). However, there is disagreement among the courts as to whether an employee who is injured by a fellow employee has a claim for negligent retention. See Hazzis v. Modjadidi, 69 Va. Cir. 385, 390-91 (Norfolk Cir. Ct. December 19, 2005). Additionally, there is disagreement as to whether there must be an allegation and proof of physical injury in order to maintain a cause of action for negligent retention. Investors Title Ins. Co. v. Lawson, 68 Va. Cir. 337, 338 (Henry Cir. Ct. August 5, 2005).

In Chesapeake & Potomac Tel. Co. v. Dowdy, the Virginia Supreme Court held that "there is no duty of reasonable care imposed upon an employer in the supervision of its employees," but then seemingly limited its holding to the circumstances of that particular case. 235 Va. 55, 61, 365 S.E.2d 751, 754 (1988). Dowdy has led to inconsistent results among Virginia trial courts as to whether negligent supervision is actionable in Virginia. See Wolf v. Fauquier County Bd. of Supervisors, 2007 U.S. Dist. LEXIS 67362, *21-22 (E.D. Va. September 12, 2007), Millman v. Snyder, 65 Va. Cir. 62, 65 (Fairfax Cir. Ct. May 4, 2004) and Gilbertson v. Purdham, 78 Va. Cir. 295, 298 (Roanoke Cir. Ct. 2009) (discussing conflicting authority). In Kellermann v. McDonough, the Virginia Supreme Court held that when a parent relinquishes the supervision and care of a child to an adult who agrees to supervise and care for that child, the supervising adult must discharge that duty with reasonable care. 278 Va. 478, 487, 684 S.E.2d 786, 790 (2009).

B. Intentional Infliction of Emotional Distress

1. ***Elements.*** To plead a tort of intentional infliction of emotional distress, facts must be alleged to support four elements: The act causing the distress must be (1) intentional and reckless, and (2) outrageous and intolerable; there must be a (3) causal connection between the act and the distress, and (4) the emotional distress must be severe. Womack v. Eldridge, 215 Va. 338, 342, 210 S.E.2d 145, 148 (1974). Under the first prong, emotional distress must be the defendant's "specific purpose." Ely v. Whitlock, 238 Va. 670, 677, 385 S.E.2d 893, 897 (1989). Further, the conduct must be "beyond all possible bounds of decency, and to be regarded as atrocious and utterly intolerable in a civilized community." Russo v. White, 241 Va. 23, 27, 400 S.E.2d 160, 162 (1991). A claim does not lie for "mere insults, indignities, threats, annoyances, petty oppressions or other trivialities." Gaiters v. Lynn, 831 F.2d 51, 53 (4th Cir. 1987). Finally, "[b]ecause injury to the mind or emotions can be easily feigned, actions for intentional infliction of emotional distress are not favored in Virginia." Michael v. Sentara Health Sys., 939 F. Supp. 1220, 1233 (E.D. Va. 1996) (citing Ruth v. Fletcher, 237 Va. 366, 373, (1989). Such a claim fails in the absence of any objective, verifiable evidence of the plaintiff's severe emotional distress. Russo, 241 Va. at 28, 400 S.E.2d at 163.

The standard for negligent infliction of emotional distress is even more rigorous than the standard for intentional infliction of emotional distress. To survive a motion to dismiss in a claim for negligent infliction of emotional distress without physical impact, a plaintiff must plead that the conduct caused the plaintiff both emotional disturbance and physical injury. See Myseros v. Sissler, 239 Va. 8, 12, 387 S.E.2d 463 (1990); Hughes v. Moore, 214 Va. 27, 34, 197 S.E.2d 214 (1973). The plaintiff must put forth clear and convincing evidence of "symptoms" or "manifestations" of physical injury; symptoms of emotional disturbance alone provide no basis for recovery. Id. See also Michael, 939 F. Supp. at 1235.

2. ***Claims Based on Statements.*** In Russo, supra, a single parent failed in her claim against an acquaintance with whom she had been on one date, alleging that he had made over 340 "hang up" phone calls to her residence over a nine month period. The City of Fredericksburg Circuit Court has found that statements accusing a student of improper sexual relationships at a school - in fact, of rape - were not sufficiently outrageous where they were made after an investigation and in a context where the declarant had a duty to supervise its employees. Abrams v. Mary Washington College, 33 Va. Cir. 449 (Fredericksburg Cir. Ct. 1994). In Webb v. Baxter Healthcare Corp., 57 F.3d 1067 (4th Cir. 1995), the plaintiff alleged that a male supervisor's continuous gender-based ridicule and harassment of the plaintiff, who was the only female sales representative in the region, over a two-year period resulted in the plaintiff's hospitalization in a psychiatric hospital for depression and abuse of prescription drugs. Id. The Webb Court held that the defendant's conduct "may violate contemporary standards of appropriate behavior in the workplace, but we cannot label it an atrocity or 'utterly intolerable in a civilized society.'" Id.

C. Interference with Economic Advantage

1. ***Elements.*** Virginia recognizes the tort of interference with prospective economic advantage – a tort which includes within its ambit interference with prospective contract, business expectancy or a contract terminable at will, all of which are distinct from the tort of interference with a contract not terminable at will. To prove that a defendant wrongfully interfered with the plaintiff's prospective economic advantage, the plaintiff must prove (1) existence of a valid contractual relationship or business expectancy; (2) defendant's knowledge of the relationship or expectancy; (3) intentional interference (4) through improper methods that induced or caused a termination of the relationship or expectancy; and (5) resultant damage to the plaintiff's relationship or expectancy. See, e.g., Maximus, Inc. v. Lockheed Information Mgmt. Sys. Co., Inc., 254 Va. 408, 414, 493 S.E.2d 375, 378 (1997); Duggin v. Adams, 234 Va. 221, 226-27, 360 S.E.2d 832, 835-36 (1987); Smithfield Ham & Products Co. v. Portion PAC, Inc., 905 F. Supp. 346, 349 (E.D. Va. 1995). "Virginia law requires that a plaintiff plead a specific prospective economic advantage or business expectancy, and that a general expectancy . . . does not suffice." GEICO v. Google, No. 1:04CV507, 2004 U.S. Dist. LEXIS 18415, at *15 (E.D. Va. Aug. 25, 2004). Moreover, one cannot interfere with a contract that is not enforceable. Power Distribution, Inc. v. Emergency Power Engineering, Inc., 569 F. Supp. 54, 55-56, 58 (E.D. Va. 1983). Nor can one, or one's agents, interfere with one's own contracts. Fox v. Deese, 234 Va. 412, 427, 362 S.E.2d 699, 708 (1987); Ashco Int'l, Inc. v. Westmore Shopping Ctr. Assocs., 42 Va. Cir. 427, 1997 WL 1070624 (Fairfax Co. 1997); Ansari v. Pahlavi, 23 Va. Cir. 402, 1991 WL 834921 (Fairfax Co. 1991). Negligent interference is not actionable. See Philip Morris, Inc. v. Emerson, 235 Va. 380, 406-07, 368

S.E.2d 268, 282-83 (1988). That a defendant knows that an incidental effect of his conduct may be interference with plaintiff's prospective economic advantage is not sufficient; defendant must be motivated by a specific desire to interfere with plaintiff's advantage to be liable for this tort. Levine v. McLeskey, 881 F. Supp. 1030, 1055-56, (E.D. Va. 1995) aff'd in part, vacated in part on other grounds, 164 F.3d 210 (4th Cir. 1998) (E.D. Va. 1995). **Where a former employer's statements about an employee constitute the allegedly improper methods of interference, the plaintiff must allege that the statements were defamatory, illegal, independently tortious, or violated established standards of the profession. Whitaker v. WellsFargo Advisors, LLC, 2011 U.S. Dist. LEXIS 111938, * (E.D. Va. Sept. 29, 2011).** No cause of action arises where defendant's interference in plaintiff's prospective business arrangements is the result of lawful efforts to protect its own rights. See Thompson Everett, Inc. v. National Cable Advertising, 850 F. Supp. 470, 482 (E.D. Va. 1994). Virginia has recognized five affirmative defenses to claims for intentional interference with prospective economic advantage: (1) legitimate business competition; (2) financial self-interest; (3) responsibility for the welfare of a third party; (4) directing business policy; and (5) providing solicited advice. Chaves v. Johnson, 230 Va. 112, 121, 335 S.E.2d 97, 103 (1985); see also Maximus, 254 Va. at 415, 493 S.E.2d at 379; Commerce Funding Corp. v. Worldwide Sec. Services Corp., 249 F.3d 204, 210-214 (4th Cir. 2001). In addition, Virginia statutorily recognizes a claim for conspiracy to injure others in their reputation trade, business, or profession. Va. Code § 18.2-499. However, no conspiracy exists under this claim when damage to "professional reputation" is alleged. Buschi v. Kirven, 775 F.2d 1240, 1259 (4th Cir. 1985). The statute is aimed at conduct that injures a business and is to be construed to exclude employment from its scope. Id.; Loria v. Regelson, 38 Va. Cir. 283 (Richmond Cir. Ct. December 26, 1995).

2. ***Claims Based on Statements.*** "Improper" methods include those that are illegal or independently tortious, violence, threats, undue influence, misuse of confidential information, sharp dealing, overreaching, unfair competition or other conduct improper in the circumstances of the case. Duggin, 234 Va. at 227-28, 360 S.E.2d at 836-37; Maximus, 254 Va. at 414, 493 S.E.2d at 378-79; see also, e.g., Magnuson v. Peak Technical Servs., Inc., 808 F. Supp. 500, 516-17 (E.D. Va. 1992) (false statements regarding work performance); Murray v. Cees of Virginia, Inc., 29 Va. Cir. 95 (Petersburg Cir. Ct. 1992) (demeaning reference to character); Reston Pressure Seal, Inc. v. Northern Virginia Waterproofing, Inc., 19 Va. Cir. 545, 1988 WL 619281 (Fairfax Cir. Ct. 1988) (factual misrepresentations regarding competitor's product). Where plaintiff alleges interference with advantage or expectancy, rather than contract, he or she must show with reasonable certainty that, absent defendant's conduct, the advantage or expectancy would have been realized. See DSC Communications Corp. v. Pulse Communications, Inc., 976 F. Supp. 359, 366 (E.D. Va. 1997).

D. Prima Facie Tort

Virginia does not recognize an action for prima facie tort. Unlimited Screw Products, Inc. v. Malm, 781 F. Supp. 1121, 1130 (E.D. Va. 1991).

V. OTHER ISSUES

A. Statute of Limitations

Duration. Prior to 1995, Virginia included defamation suits in its "catch-all" limitations period. See Va. Code Ann. § 8.01-248. Defamation suits currently are governed by the one-year limitation period found in Virginia Code Section 8.01-247.1. The discovery rule does not apply to defamation actions; rather, the limitation period runs from the date of publication. Bass v. E.I. DuPont De Nemours & Co., No. 01-1073, 2002 U.S. App. LEXIS 474 (4th Cir. Jan. 10, 2002). Notwithstanding, Va. Code Ann. § 8.01-229 sets forth the events that may toll the running of the statute; for instance, a plaintiff may take one voluntary nonsuit and then refile within the remaining limitations period or six months, whichever is longer. The filing of a complaint with the Equal Employment Opportunity Commission ("EEOC") does not toll the statute of limitations for a defamation claim because defamation "is a state-law tort claim and is not a claim that can be addressed by the EEOC." McKamey v. Henrico County Pub. Sch., 2008 U.S. Dist. LEXIS 6866 (E.D. Va. Jan. 30, 2008), aff'd, 2008 U.S. App. LEXIS 11352 (4th Cir. May 28, 2008). Where a plaintiff sued a defendant who accused him of theft and caused his arrest, a trial court held that the § 8.01-247.1 one-year limitations period ran not from the original publication but from the date of the plaintiff's acquittal on criminal charges, since before that date the plaintiff could have been estopped from recovery by a potential conviction, which would have adjudged the accusation as true. Daniels v. Melart Jewelers, 40 Va. Cir. 254 (Fairfax Cir. Ct. of Fairfax County 1996). The trial court did not consider whether the statute would have run had a third party, such as media reporting the accusation, been sued. The defendant bears the burden of asserting the statute of limitations as an affirmative defense, even where the plaintiff fails to provide specific dates for the alleged defamatory statements. Broadnax v. Dep't of Veteran Affairs Wash. Mut. Bank, 2005 U.S. Dist. LEXIS 9549 (E.D. Va. May 19, 2005).

Single Publication Rule. In Morrissey v. William Morrow & Co., Inc., 739 F.2d 962, 10 Media L. Rep. 2305 (4th Cir. 1984), the Fourth Circuit held that Virginia recognizes the single publication rule. In August Moon v. CBS, Inc., Law No. LD-1544, 7 Va. Cir. (VCO) 68 (Richmond Cir. Ct. 1981), a Virginia trial court adopted the single publication rule. Both cases applied the then applicable one-year statute of limitations of Va. Code § 8.01-248. See also Shestul v. Moeser, 344 F. Supp. 2d 946 (E.D. Va. 2004) (involving the single publication rule and the applicable statute of limitations).

Definition of "Publication" for Limitation Purposes. In Morrissey v. William Morrow & Co., Inc., 739 F.2d 962, 10 Media L. Rep. 205 (4th Cir. 1984), the Fourth Circuit ruled that the statute of limitations does not necessarily begin to run on the "official" publication date, and affirmed a grant of summary judgment for both defendants on the basis of separate affidavits, one showing the date on which the publication was "generally available and sold to the public," and the other showing only the date on which the book was "generally available for sale to the public." Additionally, having mailed a letter is not enough for publication. The letter is published when it is opened and read by any third party, regardless of whether that party is the intended recipient of the letter. Shabazz v. Pya Monarch, LLC, 271 F. Supp. 2d 797, 804 (E.D. Va. 2003). **In Askew v. Collins, 283 Va. 482, 487, 722 S.E.2d 249, 252 (2012), the Supreme Court of Virginia found that the plaintiff's cause of action accrued when the defendant made the defamatory statement to newspaper reporters; therefore, the plaintiff suffered the emotional and reputational injury resulting from that statement at that time and the injury resulting from subsequent republication in the newspaper was a separate and distinct injury.**

B. Jurisdiction

In Blue Ridge Bank v. Veribanc, Inc., 755 F.2d 371 (4th Cir. 1985), the Fourth Circuit held that a Massachusetts company that provided financial data to a reporter who in turn published a defamatory article on a Virginia bank was subject to personal jurisdiction under Virginia's long arm statute. However, in Young v. New Haven Advocate, 315 F.3d 256 (4th Cir. 2002), personal jurisdiction was not found where a Connecticut newspaper posted an article on its Internet website about a Virginia prison. The Court found that the determining factor was whether the newspapers manifested an intent to direct their website content to a Virginia audience. Id. at 263; see also Falwell v. Cohn, No. 6:02CV00040, 2003 WL 751130 (W.D. Va. Mar. 4, 2003). **In Nathan v. Takeda Pharmaceuticals America, Inc., 83 Va. Cir. 216 (Fairfax Cir. Ct. 2011), the court held that the defendant supervisors did not commit any acts in Virginia by sending allegedly defamatory emails and making allegedly defamatory telephone calls from Illinois to Virginia. Id. at 228. Accordingly, they were not subject to personal jurisdiction under the long arm statute.** In Sweeney v. The Gazette, Inc., Law No. LE-1634 (Richmond Cir. Ct. 1982), aff'd on other grounds, The Gazette, Inc. v. Harris, 229 Va. 1, 325 S.E.2d 713, 11 Media L. Rep. 1609, cert. denied, 472 U.S. 1032 and 473 U.S. 905 (1985), the single publication rule was applied in granting a transfer of venue. In Jae-Woo Cha v. Korean Presbyterian Church, 262 Va. 604, 553 S.E.2d 511 (2001), the Court concluded that the Free Exercise Clause divested a civil court of jurisdiction to consider a defamation claim against a church and its officials who merely discharged their duties in commenting on the pastor's behavior in a meeting to decide whether he should continue preaching.

C. Worker's Compensation Exclusivity

The Virginia Workers' Compensation Act applies to injuries by accident "arising out of and in the course of" an individual's employment. Va. Code § 65.2-300. When an employee sustains such an injury, the Act provides the sole and exclusive remedy available against the employer. Rasnick v. The Pittston Co., 237 Va. 658, 660, 379 S.E.2d 353, 354 (1989). To the extent that an employee's injury does not come within the ambit of the Act, the employee's common-law remedies against his employer are preserved unimpaired. Adams v. Alliant Techsystems, Inc., 261 Va. 594, 599, 544 S.E.2d 354, 356 (2001). An injury comes within the ambit of the Act only if the injury satisfies both the "arising out of" and the "in the course of" prongs of the statutory requirements of compensability. Butler v. S. States Coop., Inc., 270 Va. 459, 466, 620 S.E.2d 768, 773 (Va. 2005). With regard to the "arising out of" prong, Virginia applies the "actual risk" test rather than the "positional risk" test, where simply being injured at work is sufficient to establish compensability, to determine whether a particular injury satisfies these statutory requirements of compensability. County of Chesterfield v. Johnson, 237 Va. 180, 185, 376 S.E.2d 73, 75-76 (1989). An injury occurring at work that in one way acts in furtherance of the employer's business does not arise "out of" the employee's employment. Butler, 270 Va. at 466, 620 S.E.2d at 773. Pleading respondeat superior liability, i.e., that the injury occurred "in the course of" the plaintiff's employment, does not preclude a finding that the injury did not arise "out of" the plaintiff's employment. Id.

"Injury by accident" within the context of the Act has been defined as "an identifiable incident or sudden precipitating event [that results] in an obvious sudden mechanical or structural change in the body." Morris v. Morris, 238 Va. 578, 589, 385 S.E.2d 858, 865 (1989). Virginia follows the rule that injury to reputation and other damages arising from published statements do not fall within the interpretation and application of 'injury' under the Act. Snead v. Harbaugh, 241 Va. 524, 528-529, 404 S.E.2d 53, 55 (1991); Williams v. Garraghty, 249 Va. 224, 239, 455 S.E.2d 209, 219 (1995).

D. Pleading Requirements

1. ***Pleading of Exact Words.*** In Federal Land Bank v. Birchfield, 173 Va. 200, 215, 3 S.E.2d 405, 410 (1939), the Supreme Court of Virginia held: "Good pleading requires that the exact words spoken or written must be set

out in the declaration in haec verba. Indeed, the pleading must go further — that is, it must purport to give the exact words." **At least one Virginia court has found that statements outside quotation marks in the complaint fail to satisfy this standard; however, this case appears to be an example of extreme enforcement of the pleading requirements. See Tomlin v. IBM, Corp., 2012 Va. Cir. LEXIS 26, *11–14 (Fairfax Cir. Ct. Feb. 13, 2012).** Notwithstanding, "details such as the time and place of the alleged communication, the name of a defendant's agent, and the names of individuals to whom the defamatory statement was purportedly communicated" need not be plead in a Motion for Judgment. Fuste v. Riverside Healthcare Ass'n., 265 Va. 127, 134, 575 S.E.2d 858, 862 (2003). However, if the complaint does not contain all of the specifics but still states a "substantial cause of action imperfectly," then a bill of particulars may supply the particulars of the allegedly defamatory statement. Government Micro Resources, Inc. v. Jackson, 271 Va. 29, 38, 624 S.E.2d 63, 67-68 (2006) (quoting Federal Land Bank v. Birchfield, 173 Va. 200, 217, 3 S.E.2d 405, 411 (1939)). Plaintiff's submission of witness affidavits in opposition to a summary judgment motion which specified the exact sentences said by the defendant was sufficient to satisfy the pleading requirement of stating the exact words. Baylor v. Comprehensive Pain Management Centers, Inc., 2011 U.S. Dist. LEXIS 37699, at *29 (W.D. Va. April 6, 2011). The Federal Rules of Civil Procedure do not require a heightened pleading standard for defamation cases. Hatfill v. The New York Times, 416 F.3d 320, 329 (4th Cir. 2005); Mann v. Heckler & Koch Def., Inc., 2008 U.S. Dist. LEXIS 79126, *21 (E.D. Va. Oct. 7, 2008). However, federal pleading requirements under Bell Atlantic Corp. v. Twombly, 550 U.S. 544, 561, 127 S. Ct. 1955, 167 L. Ed. 2d 929 (2007) and Ashcroft v. Iqbal, 129 S. Ct. 1937, 1949, 173 L. Ed. 2d 868 (2009) still apply. See Skillstorm, Inc. v. Elec. Data Sys., LLC, 666 F. Supp. 2d 610, 620 (E.D. Va. 2009) (dismissing defamation claim pursuant to Twombly and Iqbal because plaintiff "[did] not identify a speaker, the substance of the statement, when the statement was made, and why the statement [was] defamatory"). **At least one federal district court has held that a complaint need not detail the precise reasons that third parties drew defamatory inferences from statements capable of defamatory meaning in a given context to survive a Rule 12(b)(6) motion. Sewell v. Wells Fargo Bank, N.A., 2012 U.S. Dist. LEXIS 9376, *17–18 (W.D. Jan. 27, 2012).**

2. ***Issues for the Jury and Issues for the Judge.*** Whether words are capable of a defamatory meaning is for the court. See Wilder v. Johnson Publishing Co., Inc., 55 F. Supp. 622, 9 Media L. Rep. 1145 (E.D. Va. 1982); Jordan v. Kollman, 269 Va. 569, 576, 612 S.E.2d 203, 206-07 (2005). The determination of whether statements are privileged is a question of law for the court, whereas the determination of whether a privilege is abused is generally for the jury to decide. See, e.g., Bragg v. Elmore, 152 Va. 312, 147 S.E. 275 (1928); Smalls v. Wright, 241 Va. 52, 54, 399 S.E.2d 805, 807 (1991). The determination of whether a party is a public figure or public official is a matter of law to be decided by the court, see, Fleming v. Moore, 221 Va. 884, 275 S.E.2d 632, 7 Media L. Rep. 138 (1981); Fitzgerald v. Penthouse, 639 F.2d 1076, 1080, 6 Media L. Rep. 2447, 2450 (4th Cir. 1981), cert. denied, 460 U.S. 1024 (1983); Ryan v. Brooks, 634 F.2d 726, 728 n.2, 6 Media L. Rep. 2155, 2156 n.2 (4th Cir. 1980), as is the determination of whether the words make substantial danger to reputation apparent, The Gazette, Inc. v. Harris, 229 Va. 1, 15, 325 S.E.2d 713, 725, 11 Media L. Rep. 1609, 1618, cert. denied, 472 U.S. 1032 and 473 U.S. 905 (1985). Whether words are opinion is to be decided by the court. Yeagle v. Collegiate Times, 255 Va. 293, 296, 497 S.E.2d 136, 138 (1998); Chaves v. Johnson, 230 Va. 112, 119, 335 S.E.2d 97, 102 (1985). Once the court determines that a statement is capable of being proved false, and thus not opinion, it is the province of the jury to determine whether, in fact, the statement was false. Hyland v. Raytheon Tech. Servs. Co., 277 Va. 40, 48, 670 S.E.2d 746, 752 (2009).

SURVEY OF VIRGINIA EMPLOYMENT PRIVACY LAW

Michael D. Sullivan and Shaina D. Jones
Levine Sullivan Koch & Schulz, L.L.P.
1899 L. Street, N.W., Suite 200
Washington, D.C. 20036
Telephone (202) 508-1100; Facsimile (202) 861-9888

(With Developments Reported Through **November 1, 2012**)

GENERAL COMMENTS

Procedure and practice in Virginia's state court system differs markedly from that in the federal court system – and, for that matter, practice in Virginia's federal district courts, particularly the "rocket docket" Eastern District, differs in significant respects from federal practice elsewhere in the country. Counsel must consult carefully both Title 8.01 of the Virginia Code and the Rules of the Supreme Court of Virginia with respect to actions in state court, and the Local Rules with respect to actions in federal court. The state trial court of general jurisdiction is the Circuit Court. Depending upon the nature of the case, appeals are taken either to the Court of Appeals or to the Virginia Supreme Court. Appeal as of right is extremely limited in the Virginia Supreme Court. Circuit Court decisions, to the extent published at all, are to be found in Virginia Circuit Court Opinions. Appellate court opinions may be found in either the Virginia Supreme Court Reports or the Virginia Court of Appeals Reports and in the Southeastern Reporter.

SIGNIFICANT DEVELOPMENTS SINCE THE 2012 *SURVEY*

None.

I. GENERAL LAW OF PRIVACY

A. Legal Basis of Privacy Claims

Virginia does not recognize any of the common-law forms of the tort of invasion of privacy. See, e.g., WJLA-TV v. Levin, 264 Va. 140, 160 n.5, 564 S.E.2d 383, 394 n.5 (2002); Wiest v. E-Fense, Inc., 356 F. Supp. 2d 604, 605 (E.D. Va. 2005); Superperformance Int'l, Inc. v. Hartford Cas. Ins. Co., 203 F. Supp. 2d 587, 601 (E.D. Va. 2002), aff'd on other grounds, 332 F.3d 215 (4th Cir. 2003); Mansoor v. County of Albemarle, 124 F. Supp. 2d 367, 382 (W.D. Va. 2000); Brown v. ABC, 704 F.2d 1296, 1302-03 (4th Cir. 1983); Ward v. Connor, 495 F. Supp. 434, 440 (E.D. Va. 1980), rev'd on other grounds, 657 F.2d 45 (4th Cir. 1981), cert. denied, 455 U.S. 907 (1982); Evans v. Sturgill, 430 F. Supp. 1209, 1213 (W.D. Va. 1977). By statute, Virginia has created a cause of action for commercial misappropriation of name or likeness, Va. Code Ann. § 8.01-40, and Virginia imposes misdemeanor criminal penalties for such misappropriation, Va. Code Ann. § 18.2-216.1. Virginia's wiretap statute imposes liability on persons who disclose the contents of a covered communication if the discloser knows or has reason to know that the information was obtained by the unauthorized interception of such communication. Va. Code Ann. § 19.2-62. Virginia has criminalized the use of "a computer or computer network" where a person "intentionally examines without authority any employment, salary, credit or any other financial or identifying information, as defined in clauses (iii) through (xiii) of subsection C of § 18.2-186.3, relating to any other person." Va. Code Ann. § 18.2-152.5(A). Various other statutes prohibit disclosure of specific information, see, e.g., Va. Code Ann. § 16.1-309 (prohibiting disclosure of juvenile court records); Va. Code Ann. § 19.2-192 (prohibiting disclosure by grand jurors of proceedings before them); Va. Code Ann. §§ 2.2-3800-2.2-3809 (prohibiting disclosure by government agencies of certain information), but these statutes generally impose penalties for violations only on those who serve as official custodians of such records.

B. Causes of Action

1. ***Misappropriation/Right of Publicity***. Virginia has, by statute, created a cause of action for commercial misappropriation of name or likeness, Va. Code Ann. § 8.01-40; Town & Country Properties, Inc. v. Riggins, 249 Va. 387, 457 S.E.2d 350, 23 Media L. Rep. 2045 (1995), and violators also are subject to misdemeanor criminal penalties, Va. Code Ann. § 18.2-216.1. The misappropriation statute provides: "Any person whose name, portrait, or picture is used without having first obtained the written consent of such person, or if dead, of the surviving consort and if none, of the next of kin, or if a minor, the written consent of his or her parent or guardian, for advertising purposes or for the purposes of trade, such persons may maintain a suit in equity against the person, firm, or corporation so using such person's name, portrait, or picture to prevent and restrain the use thereof; and may also sue and recover damages for any injuries sustained by reason of such use. And if the defendant shall have knowingly used such person's name, portrait or picture in such manner as is forbidden or declared to be unlawful by this chapter, the jury, in its discretion, may award exemplary damages." Va. Code Ann. § 8.01-40(A). Enacted in derogation of the common law, the statute is strictly construed. Falwell v. Penthouse Int'l, 521

F. Supp. 1204, 1210, 7 Media L. Rep. 1891 (W.D. Va. 1981). The statute may be invoked only by persons, not businesses. Lawson v. Lake, 36 Va. Cir. 138, 139 (Fairfax Co. 1995); Silver Ring Splint Co. v. Digisplint, Inc., 567 F. Supp. 2d 847, 855 (W.D. Va. June 18, 2008) (dismissing a corporation's misappropriation claim under the statute because "the text of § 8.01-40 makes clear that this statute applies only to natural persons"). To give rise to a cause of action, the plaintiff's name or likeness must have had pre-existing commercial value. Williams v. Nathan, 1993 WL 219516, at *9, 21 Media L. Rep. 1339, 1345 (E.D. Va. 1993). Corporate owners and officers individually may be held jointly and severally liable with the corporation for violation of this statutory right of publicity if they participated in the wrongful conduct. Buckman v. PTS Corp. Inc., 2000 WL 5240 (Va. Cir. Ct. Jan. 4, 2000) (overruling demurrer where defendant corporate owners and officers were actively involved in and stood to benefit financially from unauthorized use of plaintiff former employee's name in directory advertisement and defendants had implied in other communications that plaintiff was still affiliated with corporation), aff'd in relevant part, PTS Corp. v. Buckman, 263 Va. 613, 622, 561 S.E.2d 718, 723 (2002); Wiest v. E-Fense, Inc., 356 F. Supp. 2d 604, 612 (E.D. Va. 2005) (denying motion to dismiss complaint against corporate officers and employees where plaintiff "points to all the defendants throughout his complaint [and] is alleging that they all were engaged in tortious activities"). No cause of action arises from the unauthorized publication of an interview with a person in a magazine, as dissemination of news to the public is not to be construed as for purposes of trade, see Falwell v. Penthouse Int'l, 521 F. Supp. at 1210; Wiest, 356 F. Supp. 2d at 611 ("[i]f a name or likeness is used without consent in connection with matters that are 'newsworthy' or of 'public interest,' the statute does not apply"), nor, for the same reason, is a parody of a well-known person actionable, Falwell v. Flynt, 797 F.2d 1270, 1278, 13 Media L. Rep. 1145 (4th Cir. 1986), rev'd on other grounds, 485 U.S. 46, 14 Media L. Rep. 2281 (1988). The "newsworthiness" exception has been held not to apply where the plaintiff author attempted to generate a matter of public concern by baselessly manufacturing charges of plagiarism against a well-known author and then used the well-known author's name in connection with promotional materials for his book. Cornwell v. Sachs, 99 F. Supp. 2d 695, 711-13 (E.D. Va. 2000). However, the Virginia Supreme Court held that the newsworthiness exception does apply to promotional announcements broadcast by the defendant, "in part, to entice the public to view [a] ... news broadcast in order to increase the station's ratings during a critical 'sweeps' period and, thus, potentially increase future advertising revenue," where "it cannot reasonably be disputed that the principal purpose" of the announcements "was to promote a report' of a newsworthy event or matter of public interest. WJLA-TV v. Levin, 264 Va. 140, 161, 564 S.E.2d 383, 395 (2002) (citation omitted). The statute contains a "cutoff" provision which provides that "[n]o action shall be commenced under this section more than twenty years after the death of such person." Va. Code Ann. § 8.01-40(B) (2003). In addition, Virginia's five-year statute of limitations for injury to property applies to causes of action arising under the statute. See Va. Code Ann. § 8.01-243 (B); Lavery v. Automation Mgmt. Consultants, Inc., 234 Va. 145, 150, 360 S.E.2d 336, 339 (1987). Virginia's statute is similar to Section 51 of the New York Civil Rights Law and Virginia courts will look to New York courts for guidance in construing Section 8.01-40. E.g., Town & Country Properties, Inc. v. Riggins, 249 Va. 387, 394, 457 S.E.2d 350, 362 (1995); WJLA-TV, 264 Va. at 161, 564 S.E.2d at 395; PTS Corp., 263 Va. at 622-23,561 S.E.2d at 723-24.

2. ***False Light***. Virginia does not recognize a cause of action for false light invasion of privacy. See, e.g., WJLA-TV, 264 Va. at 160 n.5, 564 S.E.2d at 394 n.5; Falwell, 521 F. Supp. at 1206; **Christmas v. The Arc of The Piedmont, Inc., 2012 WL 2905584, at *7 (W.D. Va. July 16, 2012)**.

3. ***Publication of Private Facts***. Virginia does not recognize a cause of action for invasion of privacy by publication of private facts. See, e.g., WJLA-TV, 264 Va. at 160 n.5, 564 S.E.2d at 394 n.5; Brown v. ABC, 704 F.2d 1296, 1302 (4th Cir. 1983). However, Virginia's wiretap statute imposes liability on persons who disclose the contents of a covered communication if the discloser knows or has reason to know that the information was obtained by the unauthorized interception of such communication. Va. Code Ann. § 19.2-62. See IV, infra. Various other statutes prohibit disclosure of specific information, see, e.g., Va. Code Ann. § 16.1-309 (prohibiting disclosure of juvenile court records); Va. Code Ann. § 19.2-192 (prohibiting disclosure of grand jury records); Va. Code Ann. §§ 2.2-3800 to 2.2-3809 (prohibiting disclosure by government agencies of certain information), but these statutes generally impose penalties for violations only on those who serve as official custodians of such records.

4. ***Intrusion***. Virginia does not recognize a cause of action for invasion of privacy by intrusion. See, e.g., WJLA-TV, 264 Va. at 160 n.5, 564 S.E.2d at 394 n.5; Brown, 704 F.2d at 1302; Ward v. Connor, 495 F. Supp. 434, 439-40 (E.D. Va. 1980). Pursuant to the Interception of Wire, Electronic, or Oral Communications Act, Virginia has created a cause of action against persons who disclose the contents of a covered communication if the discloser knows or has reason to know that the information was obtained by the unauthorized interception of such communication. Va. Code Ann. § 19.2-62. See IV, infra. It is a misdemeanor for a person without "authority of law" to enter on or remain upon "the lands, buildings or premises of another, or any portion or area thereof, after having been forbidden to do so, either orally or in writing, by the owner, lessee, custodian, or the agent of any such person, or other person lawfully in charge thereof, or after having been forbidden to do so by a sign or signs posted by or at the direction of such persons or the agent of any such person." Va. Code Ann. § 18.2-119; see also Hall v. Commonwealth, 188 Va. 72, 49 S.E.2d 369, appeal dismissed, 335 U.S. 875 (1948). Virginia recognizes the common-law crime of trespass where the trespass amounts to or threatens breach of the peace. See, e.g., Snead v. Commonwealth, 212 Va. 803, 804, 188 S.E.2d 197, 198 (1972). The victim of a violation of section 18.2-119

may bring a civil action for damages against a trespasser, see, e.g., Chaffinch v. C&P Telephone Co., 227 Va. 68, 72-73, 313 S.E.2d 376, 378-79 (1984), but it appears that, if the trespass was committed accidentally, by inadvertence or mistake not the product of gross negligence, it will not be actionable, see Wood v. Weaver, 121 Va. 250, 260-61, 92 S.E. 1001, 1004 (1917). Any person who uses a computer or computer network to make "an unauthorized copy ... of computer data" commits a trespass in violation of Va. Code Ann. § 18.2-152.4. McGladrey & Pullen, L.L.P. v. Shrader, 62 Va. Cir. 401, 2003 WL 22203709, at *6 (Rockingham Co. Aug. 11, 2003); see also id. ("The case law makes clear that when a person exceeds the scope of the permission he or she has to use a computer, that use is a trespass in violation of § 18.2-152.4."); Physicians Interactive v. Lathian Sys., Inc., 2003 WL 23018270, at *7 (E.D. Va. Dec. 5, 2003) ("[t]he website invitation to Internet users to visit a website, gather information, and sign up for services is not an invitation for Internet users to hack the website's host computer file server and copy company financial statements or personnel files"); DiMaio v. Commonwealth, 46 Va. App. 755, 769, 621 S.E.2d 696, 703 (2005) (affirming former human resource director's conviction for, inter alia, computer trespass where he downloaded human resource documents onto third-party server on day he resigned and deleted those files from work computer), aff'd, 272 Va. 504, 636 S.E.2d 456 (2006). Note that "[a] person is guilty of the crime of computer invasion of privacy when he uses a computer or computer network and intentionally examines without authority any employment, salary, credit or any other financial or identifying information, as defined in clauses (iii) through (xiii) of subsection C of § 18.2-186.3, relating to any other person." Va. Code Ann. § 18.2-152.5(A).

C. Other Privacy-Related Actions

1. ***Intentional Infliction of Emotional Distress.*** Virginia recognizes the tort of intentional infliction of emotional distress ("IIED"), but looks upon it with disfavor. Harris v. Kreutzer, 271 Va. 188, 203-04, 624 S.E.2d 24, 33 (2006); Denny v. Elizabeth Arden Salons, Inc., 456 F.3d 427, 436 (4th Cir. 2006); Ruth v. Fletcher, 237 Va. 366, 373, 377 S.E.2d 412, 415-16 (1989); Hager v. First Va. Banks, Inc., 2002 WL 57249, at *10 (W.D. Va. Jan. 10, 2002); Garland v. Travco Ins. Co., 2002 WL 485702, at *3 (W.D. Va. Mar. 18, 2002). A plaintiff must prove, generally by clear and convincing evidence, (1) that the defendant specifically intended to cause the plaintiff emotional distress, or that he or she knew or should have known that emotional distress would likely result from his intentional conduct; (2) that the conduct complained of was outrageous and intolerable; (3) that the conduct complained of was the proximate cause of the distress; and (4) that the distress was severe. See, e.g., Womack v. Eldridge, 215 Va. 338, 342, 210 S.E.2d 145, 148 (1974); Harris v. Kreutzer, 271 Va. at 203, 624 S.E.2d at 33; Russo v. White, 241 Va. 23, 26, 400 S.E.2d 160, 162 (1991); Hatfill v. New York Times Co., 416 F.3d 320, 336 (4th Cir.), reh'g en banc denied, 427 F.3d 253 (4th Cir. 2005), cert. denied, 126 S.Ct. 1619 (2006). Virginia does not, however, recognize a cause of action for conspiracy to intentionally inflict emotional distress. Almy v. Grisham, 273 Va. 68, 81, 639 S.E.2d 182, 189 (2007).

For IIED to be actionable, the resulting distress must be "so severe that no reasonable person could be expected to endure it." Russo, 241 Va. at 27, 400 S.E.2d at 163. Courts applying Virginia law have tended to closely scrutinize allegations and evidence of severe distress. See, e.g., **Torabipour v. Cosi, Inc., 2012 WL 2153168, at *5 (E.D. Va. June 12, 2012) (allegation that plaintiff suffered "humiliation, embarrassment and indignity to h[is] feelings" insufficient to allege severity); Long v. Teradata Corp., 2012 WL 3947811, at *5 (E.D. Va. Sept. 10, 2012) (allegations of "ongoing anorexia, alopecia, accelerated hypertension, and stress related insomnia with endogenous depression," were "stress and stress-related symptoms" that "[did] not sufficiently support pleading the requisite severity of distress");** Ortiz v. Panera Bread Co., 2011 WL 3353432, at *7 (E.D. Va. Aug. 2, 2011) (claim that plaintiff experienced "emotional pain and suffering, loss of enjoyment, and other damages," and "severe mental and emotional distress," insufficient); Weth v. O'Leary, 796 F. Supp. 2d. 766, 774 (E.D. Va. 2011) (allegation that plaintiff "suffered severe emotional anguish as a result of her termination" insufficient); McKelvy v. Capital One Servs., LLC, 2010 WL 3418228, at *9 (E.D. Va. Aug. 20, 2010) (loss of sleep, focus, and productivity "do not rise to the level of severe emotional distress" even where plaintiff sought medical attention and was prescribed an anti-depressant), aff'd, 2011 WL 1625018 (4th Cir. 2011); Earley v. Marion, 540 F. Supp. 2d 680, 690 (W.D. Va. 2008) (allegations that plaintiff "suffered from renewed anxiety, was forced to resume taking anti-anxiety medication, and lost approximately ten pounds in weight" failed to "suggest emotional distress so severe that no reasonable person could be expected to endure it"), aff'd, 340 F. App'x 169 (4th Cir. 2009); Russo, 241 Va. at 27, 400 S.E.2d at 163 (where defendant allegedly had stalked plaintiff and telephoned her hundreds of times over a period of months but the resulting "stress" and loss of sleep did not cause plaintiff to seek medical attention or to sustain physical injury, distress was not sufficiently severe to be actionable); Harris v. Kreutzer, 271 Va. at 204-05, 624 S.E.2d at 34 (plaintiff failed to sufficiently allege severity where she alleged "nightmares, difficulty sleeping, extreme loss of self-esteem and depression, requiring additional counseling," and "claims to have suffered mortification, humiliation, shame, disgrace, and injury to reputation"); Denny, 456 F.3d at 436 (plaintiffs "failed to present evidence that they suffered sufficiently severe distress" where they alleged that the "defendant's conduct made them nervous, caused them stress, and resulted in an inability to adequately sleep and eat," but made "no claim 'that [they] had any objective physical injury caused by the stress, that [they] sought medical attention, that [they were] confined at home or in a hospital, or that [they] lost income'") (citation omitted); Harris v. Americredit Fin. Servs., Inc., 2005 WL 2180477, at *4 (W.D. Va. Sept. 9, 2005) (plaintiff's alleged "nightmares, loss of self esteem, depression, and nightly episodes of crying ... are not so severe that no one could expect to endure them"); Hall v. Wal-Mart Stores East, Inc., 2003 WL 22757942, at *5 (W.D. Va. Nov. 21, 2003) (plaintiff acquitted of shoplifting charges who alleged injuries consisting of anxiety attacks, irregular appetite, stress and inability to engage in certain activities, including shopping, "for fear of being wrongly accused again," failed to allege injuries that "rise to the severity that would be actionable and recoverable in tort"); Veney v. Ojeda, 321 F. Supp. 2d 733, 748-49 (E.D. Va. 2004) (plaintiff's allegations "that he 'didn't feel right' after the incident and that he felt depressed for a couple days, but that these feelings did not interfere with his activities" not actionable); Glover v. Oppelman, 178 F. Supp. 2d 622, 643 (W.D. Va. 2001) (plaintiff's injuries consisting of sleeplessness, fatigue, anxiety and loss of enjoyment, "while unfortunate and compensable under Title VII, [are] simply not severe enough to support her emotional distress claim"); Collins v. Franklin, 2001 WL 589029, at *3 (W.D. Va. May 29, 2001) ("The Virginia Supreme Court has held that sleeplessness, stress, withdrawal, and an inability to concentrate are not sufficient to establish severe emotional harm under the law."). But see Almy, 273 Va. at 80, 639 S.E.2d at 188 (allegations of severe distress sufficient to survive demurrer where complaint claimed plaintiff had to "seek professional counseling" and became "functionally incapable of carrying out any of her work or family responsibilities") (distinguishing Russo and Harris); Hazzis v. Modjadidi, 2005 WL 3462257, at *3 (Va. Cir. Ct. Dec. 19, 2005) ("plaintiff's claims of emotional distress to the point of vomiting blood[] are sufficient to overrule the Defendants' demurrers"); Hatfill v. New York Times Co., 416 F.3d 320, 337 (4th Cir. 2005) (plaintiff's allegations that he "suffered severe and ongoing loss of reputation and professional standing, loss of employment, past and ongoing financial injury, severe emotional distress and other injury" and that defendants inflicted "grievous emotional distress" sufficient to survive motion to dismiss under Federal Rules of Civil Procedure); Cobbs v. Commonwealth, 2001 WL 322728, at *6 (Va. Cir. Ct. Chesterfield Co. Jan. 31, 2001) (plaintiff's allegations that she received psychological and medical treatment and suffered loss of income and employment opportunities as result of defendants' conduct sufficient to survive motion to dismiss); Thompson v. Town of Front Royal, 117 F. Supp. 2d 522, 532 (W.D. Va. 2000) (denying defendants' motion for summary judgment where plaintiff submitted reports of several doctors in support of emotional distress claim). Although the Virginia Supreme Court has held that physical injury is not required for an IIED claim, Womack v. Eldridge, 215 Va. 338, 342, 210 S.E.2d 145, 148 (1974), one state court has said that "there must be some accompanying objective physical injury" for such a claim to lie, Robinson v. Phi Beta Sigma Fraternity, Inc., 60 Va. Cir. 452, 2003 WL 1870097, at *1 (Norfolk Jan. 10, 2003).

In any event, the plaintiff must plead and prove the "particulars of her suffering" to survive a motion to dismiss or for summary judgment, Baradell v. Board of Soc. Servs., 970 F. Supp. 489, 495 (W.D. Va. 1997); see also **Tohotcheu v. Harris Teeter, Inc., 2011 WL 5873074, at *5 (E.D. Va. Nov. 22, 2011) (dismissing claim where plaintiff alleged only conclusory statement that he suffered "emotional distress," and "[did] not provide factual support for any element" of the claim)**; Gallo v. U.S. Investigations Servs., 2006 WL 1647194, at *2 (E.D. Va. June 8, 2006) (dismissing claim where "[p]laintiff's allegations of emotional distress are not based on factual assertions, but are simply conclusory legal statements"); Gedrich v. Fairfax County Dep't of Family Servs., 282 F. Supp. 2d 439, 474 (E.D. Va. 2003) (granting motion to dismiss where "[p]laintiff's cursory intentional infliction of emotional distress claim is made in one lone sentence with no factual elaboration"); Morrissey v. Jennings, 60 Va. Cir. 179, 2002 WL 31264414, at *7 (Richmond Sept. 30, 2002) (plaintiff's "bald assertion" that 'defendant wrongly and intentionally inflicted great, severe and permanent emotional distress on plaintiff. . .' do[es] not come close to surviving demurrer") (citation omitted); Barrett v. The Applied Radiant Energy Corp., 240 F.3d 262, 269 (4th Cir. 2001) (dismissing plaintiff's claims for severe emotional distress where "her specific allegations do not reach the high threshold of severe and specific injury required to make out this claim"). However, at least one court has held that "[e]motional distress is sufficiently severe to survive a motion to dismiss where it fundamentally affects the plaintiff's interactions with her closest family members and outlook for her offspring's future." Pennell v. Vacation Reservation Ctr., LLC, 783 F. Supp. 2d 819, 824-25 (E.D. Va. 2011) (plaintiff's claim that supervisor's running commentary about her dwarfism resulted in failure to manage day-to-day activities; fear of applying for other jobs; fear of leaving the house; and fear of preparing her child, also a dwarf, for the workplace sufficient to allege severity); See also Hatfill, 416 F.3d at 337 (although "[a] plaintiff in Virginia state court must plead 'with the requisite degree of specificity' the facts giving rise to his claim of severe emotional distress, ... [Federal] Rule [of Civil Procedure] 8 – applicable in [a] diversity case – did not require him" to plead claim in "such specific terms," but only "to give the [defendant] 'fair notice of what [plaintiff's] claim is and the grounds upon which it rests'"); Harris v. Americredit Fin. Servs., Inc., 2005 WL 2180477, at *3 (because "the liberal pleading standard of Rule 8 ... applies even to claims in diversity cases which are subject to stricter pleading requirements under state law, ... the plaintiff's claim for intentional infliction of emotional distress, a disfavored action under Virginia law, need not be pled with the degree of specificity required by Virginia courts"); Perk v. Warden, 475 F. Supp. 2d 565, 571 (E.D. Va. 2007) (same); Wain v. Trammell Hotel Invs., LLC, 2005 WL 2044950, at *3 (W.D. Va. Aug. 24, 2005) (plaintiff's allegations "that she suffered 'severe emotional distress in the form of mental suffering' ... is enough, under Federal Rule of Civil Procedure 8, to put the defendants on notice of the nature of [plaintiff's] claim and the ground upon which it rests").

In addition, the plaintiff must show that the conduct complained of was "so outrageous in character and so extreme in degree, as to be beyond all possible bounds of decency, and to be regarded as atrocious and utterly intolerable in a civilized community." Russo v. White, 241 Va. 23, 27, 400 S.E.2d 160, 162 (1991) (citation omitted). "[L]iability clearly does not extend to mere insults, indignities, threats, annoyances, petty oppressions or other trivialities," Simmons v. Norfolk & W. Ry. Co., 734 F. Supp. 230, 231 (W.D. Va. 1990) (quoting Restatement (2d) of Torts § 46); Hall v. Wal-Mart Stores East, Inc., 2003 WL 22757942, at *4 (W.D. Va. Nov. 21, 2003) ("[t]ort actions based on emotional harm ... are available only in those cases where the facts allege inordinately shocking or unconscionable conduct"); see also, e.g., Moore v. Williamsburg Reg'l Hosp., 560 F.3d 166, 176 (4th Cir.) (hospital's suspension of doctor's privileges based on allegations he sexually abused daughter did not clear outrageousness bar because "attempt by the hospital to protect its minor patients, even if ultimately misguided, surely does not 'exceed all possible bounds of decency'"), cert. denied, 130 S. Ct. 201 (2009); Hatfill v. New York Times Co., 416 F.3d 320, 336 (4th Cir. 2005) (allegations that defendants intentionally published false charges accusing plaintiff of being responsible for anthrax mailings that resulted in five deaths without giving plaintiff opportunity to respond held to allege extreme or outrageous conduct sufficient to survive motion to dismiss); **Coles v. Carilion Clinic, 2012 WL 2884917, at *10 (W.D. Va. July 13, 2012) (claim that plaintiff used racially abusive language and symbols and persistently refused to promote plaintiff, an African-American, while electing to promote white males instead, insufficient to allege extreme or outrageous conduct); Torabipour v. Cosi, Inc., 2012 WL 2153168, at *5 (E.D. Va. June 12, 2012) (questions to employee regarding another employee's alleged illicit relations with female employee in store's basement, while "distressful and unsettling" to plaintiff, not outrageous conduct); Ainsworth v. Loudon County Sch. Bd., 851 F. Supp. 2d 963, 982 (E.D. Va. 2012) (allegations that officials branded plaintiff a "problem employee" with "issues," criticized her work performance, and otherwise treated her negatively did not rise to level of outrageous conduct);** Pennell, 783 F. Supp. 2d at 823 (conduct sufficiently alleged as "outrageous" and "understood to humiliate or disparage" where supervisor publicly and pervasively addressed employee as "Shorty," referring to her dwarfism); Rasi v. Dep't of Corrections, 2009 WL 102530, at *10 (W.D. Va. Jan. 14, 2009) (not "outrageous" for prison warden to repeat allegation that employee accepted money from supervisor following alleged sexual encounter when allegation was based upon internal investigator's report); McHugh v. Check Investors, Inc., 2003 WL 21283288, at *4 (W.D. Va. May 21, 2003) (awarding damages for emotional distress caused by "overzealous, deceitful" debt collector who threatened that plaintiff would be criminally prosecuted and jailed for up to six months if she did not pay alleged debt by end of day); Harris v. Kreutzer, 271 Va. 188, 204, 624 S.E.2d 24, 33-34 (2006) (psychologist's conduct in examining plaintiff in connection with unrelated personal injury litigation, although "[i]nsensitive and demeaning ... does not equate to outrageous behavior" where plaintiff alleged that he "verbally abused [her], raised his voice to her, caused her to break down into tears ... , stated she was 'putting on a show,' and accused her of being a faker and malingerer"); Morrissey v. Jennings, 60 Va. Cir. 179, 2002 WL 31264414, at *6 (Richmond Sept. 30, 2002) (court-appointed guardian's alleged conduct in arranging admissions to and discharges from hospital and nursing home do not rise to level of intentional infliction of emotional distress where they would not "prompt an average member of the community to exclaim 'Outrageous!'"); Hickman v. Lab. Corp. of Am. Holdings, Inc., 2005 WL 2475733, at *5 (W.D. Va. Oct. 6, 2005) (plaintiff's "blanket accusations" and "conclusional" allegations that defendant knew or should have known that its conduct in erroneously reporting that plaintiff was HIV-positive "would cause extreme fright, shock and emotional disturbance and resulting physical injury and illness" did not support a finding of extreme or outrageous conduct"); Poole v. Pass, 351 F. Supp. 2d 473, 482 (E.D. Va. 2005) (alleged harassment by police officers who detained plaintiff on suspicion of towing car, "including [their] suggestion that her children might be taken from her, is plainly inappropriate, even reprehensible, [but] ... simply cannot be said to be beyond all possible bounds of decency").

It is, at least as an initial matter, a question of law for the court whether defendant's alleged conduct was sufficiently extreme and outrageous as to present a jury question. E.g., Harris v. Kreutzer, 271 Va. at 204, 624 S.E.2d at 33; Womack v. Eldridge, 215 Va. 338, 342, 210 S.E.2d 145, 148 (1974); Hickman, 2005 WL 2475733, at *5; Hall, 2003 WL 22757942, at *5; Garland v. Travco Ins. Co., 2002 WL 485702, at *3 (W.D. Va. Mar. 18, 2002); Owens v. Ashland Oil, Inc., 708 F. Supp. 757, 760 (W.D. Va. 1989); Lewis v. First Nat'l Bank of Stuart, 645 F. Supp. 1499, 1506 (W.D. Va. 1986), aff'd, 818 F.2d 861 (4th Cir. 1987); but compare Hager v. First Va. Banks, Inc., 2002 WL 57249, at *10 (W.D. Va. Jan. 10, 2002) (denying without prejudice defendant's motion to dismiss emotional distress claim where "Plaintiff's claim satisfies the minimal requirements of notice pleading, but the court lacks sufficient facts to determine whether the alleged conduct satisfies the stringent standard required for an intentional infliction of emotional distress claim"), with Hager v. First Va. Bank-Southwest, 2002 WL 31373439, at *4 (W.D. Va. Oct. 18, 2002) ("Hager II") (granting defendant's motion for summary judgment on emotional distress claim where, "[h]owever else [defendant's] alleged actions may be characterized, they do not rise to the level of 'intolerable conduct' that 'offends... standards of decency and morality'") (alteration in original) (citation omitted). Similarly, the Fourth Circuit has held in an unpublished opinion that a court may grant judgment for the defendant as a matter of law where plaintiff fails to provide either "direct or circumstantial evidence from which a jury could conclude that the conduct was intentional." Combs v. Wal-Mart Stores, Inc., 61 Fed. App'x 61, 62, 2003 WL 1426364, at *1 (4th Cir. Mar. 21, 2003).

In Virginia, plaintiffs who allege IIED claims based on employment actions face a sizeable bar to recovery. See Musselman v. Merck & Co. Inc., 2006 WL 2645174, at *5 (E.D. Va. Sept. 13, 2006) (series of employment actions, including employer's demands that plaintiff "return to work, denial of her requests for an extended leave of absence, disapproval of her request to telecommute, rejection of her request to secure a new position through her own contacts, and [her] ultimate termination" did not give rise to claim); see also, e.g., Hall v. Autozoners, 2011 WL 2414534, at *3 (E.D. Va. June 13, 2011) (allegation of employer grabbing his testicles and referring to them as "nuts" for the plaintiff; stating that he wanted to have sexual intercourse with customers; and that he would make plaintiff's life "hell" insufficient to establish outrageousness); Taylor v. CNA Corp., 782 F. Supp. 2d 182 (E.D. Va. Aug. 27, 2010) (employer's requirement that plaintiff attend sexual harassment training and work with counselor in response to staff complaints was not "outrageous conduct"); Nigro v. Va. Commonwealth Univ. Med. Coll. of Va., 2010 WL 2262539, at *14-15 (W.D. Va. June 4, 2010) (allegations that supervisors falsely accused physician trainee of criminal conduct, made other defamatory statements about her, refused to provide her with counseling, and threatened termination were insufficient to support a finding of outrageous conduct), aff'd, 2012 WL 2354635 (4th Cir. June 21, 2012); Twigg v. Triple Canopy, Inc., 2010 WL 2245511, at *1, *7 (E.D. Va. June 2, 2010) (employer's transmittal to client of letter accusing ex-employee of, *inter alia*, "pattern of poor leadership and poor judgment" cannot support IIED claim where letter was neither sent to ex-employee nor made public); Law v. AutoZone Stores, Inc., 2009 WL 4349165, at *3 (W.D. Va. Nov. 25, 2009) (single use of racial epithet by plaintiff's manager cannot, standing alone, support finding of outrageous and intolerable conduct, though it "certainly violated well-established norms of etiquette and decency"); Earley v. Marion, 540 F. Supp. 2d 680, 690 (W.D. Va. 2008) (employer's alleged conduct, including, "wrongly suspend[ing]" employee and subjecting her to "mean-spirited rumors about her emotional and mental fitness," was not "outrageous or intolerable" even though it may have been "hasty, unkind or inconsiderate"); aff'd, 340 F. App'x 169 (4th Cir. 2009). **Generally, allegations of discrimination do not rise to the level of outrageousness required to state an IIED claim. Long v. Teradata Corp., 2012 WL 3947811, at *5 (E.D. Va. Sept. 10, 2012) (allegations that employer discriminated by formulating and publicizing sexual harassment claim against plaintiff which resulted in his termination, even if sufficiently pled, not enough to plead IIED claim);** see also, Burke v. AT&T Technical Services Co. Inc., 55 F. Supp. 2d 432, 441 (E.D. Va. 1999) (demotion and termination allegedly based on racial discrimination, while "insidious and unacceptable," did not constitute outrageous conduct); Beardsley v. Isom, 828 F. Supp. 397, 401 (E.D. Va. 1993) (actions allegedly taken in retaliation for plaintiff's complaints of sexual harassment did not rise to the requisite level of severity), aff'd sub nom, Beardsley v. Webb, 30 F.3d 524 (4th Cir. 1994); Harris v. Norfolk & W. Ry. Co., 720 F. Supp. 567, 567-68 (W.D. Va. 1989) (demotion allegedly based on gender discrimination did not constitute the "unconscionable abuse" necessary to state an IIED claim under Virginia law); Gallo v. U.S. Investigations Servs., 2006 WL 1647194, at *2 (E.D. Va. June 8, 2006) (employer's conduct not outrageous and intolerable where "[t]he only specific conduct that Plaintiff alleges is that when her employment was terminated she was escorted from Defendant's premises in a humiliating manner and that the basis for her termination was conveyed to her former co-workers"); Hager II, 2002 WL 31373439, at *4 (employer's alleged failure to accommodate plaintiff's disability did not amount to intolerable conduct required to withstand summary judgment on emotional distress claim where, "[a]t worst, [employer's] actions were to refuse to move [plaintiff] from one work station to another... and to refuse to allow [plaintiff] to leave work early to see a doctor after notes from two of [her] doctors on that day made no mention of the need for [plaintiff] to see them"); Glover v. Oppelman, 178 F. Supp. 2d 622, 643 (W.D. Va. 2001) (employer's "boorish" and "inappropriate" conduct may be actionable sexual harassment under Title VII, but is not outrageous enough to support emotional distress claim); Warner v. Buck Creek Nursery, Inc., 149 F. Supp. 2d 246, 265 (W.D. Va. 2001) (employers' allegedly false statements that "[plaintiff] was fired for theft – statements that [plaintiff] contends were made with the intent to destroy his reputation in the community... simply fail to show that the defendants engaged in conduct 'so outrageous in character, and so extreme in degree, as to go beyond all possible bounds of decency'") (citation omitted); Collins v. Franklin, 2001 WL 589029, at *2 (W.D. Va. May 29, 2001) (defendant's sexually harassing comments, while "insensitive" and "boorish," not sufficiently outrageous to sustain cause of action); Owens v. Ashland Oil, Inc., 708 F. Supp. 757 (W.D. Va. 1989) (termination of employment not sufficiently outrageous to sustain cause of action). But see Rasi v. Dep't of Corrections, 2009 WL 102530, at *9 (W.D. Va. Jan. 14, 2009) (plaintiff stated IIED claim based on workplace sexual harassment and alleged sexual battery); Cobbs v. Commonwealth, 2001 WL 322728, at *5 (Va. Cir. Ct. Chesterfield Co. Jan. 31, 2001) (finding that "continually harassing a co-worker because of one's race and political beliefs is outrageous and intolerable"); Swentek v. USAIR, Inc., 830 F.2d 552 (4th Cir. 1987) (pattern of physical sexual harassment on job held sufficiently outrageous to sustain cause of action).

Federal government employees who allege they have suffered extreme workplace abuse generally cannot sue their employers for intentional infliction of emotional distress because the Civil Service Reform Act (CSRA) "provides an integrated system of administrative review for disputes small and large arising out of the employment relationship," and thus the law "precludes judicial review of personnel actions" except those expressly made actionable by federal statute. See Steeves v. United States, 2006 WL 3526911, at *2-3 (W.D. Va. Dec. 6, 2006) (dismissing IIED claim arising out of alleged searches of plaintiff's office by agency managers), aff'd, 234 F. App'x 102 (4th Cir. 2007); Gordon v. Gutierrez, 2006 WL 3760134, at *2 (E.D. Va. Dec. 14, 2006) (intentional tort claims against federal agency managers pre-empted by CSRA), aff'd, 250 F. App'x 561 (4th Cir. 2007); see also Steeves, 2006 WL 3526911, at *3 (CSRA pre-emption does not apply if alleged malfeasance "extends beyond the ordinary employer-employee relationship").

At least where the plaintiff is a public figure, he or she cannot invoke this tort to avoid the strictures of the First Amendment otherwise applicable to a defamation claim. See Hustler Magazine v. Falwell, 485 U.S. 46, 56 (1988). Indeed, at least one lower court has held that plaintiffs may not maintain a cause of action for intentional infliction of emotional distress if premised exclusively on conduct that would also constitute the tort of defamation. Smith v. Dameron, 12 Va. Cir. 105 (Stafford Co. 1987). Similarly, the Fourth Circuit has observed that where a plaintiff cannot prevail on defamation claims "because he is unable to satisfy constitutional requirements for recovery, then he likely will be unable to prove that [defendants'] misconduct was intentional or reckless or that such misconduct was sufficiently outrageous to warrant recovery." See Hatfill v. New York Times Co., 416 F.3d 320, 336-37 (4th Cir. 2005); see also Hatfill v. New York Times Co., 488 F. Supp. 2d 522, 534 (E.D. Va. 2007) (on remand, defendant entitled to summary judgment on intentional infliction of emotional distress claim because plaintiff, who failed to produce evidence of actual malice on defamation claim, lacked evidence to support jury finding of intent or outrageousness), aff'd, 532 F.3d 312 (4th Cir. 2008).

The tort is governed by Virginia's two-year personal-injury statute of limitations. Va. Code Ann. § 8.01-243(A); **Christmas v. The Arc of The Piedmont, Inc., 2012 WL 2905584, at * 6 (W.D. Va. July 16, 2012); Torabipour v. Cosi, Inc., 2012 WL 2153168, at *5 (E.D. Va. June 12, 2012);** Luddeke v. Amana Refrigeration, Inc., 239 Va. 203, 207, 387 S.E.2d 502, 504 (1990); Young v. City of Norfolk, 62 Va. Cir. 307, 2003 WL 21730724, at *6 (July 17, 2003); Samuel v. Rose's Stores, Inc., 907 F. Supp. 159, 164 (E.D. Va. 1995); Welch v. Kennedy Piggly Wiggly Stores, Inc., 63 B.R. 888, 898 (Bankr. W.D. Va. 1986).

2. ***Interference With Prospective Economic Advantage.*** Virginia recognizes the tort of interference with prospective economic advantage – a tort that includes within its ambit interference with prospective contract, business expectancy or a contract terminable at will, all of which are distinct from the tort of interference with a contract not terminable at will. To prove that a defendant wrongfully interfered with the plaintiffs' prospective economic advantage, the plaintiff must prove (1) existence of a valid contractual relationship or business expectancy; (2) defendant's knowledge of the relationship or expectancy; (3) intentional interference; (4) through improper methods that induced or caused a termination of the relationship or expectancy; and (5) resultant damage to the plaintiffs' relationship or expectancy. See, e.g., Cobbs, 2001 WL 322728, at *3; Eslami v. Global One Communications, Inc., 48 Va. Cir. 17, 1999 WL 51864 at *6 (Newport News, Jan. 11, 1999); Maximus, Inc. v. Lockheed Information Mgmt. Sys. Co., Inc., 254 Va. 408, 414, 493 S.E.2d 375, 378 (1997); Duggin v. Adams, 234 Va. 221, 226-27, 360 S.E.2d 832, 835-36 (1987); Smithfield Ham & Products Co. v. Portion PAC, 905 F. Supp. 346, 349 (E.D. Va. 1995). See also 17th St. Assocs., LLP v. Markel Int'l Ins. Co. Ltd., 373 F. Supp. 2d 584, 600, 601 (E.D. Va. 2005) (noting that "Virginia caselaw applying the tort of intentional interference with a business expectancy contain [another], unstated element to the prima facie case: a competitive relationship between the party interfered with and the interferor," and that "contact by the defendant with the source of plaintiff's business expectancy, direct or indirect, is a de facto prima facie element" of such a claim); Whitaker v. Sheild, 2006 WL 1321481, at *10 (E.D. Va. May 3, 2006) (same).

One cannot interfere with a contract that is not enforceable. Power Distribution v. Emergency Power Engineering, 569 F. Supp. 54, 55-56, 58 (E.D. Va. 1983). Nor can one, or one's agents, interfere with one's own contract, Fox v. Deese, 234 Va. 412, 427, 362 S.E.2d 699, 708 (1987); Ashco Int'l Inc. v. Westmore Shopping Ctr. Assocs., 1997 WL 1070624, 42 Va. Cir. 427 (Fairfax Co. 1997); Ansari v. Pahlavi, 23 Va. Cir. 402 (Fairfax Co. 1991); McClain & Co. v. Carucci, 2011 WL 1706810, at *9 (W.D. Va. May 4, 2011) (allegation that defendants, acting as alter egos, caused interference is insufficient); Harper Hardware Co. v. Powers Fasteners, Inc., 2006 WL 141672, at *4 (E.D. Va. Jan. 19, 2006); Secureinfo Corp. v. Telos Corp., 387 F. Supp. 2d 593, 618 (E.D. Va. 2005), except where the agent conspires with an independent, third party, Garrett v. Langley Federal Credit Union, 121 F. Supp. 2d 887, 906 (E.D. Va. 2000); Douty v. Irwin Mortgage Corp., 70 F. Supp. 2d 626, 632 (E.D. Va. 1999), or acts outside the scope of employment, Cobbs, 2001 WL 322728, at *4. "[A] corporation and its agents are regarded as a single entity under the intra-corporate immunity doctrine," and thus are incapable of conspiring with each other to interfere with contractual relationships, unless one of the agents is acting outside the scope of his or her employment during the alleged conspiracy. Id. See also Brooks v. Arthur, 2011 WL 3102791, at *15 (W.D. Va. July 26, 2011) (issuance of disciplinary notices against plaintiffs within scope of defendant's employment where defendant supervised plaintiffs and had authority to terminate them); Baylor v. Comprehensive Pain Mgmt. Ctrs., 2011 WL 1327396, at *15 (W.D. Va. Apr. 6, 2011) (summary judgment entered against plaintiff who failed to show defendants acted outside scope of employment in terminating him). Accord Williams v. AutoZone Stores, Inc., 2009 WL 3837281, at *3 (E.D. Va. Nov. 13, 2009) ("If [manager's] actions fell outside the scope of his employment, then they were his alone and he can be held liable" to subordinate employee for interference with her contract with employer.).

Negligent interference is not actionable. See Philip Morris, Inc. v. Emerson, 235 Va. 380, 406-07, 368 S.E.2d 268, 282-83 (1988). See also Ratledge v. Sci. Applications Int'l Corp., 2011 WL 652274, at *5 (E.D. Va. Feb. 10, 2011) (deactivation of plaintiff's access badge and terminating her clearance insufficient to show intentional interference). That a defendant knows that an incidental effect of his conduct may be interference with plaintiffs' prospective economic advantage is not sufficient; defendant must be motivated by a specific desire to interfere with plaintiffs' advantage to be liable for this tort. Neurology Servs., Inc. v. Fairfax Med. PWH, LLC, 67 Va. Cir. 1, 2005 WL 832160, at *7 (Fairfax Co. Jan. 3,

2005); Levine v. McLeskey, 881 F. Supp. 1030, 1055-56 (E.D. Va. 1995), aff'd in relevant part, 164 F.3d 210 (4th Cir. 1998). No cause of action arises where defendant's interference in plaintiffs' prospective business arrangements is the result of lawful efforts to protect its own rights, see Southprint, Inc. v. H3, Inc., 2005 WL 1801667, at *8 (W.D. Va. Jul. 29, 2005), adopted in full at 2005 WL 2211378 (W.D. Va. Sept. 8, 2005), aff'd, 208 Fed. App'x 249 (4th Cir. 2006); Eurotech, Inc. v. Cosmos European Travels Aktiengesellschaft, 189 F. Supp. 2d 385, 390 (E.D. Va. 2002); Thompson Everett, Inc. v. Nat'l Cable Advertising, 57 F.3d 1317, 1327 (4th Cir. 1995); or is compelled by law, see Bridge Tech. Corp. v. Kenjya Group, Inc., 65 Va. Cir. 23, 2004 WL 1318884, at *4 (Fairfax Co. Apr. 20, 2004).

"Improper" methods include those that are illegal or independently tortious, violence, threats, undue influence, misuse of confidential information, sharp dealing, overreaching, unfair competition or other conduct improper in the circumstances of the case. Warner v. Buck Creek Nursery, Inc., 149 F. Supp. 2d 246, 266 (W.D. Va. 2001); Duggin v. Adams, 234 Va. 221, 227-28, 360 S.E.2d 832, 836-37 (1987); Maximus, Inc. v. Lockheed Information Mgmt. Sys. Co., Inc., 254 Va. 408, 414, 493 S.E.2d 375, 378-79 (1997); see also, e.g., **Long v. Teradata Corp., 2012 WL 3947811 , at *8 (E.D. Va. Sept. 10, 2012) (although claim that coworker filed a false sexual harassment claim against plaintiff and that supervisors violated company's code of ethics in handling the claim could constitute improper methods, plaintiff failed to plead sufficient facts to establish link between alleged interference and plaintiff's termination); RitLabs, S.R.L. v. RitLabs, Inc., 2012 WL 3263893, at *7 (E.D. Va. Aug. 9, 2012) (finding on summary judgment that defendant employed improper methods in interfering with software distribution contract where defendant, acting on behalf of plaintiff, terminated a contract with a distribution company, then entered into a virtually identical contract with the same company on behalf of company in which he held a controlling ownership stake);** Star City Comics & Games, Inc. v. Webbed Sphere, Inc., 2010 WL 5186713, at *7 (W.D. Va. Dec. 9, 2010) (claim that company president acted unethically by misrepresenting that company would not hire former employee of competitor if he could not be released from non-compete agreement sufficient to allege improper methods); Garrett, 121 F. Supp. 2d at 907 (improper use of confidential information); Eslami v. Global One Communications, Inc., 48 Va. Cir. 17, 1999 WL 51864 at *6 (Newport News, Jan. 11, 1999) (defamatory statements regarding interpersonal skills); Magnuson v. Peak Technical Servs., Inc., 808 F. Supp. 500, 516 -17 (E.D. Va. 1992) (false statements regarding work performance); Murray v. Cees of Virginia, Inc., 29 Va. Cir. 95 (Petersburg 1992) (demeaning reference to character); Reston Pressure Seal, Inc. v. N. Va. Waterproof, Inc., 19 Va. Cir. 545 (Fairfax Co. 1988) (factual misrepresentations regarding competitor's product). **But see Preferred Sys. Solutions, Inc. v. GP Consulting, LLC, --- S.E. 2d ----, 2012 WL 4039828, at *12 (Va. Sept. 14, 2012) ("breach of a noncompete clause is not in itself an improper method or means"); Heflin v. Coleman Music & Ent'mt, LLC, 2011 WL 6130802, at *9 (E.D. Va. Dec. 5, 2011) (filing of a lawsuit to enforce a patent, even if infringement claims were ultimately found to be meritless, did not constitute an "improper method" where there was no bad faith or improper purpose in bringing the suit);** Lewis-Gale Med. Ctr, LLC v. Alldredge, 282 Va. 141, 152, 710 S.E.2d 716, 721 (2011) (referring to physician as "organizational terrorist" insufficient to allege improper method of inducing company to terminate her); Dunn, McCormack & MacPherson v. Connolly, 281 Va. 553, 560, 708 S.E.2d 867, 871 (2011) (claim that defendant was motivated solely "by personal spite, ill will, and malice" insufficient to allege improper methods).

Where plaintiff alleges interference with advantage or expectancy, rather than contract, he or she must show with reasonable certainty that, absent defendant's conduct, the advantage or expectancy would have been realized. See American Chiropractic Ass'n, Inc. v. Trigon Healthcare, Inc., 367 F.3d 212, 228 (4th Cir.), cert. denied, 125 S.Ct. 479 (2004); DSC Commc'ns Corp. v. Pulse Commc'ns, Inc., 976 F. Supp. 359, 366 (E.D. Va. 1997), aff'd in relevant part, 170 F.3d 1354 (Fed. Cir.), cert. denied, 528 U.S. 923, 120 S. Ct. 286 (1999). "The evidence of an expectancy must establish expectancy by and between two parties at least, based upon something that is a concrete move in that direction," and not merely "plaintiff's hope." Moore v. United Int'l Investigative Servs., Inc., 209 F. Supp. 2d 611, 619-20 (E.D. Va. 2002); see also Eurotech, Inc., 189 F. Supp. 2d at 390-91 (same); H.E.R.C. Products, Inc. v. Turlington, 62 Va. Cir. 489, 2003 WL 23162378, at *4 (Norfolk, Sept. 17, 2003) ("plaintiff's belief and hope that a business relationship will continue is inadequate to sustain the cause of action") (quoting Commercial Bus. Sys., Inc. v. Halifax Corp., 253 Va. 292, 302, 484 S.E.2d 892, 897 (1997)); **Velocity Micro, Inc. v. JAZ Marketing, Inc., 2012 WL 3948018, at *6 (E.D. Va. Sept. 10, 2012) ("bald assertion" that plaintiff was "aware of no other reason why" business relationships ended insufficient to establish interference with contractual expectancy); East West, LLC v. Rahman, --- F. Supp. 2d ----, 2012 WL 2046151, at *10 (E.D. Va. June 5, 2012) ("bare assertions" which failed to establish which customer relationships defendants allegedly interfered with, "fail[ed] to raise [plaintiff's] relief above the speculative level"); Heflin, 2011 WL 6130802, at *10 (rejecting interference with business expectancy counterclaim alleging only that defendants were "attempting to persuade certain individuals and businesses to enter into businesses with Defendants" without any additional facts);** Jackson v. BECCM Co., Inc., 2010 WL 56077, at *6 (W.D. Va. Jan. 5, 2010) (plaintiff's speculation, based on past experience, that it likely would have received subsequent contracts is not "a valid business expectancy"); Ford v. Wellmont Health Sys., 2009 WL 4544099, at *9 (W.D. Va. Nov. 30, 2009) (physician's expectation of future professional relationship with his patients was insufficiently certain to support finding that solicitation sent to patients by physician's former colleagues interfered with business expectancy); Harper Hardware Co. v. Powers Fasteners, Inc., 2006 WL 141672, at *4 (E.D. Va. Jan. 19, 2006) (dismissing tortious interference claim where plaintiff made only "a general claim about [defendant's] conduct intentionally damaging [plaintiff's] business relationship," and failed to plead "a specific, existing contract or expectancy with a specific party"); GEICO v. Google, Inc., 330 F. Supp. 2d 700, 705-06 (E.D. Va. 2004) (same); Masco Contractor Servs. East, Inc. v. Beals, 279 F. Supp. 2d 699, 710 (E.D. Va. 2003) ("there must be a particular expectancy which [claimant] is reasonably certain will be realized") (citation omitted). A total loss of expected business is not necessary to maintain a claim for interference with prospective economic advantage. See, e.g., Ford. v. Torres, 2009 WL 537563, at *5-6 (E.D. Va. March 3, 2009) (even where plaintiff ultimately secured anticipated contract, notwithstanding alleged interference by its former employee, plaintiff stated claim based on theory that it had a valid expectancy interest in a more immediate relationship, such that "having the contract ... immediately rather than at some unknown point in the future constituted an economic advantage that was terminated").

Virginia has recognized five affirmative defenses to claims for intentional interference with prospective economic advantage: (1) legitimate business competition; (2) financial self-interest; (3) responsibility for the welfare of a third party; (4) directing business policy; and (5) providing solicited advice. Chaves v. Johnson, 230 Va. 112, 121, 335 S.E.2d 97, 103 (1985); see also Maximus, Inc. v. Lockheed Info. Mgmt. Sys. Co., Inc., 254 Va. 408, 415, 493 S.E.2d 375, 379 (1997). In addition, the Commonwealth has adopted statutory protection for an employer who discloses information regarding an employee in certain circumstances: "Any employer who, upon request by a person's prospective or current employer, furnishes information about that person's professional conduct, reasons for separation or job performance, including, but not limited to, information contained in any written performance evaluations, shall be immune from civil liability for furnishing such information, provided that the employer is not acting in bad faith. An employer shall be presumed to be acting in good faith. The presumption of good faith shall be rebutted if it is shown by clear and convincing evidence that the employer disclosed such information with knowledge that it was false, or with reckless disregard for whether it is false or not, or with the intent to deliberately mislead." Va. Code Ann. § 8.01-46.1.

The Virginia courts do not appear to have definitively settled the question of which statutes of limitations apply to which branches of the tort. Compare Worrie v. Boze, 198 Va. 533, 535-36, 95 S.E.2d 192, 195-96 (1956) (applying five-year statute), Welch v. Kennedy Piggly Wiggly Stores, Inc., 63 B.R. 888, 898 (Bankr. W.D. Va. 1986) (same), Guthrie v. Shield, 2005 WL 2050472, at *2 (Va. Cir. Ct. Richmond, Aug. 24, 2005) (same); Whitaker v. Sheild, 2006 WL 1321481, at *8 (E.D. Va. May 3, 2006) (same), and Williams v. Reynolds, 2006 WL 3198968 (W.D. Va. 2006) (acknowledging "some confusion" regarding applicable limitations period, but concluding that "Virginia courts have consistently applied a five year statute of limitations to tortious interference claims") with Johnson v. Plaisance, 25 Va. Cir. 264 (Charlottesville 1991) (one-year statute); Unlimited Screw Products, Inc. v. Malm, 781 F. Supp. 1121, 1127-28 (E.D. Va. 1991) (two-year statute) and Douty v. Irwin Mortgage Corp., 70 F. Supp. 2d 626, 630-31 (E.D. Va. 1999) (two-year statute).

Virginia has, by statute, created a cause of action for conspiracy to injure another's business. Va. Code Ann. § 18.2-499. A conspiracy is defined as the combination of two or more people acting in concert for the purpose of "willfully and maliciously injuring another in his reputation, trade, business or profession by any means whatever." Id. A party injured by violation of the statute is entitled to recover treble damages and attorney's fees. Id. "[B]usiness conspiracy, like fraud, must be pleaded with particularity, and with more than 'mere conclusory language.'" GEICO, 330 F. Supp. 2d at 705 (citation omitted). See Harper Hardware Co. v. Powers Fasteners, Inc., 2006 WL 141672, at *5 (E.D. Va. Jan. 19, 2006) (dismissing claim where "[p]laintiff's broad allegations provide no factual basis to discern the method of the alleged conspiracy or how it was carried out"); Scharpenberg v. Carrington, 686 F. Supp. 2d 655, 662 (E.D. Va. 2010) ("plaintiffs' broad brush general allegations and statements of mere parallel conduct" lacked sufficient particularity to support conspiracy claim under § 18.2-499). The Virginia Supreme Court has held that, to prevail under the statute, a plaintiff need not prove that the conspirators' primary purpose was to injure another in his trade or business. Advanced Marine Enters., Inc. v. PRC Inc., 256 Va. 106, 117, 501 S.E.2d 148, 154-55 (1998). A plaintiff need prove only that the conspirators acted "intentionally, purposefully, and without lawful justification." Id.; James, Ltd. v. Saks Fifth Ave., Ltd., 67 Va. Cir. 126, 2005 WL 603131, at *11 (Arlington Co. Mar. 8, 2005), rev'd on other grounds, 630 S.E.2d 304 (Va. 2006); Harper Hardware Co., 2006 WL 141672, at *5 ("In order to sustain a claim for statutory business conspiracy, the plaintiff must prove by clear and convincing evidence that the defendants acted intentionally, purposefully, and without lawful justification, and that such actions injured the plaintiff's business."). Under the intracorporate immunity doctrine, "a conspiracy 'requires two or more persons and ... because a corporation and its agents comprise a single legal entity, they are legally incapable of conspiracy.'" Secureinfo Corp. v. Telos Corp., 387 F. Supp. 2d 593, 616 (E.D. Va. 2005) (citation omitted); Phoenix Renovation Corp. v. Rodriguez, 403 F. Supp. 2d 510, 517 (E.D. Va. 2005) ("The intracorporate immunity doctrine holds that a conspiracy between a corporation and agents of that corporation acting within the scope of their employment is a legal impossibility."). "However, the doctrine of intracorporate immunity is excepted under two circumstances: (1) when an agent of the corporation has an independent personal stake in achieving the corporation's illegal objective, or (2) when the agent is engaged in unauthorized acts." Whitaker, 2006 WL 1321481, at *11; see id. at *12 (intracorporate immunity doctrine did not bar conspiracy claims where plaintiffs alleged that defendant attorneys "stood to benefit independently" because they would gain additional work if the deal being negotiated came to fruition, and where they "participated in unauthorized acts" by "represent[ing] adverse parties in the same transaction").

3. ***Prima Facie Tort.*** Virginia has not recognized a cause of action for prima facie tort. Unlimited Screw Products, 781 F. Supp. at 1130.

II. EMPLOYER TESTING OF EMPLOYEES

A. Psychological or Personality Testing

1. ***Common Law and Statutes.*** Although Virginia courts do not appear to have addressed the subject of psychological or personality testing in the employment context through the common law, in Mansoor v. County of Albemarle, 124 F. Supp. 2d 367, 384 (W.D. Va. 2000), the court held that a police officer who was required to undergo psychological testing purportedly as a prerequisite to being reimbursed for sick leave and counseling for a panic disorder stated a claim under § 2.1-378(B)(4) of the Virginia Privacy Protection Act (now, the Government Data Collection and Dissemination Practices Act § 2.2-3800 et seq.), where he alleged that "the true purpose was to obtain a method for chilling his future speech." See id. ("Allegations that the defendants induced the plaintiff to see [the psychologist] based on what they knew to be false premises are sufficient to sustain a claim that the psychological information about him 'was obtained by fraudulent or unfair means.'"). A discussion of federal statutes and the case law construing them is beyond the scope of this survey.

2. ***Private Employers.*** See II.A.1, supra.

3. ***Public Employers.*** See II.A.1, supra. In Reynolds v. Fairfax Co. School Bd., 985 F.2d 553 (4th Cir. 1993) (table, text available in Westlaw), a teacher challenged her dismissal by her employer after an incident in her classroom prompted supervisors to subject her to a battery of personality and psychological tests. It does not appear that plaintiff challenged the propriety of the tests, and the Fourth Circuit appears to have assumed, without discussion, that the testing was authorized. In Earley v. Marion, 540 F. Supp. 2d 680, 688 (W.D. Va. 2008), aff'd, 340 F. App'x 169 (4th Cir. 2009), the court found "no constitutional deprivation of [the] substantive due process" rights of a teacher who was suspended with pay pending psychological evaluation because "there was ample evidence supporting the defendants' decision." In Mansoor, 124 F. Supp. 2d at 384, the court held that "[c]ollecting, using, and disseminating private information" – including, in that case, the results of a psychological evaluation by a psychologist hired by the county – "to chill an individual's right to freedom of speech is not a proper purpose for collecting that information" and constitutes a violation of § 2.1-380(A)(1) of the Virginia Privacy Protection Act (now, the Government Data Collection and Dissemination Practices Act § 2.2-3800 et seq.).

B. Drug Testing

1. ***Common Law and Statutes.*** Except with regard to qualification for unemployment benefits, Virginia does not appear to have addressed the subject of drug testing in the employment context by statute. In certain circumstances, a person who fails a drug test is disqualified from receiving unemployment benefits. Va. Code Ann. § 60.2-618 2(b)(1); (3)(d). For the few Virginia cases involving other aspects of drug testing, see IIB.2 and IIB.3, infra. A discussion of federal statutes concerning drug testing and case law construing them is beyond the scope of this survey.

2. ***Private Employers.*** Where a collective bargaining agreement governs the employer's right to conduct drug testing, disputes over implementation of such testing will be resolved with reference to federal labor law, and federal labor law preempts the employee's state law claims based on allegedly negligent testing procedures and wrongful discharge following improper testing. Clark v. Newport News Shipbuilding & Dry Dock Co., 937 F.2d 934 (4th Cir. 1991). The appellate court noted that the plaintiff had been unable to cite to any "independent state law or public policy regarding drug testing standards or procedures in the private employment sector that create rights or obligations beyond those which can be the subject of a private agreement." Id. at 937-38; see also District 28 v. Consolidation Coal Co., 108 F.3d 1371, 1997 WL 107455 (4th Cir. 1997) (table, text available in Westlaw) (affirming decision of arbitrator pursuant to collective bargaining agreement that employee was terminated for just cause in view of positive drug use tests). Where an employee is discharged for failure to comply with a drug testing policy and then seeks unemployment benefits based on alleged wrongful discharge, an employer bears the burden of proving that the employee "deliberately or willfully" violated the prescribed testing procedures. Bell Atlantic Network Servs. v. Va. Employment Comm'n, 16 Va. App. 741, 745, 433 S.E.2d 30, 32 (1993); see also Carter v. Extra's Inc., 15 Va. App. 648, 427 S.E.2d 197 (1993) (en banc) (affirming, without opinion by an equally divided court, judgment of trial court disqualifying employee for unemployment benefits where he was discharged for refusal to sign acknowledgment of employer's drug testing policy).

3. ***Public Employers.*** In Roberts v. City of Newport News, 36 F.3d 1093, 1994 WL 520948 (4th Cir. 1994) (table, text available in Westlaw), the Fourth Circuit discussed in general terms the circumstances under which a municipal government may impose drug tests on its employees. A firefighter refused to submit to a urinalysis and blood test for drugs and was terminated. He brought an action against the city and others pursuant to 42 U.S.C. § 1983. In the context of

an appeal from the trial court's order rejecting certain defendants' defense of qualified immunity, the Fourth Circuit observed that, as a search governed by the Fourth Amendment, "[a]ny government order for urinalysis must be reasonable." 1994 WL 520948 at *2. What is reasonable will depend upon the particular circumstances of the case and a court must balance "the individual's legitimate expectations of privacy against the government's need to conduct the testing in the manner it proposes." Id. "Urinalysis can be required where the testing is carried out under a specific plan and is applied either randomly or routinely to government employees, or private employees tested in satisfaction of government regulations, who occupy particularly sensitive positions." Id. Although the touchstone in these circumstances is the limited discretion afforded the employer to single out particular employees for tests, "[r]egardless of whether any drug testing plan is in place, a government employer may require an employee to submit to urinalysis where the employer has reasonable, articulable grounds to suspect an employee of illegal drug involvement. This would require individualized suspicion, specifically directed to the person who is targeted for the urinalysis test." Id. The Fourth Circuit ruled that the fire chief did not have reasonable grounds to suspect drug use by the plaintiff, since the only basis for his request that plaintiff submit to the test were two anonymous telephone calls, one from a tipster who, at the time, admitted she had never actually seen the plaintiff use illegal drugs, but merely believed that he had a "problem other than with alcohol." Id. at *3. See also Op. Va. Att'y Gen. Feb. 27, 1987 (Drug Testing: Employer May Administer Drug Test To Public Safety Employees on Reasonable Suspicion). Cf. Hassell v. City of Chesapeake, 64 F. Supp. 2d 573, 577 (E.D. Va. 1999) ("even if it could be found that one co-worker's observation that Plaintiff smelled of marijuana was outweighed by the undisputed observations [to the contrary] of several other co-workers, when the Court weighs the highly sensitive nature of the Plaintiff's position [as Children's Counselor and Senior Parole Officer at juvenile detention facility] against his reasonable expectation of privacy, the totality of facts support the [drug] testing order"), aff'd, 230 F.3d 1352, 2000 WL 1339232 (4th Cir. 2000) (holding that City could not be held liable for drug testing where "there is no evidence that Chesapeake agencies customarily test their employees in similar circumstances or that city policymakers are aware of such a custom") (table, text available in Westlaw); Carroll v. City of Westminster, 233 F.3d 208, 212 (4th Cir. 2000) (police chief "had reasonable individualized suspicion that [plaintiff police officer] was abusing drugs" where he received tip from acquaintance of plaintiff whose credibility "was enhanced by his willingness to use his own name and to provide a work phone number where he could be reached"). The Fourth Circuit has noted "that courts have long recognized that individuals in certain safety-sensitive professions, such as law enforcement, have a reduced expectation of privacy." Id. at 212.

C. Medical Testing

1. ***Common Law and Statutes***. Employers may not require applicants or employees to pay the cost of a medical examination or of furnishing medical records; such costs must be borne by the employer. Va. Code Ann. § 40.1-28 (2002). Virginia has adopted legislation restricting the use of genetic information by employers and insurers. Employers may not require applicants or employees to take a genetic test as a condition of employment, or take adverse action against such individuals solely on the basis of a genetic characteristic, regardless of how the employer obtained the information. Va. Code Ann. § 40.1-28.7:1 (A). The statute gives employees a private right of action against employers who violate its provisions. Va. Code Ann. § 40.1-28.7:1 (B). Virginia does not appear to have addressed other relevant aspects of medical testing in the employment context either by statute or through the common law. A discussion of federal statutes and case law construing them is beyond the scope of this survey.

2. ***Private Employers***. See II.C.l, supra.

3. ***Public Employers***. See II.C.l, supra. When an incident involving a public safety employee or certain other persons assisting a public safety employee may have resulted in the exposure of any of such persons or third parties to the bodily fluids of another, affected persons may request the other's consent to be tested for Hepatitis B, Hepatitis C and HIV and, where consent is refused, the affected person may file a petition in District Court seeking a judicial order requiring such tests. Va. Code Ann. § 32.1-45.2.

D. Polygraph Tests

Neither public nor private employers in Virginia may, as a condition of employment, require a prospective employee to answer questions during a polygraph examination concerning his or her sexual activities unless the applicant has been convicted of a sexual crime in Virginia. See Va. Code Ann. §§ 40.1-51.4:3, 54.1-1806. Written records of any polygraph examination given to a prospective employee must be destroyed or maintained in confidence and can be released only with the prospective employee's agreement. Va. Code Ann. § 40.1-51.4:3. Law enforcement agencies may not require an employee to submit to a polygraph examination or discriminate on the basis of a refusal to so submit, except where the chief executive officer of an agency issues a written order requiring an employee to submit to an examination in connection with an internal administrative investigation of criminal or other misconduct. Va. Code Ann. § 40.1-51.4:4. Law enforcement agencies may not take any adverse employment action based solely on the result of such an examination. Id. In the context of an action brought by former police officers against the City of Chesapeake and others pursuant to 42 U.S.C. § 1983, the federal appellate court ruled that the police chief's decision to terminate the officers after they refused to submit to polygraph examinations did not violate the officers' due process rights, at least where the officers' employment agreement included a provision for such examinations and they were informed at the time the examination was requested that they would be terminated if they refused to comply. Kersey v. Shipley, 673 F.2d 730 (4th Cir.), cert. denied, 459 U.S. 836 (1982). A discussion of federal statutes, including the Employee Polygraph Protection Act of 1988, 29 U.S.C. § 2001 et seq., is beyond the scope of this survey, and Virginia courts have rarely been called upon to construe the Act. But see Harmon v. CB Squared Servs., 624 F. Supp. 2d 459 (E.D. Va. 2009) (granting plaintiff-employee partial summary judgment in action alleging violation of EPPA based on defendant-employer's use of polygraph test).

E. Fingerprinting

Several classes of employees in Virginia are required to submit to fingerprinting as a condition of employment. See Va. Code Ann. §§ 9.1-139 (certain persons accepting employment in private security services businesses), 18.2-308.2:3 (certain persons accepting employment selling firearms), 22.1-296.2 (certain persons accepting employment in public schools), 22.1-296.3 (certain persons accepting employment in private and parochial schools), 37.2-416 (certain persons accepting employment at mental health facilities), 37.2-506 (certain persons accepting employment to provide mental health care to consumers), 37.2-416 (same), 59.1-371 (2000) (certain persons employed or otherwise participating in horse racing), 58.1-4008 (2004) (all persons employed by State Lottery Department), 63.2-1726 (certain persons employed, volunteering or providing services to juvenile residential facilities). Virginia does not appear to otherwise have addressed the subject of fingerprinting in the employment context, either by statute or through the common law.

III. SEARCHES

Virginia does not appear to have addressed in a pertinent context the subject of employer-conducted searches of employees and/or their work area or property, either by statute or through the common law. Of course, the Fourth Amendment to the United States Constitution, made applicable to the states by the Fourteenth Amendment, limits the right of public employers to conduct such searches. The protection against unreasonable searches by government officers afforded by Va. Code Ann. § 19.2-59 is the same as that provided by the Fourth Amendment. See, e.g., Buonocore v. Chesapeake & Potomac Tel. Co., 254 Va. 469, 473, 492 S.E.2d 439, 441 (Va. 1997). A discussion of Fourth Amendment jurisprudence is beyond the scope of this survey, but a helpful discussion of the federal constitutional concepts in the context of warrantless searches of computer files and computer drives as part of an investigation of potential public employee wrongdoing may be found in United States v. Simons, 206 F.3d 392 (4th Cir. 2000).

A. Employee's Person

1. ***Private Employers***. The federal appellate court has noted that, where a collective bargaining agreement applies, whether a search of an employee's person by his employer is wrongful will be governed by the terms of that agreement. McCormick v. AT&T Technologies, Inc., 934 F.2d 531, 538 (4th Cir. 1991). In a closely regulated industry, such as mining, governing regulations may authorize warrantless searches of the workplace, but authority limited to searches of the workplace does not extend to searches of an employee's person. Commonwealth v. Burgan, 19 Va. App. 172, 450 S.E.2d 177 (1994). See also III, supra.

2. ***Public Employers***. See III, supra.

B. Employee's Work Area

Although Virginia courts apparently have not addressed the availability of civil remedies for searches conducted by an employer of an employee's work area, case law suggests that employers have broad discretion to limit workers' expectations of privacy in their workspaces, such as through company computer-use policies. For example, in affirming a jury verdict for breach of a fiduciary duty and tortious interference with business relations against a company's former sales manager arising out of the manager's actions in leaving the company to start a competing business, the Virginia Supreme Court found that, in light of language in an employee handbook, the manager had "no expectation of privacy" in a document that he had maintained on his former work computer and that was recovered through forensic analysis. Banks v. Mario Indus. of Virginia, Inc., 274 Va. 438, 454, 650 S.E.2d 687, 696 (Sept. 14, 2007). Thus, even though the document was prepared exclusively for the purpose of seeking legal advice from the manager's attorney and deleted by the manager before he left the company, the manager had waived any claim to attorney-client privilege by storing the document on his work computer. Id. See also III, supra.

C. Employee's Property

1. ***Private Employers***. Whether it is actionable that an employer opened an employee's locker after termination in order to retrieve its property, and subsequently disposed of employee's personal property, will be governed by

collective bargaining agreement where such agreement applies. McCormick v. AT&T Technologies, Inc., 934 F.2d 531, 538 (4th Cir. 1991).

2. ***Public Employers***. See III, supra.

IV. MONITORING OF EMPLOYEES

Virginia statutes and pertinent case law are discussed below. A discussion of federal wiretap and related statutory and decisional law is beyond the scope of this survey.

A. Telephones and Electronic Communications

1. ***Wiretapping.*** The Virginia Interception of Wire, Electronic or Oral Communications Act, Va. Code Ann. § 19.2-61 et seq., prohibits interception not only of "wire communications," defined as any aural transfer made in whole or in part, through wire, cable or like facilities, including switching stations, but also "electronic communications," defined to include radio and several other forms of wireless transmission, and "oral communications," defined as any utterance by a person exhibiting an expectation that the communication is not subject to interception under circumstances justifying such an expectation. Va. Code Ann. § 19.2-61. "[T]he justifiable expectation of noninterception contained in the statutory definition of the term "oral communication" is equivalent to the constitutional expectation of privacy." Belmer v. Commonwealth, 36 Va. App. 448, 455, 553 S.E.2d 123, 126 (2001) (citation omitted). The statute makes it a felony (1) to intentionally intercept, endeavor to intercept, or procure another person to intercept any wire, electronic or oral communication; (2) to intentionally use, endeavor to use, or procure another person to use any device to intercept an oral communication; (3) to intentionally disclose or endeavor to disclose to any other person the contents of any wire, electronic or oral communication with reason to know that the information was obtained through interception of such communication; and (4) to intentionally use or endeavor to use the contents of any wire, electronic or oral communication with reason to know that the information was obtained through the interception of such communication. Va. Code Ann. § 19.2-62. "Intercept" is defined as "any aural or other means of acquisition of the contents of any wire, electronic or oral communication through the use of any electronic, mechanical or other device." Va. Code Ann. § 19.2-61. It is not a violation of the statute "for a person to intercept a wire, electronic or oral communication, where such person is a party to the communication or one of the parties to the communication has given prior consent to such interception." Va. Code Ann. § 19.2-62(B)(2); see also, e.g., Watkins v. Commonwealth, 238 Va. 341, 347, 385 S.E.2d 50, 53-54 (1989) (where police persuaded criminal suspect's girlfriend to permit recording device to be placed on her telephone, there was no violation of the Act because "a telephone conversation recorded by or with the consent of one of the parties to the communication is not an 'interception' within the meaning of the wiretap statutes"), cert. denied, 494 U.S. 1074 (1990); Hulcher v. City of Richmond, 31 Va. Cir. 468 (Richmond 1993) (same with respect to employee whose telephone conversations were recorded). The Act provides certain other limited exceptions to liability. See Va. Code Ann. § 19.2-62(B)(3). A person whose wire, electronic or oral communication has unlawfully been intercepted, disclosed or used in violation of the Act may bring a civil action against the violator and recover actual damages or liquidated damages of up to $1,000, punitive damages, and reasonable attorney's fees and costs. Va. Code Ann. § 19.2-69. It does not appear that the Virginia appellate courts have considered what statute of limitations would apply to actions alleging violations of section 19.2-69, which does not itself provide a limitations period. However, Virginia's catch-all statute provides a limitations period of two years, Va. Code Ann. § 8.01-248, and one trial court considering an emotional distress claim arising out of an alleged violation of the Act ruled that the two-year period applied, Eshaghi v. Kunz, 41 Va. Cir. 476 (Chesterfield Co. 1997).

2. ***Electronic Communications.*** "A person is guilty of the crime of computer invasion of privacy when he uses a computer or computer network and intentionally examines without authority any employment, salary, credit or any other financial or identifying information, as defined in clauses (iii) through (xiii) of subsection C of § 18.2-186.3, relating to any other person." Va. Code Ann. § 18.2-152.5(A). A discussion of Fourth Amendment jurisprudence is beyond the scope of this survey, but a helpful discussion of the federal constitutional concepts in the context of warrantless searches of computer files and computer drives as part of an investigation of potential public employee wrongdoing may be found in United States v. Simons, 206 F.3d 392 (4th Cir. 2000). See also IV.A.1, supra.

3. ***Other Electronic Monitoring.*** It does not appear that Virginia has addressed the subject of other forms of electronic monitoring in the employment context either through the common law or by statute. A discussion of federal law on the subject is beyond the scope of this survey.

B. Mail

Virginia does not appear to have addressed the subject of employees' privacy interests in their mail either by statute or through the common law. A discussion of federal law on the subject is beyond the scope of this survey.

C. Surveillance/Photographing

For a discussion of the Virginia Interception of Wire, Electronic or Oral Communications Act, Va. Code Ann. § 19.2 -61 et seq., see IV.A.I, supra. It is a misdemeanor in Virginia to enter another's property and "peep, spy or attempt to peer or spy into or through a window, door or other aperture of any building ... intended for occupancy as a dwelling." Va. Code Ann. § 18.2-130. It also is a misdemeanor to videotape, photograph or film any nonconsenting person while that person is nude, clad in undergarments, or in a state of undress such that genitals, buttocks or female breasts are exposed in a restroom, dressing room, locker room, hotel room, or other location, if the circumstances are such that the person had a reasonable expectation of privacy. Va. Code Ann. § 18.2-386.1. Virginia has adopted an anti-stalking statute, Va. Code Ann. § 18.2-60.3, but it does not appear likely to be pertinent to most employment-related situations.

V. ACTIVITIES OUTSIDE THE WORKPLACE

A. Statute or Common Law

See V.B, infra.

B. Employees' Personal Relationships

1. ***Romantic Relationships Between Employees***. It does not appear that Virginia has addressed the subject of romantic relationships between employees either by statute or through the common law.

2. ***Sexual Orientation***. The Virginia legislature has declined to recognize sexual orientation as a protected class in Virginia. However, neither public nor private employers in Virginia may, as a condition of employment, require a prospective employee to answer questions during a polygraph examination concerning his or her sexual activities unless the applicant has been convicted of a sexual crime in Virginia. See Va. Code Ann. §§ 40.1-51.4:3, 54.1-1806.

Former Governors Mark Warner and Timothy Kaine each had issued executive orders banning discrimination in state employment on the basis of sexual orientation. See Va. Exec. Order No. 1 (Jan. 14, 2006); see also Va. Exec. Order No. 1, 18:11 Va. Reg. Regs. 1431 (Feb. 11, 2002), revised 22:10 Va. Reg. Regs. 1701 (Jan. 23, 2006). In 2010, when Governor Robert McDonnell took office, he rescinded his predecessor's order. See Va. Exec. Order No. 6 (Feb. 5, 2010). McDonnell, in his prior role as the state's Attorney General, had concluded that the Warner-Kaine orders exceeded the scope of executive authority and were therefore unconstitutional. See Va. Att'y Gen. Op. No. 05-094 (Feb. 24, 2006).

3. ***Marital Status***. The Virginia Human Rights Act prohibits discrimination in employment on the basis of marital status. See Va. Code Ann. §§ 2.2-3900 to 2.2-3902. There do not appear to by any judicial opinions discussing this provision.

C. Smoking

It does not appear that Virginia has addressed the subject of smoking in an employment-related context, either by statute or through the common law. Some local jurisdictions regulate smoking by ordinance.

D. Blogging

It does not appear that Virginia has addressed the subject of employee blogging, either with or without employer approval, by statute or through the common law.

VI. RECORDS

A discussion of federal statutes and decisional law concerning record-keeping and confidentiality requirements is beyond the scope of this survey.

A. Personnel Records

The Government Data Collection and Dissemination Practices Act, Va. Code Ann. § 2.2-3800 et seq. (formerly, the Virginia Privacy Protection Act, Va. Code Ann. § 2.1-377 et seq. (repealed)), has been applied to records of an internal investigation conducted by a police department, and an officer whose personnel records were released to persons not authorized by the Act to receive them obtained an injunction against further dissemination. Hinderliter v. Humphries, 224 Va. 439, 297 S.E.2d 684 (1982); see also Mansoor v. County of Albemarle, 124 F. Supp. 2d 367, 384 (W.D. Va. 2000). An employee who was reprimanded for contributing to a hostile work environment was entitled under the Government Data Collection and Dissemination Practices Act to access records of the investigation into his alleged conduct, including information concerning the identities of complainants, informants, and others involved in the investigation or mentioned in the final investigatory report, even though the investigatory materials leading up to the final report would have been exempt from disclosure under the Virginia Freedom of Information of Act. McChrystal v. Fairfax County Bd. of Supervisors, 67 Va. Cir. 171, 2005 WL 832242, at *10 (Fairfax Co. Mar. 22, 2005). The Virginia Freedom of Information Act, Va. Code Ann. § 2.2-3700 et seq., which excludes from its disclosure requirements "[p]ersonnel records containing information concerning identifiable individuals," Va. Code Ann. § 2.2-3705.1, has been invoked successfully to preserve the confidentiality of materials generated during a city investigation into wrongdoing by a plumbing inspector, Moore v. Maroney, 258 Va. 21, 516 S.E.2d 9 (1999) (affirming, expressly without approving or disapproving order on ground that appellate record was incomplete, trial court's order denying request for release of information). Virginia provides a safe harbor to employers who disclose personnel information in certain circumstances: "Any employer who, upon request by a person's prospective or current employer, furnishes information about that person's professional conduct, reasons for separation or job performance, including, but not limited to, information contained in any written performance evaluations, shall be immune from civil liability for furnishing such information, provided that the employer is not acting in bad faith. An employer shall be presumed to be acting in good faith. The presumption of good faith shall be rebutted if it is shown by clear and convincing evidence that the employer disclosed such information with knowledge that it was false, or with reckless disregard for whether it is false or not, or with the intent to deliberately mislead." Va. Code Ann. § 8.01-46.1.

Virginia does not appear to have directly addressed the subject of personnel records through the common law. However, in Muhammad v. VSI Group, 2001 WL 506161, at *1 (Va. Ct. App. May 15, 2001), the court held that the Workers' Compensation Commission did not err in finding that an employee who was fired "because she looked in another employee's personnel file and took a copy of that person's driver's license" was terminated for cause. "[T]he claimant's conduct was wrongful and in violation of the employer's legitimate business interest in protecting the privacy of its employees." Id.

B. Medical Records

Virginia recognizes a cause of action in tort against health care providers for disclosure of patient records without the patient's authorization and permits the recovery of emotional distress damages in such cases. Fairfax Hosp. v. Curtis, 254 Va. 437, 492 S.E.2d 642 (1997). Employers may not require applicants or employees to pay the cost of furnishing copies of medical records; such costs must be borne by the employer, Va. Code Ann. § 40.1-28. Note that "[a] person is guilty of the crime of computer invasion of privacy when he uses a computer or computer network and intentionally examines without authority any employment, salary, credit or any other financial or identifying information, as defined in clauses (iii) through (xiii) of subsection C of § 18.2-186.3, relating to any other person." Va. Code Ann. § 18.2-152.5(A). Virginia does not otherwise appear to address the subject of medical records in the employment context.

C. Criminal Records

In general, most private and many public employers are excluded from the list of those entities entitled to receive copies of records from the state's Central Criminal Records Exchange. See Va. Code Ann. § 19.2-389(A). Criminal justice agencies and persons, moreover, are prohibited from confirming the existence or nonexistence of criminal history record information in response to most employers' inquiries. Va. Code Ann. § 19.2-389(C). Non-profit institutions of higher education, however, are among those entities that are entitled to obtain such criminal records under state law, so long as it is to be used "for the purpose of screening individuals who are offered or accept employment," and Virginia's attorney general has therefore concluded in an advisory opinion that such institutions – including private universities – may require criminal background searches as a condition of employment. Va. Att'y Gen. Op. No. 06-046 (Aug. 8, 2006). In certain circumstances, liability may arise if an employer could have conducted a criminal background check but did not. Indeed, the Fourth Circuit held that a janitorial staffing company was not entitled to summary judgment on a negligent hiring and retention claim where the company was contractually obligated to a public college to conduct background checks on its employees, failed to do so prior to hiring an employee who subsequently committed a violent assault at the college, and the check arguably would have revealed that the employee had been the subject of a prior criminal complaint and protective order and thus would not have been placed at the college. See Blair v. Defender Servs., Inc., 386 F.3d 623, 630 (4th Cir. 2004). Employers, however, may not require applicants to disclose information concerning an arrest or criminal charge that has been expunged. Va. Code Ann. § 19.2-392.4. Note also that "[a] person is guilty of the crime of computer invasion of privacy when he uses a computer or computer network and intentionally examines without authority any employment, salary, credit or any other financial or identifying information, as defined in clauses (iii) through (xiii) of subsection C of § 18.2-186.3, relating to any other person." Va. Code Ann. § 18.2-152.5(A); see also Plasters v. Commonwealth, 2000 WL 827940 (Va. Ct. App. June 27, 2000) (affirming conviction under this statute of public employee who accessed criminal history information without authorization).

D. Subpoenas / Search Warrants

It does not appear that Virginia has addressed the subject of search warrants served on employers seeking to search employee files or an employee's workspace.

There is limited case law in Virginia on subpoenas served on employers for information relating to employees. In United States v. Doe, 434 F. Supp. 2d 377 (E.D. Va. 2006), the court quashed a grand jury subpoena seeking records from a city police department's internal affairs office containing statements made by police officers during an internal investigation of a possible target of the grand jury investigation. The statements had been obtained pursuant to the police chief's decree that cooperation in internal investigations was a condition of employment for all officers, and his written assurance that any information thus obtained could be used in departmental administrative actions, but not in any criminal proceeding. Id. at 378. The court cited three critical factors: "First, the availability of an exceedingly simple alternative to obtaining this information, subpoenaing the officers directly; second, the risk that, if the motion to quash is denied, the officers' privileges against self-incrimination will be offended; and third, the effect the erosion of secrecy may have on the internal affairs office's ability to police the police." Id. at 381. Concluding that "the law enforcement interests of the City outweigh those of the federal government," the court quashed the subpoena pursuant to Federal Rule of Criminal Procedure 17(c). Id.

VII. ACTIONS SUBSEQUENT TO EMPLOYMENT

A. References

Virginia provides a safe harbor to employers who provide references in certain circumstances: "Any employer who, upon request by a person's prospective or current employer, furnishes information about that person's professional conduct, reasons for separation or job performance, including, but not limited to, information contained in any written performance evaluations, shall be immune from civil liability for furnishing such information, provided that the employer is not acting in bad faith. An employer shall be presumed to be acting in good faith. The presumption of good faith shall be rebutted if it is shown by clear and convincing evidence that the employer disclosed such information with knowledge that it was false, or with reckless disregard for whether it is false or not, or with the intent to deliberately mislead." Va. Code Ann. § 8.01-46.1. There do not appear to be any cases applying this statute, which was enacted in 2000, and applies to any cause of action accruing after July 1, 2000.

B. Non-Compete Agreements

Non-compete agreements "are not favored, will be strictly construed, and, in the event of an ambiguity, will be construed in favor of the employee." Modern Env'ts, Inc. v. Stinnett, 263 Va. 491, 493, 561 S.E.2d 694, 695 (2002); see also Omniplex World Servs. Corp. v. US Investigations Servs., Inc., 270 Va. 246, 249, 618 S.E.2d 340, 342 (2005) ("Because such restrictive covenants are disfavored restraints on trade, the employer bears the burden of proof and any ambiguities in the contract will be construed in favor of the employee."). Thus, when an employee resists enforcement of a non-compete agreement as facially invalid, courts generally will presume that ambiguous provisions of the covenant have "the broadest logical meaning and the [meaning] most restrictive on the employee." See Capital One Financial Corp. v. Kirkpatrick, 2007 WL 2247599 (E.D. Va. 2007). But see Strategic Enter. Solutions, Inc. v. Ikuma, 2008 Va. Cir. LEXIS 144, at *6 (Fairfax Co. Oct. 7, 2008) (finding non-compete agreement's geographic limitation of "100 square mile radius" to be ambiguous because it "is a mathematical impossibility, containing both a linear measurement and an area measurement"; term construed to confine non-compete area to a 5.642-mile radius because "a circle with an area of 100 square miles has a radius of 5.642 miles"); McClain & Co. v. Carucci, 2011 WL 1706810, at *6 (W.D. Va. May 4, 2011) (non-compete agreement formed *after* employment relationship terminated held to less restrictive standard of reasonableness, where agreement was result of arms-length negotiation and former employee was represented by counsel).

Virginia courts usually decline to engage in "blue penciling" of otherwise unambiguous agreements, and thus reject requests to narrow overly broad restrictions to make them enforceable. See, e.g., Strategic Enter. Solutions, Inc., 2008 Va. Cir. LEXIS 144, at *12-13 ("[I]t is clear from the restrictive covenant jurisprudence in Virginia that the [Virginia Supreme] Court does not entertain the notion that these disfavored restraints on trade should be reformed by the judiciary[.]") (collecting cases); Better Living Components, Inc. v. Coleman, 2005 WL 771592, at *5 (Va. Cir. Ct. Albemarle Co. Apr. 6, 2005) (circuit courts in Virginia "have uniformly denied the existence" of judicial power to "blue pencil" a non-compete agreement to render it enforceable).

In Virginia, the enforceability of a restrictive covenant is a question of law. **Preferred Systems Solutions, Inc. v. GP Consulting, LLC, --- S.E.2d ----, 2012 WL 4039828, at *2 (Va. 2012);** Phoenix Renovation Corp. v. Rodriguez, 439 F. Supp. 2d 510, 520 (E.D. Va. 2006). In determining whether a non-compete agreement between an employer and employee should be enforced, courts consider the following factors: "(1) Is the restraint, from the standpoint of the employer, reasonable in the sense that it is no greater than necessary to protect the employer in some legitimate business interest? (2) From the standpoint of the employee, is the restraint reasonable in the sense that it is not unduly harsh and oppressive in curtailing his legitimate efforts to earn a livelihood? (3) Is the restraint reasonable from the standpoint of a sound public policy?" Advanced Marine Enters., Inc. v. PRC Inc., 256 Va. 106, 118, 501 S.E.2d 148, 155 (1998); Cantol, Inc. v. McDaniel, 2006 WL 1213992, at *4 (E.D. Va. Apr. 28, 2006); accord Modern Env'ts, Inc., 263 Va. at 493, 561 S.E.2d at 695 ("the employer bears the burden to show that the restraint is no greater than necessary to protect a legitimate business interest, is not unduly harsh or oppressive in curtailing an employee's ability to earn a livelihood, and is reasonable in light of sound public policy"). These factors must not be considered as separate and distinct issues; rather, they must be considered together. Phoenix Renovation Corp., 439 F. Supp. 2d at 520 (citation omitted). Furthermore, the employer has the burden of proving that the restraint is reasonable and the contract is valid. Id.

In at-will employment relationships, continued employment has been held to be adequate consideration for a promise not to compete made by the employee after the initial formation of the employment relationship. See James, Ltd. v. Saks Fifth Ave., Inc., 67 Va. Cir. 126, 2005 WL 603131, at *9 (Arlington Co. Mar. 8, 2005) ("When a company continues to employ at-will employees and provides them with access to valuable information after they sign non-competition agreements, courts have held that requisite and sufficient consideration for the promise not to compete has been given."), rev'd on other grounds, 630 S.E.2d 304 (Va. 2006). Non-compete agreements do not alter an employee's at-will status. Devnew v. Brown & Brown, Inc., 396 F. Supp. 2d 665, 672 (E.D. Va. 2005) ("a non-compete clause has no effect on the ability of an employer to terminate an at-will employee with or without cause"); **See also Capital One Fin. Corp. v. Kanas, --- F. Supp. 2d ----, 2012 WL 1806138, at *7 (E.D. Va. May 17, 2012) ("unprecedented" consideration of $42 million in restricted stock to defendants, executives responsible for growing a small town bank into a "corporate behemoth," with obvious equal bargaining power and sophistication, held as valid consideration).**

Non-compliance with contractual formalities will typically result in an unenforceable agreement in Virginia courts. See, e.g., Workflow Solutions v. Lewis, 2008 Va. Cir. LEXIS 186, at *9 (Norfolk Dec. 12, 2008) (although parties had agreed, as a condition of defendant's renewed employment, that defendant would "execute a new employment agreement continuing ... [certain] restrictive covenants," no such agreement was ever executed; thus, court could not restrain defendant from competing, "even though he benefited from working [for plaintiff]").

Courts have declined to enforce non-compete agreements that broadly prohibit professional activities by the employee without any limiting language on the types of activities restricted. See **Home Paramount Pest Control Companies, Inc. v. Shaffer, 718 S.E.2d 762,765-66, 282 Va. 412, 418 (2011) (non-compete agreement barring employee from working for any other business in pest control industry in any capacity overbroad and unenforceable, where it was not confined to those activities in which the employer actually engaged) (overruling Paramount Termite Control Co., v. Rector, 238 Va. 171, 380 S.E.2d 922 (1989));** Nortec Commc'ns, Inc. v. Lee-Llacer, 548 F. Supp. 2d 226, 228 (E.D. Va. 2008) (holding that employment contract's "non-competition and non-solicitation provisions" were "invalid and unenforceable" because provisions were "not limited to the performance of the same work that [defendant] did as [an] employee" for plaintiff and contained "several undefined key terms"); Omniplex World Servs. Corp., 270 Va. at 250, 618 S.E.2d at 342-43 (declining to enforce clause that prohibited former employee from performing "any services for any other employer in a position supporting" employer's customer, and was "not limited to employment that would be in competition" with kinds of services employer provided to that customer); Strategic Enter. Solutions, Inc., 2008 Va. Cir. LEXIS 144, at *6-8 (finding overly broad, and therefore unenforceable, agreement that employee not "actively engage ... in any business in competition" because it would prevent employee from working in any capacity for competitor, without regard to function to be performed by employee); Better Living Components, Inc. v. Coleman, 2005 WL 771592, at *3 (Va. Cir. Ct. Albemarle Co. Apr. 6, 2005) (clause that prevented employee from working in any capacity for wide variety of companies dealing in types of products in which employer deals unenforceable); Modern Env'ts, Inc., 263 Va. at 493-94, 561 S.E.2d at 695 (clause that prevented employee from working in any capacity for competitor of former employer unenforceable); Strategic Resources, Inc. v. Nevin, 2005 WL 3143941, at *3 (E.D. Va. Nov. 23, 2005) (declining to enforce clause whose scope "extends beyond employment with which [company] is or potentially would be competitive"); Rodriguez, 439 F. Supp. 2d at 521-22 (finding one-year non-solicitation clauses to be overbroad, unduly burdensome, and contrary to Virginia's public policy where the clauses had no express geographic limitation, but, rather, prevented the solicitation for service of "'any present or prospective customer or client of the Company,'" a clause which the court construed to cover anyone in the thirty-eight states where the employer conducted business, while the defendants had only worked for the employer in the metropolitan D.C. area); Alston Studios, Inc. v. Lloyd V. Gress & Assocs., 492 F.2d 279, 283 (4th Cir. 1974) (clause that encompassed activities in which employee was not engaged unenforceable); see also Cantol, Inc., 2006 WL 1213992, at *4 ("the Virginia Supreme Court upholds covenants not to compete ... only to the extent that the proscribed functions are the same functions as were performed for the former employer"). **But see Capital One Fin. Corp., 2012 WL 1806138, at *9 (covenant was not overbroad given former bank executives "proven ability to start from scratch and grow a bank from the ground up," their access to confidential information regarding plaintiff's business, and given that while at bank, executives' abilities and customer relationships "rendered them a unique competitive threat" to plaintiff);** Brainware v. Mahan, 808 F. Supp. 2d. 820, 827 (E.D. Va. 2011) (clause precluding defendant from producing products competitive with plaintiff's products not overly broad due to plaintiff's "small product line" and defendant's "extensive knowledge" of plaintiff's business strategy and other confidential information); Star City Comics & Games, Inc. v. Webbed Sphere, Inc., 2010 WL 5186713, at *4 (W.D. Va. Dec. 9, 2010) (clause prohibiting defendant from "competing directly with [plaintiff] or otherwise managing a direct competitor" enforceable where it did not bar defendant from accepting management position with unrelated business); Blue Ridge Anesthesia & Critical Care, Inc. v. Gidick, 239 Va. 369, 373-74, 389 S.E.2d 467, 469-70 (1990) (clause prohibiting employee "from working ... in some role which would compete with the business of [the employer]" enforceable).

Geographical limitations restricting employees from competing within the territories serviced by the employee generally have been enforced. **See Preferred Sys. Solutions, Inc. v. GP Consulting, LLC, --- S.E.2d----, 2012 WL 4039828, at *3-4 (Va. Sept. 14, 2012) (noncompetition agreement between contractor and former subcontractor not overbroad even though agreement lacked specific geographical limitation where it was narrowly drawn to limit work on one particular project and work with a handful of direct competitors for 12 months);** see also Better Living Components, Inc. v. Coleman, 2005 WL 771592, at *2 (Va. Cir. Ct. Albemarle Co. Apr. 6, 2005) (citing Blue Ridge Anesthesia & Critical Care, Inc., 239 Va. at 373-74, 389 S.E.2d at 469-70). Courts have enforced non-compete agreements that prohibited engineers from competing with an employer for eight months following termination within a fifty-mile radius of the employer's office, Advanced Marine Enters., Inc., 256 Va. at 118, 501 S.E.2d at 155, prohibited a disc jockey from engaging in a competing business within 60 miles of the employer's radio station for twelve months after termination of employment, New River Media Group, Inc. v. Knighton, 245 Va. 367, 369-70, 429 S.E.2d 25, 26-27 (1993), prohibited a corporate officer from competing with his employer for three years in any similar business located in Virginia or North Carolina that covered the same sales area serviced by the employer, Roanoke Eng'g Sales v. Rosenbaum, 223 Va. 548, 553, 290 S.E.2d 882, 885 (1990), and prohibited a limousine service employee from providing similar services for one year within a seventy-five mile radius or for any customers with whom he did business during his employment, Int'l Limousine Serv., Inc. v. Reston Limousine & Travel Serv., Inc., 68 Va. Cir. 84, 2005 WL 1026985, at *2 (Loudoun Co. May 3, 2005) (applying Maryland law, which is "substantially similar to Virginia's law" governing non-compete provisions). See also **Capital One Fin. Corp, 2012 WL 1806138, at *10 (covenant limiting executives' noncompete to tri-state area, the same market in which executives operated company for 30 years, for a five year period was not unreasonable);** James, Ltd. v. Saks Fifth Ave., Ltd., 67 Va. Cir. 126, 2005 WL 603131, at *8 (Arlington Co. Mar. 8, 2005) (agreement restricting high-end men's clothing salesmen from selling men's clothes within one mile radius for three years not overbroad or excessive), rev'd on other grounds, 630 S.E. 2d 304 (Va. 2006). However, "the Supreme Court of Virginia has never upheld a restrictive covenant, which was ancillary to an employer-employee relationship, when the restrictive covenant could be applied to a geographic area in which the employee performed no function for the employer." Cantol, Inc. v. McDaniel, 2006 WL 1213992, at *4 (E.D. Va. Apr. 28, 2006).

As in other contexts, a preliminary injunction to enforce a non-compete agreement requires consideration of (1) the likelihood of irreparable harm to the plaintiff if the injunction is denied; (2) the likelihood of harm to the defendant if the injunction is granted; (3) the plaintiff's likelihood of success on the merits; and (4) the public interest. Signature Flight Support Corp. v. Landow Aviation L.P., 2009 WL 111603, at *2 (E.D. Va. Jan. 14, 2009); Int'l Limousine Serv., Inc., 68 Va. Cir. at 85-86. Such case-by-case balancing makes generalization difficult, but courts appear hesitant to enter preliminary injunctions against former employees. See, e.g., **Preferred Sys. Solutions, Inc., 2012 WL 4039828, at *11 (affirming denial of injunction where contractor did not show that it lacked an adequate remedy in law for former subcontractor's breach of noncompetition agreement);** Signature Flight Support Corp., 2009 WL 111603, at *2-13 (injunction denied despite fact that plaintiff had demonstrated "some likelihood of success on the merits" and that "the public interest slightly favor[ed]" issuance, because plaintiff had made only a "limited showing of irreparable harm," in the loss of a small percentage of customers and some goodwill, had failed to "demonstrate[] that the quantum of harm [would] be substantial," and had delayed bringing suit, and because injunction "would severely affect the way [defendant] did business and could ultimately threaten the viability" of that business); Deltek, Inc. v. Iuvo Sys., Inc., 2009 WL 1073196 (E.D. Va. April 20, 2009) (injunction denied where plaintiff lost some business from at least two customers, but had over 11,000 customers, and where there were "questions that go to the merits of the validity and enforceability of the noncompete provisions").

VIII. OTHER ISSUES

A. Statutes of Limitations

(1) Virginia's five-year statute of limitations for injury to property applies to causes of action for misappropriation of name or likeness. See Va. Code Ann. § 8.01-243(B); Lavery v. Automation Mgmt. Consultants, Inc., 234 Va. 145, 150, 360 S.E.2d 336, 339 (1987). (2) The tort of intentional infliction of emotional distress is governed by Virginia's two-year personal -injury statute of limitations. Va. Code Ann. § 8.01-243(A); Luddeke v. Amana Refrigeration, Inc., 239 Va. 203, 207, 387 S.E.2d 502, 504 (1990); Samuel v. Rose's Stores, Inc., 907 F. Supp. 159, 164 (E.D. Va. 1995); Welch v. Kennedy Piggly Wiggly Stores, Inc., 63 B.R. 888, 898 (Bankr. W.D. Va. 1986). (3) The Virginia courts do not appear to have definitively settled the question of which statutes of limitations apply to which branches of the tort of interference with prospective economic advantage. Compare Worrie v. Boze, 198 Va. 533, 535-36, 95 S.E.2d 192, 195-96 (1956) (applying five-year statute), Welch, 63 B.R. at 898 (same), Guthrie v. Shield, 2005 WL 2050472, at *2 (Va. Cir. Ct. Richmond, Aug. 24, 2005) (same); Whitaker v. Sheild, 2006 WL 1321481, at *8 (E.D. Va. May 3, 2006) (same), and Williams v. Reynolds, 2006 WL

3198968 (W.D. Va. 2006) (noting "some confusion" regarding applicable limitations period, but concluding that "Virginia courts have consistently applied a five year statute of limitations to tortious interference claims") with Johnson v. Plaisance, 25 Va. Cir. 264 (Charlottesville 1991) (one-year statute); Unlimited Screw Products, Inc. v. Malm, 781 F. Supp. 1121, 1127-28 (E.D. Va. 1991) (two-year statute) and Douty v. Irwin Mortgage Corp., 70 F. Supp. 2d 626, 630-31 (E.D. Va. 1999) (two-year statute). (4) Claims to enforce non-compete agreements are subject to Virginia's five-year statute of limitations. See State Analysis, Inc. v. American Fin. Servs. Assoc., 621 F. Supp. 2d 309, 321-22 (E.D. Va. 2009) (citing Va. Code Ann. § 8.01-246(2)). (5) Virginia's catch-all statute provides a limitations period of two years for "[e]very personal action accruing on or after July 1, 1995, for which no limitation is otherwise prescribed." Va. Code Ann. § 8.01-248. Causes of action accruing before July 1, 1995 are subject to the pre-amendment limitations period of one year. E.g., Michael v. Sentara Health Sys., 939 F. Supp. 1220, 1229 (E.D. Va. 1996).

B. Jurisdiction

In Virginia, the Circuit Courts have original jurisdiction over all civil actions other than those that seek money damages of $4,500 or less, for which exclusive jurisdiction lies in the General District Courts, subject to Circuit Court review. Va. Code Ann. §§ 16.1-77, 17.1-513. The General District and Circuit Courts have concurrent jurisdiction in cases seeking damages of more than $4,500 but less than $25,000. Va. Code Ann. § 16.1-77(1). The Court of Appeals has limited appellate jurisdiction, including review of decisions of the Workers' Compensation Commission. Va. Code Ann. § 17.1-405. In most civil cases, the Supreme Court of Virginia is the only tribunal with appellate jurisdiction, and it is discretionary. Va. Code Ann. § 8.01-670(3). If the requirements for federal-question or diversity jurisdiction are met, claims may be brought in the federal district courts. 28 U.S.C. §§ 1331-1332.

C. Pleading Requirements

Except to the extent discussed above in connection with specific torts, the Virginia courts do not appear expressly to have addressed this subject in relevant contexts.

SURVEY OF WASHINGTON EMPLOYMENT LIBEL LAW

Kari Vander Stoep, Esq.
K&L Gates LLP
925 Fourth Avenue, Suite 2900
Seattle, WA 98104-1158
Telephone: (206) 370-7804

(With Developments Reported Through **November 1, 2012**)

GENERAL COMMENTS

None.

SIGNIFICANT DEVELOPMENTS SINCE THE 2012 *SURVEY*

None.

I. GENERAL LAW

A. General Employment Law

1. ***At-Will Employment.*** In Washington, employment that is indefinite in duration may be terminated at will by either party. Roberts v. ARCO, 88 Wn.2d 887, 894, 568 P.2d 764 (1977). In order to establish an equitable exception to the at-will rule, an employee must prove that the employer promised specific treatment in specific situations, that he or she justifiably relied upon such promises, and that the employer breached its promises, causing him or her damage. Klontz v. Puget Sound Power & Light Co., 90 Wn. App. 186, 951 P.2d 280 (1998) (addressing claim of breach of implied employment contract); Thompson v. St. Regis Paper Co., 102 Wn.2d 219, 685 P.2d 1081 (1984) (general statements of company policy do not create binding contracts). A wrongful discharge claim may be based upon termination in violation of a clear public policy shown in constitutional, statutory or regulatory law. Thompson, 102 Wn.2d at 232. State statutory law also provides causes of action for wrongful discharge based upon unlawful discrimination, RCW 49.60.180(2), or in retaliation for opposing unlawful discrimination, RCW 49.60.210.

B. Elements of Libel Claim

1. ***Basic Elements.*** The essential elements of a cause of action for libel (more commonly called defamation in Washington) are: (1) a false statement, (2) an unprivileged publication of the statement, (3) fault, and (4) damages. LaMon v. Butler, 112 Wn.2d 193, 197, 770 P.2d 1027 (1989); Momah v. Bharti, 144 Wn. App. 731, 748, 182 P.3d 455 (2008). Courts consider three factors in deciding whether an allegedly defamatory statement is actionable: (1) the medium and context in which the statement was published, (2) the audience to whom it was published, and (3) whether the statement implied undisclosed facts. Dunlap v. Wayne, 105 Wn.2d 529, 539, 716 P.2d 842 (1986).

2. ***Fault.*** The level of fault that must be shown depends upon whether the plaintiff is a public or a private figure, and on whether a privilege existed as to the defendant's statement. LaMon, 112 Wn.2d at 197, 213.

a. **Private-Figure Plaintiff/Matter of Public Concern.** There appears to be conflicting authority in Washington as to whether a private-figure plaintiff seeking damages for a statement pertaining to an issue of public concern must prove negligence or actual malice in order to recover on a claim for defamation. Momah v. Bharti, 144 Wn. App. 731, 743-745, 182 P.3d 455 (Wash. Ct. App. Div. II 2008) (negligence); Alpine Indus., Computers, Inc. v. Cowles Publ'g Co., 114 Wn. App. 371, 392-93, 57 P.3d 1178 (Wash. Ct. App. Div. III 2002), as amended by 64 P.3d 49, 31 Media L. Rep. 1527 (2003) ("[A]n actual malice standard of fault should apply where a private figure plaintiff is allegedly defamed by a statement pertaining to a matter of public concern."); Mohr v. Grant, 153 Wn.2d 812, 822 n.8, 108 P.3d 768 (2005) (Washington Supreme Court saves "for another day" its review of this issue); **U.S. ex rel. Klein v. Omeros Corp., --- F. Supp. 2d ---, 2012 WL 4874031, at *9 (W.D. Wash. Oct. 15, 2012) (citing Alpine to conclude that an actual malice standard of fault should apply to a private figure allegedly defamed by statements pertaining to matters of public concern, including executive pay and adherence to tax laws, and the false recording of time on a grant from the U.S. government)**. Negligence means that the defendant knew or, in the exercise of reasonable care, should have known, that the statement was false or would create a false impression in some material respect. Vern Sims Ford, Inc. v. Hagel, 42 Wn. App. 675, 680, 713 P.2d 736, 12 Media L. Rep. 2248 (1986). Negligence is established by a preponderance of the evidence. Haueter v. Cowles Publ'g Co., 61 Wn. App. 572, 584, 811 P.2d 231, 19 Media L. Rep. 2107 (1991). In contrast, actual malice requires knowledge of the falsity or reckless disregard of the truth or falsity of the statement, which must be shown by clear and convincing evidence. Herron v. KING Broad. Co., 112 Wn.2d 762, 775-76, 776 P.2d 98, 17 Media L. Rep. 1289 (1989).

b. **Private Figure Plaintiff/Matter of Private Concern.** A private-figure plaintiff must prove negligence in order to recover on a claim for defamation. LaMon, 112 Wn.2d at 197.

c. **Public-Figure Plaintiff/Matter of Public Concern.** In defamation, whether the plaintiff is a public figure is a question of law for the court to decide. Clawson v. Longview Publ'g Co., 91 Wn.2d 408, 413, 589 P.2d 1223 (1979). The two factors courts consider in this determination are the plaintiff's (1) ease of access to the press and (2) assumption of the risk of public scrutiny, with much greater emphasis on the latter. Id. at 414. Washington courts have found that a public official is a public figure when the defamation action involves the manner in which the public official performed his or her duties. Corbally v. Kennewick Sch. Dist., 94 Wn. App. 736, 741, 973 P.2d 1074 (1999); Valdez-Zontek v. Eastmont Sch. Dist., 154 Wn. App. 147, 161, 225 P.3d 339 (2010) (public employee was a private figure for purposes of defamation action arising from employee's alleged affair, because affair was unrelated to employee's job performance).

A public-figure seeking damages for defamation must prove that the defendant acted with actual malice. Herron, 112 Wn.2d at 774-75. The actual malice standard applies to any aspect of a public official's life reflecting upon his or her fitness for the position. Clawson, 91 Wn.2d at 416-17. The scope of this standard of proof for public officials varies with the power and importance of the official. Thus, for a less powerful official, the standard of proof applies only to matters more closely connected to the official's job performance. Eubanks v. N. Cascades Broad., 115 Wn. App. 113, 122, 61 P.3d 368 (2003).

If a private individual who is involved in a matter of public or general concern becomes a limited-purpose public figure, he or she must prove actual malice. Washington courts have adopted a non-exclusive five-part test to determine whether an individual has become a limited-purpose public figure: (1) the plaintiff had access to the media; (2) the plaintiff voluntarily assumed a role of special prominence in the public controversy; (3) the plaintiff sought to influence the resolution or outcome of the controversy; (4) the controversy existed prior to the publication of the defamatory statement; and (5) the plaintiff retained public-figure status at the time of the alleged defamation. Clardy v. Cowles Publ'g, 81 Wn. App. 53, 62-65, 912 P.2d 1078 (1996); Duc Tan v. Le, 161 Wn. App. 340, 254 P.3d 904 (2011) (teacher and political activist in Vietnamese community was a public figure).

3. ***Falsity.*** To be false, a statement must falsely express or imply provable facts, either as a statement of fact or in the form of an opinion, but there are no false ideas. Schmalenberg v. Tacoma News, 87 Wn. App. 579, 590-91, 943 P.2d 350 (1997). If a direct statement of facts would be defamatory, then a statement of an opinion implying the existence of those false facts supports a defamation action. Henderson v. Pennwalt Corp., 41 Wn. App. 547, 557, 704 P.2d 1256 (1985). In a defamation by omission case, the plaintiff must show that the communication left a false impression that would be contradicted by the inclusion of omitted facts. Mohr v. Grant, 153 Wn.2d 812, 827, 108 P.3d 768 (2005). Merely omitting facts favorable to the plaintiff or facts that the plaintiff thinks should have been included does not make a publication false and subject to defamation liability. Id. at 828. There appears to be a split of authority among Washington courts as to whether the law recognizes defamation by implication, which occurs when the declarant juxtaposes a series of facts or omits facts so as to imply a defamatory connection. Yeakey v. Hearst Communications, Inc., 156 Wn. App. 787, 792, 232 P.3d 332 (Wash. Ct. App. Div. II 2010) (no such claim); Corey v. Pierce County, 154 Wn. App. 752, 761-62, 225 P.3d 367, 38 Media L. Rep. 1297 (Wash. Ct. App. Div. II 2010) (recognizing claim).

4. ***Defamatory Statement of Fact.*** A communication is defamatory if it tends to harm the reputation of another and lower that party in the estimation of the community or deter third persons from associating or dealing with that party. LaMon v. Butler, 44 Wn. App. 654, 658, 722 P.2d 1373 (1986). Mere vulgar name-calling is not defamatory where the insults are non-actionable opinions. Robel v. Roundup Corp., 148 Wn.2d 35, 55-58, 59 P.3d 611 (2002); **Davis v. Fred's Appliance, Inc., --- P.3d ---, 2012 WL 5208505, at *8-9 (Wash. Ct. App. Div. III Oct. 23, 2012) (coworker's references to plaintiff by an offensive name suggesting homosexuality were not statements of fact as necessary to support a defamation claim)**. Defamation does not exist if the audience members know the facts underlying an assertion and can judge the truthfulness of the alleged defamatory statement themselves. Dunlap v. Wayne, 105 Wn.2d 529, 540, 716 P.2d 842 (1986).

5. ***Of and Concerning Plaintiff.*** The recipient of a defamatory statement must be able to reasonably conclude that the plaintiff is the object of the statement. Sims v. KIRO, Inc., 20 Wn. App. 229, 580 P.2d 642, 4 Media L. Rep. 1149 (1978). That the defamatory statement concerns the plaintiff must be certain and apparent from the words themselves. Camer v. Post-Intelligencer, 45 Wn. App. 29, 37, 723 P.2d 1195, 13 Media L. Rep. 1481 (1986).

6. ***Publication.*** To be actionable, a defamatory statement must be published to a third party. Galbraith v. Tapco Credit Union, 88 Wn. App. 939, 946 P.2d 1242 (1997).

a. **Intracorporate Communication.** Intracorporate communications are subject to a conditional privilege for purposes of defamation. Doe v. Gonzaga Univ., 143 Wn.2d 687, 702-704, 24 P.3d 390 (2001), rev'd on other grounds, 536 U.S. 273 (2002) (communications between employees acting in the ordinary course of their work are not "published"); Charnholm v. Bartell Drug Co., 2007 WL 316784 2007, *4, 137 Wn. App. 1002 (2007) (unpublished opinion). In the context of privileged communications, Washington has recognized specifically that an employer has a qualified privilege to communicate with its employees about matters of common interest, including potentially defamatory matter. Messerly v. Asamera Minerals, 55 Wn. App. 811, 780 P.2d 1327 (1989) (termination of employees for illegal drug use).

b. **Compelled Self-Publication.** Washington does not recognize compelled self-publication of a defamatory matter as supporting a cause of action. Hill v. J.C. Penney, 70 Wn. App. 225, 239, 852 P.2d 1111 (1993).

c. **Republication.** Washington has adopted the single publication rule that any one edition of a book or newspaper, or any one radio or television broadcast, is a single publication. Momah v. Bharti, 144 Wn. App. 731, 182 P.3d 455 (2008). Republication of materials that were subject to privilege in a judicial proceeding is not privileged and may make the second publisher liable. LaMon v. Westport, 44 Wn. App. 664, 668, 723 P.2d 470 (1986). In this case, however, the court concluded that the placing of the court materials behind the checkout desk in the library, where access was available only through the librarian and no evidence showed that anyone had actually read the allegedly defamatory content, did not prove that a republication had occurred. Id. at 669. **Providing a link to a URL where a defamatory publication is located is not publication of the contents of the materials referred to. U.S. ex rel. Klein v. Omeros Corp., --- F. Supp. 2d ---, 2012 WL 4874031, at *11 (W.D. Wash. Oct. 15, 2012) ("a mere reference or URL is not a publication of the contents of the materials referred to").**

7. ***Statements versus Conduct.*** While Washington courts have not directly resolved the question of whether a defamation claim can be based upon conduct, a "statement" is an essential element of a defamation claim. LaMon v. Butler, 112 Wn.2d 193, 197, 770 P.2d 1027 (1989). In one case, plaintiffs alleged that police conduct amounted to defamation where plaintiffs were stopped at gunpoint, publicly handcuffed and frisked. McKinney v. City of Tukwila, 103 Wn. App. 391, 13 P.3d 631 (2000). The court did not decide whether this conduct could be defamatory, because the plaintiffs failed to prove that the conduct was negligent and thus failed to prove an essential element of defamation. Id.

8. ***Damages.*** No punitive damages are available in Washington, but a plaintiff may recover compensatory damages for harm factually caused by defamation. Schmalenberg v. Tacoma News, 87 Wn. App. 579, 943 P.2d 350 (1997). Upon a showing of causation, general damages are available for loss of reputation, humiliation and emotional distress, as are provable special damages, such as lost earnings or business income. Id. at 589 n.23 and 599 n.56.

a. **Presumed Damages and Libel *Per Se*.** In an action involving libel *per se*, special damages can be recovered upon a showing of actual malice. Demopolis v. Peoples Nat'l Bank, 59 Wn. App. 105, 116, 796 P.2d 426 (1990). Damages for defamation of a public official can be presumed upon a showing of actual malice. Richmond v. Thompson, 130 Wn.2d 368, 387, 922 P.2d 1343 (1996). Washington courts follow Gertz v. Robert Welch, Inc., 418 U.S. 323 (1974), and Dun & Bradstreet, Inc. v. Greenmoss Builders, Inc., 472 U.S. 749 (1985), except that no punitive damages are allowed in Washington. Haueter v. Cowles Publ'g Co., 61 Wn. App. 572, 592, 811 P.2d 231, 19 Media L. Rep. 2107 (1991). A defamatory communication is defamation *per se* if it injures the plaintiff in his or her profession or creates the imputation of unchastity, and the declarant knew the communication was false or acted with reckless disregard for the truth or falsity of the communication. Valdez-Zontek v. Eastmont Sch. Dist., 154 Wn. App. 147, 164-65, 225 P.3d 339 (2010); **Davis v. Fred's Appliance, Inc., --- P.3d ---, 2012 WL 5208505, at *9 (Wash. Ct. App. Div. III Oct. 23, 2012) (imputation of homosexuality is not defamatory per se so as to permit recovery of general damages).** If a statement is defamation *per se,* then the plaintiff may recover presumed damages, reflecting noneconomic loss, such as harm to reputation and emotional distress. Id. Where no matters of public concern are involved, a private plaintiff may be able to recover presumed damages without proof of actual malice. Maison De France Ltd. v. Mais Oui!, Inc., 126 Wn. App. 34, 54, 108 P.3d 787 (2005). A plaintiff is not entitled to presumed damages unless the damages are solely attributable to the false statement. Wiseman v. Wendel, 2006 WL 302763, *6, 131 Wn. App. 1033 (2006) (unpublished opinion).

(1) **Employment-Related Criticism.** Statements critical of an employee's work are subject to the standard test for defamation; for example, the plaintiff must show falsity and lack of privilege. See, e.g., Klontz v. Puget Sound Power & Light, 90 Wn. App. 186, 951 P.2d 280 (1998) (statement by an employee that plaintiff had not adequately supervised an employee who engaged in sexual harassment of another employee was neither false nor unprivileged); Valdez-Zontek v. Eastmont Sch. Dist., 154 Wn. App. 147, 168, 225 P.3d 339 (2010) (dissemination of admittedly false information regarding an employee no longer privileged when communicated to numerous individuals outside the scope of any common interest); Woody v. Stapp, 146 Wn. App. 16, 21-22, 189 P.3d 807 (2008) (defamation claim dismissed where plaintiff failed to prove falsity of conditionally privileged statements by co-workers regarding his workplace conduct).

(2) **Single-Instance Rule.** No Washington cases address a "single-instance rule" as to statements relating to a single instance of professional or business malfeasance.

b. **Punitive Damages.** No punitive damages are available in Washington. Haueter v. Cowles Publ'g Co., 61 Wn. App. 572, 590, 811 P.2d 231, 19 Media L. Rep. 2107 (1991).

II. PRIVILEGES AND DEFENSES

A. Scope of Privileges

1. ***Absolute Privilege.*** Because an absolute privilege absolves the defendant of all liability for defamatory statements, it is generally limited to "cases in which the public service and administration of justice require complete immunity." Wood v. Battle Ground Sch. Dist., 107 Wn. App. 550, 27 P.3d 1208 (2001). Defamatory communications made by a party or counsel in the course of a judicial proceeding are absolutely privileged if they are pertinent or material to the redress or relief sought. McNeal v. Allen, 95 Wn.2d 265, 267, 621 P.2d 1285 (1980). This includes publication of defamatory material that is required by law, as when released pursuant to court order. For example, an employer's investigation file concerning alleged misconduct by a teacher was sought by the news media and released by court order; this release was absolutely privileged. Corbally v. Kennewick Sch. Dist., 94 Wn. App. 736, 973 P.2d 1074 (1999). The absolute judicial privilege extends to administrative boards acting in their quasi-judicial capacity. LaBrec v. State, Employment Sec. Dept., 52 Wn. App. 188, 758 P.2d 501 (1988) (statements in an administrative decision regarding unemployment compensation were absolutely privileged). Bruce v. Byrne-Stevens & Assocs. Eng'rs, Inc., 113 Wn.2d 123, 125, 776 P.2d 666 (1989), extended the privilege, holding that an expert witness cannot be found civilly liable for any action done as part of a judicial function. The absolute privilege did not, however, extend to a witness in a later professional misconduct administrative review board hearing, based upon the witness's misconduct in giving expert testimony at trial. Deatherage v. Bd. of Psychology, 134 Wn.2d 131, 948 P.2d 828 (1997). Immunity from civil liability for statements on matters of public or governmental concern may also be available under certain circumstances pursuant to Washington's Anti-SLAPP statutes. See III.E, infra.

Executive government officials have an absolute privilege as to authorized communications made in the performance of their official duties. Taskett v. KING Broad. Co., 86 Wn.2d 439, 458, 546 P.2d 81, 1 Media L. Rep. 1716 (1976). A government regulator is also absolutely privileged to make defamatory statements in the course of official duties if (1) the regulator is among that class of public officials absolutely privileged to publish defamatory matter and (2) the publication has more than a tenuous relationship to the regulator's official capacity. Aitken v. Reed, 89 Wn. App. 474, 491, 949 P.2d 441 (1998) (state supervisor of credit unions absolutely privileged to make statements critical of plaintiff's operation of credit union).

2. ***Qualified Privilege.*** A qualified privilege protects the maker from liability for a defamatory statement unless the privilege was abused. Bender v. Seattle, 99 Wn.2d 582, 600, 664 P.2d 492 (1983). The burden of establishing an abuse of a qualified privilege rests on the defamed party, who must show that the speaker acted with actual malice (*i.e.*, that he or she knew the statement was false or had a reckless disregard for its truth or falsity). Demopolis v. Peoples Nat'l Bank, 59 Wn. App. 105, 114, 796 P.2d 426 (1990); Brecht v. Fisher Communications, Inc., 2011 WL 1120506, *2-3, 160 Wn. App. 1040 (2011) (unpublished opinion). The police have a qualified privilege in releasing information to the public in the course of a criminal investigation. Stansfield v. Douglas County, 107 Wn. App. 20, 26 P.3d 935 (2001), aff'd on other grounds, 146 Wn.2d 116, 43 P.3d 498 (2002). Inferior state officers, such as school board presidents, have a qualified privilege. Wood v. Battle Ground Sch. Dist., 107 Wn. App. 550, 27 P.3d 1208 (2001). The existence of a qualified privilege does not create a duty to disclose information. Richland Sch. Dist. v. Mabton Sch. Dist., 111 Wn. App. 377, 390, 45 P.3d 580 (2002) (privilege is a shield against slander, but cannot be used as a sword, where former employer had a common interest privilege but failed to disclose former employee's arrest for child molestation). The fair reporting privilege applies where the communication is attributed properly to an official proceeding and the report is an accurate report of that proceeding or a fair abridgement. Alpine Indus., Computers, Inc. v. Cowles Publ'g Co., 114 Wn. App. 371, 384, 57 P.3d 1178 (2002), as amended by 64 P.3d 49 (2003); Momah v. Bharti, 144 Wn. App. 731, 182 P.3d 455 (2008).

a. **Common Interest.** The common interest privilege applies when the declarant and the recipient have a common interest in the subject matter of the communication. Moe v. Wise, 97 Wn. App. 950, 957-59, 989 P.2d 1148 (1999). The parties sharing the information need not be allied with each other, but they must share the common interest. Id. Statements made in the course of an investigation of a charge of sexual harassment are conditionally privileged, because an employer and its employees have a common interest in a workplace free of sexual harassment. Lawson v. Boeing Co., 58 Wn. App. 261, 267, 792 P.2d 545 (1990). Similarly, a past employer and a prospective employer have a common interest and a qualified privilege against an action for defamation by an employee. Bankhead v. Tacoma, 23 Wn. App. 631, 597 P.2d 920 (1979). A school official and a parent have a common interest in the welfare and safety of a child, and statements concerning improper touching of a child by a teacher were thus subject to a conditional privilege. Hitter v. Bellevue Sch. Dist., 66 Wn. App. 391, 832 P.2d 130 (1992). Corporate employees have a qualified privilege to share information in the ordinary course of the employees' work in which there is a common interest. Doe v. Gonzaga Univ., 143

Wn.2d 687, 24 P.3d 390 (2001), rev'd on other grounds, 536 U.S. 273 (2002). A Chapter 11 bankruptcy debtor and its creditors share a common interest with regard to subjects pertinent to the financial health of the debtor. Moe, 97 Wn. App. at 961.

b. **Duty.** Executive government officials have an absolute privilege as to authorized communications made in the performance of their official duties. Taskett v. KING Broad. Co., 86 Wn.2d 439, 458, 546 P.2d 81, 1 Media L. Rep. 1716 (1976). The communication must have more than a tenuous relationship to the speaker's official capacity. Aitken v. Reed, 89 Wn. App. 474, 491, 949 P.2d 441 (1998).

c. **Criticism of Public Employee.** Criticism of a public employee is subject to a qualified privilege. Richmond v. Thompson, 130 Wn.2d 368, 922 P.2d 1343 (1996) (state trooper proved actual malice as to defamatory statements about him to public officials by a person he had stopped for speeding). For example, a public schoolteacher is a public official for purposes of a libel claim if the claim involves the manner in which the teacher performed duties pursuant to a public contract. Corbally v. Kennewick Sch. Dist., 94 Wn. App. 736, 741, 973 P.2d 1074 (1999). Criticisms of public employees may also be protected by Washington's Anti-SLAPP statutes if the criticisms relate to matters of public or governmental concern. See III.E, infra; Castello v. City of Seattle, No. C10–1456MJP, 2010 WL 4857022, 39 Media L. Rep. 1591 (W.D. Wash. Nov. 22, 2010) (slip copy) (striking fire department employee's defamation claims based on various statements made by co-workers regarding employee's conduct and performance, including statements made during internal investigations and disciplinary proceedings and statements made to television news station).

d. **Limitation on Qualified Privilege.** A conditional privilege is lost if abused, as by a showing that the defendant acted with actual malice. Doe, 143 Wn.2d 687; Richmond, 130 Wn.2d 368; Herron v. Tribune Publ'g Co., 108 Wn.2d 162, 183, 746 P.2d 249 (1990). Mere negligence is not sufficient to show abuse of a conditional privilege. Moore v. Smith, 89 Wn.2d 932, 578 P.2d 26 (1978). The qualified privilege is abused if the person claiming the privilege (1) knows the matter to be false or acts in reckless disregard as to its truth or falsity, (2) does not act for the purpose of protecting the interest that is the reason for the existence of the privilege, (3) knowingly publishes the matter to a person to whom its publication is not otherwise privileged, (4) does not reasonably believe the matter to be necessary to accomplish the purpose for which the privilege is given, or (5) publishes unprivileged as well as privileged matter. Moe v. Wise, 97 Wn. App. at 963.

(1) **Constitutional or Actual Malice.** A plaintiff must prove actual malice to overcome a qualified privilege. Richmond, 130 Wn.2d 368. Actual malice exists when a statement is made with knowledge of its falsity or reckless disregard for its truth or falsity. Doe, 143 Wn.2d 687. Thus, proof of knowledge of, or reckless disregard as to, the falsity of the statements is required to establish abuse of the conditional privilege. Lawson v. Boeing Co., 58 Wn. App. 261, 267, 792 P.2d 545 (1990).

(2) **Common Law Malice.** It does not appear that proof of common law malice is sufficient to overcome a qualified privilege.

(3) **Other Limitations on Qualified Privileges.** See generally II.A.2, supra.

e. **Question of Fact or Law.** Whether a statement is subject to a qualified privilege is a question of law for the court. Liberty Bank v. Henderson, 75 Wn. App. 546, 878 P.2d 1259 (1994); Parry v. George H. Brown & Assocs., Inc., 46 Wn. App. 193, 196, 730 P.2d 95 (1986).

f. **Burden of Proof.** Once the plaintiff alleges defamation, the defendant has the burden of asserting the defense of privilege. The plaintiff has the burden of proving that the defendant abused the privilege, by clear and convincing evidence. Havsy v. Flynn, 88 Wn. App. 514, 945 P.2d 221 (1997); Hitter v. Bellevue Sch. Dist., 66 Wn. App. 391, 832 P.2d 130 (1992). Demonstrating the falsity of the statement is not sufficient to prove abuse of the privilege. Mark v. Seattle Times, 96 Wn.2d 473, 486, 635 P.2d 1081 (1981), cert. denied, 457 U.S. 1124 (1982). The plaintiff must show by clear and convincing evidence that the defendant knew the communication was false or acted with reckless disregard as to its truth or falsity. Right-Price Recreation, LLC v. Connells Prairie Cmty. Council, 146 Wn.2d 370, 46 P.3d 789 (2002).

B. Standard Libel Defenses

1. ***Truth.*** Truth is a defense to a charge of falsity in a defamation action. The defendant need not prove the literal truth of the statement, only that the statement is substantially true or the "gist" of the statement is true. Herron v. KING Broad. Co., 112 Wn.2d 762, 769-74, 776 P.2d 98 (1989). A false statement among true statements affects the sting of the report if it adds significant opprobrium, and a separate and damaging implication, than the report would have had without the falsehood. Id. Inaccuracies are not actionable if the report of the literal truth would not have a materially different impact on the reputation of the plaintiff. Mark, 96 Wn.2d 473.

2. ***Opinion.*** A defamatory communication may consist of a statement in the form of an opinion, but a statement of this nature is actionable only if it implies the allegation of undisclosed defamatory facts as the basis for the opinion. Dunlap v. Wayne, 105 Wn.2d 529, 716 P.2d 842 (1986). Whether an opinion is capable of being defamatory is a question of law. Hoppe v. Hearst Corp., 53 Wn. App. 668, 672, 770 P.2d 203, 16 Media L. Rep. 2076 (1989). Washington follows Milkovich v. Lorain Journal Co., 497 U.S. 1, 17 Media L. Rep. 2009 (1990), in that there is no separate opinion privilege; a statement must be provably false to be actionable. Duc Tan v. Le, 161 Wn. App. 340, 352-353, 254 P.3d 904 (2011).

3. ***Consent.*** Consent to the defamation creates an absolute privilege. Jolly v. Fossum, 63 Wn.2d 537, 541, 388 P.2d 139 (1964).

4. ***Mitigation.*** As a general rule, in a defamation action, the defendant may offer evidence that a plaintiff's reputation in the community is already bad, in spite of the alleged defamation, in order to mitigate damages. Corey v. Pierce County, 154 Wn. App. 752, 772-73, 225 P.3d 367 (2010).

III. RECURRING FACT PATTERNS

A. Statements in Personnel File

Statements by an employer in an employee's personnel file are conditionally privileged. Lillig v. Becton-Dickinson, 105 Wn.2d 653, 717 P.2d 1371 (1986) (plaintiff failed to show an abuse of the conditional privilege where there was no showing that the employer lacked a good faith belief that the employee had lied to a customer).

B. Performance Evaluations

Washington courts have not yet recognized a cause of action for allegedly defamatory statements in performance evaluations of employees and have cautioned against judicial interference in this area. Murphy v. City of Kirkland, 2009 WL 1110884, 149 Wn. App. 1064 (2009) (unpublished opinion).

C. References

A Washington statute protects employers that provide reference information. RCW 4.24.730. Under the statute, an employer that discloses information about a current or former employee to a prospective employer or employment agency, at the request of the prospective employer or employment agency, is presumed to be acting in good faith and is immune from civil and criminal liability for the disclosure if the information relates to (i) the employee's ability to perform the job, (ii) the employee's diligence, skill, or reliability in carrying out job duties, or (iii) illegal or wrongful acts committed by the employee when related to the job duties. Id. The presumption of good faith may be rebutted only by clear and convincing evidence that the information disclosed by the employer was knowingly false, deliberately misleading, or made with reckless disregard for the truth. Id. The statute also requires the employer to retain a written record in the personnel file of the employee or former employee, showing the identity of the person or entity to which information is disclosed. Id. Other Washington statutes give the employee or former employee the right to inspect and dispute the contents of the employee's personnel file. RCW 49.12.240-.260.

Washington case law is consistent with RCW 4.24.730. Bankhead v. Tacoma, 23 Wn. App. 631, 597 P.2d 920 (1979) (past employer and a prospective employer have a common interest and a qualified privilege against an action for defamation by the employee based upon a job reference); Wiseman v. Wendel, 2006 WL 302763, *4, 131 Wn. App. 1033 (2006) (unpublished opinion) (qualified privilege applied where former employer had a basis in fact for making statements to potential employers that former employee's personal life interfered with her work).

D. Intracorporate Communication

Intracorporate communications are subject to a conditional privilege. Doe v. Gonzaga Univ., 143 Wn.2d 687, 24 P.3d 390 (2001), rev'd on other grounds, 536 U.S. 273 (2002). Washington has recognized that an employer has a qualified privilege to communicate with its employees about matters of common interest, including potentially defamatory matter. Messerly v. Asamera Minerals, 55 Wn. App. 811, 780 P.2d 1327 (1989) (termination of employees for illegal drug use); Lambert v. Morehouse, 68 Wn. App. 500, 506, 843 P.2d 1116 (1993) (sexual harassment investigation); Woody v. Stapp, 146 Wn. App. 16, 21-22, 189 P.3d 807 (2008) (same). **Intracorporate communications are not absolutely privileged; the privilege may be lost if the employee publishes a defamatory statement to a co-employee not in the ordinary course of his or her work or if the employee made the statement with actual malice. Armijo v. Yakima HMA, LLC, --- F. Supp. 2d ---, 2012 WL 1205867, at *7 (E.D. Wash. Apr. 11, 2012).**

E. Statements to Government Regulators

Citizen complaints to a governmental agency have been held absolutely privileged. Story v. Shelter Bay Co., 52 Wn. App. 334, 760 P.2d 368 (1988) (defamatory statements to HUD were absolutely privileged); Gilman v. McDonald, 74

Wn. App. 733, 875 P.2d 697 (1994) (communication to a public officer who is authorized to act on the communication is subject to a qualified privilege).

Anti-SLAPP Statutes. Since 1989, Washington has had in effect a statute intended to curb strategic lawsuits against public participation (an "Anti-SLAPP" statute). RCW 4.24.500-.520. The statute provides that a person who communicates a complaint or information to any branch or agency of federal, state, or local government, or self-regulatory agency involved in securities under the oversight of a government agency, is immune from civil liability for claims based on the communication to the agency or organization regarding any matter reasonably of concern to that agency or organization. RCW 4.24.510; see also, e.g., Phoenix Trading, Inc. v. Kayser, No. C10–0920JLR, 2011 WL 3158416 (W.D. Wash. July 25, 2011) (slip copy) (defendants immune from civil liability for statements to mayor, city officials and customs agency regarding concerns about plaintiff's products). A person prevailing on this immunity defense may recover expenses and attorneys fees, and $10,000 in statutory damages, unless the complaint or communication was made in bad faith. RCW 4.24.525(6)(a).

Matters of Public or Governmental Concern. In 2010, the Washington legislature enacted an additional Anti-SLAPP statute that expanded the scope of protected communication and created a procedural device to quickly halt any litigation found to be targeted at persons lawfully communicating on matters of public or governmental concern. RCW 4.24.525; see also, e.g., Castello v. City of Seattle, No. C10–1456MJP, 2010 WL 4857022, 39 Media L. Rep. 1591 (W.D. Wash. Nov. 22, 2010) (slip copy) (striking fire department employee's defamation claims). The statute provides that a party may bring a special motion to strike any claim that is based on an action involving public participation and petition. RCW 4.24.525(4)(a). An action involving public participation and petition is defined as "[a]ny oral statement made, or written statement or other document submitted" (1) "in a legislative, executive, or judicial proceeding or other governmental proceeding authorized by law," (2) "in connection with an issue under consideration or review by a legislative, executive, or judicial proceeding or other governmental proceeding authorized by law," (3) "that is reasonably likely to encourage or to enlist public participation in an effort to effect consideration or review of an issue in a legislative, executive, or judicial proceeding or other governmental proceeding authorized by law," or (4) "in a place open to the public or a public forum in connection with an issue of public concern." RCW 4.24.525(2)(a)-(d); see also, e.g., Brawley v. Rouhfar, 2011 WL 2993467, 162 Wn. App. 1058 (2011) (unpublished opinion) (reports by parents to police and state agency of alleged child abuse by nanny were absolutely privileged; defamation claims premised on such statements properly dismissed pursuant to statute). In addition, the statute contains a catch-all provision that includes "any other lawful conduct in furtherance of the exercise of the constitutional right of free speech in connection with an issue of public concern, or in furtherance of the exercise of the constitutional right of petition." RCW 4.24.525(2)(e); see also, e.g., Phoenix Trading, Inc. v. Kayser, No. C10–0920JLR, 2011 WL 3158416 (W.D. Wash. July 25, 2011) (slip copy) (defendants' statements to media outlets and non-profit public interest or trade group that addresses counterfeiting and piracy issues were covered by "public form" and catch-all provisions of statute).

The Anti-SLAPP statute assigns a moving party the initial burden of demonstrating by a preponderance of the evidence that the claim or claims concern an action involving public participation and petition. RCW 4.24.525(4)(b). Once that burden is met, the burden shifts to the plaintiff to establish by clear and convincing evidence a probability of proving the claim or claims. Id. The statute provides that a moving party who prevails in whole or in part on a motion to strike is entitled to a mandatory award of costs and reasonable attorney fees and a further mandatory penalty of $10,000. RCW 4.24.525(6)(a); but see Phillips v. KIRO-TV, Inc., 817 F. Supp. 2d 1317 (W.D. Wash. 2011) (order granting defamation defendant's motion to dismiss claims, but denying as moot defendant's accompanying anti-SLAPP motion to strike, despite potential availability of costs, attorney's fees and statutory penalty, because such potential recovery should defendant prevail was "outweighed by the burden on the parties and the Court" that would be necessary to address plaintiff's challenge to the constitutionality of the Anti-SLAPP statute). The statute also requires a similar award to a prevailing plaintiff if the court finds that a motion to strike was frivolous or solely intended to cause unnecessary delay. RCW 4.24.525(6)(b).

F. Reports to Auditors and Insurers

A report to an insurer, even if subsequently used in a judicial proceeding, does not merit absolute privilege. Such reports are subject to a qualified privilege. Bruce v. Byrne-Stevens & Assocs., 113 Wn.2d 123, 776 P.2d 666 (1989). Reports to auditors are likely also subject to a qualified privilege based on common interest, provided the information at issue falls within the scope of an auditor's duties. See Valdez-Zontek v. Eastmont Sch. Dist., 154 Wn. App. 147, 161, 164, 225 P.3d 339 (2010).

G. Vicarious Liability of Employers for Statements Made by Employees

An employer is liable for the torts of its employees only if committed in the furtherance of the employer's business and within the course and scope of employment. Henderson v. Pennwalt Corp., 41 Wn. App. 547, 704 P.2d 1256 (1985) (management was aware of defendant supervisor's ongoing slander of the plaintiff employee and failed to remedy the situation; remanded for trial as to whether slander was "authorized"). A client is not liable for his or her attorney's defamatory statements, unless the statements are made within the scope of the attorney's employment and with the client's knowledge and consent. Demopolis v. Peoples Nat'l Bank, 59 Wn. App. 105, 118, 796 P.2d 426 (1990).

1. ***Scope of Employment.***

a. Blogging. No cases on point.

2. ***Damages.*** There appear to be no Washington cases on the specific issue of whether available damages for defamation could vary depending on whether an employer's liability for the defamation is vicarious or direct.

H. Internal Investigations

Complaints of sexual harassment made in the context of an investigation are conditionally privileged. Lambert v. Morehouse, 68 Wn. App. 500, 506, 843 P.2d 1116 (1993). Moreover, there can be no liability for defamation arising out of an investigation into employee misconduct absent specific evidence of falsity of the statement sufficient for a reasonable trier of fact to find clear and convincing evidence of actual malice; a plaintiff's conclusory denials are not enough. Charnholm v. Bartell Drug Co., 2007 WL 316784 2007, *4, 137 Wn. App. 1002 (2007) (unpublished opinion). See also I.B.6(a) and III.D, supra.

IV. OTHER ACTIONS BASED ON STATEMENTS

A. Negligent Hiring, Retention, and Supervision

Washington recognizes the torts of negligent hiring and supervision. Lynn v. Labor Ready Inc., 136 Wn. App. 295, 306-07, 151 P.3d 201 (2006); Rucshner v. ADT Sec. Sys., Inc., 149 Wn. App. 665, 204 P.3d 271 (2009). Washington courts addressing cases where a plaintiff has brought such a negligence claim as well as a claim of defamation based on statements made by the employee who is the subject of the negligent hiring or supervision claim have generally examined these claims separately on their merits and have not expressly addressed whether or when such claims might be duplicative or mutually exclusive. Wilson v. City of Longview, 2002 WL 1831981, 113 Wn. App. 1007 (2002) (unpublished opinion).

B. Intentional Infliction of Emotional Distress

Intentional infliction of emotional distress is called "outrage" in Washington. The tort requires (1) intent or recklessness that (2) causes severe emotional distress through (3) extreme and outrageous conduct. Reid v. Pierce County, 136 Wn.2d 195, 961 P.2d 333 (1998); Womack v. Rardon, 133 Wn. App. 254, 260-61, 135 P.3d 542 (2006). The behavior must go beyond all reasonable bounds of decency. Contreras v. Crown Zellerbach, 88 Wn.2d 735, 737, 565 P.2d 1173 (1977). While emotional distress damages are available as general or compensatory damages for defamation, Cagle v. Burns and Roe, 106 Wn.2d 911, 726 P.2d 434 (1986), statements that are privileged or otherwise not actionable as defamation most likely also cannot form the basis for a claim of outrage. **Phillips v. World Publ'g Co., 822 F. Supp. 2d 1114, 1120, 40 Media L. Rep. 1048 (W.D. Wash. 2011) ("An emotional distress claim based on the same facts as an unsuccessful defamation claim 'cannot survive as an independent cause of action.'" (quoting Harris v. City of Seattle, 315 F. Supp. 2d 1105, 1112 (W.D. Wash. 2004)))**; Hoppe v. Hearst Corp., 53 Wn. App. 668, 672, 770 P.2d 203, 16 Media L. Rep. 2076 (1989).

Washington also recognizes a cause of action for false light. A false light invasion of privacy claim arises when someone publicizes a matter that places another in a false light if the false light would be highly offensive to a reasonable person and the actor knew of or recklessly disregarded the falsity of the publication and the false light in which the other would be placed. Corey v. Pierce County, 154 Wn. App. 752, 762-63, 225 P.3d 367, 38 Media L. Rep. 1297 (2010). False light differs from defamation in that it focuses on compensation for mental suffering, rather than reputation. Eastwood v. Cascade Broad. Co., 106 Wn.2d 466, 471, 722 P.2d 1295, 13 Media L. Rep. 1136 (1986). False light and defamation overlap when the statement complained of is both false and defamatory; a person need not be defamed, however, to bring a false light action. Id. A plaintiff can proceed upon either theory, or both, but can have only one recovery for a single instance of publicity. Id. False light claims, like defamation claims, are subject to a two-year statute of limitations. Id. at 474.

C. Interference with Economic Advantage

Washington recognizes a cause of action for tortious interference with a business expectancy or contract. The elements are (1) existence of a contract or business expectancy, (2) knowledge of the relationship, (3) intentional interference, (4) improper purpose, and (5) damages from breach of the contract or expectancy. Commodore v. Univ. Mech. Contractors, Inc., 120 Wn.2d 120, 137, 839 P.2d 314 (1992). A party can have no valid business expectancy from a party in violation of the law. To-Ro Trade Shows v. Collins, 144 Wn.2d 403, 27 P.3d 1149 (2001).

A claim of interference with a business relationship may be considered separately from defamation as to damages. See Koehler v. Wales, 16 Wn. App. 304, 556 P.2d 203 (1976) (trial court awarded actual damages for business interference and nominal damages for libel *per se*). There is no liability for tortious interference with a business by defamation if the defamation is privileged. Lawson v. Boeing Co., 58 Wn. App. 261, 269, 792 P.2d 545 (1990).

D. Prima Facie Tort

Washington has adopted a redefinition of a prima facie tort as tortious interference with economic relationships. Pleas v. Seattle, 112 Wn.2d 794, 774 P.2d 1158 (1989). A cause of action arises when interference causing injury to another is wrongful beyond the fact of the interference itself. Id.; Cleverley v. Campbell, No. 40788–4–II, 2011 WL 3907127, *5 (Sept. 7, 2011) (unpublished opinion); see also IV.C, supra.

V. OTHER ISSUES

A. Statute of Limitations

The statute of limitations for defamation is two years. RCW 4.16.100(1); Milligan v. Thompson, 90 Wn. App. 586, 592, 953 P.2d 112 (1998). A limitation period begins to run when the plaintiff's cause of action accrues. Crisman v. Crisman, 85 Wn. App. 15, 20, 931 P.2d 163 (1997). Generally, this occurs when the plaintiff suffers actual injury or damage and has the right to apply to a court for relief. Gazija v. Nicholas Jerns Co., 86 Wn.2d 215, 219, 543 P.2d 338 (1975). Some authority suggests that the statute of limitations for a defamation action does not being to accrue until the plaintiff discovers or reasonably should have discovered that an allegedly defamatory statement has been made. Lang v. City of Spokane Valley, No. CV-08-383-RHW, 2010 WL 3583939, *2 (E.D. Wash. Sept. 8, 2010) (slip copy); Blackledge v. City of Tacoma, 2003 WL 22391016, *3, 118 Wn. App. 1078 (2003) (unpublished opinion). **In the internet context, the statute of limitations begins to run when the allegedly defamatory material is first posted on the internet. Phillips v. World Publ'g Co., 822 F. Supp. 2d 1114, 1122 (W.D. Wash. 2011).**

B. Jurisdiction

Where defendants committed no acts in Washington, but were alleged to be part of a Washington-based conspiracy to defame a resident of another state, no long-arm personal jurisdiction existed. Hewitt v. Hewitt, 78 Wn. App. 447, 896 P.2d 1312 (1995).

C. Worker's Compensation Exclusivity

No Washington cases on point.

D. Pleading Requirements

Malice may be pleaded generally. CR 9(b). Special damages, if sought, must be specifically stated. CR 9(g). Although Washington is a notice pleading state, if new claims are added to a complaint by amendment that arose out of the conduct, transaction, or occurrence set forth in the original pleading, the amendment relates back to the date of the original pleading. CR 15. Claims such as defamation and outrage can, therefore, be added by amendment later without other notice if they arose from the facts underlying the original complaint, such as, for example, tortious interference with economic advantage. Caruso v. Local 690, 33 Wn. App. 201, 211, 653 P.2d 638 (1982), rev'd on other grounds, 100 Wn.2d 343 (1983).

SURVEY OF WASHINGTON EMPLOYMENT PRIVACY LAW

Robert Blackstone
Angela Galloway
Davis Wright Tremaine
Suite 2200
1201 Third Avenue
Seattle, Washington 98101-3045
Telephone: (206) 622-3150; Facsimile: (206) 757-7700

(With Developments Reported Through **November 1, 2012**)

GENERAL COMMENTS

None.

SIGNIFICANT DEVELOPMENTS SINCE THE 2012 *SURVEY*

On Nov. 6, 2012, Washington voters approved a ballot initiative partially legalizing marijuana growth and possession. Initiative No. 502 removed some state criminal and civil prohibitions against manufacturing, distributing, and possessing marijuana. It applies only to limited quantities of marijuana grown or possessed by persons at least 21 years old. The measure also establishes a state licensing and regulatory scheme. Washington voters decriminalized medicinal use of marijuana in 2007. RCW § 69.5A.060. The statute directs that employers are not required to accommodate on-site use. Id. In 2011, the Washington Supreme Court held employers may terminate an employee for exclusively at-home use of medicinal marijuana. Roe v. TeleTech Customer Care Mgt., LLC, 171 Wn.2d 736, 743, 257 P.3d 586 (2011).

The Washington Court of Appeals held that state ferry system employees' drug and alcohol test results are not subject to disclosure under the Public Records Act (PRA) because they are shielded by a federal law that protects the confidentiality of such tests performed on certain public transportation employees. Freedom Found. v. Wash. State Dep't. of Transp., Div. of Wash. State Ferries, 276 P.3d 341, 343, 168 Wn. App. 278 (May 10, 2012). Federal laws qualify for an exception under the "other statute" exemption provided by the PRA. Id.

I. GENERAL LAW OF PRIVACY

A. Legal Basis of Privacy Claims

1. ***Constitutional Law.*** The Washington state constitution contains an explicit privacy right that states, "[n]o person shall be disturbed in his private affairs, or his home invaded, without authority of law." Wash. Const. art. 1, § 7. The provision requires state action and does not regulate the behavior of private persons. State v. Clark, 48 Wn. App. 850, 855, 743 P.2d 822, rev. denied, 109 Wn.2d 1015 (1987). Article 1, section 7 grants broader protection than the U.S. Constitution's Fourth Amendment. Am. Legion Post. No. 149 v. Dep't of Health, 164 Wn.2d 570, 597, 192 P.3d 306 (2008); State v. Gunwall, 106 Wn.2d 54, 720 P.2d 808 (1986). The Washington Supreme Court has noted that the state constitution clearly recognizes an individual's right to privacy with no express limitations. State v. Simpson, 95 Wn.2d 170, 178, 622 P.2d 1199 (1980); see also State v. Eisfeldt, 163 Wn.2d 628, 636, 185 P.3d 580 (2008). However, the Court has declined to decide whether a plaintiff can maintain a civil cause of action for constitutional privacy violations, holding instead that common law causes of action more appropriately address privacy rights. Reid v. Pierce County, 136 Wn.2d 195, 213-14, 961 P.2d 333 (1998). A U.S. District Court in Washington has also declined to recognize a civil cause of action for a violation of art. 1, sec. 7 of the Washington Constitution. Fowler v. U.S. Bank Nat'l Ass'n., No. C07-5589 RBL, 2007 WL 4562900, at *4 (W.D. Wash. Dec. 20, 2007) (unpublished), aff'd, 362 Fed. App'x 682 (9th Cir. 2010).

2. ***Statutory Law.*** Several Washington statutes affect privacy in the employment setting. Among the most important are:

The Privacy Act, RCW §§ 9.73.010-9.73.260. The Privacy Act bans the interception or recording of private conversations without the consent of all parties. RCW § 9.73.030. The statute creates a civil cause of action and criminal sanctions for violations of the Act. RCW § 9.73.080 (gross misdemeanor); RCW § 9.73.060 (civil liability). The Privacy Act provides broader protection than the state constitution, and it applies to private citizens. State v. Corliss, 123 Wn.2d 656, 661, 870 P.2d 317 (1994). In State v. Townsend, email messages and real-time internet client-to-client messages with an undercover police officer were considered "private communications" recorded by a "device" that fell within the scope of the Privacy Act. 147 Wn.2d 666, 674-75, 57 P.3d 255 (2002). However, the Court found that under the circumstances, the sender of such messages gave implied permission for the recipient to record them. Id. at 676. **The Washington Court of Appeals recently extended that rationale to text messages delivered via cell phone. State v. Roden, 169 Wn. App. 59,**

279 P.3d 461 (June 26, 2012). The court held that someone who voluntarily sends text messages impliedly consents to their recording. Id. at 67. In a separate case decided on the same day, the court held that the interception of such messages does not violate Wash. Const. art. 1, § 7's privacy protections, nor the Fourth Amendment of the U.S. Constitution. State v. Hinton, 169 Wash.App. 28, 34 – 39, 280 P.3d 476 (June 26, 2012). Text messages warrant privacy protection similar to that provided to letters: any expectation of privacy expires once the letter is mailed. Id. at 43.

Polygraph Testing, RCW § 49.44.120. State law bars public and private employers from requiring employees or job candidates to take a lie detector test. Violators can face criminal sanctions and a civil lawsuit. RCW § 49.44.120 (misdemeanor); RCW § 49.44.135 (civil action). The restriction applies to both employee candidates and current employees; law enforcement agencies, drug manufacturers, and organizations related to national security are exempt. RCW § 49.44.120. See II.D, infra. Employers in law enforcement agencies and juvenile court services agencies may require initial applicants or those who return after a break of more than two years in service to take lie detector tests. Id. See II.D, infra.

Washington Law Against Discrimination, RCW § 49.60 (WLAD). The WLAD deems it an "unfair practice" Wn. App.for employers to base hiring, firing, or compensation decisions on age, sex, marital status, sexual orientation, race, creed, color, national origin, disability, or military status. RCW § 49.60.180(1). Military status is defined as a veteran or an "active or reserve member in any branch of the armed forces of the United States, including the national guard, coast guard, and armed forces." RCW § 49.60.040(25); RCW § 41.04.007. Unfair practice within WLAD includes asking prospective employees questions about these protected subjects. WAC 162-12-140. In Brown v. Scott Paper Worldwide Co., the Washington Supreme Court held that managers could be sued individually for employment discrimination and held liable under the WLAD for asking an employee questions about subject matter prohibited by the Act. 143 Wn.2d 349, 358, 20 P.3d 921 (2001). In 2009, WLAD was expanded to protect mothers who breastfeed in public. See RCW §§ 49.60.030(1)(g), 49.60.215. However, in 2011, Washington became the first state to pass legislation expressly permitting private employers to give a hiring preference to certain veterans and their spouses. 2011 Wash. Sess. Laws ch. 144. The law expressly provides that such preference will not violate local equal employment opportunity law, including the WLAD. Id. Presumably, employers may now inquire into a prospective employee's military status without running afoul of the WLAD.

Washington Anti-SLAPP Statutes, RCW §§ 4.24.510; 4.24.525. In 1989, Washington passed the first anti-SLAPP statute (Strategic Lawsuit Against Public Participation), providing defendants procedural protections and fee awards for unfounded defamation suits and similar claims based on the defendant's speech activities. RCW § 4.24.510. That law granted immunity to a person who (1) "communicates a complaint or information to any branch or agency of federal, state, or local government, or to any self-regulatory organization" and (2) such complaint regards matter "reasonably of concern to that agency." See Bailey v. State, 147 Wn. App. 251, 261, 191 P.3d 1285 (2008) (quoting RCW § 4.24.510). In 2010, the Legislature significantly expanded anti-SLAPP protection to statements made outside government agencies, including those in "a public forum in connection with an issue of public concern." RCW § 4.24.525(2). Courts have applied the anti-SLAPP statutes to bar claims in the employment context. See I.B.2. infra. However, the Washington Supreme Court held recently that a government agency does not qualify as a "person" entitled to anti-SLAPP immunity. Segaline v. Dep't of Labor & Indus., 169 Wn.2d 467, 238 P.3d 1107 (2010) (reasoning that RCW § 4.24.510 is meant "to protect free speech rights and a government agency has no such rights to protect").

RFID Legislation, RCW §§ 19.300.010-19.300.030. In 2008, the Washington legislature enacted a statute that makes intentional remote scanning of another person's "identification device" without the person's knowledge and consent, "for the purpose of fraud, identity theft, or for any other illegal purpose," a class C felony. RCW § 19.300.020. Identification devices include radio frequency identification ("RFID") tags, such as those embedded in new enhanced driver's licenses or employer ID cards, as well as facial recognition systems. RCW § 19.300.010. The use of RFID devices in commercial transactions is strictly limited, notwithstanding several exceptions for emergencies, law enforcement needs, or consensual transactions. RCW § 19.300.030.

3. ***Common Law.*** In 1998, the Washington Supreme Court finally settled decades of confusion over the tort of invasion of privacy by explicitly recognizing a common law cause of action. Reid v. Pierce County, 136 Wn.2d 195, 206, 961 P.2d 333 (1998). The Reid court allowed families of deceased persons to proceed with a disclosure of private facts claim after county workers displayed autopsy photos at social functions. Id. In doing so, the court adopted the test for public disclosure claims outlined in the Restatement (Second) of Torts. Id. at 205. The decision ended years of speculation and overruled an appellate case that had rejected the tort of invasion of privacy. See Doe v. Grp. Health Coop. of Puget Sound, Inc., 85 Wn. App. 213, 223, 932 P.2d 178, 183 (1997). Previously, the Washington Supreme Court had assumed the tort existed but had declined to rule directly on the issue. See, e.g., Eastwood v. Cascade Broad. Co., 106 Wn.2d 466, 474, 722 P.2d 1295, 13 Media L. Rep. 1136 (1986); Mark v. Seattle Times, 96 Wn.2d 473, 635 P.2d 1081, 7 Media L. Rep. 2209 (1981), cert. denied, 457 U.S. 1124 (1982). In one of the first applications of Reid, the Washington Court of Appeals reversed the summary dismissal of a public teacher's common law invasion of privacy claim stemming from the school's

investigation of alleged misconduct by the teacher and comments about the teacher made to the local newspaper by school officials. Corbally v. Kennewick Sch. Dist., 94 Wn. App. 736, 973 P.2d 1074 (1999). Similarly, the Washington Court of Appeals reversed a grant of summary judgment in favor of a public employer in a case where the employer disclosed medical information about an employee, a deputy town marshal, to a local newspaper. White v. Town of Winthrop, 128 Wn. App. 588, 116 P.2d 1034 (2005). The court held that a jury should decide whether the public had a legitimate concern with the details of the employee's medical condition. Id. at 597. The extent of the right to privacy tort in other areas remains unclear.

The U.S. District Courts for both the Western and Eastern districts of Washington have affirmed the recognition of a common law cause of action for the tort of invasion of privacy. Fowler v. U.S. Bank Nat'l Ass'n., No. C07-5589 RBL, 2007 WL 4562900, at *4 (W.D. Wash. Dec. 20, 2007) (unpublished); Nealey v. BNSF Ry. Co., No. CV-06-5057 -FVS, 2007 WL 4287272 (E.D. Wash. Dec. 4, 2007) (unpublished). In Nealey, the court noted that a person may be liable for invasion of privacy by giving publicity to a matter concerning the private life of another if the matter is highly offensive to a reasonable person and is not of legitimate public concern. Id. (citing White, 128 Wn. App. at 593).

B. Causes Of Action

1. ***Misappropriation/Right of Publicity.*** The Washington State Supreme Court has ruled only once on the issue of misappropriation/right of publicity, and it did not discuss either the tort of misappropriation or the right to privacy in its decision. State ex. rel. LaFollette v. Hinkle, 131 Wash. 86, 229 P. 317 (1924). The court held that a political party could not use a person's name without permission because "[n]othing so exclusively belongs to a man or is so personal and valuable to him as his name." Id. at 93. The court presumed damages and authorized an injunction. Id. The court did not address the statute of limitations, but the limit for defamation and related privacy torts is two years. RCW § 4.16.100(1).

2. ***Defamation.*** A successful claim of defamation requires proof that (1) the defendant's statement was false; (2) it was unprivileged; (3) fault; and (4) the statement proximately caused injury. Mohr v. Grant, 153 Wn.2d 812, 822, 108 P.3d 768 (2005). Washington also recognizes a cause of action for defamation by implication when a defendant "juxtaposes a series of facts so as to imply a defamatory connection between them, or creates a defamatory implication by omitting facts." Corey v. Pierce County, 154 Wn. App. 752, 225 P.3d 367, 38 Media L. Rep. 1297 (2010), rev. denied, 170 Wn.2d 1016, 245 P.3d 775 (2010). One recent court has held that a defamation by implication claim may not be sustained, however, when all of the published statements are true and a false impression could not have been contradicted by omitted facts. Yeakey v. Hearst Comm., Inc., 156 Wn. App. 787, 234 P.3d 332 (2010). To sustain a claim of defamation against a public figure, proof of actual malice is required. Corey, 154 Wn. App. at 762 (citing Herron v. KING Broad. Co., 109 Wn.2d 514, 523, 746 P.2d 295 (1987)).

An employment relationship creates a conditional privilege for an employee who reports another employee's alleged criminal acts to supervisors or to the police. Wilson v. City of Longview, No. 27740-9-II, 2002 WL 1831981, at *13-14 (Wash. Ct. App. Aug. 9, 2002) (unpublished). In addition, the Washington Court of Appeals has held that an otherwise defamatory statement may be privileged under a "common interest" qualified privilege if "the declarant and the recipient have a common interest in the subject matter of the communication." Vande Hey v. Walla Walla Cmty. Hospice, No. 26216-2-III, 2008 WL 152595, at *2 (Wash. Ct. App. Jan. 17, 2008) (unpublished) (quoting Moe v. Wise, 97 Wn. App. 950, 957-58, 989 P.2d 1148 (1999)). In Vande Hey, the court held that an internal memo from a hospice worker, posted for the review of co-workers, was not a "published" statement. Id. at *3. As a general rule, intra-corporate communications are not "published" because such communications are essentially communication of the corporation with itself. Charnholm v. Bartell Drug Co., No. 57912-6-I, 2007 WL 316784, at *4 (Wash. Ct. App. Feb. 5, 2007) (unpublished). However, the qualified protection afforded to intra-corporate communication can be lost if the defamatory publication is either made outside the ordinary course of work or made with actual malice. Id. (citing Doe v. Gonzaga Univ., 143 Wn.2d 687, 701, 702-03, 24 P.3d 390 (2001), rev'd on other grounds, 536 U.S. 273 (2002)). Similarly, the common interest privilege can be lost if the defamatory statements are spread beyond the persons and interests protected by the privilege or if the statements are published with actual malice. Valdez-Zontek v. Eastmont Sch. Dist., 154 Wn. App. 147, 163-65, 225 P.3d 339 (2010).

Courts have applied Washington's anti-SLAPP statutes, RCW §§ 4.24.510 and 4.24.525, to bar defamation claims in the employment context. In one case, a nanny sued her former employer – parents of a child in the nanny's care – for defamation based on the parents' communication to police and Child Protective Services that the nanny abused the child. Brawley v. Roufar, 162 Wn. App. 1058, 2011 WL 2993467, at *1 (2011) (unpublished). The court granted summary judgment in favor of the parents, agreeing their statements to those government agencies were absolutely privileged under RCW § 4.24.510. Another court dismissed a paramedic's defamation claim against former colleagues who made statements to a news station about the paramedic's misconduct. Castello v. City of Seattle, 39 Media L. Rep. 1591, 2010 WL 4857022, *6-9 (W.D. Wash. 2010) (unpublished). The court concluded the news broadcast was a "public forum" under RCW

§ 4.24.525 and that the colleagues' statements were privileged due to the public's concern with how the fire department handled unrest and morale issues. Id. at*6.

Washington also recognizes a fair reporting privilege that affords protection to news media defendants for reporting on defamatory statements contained in official records and proceedings. Clapp v. Olympic View Pub. Co., L.L.C., 137 Wn. App. 470, 477, 154 P.3d 230 (2007). In construing this privilege, the Clapp court held that the privilege applied to defamatory statements printed in a newspaper article which directly and accurately quoted an employee's allegation that her former employer "trampled" her infant child, although the substance of the allegations were later proved false. Id.

3. ***False Light.*** Until recently, it was an unsettled question as to what extent Washington courts recognized the tort of false light. Although the Washington Supreme Court has noted that the tort addresses compensation for mental suffering rather than reputation, it expressly declined to consider whether the claim should be recognized. Eastwood v. Cascade Broad. Co., 106 Wn.2d 466, 471, 722 P.2d 1295, 13 Media L. Rep. 1136 (1986) (holding that a potential false light claim was barred by the statute of limitations). Some courts have indicated in dicta that the claim is not actionable in Washington. Hoppe v. Hearst Corp., 53 Wn. App. 668, 677 n 5, 770 P.2d 203 (1989). Other courts have agreed on the elements required to establish the claim but have declined to permit recovery because the required elements were not proved. See, e.g., Patterson v. Little, Brown & Co., 502 F. Supp. 2d 1124 (W.D. Wash. 2007) (no proof of actual malice); LaMon v. City of Westport, 44 Wn. App. 664, 669, 723 P.2d 470, 474 (1986), rev. denied, 112 Wn.2d 1024 (1989) (no publication). However, the Washington State Court of Appeals recently upheld a jury verdict in favor of a former deputy county prosecutor on her false light claim against her former employer based on inaccurate statements made to a local newspaper about the grounds for her termination. Corey v. Pierce County, 154 Wn. App. 752, 225 P.3d 367, 38 Media L. Rep. 1297 (2010), rev. denied, 170 Wn.2d 1016, 245 P.3d 775 (2010).

A false light claim arises when "someone publicizes a matter that places another in a false light if (a) the false light would be highly offensive to the reasonable person and (b) the actor knew of or recklessly disregarded the falsity of the publication and the false light in which the other would be placed." Corey, 154 Wn. App. at 762 (quoting Eastwood, 106 Wn.2d at 470-71). Because most cases addressing false light claims have involved public officials, plaintiffs have been required to prove actual malice (as required with defamation claims). See, e.g., Corey, 154 Wn. App. at 762; Hoppe v. Hearst Corp., 53 Wn. App. at 677. Although one of the tort's elements is the defendant's knowledge or reckless disregard of the false light, Washington courts have yet to explicitly decide whether a private (non-public figure) plaintiff must show actual malice when asserting a false light claim. In Harris v. City of Seattle, the court noted the unresolved question but declined to determine the issue because the plaintiff was a public official. 315 F. Supp. 2d 1105, 32 Media L. Rep. 1572 (W.D. Wash. 2004), aff'd, 152 Fed. Appx. 565, 33 Media L. Rep. 2473 (9th Cir. 2005).

Matters of public record cannot satisfy the publication requirement. LaMon v. City of Westport, 44 Wn. App. 664, 669, 723 P.2d 470, 474 (1986), rev. denied, 112 Wn.2d 1024 (1989), cert. denied, 493 U.S. 1074 (1990). Courts recognize the overlap between defamation and false light by allowing parties to allege both torts yet recover for only one. Brink v. Griffith, 65 Wn.2d 253, 259, 396 P.2d 793 (1964). The statute of limitations is two years. Eastwood, 106 Wn.2d at 474.

4. ***Publication of Private Facts.*** In 1998, the Washington Supreme Court recognized this type of invasion of privacy tort. Reid v. Pierce County, 136 Wn.2d 195, 206, 961 P.2d 333 (1998). A plaintiff may sue for damages if the defendant publicizes information that (1) would be highly offensive to a reasonable person and (2) is not of legitimate concern to the public. Id. at 205.

As with false light claims, Washington has adopted the Restatement's view of "publication" for the purposes of publication of private facts claims: the publication must result in "unreasonable publicity, of a kind highly offensive to the ordinary reasonable [person]." See I.B.3, infra; Restatement (Second) of Torts § 652D (1977); Fisher v. State ex rel. Dep't of Health, 125 Wn. App. 869, 879, 106 P.3d 836 (2005). Communication of "a fact concerning the plaintiff's private life to a single person or even a small group of persons" will not give rise to an invasion of privacy claim. Doe v. State, No. 35130-7-II, 2008 WL 929885, at *13 (Wash. Ct. App. Apr. 8, 2008) (quoting Restatement § 652D cmt. c at 387 (1977)) In Doe, a state employee disclosed an extensive pattern of sexual harassment by a co-worker to an investigator under the expectation of confidentiality; however, the state included the complaining employee's name in the harasser's termination letter. Id., at *1-2. The court upheld the dismissal of the plaintiff's invasion of privacy claim, finding that the inclusion of her name in the termination letter was not "publication." Id., at *13.

A claim is not foreclosed because the private conduct occurred on the job. One court held that there was prima facie evidence supporting a plaintiff's invasion of privacy claim after his employer disclosed to the media an argument between the plaintiff and his wife at a company picnic, as well as a statement that the plaintiff had an extramarital affair with a subordinate. White v. Woodinville Water Dist., No. 52015-6-I, 2004 WL 1444556, at *8 (Wash. Ct. App. June 28, 2004) (unpublished). Given the nature of the matters concerned and the lack of reasonable public concern about them, the court held it did not matter, as the district contended, that the matters occurred on "district time." Id. In White v. Town of Winthrop, town officials allegedly disclosed to a local newspaper that one of the town's former deputy marshals resigned because he had epilepsy. 128 Wn. App. 588, 116 P.2d 1034 (2005). Reversing the trial court's grant of summary judgment in favor of the town, the Washington Court of Appeals held that there was an issue of fact regarding whether the deputy's seizure disorder was an "unpleasant or disgraceful or humiliating illness one would not wish announced in a newspaper." Id. at 594. The court held that a jury should decide whether the public had a legitimate concern in the details of the employee's medical condition. Id. at 597.

The Washington Court of Appeals affirmed a trial court's dismissal of an invasion of privacy claim holding that the employee waived her right to medical privacy by putting her health at issue when she applied for workers' compensation. Mayer v. Huesner, 126 Wn. App. 114, 122, 107 P.3d 152 (2005).

Washington courts will look to the Restatement (Second) of Torts for the "guiding principles" on invasion of privacy. Reed, 136 Wn.2d at 206. A claim may be brought by certain third parties, such as family members injured by the disclosures. Id. at 212. Some examples of private information that could result in liability if disclosed include family quarrels, unpleasant illnesses, sexual relations, intimate letters, and a person's past history. Id. at 210. In Reed, the court found an expectation of privacy in autopsy reports, citing statutes that require confidentiality. Id. at 211-12 (citing RCW § 68.50.105). This raises questions about whether other statutes requiring confidentiality could lead to implied causes of action for invasion of privacy.

Courts will typically apply the Restatement's approach to damages. Id. at 204 n.4 (plaintiff can recover for harm to his or her interests, mental distress, and special damages); see also White, 128 Wn. App. at 597. The statute of limitations does not exceed the two years allowed for defamation, as the claims are similar. Moloney v. Tribune Publ'g Co., 26 Wn. App. 357, 362-63, 613 P.2d 1179, 6 Media L. Rep. 1426 (1980), overruled on other grounds, Bender v. City of Seattle, 99 Wn.2d 582, 664 P.2d 492, 9 Media L. Rep. 2101 (1983); see also Eastwood, 106 Wn.2d at 474 (false light claim has two year statute of limitations because of similarity to defamation).

5. ***Intrusion.*** Washington courts have assumed the tort of intrusion exists but have not ruled in favor of a plaintiff. Mark v. Seattle Times, 96 Wn.2d 473, 497, 635 P.2d 1081, 7 Media L. Rep. 2209, cert. denied, 457 U.S. 1124 (1982); LaMon, 44 Wn. App. at 669. The tort of intrusion requires (1) intrusion (2) into another's private affairs (3) that is offensive and objectionable to the ordinary person. Mark, 96 Wn.2d at 497. Matters of public record cannot support a claim. LaMon, 44 Wn. App. at 669. Cases have not addressed the potential statute of limitations.

C. Other Privacy-Related Actions

1. ***Intentional Infliction of Emotional Distress.*** To establish the tort of outrage, a plaintiff must show (1) extreme and outrageous conduct, (2) intentional or reckless infliction of emotional distress, and (3) severe emotional distress on the part of the plaintiff. Reid v. Pierce County, 136 Wn.2d 195, 202, 961 P.2d 333 (1998) (citing Dicomes v. State, 113 Wn.2d 612, 630, 782 P.2d 1002 (1989)). Washington expressly recognizes the tort in the employment setting. Contreras v. Crown Zellerbach Corp., 88 Wn.2d 735, 565 P.2d 1173 (1977). However, a claim that stems from an injury or occupational disease that occurs in the ordinary course of employment is not actionable, as it is covered by the exclusive remedy provisions of Washington's Industrial Insurance Act. See VIII.C, infra. An employer can be held vicariously liable for the tort of outrage if the wrongful conduct occurs while a tortfeasing employee is acting within the scope of employment, regardless of whether the conduct furthers the employer's business or whether the employer was aware of the wrongful conduct. Robel v. Roundup Corp., 148 Wn.2d 35, 59 P.3d 611 (2002). Nonetheless, Washington courts will not recognize a claim against an employer for intentional infliction of emotional distress when the only factual basis for the claim is the same as for discrimination claim. See Goodman v. The Boeing Co., 127 Wn.2d 401, 407, 899 P.2d 1265 (1995) (applying a separate injury analysis to allow an employee's claims based on verbal harassment); Haubry v. Snow, 106 Wn. App. 666, 678, 31 P.3d 1186 (2001).

To qualify as extreme and outrageous, the wrongful conduct must go "beyond all reasonable bounds of decency." Contreras, 88 Wn.2d at 737, 565 P.2d at 1174 (quoting the Restatement (Second) of Torts). Insults and indignities causing mere embarrassment or humiliation are not enough to support a claim. Rich v. Fiberweb Washougal, Inc., 1999 WL 221562, at *7 (1999), rev. denied, 139 Wn.2d 1025, 994 P.2d 845 (2000). In addition, the Washington Court of Appeals has held that the intent element requires a specific intent or recklessness to cause harm rather than simply an intent to act. Henson v. Crisp, 88 Wn. App. 957, 961, 946 P.2d 1252 (1997), rev. denied, 135 Wn.2d 1010, 960 P.2d 937 (1998). However, the analysis of an emotional distress claim requires a case-by-case approach that examines factors such as the defendant's position and whether the defendant knew of the plaintiff's unique susceptibility to certain conduct. Reid, 136 Wn.2d at 202; Contreras, 88 Wn.2d at 742 (lesser behavior satisfied the outrageous conduct element because employer knew of employee's susceptibility to racist comments). In a recent unpublished decision, one court found that a former city employee could not sustain an intentional infliction of emotional distress claim against her former employer based on the manner in which she was terminated, although the court did not foreclose the possibility that such a claim was possible. Beahm v. City of Bremerton, No. C09-5048 RJB, 2010 WL 1141476 (W.D. Wash. Mar. 22, 2010) (unpublished).

Courts have held that the extreme nature of an act can provide evidence that severe harm occurred. Brower v. Ackerly, 88 Wn. App. 87, 102, 943 P.2d 1141 (1997), rev. denied, 134 Wn.2d 1021, 958 P.2d 315 (1998). The tort does not require a showing of bodily harm, but the plaintiff must show he or she at least witnessed the outrageous conduct. Reid, 136 Wn.2d at 203, 961 P.2d at 337-38. If the conduct was directed at someone other than the plaintiff, the plaintiff must show that they are an immediate family member of the person at whom the conduct was directed, and be present at the time of the conduct. Stafford v. Benjamin, 1999 WL 528153, at *3 (1999), rev. denied, 139 Wn.2d 1019, 994 P.2d 848 (2000) (citing Reid, 136 Wn.2d at 202).

The Washington Supreme Court has declined to determine the statute of limitations for outrage. Doe v. Finch, 133 Wn.2d 96, 101, 942 P.2d 359 (1997). Courts have held that outrage can overlap with other causes of action, but double recovery is not permitted when the alternate cause of action permits recovery for emotional distress. See Rice v. Janovich, 109 Wn.2d 48, 742 P.2d 1230 (1987) (no double recovery with assault); Anaya v. Graham, 89 Wn. App. 588, 950 P.2d 16 (1998) (no double recovery with disability claim under WLAD); Sedlacek v. Hillis, 104 Wn. App. 1, 25, 3 P.3d 767 (2000), rev'd on other grounds, 145 Wn.2d 379, 36 P.3d 1014 (no double recovery with wrongful discharge in violation of public policy claim).

2. ***Negligent Infliction of Emotional Distress.*** Washington explicitly recognizes a claim for negligent infliction of emotional distress in an employment context. Chea v. Men's Wearhouse, Inc., 85 Wn. App. 405, 412, 932 P.2d 1261, rev. denied, 134 Wn.2d 1002, 953 P.2d 96 (1998). A plaintiff must show that (1) he or she was injured by an employer's negligent acts, (2) the acts were not a workplace dispute or employee discipline, (3) the injury is not covered by the Industrial Insurance Act, and (4) the dominant feature of the claim is emotional injury. Little v. Windermere Relocation, Inc., 301 F.3d 958, 972 (9th Cir. 2002) (citing Snyder v. Med. Serv. Corp. of E. Wash., 98 Wn. App. 315, 988 P.2d 1023 (1999). A supervisor's intentional actions designed to force an employee to resign can give rise to a claim of negligent infliction of emotional distress against the employer. Schraum v. Riviera Cmty. Club, No. 25003-9-II, 2001 WL 112326 (Wash. Ct. App. Feb. 9, 2001) (unpublished). However, Washington courts do not recognize a negligent infliction claim when the factual basis for the emotional distress provides the same basis for a discrimination claim. Little, 301 F.3d at 972 (citing Robel v. Roundup Corp., 103 Wn. App. 75, 10 P.3d 1104 (2000)).

Washington courts have not clearly defined the boundaries of the "workplace dispute" element of the claim. For example, a supervisor's demeaning comments and jokes about an employee's hair color, the house she purchased, and her husband's employment were not part of a "workplace dispute" although the supervisor's conduct occurred in the workplace. Strong v. Terrell, 147 Wn. App. 376, 388-89, 195 P.3d 977 (2008). Those facts, in combination with the supervisor spitting on the employee and threatening a battery, were sufficient to allow the employee's claim of negligent infliction of emotional distress to go to trial. Strong, 147 Wn. App. at 389, 195 P.3d at 984. The Washington Court of Appeals has held, however, that "absent a statutory or public policy mandate, employers do not owe employees a duty to use reasonable care to avoid the inadvertent infliction of emotional distress when responding to workplace disputes." Francom v. Costco Wholesale Corp., 98 Wn. App. 845, 864, 991 P.2d 1182, rev. denied, 141 Wn.2d 1017, 10 P.3d 1071 (2000).

One recent court considered a negligent infliction of emotional distress claim brought by a state contractor. Segaline v. State Dep't of Labor and Indus., 144 Wn. App. 312, 182 P.3d 480 (2008), rev'd on other grounds, 169 Wn.2d 467, 238 P.3d 1107 (2010). The court applied the same test used for employee-based claims, but it held that the contractor failed to show that he would develop objective symptoms of emotional stress as a result of being served a no trespass notice and being removed from state property. Id.

3. ***Interference With Prospective Economic Advantage.*** Washington does recognize interference with contract claims. Calbom v. Knudtzon, 65 Wn.2d 157, 396 P.2d 148 (1964). The elements are (1) existence of a contract or business expectancy, (2) knowledge of the relationship, (3) intentional interference, (4) improper purpose, and (5) resultant damages. Id. at 162, 396 P.2d at 151; Leingang v. Pierce County Med. Bureau, 131 Wn.2d 133, 157, 930 P.2d 288 (1997); Goodyear Tire & Rubber Co., 86 Wn. App. 732, 745, 935 P.2d 628, 636 (1997), rev. denied, 133 Wn.2d 1033, 950 P.2d 477 (1998); Vasquez v. State Dep't of Soc. & Health Servs., 94 Wn. App. 976, 989, 974 P.2d 348, 355, rev. denied, 138 Wn.2d 1019, 989 P.2d 1143 (1999).

The U.S. District Court recently adhered to the Washington Supreme Court's holding that where interference with business is a mere incidental consequence of a breach in contract, a tortious interference claim is properly dismissed. Manay v. Academic Exch. of Am., No. C07-5071 RBL, 2008 WL 820097 (W.D. Wash. Mar. 25, 2008) (unpublished). In another case, the U.S. District Court also adhered to the Washington Supreme Court's holding that a tortious interference claim requires an "intermeddling third party", and thus such a claim cannot be supported in a claim involving only two parties. Ellis v. Smithkline Beecham Corp., No. C07-5302 RJB, 2008 WL 618631 (W.D. Wash. Mar. 3, 2008) (unpublished) (citing Houser v. City of Redmond, 91 Wn.2d 36, 39, 586 P.2d 482 (1978)).

The aggrieved party receives tort damages rather than contract damages. Calbom, 65 Wn.2d at 167; **See also I.C.4. infra (discussing the "economic loss rule").** The statute of limitations is three years. City of Seattle v. Blume, 134 Wn.2d 243, 250-51, 947 P.2d 223 (1997). The courts have not ruled whether interference with contract overlaps with any privacy torts.

4. ***Prima Facie Tort.*** Washington courts have reformulated the prima facie tort into "wrongful interference with economic relationships." Pleas v. City of Seattle, 112 Wn.2d 794, 803, 774 P.2d 1158 (1989). A cause of action for tortious interference requires a showing that the interference was "wrongful" or that the party had a duty of non-interference. Id. at 804. Courts have some difficulty in agreeing on a label for this tort, as courts addressing wrongful interference after the redefinition discuss what they term "tortious interference with a business expectancy." See To-Ro Trade Shows v. Collins, 100 Wn. App. 483, 997 P.2d 960 (2000); aff'd, 144 Wn.2d 403, 27 P.3d 1149 (2001); Hudson v. City of Wenatchee, 94 Wn. App. 990, 974 P.2d 342 (1999).

In order to establish a claim, the plaintiff must prove: (1) the existence of a valid contractual relationship or business expectancy; (2) that defendants had knowledge of that relationship; (3) an intentional interference inducing or causing a breach or termination of the relationship or expectancy; (4) that defendants interfered for an improper purpose or used improper means; and (5) resultant damages. Commodore v. Univ. Mech. Contractors, Inc., 120 Wn.2d 120, 137, 839 P.2d 314 (1992). Specifically, to satisfy the fourth element, the plaintiff must show that the defendant pursued an improper objective of harming the plaintiff or used wrongful means that caused the injury to contractual or business relationships. Pleas, 112 Wn.2d at 803-04. Once the plaintiff has established all elements, the burden of proof shifts to the defendant to justify the interference or otherwise show that the actions were privileged. Commodore, 120 Wn.2d at 137 (citing Pleas, 112 Wn.2d at 800).

In Galactic Ventures, LLC v. King County, the defendant attempted to argue that even if all of the elements of the tortious interference with a business expectancy had been met, its conduct was privileged. No. C05-1054RSM, 2006 WL 1587415, at *4 (W.D. Wash. Jun. 7, 2006) (unpublished). The defendant relied on the Cherberg court's holding that in some instances, intentional interference with a business expectancy may be 'privileged,' and therefore not a basis for tort recovery, if the interferor's conduct is deemed justifiable. Cherberg v. Peoples Nat'l Bank, 88 Wn.2d 595, 564 P.2d 1137 (1977). The Cherburg court provided several such factors for consideration: the nature of the interferor's conduct; the character of the expectancy with which the conduct interferes; the relationship between the various parties; the interest sought to be advanced by the interferor; and the social desirability of protecting the expectancy or the interferor's freedom of action. Id. at 604-05. However, the Galactic court was persuaded by the plaintiff that in the context of Cherberg, the "privilege" discussion was really intended to determine whether improper purpose or means were present. Galactic, 2006 WL 1587415, at *4; see also Calbom v. Knudtson, 65 Wn.2d 157, 163 (1964) ("The basic issue raised by the assertion of the [privilege] is whether, under the circumstances of the particular case, the interferor's conduct is justifiable[.]").

A plaintiff does not have to show the existence of an enforceable contract or breach of a contract to raise a claim of tortious interference with a business relationship, Commodore, 120 Wn.2d at 138. A plaintiff can instead point to a "business expectancy," an expectation of business by a third party that was interfered with by the defendant. Graham v. Cingular Wireless, LLC, No. C05-1810JLR, 2006 WL 354969 (W.D. Wash. Feb. 14, 2006) (unpublished). A plaintiff must also show that the future opportunities and profits are based on a reasonable expectation and not based on wishful thinking. Sea-Pac Co., Inc. v. United Food & Commercial Workers Local 44, 103 Wn.2d 800, 805, 699 P.2d 217 (1985).

Because the tort is directed at interfering third parties rather than parties to a contract or expectancy (who would instead be subject to a breach of contract claim), a plaintiff–employee usually may not bring a tortious interference claim against other employees or agents of the same employer due to the termination of an employment contract. Houser, 91 Wn.2d at 39; Daniels v. City of Spokane, No. 27160-9-III, 2009 WL 891823 (Wash. Ct. App. Apr. 2, 2009) (unpublished), rev. denied, 166 Wn.2d 1038 (2009).

Washington case law is unclear whether at-will employees have an expectancy in continued employment. Some courts seem to conclude that at-will employees have no such expectancy. See, e.g., Woody v. Stapp, 146 Wn. App. 16, 24, 189 P.3d 807 (2008); Raymond v. Pac. Chem., 98 Wn. App. 739, 992 P.2d 517 (1999), rev'd sub nom. on other grounds, Brown v. Scott Paper Worldwide Co., 143 Wn.2d 349, 20 P.3d 921 (2001). Other courts apparently reject that premise. See, e.g., Lincor v. Contractors, Ltd. v. Hyskell, 39 Wn. App. 317, 323, 692 P.2d 903 (1984) (holding that a third party could tortuously interfere with an at-will contract "so long as neither party of the parties had elected to terminate it"); Island Air,

Inc. v. LaBar, 18 Wn. App. 129, 140, 566 P.2d 972 (1977) ("[T]he fact that a party's terminable at will contract is ended in accordance with its terms does not defeat that party's claim for damages caused by unjustifiable interference[.]"). A federal district court acknowledged this uncertainty in Washington law and squarely held that an "at-will employment relationship can satisfy the first element of the tort of intentional interference with contract or business expectancy." Tamosaitis v. Bechtel Nat'l, Inc., 2011 WL 321726, at *3 (E.D. Wash. 2011).

Tort vs. Contract Remedies. In November 2010, the Washington Supreme Court clarified the proper division between tort and contract remedies in a decision that will likely affect employment disputes implicating both tort and contract theories. Eastwood v. Horse Harbor Found., Inc., 170 Wn.2d 380, 241 P.3d 1256 (2010). In Eastwood, a lease required the tenant to maintain the property in good condition. Id. at 383. When the property deteriorated, the landlord sued for breach of lease and the tort of waste. Id. at 384. The Court of Appeals denied recovery on the waste claim by applying the so-called "economic loss rule," which purportedly prevents recovery of economic losses in tort whenever such losses arose out of a relationship governed by contract. Id. at 385. Reversing, the Washington Supreme Court held that "[a]n injury is remedial in tort if it traces back to the breach of the tort duty arising independently of the terms of the contract." Id. at 389. Courts are to examine on a case-by-case basis whether an independent duty of care exists as a matter of law, thereby allowing recovery in tort. Id. To help clarify this approach, the court redenominated the "economic loss rule" into the "independent duty doctrine." Id. at 394. The Eastwood court acknowledged that this doctrine likely has an impact in the employment context in that, for instance, economic losses have been recoverable through the torts of interference with business expectancy and wrongful discharge in violation of public policy. Id. at 388.

II. EMPLOYER TESTING OF EMPLOYEES

A. Psychological or Personality Testing

1. ***Common Law and Statutes.*** Subject to potential disability issues (discussed infra), employers in Washington appear free to require psychological or personality tests from employees and prospective employees. The Washington statute barring employment polygraph tests states "[n]othing in this section shall be construed to prohibit the use of psychological tests. . . ." RCW § 49.44.120. A separate statute defines psychological testing. RCW § 18.83.010. Research tests and drug trials are excluded from the list of permissible activities. Id.

Very little case law exists on the subject of psychological or personality testing. The Washington Court of Appeals has previously held that an employee cannot sue for wrongful termination under a constructive discharge theory based on an employer's order to undergo psychological evaluation. Micone v. Town of Steilacoom Civil Serv. Comm'n, 44 Wn. App. 636, 643, 722 P.2d 1369, overruled on other grounds, Riccobono v. Pierce County, 92 Wn. App. 254, 966 P.2d 327 (1998). The court also rejected the employee's claim that the order made his resignation involuntary, although the court did not explicitly address the privacy rights of the employee. Id. at 642.

Although state law does not bar psychological or personality testing directly, tests designed to elicit information about mental illnesses could conflict with the protection from disability discrimination provided by the Washington Law Against Discrimination (WLAD). RCW § 49.60.180. The WLAD and accompanying administrative provisions bar pre-employment screening for disability. RCW § 49.60.180; WAC 162-12-140 (prohibiting questions about protected subjects); see also V.B.II, infra (state legislature's recently adopted definition of "disability").

2. ***Private Employers.*** See II.A.1, supra.

3. ***Public Employers.*** See II.A.1, supra.

B. Drug Testing

1. ***Common Law and Statutes.*** See II.B.2.-3, infra.

2. ***Private Employers.*** No statutes directly forbid drug testing by private employers. In 2007, Washington voters approved the Medical Use of Marijuana Act (MUMA), decriminalizing medicinal marijuana use by patients with terminal or debilitating illnesses, but expressly stating employers are not required to accommodate on-site use. RCW § 69.5A.060. Recent amendments to the act also reiterate that "[e]mployers may establish drug-free work policies" and are not required to accommodate medical use of marijuana if the employer has a drug-free work place. 2011 Wash. Sess. Laws ch. 181.

In 2011, the Washington Supreme Court confirmed employers may terminate an employee for exclusively at-home use of medicinal marijuana. Roe v. TeleTech Customer Care Mgt., LLC, 171 Wn.2d 736, 743, 257 P.3d 586 (2011). In Roe, the employer terminated an employee who tested positive for medicinal marijuana on a company drug test. Id. at 743. Denying the employee's wrongful termination claims, the court held MUMA neither creates a private cause of action for wrongful termination nor establishes public policy supporting an action for wrongful discharge in violation of public policy based on medicinal marijuana use. Id. at 754, 759-60. Appellate courts have also upheld random drug testing programs by private employers because the Washington constitution requires state action before its provisions apply. Roe v. Quality Transp. Serv., 67 Wn. App. 604, 838 P.2d 128 (1992) (dismissing wrongful discharge action and finding no public policy against drug testing). Mandatory drug testing also does not create grounds for constructive discharge. Olsen v. Payless Drug Stores Nw., No. 21531-4-II, 1998 WL 386196 (Wash. Ct. App. July 10, 1998) (unpublished), rev. denied, 137 Wn.2d 1016, 978 P.2d 1097 (1999).

On the issue of alcohol testing, the Washington Supreme Court has declined to decide as a matter of law whether alcoholism is a disability protected by the Washington Law Against Discrimination (WLAD) or the Americans With Disabilities Act (ADA). Phillips v. City of Seattle, 111 Wn.2d 903, 910, 766 P.2d 1099 (1989); Brady v. Daily World, 105 Wn.2d 770, 777, 718 P.2d 785 (1986). The court has similarly held that the question of whether drug abuse constitutes a disability is the province of the fact-finder. Rhodes v. URM Stores, Inc., 95 Wn. App. 794, 977 P.2d 651, rev. denied, 139 Wn.2d 1006, 989 P.2d 1141 (1999).

On Nov. 6, 2012, Washington voters approved a ballot initiative partially legalizing marijuana growth and possession. Initiative No. 502 removed some state criminal and civil prohibitions against manufacturing, distributing, and possessing marijuana. It applies only to limited quantities of marijuana grown or possessed by persons at least 21 years old. The measure also establishes a state licensing and regulatory scheme.

3. ***Public Employers.*** The state constitution protects individual privacy from state intrusion. Wash. Const. art. 1, § 7 ("No person shall be disturbed in his private affairs, or his home invaded, without authority of law"). The Washington Supreme Court has held that urinalysis of public employees is a search within the U.S. Constitution's Fourth Amendment. Alverado v. Wash. Pub. Power Supply Sys., 111 Wn.2d 424, 759 P.2d 427 (1988), cert. denied, 409 U.S. 1004, 109 S. Ct. 1637, 104 L. Ed. 2d 153 (1989). The court upheld pre-employment testing at a nuclear power plant as a permissible administrative search, citing the highly regulated and dangerous nature of the industry. Id. at 438-39. However, one court struck down a municipality's pre-employment urinalysis drug test as an unconstitutional violation of privacy. Robinson v. City of Seattle, 102 Wn. App 795, 10 P.3d 452 (2000). The city required drug testing of city employees who were employed in "safety related positions", a classification the court found so broad as to encompass more than half of the city's jobs. Id. at 801, 823. State administrative regulations prohibit agencies from disciplining employees based solely on drug test results. WAC 356-46-125(2).

In York v. Wahkiakum School District No. 200, the Washington Supreme Court held that a school district's policy providing for random and suspicion-less drug testing of student athletes violated the students' state constitutional rights. 163 Wn.2d 297, 178 P.3d 995 (2008). One concurring opinion noted that the decision appears to contradict the court's prior decision in State v. Athan, in which the court held that use of saliva samples for DNA testing was neither an invasion of privacy nor involuntary when the method used to obtain the samples was not invasive. 160 Wn.2d 354, 158 P.3d 27 (2007). While York does not concern testing in the context of employment, the court's holding on the privacy issue may be relevant in an employment setting.

In Freedom Found. v. Wash. State Dep't. of Transp., Div. of Wash. State Ferries, 276 P.3d 341, 343, 168 Wn. App. 278 (May 10, 2012), the Washington Court of Appeals held that state ferry system employees' drug and alcohol test results are not subject to disclosure under the Public Records Act (PRA) because they are shielded by a federal law that protects the confidentiality of such tests performed on certain public transportation employees. Federal laws qualify under the PRA's "other statute[s]" exemption for record-protection laws. Id.

C. Medical Testing

The WLAD and its accompanying regulations prohibit pre-employment questions about disability. RCW § 49.60.180; WAC 162-12-140(3). Discrimination in benefits and termination based on disability also are barred. RCW § 49.60.180(2)(3). The law allows medical exams only after an employer makes a conditional offer of employment, but if the employer uses the exam to screen for disabilities, the procedure could conflict with the WLAD and the ADA. If employers obtain disability information for accommodation purposes, they must prevent improper use by maintaining those records in a manner accessible only on a need to know basis. WAC 162-12-180; see also V.B.II, infra (State legislature revises definition of "disability").

AIDS/HIV Testing. A comprehensive state law regulates HIV testing in the workplace. RCW § 49.60.172. Public and private employers cannot require HIV tests as "a condition of hiring, promotion, or continued employment unless the absence of HIV infection is a bona fide occupational qualification for the job in question." RCW § 49.60.172(1). Employers cannot release HIV test results or the fact that a person has AIDS, except to some health care and insurance providers. RCW

§ 70.24.105. They also cannot discriminate based on HIV status. RCW § 49.60.172(2); Lins v. Children's Discovery Ctrs. of Am., Inc., 95 Wn. App. 486, 490-91, 976 P.2d 168, 171 (1999). Finally, the statute protects employers from lawsuits if their employees transmit HIV to other employees or the public, unless the employer acted with gross negligence. RCW § 49.60.172(5).

D. Polygraph Tests

State law strictly prohibits lie detector tests by both public and private employers unless they obtain the employee's consent. RCW § 49.44.120. The restriction applies to both employee candidates and current employees, with an exception for law enforcement agencies, drug manufacturers, and organizations related to national security. RCW § 49.44.120. Effective July 22, 2007, law enforcement agencies and juvenile court services agencies may require initial applicants or those who return after a break of at least two years in service to take lie detector tests. 2007 Wash. Sess. Laws ch. 14, § 1; RCW § 49.44.120. Previously, lie detector tests were allowed only on initial applications to law enforcement agencies. Id. The Washington Supreme Court has rejected equal protection challenges to the law enforcement exception. O'Hartigan v. Dep't of Pers., 118 Wn.2d 111, 821 P.2d 44 (1991). However, the agencies must carefully tailor questions to relate only to the employment situation. Id. at 120, 821 P.2d at 49. The statute specifically excludes psychological testing from coverage. RCW § 49.44.120. Drug testing also does not fall within the statute's prohibitions. Roe v. Quality Transp. Servs., 67 Wn. App. 604, 838 P.2d 128 (1992). Violations can lead to criminal convictions. RCW § 49.44.120(3). Employees forced "directly or indirectly" to undergo a polygraph can sue for damages, a $500 penalty, and attorneys' fees. RCW § 49.44.135.

E. Fingerprinting

State law requires fingerprinting of school employees and contractors who will have regularly scheduled, unsupervised access to children. RCW § 28A.400.303. The employees must be allowed to review their record checks, and the school districts cannot release the information to the public or to other employees. WAC 392-300-025, 392-300-045. Until recently, private schools were unable to obtain copies of employee background check results; however, in 2010, the Washington State Legislature amended the statute to permit distribution of the background reports to approved private schools. 2010 Wash. Sess. Laws ch. 100, § 1; RCW 28A.400.305. Employees of secured facilities for sexually violent predators must also undergo fingerprint checks. RCW § 71.09.115. Any facility that "educates, trains, treats, supervises, houses or provides recreation" to children, vulnerable adults, or the disabled must check the criminal background of potential employees or volunteers who will have unsupervised access to clients. RCW § 43.43.832; RCW § 43.43.834. These background checks may involve fingerprinting, and if so the employer must notify the applicant about any inquiry made to the Washington State Patrol or any Federal law enforcement agency. RCW § 43.43.834(1). A similar provision applies to nursing homes and health care facilities. RCW § 43.43.832. A 2009 requires the Department of Licensing to obtain fingerprints and to do background checks of current or prospective employees who process applications for enhanced drivers' licenses. RCW 46.01.130(2).

There are no statutes limiting private employers from fingerprinting employees. In fact, state law outlines procedures for the State Patrol when taking fingerprints and submitting record checks to employers. RCW § 43.43.760. The only case to address fingerprinting in employment upheld a Seattle city ordinance that required temporary police officers to provide fingerprints for background checks. Surry v. City of Seattle, 14 Wn.2d 350, 128 P.2d 322 (1942). The court held that the ordinance was a valid exercise of the police power. Id. at 359, 128 P.2d at 326. However, the Ninth Circuit Court of Appeals has previously noted that collection of fingerprints from "free persons" constitutes a "significant interference with individual expectations of privacy." Rise v. Oregon, 59 F.3d 1556, 1559-60 (1995), cert. denied, 517 U.S. 1160 (1996), overruled on other grounds, Ferguson v. City of Charleston, 532 U.S. 67 (2001) and City of Indianapolis v. Edmond, 531 U.S. 32 (2000). The Rise court's sharp distinction between the privacy interests invoked by fingerprinting a person in custody, as opposed to a person out of custody, has been acknowledged with tacit agreement by some Washington courts. See, e.g., State v. Bachman, No. 38256-3-II, 2009 WL 3756790 (Wash. Ct. App. Nov. 10, 2009) (unpublished), rev. granted by, remanded by 172 Wn.2d 1009 (2011).

In Ino Ino, Inc. v. City of Bellevue, the Washington Supreme Court held that the City of Bellevue's requirement of fingerprinting for entertainers and managers at an adult entertainment club did not violate article I, section 7 of the Washington State Constitution. 132 Wn.2d 103, 937 P.2d 154 (1997), cert. denied, 522 U.S. 1077, 118 S. Ct. 856, 139 L. Ed. 2d 755 (1998). The court held that fingerprinting need only meet a rational basis test because the interest in confidentiality of personal information is not a fundamental right, finding that the licensing requirements advanced several legitimate goals and that the disclosure required only the type of information necessary to advance those goals. As of 2010, all counties and municipalities cities within the state may, by ordinance, require state and federal background checks (including fingerprinting) for any license applicants or licensees seeking a locally-issued occupational license not otherwise issued by the state. See RCW § 36.01; RCW § 35.21; RCW § 35A.21.

F. Genetic Testing

In 2004, Washington enacted a law that prohibits "any person, firm, corporation, or the state of Washington, its political subdivisions, or municipal corporations to require, directly or indirectly, that any employee or prospective employee submit genetic information or submit to screening for genetic information as a condition of employment or continued employment." RCW § 49.44.180. "Genetic information" includes information about inherited characteristics that can be derived from a DNA-based or other laboratory test, family history, or medical examination, but does not include: (1) routine physical measurements, including chemical, blood, and urine analysis, unless conducted purposefully to diagnose genetic or inherited characteristics; and (2) results from tests for abuse of alcohol or drugs or for the presence of HIV.

Recently, the Washington Supreme Court held there is no inherent privacy interest in saliva. State v. Athan, 160 Wn.2d 354, 158 P.3d 27 (2007). In Athan, the defendant appealed a conviction of second degree murder based on the claim that his DNA was collected in violation of the Washington State Constitution. Id. Police detectives, pretending to be a law firm, induced the defendant to mail a letter to the firm and extracted his DNA from the letter. The defendant relied on Robinson v. City of Seattle, 102 Wn. App. 795, 10 P.3d 452 (2000), which held that a pre-employment urinalysis drug test violated the Washington State Constitution. See II.B.3., supra. In Athan, the court distinguished Robinson, explaining that unlike forced urine or blood testing, the process for obtaining the saliva in this case was not invasive or involuntary. Athan, 160 Wn.2d at 367, 158 P.3d at 33. The court held that when a person licks an envelope and mails it, that person does not retain any privacy interest in his saliva. Id.

III. SEARCHES

A. Employee's Person

1. ***Private Employers.*** No authority addresses physical searching of private employees. The state constitution applies only to state action and does not bar searches by private employers. However, employers could open themselves up to actions for intrusion or outrage, despite the lack of clarity in those areas of law. See I.C.4, supra; VII.A, infra.

2. ***Public Employers.*** The Washington Supreme Court has held that urinalysis of public employees is a search within the meaning of the U.S. Constitution. Alvaredo v. Wash. Pub. Power Supply Sys., 111 Wn.2d 424, 759 P.2d 427 (1988), cert. denied, 490 U.S. 1004 (1989). The Alvaredo court indicated that bodily searches of public employees require more than a showing that government need outweighs the employee's expectation of privacy. Alvaredo, 111 Wn.2d at 439-40. Additional evidence of need and the presence of procedural safeguards are required even in heavily regulated industries. Id. Although the court has not interpreted the state constitution's privacy provision in employee bodily search cases, it has held that the provision provides more protection than the federal Constitution. State v. Clark, 48 Wn. App. 850, 855, 743 P.2d 822, rev. denied, 109 Wn.2d 1015 (1987).

B. Employee's Work Area

Constitutional protections apply to government searches of a person's belongings and turn on whether the worker has a reasonable expectation of privacy. State v. Kealey, 80 Wn. App. 162, 907 P.2d 319 (1995), rev. denied, 129 Wn.2d 1021, 919 P.2d 599 (1996). The Washington Supreme Court has not interpreted the state constitution as applied to searches of workspaces. There are no statutes or case law prohibiting private employers from searching workspaces. However, an employer could face a conversion claim if he or she takes the employee's property when searching it. Walling v. S. Birch & Sons Constr. Co., 35 Wn.2d 435, 213 P.2d 478 (1950). An employer who searches private mail would violate state law and could face civil or criminal sanctions. RCW § 9.73.020; RCW § 9.73.010 (misdemeanor); 9.73.060 (civil cause of action).

C. Employee's Property

See III.B, supra.

IV. MONITORING OF EMPLOYEES

A. Telephones and Electronic Communications

1. ***Wiretapping.*** Washington's Privacy Act prohibits intercepting or recording any "private communication transmitted by telephone, telegraph, radio, or other device." without the consent of all parties. RCW § 9.73.030(1)(a). The law applies to all persons. State v. Cunningham, 93 Wn.2d 823, 613 P.2d 1139. In Kitsap County v. Smith, the Washington Court of Appeals held that a public employer (a county) had a legitimate interest in advising its employees and the public of the possibility that their conversations might be recorded. 143 Wn. App. 893, 180 P.3d 834, rev. denied, 164 Wn.2d 1036, 197 P.3d 1185 (2008). The court found that the question of whether the Washington Privacy Act applies to conversations with public employees is one "of great public importance." Id. The courts have extended protection

to cordless telephone conversations and have barred pen registers. State v. Faford, 128 Wn.2d 476, 910 P.2d 447 (1996) (cordless phones); State v. Gunwall, 106 Wn.2d 54, 720 P.2d 808 (1986) (pen register). Taking a number off a pager, however, does not violate the statute. State v. Wojtyna, 70 Wn. App. 689, 695, 855 P.2d 315 (1993), rev. denied, 123 Wn.2d 1007, 869 P.2d 1084 (1994). **In 2012, the Washington Court of Appeals held that the same logic applies in all electronic communications, including text messages sent to a cellular phone: any expectation of privacy evaporates upon delivery to the recipient. State v. Hinton, 169 Wn. App. 28, 45, 280 P.3d 476 (June 26, 2012).** "Private" is determined on a case-by -case basis by examining both the parties' subjective expectations and those of a reasonable person. State v. Clark, 129 Wn.2d 211, 224-25, 916 P.2d 384 (1996). Interception of a conversation through a device for purposes of RCW § 9.73 includes surreptitiously listening to a private telephone conversation by use of the speakerphone function on a cordless telephone base. State v. Christensen, 153 Wn.2d 186, 102 P.3d 789 (2004). There is no reasonable expectation of privacy at a meeting where others could reveal what transpired. Id. at 226.

Recording of private oral conversations also is barred by the Privacy Act unless all parties to the conversation consent. RCW § 9.73.030(1)(b). However, divulging private conversations is not a violation of the statute. Kearney v. Kearney, 95 Wn. App. 405, 974 P.2d 872, rev. denied, 95 Wn.2d 1022, 989 P.2d 1137 (1999) (offering transcript of illegally recorded phone conversations into evidence held not to violate Privacy Act). The statute prohibits both recording and transmitting by "any device electronic or otherwise." RCW § 9.73.030(1)(b). In State v. Bonilla, a police officer listened on an extension line as the defendant told a dispatcher that he shot and killed his wife, and the court held there was no violation because the police officer only overheard the conversation on an ordinary extension phone. 23 Wn. App. 869, 598 P.2d 783 (1979). However, a later court reached a different conclusion, noting that the Bonilla court did not determine whether an extension phone is a "device" under the statute. State v. Christensen, 153 Wn.2d 186, 197, 102 P.3d 789 (2004).

The Privacy Act contains exceptions for emergencies and for cases when the communications are threatening. RCW § 9.73.030(2). However, the statute does not contain an extension phone exception for employers similar to the exception provided for in the federal Electronic Communications Privacy Act. See 18 U.S.C. § 2511(2)(a). Police recordings of conversations that are part of a bona fide criminal drug investigation are exempted from the statute. State v. Cibrian, No. 41581-6-I, 1999 WL 458974, at *2 (Wash. Ct. App. Jul. 6, 1999) (unpublished). The statute also allows intercepting and recording if all parties present to the conversation consent, and consent exists when one party to the conversation announces to all others that the conversation or communication will be recorded. RCW § 9.73.030(3).

The Washington Supreme Court has cautioned that "[i]ntercepting or recording telephone calls violates the privacy act except under narrow circumstances," creating a broad presumption of protection. State v, 164 Wn.2d 83, 186 P.3d 1062 (2008). In particular, the court noted that a private conversation does not lose the protection of the Privacy Act simply because the participants know it will (or might be) recorded or intercepted, and signs indicating that calls may be monitored or recorded do not by themselves defeat a reasonable expectation of privacy. Id. (holding instead that the defendant's presence in jail at the time defeated his reasonable expectation of privacy).

One court recently held that a former county employee was ineligible for state unemployment benefits after the employee was terminated for violating the Privacy Act by secretly creating audio recordings of co-workers in the workplace. Smith v. Emp't Sec. Dep't, 155 Wn. App. 24, 226 P.3d 263 (2010).

A person who suffers injury to "his business, his person, or his reputation" from violations of the chapter can bring a cause of action against violators. RCW § 9.73.060. A person cannot evade liability by having another party do the actual intercepting, recording, or divulging of private communications. RCW § 9.73.060. Successful plaintiffs will receive attorneys' fees and either actual damages, including pain and suffering, or liquidated damages of $100 per day of violation. RCW § 9.73.060. Violators also can face criminal charges for gross misdemeanor. RCW § 9.73.080. The statute of limitations is three years for a civil lawsuit and two years for criminal cases. RCW § 4.16.080 (civil claims); RCW § 4.16.115; RCW § 9A.04.080.

2. ***Electronic Communications.*** Internal policies against use of state-provided Internet access other than for state business, or to promote personal religious beliefs, business interests, or commercial use, do not violate state privacy laws and are not prohibited by RCW § 49.60.180. Evans v. State, No. 35941-3-II, 2008 WL 186785 (Wash. Ct. App. Jan. 23, 2008) (unpublished). See IV.A.1, supra. **Attorney-client privilege does not attach to an employee's personal electronic records if they are produced or stored in a manner indicating no reasonable expectation of privacy, e.g., on a computer that belongs to an employer with a disclosed policy reserving rights to the records, or where the employee has waived any privilege by relinquishing a laptop to the employer. Aventa Learning, Inc. v. K12, Inc., 830 F. Supp.2d 1083, 1106 – 1110 (W.D. Wash. Nov. 8, 2011).**

Public employer-provided email systems are not private because they are limited to official business and all emails generated on a city email system are city property. Kirby v. City of Tacoma, 124 Wn. App. 454, 98 P.3d 827 (2004), rev. denied, 154 Wn.2d 1007, 114 P.3d 1198 (2005). A police officer alleged his supervisor had seized his email account and conducted an illegal search of his emails without a warrant in retaliation for raising an issue with the supervisor's superiors. The court held that the information on the city's email system can be considered a public record, subject to disclosure, and therefore the search did not violate privacy laws. While email is considered private under the Act, the party sending the email implicitly consents to having the email recorded on the receiving party's computer, thereby eliminating the reasonable expectation of privacy. Id.

3. ***Electronic Monitoring.*** In 2008, the Washington legislature enacted a statute that makes intentional remote scanning of another person's "identification device" without the person's knowledge and consent, "for the purpose of fraud, identity theft, or for any other illegal purpose" a class C felony. RCW § 19.300.020. Identification devices include radio frequency identification ("RFID") tags, such as those embedded in new enhanced driver's licenses or employer ID cards, as well as facial recognition systems. RCW § 19.300.010. The use of RFID devices in commercial transactions is strictly limited, notwithstanding several exceptions for emergencies, law enforcement needs, or consensual transactions. RCW § 19.300.030.

Under the Washington Public Records Act, public transit agencies are permitted under certain circumstances to release information about individuals who acquire and use transit passes. RCW § 42.56.330(5). In 2010, the statute was amended to permit disclosure of the pass-holder's personally identifying information to an employer or other sponsoring organization "for the purpose of preventing fraud, or to the news media when reporting on public transportation or [safety]." Id. The information may also be released to law enforcement agencies if required by a court order, or it may be disclosed in aggregate form if the data does not contain personally identifying information. Id.

B. Mail

A Washington statute from 1909 makes any person who "shall willfully open or read, or cause to be opened or read, any sealed message, letter or telegram intended for another person . . . ." guilty of a misdemeanor. RCW § 9.73.020. A person also breaks the law by publishing any portion of the message if he or she knows it has been opened without consent. Id. The only case interpreting this statute states the expectation of privacy lessens when a common carrier delivers the letter as opposed to first-class mail. State v. Wolohan, 23 Wn. App. 813, 598 P.2d 421 (1979), rev. denied, 93 Wn.2d 1008 (1980). A similar statute says anyone who improperly obtains or divulges the contents of another person's telegram commits a misdemeanor. RCW § 9.73.010. Violators can face the same civil liability as under the Privacy Act. See IV.A.4, supra.

C. Surveillance/Photographing

The Privacy Act does not bar employers from monitoring employees with soundless video recordings or photographs. State v. Clark, 129 Wn.2d 211, 916 P.2d 384 (1996); State v. Raymer, 61 Wn. App. 516, 810 P.2d 1383, rev. denied, 117 Wn.2d 1022, 818 P.2d 1098 (1991). However, if the video includes sound, it could violate the private conversation portion of the Privacy Act. RCW § 9.73.030(1)(b). The Washington Supreme Court has held in a criminal case that the installation of global positioning system (GPS) devices on a defendant's impounded vehicle involved a search and seizure under article I, section 7, the privacy provision of the Washington State Constitution, and required a warrant. State v. Jackson, 150 Wn.2d 151, 76 P. 3d 217 (2003). The court noted that there was no issue as to whether the state Privacy Act was violated by the installation and use of the GPS device, as RCW 9.73.260(1)(b)(iii) provides that tracking devices are not communications within the Privacy Act. 150 Wn.2d, at 259 n.1.

V. ACTIVITIES OUTSIDE THE WORKPLACE

A. Statute or Common Law

The Washington legislature has declared a "policy" of encouraging rehabilitated felons to enter the workforce. RCW § 9.96A.010. However, the Washington Court of Appeals has held the policy does not prevent private employers from dismissing employees solely because of convictions. Selix v. Boeing Co., 82 Wn. App. 736, 919 P.2d 620 (1996), rev. denied, 130 Wn.2d 1024, 930 P.2d 1230 (1997). The Washington Administrative Code previously contained regulations prohibiting employment discrimination based on convictions. WAC 162-16-060. However, the regulations were repealed in 1999. Wash. St. Reg. 99-15-025; see also VI.C, infra.

Former Human Rights Commission regulations, also repealed, declared that it was an unfair practice for any employer to "refuse to hire or otherwise discriminate against a person in employment because he or she has been arrested." WAC 162-16-050(1). These regulations barred pre-employment inquiries about arrests. WAC 162-16-050(3). In the face of criticism by the Washington Court of Appeals that the Commission had exceeded its authority by creating a new protected class, the Commission repealed the regulations in 1999. Wash. St. Reg. 99-15-025; Gugin v. Sonico, 68 Wn. App. 826, 846 P.2d 571 (1993).

Some city or county ordinances extend additional protection to employee activity outside of the workplace. For example, a Seattle ordinance prohibits employers from discriminating on grounds of political ideology among other protected activities. Seattle Mun. Code § 14.04.020(A) (protected classes); Seattle Mun. Code § 14.04.040(C) (non-discrimination provision).

In State v. Hirschfelder, the Washington Court of Appeals held that the statute criminalizing sexual contact between school employees and students only applied to 16- and 17-year-old students. State v. Hirschfelder, 148 Wn. App. 328, 331, 199 P.3d 1017 (2009); see RCW § 9A.44.093(1)(b) (2008). Thus, a high school choir teacher did not commit a crime when he had sex with an 18-year-old student. Id. In 2010, the Washington Supreme Court reversed, concluding that "minor" included registered students up to 21 years old. 170 Wn.2d 536, 542-43, 242 P.3d 876 (2010). In the intervening time before that decision, the Legislature amended RCW § 9A.44.093 and RCW § 9A.44.096 to explicitly prohibit a school employee from having sexual contact with students between the ages of 16 and 21. 2010 Wash. Sess. Laws ch. 324, § 1.

See also V.B, infra.

See also II.B.2, supra (discussing medicinal marijuana).

B. Employees' Personal Relationships

1. ***Romantic Relationships Between Employees.*** The Washington Law Against Discrimination (WLAD), RCW § 49.60.180, does not apply to cohabitating, dating, or other social relationships. Waggoner v. Ace Hardware Corp., 134 Wn.2d 748, 953 P.2d 88 (1998). In Waggoner, the court held that the plain meaning of marital status excludes cohabitation by employees, and the court deferred to the legislature to protect those relationships. Id. at 756, 953 P.2d at 92.

2. ***Sexual Orientation.*** Formerly, the WLAD did not include sexual orientation, although both King County and the City of Seattle prohibited such discrimination by employers. King County Code §§ 12.18.010-030; Seattle Mun. Code § 14.04.040(C). In 2006, the WLAD added "sexual orientation" to its list of protected classes. The WLAD already prohibits discrimination on the basis of race, creed, color, national origin, families with children, sex, marital status, age, the presence of any sensory, mental or physical disability, or disabled persons using a training dog guide or service animal. The addition of "sexual orientation" encompasses "heterosexuality, homosexuality, and bisexuality" as well as "gender expression or identity." Gender expression or identity is defined by the statute as "having or being perceived as having a gender identity, self-image, appearance, behavior, or expression, whether or not that gender identity, self-image, appearance, behavior or expression is different from that traditionally associated with the sex assigned to that person at birth." The addition of "sexual orientation" was intended to cover discrimination against transsexuals (individuals who have or are in the process of sex reassignment), intersexuals (also known as hermaphrodites), discrimination because of gender stereotypes, and discrimination based on actual or perceived sexual orientation. However, the law still allows employers to segregate bathrooms based on biological gender. RCW § 49.60.180. The law expressly states that it should not be construed to modify or supersede state law regarding marriage. RCW § 49.60.020. An "employer" includes any person acting in the interest of an employer, directly or indirectly, who employs eight or more persons, and does not include any religious or sectarian organization not organized for private profit. RCW § 49.60.040. The WLAD prohibits discrimination in employment, credit and insurance transactions, places of public accommodation, and real property transactions.

In May 2009, Washington enacted legislation significantly expanding the rights of registered domestic partners under state law (nicknamed the "Everything But Marriage" bill). 2009 Wash. Sess. Laws ch. 521. State agencies are required to amend their rules to ensure that all rights, benefits, privileges and immunities granted or imposed by statute apply equally to registered domestic partners as marital spouses. Id., § 2. The law was ratified in a voter referendum in November 2009.

An executive order issued by the Mayor of Seattle requiring city departments to recognize "same sex marriages" of city employees in the same manner as opposite-sex marriages for purposes of employee benefits did not directly conflict with the state's Defense of Marriage Act. Leskovar v. Nickels, 140 Wn. App. 770, 166 P.3d 1251 (2007), rev. denied, 163 Wn.2d 1043, 187 P.3d 270 (2008). The court held that the order determined only who was eligible for employee benefits and did not give legal effect to same sex marriages.

In Deo v. King Broadcasting Co., 122 Wn. App. 1034, 2004 WL 1598862 (Wash. Ct. App. Jul. 19, 2004) (unpublished opinion), where the plaintiff's coworkers allegedly made offensive comments because of the plaintiff's sexual orientation, the court examined the defendant's conduct in light of the provisions of the Seattle Municipal Code prohibiting discrimination on the basis of sexual orientation. Using only the Seattle Municipal Code provisions (because the plaintiff's references to King County ordinances were unsupported by citation), the court found that the isolated remarks of coworkers were insufficient to show that the defendant used pretextual reasons to fire the plaintiff. Id. at 3-4. The King County provision makes it an unfair practice to discriminate "against any person on the basis of race, color, age, sex, marital status, sexual orientation, religion, ancestry, national origin, or the presence of any sensory, mental or physical handicap." King

County Code 12.18.010. The section applies to employers of eight or more persons. King County Code 12.18.020(D). Seattle's ordinance applies to those with one or more employees. Seattle Mun. Code § 14.04.030(H). The ordinance bars discrimination based on "race, color, age, sex, marital status, sexual orientation, gender identity, political ideology, creed, religion, ancestry, national origin, or presence of any sensory, mental or physical disability." Seattle Mun. Code § 14.04.020 (A) (protected classes); Seattle Mun. Code § 14.04.040(C) (anti-discrimination provisions).

In Pedersen v. Snohomish County Center for Battered Women, the Court of Appeals held that isolated comments by a supervisor concerning dissatisfaction with the dress habits of lesbian women and the sexual orientation of a lesbian woman the supervisor later hired for a management position were insufficient to support a complaint of a hostile work environment. No. 60275-6-I, 2008 WL 1934846 (Wash. Ct. App. May 5, 2008) (unpublished). The court concluded that the incidents did not unreasonably interfere with the employee's work performance and therefore did not support a claim of a hostile work environment. Id.

City and county codes barring discrimination on the basis of sexual orientation do not establish a clear mandate of statewide public policy and are thus not sufficient to support a common law claim of wrongful discharge in violation of public policy. Webb v. Puget Sound Broad. Co., No. 41228-2-I, 1998 WL 898788 (Wash. Ct. App. Dec. 28, 1998) (unpublished).

Transsexualism. A Seattle ordinance makes it an unfair practice for employers to discriminate on the basis of gender identity. Seattle Mun. Code § 14.04.020; RCW § 14.04.040. In addition, transsexualism is now included as a protected trait under the Washington Law Against Discrimination (WLAD), RCW § 49.60.180. See Sexual Orientation, infra. Moreover, the Washington Supreme Court has indicated that the WLAD provision for disability may protect employees suffering from gender dysphoria. Doe v. Boeing Co., 121 Wn.2d 8, 846 P.2d 531 (1993). The court recognized that gender dysphoria is an abnormal medical condition. Id. at 14 (holding, however, the employee failed to prove discrimination).

On July 6, 2006, the Washington Supreme Court interpreted the definition of "disability" under the WLAD to be identical to the definition of "disability" in the federal Americans with Disabilities Act of 1990 (ADA), 42 U.S.C. §§ 12101-12209. McClarty v. Totem Electric, Int'l, 157 Wn.2d, 214, 137 P.3d 844 (2006). In response, the state legislature amended WLAD to explicitly define "disability", using a broader definition than the ADA provides. 2007 Wash. Sess. Laws ch. 317, § 2. Under the revised definition, for purposes of protection from discrimination, "disability" means an impairment that: (1) is cognizable or diagnosable; or (2) exists as a record or history; or (3) is perceived to exist. RCW § 49.60.040(25) (a). This definition is broader than the definition in the ADA because it includes disabilities that are "temporary or permanent, common or uncommon, mitigated or unmitigated." RCW § 49.60.040(25)(b).

However, for purposes of qualifying for reasonable accommodation in employment, the revised definition of "disability" is narrower than the ADA definition. The condition must substantially limit job performance or access to equal privileges or terms of employment, rather than simply impacting a major life activity. RCW § 49.60.040(25)(d). Under the new definition, the impairment must: (1) be known or shown through an interactive process and (2) substantially limit the employee's ability to perform the job. Id. Furthermore, medical documentation must establish a reasonable likelihood that engaging in job functions without an accommodation would aggravate the impairment and have a substantially limiting effect on job performance. Id. This definition also explicitly excludes impairments that have "only a trivial effect." RCW § 49.60.040(25)(e). This may change an employee's ability to establish gender dysphoria as a disability under the WLAD.

3. ***Marital Status.*** The WLAD makes it an unfair practice for employers to fire, refuse to hire, or discriminate in compensation and terms of employment based on a person's marital status. RCW §§ 49.60.180(1)-(3). The statute applies to any employer with eight or more employees. RCW § 49.60.040(3); Griffin v. Eller, 130 Wn.2d 58, 922 P.2d 788 (1996). However, the Washington Supreme Court has extended the discrimination provisions to employers with fewer than eight employees if the plaintiff brings a cause of action that is implied in, or based on, common law, or based on a different statute. Bennett v. Hardy, 113 Wn.2d 912, 929, 784 P.2d 1258, 1266 (1990). The Washington Supreme Court has recognized the tort of wrongful discharge in violation of public policy for gender discrimination by an employer of fewer than eight employees. Roberts v. Dudley, 140 Wn.2d 58, 993 P.2d 901 (2000). The court expressly noted that the technical statutory definition of employer to mean one employing eight or more employees did not apply to the common law cause of action. Id. at 911. The WLAD prevents employers from creating anti-nepotism policies that would force one spouse to quit. Wash. Water Power Co. v. Wash. State Human Rights Comm'n, 91 Wn.2d 62, 69, 586 P.2d 1149 (1978). Administrative regulations also bar any pre-employment inquiries about marital status unless a bona fide occupational qualification exists. WAC 162-12-140(1), (2)(a). The rules also prevent questioning of third parties, such as a credit reporting service. WAC 162 -12-140(1). An employee bringing a claim must establish that marital status was a "substantial factor" in the adverse employment decision. Magula v. Benton Franklin Title Co., Inc., 131 Wn.2d 171, 176, 930 P.2d 307 (1997). The employer can justify the discrimination through "business necessity." Id. The legislature defined marital status in 1993 as "the legal status of being married, single, separated, divorced, or widowed." RCW § 49.60.040(7). See also Waggoner v. Ace

Hardware Corp., Wn.2d 748, 755, 953 P.2d 88 (1998) (refusing to expand the definition of marital status to include the legal status of cohabitating or dating).

4. ***Domestic Partnerships.*** In 2007, the state legislature extended certain rights and benefits to registered same-sex domestic partners of any age, and to opposite-sex partners with one partner who is at least 62 years of age. The revised laws provide processes for registering the domestic partnership with the Secretary of State and terminating the domestic partnership. This legislation allows domestic partners to give informed consent for medical procedures. RCW § 7.70.065. Domestic partners also have the same hospital visitation rights as spouses and now may also bring lawsuits for wrongful death. RCW § 4.20.020.

In May 2009, Washington enacted legislation significantly expanding the rights of registered domestic partners under state law (nicknamed the "Everything But Marriage" bill). 2009 Wash. Sess. Laws ch. 521. State agencies are required to amend their rules to ensure that all rights, benefits, privileges and immunities granted or imposed by statute apply equally to registered domestic partners as marital spouses. Id., § 2. The law was ratified in a voter referendum in November 2009.

5. ***Childbearing.*** The Washington Court of Appeals held that if an employer terminates an employee based on her potential to become pregnant, the employer has committed sex discrimination prohibited by the Washington Law Against Discrimination (WLAD), RCW § 49.60. Kuest v. Regent Assisted Living, Inc., 111 Wn. App. 36, 43, 43 P.3d 23 (2002); see also WAC 162-30-020. In Kuest, a former employee appealed a lower court's grant of summary judgment to her employer on an action alleging sex discrimination and wrongful termination. Kuest, 111 Wn. App. at 41. The Kuest court determined that it is an unfair practice for an employer to discharge a woman, penalize her in terms or conditions of employment, or in any way limit the job opportunities of a woman because she is pregnant or may require time away from work for childbearing. Id. at 43. The court also noted that evidence that the employee was discharged soon after supervisors asked the employee about childbearing plans, and evidence of the employee's history of satisfactory performance reviews were sufficient to establish a prima facie case of sexual discrimination and raise a material issue of fact as to whether the employee was a victim of discrimination. Id. at 45.

As of July 2009, a mother's right to breastfeed in public is protected under the WLAD. See RCW 49.60.030(1)(g); RCW 49.60.215.

C. Smoking

There is no authority barring employers from discriminating against employees who smoke outside the workplace. However, state rules and some county and city ordinances require employers to eliminate smoking at the workplace.

In 2005, Washington voters passed Initiative 901, amending RCW § 70.160. The former law, the Washington Clean Indoor Air Act (WCIAA) of 1985, prohibited smoking in a "public place," except within designated smoking areas. The former law allowed bars, taverns, restaurants, and bowling alleys to designate smoking areas. As amended by Initiative 901, RCW § 70.160 now prohibits smoking in "public places" and "places of employment." The definition of "public places" includes, among others, bars, taverns, bowling alleys, schools, skating rinks, and (non-tribal) casinos. RCW § 70.160.020(2). Additionally, at least 75 percent of the sleeping quarters in a hotel or motel rented to guests must be smoke-free. The law is not intended to restrict smoking in private facilities which are occasionally open to the public except upon the occasions when the facility is open to the public. Id. A "place of employment" includes "any area under the control of a public or private employer which employees are required to pass through during the course of employment," including, but not limited to: entrances and exits, work areas, restrooms, conference and class rooms, break rooms and cafeterias, and "other common areas." RCW § 70.160.020(3). Owners and employers must post "smoking prohibited" signs conspicuously at each building entrance. Additionally, retail stores and service establishments must post smoking prohibited signs conspicuously throughout their businesses. Smoking is banned within 25 feet of any entrance, exit, windows that open, or ventilation intakes of "public places" and "places of employment." RCW § 70.160.050. The initiative defines 25 feet as a "presumptively reasonable minimum distance." RCW § 70.160.075. Those passing by on a sidewalk are not in violation of the law.

The Washington Supreme Court held in American Legion Post No. 149 v. Dep't of Health that under the Smoking in Public Places Act, RCW § 70.160, smoking is prohibited in a place of employment, regardless of whether it is a private facility. 164 Wn.2d 570, 192 P.3d 306 (2008). Although the plaintiff in that case was a nonprofit, private fraternal organization that owned and operated a private club, the court held that the Smoking in Public Place Act applied because the club employed seven people. Am. Legion, 164 Wn.2d at 613.

D. Blogging

In one of the very few Washington cases addressing blogging in the context of employment issues, a court held that a school district employee could not maintain a civil rights claim under 42 U.S.C. § 1983 when the district demoted her based on the content of several of her personal blog entries. Richerson v. Beckon, No. C07-5590 JKA, 2008 WL 833076 (W.D. Wash. Mar. 27, 2008) (unpublished). The court determined the plaintiff's mean-spirited and offensive comments about co-workers on her blog did not "substantially involve matters of public concern"; therefore, she was not entitled to First Amendment protection by virtue of her position as a government employee. Id., at *3 (citing Connick v. Myers, 461 U.S. 138, 103 S. Ct. 1684, 75 L. Ed. 2d 686 (1994)).

VI. RECORDS

A. Personnel Records

1. ***Private Employers.*** All employers must record every employee's name, address, occupation, dates of employment, pay level, and hours worked. WAC 296-126-050(1) (1989). Employers must save these records for at least three years. Id. Employees have a right to inspect these records at any reasonable time. WAC 296-126-050(2). Employers may record the "race, creed, color, national origin, sex, marital status, disability, or age" of any employee, but these records must be separated from the personnel files in order to prevent improper usage.

Employees may examine their own personnel files at least once annually. RCW § 49.12.240 (1985). These include files that are "regularly maintained by the employer as a part of his business or are subject to reference for information given to persons outside of the company." RCW § 49.12.250(2) (1985). The employer may remove "irrelevant or erroneous" information, but the employee may challenge the employer's determination of what is irrelevant or erroneous and place a rebuttal in the file. Id. Former employees also can rebut or correct their files up to two years after they leave. RCW § 49.12.250(3). The employer does not have to allow copying of items other than payroll information. WAC 296-128-025 (1989). The employee's inspection rights do not apply to records regarding investigations of possible crimes or to records kept in preparation for litigation. RCW § 49.12.260 (1985).

In one recent case, a court upheld a jury verdict awarding an employee $500 because of her employer's delay in allowing her to examine her personnel file. Sheffield v. Goodyear Tire & Rubber Co., No. 61238-7-I, 2009 WL 2586619, at *11 (Wash. Ct. App. Aug. 24, 2009) (unpublished), rev. denied, 168 Wn.2d 1023, 231 P.3d 165 (2010). The court held that the employee was entitled to reasonable attorney's fees as she was "put to the inconvenience of hiring counsel to enforce her right." Id.

In order to protect individuals from identity theft, a Washington statute requires employers to "take all reasonable steps to destroy, or arrange for the destruction of, personal financial and health information and personal identification numbers issued by government entities in an individual's records within its custody or control when the entity is disposing of records that it will no longer retain." RCW § 19.215. Thus, employers must take special care when disposing of employee personnel, payroll, and medical files, and any other documents that may contain personal identifying information such as a social security numbers.

2. ***Public Employers.*** **The Public Records Act, RCW §§ 42.56.001 – 42.56.902.** In 2005 and 2006, the state legislature enacted significant changes to the Washington Public Disclosure Act (PDA), former RCW §§ 42.17.010 – 42.17.348 (2004). Effective July 1, 2006, the PDA statutes were reorganized into several discrete topics and became the Public Records Act (PRA), RCW §§ 42.56.001 – 42.56.902. Although the 2005 amendment contained substantive changes to the Act, including prohibiting public agencies from denying a request for identifiable records solely on the basis that the request was overbroad, the 2006 amendment recodified existing PDA statutes without any substantive changes. A listing of the primary exemptions can be found in RCW § 42.56.230 through RCW § 42.56.480; however numerous other exemptions and disclosure prohibitions exist throughout the statutes.

The PRA requires state and local agencies to make a variety of records available for public inspection. RCW § 42.56.070. The Washington Supreme Court has consistently held that the PDA "is a strongly worded mandate for broad disclosure of public records." Limstrom v. Ladenburg, 136 Wn.2d 595, 603, 963 P.2d 869 (1998). The statute contains several exemptions relevant to employers, but public employers are not liable for wrongly disclosing information if they acted in good faith while attempting to comply with the PRA. RCW § 42.56.060. Persons named in the records may seek an injunction to prevent disclosure if releasing the information "would clearly not be in the public interest and would substantially and irreparably damage any person." RCW § 42.56.540. Additionally, a person who fails to object to a single records request does not waive their right to privacy as to all future requests. Bainbridge Island Police Guild v. City of Puyallup, 172 Wn.2d 398, 259 P.3d 190 (2011). However, a divided Washington Supreme Court has held that the individual requesting the record has a right to intervene in the lawsuit to advocate for disclosure if the agency maintaining the record is not a strong proponent of disclosure. Burt v. Wash. State Dep't of Corrs., 168 Wn.2d 828, 231 P.3d 191 (2010).

When making a request under the PRA, a party must, at minimum, provide notice that the request is made pursuant to the PRA, and documents must be identified with reasonable clarity to allow the agency to locate them. Wood v.

Lowe, 102 Wn. App. 872, 878, 10 P.3d 494 (2000). **Washington law offers no clear definition of "fair notice" for PRA purposes; courts evaluate sufficiency according to the (1) characteristics of the request; and (2) the characteristic of the records sought. Germeau v. Mason Cnty., 166 Wn. App. 789, 805, 271 P.3d 932 (Feb. 28, 2012), review denied by Germeau v. Mason County, 2012 Wash. LEXIS 525 (Wash., July 10, 2012).** The request need be made in writing, as long as it is recognizable as a PRA request. Beal v. City of Seattle, 150 Wn. App. 865, 876, 209 P.3d 872 (2009). The PRA requires agencies to produce only "identifiable public records." RCW § 42.56.040. "Public record" also includes "metadata" associated with an electronic version of a responsive record, if specifically requested. O'Neill v. City of Shoreline, 170 Wn.2d 138, 147-48, 240 P.3d 1149, 38 Media L. Rep. 2345 (2010). If a request is too vague, an agency can request clarification. RCW §42.56.520. The PRA prohibits agencies from denying a request for identifiable public records solely on the basis that the request is overbroad. RCW § 42.56.080 (superseding in part Hangartner v. City of Seattle, 151 Wn.2d 439, 90 P.3d 26 (2004)). However, the PRA does not provide for "standing records requests"; after responding to a request, an agency need not monitor for "newly created or newly nonexempt" records covered by the prior request. A party must refresh his request. Sargent v. Seattle Police Dep't, 260 P.3d 1006, 1012 (2011), appeal granted, 175 Wn.2d 1001, 285 P.3d 884 (Wash. Sept 5, 2012). **Also, not all records produced on behalf of a public agency are public records; the Washington Court of Appeals recently held that a "writing" produced by an agency's insurer-appointed lawyers is not necessarily a public record. West v. Thurston Cnty., 168 Wn. App. 162, 184, 275 P.3d 1200, 1212 (May 8, 2012).**

In 2011, the Washington Supreme Court established the standards for an "adequate search" under the PRA. Neighborhood Alliance of Spokane Cty. v. Spokane County, 172 Wn.2d 702, 261 P.3d 119 (2011). Adopting the federal Freedom of Information Act (FOIA) standards, the court held a PRA search "must be reasonably calculated to uncover all relevant documents." Id. at *7. Agencies must "make more than a perfunctory search, and follow obvious leads as they are uncovered," shall not limit the search "to one or more places if there are additional sources for the information requested," and must search places where a requested record "is reasonably likely to be found." Id. An inadequate search violates the PRA and an agency bears the burden of showing its search was adequate. Id. at *8. Additionally, an inadequate search is an "aggravating factor" in setting daily penalties for PRA violations; however, the court declined to answer whether the PRA permits a "freestanding" daily penalty where the agency performs an inadequate search, but produces no records. Id. at *9-10.

Public agencies can respond to records requests on a partial or installment basis as records that are part of a larger set of requested records are assembled, and if an installment is not retrieved or reviewed, public agencies are not obligated to fulfill the balance of the request. RCW § 42.56.080; RCW § 42.56.120. An agency is not obligated to provide records electronically, but may be required to do so if a court determines such format is "reasonable and feasible." Mitchell v. Wash. State Dep't of Corrs., 164 Wn. App. 597, 277 P.3d 670 (2011). Each state and local agency must appoint and publicly identify a public records officer who serves as a point of contact for members of the public requesting disclosure of public records and oversees the agency's compliance with the PRA. A state or local agency's public records officer may appoint an employee or official of another agency as its public records officer. RCW § 42.56.580. A one year statute of limitations applies. RCW § 42.56.550(6).

Personal Information. The PRA exempts personal information about public employees "to the extent that disclosure would violate their right to privacy." RCW § 42.56.230(2). See also Bellevue John Does 1–11 v. Bellevue Sch. Dist. No. 405, 164 Wn.2d 199, 210-11, 189 P.3d 139 (2008). To fall under this exemption, (1) the information must constitute personal information, (2) the employee must have a right to privacy in the information, and (3) disclosure of such would violate the employee's right to privacy. See Does, 164 Wn.2d at 210. "Personal information" is "information relating to or affecting a particular a particular individual, information associated with private concerns, or information that is not public or general." Id. at 211, 259 P.3d 190. Disclosure violates the right to privacy if it would be highly offensive to a reasonable person and is not of legitimate public concern. RCW § 42.56.050. When disclosing documents that contain some exempt information, agencies must redact identifying details that might involve an "unreasonable invasion of personal privacy interests." RCW § 42.56.070(1). A person may have a right to privacy in identifying details even if there is media coverage of the information; an agency must consider the contents of the record, not the knowledge of third parties, in determining whether information is private. Bainbridge Island Police Guild v. City of Puyallup, 172 Wn.2d 398, 259 P.3d 190 (2011).

In King County v. Sheehan, the court held that a website's inclusion of a list of county police officers' full names did not constitute "specific intelligence information," within the meaning of the PDA's disclosure exemption and thus did not violate an officer's right to privacy. 114 Wn. App. 325, 57 P.3d 307 (2002). The court reemphasized the PDA's disclosure exemption for personal information in files maintained for public employees, to the extent that disclosure would violate their right to privacy, applies to personal information that employees would not normally share with strangers. Id. In response to the Sheehan decision, the Legislature enacted RCW §§ 4.24.680 – .700, a statute prohibiting the publication or distribution of personal information of law enforcement, corrections, and court employees without permission. The statute was subsequently invalidated on First Amendment grounds. Sheehan v. Gregoire, 272 F. Supp. 2d 1135 (W.D. Wash. 2003). In 2010, the Legislature again extended limited protection to workers and employees of criminal justice agencies (including law enforcement, corrections, and court employees) by exempting photographs and dates of birth contained within employment records from disclosure. 2010 Wash. Sess. Laws ch. 257, § 1; RCW § 42.56.250. The statute permits news media to obtain the information, but it excludes any individual in the custody of a criminal justice agency from qualifying as news media. Id.

State and local agencies may choose not to disclose any application for public employment. RCW § 42.56.250(2). The exemption includes the applicant's name, resume, and any other material submitted, RCW § 42.56.250(2), as well as information about the applicant's personal life and past activities, Wash. State Human Rights Comm'n v. City of Seattle, 25 Wn. App. 364, 369-70, 607 P.2d 332 (1980). A requestor can obtain the name, salary, job title, and benefits of current employees. Tacoma Pub. Library v. Woessner, 90 Wn. App. 205, 951 P.2d 357 (1998). Residential addresses, email addresses, and telephone numbers of state and local agency employees or volunteers may be withheld if they are in agency "personnel records, employment or volunteer rosters, or mailing lists of employees or volunteers." RCW § 42.56.250(3). However, a city employee's town of residence is not exempt from disclosure. Kitsap Cnty. Prosecuting Att'ys Guild v. Kitsap County, 156 Wn. App. 110, 231 P.3d 219 (2010) (upholding an award of attorney's fees based on the county's failure to disclose the information in a timely fashion). In addition, if the otherwise protected information is not contained in a personnel record but rather in email communication, it may not be exempt from disclosure. Mechling v. City of Monroe, 152 Wn. App. 830, 222 P.3d 808 (2009), rev. denied, 169 Wn.2d 1007, 236 P.3d 206 (2010)(requiring disclosure of city council members' personal email addresses because they were present in otherwise non-exempt emails sent between the members' personal accounts that contained discussions of city business).

Performance Evaluations. Performance evaluations are exempt from disclosure if they do not contain specific instances of misconduct or relate to public performance. Dawson v. Daly, 120 Wn.2d 782, 797, 845 P.2d 995 (1993) (prosecutor's evaluations contained no misconduct); Tibernino v. Spokane County, 103 Wn. App. 680, 13 P.3d 1104 (2000) (contents of employee's personal emails, for which the employee was terminated, was exempt from disclosure because of an absence of legitimate public interest). However, information about public job performance is not exempt from disclosure. Ollie v. Highland Sch. Dist. No. 203, 50 Wn. App. 639, 645, 749 P.2d 757, rev. denied, 110 Wn.2d 1040 (1988). In Richland Sch. Dist. v. Mabton School Dist., the Washington Court of Appeals held that the PDA does not require a former employer to include information concerning discipline problems or alleged misconduct in letters of recommendation; such a duty is required only when information is specifically requested. 111 Wn. App. 377, 392, 45 P.3d 580 (2002), rev. denied, 148 Wn.2d 1002 (2003).

In Spokane Research & Defense Fund v. City of Spokane, the Court of Appeals held that the performance evaluations of a Spokane City Manager were subject to public disclosure despite the fact that the performance evaluations did not discuss any specific instances of misconduct or any performance of public duties. Spokane Research & Defense Fund v. City of Spokane, 99 Wn. App. 452, 994 P.2d 267 (2000). The evaluation in question was a summary of the results of 125 questionnaires sent out to a broad spectrum of the community regarding the City Manager's performance. Id. at 453. The court further held that the public has a legitimate interest in the disclosure of the city manager's performance evaluation, and thus, the information was not exempt even if it would otherwise qualify for the employee privacy exemption. Id. at 458.

Records of Misconduct & Workplace Investigations. Investigations by the Washington Department of Corrections (DOC) into misconduct by prison medical staff were not conducted for purposes of "law enforcement," within the meaning of the state public disclosure act's (PDA) disclosure exemption for specific investigative records compiled by penology agencies essential to effective law enforcement. Prison Legal News, Inc. v. Dep't of Corrs., 154 Wn.2d 628, 115 P.3d 316 (2005). The court held that the investigations were undertaken for the purpose of improving patient care and disciplinary actions against medical employees, and not for purposes of law enforcement. Furthermore, the court held that medical details in medical records could not be redacted based on RCW § 70.02 (covering privacy of medical information) and privacy grounds when the names of the patients were redacted, absent a showing that each separately redacted piece of information would identify the patient to the general public. Id.

The Washington Supreme Court has recently held that a public employee has a right to privacy in false or unsubstantiated allegations of misconduct. Bellevue John Does 1–11 v. Bellevue Sch. Dist. No. 405, 164 Wn.2d 199, 189 P.3d 139, 36 Media L. Rep. 2217 (2008). The court held that an educator's identity should only be made public when the allegations of misconduct are substantiated or when the teacher's conduct results in disciplinary action. Id. The court concluded that the contents of a public employee's personnel file guiding future performance or containing feedback are exempt from public disclosure. Id. That exemption applies to the Public Records Act, but does not create a sweeping right of privacy in such situations. Cawley-Herrmann v. Meredith Corp., 654 F. Supp.2d 1264, 37 Media L. Rep. 2396 (2009). Records of a city's investigation into allegations of misconduct by an elected judge – including complaints that he created a hostile work environment and made inappropriate sexual comments – were held to be subject to disclosure under the PRA because the allegations were substantiated and there was a substantial public interest in the availability of the information. Morgan v. City of Federal Way, 166 Wn.2d 747, 213 P.3d 596 (2009).

Records concerning unsubstantiated employee misconduct are not necessarily exempt in their entirety if there is a substantial public interest in some of the information. In one recent case, internal investigations exonerated a police officer of alleged sexual misconduct, but the court held that redacted versions of the reports should be disclosed due to the public's "legitimate interest in how a police department responds to and investigates" alleged misconduct. Bainbridge Island Police Guild v. City of Puyallup, 172 Wn.2d 398, 259 P.3d 190 (2011).

The PRA allows agencies to destroy information about employee misconduct "to the extent necessary to ensure fairness to the employee." RCW § 42.56.110. Each agency also must implement procedures for destroying employee misconduct information that is false or irrelevant. RCW § 41.06.450. Agencies may choose to destroy other employee records that are not disclosable under the PDA. RCW § 41.06.455.

Litigation & Discovery. Recently, the Washington Supreme Court clarified that the civil rules control discovery in a PRA action. Neighborhood Alliance of Spokane Cty. v. County of Spokane, 172 Wn.2d 702, 261 P.3d 119 (2011). Generally, all relevant unprivileged matter is discoverable. See id. The Washington Supreme Court has held that under the Public Disclosure Act (PDA), litigation files of a public prosecutor "are subject to disclosure only upon a showing that the party seeking disclosure of the documents actually has substantial need of the materials and that the party is unable, without undue hardship, to obtain the substantial equivalent of the materials by other means." Limstrom v. Ladenburg, 136 Wn.2d 595, 612, 963 P.2d 869 (1998). However, materials protected by the work product doctrine are exempt from disclosure. Id. at 613-14. Another exemption prevents persons from using the PDA as a discovery device. The requestor cannot obtain information about a contested matter if court discovery rules would bar access to the records. RCW § 42.56.290; see also Soter v. Cowles Publ'g Co., 131 Wn. App. 882, 130 P.3d 840, 34 Media L. Rep. 1598 (2006), aff'd, 162 Wn.2d 716, 174 P.3d 60, 36 Media L. Rep. 1 (2007) (discussing newspaper denied access to records of a school district's investigation of the death of a student under the PDA after a settlement was reached between the district and the student's parents).

Other Exemptions. In Evergreen Freedom Found. v. Locke, the Court of Appeals addressed the "research data" and "business siting" exemptions, which include "financial and proprietary information" provided to a public agency that relates to the siting, relocation, or expansion of that person's business. 127 Wn. App. 243, 248-50, 110 P.3d 858 (2005). At issue were certain redacted portions of an Agreement between the State and The Boeing Company that contained design specifications and budgetary information for a proposed manufacturing facility. The Court of Appeals affirmed the lower court's holding that the information constituted Boeing's trade secrets and valuable research data and thus was exempt. Id.; see RCW §§ 42.56.070(1), 56.270(12)(a)(ii).

In 2010, the Legislature amended several pre-existing disclosure exemptions. 2010 Wash. Sess. Laws ch. 128. Under the revised statutes, transit agencies may disclose personally identifying information about transit pass holders to employers or sponsoring organizations for the purposes of preventing fraud, or to the news media when reporting on public transportation or safety. RCW § 42.56.330(5). Also of note, the disclosure of workplace discrimination investigations was previously exempted if the investigation was "current"; the Legislature narrowed the exemption to only "active and ongoing" investigations. RCW § 42.56.250(5). **In 2012, the Legislature amended the statute to clarify that "personally identifying information" includes "acquisition or use information pertaining to a specific, individual transit pass or fare payment media." 2012 Wash. Sess. Laws ch. 68.**

B. Medical Records

HIV Records. State statute protects the confidentiality of testing and treatment for HIV or other sexually transmitted diseases. RCW § 70.24.105 (1997). The provisions apply to anyone who has information about a person's status, including employers. RCW §§ 70.24.105(1), (2) ("no person may disclose"). The statute does allow disclosure to insurers, but the insurer cannot release the information to persons not handling medical claims. RCW § 70.24.105(2)(j) (2001). If a person's confidentiality rights are violated, he or she may sue for damages and attorneys' fees. The statute also allows the person to pursue relief under common law theories as well. RCW §§ 70.24.084(1), (3) (2001). The statute of limitations for the statutory cause of action is three years. RCW § 70.24.084(2). The Washington Law Against Discrimination (WLAD) bars employers from requiring HIV tests. See II.C.2, supra.

Other Medical Records. Under the Health Care Disclosure Act (HCDA), health care providers may disclose records only if they have authorization from the employee or if the request meets narrow exceptions. RCW § 70.02.050 (1998). A similar statute protects the confidentiality of mental illness records. RCW § 71.05.390 (2000). An employer who requests employees sign medical releases could risk violating the WLAD's provisions covering disabilities. See II.A.-C, supra. The Washington Court of Appeals held in Hines v. Todd Pacific Shipyards Corp. that an employer did not violate RCW § 70.02.010 when it disclosed the results of an employee's drug screening test to one of its subcontractors. 127 Wn. App. 356, 112 P.3d 522 (2005). The court concluded that the employer was not covered by the HCDA, the drug screening test results were not "health care information" under the statute, and the employee was not a "patient" under the statute as the drug screening test was a condition of his employment. Id. at 367-69.

The Washington Court of Appeals has held that employees waive their right to patient confidentiality and medical privacy when they put their health at issue by applying for workers' compensation. Mayer v. Huesner, 126 Wn. App. 114; 107 P.3d 15 (2005).

C. Criminal Records

Arrest Records. Pre-1999 regulations of the Human Rights Commission stated that employers could not access arrest records of prospective employees because such inquiries were "unfair practices." WAC 162-16-050(3) (1975) (repealed in 1999). Employers also were to avoid obtaining arrest records of current employees, as the regulations prohibited discrimination based on arrests. WAC 162-16-050(1) (1975) (repealed in 1999). These rules were eliminated in light of Gugin v. Sonico, in which the court held the Commission lacked authority to create a new protected class of former felons. 68 Wn. App. 826, 846 P.2d 571 (1993); Wash. St. Reg. 99-15-025; see also V.A, supra. Where the Prison Legal News made a request to the Department of Corrections for the names of DOC employees with arrest records, the court failed to specifically comment on whether such records are exempt from the Public Disclosure Act, but affirmed the trial court holding that DOC's provision of the names did not violate the PDA. The court further held that records of DOC investigations and disciplinary actions for misconduct of DOC employees were not exempt from disclosure. Prison Legal News, Inc. v. Department of Corrections, 154 Wn.2d 628, 115 P.3d 316 (2005).

Conviction Records. State statutes require some employers to check the conviction records of employees or prospective employees, including volunteers. One category applies to anyone who will have unsupervised access to children, developmentally disabled persons or vulnerable adults at a facility that "educates, trains, treats, supervises, houses or provides recreation." RCW § 43.43.834; see also Forrestal v. Tukwila Sch. Dist., No. 44259-7-I, 2000 WL 1346818 (Wash. Ct. App. Sept. 18, 2000) (holding school districts are required to conduct criminal record checks of applicants for certain positions, such as school counselors, prior to hiring). Each prospective employee must disclose any crimes or civil lawsuits to their prospective employer. RCW § 43.43.834(2). Employers must inform the applicant that they are obtaining conviction information. RCW § 43.43.834(1). The information can be used only when making the initial employment decision. RCW § 43.43.834(5). A similar statute applies to nursing homes and other health care facilities. RCW § 43.43.832(6)(g). A school volunteer may alert a school district that the volunteer has had a criminal records check in accordance with state law in the past two years. RCW § 28A.320.155. The school may then request that the volunteer furnish a copy of the records check or sign a release allowing the entity that originally requested the criminal history information to convey those records to the school. Id. Once the school requests the information it must be released and the releasing entity is immune from criminal or civil liability for dissemination of the information. Id.

In May 2007, the state legislature amended RCW § 43.43.832 to give the director of the department of early learning authority to investigate the criminal records of current employees and any person being considered for a position with the department who may have unsupervised access to children. "Considered for any position" means decisions about "initial hiring, layoffs, reallocations, transfers, promotions, or demotions," or other decisions that could result in a person having unsupervised access to children "as an employee, an intern, or a volunteer." RCW § 43.43.832.

State law allows other employers to access the conviction records of employees or prospective employees for broad purposes. RCW § 43.43.815. Valid reasons are to (1) secure a bond required for employment, (2) conduct screening of potential or current employees who might have access to "information affecting national security, trade secrets, confidential or proprietary business information, money or items of value" or (3) investigate employee misconduct that also might be criminal. RCW § 43.43.815(1)(a)-(c). For example, a new amendment in 2009 requires the Department of Licensing to obtain fingerprints and background checks of current or prospective employees who process applications for enhanced drivers' licenses. RCW 46.01.130(2). Only people involved in the hiring or the background investigation may see the information. RCW § 43.43.815(4). The employer must notify the employee of the record within 30 days of receiving the report and allow the employee to review the material. RCW § 43.43.815(2). Employers who violate the statute can face misdemeanor charges or a civil lawsuit for damages and attorneys' fees. RCW § 43.43.815(5). Despite these restrictions on the use of records, a separate statute states, "[c]onviction records may be disseminated without restriction." RCW § 10.97.050(1) (1990). There is no authority reconciling the two statutes. The Washington Administrative Code regulations prohibiting employment discrimination based on conviction records were also repealed in 1999. Wash. St. Reg. 99-15-025; see also V.A, VI.C, supra.

D. Subpoenas / Search Warrants

No Washington cases on point.

E. Credit Records

Washington has enacted a Fair Credit Reporting Act, RCW § 19.182.010 et seq. (FCRA), to complement its federal counterpart of the same name. The Act identifies two types of reports: (1) "consumer reports" evaluate a person's credit worthiness and character by obtaining information from a reporting agency and (2) "investigative consumer reports" obtain information by interviewing people who know the applicant. RCW § 19.182.010(4)(a) (1993). It is permissible for employers to obtain either type of report for employment purposes. RCW § 19.182.020(1)(c)(ii). However, the employer first must give the consumer written notice or obtain consent. Cf. RCW § 19.182.020(2)(b) and RCW 19.182.050(1) with 15.U.S.C. § 1681(b) (requiring both notice and consent). Employers must give the employee a "reasonable opportunity" to respond to the report before making adverse employment decisions. RCW § 19.182.020(2)(c). The Act also places restrictions on reporting agencies by prohibiting them from disclosing obsolete information unless it involves a highly-paid employee. RCW § 19.182.040. Agencies also must provide the employee access to the report if requested and must keep records of all persons who request copies of the report. RCW § 19.182.060 (tracking of requests); RCW § 19.182.070 (disclosure to consumer). Violators can face criminal charges or a civil action for damages and attorneys' fees. RCW § 19.182.140 (criminal sanctions); RCW § 19.182.150 (civil suit). The statute of limitations is two years. RCW § 19.182.120.

In 2007, the state legislature revised the FCRA to limit the circumstances in which an employer may seek credit checks on job applicants and employees. The law permits employers to perform credit checks only when the credit information is (1) substantially job related and the employer's reasons for using the information are disclosed to the consumer or (2) required by law. RCW § 19.182.020.

The FCRA specifically bars consumers from bringing claims "in the nature of defamation, invasion of privacy, or negligence with respect to the reporting of information against a consumer reporting agency." RCW § 19.182.080(6). This protection only apples if the credit report is lawfully furnished under the statute with no "malice or willful intent to injure the consumer". Id. In a recent case, the Washington Court of Appeals held that this statutory provision bars prospective employees from bringing claims against credit reporting agencies for furnishing incorrect information to a prospective employer. Van Hoven v. Pre-Employee.com, Inc., 156 Wn. App. 879, 234 P.3d 1183 (2010).

VII. ACTIONS SUBSEQUENT TO EMPLOYMENT

A. References

1. ***Qualified Immunity Statute for Employment References.*** An employer may face liability for disclosing private information about employees or former employees, such as in a request for a reference, to outside third parties. However, Washington RCW § 4.24.730 provides that employers who disclose information about a former or current employee to a prospective employer or employment agency, at the request of the same, are presumed to be acting in good faith and are immune from civil or criminal liability when the disclosed information relates to (1) the employee's ability to perform his or her job; (2) the diligence, skill, or reliability with which the employee carried out the duties of his or her job; or (3) any illegal or wrongful act committed by the employee when related to the duties of his or her job. The presumption of good faith is lost if that disclosure is knowingly false, deliberately misleading, or made with reckless disregard for the truth. RCW § 4.24.730(3). Employers should retain a written record of the identity of the person or entity to which information is disclosed under this section for a minimum of two years from the date of disclosure, which should become part of the employee's personnel file. RCW § 4.24.730(2). The employee has a right to inspection of this information upon written request. Id.

B. Noncompete Agreements

In Washington, courts will enforce noncompetition and nonsolicitation agreements which are reasonable, supported by consideration, and otherwise validly formed. Labriola v. Pollard Group, Inc., 152 Wn.2d 828, 100 P.3d 791 (2004). Wood v. May, 73 Wn.2d 307, 438 P.2d 587 (1968); Racine v. Bender, 141 Wash. 606, 252 P. 115 (1927). There is no statute in Washington which specifically governs the enforceability of covenants not to compete.

Whether a noncompete is reasonable is a matter of law to be decided by the courts. Knight, Vale & Gregory v. McDaniel, 37 Wn. App. 366, 368-69, 680 P.2d 448, rev. denied, 101 Wn.2d 1025 (1984). Whether a covenant is reasonable involves consideration of three factors: (1) whether the restraint is necessary for the protection of the business or goodwill of the employer, (2) whether it imposes upon the employee any greater restraint than is reasonably necessary to secure the employer's business or goodwill, and (3) whether the degree of injury to the public is such a loss of the service and skill of the employee as to warrant non-enforcement of the covenant not to compete. Racine, 141 Wash. at 612; see also Knight, Vale & Gregory, 37 Wn. App. at 368. Agreements cannot be more restrictive than is reasonably necessary to protect the legitimate business interest of employers. Racine, 141 Wash. at 612. The employer has the burden of showing that a restriction is reasonable. Sheppard v. Blackstock Lumber Co., Inc., 85 Wn.2d 929, 933, 540 P.2d 1373 (1975).

In Labriola v. Pollard Group, Inc., the Washington Supreme Court clarified that noncompete agreements entered into after the commencement of employment will be enforced if they are supported by independent consideration, i.e. new promises or obligations which were previously not required. 152 Wn.2d 828, 100 P. 791. Continued employment and subsequent training did not serve as independent consideration for a noncompete agreement signed five years after the commencement of employment. Id.

Washington courts will partially enforce or re-word an otherwise overbroad covenant where doing so is possible without injury to the public and without injustice to the parties. Sheppard, 85 Wn.2d at 934. Wood v. May, 73 Wn.2d 307, 310-11, 438 P.2d 587 (1968). Washington courts will allow a customer base restriction to substitute for or complement a geographic restriction. Perry v. Moran, 109 Wn.2d 691, 702, 748 P.2d 224 (1987), aff'd. as modified, 111 Wn.2d 885, 766 P.2d 1096; see also Pac. Aerospace & Elecs., Inc. v. Taylor, 295 F. Supp. 2d 1205 (E.D. Wash. 2003).

To determine whether the length of time of the restriction is reasonable, the court will evaluate whether it is reasonably necessary and calculated to protect the legitimate interests of the employer without imposing undue hardship on the employee. Perry, 109 Wn.2d at 700. Although a three-year restriction was upheld in Knight, Vale & Gregory, generally the courts find one to two years reasonable. See Pac. Aerospace & Elecs., Inc., 295 F. Supp. 2d at 1218. However, in upholding a five-year restriction in a contract for the sale of shares in a taxi company, the court noted that "[a] covenant that is unreasonable as applied to an employment contract may be reasonable as applied to the sale of a business. Hieronymus v. Parslow, No. 19436-1-III, 2001 WL 564213, at *3 (Wash. Ct. App. May 24, 2001) (citing Alexander & Alexander v. Wohlman, 19 Wn. App. 670, 685, 578 P.2d 530 (1978), rev. denied, 91 Wn.2d 1006 (1978)).

A covenant not to compete may be breached even where the covenanter does not derive profits from a competing business. Evergreen Crane Servs., Inc. v. Ford, 144 Wn. App. 1015, 2008 WL 1851089 (2008). While simply providing financial assistance to a competitor is generally insufficient to constitute a breach of a generic noncompetition covenant, when that financial assistance is coupled with giving advice, providing labor, customer referrals, or making purchases for the competitor, particularly when the language of the noncompete is broadly worded ("directly or indirectly, in any manner or capacity, . . . as creditor or otherwise"), a breach of the noncompete will be found. Id.

VIII. OTHER ISSUES

A. Statute of Limitations

Information on the statute of limitations is included above in the sections describing the individual causes of action.

B. Jurisdiction

C. Worker's Compensation Exclusivity

The Washington Industrial Insurance Act (IIA), chapter 51 RCW, provides the exclusive remedy for employees' injuries occurring in the course of employment, or for industrial or occupational diseases. RCW § 51.04.010. However, "an injury that is of a different nature, arises at a different time, and stems from different causes than a workplace injury is not barred by the IIA, even though it may result from actions by an employer that injure an employee." Birklid v. The Boeing Co., 127 Wn.2d 853, 870, 904 P.2d 278 (1995). Similarly, Washington courts have held that the IIA does not bar a civil action for a separate physical injury resulting from a discriminatory response to an IIA-compensable injury. Id.; see also Goodman v. The Boeing Co., 127 Wn.2d 401, 405, 899 P.2d 1265 (1995). Recently, in Rothwell v. Nine Mile Falls School District, a school employee sued the school district and superintendent for intentional and negligent infliction of emotional distress, alleging she suffered post-traumatic stress disorder (PTSD) from being ordered to clean up after a student killed himself at the high school. 149 Wn. App. 771, 774-76, 206 P.3d 347 (2009). The Court of Appeals held the employee's claims were not barred by the exclusivity provisions of the IIA because her PTSD did not result from a single traumatic event and therefore was not an injury or occupational disease under the Act. Rothwell, 149 Wn. App. at 782.

D. Pleading Requirements

Washington is a notice pleading state. Pleadings must contain (1) a short and plain statement of the claim and (2) a demand for judgment. CR 8(a). Parties may request alternative forms of relief. Id. Parties also may make claims in the alternative. CR 8(e)(2).

SURVEY OF WEST VIRGINIA EMPLOYMENT LIBEL LAW

Ashley C. Pack
Katherine A. Brings
Dinsmore & Shohl LLP
900 Lee Street
Huntington Square, Suite 600
Charleston, West Virginia 25301
Telephone (304) 357-0900 Facsimile (304) 357-0919
ashley.pack@dinsmore.com
katherine.brings@dinsmore.com

(With Developments Reported Through **November 1, 2012**)

GENERAL COMMENTS

West Virginia has a two-tiered court system consisting of circuit courts at the trial level with the right of only discretionary appeal to the West Virginia Supreme Court of Appeals. There is no intermediate court of appeals. Circuit court decisions are not reported. The Supreme Court of Appeals' decisions are published in the Southeastern Reporter.

SIGNIFICANT DEVELOPMENTS SINCE THE 2012 *SURVEY*

None.

I. GENERAL LAW

A. General Employment Law

1. ***At Will Employment.*** West Virginia has long recognized the employment at-will doctrine. Wright v. Standard Ultramarine & Color Co., 141 W. Va. 368, 90 S.E.2d 459 (1955). The only exceptions to this general doctrine are a public policy exception and implied contract exception based upon employee handbooks. According to the West Virginia Supreme Court of Appeals, the general principle that an employee may be discharged at any time for any reason should be tempered when the reason for that termination contravenes a substantial public policy. See Harless v. First Nat'l Bank in Fairmont, 162 W. Va. 116, 246 S.E.2d 270 (1981) (employee discharged for attempting to make employer comply with consumer protection laws); Shanholtz v. Monongahela Power Co., 165 W. Va. 305, 270 S.E.2d 178 (1980) (discharge of employee for filing workers' compensation claim); Wiggins v. E. Associated Coal Corp., 178 W. Va. 63, 357 S.E.2d 745 (1987) (discharge of employee for complaining about unsafe mining practices).

The other exception to the employment at-will doctrine was carved out in Cook v. Heck's, Inc., 176 W. Va. 368, 342 S.E.2d 453 (1986). In Cook, the court held that an employee handbook may form the basis of a unilateral contract if there is a definite promise therein by the employer not to terminate employees except for specified reasons.

B. Elements of Libel Claim

In West Virginia, a libel plaintiff's status sets the standard for assessing the elements of liability. Essentially, private figures need only show that the defendant was negligent in publishing the false and defamatory statement. In contrast, public officials and public figures must establish that the defendant made the defamatory statement with knowledge that it was false or with reckless disregard of whether it was false. Moreover, West Virginia recognizes the concept of a "limited purpose public figure" when the libel plaintiff has voluntarily engaged in significant efforts to influence public debate on a matter of public concern.

1. ***Basic Elements.*** The essential elements of a defamation claim by a private individual are: (1) a defamatory statement; (2) a non-privileged communication to a third party (publication); (3) falsity; (4) reference to the plaintiff; (5) negligence at least on the part of the publisher; and (6) resulting injury. See Crump v. Beckley Newspapers, Inc., 173 W. Va. 699, 320 S.E.2d 70, 10 Media L. Rep. 2225 (1984); Rand v. Miller, 185 W. Va. 705, 408 S.E.2d 655 (1991); Crain v. Lightner, 178 W. Va. 765, 364 S.E.2d 778 (1987); Bryan v. Massachusetts Mut. Life Ins. Co., 178 W. Va. 773, 364 S.E.2d 786 (1987); Bell v. Nat'l Republican Cong. Comm., 187 F. Supp. 2d 605 (S.D. W.Va. 2002).

In order for a public official to sustain an action for libel, he must prove, by clear and convincing evidence, that: (1) the statements were false or misleading; (2) the statements tended to defame the plaintiff and reflect "shame, contumely and disgrace upon him"; (3) the statements were published with knowledge at the time of publication that they were false or misleading or were published with a reckless and willful disregard for the truth (malice); and (4) the publisher intended to injure the plaintiff through the knowing or reckless publication of the alleged libelous material. See Sprouse v. Clay Communication, Inc., 158 W. Va. 427, 211 S.E.2d 674, 1 Media L. Rep. 1695 (1975); Neal v. Huntington Publishing Co., 159 W. Va. 556, 223 S.E.2d 792 (1976); Pritt v. Republican Nat'l Comm., 210 W.Va. 446, 557 S.E.2d 853 (W. Va. 2001).

2. ***Fault.***

a. **Private Figure Plaintiff/Matter of Public Concern.** As indicated above, a private individual may recover for defamation by establishing mere negligence on the part of the publisher. Echoing the Restatement (Second) of Torts, the West Virginia Supreme Court of Appeals has thus held that the conduct of the defendant is to be measured against what a reasonably prudent person would have done under the same or similar circumstances. Crump v. Beckley Newspapers, Inc., 173 W. Va. 699, 320 S.E.2d 70, 10 Media L. Rep. 2225 (1984); Havalunch v. Mazza, 170 W. Va. 268, 294 S.E.2d 70 (1981); Restatement (Second) of Torts § 283. In Havalunch, the Court characterized a family restaurant, claiming defamation by a student newspaper's slanderous review, as a private person able to recover against a media defendant upon a showing of simple negligence. Nevertheless, the Court ultimately concluded that the newspaper's comment was protected by the doctrine of fair comment, a form of qualified privilege. See II.A.2, infra.

A qualified privilege of fair comment on matters of public concern is defeated if the speaker acts with malice. Malice requires that the private figure prove that the defendant had a subjective appreciation at the time of publication that either (1) the defamatory statement is false, or (2) the defamatory statement is being published in reckless disregard of whether it is false. See Tomblin v. WCHS-TV8, 2011 U.S. App. LEXIS 9752, 39 Media L. Rep. 1753 (4th Cir. May 11, 2011).

b. **Private Figure Plaintiff/Matter of Private Concern.** As indicated above, a private individual may recover for defamation by establishing mere negligence on the part of the publisher. See I.B.2.a, supra.

c. **Public Figure Plaintiff/Matter of Public Concern.** As indicated earlier, West Virginia law subscribes to the general rule, as announced by the United States Supreme Court in New York Times Co. v. Sullivan, 376 U.S. 254, 1 Media L. Rep. 1527 (1964), that a public official's right to sue for libel is properly curtailed in view of First Amendment considerations militating that the media be permitted its constitutional right to freedom of the press where the speech involves an area of public concern. Thus, a public official can recover only if he proves that the statement was made with "actual malice"—that is, with knowledge that it was false or with reckless disregard as to whether it was false. See Long v. Egnor, 176 W. Va. 628, 346 S.E.2d 778, 13 Media L. Rep. 1855 (1986) (challenged memorandum of State Education Association did not constitute libel as a matter of law; statements of opinion are absolutely protected under the First Amendment); Sprouse v. Clay Communications, Inc., 158 W. Va. 427, 211 S.E.2d 674, 1 Media L. Rep. 1695, cert. denied, 423 U.S. 882, reh'g denied, 423 U.S. 991 (1975) (plaintiff, an unsuccessful gubernatorial candidate, proved that newspaper story was false or misleading and that it was published with the knowledge it was false or misleading); Hinerman v. Daily Gazette Co., 188 W. Va. 157, 423 S.E.2d 560, 20 Media L. Rep. 2169 (1992) (plaintiff met burden of establishing actual malice given the fact that newspaper intentionally avoided the truth in its investigatory techniques or omitted facts in order to distort the truth); Tomblin v. WHCS-TV8, 2011 U.S. App. LEXIS 9752, 39 Media L. Rep. 1753 (4th Cir. May 11, 2011) (where the defendant finds internal consistencies or apparently reliable information that contradicts its libelous assertions, but nevertheless publishes those statements anyway, the New York Times actual malice test can be met).

In a claim for defamation, West Virginia recognizes three categories of public figures: (1) "involuntary public figures"; (2) "all-purpose public figures"; and (3) "limited purpose public figures." See Wilson v. The Daily Gazette Co., 214 W. Va. 208, 588 S.E.2d 197 (2003).

In order to prove that a plaintiff is an "all-purpose public figure," the defendant must produce clear evidence of the plaintiff's general fame and notoriety in the state and pervasive involvement in the affairs of society. In determining whether a plaintiff is an all-purpose public figure, a trial court may consider: (1) statistical survey data concerning the plaintiff's name recognition; (2) evidence of previous coverage of the plaintiff by the media; (3) evidence that others alter or reevaluate their conduct or ideas in light of the plaintiff's actions; and (4) any other relevant evidence. See Wilson, supra.

In Wilson, supra, the plaintiff, a prominent high school athlete, sued the defendant newspaper in connection with an article it published, claiming that the article defamed him by indicating that he had exposed himself in public during a post-game victory celebration. The West Virginia Supreme Court of Appeals concluded that the newspaper failed to prove that the plaintiff was an all-purpose public figure because the evidence merely showed that the plaintiff had achieved notoriety in limited circles, namely athletics, not that he had achieved general fame and notoriety in the community at large.

In order to prove that a plaintiff is an "involuntary public figure," the defendant must demonstrate by clear evidence that: (1) the plaintiff has become a central figure in a significant public controversy; (2) that the allegedly defamatory statement has arisen in the course of discourse regarding the public matter; and (3) the plaintiff has taken some action, or failed to act when action was required, in circumstances in which a reasonable person would understand that publicity would likely inhere. See Wilson, supra.

In Wilson, supra, the Court concluded that the plaintiff was not an "involuntary public figure" because nothing in the record suggested that the plaintiff was a central figure in any purported public controversy involving sportsmanship that existed prior to the publication of the allegedly defamatory article.

In addition, West Virginia recognizes the concept of a "limited purpose public figure" under certain circumstances. Generally, West Virginia has adopted an approach which relies upon the twin rationales, identified in Gertz v. Robert Welch, 418 U.S. 323, 1 Media L. Rep. 1633 (1974). The most significant of the two is the concept that public figures have voluntarily exposed themselves to increased risk of injury from defamatory falsehood by abandoning their anonymity. Secondarily, public figures have ready outlets to respond to attacks. Accordingly, the West Virginia Supreme Court of Appeals has held that a libel plaintiff who might otherwise be considered a private figure plaintiff is a limited purpose public figure if the defendant can prove the following: (1) that the plaintiff voluntarily engaged in significant efforts to influence public debate, or voluntarily assumed a position that would propel him to the forefront of a public debate, on a matter of public concern; (2) the public debate or controversy and the plaintiff's involvement in it existed prior to the publication of the allegedly libelous statement; and (3) the plaintiff had reasonable access to channels of communication that would permit him to make an effective response to the defamatory statement in question. Syllabus Point 3, State ex rel. Suriano v. Gaughan, 198 W. Va. 339, 480 S.E.2d 548 (1996). In Suriano, the West Virginia Supreme Court of Appeals examined the case of a physician who sued the county education association and its president in connection with a newspaper advertisement and article, claiming that the article defamed him by indicating that the physician had denied health services to public teachers. The Court concluded that the physician was a limited purpose public figure because the issues involved were matters of public controversy into which the plaintiff had voluntarily thrust himself. See also Wilson, supra, wherein the Court held that the defendant failed to prove that the plaintiff was a limited purpose public figure because: (1) there was no evidence that the plaintiff voluntarily injected himself into a controversy involving sportsmanship; and, (2) there was no evidence of a controversy that existed prior to the publication of the articles. The Court also rejected the defendant's argument that amateur athletes become "limited purpose public figures" simply by participating voluntarily in public sporting events.

3. ***Falsity.*** West Virginia law has adopted the U.S. Supreme Court's analysis regarding the requisite falsity necessary to prove defamation. So long as the communication is "substantially true," minor inaccuracies are overlooked and the communication is not defamatory. See State ex rel. Suriano v. Gaughan, 198 W. Va. 339, 480 S.E.2d 548 (1996) (newspaper advertisement was substantially true and thus protected speech); Kinney v. Daniels, 574 F. Supp. 542 (S.D. W. Va. 1983) (letter written by chief of hospital's medical service about a physician in the context of a health care peer review procedure was substantially true).

4. ***Defamatory Statement of Fact.*** Echoing the Restatement (Second) of Torts § 559 (1977), West Virginia's courts have held that statements may be described as defamatory if they tend to harm the reputation of another as to lower him in the estimation of the community, to deter third persons from associating or dealing with him, or if they tend to "reflect shame, contumely and disgrace" upon the plaintiff. See Crump v. Beckley Newspapers, 173 W. Va. 699, 320 S.E.2d 70, 10 Media L. Rep. 2225 (1984); Sprouse v. Clay Communications, Inc., 158 W. Va. 427, 211 S.E.2d 674, 1 Media L. Rep. 1695 (1975), cert. denied, 423 U.S. 882 (1976).

Direct defamatory statements are not an absolute prerequisite to recovery, however, West Virginia law permits defamation to be accomplished through inference, implication, innuendo, or insinuation. See Crump, supra.

Moreover, a statement of opinion may be actionable if it implies the existence of facts known to the publisher but undisclosed to the recipient which would inevitably lead to a false, but defamatory conclusion in the recipient's mind. In other words, if a statement of opinion implies the allegation of undisclosed defamatory facts as the basis of the opinion, it may be actionable. See Havalunch v. Mazza, 170 W. Va. 268, 294 S.E.2d 70 (1981), citing Restatement (Second) of Torts, § 566 (1977); see also Long v. Egnor, 176 W. Va. 628, 346 S.E.2d 778, 13 Media L. Rep. 1855 (1986) (statements of opinion are absolutely protected under the First Amendment).

5. ***Of and Concerning Plaintiff.*** In an action for libel, the defamatory words must refer to some ascertained or ascertainable person and that person must be the plaintiff. If the words used really contain no reflection on any particular individual, no innuendo can make them defamatory. An innuendo cannot make the person certain who was uncertain before. See Argabright v. Jones, 46 W. Va. 144, 32 S.E. 995 (1899); see also Neal v. Huntington Publishing Co.,

159 W. Va. 556, 223 S.E.2d 792 (1976) (fact that a defamatory statement refers to a particular person could be proven by extrinsic evidence).

6. ***Publication.*** Traditional defamation law has always required the injured party to prove publication of the defamatory statement. West Virginia also has enacted an anti-dueling statute, which remains viable to date. W. Va. Code § 55-7-2. Known as the "insulting words" statute, this claim is supplemental to traditional common law defamation claims, and provides a cause of action for insulting words which are published only to the victim and which would not provide recovery under defamation law unless proof of special damages was offered. See Mauck v. City of Martinsburg, 167 W. Va. 332, 280 S.E.2d 216 (1981) (law under insulting words statute to be interpreted in accord with defamation law in all other respects).

a. **Intracorporate Communication.** Although West Virginia law would likely recognize the concept that dissemination of the defamatory statement within the corporation does not constitute publication, the Supreme Court of Appeals' decisions usually frame this issue in terms of the existence of a qualified privilege within the corporation. See Mutafis v. Erie Ins. Exchange, 174 W. Va. 660, 328 S.E.2d 675 (1985), citing Mauck v. City of Martinsburg, 167 W. Va. 332, 280 S.E.2d 216 (1981); see also Moore v. Am. Express Co., 663 F. Supp. 97 (S.D. W. Va. 1987) (no publication under West Virginia law where communication remained entirely within the corporation). The Court in Mutafis ruled that the facts supported a finding that the defendant insurance company had violated the state Unfair Trade Practices Act's prohibition against defamatory statements, including insertion of such statements into corporate files. Although recognizing a defense of qualified privilege coexistent with the privilege under traditional common law defamation, the Court concluded that the statement was made without any factual foundation whatsoever and in willful and reckless disregard for its truth or falsity, thus no privilege could be claimed by the publishers.

b. **Compelled Self-Publication.** West Virginia law has not recognized a cause of action for compelled self-publication.

c. **Republication.** Although the writers are aware of cases decided in trial courts involving republication of material originally published by others, such as wire services, there are no reported cases in this general area except Sprouse v. Clay Communications, Inc., 158 W. Va. 427, 211 S.E.2d 674, 1 Media L. Rep. 1695 (1975), cert. denied, 423 U.S. 882, reh'g denied, 423 U.S. 991 (1976). In Sprouse, the defendant contended that it was under no duty to subject statements of plaintiff's opponent for the office of governor to any test of truth. The court, while stating that "in general a newspaper is not liable for publishing in good faith statements of political candidates during an election campaign, ... the evidence in this case reasonably implies . . . [that defendant] knew that the accusations made by Moore were false." Sprouse, supra.

7. ***Statements versus Conduct.*** West Virginia case law has not analyzed the issue of the publisher's conduct constituting defamation.

8. ***Damages.*** Under West Virginia law a plaintiff may recover such compensatory damages or actual damages as he/she is able to establish at trial. See Sprouse, supra. Adopting language from Gertz, the Sprouse Court acknowledged that such damages would include impairment of reputation and standing in the community, as well as the more traditional elements of mental anguish, insult, indignity and humiliation. The determination of such intangible and subjective damages is the exclusive province of the jury, subject to the rule that awards in these areas not be excessive. The Sprouse Court concluded that a $250,000 award for actual damages was not excessive.

a. **Presumed Damages and Libel Per Se.** West Virginia has traditionally followed the common law rule that imposed strict liability for certain false statements. Thus, a plaintiff had only to show that certain actionable statements were made in order to entitle him to general damages. See Denoff v. Fama, 102 W. Va. 494, 135 S.E. 578 (1926); Hancock v. Mitchell, 83 W.Va. 156, 98 S.E. 65 (1919) (a writing charging one "with incompetence in his profession and office, neglect of duty and misconduct" is actionable without establishing special damage); Milan v. Long, 78 W. Va. 102, 88 S.E. 618 (1916) (general damages awardable where words are actionable per se; special damages, however, require a specific allegation of harm and proof thereof); see also Mauck v. City of Martinsburg, 167 W. Va. 332, 280 S.E.2d 216 (1981) (confirming that a victim need not prove actual pecuniary damages for statements that are defamatory per se under the insulting words statute).

Cases suggest that West Virginia has adopted the rationale of Gertz v. Welch, 418 U.S. 323, 1 Media L. Rep. 1633 (1974). These cases suggest that a defamation plaintiff must always demonstrate the element of resulting injury from the publication of the defamatory statement. In Sprouse, supra, the Court adopted the Gertz Court's language regarding the necessity of proving injury by competent evidence, even though it need not be evidence which assigns an actual dollar value to the injury. Likening the damages in a defamation action to those of intentional torts, the Court ruled that a defamation plaintiff in West Virginia is entitled to have such elements as mental anguish, insult, indignity and humiliation considered by the jury in arriving at an award of actual damages. The Court therefore concluded that the $250,000 award of actual damages was not excessive in Sprouse. See Havalunch v. Mazza, 170 W. Va. 268, 294 S.E.2d 70 (1981) (citing Gertz in libel action against newspaper, holding that presumed damages and punitive damages may be recovered only upon a showing of malice).

In the employment context, West Virginia has similarly applied the requirement of proof of resulting injury from defamatory statements. See Miller v. City Hosp., Inc., 197 W. Va. 403, 475 S.E.2d 495 (1996) (essential element of private employee's claim against her former employer is resulting injury to reputation).

(1) **Employment-Related Criticism.** The cases interpreting West Virginia law concerning employment-related criticism apply a qualified privilege with respect to statements made by an employer or its agents regarding the employee-plaintiff's questionable behavior. See McKinney v. K-Mart Corp., 649 F. Supp. 1217 (S.D. W. Va. 1986) (employer's security guard had qualified privilege with regard to statement to another guard that plaintiff had experienced cash shortage); Mauck v. City of Martinsburg, 167 W. Va. 332, 280 S.E.2d 216 (1981) (letter by city manager regarding former employee's incompetence sent to appropriate city officials was protected by qualified privilege).

(2) **Single Instance Rule.** No such cases have been decided in West Virginia.

b. **Punitive Damages.** West Virginia cases concerning the imposition of punitive damages have related to media defendants, not private employers. Punitive damages are not awardable unless the plaintiff has shown that the media defendant knew the reported information was false or had a reckless disregard for its truth. Havalunch v. Mazza, 170 W. Va. 268, 294 S.E.2d 70 (1981). The public policy behind permitting such awards permits punitive damages where the award of actual damages is insufficient to dissuade others in like circumstances from committing similar acts in the future. See Sprouse, supra (reversing an award of $500,000 in punitive damages as having a chilling effect upon the legitimate exercise of First Amendment rights); see also Hinerman v. Daily Gazette Co., 188 W. Va. 157, 423 S.E.2d 560, 20 Media L. Rep. 2169 (1992) (award of punitive damages upheld where newspaper failed to offer prompt, prominent, abject apology combined with offer to pay reasonable damages).

II. PRIVILEGES AND DEFENSES

A. Scope of Privileges

1. ***Absolute Privilege.*** Generally, an absolute privilege which protects one who issues a defamatory communication is practically limited to legislative, judicial and quasi-judicial proceedings and other acts of the State. See Porter v. Eyster, 294 F.2d 613 (4th Cir. 1961) (interpreting West Virginia law); Clark v. Druckman, 218 W.Va. 427, 624 S.E.2d 864 (2005) (absolute indemnity must be afforded to any act occurring during the course of a judicial proceeding, regardless of whether the act involves a defamatory statement or other tortious behavior, so long as the act has some relation to other proceeding.); City of Mullens v. Davidson, 133 W. Va. 557, 57 S.E.2d 1 (1949); Parker v. Appalachian Elec. Power Co., 126 W. Va. 666, 30 S.E.2d 1 (1944); Collins v. Red Roof Inns, Inc., 248 F. Supp. 2d 512 (S.D. W. Va. 2003) (holding that prior to the filing of a prospective judicial proceeding, a party to a dispute is absolutely privileged to publish defamatory matter about a third person who is not a party to the dispute only wherein: (1) the prospective judicial action is contemplated in good faith and is under serious consideration; (2) the defamatory statement is related to the prospective judicial proceeding; and, (3) the defamatory matter is published only to persons with an interest in the prospective judicial proceeding). But see Yoder v. Workman, 224 F.Supp. 2d 1077 (S.D. W. Va. 2002) (holding that a judge is not performing an act normally performed by a judge when publishing a press release on the court's website; therefore, the statements are not privileged).

West Virginia courts have also suggested that absolute privilege situations could include those situations where a plaintiff has consented to the defamation or instigated the publication of defamatory statements, where the broadcast of statements made by political candidates is involved, or where a petitioning of the government for redress of grievances protected by the First Amendment is involved. See Crump v. Beckley Newspapers, Inc., 173 W. Va. 699, 320 S.E.2d 70, 10 Media L. Rep. 2225 (1984).

In the employment context, West Virginia has enacted a statute prohibiting any action for defamation based upon information furnished by an employer (or employee) to the State Bureau of Unemployment Compensation. W. Va. Code § 21A-10-11. This statute has consistently been interpreted to bestow an absolute privilege upon employers, thus providing protection even if the statement was false or maliciously made. See Thacker v. Peak, 800 F. Supp. 372 (S.D. W. Va. 1992) (rejecting plaintiff's argument that the privilege does not extend to an employer who discharges an employee for one reason but records another reason on his records).

W. Va. Code § 55-7-18a provides employers immunity from liability for disclosing information regarding former or current employees. Specifically, the statute provides that any employer or his or her designated agent who discloses job-related information that may be reasonably considered adverse about a former or current employee is presumed to be acting in good faith and is immune from civil liability for the disclosure or its consequences. The disclosure must be in writing and a copy must be provided to the employee at the time of the disclosure. The presumption of good faith may be rebutted upon a showing that the information disclosed was: (1) knowingly false; (2) disclosed with reckless disregard for the truth; (3) deliberately misleading; (4) rendered with malicious purpose toward the former or current employee; or (5) disclosed in violation of a nondisclosure agreement or applicable law. W. Va. Code § 55-7-18a(b).

2. ***Qualified Privileges.***

a. **Common Interest.** In West Virginia, a qualified privilege exists where a person publishes a statement in good faith about a subject in which he has an interest or duty and limits the publication to those persons who have a legitimate interest in the subject matter. See Crump, supra; Swearingen v. Parkersburg Sentinel Co., 125 W. Va. 731, 26 S.E.2d 209 (1943).

Thus, West Virginia courts have often held that a qualified privilege extends to employer-employee relations. The focus in applying this privilege is whether the communication dealt with facts which affect a sufficiently important interest of the publisher and whether the recipient's knowledge of the defamatory matter will be of service in the lawful protection of the interest. Stated another way, the test is whether the publisher limited the publication to the parties to whom he owes a duty or to parties who may be concerned with him in the protection of a legitimate interest. See Mauck v. City of Martinsburg, 167 W. Va. 332, 280 S.E.2d 216 (1981) (letter by city manager to former employee was protected by qualified privilege where sent only to those people who had lawful interest in the dismissal); see also Parker, supra (letter from plaintiff's former employer to agent of Division of Vocational Rehabilitation discussing why employer would not rehire plaintiff protected by qualified privilege); Straitwell v. Nat'l Steel Corp., 869 F.2d 248, 16 Media L. Rep. 1329 (4th Cir. 1989) (news release protected by qualified privilege under West Virginia law); McKinney v. K-Mart Corp., 649 F. Supp. 1217 (S.D. W. Va. 1986) (employer's security guard had qualified privilege against defamation with regard to statements made to another security officer regarding cash shortage); Belcher v. Wal-Mart Stores, Inc., 211 W. Va. 712, 568 S.E.2d 19 (2002) (managers had qualified privilege against defamation with regard to statements made to a police officer in the course of an investigation of criminal activity by a customer); Rand v. Miller, 185 W. Va. 705, 408 S.E.2d 655 (1991) (physician hired by employer to make such medical report regarding prospective employee's health may have a qualified privilege); Spano v. Metro. Life Ins. Co., 2011 U.S. Dist. LEXIS 60020 (S.D. W. Va. June 2, 2011) (employer had qualified privilege to report investigation into employee's alleged misconduct to self-regulatory industry group when it was under a legal duty to report).

b. **Duty.** See II.A.2.a, supra.

c. **Criticism of Public Employee.** West Virginia recognizes the privilege of "fair comment" which protects editorial opinion of public figures or employees. Moreover, West Virginia recognizes a media privilege in reporting official proceedings or public meetings, in accordance with the Restatement (Second) of Torts (1977). See Hinerman v. Daily Gazette Co., 188 W. Va. 157, 423 S.E.2d 560, 20 Media L. Rep. 2169 (1992) (recognizing that the publication must be accurate and complete or at least a fair representation of the occurrence reported).

d. **Limitation on Qualified Privileges.**

(1) **Constitutional or Actual Malice.** Unlike an absolute privilege, a qualified privilege may be defeated by a showing of actual malice. As interpreted by the Supreme Court of Appeals of West Virginia, this showing would include a showing that the publisher had intentionally published false, defamatory material, had published such material in reckless disregard for its truth or falsity, had published such material with a primary purpose unrelated to the purpose of the privilege or to persons who have no reason to receive the information, or a publication with a primary purpose unrelated to the purpose of the privilege. See Crump v. Beckley Newspapers, Inc., 173 W. Va. 699, 320 S.E.2d 70, 10 Media L. Rep. 2225 (1984).

(2) **Common Law Malice.** No distinction between constitutional versus common law malice has been discussed by West Virginia courts.

e. **Question of Fact or Law.** Where the facts are not in dispute, the question of privilege is entirely one of law for the Court. See Higgins v. Williams Pocahontas Coal Co., 103 W. Va. 504, 138 S.E. 112 (1927); Thacker v. Peak, 800 F. Supp. 372 (S.D. W. Va. 1992); see also Belcher v. Wal-Mart Stores, Inc., 211 W. Va. 712, 568 S.E.2d 19 (2002).

f. **Burden of Proof.** While the defendant-employer bears the burden of proof on the existence of a qualified privilege, the burden remains with the plaintiff-employee to demonstrate that the privilege was lost through abuse. This question is a question of law for the Court. See Thacker, supra.

B. Standard Libel Defenses

West Virginia law permits the traditional defenses against defamation, including truth, opinion, consent and mitigation.

1. ***Truth***. The traditional, common law defense of truth is modified in West Virginia by virtue of the West Virginia Constitution. In actions of libel at common law or under the statute of insulting words (but not actions for slander), a defendant must not only establish the truth of the statements made, but also that he published them "with good intent and for justifiable ends." W. Va. Const., Article III, § 8. See England v. Daily Gazette Co., 143 W. Va. 700, 104 S.E.2d 306 (1958). If these three criteria are established, even if the communication complained of is defamatory and actual malice is present, the plaintiff cannot recover. See Crump, supra. This provision is not applicable to actions for slander. See McClaugherty v. Cooper, 39 W. Va. 313, 19 S.E. 415 (1894). Thus, in actions for slander, truth alone is a complete defense. See Burdette v. FMC Corp., 566 F. Supp. 808 (S.D. W. Va. 1983); McClaugherty, supra.

As indicated earlier, West Virginia has adopted the U.S. Supreme Court's analysis regarding the issue of substantial truth/substantial falsity. So long as the communication is "substantially true," minor inaccuracies are overlooked and the communication is not defamatory. See Kinney v. Daniels, 574 F. Supp. 542 (S.D. W. Va. 1983); State ex rel. Suriano v. Gaughn, 198 W. Va. 339, 480 S.E.2d 548 (1996).

2. ***Opinion.*** The West Virginia Supreme Court of Appeals has adopted the U.S. Supreme Court's reasoning from Gertz v. Welch, 418 U.S. 323, 1 Media L. Rep. 1633 (1974), regarding the defamatory nature of a statement that constitutes opinion. As the Gertz Court held, there is no such thing as a "false opinion." See Maynard v. Daily Gazette Co., 191 W. Va. 601, 447 S.E.2d 293 (1994) ("A statement of opinion that does not prove false assertion of fact is entitled to full constitutional protection . . ."); Long v. Egnor, 176 W. Va. 628, 346 S.E.2d 778, 13 Media L. Rep. 1855 (1986) (statements in memoranda no more than an expression of opinion). Therefore, West Virginia law affirms that statements of opinion are absolutely protected under the First Amendment and cannot serve as a basis for a defamation action.

However, the West Virginia Supreme Court of Appeals has also adopted the reasoning of § 566 of the Restatement (Second) of Torts, that permits a defamation action if an opinion implies an allegation of undisclosed defamatory facts as the basis for the opinion. See Havalunch, Inc. v. Mazza, 170 W. Va. 268, 294 S.E.2d 70 (1981) (student newspaper article humorously portraying restaurant as equivalent of truck stop is also protected by common law doctrine of fair comment).

3. ***Consent.*** Although no West Virginia cases are directly on point, the West Virginia Supreme Court of Appeals has suggested in dicta that consent to publication may constitute absolute privilege to defamatory statements. See Crump v. Beckley Newspapers, Inc., 173 W. Va. 699, 320 S.E.2d 70, 10 Media L. Rep. 2225 (1984), citing Walters v. Litkof, 559 F. Supp. 1231, 9 Media L. Rep. 1477 (D. Colo. 1983) (allegedly defamatory statements made in response to requests for comment and public participation).

4. ***Mitigation.*** One important partial defense in actions for defamation is that of mitigation. Three types of mitigating circumstances have been recognized in West Virginia. Intoxication of the defendant at the time of his use of slanderous words is a mitigating circumstance proper for jury consideration. See Crump, supra. Another mitigating circumstance is provocation by the plaintiff, indicating the utterance of slanderous words. Finally, West Virginia recognizes that a retraction or apology, while not exonerating a defendant, is a mitigating factor. See Crump, supra; Milan v. Long, 78 W. Va. 102, 88 S.E. 618 (1916). West Virginia has provided that a defendant, after notice in writing of his intention to do so, may submit as evidence of mitigation showing that he made or offered an apology before the commencement of the action or as soon after as he had an opportunity to do so. See W. Va. Code § 57-2-4.

III. RECURRING FACT PATTERNS

A. Statements in Personnel File

The Supreme Court of Appeals of West Virginia has not addressed defamation or privacy issues in private employer personnel files. A federal court interpreting West Virginia law concluded that employees have no property right in their personnel files and that false statements entered by an employer into an employee's personnel file would not constitute defamation under West Virginia law. Councell v. Homer Laughlin China Co., 823 F. Supp. 2d 370 (N.D. W. Va. 2011).

B. Performance Evaluations

None.

C. References

W. Va. Code § 55-7-18a provides employers immunity from liability for disclosing information regarding former or current employees. Specifically, the statute provides that any employer or his or her designated agent who discloses job-related information that may be reasonably considered adverse about a former or current employee is presumed to be acting in good faith and is immune from civil liability for the disclosure or its consequences. The disclosure must be in writing and a copy must be provided to the employee at the time of the disclosure. The presumption of good faith may be rebutted upon a showing that the information disclosed was: (1) knowingly false; (2) disclosed with reckless disregard for the truth; (3) deliberately misleading; (4) rendered with malicious purpose toward the former or current employee; or (5) disclosed in violation of a nondisclosure agreement or applicable law. W. Va. Code § 55-7-18(a)(b).

D. Intracorporate Communication

See I.B.6.a, supra.

E. Statements to Government Regulators

The Supreme Court of Appeals of West Virginia has not addressed this issue. A federal district court interpreting West Virginia law determined that an employer who reported alleged misconduct of an employee to the Financial Industry Regulatory Authority had a qualified privilege to do so and did not defame the employee because it had a legal duty to report the alleged misconduct. Spano v. Metro. Life Ins. Co., 2011 U.S. Dist. LEXIS 60020 (S.D. W. Va. June 2, 2011).

F. Reports to Auditors and Insurers

West Virginia's Unfair Trade Practices Act specifically prohibits any person or company from publishing, disseminating or circulating, either directly or indirectly, or otherwise encouraging any oral or written statement which is false or maliciously critical of or derogatory to the financial condition of any person and which is calculated to injure such person. W. Va. Code § 33-11-4(3). See Mutafis v. Erie Ins. Exch., 561 F. Supp. 192 (N.D. W. Va. 1983), aff'd 775 F.2d 593, 12 Medial L. Rep. 1279 (4th Cir. 1985) (assertion that a person is closely associated with the Mafia which was inserted into a business file without any factual foundation gives rise to private cause of action under W. Va. Code § 33-11-4(3)).

G. Vicarious Liability of Employers for Statements Made by Employees

1. ***Scope of Employment.*** Under West Virginia law, a corporation is not liable for defamatory statements published by one of its agents unless he was authorized thereto, or his acts were subsequently ratified. See Miller v. City Hosp., Inc., 197 W. Va. 403, 475 S.E.2d 495 (1996) (plaintiff failed to meet her burden of providing specific facts to demonstrate publisher was authorized or was ratified by his employer); Barger v. Hood, 87 W. Va. 78, 104 S.E. 280 (1920) (agent and corporation who ratified defamation would both be liable).

a. **Blogging.** No West Virginia reported cases.

2. ***Damages.*** Under West Virginia law, employers may be liable for damages for their employee's defamatory statements if authorized or ratified by the corporation. See Barger, supra.

H. Internal Investigations

No West Virginia reported cases.

IV. OTHER ACTIONS BASED ON STATEMENTS

A. Negligent Hiring, Retention, and Supervision

A principal may be held liable to a third party for civil damages if the principal is negligent in the selection and retention of a contractor, and if such negligence proximately causes harm to the third party. Thomson v. McGinnis, 195 W. Va. 465, 465 S.E.2d 922 (1995). Accordingly, in West Virginia an employer is subject to liability for physical harm to third persons caused by the employer's failure to exercise reasonable care to employ a competent and careful contractor to do work which will involve a risk of physical harm unless it is skillfully and carefully done, or to perform any duty which the employer owes to third persons. See Sipple v. Starr, 205 W. Va. 717, 520 S.E.2d 884 (1999) (adopting Restatement (Second) of Torts § 411).

B. Intentional Infliction of Emotional Distress

West Virginia's law regarding the intentional infliction of emotional distress (also referred to as the tort of outrage) is well-developed, especially in the employment area. The Supreme Court of Appeals has adopted the Restatement's general standard of liability requiring "extreme or outrageous conduct intentionally or recklessly causing severe emotional distress where the conduct is so outrageous in character and so extreme in degree as to go beyond all possible bounds of decency and to be regarded as atrocious and utterly intolerable in a civilized community." See Hines v. Hills Dep't Stores, Inc., 193 W. Va. 91, 454 S.E.2d 385 (1994).

Generally, plaintiffs have joined an outrage claim to their defamation claim, although the Supreme Court of Appeals has rarely concluded that the conduct was sufficiently outrageous to impose liability. See, e.g., Hines v. Hills Dep't Stores, Inc., 193 W. Va. 91, 454 S.E.2d 385 (1994), Tanner v. Rite Aid of West Virginia, Inc., 194 W. Va. 643, 461 S.E.2d 149 (1995); Tudor v. Charleston Area Med. Ctr., 203 W. Va. 111, 506 S.E.2d 554 (1997); Travis v. Alcon Labs., 202 W. Va. 369, 504 S.E.2d 419 (1998); Greenfield v. Schmidt Baking Co., 199 W. Va. 447, 485 S.E.2d 391 (1997).

C. Interference with Economic Advantage

West Virginia permits a cause of action for tortious interference with business relationships. First enumerated in Torbett v. Wheeling Dollar Savings & Trust Co., 173 W. Va. 210, 314 S.E.2d 166 (1983), the elements of this action are: (1) existence of a contractual or business relationship or expectancy; (2) an intentional act of interference by a party outside that relationship or expectancy; (3) proof that the interference caused the harm sustained; and (4) damages.

On several occasions, plaintiffs have joined tortious interference claims with defamation claims. See Bryan v. Massachusetts Mutual Life Ins., 178 W. Va. 773, 364 S.E.2d 786 (1987) (summary judgment properly granted; letter in question was truthful; and defendants had legitimate financial interests in business); Cutright v. Metro. Life Ins., 201 W. Va. 50, 491 S.E.2d 308 (1997) (summary judgment also affirmed).

D. Prima Facie Tort

No West Virginia reported cases.

V. OTHER ISSUES

A. Statute of Limitations

Actions for defamation, including both libel and slander, have a one-year statute of limitations by virtue of W. Va. Code § 55-5-12(c). See Snodgrass v. Sisson's Mobile Home Sales, Inc., 161 W. Va. 588, 244 S.E.2d 321 (1978); Duffy v. Ogden Newspapers, Inc., 170 W. Va. 318, 294 S.E.2d 121, 8 Media L. Rep. 1879 (1982); Cavendish v. Moffitt, 163 W. Va. 38, 253 S.E.2d 558 (1979).

In defamation actions, the period of the statute begins to run when the fact of the defamation becomes known, or reasonably should have become known to the plaintiff. Padon v. Sinns, Roelneck & Co., 186 W. Va. 102, 411 S.E.2d 245 (1991).

Other tort claims often joined with defamation actions take a two-year statute of limitations. See Courtney v. Courtney, 190 W. Va. 126, 437 S.E.2d 436 (1993) (intentional infliction of emotional distress); Garrison v. Herbert J. Thomas Mem'l Hosp., 190 W. Va. 214, 438 S.E.2d 6 (1993) (tortious interference with business relationships).

B. Jurisdiction

Defamation claims are properly brought in the courts of law in the county where the defamatory statement is published. See Sprouse v. Clay Communications, Inc., 158 W. Va. 427, 211 S.E.2d 674, 1 Media L. Rep. 1695, cert. denied, 423 U.S. 882, reh'g denied, 423 U.S. 991 (1975) (for purposes of suing newspaper, venue is proper in any county in which newspaper is circulated).

C. Worker's Compensation Exclusivity

In West Virginia, the workers' compensation system is the exclusive recourse for employees of qualified employers who are injured in the workplace. W.Va. Code § 23-2-6. However, injuries that resulted from the employer's "deliberate intent" are excluded from this provision for employer immunity. W.Va. Code §23-4-2(d).

D. Pleading Requirements

In West Virginia, the rule appears to be that for a cause of action for libel and slander to be correctly pleaded, the exact words spoken or material published must be alleged with particularity. See Kondos v. West Virginia Bd. of Regents, 318 F. Supp. 394 (S.D. W. Va. 1920), aff'd, 441 F.2d 1172 (4th Cir. 1971) (interpreting West Virginia law). It is up to the Court to initially decide whether, as a matter of law, the challenged statements are capable of a defamatory meaning. Furthermore, since statements of opinion are absolutely protected under the First Amendment, the Court must initially decide whether the statement is one of fact or opinion. See Long v. Egnor, 176 W. Va. 628, 346 S.E.2d 778, 13 Media L. Rep. 1855 (1986).

SURVEY OF WEST VIRGINIA EMPLOYMENT PRIVACY LAW

Ashley C. Pack
Katherine A. Brings
Dinsmore & Shohl LLP
900 Lee Street
Huntington Square, Suite 600
Charleston, West Virginia 25301
Telephone (304) 357-0900 Facsimile (304) 357-0919
ashley.pack@dinsmore.com
katherine.brings@dinsmore.com

(With Developments Reported Through **November 1, 2012**).

GENERAL COMMENTS

West Virginia has a two-tiered court system consisting of circuit courts at the trial level with only discretionary appeal to the West Virginia Supreme Court of Appeals. There is no intermediate court of appeals. Circuit court decisions are not reported. Decisions of the West Virginia Supreme Court of Appeals are published in the Southeastern Reporter.

SIGNIFICANT DEVELOPMENTS SINCE THE 2012 *SURVEY*

None.

I. GENERAL LAW OF PRIVACY

A. Legal Basis of Privacy Claims

In West Virginia, public employees are protected by the Fourth Amendment to the United States Constitution, and Article III, Section 6 of the West Virginia Constitution, both of which prohibit the government from unreasonable searches and seizures. These constitutional provisions have been interpreted to create a right of privacy for public employees. See, e.g., Orr v. Crowder, 173 W. Va. 335, 315 S.E.2d 593 (1983) (public employees granted constitutional right to free speech; constitutional right to privacy does not apply to private sector employees). See also Tiernan v. Charleston Area Med. Ctr, Inc., 203 W.Va. 135, 506 S.E.2d 578 (1998) (private sector employees do not have a cause of action against their employers who terminate them because of their exercise of the employee's state constitutional right of free speech). Thus, private sector employees are limited to the common law remedies recognizing the tort of invasion of privacy. See I.B, infra.

B. Causes of Action

West Virginia has recognized the standard four types of invasion of privacy claims, as adopted by most states and the Restatement (Second) of Torts. For a lengthy discussion of the development of the tort of invasion of privacy and its elements, reference should be made to the West Virginia Supreme Court of Appeals opinion in Crump v. Beckley Newspapers, Inc., 173 W. Va. 699, 320 S.E.2d 70, 10 Media L. Rep. 2225 (1984).

1. ***Misappropriation/Right of Publicity.*** This privacy theory primarily serves to prevent the emotional harm which results from the unauthorized use of an individual's name or likeness to promote a particular product or service. The prohibition also extends to other situations in which a person's name or likeness is appropriated to the non-commercial advantage of another. See Crump, supra. This prohibition is subject to the limitations imposed by First Amendment considerations. Therefore, in order for a communication to constitute appropriation, mere publication of a person's name or likeness is not enough, and the defendant must take, for his own use or benefit the reputation, prestige or commercial standing, public interest or other value associated with the name or likeness published. The Court in Crump concluded that the plaintiff's photograph was not published because it was her likeness, but because it was the likeness of a woman coal miner, the subject matter of the newspaper article. Therefore, the Court concluded that the plaintiff was not entitled to recover under the appropriation theory as a matter of law.

2. ***False Light.*** The Crump case also discussed a second privacy theory, that of publicity which unreasonably places another in a false light before the public. As indicated by the Court in Crump, the plaintiff must establish that the matter publicized as to the plaintiff constitutes an untrue characterization. Additionally, although the false light need not be defamatory, it must be offensive to a reasonable person. Finally, the publicized material must be publicized in a widespread manner. See Benson v. AJR, Inc., 599 S.E.2d 747 (W. Va. 2004) (no invasion of privacy when defendant disclosed the results of plaintiff's drug test to three individuals, all of whom were AJR employees, officers, or creditors). As in defamation actions, if a privileged communication is involved, the actual malice or abuse of privilege standard will apply.

The determination of whether the plaintiff is placed in a false light is one for the jury. See Crump v. Beckley Newspapers, Inc., 173 W. Va. 699, 320 S.E.2d 70 (1984).

3. ***Publication of Private Facts.*** As indicated by the Supreme Court in Crump, West Virginia recognizes this third type of invasion of privacy claim. In the employment arena, this issue has most often arisen in the context of disclosure of employee medical or personnel records. See, e.g., Grant v. Monsanto Company, 151 F.R.D. 285 (S.D. W. Va. 1993) (federal court rejecting West Virginia invasion of privacy cases as applicable in determining the discoverability of employee medical records); E.I. duPont deNemours & Co. v. Finklea, 442 F. Supp. 821 (S.D. W. Va. 1977) (although medical records of employees were protected by a constitutional right of privacy, disclosure of such records pursuant to subpoenas would not abridge such right). See also Jordan v. Town of Pratt, 886 F. Supp. 555 (S.D. W. Va. 1995) (plaintiff failed to establish invasion of privacy claim against police officer under West Virginia law for not keeping confidential information regarding an assault of her daughter); Davis v. Monsanto Co., 627 F. Supp. 418 (S.D. W. Va. 1986) (employer's limited disclosure of information suggesting employee's mental instability did not constitute publication necessary to establish cause of action for public disclosure of private facts) (cited by Benson v. AJR, Inc., supra); Copley v. Northwestern Mutual Life Ins. Co., 295 F. Supp. 93 (S.D. W. Va. 1968) (protection of the right of privacy afforded by law is primarily designed to protect personal feelings, rather than business or pecuniary interests which are not entitled to such protection); Martino v. Barnett, 215 W. Va 123, 595 S.E.2d 65 (2004) (non-public personal information could be subject to release pursuant to judicial process under the exceptions to the privacy provisions of the Gramm-Leach-Bliley Act and the privacy rule of the West Virginia Insurance Commission); Keplinger v. Virginia Elec. & Power Co., 208 W. Va. 11, 537 S.E.2d 632 (2000) (Morris, infra, cause of action not extended to discovery violations); Greenfield v. Schmidt Baking Co., Inc., 199 W. Va. 447, 485 S.E.2d 391 (1997) (state law claim for unreasonable publicity of private facts and false light not preempted by federal law); Morris v. Consolidation Coal Co., 191 W. Va. 426, 446 S.E.2d 648 (1994) (patient has cause of action against third party employer representative who induces his physician to breach his fiduciary relationship by disclosing confidential information).

4. ***Intrusion.*** The tort of invasion of privacy was first recognized in West Virginia in 1958 by an intrusion case, which held that the right of privacy included the right of an individual to be let alone and to keep secret his private communications, conversations and affairs. See Roach v. Harper, 143 W. Va. 869, 105 S.E.2d 564 (1958) (claim for right of privacy would be recognized in action filed by tenant against landlord who caused a listening device to be installed in tenant's apartment); Sutherland v. Kroger Co., 144 W. Va. 673, 110 S.E.2d 716 (1959) (an illegal search by a private individual is a trespassing violation of the right of privacy); State ex rel. State Farm Fire & Cas. Co. v. Madden, 192 W. Va. 155, 451 S.E.2d 721 (1994) (investigator's surveillance of observing plaintiff in public not illegal because plaintiff had no legitimate expectations of privacy in a public setting). A person has no expectation of privacy in a public place, however, and thus an invasion of privacy claim cannot arise from an alleged intrusion into his or her privacy while in public. O'Dell v. Stegall, 226 W. Va. 590, 703 S.E.2d 561 (2010).

In the employment area, West Virginia has recognized a claim for intrusion where the employer was responsible for placing a listening device in the ceiling of the plaintiff's office. See Slack v. Kanawha County Hous. & Redev. Auth., 188 W. Va. 144, 423 S.E.2d 547 (1992).

C. Other Privacy-Related Actions

1. ***Intentional Infliction of Emotional Distress.*** West Virginia's law regarding the intentional infliction of emotional distress (also referred to as the tort of outrage) is well developed, especially in the employment area. The Supreme Court of Appeals has adopted the Restatement's general standard of liability requiring, "extreme or outrageous conduct intentionally or recklessly causing severe emotional distress where the conduct is so outrageous in character and so extreme in degree as to go beyond all possible bounds of decency and to be regarded as atrocious and utterly intolerable in a civilized community." See Hines v. Hills Dep't Stores, Inc., 193 W. Va. 91, 454 S.E.2d 385 (1994). A plaintiff must prove four elements: (1) conduct so "atrocious, intolerable, and so extreme and outrageous as to exceed the bounds of decency;" (2) intent to inflict emotional distress or recklessness when certain or substantially certain emotional distress would result; (3) actual emotional distress; and, (4) severity of emotional distress such "that no reasonable person could be expected to endure it." O'Dell v. Stegall, 226 W. Va. 590, 703 S.E.2d 561 (2010); Travis v. Alcon Laboratories, Inc., 202 W.Va. 369, 504 S.E.2d 419 (1998).

In the employment context, the fact of discharge cannot in and of itself rise to the level of intentional infliction of emotional distress, although a discharge carried out in a particularly outrageous manner could support a claim for intentional infliction of emotional distress. Roth v. Defelicecare, Inc., 226 W. Va. 214 , 700 S.E.2d 183 (2010); Dzinglski v. Weirton Steel Corp., 191 W. Va. 278, 445 S.E.2d 219 (1994).

Plaintiffs have often joined outrage claims to their claims of invasion of privacy. See, e.g., O'Dell v. Stegall, 226 W. Va. 590, 703 S.E.2d 561 (2010); Greenfield v. Schmidt Baking Co., 199 W. Va. 447, 485 S.E.2d 391 (1997).

2. ***Interference With Prospective Economic Advantage.*** West Virginia permits a cause of action for tortious interference with prospective business relationships. First enumerated in Torbett v. Wheeling Dollar Savings & Trust Co., 173 W. Va. 210, 314 S.E.2d 166 (1983), the elements of this action are: (1) the existence of a contractual or business relationship or expectancy; (2) an intentional act of interference by a party outside that relationship or expectancy; (3) proof that the interference caused the harm sustained; and (4) damage.

An employer may defend by proving justification or privilege, both of which are affirmative defenses. See Bryan v. Massachusetts Mut. Life Ins. Co., 178 W. Va. 773, 364 S.E.2d 786 (1987). Moreover, defendants are not liable for interference that is negligent, rather than intentional, or if defendants demonstrate defenses of legitimate competition between the plaintiff and themselves, their financial interest in the induced party's business, their responsibility for another's welfare, their intention to influence another's business policies in which they have interest, their giving of honest, truthful requested advice, or other factors that show the interference was proper.

3. ***Prima Facie Tort.*** No cases.

II. EMPLOYER TESTING OF EMPLOYEES

A. Psychological or Personality Testing

1. ***Common Law and Statutes.*** No statute in West Virginia concerns either psychological or personality testing by employers. However, by virtue of decisional authority, all correctional officers for the state of West Virginia Department of Correction Systems must undergo psychological testing before they are employed and at least annually throughout their employment. See Harrah v. Leverette, 165 W. Va. 665, 271 S.E.2d 322 (1980).

2. ***Private Employers.*** None.

3. ***Public Employers.*** See II.A.1, supra.

B. Drug Testing

1. ***Common Law and Statutes.*** The West Virginia legislature recently passed a statute that will take effect on January 1, 2013. W. Va. Code § 22A-1-1 will require that every employer of miners in West Virginia implement a substance abuse screening policy and program. The policy and program must include a preemploymnet urine test and a random substance abuse testing program.

The Supreme Court of Appeals of West Virginia has ruled that, because of an employee's common law right of privacy, it is contrary to public policy for an employer to require an employee to submit to drug testing. In Twigg v. Hercules Corp., 185 W. Va. 155, 406 S.E.2d 52 (1990), the court ruled that drug testing is unlawful in West Virginia except in two very limited circumstances: (1) where the employer has a reasonable good faith, objective suspicion of an employee's drug use; or (2) when an employee's job responsibility involves public safety or the safety of others ("safety sensitive"). See also Rohrbaugh v. Wal-Mart Stores Inc., 212 W. Va. 358 572 S.E.2d 881 (2002). A private employer may conduct pre-employment drug screening of applicants because the applicant, as opposed to a current employee, has a lowered expectation of privacy. See Baughman v. Wal-Mart Stores, Inc., 215 W.Va. 45, 592 S.E.2d 824 (2003).

2. ***Private Employers.*** See II.B.1, supra.

3. ***Public Employers.*** See II.B.1, supra.

C. Medical Testing

1. ***Common Law and Statutes.*** W. Va. Code § 21-3-17 makes it unlawful for an employer to require an employee or applicant for employment to pay the costs of a medical examination as a condition of employment. Any employer who violates this provision shall be liable to a penalty of not more than one hundred dollars for every violation.

2. ***Private Employers.*** No cases.

3. ***Public Employers.*** No cases.

D. Polygraph Tests

Although federal law permits private employees to conduct polygraph examinations where there is a reasonable suspicion of employee theft, West Virginia law does not. The Supreme Court of Appeals of West Virginia has held that polygraph tests of employees are contrary to the state public policy protecting individual privacy interests. Cordle v. General Hugh Mercer Corp., 174 W. Va. 321, 325 S.E.2d 111 (1984). Additionally, W. Va. Code §21-5-5D prohibits employers from requiring or requesting employees or applicants to submit to polygraph examinations. Like the federal statute, however, the state statute does not apply to employers authorized to manufacture, distribute, or dispense controlled substances.

E. Fingerprinting

State law provides the director of the State Lottery Commission with the authority to conduct pre-employment background checks, including fingerprinting, of professional, clerical, technical and administrative personnel. W. Va. Code § 29-25-4.

III. SEARCHES

A. Employee's Person

1. ***Private Employers.*** There are no cases specifically involving searches of private employees in West Virginia, although one case concerns a grocery store's search of a customer's package. See Sutherland v. Kroger, 144 W. Va. 673, 110 S.E.2d 716 (1959).

2. ***Public Employers.*** There are no cases specifically involving searches of public employees, although it is clear that public employees are accorded full constitutional rights by both the U.S. and West Virginia Constitutions.

B. Employee's Work Area

No cases.

C. Employee's Property

1. ***Private Employers.*** No cases.

2. ***Public Employers.*** No cases.

IV. MONITORING OF EMPLOYEES

A. Telephones and Electronic Communications

1. ***Wiretapping.*** West Virginia has enacted a state law governing wiretapping known as the West Virginia Wiretapping and Electronic Surveillance Act, W. Va. Code §62-1D-1. Pursuant to this law, it is lawful for one party to intercept a communication where that person is a party to the communication or where one of the parties to the communication has given prior consent to the interception, unless the communication is intercepted for the purpose of committing criminal acts. See W. Va. Code §62-1D-3. In addition to criminal penalties, this law provides for civil liability permitting victims to recover actual damages, punitive damages and attorney's fees. See W. Va. Code § 62-1D-12, as discussed in Slack v. Kanawha County Hous. & Redev. Auth., 188 W. Va. 144, 423 S.E.2d 547 (1992) (employee plaintiff has no cause of action based on this statute where the interceptions occurred before the effective date of the statute).

2. ***Electronic Communications.*** In addition to the provisions of the West Virginia Wiretapping and Electronic Surveillance Act discussed above, West Virginia also has a Computer Crime and Abuse Act which prohibits any person from knowingly, willfully and without authorization accessing a computer or computer network to examine any employment, salary, credit or any other financial or personal information relating to any other person. See W. Va. Code § 61-3C-12. In addition to criminal violations, this Act also provides a private right of action and expressly permits the recovery of punitive damages. W. Va Code § 61-3C-16.

In Bowyer v. HI-LAD, Inc., 216 W.Va. 634, 609 S.E.2d 895 (2004), the plaintiff, a hotel employee, sued the owner of the hotel-employer, alleging the defendant had subjected him to illegal audio surveillance and monitoring in violation of the West Virginia Wiretapping and Electronic Surveillance Act. In a per curiam opinion, the Supreme Court of Appeals of West Virginia upheld a jury verdict holding the defendant hotel owner liable for intercepting the private conversations of the plaintiff through hidden microphones in the workplace. The Supreme Court of Appeals of West Virginia upheld an award of $100,000 in compensatory damages even absent direct evidence that the defendant had intercepted the plaintiff's conversation within the hotel. At trial, the plaintiff introduced videotape evidence from the hotel's surveillance equipment containing over four hours of video and audio of hotel employees and the public speaking near the hotel's front desk and bar. Thus, the court ruled sufficient circumstantial evidence existed that the jury could conclude that the defendant intercepted the plaintiff's communications, as well.

The court also upheld the jury's award of $400,000 in punitive damages. On multiple occasions, an assistant manager of the hotel told the plaintiff microphones were hidden in the hotel but were disconnected. According to the court, the jury could rightly conclude that the defendant had, for at least two years, secretly monitored verbal communications of employees and hotel guests, had attempted to conceal its actions, and had made no effort to make amends for its transgressions.

3. ***Other Electronic Monitoring.*** No Cases.

B. Mail

No cases.

C. Surveillance/Photographing

Employers are prohibited from electronically surveilling (by videotape, closed-circuit TV, etc.) employee activities in areas designed for their health or personal comfort such as restrooms, locker rooms, and employee lounges. Conviction under this misdemeanor statute carries monetary penalties. W. Va. Code § 21-3-20. Presumably, surveillance outside the workplace would not constitute an invasion of privacy so long as the employee does not have a reasonable expectation of privacy. Even if the employee is found to have a reasonable expectation of privacy, courts will also consider whether the employer has a reasonable justification for the surveillance which outweighs the employee's expectations of privacy. See State ex rel. State Farm Fire & Cas. Co. v. Madden, 192 W. Va. 155, 451 S.E.2d 721 (1994) (private investigator hired by insurer committed no illegal acts by merely visually surveying and photographing plaintiff engaged in activities which occurred in full view of the general public).

V. ACTIVITIES OUTSIDE THE WORKPLACE

A. Statute or Common Law

Other than the anti-discrimination provision regarding smoking, West Virginia has no statutes pertaining to an employer's reliance upon employee activities outside the workplace. With respect to public employees, however, the Supreme Court has construed a West Virginia statute as authorizing county boards of education to terminate teachers for, among other things, "immorality." See W. Va. Code § 18A-2-8. In Golden v. Bd. of Educ. of Harrison County, 169 W. Va. 63, 285 S.E.2d 665 (1981), the Supreme Court held that the dismissal of a school teacher on the basis of immorality for shoplifting could be upheld only upon a showing of a rational nexus between the conduct and the teacher's ability to perform duties, a nexus that the majority held was not established. Where a school board employee commits a criminal act that directly involves the employee's occupational responsibilities, however, a rational nexus exists, and the employee may be directly dismissed. See Bledsoe v. Wyoming County Bd. of Educ., 183 W. Va. 190, 193–94, 394 S.E.2d 885 (1990).

B. Employees' Personal Relationships

No West Virginia laws or cases concern an employer's prohibitions regarding employees' personal relationships outside the workplace.

1. ***Romantic Relationships Between Employees.*** No cases.

2. ***Sexual Orientation.*** No cases.

3. ***Marital Status.*** No cases.

C. Smoking

West Virginia law prohibits any employer from discriminating against any applicant or employee solely because the individual uses tobacco products off the premises of the employer during nonworking hours. See W. Va. Code § 21-3-19.

D. Blogging

There are no cases in West Virginia on this issue. Federal law, however, limits employers' abilities to regulate their employees' internet communications. For instance, the Stored Communications Act ("SCA") prohibits third parties from accessing electronically stored communications. 18 U.S.C. § 2701; see also Pietrylo v. Hillstone Restaurant Group d/b/a Houston's, No. 06-5754, 2008 U.S. Dist. LEXIS 108834 (D.N.J. July 25, 2008). Employers also should recognize the potential liabilities under the National Labor Relations Act ("NLRA"). Employers monitoring employees' social networking sites may have a chilling effect on employees' communications regarding the terms and conditions of their employment, and thus, employers should exercise caution in monitoring employees' online activities. Endicott Interconnect Technologies, Inc., 345 NLRB No. 28 (Aug. 27, 2005).

VI. RECORDS

A. Personnel Records

No West Virginia law permits public access to personnel records. The West Virginia Freedom of Information Act exempts from disclosure information of a personal nature if the public disclosure thereof would constitute an unreasonable invasion of privacy, unless the public interest by clear and convincing evidence requires disclosure in a particular instance. W. Va. Code § 29B-1-4(2). See also Manns v. City of Charleston Police Dep't., 209 W. Va. 620, 550 S.E.2d 598 (2001).

Public documents relating to such matters as names of public employees, their designation, an employee number, payroll records, time sheets, salary amounts, attendance records, numerical data dealing with a public employee's vacation or sick leave records, retirement service credit, and statutorily withheld federal, state and city taxes, are clearly public records and subject to disclosure. See In re Gazette FOIA Request, 222 W. Va. 771, 783, 671 S.E.2d 771 (2008).

B. Medical Records

West Virginia law strictly prohibits the disclosure of confidential information relating to mental health records. See W. Va. Code § 27-3-1. See also Allen v. Smith, 179 W. Va. 360, 368 S.E.2d 924 (1988) (private cause of action for violation of the protective provisions of this chapter). As indicated above, several cases interpreting West Virginia law have concerned common law invasion of privacy claims where an employer has disclosed confidential employee medical files. See I.B.3, supra.

C. Criminal Records

Criminal records are considered to be public and may generally be accessed by any individual upon request.

D. Subpoenas / Search Warrants

Rule 45 of the West Virginia Rules of Civil Procedure applies to the use of subpoenas in civil trials. W.Va.R.Civ.Proc. 45. In addition, Rule 45 may be used as a discovery tool pursuant to Rule 34. See W.Va.R.Civ.Proc. 34. When Rule 45 is used as a discovery device pursuant to Rule 34, however, Rule 45 is subject to all of the discovery provisions, including, but not limited to, the scope of discovery outlined in W.Va.R.Civ.Proc. 26(b)(1). Syl. Pt. 4, Keplinger v. Virginia Elec. & Power Co., 208 W.Va. 11, 537 S.E.2d 632 (2000). Furthermore, special rules apply to the production of hospital records via subpoena. Any time a subpoena duces tecum is issued to require the production of hospital records as defined in W.Va. Code § 57-5-4a(a), regardless of the purpose for which the records are sought, the requirements of W.Va. Code §§ 57-5-4a to 57-5-4j apply and must be followed. Syl. Pt. 3, Keplinger, supra. Moreover, when a party to a civil action seeks to utilize Rule 45 to subpoena an opposing party's medical records, notice to the party/patient must occur sufficiently in advance of service of the subpoena to provide a reasonable opportunity for the patient/party to object to the request. Syl. Pt. 4, Keplinger, supra. Lastly, a party may not use Rule 45, or any other discovery device, to pursue discovery of items that are the subject of an ongoing discovery dispute that has not yet been resolved by the parties or decided by the trial court. Syl. Pt. 6, Keplinger, supra.

VII. ACTIONS SUBSEQUENT TO EMPLOYMENT

A. References.

There are no cases concerning references in West Virginia. W. Va. Code § 55-7-18a provides employers immunity from liability for disclosing information regarding former or current employees. Specifically, the statute provides that any employer or his or her designated agent who discloses job-related information that may be reasonably considered adverse about a former or current employee is presumed to be acting in good faith and is immune from civil liability for the disclosure or its consequences. The disclosure must be in writing and a copy must be provided to the employee at the time of the disclosure. The presumption of good faith may be rebutted upon a showing that the information disclosed was: (1) knowingly false; (2) disclosed with reckless disregard for the truth; (3) deliberately misleading; (4) rendered with malicious purpose toward the former or current employee; or (5) disclosed in violation of a nondisclosure agreement or applicable law. W. Va. Code § 55-7-18a(b).

B. Non-Compete Agreements

In West Virginia, a contractual covenant between an employer and employee, restricting the employee from engaging in business similar to that of the employer within a designated time and territory after the employment should cease, will be inferred if the restriction is reasonably necessary for the protection of the employer and does not impose undue hardship on the employee. Syl. Pt. 1, Voorhees v. Guyan Mach. Co., 191 W.Va. 450, 446 S.E.2d 672 (1994). In Reddy v. Cmty. Health Found. of Man, 171 W.Va. 368, 298 S.E.2d 906 (1982), the seminal case on this subject, the West Virginia

Supreme Court of Appeals outlined the standards governing the enforcement of restrictive covenants not to compete. An employee covenant not to compete is unreasonable on its face if its time or area limitations are excessively broad, or where the covenant appears designed to intimidate employees rather than to protect the employer's business, and a court should hold any such covenant void and unenforceable and not undertake even a partial enforcement of it, bearing in mind, however, that a standard of "unreasonable on its face" is to be distinguished from the standard of "reasonableness" used in inquiries adopted by other authorities to address the minor instances of over-breadth to which restrictive covenants are naturally prone. Syl. Pt. 2, Reddy, supra. An inherently reasonable restrictive covenant is presumptively enforceable in its entirety upon a showing by the employer that he has interests requiring protection from the employee. Syl. Pt. 3, Reddy, supra. An employee may rebut the presumptive enforceability of a restrictive covenant by showing: (1) that he has no "trade assets" of the employer to convert; (2) that such "trade assets" as he has belong to him and not to the employer; (3) that the employer could be equally well protected by a narrowed covenant; or (4) that the employer has had time to recoup any extraordinary investment in the employee. Reddy, supra. See also Cook v. Robinson, 2011 U.S. Dist. LEXIS 114689 (N.D. W. Va. Oct. 4, 2011); Huntington Eye Assocs. Inc. v. LoCascio, 210 W.Va. 76, 553 S.E.2d 773 (2001). In addition, if a covenant not to compete is contracted after employment has been commenced, there must be new consideration to support its enforcement. Envtl Prods. Co., Inc. v. Duncan, 168 W.Va. 349, 285 S.E.2d 889 (1982).

In addition, West Virginia law recognizes a difference between non-compete agreements and non-piracy/non-solicitation agreements. According to the West Virginia Supreme Court of Appeals, a covenant not to compete in an employment agreement between an employer and an employee restricts the employee from engaging in business similar to that of the employer within a designated time and territory after the employment ends; a non-piracy provision, also known as a non-solicitation or hand-off provision, in an employment agreement, restricts the employee, should the employment cease, from soliciting the employer's customers or making use of the employer's confidential information. Wood v. Acordia of West Virginia, Inc., 217 W.Va. 406, 618 S.E.2d 415 (2005). Although both covenants not to compete and non-piracy provisions are utilized to safeguard an employer's protectable business interests, non-piracy provisions, which ordinarily do not include territorial limits, are less restrictive on the employee and the economic forces of the marketplace. Wood, 217 W.Va. 406, 618 S.E.2d 415 (2005).

In Wood, the Supreme Court of Appeals held that the validity of non-solicitation/non-piracy provisions are dependent upon: (1) Whether the employer has a protectable business interest to be safeguarded in relation to the employee, (2) the extent to which the non-piracy provision reasonably and fairly protects that interest and (3) whether the non-piracy provision unjustly restricts the employee from engaging in the business activity he or she seeks to pursue. Wood, supra. Whereas the burden is on the employer with regard to factors (1) and (2) above concerning the showing of a protectable business interest and the reasonableness of the non-piracy provision, the burden is on the employee with regard to factor (3) concerning whether the provision constitutes an unjust restriction. Wood, supra.

VIII. OTHER ISSUES

A. Statutes of Limitations

The West Virginia Supreme Court has ruled that the applicable statute of limitations for invasion of privacy actions is one-year. Slack v. Kanawha County Hous. & Redev. Auth., 188 W. Va. 144, 423 S.E.2d 547 (1992) (invasion of privacy is a personal action that does not survive the death of an individual at common law and is therefore governed by a one-year statute of limitations). The discovery rule has been held applicable to invasion of privacy claims in West Virginia, thus delaying the running of the statute of limitations until such time as the plaintiff knew or reasonably should have known of the injury and its cause. See Slack, supra.

Claims of intentional infliction of emotional distress have a two-year statute of limitations in West Virginia. See Courtney v. Courtney, 190 W. Va. 126, 437 S.E.2d 436 (1993). Actions for tortious interference with business relationships also have a two-year statute of limitations. See Garrison v. Herbert J. Thomas Mem'l Hosp., 190 W. Va. 214, 438 S.E.2d 6 (1993).

The West Virginia Supreme Court has ruled that the applicable statute of limitations for breach of confidentiality actions in violation of a statute is one year. Thompson v. Branches-Domestic Violence Shelter of Huntington, W. Va., Inc., 207 W. Va. 479, 534 S.E.2d 33 (2000). Also, the discovery rule has been held applicable to breach of confidentiality actions in West Virginia. See Thompson, supra.

B. Jurisdiction

In West Virginia, the circuit courts are the courts of general jurisdiction and can hear all cases where the amount in controversy exceed $2,500. W. Va. Code § 51-2-2(b). Venue is proper in the circuit court of the county in which any of the defendants reside or the cause of action arose. W. Va. Code § 56-1-1(a).

C. Workers' Compensation Exclusivity

In West Virginia, the workers' compensation system is the exclusive recourse for employees of qualified employers who are injured in the workplace. W.Va. Code § 23-2-6. However, injuries that resulted from the employer's "deliberate intent" are excluded from this provision for employer immunity. W.Va. Code §23-4-2(d).

D. Pleading Requirements

The seminal West Virginia case on invasion of privacy sets forth the pleading requirements and defenses, including privilege, for invasion of privacy cases in West Virginia, as well as defamation cases. See Crump v. Beckley Newspapers, Inc., 173 W. Va. 699, 320 S.E.2d 70, 10 Media L. Rep. 2225 (1984).

SURVEY OF WISCONSIN EMPLOYMENT LIBEL LAW

Brady C. Williamson
Robert J. Dreps
James A. Friedman
Sherry D. Coley
Godfrey & Kahn, S.C.
One East Main Street, Suite 500
Madison, Wisconsin 53703
Telephone: (608) 257-3911; Facsimile: (608) 257-0609

(With Developments Reported Through **November 1, 2012**)

GENERAL COMMENTS

Wisconsin has both an intermediate court of appeals and a Supreme Court. The court of appeals is divided into four geographic districts, but it acts as one court for purposes of precedent. Litigants have a right to appeal final judgments or orders only to the court of appeals. The Wisconsin Supreme Court has seven justices - Chief Justice Shirley S. Abrahamson and Justices Ann Walsh Bradley, N. Patrick Crooks, Michael J. Gableman, David T. Prosser, Jr., Patience D. Roggensack, and Annette K. Ziegler. The Court has complete discretion to decide the cases it will hear each term.

The Wisconsin Supreme Court publishes all of its decisions, but the Court of Appeals publishes only a small percentage of its decisions. Only published opinions have precedential value. As of July 1, 2009, however, authored court of appeals opinions may be cited for persuasive value. §§ 752.41 and 809.23, Wis. Stats. The first citation to a Wisconsin appellate opinion must include a reference to the volume and page number of both the Wisconsin Reports and the Northwestern Reporter in which the opinion is published. Subsequent citations must include references to the volume and page number of at least one of these publications. Supreme Court Rule 80.02.

All Wisconsin appellate opinions issued on or after January 1, 2000 include a public domain citation. The first citation to these opinions also must include a reference to the public domain citation. Subsequent citations may refer to either of the publications or to the public domain citation. Id.

SIGNIFICANT DEVELOPMENTS SINCE THE 2012 *SURVEY*

There have been no significant developments in Wisconsin employment libel law since the 2012 survey.

I. GENERAL LAW

A. General Employment Law

1. ***At Will Employment.*** The Wisconsin Supreme Court first recognized the at will employment doctrine in 1871. Prentiss v. Ledyard, 28 Wis. 131, 133 (1871). "[T]he doctrine generally allows an employer to discharge an employee 'for good cause, for no cause, or even for cause morally wrong, without being thereby guilty of legal wrong.'" Hausman v. St. Croix Care Center, 214 Wis. 2d 654, 662, 571 N.W.2d 393, 396 (1997) (citation omitted). In Brockmeyer v. Dun & Bradstreet, 113 Wis. 2d 561, 573, 335 N.W.2d 834, 840 (1983), the Supreme Court recognized a narrow exception to the doctrine: "a wrongful discharge is actionable when the termination clearly contravenes the public welfare and gravely violates paramount requirements of public interest." Pursuant to this exception, an employer cannot legally fire an employee for refusing to violate the state or federal constitution, a statute, or an administrative rule. See Hausman, 214 Wis. 2d at 663, 571 N.W.2d at 396. While Wisconsin courts do not recognize a general "whistle-blower" exception to the at will employment rule, the Wisconsin Supreme Court, in Hausman, held that "[w]here the law imposes an affirmative obligation upon an employee to prevent abuse or neglect of nursing home residents and the employee fulfills that obligation by reporting the abuse, an employer's termination of employment for fulfillment of the legal obligation exposes the employer to a wrongful termination action." Id. at 668, 571 N.W.2d at 398. Discharging an employee for failing to sign an unreasonable non-compete agreement, on the other hand, does not give rise to a wrongful discharge claim. Tatge v. Chambers & Owen, Inc., 219 Wis. 2d 99, 579 N.W.2d 217 (1998).

B. Elements of Libel Claim

1. ***Basic Elements.*** "The elements of a defamatory communication are: (1) a false statement; (2) communicated by speech, conduct or in writing to a person other than the person defamed; and, (3) the communication is unprivileged and tends to harm one's reputation so as to lower him or her in the estimation of the community or to deter third persons from associating or dealing with him or her." Torgerson v. Journal/Sentinel, Inc., 210 Wis. 2d 524, 534, 563 N.W.2d

472, 477, 25 Media L. Rep 2249 (1997). Wisconsin courts adhere to the definition of defamatory meaning noted in the Restatement (Second) of Torts § 559 (1977). See Tatur v. Solsrud, 174 Wis. 2d 735, 741, 498 N.W.2d 232, 233-34 (1993).

In addition, the Wisconsin Court of Appeals has "conclude[d] that 'negligent defamation' is not a contradiction in terms and [that] Wisconsin law recognizes the possibility of recovery by a plaintiff even where the defendant does not deliberately and intentionally defame the plaintiff." Baumann v. Elliott, 2005 WI App 186, ¶ 1, 286 Wis.2d 667, 704 N.W.2d 361. Negligent defamation typically only justifies compensatory damages, "whereas punitive damages require a showing of various types of ill will or corrupt motives that demonstrate malice in fact." Id., ¶ 23.

2. ***Fault.***

a. **Private Figure Plaintiff/Matter of Public Concern.** No Wisconsin court has addressed the level of fault a private figure libel plaintiff must prove to prevail where the speech is on a matter of public concern since the U.S. Supreme Court's decision on that issue in Dun & Bradstreet, Inc. v. Greenmoss Builders, Inc., 472 U.S. 749 (1985). In Denny v. Mertz, 106 Wis. 2d 636, 318 N.W.2d 141, 4 Media L. Rep. 1153 (1982), the Wisconsin Supreme Court suggested that in private figure plaintiff cases, it would not differentiate between speech concerning public controversies and speech on private concerns. Wisconsin courts, addressing the limited purpose public figure test, have found the following issues matters of public concern: an inmate's attempted suicide, which may have exposed jail personnel to the AIDS virus, Van Straten v. Milwaukee Journal Newspaper-Publisher, 151 Wis. 2d 905, 447 N.W.2d 105, 16 Media L. Rep. 2408 (Ct. App. 1989); pollution problems in a Wisconsin lake, Wiegel v. Capital Times Co., 145 Wis. 2d 71, 426 N.W.2d 43, 15 Media L. Rep. 1569 (Ct. App. 1988); financing of pollution control measures, Polzin v. Helmbrecht, 54 Wis. 2d 578, 196 N.W.2d 685 (1972); and, cryptosporidium contamination of the public water supply, Bay View Packing Co. v. Taff, 198 Wis. 2d 653, 543 N.W.2d 522, 24 Media L. Rep. 1289 (Ct. App. 1995). In Denny, 106 Wis. 2d at 650, 318 N.W.2d at 147, on the other hand, the Wisconsin Supreme Court took a restrictive view of public concern, finding that a stockholder dispute involving a Fortune 500 company "did not have an impact outside of those immediately interested in the [] corporation."

b. **Private Figure Plaintiff/Matter of Private Concern.** In Denny, 106 Wis. 2d at 654, 318 N.W.2d at 150, the court held "that a private individual need only prove that a media defendant was negligent in broadcasting or publishing a defamatory statement" on a matter of private concern. Still, the plaintiff is not entitled to punitive or presumed damages unless he can prove actual malice. Id. at 659, 318 N.W.2d at 152. Under the same circumstances, however, a nonmedia defendant is strictly liable for defamation under the common law. Id. at 661, 318 N.W.2d at 153.

c. **Public Figure Plaintiff/Matter of Public Concern.** When the defendant is a member of the news media, of course, public figure plaintiffs must always prove actual malice to satisfy the fault element of their defamation claims. See, e.g., Bay View Packing, 198 Wis. 2d at 676, 543 N.W.2d at 530; In re Storms v. Action Wisconsin, Inc., 2008 WI 56, ¶ 38, 309 Wis.2d 704, 750 N.W.2d 739. Whether the actual malice standard applies to nonmedia defendants alleged to have libeled public figures is an open question in Wisconsin. See id. at 674-75 n. 5, 543 N.W.2d at 529 n. 5. A federal district court recently held that a limited purpose public figure plaintiff had to prove actual malice against a nonmedia defendant. Framsted v. Municipal Ambulance Service, Inc., 347 F. Supp. 2d 638, 663 (W.D. Wis. 2004). Two other federal court decisions applying Wisconsin law are in conflict on the issue. Compare Underwager v. Salter, 22 F.3d 730, 734, 22 Media L. Rep. 1852 (7th Cir. 1994) ("Cases since Denny have made it clear that a public figure must establish that the defendant acted with actual malice. None of the cases we could find suggests that Wisconsin imposes a lesser burden on a public figure suing a psychologist or prosecutor than on one suing a reporter"); with Harris v. Quadracci, 856 F. Supp. 513, 519, 22 Media L. Rep. 2147 (E.D. Wis. 1994), aff'd, 48 F.3d 247, 23 Media L. Rep. 1296 (7th Cir. 1995) ("Wisconsin case law indicates that a Wisconsin court would not afford the New York Times malice standard to nonmedia defendants"), citing Denny, 106 Wis. 2d at 660-61.

3. ***Falsity.*** "Truth is a complete defense to a libel action." Lathan v. Journal Co., 30 Wis. 2d 146, 158, 140 N.W.2d 417, 423 (1966). "Nor is it necessary that the article or statement in question be true in every particular. All that is required is that the statement be substantially true." Id.; see Torgerson, 210 Wis. 2d at 534-35, 563 N.W.2d at 477 ("If the challenged statements as a whole are not capable of a false and defamatory meaning, or are substantially true, a libel action will fail"). In Torgerson, 210 Wis. 2d at 543, 563 N.W.2d at 481, the Wisconsin Supreme Court applied Philadelphia Newspapers, Inc. v. Hepps, 475 U.S. 767 (1986), and held that, at least with media defendants, the plaintiff has the burden of proving falsity in both public figure and private plaintiff defamation actions.

4. ***Defamatory Statement of Fact.*** Wisconsin applies the Restatement's definition of defamatory meaning. "A communication is defamatory if it tends so to harm the reputation of another as to lower him in the estimation of the community or to deter third persons from associating or dealing with him." Tatur, 174 Wis. 2d at 741, 498 N.W.2d at 233-34 (quoting Restatement (Second) of Torts § 559 (1977)). "If the statements complained of are capable of a

nondefamatory meaning as well as a defamatory meaning, then a jury question is presented." Converters Equipment Corp. v. Condes Corp., 80 Wis. 2d 257, 262-63, 258 N.W.2d 712, 715 (1977). "[W]ords spoken of an individual or a corporation which charge dishonorable, unethical or unprofessional conduct in a trade, business or profession are capable of a defamatory meaning . . . . A statement is also defamatory if, in its natural and ordinary sense, it imputes to the person charged commission of a criminal act." Id. at 263, 258 N.W.2d at 715. In the employment context, the Wisconsin Supreme Court held it is defamatory to report that a corporate officer was "fired" from his position. Denny, 84 Wis. 2d 654, 267 N.W.2d 304. It is also defamatory to describe a business as "masquerading as a charitable enterprise," Fields Foundation, Ltd. v. Christensen, 103 Wis. 2d 465, 483, 309 N.W.2d 125, 134 (Ct. App. 1981); to state that the plaintiff reneged on paying the defendant, Milsap v. Journal/Sentinel, Inc., 100 F.3d 1265, 25 Media L. Rep. 1046 (7th Cir. 1996) (applying Wisconsin law); or that the plaintiff "assaulted" her ex-husband, Maguire v. Journal/Sentinel, Inc., 1995 WL 672534, *2 (Ct. App. 1995) (unpublished opinion). It is not defamatory, on the other hand, to report that a court entered a civil judgment against the plaintiff, Stern v. Credit Bureau of Milwaukee, 105 Wis. 2d 647, 315 N.W.2d 511 (Ct. App. 1981); to misstate a political candidate's voting record, Tatur, 174 Wis. 2d 735, 498 N.W.2d 232; or to accuse the plaintiff of being a "fast talker who generated excitement," Milsap v. Journal/Sentinel, Inc., 897 F. Supp. 406, 411 (E.D. Wis. 1995) (applying Wisconsin law). Wisconsin courts recognize claims for libel by implication. Mach v. Allison, 259 Wis. 2d 686, 698-99, 656 N.W.2d 766, 772 (Ct. App. 2002). "The court decides, as a matter of law, whether an alleged defamatory implication is fairly and reasonably conveyed by the words and pictures of the publication or broadcast. If the court decides it is not, the defendant is entitled to summary judgment. If the court decides the alleged defamatory implication is fairly and reasonably conveyed but there is also a nondefamatory implication, it is the jury's role to decide which the publication or broadcast implies." Id. at 712, 656 N.W.2d at 778.

5. ***Of and Concerning Plaintiff.*** "[A] victim of defamation need not be identified by name. Rather, it is sufficient if the defamatory statement refers to a person whose identity is ascertainable." Wildes v. Prime Manufacturing Corp., 160 Wis. 2d 443, 448, 465 N.W.2d 835, 838 (Ct. App. 1991); see De Witte v. Kearney & Trecker Corp., 265 Wis. 132, 60 N.W.2d 748 (1953). Furthermore, a member of a defamed group has a cause of action only if the group is sufficiently small that the statement may reasonably be understood as referring to that individual. See, e.g., Ogren v. Employers Reinsurance Corp., 119 Wis. 2d 379, 350 N.W.2d 725, 10 Media L. Rep. 2043 (Ct. App. 1984); see also Williams v. Journal Co., 211 Wis. 362, 247 N.W. 435 (1933) (holding that assistant city attorney on small staff had no claim arising out of an article concerning "a member" of the staff); but see De Witte, 265 Wis. 132, 60 N.W.2d 748 (holding an article critical of "the small group" of union officers defamatory of each individual officer).

6. ***Publication.*** To satisfy the publication element of a defamation claim in Wisconsin, the plaintiff must prove that the defendant communicated the allegedly defamatory statement by speech, conduct, or in writing to a person other than the person defamed. Torgerson, 210 Wis. 2d at 534, 563 N.W.2d at 477.

a. **Intracorporate Communication.** Wisconsin courts have not explicitly addressed the forms of intracorporate communication that can constitute publication. In Zinda v. Louisiana Pacific Corp., 149 Wis. 2d 913, 440 N.W.2d 548 (1989), the defendant published the allegedly defamatory statements in a company newsletter distributed to employees in the lunchroom. The company did not restrict employees from taking the newsletter home, and testimony indicated that it reached the plaintiff's wife at a local hospital where she worked. Id. at 919, 440 N.W.2d at 551. In Olson v. 3M Co., 188 Wis. 2d 25, 523 N.W.2d 578 (Ct. App. 1994), the employer issued a news release on allegations about two employees' sexual harassment. In both Zinda and Olson, the courts held the defendants did not, at least as a matter of law, abuse their conditional privilege by overpublication. See II.A.2, infra.

b. **Compelled Self-Publication.** No Wisconsin court has addressed the merits of a defamation by self-publication claim. In Wolf v. F&M Banks, 193 Wis. 2d 439, 534 N.W.2d 877 (Ct. App. 1995), F&M fired Wolf after another employee accused him of sexual harassment. Wolf claimed that he would be defamed by self-publication because he would be required to reveal his discharge to prospective employers. Id. at 449, 534 N.W.2d at 880. The Wisconsin Court of Appeals held that Wolf's claim was preempted by the Workers Compensation Act, § 102.03, Wis. Stat. Id at 455, 534 N.W.2d at 883. **The Workers Compensation Act does not preclude a defamation claim, however, when the plaintiff had resigned before the employer made the allegedly defamatory statement. Anderson v. Herbert, 2011 WI App 56, 332 Wis. 2d 432, 798 N.W.2d 275.**

c. **Republication.** In Wisconsin, all persons directly involved in the publication of a defamatory statement are theoretically liable for any defamation. Pfister v. Sentinel Co., 108 Wis. 572, 84 N.W. 887 (1901). "It is an elementary rule of defamation law that the author of a libelous statement is liable for any secondary publication which is the natural consequence of his or her act. Secondary publication by a newspaper, magazine, or periodical may expose such a publisher to liability as well, but it does not relieve the original author from liability for the secondary publication." Hucko v. Joseph Schlitz Brewing Co., 100 Wis. 2d 372, 377, 302 N.W.2d 68, 72 (Ct. App. 1981); Hart v. Bennet, 2003 WI App 231, 267 Wis. 2d 919, 672 N.W.2d 306. "[N]ewspapers that rely on the accuracy of a wire service release are not negligent as a matter of law," however. Van Straten, 151 Wis. 2d at 920, 447 N.W.2d at 112. In Torgerson, 210 Wis. 2d 524, 563 N.W.2d 472, the trial court held that a defamation plaintiff, to comply with the mandatory retraction demand statute, § 895.05(2), Wis. Stat., must give a retraction notice for all related publications before filing a claim based on any of the publications. Neither the Wisconsin Court of Appeals nor the Wisconsin Supreme Court addressed the issue, however. The printer of a defamatory publication is not liable for the publication unless it knew or had reason to know of the libel. Maynard v. Port Publications, Inc., 98 Wis. 2d 555, 297 N.W.2d 500, 6 Media L. Rep. 2239 (1980).

7. ***Statements versus Conduct.*** No cases in Wisconsin.

8. ***Damages.*** Slander is not actionable without proof of special damages except when the slander falls within one of the traditional per se categories — allegations of a criminal offense, a loathsome disease, or unchastity, and defamatory language affecting the plaintiff's business, trade, or profession. Starobin v. Northridge Lakes Development Co., 94 Wis. 2d 1, 13, 287 N.W.2d 747, 752 (1980). A libel plaintiff need not prove special damages but may recover general damages for injury to reputation and mental suffering caused by the defamatory statement. Badger Bearing Inc. v. Drives & Bearings, Inc., 111 Wis. 2d 659, 331 N.W.2d 847 (Ct. App. 1983).

a. **Presumed Damages and Libel Per Se.** Based on Gertz v. Robert Welch, Inc., 418 U.S. 323 (1974), the Wisconsin Supreme Court has held that a plaintiff may not recover presumed damages against a news media defendant absent proof of actual malice. Denny v. Mertz, 106 Wis. 2d 636, 659, 318 N.W.2d 141, 152, 4 Media L. Rep. 1153 (1982). No Wisconsin court has addressed presumed damages in light of Dun & Bradstreet, Inc. v. Greenmoss Builders, Inc., 472 U.S. 749 (1985).

(1) **Employment-Related Criticism.** In Zinda, 149 Wis. 2d at 933, 440 N.W.2d at 556, the Wisconsin Supreme Court held that the trial court should not have instructed the jury that in assessing damages it could consider the defendant's refusal to retract the statement at issue.

(2) **Single Instance Rule.** No cases in Wisconsin.

b. **Punitive Damages.** Pursuant to § 895.043, Wis. Stat., a plaintiff may only recover punitive damages if the defendant acted maliciously or intentionally disregarded the plaintiff's rights. "[T]he phrase 'intentional disregard of the rights of the plaintiff' in Wis. Stat. § 895.043(3) can only be reasonably interpreted to require either an intent by a defendant to cause injury to the plaintiffs or knowledge that the defendant's conduct was practically certain to cause the accident or injury to the plaintiffs." Wischer v. Mitsubishi Heavy Industries America, Inc., 2003 WI App 202 ¶ 5, 267 Wis. 2d 638, 647, 673 N.W.2d 303, 308. A libel plaintiff may not recover punitive damages against a defendant who timely publishes a correction. § 895.05 (2), Wis. Stat. To recover punitive damages from a news media defendant, a plaintiff must prove actual malice by clear and convincing evidence. Denny, 106 Wis. 2d at 659, 318 N.W.2d at 152.

In cases not involving First Amendment protections, plaintiffs may only recover punitive damages upon proof, by a mere preponderance of the evidence, of express malice — that is, ill-will, spite, or corrupt motive. Calero v. Del Chemical Corp. 68 Wis. 2d 487, 228 N.W.2d 737, 745 (1975); Gibson v. Overnite Transp. Co., 2003 WI App 210, 267 Wis. 2d 429, 439-40, 671 N.W.2d 388, 393-94 (upholding punitive damages of $250,000 and compensatory damages of $33,000 where the ex-employer supplied an expressly malicious employment reference). In deciding whether to award punitive damages, the court considers the grievousness of the defendant's conduct, the degree of malicious intention, the potential and actual damage to the plaintiff, and the defendant's ability to pay. Badger Bearing, 111 Wis. 2d 659, 331 N.W.2d 847. In Wisconsin, a plaintiff who receives no compensatory damages is entitled to no punitive damages. Tucker v. Marcus, 142 Wis. 2d 425, 438-39, 418 N.W.2d 818, 822-23 (1988).

II. PRIVILEGES AND DEFENSES

A. Scope of Privileges

1. ***Absolute Privilege.*** Wisconsin courts have recognized an absolute privilege against defamation liability for statements by participants in a judicial proceeding, Spoehr v. Mittelstadt, 34 Wis. 2d 653, 150 N.W.2d 502 (1967), statements made to a grand jury or to a district attorney, Bergman v. Hupy, 64 Wis. 2d 747, 221 N.W.2d 898 (1974), statements made by high-ranking executive government officials in carrying out their duties, Ranous v. Hughes, 30 Wis. 2d 452, 141 N.W.2d 251 (1966), and statements by participants in quasi-judicial proceedings, such as statements made to a real estate broker's board, Schier v. Denny, 12 Wis. 2d 544, 107 N.W.2d 611 (1961), and petitions to the governor for removal of a sheriff, Larkin v. Noonan, 19 Wis. 93 (1865). Statements of witnesses before a legislative body, however, are not absolutely privileged in Wisconsin. Vultaggio v. Yasko, 215 Wis. 2d 325, 342, 572 N.W.2d 450, 457 (1998). "[F]or the absolute privilege to attach the statement at issue must have been published on an occasion or in a context which is an integral part of the . . . proceeding involved," Converters Equipment Corp. v. Condes Corp., 80 Wis. 2d 257, 267, 258 N.W.2d 712,

717 (1977) (holding no absolute privilege attached to letters sent by plaintiff's attorneys to customers accusing defendants of infringing plaintiff's intellectual property rights), and the statements must "bear a proper relationship to the issues addressed" in the proceeding, Vultaggio, 215 Wis. 2d at 333, 572 N.W.2d at 453. Section 895.05(1), Wis. Stat., provides an absolute privilege for true and fair reports of judicial, legislative, or other public official proceedings. The privilege does not extend to headlines, id., and may not protect reports of judicial pleadings when no judicial action has been taken, Ilsley v. Sentinel Co., 133 Wis. 20, 113 N.W. 425 (1907).

2. ***Qualified Privileges.*** "Defamatory conduct otherwise actionable may escape liability because the defendant acts in furtherance of an interest of social importance — an interest that is entitled to protection even at the expense of uncompensated harm to the plaintiff." Olson v. 3M Co., 188 Wis. 2d 25, 36, 523 N.W.2d 578, 582 (Ct. App. 1994). "In the area of conditional privilege," Wisconsin courts "have endorsed the language of the Restatement of Torts." Zinda, 149 Wis. 2d at 922, 440 N.W.2d at 552. Wisconsin courts have found conditionally privileged statements to law enforcement officers, Bergman, 64 Wis. 2d 747, 221 N.W.2d 898; letters of recommendation from an ex-employer to a prospective employer, Calero, 68 Wis. 2d 487, 228 N.W.2d 737; statements by an educator to a prospective employer, Talens v. Bernhard, 669 F. Supp. 251 (E.D. Wis. 1987) (applying Wisconsin law); credit bureau reports, Stern v. Credit Bureau of Milwaukee, 105 Wis. 2d 647, 315 N.W.2d 511 (Ct. App. 1981); statements made by all but the most high-ranking public officials in carrying out their duties, Ranous, 30 Wis. 2d 452, 141 N.W.2d 251; statements made by witness at legislative proceedings, Vultaggio, 215 Wis. 2d 325, 572 N.W.2d 450; and communications between persons with a common interest, Olson, 188 Wis. 2d 25, 523 N.W.2d 578.

a. **Common Interest.** A conditional privilege applies to statements made on a subject matter in which the person making the statement and the person to whom it is made have a legitimate common interest. Zinda, 149 Wis. 2d at 922, 440 N.W.2d at 552 (applying conditional privilege to statements about former employee made by employer in company newsletter); see Olson, 523 N.W.2d 578, 188 Wis. 2d 25 (applying conditional privilege to news release by employer about workplace sexual harassment); Hett v. Ploetz, 20 Wis. 2d 55, 121 N.W.2d 270 (1963) (applying conditional privilege to letter of recommendation from former employer to prospective employer); Calero, 68 Wis. 2d 487, 228 N.W.2d 737; Wildes v. Prime Manufacturing Corp., 160 Wis. 2d 443, 465 N.W.2d 835 (Ct. App. 1991) (applying conditional privilege to statements made during meeting with other employees and during interview with prospective employee); Fischer v. Mt. Olive Lutheran Church, Inc., 207 F. Supp. 2d 914, 929-930 (W.D. Wis. 2002) (conditional privilege could apply to communications among members of religious organizations concerning the qualifications of the officers and members and their participation in the society's activities) Riley v. Schultz, 2007 WI App 216, ¶¶ 9-15, 305 Wis. 2d 656, 739 N.W.2d 492 (unpublished) (concluding employer's statements at meeting wherein employer labeled an ex-employee a criminal and terrorist was not an abuse of this common interest privilege under the standard established in Olson, 188 Wis. 2d at 38); see also § 895.487, Wis. Stat.; III.C, infra.

b. **Duty.** "[A] defamatory communication if made in good faith, upon a subject matter concerning which the person communicating has a duty or interest, is privileged, if made to one having a corresponding duty or interest." Otten v. Schutt, 15 Wis. 2d 497, 500, 113 N.W.2d 154 (1962).

c. **Criticism of Public Employee.** No cases in Wisconsin.

d. **Limitation on Qualified Privileges.**

(1) **Constitutional or Actual Malice.** The defendant's actual malice is an abuse of the qualified privilege. Zinda, 149 Wis. 2d at 924, 440 N.W.2d at 553.

(2) **Common Law Malice.** Common law malice is not one of the conditions constituting an abuse of a conditional privilege. See id.

(3) **Other Limitations on Qualified Privileges.** Qualified privileges are not absolute and may be forfeited if abused. Id. Wisconsin applies the five conditions on the privileges which may constitute abuse from the Restatement (Second) of Torts. Id. The privilege may be abused: (1) because of the defendant's knowledge or reckless disregard of the falsity of the statement; (2) because the defamatory matter is published for some purpose other than that for which the privilege is given; (3) because the publication is made to some person not reasonably believed to be necessary to accomplish the purpose of the particular privilege; (4) because the publication includes defamatory matter not reasonably believed to be necessary to accomplish the purpose of the privilege; or (5) because the publication includes unprivileged matter as well as privileged matter. Id.

e. **Question of Fact or Law.** Whether the defendant abused a conditional privilege is an issue of fact. Wildes, 160 Wis. 2d at 451, 465 N.W.2d at 839. Whether a party has met its burden of establishing a prima facie case of abuse, however, is a question of law. Id. at 452, 465 N.W.2d at 839.

f. **Burden of Proof.** The burden is on the defendant to prove privilege as a defense to an action for defamation. Otten, 15 Wis. 2d at 504, 113 N.W.2d at 156. Once the defendant has established a prima facie case of privilege, the burden shifts to the plaintiff to rebut this showing with a prima facie showing that the defendant abused the privilege. Id.

B. Standard Libel Defenses

1. ***Truth.*** See I.B.3, supra. "On the defense of truth, this dispute as to what actually occurred is not peripheral." DiMiceli v. Klieger, 58 Wis. 2d 359, 364, 206 N.W.2d 184, 187 (1973) (denying summary judgment because of conflict between statements in allegedly defamatory letter and plaintiff's affidavit). In John v. Journal Communications, Inc., 801 F. Supp. 210, 212-13, 20 Media L. Rep. 1833 (E.D. Wis. 1992), a federal district court, applying Wisconsin law, held that although the description of how the plaintiff violated the securities laws was inaccurate, because a violation did occur, the inaccuracy did not amount to falsity since the substance, gist, or sting of the accusation was true.

2. ***Opinion.*** No Wisconsin court has ruled on the pure opinion issue in a published decision since Gertz v. Robert Welch, Inc., 418 U.S. 323 (1974), and no court has set forth a test to distinguish opinion from facts. The U.S. Court of Appeals for the Seventh Circuit, applying Wisconsin law, explained that "a communication that blends an expression of opinion with an expression of fact is actionable in Wisconsin 'if it implies the assertion of undisclosed defamatory facts as a basis of the opinion.'" Milsap v. Journal/Sentinel, Inc., 100 F.3d 1265, 1268, 25 Media L. Rep. 1046 (7th Cir. 1996). In Milsap, the court held that the statement that the plaintiff "simply reneged on paying people" did not imply that the plaintiff failed to pay persons other than the author; it did imply the objective fact that the plaintiff reneged on paying the author and, to that extent, the statement was actionable. One judge from the Wisconsin Court of Appeals relied on Milkovich v. Lorain Journal Co., 497 U.S. 1 (1990), in a dissenting opinion, to argue that the statement that a college basketball player was a "disgrace" to the team and the university was actionable because, in context, it implied the player engaged in an improper relationship with an assistant coach and, therefore, could be proved false. Bauer v. Murphy, 191 Wis. 2d 517, 530 N.W.2d 1 (Ct. App. 1995) (Sundby, J., dissenting); see Wildes, 160 Wis. 2d at 449 n. 1, 465 N.W.2d at 838 n. 1 (citing Milkovich for observation that statement "damn you, that's bullshit" could, but need not be, construed as an assertion that the plaintiff was lying). In Dilworth v. Dudley, 75 F.3d 307, 309 (7th Cir. 1996) (applying Wisconsin law), the Seventh Circuit held that, based on Milkovich, referring to an academic as "a crank" is mere rhetorical hyperbole, "a well recognized category of, as it were, privileged defamation."

3. ***Consent.*** Publication of false and defamatory matter with the consent of the subject is absolutely privileged. Ranous v. Hughes, 30 Wis. 2d 452, 462, 141 N.W.2d 251, 256 (1966); see § 942.01, Wis. Stat. (criminal defamation).

4. ***Mitigation.*** Pursuant to § 895.05(2), Wis. Stat., if a defendant timely publishes a correction of allegedly defamatory statements published in a newspaper, magazine, or periodical (but not broadcast stations), the plaintiff may only recover actual damages and the retraction is "competent and material in mitigation of actual damages to the extent the correction published does so mitigate them." See Hucko v. Joseph Schlitz Brewing Co., 100 Wis. 2d 372, 379 n.5, 302 N.W.2d 68, 73 (Ct. App. 1981) ("Mitigation is facilitated where the speaker is promptly informed of the content of the allegedly defamatory articles, which statements are claimed to be false, and what is claimed to be the truth"). Before initiating a libel suit based on statements published in a newspaper, magazine or periodical, the potential plaintiff must give notice in writing to each defendant identifying the alleged defamatory statements. § 895.05 (2), Wis. Stat. This provision applies whether or not the potential defendant is a member of the news media. See Hucko, supra. Dismissal, with prejudice, is the remedy when a plaintiff commences a defamation action without first satisfying the statute's notice requirements. DeBraska v. Quad Graphics, Inc., 2009 WI App 23, ¶ 26, 316 Wis. 2d 386, 763 N.W.2d 219.

III. RECURRING FACT PATTERNS

A. Statements in Personnel File

No cases in Wisconsin.

B. Performance Evaluations

In 2008, the Wisconsin Supreme Court held that the statute granting civil immunity from damages for the medical "peer review" system, § 146.37, Wis. Stat., applies to a defamation claim. Rechsteiner v. Hazelden, 2008 WI 97, 313 Wis. 2d 542, 753 N.W.2d 496. The court applied the immunity provision to a doctor's defamation claim against the hospital for statements made by members of the hospital's board of directors and administration to the staff at the treatment facility where the doctor was being assessed and treated for alcoholism.

C. References

Pursuant to § 134.02, Wis. Stat., an employer may be fined for blacklisting or otherwise seeking to prevent any person from obtaining employment. "Nothing in this section shall prohibit any employer from giving any other employer, to whom a discharged employee has applied for employment . . . a truthful statement of the reasons for the employee's discharge, when requested to do so by . . . [t]he discharged employee [or] [t]he person to whom the discharged employee has applied for employment." § 134.02(2)(a), Wis. Stat. Furthermore, "[a]n employer who, on the request of an employee or a prospective employer of the employee, provides a reference to that prospective employer is presumed to be acting in good faith and, unless lack of good faith is shown by clear and convincing evidence, is immune from all civil liability that may result from providing that reference." § 895.487(2), Wis. Stat.

Section 895.487, Wis. Stat., codified the common law in Wisconsin. See Hett v. Ploetz, 20 Wis. 2d 55, 121 N.W.2d 270 (1963). See also Calero v. Del Chemical Corp., 68 Wis. 2d 487, 228 N.W.2d 737 (1975); Gibson v. Overnite Transp. Co., 267 Wis. 2d 429, 438, 671 N.W.2d 388, 393 (Ct. App. 2003). In Hett, a speech therapist in a public school system resigned when the superintendent of schools informed him that his contract would not be renewed. The speech therapist listed the superintendent as a reference on a job application and, in response to an inquiry about the application, the superintendent explained the circumstances underlying the speech therapist's resignation. Hett, 20 Wis. 2d at 57-58, 121 N.W.2d at 271. The Wisconsin Supreme Court held that the letter of recommendation was conditionally privileged and the superintendent did not abuse the privilege because the letter was reasonably calculated to accomplish the privileged purpose and was made without malice. Id. at 59-61, 121 N.W.2d at 271-72.

Interpreting § 895.487, Wis. Stat., for the first time, a Wisconsin court held that a reference made with actual malice, express malice, or a discriminatory or retaliatory purpose abuses the conditional privilege against liability for defamation. See Gibson v. Overnite Transp. Co., 2003 WI App 210, 267 Wis. 2d 429, 438-39, 671 N.W.2d 388, 393-94. In Gibson, the jury found that the defendant had acted with express malice when one of its employees gave a severely negative, baseless employment reference. 267 Wis. 2d at 439, 671 N.W.2d at 393-94. Accordingly, the Wisconsin Court of Appeals upheld the jury's finding of defamation and affirmed the award of compensatory and punitive damages.

D. Intracorporate Communication

See § I.B.6.a, supra. In Zinda v. Louisiana Pacific Corp., 149 Wis. 2d 913, 440 N.W.2d 548 (1989), the plaintiff indicated on the "personal health history" portion of an employment application that he had no back trouble. He later filed a products liability action against his employer seeking compensation for back and other injuries resulting from a fall from his roof that occurred before he completed the employment application. Id. at 917-18, 440 N.W.2d at 550. The employer fired the plaintiff and distributed a newsletter to employees that indicated he was terminated for falsifying his employment application. Id. The Wisconsin Supreme Court held that "the company newsletter was conditionally privileged as a communication of common interest concerning the employer-employee relationship." Id. at 921, 440 N.W.2d at 552. Whether the employer abused the privilege by excessively publishing the newsletter, the Court determined, was a question of fact for the jury. Id.

In Olson v. 3M Co., 188 Wis. 2d 25, 523 N.W.2d 578 (Ct. App. 1994), the employer terminated two employees after a co-employee accused them of sexual harassment. The company then issued a news release concerning the investigation of the charges and termination of the two employees. Id. at 34, 523 N.W.2d at 581. The Wisconsin Court of Appeals held that the employer had a conditional privilege to issue the news release and it did not abuse that privilege. Id. at 36-46, 523 N.W.2d at 582-586 ("We conclude that 3M had an interest in common with its employees in maintaining a work environment free of harassment, including sexual harassment . . . . 3M had an important interest in letting the community know that it took seriously its obligation to provide a harassment-free work place . . . . No facts on this record, and no reasonable inferences from those facts, show 3M abused its conditional privilege . . . ."); see Wildes, 160 Wis. 2d 443, 465 N.W.2d 835 (holding privileged statements made at a meeting of co-employees and statements made to a candidate for employment).

E. Statements to Government Regulators

No cases in Wisconsin.

F. Reports to Auditors and Insurers

No cases in Wisconsin.

G. Vicarious Liability of Employers for Statements Made by Employees

1. ***Scope of Employment.*** In Wisconsin, "employers can be held vicariously liable for the negligent acts of their employees while they are acting within the scope of their employment. The touchstone of scope-of-employment

issues . . . is employer control over the employee." DeRuyter v. Wisconsin Electric Power Co., 200 Wis. 2d 349, 360, 546 N.W.2d 534, 539-40 (Ct. App. 1996). Courts also must examine the employee's intent when reviewing the scope-of-employment issue. "[A]n employee may be found to have acted within the scope of his or her employment as long as the employee was at least partially actuated by a purpose to serve the employer. There is no requirement that serving the employer must be the employee's only purpose or even the employee's primary purpose." Olson v. Connerly, 156 Wis. 2d 488, 499, 457 N.W.2d 479, 483 (1990). There are no Wisconsin cases regarding employers' vicarious liability for statements by employees.

a. **Blogging.** No cases in Wisconsin.

2. ***Damages.*** No cases in Wisconsin.

H. Internal Investigations

No cases in Wisconsin.

IV. OTHER ACTIONS BASED ON STATEMENTS

A. Negligent Hiring, Retention, and Supervision

Until 1998, no Wisconsin court had explicitly recognized a claim for negligent hiring, retention, or supervision. See, e.g., L.L.N. v. Clauder, 209 Wis. 2d 674, 685, 563 N.W.2d 434, 439 (1997) ("This court has not determined whether a claim for negligent supervision exists . . . . However, for purposes of this case, we assume that such a claim exists, without deciding the issue"). In Miller v. Wal-Mart Stores, Inc., 219 Wis. 2d 250, 257, 580 N.W.2d 233, 237 (Wis. 1998), the Wisconsin Supreme Court finally held "that negligent hiring, training or supervision is a valid claim in Wisconsin." To state a claim for these torts, the plaintiff must allege that the employer had a duty of care, that the employer breached that duty, that the act or omission of the employee was a cause-in-fact of the plaintiff's injury, and that the act or the omission of the employer was a cause-in-fact of the wrongful act of the employee. Id. at 267-68, 580 N.W.2d at 241. The employee's wrongful act need not be a tort. Id. at 263, 580 N.W.2d at 239. A plaintiff may recover punitive damages for negligent hiring, training, or supervision. Id. at 270, 580 N.W.2d at 273. There are no Wisconsin cases indicating whether a plaintiff may circumvent the requirements of defamation law using a claim for negligent hiring, retention, or supervision.

A plaintiff cannot bring a claim of negligent hiring, training, or supervision against an employer, however, unless there is wrongful conduct by its employee. John Doe 1 v. Archdiocese of Milwaukee, 2007 WI 95, ¶¶ 29-32, 303 Wis. 2d 34, 734 N.W.2d 827. Negligent supervision is not a matter of vicarious liability, and it does not fall within the principles of agency law; an employer's liability arises out of the negligence of the *employer's* actions or inactions, not the employer-employee relationship. Id., ¶¶ 32-33. In addition, an employer cannot be liable if the employee was not acting within the scope of his or her employment at the time of the offending activity, Manning v. Necedah Area School District, 2007 WI App 230, 306 Wis.2d 124,, 740 N.W.2d 901 (unpublished), and governmental employers cannot be liable for negligent supervision, training or investigation unless the situation triggered the employer's "ministerial duty" or "known and present danger" exceptions to governmental immunity. Id., ¶ 17. An affirmative act of negligence is required for a contract employer's liability for its contract employee. Danks v. Stock Building Supply, Inc., 2006 WI App 8, ¶¶ 27, 35, 298 Wis. 2d 348, 727 N.W.2d 846. Importantly, a contractor's failure to train its employees, by itself, cannot constitute an affirmative act of negligence. Id.

B. Intentional Infliction of Emotional Distress

Wisconsin has recognized the tort of intentional infliction of emotional distress at least since 1963. Alsteen v. Gehl, 21 Wis. 2d 349, 124 N.W.2d 312 (1963). A plaintiff must establish the four basic factors of intentional infliction of emotional distress recognized in most other jurisdictions — intentional or reckless conduct, extreme and outrageous conduct, severe emotional distress, and causation. To establish the first element, the plaintiff must show that "the defendant behaved as he did for the purpose of causing emotional distress for the plaintiff." Id. at 359, 124 N.W.2d at 318. For the defendant's conduct to be extreme and outrageous, "[t]he average member of the community must regard the defendant's conduct in relation to the plaintiff as being a complete denial of the plaintiff's dignity as a person . . . ." Id. at 350-60, 124 N.W.2d at 318. Severe emotional distress is "an extreme disabling emotional response to the defendant's conduct . . . . The plaintiff must demonstrate that he was unable to function in his other relationships because of the emotional distress caused by defendant's conduct. Temporary discomfort cannot be the basis of recovery." Id. at 360-61, 124 N.W.2d at 318. Finally, "the plaintiff must demonstrate that the defendant's conduct was a cause-in-fact of his injury . . . ." Id. at 360, 124 N.W.2d at 318.

Plaintiffs may recover punitive damages based on intentional infliction of emotional distress. Gianoli v. Pfleiderer, 209 Wis. 2d 509, 563 N.W.2d 562 (Ct. App. 1997). Workers compensation is the exclusive remedy for a claim of intentional infliction of emotional distress in connection with a claim for wrongful discharge. See Jenson v. Employers Mut. Cas. Co.,

161 Wis. 2d 253, 468 N.W.2d 1 (1991); Torres v. Roundy's Supermarkets, Inc., 2009 WL 129595, 316 Wis. 2d 413, 763 N.W.2d 560 (Ct. App. 2009) (unpublished) (claims for defamation and intentional infliction of emotional distress barred by Wisconsin Workers' Compensation Act); see also Farady-Sultze v. Aurora Medical Center, 2010 WI App 99, 327 Wis. 2d 110, 787 N.W.2d 433. There are no Wisconsin cases indicating whether a plaintiff may circumvent the requirements of defamation law using a claim for intentional infliction of emotional distress.

C. Interference with Economic Advantage

No Wisconsin court has recognized the claim of interference with prospective economic advantage. The Wisconsin Court of Appeals, in Cudd v. Crownhart, 122 Wis. 2d 656, 364 N.W.2d 158 (Ct. App. 1995), first recognized a claim for interference with prospective contractual relations based on the Restatement (Second) of Torts, § 766B. "Sec. 766B provides that one who intentionally and improperly interferes with another's prospective contractual relation is subject to liability to the other for his pecuniary harm resulting from the loss of the benefits of the relation when the interference consists of (a) inducing or otherwise causing a third person not to enter into or continue the prospective relation or (b) preventing the other from acquiring or continuing the prospective relation." Id. at 659-60, 364 N.W.2d at 160. To be actionable, the interference must be both intentional and improper. "[T]o have the requisite intent, the defendant must act with a purpose to interfere with the contract. If the actor does not have this purpose, his conduct does not subject him to liability even if it has the unintended effect of deterring the third person from dealing with the other." Id. at 660, 364 N.W.2d at 160. Courts balance a series of factors to determine whether an alleged interference is improper.

Providing truthful information to a third party can never constitute interference with a prospective contractual relation. Liebe v. City Finance Co., 98 Wis. 2d 10, 13, 295 N.W.2d 16, 17 (Ct. App. 1980). In Magnum Radio, Inc. v. Brieske, 217 Wis. 2d 130, 577 N.W.2d 377 (Ct. App. 1998), the defendant claimed First Amendment protection against an interference with prospective contract claim for statements he made in a letter to the FCC contesting the sale of two radio stations. The Wisconsin Court of Appeals did not address the merits of the defendant's privilege argument but remanded it to the trial court because there were material factual issues in dispute. Id. at *5.

The statute of limitations for interference with contract in Wisconsin is six years. Segall v. Hurwitz, 114 Wis. 2d 471, 339 N.W.2d 333 (Ct. App. 1983). An interference with contract claim is not preempted by Wisconsin's Workers Compensation Act. Wolf v. F&M Banks, 193 Wis. 2d 439, 534 N.W.2d 877 (Ct. App. 1995). There are no Wisconsin cases indicating whether a plaintiff may circumvent the requirements of defamation law using a claim for interference with economic advantage.

D. Prima Facie Tort

No cases in Wisconsin.

V. PROCEDURAL ISSUES

A. Statute of Limitations

In Wisconsin, the statute of limitations for both libel and slander is three years. § 893.57, Wis. Stat. Wisconsin applies its borrowing statute, § 893.07, Wis. Stat., when there are conflicting statutes of limitation that could apply to a claim in a Wisconsin court. Under the borrowing statute, Wisconsin applies the shortest potentially applicable limitation period when the claim involves a "foreign cause of action." And a claim involves a "foreign cause of action" when the plaintiff has alleged injury suffered outside Wisconsin. Guertin v. Harbour Assurance Co. of Bermuda, Ltd., 141 Wis. 2d 622, 632, 415 N.W.2d 831, 835 (1987). In Faigin v. Doubleday Dell Publishing Group, Inc., 98 F.3d 268, 24 Media L. Rep. 2590 (7th Cir. 1996), the Seventh Circuit, applying the Wisconsin borrowing statute, held that a libel action involving publication inside Wisconsin and elsewhere is not a foreign cause of action even when just a small fraction of a book's distribution occurred in Wisconsin.

For purposes of determining the limitations period, a claim against an employer for negligent supervision of an employee begins to accrue at the time the employer knew or should have reasonably known that the employee engaged in the offending behavior. John Doe, 2007 WI 95, ¶¶ 2, 10, 36.

B. Jurisdiction

No Wisconsin state court has addressed personal jurisdiction in a defamation case.

C. Pleading Requirements

"In an action for libel or slander, the particular words complained of shall be set forth in the complaint, but their publication and their application to the plaintiff may be stated generally." § 802.03(6), Wis. Stat.

In Lassa v. Rongstad, 2006 WI 105, ¶¶ 42-52, 249 Wis. 2d 187, 718 N.W.2d 673, the Wisconsin Supreme Court held that courts should decide a motion to dismiss for failure to state a claim before ordering disclosure of information identifying an anonymous speaker. According to the court, "[w]hen faced with an assertion of constitutional privilege against disclosure of information identifying otherwise-anonymous organization members, the circuit court should decide a pending motion to dismiss for failure to state a claim before sanctioning the party for refusing to disclose that information." Id., ¶ 52.

In 2009, the Wisconsin Court of Appeals reversed the lower court's decision and remanded with instructions to dismiss the plaintiff's complaint with prejudice for failing to satisfy the conditions precedent to bringing an action under the retraction demand statute, § 895.05(2), Wis. Stat. See DeBraska v. Quad Graphics, Inc., 2009 WI App 23, 316 Wis. 2d 386, 763 N.W.2d 219. DeBraska's pre-suit notice failed to include a statement of what he claimed to be true facts. Id. at ¶ 22. Furthermore, the Court held DeBraska could not revive his claim. Id. at ¶ 26.

SURVEY OF WISCONSIN EMPLOYMENT PRIVACY LAW

Brady C. Williamson
Robert J. Dreps
James A. Friedman
Sherry D. Coley
Godfrey & Kahn, S.C.
One East Main Street, Suite 500
Madison, Wisconsin 53703
Telephone: (608) 257-3911; Facsimile: (608) 257-0609

(With Developments Reported Through **November 1, 2012**)

GENERAL COMMENTS

Wisconsin has both an intermediate court of appeals and a Supreme Court. The court of appeals is divided into four geographic districts, but it acts as one court for purposes of precedent. Litigants have a right to appeal final judgments or orders only to the court of appeals. The Wisconsin Supreme Court has seven justices - Chief Justice Shirley S. Abrahamson and Justices Ann Walsh Bradley, N. Patrick Crooks, Michael J. Gableman, David T. Prosser, Jr., Patience D. Roggensack, and Annette K. Ziegler. The Court has complete discretion to decide the cases it will hear each term.

The Wisconsin Supreme Court publishes all of its decisions, but the court of appeals publishes only a small percentage of its decisions. Only published opinions have precedential value. As of July 1, 2009, however, authored court of appeals opinions may be cited for persuasive value. §§ 752.41 and 809.23, Wis. Stats. The first citation to a Wisconsin appellate opinion must include a reference to the volume and page number of both the Wisconsin Reports and the Northwestern Reporter in which the opinion is published. Subsequent citations must include references to the volume and page number of at least one of these publications. Supreme Court Rule 80.02.

All Wisconsin appellate opinions issued on or after January 1, 2000 include a public domain citation. The first citation to these opinions also must include a reference to the public domain citation. Subsequent citations may refer to either of the publications or to the public domain citation. Id.

SIGNIFICANT DEVELOPMENTS SINCE THE 2012 *SURVEY*

There have been no significant developments in Wisconsin employment privacy law since the 2012 survey.

I. GENERAL LAW OF PRIVACY

A. Legal Basis of Privacy Claims

Wisconsin recognizes by statute three of the four traditional branches of the privacy tort. § 995.50, Wis. Stat. Wisconsin's right of privacy statute protects against publication of private facts, physical intrusion, and commercial misappropriation. Neither the Wisconsin legislature nor the courts have adopted the tort of false light. The Wisconsin Supreme Court did not acknowledge invasion of privacy as an actionable tort at common law. See Yoeckel v. Samonig, 272 Wis. 430, 75 N.W.2d 925 (1956); but see Hirsch v. S.C. Johnson & Son, Inc., 90 Wis. 2d 379, 397, 280 N.W.2d 129 (1979) (recognizing, in an action predating the privacy statute, a claim for commercial misappropriation separate and distinct from invasion of privacy). The Wisconsin legislature enacted its privacy statute, § 995.50, Wis. Stat., in 1977. The statute of limitation for invasion of privacy is three years. § 893.57, Wis. Stat. Section 995.01(1), Wis. Stat., provides that claims for invasion of privacy survive death.

B. Causes of Action

1. ***Misappropriation/Right of Publicity.*** In Hirsch, 90 Wis. 2d 379, 280 N.W.2d 129, the state's most celebrated privacy case, the Wisconsin Supreme Court recognized the tort of commercial misappropriation at common law. Although the Wisconsin legislature already had codified this tort, the events at issue in Hirsch preceded the passage of the law and, thus, necessitated the application of the state's common law. In determining that Wisconsin common law encompassed the right of publicity, the Wisconsin Supreme Court repeatedly distinguished the three other privacy torts, asserting that the other torts protect primarily the mental interest in being let alone, while misappropriation protects primarily the property interest in the publicity value of one's name. Id. at 387, 280 N.W.2d at 132. While Wisconsin courts had explicitly rejected the other three privacy torts at common law, the cases did not eliminate the tort of misappropriation.

The Wisconsin legislature also included this tort in its general privacy law. See § 995.50(2)(b), Wis. Stat. The statute forbids "[t]he use, for advertising purposes or for purposes of trade, of the name, portrait or picture of any living person, without first having obtained the written consent of the person . . . ." The fact that the name appropriated is a nickname, rather than the plaintiff's formal name, does not preclude a claim as long as the misappropriated name clearly identifies the wronged person. Hirsch, 90 Wis. 2d at 397, 280 N.W.2d at 137.

The Hirsch court required the former football star plaintiff, upon retrial, to prove that the appropriated nickname, "Crazylegs," identified him and to show as well that he had suffered damages based either on his loss or on the defendant's unjust enrichment. Id. at 403, 280 N.W.2d at 140. Section 995.50(2)(b), Wis. Stat., only recognizes a right of publicity for living persons. Hagen v. Dahmer, 1995 WL 822644, *4, 24 Media L. Rep. 1311, 1314 (E.D. Wis. 1995) (unpublished decision).

2. ***False Light.*** Wisconsin does not recognize this tort. Zinda v. Louisiana Pacific Corp., 149 Wis. 2d 913, 929, 440 N.W.2d 548, 555 (1989). While Wisconsin's privacy statute includes the other three traditional privacy torts, false light is conspicuously absent. See § 995.50, Wis. Stat.; see also Jacqueline Hanson Dee, Comment, The Absence of False Light from the Wisconsin Privacy Statute, 66 Marq. L. Rev. 99 (1982) (explaining that the false light tort, while initially included in the proposed privacy legislation, was specifically deleted by amendment).

3. ***Publication of Private Facts.*** Wisconsin recognizes this tort by statute. See § 995.50(2)(c), Wis. Stat. The statute forbids publicity concerning the private life of another that a reasonable person would find "highly offensive," if the defendant has acted "either unreasonably or recklessly as to whether there was a legitimate public interest in the matter involved, or with actual knowledge that none existed." The Wisconsin statute reflects § 652D of the Restatement (Second) of Torts (1977). A plaintiff must prove four elements to establish a claim for publication of private facts: (1) a public disclosure of facts regarding the plaintiff; (2) the facts disclosed must be private facts; (3) the private matter made public must be one that would be highly offensive to a person of ordinary sensibilities; and, (4) the defendant must either act unreasonably or recklessly as to whether there was a legitimate public interest in the matter or with actual knowledge that none existed. Zinda, 149 Wis. 2d at 929-30, 440 N.W.2d at 555; see Pachowitz v. Ledoux, 2003 WI App 120, 265 Wis. 2d 631, 648-50, 666 N.W.2d 88, 96-97 (holding that disclosure of private information to a single person can constitute a public disclosure); Olson v. Red Cedar Clinic, 2004 WI App 102, 273 Wis. 2d 728, 681 N.W.2d 306 (finding "public disclosure" to mean communicating the matter to the public at large, or to so many persons that the matter may be regarded as substantially certain to become one of public knowledge, or where there is a "special relationship" between the plaintiff and the "public" to whom the information has been disclosed); Hillman v. Columbia County, 164 Wis. 2d 376, 393, 474 N.W.2d 913, 919-20 (Ct. App. 1991); Helland v. Kurtis A. Froedtert Memorial Lutheran Hospital, 229 Wis. 2d 751, 601 N.W.2d 318 (Ct. App. 1999). See also Marino v. Arandell Corp., 1 F. Supp. 2d 947 (E.D. Wis. 1998).

Where there is no injury to the plaintiff's reputation from the disclosure of private facts, the plaintiff has no claim under Wisconsin privacy law. See Albertson v. Tak Communications, Inc., 1989 WL 129270 (Wis. Ct. App. 1989) (unpublished decision). Pursuant to the statute, "[i]t is not an invasion of privacy to communicate any information available to the public as a matter of public record." § 995.50(2)(c), Wis. Stat.; see Newspapers, Inc. v. Breier, 89 Wis. 2d 417, 432, 279 N.W.2d 179, 186, 5 Media L. Rep. 1524 (1979) (explaining in dicta that an individual could not bring a claim for invasion of privacy under Wisconsin law on the basis of a news report concerning his arrest). The finding of a public controversy for purposes of the limited purpose public figure test in defamation also satisfies the definition of "legitimate public interest" in an invasion of privacy suit. Van Straten v. Milwaukee Journal Newspaper-Publisher, 151 Wis. 2d 905, 921, 447 N.W.2d 105, 112 (Ct. App. 1989).

The statute expressly states that "[i]t is not an invasion of privacy to communicate any information available to the public as a matter of public record." § 995.50(2)(c). Accordingly, the Seventh Circuit held it was not an invasion of privacy for the Milwaukee County Sheriff to disclose a deputy's disciplinary history on a radio call-in program, in response to the deputy's criticism of the sheriff on the same program. Hutchins v. Clarke, 661 F.3d 947, 952 (7th Cir. 2011).

4. ***Intrusion.*** Wisconsin included physical intrusion in its general privacy statute. See § 995.50(2)(a), Wis. Stat. The statute makes actionable intrusions of "a nature highly offensive to a reasonable person, in a place that a reasonable person would consider private or in a manner which is actionable for trespass." Id.; see Munson v. Milwaukee Board of School Directors, 969 F.2d 266, 271 (7th Cir. 1992) (applying Wisconsin law). In Hillman, 164 Wis. 2d at 391, 474 N.W.2d at 919, the Wisconsin Court of Appeals addressed an inmate's claim that jail employees violated the statute by reviewing the inmate's confidential medical records. The court held that the plaintiff had not stated a claim for intrusion because a file of medical records does not constitute a "place" under the statute. Id.; but see Fischer v. Mt. Olive Lutheran Church, 207 F.Supp.2d 914 (W.D. Wis. 2002) (stating that the term "place" as used in § 995.50(2)(a) is not limited to physical environment, but may also include a person's private belongings, such as a youth minister's off-site email account).

In a case before the passage of Wisconsin's privacy statute, the Wisconsin Court of Appeals found television reporters potentially liable for common law trespass when they entered private property, without permission, to film a police investigation of the premises and interview the owner. Prahl v. Brosamle, 98 Wis. 2d 130, 295 N.W.2d 768 (Ct. App. 1980). Placing a school principal under surveillance, on the other hand, did not constitute intrusion according to the U.S. Court of Appeals for the Seventh Circuit. Munson, 969 F.2d at 271. Based on suspicions that the principal did not reside in Milwaukee County, in violation of the school board's residency requirement, the board sent school safety aides to the principal's suspected residence. The safety aides who conducted the surveillance never trespassed on private property and operated only from areas designated as public streets or highways. Id. The district court dismissed the intrusion claim and awarded the defendant costs and attorney fees because the claim was frivolous, and the court of appeals affirmed. Id. The same court, applying either Wisconsin or Indiana law, held that ABC Television was not liable for trespass for using hidden cameras to videotape consultations between individuals posing as patients and the treating physicians at the plaintiff's eye clinics. Desnick v. ABC, 44 F.3d 1345, 23 Media L. Rep. 1161 (7th Cir. 1995). There was no trespass, the court stated, because the clinics are places of business open to the public and "the entry was not invasive in the sense of infringing the kind of interest of the plaintiffs that the law of trespass protects . . . ." Id. at 1352-53.

C. Other Privacy-Related Actions

1. ***Intentional Infliction of Emotional Distress.*** Wisconsin has recognized the tort of intentional infliction of emotional distress at least since 1963. Alsteen v. Gehl, 21 Wis. 2d 349, 124 N.W.2d 312 (1963). A plaintiff must establish the four basic factors of intentional infliction of emotional distress recognized in most other jurisdictions — intentional or reckless conduct, extreme and outrageous conduct, severe emotional distress, and causation. To establish the first element, the plaintiff must show that "the defendant behaved as he did for the purpose of causing emotional distress for the plaintiff." Id. at 359, 124 N.W.2d at 318. For the defendant's conduct to be extreme and outrageous, "[t]he average member of the community must regard the defendant's conduct in relation to the plaintiff, as being a complete denial of the plaintiff's dignity as a person . . . ." Id. at 359-60, 124 N.W.2d at 318. Severe emotional distress is "an extreme disabling emotional response to the defendant's conduct . . . . The plaintiff must demonstrate that he was unable to function in his other relationships because of the emotional distress caused by defendant's conduct. Temporary discomfort cannot be the basis of recovery." Id. at 360-61, 124 N.W.2d at 318. Finally, "[t]he plaintiff must demonstrate that the defendant's conduct was a cause-in-fact of his injury . . . ." Id. at 360, 124 N.W.2d at 318.

Wrongful discharge cannot be the basis of a separate claim for intentional infliction of emotional distress. Helland v. Kurtis A. Froedtert Memorial Lutheran Hospital, 229 Wis. 2d 751, 601 N.W.2d 318 (Ct. App. 1999).

Plaintiffs may recover punitive damages based on intentional infliction of emotional distress. Gianoli v. Pfleiderer, 209 Wis. 2d 509, 563 N.W.2d 562 (Ct. App. 1997). There are no Wisconsin cases concerning privileges or defenses to the claim.

The exclusivity provision of the Wisconsin Worker's Compensation Act, § 102.03, Wis. Stat., bars claims for intentional infliction of emotional distress in the workplace. Farady-Sultze v. Aurora Medical Center of Oshkosh, 2010 WI App 99, 327 Wis. 2d 110, 787 N.W.2d 433.

2. ***Interference With Prospective Economic Advantage.*** The Wisconsin Court of Appeals, in Cudd v. Crownhart, 122 Wis. 2d 656, 364 N.W.2d 158 (Ct. App. 1985), first recognized a claim for interference with prospective contractual relations based on the Restatement (Second) of Torts, § 766B. "Sec. 766B provides that one who intentionally and improperly interferes with another's prospective contractual relation is subject to liability to the other for his pecuniary harm resulting from the loss of the benefits of the relation when the interference consists of (a) inducing or otherwise causing a third person not to enter into or continue the prospective relation or (b) preventing the other from acquiring or continuing the prospective relation." Id. at 659-60, 364 N.W.2d at 160. To be actionable, the interference must be both intentional and improper. "[T]o have the requisite intent, the defendant must act with a purpose to interfere with the contract. If the actor does not have this purpose, his conduct does not subject him to liability even if it has the unintended effect of deterring the third person from dealing with the other." Id. at 660, 364 N.W.2d at 160. Courts balance a series of factors to determine whether an alleged interference is improper. In addition, an employer's actions do not constitute interference with a former employee's prospective contract of employment if the employer fails to perform an act that it has no duty to perform. Schindler v. Marshfield Clinic, No. 05-C-705, 2006 WL 1236720 (W.D. Wis. May 2, 2006) (vacated in part, Schindler v. Marshfield Clinic, No. 05-C-705, 2006 WL 1589647 (W.D. Wis. June 2, 2006) (employer did not tortiously interfere with a former employee's prospective employment by failing to verify the dates during which he was affiliated with the employer)).

Providing truthful information to a third party can never constitute interference with a prospective contractual relation. Liebe v. City Finance Co., 98 Wis. 2d 10, 13, 295 N.W.2d 16, 18 (Ct. App. 1980). In Magnum Radio, Inc. v. Brieske, 217 Wis. 2d 130, 142, 577 N.W.2d 377 (Ct. App. 1998), the defendant claimed First Amendment protection for statements he made in a letter to the FCC contesting the sale of two radio stations. The Wisconsin Court of Appeals did not address the merits of the defendant's privilege arguments, but remanded the case to the trial court because there were material factual issues in dispute. Id. at *5.

The statute of limitations for interference with contract in Wisconsin is six years. Segall v. Hurwitz, 114 Wis. 2d 471, 339 N.W.2d 333 (Ct. App. 1983). An interference with contract claim is not preempted by Wisconsin's Workers Compensation Act. Wolf v. F&M Banks, 193 Wis. 2d 439, 534 N.W.2d 877 (Ct. App. 1995).

3. ***Prima Facie Tort.*** No cases in Wisconsin

II. EMPLOYER TESTING OF EMPLOYEES

A. Psychological or Personality Testing

1. ***Common Law and Statutes.*** Wisconsin law does not explicitly address whether employers may use psychological or personality tests. In Pluskota v. Roadrunner Freight Systems, Inc., 188 Wis. 2d 288, 297, 524 N.W.2d 904, 908 (Ct. App. 1994), the court held that a pen and paper honesty test, which does not measure physiological responses to questions, does not violate the restrictions in § 111.37(2), Wis. Stat., regarding honesty testing devices and, hence, Wisconsin employers may require employees to take these tests. The Wisconsin Fair Employment Act, like the Americans With Disabilities Act, prohibits employment discrimination based on a disability, including mental impairment. See §§ 111.31-111.395, Wis. Stats. Therefore, an employer may not use the results of psychological testing in the hiring process if it may have a disparate impact on applicants with disabilities unless "the disability is reasonably related to the individual's ability to adequately undertake the job-related responsibilities . . . ." See § 111.34(2)(a), Wis. Stat.

2. ***Private Employers.*** No cases in Wisconsin.

3. ***Public Employers.*** No cases in Wisconsin.

B. Drug Testing

1. ***Common Law and Statutes.*** Wisconsin has no law that expressly regulates drug or alcohol testing in the workplace. Recently, in a case specifically addressing whether an employer violated the Wisconsin Fair Employment Act when it fired an employee based on her arrest and conviction record, the Wisconsin Court of Appeals stated in dicta that "there is nothing in this opinion, which suggests that an employer may not take appropriate action against an employee who is discovered to have violated an employer's policies regarding drug use during the term of his or her employment." Wal-Mart Stores, Inc. v. Labor and Industry Review Commission, 1998 WL 286332 (Wis. Ct. App. June 4, 1998) (unpublished decision). Wisconsin courts consider alcoholism a disability, as that term is defined in § 111.32(8), Wis. Stat., and drug addiction may also constitute a disability. See Connecticut General Life Insurance Co. v. Department of Industry, Labor & Human Relations, 86 Wis. 2d 393, 273 N.W.2d 206 (1979); see also Squires v. Labor and Industry Review Commission, 97 Wis. 2d 648, 294 N.W.2d 48 (Ct. App. 1980). Wisconsin employers may, as a result, be subject to disability discrimination claims if they improperly use drug tests.

2. ***Private Employers.*** No cases in Wisconsin.

3. ***Public Employers.*** No cases in Wisconsin.

C. Medical Testing

1. ***Common Law and Statutes.*** While the Americans with Disabilities Act expressly states that drug testing is not medical testing, there is no express exception under the Wisconsin Fair Employment Act. Nothing in Wisconsin law generally prohibits medical testing of prospective and current employees. An employer may not, however, require an applicant or employee "to pay the cost of a medical examination required by the employer as a condition of employment." § 103.37(1), Wis. Stat. Furthermore, employers may not require an HIV test nor a genetic test as a condition of employment. §§ 103.15 and 111.372, Wis. Stats., respectively. In fact, it is a crime to require or administer a genetic test without the prior written and informed consent of the employee or to disclose to an employer that an employee took a genetic test and the results of that test. § 942.07(2)(3), Wis. Stat.

2. ***Private Employers.*** No cases in Wisconsin.

3. ***Public Employers.*** No cases in Wisconsin.

D. Polygraph Tests

Pursuant to § 111.37(2)(a), Wis. Stat., no employer may "[d]irectly or indirectly require, request, suggest or cause an employee or prospective employee to take or submit to a lie detector test." Section 942.06, Wis. Stat., requires written and informed consent to both administer and disclose the results of the test. Furthermore, employers may not use the results of lie detector tests, or an employee's refusal to take one, as a condition of employment. § 111.37(2)(b)-(d), Wis. Stats. The statute defines "lie detector" as "a polygraph, deceptograph, voice stress analyzer, psychological stress evaluator or other similar device, whether mechanical or electrical, that is used, or the results of which are used, to render a diagnostic opinion about the honesty or dishonesty of an individual." § 111.37(1)(b), Wis. Stat. A paper and pencil test designed to measure a person's honesty, however, does not violate the statute "because it [does] not measure physiological responses of the subject during the test . . . ." Pluskota, 188 Wis. 2d at 297, 524 N.W.2d at 908.

E. Fingerprinting

No cases in Wisconsin.

III. SEARCHES

There is no Wisconsin law specifically addressing workplace searches. Article I, § 11 of the Wisconsin Constitution provides that "[t]he right of the people to be secure in their persons, houses, papers, and effects against unreasonable searches and seizures shall not be violated . . . ." And § 968.10, Wis. Stat., lists those instances when searches are appropriate: (1) incident to a lawful arrest; (2) with consent; (3) pursuant to a valid search warrant; (4) with the authority and within the scope of a right of lawful inspection; (5) pursuant to a search during an authorized temporary questioning; and (6) as otherwise authorized by law. The privacy statute, § 995.50(2)(a), Wis. Stat., makes actionable certain intrusions.

A. Employee's Person

1. ***Private Employers.*** No cases in Wisconsin.

2. ***Public Employers.*** No cases in Wisconsin.

B. Employee's Work Area

No cases in Wisconsin.

C. Employee's Property

1. ***Private Employers.*** No cases in Wisconsin.

2. ***Public Employers.*** No cases in Wisconsin.

IV. MONITORING OF EMPLOYEES

A. Telephones and Electronic Communications

Section 968.31, Wis. Stat., prohibits the intentional interception, use, disclosure, or alteration of any wire, electronic, or oral communication. The statute also forbids attempts to procure others to perform these acts. But Wisconsin is a one-party consent state. Section 968.31(2)(b), Wis. Stat., permits eavesdropping by a party to the communication where one of the parties to the communication has given prior consent to the interception. See Griffin v. City of Milwaukee, 74 F.3d 824 (7th Cir. 1996) (employee implicitly consented to monitoring of personal telephone calls where employer had given notice that calls might be monitored and equipment was in plain view). Even consensual interceptions are not allowed, however, if they are "for the purpose of committing any criminal or tortious act in violation of the constitution or laws of the United States or of any state or for the purpose of committing any other injurious act." § 968.31(2)(c), Wis. Stat. According to the United States Court of Appeals for the Seventh Circuit, the one-party consent rule applies when a reporter records a conversation using a hidden camera, even when the resulting video is used for a potentially defamatory broadcast, as long as the reporter does not intend to commit a crime or tort when recording the conversation. Desnick v. ABC, 44 F.3d 1345, 23 Media L. Rep. 1161 (7th Cir. 1995).

A person who violates the eavesdropping statute may be subject to both criminal sanctions and civil claims. See § 968.31(1), (2m), Wis. Stat. Because § 968.31, Wis. Stat., does not specify a statute of limitations, Wisconsin courts probably would apply the two-year limit generally applicable to intentional torts including defamation and invasion of privacy. See § 893.57, Wis. Stat. Although one-party consent recordings are lawful, they are not admissible as evidence in criminal proceedings unless obtained pursuant to procedures specified in § 968.30, Wis. Stat. See State v. Waste Management, 81 Wis. 2d 555, 261 N.W.2d 147 (1978); see also § 885.365, Wis. Stat. (referring specifically to the use of recorded telephone conversations in civil actions). In State v. Duchow, 2008 WI 57, 310 Wis.2d 1, 749 N.W.2d 913, the Supreme Court determined whether a bus driver's threatening statements to a disabled child aboard a public school bus that were surreptitiously recording using a voice-activated tape recorder were "oral communications" within the meaning of the Electronic Surveillance Control Law, §§ 968.27-.33, Wis. Stats. The court concluded that the bus driver did not have a reasonable expectation of privacy when making the statements on the public school bus, therefore, the statements were not "oral communications" within the meaning of the statute and admissible in evidence.

1. ***Wiretapping.*** See IV.A, supra.

2. ***Electronic Communications.*** For purposes of Fourth Amendment seizures, Wisconsin law recognizes a "reasonable expectation of privacy" in e-mail and electronically stored information created and stored at work. In re John Doe Proceeding, 2004 WI 65, 272 Wis. 2d 208, 238-39, 680 N.W.2d 792, 806. In In re John Doe Proceeding, the court held that a subpoena seeking, among other things, electronic communications, issued as part of a John Doe proceeding to investigate possible crimes by Wisconsin legislators was an unreasonable search in violation of the Fourth Amendment. 272 Wis. 2d at 240, 680 N.W.2d at 807. But the court held that the scope of the privacy interest is limited. See id. at 242, 680 N.W.2d at 808 (Any documents that could be described with reasonable particularity and which are "supported by probable cause to believe that the documents sought will produce evidence of a crime" could be compelled.). Sections 968.31 and 943.70, Wis. Stats., prohibit unauthorized interception or accessing of "stored" electronic or computer communications. See Burbank Grease Services, LLC v. Sokolowski, 2006 WI 103, ¶ 39, 294 Wis. 2d 274, 717 N.W.2d 781 (employee's taking of employer's computer data is not a violation of § 943.70, Wis. Stat., because statute does not prohibit unauthorized *disclosure* of data if that data is *obtained* with authorization). The Wisconsin Supreme Court recently held that public employee personal emails, though sent through government email accounts and government-owned computers, are not public records. Schill v. Wisconsin Rapids Sch. Dist., 2010 WI 86, 786 N.W.2d 177.

3. ***Other Electronic Monitoring***. No cases in Wisconsin.

B. Mail

It is a crime, without the consent of either the sender or the addressee, to open intentionally any sealed letter or package or publish the contents of an unlawfully opened letter or package. § 942.05, Wis. Stat.

C. Surveillance/Photographing

Wisconsin criminal law prohibits improper surveillance of "nude" or "partially nude" persons (§ 942.08, Wis. Stat.), capturing, displaying, reproducing, possessing, and distributing "representations" of nudity made without knowledge or consent and in a manner in which the subject has a reasonable expectation of privacy (§ 942.09, Wis. Stat.), and "stalking," which is a "course of conduct" of two or more acts showing a continuity of purpose, such as photographing, videotaping, audiotaping or electronic monitoring of a person (§ 940.32, Wis. Stat.). The Seventh Circuit, interpreting Wisconsin law, found frivolous a claim for invasion of privacy when an employer placed an employee under surveillance outside of his home. Munson v. Milwaukee Board of School Directors, 969 F.2d 266 (7th Cir. 1992). In Munson, the Milwaukee Board of School Directors learned that a school principal was living outside Milwaukee County, in violation of the school board's residency policy. To confirm the board's suspicions, school safety aides began periodic surveillance of the principal's residence. Id. at 268. The principal filed an action against the school board claiming, amongst other things, that the surveillance violated Wisconsin's intrusion statute, § 995.50(2)(a), Wis. Stat. The Seventh Circuit found the claim frivolous. "As the district court found, [the principal] neither pleaded nor advanced evidence of a legitimate expectation of privacy violated by the defendants' investigation. The MBSD safety aides who conducted the surveillance never trespassed onto [the principal's] private property and operated only from areas designated as public streets or highways." Id. at 271.

V. ACTIVITIES OUTSIDE THE WORKPLACE

A. Statute or Common Law

The Wisconsin Fair Employment Act, §§ 111.31-111.395, Wis. Stats., generally prohibits discrimination in the workplace based on, among other things, marital status, sexual orientation, arrest and conviction records, membership in the military, and the use of lawful products off the employer's premises during non-working hours.

In Bowen v. Labor and Industry Review Comm'n, 2007 WI App 164, ¶¶ 12-16, 299 Wis. 2d 800, 730 N.W.2d 164, the Wisconsin Court of Appeals evaluated of an employee's claim that he was subjected to a hostile work environment because of his sexual orientation. The Court concluded that the Labor and Industry Review Commission should have considered acts that fell outside the 300 day statutory time period under § 111.39(1), Wis. Stat., because at least one of the acts contributing to the hostile work environment occurred within the 300 days, and those acts that fell outside the 300-day period were not "unduly remote" from those within the limitations period. Id.

B. Employees' Personal Relationships

1. ***Romantic Relationships Between Employees.*** Employers can prohibit romantic associations in the workplace, provided that the workplace rules do not impermissibly discriminate. See Federated Rural Electric Insurance,

Co. v. Kessler, 131 Wis.2d 189, 192, 388 N.W.2d 553 (1986) (employer's rule prohibiting the romantic association of any employee with married employee of the opposite sex did not constitute discrimination on the basis of marital status).

2. ***Sexual Orientation.*** No employer may discriminate against any individual on the basis of sexual orientation. § 111.321, Wis. Stat. Discrimination includes refusing to hire, terminating from employment, and discriminating in promotion, compensation, or terms and conditions of employment. § 111.36(1)(d), Wis. Stat.

3. ***Marital Status.*** Section 111.321, Wis. Stat., prohibits employment discrimination based on marital status. "[I]t is not employment discrimination because of marital status to prohibit an individual from directly supervising or being directly supervised by his or her spouse." § 111.345, Wis. Stat.; see Bammert v. LIRC, 2000 WI App 28, 232 Wis. 2d 365, 606 N.W.2d 620 (marital status discrimination does not include employer's actions based on identity or particular characteristics of employee's spouse); Federated Elec. v. Kessler, 131 Wis. 2d 189, 388 N.W.2d 553 (1986) (holding that employer's rule prohibiting any person from associating with married coemployees does not impermissibly discriminate against class of married employees).

C. Smoking

Pursuant to § 111.321, Wis. Stat., the "use or nonuse of lawful products off the employer's premises during nonworking hours" is a prohibited basis of discrimination. The prohibition does not apply to "a nonprofit corporation that, as one of its primary purposes or objectives, discourages the general public from using a lawful product . . . ." § 111.35(1)(a), Wis. Stat. Furthermore, employers may discriminate based on the use of a lawful product, including tobacco, if it impairs an individual's ability to perform job-related duties, creates a real or apparent conflict of interest with job-related duties, conflicts with a bona fide occupational qualification that is reasonably related to the job, or violates any federal or state law. § 111.35(2), Wis. Stat.

D. Blogging

No cases in Wisconsin.

VI. RECORDS

Wisconsin law establishes few record-keeping requirements for private employers. Pursuant to Wis. Admin. Code § DWD 274.06, employers must maintain records for at least three years showing the name, address, hours of employment, and wages of each employee. For purposes of workers' compensation, § 102.37, Wis. Stat., requires employers to "keep a record of all accidents causing death or disability of any employee while performing services growing out of and incidental to the employment."

The Wisconsin Court of Appeals recently concluded that an employer did not violate the prohibition on destroying requested records when the employer only destroyed copies of records it had already provided to the requestor. Stone v. Board of Regents of the University of Wisconsin System, 2007 WI App 223, 305 Wis. 2d 679, 741 N.W.2d 774.

The Wisconsin Open Records Law, §§ 19.31-19.39, Wis. Stats., begins with a "presumption of complete public access" to government records. § 19.31, Wis. Stat. Record custodians may only deny access to public records in three circumstances: (1) where there is a clear statutory exception; (2) based on a common law limitation to access; or (3) when the public interest in confidentiality outweighs the public interest in openness. Wisconsin Newspress, Inc. v. School District of Sheboygan Falls, 199 Wis. 2d 768, 546 N.W.2d 143 (1996); see Hempel v. City of Baraboo, 2005 WI 120, 699 N.W.2d 551 (police officer, a subject of sexual harassment investigation, was denied open records request because records were "in connection with a complaint" and disclosure would expose names with statements of informants who were promised confidentiality for their cooperation in the internal investigation); see also Schill, 2010 WI 86 (holding personal emails of government employees are not public records subject to disclosure under the Open Records Law).

The Wisconsin Supreme Court recently held that confidentiality provisions in a legislatively ratified collective bargaining agreement did not amend or pre-empt the presumption of public access to names of public employees represented by state employees union. See Milwaukee Journal Sentinel v. Wisconsin Dept. of Admin., 2009 WI 79, ¶¶ 11-13, 319 Wis. 2d 439, 768 N.W.2d 700.

A. Personnel Records

"[T]here is no blanket exception under the open records law for public employee disciplinary or personnel records . . . ." Newspress, 199 Wis. 2d at 781; 546 N.W.2d at 148. Where public records reveal "illegal conduct on the part of public employees, the public is entitled to that information . . . ." State ex rel. Ledford v. Turcotte, 195 Wis. 2d 244, 251, 536 N.W.2d 130, 132 (Ct. App. 1995). Subject to certain limited exceptions, employers must permit current and former employees to inspect their own personnel files. § 103.13, Wis. Stat. The Wisconsin Court of Appeals recently concluded that the provision in the Open Records Law that exempts from disclosure information used "for staff management planning," Wis. Stat. § 19.36(1)(d), does not apply to records pertaining to a misconduct investigation or disciplinary action and that these records are available for public review, subject to the balancing test. Kroeplin v. Wisconsin Dept. of Natural Resources, 2006 WI App 227, ¶ 32, 297 Wis. 2d 254, 725 N.W.2d 286. The Court also determined that this provision does not exempt from disclosure evaluative judgments – as compared to factual information – included in an employee's records. Id., ¶ 35.

In Woznicki v. Erickson, 202 Wis. 2d 178, 549 N.W.2d 699 (1996), the Wisconsin Supreme Court, for the first time, required that a district attorney, before releasing records from an investigative file, notify the subject of the records of their imminent release so that the subject could seek judicial review of the district attorney's decision to release the records. The court "extended" the Woznicki notice and review procedures to "all cases in which a record custodian decides to disclose information implicating the privacy and/or reputational interests of an individual public employee, regardless of the identity of the record custodian" in Milwaukee Teachers Education Association v. Milwaukee Board of School Directors, 227 Wis. 2d 779, 596 N.W.2d 403 (1999).

The legislature narrowed the procedural requirements of Woznicki in 2003. Section 19.356 now limits the right to notice and review to three categories of records: 1) public employee disciplinary records; 2) records obtained through a subpoena or search warrant; and, 3) records relating to private employees. Beyond these categories, however, "no person is entitled to judicial review of the decision of an authority to provide a requester with access to a record." § 19.356(1), Wis. Stat.

B. Medical Records

In general, "[a]ll patient health care records shall remain confidential." § 146.82(1), Wis. Stat. Similarly, mental health "treatment records shall remain confidential and are privileged to the subject individual." § 51.30(4), Wis. Stat.; see Milwaukee Deputy Sheriffs Assoc. v. City of Wauwatosa, 2010 WI App 95, 327 Wis. 2d 206, 787 N.W.2d 438 (holding that § 51.30(4) barred city from disclosing to county sheriff's department an emergency detention report and a police department incident report containing mental health information concerning a deputy sheriff). Record custodians who knowingly and willfully violate this confidentiality may be subject to both civil and criminal sanctions. § 146.84, Wis. Stat. Patients themselves, upon submitting a statement of informed consent, have the right to inspect their own healthcare records. § 146.83, Wis. Stat.; see also § 103.13(5), Wis. Stat. "If the employer believes that disclosure of an employee's medical records would have a detrimental effect on the employee, the employer may release the medical records to the employee's physician . . . ." Id. With limited exceptions, an employer may not disclose the results of an employee's HIV test. See § 252.15, Wis. Stats. The Wisconsin Family Medical Leave statute restricts the amount of information that an employer can receive to certify a request for leave. § 103.10(7)(b), Wis. Stat. In addition, § 995.50, Wis. Stat., may apply to the unauthorized disclosure of medical information. See, e.g., Pachowitz v. LeDoux, 2003 WI App 120, 265 Wis. 2d 631, 666 N.W.2d 88 (emergency medical technician's disclosure of private medical information to single individual constituted 'publicity' under statute).

C. Criminal Records

In Wisconsin, arrest records, Newspapers, Inc. v. Breier, 89 Wis. 2d 417, 279 N.W.2d 179 (1979), and conviction records, see generally §§ 19.35(1) and 757.14, Wis. Stats., are available for public inspection, while a prosecutor's investigative files are not, State ex rel. Richards v. Foust, 165 Wis. 2d 429, 477 N.W.2d 608 (1991). Law enforcement records concerning juveniles, defined as anyone under 17 years of age, are generally confidential, § 938.396(1), Wis. Stat., although there are significant exceptions for serious, violent crimes. This confidentiality "does not apply to representatives of the news media who wish to obtain information for the purpose of reporting news without revealing the identity of the juvenile involved . . . ." Id.

Section 111.321, Wis. Stat., prohibits employment discrimination based on an arrest or conviction record. It is not employment discrimination, however, to refuse to employ an individual who has been convicted of a crime "which substantially relate[s] to the circumstances of the particular job . . . ." § 111.335(1)(c)1, Wis. Stat. To determine whether the circumstances of the crime substantially relate to the job, an employer need not, in all cases, conduct a detailed inquiry into the facts of the offense. Milwaukee County v. Labor & Industry Review Commission, 139 Wis. 2d 805, 823-24, 407 N.W.2d 908, 916 (1987). The employer should inquire into the circumstances that fostered the criminal activity, however. Id.

D. Subpoenas / Search Warrants

The Wisconsin Supreme court ruled that the custodian of electronic information created and maintained by the Wisconsin legislature was required to comply with the subpoena duces tecum of the John Doe judge, who requested the release of documents created by people working in the Democratic and Republican caucuses. In re John Doe Proceeding, 2004 WI 65, 272 Wis. 2d 208, 680 N.W.2d 792. According to the court, a statutory requirement obligating the custodian to treat all information within his possession as confidential did not create a privilege and therefore did not supersede the subpoena. Id.

The Wisconsin Court of Appeals recently upheld a search warrant for financial records maintained in an employee's office. In State v. LaCount, 2007 WI App 116, 301Wis. 2d 472, 732 N.W.2d 29, the employee asserted that the execution of a search warrant was invalid because the police, in searching for documents relating to specific clients, discovered and seized records relating to additional crimes involving other clients not named in the warrant. Id., ¶¶ 3-4. The Court held the search valid, concluding that the warrant authorized the police to search the employer's office, which included the employee's office. Id., ¶ 11.

VII. ACTIONS SUBSEQUENT TO EMPLOYMENT

A. References

An employer is not deemed to have interfered with a former employer's prospective employment opportunities for failing to verify the dates during which a former employee was affiliated with the employer unless the employer has a duty to do so. Schindler v. Marshfield Clinic, 2006 WL 1236720 (W.D. Wis. May 2, 2006) (vacated in part, Schindler v. Marshfield Clinic, 2006 WL 1589647 (W.D. Wis. Jun 2, 2006)).

B. Non-Compete Agreements

Section 103.465 permits covenants not to compete so long as the restrictions imposed are "reasonably necessary for the protection of the employer or principal." In general, however, Wisconsin courts regard covenants not to compete with "suspicion" because of the restraints they place on worker mobility. See, e.g., GreenStone Farm Credit Services v. Giesler, 2005 WI App 126, 699 N.W.2d 253 (finding covenant not void for prohibiting former employee from servicing any of the employer's clients who had been employee's customers within the year preceding his termination and who were also serviced within the year). Wisconsin courts make five inquiries when evaluating the enforceability of a covenant not to compete. Specifically, a court asks whether the covenant: 1) is necessary for the protection of the employer or principal; 2) provides a reasonable time restriction; 3) provides a reasonable territorial limit; 4) is not harsh or oppressive to the employee; and 5) is not contrary to public policy. Id. See H&R Block Eastern Enter, Inc. v. Swenson, 2008 WI App 3, ¶ 23, 307 Wis. 2d 390, 745 N.W.2d 421 (holding noncompetition clause void and unenforceable because extension provision was unreasonable).

VIII. PROCEDURAL ISSUES

A. Statutes of Limitations

For most intentional torts in Wisconsin, including defamation and invasion of privacy, the statute of limitations is three years. § 893.57, Wis. Stat.

B. Jurisdiction.

No cases in Wisconsin.

C. Pleading Requirements.

No cases in Wisconsin.

SURVEY OF WYOMING EMPLOYMENT LIBEL LAW

Bradley T. Cave and Joanna R. Vilos
Holland & Hart LLP
2515 Warren Avenue, Suite 450
Cheyenne, WY 82001

(With Developments Reported Through **November 1, 2012**)

GENERAL COMMENTS

For cases decided between Jan. 1, 2001 and Jan. 1, 2003, the Wyoming Supreme Court requires citation to a public domain citation format in addition to the West Reporting System. For cases decided after Jan. 1, 2003, only citation to the public domain system is required. See In the Matter of Adopting A Public Domain, Neutral-Format Citation Format (Wyo. order issued Oct. 2000), available at courts.state.wy.us.

SIGNIFICANT DEVELOPMENTS SINCE THE 2012 *SURVEY*

None.

I. GENERAL LAW

A. General Employment Law

1. ***At Will Employment.*** In Wyoming, employment is presumed to be at-will and, thus, may be terminated at any time and for any reason, unless an express or implied contract establishes employment that may only be terminated for cause. Davis v. Wyoming Med. Ctr., Inc., 934 P.2d 1246 (Wyo. 1997)**; Kuhl v. Wells Fargo Bank, N.A., 2012 WY 85, 281 P.3d 716 (Wyo. 2012)**. Notwithstanding Wyoming's presumption of at-will employment, it has recognized all three of the common exceptions to the doctrine. Wilder v. Cody Country Chamber of Commerce, 868 P.2d 211 (Wyo. 1994).

a. **Implied-in-fact exception.** Employee handbooks, personnel policies, letters of employment, performance evaluations, and a course of dealing may create an implied-in-fact contract if such communication manifests an intent to create an expectation that employment will not be terminated except for cause. Ormsby v. Dana Kepner Co. of Wyo., Inc., 997 P.2d 465 (Wyo. 2000). The Wyoming Supreme Court defined "cause" as "a reasoned conclusion...supported by substantial evidence gathered through an adequate investigation that includes notice of the claimed misconduct and a chance for the employee to respond." Life Care Centers of America, Inc. v. Dexter, 2003 WY 38, 65 P.3d 385 (Wyo. 2003). Employers can use clearly worded, conspicuous disclaimers within its communications with employees to prevent the creation of an implied contract of employment. Bouwens v. Centrilift, 974 P.2d 941 (Wyo. 1999). When employment is governed by an employee handbook requiring just cause for termination, new consideration must be given to the employee in order to modify that relationship to at-will employment. Reynolds v. West Park Hosp. District, 2010 WY 69; see also Brodie v. Gen. Chem. Corp., 934 P.2d 1263 (Wyo. 1997). In Reynolds v. West Park Hosp. District, 2010 WY 69, the plaintiff-employee resigned her employment with the defendant-employer and signed a release waiving all rights under the handbook that had governed her employment. She was later rehired for a new position with the employer. The Wyoming Supreme Court ruled that the plaintiff-employee's new employment was subject to the employer's new handbook, which had reinstated employment at will.

In Trabing v. Kinko's, Inc., 2002 WY 171, 57 P.3d 1248 (Wyo. 2002), the plaintiff-employee was given an employee handbook to read and sign at the time of her hire. The handbook contained one provision that implied that just cause was required for termination, as well as a seemingly contradictory provision that stated that nothing in the handbook was intended to create a contract and employment remained at-will. Id. Several days after her hire, the employee was asked to read and sign a separate agreement that specifically stated that she was an at-will employee. Id. The Wyoming Supreme Court found that, although the handbook did not contain a conspicuous disclaimer (and the handbook provisions were ambiguous), the subsequent agreement accomplished the same purpose as would a conspicuous disclaimer— it clearly informed the employee of her at-will employment status. Id.

In Hoff v. City of Casper-Natrona County Health Department, 2001 WY 97, 33 P.3d 99 (Wyo. 2001), a terminated public employee filed breach of contract, breach of implied covenant of good faith and fair dealing, and public policy tort claims against his former employer. The Wyoming Supreme Court held that the statement that the agency's handbook was not a contract showed that the employer had clearly not intended to enter into a contract with its employees and that the plaintiff could not have reasonably believed otherwise. The Wyoming Supreme Court also held that the

Wyoming Governmental Claims Act abrogated sovereign immunity only for the torts expressly recognized in the act itself, and did not expressly waive immunity for the public policy tort or the implied covenant of good faith and fair dealing tort.

b. **Implied-in-law exception.** A covenant of good faith and fair dealing, which could lead to tort liability, arises only when a special relationship is created between the employer and the employee. Wilder v. Cody Country Chamber of Commerce, 868 P.2d 211 (Wyo. 1994). Without a special relationship, the covenant of good faith and fair dealing is incompatible with at-will employment and does not apply. Scherer Constr., LLC v. Hedquist Constr., LLC, 2001 WT 23, 18 P.3d 645 (Wyo. 2001). This special relationship can be based on common law, statutes, separate consideration or longevity of service. For example, 15 years of service in a position that was considered important to the employer, coupled with oral assurances of job security made by management, created a special relationship in Worley v. Wyoming Bottling Co. Inc., 1 P.3d 615 (Wyo. 2000). A long tenure of employment, standing alone, is not sufficient to form the requisite "special relationship." Garcia v. UniWyo Fed. Credit Union, 920 P.2d 642 (Wyo. 1996). If a special relationship is shown, a plaintiff must further show that the employer terminated the employee to deny benefits or compensation already accrued. Worley v. Wyoming Bottling Co., Inc., 1 P.3d 615 (Wyo. 2000).

c. **Public Policy Tort.** Wyoming has recognized the public policy tort as an exception to the presumption of at-will employment in only one area. In Griess v. Consolidated Freightways, 776 P.2d 752 (Wyo. 1989) the Wyoming Supreme Court found that it was against the public policy of Wyoming to terminate an employee in retaliation for exercising his rights under the Wyoming Worker's Compensation Act. See also McLean v. Hyland Enterprises, Inc., 2001 WY 111, 34 P.3d 1262 (Wyo. 2001). Several attempts to expand this holding outside the area of worker's compensation have failed. Dynan v. Rocky Mountain Federal Savings and Loan, 792 P.2d 631 (Wyo. 1990); Bitner v. Burlington Northern, 857 F.Supp. 1482 (D. Wyo. 1995); Hemreck v. United Parcel Service, 938 P.2d 863 (Wyo. 1997); Sears v Amoco Production, 967 F.Supp 1222 (D. Wyo. 1997); Boone v. Frontier Refining, 987 P.2d 681 (Wyo. 1999).

Termination of an at-will employee could violate Wyoming public policy if (1) the termination violates some well-established policy and (2) there is no remedy to protect the employee or the public at large. Dynan v. Rocky Mountain Fed. Sav. and Loan, 792 P.2d 631 (Wyo. 1990). There can be no claim for wrongful termination in violation of public policy if there exists an administrative remedy. McLean v. Hyland Enterprises, Inc., 2001 WY 111, 34 P.3d 1262 (Wyo. 2001).

In Drake v. Cheyenne Newspapers, Inc., 891 P.2d 80 (Wyo. 1995) a newspaper editor was terminated when he refused to wear a button urging employees to vote "no" on the creation of a union at a Cheyenne newspaper. The plaintiff argued that his termination violated public policy because it infringed on his right to free speech. The Wyoming Supreme Court found no public policy tort because the right to free speech does not extend to private property. In McGarvey v. Key Property Management LLC, 2009 WY 84 (Wyo. 2009), the Wyoming Supreme Court affirmed that speech on an employer's private property is not constitutionally protected and discharge based on that speech does not violate any well-established public policy. Id. at ¶ 22. This exception is not applicable to public employer-employee situations. See Hoff v. City of Casper-Natrona County Health Department, 2001 WY 97, 33 P.3d 99 (Wyo. 2001).

2. ***Promissory Estoppel.*** In Worley v. Wyoming Bottling Co. Inc., 1 P.3d 615 (Wyo. 2000) the Wyoming Supreme Court adopted promissory estoppel as a theory of recovery in a cause of action for wrongful termination. However, a conspicuous disclaimer in an employee handbook that provides for at-will employment defeats an employee's promissory estoppel claim because the disclaimer makes the employee's belief that he could only be terminated for cause unreasonable. Trabing v. Kinko's, Inc., 2002 WY 171, 57 P.3d 1248 (Wyo. 2002).

B. Elements of Defamation Claim

1. ***Basic Elements.*** The basic elements of a defamation claim are (1) a false statement; (2) which is published to a third party; (3) that causes harm to the plaintiff's reputation. Tschirgi v. Lander Wyo. State Journal, 706 P.2d 1116 (Wyo. 1985). A libel is any writing, picture, or other like representation of a nature to blacken a person's reputation, or hold him up to contempt or ridicule while slander is an oral defamation. In re McDonald, 33 P. 18, 4 Wyo. 150 (1893). A defamatory communication is one which tends to hold the plaintiff up to hatred, contempt, ridicule, or scorn, or which causes him to be shunned or avoided, one that tends to injure his reputation as to diminish the esteem, respect, good will, or confidence in which he is held. Davis v. Big Horn Basin Newspapers, Inc., 884 P.2d 979, 983 (Wyo. 1994); Lever v. Community First Bancshares, Inc., 989 P.2d 634 (Wyo. 1999).

2. ***Fault.***

a. **Private Figure Plaintiff/Matter of Public Concern.** Wyoming has adopted a negligence standard for private figures and issues of public concern. See Davis v. Big Horn Basin Newspapers, Inc., 884 P.2d

979 (Wyo. 1994). A private figure who has been libeled by the publication of a false statement on a matter of public concern must prove that the defendant was negligent in publishing the false statement. Id.; Spence v. Flynt, 816 P.2d 771 (Wyo. 1991).

b. **Private Figure Plaintiff/Matter of Private Concern.** There is no authority in Wyoming for this issue.

c. **Public Figure Plaintiff/Matter of Public Concern.** Wyoming follows the actual malice standard of New York Times Co. v. Sullivan in cases involving public officials and public figures. Actual malice has been defined as publication with actual knowledge of falsity or publication with reckless disregard of whether it was false or not. Davis v. Big Horn Basin Newspapers, Inc., 884 P.2d 979, 984, 23 Media L. Rep. 1345 (Wyo. 1994). Actual malice must be shown with convincing clarity and the testimony of publishers is not controlling, though it cannot be ignored if unrefuted. McMurry v. Howard Publications, Inc., 612 P.2d 14, 6 Media L. Rep. 1814 (Wyo. 1980). Where publisher and plaintiff disagreed as to interpretation and perception, subjective awareness of probable falsity cannot be demonstrated. Id.

In Spence v. Flynt, 816 P.2d 771 (Wyo. 1991), the Wyoming Supreme Court held that the public figure subject to defamatory criticism is one who is involved in the resolution of important public questions, or who by reason of fame, shapes events in areas of concern to society, and who injects himself into the vortex of controversy. Id. at 776. The Spence court also held that an individual may be a public figure for some purposes but not for others, and that an attorney "who is merely advocating for a famous or controversial client is not a public figure, merely because he has taken on the cause of an advocate." Id. at 777.

In Martin v. Committee for Honesty and Justice at Star Valley Ranch, 101 P.3d 123 (Wyo. 2004), the Wyoming Supreme Court held that a member of the Board of Directors of a homeowner's association was a limited public figure when he voluntarily injected himself into the controversy surrounding the termination of the association's general manager. Id. at 131. This dispute was a public controversy because it "had ramifications for persons who were not direct participants in it," specifically the other lot owners within the homeowner's association. Id. at 128. The Supreme Court also held that the plaintiff had not successfully proven the necessary element of actual malice, since he had failed "to present any argument as to the Defendants' knowledge of [the statements'] falsity." Id. at 132.

3. ***Falsity.*** In Dworkin v. L.F.P., Inc., 839 P.2d 903, 920 (Wyo. 1992), the Wyoming Supreme Court invalidated a portion of Article 1, Section 20 of the Wyoming Constitution, which states that "the truth, when published with good intent, and for justifiable ends, shall be a sufficient defense." The Court held that in cases involving public figures or public officials, and a media defendant, it is repugnant to the First Amendment of the United States Constitution to condition the defense of truth on the presence of good motives and justifiable ends. Id. In Tschirgi v. Lander, Wyoming State Journal, 706 P.2d 1116 (Wyo. 1985), the Wyoming Supreme Court held that the truth is a sufficient defense if the matter published is substantially true, as opposed to literally true. In Tschirgi, the Court cited Restatement (Second) of Torts, § 581A for the proposition that slight inaccuracies of expression are immaterial, provided that the defamatory charge is true in substance. In Davis v. Big Horn Basin Newspapers, Inc., 884 P.2d 979, 984 (Wyo. 1994), the Wyoming Supreme Court stated, with regard to a public figure and a matter of public concern, inaccuracy without malice is not actionable.

4. ***Defamatory Statement of Fact.*** A defamatory communication is one which tends to hold the plaintiff up to hatred, contempt, ridicule, or scorn, or which causes him to be shunned or avoided; one that tends to injure his reputation as to diminish the esteem, respect, good will, or confidence in which he is held. Davis v. Big Horn Basin Newspapers, Inc., 884 P.2d 979, 983 (Wyo. 1994); see also Lever v. Community First Bancshares, Inc., 989 P.2d 634 (Wyo. 1999). Statements that cannot reasonably be interpreted as stating actual facts about an individual are not actionable. See Dworkin v. L.F.P., Inc., 839 P.2d 903 (Wyo. 1992). Statements that an ex-employee was sneaky, lazy, a good-for-nothing, a thief, as well as other disparaging terms are offensive, but not actionable where they do not affect the person referred to in some way that is peculiarly harmful to one engaged in his trade or profession. Wilder v. Cody Country Chamber of Commerce, 868 P.2d 211 (Wyo. 1994).

5. ***Of and Concerning Plaintiff.*** Whether a publication is of and concerning a plaintiff goes to the identification of the plaintiff. Pring v. Penthouse, 695 F.2d 438 (10th Cir. 1983). Defamatory words are actionable only if they refer to some ascertained or ascertainable person. Cinker, Inc. v. Northern Gas Company, Inc., 578 F. Supp. 112 (D. Wyo. 1983).

6. ***Publication.*** The plaintiff must allege and prove that the defamatory statement was published. Evidence a third person handed a libelous letter to the plaintiff was sufficient to give rise to an inference that a third person had, in fact, read the letter. Sylvester v. Armstrong, 53 Wyo. 382, 84 P.2d 729 (1938).

a. **Intracorporate Communication.** Where one person has an interest in the subject matter of the communication and the person to whom the communication is made has a corresponding interest, every communication honestly made in order to protect such common interest is conditionally privileged by reason of the occasion. Sylvester v. Armstrong, 53 Wyo. 382, 84 P.2d 729 (1938).For example, where the writer of an allegedly libelous letter concerning conduct of a manager of a hotel owned 40% of the stock in the hotel corporation, and the receiver of the letter owned 60% of the stock, the occasion was a privileged one, and the letter was conditionally or qualifiedly privileged. Id. The communication is presumed to be made without malice, and the person alleging defamation bears the burden to show malice to remove the communication from the protective umbrella of conditional privilege. Lever v. Community First Bancshares, Inc., 989 P.2d 634 (Wyo. 1999).

b. **Compelled Self-Publication.** There is no authority on this issue in Wyoming.

c. **Republication.** One who only delivers or transmits defamatory materials published by a third person is subject to liability if, but only if, he knows or has reason to know, of its defamatory character. Dworkin v. Hustler Magazine, Inc., 611 F. Supp. 781 (D. Wyo. 1985) (citing Restatement (Second) of Torts, § 581). In Setlaff v. Memorial Hospital, 850 F.2d 1384 (10th Cir. 1988), the Tenth Circuit Court of Appeals, interpreting Wyoming law, held that a review of the plaintiff's personnel file by the hospital Board of Trustees was not republication, for statute of limitations purposes.

7. ***Statements versus Conduct.*** There is no authority in Wyoming on this subject.

8. ***Damages.***

a. **Presumed Damages and Libel Per Se.** Defamation "per se" is a statement that is defamatory on its face and, thus, does not require a showing of specific damages or harm. Hoblyn v. Johnson, 2002 WY 152, 55 P.3d 1219 (Wyo. 2002). Defamation per se consists of statements which impute: (1) a criminal offense; (2) a loathsome disease; (3) a matter incompatible with business, trade, profession, or office; or (4) serious sexual misconduct. Id.

A person must show special damages to recover for libel upon property. Brannen v. Laramie Newspapers, Inc., 493 P.2d 1044 (Wyo. 1972). The Wyoming Constitution prohibits limiting the amount of damages to be recovered for causing injury to a person. Article X, Section 4.

(1) **Employment-Related Criticism.** In Sylvester, the defendant called the plaintiff a drunk and whoremonger and commented that the plaintiff should be discharged if the hotel was to operate properly. The Court ruled in favor of the defendant because it found that this language could have easily been made because of a bona fide concern about the operations of the hotel rather than with malice. Sylvester v. Armstrong, 53 Wyo. 382, 84 P.2d 729 (1938). Where an employer-defendant alleged that the employee-plaintiff might steal corporate secrets, and termed the employee sneaky, lazy, good-for-nothing, and a son-of-a-bitch, the Wyoming Supreme Court ruled that the tenor of the language is disparaging and offensive, but is not actionable as defamation. Wilder v. Cody Country Chamber of Commerce, 868 P.2d 211 (Wyo. 1994).

(2) **Single Instance Rule.** No reported cases.

b. **Punitive Damages.** Punitive damages in Wyoming are awarded for willful and wanton misconduct, and are to be determined in a bifurcated proceeding only after a jury properly instructed determines that such damages are appropriate. Campen v. Stone, 635 P.2d 1121 (Wyo. 1981).

II. PRIVILEGES AND DEFENSES

A. Scope of Privileges

1. ***Absolute Privilege.*** In Casteel v. News-Record, Inc., 875 P.2d 21, 23 (Wyo. 1994), the Wyoming Supreme Court noted, "an absolute privilege protects the speaker or publisher without reference to his motives or the falsity of his statement." In Abromats v. Wood, 2009 WY 100 (Wyo. 2009), the Wyoming Supreme Court recognized that an absolute privilege applied to a statement by crime victims to a non-profit victim services organization, as well as the prosecuting attorney, court staff and judge.

2. ***Qualified Privileges.*** When applying a conditional privilege, absence of malice is presumed, and the plaintiff must prove malice on the part of the defendant. Casteel v. News-Record, Inc., 875 P.2d 21 (Wyo. 1994). Reply in a political campaign is appropriate, and does not occupy a qualified privilege. Pfifer v. Foe, 443 P.2d 870 (Wyo. 1978). A conditional privilege attached to a statement made by a title insurance company officer to a bank officer regarding the financial stability of plaintiff, who was applying for title insurance. William v. Blount, 741 P.2d 595 (Wyo. 1987).

By statute, publication of criminal and civil proceedings are conditionally privileged. Id.; Wyo. Stat. § 1-29 -105 (2002). An employer who discloses information about a former employee's job performance to an employer or prospective employer of the employee, is presumed to be acting in good faith, unless actual malice is demonstrated. Wyo. Stat. § 27-1-113; Beus v. Uinta County Bd. of County Comm'rs, 143 Fed.Appx. 945 (Wyo. 2005).

a. **Common Interest.** Where both the party making and the party receiving the communication have an interest in it, the communication is privileged. Sylvester v. Armstrong, 84 P.2d 729 (Wyo. 1938). A defamatory publication made purely in the interests of one's own business for the purpose of securing an advantage over a rival is not privileged. Id.; Lever v. Community First Bancshares, Inc., 989 P.2d 634 (Wyo. 1999) (qualified privilege attached to statements made in the course of a "routine business transaction in which both parties had a pecuniary interest").

b. **Duty.** No reported cases.

c. **Criticism of Public Employee.** Statements in reference to acts of a "public officer and with respect to his official conduct in which the public was interested" are qualifiedly privileged. Kutcher v. Post Printing Co., 149 P. 552, 553 (Wyo. 1915). This means that publication of such criticism, when false, is privileged only when made in good faith and without malice. Id. In the public employment setting, criticism of a public employee by other public employees is not actionable; the public employees are immune under the Wyoming Governmental Claims Act if discussion of staffing concerns and personnel evaluations fall within the scope of employment duties. Beus v. Uinta County Bd. of County Comm'rs, 143 Fed.Appx. 945 (10th Cir. 2005) (applying Wyoming law). See also Deutsch v. Jordan, 2009 U.S. Dist. LEXIS 129670, at *8-9 (D. Wyo. Apr. 13, 2009).

d. **Limitation on Qualified Privileges.** When applying a conditional privilege, absence of malice is presumed, and the plaintiff must prove malice on the part of the defendant. Lever v. Community First Bancshares, Inc., 989 P.2d 634 (Wyo. 1999); Casteel v. News Record, Inc., 875 P.2d 21 (Wyo. 1994).

(1) **Constitutional or Actual Malice.** In Lever v. Community First Bancshares, Inc., 989 P.2d 634 (Wyo. 1999), the Wyoming Supreme Court noted that while the state's prior precedent uses a common law malice standard, the Restatement (Second) of Torts uses an "actual knowledge or reckless disregard as to falsity" standard. The court also noted that "[n]either party advocated a change in our precedent, and we decline to raise the issue on our own initiative." Id.

(2) **Common Law Malice.** According to the Wyoming Supreme Court in Lever, evidence of common law malice is required to defeat a qualified privilege. Id.

e. **Question of Fact or Law.** Whether a privilege or immunity exists over a particular statement is a question of law. Abromats v. Wood, 2009 WY 100 (Wyo. 2009); Lever v. Community First Bancshares, Inc., 989 P.2d 634 (Wyo. 1999). In a libel action, it is the court's duty to determine as a matter of law whether language used in a qualifiedly privileged communication is such as tends to show malice. Sylvester v. Armstrong, 84 P.2d 729 (1938). Although an utterance that is slander per se is a jury question, the court will practically instruct them that the words are actionable and that they should find for the plaintiff. Nash v. Fisher, 162 P. 933 (1917). A trial court in a defamation action is not precluded by the Wyoming Constitution from the use of a summary judgment procedure. Dworkin v. L.F.P., Inc., 839 P.2d 903 (Wyo. 1992); Wilder v. Cody Country Chamber of Commerce, 868 P.2d 211 (Wyo. 1994); Davis v. Big Horn Newspapers, Inc., 884 P.2d 979 (Wyo. 1994). In the context of a conditionally privileged communication, the absence of malice entitles the defendant to judgment as a matter of law. Lever v. Community First Bancshares, Inc., 989 P.2d 634 (Wyo. 1999).

f. **Burden of Proof.** The absence of malice is presumed in a conditionally privileged communication. Lever v. Community First Bancshares, Inc., 989 P.2d 634 (Wyo. 1999). Thus, the plaintiff has the burden of proving malice on the part of the defendant. Id.

B. Standard Libel Defenses

1. ***Truth.*** The Wyoming Constitution states that truth, when published with good intent and for justifiable ends, shall be a sufficient defense. Wyo. Const. art. 1, § 20. But in Dworkin v. L.F.P., Inc., 839 P.2d 903 (Wyo. 1992), the Court held that in cases involving public figures or public officials and a media defendant, it is repugnant to the First Amendment of the United States Constitution to condition the defense of truth on the presence of good motives and justifiable ends. In Tschirgi v. Lander Wyoming State Journal, the Court held that truth is a sufficient defense if the matter published is substantially true as opposed to literally true.

2. ***Opinion.*** In Dworkin v. L.F.P., Inc., 839 P.2d 903, 914, 20 Media L. Rep. 2001, 2009 (Wyo. 1992), the Wyoming Supreme Court noted that the United States Supreme Court in Milkovich v. Lorain Journal Company, 497 U.S. 1 (1990) refused to recognize a First Amendment-based protection for defamatory statements that are characterized as opinion as opposed to fact. The Dworkin court cited Milkovich for the proposition that "the breathing space which

freedoms of expression require in order to survive . . . is adequately secured by existing constitutional doctrine without the creation of an artificial dichotomy between opinion and fact." Id. In Spence v. Flynt, 816 P.2d 771, 775, 19 Media L. Rep. 1129, 1132 (Wyo. 1991) the Wyoming Supreme Court also adopted the Milkovich approach to "fair comment" determination. Cf. Cinker, Inc. v. Northern Gas Company, Inc., 578 F. Supp. 112, 114 (D. Wyo. 1993) (citing Gertz v. Robert Welch, Inc., 418 U.S. 323 (1974), and its progeny with approval with regard to the fact-opinion dichotomy). Under the "fair comment" privilege, an expression of opinion on matters of legitimate public interest not made solely for the purpose of causing harm would appear to remain constitutionally protected. See Spence v. Flynt, 816 P.2d at 775, 19 Media L. Rep. at 1132 (citing Milkovich, 110 S. Ct. at 2703).

The Dworkin court applied the Milkovich analysis to determine whether the allegedly defamatory statements were protected, by examining: (1) the type of language used; (2) the meaning of the statement in context; (3) the verifiability of the statements; and (4) the broader social circumstances of the statements. Id. at 915-20. For example, the context of the statement, such as an editorial page, may indicate that the statement does not purport to state or imply actual known facts. Id. at 915.

3. ***Consent.*** No reported cases.

4. ***Mitigation.*** No reported cases.

III. RECURRING FACT PATTERNS

A. Statements in Personnel File

No reported cases.

B. Performance Evaluations

No reported cases.

C. References

Wyoming has statutory employer immunity for disclosure of certain employee information. Wyo. Stat. § 27-1-113 (2009) provides:

> (a) An employer who discloses information about a former employee's job performance to a prospective employer or to an employer of the former employee is presumed to be acting in good faith. Unless lack of good faith is shown by a preponderance of evidence, the employer is immune from civil liability for the disclosure or for the consequences resulting from the disclosure.
>
> (b) For purposes of subsection (a) of this section, the presumption of good faith is rebutted upon a showing that the information disclosed by the former employer was knowingly false or deliberately misleading or was rendered with malicious purpose.

D. Intracorporate Communication

In Sylvester v. Armstrong, the writer of a libelous letter concerning a hotel manager owned 40% of the hotel stock, and the receiver of the letter owned 60% of the stock. The Wyoming Supreme Court held that the occasion was a privileged one, and the letter was conditionally or qualifiedly privileged. Sylvester v. Armstrong, 84 P.2d 729 (1938).

E. Statements to Government Regulators

No reported cases. But see Abromats v. Wood, 2009 WY 100, where statements made to a public or non-profit crime victim service provider, with a statutorily defined role, for the purpose of submitting the statements to the court in a criminal case were absolutely privileged.

F. Reports to Auditors and Insurers

No reported cases.

G. Vicarious Liability of Employers for Statements Made by Employees

1. ***Scope of Employment.*** No reported cases. But see Century Ready-Mix Co. v. Campbell Co. Sch. Dist., 816 P.2d 795 (Wyo. 1991) where relationship between school board and materials tester it had hired did not create an agency relationship sufficient to make defendant school board liable for statements made. Id. at 799.

a. **Blogging.** No reported cases.

2. ***Damages.*** No reported cases.

H. Internal Investigations

No reported cases.

IV. OTHER ACTIONS BASED ON STATEMENTS

A. Negligent Hiring, Retention, and Supervision

1. ***Elements.*** A person conducting an activity through servants or other agents is subject to liability for harm resulting from his conduct if he is negligent or reckless in the employment of improper persons in work involving the risk of harm to others. Cranston v. Weston County Weed & Pest Board, 826 P.2d 251 (Wyo. 1992). Cranston adopted the definition of negligent hiring set forth in Restatement (Second) of Agency § 213 (1958). The plaintiff must show the employer was negligent in selecting the employee; the employee caused plaintiff's injuries; and the employer's negligence was the proximate cause of the plaintiff's injuries. Cranston, 826 P.2d 251; see also Beavis ex. rel. Beavis v. Campbell County Mem. Hosp., 2001 WY 32, 20 P.3d 508 (Wyo. 2001).

2. ***Claims Based on Statements.*** No reported cases.

B. Intentional Infliction of Emotional Distress

1. ***Elements.*** A person, by extreme and outrageous conduct, who intentionally or recklessly causes severe emotional distress to another, may be liable. See Restatement (Second) of Torts, § 46. This tort was adopted in Leithead v. American Colloid Company, 721 P.2d 1059 (Wyo. 1986).

The at-will employment relationship provides a complete defense to an employee's claim of intentional infliction of emotional distress that is caused solely by his or her termination. Trabing v. Kinko's, Inc., 2002 WY 171, 57 P.3d 1248 (Wyo. 2002).

2. ***Claims Based on Statements.*** Offensive remarks, although annoying, insulting, or insensitive, are not actionable. Actionable remarks must be beyond all possible bounds of decency, atrocious, or utterly intolerable in a civilized community. Garcia v. Lawson, 928 P.2d 1164 (Wyo. 1996). Wyoming has adopted a tort of negligent infliction of emotional distress. Gates v. Richardson, 719 P.2d 193 (Wyo. 1986). But this tort has been limited to a narrow range of situations, including intentional torts; violation of constitutional rights; and breach of the covenant of good faith and fair dealing.

C. Interference with Contract or Economic Advantage

Wyoming has adopted the Restatement (Second) of Torts, § 766B, in recognizing intentional interference with prospective advantage. There must be a business expectancy or contract; the defendant must have knowledge of the expectancy or contract; there must be intentional and improper interference resulting in a termination of the expectancy or breach of the contract by the third party; and there must be consequent damages. Bear v. Volunteers of America, Wyoming, Inc., 964 P.2d 1245 (Wyo. 1998) (providing the elements of the tort of interference with contract); Martin v. Wing, 667 P.2d 1159 (Wyo. 1983) (providing the elements of the tort of interference with economic advantage). Truthful statements are not actionable as intentional interference. Four Nines Gold, Inc. v. 71 Construction, Inc., 809 P.2d 236 (Wyo. 1991). Interference is permitted when the interferor acts in good faith to protect an economic interest. Id.; see also Lever v. Community First Bancshares, Inc., 989 P.2d 634 (Wyo. 1999) (plaintiff failed to show that intent was improper). A claim for intentional interference with contract will fail if it involves an assertion that an agent for a party to the contract interfered with it. Excel Constr. , Inc. v. HKM Eng'g, Inc., 2010 WY 34.

D. Prima Facie Tort

No reported cases.

V. OTHER ISSUES

A. Statute of Limitations

Wyoming has a one-year statute of limitations relating to libel and slander. Wyo. Stat. § 1-3-105(a)(v)(A). An action for libel does not survive the death of either of the parties thereto. Wyo. Stat. § 1-4-102. In Setlaff v. Memorial

Hospital, 850 F.2d 1384 (10th Cir. 1988), the Tenth Circuit Court of Appeals, interpreting Wyoming law, held that a review of the plaintiff's personnel file by the hospital Board of Trustees was not republication, for statute of limitations purposes.

B. Jurisdiction

Under Wyo. Stat. § 5-1-107, Wyoming courts may exercise personal jurisdiction over a non-resident on any basis not inconsistent with the Wyoming or United States Constitutions. This statute extends the jurisdiction of Wyoming courts to the constitutional limit of the Fourteenth Amendment, and incorporates the concepts of fair play and substantial justice set forth in International Shoe Company v. Washington, 326 U.S. 310 (1945). See also Amoco v. EM Partnership Co., 886 P.2d 265 (Wyo. 1994).

C. Worker's Compensation Exclusivity

No reported cases address whether injury to reputation can form the basis of a workers compensation claim, and therefore be subject to the exclusivity provisions under the Wyoming Workers Compensation Act. However, the Wyoming Workers' Compensation Act indicates that there is no workers' compensation coverage for a mental injury unless it is caused by a physical injury and meets other diagnostic requirements. Wyo. Stat. 27-14-102(a)(xi)(J).

D. Pleading Requirements

In Wyoming, notice pleading is sufficient. Wyo. R. Civ. P. 8. A complaint need only contain a short, plain statement of the claim showing that the pleader is entitled to relief. Wyo. R. Civ. P. 8(a). Special damages must be specifically stated. Wyo. R. Civ. P. 9(g).

SURVEY OF WYOMING EMPLOYMENT PRIVACY LAW

Bradley T. Cave and Joanna R. Vilos
Holland & Hart LLP
2515 Warren Avenue, Suite 450
Cheyenne, WY 82001

(With Developments Reported Through **November 1, 2012**)

GENERAL COMMENTS

For cases decided between Jan. 1, 2001 and Jan. 1, 2003, the Wyoming Supreme Court requires citation to a public domain citation format in addition to the West Reporting System. For decisions after Jan. 1, 2003, only citation to the public domain system will be required. See In the Matter of Adopting A Public Domain, Neutral-Format Citation Format (Wyo. order issued Oct. 2000), available at courts.state.wy.us.

SIGNIFICANT DEVELOPMENTS SINCE THE 2012 *SURVEY*

Personnel Records: In Laramie County School District No. One v. Cheyenne Newspapers, Inc., 2011 WY 55, 250 P.3d 522 (Wyo. 2011), the Wyoming Supreme Court held that the school district was obligated to allow inspection of employment contracts listing employees' names and salaries. Although the school district argued that these documents were exempt from disclosure under the Wyoming Education Code, the Court held that no such exemption existed and the Wyoming Public Records Act required disclosure.

Actions Subsequent to Employment: No additional consideration beyond continuation of the at-will employment relationship is necessary to support an agreement whereby the employee assigns to the employer his/her intellectual property. Preston v. Marathon Oil Co., 2012 WY 66, 277 P.3d 81 (Wyo. 2012). There is a fundamental difference between non-compete agreements and intellectual property assignment agreements. Since an intellectual property assignment agreement does not affect an employee's right to earn a living or otherwise impose an improper restraint on trade, the holding in Hopper v. All Pet Animal Clinic, Inc., 861 P.2d 531, 539 (Wyo. 1993) requiring additional consideration to support a post-employment non-compete agreement does not carry over to the post-employment execution of an intellectual property assignment agreement. Preston, 277 P.3d at 87. If the employee does not wish to modify the terms of his/her employment relationship by assigning his/her intellectual property rights, he/she is free to terminate the employment relationship without any penalties. Id. at 88.

I. GENERAL LAW OF PRIVACY

A. Legal Basis of Privacy Claims

The law of privacy in Wyoming is not well developed and is primarily based on the common law. The Wyoming Supreme Court has addressed the issue of invasion of privacy in only a small handful of cases. The Court defined invasion of privacy in Houghton v. Franscell, 870 P.2d 1050, 1055 (Wyo. 1994), as an "unwarranted publicity, unwarranted appropriation or exploitation of one's personality, or the publicizing of one's private affairs with which the public has no legitimate concern."

In Jewell v. North Big Horn Hosp. Dist., 953 P.2d 135 (Wyo. 1998), the Wyoming Supreme Court held that an employee could not bring an invasion of privacy claim against her employer based on the employer's comments regarding the manner and reasons for the plaintiff's discharge.

B. Causes of Action

1. ***Misappropriation/Right of Publicity***. No reported cases.

2. ***False Light.*** Wyoming does not clearly recognize a separate cause of action called "false light." However, in Wagner v. Campbell County, Wyoming, 695 F. Supp. 512 (D. Wyo. 1988), the U.S. District Court for the District of Wyoming held that a plaintiff's claim for invasion of privacy was based upon "his being placed in a false light resulting in damage to his good name and reputation." Id. at 517. The court also found that invasion of privacy by placing the plaintiff in a false light resulting in damage to his good name and reputation is governed by the one (1) year limitations period for libel and slander. Id.; Wyo. Stat. § 1-3-105(a)(v).

3. ***Publication of Private Facts***. No reported cases.

4. ***Intrusion.*** The Supreme Court has not explicitly accepted or rejected the tort of intrusion. The only related Wyoming Supreme Court cases deal with the application of Wyoming's wiretap statute, Wyo. Stat. § 7-3-602 et.

seq. See Clark v. Alexander, 953 P.2d 145 (Wyo. 1998); Wells v. State, 846 P.2d 589 (Wyo. 1992); Saldana v. State, 846 P.2d 604 (Wyo. 1993).

C. Other Privacy-Related Actions

1. ***Intentional Infliction of Emotional Distress.*** Wyoming has adopted the Restatement (Second) of Torts § 46. The elements of this tort are (1) extreme and outrageous conduct; (2) intentionally or recklessly causing severe emotional distress. Leithead v. American Colloid Co., 721 P.2d 1059 (Wyo. 1986). The conduct must be "beyond all possible bounds of decency, atrocious, or utterly intolerable in a civilized community." Garcia v. Lawson, 928 P.2d 1164 (Wyo. 1996).

Wyoming also recognizes claims for third party intentional infliction of emotional distress, as described in Restatement (Second) of Torts § 46. The elements of this tort are: (1) extreme and outrageous conduct (2) directed at (a) a member of such person's immediate family who is present at the time, whether or not such distress results in bodily harm, or (b) any other person who is present at the time, if such distress results in bodily harm, which (3) causes severe emotional distress. Cook v. Shoshone First Bank, 2006 WY 13, ¶¶ 21–22 (2006).

The at-will employment relationship provides a complete defense to an employee's claim of intentional infliction of emotional distress that is caused solely by his or her termination. Trabing v. Kinko's, Inc., 2002 WY 171, 57 P.3d 1248 (Wyo. 2002).

Wyoming has also adopted the tort of negligent infliction of emotional distress. Gates v. Richardson, 719 P.2d 193 (Wyo. 1986). This tort is available only for parents, spouses, children, and siblings who: (1) observe the infliction of serious bodily harm or death, or its immediate aftermath, (2) without material change in the condition and location of the victim, (3) the bodily harm or death was caused by negligence, and (4) such negligence causes the emotional distress. Hedricks v. Hurley, 2008 WY 57, ¶¶ 26–29 (2008). This tort has been limited to a narrow range of situations, including intentional torts, violation of constitutional rights, and breach of the covenant of good faith and fair dealing.

2. ***Interference With Prospective Economic Advantage.*** Wyoming has adopted the Restatement (Second) of Torts § 766B. The elements of the tort of interference with prospective economic advantage are (1) a business expectancy (no contract is required); (2) defendant's knowledge of the business expectancy; (3) intentional and improper interference resulting in the termination of the expectancy by the third party; and (4) damages. Shaeffer v. State ex rel. Univ. of Wyo. ex rel. Bd. or Trustees, 2009 WY 19, ¶¶ 51–53 (2009); Martin v. Wing, 667 P.2d 1159 (Wyo. 1983); see also Bear v. Volunteers of America, Wyoming, Inc., 964 P.2d 1245 (Wyo. 1998) (outlining the elements for the related tort of interference with contract). Truth is a defense to a claim of interference with prospective economic advantage. Four Nines Gold, Inc. v. 71 Construction, Inc., 809 P.2d 236 (Wyo. 1990). Good faith interference for protection of an economic interest is permitted. Id. See also Lever v. Community First Bancshares, Inc., 989 P.2d 634 (Wyo. 1999) (plaintiff failed to show that intent was improper).

3. ***Prima Facie Tort.*** Wyoming does not recognize a prima facie tort cause of action for employment terminations. Townsend v. Living Centers Rocky Mountain, Inc., 947 P.2d 1297, 1299 (Wyo. 1997).

II. EMPLOYER TESTING OF EMPLOYEES

A. Psychological or Personality Testing

No reported cases.

B. Drug Testing

1. ***Common Law and Statutes.*** In Employment Sec. Comm'n v. Western Gas Processors, Ltd., 786 P.2d 866 (Wyo. 1990), an employee filed a claim for unemployment benefits after quitting his job rather than submitting to a urine drug test. The Wyoming Supreme Court held that the employee had been constructively discharged and was entitled to unemployment compensation. The Court also held that the demand to submit to a drug test was unreasonable given the circumstances. As for the employee's right to privacy, the Court stated that "we regard highly the federal constitutional guarantees to privacy as well as the right to privacy in Wyoming ...." Id. at 873. However, the Court avoided and did not rule on the privacy issue at hand. Id. But see Horne v. J. W. Gibson Well Service Co., 894 F.2d 1194 (10th Cir. 1990) (former employee filed suit for wrongful discharge due to employee's drug policy violation, alleging the discharge violated public policy of protecting employees from unreasonable invasions of privacy; the Tenth Circuit Court of Appeals affirmed summary judgment for the employer, holding that Wyoming public policy does not prohibit an employer from insuring a drug free workplace); Greco v. Halliburton Company, 674 F. Supp. 1447 (D. Wyo. 1987) (holding urine analysis tests required by an employer do not violate public policy against invasions of privacy).

Applying Wyoming employment contract law, in Tobey Anderson v. Exxon Coal U.S.A., Inc., 110 F.3d 73 (10th Cir. 1997) (unpublished opinion), the Tenth Circuit Court of Appeals reversed a judgment entered in favor of an employee who was fired after failing a "for cause" drug test. The Tenth Circuit agreed that the jury should have been permitted to decide if the plaintiff had a contract of employment but that the termination was not a breach of contract. The court noted that the drug policy did not specifically require any investigation of an employee before a drug test was requested. The court held that the defendant's drug policy allowed testing if there was "cause to suspect" drug use and that this definition established an extremely low threshold and this threshold was met prior to testing. The plaintiff also argued that summary discharge for violation of the drug policy was a breach of the employment contract which provided for progressive discipline, required the employer to "weigh extenuating circumstances" and to treat employees fairly. The court disagreed finding that the specific provisions of the drug policy that allowed the company to terminate employment after a positive test controlled over more general provisions not directly related to the drug policy. At trial the plaintiff also argued that the drug test was an invasion of her privacy. The trial judge dismissed that claim and that decision was not appealed.

In Duncan v. Afton, Inc., 991 P.2d 739 (Wyo. 1999), the Wyoming Supreme Court held that "[a] company collecting urine specimens as part of an employer's substance abuse testing program owes a duty of care to the employee who submits a specimen." Accordingly, the court reversed the dismissal of the plaintiff's negligence claim against the company his former employer had contracted with to collect urine samples from employees.

2. ***Private Employers.*** See II.B.1, supra.

3. ***Public Employers.*** See II.B.1, supra.

C. Medical Testing

No reported cases.

D. Polygraph Tests

No reported cases.

E. Fingerprinting

No reported cases.

III. SEARCHES

A. Employee's Person

1. ***Private Employers.*** The Wyoming "constitutional [prohibition] against unreasonable searches and seizures" only limits the "powers of government". State v. George, 231 P. 683 (1924). In Wagner v. Campbell County, Wyoming, 695 F. Supp. 512 (D. Wyo. 1988), a railroad employee brought a § 1983 action against Campbell County, Wyoming, together with an invasion of privacy action against his employer, Burlington Northern Railroad Company. Id. The plaintiff claimed that his privacy had been invaded by a forced drug search by the Campbell County undersheriff and Burlington Northern officials. Id. at 514. The District Court observed that the plaintiff based his invasion of privacy claim upon being placed in a false light, thus resulting in damage to his name and reputation; however, the Court applied Wyoming's one-year libel and slander statute of limitations (Wyo. Stat. § 1-3-105(a)(v)) and found that the plaintiff failed to timely assert the invasion of privacy claim. Id. at 517.

2. ***Public Employers.*** The Wyoming Constitution has a provision providing for security against search and seizures which closely parallels the Fourth Amendment of the U.S. Constitution. Wyo. Const., Art. 1, § 4 (1997). The constitutional mandate of the United States against unreasonable searches and seizures is essentially the same as the parallel constitutional restriction in the Wyoming constitution. State v. Hiteshew, 292 P. 2 (1930). The Wyoming provision is somewhat stronger than its federal counterpart because the search warrant must be issued upon affidavit. Hall v. State, 911 P.2d 1364 (Wyo. 1996).

B. Employee's Work Area

No reported cases.

C. Employee's Property

No reported cases.

IV. MONITORING OF EMPLOYEES

A. Telephones and Electronic Communications

1. ***Wiretapping.*** It is unlawful to intercept any wire, oral, or electronic communication. Wyo. Stat. § 7-3-702 (a)(i) (2009). But this law does not prohibit any person from intercepting an oral, wire or electronic communication where the person is a party to the communication or where one of the parties to the communication has given prior consent to the interception unless the communication is intercepted for the purpose of committing any criminal or tortious act. Wyo. Stat. § 7-3-702(b)(iv). Violation of this statute is a felony punishable by fine of not more than one thousand dollars ($1,000.00), imprisonment for not more than five years, or both. Wyo. Stat. § 7-3-702(f). Violation of this statute can also support a private cause of action for civil damages of actual damages (but not less than one thousand dollars ($1,000.00) per day for each day of violation), punitive damages, and reasonable attorney's fees and litigation costs. Wyo. Stat. § 7-3-710. Oral communication means "any oral communication uttered by a person who reasonably expects and circumstances justify the expectation that the communication is not subject to interception but does not include any electronic communication." Wyo. Stat. § 7-3-701(a)(xi).

There are no reported cases on this issue.

2. ***Electronic Communications.*** The term electronic communications in the above statute is defined as "any transfer of signs, signals, writing, images, sounds, data or intelligence of any nature transmitted in whole or in party by a wire, radio, electromagnetic, photo electronic or photo optical system that affects interstate or foreign commerce" but excludes communications made through a tracking device or tone-only paging device, or "electronic fund transfer information stored by a financial institution", and wire or oral communications. Wyo. Stat. § 7-3-701 (a)(v) (2001).

There are no reported cases on this issue.

3. ***Other Electronic Monitoring.*** There are no reported cases on this issue.

B. Mail

There are no reported cases or statutes on this issue.

C. Surveillance/Photographing

Wyoming has both civil and criminal stalking statutes. Wyo. Stat. § 6-2-506 provides that a person commits the crime of stalking if, with intent to harass another person, the person engages in a course of conduct reasonably likely to harass that person, including, but not limited to, any combination of communicating with another person in a manner that harasses; following another person; placing another person under surveillance; or otherwise engaging in a course of conduct that harasses another person. Wyo. Stat. § 1-1-126 creates a private cause of action for a victim of stalking, authorizing the victim to maintain a civil action against the individual who engages in a course of conduct prohibited by Wyo. Stat. § 6-2-506. A plaintiff may recover damages, punitive damages, attorney's fees and costs. Wyo. Stat. § 1-1-126. Veile v. Martenson, 258 F.3d 1180 (10th Cir. 2001); Luplow v. State, 897 P.2d 463 (Wyo. 1995); see generally Comment, Utilizing the Tools: Successfully Implementing the Stalking Statutes, 35 Land & Water L. Rev. 521 (2000).

V. ACTIVITIES OUTSIDE THE WORKPLACE

A. Statute or Common Law

This area could be controlled by both statute and common law.

B. Employees' Personal Relationships

1. ***Romantic Relationships Between Employees***. No reported cases.

2. ***Sexual Orientation.*** The Wyoming Constitution provides: "In their inherent right to life, liberty and the pursuit of happiness, all members of the human race are equal." Wyo. Const., Art. 1, § 2. This provision may provide broader protections than its federal counterpart in the Fourteenth Amendment. Wyoming's Fair Employment Practices Act, Wyo. Stat. § 27-9-105, et seq. (2002), does not list sexual orientation as a protected class.

3. ***Marital Status.*** All marriages which are valid by the laws of another state are valid in Wyoming.. Wyo. Stat. 2-1-111. Although Wyoming does not recognize common-law marriages, it will recognize common-law marriage established under laws of another jurisdiction, and give such marriage same binding effect it would have in state in which it was consummated. Bowers v. Wyo. State Treasurer ex rel. Workmen's Comp. Div., 593 P.2d 182 (Wyo. 1979).

C. Smoking

It is a discriminatory or unfair employment practice "[f]or an employer to require as a condition of employment that any employee or prospective employee use or refrain from using tobacco products outside the course of his employment, or otherwise to discriminate against any person in matters of compensation or the terms, conditions or privileges of employment on the basis of use or nonuse of tobacco products outside the course of his employment unless it is a bona fide occupational qualification that a person not use tobacco products outside the workplace." Wyo. Stat. § 27-9-105(a)(iv) (2009). Employers may however impose differential rates on health, life or disability insurance based on tobacco usage. Id.

D. Blogging

There are no reported cases on this issue.

VI. RECORDS

A. Personnel Records

"An employer who discloses information about a former employee's job performance to a prospective employer or to an employer of the former employee is presumed to be acting in good faith. Unless lack of good faith is shown by a preponderance of evidence, the employer is immune from civil liability for the disclosure or for the consequences resulting from the disclosure." Wyo. Stat. § 27-1-113 (2009).

In Wyoming Dept. of Transportation v. Union of Operating Engineers Local Union 800, 908 P.2d 970, 974 (Wyo. 1995), the Wyoming Department of Transportation opposed disclosure of federal payroll records sought by a local union. The department contended that releasing the records "would constitute an unwarranted invasion of privacy." Id. The Wyoming Supreme Court held that no privacy interest was at stake. The Court also observed that the record made no suggestion that any employees listed in the payroll records had complained about the potential release, and that any such complaints could not overcome the public records act requirement to release information. Id. at 975.

In Laramie County School District No. One v. Cheyenne Newspapers, Inc., 2011 WY 55, 250 P.3d 522 (Wyo. 2011), the Wyoming Supreme Court held that the school district was obligated to allow inspection of employment contracts listing employees' names and salaries. Although the school district argued that these documents were exempt from disclosure under the Wyoming Education Code, the Court held that no such exemption existed and the Wyoming Public Records Act required disclosure.

In many cases, public record custodians are statutorily required to refuse an individual's request to inspect public employees' and officials' personnel files. Wyo. Stat. § 16-4-203 (2002).

B. Medical Records

Hospital records generally cannot be disclosed without patient authorization. Wyo. Stat. § 35-2-605 to -617 (1997). This statute provides several exceptions. Id. In Harston v. Campbell County Memorial Hospital, 913 P.2d 870 (Wyo. 1996), the Wyoming Supreme Court determined an *in camera* inspection of materials requested during discovery is the proper vehicle for the evaluation of one of the enumerated exceptions: medical records are discoverable if the party seeking the information can show the interest in access outweighs the patient's privacy interest.

C. Criminal Records

"No criminal history record information released to an authorized recipient shall be released, used or disseminated by that recipient to any other person for any purpose not included in the original request except that the record subject may make further dissemination in his discretion." Wyo. Stat. § 7-19-106(j) (2009).

D. Subpoenas / Search Warrants

There are no reported cases on this issue.

VII. ACTIONS SUBSEQUENT TO EMPLOYMENT

A. References

There are no reported cases on this issue.

B. Non-Compete Agreements

Wyoming employers are generally permitted to seek protection from improper and unfair competition from a former employee but are not entitled to protection against ordinary competition. Hopper v. All Pet Animal Clinic, Inc., 861 P.2d

531, 539 (Wyo. 1993). When an employee enters into a non-compete agreement after the employment relationship has commenced, separate consideration beyond continued at-will employment must be provided to the employee. Id. at 541. The separate consideration necessary to support an employee's post-employment execution of a non-compete agreement "would include promotion, pay raise, special training, employment benefits or other advantages for the employee." Id.

In order to be considered reasonable, the restraint must only afford fair protection of the interests of the employer and must not be so large a restraint as to interfere with the interests of the public. Tench v. Weaver, 374 P.2d 27, 29 (Wyo. 1962). This requires a showing that the covenant is: (1) in writing; (2) part of the contract for employment; (3) based on reasonable consideration; (4) reasonable in durational and geographical limitation; and (5) not against public policy. Hopper, 861 P.2d at 540. Generally, lost net profits are a proper element of recovery for breaches of covenants not to compete. Id. at 547.

A covenant not to compete entered contemporaneously with employment is enforceable and supported by consideration. CBM Geosolutions, Inc. v. Gas Sensing Tech. Corp., 2009 WY 113, ¶ 13. The reasonableness of non-compete agreement is a fact-specific inquiry and a court will consider: degree of inequality in bargaining power; the risk of the employer losing customers; the extent of respective participation by the parties in securing and retaining customers; the good faith of the employer; the existence of sources or general knowledge pertaining to the identity of customers; the nature and extent of the business position held by the employee; the employee's training, health, education, and needs of his family; the current conditions of employment; the necessity of the employee changing his calling or residence; and the correspondence of the restraint with the need for protecting the legitimate interests of the employee. Id.

No additional consideration beyond continuation of the at-will employment relationship is necessary to support an agreement whereby the employee assigns to the employer his/her intellectual property. Preston v. Marathon Oil Co., 2012 WY 66, 277 P.3d 81 (Wyo. 2012). There is a fundamental difference between non-compete agreements and intellectual property assignment agreements. Since an intellectual property assignment agreement does not affect an employee's right to earn a living or otherwise impose an improper restraint on trade, the holding in Hopper requiring additional consideration to support a post-employment non-compete agreement does not carry over to the post-employment execution of an intellectual property assignment agreement. Id. at 87. If the employee does not wish to modify the terms of his/her employment relationship by assigning his/her intellectual property rights, he/ she is free to terminate the employment relationship without any penalties. Id. at 88.

VIII. OTHER ISSUES

A. Statutes of Limitations

The general statute of limitations for torts is four (4) years. Wyo. Stat. § 1-3-105 (2009). Liability created by federal statute has a two (2) year statute of limitations. Wyo. Stat. § 1-3-115. Libel and slander have a one (1) year statute of limitations. Wyo. Stat. § 1-3-105(a)(v). False light and invasion of privacy also have a one (1) year statute of limitations. Wagner v. Campbell County, Wyo., 695 F. Supp. 512, 517 (D. Wyo. 1988).

B. Jurisdiction

Under Wyo. Stat. § 5-1-107, Wyoming courts may exercise personal jurisdiction over a non-resident on any basis not inconsistent with the Wyoming or United States Constitutions. This statute extends the jurisdiction of Wyoming courts to the constitutional limit of the Fourteenth Amendment, and incorporates the concepts of fair play and substantial justice set forth in International Shoe Company v. Washington, 326 U.S. 310 (1945). See also Amoco v. EM Partnership Co., 886 P.2d 265 (Wyo. 1994).

C. Worker's Compensation Exclusivity

Worker's compensation benefits take the place of any and all causes of action which the injured or deceased worker might otherwise have had against his or her employer, so long as that employer was a participating member of the compensation fund. E.g., Jackson v. Dravo Corp., 603 F.2d 157 (10th Cir. 1979). However, there are no Worker's Compensation cases relating to privacy torts. The Wyoming Workers' Compensation Act indicates that there is no workers' compensation coverage for a mental injury unless it is caused by a physical injury and meets other diagnostic requirements. Wyo. Stat. § 27-14-102(a)(xi)(J).

D. Pleading Requirements

In Wyoming, notice pleading is sufficient. Wyo. R. Civ. P. 8. A complaint need only contain a short, plain statement of the claim showing that the pleader is entitled to relief. Wyo. R. Civ. P. 8(a). Special damages must be specifically stated. Wyo. R. Civ. P. 9(g).

INDEX OF ISSUES IN STATE SURVEYS

Defenses, Libel — Truth, Opinion, Consent, Mitigation, continued

Falsity

Fault

Fingerprinting

Intracorporate Communication — As Publication/Fact Pattern, continued

Intrusion

Jurisdiction — Libel/Privacy

Publication of Private Facts, continued

References - Libel/Privacy

Republication — *See* Publication

Reports to Auditors and Insurers

Romantic Relationships Between Employees — *See* Activities Outside the Workplace

Searches

Vicarious Liability

Wiretapping — *See* Monitoring of Employees

Workers' Compensation Exclusivity - Libel/Privacy